COLLINS COBUILD ENGLISH DICTIONARY

HarperCollins*Publishers*

HarperCollins Publishers
77-85 Fulham Palace Road
London W6 8JB

COBUILD is a trademark of William Collins Sons & Co. Ltd

This edition, first published in Great Britain 1995

Reprinted 1995

10 9 8 7 6 5 4 3 2

ISBN 0 00 370941 8 paperback
ISBN 0 00 375029 9 hardback
Norway ISBN 0 00 375054 X hardback

Computer Typeset by
Morton Word Processing, Scarborough, England
Printed in Great Britain by HarperCollins Manufacturing

Corpus Acknowledgements

We would like to acknowledge the assistance of the many hundreds of individuals and companies who have kindly given permission for copyright material to be used in The Bank of English. The written sources include many national and regional newspapers in Britain and overseas; magazine and periodical publishers; and book publishers in Britain, the United States and Australia. Extensive spoken data has been provided by radio and television broadcasting companies; research workers at many universities and other institutions; and numerous individual contributors. We are grateful to them all.

Note

Entered words that we have reason to believe constitute trademarks have been designated as such. However, neither the presence nor absence of such designation should be regarded as affecting the legal status of any trademark.

legal: used mainly in legal documents, in law courts, and by the police in official situations; e.g. *breach of the peace, de jure.*

> **breach of the peace, breaches of the peace.** A **breach of the peace** is noisy or violent behaviour in a public place which is illegal because it disturbs other people; a legal term. *He admitted causing a breach of the peace... Four men were found guilty of breach of the peace.* N-VAR

literary: used mainly in novels, poetry, and other forms of literature; e.g. *beatific, forsaken.*

> **beatific** /biːətɪfɪk/. A **beatific** expression shows or expresses great happiness and calmness; a literary word. *He smiled an almost beatific smile.* ADJ-GRADED: usu ADJ n =blissful

medical: used mainly in medical texts, and by doctors in official situations; e.g. *anterior, duodenum.*

> **duodenum** /djuːoʊdiːnəm, AM duː-/ **duodenums.** Your **duodenum** is the part of your small intestine that is just below your stomach; a medical term. N-COUNT

offensive: likely to offend people, or to insult them; words labelled **offensive** should therefore usually be avoided; e.g. *berk, commie.*

> **berk** /bɜːʳk/ **berks.** If you call someone a **berk**, you mean that you think they are stupid or irritating; an informal and offensive word in British English. N-COUNT PRAGMATICS

old-fashioned: generally considered to be old-fashioned, and no longer in common use; e.g. *bawdy, frock.*

> **frock** /frɒk/ **frocks.** A **frock** is a woman's or girl's dress; an old-fashioned word. ◆◇◇◇◇ N-COUNT

spoken: used mainly in speech rather than in writing; e.g. *school kid, whoops.*

> **whoops** /ʰwʊps/. People say **'whoops'** when they have had a slight accident or made a mistake; used in spoken English. *Whoops, that was a mistake... Whoops, it's past 11, I'd better be off home.* EXCLAM PRAGMATICS

technical: used mainly when talking or writing about objects, events, or processes in a specialist subject, such as business, science, or music; e.g. *amortize, electrolyte, fugue.*

> **electrolyte** /ɪlektrəlaɪt/ **electrolytes.** An **electrolyte** is a substance, usually a liquid, which electricity can pass through; a technical use in science. N-COUNT

written: used mainly in writing rather than in speech; e.g. *animus, bespectacled.*

> **bespectacled** /bɪspektəkəld/. Someone who is **bespectacled** is wearing spectacles; used in written English. *Mr Merrick was a slim, quiet, bespectacled man.* ADJ: usu ADJ n

Examples

Examples of how words have been used form a very important part of COBUILD dictionaries. Indeed, we know from research that COBUILD has done that users of a dictionary often read the examples first – that is, even before they read the definitions. They are looking for an example that is similar to one that they have heard or read, or that will confirm the way they want to use the word. For instance, users might be unsure which verb to use with the noun **homework**: should it be 'do your homework' or 'make your homework', or a different verb altogether? If they look at the dictionary entry for 'homework' (which is shown below), they will see that the example shows that it is right to use the verb 'do'.

homework /hoʊmwɜːʳk/ ◆◇◇◇◇
1 Homework is school work that teachers give to pupils to do at home in the evening or at the weekend. *Have you done your homework, Gemma?* N-UNCOUNT

This means, of course, that the examples given in a dictionary should be characteristic of the ones that users will come across. The examples given in this dictionary have been carefully chosen to show typical contexts in which the word, is used. For most words and phrases, we have hundreds, or even thousands, of instances in The Bank of English, and we have selected those which show typical grammatical patterns, typical vocabulary, and typical contexts. For instance, we give four examples for meaning 1 of the adjective **steady**. These examples show the kinds of situation and context where this meaning of **steady** can be used:

steady /stedi/ **steadier, steadiest; steadies, steadying, steadied** ◆◆◆◇◇
1 A **steady** situation continues or develops gradually without any interruptions and is not likely to change quickly. *Despite the steady progress of building work, the campaign against it is still going strong... The improvement in standards has been steady and persistent, but has attracted little comment from educationalists... Despite the steady rain, the mood was friendly and festive... A student doesn't have a steady income.* ADJ-GRADED =constant
♦ **steadily** /stedɪli/ *Relax as much as possible and keep breathing steadily... The company has steadily been losing market share to Boeing and Airbus.* ADV-GRADED: ADV with v

The majority of the examples in the dictionary are taken word for word from one of the texts in The Bank of English. Occasionally, we have made very minor changes to them, so that they are more successful as dictionary examples.

Throughout the whole dictionary, there are about 100,000 examples. Because this is a completely new edition of the dictionary, we have chosen examples which we have never used before in any of our dictionaries or other reference books. This makes the dictionary a valuable resource for both students and teachers, showing how the words have been used in books, newspapers, magazines, broadcasting, and conversation. Nearly all the words and meanings in the dictionary have at least one example. The main exceptions are concrete nouns such as **bathmat**, **seahorse,** and **trombone,** and a few other words where an example would add nothing to the information given in the definition.

All the examples in the dictionary have been chosen with care, and, as we have said, they contain important information about the typical patterning associated with a word. In the case of verbs, we give examples for all the main grammatical structures in which they are used. The examples are given in the same order as the patterns shown in the Extra Column. These patterns are explained in the **Grammar** section on pages xxiv-xxxiii. For instance, here are the first four meanings of the verb **melt**:

melt /melt/ **melts, melting, melted** ◆◆◇◇◇
1 When a solid substance **melts** or when you **melt** it, it changes to a liquid, usually because it has been heated. *The snow had melted, but the lake was still frozen solid... Meanwhile, melt the white chocolate in a bowl suspended over simmering water... Add the melted butter, molasses, salt, and flour.* V-ERG; V; V n; V-ed
2 If something such as your feelings **melt**, they suddenly disappear and you no longer feel them; a literary use. *His anxiety about the outcome melted, to return later but not yet... He would have struggled but his strength had melted.* VERB; V
▶ **Melt away** means the same as **melt**. *When he heard these words, Shinran felt his inner doubts melt away.* PHRASAL VERB; V P
3 If a person or thing **melts into** something such as darkness or a crowd of people, they become difficult to see, for example because they are moving away from you or are the same colour as the background; a literary use. *The youths dispersed and melted into the darkness... The squadron's armour is draped in sand-coloured nets that melt into the landscape.* VERB =disappear; V into n
4 If someone or something **melts** your heart, or if your heart **melts,** you start to feel loving or tender towards them. *When his lips break into a smile, it is enough to melt any woman's heart... When a bride walks down the aisle to a stirring tune, even the iciest of hearts melt.* V-ERG; V n; V

The grammatical patterns in the examples are set out clearly in the Extra Column. In this way, users will find it easy to understand and follow the grammatical behaviour of verbs, as shown in the examples.

Editorial Team

Editor in Chief
John Sinclair

Editorial Director
Gwyneth Fox

Editorial Manager
Stephen Bullon

Senior Editor
Elizabeth Manning

Editors

Jane Bradbury
Rosalind Combley
Ramesh Krishnamurthy
Carole Murphy
Michael Murphy
Elizabeth Potter
Christina Rammell
Jenny Watson
Laura Wedgeworth
John Williams

Assistant Editors

Michael Lax
Dawn McKen
Deborah Orpin
Luisa Plaja
Jim Ronald
Miranda Timewell

Grammar
Gill Francis
Susan Hunston

Pragmatics
Joanna Channell
Alice Deignan

Pronunciation
Jonathan Payne

Computer Staff
Jeremy Clear
Zoe James
Tim Lane
Andrea Lewis

The Bank of English
Sue Smith

Secretarial Staff
Sue Crawley
Michelle Devereux

Publishing Manager
Debbie Seymour

Design and Production
Ted Carden
Jill McNair

Managing Director, Collins Dictionaries
Richard Thomas

We would especially like to thank Rosamund Moon, Editorial Manager at COBUILD, for her invaluable contribution to all aspects of this project during its latter stages.

We would also like to thank Diana Bankston, Julia Penelope, Julie Plier, Debbie Posner, and Lynda Thomas for their advice and assistance on American English.

We gratefully acknowledge the editorial assistance of Catherine Brown, Helen Bruce, Jane Clarke, Ann Hewings, Ceri Hewitt, David Lee, Annelet Lykles, Sean Lynch, Clare Marson, Héloïse McGuinness, David Morrow, and Michael Stocks.

We also owe a debt of gratitude for editorial assistance to the following people from Collins Bilingual Dictionaries: Harry Campbell, Phyllis Gautier, Janet Gough, Bob Grossmith, Gavin Killip, Cordelia Lilly.

We would also like to thank Fred Karlsson and his team at the University of Helsinki for their work on tagging and parsing The Bank of English.

We have continued to receive academic support from our colleagues in the School of English, University of Birmingham, in particular from Malcolm Coulthard. Two visiting scholars contributed significantly to the development of our editorial policies: Flor Aarts of the Katholieke Universiteit, Nijmegen, and Bill Louw of the University of Zimbabwe.

Staff and students of the following institutions kindly took part in a research project on dictionary use, the results of which were used in the writing of this dictionary: English for Overseas Students Unit, University of Birmingham; Formalangues, Paris; Languacom, Paris; Ecole de Langues de Nouvelles Frontières, Paris; International Language Centre, Paris; International Language Centre, Hastings; E.F. International, Brighton; Swan School, Stratford-upon-Avon.

From the First Edition (1987)

EDITORIAL TEAM

EDITOR IN CHIEF
John Sinclair

MANAGING EDITOR
Patrick Hanks

EDITORS
Gwyneth Fox
Rosamund Moon
Penny Stock

SENIOR COMPILERS
Andrew Delahunty
Sheila Dignen
Ramesh Krishnamurthy
Elaine Pollard

COMPILERS
Stephen Bullon
Deborah Kirby
Helen Liebeck
Elizabeth Manning
John Todd

SENIOR COMPUTING OFFICER
Jeremy Clear

COMPUTING OFFICER
Eileen Fitzgerald

CLERICAL STAFF
Lynne Farrow
Janice Johnson
Brenda Nicholls
Pat Smith

COLLINS PUBLISHING DIRECTOR
Richard Thomas

Foreword

The Project Team

The final project team is set out above. Several other colleagues made a notable contribution in the early years, and continued to provide support throughout the life of the project. Antoinette Renouf, the original Project Co-ordinator led the team from 1980-83 and established the text corpus and maintained and developed corpus work. Dr Michael Hoey gave a great deal of help in administration and policy guidance in the early period and continued with strong academic guidance. From Collins, Beryl T Atkins played a formative role in the design of the project and in the general training; continuing in her capacity as General Editor she commented on draft dictionary texts throughout.

Some members of the team moved on before the work was completed. Wendy Morris and Clive Upton were two of the original editors. Nigel Turton, Martin Manser, Dieter Wachendorff, Judy Amanthis, Duncan Marshall, Emily Driver, Kathy Kavanagh and Michael Rundell were compilers for substantial periods. Ian Sedwell helped with the computing. Heather Champion, Lorraine Dove, Cheryl Evans and Sue Smith were secretaries.

The project has also benefited greatly from people who, while not regular members of the team, acted in a consultative capacity or provided a specialist service. In particular Marcel Lemmens, grammar consultant, must be mentioned, Cathy Emmott, who helped with the Extra Column, and also Ela Bullon, Helmut Hirschmüller, Debbie Krishnamurthy, Clare Ramsey, and Louise Ravelli.

Acknowledgements

I would like to thank many other people whose names do not appear on the team credits but who made a significant contribution to the compilation of the dictionary.

This project was part of the work of the English Department and its successful completion owes much to the support of the Head of the Department throughout, Professor J T Boulton. In various ways every one of the staff helped and encouraged the work and one or two must be singled out for specific contributions. Dr David Brazil devised the system of recording pronunciations, and transcribed most of them. Tim Lane ensured their transfer to electronic form and gave support on the computational side. Tim Johns encouraged the use of real examples and made experimental classes available. Chris Kennedy, Tony Dudley-Evans, Dr Mike McCarthy, Charles Owen, Phillip King, Dr Kirsten Malmkjaer and Martin Hewings all read drafts, picked holes in them and offered many suggestions for improvement.

Many colleagues in the University of Birmingham contributed notably to the project. Three Pro-Vice Chancellors in turn guided the project through various committees; Professor Harry Prime, Professor John Fage and Professor John Samuels. The Centre for Computing and Computer Sciences was deeply involved throughout and eased problems in the complex final editing.

I would also like to thank the past and present members of Collins staff who have helped in the project.

This dictionary is based on evidence and the evidence comes from hundreds of documents and conversations, kindly made available by the copyright holders. A full list is provided on page xxii.

Such a fundamental re-appraisal of a language requires a high degree of teamwork and large-scale co-ordination of resources. The success of this book and other books to come will owe a great deal to the people and groups mentioned above, and I am very grateful to them for their contributions.

John M Sinclair
Professor of Modern English Language
Editor in Chief

Contents

Introduction

A new dictionary

This is a new book, a completely new edition of the Collins COBUILD English Language Dictionary, which was published in 1987. That dictionary was based on a corpus of 20 million words of the English of the 1980s. Since then we have built a new corpus, The Bank of English, which now stands at over 200 million words of English of the 1990s. So we have analysed every word again, looking at our new corpus data, and this book is the result.

The method which we worked out for the original dictionary, and which we explained in detail in *Looking Up* (HarperCollins 1987), proved very successful. But the opportunities of today's technology have made it possible to improve the method. Looking at the new corpus data, we decided which words and phrases to put in, and then we examined the language word by word and phrase by phrase, in order to give a clear account of each meaning and use. We then wrote a definition, chose typical examples, and added information about the pronunciation, grammar, semantics, pragmatics, and frequency to complete the entry.

So the information about English in this book is either new, or it has been recently checked against the large amount of corpus data that gives COBUILD its reliability and authority. In general, the new analysis confirms the picture of the language that we gave in 1987, but the larger corpus enables us to make statements about the meanings, patterns, and uses of words with much greater confidence and accuracy of detail.

Although the changes in a huge vocabulary like that of English are not dramatic over a decade or so, when you get down to detail there are a lot of points to make. Even core words can acquire new uses, and new words and combinations are constantly entering the mainstream of the language. Many words for which we had very little evidence in the 20 million word corpus have been included in this dictionary because we now have much more information about them.

In the compilation and editing, all the policies of the 1987 Dictionary have been reconsidered. Although we have retained most of them, there has been a lot of detailed updating and improvement. We have looked carefully at the many comments made by reviewers and correspondents about the original dictionary. Many users have written to me, and COBUILD has taken all their points into account. I think this new dictionary is much improved as a result.

The evidence

A dictionary must start with its evidence, its facts. Speakers of a language know a lot about it, since they read and speak it effortlessly for hours every day. But they may not be able to explain what they do, any more than they can explain how they walk, without falling over. Using a language is a skill that most people are not conscious of; they cannot examine it in detail, but simply use it to communicate.

Those who learn to observe language carefully can express and organize some of the facts about it on the basis of their experience, and that is the origin of many descriptions of English through the centuries. However, there are many facts about language that cannot be discovered by just thinking about it, or even reading and listening very intently, and COBUILD was established in 1980 to use computers to identify them.

A corpus

The result of this was that COBUILD established a new kind of evidence for English in the 80s – a collection of English texts called a corpus, held in a computer so that they can be consulted instantly. We knew that we needed millions of words of recent English, spoken and written, British and American, formal and informal, fact and fiction, and so on. This evidence, gathered over several years, allowed us to find out which words and expressions were most commonly used at the time. Where a word has many meanings – like several on each page of this Dictionary – we were able to see which were the important ones, and which phrases we should be sure to put in.

We learned an early lesson in lexicography from this work. It made us aware that all the details of a natural use of a word were essential, and cannot be faked. We realized that we would have to use real examples, in the tradition of the great English lexicographers, rather than make them up. It is not always easy to find suitable examples, but we thought that it was worthwhile, and it is now a cornerstone of the COBUILD approach to language.

At that time, 20 million words was so much bigger than any other corpus that it seemed like the ultimate in modern technology. However, by going through this process, COBUILD realized that with more evidence the job could be done even better. There would be more examples to choose from, so that the ones chosen would be simpler and more typical of the patterning; there would be more instances of the less common words, so that their definitions could be checked and refined; the idiomatic phrases would be easier to find and explain accurately.

The Bank of English

This book has been written using the evidence of over *two hundred* million words – ten times the corpus made for the original dictionary. The new corpus is called The Bank of English, and it covers a vast range of current English. As a result the definitions and examples in this book are even clearer and more authoritative than in our previous works.

A few years ago it became much easier to gather large quantities of spoken and written English. The publishers of books, magazines, and newspapers became aware that large amounts of language passed through their hands, and there could be many good reasons for keeping it in electronic form as well as printing it out in what is now known as 'hard copy'. A market grew up for electronic language among people who want to find or check statements, particularly in news, magazines, and legal language. Gradually, with the emergence of compact disks – the CD-ROMs that are now familiar – words in their millions became available to students of language. Nowadays the problem is not finding the language, but managing and controlling it, and making sensible and balanced selections for the analytical tasks that COBUILD has to do.

There are about five hundred million words in the COBUILD archives, most of them from newspapers or the radio. In designing the present shape of The Bank of English we balanced a number of factors – spoken and written, UK, USA and other varieties from predominantly native speaker communities, books and magazines, and other classifications within those.

Within the spoken component, the most difficult kind of language to collect was, as always, the informally recorded conversations of people going about their daily lives, without thought of their language being preserved in a corpus. Each conversation has to be recorded and transcribed by experts, and then entered in the computer – the technology for this has hardly advanced since corpora began. Nevertheless, this kind of impromptu language is of particular interest to dictionary makers. The Bank of English, with a total of 15 million words of this kind of recorded speech, has the most extensive evidence available.

The headword list

It is much easier to decide which words and phrases to include, and which to omit, when we have accurate figures from such a large amount of language. Our computers can instantly check the language activity of thousands of speakers and writers, rather than just a handful of experts. A dictionary – even a big dictionary – is able to choose only the most important facts of the language to present, and the compilers need good evidence for their selections.

For this edition, COBUILD made available a lot of space for new and additional entries, by increasing the size of the book and also the efficiency of presentation. You will find many new words such as *care worker, carjacking,* and *multimedia; hand-held, multi-tasking,* and *video conferencing; neural network, photo opportunity,* and *talking head; imaging, off-the-wall,* and *wetland* – many more than we were able to include in 1987. These are all words that have occurred recently, often enough, and in a sufficient variety of sources to earn their place; we do not include words just because they are odd or interesting. COBUILD specializes in presenting the words and phrases that are frequent in everyday use, and everything in the book is worth learning for mastery of contemporary English. COBUILD is <u>not</u> a historical record of the language, and it is <u>not</u> a list of all the peculiar words that help you finish a crossword.

Frequency

For the first time in a major dictionary, COBUILD gives information about the frequency of the headwords. Five frequency bands have been established (details are on page xiii). Starting with the very common words, we move through a basic vocabulary to an intermediate one, and on until we have covered the core vocabulary of the language. Headwords with no frequency marker are less common, but are still worth including in the dictionary. If you look at any page of the dictionary, you will see that we have included a large number of these words, unmarked for frequency.

The point is that English uses a fairly small number of words for most purposes, but it also has available a large and rich vocabulary when that is needed. So you will find that *be* is quite naturally in the commonest band, as is *because,* a common function word. Words like *barracuda, basalt, bas-relief* and *bassoon* are not frequent, and are not placed in a band. They are clearly of the type that are only used on particular occasions. Again I must emphasize that these too have been chosen for their relative usefulness from many thousands of possible entries.

So, if you see that a headword is marked for frequency, you will know that it is worth learning; if it has two or more black diamonds it is part of the essential core vocabulary of the language; the more marked it is, the more frequently you will come across it.

Examples

All of the examples in this book are newly selected from The Bank of English. As before, the examples are chosen carefully to show the patterns that are frequently found alongside a word or phrase. The compiler has dozens, hundreds or thousands of examples available, and quickly picks out the *collocates* – the particular words that are found near the headword – and the typical structures in which the word or phrase is most often found.

This means that the examples perform several functions. Of course, they help to show the meaning of the word by showing it in use. Research suggests that a large number of users start with the examples as a short cut to the meaning anyway; but in the COBUILD style of defining, the definitions ought to be clear enough in themselves, and the examples can be used to show the characteristic phrasing round the word. Since the examples are genuine pieces of text, and they have been chosen against the background of a full display of the usage of the word, they can be trusted to show the word in use in a natural context.

Coverage

A language used by many people has many varieties, and part of the use of a corpus is to study the kinds of variation that occur. The Bank of English is divided into 15 components, and the compilers can see the coverage of a word every time they look it up in the corpus. They can readily see if a usage is characteristic of just one or two varieties, and if so they can make a note that this is American, or informal, or the like.

As far as possible COBUILD gives priority to the English of most general utility worldwide. Dialect words are not featured, nor is the language of small social groups or specialists; instead space is reserved for international English, predominantly British English but with a lot of American usage recorded.

English is the most widespread language in the world and is used by hundreds of millions of speakers who have another mother tongue. This makes the core vocabulary very important, because it is likely to be shared by most users of English. The value of COBUILD'S frequency information is that we can list the words that a worldwide user is most likely to need.

Adaptability

The Bank of English also makes it possible to study the way words and their surrounding patterns fit together into connected speech or writing. The large amount of evidence makes it possible to see what makes a natural utterance, and what can be changed around or omitted altogether. This feature is one of the most important advances in preparing this new dictionary – the ability to see the regular patterns in the midst of all the natural variation.

The entries always begin by pointing out the main patterns, and illustrating them with examples; where there is some room for variation you will probably find it in the later examples. So, for example, **true** 5 has the regular pattern *It is true that...*, but in the third example the use of the word *true* on its own or repeated at the beginning of a sentence is shown to be a short form of the phrase: *'Things are a bit different in my country.' 'True, true, but we're not in your country, are we?'.*

Phraseology

For the first time the compilers have been able to see the phraseology of the language clearly. There are many idioms in a language, and many more expressions which are more common and more ordinary than idioms. But combinations of words are much less frequent than the individual words, so a large corpus is necessary to define them accurately. Without it, we might not have found that your *true feelings* are usually hidden – the occurrence of verbs like *express, show,* and *reveal* indicate that (see **true** 2). Another example is **lap** 1, where both a preposition and a possessive adjective must come in front of the word in natural use: *She waited quietly with her hands in her lap... Hugh glanced at the child on her mother's lap.*

Bold face

The word or phrase being defined in each paragraph is printed in **bold face**. This convention allows us to point out where words other than the headword are really part of the expression being defined. The corpus makes it clear when such an action is justified, and the user is helped in several ways. Principally, the association between the exact phrasing and the meaning is a big help to recognition and learning – there is nothing more daunting than a word that has several meanings, with nothing to tell you which one is relevant to your needs on a particular occasion. For example in the entry for **count**, sense 11 deals with recording or remembering things. Nearly always this meaning occurs with the verb **keep** or **lose**, so these words also are put in bold face to emphasize the collocation.

Long entries

The commonest words of a language have many uses, and to explain them in a dictionary results in some very long entries. Many users of the original COBUILD Dictionary felt that the long entries were particularly difficult to understand. We therefore studied this problem, and made a number of changes in order to make it easier to find the information you need even in the longest and most complicated entry. As mentioned above, we have tried to print more words in bold face to help you find the sense you are looking for. For example, the entry for **thing** is long, and many of the meanings and uses of the word are difficult to explain and recognize. Notice how often there are one or more other words in bold face in that entry – senses 3 and 5 indicate some variable expressions, and then from sense 18 to the end there are a large number of relatively fixed phrases.

Superheadwords

This is a new feature. One of the most controversial features that COBUILD has become committed to is the strict policy of 'one word, one entry'. It is common practice in dictionaries to have two different entries for *call*, noun, and *call*, verb, even though the meanings overlap a lot. Also it is normal where there are two pronunciations, like *bow* (rhyming with *cow* or *toe*) to have two entries. Some dictionaries have several separate entries for the same word.

COBUILD decided on the opposite policy, so that the user can have confidence that all the information about a word will be there in a single entry. This resulted in some features that occasionally irritated users – for example, the verb forms *mean, means, meaning, meant* were put together with the adjective forms *mean, meaner, meanest,* and so on.

For these cases we have devised a 'superheadword' structure. There is, as before, only one entry, so you will not have to look anywhere else, but the entry is divided into several sub-entries, each of which gives a list of forms and has all the features of a regular entry. We have considered every entry that has ten or more senses for superheadword status, as well as the obvious ones. So **mean** is now divided into three sections, corresponding to its verb, adjective, and noun uses.

The same principle is used for a word like **fancy**, where there is a fairly major sense distinction running through its uses. One group of meanings deals with liking and preference, and the other group with elaborateness and expensiveness. Where a word such as **do** has quite distinct uses as an auxiliary verb and a main verb, this is also set out as a superheadword.

If this feature is found to be helpful we hope to extend it in the future. It makes the structure of an entry more flexible, and allows us to give a general guide to the longer and more complex or unusual entries.

Grammatical words

These are the most difficult words for compilers, because they are usually very frequent and have a lot of meanings and uses, but are extremely difficult to define. At first we tried to set out each word in all its detail, and we set aside a large proportion of the dictionary for this. But since we have now published two grammar books that treat the grammar words in an organized sequence of structural patterns, in this dictionary we talk mainly about their usage.

We therefore present a summary of the most prominent uses of the grammar words in the dictionary, and we hope that the user will refer to the grammars for all the structural details. We have tried very hard to make these entries really useful as dictionary entries. Consider the new entry for **down**, for example.

Grammatical information

Almost every sense of every entry in this dictionary has alongside it a grammatical classification, usually a word class, and often a structural note as well. For this information COBUILD has established an Extra Column so that the technical information can be set out economically in notes, separate from the definitions. This feature has been well received, and we have concentrated on simplifying and improving the grammar notes in this new Edition.

A few notes are quite long, but it is worth understanding them because they are important in the way a word is used to give a particular meaning. So one pattern under **mean** 3 reads '*it* V amount to-inf'. This means that the word *it* is followed by the verb *means* and a word or phrase that expresses an amount of something, such as *a lot*. In turn this is followed by a to-infinitive. This pattern is also shown in the example: *It would mean a lot to them to win.*

The conventions used in the grammatical notes are set out on the inside of the cover. They compress a lot of very helpful information into a small space, and the abbreviations that are used are nearly all familiar to any learner.

Pragmatics

Many uses of words need more than a statement of meaning to be properly explained. People use words to do many things: to make invitations, to express their feelings, to emphasize what they are saying, and so on. The corpus gives us evidence for such uses that are difficult to get from any other source, because we only notice them when we see many examples of them gathered together.

The study and description of the ways in which people use language to do things is called pragmatics. This aspect of language is very important, and easy to miss. This is where the language is giving added meaning. COBUILD has always had a lot of information on pragmatics in its pages, but we have not previously drawn attention to it except in the case of insults, swear words, and things like that. In this new Edition we frequently use a 'pragmatics' sign in the Extra Column, and if you look carefully at such entries you will see the point being made. For example, you will find the phrase used above in this paragraph *and things like that* explained at **thing** 2, where we say that it is used to widen the range of a list. This use has the 'pragmatics' sign in the Extra Column. Indeed, many of the senses of **thing** have a 'pragmatics' sign.

Defining style

The most distinctive feature of the original dictionary was the use of full English sentences in the definitions, setting out the meaning in the way one ordinary person might explain it to another. We had a lot of favourable comments on this feature, and we have revised and extended it in this new edition.

For some users who expected the brief traditional definitions, COBUILD definitions were so generous that they seemed almost wasteful. But when you look closely at the way the definitions are phrased you will see that every word is chosen to illustrate some aspect of the meaning. And as far as possible, the words used in a definition are more frequent than the word being defined.

Shorter definitions just do not tell you as much. For example, the first verb sense of **mean** might be defined as just 'signify', which is true, but is not all that can be said. The COBUILD Dictionary puts this in the setting 'If you want to know...' – that is to say such a sense arises when someone is seeking information. The word 'if' indicates that this is an option, but a perfectly normal one, and 'you' tells us that it is not characteristic of any particular group of people (compare 'If a *policeman* arrests you...'). Then the definition says that you may want to know the meaning of a 'word, code, signal or gesture', indicating that these are the typical kinds of subject that this sense of **mean** will be found with. Only after all this information do we come to the equivalent of 'signify': 'what it refers to or what message it conveys'. So there are 12 words before the headword in this sense, but every one of them conveys vital information that would be very difficult to put into a shorter definition.

Hence there is no apology for full sentence definitions – far from it. Users expect more and more from their dictionaries, and in particular want to gain confidence in using a word by looking it up in a dictionary. The kind of help that the COBUILD definitions give is of great importance.

I hope, then, that this new edition is found to be even more useful, and easier to use, than the one it replaces; there are more words and more senses, simplified notes on grammar, new features showing frequency and pragmatics. Above all, it refers throughout to the massive authority of The Bank of English, and so I can offer it with confidence.

No book is perfect, however, and I would like to repeat my request for comments and criticisms of this new book. We have established an e-mail address (editors @ cobuild. collins. co. uk) to make it easier for users to correspond with us.

I would also like to thank personally all those who have allowed their texts to be placed in The Bank of English. Without them there would be no dictionary.

John Sinclair
Editor in Chief
Professor of Modern English Language
University of Birmingham

The Bank of English

The Bank of English is a collection, or corpus, of over 200 million words of written and spoken English held on computer for the study of language use. The first edition of the Collins COBUILD English Language Dictionary (1987) was the first dictionary to present a comprehensive account of English vocabulary derived from direct observation of the way the language is being used. Since then, the COBUILD team has continued to collect texts from all kinds of sources to create the largest English corpus of its kind in the world – The Bank of English.

The Bank of English contains a wide range of different types of writing and speech from hundreds of different sources. The material is up to date, with most of the texts dating from 1990 onwards. Although most of the sources are British, approximately 25% of our data comes from American English sources, and about 5% from other native varieties of English – such as Australian and Singapore.

Written texts come from newspapers, magazines, fiction and non-fiction books, brochures, leaflets, reports, and letters. Two-thirds of the corpus is made up of media language: newspapers, magazines, radio and TV; this is a significant category in view of the millions of people who read and listen to the language presented in the media. International, national, and local publications are included to capture a broad range of subject matter and style. There are thousands of books and special interest magazines in The Bank of English which reflect hundreds of topics of general interest, from aerobics to zoology. However, technical or scientific textbooks, manuals, directories, and so on are not included in the corpus.

Informal spoken language is represented by recordings of everyday casual conversation, meetings, interviews, and discussions. Currently, about 15 million words of The Bank of English are transcriptions of spoken language of this kind. These are selected to include a wide range of subject matter and speech situations.

Using The Bank of English

The purpose of collecting all this valuable data on our computers was to enable the lexicographers – the dictionary writers – to have access to as much information as possible about each of the words being defined. Of course, lexicographers are chosen because of their skill with language, but even the most experienced lexicographer cannot deduce from his or her own intuition all the relevant facts about all the words in the language. The corpus, and the software we use to analyse it, helps the COBUILD team to sort through the information and gain valuable insights into the way words are actually used: their meanings, their typical grammar patterns, and the ways in which they relate to other words.

The corpus lies at the heart of each entry. As a lexicographer begins writing an entry, he or she can call up onto the computer screen all the occurrences of the word in question. These appear in the form of concordance lines, and the lines can be examined in a number of different ways to show different aspects of the word's behaviour.

Here, for example, are some concordance lines for **play**, **plays**, **playing**, and **played**. This is, of course, only a small sample of the thousands of lines available, but you will see how lexicographers are able to use the lines to see the behaviour of a word. For example, this sample seems to shows that **play** often occurs with *role* or *part*, in the expressions *play a role* and *play a part*.

Further investigation confirms this finding, and shows that *important* or words that mean 'important' often occur in front of *role* or *part*.

```
     ...It would appear that hormones play a crucial role in precipitating...
         ...area, and politics has to play a part in the Deputy Speaker's...
       ...it wasn't him. He obviously played a role, but it was those young...
           ...on this issue would He's playing a waiting-game He'll hope to...
   ...unknown, but hereditary factors play an important part in triggering...
 ...take such a step if it wanted to play an active part in the search for...
      ..Every day this week we'll be playing an exclusive track from the...
...developments.New Zealand has been playing an active role in getting the...
     ...An eccentric cricket game was played at Timsgarry in the Outer...
         ...Butcher was forced to quit playing because of a knee injury after...
     ...keeps the same tunes the band played before Sandmelle was born...
        ...and most popularly used to play computer games...
     ...teams. Our top teams already play far too many games and need to...
     ...the full England squad.Taylor plays for Northamptonshire; Ilott for...
     ...role that the government has played in gathering investment...
        ...eyes. 'He bet on games he played in. Sometimes he bet on his...
```

Many words have more than one grammatical word class and it is often helpful for the lexicographers to look at only one word class at a time. In order to help them do this, software has been developed which shows the word class of the keyword in each corpus line. The lexicographers can look at either all the data, with the word class code , or they can ask to see only verbs, nouns, and so on. This is how we arrived at the lines for play you saw above. Here are some lines for the word light, which are coded according to their word class. In the sample, NN means 'noun', JJ means 'adjective' and VB means 'verb'.

```
NN        ...their car at a traffic light, stripped and beaten, and shot...
NN     ...Later, alone, by lantern light and by flashlight she strained...
JJ       ...Possessed of a lovely, light gracefulness, Brook's...
NN          ...as are all tips. If light conditions change, simply slot...
NN      ...on the river. There was light and air to be sure, big...
JJ               ...4.50 metre,looks light and fresh and is also...
NN        ...the Haggadah in a new light. And whenever we do, we find...
VB     ...pile it up with peat and light it you see. Er er er...
NN      ...Photograph. AS the cold light of dawn slowly broke over...
```

Software such as this allows lexicographers to make decisions about the different senses of words, the language of the definitions, the choice of examples, and the grammatical information given. We could, of course, make statements about these things without a corpus, but having a corpus enables us to make them with confidence and accuracy. And the larger the corpus, the more confident and accurate we can be.

The result is a dictionary which describes with authority the way the English language works in the 1990s.

Frequency bands

In this dictionary, we have added some new information from The Bank of English – information on frequency. This means that when you look up a word, you can immediately see how important it is.

There are five frequency bands, shown by black diamonds in the Extra Column. The most frequent words have five black diamonds, the next most frequent four, and so on. Words which occur less frequently, but which still deserve an entry in the dictionary, do not have any black diamonds.

Note that the individual sections of words which have been treated as superheadwords are given their own frequency bands. Words which belong to recognizable sets, such as nationality adjectives, have generally been put into the same band.

◆◆◆◆◆ Many of the words in this band are the common grammar words such as **the**, **and**, **of**, and **to,** which are an essential part of the way we put words together. Also in this band are the very frequent vocabulary items, such as **like**, **go**, **paper**, **return**, and so on. There are approximately 700 words in this band.

◆◆◆◆◇ This band includes words such as **argue**, **bridge**, **danger**, **female**, **obvious**, and **sea**. There are approximately 1200 words in this band.

The words in the top two bands account for approximately 75% of all English usage – so their importance is obvious.

◆◆◆◇◇ This band includes words such as **aggressive**, **medicine**, and **tactic**. There are approximately 1500 words in this band.

Knowing the words in this band extends the range of topics which you can talk about.

◆◆◇◇◇ This band includes words such as **accuracy**, **duration**, **miserable**, **puzzle**, and **rope**. There are approximately 3200 words in this band.

◆◇◇◇◇ This band includes words such as **abundant**, **crossroads**, **fearless**, and **missionary**. There are approximately 8100 words in this band.

The bottom two bands contain words which you are likely to use less frequently than words in the other bands, but which are still important.

The entries that have no frequency diamond are words which you will probably read or hear rather than words which you will often need to use yourself. They are mostly nouns, verbs, and adjectives. Of course, there are thousands of words which we could have included in the dictionary, but because it is based on a corpus you can be sure that we have chosen only those which you are most likely to come across.

The words in the five frequency bands are of immense importance to learners because they make up 95% of all spoken and written English. These frequency bands therefore will be an invaluable aid to anyone who is interested in using natural English.

Guide to the Dictionary Entries

Romeo
romp
romper suit
roof

Order of entries: in alphabetical order, taking no notice of capital letters, hyphens, apostrophes, accents, or spaces between words.

reflector /rɪflektə/ **reflectors**
1 A **reflector** is a small piece of specially patterned glass or plastic which is fitted to the back of a bicycle or car or to a post beside the road, and which glows when light shines on it.

Headwords: the main form of the headword appears in large bold face letters, starting in the left hand margin.

rabbinical /ræbɪnɪkəl/ or **rabbinic** /ræbɪnɪk/.

Variant forms of a headword are given after the headword, in smaller bold face letters.

re-form, re-forms, re-forming, re-formed; also spelled **reform.**

Alternative spellings are given at the end of the information about the headword.

reformist /rɪfɔːmɪst/ **reformists.**

refrain /rɪfreɪn/ **refrains, refraining, refrained**

runny /rʌni/ **runnier, runniest**

Inflected forms: given in smaller bold face letters, for noun, verb, adjective, and adverb forms.

revel /revəl/ **revels, revelling, revelled;** spelled **reveling, reveled** in American English.

run /rʌn/ **runs, running, ran.** The form **run** is used in the present tense and is also the past participle of the verb.

Notes about inflected forms.

refresh /rɪfreʃ/ **refreshes, refreshing, refreshed**

Pronunciation: see pages xxviii-xxxix for details.

rewind, rewinds, rewinding, rewound. The verb is pronounced /riːwaɪnd/. The noun is pronounced /riːwaɪnd/.

Notes about pronunciation.

refreshing /rɪfreʃɪŋ/
1 You say that something is **refreshing** when it is pleasantly different from what you are used to. *It's refreshing to hear somebody speaking common sense... It made a refreshing change to see a good old-fashioned movie.* ♦ **refreshingly** *He was refreshingly honest.*
2 A **refreshing** bath or drink makes you feel energetic or cool again after you have been uncomfortably tired or hot. *Herbs have been used for centuries to make refreshing drinks.*

Paragraph numbers: for words with more than one meaning or use.

Definitions: given in full sentences, showing the commonest ways in which the headword is used. See pages xviii-xix for details.

5 A **radio** is a piece of equipment that is used for sending and receiving messages. *Judge Bruce Laughland praised the courage of the young constable, who managed to raise the alarm on his radio... The radio message was brief.*
6 If you **radio** someone, you send a message to them by radio. *The officer radioed for advice... A few minutes after take-off, the pilot radioed that a fire had broken out.*

Examples: in italics, taken from The Bank of English. See pages xxii-xxiii for details.

refusal /rɪfjuːzᵊl/ **refusals**
1 Someone's **refusal** to do something or **refusal** of something is the fact of them showing or saying that they will not do it, allow it, grant it, or accept it. *Her country suffered through her refusal to accept change... His letter in response to her request had contained a firm refusal. ...the Council's refusal of planning permission for a major shopping centre... We would appreciate confirmation of your refusal of our invitation to take part.*

play /pleɪ/ **plays, playing, played**
17 If something or someone **plays a part** or **plays a role** in a situation, they are involved in it and have an effect on it. *They played a part in the life of their community... The UN would play a major role in monitoring a ceasefire. ...the role played by diet in disease.*

Derived words: formed with common suffixes such as '-ly' or '-ness' and not involving a change in meaning are given after the diamond symbol ♦.

regal /riːgᵊl/. If you describe something as **regal**, you mean that it is suitable for a king or queen, because it is very splendid or dignified. *He sat with such regal dignity... Never has she looked more regal.* ♦ **regally** *He inclined his head regally.*

raw /rɔː/ **rawer, rawest**
5 If you describe something as **raw**, you mean that it is simple, powerful, and real. *...the raw power of instinct. ...the raw vitality of his earlier painting.* ♦ **rawness** *Recorded almost live, there's a certain seductive rawness about the whole thing.*

Changes in word class which do not involve any change in meaning are introduced by a triangle symbol ►.

1 If something **reeks** of something else, usually something unpleasant, it smells very strongly of it. *Your breath reeks of stale cigar smoke... The entire house reeked for a long time.* ► Also a noun. *He smelt the reek of whisky.*

The triangle symbol ► is also used to introduce a meaning which is closely connected with another meaning.

rand /rænd/ **rands; rand** can also be used as the plural form. The **rand** is the unit of currency used in South Africa. *...12 million rand.* ► **The rand** is also used to refer to the South African currency system. *The rand slumped by 22% against the dollar.*

The triangle symbol ► is also used to introduce phrasal verbs which have the same meaning as the verb which is the headword.

6 When a horse **rears**, it moves the front part of its body upwards, so that its front legs are high in the air and it is standing on its back legs. *The horse reared and threw off its rider.* ► **Rear up** means the same as **rear**. *...an army pony that didn't rear up at the sound of gunfire.*

6 You can use **as regards** to indicate the subject that is being talked or written about. *As regards the war, Haig believed in victory at any price.*
7 You can use **with regard to** or **in regard to** to indicate the subject that is being talked or written about. *The department is reviewing its policy with regard to immunisation.*
8 You can use **in this regard** or **in that regard** to refer back to something you have just said. *In this regard nothing has changed... I may have made a mistake in that regard.*

Phrases: usually the last paragraph or paragraphs of an entry, before phrasal verbs.

5 Reflection is careful thought about a particular topic. Your **reflections** are your thoughts about a particular topic. *After days of reflection she decided to write back... He paused, absorbed by his reflections.* • If someone admits or accepts something **on reflection**, they admit or accept it after having thought carefully about it. *On reflection, he says, he very much regrets the comments.*

If the phrase is closely connected with another use or meaning, it may be included within the same paragraph, after the symbol •.

reel in. If you **reel in** something such as a fish, you pull it towards you by winding around a reel the wire or line that it is attached to. *Gleacher reeled in the first fish... The crew of the US space shuttle Atlantis were preparing to reel in the craft.*
reel off. If you **reel off** information, you repeat it from memory quickly and easily. *She reeled off the titles of a dozen or so of the novels.*

Phrasal verbs: in alphabetical order at the end of an entry. Sometimes phrasal verbs are explained earlier in the entry, after the symbol ► (see above).

2 If you **rustle** something **up**, you provide or obtain it quickly, with very little planning; an informal use.

rutabaga /ruːtəbeɪgə/ **rutabagas.** In American English, a **rutabaga** is a round yellow root vegetable with a brown or purple skin. The usual British word is **swede.**

Style and usage: information about who uses a word or expression, and in what situation. See pages xx-xxi for details.

rata /rɑːtə/. See **pro rata.**

1 Rustling is the activity of stealing farm animals, especially cattle; used especially in American English. *Her thievery was confined mostly to cattle rustling and horse stealing.*
2 See also **rustle.**

5 • to **rant and rave**: see **rant.**

59 • to **run amok**: see **amok.** • to **make your blood run cold**: see **blood.** • to **run counter to** something: see **counter.** • to **run** its **course**: see **course.** • to **cut and run**: see **cut.** • to **run deep**: see **deep.** • to **run** someone **to earth**: see **earth.**

Cross-references: indicating that relevant information can be found at another entry.

Cross-references often follow the symbol •.

Extra Column

In this dictionary, as in some other COBUILD dictionaries, we have given certain information in the Extra Column so that it does not interfere with the explanations and examples. This makes all the information easier to find and read.

Frequency information: see page xiii for details.

refrigerator /rɪfrɪdʒəreɪtəʳ/ **refrigerators.** A **refrigerator** is a large container which is kept cool inside, usually by electricity, so that the food and drink in it stays fresh. ◆◇◇◇◇ N-COUNT =fridge

reggae /reɡeɪ/. **Reggae** is a kind of West Indian popular music with a very strong beat. *Many people will remember Bob Marley for providing them with their first taste of Reggae music.* ◆◆◇◇◇ N-UNCOUNT: oft N n

regime /reɪʒiːm/ **regimes** ◆◆◆◇◇
1 If you refer to a government or system of running a country as a **regime**, you are critical of it because you think it is not democratic and uses unacceptable methods. *...the collapse of Communist regimes in Eastern Europe... Pujol was imprisoned and tortured under the Franco regime.* N-COUNT: oft supp N PRAGMATICS

Grammar: see pages xxiv-xxxiii for details, where all word classes, restrictions, extensions, and patterns are explained.

1 **Relations** between people, groups, or countries are contacts between them and the way in which they behave towards each other. *Greece has established full diplomatic relations with Israel... Apparently relations between husband and wife had not improved... The company has a track record of good employee relations.* N-COUNT: usu pl

2 If organs or tissues **regenerate** or if something **regenerates** them, they heal and grow again after they have been damaged. *Nerve cells have limited ability to regenerate if destroyed... Newts can regenerate their limbs.* ♦ **regeneration** *Vitamin B assists in red-blood-cell regeneration.* V-ERG V V n N-UNCOUNT

Synonyms: words which mean approximately the same as the word being explained are given after the symbol =.

re-examine, re-examines, re-examining, re-examined. If a person or group of people **re-examines** their ideas, beliefs, or attitudes, they think about them carefully because they are no longer sure if they are correct. ◆◇◇◇◇ VERB =reassess V n

Antonyms: words which mean approximately the opposite of the word being explained are given after the symbol ≠.

radicalism /rædɪkəlɪzəm/. **Radicalism** is radical beliefs, ideas, or behaviour. *Williams himself was a rather curious mixture of radicalism and conservatism.* ◆◇◇◇◇ N-UNCOUNT ≠conservatism

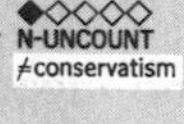

Pragmatics: see pages xxxiv-xxxvii for details.

2 If you say that something **reeks** of unpleasant ideas, feelings, or practices, you disapprove of it because it gives a firm impression that it involves those ideas, feelings, or practices. *The whole thing reeks of hypocrisy.* VERB PRAGMATICS V of n

Definitions

Most books are written in sentences, not phrases. This book is no exception. Indeed, it is a feature of all COBUILD dictionaries that the definitions (or explanations, as we often call them) are written in full sentences, using vocabulary and grammatical structures that occur naturally with the word being explained. We have chosen to explain words in this way because we think that this makes them much easier to read and understand. It also enables us to give a lot of information about the way a word or meaning is used by speakers of the language.

The definitions are written in the sort of direct and informal style that teachers use when explaining words, or that friends use with each other. Whenever possible, words are explained using simpler and more common words. This gives us a natural defining vocabulary with most words in our definitions being amongst the 2,500 commonest words of English.

The use of bold face

The word, expression, or use being explained is in **bold face**. Here are the definitions for **cloudburst**, **acetic acid**, and the phrase **spill the beans**:

> A **cloudburst** is a sudden, very heavy fall of rain.
>
> **Acetic acid** is a colourless acid. It is the main substance in vinegar.
>
> If you **spill the beans**, you tell someone something that people have been trying to keep secret.

When a word is always used with a particular determiner or preposition, the determiner or preposition is also in bold face. For example, you always use the word **standstill** with the indefinite article **a**:

> If movement or activity comes to or is brought to **a standstill**, it stops completely.

And meaning 2 of **keen** is always used with the preposition **on**:

> If you are **keen on** something, you like it a lot and are very enthusiastic about it.

Information about collocates and structures

In our definitions, we try to show the typical collocates of a word: that is, the other words that are used with the word we are defining. For example, the definition of meaning 2 of the adjective **savoury** says:

> **Savoury** food has a salty or spicy flavour rather than a sweet one.

This shows that you use the adjective **savoury** to describe food, rather than other kinds of thing.

Meaning 1 of the adjective **bitter** says:

> In a **bitter** argument or conflict, people argue very angrily or fight very fiercely.

The definition shows that this meaning of **bitter** is used to describe arguments and conflicts, and so it is used with words that mean 'argument' or 'conflict'.

Meaning 32 of the verb **take** says:

> If you **take** a test or examination, you do it in order to obtain a qualification.

This shows that you use a human subject with the verb, and the object is a word such as 'test' or 'examination', or a word that means the same as 'test' or 'examination'.

Finally, meaning 1 of the verb **wag** says:

> When a dog **wags** its tail, it repeatedly waves its tail from side to side.

This shows that the subject of meaning 1 of **wag** refers to a dog, rather than a human or any other kind of animal, and the object of the verb is 'tail'.

Information about grammar

The definitions also give information about the grammatical structures that a word is used with, by explaining the word as it occurs in its typical grammatical structure or structures. For example, meaning 1 of **unaffected** says:

> If someone or something is **unaffected** by an event or occurrence, they are not changed by it in any way.

This shows **unaffected** in its typical structure, after a link verb such as 'be', and followed by a prepositional phrase with 'by'. It also shows that both people and things can be **unaffected** by events.

Similarly, meaning 1 of the adjective **candid** says:

> When you are **candid** about something or with someone, you speak honestly.

This shows that you use **candid** with the preposition 'about' when you are mentioning the thing that you are speaking honestly about. You also use **candid** with the preposition 'with' when you are mentioning the person who you are speaking to.

Other definitions show other kinds of structure. Meaning 1 of the verb **soften** says:

> If you **soften** something or if it **softens**, it becomes less hard, stiff, or firm.

This shows that the verb, which is an ergative verb, is used both transitively and intransitively in this meaning. In the transitive use, you have a human subject and a non-human object. In the intransitive use, you have a non-human subject.

Finally, meaning 1 of **compel** says:

> If a situation, a rule, or a person **compels** you to do something, they force you to do it.

This shows you what kinds of subject and object to use with **compel**, and it also shows that you typically use the verb in a structure with a to-infinitive.

The important grammatical information contained in the definitions is also set out in the Extra Column.

Information about context and usage

In addition to information about collocation and grammar, definitions also give information about contexts of use. For example, meaning 4 of **ace** shows that it is used when you are talking about tennis:

> In tennis, an **ace** is a serve which is so fast that the other player cannot reach the ball.

Meaning 3 of **absentee** shows that this use relates to elections in the United States:

> In the United States, if you vote by **absentee** ballot, you vote in advance because you will be away on the day of an election.

Other definitions show that a word or expression is mainly used to convey your evaluation of something, for example to express your approval or disapproval. For example, here are the definitions of **tiresome** and **unforgivable**:

> If you describe someone or something as **tiresome**, you mean that you find them irritating or boring.

> If you say that something is **unforgivable**, you mean that it is very bad, cruel, or socially unacceptable.

In these definitions, the expressions 'if you describe', 'if you say that', and 'you mean that' indicate that these words are used subjectively, rather than objectively. More information about this is given in the section on **Pragmatics**, on pages xxxiv-xxxvii.

Other kinds of definition

We sometimes explain grammatical words and other function words by paraphrasing the word in context. For example, meaning 3 of **through** says:

> To go **through** a town, area, or country means to travel across it or in it.

In many cases, it is impossible to paraphrase the word, and so we explain its function instead. For example, meaning 1 of **the** says:

> You use **the** at the beginning of noun groups to refer to someone or something that you have already mentioned or identified.

The definition of meaning 1 of **sorry** says:

> You say **'Sorry'** or **'I'm sorry'** as a way of apologizing to someone for something that you have done which has upset them or caused them difficulties.

Similarly, the definition of **unfortunately** explains its function as well as its meaning:

> You can use **unfortunately** to introduce or refer to a statement when you consider that it is sad or disappointing, or when you want to express regret.

Lastly, some definitions are expressed as if they are cross-references. For example:

> **esp.** is a written abbreviation for **especially**.

If you need to know more about the word **especially**, you look at the entry for that word.

Style and Usage

Some words or meanings are used mainly by particular groups of people, or in particular social contexts. In this dictionary, when it is relevant, the definitions also give information about the kind of people who are likely to use a word or expression, and the type of social situation in which it is used. This information is usually placed at the end of the definition.

> A **blockbuster** is a film or book that is very popular and successful, usually because of the exciting or sensational events featured in it; an informal word.
>
> **Verve** is lively and forceful enthusiasm; used in written English.

aubergine /oʊbəʳʒiːn/ **aubergines.** In British English, an **aubergine** is a vegetable with a smooth, dark purple skin. The usual American word is **eggplant**. ◆◇◇◇◇ N-VAR

bookstore /bʊkstɔːʳ/ **bookstores.** A **bookstore** is a shop where books are sold; used mainly in American English. The usual British word is **bookshop**. ◆◇◇◇◇ N-COUNT

demonstrable /dɪmɒnstrəbᵊl/. A **demonstrable** fact or quality can be shown to be true or to exist; a formal word. *An additive is permitted in food only where there is a genuine demonstrable need for it... Despite its demonstrable speed and safety, the boat failed to become popular.* ADJ: usu ADJ n
♦ **demonstrably** /dɪmɒnstrəbli/. *...demonstrably false statements.* ADV

decaf /diːkæf/ **decafs;** also spelled **decaff. Decaf** is decaffeinated coffee; an informal word. *He only drinks decaf.* N-MASS

cash-starved. A **cash-starved** company or organization does not have enough money to operate properly, usually because another organization, such as the government, is not giving them the money that they need; used in journalism. *We are heading for a crisis, with cash-starved councils forced to cut back on vital community services.* ADJ: usu ADJ n

Although English is spoken as a first language in many parts of the world, two groups of speakers are especially important, those who speak British English and those who speak American English. Most of the books, newspapers, radio and TV programmes, and teaching materials for international use are produced in Britain or the USA.

In general, this dictionary focuses on British English, but when there is sufficient evidence in the Bank of English, differences in British and American usage are indicated.

Geographical labels

British: used mainly by speakers and writers in Britain, and in other places where British English is used or taught; e.g. *aubergine, bookshop, unit trust.*

American: used mainly by speakers and writers in the USA, and in other places where American English is used or taught; e.g. *bookstore, eggplant, mutual fund.*

Style labels

formal: used mainly in official situations, or by political and business organizations, or when speaking or writing to people in authority; e.g. *belated, demonstrable.*

informal: used mainly in informal situations, conversations, and personal letters; e.g. *decaf, elbow room.*

journalism: used mainly in journalism; e.g. *abuzz, cash-starved.*

Here is the entry from the dictionary for the word **motive**:

> **motive** /moʊtɪv/ **motives**. Your **motive** for doing something is your reason for doing it. *Police have ruled out robbery as a motive for the killing. ...the motives and objectives of British foreign policy... The doctor's motive was to bring an end to his patient's suffering.*
>
> ◆◆◇◇◇ N-COUNT: oft N prep

As you will see there are three examples, each one showing a different grammatical pattern. Below are some concordance lines from the Bank of English for the word **motive**. Notice that the computer has arranged the extracts so that the word **motive** is in the middle of each line. The actual examples used in the dictionary entry are highlighted so that you can see how the entry has been compiled

```
...source that might help explain a motive for the attack, which killed at...
  ...not so far been able to find a motive for the attacks -  The most...
 ...that Houston was seeking for a motive for the deaths of Gil and Hilton...
   ...that way. It also gives us a motive for the killing on the island...
      ...A UNICEF spokesman said a motive for the killing had yet to be...
   ...have ruled out robbery as a motive for the killing. Commandant...
   ...Chief F.L. Giacomozzi says a motive for the killings may never be...
  ...a word of it. But I've got a motive for the murder that may not have...
      ...unable to come up with a motive for the murder in Bedford...
        ...ruled out robbery as a motive for the murder of British mother...

   ...and at worst trivialises the motives and merits of education. This...
 ...acquisition of land obeyed only motives and objectives of a rigorously...
  ...to Bismarck, p. 297.99 On the motives and objectives of British...
    ...particular attention to the motives and objectives of Hitler within...
  ...deal of speculation about the motives and objectives of Adenauer and...
       ...in a different form, the motives and passions of the first...
  ...what they showed but also the motives and predicaments of the artists...
     ...types but also examine the motives and strategies of others in an...

    ...advancement of science, the motive was the `project'. When uteri...
     ...too vague - But the actual motive was to prevent the Soviet ship...
 ...prosecution, said the doctor's motive was to bring an end" to his...
        ...most people reckon the motive was to provoke a confrontation...
      ...of  2,500, said her prime motive was to protect her family...
       ...but Sharon says her only motive was to `make someone happy. I don't...
 ...When the stamps were sold, the motive was to achieve liquidity. The...
         ...Front. He said his main motive was to win a share of government...
...Colin alleged that Mr Branson's motive was to `secure publicity'...
 ...be some dispute as to what the motive was ... whether it was a communal...
```

You can see from these sets of lines that the examples given in the dictionary are typical of how the word **motive** has been used in the texts in The Bank of English.

The first example shows that we often use **motive** in the pattern 'a motive for', followed by a noun which expresses a violent action such as a **killing**.

The second example shows the pattern 'the motives of', followed by a noun group which describes a person or organization, or their ideas and plans.

The third example shows that **motive** can also be followed by a link verb such as **be**, and a to-infinitive structure which states what the motive is.

At COBUILD, great emphasis is placed on describing and explaining the language accurately, through the evidence in our corpus. The Bank of English helps our dictionaries to be more effective and reliable. Our choices of representative examples, taken from the corpus, will give students and teachers information which, we believe, they will find very useful.

Grammar

Introduction

For each use of each word in this dictionary, there is grammar information in the Extra Column. For a very few words, such as abbreviations, contractions and some words of foreign origin, no grammar is given, because the words do not belong to any word class, or are used so freely that every example could be given a different word class, e.g. *AD, ditto, mpg, must've.*

The grammar information that is given is of three types:

1. the word class of the word: e.g. **VERB, N-COUNT, ADJ, ADJ-GRADED, QUANT**
2. restrictions or extensions to its behaviour, compared to other words of that word class: e.g. **usu passive, usu sing, also no det**
3. the patterns that the word most frequently occurs in: e.g. **V n, N *of* n, ADJ that, ADV with v**

For all word classes except verbs, the patterns are given immediately after the word class and any restrictions or extensions. For verbs, the patterns are given next to the examples and in the same order as the examples, so that they are easier to see and understand.

The word class of the word being explained is in CAPITAL LETTERS. The order of items in a pattern is the order in which they normally occur in a sentence. Words in *italics* are words (not word classes) that occur in the pattern. Alternatives are separated by a slash (/). For example:

V n means that the word being explained is a verb (**V**), and it is followed in the sentence by a noun group (**n**).

N *of* n means that the word being explained is a noun (**N**), and it is followed in the sentence by the word *of* and another noun or noun group (**n**).

ADV adj/adv means that the word being explained is an adverb (**ADV**), and it is followed in the sentence by an adjective (**adj**) or (/) another adverb (**adv**).

Word classes

ADJ **ungraded adjective**

An ungraded adjective is never or very rarely used with an adverb or phrase indicating degree, e.g. *He has been absent from his desk for two weeks.*

ADJ-COMPAR **comparative adjective**

A comparative adjective is an adjective that must be in the comparative form, e.g. *Earlier reports of gunshots have not been substantiated.*

ADJ-GRADED **graded adjective**

A graded adjective is sometimes used with an adverb or phrase indicating degree, such as *a bit, as...as, enough, equally, how, less, more, most, particularly, very, rather, so, too;* e.g. *Police have stressed that this is the most accurate description of the killer to date.* Many graded adjectives have comparative and superlative forms, usually made by adding *-er* and *-est* to the base form of the adjective, e.g. *cold, colder, coldest.*

ADJ-SUPERL **superlative adjective**

A superlative adjective is an adjective that must be in the superlative form, e.g. *The eldest child was a daughter called Fiona.*

Adjective patterns

ADJ n The adjective is always used before a noun, e.g. *...a governmental agency for providing financial aid to developing countries.*

usu ADJ n The adjective is usually used before a noun. It is sometimes used after a link verb.

v-link ADJ The adjective is used after a link verb such as *be* or *feel*, e.g. *She was feeling unwell.* Adjectives with this label are sometimes used in other positions such as after the object of a verb such as *make* or *keep*, but never before a noun.

usu v-link ADJ The adjective is usually used after a link verb. It is sometimes used before a noun.

ADJ after v The adjective is used after a verb that is not a link verb, e.g. *Alan came running barefoot through the house.*

n ADJ The adjective comes immediately after a noun e.g. *...a trade union leader not a politician proper.*

det ADJ The adjective comes immediately after a determiner and before any other adjectives, and sometimes comes before numbers, e.g. *...a product which cannot be traded outside a certain limited geographic area.*

If the dictionary does not show that an adjective is used only or mainly in the pattern **ADJ n** and **v-link ADJ**, this means that the adjective is used freely in both patterns.

These main adjective patterns are sometimes combined with other patterns, using the notations shown on the inside of the cover. For example, **ADJ-GRADED: oft ADJ *to* n** means that the adjective has both the **ADJ n** and the **v-link ADJ** patterns, and when it follows a link verb it often has the pattern **ADJ *to* n**, e.g. *They want to write literary books that are accessible to a general audience.*

ADV **ungraded adverb**

An ungraded adverb is never or very rarely used with an adverb or phrase indicating degree, e.g. *Much of our behaviour is biologically determined.*

ADV-BRD-NEG **broad negative adverb**

A broad negative adverb is an adverb that is nearly negative in meaning, e.g. *I hardly know you.*

ADV-COMPAR **comparative adverb**

A comparative adverb is an adverb that must be in the comparative form, e.g. *Inflation is below 5% and set to fall further.*

ADV-GRADED **graded adverb**

A graded adverb is sometimes used with an adverb or phrase indicating degree, such as *a bit, as...as, enough, equally, how, less, more, rather, so, too, very*. A few graded adverbs have comparative and superlative forms e.g. *She blinked hard. You must work harder. ...countries hardest hit by the rise in oil prices.*

ADV-INDEF **indefinite adverb**

An indefinite adverb is an adverb with an indefinite meaning, such as *somewhere, everywhere.*

ADV-SUPERL **superlative adverb**

A superlative adverb is an adverb that must be in the superlative form, e.g. *The risk of thunder is greatest in those areas furthest from the coast.*

Adverb patterns

For the more frequent adverbs in this dictionary, you will see in the Extra Column all the patterns that the adverb occurs in. For some less common adverbs, only the most usual patterns are given, e.g. **ADV-GRADED:** usu **ADV** after **V**. If no patterns are given, the example shows the most frequent pattern.

For some adverbs in this dictionary, you will see two sets of patterns, the second set introduced by *usu* or *oft*, e.g. everywhere 1: **n ADV, ADV after v, *be* ADV, oft *from* ADV, ADV cl/group**. This means that any of the patterns in the second set can occur in combination with any of the patterns in the first set.

AUX **auxiliary verb**

An auxiliary verb is used with another verb to add particular meanings to that verb, for example, to form the continuous aspect or the passive voice, or to form negatives and interrogatives. The verbs *be, do, get* and *have* have some senses in which they are auxiliary verbs.

COLOUR **colour word**

A colour word refers to a colour. It is like an adjective, e.g. *the blue sky... The sky was blue*, and also like a noun, e.g. *She was dressed in red. ...several shades of yellow.*

COMB **combining form**

A combining form is a word which is joined with another word, usually with a hyphen, to form compounds, e.g. *grey-haired, lemon-flavoured, heat-resistant.* The word class of the compound is also given, e.g. **COMB in ADJ-GRADED, COMB in N-UNCOUNT.**

CONJ-COORD **co-ordinating conjunction**

A co-ordinating conjunction usually links elements of the same grammatical type, such as two clauses, two groups, or two words, e.g. *She and Simon had already gone... It is completely waterproof, yet light and comfortable.*

CONJ-COORD-NEG **negative co-ordinating conjunction**

A negative co-ordinating conjunction is a co-ordinating conjunction with a negative meaning. The two negative co-ordinating conjunctions are *neither* and *nor.*

CONJ-SUBORD **subordinating conjunction**

A subordinating conjunction is used at the beginning of a subordinate clause. A subordinate clause is a clause which cannot normally be a complete sentence on its own. E.g. *She gets very upset if I exclude her from anything... Racing was halted for an hour while the track was repaired.*

CONVENTION **convention**

A convention is a word or a fixed phrase which is used in conversation, for example when greeting someone, apologizing, or replying, e.g. *hello, sorry, no comment.*

DET **determiner**

A determiner is a word that is used at the beginning of a noun group, e.g. *a tray, more time, some books, this amount.*

DET-NEG **negative determiner**

A negative determiner is a determiner with a negative meaning. The two negative determiners are *no* and *neither.*

DET-POSS **possessive determiner**

A possessive determiner is a determiner which is used to say who or what something belongs or relates to, e.g. *his face, my flat.*

DET-POSS-QUEST **question possessive determiner**

A question possessive determiner is a possessive determiner which is used to begin a question. The only word of this kind is *whose, e.g. Whose car are they in?*

DET-QUEST **question determiner**

A question determiner is a determiner which begins a question, e.g. *Which book do you want?*

ERG see **V-ERG**

EXCLAM **exclamation**

An exclamation is a word or phrase which is spoken suddenly, loudly, or emphatically in order to express a strong emotion such as shock or anger. Exclamations are often followed by exclamation marks, e.g. *good heavens! ouch!*

FRACTION **fraction**

A fraction is used in numbers, e.g. *three and a half, two and two thirds*; before *of* and a noun group, e.g. *half of the apple, a third of the biscuits, three eighths of the pie*; after *in* or *into*, e.g. *in half, into thirds*. A fraction is also used like a count noun, e.g. *two halves, the first quarter of the year*.

LINK see **V-LINK**

MODAL **modal**

A modal is used before the infinitive form of a verb, e.g. *You may go*. In questions, it comes before the subject, e.g. *Must you speak?* In negatives, it comes before the negative word, e.g. *They would not like this*. It does not inflect, for example, it does not take an *-s* in the third person singular, e.g. *She can swim*.

N-COUNT **count noun**

A count noun has a plural form, usually made by adding *-s*. When it is singular, it must have a determiner in front of it, such as *the, her,* or *such*, e.g. *My cat is getting fatter... She's a good friend*.

N-COUNT-COLL **collective count noun**

A collective count noun is a count noun which refers to a group of people or things. It behaves like a count noun, but when it is in the singular form it can be used with either a singular or plural verb, e.g. *Their audience are much younger than the average... The British audience has a huge appetite for serials... Audiences are becoming more selective.*

N-FAMILY **family noun**

A family noun refers to a member of a family, e.g. *father, mummy,* and *granny*. Family nouns are count nouns which are typically used in the singular, usually follow a possessive determiner. They are also vocative nouns. They are also proper nouns, used with no determiner, e.g. *My mummy likes marzipan... Tell them I didn't do it, Mummy... Mummy's always telling me I'm too old for dolls.*

N-IN-NAMES **noun in names**

The noun occurs in names of people, things, or institutions.

N-MASS **mass noun**

A mass noun typically combines the behaviour of both count and uncount nouns in the same sense. It is used like an uncount noun to refer to a substance. It is used like a count noun to refer to a brand or type, e.g. *Rinse in cold water to remove any remaining detergent...Wash it in hot water with a good detergent... We used several different detergents in our stain-removal tests*. Other examples of mass nouns are: *shampoo, butter, bleach.*

N-PLURAL **plural noun**

A plural noun is always plural, and is used with plural verbs. If a pronoun is used to stand for the noun, it is a plural pronoun such as *they* or *them*, e.g. *These clothes are ready to wear... He expressed his condolences to the families of people who died in the incident*. Plural nouns which end in *-s* usually lose the *-s* when they come in front of another noun, e.g. *trousers, trouser pocket*. If they refer to a single object which has two main parts, such as *jeans* and *glasses*, the expression *a pair of* is sometimes used, e.g. *a pair of jeans* or *a pair of glasses*. This is shown as **N-PLURAL: also *a pair of* N**.

N-PROPER **proper noun**

A proper noun refers to one person, place, thing, or institution, and begins with a capital letter. Many proper nouns are used without a determiner, e.g. *...higher education in America, ...Father Christmas*; some must be used with *the*, and this is indicated: **N-PROPER: *the* N**, e.g. *the Ice Age*.

N-PROPER-COLL **collective proper noun**

A collective proper noun is a proper noun which refers to a group of people or things. It can be used with either a singular or a plural verb, e.g. *The Boy Scouts is sending a message to all of these kids... The Boy Scouts have a different view.*

N-SING **singular noun**

A singular noun is always singular, and needs a determiner, e.g. *...damage to the environment. He looks the epitome of personal and professional contentment*. When only *a* or *the* is used, this is indicated: **N-SING: *a* N** or **N-SING: *the* N**, e.g. *Production is more or less at a standstill. ...a come-down, the vicinity, the aisle*.

Nouns: untypical uses

Some nouns are sometimes used in ways that are not typical of their word class. For example, a count noun such as *train* is used without a determiner, unlike a typical count noun, but only when it follows *by*, e.g. *...travelling by train*. This is shown as **N-COUNT: also *by* N**. Here are some other examples of patterns indicating untypical noun behaviour:

farce 3 **N-SING**: also no det *The elections have been reduced to a farce... Some aspects of the scheme descend into farce.*

gossip 1 **N-UNCOUNT**: also *a* **N** *We spent an hour talking gossip... They usually stopped for a gossip.*

flu **N-UNCOUNT**: also *the* **N** *I got flu... He had come down with the flu.*

accommodation **N-UNCOUNT**: also **N** in pl *We will provide temporary accommodation... Rates are higher for deluxe accommodations.*

N-SING-COLL **collective singular noun**

A collective singular noun is a singular noun which refers to a group of people or things. It behaves like a singular noun, but can be used with either a singular or plural verb, e.g. *Her shop clientele are mostly women with babies... The clientele is a mixed bunch.*

N-TITLE **title noun**

A title noun is used to refer to someone who has a particular role or position. Titles come before the name of the person and begin with a capital letter, e.g. *Sir Isaac Newton, Lady Macbeth.*

N-UNCOUNT **uncount noun**

An uncount noun refers to things that are not normally counted or considered to be individual items. Uncount nouns do not have a plural form, and are used with a singular verb. They do not need determiners, e.g. *...an area of outstanding natural beauty.*

N-UNCOUNT-COLL **collective uncount noun**

A collective uncount noun is an uncount noun which refers to a group of people or things. It behaves like an uncount noun, but can be used with either a singular or plural verb, e.g. *...in a country where livestock outnumber people by ten to one... Any kind of livestock is totally dependent on its owner for all its needs.*

N-VAR **variable noun**

A variable noun typically combines the behaviour of both count and uncount nouns in the same sense (see **N-COUNT, N-UNCOUNT**). The singular form occurs freely both with and without determiners. Variable nouns also have a plural form, usually made by adding *-s*. Some variable nouns when used like uncount nouns refer to abstract things like *hardship* and *injustice*, and when used like count nouns refer to individual examples or instances of that thing, e.g. *He is not afraid to protest against injustice... It is never too late to correct an injustice. ...the injustices of world poverty.* Others refer to objects which can be mentioned either individually or generally, like *potato* and *salad*: you can talk about *a potato, potatoes*, or *potato*.

N-VAR-COLL **collective variable noun**

A collective variable noun is a variable noun which refers to a group of people or things. It behaves like a variable noun, but when it is singular it can be used with either a singular or a plural verb, e.g. *...the recent fall in party membership.*

N-VOC **vocative noun**

A vocative noun is used when speaking directly to someone or writing to them. Vocative nouns do not need a determiner, but some may be used with a possessive determiner, e.g. *I want you to enjoy yourself, darling... How are you, my darling?*

NUM **number**

A number is a word such as *three* and *hundred.* Numbers such as *one, two, three* are used like determiners, e.g. *three bears*; like adjectives, e.g. *the four horsemen*; like pronouns, e.g. *She has three cases and I have two*; and like quantifiers, e.g. *Six of the boys stayed behind.* Numbers such as *hundred, thousand, million* always follow a determiner or another number, e.g. *two hundred bears, the thousand horsemen, She has a thousand dollars and I have a million, A hundred of the boys stayed behind.*

ORD **ordinal**

An ordinal is a type of number. Ordinals are used like adjectives, e.g. *He was the third victim*; like pronouns, e.g. *She took the first plate and I took the second. ...the second of the two teams;* like adverbs, e.g. *The other team came first*; and like determiners, e.g. *Fourth place goes to Timmy.*

PASSIVE see **V-PASSIVE**

PHRASAL VERB **phrasal verb**

A phrasal verb consists of a verb and one or more particles, e.g. *look after, look back, look down on.* Some phrasal verbs are ergative, reciprocal, link or passive verbs. See **V-ERG, V-RECIP, V-RECIP-ERG, V-LINK** and **V-PASSIVE.**

PHRASE **phrase**

Phrases are groups of words which are used together with little variation and which have a meaning of their own, e.g. *They are reluctant to upset the applecart.*

PHR-CONJ-COORD **phrasal co-ordinating conjunction**

A phrasal co-ordinating conjunction is a phrase which behaves like a co-ordinating conjunction (see **CONJ-COORD**), e.g. *Make sure you are strapped in very well, or else you will fall out.*

PHR-CONJ-SUBORD **phrasal subordinating conjunction**

A phrasal subordinating conjunction is a phrase which behaves like a subordinating conjunction (see **CONJ-SUBORD**), e.g. *Just because it has a good tune does not mean it is great music... In case anyone was following me, I made an elaborate detour.*

PHR-ERG **ergative phrase**

An ergative phrase is a phrase which includes a verb and is used like an ergative verb (see **V-ERG**), e.g. *The true facts will turn your stomach... Her stomach turned and he pulled her away roughly.*

PHR-MODAL **phrasal modal**

Phrasal modals are phrases which, like modals, occur before the infinitive form of a verb, e.g. *The company say they're able to keep pricing competitive.* To make a question with most phrasal modals, you put the subject after the first word in the phrase. e.g. *Are they going to be alright?* Used to also has a question form with *do*, e.g. *What did you used to do when you were bored?* To make a negative with most phrasal modals, you put the negative word after the first word in the phrase, e.g. *We ought not to be quarrelling now.* Used to also has a negative form with *do,* e.g. *He didn't used to like anyone walking on the lawns.* With *had best* and *had better* the negative word comes after the whole phrase, e.g. *He'd better not try to fool me.* Phrasal modals beginning with *be* and *have* inflect; the other phrasal modals do not, e.g. *Public spending is supposed to fall in the next few years.* Where phrasal modals have additional patterns, these are shown in the Extra Column.

PHR-PREP **phrasal preposition**

A phrasal preposition is a phrase which behaves like a preposition, e.g. *He drew abreast of the man. ...according to local gossip.*

PHR-RECIP **reciprocal phrase**

A reciprocal phrase is a phrase which includes a verb, and behaves like a reciprocal verb. It occurs in the patterns **pl-n PHR** and **PHR *with* n**, e.g. *The rival gangs settled their accounts... He would one day settle accounts with his former colleagues.*

PREDET **predeterminer**

A predeterminer is used in a noun group before *a, the,* or another determiner, e.g. *What a busy day! ... both the parents. ...all his skill.*

PREFIX **prefix**

A prefix is a letter or group of letters, such as *un-* or *multi-*, which is added to the beginning of a word in order to form another word. For example, the prefix *un-* is added to *happy* to form *unhappy.*

PREP **preposition**

A preposition begins a prepositional phrase and is followed by a noun group or a present participle. Patterns for prepositions are shown in the dictionary only if they are restricted in some way. For example, if a preposition occurs only before a present participle, it is shown as **PREP -ing**.

PRON **pronoun**

Pronouns are used like noun groups, to refer to someone or something that has already been mentioned or whose identity is known, e.g. *They produced their own shampoos and hair-care products, all based on herbal recipes... She began to consult doctors, and each had a different diagnosis.* Some pronouns are further classified, for example as PRON-EMPH, PRON-INDEF, and so on.

PRON-EMPH **emphatic pronoun**

Emphatic pronouns are words like *all, both,* and *each,* when they are used to emphasize another noun or pronoun, e.g. *We each have different needs and interests... 'Well, I'll leave you both, then,' said Gregory.*

PRON-INDEF **indefinite pronoun**

Indefinite pronouns are words like *anyone, anything, everyone,* and *something,* e.g. *Why would anyone want that job?... Cathy thought that she had the answer to everything.*

PRON-INDEF-NEG **negative indefinite pronoun**

Negative indefinite pronouns are words like *none, no-one,* and *nothing,* e.g. *He searched for a sign of recognition on her face, but there was none... Do our years together mean nothing?*

PRON-PLURAL **plural pronoun**

Plural pronouns are the plural personal pronouns, which include *we, us, they,* and *them,* e.g. *Neither of us forgot about it.*

PRON-POSS **possessive pronoun**

A possessive pronoun is used to say who or what something belongs to or relates to. The possessive pronouns are *mine, yours, his, hers, ours* and *theirs,* e.g. *That wasn't his fault, it was mine... The author can report other people's results which more or less agree with hers.*

PRON-RECIP **reciprocal pronoun**

The reciprocal pronouns are *each other* and *one another,* e.g. *We looked at each other in silence.*

PRON-REFL **reflexive pronoun**

Reflexive pronouns are pronouns which are used as the object of a verb or preposition when they refer to the same person or thing as the subject of the verb. They are used in the same positions as other pronouns. The reflexive pronouns are *myself, yourself, himself, herself, itself, oneself, ourselves, yourselves,* and *themselves,* e.g. *I would like to see myself as an enlightened parent... One* of *the best measures of mental health is the ability to laugh at oneself.*

PRON-REFL-EMPH **emphatic reflexive pronoun**

Emphatic reflexive pronouns are reflexive pronouns which are used for emphasis, often after another pronoun or at the end of a clause, e.g. *I've been wondering if you yourselves have any idea why she came... The Prime Minister himself is on a visit to Peking... I'm fond of cake, myself.*

PRON-REL **relative pronoun**

Relative pronouns are words like *which* and *who,* that introduce relative clauses. They are the subject or object of the verb in the relative clause, or the object of a preposition, e.g. *Old people who don't get out much are especially likely to be short of vitamin D... I'm no longer allowed to smoke in any room which he currently occupies.*

PRON-SING **singular pronoun**

Singular pronouns are the singular personal pronouns, which include *I, me, he, him, she, her, it,* and *one,* e.g. *My dog Rex did all sorts of tricks. I cried when he died.*

QUANT **quantifier**

A quantifier comes before *of* and a noun group, e.g. *most of the house.* If there are any restrictions on the type of noun group, this is indicated: **QUANT *of*def-n** means that the quantifier occurs before *of* and a definite noun group, e.g. *Most of the houses in the capital have piped water.*

QUEST **question word**

A question word is a wh-word that is used to begin a question, e.g. *Why do you say that?*

RECIP see **V-RECIP**

RECIP-ERG see **V-RECIP-ERG**

SOUND **sound word**

Sound words are used before verbs such as *go* and *say*, e.g. *Bang went the door.*; or after those verbs, e.g. *It went bang.*

SUFFIX **suffix**

A suffix is a letter or group of letters such as *-ly* or *-ness*, which is added to the end of a word in order to form a new word, usually of a different word class, e.g. *quick, quickly.*

VB, VERB **verb**

V-ERG **ergative verb**

An ergative verb is used both in the pattern **v** and in the pattern **v n**, e.g. *The vase broke* and *Fred broke the lamp*. The noun group that is the subject in the **v** pattern refers to the same kind of thing as the noun group **n** in the **v n** pattern. For example, *vase* and *lamp* in the examples above are both breakable objects. Ergative verbs allow you to describe an action from the point of view of the performer of the action or from the point of view of something which is affected by the action.

Some phrasal verbs are ergative verbs, e.g. *Powdering a sweaty nose will only block up the pores* (**v P n**); *With this disease the veins in the liver can block up* (**v P**).

V-LINK **link verb**

A link verb connects a subject and a complement. Link verbs most commonly occur in the patterns **v adj** and **v n**. Most link verbs do not occur in the passive voice, e.g. *be, become, taste, feel.*

Some phrasal verbs are link verbs, e.g. *I was sure things were going to turn out fine* (**v adj**); *Sometimes things don't turn out the way we think they are going to* (**v n**).

V-LINK-ERG **ergative link verb**

An ergative link verb sometimes behaves like a link verb, connecting a subject and a complement, e.g. *The sea turned pink* (**v colour**); *To keep warm they burned wood in an oil barrel* (**v adj**). As well as these link verb patterns it also occurs in non-link **v n** patterns, e.g. *The lenses turned her eyes green* (**v n colour**); *The noise kept him awake* (**v n adj**). In this way it is like an ergative verb. See **V-LINK, V-ERG.**

V-PASSIVE **passive verb**

A passive verb occurs in the passive voice only, e.g. *His parents are rumoured to be on the verge of splitting up.*

Some phrasal verbs are passive verbs, e.g. *The civilians were just caught up in the conflict.*

V-RECIP **reciprocal verb**

Reciprocal verbs describe processes in which two or more people, groups, or things interact mutually: they do the same thing to each other, or participate jointly in the same action or event. Reciprocal verbs are used in the pattern **pl-n v**, e.g. *Fred and Sally met*, where the subject is both participants. The participants can also be referred to separately in other patterns, e.g. **v n** *Fred met Sally*, and **v *with* n** *Fred argued with Sally*. These patterns are reciprocal because they also mean that *Sally met Fred* and *Sally argued with Fred.* Note that many reciprocal verbs can also be used in a way that is not reciprocal. For example, *Fred and Sally kissed* is reciprocal, but *Fred kissed Sally* is not reciprocal (because it does not mean that Sally also kissed Fred). Non-reciprocal uses of reciprocal verbs are shown as **non-recip**.

Some phrasal verbs are reciprocal verbs, e.g. *He felt appalled by the idea of marriage so we broke up...* (**pl-n v P**) *My girlfriend broke up with me.* (**v P *with* n**).

V-RECIP-ERG **ergative reciprocal verb**

An ergative reciprocal verb behaves both like an ergative verb and a reciprocal verb. Like an ergative verb, it occurs in the patterns **v** and **v n** (see **V-ERG**). Like a reciprocal verb, it occurs in patterns which include **pl-n v** and **v with n** (see **V-RECIP**). The typical ergative-reciprocal patterns are therefore **pl-n v**, **v *with* n**, **v pl-n** and **v n *with* n**, e.g. *The three plays will alternate throughout the tour... Love songs alternated with folk songs... You alternate layers of the mixture... The band alternated love songs with folk songs.*

Some phrasal verbs are ergative reciprocal verbs, e.g. *Men and girls pair up to dance* (**pl-n v P**); *They asked us to pair up with the person next to us* (**v P *with* n**); *They paired up smokers and non-smokers* (**v P pl-n**); *They paired smokers up with non-smokers* (**v n P *with* n**).

Words and notations used in patterns

In a pattern, the element in capital letters represents the word in the entry. For example, the adjective *afraid* sometimes occurs in expressions such as *afraid of the boys*. In the pattern indicating this, **ADJ** is in capitals: **ADJ *of* n**. All the other elements are in small letters. Items in italics show the actual word that is used, such as ***of***. Items in roman print show the word class or type of clause that is used, such as **n**.

When the word in the entry occurs in a pattern, the element in capital letters is **V** for a verb, **N** for any kind of noun, **ADJ** for any kind of adjective, and so on. **PHR** is used for a phrase, and **V** and **N** are used to represent verbs and nouns in phrases. For phrasal verbs, **V** and **P** are used to represent the verb and the particle(s) respectively.

The following words are used to structure information in patterns.

oft: used to indicate that a word or phrase often occurs in a particular pattern or behaves in a particular way.

usu: used to indicate that a word or phrase usually occurs in a particular pattern or behaves in a particular way.

also: used with some nouns to show that the word is used in a way that is not typical of that type of noun (see page xxvi). For example, **N-UNCOUNT: also N in pl** means that unlike most uncount nouns, this noun also has a plural form and use. **Also** is used with some adverbs and adjectives to show a pattern that is less common than the other patterns mentioned. For example, **ADV: usu ADV with v, also ADV adj** means that the adverb is usually used with a verb but is also used before an adjective. Also is used before less common verb patterns which do not have examples.

no: used to indicate that a verb is not used in a particular way, for example **no passive**, or that a singular noun is also used without a determiner: **N-SING: also no det**.

only: used to indicate that a verb is always used in a particular way, for example **only cont**.

after: after v means after a verb. The word is used either immediately after the verb, or after the verb and another word or phrase, or in a marked position at the beginning of the clause. For example, the adverb **mildly** at **mild 2** is used:

- immediately after a verb: *'I'm not meddling,' Kenworthy said mildly, 'I'm just curious'*;
- after a verb and its object: *'That's enough, Hunter,' his father said, reproaching him mildly with raised eyebrows*;
- at the beginning of a clause: *Mildly, Amy said that she was sorry about the hospital smell.*

The phrase **on alert** at **alert 6** is used:

- immediately after a verb: *Soldiers and police have been put on alert*;
- after a verb and its object: *Slovenia is keeping its own defence forces on alert.*

before: before v means before a verb. The word is used before the main element in a verb group. For example, the adverb **already** 1 is used:

- before the whole verb group: *those who already know of the delights of skiing*;
- immediately before the main element in the group: *They had already voted for him at the first ballot.*

with: with is used when the position of a word or phrase is not fixed. This means that the word or phrase sometimes comes before the named word class and sometimes comes after it. For example, **quickly** at **quick 1** has the pattern **ADV with v**. It occurs:

- after the verb: *Cussane worked quickly and methodically*;
- before the verb: *Hold your skin taut and quickly pull out each hair in the direction it grows.*

bring 1 has the pattern **V n with adv**. The adverb occurs:

- after the noun group: *He had to bring a bed down to the front room of the cottage*;
- before the noun group: *Someone brought down a huge kettle.*

In addition, **with cl** and **with quote** are used when the word sometimes occurs at the beginning of the clause or quote, sometimes at the end, and sometimes in the middle. For example, **ask** 1 has the pattern **V with quote**. It occurs:

- after the quote: *'How is Frank?' he asked*;
- before the quote: *Estela asked: 'Does my father know?'*;
- in the middle of the quote: *'What are you doing?' Suzanne asked. 'Is something wrong?'*

inflects: used to show that an element in a phrase inflects. **V inflects** means that the form of the verb in the phrase is not fixed but changes according to the subject of the verb or its tense. **N inflects** means that the noun in the phrase is used in the singular and the plural forms. If a phrase has two verbs, but only one inflects, or two nouns, but only one inflects, that verb or noun is given in italics, e.g. for the phrase **a change of heart** the Extra Column says: *change* inflects.

The following elements are used in patterns:

adj: stands for **adjective group**. This may be one word, such as 'happy', or a group of words, such as 'very happy' or 'as happy as I have ever been'.
e.g. **adj N**

> **acclaim 2** ... *Angela Bassett has won critical acclaim for her excellent performance.*

adj-compar: stands for **comparative adjective**. This is used to indicate an adjective group with the comparative form of the adjective.
e.g. **V adj-compar**

> **close** 9 ... *The US dollar closed higher in Tokyo today.*

adj-superl: stands for **superlative adjective**. It is used to indicate an adjective group with the superlative form of the adjective.
e.g. PREP **poss adj-superl**
at 15 ... *He was at his happiest whilst playing cricket.*

adv: stands for **adverb group**. This may be one word, such as 'slowly', or a group of words, such as 'extremely slowly' or 'more slowly than ever'.
e.g. **adv** ADJ
accepted ... *There is no generally accepted definition of life.*

amount: means **word or phrase indicating an amount of something**, such as 'a lot', 'nothing', 'three percent', 'four hundred pounds', 'more', or 'much'.
e.g. V **amount** ***for*** **n**
budget 4 ... *The company has budgeted $3 million for the advertising.*
ADV **amount**
fully 4 ... *Fully 30% of the people were unable to afford adequate housing.*

as if: stands for **clause beginning with 'as if' or 'as though'**.
e.g. V **as if**
look 1 ... *He looked as if he was going to smile.*

be: stands for any form of the verb 'be'. It is used in passive verb patterns.
e.g. ***be*** **V-ed to-inf**
think 2 ... *The storm is thought to be responsible for as many as four deaths.*

brd-neg: stands for **broad negative**, that is, a clause which is negative in meaning. It may contain a negative element such as 'no-one', 'never', or 'hardly', or may show that it is negative in some other way.
e.g. VB: **with brd-neg**
abide 1 ... *She couldn't abide his success.*
PHR: **with brd-neg**
do things by halves at **half** 15 ... *In Italy they rarely do things by halves.*

cl: stands for **clause**.
e.g. PHR **with cl**
in addition at **addition** 1 ... *Hong Kong has some of the largest buses in the world. In addition, the city has underground trains and a rapid surface railway.*
cl ADV
anyway 4 ... *What do you want from me, anyway.*

colour: means **colour word**, such as 'red', 'green', or 'blue'.
e.g. V **colour**
blush 1 ... *I blushed scarlet at my stupidity.*

compar: stands for **comparative form of an adjective or adverb**.
e.g. ADV **compar**
even 2 ... *The other incident was even more spectacular... Stan was speaking even more slowly than usual.*

cont: stands for **continuous**. It is used when indicating that a verb is always, usually, or never used in the continuous.
e.g. VB: **only cont**
die 8 ... *I'm dying for a breath of fresh air.*
VB: **no cont**
adore 2 ... *I adore good books and the theatre.*

def-n: stands for **definite noun group**. A definite noun group is a noun group that refers to a specific person or thing, or a specific group of people or things, that is known and identified.
e.g. QUANT ***of*** **def-n**
whole 1 ... *I was cold throughout the whole of my body.*

def-n-uncount: stands for **definite noun group with an uncount noun**. An uncount noun is a noun which has no plural form and which is sometimes used without a determiner.
e.g. QUANT ***of*** **def-n-uncount**
much 5 ... *She does much of her work abroad.*

def-pl-n: stands for **definite noun group with a noun in the plural**.
e.g. QUANT ***of*** **def-pl-n**
a few at **few** 1 ... *a little tea-party I'm giving for a few of the teachers.*

det: stands for **determiner**. A determiner is a word that comes at the beginning of a noun group, such as 'the', 'her', or 'those'.
e.g. **det** ADJ
final 1 ... *I received a final letter from Clive.*

det-poss: stands for **possessive determiner**. A possessive determiner is a determiner that shows possession, such as 'my', 'his', or 'their'.
e.g. **det-poss** N
Ladyship ... *Her Ladyship's expecting you, sir.*

-ed: stands for **past participle of a verb**, such as 'decided', 'gone', or 'taken'.
e.g. ADV **-ed**
centrally at **central** 1 ... *This is a centrally planned economy.*
V n -ed
hear 2 ...*if she can hear it played by a professional orchestra.*
AUX **-ed**
be 2 ... *Her husband was killed in a car crash.*

get: stands for any form of the verb 'get'. It is used in passive verb patterns.
e.g. ***get*** **V-ed**
change 5 ... *I've got to get changed first.*

group: stands for **noun group, adjective, adverb, or prepositional phrase**.
e.g. ADV **group**
altogether 3 ... *'I'm not altogether a fool,' she said... We were not altogether sure that the comet would miss the Earth.*
group PHR
to the last at **last** 25 ... *Armstrong was tall and handsome to the last.*

imper: stands for **imperative.** It is used when indicating that a verb is always or usually used in the imperative.
e.g. **only imper**
fire away ... *'May I ask you something?' 'Sure. Fire away.'*

inf: stands for **infinitive form of a verb,** such as 'decide', 'go', or 'sit'.
e.g. **V n inf**
make 1 ... *Grit from the highway made him cough.*
PHR inf
cannot but at **but** 8 ... *She couldn't but congratulate him.*

-ing: stands for **present participle of a verb,** such as 'deciding', 'going', or 'taking'.
e.g. **V n -ing**
catch 7 ... *He caught a youth breaking into his car.*
V n *into* -ing
nudge 3 ... *Bit by bit Bob had nudged Fitz into selling his controlling interest.*
N *of* -ing
custom 1 ...*the custom of lighting the Olympic flame.*

it: means an 'introductory' or 'dummy' *it. It* does not refer to anything in a previous sentence or in the world; it may refer to what is coming later in the clause or it may refer to things in general.
e.g. ***it* V-link ADJ to-inf**
easy 1 ... *It is easy to get a seat at the best shows in town.*
V *it* P
brazen out ... *If you are caught, simply brazen it out.*

like: means **clause beginning with 'like'**.
e.g. **V like**
feel 1 ... *I felt like I was being kicked in the teeth every day.*

n: stands for **noun** or **noun group**. If the **n** element occurs in a pattern with something that is part of a noun group, such as an adjective or another noun, it represents a noun. If the **n** element occurs in a pattern with something that is not part of a noun group, such as a verb or preposition, it represents a noun group. The noun group can be of any kind, including a pronoun.
e.g. **n N**
collector 2 ... *He earned his living as a tax collector.*
V *for* n
advertise 2 ... *We advertised for staff in a local newspaper.*

n (not pron): stands for a **noun group** of some kind, but **not a personal pronoun**. It is used in phrasal verb patterns where the particle is an adverb.
e.g. **V P n (not pron)**
burn down ... *Anarchists burnt down a restaurant.*

names: means **names of places or institutions.**
e.g. **N-COUNT: oft in names**
lake ...*Lake Victoria.*

neg: stands for **negative word,** such as 'not', or 'never'.
e.g. **VB: with neg**
agree 6 ... *I don't think the food here agrees with me.*

non-recip: stands for **verb pattern with no reciprocal meaning**. It is used when the verb is a reciprocal verb (see the explanation for V-RECIP in **Word classes** on page xxix).
e.g. **V n (non-recip)**
hug 1 ... *She had hugged him exuberantly.*

n-proper: stands for **proper noun**. A proper noun is the name of a particular person or thing.
e.g. **n-proper N**
look-alike ...*a Marilyn Monroe look-alike.*

num: stands for **number**.
e.g. **num N**
dollar ... *She gets paid seven dollars an hour.*

n-uncount: stands for **uncount noun** or **noun group with an uncount noun**. An uncount noun is a noun which has no plural form and which is sometimes used with no determiner.
e.g. **DET n-uncount**
little 1 ... *I had little money and little free time.*

ord: stands for **ordinal**, such as 'first', or 'second'.
e.g. **ord N**
century 1 ...*the late eighteenth century.*

P: stands for **particle**. It is used in phrasal verb patterns to represent the particle. Particles may be either adverbs or prepositions.
e.g. **V P n**
look after 1 ... *I love looking after the children.*

passive: stands for **passive voice**. It is used when indicating that a verb usually or never occurs in the passive voice.
e.g. **VB: usu passive**
expel 1 ... *More than five-thousand secondary school students have been expelled for cheating.*

pl: stands for **plural**.

pl-n: stands for **noun in the plural, plural noun group, or co-ordinate noun group** (two or more noun groups joined by a co-ordinating conjunction).
e.g. **DET pl-n**
these 1 ... *These people can make decisions in ten minutes which would usually take us months.*
pl-n V
argue 5 ... *They were still arguing; I could hear them down the road.*

poss: stands for **possessive**. Possessives which come before the noun may be a possessive determiner, such as 'my', 'her', or 'their', or a possessive formed from a noun group, such as 'the horse's'. Possessives which come after the noun are of the form '*of* n', such as 'of the horse'.

e.g. **poss N**

betters at **better** 7 ... *Sit down and be quiet in front of your elders and betters.*

with poss

ancestor 1 *...an ancestor of Eleonora Massimo.*

prep: stands for **prepositional phrase** or **preposition**.

e.g. **V prep**

advance 1 ... *Rebel forces are advancing on the capital.*

prep PRON

him 1 ... *Is Sam there? Let me talk to him.*

pron: stands for **pronoun**. A pronoun is a word such as 'I', 'it', or 'them' which is used like a noun group. It refers to someone or something that has already been mentioned or whose identity is known.

e.g. **PREP pron**

before 12 ... *Everyone in the room knew it was the single hardest task before them.*

V pron

kill 5 ... *My feet are killing me.*

pron-recip: stands for **reciprocal pronoun**. The reciprocal pronouns are 'each other' and 'one another'.

e.g. **pl-n V *with* pron-recip**

compete 1 ... *The stores will inevitably end up competing with each other.*

pron-refl: stands for **reflexive pronoun,** such as 'yourself', 'herself', or 'ourselves'.

e.g. **V pron-refl *to* n**

attach 2 ... *Natasha attached herself to the film crew filming at her orphanage.*

quest: stands for **question word.** A question word is a wh-word such as 'what', 'how', or 'why' which is used to begin a question.

e.g. **quest PHR**

on earth at **earth** 7 ... *How on earth did that happen?*

quote: means **direct speech**. Direct speech is often found in quotation marks.

e.g. **V with quote**

announce 2 ... *'I'm having a bath and going to bed,' she announced.*

sing: stands for **singular**.

sing-n: stands for **noun in the singular**.

e.g. **DET sing-n**

this 1 ... *During this delay, the centre carries on cooking.*

supp: stands for **supplementary information accompanying a noun.** Supplementary information that comes before a noun may be given by a determiner, possessive, adjective, or noun modifier. Supplementary information that comes after the noun may be given by a prepositional phrase or a clause.

e.g. **supp N**

belief 2 ... *He refuses to compete on Sundays because of his religious beliefs... What the public really wants is a fearless politician who states honestly his or her beliefs and then sticks to them.*

with supp

aspect 1 ... *Climate and weather affect every aspect of our lives... Monroe described the financial aspect as crucial.*

that: stands for **'that'-clause**. The clause may begin with the word 'that', but does not necessarily do so.

e.g. **V n that**

tell 1 ... *I returned to tell Phyllis our relationship was over.*

N that

suggestion 2 ... *We reject any suggestion that the law needs amending.*

***it* V-link ADJ that**

likely 1 ... *It's far more likely that you'll get to the hospital too early.*

to-inf: stands for **to-infinitive form of a verb**.

e.g. **V to-inf**

want 1 ... *People wanted to know who this talented designer was.*

N to-inf

promise 3 ... *The program has lived up to its promise to promote family welfare.*

V: stands for **verb** or **verb group.** It is not used to represent a link verb. See also the explanations of **after, before** and **with.**

e.g. **V PRON**

her 1 ... *I told her I had something to say.*

V PHR

bolt upright at **bolt** 12 ... *Trevor was sitting bolt upright in bed.*

V PREP n

at 10 ... *She opened the door and stood there, frowning at me.*

V-ed: stands for **past participle** of the verb explained in the entry.

V-ing: stands for **present participle** of the verb explained in the entry.

V-link: stands for **link verb.** A link verb is a verb such as 'be' which connects a subject and a complement.

e.g. **V-link PHR**

alive and kicking at **alive** 9 ... *There are growing worries that the secret police may still be alive and kicking.*

way: means the noun 'way' preceded by a possessive determiner.

e.g. **V *way* prep/adv**

push 2 ... *He pushed his way towards her.*

wh: stands for **wh-word, or clause beginning with a wh-word,** such as 'what', 'why', 'when', 'how', 'if', or 'whether'.

e.g. **V wh to-inf**

know 7 ... *We know what to do to make it work.*

V wh

ask 1 ... *If Daniel asks what happened in court we will tell him.*

Pragmatics

People use language to achieve different goals – they invite, give compliments, give warnings, show their emotions, tell lies, and make commitments. The ability to use language effectively to fulfil intentions and goals is known as pragmatic competence, and the study of this ability is called pragmatics. The analysis of language which has been used to prepare this dictionary is based on the idea that speakers and writers plan and fulfil goals as they use language. This in turn entails choices. Speakers choose their goals and they choose appropriate language for their goals.

Different languages use different pragmatic strategies. In order to use a language effectively, and be successful in achieving your goals, you need to know what the pragmatic conventions are for that particular language. It is therefore important that learners of English are given as much information as possible about the ways in which English speakers use their language to communicate.

Because of the large amounts of data in The Bank of English, COBUILD is uniquely placed to help learners with pragmatics. We have analyzed the data and have found, for example, the ways in which English speakers invite friends to parties, compliment someone on their appearance, or promise to do something.

In this dictionary, we draw attention to the pragmatic aspects of words and phrases of English, paying special attention to those that, for cultural or linguistic reasons, may be confusing to learners.

For every word sense where there is pragmatic information which is important for correct use, we

(a) show this in the extra column with the word PRAGMATICS and
(b) include additional information in the definition about how, when, and why the word or expression is used.

There are several types of pragmatic information which are given in the dictionary. The following extracts from dictionary entries show how to understand and make use of the pragmatic information provided.

Functions

1 People often use language to try to get someone else to do something, for example when giving an order, persuading, or advising someone.

suppose

You can use 'do you suppose'	This shows that this phrase has a functional use.
as a polite way of	This gives the intention or goal the speaker wants to accomplish.
suggesting or requesting that someone does something.	This gives information about the appropriate situation where the phrase can be used.
Do you suppose we could get together for a little chat sometime soon?	An example showing typical use in context.

advise

if an official document states that you **are advised** to do something,	This tells you where you will find this use.
it is telling you the correct or appropriate thing to do;	This gives the intention or goal the writer wants to accomplish.
a formal use.	This gives information about the appropriate situation where the phrase can be used.
Candidates in India are advised to submit their applications through the overseas student office in London.	An example showing typical use in context.

2 Another function is to express feelings.

	hate
This shows that these phrases have a functional use.	You can use **hate** in expressions like **I hate to trouble you** or **I hate to bother you**
This gives the intention or goal the speaker wants to accomplish.	when you are apologizing to someone
This gives information about the appropriate situation where the phrase can be used.	for interrupting them or asking them to do something.
An example showing typical use in context.	*I hate to rush you but I have another appointment later on.*

3 Another function is to state your response to a request or question.

	ask
This shows the function of this phrase.	You reply **'don't ask me'**
This gives the main meaning the speaker wants to communicate.	when you do not know the answer to a question,
This gives information about the speaker's feelings.	usually when you are annoyed or surprised that you have been asked.
An example showing typical use in context.	*'She's got other things on her mind, wouldn't you think?' 'Don't ask me,' murmured Chris. 'I've never met her.'*

Discourse organizers

Discourse organizers are words and phrases which help to organize speech or writing so that it is easy for hearers or readers to understand. They are sometimes called 'signposts' or 'link words'. Some discourse organizers also give information about the writer's or speaker's attitude.

	story
This shows that this phrase has a functional use.	You use **to cut a long story short**
This gives the intention or goal the speaker wants to accomplish.	to indicate that you are going to state the final result of an event and not give any more details;
This gives information about the appropriate situation where the phrase can be used.	used in spoken English.
An example showing typical use in context.	*To cut a long story short, I ended up as managing director.*

	happen
This shows that this phrase has a functional use.	You use **as it happens**
This gives the intention or goal the speaker wants to accomplish.	in order to introduce a statement,
This gives information about the speaker's belief or attitude.	especially one that is rather surprising.
An example showing typical use in context.	*She called Amy to see if she had any idea of her son's whereabouts. As it happened, Amy had.*

Speaker/hearer relationship

Some words and phrases are chosen by a speaker because of the relationship or feelings they have towards the person they are speaking to.

son

Some people use **son** as a form of address	This gives information about the function of this word.
when they are showing kindness or affection	This describes the attitude of the speaker.
to a boy or a man who is younger than them; an informal use.	This gives information about the relationship of speaker to hearer.
Don't be frightened by failure, son.	An example showing typical use in context.

Attitudes and feelings

You can also choose words and expressions to express your attitude to the person or thing that you are talking about.

plain-spoken

If you say that someone is **plain-spoken**, you mean that	This shows that the word has a functional use.
they say exactly what they think, even when they know that what they say may not please other people;	This shows the reason for the speaker's attitude or point of view.
used showing approval.	This shows that the speaker's attitude, if they choose this word, is positive and favourable.

pig-headed

If you describe someone as **pig-headed**, you are critical of them	This shows that the speaker's attitude, if they choose this word, is negative or unfavourable.
because they refuse to change their mind about things.	This shows the reason for the speaker having that attitude or point of view.
She, in her pigheaded way, insists that she is right and that everyone else is wrong.	An example showing typical use in context.

Emphasis

Many words and expressions are used to emphasize the point that you are making.

scot-free

If you say that someone got away **scot-free**,	
you are emphasizing	This shows that this word is used for emphasis.
that they escaped punishment for something that you believe they should have been punished for.	This shows the attitude or point of view of someone who uses this word.
Others who were guilty were being allowed to get off scot-free.	An example showing typical use in context.

This shows that this phrase is used for emphasis.

This shows the attitude or point of view of someone who uses this phrase.

An example showing typical use in context.

fact

You say **the fact remains that** something is the case

when you want to emphasize

that the situation must be realized and accepted.

The fact remains that inflation, however you measure it, is unacceptably high.

Expressing certainty and uncertainty

Many words and expressions in English allow speakers and writers to show how certain they are about the truth or validity of their statements. This is sometimes called 'hedging' or 'modality'.

This shows that the phrase has a functional use.

This gives information about the speaker's degree of certainty.

This gives information about the appropriate situation where the phrase can be used.

An example showing typical use in context.

guess

You say **I guess**

to indicate slight uncertainty or reluctance about what you are saying;

an informal expression, used mainly in American English.

I guess she thought that was pretty smart.

This shows that this phrase has a functional use.

This gives information about the speaker's degree of certainty.

This gives information about the appropriate situation where the phrase can be used.

An example showing typical use. The second sentence contrasts with the first sentence.

actuality

You can use **in actuality**

to emphasize that what you are saying is true

when it contradicts or contrasts with what you have previously said.

It would have been a monumental feat of self-control for him to change the habits of a lifetime. In actuality, he seems to have made very little effort to do so.

We hope that you will enjoy learning about pragmatics in the English language. Pragmatics, in any language, is central to communication. When you can understand the context and subtle meanings of a word, you can give and receive accurate messages. This should enable you to achieve your pragmatic goals whether you are intending to criticize, to complain, to persuade, and so on. Good communication is vital. We hope that by giving you a great deal of pragmatic information in this dictionary we will encourage you to improve your communication skills.

Pronunciation

Information on pronunciation is an important part of any learner's dictionary. Our aim has been to provide a pronunciation key that is accurate, clear, and simple.

The basic principle underlying the suggested pronunciations is 'If you pronounce it like this, most people will understand you'. The pronunciations are therefore broadly based on the two most widely taught accents of English, RP or Received Pronunciation for British English, and GenAm or General American for American English.

For the majority of words, a single pronunciation is given, as most differences between British and American pronunciation are systematic. Where the usual American pronunciation differs from the usual British pronunciation more significantly, a separate transcription is given of the part of the word that is pronounced differently in American English after the code AM. Where more than one pronunciation is common in British English, alternative pronunciations are also given.

The pronunciations are the result of a programme of monitoring spoken English and consulting leading reference works. For American English, the advice and helpful criticism of Debbie Posner is gratefully acknowledged.

The transcription system has developed from original work by Dr David Brazil for the Collins COBUILD English Language Dictionary. The symbols used in the dictionary are adapted from those of the International Phonetic Alphabet (IPA), as standardized in the English Pronouncing Dictionary by Daniel Jones (14th Edition, revised by AC Gimson and SM Ramsaran 1988), for representing RP.

IPA symbols

Vowel Sounds

ɑː	calm, ah	ɒ	lot, spot
ɑːʳ	heart, far	oʊ	note, coat
æ	act, mass	ɔː	claw, faun
aɪ	dive, cry	ɔʳ	more, cord
aɪəʳ	fire, tyre	ɔɪ	boy, joint
aʊ	out, down	ʊ	could, stood
aʊəʳ	flour, sour	uː	you, use
e	met, lend, pen	ʊəʳ	lure, pure
eɪ	say, weight	ɜːʳ	turn, third
eəʳ	fair, care	ʌ	fund, must
ɪ	fit, win	ə	the first vowel in about
iː	feed, me	əʳ	the first vowel in forgotten
ɪəʳ	near, beard	i	the second vowel in very
		u	the second vowel in actual

Consonant Sounds

b	bed, rub	s	soon, bus
d	done, red	t	talk, bet
f	fit, if	v	van, love
g	good, dog	w	win, wool
h	hat, horse	ʰw	why, wheat
j	yellow, you	x	loch
k	king, pick	z	zoo, buzz
l	lip, bill	ʃ	ship, wish
ᵊl	handle, panel	ʒ	measure, leisure
m	mat, ram	ŋ	sing, working
n	not, tin	tʃ	cheap, witch
ᵊn	hidden, written	θ	thin, myth
p	pay, lip	ð	then, bathe
r	run, read	dʒ	joy, bridge

Notes

/ɑː/ or /æ/

There are a number of words which are shown in the dictionary with alternative pronunciations with /ɑː/ and /æ/, such as 'path' /pɑːθ, pæθ/. In this case, /pɑːθ/ is the RP pronunciation. However, in most other accents of English, including GenAm, the pronunciation is /pæθ/.

/ʳ/

One of the main ways in which RP differs from most other accents of English is that 'r' is only pronounced as /r/ when the next sound is a vowel. Thus, in RP, 'far gone' is pronounced /fɑː gɒn/ but 'far out' is pronounced /fɑːr aʊt/. In other accents of English, including GenAm, the 'r' in 'far' is always pronounced.

The /ʳ/ superscript shows that
i) in RP, /r/ is pronounced only when it is followed by a vowel;
ii) in GenAm, /r/ is always pronounced

Some of the complex vowel sounds shown in the table above are simplified in GenAm. The vowel sound in 'fire' is shown as /aɪəʳ/. This represents the pronunciation /aɪə/ in RP, but in GenAm the pronunciation is not /aɪər/, but /aɪr/. So 'fire', 'flour', 'fair', 'near' and 'lure' are pronounced /faɪə/, /flaʊə/, /feə/, /nɪə/ and /lʊə/ in RP, but /faɪr/, /flaʊr/, /fer/, /nɪr/ and /lʊr/ in GenAm.

/ɒ/

In GenAm, this symbol represents the same sound as the symbol /ɑː/, so that the first syllable of 'common' sounds like 'calm'. In RP, the sounds are different.

/oʊ/

This symbol is used to represent the sound /əʊ/ in RP, and also the sound /o/ in GenAm, as these sounds are almost entirely equivalent.

/i/ and /u/

These are short vowels which only occur in unstressed syllables:

/i/ has a sound like /iː/, but is short like /ɪ/: **very** /veri/ **create** /krieɪt/

/u/ has a sound like /uː/, but is short like /ʊ/: **actual** /æktʃuəl/

/ᵊl/ and /ᵊn/

These show that /l/ and /n/ are pronounced as separate syllables:

handle /hændᵊl/ **hidden** /hɪdᵊn/

/ʰw/

This shows that some people say /w/, and others, including many American speakers, say /hw/: **why** /ʰwaɪ/

Stress

Stress is shown by underlining the vowel in the stressed syllable:

two /tuː/ **result** /rɪzʌlt/ **disappointing** /dɪsəpɔɪntɪŋ/

When a word is spoken in isolation, stress falls on the syllables which have vowels which are underlined. If there is one syllable underlined, it will have primary stress.

'TWO' 'reSULT'

If two syllables are underlined, the first will have secondary stress, and the second will have primary stress:

'DISapPOINTing'

A few words are shown with three underlined syllables, for example 'disqualification' /dɪskwɒlɪfɪkeɪʃᵊn/. In this case, the third underlined syllable will have primary stress, while the secondary stress may be on the first or second syllable:

'DISqualifiCAtion' or 'disQUALifiCAtion'

RP tends to prefer 'DIS-', while GenAm usually prefers 'dis-'.

In the case of compound words, where the pronunciation of each part is given separately, the stress pattern is shown by underlining the headword: 'off-peak', 'first-degree', but 'off season'.

Words in context

Stressed syllables

When words are used in context, the way in which they are pronounced depends upon the information units that are constructed by the speaker. For example, a speaker could say:

1) 'the reSULT was disapPOINTing'
2) 'it was a DISappointing reSULT'
3) 'it was VERy disappointing inDEED'

In (3), neither of the two underlined syllables in disappointing /dɪsəpɔɪntɪŋ/ receives either primary or secondary stress. This shows that it is not possible for a dictionary to predict whether a particular syllable will be stressed in context.

It should be noted, however, that in the case of adjectives with two stressed syllables, the second syllable often loses its stress when it is used before a noun:

'an OFF-peak FARE'

'a FIRST-degree BURN'

Two things should be noted about the marked syllables:

1) They can take primary or secondary stress in a way that is not shared by the other syllables.

2) Whether they are stressed or not, the vowel must be pronounced distinctly; it cannot be weakened to /ə/, /ɪ/, or /ʊ/.

These features are shared by most of the one-syllable words in English, which are therefore transcribed in this dictionary as stressed syllables:

two /tuː/ **inn** /ɪn/ **tree** /triː/

Unstressed syllables

It is an important characteristic of English that vowels in unstressed syllables tend not to be pronounced clearly. Many unstressed syllables contain the vowel /ə/, a neutral vowel which is not found in stressed syllables. The vowels /ɪ/ and /ʊ/, which are relatively neutral in quality, are also common in unstressed syllables.

Some unstressed syllables, although they may often have a distinct quality, can also be pronounced with /ə/. This means that the vowel quality can vary in these syllables. In this dictionary, these syllables are indicated by their vowels being transcribed in italic script. Thus, the pronunciation of 'abdominal' is given as /æbdɒm*ɪ*nᵊl/, to show that although it is possible to pronounce this word /æbdɒmɪnᵊl/, it is equally possible, particularly in informal English, to pronounce it /əbdɒmənᵊl/.

Single-syllable grammatical words such as 'shall' and 'at' require a different approach.

Although such words are often pronounced with a weak vowel such as /ə/, some of them are pronounced with a more distinct vowel under certain circumstances, for example when they occur at the end of a sentence. This distinct pronunciation is generally referred to as the strong form, and is given in this dictionary after the word STRONG.

shall /ʃəl, STRONG ʃæl/ **at** /ət, STRONG æt/

A a

A, a /eɪ/ **A's, a's**

1 **A** is the first letter of the English alphabet. N-VAR

2 In music, **A** is the sixth note in the scale of C major. N-VAR

3 If you get an **A** as a mark for a piece of work or in an exam, your work is extremely good. *Gifted students frequently get A's without doing much work.* N-VAR

4 **A** or **a** is used as an abbreviation for words beginning with a, such as 'acceleration', 'ampere', or 'answer'.

5 People talk about getting **from A to B** when they are referring generally to journeys they need to make, without saying where the journeys will take them. *Cars are for getting people from A to B in maximum safety.* PHRASE: PHR after v

a /ə, STRONG eɪ/ **an** /ən, STRONG æn/ ◆◆◆◆◆

A or **an** is the indefinite article. It is used at the beginning of noun groups which refer to only one person or thing. The form **an** is used in front of words that begin with vowel sounds.

1 You use **a** or **an** when you are referring to someone or something for the first time and you cannot assume that your listener or reader knows which particular thing you are talking about. *A waiter entered with a tray bearing a glass and a bottle of whiskey... Just before Barnes Bridge the path crosses the front of a boathouse... Today you've got a new teacher taking you... I manage a hotel.* DET: DET sing-n

2 You use **a** or **an** when you are referring to any person or thing of a particular type and do not want to be specific. *...expensive make-up that we saw being advertised by a beautiful model... There is a Mortgage Adviser in every branch... Bring a sleeping bag. ...waiting for a bus.* DET: DET sing-n

3 You use **a** or **an** in front of an uncount noun when that noun follows an adjective, or when the noun is followed by words that describe it more fully. *The islanders exhibit a constant happiness with life... He did have a real knowledge of the country... Baseball movies have gained an appreciation that far outstrips those dealing with any other sport.* DET: DET n-uncount with supp

4 You use **a** or **an** in front of a mass noun when you want to refer to a single type, or brand of something. *Bollinger 'RD' is a rare, highly prized wine.* DET: DET n-mass

5 You use **a** in quantifiers such as **a lot, a little**, and **a bit**. *I spend a lot on expensive jewelry and clothing... I've come looking for a bit of advice.* DET: DET in quant

6 You use **a** or **an** to refer to someone or something as a representative member of a group, class, or type of person or thing. *Some parents believe a boy must learn to stand up and fight like a man. ...the operation a patient has had.* DET: DET sing-n

7 You use **a** or **an** in front of the names of days, months, or festivals when you are referring to one particular instance of that day, month, or festival. *The interview took place on a Friday afternoon... It was a Christmas when shoppers passed by expensive silks in favor of more practical gifts.* DET: DET sing-n

8 You use **a** or **an** when you are saying what someone is or what job they have. *I explained that I was an artist, but that I was sometimes a plumber as well... He was now a teacher and a respectable member of the community.* DET: DET sing-n

9 You use **a** or **an** in front of the names of people as a way of indicating that you do not know them or anything about them and you are saying their name for the first time. *The full address on a stick-on label was that of a Mrs P. R. Slater of Peterborough... A Dr Matthew Owens was reported missing while on an expedition to north-eastern Turkey.* DET: DET n-proper

10 You use **a** or **an** in front of the names of people when you want to refer to someone else who has the same qualities or character as the person named. *It would be wrong to see the Prime Minister as simply a Mrs Thatcher in disguise.* DET: DET n-proper

11 You use **a** or **an** in front of a surname when want to refer to someone who belongs to the family with that surname. *As far as I can recall, Patti was a Smith... He suspects that the jury will clear him because he is a Kennedy.* DET: DET n-proper

12 You use **a** or **an** in front of the names of painters and sculptors to refer to one individual painting or sculpture created by them. *Most people have very little difficulty in seeing why a Van Gogh is a work of genius... The value of a Rodin work depends on age, condition, authenticity and rarity.* DET: DET n-proper

13 You use **a** or **an** instead of the number 'one', especially with words of measurement such as 'hundred', 'hour', and 'metre', and with fractions such as 'half', 'quarter', and 'third'. *...more than a thousand acres of land. ...a quarter of an hour... The skirts were shortened an inch or two.* DET: DET sing-n

14 You use **a** or **an** in expressions such as **eight hours a day** to express a rate or ratio. *Prices start at £13.95 a metre for printed cotton... The helicopter can zip along at about 150 kilometres an hour... I get an income of thirteen and a half thousand a year.* DET: num DET sing-n

a- /eɪ-/. **A-** is added to the beginning of some adjectives in order to form adjectives that describe someone or something that does not have the feature or quality indicated by the original word. *I'm a completely apolitical man... She was amoral but honest. ...her new asymmetrical haircut.* PREFIX

aah /ɑː/. See **ah**.

aback /əbæk/. If you are **taken aback** by something, you are surprised or shocked by it and you cannot respond at once. *Roland was taken aback by our strength of feeling... Derek was taken aback when a man answered the phone.* ◆◇◇◇◇ PHRASE: usu v-link PHR, oft PHR *by* n

abacus /æbəkəs/ **abacuses.** An **abacus** is a frame used for counting. It has rods with sliding beads on them. N-COUNT

abandon /əbændən/ **abandons, abandoning, abandoned** ◆◆◆◇◇

1 If you **abandon** a place, thing, or person, you leave the place, thing, or person permanently or for a long time, especially when you should not do so. *He claimed that his parents had abandoned him... The road is strewn with abandoned vehicles.* VERB ≠stay with V n V-ed

2 If you **abandon** an activity or piece of work, you stop doing it before it is finished. *The authorities have abandoned any attempt to distribute food in an orderly fashion... The scheme's investors, fearful of bankruptcy, decided to abandon the project.* VERB =give up ≠continue V n

3 If you **abandon** an idea or way of thinking, you stop having that idea or thinking in that way. *Logic had prevailed and he had abandoned the idea.* VERB =give up V n

4 If you **abandon** yourself to an emotion, you think about it a lot and feel it strongly. *We are scared to abandon ourselves to our feelings in case we seem weak or out of control.* VERB V pron-refl *to* n

5 If you say that someone does something with **abandon**, you mean that they behave in a wild, uncontrolled way and do not think or care about how they should behave; used showing disapproval. *He has splashed dollars around with gay abandon... Their permissiveness toward their children reflects the wild abandon of their own lives.* N-UNCOUNT: usu *with* N PRAGMATICS

6 See also **abandoned**.

7 If people **abandon ship**, they get off a ship be- PHRASE:

cause it is sinking. *The officers and crew prepared to abandon ship in an orderly fashion.* V inflects

abandoned /əbændənd/. An **abandoned** place or building is no longer used or occupied. *All that digging had left a network of abandoned mines and tunnels. ...abandoned buildings that become a breeding ground for crime.* ◆◆◆◇◇ ADJ: usu ADJ n

abandonment /əbændənmənt/ ◆◇◇◇◇

1 The **abandonment** of a place, thing, or person is the act of leaving it permanently or for a long time, especially when you should not do so. *...memories of her father's complete abandonment of her.* N-UNCOUNT: oft N *of* n

2 The **abandonment** of a piece of work or activity is the act of stopping doing it before it is finished. *Constant rain forced the abandonment of the next day's competitions.* N-UNCOUNT: oft N *of* n

3 The **abandonment** of an idea or way of thinking is the act of stopping having the idea or of stopping thinking in that way. *...the government's abandonment of Marxism.* N-UNCOUNT: oft N *of* n

abashed /əbæʃt/. If you are **abashed**, you feel embarrassed and ashamed; used in written English. *He seemed both abashed and secretly delighted at Dan's gift.* ADJ-GRADED: usu v-link ADJ

abate /əbeɪt/ **abates, abating, abated.** If something **abates**, it becomes much less strong or widespread; a formal word. *The storms had abated by the time they rounded Cape Horn. ...a crime wave that shows no sign of abating.* ◆◇◇◇◇ VERB =die down V

abatement /əbeɪtmənt/. **Abatement** means a reduction in the strength or power of something or the reduction of it; a formal word. *It was not an environment conducive to the abatement of his hypochondria. ...noise abatement.* N-UNCOUNT: also *a* N

abattoir /æbətwɑːʳ/ **abattoirs.** An **abattoir** is a place where animals are killed in order to provide meat. N-COUNT =slaughterhouse

abbess /æbes/ **abbesses.** An **abbess** is the nun who is in charge of the other nuns in a convent. N-COUNT

abbey /æbi/ **abbeys.** An **abbey** is a church with buildings attached to it in which monks or nuns live or used to live. ◆◆◇◇◇ N-COUNT

abbot /æbət/ **abbots.** An **abbot** is the monk who is in charge of the other monks in a monastery or abbey. N-COUNT

abbreviate /əbriːvieɪt/ **abbreviates, abbreviating, abbreviated.** If you **abbreviate** something, especially a word or a piece of writing, you make it shorter. *He persuaded his son to abbreviate his first name to Alec.* ♦ **abbreviated** *It was an abbreviated document without detailed proposals.* VERB =shorten V n *to* n Also V n ADJ-GRADED: usu ADJ n

abbreviation /əbriːvieɪʃᵊn/ **abbreviations.** An **abbreviation** is a short form of a word or phrase, made by leaving out some of the letters or by using only the first letter of each word. *The postal abbreviation for Kansas is KS.* N-COUNT

ABC /eɪ biː siː/ **ABCs** ◆◆◇◇◇

1 The **ABC** of a subject or activity is the parts of it that you have to learn first because they are the most important and basic. *...the ABC of Marxism.* N-SING: N *of* n

2 Children who have learned their **ABC** or their **ABCs** have learned to recognize, write, or say the alphabet; an informal use. *...encouraging him to learn his ABC.* N-COUNT: poss N

abdicate /æbdɪkeɪt/ **abdicates, abdicating, abdicated**

1 If a king or queen **abdicates**, he or she resigns. *The last French king was Louis Philippe, who abdicated in 1848.* ♦ **abdication** /æbdɪkeɪʃᵊn/ *...the most serious royal crisis since the abdication of Edward VIII.* VERB V Also V n N-UNCOUNT: usu with poss

2 If you **abdicate** your responsibility for something, you refuse to accept the responsibility for it any longer. *Many parents simply abdicate all responsibility for their children.* ♦ **abdication** *There had been a complete abdication of responsibility.* VERB V n N-UNCOUNT: N *of* n

abdomen /æbdəmən, AM æbdoʊ-/ **abdomens.** Your **abdomen** is the part of your body below your chest where your stomach and intestines are; a formal word. *He went into hospital to undergo tests for a pain in his abdomen.* ◆◇◇◇◇ N-COUNT: oft poss N

abdominal /æbdɒmɪnᵊl/. **Abdominal** is used to describe something that is situated in the abdomen or forms part of it; a formal word. *...vomiting, diarrhoea and abdominal pain.* ◆◇◇◇◇ ADJ: ADJ n

abdominals /æbdɒmɪnᵊlz/. Your abdominal muscles can be referred to as your **abdominals** when you are talking about exercise. *One exercise for abdominals is the curl up, lying on the floor.* N-PLURAL

abduct /æbdʌkt/ **abducts, abducting, abducted.** If someone is **abducted** by another person, he or she is taken away illegally, usually using force. *He was on his way to the airport when his car was held up and he was abducted by four gunmen... She was sent for trial yesterday charged with abducting a six-month-old child.* ♦ **abduction** /æbdʌkʃᵊn/ **abductions** *...the abduction of four black youths from a church hostel in Soweto.* ♦ **abductor, abductors** *She cooperated with her abductor for fear that something might happen to the child.* ◆◇◇◇◇ VERB =kidnap be V-ed V n N-VAR N-COUNT

aberrant /æberənt/. **Aberrant** means unusual and not socially acceptable; a formal word. *Ian's rages and aberrant behavior worsened.* ADJ-GRADED: usu ADJ n

aberration /æbəreɪʃᵊn/ **aberrations** ◆◇◇◇◇

1 An **aberration** is an incident or way of behaving that is not typical. *It became very clear that the incident was not just an aberration, it was not just a single incident... Right-wing victories of 1974 and 1978 were written off as some form of aberration.* N-VAR

2 If you describe a person or their behaviour as an **aberration**, you believe that they are strange and not socially acceptable. *Single people are treated as an aberration and made to pay a supplement. ...sexual aberration.* N-VAR

abet /əbet/ **abets, abetting, abetted.** If one person **abets** another person, they help or encourage them to do something wrong. Aiding and abetting a criminal or aiding and abetting a crime is a criminal offence. *His wife was sentenced to seven years imprisonment for aiding and abetting him... We shall strike hard, without flinching, at terrorists and those who abet them.* VERB V n

abeyance /əbeɪəns/. If something is **in abeyance**, it is not operating or being used at the present time; a formal expression. *The Russian threat is, at the least, in abeyance... The matter was left in abeyance until Haig saw French.* PHRASE: v-link PHR, PHR after v

abhor /æbhɔːʳ/ **abhors, abhorring, abhorred.** If you **abhor** something, you hate it very much, especially for moral reasons; a formal word. *He was a man who abhorred violence and was deeply committed to reconciliation... If nature abhors a vacuum, journalists abhor a transition, when there is little news to cover.* VERB =detest V n

abhorrence /æbhɒrəns, AM -hɔːr-/. Someone's **abhorrence** of something is their strong hatred of it; a formal word. *They are anxious to show their abhorrence of racism.* N-UNCOUNT: usu with supp, oft poss N, N *of* n =hatred

abhorrent /æbhɒrənt, AM -hɔːr-/. If something is **abhorrent** to you, you hate it very much or consider it completely unacceptable; a formal word. *Racial discrimination is abhorrent to my council and our staff... There are many people who still find the act of abortion abhorrent.* ADJ-GRADED: usu v-link ADJ, oft ADJ *to* n

abide /əbaɪd/ **abides, abiding, abided.** If you can't **abide** someone or something, you dislike them very much. *I can't abide people who can't make up their minds... She couldn't abide his success.* ● See also **abiding**, **law-abiding**. ◆◇◇◇◇ VB: no passive, with brd-neg V n

abide by. If you **abide by** a law, agreement, or decision, you do what it says you should do. *They have got to abide by the rules... The group insisted that it was abiding by the code.* PHRASAL VERB V P n

abiding /əbaɪdɪŋ/. An **abiding** feeling, memory, or interest is one that you have for a very long time. *He has a genuine and abiding love of the craft... One of my abiding memories of him is of his singing to a small private party... The folksong world was another of his abiding interests.* ◆◇◇◇◇ ADJ-GRADED: ADJ n =lasting ≠short-lived

ability /əbɪlɪti/ **abilities** ◆◆◆◆◇

1 Your **ability** to do something is the fact that you can do it. *The public never had faith in his ability to* N-SING: N to-inf, oft with poss

handle the job... He has the ability to bring out the best in others. =capability

2 Your **ability** is the quality or skill that you have which makes it possible for you to do something. *Her drama teacher spotted her ability... I have confidence in the ability of the players... They repeatedly questioned his leadership abilities... Does the school cater for all abilities?* N-VAR: oft with poss

3 If you do something **to the best of** your **abilities** or **to the best of** your **ability**, you do it as well as you can. *I take care of them to the best of my abilities... They tackled them to the best of their ability.* PHRASE

-ability /-əbɪ̲lɪti/ **-abilities. -ability** replaces '-able' at the end of adjectives to form nouns. Nouns formed in this way refer to the state or quality described by the adjectives. *...the desirability of much closer political union... No one ever questioned her capability.* SUFFIX

abject /æbdʒekt/ ◆◇◇◇◇

1 You use **abject** to emphasize that a situation or quality is shameful or depressing. *Both of them died in abject poverty... This scheme was an abject failure.* ♦ **abjectly** *Both have failed abjectly.* ADJ-GRADED: usu ADJ n PRAGMATICS =total ADV-GRADED

2 If you describe someone as **abject**, you think they have no self-respect or courage *He sounded abject and eager to please... He looked back at the abject, silent girl and repeated his question.* ADJ-GRADED

abjure /æbdʒʊə̲ʳ/ **abjures, abjuring, abjured.** If you **abjure** something such as a belief or way of life, you state publicly that you will give it up or that you reject it; a formal word. *He abjured the Protestant faith and became King in 1594. ...countries whose officials abjure bribery.* VERB V n

ablaze /əbleɪ̲z/ ◆◇◇◇◇

1 Something that is **ablaze** is burning fiercely. *Shops, houses, and vehicles were set ablaze.* ADJ: v n ADJ, v-link ADJ

2 If a place is **ablaze** with lights or colours, it is very bright because of them. *The chamber was ablaze with light... In spring, the valleys are ablaze with colour.* ADJ: v-link ADJ, usu ADJ *with* n

3 If someone is **ablaze**, or if their eyes are **ablaze**, their expression shows that they are feeling a strong emotion, such as great excitement or anger. *He was ablaze with enthusiasm... Her voice is passionate. Her eyes are ablaze.* ADJ: v-link ADJ, oft ADJ *with* n

able /eɪ̲bəl/ **abler** /eɪ̲bləʳ/ **ablest** /eɪ̲blɪst/ ◆◆◆◆◆

1 If someone or something **is able to** do something, they have skills or qualities which make it possible for them to do it. *The older child should be able to prepare a simple meal... The company say they're able to keep pricing competitive... They seemed able to work together very efficiently.* PHR-MODAL =can ≠be unable to

2 If someone or something **is able to** do something, they have enough freedom, power, time, or money to do it. *You'll be able to read in peace... Have you been able to have any kind of contact?... It would be nice to be able to afford to retire earlier.* PHR-MODAL =can ≠be unable to

3 Someone who is **able** is very clever or very good at doing something. *...one of the brightest and ablest members of the government... They are bright, intelligent, able and confident.* ADJ-GRADED =clever, gifted

-able /-əbəl/. **-able** combines with verbs to form adjectives. Adjectives formed in this way describe someone or something that can have a particular thing done to them. For example, if something is avoidable, it can be avoided. *Tragic as these deaths are, they are avoidable... He was an admirable chairman.* SUFFIX

able-bodied /eɪ̲bəl bɒ̲did/. An **able-bodied** person is physically strong and healthy, rather than weak or disabled. *The gym can be used by both able-bodied and disabled people.* ► **The able-bodied** are people who are able-bodied. *The able-bodied had fled.* ADJ-GRADED ≠disabled N-PLURAL: the N

ablutions /əblu̲ːʃənz/. **Ablutions** is a formal or humorous word for the activity of washing yourself. *Doubtless Manny was meticulous about his ablutions.* N-PLURAL: oft poss N

ably /eɪ̲bli/. **Ably** means skilfully and successfully. *He was ably assisted by a number of members from the Middlesex branches.* ADV-GRADED: ADV with v

abnormal /æbnɔ̲ːʳməl/. Someone or something that is **abnormal** is unusual, especially in a way that is worrying; a formal word. *...abnormal heart rhythms and high anxiety levels. ...a child with an abnormal fear of strangers.* ♦ **abnormally** *...abnormally high levels of glucose... This stops the cells from growing abnormally.* ◆◇◇◇◇ ADJ-GRADED ADV: usu ADV adj/adv, also ADV with v

abnormality /æbnɔːʳmæ̲lɪti/ **abnormalities.** An **abnormality** in something, especially in a person's body or behaviour, is an unusual part or feature of it that may be worrying or dangerous; a formal word. *Further scans are required to confirm the diagnosis of an abnormality... Genetic abnormalities are more often associated with faults in paternal DNA than in maternal DNA.* ◆◇◇◇◇ N-VAR

aboard /əbɔ̲ːʳd/. If you are **aboard** a ship or plane, you are on it or in it. *She invited 750 people aboard the luxury yacht, the Savarona... Mrs Parrish had left Baghdad aboard a plane for the Zambian capital, Lusaka.* ► Also an adverb. *It had taken two hours to load all the people aboard... The United States has a naval task force offshore, with two thousand marines aboard.* ◆◆◇◇◇ PREP =on board ADV: ADV after v =on board

abode /əbo̲ʊd/ **abodes**

1 Your **abode** is the place where you live; a formal word. *I went round the streets and found his new abode.* N-COUNT

2 In law, the term **no fixed abode** is used to refer to people who are homeless. *In any local hospital 30 per cent of psychiatric beds are occupied by people of no fixed abode.* PHRASE: oft *of* PHR

3 If someone is given the **right of abode** in a particular country, they are legally allowed to live there; a legal term. *Some 225,000 Hong Kong residents will be given right of abode in Britain.* PHRASE: oft PHR *in* n

abolish /əbɒ̲lɪʃ/ **abolishes, abolishing, abolished.** If someone in authority **abolishes** a system or practice, they formally put an end to it. *The following year Parliament voted to abolish the death penalty for murder... The whole system should be abolished.* ◆◆◇◇◇ VERB V n

abolition /æ̲bəlɪʃən/. The **abolition** of something such as a system or practice is its formal ending. *Mr Botha said President de Klerk's commitment to the abolition of apartheid was irreversible... Energetic campaigning against the legislation led to its abolition in the early 1980s.* ◆◇◇◇◇ N-UNCOUNT: also a N, usu with supp, oft N *of* n

abolitionist /æbəlɪ̲ʃənɪst/ **abolitionists.** An **abolitionist** is someone who campaigns for the abolition of a particular system or practice. *By 1838, the abolitionists had shamed parliament into ending slavery in British colonies... As long as most people are happy to have the monarchy, the abolitionist position is an arrogant fantasy.* N-COUNT: oft N n

A-bomb /e̲ɪ bɒm/ **A-bombs.** An **A-bomb** is an atomic bomb. N-COUNT

abominable /əbɒ̲mɪnəbəl/. Something that is **abominable** is very unpleasant or very bad. *The President described the killings as an abominable crime... English food can be wonderful but the normal English diet is abominable.* ♦ **abominably** /əbɒ̲mɪnəbli/. *Chloe has behaved abominably... Wallis was harsh, dominating, often abominably rude.* ADJ-GRADED =detestable ADV: ADV after v, ADV -ed/adj

abomination /əbɒmɪne̲ɪʃən/ **abominations.** If you say that something is an **abomination**, you think that it is completely unacceptable; a formal word. *What is happening is an abomination.* N-COUNT PRAGMATICS =outrage

aboriginal /æbərɪ̲dʒɪnəl/ **aboriginals** ◆◇◇◇◇

1 An **Aboriginal** is an Australian Aborigine. *He remained fascinated by the Aboriginals' tales.* N-COUNT =Aborigine

2 **Aboriginal** means belonging or relating to the Australian Aborigines. *For many aboriginal people such measures don't go far enough. ...Aboriginal art. ...a protest over aboriginal land rights.* ADJ: ADJ n

3 The **aboriginal** people or animals of a place are ones that have been there from the earliest known times or that were there before Europeans arrived. *Most Canadians acknowledge that the aboriginal people have had a rotten deal.* ADJ: ADJ n =native, indigenous

Aborigine /æbərɪdʒɪni/ **Aborigines. Aborigines** are members of the tribes that were living in Australia when Europeans arrived there. N-COUNT: usu pl =Aboriginal

abort /əbɔːʳt/ **aborts, aborting, aborted** ◆◇◇◇◇
1 If an unborn baby **is aborted**, the pregnancy is ended deliberately and the baby is not born alive; a formal use. *Ruth Ellis gunned down the lover who walked out on her after she had aborted their child. ...the latest date at which a foetus can be aborted. ...tissue from aborted fetuses.* VERB V n V-ed Also V
2 If someone **aborts** a process, plan, or activity, they stop it before it has been completed. *When the decision was made to abort the mission, there was great confusion... The take-off was aborted... A military guard was injured in the aborted coup.* VERB V n V-ed

abortion /əbɔːʳʃᵊn/ **abortions.** If a woman has an **abortion**, she ends her pregnancy deliberately so that the baby is not born alive. *He and his girlfriend had been going out together for a year when she had an abortion. ...anti-abortion groups... He and his wife both strongly support abortion rights.* ◆◆◆◇◇ N-VAR

abortionist /əbɔːʳʃənɪst/ **abortionists.** An **abortionist** is someone who performs abortions, usually illegally. *She knew who to ask about finding an abortionist.* ● See also **anti-abortionist**. N-COUNT

abortive /əbɔːʳtɪv/. An **abortive** attempt or action is unsuccessful; a formal word. *...the abortive attempt to grow groundnuts in Tanganyika. ...the abortive coup attempt in August 1991.* ◆◇◇◇◇ ADJ: usu ADJ n =failed

abound /əbaʊnd/ **abounds, abounding, abounded.** If things **abound**, or if a place **abounds** with things, there are very large numbers of them; a formal word. *Stories abound about when he was in charge... Venice abounds in famous hotels... The book abounds with close-up images from space.* ◆◇◇◇◇ VERB V V *in* n V *with* n

about /əbaʊt/ ◆◆◆◆◆
In addition to the uses shown below, **about** is used after some verbs, nouns, and adjectives to introduce extra information. **About** is also often used after verbs of movement, such as 'walk' and 'drive', and in phrasal verbs such as 'mess about' and 'set about', especially in British English.
1 You use **about** to introduce who or what something relates to or concerns. *She came in for a coffee, and told me about her friend Shona... She knew a lot about food. ...advice about exercise, and diet... He never complains about his wife.* PREP
2 When you mention the things that an activity or institution is **about**, you are saying what it involves or what its aims are. *Leadership is about the ability to implement change.* PREP
3 You use **about** after some adjectives to indicate the person or thing that a feeling or state of mind relates to. *'I'm sorry about Patrick,' she said... I feel so guilty and angry about the whole issue.* PREP
4 If you do something **about** a problem, you take action in order to solve it. *Rachel was going to do something about Jacob... He said he'd ask Nina for a divorce, but he never did anything about it.* PREP
5 When you say that there is a particular quality **about** someone or something, you mean that they have this quality but you can't specify it exactly. *There was a dreary absence of originality about Curtis... I think there's something a little peculiar about the results of your test.* PREP
6 **About** is used in front of a number to show that the number is not exact. *In my local health centre there's about forty parking spaces... The rate of inflation is running at about 2.7 percent... When I was about nine I started to have very vivid dreams.* ADV: ADV num =approximately ≠precisely
7 If someone or something moves **about**, they keep moving in different directions. *The house isn't big, what with three children running about.* ► Also a preposition. *From 1879 to 1888 he wandered about Germany, Switzerland, and Italy... His hair was drifting about his shoulders like dirty snow.* ADV: ADV after v =around PREP: v PREP n =around
8 If you put something **about** a person or thing, you put it around them. *Helen threw her arms about him... She was elegantly dressed with a double strand of pearls about her neck.* PREP =round, around
9 If someone or something is **about**, they are present or available. *There's lots of money about these days for schemes like this.* ADJ: v-link ADJ
10 If you are **about** to do something, you are going to do it very soon. If something is **about** to happen, it will happen very soon. *I think he's about to leave... Argentina has lifted all restrictions on trade and visas are about to be abolished... The film was about to start.* ADJ: v-link ADJ to-inf
11 ● **how about**: see **how**. ● **what about**: see **what**. ● **just about**: see **just**.
12 If someone is **out and about**, they are available after being unavailable or are outdoors after being indoors for some time, for example because of illness. *Despite considerable pain she has been getting out and about almost as normal... The regulations were relaxed and the prisoners could get out and about a bit.* PHRASES usu PHR after v, also v-link PHR
13 If someone is **out and about**, they are travelling from one place to another, often as part of their job. *They knew that I was again on the scene because they saw me out and about... Get out and about – it's amazing how many stylists get work through meeting artists at bars, clubs and parties.* usu PHR after v, also v-link PHR

about-face, about-faces. An **about-face** is the same as an **about-turn**. *Few observers believe the president will do an about-face and start spending more.* N-COUNT =about-turn, volte-face

about-turn, about-turns. An **about-turn** is a complete change of attitude or opinion. *The decision was seen as an about-turn for the Government.* N-COUNT =about-face

above /əbʌv/ ◆◆◆◆◇
1 If one thing is **above** another one, it is directly over it or higher than it. *He lifted his hands above his head... Apartment 46 was a quiet apartment, unlike the one above it... He was staring into the mirror above him.* ► Also an adverb. *A long scream sounded from somewhere above. ...a picture of the new plane as seen from above... There are five bedrooms, a large attic above, and wine cellars below.* PREP ADV: ADV after v, *from* ADV ≠below
2 In writing, you use **above** to refer to something that has already been mentioned or illustrated. *Several conclusions could be drawn from the results described above... Full details are in the table above.* ► Also a noun. *For additional information, contact any of the above.* ► Also an adjective. *For a copy of their brochure, write to the above address.* ADV: ADV after v, n ADV PRAGMATICS ≠below N-SING-COLL: *the* N ADJ: ADJ n
3 If an amount or measurement is **above** a particular level, it is greater than that level. *The temperature crept up to just above 40 degrees... Victoria Falls has had above average levels of rainfall this year... These plants must be stored in the light at above freezing temperature... Government spending is planned to rise 3 per cent above inflation.* ► Also an adverb. *Banks have been charging 25 percent and above for unsecured loans.* PREP ≠below ADV: amount *and* ADV
4 If you hear one sound **above** another, it is louder or clearer than the second one. *...trying to talk above the noise to Dwight Perkins... Then there was a woman's voice, rising shrilly above the barking.* PREP =over
5 If someone is **above** you, they are in a higher social position than you or in a position of authority over you. *I know you're above me socially, but I must say I find your attitude offensive... I married above myself – rich county people... Look at the people above you in the positions of power and see what type of characters they are.* ► Also an adverb. *The policemen admitted beating the student, but said they were acting on orders from above.* PREP ≠below ADV: *from* ADV
6 If you say that someone **is getting above themselves**, you disapprove of them because they think they are better than everyone else. *I just think you're getting a little bit above yourself.* PHRASE: V inflects PRAGMATICS
7 If someone thinks that they are **above** something, they think that they are too good or too important for it; used showing disapproval. *This was clearly a failure by someone who thought he was above failure... He was one of those men who live above their own rules.* PREP PRAGMATICS
8 If someone is **above** criticism or suspicion, they cannot be criticized or suspected because of their PREP: v-link PREP n =beyond

good qualities or their position. *The Queen remains above criticism, apart from the issue of her tax liability... He was a respected academic and above suspicion.*

9 If you value one person or thing **above** any other, you value them more or consider that they are more important. *...his tendency to put the team above everything... I want to be honest, honest above everything else.* PREP

10 • **over and above**: see **over**. • **above the law**: see **law**. • **above board**: see **board**.

abracadabra /æbrəkədæbrə/. **Abracadabra** is a word that someone says when they are performing a magic trick in order to make the magic happen. EXCLAM

abrade /əbreɪd/ **abrades, abrading, abraded.** If something rough **abrades** something else, it scratches it or wears it down by rubbing against it; a formal word. *...the grazed patches on her hands where the brutally rough rock has abraded the skin.* VERB; V n

abrasion /əbreɪʒ^{ə}n/ **abrasions.** An **abrasion** is an area on a person's body where the skin has been scraped; a formal word. *He had severe abrasions to his right cheek.* N-COUNT =graze, cut

abrasive /əbreɪsɪv/ **abrasives** ◆◇◇◇◇

1 Someone who has an **abrasive** manner is unkind and rude. *His abrasive manner has won him an unenviable notoriety... Pamela was unrepentant about her strong language and abrasive remarks.* ADJ-GRADED =harsh

2 An **abrasive** substance is rough and can be used to clean hard surfaces. *Abrasive cleaners will scratch and dull the surface.* ADJ-GRADED

3 An **abrasive** is a substance that is rough and can be used to clean hard surfaces. *Avoid abrasives, which can damage the tiles.* N-MASS

abreast /əbrest/ ◆◇◇◇◇

1 If people or things walk or move **abreast**, they are next to each other, side by side, and facing in the same direction. *The steep pavement was too narrow for them to walk abreast. ...a group of youths riding their motorbikes four abreast.* ADV: ADV after v, num ADV

2 If you are **abreast of** someone or something, you are level with them or in line with them. *As he drew abreast of the man he pretended to stumble.* PHR-PREP

3 If you keep **abreast of** a subject, you know all the most recent facts about it. *He will be keeping abreast of the news... We'll keep you abreast of developments.* PHR-PREP

abridge /əbrɪdʒ/ **abridges, abridging, abridged.** If a writer or editor **abridges** a book, play, or article, they make it shorter by removing some parts of it. *You've scripted a film about him; you've abridged 'Finnegan's Wake'; you've done a musical.* VERB =shorten; V n

abridged /əbrɪdʒd/. A book or play that is **abridged** has been made shorter by removing some parts of it. *This is an abridged version of her new novel 'The Queen and I'.* ADJ-GRADED: usu ADJ n =shortened

abroad /əbrɔːd/ ◆◆◆◇◇

1 If you go **abroad**, you go to a foreign country, usually one which is separated from the country where you live by an ocean or a sea. *I would love to go abroad this year, perhaps to the South of France. ...public opposition here and abroad... He will stand in for Mr Goh when he is abroad... About 65 per cent of its sales come from abroad.* ADV: ADV after v, n ADV, be ADV, from ADV =overseas

2 If there is a story or feeling **abroad**, people generally know about it or feel it. *There'll still be a feeling abroad that this change has to be recognised.* ADV: n ADV =around

abrogate /æbrəgeɪt/ **abrogates, abrogating, abrogated.** If someone in a position of authority **abrogates** something such as a law, agreement, or practice, they put an end to it; a formal word. *Our information is that the next prime minister could abrogate the treaty.* ♦ **abrogation** /æbrəgeɪʃ^{ə}n/ *Mr Pehoua criticised the abrogation of trade union rights by the government.* VERB =revoke; V n; N-UNCOUNT: N of n

abrupt /əbrʌpt/ ◆◆◇◇◇

1 An **abrupt** change or action is very sudden, often in a way which is unpleasant. *Rosie's idyllic world came to an abrupt end when her parents' marriage broke up... The recession brought an abrupt halt to this happiness... His abrupt departure is bound to raise questions.* ♦ **abruptly** *He stopped abruptly and looked my way.* ADJ-GRADED =unexpected; ADV-GRADED: ADV with v =suddenly

2 Someone who is **abrupt** speaks in a rather rude, unfriendly way. *He was abrupt to the point of rudeness... Cross was a little taken aback by her abrupt manner.* ♦ **abruptly** *'Good night, then,' she said abruptly.* ♦ **abruptness** *I think Simon was hurt by your abruptness this afternoon.* ADJ-GRADED =offhand; ADV-GRADED; N-UNCOUNT

abscess /æbses/ **abscesses.** An **abscess** is a painful swelling, containing pus. *I soon discovered that I had an abscess at the base of my tooth.* N-COUNT

abscond /æbskɒnd/ **absconds, absconding, absconded**

1 If someone **absconds** from somewhere such as a prison, they escape from it or leave it without permission; a formal use. *He was remanded in care and ordered to appear the following day, but absconded... A dozen inmates have escaped or absconded from Forest Jail in the past year.* VERB =run away; V; V from n

2 If someone **absconds** with something, they leave and take it with them, although it does not belong to them; a formal use. *Unfortunately, his partners were crooks and absconded with the funds.* VERB =run off; V with n

abseil /æbseɪl/ **abseils, abseiling, abseiled.** In British English if mountain climbers **abseil** down a cliff or rock face, they go down it by sliding in a controlled way down a rope, with their feet against the cliff or rock. The usual American word is **rappel**. *Dave Thompson and his teenage son Mark had abseiled down the sheer 200 ft cliffs at Mewsford, Dyfed.* VERB; V down n

absence /æbs^{ə}ns/ **absences** ◆◆◆◇◇

1 Someone's **absence** from a place is the fact that they are not there. *...a bundle of letters which had arrived for me in my absence... Eleanor would later blame her mother-in-law for her husband's frequent absences.* N-VAR: with supp ≠presence

2 The **absence** of something from a place is the fact that it is not there or does not exist. *The presence or absence of clouds can have an important impact on heat transfer... In the absence of a will the courts decide who the guardian is.* N-SING: with supp =lack ≠presence

3 See also **leave of absence**. • **conspicuous by** one's **absence**: see **conspicuous**.

absent, absents, absenting, absented. The adjective and preposition are pronounced /æbs^{ə}nt/. The verb is pronounced /æbsent/. ◆◆◇◇◇

1 If someone or something is **absent** from a place or situation, they are not there. *He has been absent from his desk for two weeks... The pictures, too, were absent from the walls... Any soldier failing to report would be considered absent without leave and punished accordingly.* ADJ: usu v-link ADJ, oft ADJ from n

2 If someone appears **absent**, they are not paying attention because they are thinking about something else. *'Nothing,' Rosie said in an absent way.* ♦ **absently** /æbs^{ə}ntli/ *He nodded absently.* ADJ-GRADED =inattentive; ADV-GRADED

3 If someone **absents** themselves from a place, they do not go there or they do not stay there; a formal use. *She was old enough to absent herself from the lunch table if she chose... He pleaded guilty before a court martial to absenting himself without leave.* VERB; V pron-refl from n; V pron-refl

4 In formal American English, if you say that **absent** one thing, another thing will happen, you mean that if the first thing does not happen, the second thing will happen. *Absent a solution, people like Sue Godfrey will just keep on fighting.* PREP =without

absentee /æbs^{ə}ntiː/ **absentees** ◆◇◇◇◇

1 An **absentee** is a person who is expected to be in a particular place but who is not there. *I was expecting far more in the classes but there are a lot of absentees.* N-COUNT

2 **Absentee** is used to describe someone who is not there to do a particular job in person. *Absentee fathers will be forced to pay child maintenance. ...an absentee landlord.* ADJ: ADJ n

3 In the United States, if you vote by **absentee** ballot, you vote in advance because you will be away on the day of an election. *He has already voted by* ADJ: ADJ n =proxy

absentee ballot... The deadline for absentee voting in Louisiana was Saturday.

absenteeism /æbsəntiːɪzəm/. **Absenteeism** is the fact or habit of frequently being away from work or school, usually without a good reason. *...the high rate of absenteeism.* N-UNCOUNT =truancy ≠attendance

absentia /æbsentiə, AM -senʃə/. If something is done to you **in absentia**, it is done to you when you are not present; a formal expression. *He was tried in absentia and sentenced to seven years in prison.* PHRASE: PHR after v

absent-minded; also spelled **absentminded.** Someone who is **absent-minded** forgets things or does not pay attention to what they are doing, often because they are thinking about something else. *Malcolm is a genius, but he's the absent-minded professor type... In his later life he became even more absent-minded.* ADJ-GRADED =forgetful ♦ **absent-mindedly** *Elizabeth absent-mindedly picked a thread from his lapel... Absent-mindedly, she took the milk pan from Marcus and started making breakfast.* ADV-GRADED: ADV with v ♦ **absent-mindedness** *You will have to put up with Grace's absent-mindedness.* N-UNCOUNT: oft with poss

absinthe /æbsɪnθ/. **Absinthe** is a very strong alcoholic drink. It is green in colour and bitter in taste. N-UNCOUNT

absolute /æbsəluːt/ **absolutes** ♦♦♦◇◇

1 Absolute means total and complete. *It's not really suited to absolute beginners... A sick person needs absolute confidence and trust in a doctor.* ADJ: usu ADJ n =complete

2 You use **absolute** to emphasize something that you are saying. *About 12 inches wide is the absolute minimum you should consider... I think it's absolute nonsense.* ADJ: ADJ n PRAGMATICS =complete

3 An **absolute** ruler has complete power and authority over his or her country. *He ruled with absolute power. ...the doctrine of absolute monarchy based upon divine right.* ADJ: ADJ n

4 Absolute is used to say that something is definite and will not change even if circumstances change. *John brought the absolute proof that we needed... They had given an absolute assurance that it would be kept secret.* ADJ: usu ADJ n

5 An amount that is expressed in **absolute** terms is expressed as a fixed amount rather than being expressed with reference to variable factors such as what you earn or the effects of inflation. *They might be just as badly in debt, both in absolute terms and as a proportion of their incomes.* ADJ: ADJ n ≠real

6 Absolute rules and principles are believed to be true, right, or relevant in all situations. *There are no absolute rules. ...certain assumptions which are accepted without question as absolute truths.* ADJ: usu ADJ n

7 An **absolute** is a rule or principle that is believed to be true, right, or relevant in all situations. *We tend to think in absolutes.* N-COUNT

8 See also **decree absolute**.

absolutely /æbsəluːtli/ ♦♦♦♦◇

1 Absolutely means totally and completely. *Jill is absolutely right... I absolutely refuse to get married... There is absolutely no difference!* ADV: usu ADV adj/adv, also ADV with v

2 Some people say **absolutely** as an emphatic way of saying yes or of agreeing with someone. They say **absolutely not** as an emphatic way of saying no or of disagreeing with someone. *'It's worrying that they're doing things without training though, isn't it?'—'Absolutely.'... 'Did they approach you?'—'No, absolutely not.'* ADV: ADV as reply PRAGMATICS

absolute majority, absolute majorities. If a political party wins an **absolute majority**, they obtain more seats or votes than the total number of seats or votes gained by their opponents in an election. *Mr Demirel failed to win an absolute majority in that election.* N-COUNT: usu sing

absolute zero. **Absolute zero** is a theoretical temperature that is thought to be the lowest possible temperature. N-UNCOUNT

absolution /æbsəluːʃən/. If someone is given **absolution**, they are forgiven for something wrong that they have done; a formal or religious word. *She felt as if his words had granted her absolution.* N-UNCOUNT =forgiveness

absolutism /æbsəluːtɪzəm/

1 Absolutism is a political system in which one ruler or leader has complete power and authority over a country; used showing disapproval. *...the triumphal reassertion of royal absolutism.* N-UNCOUNT PRAGMATICS

2 You describe someone's beliefs as **absolutism** if they are believed to be true, right, or relevant in all situations, without any allowances being made for different circumstances; used showing disapproval. *They are saying, with varying degrees of absolutism, that animals should not be exploited at all.* N-UNCOUNT PRAGMATICS ♦ **absolutist** *This absolutist belief is replaced by an appreciation that rules can vary.* ADJ

absolve /æbzɒlv/ **absolves, absolving, absolved.** If a report or investigation **absolves** someone from blame or responsibility, it formally states that he or she is not guilty or is not to blame. *The announcement follows a police investigation yesterday which absolved the police of all blame in the incident... The programme was critical of the judicial inquiry which absolved the soldiers.* VERB =excuse, vindicate V n of/from n V n

absorb /əbzɔːʳb/ **absorbs, absorbing, absorbed** ♦♦◇◇◇

1 If something **absorbs** a liquid, gas, or other substance, it soaks it up or takes it in. *Plants absorb carbon dioxide from the air and moisture from the soil... Refined sugars are absorbed into the bloodstream very quickly.* VERB =soak up V n be V-ed into n

2 If something **absorbs** light, heat, or another form of energy, it takes it in. *A household radiator absorbs energy in the form of electric current and releases it in the form of heat.* VERB V n

3 If a group **is absorbed** into a larger group, it becomes part of the larger group. *The Colonial Office was absorbed into the Foreign Office... President Bush had promised more American money to help Israel absorb Soviet immigrants.* VERB be V-ed into n V n

4 If something **absorbs** a force or shock, it reduces its effect. *...footwear which does not absorb the impact of the foot striking the ground.* VERB V n

5 If a system or society **absorbs** changes, effects, or costs, it is able to deal with them without being badly affected. *The banks would be forced to absorb large losses... We can't absorb those costs.* VERB =cope with V n

6 If something **absorbs** something such as money, space, or time, it uses up a great deal of it. *It absorbed vast amounts of capital that could have been used for investment... It might help if campaigning didn't absorb so much time and money.* VERB =eat up V n

7 If you **absorb** information, you learn and understand it. *Too often he only absorbs half the information in the manual... We closed our offices at 2:00 p.m. to give employees time to absorb the bad news.* VERB =digest, take in V n

8 If something **absorbs** you, it interests you a great deal and takes up all your attention and energy. *...a second career which absorbed her more completely than her acting ever had.* ● See also **absorbed, absorbing**. VERB =grip V n

absorbed /əbzɔːʳbd/. If you are **absorbed** in something or someone, you are very interested in them and they take up all your attention and energy. *They were completely absorbed in each other... He had discovered politics and was rapidly becoming absorbed by it... I get so absorbed in doing something that I am unaware of things happening round me.* ♦◇◇◇◇ ADJ-GRADED: v-link ADJ, usu ADJ in/by n =engrossed

absorbent /əbzɔːʳbənt/. **Absorbent** material soaks up liquid easily. *The towels are highly absorbent.* ADJ-GRADED ≠water-repellent ♦ **absorbency** /əbzɔːʳbənsi/ *You can use two nappies for extra absorbency at night.* N-UNCOUNT

absorber /əbzɔːʳbəʳ/. See **shock absorber**.

absorbing /əbzɔːʳbɪŋ/. An **absorbing** task or activity interests you a great deal and takes up all your attention and energy. *'Two Sisters' is an absorbing read... Children will find other exhibits equally absorbing.* ♦◇◇◇◇ ADJ-GRADED =captivating

absorption /əbzɔːʳpʃən/ ♦◇◇◇◇

1 The **absorption** of a liquid, gas, or other substance is the process of it being soaked up or taken in. *This controls the absorption of liquids... Vitamin C increases the absorption of iron from food.* N-UNCOUNT: oft N of n

2 The **absorption** of a group into a larger group is the process of it becoming part of the larger group. *...East Germany's absorption into the Federal Republic... He has special responsibility for the absorption of Soviet immigrants.*
N-UNCOUNT: usu with poss, oft N *into/by* n

3 Someone's **absorption** in something is the fact that they are very interested in it and that it takes up all their attention and energy. *He was struck by the artists' total absorption in their work... My boyhood absorption with soccer and cricket continued.*
N-UNCOUNT: poss N *in/with* n

abstain /æbste͟ɪn/ **abstains, abstaining, abstained** ◆◇◇◇◇

1 If you **abstain** from something, usually something you want to do, you deliberately do not do it; a formal word. *Abstain from sex or use condoms... After six months, fewer than one-third of smokers who try nicotine patches will still be abstaining.*
VERB
V *from* n
V

2 If you **abstain** during a vote, you do not use your vote. *Three Conservative MPs abstained in the vote on the second reading of the Railways Bill... The voting was twelve to two, with Cuba and Yemen opposing the move and China abstaining.*
VERB
V

abstemious /æbsti͟ːmiəs/. Someone who is **abstemious** avoids doing too much of something enjoyable such as eating or drinking; a formal word.
ADJ-GRADED
=temperate

abstention /æbste͟nʃᵊn/ **abstentions** ◆◇◇◇◇

1 **Abstention** is a formal act of not voting either for or against a proposal. *...a vote of sixteen in favor, three against, and one abstention... The number of abstentions is likely to be crucial... Abstention is traditionally high in Colombia.*
N-VAR

2 **Abstention** is the same as abstinence; a formal word. *The goal is complete abstention from all mind-altering substances.*
N-UNCOUNT: oft N *from* n
=abstinence

abstinence /æ͟bstɪnəns/. **Abstinence** is the practice of abstaining from something such as alcoholic drink or sex, often for health or religious reasons. *...six months of abstinence. ...total abstinence from alcohol.*
◆◇◇◇◇
N-UNCOUNT
=abstention
≠indulgence

abstract, abstracts, abstracting, abstracted. The adjective and noun are pronounced /æ͟bstrækt/. The verb is pronounced /æbstræ͟kt/. ◆◆◇◇◇

1 An **abstract** idea or way of thinking is based on general ideas rather than on real things and events. *...starting with a few abstract principles... It's not a question of some abstract concept of justice. ...the faculty of abstract reasoning.* ♦ **abstractly** *It is hard to think abstractly in these conditions.*
ADJ-GRADED
=theoretical
ADV-GRADED

2 When you talk or think about something **in the abstract**, you talk or think about it in a general way, rather than considering particular things or events. *Money was a commodity she never thought about except in the abstract... In the abstract there is nothing wrong with taking risks and assuming debts.*
PHRASE: PHR with cl/group

3 In grammar, an **abstract** noun refers to a quality or idea rather than to a physical object. *...abstract words such as glory, honor, and courage.*
ADJ: ADJ n
≠concrete

4 **Abstract** art makes use of shapes and patterns rather than showing people or things as they actually are. *A modern abstract painting takes over one complete wall.*
ADJ-GRADED: usu ADJ n
≠figurative

5 An **abstract** is an abstract work of art. *He persuaded her to change from abstracts to portraits.*
N-COUNT

6 An **abstract** of an article, document, or speech is a short piece of writing that summarizes the main points of it. *I was sent to pick up an abstract of the specifications.*
N-COUNT: oft N *of* n
=summary

7 If you **abstract** something from a place, you take it from there; a formal use. *...a licence to abstract water from the River Axe... The author has abstracted poems from earlier books.*
VERB
V n *from* n
Also V n

abstracted /æbstræ͟ktɪd/. Someone who is **abstracted** is thinking so deeply that they are not fully aware of what is happening around them; used in written English. *Meg was so abstracted she scarcely noticed that the train had stopped... The same abstracted look was still on his face.* ♦ **abstractedly** *'I suppose so,' she said abstractedly.*
ADJ-GRADED
=preoccupied
ADV-GRADED: ADV with v

abstraction /æbstræ͟kʃᵊn/ **abstractions** ◆◇◇◇◇

1 An **abstraction** is a general idea rather than one relating to a particular object, person, or situation; a formal use. *Is it worth fighting a big war, in the name of an abstraction like sovereignty?*
N-VAR
=concept

2 **Abstraction** is the state of being very deep in thought; used in written English. *Andrew noticed her abstraction and asked, 'What's bothering you?'*
N-UNCOUNT
=preoccupation

3 **Abstraction** is the use of shapes and patterns in art; a technical use. *For almost 100 years, artists have experimented with abstraction.*
N-UNCOUNT

abstruse /æbstru͟ːs/. If you describe something as **abstruse**, you mean that it is difficult to understand; a formal word which is often used showing disapproval. *Meanwhile meetings keep reverting to fruitless discussions about abstruse resolutions.*
ADJ-GRADED
PRAGMATICS

absurd /æbsɜ͟ːʳd/. If you say that something is **absurd**, you are criticizing it because you think that it is ridiculous or that it does not make sense. *It is absurd to be discussing compulsory redundancy policies for teachers... I've known clients of mine go to absurd lengths, just to avoid paying me a few pounds... That's absurd.* ► **The absurd** is something that is absurd. *Parkinson had a sharp eye for the absurd.* ♦ **absurdly** *Prices were still absurdly low, in his opinion... Absurdly, it makes shoppers overpay farmers to grow too much food.* ♦ **absurdity** /æbsɜ͟ːʳdɪti/ **absurdities** *I find myself growing increasingly angry at the absurdity of the situation. ...the absurdities of fashionable childcare methods.*
◆◆◇◇◇
ADJ-GRADED: oft *it* v-link ADJ to-inf/that
PRAGMATICS
=ridiculous
N-SING: *the* N
ADV-GRADED
N-VAR

absurdist /æbsɜ͟ːʳdɪst/. An **absurdist** play or other work shows the absurdity of some aspect of society or human behaviour. *...'La Peste', the last volume in the absurdist trilogy.*
ADJ: usu ADJ n

abundance /əbʌ͟ndəns/. An **abundance** of something is a large quantity of it. *This area of France has an abundance of safe beaches and a pleasing climate. ...the variety and abundance of wildlife found in Florida... Food was in abundance.*
◆◇◇◇◇
N-SING-COLL: usu N *of* n, also *in* N
=wealth

abundant /əbʌ͟ndənt/. Something that is **abundant** is present in large quantities. *There is an abundant supply of cheap labour... Birds are abundant in the tall vegetation by the canal.*
◆◇◇◇◇
ADJ-GRADED
=plentiful

abundantly /əbʌ͟ndəntli/

1 If something is **abundantly** clear, it is extremely obvious. *He made it abundantly clear that anybody who disagrees with his policies will not last long.*
ADV: ADV adj
=manifestly

2 Something that occurs **abundantly** is present in large quantities. *...a plant that grows abundantly in the United States... All the pages are abundantly illustrated with colour photographs.*
ADV-GRADED: usu ADV with v, also ADV adj

abuse, abuses, abusing, abused. The noun is pronounced /əbju͟ːs/. The verb is pronounced /əbju͟ːz/. ◆◆◆◆◇

1 **Abuse** of someone is cruel and violent treatment of them. *...investigation of alleged child abuse. ...victims of sexual and physical abuse. ...controversy over human rights abuses.*
N-UNCOUNT: also N in pl, usu with supp

2 **Abuse** is extremely rude and insulting things that people say when they are angry. *I was left shouting abuse as the car sped off... Raft repeatedly hurled verbal abuse at his co-star.*
N-UNCOUNT
=insults

3 **Abuse** of something is the use of it in a wrong way or for a bad purpose. *What went on here was an abuse of power. ...drug and alcohol abuse.*
N-VAR: with supp

4 If someone **is abused**, they are treated cruelly and violently. *Janet had been abused by her father since she was eleven. ...parents who feel they cannot cope or might abuse their children. ...those who work with abused children.* ♦ **abuser, abusers** *...a convicted child abuser.*
VERB
be V-ed
V n
V-ed
N-COUNT

5 You can say that someone **is abused** if extremely rude and insulting things are said to them. *He alleged that he was verbally abused by other soldiers.*
VERB
=insult
be V-ed
Also V n

6 If you **abuse** something, you use it in a wrong way or for a bad purpose. *He showed how the rich and powerful can abuse their position.* ♦ **abuser** *...the treatment of alcohol and drug abusers.*
VERB
V n
N-COUNT

abusive /əbjuːsɪv/ ◆◇◇◇◇

1 Someone who is **abusive** behaves in a cruel and violent way towards other people. *He became violent and abusive toward Ben's mother. ...her cruel and abusive husband.* ADJ-GRADED

2 Abusive language is extremely rude and insulting. *He was alleged to have used abusive language.* ADJ-GRADED =insulting ≠polite

abut /əbʌt/ **abuts, abutting, abutted.** When land or a building **abuts** something or **abuts on** something, it is next to it; a formal word. *One edge of the garden abutted on an old entrance to the mine... He was born in 1768 in the house abutting our hotel.* VERB =adjoin V *on* n V n

abuzz /əbʌz/. If someone says that a place is **abuzz** with rumours or plans, they mean that everyone there is excited about them; used in journalism. *Washington has been abuzz with stories about disarray inside the White House.* ADJ: v-link ADJ, usu ADJ *with* n

abysmal /əbɪzməl/. If you describe a situation or the condition of something as **abysmal**, you think that it is very bad or very poor in quality. *Our abysmal record at producing scientifically trained and numerate manpower will cripple us... The general standard of racing was abysmal.* ADJ-GRADED PRAGMATICS =dismal

♦ **abysmally** *The group for the most part found the standard of education abysmally low... As the chart shows, it has failed abysmally.* ADV-GRADED: ADV adj, ADV after v =dismally

abyss /æbɪs/ **abysses** ◆◇◇◇◇

1 An **abyss** is a very deep hole in the ground; a literary use. N-COUNT: usu sing

2 If someone is on the edge or brink of an **abyss**, they are about to enter into a very frightening or threatening situation; a literary use. *He felt he was on the edge of an abyss; one false move and he was done for... The country was on the brink of an abyss.* N-COUNT: usu sing

3 A very great difference between two people, things, or groups can be referred to as an **abyss**; a literary use. *How big is the abyss between what you think you are and what you actually are?* N-COUNT: usu sing, with supp =gap, gulf

AC /eɪ siː/. **AC** is used to refer to an electric current that continually changes direction as it flows. **AC** is an abbreviation for 'alternating current'. *In Europe, AC is usually generated at 50 Hz. ...a portable AC generator.* ◆◇◇◇◇ N-UNCOUNT: oft N n

acacia /əkeɪʃə/ **acacias.** The form **acacia** can also be used for the plural. An **acacia** or an **acacia tree** is a tree which grows in warm countries and which usually has small yellow or white flowers. N-COUNT

academe /ækədiːm/. The academic world of universities is sometimes referred to as **academe**; a formal word. *The hallowed portals of academe were slowly and grudgingly opening to women.* N-UNCOUNT

academia /ækədiːmiə/. **Academia** refers to all the academics in a particular country or region, the institutions they work in, and their work. *...the importance of strong links between industry and academia.* N-UNCOUNT

academic /ækədemɪk/ **academics** ◆◆◆◇◇

1 Academic is used to describe things that relate to the work done in schools, colleges, and universities, especially work which involves studying and reasoning rather than practical or technical skills. *Their academic standards are high... I was terrible at school and left with few academic qualifications... Her academic work suffered and she fell behind.* ADJ: ADJ n

♦ **academically** /ækədemɪkli/ *He is academically gifted... I was only average academically, but was good at sports.* ADV

2 Academic is used to describe things that relate to schools, colleges, and universities. *...the start of the last academic year... I'd had enough of academic life.* ADJ: ADJ n

3 Academic is used to describe work, or a school, college, or university, that places emphasis on studying and reasoning rather than on practical or technical skills. *The author has settled for a more academic approach... Different schools teach different types of syllabus, from the highly academic to the broadly vocational.* ADJ-GRADED

4 Someone who is **academic** is good at studying. *The system is failing most disastrously among less academic children.* ADJ-GRADED =scholarly

5 An **academic** is a member of a university or college who teaches or does research. *The move has upset many prominent academics.* N-COUNT =scholar

6 You say that you think a particular point is **academic** when you want to indicate that you think it has no real relevance or effect. *This was not an academic exercise – soldiers' lives were at risk... Such is the size of the problem that these arguments are purely academic.* ADJ-GRADED =theoretical

academician /əkædəmɪʃən, AM ækədə-/ **academicians.** An **academician** is a member of an academy, usually one which has been formed to promote and maintain standards in a particular field. *He was elected a Royal Academician at the age of 53.* N-COUNT

academy /əkædəmi/ **academies.** ◆◆◇◇◇

1 Schools and colleges, especially those specializing in particular subjects or skills, sometimes have **academy**, as part of their name. *If you want to be a musician, you go to the Royal Academy of Music. ...her experience as a police academy instructor.* N-COUNT: usu with supp, oft in names

2 Academy appears in the names of some societies formed to promote and maintain standards in a particular field. *...the American Academy of Psychotherapists... The British Academy of Film and Television Arts.* N-IN-NAMES

accede /æksiːd/ **accedes, acceding, acceded**

1 If you **accede to** someone's request, you do what they ask; a formal word. *The Prime Minister would have to accede to any request by the opposition to recall parliament... I never understood why he didn't just accede to our demands at the outset.* VERB V *to* n

2 When a member of a royal family **accedes to** the throne, they become king or queen; a formal use. *When Henry VIII acceded to the throne, More soon came to the attention of both him and Wolsey.* VERB V *to* n Also V

accelerate /ækseləreɪt/ **accelerates, accelerating, accelerated** ◆◆◇◇◇

1 If someone or something **accelerates** a process or the rate of something, or if the process or rate **accelerates**, it gets faster and faster. *The government is to accelerate its privatisation programme... Growth will accelerate to 2.9 per cent next year.* V-ERG V n V

2 When a moving vehicle **accelerates**, it goes faster and faster. *Suddenly the car accelerated... She accelerated away from the kerb.* VERB V V prep/adv

acceleration /ækseləreɪʃən/ ◆◇◇◇◇

1 The **acceleration** of a process or change is the fact that it is getting faster and faster. *He has also called for an acceleration of political reforms... The sharp acceleration in job losses has led to a change of heart.* N-UNCOUNT: oft N *of/in* n

2 Acceleration is the rate at which a car or other vehicle can increase its speed, often seen in terms of the time that it takes to reach a particular speed. *Acceleration to 60 mph takes a mere 5.7 seconds.* N-UNCOUNT

3 Acceleration is the rate at which the speed of an object is increasing; a technical use in physics. *Force equals mass times acceleration.* N-UNCOUNT

accelerator /ækseləreɪtəʳ/ **accelerators.** The **accelerator** in a car or other vehicle is the pedal which you press with your foot in order to make the vehicle go faster. *He eased his foot off the accelerator.* ◆◇◇◇◇ N-COUNT

accent, accents, accenting, accented. The noun is pronounced /æksənt/. The verb is pronounced /æksent/. ◆◆◇◇◇

1 Someone who speaks with a particular **accent** pronounces the words of a language in a distinctive way that shows which country, region, or social class they come from. *He had developed a slight American accent.* N-COUNT

2 An **accent** is a short line or other mark which is written above certain letters in some languages and which indicates the way those letters are pronounced. N-COUNT

3 If you put the **accent** on a particular feature of something, you emphasize it or give it special importance. *He is putting the accent on military* N-SING: oft N *on* n =emphasis *readiness... There is often a strong accent on material success.*

4 If something **is accented** by something else, especially something contrasting, it is emphasized by it; used in written English. *...a white dress accented by a ribbon... The classical choreography is accented by steps from Hungarian folk dances.*
VB: no cont — V-ed — *be* V-ed — Also V n

accented /æksentɪd/. Language or speech that is **accented** is spoken with a particular accent. *I spoke rather good, but heavily accented English... 'Don't do that,' he says in his soft, accented voice.* • See also **accent**.
ADJ-GRADED

accentuate /æksentʃueɪt/ **accentuates, accentuating, accentuated.** To **accentuate** something means to emphasize it or make it more noticeable. *His shaven head accentuates his large round face... The whole air of menace was accentuated by the fact that he was so cordial and soft-voiced.*
◆◇◇◇◇ VERB =intensify — V n

accept /æksept/ **accepts, accepting, accepted** ◆◆◆◆◆

1 If you **accept** something that you have been offered, you say yes to it or agree to take it. *Eventually Stella persuaded her to accept an offer of marriage... Your old clothes will be gratefully accepted by jumble sale organisers... All those invited to next week's peace conference have accepted.*
VERB — V n — V

2 If you **accept** an idea, statement, or fact, you believe that it is true or valid. *I do not accept that there is any kind of crisis in British science... I don't think they would accept that view... He did not accept this reply as valid. ...a workforce generally accepted to have the best conditions in Europe.*
VERB =acknowledge — V that — V n — V n *as* adj/n — V-ed

3 If you **accept** a plan or an intended action, you agree to it and allow it to happen. *...Britain's reluctance to accept a proposal for a single European currency... The Council will meet to decide if it should accept his resignation.*
VERB ≠reject — V n

4 If you **accept** an unpleasant fact or situation, you get used to it or recognize that it cannot be changed. *People will accept suffering that can be shown to lead to a greater good... Urban dwellers often accept noise as part of city life... I wasn't willing to accept that her leaving was a possibility.*
VERB — V n — V n *as* n/adj — V that

5 If a person, company, or organization **accepts** something such as a document, they recognize that it is genuine, correct, or satisfactory and agree to consider it or handle it. *We took the unusual step of contacting newspapers to advise them not to accept the advertising... Cheques can only be accepted up to the value guaranteed on the card... Proof of postage will not be accepted as proof of receipt.*
VERB ≠reject — V n — *be* V-ed *as* n — Also V n *as* n/adj

6 If an organization or person **accepts** you, you are allowed to join the organization or use the services that are offered. *Should the British Army accept gays?... All-male groups will not be accepted. ...incentives to private landlords to accept young people as tenants.*
VERB ≠reject — V n — V n *as* n — Also V n *into* n

7 If a person or a group of people **accepts** you, they begin to be friendly towards you or to think of you as part of the group. *As far as my grandparents were concerned, they've never had a problem accepting me... We should accept her for what she is, an accomplished, hard-working woman... Many men still have difficulty accepting a woman as a business partner... Stephen Smith was accepted into the family like an adopted brother.*
VERB ≠reject — V n — V n *for/as* n — V n *into* n

8 If you **accept** the responsibility or blame for something, you recognize that you are responsible for it. *The company cannot accept responsibility for loss or damage.*
VERB ≠reject — V n

9 If you **accept** someone's advice or suggestion, you agree to do what they say. *An older man, for instance, would never accept orders from a younger woman... Don't automatically accept the solicitor recommended by the broker.*
VERB ≠reject — V n

10 If someone's body **accepts** a transplanted organ, the organ becomes part of the body and starts to function normally. *...drugs which will fool the body into accepting transplants.*
VERB ≠reject — V n

11 If a machine **accepts** a particular kind of thing, it is designed to take it and deal with it or process it. *The telephone booths accept 10 and 20 pence coins... The images were digitised in a form that could be accepted by a computer.*
VERB — V n

12 See also **accepted**.

acceptable /ækseptəbᵊl/ ◆◆◆◇◇

1 **Acceptable** activities and situations are those that most people approve of or consider to be normal. *It is becoming more acceptable for women to drink... The air pollution exceeds most acceptable levels by 10 times or more.* ♦ **acceptability** /ækseptəbɪlɪti/ *This assumption played a considerable part in increasing the social acceptability of divorce.* ♦ **acceptably** /ækseptəbli/ *The aim of discipline is to teach children to behave acceptably.*
ADJ-GRADED ≠unacceptable — N-UNCOUNT: usu N *of* n — ADV-GRADED ≠unacceptably

2 If something is **acceptable** to someone, they agree to consider it, use it, or allow it to happen. *They have thrashed out a compromise formula acceptable to Moscow... They recently failed to negotiate a mutually acceptable new contract... All entries must be on Kodak film, but slides and prints in mono or colour are equally acceptable.*
ADJ-GRADED: oft ADJ *to* n ≠unacceptable

3 If you describe something as **acceptable**, you mean that it is good enough or fairly good. *On the far side of the street was a restaurant that looked acceptable... We've made an acceptable start, but it could've been better.* ♦ **acceptably** *...a method that provides an acceptably accurate solution to a problem... These exercises will result in your being able to hit the ball quite acceptably.*
ADJ-GRADED =passable — ADV-GRADED: ADV adj, ADV with v

acceptance /ækseptəns/ **acceptances** ◆◆◇◇◇

1 **Acceptance** of an offer or a proposal is the act of saying yes to it or agreeing to it. *The Party is being degraded by its acceptance of secret donations... I sent them more than 6,000 cartoons before I had my one and only acceptance by them... Several shareholders have withdrawn earlier acceptances of the offer. ...a letter of acceptance. ...his acceptance speech for the Nobel Peace Prize.*
N-VAR: usu with supp, oft poss N, N *of* n ≠rejection

2 If there is **acceptance** of an idea, most people believe or agree that it is true. *...a theory that is steadily gaining acceptance... There's a general acceptance that the US defence budget will shrink considerably over the next few years.*
N-UNCOUNT

3 Your **acceptance** of a situation, especially an unpleasant or difficult one, is an attitude or feeling that you cannot change it and that you must get used to it. *Popular acceptance of authority had been an early aim of the Nationalists... The most impressive thing about him is his calm acceptance of whatever comes his way.*
N-UNCOUNT: usu N *of* n ≠rejection

4 If there is **acceptance** of a new product, people start to like it and get used to it. *Car manufacturers are already producing small numbers of electric vehicles to test customer acceptance... Avant-garde music to this day has not found general public acceptance.*
N-UNCOUNT: usu with supp ≠rejection

5 **Acceptance** of someone into a group means beginning to think of them as part of the group and to act in a friendly way towards them. *A very determined effort by society will ensure that the disabled achieve real acceptance and integration.*
N-UNCOUNT =recognition ≠rejection

accepted /ækseptɪd/. **Accepted** ideas are agreed by most people to be correct or reasonable. *There is no generally accepted definition of life... It is accepted wisdom that the rise of science has been partly responsible for the decline of religious beliefs.* • See also **accept**.
◆◆◆◆◇ ADJ: oft adv ADJ

access /ækses/ **accesses, accessing, accessed** ◆◆◆◇◇

1 If you have **access** to a building or other place, you are able or allowed to go into it. *The facilities have been adapted to give access to wheelchair users... For logistical and political reasons, scientists have only recently been able to gain access to the area... The Mortimer Hotel in Shepherd's Bush offers easy access to central London.*
N-UNCOUNT: usu N *to* n

2 If you have **access** to something such as information or equipment, you have the opportunity or right to see it or use it. *...a Code of Practice that would give patients right of access to their medical records. ...whether one has access to a dish and the other accoutrements needed to watch satellite TV.*
N-UNCOUNT: usu N *to* n

3 If you have **access** to a person, you have the opportunity or right to see them or meet them. *He was not allowed access either to a lawyer, or to officials of the British High Commission... My ex-wife deliberately sabotages my access to the children.*
N-UNCOUNT: usu N *to* n

4 If you **access** something, especially information held on a computer, you succeed in finding or obtaining it. *You've illegally accessed and misused confidential security files.*
VERB
V n

access course, access courses. In Britain, an **access course** is an educational course which prepares adults with few or no qualifications for study at a university or other place of higher education.
N-COUNT

accessible /æksesɪbᵊl/ ◆◆◇◇◇

1 If a place or building is **accessible** to people, it is easy for them to reach it or get into it. If an object is **accessible**, it is easy to reach. *The Gateshead Shopping Centre is easily accessible to virtually all the population of Tyne and Wear... The premises are wheelchair accessible... I had to keep the video camera readily accessible in case I saw something that needed to be filmed.* ♦ **accessibility** /æksesɪbɪlɪti/ *Unlike the other South Western reservoirs it has uniquely easy accessibility.*
ADJ-GRADED: oft ADJ *to* n
N-UNCOUNT

2 If something is **accessible** to people, they can easily use it or obtain it. *The aim of any reform of legal aid should be to make the system accessible to more people... This device helps make virtual reality a more usable and accessible technology.* ♦ **accessibility** *...growing public concern about the cost, quality and accessibility of health care.*
ADJ-GRADED: oft ADJ *to* n
N-UNCOUNT

3 If you describe a book, painting, or other work of art as **accessible**, you approve of it because it is simple enough for people to understand and appreciate easily. *Both say they want to write literary books that are accessible to a general audience. ...their reputation for providing exciting and accessible theatre for young people.* ♦ **accessibility** *Seminar topics are chosen for their accessibility to a general audience.*
ADJ-GRADED: oft ADJ *to* n
PRAGMATICS
N-UNCOUNT

accession /ækseʃᵊn/

1 **Accession** is the act of taking up a position as the ruler of a country; a formal word. *...the 40th anniversary of the Queen's accession to the throne. ...the accession of Mikhail Gorbachev in 1985.*
N-UNCOUNT: with poss, oft N *to* n

2 A country's **accession** to a group of countries or to an association is its joining that group of countries or association; a formal word. *...Namibia's accession to the Lome convention. ...our accession to Europe under the Maastricht treaty.*
N-UNCOUNT: oft with poss, N *to* n

accessorize /æksesəraɪz/ **accessorizes, accessorizing, accessorized;** also spelled **accessorise** in British English. To **accessorize** something such as a set of furniture or clothing means to add other things to it in order to make it look more attractive; used in written English. *Adding extra fabrics and linens is one of the easiest ways to accessorise your bedroom.*
VERB
V n
Also V n *with* n

accessory /æksesəri/ **accessories** ◆◆◇◇◇

1 **Accessories** are items of equipment that are not usually essential, but which can be used with or added to something else in order to make it more efficient, useful, or decorative. *...an exclusive range of hand-made bedroom and bathroom accessories.*
N-COUNT: usu pl

2 **Accessories** are articles, such as belts and handbags, which you wear or carry but which are not part of your main clothing; used in written English. *...varying reductions up to 50 per cent on most clothing, shoes and accessories.*
N-COUNT: usu pl

3 If someone is guilty of being an **accessory** to a crime, they helped the person who committed it, or knew it was being committed but did not tell the police; a legal use. *She had been charged with being an accessory to the embezzlement of funds from a co-operative farm.*
N-COUNT: usu N *to* n =accomplice

4 You can use **accessory** to describe something which contributes to an activity or process, but is not the most essential or important part of it; a formal use. *Forster established the essentiality of minerals as accessory food factors required for maintaining life.*
ADJ: usu ADJ n

access road, access roads. An **access road** is a road which enables traffic to reach a particular place or area. *...the access road to the airport.*
N-COUNT

accident /æksɪdənt/ **accidents** ◆◆◆◇◇

1 An **accident** happens when a vehicle hits a person, an object, or another vehicle, causing injury or damage. *She was involved in a serious car accident last week... The train driver failed to brake in time, according to the official report into the accident.*
N-COUNT

2 If someone has an **accident**, something unpleasant happens to them that was not intended, sometimes causing injury or death. *I had an accident at work and I got a cheque for £600... The police say the killing of the young man was an accident. ...the accident and emergency department of York district hospital.*
N-COUNT

3 If something happens by **accident**, it happens completely by chance. *She discovered the problem by accident during a visit to a nearby school... Almost like an accident of nature, this family has produced more talent than seems possible.*
N-VAR: usu *by* N =chance

4 If you describe something or someone as **an accident waiting to happen**, you mean that they are likely to be a cause of danger in the future, for example because they are in poor condition or behave in an unpredictable way. *A lot of the city's buildings are accidents waiting to happen.*
PHRASES
N inflects, v-link PHR

5 You begin a sentence with **'it's no accident'** if you want to suggest that something was done deliberately or has a logical explanation, although it might give the impression of having happened by chance. *It's no accident that the boom in police series on TV coincided with the decline of the Western.*
usu PHR that

accidental /æksɪdentᵊl/. An **accidental** event happens by chance or as the result of an accident, and is not deliberately intended. *Video evidence was shown to the inquest jury, before it returned a verdict of accidental death... His hand brushed against hers; it could have been either accidental or deliberate.* ♦ **accidentally** /æksɪdentli/. *A policeman accidentally killed his two best friends with a single bullet... A special locking system means the door cannot be opened accidentally.*
◆◆◇◇◇
ADJ ≠deliberate
ADV: ADV with v ≠deliberately

accident prone; also spelled **accident-prone.** If you describe someone or something as **accident prone**, you mean that a lot of accidents or other unpleasant things happen to them.
ADJ-GRADED

acclaim /əkleɪm/ **acclaims, acclaiming, acclaimed** ◆◆◇◇◇

1 If someone or something **is acclaimed**, they are praised enthusiastically; a formal word. *More recently she has been acclaimed for the TV dramas 'Prime Suspect' and 'Civvies'... He was acclaimed as England's greatest modern painter... He too, had been acclaimed a hero during the Gulf war.* ♦ **acclaimed** *She has published six highly acclaimed novels.*
VB: usu passive
be V-ed *for* n/-ing
be V-ed *as* n
be V-ed n
ADJ-GRADED

2 **Acclaim** is public praise for someone or something; a formal word. *Angela Bassett has won critical acclaim for her excellent performance... All this equipment has received international acclaim from the specialist hi-fi press.*
N-UNCOUNT: usu with supp, oft adj N =praise

acclamation /ækləmeɪʃᵊn/

1 **Acclamation** is a noisy or enthusiastic expression of approval for someone or something; a formal use. *The event went ahead to universal acclamation from spectators and participants alike.*
N-UNCOUNT =applause

2 If someone is chosen or elected by **acclamation**, they are elected as a result of an oral vote; a formal use. *...Al Gore was nominated by acclamation for vice president.*
N-UNCOUNT

acclimatize /əklaɪmətaɪz/ **acclimatizes, acclimatizing, acclimatized;** also spelled **acclimatise** in British English. When you **acclimatize** or **are acclimatized** to a new situation, place, or climate, you become used to it; a formal word. *The athletes are acclimatising to the heat by staying in Monte Carlo... This year he has left for St Louis early to acclimatise himself... They have been travelling for two days and will need some time to acclimatise.* ♦ **acclimatization** /əklaɪmətaɪzeɪʃᵊn/
V-ERG
V *to* n
V pron-refl
V
Also V n *to* n
N-UNCOUNT

Acclimatization to higher altitudes may take several weeks. ♦ **acclimatized** *She figured that it would take her two years to get acclimatized to her new surroundings... I'm not acclimatized to English temperatures yet.* ADJ-GRADED: usu v-link ADJ, oft ADJ *to* n

accolade /ækəleɪd/ **accolades.** If someone is given an **accolade**, something is done or said about them which shows how much people admire them; a formal word. *To ride for one's country is the ultimate accolade... Ari Hart recently received the accolade of being represented in the Museum of Modern Art.* ◆◇◇◇◇ N-COUNT =honour, award, tribute

accommodate /əkɒmədeɪt/ **accommodates, accommodating, accommodated** ◆◆◇◇◇

1 If a building or space can **accommodate** someone or something, it has enough room for them. *The school in Poldown was not big enough to accommodate all the children... The CD-ROMS will accommodate the works of all English poets from 600 to 1900.* VB: no cont; V n

2 To **accommodate** someone means to provide them with a place to live or stay. *...a hotel built to accommodate guests for the wedding of King Alfonso... Students are accommodated in homes nearby.* VERB; V n; *be* V-ed prep/adv

3 If something is planned or changed to **accommodate** a particular fact or situation, it is planned or changed in such as way as to take this fact or situation into account. *The roads are built to accommodate gradual temperature changes... The way that American history is taught may change in order to accommodate some more of those cultures.* VERB; V n

4 If you do something to **accommodate** someone, you do it with the main purpose of pleasing or satisfying them. *He has never put an arm around his wife to accommodate photographers... He's already altered several of the proposals in his economic plan to accommodate demands of special interests.* VERB =oblige; V n

5 If you **accommodate** to something new, you change your behaviour or ideas so that you are able to deal with it; a formal use. *Some animal and plant species cannot accommodate to the rapidly-changing conditions... She walked slowly to accommodate herself to his pace.* VERB =adapt; V *to* n; V pron-refl *to* n

accommodating /əkɒmədeɪtɪŋ/. If you describe someone as **accommodating**, you mean that they are willing to do things in order to please you or help you. ADJ-GRADED =obliging, co-operative

accommodation /əkɒmədeɪʃən/ **accommodations** ◆◆◇◇◇

1 In British English, **accommodation** is used to refer to buildings or rooms where people live or stay. The usual American word is **accommodations.** *The government will provide temporary accommodation for up to three thousand people sleeping rough in London... Prices start at £2,095 per person, including flights, hotel accommodation and various excursions... Rates are higher for deluxe accommodations and lower in the off-season.* N-UNCOUNT: also N in pl

2 **Accommodation** is space in buildings or vehicles that is available for certain things, people, or activities; a formal use. *The school occupies split-site accommodation on the main campus... Some trains carry bicycles, but accommodation is restricted so a reservation is essential.* N-UNCOUNT

3 An **accommodation** is an agreement or compromise between different people or groups which enables them to exist together without trouble; a formal use. *Mr Gorbachev and Mr Bush had begun to seek a possible accommodation... Religions, to survive, must make accommodations with the larger political structures that nurture them.* N-COUNT: oft N *with* n, N *between* pl-n

accompaniment /əkʌmpnɪmənt/ **accompaniments** ◆◇◇◇◇

1 The **accompaniment** to a song or tune is the music that is played at the same time as it and forms a background to it. *He sang 'My Funny Valentine' and 'Wanted' to musical director Jim Steffan's piano accompaniment.* N-COUNT: usu with supp

2 An **accompaniment** is something which goes with another thing. *This recipe makes a good accompaniment to ice-cream.* N-COUNT: usu with supp ● If one thing happens **to the accompaniment of** another, they happen at the same time. *The two teams took a lap of honour together to the accompaniment of fireworks.* PHR-PREP

accompanist /əkʌmpənɪst/ **accompanists.** An **accompanist** is a musician, especially a pianist, who plays one part of a piece of music while someone else sings or plays the main tune. N-COUNT

accompany /əkʌmpəni/ **accompanies, accompanying, accompanied** ◆◆◆◇◇

1 If you **accompany** someone, you go somewhere with them; a formal use found mainly in written English. *Ken agreed to accompany me on a trip to Africa... She was accompanied by her younger brother... The Prime Minister, accompanied by the governor, led the President up to the house.* VERB; V n; V-ed

2 If one thing **accompanies** another, it happens or exists at the same time, or as a result of it; a formal use found mainly in written English. *This volume of essays was designed to accompany an exhibition in Cologne... The proposal was instantly voted through with two to one in favour, accompanied by enthusiastic applause... Perhaps the accompanying illustration will explain it.* VERB; V n; V-ed; V-ing

3 If you **accompany** a singer or a musician, you play one part of a piece of music while they sing or play the main tune. *On Meredith's new recording, Eddie Higgins accompanies her on all but one song... We ended with Blake's Jerusalem, accompanied on the organ by Herbert Wiseman.* VERB; V n; V-ed

accompli /æ kɒmpliː/. See **fait accompli.**

accomplice /əkʌmplɪs, AM əkɒm-/ **accomplices.** Someone's **accomplice** is a person who helps them to commit a crime. *Witnesses said the gunman immediately ran to a motorcycle being ridden by an accomplice... His accomplice was arrested after a high-speed police chase.* ◆◇◇◇◇ N-COUNT: oft poss N

accomplish /əkʌmplɪʃ, AM əkɒm-/ **accomplishes, accomplishing, accomplished.** If you **accomplish** something, you succeed in doing it. *If we'd all work together, I think we could accomplish our goal... They are skeptical about how much will be accomplished by legislation.* ◆◆◇◇◇ VERB =realize; V n

accomplished /əkʌmplɪʃt, AM əkɒm-/. If someone is **accomplished** at something, they are very good at it; a formal word. *She is an accomplished painter and a prolific author of stories for children. ...one of the most accomplished composers of our time.* ◆◆◇◇◇ ADJ-GRADED

accomplishment /əkʌmplɪʃmənt, AM əkɒm-/ **accomplishments** ◆◇◇◇◇

1 An **accomplishment** is something remarkable that has been done or achieved. *For a novelist, that's quite an accomplishment... By any standards, the accomplishments of the past year are extraordinary.* N-COUNT =achievement

2 Your **accomplishments** are the things that you can do well or the important things that you have done; a formal word. *The list of her accomplishments is staggering... Needlepoint was an accomplishment any nineteenth-century girl learnt.* N-COUNT: usu pl, oft poss N

3 The **accomplishment** of something is the fact of achieving or finishing it. *He wished Mr Walesa success in the accomplishment of his highly important mission... I look outside and feel a sense of accomplishment.* N-UNCOUNT =accomplishing

accord /əkɔːʳd/ **accords, according, accorded** ◆◆◆◆◆

1 An **accord** between countries or groups of people is a formal agreement, for example to end a war. *...UNITA, legalised as a political party under the 1991 peace accords... The one-hundred members of GATT are trying to reach an accord on reforming international world trade.* N-COUNT: usu with supp, oft n N

2 If you **are accorded** a particular kind of treatment, people act towards you or treat you in that way; a formal use. *His predecessor was accorded an equally tumultuous welcome... On his return home, the government accorded him the rank of Colonel... The treatment accorded to a United Nations official, was little short of insulting.* VERB =grant; *be* V-ed n; V n n; V-ed; Also V n *to* n

3 If one fact, idea, or condition **accords with** another, they are in agreement and there is no con- VERB =correspond

flict between them; a formal use. *Such an approach accords with the principles of socialist ideology. ...scientific evidence that did not fully accord with the facts uncovered by the police.*
V *with* n

4 See also **according to**.

5 If one person, action, or fact is **in accord with** another, they are in agreement and there is no conflict between them. You can also say that two people or things are **in accord**; a formal expression. *...this military action, taken in accord with United Nations resolutions... Old enemies can become new friends even if all their national interests are not in complete accord.*
PHRASES v-link PHR, PHR after v, oft PHR *with* n

6 If something happens **of** its **own accord**, it seems to happen automatically, without anybody making it happen. *In many cases the disease will clear up of its own accord.*
PHR after v

7 If you do something **of** your **own accord**, you do it because you want to, without being asked or forced. *He did not quit as France's prime minister of his own accord.*
PHR after v =voluntarily

8 If a number of people do something **with one accord**, they do it together or at the same time, because they agree about what should be done; a literary use. *With one accord they turned and walked back over the grass.*

accordance /əkɔ:ʳdəns/. If something is done **in accordance with** a particular rule or system, it is done in the way that the rule or system says that it should be done. *Entries which are illegible or otherwise not in accordance with the rules will be disqualified.*
◆◇◇◇◇ PHR-PREP

accordingly /əkɔ:ʳdɪŋli/
◆◆◇◇◇

1 You use **accordingly** to introduce a fact or situation which is a result or consequence of something that you have just referred to. *We have a different background, a different history. Accordingly, we have the right to different futures... The workforce have recently been calling for their working hours to be reduced. Many companies have accordingly switched to a five-day week.*
ADV: usu ADV with cl, also ADV with v PRAGMATICS =therefore, consequently

2 If you consider a situation and then act **accordingly**, the way you act depends on the nature of the situation. *It is a difficult job and they should be paid accordingly... The new government will make a judgment about its interests and act accordingly.*
ADV: ADV after v

according to
◆◆◆◆◆

1 If someone says that something is true **according to** a particular person, book, or other source of information, they are indicating where they got their information. *Philip stayed at the hotel, according to Mr Hemming... He and his father, according to local gossip, haven't been in touch for years.*
PHR-PREP

2 If something is done **according to** a particular set of principles, these principles are used as a basis for the way it is done. *They both played the game according to the rules... They must take their own decision according to their own legal advice.*
PHR-PREP

3 If something varies **according to** a changing or variable factor, it varies in a way that is determined by this factor. *Prices vary according to the quantity ordered... The route that the boatmen choose varies according to the water level.*
PHR-PREP

4 If something happens **according to plan**, it happens exactly in the way that it was intended to happen. *If all goes according to plan, the first concert will be Tuesday evening.*
PHRASE: usu PHR after v

accordion /əkɔ:ʳdiən/ **accordions.** An **accordion** is a musical instrument in the shape of a fairly large box which you hold in your hands. You play the accordion by pressing keys or buttons on either side while moving the two sides together and apart. Accordions are used especially to play traditional popular music.
◆◇◇◇◇ N-COUNT =squeezebox

accost /əkɒst, AM əkɔ:st/ **accosts, accosting, accosted.** If someone **accosts** another person, especially a stranger, they stop them or go up to them and speak to them; a formal word which is often used showing disapproval. *I went up to the policeman and complained that this man had accosted me in the street.*
VERB PRAGMATICS V n

account /əkaʊnt/ **accounts, accounting, accounted**
◆◆◆◆◆

1 If you have an **account** with a bank or a similar organization, you have an arrangement to leave your money there and take some out when you need it. *Some banks make it difficult to open an account... He paid £20 into his savings account.*
N-COUNT

2 In business, a regular customer of a company, can be referred to as an **account**, especially when the customer is another company. *Biggart Donald, the Glasgow-based marketing agency, has won two Edinburgh accounts... I spent the rest of the afternoon calling all the Remington accounts in England.*
N-COUNT

3 **Accounts** are detailed records of all the money that a person or business receives and spends. *He kept detailed accounts. ...Rolls-Royce's profit and loss account. ...an account book.*
N-COUNT: usu pl

4 An **account** is a written or spoken report of something that has happened. *He gave a detailed account of what happened on the fateful night... According to police accounts, Mr and Mrs Hunt were found dead on the floor of their kitchen.*
N-COUNT: with supp, usu N *of* n =statement

5 An **account** of something is a theory which is intended to explain or describe it; a formal use. *This basic utilitarian model gives a relatively unsophisticated account of human behaviour... Science, on Weber's account, is an essentially value-free activity.*
N-COUNT: usu N *of* n, oft poss N

6 If you say that something **is accounted** a particular thing, you are reporting someone's judgment or opinion that it is that thing; a formal use. *The opening day of the battle was, nevertheless, accounted a success. ...homosexuals, whose sexual behaviour is still accounted sinful by the church.*
VB: usu passive *be* V-ed n *be* V-ed adj

7 See also **accounting, bank account, current account, deposit account, joint account.**

8 If you say that something is true **by all accounts** or **from all accounts**, you believe it is true because other people say so. *He is, by all accounts, a superb teacher.*
PHRASES PHR with cl

9 If you say that someone **gave a good account of** themselves in a particular situation, you mean that they performed well, although they may not have been completely successful. *We have been hindered by our lack of preparation, but I'm sure we will give a good account of ourselves.*
V inflects

10 If you say that something is **of no account** or **of little account**, you mean that it is very unimportant and is not worth considering; a formal use. *These obscure groups were of little account in either national or international politics.*
v-link PHR

11 If you buy or pay for something **on account**, you pay nothing or only part of the cost at first, and pay the rest later. *He was ordered to pay the company £500,000 on account pending a final assessment of his liability.*
PHR after v

12 You use **on account of** to introduce the reason or explanation for something. *The President declined to deliver the speech himself, on account of a sore throat... A newly-married couple, he thought, on account of their walking so close together.*
PREP PRAGMATICS =because of

13 Your feelings **on** someone**'s account** are the feelings you have about what they have experienced or might experience, especially when you imagine yourself to be in their situation. *Mollie told me what she'd done and I was really scared on her account.*
usu adj/n PHR =on someone's behalf

14 If you tell someone not to do something **on** your **account**, you mean that they should do it only if they want to, and not because they think it will please you; used in spoken English. *Don't leave on my account.*
PHR after v PRAGMATICS =for your sake

15 If you say that something should **on no account** be done, you are emphasizing that it should not be done under any circumstances. *On no account should finches and lovebirds be housed together.*
PRAGMATICS =under no circumstances

16 You can use **on that account** or **on this account** when you want to say that something happens for the reason you have just mentioned. *Wine is radioactive but few people stop drinking it on that account.*
usu PHR after v, PHR with cl PRAGMATICS

17 If you say that something concerning a particular person is true **by** his or her **own account**, you mean that you believe it because that person has said it is true. *He was by his own account an ambitious workaholic.*

18 If you take part in a business activity **on** your **own account**, you do it for yourself, and not as a representative or employee of a company. *She had plans to set up in business on her own account.*
PHR after v

19 If you do something **on** your **own account**, you do it because you want to and without being asked, and you take responsibility for your own action. *I told him if he withdrew it was on his own account.*
PHR after v

20 If you **settle accounts**, or **settle** your **accounts**, with an enemy or opponent, you bring your conflict or quarrel to an end by defeating them. You can also say that two enemies or opponents **settle accounts**, or **settle** their **accounts**. *...until the great day came when the Germans could finally settle accounts with the British... Their sleep is regularly disturbed by the sound of gunfire as criminal gangs settle their nightly accounts.*
RECIP: V inflects, PHR *with* n, pl-n PHR

21 If you **take** something **into account**, or **take account of** something, you consider it when you are thinking about a situation or deciding what to do. *The defendant asked for 21 similar offences to be taken into account... Urban planners in practice have to take account of many interest groups in society.*
V inflects =consider

22 If someone **is called, held,** or **brought to account** for something they have done wrong, they are made to explain why they did it, and are often criticized or punished for it. *Individuals who repeatedly provide false information should be called to account for their actions.*
V inflects, oft PHR *for* n

account for
PHRASAL VERB

1 If a particular thing **accounts for** a part or proportion of something, that part or proportion consists of that thing, or is used or produced by it. *Computers account for 5% of the country's commercial electricity consumption.*
V P n

2 If something **accounts for** a particular fact or situation, it causes or explains it. *Now, the gene they discovered today doesn't account for all those cases.*
=explain V P n

3 If you can **account for** something, you can explain it or give the necessary information about it. *How do you account for the company's alarmingly high staff turnover?... He said only 200 of the train's 600 passengers had been accounted for.*
=explain V P n

4 If someone has to **account for** an action or policy, they are responsible for it, and may be required to explain it to other people or be punished if it fails. *The President and the President alone must account for his government's reforms.*
=answer for V P n

5 If a sum of money **is accounted for** in a budget, it has been included in that budget for a particular purpose. *The really heavy redundancy costs have been accounted for.*
be V-ed P Also V P n

6 If you **account for** an enemy or opponent, you defeat them. *In the first ten days of May our squadron accounted for at least seven enemy aircraft... In the final they accounted for Brentford by three goals to two.*
V P n

accountable /əkaʊntəbᵊl/. If you are **accountable** to someone for something that you do, you are responsible for it and must be prepared to justify your actions to that person. *Public officials can finally be held accountable for their actions... The major service industries should be accountable to their customers.* ♦ **accountability** /əkaʊntəbɪlɪti/ *...an impetus towards democracy and greater accountability.*
◆◆◇◇◇ ADJ-GRADED: usu v-link ADJ, oft ADJ *to/for* n =answerable; N-UNCOUNT

accountancy /əkaʊntənsi/. **Accountancy** is the theory or practice of keeping financial accounts. *He's sitting his final exams in accountancy.*
◆◇◇◇◇ N-UNCOUNT

accountant /əkaʊntənt/ **accountants.** An **accountant** is a person whose job is to keep financial accounts.
◆◆◇◇◇ N-COUNT

accounting /əkaʊntɪŋ/. **Accounting** is the activity of keeping detailed records of the amounts of money a business or person receives and spends. *...allegations of theft, forgery and false accounting. ...the accounting firm of Leventhal & Horwath.* ● See also **account**.
◆◆◇◇◇ N-UNCOUNT

accoutrement /əkuːtrəmənt/ **accoutrements.** **Accoutrements** are all the things you have with you when you travel or when you take part in a particular activity; an old-fashioned or humorous word. *I loved stationery and all the accoutrements of writing.*
N-COUNT: usu pl, usu with supp, oft N *of* n =paraphernalia

accredit /əkredɪt/ **accredits, accrediting, accredited**
◆◇◇◇◇

1 If an educational qualification or institution **is accredited**, it is officially declared to be of an approved standard; a formal use. *This degree programme is fully accredited by the Institution of Electrical Engineers. ...an accredited college of Brunel University.* ♦ **accreditation** /əkredɪteɪʃᵊn/ *...the Council for the Accreditation of Teacher Education.*
VB: usu passive =endorse be V-ed V-ed; N-UNCOUNT

2 If someone such as a diplomat or journalist **is accredited** to a particular job or place, they are officially recognized as having that job, or the right to be in that place; a formal use. *The President proposed that Russian diplomats could be accredited to NATO headquarters... Some of the organisations taking part protested that the delegates they had chosen were not being accredited. ...fully accredited diplomats.* ♦ **accreditation** *Media representatives should arrive at the Press Centre by 11:40 to obtain accreditation.*
VB: usu passive be V-ed to n be V-ed V-ed; N-UNCOUNT

accretion /əkriːʃᵊn/ **accretions**

1 An **accretion** is an addition to something, usually one that has been added over a period of time; a formal use. *...the mythical structure has been overlaid by literary accretions.*
N-COUNT

2 Accretion is the process of new layers or parts being added to something so that it increases in size; a formal use. *The question arises as to whether the accretion of more powers is the answer.*
N-UNCOUNT

accrual /əkruːəl/ **accruals.** The **accrual** of something such as interest or investments is the adding together of interest or different investments over a period of time; used mainly in banking. *...the accrual of funds used during construction. ...an accrual method of accounting.*
N-COUNT: usu sing, oft N n =accumulation

accrue /əkruː/ **accrues, accruing, accrued**
◆◇◇◇◇

1 If money or interest **accrues** or if it **is accrued**, it gradually increases in amount over a period of time. *I owed £5,000 - part of this was accrued interest... While they may use a credit card for convenience, affluent people never let interest charges accrue... Officials say the options will offer investors a longer time in which to accrue profits.*
V-ERG =accumulate V-ed V V n

2 If things such as profits or benefits **accrue** to someone or if they **are accrued**, they accumulate over a period of time; a formal use. *Financial economies may accrue through more advantageous bulk-buying discounts... Vietnam's need for normal relations, and the economic benefits that accrue, is becoming increasingly acute... In many cases, the fee structure alone will exceed the tax benefits accrued.*
V-ERG V V-ed

accumulate /əkjuːmjʊleɪt/ **accumulates, accumulating, accumulated.** When you **accumulate** things or when they **accumulate**, they collect or are gathered over a period of time. *It suggests that households accumulate wealth across a broad spectrum of assets... Lead can accumulate in the body until toxic levels are reached.*
◆◆◇◇◇ V-ERG =build up V n V

accumulation /əkjuːmjʊleɪʃᵊn/ **accumulations**
◆◇◇◇◇

1 An **accumulation** of something is a large number of things which have been collected together or acquired over a period of time. *Gamekeeping is not some sort of science, but an accumulation of experience and knowledge. ...accumulations of dirt.*
N-COUNT: oft N *of* n

2 Accumulation is the collecting together of things over a period of time. *...the accumulation of capital and the distribution of income... The rate of accumulation decreases with time.*
N-UNCOUNT: oft N *of* n =growth

accumulative /əkjuːmjʊlətɪv, AM -leɪtɪv/. If something is **accumulative,** it becomes increasingly great in amount, number, or intensity over
ADJ =cumulative

a period of time. *The consensus is that risk factors have an accumulative effect.*

accumulator /əkjuːmjʊleɪtəʳ/ **accumulators.** In Britain, an **accumulator** is a betting system in horse racing in which any money won in one race is automatically bet on other races. [N-COUNT: usu sing]

accuracy /ækjʊrəsi/ ◆◆◇◇◇

1 The **accuracy** of information or measurements is their quality of being true or correct, even in small details. *The preceding text cannot be guaranteed as to the accuracy of speakers' words or spelling.* [N-UNCOUNT: oft N of n ≠inaccuracy]

2 If someone or something performs a task, for example hitting a target, with **accuracy**, they do it in an exact way without making a mistake. *...weapons that could fire with accuracy at targets 3,000 yards away... Every bank pays close attention to the speed and accuracy of its staff.* [N-UNCOUNT: oft with N ≠inaccuracy]

accurate /ækjʊrət/ ◆◆◆◇◇

1 **Accurate** information, measurements, and statistics are correct to a very detailed level. An **accurate** instrument is able to give you information of this kind. *Police have stressed that this is the most accurate description of the killer to date... This may provide a quick and accurate way of monitoring the amount of carbon dioxide in the air... Quartz timepieces are very accurate, to a minute or two per year.* [ADJ-GRADED =precise ≠inaccurate] ♦ **accurately** *The test can accurately predict what a bigger explosion would do.* [ADV-GRADED]

2 An **accurate** statement or account gives a true or fair judgment of something. *Joseph Stalin gave an accurate assessment of the utility of nuclear weapons... They were accurate in their prediction that he would change her life drastically.* [ADJ-GRADED ≠inaccurate] ♦ **accurately** *What many people mean by the word 'power' could be more accurately described as control.* [ADV-GRADED: ADV with v ≠inaccurately]

3 You can use **accurate** to describe the results of someone's actions when they do or copy something correctly or exactly. *This summer's exam results are the first to be weighted for accurate spelling and punctuation. ...his maliciously accurate imitation of Hubert de Burgh.* [ADJ-GRADED ≠inaccurate]

4 An **accurate** weapon or throw reaches the exact point or target that it was intended to reach. You can also describe a person as **accurate** if they fire a weapon or throw something in this way. *The rifle was extremely accurate... The pilots, however, were not as accurate as they should be.* [ADJ-GRADED =precise ≠inaccurate] ♦ **accurately** *The more accurately you can aim bombs from aircraft, the fewer civilians you will kill.* [ADV-GRADED: ADV with v =precisely ≠inaccurately]

accursed /əkɜːʳsɪd, əkɜːʳst/

1 Some people use **accursed** to describe something which they are very annoyed about; an old-fashioned use. *How I wish I'd never come to this accursed muckheap.* [ADJ: ADJ n PRAGMATICS =damned]

2 If a person is **accursed**, they have a curse on them; a literary use. *Boundary stones were set up and were then regarded as sacred and anyone removing them was accursed.* [ADJ: v-link ADJ =damned]

accusation /ækjʊzeɪʃᵊn/ **accusations** ◆◆◇◇◇

1 If you make an **accusation** against someone, you criticize them or express the belief that they have done something wrong. *Kim rejects accusations that Country music is over-sentimental... Another accusation levelled at the Minister is that he does not understand ordinary people... She was surprised that he had no words of blame or accusation for her.* [N-VAR: oft N that, N of n/-ing =charge]

2 An **accusation** is a statement or claim by a witness or someone in authority that a particular person has committed a crime, although this has not yet been proved. *...people who have made public accusations of rape... The government denied the accusation that it was involved in the murders.* [N-COUNT: oft N of n, N that]

accusative /əkjuːzətɪv/. In the grammar of some languages, **the accusative**, or **the accusative case**, is the case used for a noun when it is the direct object of a verb, or the object of some prepositions. In English, only the pronouns 'me', 'him', 'her', 'us', and 'them' are in the accusative. Compare **nominative**. [N-SING: the N]

accusatory /əkjuːzətəri, AM -tɔːri/. An **accusatory** look, remark, or tone of voice suggests blame or criticism; used in written English. *Her blue eyes took on an unblinking, accusatory stare.* [ADJ-GRADED =accusing]

accuse /əkjuːz/ **accuses, accusing, accused** ◆◆◆◆◇

1 If you **accuse** someone of doing something wrong or dishonest, you say or tell them that you believe that they did it. *My mum was really upset because he was accusing her of having an affair with another man... Talk things through in stages. Do not accuse or apportion blame.* [VERB V n of n/-ing V Also V n]

2 If you **are accused** of a crime, a witness or someone in authority states or claims that you did it, and you may be formally charged with it and put on trial. *Her assistant was accused of theft and fraud by the police... He faced a total of seven charges, all accusing him of lying in his testimony... The accused men have been given relatively light sentences.* [VERB be V-ed of n V n of n V-ed Also V n]

3 See also **accused, accusing.**

4 If someone **stands accused** of something, they have been accused of it. *The candidate stands accused of breaking promises even before he's in office... Today, Rostov stands accused of extortion and racketeering.* [PHRASE: V inflects, PHR of n/-ing]

accused /əkjuːzd/; **accused** is both the singular and the plural form. You can use **the accused** to refer to a person or a group of people charged with a crime or on trial for it; a legal term. *The accused is alleged to be a member of a right-wing gang... The fifteen accused, young men from different parts of England, denied the charges.* ◆◇◇◇◇ [N-COUNT: the N =defendant]

accuser /əkjuːzəʳ/ **accusers.** An **accuser** is a person who says that another person has done something wrong, especially that he or she has committed a crime. *...a criminal proceeding where defendants have the right to confront their accusers.* [N-COUNT: usu poss N]

accusing /əkjuːzɪŋ/. If you look at someone with an **accusing** expression or speak to someone in an **accusing** tone of voice, it shows that you think that they have done something wrong. *The accusing look in her eyes conveyed her sense of betrayal.* [ADJ-GRADED] ♦ **accusingly** *'Where have you been?' he asked Blake accusingly.* [ADV-GRADED: ADV after v] ● See also **accuse.**

accustom /əkʌstəm/ **accustoms, accustoming, accustomed.** If you **accustom** yourself or someone else to something, you make yourself or them experience it or learn about it, so that it becomes familiar or natural; a formal word. *...while his team accustoms itself to the pace and style of first division rugby... Shakespeare has accustomed us to a mixture of humor and tragedy in the same play.* ● See also **accustomed.** ◆◇◇◇◇ [VERB =familiarize V pron-refl to n V n to n]

accustomed /əkʌstəmd/ ◆◇◇◇◇

1 If you are **accustomed to** something, you know it so well or have experienced it so often that it seems natural, unsurprising, or easy to deal with. *I was accustomed to being the only child at a table full of adults... She had not yet become accustomed to the fact that she was a rich woman.* [ADJ-GRADED: v-link ADJ to n/-ing =used ≠unaccustomed]

2 When your eyes become **accustomed** to darkness or bright light, they adjust so that you start to be able to see things, after not being able to see properly at first. *My eyes were becoming accustomed to the gloom and I was able to make out a door at one side of the room.* [ADJ: v-link ADJ to n]

3 You can use **accustomed** to describe an action that someone usually does, a quality that they usually show, or an object that they usually use. *He took up his accustomed position with his back to the fire... Freed acted with his accustomed shrewdness. ...his accustomed glass of whisky.* [ADJ: poss ADJ n =usual, habitual]

ace /eɪs/ **aces** ◆◆◇◇◇

1 An **ace** is a playing card with a single symbol on it. In most card games, the ace of a particular suit has either the highest or the lowest value of the cards in that suit. *...the ace of hearts.* [N-COUNT: oft N of n]

2 If you describe someone such as a sports player as an **ace**, you mean that they are very good at what they do; used in journalism. *...former motor-racing ace Stirling Moss.* [N-COUNT: usu with supp, oft n N] ► Also an adjective. *...ace horror-film producer Lawrence Woolsey.* [ADJ: ADJ n]

3 If you say that something is **ace**, you think that it is good and you like it a lot; an informal use. *It's* [ADJ PRAGMATICS]

been a while since a really ace film came out of Germany.

4 In tennis, an **ace** is a serve which is so fast that the other player cannot reach the ball. *The American served three aces in the opening game of the set.* N-COUNT

5 If you say that someone **holds all the aces**, you mean that they have all the advantages in a contest or situation. *'When I was an adolescent,' says a thirty-one-year-old man, 'I thought girls held all the aces.'* PHRASES V inflects

6 Something that is an **ace in the hole** is an advantage which you have over an opponent or rival, and which you can use if necessary. *Our superior technology is our ace in the hole.* v-link PHR, PHR after v

7 If you **come within an ace of** doing something, or you **are within an ace of** doing something, you very nearly do or experience it. *He was intent on murder and he came within an ace of succeeding.* V inflects, PHR -ing/n

acerbic /əsɜːʳbɪk/. If you describe someone's sense of humour or the things they say as **acerbic**, you approve of it because it is critical and direct; a formal word. *...his acerbic wit and repartee... His lyrics are as acerbic and poignant as they ever have been.* ADJ-GRADED PRAGMATICS =sharp

acerbity /əsɜːʳbɪti/. **Acerbity** is a kind of bitter wit or humour; a formal word. *...her usual cool acerbity.* N-UNCOUNT

acetate /æsɪteɪt/. **Acetate** is a shiny man-made material, sometimes used for making clothes or records. *The jacket is lined with acetate satin.* N-UNCOUNT

acetic acid /əsiːtɪk æsɪd/. **Acetic acid** is a colourless acid. It is the main substance in vinegar. N-UNCOUNT

acetone /æsɪtoʊn/. **Acetone** is a type of solvent. N-UNCOUNT

acetylene /əsetɪliːn/. **Acetylene** is a colourless gas which burns with a very hot bright flame. It is often used in lamps and for cutting and welding metal. *The gang worked for up to ten hours with acetylene torches to open the vault.* N-UNCOUNT: oft N n

ach /æx/. **Ach** is the same as **och**. *Ach, she's too late for lunch now, man.* EXCLAM

ache /eɪk/ **aches, aching, ached** ◆◆◇◇◇

1 If you **ache** or a part of your body **aches**, you feel a steady, fairly strong pain. *The glands in her neck were swollen, her head was throbbing and she ached all over... My leg is giving me much less pain but still aches when I sit down... The weary holidaymakers soothed their aching feet in the sea.* VERB V adv/prep V V-ing

2 An **ache** is a steady, fairly strong pain in a part of your body. *You feel nausea and aches in your muscles... Poor posture can cause neck ache, headaches and breathing problems.* • See also **backache, headache, heartache, stomach ache.** N-COUNT: usu with supp, oft N *in* n, n N

3 If you **ache** for something or your heart **aches**, you want something very much, and feel very unhappy because you cannot have it; used in written English. *She still ached for the lost intimacy and sexual contact of marriage... But Spain was a country aching to get away from its past... It was quite an achievement to keep smiling when his heart must have been aching.* ► Also a noun. *You also feel an overwhelming ache for support from others which you cannot put into words.* VERB =long V *for* n V to-inf V N-SING: N *for* n

4 You can use **aches and pains** to refer in a general way to any minor pains that you feel in your body. *It seems to ease all the aches and pains of a hectic and tiring day.* PHRASE

achievable /ətʃiːvəbəl/. If you say that something you are trying to do is **achievable**, you mean that it is possible for you to succeed in doing it. *A 50% market share is achievable... It is often a good idea to start with smaller, easily achievable goals.* ADJ-GRADED =attainable

achieve /ətʃiːv/ **achieves, achieving, achieved.** If you **achieve** a particular aim or effect, you succeed in doing it or causing it to happen, usually after a lot of effort. *There are many who will work hard to achieve these goals... We have achieved what we set out to do.* ◆◆◆◆◇ VERB =accomplish V n

achievement /ətʃiːvmənt/ **achievements** ◆◆◆◇◇

1 An **achievement** is something which someone has succeeded in doing, especially after a lot of effort. *It was a great achievement that a month later a global agreement was reached... The Conference will be a celebration of women's achievements.* N-COUNT =accomplishment

2 **Achievement** is the process of achieving something. *It is only the achievement of these goals that will finally bring lasting peace.* N-UNCOUNT: oft N *of* n

achiever /ətʃiːvəʳ/ **achievers.** An **achiever** is someone who is successful in their studies or their work, usually as a result of their efforts. A low **achiever** is someone who achieves less than those around them. *High achievers at British Airways are in line for cash bonuses... In school, he was not one of the achievers. ...a way to keep low achievers from dropping out.* ◆◇◇◇◇ N-COUNT

Achilles heel /əkɪliːz hiːl/. Someone's **Achilles heel** is the weakest point in their character or nature, where it is easiest for other people to attack or criticize them. *Horton's Achilles heel was that he could not delegate.* N-SING: usu poss N

Achilles tendon /əkɪliːz tendən/ **Achilles tendons.** Your **Achilles tendon** or your **Achilles** is the tendon inside the back of your leg just above your heel. *Barnes ruptured an achilles tendon during England's 2-1 win over Finland in Helsinki. ...a serious Achilles injury.* N-COUNT

achingly /eɪkɪŋli/. You can use **achingly** for emphasis when you are referring to things that inspire feelings of wanting something very much, but of not being able to have it; used in written English. *...three achingly beautiful ballads... Go out to eat instead of staying in the hotel, where the service is achingly slow.* ADV-GRADED: ADV adj/adv PRAGMATICS

achy /eɪki/. If you feel **achy**, your body aches; an informal word used mainly in spoken English. *I feel achy all over.* ADJ-GRADED: usu v-link ADJ

acid /æsɪd/ **acids** ◆◆◆◇◇

1 An **acid** is a chemical substance, usually a liquid, which contains hydrogen and can react with other substances to form salts. Some acids burn or dissolve other substances that they come into contact with. *...citric acid... Enzymes in the saliva as well as acids in the stomach destroy the virus.* N-MASS ≠alkali

2 An **acid** substance contains acid. *These shrubs must have an acid, lime-free soil.* ♦ **acidity** /æsɪdɪti/ *...the acidity of rainwater.* ADJ-GRADED N-UNCOUNT: oft N *of* n

3 An **acid** fruit or drink has a sour or sharp taste. *These wines may taste rather hard and somewhat acid.* ♦ **acidity** *...a finely balanced wine with ripe acidity and soft fruit flavours.* ADJ-GRADED =acidic N-UNCOUNT

4 An **acid** remark, or **acid** humour, is very unkind or critical. *This comedy of contemporary manners is told with compassion and acid humour.* ♦ **acidly** *'You don't know how to be a mother and you never did,' she said acidly.* ADJ-GRADED ADV-GRADED: usu ADV with v, also ADV adj

5 The drug **LSD** is sometimes referred to as **acid**; an informal use. N-UNCOUNT

6 See also **amino acid, hydrochloric acid, nitric acid, nucleic acid, sulphuric acid.**

acid house. **Acid house** is a type of electronic dance music with a strong, repetitive rhythm. N-UNCOUNT

acidic /əsɪdɪk/ ◆◇◇◇◇

1 **Acidic** substances contain acid. *Dissolved carbon dioxide makes the water more acidic.* ADJ-GRADED ≠alkaline

2 An **acidic** taste is sour and sharp. *If the sprouts smell, or taste, mouldy or acidic do not eat them.* ADJ-GRADED =acid

acid rain. **Acid rain** is rain polluted by acid released into the atmosphere from factories and other industrial processes. Acid rain damages plants and trees, and is harmful to the environment. *Air pollution, acid rain and toxic waste are already a problem in this country.* ◆◇◇◇◇ N-UNCOUNT

acid test. The **acid test** of something is an important aspect or result that it might have, which allows you to decide whether it is true or successful. *The perception of fairness is the acid test for a democracy.* N-SING: *the* N

acknowledge /æknɒlɪdʒ/ **acknowledges, acknowledging, acknowledged** ◆◆◆◇◇

1 If you **acknowledge** a fact or a situation, you accept or admit that it is true or that it exists; a formal use. *Naylor acknowledged, in a letter to the judge, that he was a drug addict... Belatedly, the govern-* VERB =admit V that V n V-ed

ment has acknowledged the problem... There is an acknowledged risk of lung cancer from radon. Also V n to-inf, V n as n/adj

2 If someone's achievements, status, or qualities **are acknowledged**, they are known about and recognized by a lot of people, or by a particular group of people. *He is also acknowledged as an excellent goal-keeper... Some of the clergy refused to acknowledge the new king's legitimacy.* VERB =recognize; be V-ed as n; V n; Also V n to-inf

3 If you **acknowledge** a message or letter, you write to the person who sent it in order to say that you have received it. *The army sent me a postcard acknowledging my request.* VERB; V n

4 If you **acknowledge** someone, for example with a nod or a smile, you show that you have seen and recognized them. *She never even acknowledged the man who opened the door for her.* VERB; V n

5 If you **acknowledge** someone's applause or compliments, you make a gesture in order to thank them or show your appreciation. *Doran stuck his head out of the window to acknowledge the cheering... He acknowledged the applause with a small bow.* VERB; V n; V n with n

acknowledgement /æknɒlɪdʒmənt/ **acknowledgements;** also spelled **acknowledgment**. ◆◇◇◇◇

1 An **acknowledgement** is a statement or action which recognizes that something exists or is true. *The President's resignation appears to be an acknowledgment that he has lost all hope of keeping the country together... He appreciated her acknowledgement of his maturity.* N-SING: also no det, usu with supp, oft N that, N of n =recognition

2 The **acknowledgements** in a book are the section in which the author thanks all the people who have helped him or her. N-PLURAL

3 A gesture of **acknowledgement**, such as a nod or a smile, shows someone that you have seen and recognized them. *Farling smiled in acknowledgement and gave a bow... Mitzi nodded a perfunctory acknowledgement as her glass was filled.* N-UNCOUNT: also a N

4 An **acknowledgement** is a published statement in which you express your gratitude for or appreciation of something. *The benefit to the donor was an acknowledgment of the donation in a printed bulletin... Grateful acknowledgment is made for permission to reprint.* N-VAR

5 An **acknowledgement** is a letter or message that you receive from someone, telling you that something you have sent to them has arrived. *I have received neither an acknowledgment nor a reply.* N-COUNT

acme /ækmi/. The **acme** of something is its highest point of achievement or excellence; a formal word. *His work is considered the acme of cinematic art.* N-SING: usu the N of n =height

acne /ækni/. If someone has **acne**, they have a lot of spots on their face and neck. Acne is common among teenagers. ◆◇◇◇◇ N-UNCOUNT

acolyte /ækəlaɪt/ **acolytes**

1 An **acolyte** is a follower or assistant of an important person; a formal use. *Richard Brome, an acolyte of Ben Jonson's, wrote 'The Jovial Crew' in 1641. ...Mr Bossi and his acolytes.* N-COUNT

2 An **acolyte** is someone who assists a priest in performing certain religious services. *When the barge reached the shrine, acolytes removed the pall.* N-COUNT

acorn /eɪkɔːʳn/ **acorns.** An **acorn** is a pale oval nut that is the fruit of an oak tree. N-COUNT

acoustic /əkuːstɪk/ **acoustics** ◆◆◇◇◇

1 An **acoustic** guitar or other instrument is one whose sound is natural and not made louder by electrical apparatus. ♦ **acoustically** /əkuːstɪkli/ *It's a very exciting time, I think, to be writing acoustically based music.* ADJ: ADJ n; ADV: oft ADV with cl

2 If you refer to the **acoustics** or the **acoustic** of a space, you are referring to the structural features which determine how well you can hear music or speech in it. *In this performance, Rattle had the acoustic of the Symphony Hall on his side.* ♦ **acoustically** *The church is fully air-conditioned and acoustically perfect.* N-COUNT; ADV: ADV adj

3 **Acoustics** is the scientific study of sound. N-UNCOUNT

4 **Acoustic** or **acoustical** means relating to sound or hearing. *...acoustic signals.* ADJ: ADJ n

acoustical /əkuːstɪkəl/. **Acoustical** means relating to sound or hearing. *...an ideal acoustical experience.* ADJ

acquaint /əkweɪnt/ **acquaints, acquainting, acquainted.** If you **acquaint** someone with something, you tell them about it so that they know it or become familiar with it. If you **acquaint** yourself with something, you learn it or become familiar with it; a formal word. *Have steps been taken to acquaint breeders with their right to apply for licences?... I want to acquaint myself with your abilities, your strengths and weaknesses.* • See also **acquainted.** ◆◇◇◇◇ VERB =familiarize; V n with n; V pron-refl with n

acquaintance /əkweɪntəns/ **acquaintances** ◆◆◇◇◇

1 An **acquaintance** is someone who you have met and know slightly, but not well. *He exchanged a few words with the proprietor, an old acquaintance of his... I have a large circle of friends and acquaintances engaged in photography.* N-COUNT: oft with poss =associate

2 If you have an **acquaintance** with someone, you have met them and you know them. *...a writer who becomes involved in a real murder mystery through his acquaintance with a police officer... On first acquaintance she is cool and slightly distant.* N-VAR: oft poss N, N with n, on N =association

3 Your **acquaintance** with a subject is your knowledge or experience of it; a formal use. *They had little or no acquaintance with Chinese philosophy or history... Nurses have an intimate acquaintance with the male body.* N-UNCOUNT: usu with supp, oft N with n

4 When you **make** someone's **acquaintance**, you meet them for the first time and get to know them a little; a formal expression. *I first made his acquaintance and that of his wife and young family in the early 1960s... I am so pleased to make your acquaintance, Mr Tweed.* PHRASES V inflects

5 A person **of** your **acquaintance** is someone who you have met and know; a formal expression. *...a highly cultivated woman of our acquaintance.* n PHR

acquaintanceship /əkweɪntənsʃɪp/ **acquaintanceships.** Your **acquaintanceship** with a person is your acquaintance with them; a formal word. *Gibb's acquaintanceship with Getty dates back to the Sixties.* N-VAR: usu with supp, oft poss N, N with n

acquainted /əkweɪntɪd/

1 If you are **acquainted** with something, you know about it because you have learned it or experienced it; a formal use. *He was well acquainted with the literature of France, Germany and Holland... I am also looking forward to getting more acquainted with immigration law.* ADJ-GRADED: v-link ADJ with n =familiar with

2 If you are **acquainted** with someone, you have met them and you know them. You can also say that two people are **acquainted**; a formal use. *No-one personally acquainted with the couple was permitted to talk to the Press... It's true we were acquainted, but no more than that.* ADJ-GRADED: v-link ADJ, usu ADJ with n

3 If you get or become **acquainted** with someone that you do not know, you talk to each other or do something together so that you get to know each other. You can also say that two people get or become **acquainted**. *At first the meetings were a way to get acquainted with each other. ...an opportunity for the leaders to become better acquainted.* ADJ-GRADED: v-link ADJ, oft ADJ with n

4 See also **acquaint**.

acquiesce /ækwies/ **acquiesces, acquiescing, acquiesced.** If you **acquiesce** to something, you agree to do what someone wants or to accept what they do; a formal word. *Steve seemed to acquiesce in the decision... He has gradually acquiesced to the demands of the opposition... When her mother suggested that she should not go far from the hotel, Alice willingly acquiesced.* VERB =give in, submit ≠resist; V in/to n; V

acquiescence /ækwiesəns/. **Acquiescence** is agreement to do what someone wants, or acceptance of what they do even though you do not agree with it. *Deirdre smiled her acquiescence and resumed her seat... Fear of rapid social change made temporary acquiescence in slavery tolerable in the South.* N-UNCOUNT: with supp, oft N in/to n ≠resistance

acquiescent /ækwiesənt/. Someone who is **acquiescent** is ready to agree to do what someone wants, or to accept what they do. *The other men* ADJ-GRADED =submissive *were acquiescent, but Trevor had an independent streak.*

acquire /əkwaɪəʳ/ **acquires, acquiring, acquired** ◆◆◆◇◇

1 If you **acquire** something, you buy or obtain it for yourself, or someone gives it to you; a formal use. *General Motors acquired a 50% stake in Saab for about $400m... I recently acquired some wood from a holly tree which has been felled... She was sitting in her newly-acquired wheelchair.*
VERB · V n · V n *from* n · V-ed

2 If you **acquire** something such as a skill or a habit, you learn it, or develop it through your daily life or experience. *I've never acquired a taste for wine... Having read the book, she will be able to pass on the acquired knowledge to trainee teachers.*
VERB · V n · V-ed

3 If someone or something **acquires** a certain reputation, they start to have that reputation. *He has begun to acquire a reputation among some critics as perhaps this country's premier solo violinist.*
VERB · V n

4 If you describe something as an **acquired taste**, you mean that a lot of people do not like it when they first experience it, but often start to like it more when they get to know it better. *Tibetan tea is most definitely an acquired taste.*
PHRASE: usu v-link PHR

acquired immune deficiency syndrome. **Acquired immune deficiency syndrome** is the same as **AIDS**.
N-UNCOUNT

acquirer /əkwaɪərəʳ/ **acquirers.** An **acquirer** is a company or person who buys another company; a technical term in business. *...the ability of corporate acquirers to finance large takeovers with the help of junk bond sales.*
N-COUNT

acquisition /ækwɪzɪʃᵊn/ **acquisitions** ◆◆◆◇◇

1 If a company or business person makes an **acquisition**, they buy another company or part of a company; a technical use in business. *...the acquisition of a profitable paper recycling company. ...the number of mergers and acquisitions made by Europe's 1,000 leading firms.*
N-VAR: oft N *of* n

2 If you make an **acquisition**, you buy or obtain something, often to add to things that you already have. *How did you go about making this marvellous acquisition then? ...the President's recent acquisition of a helicopter.*
N-COUNT: oft N *of* n =purchase

3 You can use **acquisition** to refer to an object that you buy or obtain, often to add to things that you already have. *She pulls my latest acquisition from the tall bottom shelf and gazes at the cover.*
N-COUNT =purchase

4 The **acquisition** of a skill or a particular type of knowledge is the process of learning it or developing it. *...hypotheses about children's conceptual structure and how it feeds into language acquisition.*
N-UNCOUNT: n N, N *of* n

acquisitive /əkwɪzɪtɪv/. If you describe a person or an organization as **acquisitive**, you mean that they like getting new possessions; used showing disapproval. *We live in an acquisitive society... The most acquisitive firms tend to be engineering groups.* ♦ **acquisitiveness** *His villa is filled with evidence of his acquisitiveness.*
ADJ-GRADED: usu ADJ n · PRAGMATICS · N-UNCOUNT

acquit /əkwɪt/ **acquits, acquitting, acquitted** ◆◇◇◇◇

1 If someone **is acquitted** of a crime in a court of law, they are formally declared not to have committed the crime. *Mr Ling was acquitted of disorderly behaviour by magistrates... Mr Hope was initially convicted but then was acquitted on appeal.*
VB: usu passive =clear ≠convict · *be* V-ed *of* n · *be* V-ed

2 If you **acquit** yourself well or admirably in a particular situation, other people feel that you have behaved well or admirably; a formal use. *Most officers and men acquitted themselves well throughout the action.*
VERB · V pron-refl adv

acquittal /əkwɪtᵊl/ **acquittals.** **Acquittal** is a formal declaration in a court of law that someone who has been accused of a crime is innocent. *...the acquittal of six police officers charged with the beating of an alleged drug dealer... The jury voted 8-to-4 in favor of acquittal... The trial resulted in acquittals on all but one count.*
◆◇◇◇◇ N-VAR ≠conviction

acre /eɪkəʳ/ **acres.** An **acre** is an area of land measuring 4840 square yards or 4047 square metres. *The property is set in two acres of land.*
◆◆◆◇◇ N-COUNT

acreage /eɪkərɪdʒ/ **acreages.** **Acreage** is a large area of agricultural land; a formal word. *He has sown coffee on part of his acreage... Enormous acreages of soya beans are grown in the United States.*
N-VAR

acrid /ækrɪd/. An **acrid** smell or taste is strong and sharp, and usually unpleasant. *The room filled with the acrid smell of tobacco... The plant has an unpleasant odour and an acrid taste.*
ADJ-GRADED: usu ADJ n =pungent, bitter

acrimonious /ækrɪmoʊniəs/. **Acrimonious** words or quarrels are bitter and angry; a formal word. *The acrimonious debate on the agenda ended indecisively.* ♦ **acrimoniously** *Our relationship ended acrimoniously.*
◆◇◇◇◇ ADJ-GRADED: usu ADJ n =bitter · ADV-GRADED: ADV with v

acrimony /ækrɪməni, AM -moʊni/. **Acrimony** is bitter and angry words or quarrels; a formal word. *The council's first meeting ended in acrimony.*
N-UNCOUNT

acrobat /ækrəbæt/ **acrobats.** An **acrobat** is an entertainer who performs difficult jumps, somersaults, and balancing acts. *In his youth he had briefly been a circus acrobat.*
N-COUNT =tumbler

acrobatic /ækrəbætɪk/. An **acrobatic** movement or display involves difficult jumps, somersaults, and balancing acts. *He performed a sensational acrobatic feat.*
ADJ-GRADED: usu ADJ n

acrobatics /ækrəbætɪks/. **Acrobatics** are acrobatic movements that involve difficult jumps, somersaults, and balancing acts. *A young girl performed acrobatics on a palomino horse.*
N-PLURAL

acronym /ækrənɪm/ **acronyms.** An **acronym** is a word composed of the initial letters of the words in a phrase, especially when this is used as the name of something. An example of an acronym is NATO which is made up of the first letters of 'the North Atlantic Treaty Organization'.
◆◇◇◇◇ N-COUNT

across /əkrɒs, AM əkrɔːs/ ◆◆◆◆◆

In addition to the uses shown below, **across** is used in phrasal verbs such as 'come across', 'get across', and 'put across'.

1 If someone or something goes **across** a place or a boundary, they go from one side of it to the other. *She walked across the floor and lay down on the bed... He watched Karl run across the street to Tommy. ...an expedition across Africa.* ► Also an adverb. *Richard stood up and walked across to the window.*
PREP · ADV: ADV after v

2 If something is situated or stretched **across** something else, it is situated or stretched from one side of it to the other. *...the floating bridge across Lake Washington in Seattle... He scrawled his name across the bill... Lucy had strung a banner across the wall saying 'Welcome Home Daddy'.* ► Also an adverb. *Trim toenails straight across using nail clippers.*
PREP · ADV: ADV after v

3 If something is lying **across** an object or place, it is resting on it and partly covering it. *She found her clothes lying across the chair... The wind pushed his hair across his face.*
PREP =over

4 Something that is **across** something such as a street, river, or area is on the other side of it. *Anyone from the houses across the road could see him... When I saw you across the room I knew I'd met you before.* ► Also an adverb. *They parked across from the Castro Theatre... He pulled up a chair and sat down across from Michael.*
PREP · ADV: ADV after v, usu ADV *from* n

5 If you look **across** at a place, person, or thing, you look towards them. *He glanced across at his sleeping wife... She rose from the chair and gazed across at him. ...breathtaking views across to the hills.*
ADV: ADV after v, oft ADV prep

6 You use **across** to say that a particular expression is shown on someone's face. *An enormous grin spread across his face... For a moment a shadow seemed to pass across Roy's face.*
PREP =over

7 If someone hits you **across** the face or head, they hit you on that part. *Graham hit him across the face with the gun, then pushed him against the wall.*
PREP

8 When something happens **across** a place or organization, it happens equally everywhere within it. *The film 'Hook' opens across America on December 11... Thousands of farmers from across Europe have held a huge demonstration in the centre of*
PREP

Brussels... 2,000 workers across all state agencies are to be fired by March 31st.

9 When something happens **across** a political, religious, or social barrier, it involves people in different groups. *...parties competing across the political spectrum... We want to promote cosmetics that appeal across the colour barrier.* ● **across the board**: see **board**.
PREP

10 **Across** is used in measurements to show the width of something. *This hand-decorated plate measures 30cm across and costs £11.50... The snails are no larger than one centimetre across.*
ADV: amount ADV

acrylic /ækrɪlɪk/ **acrylics** ◆◇◇◇◇

1 **Acrylic** material is man-made and manufactured by a chemical process. *One of my fears was that Mike would wear one of his acrylic jumpers.*
N-UNCOUNT: usu N n

2 **Acrylics** or **acrylic paint** is a type of paint used by artists. *I use watercolours much less than I do oils or acrylics... He never uses acrylic paint.*
N-MASS

act /ækt/ **acts, acting, acted** ◆◆◆◆◆

1 When you **act**, you do something for a particular purpose. *The deaths occurred when police acted to stop widespread looting and vandalism... I have no reason to doubt that the bank acted properly in the best interests of the depositors.*
VERB V V adv/prep

2 If you **act on** advice or information, you do what has been advised or suggested. *A patient will usually listen to the physician's advice and act on it.*
VERB V *on/upon* n

3 If someone **acts** in a particular way, they behave in that way. *...a gang of youths who were acting suspiciously... He acted as if he hadn't heard any of it... Open wounds act like a magnet to flies in hot weather.*
VERB =behave V adv V as if V *like* n

4 If someone or something **acts as** a particular thing, they have that role or function. *Among his other duties, he acted both as the ship's surgeon and as chaplain for the men. ...the Cunard Princess, which acted as a support ship for American forces.*
VERB V *as/like* n

5 If someone **acts** in a particular way, they pretend to be something that they are not. *Chris acted astonished as he examined the note... Kenworthy had tried not to act the policeman.*
VERB V adj V n

6 When professionals such as lawyers or estate agents **act for** you, or **act on** your **behalf**, they are employed by you to deal with a particular matter. *Daniel Webster acted for Boston traders while still practicing in New Hampshire... Because we travelled so much, Sam and I asked a broker to act on our behalf.*
VERB V *for* n V prep

7 If a force or substance **acts on** someone or something, it has a certain effect on them. *He's taking a dangerous drug: it acts very fast on the central nervous system... A hypnotist can act upon the unconscious mind directly.*
VERB V *on/upon* n Also V

8 If you **act**, or **act** a part in a play or film, you have a part in it. *She confessed to her parents her desire to act... Roberto introduced Ingrid to Helen, whose husband was acting in Roberto's films.*
VERB V V *in* n Also V n

9 An **act** is a single thing that someone does; a formal use. *Language interpretation is the whole point of the act of reading... My insurance excludes acts of sabotage and damage done by weapons of war.*
N-COUNT: oft N *of* n

10 If you say that someone's behaviour is an **act**, you mean that it does not express their real feelings. *There were moments when I wondered: did she do this on purpose, was it all just a game, an act?... His anger was real. It wasn't an act.*
N-SING =pretence

11 An **Act** is a law passed by the government. *Until 1857 a woman could not sue for divorce except by an Act of Parliament.*
N-COUNT

12 An **act** in a play, opera, or ballet is one of the main parts into which it is divided. *Act II contained one of the funniest scenes I have ever witnessed... The Juniper Tree is an opera in two acts.*
N-COUNT: oft N num

13 An **act** in a show is a short performance which is one of several in the show. *The Comedy Shack is a great night out, featuring some of the best new comedy acts... The Orange Ball will feature live acts, a celebrity fashion show and a non-stop party.*
N-COUNT

14 If you **catch** someone **in the act**, you discover them doing something wrong or committing a crime. *The men were caught in the act of digging up buried explosives.*
PHRASES V inflects

15 If someone who has been behaving badly **cleans up** their **act**, they start to behave in a more acceptable or responsible way; an informal expression. *The nation's advertisers need to clean up their act.*
V inflects

16 If you **get in on the act**, you take part in or take advantage of something that was started by someone else; an informal expression. *In the 1970s Kodak, anxious to get in on the act, launched its own instant camera.*
V inflects

17 You say that someone was **in the act of** doing something to indicate what they were doing when they were seen or interrupted. *Ken was in the act of paying his bill when Neil came up behind him.*
v-link PHR -ing

18 When you **get your act together**, you organize your life or your affairs so that you are able to achieve what you want or to deal with something effectively; an informal expression. *The Government should get its act together... We have to get our act together – we have to organize ourselves.*
V inflects

19 ● **act one's age**: see **age.** ● **act the fool**: see **fool**.

act out. If you **act out** an event which has happened, you copy the actions which took place and make them into a play. *The group acts out the stories in such a way that the members experience really being there.*
PHRASAL VERB V P n (not pron) Also V n P

act up
PHRASAL VERB

1 If something **is acting up**, it is not working properly; an informal expression. *She was messing with the coffee pot, which was acting up again.*
usu cont V P

2 If a child **is acting up**, he or she is behaving badly. *I could hear Jonathan acting up downstairs.*
usu cont V P

acting /æktɪŋ/ ◆◆◇◇◇

1 **Acting** is the activity or profession of performing in plays or films. *Saffron Burrows returned to London to pursue her acting career after four years of modelling.*
N-UNCOUNT

2 You use **acting** before the title of a job to indicate that someone is doing that job temporarily. *The new acting President has a reputation of being someone who is independent.*
ADJ: ADJ n

action /ækʃᵊn/ **actions** ◆◆◆◆◆

1 **Action** is doing something for a particular purpose. *She claimed she was anxious to avoid any action which might harm him... The government is taking emergency action to deal with a housing crisis... What was needed, he said, was decisive action to halt what he called these savage crimes.*
N-UNCOUNT: usu with supp

2 An **action** is something that you do on a particular occasion. *As always, Peter had a reason for his action... Jack was the sort of man who did not like his actions questioned.*
N-COUNT

3 A legal **action** is an attempt to get a court order to stop someone doing something or to pay compensation for damage they have caused; a legal use. *Two leading law firms are to prepare legal actions against tobacco companies. ...a libel action brought by one of France's bureaucrats.*
N-COUNT =suit, case

4 The **action** of a chemical is the way in which it works, or the effects that it has. *Her description of the nature and action of poisons is amazingly accurate.*
N-UNCOUNT

5 **The action** is all the important and exciting things that are happening in a situation. *Hollywood is where the action is now.*
N-SING: *the* N

6 The fighting which takes place in a war can be referred to as **action**. *Leaders in America have generally supported military action if it proves necessary... 13 soldiers were killed and 10 wounded in action.*
N-UNCOUNT: oft *in* N

7 If someone or something is **out of action**, they are injured or damaged and cannot work or be used. *He's been out of action for 16 months with a serious knee injury... They were trapped after the lifts went out of action.*
PHRASES v-link PHR, PHR after v

8 If someone wants to have **a piece of the action** or **a slice of the action**, they want to take part in an exciting activity or situation, usually in order to make money or become more important. *Holiday*

spots have seen a dramatic revival and tourist chiefs are competing for a slice of the action.

9 If you **put** an idea or policy **into action**, you begin to use it or cause it to operate. *They have excelled in learning the lessons of business management theory, and putting them into action.* V inflects

actionable /ækʃənəbəl/. If something that you do or say to someone is **actionable**, it gives them a valid reason for bringing a legal case against you. ADJ: usu v-link ADJ

action replay, action replays. An **action replay** is a repeated showing, usually in slow motion, of an event that has just been on television. N-COUNT

activate /æktɪveɪt/ **activates, activating, activated.** ◆◇◇◇◇ If a device or process is **activated**, something causes it to start working. *Video cameras with night vision can be activated by movement... She has written two books on her voice-activated computer.* VB: usu passive be V-ed V-ed

active /æktɪv/ ◆◆◆◆◇

1 Someone who is **active** moves around a lot or does a lot of things. *Compared to other women your age, how physically active are you?... Having an active youngster about the house can be quite wearing. ...a long and active life.* ADJ-GRADED ≠sedentary

2 If you have an **active** mind or imagination, you are always thinking of new things. *His mind was always active and his country home bore evidence of this in many innovations.* ADJ-GRADED =lively

3 If someone is **active** in an organization, cause, or campaign, they do things for it rather than just give it their support. *The supervisor played an active role in communicating the EFE's goals... I am an active member of the Conservative Party. ...politically active students... He is active on Tyler's behalf.* ADJ-GRADED: oft ADJ prep ≠passive

♦ **actively** *They actively campaigned for the vote.* ADV

4 **Active** is used to emphasize that someone is taking action in order to achieve something, rather than just hoping for it or achieving it in an indirect way. *...if companies do not take active steps to increase exports. ...active discouragement from teachers.* ADJ: ADJ n PRAGMATICS =positive ♦ **actively** *They have never been actively encouraged to take such risks. ...the White House says the president is not actively considering such a move.* ADV: usu ADV with v

5 If you say that a person or animal is **active** in a particular place or at a particular time, you mean that they are performing their usual activities or performing a particular activity. *Guerrilla groups are active in the province. ...animals which are active at night. ...men who are sexually active.* ADJ: usu v-link ADJ, usu ADJ prep

6 An **active** volcano has erupted recently or is expected to erupt quite soon. *...molten lava from an active volcano.* ADJ: usu ADJ n ≠extinct

7 An **active** substance has a chemical or biological effect on things. *The active ingredient in some of the mouthwashes was simply detergent.* ADJ: usu ADJ n

8 In grammar, **the active** or **the active voice** means the forms of a verb which are used when the subject refers to a person or thing that does something. For example, in 'I saw her yesterday', the verb is in the active. Compare **passive**. N-SING: the N

active duty. **Active duty** means the same as **active service**; used mainly in American English. *There would be little holiday leave for troops on active duty.* N-UNCOUNT: oft on N

active service. Someone who is on **active service** is taking part in a war as a member of the armed forces; used mainly in British English. *In April 1944 he was killed on active service... Bush is one of the last western leaders to have seen active service.* N-UNCOUNT: oft on N

activism /æktɪvɪzəm/. **Activism** is the process of campaigning in public or working for an organization in order to bring about political or social change. *He believed in political activism to achieve justice.* ◆◇◇◇◇ N-UNCOUNT

activist /æktɪvɪst/ **activists.** An **activist** is a person who works to bring about political or social changes by campaigning in public or working for an organization. *The police say they suspect the attack was carried out by animal rights activists.* ◆◆◆◇◇ N-COUNT =agitator

activity /æktɪvɪti/ **activities** ◆◆◆◆◇

1 **Activity** is a situation in which a lot of things are happening or being done. *We will see an extraordinary level of activity in the market for UK government bonds. ...the electrical activity of the brain.* N-UNCOUNT

2 An **activity** is something that you spend time doing. *For lovers of the great outdoors, activities range from canoeing to bird watching.* N-COUNT

3 The **activities** of a group are the things that they do in order to achieve their aims. *...a jail term for terrorist activities... Moscow city council has suspended the activities of the city's Communist party.* N-PLURAL: with supp =actions

act of God, acts of God. An **act of God** is an event that is beyond human control, especially one in which something is damaged or someone is hurt. *The President described the disaster as an act of God.* N-COUNT

actor /æktər/ **actors.** An **actor** is someone whose job is acting in plays or films. 'Actor' in the singular usually refers to a man, but some women who act prefer to be called 'actors' rather than 'actresses'. *His father was an actor in the Cantonese Opera Company... You have to be a very good actor to play that part.* ◆◆◆◇◇ N-COUNT

actress /æktrəs/ **actresses.** An **actress** is a woman whose job is acting in plays or films. *She's not only a very great dramatic actress but she's also very funny.* ◆◆◆◇◇ N-COUNT

actual /æktʃuəl/ ◆◆◆◇◇

1 You use **actual** to emphasize that you are referring to something real or genuine. *The segments are filmed using either local actors or the actual people involved... Officials admit the actual number of AIDS victims is much higher than statistics reflect... The difference between their final figures and the actual result was 1.4%.* ADJ: ADJ n PRAGMATICS =real, genuine

2 You use **actual** to contrast the important aspect of something with a less important aspect. *She had compiled pages of notes, but she had not yet gotten down to doing the actual writing... The exercises in this chapter can guide you, but it will be up to you to do the actual work.* • **in actual fact**: see **fact**. ADJ: ADJ n PRAGMATICS

actuality /æktʃuælɪti/ **actualities** ◆◇◇◇◇

1 You can use **in actuality** to emphasize that what you are saying is true, when it contradicts or contrasts with what you have previously said. *It would have been a monumental feat of self-control for him to change the habits of a lifetime. In actuality, he seems to have made very little effort to do so... The woman he had seen shining onstage was in actuality quite older than she had seemed.* PHRASE: PHR with cl PRAGMATICS =in reality, actually

2 **Actuality** is the state of really existing rather than being imagined. *It exists in dreams rather than actuality.* N-UNCOUNT =reality

3 An **actuality** is a fact or condition that really exists; a formal use. *To stop the fighting there requires the threat and probably the actuality of military force... While economists are free to theorise, company chairmen are concerned with actualities.* N-COUNT

actually /æktʃuəli/ ◆◆◆◆◆

1 You use **actually** to indicate that a situation exists or happened, or to emphasize that it is true or correct, especially when its existence or truth is surprising. *One afternoon, I grew bored and actually fell asleep for a few minutes... Although she trained as a marine biologist, she actually studied botany at university... Interest is only payable on the amount actually borrowed... The appearance of my body is actually awful.* ADV: ADV before v, ADV group PRAGMATICS

2 You use **actually** when you are correcting or contradicting someone. *No, I'm not a student. I'm a doctor, actually... 'So it's not a family show then?'—'Well, actually, I think that's exactly what it is.'* ADV: ADV with cl PRAGMATICS

3 You can use **actually** when you are expressing an opinion that other people might not have expected from you in a polite way. *'Do you think it's a good idea to socialize with one's patients?'—'Actually, I do, I think it's a great idea.'... I would be surprised, actually, if he left Birmingham.* ADV: ADV with cl PRAGMATICS

4 You use **actually** to introduce a new topic into a conversation. *Well actually, John, I rang you for some advice... Actually, let's just read this little bit where you've made them bump into each other.*
ADV: ADV with cl PRAGMATICS

actuarial /æktʃueəriəl/. **Actuarial** means relating to the work of an actuary. *The company's actuarial report must be made available on demand.*
ADJ: ADJ n

actuary /æktʃuəri, AM -tʃueri/ **actuaries.** An **actuary** is a person who is employed by insurance companies to calculate how much they should charge their clients for insurance.
N-COUNT

actuate /æktʃueɪt/ **actuates, actuating, actuated.** If a person is **actuated** by an emotion, that emotion makes them act in a certain way. If something **actuates** a device, the device starts working. *They were actuated by desire... As the aircraft became airborne, the engines overheated, actuating the fire extinguishers.*
VERB =activate be V-ed V n

acuity /əkjuːɪti/. **Acuity** is sharpness or quickness of vision, hearing, or thought; a formal word. *Caffeine gives a boost of energy and temporarily sharpens mental acuity.*
N-UNCOUNT

acumen /ækjʊmen, AM əkjuːmən/. **Acumen** is the ability to make good judgements and quick decisions. *His sharp business acumen meant he quickly rose to the top.*
N-UNCOUNT: usu supp N

acupressure /ækjʊpreʃəʳ/. **Acupressure** is the treatment of pain by a type of massage in which pressure is put on certain areas of a person's body. *Acupressure is used to release tension spots in the shoulders and neck.*
N-UNCOUNT

acupuncture /ækjʊpʌŋktʃəʳ/. **Acupuncture** is the treatment of a person's illness or pain by sticking small needles into their body at certain places. *All of those who received the true acupuncture experienced pain relief.*
◆◇◇◇◇ N-UNCOUNT

acupuncturist /ækjʊpʌŋktʃərɪst/ **acupuncturists.** An **acupuncturist** is a person who performs acupuncture.
N-COUNT

acute /əkjuːt/ ◆◆◇◇◇

1 An **acute** situation or feeling is very severe or intense. *The war has aggravated an acute economic crisis... The report has caused acute embarrassment to the government... The labour shortage is becoming acute.*
ADJ-GRADED =severe

2 An **acute** illness is one that becomes severe very quickly but does not last very long; a medical use. Compare **chronic**. *...a patient with acute rheumatoid arthritis. ...an acute case of dysentery.*
ADJ: ADJ n

3 If a person's or animal's sight, hearing, or sense of smell is **acute**, it is sensitive and powerful. *I like how in the dark my sense of smell and hearing become so acute.*
ADJ-GRADED =keen

4 If you say that someone is **acute** or has an **acute** mind, you mean that they are quick to notice things and are able to understand them clearly. *Into her nineties, her thinking remained acute and her character forceful... His relaxed exterior hides an extremely acute mind.* ♦ **acuteness** *Everything he writes demonstrates the acuteness of his intelligence.*
ADJ-GRADED =keen, perceptive N-UNCOUNT: oft *the* N *of* n

5 An **acute** angle is less than 90°.
ADJ-GRADED

6 An **acute** accent is a symbol that is placed over vowels in some languages in order to indicate how that vowel is pronounced or over one letter in a word to indicate where it is stressed. You refer to a letter with this accent as, for example, e **acute**. For example, there is an acute accent over the letter 'e' in the French word 'cité'.
ADJ: ADJ n, n ADJ

acutely /əkjuːtli/ ◆◇◇◇◇

1 If you feel or notice something **acutely**, you feel or notice it very strongly. *He was acutely aware of the odour of cooking oil... Those tensions have been felt most acutely by women.*
ADV-GRADED: ADV adj, ADV with v =keenly

2 If a feeling or quality is **acutely** unpleasant, it is extremely unpleasant. *It was an acutely uncomfortable journey back to London.*
ADV-GRADED: ADV adj, ADV with v =intensely

ad /æd/ **ads.** An **ad** is an advertisement; an informal use. *She replied to a lonely hearts ad she spotted in the New York Times.*
◆◆◆◇◇ N-COUNT

AD /eɪ diː/. You use **AD** in dates to indicate the number of years or centuries that have passed since the year in which Jesus Christ is believed to have been born. *The cathedral was destroyed by the Great Fire of 1136 AD... The original castle was probably built about AD 860... The Roman Empire was divided in the fourth century AD.*
◆◇◇◇◇

adage /ædɪdʒ/ **adages.** An **adage** is something which people often say and which expresses a general truth about some aspect of life; an old-fashioned word. *The old adage, 'Every baby brings its own love' usually turns out to be true.*
N-COUNT =maxim, saying

adagio /ədɑːdʒioʊ, AM -dʒoʊ/ **adagios**

1 **Adagio** written above a piece of music means that it should be played slowly.
ADV-GRADED: ADV after v

2 An **adagio** is a piece of music that is played slowly. *...Samuel Barber's Adagio For Strings. ...the Adagio movement of his Sixth Symphony.*
N-COUNT: usu sing

adamant /ædəmənt/. If someone is **adamant** about something, they are determined not to change their mind about it. *The prime minister is adamant that he will not resign... Sue was adamant about that job in Australia.* ♦ **adamantly** *She was adamantly opposed to her husband travelling to Brussels.*
◆◇◇◇◇ ADJ-GRADED: usu v-link ADJ, oft ADJ that, ADJ *about* n/-ing ADV-GRADED: usu ADV with v, also ADV adj

Adam's apple /ædᵊmz æpᵊl/ **Adam's apples.** Your **Adam's apple** is the lump that sticks out of the front of your neck below your throat.
N-COUNT

adapt /ədæpt/ **adapts, adapting, adapted** ◆◆◇◇◇

1 If you **adapt** to a new situation or **adapt** yourself to it, you change your ideas or behaviour in order to deal with it successfully. *The world will be different, and we will have to be prepared to adapt to the change... They have been tightening their belts for months, adapting themselves to a war economy.*
VERB =adjust V *to* n V pron-refl *to* n Also V

2 If you **adapt** something, you change it to make it suitable for a new purpose or situation. *Shelves were built to adapt the library for use as an office.*
VERB =modify V n Also V n *to* n

3 If you **adapt** a book or play, you change it so that it can be made into a film or a television programme. *The scriptwriter helped him to adapt his novel for the screen... The film has been adapted from a play of the same title.*
VERB V n

4 See also **adapted**.

adaptable /ədæptəbᵊl/. If you describe a person or animal as **adaptable**, you mean that they are able to change their ideas or behaviour in order to deal with new situations. *By making the workforce more adaptable and skilled, he hopes to attract foreign investment... They are adaptable foragers that learn to survive on a wide range of food sources.* ♦ **adaptability** /ədæptəbɪlɪti/ *The adaptability of wool is one of its great attractions.*
◆◇◇◇◇ ADJ-GRADED =flexible ≠unadaptable N-UNCOUNT =flexibility

adaptation /ædæpteɪʃᵊn/ **adaptations** ◆◇◇◇◇

1 An **adaptation** of a novel or play is a play or film that is based on it. *Branagh won two awards for his screen adaptation of Shakespeare's Henry the Fifth.*
N-COUNT

2 **Adaptation** is the act of changing something or changing your behaviour to make it suitable for a new purpose or situation. *Most living creatures are capable of adaptation when compelled to do so.*
N-UNCOUNT

adapted /ədæptɪd/. If something is **adapted** to a particular situation or purpose, it is especially suitable for it. *The camel's feet, well adapted for dry sand, are useless on mud.*
ADJ-GRADED: v-link ADJ *to/for* n =suited

adaption /ədæpʃᵊn/ **adaptions. Adaption** means the same as **adaptation.**
N-VAR

adaptive /ədæptɪv/. **Adaptive** means having the ability or tendency to adapt to different situations; a formal word. *Societies need to develop highly adaptive behavioural rules for survival.*
ADJ-GRADED

adaptor /ədæptəʳ/ **adaptors;** also spelled **adapter.** An **adaptor** is a device for connecting two or more electrical plugs to the same socket or for connecting a device with a plug that does not fit into the socket.
N-COUNT

add /æd/ **adds, adding, added** ◆◆◆◆◆

1 If you **add** one thing to another, you put it in or on the other thing, to increase, complete, or improve it. *Add the grated cheese to the sauce... Since 1908, chlorine has been added to drinking water...*
VERB V n *to* n Also V n

He wants to add a huge sports complex to Binfield Manor.

2 If you **add** numbers or amounts together, you calculate their total. *Banks add all the interest and other charges together... Two and three added together are five.* ▶ **Add up** means the same as **add**. *More than a quarter of seven year-olds cannot add up properly... We just added all the numbers up and divided one by the other... His task had been one of administration, shuffling the numbers so they added up.* VERB ≠subtract V pl-n with together PHRASAL VERB ERG V P V pl-n P V P

3 If one thing **adds** to another, it makes the other thing greater in degree or amount. *Overnight bedrest in a clinic adds substantially to the cost of cosmetic surgery... Smiles, nods, and cheerful faces added to the general gaiety.* VERB V to n

4 To **add** a particular quality to something means to cause it to have that quality. *The generous amount of garlic adds flavour... A delicious blend of cider and delicate fruit juices adds a little sparkle to any occasion.* VERB V n V n to n

5 If you **add** something when you are speaking, you say something more. *'You can tell that he is extremely embarrassed,' Mr Brigden added... The Italian central bank added that the aim was to provide stability... Hunt added his congratulations, saying 'Nigel has made a cracking job of it'.* VERB V with quote V that V n

6 You use **added to this** or **added to that** to introduce a fact that supports or expands what you are saying. *More than 750 commercial airliners were involved in fatal accidents last year. Added to that were the 1,550 smaller aircraft.* • **add insult to injury**: see **insult**. PHRASE: V inflects PRAGMATICS

add in. If you **add in** something, you include it as a part of something else. *Once the vegetables start to cook add in a couple of tablespoons of water.* PHRASAL VERB V P n (not pron)

add on PHRASAL VERB

1 If something **is added on**, it is attached to something else, or is made a part of something else. *The colour is either drab or garish and is obviously added on.* usu passive be V-ed P

2 If you **add on** an extra amount or item to a list or total, you include it in the list or total. *Many loan application forms automatically add on insurance.* V P n (not pron) Also V n P

3 If you **add on** to something, especially a building, you make it larger by including or attaching an extra part or thing. *That's only a two bedroom home, so you might want to add on.* V P Also V P to n

add up PHRASAL VERB

1 See **add** 2.

2 If facts or events do not **add up**, they make you confused about a situation because they do not seem to be consistent. If something that someone has said or done **adds up**, it is reasonable and sensible. *Police said they arrested Olivia because her statements did not add up... Well, I could be wrong, but it all seems to add up.* usu with neg V P

3 If small amounts of something **add up**, they gradually increase. *Even small savings, 5 pence here or 10 pence there, can add up... It's the little minor problems that add up.* V P

add up to. If amounts **add up to** a particular total, they result in that total when they are put together. *For a hit show, profits can add up to millions of dollars.* PHRASAL VERB =amount to V P P n

added /ædɪd/. You use **added** to say that something has more of a particular thing or quality. *For added protection choose moisturising lipsticks with a sun screen.* ◆◇◇◇◇ ADJ: ADJ n =extra

added value. In marketing, **added value** is something which is added to a product to increase its value and make it more appealing to the consumer. *We tried to find new services which were sophisticated and had added value.* N-UNCOUNT

addendum /ədendəm/ **addenda** /ədendə/. An **addendum** is an additional section at the end of a book or document. N-COUNT =appendix

adder /ædəʳ/ **adders.** An **adder** is a small poisonous snake that has a black zigzag pattern on its back. N-COUNT =viper

addict /ædɪkt/ **addicts** ◆◆◇◇◇

1 An **addict** is someone who takes harmful drugs and cannot stop taking them. *He's only 24 years old and a drug addict.* N-COUNT: oft supp N

2 If you say that someone is an **addict**, you mean that they like a particular activity very much and spend as much time doing it as they can. *She is a TV addict and watches as much as she can.* N-COUNT: usu supp N

addicted /ədɪktɪd/ ◆◇◇◇◇

1 Someone who is **addicted** to a harmful drug cannot stop taking it. *Many of the women are addicted to heroin and cocaine... After about three months, I was no longer addicted to nicotine.* ADJ-GRADED: usu v-link ADJ, usu ADJ to n =hooked on

2 If you say that someone is **addicted** to something, you mean that they like it very much and want to spend as much time doing it as possible. *I went through about four years of being addicted to video games... She had become addicted to golf.* ADJ-GRADED: usu v-link ADJ, usu ADJ to n

addiction /ədɪkʃᵊn/ **addictions** ◆◆◇◇◇

1 **Addiction** is the condition of taking harmful drugs and being unable to stop taking them. *She helped him fight his drug addiction. ...long-term addiction to nicotine.* N-VAR: oft n N, N to n

2 An **addiction** to something is a very strong desire or need for it. *He needed money to feed his addiction to gambling... I discovered an addiction to housework which I had never felt before.* N-VAR: oft N to n

addictive /ədɪktɪv/ ◆◇◇◇◇

1 If a drug is **addictive**, people who take it cannot stop taking it. *Cigarettes are highly addictive... Crack is the most addictive drug on the market.* ADJ-GRADED

2 Something that is **addictive** is so enjoyable that it makes you want to do it or have it a lot. *Video movie-making can quickly become addictive.* ADJ-GRADED

3 If someone has an **addictive** personality, they easily become addicted to something. *I have an eating disorder and an addictive personality.* ADJ-GRADED: usu ADJ n

addition /ədɪʃᵊn/ **additions** ◆◆◆◆◇

1 You use **in addition** when you want to mention another item connected with the subject you are discussing. *Hong Kong has some of the largest buses in the world. In addition, the city has underground trains and a rapid surface railway... There's a postage and packing fee in addition to the repair charge.* PHRASE: PHR with cl, oft PHR to n PRAGMATICS

2 An **addition** to something is a thing which is added to it. *This is a fine book; a worthy addition to the Cambridge Encyclopedia series... This plywood addition helps to strengthen the structure.* N-COUNT: usu with supp, oft N to n

3 The **addition** of something is the fact that it is added to something else. *It was completely refurbished in 1987, with the addition of a picnic site.* N-UNCOUNT: the N of n ≠removal

4 **Addition** is the process of calculating the total of two or more numbers. *...simple addition and subtraction problems using whole numbers.* N-UNCOUNT

additional /ədɪʃənᵊl/. **Additional** things are extra things apart from the ones already present. *The US is sending additional troops to the region... The insurer will also have to pay the additional costs of the trial.* ◆◆◆◇◇ ADJ: usu ADJ n =supplementary

additionally /ədɪʃənəli/ ◆◇◇◇◇

1 You use **additionally** to introduce something extra such as an extra fact or reason; a formal use. *All teachers are qualified to teach their native language. Additionally, we select our teachers for their engaging personalities... The maintenance programme will additionally seek to keep the sites free of graffiti.* ADV: ADV with cl PRAGMATICS =further

2 **Additionally** is used to say that something happens to a greater extent than before. *The birds are additionally protected in the reserves at Birsay... He will sign a personal guarantee to additionally secure the loan.* ADV: ADV with v

additive /ædɪtɪv/ **additives.** An **additive** is a substance which is added in small amounts to foods or other things in order to improve them or to make them last longer. *Strict safety tests are carried out on food additives. ...additive-free baby foods.* ◆◇◇◇◇ N-COUNT

addle /ædᵊl/ **addles, addling, addled.** If something **addles** someone's mind or brain, they become confused and unable to think properly. *I suppose the shock had addled his poor old brain.* VERB =befuddle V n

addled /ædᵊld/. If you describe someone as **addled**, you mean that they are confused or unable ADJ-GRADED: usu ADJ n =befuddled to think properly. *She wore a sweet and slightly addled expression... You're talking like an addled romantic.*

add-on, add-ons. An **add-on** is an extra piece of equipment that can be added to a larger one which you already own in order to improve its performance or its usefulness; used especially to refer to computer equipment. *In most electronics shops, active speakers are sold as add-ons for personal stereos... Nintendo hopes to price the add-on modem at less than $200.* N-COUNT: oft N n

address /ədres, AM ædres/ **addresses, addressing, addressed** ◆◆◆◆◇

1 Your **address** is the number of the house, and the name of the street and the town where you live or work. *The address is 2025 M Street, Northwest, Washington, DC, 20036... We require details of your name and address.* N-COUNT: usu poss N

2 If a letter, envelope, or parcel **is addressed to** you, your name and address have been written on it. *Applications should be addressed to: The business affairs editor.* VB: usu passive; be V-ed to n

3 If you **address** a group of people, you give a speech to them. *Nelson Mandela is due to address a gathering of supporters here shortly.* ► Also a noun. *He had scheduled an address to the American people for the evening of May 27.* VERB; V n; N-COUNT

4 If you **address** someone or **address** a remark to someone, you say something to them. *The two foreign ministers did not address each other directly when they last met... Needless to say, I will address this complaint to the bank concerned.* VERB; V n; V n to n

5 If you **address** someone by a name or a title such as 'sir', you call them that name or title when you talk or write to them. *I heard him address her as darling... The Duchess should be addressed as Your Grace.* VERB; V n as n

6 If you **address** a problem or task or if you **address** yourself to it, you try to understand it or deal with it. *Mr King sought to address those fears when he spoke at the meeting... Throughout the book we have addressed ourselves to the problem of ethics.* VERB ≠ignore; V n; V pron-refl to n

address book, address books. An **address book** is a book in which you write people's names and addresses. N-COUNT

addressee /ædresiː/ **addressees.** The **addressee** of a letter or parcel is the person or company that it is addressed to; a formal word. N-COUNT: usu the N in sing

adduce /ədjuːs, AM -duːs/ **adduces, adducing, adduced.** If you **adduce** something such as a fact or reason, you mention it in order to support an argument; a formal word. *The evidence she adduces to back up her arguments is usually authoritative.* VERB =cite; V n

adenoidal /ædɪnɔɪdᵊl/. If someone has an **adenoidal** voice, they speak in a nasal way because they have swollen adenoids. ADJ: ADJ n

adenoids /ædɪnɔɪdz/. **Adenoids** are soft lumps of flesh at the back and top of a person's throat that sometimes become swollen and have to be removed. N-PLURAL

adept, adepts. The adjective is pronounced /ædept/. The noun is pronounced /ædept/. Someone who is **adept** at something can do it skilfully. *He's usually very adept at keeping his private life out of the media... He is an adept guitar player.* ► An **adept** is someone who is adept at something. *Kitzi was an adept at getting people to talk confidentially to him.* ♦ **adeptly** /ædeptli/ *Mrs Marcos' lawyer adeptly exploited the prosecution's weakness.* ◆◇◇◇◇ ADJ-GRADED: usu v-link ADJ, usu ADJ at -ing/n; N-COUNT; ADV-GRADED: ADV with v

adequacy /ædɪkwəsi/. **Adequacy** is the quality of being good enough or great enough in amount to be acceptable or usable. *I am very critical of the adequacy of Britain's race laws... Several studies point to a real cause for concern over the adequacy of the diet eaten by British children.* N-UNCOUNT: usu N of n ≠inadequacy

adequate /ædɪkwət/. If something is **adequate**, there is enough of it or it is good enough to be used or accepted. *One in four people worldwide are without adequate homes... She is prepared to offer me an amount adequate to purchase another house... The western diet should be perfectly adequate for most people.* ♦ **adequately** *Many students are not adequately prepared for higher education... I speak the language adequately.* ◆◆◆◇◇ ADJ-GRADED: oft ADJ to-inf, ADJ for n =suitable ≠inadequate; ADV-GRADED: ADV with v

adhere /ædhɪəʳ/ **adheres, adhering, adhered** ◆◇◇◇◇

1 If you **adhere** to a rule or agreement, you act in the way that it says you should. *All members of the association adhere to a strict code of practice... She adhered to the strict Islamic dress code.* VERB =keep; V to n

2 If you **adhere** to an opinion or belief, you support or hold it. *He urged them to adhere to the values of Islam which defend the dignity of man.* VERB; V to n

3 If something **adheres** to something else, it sticks firmly to it. *Small particles adhere to the seed... This sticky compound adheres well on this surface.* VERB; V to n; V adv/prep; Also V

adherence /ædhɪərəns/. **Adherence** is the fact of adhering to a particular rule, agreement, or belief. *...strict adherence to the constitution and respect for our laws.* ◆◇◇◇◇ N-UNCOUNT: usu N to n

adherent /ædhɪərənt/ **adherents.** An **adherent** is someone who holds a particular belief or supports a particular person or group. *Communism was gaining adherents in Latin America.* N-COUNT =follower, supporter

adhesion /ædhiːʒᵊn/. **Adhesion** is the ability of one thing to stick firmly to another; a formal use. *Better driving equipment will improve track adhesion in slippery conditions.* N-UNCOUNT

adhesive /ædhiːsɪv/ **adhesives** ◆◇◇◇◇

1 An **adhesive** is a substance such as glue, which is used to make things stick firmly together. *Glue the mirror in with a strong adhesive.* N-MASS

2 An **adhesive** substance is able to stick firmly to something else. *...adhesive tape.* ADJ-GRADED: usu ADJ n

ad hoc /æd hɒk/. An **ad hoc** activity or organization is done or formed only because a situation has made it necessary and is not planned in advance. *'I would accept opportunities in TV on an ad hoc basis,' he said. ...ad hoc committees to examine specific problems.* ◆◇◇◇◇ ADJ: usu ADJ n =makeshift ≠planned

adieu /ədjuː/ **adieus. Adieu** means the same as **goodbye**; a literary or old-fashioned word. *'Gentlemen, I bid you adieu.'* CONVENTION

ad infinitum /æd ɪnfɪnaɪtəm/. If something happens **ad infinitum**, it is repeated again and again in the same way. *This cycle repeats itself ad infinitum.* ADV: ADV after v

adj. Adj is a written abbreviation for **adjective**. =adjective

adjacent /ədʒeɪsᵊnt/. If one thing is **adjacent** to another, the two things are next to each other. *He sat in an adjacent room and waited... The schools were adjacent but there were separate doors. ...offices adjacent to the museum.* ◆◇◇◇◇ ADJ: oft ADJ to n

adjectival /ædʒɪktaɪvᵊl/. **Adjectival** means relating to adjectives or like an adjective. *...an adjectival phrase.* ADJ: usu ADJ n

adjective /ædʒɪktɪv/ **adjectives.** An **adjective** is a word such as 'big', 'dead', or 'financial' that describes a person or thing, or gives extra information about them. Adjectives usually come before nouns or after link verbs. ◆◇◇◇◇ N-COUNT

adjective group, adjective groups. An **adjective group** or **adjectival group** is a group of words based on an adjective, such as 'very nice' or 'interested in football'. An adjective group can also consist simply of an adjective. N-COUNT

adjoin /ədʒɔɪn/ **adjoins, adjoining, adjoined.** If one room, place, or object **adjoins** another, they are next to each other; a formal word. *Fields adjoined the garden and there were no neighbours... We waited in an adjoining office.* ◆◇◇◇◇ VERB; V n; V-ing

adjourn /ədʒɜːʳn/ **adjourns, adjourning, adjourned.** If a meeting or trial **is adjourned** or if it **adjourns**, it is stopped for a short time. *The proceedings have now been adjourned until next week... I am afraid the court may not adjourn until three or even later.* ◆◇◇◇◇ V-ERG; be V-ed; V

adjournment /ədʒɜːʳnmənt/ **adjournments.** An **adjournment** is a temporary stopping of a trial, enquiry, or other meeting. *The court ordered a four month adjournment.* N-COUNT =suspension

adjudge /ədʒʌdʒ/ **adjudges, adjudging, adjudged.** If someone is **adjudged** to be some- VERB =decree thing, they are judged or considered to be that thing; a formal word. *He was adjudged to be guilty... At college he was adjudged the Best Speaker in a number of annual debating competitions.* — be V-ed to-inf; be V-ed n

adjudicate /ədʒuːdɪkeɪt/ **adjudicates, adjudicating, adjudicated.** If you **adjudicate** on a dispute or problem, you make an official judgement or decision about it. *...a commissioner to adjudicate on legal rights... The international court of justice might be a suitable place to adjudicate claims.* ♦ **adjudication** /ədʒuːdɪkeɪʃən/ **adjudications** *...unbiased adjudication of cases of unfair dismissal.* ♦ **adjudicator** /ədʒuːdɪkeɪtəʳ/ **adjudicators** *...an independent adjudicator.* — VERB =decide; V prep; V n; Also V; N-VAR =decision; N-COUNT

adjunct /ædʒʌŋkt/ **adjuncts**

1 Something that is an **adjunct** to something larger or more important is connected with it or helps to perform the same task. *Physical therapy is an important adjunct to drug treatments... The Party was certainly not an official adjunct of the police department.* — N-COUNT: oft N *to/of* n =appendage

2 In grammar, an **adjunct** is a word or group of words which indicates the circumstances of an action, event, or situation. An adjunct is usually a prepositional phrase or an adverb group. — N-COUNT

adjust /ədʒʌst/ **adjusts, adjusting, adjusted** ◆◆◆◇◇

1 When you **adjust** to a new situation, you get used to it by changing your behaviour or your ideas. *We have been preparing our fighters to adjust themselves to civil society... I felt I had adjusted to the idea of being a mother very well... It has been hard to adjust but now I'm getting satisfaction from my work.* ● See also **well-adjusted.** — VERB; V n *to* n; V *to* n; V; Also V adv

2 If you **adjust** something, you change it so that it is more effective or appropriate. *To attract investors, Panama has adjusted its tax and labour laws.* — VERB; V n

3 If you **adjust** something such as your clothing or a machine, you correct or alter its position or setting. *She adjusted her head scarf fussily... Liz adjusted her mirror and then edged the car out of its parking bay.* — VERB; V n

4 If you **adjust** your vision or if your vision **adjusts**, the muscles of your eye or the pupils alter to cope with changes in light or distance. *He stopped to try to adjust his vision to the faint starlight... We stood in the doorway until our eyes adjusted... It was a few moments before his eyes became adjusted to the bright glare of the sun.* — V-ERG; V n; V; V-ed

adjustable /ədʒʌstəbəl/. If something is **adjustable**, it can be changed to different positions or sizes. *The bags have adjustable shoulder straps... The seats are fully adjustable.* — ◆◇◇◇◇ ADJ ≠fixed, unadjustable

adjuster /ədʒʌstəʳ/ **adjusters;** also spelled **adjustor.**

1 An **adjuster** is someone who is employed by an insurance company to investigate claims. He or she judges the value of the loss and the validity of the claim. — N-COUNT

2 An **adjuster** is a device which allows you to alter a piece of equipment's position or setting. *...a seat belt adjuster.* — N-COUNT

adjustment /ədʒʌstmənt/ **adjustments** ◆◆◇◇◇

1 An **adjustment** is an alteration or correction made to something such as a machine or a way of doing something. *Compensation could be made by adjustments to taxation... Investment is up by 5.7% after adjustment for inflation.* — N-COUNT: oft N *to/for/in* n

2 An **adjustment** is a change in a person's behaviour or thinking. *He will have to make major adjustments to his thinking if he is to survive in office.* — N-COUNT: oft N *to* n

adjutant /ædʒʊtənt/ **adjutants.** An **adjutant** is an officer in the army who deals with administrative work. — N-COUNT

ad-lib, ad-libs, ad-libbing, ad-libbed; also spelled **ad lib.**

1 If you **ad-lib** something in a play or a speech, you say something which has not been planned or written beforehand. *He began comically ad-libbing a script... Audiences giggled while Moody ad-libbed his way through the revue... He is rather disjointed when he ad-libs. ...ad-libbed phrases.* — VERB =improvise; V n; V *way* prep; V; V-ed

2 An **ad-lib** is something which is said without having been planned or written beforehand. *Every time I fluffed a line Lenny got me out of trouble with a brilliant ad-lib.* ► Also an adverb. *I spoke from the pulpit ad lib.* — N-COUNT =improvisation; ADV: ADV after v

adman /ædmæn/ **admen.** An **adman** is someone who works in advertising; an informal word. *He was the most brilliant adman that any of us knew.* — N-COUNT

admin /ædmɪn/. **Admin** is the activity or process of organizing an institution or organization; an informal word. *I have two assistants who help with the admin. ...the prison's admin staff.* — N-UNCOUNT: oft N n =administration

administer /ædmɪnɪstəʳ/ **administers, administering, administered** ◆◆◇◇◇

1 If someone **administers** something such as a country, the law, or a test, they take responsibility for organizing and supervising it. *The plan calls for the UN to administer the country until elections can be held... We hope that they're going to administer justice impartially... Next summer's exams would be straightforward to administer and mark.* — VERB; V n; Also V n *to* n

2 If a doctor or a nurse **administers** a drug, they give it to a patient; a formal use. *Sister came to watch the staff nurse administer the drugs.* — VERB =give; V n; Also V n *to* n

3 If someone **administers** a punch or a kick, they punch or kick someone; a formal use. *He is shown in the tape of the beating as administering most of the blows.* — VERB; V n

administration /ædmɪnɪstreɪʃən/ ◆◆◆◆◇

1 **Administration** is the range of activities connected with organizing and supervising the way that an organization or institution functions. *Too much time is spent on administration. ...a master's degree in business administration.* — N-UNCOUNT

2 The **administration** of something is the process of organizing and supervising it. *Standards in the administration of justice have degenerated... The cost of administration is around £500.* — N-UNCOUNT

3 **The administration** of a company or institution is the group of people who organize and supervise it. *They would like the college administration to exert more control over the fraternity.* — N-SING: *the* N, usu n N

4 You can refer to a country's government as the **administration**; used especially in the United States. *O'Leary served in federal energy posts in both the Ford and Carter administrations... Congress is to raise questions about the administration's handling of the post-Gulf War situation.* — N-COUNT: oft *the* n N

administrative /ædmɪnɪstrətɪv, AM -streɪt-/. **Administrative** work involves organizing and supervising an organization or institution. *Other industries have had to sack managers to reduce administrative costs... The project will have an administrative staff of 12.* ♦ **administratively** *Cuba is politically and administratively divided into 14 provinces.* — ◆◆◇◇◇ ADJ: usu ADJ n =management; ADV: ADV with v, ADV adj, ADV with cl

administrator /ædmɪnɪstreɪtəʳ/ **administrators.** An **administrator** is a person whose job involves helping to organize and supervise the way that an organization or institution functions. — ◆◆◇◇◇ N-COUNT

admirable /ædmɪrəbəl/. An **admirable** quality or action is one that deserves to be praised and admired. *Beyton is an admirable character... The film tells its story with admirable economy.* ♦ **admirably** /ædmɪrəbli/ *Peter had dealt admirably with the sudden questions about Keith... Johnstone's research is admirably wide-ranging.* — ◆◆◇◇◇ ADJ-GRADED =excellent, estimable; ADV-GRADED: ADV with v, ADV adj/adv

admiral /ædmərəl/ **admirals.** An **admiral** is a very senior officer who commands a navy or fleet of ships. *...Admiral Hodges.* — ◆◆◇◇◇ N-COUNT; N-TITLE

Admiralty /ædmərəlti/. In Britain, **the Admiralty** is the government department that is in charge of the navy. *The loss of the biggest ship in the Royal Navy shocked the Admiralty.* — N-PROPER: *the* N

admiration /ædmɪreɪʃən/. **Admiration** is a feeling of great liking and respect for a person or thing. *I have always had the greatest admiration for him... Meg's eyes widened in admiration.* — ◆◆◇◇◇ N-UNCOUNT: oft N *for/of* n, *in* N

admire /ədmaɪəʳ/ **admires, admiring, admired** ◆◆◆◇◇

1 If you **admire** someone or something, you like and respect them very much. *I admired her when I* — VERB; V n

first met her and I still think she's marvellous... He admired the way she had coped with life... All those who knew him will admire him for his work.
V n *for* n/-ing

2 If you **admire** someone or something, you look at them with pleasure. *We took time to stop and admire the view.*
VERB =appreciate V n

3 See also **admiring**.

admirer /ədmaɪərəʳ/ **admirers** ◆◇◇◇◇

1 If you are an **admirer** of someone, you like and respect them or their work very much. *He was an admirer of her grandfather's paintings.*
N-COUNT

2 A woman's **admirers** are the men who are attracted to her. *Johnny was the most persistent and most harmless of her admirers.*
N-COUNT =suitor

admiring /ədmaɪərɪŋ/. An **admiring** expression indicates a person's liking and respect for someone or something. An **admiring** person is someone who likes or respects another person or thing. *He cast her admiring glances all the way down the stairs... Within moments, he'd attracted an admiring audience.* ♦ **admiringly** *He glanced admiringly at the design.* ● See also **admire**.
ADJ-GRADED: usu ADJ n =appreciative; ADV-GRADED: ADV with v

admissible /ædmɪsɪbᵊl/. If evidence is **admissible**, it is allowed in a court of law. *Convictions will rise steeply now photographic evidence is admissible.*
ADJ: usu v-link ADJ ≠inadmissable

admission /ædmɪʃᵊn/ **admissions** ◆◆◇◇◇

1 **Admission** is permission given to a person to enter a place or to a country to enter an organization. **Admission** is also the act of entering a place. *Students apply for admission to a particular college... Poland and Czechoslovakia have vigorously pursued admission to the European Community... There have been substantial increases in hospital admissions of children.*
N-VAR: oft N *to* n =admittance

2 **Admission** or an **admission fee** at a park, museum, or other place is the amount of money that you pay to enter it. *Gates open at 10.30am and admission is free.*
N-UNCOUNT =entrance

3 An **admission** is a statement that something bad, unpleasant, or embarrassing is true. *By his own admission, he is not playing well... She wanted some admission of guilt from her father.*
N-VAR: oft N *of* n, N that

admit /ædmɪt/ **admits, admitting, admitted** ◆◆◆◆◇

1 If you **admit** that something bad, unpleasant, or embarrassing is true, you agree, often reluctantly, that it is true. *I am willing to admit that I do make mistakes... Up to two thirds of 14 to 16 year olds admit to buying drink illegally... I'd be ashamed to admit feeling jealous... None of these people will admit responsibility for their actions... 'Actually, most of my tennis is at club level,' he admitted.*
VERB =confess ≠deny V that, V *to*-ing/n, V-ing, V n, V with quote

2 If someone **is admitted** to hospital, they are taken into hospital for treatment and kept there until they are well enough to go home. *She was admitted to hospital with a soaring temperature... He was admitted yesterday for treatment of blood clots in his lungs.*
VB: usu passive *be* V-ed *to* n, *be* V-ed

3 If someone **is admitted** to an organization or group, they are allowed to join it. *He won the gold medal for fish cookery and was admitted to the Academie Culinaire de France... The Parachute Regiment could be forced to admit women.*
VERB *be* V-ed *to* n, V n

4 To **admit** someone to a place means to allow them to enter it. *Embassy security personnel refused to admit him or his wife... Journalists are rarely admitted to the region.*
VERB V n, V n *to* n

admittance /ædmɪtᵊns/. **Admittance** is the act of entering a place or institution or the right to enter it. *Dr Patel had a similar experience trying to gain admittance into medical school in Britain.*
N-UNCOUNT: oft N *into/to* n =admission

admittedly /ædmɪtɪdli/. You use **admittedly** when you are saying something which weakens the importance or force of your statement. *It's only a theory, admittedly, but the pieces fit together... Sometimes, avoidance of one particular food will have this beneficial effect, though admittedly rarely.*
◆◇◇◇◇ ADV: ADV with cl/group PRAGMATICS

admixture /ædmɪkstʃəʳ/. **Admixture** means the same as **mixture**; a formal word. *Seaton's heart beat with the admixture of aversion and thrill.*
N-SING: usu N *of* n =mixture

admonish /ædmɒnɪʃ/ **admonishes, admonishing, admonished.** If you **admonish** someone, you tell them sternly that they have done something wrong; a formal word. *They told me I was a fool and admonished me for taking risks with my health... She admonished him gently, 'You should rest, not talk so much.'* ♦ **admonishment, admonishments** *The admonishment in his normally mild voice surprised his wife.*
VERB =rebuke V n *for* n/-ing, V n with quote, Also V n, V n to-inf; N-COUNT

admonition /ædmənɪʃᵊn/ **admonitions.** An **admonition** is a warning or rebuke about someone's behaviour; a formal word. *She is full of admonitions about smoking, now that she has given it up.*
N-VAR =reproof

ad nauseam. If someone does something **ad nauseam**, they do it repeatedly and over a long period of time so that it becomes annoying or boring. *We discussed it ad nauseam.*
PHRASE: PHR after v =endlessly

ado /ədu:/. If you do something **without further ado** or **without more ado**, you do it at once and do not discuss or delay it any longer; an old-fashioned expression. *'And now, without further ado, let me introduce our benefactor.'*
PHRASE: PHR with v

adobe /ədoʊbi/. **Adobe** is a mixture of mud and straw that is dried into bricks in the sun and used for building, especially in hot countries. *...a few blocks of adobe houses.*
N-UNCOUNT: usu N n

adolescence /ædəlesᵊns/. **Adolescence** is the period of your life in which you develop from being a child into being an adult. *Some young people suddenly become self-conscious and tongue-tied in early adolescence.*
◆◇◇◇◇ N-UNCOUNT

adolescent /ædəlesᵊnt/ **adolescents. Adolescent** is used to describe young people who are no longer children but who have not yet become adults. It also refers to their behaviour. *It is important that an adolescent boy should have an adult in whom he can confide... He spent his adolescent years playing guitar in the church band. ...adolescent rebellion.* ► An **adolescent** is an adolescent boy or girl. *Young adolescents are happiest with small groups of close friends.*
◆◆◇◇◇ ADJ: usu ADJ n =teenage; N-COUNT =teenager

adopt /ədɒpt/ **adopts, adopting, adopted** ◆◆◆◆◇

1 If you **adopt** a new attitude, plan, or way of behaving, you begin to have it. *The United Nations has adopted a resolution that calls for sending UN observers to Yugoslavia... Pupils should be helped to adopt a positive approach to the environment.* ♦ **adoption** /ədɒpʃᵊn/ *...the adoption of Japanese management practices by British manufacturing.*
VERB V n, Also V n *as* n; N-UNCOUNT

2 If you **adopt** someone else's child, you take it into your own family and make it legally your son or daughter. Compare **foster**. *There are hundreds of people desperate to adopt a child... The adopted child has the right to see his birth certificate.* ♦ **adopter, adopters** *A social worker is appointed to interview the prospective adopters.* ♦ **adoption, adoptions** *They gave their babies up for adoption... The majority of adoptions are successful.*
VERB V n, V-ed, Also V; N-COUNT; N-VAR

3 If you **adopt** a physical position, you move yourself into it; a formal use. *I tried to adopt a foetal position to avoid damaging my limbs.*
VERB V n

4 If you **adopt** a country, you choose it as a place to live. *Podulski had joined the U.S. Navy as an aviator, adopting a new country and a new profession. ...their adopted home in England.*
VERB V n, V-ed

5 If you **adopt** an accent or a particular tone of voice, you speak differently from normal, especially to create an effect in a particular situation. *He has adopted the accent of a Second World War newscaster... The girl was uncertain what to do, or what tone of voice to adopt.*
VERB V n

adorable /ədɔːrəbᵊl/. If you say that someone or something is **adorable**, you emphasize that they are very attractive and you feel great affection for them. *By the time I was 30, we had three adorable children.*
◆◇◇◇◇ ADJ-GRADED PRAGMATICS =wonderful

adoration /ædɔːreɪʃᵊn/. **Adoration** is a feeling of great admiration and love for someone or something. *She needs and wants to be loved with overwhelming passion and adoration... He had been used to female adoration all his life.*
N-UNCOUNT

adore /ədɔːʳ/ **adores, adoring, adored** ◆◇◇◇◇
1 If you **adore** someone, you feel great love and admiration for them. *She adored her parents and would do anything to please them.* VB: no cont V n
2 If you **adore** something, you like it very much; an informal use. *My mother adores bananas and eats two a day... I adore good books and the theatre.* VB: no cont V n

adoring /ədɔːrɪŋ/. An **adoring** person is someone who loves and admires another person very much. *She can still pull in adoring audiences.* ◆◇◇◇◇ ADJ-GRADED
♦ **adoringly** *She gazes adoringly at her husband.* ADV-GRADED

adorn /ədɔːʳn/ **adorns, adorning, adorned.** If something **adorns** a place or an object, it makes it look more beautiful. *His watercolour designs adorn a wide range of books... Several magnificent oil paintings adorn the walls.* ◆◇◇◇◇ VERB =decorate V n

adornment /ədɔːʳnmənt/ **adornments**
1 An **adornment** is something that is used to make someone or something more beautiful. *It was a building without any adornment or decoration.* N-VAR
2 **Adornment** is the process of making something more beautiful by adding something to it. *Cosmetics are used for adornment.* N-UNCOUNT

adrenalin /ədrenəlɪn/; also spelled **adrenaline. Adrenalin** is a substance which your body produces when you are angry, scared, or excited. It makes your heart beat faster and gives you more energy. *That was my first big game in months and the adrenalin was going.* ◆◇◇◇◇ N-UNCOUNT

adrift /ədrɪft/ ◆◇◇◇◇
1 If a boat is **adrift**, it is floating on the water and is not tied to anything or controlled by anyone. *They were spotted after three hours adrift in a dinghy.* ADJ: v-link ADJ, v n ADJ
2 If someone is **adrift**, they feel alone with no clear idea of what they should do. *Amy had the growing sense that she was adrift and isolated.* ADJ-GRADED: v-link ADJ, v n ADJ
3 If something comes **adrift**, it is no longer attached to an object that it should be part of. *My doll lost her arm when the stitching came adrift... Three insulating panels had come adrift from the base of the vehicle.* ADJ: v-link ADJ, ADJ after v =loose
4 In sporting competitions, if a team or a player is **adrift** of their rivals, they are behind them, usually by a specified number of points or by a specified distance. *Aberdeen are nine points adrift of Rangers at the top of the Scottish League.* ADJ-GRADED: v-link ADJ, usu ADJ *of* n
5 If something has gone **adrift**, it is no longer happening in the way that was intended. *We have seen this as an attempt to place the blame for a policy that has gone adrift.* ADJ-GRADED: v-link ADJ =awry

adroit /ədrɔɪt/. Someone who is **adroit** is quick and skilful in their thoughts, behaviour, or actions. *She is a remarkably adroit and determined politician.* ADJ-GRADED =adept ♦ **adroitly** *He drove adroitly.* ADV-GRADED: ADV with v ♦ **adroitness** *He governed with an adroitness that gained him the nickname 'the old fox'.* N-UNCOUNT

adulation /ædʒʊleɪʃᵊn/. **Adulation** is uncritical admiration and praise of someone or something. *The book was received with adulation by critics.* N-UNCOUNT =acclaim

adulatory /ædʒʊleɪtəri, AM -tɔːri/. If someone makes an **adulatory** comment about someone, they praise them. *...adulatory reviews.* ADJ-GRADED: usu ADJ n =laudatory

adult /ædʌlt, AM ədʌlt/ **adults** ◆◆◆◆◇
1 An **adult** is a mature, fully developed person. An adult has reached the age when they are legally responsible for their actions. *Becoming a father signified that he was now an adult... Children under 14 must be accompanied by an adult.* N-COUNT =grown up ≠minor
2 An **adult** is a fully developed animal. *The adult trout that were left were unable to reproduce. ...a pair of adult birds.* N-COUNT ≠juvenile
3 **Adult** means relating to the time when you are an adult, or typical of adult people. *I've lived most of my adult life in London.* ADJ: ADJ n
4 If you say that someone is **adult** about something, you think that they act in a mature, intelligent way, especially when faced with a difficult situation. *We were very adult about it. We discussed it rationally over a drink. ...dealing with emerging sexuality in an adult way.* ADJ-GRADED: v-link ADJ =grown up
5 You can describe things such as films or books as **adult** when they contain sexually explicit material. *...an adult movie.* ADJ

adult education. **Adult education** is education for adults in a variety of subjects, most of which are practical, not academic. Classes are often held in the evenings. *Adult education centres offer many courses in cooking and dressmaking.* N-UNCOUNT

adulterate /ədʌltəreɪt/ **adulterates, adulterating, adulterated.** If something such as food or drink **is adulterated**, someone has made its quality worse by adding water or cheaper products to it. *The food had been adulterated to increase its weight... There is a regulation against adulterated cosmetics.* VB: usu passive *be* V-ed V-ed ♦ **adulteration** /ədʌltəreɪʃᵊn/ *The Laboratory was set up with the prime purpose of detecting the adulteration of tobacco.* N-UNCOUNT

adulterer /ədʌltərəʳ/ **adulterers.** An **adulterer** is someone who commits adultery. N-COUNT

adulteress /ədʌltrɪs/ **adulteresses.** An **adulteress** is a woman who commits adultery. N-COUNT

adulterous /ədʌltərəs/. An **adulterous** relationship is a sexual relationship between a married person and someone they are not married to. An **adulterous** person is someone who commits adultery. ADJ: usu ADJ n

adultery /ədʌltəri/. If a married person commits **adultery**, they have sex with someone that they are not married to. *She is going to divorce him on the grounds of adultery.* ◆◇◇◇◇ N-UNCOUNT

adulthood /ædʌlthʊd, AM ədʌlt-/. **Adulthood** is the state of being an adult. *Few people nowadays are able to maintain friendships into adulthood.* ◆◇◇◇◇ N-UNCOUNT

adv. Adv is a written abbreviation for **adverb.** =adverb

advance /ædvɑːns, -væns/ **advances, advancing, advanced** ◆◆◆◆◇
1 To **advance** means to move forward, often in order to attack someone. *Reports from Chad suggest that rebel forces are advancing on the capital... According to one report, the water is advancing at a rate of between 5cm and 7cm a day... The Daily Telegraph carries a picture of a man throwing himself before an advancing tank.* VERB V prep/adv V V-ing
2 To **advance** means to make progress, especially in your knowledge of something. *Now that medical technology has advanced to its present state, more people are aware of how long one can be kept alive... Japan has advanced from a rural, feudal society to an urban, industrial power.* • See also **advanced.** VERB =progress V
3 If you **advance** someone a sum of money, you lend it to them, or pay it to them earlier than arranged. *I advanced him some money, which he would repay on our way home... The bank advanced $1.2 billion to help Mexico with debt repayments.* VERB =lend V n n V n
4 An **advance** is money which is lent or paid to someone before they are due to receive it. *She was paid a £100,000 advance for her next two novels.* N-COUNT
5 To **advance** an event, or the time or date of an event, means to bring it forward to an earlier time or date. *Too much protein in the diet may advance the ageing process... The country's election commission has advanced the date of parliamentary elections by three days.* VERB =bring forward ≠put back V n
6 If you **advance** a cause, interest, or claim, you support it and help to make it successful. *When not producing art of his own, Oliver was busy advancing the work of others.* VERB =further ≠hinder V n
7 When a theory or argument **is advanced**, it is put forward for discussion. *Many theories have been advanced as to why some women suffer from depression... An important set of ideas have been advanced by the biologist Rupert Sheldrake.* VB: usu passive =put forward *be* V-ed
8 An **advance** is a forward movement of people or vehicles, usually as part of a military operation. *In an exercise designed to be as real as possible, they simulated an advance on enemy positions... The defences are intended to obstruct any advance by tanks and other vehicles.* N-VAR =attack ≠retreat
9 If you make **advances** to someone, you try to start a sexual relationship with them; a literary use. *Mark had for some time been making advances to-* N-PLURAL =overtures

wards her... She rejected his advances during the trip to Cannes.

10 An **advance** in a particular subject or activity is progress in understanding it or in doing it well. *Air safety has not improved since the dramatic advances of the 1970s... Their progress at work was mirrored by their children's educational advance.* N-VAR =development

11 If something is an **advance** on what was previously available or done, it is better in some way. *This could be an advance on the present situation.* N-SING: usu *a* N *on* n

12 Advance booking, notice, or warning is done or given before an event happens. *They don't normally give any advance notice about which building they're going to inspect... The event received little advance publicity.* ADJ: ADJ n

13 An **advance** party or group is a small group of people who go on ahead of the main group. *So far the United Nations has sent an advance party to Cambodia of little more than 200 troops.* ADJ: ADJ n =expeditionary

14 If one thing happens or is done **in advance of** another, it happens or is done before the other thing. *I had asked everyone to submit questions in advance of the meeting.* PHRASES PREP =ahead

15 If you do something **in advance**, you do it before a particular date or event. *The subject of the talk is announced a week in advance, but the name of the speaker is not.* PHR after v

advanced /ædvɑːnst, -vænst/ ◆◆◆◇◇

1 An **advanced** system, method, or design is modern and has been developed from an earlier version of the same thing. *Many are afraid that without more training or advanced technical skills, they'll lose their jobs. ...the most advanced optical telescope in the world.* ADJ-GRADED: usu ADJ n =up-to-date

2 A country that is **advanced** has reached a high level of industrial or technological development. *A crucial element of Mr Patten's review should be a study of the educational levels reached in other advanced countries.* ADJ-GRADED

3 An **advanced** student has already learned the basic facts of a subject and is doing more difficult work. An **advanced** course of study is designed for such students. *The course is suitable for beginners and advanced students... The lab has recently been updated to allow for more advanced courses.* ADJ-GRADED: usu ADJ n ≠elementary

4 Something that is at an **advanced** stage or level is at a late stage of development. *'Medicare' is available to victims of advanced kidney disease... His ideas should be more advanced by the time the Committee meets in Edinburgh in October.* ADJ-GRADED

5 If you say that someone is of **advanced** years or is **advanced** in age, you are saying in a polite way that they are old; a formal use. *The gentleman, despite his advanced years, helped Kathryn back to her seat.* ADJ-GRADED PRAGMATICS =mature

advancement /ædvɑːnsmənt, -væns-/ **advancements** ◆◇◇◇◇

1 Advancement is promotion in your job or to a higher social class. *He cared little for social advancement.* N-UNCOUNT: oft adj N =preferment

2 The **advancement** of something is the process of helping it to progress or the result of its progress. *Her work for the advancement of the status of women in India was recognised by the whole nation.* N-VAR: oft N *of* n =progress

advantage /ædvɑːntɪdʒ, -væn-/ **advantages** ◆◆◆◆◇

1 An **advantage** is something that puts you in a better position than other people. *They are deliberately flouting the law in order to obtain an advantage over their competitors... A good crowd will be a definite advantage to me and the rest of the team.* N-COUNT ≠disadvantage

2 Advantage is the state of being in a better position than others who are competing against you. *Men have created a social and physical position of advantage for themselves over women.* N-UNCOUNT

3 An **advantage** is a way in which one thing is better than another. *The great advantage of home-grown oranges is their magnificent flavour... This custom-built kitchen has many advantages over a standard one.* N-COUNT: oft N *of* n ≠disadvantage

4 If you **take advantage of** something, you make good use of it while you can. *I intend to take full advantage of this trip to buy the things we need.* PHRASES V inflects, PHR n

5 If someone **takes advantage of** you, they treat you unfairly for their own benefit. *She took advantage of him even after they were divorced.* V inflects, PHR n

6 If you use or turn something **to your advantage**, you exploit it in order to benefit from it. *The government have not been able to turn today's demonstration to their advantage.* PHR after v

7 If something is shown **to good advantage** or **to best advantage**, it is shown in a way that highlights its best features. *The walls were painted in muted tones to show the pictures to good advantage.* PHR after v

advantaged /ædvɑːntɪdʒd, -væn-/. A person or place that is **advantaged** is in a better social or financial position than other people or places. *Some cities are always going to be more advantaged.* ADJ-GRADED =privileged ≠disadvantaged

advantageous /ædvənteɪdʒəs/. If something is **advantageous** to you, it is likely to benefit you. *Free exchange of goods was advantageous to all. ...an opportunity to purchase a set of tools at very advantageous prices.* ◆◇◇◇◇ ADJ-GRADED: oft ADJ *to* n =favourable ≠unfavourable ♦ **advantageously** *They acquire the land in order to be able to sell it advantageously to the government.* ADV-GRADED: ADV with v =favourably ≠unfavourably

advent /ædvent/ ◆◇◇◇◇

1 The **advent** of an important event, invention, or situation is the fact of it starting or coming into existence; a formal use. *The advent of the computer has brought this sort of task within the bounds of possibility... The advent of war led to a greater austerity.* N-UNCOUNT: usu *the* N *of* n =appearance

2 The **advent** of a person at a place is their arrival there; a literary use. *Deptford had come alive with the advent of the new priest at St Paul's.* N-UNCOUNT: usu *the* N *of* n =arrival

Advent. In the Christian church, **Advent** is the period between Advent Sunday, the Sunday closest to the 30th of November, and Christmas Day. N-UNCOUNT

adventure /ædventʃəʳ/ **adventures, adventuring, adventured** ◆◆◇◇◇

1 If someone has an **adventure**, they become involved in an unusual, exciting, and rather dangerous journey or series of events. *I set off for a new adventure in the United States on the first day of the new year.* N-COUNT

2 Adventure is excitement and willingness to do new, unusual, or rather dangerous things. *Their cultural backgrounds gave them a spirit of adventure. ...a feeling of adventure and excitement.* N-UNCOUNT

3 If you **adventure** somewhere, you go somewhere new, unusual, and exciting. *The group has adventured as far as the Austrian alps.* VERB V prep/adv

adventure playground, adventure playgrounds. In Britain, an **adventure playground** is an area of land for children to play in, usually in cities or in a park. It has wooden structures and equipment such as ropes, nets, and rubber tyres. N-COUNT

adventurer /ædventʃərəʳ/ **adventurers** ◆◇◇◇◇

1 An **adventurer** is a person who enjoys going to new, unusual, and exciting places. *...the Amazon Rain Forest, a true adventurer's paradise.* N-COUNT

2 If you describe someone as an **adventurer**, you disapprove of them because they are using dishonest or immoral methods to gain money or power. *...unprincipled opportunists and ambitious political adventurers.* N-COUNT PRAGMATICS =shark

adventurism /ædventʃərɪzəm/. **Adventurism** is a willingness to take risks, especially in order to obtain an unfair advantage in politics or business; used showing disapproval. *Lenin dismissed guerrilla warfare as 'left adventurism.'* N-UNCOUNT PRAGMATICS

adventurist /ædventʃərɪst/ **adventurists.** If you describe someone or something as **adventurist**, you disapprove of them because they are willing to take risks in order to gain an unfair advantage in business or politics. *...aggressive and adventurist foreign policy.* ADJ PRAGMATICS ▶ An **adventurist** is someone who is adventurist. *...political adventurists.* N-COUNT

adventurous /ædventʃərəs/ ◆◇◇◇◇

1 Someone who is **adventurous** is willing to take risks and to try new methods. Something that is **adventurous** involves new things or ideas. *Warren was an adventurous businessman... The menu seemed far more adventurous before the festival started.* ADJ-GRADED =daring ≠unadventurous

2 Someone who is **adventurous** is eager to visit new places and have new experiences. *He had always wanted an adventurous life in the tropics.* — ADJ-GRADED ≠unadventurous

adverb /ˈædvɜːʳb/ **adverbs.** An **adverb** is a word such as 'slowly', 'now', 'very', 'politically', or 'fortunately' which adds information about the action, event, or situation mentioned in a clause. — N-COUNT

adverb group, adverb groups. An **adverb group** or **adverbial group** is a group of words based on an adverb, such as 'very slowly' or 'fortunately for us'. An adverb group can also consist simply of an adverb. — N-COUNT

adverbial /ædvɜːʳbiəl/. **Adverbial** means relating to adverbs or like an adverb. *...an adverbial expression.* — ADJ: usu ADJ n

adversarial /ædvəʳseəriəl/. If you describe something as **adversarial**, you mean that it involves two or more people or organizations who are opposing each other; a formal use. *In our country there is an adversarial relationship between government and business. ...an adversarial legal system.* — ADJ-GRADED

adversary /ˈædvəʳsəri, AM -seri/ **adversaries.** Your **adversary** is someone you are competing with, or arguing or fighting against. *Elliott crossed the finish line just half a second behind his adversary... His political adversaries were creating a certain amount of trouble for him.* — ◆◇◇◇◇ N-COUNT: usu with supp =opponent, enemy ≠allies

adverse /ˈædvɜːʳs, AM ædvɜːrs/. **Adverse** decisions, conditions, or effects are unfavourable to you. *The police said Mr Hadfield's decision would have no adverse effect on the progress of the investigation... Despite the adverse conditions, the road was finished in just eight months.* ♦ **adversely** *Price changes must not adversely affect the living standards of the people.* — ◆◆◇◇◇ ADJ-GRADED: usu ADJ n ≠favourable; ADV-GRADED: ADV with v

adversity /ædvɜːʳsɪti/ **adversities. Adversity** is a very difficult or unfavourable situation. *He showed courage in adversity... He has not yet shown himself to be a really strong character in the face of adversity.* — ◆◇◇◇◇ N-VAR: oft *in/of*N =misfortune

advert /ˈædvɜːʳt/ **adverts** — ◆◆◇◇◇

1 An **advert** is an announcement in a newspaper, on television, or on a poster about something such as a product, event, or job vacancy; used in British English. The usual American word is **ad**. *I saw an advert for a transport job with a large steel and engineering company... Many caravans are let by private individuals through adverts in papers or shop windows.* — N-COUNT: oft N *for*n =ad, advertisement

2 If you say that an example of something is an **advert** for that thing in general, you mean that it shows how good that thing is; used in British English. *This courtroom battle has been a poor advert for English justice.* — N-COUNT: usu *a*N *for*n =advertisement

3 **The adverts** can refer to the interval in a commercial television programme, or between programmes, during which advertisements are shown; an informal use in British English. *After the adverts, Terry Christian tried to pretend that everything was back to normal.* — N-PLURAL: *the*N =commercials

advertise /ˈædvəʳtaɪz/ **advertises, advertising, advertised** — ◆◆◆◇◇

1 If you **advertise** something such as a product, an event, or a job, you tell people about it in newspapers, on television, or on posters in order to encourage them to buy the product, go to the event, or apply for the job. *The players can advertise baked beans, but not rugby boots... In 1991, the house was advertised for sale at $49,000... Religious groups are currently not allowed to advertise on television.* — VERB; V n; V

2 If you **advertise** for someone to do something for you, for example to work for you or share your accommodation, you announce it in a newspaper, on television, or on a notice board. *We advertised for staff in a local newspaper... I shall advertise for someone to go with me.* — VERB; V *for*n

3 If someone or something **advertises** a particular quality, they show it in their appearance or behaviour; a literary use. *His hard sinewy body advertised his ruthlessness of purpose.* — VERB =emphasize; V n

4 If you do not **advertise** the fact that something is the case, you try not to let other people know about it. *There is no need to advertise the fact that you are a single woman... I didn't want to advertise the fact that he hadn't driven me to the airport.* • See also **advertising.** — VB: usu with brd-neg; V n

advertisement /ædvɜːʳtɪsmənt, AM ædvəʳtaɪz-/ **advertisements** — ◆◆◇◇◇

1 An **advertisement** is an announcement in a newspaper, on television, or on a poster about something such as a product, event, or job vacancy; used mainly in written English. *Miss Parrish recently placed an advertisement in the local newspaper... We run regular Aids awareness advertisements.* — N-COUNT: oft N *for*n =advert, ad

2 If you say that an example of something is an **advertisement** for that thing in general, you mean that it shows how good that thing is; used mainly in British English. *The Treviso team were an effective advertisement for the improving state of Italian club rugby... That would not be a good advertisement for Hungary's emerging democracy.* — N-COUNT: usu *a*N *for*n

advertiser /ˈædvəʳtaɪzəʳ/ **advertisers** — ◆◇◇◇◇

1 An **advertiser** is a person or company that pays for a product, event, or job vacancy to be advertised in a newspaper, on television, or on posters. *To reach the millions of people who watch television, advertisers are willing to pay big money... We became the first advertiser ever to put inserts into major magazines.* — N-COUNT

2 **Advertiser** is used in the name of some local newspapers. *Taylor became editor of the Croydon Advertiser in 1950.* — N-IN-NAMES

advertising /ˈædvəʳtaɪzɪŋ/. **Advertising** is the activity of telling people about products, events, or job vacancies, and making them want to buy the products, go to the events, or apply for the jobs. *Tobacco advertising in women's magazines... The zoo launched an advertising campaign to attract more people.* — ◆◆◇◇◇ N-UNCOUNT

advertorial /ædvɜːʳtɔːriəl/ **advertorials.** An **advertorial** is an advertisement that uses the style of newspaper or magazine articles or television documentary programmes, so that it appears to be giving facts and not trying to sell a product. *The current ethical debate in the industry is prompted by the increasing use of the advertorial... Our magazines have turned away advertorials for products that they simply could not endorse.* — N-VAR

advice /ædvaɪs/ — ◆◆◆◆◇

1 If you give someone **advice**, you tell them what you think they should do in a particular situation. *Don't be afraid to ask for advice about ordering the meal... Your community officer can give you advice on how to prevent crime in your area. ...take my advice and stay away from him! ...most foreign nationals have now left the country on the advice of their governments.* — N-UNCOUNT: oft N *on/about* n/wh/-ing

2 If you **take advice** or **take legal advice**, you ask a lawyer for his or her professional opinion on a situation; a formal expression. *He requested a two-week adjournment to prepare the case and take further advice on the matter... If you are prosecuted by the police, then it is essential that you take specialist legal advice.* — PHRASE: V inflects

advisable /ædvaɪzəbᵊl/. If you tell someone that it is **advisable** to do something, you are suggesting that they should do it, because it is sensible or is likely to achieve the result they want; a formal word. *Because of the popularity of the region, it is advisable to book hotels or camp sites in advance... It is generally not advisable for expectant mothers to travel by air after the 28th week of pregnancy.* ♦ **advisability** /ædvaɪzəbɪlɪti/ *He is doubtful about the advisability of any interference with the immune system.* — ◆◇◇◇◇ ADJ-GRADED: v-link ADJ, oft *it* v-link ADJ to-inf PRAGMATICS =wise ≠inadvisable; N-UNCOUNT: *the*N *of*n ≠inadvisability

advise /ædvaɪz/ **advises, advising, advised** — ◆◆◆◇◇

1 If you **advise** someone to do something, you tell them what you think they should do. *The minister advised him to leave as soon as possible... Herbert would surely advise her how to approach the* — VERB; V n to-inf; V n wh; V *against*n; V that

bank... I would strongly advise against it... Doctors advised that he should be transferred to a private room. Also V with quote

2 If an expert **advises** people on a particular subject, he or she gives them help and information on that subject. *...an officer who advises undergraduates from London's City University on money matters... A family doctor will be able to advise on suitable birth control.* VERB V n *on* n V *on* n

3 If you **advise** someone of a fact or situation, you tell them the fact or explain what the situation is; a formal use. *...the decision requiring police to advise suspects of their rights... I think it best that I advise you of my decision to retire.* VERB =inform, apprise V n *of* n

4 If an official document states that you **are advised** to do something, it is telling you the correct or appropriate thing to do; a formal use. *Candidates in India are advised to submit their applications through the overseas student office in London... Residents are advised not to put their rubbish bags on the pavement outside their houses.* V-PASSIVE PRAGMATICS *be* V-ed to-inf

5 See also **ill-advised**, **well advised**.

advisedly /ædvaɪzɪdli/. If you say that you are using a word or expression **advisedly**, you mean that you have deliberately chosen to use it, even though it may sound unusual, wrong, or offensive, because it draws attention to what you are saying. *I say 'boys' advisedly because we are talking almost entirely about male behaviour... The phrase 'seemingly effortless' is used advisedly, because his dazzling results were the product of a great deal of hard graft.* ADV: ADV after v PRAGMATICS

advisement /ædvaɪzmənt/. If someone in authority **takes** a matter **under advisement**, they decide that the matter needs to be considered more carefully, often by experts; used in formal American English. *I think this is too important for a snap decision. I will take it under advisement and give you an answer in twenty-four hours.* PHRASE: V inflects

adviser /ædvaɪzəʳ/ **advisers;** also spelled **advisor**. An **adviser** is an expert whose job is to give advice to another person or to a group of people. *In Washington, the President and his advisers spent the day in meetings... He became an adviser to the government on American affairs. ...a careers adviser.* ◆◆◆◇◇ N-COUNT: usu with supp, oft N *to* n =counsellor

advisory /ædvaɪzəri/ **advisories** ◆◆◇◇◇

1 An **advisory** group, or a group or person with an **advisory** role, regularly gives suggestions and help to people or organizations, especially about a particular subject or area of activity; a formal use. *...members of the advisory committee on the safety of nuclear installations... Now my role is strictly advisory.* ADJ: usu ADJ n

2 In American English, an **advisory** is an official announcement or report that warns people about bad weather, diseases, or other dangers or problems. *Both the Missouri and Kansas Highway Patrols have issued travel advisories for tonight... 26 states have issued health advisories.* N-COUNT: usu supp N =warning

advocacy /ædvəkəsi/ ◆◇◇◇◇

1 Someone's **advocacy** of a particular action or plan is their act of recommending it publicly; a formal use. *I support your advocacy of free trade. ...the president's advocacy of higher taxes.* N-SING: usu poss N *of* n =support for

2 **Advocacy** is the way in which lawyers deal with cases in court; a formal use. *Sir Peter would also like to see the current adversarial system of advocacy examined by the royal commission.* N-UNCOUNT

3 In American English, an **advocacy** group or organization is one that tries to influence the decisions of a government or other authority. *Consumer advocacy groups are not so enthusiastic about freeing up the telephone companies.* N-UNCOUNT: usu N n =lobby

advocate, advocates, advocating, advocated. The verb is pronounced /ædvəkeɪt/. The noun is pronounced /ædvəkət/. ◆◆◆◇◇

1 If you **advocate** a particular action or plan, you recommend it publicly; a formal use. *Mr Williams is a conservative who advocates fewer government controls on business. ...the Europe-wide strategy advocated by Jacques Delors to get people back to work.* VERB =recommend V n

2 An **advocate** of a particular action or plan is someone who recommends it publicly; a formal use. *He was a strong advocate of free market policies and a multi-party system.* N-COUNT: oft N *of* n =proponent

3 An **advocate** is a lawyer who speaks in favour of someone or defends them in a court of law; a legal term. *His failure to be made a full-time judge disappointed and perplexed his fellow advocates.* N-COUNT =lawyer

4 An **advocate** for a particular group is a person who works for the interests of that group; used mainly in American English. *...advocates for the homeless... Consumer advocates claim that some oil companies are exploiting the Persian Gulf crisis.* N-COUNT: with supp

• See also **devil's advocate**.

aegis /iːdʒɪs/. Something that is done **under the aegis of** a person or organization is done with their official support and backing; a formal expression. *The military space programme will continue under the aegis of the joint strategic armed forces... She went to Sheffield University as a lecturer, under the aegis of Boris Ford.* PHR-PREP =under the auspices of

aeon /iːɒn/ **aeons;** spelled **eon** in American English. An **aeon** is an extremely long period of time. *Aeons ago, there were deserts where there is now fertile land.* N-COUNT =age

aerate /eəreɪt/ **aerates, aerating, aerated.** To **aerate** a substance means to cause air or gas to pass through it. *Aerate the soil by spiking with a fork. ...fresh crab and lobster, transported south in tanker loads of aerated salted water.* VERB =oxygenate V n V-ed

aerial /eəriəl/ **aerials** ◆◇◇◇◇

1 You talk about **aerial** attacks and **aerial** photographs to indicate that people or things on the ground are attacked or photographed by people in aeroplanes. *Weeks of aerial bombardment had destroyed factories and highways... Patterns that are invisible on the ground can be the most striking part of an aerial photograph... The film begins with an aerial view of the Great Basin of Nevada.* ADJ: ADJ n

2 You can use **aerial** to describe things that exist or happen above the ground or in the air. *The seagulls swirled in aerial combat over the barges.* ADJ: ADJ n

3 An **aerial** is a device or a piece of wire that receives television or radio signals and is usually attached to a radio, television, car, or building; used mainly in British English. The usual American word is **antenna**. *...a saucer-shaped satellite television aerial. ...the radio aerials of taxis and cars.* N-COUNT

aero- /eərəʊ-/

1 **aero-** is used at the beginning of words, especially nouns, that refer to things or activities connected with air or movement through the air. PREFIX

2 **aero-** combines with nouns to form nouns relating to aeroplanes. *...the British aero-engine maker, Rolls-Royce.* COMB in N-COUNT

aerobatics /eərəbætɪks/; the form **aerobatic** is used as a modifier. **Aerobatics** are skilful and spectacular movements made by aeroplanes, usually to entertain people watching from the ground. *He denies that it is the risk involved which attracts him and other pilots to performing aerobatics. ...one of the greatest aerobatic display pilots of his generation.* N-PLURAL

aerobic /eəroʊbɪk/. **Aerobic** activity exercises and strengthens your heart and lungs. *Aerobic exercise gets the heart pumping and helps you to burn up the fat.* ◆◇◇◇◇ ADJ-GRADED: usu ADJ n

aerobics /eəroʊbɪks/. **Aerobics** is a form of exercise which increases the amount of oxygen in your blood, and strengthens your heart and lungs. The verb that follows **aerobics** may be either singular or plural. *I'd like to join an aerobics class to improve my fitness.* ◆◇◇◇◇ N-PLURAL: oft N n

aerodrome /eərədroum/ **aerodromes.** An **aerodrome** is a place or area where small aeroplanes can land and take off; used mainly in British English. N-COUNT: oft in names =airfield

aerodynamic /eərəʊdaɪnæmɪk/. If something such as a car has an **aerodynamic** shape or de- ADJ-GRADED: usu ADJ n sign, it goes faster and uses less fuel than other cars because the air passes over it more easily. *The secret of the machine lies in the aerodynamic shape of the one-piece, carbon-fibre frame.* ♦ **aerodynamically** *The whole cheetah is aerodynamically built, from the tip of its nose to the tip of its tail.* ADV: ADV adj, ADV with v

aerodynamics /eəroʊdaɪnæmɪks/; the form **aerodynamic** is used as a modifier. **Aerodynamics** is the study of the way in which objects move through the air. The verb that follows **aerodynamics** maybe either singular or plural. *According to the laws of aerodynamics, bumble bees shouldn't be able to fly. ...sound aerodynamic principles.* N-PLURAL

aeronautical /eərənɔːtɪkəl/. **Aeronautical** means involving or relating to the design and construction of aeroplanes. *...the biggest aeronautical research laboratory in Europe.* ADJ: ADJ n

aeronautics /eərənɔːtɪks/. **Aeronautics** is the science of designing and constructing aeroplanes. *Cuts in the military budget cost thousands of jobs in the aeronautics industry.* N-UNCOUNT

aeroplane /eərəpleɪn/ **aeroplanes.** In British English, an **aeroplane** is a vehicle with wings and one or more engines that enable it to fly through the air. The usual American word is **airplane**. ◆◆◇◇◇ N-COUNT =plane, aircraft

aerosol /eərəsɒl, AM -sɔːl/ **aerosols.** An **aerosol** is a small container in which a liquid such as paint or deodorant is kept under pressure. When you press a button, the liquid is forced out as a fine spray or foam. *...a small aerosol can of black paint.* ◆◇◇◇◇ N-COUNT: oft N n

aerospace /eəroʊspeɪs/. **Aerospace** companies are involved in developing and making rockets, missiles, space vehicles, and related equipment. *The US government also helps its aerospace industry, chiefly via the space agency, Nasa.* ◆◆◇◇◇ N-UNCOUNT: usu N n

Aertex /eəʳteks/. **Aertex** is a loosely woven cotton material which is used for making shirts, underwear, and sports clothes. **Aertex** is a trademark. *...blue Aertex shirts.* N-UNCOUNT

aesthete /iːsθiːt, AM es-/ **aesthetes.** An **aesthete** is someone who loves and appreciates works of art and beautiful things. N-COUNT ≠philistine

aesthetic /iːsθetɪk, AM es-/; spelled **esthetic** in American English. **Aesthetic** involves beauty or art, and people's appreciation of beautiful things. *...products chosen for their aesthetic appeal as well as their durability and quality.* ► The **aesthetic** of a work of art is its aesthetic quality. *He responded very strongly to the aesthetic of this particular work.* ♦ **aesthetically** /iːsθetɪkli, AM es-/ *A statue which is aesthetically pleasing to one person, however, may be repulsive to another.* ◆◆◇◇◇ ADJ-GRADED; N-SING: the N; ADV-GRADED: oft ADV with cl

aesthetics /iːsθetɪks, AM es-/. **Aesthetics** is a branch of philosophy concerned with the study of the concept of beauty. ◆◇◇◇◇ N-UNCOUNT

aetiology /iːtiɒlədʒi/. See **etiology**.

afar /əfɑːʳ/. **Afar** means a long way away; a literary word. *Seen from afar, its towering buildings beckon the visitor in. ...a stranger who has loved her from afar for 23 years.* ADV: usu *from* ADV, also ADV after v

affable /æfəbəl/. Someone who is **affable** is pleasant and friendly. *Mr Brooke is an extremely affable and approachable man.* ♦ **affability** /æfəbɪlɪti/ *Beneath the surface affability there was a sort of struggle for power.* ♦ **affably** *'Ah, Captain Fox,' Martin McGuinness said affably. 'Nice to see you again.'* ◆◇◇◇◇ ADJ-GRADED =amicable; N-UNCOUNT; ADV-GRADED: usu ADV with v, also ADV adj

affair /əfeəʳ/ **affairs** ◆◆◆◆◇

1 If an event or a series of events has been mentioned and you want to talk about it again, you can refer to it as **the affair**. *The government has mishandled the whole affair... The affair began when customs officials inspected a convoy of 60 tankers... The industry minister described the affair as 'an absolute scandal'.* N-SING: the N =business, matter

2 Journalists often refer to an important or interesting event or situation as '**the ... affair**'. *...the damage caused to the CIA and FBI in the aftermath of the Watergate affair. ...confidential Bank of England documents relating to the BCCI affair.* N-SING: usu the n-proper N

3 You can describe the main quality of an event by saying that it is a particular kind of **affair**. *Michael said that his planned 10-day visit would be a purely private affair... Breakfast will be a cheerless affair for the Prime Minister this morning.* N-SING: usu supp N

4 You can describe an object as a particular kind of **affair** when you want to draw attention to a particular feature, or indicate that it is unusual; an old-fashioned use. *All their beds were distinctive; Mac's was an iron affair with brass knobs... He tried dividing it into two bundles, tying them to his walking stick, and slinging the whole affair across his back.* N-SING: supp N

5 If two people who are not married to each other have an **affair**, they have a sexual relationship. *Married male supervisors were carrying on affairs with female subordinates in the office.* • See also **love affair**. N-COUNT

6 You can use **affairs** to refer to all the important facts or activities that are connected with a particular subject. *He does not want to interfere in the internal affairs of another country... With more details, here's our foreign affairs correspondent.* • See also **current affairs, state of affairs**. N-PLURAL: usu supp N

7 Your **affairs** are all the matters connected with your life which you consider to be private and normally deal with yourself. *He was rational and consistent in the conduct of his affairs... The unexpectedness of my father's death meant that his affairs were not entirely in order.* N-PLURAL: usu poss N

8 If you say that a decision or situation is someone's **affair**, you mean that it is their responsibility, and other people should not interfere; used mainly in old-fashioned British English. *If you wish to make a fool of yourself and damage your career here, that is your affair... If they want to stay and fight, then I guess that's their affair.* N-SING: poss N =business

affect /əfekt/ **affects, affecting, affected** ◆◆◆◆◇

1 If something **affects** someone or something else, it influences them or causes them to change in some way. *Nicotine adversely affects the functioning of the heart and arteries... More than seven million people have been affected by drought. ...the worst affected areas of East Central China.* VERB V n V-ed

2 If a disease **affects** someone, it causes them to become ill. *AIDS seems to affect men and women in equal numbers... Arthritis is a crippling disease which affects people all over the world.* VERB =afflict V n

3 If something or someone **affects** you, they make you feel a strong emotion, especially sadness or pity. *If Jim had been more independent, the divorce would not have affected him as deeply... Gregor loved his sister, and her loss clearly still affects him.* VERB =touch V n

4 If you **affect** a particular characteristic or way of behaving, you pretend that it is genuine, or natural for you; a literary use. *He listened to them, affecting an amused interest... Ms. Redgrave affects a heavy Italian accent.* VERB V n Also V to-inf

affectation /æfekteɪʃən/ **affectations.** If you say that someone's attitude or behaviour is an **affectation**, you disapprove of the fact that it is not genuine or natural, but is intended to impress other people. *Although it is long after dark, he is wearing black sunglasses. With anyone else you might think it was an affectation... Lawson writes so well: in plain English, without fuss or affectation.* N-VAR PRAGMATICS =mannerism

affected /əfektɪd/. If you describe someone's behaviour as **affected**, you disapprove of the fact that they behave in an unnatural way that is intended to impress other people; an old-fashioned literary word. *She passed along with an affected air and a disdainful look.* ADJ: usu ADJ n PRAGMATICS =mannered ≠genuine

affecting /əfektɪŋ/. If you describe something such as a story or a piece of music as **affecting**, you mean that you like it because it makes you feel a strong emotion, especially sadness or pity; a literary word. *One of the most affecting pieces of film shows soldiers standing round a mass grave.* ADJ-GRADED PRAGMATICS =moving, touching

affection /əfe̲kʃən/ **affections** ◆◆◇◇◇

1 If you regard someone or something with **affection**, you like them and are fond of them. *She thought of him with affection... She had developed quite an affection for the place. ...trying to win their affection.* N-UNCOUNT: oft N *for/of* n =love

2 Your **affections** are your feelings of love or fondness for someone. *The distant object of his affections is Caroline... Jack Russell has a special place in the affections of the cricketing public. ...her fear of being replaced in his affections.* N-PLURAL: with poss

affectionate /əfe̲kʃənət/. If you are **affectionate**, you show your love or fondness for another person in the way that you behave towards them. *They seemed devoted to each other and were openly affectionate... She gave me a very long and affectionate hug.* ♦ **affectionately** *He looked affectionately at his niece.* ◆◇◇◇◇ ADJ-GRADED =loving; ADV-GRADED: ADV with v =fondly

affidavit /æfɪde̲ɪvɪt/ **affidavits.** An **affidavit** is a written statement which you swear is true and which may be used as evidence in a court of law. *Mr Smith has put his information in a sworn affidavit, which has been given to the police.* ◆◇◇◇◇ N-COUNT

affiliate, affiliates, affiliating, affiliated. The noun is pronounced /əfɪ̲liət/. The verb is pronounced /əfɪ̲lieɪt/. ◆◆◇◇◇

1 An **affiliate** is an organization which is officially connected with another, larger organization or is a member of it; a formal use. *...twelve companies, including three affiliates of a Texas oil firm... The World Chess Federation has affiliates in around 120 countries.* N-COUNT: oft with poss

2 If an organization **affiliates to** or **with** another larger organization, it forms a close connection with the larger organization or becomes a member of it; a formal use. *All youth groups will have to affiliate to the National Youth Agency... The Government will not allow the staff association to affiliate with outside unions.* VERB; V *to/with* n; Also V

3 If a professional person, such as a lawyer or doctor, **affiliates** with an organization, they become officially connected with that organization or do some official work for it; used especially in formal American English. *He said he wanted to affiliate with a U.S. firm because he needed 'expert advice and counsel in legal affairs'.* VERB; V *with* n

affiliated /əfɪ̲lieɪtɪd/ ◆◇◇◇◇

1 If an organization is **affiliated** with another larger organization, it is officially connected with the larger organization or is a member of it; a formal use. *Their country is not affiliated to the Organisation of African Unity. ...the United Nations and its affiliated organisations.* ► **-affiliated** combines with nouns to form adjectives that describe which organization something or someone is affiliated to. *...church-affiliated schools in Oregon.* ADJ: v-link ADJ *to/with* n, ADJ n; COMB in ADJ =associated

2 If a professional person, such as a lawyer or doctor, is **affiliated** with an organization, they are officially connected with that organization or do some official work for it; a formal use. *He will remain affiliated with the firm as a special associate director. ...our affiliated members.* ADJ: v-link ADJ *with/to* n, ADJ n

affiliation /əfɪlie̲ɪʃən/ **affiliations** ◆◇◇◇◇

1 If one group has an **affiliation** with another group, it has a close or official connection with it; a formal use. *The group has no affiliation to any political party... The officer cited the federation's rule on affiliation.* N-VAR: oft N *with/to* n

2 If you have an **affiliation** with a group or another person, you have a close or official connection with them; a formal use. *...Johnson's affiliation with shoe company Nike... They nodded their approval, then asked what her political affiliations were.* N-VAR: oft N *with/to* n

affinity /əfɪ̲nɪti/ **affinities** ◆◇◇◇◇

1 If you have an **affinity** with someone or something, you feel that you are similar to them and understand them very well. *He has a close affinity with the landscape he knew when he was growing up... There is a natural affinity between British and Asian women.* N-SING: also no det, with supp =rapport

2 If people or things have an **affinity** with each other, they are similar in some ways; a formal use. *The two plots share certain obvious affinities.* N-COUNT =similarity

affirm /əfɜ̲ːʳm/ **affirms, affirming, affirmed** ◆◆◇◇◇

1 If you **affirm** that something is true or that something exists, you state firmly and publicly that it is true or exists; a formal use. *The European Community has repeatedly affirmed that it's in agreement with the Americans on this point. ...a speech in which he affirmed a commitment to lower taxes... 'This place is a dump,' affirmed Miss T.* ♦ **affirmation** /æfəʳme̲ɪʃən/ **affirmations** *After the meeting, the ministers issued a robust affirmation of their faith in the European Monetary System.* VERB =assert; V that; V n; V with quote; Also V n to-inf; N-VAR

2 If an event **affirms** something, it shows that it is true or exists; a formal use. *Everything I had accomplished seemed to affirm that opinion.* ♦ **affirmation** *The high turnout was an eloquent affirmation of the importance that the voters attached to the election.* VERB =confirm; V n; N-UNCOUNT: also a N

affirmative /əfɜ̲ːʳmətɪv/ ◆◇◇◇◇

1 An **affirmative** word or gesture indicates that you agree with what someone has said or that the answer to a question is 'yes'; a formal use. *Haig was desperately eager for an affirmative answer... Dr Sinclair's affirmative nod seemed a shade reluctant.* ♦ **affirmatively** *'Is that clear?' Bob nodded his head affirmatively.* ADJ ≠negative; ADV: ADV with v

2 If you reply to a question **in the affirmative**, you say 'yes' or make a gesture that means 'yes'; a formal expression. *He asked me if I was ready. I answered in the affirmative.* PHRASE: PHR after v ≠in the negative

3 In grammar, an **affirmative** clause is positive and does not contain a negative word. ADJ ≠negative

affirmative a̲ction. In American English, **affirmative action** means making sure that members of disadvantaged groups, such as racial minorities or women, get an appropriate share of the opportunities available. The British term is **positive discrimination.** *A growing number of whites are challenging affirmative action policies.* ◆◇◇◇◇ N-UNCOUNT

affix, affixes, affixing, affixed. The verb is pronounced /əfɪ̲ks/. The noun is pronounced /æ̲fɪks/.

1 If you **affix** one thing to another, you stick it or attach it to the other thing; a formal use. *Complete the form and affix four tokens to its back... I covered the scroll in sealing wax, and affixed a red ribbon. ...special storage racks affixed to the sides of buses.* VERB; V n *to* n; V n; V-ed; Also V n prep/adv

2 An **affix** is a letter or group of letters, for example 'un-' or '-y', which is added to either the beginning or the end of a word to form a different word with a different meaning. For example, 'un-' is added to 'kind' to form 'unkind'. Compare **prefix** and **suffix.** N-COUNT

afflict /əflɪ̲kt/ **afflicts, afflicting, afflicted.** If you **are afflicted** by pain, illness, or disaster, it affects you badly and makes you suffer; a formal word. *Italy has been afflicted by political corruption for decades... There are two main problems which afflict people with hearing impairments... The afflicted person should keep off solid foods and drink plenty of fluids.* ► **The afflicted** are people who are afflicted. *It is food that the afflicted want now.* ◆◇◇◇◇ VERB =affect; be V-ed *by/with* n; V n; V-ed; N-PLURAL: *the* N

affliction /əflɪ̲kʃən/ **afflictions.** An **affliction** is something which causes physical or mental suffering; a formal word. *Hay fever is an affliction which arrives at an early age. ...the afflictions of modern society.* ◆◇◇◇◇ N-VAR =misfortune

affluence /æ̲fluəns/. **Affluence** is the state of having a lot of money or a high standard of living; a formal word. *The postwar era was one of new affluence for the working class.* N-UNCOUNT =prosperity ≠poverty

affluent /æ̲fluənt/. If you are **affluent**, you have a lot of money. *Cigarette smoking used to be commoner among affluent people. ...the affluent neighborhoods of Malibu.* ► **The affluent** are people who are affluent. *The diet of the affluent has not changed much over the decades.* ◆◇◇◇◇ ADJ-GRADED =prosperous, wealthy ≠poor; N-PLURAL: *the* N

afford /əfɔ̲ːʳd/ **affords, affording, afforded** ◆◆◆◇◇

1 If you **cannot afford** something, you do not have enough money to pay for it. *My parents can't even afford a new refrigerator... The arts should be avail-* VERB; V n; V to-inf

able to more people at prices they can afford... We couldn't afford to buy a new rug.

2 If you say that you cannot **afford** to do something or allow it to happen, you mean that you must not do it or must prevent it from happening because it would be harmful or embarrassing to you. *We can't afford to wait... The country could not afford the luxury of an election.*
VERB
V to-inf
V n

3 If someone or something **affords** you an opportunity or protection, they give it to you; a formal use. *This affords us the opportunity to ask questions about how the systems might change... It was a cold room, but it afforded a fine view of the Old City. ...the protection afforded by the police.*
VERB
V n n
V n
V-ed

affordable /əfɔːʳdəbᵊl/. If something is **affordable**, people have enough money to buy it. *...the availability of affordable housing... Clinton promised he would make health care affordable for poor families.* ♦ **affordability** /əfɔːʳdəbɪlɪti/ *...research into homelessness and housing affordability. ...the affordability of highly sophisticated weapons.*
◆◇◇◇◇
ADJ-GRADED
N-UNCOUNT

afforestation /æfɒrɪsteɪʃᵊn, AM -fɔːr-/. **Afforestation** is the process of planting large numbers of trees on land which has few or no trees on it. *Since the Sixties, afforestation has changed the Welsh countryside.*
N-UNCOUNT

affray /əfreɪ/. An **affray** is a noisy and violent fight, especially in a public place; a formal word. *Barnstaple crown court was told he caused an affray at a pub in Braunton, Devon... They were convicted of affray and received community service sentences.*
N-SING: also no det
=disorder

affront /əfrʌnt/ **affronts, affronting, affronted**
◆◇◇◇◇

1 If something **affronts** you, you feel insulted and hurt because of it; a formal use. *One recent example, which particularly affronted Kasparov, was at the European team championship in Hungary.* ♦ **affronted** *He pretended to be affronted, but inwardly he was pleased... Reggie reacted with the same affronted horror Midge had felt.*
VERB
V n
ADJ-GRADED: usu v-link ADJ

2 If something is an **affront** to you, it is an obvious insult to you. *It's an affront to human dignity to keep someone alive like this... She has taken my enquiry as a personal affront.*
N-COUNT: usu sing, usu N to n
=insult

Afghan /æfgæn/ **Afghans. Afghan** means belonging or relating to Afghanistan, or to its people or language. *...the Afghan capital, Kabul.* ► An **Afghan** is a person who comes from Afghanistan.
◆◆◆◆◇
ADJ
N-COUNT

aficionado /əfɪʃiənɑːdoʊ/ **aficionados.** If someone is an **aficionado** of something, they like it and know a lot about it. *I happen to be an aficionado of the opera and symphony, and I love art museums... You are obviously a jazz aficionado.*
N-COUNT: usu with supp, oft N of n
=buff

afield /əfiːld/
◆◇◇◇◇

1 **Further afield** or **farther afield** means in places or areas other than the nearest or most obvious one. *They enjoy participating in a wide variety of activities, both locally and further afield... You are not allowed to bring plants in from further afield without a licence.*
PHRASES
oft from PHR

2 If someone comes from **far afield**, they come from a long way away. *Many of those arrested came from far afield.*
oft from PHR

afire /əfaɪəʳ/

1 If something is **afire** or is set **afire**, it is on fire or looks as if it is on fire. *The houses were set afire but there were only minor injuries to seven personnel... The sun has already set, leaving the sky afire with orange and green light.*
ADJ: v-link ADJ, v n ADJ
=alight

2 If someone is **afire** with emotion, they are extremely enthusiastic and excited about something; a literary use. *All Dan's senses were afire... Sydney is afire with Olympic enthusiasm.*
ADJ: v-link ADJ, oft ADJ with n

aflame /əfleɪm/

1 If something is on fire, you can say it is **aflame**; a literary use. *Hundreds of tightly rolled newspapers were set aflame among the 50,000 crowd.*
ADJ: v-link ADJ, v n ADJ

2 If you say that something is **aflame**, you mean it is filled with light or colour; a literary use. *The shop windows were aflame with Christmas lights.*
ADJ: v-link ADJ, oft ADJ with n
=aglow

afloat /əfloʊt/
◆◇◇◇◇

1 When someone or something is **afloat**, they remain partly above the surface of water and do not sink. *They talked modestly of their valiant efforts to keep the tanker afloat... Three hours is a long time to try to stay afloat in these conditions.*
ADV: usu ADV after v, also v-link ADV, n ADV

2 If a person, business, or country stays **afloat** or is kept **afloat**, they have just enough money to pay their debts and not become bankrupt. *A number of efforts were being made to keep the company afloat... They are borrowing just to stay afloat, not for investment.*
ADV: usu ADV after v, also v-link ADV, n ADV
=solvent, viable

afoot /əfʊt/. If you say that a plan or scheme is **afoot**, it is already happening or being planned, but you do not know much about it. *Everybody knew that something awful was afoot.*
◆◇◇◇◇
ADJ: v-link ADJ

aforementioned /əfɔːʳmenʃᵊnd/. When you refer to **the aforementioned** person or subject, you mean the person or subject that has already been mentioned; a formal word. *The aforementioned Mr Boylett had been based on a real-life member of the staff at Radley.*
◆◇◇◇◇
ADJ: det ADJ, usu *the* ADJ n
=aforesaid

aforesaid /əfɔːʳsed/. **Aforesaid** means the same as **aforementioned**; a formal word. *...the aforesaid organizations and institutions.*
ADJ: det ADJ, usu *the* ADJ n
=aforementioned

afoul /əfaʊl/. If you **run afoul of** someone or something, you do something which gets you into trouble with them; used mainly in American English. *...an otherwise law-abiding citizen who, if left to his own devices, would never have run afoul of the law.*
PHRASE: V inflects, PHR n
=fall foul of

afraid /əfreɪd/
◆◆◆◇◇

1 If you are **afraid** of someone or **afraid** to do something, you are frightened because you think that something very unpleasant is going to happen to you. *She did not seem at all afraid... I was afraid of the other boys... I'm still afraid to sleep in my own bedroom.*
ADJ-GRADED: v-link ADJ, oft ADJ of n, ADJ to-inf
=frightened

2 If you are **afraid** for someone else, you are worried that something horrible is going to happen to them. *She's afraid for her family in Somalia.*
ADJ-GRADED: v-link ADJ, usu ADJ for n

3 If you are **afraid** that something unpleasant will happen, you are worried that it may happen and you want to avoid it. *I was afraid that nobody would believe me... The Government is afraid of losing the election... Don't be afraid to ask questions.*
ADJ-GRADED: v-link ADJ, ADJ that, ADJ of-ing, ADJ to-inf

4 When you want to apologize to someone or to disagree with them in a polite way, you can say **I'm afraid**; used mainly in spoken English. *We don't have anything like that, I'm afraid... I'm afraid I can't help you... 'Bad news?'—'I'm afraid so.'*
PHRASE: PHR with cl, PHR that
PRAGMATICS

afresh /əfreʃ/. If you do something **afresh**, you do it again in a different way. *They believe that the only hope for the French left is to start afresh... Only one expert source seemed prepared to analyse the problem afresh, from first principles.*
ADV: ADV after v
=anew

African /æfrɪkən/ **Africans**
◆◆◆◆◇

1 **African** means belonging or relating to the continent of Africa, or to its countries or people. *...the African continent... Some African countries have also expressed the wish to participate.*
ADJ

2 **African** means belonging or relating to black people who come from Africa. *...traditional African culture. ...dance music with African roots.*
ADJ

3 **African** is used to describe someone, usually a black person, who comes from Africa. *...African women.* ► An **African** is someone who is African. *Fish is a staple in the diet of many Africans.*
ADJ
N-COUNT

Afrikaans /æfrɪkɑːns/. **Afrikaans** is one of the official languages of South Africa. *...a radical Afrikaans newspaper.*
N-UNCOUNT: oft N n

Afrikaner /æfrɪkɑːnəʳ/ **Afrikaners. Afrikaner** means belonging or relating to the white people in South Africa whose ancestors were Dutch. *Several thousand gun-carrying Afrikaner farmers gathered to listen to Mr Viljoen last week.* ► An **Afrikaner** is someone who is Afrikaner.
ADJ
N-COUNT

Afro /æfroʊ/ **Afros**
◆◇◇◇◇

1 **Afro** hair is very tightly curled and sticks out all around your head. *She looks great in her Afro wig.*
ADJ

2 An **Afro** is an Afro hairstyle.
N-COUNT

Afro- /æfroʊ-/. **Afro-** is used to form adjectives and nouns that describe something that is connected with Africa. *...very well known Afro-American family. ...an Afro-centric fashion show.* COMB in ADJ and N-COUNT

Afro-Caribbean, Afro-Caribbeans. ◆◇◇◇◇ **Afro-Caribbean** refers to people of African descent who come from the Caribbean. *...Britain's Afro-Caribbean community.* ADJ ► An **Afro-Caribbean** is someone who is Afro-Caribbean. N-COUNT

aft /ɑːft, æft/ ◆◇◇◇◇

1 If you go **aft** in a boat or plane, you go to the back of it. If you are **aft**, you are in the back. *Clark shook hands with the pilot and walked aft to find his way off the ship.* ADV: ADV after v, be ADV, oft ADV of n ≠fore

2 The **aft** end on a boat or plane is towards the back of it. *Getting into the aft cabin involves a slight step down from saloon level.* ADJ: ADJ n

after /ɑːftəʳ, æftəʳ/ ◆◆◆◆◆

In addition to the uses shown below, **after** is used in phrasal verbs such as 'ask after', 'look after', and 'take after'.

1 If something happens **after** a particular date or event, it happens during the period of time that follows it. *After 19 May, strikes were occurring on a daily basis... After breakfast Amy ordered the local taxi to take her to the station... It wasn't until after Christmas that I met Paul.* PREP ≠before ► Also a conjunction. *After Don told me this, he spoke of his mother... Marina cared for him after he seriously injured his eye several years ago.* CONJ-SUBORD

2 If you do something **after** doing something else, you do it during the period of time that follows it. *After completing and signing it , please return the form to us in the envelope provided. ...women who have changed their mind after deciding not to have children... After flying from Los Angeles to London, allow four full days to adjust.* PREP: PREP -ing ≠before

3 You use **after** when you are talking about time. For example, if something will happen during **the day after** or **the weekend after** a particular date or event, it will happen during the next day or during the next weekend. *She's leaving the day after tomorrow. ...the party's annual conference, to be held the week after next.* PREP: n PREP n ► Also an adverb. *Tomorrow. Or the next day. Or the day after.* ADV: ADV after v

4 If you go **after** someone, you follow or chase them. *Alice said to Gina, 'Why don't you go after him, he's your son.' ...people who were after him for large amounts of money.* PREP

5 If you are **after** something, you are trying to get it. *They were after the money... I did eventually find what I was after.* PREP

6 If you call, shout, or stare **after** someone, you call, shout, or stare at them as they move away from you. *'Come back!' he called after me... Claire stared after him until he disappeared around a corner.* PREP

7 If you do something **after** someone, you do it for them, because they cannot or will not do it for themselves. *She used to mess up the floor and I had to clean up after her.* PREP =for

8 If you tell someone that one place is a particular distance **after** another, you mean that it is situated beyond the other place and further away from you. *Seven kilometres after the drastic hairpin bends and before the village of Piccione, turn right to Montelabate.* PREP =past ≠before

9 If something is written **after** something else on a page, it is written following it or underneath it. *I wrote my name after Penny's at the bottom of the page.* PREP

10 You use **after** in order to give the most important aspect of something when comparing it with another aspect. *After Germany, America is Britain's second-biggest customer... Methane is often regarded as the second most important greenhouse gas after carbon dioxide.* PREP

11 To be named **after** someone means to be given the same name as them. *Phillimore Island is named after Sir Robert Phillimore... He persuaded Virginia to name the baby after him.* PREP

12 If you say **after you** to someone, you are being polite and allowing them to go in front of you or through a doorway before you do. *'After you.'—'Not at all, Mr Bird, after you.'* CONVENTION PRAGMATICS

13 In American English, **after** is used when telling the time. If it is, for example, **ten after six**, the time is ten minutes past six. PREP =before

14 ● **after all**: see **all**.

15 If you do something to several things **one after the other** or **one after another**, you do it to one, then the next, and so on, with no break between your actions. *Sybil ate three ginger biscuits, one after the other, greedily... Caroline was trying on one outfit after another.* PHRASES

16 If something happens **day after day** or **year after year**, it happens every day or every year, for a long time. *I waited for news, day after day, expecting to hear. ...people who'd been coming here year after year.*

after- /ɑːftəʳ-, æftəʳ-/. **After-** is added to nouns to form adjectives which indicate that something takes place or exists after an event or process. *...an after-dinner speech. ...a delicious after-show supper at a restaurant in Gerard Street... After-tax profit fell by 28 percent.* COMB in ADJ: ADJ n ≠pre-

after-care; also spelled **after care. After-care** is the nursing and care of people who have been treated in hospital, and who are now recovering. *As part of the treatment, he attended 15 weeks of after-care... Mr Lloyd specialised in after-care services.* N-UNCOUNT

after-effect, after-effects. The **after-effects** of an event, experience, or substance are the conditions which result from it. *...people still suffering from the after-effects of the world's worst nuclear accident... He was suffering from shock as well as the after-effects of drugs.* N-COUNT: usu pl

afterglow /ɑːftəʳgloʊ, æf-/

1 The **afterglow** is the glow that remains after a light has gone, for example after sunset. *The clifftops glowed with the light of the sunset's afterglow.* N-UNCOUNT: oft with poss

2 You can refer to the good feeling or effects that remain after an event as the **afterglow**. *In the afterglow of agreement, the negotiators blithely say such details can be worked out later.* N-UNCOUNT: oft N of n

after-hours. ◆◇◇◇◇ You use **after-hours** to describe activities which happen after the end of the usual time for them. *An attempt by a high court judge to get an after-hours drink led to his arrest... In after-hours trading, shares surged by another estimated 30 points or more.* ADJ: ADJ n

afterlife /ɑːftəʳlaɪf, æf-/ **afterlives;** also spelled **after-life.** The **afterlife** is a life that some people believe begins when you die, for example a life in heaven or as another person or animal. *I am not religious, so do not believe an afterlife.* N-COUNT: usu sing

aftermath /ɑːftəʳmɑːθ, æftəʳmæθ/. ◆◆◇◇◇ The **aftermath** of an important event, especially a harmful one, is the situation that results from it. *In the aftermath of the coup, the troops opened fire on the demonstrators... The human costs of the Gulf War and its aftermath will never be fully known.* N-SING: with supp, oft the N of n

afternoon /ɑːftəʳnuːn, æf-/ **afternoons.** ◆◆◆◆◇ The **afternoon** is the part of each day which begins at lunchtime and ends at about six o'clock. *He's arriving in the afternoon... He had stayed in his room all afternoon. ...an afternoon news conference.* N-VAR

afternoon tea, afternoon teas. Afternoon tea is a meal you can have in the afternoon. It includes a cup of tea and food such as sandwiches and cakes. *Occasionally they'll drop in for afternoon tea at the Imperial Hotel.* N-VAR

after-school. ◆◇◇◇◇ **After-school** activities are those that are organized for children in the afternoon or evening after they have finished school. *...an after-school childcare scheme.* ADJ: ADJ n

aftershave /ɑːftəʳʃeɪv, æf-/ **aftershaves;** also spelled **after-shave. Aftershave** is a liquid with a pleasant smell that men sometimes put on their faces after shaving. N-MASS =cologne

aftershock /ɑːftəʳʃɒk, æf-/ **aftershocks**

1 Aftershocks are smaller earthquakes which oc- N-COUNT

cur after a large earthquake. *Early this morning, a second strong aftershock struck Northern California.*

2 Journalists sometimes refer to the effects of a important event, especially a bad one, as an **aftershock**. *They were already under stress, thanks to the aftershock of last year's drought.* N-COUNT: usu with supp

aftertaste /ɑːftəʳteɪst, æf-/; also spelled **after-taste**. An **aftertaste** is a taste that remains in your mouth after you have finished eating or drinking something. *It is very thick and creamy with no bitter aftertaste.* N-SING: usu with supp

afterthought /ɑːftəʳθɔːt, æf-/ **afterthoughts.** If you do or say something as an **afterthought**, you do or say it after something else as an addition, perhaps without careful thought. *Almost as an afterthought he added that he missed her.* N-COUNT: usu sing, usu *a* N

afterwards /ɑːftəʳwəʳdz, æf-/. The form **afterward** is also used, mainly in American English. If you do something or if something happens **afterwards**, you do it or it happens after a particular event or time that has already been mentioned. *Shortly afterwards, police arrested four suspects... James was taken to hospital but died soon afterwards... Not long afterward she received five calls in one day.* ◆◆◆◇◇ ADV: ADV with cl

again /əgen, əgeɪn/ ◆◆◆◆◆

1 You use **again** to indicate that something happens a second time, or after it has already happened before. *He kissed her again... Again there was a short silence... I don't ever want to go through anything like that again.* ADV: ADV with v, ADV with cl

2 You use **again** to indicate that something is now in a particular state or place that it used to be in. *He opened his attache-case, removed a folder, then closed it again... I started to feel good about myself again.* ADV: ADV after v

3 You can use **again** when you want to point out that there is a similarity between the subject that you are talking about now and a previous subject. *Again the pregnancy was very similar to my previous two... With the new artists, you see a more dynamic stage show than you used to see. And again, that's probably part of the progress of technology.* ADV: ADV cl PRAGMATICS

4 You can use **again** in expressions such as **but again, then again**, and **there again** when you want to introduce a remark which contrasts with or weakens something that you have just said. *You may be happy to buy imitation leather, and then again, you may wonder what you're getting for your money... They may, but there again they may not.* ADV: ADV with cl PRAGMATICS

5 You can add **again** to the end of your question when you are asking someone to tell you something that you have forgotten or that they have already told you; used in spoken English. *Sorry, what's your name again?.* ADV: cl ADV PRAGMATICS

6 You use **again** in expressions such as **half as much again** when you are indicating how much greater one amount is than another amount that you have just mentioned or are about to mention. *40% of the state's general fund has to go to education. Nearly as much again is mandated to various health and welfare programmes... Sherry is half as strong again as table wine.* ADV: amount ADV PRAGMATICS

7 You can use **again and again** or **time and again** to emphasize that something happens many times. *He would go over his work again and again until he felt he had it right... Time and again political parties have failed to tackle this issue.* PHRASE: usu PHR after v PRAGMATICS =repeatedly

8 • **now and again**: see **now**. • **once again**: see **once**.

against /əgenst, əgeɪnst/ ◆◆◆◆◆

In addition to the uses shown below, **against** is used in phrasal verbs such as 'come up against', 'guard against', and 'hold against'.

1 If something is leaning or pressing **against** something else, it is touching it. *She leaned against him... On a table pushed against a wall there were bottles of beer and wine. ...the rain beating against the window panes.* PREP

2 If you are **against** something such as a plan, policy, or system, you think it is wrong, bad, or stupid. *Taxes are unpopular – it is understandable that voters are against them... Joan was very much against commencing drug treatment. ...a march to protest against job losses.* ► Also an adverb. *The vote for the suspension of the party was 283 in favour with 29 against.* PREP ≠in favour of, for; ADV: ADV after v

3 If you compete **against** someone in a game, you try to beat them. *The tour will include games against the Australian Barbarians... Billy Hardy has pulled out of his second fight against Noel Carroll after a training accident.* PREP

4 If you take action **against** someone or something, you try to harm them. *Security forces are still using violence against opponents of the government. ...an upsurge in racism against immigrants... The demonstration itself was against the Government's new Community Charge.* PREP

5 If you take action **against** a possible future event, you try to prevent it. *Experts have been discussing how to improve the fight against crime... They are arguing against hospital closures... I must warn you against raising your hopes.* PREP

6 If you do something **against** someone's wishes, advice, or orders, you do not do what they want you to do or tell you to do. *He didn't want to go against the wishes of the German government... He discharged himself from hospital against the advice of doctors.* PREP

7 If you do something in order to protect yourself **against** something unpleasant or harmful, you do something which will make its effects on you less serious if it happens. *Any business needs insurance against ordinary risks such as fire, flood, and breakage... It has been claimed that wine helps protect against heart disease.* PREP

8 If you **have** something **against** someone, you dislike them, often because you know something unpleasant about them or because they have done something unpleasant to you. *Have you got something against women, Les?... I have nothing against foreigners.* PHRASE: V inflects, PHR n

9 If something is **against** the law or **against** the rules, there is a law or a rule which says that you must not do it. *It is against the law to detain you against your will for any length of time... We thought cheating was against the rules.* PREP

10 If you are moving **against** a current, tide, or wind, you are moving in the opposite direction to it. *...swimming upstream against the current... They were going to sail around the little island, against the tide.* PREP ≠with

11 If something happens or is considered **against** a particular background of events, it is considered in relation to those events, because those events are relevant to it. *The Pope has sent a message appealing for unity in his homeland, against a background of divisions in the Solidarity movement... The profits rise was achieved against a backdrop of falling metal prices.* PREP

12 If something is measured or valued **against** something else, it is measured or valued by comparing it with the other thing. *Our policies have to be judged against a clear test: will it improve the standard of education?... Check the operator's productivity against agreed targets... The US dollar is down against most foreign currencies today.* PREP

13 If you discuss a particular set of facts or figures **as against** another set, you are comparing or contrasting the two sets of facts or figures. *Only about 60% of voters were firm in their intention at the start of the campaign, as against 80% before.* PHRASE

14 The chances or odds **against** something happening are the chances or odds that it will not happen. *One's chances against cancer depend on smoking, obesity, and poor diet... The odds against him surviving are incredible.* ► Also an adverb. *What were the odds against?* PREP: n PREP ≠for; ADV: n ADV ≠for

15 • **up against**: see **up**. • **against the clock**: see **clock**.

agape /əgeɪp/. If you describe someone as having their mouth **agape**, their mouth is open very wide, often because they are very surprised by ADJ: v-link ADJ something; used in written English. *She stood looking at Carmen with her mouth agape.*

agate /ægɪt/ **agates. Agate** is a very hard stone which is used to make jewellery. N-VAR

age /eɪdʒ/ **ages, ageing** or **aging, aged** ◆◆◆◆◆

1 Your **age** is the number of years that you have lived. *She has a nephew who is just ten years of age... At the age of sixteen he qualified for a place at the University of Hamburg... I admired him for being so confident at his age.* N-VAR

2 The **age** of a thing is the number of years since it was made. *Everything in the room looks in keeping with the age of the building.* N-VAR =period

3 **Age** is the state of being old or the process of becoming older. *Perhaps he has grown wiser with age... This cologne, like wine, improves with age... The worst sign of age was in the fabric which looked decidedly ancient.* N-UNCOUNT ≠youth

4 When someone **ages**, or when something **ages** them, they seem much older and less strong or less alert. *He had always looked so young, but he seemed to have aged in the last few months... He was only in his mid-thirties, but already worry had aged him.* V-ERG V V n

5 An **age** is a period in history. *...the age of steam and steel. ...items of Bronze Age pottery.* N-COUNT: usu with supp

6 You can say **an age** or **ages** to mean a very long time; an informal use. *He waited what seemed an age... The bus took absolutely ages to arrive.* N-COUNT =forever, years

7 See also **aged, ageing, coming-of-age, dark age, golden age, ice age, Iron Age, middle age, Stone Age.**

8 If someone tells you to **act** your **age**, they are telling you to behave in a way that is suitable for someone your age, because they think you are behaving in a childish way. PHRASES V inflects PRAGMATICS

9 If something **comes of age**, it reaches an important stage of development and is accepted by a large number of people. *Recycling is an issue that has come of age in Britain in the last decade.* V inflects =mature

10 When someone **comes of age**, they become legally an adult. *The company was now officially owned by Eddie, but held in trust until he came of age.* V inflects

11 Someone who is **under age** is not legally old enough to do something, for example to buy an alcoholic drink. *Because she was under age, her parents were still responsible for her. ...under age smoking.* usu v-link PHR, PHR n

aged. Pronounced /eɪdʒd/ for meaning 1, and /eɪdʒɪd/ for meanings 2 and 3. ◆◆◇◇◇

1 You use **aged** followed by a number to say how old someone is. *Alan has two children, aged eleven and nine.* ADJ: usu n ADJ num

2 **Aged** means very old. *She has an aged parent who's capable of being very difficult.* ADJ: ADJ n

3 You can refer to all people who are very old as **the aged**. *The American Society on Aging provides resource services to those dealing with the aged.* N-PLURAL: the N =the elderly

4 See also **middle-aged.**

age group, age groups. An **age group** is the people in a place or organization who were born during a particular period of time, for example all the people aged between 18 and 25. *...a style that would appeal to all age groups.* ◆◇◇◇◇ N-COUNT

ageing /eɪdʒɪŋ/; also spelled **aging.** ◆◆◇◇◇

1 Someone or something that is **ageing** is becoming older and less healthy or efficient. *John lives with his ageing mother... Ageing aircraft need more frequent safety inspections.* ADJ: usu ADJ n

2 **Ageing** is the process of becoming old or becoming worn out. *Inadequate fluid intake and poor diet all contribute to ageing.* N-UNCOUNT

ageism /eɪdʒɪzəm/. **Ageism** is the behaviour that occurs as a result of the belief that older people are of less value than younger people; used showing disapproval. N-UNCOUNT

ageist /eɪdʒɪst/. **Ageist** behaviour is based on the belief that older people are of less value than younger people; used showing disapproval. *...his efforts to find work in the face of ageist bias from employers.* ADJ-GRADED PRAGMATICS

ageless /eɪdʒləs/

1 If you describe someone as **ageless**, you mean that they never seem to look any older; a literary use. *She was rich, beautiful and seemingly ageless.* ADJ

2 If you describe something as **ageless**, you mean that it is impossible to tell how old it is, or that it seems to have existed for ever; a literary use. *...the ageless oceans out of which had emerged the first living things.* ADJ

age limit, age limits. An **age limit** is the oldest or youngest age at which you are allowed under particular regulations to do something. *In some cases there is a minimum age limit.* N-COUNT

agency /eɪdʒənsi/ **agencies** ◆◆◆◆◇

1 An **agency** is a business which provides a service on behalf of other businesses. *We had to hire maids through an agency. ...a successful advertising agency.* ● See also **employment agency, press agency, travel agency.** N-COUNT: oft supp N

2 An **agency** is a government organization responsible for a certain area of administration. *...the government agency which monitors health and safety at work in Britain... Webster is retiring as head of the Central Intelligence Agency (CIA).* N-COUNT: oft supp N

agenda /ədʒendə/ **agendas** ◆◆◆◇◇

1 You can refer to the political issues which are important at a particular time as an **agenda**. *Does television set the agenda on foreign policy?... Many of the coalition members could have their own political agendas... There are signs that the Danish presidency will attempt to put environmental issues high on its agenda.* ● See also **hidden agenda.** N-COUNT: with supp

2 An **agenda** is a list of the items that have to be discussed at a meeting. *This is sure to be an item on the agenda next week... High on the agenda of tomorrow's meeting will be the turmoil in Japan.* N-COUNT

agent /eɪdʒənt/ **agents** ◆◆◆◆◇

1 An **agent** is a person who looks after someone else's business affairs or does business on their behalf. *You are buying direct, rather than through an agent. ...a written declaration by someone, authorizing another person to act as his agent.* ● See also **estate agent, press agent, travel agent.** N-COUNT =representative, rep

2 An **agent** in the arts world is a person who gets work for an actor or musician, or who sells the work of a writer to publishers. N-COUNT

3 An **agent** is a person who works for a country's secret service. *All these years he's been an agent for the East... He was convinced he was surrounded by secret agents out to murder him.* N-COUNT

4 If you refer to someone or something as the **agent** of a particular effect, you mean that they cause this effect. *He identifies Gorbachev as the key agent of change.* N-COUNT: N of n =instrument

5 A chemical that has a particular effect or is used for a particular purpose can be referred to as a particular kind of **agent**. *...the bleaching agent in white flour. ...fibrinogen, a blood clotting agent.* N-COUNT: supp N

agent provocateur /æʒɒn prɒvɒkətɜːʳ/ **agents provocateurs.** An **agent provocateur** is a person who is employed by the government or the police to encourage certain groups of people to break the law, because the government or police want to arrest those people or want them to lose public support. *Many are convinced that agents provocateurs are seeking to discredit the opposition.* N-COUNT

age of consent. The **age of consent** is the age at which a person can legally agree to having a sexual relationship. *He was under the age of consent.* ◆◇◇◇◇ N-SING: the N

age-old. An **age-old** story, tradition, or problem has existed for many generations or centuries; used in written English. *This age-old struggle for control had led to untold bloody wars.* ◆◇◇◇◇ ADJ: usu ADJ n =ancient

agglomeration /əglɒməreɪʃən/ **agglomerations.** An **agglomeration** of things is a lot of different things gathered together, often in no particular order or arrangement; a formal word. *The towns are on the way to becoming agglomerations of desperately poor people... The album is a bizarre agglomeration of styles.* N-VAR: usu with supp =accumulation

aggrandize /əɡrændaɪz/ **aggrandizes, aggrandizing, aggrandized;** also spelled **aggrandise** in British English. To **aggrandize** someone means to make them seem richer, more powerful, and more important than they really are. To **aggrandize** a building means to make it more impressive; used showing disapproval. *At the dinner table, my father would go on and on, showing off, aggrandising himself... In 1864 they set about alterations to aggrandise the building.*
VERB PRAGMATICS — V pron-refl, V n

aggrandizement /əɡrændɪzmənt/; also spelled **aggrandisement**. If someone does something for **aggrandizement**, they do it in order to get power, wealth, and importance for themselves; a formal word used showing disapproval. *It would be the first time in human history that economic necessity has prevailed over military aggrandizement.* ● See also **self-aggrandizement**.
N-UNCOUNT: usu with supp PRAGMATICS =growth, cumulation

aggravate /æɡrəveɪt/ **aggravates, aggravating, aggravated** ◆◇◇◇◇

1 If someone or something **aggravates** a situation, they make it worse. *Stress and lack of sleep can aggravate the situation... He would only aggravate the injury by rubbing it.*
VERB =worsen ≠alleviate V n

2 If someone or something **aggravates** you, they make you annoyed; an informal use. *What aggravates you most about this country?* ♦ **aggravating** *You don't realise how aggravating you can be.* ♦ **aggravation** /æɡrəveɪʃən/ **aggravations** *I just couldn't take the aggravation.*
VERB =annoy V n; ADJ-GRADED =annoying; N-VAR =annoyance

aggravated /æɡrəveɪtɪd/. **Aggravated** is used to describe a serious crime which involves violence; a legal term. *He was jailed for 10 years after admitting aggravated assault.*
ADJ: ADJ n

aggregate, aggregates, aggregating, aggregated. The adjective and noun are pronounced /æɡrɪɡət/. The verb is pronounced /æɡrɪɡeɪt/. ◆◆◇◇◇

1 An **aggregate** amount or score is made up of several smaller amounts or scores added together; a technical use in economics and sport. *The rate of growth of GNP will depend upon the rate of growth of aggregate demand... England have beaten the Welsh three times in succession with an aggregate score of 83-12.* ► Also a noun. *The highest aggregate came in the third round where Leeds and Middlesbrough drew 4-4.*
ADJ: ADJ n; N-COUNT: usu sing

2 An **aggregate** is a number of people or things that are being considered as a single thing; a formal use. *...society viewed as an aggregate of individuals.*
N-COUNT

3 If amounts or things **are aggregated**, they are added together and considered as a single amount or thing; a formal use. *...if the results were to be aggregated into national league tables... We should never aggregate votes to predict results under another system.* ♦ **aggregation** /æɡrɪɡeɪʃən/ *A bigger objection is that aggregation of the results invites distortion.*
VERB be V-ed into n, V pl-n, Also V pl-n into n; N-UNCOUNT: usu N of n

4 If a number of different things or amounts are considered **in aggregate**, or **in the aggregate**, they are considered as a single thing or amount; a formal expression. *Expenses are deductible only to the extent that in aggregate they exceed 7 percent of gross income.*
PHRASES =in total

5 If one team beats another **on aggregate**, it wins because it has a higher total score than the other team after a series of games. *United won 5-3 on aggregate.*
PHR after v

aggression /əɡreʃən/ **aggressions** ◆◆◇◇◇

1 **Aggression** is a quality of anger and determination that makes you ready to attack other people. *Aggression is by no means a male-only trait.*
N-UNCOUNT =belligerence ≠gentleness

2 **Aggression** is violent and attacking behaviour. *The raid was an unjustifiable act of aggression. ...the threat of massive military aggression.*
N-VAR

aggressive /əɡresɪv/ ◆◆◆◇◇

1 An **aggressive** person or animal has a quality of anger and determination that makes them ready to attack other people. *Some children are much more aggressive than others... These fish are very aggressive... Aggressive behaviour is a sign of emotional distress.* ♦ **aggressively** *They'll react aggressively.* ♦ **aggressiveness** *Her aggressiveness made it difficult for him to explain his own feelings.*
ADJ-GRADED =belligerent; ADV-GRADED; N-UNCOUNT =aggression

2 People who are **aggressive** in their work or other activities behave in a forceful way because they are very eager to succeed. *He is respected as a very aggressive and competitive executive... The Zambian game is much more aggressive than European soccer.* ♦ **aggressively** *...countries noted for aggressively pursuing energy efficiency.*
ADJ-GRADED; ADV-GRADED: usu ADV with v

aggressor /əɡresəʳ/ **aggressors.** The **aggressor** in a fight or battle is the person, group, or country that starts it. *They have been the aggressors in this conflict.* ◆◇◇◇◇
N-COUNT

aggrieved /əɡriːvd/. If you feel **aggrieved**, you feel upset and angry because of the way in which you have been treated. *I really feel aggrieved at this sort of thing.* ◆◇◇◇◇
ADJ-GRADED =resentful, bitter

aggro /æɡroʊ/

1 **Aggro** is the difficulties and problems that are involved in something; used in informal British English. *Simply phone the ticket hot-line and all that aggro will be a thing of the past.*
N-UNCOUNT =hassle

2 **Aggro** is aggressive or violent behaviour; used in informal British English. *They could see there wasn't going to be any aggro and they left us to it.*
N-UNCOUNT =aggression

aghast /əɡɑːst, əɡæst/. If you are **aghast**, you are filled with horror and surprise; a formal word. *While she watched, aghast, his eyes glazed over as his life flowed away... His colleagues were aghast at the sackings... Tania stared at him aghast, unable to speak.*
ADJ-GRADED: ADJ after v, v-link ADJ, oft ADJ at n, ADJ n =horrified

agile /ædʒaɪl, AM -dʒəl/ ◆◇◇◇◇

1 Someone who is **agile** can move with great or surprising ease and speed. *He is very agile for a big man and covers a large area quickly.* ♦ **agility** /ədʒɪlɪti/ *She blinked in surprise at his agility.*
ADJ-GRADED =nimble ≠clumsy; N-UNCOUNT

2 If you have an **agile** mind, you think quickly and intelligently. *She was quick-witted and had an extraordinarily agile mind.* ♦ **agility** *His intellect and mental agility have never been in doubt.*
ADJ-GRADED; N-UNCOUNT

aging /eɪdʒɪŋ/. See **age, ageing**.

agitate /ædʒɪteɪt/ **agitates, agitating, agitated** ◆◇◇◇◇

1 If people **agitate** for something, they protest or take part in political activity in order to get it. *The women who worked in these mills had begun to agitate for better conditions.* ♦ **agitation** /ædʒɪteɪʃən/ *At least seventy students were injured in the continuing agitation against the decision.*
VERB V for n, Also V, V for n to-inf; N-UNCOUNT: oft N for/against/over n

2 If you **agitate** something, you shake it so that it moves about; a formal use. *All you need to do is gently agitate the water with a finger or paintbrush... Its molecules can be agitated by microwave energy.* ♦ **agitation** *Temperature is a measure of the agitation of the molecules of matter.*
VERB V n; N-UNCOUNT

3 If something **agitates** you, it worries you and makes you unable to think clearly or calmly. *Carl and Martin may inherit their grandmother's possessions when she dies. The thought agitates her.*
VERB V n

4 See also **agitation**.

agitated /ædʒɪteɪtɪd/. If someone is **agitated**, they are very worried or upset, and show this in their behaviour, movements, or voice. *Susan seemed agitated about something... The man in the house was in a very excited and agitated state.*
ADJ-GRADED =upset, disturbed

agitation /ædʒɪteɪʃən/. If someone is in a state of **agitation**, they are very worried or upset, and show this in their behaviour, movements, or voice. *Danny returned to Father's house in a state of intense agitation... Diane lit a cigarette, trying to mask her agitation.* ● See also **agitate**.
N-UNCOUNT =anxiety

agitator /ædʒɪteɪtəʳ/ **agitators.** If you describe someone involved in politics as an **agitator**, you disapprove of them because of the trouble they cause in organizing campaigns and protests. *...a famous actress who was accused of being a Communist agitator.*
N-COUNT: oft supp N PRAGMATICS

agitprop /ædʒɪtprɒp/; also spelled **agit-prop**. **Agitprop** is the use of artistic forms such as drama or posters to further political aims. *Audiences expecting an evening of fiery agitprop had best look elsewhere.*
N-UNCOUNT

aglow /əglou/

1 If something is **aglow**, it is shining and bright with a soft, warm light; a literary use. *The night skies will be aglow with fireworks.* [ADJ: v-link ADJ, oft ADJ *with* n]

2 If someone is **aglow** or if their face is **aglow**, they look excited; a literary use. *'It was incredible,' Kurt says, suddenly aglow.* [ADJ: v-link ADJ, oft ADJ *with* n]

AGM /eɪ dʒiː em/ **AGMs;** also spelled **agm**. The **AGM** of a company or organization is a meeting which it holds once a year in order to discuss the previous year's accounts and activities. **AGM** is an abbreviation for 'Annual General Meeting'. [◆◇◇◇◇ N-COUNT]

agnostic /ægnɒstɪk/ **agnostics**

1 An **agnostic** believes that it is not possible to know whether God exists or not. *Vasari claimed with horror that he was, if not an atheist, then an agnostic.* [N-COUNT =unbeliever]

2 **Agnostic** means relating to agnostics or to their beliefs. *You grew up in an agnostic household and have never been able to bring yourself to believe in God.* [ADJ]

agnosticism /ægnɒstɪsɪzəm/. **Agnosticism** is the belief that it is not possible to say definitely whether or not there is a God. [N-UNCOUNT]

ago /əgou/. You use **ago** when you are referring to past time. For example, if something happened one year **ago**, it is one year since it happened. If it happened a long time **ago**, it is a long time since it happened. *He was killed a few days ago in a skiing accident... The meeting is the first ever between the two sides since the war there began 14 years ago... Harry's daughter is dead. She died long ago.* [◆◆◆◆◆ ADV: ADV with v, n ADV, *long* ADV]

agog /əgɒg/. If you are **agog**, you are excited about something, and eager to know more about it. *The city was agog with rumours last night that the two had been executed.* [ADJ: usu v-link ADJ, oft ADJ prep]

agonize /ægənaɪz/ **agonizes, agonizing, agonized;** also spelled **agonise** in British English. If you **agonize** over something, you feel very anxious about it and spend a long time thinking about it. *Perhaps he was agonizing over the moral issues involved... She only made the decision to apply for training after years of agonizing.* [VERB; V *over/about* n; V-ing; Also V]

agonized /ægənaɪzd/; also spelled **agonised**. **Agonized** describes something that you say or do when you are in great physical or mental pain. *The agonised look on his face said he wouldn't be staying at the front much longer.* [ADJ-GRADED: usu ADJ n]

agonizing /ægənaɪzɪŋ/; also spelled **agonising**. [◆◇◇◇◇]

1 Something that is **agonizing** causes you to feel great physical or mental pain. *He did not wish to die the agonizing death of his mother and brother... In the heat of Rome, the wait was agonizing.* [ADJ-GRADED =excruciating] ♦ **agonizingly** *Progress was agonizingly slow.* [ADV]

2 **Agonizing** decisions and choices are very difficult to make. *He now faced an agonizing decision about his immediate future.* [ADJ-GRADED]

agony /ægəni/ **agonies. Agony** is great physical or mental pain. *A new machine may save thousands of animals from the agony of drug tests... They sat and listened as she called out in agony... As a young man he suffered agonies of religious doubt.* [◆◆◇◇◇ N-UNCOUNT: also N in pl =torment]

agony aunt, agony aunts. In British English, an **agony aunt** is a person who writes a column in a newspaper or magazine in which they reply to readers who have written to them for advice on their personal problems. The usual American term is **advice columnist**. [N-COUNT =advice columnist]

agony column, agony columns. The **agony column** in a British newspaper or magazine is the part where letters from readers about their personal problems are printed and where advice about these problems is given. The usual American term is **advice column**. [N-COUNT =advice column]

agoraphobia /ægərəfoubiə/. **Agoraphobia** is the fear of open or public places; a technical term in psychiatry. [N-UNCOUNT]

agoraphobic /ægərəfoubɪk/ **agoraphobics.** Someone who is **agoraphobic** suffers from agoraphobia; a technical term in psychiatry. [ADJ-GRADED: usu v-link ADJ] ▸ An **agoraphobic** is someone who suffers from agoraphobia. [N-COUNT]

agrarian /əgreəriən/. **Agrarian** means relating to the ownership and use of land, especially farmland, or relating to the part of a society or economy that is concerned with agriculture. *...a rich area with a highly developed agrarian economy.* [◆◇◇◇◇ ADJ: usu ADJ n]

agree /əgriː/ **agrees, agreeing, agreed** [◆◆◆◆◆]

1 If people **agree** with each other about something, they have the same opinion about it or say that they have the same opinion. *If we agreed all the time it would be a bit boring, wouldn't it?... Both the House and Senate have agreed on the need for the money... So we both agree there's a problem?... I see your point but I'm not sure I agree with you... I agree with you about the gun situation... I agree with you that the open system is by far the best... 'It's appalling.'—'It is. I agree.'... I agree that the demise of London zoo would be terrible... I agree with every word you've just said... 'Frankly I found it rather frightening.' 'A little startling,' Mark agreed.* [V-RECIP =concur ≠disagree; pl-n V; pl-n V that; V *with* n; V *with* n that; NON-RECIP: V; V that; V *with* n; V with quote]

2 If you **agree** to do something or **agree** to a proposal, you say that you will do what someone wants, or that you will let something be done. *He agreed to pay me for the drawings... Donna agreed to both requests... All 100 senators agree to a postponement.* [VERB =consent; V to-inf; V *to* n; Also V]

3 If people **agree** on something or **agree** something, they all decide to have or do something. *The warring sides have agreed on an unconditional ceasefire... We never agreed a date... The court had given the unions until September 11 to agree terms with a buyer.* [V-RECIP; pl-n V *on/upon* n; pl-n V n; V n *with* n; Also pl-n V to-inf] • If two people who are arguing about something **agree to disagree** or **agree to differ**, they decide to stop arguing because neither of them is going to change their opinion. *You and I are going to have to agree to disagree then.* [PHRASE: V inflects, pl-n PHR]

4 If you **agree** with an action or suggestion, you approve of it. *You didn't want to ask anybody whether they agreed with what you were doing... In his heart he knew they'd agree with his stand.* [VERB ≠disagree; V *with* n]

5 If one account of an event or one set of figures **agrees** with another, the two accounts or sets of figures are the same or are consistent with each other. *His second statement agrees with facts as stated by the other witnesses.* [V-RECIP =tally; V *with* n; Also V]

6 If some food that you eat **does not agree with** you, it makes you feel ill. *I have an upset stomach. I don't think the food here agrees with me.* [VB: with neg; V *with* n]

7 If a place or experience **agrees with** you, it makes you feel healthy and happy. *You look great, Brian. The Bahamas certainly agree with you.* [VERB; V *with* n]

8 In grammar, if a word **agrees** with a noun or pronoun, it has a form appropriate to the number or gender of the noun or pronoun. For example, in 'He hates it', the singular verb agrees with the singular pronoun 'he'. You can also say that two words **agree**. [V-RECIP: V *with* n, pl-n V]

9 See also **agreed**.

agreeable /əgriːəbᵊl/ [◆◇◇◇◇]

1 If something is **agreeable**, it is pleasant and you enjoy it. *...workers in more agreeable and better paid occupations. ...an agreeable surprise.* [ADJ-GRADED =nice ≠disagreeable] ♦ **agreeably** *At first we chatted agreeably about his trips to London and Paris... The sisters were agreeably surprised to find out that the King of Spain had been their rescuer.* [ADV-GRADED]

2 If someone is **agreeable**, they are pleasant and try to please people. *...sharing a bottle of wine with an agreeable companion... I've gone out of my way to be agreeable to his friends.* [ADJ-GRADED =nice]

3 If you are **agreeable** to something or if it is **agreeable** to you, you are willing to do it or to allow it to happen; a formal use. *She was agreeable to the project... If you are agreeable, my husband's office will make all the necessary arrangements. ...a solution that would be agreeable to all.* [ADJ-GRADED: v-link ADJ, oft ADJ *to* n]

agreed /əgriːd/ [◆◇◇◇◇]

1 If people are **agreed** on something, they have reached a joint decision on it or have the same opinion about it. *Okay, so are we agreed on going* [ADJ: v-link ADJ, oft ADJ *on* n, ADJ that]

north?... All twelve member states are agreed that something needs to be done about the situation.

2 When you are discussing something formally, you can say '**Agreed?**' to check whether the other people agree with what you have just said. You can say '**Agreed**' if you agree with what someone has just said. *'That means we move out today. Agreed?'—'Agreed.'... 'One thing you can never insure against is corruption among your staff.'—'Agreed.'* CONVENTION PRAGMATICS =o.k.

3 See also **agree**.

agreement /əgriːmənt/ **agreements** ◆◆◆◆◇

1 An **agreement** is a formal decision about future action which is made by two or more countries, groups, or people. *It looks as though a compromise agreement has now been reached... The two countries signed an agreement in 1988 to jointly launch and develop satellites. ...a new defence agreement between Greece and the United States.* N-COUNT: oft N to-inf, N prep

2 **Agreement** on something is a joint decision that a particular course of action should be taken. *A spokesman said, however, that the two men had not reached agreement on the issues discussed... But instead of ending in agreement, the talks broke up in acrimony at the end of the week.* N-UNCOUNT: oft N on n ≠disagreement

3 **Agreement** with someone means having the same opinion as they have. *The judge kept nodding in agreement... There was general agreement that every effort should be made to prevent the war from spreading.* N-UNCOUNT ≠disagreement • If you are **in agreement** with someone, you have the same opinion as they have. *Not all scholars are in agreement with her, however... We were in basic agreement on this point.* PHRASE: usu v-link PHR, v PHR, oft PHR *with* n

4 **Agreement** to a course of action means allowing it to happen or giving it your approval. *The clinic doctor will then write to your GP to get his agreement.* N-UNCOUNT =consent • If you are **in agreement** with a plan or proposal, you approve of it. *The president was in full agreement with the proposal.* PHRASE: v-link PHR, usu PHR *with* n

5 If there is **agreement** between two accounts of an event or two sets of figures, they are the same or are consistent with each other. *Many other surveys have produced results essentially in agreement with these figures.* N-UNCOUNT =concurrence

6 In grammar, **agreement** refers to the way that a word has a form appropriate to the number or gender of the noun or pronoun it relates to. N-UNCOUNT =concord

agribusiness /ægribɪznɪs/ **agribusinesses. Agribusiness** is the various businesses that produce, sell, and distribute farm products, especially on a large scale. *Many of the old agricultural collectives are now being turned into agribusiness corporations.* N-UNCOUNT: also N in pl, oft N n

agricultural /ægrɪkʌltʃərəl/ ◆◆◆◇◇

1 **Agricultural** means involving or relating to agriculture. *Farmers struggling for survival strip the forests for agricultural land. ...corn and other agricultural products.* ADJ: usu ADJ n

2 An **agricultural** place or society is one in which agriculture is important or highly developed. *Large families are more common in traditional agricultural societies than in cities.* ADJ: usu ADJ n

agriculturalist /ægrɪkʌltʃərəlɪst/ **agriculturalists.** An **agriculturalist** is someone who is an expert on agriculture and who advises farmers. N-COUNT

agriculture /ægrɪkʌltʃəʳ/. **Agriculture** is farming and the methods that are used to raise and look after crops and animals. *Strong both in industry and agriculture, the Ukraine produces much of the grain for the nation.* ◆◆◆◇◇ N-UNCOUNT

agro- /ægroʊ-/. **Agro-** is used to form nouns and adjectives which refer to things relating to agriculture, or to agriculture combined with another activity. *Some land may take up to 20 years to be free from agro-chemical residues.* PREFIX

agronomist /əgrɒnəmɪst/ **agronomists.** An **agronomist** is someone who studies the cultivation of land in order to produce crops. N-COUNT

aground /əgraʊnd/. If a ship runs **aground**, it touches the ground in a shallow part of a river, lake, or the sea, and gets stuck. *The ship ran aground where there should have been a depth of 35ft.* ◆◇◇◇◇ ADV: ADV after v

ah /ɑː/. **Ah** is used in writing to represent a noise that people make in conversation, for example to acknowledge or draw attention to something, or to express surprise or disappointment. *I'm meeting Anna Langenbach. Ah, this seems to be the train now... Ah, so many questions, so little time.* ◆◆◆◇◇ EXCLAM PRAGMATICS

aha /ɑːhɑː/. **Aha** is used in writing to represent a noise that people make in conversation, for example to acknowledge something, or to express satisfaction, triumph, or surprise. *'Do I rub some more in tomorrow?'—'Aha,' Glyn nodded... Aha! Here at last, the answer to the question that has baffled scholars through the centuries.* EXCLAM PRAGMATICS

ahead 1 adverb uses

ahead /əhed/ ◆◆◆◆◇

In addition to the uses shown below, **ahead** is used in phrasal verbs such as 'get ahead', 'go ahead', and 'press ahead'.

1 Something that is **ahead** is in front of you. If you look **ahead**, you look directly in front of you. *Brett looked straight ahead... I peered ahead through the front screen... The road ahead was now blocked solid... Ahead, he saw the side railings of First Bridge over Crooked Brook.* ADV: ADV after v, n ADV, ADV with cl =in front ≠behind

2 You use **ahead** with verbs such as 'push', 'move', and 'forge' to indicate that a plan, scheme, or organization is making fast progress. *Western countries were moving ahead with plans to send financial aid to all of the former Soviet republics... Now BBC World Television is forging ahead on its own.* ADV: ADV after v =forward

3 If you are **ahead** in your work or achievements, you have made more progress than you expected to and are performing well. *The North Korean economy was pretty strong in its time, and was ahead until maybe 1970... First half profits have charged ahead from £127.6m to £134.2m... Children in small classes were 1.5 months ahead in reading and 2.5 months ahead in mathematics.* ADV: *be* ADV, ADV after v, oft amount ADV

4 If a person or a team is **ahead** in a competition, they are winning. *Australia were ahead throughout the game. ...an ICM poll today showing Labour ahead as the party considered to have the best policies on crime... A goal would have put Dublin 6-1 ahead.* ADV: *be* ADV, ADV after v, oft amount ADV

5 **Ahead** also means in the future. *A much bigger battle is ahead for the president... Anne Garrels reports there are still difficult times ahead for Poland... Now I can remember without mourning, and begin to look ahead... Talking about the days ahead, Mr Hurd said his aim in standing was to unify the party... The task ahead is huge.* ADV: v-link ADV, ADV after v, n ADV

6 If you prepare or plan something **ahead**, you do it some time before a future event so that everything is ready for that event to take place. *The government wants figures that help it to administer its policies and plan ahead... Do book ahead as the restaurant is very popular... Summer weddings are very popular and need to be arranged months ahead.* ADV: ADV after v =in advance

7 If you go **ahead**, or if you go on **ahead**, you go in front of someone who is going to the same place so that you arrive there some time before they do. *I went ahead and waited with Sean... You just go on ahead. I'll come by later... I'd have to send Tina on ahead with Rachael.* ADV: ADV after v

ahead 2 preposition uses

ahead of ◆◆◆◇◇

1 If someone or something is **ahead of** you, they are directly in front of you. If someone or something is moving **ahead of** you, they are in front of you and moving in the same direction. *I saw a man in a blue jacket thirty metres ahead of me... She walked ahead of Helene up the steps into the hotel.* PHR-PREP

2 If an event or period of time lies **ahead of** you, it is going to happen or take place soon or in the future. *I tried to think about all the problems that were ahead of me tomorrow... Catherine had been awake all night thinking about the future that lay ahead of her... We have a very busy day ahead of us today.* PHR-PREP: PREP pron =before

3 In a competition, if a person or team does some- PHR-PREP:

thing **ahead of** someone else, they do it before the second person or team. *Robert Millar finished 1 minute and 35 seconds ahead of the Frenchman Thierry Claveyrolat.* oft n PREP n

4 If something happens **ahead of** an event or time, it happens before that event or time. *The Prime Minister was speaking ahead of today's meeting.* PHR-PREP

5 If something happens **ahead of** schedule or **ahead of** time, it happens earlier than was planned. *The election was held six months ahead of schedule... This dish may be prepared a day ahead of time and refrigerated.* PHR-PREP ≠behind

6 If someone is **ahead of** someone else, they have made more progress and are more advanced in what they are doing. *Henry generally stayed ahead of the others in the academic subjects.* PHR-PREP

7 • **one step ahead**: see **step**. • **ahead of one's time**: see **time**.

ahem; usually pronounced as two short coughs. Writers put **ahem** to show that someone who is speaking is about to say something that is in some way difficult, embarrassing, or amusing. Writers also put **ahem** to show that the thing that they are about to say is not exactly true or accurate. *It can be a dangerous course of action which might be sound in theory but – ahem – perhaps a trifle risky in practice... It is not unknown for valuable display items to go, ahem, missing.* CONVENTION PRAGMATICS

ahold /əhoʊld/

1 If you **get ahold of** someone or something, you manage to contact, find, or get them; used mainly in American English. *I tried again to get ahold of my cousin Joan, and I got her on the phone.* PHRASE: V inflects, PHR n =get hold of

2 If you **get ahold of** yourself, you force yourself to become calm and sensible after a shock or in a difficult situation; used mainly in American English. *I'm going to have to get ahold of myself.* PHRASE: V inflects, PHR pron-refl

ahoy /əhɔɪ/. **Ahoy** is something that people in boats shout in order to attract attention. *Ahoy there!... Ship ahoy!* EXCLAM PRAGMATICS

AI /eɪ aɪ/. **AI** is an abbreviation for **artificial intelligence**, or **artificial insemination**. N-UNCOUNT

aid /eɪd/ **aids, aiding, aided** ◆◆◆◆◆

1 **Aid** is money, equipment, or services that are provided for people, countries, or organizations who need them but cannot provide them for themselves. *...regular flights carrying humanitarian aid to Cambodia... They have already pledged billions of dollars in aid. ...food aid convoys.* N-UNCOUNT: oft supp N, N *to* n

2 To **aid** a country, organization, or person means to provide them with money, equipment, or services that they need. *...US efforts to aid Kurdish refugees. ...a charitable organization that has spent millions aiding pharmaceutical research.* ♦ **-aided** *...grant-aided factories. ...state-aided schools.* VERB V n COMB in ADJ

3 To **aid** someone means to help or assist them; used in written English. *...a software system to aid managers in advanced decision-making... The hunt for her killer will continue, with police aided by the army and air force.* ► Also a noun. *He was forced to turn for aid to his former enemy.* VERB =help, assist V n V-ed Also V n to-inf N-UNCOUNT =assistance

4 If you perform a task with the **aid** of something, you need or use it to perform that task. *He succeeded with the aid of a completely new method he discovered... Gently raise your upper body to a sitting position, without the aid of your hands.* N-UNCOUNT: usu *with/without the* N *of* n

5 An **aid** is an object, device, or technique that makes something easier to do. *The new law gives authorities a responsibility to provide aids to the disabled... The book is an invaluable aid to teachers of literature... Colonel Hardy would like to see every tank with a computerized aid.* N-COUNT: oft N *to* n

6 If something **aids** a process, it makes it easier or more likely to happen. *The survey suggests that the export sector will continue to aid the economic recovery... Calcium may aid in the prevention of colon cancer.* VERB V n V *in* n/-ing

7 See also **Band-aid, first aid, hearing aid, legal aid**.

8 An activity or event **in aid of** a particular cause or charity is intended to raise money for that cause or charity; used mainly in British English. *...a charity performance in aid of Great Ormond Street Children's Hospital.* PHRASES PHR n

9 If you **come** or **go to** someone's **aid**, you try to help them when they are in danger or difficulty. *We're coming to the aid of the people of Somalia at the request of the United Nations... Horrified neighbours rushed to his aid as he fell.* V inflects

aide /eɪd/ **aides.** An **aide** is an assistant to someone who has an important job, especially in government or in the armed forces. *A close aide to the Prime Minister repeated that Israel would never accept it.* ◆◆◇◇◇ N-COUNT

aide-de-camp /eɪd də kɒm/ **aides-de-camp.** An **aide-de-camp** is an officer in the armed forces who helps an officer of higher rank. *...a colonel in the Greek army who had been aide-de-camp to the king.* N-COUNT

aide-memoire /eɪd memwɑːʳ/ **aide-memoires;** also spelled **aide-mémoire**. An **aide-memoire** is something such as a list that you use to remind you of something. *A beginner might use such a checklist as an aide-memoire.* N-COUNT =reminder

AIDS /eɪdz/. **AIDS** is a disease which destroys the natural system of protection that the body has against other diseases. **AIDS** is an abbreviation for **acquired immune deficiency syndrome**. ◆◆◆◆◇ N-UNCOUNT

ail /eɪl/ **ails, ailing, ailed**

1 If something **ails** a group or area of activity, it is a problem or source of trouble for that group or for people involved in that activity. *A full-scale debate is under way on what ails the industry.* VERB V n

2 If something **ails** someone, they are ill; an old-fashioned use. *'What ails you?' he asked.* VERB V n

aileron /eɪlərɒn/ **ailerons.** An **aileron** is a flap on the back edge of the wing of an aeroplane that can be raised or lowered in order to control the plane's movement. N-COUNT

ailing /eɪlɪŋ/ ◆◇◇◇◇

1 An **ailing** organization or society is in difficulty and is becoming weaker. *The rise in overseas sales is good news for the ailing American economy.* ADJ: usu ADJ n ≠thriving

2 If someone is **ailing**, they are ill and are not getting better. *He is said to be ailing at his home in Washington.* ADJ

ailment /eɪlmənt/ **ailments.** An **ailment** is an illness, especially one that is not very serious. *The pharmacist can assist you with the treatment of common ailments.* ◆◇◇◇◇ N-COUNT =affliction

aim /eɪm/ **aims, aiming, aimed** ◆◆◆◆◇

1 If you **aim** for something or **aim** to do something, you plan or hope to achieve it. *He said he would aim for the 100 metres world record at the world championships in August... Businesses will have to aim at long-term growth. ...an appeal which aims to raise funds for children with special needs.* VERB V *for/at* n/-ing V to-inf

2 The **aim** of something that you do is the purpose for which you do it or the result that it is intended to achieve. *The aim of the festival is to increase awareness of Hindu culture and traditions. ...a research programme that has largely failed to achieve its principal aims.* N-COUNT: oft with poss =objective

3 If an action or plan **is aimed** at achieving something, it is intended or planned to achieve it. *The new measures are aimed at tightening existing sanctions. ...talks aimed at ending the nine year old war in Mozambique.* V-PASSIVE *be* V-ed *at* n/-ing V-ed

4 If your actions or remarks **are aimed** at a particular person or group, you intend that the person or group should notice them and be influenced by them. *His message was aimed at the undecided middle ground of Israeli politics... Advertising aimed at children should be curbed.* VB: usu passive *be* V-ed *at* n V-ed

5 If you **aim** a weapon or object **at** something or someone, you point it towards them before firing or throwing it. *When he appeared again, he was aiming the rifle at Wade. ...a missile aimed at the arms factory... I didn't know I was supposed to aim at the same spot all the time.* VERB V n *at* n V-ed V *at* n Also V

6 Your **aim** is your skill or action in pointing a weapon or other object at its target. *He stood with the gun gripped in his right hand and his left hand steadying his aim.* N-SING: oft poss N

7 If you **aim** a kick or punch at someone, you try to kick or punch them. *They set on him, punching him in the face and aiming kicks at his shins.* — VERB; V n prep/adv; Also V n

8 When you **take aim**, you point a weapon or object at someone or something, before firing or throwing it. *She had spotted a man with a shotgun taking aim.* — PHRASES; V inflects

9 In American English, if you **take aim at** someone or something, you criticize them strongly. *Republican strategists are taking particular aim at Democratic senators in the Carolinas.* — V inflects, PHR n

aimless /eɪmləs/. A person or activity that is **aimless** has no clear purpose or plan. *Peters had been adrift and aimless... After several hours of aimless searching they were getting low on fuel.* ♦ **aimlessly** *I wandered around aimlessly.* ♦ **aimlessness** *His sense of aimlessness increased.* — ◆◇◇◇◇; ADJ-GRADED; ≠purposeful; ADV-GRADED: ADV after v; N-UNCOUNT

ain't /eɪnt/. **Ain't** is used in some dialects of English instead of 'am not', 'aren't', 'isn't', 'haven't', and 'hasn't'. *Well, it's obvious, ain't it?... I ain't got kids, but I have to pay towards the schools.* — ◆◆◇◇◇

air /eəʳ/ **airs, airing, aired** — ◆◆◆◆◆

1 **Air** is the mixture of gases which forms the earth's atmosphere and which we breathe. *Draughts help to circulate air... Keith opened the window and leaned out into the cold air. ...water and air pollutants.* — N-UNCOUNT

2 The **air** is the space around things or above the ground. *Government troops broke up the protest by firing their guns in the air... People's cigarette smoke seemed to hang in the air.* — N-SING: the N

3 **Air** is used to refer to travel in aircraft. *Air travel will continue to grow at about 6% per year until 2000... The United Nations have been unable to distribute food around the country, other than by air.* — N-UNCOUNT: usu N n, by N

4 An **air** is a simple tune which can be easily recognized and remembered; an old-fashioned use. — N-COUNT: usu with supp

5 If you say that someone or something has a particular **air**, you mean that they give this general impression. *Jennifer took a drag on her cigarette, regarding him with an air of faint amusement... The meal gave the occasion an almost festive air.* — N-SING: with supp, oft N of n

6 In American English, if a broadcasting company **airs** a television or radio programme, they show it on television or broadcast it on the radio. *The largest television network in France has aired a number of stories on Clarence Thomas this week.* ♦ **airing** *Switzer said his program and his university could not tolerate the airing of this material.* — VERB; =broadcast; V n; N-SING

7 If you **air** your opinions, you make them known to people. *They sat for more than six hours, and both sides agreed they had aired all their differences... The whole issue was thoroughly aired at the meeting.* ♦ **airing** *While we're able to broach the subject of sex, money rarely gets an airing.* — VERB; =express; V n; N-SING: a N

8 If you **air** a room or building, you let fresh air into it. *One day a week her mother systematically cleaned and aired each room.* ♦ **airing** *Open all the windows of the bedroom and give it a good airing.* — VERB; V n; N-SING: a N

9 If you **air** clothing or bedding, you put it somewhere warm to make sure that it is completely dry. *When the shirts were clean, I ironed them myself, aired them and placed them in drawers in his room.* — VERB; V n

10 If you do something to **clear the air**, you do it in order to get rid of any misunderstandings that there might be. *...an inquiry just to clear the air and settle the facts of the case.* — PHRASES; V inflects

11 If you refer to someone's **airs and graces**, you mean that they behave in a way that shows that they think they are more important than other people; used showing disapproval. *The old cliche of the customer being always right is what gives them airs and graces.* — PRAGMATICS

12 If something is **in the air** it is felt to be present, but it is not talked about. *There was great excitement in the air... She walked away and left the question hanging in the air.*

13 If someone is **on the air**, they are broadcasting on radio or television. If a programme is **on the air**, it is being broadcast on radio or television. If it is **off the air**, it is not being broadcast. *Singer Dani Behr, 17, is going on the air as presenter of Channel 4's 'The Word'... Rockwell hopes the program can be on the air within a year... This message did not reach me until after the programme went off the air.* — v-link PHR, PHR after v

14 If someone or something disappears **into thin air**, they disappear completely. If someone or something appears **out of thin air**, they appear suddenly and mysteriously. *'But where could they have gone?' he demanded. 'They can't just vanish into thin air!'... He had materialized out of thin air; I had not seen or heard him coming.* — PHR after v

15 If you say that a decision or a situation is **up in the air**, you mean that it has not yet been completely settled or planned. *He told reporters today that the president's trip to Moscow is up in the air.* — v-link PHR; =undecided; ≠settled

16 If you say that you are **walking on air** or **floating on air**, you mean that you feel extremely happy about something. *As soon as I know I'm in the team it's like I'm walking on air.* — V inflects

airbag /eəʳbæg/ **airbags;** also spelled **air bag**. An **airbag** is a safety device in a car which inflates automatically if the car crashes to protect the people travelling in the car when they are thrown forward. — N-COUNT

air base, air bases; also spelled **airbase**. An **air base** is a centre where military aircraft take off or land and are serviced, and where many of the centre's staff live. *She was stationed at the American air base at Mildenhall, Suffolk.* — ◆◇◇◇◇; N-COUNT

airbed /eəʳbed/ **airbeds.** An **airbed** is a plastic or rubber mattress which can be folded or stored flat and which you fill with air before you use it. — N-COUNT

airborne /eəʳbɔːʳn/ — ◆◇◇◇◇

1 If an aircraft is **airborne**, it is in the air and flying. *The pilot did manage to get airborne.* — ADJ: v-link ADJ

2 **Airborne** troops use parachutes to get into enemy territory. *The allies landed thousands of airborne troops.* — ADJ: ADJ n

3 **Airborne** means in the air or carried in the air. *Many people are allergic to airborne pollutants such as pollen.* — ADJ: usu ADJ n

air brake, air brakes. Air brakes are brakes which are used on heavy vehicles such as buses and trains and which are operated by means of compressed air. — N-COUNT

airbrush /eəʳbrʌʃ/ **airbrushes, airbrushing, airbrushed**

1 An **airbrush** is an artist's tool which sprays paint onto a surface. — N-COUNT

2 To **airbrush** a photograph or other image means to change it using an airbrush, especially to make it more beautiful or perfect. *...perfect airbrushed bodies. ...bits of photographs cut, pasted and then airbrushed to create a convincing whole.* — VERB; V-ed; Also V n

Airbus /eəʳbʌs/ **Airbuses.** An **Airbus** is an aeroplane which is designed to carry a large number of passengers for fairly short distances. **Airbus** is a trademark. — N-COUNT

air-conditioned. If a room or vehicle is **air-conditioned**, the air in it is kept cool and dry by means of a special machine. *...spacious air-conditioned offices.* — ◆◇◇◇◇; ADJ

air-conditioner, air-conditioners; also spelled **air conditioner**. An **air-conditioner** is a machine which keeps the air in a building cool and dry. — N-COUNT

air-conditioning; also spelled **air conditioning. Air-conditioning** is a method of providing buildings and vehicles with cool dry air. *The air-conditioning systems rarely work effectively.* — ◆◇◇◇◇; N-UNCOUNT: oft N n

aircraft /eəʳkrɑːft, -kræft/; **aircraft** is both the singular and the plural form. An **aircraft** is a vehicle which can fly, for example an aeroplane or a helicopter. *The return flight of the aircraft was delayed... At least three military aircraft were destroyed.* — ◆◆◆◆◇; N-COUNT

aircraft carrier, aircraft carriers. An **aircraft carrier** is a warship with a long, flat deck where aircraft can take off and land. — ◆◇◇◇◇; N-COUNT

aircrew /eəʳkruː/ **aircrews;** also spelled **air crew**. The **aircrew** on a plane are the pilot and — N-COUNT-COLL other people who are responsible for flying it and for looking after any passengers who are on it.

air-drop, air-drops, air-dropping, air-dropped; also spelled **air drop**.

1 An **air-drop** is a delivery of supplies by aircraft to an area that is hard to get to. The supplies are dropped from the aircraft on parachutes. *...the proposed US air-drops of relief supplies in Bosnia.* N-COUNT

2 When a country or organization **air-drops** supplies to a place, it drops supplies there from aircraft. *Meanwhile, United Nations plans to start air dropping food to rural villages are being held up.* VERB V n to/into n Also V n

airfare /eəʳfeəʳ/ **airfares.** The **airfare** to a place is the amount it costs to fly there. N-COUNT

airfield /eəʳfiːld/ **airfields.** An **airfield** is an area of ground where aircraft take off and land. It is smaller than an airport. ◆◇◇◇◇ N-COUNT

air force, air forces; also spelled **airforce**. An **air force** is the part of a country's armed forces that is concerned with fighting in the air. *...the United States Air Force... Jack Mann was a Royal Air Force fighter pilot during World War II.* ◆◆◆◇◇ N-COUNT

airframe /eəʳfreɪm/ **airframes.** The **airframe** of an aircraft is its body excluding the engines. N-COUNT

air freshener, air fresheners. An **air freshener** is a product people can buy which is meant to make rooms smell pleasant. N-VAR

airgun /eəʳgʌn/ **airguns;** also spelled **air gun**. An **airgun** is a gun which is fired by means of air pressure. N-COUNT

airhead /eəʳhed/ **airheads.** If you describe someone, especially a young woman, as an **airhead**, you are critical of them because you think they are not at all clever and are interested only in unimportant things. *Her antics may have fueled the popular perception of her as an ambitious, pretty airhead.* N-COUNT PRAGMATICS

air hostess, air hostesses. An **air hostess** is a woman who looks after the passengers in an aircraft. N-COUNT =stewardess

airing cupboard, airing cupboards. In British houses, an **airing cupboard** is a warm cupboard where you put clothes and other things that have been washed and partly dried, to make sure they are completely dry. N-COUNT

airless /eəʳləs/. If a place is **airless**, there is no fresh air in it. *...a dark, airless room... The afternoon was hot, sticky and airless.* ADJ-GRADED

airlift /eəʳlɪft/ **airlifts, airlifting, airlifted** ◆◆◇◇◇

1 An **airlift** is an operation to move people, troops, or goods by air, especially in a war or when land routes are closed. *President Garcia has ordered an airlift of food, medicines and blankets.* N-COUNT

2 If people, troops, or goods **are airlifted** somewhere, they are carried by air, especially in a war or when land routes are closed. *The injured were airlifted to hospital in Prestwick... Other nationalities, such as Pakistanis, were being airlifted out by their governments... The government is trying to replenish supplies by airlifting food.* VERB be V-ed to n be V-ed adv/prep V n

airline /eəʳlaɪn/ **airlines.** An **airline** is a company which provides regular services carrying people or goods in aeroplanes. *Eleven of Europe's 15 busiest routes are controlled by only two national airlines.* ◆◆◆◆◇ N-COUNT: oft in names

airliner /eəʳlaɪnəʳ/ **airliners.** An **airliner** is a large aeroplane that is used for carrying passengers. ◆◇◇◇◇ N-COUNT

airlock /eəʳlɒk/ **airlocks;** also spelled **air lock**.

1 An **airlock** is a compartment between places which do not have the same air pressure, for example in a spacecraft or submarine. *Three astronauts left the shuttle's air lock yesterday afternoon.* N-COUNT

2 An **airlock** is a blockage in a pipe which is caused by a bubble of air that prevents liquid from flowing through. *Sometimes airlocks prevent radiators from heating up properly.* N-COUNT

airmail /eəʳmeɪl/. **Airmail** is the system of sending letters, parcels, and goods by air. *...an airmail letter... Goods are generally shipped by airmail.* N-UNCOUNT: oft N n, by N

airman /eəʳmən/ **airmen.** An **airman** is a man who serves in his country's air force. *...an English airman.* ◆◇◇◇◇ N-COUNT: oft supp N

airplane /eəʳpleɪn/ **airplanes.** In American English, an **airplane** is a vehicle with wings and one or more engines that enable it to fly through the air. The usual British word is **aeroplane**. ◆◆◇◇◇ N-COUNT

airplay /eəʳpleɪ/. The **airplay** which a piece of popular music receives is the number of times it is played on the radio. *We were fortunate enough to get a lot of Radio 1 airplay with our first single.* N-UNCOUNT: oft supp N

airport /eəʳpɔːʳt/ **airports.** An **airport** is a place where aircraft land and take off, which has buildings and facilities for passengers. *...Heathrow Airport, the busiest international airport in the world.* ◆◆◆◆◇ N-COUNT: oft in names

air power; also spelled **airpower**. A nation's **air power** is the strength of its air force. *The U.S. says it will use air power to protect the peacekeepers if they call for help.* ◆◇◇◇◇ N-UNCOUNT

air raid, air raids. An **air raid** is an attack by military aircraft in which bombs are dropped. This expression is usually used by the country or group that is suffering the attack. Compare **air strike**. *The war began with overnight air raids on Baghdad and Kuwait. ...an underground air raid shelter.* ◆◇◇◇◇ N-COUNT: oft N on n, N n

air rifle, air rifles. An **air rifle** is a rifle which is fired by means of air pressure. N-COUNT

airship /eəʳʃɪp/ **airships.** An **airship** is an aircraft that consists of a large balloon filled with gas with a compartment underneath for passengers that is powered by an engine. ◆◇◇◇◇ N-COUNT

airshow /eəʳʃoʊ/ **airshows;** also spelled **air show**. An **airshow** is an event at which aeroplane pilots entertain spectators by performing very skilful and complicated manoeuvres in the sky. N-COUNT

airspace /eəʳspeɪs/; also spelled **air space**. A country's **airspace** is the part of the sky that is over that country and is considered to belong to it. *Forty minutes later, they left Colombian airspace.* N-UNCOUNT: usu with supp

airspeed /eəʳspiːd/ **airspeeds;** also spelled **air speed**. An aircraft's **airspeed** is the speed at which it travels through the air. N-COUNT

air strike, air strikes; also spelled **airstrike**. An **air strike** is an attack by military aircraft in which bombs are dropped. This expression is usually used by the country or group that is carrying out the attack. Compare **air raid**. *A senior defence official said last night that they would continue the air strikes.* ◆◇◇◇◇ N-COUNT

airstrip /eəʳstrɪp/ **airstrips.** An **airstrip** is a stretch of land which has been cleared so that aircraft can take off and land. *We landed on a grass airstrip, fifteen minutes after leaving Mahe.* ◆◇◇◇◇ N-COUNT

air terminal, air terminals. An **air terminal** is a building in which passengers wait before they get on to their aeroplane; used mainly in British English. N-COUNT

airtight /eəʳtaɪt/; also spelled **air-tight**. If a container is **airtight**, its lid fits so tightly that no air can get in or out. *Store the cookies in an airtight tin.* ADJ

air time; also spelled **airtime**. The **airtime** that something gets is the amount of time taken up with broadcasts about it. *Even the best women's teams get little air time... They devoted their entire airtime to covering the storm.* N-UNCOUNT

air-to-air. **Air-to-air** combat is a battle between military aeroplanes where rockets or bullets are fired at one aeroplane from another. *...air-to-air missiles.* ADJ: ADJ n

air traffic control

1 **Air traffic control** is the activity of organizing the routes that aircraft should follow, and telling pilots by radio which routes they should take. *...the nation's overburdened air-traffic-control system.* N-UNCOUNT: oft N n

2 **Air traffic control** is the group of people who organize the routes aircraft take. *They have to wait for clearance from air traffic control.* N-UNCOUNT-COLL

air traffic controller, air traffic controllers. ◆◇◇◇◇ An **air traffic controller** is someone whose job is to organize the routes that aircraft should follow, and to tell pilots by radio which routes they should take. [N-COUNT]

airwaves /eəʳweɪvz/; also spelled **air waves.** ◆◇◇◇◇
1 **The airwaves** is used to refer to the activity of broadcasting on radio and television. For example, if someone says something over the **airwaves** or on the **airwaves**, they say it on the radio or television; used in journalism. *The election campaign has been fought not in street rallies but on the airwaves... The song was banned from the airwaves.* [N-PLURAL: usu *the*N]
2 **Airwaves** are the radio waves which are used in radio and television broadcasting. *The airwaves which carry TV signals are already pretty full with only four national channels.* [N-PLURAL]

airway /eəʳweɪ/ **airways** ◆◆◇◇◇
1 **Airways** is used in the name of some airlines. *...British Airways.* [N-IN-NAMES]
2 A person's **airways** are the passages from their nose and mouth down to their lungs, through which air enters and leaves their body; a medical use. *...an inflammation of the airways.* [N-COUNT]

airwoman /eəʳwʊmən/ **airwomen.** An **airwoman** is a woman who serves in her country's air force. [N-COUNT]

airworthy /eəʳwɜːʳði/. If an aircraft is **airworthy**, it is safe to fly. *The mechanics try to keep the helicopters airworthy, but they're suffering from a lack of spare parts.* [ADJ-GRADED] ♦ **airworthiness** *All our aircraft have certificates of airworthiness.* [N-UNCOUNT]

airy /eəri/ **airier, airiest** ◆◇◇◇◇
1 If a building or room is **airy**, it has plenty of fresh air inside, usually because it is very spacious. *The bathroom has a light and airy feel.* [ADJ-GRADED ≠stuffy]
2 You can use **airy** to describe someone's behaviour when they are light-hearted and casual about things which some people take seriously. *Giving them an airy wave of his hand, the Commander sailed past.* [ADJ-GRADED: ADJ n =casual ≠serious] ♦ **airily** /eərɪli/ *'I'll be all right,' he said airily. 'It was only a thought.'* [ADV-GRADED: ADV with v]

airy-fairy. If you describe someone's ideas as **airy-fairy**, you are critical of them because you think the ideas are vague, impractical, and unrealistic; used in British English. *...their airy-fairy principles.* [ADJ-GRADED PRAGMATICS]

aisle /aɪl/ **aisles** ◆◇◇◇◇
1 An **aisle** is a long narrow gap that people can walk along between rows of seats in a public building such as a church or between rows of shelves in a supermarket. *He started down the centre aisle. ...the frozen food aisle.* [N-COUNT]
2 **The aisle** is used in expressions such as **walking down the aisle** to refer to the activity of getting married. *He was in no hurry to walk down the aisle.* [N-SING: *the*N]

ajar /ədʒɑːʳ/. If a door is **ajar**, it is slightly open. *He left the door ajar in case I needed him.* [ADJ: v-link ADJ]

aka. **aka** is an abbreviation for 'also known as'. **aka** is used especially when referring to a nickname or a stage name. *From the very beginning, Stuart Leslie Goddard, aka Adam Ant, knew he was going to be a star.* ◆◇◇◇◇

akimbo /əkɪmboʊ/. If you stand **arms akimbo** or **with arms akimbo**, you stand with your hands on your hips and your elbows pointing outwards; an old-fashioned expression. [PHRASE: usu PHR after v]

akin /əkɪn/. If one thing is **akin** to another, it is similar to it in some way; a formal word. *Cooking is a physical activity, more akin to woodwork or gardening than to reading or listening to music.* ◆◇◇◇◇ [ADJ-GRADED: v-link ADJ *to*n]

à la /ɑː lɑː/. If you do something **à la** a particular person, you do it in the same style or in the same way that they would do it. *Choose a crisp, tailored dress à la Audrey Hepburn in Breakfast At Tiffany's.* [PHR-PREP: PREP n-proper]

alabaster /æləbɑːstəʳ, -bæs-/
1 **Alabaster** is a white stone that is used for making statues, vases, and ornaments. *...four carved alabaster figures of maidens.* [N-UNCOUNT: usu N n]
2 If you say that somebody has **alabaster** skin, you mean that their skin is very beautiful because it is so white and smooth; a literary use. *She wore a fine chain about her alabaster neck.* [ADJ: usu ADJ n]

à la carte /ɑː lɑː kɑːʳt/. An **à la carte** menu in a restaurant offers you a selection of individually priced dishes for each course. *You could choose as much or as little as you wanted from an à la carte menu.* [ADJ: ADJ n] ► Also an adverb. *Choose a light snack in the cafe or eat à la carte in the elegant dining room.* [ADV: ADV after v]

alacrity /əlækrɪti/. If you do something with **alacrity**, you do it quickly and eagerly; a formal word. *As you can imagine, I accepted with alacrity.* [N-UNCOUNT: usu *with*N]

alarm /əlɑːʳm/ **alarms, alarming, alarmed** ◆◆◆◇◇
1 **Alarm** is a feeling of fear or anxiety that something unpleasant or dangerous might happen. *The news was greeted with alarm by MPs... She sat up in alarm... The moves reflect growing alarm over recent events.* [N-UNCOUNT: oft *with/in*N, N *over/about*n =apprehension]
2 If something **alarms** you, it makes you afraid or anxious that something unpleasant or dangerous might happen. *We could not see what had alarmed him.* [VERB =frighten V n]
3 An **alarm** is an automatic device that warns you of danger, for example by ringing a bell. *He heard the alarm go off. ...an extremely sophisticated alarm system... The other man rang the alarm bell.* [N-COUNT]
4 An **alarm** is the same as an **alarm clock**. [N-COUNT]
5 See also **alarming, alarmed, burglar alarm, car alarm, false alarm, fire alarm, smoke alarm.**
6 If you say that something sets **alarm bells** ringing, you mean that it makes people feel worried or concerned about something. *This has set the alarm bells ringing in Moscow... Alarm bells are beginning to sound at Westminster.* [PHRASES N inflects =warning bells]
7 If you **raise the alarm** or **sound the alarm**, you warn people of danger. *His family raised the alarm when he had not come home by 9pm.* [V inflects]

alarm clock, alarm clocks. An **alarm clock** is a clock that you can set to make a noise so that it wakes you up at a particular time. *I set my alarm clock for 4.30.* [N-COUNT =alarm]

alarmed /əlɑːʳmd/. If someone is **alarmed**, they feel afraid or anxious that something unpleasant or dangerous might happen. *They should not be too alarmed by the press reports... The Americans are alarmed at this prospect.* ◆◇◇◇◇ [ADJ-GRADED: usu v-link ADJ, oft ADJ *by/at*n]

alarming /əlɑːʳmɪŋ/. Something that is **alarming** makes you feel afraid or anxious that something unpleasant or dangerous might happen. *The disease has spread at an alarming rate. ...the alarming increase in crime.* ◆◆◇◇◇ [ADJ-GRADED =worrying] ♦ **alarmingly** *...the alarmingly high rate of heart disease.* [ADV-GRADED]

alarmist /əlɑːʳmɪst/ **alarmists**
1 Someone or something that is **alarmist** causes unnecessary fear or anxiety that something unpleasant or dangerous might happen. *The change is not as dramatic as some of the more alarmist reports would have us believe.* [ADJ-GRADED]
2 An **alarmist** is someone who causes unnecessary fear or anxiety that something unpleasant or dangerous might happen. [N-COUNT]

alas /əlæs/. You use **alas** to say that you think that the facts you are talking about are sad, unfortunate, or regrettable. *Such scandals have not, alas, been absent... Alas, it's not that simple.* ◆◇◇◇◇ [ADV: ADV with cl PRAGMATICS =sadly]

Albanian /ælbeɪniən/ **Albanians** ◆◆◆◆◇
1 **Albanian** means belonging or relating to Albania, its people, language, or culture. *Her parents were Albanian. ...the Albanian coast.* [ADJ]
2 An **Albanian** is an Albanian citizen or a person of Albanian origin. [N-COUNT]
3 **Albanian** is the language spoken by people who live in Albania. [N-UNCOUNT]

albatross /ælbətrɒs, AM -trɔːs/ **albatrosses**
1 An **albatross** is a very large white seabird. [N-COUNT]
2 If you describe something or someone as an **albatross** around your neck, you mean that they cause you great problems from which you cannot escape, or they prevent you from doing what you want to do. *Privatization could become a political albatross for the ruling Tories.* [N-COUNT: usu with supp]

albeit /ɔːlbiːɪt/. You use **albeit** to introduce a fact or comment which reduces the force or significance of what you have just said; a formal word. *Charles's letter was indeed published, albeit in a somewhat abbreviated form.* ◆◆◇◇◇ ADV: ADV with cl/group PRAGMATICS =although

albino /ælbiːnoʊ, AM -baɪn-/ **albinos.** An **albino** is a person or animal with very white skin, white hair, and pink eyes. ► Also an adjective. *There were three albino deer in his yard.* N-COUNT ADJ: ADJ n

album /ælbəm/ **albums** ◆◆◆◆◇

1 An **album** is a record with about 25 minutes of music on each side. You can also refer to a collection of songs that is available on an LP, cassette, or CD as an **album**. *Chris likes music and has a large collection of albums and cassettes.* N-COUNT =LP

2 An **album** is a book in which you keep things such as photographs or stamps that you have collected. *Theresa showed me her photo album.* N-COUNT: oft n N

albumen /ælbjʊmɪn, AM ælbjuːmən/. **Albumen** is the same as **albumin**. N-UNCOUNT =albumin

albumin /ælbjʊmɪn, AM ælbjuːmɪn/. **Albumin** is a protein that is found in blood plasma, egg white, and some other substances. N-UNCOUNT =albumen

alchemical /ælkemɪkəl/. **Alchemical** means relating to the science of alchemy. *...alchemical experiments. ...Ruland's Alchemical Dictionary.* ADJ: ADJ n

alchemist /ælkəmɪst/ **alchemists.** An **alchemist** was a scientist in the Middle Ages who tried to discover how to change ordinary metals into gold. N-COUNT

alchemy /ælkəmi/

1 **Alchemy** was a form of chemistry studied in the Middle Ages, which was concerned with trying to discover ways to change ordinary metals into gold. *He was very interested in alchemy and astrology.* N-UNCOUNT

2 **Alchemy** is the power to change or create things in a way which seems mysterious and magical; a literary use. *Let us imagine that by some political alchemy it had been possible to make all men equal.* N-UNCOUNT =wizardry

alcohol /ælkəhɒl, AM -hɔːl/ **alcohols** ◆◆◆◇◇

1 Drinks that can make people drunk, such as beer, wine, and whisky, can be referred to as **alcohol**. *Do either of you smoke cigarettes or drink alcohol?... No alcohol is allowed on the premises.* N-UNCOUNT

2 **Alcohol** is a colourless liquid that is found in drinks such as beer, wine, and whisky. It is also used in products such as perfumes and cleaning fluids. *...low-alcohol beer... Products for dry skin have little or no alcohol.* N-MASS

alcoholic /ælkəhɒlɪk, AM -hɔːl-/ **alcoholics** ◆◆◇◇◇

1 An **alcoholic** is someone who cannot stop drinking large amounts of alcohol, even when this is making them ill. *He showed great courage by admitting on television that he is an alcoholic.* N-COUNT

2 **Alcoholic** drinks are drinks that contain alcohol. *The serving of alcoholic drinks was forbidden after six o'clock. ...tea, coffee, and alcoholic beverages.* ADJ-GRADED

alcoholism /ælkəhɒlɪzəm/. People who suffer from **alcoholism** cannot stop drinking large quantities of alcohol. *...a physician who specialized in the problems of alcoholism.* ◆◇◇◇◇ N-UNCOUNT

alcove /ælkoʊv/ **alcoves.** An **alcove** is a small area of a room which is formed by one part of a wall being built further back than the rest of the wall. *In the alcoves on either side of the fire were bookshelves.* ◆◇◇◇◇ N-COUNT =niche

al dente /æl denteɪ/. If you cook pasta or a vegetable until it is **al dente**, you cook it just long enough so that it is neither hard nor soft but is firm and slightly chewy. ADJ: usu v-link ADJ

alder /ɔːldəʳ/ **alders.** An **alder** is a tree or shrub that grows in Northern temperate areas, often in damp places. It has cones, and its leaves have small points along the edges. N-VAR

alderman /ɔːldəʳmən/ **aldermen**

1 In the United States and Canada, an **alderman** is a member of the governing body of a city. N-COUNT; N-TITLE

2 Until 1974 in England and Wales, an **alderman** was a senior member of a local council who was elected by other councillors. N-COUNT; N-TITLE

ale /eɪl/ **ales.** **Ale** is a kind of strong beer served in British pubs. *...our selection of ales and spirits.* ● See also **ginger ale, real ale.** ◆◇◇◇◇ N-MASS

alec /ælɪk/ **alecs.** See **smart alec.**

aleck /ælɪk/ **alecks.** See **smart alec.**

alehouse /eɪlhaʊs/ **alehouses;** also spelled **ale-house.** An **alehouse** is a pub; an old-fashioned, informal word. N-COUNT

alert /əlɜːʳt/ **alerts, alerting, alerted** ◆◆◆◇◇

1 If you are **alert**, you are paying full attention to things around you and are able to deal with anything that might happen. *We all have to stay alert... He had been spotted by an alert neighbour.* ADJ-GRADED =attentive ≠unprepared

♦ **alertness** *The drug improved mental alertness.* N-UNCOUNT

2 If you are **alert** to something, you are fully aware of it. *The bank is alert to the danger.* ADJ-GRADED: v-link ADJ *to* n

3 An **alert** is a situation in which people prepare themselves for something dangerous that might happen soon. *Due to a security alert, this train will not be stopping at Oxford Circus.* N-COUNT

4 If you **alert** someone to a situation, especially a dangerous or unpleasant situation, you tell them about it. *He wanted to alert people to the activities of the group... I was hoping he'd alert the police.* VERB V n *to* n V n

5 See also **red alert.**

6 If soldiers or police are **on alert**, they are ready to deal with anything that may happen. *Soldiers and police have been put on alert.* PHRASES PHR after v, v-link PHR

7 If you are **on the alert** for something, you are ready to deal with it if it happens. *They want to be on the alert for similar buying opportunities.* PHR after v, v-link PHR

A level /eɪ levəl/ **A levels.** **A levels** are British educational qualifications which schoolchildren take when they are seventeen or eighteen years old. People usually need A levels if they want to go to university in Britain. *He left school with four A levels... Laura is taking A levels next summer in theatre and religious studies.* ◆◆◇◇◇ N-VAR

alfalfa /ælfælfə/. **Alfalfa** is a plant that is used for feeding farm animals. The shoots that develop from its seeds are sometimes eaten as a vegetable. N-UNCOUNT =lucerne

alfresco /ælfreskoʊ/; also spelled **al fresco**. An **alfresco** activity, especially a meal, is one that takes place in the open air. *We woke to a wonderful al fresco breakfast of dates, figs and melon.* ADJ: ADJ n =outdoor

► Also an adverb. *He came across the man shaving alfresco.* ADV: ADV after v

algae /ældʒi, ælgaɪ/. **Algae** is a type of plant with no stems or leaves that grows in water or on damp surfaces. ◆◇◇◇◇ N-UNCOUNT-COLL

algal /ælgəl/. **Algal** means relating to algae. *Sewage nutrients do increase algal growth in the harbour.* ADJ: ADJ n

algebra /ældʒɪbrə/. **Algebra** is a type of mathematics in which letters are used to represent possible quantities. N-UNCOUNT

algebraic /ældʒɪbreɪɪk/. **Algebraic** equations, expressions, and principles are based on or use algebra. ADJ: ADJ n

Algerian /ældʒɪəriən/ **Algerians.** ◆◆◆◆◇

1 **Algerian** means belonging or relating to Algeria, or its people or culture. *...the Algerian desert. ...a young Algerian actor.* ADJ

2 An **Algerian** is an Algerian citizen or a person of Algerian origin. N-COUNT

algorithm /ælgərɪðəm/ **algorithms.** An **algorithm** is a series of mathematical steps, especially in a computer programme, which will give you the answer to a particular kind of problem or question. N-COUNT

alia /eɪliə/. See **inter alia.**

alias /eɪliəs/ **aliases** ◆◇◇◇◇

1 An **alias** is a false name, especially one used by a criminal. *Using an alias, he had rented a house in Fleet, Hampshire.* N-COUNT

2 You use **alias** when you are mentioning another name that someone, especially a criminal or an actor, is known by. *Richard Thorp, alias Alan Turner, said yesterday: 'It is a sad time for both of us.'* PREP: n-proper PREP n-proper

alibi /ælɪbaɪ/ **alibis.** If you have an **alibi**, you can prove that you were somewhere else when a ◆◇◇◇◇ N-COUNT crime was committed. *The police had a suspect but he later proved to have an alibi.*

alien /eɪliən/ **aliens** ◆◆◇◇◇

1 **Alien** is used to describe someone or something that belongs to a different country, race, or group. This use usually indicates disapproval, and is considered offensive by some people. *He said they were opposed to what he described as the presence of alien forces in the region.*
ADJ: usu ADJ n PRAGMATICS =foreign

2 You use **alien** to describe something that seems strange and perhaps frightening, because it is not part of your normal experience. *Alone in an alien culture, Avik befriends Albertine.*
ADJ-GRADED: usu ADJ n PRAGMATICS =strange

3 If something is **alien** to you or to your normal feelings or behaviour, it is not the way you would normally feel or behave. *Such an attitude is alien to most businessmen.*
ADJ-GRADED: v-link ADJ *to* n =foreign

4 An **alien** is someone who is not a legal citizen of the country in which they live; a legal use, which is considered offensive by some people. *Both women had hired illegal aliens for child care... When war broke out, he was interned as an enemy alien.*
N-COUNT PRAGMATICS =foreigner

5 In science fiction, an **alien** is a creature from outer space.
N-COUNT

alienate /eɪliəneɪt/ **alienates, alienating, alienated** ◆◆◇◇◇

1 If you **alienate** someone, you make them become unfriendly or unsympathetic towards you. *The government cannot afford to alienate either group.*
VERB V n

2 If someone or something **alienates** a person from someone or something that they are normally linked with, they cause them to be emotionally or intellectually separated from them. *His second wife, Alice, was determined to alienate him from his two boys.* ♦ **alienated** *He felt alienated from his peers.* ♦ **alienation** /eɪliəneɪʃən/ *...the alienation of many from the political process... Her sense of alienation from the world disappeared.*
VERB V n *from* n
ADJ-GRADED: usu v-link ADJ, oft ADJ *from* n
N-UNCOUNT: oft N *of/from* n

alight /əlaɪt/ **alights, alighting, alighted** ◆◇◇◇◇

1 If something is **alight**, it is burning. *Several buildings were set alight... The gas fire was still alight.*
ADJ: v n ADJ, v-link ADJ

2 If someone's eyes are **alight** or if their face is **alight**, the expression in their eyes or on their face shows that they are feeling a strong emotion such as excitement or happiness. *Her eyes were alight with a girlish enjoyment of life... She paused and turned, her face alight with happiness.*
ADJ: v-link ADJ, oft ADJ *with* n =alive

3 If a bird or insect **alights** somewhere, it lands there; a literary use. *A thrush alighted on a branch of the pine tree.*
VERB V prep/adv

4 When you **alight** from a train, bus, or other vehicle, you get out of it after a journey; a formal use. *Two men alighted from the vehicle.*
VERB =get off V prep/adv Also V

5 If someone **alights** on something, they suddenly see it, think of it, or take an interest in it; a literary use. *He would then suddenly alight on the tune he really wanted to play.*
VERB =hit upon V *on/upon* n

align /əlaɪn/ **aligns, aligning, aligned** ◆◇◇◇◇

1 If you **align** yourself with a particular group, you support them because you have the same political aim. *Of late, though, there have been signs that the prime minister is aligning himself with the liberals... He has attempted to align the Socialists with the environmental movement.*
VERB V pron-refl prep V n prep Also V prep

2 If you **align** something, you place it in a certain position in relation to something else, usually parallel to it. *A tripod will be useful to align and steady the camera... Keep the rough edge of the fabric aligned with the raw edge of the piping.*
VERB V n V-ed Also V n prep

alignment /əlaɪnmənt/ **alignments** ◆◇◇◇◇

1 An **alignment** is support for a particular group, especially in politics, or for a side in a quarrel or struggle. *He refused to compromise the church by a particular political alignment... His increasing alignment with the Reagan administration nearly cost him re-election.*
N-VAR =affiliation

2 The **alignment** of something is its position in relation to something else or to its correct position. *They shunned the belief that there is a link between the alignment of the planets and events on the Earth.*
N-UNCOUNT =position

alike /əlaɪk/ ◆◆◇◇◇

1 If two or more things are **alike**, they are similar in some way. *We looked very alike.*
ADJ-GRADED: v-link ADJ ≠different

2 **Alike** means in a similar way. *They even dressed alike. ...their assumption that all men and women think alike.*
ADV-GRADED: ADV after v ≠differently

3 You use **alike** after mentioning two or more people, groups, or things in order to emphasize that you are referring to both or all of them. *The techniques are being applied almost everywhere by big and small firms alike.*
ADV: n *and* n ADV PRAGMATICS =equally

4 See also **look-alike**.

alimentary canal /ælɪmentri kənæl/ **alimentary canals.** The **alimentary canal** in a person or animal is the passage in their body through which food passes from their mouth to their anus.
N-COUNT

alimony /ælɪməni, AM -mouni/. **Alimony** is money that a court of law orders someone to pay regularly to their former wife or husband after they have got divorced. *A great deal of Jeff's money went in alimony to his three former wives.*
N-UNCOUNT

alive /əlaɪv/ ◆◆◆◇◇

1 If people or animals are **alive**, they have life. *She does not know if he is alive or dead... They kept her alive on a life support machine.*
ADJ: v-link ADJ, *keep* n ADJ ≠dead

2 If you say that someone seems **alive**, you mean that they seem to be very lively and to enjoy everything that they do. *She seemed more alive and looked forward to getting up in the morning... I never expected to feel so alive in my life again.*
ADJ-GRADED: usu v-link ADJ

3 If an activity, organization, or situation is **alive**, it continues to exist or function. *The big factories are trying to stay alive by cutting costs... Both communities have a tradition of keeping history alive.*
ADJ-GRADED: v-link ADJ, *keep* n ADJ ≠dead

4 If a place is **alive** with something, there are a lot of people or things there and it seems busy or exciting. *The river was alive with birds... The street was alive with the sounds of the soldiers.*
ADJ: v-link ADJ, usu ADJ *with* n

5 If you are **alive** to a situation or problem, you are aware of it and realize how important it is. *You must be alive to opportunity!... He was alive to what he was doing.*
ADJ: v-link ADJ *to* n/wh

6 If people, places, or events **come alive**, they start to be active or lively again after a quiet or dull period. If someone or something **brings** them **alive**, they cause them to come alive. *The doctor's voice had come alive and his small eyes shone. ...the songs of birds that bring the garden alive.*
PHRASES V inflects

7 If a story or description **comes alive**, it becomes interesting, lively, or realistic. If someone or something **brings** it **alive**, they cause it to come alive. *She made history come alive with tales from her own memories... From here on he brings the character confidently alive.*
V inflects

8 If someone **eats** you **alive**, they defeat you very easily in an argument or contest, tell you off very severely, or ridicule you a great deal; an informal expression. *He was certain Sid would be eaten alive by the hardened criminals in the jail.*
V inflects

9 If you say that someone or something is **alive and kicking**, you are emphasizing not only that they continue to survive, but also that they are very active. *There are growing worries that the secret police may still be alive and kicking.*
v-link PHR PRAGMATICS

10 If you say that someone or something is **alive and well**, you are emphasizing that they continue to survive. *A Yorkshire farmer who went missing yesterday during a blizzard has been found alive and well.*
v-link PHR PRAGMATICS

alkali /ælkəlaɪ/ **alkalis.** An **alkali** is a substance with a pH value of more than 7. Alkalis form chemical salts when they are combined with acids.
N-MASS ≠acid

alkaline /ælkəlaɪn/. Something that is **alkaline** contains an alkali or has a pH value of more than 7. *Some soils are actually too alkaline for certain plant life.* ♦ **alkalinity** /ælkəlɪnɪti/ *A pH test measures the acidity or alkalinity of a substance.*
◆◇◇◇◇ ADJ-GRADED ≠acidic
N-UNCOUNT ≠acidity

all /ɔːl/ ◆◆◆◆◆

1 You use **all** to indicate that you are referring to the whole of a particular group or thing or to every-
PREDET: PREDET det pl-n/n-uncount

one or everything of a particular kind. *He felt betrayed by his mother, and this anger twisted all his later relationships... President Bush will need all his skill in the coming weeks to carry American public opinion with him.* ► Also a determiner. *There is built-in storage space in all bedrooms... 85 percent of all American households owe money on mortgages... Germany, like all great nations, will not change its personality... He was passionate about all literature.* ► Also a quantifier. *He was told to pack up all of his letters and personal belongings... He was talking to all of us.* ► Also a pronoun. *Molton Brown was the only salon producing its own shampoos and hair-care products, all based on herbal recipes... I'd spent all I had, every last penny.* ► Also an emphasizing pronoun. *Milk, oily fish and egg all contain vitamin D... We all admire professionalism and dedication.*

DET: DET pl-n/n-uncount
QUANT: QUANT *of* def-pl-n/def-n-uncount
PRON
PRON-EMPH: n PRON v

2 You use **all** to refer to the whole of a particular period of time. *George had to cut grass all afternoon... She's been feeling bad all week.* ► Also a predeterminer. *She's worked all her life... He was looking at me all the time.* ► Also a quantifier. *Mr Vance and Lord Owen spent all of yesterday in talks with the Serbs... Two-thirds of the women interviewed think about food a lot or all of the time.*

DET: DET sing-n
PREDET: PREDET det sing-n
QUANT: QUANT *of* def-n

3 You use **all** to refer to a situation or to life in general. *All is silent on the island now... As you'll have read in our news pages, all has not been well of late.*

PRON

4 You use **all** to emphasize that something is completely true, or happens everywhere or always, or on every occasion. *He loves animals and he knows all about them... There are an equal number of Hong Kong students at foreign universities all round the world... I got scared and I ran and left her all alone... He was doing it all by himself... All around he could hear people calling out his name.*

ADV: ADV prep/adv
PRAGMATICS

5 You use **all** at the beginning of a clause when you are emphasizing that something is the only thing that is important. *He said all that remained was to agree to a time and venue... All you ever want to do is go shopping!... All I could say was, 'I'm sorry'.*

PRON
PRAGMATICS

6 You use **all** in expressions such as **in all sincerity** and **in all probability** when you are emphasizing that you are being sincere or that something is very probable. *In all fairness he had to admit that she was neither dishonest nor lazy... If the pool was open, we'd in all probability still be swimming in it... In all seriousness, there is nothing else I can do.*

DET: *in* DET n-uncount
PRAGMATICS

7 In spoken English, you use **all** in front of an adjective when you want to emphasize a quality that affects someone or something temporarily; an informal use. *You've gone all chatty... He came over all dizzy when he stood up.*

ADV: v-link ADV adj-graded
PRAGMATICS

8 You use **all** when you are talking about an equal score in a game. For example, if the score is three **all**, both players or teams have three points.

ADV: amount ADV

9 **All** is used in structures such as **all the more** or **all the better** to mean even more or even better than before. *The living room is decorated in pale colours that make it all the more airy... 'How are you?'—'All the better for seeing you.'*

ADV: ADV *the* adv/adj-compar
=even

10 You use **all** in expressions such as **seen it all** and **done it all** to emphasize that someone has had a lot of experience of something. *Pauline appeared to have it all; a happy marriage, a comfortable home and beautiful children... Here's a man who has seen it all, tasted and heard it all.*

PRON-EMPH
PRAGMATICS

11 You say **above all** to indicate that the thing you are mentioning is the most important point. *Above all, chairs should be comfortable... Social services departments must accept, above all, the role of the parents.*

PHRASES
PHR with cl/group
PRAGMATICS

12 You use **after all** when introducing a statement which supports or helps explain to something you have just said. *I thought you might know somebody. After all, you're the man with connections.*

PHR with cl
PRAGMATICS

13 You use **after all** when you are saying that something that you thought might not be the case is in fact the case. *I came out here on the chance of finding you at home after all... The Social Democrats say they are ready after all to begin talks on joining a coalition government.*

14 You use **and all** when you want to emphasize that what you are talking about includes the thing mentioned, especially when this is surprising or unusual. *He dropped his sausage on the pavement and someone's dog ate it, mustard and all.*

n PHR
PRAGMATICS

15 You use **all in all** to introduce a summary or generalization. *We both thought that all in all it might not be a bad idea... All in all, it appeared that a pretty depressing summer awaited Jones.*

PHR with cl
PRAGMATICS

16 You use **at all** at the end of a clause to give emphasis in negative statements, conditional clauses, and questions. *Robin never really liked him at all... There were no roads at all... Surely if the woman had any decency at all, she'd have withdrawn at once... 'Are you dizzy at all?' he asked her.*

PRAGMATICS

17 **All but** a particular person or thing means everyone or everything except that person or thing. *The general was an unattractive man to all but his most ardent admirers... The plant will stand all but the worst winters out of doors.*

PHR n

18 You use **all but** to say that something is almost the case. *The concrete wall that used to divide this city has now all but gone... He has been all but forgotten.*

PHR -ed

19 You use **for all** to indicate that the thing mentioned does not affect or contradict the truth of what you are saying. *For all its beauty, Prague could soon lose some of the individuality that the communist years helped to preserve.*

PHR n
PRAGMATICS
=despite

20 You use **for all** in phrases such as **for all I know**, and **for all he cares**, to emphasize that you don't know something or that something does not really matter to someone. *They chose to decide that Margaret was lying, and for all I know or care, they were right.*

PHR with cl
PRAGMATICS

21 If you **give** your **all** or **put** your **all** into something, you make the maximum effort possible. *He puts his all into every game.*

V inflects

22 **In all** means in total. *In all some 15 million people live in the selected areas... There was evidence that thirteen people in all had taken part in planning the murder.*

PHR with cl, amount PHR

23 In spoken English, if you say that you are **all in**, you mean that you are extremely tired; an informal use. *'Have you eaten? – You look all in!'*

v-link PHR

24 If something such as an activity is a particular price **all in**, that price includes everything that is offered; mainly used in informal British English. *Dinner is about £25 all in.*

amount PHR, PHR with cl

25 You use **of all** to emphasize the words 'first' or 'last', or a superlative adjective or adverb. *First of all, answer these questions... Now she faces her toughest task of all.*

PHR with superl
PRAGMATICS

26 You use **of all** in expressions such as **of all people** or **of all things** when you want to emphasize someone or something surprising. *One group of women, sitting on the ground, was singing, of all things, 'Greensleeves'.*

PHR n
PRAGMATICS

27 You use **all** in expressions like **of all the cheek** or **of all the luck** to emphasize how angry or surprised you are at what someone else has done or said. *Of all the lazy, indifferent, unbusinesslike attitudes to have!*

PRAGMATICS

28 You use **all of** before a number to emphasize how small or large an amount is. *It took him all of 41 minutes to score his first goal... I'm just checking up on Kim. It'll take me all of five minutes.*

PHR amount
PRAGMATICS

29 **One and all** means everyone present or everyone in a particular group; an old-fashioned use. *Being in charge of the National Health Service reforms did not endear you to one and all.*

=everyone

30 You use **all that** in statements with negative meaning when you want to weaken the force of what you are saying; used mainly in spoken English. *He wasn't all that older than we were... He said it would not be all that difficult to reach a peaceful conclusion to the conflict.*

PHR with brd-neg, PHR adj/adv
PRAGMATICS

31 You can say **that's all** at the end of a sentence when you are explaining something and want to emphasize that nothing more happens or is the

cl PHR
PRAGMATICS

case. *'Why do you want to know that?' he demanded.—'Just curious, that's all.'... 'I had no desire at all to be a mother – I had a child, that's all.'*

32 You use **all very well** in structures where you are suggesting that you do not really approve of it or think that it is unreasonable. *It is all very well to urge people to give more to charity when they have less, but is it really fair?* — V-link PHR; PRAGMATICS

all- /ɔːl-/

1 All- is added to nouns or adjectives in order to form adjectives which describe something as consisting only of the thing mentioned or as having only the quality indicated. *An all-star cast gathered at London's Savoy Hotel for the Evening Standard Awards... It is often very hard to compare all-male and all-female jobs. ...all-cotton sheeting.* — COMB in ADJ: usu ADJ n

2 All- is added to present participles or adjectives in order to form adjectives which describe something as including or affecting everything or everyone. *Nursing a demented person is an all-consuming task... There are no all-embracing EC directives on race equality.* — COMB in ADJ-GRADED: usu ADJ n

3 All- is added to nouns in order to form adjectives which describe something as being suitable for or including all types of a particular thing. *He wanted to form an all-party government of national unity... Jeans, the all-purpose denim trousers, have been around for over a hundred years.* — COMB in ADJ: usu ADJ n

Allah /ælə, ælɑː/. **Allah** is the name of God in Islam. — ◆◇◇◇◇ N-PROPER

all-American. If you describe someone as an **all-American** boy or girl, you mean that they seem to have all the typical qualities that are valued by ordinary Americans, such as good looks and patriotism. *...the image of the standard all-American boy.* — ◆◇◇◇◇ ADJ: ADJ n

allay /əleɪ/ **allays, allaying, allayed.** If you **allay** someone's fears or doubts, you stop them feeling afraid or doubtful; a formal word. *He did what he could to allay his wife's myriad fears.* — ◆◇◇◇◇ VERB =calm V n

all clear

1 The **all clear** is a signal that a dangerous situation, for example an air raid, has ended. *The all clear was sounded about 10 minutes after the alert was given.* ▶ Also a convention. *'All clear,' Misha growled.* — N-SING: the N; CONVENTION

2 If someone in authority gives you the **all clear**, they give you permission to continue with a plan or activity, usually after a problem has been sorted out. *I hope to be given the all clear to resume playing when I see the specialist in three weeks.* — N-SING: the N =go-ahead

all-comers; also spelled **allcomers**. You use **all-comers** to refer to everyone who wants to take part in an activity, especially a competition. *This offer is open to allcomers, so long as they own a home.* — N-PLURAL

allegation /ælɪgeɪʃən/ **allegations.** An **allegation** is a statement saying that someone has done something wrong. *The company has denied the allegations... Allegations of brutality and theft have been levelled at the army.* — ◆◆◆◇◇ N-COUNT =claim

allege /əledʒ/ **alleges, alleging, alleged.** If you **allege** that something bad is true, you say it but do not prove it; a formal word. *She alleged that there was rampant drug use among the male members of the group... The accused is alleged to have killed a man... It was alleged that the restaurant discriminated against black customers.* — ◆◆◇◇◇ VERB =claim V that; be V-ed to-inf; it be V-ed that; Also V with quote

alleged /əledʒd/. An **alleged** fact has been stated but has not been proved to be true; a formal word. *They have begun a hunger strike in protest at the alleged beating. ...a list of alleged war criminals.* ♦ **allegedly** /əledʒɪdli/ *His van allegedly struck the two as they were crossing a street.* — ◆◆◆◆◇ ADJ: ADJ n; ADV

allegiance /əliːdʒəns/ **allegiances.** Your **allegiance** is your support for and loyalty to a particular group, person, or belief. *My allegiance to Kendall and his company ran deep. ...a community driven by strong ties and allegiances.* — ◆◇◇◇◇ N-VAR: oft N to n

allegorical /ælɪgɒrɪkəl, AM -gɔːr-/. An **allegorical** story, poem, or painting uses allegory. *...his curious allegorical fairy-tale.* — ADJ-GRADED =symbolic

allegory /ælɪgəri, AM -gɔːri/ **allegories**

1 An **allegory** is a story, poem, or painting in which the characters and events are symbols of something else. Allegories are often moral, religious, or political. *The book is a kind of allegory of Latin American history.* — N-COUNT: oft N of n =parable

2 Allegory is the use of characters and events in a story, poem, or painting to represent other things. *The poem's comic allegory was transparent.* — N-UNCOUNT =symbolism

allegro /əlegroʊ/ **allegros.** An **allegro** is a piece of classical music that should be played in a brisk, lively way. — N-COUNT: oft in names

alleluia /ælɪluːjə/. **Alleluia** means the same as **hallelujah**. — EXCLAM

all-embracing. Something that is **all-embracing** includes or affects everyone or everything. *His hospitality was instantaneous and all-embracing.* — ADJ-GRADED =all-encompassing

allergen /ælərdʒen/ **allergens.** An **allergen** is a substance that causes an allergic reaction in someone; a technical term. *Allergens include pollen, dust-mite, feathers and fabrics.* — N-COUNT

allergic /əlɜːrdʒɪk/ — ◆◇◇◇◇

1 If you are **allergic** to something, you become ill or get a rash when you eat it, smell it, or touch it. *I'm allergic to cats.* — ADJ-GRADED: v-link ADJ to n

2 If you have an **allergic** reaction to something, you become ill or get a rash when you eat it, smell it, or touch it. *Soya milk can cause allergic reactions in some children.* — ADJ: ADJ n

3 If you say that you are **allergic** to something or someone, you mean that you dislike them very strongly and try to avoid them; an informal use. *He was allergic to risk.* — ADJ-GRADED: v-link ADJ to n =averse

allergist /ælərdʒɪst/ **allergists.** An **allergist** is a doctor who specializes in treating people with allergies. — N-COUNT

allergy /ælərdʒi/ **allergies** — ◆◆◇◇◇

1 If you have a particular **allergy**, you become ill or get a rash when you eat, smell, or touch something that does not normally make people ill. *Food allergies can result in an enormous variety of different symptoms... Allergy to cats is one of the commonest causes of asthma.* — N-VAR

2 If you say that you have got an **allergy** to something or someone, you mean that you dislike them very strongly and try to avoid them; an informal use. *I developed a temporary allergy to the company of couples.* — N-COUNT: N to n

alleviate /əliːvieɪt/ **alleviates, alleviating, alleviated.** If you **alleviate** pain, suffering, or an unpleasant condition, you make it less intense or severe; a formal word. *Nowadays, a great deal can be done to alleviate back pain. ...the problem of alleviating mass poverty.* ♦ **alleviation** /əliːvieɪʃən/ *Their energies were focussed on the alleviation of the refugees' misery.* — ◆◇◇◇◇ VERB =ease ≠aggravate V n; N-UNCOUNT: usu N of n

alley /æli/ **alleys.** An **alley** is a narrow passage or street with buildings or walls on both sides. • See also **blind alley**, **bowling alley**. — ◆◇◇◇◇ N-COUNT =alleyway

alley cat, alley cats. An **alley cat** is a cat that lives in the streets of a town, is rather fierce, and is usually one not owned by anyone. — N-COUNT

alleyway /æliweɪ/ **alleyways;** also spelled **alley-way**. An **alleyway** is the same as an **alley**. — ◆◇◇◇◇ N-COUNT =alley

alliance /əlaɪəns/ **alliances** — ◆◆◆◇◇

1 An **alliance** is a group of countries or political parties that are formally united and working together because they have similar aims. *The two parties were still too much apart to form an alliance.* — N-COUNT =coalition

2 An **alliance** is a relationship in which two countries, political parties, or organizations work together for some purpose. *The Socialists' electoral strategy has been based on a tactical alliance with the Communists... They are now in a position to govern the state in alliance with either the Free Democrats or the Green Party.* — N-COUNT: oft N with/between n, also in N with n =partnership

allied /ælaɪd, AM əlaɪd/ — ◆◆◆◇◇

1 Allied forces or troops are armies from different countries who are fighting on the same side in a — ADJ: ADJ n war. *...the approaching Allied forces... They're backed by allied warplanes and tanks.*

2 **Allied** countries, troops, or political parties are united by a political or military agreement. *...forces from three allied nations. ...a think-tank allied to the right wing of the Democratic Party.* — ADJ: ADJ n, v-link ADJ *to* n

3 If one thing or group is **allied** to another, it is related to it because the two things have particular qualities or characteristics in common. *...lectures on subjects allied to health, beauty and fitness... Only now have doctors, and allied medical professionals, come to appreciate this.* — ADJ: v-link ADJ *to/with* n, ADJ n =associated

4 Something that is **allied** to another thing occurs with the other thing; a formal use. *He possessed a raw energy allied to a feeling of something special. ...a disastrous rise in interest rates allied with a stock market slump.* — ADJ: v-link ADJ *to/with* n =coupled

alligator /ælɪgeɪtəʳ/ **alligators** ◆◇◇◇◇

1 An **alligator** is a large reptile with short legs, a long tail and very powerful jaws. — N-COUNT

2 **Alligator** boots and bags are made from the skin of an alligator. *...alligator cowboy boots.* — ADJ

all-inclusive. **All-inclusive** is used to indicate that a price, especially the price of a holiday, includes all the charges and all the services offered. *An all-inclusive two-week holiday costs around £2880 per person.* — ADJ: usu ADJ n

alliteration /əlɪtəreɪʃən/ **alliterations.** **Alliteration** is the use in speech or writing of several words close together which all begin with the same letter or sound; a technical term. — N-VAR

alliterative /əlɪtərətɪv, AM -təreɪtɪv/. **Alliterative** means relating to or connected with alliteration. *Her campaign slogan, 'a president for the people', was pleasantly alliterative but empty.* — ADJ

allocate /æləkeɪt/ **allocates, allocating, allocated.** If one item or share of something **is allocated** to a particular person or for a particular purpose, it is given to that person or used for that purpose. *Tickets are limited and will be allocated to those who apply first... The 1985 federal budget allocated $7.3 billion for development programmes... Our plan is to allocate one member of staff to handle appointments.* — ◆◆◇◇◇ VERB =assign; *be* V-ed *to* n; V n *for/to* n; V n to-inf; Also V n n, V n

allocation /æləkeɪʃən/ **allocations** ◆◇◇◇◇

1 An **allocation** is an amount of something, especially money, that is given to a particular person or used for a particular purpose. *A State Department spokeswoman said that the aid allocation for Pakistan was still under review... During rationing we had a sugar allocation.* — N-COUNT

2 The **allocation** of something is the decision that it should be given to a particular person or used for a particular purpose. *His sons quarrelled bitterly over the allocation of family resources... Town planning and land allocation had to be coordinated.* — N-UNCOUNT: usu with supp

allot /əlɒt/ **allots, allotting, allotted.** If something **is allotted** to someone, it is given to them as their share. *The seats are allotted to the candidates who have won the most votes... We were allotted half an hour to address the committee.* — ◆◇◇◇◇ VB: usu passive =assign; *be* V-ed *to* n; *be* V-ed n

allotment /əlɒtmənt/ **allotments** ◆◇◇◇◇

1 In Britain, an **allotment** is a small area of land in a town which a person rents to grow vegetables on. — N-COUNT =plot

2 An **allotment** of something is a share or amount of it that is given to someone. *His meager allotment of gas had to be saved for emergencies.* — N-COUNT: oft N *of* n =allocation

all-out. You use **all-out** to describe actions that are carried out in a very energetic and determined way, using all the resources available. *He launched an all-out attack on his critics. ...an all-out effort to bring the fire under control.* — ◆◇◇◇◇ ADJ: ADJ n

▶ Also an adverb. *We will be going all out to ensure it doesn't happen again.* — ADV: ADV after v

allow /əlaʊ/ **allows, allowing, allowed** ◆◆◆◆◆

1 If someone **is allowed** to do something, it is all right for them to do it and they will not get into trouble. *The children are not allowed to watch violent TV programmes... The Government will allow them to advertise on radio and television... They will be allowed home... Smoking will not be allowed.* — VERB =permit, let ≠forbid; *be* V-ed to-inf; V n to-inf; *be* V-ed adv/prep; *be* V-ed; Also V n/-ing

2 If you **are allowed** something, you are given permission to have it or are given it. *Gifts like chocolates or flowers are allowed... He should be allowed the occasional treat.* — VERB =permit ≠forbid; *be* V-ed; *be* V-ed n

3 If you **allow** something to happen, you do not prevent it. *He won't allow himself to fail... If the soil is allowed to dry out the tree could die.* — VERB =permit ≠prevent; V n to-inf

4 If something **allows** something to happen, it gives the opportunity for it to happen. *The compromise will allow him to continue his free market reforms. ...an attempt to allow the Moslem majority a greater share of power... She said this would allow more effective planning.* — VERB =permit, let ≠prevent; V n to-inf; V n n; V n

5 If you **allow** a particular length of time or a particular amount of something for a particular purpose, you include it in your planning. *Please allow 28 days for delivery... Allow about 75ml (3fl oz) per six servings.* — VERB; V n *for* n; V n

6 If you **allow** that something is true, you admit or agree that it is true; a formal use. *Warren also allows that capitalist development may, in its early stages, result in increased social inequality.* — VERB =acknowledge; V that

7 Some people say **'Allow me'** as a polite way of offering to do something for someone; a formal expression. *Allow me to buy you a drink at the bar.* — PHRASES PRAGMATICS =permit me

8 Some people use **Allow me to...** as a way of introducing something that they want to say; a formal expression. *Allow me to introduce Dr Amberg.* — PRAGMATICS =permit me to

allow for. If you **allow for** certain problems or expenses, you include some extra time or money in your planning so that you can deal with them if they occur. *You have to allow for a certain amount of error... The Agency's budget simply did not allow for such a massive increase.* — PHRASAL VERB; V P n

allowable /əlaʊəbəl/

1 If people decide that something is **allowable**, they let it happen without trying to stop it. *It ought not to be allowable in law for any parent to remove a child from another parent without consent.* — ADJ =permissible

2 **Allowable** amounts are amounts of money that are deducted from your earnings before the amount of income tax that you have to pay is calculated; a technical use in taxation. *Her expenses were allowable deductions.* — ADJ

allowance /əlaʊəns/ **allowances** ◆◆◇◇◇

1 An **allowance** is money that is given to someone, usually on a regular basis, in order to help them pay for the things that they need. *...the severe disablement allowance of £26.20 per week... She gets an allowance for looking after Lillian.* — N-COUNT: usu with supp, oft N *of* amount

2 In American English, a child's **allowance** is money that is given to him or her every week or every month by his or her parents. The usual British term is **pocket money**. — N-COUNT: usu poss N

3 In Britain, your tax **allowance** is the amount of money that you are allowed to earn before you have to start paying income tax. *...those earning less than the basic tax allowance.* — N-COUNT: usu with supp

4 A particular type of **allowance** is an amount of something that you are allowed in particular circumstances. *Most of our flights have a baggage allowance of 44lbs per passenger.* — N-COUNT: with supp

5 If you **make allowances** for something, you take it into account in your decisions, plans, or actions. *They'll make allowances for the fact it's affecting our performance... The raw exam results make no allowance for social background.* — PHRASES V and N inflect, oft PHR *for* n

6 If you **make allowances** for someone, you accept behaviour which you would not normally accept or deal with them less severely than you would normally, because of a problem that they have. *He's tired so I'll make allowances for him.* — V inflects, oft PHR *for* n

alloy /ælɔɪ/ **alloys.** An **alloy** is a metal that is made by mixing two or more types of metal together. *Bronze is an alloy of copper and tin... The company produces titanium alloy.* — ◆◇◇◇◇ N-MASS

all-powerful. An **all-powerful** person or organization has the power to do anything they want. *...the all-powerful labour unions.* — ADJ

all-purpose. You use **all-purpose** to refer to things that have lots of different uses or can be used in lots of different situations. *You can sub-* — ADJ: ADJ n *stitute all-purpose flour if you cannot find pastry flour.*

all right; also spelled **alright.** ◆◆◆◆◇

1 If you say that someone or something is **all right**, you mean that you find them satisfactory or acceptable. *I consider you a good friend, and if it's all right with you, I'd like to keep it that way... 'How was this school you attended?'—'It was all right.'* ADJ: v-link ADJ =okay

2 If you say that something happens or goes **all right**, you mean that it happens in a satisfactory or acceptable manner. *Things have thankfully worked out all right... 'Can you walk all right?' the nurse asked him.* ADV: ADV after v =okay

3 If someone or something is **all right**, they are well or safe. *All she's worried about is whether he is all right... Are you feeling all right now?* ADJ: v-link ADJ =okay

4 If you say that something is true **all right** or something will happen **all right**, you are emphasizing that there is no doubt that it is true or that it will happen. *It's an isolated spot all right... That looks like a prescription number all right... I remember him, all right.* PHRASE: cl PHR PRAGMATICS

5 You say **'all right'** when you are agreeing to something. *'I think you should go now.'—'All right.'... 'I'll explain later.'—'All right then.'* CONVENTION PRAGMATICS =okay

6 You say **'all right?'** after you have given an instruction or explanation to someone when you are checking that they have understood what you have just said, or checking that they agree with or accept what you have just said. *Peter, you get half the fees. All right?... I'll see you tomorrow, all right?... 'We'll see what other prisoner officers think, all right?'* CONVENTION PRAGMATICS =okay

7 If someone in a position of authority says **'all right'**, and suggests talking about or doing something else, they are indicating that they want you to end one activity and start another. *All right, Bob. You can go now... All right, boys and girls, let's meet again next week same time and place.* CONVENTION PRAGMATICS

8 You say **'all right'** during a discussion to show that you understand something that someone has just said, and to introduce a statement that relates to it. *I said there was no room in my mother's house, and he said, 'All right, come to my studio and paint.'* CONVENTION PRAGMATICS =okay

9 You say **all right** before a statement or question to indicate that you are challenging or threatening someone. *All right, who are you and what are you doing in my office?... All right, let's stop playing games. Hand over the goods right now.* CONVENTION PRAGMATICS =okay, well

all-rounder, all-rounders. In British English, someone who is an **all-rounder** is good at a lot of different skills, academic subjects, or sports. *I class myself as an all-rounder and a team man at heart.* ◆◇◇◇◇ N-COUNT

all-seater An **all-seater** stadium has enough seats for all the spectators who are in it, rather than having some areas without seats where spectators stand to watch the match. ADJ: usu ADJ n

allspice /ɔːlspaɪs/. **Allspice** is a powder used as a spice in cooking, which is made from the berries of a tropical American tree. N-UNCOUNT =pimento

all-star. An **all-star** cast, performance, or game is one which contains only famous or extremely good performers or players. ◆◇◇◇◇ ADJ-GRADED: ADJ n

all-time. **All-time** is used when you are comparing all the things of a particular type that there have ever been. For example, if you say that something is the **all-time** best, you mean that it is the best thing of its type that there has ever been. *The president's popularity nationally is at an all-time low... Duane Eddy is John Peel's all-time favourite artist.* ◆◇◇◇◇ ADJ: ADJ n

allude /əluːd/ **alludes, alluding, alluded.** If you **allude** to something, you mention it in an indirect way; a formal word. *With friends, she sometimes alluded to a feeling that she herself was to blame for her son's predicament.* ◆◇◇◇◇ VERB =refer V *to*n

allure /æljʊəʳ, AM əlʊr/. The **allure** of something or someone is the pleasing or exciting quality that they have. *It's a game that has really lost its allure. ...the captivating allure of Isabelle Adjani.* ◆◇◇◇◇ N-UNCOUNT: usu with supp =attraction

alluring /æljʊərɪŋ, AM əlʊrɪŋ/. Someone or something that is **alluring** is very attractive. *Why are the contents of the next person's shopping trolley always more alluring than one's own? ...the most alluring city in South-East Asia.* ◆◇◇◇◇ ADJ-GRADED =interesting, fascinating

♦ **alluringly** *She turned and smiled alluringly at Douglas.* ADV-GRADED: ADV after v, ADV adj/adv

allusion /əluːʒᵊn/ **allusions.** An **allusion** is an indirect reference to someone or something. *This last point was understood to be an allusion to the long-standing hostility between the two leaders.* ◆◇◇◇◇ N-VAR: oft N *to*n

allusive /əluːsɪv/. **Allusive** speech, writing, or art is full of indirect references to people or things. *His new play, Arcadia, is as intricate, elaborate and allusive as anything he has yet written.* ADJ-GRADED

alluvial /əluːviəl/. **Alluvial** soils are soils which consist of earth and sand left behind on land which has been flooded or where a river once flowed; a technical term in geography. ADJ

ally, allies, allying, allied. The noun is pronounced /ælaɪ/. The verb is pronounced /əlaɪ/. ◆◆◆◆◇

1 A country's **ally** is another country that has an agreement to support it, especially in war. *Washington would not take such a step without its allies' approval... Cuba has traditionally been a staunch ally of the Soviet Union.* N-COUNT: with supp ≠enemy

2 **The Allies** were the armed forces that fought against Germany and Japan in the Second World War. *He reluctantly agreed to the Allies' wishes.* N-PLURAL

3 If you describe someone as your **ally**, you mean that they help and support you, especially when other people are opposing you. *He is a close ally of the Prime Minister... She will regret losing a close political ally.* N-COUNT: with supp =supporter, friend ≠enemy

4 If you **ally** yourself with someone or something, you give your support to them. *He will have no choice but to ally himself with the new movement.* VERB V pron-refl *with* n

5 See also **allied.**

alma mater /ælmə mɑːtəʳ, - meɪtəʳ/ **alma maters.** Your **alma mater** is the school or university which you went to; a formal expression. N-COUNT: usu sing, usu with poss

almanac /ɔːlmənæk/ **almanacs;** also spelled **almanack.**

1 An **almanac** is a book published every year which contains information about the movements of the planets, the phases of the moon and the tides, and the dates of important anniversaries. N-COUNT: oft in names

2 An **almanac** is a book published every year which contains information about events connected with a particular subject or activity, and facts and figures about the activity; an old-fashioned use. N-COUNT: oft in names

almanack /ɔːlmənæk/ **almanacks.** See **almanac.**

almighty /ɔːlmaɪti/ ◆◇◇◇◇

1 **The Almighty** is another name for God. You can also refer to **Almighty God**. *Adam sought guidance from the Almighty... Let us now confess our sins to Almighty God.* N-PROPER

2 People sometimes say **God Almighty** or **Christ Almighty** to express their surprise, anger, or horror; some people are offended by this use. EXCLAM PRAGMATICS

3 **Almighty** means very serious or great in extent; an informal use. *I had the most almighty row with the waitress... I heard an almighty bang.* ADJ-GRADED: ADJ n PRAGMATICS =enormous

almond /ɑːmənd/ **almonds** ◆◇◇◇◇

1 **Almonds** are pale oval nuts. They are often used in cooking. *...sponge cake flavoured with almonds.* N-VAR

• See also **sugared almond.**

2 An **almond** or an **almond tree**, is a tree on which almonds grow. The plural of **almond** is either 'almonds' or 'almond'. *On the left was a plantation of almond trees. ...groves of almond and cherry.* N-VAR

almoner /ɑːmənəʳ, AM ælm-/ **almoners.** In Britain, an **almoner** is a social worker who works in a hospital; an old-fashioned word. N-COUNT

almost /ɔːlmoust/. You use **almost** to indicate that something is not completely the case but is nearly the case. *The couple had been dating for almost three years... Storms have been hitting almost all of Britain recently... The effect is almost impossible to describe... He was almost as tall as Pete, but skinnier... The arrested man will almost certainly be kept at this police station... He contracted Spanish flu, which almost killed him.* ◆◆◆◆◆ ADV: ADV group, ADV before v =nearly

alms /ɑːmz/. **Alms** are gifts of money, clothes, or food to poor people; an old-fashioned word. *Alms were distributed to those in need.* N-PLURAL

almshouse /ɑːmzhaʊs/ **almshouses;** also spelled **alms-house**. **Almshouses** are houses which were built and run by charities to provide accommodation for poor or old people who could not afford to pay rent. N-COUNT

aloe vera /æloʊ vɪərə/. **Aloe vera** is a substance that contains a lot of vitamins and minerals and is often used in lotions, creams, and ointments. **Aloe vera** is also the name of the plant from which this substance is extracted. N-UNCOUNT: oft N n

aloft /əlɒft, AM əlɔːft/. Something that is **aloft** is in the air or off the ground; a literary word. *As they emerged from the court they held their arms aloft before crowds of cheering well-wishers... Four of the nine starting balloons were still aloft the next day.* ◆◇◇◇◇ ADV: ADV after v, be ADV

alone /əloʊn/ ◆◆◆◆◇

1 When you are **alone**, you are not with any other people. *There is nothing so fearful as to be alone in a combat situation... He was all alone in the middle of the hall, looking at no-one.* ADJ: v-link ADJ ▶ Also an adverb. *She has lived alone in this house for almost five years now... He was sitting alone at a table in a wine bar, smoking a big cigar.* ADV: ADV after v

2 If one person is **alone** with another person, or if two or more people are **alone**, they are together, without anyone else present. *I couldn't imagine why he would want to be alone with me... My brother and I were alone with Vincent.* ADJ: v-link ADJ, oft ADJ *with* n

3 If you say that you are **alone** or feel **alone**, you mean there is no-one with you, or no-one at all, who cares about you. *Never in her life had she felt so alone, so abandoned... He found himself alone in a hostile world.* ADJ-GRADED: v-link ADJ

4 You say that one person or thing **alone** does something when you are emphasizing that only one person or thing is involved. *You alone should determine what is right for you... They were convicted on forensic evidence alone.* ADV: n ADV PRAGMATICS

5 If you say that one person or thing **alone** is responsible for part of an amount, you are emphasizing the size of that part and the size of the total amount. *The BBC alone is sending 300 technicians, directors and commentators... Megastars like Jack Nicholson, who made £50 million from Batman alone, are unlikely to be affected.* ADV: n ADV PRAGMATICS

6 If you say that someone or something is **alone** in doing something, you mean that they are the only person or thing that does it, and so are different from other people or things. *Newcastle is far from alone. Colleges around the country have developed programmes of student support... Burns was not alone in thinking that the Prince was unduly preoccupied with the unfortunate and the underprivileged... Am I alone in recognising that these two statistics have quite different implications?* ADJ: v-link ADJ, oft ADJ *in* -ing/n =unique ▶ Also an adverb. *Alone among the major candidates, Gaviria expressed a determination to continue the campaign to defeat the drugs cartels... I alone was sane, I thought, in a world of crazy people.* ADV: ADV prep, n ADV

7 When someone does something **alone**, they do it without help from other people. *Bringing up a child alone should give you a sense of achievement... He was working alone and did not have an accomplice.* ADV: ADV after v

8 If you **go it alone**, you do something without any help from other people; an informal expression. *I missed the stimulation of working with others when I tried to go it alone.* PHRASE: V inflects ● **leave** someone or something **alone**: see **leave**. ● **let alone**: see **let**.

along /əlɒŋ, AM əlɔːŋ/ ◆◆◆◆◆

In addition to the uses shown below, **along** is used in phrasal verbs such as 'go along with', 'play along', and 'string along'.

1 If you move or look **along** something such as a road, you move or look towards one end of it. *Newman walked along the street alone... The young man led Mark Ryle along a corridor... I looked along the length of the building.* PREP

2 If something is situated **along** a road, river, or corridor, it is situated in it or beside it. *...enormous traffic jams all along the roads. ...houses built on piles along the river... Along each wall stretched green metal filing cabinets.* PREP

3 When someone or something moves **along**, they keep moving in a particular direction. *She skipped and danced along... He raised his voice a little, talking into the wind as they walked along... The wide road was blocked solid with traffic that moved along sluggishly.* ADV: ADV after v

4 If you say that something is going **along** in a particular way, you mean that it is progressing in that way. *...the negotiations which have been dragging along interminably... Everything was coming along fine after all... My life is going along nicely.* ADV: ADV after v

5 If you take someone or something **along** when you go somewhere, you take them with you. *This is open to women of all ages, so bring along your friends and colleagues... Some of the men would take their wives along... Wives will have to bring along their marriage certificate.* ADV: ADV after v

6 If someone or something is coming **along** or is sent **along**, they are coming or being sent to a particular place. *She invited everyone she knew to come along... He had the material tested and sent along the results.* ADV: ADV after v

7 You use **along with** to mention someone or something else that is also involved in an action or situation. *The baby's mother escaped from the fire along with two other children... There are 32 different kinds of chocolate on sale along with the bread and cakes.* PHR-PREP

8 If something has been true or been present **all along**, it has been true or been present throughout a period of time. *I've been fooling myself all along... I think she had been planning all along to leave Hungary.* PHRASE: PHR with cl, PHR after v

9 ● **along the way**: see **way**.

alongside /əlɒŋsaɪd, AM -lɔːŋ-/ ◆◆◆◇◇

1 If something is **alongside** something else, it is next to it. *He crossed the street and walked alongside Central Park... Much of the industry was located alongside rivers.* PREP ▶ Also an adverb. *He waited several minutes for a car to pull up alongside.* ADV: ADV after v

2 If you work **alongside** other people, you work in the same place and co-operate with them. *He had worked alongside Frank and Mark and they had become friends... Men aged 60 are fighting alongside young boys.* PREP =together with

3 If one thing exists or develops **alongside** another, the two things exist or develop together at the same time. *As she makes progress, her personal self-confidence will develop alongside her technique... Alongside the Job Creation Programme they launched a Work Experience Programme.* PREP =together with

aloof /əluːf/ ◆◇◇◇◇

1 If you say that someone is **aloof**, you are critical of them because they do not like to socialize and are not very friendly towards other people. *He seemed aloof and detached.* ADJ-GRADED: usu v-link ADJ PRAGMATICS =distant ♦ **aloofness** *He had an air of aloofness about him.* N-UNCOUNT

2 If someone stays **aloof** from something, they do not become involved with it; a formal use. *The Government is keeping aloof from the controversy... I will hold myself aloof from wrong and corruption.* ADJ-GRADED: v-link ADJ *from* n

aloud /əlaʊd/ ◆◇◇◇◇

1 When you say something, read, or laugh **aloud**, you speak or laugh so that other people can hear you. *When we were children, our father read aloud to us... 'The bastard,' she said aloud.* ADV: ADV after v =out loud ≠silently

2 If you **think aloud**, you express your thoughts as they occur to you, rather than thinking first and then speaking. *He really must be careful about thinking aloud. Who knew what he might say?* PHRASE: V inflects =out loud

alpaca /ælpækə/ **alpacas**

1 **Alpaca** is a type of soft wool. *He was wearing a light-grey alpaca suit.* N-UNCOUNT: oft N n

2 **Alpacas** are South American animals similar to llamas. Their hair is the source of alpaca wool. N-COUNT

alphabet /ælfəbet/ **alphabets.** An **alphabet** is a set of letters usually presented in a fixed order ◆◇◇◇◇ N-COUNT which is used for writing the words of a particular language or group of languages. *The modern Russian alphabet has 31 letters... By two and a half he knew the alphabet.*

alphabetical /ælfəbetɪkəl/. **Alphabetical** means arranged according to the normal order of the letters in the alphabet. *Their herbs and spices are arranged in alphabetical order on narrow open shelves.* ADJ: ADJ n ♦ **alphabetically** /ælfəbetɪkli/. *The catalog is organized alphabetically by label name.* ADV

alpine /ælpaɪn/. ◆◇◇◇◇ **Alpine** means existing in or relating to mountains, especially the ones in Switzerland. *...grassy, alpine meadows. ...picturesque alpine villages.* ADJ: usu ADJ n

alpines /ælpaɪnz/. **Alpines** are small flowering plants that grow high up on mountains and are sometimes grown in gardens. There are many different types of alpines. N-PLURAL

already /ɔːlredi/ ◆◆◆◆◆

1 You use **already** to focus on the fact that something has happened, or that something had happened before the moment you are referring to. Speakers of British English use **already** with a verb in a perfect tense, putting it after 'have', 'has', or 'had', or at the end of a clause. Some speakers of American English use **already** with the simple past tense of the verb instead of a perfect tense. *They had already voted for him at the first ballot... The group has already shed 10,000 jobs... She says she already told the neighbors not to come over for a couple of days... They've spent nearly a billion dollars on it already.* ADV: ADV before v, cl ADV

2 You use **already** to focus on the fact that a situation exists at this present moment or that it exists at an earlier time than expected. You use **already** after the verb 'be' or an auxiliary verb, or before a verb if there is no auxiliary. When you want add emphasis, you can put **already** at the beginning of a sentence. *The authorities believe those security measures are already paying off... He was already rich... He was already late for his appointment... She also tried to make a mockery of our already tarnished justice system... Already, he has a luxurious, secluded villa in the swish community of Formello.* ADV: ADV before v, ADV with group

alright /ɔːlraɪt/. See **all right**. ◆◇◇◇◇

Alsatian /ælseɪʃən/ **Alsatians.** An **Alsatian** is a large, usually fierce dog that is often used to guard buildings or by the police to help them find criminals; used in British English. N-COUNT =German shepherd

also /ɔːlsoʊ/ ◆◆◆◆◆

1 You can use **also** to give more information about a person or thing, or to add another relevant fact. *It is the work of Ivor Roberts-Jones, who also produced the statue of Churchill in Parliament Square... He is an asthmatic who was also anaemic three months ago... She has a reputation for brilliance. Also, she is gorgeous.* ADV: ADV before v, ADV with cl/group PRAGMATICS

2 You can use **also** to indicate that something you have just said or implied about one person or thing is true of someone or something else. *General Geichenko was a survivor. His father, also a top-ranking officer, had perished during the war... This rule has also been applied in the case of a purchase of used tires and tubes... Not only cancer, but also heart and lung disease are influenced by smoking.* ADV: ADV before v, ADV with group PRAGMATICS

also-ran, also-rans. If you describe someone as an **also-ran**, you mean that they have been or are likely to be unsuccessful in a contest; used showing disapproval. N-COUNT PRAGMATICS

altar /ɔːltəʳ/ **altars** ◆◇◇◇◇

1 An **altar** is a holy table in a church or temple. *...the high altar at Chichester Cathedral.* N-COUNT

2 If you say that someone or something **is sacrificed on the altar** or **sacrificed at the altar of** another thing, you mean they suffer because of that thing or are disadvantaged by it. *Napoleon's army was sacrificed on the altar of folly in the disastrous Russian campaign.* PHRASE: V inflects, oft PHR n

alter /ɔːltəʳ/ **alters, altering, altered.** ◆◆◆◇◇ If something **alters** or if you **alter** it, it changes. *Little had altered in the village... They have never altered their programmes by a single day.* V-ERG =change V V n

alteration /ɔːltəreɪʃən/ **alterations** ◆◇◇◇◇

1 An **alteration** is a change in or to something. *Making some simple alterations to your diet will make you feel fitter... The structural alterations made to the house were planned with Gail's help.* N-COUNT: usu N *to/in/of* n =change

2 The **alteration** of something is the process of changing it. *Her pink jacket and black skirt were still in the Ruffles boutique waiting for alteration.* N-UNCOUNT

altercation /ɔːltəʳkeɪʃən/ **altercations.** An **altercation** is a noisy argument or disagreement; a formal word. *I had a slight altercation with some people who objected to our filming.* N-COUNT: oft N *with/between* n =dispute

alter ego, alter egos

1 Your **alter ego** is the other side of your personality from the one which people normally see. N-COUNT: usu with supp

2 You can describe the character that an actor usually plays on television or in films as his or her **alter ego**. *Barry Humphries's alter ego Dame Edna has taken the US by storm.* N-COUNT: usu with supp

3 An **alter ego** is a very close and intimate friend whose character is often the opposite of your own. *She is, first and foremost, her husband's alter ego.* N-COUNT: usu poss N =counterpart

alternate, alternates, alternating, alternated. ◆◆◇◇◇ The verb is pronounced /ɔːltəʳneɪt/. The adjective is pronounced /ɔːltɜːʳnət/.

1 When you **alternate** two things, you keep using one then the other. When one thing **alternates** with another, the first regularly occurs after the other. *Her aggressive moods alternated with gentle or more co-operative states... The three acts will alternate as headliners throughout the tour... Now you just alternate layers of that mixture and eggplant. ...a German big band that alternated romantic American love songs with bouncy Bavarian numbers. ...an imaginative novel, with alternating chapters presenting each partner's point of view.* V-RECIP-ERG V *between/with* n pl-n V V pl-n V n *with* n V-ing ♦ **alternation** /ɔːltəʳneɪʃən/ **alternations** *The alternation of sun and snow continued for the rest of our holiday.* N-VAR

2 **Alternate** actions, events, or processes regularly occur after each other. *They were streaked with alternate bands of colour.* ADJ: ADJ n ♦ **alternately** *He could alternately bully and charm people... She became alternately angry and calm.* ADV: ADV with v, ADV adj

3 You use **alternate** to describe a plan, idea, or system which is different from the one already in operation and can be used instead of it. *His group was forced to turn back and take an alternate route. ...alternate forms of medical treatment.* ADJ: ADJ n =alternative

4 If something happens on **alternate** days, it happens on one day, then happens on every second day after that. In the same way, something can happen in **alternate** weeks, years, or other periods of time. *Lesley had agreed to Jim going skiing in alternate years.* ADJ: ADJ n =every other

alternating current, alternating currents. An **alternating current** is an electric current that continually changes direction as it flows. The abbreviation 'AC' is also used. N-VAR

alternative /ɔːltɜːʳnətɪv/ **alternatives** ◆◆◆◆◇

1 If one thing is an **alternative** to another, the first can be found, used, or done instead of the second. *New ways to treat arthritis may provide an alternative to painkillers.* N-COUNT: oft N *to* n =option

2 An **alternative** plan or offer is different from the one that you already have, and can be done or used instead. *There were alternative methods of travel available... They had a right to seek alternative employment.* ADJ: ADJ n =other

3 **Alternative** is used to describe something that is very different from the usual things of its kind, especially when it contrasts with traditional things that are available to you or traditional ways of doing something. *...alternative health care.* ADJ: ADJ n ≠conventional

alternatively /ɔːltɜːʳnətɪvli/. ◆◆◇◇◇ You use **alternatively** to introduce a suggestion or to mention something different to what has just been stated. *Allow about eight hours for the drive from Calais. Alternatively, you can fly to Brive.* ADV: ADV with cl PRAGMATICS =otherwise

alternator /ɔːltəʳneɪtəʳ/ **alternators.** An **alternator** is a device, used especially in a car, that cre- N-COUNT ates an electrical current that changes direction as it flows.

although /ɔːlðoʊ/ ◆◆◆◆◆

1 You use **although** to introduce a subordinate clause which contains a statement which contrasts with the statement in the main clause. *Although he is known to only a few, his reputation among them is very great... Although the shooting has stopped for now, the destruction left behind is enormous.* CONJ-SUBORD PRAGMATICS

2 You use **although** to introduce a subordinate clause which contains a statement which makes the main clause of the sentence seem surprising or unexpected. *Although I was only six, I can remember seeing it on TV... Although he was twice as old as us, he became the life and soul of the company.* CONJ-SUBORD PRAGMATICS =though

3 You use **although** to introduce a subordinate clause which gives some information that is relevant to the main clause but modifies the strength of that statement. *He was in love with her, although a man seldom puts that name to what he feels.* CONJ-SUBORD PRAGMATICS =though

4 You use **although** when admitting a fact about something which you regard as less important than a contrasting fact. *Although they're expensive, they last forever and never go out of style... Although not ideal, this attitude is not entirely destructive.* CONJ-SUBORD PRAGMATICS

altimeter /æltɪmiːtəʳ, AM æltɪmɪtəʳ/ **altimeters.** An **altimeter** is an instrument in an aircraft that shows the height of the aircraft above the ground. N-COUNT

altitude /æltɪtjuːd, AM -tuːd/ **altitudes.** If something is at a particular **altitude**, it is at that height above sea level. *The aircraft had reached its cruising altitude of about 39,000 feet... The following day I ran my first race at high altitude.* ◆◇◇◇◇ N-VAR: oft N *of* n

alto /æltoʊ/ **altos**

1 An **alto** is a woman who has a low singing voice. *...the altos, the tenors, the sopranos. ...the famous alto aria 'Have Mercy Lord on me'.* N-COUNT: oft N n =contralto

2 An **alto** or **male alto** is a man who has the highest male singing voice. *In the recording I have today, it is sung by a male alto.* N-COUNT =counter-tenor

3 An **alto** musical instrument has a range of notes of medium pitch. *...the alto saxophone.* ADJ: ADJ n

altogether /ɔːltəgeðəʳ/ ◆◆◆◇◇

1 You use **altogether** to emphasize that something has stopped, been done, or finished completely. *When Artie stopped calling altogether, Julie found a new man... His tour may have to be cancelled altogether... Mr Kanemaru announced he was leaving politics altogether.* ADV: ADV after v PRAGMATICS

2 You use **altogether** in front of an adjective or adverb to emphasize that someone or something has more of a quality than, or is different from, other people or things. *The choice of language is altogether different... Today's celebrations have been altogether more sedate... This wine has an altogether stronger, more pronounced flavour than their other white wines.* ADV: ADV adj/adv PRAGMATICS

3 You use **altogether** to modify a negative statement and make it less forceful. *We were not altogether sure that the comet would miss the Earth... The fashion business, he claims, not altogether convincingly, is more real than the film business... 'I'm not altogether a fool,' she said gruffly.* ADV: with neg, ADV group PRAGMATICS

4 You can use **altogether** to introduce a summary or evaluation of what you have been saying. *Altogether, it was a delightful town garden, peaceful and secluded.* ADV: ADV with cl PRAGMATICS

5 If several amounts add up to a particular amount **altogether**, that amount is their total. *Britain has a dozen warships in the area, with a total of five thousand military personnel altogether... Altogether seven inmates escaped by scaling a wall and climbing down scaffolding.* ADV: ADV with amount =in total

altruism /æltruɪzəm/. **Altruism** is unselfish concern for other people's happiness and welfare. N-UNCOUNT

altruistic /æltruɪstɪk/. If your behaviour or motives are **altruistic**, you show concern for the happiness and welfare of other people rather than for yourself. *...motives and ambitions that are not entirely altruistic.* ADJ-GRADED =selfless ≠selfish

aluminium /æluːmɪniəm/. In British English, **aluminium** is a lightweight metal used, for example, for making cooking equipment and aircraft parts. The usual American word is **aluminum**. *...aluminium cans.* ◆◆◇◇◇ N-UNCOUNT

aluminum /əluːmɪnəm/. See **aluminium**.

alumnus /əlʌmnəs/ **alumni** /əlʌmnaɪ/. In American English, the **alumni** of a school, college, or university are the people who used to be students there. ◆◇◇◇◇ N-COUNT

always /ɔːlweɪz/ ◆◆◆◆◆

1 If you **always** do something, you do it whenever a particular situation arises. If you **always** did something, you did it whenever a particular situation arose. *Whenever I get into a relationship, I always fall madly in love... She's always late for everything... We've always done it this way. In fact, we've never done it any other way... Always lock your garage.* ADV: ADV before v ≠never

2 If something is **always** the case, was **always** the case, or will **always** be the case, it is, was, or will be the case all the time, continuously. *We will always remember his generous hospitality... He has always been the family solicitor... He was always cheerful.* ADV: ADV before v, ADV group ≠never

3 If you say that something is **always** happening, especially something which annoys you, you mean that it happens repeatedly. *She was always moving things around.* ADV: ADV before v-cont =forever

4 You use **always** in expressions such as **can always** or **could always** when you are making suggestions or suggesting an alternative approach or method. *If you can't find any decent apples, you can always try growing them yourself... 'What are you going to do?'—'I don't know. I could always go back in the Navy or something.'* ADV: *can/could* ADV inf PRAGMATICS

5 You can say that someone **always** was, for example, awkward or lucky to indicate that you are not surprised about what they are doing or have just done. *She's going to be fine. She always was pretty strong... You always were a good friend.* ADV: ADV before v PRAGMATICS

Alzheimer's Disease /æltshaɪməʳz dɪsiːz/. **Alzheimer's Disease** is a condition in which a person's brain and body gradually stop working properly. ◆◇◇◇◇ N-UNCOUNT

am /əm, STRONG æm/. **Am** is the first person singular of the present tense of **be. Am** is often contracted to **'m**. The negative of am is **am not**, which in questions and tags is usually abbreviated to **aren't**.

Am. **Am.** is a written abbreviation for **American**.

a.m. /eɪ em/. **a.m.** is used after a number to show that you are referring to a particular time between midnight and noon. *The program starts at 9 a.m.* ◆◆◇◇◇

amalgam /əmælgəm/ **amalgams** ◆◇◇◇◇

1 Something that is an **amalgam** of two or more things is a mixture of them. *Marlene Dietrich was a complex amalgam of a great number of women.* N-COUNT: oft N *of* pl-n =mixture

2 **Amalgam** is a mixture of mercury and another metal, usually silver, that is used in dentistry to make fillings. *...amalgam fillings.* N-UNCOUNT: oft N n

amalgamate /əmælgəmeɪt/ **amalgamates, amalgamating, amalgamated.** When two or more things, especially organizations, **amalgamate** or **are amalgamated**, they become one large thing. *The firm has amalgamated with an American company... The chemical companies had amalgamated into a vast conglomerate... The Visitors' Centre amalgamates the traditions of the Old World with the technology of the New.* ◆◇◇◇◇ V-RECIP-ERG =merge V *with/into* n pl-n V V n *with/into* n Also V pl-n

♦ **amalgamation** /əmælgəmeɪʃən/ **amalgamations** *Athletics South Africa was formed by an amalgamation of two organisations.* N-VAR: oft N *of* n =merger

amass /əmæs/ **amasses, amassing, amassed.** If you **amass** something such as money or information, you gradually get a lot of it. *It was better not to enquire too closely into how he had amassed his fortune.* ◆◇◇◇◇ VERB =accumulate, accrue V n

amateur /æmətəʳ, AM -tʃɜːr/ **amateurs** ◆◆◆◇◇

1 An **amateur** is someone who does something as a hobby and not as a job. *Jerry is an amateur who* N-COUNT: oft N n ≠professional

dances because he feels like it... Taylor began his playing career as an amateur goalkeeper.
2 Amateur sports or activities are done by people as a hobby and not as a job. *She'd particularly like to join the local amateur dramatics society... At college he studied English and did amateur boxing.* [ADJ: ADJ n]

amateurish /æmətərɪʃ, AM -tʃɜːrɪʃ/. If you describe something as **amateurish**, you think that it is not skilfully made or done. *We have to develop a less amateurish approach to our organisations... The rock press can be very childish, sloppy and amateurish.* [ADJ-GRADED; PRAGMATICS]

amateurism /æmətərɪzəm, AM -tʃɜːr-/. **Amateurism** is the belief that people should take part in sports and other activities as a hobby, for pleasure, rather than as a job, for money. *He is a staunch supporter of amateurism.* [N-UNCOUNT; ≠professionalism]

amaze /əmeɪz/ **amazes, amazing, amazed.** If something **amazes** you, it surprises you very much. *He amazed us by his knowledge of Welsh history... The Riverside Restaurant promises a variety of food that never ceases to amaze!* [◆◆◇◇◇; VERB; =astonish; V n; V; Also *it* V n that/wh]
♦ **amazed** *He said most of the cast was amazed by the play's success... I was amazed to learn she was still writing her stories... She is amazed that people still risk travelling without insurance.* [ADJ-GRADED: usu v-link ADJ; =astonished]

amazement /əmeɪzmənt/. **Amazement** is the feeling you have when something surprises you very much. *I stared at her in amazement.* [◆◇◇◇◇; N-UNCOUNT: oft *in* N; =astonishment]

amazing /əmeɪzɪŋ/. You say that something is **amazing** when it is very surprising and makes you feel pleasure, approval, or wonder. *It's amazing what we can remember with a little prompting... This movie has some of the most amazing stunts you're ever likely to see.* [◆◆◆◇◇; ADJ-GRADED: oft *it* v-link ADJ wh/that; =astonishing]
♦ **amazingly** *She was an amazingly good cook.* [ADV-GRADED]

Amazon /æməzən/ **Amazons**
1 In Greek mythology, the **Amazons** were a tribe of women warriors. [N-COUNT: usu pl]
2 A tall, strong, assertive woman is sometimes referred to as an **Amazon**. *In China Grace Thompson observed the great variety of loads that were carried by 'slim, erect but muscular Amazons'.* [N-COUNT]

Amazonian /æməzoʊniən/
1 A tall, strong woman can be referred to as **Amazonian**. *The Amazonian Geena Davis gives a regal performance as a great baseball player.* [ADJ: usu ADJ n]
2 An **Amazonian** woman or thing belongs to or is connected with a tribe of women warriors in Greek mythology. *...Amazonian queens. ...Amazonian mythology.* [ADJ: usu ADJ n]

ambassador /æmbæsədəʳ/ **ambassadors.** An **ambassador** is an important official who lives in a foreign country and represents his or her own country's interests there. *...the German ambassador to Poland.* [◆◆◆◇◇; N-COUNT: oft adj N, N *to* n]

ambassadorial /æmbæsədɔːriəl/. **Ambassadorial** means belonging or relating to an ambassador. *His three ambassadorial posts were in Djakarta, Rekyjavik and Dublin.* [ADJ: ADJ n]

amber /æmbəʳ/
1 **Amber** is a hard yellowish-brown substance used for making jewellery. *...an amber choker with matching earrings. ...a Victorian cigar holder of amber and sterling silver.* [◆◇◇◇◇; N-UNCOUNT: usu N n]
2 **Amber** is used to describe things that are yellowish-brown in colour. *A burst of sunshine sent a beam of amber light through the window... He shook the amber bottle vigorously.* [COLOUR: usu COLOUR n]

ambergris /æmbəʳgriːs/. **Ambergris** is a waxy substance produced by sperm whales. It is used to make some perfumes. *...a sweet fragrance which suggests a blend of ambergris and lavender.* [N-UNCOUNT]

ambiance /æmbiəns/. See **ambience**.

ambidextrous /æmbidekstrəs/. Someone who is **ambidextrous** can use both their right hand and their left hand equally skilfully. [ADJ: usu v-link ADJ]

ambience /æmbiəns/; also spelled **ambiance**. The **ambience** of a place is the character and atmosphere that it seems to have; a literary word. *The overall ambience of the room is cosy.* [◆◇◇◇◇; N-SING: also no det, oft N *of* n; =atmosphere]

ambient /æmbiənt/
1 The **ambient** temperature is the temperature of the air above the ground in a particular place; a technical use. [ADJ: ADJ n]
2 **Ambient** sound or light is the sound or light which is all around you; a formal use. *...ambient sounds of children in the background.* [ADJ-GRADED: usu ADJ n]

ambiguity /æmbɪgjuːɪti/ **ambiguities** [◆◇◇◇◇]
1 If you say that there is **ambiguity** in something, you mean that it is unclear or confusing, or it can be understood in more than one way. *Mr Yeltsin is keen that there is no ambiguity over the issue of who owns a republic's natural resources. ...the ambiguities of language.* [N-VAR; =vagueness; ≠clarity]
2 If you say that there is an **ambiguity** in a situation or in someone's character, you mean that it contains several different qualities or attitudes which do not fit well together. *The author's style suggests a certain ambiguity in his moral view.* [N-VAR; =contradiction]

ambiguous /æmbɪgjuəs/ [◆◇◇◇◇]
1 If you describe something as **ambiguous**, you mean that it is unclear or confusing because it can be understood in more than one way. *This agreement is very ambiguous and open to various interpretations... The Foreign Secretary's remarks clarify an ambiguous statement issued earlier this week.* [ADJ-GRADED; =vague; ≠obvious, clear]
♦ **ambiguously** *Zaire's national conference on democracy ended ambiguously.* [ADV-GRADED: usu ADV with v, also ADV adj]
2 If you describe something as **ambiguous**, you mean that it contains several different ideas or attitudes that do not fit well together. *Students have ambiguous feelings about their role in the world.* [ADJ-GRADED]

ambit /æmbɪt/. The **ambit** of something is its range or extent; a formal word. *Her case falls within the ambit of moral law.* [N-SING: usu with poss; =scope]

ambition /æmbɪʃᵊn/ **ambitions** [◆◆◆◇◇]
1 If you have an **ambition** to do or achieve something, you want very much to do it or achieve it. *His ambition is to sail round the world... He harboured ambitions of becoming a Tory MP.* [N-COUNT: oft N to-inf; =goal]
2 **Ambition** is the desire to be successful, rich, or powerful. *Even when I was young I never had any ambition. ...a mixture of ambition and ruthlessness.* [N-UNCOUNT]

ambitious /æmbɪʃəs/ [◆◆◇◇◇]
1 Someone who is **ambitious** has a strong desire to be successful, rich, or powerful. *Chris is so ambitious, so determined to do it all... He's a very ambitious lad and he wants to play at the highest level.* [ADJ-GRADED; ≠unambitious]
2 An **ambitious** idea or plan is on a large scale and needs a lot of work to be carried out successfully. *The ambitious project was completed in only nine months... Their goal was extraordinarily ambitious.* [ADJ-GRADED]
♦ **ambitiously** *Its trade and industrial policies should be used more ambitiously... He is working on his life story, ambitiously planned as a 50-volume work.* [ADV-GRADED: ADV with v, ADV adj]

ambivalent /æmbɪvələnt/. If you say that someone is **ambivalent** about something, they seem to be uncertain whether they really want it, or whether they really approve of it. *She remained ambivalent about her marriage... He maintained an ambivalent attitude to the Church throughout his long life.* [◆◇◇◇◇; ADJ-GRADED; =unsure]
♦ **ambivalence** /æmbɪvələns/ **ambivalences** *I've never lied about my feelings, including my ambivalence about getting married again.* [N-VAR: usu with supp, oft N *about/towards* n]
♦ **ambivalently** *They ambivalently condemn both the disorders and the jury verdict that touched off the disorders.* [ADV-GRADED: ADV with v]

amble /æmbᵊl/ **ambles, ambling, ambled.** When you **amble**, you walk slowly and in a relaxed manner. *We ambled along in front of the houses... Slowly they ambled back to the car.* [VERB; =stroll; V adv/prep]
► Also a noun. *...an afternoon's amble around the oldest parts of Paris.* [N-SING]

ambrosia /æmbroʊziə, AM -ʒiə/. In Greek mythology, **ambrosia** is the food of the gods. [N-UNCOUNT]

ambulance /æmbjʊləns/ **ambulances.** An **ambulance** is a vehicle for taking people to and from hospital. *His wife called for an ambulance when he collapsed... He was taken to hospital by ambulance.* [◆◆◇◇◇; N-COUNT: also *by* N]

ambulanceman /æmbjʊlənsmæn/ **ambulancemen.** An **ambulanceman** is a person who drives an ambulance or takes care of sick people in an ambulance on the way to hospital. *By the time ambulancemen arrived he was unconscious.*
N-COUNT

ambush /æmbʊʃ/ **ambushes, ambushing, ambushed** ◆◆◇◇◇

1 If a group of people **ambush** their enemies, they attack them after hiding and waiting for them. *The Guatemalan army says rebels ambushed and killed 10 patrolmen.*
VERB =waylay V n

2 An **ambush** is an attack on someone by people who have been hiding and waiting for them. *A policeman has been shot dead in an ambush in County Armagh.*
N-VAR

3 If someone is lying **in ambush**, they are hiding and waiting for someone, usually to attack them. *The gunmen, lying in ambush, opened fire, killing the driver.*
PHRASE: PHR after v

ameliorate /əmiːliəreɪt/ **ameliorates, ameliorating, ameliorated.** If someone or something **ameliorates** a situation, they make it better or easier in some way; a formal word. *Nothing can be done to ameliorate the situation... He expected me to do something to ameliorate his depression.*
VERB =alleviate ≠exacerbate V n
♦ **amelioration** /əmiːliəreɪʃən/ *...a demand for amelioration of conditions.*
N-UNCOUNT: usu N *of* n

amen /ɑːmen, eɪ-/. **Amen** is said by Christians at the end of a prayer. *In the name of the Father and of the Son and of the Holy Ghost, Amen.*
CONVENTION

amenable /əmiːnəbəl/. If you are **amenable** to something, you are willing to do it or accept it. *The Jordanian leader seemed amenable to attending a conference... I never had a long-term relationship as I wasn't good enough, or interesting or amenable enough.*
ADJ-GRADED: usu v-link ADJ, oft ADJ *to* n/-ing =agreeable

amend /əmend/ **amends, amending, amended** ◆◆◇◇◇

1 If you **amend** something that has been written such as a law, or something that is said, you change it in order to improve it or make it more accurate. *Kaunda agreed to amend the constitution and allow multi-party elections... 'You must admit that the man has got charm,' said Nicolson. 'Glamour,' amended Wells. ...the amended version of the Act.*
VERB =revise V n V with quote V-ed

2 If you **make amends** when you have harmed someone, you show that you are sorry by doing something to please them. *He wanted to make amends for causing their marriage to fail.*
PHRASE: V inflects, oft PHR *for* n/-ing =atone

amendment /əmendmənt/ **amendments** ◆◆◆◇◇

1 An **amendment** is a section that is added to a law or rule in order to change it. *...an amendment to the defense bill. ...a constitutional amendment... Parliament gained certain rights of amendment.*
N-VAR

2 An **amendment** is a change or correction to a piece of writing. *I showed him the script and he made loads of amendments and corrections.*
N-COUNT =improvement

amenity /əmiːnɪti, AM -men-/ **amenities.** **Amenities** are things such as shopping centres or sports facilities that are provided for people's convenience, enjoyment, or comfort. *The hotel amenities include health clubs, conference facilities, and banqueting rooms.*
◆◇◇◇◇ N-COUNT: usu pl =facilities

America /əmerɪkə/ **Americas** ◆◆◆◆◇

1 **America** is the continent containing North, South, and Central America. In former times this continent was also known as **the Americas**.
N-PROPER

2 The United States of America is often referred to as **America**.
N-PROPER

American /əmerɪkən/ **Americans.** An **American** person or thing belongs to or comes from the United States of America. *...the American Ambassador at the United Nations... It was very pleasant to sit in the summer in open air theaters and see American movies.* ● See also **Latin American.** ► An **American** is someone who is American. *The 1990 Nobel Prize for medicine was won by two Americans.*
◆◆◆◆◇ ADJ; N-COUNT

Americana /əmerɪkɑːnə/. Objects that come from or relate to America are referred to as **Americana**, especially when they are in a collection. *...1950s Americana.*
N-UNCOUNT

American football, American footballs ◆◇◇◇◇

1 **American football** is a game similar to rugby that is played between two teams of eleven players. *...the World League of American Football.*
N-UNCOUNT

2 An **American football** is an oval shaped ball used for playing American football; used in British English.
N-COUNT

American Indian, American Indians. American Indian people or things belong to or come from one of the native peoples of America. *There's a lot of similarity between American Indian languages.* ► An **American Indian** is someone who belongs to or comes from one of the native peoples of America.
ADJ: usu ADJ n; N-COUNT

Americanism /əmerɪkənɪzəm/ **Americanisms**

1 An **Americanism** is an expression that is typical of people living in the United States of America. *He was, to adopt an Americanism 'an empty suit'.*
N-COUNT

2 **Americanism** is the quality or state of being American. *I liked the film's Americanism. ...his deep-seated Americanism.*
N-UNCOUNT: oft with poss

Americanize /əmerɪkənaɪz/ **Americanizes, Americanizing, Americanized;** also spelled **Americanise** in British English. If someone **Americanizes** someone or something, they make them follow American customs and practice. *He hated the climate, the food, and the people, especially those who tried to Americanize him.*
VERB V n
♦ **americanization** /əmerɪkənaɪzeɪʃən/ **americanizations** *...the americanization of French culture.*
N-VAR

Amerindian /æmərɪndiən/ **Amerindians. Amerindian** means the same as **American Indian.**

amethyst /æməθɪst/ **amethysts**

1 **Amethysts** are clear purple stones, sometimes used to make jewellery. *The necklace consisted of amethysts set in gold. ...rows of amethyst beads... Amethyst was believed by the Greeks to protect a person from drunkenness.*
N-VAR

2 **Amethyst** is used to describe things that are pale purple in colour. *She had watched the colours changing from green to amethyst. ...amethyst glass.*
COLOUR

amiability /eɪmiəbɪlɪti/. **Amiability** is the quality of being friendly and pleasant; used in written English. *I found his amiability charming.*
N-UNCOUNT =friendliness

amiable /eɪmiəbəl/. Someone who is **amiable** is friendly and pleasant to be with; used in written English. *She had been surprised at how amiable and polite he had seemed.* ♦ **amiably** *We chatted amiably about old friends.*
◆◇◇◇◇ ADJ-GRADED =friendly; ADV-GRADED: ADV with v

amicable /æmɪkəbəl/. When people have an **amicable** relationship, they are pleasant to each other and solve their problems without quarrelling. *The meeting ended on reasonably amicable terms... Our discussions were amicable and productive.* ♦ **amicably** /æmɪkəbli/ *He hoped the dispute could be settled amicably.*
◆◇◇◇◇ ADJ-GRADED =friendly ≠hostile; ADV-GRADED: ADV with v

amid /əmɪd/. The form **amidst** is also used, but is more literary. ◆◆◆◇◇

1 If something happens **amid** noises or events of some kind, it happens while the other things are happening. *A senior leader cancelled a trip to Britain yesterday amid growing signs of a possible political crisis... Children were changing classrooms amid laughter and shouts.*
PREP =amidst

2 If something is **amid** other things, it is surrounded by them; a literary use. *...a tiny bungalow amid clusters of trees.*
PREP

amidships /əmɪdʃɪps/. **Amidships** means halfway along the length of a ship. *We'd hit a fishing boat amidships, cutting it in half.*
ADV: ADV after v

amidst /əmɪdst/. **Amidst** means the same as **amid**, but is a more literary word.
◆◇◇◇◇ PREP =amid

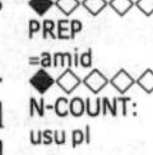

amino acid /əmiːnəʊ æsɪd/ **amino acids. Amino acids** are substances containing nitrogen and hydrogen which are found in proteins, and which occur naturally in the body; a technical term in chemistry.
◆◇◇◇◇ N-COUNT: usu pl

Amir /eɪmɪər/ **Amirs. Amir** means the same as **Emir**.

amiss /əmɪs/

1 If you say that something is **amiss**, you mean there is something wrong. *Their instincts warned them something was amiss... Something is radically amiss in our health care system.*
ADJ GRADED: v-link ADJ

2 If you say that something **would not go amiss** or **would not come amiss**, you mean that it would be pleasant and useful. *A bit of charm and humour would not go amiss... The cracks are showing in the walls and a lick of paint would not come amiss.*
PHRASE: V inflects

amity /æmɪti/. **Amity** is peaceful, friendly relations between people or countries; a formal word. *Over the past two decades the two countries have lived in amity with each other.*
N-UNCOUNT =peace ≠enmity

ammo /æmoʊ/. **Ammo** is ammunition for guns and other weapons; an informal word.
N-UNCOUNT

ammonia /əmoʊniə/. **Ammonia** is a colourless liquid or gas with a strong, sharp smell. It is used in making household cleaning substances.
◆◇◇◇◇ N-UNCOUNT

ammunition /æmjʊnɪʃᵊn/
◆◆◇◇◇

1 **Ammunition** is bullets and rockets that are made to be fired from guns. *He had only seven rounds of ammunition for the revolver.*
N-UNCOUNT

2 You can describe information that you can use against someone in an argument or discussion as **ammunition**. *The improved trade figures have given the government fresh ammunition.*
N-UNCOUNT

amnesia /æmniːziə, -ʒə/. If someone is suffering from **amnesia**, they have lost their memory. *People suffering from amnesia don't forget their general knowledge of objects.*
N-UNCOUNT

amnesiac /æmniːziæk/ **amnesiacs.** Someone who is **amnesiac** has lost their memory. *Rachel had been found, wandering, apparently amnesiac and shocked.* ► An **amnesiac** is someone who is amnesiac. *Even profound amnesiacs can usually recall how to perform daily activities.*
ADJ / N-COUNT

amnesty /æmnɪsti/ **amnesties**
◆◆◇◇◇

1 An **amnesty** is an official pardon granted to a group of prisoners by the state. *Activists who were involved in crimes of violence will not automatically be granted amnesty.*
N-VAR =pardon

2 An **amnesty** is a period of time during which people can confess to a crime or give up weapons without being punished. *The government has announced an immediate amnesty for rebel fighters.*
N-COUNT

amniocentesis /æmnioʊsentiːsɪs/. When a pregnant woman has an **amniocentesis**, fluid is removed from her womb in order to check that her unborn baby is healthy.
N-UNCOUNT

amoeba /əmiːbə/ **amoebae** /əmiːbi/ or **amoebas.** An **amoeba** is the smallest kind of living creature. Amoebae consist of only one cell, and are found in water or soil.
N-COUNT

amok /əmʌk, əmɒk/. If a person, animal, or machine **runs amok**, they behave in a violent and uncontrolled way. *A soldier was arrested after running amok with a vehicle through Berlin.*
PHRASE: V inflects

among /əmʌŋ/. The form **amongst** is also used, but is more literary.
◆◆◆◆◆

1 Someone or something that is situated or moving **among** a group of things or people is surrounded by them. *...youths in their late teens sitting among adults... They walked among the crowds in Red Square. ...a garden of semi-tropical vegetation set among pools and waterfalls.*
PREP =amidst

2 If you are **among** people of a particular kind, you are with them and having contact with them. *Things weren't so bad, after all. I was among friends again... I was brought up among people who read and wrote a lot.*
PREP

3 If someone or something is **among** a group, they are a member of that group and share its characteristics. *A fifteen year old girl was among the injured... Also among the speakers was the new American ambassador to Moscow.*
PREP

4 If you want to focus on something that is happening within a particular group of people, you can say that it is happening **among** that group. *Homicide is the leading cause of death among black men. ...discussions among the world leaders who are in Paris for the European security conference.*
PREP

5 If something happens **among** a group of people, it happens within the whole of that group or between the members of that group. *The calls for reform come as intense debate continues among the leadership over the next five-year economic plan... Much of the talk of political disaster had been among intellectuals.*
PREP

6 If something such as a feeling, opinion, or situation exists **among** a group of people, most of them have it or experience it. *There was some concern among book and magazine retailers after last Wednesday's news... The resort is popular among ski enthusiasts.*
PREP

7 You use **among** before a noun to mention a group when talking about a smaller group within it. *Among those 18 and over, 510,000 benefit claimants were not unemployed... Among the varieties available, my preference stays with the old and lovely pink-flowered variety, 'Apple Blossom'.*
PREP

8 If something applies to a particular person or thing **among** others, it also applies to other people or things. *...a news conference attended among others by our foreign affairs correspondent... She knew many theatrical personalities and had worked, among others, with George Bernard Shaw.*
PREP

9 If something is shared **among** a number of people, some of it is given to all of them. *Most of the furniture was left to the neighbours or distributed among friends... She tried to ensure her affection was equally shared among all three children.*
PREP

10 If people talk, fight, or agree **among** themselves, they do it together, without involving anyone else. *European farm ministers disagree among themselves... The directors have been arguing among themselves.*
PREP: PREP pron-refl =amongst

amongst /əmʌŋst/. **Amongst** means the same as **among**, but is a more literary word.
◆◆◇◇◇ PREP =among

amoral /eɪmɒrəl, AM -mɔːr-/. An **amoral** person does not care whether people consider that what they do is right or wrong; used showing disapproval. *...a society threatened by amoral and often random violence... The film was violent and amoral.* ♦ **amorality** /eɪməræləti/ *Anita envied her sister's amorality and contempt for public opinion.*
ADJ-GRADED PRAGMATICS ≠moral / N-UNCOUNT ≠morality

amorous /æmərəs/. If you describe someone's feelings or actions as **amorous**, you mean that they involve sexual desire. *The object of his amorous intentions is Martina.*
ADJ-GRADED: usu ADJ n =passionate

amorphous /əmɔːʳfəs/. Something that is **amorphous** has no clear shape or structure. *A dark, strangely amorphous shadow filled the room. ...the amorphous mass of the unemployed.*
ADJ-GRADED: usu ADJ n =shapeless

amortize /əmɔːʳtaɪz, AM æmər-/ **amortizes, amortizing, amortized;** also spelled **amortise** in British English. If you **amortize** a debt, you pay it back in regular payments; a technical term in economics. *He may elect to amortize the premium over the life of the bond.*
VERB =pay off / V n over n Also V n

amount /əmaʊnt/ **amounts, amounting, amounted**
◆◆◆◆◇

1 The **amount** of something is how much there is, or how much you have, need, or get. *He needs that amount of money to survive... I still do a certain amount of work for them... Postal money orders are available in amounts up to $700.*
N-VAR: usu N of n

2 If something **amounts** to a particular total, all the parts of it add up to that total. *Consumer spending on sports-related items amounted to £9.75 billion.*
VERB / V to amount

3 If you say that there is **any amount of** something, there is a lot of it. If you say that there are **any amount of** people or things, there are many people or things. *I'm able to lay my hands on any amount of cash at a minute's notice... There are any amount of clubs you could join.*
PHRASE

amount to. If you say that one thing **amounts to** something else, you consider the first thing to be the same as the second thing. *The banks have what amounts to a monopoly. ...a schoolboy comedy, which amounted to little more than slapstick.*
PHRASAL VERB LINK PRAGMATICS / V P n

amour /æmʊəʳ/ **amours.** An **amour** is a love affair, especially one which is kept secret; an old-fashioned or literary word. N-COUNT

amp /æmp/ **amps**

1 An **amp** is the same as an **ampère**. *Use a 3 amp fuse for equipment up to 720 watts.* N-COUNT

2 An **amp** is the same as an **amplifier**; an informal use. N-COUNT

3 An **amp** is the same as an **ampoule**. N-COUNT

ampère /æmpeəʳ, AM -pɪəʳ/ **ampères;** also spelled **ampere**. An **ampère** is a unit which is used for measuring electric current. The abbreviation **amp** is also used. N-COUNT

amphetamine /æmfetəmiːn/ **amphetamines.** Amphetamine is a drug which increases people's energy, makes them excited, and reduces their appetite. ◆◇◇◇◇ N-MASS =speed

amphibian /æmfɪbiən/ **amphibians**

1 **Amphibians** are animals such as frogs and toads that can live both on land and in water. N-COUNT

2 An **amphibian** is a vehicle which is able to move on both land and water, or an aeroplane which can land on both land and water. N-COUNT

amphibious /æmfɪbiəs/ ◆◇◇◇◇

1 In an **amphibious** military operation, army and navy forces attack a place from the sea. *A third brigade is at sea, ready for an amphibious assault.* ADJ: ADJ n

2 An **amphibious** vehicle is able to move on both land and water. *...an amphibious landing craft which can carry helicopters and up to 2,000 troops.* ADJ: ADJ n

3 **Amphibious** animals are animals such as frogs and toads that can live both on land and in water. ADJ

amphitheatre /æmfiθɪətəʳ/ **amphitheatres;** spelled **amphitheater** in American English.

1 An **amphitheatre** is a large open area surrounded by rows of seats sloping upwards. Amphitheatres were built mainly in Greek and Roman times for the performance of plays. N-COUNT

2 You can describe land which partly or completely surrounds an open area as an **amphitheatre**. *...a natural amphitheatre of mountains.* N-COUNT

ample /æmpᵊl/ **ampler, amplest** ◆◆◇◇◇

1 If there is an **ample** amount of something, there is enough of it and usually some extra. *There'll be ample opportunity to relax, swim and soak up some sun... The design of the ground floor created ample space for a good-sized kitchen.* ♦ **amply** *This collection of his essays and journalism amply demonstrates his commitment to democracy.* ADJ-GRADED: usu ADJ n; ADV-GRADED: usu ADV with v, also ADV adj

2 If you describe someone's figure as **ample**, you mean that they are large in a pleasant or attractive way; used in written English. *...a young mother with a baby resting against her ample bosom.* ADJ-GRADED

amplifier /æmplɪfaɪəʳ/ **amplifiers.** An **amplifier** is an electronic device in a radio or stereo system which causes sounds or signals to get louder. ◆◇◇◇◇ N-COUNT

amplify /æmplɪfaɪ/ **amplifies, amplifying, amplified** ◆◇◇◇◇

1 If you **amplify** a sound, you make it louder, usually by using electronic equipment. *This landscape seemed to trap and amplify sounds... The music was amplified with microphones... 'This is the police,' came the amplified voice from the helicopter.* ♦ **amplification** /æmplɪfɪkeɪʃᵊn/ *...a voice that needed no amplification.* VERB V n V-ed; N-UNCOUNT

2 To **amplify** something means to increase its strength or intensity. *The mist had been replaced by a kind of haze that seemed to amplify the heat... Her anxiety about the world was amplifying her personal fears about her future.* ♦ **amplification** *...that amplification of the elements in his character that made him able to dominate her.* VERB V n; N-UNCOUNT

amplitude /æmplɪtjuːd, AM -tuːd/ **amplitudes**

1 The **amplitude** of a sound wave or electrical signal is its strength; a technical use in physics. *As we fall asleep the amplitude of brain waves slowly becomes greater.* N-VAR

2 **Amplitude** is the quality of being large in size or quantity; a formal use. *...a man of nineteenth-century amplitude.* N-UNCOUNT

ampoule /æmpuːl/ **ampoules;** spelled **ampule** in American English. An **ampoule** is a small container, usually made of glass, that contains a drug which will be injected into someone. The abbreviation **amp** is also used. N-COUNT =phial

amputate /æmpjʊteɪt/ **amputates, amputating, amputated.** If a surgeon **amputates** someone's arm or leg, he or she cuts all or part of it off in an operation because it is diseased or badly damaged. *To save his life, doctors amputated his legs... He had to have one leg amputated above the knee.* ♦ **amputation** /æmpjʊteɪʃᵊn/ **amputations** *He lived only hours after the amputation.* ◆◇◇◇◇ VERB V n *have* n V-ed Also V; N-VAR

amputee /æmpjʊtiː/ **amputees.** An **amputee** is someone who has had all or part of an arm or a leg amputated. N-COUNT

amulet /æmjʊlət/ **amulets.** An **amulet** is a small object that you wear or carry because you think it will bring you good luck and protect you from evil or injury. *She touched the crystal amulet around her neck.* N-COUNT =charm, talisman

amuse /əmjuːz/ **amuses, amusing, amused** ◆◇◇◇◇

1 If something **amuses** you, it makes you want to laugh or smile. *The thought seemed to amuse him... Their antics never fail to amuse.* VERB =delight ≠depress V n

2 If you **amuse** yourself, you do something in order to pass the time and not become bored. *I need distractions. I need to amuse myself so I won't keep thinking about things... Put a selection of baby toys in his cot to amuse him if he wakes early.* VERB =entertain V pron-refl V n

3 See also **amused, amusing**.

amused /əmjuːzd/ ◆◇◇◇◇

1 If you are **amused** by something, it makes you want to laugh or smile. *Sara was not amused by Franklin's teasing... We were amused to see how assiduously the animal groomed its fur.* ADJ-GRADED: usu v-link ADJ, oft ADJ *by/at* n, ADJ to-inf

2 If you **keep** someone **amused**, you find things to do which stop them getting bored. *Having pictures to colour will keep children amused for hours... Archie kept us amused with his stories.* PHRASE: V inflects =keep someone entertained

amusement /əmjuːzmənt/ **amusements** ◆◇◇◇◇

1 **Amusement** is the feeling that you have when you think that something is funny or amusing. *He stopped and watched with amusement to see the child so absorbed... Steamers tooted at us as sailors on deck waved in amusement.* N-UNCOUNT

2 **Amusement** is the pleasure that you get from being entertained or from doing something interesting. *I stumbled sideways before landing flat on my back, much to the amusement of the rest of the lads... She excelled at impersonations, which provided great amusement for him and his friends.* N-UNCOUNT =enjoyment, delight

3 **Amusements** are ways of passing the time pleasantly. *People had very few amusements to choose from. There was no radio, or television.* N-COUNT: usu pl =pastime

4 **Amusements** are games, rides on roundabouts, and other things that you can enjoy at a fairground or holiday resort. *...a place full of swings and amusements and the shrieks of children splashing in water.* N-PLURAL

amusement arcade, amusement arcades. In Britain, an **amusement arcade** is a large room in which you can play games on machines which work when you put money in them, such as fruit machines and electronic games. N-COUNT

amusement park, amusement parks. An **amusement park** is the same as a **funfair**; used mainly in American English. N-COUNT

amusing /əmjuːzɪŋ/. Someone or something that is **amusing** makes you laugh or smile. *He had a terrific sense of humour and could be very amusing... They recounted amusing stories about their first sexual experiences.* ♦ **amusingly** *It must be amusingly written... Recline & Sprawl is an amusingly named furniture shop in London.* ◆◆◇◇◇ ADJ-GRADED =entertaining; ADV-GRADED: ADV with v, ADV adj

an /ən STRONG æn/. **An** is used instead of 'a', the indefinite article, in front of words that begin with vowel sounds: see **a**. DET

-an /-ən/ **-ans**

1 **-an** is added to the names of some places in order to form adjectives or nouns that describe or refer to someone or something that comes from that place. *The Australian foreign minister... Glaswegians* SUFFIX

smoke more and eat fewer fresh vegetables and fruit than people in Edinburgh.

2 **-an** is added to the names of famous people in order to form adjectives or nouns that describe or refer to something or someone that is connected with or typical of that person's work or the time at which they lived. *...a great Shakespearean actor. ...a fascinating exhibition of fine Victorian and Edwardian furniture. ...a tradition perfected by the Elizabethans.*
SUFFIX

anabolic steroid /ænəbɒlɪk stɛrɔɪd, stɪər-/ **anabolic steroids.** **Anabolic steroids** are drugs which people, especially athletes, take to make their muscles bigger and to give them more strength. *He was stripped of his Olympic title after testing positive for anabolic steroids.*
N-COUNT

anachronism /ənækrənɪzəm/ **anachronisms**

1 You say that something is an **anachronism** when you think that it is out of date or old-fashioned. *In this day and age the dowry with all its attendant cruelties is an anachronism.*
N-COUNT

2 An **anachronism** is something in a book, play, or film that is wrong because it did not exist at the time the book, play, or film is set. *We had to stick to the period; any anachronisms, particularly in the dance, would be wrong.*
N-COUNT

anachronistic /ənækrənɪstɪk/. You say that something is **anachronistic** when you think that it is out of date or old-fashioned. *My children regard handwriting as some lost, anachronistic art.*
ADJ-GRADED

anaemia /əniːmiə/ **anaemias;** spelled **anemia** in American English. **Anaemia** is a medical condition in which there are too few red cells in your blood, so that you feel tired and look pale. *She suffered from anaemia and even required blood transfusions.*
◆◇◇◇◇ N-UNCOUNT: also N in pl

anaemic /əniːmɪk/; spelled **anemic** in American English.

1 Someone who is **anaemic** suffers from anaemia. *Losing a lot of blood makes you tired and anaemic.*
ADJ-GRADED: usu v-link ADJ

2 If you describe something as **anaemic**, you mean that it is not as strong or effective as you think it should be. *We will see some economic recovery, but it will be very anaemic... They insist on tastier chocolate than the anaemic British stuff.*
ADJ-GRADED PRAGMATICS =weak ≠strong

anaesthesia /ænɪsθiːziə, -ʒə/; also spelled **anesthesia**. **Anaesthesia** is the use of anaesthetics in medicine and surgery. *The operation can be done under local anaesthesia.*
N-UNCOUNT

anaesthetic /ænɪsθetɪk/ **anaesthetics;** also spelled **anesthetic**. **Anaesthetic** is a substance that doctors use to stop you feeling pain during an operation, either in the whole of your body when you are unconscious, or in a part of your body when you are awake. *The operation is carried out under a general anaesthetic.*
◆◇◇◇◇ N-MASS: oft *under* N

anaesthetist /əniːsθətɪst/ **anaesthetists;** also spelled **anesthetist**.

1 In British English, an **anaesthetist** is a doctor who specializes in giving anaesthetics to patients. The usual American word is **anesthesiologist**.
N-COUNT

2 In American English, an **anesthetist** is a nurse or other person who gives an anaesthetic to a patient.
N-COUNT

anaesthetize /əniːsθətaɪz/ **anaesthetizes, anaesthetizing, anaesthetized;** also spelled **anaesthetise** in British English, and **anesthetize** in American English.

1 When a doctor or other trained person **anaesthetizes** a patient, they make the patient unconscious or unable to feel pain by giving them an anaesthetic. *The operation involves anaesthetising the eye.*
VERB; V n

2 If something such as a drug **anaesthetizes** part or all of your body, it makes you unable to feel anything in that part of your body. *Alcohol is a potent drug that anaesthetizes the brain.*
VERB =numb; V n

anagram /ænəgræm/ **anagrams.** An **anagram** is a word or phrase formed by changing the order of the letters in another word or phrase. For example, 'triangle' is an anagram of 'integral'.
N-COUNT

anal /eɪnəl/. **Anal** means relating to the anus of a person or animal.
◆◇◇◇◇ ADJ: usu ADJ n

analgesic /ænəldʒiːzɪk/ **analgesics.** An **analgesic** drug lessens the effect of pain; a formal use. *Aloe may have an analgesic effect on inflammation and minor skin irritations.* ► An **analgesic** is an analgesic drug. *The hospital advised an analgesic for chest and shoulder pains.*
ADJ-GRADED: usu ADJ n =painkilling; N-COUNT =painkiller

analogous /ənæləgəs/. If one thing is **analogous** to another, the two things are similar in some way; a formal word. *Marine construction technology like this is very complex, somewhat analogous to trying to build a bridge under water.*
ADJ-GRADED: usu v-link ADJ *to* n =equivalent

analogue /ænəlɒg, AM -lɔːg/ **analogues;** spelled **analog** in American English. British English also uses the spelling **analog** for meaning 3.
◆◇◇◇◇

1 If one thing is an **analogue** of another, it is similar in some way; a formal use. *No model can ever be a perfect analogue of nature itself.*
N-COUNT: oft N *of* n

2 An **analogue** watch or clock shows what it is measuring with a pointer on a dial rather than with a number display. Compare **digital**.
ADJ: usu ADJ n

3 **Analogue** technology involves measuring, storing, or recording an infinitely variable amount of information by using physical quantities such as voltage. Compare **digital**. *The analogue signals from the video tape are converted into digital code.*
ADJ: usu ADJ n

analogy /ənælədʒi/ **analogies.** If you make or draw an **analogy** between two things, you show that they are alike in some way. *The analogy between music and fragrance has stuck.*
◆◇◇◇◇ N-COUNT: oft N *between/with* n =similarity

analyse /ænəlaɪz/ **analyses, analysing, analysed;** spelled **analyze** in American English.
◆◆◇◇◇

1 If you **analyse** something, you consider it carefully or use statistical methods in order to fully understand it. *McCarthy was asked to analyse the data from the first phase of trials of the vaccine... This book teaches you how to analyse what is causing the stress in your life.*
VERB; V n; V wh

2 If you **analyse** something, you examine it using scientific methods in order to find out what it consists of. *We haven't had time to analyse those samples yet... They had their tablets analysed to find out whether they were getting the real drug or not.*
VERB; V n; *have* n V-ed; Also V wh

analyser /ænəlaɪzər/ **analysers;** spelled **analyzer** in American English.

1 An **analyser** is a piece of equipment which is used to analyse the substances that are present in something such as a gas. *...an oxygen analyser.*
N-COUNT: usu n N

2 An **analyser** is someone who analyses information.
N-COUNT =analyst

analysis /ənælɪsɪs/ **analyses** /ənælɪsiːz/
◆◆◆◇◇

1 **Analysis** is the process of considering something carefully or using statistical methods in order to understand it or explain it. *Her criteria defy analysis... We did an analysis of the way that government money has been spent in the past.*
N-VAR

2 **Analysis** is the scientific process of examining something in order to find out what it consists of. *They collect blood samples for analysis at a national laboratory... Jacobsen based his conclusion on an analysis of the decay of samarium-147 into neodymium-143.*
N-VAR

3 An **analysis** is an explanation or description that results from considering something carefully. *The census provides a considerable amount of detail in its analysis of internal movement in France.*
N-COUNT

4 You use the expression **in the final analysis** or **in the last analysis** to indicate that the statement you are making is the most important or basic aspect of an issue. *I'm on the right track and I think in the final analysis people will understand that... Violence in the last analysis produces more violence.*
PHRASE: PHR with cl PRAGMATICS =in the end

analyst /ænəlɪst/ **analysts**
◆◆◆◆◇

1 An **analyst** is a person whose job is to analyse a subject and give opinions about it. *...a political analyst.*
N-COUNT

2 An **analyst** is someone, usually a doctor, who examines and treats people who are emotionally disturbed.
N-COUNT =psychoanalyst

analytic /ænəlɪtɪk/. **Analytic** means the same as **analytical**.
ADJ-GRADED

analytical /ænəlɪtɪkəl/
◆◇◇◇◇

1 An **analytical** way of doing something involves
ADJ-GRADED

the use of logical reasoning. *I have an analytical approach to every survey.* ♦ **analytically** /ænəlɪtɪkli/ *A teacher can encourage children to think analytically.* ADV-GRADED: ADV with v, ADV adj

2 **Analytical** research involves using chemical analysis. *All raw materials are subjected to our latest analytical techniques.* ADJ: ADJ n

analyze /ænəlaɪz/. See **analyse**.

anarchic /ænɑːʳkɪk/. If you describe someone or something as **anarchic**, you disapprove of them because they do not recognize or obey any rules or laws. *...anarchic attitudes and complete disrespect for authority.* ♦◇◇◇◇ ADJ-GRADED: usu ADJ n PRAGMATICS =lawless

anarchism /ænəʳkɪzəm/. **Anarchism** is the belief that the laws and power of governments should be replaced by people working together freely. *He advocated anarchism as the answer to social problems.* N-UNCOUNT

anarchist /ænəʳkɪst/ **anarchists** ♦◇◇◇◇

1 An **anarchist** is a person who believes in anarchism. *West Berlin always had a large anarchist community. ...a well-known anarchist poet.* N-COUNT: oft N n

2 If someone has **anarchist** beliefs or views, they believe in anarchism. *He was apparently quite converted from his anarchist views.* ADJ: ADJ n

3 If you say that someone is an **anarchist**, you disapprove of them because they seem to pay no attention to the rules or laws that everyone else obeys. *He was a true misanthrope, a social anarchist.* N-COUNT PRAGMATICS

anarchistic /ænəʳkɪstɪk/

1 An **anarchistic** person believes in anarchism. **Anarchistic** activity or literature promotes anarchism. *Their political beliefs led them to anarchistic revolt.* ADJ: usu ADJ n

2 If you describe someone as **anarchistic**, you disapprove of them because they pay no attention to the rules or laws that everyone else obeys. *The Hells Angels were once the most notorious and anarchistic of bike gangs.* ADJ-GRADED: usu ADJ n PRAGMATICS

anarcho- /ænɑːʳkoʊ-/. **Anarcho-** combines with nouns and adjectives to form words indicating that something is both anarchistic and the other thing that is mentioned. *In France there was a long tradition of anarcho-syndicalism.* COMB in ADJ and N

anarchy /ænəʳki/. If you describe a situation as **anarchy**, you mean that nobody seems to be paying any attention to rules or laws. *The school's liberal, individualistic traditions were in danger of slipping into anarchy... In June, 1960, the Congo was plunged into five years of civil war and political anarchy.* ♦◇◇◇◇ N-UNCOUNT PRAGMATICS =chaos

anathema /ənæθəmə/. If something is **anathema** to you, you strongly dislike it. *Violence was anathema to them.* ♦◇◇◇◇ N-UNCOUNT: usu N to n

anatomical /ænətɒmɪkᵊl/. **Anatomical** means relating to the structure of the bodies of people and animals. *...minute anatomical differences between insects.* ♦ **anatomically** /ænətɒmɪkli/. *I need my pictures to be anatomically correct.* ADJ: usu ADJ n ADV

anatomist /ənætəmɪst/ **anatomists.** An **anatomist** is an expert in anatomy. N-COUNT

anatomize /ənætəmaɪz/ **anatomizes, anatomizing, anatomized;** also spelled **anatomise** in British English. If you **anatomise** a subject or an issue, you examine it in great detail; a formal word. *The Public Interest is a magazine devoted to anatomizing the inadequacies of liberalism.* VERB Vn

anatomy /ənætəmi/ **anatomies** ♦◇◇◇◇

1 **Anatomy** is the study of the structure of the bodies of people or animals. N-UNCOUNT

2 You can refer to your body as your **anatomy**. *The ball hit him in the most sensitive part of his anatomy.* N-COUNT: usu poss N

3 An animal's **anatomy** is the structure of its body. *He had worked extensively on the anatomy of living animals.* N-COUNT: oft with poss

4 The **anatomy** of a subject or an idea is an examination or investigation of it. *This was a troubling essay on the anatomy of nationhood.* N-SING: usu the N of n =analysis

ancestor /ænsestəʳ/ **ancestors** ♦♦◇◇◇

1 Your **ancestors** are the people from whom you are descended. *...our daily lives, so different from those of our ancestors... He could trace his ancestors back seven hundred years.* N-COUNT: usu pl, with poss ≠descendant

2 An **ancestor** of something modern is an earlier thing from which it developed. *The direct ancestor of the modern cat was the Kaffir cat of ancient Egypt... The immediate ancestor of rock 'n' roll is rhythm-and blues.* N-COUNT: usu N of n ≠descendant

ancestral /ænsestrəl/. You use **ancestral** to refer to a person's family in former times, especially when the family is important and has property or land which they have had for a long time. *...the family's ancestral home in southern Germany. ...the ancestral portraits in the hallway.* ♦◇◇◇◇ ADJ: usu ADJ n

ancestry /ænsestri/ **ancestries.** Your **ancestry** is the fact that you are descended from certain people. *...a family who could trace their ancestry back to the sixteenth century.* ♦◇◇◇◇ N-COUNT: usu with supp

anchor /æŋkəʳ/ **anchors, anchoring, anchored** ♦♦◇◇◇

1 An **anchor** is a heavy hooked object that is dropped from a boat into the water at the end of a chain in order to make the boat stay in one place. *Joe pulled up the anchor and turned for home.* N-COUNT

2 When a boat **anchors** or when you **anchor** it, its anchor is dropped into the water in order to make it stay in one place. *We could anchor off the pier... They anchored the boat.* V-ERG V Vn

3 If you **anchor** an object somewhere, you fix it to something to prevent it moving from that place. *The roots anchor the plant in the earth... The child seat belt was not properly anchored to the car.* VERB =fix V n prep V-ed

4 If one thing is the **anchor** for something else, it makes that thing stable and secure. *He provided an emotional anchor for her... Mr Deng remains the anchor of China's fragile political balance.* N-COUNT: oft N of/for n

5 If something **is anchored in** something or **to** something, it has strong links with it. *A united Germany must be firmly anchored in NATO if Europe is to remain stable... His basic outlook remains anchored in the liberal tradition.* VB: usu passive =rooted in be V-ed in/to n V-ed

6 The person who **anchors** a television or radio programme presents it and acts as a link between interviews and reports which come from other places or studios; used mainly in American English. *Viewers saw him anchoring a five-minute summary of regional news. ...a series of cassettes on the Vietnam War, anchored by Mr. Cronkite.* VERB Vn V-ed

7 The **anchor** on a television or radio programme, such as a news programme, is the person who presents it; used mainly in American English. *He worked in the news division of ABC – he was the anchor of its 15-minute evening newscast.* N-COUNT =anchorman, anchorwoman

8 If a boat is **at anchor**, it is floating in a particular place and is prevented from moving by its anchor. *Sailing boats lay at anchor in the narrow waterway.* PHRASES

9 When the people on a boat **drop anchor** or **cast anchor**, they drop the boat's anchor into the water in order to prevent the boat from moving. *We dropped anchor in a sheltered spot.* V inflects

10 When the people on a boat **weigh anchor** or **up anchor**, they pull the anchor of the boat out of the water so that they can sail away. V inflects

anchorage /æŋkərɪdʒ/ **anchorages.** An **anchorage** is a place where a boat can anchor safely. *The nearest safe anchorage was in Halifax, Nova Scotia... The vessel yesterday reached anchorage off Dubai.* ♦◇◇◇◇ N-VAR

anchorman /æŋkəʳmæn/ **anchormen;** also spelled **anchor man**. The **anchorman** on a television or radio programme, such as a news programme, is the person who presents it. N-COUNT

anchorwoman /æŋkəʳwʊmən/ **anchorwomen.** The **anchorwoman** on a television or radio programme, such as a news programme, is the woman who presents it. N-COUNT

anchovy /æntʃəvi, AM -tʃoʊvi/ **anchovies. Anchovies** are very small fish with a strong salty taste. *...a tin of anchovies. ...anchovy fillets.* ♦◇◇◇◇ N-VAR: oft N n

ancien regime /ɑːnsjɒn reɪʒiːm/

1 The **ancien regime** was the political and social system in France before the revolution of 1789. N-SING: usu the N

2 If a country has had the same political system for a long time and you disapprove of it, you can refer to it as the **ancien regime**. *The Chinese and Vietnamese parties attempted to maintain the ancien regime.* N-SING: usu *the* N PRAGMATICS

ancient /eɪnʃənt/ **ancients** ◆◆◆◇◇

1 Ancient means belonging to the distant past, especially to the period in history before the end of the Roman Empire. *They believed ancient Greece and Rome were vital sources of learning.* ADJ-GRADED: ADJ n
♦ **anciently** *Salisbury Plain was known anciently as Ellendune.* ADV

2 Ancient means very old, or having existed for a long time. *...ancient Jewish tradition. ...ancient fishing rights. ...a few acres of ancient woodland.* ADJ-GRADED: usu ADJ n

3 The ancients are the people of an old civilization, especially classical Greece or Rome. *The ancients knew more than we do about the heavens.* N-PLURAL: *the* N

ancient history

1 Ancient history is the history of ancient civilizations, especially Greece and Rome. N-UNCOUNT

2 If you describe something as **ancient history**, you mean that it happened in the past and is no longer relevant to the present. *It does not bother me now at all. It is all ancient history.* N-UNCOUNT

ancillary /ænsɪləri, AM ænsəleri/

1 The **ancillary** workers in an institution are the people such as cleaners and cooks whose work supports the main work of the institution. *...ancillary staff... Ancillary services like cleaning are put up for competitive tender.* ADJ: ADJ n =auxiliary

2 Ancillary means additional to something else. *Ancillary charges are at least $30 per day... Scientific development meant the growth of numerous professions ancillary to medicine.* ADJ: usu ADJ n =supplementary, subsidiary

and /ənd, STRONG ænd/ ◆◆◆◆◆

1 You use **and** to link two or more words, groups, or clauses. *When he returned, she and Simon had already gone... Between 1914 and 1920 large parts of Albania were occupied by the Italians... I'm going to write good jokes and become a good comedian... I'm 53 and I'm very happy.* CONJ-COORD

2 You use **and** to link two identical words or phrases in order to emphasize the degree of something or to suggest that something continues or increases over a period of time. *Learning becomes more and more difficult as we get older... Day by day I am getting better and better... We talked for hours and hours... He lay down on the floor and cried and cried.* CONJ-COORD PRAGMATICS

3 You use **and** to link two statements about events when one of the events follows the other. *I waved goodbye and went down the stone harbour steps... He asked for ice for his whiskey and proceeded to get drunk.* CONJ-COORD =then

4 You use **and** to link two statements when the second statement continues the point that has been made in the first statement. *You could only really tell the effects of the disease in the long term, and five years wasn't long enough... The cure for bad teaching is good teachers, and good teachers cost money.* CONJ-COORD

5 You use **and** to link two clauses when the second clause is a result of the first clause. *All through yesterday crowds have been arriving and by midnight thousands of people packed the square.* CONJ-COORD

6 You use **and** to interrupt yourself in order to make a comment on what you are saying. *As Downing claims, and as we noted above, reading is best established when the child has an intimate knowledge of the language... Finally – and I really ought to stop in a minute – I wish to make the following recommendations.* CONJ-COORD PRAGMATICS

7 You use **and** at the beginning of a sentence to introduce something else that you want to add to what to have just said. Some people think that starting a sentence with **and** is ungrammatical, but it is now quite common in both spoken and written English. *Commuter airlines fly to out-of-the-way places. And business travelers are the ones who go to those locations.* CONJ-COORD PRAGMATICS

8 You use **and** to introduce a question which follows logically from what someone has just said. *'He used to be so handsome.'—'And now?'... 'Well, of course, they haven't won a football game.'—'And what would you expect?'.* CONJ-COORD PRAGMATICS

9 And is used by broadcasters and people making announcements to change a topic or to start talking about a topic they have just mentioned. *And now the drought in Sudan... Football, and Aston Villa will reclaim their lead at the top of the English First Division.* CONJ-COORD PRAGMATICS

10 You use **and** to indicate that two numbers are to be added together. *What does two and two make?* CONJ-COORD =plus

11 And is used before a fraction that comes after a whole number. *McCain spent five and a half years in a prisoner of war camp in Vietnam. ...fourteen and a quarter per cent.* CONJ-COORD

12 You use **and** in numbers larger than one hundred, after the words 'hundred' or 'thousand' and before other numbers. *We printed two hundred and fifty invitations. ...three thousand and twenty-six pounds.* CONJ-COORD

andante /ændænti/ **andantes**

1 Andante written above a piece of music means that it should be played fairly slowly. ADV-GRADED: ADV after v

2 An **andante** is a piece of music that is played fairly slowly. *...the lovely central Andante. ...the violas' Andante theme.* N-COUNT: usu sing

androgynous /ændrɒdʒɪnəs/

1 An **androgynous** person, animal, or plant has both male and female sexual characteristics; a technical use in biology. ADJ: usu ADJ n =hermaphrodite

2 If you describe someone or something as **androgynous**, you mean that they are not distinctly masculine or feminine in appearance or in behaviour. *Belinda was always attracted to men with an androgynous quality to them... The style was quite androgynous.* ADJ-GRADED: usu ADJ n

androgyny /ændrɒdʒɪni/. **Androgyny** is the state of being neither distinctly masculine nor distinctly feminine. *Androgyny is no longer the height of fashion.* N-UNCOUNT

android /ændrɔɪd/ **androids.** In science fiction books and films, an **android** is a robot that looks like a human being. N-COUNT

anecdotal /ænɪkdoʊtəl/ ◆◇◇◇◇

1 Anecdotal evidence is based on individual accounts, rather than on reliable research or statistics, and so may not be valid. *Anecdotal evidence suggests that sales in Europe have slipped. ...countless anecdotal reports.* ADJ-GRADED

2 Anecdotal speech or writing is full of anecdotes or is based on anecdotes. *Gray's book is anecdotal and entertaining.* ADJ-GRADED

anecdote /ænɪkdoʊt/ **anecdotes** ◆◇◇◇◇

1 An **anecdote** is a short, amusing account of something that has happened. *Pete was telling them an anecdote about their mother... He has a talent for recollection and anecdote.* N-VAR: oft N *about* n

2 Anecdotes are individual accounts that are not reliable evidence. *The image of the fox as a pest is grossly exaggerated in anecdote and folklore. ...apocryphal anecdotes.* N-VAR

anemia /əniːmiə/. See **anaemia**.

anemic /əniːmɪk/. See **anaemic**.

anemone /ənemən i/ **anemones.** An **anemone** is a garden plant with red, purple, or white flowers. N-COUNT

anesthesia /ænɪsθiːziə, -ʒə/. See **anaesthesia**.

anesthesiologist /ænɪsθiːziɒlədʒɪst/ **anesthesiologists.** In American English, an **anesthesiologist** is a doctor who specializes in giving anaesthetics to patients. The usual British word is **anaesthetist**. N-COUNT

anesthetic /ænɪsθetɪk/. See **anaesthetic**.

anesthetist /əniːsθətɪst/. See **anaesthetist**.

anesthetize /əniːsθətaɪz/. See **anaesthetize**.

anew /ənjuː, AM ənuː/. If you do something **anew**, you do it again, often in a different way from before; used in written English. *She's ready to start anew... He began his work anew.* ◆◇◇◇◇ ADV: ADV after v =afresh

angel /eɪndʒəl/ **angels** ◆◆◇◇◇

1 Angels are spiritual beings that some people be- N-COUNT lieve are God's messengers and servants in heaven. *She is in heaven with the angels.*

2 You can call someone you like very much an **angel** in order to show affection, especially when they have been kind to you or done you a favour. *Thank you a thousand times, you're an angel.* — N-COUNT PRAGMATICS

3 If you describe someone as an **angel**, you mean that they seem to be very kind and considerate. *Poppa thought her an angel... He was such an angel to put up with it.* — N-COUNT

4 If you say that someone is **on the side of the angels**, you are saying that you believe very firmly that what they are doing is right. *On this issue Chancellor Helmut Kohl is on the side of the angels.* — PHRASES; usu v-link PHR; PRAGMATICS

5 If you say that someone **rushes in where angels fear to tread**, you are criticising them gently because they get themselves into dangerous or difficult situations without thinking carefully enough about what they are doing. *Martin is inclined to rush in where angels fear to tread.* — *rush* inflects; PRAGMATICS

angelic /ændʒelɪk/

1 You can describe someone as **angelic** when they are, or seem to be, very good, kind, and gentle. *...an angelic face... He looked angelic.* — ADJ-GRADED: usu ADJ n; =saintly

2 Angelic means like angels or relating to angels. *...angelic choirs.* — ADJ: ADJ n

angelica /ændʒelɪkə/. **Angelica** is the candied stems of the angelica plant which can be used in making cakes or sweets. — N-UNCOUNT

anger /æŋgəʳ/ **angers, angering, angered** ◆◆◆◇◇

1 Anger is the strong emotion that you feel when you think that someone has behaved in an unfair, cruel, or unacceptable way. *He cried with anger and frustration... Ellen felt both despair and anger at her mother.* — N-UNCOUNT: oft N *at* n/-ing; =rage

2 If something **angers** you, it makes you feel angry. *The decision to allow more offshore oil drilling angered some Californians.* — VERB; =enrage; V n

angina /ændʒaɪnə/. **Angina** is severe pain in the chest and left arm, caused by heart disease. ◆◇◇◇◇ N-UNCOUNT

angle /æŋgᵊl/ **angles, angling, angled** ◆◆◆◇◇

1 An **angle** is the difference in direction between two lines or surfaces. Angles are measured in degrees. *The boat is now leaning at a 30 degree angle.* — N-COUNT
• See also **right angle**.

2 An **angle** is the shape that is created where two lines or surfaces join together. *...the angle of the blade. ...brackets to adjust the steering wheel's angle.* — N-COUNT: usu *the* N *of* n

3 An **angle** is the direction from which you look at something. *Thanks to the angle at which he stood, he could just see the sunset... His face will be discreetly concealed by camera angles.* — N-COUNT

4 You can refer to a way of presenting something or thinking about it as a particular **angle**. *We had to do the scene over and over again, from different angles... He was considering the idea from all angles.* — N-COUNT: supp N

5 If someone **is angling for** something, they are trying to make someone offer it to them without asking for it openly and directly. *It sounds as if he's just angling for sympathy.* — VB: usu cont; V *for* n

6 If you **angle** something or if it **angles** in a particular direction, it faces or points in that direction. *You can open the slats for a bright light or angle them for more shade... The path angled downhill and northwards... David Auld scored their equaliser with an acutely angled shot.* — V-ERG; V n; V adv/prep; V-ed

7 See also **angling**.

8 If something is **at an angle**, it is leaning in a particular direction so that it is not straight, horizontal, or vertical. *An iron bar stuck out at an angle... The wall's at a slight angle.* — PHRASE: PHR after v, v-link PHR

angler /æŋgləʳ/ **anglers.** An **angler** is someone who fishes with a fishing rod as a hobby. ◆◆◇◇◇ N-COUNT

Anglican /æŋglɪkən/ **Anglicans**

1 Anglican means belonging or relating to the Church of England. *...the Anglican Church. ...an Anglican priest. ...the Anglican community.* — ADJ: usu ADJ n

2 An **Anglican** is a Christian who is a member of the Church of England. *Both my parents were devout Anglicans.* — N-COUNT

Anglicanism /æŋglɪkənɪzəm/. **Anglicanism** is the beliefs and practices of the Church of England. — N-UNCOUNT

anglicize /æŋglɪsaɪz/ **anglicizes, anglicizing, anglicized;** also spelled **anglicise** in British English. If you **anglicize** something, you change it so that it resembles or becomes part of the English language or English culture. *He had anglicized his surname... When Dutch colonial rule ended in the 19th century the civil service was anglicised.* — VERB; V n
♦ **anglicized** *While 'Llywelyn' is the purest Welsh form of the name, I chose a slightly Anglicized version.* — ADJ-GRADED

angling /æŋglɪŋ/. **Angling** is the activity or sport of fishing with a fishing rod. ◆◇◇◇◇ N-UNCOUNT

Anglo- /æŋgloʊ-/

1 Anglo- combines with adjectives indicating nationality to form adjectives which describe something connected with relations between Britain and another country. *...the future of Anglo-American relations. ...the Anglo-Irish Agreement.* — COMB in ADJ: ADJ n

2 Anglo- combines with adjectives indicating nationality to form adjectives which describe a person who has one British parent and one non-British parent. *Born of Anglo-American parentage, Clarke was raised and educated in both countries.* — COMB in ADJ: ADJ n

Anglo-Asian, Anglo-Asians. An **Anglo-Asian** person is someone of Indian, Pakistani, or Bangladeshi origin who has grown up in Britain. *...the Anglo-Asian community.* — ADJ: usu ADJ n; =British Asian
► An **Anglo-Asian** is someone who is Anglo-Asian. — N-COUNT; =British Asian

Anglo-Catholic, Anglo-Catholics

1 The **Anglo-Catholic** part of the Church of England is the part of it whose beliefs and practices are similar to those of the Catholic Church. *Anglo-Catholic opponents of women priests are divided about moves to seek special links with Rome.* — ADJ: ADJ n

2 An **Anglo-Catholic** is a Christian who belongs to the Anglo-Catholic section of the Church of England. — N-COUNT

Anglo-Indian, Anglo-Indians

1 An **Anglo-Indian** person is someone who is of mixed British and Indian descent. *...Anglo-Indian writer Amitav Ghosh.* — ADJ: usu ADJ n

2 An **Anglo-Indian** is someone who is Anglo-Indian. — N-COUNT

Anglophile /æŋgloʊfaɪl/ **Anglophiles.** If you describe a non-British person as **Anglophile**, you mean that they are very interested in Britain and British culture. *Clinton is the most Anglophile President ever to enter the Oval Office.* — ADJ-GRADED
► Also a noun. *He became a fanatical Anglophile.* — N-COUNT

Anglophone /æŋgləfoʊn/ **Anglophones**

1 Anglophone communities are English-speaking communities in areas where more than one language is commonly spoken. *...anglophone Canadians. ...anglophone Africa.* — ADJ: ADJ n

2 Anglophones are people whose native language is English or who speak English because they live in a country where English is one of the official languages. *It's felt there's no future for Anglophones in the province. ...sub-Sahara Anglophones.* — N-COUNT: usu pl

Anglo-Saxon, Anglo-Saxons

1 The **Anglo-Saxon** period is the period of English history from the fifth century A.D. to the Norman Conquest in 1066. *Excavations have revealed Roman and Anglo-Saxon remains in the area. ...the grave of an early Anglo-Saxon king.* — ADJ: usu ADJ n
► An **Anglo-Saxon** was someone who was Anglo-Saxon. *The Anglo-Saxons did not have a letter V.* — N-COUNT

2 Anglo-Saxon people are members of or are descended from the English race. *...white Anglo-Saxon Protestant men.* — ADJ
► Also a noun. *The difference is, you are Anglo-Saxons, we are Latins.* — N-COUNT

3 Anglo-Saxon attitudes or ideas have been strongly influenced by English culture. *Debilly had no Anglo-Saxon shyness about discussing money.* — ADJ: usu ADJ n

4 Anglo-Saxon is the language that was spoken in England between the fifth century A.D. and the Norman Conquest in 1066. — N-UNCOUNT

Angolan /æŋgoʊlᵊn/ **Angolans** ◆◆◆◆◇

1 Angolan means belonging or relating to Angola — ADJ:

or its people. *The Angolan government is under serious pressure.* usu ADJ n
2 An **Angolan** is someone who comes from Angola. *Angolans are worrying about a return to war.* N-COUNT

angora /æŋgɔːrə/
1 An **angora** goat or rabbit is a particular breed that has long silky hair. ADJ: ADJ n
2 **Angora** cloth or clothing is made from the hair of the angora goat or rabbit. *...an angora sweater.* N-UNCOUNT: usu N n

angry /æŋgri/ **angrier, angriest** ◆◆◆◇◇
1 When you are **angry**, you feel strong dislike or impatience about something. *She had been very angry at the person who stole her new bike... Are you angry with me for some reason?... I was angry about the rumours... He's angry that people have called him a racist... An angry mob gathered outside the courthouse.* ADJ-GRADED: usu v-link ADJ, oft ADJ *at/with/about* n ♦ **angrily** /æŋgrɪli/ *Officials reacted angrily to those charges... Health workers are angrily demanding higher pay.* ADV-GRADED: ADV with v
2 An **angry** wound or rash is inflamed and painful. *He was badly concussed, the glass leaving two angry cuts across his forehead.* ADJ-GRADED
3 If you describe the sky or sea as **angry**, you mean that it is dark and stormy; a literary use. *Under the angry red sky he ran, into the thickening darkness.* ADJ-GRADED =threatening

angst /æŋst/. **Angst** is a feeling of anxiety and worry; used mainly in journalism. *Many kids suffer from acne and angst.* ◆◇◇◇◇ N-UNCOUNT

anguish /æŋgwɪʃ/. **Anguish** is great mental suffering or physical pain; used in written English. *A cry of anguish burst from her lips... Mark looked at him in anguish.* ◆◇◇◇◇ N-UNCOUNT

anguished /æŋgwɪʃt/. **Anguished** means showing or feeling great mental suffering or physical pain; used in written English. *She let out an anguished cry. ...an anguished mother.* ◆◇◇◇◇ ADJ-GRADED: usu ADJ n =tormented

angular /æŋgjʊləʳ/. **Angular** things have shapes that seem to contain a lot of straight lines and sharp points. *He had an angular face with prominent cheekbones.* ◆◇◇◇◇ ADJ-GRADED: usu ADJ n ♦ **angularity** /æŋgjulærɪti/ *...the angularity of her face.* N-UNCOUNT

animal /ænɪməl/ **animals** ◆◆◆◆◇
1 An **animal** is a living creature such as a dog, lion, or rabbit, rather than a bird, fish, insect, or human being. *He was attacked by wild animals... He had a real knowledge of animals, birds and flowers.* N-COUNT
2 Any living creature other than a human being can be referred to as an **animal**. *Language is something which fundamentally distinguishes humans from animals. ...a habitat for plants and animals.* N-COUNT
3 Any living creature, including a human being, can be referred to as an **animal**. *Watch any young human being, or any other young animal.* N-COUNT
4 **Animal** products come from animals rather than from plants. *The illegal trade in animal products continues to flourish... Cut down on animal fats found in red meat, hard cheeses and so on.* ADJ
5 If you say that someone is an **animal**, you find their behaviour disgusting or very unpleasant. *This man is an animal, a beast... He was an animal in his younger days.* N-COUNT
6 **Animal** qualities, feelings, or abilities relate to someone's physical nature and instincts rather than to their mind. *There was no doubting the animal magnetism of the man... You feel an animal panic to run and hide.* ADJ
7 You can refer to someone as a particular type of **animal** in order to say what their interests are or what their typical behaviour is. *You're quite a party animal aren't you, out there every night... The entrepreneur at twenty-five is a different animal from the entrepreneur at fifty.* N-COUNT: supp N

animal rights. People who are concerned with **animal rights** believe very firmly that animals should not be exploited or abused by humans. *To the delight of the animal rights movement, Britain's trade in fur is in drastic decline.* ◆◇◇◇◇ N-UNCOUNT: oft N n

animate, animates, animating, animated. The adjective is pronounced /ænɪmət/. The verb is pronounced /ænɪmeɪt/.
1 Something that is **animate** has life, in contrast to things like stones and machines which do not. *Natural philosophy involved the study of all aspects of the material world, animate and inanimate.* ADJ =living ≠inanimate
2 To **animate** something means to make it lively or more cheerful. *There was precious little about the cricket to animate the crowd... The girls watched, little teasing smiles animating their faces.* VERB =enliven V n

animated /ænɪmeɪtɪd/ ◆◇◇◇◇
1 Someone who is **animated** or who is having an **animated** conversation is lively and expressive. *She was seen in animated conversation with the singer Yuri Marusin... Everyone became more animated.* ADJ-GRADED ♦ **animatedly** *Sammy was standing close to Ned, talking animatedly with him.* ADV-GRADED: ADV with v
2 An **animated** film is one in which puppets or drawings appear to move. *Disney has returned to what it does best: making full-length animated feature films.* ADJ: ADJ n

animation /ænɪmeɪʃən/ **animations** ◆◇◇◇◇
1 **Animation** is the process of making films in which drawings or puppets appear to move. *The films are a mix of animation and full-length features. ...computer animation.* N-UNCOUNT
2 An **animation** is a film in which drawings or puppets appear to move. *This film is the first British animation sold to an American network.* N-COUNT =cartoon
3 Someone with **animation** shows liveliness in the way that they speak, look, or behave. *They both spoke with animation.* N-UNCOUNT =enthusiasm
4 See also **suspended animation**.

animator /ænɪmeɪtəʳ/ **animators.** An **animator** is a person who makes films by means of animation. N-COUNT

animosity /ænɪmɒsɪti/ **animosities. Animosity** is a strong feeling of dislike and anger. **Animosities** are feelings of this kind. *There's a long history of animosity between the Cambodians and the Vietnamese... Sir Geoffrey had no personal animosity towards the Prime Minister. ...the age-old animosities in the Middle East.* ◆◇◇◇◇ N-UNCOUNT: also N in pl =hostility

animus /ænɪməs/. If a person has an **animus** against someone, they have a strong feeling of dislike for them, even when there is no good reason for it; used in written English. *Perot is known to harbor a deep animus against Mr. Bush. ...Mr Milner's animus towards Mr Stevens.* N-UNCOUNT: usu N prep =animosity

anise /ænɪs/. **Anise** is a plant with seeds that smell and taste of liquorice. It is often made into an alcoholic drink. N-UNCOUNT

aniseed /ænɪsiːd/. **Aniseed** is a substance made from the seeds of the anise plant. It tastes of liquorice and is used as a flavouring in sweets, drinks, and medicines. *Fennel has a very distinctive aniseed flavour.* N-UNCOUNT

ankle /æŋkəl/ **ankles.** Your **ankle** is the joint where your foot joins your leg. *John twisted his ankle badly.* ◆◆◇◇◇ N-COUNT: usu poss N

annals /ænəlz/
1 If something is in the **annals** of a nation or field of activity, it is recorded as part of its history. *He has become a legend in the annals of military history.* N-PLURAL: usu *in the* N *of* n
2 You can refer to the journal of a particular field of academic research as its **annals**. *It was published in the 'Annals of Internal Medicine'.* N-PLURAL: with supp, usu *the* N *of* n

annex, annexes, annexing, annexed. Also spelled **annexe**. The verb is pronounced /æneks/. The noun is pronounced /æneks/. ◆◇◇◇◇
1 If a country **annexes** another country or an area of land, it seizes it and takes control of it. *The King knew nothing of the plan to invade and annex Kuwait. ...the idea of annexing Abkhazia to Russia.* VERB V n V n *to* n ♦ **annexation** /ænekseɪʃən/ **annexations** *Indonesia's annexation of East Timor has never won the acceptance of the United Nations.* N-COUNT: usu sing, usu N *of* n
2 An **annex** is the same as an **annexe**. N-COUNT

annexe /æneks/ **annexes;** also spelled **annex**.
1 An **annexe** is a building which is joined to or is next to a larger main building. *...setting up a museum in an annexe to the theatre.* N-COUNT
2 An **annexe** to a document is a section added to it at the end. *The Annex lists and discusses eight titles.* N-COUNT
3 See also **annex**.

annihilate /ənaɪɪleɪt/ **annihilates, annihilating, annihilated** ◆◇◇◇◇

1 To **annihilate** something means to destroy it completely. *There are lots of ways of annihilating the planet... The Army was annihilated.* VERB Vn
♦ **annihilation** /ənaɪɪleɪʃən/ *Muslim political leaders fear the annihilation of their people.* N-UNCOUNT: oft N ofn

2 If you **annihilate** someone in a contest or argument, you totally defeat them. *The Dutch annihilated the Olympic champions 5-0.* VERB Vn

anniversary /ænɪvɜːʳsəri/ **anniversaries.** An **anniversary** is a date which is remembered or celebrated because a special event happened on that date in a previous year. *Vietnam is celebrating the one hundredth anniversary of the birth of Ho Chi Minh.* ◆◆◆◇◇ N-COUNT: usu ord N, the N ofn

annotate /ænoʊteɪt/ **annotates, annotating, annotated.** If you **annotate** written work or a diagram, you add notes to it, especially in order to explain it. *Historians annotate, check and interpret the diary selections. ...an annotated bibliography.* VERB Vn V-ed

annotation /ænoʊteɪʃən/ **annotations**

1 **Annotation** is the activity of annotating something. *She retained a number of copies for further annotation.* N-UNCOUNT

2 An **annotation** is a note that is added to a text or diagram, often in order to explain it. *He supplied annotations to nearly 15,000 musical works.* N-COUNT: usu pl =glosses, footnotes

announce /ənaʊns/ **announces, announcing, announced** ◆◆◆◆◆

1 If you **announce** something, you tell people about it publicly or officially. *He will announce tonight that he is resigning from office... She was planning to announce her engagement to Peter... It was announced that the groups have agreed to a cease-fire.* VERB V that Vn it be V-ed that

2 If you **announce** a piece of news or an intention, especially something that people may not like, you say it loudly and clearly, so that everyone you are with can hear it. *Peter announced that he had no intention of wasting his time at any university... 'I'm having a bath and going to bed,' she announced, and left the room.* VERB =declare V that V with quote

3 If an airport or railway employee **announces** something, they tell the public about it by means of a loudspeaker system. *Station staff announced the arrival of the train over the tannoy... They announced his plane was delayed.* VERB Vn V that

4 If a letter, sound, or sign **announces** something, it informs people about it. *The next letter announced the birth of another boy... His entrance was announced by a buzzer connected to the door.* VERB Vn

5 If a meal or a guest **is announced** by a servant at a formal party, the servant says clearly that the meal is ready or the guest has arrived. *Dinner was announced, and served.* VB: usu passive be V-ed

announcement /ənaʊnsmənt/ **announcements** ◆◆◆◇◇

1 An **announcement** is a statement made to the public or to the media which gives information about something that has happened or that will happen. *Mr Shevardnadze made the announcement that he was to step down... There has been no formal announcement by either government.* N-COUNT: oft supp N, N that =declaration

2 The **announcement** of something that has happened is the act of telling people about it. *From his first meeting with Veronica to the announcement of the engagement was just under eight weeks... There has been no official announcement of the arrests.* N-SING: usu N ofn

3 An **announcement** in a public place, such as a newspaper or the window of a shop, is a short piece of writing telling people about something or asking for something. *He will place an announcement in the personal column of The Daily Telegraph.* N-COUNT

announcer /ənaʊnsəʳ/ **announcers** ◆◇◇◇◇

1 An **announcer** is someone who introduces programmes on radio or television or who reads the text of a radio or television advertisement. *The radio announcer said it was nine o'clock... In the commercial an announcer interviews a Texan.* N-COUNT

2 The **announcer** at a railway station or airport is the person who makes the announcements. *The announcer apologised for the delay.* N-COUNT

annoy /ənɔɪ/ **annoys, annoying, annoyed.** If someone or something **annoys** you, it makes you fairly angry and impatient. *Try making a note of the things which annoy you... It annoyed me that I didn't have time to do more ironing... It just annoyed me to hear him going on.* • See also **annoyed**, **annoying**. ◆◇◇◇◇ VERB =irritate Vn it V n that it V n to-inf Also V

annoyance /ənɔɪəns/ **annoyances** ◆◇◇◇◇

1 **Annoyance** is the feeling that you get when someone makes you feel fairly angry or impatient. *To her annoyance the stranger did not go away... He denied there was any annoyance with the British among other EC members.* N-UNCOUNT: oft with poss =irritation

2 An **annoyance** is something that makes you feel angry or impatient. *Snoring can be more than an annoyance.* N-COUNT: usu sing

annoyed /ənɔɪd/. If you are **annoyed**, you are fairly angry about something. *She tapped her forehead and looked annoyed with herself... Syria is annoyed that the PLO called last month's Arab summit in Baghdad.* • See also **annoy**. ◆◇◇◇◇ ADJ-GRADED: usu v-link ADJ, oft ADJ prep, ADJ that =irritated

annoying /ənɔɪɪŋ/. Someone or something that is **annoying** makes you feel fairly angry and impatient. *You must have found my attitude annoying... The annoying thing about the scheme is that it's confusing.* ♦ **annoyingly** *Alex looked annoyingly cheerful.* • See also **annoy**. ◆◇◇◇◇ ADJ-GRADED =irritating ADV-GRADED: usu ADV adj

annual /ænjuəl/ **annuals** ◆◆◆◆◇

1 **Annual** events happen once every year. *...the annual conference of Britain's trade union movement... In its annual report, UNICEF says at least 40,000 children die every day.* ♦ **annually** *Companies report to their shareholders annually.* ADJ: ADJ n =yearly ADV: ADV with v

2 **Annual** quantities or rates relate to a period of one year. *Annual costs, tuition and fees, £1,600... The electronic and printing unit has annual sales of about $80 million.* ♦ **annually** *El Salvador produces 100,000 tons of refined copper annually... Holiday World hires 300 new employees annually.* ADJ: ADJ n =yearly ADV: ADV with v, amount ADV

3 An **annual** is a book or magazine that is published once a year. *I looked for Wyman's picture in my high-school annual... He tried the various almanacs, annuals and gazettes which were held in the library.* N-COUNT

4 An **annual** is a plant that grows and dies within one year. *The simplest way to deal with these hardy annuals is to sow them where they are to flower.* N-COUNT

annuity /ənjuːɪti, AM ənuːɪti/ **annuities.** An **annuity** is an investment or insurance policy that pays someone a fixed sum of money each year. ◆◇◇◇◇ N-COUNT =endowment

annul /ənʌl/ **annuls, annulling, annulled.** If an election or a contract **is annulled**, it is declared invalid, so that legally it is considered never to have existed. *Opposition party leaders are now pressing for the entire election to be annulled... The marriage was annulled last month.* VB: usu passive be V-ed

annulment /ənʌlmənt/ **annulments.** The **annulment** of a contract or marriage is an official declaration that it is invalid, so that legally it is considered never to have existed. *...the annulment of the elections... He may appeal to the Pope for an annulment of his 24-year marriage.* N-VAR

annum /ænəm/. See **per annum**.

Annunciation /ənʌnsieɪʃən/. In Christian belief, the **Annunciation** was the announcement by the Archangel Gabriel to the Virgin Mary that she was going to give birth to the son of God. N-PROPER: the N

anode /ænoʊd/ **anodes.** An **anode** is the positive electrode in a cell such as a battery; a technical term in electronics. Compare **cathode**. N-COUNT

anodyne /ænədaɪn/. Something that is **anodyne** is neutral and not dangerous or distressing. *Their quarterly meetings were anodyne affairs.* ADJ-GRADED

anoint /ənɔɪnt/ **anoints, anointing, anointed**

1 If someone **anoints** a person or a part of their body, they put oil or another liquid on a part of that person's body, usually for religious or ceremonial reasons. *He anointed my forehead... The Pope has anointed him as Archbishop. ...the anointed king.* VERB Vn Vn as n V-ed

2 If someone in a position of authority **anoints** someone as something, they choose that person to do a particular important job. *...anointing Mr Wasmosy as the Colorado candidate... Mr. Olsen has always avoided anointing any successor... His message about moderation and the middle class captured the attention of the press, which anointed him front-runner.* VERB V n *as* n V n V n n

anomalous /ənɒmələs/. Something that is **anomalous** is different from what is usual or expected; a formal word. *For years this anomalous behaviour has baffled scientists... His position here is anomalous.* ADJ-GRADED =unusual

anomaly /ənɒməli/ **anomalies.** If something is an **anomaly**, it is different from what is usual or expected; a formal word. *The British public's wariness of opera is an anomaly in Europe.* ◆◇◇◇◇ N-COUNT =oddity

anon /ənɒn/. **Anon** means quite soon; a literary word. *You shall see him anon.* ADV: ADV after v

anon. /ənɒn/. **Anon.** is often written after poems or other writing to indicate that the author is not known. **Anon.** is an abbreviation for 'anonymous'.

anonymous /ənɒnɪməs/ ◆◆◇◇◇

1 If you remain **anonymous** when you do something, you do not let people know that you were the person who did it. *You can remain anonymous if you wish... An anonymous benefactor stepped in to provide the prize money. ...anonymous phone calls.* ADJ ≠known, named
♦ **anonymity** /ænɒnɪmɪti/ *Both mother and daughter, who have requested anonymity, are doing fine.* N-UNCOUNT ♦ **anonymously** *The latest photographs were sent anonymously to the magazine's Paris headquarters.* ADV

2 Something that is **anonymous** does not reveal who you are. *Of course, that would have to be by anonymous vote.* ADJ: usu ADJ n ♦ **anonymity** *He claims many more people would support him in the anonymity of a voting booth.* N-UNCOUNT: with supp

3 If you describe a place as **anonymous** you dislike it because it has no unusual or interesting features and seems unwelcoming. *...the most anonymous part of north-west Washington... It's nice to stay in a home rather than in an anonymous holiday villa.* ADJ-GRADED PRAGMATICS
♦ **anonymity** *...the anonymity of the rented room.* N-UNCOUNT

anorak /ænəræk/ **anoraks.** An **anorak** is a warm waterproof jacket, usually with a hood; used mainly in British English. ◆◇◇◇◇ N-COUNT

anorexia /ænəreksiə/. **Anorexia** or **anorexia nervosa** is an illness in which a person has an overwhelming fear of becoming fat, and so refuses to eat enough and becomes thinner and thinner. ◆◇◇◇◇ N-UNCOUNT

anorexic /ænəreksɪk/ **anorexics.** If someone is **anorexic**, they are suffering from anorexia and so are very thin. *Claire had been anorexic for three years. ...an anorexic teenager.* ADJ ► Also a noun. *Not eating makes an anorexic feel in control.* N-COUNT

another /ənʌðəʳ/ ◆◆◆◆◆

1 **Another** thing or person means an additional thing or person of the same type as one that already exists. *Divers this morning found the body of another American sailor drowned during yesterday's ferry disaster... We're going to have another baby.* DET: DET sing-n ► Also a pronoun. *The demand generated by one factory required the construction of another... MPs have one free trip to Brussels and another to Strasbourg, headquarters of the EC, each year.* PRON

2 You use **another** when you want to emphasize that an additional thing or person is different to one that already exists. *I think he's just going to deal with this problem another day... The counsellor referred her to another therapist.* DET: DET sing-n PRAGMATICS ► Also a pronoun. *He said one thing when he came here, and he's gone back to Washington and done quite another... He didn't really believe that any human being could read another's mind.* PRON

3 You use **another** at the beginning of a statement to link it to a previous statement. *Another time of great excitement for us boys was when war broke out... Another change that Sue made was to install central heating.* DET: DET sing-n PRAGMATICS

4 You use **another** before a word referring to a distance, length of time, or other amount, to indicate an additional amount. *Continue down the same road for another 2 kilometres until you reach the church of Santa Maria... He believes prices will not rise by more than another 4 per cent.* DET: DET amount =further, additional

5 You use **another** in front of the name of a well-known person, place, or event to indicate that you think they are just like that person, place, or event. *There is another Maradona in this year's World Cup: Romania's 25-year old star midfielder Hagi.* DET: DET n-proper

6 You use **one another** to indicate that each member of a group does something to or for the other members. *...women learning to help themselves and one another... Central planning has made the Soviet republics highly dependent on trade with one another.* PRON-RECIP: v PRON, prep PRON =each other

7 If you talk about **one** thing **after another**, you are referring to a series of repeated or continuous events. *They had faced one difficulty after another with bravery and dedication... They kept going, destroying one store after another.* PHRASES PHR after v

8 You use **or another** in expressions such as **one kind or another** when you do not want to be precise about which of several alternatives or possibilities you are referring to. *...family members and visiting artists of one kind or another crowding the huge kitchen... All of these industries have at one time or another been linked to cancer.* usu n PHR =or other

answer /ɑːnsəʳ, æn-/ **answers, answering, answered** ◆◆◆◆◆

1 When you **answer** someone who has asked you something, you say something back to them. *I knew Ben was lying when he answered me... Just answer the question... He paused before answering... 'When?' asked Alba, 'Tonight', answered Tom... Williams answered that he had no specific proposals yet.* VERB =reply, respond V n V V with quote V that

2 An **answer** is something that you say when you answer someone. *Without waiting for an answer, he turned and went in through the door... I don't quite know what to say in answer to your question.* N-COUNT: also *in* N *to* n =reply, response

3 If you say that someone will not **take no for an answer**, you mean that they go on trying to make you agree to something even after you have refused. *She is tough, unwilling to take no for an answer... He would never take no for an answer.* PHRASE: with brd-neg

4 If you **answer** a letter or advertisement, you write to the person who wrote it. *Did he answer your letter?... She answered an advert for a job as a cook.* VERB =reply to V n Also V

5 An **answer** is a letter that you write to someone who has written to you. *I wrote to him but I never had an answer back... She wrote to Roosevelt's secretary in answer to his letter of the day before.* N-COUNT: also *in* N *to* n =reply, response

6 When you **answer** the telephone, you pick it up when it rings. When you **answer** the door, you open it when you hear a knock or the bell. *She answered her phone on the first ring... A middle-aged woman answered the door.* VERB V n Also V ► Also a noun. *I knocked at the front door and there was no answer.* N-COUNT: usu sing

7 An **answer** to a problem is a solution to it. *There are no easy answers to the problems facing the economy... Prison is not the answer for most young offenders... Legislation is only part of the answer.* N-COUNT: oft N *to* n

8 Someone's **answer** to a question in a test or quiz is what they write or say in an attempt to give the facts that are asked for. The **answer** to a question is the fact that was asked for. *Simply marking an answer wrong will not help the pupil to get future examples correct... Below are printed the answers to the Brain of Soccer 1993 quiz.* N-COUNT: oft N *to* n

9 When you **answer** a question in a test or quiz, you write or say something in an attempt to give the facts that are asked for. *To obtain her degree, she answered 81 questions over 10 papers.* VERB V n

10 Your **answer** to something that someone has said or done is what you say or do in response to it or in defence of yourself. *In answer to speculation that she wouldn't finish the race, she boldly declared her intention of winning it.* N-COUNT: also *in* N *to* n =reply, response

11 If you **answer** something that someone has said or done, you respond to it. *He answered her smile* VERB =counter V n *with* n

with one of his own... That statement seemed designed to answer criticism of allied bombing missions.
V n
Also V n *by*-ing

12 If you say that something is a place's **answer** to a famous thing, you mean that the first thing is the equivalent of the second in that place; used mainly in journalism. *Cachaca is Brazil's answer to tequila.*
N-SING: poss N *to* n

13 If something **answers** a need or purpose, it satisfies it, because it has the right qualities. *Would communism answer their needs?*
VERB =satisfy
V n

14 If someone or something **answers** a particular description or **answers to** it, they have the characteristics described. *Two men answering the description of the suspects tried to enter Switzerland... The Japanese never built any aircraft remotely answering to this description.*
VERB =fit
V n
V *to* n

answer back. If someone, especially a child, **answers back**, they speak rudely to you when you speak to them. *She was beaten by teachers for answering back... I always answered him back when I thought he was wrong.*
PHRASAL VERB
V P
V n P

answer for
PHRASAL VERB

1 If you have to **answer for** something bad or wrong you have done, you are punished for it. *He must be made to answer for his terrible crimes.*
=pay
V P n

2 If you say that someone **has a lot to answer for**, you are saying that their actions have led to problems which you think they are responsible for.
have inflects

answerable /ɑːnsərəbəl, æn-/

1 If you are **answerable** to someone, you have to report to them and explain your actions. *Councils should be answerable to the people who elect them... All ministers, including the prime minister, will be answerable directly to him.*
ADJ: v-link ADJ *to* n

2 If you are **answerable** for your actions or for someone else's actions, you are considered to be responsible for them and must undergo any punishment that is justified. *He must be made answerable for these terrible crimes.*
ADJ: v-link ADJ, usu ADJ *for* n =responsible, accountable

answering machine, answering machines. An **answering machine** is a device which you connect to your telephone and which records telephone calls while you are out.
◆◇◇◇◇ N-COUNT =answerphone

answerphone /ɑːnsərfoʊn/ **answerphones.** In British English, an **answerphone** is the same as an answering machine.
N-COUNT =answering machine

ant /ænt/ **ants. Ants** are small crawling insects that live in large groups. *Ants swarmed up out of the ground and covered her shoes and legs.*
◆◇◇◇◇ N-COUNT

antacid /æntæsɪd/ **antacids. Antacid** is a substance that reduces the level of acid in the stomach.
N-MASS

antagonise /æntægənaɪz/. See **antagonize**.

antagonism /æntægənɪzəm/ **antagonisms. Antagonism** between people is hatred or hostility between them. **Antagonisms** are instances of this. *There is still much antagonism between trades unions and the oil companies... Old antagonisms resurfaced.*
◆◇◇◇◇ N-UNCOUNT: also N in pl =resentment

antagonist /æntægənɪst/ **antagonists.** Your **antagonist** is your opponent or enemy. *Spassky had never previously lost to his antagonist.*
◆◇◇◇◇ N-COUNT

antagonistic /æntægənɪstɪk/. If a person is **antagonistic** to someone or something, they show hatred or hostility towards them. *Nearly all the women I interviewed were aggressively antagonistic to the idea.*
ADJ-GRADED: usu v-link ADJ, oft ADJ *to/towards* n

antagonize /æntægənaɪz/ **antagonizes, antagonizing, antagonized;** also spelled **antagonise** in British English. If you **antagonize** someone, you make them feel angry or hostile towards you. *He didn't want to antagonize her.*
◆◇◇◇◇ VERB =aggravate
V n

Antarctic /æntɑːrktɪk/. The **Antarctic** is the area around the South Pole.
◆◇◇◇◇ N-PROPER: *the* N

ante /ænti/ **antes, anted.** If you **up the ante** or **raise the ante**, you increase your demands when you are in dispute or fighting for something; used mainly in journalism.
◆◇◇◇◇ PHRASE: V inflects

ante up. In American English, if you **ante up** an amount of money, you pay it, sometimes reluctantly; an informal expression. The usual British term is **cough up**. *Paul Reichmann offered to ante up $2 million.*
PHRASAL VERB no cont
V P n

anteater /æntiːtər/ **anteaters;** also spelled **ant-eater.** An **anteater** is an animal with a long snout that eats termites or ants. Anteaters live in warm countries.
N-COUNT

antecedent /æntɪsiːdənt/ **antecedents**

1 An **antecedent** of something happened or existed before it and was similar to it in some way; a formal use. *We shall first look briefly at the historical antecedents of this theory.*
N-COUNT: usu with supp =precursor, precedent

2 An **antecedent** thing or event happened or existed before another related thing or event; a formal use. *It was permissible to take account of antecedent legislation.*
ADJ: usu ADJ n =previous

3 Your **antecedents** are your ancestors; a formal use. *...a Frenchman with Irish antecedents.*
N-COUNT: usu pl

antechamber /æntitʃeɪmbər/ **antechambers;** also spelled **ante-chamber.** An **antechamber** is a small room leading into a larger room. *Her office was an antechamber to UNACO headquarters.*
N-COUNT =anteroom

antediluvian /æntidɪluːviən/. People sometimes describe old or old-fashioned things as **antediluvian** when they are trying to be funny. *...those antediluvian days before telephone answering machines.*
ADJ PRAGMATICS

antelope /æntɪloʊp/ **antelopes.** An **antelope** is an animal like a deer, with long legs and horns, that lives in Africa or Asia. Antelopes are graceful and can run fast. There are many different types of antelope. The plural is either 'antelope' or 'antelopes'.
N-COUNT

antenatal /æntineɪtəl/; also spelled **ante-natal. Antenatal** means relating to the medical care of women when they are expecting a baby. *...antenatal classes. ...antenatal care.*
ADJ: ADJ n ≠postnatal

antenna /æntenə/ **antennae** /ænteniː/ or **antennas. Antennas** is the usual plural form for meaning 2.
◆◇◇◇◇

1 The **antennae** of something such as an insect or crustacean are the two long, thin parts attached to its head that it uses to feel things with. *...a large crustacean that looks like a lobster but has two huge antennae instead of claws.*
N-COUNT: usu pl

2 An **antenna** is a device that sends and receives television or radio signals. *...engineers using radio antennas for satellite communication.*
N-COUNT =aerial

anterior /æntɪəriər/. **Anterior** describes a part of the body that is situated at or towards the front of another part; a medical term. *...the left anterior descending artery.*
ADJ: usu ADJ n ≠posterior

anteroom /æntiruːm/ **anterooms;** also spelled **ante-room.** An **anteroom** is a small room leading into a larger room. *I was waiting in the anteroom of a BBC radio studio to interview Mr Follows.*
N-COUNT =antechamber

anthem /ænθəm/ **anthems.** An **anthem** is a song which is used to represent a particular nation, society, or group and which is sung on special occasions. *The band played the Czech anthem. ...the Olympic anthem.* • See also **national anthem**.
◆◇◇◇◇ N-COUNT

anthill /ænthɪl/ **anthills;** also spelled **ant-hill.** An **anthill** is a mound of earth formed by ants when they are making a nest.
N-COUNT

anthology /ænθɒlədʒi/ **anthologies.** An **anthology** is a collection of writings by different writers published together in one book. *...an anthology of poetry.*
◆◇◇◇◇ N-COUNT

anthracite /ænθrəsaɪt/. **Anthracite** is a type of very hard coal which burns slowly, producing a lot of heat and very little smoke.
N-UNCOUNT

anthrax /ænθræks/. **Anthrax** is a disease of cattle and sheep, in which they get painful sores and a fever. Anthrax is sometimes used as a weapon in biological warfare.
N-UNCOUNT

anthropology /ænθrəpɒlədʒi/. **Anthropology** is the scientific study of people, society, and culture. ♦ **anthropologist** /ænθrəpɒlədʒɪst/ **anthropologists** *...an anthropologist who had been in China for three years.* ♦ **anthropological** /ænθrəpəlɒdʒɪkəl/ *...anthropological research.*
◆◇◇◇◇ N-UNCOUNT
N-COUNT
ADJ: ADJ n

anthropomorphic /ænθrəpəmɔːʳfɪk/. **Anthropomorphic** means relating to the idea that an animal, a god, or an object has feelings or characteristics like those of a human being. *...the anthropomorphic attitude to animals... The world of the gods is anthropomorphic, an imitative projection of ours.* ADJ

anthropomorphism /ænθrəpəmɔːʳfɪzəm/. **Anthropomorphism** is the idea that an animal, a god, or an object has feelings or characteristics like those of a human being. N-UNCOUNT

anti /ænti/ **antis**

1 In informal English, you can refer to people who are opposed to a particular activity or idea as **antis**. *The antis will not be able to resist a touch of 'I told you so'.* N-COUNT: usu pl, oft *the* N

2 If someone is opposed to something you can say that they are **anti** it; used especially in informal spoken English. *That's why you're so anti other people smoking.* ADJ-GRADED: v-link ADJ =against ≠for

anti- /ænti-/

1 **Anti-** is used to form adjectives and nouns that describe someone or something that is opposed to a particular system, practice, or group of people. *...anti-government demonstrations. ...anti-racist campaigners. ...anti-Fascists.* PREFIX

2 **Anti-** is used to form adjectives and nouns that describe things that are intended to destroy something harmful or to prevent something from happening. *Anti-aircraft and anti-tank guns were exported with forged papers. ...anti-discrimination legislation. ...anti-inflammatory drugs.* PREFIX

anti-abortionist, anti-abortionists. An **anti-abortionist** is someone who wants to limit or prevent the legal availability of abortions. *An attempt by anti-abortionists to tighten the rules was defeated.* N-COUNT

antibiotic /æntibaɪɒtɪk/ **antibiotics. Antibiotics** are drugs that are used in medicine to kill bacteria and infections. *Your doctor may prescribe a course of antibiotics.* ◆◆◇◇◇ N-COUNT: usu pl

antibody /æntibɒdi/ **antibodies. Antibodies** are substances which a person's or an animal's body produces in their blood in order to destroy substances which carry disease. ◆◆◇◇◇ N-COUNT: usu pl

anticipate /æntɪsɪpeɪt/ **anticipates, anticipating, anticipated** ◆◆◇◇◇

1 If you **anticipate** an event, you realize in advance that it may happen and you are prepared for it. *At the time we couldn't have anticipated the result of our campaigning... It is anticipated that the equivalent of 192 full-time jobs will be lost... Officials anticipate that rivalry between leaders of the various drug factions could erupt into full scale war.* VERB =expect V n *it be* V-ed that V that Also V

2 If you **anticipate** a question, request, or need, you do what is necessary or required before the question, request, or need occurs. *What Jeff did was to anticipate my next question... Do you expect your partner to anticipate your needs?* VERB V n

3 If you **anticipate** something, you do it, think it, or say it before someone else does. *In the 50s, Rauschenberg anticipated the conceptual art movement of the 80s.* VERB V n

anticipated /æntɪsɪpeɪtɪd/. If an event, especially a cultural event, is eagerly **anticipated**, people expect that it will be very good, exciting, or interesting. *...the most eagerly anticipated rock event of the year. ...one of the conference's most keenly anticipated debates... The long-anticipated study drew criticism from the tobacco industry.* ADJ-GRADED =awaited

anticipation /æntɪsɪpeɪʃᵊn/ ◆◇◇◇◇

1 **Anticipation** is a feeling of excitement about something pleasant or exciting that you know is going to happen. *There's been an atmosphere of anticipation around here for a few days now... We await the next volume of this superb edition with keen anticipation.* N-UNCOUNT

2 If something is done **in anticipation of** an event, it is done because people believe that event is going to happen. *Troops in the Philippines have been put on full alert in anticipation of trouble during a planned general strike.* PHRASE: PHR n

anticipatory /æntɪsɪpeɪtəri, AM -pətɔːri/. An **anticipatory** feeling or action is one that you have or do because you are expecting something to happen soon; a formal word. *...anticipatory excitement at the prospect of cooking and eating such delights.* ADJ: usu ADJ n

anticlimax /æntiklaɪmæks/ **anticlimaxes.** You can describe something as an **anticlimax** if it disappoints you because it happens after something that was very exciting, or because it is not as exciting as you expected. *Barry's speech followed Dirk Bogarde's appearance, and was an inevitable anticlimax... It was sad that his international career should end in such anticlimax.* N-VAR =disappointment

anticlockwise /æntiklɒkwaɪz/; also spelled **anti-clockwise**. In British English, if something is moving **anticlockwise**, it is moving in the opposite direction to the direction in which the hands of a clock move. The usual American word is **counterclockwise**. *The cutters are opened by turning the knob anticlockwise.* ▸ Also an adjective. *...an anticlockwise route around the coast.* ADV: ADV after v ≠clockwise; ADJ: ADJ n

antics /æntɪks/. **Antics** are funny, silly, or unusual ways of behaving. *Elizabeth tolerated Sarah's antics.* ◆◇◇◇◇ N-PLURAL

anticyclone /æntisaɪkloʊn/ **anticyclones.** An **anticyclone** is an area of high atmospheric pressure which causes settled weather conditions and, in summer, clear skies and high temperatures. N-COUNT

antidote /æntidoʊt/ **antidotes** ◆◇◇◇◇

1 An **antidote** is a chemical substance that stops or controls the effect of a poison. *When he returned, he noticed their sickness and prepared an antidote.* N-COUNT =remedy

2 Something that is an **antidote** to a difficult or unpleasant situation helps you to overcome the situation. *Massage is a wonderful antidote to stress.* N-COUNT: usu N *to* n =cure, remedy

antifreeze /æntifriːz/. **Antifreeze** is a liquid which is added to water to stop it freezing. It is used in car radiators in cold weather. N-UNCOUNT: also *a* N

anti-hero, anti-heroes; also spelled **antihero**. An **anti-hero** is the main character in a novel, play, or film who behaves in a completely different way from the way that people expect a hero to behave. *Clark is a tough, belligerent anti-hero.* N-COUNT ≠hero

antihistamine /æntihɪstəmɪn/ **antihistamines;** also spelled **anti-histamine**. An **antihistamine** is a drug that is used to treat illnesses, such as hay fever, that are caused by allergies. N-COUNT

antimatter /æntimætəʳ/. According to scientific theory, **antimatter** is a form of matter whose particles have characteristics and properties opposite to those of ordinary matter; a technical term in science. N-UNCOUNT

antipathy /æntɪpəθi/. **Antipathy** is a strong feeling of dislike or hostility. *Gyles and Michael have shown their patent antipathy to my smoking.* ◆◇◇◇◇ N-UNCOUNT: usu N prep =aversion

Antipodean /æntɪpədiːən/; also spelled **antipodean**. **Antipodean** describes people or things that come from or relate to Australia and New Zealand; used mainly in British journalism. *New Zealand's Cloudy Bay winery produces some of the best antipodean wines.* ADJ: usu ADJ n

Antipodes /æntɪpədiːz/. In British English, people sometimes refer to Australia and New Zealand as **the Antipodes**. N-PROPER: *the* N

antiquarian /æntɪkweəriən/ **antiquarians**

1 **Antiquarian** means concerned with old and rare objects. *...an antiquarian bookseller. ...antiquarian and second-hand books.* ADJ: ADJ n

2 An **antiquarian** is the same as an **antiquary**. N-COUNT

antiquary /æntɪkwəri, AM -kweri/ **antiquaries.** An **antiquary** is a person who studies the past, or who collects or buys and sells old and valuable objects. N-COUNT =antiquarian

antiquated /æntɪkweɪtɪd/. If you describe something as **antiquated**, you disapprove of it because it is very old or old-fashioned. *Many factories are so antiquated they are not worth sav-* ◆◇◇◇◇ ADJ-GRADED PRAGMATICS =out-moded *ing... Do we really want a return to an antiquated system of privilege and elitism?*

antique /æntiːk/ **antiques.** An **antique** is an old object such as a piece of china or furniture which is valuable because of its beauty or rarity. *...a genuine antique. ...antique silver jewellery... He deals in antiques and fine art.* ◆◆◆◇◇ N-COUNT: oft N n

antiqued /æntiːkt/. An **antiqued** object is modern but has been made to look like an antique. *Both rooms have antiqued pine furniture.* ADJ

antique shop, antique shops. An **antique shop** is a shop where antiques are sold. N-COUNT

antiquity /æntɪkwɪti/ **antiquities** ◆◇◇◇◇

1 **Antiquity** is the distant past, especially the time of the ancient Egyptians, Greeks, and Romans. *...famous monuments of classical antiquity... The town was famous in antiquity for its white bulls.* N-UNCOUNT

2 **Antiquities** are things such as buildings, statues, or coins that were made in ancient times and have survived to the present day. *...collectors of Roman antiquities.* N-COUNT: usu pl

3 The **antiquity** of something is its great age. *...a town of great antiquity... It indicates the antiquity of the tradition.* N-UNCOUNT: with supp

anti-Semite /ænti siːmaɪt, AM - sem-/ **anti-Semites.** An **anti-Semite** is someone who strongly dislikes and is prejudiced against Jewish people. N-COUNT

anti-Semitic; also spelled **antisemitic**. Someone or something that is **anti-Semitic** is hostile to or prejudiced against Jewish people. *His anti-Semitic beliefs were well-known in America.* ◆◇◇◇◇ ADJ-GRADED

anti-Semitism /ænti semɪtɪzəm/. **Anti-Semitism** is hostility to and prejudice against Jewish people. *The extreme right-wing National Front promoted anti-semitism.* ◆◇◇◇◇ N-UNCOUNT

antiseptic /æntiseptɪk/ **antiseptics** ◆◇◇◇◇

1 **Antiseptic** is a substance that kills germs and harmful bacteria. *She bathed the cut with antiseptic.* N-MASS =disinfectant

2 Something that is **antiseptic** kills germs and harmful bacteria. *These vegetables and herbs have strong antiseptic qualities.* ADJ

anti-social; also spelled **antisocial**. ◆◇◇◇◇

1 Someone who is **anti-social** is unwilling to meet and be friendly with other people. *Britain is breeding a nation of teenagers who will become aggressive and anti-social.* ADJ-GRADED ≠out-going, gregarious

2 **Anti-social** behaviour is annoying or upsetting to other people. *Playing these games can lead to anti-social behaviour.* ADJ-GRADED

antithesis /æntɪθəsɪs/ **antitheses** /æntɪθəsiːz/

1 The **antithesis** of something is its exact opposite; a formal use. *The antithesis of the Middle Eastern buyer is the Japanese.* N-COUNT: usu *the* N *of* n =opposite

2 If there is an **antithesis** between two things, there is a contrast between them; a formal use. *...the antithesis between instinct and reason.* N-COUNT =opposition

antithetical /æntɪθetɪkəl/. Something that is **antithetical** to something else is the opposite of it and is unable to exist with it; used in written English. *The oppressive use of power is antithetical to our democratic ideals.* ADJ: usu v-link ADJ *to* n

antitrust /æntitrʌst/. In the United States, **antitrust** laws are intended to stop large firms taking over their competitors, fixing prices with their competitors, or interfering with free competition in any way. *The jury found that the NFL had violated antitrust laws, as the USFL claimed.* ◆◇◇◇◇ ADJ: ADJ n

antler /æntləʳ/ **antlers.** A male deer's **antlers** are the branched horns on its head. N-COUNT

antonym /æntənɪm/ **antonyms.** The **antonym** of a word is a word which means the opposite; a formal word. N-COUNT ≠synonym

antsy /æntsi/. In informal American English, if someone is **antsy**, they are easily irritated or slightly angry about something. *This is the end of a tour so I'm a little antsy, I guess.* ADJ-GRADED: usu v-link ADJ =tetchy

anus /eɪnəs/ **anuses.** A person's **anus** is the hole between their buttocks, from which faeces leave their body; a medical term. N-COUNT

anvil /ænvɪl/ **anvils**

1 An **anvil** is a heavy iron block on which hot metals are beaten into shape. N-COUNT

2 If you refer to something as an **anvil**, you mean that it is a difficult experience or circumstance that changes someone or produces something good; a literary use. *His independence had been forged on the anvil of a harsh environment.* N-COUNT: usu sing

anxiety /æŋzaɪɪti/ **anxieties. Anxiety** is a feeling of nervousness or worry. *Her voice was full of anxiety... Many editorials express their anxieties about the economic chaos in the country.* ◆◆◆◇◇ N-UNCOUNT: also N in pl

anxious /æŋkʃəs/ ◆◆◆◇◇

1 If you are **anxious** to do something or **anxious** that something should happen, you very much want to do it or very much want it to happen. *Both the Americans and the Russians are anxious to avoid conflict in South Asia... He is anxious that there should be no delay... Those anxious for reform say that the present system is too narrow.* ADJ-GRADED: v-link ADJ, ADJ to-inf, ADJ that, ADJ prep =eager

2 If you are **anxious**, you are nervous or worried about something. *The foreign minister admitted he was still anxious about the situation in the country... A friend of mine is a very anxious person.* ADJ-GRADED =concerned

♦ **anxiously** *They are waiting anxiously to see who will succeed him.* ADV-GRADED: ADV with v

3 An **anxious** time or situation is one during which you feel nervous and worried. *The Prime Minister faces anxious hours before the votes are counted tomorrow night.* ADJ-GRADED: ADJ n =uneasy

any /eni/ ◆◆◆◆◆

1 You use **any** in statements with negative meaning to indicate that no thing or person of a particular type exists, is present, or is involved in a situation. *I never make any big decisions... I'm not making any promises... We are doing this all without any support from the hospital... Earlier reports were unable to confirm that there were any survivors... It is too early to say what effect, if any, there will be on the workforce.* ► Also a quantifier. *You don't know any of my friends... There was nothing you could do, nothing any of us could do.* ► Also a pronoun. *The children needed new school clothes and Kim couldn't afford any.* DET: DET pl-n/n-uncount; QUANT: QUANT *of* def-n-uncount/def-pl-n; PRON: PRON after v

2 You use **any** in questions and conditional clauses to ask whether there is some of a particular thing or some of a particular group of people, or to suggest that there might be. *Do you speak any foreign languages?... Are there any ladies in the audience?... Have you got any cheese I can have with this bread?* ► Also a quantifier. *Introduce foods one at a time and notice if you feel uncomfortable with any of them... Have you ever used a homeopathic remedy for any of the following reasons?* ► Also a pronoun. *If any bright thoughts occur to you pass them straight to me. Have you got any?... The plants are inspected for insects and if I find any, they are squashed.* DET: DET pl-n/n-uncount; QUANT: QUANT *of* def-n-uncount/def-pl-n; PRON: PRON after v

3 You use **any** in positive statements when you are referring to someone or something of a particular kind that might exist, occur, or be involved in a situation, when their exact identity or nature is irrelevant. *Any actor will tell you that it is easier to perform than to be themselves... I'm prepared to take any advice... I would overcome any weakness, any despair, any fear.* ► Also a quantifier. *Nealy disappeared two days ago, several miles away from any of the fighting... It had been the biggest mistake any of them could remember.* ► Also a pronoun. *Clean the mussels and discard any that do not close. ...mangoes, bananas, pineapples, pears, and grapes as delicious as any you have ever eaten.* DET; QUANT: QUANT *of* def-n-uncount/def-pl-n; PRON

4 You can also use **any** to emphasize a comparative adjective or adverb in a negative statement. *I can't see things getting any easier for graduates... Anne's not getting any younger.* ADV: ADV compar PRAGMATICS

5 If you say that someone or something is **not just any** person or thing, you mean that they are special in some way. *Finzer is not just any East Coast businessman... It's fashionable for young people to wear training shoes, but not just any trainers.* PHRASES PHR n

6 If something does not happen or is not true **any** PHR after v

more or **any longer**, it has stopped happening or is no longer true. *I don't want to see her any more... We felt we had no home any more, no family, nothing... I couldn't keep the tears hidden any longer.*

7 • **in any case**: see **case**. • **by any chance**: see **chance**. • **in any event**: see **event**. • **by any means**: see **means**. • **any old**: see **old**. • **at any rate**: see **rate**.

anybody /ˈenibɒdi/. **Anybody** means the same as **anyone**. ◆◆◆◇◇ PRON-INDEF

anyhow /ˈenihaʊ/ ◆◇◇◇◇

1 **Anyhow** means the same as **anyway**. ADV

2 If you do something **anyhow**, you do it in a careless or untidy way; used in informal British English. *...her long legs which she displayed all anyhow getting in and out of her car.* ADV: ADV after v

anymore /ˈenimɔːr/. If something does not happen or is not true **anymore**, it has stopped happening or is no longer true. Some people think this spelling is incorrect and prefer to use **any more**. *I don't ride my motorbike much anymore... I couldn't trust him anymore... People are not interested in movies anymore.* ◆◆◇◇◇ ADV: ADV after v =any longer

anyone /ˈeniwʌn/. The form **anybody** is also used. ◆◆◆◆◇

1 You use **anyone** or **anybody** in statements with negative meaning to indicate in a general way that nobody is present or involved in an action. *I won't tell anyone I saw you here... You needn't talk to anyone if you don't want to... He was far too scared to tell anybody... Presidents are not any different from anybody else; they're human beings.* PRON-INDEF

2 You use **anyone** or **anybody** in questions and conditional clauses to ask or talk about whether someone is present or doing something. *Why would anyone want that job?... How can anyone look sad at an occasion like this?... If anyone deserves to be happy, you do.* PRON-INDEF

3 You also use **anyone** and **anybody** before words which indicate the kind of person you are talking about. *I always had been the person who achieved things before anyone else at my age... It's not a job for anyone who is slow with numbers... Anybody interested in pop culture at all should buy 'Pure Cult'.* PRON-INDEF: PRON cl/group

4 You use **anyone** or **anybody** to refer to a person when you are emphasizing that it could be any person out of a very large number of people. *Anyone could be doing what I'm doing... Al Smith could make anybody laugh.* PRON-INDEF

5 You use **anyone who is anyone** and **anybody who is anybody** to refer to people who are important or influential. *It seems anyone who's anyone in business is going to the conference.* PHRASE

anyplace /ˈenipleɪs/. In American English, **anyplace** means the same as **anywhere**. *She didn't have anyplace to go... You can go anyplace to get the car serviced.* ADV: ADV after v

anything /ˈeniθɪŋ/ ◆◆◆◆◆

1 You use **anything** in statements with negative meaning to indicate in a general way that nothing is present or that an action or event does not or cannot happen. *We can't do anything... Dad sat, not saying anything... She couldn't see or hear anything at all... By the time I get home, I'm too tired to do anything active... I couldn't manage anything without you.* PRON-INDEF: v PRON, oft PRON adj

2 You use **anything** in questions and conditional clauses to ask or talk about whether something is present or happening. *What happened, is anything wrong?... Did you find anything?... Is there anything you can do to help?... If there's anything I could do for him, I would.* PRON-INDEF: oft PRON adj

3 You can use **anything** before words which indicate the kind of thing you are talking about. *More than anything else, he wanted to become a teacher... Anything that's cheap this year will be even cheaper next year... She collects anything that has charm.* PRON-INDEF: PRON cl/group

4 You use **anything** to emphasize a possible thing, event, or situation, when you are saying that it could be any one of a very large number of things. *He is young, fresh, and ready for anything... At that point, anything could happen... He is convinced he just has to say 'please' and he can have anything.* PRON-INDEF PRAGMATICS

5 You use **anything** in expressions such as **anything near**, **anything close to** and **anything like** to emphasize a statement that you are making. *Doctors have decided the only way he can live anything near a normal life is to give him an operation... Only Cowans played anything close to his true form... Plainer examples of the early period do not fetch anything like these sums.* PRON-INDEF: PRON prep PRAGMATICS

6 When you do not want to be exact, you use **anything** to talk about a particular range of things or quantities. *Factory farming has turned the cow into a milk machine, producing anything from 25 to 40 litres of milk per day... Fights with his father lasted anything between fifteen minutes and an hour.* PRON-INDEF: PRON *from* n *to* n, PRON *between* n *and* n

7 In informal spoken English, you use **as anything** after an adjective to emphasize a quality that someone has. *He used to be as smart as anything... She opened the door and jumped out, quick as anything.* PHRASES adj PHR PRAGMATICS

8 You use **anything but** in expressions such as **anything but quiet** and **anything but attractive** to emphasize that something is not the case. *I will be anything but quiet on Saturday night!... What existed in central and eastern Europe was anything but democratic socialism... The Los Angeles police chief was not always so insulated from politicians; anything but.* v-link PHR, usu PHR adj/n PRAGMATICS

9 In informal spoken English, you can say that you **would not** do something **for anything** to emphasize that you definitely would not want to do or be a particular thing. *I wouldn't want to move for anything in the world... I wouldn't have missed this summer in England for anything... I wouldn't be without Matthew for anything.* PRAGMATICS

10 You use **if anything**, especially after a negative statement, to introduce a statement that adds to what you have just said. *I never had to clean up after him. If anything, he did most of the cleaning.* PHR with cl PRAGMATICS

11 In informal spoken English, you can add **or anything** to the end of a clause or sentence in order to refer vaguely to other things that are or may be similar to what has just been mentioned. *Listen, if you talk to him or anything make sure you let us know, will you... He didn't cry or scream or anything.* PRAGMATICS

anytime /ˈenitaɪm/. You use **anytime** to mean at an unspecified point in time. *The college admits students anytime during the year... He can leave anytime he wants... He can call me anytime.* ◆◇◇◇◇ ADV-INDEF: ADV with v, oft ADV prep/cl =whenever

anyway /ˈeniweɪ/. The form **anyhow** is also used. ◆◆◆◆◇

1 You use **anyway** or **anyhow** to indicate that a statement explains or supports a previous point. *I'm certain David's told you his business troubles. Anyway, it's no secret that he owes money... Mother certainly won't let him stay with her and anyhow he wouldn't.* ADV: ADV with cl =besides

2 You use **anyway** or **anyhow** to suggest that a statement is true or relevant in spite of other things that have been said. *I don't know why I settled on Aberdeen, but anyway I did... I wasn't qualified to apply for the job really but I got it anyhow.* ADV: ADV with cl

3 You use **anyway** or **anyhow** to correct or modify a statement, for example to limit it to what you definitely know to be true. *Mary Ann doesn't want to have children. Not right now, anyway.* ADV: cl/group ADV PRAGMATICS

4 You use **anyway** or **anyhow** to indicate that you are asking what the real situation is or what the real reason for something is. *What do you want from me, anyway?... Where the hell was Bud, anyhow?* ADV: cl ADV

5 You use **anyway** or **anyhow** to indicate that you are missing out some details in a story and are passing on to the next main point or event. *I was told to go to Reading for this interview. It was a very amusing affair. Anyhow, I got the job.* ADV: ADV with cl PRAGMATICS =well

6 You use **anyway** or **anyhow** to change the topic or return to a previous topic. *'I've got a terrible cold.'—'Have you? Oh dear. Anyway, so you're not going to go away this weekend?'* ADV: ADV cl PRAGMATICS =well

7 You use **anyway** or **anyhow** to indicate that you ADV:

want to end the conversation. *'Anyway, I'd better let you have your dinner. Give our love to Francis. Bye.'... 'Anyhow, thanks a lot. Bye bye.'* ADV cl PRAGMATICS =well

anyways /eniweɪz/. In spoken American English, some people use **anyways** instead of **anyway**. ADV

anywhere /enihweəʳ/ ◆◆◆◇◇

1 You use **anywhere** in statements with negative meaning to indicate that a place does not exist. *I haven't got anywhere to live... There had never been such a beautiful woman anywhere in the world.* ADV-INDEF: ADV after v, *be* ADV, oft ADV cl/group

2 You use **anywhere** in questions and conditional clauses to ask or talk about a place without saying exactly where you mean. *Did you try to get help from anywhere?... If she wanted to go anywhere at all she had to wait for her father to drive her.* ADV-INDEF: ADV after v, *be* ADV, *from* ADV, oft ADV cl/group

3 You use **anywhere** before words that indicate the kind of place you are talking about. *In America most leisure-time activities are about a million times better than anywhere else... He'll meet you anywhere you want... Let us know if you come across anywhere that has something special to offer.* ADV-INDEF: ADV cl/group =anyplace

4 You use **anywhere** to refer to a place when you are emphasizing that it could be any of a large number of places. *Rachel would have known Julia Stone anywhere. ...jokes that are so funny they always work anywhere.* ADV-INDEF: ADV after v, *be* ADV PRAGMATICS

5 When you do not want to be exact, you use **anywhere** to refer to a particular range of things. *His shoes cost anywhere from $200 up... My visits lasted anywhere from three weeks to two months.* ADV-INDEF: ADV *from/to* n, ADV *between* pl-n, ADV *up*

6 You use **anywhere** in expressions such as **anywhere near** and **anywhere close to** to emphasize a statement that you are making. *There weren't anywhere near enough empty boxes... The only one who's anywhere close to the truth is my mother.* ADV-INDEF: ADV adj/adv PRAGMATICS

7 If you say that someone or something **is not getting anywhere** or **is not going anywhere**, you mean that they are not making progress or achieving a satisfactory result. *The conversation did not seem to be getting anywhere... I didn't see that my career as a filmmaker was going anywhere.* PHRASE: V inflects

aorta /eɪɔːʳtə/ **aortas.** Your **aorta** is the main artery through which blood leaves your heart before it flows through the rest of your body. N-COUNT

apace /əpeɪs/. If something develops or continues **apace**, it is developing or continuing quickly; a formal word. *Land reclamation continues apace... The plan is proceeding apace, with another 13 superstores opened in the first half of this year.* ADV: ADV after v =speedily, swiftly

apart 1 positions and states

apart /əpɑːʳt/ ◆◆◆◆◇

In addition to the uses shown below, **apart** is used in phrasal verbs such as 'grow apart' and 'take apart'.

1 When someone or something is positioned **apart** from someone or something else, they are some distance from that person or thing. *He was standing a bit apart from the rest of us, watching us... She saw Sheila standing some distance apart.* ADV: ADV after v, oft ADV *from* n

2 If two people or things are positioned **apart**, there is a space or a distance between them. *Ray and sister Renee lived just 25 miles apart from each other. ...regions that were too far apart to have any way of knowing about each other... He was standing, feet apart.* ADV: ADV after v, n ADV

3 If two people or things move **apart** or are pulled **apart**, they move away from each other. *John and Isabelle moved apart, back into the sun... He tried in vain to keep the two dogs apart before the neighbour intervened.* ADV: ADV after v

4 If two people are **apart**, they are no longer living together or spending time together, either permanently or just for a short time. *It was the first time Jane and I had been apart for more than a few days... Mum and Dad live apart.* ADV: *be* ADV, ADV after v

5 If you take something **apart**, you separate it into the pieces that it is made of. If it comes or falls **apart**, its parts separate from each other. *When the clock stopped he took it apart, found what was wrong, and put the whole thing together again... Many school buildings are unsafe, and some are falling apart.* ADV: ADV after v

6 If something such as an organization or relationship falls **apart**, or if something tears it **apart**, it can no longer continue because it has serious difficulties. *Any manager knows that his company will start falling apart if his attention wanders... Her marriage to film producer Michael Greenburg fell apart.* ADV: ADV after v

7 If something sets someone or something **apart**, it makes them different from other people or things. *What really sets Mr Thaksin apart is that he comes not from Southern China, but from northern Thailand... Health spending tends to rise disproportionately as countries become richer; but even adjusting for this, America is a case apart.* ADV: ADV after v, n ADV

8 If people or groups are a long way **apart** on a particular topic or issue, they have completely different views and disagree about it. *Officials say they're so far apart on such a wide range of issues there's no telling how long the talks could drag on... Their concept of a performance and our concept were miles apart.* ADJ: v-link amount ADJ, oft ADJ *on* n

9 If you **can't tell** two people or things **apart**, they look exactly the same to you. *I can still only tell Mark and Dave apart by the colour of their shoes!... Free range and battery eggs, boiled for four minutes, were hard to tell apart.* PHRASE: V inflects, usu with brd-neg

apart 2 indicating exceptions and focusing

apart /əpɑːʳt/ ◆◆◆◇◇

1 You use **apart from** when you are making an exception to a general statement. *The room was empty apart from one man seated beside the fire... She was the only British competitor apart from Richard Meade.* PHR-PREP =except for

2 You use **apart** when you are making an exception to a general statement. *This was, New York apart, the first American city I had ever been in where people actually lived downtown.* ADV: n ADV =excepted

3 You use **apart from** to indicate that you are aware of one aspect of a situation, but that you are going to focus on another aspect. *Illiteracy threatens Britain's industrial performance. But, quite apart from that, the individual who can't read or write is unlikely to get a job... There was always something to look forward to, apart from Rachel's visits.* PHR-PREP PRAGMATICS

4 You use **apart** to indicate that you are aware of one aspect of a situation, but that you are going to focus on another aspect. *That argument apart, it is for the Germans themselves to work out how their forces should come together.* ADV: n ADV PRAGMATICS =aside

apartheid /əpɑːʳthaɪt/. **Apartheid** was a political system in South Africa in which people were divided into racial groups and kept apart by law. *He praised her role in the struggle against apartheid. ...the anti-apartheid movement.* ◆◆◇◇◇ N-UNCOUNT

apartment /əpɑːʳtmənt/ **apartments** ◆◆◆◇◇

1 An **apartment** is a set of rooms for living in, usually on one floor of a large building. The usual British word is **flat**. *Christina has her own apartment, with her own car. ...a high-rise apartment building. ...bleak cities of concrete apartment blocks.* N-COUNT

2 The **apartments** of an important person such as a king, queen, or president are a set of large rooms, usually richly furnished, which are used by them. *Mr Major was ushered into the Queen's apartments for his first briefing.* N-PLURAL

apartment house, apartment houses. In American English, an **apartment house** is a tall building which contains different apartments on different floors. The British expression is **block of flats**. *...the Manhattan apartment house where they live.* N-COUNT

apathetic /æpəθetɪk/. If you describe someone as **apathetic**, you mean that they are not interested in doing anything; used showing disapproval. *Even the most apathetic students are beginning to sit up and listen... Others feel apathetic about the candidates in both parties.* ADJ-GRADED PRAGMATICS

♦ **apathetically** /æpəθetɪkli/ *The men were trudging along apathetically.* ADV-GRADED

apathy /æpəθi/. **Apathy** is a state of mind in which someone is not interested in or enthusiastic about anything; often used showing disapproval. *They told me about isolation and public apathy. ...the political apathy and emotional uncertainty of young Americans.* ◆◇◇◇◇ N-UNCOUNT PRAGMATICS

ape /eɪp/ **apes, aping, aped** ◆◇◇◇◇
1 **Apes** are chimpanzees, gorillas, and other animals in the same family. *...the theory that man is descended from the apes.* N-COUNT
2 If you **ape** someone's speech or behaviour, you imitate it. *Modelling yourself on someone you admire is not the same as aping all they say or do. ...French films which merely aped Hollywood.* VERB =copy, imitate V n

aperitif /æperɪtiːf/ **aperitifs.** An **aperitif** is an alcoholic drink that you have before a meal. *...a garden terrace where you can drink your aperitifs.* N-COUNT

aperture /æpəʳtʃəʳ/ **apertures** ◆◇◇◇◇
1 An **aperture** is a narrow hole or gap; a formal use. *Through the aperture he could see daylight.* N-COUNT
2 In photography, the **aperture** of a camera is the size of the hole through which light passes to reach the film. *Use a small aperture and position the camera carefully... The camera has a 32mm lens with a maximum aperture of f/4.5 and a fixed shutter speed of 1/100sec.* N-COUNT

apex /eɪpeks/ **apexes**
1 The **apex** of an organization or system is the highest and most important position in it. *At the apex of the party was its central committee.* N-SING: usu *the* N *of* n =top
2 The **apex** of something is its pointed top or end. *Georgeanne Woods led me up a gloomy corridor to the apex of the pyramid.* N-COUNT: usu sing, oft *the* N *of* n

Apex; also spelled **APEX**. An **Apex** or an **Apex ticket** is a ticket for a journey by air or rail which costs less than the standard ticket, but which you have to book a specified period in advance. *The Apex fare is £195 return.* N-SING: usu N n

aphasia /əfeɪziə, -ʒə/. **Aphasia** is a mental condition in which people are often unable to remember simple words or communicate; a medical term. N-UNCOUNT

aphid /eɪfɪd/ **aphids. Aphids** are very small insects which live on plants and suck their juices. They are common garden pests. *Spray the plants against aphids, whitefly and red spider mite.* ◆◇◇◇◇ N-COUNT: usu pl

aphorism /æfərɪzəm/ **aphorisms.** An **aphorism** is a short witty sentence which expresses a general truth or observation; a formal word. *'What if they gave a war and nobody came?' was one of his generation's favored aphorisms.* N-COUNT =witticism

aphrodisiac /æfrədɪziæk/ **aphrodisiacs.** An **aphrodisiac** is a food, drink, or drug which is said to make people want to have sex. *Asparagus is reputed to be an aphrodisiac.* N-COUNT ► Also an adjective. *...plants with narcotic or aphrodisiac qualities.* ADJ-GRADED

apiece /əpiːs/ ◆◇◇◇◇
1 If people have a particular number of things **apiece**, they have that number each. *He and I had two fish apiece... The World Series between the Atlanta Braves and Toronto Blue Jays is tied at one game apiece.* ADV: amount ADV =each
2 If a number of similar things are for sale at a certain price **apiece**, that is the price for each one of them. *Corey found the shells at a yard sale priced at 35 cents apiece.* ADV: amount ADV =each

aplenty /əplenti/. If you have something **aplenty**, you have plenty of it. *There were chances aplenty to win the game but United showed as much killer instinct as a toy poodle.* ADV: n ADV

aplomb /əplɒm/. If you do something with **aplomb**, you do it with confidence in a relaxed way; a formal word. *The whole cast executed the production with truly professional aplomb.* N-UNCOUNT: usu *with* N =poise

apocalypse /əpɒkəlɪps/. The **apocalypse** is the total destruction and end of the world. *We live in the shadow of the apocalypse, of a catastrophe that will mean the end of the world itself.* ◆◇◇◇◇ N-SING: usu *the* N

apocalyptic /əpɒkəlɪptɪk/ ◆◇◇◇◇
1 **Apocalyptic** means relating to the total destruction of something, especially of the world. *A young Mongolian journalist saw the news from Moscow in apocalyptic terms.* ADJ: usu ADJ n
2 **Apocalyptic** means relating to or involving prophecy about future disasters and the destruction of the world. *The Bible's Book of Revelation is an apocalyptic vision about the second coming of Christ.* ADJ-GRADED: usu ADJ n

apocryphal /əpɒkrɪfəl/. An **apocryphal** story is one which is not generally thought to be true or to have happened but which may convey a true picture of someone or something. *This may well be an apocryphal story... There is a story, probably apocryphal, about a British motorcyclist on holiday in America.* ADJ

apogee /æpədʒiː/. The **apogee** of something such as a culture or a business is its highest or its greatest point; a formal word. *The Alliance for Progress reached its apogee during the first half of the decade.* N-SING: with supp =apex, peak

apolitical /eɪpəlɪtɪkəl/
1 Someone who is **apolitical** is not interested in politics. *As a musician, you cannot be apolitical.* ADJ-GRADED ≠political
2 If you describe an organization or an activity as **apolitical**, you mean that it is not linked to a particular political party. *...the normally apolitical European Commission... Others maintain the violence is apolitical and the perpetrators are just gangs bent on defying authority.* ADJ

apologetic /əpɒlədʒetɪk/. If you are **apologetic**, you show or say that you are sorry for causing trouble for someone, for hurting them, or for disappointing them. *The hospital staff were very apologetic but that couldn't really compensate... They were almost apologetic about the improvements they'd made... 'I don't follow football,' she said with an apologetic smile.* ◆◇◇◇◇ ADJ-GRADED ♦ **apologetically** /əpɒlədʒetɪkli/ *'It's of no great literary merit,' he said, almost apologetically.* ADV-GRADED: ADV with v

apologia /æpəloʊdʒiə/ **apologias.** An **apologia** is a statement in which you defend something that you strongly believe in, for example a way of life, a person's behaviour, or a philosophy; a formal word. *The left have seen the work as an apologia for privilege and property.* N-COUNT: usu sing

apologise /əpɒlədʒaɪz/. See **apologize**.

apologist /əpɒlədʒɪst/ **apologists.** An **apologist** is a person who writes or speaks in defence of a belief, a cause, or a person's life; a formal word. *'I am no apologist for Hitler,' observed Pyat. ...the great Christian apologist Origen.* N-COUNT

apologize /əpɒlədʒaɪz/ **apologizes, apologizing, apologized;** also spelled **apologise** in British English. When you **apologize** to someone, you say that you are sorry that you have hurt them or caused trouble for them. You can say **'I apologize'** as a formal way of saying sorry. *Two years ago, Congress formally apologized for the internment... I apologize for being late, but I have just had a message from the hospital... Costello later apologized, saying he'd been annoyed by the man... He apologized to the people who had been affected.* ◆◆◇◇◇ VERB PRAGMATICS V *for* n/-ing V V *to* n Also V with quote

apology /əpɒlədʒi/ **apologies** ◆◆◇◇◇
1 An **apology** is something that you say or write in order to tell someone that you are sorry that you have hurt them or caused trouble for them. *I didn't get an apology... We received a letter of apology... He made a public apology for the team's performance.* N-VAR
2 If you offer or make your **apologies**, you apologize; a formal use. *His mother offered her apologies to the Jones family... When Mary finally appeared, she made her apologies to Mrs Madrigal.* N-PLURAL: usu poss N
3 If you say that you **make no apologies** for what you have done, you are emphasizing that you feel that you have done nothing wrong. *It was a battling performance and I make no apologies for the way we played.* PHRASE: V inflects

apoplectic /æpəplektɪk/. If someone is **apoplectic**, they are extremely angry about something; a ADJ =furious, incensed formal word. *It's enough to make them choke with apoplectic rage... My father was apoplectic when he discovered the truth.*

apoplexy /æpəpleksi/

1 **Apoplexy** is a heart attack; an old-fashioned use.
N-UNCOUNT

2 **Apoplexy** is extreme anger; a formal use. *He has already caused apoplexy with his books on class and on war.*
N-UNCOUNT

apostasy /əpɒstəsi/. If someone is accused of **apostasy**, they are accused of abandoning their religious faith, political loyalties, or principles; a formal word. *...a charge of apostasy.*
N-UNCOUNT

apostate /əpɒsteɪt/ **apostates.** An **apostate** is someone who has abandoned their religious faith, political loyalties, or principles; a formal word.
N-COUNT =renegade, defector ≠follower

apostle /əpɒsᵊl/ **apostles**

1 The **apostles** were the followers of Jesus Christ who went from place to place telling people about him and trying to persuade them to become Christians. *...the twelve apostles.*
N-COUNT =disciples

2 An **apostle** of a particular philosophy, policy, or cause is someone who strongly believes in it and works hard to promote it. *Even though we present ourselves as the apostles of free trade, we still protect our producers in many ways.*
N-COUNT: usu N *of* n =defender

Apostolic /æpɒstɒlɪk/

1 **Apostolic** means belonging or relating to a Christian religious leader, especially the Pope, who is considered to inherit authority from Christ's early followers. *He was appointed Apostolic Administrator of Minsk by Pope John Paul II.*
ADJ

2 **Apostolic** means belonging or relating to the early followers of Christ and to their teaching. *He saw his vocation as one of prayer and apostolic work.*
ADJ

apostrophe /əpɒstrəfi/ **apostrophes.** An **apostrophe** is the mark **'**, written to indicate that one or more letters have been omitted from a word, as in 'isn't' and 'we'll'. It is also added to nouns to form possessives, as in 'Mike's car'; see also **'s**.
N-COUNT

apothecary /əpɒθɪkri, AM -keri/ **apothecaries.** An **apothecary** was a person who prepared medicines for people; an old-fashioned word.
N-COUNT

apotheosis /əpɒθioʊsɪs/

1 If something is the **apotheosis** of something else, it is an ideal or typical example of it; a formal use. *The Oriental in Bangkok is the apotheosis of the grand hotel.*
N-SING: oft N *of* n =epitome

2 If you describe an event or a time as someone's **apotheosis**, you mean that it was the high point in their career or their life; a formal use. *This was the time of Elizabeth Taylor's apotheosis.*
N-SING: with poss

appal /əpɔːl/ **appals, appalling, appalled;** spelled **appall** in American English. If something **appals** you, it disgusts you because it seems so bad or unpleasant. *The new-found strength of Hindu militancy appals many observers... My wife now looks like her mother, which appals me.*
◆◆◇◇◇ VERB =horrify V n Also V

appalled /əpɔːld/. If you are **appalled** by something, you feel disgust or dismay because it seems so bad or unpleasant. *She said that the Americans are appalled at the statements made at the conference... We are all, of course, appalled that such items are still on sale in the shops.*
◆◇◇◇◇ ADJ-GRADED: usu v-link ADJ, usu ADJ *by/at* n =horrified

appalling /əpɔːlɪŋ/
◆◆◇◇◇

1 Something that is **appalling** is so bad or unpleasant that it shocks you. *They have been living under the most appalling conditions for two months.*
ADJ-GRADED =dreadful
♦ **appallingly** *He says that he understands why they behaved so appallingly... The detection rate for racial crimes is appallingly low.*
ADV-GRADED

2 You can use **appalling** to emphasize that something is very great or severe. *I developed an appalling headache.* ♦ **appallingly** *It's been an appallingly busy morning.*
ADJ-GRADED PRAGMATICS ADV-GRADED

3 See also **appal**.

apparatchik /æpərætʃɪk/ **apparatchiks.** An **apparatchik** is an active long-term member of a political party; a formal word which is often used showing disapproval. *Political party apparatchiks are appointed to every office of social authority.*
N-COUNT PRAGMATICS

apparatus /æpəreɪtəs, -ræt-/ **apparatuses**
◆◇◇◇◇

1 The **apparatus** of an organization or system is its structure and method of operation. *For 74 years, Russia had been buried under the apparatus of Soviet power. ...a massive bureaucratic apparatus.*
N-VAR: with supp

2 **Apparatus** is the equipment, such as tools and machines, which is used to do a particular job or activity. *One of the boys had to be rescued by firemen wearing breathing apparatus.*
N-VAR: oft supp N

apparel /əpærəl/. **Apparel** is a formal word for clothes, especially formal clothes worn on an important occasion; used mainly in American English. *Women's apparel is offered in petite, regular, and tall models.*
◆◇◇◇◇ N-UNCOUNT =clothing

apparent /əpærənt/
◆◆◆◇◇

1 An **apparent** situation, quality, or feeling seems to exist, although you cannot be certain that it does exist. *These workers don't apologize for their apparent good fortune... There is at last an apparent end to the destructive price war.*
ADJ: ADJ n

2 If something is **apparent** to you, it is clear and obvious to you. *It has been apparent that in other areas standards have held up well... The presence of a star is already apparent in the early film.*
ADJ-GRADED: v-link ADJ, oft *it* v-link ADJ that =clear

3 If you say that something happens **for no apparent reason**, you cannot understand why it happens. *The person may become dizzy for no apparent reason.*
PHRASE

apparently /əpærəntli/
◆◆◆◆◇

1 You use **apparently** to indicate that the information you are giving is something that you have heard, but you are not certain that it is true. *Apparently the girls are not at all amused by the whole business... Many young men are not being allowed out, apparently because of fears that they may join the army in exile.*
ADV: ADV with cl/group, ADV before v PRAGMATICS

2 You use **apparently** to refer to something that the facts which are currently available suggest is the case. *...The recent deterioration has been caused by an apparently endless recession. ...Rudolph said no more. Apparently he was a man of few words.*
ADV: ADV with cl/group, ADV before v

apparition /æpərɪʃᵊn/ **apparitions.** An **apparition** is someone you see or think you see but who is not really there as a physical being; a formal word. *The patient recognized one of the women as the apparition she had seen. ...these apparitions of the Virgin.*
N-COUNT

appeal /əpiːl/ **appeals, appealing, appealed**
◆◆◆◆◇

1 If you **appeal** to someone to do something, you make a serious and urgent request to them. *Deng Xiaoping recently appealed for students to return to China... He will appeal to the state for an extension of unemployment benefits... The United Nations has appealed for help from the international community.*
VERB V *to/for* n to-inf V *to* n *for* n V *for* n

2 An **appeal** is a serious and urgent request. *He has a message from King Fahd, believed to be an appeal for Arab unity... Romania's government issued a last-minute appeal to him to call off his trip.*
N-COUNT: oft N *for/to* n, N to-inf =petition

3 An **appeal** is an attempt to raise money for a charity or for a good cause. *...an appeal to save a library containing priceless manuscripts... This is not another appeal for famine relief.*
N-COUNT: oft N to-inf, N *for* n

4 If you **appeal** to someone in authority against a decision, you formally ask them to change it. In British English, you **appeal against** something. In American English, you **appeal** something. *He said they would appeal against the decision... We intend to appeal the verdict... Maguire has appealed to the Supreme Court to stop her extradition.*
VERB V *against* n V n V *to* n to-inf

5 An **appeal** is a formal request for a decision to be changed. *Heath's appeal against the sentence was later successful... The jury agreed with her, but she lost the case on appeal.* ● See also **court of appeal**.
N-VAR

6 If something **appeals** to you, you find it attractive or interesting. *On the other hand, the idea appealed to him... The range has long appealed to all tastes.*
VERB V *to* n Also V

7 The **appeal** of something is a quality that it has which people find attractive or interesting. *Its new title was meant to give the party greater public appeal... Johnson's appeal is to people in all walks of life.* ● See also **sex appeal**.
N-UNCOUNT: with supp =attraction

8 See also **appealing**.

appealing /əpiːlɪŋ/ ◆◇◇◇◇

1 Someone or something that is **appealing** is pleasing and attractive. *There was a sense of humour to what he did that I found very appealing... That's a very appealing idea.* ♦ **appealingly** *Irish whiskeys, rather like the Irish themselves, have an appealingly direct charm about them.*
ADJ-GRADED =attractive ≠unappealing
ADV-GRADED: ADV adj/-ed, ADV after v

2 An **appealing** expression or tone of voice indicates to someone that you want help, advice, or approval. *She gave him a soft appealing look that would have melted solid ice.* ♦ **appealingly** *Dena looked appealingly at Blair, hoping to hear a contrary opinion.*
ADJ =enticing
ADV: ADV after v

3 See also **appeal**.

appear /əpɪəʳ/ **appears, appearing, appeared** ◆◆◆◆◆

1 If you say that something **appears** to be the way you describe it, you are reporting what you believe or what you have been told, though you cannot be sure it is true. *There appears to be increasing support for the leadership to take a more aggressive stance... The aircraft appears to have crashed near Katmandu... It appears that some missiles have been moved... It appears unlikely that the UN would consider making such a move... The executive presidency is beginning to appear a political irrelevance... Nine months later, those talks appear as distant as ever... He appeared willing to reach an agreement.*
V-LINK: no cont PRAGMATICS =seem
there V to-inf / V to-inf / *it* V that / *it* V adj that/to-inf / V n / V adj / V adj to-inf

2 If someone or something **appears** to have a particular quality or characteristic, they give the impression of having that quality or characteristic. *She did her best to appear more self-assured than she felt... He is anxious to appear a gentleman... Under stress these people will appear to be superficial, over-eager and manipulative.*
V-LINK: no cont =seem
V adj / V n / V to-inf

3 When someone or something **appears**, they move into a position where you can see them, for example when they arrive somewhere. *A woman appeared at the far end of the street... Last night some of the prisoners appeared on the roof.*
VERB
V / Also *there* V n

4 When something new **appears**, it begins to exist or reaches a stage of development where its existence can be noticed. *...small white flowers which appear in early summer. ...a test which can reveal infection at an early stage, before symptoms appear... Slogans have appeared on walls around the city.*
VERB
V / Also *there* V n

5 When something such as a book **appears**, it is published or becomes available for people to buy. *I could hardly wait for 'Boys' World' to appear each month. ...a poem which appeared in his last collection of verse.*
VERB
V

6 When someone **appears** in something such as a play, a show, or a television programme, they take part in it. *Jill Bennett became John Osborne's fourth wife, and appeared in several of his plays... Student leaders appeared on television to ask for calm.*
VERB
V *in* n / V *on/at* n

7 When someone **appears** before a court of law or before an official committee, they go there in order to answer charges or to give information as a witness. *Two other executives appeared at Worthing Magistrates' Court charged with tax fraud... The American will appear before members of the disciplinary committee at Portman Square.*
VERB
V *in/at* n / V *before* n

appearance /əpɪərəns/ **appearances** ◆◆◆◆◇

1 When someone makes an **appearance** at a public event or in a broadcast, they take part in it. *It was the president's second public appearance to date... Keegan made 68 appearances in two seasons for Southampton, scoring 37 times.*
N-COUNT: usu with supp, oft supp N

2 Someone's or something's **appearance** is the way that they look. *She used to be so fussy about her appearance... He had the appearance of a college student... A flat-roofed extension will add nothing to the value or appearance of the house.*
N-SING: with supp

3 The **appearance** of someone or something in a place is their arrival there, especially when it is unexpected. *The sudden appearance of a few bags of rice could start a riot. ...last Christmas, when there'd been the welcome appearance of Cousin Fred.*
N-SING: with supp, oft N *of* n

4 The **appearance** of something new is its coming into existence or use. *Flowering plants were making their first appearance, but were still a rarity... Fears are growing of a cholera outbreak following the appearance of a number of cases in the city.*
N-SING: with supp, oft N *of* n

5 If something has the **appearance** of a quality, it seems to have that quality. *We tried to meet both children's needs without the appearance of favoritism or unfairness... The US president risked giving the appearance that the US was taking sides.*
N-SING: with supp

6 If something is true **to all appearances, from all appearances**, or **by all appearances**, it seems from what you observe or know about it that it is true. *He was a small and to all appearances an unassuming man.*
PHRASES PHR with cl/group

7 If you **keep up appearances**, you try to behave and dress in a way that people expect of you, even if you can no longer afford it. *His parents' obsession with keeping up appearances haunted his childhood.*
V inflects

8 If you **put in an appearance** at an event, you go to it for a short time although you may not really want to, but do not stay. *You must put in an appearance, at least, or she'll think you're avoiding her.*
V inflects =show your face

appearance money. **Appearance money** is money paid to a famous person such as a sports star or film star for taking part in a public event.
N-UNCOUNT

appease /əpiːz/ **appeases, appeasing, appeased.** If you try to **appease** someone, you try to stop them being angry by giving them what they want; often used showing disapproval. *Gandhi was accused by some of trying to appease both factions of the electorate... The offer has not appeased separatists.* ♦ **appeaser, appeasers** *Not many such appeasers were left in 1941.*
◆◇◇◇◇ VERB PRAGMATICS =placate V n
N-COUNT

appeasement /əpiːzmənt/. **Appeasement** means giving people what they want to prevent them from harming you or being angry with you; a formal word which is used showing disapproval. *He denied there is a policy of appeasement... They have already been accused of appeasement by more militant organisations.*
◆◇◇◇◇ N-UNCOUNT PRAGMATICS

appellant /əpelənt/ **appellants.** An **appellant** is someone who is appealing against a court's decision after they have been judged guilty of a crime; a legal term. *The Court of Appeal upheld the appellants' convictions.*
N-COUNT

appellate court /əpelɪt kɔːʳt/ **appellate courts.** In the United States, an **appellate court** is a special court where people who have been convicted of a crime can appeal against their conviction. The usual British term is **court of appeal**. *A racially mixed jury in Miami convicted Lozano of manslaughter, but an appellate court overturned the convictions.*
N-COUNT

appellation /æpəleɪʃən/ **appellations.** An **appellation** is a name or title that a person, place, or thing is given; a formal word. *His critics called him 'the King of Pork'. Burdick never minded the appellation.*
◆◇◇◇◇ N-COUNT =epithet

append /əpend/ **appends, appending, appended.** When you **append** something to something else, especially a piece of writing, you attach it or add it to the end of it; a formal word. *Violet appended a note at the end of the letter... It was a relief that his real name hadn't been appended to the manuscript.*
VERB
V n / *be* V-ed *to* n

appendage /əpendɪdʒ/ **appendages.** An **appendage** is something that is joined to or connected with something larger or more important; a formal word. *Upon marriage she automatically lost most of her legal rights and became an appendage of her husband... Macmillan must have loathed being judged as a mere appendage to domestic politics.*
N-COUNT: oft N *of/to* n

appendices /əpendɪsiːz/. **Appendices** is a plural of **appendix**.

appendicitis /əpendɪsaɪtɪs/. **Appendicitis** is an illness in which a person's appendix is infected and painful. *He is recovering in hospital after an operation for acute appendicitis.*
N-UNCOUNT

appendix /əpendɪks/ **appendices** /əpendɪsiːz/ or **appendixes** ◆◇◇◇◇

1 Your **appendix** is a small closed tube inside your body which is attached to your digestive system. It has no particular function. *Phil Tufnell is still recovering from a burst appendix.* N-COUNT

2 An **appendix** to a book is extra information that is placed after the end of the main text. *These data are elaborated upon in the Appendix... The appendices provide a brief history of computing.* N-COUNT

appetite /æpɪtaɪt/ **appetites** ◆◆◇◇◇

1 Your **appetite** is your desire to eat. *He has a healthy appetite... Symptoms are a slight fever, headache and loss of appetite.* N-VAR

2 Someone's **appetite** for something is their strong desire for it. *...his appetite for success. ...Americans' growing appetite for scandal... She gave him just enough information to whet his appetite.* N-COUNT: oft N *for*n

appetizer /æpɪtaɪzəʳ/ **appetizers;** also spelled **appetiser** in British English. An **appetizer** is the first course of a meal. It consists of a small amount of food. *Seafood soup is a good appetizer.* N-COUNT

appetizing /æpɪtaɪzɪŋ/; also spelled **appetising** in British English. **Appetizing** food looks and smells good, so that you want to eat it. *...the appetising smell of freshly baked bread... Kippers are dyed yellow to make them more appetizing.* ADJ-GRADED ♦ **appetizingly** *It is simply and appetisingly laid out.* ADV-GRADED: ADV adj/-ed

applaud /əplɔːd/ **applauds, applauding, applauded** ◆◆◇◇◇

1 When a group of people **applaud**, they clap their hands in order to show approval, for example when they have enjoyed a play or concert. *The audience laughed and applauded... Every person stood to applaud his unforgettable act of courage.* VERB V Vn

2 When an attitude or action **is applauded**, people praise it. *He should be applauded for his courage... This last move can only be applauded... She applauds the fact that they are promoting new ideas.* VERB be V-ed *for*n be V-ed Vn

applause /əplɔːz/. **Applause** is the noise made by a group of people clapping their hands to show approval. *They greeted him with thunderous applause. ...a round of applause.* ◆◆◇◇◇ N-UNCOUNT

apple /æpəl/ **apples** ◆◆◆◇◇

1 An **apple** is a round fruit with smooth green, yellow, or red skin and firm white flesh. *I want an apple. ...2kg cooking apples. ...his ongoing search for the finest varieties of apple. ...a large garden with apple trees in it.* ● See also **Adam's apple, Big Apple, crab apple, toffee apple.** N-VAR

2 If you say that someone is **the apple of** your **eye**, you mean that they are very important to you and you are extremely fond of them. *Penny's only son was the apple of her eye.* PHRASE: usu v-link PHR

applecart /æpəlkɑːʳt/. If you **upset the applecart**, you do something which causes a plan, system, or arrangement to go wrong. *They may also be friends of the chairman, so they are reluctant to upset the applecart.* PHRASE: V inflects

apple pie, apple pies.

1 An **apple pie** is a kind of pie made with apples. N-COUNT

2 If a room or a desk is **in apple pie order**, it is neat and tidy, and everything is where it should be. *They found everything in apple-pie order.* PHRASE: v-link PHR

3 If you say that something is **as American as apple pie**, you mean that it is typically American. *Jeans are as American as apple pie.* PHRASE: v-link PHR

appliance /əplaɪəns/ **appliances** ◆◆◇◇◇

1 An **appliance** is a device or machine in your home that you use to do a job such as cleaning or cooking. Appliances are often electrical; a formal word. *He could also learn to use the vacuum cleaner, the washing machine and other household appliances. ...Maytag, one of America's biggest domestic appliance manufacturers.* N-COUNT

2 The **appliance** of a skill or of knowledge is its use for a particular purpose. *They were the result of the intellectual appliance of science.* N-SING: usu N *of*n

applicable /æplɪkəbəl, əplɪkə-/. Something that is **applicable** to a particular situation is relevant to it or can be applied to it. *What is a reasonable standard for one family is not applicable for another... It should include a review of energy usage and, where applicable, the production and disposal of waste.* ◆◇◇◇◇ ADJ-GRADED: usu v-link ADJ, oft ADJ *to*n =relevant ♦ **applicability** /əplɪkəbɪlɪti/ *Piaget himself wrote relatively little about the applicability of his theories to education.* N-UNCOUNT: oft N *of*n =relevance

applicant /æplɪkənt/ **applicants.** An **applicant** for something such as a job or a place at a college is someone who makes a formal written request to be given it. *He is one of thirty applicants for the manager's job. ...the number of applicants for university places.* ◆◆◇◇◇ N-COUNT

application /æplɪkeɪʃən/ **applications** ◆◆◆◇◇

1 Someone's **application** for something such as a job or membership of an organization is a formal written request to be allowed to have it. *His application for membership of the organisation was rejected. ...Turkey's application to join the European Community... Applications should be submitted as early as possible... Tickets are available on application.* N-COUNT: usu with supp, oft N *for*n, N to-inf, also *on/upon* N

2 The **application** of a rule or piece of knowledge is the use of it in a particular situation. *Students learned the practical application of the theory they had learned in the classroom... Simon's book provides a succinct outline of artificial intelligence and its application to robotics.* N-VAR: oft N *of/to*n

3 **Application** is hard work and concentration on what you are doing over a period of time. *...his immense talent, boundless energy and unremitting application.* N-UNCOUNT =diligence

4 The **application** of something to a surface is the act or process of putting it on or rubbing it into the surface. *With repeated applications of weedkiller, the weeds were overcome.* N-VAR: oft N *of*n

applicator /æplɪkeɪtəʳ/ **applicators**

1 An **applicator** is something such as a brush or sponge which is used to apply a powder or liquid to a surface. *...eye-shadows with sponge applicators.* N-COUNT

2 An **applicator** is a tube or other device which is used to insert tampons or pessaries into the vagina. N-COUNT

applied /əplaɪd/. An **applied** subject of study has a practical use, rather than being concerned only with theory. *...Applied Physics. ...plans to put more money into applied research.* ADJ: ADJ n ≠pure

applique /əpliːkeɪ, AM æplɪkeɪ/ also spelled **appliqué**. **Applique** is the craft of sewing fabric shapes onto larger pieces of cloth. You can also use applique to refer to things you make using this craft. *Beadwork, applique and embroidery add a uniquely feminine touch.* N-UNCOUNT

appliqued /əpliːkeɪd, AM æplɪkeɪd/; also spelled **appliquéd**. **Appliqued** shapes or fabric are formed from pieces of fabric which are stitched on to clothes or larger pieces of cloth. *...a centrepiece of appliqued flowers and birds. ...a magnificent appliqued bedspread.* ADJ

apply /əplaɪ/ **applies, applying, applied** ◆◆◆◆◇

1 If you **apply** for something such as a job or membership of an organization, you write a letter or fill in a form in order to ask formally for it. *I am continuing to apply for jobs... They may apply to join the organization.* VERB V *for*n V to-inf Also V *to*n *for*n

2 If you **apply** yourself to something or **apply** your mind to something, you concentrate hard on doing it or on thinking about it. *Faulks has applied himself to this task with considerable energy... In spare moments he applied his mind to how rockets could be used to make money.* VERB V pron-refl *to* n/-ing V n *to*n/wh Also V pron-refl

3 If something such as a rule or a remark **applies** to a person or in a situation, it is relevant to the person or the situation. *The convention does not apply to us... The rule applies where a person owns stock in a corporation.* VB: no cont V *to*n V

4 If you **apply** something such as a rule, system, or skill, you use it in a situation or activity. *The Government appears to be applying the same principle... His project is concerned with applying the technology to practical business problems.* VERB Vn Vn *to*n

5 A name that **is applied** to someone or something VERB

is used to refer to them. *...a biological term which cannot be applied to a whole culture.* be V-ed to n

6 If you **apply** something to a surface, you put it on or rub it into the surface. *The right thing would be to apply direct pressure to the wound... Applying the dye can be messy, particularly on long hair.* VERB V n to n V n

7 When the driver of a vehicle **applies** the brakes, he or she uses them to slow the vehicle down or to stop it from moving; a formal use. *They forgot to apply the handbrake and the car rolled 60ft into the river.* VERB V n

8 See also **applied**.

appoint /əpɔɪnt/ **appoints, appointing, appointed.** If you **appoint** someone to a job or official position, you formally choose them for it. *It made sense to appoint a banker to this job... The commission appointed a special investigator to conduct its own inquiry... The Prime Minister has appointed a civilian as defence minister... In 1958 she was appointed a US delegate to the United Nations.* • See also **appointed**. ◆◆◆◇◇ VERB =assign V n to n V n to-inf V n as n be V-ed n Also V n n, V n

appointed /əpɔɪntɪd/. If something happens at the **appointed** time, it happens at the time that was decided in advance; a formal word. *The appointed hour of the ceremony was drawing nearer.* ADJ: ADJ n

-appointed /-əpɔɪntɪd/. **-appointed** combines with adverbs to form adjectives such as **well-appointed** that describe a building or room that is equipped or furnished in the way that is mentioned; used in written English. *Sloan looked round the well-appointed kitchen... We ended up in a tastefully appointed sitting room.* • See also **self-appointed.** COMB in ADJ-GRADED

appointee /əpɔɪntiː/ **appointees.** An **appointee** is someone who has been chosen for a particular job or position of responsibility; a formal word. *...Becket, a recent appointee to the Supreme Court. ...Diane Ravitch, a political appointee in charge of federal education research.* ◆◇◇◇◇ N-COUNT

appointment /əpɔɪntmənt/ **appointments** ◆◆◆◇◇

1 The **appointment** of a person to a particular job is the choice of that person to do it. *His appointment to the Cabinet would please the right-wing. ...his appointment as foreign minister in 1985.* N-VAR: usu with poss, oft N to/as n

2 An **appointment** is a job or position of responsibility. *Mr Fay is to take up an appointment as a researcher with the Royal Society.* N-COUNT =post

3 If you have an **appointment** with someone, you have arranged to see them at a particular time, usually in connection with their work or for a serious purpose. *She has an appointment with her accountant... I made an appointment to see a specialist. ... a dental appointment.* N-COUNT: oft N with n, N to-inf

4 If something can be done **by appointment**, people can arrange in advance to do it at a particular time. *Viewing is by appointment only.* PHRASE

apportion /əpɔːʳʃᵊn/ **apportions, apportioning, apportioned.** When you **apportion** something such as blame, you decide how much of it different people deserve or should be given; a formal word. *The experts are even-handed in apportioning blame among EC governments... The allowable deduction is apportioned between the estate and the beneficiaries.* ♦ **apportionment** *...the apportionment of resources.* VERB V n prep Also V n N-UNCOUNT

apposite /æpəzɪt/. Something that is **apposite** is suitable for or appropriate to what is happening or being discussed; a formal word. *The events of recent days have made his central theme even more apposite... She thought in both languages, and selected the most apposite phrase from either.* ADJ-GRADED =relevant, apt

apposition /æpəzɪʃᵊn/. If two noun groups referring to the same person or thing are in **apposition**, one is placed immediately after the other, with no conjunction joining them, as in 'Her father, Nigel, left home three months ago.' N-UNCOUNT: usu in N

appraisal /əpreɪzᵊl/ **appraisals** ◆◇◇◇◇

1 If you make an **appraisal** of something, you consider it carefully and form an opinion about it. *What is needed in such cases is a calm appraisal of the situation... Self-appraisal is never easy.* N-VAR: oft N of n =evaluation

2 **Appraisal** is an official or formal evaluation of the strengths and weaknesses of someone or something. Appraisal often involves observation or some kind of testing. *In Britain and many other countries appraisal is now a tool of management. ...an appraisal of your financial standing.* N-VAR: oft N of n =evaluation

appraise /əpreɪz/ **appraises, appraising, appraised.** If you **appraise** something or someone, you consider them carefully and form an opinion about them; a formal word. *This prompted many employers to appraise their selection and recruitment policies... Gloria slid an appraising eye over the rest of the rack before reaching for the dress.* ◆◇◇◇◇ VERB =evaluate V n V-ing

appraiser /əpreɪzəʳ/ **appraisers.** In American English, an **appraiser** is someone whose job is to estimate the cost or value of something such as property. The usual British word is **valuer.** N-COUNT

appreciable /əpriːʃəbᵊl/. An **appreciable** amount or effect is large enough to be important or clearly noticed; a formal word. *It contains less than 1 per cent fat, an appreciable amount of protein, and a high content of minerals... This has not had an appreciable effect on production.* ♦ **appreciably** /əpriːʃəbli/ *Travel had not mellowed him appreciably... Summer temperatures are appreciably more comfortable there.* ADJ-GRADED: usu ADJ n =significant ADV: ADV with v, ADV adj

appreciate /əpriːʃieɪt/ **appreciates, appreciating, appreciated** ◆◆◆◇◇

1 If you **appreciate** something, for example a piece of music or good food, you like it because you recognize its good qualities. *Anyone can appreciate our music... In time you'll appreciate the beauty and subtlety of this language.* VERB V n

2 If you **appreciate** a situation or problem, you understand it and know what it involves. *She never really appreciated the depth and bitterness of the Irish conflict... He appreciates that co-operation with the media is part of his professional duties.* VERB V n V that

3 If you say that you **appreciate** something that someone has done for you, you mean that you are grateful to them for it. *Peter stood by me when I most needed it. I'll always appreciate that... Do all you can to show you appreciate her efforts.* VERB V n

4 When you want to thank someone or ask someone for something, you can use **appreciate** to say that you are grateful. *Thanks, lads. I appreciate it... I'd appreciate it if you wouldn't mention it.* VERB PRAGMATICS V n V it if

5 If something that you own **appreciates** over a period of time, its value increases. *They don't have any confidence that houses will appreciate in value.* VERB =go up ≠depreciate V

appreciation /əpriːʃieɪʃᵊn/ **appreciations** ◆◆◇◇◇

1 Someone's **appreciation** of something is their recognition and enjoyment of its good qualities. *...an investigation into children's understanding and appreciation of art... Brian whistled in appreciation.* N-SING: also no det, oft N of n

2 Your **appreciation** for something that someone does for you is your gratitude for it. *He expressed his appreciation for what he called Saudi Arabia's moderate and realistic oil policies. ...the gifts presented to them in appreciation of their work.* N-SING: also no det, oft with poss, N for n =gratitude

3 An **appreciation** of a situation or problem is an understanding of what it involves. *They have a stronger appreciation of the importance of economic incentives.* N-SING: also no det, with supp, oft N of n =grasp

4 **Appreciation** in the value of something is an increase in its value over a period of time. *You have to take capital appreciation of the property into account.* N-UNCOUNT ≠depreciation

5 An **appreciation** of an artist or performer or of their work is a speech or piece of writing in which they are discussed and evaluated. *I had written an appreciation of Hernandez for a magazine.* N-COUNT: usu N of n =review, critique

appreciative /əpriːʃətɪv/ ◆◇◇◇◇

1 An **appreciative** reaction or comment shows the enjoyment that you are getting from something. *There is a murmur of appreciative laughter... Mrs Hastings' eyes grow warmer and more appreciative with my every word.* ♦ **appreciatively** *She looked appreciatively at Blair's lovely pictures.* ADJ-GRADED ADV-GRADED: ADV with v

2 If you are **appreciative** of something, you are grateful for it. *We have been very appreciative of* ADJ-GRADED: oft ADJ of n

their support... I am most appreciative of your writing as you did.

apprehend /æprɪhend/ **apprehends, apprehending, apprehended** ◆◇◇◇◇

1 If the police **apprehend** someone, they catch them and arrest them; a formal use. *Police have not apprehended her killer.* VERB =catch V n

2 If you **apprehend** something, you understand it fully; a literary use. *Only now can I begin to apprehend the power of these forces.* VERB =grasp V n

apprehension /æprɪhenʃᵊn/ **apprehensions** ◆◇◇◇◇

1 **Apprehension** is a feeling of fear that something bad may happen; a formal use. *It reflects real anger and apprehension about the future... I tensed every muscle in my body in apprehension.* N-VAR =worry

2 The **apprehension** of someone who is thought to be a criminal is their capture or arrest by the police; a formal use. *...information leading to the apprehension of the alleged killer.* N-UNCOUNT: oft N *of* n

3 The **apprehension** of something is awareness and understanding of it; a literary use. *...the sudden apprehension of something familiar as something alien.* N-UNCOUNT: oft N *of* n =comprehension

apprehensive /æprɪhensɪv/. Someone who is **apprehensive** is afraid that something bad may happen. *People are still terribly apprehensive about the future.* ♦ **apprehensively** *I waited apprehensively for him to comment.* ◆◇◇◇◇ ADJ-GRADED: usu v-link ADJ, oft ADJ *about* n/-ing ADV-GRADED: ADV with v

apprentice /əprentɪs/ **apprentices, apprenticing, apprenticed** ◆◇◇◇◇

1 An **apprentice** is a young person who works for someone in order to learn their skill. *I started off as an apprentice and worked my way up... He left school at 15 and trained as an apprentice carpenter.* N-COUNT: oft N n

2 If a young person **is apprenticed** to someone, they go to work for them in order to learn their skill. *I was apprenticed to a builder when I was fourteen.* VB: usu passive *be* V-ed *to* n

apprenticeship /əprentɪsʃɪp/ **apprenticeships.** Someone who has an **apprenticeship** works for a fixed period of time for a person who has a particular skill in order to learn the skill. **Apprenticeship** is the system of learning a skill like this. *After serving his apprenticeship as a toolmaker, he became a manager. ...a period of apprenticeship.* ◆◇◇◇◇ N-VAR

apprise /əpraɪz/ **apprises, apprising, apprised.** When you **are apprised** of something, someone tells you about it; a formal word. *Have these customers been fully apprised of the advantages?... I thought I needed to apprise the students of the dangers that may be involved.* VERB =notify *be* V-ed *of* n V n *of* n

approach /əprəʊtʃ/ **approaches, approaching, approached** ◆◆◆◆◇

1 When you **approach** something, you get closer to it. *He didn't approach the front door at once... When I approached, they grew silent... We turned to see the approaching car slow down.* ► Also a noun. *At their approach the little boy ran away and hid. ...the approach of a low-flying helicopter.* VERB V n V V-ing N-COUNT: usu sing, with supp =advance

2 An **approach** to a place is a road, path, or other route that leads to it. *The path serves as an approach to the boat house.* N-COUNT: usu N *to* n

3 If you **approach** someone about something, you speak to them about it for the first time, often making an offer or request. *When Chappel approached me about the job, my first reaction was of disbelief... He approached me to create and design the restaurant... Anna approached several builders and was fortunate to come across Eddie.* ► Also a noun. *There had already been approaches from buyers interested in the whole of the group.* VB: no cont V n prep V n to-inf V n N-COUNT: oft N *from/to* n

4 When you **approach** a task, problem, or situation in a particular way, you deal with it or think about it in that way. *The Bank has approached the issue in a practical way... Employers are interested in how you approach problems.* VERB =tackle V n prep/adv

5 Your **approach** to a task, problem, or situation is the way you deal with it or think about it. *We will be exploring different approaches to gathering information. ...the adversarial approach of the British legal system.* N-COUNT: usu with supp, oft N *to*-ing/n

6 As a future time or event **approaches**, it gradually gets nearer as time passes. *As autumn approached, the plants and colours in the garden changed. ...the approaching crisis.* ► Also a noun. *The approach of crucial elections has forced Mr Markovic to act.* VERB V V-ing N-SING: usu N *of* n

7 As you **approach** a future time or event, time passes so that you get gradually nearer to it. *There is a need for understanding and co-operation as we approach the 21st century.* VERB V n

8 If something **approaches** a particular level or state, it almost reaches that level or state. *Oil prices have approached their highest level for almost ten years... Mansell will race at average speeds approaching 200mph.* VERB =come close to V n

approachable /əprəʊtʃəbᵊl/

1 If you describe someone as **approachable**, you think that they are friendly and easy to talk to. *We found him very approachable and easy to talk with.* ADJ-GRADED ≠aloof, unapproachable

2 If you describe an idea or piece of work as **approachable**, you think that it is presented in a way which people find enjoyable and easy to understand. *The text is approachable, coping well with quite complicated subjects.* ADJ-GRADED =accessible

approbation /æprəbeɪʃᵊn/. **Approbation** is approval of something or agreement to it; a formal word. *Julian Lloyd Webber thinks his brother would like the approbation of serious critics... The result has not met universal approbation.* N-UNCOUNT =approval

appropriate, appropriates, appropriating, appropriated. The adjective is pronounced /əprəʊpriət/. The verb is pronounced /əprəʊprieɪt/. ◆◆◆◇◇

1 Something that is **appropriate** is suitable or acceptable for a particular situation. *It is appropriate that Irish names dominate the list... Dress neatly and attractively in an outfit appropriate to the job... The teacher can then take appropriate action.* ♦ **appropriately** *Dress appropriately and ask intelligent questions... It's entitled, appropriately enough, 'Art for the Nation'.* ♦ **appropriateness** *He wonders about the appropriateness of each move he makes.* ADJ-GRADED: oft *it* v-link ADJ that/to-inf, ADJ *for/to* n ≠inappropriate ADV-GRADED: ADV with v, ADV with cl/group N-UNCOUNT: oft N *of* n

2 If someone **appropriates** something which does not belong to them, they take it, usually without the right to do so; a formal use. *Several other newspapers have appropriated the idea... The land was simply appropriated by the Communists.* VERB =purloin V n

3 If a government or organization **appropriates** an amount of money for a particular purpose, it reserves it for that purpose; a formal use. *Senator Lugar is skeptical that Congress will appropriate more funding for this purpose.* VERB =earmark V n

appropriation /əprəʊprieɪʃᵊn/ **appropriations** ◆◇◇◇◇

1 An **appropriation** is an amount of money that a government or organization reserves for a particular purpose; a formal use. *The government raised defence appropriations by 12 per cent.* N-COUNT: usu with supp =allocation

2 **Appropriation** of something that belongs to someone else is the act of taking it, usually without having the right to do so; a formal use. *Other charges filed against the family include fraud and illegal appropriation of land.* N-UNCOUNT: also *a* N, usu N *of* n

approval /əpruːvᵊl/ **approvals** ◆◆◆◇◇

1 If you win someone's **approval** for something that you ask for or suggest, they agree to it. *...efforts to win congressional approval for an aid package for Moscow... The chairman has also given his approval for an investigation into the case... Mr Clinton could not change present policy without the approval of Congress.* N-UNCOUNT: usu with supp, oft with poss, N *for* n =sanction

2 **Approval** is a formal or official statement that something is acceptable. *The testing and approval of new drugs will be speeded up.* N-VAR

3 If someone or something has your **approval**, you like and admire them. *His son had an obsessive drive to gain his father's approval... The president's approval rating had risen.* N-UNCOUNT: usu with poss

4 If a person or organization gives something their **seal of approval** or their **stamp of approval**, they officially say that they admire or like it, or that they think it is acceptable. *Ministers have put their seal of approval on the proposal... Last November the commission gave its stamp of approval to the deal.* PHRASE: PHR after v

approve /əpruːv/ **approves, approving, approved** ◆◆◆◆◇
1 If you **approve of** an action, event, or suggestion, you like it or are pleased about it. *Not everyone approves of the festival... I approved of the proposal.* VB: oft with brd-neg V *of* n
2 If you **approve of** someone or something, you like and admire them. *You've never approved of Henry, have you?... I didn't approve of his manner.* VB: oft with brd-neg V *of* n
3 If someone in a position of authority **approves** a plan or idea, they formally agree to it and say that it can happen. *The Russian Parliament has approved a program of radical economic reforms... MPs approved the Bill by a majority of 97.* VERB =sanction V n
4 If a product or person **is approved** by an official organization, they are declared to be of a good enough standard to be used or employed. *We have three suppliers in all who are approved by the Organic Farm Food Association.* VERB =authorized be V-ed Also V n
5 See also **approved, approving**.

approved /əpruːvd/. An **approved** method or course of action is officially accepted as appropriate in a particular situation. *The approved method of cleaning is industrial sand-blasting.* ADJ-GRADED: usu ADJ n

approved school, approved schools. In Britain, an **approved school** was a boarding school where young people could be sent to stay if they had been found guilty of a crime. Approved schools were abolished in 1971. N-COUNT

approving /əpruːvɪŋ/. An **approving** reaction or remark shows support for something, or satisfaction with it. *Helen got the benefit of an approving nod.* ADJ-GRADED: usu ADJ n ≠disapproving ♦ **approvingly** *He nodded approvingly.* ADV-GRADED

approx. Approx. is a written abbreviation for **approximately**. *Group Size: Approx. 12 to 16.*

approximate, approximates, approximating, approximated. The adjective is pronounced /əprɒksɪmət/. The verb is pronounced /əprɒksɪmeɪt/. ◆◆◇◇◇
1 An **approximate** number, time, or position is close to the correct number, time, or position, but is not exact. *The approximate cost varies from around £150 to £250... The times are approximate only.* ADJ-GRADED =rough ≠exact ♦ **approximately** *Approximately $150 million is to be spent on improvements.* ADV: ADV num
2 An idea or description that is **approximate** is not intended to be precise or accurate, but to give some indication of what something is like. *They did not have even an approximate idea what the Germans really wanted.* ADJ-GRADED
3 If something **approximates** to something else, it is similar to it but is not exactly the same. *Something approximating to a just outcome will be ensured... The mixture described below will approximate it, but is not exactly the same.* VERB =resemble V *to* n V n

approximation /əprɒksɪmeɪʃən/ **approximations**
1 An **approximation** is a fact, object, or description which is similar to something else, but which is not exactly the same. *That is a fair approximation of the way in which the next boss is being chosen.* N-COUNT: oft N *of/to* n
2 An **approximation** is a number, calculation, or position that is close to a correct number, time, or position, but is not exact. *Clearly that's an approximation, but my guess is there'll be a reasonable balance.* N-COUNT =estimate

appt. Appt is a written abbreviation for **appointment**.

Apr. Apr. is a written abbreviation for **April**. *An agreement was reached on Apr. 27.* ◆◆◇◇◇

apres-ski /æpreɪ skiː/; also spelled **après-ski**. **Apres-ski** is evening entertainment and social activities which take place in ski resorts. *Most apres-ski in Geilo takes place within the hotels. ...a typical Vermont apres-ski place.* N-UNCOUNT: oft N n

apricot /eɪprɪkɒt/ **apricots** ◆◇◇◇◇
1 An **apricot** is a small, soft, round fruit with yellowish-orange flesh and a stone inside. *...12 oz apricots, halved and stoned. ...apricot tart.* N-VAR
2 **Apricot** is used to describe things that are yellowish-orange in colour. *The bridesmaids wore apricot and white organza... The heavy curtains were a warm apricot.* COLOUR

April /eɪprɪl/ **Aprils. April** is the fourth month of the year in the Western calendar. *The changes will be introduced in April... They were married on 7 April 1927 at Paddington Register Office.* ◆◆◆◆◇ N-VAR

April Fool, April Fools
1 An **April Fool** is a trick that is played on April Fool's Day. N-COUNT
2 You say **'April Fool!'** to someone who has just been deceived by an April Fool's Day trick in order to tell them it was a trick and to make fun of them. EXCLAM PRAGMATICS

April Fool's Day. April Fool's Day is the 1st of April, the day on which people traditionally play tricks on each other up until midday. N-UNCOUNT

a priori /eɪ praɪɔːraɪ/. An **a priori** argument, reason, or probability is based on an assumed principle or fact, rather than on actual observed facts. *In the absence of such evidence, there is no a priori hypothesis to work with.* ADJ: usu ADJ n ► Also an adverb. *One assumes, a priori, that a parent would be better at dealing with problems.* ADV: usu ADV *with* cl, also ADV after v

apron /eɪprən/ **aprons** ◆◇◇◇◇
1 An **apron** is a piece of clothing that you put on over the front of your normal clothes and tie round your waist, especially when you are cooking, in order to prevent your clothes from getting dirty. *She came bustling out, wiping her hands on her apron.* N-COUNT
• If you say that someone is tied to another person's **apron strings**, you mean that they are controlled or influenced too much by the other person. *If you try to keep him under control and tethered to your apron strings there will almost certainly be a row.* PHRASE
2 At an airport, the **apron** is an area of concrete or tarmac where aircraft are parked. *The Lear jet was waiting on the apron by the control tower.* N-COUNT: usu *the* N in sing

apropos /æprəpoʊ/
1 Something which is **apropos**, or **apropos of**, a subject or event, is connected with it or relevant to it; a formal use. *All my suggestions apropos the script were accepted... George Orwell once asked, apropos of publishers, 'Why don't they just say, "We don't want your poems"?'* PREP =with reference to
2 **Apropos** or **apropos of** is used to introduce something that you are going to say which is related to the subject you have just been talking about; a formal use. *Apropos Dudley Moore living in California he said, 'He loves the space, Californians have a lot of space.'* PREP PRAGMATICS
3 Something that is **apropos** is very suitable in a particular situation; a formal use. *It seems entirely apropos to show the attempts by such as Lissitzky and Antal in revolutionary Russia to evolve a modern Jewish style.* ADJ-GRADED: v-link ADJ =appropriate

apt /æpt/ ◆◆◇◇◇
1 An **apt** remark, description, or choice is especially suitable. *The words of this report are as apt today as in 1929. ...an apt description of the situation.* ADJ-GRADED =apposite ♦ **aptly** *...the beach in the aptly named town of Oceanside.* ADV-GRADED
2 If someone or something is **apt** to do something, they often do it and so it is likely that they will do it again. *She was apt to raise her voice and wave her hands about... This type of weather is apt to be more common in winter.* ADJ-GRADED: v-link ADJ to-inf

aptitude /æptɪtjuːd, AM -tuːd/ **aptitudes.** Someone's **aptitude** for a particular kind of work or activity is their ability to learn it quickly and to do it well. *He drifted into publishing and discovered an aptitude for working with accounts... Some students have more aptitude for academic work than others.* ◆◇◇◇◇ N-VAR: usu N *for* n/-ing

aptitude test, aptitude tests. An **aptitude test** is a test that is specially designed to find out how easily and how well you can do something. N-COUNT

aqua /ækwə/. **Aqua** is the same as the colour **aquamarine**. *...floor-length curtains in restful aqua and lavender colours.* ◆◇◇◇◇ COLOUR

aquamarine /ækwəməriːn/ **aquamarines**
1 **Aquamarines** are clear, greenish-blue stones, sometimes used to make jewellery. *A necklace set with aquamarines. ...a large aquamarine ring.* N-VAR
2 **Aquamarine** is used to describe things that are COLOUR

greenish-blue in colour. ...*warm aquamarine seas and white beaches.* ...*huge aquamarine eyes.*

aquarium /əkweəriəm/ **aquariums** or **aquaria** /əkweəriə/ ◆◇◇◇◇
1 An **aquarium** is a building, often in a zoo, where fish and underwater animals are kept. N-COUNT
2 An **aquarium** is a glass tank filled with water, in which people keep fish. N-COUNT

Aquarius /əweəriəs/ ◆◆◇◇◇
1 **Aquarius** is one of the twelve signs of the zodiac. Its symbol is a person pouring water. People who are born approximately between 20th January and 18th February come under this sign. N-UNCOUNT
2 **An Aquarius** is a person whose sign of the zodiac is Aquarius. N-SING: aN

aquatic /əkwætɪk/ ◆◇◇◇◇
1 An **aquatic** animal or plant lives or grows on or in water. *The pond is quite small but can support many aquatic plants and fish.* ...*aquatic birds.* ADJ: usu ADJ n
2 **Aquatic** means relating to water. ...*aquatic consultant Ben Tucker.* ...*our aquatic resources.* ADJ

aqueduct /ækwɪdʌkt/ **aqueducts**
1 An **aqueduct** is a long bridge with many arches, which carries a water supply or a canal over a valley. ...*an old Roman aqueduct.* N-COUNT
2 An **aqueduct** is a large pipe or canal which carries a water supply to a city or a farming area. ...*a nationwide system of aqueducts to carry water to the arid parts of this country.* N-COUNT

aqueous /eɪkwiəs/. An **aqueous** solution or cream has water as its base; a technical term in chemistry. ...*an aqueous solution containing various sodium salts.* ...*a soap substitute such as an aqueous cream, available from chemists.* ADJ: ADJ n =water-based

aquifer /ækwɪfəʳ/ **aquifers.** An **aquifer** is rock underneath the surface of the earth which absorbs and holds water, making it a valuable source of water; a technical term in geology. ...*the discovery of the aquifer in the Thar desert.* N-COUNT

aquiline /ækwɪlaɪn/. If someone has an **aquiline** nose or profile, their nose is large, thin, and usually curved; a formal word. *He had black hair, a thin aquiline nose, and deep-set brown eyes.* ADJ-GRADED: usu ADJ n PRAGMATICS

Arab /ærəb/ **Arabs**
1 **Arabs** are the major ethnic group in the Middle East and parts of North Africa. N-COUNT
2 **Arab** means belonging or relating to Arabs or to their countries or customs. *On the surface, it appears little has changed in the Arab world.* ADJ: usu ADJ n

arabesque /ærəbesk/ **arabesques**
1 An **arabesque** is a position in ballet dancing. The dancer stands on one leg with their other leg lifted and stretched out backwards, and their arms stretched out in front of them. *The ballerina remained suspended in a faultless arabesque.* N-COUNT
2 In art, an **arabesque** is a design of flowing lines. ...*a clay water jug decorated with painted arabesques.* N-COUNT

Arabian /əreɪbiən/. **Arabian** means belonging or relating to Arabia, especially to Saudi Arabia. ...*the Arabian Peninsula.* ... *an Arabian stallion.* ◆◆◆◆◇ ADJ

Arabic /ærəbɪk/
1 **Arabic** is a language that is spoken in the Middle East and in parts of North Africa. N-UNCOUNT
2 Something that is **Arabic** belongs or relates to the language, writing, or culture of the Arabs. ...*a large tapestry with swirling Arabic script.* ...*the development of modern Arabic literature.* ...*Arabic music.* ADJ
3 An **Arabic** numeral is one of the written figures such as 1, 2, 3, or 4. *The clock is available with either Roman or Arabic numerals.* ADJ: ADJ n

Arabist /ærəbɪst/ **Arabists.** An **Arabist** is a person who supports Arab interests or knows a lot about the Arabic language. ...*a leading Arabist.* N-COUNT

arable /ærəbᵊl/. **Arable** farming involves the growing of crops such as wheat and barley rather than the keeping of animals or the growing of fruit and vegetables. **Arable** land is land that is used for arable farming. *The big arable farmers did very well.* ...*arable crops.* ADJ: usu ADJ n

arbiter /ɑːʳbɪtəʳ/ **arbiters** ◆◇◇◇◇
1 An **arbiter** is a person or institution that judges and settles a quarrel between two other people or groups; a formal use. *He was the ultimate arbiter on both theological and political matters.* ...*the court's role as arbiter in the law-making process.* N-COUNT =adjudicator
2 An **arbiter** of taste or style is someone who has a lot of influence in deciding what is fashionable or socially desirable; a formal use. *Sequins have often aroused the scorn of arbiters of taste.* N-COUNT: usu N of n

arbitrage /ɑːʳbɪtrɑːʒ/. In finance, **arbitrage** is the activity of buying shares or currency in one financial market and selling it at a profit in another. ◆◇◇◇◇ N-UNCOUNT: oft N n

arbitrager /ɑːʳbɪtrɑːʒɜːʳ/ **arbitragers;** also spelled **arbitrageur.** In economics, an **arbitrager** is someone who buys currencies, securities, or commodities on one country's market in order to make money by immediately selling them at a profit on another country's market. N-COUNT

arbitrary /ɑːʳbɪtri, AM -treri/. If you describe an action, rule, or decision as **arbitrary**, you think that it is not based on any principle, plan, or system. It often seems unfair because of this. *Arbitrary arrests and detention without trial were common.* ♦ **arbitrarily** /ɑːʳbɪtreərɪli/ *The victims were not chosen arbitrarily.* ♦ **arbitrariness** /ɑːʳbɪtrərinəs, AM -trer-/ *He is horrified by the apparent arbitrariness by which she sets the prices.* ◆◇◇◇◇ ADJ-GRADED PRAGMATICS; ADV-GRADED: ADV with v; N-UNCOUNT

arbitrate /ɑːʳbɪtreɪt/ **arbitrates, arbitrating, arbitrated.** When someone in authority **arbitrates** between two people or groups who are in dispute, they consider all the facts and make an official decision about who is right. *He arbitrates between investors and members of the association... The tribunal had been set up to arbitrate in the dispute.* ♦ **arbitrator** /ɑːʳbɪtreɪtəʳ/ **arbitrators** *He served as an arbitrator in a series of commercial disputes in India.* VERB =adjudicate; V *between* pl-n; V; N-COUNT

arbitration /ɑːʳbɪtreɪʃᵊn/. **Arbitration** is the judging of a dispute between people or groups by someone who is not involved. ...*the independent arbitration service, ACAS... The matter is likely to go to arbitration.* ◆◇◇◇◇ N-UNCOUNT: oft N n

arboreal /ɑːʳbɔːriəl/
1 **Arboreal** animals live in trees; a technical use. *This clear tract in the deep forest gave him wonderful views of the arboreal birds.* ADJ: usu ADJ n
2 **Arboreal** means relating to trees; a formal use. ...*the arboreal splendor of the valley.* ADJ: usu ADJ n

arboretum /ɑːʳbəriːtəm/ **arboreta** /ɑːʳbəriːtə/ or **arboretums.** An **arboretum** is a specially designed garden of different types of trees. N-COUNT

arbour /ɑːʳbəʳ/ **arbours;** spelled **arbor** in American English. An **arbour** is a shelter in a garden which is formed by leaves and stems of plants growing close together over a light framework. N-COUNT =bower

arc /ɑːʳk/ **arcs, arcing, arced** ◆◇◇◇◇
1 An **arc** is a smoothly curving line or movement. *His 71 offices are spread through the Thames Valley and in an arc around north London.* N-COUNT
2 In geometry, an **arc** is a part of the line that forms the outside of a circle. N-COUNT
3 If something **arcs** in a particular direction, it makes a smoothly curving line or movement; a literary use. *A rainbow arced gracefully over the town.* VERB =curve; V prep/adv

arcade /ɑːʳkeɪd/ **arcades** ◆◇◇◇◇
1 An **arcade** is a covered passage where there are shops or market stalls. ...*a shopping arcade.* N-COUNT
2 An **arcade** is the same as an **amusement arcade**. ...*13 year-olds spending their pocket money on fruit machines in arcades.* N-COUNT

arcade game, arcade games. An **arcade game** is a computer game of the type that is often played in amusement arcades. N-COUNT

arcane /ɑːʳkeɪn/. Something that is **arcane** is secret or mysterious; a formal word. *Until a few months ago few people outside the arcane world of contemporary music had heard of Gorecki.* ◆◇◇◇◇ ADJ-GRADED

arch /ɑːʳtʃ/ **arches, arching, arched** ◆◆◇◇◇
1 An **arch** is a structure that is curved at the top and is supported on either side by a pillar, post, or wall. *They walked through the arch and into the cobbled courtyard... They slept under railway arches.* N-COUNT

2 An **arch** is a curved line or movement. *Her eyebrows were two perfect arches.* N-COUNT =arc

3 The **arch** of your foot is the curved section of bone at the top. *I suffer from fallen arches.* N-COUNT

4 If you **arch** a part of your body such as your back or if it **arches**, you bend it so that it forms a curve. *Don't arch your back, keep your spine straight.* V-ERG V n Also V

5 If you **arch** your eyebrows or if they **arch**, you raise your eyebrows as a way of showing surprise or disapproval. *'Oh really?' he said, arching an eyebrow.* V-ERG =raise V n Also V

6 If something **arches** in a particular direction, it makes a curved line or movement. *I gazed up at the domed ceiling arching overhead.* VERB V adv/prep

7 An **arch** look is mysterious and mischievous. *Both of them looked at him with that curious, slightly amused and even arch expression.* ADJ-GRADED: usu ADJ n ♦ **archly** *She looked at me rather archly.* ADV-GRADED

8 If you say that someone says something in an **arch** tone of voice, you are critical of them because they say it in a way that suggests they think they are better or more important than other people. *Their attempts to be casual have so far just looked arch or patronising.* ADJ-GRADED PRAGMATICS =superior ♦ **archly** *'You can't fool me,' Shirley said archly.* ADV-GRADED

9 See also **arched**.

arch- /ɑːʳtʃ-/. **Arch-** combines with nouns that refer to people, usually people who are opposed to something or who are considered bad, to form new nouns that refer to people who are extreme representatives of something. For example, your **arch-rival** is the rival you most want to beat. *Neither he nor his arch-rival, Giuseppe De Rita, won. ...his arch-enemy.* COMB in N-COUNT

archaeology /ɑːʳkiɒlədʒi/; also spelled **archeology**. **Archaeology** is the study of the societies and peoples of the past, by examining the remains of their buildings, tools, and other artefacts. *One of the attractive aspects of archaeology is the element of surprise.* ◆◆◇◇◇ N-UNCOUNT ♦ **archaeological** /ɑːʳkiəlɒdʒɪkəl/ *...one of the region's most important archaeological sites.* ADJ: ADJ n ♦ **archaeologist** /ɑːʳkiɒlədʒɪst/ **archaeologists** *The archaeologists found a house built around 300 BC, with a basement and attic.* N-COUNT

archaic /ɑːʳkeɪɪk/. **Archaic** means extremely old or extremely old-fashioned. *...archaic laws that are very seldom used... Archaic practices such as these are usually put forward by people of limited outlook. ...archaic sculpture and porcelain.* ◆◇◇◇◇ ADJ-GRADED: usu ADJ n =antiquated

archangel /ɑːʳkeɪndʒəl/ **archangels.** An **archangel** is an angel of the highest rank. *The archangel's triumph landed the satanic forces in hell. ...the Archangels Gabriel and Michael.* N-COUNT; N-TITLE: the N

archbishop /ɑːʳtʃbɪʃəp/ **archbishops.** In the Roman Catholic, Orthodox, and Anglican Churches, an **archbishop** is a bishop of the highest rank, who is in charge of all the bishops and priests in a particular country or region. *The archbishops renewed pledges that there would be no discrimination. ...the Archbishop of Canterbury. ...Archbishop Desmond Tutu.* N-COUNT; N-TITLE

archdeacon /ɑːʳtʃdiːkən/ **archdeacons.** An **archdeacon** is a high-ranking clergyman who works as an assistant to a bishop, especially in the Anglican church. *...the Right Rev James Adams, the Archdeacon of Colchester.* N-COUNT; N-TITLE

archdiocese /ɑːʳtʃdaɪəsɪs/ **archdioceses** /ɑːʳtʃdaɪəsiːz/. An **archdiocese** is the area over which an archbishop has control. *...the archdiocese of Toledo.* N-COUNT

arched /ɑːʳtʃt/ ◆◇◇◇◇

1 An **arched** roof, window, or doorway is curved at the top. *We came to a large arched doorway.* ADJ: usu ADJ n

2 An **arched** bridge has arches as part of its structure. *...a fortified arched bridge spanning the River Severn.* ADJ: usu ADJ n

3 You use **arched** to describe something that is curved like an arch. *A frown formed between her arched brows.* ADJ: usu ADJ n

archeology /ɑːʳkiɒlədʒi/. See **archaeology**.

archer /ɑːʳtʃəʳ/ **archers.** An **archer** is someone who shoots arrows using a bow. N-COUNT

archery /ɑːʳtʃəri/. **Archery** is a sport in which people shoot arrows at a target using a bow. *...a traditional national festival of horse racing, wrestling and archery.* N-UNCOUNT

archetypal /ɑːʳkɪtaɪpəl/. Someone or something that is **archetypal** has all the most important characteristics of a particular kind of person or thing and is a perfect example of it; a formal word. *Cricket is the archetypal English game, and probably the most arcane recreation yet invented.* ◆◇◇◇◇ ADJ-GRADED: usu ADJ n

archetype /ɑːʳkɪtaɪp/ **archetypes.** An **archetype** is something that is considered to be a perfect or typical example of a particular kind of person or thing, because it has all their most important characteristics; a formal word. *He came to this country 20 years ago and is the archetype of the successful Asian businessman.* ◆◇◇◇◇ N-COUNT =epitome

archetypical /ɑːʳkɪtɪpɪkəl/. **Archetypical** means the same as **archetypal**. *...an archetypical BBC voice.* ADJ: usu ADJ n

archipelago /ɑːʳkɪpeləgəʊ/ **archipelagos** or **archipelagoes.** An **archipelago** is a group of islands, especially small islands. *...the Azores, a rugged, volcanic archipelago of nine islands.* N-COUNT

architect /ɑːʳkɪtekt/ **architects** ◆◆◇◇◇

1 An **architect** is a person who designs buildings. *...the American architect Michael Gabellini.* N-COUNT

2 A person who plans the design of large projects such as landscaping or railways can be referred to as an **architect** of a particular kind. *...Merrick Denton-Thompson, the landscape architect for Hampshire county council. ...Paul Andreu, chief architect of French railways.* N-COUNT: with supp, oft N of n

3 The **architect** of an idea, event, or institution is the person who invented it or made it happen; a formal use. *...Russia's chief architect of economic reform.* N-COUNT: oft N of n

architectural /ɑːʳkɪtektʃərəl/. **Architectural** means relating to the design and construction of buildings. *...Tibet's architectural heritage. ...the unique architectural style of towns like Lamu.* ◆◆◇◇◇ ADJ: usu ADJ n ♦ **architecturally** *...the most architecturally stunning hotels in India... Architecturally, the chapel would be the perfect match for the school.* ADV: ADV adj, ADV with cl

architecture /ɑːʳkɪtektʃəʳ/ **architectures** ◆◆◇◇◇

1 **Architecture** is the art of planning, designing, and constructing buildings. *He studied classical architecture and design in Rome.* N-UNCOUNT

2 The **architecture** of a building is the style in which it is designed and constructed. *...modern architecture. ...a fine example of Moroccan architecture. ...the architecture of the city's buildings.* N-UNCOUNT: with supp

3 The **architecture** of something is its structure; a formal use. *...the crumbling intellectual architecture of modern society. ...the architecture of muscle fibres.* N-UNCOUNT: also N in pl, N of n

archival /ɑːʳkaɪvəl/. **Archival** means belonging or relating to archives. *...his extensive use of archival material.* ADJ: usu ADJ n

archive /ɑːʳkaɪv/ **archives** ◆◆◇◇◇

1 The **archive** or **archives** are a collection of documents and records that contain historical information. You can also use **archives** to refer to the place where archives are stored. *...the archives of the Imperial War Museum... I decided I would go to the Archive the next day and look up the appropriate issue.* N-COUNT: usu pl

2 **Archive** material is information that comes from archives. *...archive material. ...pieces of archive film.* ADJ: ADJ n

archivist /ɑːʳkɪvɪst/ **archivists.** An **archivist** is a person whose job is to collect, sort, and preserve historical documents and records. N-COUNT

archway /ɑːʳtʃweɪ/ **archways.** An **archway** is a passage or entrance that has a curved roof. *Access was via a narrow archway.* N-COUNT

arc light, arc lights. Arc lights are a type of very bright electric light. *...the brilliant glare of the arc lights.* N-COUNT: usu pl

arctic /ɑːʳktɪk/ ◆◇◇◇◇
1 **The Arctic** is the area of the world around the North Pole. It is extremely cold and there is very little light in winter and very little darkness in summer. *...winter in the Arctic. ...Arctic ice.* N-PROPER: *the* N ≠Antarctic
2 If you describe a place or the weather as **arctic**, you are emphasizing that it is extremely cold; an informal use. *The bathroom, with its spartan pre-war facilities, is positively arctic.* ADJ-GRADED PRAGMATICS =freezing

Arctic Circle. **The Arctic Circle** is an imaginary line drawn around the northern part of the world at approximately 66° North. N-PROPER: *the* N

ardent /ɑːʳdᵊnt/. **Ardent** is used to describe someone who has extremely strong feelings about something or someone. *He's been one of the most ardent supporters of the administration's policy. ...an ardent opponent of the Vietnam War.* ◆◇◇◇◇ ADJ-GRADED: usu ADJ n =fervent, passionate
♦ **ardently** *Why had Hilton defended him so ardently?... His reports are often ardently pro-Russian.* ADV-GRADED: usu ADV with v, also ADV adj

ardor /ɑːʳdəʳ/. See **ardour**.

ardour /ɑːʳdəʳ/; spelled **ardor** in American English. **Ardour** is an intense, passionate feeling of love or enthusiasm for someone or something; a literary word. *The sexual ardour had cooled. ...my ardor for football.* N-UNCOUNT: also N in pl =passion, fervour

arduous /ɑːʳdʒuəs/. Something that is **arduous** is difficult and tiring, and involves a lot of effort. *...a long, hot and arduous journey... The task was more arduous than he had calculated.* ◆◇◇◇◇ ADJ-GRADED

are /əʳ, STRONG ɑːʳ/. **Are** is the plural and the second person singular of the present tense of the verb **be**. **Are** is often abbreviated to **'re** after pronouns.

area /eəriə/ **areas** ◆◆◆◆◆
1 An **area** is a particular part of a town, a country, a region, or the world. *...the large number of community groups in the area... 60 years ago half the French population still lived in rural areas. ...mountainous areas of Europe, Asia, North and South America.* N-COUNT
2 Your **area** is the part of a town, country, or region where you live. An organization's **area** is the part of a town, country, or region that it is responsible for. *Local authorities have been responsible for the running of schools in their areas... If there is an election in your area, you should go and vote.* N-COUNT: poss N
3 A particular **area** is a piece of land or part of a building that is used for a particular activity. *...a picnic area. ...the main check-in area located in Terminal 1.* N-COUNT: supp N
4 An **area** is a particular place on a surface or object, for example an external part of your body. *Massage may help to increase blood flow to specific areas of the body.* N-COUNT: with supp
5 The **area** of a surface such as a piece of land is the amount of flat space or ground that it covers, measured in square units. *The islands cover a total area of 625.6 square kilometers... Although large in area, the flat did not have many rooms.* N-VAR
6 You can use **area** to refer to a particular subject or topic, or to a particular part of a larger, more general situation or activity. *...the politically sensitive area of old age pensions. ...the internationalization of the economy and all other areas of society... She wants to be involved in every area of your life.* N-COUNT: usu with supp
7 In football, **the area** is the same as the **penalty area**; an informal use. *He fouled Paul Williams near the edge of the area.* N-COUNT: usu sing, *the* N =box
8 See also **catchment area, disaster area, grey area, penalty area.**

area code, area codes. The **area code** for a particular city or region is a series of numbers that you have to dial if you are making a telephone call to that place from a different area; used mainly in American English. *The area code for western Pennsylvania is 412.* N-COUNT

arena /əriːnə/ **arenas** ◆◆◇◇◇
1 An **arena** is a place where sports, entertainments, and other public events take place. It has seats around it where people sit and watch. *...the largest indoor sports arena in the world.* N-COUNT =stadium
2 You can refer to a field of activity, especially one where there is a lot of conflict or action, as an **arena** of a particular kind. *He made it clear he had no intention of withdrawing from the political arena... Oil speculation proved a natural arena for his skills.* N-COUNT: usu with supp

aren't /ɑːʳnt, AM also ɑːrənt/ ◆◆◆◆◇
1 In informal English, **are not** is usually said or written as **aren't**.
2 **Aren't** is the form that is usually used instead of **am not** in negative question tags.

Argentine /ɑːʳdʒəntaɪn/ **Argentines. Argentine** means the same as **Argentinian**. *...Argentine agricultural products.* ADJ =Argentinian ► An **Argentine** is the same as an **Argentinian**. N-COUNT =Argentinian

Argentinian /ɑːʳdʒəntɪniən/ **Argentinians. Argentinian** means belonging or relating to Argentina or its people. *...the Argentinian capital, Buenos Aires.* ◆◆◆◆◇ ADJ =Argentine ► An **Argentinian** is someone who comes from Argentina. N-COUNT =Argentine

argon /ɑːʳgɒn/. **Argon** is an inert gas which occurs in very small amounts in the atmosphere. It is used in electric lights. N-UNCOUNT

argot /ɑːʳgoʊ/ **argots.** An **argot** is a special vocabulary used by a particular group of people, which other people find difficult to understand; a formal word. *...the argot of the university campus. ...footballing argot.* N-VAR: usu with supp =slang

arguable /ɑːʳgjuəbᵊl/
1 If you say that it is **arguable** that something is true, you believe that it can be supported by evidence and that many people would agree with it; a formal use. *It is arguable that this was not as grave a handicap as it might appear... The judges said there was at least a good arguable case of negligence to answer.* ADJ-GRADED: oft *it* v-link ADJ that
2 An idea, point, or comment that is **arguable** is not obviously true or correct and should be questioned; a formal use. *It is arguable whether he ever had much control over the real economic power... He said that her remarks disgusted every practising Christian. That claim is arguable.* ADJ-GRADED: usu v-link ADJ, oft *it* v-link ADJ whether =debatable

arguably /ɑːʳgjuəbli/. You can use **arguably** when you are stating your opinion or belief, as a way of giving more authority to it. *They are arguably the most important band since The Rolling Stones... Arguably, 1932 was the year of greatest achievement at the Laboratories.* ◆◇◇◇◇ ADV: ADV with cl/group, ADV before v PRAGMATICS

argue /ɑːʳgjuː/ **argues, arguing, argued** ◆◆◆◆◇
1 If you **argue** that something is true, you state it and give the reasons why you think it is true. *His lawyers are arguing that he is unfit to stand trial... It could be argued that the British are not aggressive enough.* VERB V that *it be* V-ed that Also V with quote, V n
2 If you **argue for** or **against** an idea or policy, you state the reasons why you support or oppose it, in order to persuade people that it is right or that it is wrong. *The report argues against tax increases... I argued the case for an independent central bank.* VERB V *for/against* n V n
3 If you **argue**, you support your opinions with evidence in an ordered or logical way. *I've argued deductively from the text... I'd like to argue in a framework that is less exaggerated.* VERB V adv/prep Also V
4 If you **argue** with someone about something, you discuss or debate it with them, with each of you giving your different or opposing opinions. You can also say that two people **argue** about something. *He was arguing with the King about the need to maintain the cavalry at full strength... They are arguing over foreign policy... The two of them sitting in their office were arguing this point.* V-RECIP V *with* n *about/over* n pl-n V *about/over* n pl-n V n
5 If one person **argues** with another, they speak angrily to each other about something that they disagree about. You can also say that two people **argue**. *The committee is concerned about players' behaviour, especially arguing with referees... They were still arguing; I could hear them down the road.* V-RECIP V *with* n pl-n V Also V *about/over* n
6 If you tell someone not to **argue** with you, you want them to do or believe what you say without protest or disagreement. *Don't argue with me... The children go to bed at 10.30. No one dares argue.* VB: usu imper with neg PRAGMATICS V *with* n V
7 If you say that no-one can **argue** with a particular VB: with brd-neg

fact or opinion, you are emphasizing that it is obviously true and so everyone must accept it; used in spoken English. *We produced the best soccer of the tournament. Nobody would argue with that.* neg PRAGMATICS V with n Also V that

8 • **argue the toss**: see **toss**.

argue out. If two or more people **argue** something **out**, they discuss it or thoroughly in order to reach a conclusion or decision. *If there's a dispute we argue it out... The question of divorce was discussed and argued out in the frankest tones.* PHRASAL VERB V n P Also V P n (not pron)

argument /ɑːʳgjʊmənt/ **arguments** ◆◆◆◆◇

1 An **argument** is a statement or set of statements that you use in order to try to convince people that your opinion about something is correct. *There's a strong argument for lowering the price... The doctors have set out their arguments against the proposals... It is better to convince by argument than seduce by example.* N-VAR: oft N for/against n/-ing, N that

2 An **argument** is a discussion or debate in which a number of people put forward different or opposing opinions. *The incident has triggered fresh arguments about the role of the extreme right in France... The issue has caused heated political argument.* N-VAR: oft N about/over n =debate

3 An **argument** is a conversation in which people disagree with each other angrily or noisily. *Anny described how she got into an argument with one of the marchers. ...a heated argument.* N-COUNT: oft N with n, N between pl-n

4 If you accept something without **argument**, you do not question it or disagree with it. *He complied without argument... It should of course be given back. There is no argument about that.* N-UNCOUNT: with brd-neg =question

5 See also **counter-argument**.

argumentation /ɑːʳgjʊmenteɪʃən/. **Argumentation** is the process of arguing in a systematic or logical way, for example in philosophy; a formal word. *They had little trouble showing the fallacy in this line of argumentation.* N-UNCOUNT =argument, debate

argumentative /ɑːʳgjʊmentətɪv/. If you describe someone as **argumentative**, you disapprove of them because they are always ready to disagree or start quarrelling with other people. *Great chess players have a reputation for being both eccentric and argumentative... You're in an argumentative mood today!* ADJ-GRADED PRAGMATICS =quarrelsome

aria /ɑːriə/ **arias.** An **aria** is a song for one of the leading singers in an opera or choral work. *...Alfredo's aria from the opera, La Traviata.* ◆◇◇◇◇ N-COUNT

arid /ærɪd/ ◆◇◇◇◇

1 **Arid** land is so dry that very few plants can grow on it. *...new strains of crops that can withstand arid conditions. ...the arid zones of the country.* ADJ-GRADED: usu ADJ n

2 If you describe something such as a period of your life or an academic subject as **arid**, you mean that it has so little interest, excitement, or purpose that it makes you feel bored or unhappy. *She had given him the only joy his arid life had ever known. ...the politically arid years of military dictatorship in the 1960s and '70s.* ADJ-GRADED: usu ADJ n

Aries /eəriːz/ ◆◆◇◇◇

1 **Aries** is one of the twelve signs of the zodiac. Its symbol is a ram. People who are born approximately between 21st March and 19th April come under this sign. N-UNCOUNT

2 **An Aries** is a person whose sign of the zodiac is Aries. N-SING: a N

arise /əraɪz/ **arises, arising, arose, arisen** /ərɪzən/ ◆◆◆◇◇

1 If a situation or problem **arises**, it begins to exist or people start to become aware of it. *...if a problem arises later in the pregnancy... The birds also attack crops when the opportunity arises.* VERB =occur V

2 If something **arises from** a particular situation, or **arises out of it**, it is created or caused by the situation. *This serenity arose in part from Rachel's religious beliefs... The charges arise out of a long-running fraud enquiry by Merseyside police.* VERB V from/out of n

3 If something such as a new species, organization, or system **arises**, it begins to exist and develop. *New biological species arise only after the passage of millennia.* VERB V

4 When you **arise**, you get out of bed in the morning; a formal use. *He arose at 6:30 a.m. as usual.* VERB V

5 When you **arise** from a chair or a kneeling position, you stand up; a formal use. *When I arose from the chair, my father and Eleanor's father were in deep conversation... Arise, Sir William.* VERB V

6 If someone tells a group of people to **arise**, they are urging them to protest and struggle together in order to obtain something such as political rights or freedom; a literary use. *Lenin could not abandon the call 'Proletarians arise!' for oppressed nations.* VB: usu imper =rise up V

7 You can say that something tall such as a building or mountain **arises** from the ground around it; a literary use. *...the flat terrace, from which arises the cubic volume of the house.* VERB =rise up V from n

aristocracy /ærɪstɒkrəsi/ **aristocracies.** The **aristocracy** is a class of people in some countries who have a high social rank and special titles. *...a member of the aristocracy.* ◆◇◇◇◇ N-COUNT-COLL =nobility

aristocrat /ærɪstəkræt, ərɪst-/ **aristocrats.** An **aristocrat** is someone whose family has a high social rank, especially someone who has a title. ◆◇◇◇◇ N-COUNT

aristocratic /ərɪstəkrætɪk/. **Aristocratic** means belonging to or typical of the aristocracy. *...a wealthy, aristocratic family... He laughed it off with aristocratic indifference.* ◆◇◇◇◇ ADJ-GRADED: usu ADJ n

arithmetic. The noun is pronounced /ərɪθmɪtɪk/. The adjective is pronounced /ærɪθmetɪk/. ◆◇◇◇◇

1 **Arithmetic** is the part of mathematics that is concerned with the addition, subtraction, multiplication, and division of numbers. *...teaching the basics of reading, writing and arithmetic. ...an arithmetic test.* N-UNCOUNT

2 You can use **arithmetic** to refer to the process of doing a particular sum or calculation. *4,000 women put in ten rupees each, which if my arithmetic is right adds up to 40,000 rupees.* N-UNCOUNT: oft poss N

3 If you refer to the **arithmetic** of a situation, you are concerned with those aspects of it that can be expressed in numbers, and how they affect the situation. *The budgetary arithmetic for 1993 suggests that government borrowing is set to surge... The arithmetic is finely balanced: the socialists and their allies do not have an overall majority.* N-UNCOUNT: usu the N

4 **Arithmetic** means relating to or consisting of calculations involving numbers. *...a processor which performs simple arithmetic operations such as adding or multiplying numbers.* ADJ: ADJ n =arithmetical

arithmetical /ærɪθmetɪkəl/. **Arithmetical** calculations, processes, or skills involve the addition, subtraction, multiplication, or division of numbers. *...complex arithmetical formulae.* ADJ: usu ADJ n

ark /ɑːʳk/. In the Bible, the **ark** was a large boat which Noah built in order to save his family and two of every kind of animal from the Flood. ◆◇◇◇◇ N-SING: usu the N

arm 1 part of your body or of something else

arm /ɑːʳm/ **arms** ◆◆◆◆◆

1 Your **arms** are the two long parts of your body that are attached to your shoulders and that have your hands at the end. *She stretched her arms out... He had a large parcel under his left arm.* N-COUNT

2 The **arm** of a piece of clothing is the part of it that covers your arm. N-COUNT =sleeve

3 The **arm** of a chair is the part on which you rest your arm when you are sitting down. N-COUNT

4 An **arm** of an object is a long thin part of it that sticks out from the main part. *...the lever arm of the machine. ...the arms of the doctor's spectacles.* N-COUNT: usu N of n

5 An **arm** of land or water is a long thin area of it that is joined to a broader area. *At the end of the other arm of Cardigan Bay is Bardsey Island.* N-COUNT: usu N of n

6 An **arm** of an organization is a section of it that operates in a particular country or that deals with a particular activity. *Millicom Holdings is the British arm of an American company. ...the research arm of Congress.* N-COUNT: usu sing, usu N of n =wing

7 If two people are walking **arm in arm**, they are walking together with their arms linked. *He walked from the court arm in arm with his wife.* PHRASES usu v PHR, oft PHR with n

8 If you say that something costs **an arm and a leg**, you mean that it is very expensive; an informal ex- PHR after v

pression. *A week at a health farm can cost an arm and a leg.*

9 If you hold something **at arm's length**, you hold it away from your body with your arm straight. *He struck a match, and held it at arm's length.* usu PHR after v

10 If you **keep** someone **at arm's length**, you avoid becoming too friendly or involved with them. *She had always kept the family at arm's length.*

11 If you say that a list is **as long as your arm**, you emphasize that it is very long; an informal expression. usu v-link PHR PRAGMATICS

12 If you welcome some action or change **with open arms**, you are very pleased about it. If you welcome a person **with open arms** you are very pleased about their arrival. *They would no doubt welcome the action with open arms... Many Panamanians welcomed the troops with open arms.* PHR after v PRAGMATICS

13 If you **twist** someone's **arm**, you persuade them to do something; an informal expression. *She had twisted his arm to get him to invite her.* V and N inflect

arm 2 weapons

arm /ɑːʳm/ **arms, arming, armed** ◆◆◆◆◆

1 **Arms** are weapons, especially bombs and guns; a formal use. *The IRA had extensive supplies of arms. ...arms control.* N-PLURAL: oft N n =armaments

2 If you **arm** someone with a weapon, you provide them with a weapon. *She'd been so terrified that she had armed herself with a loaded rifle... Arming the police doesn't deter crime.* VERB V n *with* n V n

3 If you **arm** someone with something that will be useful in a particular situation, you provide them with it. *She thought that if she armed herself with all the knowledge she could gather she could handle anything... Armed only with a BBC microphone, I travelled across South Africa meeting writers.* VERB V n *with* n V-ed

4 The **arms** of a city or of a noble family are its coat of arms. **Arms** is often used in the names of pubs. *...china painted with the arms of Philippe V. ...his local pub, the Abercorn Arms.* N-PLURAL

5 See also **armed**, **-armed**, **coat of arms**, **comrade-in-arms**, **small arms**.

6 If soldiers **lay down their arms**, they stop fighting and surrender; an old-fashioned expression. PHRASES V inflects

7 If one group or country **takes up arms** against another, they prepare to attack and fight them. *They threatened to take up arms against the government if their demands were not met.* V inflects, oft PHR *against* n

8 If a country has people **under arms**, it has people trained to use weapons and to fight a war. *There are nearly four million soldiers under arms in this country.*

9 If people are **up in arms** about something, they are very angry about it and are protesting strongly against it. *Environmental groups are up in arms about plans to sink an oil well close to Hadrian's Wall.* usu v-link PHR

armada /ɑːʳmɑːdə/ **armadas.** An **armada** is a large fleet of warships. *An armada of U.S. Navy ships participated in the invasion. ...the defeat of the Spanish Armada, 1588.* N-COUNT: oft N *of* n

armadillo /ɑːʳmədɪloʊ/ **armadillos.** An **armadillo** is a small animal which has a body covered with large bony scales and which rolls itself into a ball when it is attacked. Armadillos live in South America. N-COUNT

Armageddon /ɑːʳmægedᵊn/. When people refer to **Armageddon**, they are referring to a terrible battle or war that will lead to the total destruction of the world or the human race. *We may be the generation that sees Armageddon.* N-UNCOUNT

Armagnac /ɑːʳmənjæk/ **Armagnacs. Armagnac** is a type of brandy made in south-west France. N-MASS

armament /ɑːʳməmənt/ **armaments** ◆◇◇◇◇

1 **Armaments** are weapons and military equipment belonging to an army or country. *...global efforts to reduce nuclear and other armaments. ...the armaments industry.* N-PLURAL =arms

2 **Armament** is used to refer to weapons and bombs carried by an aircraft or other military vehicle; a technical military term. *...a bomber with twin engines and heavy defensive armament.* N-VAR

3 A country's increase in the number and effectiveness of its weapons is its **armament**. *...the pursuit of national security through national armament... The fears have prompted several countries to embark on massive armament plans.* N-UNCOUNT ≠disarmament

armband /ɑːʳmbænd/ **armbands**

1 An **armband** is a band of fabric that you wear round your arm in order to show that you have an official position or belong to a particular group. Some people also wear a black armband to show that a friend or relation has died. *...volunteer guards equipped with official armbands.* N-COUNT

2 **Armbands** are air-filled plastic rings that people who are learning to swim wear on their arms to help them float. N-COUNT: usu pl =water wings

armchair /ɑːʳmtʃeəʳ/ **armchairs** ◆◇◇◇◇

1 An **armchair** is a big comfortable chair which has a support on each side for your arms. *She was sitting in an armchair with blankets wrapped round her.* N-COUNT

2 An **armchair** critic, fan, or traveller knows about a particular subject from what he or she has read or heard about rather than from practical experience; sometimes used showing disapproval. *The last thing we need are words of wisdom from an armchair critic... This great book is ideal for both the travelling supporter and the armchair fan.* ADJ: ADJ n PRAGMATICS

3 If a bank or shop provides an **armchair** service, their customers can carry out financial transactions or order goods from home, using the telephone, a computer, or the postal service, rather than having to go into the bank or shop. ADJ: ADJ n

armed /ɑːʳmd/ ◆◆◆◆◇

1 Someone who is **armed** is carrying a weapon, usually a gun. *A third man escaped and police believe he may be armed. ...a barbed-wire fence patrolled by armed guards... The rebels are well organised, disciplined and very well armed.* ADJ

2 An **armed** attack or conflict involves people fighting with guns or carrying weapons. *I call on everyone to renounce the use of violence and armed struggle... They had been found guilty of armed robbery.* ADJ: ADJ n ≠unarmed

3 See also **arm**, **-armed**.

-armed /-ɑːʳmd/

1 **-armed** is used with adjectives to indicate what kind of arms someone has. *...plump-armed women in cotton dresses.* COMB in ADJ-GRADED

2 **-armed** is used with adjectives such as 'nuclear' and nouns such as 'missile' to form adjectives that indicate what kind of weapons an army or person has. *The government is not willing to forsake its status as a nuclear-armed power.* COMB in ADJ-GRADED

3 See also **armed**.

armed forces. The **armed forces** or the **armed services** of a country are its military forces, usually the army, navy, and air force. ◆◆◆◇◇ N-PLURAL

armful /ɑːʳmfʊl/ **armfuls.** An **armful** of something is the amount of it that you can carry fairly easily. *He hurried out with an armful of brochures.* N-COUNT: usu N *of* n =armload

armhole /ɑːʳmhoʊl/ **armholes.** The **armholes** of something such as a shirt or dress are the openings through which you put your arms, or the places where the sleeves are attached. *...a T-shirt with a round neck and deep armholes for comfort.* N-COUNT

armistice /ɑːʳmɪstɪs/. An **armistice** is an agreement between countries who are at war with one another to stop fighting and to discuss ways of making a peaceful settlement. *Finally, the Bolsheviks signed an armistice with Germany.* N-SING

armload /ɑːʳmloʊd/ **armloads.** An **armload** of something is the same as an **armful** of something. *Troy came rushing back in with an armload of kindling wood.* N-COUNT: usu N *of* n =armful

armor /ɑːʳməʳ/. See **armour**.

armored /ɑːʳməʳd/. See **armoured**.

armorer /ɑːʳmərəʳ/ **armorers.** See **armourer**.

armory /ɑːʳməri/ **armories.** See **armoury**.

armour /ɑːʳməʳ/; spelled **armor** in American English. ◆◆◇◇◇

1 **Armour** consists of tanks and other military vehi- N-UNCOUNT cles used in battle; a technical military use. *...the biggest movement of heavy British armour since the Second World War.*

2 **Armour** is a hard, usually metal, covering that protects a vehicle against attack. *...a formidable warhead that can penetrate the armour of most tanks. ...armour-piercing missiles.* N-UNCOUNT

3 In former times, **armour** was special metal clothing that soldiers wore for protection in battle. *...the collection of weapons and armour in the historic White Tower. ...knights in armour. ...a medieval suit of armour.* N-UNCOUNT

4 See also **body armour.** • **a chink in someone's armour**: see **chink.** • **a knight in shining armour**: see **knight.**

armoured /ɑːʳməʳd/; spelled **armored** in American English. ◆◆◇◇◇

1 **Armoured** vehicles are fitted with a hard metal covering in order to protect them from gunfire and other missiles. *More than forty armoured vehicles carrying troops have been sent into the area.* ADJ: usu ADJ n

2 **Armoured** troops are troops in armoured vehicles. *These front-line defences are backed up by armoured units in reserve.* ADJ: usu ADJ n

armourer /ɑːʳmərəʳ/ **armourers;** spelled **armorer** in American English. An **armourer** is someone who makes or supplies weapons. N-COUNT

armour-plated; spelled **armor-plated** in American English. An **armour-plated** vehicle or building has a hard metal covering in order to protect it from gunfire and other missiles. *He has taken to travelling in an armour-plated car.* ADJ: usu ADJ n

armour-plating; spelled **armor-plating** in American English. The **armour-plating** on a vehicle or building is the hard metal covering which is intended to protect it from gunfire and other missiles. N-UNCOUNT

armoury /ɑːʳməri/ **armouries;** spelled **armory** in American English. ◆◇◇◇◇

1 You can refer to a large number of things which someone has available for a particular purpose as their **armoury.** *The strongest weapon in the government's armoury is the price cuts announced on Saturday... Modern medicine has a large armoury of drugs for the treatment of mental illness.* N-COUNT: usu sing, with supp =arsenal

2 A country's **armoury** is all the weapons and military equipment that it has. *Nuclear weapons will play a less prominent part in NATO's armoury in the future... Delegates signed a treaty to reduce the armouries of conventional weapons in Europe.* N-COUNT: usu supp N

3 An **armoury** is a place where weapons, bombs, and other military equipment are stored. N-COUNT =arsenal

armpit /ɑːʳmpɪt/ **armpits.** Your **armpits** are the areas of your body under your arms where your arms join your shoulders. *The nurse shook the thermometer and put it under my armpit.* ◆◇◇◇◇ N-COUNT

armrest /ɑːʳmrest/ **armrests;** also spelled **arm rest.** The **armrests** on a chair are the two pieces on either side that support your arms when you are sitting down. N-COUNT

arms race. An **arms race** is a situation in which two countries or groups of countries are continually trying to get more and better weapons than each other. *...a conference on ways to control the arms race in the region.* ◆◇◇◇◇ N-SING

army /ɑːʳmi/ **armies** ◆◆◆◆◆

1 An **army** is a large organized group of people who are armed and trained to fight on land in a war. Most armies are organized and controlled by governments. *After returning from France, he joined the army... The army is about to launch a major offensive. ...a top-ranking army officer.* N-COUNT-COLL

2 An **army** of people, animals, or things is a large number of them, especially when they are regarded as a force of some kind. *...data collected by an army of volunteers. ...armies of ants. ...the army of television cameras outside his house.* N-COUNT-COLL: N of n

A-road **A-roads.** In Britain, an **A-road** is a major road. A-roads are narrower than motorways but are wider and straighter than B-roads. *Ignore the tempting motorway signs and stick to the A-roads.* ◆◇◇◇◇ N-COUNT

aroma /əroʊmə/ **aromas.** An **aroma** is a strong, pleasant smell. *...the wonderful aroma of freshly baked bread.* ◆◇◇◇◇ N-COUNT: usu with supp

aromatherapist /əroʊməθerəpɪst/ **aromatherapists.** An **aromatherapist** is a person who is qualified to practise aromatherapy. N-COUNT

aromatherapy /əroʊməθerəpi/. **Aromatherapy** is a type of treatment, used especially to relieve tension, which involves massaging the body with special fragrant oils. ◆◇◇◇◇ N-UNCOUNT

aromatic /ærəmætɪk/. An **aromatic** plant or food has a strong, pleasant smell of herbs or spices. *...an evergreen shrub with deep green, aromatic leaves... An aromatic beef stew waited on the stove.* ◆◇◇◇◇ ADJ-GRADED =fragrant

arose /əroʊz/. **Arose** is the past tense of **arise.**

around /əraʊnd/ ◆◆◆◆◆

Around is an adverb and a preposition. In British English, the word 'round' is often used instead. **Around** is often used with verbs of movement, such as 'walk' and 'drive', and also in phrasal verbs such as 'get around' and 'hand around'.

1 To be positioned **around** a place or object means to surround it or be on all sides of it. To move **around** a place means to go along its edge, back to your starting point. *She looked at the papers around her... Today she wore her hair down around her shoulders. ...a prosperous suburb built around a new mosque.* ► Also an adverb. *...a village with a rocky river, a ruined castle and hills all around... The Memorial seems almost ugly, dominating the landscape for miles around.* PREP; ADV: n ADV

2 If you move **around** a corner or obstacle, you move to the other side of it. If you look **around** a corner or obstacle, you look to see what is on the other side. *The photographer stopped clicking and hurried around the corner... I peered around the edge of the shed – there was no sign of anyone else.* PREP

3 If you turn **around**, you turn so that you are facing in the opposite direction. *I turned around and wrote the title on the blackboard... He straightened up slowly and spun around on the stool to face us.* ADV: ADV after v

4 If you move **around** a place, you travel through it, going to most of its parts. If you look **around** a place, you look at every part of it. *I've been walking around Moscow and the town is terribly quiet... He glanced discreetly around the room at the other people.* ► Also an adverb. *He backed away from the edge, looking all around at the flat horizon.* PREP; ADV: ADV after v

5 If someone moves **around** a place, they move through various parts of that place without having any particular destination. *These days much of my time is spent weaving my way around drinks parties... They milled around the ballroom with video cameras.* ► Also an adverb. *My mornings are spent rushing around after him. ...a scruffy youth wandering around looking lost.* PREP; ADV: ADV after v

6 If you go **around** to someone's house, you visit them. *She helped me unpack my things and then we went around to see the other girls.* ADV: ADV after v

7 You use **around** in expressions such as **sit around** and **hang around** when you are saying that someone is spending time in a place and not doing anything very important. *I'm just going to be hanging around twiddling my thumbs... After breakfast the next morning they sat around for an hour discussing political affairs.* ► Also a preposition. *He used to skip lessons and hang around the harbor with some other boys.* ADV: ADV after v; PREP

8 If you move things **around**, you move them so that they are in different places. *Furniture in the classroom should not be changed around without warning the blind child... She moved things around so the table was beneath the windows.* ADV: ADV after v

9 If a wheel or object turns **around**, it turns on its axis. *The boat started to spin around in the water.* ADV: ADV after v

10 You use **around** to say that something happens in or relates to different parts of a place or area, or is near a place or area. *Police in South Africa say ten people have died in scattered violence around the country... Elephants were often to be found in swamp in eastern Kenya around the Tana River.* PREP

...pests and diseases around the garden. ► Also an adverb. *What the hell do you think you're doing following me around?... Giovanni has the best Parma ham for miles around.*
ADV: ADV after v, n ADV

11 If someone or something is **around**, they exist or are present in a place. *You haven't seen my publisher anywhere around, have you?... Just having lots of people around that you can talk to is important... You see very little of this wine around these days.*
ADV

12 The people **around** you are the people who you come into contact with, especially your friends, colleagues, and relatives. *We change our behaviour by observing the behaviour of those around us... Those around her would forgive her for weeping.*
PREP

13 If something such as a film, a discussion, or a plan is based **around** something, that thing is its main theme. *...the gentle comedy based around the Larkin family... The discussion centered around four subjects. ...a government whose economic policy was built around low interest rates.*
PREP

14 You use **around** in expressions such as **this time around** or **to come around** when you are describing something that has happened before or things that happen regularly. *Senator Bentsen has declined to get involved this time around... When July Fourth comes around, the residents of Columbia City throw a noisy party.*
ADV: n ADV, ADV after v

15 When you are giving measurements, you can use **around** to mention the circumference of something. *She was 5 foot 4 inches, 38 around the chest, 28 around the waist and 40 around the hips.*
PREP

16 **Around** means approximately. *My salary was around £19,000 plus a car and expenses... Rolls Royce produces around 1,000 extremely desirable cars a year.* ► Also a preposition. *He expects the elections to be held around November.*
ADV =about; PREP

17 In spoken English, **around about** means approximately. *There is an outright separatist party but it only scored around about 10 percent in the vote... He's charging you around about a hundred pounds an hour for his services.*
PHRASES PREP

18 You say **all around** to indicate that something affects all parts of a situation or all members of a group. *He compared the achievements of the British and the French during 1916 and concluded that the latter were better all around.*
cl PHR

19 If someone **has been around**, they have had a lot of experience of different people and situations; an informal expression. *He knows what to do. He's been around... He's been around a long time and has acquired a number of skills.*

20 • **the other way around**: see **way**. • **get your tongue around something**: see **tongue**.

around-the-clock. See **clock**.

arousal /əraʊzəl/ ◆◇◇◇◇

1 **Arousal** is the state of being sexually excited. *...sexual arousal... Use this technique to control your level of arousal.*
N-UNCOUNT

2 **Arousal** is a state in which you feel excited or very alert, for example as a result of fear, stress, or anger. *Thinking angry thoughts can provoke strong physiological arousal.*
N-UNCOUNT

arouse /əraʊz/ **arouses, arousing, aroused** ◆◆◇◇◇

1 If something **arouses** a particular reaction or attitude in people, it causes them to have that reaction or attitude. *His revolutionary work in linguistics has aroused intense scholarly interest. ...the deep public anger you have aroused.*
VERB; V n

2 If something **arouses** a particular feeling or instinct that exists in someone, it causes them to experience that feeling or instinct strongly. *There is nothing quite like a crisp, dry sherry to arouse the appetite... He aroused her mothering instincts.*
VERB; V n; Also V n *in* n

3 If you **are aroused** by something, it makes you feel sexually excited. *Some men are aroused when their partner says erotic words to them.* ♦ **aroused** *Some men feel that they get most sexually aroused in the morning.* ♦ **arousing** *Being stroked by a partner is usually more arousing than stroking yourself.*
VB: usu passive; *be* V-ed; ADJ-GRADED: usu v-link ADJ; ADJ-GRADED

4 If something **arouses** you, it makes you feel angry. *He apologized, saying this subject always aroused him.*
VERB; V n

5 If something **arouses** you from sleep, it wakes you up; used in written English. *At dawn the loud peal of cannons aroused us... About two o'clock, we were aroused from our sleep by a knocking at the door.*
VERB =awaken; V n

arr.

1 **Arr.** is a written abbreviation for 'arrives'. It is used on timetables to indicate what time a bus, train, or plane will reach a place. *...dep. Victoria 1927, arr. Ramsgate 2110.*
=arrives

2 **Arr.** is a written abbreviation for **arranged**. It is used to show that a piece of music written by one person has been rewritten in a different way or for different instruments by another person. *'A Good New Year', sung by Kenneth McKellar, (Trad., Arr. Knight).*

arraign /əreɪn/ **arraigns, arraigning, arraigned.** If someone **is arraigned** on a particular charge, they are brought before a court of law to answer that charge; a legal term. *She was arraigned today on charges of assault and kidnapping... He was arraigned for criminally abetting a traitor.*
VB: usu passive; *be* V-ed; *be* V-ed *for* n/-ing

arraignment /əreɪnmənt/ **arraignments.** **Arraignment** is when someone is brought before a court of law to answer a particular charge; a legal term. *Keating and his associates are scheduled for arraignment October 5th... Crowds appeared at the arraignments, prompting more clashes with security forces.*
N-VAR

arrange /əreɪndʒ/ **arranges, arranging, arranged** ◆◆◆◇◇

1 If you **arrange** an event or meeting, you make plans for it to happen. *She arranged an appointment for Friday afternoon at four-fifteen... This time it was a friend ringing to try to arrange a fishing trip in Scotland... The Russian leader threw the carefully arranged welcome into chaos.*
VERB; V n; V-ed

2 If you **arrange** with someone to do something, you make plans with them to do it. *I've arranged to see him on Friday morning... It was arranged that the party would gather for lunch in the Royal Garden Hotel... He had arranged for the boxes to be stored until they could be collected.*
VERB; V to-inf; *it be* V-ed that; V *for* n to-inf; Also V that

3 If you **arrange** something for someone, you make it possible for them to have it or to do it. *I will arrange for someone to take you round... The hotel manager will arrange for a baby-sitter... I've arranged your hotels for you... Transport is not included but can be arranged.*
VERB; V *for* n to-inf; V *for* n; V n; *be* V-ed

4 If you **arrange** things somewhere, you place them in a particular position, usually in order to make them look attractive or tidy. *When she has a little spare time she enjoys arranging dried flowers... He started to arrange the books in piles... A number of seats have been arranged in front of the painting.*
VERB; V n; V n prep

5 If a piece of music is **arranged** by someone, it is changed or adapted so that it is suitable for particular instruments or voices, or for a particular performance. *The songs were arranged by another well-known bass player, Ron Carter.*
VB: usu passive; *be* V-ed

arranged /əreɪndʒd/. If you say how things are **arranged**, you are talking about their position in relation to each other or to something else. *The house itself is three stories high and arranged around a courtyard... They lived in neatly-arranged little houses.*
ADJ =planned

arranged marriage, arranged marriages. In an **arranged marriage**, the parents choose the person who their son or daughter will marry.
N-COUNT

arrangement /əreɪndʒmənt/ **arrangements** ◆◆◆◇◇

1 **Arrangements** are plans and preparations which you make so that something will happen or be possible. *The staff is working frantically on final arrangements for the summit... She telephoned Ellen, but made no arrangements to see her... I am in charge of all the travel arrangements.*
N-COUNT: usu pl, oft N *for* n, N to-inf

2 An **arrangement** is an agreement that you make with someone to do something. *The caves can be*
N-COUNT: also *by* N

visited only by prior arrangement... Her class teacher made a special arrangement to discuss her progress at school once a month.

3 An **arrangement** of things, for example flowers or furniture, is a group of them displayed in a particular way. *The house was always decorated with imaginative flower arrangements. ...an arrangement of dark-blue armchairs around a coffee table.* *N-COUNT: with supp*

4 If someone makes an **arrangement** of a piece of music, they change it so that it is suitable for particular voices or instruments, or for a particular performance. *...an arrangement of a well-known piece by Mozart... Glen Bronka wrote his own orchestral arrangements.* *N-COUNT: usu with supp*

arranger /əreɪndʒəʳ/ **arrangers**

1 An **arranger** is a musician who arranges music by other composers, either for particular instruments or voices, or for a particular performance. *By the age of 17, he had already joined Lionel Hampton's band as both a trumpeter and arranger.* *N-COUNT*

2 An **arranger** is a person who arranges things for other people. *What he really required, John soon decided, was a letter-opener, an arranger, but, also, a friend.* *N-COUNT*

arrant /ærənt/. **Arrant** is used to emphasize that something or someone is very bad in some way; a formal word, used showing disapproval. *That's the most arrant nonsense I've ever heard. ...an arrant coward.* *ADJ: ADJ n; PRAGMATICS; =unmitigated*

array /əreɪ/ **arrays** ◆◆◇◇◇

1 An **array** of different things or people is a large number or wide range of them. *As the deadline approached she experienced a bewildering array of emotions... A dazzling array of celebrities are expected at the Mayfair gallery to see the pictures.* *N-COUNT-COLL: usu sing, N of n*

2 An **array** of objects is a collection of them that is displayed or arranged in a particular way. *There was an impressive array of pill bottles stacked on top of the fridge... We visited the local markets and saw wonderful arrays of fruit and vegetables.* *N-COUNT: usu sing, N of n*

3 An **array** of instruments such as telescopes or solar panels is a number of them that are connected together to form a single unit. *The solar arrays are very fragile and they are also very big.* *N-COUNT: usu with supp, oft adj N, N of n*

4 An **array** of things such as atoms or numbers is a regular pattern or structure that is formed by them; a technical use in science and mathematics. *...methods which can be used to create an ordered array of molecules within materials... The image is then stored on the computer hard disk as a vast array of black or white dots.* *N-COUNT: usu N of n*

arrayed /əreɪd/

1 If things are **arrayed** in a particular way, they are arranged or displayed in that way; a formal use. *Cartons of Chinese food were arrayed on a large oak table. ...how molecules are arrayed in materials such as plastics and other polymers.* *ADJ: v-link ADJ, usu ADJ prep/adv*

2 If something such as a military force is **arrayed against** someone, it is ready and able to be used against them; a formal use. *The trouble with all such proposals is that so many powerful interests are arrayed against them... Napoleon ultimately failed in his plan to defeat the two armies arrayed against him.* *ADJ: v-link ADJ against n*

3 If someone is **arrayed** in particular clothes, especially attractive or beautiful ones, they are dressed in those clothes; a literary use. *Sabrina has discarded her habitual boilersuit and is arrayed in black mini and tights. ...gorgeously arrayed priests.* *ADJ: v-link ADJ prep/adv, adv ADJ; =clothed*

arrears /ərɪəʳz/ ◆◇◇◇◇

1 Arrears are amounts of money that you owe, especially regular payments that you should have made earlier. *They have promised to pay the arrears over the next five years... These 50,000 arrears cases represent a tiny fraction of all home owners.* *N-PLURAL*

2 If someone is **in arrears** with their payments, or has got **into arrears**, they have not paid the regular amounts of money that they should have paid. *...the 300,000 households who are more than six months in arrears with their mortgages. ...debtor countries which fall into arrears with the banks.* *PHRASES: v-link PHR, PHR after v, oft amount PHR, PHR with/on n*

3 If sums of money such as wages or taxes are paid **in arrears**, they are paid at the end of the period of time to which they correspond, for example after a job has been done and the wages have been earned. *Unemployment benefit is paid fortnightly in arrears.* *PHR after v; ≠in advance*

4 If someone is **in arrears** in a sports match or race, they are not winning, because they have a lower score or slower time than other competitors; used in journalism. *Gary Baker took third place, a further minute in arrears.* *=behind*

arrest /ərest/ **arrests, arresting, arrested** ◆◆◆◆◇

1 If the police **arrest** you, they take charge of you and take you to a police station, because they believe you may have committed a crime. *Police arrested five young men in connection with one of the attacks... The police say seven people were arrested for minor offences.* ► Also a noun. *...a substantial reward for information leading to the arrest of the bombers... Police chased the fleeing terrorists and later made two arrests... Murder squad detectives approached the man and placed him under arrest.* *VERB; V n; be V-ed for n; Also V n for n; N-VAR: oft under N*

2 If something or someone **arrests** a process, they stop it continuing; a formal use. *The sufferer may have to make major changes in his or her life to arrest the disease... The law could arrest the development of good research if applied prematurely.* *VERB; V n*

3 If something interesting or surprising **arrests** your attention, you suddenly notice it and then continue to look at it or consider it carefully; a formal use. *The work of an architect of genius always arrests the attention no matter how little remains... As he reached the hall after her, he saw what had arrested her.* ♦ **arresting** *The most arresting feature is the painted wall decoration.* *VERB; V n; ADJ-GRADED*

4 See also **house arrest**.

arrival /əraɪvəl/ **arrivals** ◆◆◆◇◇

1 When a person or vehicle arrives at a place, you can refer to their **arrival**. *...the day after his arrival in England... He was dead on arrival at the nearby hospital. ...the airport arrivals hall.* *N-VAR: oft with poss, on N; ≠departure*

2 When someone starts a new job, you can refer to their **arrival** in that job. *...the power vacuum created by the arrival of a new president... The company had eight departures and 11 new arrivals on its management board in 1980-89.* *N-VAR: oft with poss; ≠departure*

3 When something is brought to you or becomes available, you can refer to its **arrival**. *I was flicking idly through a newspaper while awaiting the arrival of orange juice and coffee... The coronation broadcast marked the arrival of television.* *N-SING: usu with poss*

4 When a particular time comes or a particular event happens, you can refer to its **arrival**. *He celebrated the arrival of the New Year with a bout of drinking that nearly killed him.* *N-SING: usu N of n; =coming*

5 You can refer to someone who has just arrived at a place as a new **arrival**. *A high proportion of the new arrivals are skilled professionals... He was the most junior and most recent arrival at the embassy.* *N-COUNT: usu adj N; =newcomer*

6 When a baby is born, you can refer to its **arrival**. *...a couple anticipating the arrival of a new child.* *N-SING: usu with poss; =birth*

7 You can refer to a baby who has just been born as a new **arrival**. *Her father was besotted with the new arrival.* *N-COUNT: usu adj N*

arrive /əraɪv/ **arrives, arriving, arrived** ◆◆◆◆◇

1 When a person or vehicle **arrives** at a place, they come to it at the end of a journey. *Fresh groups of guests arrived. ...a small group of commuters waiting for their train, which arrived on time... The Princess Royal arrived at Gatwick this morning from Jamaica.* *VERB; ≠depart; V; V prep/adv*

2 When you **arrive** at a place, you come to it for the first time in order to stay, live, or work there. *...in the old days before the European settlers arrived in the country. ...a young student newly arrived in England from New Zealand.* *VERB; V prep/adv; V-ed; Also V*

3 When something such as letter or meal **arrives**, it is brought or delivered to you. *Any entry arriving after the closing date will not be considered... Breakfast arrived while he was in the bathroom.* *VERB; V*

4 When something such as a new product or invention **arrives**, it becomes available. *Several long-awaited videos will finally arrive in the shops this* *VERB; =appear; V* *month... They'll be ready to embrace the new technology when it arrives.*

5 When a particular moment or event **arrives**, it happens, especially after you have been waiting for it or expecting it. *The time has arrived when I need to give up smoking. ...the belief that the army would be much further forward before winter arrived.* VERB V

6 When you **arrive at** something such as a decision or a conclusion, you decide or conclude something, after thinking about it or discussing it. *...if the jury cannot arrive at a unanimous decision... These figures are arrived at on the basis of dentists' receipts for 1991-2.* VERB V at n

7 When a baby **arrives**, it is born. *It's very unlikely that your baby will arrive before you get to hospital.* VERB V

8 If you say that someone **has arrived**, you mean that they have become successful or famous; an informal use. *You know you've arrived when you get your own logo at the end of your shows.* VERB =make it V

arriviste /æriviːst/ **arrivistes.** You describe someone as an **arriviste** when you are criticising them because they are trying very hard to belong to an influential or important social group which you feel they have no right to belong to. *A woman regarded by some as a pushy arriviste... The new arrivals would not be political arrivistes.* N-COUNT PRAGMATICS

arrogant /ærəgənt/. Someone who is **arrogant** behaves in a proud, unpleasant way towards other people because they believe that they are more important than others. *He was so arrogant... That sounds arrogant, doesn't it? ...an air of arrogant indifference.* ◆◆◇◇◇ ADJ-GRADED ♦ **arrogance** *At times the arrogance of those in power is quite blatant.* N-UNCOUNT ♦ **arrogantly** *Later, Simpson arrogantly claimed: 'We won't lose another game.'* ADV-GRADED: ADV with v, ADV adj

arrogate /ærəgeɪt/ **arrogates, arrogating, arrogated.** If someone **arrogates to** themselves something such as a responsibility or privilege, they claim or take it even though they have no right to do so; a formal word, used showing disapproval. *The assembly arrogated to itself the right to alter the relationships within the Federation... He arrogated the privilege to himself alone.* VERB PRAGMATICS V to pron-refl n V n to pron-refl

arrow /ærou/ **arrows** ◆◆◇◇◇

1 An **arrow** is a long thin weapon which is sharp and pointed at one end and which often has feathers at the other end. An arrow is shot from a bow. *Warriors armed with bows and arrows and spears have invaded their villages.* N-COUNT

2 An **arrow** is a written or printed sign that consists of a straight line with another line bent at a sharp angle at one end. This is a printed arrow: →. The arrow points in a particular direction to indicate where something is. *A series of arrows points the way to the modest grave of Andrei Sakharov.* N-COUNT

3 • **slings and arrows**: see **sling**.

arrowhead /ærouhed/ **arrowheads;** also spelled **arrow-head**. An **arrowhead** is the sharp, pointed part of an arrow. N-COUNT

arrowroot /ærouruːt/. **Arrowroot** is a starch obtained from a West Indian plant. It is used in cooking, for example for thickening sauces or in making biscuits. N-UNCOUNT

arse /ɑːʳs/ **arses, arsing, arsed.** In British English, your **arse** is your bottom; an informal word which some people find offensive. The usual American word is **ass.** • **a pain in the arse**: see **pain.** ◆◇◇◇◇ N-COUNT

arse around or **arse about.** If you say that someone **is arsing around** or **arsing about**, you mean that they are behaving in a silly, irritating way instead of getting something done; an informal British expression which some people find offensive. PHRASAL VERB usu cont, V P

arsehole /ɑːʳshoul/ **arseholes.** If one person calls another person an **arsehole**, they think that person is extremely stupid or has behaved in a stupid way; a rude and offensive word used mainly in British English. N-COUNT PRAGMATICS

arsenal /ɑːʳsənᵊl/ **arsenals** ◆◇◇◇◇

1 An **arsenal** is a large collection of weapons and military equipment held by a country, group, or person. *Russia and the other republics are committed to destroying most of their nuclear arsenals... They possess a formidable arsenal of rifles, machine guns, landmines and teargas.* N-COUNT: usu with supp

2 An **arsenal** is a building where weapons and military equipment are stored. *The murder weapon was part of a haul stolen in a raid on a South African air-force arsenal in 1990.* N-COUNT =armoury

3 You can use **arsenal** to refer to a large number of tools, methods, or resources that someone has available to help them achieve what they want they want to do. *Managers use a full arsenal of motivational techniques to get employees to take risks... He has more punches in his arsenal than other boxers.* N-COUNT: usu sing, with supp

arsenic /ɑːʳsənɪk/. **Arsenic** is a very strong poison which can kill people. N-UNCOUNT

arson /ɑːʳsᵊn/. **Arson** is the crime of deliberately setting fire to a building or vehicle. *...a terrible wave of rioting, theft and arson... They vented their anger by carrying out arson attacks.* ◆◇◇◇◇ N-UNCOUNT

arsonist /ɑːʳsənɪst/ **arsonists.** An **arsonist** is a person who deliberately sets fire to a building or vehicle. N-COUNT

art /ɑːʳt/ **arts** ◆◆◆◆◆

1 **Art** consists of paintings, sculpture, and other pictures or objects which are created for people to look at and admire or think deeply about. *...the first exhibition of such art in the West. ...contemporary and modern American art. ...Whitechapel Art Gallery.* N-UNCOUNT

2 **Art** is the activity or educational subject that consists of creating paintings, sculptures, and other pictures or objects for people to look at and admire or think deeply about. *...a painter, content to be left alone with her all-absorbing art. ...Farnham College of Art and Design. ...art lessons.* N-UNCOUNT

3 The **arts** are activities such as music, painting, literature, cinema, and dance, which people can take part in for enjoyment, or to create works which express serious meanings or ideas of beauty. *Catherine the Great was a patron of the arts and sciences. ...the Arts Council of Great Britain. ...the Wexner Centre for the Visual Arts. ...the art of cinema.* N-VAR: usu *the* N in pl

4 At a university or college, **arts** are subjects such as history, literature, or languages in contrast to scientific subjects. *...arts and social science graduates. ...the Faculty of Arts.* N-PLURAL: oft N n ≠sciences

5 **Arts** or **art** is used in the names of theatres or cinemas which show plays or films that are intended to make the audience think deeply about the content, and not simply to entertain them. *...the Cambridge Arts Cinema.* ADJ: ADJ n

6 If you describe an activity as an **art**, you mean that it requires skill and that people learn to do it by instinct or experience, rather than by learning facts or rules. *...pioneers who transformed clinical medicine from an art to a science. ...the unscientific arts of seduction and romance.* N-COUNT

7 **Art** is an old-fashioned form of the second person singular of the present tense of the verb **be**. *Father, I know thou art aware of me at all times.*

8 See also **Bachelor of Arts, fine art, martial art, Master of Arts, state-of-the-art, work of art.**

Art Deco /ɑːʳt dekou/; also spelled **art deco**. **Art Deco** is a style of decoration and architecture that was common in the 1920s and 30s. It is characterized by simple, bold, geometric designs and the use of plastic and glass. *...art deco lamps.* N-UNCOUNT: oft N n

artefact /ɑːʳtɪfækt/ **artefacts;** spelled **artifact** in American English. An **artefact** is an ornament, tool, or other object that is made by a human being, especially one that has archaeological or cultural interest. *They discovered almost fifty priceless artefacts, including jewellery and a wine vessel from the time of the Trojan Wars.* ◆◇◇◇◇ N-COUNT

arterial /ɑːʳtɪəriəl/

1 **Arterial** means involving or relating to your arteries and the movement of blood through your body. *...people with arterial disease.* ADJ: ADJ n

2 An **arterial** road or railway is a main road or rail- ADJ:

way within a complex road or railway system. ...*one of the main arterial roads through the city.* ADJ n

arteriosclerosis /ɑːˈtɪərioʊskləroʊsɪs/. **Arteriosclerosis** is a medical condition in which the walls of your arteries become hard and thick, so your blood cannot flow through them properly; a medical term. N-UNCOUNT

artery /ɑːˈtəri/ **arteries** ◆◆◇◇◇

1 Your **arteries** are the tubes in your body that carry blood from your heart to the rest of your body. ...*patients suffering from blocked arteries.* N-COUNT

2 You can refer to an important main route within a complex road, railway, or river system as an **artery**. *Clarence Street was one of the north-bound arteries of the central business district. ...the point where the Ohio River, itself a great artery, joins the Mississippi.* N-COUNT

art form, art forms. If you describe an activity as an **art form**, you mean that it is concerned with creating objects, works, or performances that are beautiful or have a serious meaning. *Graffiti is now an art form in Northampton. ...Indian dance and related art forms.* ◆◇◇◇◇ N-COUNT

artful /ɑːˈtfʊl/ ◆◇◇◇◇

1 If you describe someone as **artful**, you mean that they are clever and skilful at achieving what they want, especially by deceiving people. ...*the smiles and artifices of a subtle artful woman... Some politicians have realised that there are more artful ways of subduing people than shooting or jailing them.* ADJ-GRADED: usu ADJ n =crafty

♦ **artfully** *He artfully inveigled the Prime Minister into committing his government to the venture.* ADV-GRADED: ADV before v =craftily

2 If you use **artful** to describe the way someone has done or arranged something, you approve of it because it is clever or elegant; a formal use. *There is also an artful contrast of shapes... Despite some artful editing, the anthology is a weak one.* ADJ-GRADED: usu ADJ n PRAGMATICS

♦ **artfully** ...*artfully arranged flowers.* ADV-GRADED: ADV with v

artful dodger, artful dodgers. If you describe someone as an **artful dodger**, you mean that they are clever, dishonest, and very good at escaping from difficult situations. *The Health Minister has stepped in to halt the criminal career of an 11-year-old Artful Dodger.* N-COUNT

art-house. An **art-house** film is an unusual, experimental film that is intended to be a serious artistic work rather than a piece of popular entertainment. ...*a quirky art-house film... The movies he made became art-house classics.* ADJ: ADJ n

arthritic /ɑːˈθrɪtɪk/

1 **Arthritic** is used to describe the condition, the pain, or the symptoms of arthritis. *I developed serious arthritic symptoms and chronic sinusitis.* ADJ: ADJ n

2 An **arthritic** person is suffering from arthritis, and cannot move his or her body very easily. You can also use **arthritic** to describe a part of someone's body that is affected by arthritis. ...*an elderly lady who suffered with arthritic hands.* ADJ-GRADED

arthritis /ɑːˈθraɪtɪs/. **Arthritis** is a medical condition in which the joints in someone's body are swollen and painful. *I have a touch of arthritis in the wrist.* ● See also **rheumatoid arthritis**. ◆◇◇◇◇ N-UNCOUNT

artichoke /ɑːˈtɪtʃoʊk/ **artichokes** ◆◇◇◇◇

1 **Artichokes** or **globe artichokes** are round green vegetables that have fleshy leaves arranged like the petals of a flower. Each leaf can be removed and the fleshy bottom part of it eaten. N-VAR

2 **Artichokes** or **Jerusalem artichokes** are small, yellowish-white vegetables that grow underground and look like potatoes. N-VAR

article /ɑːˈtɪkəl/ **articles** ◆◆◆◆◇

1 An **article** is a piece of writing that is published in a newspaper or magazine. ...*a newspaper article. ...a travel article... According to an article in The Economist the drug could have side effects. ...Canning's article about the Buxton Festival.* N-COUNT: oft N prep

2 You can refer to objects as **articles** of some kind; a formal use. ...*articles of clothing... He had stripped the house of all articles of value. ...household articles.* N-COUNT: oft N of n

3 If you describe something as **the genuine article**, you are emphasizing that it is genuine, and often that it is very good. *The vodka was the genuine article.* PHRASE: v-link PHR, PHR after v PRAGMATICS

4 An **article** of a formal agreement or document is a section of it which deals with a particular point. *The country appears to be violating several articles of the convention. ...Article 50 of the UN charter.* N-COUNT: oft N of n, N num

5 Someone who is in **articles** is being trained as a lawyer or accountant by a firm with whom they have a written agreement. *In 1986, 44 per cent of those admitted to articles were women.* N-PLURAL: usu prep N

6 In grammar, an **article** is a kind of determiner. In English, 'a' and 'an' are called **the indefinite article**, and 'the' is called **the definite article**. N-COUNT

articled /ɑːˈtɪkəld/. In Britain, someone who is **articled** to a firm of lawyers or accountants is employed by the firm and is training to become qualified. *He was initially articled to a solicitor. ...an articled clerk.* ADJ: v-link ADJ to n, ADJ n

article of faith, articles of faith. If something is an **article of faith** for a person or group, they believe in it totally. *It used to be an article of faith that a man's career was more important than the convenience of his family.* N-COUNT

articulate, articulates, articulating, articulated. The adjective is pronounced /ɑːˈtɪkjʊlət/. The verb is pronounced /ɑːˈtɪkjʊleɪt/. ◆◆◇◇◇

1 If you describe someone as **articulate**, you mean that they are able to express their thoughts and ideas easily and well. *She is an articulate young woman... The child was unable to offer an articulate description of what she had witnessed.* ADJ-GRADED

♦ **articulacy** /ɑːˈtɪkjʊləsi/ *To start a revolution, you need discipline, incisiveness and articulacy.* N-UNCOUNT

2 When you **articulate** your ideas or feelings, you express them clearly in words; a formal use. *The president has been accused of failing to articulate an overall vision in foreign affairs.* VERB V n/wh

3 If you **articulate**, you speak very clearly, so that each word or syllable can be heard. *He articulated very clearly... He articulated each syllable.* VERB V, V n

articulated /ɑːˈtɪkjʊleɪtɪd/. An **articulated** vehicle, especially a lorry, is made in two or more sections which are joined together by metal bars, so that the vehicle can turn more easily; used mainly in British English. ADJ: usu ADJ n

articulation /ɑːˈtɪkjʊleɪʃən/

1 **Articulation** is the action of producing a sound or word clearly, in speech or music; a formal use. ...*a singer able to sustain a full tone and clear articulation over extremely long periods.* N-UNCOUNT

2 The **articulation** of an idea or feeling is the expression of it, especially in words; a formal use. *This was seen as a way of restricting women's articulation of grievances.* N-UNCOUNT: usu N of n

3 The **articulation** of a structure or system is the way in which its different parts or elements are connected; a formal use. *Capitalist social formations reflect the interaction, or articulation, of different modes of production.* N-UNCOUNT: usu N of n

artifact /ɑːˈtɪfækt/. See **artefact**.

artifice /ɑːˈtɪfɪs/ **artifices. Artifice** is the clever use of tricks and devices; a formal word. *Weegee's photographs are full of artfulness, and artifice.* N-VAR

artificial /ɑːˈtɪfɪʃəl/ ◆◆◇◇◇

1 **Artificial** objects, materials, or processes do not occur naturally and are created by human beings, for example using science or technology. ...*a wholefood diet free from artificial additives, colours and flavours... The city is dotted with small lakes, natural and artificial... He did not want his life to be prolonged by artificial means.* ADJ =synthetic ≠natural

♦ **artificially** ...*artificially sweetened lemonade. ...drugs which artificially reduce heart rate.* ADV: usu ADV with v, also ADV adj

2 An **artificial** state or situation exists only because someone has created it, and therefore often seems unnatural or unnecessary. *Even in the artificial environment of an office, our body rhythms continue to affect us... He foresaw an open society without artificial barriers of background, religion or race.* ADJ-GRADED: usu ADJ n

♦ **artificiality** /ɑːˈtɪfɪʃiælɪti/ ...*another example of the capriciousness and artificiality of our adversar-* N-UNCOUNT: oft N of n

ial system of justice. ♦ **artificially** *...state subsidies that have kept retail prices artificially low.*
ADV-GRADED: ADV adj, ADV with v

3 If you describe someone or their behaviour as **artificial**, you disapprove of them because they pretend to have attitudes and feelings which they do not really have. *The voice was patronizing and affected, the accent artificial.* ♦ **artificiality** *...the novel's use of homosexuality to suggest the artificiality of all relationships in that nervous city.*
ADJ-GRADED PRAGMATICS
N-UNCOUNT: oft N *of* n

4 If you say that food tastes or looks **artificial**, you do not like it because its taste or appearance does not seem genuine, and seems to be created by added substances. *The meat was chewy and the sauce was glutinous and tasted artificial. ...complaints that their tinned peas were an artificial shade of green.*
ADJ-GRADED

artificial insemination. **Artificial insemination** is a medical technique for making a woman pregnant which consists of injecting previously stored sperm into her womb. Female animals can also be made pregnant by artificial insemination. *...103 children conceived by artificial insemination.*
N-UNCOUNT =AI

artificial intelligence. **Artificial intelligence** is a type of computer technology which is concerned with making machines work in an intelligent way, similar to the way that the human mind works.
◆◇◇◇◇ N-UNCOUNT =AI

artificial respiration. **Artificial respiration** is the forcing of air into the lungs of someone who has stopped breathing, usually by blowing through their mouth or nose, in order to keep them alive and to help them to start breathing again. *She was given artificial respiration and cardiac massage.*
N-UNCOUNT

artillery /ɑːʳtɪləri/
◆◆◇◇◇

1 **Artillery** consists of large, powerful guns which are transported on wheels and used by an army. *Using tanks and heavy artillery, they seized the town. ...the sound of artillery fire.*
N-UNCOUNT: oft N n

2 **The artillery** is the section of an army which is trained to use large, powerful guns. *At some stage he left the Artillery to command a radar unit.*
N-SING-COLL: *the* N

artilleryman /ɑːʳtɪlərimæn/ **artillerymen.** An **artilleryman** is a soldier in the artillery.
N-COUNT

artisan /ɑːʳtɪzæn, AM -zən/ **artisans.** People who had jobs that required skill with their hands used to be referred to as **artisans**. *They were skilled farmers, artisans and merchants.*
◆◇◇◇◇ N-COUNT =craftsman

artist /ɑːʳtɪst/ **artists**
◆◆◆◆◇

1 An **artist** is someone who draws or paints pictures or creates sculptures as a job or a hobby. *...the studio of a great artist... Each poster is signed by the artist... I'm not a good artist.*
N-COUNT

2 An **artist** is a person who creates novels, poems, films, or other things which can be considered as works of art. *His books are enormously easy to read, yet he is a serious artist... Engel is quoted as saying that balanced people do not become artists.*
N-COUNT

3 An **artist** is a performer such as a musician, actor, or dancer. *...a popular artist who has sold millions of records.*
N-COUNT

4 If you say that someone is an **artist** at a particular activity, you mean they are very skilled at it. *Jack is an outstanding barber, an artist with shears.*
N-COUNT: usu with supp

artiste /ɑːʳtiːst/ **artistes.** An **artiste** is a professional entertainer, for example a singer or a dancer; used mainly in British English. *...a Parisian cabaret artiste.*
N-COUNT: oft supp N

artistic /ɑːʳtɪstɪk/
◆◆◇◇◇

1 Someone who is **artistic** is good at drawing or painting, or arranging things in a beautiful way. *They encourage boys to be sensitive and artistic... Mary's got it all so nice – you remember how artistic she always was with colors.*
ADJ-GRADED

2 **Artistic** means relating to art or artists. *...the campaign for artistic freedom. ...their 1,300 year old artistic traditions.* ♦ **artistically** /ɑːʳtɪstɪkli/ *...artistically gifted children... Artistically, the photographs are stunning.*
ADJ: usu ADJ n
ADV: usu ADV adj/-ed, ADV with cl

3 An **artistic** design or arrangement is beautiful. *...an artistic arrangement of stone paving.* ♦ **artistically** *...artistically carved vessels. ...vegetarian dishes which can be presented artistically.*
ADJ-GRADED
ADV-GRADED: ADV after v, ADV -ed

artistry /ɑːʳtɪstri/

1 **Artistry** is the creative skill of an artist, writer, actor, or musician. *...his artistry as a cellist. ...portrait sculptors of considerable skill and artistry.*
N-UNCOUNT: oft with poss

2 You can use **artistry** to refer to a high level of skill in a profession or sport. *...professions that required skill, even artistry, in public speaking. ...his dazzling contribution of pace and artistry.*
N-UNCOUNT

artless /ɑːʳtləs/. Someone who is **artless** is simple and honest, and does not think of deceiving other people. *She was curiously artless. ...Hemingway's artless air and charming smile.*
ADJ-GRADED =genuine

Art Nouveau /ɑːʳt nuːvoʊ/; also spelled **art nouveau. Art Nouveau** is a style of decoration and architecture that was common in the 1890s. It is characterized by flowing lines and patterns of flowers and leaves. *...the Art Nouveau posters of Alphonse Mucha... We lunched at the stunning art nouveau Café American.*
N-UNCOUNT: oft N n

artsy /ɑːʳtsi/. **Artsy** means the same as **arty**; an informal word.
ADJ-GRADED PRAGMATICS

artwork /ɑːʳtwɜːʳk/ **artworks**
◆◇◇◇◇

1 **Artwork** is drawings and photographs that are prepared in order to be included in something such as a book or advertisement. *The artwork for the LP was done by Bill Hofstadter.*
N-UNCOUNT

2 **Artworks** are paintings or sculptures which are of high quality. *The museum contains 6,000 contemporary and modern artworks. ...a magnificent collection of artwork, including works by such masters as Titian, Vermeer and Goya.*
N-VAR =work of art

arty /ɑːʳti/. Someone who is **arty** seems very interested in drama, film, music, poetry, or painting. People often describe someone as **arty** when they want to suggest that the person is pretentious; an informal word. *Didn't you find her a little bit too arty? ...an arty French film no one's going to see.*
ADJ-GRADED =artsy

as 1 conjunction and preposition uses

as /əz, STRONG æz/
◆◆◆◆◆

1 If something happens **as** something else happens, it happens at the same time. *Another policeman has been killed and several others injured as fighting continued this morning... All the jury's eyes were on him as he continued... The play started as I got there.*
CONJ-SUBORD

2 You use the structure **as...as** when you are comparing things. *I never went through a final exam that was as difficult as that one... There was no obvious reason why this could not be as good a film as the original.* ► Also a conjunction. *I've learned that being a mother isn't as bad as I thought at first!... I don't think he was ever as fit as he should have been.*
PHR-CONJ-COORD
PHR-CONJ-SUBORD

3 You use **as...as** to emphasize amounts of something. *You can look forward to a significant cash return by saving from as little as £10 a month... She gets as many as eight thousand letters a month.*
PHR-CONJ-COORD

4 You use **as** when you are indicating what someone or something is or is thought to be, or what function they have. *He has worked as a diplomat in the US, Sudan and Saudi Arabia... The news apparently came as a complete surprise... I had natural ability as a footballer.*
PREP

5 If you do something **as** a child or **as** a teenager, for example, you do it when you are a child or a teenager. *She loved singing as a child and started vocal training at 12.*
PREP

6 You use **as** when you are mentioning the way that something happens or is done, or to indicate that something happens or is done in the same way as something else. *I'll behave toward them as I would like to be treated... Today, as usual, he was wearing a three-piece suit... The book was banned in the US, as were two subsequent books.*
CONJ-SUBORD

7 You use **as** in expressions like **as a result** and **as a consequence** to indicate how two situations or events are related to each other. *As a result of the growing fears about home security, more people are arranging for someone to stay in their home when they're away... In this changing business environ-*
PREP

ment, different demands are being placed on employees. As a consequence, the education system needs to change.

8 You use **as** to introduce short clauses which show why you believe something to be the case, or why someone else might believe something to be the case. *As you can see, we're still working... We were sitting, as I remember, in a riverside restaurant.* CONJ-SUBORD

9 You can use **as** to mean 'because' when you are explaining the reason for something. *They are regularly sent booklets and personal safety, but they barely read them as they have so much paperwork to deal with... Enjoy the first hour of the day. This is important as it sets the mood for the rest of the day.* CONJ-SUBORD =since

10 You say **as it were** in order to make what you are saying sound less definite. *I'd understood the words, but I didn't, as it were, understand the question.* PHRASES PHR with cl PRAGMATICS

11 You use expressions such as **as it is**, **as it turns out**, and **as things stand** when you are making a contrast between a possible situation and what actually happened or is the case. *I want to work at home on a Tuesday but as it turns out sometimes it's a Wednesday or a Thursday.* PRAGMATICS

12 • **as against**: see **against**. • **as ever**: see **ever**. • **as a matter of fact**: see **fact** • **as follows**: see **follow**. • **as long as**: see **long**. • **as opposed to**: see **opposed**. • **as regards**: see **regard**. • **as soon as**: see **soon**. • **as such**: see **such**. • **as well**: see **well**. • **as well as**: see **well**. • **as yet**: see **yet**.

as 2 used with other prepositions and conjunctions

as /əz, STRONG æz/ ◆◆◆◆◆

1 You use **as for** and **as to** at the beginning of a sentence in order to introduce a slightly different subject that is still connected to the previous one. *I feel that there's a lot of pressure put on policemen. And as for putting guns in their hands, I don't think that's a very good idea at all.* PHR-PREP: PREP n/-ing

2 You use **as to** to indicate what something refers to. *They should make decisions as to whether the student needs more help... Andy sat down at the table and inquired as to what the problem was.* PHR-PREP: PREP wh

3 If you say that something will happen **as of** or **as from** a particular date or time, you mean that it will happen from that time onwards. *The border, effectively closed since 1981, will be opened as of January the 1st... She is to retire as from 1 October.* PHR-PREP

4 You use **as if** and **as though** when you are giving a possible explanation for something or saying that something appears to be the case when it is not. *Anne shrugged, as if she didn't know... He burst into a high-pitched laugh, as though he'd said something funny.* PHR-CONJ-SUBORD

asap /eɪ es eɪ piː/. **asap** is an abbreviation for 'as soon as possible'. *The colonel ordered, 'I want two good engines down here asap.'* ADV: ADV after v

asbestos /æsbestɒs/. **Asbestos** is a grey material which does not burn and which is used as a protection against fire or heat. Clothing and mats are sometimes made from it. *...asbestos gloves.* ◆◇◇◇◇ N-UNCOUNT: oft N n

ascend /əsend/ **ascends, ascending, ascended** ◆◇◇◇◇

1 If you **ascend** a hill or staircase, you go up it; used in written English. *Mrs Clayton had to hold Lizzie's hand as they ascended the steps... Then we ascend steeply through forests of rhododendron.* VERB ≠descend V n V prep/adv Also V

2 If a staircase or path **ascends**, it leads upwards to a higher position; used in written English. *A number of staircases ascend from the cobbled streets onto the ramparts. ...an ascending spiral path leading to a tower.* VERB ≠descend V prep/adv V-ing Also V, V n

3 If something **ascends**, it moves upwards, usually vertically or into the air; used in written English. *Keep the drill centred in the borehole while it ascends and descends... Nott and Dickinson set a new altitude record when they ascended 55,900 feet in their balloon.* VERB ≠descend V V amount

4 If someone **ascends** to an important position, they achieve it or are appointed to it. When someone **ascends** a throne, they become king, queen, or pope; a formal use. *...the same year he ascended to power... Before ascending to the bench, she was a lawyer in a large New York firm. ...a few years before Sixtus V ascended the papal throne.* VERB V to n V n

5 If you **ascend** in your career or in society, you gradually achieve success or a higher status; used in written English. *Mobutu ascended through the ranks, eventually becoming commander of the army... They move freely from one department to another as they ascend the civil service ladder.* VERB =climb V prep/adv V n

6 In some religions, when a divine being or a person's soul goes to heaven, you can say that they **ascend** to heaven. *...the belief that the souls of the faithful and virtuous would ascend to heaven. ...the land from which the Buddha ascended into nirvana.* VERB V to/into n

7 If something or someone **ascends** to a higher level, they reach a state that is better than the one they were in before; a literary use. *The story ascends from a gothic tragedy to a miraculous fairy-tale.* VERB ≠descend V from/to n

8 See also **ascending**.

ascendancy /əsendənsi/; also spelled **ascendency**. If one group has **ascendancy** over another group, it has more power or influence than the other group; a formal word. *Although geographically linked, the two provinces have long fought for political ascendancy... The extremists are gaining ascendancy.* N-UNCOUNT =dominance

ascendant /əsendənt/. If someone or something is **in the ascendant**, they have more power, influence, or popularity than other people or things, or they are increasing in power, influence, or popularity; a formal expression. *Radical reformers are once more in the ascendant... Why are Geography, Drama, Art and English in the ascendant?* ◆◇◇◇◇ PHRASE: v-link PHR

ascendency /əsendənsi/. See **ascendancy**.

ascending /əsendɪŋ/. If a group of things is arranged in **ascending** order, each thing is bigger, greater, or more important than the thing before it. *Now draw or trace ten dinosaurs in ascending order of size. ...an ascending spiral of antisocial behaviour.* • See also **ascend**. ADJ: ADJ n

ascension /əsenʃən/

1 In some religions, when someone goes to heaven, you can refer to their **ascension** to heaven. *...the crucifixion, resurrection and ascension of Jesus Christ. ...the two-day holiday marking the Prophet's ascension to heaven.* N-SING: with poss

2 The **ascension** of a person to a high rank or important position is the act of reaching this position; used in written English. *...50 years after his ascension to the Cambodian throne.* N-SING: with poss, usu N to n

Ascension Day. **Ascension Day** is the day when Christians remember how Jesus Christ was taken up to heaven at the end of his time on earth. It is the Thursday forty days after Easter Sunday. N-UNCOUNT

ascent /əsent/ **ascents** ◆◇◇◇◇

1 An **ascent** is an upward journey, especially when you are walking or climbing. *In 1955 he led the first ascent of Kangchenjunga, the world's third highest mountain.* N-COUNT: oft N of n ≠descent

2 An **ascent** is an upward slope or path, especially when you are walking or climbing. *It was a tough course over a gradual ascent before the big climb of Bluebell Hill.* N-COUNT ≠descent

3 An **ascent** is an upward, vertical movement. *Burke pushed the button and the elevator began its slow ascent.* N-COUNT: usu sing, oft poss N ≠descent

4 The **ascent** of a person to a more important or successful position is the process of reaching this position; used in written English. *...while his own career continues its inexorable ascent. ...an internal revolution as daunting as their ascent to power.* N-SING: usu with supp =rise

5 In some religions, when someone goes to heaven, you can refer to their **ascent** to heaven. *...Elijah's ascent to heaven in a chariot of fire.* N-COUNT: usu sing, N prep

ascertain /æsəˈteɪn/ **ascertains, ascertaining, ascertained.** If you **ascertain** the truth about something, you find out what it is, especially by making a deliberate effort to do so; a formal word. *Through doing this, the teacher will be able* ◆◇◇◇◇ VERB =establish V n *to ascertain the extent to which the child understands what he is reading... Once they had ascertained that he was not a spy, they agreed to release him... Take time to ascertain what services your bank is providing, and at what cost.* V that V wh

ascetic /əsetɪk/ **ascetics.** An **ascetic** person has a way of life that is simple and strict, usually because of their religious beliefs. *She has never been close to her ascetic, workaholic father. ...priests practising an ascetic life. ...his bony, ascetic face.* ADJ-GRADED: usu ADJ n
▶ An **ascetic** is someone who is ascetic. *He left the luxuries of the court for the life of an ascetic.* N-COUNT

asceticism /əsetɪsɪzəm/. **Asceticism** is a simple, strict way of life with no luxuries or physical pleasures. People usually embrace asceticism because of their religious beliefs. *It was by his personal asceticism and good example that he won converts to his preaching.* N-UNCOUNT

ascorbic acid /æskɔːʳbɪk æsɪd/. **Ascorbic acid** is another name for vitamin C; a technical term. N-UNCOUNT =vitamin C

ascribe /əskraɪb/ **ascribes, ascribing, ascribed** ◆◇◇◇◇

1 If you **ascribe** an event or condition **to** a particular cause, you say or consider that it was caused by that thing. *An autopsy eventually ascribed the baby's death to sudden infant death syndrome.* VERB =attribute V n to n

2 If you **ascribe** a quality **to** someone, you consider that they possess it. *We do not ascribe a superior wisdom to government or the state.* VERB =attribute V n to n

3 If you **ascribe** something such as a quotation or a work of art **to** someone, you say that they said it or created it. *He mistakenly ascribes the expression 'survival of the fittest' to Charles Darwin.* VERB =attribute V n to n

4 If you **ascribe to** a particular belief or opinion, you hold that belief or opinion. *He ascribes to a philosophy that permeates every part of his life.* VERB V to n

asexual /eɪsekʃuəl/

1 Something that is **asexual** involves no sexual activity. *Their relationship was totally asexual. ...asexual reproduction.* ♦ **asexually** *Many fungi can reproduce asexually.* ADJ; ADV: usu ADV with v, also ADV adj

2 **Asexual** creatures and plants have no gender. *...asexual parasites.* ADJ

3 Someone who is **asexual** is not sexually attracted to other people. *It is another unfortunate myth of our culture that older people are asexual.* ADJ

ash /æʃ/ **ashes** ◆◆◇◇◇

1 **Ash** is the grey or black powdery substance that is left after something is burnt. You can also refer to this substance as **ashes**. *A cloud of volcanic ash is spreading across wide areas of the Philippines... He brushed the cigarette ash from his sleeve... He ordered their villages burned to ashes.* N-UNCOUNT: also N in pl

2 A dead person's **ashes** are their remains after their body has been cremated. *He made me promise to sprinkle his ashes from Putney Bridge.* N-PLURAL: usu poss N

3 An **ash** is a tree that has a smooth grey bark and winged seeds. *...a high forest of oak and ash.* N-VAR ▶ **Ash** is the wood from this tree. *The rafters are made from ash.* N-UNCOUNT

ashamed /əʃeɪmd/ ◆◆◇◇◇

1 If someone is **ashamed**, they feel embarrassed or guilty because of something they do or they have done, or because of their appearance. *I felt incredibly ashamed of myself for getting so angry... She was ashamed that she looked so shabby... I'm a lesbian and I'm not ashamed about it.* ADJ-GRADED: v-link ADJ, usu ADJ of/about n, ADJ that ≠proud

2 If you are **ashamed** of someone, you feel embarrassed to be connected with them, often because of their appearance or because you disapprove of something they have done. *I've never told this to anyone, but it's true, I was terribly ashamed of my mum.* ADJ-GRADED: v-link ADJ of n ≠proud

3 If someone is **ashamed** to do something, they do not want to do it because they feel embarrassed about it. *Women are often ashamed to admit they are being abused.* ADJ-GRADED: v-link ADJ to-inf ≠proud

ashen /æʃən/. Someone who is **ashen** looks very pale, especially because they are ill, shocked, or frightened. *He was ashen and trembling... He fell back, shocked, his face ashen.* ADJ =pallid

ashen-faced. Someone who is **ashen-faced** looks very pale, especially because they are ill, shocked, or frightened. *Beside her, Grace sat ashen-faced, complaining of feeling sick.* ADJ

ashore /əʃɔːʳ/. Someone or something that comes **ashore** comes from the sea onto the shore. *Oil has come ashore on a ten mile stretch to the east of Plymouth... Once ashore, the vessel was thoroughly inspected.* ◆◇◇◇◇ ADV: ADV after v, be ADV

ashtray /æʃtreɪ/ **ashtrays.** An **ashtray** is a small dish in which smokers can put the ash from their cigarettes and cigars. ◆◇◇◇◇ N-COUNT

Ash Wednesday. **Ash Wednesday** is the first day of Lent. N-UNCOUNT

Asian /eɪʒən/ **Asians.** Someone or something that is **Asian** comes from or is associated with Asia. British people use this term especially when they are referring to people or things that come from India, Pakistan, and Bangladesh. Americans use this term especially when they are referring to people or things that come from China, Korea, Thailand, Japan, or Vietnam. *...Asian music. ...the Asian community in San Francisco.* ◆◆◆◆◇ ADJ ▶ An **Asian** is a person who comes from or is associated with a country or region in Asia. *Many of the shops were run by Asians.* N-COUNT

Asiatic /eɪʒiætɪk/. **Asiatic** means belonging or relating to Asia or its people; an old-fashioned word. *...his placid Asiatic face.* ADJ: ADJ n =Asian

aside 1 adverb and noun uses

aside /əsaɪd/ **asides** ◆◆◆◇◇

In addition to the uses shown below, **aside** is used in phrasal verbs such as 'cast aside', 'stand aside', and 'step aside'.

1 If you move something **aside**, you move it to one side of you. *Sarah closed the book and laid it aside.* ADV: ADV after v

2 If you take or draw someone **aside**, you take them a little way away from a group of people in order to talk to them in private. *Billy Ewing grabbed him by the elbow and took him aside... Will looked put his arm around her shoulders and drew her aside.* ADV: ADV after v =to one side

3 If you move **aside**, you get out of someone's way. *She had been standing in the doorway, but now she stepped aside to let them pass.* ADV: ADV after v

4 If you set something such as time, money, or space **aside** for a particular purpose, you save it and do not use it for anything else. *She wants to put her pocket-money aside for holidays. ...the ground set aside for the new cathedral.* ADV: ADV after v

5 If you brush or sweep **aside** a feeling or suggestion, you reject it. *Talk to a friend who will really listen and not brush aside your feelings... Mr Major yesterday swept aside any doubts about a Tory victory.* ADV: ADV after v =banish

6 You use **aside** to indicate that you have finished talking about something, or that you are leaving it out of your discussion, and that you are about to talk about something else. *Leaving aside the tiny minority who are clinically depressed, most people who have bad moods also have very good moods... Emotional arguments aside, here are the facts.* ADV: ADV after v, n ADV PRAGMATICS =apart

7 An **aside** is a comment that a character in a play makes to the audience, which the other characters are supposed not to be able to hear. *Exasperated with her children, she rolls her eyes and mutters an aside to the camera, 'No wonder I drink!'.* N-COUNT

8 An **aside** is something that you say that is not directly connected with what you are talking about. *He'll begin one thought, inject several fascinating asides, then pick up his original idea minutes later.* N-COUNT =digression

aside 2 preposition use

aside from. **Aside from** means the same as **apart from**. This form is more usual in American English. ◆◇◇◇◇ PHR-PREP =apart from

asinine /æsɪnaɪn/. If you describe something or someone as **asinine**, you mean that they are very foolish; a formal word. *I have never heard such an asinine discussion.* ADJ-GRADED PRAGMATICS =idiotic, moronic

ask /ɑːsk, æsk/ **asks, asking, asked** ◆◆◆◆◆

1 If you **ask** someone something, you say something to them in the form of a question because you want to know the answer. *'How is Frank?' he* VERB V with quote

asked... I asked him his name... I wasn't the only one asking questions... She asked me if I'd enjoyed my dinner... If Daniel asks what happened in court we will tell him... You will have to ask David about that... 'I'm afraid to ask what it cost.'—'Then don't ask.' V n / V n / V n wh / V wh / V n *about* n / V / Also V *about* n

2 If you **ask** someone to do something, you tell them that you want them to do it. *We had to ask him to leave... She said she had been asked to take two suitcases to Africa by a man called Sean.* VERB / V n to-inf

3 If you **ask** to do something, you tell someone that you want to do it. *I asked to see the Director.* VERB / V to-inf

4 If you **ask for** something, you say that you would like it. *I decided to go to the next house and ask for food... Who asked for your opinion?* VERB / V *for* n

5 If you **ask for** someone, you say that you would like to speak to them. *There's a man at the gate asking for you.* VERB / V *for* n

6 If you **ask** someone's permission, opinion, or forgiveness, you try to obtain it by putting a question to them. *Please ask permission from whoever pays the phone bill before making your call.* VERB / =get / V n

7 If you **ask** someone to an event or place, you invite them to go there. *Couldn't you ask Jon to the party?... She asked me back to her house.* VERB / V n *to/for* n / V n adv

8 If someone **is asking** a particular price for something, they are selling it for that price. *Mr Pantelaras was asking £6,000 for his collection.* VERB / V n *for* n / Also V n

9 You reply **'don't ask me'** when you do not know the answer to a question, usually when you are annoyed or surprised that you have been asked. *'She's got other things on her mind, wouldn't you think?' 'Don't ask me,' murmured Chris. 'I've never met her.'* PHRASES / CONVENTION / PRAGMATICS

10 If something is yours **for the asking**, you could get it very easily if you wanted to. *He knew the nomination was his for the asking.*

11 If you say **'I ask you'**, you are emphasizing how much you disapprove of someone or something. *That silly old bat. I ask you, who'd she think she was?* EXCLAM / PRAGMATICS

12 You can say **'may I ask'** as a formal way of asking a question, which shows you are annoyed or suspicious about something. *May I ask where you're going, sir?* PRAGMATICS

13 You can say '**if you ask me**' to emphasize that you are stating your personal opinion. *He was nuts, if you ask me.* PHR with cl / PRAGMATICS

14 If you say that someone **is asking for trouble** or **is asking for it**, you mean that they are behaving in a way that makes it very likely that they will get into trouble. *To go ahead with the match after such clear advice had been asking for trouble.* V inflects

ask after. If someone **asks after** you, they ask someone how you are. *I had a letter from Jane. She asks after you.* PHRASAL VERB / V P n

ask around or **ask round.** If you **ask around** or **ask round**, you ask several people a question. *Ask around to see what others living in your area think about their doctors.* PHRASAL VERB / V P

askance /əskæns/

1 If you **look askance** at someone or something, you have a doubtful or suspicious attitude towards them. *They have always looked askance at the western notion of democracy.* PHRASE: V inflects, usu PHR *at* n

2 If you **look askance** at someone, you look at them in a doubtful or suspicious way. *'Do you play chess?' he asked, looking askance at Miguel.* PHRASE: V inflects, usu PHR *at* n

askew /əskjuː/. Something that is **askew** is not straight or not level with what it should be level with. *She stood there, hat askew... There were no shutters at the windows, and some of the doors hung askew.* ADJ-GRADED: v-link ADJ

asking price, asking prices. The **asking price** of something is the price which the person selling it says that they want for it, although they may accept less. *Offers 15% below the asking price are unlikely to be accepted.* ◆◇◇◇◇ N-COUNT: usu sing

asleep /əsliːp/ ◆◆◇◇◇

1 Someone who is **asleep** is sleeping. *My four year-old daughter was asleep on the sofa.* ADJ: v-link ADJ ≠awake

2 When you **fall asleep**, you start sleeping. *Sam snuggled down in his pillow and fell asleep.* PHRASES / V inflects

3 Someone who is **fast asleep** or **sound asleep** is sleeping deeply. *They were both fast asleep in their cots... Turning over, she was soon sound asleep again.* v-link PHR / ≠wide awake

asparagus /əspærəgəs/. **Asparagus** is a vegetable that is long and green and has small shoots at one end. It is cooked and served whole. ◆◇◇◇◇ N-UNCOUNT

aspect /æspekt/ **aspects** ◆◆◆◆◇

1 An **aspect** of something is one of the parts of its character or nature. *Climate and weather affect every aspect of our lives... He was interested in all aspects of the work here... Monroe described the financial aspect as crucial.* N-COUNT: usu with supp

2 The **aspect** of a building or window is the direction in which it faces; a formal use. *The house had a south-west aspect.* N-COUNT: usu sing, usu with supp

3 If something begins to have a new **aspect**, it begins to have a new appearance or quality. *Our journey had taken on a new aspect. The countryside was no longer familiar... The snowy street, like the church, assumed a dumb, lifeless aspect.* N-SING: with supp =outlook

4 In grammar, **aspect** is the way that a verb group shows whether an activity is continuing, is repeated, or is completed. For example, in 'They were laughing', the verb is in the progressive aspect and shows that the action was continuing. Compare **tense**. N-UNCOUNT

aspen /æspən/ **aspens.** An **aspen** is a tall kind of poplar tree with leaves that rustle a lot in the wind. ◆◇◇◇◇ N-VAR

asperity /æsperɪti/. **Asperity** is impatience and sternness that you express in your tone of voice; a formal word. *'I told you Preskel had no idea,' remarked Kemp with some asperity.* N-UNCOUNT: oft *with* N =sharpness

aspersions /əspɜːʳʃənz, AM -ʒənz/. If you **cast aspersions** on someone or something, you suggest that they are not very good in some way; a formal expression. *He has flatly denied casting aspersions on the rabbi's behaviour.* PHRASE: V inflects, usu PHR *on* n

asphalt /æsfælt, -fɔːlt/. **Asphalt** is a black substance used to make the surfaces of things such as roads and playgrounds. *...the school's asphalt driveway.* N-UNCOUNT: oft N n =tarmac

asphyxia /æsfɪksiə/. **Asphyxia** is death or loss of consciousness caused by being unable to breathe properly; a medical term. *Most deaths occurred from asphyxia through smoke inhalation.* N-UNCOUNT =suffocation

asphyxiate /æsfɪksieɪt/ **asphyxiates, asphyxiating, asphyxiated.** If someone **is asphyxiated**, they die or lose consciousness because they are unable to breathe properly. *Three people were asphyxiated in the crush for last week's train... John Doe died in his bath, asphyxiated by the fumes from a gas water-heater.* ♦ **asphyxiation** /æsfɪksieɪʃən/ *A post mortem examination found that she died from asphyxiation.* VB: usu passive =suffocate / *be* V-ed / V-ed / N-UNCOUNT

aspic /æspɪk/. **Aspic** is a clear shiny jelly made from meat juices. It is used in making cold savoury meat dishes. *...cold chicken in aspic.* N-UNCOUNT

aspirant /əspaɪrənt, æspɪrənt/ **aspirants**

1 Someone who is an **aspirant** to political power or to an important job has a strong desire to achieve it. *Any aspirant to the presidency here must be seriously rich... He is among the few aspirants with administrative experience.* N-COUNT

2 **Aspirant** means the same as **aspiring**. *...aspirant politicians.* ADJ: ADJ n =would-be

aspiration /æspɪreɪʃən/ **aspirations.** Someone's **aspirations** are their ambitions to achieve something. *...the needs and aspirations of our pupils... He is unlikely to send in the army to quell nationalist aspirations. ...the republic's aspiration to statehood.* 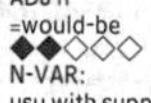 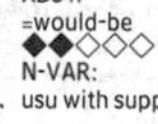 N-VAR: usu with supp

aspirational /æspɪreɪʃənəl/

1 If you describe someone as **aspirational**, you mean that they have strong hopes of moving to a higher social status; used in journalism. *...the typical tensions of an aspirational household.* ADJ-GRADED

2 If you describe a product as **aspirational**, you ADJ-GRADED

mean that it is bought or enjoyed by people who have strong hopes of moving to a higher social class; used in journalism. *Fine music, particularly opera, has become aspirational, like fine wine or foreign travel.*

aspire /əspaɪəʳ/ **aspires, aspiring, aspired.** ◆◇◇◇◇ VERB
If you **aspire to** something such as an important job, you have an ambition to achieve it. *...people who aspire to public office... They aspired to be gentlemen, though they fell far short of the ideal.* V to n/-ing; V to-inf
● See also **aspiring**.

aspirin /æspɪrɪn/ **aspirins;** the form **aspirin** can also be used for the plural. ◆◇◇◇◇ N-UNCOUNT
Aspirin is a mild drug which reduces pain and fever. It is usually in the form of white tablets. You take aspirin, for example, when you have a headache. ▶ An **aspirin** is an aspirin tablet. *She took some aspirins and went to bed.* N-COUNT

aspiring /əspaɪərɪŋ/. ◆◇◇◇◇ ADJ: ADJ n
If you use **aspiring** to describe someone who is starting a particular career, you mean that they are trying to become successful in it. *Many aspiring young artists are advised to learn by copying the masters.* ● See also **aspire**.

ass /æs/ **asses** ◆◆◇◇◇

1 An **ass** is an animal which is smaller and has long ears. N-COUNT

1 An **ass** is an animal which is related to a horse but which is smaller and has long ears. N-COUNT

2 In informal English, if you say that someone is an **ass**, you dislike them because they say or do silly things. *He was generally disliked and regarded as a pompous ass.* N-COUNT PRAGMATICS

3 In informal American English, your **ass** is the part of your body that you sit down on. The equivalent informal British word is **arse**. N-COUNT

4 To **kick ass** or to **kick** someone's **ass** means to let them know either by telling them or by using physical force that you are not pleased with them; used in informal American English. *They've really been kicking ass lately – busting places up, harassing everybody... He damn well better not try it now or he will damn well get his ass kicked.* PHRASES V inflects

5 Saying that someone can **kiss** your **ass** is a very rude way of expressing anger or disagreement; used in informal American English. Some people find this expression offensive. V inflects PRAGMATICS

6 If you say that someone **makes an ass of** themselves, you mean they behave in a way that you think is very silly. *I find no pleasure in seeing people make asses of themselves.* V and N inflect PRAGMATICS

7 ● **a pain in the ass**: see **pain**.

assail /əseɪl/ **assails, assailing, assailed** ◆◇◇◇◇

1 If someone **assails** you, they criticize you strongly; used in written English. *The opposition's newspapers assail the government each day... Mr Clinton was assailed by the very women's groups he had sought to please.* VERB =attack V n

2 If someone **assails** you, they attack you violently; used in written English. *Dividing his command, Morgan assailed both strongholds at the same time... Her husband was assailed by a young man with a knife in a Glasgow park.* VERB =attack V n

3 If you **are assailed** by something unpleasant such as fears or problems, you are greatly troubled by a large number of them; used in written English. *She is assailed by self-doubt and emotional insecurity.* VB: usu passive =beset; be V-ed

4 If you say that a loud sound or a strong smell **assails** someone's ears or nostrils, you are emphasizing that it is very intense and seems shocking or unpleasant. *The scent of burning metal assailed his nostrils.* VERB PRAGMATICS V n

assailant /əseɪlənt/ **assailants.** ◆◇◇◇◇ N-COUNT: usu poss N =attacker
Someone's **assailant** is a person who has physically attacked them; a formal word. *Other party-goers rescued the injured man from his assailant.*

assassin /əsæsɪn/ **assassins.** ◆◇◇◇◇ N-COUNT
An **assassin** is a person who assassinates someone. *He saw the shooting and memorised the number of the assassin's car.*

assassinate /əsæsɪneɪt/ **assassinates, assassinating, assassinated.** ◆◆◇◇◇ VERB
When someone important **is assassinated,** they are murdered as a political act. *Would the USA be radically different today if Kennedy had not been assassinated?... The plot to assassinate Martin Luther King had started long before he was actually killed.* be V-ed; V n
♦ **assassination** /əsæsɪneɪʃən/ **assassinations** *She would like an investigation into the assassination of her husband... He lives in constant fear of assassination. ...an assassination plot.* N-VAR: oft N of n, N n

assault /əsɔːlt/ **assaults, assaulting, assaulted** 

1 An **assault** by an army is a strong attack made on an area held by the enemy. *The rebels are poised for a new assault on the government garrisons... Most US soldiers welcomed the ground assault when the order was finally given.* N-COUNT: oft N on/upon/against n =attack

2 **Assault** weapons such as rifles are intended for soldiers to use in battle rather than for purposes such as hunting. *Gunmen opened fire with AK-47 assault rifles and 303s.* ADJ: ADJ n

3 An **assault** on a person is a physical attack on them. *The attack is one of a series of savage sexual assaults on women in the university area... At the police station, I was charged with assault.* N-VAR: oft N on/upon n

4 To **assault** someone means to physically attack them. *The gang assaulted him with iron bars... She may have been sexually assaulted by her killer.* VERB =attack V n

5 An **assault** on someone's beliefs is a strong criticism of them. *He leveled a verbal assault against his Democratic opponents.* N-COUNT: oft N on/upon/against n

assault and battery. N-UNCOUNT
Assault and battery is the crime of attacking someone and causing them physical harm; a legal expression.

assault course, assault courses. N-COUNT
An **assault course** is an area of land covered with obstacles such as walls or ditches, which people, especially soldiers, run over as an exercise to improve their skills and strength.

assay /æseɪ/ **assays.** N-COUNT
An **assay** is a test of a substance's chemical composition. It is usually carried out to find out how pure a substance is; a technical term.

assemblage /əsemblɪdʒ/ **assemblages.** N-COUNT: oft N of n
An **assemblage** of people or things is a collection of them; a formal word. *She lived with her husband, who had an assemblage of old junk cars and engine parts scattered throughout the backyard.*

assemble /əsembəl/ **assembles, assembling, assembled** ◆◆◇◇◇

1 When people **assemble** or when someone **assembles** them, they come together in a group, usually for a particular purpose such as a meeting. *There wasn't even a convenient place for students to assemble between classes... Thousands of people, mainly Zulus, assembled in a stadium in Thokoza... The assembled multitude cheered and whistled as the political leaders arrived.* V-ERG =gather; V; V in/at n; V-ed

2 To **assemble** something means to collect them together or to fit the different parts of it together. *Greenpeace managed to assemble a small flotilla of inflatable boats to waylay the ship at sea... She had been trying to assemble the bomb when it went off in her arms... He is assembling evidence concerning a murder.* VERB V n

assembler /əsembləʳ/ **assemblers.** N-COUNT
An **assembler** is a person, a machine, or a company which assembles the individual parts of a vehicle or a piece of equipment such as a computer. *The firm is an assembler of computers, not a manufacturer. ...vehicle assemblers and suppliers.*

assembly /əsembli/ **assemblies** ◆◆◆◇◇

1 An **assembly** is a large group of people who meet regularly to make decisions or laws for a particular region or country. *...the campaign for the first free election to the National Assembly. ...an assembly of party members from the Russian republic.* N-COUNT: usu sing

2 An **assembly** is a group of people gathered together for a particular purpose. *...an assembly of women Olympic gold-medal winners... He waited until complete quiet settled on the assembly.* N-COUNT =gathering

3 When you refer to rights of **assembly** or restrictions on **assembly**, you are referring to the legal right that people have to gather together; a formal N-UNCOUNT: usu prep N

use. *The US Constitution guarantees free speech, freedom of assembly and equal protection... They were accused of unlawful assembly.*

4 In a school, **assembly** is a gathering of all the teachers and pupils at the beginning of every school day. *By 9, the juniors are in the hall for assembly. ...a long room with a stage at one end for assemblies.* N-UNCOUNT: also N in pl

5 The **assembly** of a machine, device, or object is the process of fitting its different parts together. *For the rest of the day, he worked on the assembly of an explosive device. ...workers at Sao Paolo's car assembly plants.* N-UNCOUNT

assembly line, assembly lines. An **assembly line** is an arrangement of workers and machines in a factory where each worker makes only one part of a product. The product passes from one worker to another until it is finished. *...a man who works on an assembly line.* ◆◇◇◇◇ N-COUNT

assemblyman /əsemblimən/ **assemblymen.** In the United States, an **assemblyman** is an elected member of an assembly of people who make decisions and laws. *Mr Friedman is a California state assemblyman from Los Angeles... Assemblyman Gil Ferguson is a former marine colonel.* N-COUNT; N-TITLE

assemblywoman /əsembliwʊmən/ **assemblywomen.** In the United States, an **assemblywoman** is a female elected member of an assembly of people who make decisions and laws. *...Lucille Allard, a Democratic assemblywoman from Los Angeles. ...state Assemblywoman Marguerite Hudson.* N-COUNT; N-TITLE

assent /əsent/ **assents, assenting, assented** ◆◇◇◇◇

1 If someone gives their **assent** to something that has been suggested, they formally agree to it. *Both Denmark and Britain will give their final assent to the Maastricht treaty this summer... Mr Yeltsin will be unable to pass a new constitution without the assent of parliament.* N-UNCOUNT: oft with poss, N *to/for* n =agreement

2 If you **assent** to something, you agree to it or agree with it. *I assented to the request of the American publishers to write this book... 'But it's good grub,' he added. 'You're right,' Pantieri assented.* VERB V *to* n V with quote Also V

assert /əsɜːʳt/ **asserts, asserting, asserted** ◆◆◇◇◇

1 If someone **asserts** a fact or belief, they state it firmly; a formal use. *Mr. Helm plans to assert that the bill violates the First Amendment... The defendants, who continue to assert their innocence, are expected to appeal... Altman asserted, 'We were making a political statement about western civilisation and greed.'* ♦ **assertion** /əsɜːʳʃᵊn/ **assertions** *There is no concrete evidence to support assertions that the recession is truly over.* VERB =declare V that V n V with quote N-VAR

2 If you **assert** your authority, you make it clear by your behaviour that you have authority. *After the war, the army made an attempt to assert its authority in the south of the country... The people have asserted their power and that will be very difficult to reverse.* ♦ **assertion** *The decision is seen as an assertion of his authority within the company.* VERB =establish V n N-UNCOUNT: usu N *of* n

3 If you **assert** your right or claim to something, you insist that you have the right to it. *The republics began asserting their right to govern themselves.* ♦ **assertion** *These institutions have made the assertion of ethnic identity possible.* VERB V n N-UNCOUNT: usu N *of* n

4 If you **assert** yourself, you speak and act in a forceful way, so that people take notice of you. *He's speaking up and asserting himself and doing things he enjoys.* VERB V pron-refl

assertive /əsɜːʳtɪv/. Someone who is **assertive** states their needs and opinions clearly, so that people take notice. *Women have become more assertive in the past decade. ...an assertive style of management.* ♦ **assertively** *'You don't need to do that,' said Pearl assertively.* ♦ **assertiveness** *Clare's assertiveness stirred up his deep-seated sense of inadequacy. ...an assertiveness training class.* ◆◇◇◇◇ ADJ-GRADED ≠submissive ADV-GRADED: usu ADV with v N-UNCOUNT

assess /əses/ **assesses, assessing, assessed** ◆◆◆◇◇

1 When you **assess** a person, thing, or situation, you consider them in order to make a judgement about them. *Our correspondent has been assessing the impact of the sanctions... The test was to assess aptitude rather than academic achievement... It would be a matter of assessing whether she was well enough to travel.* VERB =evaluate V n V wh

2 When you **assess** the amount of money that something is worth or should be paid, you calculate or estimate it. *Ask them to send you information on how to assess the value of your belongings... What's the property's assessed value?* VERB V n V-ed Also V wh

assessment /əsesmənt/ **assessments** ◆◆◆◇◇

1 An **assessment** is a consideration of someone or something and a judgement about them. *There is little assessment of the damage to the natural environment... The tests are supposed to provide a basis for the assessment of children... Heggie was remanded to a mental hospital for assessment by doctors.* N-VAR =evaluation

2 An **assessment** of the amount of money that something is worth or that should be paid is a calculation or estimate of the amount. *Price Waterhouse have traced the losses to lenders' inflated assessments of mortgaged property. ...income assessment.* N-VAR =appraisal

assessor /əsesəʳ/ **assessors** ◆◇◇◇◇

1 An **assessor** is a person who is employed to calculate the value of something, or the amount of money that should be paid, for example in tax. N-COUNT =appraiser

2 An **assessor** is a person who is an expert in a subject, especially someone asked to advise a court of law on that subject. *Two judges and six lay assessors sentenced White to life in prison.* N-COUNT

3 An **assessor** is a person who judges the performance of someone else, for example in an exam, at an interview or at a sporting event. *...external assessors of GCSE exam results.* N-COUNT

asset /æset/ **assets** ◆◆◆◆◇

1 Something or someone that is an **asset** is considered useful or helps a person or organization to be successful. *Her leadership qualities were the greatest asset of the Conservative Party... His Republican credentials made him an asset.* N-COUNT

2 The **assets** of a company or a person are all the things that they own. *By the end of 1989 the group had assets of 3.5 billion francs.* N-PLURAL

asset-stripping. If you say that a person or company is involved in **asset-stripping**, you are critical of them because they buy companies cheaply, sell off their assets to make a profit and then close the companies down. N-UNCOUNT PRAGMATICS

asshole /æshoʊl/ **assholes.** If one person calls another person an **asshole**, they think that person is extremely stupid, or has behaved in a stupid way; a rude and offensive word, used mainly in American English. ◆◇◇◇◇ N-COUNT PRAGMATICS

assiduous /əsɪdʒuəs/. Someone who is **assiduous** works hard or does things with care and dedication. *...an assiduous student... Podulski had been assiduous in learning his adopted language.* ♦ **assiduously** *They planned their careers and worked assiduously to see them achieved... Mr Kohl has assiduously avoided discussing issues during the campaign.* ◆◇◇◇◇ ADJ-GRADED =diligent ADV-GRADED: ADV with v

assign /əsaɪn/ **assigns, assigning, assigned** ◆◆◇◇◇

1 If you **assign** a piece of work to someone, you give them the work to do. *When I taught, I would assign a topic to children which they would write about... Later in the year, she'll assign them research papers... When teachers assign homework, students usually feel an obligation to do it.* VERB V n *to* n V n n V n Also V n to-inf

2 If you **assign** something to someone, you say that it is for their use. *The selling broker is then required to assign a portion of the commission to the buyer broker... He assigned her all his land in Ireland.* VERB =allocate V n *to* n V n n

3 If someone **is assigned** to a particular place, group, or person, they are sent there, usually in order to work at that place or for that person. *I was assigned to Troop A of the 10th Cavalry... Did you choose Russia or were you simply assigned there?... Each of us was assigned a minder, someone who looked after us.* VB: usu passive =detail *be* V-ed *to* n *be* V-ed adv *be* V-ed n

4 If you **assign** a particular function or value to someone or something, you say they have it. *Under* VERB V n *to* n

Mr. Harel's system, each business must assign a value to each job... Assign the letters of the alphabet their numerical values--A equals 1, B equals 2, etc.
V n n

assignation /æsɪgneɪʃən/ **assignations.** An **assignation** is a secret meeting with someone, especially with a lover; a formal word. *She had an assignation with her boyfriend.*
N-COUNT: oft N with n

assignment /əsaɪnmənt/ **assignments** ◆◆◇◇◇

1 An **assignment** is a task or piece of work that you are given to do, especially as part of your job or studies. *The assessment for the course involves written assignments and practical tests.*
N-COUNT

2 You can refer to someone being given a particular task or job as their **assignment** to the task or job. *An Australian division scheduled for assignment to Greece was ordered to remain in Egypt... I hardly ever take photographs except on assignment.*
N-UNCOUNT: oft N to n

assimilate /əsɪmɪleɪt/ **assimilates, assimilating, assimilated** ◆◇◇◇◇

1 When people such as immigrants **assimilate** into a community or when that community **assimilates** them, they become an accepted part of it. *There is every sign that new Asian-Americans are just as willing to assimilate... His family tried to assimilate into the white and Hispanic communities... The Vietnamese are trying to assimilate themselves and become Americans... French Jews generally had been assimilated into the nation's culture.*
V-ERG =integrate; V; V into/with n; V pron-refl; be V-ed into n; Also V n, V n into n

♦ **assimilation** /əsɪmɪleɪʃən/ *They promote social integration and assimilation of minority ethnic groups into the culture.*
N-UNCOUNT: usu N of n =integration

2 If you **assimilate** new ideas, customs, or techniques, you learn them or adopt them. *My mind could only assimilate one impossibility at a time.*
VERB =absorb; V n

♦ **assimilation** *This technique brings life to instruction and eases assimilation of knowledge.*
N-UNCOUNT: usu N of n

assist /əsɪst/ **assists, assisting, assisted** ◆◆◆◇◇

1 If you **assist** someone, you help them to do a job or task by doing part of the work for them. *Julia was assisting him to prepare his speech... The family decided to assist me with my chores... Dr Amid was assisted by a young Asian nurse.*
VERB =help; V n to-inf; V n with n; be V-ed

2 If you **assist** someone, you give them information, advice, or money. *The public is urgently requested to assist police in tracing this man... Foreign Office officials assisted with transport and finance problems... The Authority will provide a welfare worker to assist you.*
VERB =help; V n in -ing; V with n; V n; Also V n to-inf

3 If something **assists** in doing a task, it makes the task easier to do. *...a chemical that assists in the manufacture of proteins... Here are some good sources of information to assist you in making the best selection... Salvage operations have been greatly assisted by the good weather conditions.*
VERB; V in/with n/-ing; V n in/with n/-ing; be V-ed; Also V n to-inf

assistance /əsɪstəns/ ◆◆◆◇◇

1 If you give someone **assistance**, you help them do a job or task by doing part of the work for them. *Since 1976 he has been operating the shop with the assistance of volunteers... She can still come downstairs with assistance but she's very weak.*
N-UNCOUNT: oft with poss =help, aid

2 If you give someone **assistance**, you give them information or advice. *Any assistance you could give the police will be greatly appreciated... Employees are being offered assistance in finding new jobs.*
N-UNCOUNT =help, aid

3 If someone gives a person or country **assistance**, they help them by giving them money. *Japan has decided to resume economic assistance to China... We shall offer you assistance with legal expenses up to $5,000.*
N-UNCOUNT: oft supp N =help, aid

4 If something is done with the **assistance** of a particular thing, that thing is helpful or necessary for doing it. *The translations were carried out with the assistance of a medical dictionary.*
N-UNCOUNT =help, aid

5 Someone or something that **is of assistance** to you is helpful or useful to you. *He was of great assistance to me in researches for my books... Can I be of any assistance?*
PHRASES; V inflects, usu modal PHR =be of help

6 If you **come to** someone's **assistance**, you take action to help them. *They are appealing to the world community to come to Jordan's assistance... Ben suffered a heart attack and Helen rushed to his assistance.*
V inflects

assistant /əsɪstənt/ **assistants** ◆◆◆◇◇

1 Assistant is used in front of titles or jobs to indicate a slightly lower rank. For example, an assistant director is one rank lower than a director in an organization. *...the assistant secretary of defense.*
ADJ: ADJ n =deputy

2 Someone's **assistant** is a person who helps them in their work. *Kalan called his assistant, Hashim, to take over while he went out... The salesman had been accompanied to the meeting by an assistant.*
N-COUNT =aide

3 An **assistant** is a person who works in a shop selling things to customers. *The assistant took the book and checked the price on the back cover... She got a job as a sales assistant selling handbags.*
N-COUNT =shop assistant

Assoc. **Assoc.** is a written abbreviation for **association** or **associated**.

associate, associates, associating, associated. The verb is pronounced /əsoʊsieɪt/. The noun and adjective are pronounced /əsoʊsiət/. ◆◆◆◇◇

1 If you **associate** someone or something with another thing, the two are connected in your mind. *Through science we've got the idea of associating progress with the future... Rap groups have been barred from large musical events because they are associated with vandalism.*
VERB; V n with n

2 If you **are associated** with a particular organization, cause, or point of view, or if you **associate** yourself with it, you support it publicly. *I haven't been associated with the project over the last year... The press feels the need to associate itself with the green movement.*
VERB =affiliate; be V-ed with n; V pron-refl with n

3 If you say that someone **is associating** with another person or group of people, you mean they are spending a lot of time in the company of people you do not approve of. *What would they think if they knew that they were associating with a murderer?... They disapproved of her dancing at discos and associating with homosexuals.*
VERB =fraternize, mix; V with n

4 Your **associates** are the people you are closely connected with, especially at work. *...the restaurant owner's business associates.*
N-COUNT: oft n N =colleague

5 Associate is used before a rank or title to indicate a slightly different or lower rank or title. *Mr Lin is associate director of the Institute... She applied for associate membership last year.*
ADJ: ADJ n

associated /əsoʊsieɪtɪd/ ◆◆◆◇◇

1 If one thing is **associated** with another, the two things are connected with each other. *These symptoms are particularly associated with migraine headaches.*
ADJ: usu v-link ADJ with n

2 Associated is used in the name of a company that is made up of a number of smaller companies which have joined together. *...the Associated Press.*
ADJ: ADJ n

association /əsoʊsieɪʃən/ **associations** ◆◆◆◆◇

1 An **association** is an official group of people who have the same occupation, aim, or interest. *...the British Olympic Association... Research associations are often linked to a particular industry.* ● See also **housing association**.
N-COUNT: oft in names

2 Your **association** with a person or a thing such as an organization is the connection that you have with them. *...the company's six-year association with retailer J.C. Penney Co... Blyth's association with the sea began in 1966... The association between the two companies stretches back thirty years.*
N-COUNT: usu N with n =affiliation

3 If something has a particular **associations** for you, it is connected in your mind with a particular memory, idea, or feeling. *He has a shelf full of things, each of which has associations for him... Black was considered inappropriate because of its associations with death.*
N-COUNT: usu pl

4 If someone does something **in association with** someone else, they do it together. *The book is published by Headmain LTD in association with the Hardy Plant Society.*
PHRASES; PHR n

5 If something is found **in association with** something else, they are found together. *Bioflavonoids are found in association with vitamin C.*
PHR n

associative /əsoʊʃətɪv, AM -ʃieɪtɪv/. **Associative** thoughts are things that you think of because
ADJ: usu ADJ n

you see, hear, or think of something that reminds you of those things or which you associate with those things. *The associative guilt was ingrained in his soul... The real picture is more horrific and stronger but one must conjure up all the associative thoughts and emotions it evokes.*

assorted /əsɔːʳtɪd/. A group of **assorted** things is a group of similar things that are of different sizes or colours or have different qualities. *It should be a great week, with overnight stops in assorted hotels in the West Highlands. ...swimsuits, sizes 12-18, in assorted colours.* ◆◇◇◇◇ ADJ: usu ADJ n =various

assortment /əsɔːʳtmənt/ **assortments.** An **assortment** is a group of similar things that are of different sizes or colours or have different qualities. *...an assortment of cheese.* ◆◇◇◇◇ N-COUNT: oft N *of* n

asst. **Asst.** is an abbreviation for **assistant**.

assuage /əsweɪdʒ/ **assuages, assuaging, assuaged**

1 If you **assuage** an unpleasant feeling that someone has, you make them feel it less strongly; a literary use. *To assuage his wife's grief, he took her on a tour of Europe... She was just trying to assuage her guilt by playing the devoted mother.* VERB =lessen, soften V n

2 If you **assuage** a need or desire for something, you satisfy it; a literary use. *The meat they'd managed to procure assuaged their hunger.* VERB V n

assume /əsjuːm, AM əsuːm/ **assumes, assuming, assumed** ◆◆◆◆◇

1 If you **assume** that something is true, you imagine that it is true, sometimes wrongly. *It is a misconception to assume that the two continents are similar... If the package is wrapped well, we assume the contents are also wonderful... If mistakes occurred, they were assumed to be the fault of the commander on the spot... 'Today?'—'I'd assume so, yeah.'* VERB =presume V that *be* V-ed to-inf V *so*

2 If someone **assumes** power or responsibility, they take power or responsibility. *Mr Cross will assume the role of Chief Executive with a team of four directors... If there is no president, power will be assumed by the most extremist forces.* VERB V n

3 If something **assumes** a particular quality, it begins to have that quality. *In his dreams, the mountains assumed enormous importance.* VERB =take on V n

4 If you **assume** a particular expression or way of behaving, you start to look or behave in this way. *He contented himself by assuming an air of superiority... Prue assumed a placatory tone of voice.* VERB =put on V n

5 You can use **let us assume** or **let's assume** when you are considering a possible situation or event, so that you can think about the consequences. *Let us assume those clubs actually win something. Then players will receive large bonuses... Let's assume for a moment that I am a litigant in your court, and I am suing Aetna.* • See also **assuming**. PHRASE: PHR that PRAGMATICS

assumed name, assumed names. If you do something under an **assumed name**, you do it using a name that is not your real name. *The articles were published in San Francisco newspapers under the assumed name of Dorothy Dodge... Kravchenko was living in New York under an assumed name.* N-COUNT: usu *under* N =pseudonym

assuming /əsjuːmɪŋ, AM -suːm-/. You use **assuming** or **assuming that** when you are considering a possible situation or event, so that you can think about the consequences. *Assuming you are a stone above your youthful weight, you probably do want to lose a few pounds... But assuming that the talks make progress, won't they do too little, too late?* ◆◆◇◇◇ CONJ-SUBORD PRAGMATICS =if

assumption /əsʌmpʃᵊn/ **assumptions** ◆◆◆◇◇

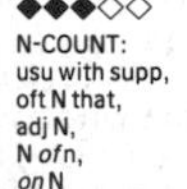

1 If you make an **assumption** that something is true or will happen, you accept that it is true or will happen, often without any real proof. *They have taken a wrong turning in their assumption that all men and women think alike... Dr Subroto questioned the scientific assumption on which the global warming theory is based... Economists are working on the assumption of an interest rate cut.* N-COUNT: usu with supp, oft N that, adj N, N *of* n, *on* N =idea, notion

2 Someone's **assumption of** power or responsibility is their taking of it. *The government have retained the support which greeted their assumption of power last March.* N-UNCOUNT: N *of* n

assurance /əʃʊərəns/ **assurances** ◆◆◇◇◇

1 If you give someone an **assurance** that something is true or will happen, you say that it is definitely true or will definitely happen, in order to make them feel less worried. *He would like an assurance that other forces will not move into the territory that his forces vacate... He will have been pleased by Marshal Yazov's assurance of the armed forces' loyalty.* N-VAR: oft N that, N *of* n =promise

2 If you do something with **assurance**, you do it with a feeling of confidence and certainty. *Masur led the orchestra with assurance... The EC is now acquiring greater assurance and authority.* N-UNCOUNT =assuredness

3 **Assurance** is insurance that provides cover in the event of the death; used mainly in British English. *...endowment assurance.* • See also **life assurance**. N-UNCOUNT

assure /əʃʊəʳ/ **assures, assuring, assured** ◆◆◇◇◇

1 If you **assure** someone that something is true or will happen, you tell them that it is definitely true or will definitely happen, often in order to make them less worried. *He hastened to assure me that there was nothing traumatic to report... 'Are you sure the raft is safe?' she asked anxiously. 'Couldn't be safer,' Max assured her confidently... Government officials recently assured Hindus of protection.* • See also **assured**. VERB =reassure V n that V n with quote V n *of* n

2 To **assure** someone of something means to make certain that they will get it. *They argued that Mr Mandela must assure himself of broad-based black support... Ways must be found to assure our children a decent start in life.* VERB =guarantee V n *of* n V n n

3 You use **I can assure you, I assure you** or **let me assure you** when you want to emphasize the truth of what you are saying, especially when expressing your confidence in something or your determination about something. *I can assure you that the animals are well cared for... This may sound trivial, but I assure you it is quite important!... And let me assure you I will use whatever force is necessary to restore order.* PHRASE: PHR that, PHR with cl PRAGMATICS =believe me

assured /əʃʊəʳd/ ◆◆◆◇◇

1 Someone who is **assured** is very confident and feels at ease. *He was infinitely more assured than in his more recent parliamentary appearances.* ADJ-GRADED =composed ♦ **assuredness** *This a lyrical work written with the authority and assuredness of an experienced writer.* N-UNCOUNT =assurance

2 If something is **assured**, it is certain to happen. *Our victory is assured; nothing can stop us... Yesterday, her future seemed assured.* ADJ: v-link ADJ ≠doubtful

3 If you **are assured of** something, you are certain to get it or achieve it. *Laura Davies is assured of a place in Europe's team... Clinton is virtually assured of winning towns like McKeesport.* ADJ-GRADED: v-link ADJ *of* n

4 If you say that someone **can rest assured** that something is the case, you mean that it is definitely the case, so they do not need to worry about it. *Their parents can rest assured that their children's safety will be of paramount importance... Rest assured, he probably has rather more common sense than you realize.* PHRASES PHR that, PHR with cl PRAGMATICS

5 You use **rest assured** when you want to emphasize your determination to do something. *I will be seeing Mr and Mrs. Johnson. And rest assured I will tell them of your rudeness... Rest assured, if you owe taxes, we will collect them.* PHR with cl PRAGMATICS

assuredly /əʃʊərɪdli/. If something is **assuredly** true, it is definitely true. *Competitiveness is, assuredly, not going to happen by leaving events to market forces alone... If he fails to win here, he will most assuredly lose the White House.* ADV-GRADED: ADV with cl/group, ADV before v =definitely

asterisk /æstərɪsk/ **asterisks.** An **asterisk** is the sign ✻. It is used especially to indicate that there is further information about something elsewhere in the text. N-COUNT

astern /əstɜːʳn/

1 Something that is **astern** is at the back of a ship or behind the back part; a technical term. *The captain was astern, pretending he was sleeping.* ADV: *be* ADV

2 A ship that is moving **astern** is moving back- ADV:

wards; a technical term. *Steering gear comes under most severe test with the yacht going astern.* ADV after v, *from* ADV

asteroid /æstərɔɪd/ **asteroids.** An **asteroid** is one of the very small planets that move around the sun between the orbits of Mars and Jupiter. ◆◇◇◇◇ N-COUNT

asthma /æsmə, AM æz-/. **Asthma** is a lung condition which causes sufferers to have difficulty breathing. ◆◆◇◇◇ N-UNCOUNT

asthmatic /æsmætɪk, AM æz-/ **asthmatics**

1 People who suffer from asthma are sometimes referred to as **asthmatics.** *I have been an asthmatic from childhood and was never able to play any sports.* ► Also an adjective. *One child in ten is asthmatic.* N-COUNT; ADJ-GRADED

2 **Asthmatic** means relating to asthma. *...asthmatic breathing.* ADJ: ADJ n

astigmatism /əstɪgmətɪzəm/. If someone has **astigmatism**, the front of their eye has a slightly irregular shape, so they cannot see properly. N-UNCOUNT

astonish /əstɒnɪʃ/ **astonishes, astonishing, astonished.** If something or someone **astonishes** you, they surprise you very much. *My news will astonish you... Her dedication constantly astonishes me.* ◆◇◇◇◇ VERB =amaze V n

astonished /əstɒnɪʃt/. If you are **astonished** by something, you are very surprised about it. *I was astonished by his stupidity... They were astonished to find the driver was a six-year-old boy.* ◆◇◇◇◇ ADJ-GRADED: oft ADJ *by/at* n, ADJ to-inf, ADJ that

astonishing /əstɒnɪʃɪŋ/. Something that is **astonishing** is very surprising. *It's astonishing, he's learned Latin in three hours! ...an astonishing display of physical strength.* ♦ **astonishingly** *Isabella was an astonishingly beautiful young woman... He was wearing, astonishingly, a frilly pink apron over shirt and trousers.* ◆◆◇◇◇ ADJ-GRADED =amazing; ADV-GRADED: ADV adj/adv, ADV with cl

astonishment /əstɒnɪʃmənt/. **Astonishment** is a feeling of great surprise. *I spotted a shooting star which, to my astonishment, was bright green in colour... 'What?' Meg asked in astonishment.* ◆◇◇◇◇ N-UNCOUNT =amazement

astound /əstaʊnd/ **astounds, astounding, astounded.** If something **astounds** you, you are very surprised by it. *He used to astound his friends with feats of physical endurance.* VERB =astonish V n Also V

astounded /əstaʊndɪd/. If you are **astounded** by something, you are shocked or amazed that it could exist or happen. *I was astounded by its beauty... I am astounded at the comments made by the Chief Superintendent.* ◆◇◇◇◇ ADJ-GRADED: oft ADJ *by/at* n, ADJ to-inf, ADJ that =astonished

astounding /əstaʊndɪŋ/. If something is **astounding**, you are shocked or amazed that it could exist or happen. *The results are quite astounding.* ♦ **astoundingly** *...astoundingly blue eyes... Astoundingly, an American had won the Tour de France.* ◆◇◇◇◇ ADJ-GRADED =amazing, astonishing; ADV-GRADED: ADV adj/adv, ADV with cl

astrakhan /æstrəkæn/. **Astrakhan** is black or grey curly fur from the skins of lambs. It is used for making coats and hats. *...a calf-length coat with astrakhan collar.* N-UNCOUNT: usu N n

astral /æstrəl/. **Astral** means relating to the stars; a formal word. ◆◇◇◇◇ ADJ

astray /əstreɪ/ ◆◇◇◇◇

1 If you are **led astray** by someone or something, they make you behave badly or foolishly. *The judge thought he'd been led astray by older children.* PHRASE: V inflects =corrupt

2 If someone or something **leads** you **astray**, they make you believe something which is not accurate or true, causing you to make a wrong decision. *The testimony would inflame the jurors, and lead them astray from the facts of the case... We drove east to Rostock, where my map led me astray.* PHRASE: V inflects

3 If something **goes astray**, it gets lost while it is being taken or sent somewhere. *Many items of mail being sent to her have gone astray.* PHRASE: V inflects =go missing

astride /əstraɪd/. If you sit or stand **astride** something, you sit or stand with one leg on each side of it. *...three youths who stood astride their bicycles and stared.* ADV: ADV after v, *be* ADV

astringent /əstrɪndʒənt/ **astringents** ◆◇◇◇◇

1 An **astringent** is a liquid that you put on your skin to make it less greasy or to make cuts stop bleeding. *Using an astringent may be too drying for some skins.* ► Also an adjective. *...an astringent lotion.* N-COUNT; ADJ: ADJ n

2 **Astringent** means forceful and critical. *Sunset Boulevard was originally conceived by Wilder as an astringent satire on Hollywood.* ADJ-GRADED =caustic

3 If something has an **astringent** taste, it is sharp or bitter; a formal use. *The fruit has a tart and astringent flavour.* ♦ **astringency** /əstrɪndʒənsi/ *The process, in which the tea develops its characteristic astringency, is known as fermentation.* ADJ-GRADED; N-UNCOUNT

astro- /æstroʊ-/. **Astro-** is used to form words which refer to things relating to the stars or to outer space. *...astro-navigation.* PREFIX

astrologer /əstrɒlədʒəʳ/ **astrologers.** An **astrologer** is a person who uses astrology in order to try to tell you things about your character and your future. ◆◇◇◇◇ N-COUNT

astrology /əstrɒlədʒi/. **Astrology** is the study of the movements of the planets, sun, moon, and stars in the belief that these movements can have an influence on people's lives. ♦ **astrological** /æstrəlɒdʒɪkəl/ *He has had a keen and lifelong interest in astrological research.* ♦ **astrologically** /æstrəlɒdʒɪkli/ *...an astrologically significant moment.* ◆◇◇◇◇ N-UNCOUNT; ADJ: ADJ n; ADV

astronaut /æstrənɔːt/ **astronauts.** An **astronaut** is a person who is trained for travelling in a spacecraft. ◆◇◇◇◇ N-COUNT =spaceman

astronomer /əstrɒnəməʳ/ **astronomers.** An **astronomer** is a scientist who studies the stars, planets, and other natural objects in space. ◆◆◇◇◇ N-COUNT

astronomical /æstrənɒmɪkəl/ ◆◇◇◇◇

1 If you describe an amount, especially the cost of something as **astronomical**, you are emphasizing that it is very large indeed. *Houses in the village are going for astronomical prices... The cost will be astronomical.* ♦ **astronomically** /æstrənɒmɪkli/ *He was astronomically wealthy... House prices had risen astronomically.* ADJ; ADV: ADV adj, ADV after v

2 **Astronomical** means relating to astronomy. *The British Astronomical Association.* ADJ: usu ADJ n

astronomy /əstrɒnəmi/. **Astronomy** is the scientific study of the stars, planets, and other natural objects in space. ◆◇◇◇◇ N-UNCOUNT

astrophysicist /æstroʊfɪzɪsɪst/ **astrophysicists.** An **astrophysicist** is someone who studies astrophysics. N-COUNT

astrophysics /æstroʊfɪzɪks/. **Astrophysics** is the study of the physical and chemical structure of the stars, planets, and other natural objects in space. N-UNCOUNT

astute /əstjuːt, AM əstuːt/. If you describe someone as **astute**, you think they show an understanding of behaviour and situations, and are skilful at using this knowledge to their own advantage. *She was politically astute... He made a series of astute business decisions.* ♦ **astutely** *Oxford, as Evelyn Waugh astutely observed, is a city best seen in early summer.* ♦ **astuteness** *Mrs Thatcher retains her political astuteness.* ◆◇◇◇◇ ADJ-GRADED =shrewd; ADV-GRADED: ADV with v =shrewdly; N-UNCOUNT =shrewdness

asunder /əsʌndəʳ/. If something tears or is torn **asunder**, it is violently separated into two or more parts or pieces; a literary word. *...a dress rent asunder from shoulder to hem... The debate is tearing Wall Street asunder.* ADV: ADV after v

asylum /əsaɪləm/ **asylums** ◆◆◇◇◇

1 An **asylum** is a mental hospital. N-COUNT

2 If a government gives a person from another country **asylum**, they allow them to stay, usually because they are unable to return home safely for political reasons. *He applied for asylum in 1987 after fleeing the police back home.* N-UNCOUNT =sanctuary

asylum seeker, asylum seekers. An **asylum seeker** is a person who is trying to get asylum in a foreign country. *Fewer than 7% of asylum seekers are accepted as political refugees.* ◆◇◇◇◇ N-COUNT

asymmetric /eɪsɪmetrɪk/. **Asymmetric** means the same as **asymmetrical.** ADJ-GRADED ≠symmetric

asymmetrical /eɪsɪmetrɪkəl/. Something that is **asymmetrical** has two sides or halves that are different in shape, size, or style. *...asymmetrical shapes.* ADJ-GRADED ≠symmetrical

asymmetry /eɪsɪmətri/ **asymmetries. Asymmetry** is the appearance that something has when N-VAR ≠symmetry its two sides or halves are different in shape, size, or style. *...the asymmetry of Van de Velde's designs of this period.*

asymptomatic /eɪsɪmptəmætɪk/. If someone with a disease is **asymptomatic**, it means that they do not show any symptoms of the disease; a medical term. *I have patients who are HIV-positive and asymptomatic.* ADJ ≠symptomatic

at /ət, STRONG æt/ ◆◆◆◆◆
In addition to the uses shown below, **at** is used after some verbs, nouns, and adjectives to introduce extra information. **At** is also used in phrasal verbs such as 'keep on at' and 'play at'.

1 You use **at** to indicate the place or event where something happens or is situated. *We had dinner at a restaurant in Attleborough... He will be at the airport to meet her... I didn't like being alone at home... Hamstrings are supporting muscles at the back of the thigh... Mr Hurd was speaking at a news conference in Jordan.* PREP

2 If someone is **at** school or college, or **at** a particular school or college, they go there regularly to study. *He was shy and nervous as a boy, and unhappy at school... It was at university that he first encountered Hopkins... I majored in psychology at Hunter College.* PREP

3 If you are **at** something such as a table or desk, a door or window, or someone's side, you are next to it or them. *An assistant sat typing away at a table beside him... Graham was already at the door... At his side was a beautiful young woman... He gave the girl at the desk the message.* PREP

4 When you are describing where someone or something is, you can say that they are **at** a certain distance, or that they are **at** an angle in relation to something else. *The two journalists followed at a discreet distance... The tree was leaning at a low angle from the ground.* PREP

5 If something happens **at** a particular time, that is the time when it happens or begins to happen. *The funeral will be carried out this afternoon at 3.00... He only sees her at Christmas and Easter.* PREP

6 If you do something **at** a particular age, you do it when you are that age. *Blake emigrated to Australia with his family at 13... Mary Martin has died at her home in California at the age of seventy-six.* PREP

7 You use **at** to express a rate, frequency, level, or price. *I drove back down the highway at normal speed... Check the oil at regular intervals, and have the car serviced regularly... The submarine lies at a depth of 6,000 feet in the Barents Sea. ...custom-designed rugs at $16 to $100 a sq ft.* PREP

8 You use **at** before a number or amount to indicate a measurement. *Weighing in at eighty tons, the B-19 was easily the largest and most sophisticated warplane in the world. ...as unemployment stays pegged at three million.* PREP: PREP amount

9 If you look **at** someone or something, you look towards them. If you direct something such as an object or a comment **at** someone, you direct it towards them. *He looked at Michael and laughed... The crowds became violent and threw petrol bombs at the police... A couple of people started shouting abuse at them as they walked past a pub.* PREP

10 You can use **at** after verbs such as smile or wave and before nouns referring to people to indicate that you have put on an expression or made a gesture which someone is meant to see or understand. *She opened the door and stood there, frowning at me... We waved at the staff to try to get the bill.* PREP: v PREP n

11 If you point or gesture **at** something, you move your arm or head in its direction so that it will be noticed by someone you are with. *He pointed at the empty bottle and the waitress quickly replaced it... He gestured at the shelves. 'I've bought many books from him.'* PREP: v PREP n

12 If you are working **at** something, you are dealing with it. If you are aiming **at** something, you are trying to achieve it. *She has worked hard at her marriage. ...a $1.04m grant aimed at improving student performance on placement examinations.* PREP

13 If something is done **at** someone's invitation or request, it is done as a result of it. *She left the light on in the bathroom at his request... I visited Japan in 1987 at the invitation of the Foreign Minister.* PREP: PREP n with poss

14 You use **at** to say that someone or something is in a particular state or condition. *I am afraid we are not at liberty to disclose that information... Their countries had been at war for nearly six weeks.* PREP: v-link PREP n

15 You use **at** before a possessive pronoun and a superlative adjective to say that someone or something has more of a particular quality than at any other time. *He was at his happiest whilst playing cricket... Howards End is old fashioned film-making at its best.* PREP: PREP poss adj-superl

16 You use **at** to say how something is being done. *Three people were killed by shots fired at random from a minibus... Mr Martin was taken out of his car at gunpoint.* PREP

17 You use **at** to indicate what someone or something is repeatedly doing something to. *She lowered the handkerchief which she had kept dabbing at her eyes... Miss Melville took a cookie and nibbled at it.* PREP: v PREP n

18 You use **at** to indicate an activity or task when saying how well someone does it. *I'm good at my work... Robin is an expert at cheesemaking... She excels at sport.* PREP: adj PREP n, n PREP n, v PREP n

19 You use **at** to indicate what someone is reacting to. *Eleanor was annoyed at having had to wait so long for him... The British team did not disguise their delight at their success... Six months ago she would have laughed at the idea.* ● **at all**: see **all**. PREP: adj PREP n, n PREP n, v PREP n

atavistic /ætəvɪstɪk/. If you describe someone's feelings or behaviour as **atavistic**, you think they are like the feelings or behaviour of your primitive ancestors; a formal word. *...an atavistic fear of thunder and lightning.* ADJ-GRADED: usu ADJ n =primordial

ate /et, eɪt/. **Ate** is the past tense of **eat**.

atelier /ətelieɪ, AM ætəljeɪ/ **ateliers.** An **atelier** is an artist's studio or workshop. N-COUNT

atheism /eɪθiɪzəm/. **Atheism** is the belief that there is no God. Compare **agnosticism**. N-UNCOUNT

atheist /eɪθiɪst/ **atheists.** An **atheist** is a person who believes that there is no God. Compare **agnostic**. ◆◇◇◇◇ N-COUNT

atheistic /eɪθiɪstɪk/. **Atheistic** means connected with or holding the belief that there is no God. *...atheistic values. ...atheistic philosophers.* ADJ

athlete /æθliːt/ **athletes** ◆◆◆◇◇
1 An **athlete** is a person who does a sport, especially athletics. *Muhammed Ali was a great athlete.* N-COUNT
2 You can refer to someone who is fit and athletic as an **athlete**. *I was no athlete.* N-COUNT

athlete's foot. **Athlete's foot** is a fungal infection in which the skin between the toes becomes cracked or peels off. N-UNCOUNT

athletic /æθletɪk/ ◆◆◇◇◇
1 **Athletic** means relating to athletes and athletics. *They have been given college scholarships purely on athletic ability... Most athletic activities are about individual effort.* ♦ **athletically** /æθletɪkli/ *...she's academically able and athletically outstanding.* ADJ: ADJ n; ADV: usu ADV adj
2 An **athletic** person is fit, and able to perform energetic movements easily. *Xandra is an athletic 36-year-old with a 21-year-old's body... He was tall, with an athletic build.* ♦ **athletically** *When Newman put in a header from 10 yards, the goalkeeper athletically tipped it over.* ADJ-GRADED; ADV-GRADED: ADV with v, ADV adj

athleticism /æθletɪsɪzəm/. A person's **athleticism** is their fitness and ability to perform well at sports or other physical activities. *Her athleticism drew the admiration of the crowd.* N-UNCOUNT

athletics /æθletɪks/. **Athletics** refers to track and field sports such as running, the high jump, and the javelin. *As the modern Olympics grew in stature, so too did athletics. ...the International Amateur Athletics Federation.* ◆◆◇◇◇ N-UNCOUNT

-ation /-eɪʃən/ **-ations. -ation** and **-ion** are added to some verbs in order to form nouns. Nouns formed in this way often refer to a state or process; for example, starvation is the process of starving, and victimization is the process of being victimized. SUFFIX

atishoo /ətɪʃuː/. **Atishoo** is used, especially in writing, to represent the sound that you make when you sneeze.

atlas /ætləs/ **atlases.** An **atlas** is a book of maps of all the areas in the world. ◆◇◇◇◇ N-COUNT

ATM /eɪ tiː em/ **ATMs.** In American English, an ATM is a machine built into the wall of a bank or other building, which allows people to take out money from their bank account by using a special card. ATM is an abbreviation for 'automated teller machine'. The usual British expression is **cash dispenser**. N-COUNT

atmosphere /ætməsfɪəʳ/ **atmospheres** ◆◆◆◇◇

1 A planet's **atmosphere** is the layer of air or other gases around it. *The shuttle Columbia will re-enter Earth's atmosphere tomorrow morning... The Partial Test-Ban Treaty bans nuclear testing in the atmosphere.* N-COUNT, usu sing

2 The **atmosphere** of a place is the air that you breathe there. *These gases pollute the atmosphere of towns and cities.* N-COUNT, usu sing

3 The **atmosphere** of a place is the general impression that you get of it. *Pale wooden floors and plenty of natural light add to the relaxed atmosphere... There's still an atmosphere of great hostility and tension in the city.* N-SING: usu with supp

4 If a place or an event has **atmosphere**, it is interesting. *The old harbour is still full of atmosphere and well worth visiting.* N-UNCOUNT =ambience

atmospheric /ætməsferɪk/ ◆◇◇◇◇

1 **Atmospheric** is used to describe something which relates to the earth's atmosphere. *...atmospheric gases. ...atmospheric pressure.* ADJ: usu ADJ n

2 If you describe a place or a piece of music as **atmospheric**, you like it because it has a particular quality which is interesting or exciting and makes you feel a particular emotion. *...beautiful, atmospheric music... One of the most atmospheric corners of Prague is the old Jewish ghetto.* ADJ-GRADED: usu ADJ n PRAGMATICS

atmospherics /ætməsferɪks/. **Atmospherics** are elements in something such as a piece of music or a book which create a certain atmosphere. *...Dickensian atmospherics.* N-PLURAL

atoll /ætɒl, AM -tɔːl/ **atolls.** An **atoll** is a ring of coral rock, or a group of coral islands surrounding a lagoon. N-COUNT

atom /ætəm/ **atoms.** An **atom** is the smallest amount of a substance that can take part in a chemical reaction. *A methane molecule is composed of one carbon atom attached to four hydrogens.* ◆◆◇◇◇ N-COUNT

atom bomb, atom bombs. An **atom bomb** or an **atomic bomb** is a bomb that causes an explosion by a sudden release of energy that results from splitting atoms. N-COUNT

atomic /ətɒmɪk/ ◆◆◇◇◇

1 **Atomic** means relating to power that is produced from the energy released by splitting atoms. *...atomic energy. ...atomic weapons.* ADJ: usu ADJ n =nuclear

2 **Atomic** means relating to the atoms of substances. ADJ: ADJ n

atonal /eɪtoʊnəl/. **Atonal** music is music that is not written or played in any key or system of scales. ADJ: usu ADJ n

atone /ətoʊn/ **atones, atoning, atoned.** If you **atone** for something that you have done, you do something to show that you are sorry you did it; a formal word. *He felt he had atoned for what he had done to his son... He atoned by apologizing... I'll never live long enough to atone.* VERB =repent V for n V by -ing V

atonement /ətoʊnmənt/. If you do something as an **atonement** for doing something wrong, you do it to show that you are sorry. *He's living in a monastery in a gesture of atonement for human rights abuses committed under his leadership... True guilt is characterized by a readiness to make atonement for having done wrong.* N-UNCOUNT: oft N for n =repentance

atop /ətɒp/. In American English and literary British English, if something is **atop** something else, it is on top of it. *Under the newspaper, atop a sheet of paper, lay an envelope.* ◆◇◇◇◇ PREP =on top of

A to Z /eɪ tə zed, AM - ziː/ **A to Zs**

1 An **A to Z** is a book of maps showing all the streets and roads in a particular city and its surrounding towns. **A to Z** is a trademark. N-COUNT

2 An **A to Z** of a particular subject is a book or programme which gives information on all aspects of it, arranging it in alphabetical order. *An A to Z of careers gives helpful information about courses.* N-SING: usu N of n

atrium /eɪtriəm/ **atriums.** An **atrium** is part of a building such as a hotel or shopping centre, which extends up through several storeys of the building and often has a glass roof. N-COUNT

atrocious /ətroʊʃəs/ ◆◇◇◇◇

1 If you describe something as **atrocious**, you are emphasizing that its quality is very bad. *I remain to this day fluent in Hebrew, while my Arabic is atrocious... The food here is atrocious.* ♦ **atrociously** *He had written the note from memory, word perfect, and spelled atrociously.* ADJ-GRADED PRAGMATICS =appalling, abominable ADV: ADV adj/-ed, ADV after v

2 If you describe someone's behaviour or their actions as **atrocious**, you mean that it is unacceptable because it is extremely violent or cruel. *The judge said he had committed atrocious crimes against women... The treatment of the prisoners by their captors is atrocious and breaks all international laws.* ADJ-GRADED

3 If you say that weather conditions are **atrocious**, you mean they are very bad, for example that it is extremely cold, wet, or windy. *...closed roads and atrocious weather: snow in the mountains, torrential rain elsewhere.* ADJ =appalling

atrocity /ətrɒsɪti/ **atrocities.** An **atrocity** is a very cruel, shocking action. *The killing was cold-blooded, and those who committed this atrocity should be tried and punished.* ◆◆◇◇◇ N-VAR

atrophy /ætrəfi/ **atrophies, atrophying, atrophied**

1 If a muscle or other part of the body **atrophies**, it decreases in size or strength, often as a result of an illness; a formal use. *Scott's muscle atrophied, his leg became stunted, and he was left lame... Patients exercised their atrophied limbs in the swimming pool.* ► Also a noun. *...exercises to avoid jelling and atrophy of cartilage.* VERB =wither shrivel V V-ed N-UNCOUNT

2 If something **atrophies**, its size, degree, or effectiveness decreases because it is not used or protected. *If you allow your mind to stagnate, this particular talent will atrophy... Many hoped he would renew the country's atrophied political system.* ► Also a noun. *...levels of consciousness which are nowadays usurped by television and in danger of atrophy.* VERB =degenerate V V-ed N-UNCOUNT

attach /ətætʃ/ **attaches, attaching, attached** ◆◆◆◇◇

1 If you **attach** something to an object, you join it or fasten it to the object. *We attach labels to things before we file them away... The gadget can be attached to any vertical surface... The astronauts will attach a motor that will boost the satellite into its proper orbit... For further information, please contact us on the attached form.* VERB V n to n V n V-ed

2 If someone **attaches** himself or herself to you, they join you and stay with you, often without being invited to do so. *Natasha attached herself to the film crew filming at her orphanage.* VERB V pron-refl to n

3 If people **attach** a quality to someone or something, or if it **attaches** to them, people consider that they have that quality. *The Chinese authorities have attached much significance to Mr Maude's visit. ...the magic that still attaches to the word 'spy'. ...the stigma attached to mental illness.* V-ERG V n to n V to n V-ed

4 If a chemical compound **attaches** to another compound or **attaches** itself to it, the molecules bond together; a medical use. *These fats are defined by the number of hydrogen atoms which attach to the carbon atoms... Monoclonal antibodies attach themselves only to a specific type of cell... You can attach radioactive materials to these antibodies and inject them into a person.* V-ERG V to n V pron-refl to n V n to n

5 If you **attach** conditions to something such as an agreement, you state that specific things must be done before the agreement is valid. *The administration is expected to attach some conditions to Chi-* VERB V n to n V n

na's Most Favored Nation status... Magistrates will be able to attach conditions when juveniles are remanded.

6 See also **attached**. • **no strings attached**: see **string**.

attaché /ætæʃeɪ, AM ætæʃeɪ/ **attachés.** An **attaché** is a member of staff in an embassy, usually with a special responsibility for something. *He was working as a cultural attache in Warsaw.* N-COUNT: usu supp N

attaché case, attaché cases. An **attaché case** is a flat, hinged, briefcase. N-COUNT

attached /ətætʃt/ ◆◆◇◇◇

1 If you **are attached to** someone or something, you are very fond of them. *She is very attached to her family and friends.* ADJ-GRADED: v-link ADJ *to* n

2 If someone **is attached to** an organization or group of people, they are working with them, often only for a short time. *Ford was attached to the battalion's first line of transport.* ADJ: v-link ADJ *to* n

3 If one organization or institution **is attached to** a larger organization, it is part of that organization and is controlled and administered by it. *At one time the schools were mainly attached to the church. ...a think-tank, attached to the Academy of Sciences.* ADJ: v-link ADJ *to* n =linked with

attachment /ətætʃmənt/ **attachments** ◆◇◇◇◇

1 If you have an **attachment** to someone or something, you are fond of them or loyal to them. *As a teenager she formed a strong attachment to one of her teachers... Mother and child form a close attachment. ...a feeling of attachment to the land where their ancestors have lived.* N-VAR: oft N *to* n

2 An **attachment** is a device that can be fixed onto a machine in order to enable it to do different jobs. *Some models come with attachments for dusting.* N-COUNT

3 If someone is on **attachment** to another company, department, or place, they are working there temporarily. *During her course she worked on attachment for six months at Kew Gardens... Before coming on my attachment to a City law firm, I spent a year at Strasbourg University.* N-VAR: usu *on* N

attack /ətæk/ **attacks, attacking, attacked** ◆◆◆◆◆

1 To **attack** a person or place means to try to hurt or damage them using physical violence. *Fifty civilians in Masawa were killed when government planes attacked the town... He bundled the old lady into her hallway and brutally attacked her... While Haig and Foch argued, the Germans attacked... The infantry would use hit and run tactics to slow attacking forces.* VERB V n V V-ing ► Also a noun. *...a campaign of air attacks on strategic targets... Refugees had come under attack from federal troops.* N-VAR: usu with supp

2 If you **attack** a person, belief, idea, or act, you criticize them strongly. *He publicly attacked the people who've been calling for secret ballot nominations... A newspaper ran an editorial attacking him for being a showman.* VERB V n V n *for*-ing Also V n *as* n/adj ► Also a noun. *The role of the state as a prime mover in planning social change has been under attack... Buthelezi responded with a blistering attack on the ANC.* N-VAR: usu with supp

3 If something such as a disease, a chemical, or an insect **attacks** something, it harms or spoils it. *The virus seems to have attacked his throat... Several key crops failed when they were attacked by pests.* VERB V n ► Also a noun. *The virus can actually destroy those white blood cells, leaving the body wide open to attack from other infections.* N-UNCOUNT: also N in pl

4 If you **attack** a job or a problem, you start to deal with it in an energetic way. *Any attempt to attack the budget problem is going to have to in some way deal with those issues.* VERB V n

5 In games such as football, when one team **attacks** the opponent's goal, they try to score a goal. *Now the US is controlling the ball and attacking the opponent's goal... The goal was just reward for Villa's decision to attack constantly in the second half.* VERB V n V ► Also a noun. *Lee was at the hub of some incisive attacks in the second half.* N-COUNT ♦ **attacking** *Manchester City will play a more attacking style of football.* ADJ-GRADED: ADJ n

6 An **attack** of an illness is a short period in which you suffer badly from it. *It had brought on an attack of asthma.* N-COUNT: with supp

7 See also **counter-attack, heart attack.**

attacker /ətækər/ **attackers.** You can refer to a person who attacks someone as their **attacker**. *There were signs that she struggled with her attacker before she was repeatedly stabbed.* ◆◆◇◇◇ N-COUNT

attain /əteɪn/ **attains, attaining, attained** ◆◇◇◇◇

1 If you **attain** something, you gain it or achieve it, often after a lot of effort; a formal word. *Jim is halfway to attaining his pilot's licence.* VERB V n

2 If you **attain** a particular state or condition, you may reach it as a result of natural development or work hard to attain this state. *...attaining a state of calmness and confidence.* VERB V n Also V *to* n

attainable /əteɪnəbᵊl/. Something that is **attainable** can be achieved. *It is unrealistic to believe perfection is an attainable goal.* ADJ-GRADED =achievable

attainment /əteɪnmənt/ **attainments** ◆◇◇◇◇

1 The **attainment** of an aim is the achieving of it; a formal use. *...the attainment of independence.* N-UNCOUNT =achievement

2 An **attainment** is a skill you have learnt or something you have achieved; a formal use. *...their educational attainments.* N-COUNT

attempt /ətempt/ **attempts, attempting, attempted** ◆◆◆◆◆

1 If you **attempt** to do something, especially something difficult, you try to do it. *The only time that we attempted to do something like that was in the city of Philadelphia... Before I could attempt a reply he added over his shoulder: 'Wait there.'* VERB V to-inf V n

2 If you make an **attempt** to do something, you try to do it, often without success. *...a deliberate attempt to destabilise the defence... It was one of his rare attempts at humour. ...their involvement in a coup attempt in September.* N-COUNT: usu with supp, oft N to-inf

3 An **attempt on** someone's life is an attempt to kill them. *...an attempt on the life of the former Iranian Prime Minister.* N-COUNT: N *on* n

4 If a sportsman or sportswoman makes an **attempt on** a sporting record, they try to beat it. *Everything is almost ready for me to make another attempt on the record.* N-COUNT: N *on* n

attempted /ətemptɪd/. An **attempted** crime or unlawful action is an unsuccessful effort to commit the crime or action. *...a case of attempted murder... The attempted coup took place in January.* ◆◆◇◇◇ ADJ: ADJ n

attend /ətend/ **attends, attending, attended** ◆◆◆◆◇

1 If you **attend** a meeting or other event, you are present at it. *Thousands of people attended the funeral... The meeting will be attended by finance ministers from many countries... We want the maximum number of people to attend to help us cover our costs.* VERB V n V

2 If you **attend** an institution such as a school, college, or church, you go there regularly. *They attended college together at the University of Pennsylvania.* VERB V n Also V

3 If you **attend** to something, you deal with it. If you **attend** to someone who is hurt or injured, you care for them. *The staff will helpfully attend to your needs... There are more pressing matters to be attended to today... The main thing is to attend to the injured.* VERB V *to* n

attendance /ətendəns/ **attendances** ◆◆◇◇◇

1 Someone's **attendance** at an event or an institution is the fact that they are present at the event or go regularly to the institution. *Her attendance at school was sporadic.* N-UNCOUNT: usu with supp

2 The **attendance** at an event is the number of people who are present at it. *Average weekly cinema attendance in February was 2.41 million... This year attendances were 28% lower than forecast... Some estimates put the attendance at 60,000.* N-VAR: usu with supp

3 If someone is in **attendance** at a place or an event, they are there. *In attendance are representatives of the parties at war in Bosnia... Police with riot gear and several fire engines are in attendance.* PHRASES

4 If someone is in **attendance** on an important person, they are accompanying that person as a servant or assistant; a formal use. *He lived in considerable style, travelling widely, usually with a cook, valet, butler and chauffeur in attendance.*

attendant /ətendənt/ **attendants** ◆◆◇◇◇

1 An **attendant** is someone whose job is to serve or help people in a place such as a petrol station, a car park, or a cloakroom. *Tony Williams was working as a car-park attendant in Los Angeles.* — N-COUNT: usu n N =assistant

2 You use **attendant** to describe something that results from a thing already mentioned or that is connected with it. *Mr Branson's victory, and all the attendant publicity, were well deserved. ...the risks attendant on the exploration of the unknown.* — ADJ: ADJ n, v-link ADJ *on/upon* n =resulting

attendee /ətendiː/ **attendees.** The **attendees** at something such as a conference are the people who are attending it; used mainly in American English. *Only one-half of the attendees could fit into the large hall at any one time.* — N-COUNT

attender /ətendəʳ/ **attenders.** The **attenders** at a particular place or event are the people who go there. *He was a regular attender at the opera.* — N-COUNT: usu adj N, oft N *at/in/of* n

attention /ətenʃᵊn/ **attentions** ◆◆◆◆◇

1 If you give something your **attention**, you look at it, listen to it, or think about it carefully. *You have my undivided attention... Later he turned his attention to the desperate state of housing in the province. ...young children with short attention spans.* — N-UNCOUNT: also N in pl, usu with poss

2 **Attention** is great interest that is shown in someone or something, particularly by the general public. *Volume Two, sub-titled 'The Lawyers', will also attract considerable attention... The conference may help to focus attention on the economy.* — N-UNCOUNT

3 If someone or something is getting **attention**, they are being dealt with or cared for. *Each year more than two million household injuries need medical attention. ...a demanding baby who seems to want attention 24 hours a day.* — N-UNCOUNT

4 You can refer to someone's efforts to help you, or the interest they show in you, as their **attentions**, especially if you dislike or disapprove of them. *The only way to escape the unwanted attentions of the local men was not to go out... The meeting was held away from the attentions of the media... Some men are flattered by the attentions of a young woman.* — N-PLURAL: usu *the* N *of* n PRAGMATICS

5 If you bring something to someone's **attention** or draw their **attention** to it, you tell them about it or make them notice it. *If we don't keep bringing this to the attention of the people, nothing will be done... We conclude by drawing attention to the issues around which the debate should focus.* — N-UNCOUNT: usu with poss

6 If someone or something **attracts** your **attention** or **catches** your **attention**, you suddenly notice them. *A faint aroma of coffee attracted his attention... He sat at one of the round tables and tried to attract her attention.* — PHRASES V inflects

7 If you **pay attention** to someone or something, you watch them, listen to them, or take notice of them. If you **pay no attention** or **pay little attention** to someone or something, you behave as if you are not aware of them or as if they do not matter. *More than ever before, the food industry is paying attention to young consumers... Other people walk along the beach at night, so I didn't pay any attention at first... I was living just for myself and paying little attention to God.* — V inflects

8 When people **stand to attention** or **stand at attention**, they stand straight with their feet together and their arms at their sides. *Soldiers in full combat gear stood at attention... The waiters stood to attention with napkins folded over their arms.* — V inflects

attentive /ətentɪv/ ◆◇◇◇◇

1 If you are **attentive**, you are paying close attention to what is being said or done. *The vast majority of the attentive audience applauded these sentiments... He wishes the government would be more attentive to detail in their response.* — ADJ-GRADED ≠inattentive
♦ **attentively** *He questioned Chrissie, and listened attentively to what she told him.* — ADV-GRADED: usu ADV after v

2 Someone who is **attentive** is helpful and polite. *At society parties he is attentive to his wife... The staff is well trained in courteous and attentive service to each and every guest.* — ADJ-GRADED: oft ADJ *to* n
♦ **attentiveness** *Anne was both flattered and surprised by Danny's attentiveness to her.* — N-UNCOUNT

attenuate /ətenjueɪt/ **attenuates, attenuating, attenuated.** To **attenuate** something means to reduce it or weaken it; a formal word. *You could never eliminate risk, but preparation and training could attenuate it... Theirs had been an increasingly attenuated relationship.* — VERB V n V-ed

attenuated /ətenjueɪtɪd/. An **attenuated** object is unusually long and thin; a formal word. *...round arches and attenuated columns.* — ADJ-GRADED

attest /ətest/ **attests, attesting, attested.** If something or someone **attests** something or **attests** to something, they show or prove that it is true; a formal word. *Police records attest to his long history of violence... I can personally attest that the cold and flu season is here... His beautifully illustrated book well attested his love of the university.* — ◆◇◇◇◇ VERB V *to* n V that V n Also V with quote

attic /ætɪk/ **attics.** An **attic** is a room at the top of a house just below the roof. — ◆◇◇◇◇ N-COUNT

attire /ətaɪəʳ/. Your **attire** is the clothes you are wearing; a formal word. *...seven women dressed in their finest attire.* — N-UNCOUNT: usu supp N, with poss

attired /ətaɪəʳd/. If you describe how someone is **attired**, you are describing how they are dressed. *He was faultlessly attired in black coat and striped trousers.* — ADJ: v-link ADJ *in* n, adv ADJ

attitude /ætɪtjuːd, AM -tuːd/ **attitudes** ◆◆◆◆◇

1 Your **attitude** to something is the way that you think and feel about it, especially when this shows in the way you behave. *...the general change in attitude towards handicapped people... Being unemployed produces negative attitudes to work... His attitude made me angry... I don't think it's fair to accuse me of having an attitude problem.* — N-VAR: usu with supp, oft N *to/towards* n

2 If you refer to someone as a person with **attitude**, you mean that they have a striking and individual style of behaviour, especially a forceful or aggressive one; used in journalism. *Patti Smith and Janis Joplin did it all years ago and they were women with attitude and talent.* — N-UNCOUNT

3 Your **attitude of mind** is your general way of thinking and feeling. *Writing calls for a critical attitude of mind that he did not possess.* — PHRASE

attitudinal /ætɪtjuːdɪnᵊl, AM -tuːd-/. **Attitudinal** means related to people's attitudes and the way they look at their life; a formal word. *Does such an attitudinal change reflect real experiences in daily life?* — ADJ: usu ADJ n

attorney /ətɜːʳni/ **attorneys.** In the United States, an **attorney** is a lawyer. *...a prosecuting attorney.* • See also **District Attorney**. — ◆◆◆◇◇ N-COUNT

Attorney General, Attorneys General. A country's **Attorney General** is its chief law officer who advises its king, queen, or government. — ◆◇◇◇◇ N-COUNT

attract /ətrækt/ **attracts, attracting, attracted** ◆◆◆◆◇

1 If something **attracts** people or animals, it has features that cause them to come to it. *The Cardiff Bay project is attracting many visitors... Warm weather has attracted the flat fish close to shore... Summer attracts visitors to the countryside.* — VERB V n V n adv/prep

2 If someone or something **attracts** you, they have particular qualities which cause you to like or admire them. If a particular quality **attracts** you to a person or thing, it is the reason why you like them. *He wasn't sure he'd got it right, although the theory attracted him by its logic... What first attracted me to her was her incredible experience of life... More people would be attracted to cycling if conditions were right.* — VERB V n V n *to* n

3 If you **are attracted** to someone, you are interested in them sexually. *In spite of her hostility, she was attracted to him... I was married to a man who had ceased to attract me.* — VERB *be* V-ed *to* n V n
♦ **attracted** *He was nice looking, but I wasn't deeply attracted to him... Men swarmed around her, attracted by her beautiful blonde looks.* — ADJ-GRADED: v-link ADJ, usu ADJ *to* n

4 If something **attracts** support, publicity, or money, it receives support, publicity, or money. *President Mwinyi said his country would also like to attract investment from private companies... Opinion polls suggest that the two rebels have attracted a lot of sympathy.* — VERB V n

5 If one object **attracts** another object, it causes the second object to move towards it. *Anything with strong gravity attracts other things to it.*
VERB V n *to* n Also V n

6 • **Attract someone's attention**: see **attention**.

attraction /ətrækʃən/ **attractions** ◆◆◇◇◇

1 **Attraction** is a feeling of liking someone, and often of being sexually interested in them. *Our level of attraction to the opposite sex has more to do with our inner confidence than how we look... It was never a physical attraction, just a meeting of minds.*
N-UNCOUNT

2 An **attraction** is a feature which makes something interesting or desirable. *...the attractions of living on the waterfront.*
N-COUNT

3 An **attraction** is something that people can go to for interest or enjoyment, for example a famous building. *The walled city is an important tourist attraction.*
N-COUNT

attractive /ətræktɪv/ ◆◆◆◇◇

1 A person who is **attractive** is pleasant to look at. *She's a very attractive woman... I thought he was very attractive and obviously very intelligent... He was always immensely attractive to women.*
ADJ-GRADED ≠unattractive
♦ **attractiveness** *Most of us would maintain that physical attractiveness does not play a major part in how we react to the people we meet.*
N-UNCOUNT

2 Something that is **attractive** has a pleasant appearance or sound. *The flat was small but attractive, if rather shabby... The creamy white flowers are attractive in the spring.*
ADJ-GRADED ≠unattractive
♦ **attractively** *It's an attractively illustrated, detailed guide that's very practical.*
ADV-GRADED: usu ADV -ed/adj
♦ **attractiveness** *The forest will enhance the attractiveness of the region.*
N-UNCOUNT

3 You can describe something as **attractive** when it seems worth having or doing. *Co-operation was more than just an attractive option, it was an obligation... Smoking is still attractive to many young people who see it as glamorous.*
ADJ-GRADED =appealing ≠unattractive
♦ **attractively** *The services are attractively priced and are tailored to suit individual requirements.*
ADV-GRADED: ADV -ed/adj
♦ **attractiveness** *The attractiveness of the schemes depends almost entirely on tax relief.*
N-UNCOUNT: oft *the* N *of* n

attributable /ətrɪbjʊtəbəl/. If something **is attributable to** an event, situation, or person, it is likely that it was caused by that event, situation or person. *10,000 deaths a year from chronic lung disease are attributable to smoking... The mess was directly attributable to a corrupt and incompetent official.*
◆◇◇◇◇ ADJ: v-link ADJ *to* n

attribute, attributes, attributing, attributed. ◆◆◇◇◇
The verb is pronounced /ətrɪbjuːt/. The noun is pronounced /ætrɪbjuːt/.

1 If you **attribute** something to an event or situation, you think that it was caused by that event or situation. *Women tend to attribute their success to external causes such as luck.*
VERB =ascribe V n *to* n

2 If you **attribute** a particular quality or feature to someone or something, you think that they have got it. *People were beginning to attribute superhuman qualities to him.*
VERB =ascribe V n *to* n
♦ **attribution** /ætrɪbjuːʃən/ *There's usually a lot of attribution of evil intent to those who have different views.*
N-UNCOUNT: oft N *of* n

3 If a piece of writing, a work of art, or a remark **is attributed** to someone, people say that they wrote it, created it, or said it. *This, and the remaining frescoes, are not attributed to Giotto. ...a Madonna and Child attributed to Pietro Lorenzetti.*
VB: usu passive *be* V-ed *to* n V-ed

4 An **attribute** is a quality or feature that someone or something has. *Cruelty is a normal attribute of human behaviour... He has every attribute you could want and could play for any team.*
N-COUNT: usu with supp =characteristic

attrition /ətrɪʃən/ ◆◇◇◇◇

1 **Attrition** is a process in which you steadily reduce the strength of an enemy by continually attacking them; a formal use. *The rebels have declared a cease-fire in their war of attrition against the government.*
N-UNCOUNT

2 At a university or place of work, **attrition** is the decrease in the number of students or employees caused by people leaving and not being replaced; used mainly in American English. *The company plans to cut a quarter of its workforce over six years through natural attrition and fewer hirings.*
N-UNCOUNT =wastage

attuned /ətjuːnd, AM ətuːnd/

1 If you **are attuned to** something, you can understand and appreciate it. *I have become attuned to Carlisle's industrial past... He seemed unusually attuned to people's feelings.*
ADJ: v-link ADJ *to* n

2 If your ears **are attuned to** a sound, you can hear it and recognize it quickly. *Their ears were still attuned to the sounds of the London suburb.*
ADJ-GRADED: v-link ADJ *to* n

atypical /eɪtɪpɪkəl/. Someone or something that is **atypical** is not typical of its kind. *The economy of the province was atypical because it was particularly small... He was an atypical English schoolboy.*
ADJ-GRADED ≠typical

aubergine /oʊbəʳʒiːn/ **aubergines.** In British English, an **aubergine** is a vegetable with a smooth, dark purple skin. The usual American word is **eggplant**.
◆◇◇◇◇ N-VAR

auburn /ɔːbəʳn/. **Auburn** hair is reddish brown. *...a tall woman with long auburn hair.*
COLOUR

auction /ɔːkʃən/ **auctions, auctioning, auctioned** ◆◆◆◇◇

1 An **auction** is a public sale where goods are sold to the person who offers the highest price. *Lord Salisbury bought the picture at auction in London some years ago... Britain's two main auction houses, Sotheby's and Christies, have been involved in valuing the works.*
N-VAR: oft *for/at* N, N n

2 If something **is auctioned**, it is sold in an auction. *Eight drawings by French artist Jean Cocteau will be auctioned next week... The airline plans to auction its international routes to former competitors... We'll auction them for charity.*
VERB *be* V-ed V n *to* n V n

auction off. If you **auction off** something, you sell it to the person who offers the most money for it, often at an auction. *Any fool could auction off a factory full of engineering machinery... It came time to auction the book off for audio rights.*
PHRASAL VERB V P n (not pron) V n P

auctioneer /ɔːkʃənɪəʳ/ **auctioneers.** An **auctioneer** is a person in charge of an auction.
◆◇◇◇◇ N-COUNT

audacious /ɔːdeɪʃəs/. Something or someone that is **audacious** takes risks in order to achieve something. *...an audacious plan to win the presidency.*
◆◇◇◇◇ ADJ-GRADED: usu ADJ n =daring
♦ **audaciously** *'What did you do?' asked Bethany audaciously... They are raking in the profits from each more audaciously violent movie.*
ADV-GRADED: ADV with v, ADV adj =daringly

audacity /ɔːdæsɪti/. **Audacity** is audacious behaviour. *I was shocked at the audacity and brazenness of the gangsters.*
N-UNCOUNT

audible /ɔːdɪbəl/. A sound that is **audible** is loud enough to be heard. *The Colonel's voice was barely audible... There was an audible sigh of relief.*
◆◇◇◇◇ ADJ-GRADED ≠inaudible
♦ **audibly** /ɔːdɪbli/ *Hugh sighed audibly.*
ADV-GRADED

audience /ɔːdiəns/ **audiences** ◆◆◆◆◇

1 The **audience** at a play, concert, film, or public meeting is the group of people watching or listening to it. *The entire audience broke into loud applause... He was speaking to an audience of students at the Institute for International Affairs.*
N-COUNT-COLL

2 The **audience** for a television or radio programme consists of all the people who watch or listen to it. *The concert will be relayed to a worldwide television audience estimated at one thousand million.* • See also **studio audience**.
N-COUNT-COLL: usu with supp

3 The **audience** of a writer, artist, or thinker is the people who read their books, look at their pictures or hear about their ideas. *Say's writings reached a wide audience during his lifetime... She began to find a receptive audience for her work.*
N-COUNT-COLL: usu sing

4 If you have an **audience** with someone important, you have a formal meeting with them. *The Prime Minister will seek an audience with the Queen later this morning.*
N-COUNT: usu sing, oft N *with* n

audio /ɔːdioʊ/. **Audio** equipment is used for recording and reproducing sound. *She uses her vocal training to record audio tapes of books for blind people.*
◆◆◇◇◇ ADJ: ADJ n

audio-typist, audio-typists. An **audio-typist** is a typist who types letters and reports that have been dictated into a tape-recorder.
N-COUNT

audio-visual; also spelled **audiovisual**. **Audio-visual** equipment and materials involve both recorded sound and pictures. *Visitors are shown an*
ADJ: ADJ n

audio-visual presentation before touring the cellars.

audit /ɔːdɪt/ **audits, auditing, audited.** When an accountant **audits** an organization's accounts, he or she examines the accounts officially in order to make sure that they have been done correctly. *Each year they audit our accounts and certify them as being true and fair.* ► Also a noun. *The bank first learned of the problem when it carried out an internal audit.* ◆◆◇◇◇ VERB; V n; N-COUNT

audition /ɔːdɪʃᵊn/ **auditions, auditioning, auditioned** ◆◇◇◇◇

1 If an actor, dancer, or musician does an **audition**, they give a short performance so that a director or conductor can decide if they are good enough to be in a play, film, or orchestra. *I used regularly to attend auditions for this or that show.* N-COUNT: oft N *for* n

2 If you **audition** or if someone **auditions** you, you do an audition. *I was auditioning for the part of a jealous girlfriend... They're auditioning for new members of the cast for 'Miss Saigon' today... I heard your record and I want you to come and audition.* V-ERG; V *for* n; V; Also V n, V n *for* n

auditor /ɔːdɪtəʳ/ **auditors.** An **auditor** is an accountant who officially examines the accounts of organizations. ◆◇◇◇◇ N-COUNT

auditorium /ɔːdɪtɔːriəm/ **auditoriums** or **auditoria** /ɔːdɪtɔːriə/ ◆◇◇◇◇

1 An **auditorium** is the part of a theatre or concert hall where the audience sits. *The Albert Hall is a huge auditorium.* N-COUNT

2 In American English, an **auditorium** is a large room, hall, or building which is used for events such as meetings and concerts. N-COUNT

auditory /ɔːdɪtri, AM -tɔːri/. **Auditory** means related to hearing; a technical word. *...the limits of the human auditory range.* ADJ: usu ADJ n

au fait /oʊ feɪ, AM ɔː -/. If you **are au fait with** something, you are familiar with it and know about it. *I am au fait with fashion.* ADJ-GRADED: v-link ADJ *with* n

Aug. **Aug.** is a written abbreviation for **August**. ◆◆◇◇◇

augment /ɔːgment/ **augments, augmenting, augmented.** To **augment** something means to make it larger, stronger, or more effective by adding something to it; a formal word. *While searching for a way to augment the family income, she began making dolls.* ♦ **augmentation** /ɔːgmenteɪʃᵊn/ *The augmentation of the army began along traditional lines.* ◆◇◇◇◇ VERB =supplement; V n; N-UNCOUNT: oft N *of* n

augur /ɔːgəʳ/ **augurs, auguring, augured.** If something **augurs** well or badly for a person or a future situation or event, it is a sign that things will go well or badly; a formal word. *The renewed violence this week in Azerbaijan hardly augurs well for smooth or peaceful change... Already there were problems. It didn't augur well.* VERB =bode; V adv *for* n; V adv; Also V n

augury /ɔːgjʊri/ **auguries.** An **augury** is a sign of what will happen in the future; a literary word. *The auguries of death are fast gathering round his head.* N-COUNT =omen

august /ɔːgʌst/. Someone or something that is **august** is dignified and impressive; a formal word. *Being so near the august person of the Empress, he was overcome with awe... The magazine held its party in the august surroundings of the Liberal Club.* ADJ-GRADED: usu ADJ n =imposing

August /ɔːgəst/ **Augusts. August** is the eighth month of the year in the Western calendar. *The world premiere took place in August 1956... The trial will resume on August the twenty-second... This August has been the wettest for four years.* ◆◆◆◆◇ N-VAR

auk /ɔːk/ **auks.** An **auk** is a bird with a heavy body and short tail that dives into the sea for its food. N-COUNT

Auld Lang Syne /oʊld læŋ zaɪn/. **Auld Lang Syne** is a Scottish song about friendship that is traditionally sung as clocks strike midnight on New Year's Eve. N-PROPER

aunt /ɑːnt, ænt/ **aunts.** Someone's **aunt** is the sister of their mother or father, or the wife of their uncle. *She wrote to her aunt in America... It was a present from Aunt Vera.* ● See also **agony aunt**. ◆◆◆◆◇ N-FAMILY; N-TITLE

auntie /ɑːnti, ænti/ **aunties;** also spelled **aunty**. Someone's **auntie** is their aunt; an informal word. *His uncle is dead, but his auntie still lives here. ...my Auntie Elsie.* N-FAMILY; N-TITLE

au pair /oʊ peəʳ, AM ɔː -/ **au pairs.** An **au pair** is a young person from a foreign country, usually a woman, who lives with a family in order to learn the language. An au pair usually helps with the children and housework in return for a small wage. *She's working as an au pair in Switzerland.* ◆◇◇◇◇ N-COUNT

aura /ɔːrə/ **auras.** An **aura** is a quality or feeling that seems to surround a person or place or to come from them. *She had an aura of authority.* ◆◇◇◇◇ N-COUNT: usu N *of* n =air

aural /ɔːrəl, aʊrəl/. **Aural** means related to the sense of hearing. Compare **oral** and **acoustic**. *He became famous as an inventor of astonishing visual and aural effects.* ◆◇◇◇◇ ADJ: usu ADJ n

auspices /ɔːspɪsɪz/. If something is done **under the auspices of** a particular person or organization, or **under** someone's **auspices**, it is done with their support and approval; a formal word. *...a walk in support of Forests of the World, under the auspices of the World Wildlife Fund. ...a peace conference under United Nations auspices.* ◆◇◇◇◇ PHRASE: PHR n

auspicious /ɔːspɪʃəs/. Something that is **auspicious** indicates that success is likely; a formal word. *His career as a playwright had an auspicious start.* ADJ-GRADED ≠inauspicious

Aussie /ɒzi, AM ɔː-/ **Aussies. Aussie** means Australian; an informal use. *...Aussie comedy actor Paul Hogan.* ► An **Aussie** is a person from Australia; an informal use. *The Aussie was in agony with a broken finger.* ◆◇◇◇◇ ADJ: ADJ n; N-COUNT

austere /ɔːstɪəʳ/ ◆◇◇◇◇

1 If you describe something as **austere**, you approve of its plain and simple appearance. *...a cream linen suit and austere black blouse... The church was austere and simple.* ADJ-GRADED PRAGMATICS

2 If you describe someone as **austere**, you disapprove of them because they are strict and serious. *I found her a rather austere, distant, somewhat cold person. ...an extraordinarily austere and puritanical organization.* ADJ-GRADED PRAGMATICS

3 An **austere** way of life is one that is simple and without luxuries. *The life of the troops was still comparatively austere.* ADJ-GRADED =harsh

4 An **austere** economic policy is one which reduces people's living standards sharply. *...a set of very austere economic measures to control inflation.* ADJ-GRADED

austerity /ɔːsterɪti/ **austerities** ◆◇◇◇◇

1 **Austerity** is a situation in which people's living standards are reduced because of economic difficulties. *...an economic austerity programme. ...the years of austerity which followed the war.* N-UNCOUNT: also N in pl, oft N n

2 If you refer to something as showing **austerity**, you like its plain and simple appearance; a formal use. *...many abandoned buildings, some of which have a compact classical austerity and dignity.* N-UNCOUNT PRAGMATICS

Australasian /ɒstrəleɪʒᵊn, AM ɔːs-/. **Australasian** means belonging or relating to Australasia or to its people. ADJ: ADJ n

Australian /ɒstreɪliən/ **Australians** ◆◆◆◆◇

1 Something that is **Australian** belongs or relates to Australia, or to its people or culture. *In the past year, Malaysia has restricted official contact with the Australian government.* ADJ

2 An **Australian** is someone who comes from Australia. N-COUNT

Austrian /ɒstriən, AM ɔːs-/ **Austrians** ◆◆◆◆◇

1 Something that is **Austrian** belongs or relates to Austria, or to its people or culture. *...the Austrian government.* ADJ

2 An **Austrian** is someone who comes from Austria. N-COUNT

Austro- /ɒstroʊ, AM ɔːstroʊ/. **Austro-** combines with adjectives indicating nationality to form adjectives which describe something connected with Austria and another country. *...the Austro-Hungarian Empire.* COMB in ADJ

authentic /ɔːθentɪk/ ◆◆◇◇◇

1 An **authentic** person, object, or emotion is genuine. *...authentic Italian food... She has authentic* ADJ: usu ADJ n =genuine,

charm whereas most people simply have nice manners... They have to look authentic. ♦ **authenticity** /ɔːθentɪsɪti/ *There are factors, however, that have cast doubt on the statue's authenticity.* ♦ **authentically** /ɔːθentɪkli/ *Consumers are increasingly interested in the authentically exotic tastes... The enamel gives new brass an authentically tarnished finish.*

real ≠fake, imitation
N-UNCOUNT: usu with poss
ADV-GRADED: usu ADV adj/-ed, also ADV after v

2 If you describe something as **authentic**, you mean that it is such a good imitation that it is almost the same as or as good as the original; used showing approval. *...patterns for making authentic frontier-style clothing.* ♦ **authentically** *The team decided to try and replicate the missing curtains as authentically as possible.*

ADJ-GRADED: usu ADJ n
PRAGMATICS
ADV-GRADED: ADV with v, ADV adj

3 An **authentic** piece of information or account of something is reliable and accurate. *I had obtained the authentic details about the birth of the organization.* ♦ **authentically** *The book authentically and intimately describes the small details of her daily life.* ♦ **authenticity** *The film's authenticity of detail has impressed critics.*

ADJ: usu ADJ n
ADV-GRADED
N-UNCOUNT: usu with poss

authenticate /ɔːθentɪkeɪt/ **authenticates, authenticating, authenticated**

1 If you **authenticate** something, you state officially that it is genuine after examining it. *He says he'll have no problem authenticating the stamp... All the antiques have been authenticated and recorded.* ♦ **authentication** /ɔːθentɪkeɪʃən/ *He had purchased a painting in reliance upon the authentication of a well-regarded expert.*

VERB
V n
Also V n *as* n
N-UNCOUNT

2 If you **authenticate** something, you prove or confirm that it is true. *Documentaries offered the chance to authenticate the accuracy of the various details in these models... There have now been well authenticated reports that the use of this drug is very occasionally responsible for heart attacks.*

VERB
V n
V-ed

author /ɔːθəʳ/ **authors, authoring, authored** ♦♦♦♦◇

1 The **author** of a piece of writing is the person who wrote it. *...Jill Phillips, author of the book 'Give Your Child Music'... The war, the authors argue, was a very special case.*

N-COUNT: oft N *of* n

2 An **author** is a person whose occupation is writing books. *Haruki Murakami is Japan's best-selling author.*

N-COUNT

3 The **author of** a plan or proposal is the person who thinks of it and works out the details. *The authors of the plan believe they can reach this point within about two years.*

N-COUNT: N *of* n

4 To **author** something means to be the author of it. *Then he opened a restaurant, authored a book, and landed his own radio show. ...a UN peace plan authored by Cyrus Vance and Lord Owen.*

VERB
V n
V-ed

5 See also **co-author**.

authoress /ɔːθəres/ **authoresses.** An **authoress** is a female author. Some female writers object to this word, preferring to be called authors.

N-COUNT
PRAGMATICS

authorial /ɔːθɔːriəl/. **Authorial** means relating to the author of something such as a book or play. *There are times when the book suffers from excessive authorial control.*

ADJ: ADJ n

authorise /ɔːθəraɪz/. See **authorize**.

authoritarian /ɔːθɒrɪteəriən, AM -θɔːr-/ **authoritarians.** If you describe a person or an organization as **authoritarian**, you are critical of them controlling everything rather than letting people decide things for themselves. *Senior officers could be considering a coup to restore authoritarian rule.* ► An **authoritarian** is someone who is authoritarian. *Don became the overly strict authoritarian he felt his brother needed.*

♦◇◇◇◇
ADJ-GRADED: usu ADJ n
PRAGMATICS
=dictatorial
N-COUNT

authoritarianism /ɔːθɒrɪteəriənɪzəm, AM -θɔːr-/. **Authoritarianism** is the state of being authoritarian or the belief that people with power, especially the State, have the right to control other people's actions; a formal word. *...the long revolt against authoritarianism.*

N-UNCOUNT

authoritative /ɔːθɒrɪtətɪv, AM əθɔːrɪteɪtɪv/ ♦◇◇◇◇

1 Someone or something that is **authoritative** gives an impression of power and importance and is likely to be obeyed. *He had a commanding presence and deep, authoritative voice... Her smile was warm but authoritative.* ♦ **authoritatively** *The man pushed his way authoritatively through the crowd.*

ADJ-GRADED
ADV-GRADED: ADV after v

2 Someone or something that is **authoritative** has a lot of knowledge of a particular subject. *The first authoritative study of polio was published in 1840... The evidence she uses is usually highly authoritative.* ♦ **authoritatively** *My own life is the only thing I can speak authoritatively about.*

ADJ-GRADED
ADV-GRADED: ADV with v

authority /ɔːθɒrɪti, AM -θɔːr-/ **authorities** ♦♦♦♦♦

1 The **authorities** are the people or organizations who have the power to make decisions, especially the government. *This provided a pretext for the authorities to cancel the elections... Croatian authorities insist, however, that they have not agreed to a surrender.*

N-PLURAL: oft *the* N

2 An **authority** is an official organization or government department that has the power to make decisions. *...the Health Education Authority... Any alterations had to meet the approval of the local planning authority.* • See also **local authority**.

N-COUNT: usu with supp, oft in names

3 **Authority** is the right to command and control other people. *Local police chiefs should re-emerge as figures of authority and reassurance in their areas... The judge had no authority to order a second trial.*

N-UNCOUNT

4 If someone has **authority**, they have a quality which makes other people take notice of what they say. *He had no natural authority and no capacity for imposing his will on others.*

N-UNCOUNT

5 **Authority** is official permission to do something. *The prison governor has refused to let him go, saying he must first be given authority from his own superiors.*

N-UNCOUNT =sanction

6 Someone who is an **authority on** a particular subject knows a lot about it. *He's universally recognized as an authority on Russian affairs.*

N-COUNT: N *on* n =expert

7 If you say you **have it on good authority** that something is true, you mean that you believe it is true because you trust the person who told you about it. *I have it on good authority that there's no way this light can cause skin cancer.*

PHRASE: V inflects, PHR that

authorize /ɔːθəraɪz/ **authorizes, authorizing, authorized;** also spelled **authorise** in British English. If someone in a position of authority **authorizes** something, they give their official permission for it to happen. *It would certainly be within his power to authorize a police raid like that... We are willing to authorize the president to use force if necessary.* ♦ **authorization** /ɔːθəraɪzeɪʃən/ **authorizations** *The United Nations will approve his request for authorization to use military force to deliver aid.*

♦♦◇◇◇
VERB =sanction
V n
V n to-inf
N-VAR

authorship /ɔːθəʳʃɪp/

1 The **authorship** of a piece of writing is the identity of the person who wrote it. *Its authorship has been disputed.*

N-UNCOUNT

2 **Authorship** is the activity or job of writing books or articles. *It was her first try at authorship and proved a great success.*

N-UNCOUNT

autism /ɔːtɪzəm/. **Autism** is a severe mental disorder that affects children and makes them unable to respond to other people.

N-UNCOUNT

autistic /ɔːtɪstɪk/. An **autistic** person suffers from autism.

ADJ

auto /ɔːtoʊ/ **autos.** In American English, an **auto** is a car. *...the auto industry.*

♦♦♦◇◇
N-COUNT: oft N n

autobahn /ɔːtoʊbɑːn/ **autobahns.** An **autobahn** is a German motorway.

N-COUNT

autobiographical /ɔːtoʊbaɪəgræfɪkəl/. An **autobiographical** piece of writing relates to events in the life of the person who has written it. *...a highly autobiographical novel of a woman's search for identity.*

♦◇◇◇◇
ADJ-GRADED

autobiography /ɔːtəbaɪɒgrəfi/ **autobiographies.** Your **autobiography** is an account of your life, which you write yourself. *He published his autobiography last autumn.*

♦♦◇◇◇
N-COUNT: usu with poss

autocracy /ɔːtɒkrəsi/ **autocracies**

1 **Autocracy** is government or management by one person who has complete power. *Many poor countries are abandoning autocracy.*

N-UNCOUNT

2 An **autocracy** is a country or organization that is ruled by one person who has complete power. *She ceded all power to her son-in-law who now runs the country as an autocracy.* N-COUNT

autocrat /ɔːtəkræt/ **autocrats.** An **autocrat** is a person in authority who has complete power. N-COUNT

autocratic /ɔːtəkrætɪk/. An **autocratic** person or organization has complete power and makes decisions without asking anyone else's advice. *The people have grown intolerant in recent weeks of the King's autocratic ways.* ◆◇◇◇◇ ADJ-GRADED: usu ADJ n

autocue /ɔːtoukjuː/ **autocues.** An **autocue** is a device used by people speaking on television or at a public event, which displays words for them to read; used mainly in British English. N-COUNT

autograph /ɔːtəgrɑːf, -græf/ **autographs, autographing, autographed** ◆◇◇◇◇

1 An **autograph** is the signature of someone famous which is specially written for a fan to keep. *He went backstage and asked for her autograph... Young autograph hunters clustered around the players' entrance.* N-COUNT: oft with poss

2 If someone famous **autographs** something, they put their signature on it. *I autographed a copy of one of my books. ...an autographed photo of Clark Gable.* VERB V n V-ed

auto-immune; also spelled **autoimmune. Auto-immune** describes medical conditions in which normal cells are attacked by the body's immune system. *...auto-immune diseases such as rheumatoid arthritis. ...an auto-immune reaction in which the body becomes sensitive to aspects of itself.* ADJ: usu ADJ n

automate /ɔːtəmeɪt/ **automates, automating, automated.** To **automate** a factory, office, or industrial process means to install machines which can do the work instead of people. *He wanted to use computers to automate the process.* ◆◇◇◇◇ VERB V n

♦ **automation** /ɔːtəmeɪʃᵊn/ *In the last ten years automation has reduced the work force here by half.* N-UNCOUNT

automated /ɔːtəmeɪtɪd/. An **automated** factory, office, or industrial process uses machines to do the work instead of people. *The equipment was made on highly automated production lines.* ◆◇◇◇◇ ADJ-GRADED: usu ADJ n

automatic /ɔːtəmætɪk/ **automatics** ◆◆◆◇◇

1 An **automatic** machine or device is one which has controls that enable it to perform a task without needing to be constantly operated by a person. **Automatic** methods and processes involve the use of such machines. *Modern trains have automatic doors.* ADJ

2 An **automatic** is a gun that keeps firing shots until you stop pulling the trigger. *He drew his automatic and began running in the direction of the sounds... The gunmen opened fire with automatic weapons.* N-COUNT

3 An **automatic** is a car in which the gears change automatically as the car's speed increases or decreases. N-COUNT

4 An **automatic** action is one that you do without thinking about it. *All of the automatic body functions, even breathing, are affected.* ADJ =instinctive

♦ **automatically** /ɔːtəmætɪkli/ *Strangely enough, you will automatically wake up after this length of time... Automatically Tommy's hand went to his forehead.* ADV-GRADED: usu ADV with v

5 If something such as an action or a punishment is **automatic**, it happens without people needing to think about it because it is the result of a fixed rule or method. *Those drivers should face an automatic charge of manslaughter... Israel offers automatic citizenship to all Jews who want it.* ADJ: usu ADJ n

♦ **automatically** *As an account customer, you are automatically entitled to a variety of benefits... Anyone giving in excess of £100 automatically becomes a member of the Trust.* ADV: usu ADV with v, also ADV n/adj

automatic pilot; the form **autopilot** is also used.

1 If you are **on automatic pilot** or **on autopilot**, you are acting without thinking about what you are doing, usually because you have done it many times before. *You've made that same trip so many times before that you're on automatic pilot... My body was on autopilot as I trailed through passport control, baggage reclaim and customs.* PHRASE: v-link PHR, PHR after v

2 An **automatic pilot** or an **autopilot** is a device in an aircraft that automatically keeps it on a particular course. N-SING

automatic transmission. A car that is fitted with **automatic transmission** has a gear system in which the gears change automatically. N-UNCOUNT

automaton /ɔːtɒmətən/ **automatons** or **automata** /ɔːtɒmətə/

1 If you say that someone is an **automaton**, you are critical of them because they behave as if they are so tired or bored that they do things without thinking. *I get sick of being thought of as a political automaton.* N-COUNT PRAGMATICS

2 An **automaton** is a small, mechanical figure that can move automatically. N-COUNT

automobile /ɔːtəməbiːl, AM -moubiːl/ **automobiles.** An **automobile** is a car; used mainly in American English. ◆◆◇◇◇ N-COUNT

automotive /ɔːtəmoutɪv/. **Automotive** is used to refer to things relating to cars. *...a chain of stores selling automotive parts.* ◆◇◇◇◇ ADJ: ADJ n

autonomous /ɔːtɒnəməs/ ◆◆◇◇◇

1 An **autonomous** country, organization, or group governs or controls itself rather than being controlled by anyone else. *They proudly declared themselves part of a new autonomous province.* ADJ-GRADED: usu ADJ n =independent

♦ **autonomously** *...a highly decentralised company, with each of its subsidiaries operating autonomously.* ADV: usu ADV after v

2 An **autonomous** person makes their own decisions rather than being influenced by somebody else. *He treated us as autonomous individuals who had to learn to make up our own minds about important issues.* ADJ-GRADED: usu ADJ n =independent

autonomy /ɔːtɒnəmi/ ◆◆◇◇◇

1 **Autonomy** is the control or government of a country, organization, or group by itself rather than by others. *Activists stepped up their demands for local autonomy last month.* N-UNCOUNT =independence

2 **Autonomy** is the ability to make your own decisions about what to do rather than being influenced by someone else or told what to do; a formal use. *Each of the area managers enjoys considerable autonomy in the running of his own area.* N-UNCOUNT =independence

autopilot /ɔːtoupaɪlət/ **autopilots.** See **automatic pilot**.

autopsy /ɔːtɒpsi/ **autopsies.** An **autopsy** is an examination of a dead body by a doctor who cuts it open in order to try to discover the cause of death. *The autopsy report gave the cause of death as poisoning.* ◆◇◇◇◇ N-COUNT =post-mortem

autumn /ɔːtəm/ **autumns. Autumn** is the season between summer and winter when the weather becomes cooler and the leaves fall off the trees. In American English, autumn is also called **fall**. *We are always plagued by wasps in autumn.* ◆◆◆◇◇ N-VAR

autumnal /ɔːtʌmnᵊl/

1 **Autumnal** means having features that are characteristic of autumn. *...the autumnal colours of the trees... We used shades of gold and green to give the room a fresh, autumnal look.* ADJ-GRADED

2 **Autumnal** means happening in autumn. *...the autumnal equinox. ...autumnal gales.* ADJ

auxiliary /ɔːgzɪljəri, AM -ləri/ **auxiliaries** ◆◇◇◇◇

1 An **auxiliary** is a person who is employed to assist other people in their work. Auxiliaries are often medical workers or members of the armed forces. *Nursing auxiliaries provide basic care, but are not qualified nurses.* N-COUNT =ancillary

2 **Auxiliary** staff and troops assist other staff and troops. *The government's first concern was to augment the army and auxiliary forces.* ADJ: ADJ n

3 **Auxiliary** equipment is extra equipment that is available for use when necessary. *...an auxiliary motor. ...auxiliary fuel tanks.* ADJ: ADJ n

4 In grammar, an **auxiliary** or **auxiliary verb** is a verb which is used with a main verb, for example to N-COUNT

form different tenses or to make the verb passive. In English, the basic auxiliary verbs are 'be', 'have', and 'do'. Modal verbs such as 'can' and 'will' are also sometimes called auxiliaries.

avail /əveɪl/ **avails, availing, availed** ◆◇◇◇◇

1 If you do something **to no avail** or **to little avail**, what you do fails to achieve what you want. *His efforts were to no avail... I apologized repeatedly, but to little avail.* PHRASE: PHR after v, v-link PHR

2 If you **avail** yourself of an offer or an opportunity, you accept the offer or make use of the opportunity; a formal use. *Guests should feel at liberty to avail themselves of your facilities.* VERB; V pron-refl of n

available /əveɪləbᵊl/ ◆◆◆◆◆

1 If something you want or need is **available**, you can find it or obtain it. *Since 1978, the amount of money available to buy books has fallen by 17%... There are three small boats available for hire... According to the best available information, the facts are these.* ♦ **availability** /əveɪləbɪlɪti/ *...the easy availability of guns.* ADJ; N-UNCOUNT: usu the N of n

2 Someone who is **available** is not busy and is therefore free to talk to you or to do a particular task. *Mr Leach is on holiday and was not available for comment.* ADJ: v-link ADJ

avalanche /ævəlɑːntʃ, -læntʃ/ **avalanches** ◆◇◇◇◇

1 An **avalanche** is a large mass of snow that falls down the side of a mountain. N-COUNT

2 You can refer to a very large quantity of things that all arrive or happen at the same time as an **avalanche** of them. *The newcomer was greeted with an avalanche of publicity.* N-SING: usu N of n

avant-garde /ævɒŋ gɑːʳd/; also spelled **avant garde**. ◆◇◇◇◇

1 **Avant-garde** art, music, theatre, and literature is very modern and experimental. *...avant-garde concert music.* ► Also a noun. *He was an enthusiast for the avant-garde.* ADJ-GRADED: usu ADJ n; N-SING: the N

2 You can refer to the artists, writers, and musicians who introduce new and very modern ideas as **the avant-garde**. *In Paris he made friends among the avant-garde.* N-SING: the N

avarice /ævərɪs/. **Avarice** is extreme greed for money and possessions; a literary word. *He paid a month's rent in advance, just enough to satisfy the landlord's avarice.* N-UNCOUNT

avaricious /ævərɪʃəs/. An **avaricious** person is very greedy for money or possessions; a literary word used showing disapproval. *He sacrificed his own career so that his avaricious brother could succeed.* ADJ-GRADED: usu ADJ n; PRAGMATICS

Ave. **Ave.** is a written abbreviation for **avenue**. *...90 Dayton Ave.* N-IN-NAMES =avenue

avenge /əvendʒ/ **avenges, avenging, avenged.** If you **avenge** a wrong or harmful act, you hurt or punish the person who is responsible for it. *He has devoted the past five years to avenging his daughter's death... She had decided to avenge herself and all the other women he had abused.* ♦ **avenger, avengers** ◆◇◇◇◇ VERB; V n; V pron-refl; N-COUNT

avenue /ævɪnjuː, AM -nuː/ **avenues** ◆◆◇◇◇

1 **Avenue** is sometimes used in the names of streets. The written abbreviation 'Ave.' is also used. *...the most expensive stores on Park Avenue.* N-IN-NAMES

2 An **avenue** is a wide, straight road, especially one with trees on either side. N-COUNT

3 An **avenue** is a way of getting something done. *Talbot was presented with 80 potential avenues of investigation... There is another avenue to pursue – it involves further negotiations.* N-COUNT: with supp, oft N of n =line

aver /əvɜːʳ/ **avers, averring, averred.** If you **aver** that something is the case, you say very firmly that it is true; a formal word. *Her girlfriends aver that men find her fascinating and alluring... 'Entertaining is something that everyone in the country can enjoy,' she averred.* VERB =state, declare; V that; V with quote; Also V

average /ævərɪdʒ/ **averages, averaging, averaged** ◆◆◆◆◇

1 An **average** is the result that you get when you add two or more numbers together and divide the total by the number of numbers you added together. *Take the average of those ratios and multiply by a hundred.* ► Also an adjective. *The average price of goods rose by just 2.2%... Of America's million millionaires in 1985, the average age was 63.* N-COUNT =mean; ADJ: ADJ n =mean

2 You use **average** to refer to a number or size that varies but is always approximately the same. *It takes an average of ten weeks for a house sale to be completed.* N-SING: a N of amount

3 An **average** person or thing is typical or normal. *The average adult man burns 1,500 to 2,000 calories per day... Packaging is about a third of what is found in an average British dustbin.* ADJ: ADJ n

4 An amount or quality that is **the average** is the normal amount or quality for a particular group of things or people. *35% of staff time was being spent on repeating work, about the average for a service industry.* ► Also an adjective. *£1.50 for a beer is average. ...a woman of average height.* N-SING: the N =norm; ADJ

5 Something that is **average** is neither very good nor very bad, usually when you had hoped it would be better. *I was only average academically.* ♦ **averagely** *Most children are not geniuses or stars. They just do averagely well... The songs are performed averagely, although the band seem to be enjoying themselves.* ADJ-GRADED; ADV: ADV adj/adv, ADV after v

6 To **average** a particular amount means to do, get, or produce that amount as an average over a period of time. *We averaged 42 miles per hour. ...pay increases averaging 9.75%.* VERB; V n

7 You say **on average** or **on an average** to indicate that a number is the average of several numbers. *American shares rose, on average, by 38%... On an average we would be spending £200 per day.* PHRASES; PHR with cl

8 If you say that something is true **on average**, you mean that it is generally true. *On average, American firms remain the most productive in the world.* PHR with cl

9 ● **law of averages**: see **law**.

average out. If a set of numbers **average out** to a particular figure or if you **average** them **out** to that figure, their average is calculated to be that figure. *There are six glasses of wine in one bottle, which averages out to 50p a glass... Averaging it out between us there's less than £10 a month each to live on.* PHRASAL VERB ERG; V P to/at n; V n P; Also V P n (not pron)

averse /əvɜːʳs/. If you say that you are not **averse** to something, you mean that you quite like it or quite want to do it; a formal word. *He's not averse to publicity, of the right kind.* ◆◇◇◇◇ ADJ-GRADED: usu with neg, v-link ADJ to n

aversion /əvɜːʳʃᵊn, AM -ʒᵊn/ **aversions.** If you have an **aversion** to someone or something, you dislike them very much. *Many people have a natural and emotional aversion to insects.* ◆◇◇◇◇ N-VAR: usu N to/for n/-ing

avert /əvɜːʳt/ **averts, averting, averted** ◆◆◇◇◇

1 If you **avert** something unpleasant, you prevent it from happening. *Talks with the teachers' union over the weekend have averted a strike... A fresh tragedy was narrowly averted yesterday.* VERB; V n

2 If you **avert** your eyes or gaze from someone or something, you look away from them. *He avoids any eye contact, quickly averting his gaze when anyone approaches... He kept his eyes averted.* VERB; V n; V-ed; Also V n from n

aviary /eɪvjəri/ **aviaries.** An **aviary** is a large cage or covered area in which birds are kept.  N-COUNT

aviation /eɪvieɪʃᵊn/. **Aviation** is the operation and production of aircraft. ◆◆◇◇◇ N-UNCOUNT

aviator /eɪvieɪtəʳ/ **aviators.** An **aviator** is a pilot of a plane, especially in the early times of aviation; an old-fashioned word. N-COUNT

avid /ævɪd/ ◆◇◇◇◇

1 You use **avid** to describe someone who is very enthusiastic about something that they do. *He misses not having enough books because he's an avid reader. ...an avid collector of art and history.* ♦ **avidly** *Thank you for a most entertaining magazine, which I read avidly each month.* ADJ-GRADED: usu ADJ n; ADV-GRADED: ADV with v

2 If you say that someone is **avid** for something, you mean that they are very eager to get it. *He was intensely eager, indeed avid, for wealth.* ♦ **avidly** *Western suppliers too are competing avidly for business abroad.* ADJ-GRADED: v-link ADJ, usu ADJ for n; ADV-GRADED: ADV with v

avionics /eɪviɒnɪks/. **Avionics** is the science of electronics used in aviation; a technical term. N-UNCOUNT

avocado /ævəkɑːdoʊ/ **avocados. Avocados** or **avocado pears** are green pear-shaped tropical ◆◇◇◇◇ N-VAR fruit. They have hard skins and contain large stones. *The ham is delicious with avocado.*

avocation /ævoukeɪʃᵊn/ **avocations.** Your **avocation** is a job or activity that you do because you are interested in it, rather than to earn your living; a formal word. *He was a printer by trade and naturalist by avocation.*
N-VAR

avoid /əvɔɪd/ **avoids, avoiding, avoided** ◆◆◆◆◇

1 If you **avoid** something unpleasant that might happen, you take action in order to prevent it from happening. *The pilots had to take emergency action to avoid a disaster... Women have to dress modestly, to avoid being harassed by the locals.*
VERB; V n; V -ing

2 If you **avoid** doing something, you choose not to do it, or you put yourself in a situation where you do not have to do it. *By borrowing from dozens of banks, he managed to avoid giving any of them an overall picture of what he was up to... The officials said North Korea was trying to avoid dialogue with the South.*
VERB; V -ing; V n

3 If you **avoid** a person or thing, you keep away from them. When talking to someone, if you **avoid** the subject, you keep the conversation away from a particular topic. *She eventually had to lock herself in the toilets to avoid him... All through lunch he had carefully avoided the subject of the house.*
VERB; V n

4 If a person or vehicle **avoids** someone or something, they change the direction they are moving in, so that they do not hit them. *The driver had ample time to brake or swerve and avoid the woman.*
VERB; V n

5 ● **Avoid someone or something like the plague**: see **plague**.

avoidable /əvɔɪdəbᵊl/. Something that is **avoidable** can be prevented from happening. *More than a quarter of the avoidable deaths in the developing world are caused by TB... The tragedy was entirely avoidable.*
ADJ-GRADED

avoidance /əvɔɪdəns/. **Avoidance** of someone or something is the act of avoiding them. *Anyone can improve his or her own health by the avoidance of stress.*
◆◇◇◇◇ N-UNCOUNT: usu N *of* n

avow /əvaʊ/ **avows, avowing, avowed.** If you **avow** something, you admit it or declare it; a formal word. *...a public statement avowing neutrality... The Prime Minister avowed that he saw no need to change his country's policies.*
VERB; V n; Also V with quote

avowed /əvaʊd/ ◆◇◇◇◇

1 If you are an **avowed** supporter or opponent of something, you have declared that you support it or oppose it; a formal use. *She is an avowed vegetarian.* ♦ **avowedly** /əvaʊɪdli/ *He remained for some years avowedly radical in his political outlook.*
ADJ: ADJ n; ADV: usu ADV adj/-ed

2 An **avowed** belief or aim is one that you have declared formally or publicly; a formal use. *...the council's avowed intention to stamp on racism.*
ADJ: ADJ n

avuncular /əvʌŋkjʊləʳ/. An **avuncular** man or a man with **avuncular** behaviour is friendly and helpful towards someone younger; a formal use. *he began to talk in his most gentle and avuncular manner.*
ADJ-GRADED: usu ADJ n

await /əweɪt/ **awaits, awaiting, awaited** ◆◆◆◇◇

1 If you **await** someone or something, you wait for them; a formal use. *Very little was said as we awaited the arrival of the chairman... He's awaiting trial, which is expected to begin early next year.*
VERB; V n

2 Something that **awaits** you is going to happen or come to you in the future; a formal use. *A nasty surprise awaited them in Rosemary Lane.*
VERB; V n

awake /əweɪk/ **awakes, awaking, awoke, awoken** ◆◆◇◇◇

1 Someone who is **awake** is not sleeping. *I don't stay awake at night worrying about that... Nightmares kept me awake all night.*
ADJ-GRADED: v-link ADJ, ADJ after v

2 Someone who is **wide awake** is fully awake and unable to sleep. *I could not relax and still felt wide awake.*
PHRASE: usu v-link PHR

3 When you **awake** or when something **awakes** you, you wake up; a literary use. *At midnight he awoke and listened to the radio for a few minutes... I awoke to the sound of the wind in the trees... The sound of many voices awoke her with a start.*
V-ERG =wake up; V; V prep; V n; Also V to-inf

awaken /əweɪkən/ **awakens, awakening, awakened** ◆◇◇◇◇

1 To **awaken** a feeling in a person means to cause them to start having this feeling; a literary use. *The aim of the cruise was to awaken an interest in and an understanding of foreign cultures.*
VERB; V n

2 When you **awaken** to a fact or when someone **awakens** you to it, you become aware of it; a literary use. *The British never awaken to peril until it is almost too late. ...the picture of the Earth, so blue and fragile, that awakened a generation to the Earth's mortality.*
V-ERG; V *to* n; V n *to* n

3 When you **awaken**, or when something or someone **awakens** you, you wake up; a literary use. *Unfortunately, Grandma always seems to awaken at awkward moments... He was snoring when Desmond awakened him.*
V-ERG =wake up; V; V n

awakening /əweɪkənɪŋ/ **awakenings**

1 The **awakening** of a feeling or realization is the start of it. *...the awakening of national consciousness in people. ...a young woman's sexual awakening.*
N-COUNT: usu sing, with supp

2 If you have a **rude awakening**, you are suddenly made aware of an unpleasant fact. *It was a rude awakening to learn after I left home that I wasn't so special anymore.*
PHRASE

award /əwɔːʳd/ **awards, awarding, awarded** ◆◆◆◆◇

1 An **award** is a prize or certificate that a person is given for doing something well. *...the Booker prize, Britain's top award for fiction... She presented a bravery award to schoolgirl Caroline Tucker.* ● See also **Academy Award**.
N-COUNT: oft supp N, N *for* n

2 In law, an **award** is a sum of money that a court decides should be given to someone. *...workmen's compensation awards.*
N-COUNT

3 A pay **award** is an increase in pay for a particular group of workers. *...this year's average pay award for teachers of just under 8%.*
N-COUNT

4 If someone **is awarded** something such as a prize or an examination mark, it is given to them. *She was awarded the prize for both films... For his dedication the Mayor awarded him a medal of merit.*
VERB; *be* V-ed n; V n n; Also V n *to* n

5 If someone such as a judge or referee **awards** something to someone, they decide that it will be given to that person. *We have awarded the contract to a British shipyard... A High Court judge had awarded him £6 million damages.*
VERB; V n *to* n; V n n

aware /əweəʳ/ ◆◆◆◆◇

1 If you are **aware** of something, you know about it. *Smokers are well aware of the dangers to their own health... He should have been aware of what his junior officers were doing... He must have been aware that my parents' marriage was breaking up.* ♦ **awareness** *The 1980s brought an awareness of green issues... There has been an increasing awareness that many people are affected by crime.*
ADJ-GRADED: v-link ADJ, ADJ *of* n, ADJ that ≠unaware; N-UNCOUNT: usu N *of/about* n, N that

2 If you are **aware** of something, you realize that it is present or is happening because you hear it, see it, smell it, or feel it. *She was acutely aware of the noise of the city... Jane was suddenly aware that she was digging her nails into her thigh.*
ADJ-GRADED: v-link ADJ, ADJ *of* n, ADJ that =conscious ≠unaware

3 Someone who is **aware** notices what is happening around them or happening in the place where they live. *They are politically very aware.* ♦ **awareness** *He introduced radio to the school to increase the children's awareness.*
ADJ-GRADED: v-link ADJ; N-UNCOUNT

awash /əwɒʃ/ ◆◇◇◇◇

1 If the ground or a floor is **awash**, it is covered in water, often because of heavy rain or as the result of an accident. *The bathroom floor was awash.*
ADJ: v-link ADJ =flooded

2 If a place is **awash** with something, it contains a large amount of it. *This, after all, is a company which is awash with cash.*
ADJ: v-link ADJ, usu ADJ *with* n

away /əweɪ/ ◆◆◆◆◆

Away is often used with verbs of movement, such as 'go' and 'drive', and also in phrasal verbs such as 'do away with' and 'fade away'.

1 If someone or something moves or is moved **away** from a place, they move or are moved so that they are no longer there. If you are **away** from a place, you are not in the place where people expect you to be. *An injured policeman was led away by*
ADV: ADV after v, *be* ADV, oft ADV prep

colleagues... He walked away from his car... She drove away before either of them could speak again... Jason was away on a business trip... Simon had been away a good deal lately.

2 If you look or turn **away** from something, you move your head so that you are no longer looking at it. *She quickly looked away and stared down at her hands... As he stands up, he turns his face away from her so that she won't see his tears.* ADV: ADV after v, oft ADV prep

3 If you put or tidy something **away**, you put it in its proper place. If you hide someone or something **away**, you put them in a place where nobody can see them or find them. *I put my journal away and prepared for bed... All her letters were carefully filed away in folders... I have $100m hidden away where no one will ever find it.* ADV: ADV after v

4 If something is **away from** a person or place, it is at a distance from that person or place. *The two women were sitting as far away from each other as possible... I was anxious to get him here, away from family and friends. ...country estate thirty miles away from town.* PHR-PREP

5 You use **away** to talk about future events. For example, if an event is a week **away**, it will happen after a week. *...the Washington summit, now only just over two weeks away... Peace it seemed might at last be no more than a few months away.* ADV: *be* amount ADV

6 When a sports team plays **away**, it plays on its opponents' ground. *...a sensational 4-3 victory for the team playing away.* ► Also an adjective. *Charlton are about to play an important away match.* ADV: ADV after v ≠at home; ADJ: ADJ n

7 You can use **away** to say that something slowly disappears, becomes less significant, or changes so that it is no longer the same. *So much snow has already melted away... His voice died away in a whisper... The Liberal Democrats support fell away at the last minute.* ADV: ADV after v

8 You use **away** to show that there has been a change or development from one state or situation to another. *British courts are increasingly moving away from sending young offenders to prison... There's been a dramatic shift away from traditional careers towards business and commerce.* ADV: ADV after v, n ADV, oft ADV prep ≠towards

9 You can use **away** to emphasize a continuous or repeated action. *He would often be working away on his word processor late into the night... She sighed, her heart banging away against her ribs as she opened the door.* ADV: ADV after v

10 You use **away** to show that something is removed. *If you take my work away I can't be happy anymore... The waitress whipped the plate away and put down my bill... Weeks of heavy rain have washed away roads and bridges.* ADV: ADV after v

11 • **right away**: see **right**. • **far and away**: see **far**.

awe /ɔː/ **awes, awed** ◆◇◇◇◇

1 **Awe** is the feeling of respect and amazement that you have when you are faced with something wonderful and often rather frightening. *She gazed in awe at the great stones... His fellow officers regarded him with awe as some sort of genius... She filled me with a sense of awe.* N-UNCOUNT

2 If you **are awed** by someone or something, they make you feel respectful and amazed, though often rather frightened. *I am still awed by David's courage... The crowd listened in awed silence.* VB: usu passive, no cont; *be* V-ed; V-ed

3 If you **are in awe of** someone or if you **stand in awe of** them, you have a lot of respect for them and are slightly afraid of them. *Caroline hardly dared talk in Alex's presence, she was so in awe of him... As little children, we stand in awe of adults who are, of course, much taller than us.* PHRASE: V inflects

awe-inspiring. If you describe someone or something as **awe-inspiring**, you are emphasizing that you think that they are remarkable and amazing, although sometimes rather frightening. *...a museum with an awe-inspiring display of jewellery... The higher we climbed, the more awe-inspiring the scenery became.* ADJ-GRADED PRAGMATICS

awesome /ɔːsəm/. An **awesome** person or thing is very impressive and often frightening. *The church in Ireland has always exercised an awesome power. ...the awesome responsibility of sending men into combat.* ♦ **awesomely** *It was quiet in the streets, awesomely quiet.* ◆◇◇◇◇ ADJ-GRADED: usu ADJ n; ADV: usu ADV adj

awestruck /ɔːstrʌk/; also spelled **awe-struck**. If someone is **awestruck**, they are very impressed and amazed by something; used in written English. *I stood and gazed at him, awestruck that anyone could be so beautiful.* ADJ-GRADED

awful /ɔːfʊl/ ◆◆◆◇◇

1 If you say that someone or something is **awful**, you dislike that person or thing or you think that they are not very good. *We met and I thought he was awful... I couldn't stand London! Bloody awful place. ...an awful smell of paint... Even if the weather's awful there's lots to do... Jeans look awful on me.* ♦ **awfulness** *The programme's awfulness has ensured it is talked about.* ADJ-GRADED PRAGMATICS =dreadful ≠wonderful; N-UNCOUNT

2 If you say that something is **awful**, you mean that it is extremely unpleasant, shocking, or bad. *Her injuries were massive. It was awful... Some of their offences are so awful they would chill the blood.* ADJ-GRADED =horrific

3 If you look or feel **awful**, you look or feel ill. *I hardly slept at all and felt pretty awful... I looked awful and felt quite shaky.* ADJ-GRADED: v-link ADJ =terrible

4 You can use **awful** with noun groups that refer to an amount in order to emphasize how large that amount is. *I've got an awful lot of work to do.* ♦ **awfully** *The caramel looks awfully good... 'I'm awfully sorry,' she told him regretfully... Would you mind awfully waiting a bit, I'll be back right away.* ADJ: ADJ n PRAGMATICS =tremendous; ADV-GRADED: usu ADV adj/adv =terribly

5 In American English, you use **awful** with adjectives that describe a quality in order to emphasize that particular quality. *Gosh, you're awful pretty... You know, 10 years sounds like an awful long time.* ADV: ADV adj PRAGMATICS =very

awhile /əʰwaɪl/. In American English, **awhile** means for a short time. In British English it is usually written 'a while': See **while**. *Authorities had been looking for him for awhile and he finally turned himself in late last night.* ► Also an adverb. *He worked awhile as a pharmacist in Cincinnati.* ◆◇◇◇◇ N-UNCOUNT; ADV: usu ADV after v

awkward /ɔːkwəʳd/ ◆◆◇◇◇

1 An **awkward** situation is embarrassing and difficult to deal with. *I was the first to ask him awkward questions but there'll be harder ones to come... There was an awkward moment as couples decided whether to stand next to their partners.* ♦ **awkwardly** *There was an awkwardly long silence. ...an awkwardly timed meeting.* ADJ-GRADED =tricky ≠easy; ADV: ADV adj/-ed

2 Something that is **awkward** to use or carry is difficult to use or carry because of its design. A job that is **awkward** is difficult to do. *It was small but heavy enough to make it awkward to carry... Full-size tripods can be awkward, especially if you're shooting a low-level subject.* ♦ **awkwardly** *The autoexposure button is awkwardly placed under the lens release button.* ADJ-GRADED: usu v-link ADJ, oft ADJ to-inf =tricky ≠easy; ADV: ADV -ed

3 An **awkward** movement or position is uncomfortable or clumsy. *Amy made an awkward gesture with her hands.* ♦ **awkwardly** *He fell awkwardly and went down in agony clutching his right knee... He lay beside her awkwardly, propped on an elbow.* ADJ-GRADED; ADV-GRADED: ADV with v

4 Someone who feels **awkward** behaves in a shy or embarrassed way. *Women frequently say that they feel awkward taking the initiative in sex... He was rather awkward with his godson.* ♦ **awkwardly** *'This is Malcolm,' the girl said awkwardly, to fill the silence.* ♦ **awkwardness** *He displayed all the awkwardness of adolescence.* ADJ-GRADED =uncomfortable ≠at ease; ADV-GRADED: ADV with v; N-UNCOUNT

5 If you say that someone is **awkward**, you are critical of them because you find them unreasonable and difficult to live with or deal with. *She's got to an age where she is being awkward.* ADJ-GRADED PRAGMATICS

awning /ɔːnɪŋ/ **awnings.** An **awning** is a piece of material attached to a caravan or building which provides shelter from the rain or sun. N-COUNT =canopy

awoke /əwoʊk/. **Awoke** is the past tense of **awake**.

awoken /əwoʊkən/. **Awoken** is the past participle of **awake**.

AWOL /eɪwɒl/

1 **AWOL** is an abbreviation for 'absent without leave'. If someone in the Armed Forces goes ADJ: usu v-link ADJ

AWOL, they leave their post without the permission of a superior officer. *The troops went AWOL to express their complaints about the camp.*

2 If you say that someone has gone **AWOL**, you mean that they have disappeared without telling anyone where they were going; an informal use. *His real father had gone AWOL about 17 years earlier, and after that his mother had remarried.* ADJ: usu v-link ADJ

awry /əraɪ/

1 If something goes **awry**, it does not happen in the way it was planned. *She was in a fury over a plan that had gone awry.* ADJ-GRADED: v-link ADJ

2 If something is **awry**, it is not in its normal or proper position; used in written English. *His dark hair was all awry.* ADJ-GRADED: v-link ADJ =askew

axe /æks/ **axes, axing, axed;** spelled **ax** in American English. ◆◆◇◇◇

1 An **axe** is a tool used for cutting wood. It consists of a heavy metal blade, usually sharpened at one edge and attached by its other edge to the end of a long handle. N-COUNT

2 If someone's job or something such as a public service or a television programme **is axed**, it is ended suddenly and without discussion. *Community projects are being axed by hard-pressed social services departments.* VB: usu passive =cut *be* V-ed

3 If a person or institution is facing **the axe**, that person is likely to lose their job or that institution is likely to be closed, usually in order to save money; used in journalism. *St Bartholomew's is one of four London hospitals facing the axe.* N-SING: *the* N

4 If you say that someone **has an axe to grind**, you mean their reason for doing something in a particular situation is motivated by selfishness; an informal expression. *Mr Rollins, who according to Mr Perot was fired, may be suspected of having an axe to grind.* PHRASE PRAGMATICS

axeman /æksmæn/ **axemen**

1 In informal English, someone who makes changes in an organization by sacking people can be referred to as an **axeman**; used especially in journalism. N-COUNT: usu adj/n N

2 Someone who attacks or murders people with a weapon such as an axe or a large knife can be referred to as an **axeman**; used in journalism. N-COUNT

axes

1 **Axes**, pronounced /æksɪz/, is the plural of **axe**.

2 **Axes**, pronounced /æksiːz/, is the plural of **axis**.

axiom /æksiəm/ **axioms.** An **axiom** is a statement or idea which people accept as being true; a formal word. *...the long-held axiom that education leads to higher income.* N-COUNT: oft N that =principle

axiomatic /æksiəmætɪk/. If something is **axiomatic**, it seems to be obviously true; a formal word. *It is axiomatic that as people grow older they generally become less agile.* ADJ: oft *it* v-link ADJ that =manifest

axis /æksɪs/ **axes** ◆◇◇◇◇

1 An **axis** is an imaginary line through the middle of something. N-COUNT

2 An **axis** of a graph is one of the two lines on which the scales of measurement are marked. N-COUNT

axle /æksəl/ **axles.** An **axle** is a rod connecting a pair of wheels on a car or other vehicle. ◆◇◇◇◇ N-COUNT

ayatollah /aɪətɒlə/ **ayatollahs.** An **ayatollah** is one of a class of Shiite religious leaders. *...Ayatollah Makarem Shirazi.* N-COUNT; N-TITLE

aye /aɪ/ **ayes;** also spelled **ay.** ◆◇◇◇◇

1 **Aye** means yes; used in some dialects of British English. *'Do you remember your first day at school?' — 'Oh aye. Yeah.'* CONVENTION

2 If you vote **aye**, you vote in favour of something. ADV:

3 **The ayes** are the people who vote in favour of something. *The Ayes to the right, 437. The Noes to the left, 35. So the Ayes have it.* N-PLURAL: *the* N ≠noes

azure /æʒuəʳ/. **Azure** is used to describe things that are bright blue; a literary word. *The sun was bright in an azure sky above them. ...warm azure seas and palm fringed beaches.* COLOUR: usu COLOUR n

B b

B, b /biː/ **B's, b's**

1 **B** is the second letter of the English alphabet. N-VAR

2 In music, **B** is the seventh note in the scale of C major. N-VAR

3 If you get a **B** as a mark for a piece of work or in an exam, your work is fairly good. N-VAR

4 **B** or **b** is used as an abbreviation for words beginning with b, for example 'born'.

BA /biː eɪ/ **BAs** ◆◇◇◇◇

1 A **BA** is a first degree in an arts or social science subject. **BA** is an abbreviation for **Bachelor of Arts**. *I did a BA in film making.* N-COUNT

2 **BA** is written after someone's name to indicate that they have a BA. *...Helen Rich, BA (Hons).*

babble /bæbəl/ **babbles, babbling, babbled** ◆◇◇◇◇

1 If someone **babbles**, they talk in a confused or excited way. *Momma babbled on and on about how he was ruining me... They all babbled simultaneously... 'Er, hello, viewers,' he babbled.* VERB V *on/away* V V with quote

2 You can refer to people's voices as a **babble** of sound when they are excited and confused, preventing you from understanding what they are saying. *Kemp knocked loudly so as to be heard above the high babble of voices... They began to curse and shout in a babble of languages.* N-SING: usu N *of* n =hubbub, babel

babe /beɪb/ **babes** ◆◇◇◇◇

1 In the United States, some people use **babe** as an affectionate way of addressing someone with whom they have an intimate relationship; an informal use. *I'm sorry, babe. I didn't mean it.* N-VOC PRAGMATICS =honey

2 Some men refer to an attractive young woman as a **babe**; used mainly in American English. N-COUNT

3 A **babe** is the same as a baby; an old-fashioned use. *...newborn babes.* N-COUNT

babel /beɪbəl/. If there is a **babel** of voices, you hear a lot of people talking at the same time, so that you cannot understand what they are saying. *The babel inside the bus was incredible.* N-SING =babble, hubbub

baboon /bæbuːn/ **baboons.** A **baboon** is a type of monkey that lives in Africa. N-COUNT

baby /beɪbi/ **babies** ◆◆◆◆◇

1 A **baby** is a very young child, especially one that cannot yet walk or talk. *She used to take care of me when I was a baby... My wife has just had a baby... Claire had to dress her baby sister.* N-COUNT

2 A **baby** animal is a very young animal. *...a baby elephant. ...baby birds.* N-COUNT: usu N n

3 **Baby** vegetables are vegetables picked when they are very small. *Serve with baby new potatoes.* ADJ: ADJ n

4 Some people use **baby** as an affectionate way of addressing someone or referring to someone; an informal use. *You have to wake up now, baby... He was confused, poor baby.* N-VOC; N-COUNT: usu sing =love

5 If you **throw the baby out with the bath water**, you lose the good parts of something as well as the bad parts, because you reject it as a whole instead of just removing what is bad; an informal expression. PHRASES V inflects

6 If you **are left holding the baby**, you are put in a situation where you are responsible for something, often in an unfair way because other people fail or refuse to take responsibility for it; an informal expression. *You go off round the world, and leave me to hold the baby.* V inflects

baby boom, baby booms. A **baby boom** is a period of time when a lot of babies are born in a particular place or country; an informal expression. *I'm a product of the postwar baby boom... In the early 1990s, China will suffer the results of the baby boom of the 1960s.* N-COUNT: usu sing

baby boomer /beɪbi buːməʳ/ **baby boomers;** also spelled **baby-boomer.** A **baby boomer** is someone who was born in Great Britain or the United States during the years 1945-1949, when there was a baby boom; an informal expression, used mainly in journalism. *...a now middle-aged baby boomer. ...baby-boomer parents shopping for children's clothing and toys.* N-COUNT: oft N n

baby buggy, baby buggies. A **baby buggy** is a small seat with wheels, which a young child can sit in and which can be pushed around. N-COUNT =pushchair

baby carriage, baby carriages. In American English, a **baby carriage** means the same as a **pram.** N-COUNT

babyhood /beɪbihʊd/. Your **babyhood** is the period of your life when you were a baby. *From babyhood, he loved to make people smile.* N-UNCOUNT

babyish /beɪbiɪʃ/. **Babyish** actions, feelings, or looks are like a baby's. *...babyish behaviour. ...a fat, babyish face... I'm ashamed of the babyish nonsense I write.* ADJ-GRADED: usu ADJ n

babysit /beɪbisɪt/ **babysits, babysitting, babysat.** If you **babysit** for someone or **babysit** their children, you look after their children while they are out. *I promised to babysit for Mrs Plunkett... My friend asked me to babysit for her six-month-old son... You can take it in turns to babysit... She had been babysitting him and his four-year-old sister.* ♦ **babysitter** *It can be difficult to find a good babysitter.* ♦ **babysitting** *Would you like me to do any babysitting?* ◆◇◇◇◇ VERB =mind; V for n; V; V n; N-COUNT; N-UNCOUNT

baby talk; also spelled **baby-talk. Baby talk** is the language used by babies when they are just learning to speak, or the way in which some adults speak when they are talking to babies. *Maria was talking baby talk to the little one.* N-UNCOUNT

baccalaureate /bækəlɔːriət/. The **baccalaureate** is a secondary school examination taken by students at the age of eighteen in France and some other countries. N-SING

bachelor /bætʃələʳ/ **bachelors.** A **bachelor** is a man who has never married. ◆◇◇◇◇ N-COUNT

Bachelor of Arts, Bachelors of Arts. A **Bachelor of Arts** is a person with a first degree in an arts or social science subject. N-COUNT

Bachelor of Science, Bachelors of Science. A **Bachelor of Science** is a person with a first degree in a science subject. N-COUNT

bachelor's degree, bachelor's degrees. A **bachelor's degree** is a first degree awarded by universities. • See also **BA, BSc.** N-COUNT

back 1 adverb uses

back /bæk/ ◆◆◆◆◆

In addition to the uses shown below, **back** is also used in phrasal verbs such as 'date back' and 'fall back on'.

1 If you move **back**, you move in the opposite direction to the one in which you are facing or in which you were moving before. *The photographers drew back to let Thorne and Abbot view the body... She stepped back from the door expectantly... He pushed her away and she fell back on the wooden bench... She pushes back her chair and stands.* ADV: ADV after v, oft ADV prep =backwards ≠forwards

2 If someone or something goes **back** somewhere, they return to the place where they were before. *I went back to bed... Mr Mandela is due back in South Africa today... Smith changed his mind and moved back home... I'll be back as soon as I can... He made a round-trip to the terminal and back.* ADV: ADV after v, *be* ADV, oft ADV prep/adv

3 If someone or something is **back** in a particular state, they were in that state before and are now in it again. *The rail company said it expected services to get slowly back to normal... Denise hopes to be back at work by the time her daughter is one... Having recently bought an old typewriter, I am now trying to bring it back into working order.* ADV: ADV after v, *be* ADV, oft ADV prep

4 If you give or put something **back**, you return it to the person who had it or to the place where it was before you took it. If you get or take something **back**, you then have it again after not having it for a while. *She handed the knife back... Put it back in the freezer... You'll get your money back.* ADV: ADV after v, oft ADV prep

5 If you put a clock or watch **back**, you change the time shown on it so that it shows an earlier time, for example when the time changes to winter time. ADV: ADV after v

6 If you write or call **back**, you write to or telephone someone after they have written to or telephoned you. If you look **back** at someone, you look at them after they have started looking at you. *They wrote back to me and they told me that I didn't have to do it... If the phone rings say you'll call back after dinner... Lee looked at Theodora. She stared back.* ADV: ADV after v, oft ADV prep

7 You can say that you go or come **back** to a particular point in a conversation to show that you are mentioning or discussing it again. *Can I come back to the question of policing once again?... To come back to what I said in the Introduction, in the nineteenth century Spain was fully a part of Europe... Going back to the school, how many staff are there?* ADV: ADV after v, ADV *to* n PRAGMATICS

8 If something is or comes **back**, it is fashionable again after it has been unfashionable for some time. *Black is back... Consensus politics could easily come back into fashion.* ADV: ADV after v, *be* ADV, oft ADV prep

9 If someone or something is kept or situated **back** from a place, they are at a distance away from it. *Keep back from the edge of the platform... I'm a few miles back from the border... He started for Dot's bedroom and Myrtle held him back.* ADV: ADV after v, *be* ADV, oft ADV *from* n

10 If something is held or tied **back**, it is held or tied so that it does not hang loosely over something. *Her hair was tied back... The curtains were held back by tassels.* ADV: ADV after v

11 If you lie or sit **back**, you move your body backwards into a relaxed sloping or flat position, with your head and body resting on something. *She lay back and stared at the ceiling... She leaned back in her chair and smiled.* ADV: ADV after v ≠forward

12 If you look or shout **back** at someone or something, you turn to look or shout at them when they are behind you. *Nick looked back over his shoulder and then stopped, frowning... He called back to her.* ADV: ADV after v, oft ADV prep

13 You use **back** in expressions like **back in London** or **back at the house** when you are giving an account, to show that you are going to start talking about what happened or was happening in the place you mention. *Meanwhile, back in London, Palace Pictures was collapsing... Later, back at home, the telephone rang.* ADV: ADV with v, ADV prep PRAGMATICS

14 If you talk about something that happened **back** in the past or several years **back**, you are emphasizing that it happened quite a long time ago. *The story starts back in 1950, when I was five... I was in St. Lucia back in January of this year... Mr Davis was wounded in that terrorist attack a few years back.* ADV: ADV with v, ADV prep, n ADV PRAGMATICS

15 If you think **back** to something that happened in the past, you remember it or try to remember it. *I thought back to the time in 1975 when my son was desperately ill... My mind flew back to stories I had heard about Vinnie.* ADV: ADV after v, ADV *to* n

16 If someone moves **back and forth**, they repeatedly move in one direction and then in the opposite direction. *He paced back and forth... Two boys were in the street, tossing a baseball back and forth.* PHRASE: PHR after v

• to **cast your mind back**: see **mind.**

back 2 opposite of front; noun and adjective uses

back /bæk/ **backs** ◆◆◆◆◆

1 A person's or animal's **back** is the part of their body between their head and their legs that is on the opposite side to their chest and stomach. *Her son was lying peacefully on his back... She turned her back to the audience... Three of the victims were shot in the back... He threw the old cloth saddle across the donkey's back.* N-COUNT: oft poss N ≠front

2 The **back** of something is the side or part of it that is towards the rear or farthest from the front. The back of something is normally not used or seen as much as the front. *...a room at the back of the* N-COUNT: usu sing, oft *the* N *of* n ≠front *shop... She raised her hands to the back of her neck... Smooth the mixture with the back of a soup spoon... Her room was on the third floor, at the back.*

3 **Back** is used to refer to the side or part of something that is towards the rear or farthest from the front. *He opened the back door... Ann could remember sitting in the back seat of their car. ...the back room of a pub in Camden. ...the path leading to the back garden.* ADJ: ADJ n ≠front

4 The **back** of a chair or settee is the part that you lean against when you sit on it. *There was a neatly folded pink sweater on the back of the chair.* N-COUNT: usu sing, with supp

5 The **back** of a piece of paper or an envelope is the side which is less important, either because it has no writing or information on it, or because the writing or information begins on the other side. *Send your answers on the back of a postcard or sealed, empty envelope... We could do catalogues, with a photograph on the front and a plan on the back.* N-COUNT: *the*N, usu sing ≠front

6 The **back** of a book is the part nearest the end, where you can find the index or the notes, for example. *The index at the back of the book lists both brand and generic names... You've given a whole list of names and addresses at the back.* N-COUNT: *the*N, usu sing ≠front

7 In spoken British English, you can use **back** in expressions such as **round the back** and **out the back** to refer generally to the area behind a house or other building. *He had chickens and things round the back... The privy's out the back.* N-SING: prep *the*N

8 In American English, you use **back** in expressions such as **in the back** and **out back** to refer to the area behind a house or other building. You also use **in back** to refer to the rear part of something, especially a car or building. *Dan informed her that he would be out back on the patio cleaning his shoes... Catlett got behind the wheel and I sat in back... She hurried to the kitchen in back of the store.* N-UNCOUNT: prep N, oft N *of*n

9 In team games such as football and hockey, a **back** is a player who is concerned mainly with preventing the other team from scoring goals, rather than scoring goals for their own team. N-COUNT =defender ≠forward

10 If you say that something was done **behind** someone**'s back**, you disapprove of it because it was done without them knowing about it, in an unfair or dishonest way. *You eat her food, enjoy her hospitality and then criticize behind her back.* PHRASES PHR after v PRAGMATICS

11 If you **break the back of** a task or problem, you do the most difficult part of what is necessary to complete the task or solve the problem. *It seems at least that we've broken the back of inflation in this country... We can deliver supplies and work to break the back of the famine.* V inflects, PHR n

12 If you are wearing something **back to front**, you are wearing it incorrectly, with the back of it at the front of your body. If you do or write something **back to front**, you do or write it the wrong way around, starting with the part that should come last. *He wears his baseball cap back to front... The picture was printed back to front.* PHR after v =backwards

13 If you tell someone to **get off** your **back**, you are telling them angrily to stop criticizing you or putting pressure on you; an informal expression. *He kept on at me to such an extent that occasionally I wished he would get off my back.* V inflects

14 If you describe a situation as a case of **'You scratch my back and I'll scratch yours'**, you mean that if one person does something to help another, especially by using the power or position that they have, the second person will do something to help them in return; an informal expression.

15 If you say that you will be glad **to see the back of** someone, you mean that you want them to leave; an informal use. *I was so badly behaved I was convinced she would be glad to see the back of me.* PHR n

16 If you **turn** your **back on** someone or something, you ignore them, leave them, or reject them. *Stacey Lattisaw has turned her back on her singing career with Motown Records to become a gospel singer... Gunnell is not the sort to turn her back on someone who has coached her for 12 years.* V inflects, PHR n =abandon

17 If someone or something **puts** your **back up** or **gets** your **back up**, they annoy you; an informal expression. *Some food labelling practices really get my back up.* V inflects =irritate

18 ● **off the back of a lorry**: see **lorry**. ● to **have your back to the wall**: see **wall**.

back 3 verb uses

back /bæk/ **backs, backing, backed** ◆◆◆◆◆

1 If a building **backs** onto something, the back of it faces in the direction of that thing or touches the edge of that thing. *We live in a ground floor flat which backs on to a busy street... His garden backs onto a school.* VERB V *onto*n V *onto*n

2 When you **back** a car or other vehicle somewhere or when it **backs** somewhere, it moves backwards. *He backed his car out of the drive... The train backed out of Adelaide Yard on to the Dublin-Belfast line... I heard the engines revving as the lorries backed and turned.* V-ERG =reverse V n prep/adv V prep/adv V Also V n

3 If you **back** a person or a course of action, you support them, for example by voting for them or giving them money. *His defence says it has found a new witness to back his claim that he is a victim of mistaken identity. ...if France cannot persuade all five permanent members of the Security Council to back the plan... The Prime Minister is backed by the civic movement, Public Against Violence.* VERB =support V n
♦ **-backed** *...government-backed loans to Egypt.* COMB in ADJ

4 If you **back** a particular person, team, or horse in a competition, you predict that they will win, and usually you bet money that they will win. *Roland Nilsson last night backed Sheffield Wednesday to win the UEFA Cup... The horse's owner Mr Hitchins backed him at 200-1 to finish in the first three... It is upsetting to discover that you have backed a loser.* VERB V n to-inf V n

5 If a singer **is backed** by a band or by other singers, they provide the musical accompaniment for the singer. *She chose to be backed by a classy trio of acoustic guitar, bass and congas.* VB: usu passive =support *be*V-ed *by*n

6 See also **backing**.

back away PHRASAL VERB

1 If you **back away** from a commitment that you made or something that you were involved with in the past, you try to show that you are no longer committed to it or involved with it. *...fears that the Soviet Union might be backing away from its support for US policy in the Gulf... He's backing away from the policies and style of his predecessor... Until yesterday, Britain had backed away because it didn't like the cost.* =retreat, withdraw V P *from*n V P

2 If you **back away**, you walk backwards away from someone or something, often because you are frightened of them. *James got to his feet and started to come over, but the girls hastily backed away.* =retreat V P Also V P *from*n

back down. If you **back down**, you withdraw a claim, demand, or commitment that you made earlier, because other people are strongly opposed to it. *The United States had no intention of backing down in its bitter row with the European Community over farm subsidies... It's too late to back down now... The Clinton Administration has backed down on its proposal to provide free vaccines to all children.* PHRASAL VERB =abandon V P V P *on/over*n

back off PHRASAL VERB

1 If you **back off**, you move away in order to avoid problems or a fight. *They backed off in horror.* V P

2 If you **back off** from a claim, demand, or commitment that you made earlier, or if you **back off** it, you withdraw it. *Mr Bryan Gould said the Conservatives were backing off from green policies... The union has publicly backed off that demand.* V P *from*n V P n

3 If you tell someone to **back off**, you are telling them to stop interfering; an informal use. *Back off, Mom, I'm old enough to make my own decisions!* usu imper V P

back out. If you **back out**, you decide not to do something that you previously agreed to do. *The Hungarians backed out of the project in 1989 on environmental grounds... Wells was supposed to put up half the money, but later backed out.* PHRASAL VERB =pull out V P *of*n V P

back up PHRASAL VERB

1 If someone or something **backs up** a statement, they supply evidence to suggest that it is true. *Ra-* =support V P n (not pron) *dio signals received from the galaxy's centre back up the black hole theory... Her views are backed up by a 1989 Home Office report on crime.* Also V n P

2 If an idea or intention **is backed up** by action, action is taken to support or confirm it. *The Secretary General says the declaration must now be backed up by concrete and effective actions... It is time the Government backed up its advert campaigns with tougher measures.* be V-ed P; V P n (not pron); Also V n P

3 If you **back** someone **up**, you show your support for them. *His employers, Norfolk social services, backed him up.* V n P; Also V P n (not pron)

4 If you **back** someone **up**, you help them by confirming that what they are saying is true, even if you know it is not true. *The girl denied being there, and the man backed her up.* V n P; Also V P n (not pron)

5 If you **back up**, the car or other vehicle that you are driving moves back a short distance. *Back up, Hans... He backed up a few feet and rolled the window down... A police van drove through the protesters and backed up to the front door of the house.* =reverse; V P; V P amount; V P *to* n

6 If vehicles **back up**, they form a stationary line of traffic which waits to be able to move on. *The supervisor didn't know whether he should use his initiative and intervene before all the traffic backed up behind... They've admitted nearly a million refugees, but cars and trucks are backed up for miles.* V P; V-ed P; Also V P n (not pron)

7 If you **back up**, you move backwards a short distance. *I backed up carefully until I felt the wall against my back... She backed up a few steps.* V P; V P amount

8 See also **backup**.

backache /bækeɪk/ **backaches. Backache** is a dull pain in your back. N-VAR

backbencher /bækbentʃəʳ/ **backbenchers.** In British English, a **backbencher** is an MP who is not a minister and who does not hold an official position in any party. *...a senior Conservative backbencher.* ◆◇◇◇◇ N-COUNT

backbenches /bækbentʃɪz/; the form **backbench** is used as a modifier. In British English, the **backbenches** are the seats in the House of Commons where backbenchers sit. The Members of Parliament who sit on the backbenches are also referred to as the **backbenches**. *It is not just the issue of Europe that is creating unrest on the backbenches. ...the Conservative Party's backbench committee on Northern Ireland.* N-PLURAL: usu *the* N

backbiting /bækbaɪtɪŋ/. If you accuse someone of **backbiting**, you mean that they say unpleasant or unkind things about someone who is not present, especially in order to stop them doing well at work. *Corporate backbiting is nothing new.* N-UNCOUNT

backbone /bækboun/ **backbones** ◆◇◇◇◇

1 Your **backbone** is the column of small linked bones down the middle of your back. N-COUNT =spine

2 The **backbone** of an organization or system is the part of it that gives it its main strength or unity. *The small business people of Britain are the economic backbone of the nation.* N-SING: usu with poss

3 If you say that someone has no **backbone**, you think they do not have the courage to do things which need to be done. *You might be taking drastic measures and you've got to have the backbone to do that.* N-UNCOUNT: oft with brd-neg =spine

back-breaking; also spelled **backbreaking. Back-breaking** work involves a lot of hard physical effort. *Many months of back-breaking work still face them.* ADJ-GRADED: usu ADJ n

back burner; also spelled **backburner**. If you put an issue on the **back burner**, you leave it in order to deal with it later because you now consider it to have become less urgent or important. *Many speculated that the US would put the peace process on the back burner... For 10 years she has looked after her three children with her career very much on the back burner.* N-SING: usu *the* N

back catalogue, back catalogues. A musical performer's **back catalogue** is the music which they recorded and released in the past rather than their latest recordings. N-COUNT: oft poss N

backcloth /bækklɒθ, AM klɔːθ/ **backcloths**

1 A **backcloth** is a large piece of cloth, often with scenery or buildings painted on it, that is hung at the back of a stage while a play is being performed; used mainly in British English. N-COUNT =backdrop

2 In British English, the **backcloth** to an event is the general situation in which it happens; a literary or journalistic use. *...schools coping with the effect of falling pupil numbers against a backcloth of financial stringency.* N-SING: with supp, oft N *of* n =backdrop

backcomb /bækkoum/ **backcombs, backcombing, backcombed;** also spelled **back-comb**. If you **backcomb** your hair, you move a comb through your hair towards your scalp instead of away from it, so that your hair looks thicker. *Take the left side section of hair, backcomb it and brush smooth. ...backcombed hair.* VERB; V n; V-ed

back copy, back copies. A **back copy** of a magazine or newspaper is the same as a **back issue**. N-COUNT

back country; also spelled **backcountry**. In American English, the **back country** is an area that is a long way from any city and has very few people living in it. *They have moved deep into the back country.* N-SING: *the* N

backdate /bækdeɪt/ **backdates, backdating, backdated;** also spelled **back-date**. If a document or an arrangement **is backdated**, it is valid from a date before the date when it is completed or signed. *The contract that was signed on Thursday morning was backdated to March 11... Anyone who has overpaid tax will be able to backdate their claim to last April.* VERB ≠post-date; be V-ed *to* n; V n *to* n; Also V n

backdoor /bækdɔːʳ/; also spelled **back door**.

1 You can use **backdoor** to describe an action or process if you disapprove of it because you think it has been done in a secret, indirect, or dishonest way. *He did the backdoor deals that allowed the government to get its budget through Parliament on time... He brushed aside talk of greedy MPs voting themselves a backdoor pay rise.* ADJ: ADJ n PRAGMATICS =underhand

2 If you say that someone is doing something through or by **the backdoor**, you disapprove of them because they are doing it in a secret, indirect, or dishonest way. *Dentists claim the Government is privatising dentistry through the back door.* N-SING: *the* N, usu prep N PRAGMATICS

backdrop /bækdrɒp/ **backdrops** ◆◇◇◇◇

1 A **backdrop** is a large piece of cloth, often with scenery painted on it, that is hung at the back of a stage while a play is being performed. N-COUNT =backcloth

2 The **backdrop** to an object or a scene is what you see behind it. *Leeds Castle will provide a dramatic backdrop to a fireworks display next Saturday... Light colours provide an effective backdrop for pictures or a mirror.* N-COUNT: usu N prep =background

3 The **backdrop** to an event is the general situation in which it happens. *The election will take place against a backdrop of increasing instability.* N-COUNT: usu N prep =background

backer /bækəʳ/ **backers.** A **backer** is someone who helps or supports a project, organization, or person, often by giving or lending money. *I was looking for a backer to assist me in the attempted buy-out.* ◆◇◇◇◇ N-COUNT =promoter

backfire /bækfaɪəʳ, AM -faɪr/ **backfires, backfiring, backfired** ◆◇◇◇◇

1 If a plan or project **backfires**, it has the opposite result to the one that was intended. *The President's tactics could backfire... It all backfired on me!* VERB; V; V *on/against* n

2 When a motor vehicle or its engine **backfires**, it produces an explosion in the exhaust pipe. *The car backfired.* VERB; V

backgammon /bækgæmən/. **Backgammon** is a game for two people, played on a board marked with long triangles. Each player has 15 wooden or plastic discs. The players throw dice and move the discs around the board. N-UNCOUNT

background /bækgraund/ **backgrounds** ◆◆◆◇◇

1 Your **background** is the kind of family you come from and the kind of education you have had. It can also refer to such things as your social and racial origins, your financial status, or the type of work experience that you have. *Moulded by his* N-COUNT: usu sing, usu with supp

background, he could not escape the traditional role of aloof Royal father... She came from a working-class Yorkshire background... His background was in engineering.

2 The **background** to an event or situation consists of the facts that explain what caused it. *The background to the current troubles is provided by the dire state of the country's economy... The meeting takes place against a background of continuing political violence. ...background information.* N-COUNT: usu sing, with supp

3 The **background** is sounds, such as music, which you can hear but which you are not listening to with your full attention. *I kept hearing the sound of applause in the background. ...police sirens wailing in the background... The background music was provided by an accordion player.* N-SING: the N ≠foreground

4 You can use **background** to refer to the things in a picture or scene that are less noticeable or important than the main things or people in it. *...roses patterned on a blue background... Paint the background tones lighter and the colours cooler.* N-COUNT: usu sing ≠foreground

• Someone who stays **in the background** avoids being noticed, although the things that they do are important or influential. *Rosemary likes to stay in the background.* PHRASE

backhand /bækhænd/ **backhands.** A **backhand** is a shot in tennis or squash, which you make with your arm across your body. *Edberg hit a backhand... She practised her backhand.* N-VAR

backhanded /bækhændɪd, AM -hændɪd/; also spelled **back-handed**.

1 A **backhanded** compliment is a remark which appears to be an insult but could also be interpreted as a compliment. A **backhanded** compliment is also a remark which appears to be a compliment but could also be interpreted as an insult. *'Even my good reviews have tended to be back-handed compliments,' he says. 'They'll say I was good and "almost unbearably grotesque".'... For once, the phrase 'The film is beautifully shot' is not intended as a back-handed compliment.* ADJ: ADJ n

2 If you say that someone is doing something in a **backhanded** way, you disapprove of their action because they are doing it in an indirect way. *In a backhanded way, Milton Friedman raises yet another objection to high excise taxes.* ADJ-GRADED: ADJ n PRAGMATICS

backhander /bækhændəʳ/ **backhanders;** also spelled **back-hander**. In informal British English, a **backhander** is an amount of money that is paid to someone illegally in order to encourage them to do something. The American word is **kickback**. *Someone in government must have taken a backhander.* N-COUNT =bribe

backing /bækɪŋ/ **backings** 

1 If someone or something has the **backing** of an organization or an important person, they receive support or money from that organization or person in order to do something. *He said the president had the full backing of his government to negotiate a deal... Mr Bach set up his own consulting business with the backing of his old boss.* N-UNCOUNT: usu N *of/for* n =endorsement

2 A **backing** is a layer of something such as cloth that is put onto the back of something in order to strengthen or protect it. N-VAR

3 The **backing** of a popular song is the music which is sung or played to accompany the main tune. *Sharon also sang backing vocals for Barry Manilow... Tapes provided the backing.* N-COUNT: oft N n =support

back issue, back issues. A **back issue** of a magazine or newspaper is an edition of it that was published some time ago and is not the most recent. N-COUNT =back number

backlash /bæklæʃ/. A **backlash** against a tendency or recent development in society or politics, is a sudden, strong reaction against it. *...the male backlash against feminism. ...a right-wing backlash.* ◆◇◇◇◇ N-SING: usu with supp =revolt

backless /bækləs/. A **backless** dress leaves most of a woman's back uncovered down to her waist. ADJ: usu ADJ n

backlog /bæklɒg, AM -lɔːg/ **backlogs.** A **backlog** is a number of things which have not yet been done but which need to be done. *There is a backlog of repairs and maintenance in schools.* ◆◇◇◇◇ N-COUNT

back number, back numbers. A **back number** of a magazine or newspaper is the same as a **back issue**. N-COUNT

backpack /bækpæk/ **backpacks.** A **backpack** is a bag with straps that go over your shoulders, so that you can carry things on your back when you are walking or climbing. N-COUNT =rucksack

backpacker /bækpækəʳ/ **backpackers.** A **backpacker** is a person who goes travelling or hiking with a backpack. *...a crowd of backpackers.* N-COUNT

backpacking /bækpækɪŋ/. If you go **backpacking**, you go travelling or hiking with a backpack. *We were going backpacking in Corfu.* N-UNCOUNT

back passage, back passages. In British English, people sometimes refer to their rectum as their **back passage**. N-COUNT

back pay. **Back pay** is money which an employer owes an employee for work that he or she did in the past. *He will receive $6,000 in back pay.* N-UNCOUNT ≠advance

back-pedal, back-pedals, back-pedalling, back-pedalled; spelled **back-pedaling, back-pedaled** in American English. Also spelled **backpedal**.

1 If you **back-pedal**, you express a different or less forceful opinion about something from the one you had previously expressed. *The General back-pedalled, saying that he had had no intention of offending the West German government... He appeared to back-pedal on that statement.* VERB =backtrack V V *on* n

2 If you say that someone **back-pedals**, you mean that you disapprove of their behaviour because they are not doing what they promised. *He's backpedaled twice already... The Federal Republic will backpedal on its earlier commitments.* VERB PRAGMATICS V V *on/from* n

♦ **back-pedalling** *The liberals were angered by Britain's back-pedalling on reforms.* N-UNCOUNT

backrest /bækrest/ **backrests.** The **backrest** of a seat or chair is the part which you rest your back on. N-COUNT

back road, back roads. A **back road** is a small country road with very little traffic. N-COUNT

back room, back rooms; also spelled **back-room** or **backroom**. ◆◇◇◇◇

1 A **backroom** is a room that is situated at the back of a building, especially a private room. *...the backroom of the officers' club.* N-COUNT

2 You can use **backroom** to refer to people in an organization who do important work but are not seen or known about by the public. You can also use **backroom** to refer a place where such people work. *He is confident the backroom can step into the temporary void... Mr Hata has emerged from the backrooms. ...Mr Smith's backroom staff.* N-COUNT

3 If you refer to a deal made by someone such as a politician as a **backroom** deal, you disapprove of it because it has been made in a secret, dishonest way. *They have been calling the Presidency decision a backroom deal.* ADJ: ADJ n PRAGMATICS

backroom boy, backroom boys; also spelled **backroom-boy**. You can refer to a man as a **backroom boy** when he does important work in an organization and has good ideas but is not seen or known about by the public. N-COUNT

back-seat driver, back-seat drivers; also spelled **backseat driver**.

1 If you refer to a passenger in a car as a **back-seat driver**, they annoy you because they constantly give you advice. N-COUNT PRAGMATICS

2 If you refer to someone, especially a politician, as a **back-seat driver**, you disapprove of them because they try to influence a situation that does not concern them. *They accused the former prime minister of trying to be a backseat driver.* N-COUNT PRAGMATICS

3 • **take a back seat**: see **seat**.

backside /bæksaɪd/ **backsides.** Your **backside** is the part of your body that you sit on; an informal word. ◆◇◇◇◇ N-COUNT =bum

back-slapping; also spelled **backslapping**. **Back-slapping** is noisy, cheerful behaviour which people, especially men, use in order to show af- N-UNCOUNT fection or congratulate each other. *Men love him for his hearty back-slapping and hand-shaking.* ► Also an adjective. *Mike Scott breaks away from a clutch of back-slapping admirers.* ADJ: ADJ n

backsliding /bækslaɪdɪŋ/. If you accuse someone of **backsliding** on something that they have agreed or promised to do, you disapprove of them because they have failed to do it. *...the government's backsliding on free market reforms.* N-UNCOUNT PRAGMATICS

backstage /bæksteɪdʒ/. In a theatre, **backstage** refers to the areas behind the stage. *He went backstage and asked for her autograph... He met Jackson backstage at his concert in Leeds.* ► Also an adjective. *...a backstage pass.* ◆◇◇◇◇ ADV: ADV after v; ADJ: ADJ n

back street, back streets; also spelled **back-street** or **backstreet.**

1 A **back street** in a town or city is a small, narrow street with very little traffic. *The small church of San Michel is tucked away in a narrow back street of Port-as-Prince. ...backstreet garages.* N-COUNT

2 The **back streets** of a town or city are the areas of small, old, poor streets rather than the richer or newer areas. *...the back streets of Berlin.* N-PLURAL

3 **Back street** activities are carried out unofficially, secretly, and often illegally. *...back street abortions.* ADJ: ADJ n

backstroke /bækstroʊk/

1 **Backstroke** is a swimming stroke that you do lying on your back. N-UNCOUNT: also the N

2 The **backstroke** is a swimming race in which the competitors swim backstroke. *...the 100 metres backstroke.* N-SING: the N

backtrack /bæktræk/ **backtracks, backtracking, backtracked;** also spelled **back-track.**

1 If you **backtrack** on a statement or decision you have made, you do or say something that shows that you no longer agree with it or support it. *The committee backtracked by scrapping the controversial bonus system... The finance minister backtracked on his decision.* ♦ **backtracking** *Some backtracking is probably inevitable... He promised there would be no backtracking on policies.* VERB =back-pedal; V; V on/from n; N-UNCOUNT

2 If you **backtrack**, you go back along a path or route you have just used. *Leonard jumped in his car and started backtracking... We had to backtrack to the corner and cross the street.* VERB; V; V prep

3 If you **backtrack** in an account or explanation, you talk about things which happened before the ones you were previously talking about. *Can we just backtrack a little bit and look at your primary and secondary education?* VERB; V

backup /bækʌp/ **backups;** also spelled **back-up.** ◆◇◇◇◇

1 **Backup** consists of extra equipment, resources, or people that you can get help or support from if necessary. *There is no emergency back-up immediately available... Alternative treatments can provide a useful back-up to conventional treatment.* N-VAR

2 If you have something such as a second piece of equipment or set of plans as **backup**, you have arranged for them to be available for use in case the first one does not work. *Every part of the system has a backup... Computer users should make regular back-up copies of their work.* N-VAR

backward /bækwəʳd/ ◆◆◇◇◇

In American English, **backward** is usually used as an adverb instead of **backwards. Backward** is also sometimes used in this way in formal British English. See **backwards** for these uses.

1 A **backward** movement or look is in the direction that your back is facing. Some people use **backwards** for this meaning. *He unlocked the door of apartment two and disappeared inside after a backward glance at Larry... He did a backward flip.* ADJ: ADJ n ≠forward

2 If someone takes a **backward** step, they do something that does not change or improve their situation, but causes them to go back a stage. *At a certain age, it's not viable for men to take a backward step into unskilled work... Many dentists will no longer treat National Health Service patients, which is a big backward step in this country.* ADJ: ADJ n =forward

3 A **backward** country or society does not have modern industries and machines. *We need to accelerate the pace of change in our backward country.* ♦ **backwardness** *I was astonished at the backwardness of our country at the time.* ADJ-GRADED ≠developed; N-UNCOUNT

4 A **backward** child has difficulty in learning. *...research into teaching techniques to help backward children... I was slow to walk and talk and my parents thought I was backward.* ♦ **backwardness** *...her backwardness in practical and physical activities.* ADJ-GRADED =slow; N-UNCOUNT

backward-looking; also spelled **backward looking.** If you describe someone or something as **backward-looking**, you disapprove of their attitudes, ideas, or actions because they are based on old-fashioned opinions or methods. *They are criticised for encouraging a stagnant, backward-looking culture... History may judge the enterprise to have been rather backward-looking.* ADJ-GRADED PRAGMATICS =regressive, reactionary ≠progressive

backwards /bækwəʳdz/; spelled **backward** in American English. ◆◆◇◇◇

1 If you move or look **backwards**, you move or look in the direction that your back is facing. *The diver flipped over backwards into the water... He took two steps backward... Bess glanced backwards... Keeping your back straight, swing one leg backwards.* ► Also an adjective. *Without so much as a backwards glance, he steered her towards the car.* ADV: ADV after v ≠forwards; ADJ: ADJ n

2 If you do something **backwards**, you do it in the opposite way to the usual way. *He works backwards, building a house from the top downwards.* ADV: ADV after v

3 You use **backwards** to indicate that something changes or develops in a way that is not an improvement, but is a return to old ideas or methods. *Greater government intervention in businesses would represent a step backwards. ...unshakable traditions that look backward rather than ahead.* ADV: ADV after v, n ADV ≠forwards

4 See also **backward.**

5 If someone or something moves **backwards and forwards**, they move repeatedly first in one direction and then in the opposite direction. *Using a gentle, sawing motion, draw the floss backwards and forwards between the teeth. ...people travelling backwards and forwards to and from London.* PHRASES PHR after v =to and fro

6 If you say that someone **knows** something **backwards**, you are emphasizing that they know it very well; used mainly in British English. *I asked about one or two things that interest me and she really did know it all backwards.* V inflects PRAGMATICS

7 • to **bend over backwards**: see **bend.**

backwash /bækwɒʃ/. The **backwash** of an event or situation is an unpleasant situation that exists after it and as a result of it. *...the backwash of the events of 1989... The Treasury had been blaming the pound's weakness on the backwash from the falling dollar.* N-SING =repercussions

backwater /bækwɔːtəʳ/ **backwaters** ◆◇◇◇◇

1 A **backwater** is a place that is isolated. *...a quiet rural backwater.* N-COUNT: usu with supp

2 If you refer to a place or institution as a **backwater**, you think it is not developing properly because it is isolated from ideas and events in other places and institutions; used showing disapproval. *Britain could become a political backwater with no serious influence in the world... This agency will be relegated to the backwaters of Washington... Quebec remained a backwater until the 1960s.* N-COUNT: usu with supp PRAGMATICS

backwoods /bækwʊdz/. If you refer to an area as the **backwoods**, you mean that it is a long way from large towns and is isolated from modern life. *I picked up two guys in the backwoods of Louisiana. ...a backwoods section of Kentucky.* N-PLURAL

backwoodsman /bækwʊdzmən/ **backwoodsmen. Backwoodsmen** are people, especially politicians, who like the old ways of doing things or are involved in an organization at a local level. *...the stubborn backwoodsmen of the Soviet Communist Party.* N-COUNT

backyard /bækjɑːʳd/ **backyards;** also spelled **back yard.** ◆◇◇◇◇

1 A **backyard** is an area of land at the back of a house. N-COUNT

2 If you refer to a country's own **backyard**, you are referring to its own territory or to somewhere that N-COUNT: with poss

is very close and where that country wants to influence events. *Economics will not stop Europe's politicians complaining when jobs are lost in their own backyard... Cuba is the largest island in the Caribbean, an area that the United States has long regarded as its own backyard.*

bacon /beɪkən/ ◆◆◇◇◇

1 **Bacon** is salted or smoked meat which comes from the back or sides of a pig. *...bacon and eggs. ...smoked streaky bacon.* N-UNCOUNT

2 If you **bring home the bacon**, you achieve what you needed to achieve; an informal expression. *Voters are interested in the representative's ability to bring home the bacon... They're sexy and recordable, but they don't bring home the musical bacon.* PHRASES V inflects

3 The person in a family who **brings home the bacon** provides the family with the money they need to live; an informal use. *Who brings up the baby and who brings home the bacon?* V inflects

4 If someone or something **saves** your **bacon**, they get you out of a dangerous or difficult situation; an informal expression, mainly used in British English. *Your mother once saved my bacon. She lent me money when I needed it.* V inflects

bacteria /bæktɪəriə/. **Bacteria** are very small organisms. Some bacteria can cause disease. *Chlorine is added to kill bacteria.* ◆◆◇◇◇ N-PLURAL

bacterial /bæktɪəriəl/. **Bacterial** is used to describe things that relate to or are caused by bacteria. *Cholera is a bacterial infection.* ◆◇◇◇◇ ADJ: ADJ n

bacteriology /bæktɪəriɒlədʒi/. **Bacteriology** is the science and the study of bacteria. N-UNCOUNT
♦ **bacteriological** /bæktɪəriəlɒdʒɪkəl/ *...the national bacteriological laboratory.* ADJ: ADJ n

bacterium /bæktɪərɪʊm/. **Bacterium** is the singular of **bacteria**.

bad /bæd/ **worse, worst** ◆◆◆◆◆

1 Something that is **bad** is unpleasant, harmful, or undesirable. *The bad weather conditions prevented the plane from landing... We have been going through a bad time... I've had a bad day at work... Divorce is bad for children... Analysts fear the situation is even worse than the leadership admits.* ADJ-GRADED ≠good

2 You use **bad** to indicate that something unpleasant or undesirable is severe or great in degree. *Glick had a bad accident two years ago and had to give up farming... This was a bad case of dangerous driving... The pain is often so bad she wants to scream... The floods are described as the worst in nearly fifty years.* ADJ-GRADED =terrible

3 A **bad** idea, decision, or method is not sensible or not correct. *Economist Jeffrey Faux says a tax cut is a bad idea... Of course politicians will sometimes make bad decisions... That's not a bad way to proceed, just somewhat different... The worst thing you can do is underestimate an opponent.* ADJ-GRADED: usu ADJ n =poor ≠good

4 If you describe a piece of news, an action, or a sign as **bad**, you mean that it is unlikely to result in benefit or success. *The closure of the project is bad news for her staff... It was a bad start in my relationship with Warr... The report couldn't have come at a worse time for the European Commission.* ADJ-GRADED: usu ADJ n ≠good

5 Something that is **bad** is of an unacceptably low standard, quality, or amount. *She was in rather a bad film about the Mau Mau... Many old people in Britain are living in bad housing... The state schools' main problem is that teachers' pay is so bad... It was absolutely the worst food I have ever had.* ADJ-GRADED =poor ≠good

6 Someone who is **bad** at doing something is not skilful or successful at it. *He had increased Britain's reputation for being bad at languages... He was a bad driver... Rose, her tone implied, was a poor cook and a worse mother.* ADJ-GRADED: v-link ADJ *at* -ing/n, ADJ n =poor ≠good

7 If you say that it is **bad** that something happens, you mean it is unacceptable, unfortunate, or wrong. *Not being able to hear doesn't seem as bad to the rest of us as not being able to see... You need at least ten pounds if you go to the cinema nowadays – it's really bad.* ADJ-GRADED: v-link ADJ, oft *it* v-link ADJ that ≠good

8 You can say that something is **not bad** to mean that it is quite good or acceptable, especially when you are rather surprised about this. *'How much is he paying you?'—'Oh, five thousand.'—'Not bad.'... 'How are you, mate?'—'Not bad, mate, how's yourself?'... He's not a bad chap, Geoffrey, quite human for an accountant... That's not a bad idea.* ADJ-GRADED: with neg ≠good

9 A **bad** person has morally unacceptable attitudes and behaviour. *I was selling drugs, but I didn't think I was a bad person... He does not think that his beliefs make him any worse than any other man.* ADJ-GRADED =wicked ≠good
♦ **badness** *They only recognise badness when they perceive it in others.* N-UNCOUNT

10 A **bad** child disobeys rules and instructions or does not behave in a polite and correct way. *You are a bad boy for repeating what I told you... Many parents find it hard to discourage bad behaviour.* ADJ-GRADED =naughty

11 If you are in a **bad** mood, you are cross and behave unpleasantly to people. *She is in a bit of a bad mood because she's just given up smoking.* ADJ-GRADED: usu ADJ n

12 If you feel **bad** about something, you feel rather sorry or guilty about it. *You don't have to feel bad about relaxing... I feel bad that he's doing most of the work... Are you trying to make me feel bad?* ADJ-GRADED: *feel* ADJ, oft ADJ *about* n, ADJ that ≠good

13 If you have a **bad** back, heart, leg, or eye, it is injured, diseased, or weak. *Alastair has a bad back so we have a hard bed.* ADJ: usu ADJ n

14 Food that has gone **bad** is not suitable to eat because it has started to decay. *They bought so much beef that some went bad.* ADJ: usu *go* ADJ, also ADJ n

15 **Bad** language is language that contains offensive words such as swear words. *I don't like to hear bad language in the street... I said a bad word.* ADJ-GRADED: usu ADJ n

16 See also **worse, worst**.

17 If you say that it is **too bad** that something is the case, you mean you are sorry or sad that it is the case. *It is too bad that Eleanor had to leave so soon... 'That's too bad,' she said with a sigh. 'Vincent can't babysit tomorrow night.'* PHRASES oft *it* v-link PHR that PRAGMATICS =a pity

18 If you say **'too bad'**, you are indicating that nothing can be done to change the situation, and that you do not feel sorry or sympathetic about this. *Too bad if you missed the bus.* CONVENTION PRAGMATICS =hard luck

19 If someone or something is **in a bad way**, they are in a bad condition or situation. *The economy is in a bad way... 'You look in a bad way,' chuckled Brad.* v-link PHR

20 If nobody has **a bad word to say about** you, you are liked or admired by everyone. *She's got beauty, wealth, and fame, and we still can't find anyone with a bad word to say about her.* with brd-neg

21 • to **make the best of a bad job**: see **best**. • **bad blood**: see **blood**. • to **be in someone's bad books**: see **book**. • **bad luck**: see **luck**. • to **get a bad press**: see **press**. • to **go from bad to worse**: see **worse**.

bad cheque, bad cheques; spelled **bad check** in American English. A **bad cheque** is a bank cheque that will not be paid because there is a mistake on it, or because there is not enough money in the account of the person who wrote the cheque. *She wrote another bad check.* N-COUNT

bad debt, bad debts. A **bad debt** is a sum of money that has been lent but is not likely to be repaid. *The bank set aside £1.1 billion to cover bad debts from business failures.* ◆◇◇◇◇ N-COUNT

baddy /bædi/ **baddies;** also spelled **baddie**. A **baddy** is a person in a story or film who is considered to be evil or wicked, or who is fighting on the wrong side; an informal word used by children. N-COUNT ≠goody

bade /bæd, beɪd/. **Bade** is a past tense of **bid**.

badge /bædʒ/ **badges** ◆◇◇◇◇

1 In British English, a **badge** is a small piece of metal or cloth which you wear on your clothes to show, for example, that you belong to a particular organisation or that you support a particular cause. The American word is **button**. *He wore a large badge on his lapel saying 'Jesus is Lord'.* N-COUNT

2 Any feature which is regarded as a sign of a particular quality can be referred to as a **badge**. *Being a Communist was a badge of honour for thousands of trade union activists.* N-SING: usu N *of* n

badger /bædʒəʳ/ **badgers, badgering, badgered** ◆◇◇◇◇

1 A **badger** is a wild animal which has a white head with two wide black stripes on it. Badgers live underground and usually come up to feed at night. N-COUNT

2 If you **badger** someone, you repeatedly tell them to do something or repeatedly ask them questions. *She badgered her doctor time and again, pleading with him to do something... They kept phoning and writing, badgering me to go back... Richard's mother badgered him into taking a Spanish wife.* VERB V n V n to-inf V n *into* n/ing

badinage /bædɪnɑːʒ, -nɑːʒ/. **Badinage** is humorous or light-hearted conversation that often involves teasing someone; a literary word. *Father Gregory tried to respond to the Bishop's light-hearted badinage.* N-UNCOUNT =banter

badly /bædli/ **worse, worst** ◆◆◆◇◇

1 If something is done **badly** or goes **badly**, it is not very successful or effective. *I was angry because I played so badly... The whole project was badly managed... The coalition did worse than expected, getting just 11.6 per cent of the vote.* ADV-GRADED: ADV with v ≠well

2 If someone or something is **badly** hurt or **badly** affected, they are severely hurt or affected. *The bomb destroyed a police station and badly damaged a church... One man was killed and another badly injured... It was a gamble that went badly wrong.* ADV-GRADED: ADV with v, ADV adj =seriously

3 If you want or need something **badly**, you want or need it very much. *Why do you want to go so badly?... Planes landed at Sarajevo airport today carrying badly needed food and medicine.* ADV-GRADED: ADV with v =much

4 If someone behaves **badly** or treats other people **badly**, they act in an unkind, unpleasant, or unacceptable way. *They have both behaved very badly and I am very hurt... I would like to know why we pensioners are being so badly treated.* ADV-GRADED: ADV with v ≠well

5 If something reflects **badly** on someone or makes others think **badly** of them, it harms their reputation. *Teachers know that low exam results will reflect badly on them... Simone de Beauvoir came out of the tales rather badly... Despite his illegal act, few people think badly of him.* ADV-GRADED: ADV after v ≠well

6 If a person or their job is **badly** paid, they are not paid very much for what they do. *You may have to work part-time, in a badly paid job with unsociable hours... This is the most dangerous professional sport there is, and the worst paid.* ADV-GRADED: usu ADV -ed, also ADV after v =poorly ≠well

7 See also **worse, worst**.

badly off, **worse off, worst off** ◆◇◇◇◇

1 If you are **badly off**, you are in a bad situation. *The average working week in Japan is 42.3 hours, compared with 41.6 in the UK, so they are not too badly off.* ADJ-GRADED: usu v-link ADJ

2 If you are **badly off**, you do not have much money. *It is outrageous that people doing well-paid jobs should moan about how badly off they are.* ADJ-GRADED: usu v-link ADJ

badminton /bædmɪntən/. **Badminton** is a game played by two or four players on a rectangular court with a high net across the middle. The players try to score points by hitting a small, feathered object, called a shuttlecock, across the net using a racket. ◆◇◇◇◇ N-UNCOUNT

bad-mouth /bædmaʊð/ **bad-mouths, bad-mouthing, bad-mouthed.** If someone **bad-mouths** you, they say unpleasant things about you, especially when you are not there to defend yourself. *If I hear one roommate bad-mouthing another, I will call her in for a talk.* VERB V n

bad-tempered. Someone who is **bad-tempered** is not very cheerful and gets angry easily. *When his headaches developed Nick became bad-tempered and even violent... They walked in bad-tempered silence.* ADJ-GRADED =irritable

baffle /bæfəl/ **baffles, baffling, baffled.** If something **baffles** you, you cannot understand it or explain it. *An apple tree producing square fruit is baffling experts.* ♦ **baffling** *I was constantly ill, with a baffling array of symptoms.* ♦ **baffled** *Police are baffled by the murder.* ◆◇◇◇◇ VERB =puzzle V n ADJ-GRADED ADJ-GRADED: usu v-link ADJ

bafflement /bæfəlmənt/. **Bafflement** is the state of being baffled. *The general response was one of understandable bafflement.* N-UNCOUNT =puzzlement

bag /bæg/ **bags, bagging, bagged** ◆◆◆◆◇

1 A **bag** is a container made of thin paper or plastic, for example one that is used in shops to put things in that a customer has bought. ► A **bag** of things is the amount of things contained in a bag. N-COUNT N-COUNT: usu N *of* n

2 A **bag** is a strong container with one or two handles, used to carry things in. *She left the hotel carrying a shopping bag.* ► A **bag** of things is the amount of things contained in a bag. N-COUNT N-COUNT: usu N *of* n

3 A **bag** is the same as a **handbag**. N-COUNT

4 If you have **bags** under your eyes, you have folds of skin there, usually because you have not had enough sleep. N-PLURAL

5 In British English, if you say there is **bags of** something, you mean that there is a large amount of it. If you say that there are **bags** of things, you mean that there are a large number of them; an informal use. *...a hotel with bags of character.* QUANT: QUANT *of* pl-n/n-uncount =heaps of

6 If someone calls a woman an old **bag** or a stupid **bag**, they are insulting her; an offensive use. N-COUNT PRAGMATICS

7 In British English, if you **bag** something that a lot of people want, you get it for yourself before anyone else can get it; an informal use. *The smart ones will have already bagged their seats by placing cards on them.* VERB V n

8 See also **bum bag, carrier bag, mixed bag, shoulder-bag, sleeping bag, tea bag**.

9 If you say that something is **in the bag**, you mean that you are certain that you will get it or achieve it; an informal expression. *'I'll get the Republican nomination,' he assured me. 'It's in the bag.'* PHRASES usu v-link PHR

10 If you **pack** your **bags**, you leave a place where you have been staying or living. *Police arrived at his hotel and ordered him to pack his bags.* V inflects

11 ● **let the cat out of the bag**: see **cat**.

bag up. If you **bag up** a quantity of something, you put it into bags. *So Sarah bagged up her old woollies and frocks and sent a parcel off to Jane.* PHRASAL VERB V P n (not pron) Also V n P

bagel /beɪgəl/ **bagels.** A **bagel** is a ring-shaped bread roll. N-COUNT

baggage /bægɪdʒ/ ◆◇◇◇◇

1 Your **baggage** consists of the suitcases and bags that you take with you when you travel. *The passengers went through immigration control and collected their baggage. ...excess baggage.* N-UNCOUNT =luggage

2 You can use **baggage** to refer to someone's emotional problems, fixed ideas, or prejudices. *How much emotional baggage is he bringing with him into the relationship? ...the ideological baggage of Fascism.* N-UNCOUNT: usu with supp

baggy /bægi/ **baggier, baggiest.** If a piece of clothing is **baggy**, it hangs loosely on your body. *...a baggy jumper.* ◆◇◇◇◇ ADJ-GRADED ≠tight

bag lady, bag ladies. A **bag lady** is a homeless woman who carries her possessions in shopping bags. N-COUNT

bagpipes /bægpaɪps/. The form **bagpipe** is used as a modifier, and sometimes as a singular. A **bagpipe** or **bagpipes** are a musical instrument consisting of a leather bag and several pipes. You play the bagpipes by blowing air through a pipe into the bag, and then squeezing the bag to force the air out through other pipes. Bagpipes are played a lot in Scotland. N-COUNT: oft *the* N

baguette /bæget/ **baguettes.** A **baguette** is a loaf of white bread which is traditionally made in France. Baguettes are long and narrow and have a crisp crust. N-COUNT

bah /bɑː, bæ/. **'Bah'** is used in writing to represent a noise that people make in order to express scorn, disappointment, or annoyance; an old-fashioned word. *Christmas? Bah! Humbug!* EXCLAM

Bahamian /bəheɪmiən/ **Bahamians**

1 **Bahamian** means belonging or relating to the Bahamas or to its people or culture. *...Bahamian Prime Minister Hubert Ingraham.* ADJ

2 **Bahamians** are people who come from the Bahamas. N-COUNT

bail /beɪl/ **bails, bailing, bailed;** also spelled **bale** for meaning 5, and for meanings 1 and 3 of the phrasal verb. ◆◆◇◇◇

1 Bail is money that must be given to a law court before an arrested person can be released while they are waiting for their trial. *He was freed on bail pending an appeal... The high court set bail at $8,000.* N-UNCOUNT: oft *on* N

2 Bail is permission for an arrested person to be released after bail has been paid. *He was yesterday given bail by South Yorkshire magistrates.* N-UNCOUNT

3 If someone **is bailed**, they are released while they are waiting for their trial, after paying an amount of money to the court. *He was bailed for probation reports... He was bailed to appear before local magistrates on 5 November.* VB: usu passive; *be* V-ed; *be* V-ed to-inf

4 In the sport of cricket, the **bails** are the two small pieces of wood that are laid across the top of the stumps to form the wicket. N-COUNT: usu pl

5 If you **bail**, you use a container to remove water from a boat or from a place which is flooded. *We kept her afloat for a couple of hours by bailing frantically.* ▶ **Bail out** means the same as **bail**. *A crew was sent down the shaft to close it off and bail out all the water... The flood waters have receded since then, but residents are still bailing out.* VERB; V; Also V n; PHRASAL VERB; V P n (not pron); V P

6 If a prisoner **jumps bail**, he or she does not come back for his or her trial after being released on bail. *He had jumped bail last year while being tried on drug charges.* PHRASE: V inflects

bail out PHRASAL VERB

1 If you **bail** someone **out**, you help them out of a difficult situation, often by giving them money. *They will discuss how to bail the economy out of its slump... He desperately needed cash to bail out the ailing restaurant... The airline had losses of $35m and was bailed out by Qantas.* V n P *of* n; V P n (not pron); Also V n P

2 If you **bail** someone **out**, you pay bail on their behalf. *He has been jailed eight times. Each time, friends bailed him out.* V n P

3 If a pilot **bails out** of an aircraft that is crashing, he or she jumps from it, using a parachute to land safely. *Reid was forced to bail out of the crippled aircraft... The pilot bailed out safely.* V P *of* n; V P

4 See **bail** 5.

bail bandit, bail bandits. In informal British English, a **bail bandit** is someone who commits a crime while they are on bail. N-COUNT

bailiff /beɪlɪf/ **bailiffs** ◆◇◇◇◇

1 In British English, a **bailiff** is a law officer who makes sure that the decisions of a court are obeyed. Bailiffs come to a person's house if they owe money, for example if they have not paid their rent, and can take their furniture or possessions away. *The bailiffs are coming this Thursday.* N-COUNT

2 In American English, a **bailiff** is a minor official in a court of law who carries messages or looks after prisoners. *The bailiff walked over to the juror, took the piece of paper and handed it to the judge.* N-COUNT

3 In Britain, a **bailiff** is a person who is employed to look after land or property for the owner. *My great-granddad was a bailiff on the Cartland Estate.* N-COUNT

bairn /beəʳn/ **bairns.** A **bairn** is a child; used mainly in Scottish English. *He's a lovely bairn.* N-COUNT

bait /beɪt/ **baits, baiting, baited** ◆◆◇◇◇

1 Bait is food which you put on a hook or in a trap in order to catch fish or animals. *...the control of cockroaches using pellets of bait... Cast past the fish and draw the bait back into their path... Chris alternated between several different baits.* N-VAR

2 When you **bait** a hook or trap, you put bait on it or in it. *He baited his hook with pie... The boys dug pits and baited them so that they could spear their prey. ...baited lures.* VERB; V n *with* n; V n; V-ed

3 If someone or something is being used as **bait**, they are being used to tempt or encourage someone to do something. *It was intended as bait to lure the security forces within range of the bomb... He was not quite sure how thoroughly his drunken friend would fall for the bait... As a bait, he offered a free holiday in Turkey.* N-UNCOUNT: also *a* N

4 If you **bait** someone, you deliberately try to make them angry by teasing them. *He delighted in baiting his mother.* VERB =needle; V n

5 If you **take the bait** or **rise to the bait**, you react to something that someone has said or done exactly as they intended you to do. *When she attempts to make you feel guilty, don't take the bait... Their behaviour may seem insulting, but it's important not to rise to the bait and get cross.* PHRASE: V inflects

-baiting /-beɪtɪŋ/

1 You use **-baiting** after nouns to refer to the activity of persecuting a particular group of people or the activity of ridiculing someone's beliefs. *...the witch-hunts and red-baiting of Senator McCarthy's Committee.* COMB in N-UNCOUNT

2 Badger-**baiting**, bear-**baiting**, and bull-**baiting** involve letting dogs attack these animals, while ensuring that they are unable to defend themselves. *...the horrific cruelties of badger-baiting.* COMB in N-UNCOUNT

baize /beɪz/. **Baize** is a thick woollen material which is used for covering things such as snooker tables and card tables. Baize is usually green. N-UNCOUNT

bake /beɪk/ **bakes, baking, baked** ◆◆◆◇◇

1 If you **bake**, you spend some time preparing and mixing together ingredients to make cakes or biscuits. You then put them in the oven to cook. *How did you learn to bake cakes?... I love to bake.* ♦ **baking** *On a Thursday she used to do all the baking.* VB: no passive; V n; V; N-UNCOUNT: also *the* N

2 When a cake or bread **bakes** or when you **bake** it, it cooks in the oven without any extra liquid or fat. *Bake the cake for 35 to 50 minutes... The batter rises as it bakes. ...freshly baked bread.* V-ERG; V n; V; V-ed

3 If places or people become extremely hot because the sun is shining very strongly, you can say that they **bake**. *If you closed the windows you baked... Britain bakes in a Mediterranean heatwave.* VERB; V

4 In British English, a vegetable or fish **bake** is a dish that is made by chopping up and mixing together a number of ingredients and cooking them in the oven so that they form a fairly dry solid mass. *...an aubergine bake.* N-COUNT: usu n N

5 See also **baking**.

baked beans. **Baked beans** are haricot beans cooked in tomato sauce. They are usually sold in tins and are very popular in Britain. N-PLURAL

Bakelite /beɪkəlaɪt/. **Bakelite** is a type of hard plastic that was used in the past for making things such as telephones and radios. **Bakelite** is a trademark. N-UNCOUNT

baker /beɪkəʳ/ **bakers** ◆◇◇◇◇

1 A **baker** is a person whose job is to bake and sell bread, pastries, and cakes. N-COUNT

2 A **baker** or a **baker's** is a shop where bread and cakes are sold. *They're freshly baked. I fetched them from the baker's this morning.* N-COUNT

bakery /beɪkəri/ **bakeries.** A **bakery** is a building where bread, pastries, and cakes are baked, or the shop where they are sold. *A smell of bread drifted from some distant bakery.* ◆◇◇◇◇ N-COUNT

bakeware /beɪkweəʳ/. Tins and trays that are used for baking can be referred to as **bakeware**. N-UNCOUNT

baking /beɪkɪŋ/. You can use **baking** to describe weather or a place that is very hot indeed. *...a baking July day... The coffins stood in the baking heat surrounded by mourners. ...the baking Jordanian desert.* ▶ Also an adverb. *...the baking hot summer of 1969.* • See also **bake**. ◆◇◇◇◇ ADJ: usu ADJ n =stifling, roasting; ADV: ADV adj

baking powder **baking powders.** **Baking powder** is an ingredient used in cake making. It causes cakes to rise when they are in the oven. N-MASS

baking soda. **Baking soda** is **bicarbonate of soda**. N-UNCOUNT

balaclava /bæləklɑːvə/ **balaclavas.** A **balaclava** is a close-fitting woollen hood that covers every part of your head except your face. N-COUNT

balance /bæləns/ **balances, balancing, balanced** ◆◆◆◆◇

1 If something or someone **balances** somewhere or if you **balance** them there, they remain steady V-ERG and do not fall over. *I balanced on the ledge... She had balanced a glass on her chest.* V prep/adv V n prep/adv

2 **Balance** is the ability to remain steady when you are standing up. *The medicines you are currently taking could be affecting your balance.* N-UNCOUNT

3 If you **balance** one thing with something different or if one thing **balances** with another, each of the things has the same strength or importance. *Balance spicy dishes with mild ones... The state has got to find some way to balance these two needs... Supply and demand on the currency market will generally balance.* ♦ **balanced** *This book is a well balanced biography.* V-RECIP-ERG V n *with* n V pl-n pl-n V Also V *with* n ADJ: usu adv ADJ

4 A **balance** is a situation or combination of things in which all the different parts or elements are equal or correct in strength or importance. *Their marriage is a delicate balance between traditional and contemporary values... There was no other way to ensure that people would get the right balance of foods. ...the ecological balance of the forest.* N-SING: with supp, oft N *between* pl-n =equilibrium ≠imbalance

5 If you say that the **balance** tips in your favour, you start winning or succeeding, especially in a conflict or contest. *...a powerful new gun which could tip the balance of the war in their favour... The balance continues to swing away from final examinations to continuous assessment.* N-SING: *the* N =scales

6 If you **balance** one thing against another, you consider its importance in relation to the other one. *She carefully tried to balance religious sensitivities against democratic freedom.* VERB V n *against* n

7 If someone **balances** their budget or if a government **balances** the economy of a country, they make sure that the amount of money that is spent is not greater than the amount that is received. *He balanced his budgets by rigid control over public expenditure.* VERB V n

8 If you **balance** your books or make them **balance**, you prove by calculation that the amount of money you have received is equal to the amount that you have spent. *...teaching them to balance the books.* V-ERG V n Also V

9 The **balance** in your bank account is the amount of money you have in it. *I'd like to check the balance in my account please.* N-COUNT: usu with supp

10 The **balance** of an amount of money is what remains to be paid for something or what remains when part of the amount has been spent. *They were due to pay the balance on delivery.* N-SING: *the* N =remainder

11 See also **bank balance**.

12 If something hangs **in the balance**, it is uncertain whether it will happen or continue. *The fate of a project which could revolutionise the use of computers in hospitals hangs in the balance.* PHRASES PHR after v, v-link PHR

13 If you **keep** your **balance**, for example when standing in a moving vehicle, you remain steady and do not fall over. If you **lose** your **balance**, you become unsteady and fall over. *She was holding onto the rail to keep her balance... He swung around, almost losing his balance.* V inflects

14 If you are **off balance**, you are in an unsteady position and about to fall. *A gust of wind knocked him off balance and he fell face down in the mud.* PHR after v, v-link PHR

15 If you are thrown **off balance** by something, you are surprised or confused by it. *She was trying to behave as if his visit hadn't thrown her off balance.* PHR after v

16 You can say **on balance** to indicate that you are stating an opinion after considering all the relevant facts or arguments. *On balance he agreed with Christine.* PHR with cl PRAGMATICS

balance out. If two or more opposite things **balance out** or if you **balance** them **out**, they become equal in amount, value, or effect. *Outgoings and revenues balanced out... The strenuous exercise undergone could balance out the increased calories.* PHRASAL VERB ERG V P V P n (not pron) Also V n P

balanced /bælənst/ ♦♦◇◇◇

1 A **balanced** report, book, or other document takes into account all the different opinions on something and presents information in a fair and reasonable way; used showing approval. *...a fair, balanced, comprehensive report.* ADJ-GRADED PRAGMATICS =objective

2 Something that is **balanced** is pleasing or beneficial because its different parts or elements are in the correct proportions; used showing approval. *...a balanced diet.* ADJ-GRADED PRAGMATICS

3 Someone who is **balanced** remains calm and thinks clearly, even in a difficult situation; used showing approval. *I have to prove myself as a respectable, balanced, person.* ADJ-GRADED PRAGMATICS

4 See also **balance**.

balance of payments, balances of payments. A country's **balance of payments** is the difference, over a period of time, between the payments it makes to other countries for imports and the payments it receives from other countries for exports. *Britain's balance of payments deficit has improved slightly.* ♦◇◇◇◇ N-COUNT: usu sing

balance of power ♦◇◇◇◇

1 The **balance of power** is a situation in which power is distributed between rival groups or countries in such a way that no single group or country can dominate the others. *World order depended on the balance of power between the United States and the Soviet Union. ...the shifting balance of power in the post-Cold War world.* N-SING

2 If a small political party holds the **balance of power** in a parliament, it is able to give a larger party a majority by supporting this larger party. *Mr Shamir owes his parliamentary majority to small religious parties which hold the balance of power.* N-SING

balance of trade, balances of trade. A country's **balance of trade** is the difference in value, over a period of time, between the goods it imports and the goods it exports. *The deficit in Britain's balance of trade in March rose to more than 532100 million pounds.* N-COUNT: usu sing

balance sheet, balance sheets. A **balance sheet** is a written statement of the amount of money and property a company has, including amounts of money that it owes or is owed. You can also use **balance sheet** to refer to the general financial state of a company. *Rolls-Royce needed a strong balance sheet.* ♦◇◇◇◇ N-COUNT

balancing act, balancing acts. If you perform a **balancing act**, you try to please two or more people or groups who are in opposition to each other. *Mr. Mandela must perform a delicate balancing act.* N-COUNT: usu sing

balcony /bælkəni/ **balconies** ♦♦◇◇◇

1 A **balcony** is a platform on the outside of a building, above ground level, with a wall or railing around it. *Fanny stood on the tiny balcony of her room.* N-COUNT

2 The **balcony** in a theatre or cinema is an area of seats upstairs, above the main seating area. *I was sitting in the balcony.* N-SING =circle

bald /bɔːld/ **balder, baldest** ♦♦◇◇◇

1 Someone who is **bald** has little or no hair on the top of their head. *The man's bald head was beaded with sweat... She is going bald.* ♦ **baldness** *He wears a cap to cover a spot of baldness.* ADJ-GRADED N-UNCOUNT

2 If a tyre is **bald**, its tread has worn down and it is no longer safe to use. *His car had a bald tyre when it was involved in a head-on collision.* ADJ-GRADED

3 A **bald** statement is made plainly and often bluntly, containing no unnecessary words. *The announcement came in a bald statement from the official news agency... The bald truth is he's just not happy.* ♦ **baldly** *'The leaders are outdated,' he stated baldly. 'They don't relate to young people.'* ADJ: ADJ n =blunt ADV-GRADED: ADV with v =bluntly

bald eagle, bald eagles. A **bald eagle** is a large white-headed eagle that lives in North America. N-COUNT

balderdash /bɔːldərdæʃ/. If you say that something that has been said or written is **balderdash**, you think it is completely untrue or very stupid; an old-fashioned word. *What a load of balderdash!* N-UNCOUNT PRAGMATICS

balding /bɔːldɪŋ/. Someone who is **balding** is beginning to lose the hair on the top of their head. *He wore a straw hat to keep his balding head from getting sunburned.* ♦◇◇◇◇ ADJ

bale /beɪl/ **bales, baling, baled** ♦◇◇◇◇

1 A **bale** is a large quantity of something such as hay, cloth, or paper, tied into a tight bundle. *The shed was filled with large round bales of hay.* N-COUNT: usu pl, usu with supp

2 If something such as hay, cloth, or paper **is baled**, it is tied together in a tight bundle. *Once hay has been cut and baled it has to go through some chemical processes.* VERB *be* V-ed Also V n
3 See also **bail**.

baleful /beɪlfʊl/. **Baleful** means harmful, or expressing harmful intentions; a literary word. *He had a baleful look.* ♦ **balefully** *He watched balefully as Cassandra walked towards him.* ADJ-GRADED: usu ADJ n ADV: ADV with v

balk /bɔːlk, AM bɔːk/ **balks, balking, balked;** also spelled **baulk**. If you **balk** at something, you are very reluctant to do it or to let it happen. *Even biology undergraduates may balk at animal experiments... Last October the bank balked, alarmed that a $24m profit had turned into a $20m deficit.* ◆◇◇◇◇ VERB =flinch, recoil V at n V

Balkanization /bɔːlkənaɪzeɪʃən/; also spelled **balkanization**. If you disapprove of the division of a country into separate independent states, you can refer to the **Balkanization** of the country. *We've never accepted that there should be that fragmentation or balkanization of the country.* N-UNCOUNT PRAGMATICS

ball /bɔːl/ **balls, balling, balled** ◆◆◆◆◇
1 A **ball** is a round object that is used in games such as tennis, cricket, and football. *I bounced a ball against the house. ...a golf ball. ...a tennis ball.* N-COUNT
2 A **ball** is something or an amount of something that has a round shape. *Thomas screwed the letter up into a ball... They heard a loud explosion and saw a ball of fire go up.* N-COUNT: oft N of n
3 When you **ball** something or when it **balls**, it becomes round and takes up less space. *He picked up the sheets of paper, and balled them tightly in his fists... His hands balled into fists... I picked up the balled socks.* ► **Ball up** means the same as **ball**. *She balled the handkerchief up and threw it at his feet... Brian's face balled up like a fist.* V-ERG V n adv/prep V adv/prep V-ed PHRASAL VERB ERG V n P V P
4 The **ball** of your foot or the **ball** of your thumb is the rounded part where your toes join your foot or where your thumb joins your hand. *Point your toes forward and walk on the balls of your feet.* N-COUNT: usu *the* N *of* n
5 A **ball** is a large formal social event at which people dance. *Tonight is Laura Ashley's 40th anniversary ball. ...a young woman in a ball gown.* N-COUNT
6 A man's **balls** are his testicles; an informal use which some people find offensive. N-COUNT: usu pl
7 See also **balls**.
8 If you say that **the ball is in** a particular person's **court**, you mean that it is his or her responsibility to take the next action or decision in a particular situation. *The ball's now in your court – you have to decide what you're going to do.* PHRASES V inflects
9 If you **get the ball rolling**, **set the ball rolling**, or **start the ball rolling**, you start something happening. *He will go to the Middle East next week to get the ball rolling again on peace talks... I just want enough cash to start the ball rolling.* V inflects
10 If you **are having a ball**, you are having a very enjoyable time; an informal expression. *Outside the boys were sitting on the ground and, going by the gales of laughter, they were having a ball.* V inflects
11 If you **keep** several **balls in the air**, you try to do several different things at once. *The detective has to discover the motive, the means and the opportunity and has to keep these three balls in the air. ...unhappy mothers trying to juggle ten balls in the air.* V inflects
12 If someone is **on the ball**, they are very alert and aware of what is happening. *She really is on the ball; she's bought houses at auctions so she knows what she's doing.* v-link PHR
13 If someone refuses to **play ball**, they are unwilling to do what someone wants them to do; an informal expression. *The association has threatened to withdraw its support if the banks and building societies refuse to play ball.* V inflects

ball up. See **ball** 3. PHRASAL VERB

ballad /bæləd/ **ballads** ◆◇◇◇◇
1 A **ballad** is a long song or poem which tells a story in simple language. *...an eighteenth century ballad about some lost children called the Babes in the Wood.* N-COUNT
2 A **ballad** is a slow, romantic, popular song. *'You Don't Know Paris' is one of the most beautiful ballads that he ever wrote.* N-COUNT

ballast /bæləst/. **Ballast** is any substance that is used in ships or hot-air balloons to make them heavier and more stable. Ballast usually consists of water, sand, or iron. ◆◇◇◇◇ N-UNCOUNT

ball bearing, ball bearings; also spelled **ball-bearing**. **Ball bearings** are small metal balls placed between the moving parts of a machine to make the parts move smoothly. N-COUNT

ball boy, ball boys. In a tennis match, the **ball boys** are the boys whose job is to pick up any balls that go into the net or off the court and to throw them back to the players. N-COUNT

ballerina /bæləriːnə/ **ballerinas.** A **ballerina** is a woman ballet dancer. ◆◇◇◇◇ N-COUNT

ballet /bæleɪ, AM bæleɪ/ **ballets** ◆◆◇◇◇
1 **Ballet** is a type of very skilled and artistic dancing with carefully planned movements. *I trained as a ballet dancer... She is also keen on the ballet.* N-UNCOUNT: also *the* N, oft N n
2 A **ballet** is an artistic work that is performed by ballet dancers. *...Rudolf Nureyev dancing in Flemming Flindt's new ballet 'The Overcoat'.* N-COUNT

balletic /bæletɪk/. If you describe someone's movements as **balletic**, you mean that they have some of the graceful qualities of ballet. *The subject seems to dance with balletic grace.* ADJ-GRADED: usu ADJ n

ball game, ball games; also spelled **ballgame**. ◆◇◇◇◇
1 **Ball games** are games that are played with a ball such as football and tennis. N-COUNT: usu pl
2 In American English, a **ball game** is a baseball match. *I'd still like to go to a ball game.* N-COUNT
3 You can use **ball game** to describe any situation or activity, especially one that involves competition. *Two of his biggest competitors are out of the ball-game... We are now in a different ball game.* N-SING
• If you say that a situation is a **new ball game**, you mean that it is completely different from, or much more difficult than, the previous situation or any situation that you have experienced before. *He finds himself faced with a whole new ball game.* PHRASE

ball girl, ballgirls. In a tennis match, the **ball girls** are the girls whose job is to pick up any balls that go into the net or off the court and to throw them back to the players. N-COUNT

ballgown /bɔːlgaʊn/ **ballgowns.** A **ballgown** is a long dress that women wear to formal dances. N-COUNT

ballistic /bəlɪstɪk/. **Ballistic** means relating to ballistics. *...ballistic missiles... Ballistic tests have matched the weapons with bullets taken from the bodies of victims.* ◆◇◇◇◇ ADJ: ADJ n

ballistics /bəlɪstɪks/. **Ballistics** is the study of the movement of objects that are shot or thrown through the air, such as bullets fired from a gun. *The weapons are undergoing ballistics tests to see whether they were used in the shootings.* N-UNCOUNT

balloon /bəluːn/ **balloons, ballooning, ballooned** ◆◆◇◇◇
1 A **balloon** is a small, thin, rubber bag that you blow air into so that it becomes larger and rounder or longer. Balloons are used as toys or decorations. *She popped a balloon with her fork.* N-COUNT
2 A **balloon** is a large, strong bag filled with gas or hot air, which can carry passengers in a basket or compartment underneath it. *They are to attempt to be the first to circle the Earth non-stop by balloon.* N-COUNT: also *by* N
3 When something **balloons**, it increases rapidly in amount. *In London, the use of the Tube has ballooned... The budget deficit has ballooned to $25 billion... Her weight ballooned from 8 stone to 11 stone.* VERB =soar, rocket V V *to* n V *from* n *to* n
4 When something **balloons**, it quickly becomes bigger in size and rounder in shape. *Paula's plaid jacket ballooned in the deep water of the creek.* VERB =billow V

balloonist /bəluːnɪst/ **balloonists.** A **balloonist** is a person who flies a hot-air balloon. N-COUNT

ballot /bælət/ **ballots, balloting, balloted** ◆◆◆◇◇
1 A **ballot** is a secret vote in which people select a candidate in an election, or express their opinion about something. *The result of the ballot will not be known for two weeks... Fifty of its members will be elected by direct ballot.* N-COUNT: also *by* N

2 A **ballot** is a piece of paper on which you indicate your choice or opinion in a ballot. *Election boards will count the ballots by hand... They succeeded in putting Perot's name on the ballot in Florida.* N-COUNT =ballot paper

3 If you **ballot** a group of people, you find out what they think about a subject by organizing a secret vote. *The union said they will ballot members on whether to strike.* ♦ **balloting** *International observers say the balloting was fair.* VERB =poll V n N-UNCOUNT

ballot box, ballot boxes ◆◇◇◇◇

1 A **ballot box** is the box into which ballot papers are put after people have voted. N-COUNT

2 You can refer to the system of democratic elections as the **ballot box**. *Martinez expressed confidence of victory at the ballot box.* N-SING: the N

ballot paper, ballot papers. A **ballot paper** is a piece of paper on which you indicate your choice or opinion in a ballot. N-COUNT: usu pl

ballot rigging; also spelled **ballot-rigging**. **Ballot rigging** is the act of illegally changing the result of an election by producing a false record of the number of votes. *The poll was widely discredited after allegations of ballot rigging.* N-UNCOUNT

ballpark /bɔːlpɑːʳk/ **ballparks;** also spelled **ball park.**

1 A **ballpark** is a park or stadium where baseball is played. N-COUNT

2 A **ballpark** figure or **ballpark** estimate is an approximate figure or estimate; used mainly in American English. *I can't give you anything more than just sort of a ballpark figure... Ballpark estimates indicate a price tag of $90 million a month.* ADJ: ADJ n

3 If you say that someone or something is in the **ballpark**, you mean that they are able to take part in a particular area of activity, especially because they are considered as good as others taking part. *This puts them in the ballpark and makes them a major player... As a general investigative agency, they're not in the same ballpark as the FBI.* N-SING: the N

ballplayer /bɔːlpleɪəʳ/ **ballplayers;** also spelled **ball player**. In American English, a **ballplayer** is a baseball player. N-COUNT

ballpoint /bɔːlpɔɪnt/ **ballpoints.** A **ballpoint** or a **ballpoint pen** is a pen with a very small metal ball at the end which transfers the ink from the pen onto a surface. N-COUNT =Biro

ballroom /bɔːlruːm/ **ballrooms.** A **ballroom** is a very large room that is used for dancing. ◆◇◇◇◇ N-COUNT

ballroom dancing. **Ballroom dancing** is a type of dancing in which a man and a woman dance together using fixed sequences of steps and movements. N-UNCOUNT

balls /bɔːlz/ **ballses, ballsing, ballsed**

1 If you say that someone has **balls**, you mean that they have courage; an informal use which some people find offensive. *To work on this show you've got to have balls... I never had the balls to do anything like this.* N-UNCOUNT: oft the N to-inf =guts

2 You can say **'balls'** or say that what someone says is **balls** when you think that it is stupid, wrong, or nonsense; an informal British use, which some people find offensive. *What complete and utter balls!* EXCLAM; N-UNCOUNT PRAGMATICS

balls up. If you **balls up** a task or activity, you do it very badly, making a lot of mistakes; an informal British expression which some people find offensive. *You have single-handedly ballsed up the most important diplomatic initiative of the decade!... I have no intention of letting you balls it up.* PHRASAL VERB V P n (not pron) V n P Also V P

balls-up, balls-ups. If you make a **balls-up** of something, you do it very badly and make a lot of mistakes; an informal British word which some people find offensive. *He was in danger of making a real balls-up of this.* N-COUNT =pig's ear

ballyhoo /bælihuː, AM -huː/. You can use **ballyhoo** to refer to great excitement or anger about something, especially when you disapprove of it because you think it is unnecessary or exaggerated. *Dr Gallo announced, amid much ballyhoo, that his laboratory had found the virus that caused AIDS.* N-UNCOUNT: also a N PRAGMATICS =to-do

balm /bɑːm/ **balms** ◆◇◇◇◇

1 **Balm** is a sweet-smelling oil that is obtained from some tropical trees and is used to make ointments that heal wounds or lessen pain. *He retired to the boundary to apply balm to his aches and pains.* N-MASS

2 If you refer to something as **balm**, you approve of it because it is comforting or soothing. *I sought the balm of a new idea... Her sentiments were a balm to the poet in my soul.* N-UNCOUNT: also a N PRAGMATICS

balmy /bɑːmi/. **Balmy** weather is fairly warm and pleasant. *...a balmy summer's evening.* ADJ-GRADED: usu ADJ n

baloney /bəloʊni/. If you say that an idea or statement is **baloney**, you disapprove of it and think it is foolish or wrong; an informal word, used mainly in American English. *That's a load of baloney.* N-UNCOUNT PRAGMATICS =rubbish, garbage

balsa /bɔːlsə/. **Balsa** or **balsa wood** is a very light wood from a South American tree. N-UNCOUNT

balsam /bɔːlsəm/. **Balsam** is a sweet-smelling oil that is obtained from certain trees or bushes and is used to make medicines and perfumes. N-UNCOUNT

balsamic vinegar /bɔːlsæmɪk vɪnɪgəʳ/. **Balsamic vinegar** is a sweet-tasting type of vinegar which is made from grape juice. N-UNCOUNT

balti /bɔːlti/ **baltis.** A **balti** is a vegetable or meat dish of Indian origin which is cooked and served in a bowl-shaped pan. It is a speciality of the West Midlands in Britain. N-VAR

balustrade /bæləstreɪd, AM -streɪd/ **balustrades.** A **balustrade** is a railing or wall on a balcony or staircase. N-COUNT

bamboo /bæmbuː/ **bamboos. Bamboo** is a tall tropical plant with hard, hollow stems. The young shoots of the plant can be eaten and the stems are used to make furniture. *...huts with walls of bamboo. ...bamboo shoots.* ◆◇◇◇◇ N-VAR

bamboozle /bæmbuːzəl/ **bamboozles, bamboozling, bamboozled.** To **bamboozle** someone means to confuse them greatly and often trick them. *He bamboozled Mercer into defeat... He was bamboozled by con men.* VERB =dupe V n *into* n be V-ed

ban /bæn/ **bans, banning, banned** ◆◆◆◆◇

1 To **ban** something means to state officially that it must not be done, shown, or used. *Canada will ban smoking in all offices later this year... Last year arms sales were banned. ...a banned substance.* ♦ **banning, bannings** *No reason was given for the banning of the magazine... Opposition groups see the bannings as the latest stage of a government clampdown.* VERB =prohibit V n V-ed N-VAR

2 A **ban** is an official ruling that something must not be done, shown, or used. *The General also lifted a ban on political parties.* N-COUNT: oft N *on* n

3 If you **are banned** from doing something, you are officially prevented from doing it. *He was banned from driving for three years.* VERB =bar be V-ed *from* n Also V n

banal /bənɑːl, -næl/. If you describe something as **banal**, you do not like it because you think that it is so ordinary that it is not at all effective or interesting. *The text is banal... Bland, banal music tinkled discreetly from hidden loudspeakers.* ► You can refer to banal things as **the banal**. *The allegations ranged from the banal to the bizarre.* ♦ **banality** /bənælɪti/ **banalities** *...the banality of life... Neil's ability to utter banalities never ceased to amaze me.* ◆◇◇◇◇ ADJ-GRADED PRAGMATICS =hackneyed N-SING: the N N-VAR

banana /bənɑːnə, -næn-/ **bananas** ◆◆◇◇◇

1 **Bananas** are long curved fruit with yellow skins. *...a bunch of bananas.* N-VAR

2 If someone is behaving in a silly or mad way, you can say that they are going **bananas**; an informal use. *People went bananas with boredom.* ADJ: v-link ADJ

3 If someone becomes extremely angry and shouts a lot, you can say that they go **bananas**. *Adamson's going to go bananas on this one.* ADJ: v-link ADJ

banana republic, banana republics. Poor, unimportant, politically unstable countries are sometimes referred to as **banana republics**; an offensive expression. N-COUNT

banana skin, banana skins. If an important or famous person slips on a **banana skin**, they say or do something that makes them look stupid N-COUNT and causes them problems; used in journalism. *She has slipped on her first ever business banana skin by opening up yet another high class hotel to compete with the rest.*

banana split, banana splits. A **banana split** is a kind of dessert. It consists of a banana cut in half along its length, with ice cream, nuts, and sauce on top. N-COUNT

band /bænd/ **bands, banding, banded** ◆◆◆◆◇

1 A **band** is a small group of musicians who play popular music such as jazz, rock, or pop. *He was a drummer in a rock band... Local bands provide music for dancing.* • See also **one-man band**. N-COUNT-COLL

2 A **band** is a group of musicians who play brass and percussion instruments. *Bands played German marches.* • See also **brass band**. N-COUNT-COLL

3 A **band** of people is a group of people who have joined together because they share an interest or belief. *Bands of government soldiers, rebels and just plain criminals have been roaming some neighborhoods. ...a small but growing band of Japanese companies taking their first steps into American publishing.* N-COUNT-COLL: with supp

4 A **band** is a flat, narrow strip of cloth which you wear round your head or wrists, or which forms part of a piece of clothing. *Almost all hospitals use a wrist-band of some kind with your name and details on it.* • See also **armband, hatband, waistband**. N-COUNT =tape

5 A **band** is a strip of something such as colour, light, land, or cloth which contrasts with the areas on either side of it. *...bands of natural vegetation between strips of crops... A band of light glowed in the space between floor and door.* N-COUNT: with supp

6 A **band** is a strip or loop of metal or other strong material which strengthens something, or which holds several things together. *Surgeon Geoffrey Horne placed a metal band around the knee cap to help it knit back together. ...a strong band of flat muscle tissue.* • See also **elastic band, rubber band**. N-COUNT =strap

7 A **band** is a range of numbers or values within a system of measurement. *For an initial service, a 10 megahertz-wide band of frequencies will be needed. ...a new tax band of 20p in the pound on the first £2,000 of taxable income.* • See also **waveband**. N-COUNT: usu with supp

8 If something such as a tax **is banded**, it is divided into bands according to the value of the thing being taxed. *They appear to rule out some of the ideas that have been mentioned – banding the tax so higher earners would pay more. ...a banding system based on property values... The choice will be between a flat-rate or a banded charge.* VERB =stream V n V-ing V-ed

9 See also **wedding band**.

band together. If people **band together**, they meet and act as a group in order to try and achieve something. *Women banded together to protect each other... They banded together in their own small communities.* PHRASAL VERB V P

bandage /bændɪdʒ/ **bandages, bandaging, bandaged** ◆◇◇◇◇

1 A **bandage** is a long strip of cloth which is wrapped around a wounded part of someone's body to protect or support it. *We put some ointment and a bandage on his knee... His chest was swathed in bandages.* N-COUNT

2 If you **bandage** a wound or part of someone's body, you tie a bandage around it. *Apply a dressing to the wound and bandage it. ...a bandaged hand.* VERB V n V-ed

▶ **Bandage up** means the same as **bandage**. *I bandaged the leg up and gave her aspirin for the pain.* PHRASAL VERB V n P Also V P n (not pron)

Band-Aid, Band-Aids; also spelled **band-aid**.

1 A **Band-Aid** is a type of sticking plaster that you use to cover small cuts on your body. **Band-Aid** is a trade mark. *She had a Band-Aid on her ankle.* N-VAR

2 If you refer to a **Band-Aid** solution to a problem, you mean that you disapprove of it because you think that it will only be effective for a short period. *What we need are long-term solutions, not short-term Band-Aid solutions.* ADJ: ADJ n PRAGMATICS =cosmetic

bandanna /bændænə/ **bandannas;** also spelled **bandana**. A **bandanna** is a large, brightly-coloured handkerchief which is worn around a person's neck or head. *He was wearing a bright yellow T-shirt and a bandanna around his neck.* N-COUNT

B&B /biː ən biː/ **B&Bs;** also spelled **b&b**.

1 **B&B** is the same as **bed and breakfast**. *...three nights b&b.* N-UNCOUNT

2 A **B&B** is the same as a **bed and breakfast**. *There are B&Bs all over the islands.* N-COUNT

banded /bændɪd/. If something is **banded**, it has one or more bands on it, often of a different colour which contrasts with the main colour. *...a stark tower, banded in dark and light stone. ...banded stripes of dyed wool.* ADJ: oft ADJ *in/with* n

-banded /-bændɪd/. **-banded** combines with colours to indicate that something has bands of a particular colour. *Tables are set with white china and gold-banded silver cutlery.* COMB in ADJ =-striped

bandit /bændɪt/ **bandits.** People sometimes refer to armed robbers as **bandits**, especially if they operate in areas where the rule of law has broken down. *Bandits shot and killed a senior army officer... This is real bandit country.* ◆◇◇◇◇ N-COUNT =outlaw

banditry /bændɪtri/. **Banditry** is used to refer to acts of robbery and violence in areas where the rule of law has broken down. *Disorder and armed banditry has made the country ungovernable.* N-UNCOUNT =outlawry

bandleader /bændliːdəʳ/ **bandleaders.** A **bandleader** is the person who conducts a band, especially a jazz band. *...a noted trumpeter, composer and bandleader.* N-COUNT

bandsman /bændzmən/ **bandsmen. Bandsmen** are musicians in military or brass bands. *Military bandsmen played music from each country represented at the summit.* N-COUNT: usu pl

bandstand /bændstænd/ **bandstands.** A **bandstand** is a platform with a roof where a military band or a brass band can play in the open air. N-COUNT: usu sing

bandwagon /bændwægən/ **bandwagons** ◆◇◇◇◇

1 You can refer to an activity or movement that has suddenly become fashionable or is attracting increasing interest or support as a **bandwagon**. If you say that a **bandwagon** is rolling, you mean that an activity, a movement, or a political campaign is attracting increasing support. *...the environmental bandwagon... Mr. Major's team believe his bandwagon is rolling with support coming not just from the right... The London media tend to turn things into bandwagons.* N-COUNT: usu sing

2 If you say that someone, especially a politician, has jumped or climbed on the **bandwagon**, you disapprove of their involvement in an activity or movement because you think they are not sincerely interested in it, but are involved in it because it is likely to succeed or because it is fashionable. *In recent months many conservative politicians have jumped on the anti-immigrant bandwagon... The main parties all jumped on Mr Segni's bandwagon... The socialists are now climbing on the bandwagon.* N-COUNT: usu sing PRAGMATICS

bandy /bændi/ **bandies, bandying, bandied.** If you **bandy** words with someone, you argue with them. *Brand shook his head. He was tired of bandying words with the man... The prosecution and defense were bandying accusations back and forth.* VERB V n *with* n V n adv

bandy about or **bandy around.** If someone's name or something such as an idea **is bandied about** or **is bandied around**, that person or that thing is discussed by many people in a casual way; used showing disapproval. *He whispered my name to newspapermen, knowing that it would be bandied about... Young players now hear various sums bandied around about how much players are getting.* PHRASAL VERB usu passive PRAGMATICS be V-ed P

bane /beɪn/ **banes.** If you say that someone or something is the **bane** of a particular person, group, or activity, or is the **bane** of a particular person's life, you mean that they cause unhappiness or distress to the people involved. *Rain is* N-COUNT: usu sing, usu *the* N *of* n *the bane of holiday-makers... Spots can be the bane of a teenager's life.*

bang /bæŋ/ **bangs, banging, banged** ◆◆◇◇◇

1 A **bang** is a sudden loud noise such as the noise of an explosion. *I heard four or five loud bangs... She slammed the door with a bang... It went bang.* [N-COUNT; SOUND]

2 If something **bangs**, it makes a sudden loud noise, once or several times. *The engine spat and banged.* [VERB: V]

3 If you **bang** a door or if it **bangs**, it closes suddenly with a loud noise. *...the sound of doors banging... All up and down the street the windows bang shut... The wind banged a door somewhere.* [V-ERG =slam: V; V adj; V n]

4 If you **bang** on something or if you **bang** it, you hit it hard, making a loud noise. *We could bang on the desks and shout till they let us out... There is no point in shouting or banging the table.* [VERB: V on n; V n]

5 If you **bang** something on something or if you **bang** it down, you quickly and violently put it on a surface, because you are angry. *She banged his dinner on the table... He banged down the telephone.* [VERB: V n prep; V n with adv]

6 If you **bang** a part of your body, you accidentally knock it against something and hurt yourself. *She'd fainted and banged her head... He hurried into the hall, banging his shin against a chair in the darkness.* ► Also a noun. *...a nasty bang on the head.* [VERB: V n; V n *against/on* n] [N-COUNT]

7 If you **bang** into something or someone, you bump or knock them hard, usually because you are not looking where you are going. *I didn't mean to bang into you... Various men kept banging into me in the narrow corridor.* [VERB =bump: V *into* n]

8 In American English, the part of someone's hair that covers their forehead and that is cut straight across is referred to as their **bangs**. The usual British word is **fringe**. *My bangs were cut short, but the rest of my hair was long.* [N-PLURAL]

9 You can use **bang** to emphasize expressions that indicate an exact position or an exact time. *...bang in the middle of the track... For once you leave bang on time for work.* [ADV: ADV prep; PRAGMATICS =right]

10 See also **big bang theory**.

11 If you say **bang goes** something, you mean that it is now obvious that it cannot succeed or be achieved. *There will be more work to do, not less. Bang goes the fantasy of retirement at 35.* [PHRASES: V inflects, PHR n]

12 If something begins or ends **with a bang**, it begins or ends very successfully, attracting a lot of attention or admiration. *Her career began with a bang in 1986.* [PHR after v]

13 • to **bang** your **head against a brick wall**: see **brick**. • to **bang two people's heads together**: see **head**.

bang on about. If someone **bangs on about** something, they keep talking about it in a boring or annoying way; an informal expression. *He has been banging on about education reform for years.* [PHRASAL VERB no passive: V P n]

bang out [PHRASAL VERB]

1 If a company **bangs out** a poor quality product, they produce large quantities of it in order to make money; used showing disapproval. *...factories that banged out the same product year after year.* [PRAGMATICS: V P n (not pron)]

2 If someone **bangs out** a tune on a musical instrument such as a piano, they play it loudly and not very well. *...the same version of 'Mr Tambourine Man' he's been banging out since the world was young.* [V P n]

bang up. When a prisoner is **banged up**, they are put in prison and locked in a cell; an informal expression. *You become a rebel if you are banged up in a cell 23 hours a day.* [PHRASAL VERB usu passive: *be* V-ed P]

banger /bæŋəʳ/ **bangers**

1 In British English, **bangers** are sausages; an informal use. *... bangers and mash.* [N-COUNT]

2 In British English, you can describe a car as an old **banger** if it is old and in very bad condition; an informal use. *...this clapped-out old banger.* [N-COUNT: usu adj N =wreck]

3 **Bangers** are fireworks that make a lot of noise. [N-COUNT]

Bangladeshi /bæŋglədeʃi/ **Bangladeshis** ◆◆◆◆◇

1 **Bangladeshi** means belonging to or relating to Bangladesh, or to its people or culture. [ADJ: usu ADJ n]

2 The **Bangladeshis** are the people who come from Bangladesh. *There were about fifteen thousand Bangladeshis working in Iraq.* [N-COUNT]

bangle /bæŋgəl/ **bangles.** A **bangle** is a decorated metal or wooden ring that you can wear round your wrist or ankle. [N-COUNT]

bang-on; also spelled **bang on.** If someone is **bang-on** with something, they are exactly right in their opinions or actions; used in informal British English. *If we are not bang-on with our preparations then we could have problems... He looks bang on with his early judgment.* [ADJ: v-link ADJ]

banish /bænɪʃ/ **banishes, banishing, banished** ◆◇◇◇◇

1 If someone or something **is banished** from a place or area of activity, they are sent away from it and prevented from entering it. *John was banished from England... I was banished to the small bedroom upstairs... They tried to banish him from politics.* [VERB =expel: *be* V-ed *from/to* n; V n *from/to* n]

2 If you **banish** something unpleasant, you get rid of it. *...a public investment programme intended to banish the recession. ...diseases like malaria that have been banished for centuries.* [VERB: V n]

3 If you **banish** the thought of something, you stop thinking about it. *He has now banished all thoughts of retirement... The past few days had been banished from his mind.* [VERB: V n; *be* V-ed *from/to* n]

banishment /bænɪʃmənt/. **Banishment** is the act of banishing someone or the state of being banished. *...banishment to 'Devil's Island'. ...banishment from political and industrial life.* [N-UNCOUNT: usu N prep]

banister /bænɪstəʳ/ **banisters;** also spelled **bannister**. A **banister** is a rail supported by posts and fixed along the side of a staircase. The plural **banisters** can be used to refer to one of these rails. *I still remember sliding down the banisters.* [N-COUNT]

banjo /bændʒoʊ/ **banjos.** A **banjo** is a musical instrument that looks like a guitar with a circular body, a long neck, and four or more strings. ◆◇◇◇◇ [N-VAR: oft *the* N]

bank 1 finance and storage

bank /bæŋk/ **banks, banking, banked** ◆◆◆◆◆

1 A **bank** is an institution where people or businesses can keep their money. *Students should look to see which bank offers them the service that best suits their financial needs... I had £10,000 in the bank.* [N-COUNT]

2 A **bank** is a building where a bank offers its services. [N-COUNT]

3 If you **bank** money, you pay it into a bank. *Once you have registered your particulars with an agency and it has banked your cheque, the process begins.* [VERB: V n]

4 If you **bank** with a particular bank, you have an account with that bank. *My husband has banked with the Co-op since before the war.* [VERB: V *with* n]

5 You use **bank** to refer to a store of something. For example, a blood **bank** is a store of blood that is kept ready for use. *...Britain's National Police Computer, one of the largest data banks in the world.* [N-COUNT: with supp, usu n N]

6 If you say that the cost of something will not **break the bank**, you mean that it will not cost a large sum of money. *Prices starting at £6 a bottle won't break the bank.* [PHRASE: V inflects]

bank 2 areas and masses

bank /bæŋk/ **banks** ◆◆◇◇◇

1 The **banks** of a river, canal, or lake are the raised areas of ground along its edge. *...30 miles of new developments along both banks of the Thames. ...an old warehouse on the banks of a canal.* [N-COUNT: usu N *of* n =side]

2 A **bank** of ground is a raised area of it with a flat top and one or two sloping sides. *...resting indolently upon a grassy bank.* [N-COUNT =knoll]

3 A **bank** of something is a long high mass of it. *On their journey south they hit a bank of fog off the north-east coast of Scotland.* [N-COUNT: N *of* n]

4 A **bank** of things, especially machines, switches, or dials, is a row of them, or a series of rows. *The typical laborer now sits in front of a bank of dials.* [N-COUNT]

5 See also **banked**.

bank 3 other verb uses

bank /bæŋk/ **banks, banking, banked.** When an aircraft **banks**, one of its wings rises higher than the other, usually when it is changing direc- ◆◇◇◇◇ [VERB] tion. *A single-engine plane took off and banked above the highway in front of him.* V

bank on. If you **bank on** something happening, you expect it to happen and rely on it happening. *The Berlin government is banking on the Olympics to save the city money... 'He's not still there, I suppose?'—'I wouldn't bank on that,' she said.* PHRASAL VERB =count on V P n

bankable /bæŋkəbᵊl/. In the entertainment industry, someone or something that is described as **bankable** is very popular and therefore likely to be very profitable. *Madonna has become the world's most bankable star.* ADJ-GRADED: usu ADJ n

bank account, bank accounts. A **bank account** is an arrangement with a bank which allows you to keep your money in the bank and to take some out when you need it. ◆◇◇◇◇ N-COUNT

bank balance, bank balances. Your **bank balance** is the amount of money that you have in your bank account at a particular time. N-COUNT

bank card, bank cards; also spelled **bankcard**. A **bank card** is a rectangular piece of plastic which the bank gives you and which you have to show when you pay for something by cheque. **Bank cards** can also be used for getting money from your bank account using an automatic machine. N-COUNT

banked /bæŋkt/

1 A **banked** stretch of road is higher on one side than the other. *He struggled to hold the bike down on the banked corners... The car took off from the banked track and went through a fence.* ADJ: usu ADJ n =sloped

2 If a place is **banked** with something, it is piled high with that thing. If something is **banked up** it is piled high. *Flowerbeds and tubs are banked with summer bedding plants... The snow was banked up along the roadside.* ADJ: v-link ADJ =piled

banker /bæŋkəʳ/ **bankers.** A **banker** is someone who works in banking at a senior level. *...an investment banker. ...a merchant banker.* ◆◆◆◇◇ N-COUNT

bank holiday, bank holidays. In British English, a **bank holiday** is a public holiday. The usual American term is **national holiday**. ◆◇◇◇◇ N-COUNT

banking /bæŋkɪŋ/. **Banking** is the business activity of banks and similar institutions. ◆◆◆◇◇ N-UNCOUNT

banknote /bæŋknoʊt/ **banknotes;** also spelled **bank note**. **Banknotes** are pieces of paper money. ◆◇◇◇◇ N-COUNT

bank rate, bank rates. The **bank rate** is the rate of interest at which a bank lends money, especially the minimum rate of interest that banks are allowed to charge, which is decided from time to time by the country's central bank. *...a sterling crisis that forced the bank rate up.* N-COUNT

bankroll /bæŋkroʊl/ **bankrolls, bankrolling, bankrolled**

1 To **bankroll** a person, organization, or project means to provide the financial resources that they need; an informal expression used mainly in American English. *The company has bankrolled a couple of local movies.* VERB =finance V n

2 A **bankroll** is the financial resources used to back a person, project, or institution; used mainly in American English. *We have a guaranteed minimum bankroll of £1.7m over the five LPs.* N-SING

bankrupt /bæŋkrʌpt/ **bankrupts, bankrupting, bankrupted** ◆◆◇◇◇

1 People or organizations that go **bankrupt** do not have enough money to pay their debts. *If the firm cannot sell its products, it will go bankrupt... He was declared bankrupt after failing to pay a £114m loan guarantee.* ADJ =insolvent

2 To **bankrupt** a person or organization means to make them go bankrupt. *The move to the market nearly bankrupted the firm and its director... Uninsured people can be bankrupted by big medical bills.* VERB V n

3 A **bankrupt** is a person who has been declared bankrupt by a court of law. N-COUNT

4 If you say that something is **bankrupt**, you are emphasizing that it lacks any value or worth. *He really thinks that European civilisation is morally bankrupt.* ADJ PRAGMATICS =deficient

bankruptcy /bæŋkrʌptsi/ **bankruptcies** ◆◆◇◇◇

1 **Bankruptcy** is the state of being bankrupt. *Pam Am is the second airline in two months to file for bankruptcy... Many established firms were facing bankruptcy.* N-UNCOUNT =insolvency

2 A **bankruptcy** is an instance of an organization or person going bankrupt. *The number of corporate bankruptcies climbed in August.* N-COUNT =insolvencies

3 If you refer to something's **bankruptcy**, you are emphasizing that it is completely lacking in value or worth. *The massacre laid bare the moral bankruptcy of the regime.* N-UNCOUNT: usu supp N PRAGMATICS =vacuum

bank statement, bank statements. A **bank statement** is a printed document showing all the money paid into and taken out of a bank account. Bank statements are usually sent by a bank to a customer at regular intervals. N-COUNT

banner /bænəʳ/ **banners** ◆◆◇◇◇

1 A **banner** is a long strip of cloth with a message or slogan on it. Banners are usually attached to two poles and carried, or stretched high above the ground, often across a street. *A large crowd of students followed the coffin, carrying banners and shouting slogans denouncing the government... A big banner was draped across one of the streets saying, 'Idaho Falls Says NO to Drugs.'* N-COUNT

2 If someone does something **under the banner of** a particular cause, idea, or belief, they do it saying that they support that cause, idea, or belief. *Russia was the first country to forge a new economic system under the banner of Marxism... Under the banner of education, we herd our children from ballet to basketball and back again.* PHRASE: PHR n

banner headline, banner headlines. A **banner headline** is a large headline in a newspaper that stretches across the front page. *Today's front page of The Sun carries a banner headline 'The adulterer, the bungler and the joker.'* N-COUNT

bannister /bænɪstəʳ/. See **banister**.

banns /bænz/. When a vicar reads or publishes the **banns**, he or she makes a public announcement in church that two people are going to be married. N-PLURAL: the N

banquet /bæŋkwɪt/ **banquets.** A **banquet** is a grand formal dinner. *Last night he attended a state banquet at Buckingham Palace.* ◆◇◇◇◇ N-COUNT

banqueting /bæŋkwɪtɪŋ/. A **banqueting** hall or room is a large room where banquets are held. ADJ: ADJ n

banquette /bæŋket/ **banquettes.** A **banquette** is a long, low, cushioned seat. Banquettes are usually long enough for more than one person to sit on at a time. N-COUNT

banshee /bænʃiː, AM bænʃi/ **banshees.** In Irish folklore, a **banshee** is a female spirit who warns you by her long, sad cry that someone in your family is going to die. N-COUNT

bantam /bæntəm/ **bantams.** A **bantam** is a breed of small chicken. N-COUNT

bantamweight /bæntəmweɪt/ **bantamweights.** A **bantamweight** is a boxer who weighs between 51 and 53.5 kilograms, or a wrestler who weighs between 52 and 57 kilograms. A bantamweight is heavier than a flyweight but lighter than a featherweight. *...the European bantamweight title-holder.* N-COUNT: usu sing, oft N n

banter /bæntəʳ/ **banters, bantering, bantered** ◆◇◇◇◇

1 **Banter** is teasing or joking talk that is amusing and friendly. *As she closed the door, she heard Tom exchanging good-natured banter with Jane.* N-UNCOUNT =badinage

2 If you **banter** with someone, you tease them or joke with them in an amusing, friendly way. *We had long discussions and bantered with one another mercilessly... He and Cosell shared a cocktail and bantered easily... All this was said in a bantering tone.* V-RECIP V with n pl-n V V-ing Also V with quote (non recip)

Bantu /bæntuː, -tuː/

1 **Bantu** means belonging or relating to a group of peoples in central and southern Africa. *The local tribe, the Tune, are Bantu people.* ADJ: ADJ n

2 **Bantu** languages belong to a group of languages spoken in central and southern Africa. ADJ: ADJ n

bap /bæ̱p/ **baps.** In some dialects of British English, a **bap** is a soft flat bread roll. N-COUNT

baptise /bæptaɪ̱z/. See **baptize.**

baptism /bæ̱ptɪzəm/ **baptisms.** A **baptism** is a Christian ceremony in which a person is baptized. Compare **christening.** *There are three baptisms tomorrow afternoon in the Parish Church... Baptists only practise adult baptism.* ◆◇◇◇◇ N-VAR

baptismal /bæptɪ̱zməl/. **Baptismal** means relating to or connected with baptism; a formal word. *...a biblical scholar who studied the origins of the baptismal ceremony.* ADJ: ADJ n

baptism of fire, baptisms of fire. If someone who has just begun a new job has a **baptism of fire**, they immediately have to cope with very many severe difficulties and obstacles. *It was Mark's first introduction to royal duties and he came through his baptism of fire unscathed.* N-COUNT: usu sing

Baptist /bæ̱ptɪst/ **Baptists**

1 A **Baptist** is a Christian who believes that baptism is necessary for a Christian, and that it should happen only to someone who is old enough to understand what they are doing. N-COUNT

2 **Baptist** means belonging or relating to Baptists. *He's pastor of a Baptist church in Tucker, Georgia.* ADJ: usu ADJ n

baptize /bæptaɪ̱z/ **baptizes, baptizing, baptized;** also spelled **baptise** in British English. When someone **is baptized**, water is sprinkled on them or they are immersed in water as a sign that their sins have been forgiven and that they have become a member of the Christian Church. Compare **christen.** *At this time she decided to become a Christian and was baptised... I think your mother was baptized a Catholic.* VB: usu passive; be V-ed

bar /bɑ̱ːʳ/ **bars, barring, barred** ◆◆◆◆◇

1 A **bar** is a place where you can buy and drink alcoholic drinks; used mainly in American English. *...Devil's Herd, the city's most popular country-western bar. ...the Brass Nickel Bar.* N-COUNT

2 A **bar** is a room in a pub or hotel where alcoholic drinks are served; used mainly in British English. *Last night in the hotel there was some talk in the bar about drugs... On the ship there are video lounges, a bar and a small duty-free shop.* N-COUNT =public bar

3 A **bar** is a counter on which alcoholic drinks are served. *Michael was standing alone by the bar when Brian rejoined him... He leaned forward across the bar.* • See also **coffee bar, public bar, singles bar, snack bar, wine bar.** N-COUNT

4 A **bar** is a long, straight, rigid piece of metal. *...a brick building with bars across the ground floor windows. ...a crowd throwing stones and iron bars.* N-COUNT

5 If you say that someone is **behind bars**, you mean that they are in prison. *Fisher was behind bars last night, charged with attempted murder... Nearly 5,000 people a year are put behind bars over motoring penalties.* PHRASE: PHR after v, v-link PHR

6 A **bar** of something is a piece of it which is roughly rectangular. *What is your favourite chocolate bar? ...a bar of soap.* N-COUNT: with supp

7 A **bar** of an electric fire is a piece of metal with wire coiled round it that glows and provides heat when the fire is switched on. *The room with its electric bar fire was quite warm.* N-COUNT: usu with supp =element

8 If you **bar** a door, you place something in front of it or a piece of wood or metal across it in order to prevent it from being opened. *For added safety, bar the door to the kitchen.* ♦ **barred** *The windows were closed and shuttered, the door was barred.* VERB =secure; V n; ADJ: usu v-link ADJ

9 If you **bar** someone's way, you prevent them from going somewhere or entering a place, by blocking their path. *Harry moved to bar his way... He stepped in front of her, barring her way.* VERB =obstruct; V n

10 If someone **is barred** from a place or from doing something, they are officially forbidden to go there or to do it. *Amnesty workers have been barred from Sri Lanka since 1982... Many jobs were barred to them.* VB: usu passive =ban; be V-ed from n; be V-ed to n

11 If something is a **bar** to doing a particular thing, it prevents someone from doing it. *One of the fundamental bars to communication is the lack of a universally spoken, common language... In industry after industry, government bodies have erected bars to competition.* • See also **colour bar.** N-COUNT: usu N to n/-ing

12 If you say that there are **no holds barred** when people are fighting or competing for something, you mean that they are no longer following any rules in their efforts to win. *It is a war with no holds barred and we must prepare to resist... When she'd get angry it was no holds barred.* PHRASE

13 You can use **bar** when you mean 'except'. For example, all the work **bar** the washing means all the work except the washing. *Bar a plateau in 1989, there has been a rise in inflation ever since the mid-1980's... The aim of the service was to offer everything the independent investor wanted, bar advice.* PREP =save

• See also **barring.** • You use **bar none** to add emphasis to a statement that someone or something is the best of their kind. *He is simply the best goalscorer we have ever had, bar none.* PHRASE =without exception

14 The **Bar** is used to refer to the profession of a barrister in England, or of any kind of lawyer in the United States. *Robert was planning to read for the Bar.* N-PROPER: *the* N

15 In music, a **bar** is one of the several short parts of the same length into which a piece of music is divided. *I can play things with eight beats to a bar, all sorts of things. ...35 bars of a Quintet for Piano and Wind Instruments.* N-COUNT

barb /bɑːʳb/ **barbs**

1 A **barb** is a sharp curved point near the end of an arrow or fish-hook which makes it difficult to pull out. N-COUNT

2 A **barb** is an unkind remark meant as a criticism of someone or something. *The barb stung her exactly the way he hoped it would.* N-COUNT =gibe

Barbadian /bɑːʳbe̱ɪdiən/ **Barbadians.** ◆◆◆◆◇

1 **Barbadian** means belonging or relating to Barbados or its people. ADJ

2 A **Barbadian** is someone who comes from Barbados. *He is now married to a Barbadian.* N-COUNT

barbarian /bɑːʳbe̱əriən/ **barbarians.** In former times, **barbarians** were members of uncivilized and violent European peoples. *...the Roman Empire was overrun by Nordic barbarians.* ◆◇◇◇◇ N-COUNT

barbaric /bɑːʳbæ̱rɪk/. If you describe someone's behaviour as **barbaric**, you strongly disapprove of it because you think that it is extremely cruel or uncivilized. *This barbaric treatment of animals has no place in any decent society. ...a particularly barbaric act of violence.* ◆◇◇◇◇ ADJ-GRADED PRAGMATICS

barbarism /bɑ̱ːʳbərɪzəm/. If you refer to someone's behaviour as **barbarism**, you strongly disapprove of it because you think that it is extremely cruel or uncivilized. *We do not ask for the death penalty: barbarism must not be met with barbarism.* N-UNCOUNT

barbarity /bɑːʳbæ̱rɪti/ **barbarities.** If you refer to someone's behaviour as **barbarity**, you strongly disapprove of it because you think that it is extremely cruel. *Rebellions were put down with appalling barbarity. ...the barbarity of war.* N-VAR PRAGMATICS =atrocity

barbarous /bɑ̱ːʳbərəs/

1 If you describe something as **barbarous**, you strongly disapprove of it because you think that it is rough and uncivilised. *He thought the poetry of Whitman barbarous.* ADJ-GRADED PRAGMATICS

2 If you describe something as **barbarous**, you strongly disapprove of it because you think that it is extremely cruel. *It was a barbarous attack on a purely civilian train.* ADJ-GRADED PRAGMATICS

barbecue /bɑ̱ːʳbɪkjuː/ **barbecues, barbecuing, barbecued** ◆◇◇◇◇

1 A **barbecue** is a piece of equipment on which you can cook food such as sausages and burgers. You use barbecues out of doors. *Don't you think it's time you lit the barbecue? ...a portable barbecue.* N-COUNT

2 If someone has a **barbecue**, they cook food such as sausages and burgers on a barbecue out of doors. People often invite friends to barbecues. *On these fine evenings we usually have a barbecue... They met at a barbecue in Virginia.* N-COUNT

3 If you **barbecue** food, especially meat, you cook it on a barbecue. *Tuna can be grilled, fried or bar-* VERB; be V-ed

becued... *Here's a way of barbecuing corn-on-the-cob that I learned in the States. ...barbecued chicken is my favourite.* V n V-ed Also V

barbecue sauce. **Barbecue sauce** is a spicy sauce used to flavour food, especially meat cooked on a barbecue N-UNCOUNT

barbed /bɑːʳbd/. A **barbed** remark or joke seems polite or humorous, but contains a cleverly hidden criticism. *...barbed comments.* ◆◇◇◇◇ ADJ-GRADED: usu ADJ n =snide

barbed wire. **Barbed wire** is strong wire with sharp points sticking out of it, which is used to make fences. *The factory was surrounded by barbed wire. ...a barbed-wire fence.* ◆◇◇◇◇ N-UNCOUNT: oft N n

barber /bɑːʳbəʳ/ **barbers** ◆◇◇◇◇

1 A **barber** is a man whose job is cutting men's hair. *...a barber's shop in south London.* N-COUNT

2 In British English, a **barber's** is a shop where a barber works. The American term is **barber shop**. *My Mom took me to the barber's.* N-SING

barber shop, barber shops; also spelled **barbershop**. In American English, a **barber shop** is a shop where a barber works. The British term is **barber's**. N-COUNT

barbie /bɑːʳbi/ **barbies**

1 A **barbie** is a piece of equipment you use out of doors and on which you can cook food such as sausages and burgers. It is an abbreviation for **barbecue**; an informal use. N-COUNT

2 If someone has a **barbie**, they cook food such as sausages and burgers on a barbecue out of doors. **Barbie** is an abbreviation for **barbecue**; an informal use. *...barbies by the pool.* N-COUNT

barbiturate /bɑːʳbɪtʃʊrɪt/ **barbiturates.** A **barbiturate** is a drug which people take to make them calm or to help them to sleep. *She was addicted to barbiturates.* N-COUNT

bar chart, bar charts. A **bar chart** is a graph which uses parallel rectangular shapes to represent changes in the size, value, or rate of something or to compare the amount of something relating to a number of different countries or groups. *The bar chart below shows the huge growth of UK car exports over the past few years.* N-COUNT

bar code, bar codes; also spelled **barcode**. A **bar code** is an arrangement of numbers and parallel lines of different widths printed on products to be sold in shops. The bar code can be electronically scanned at a checkout to register the price of the goods and to activate computer stock-checking and reordering. N-COUNT

bard /bɑːʳd/ **bards.** A **bard** is a poet; an old-fashioned or literary word. ◆◇◇◇◇ N-COUNT

Bard. People sometimes refer to the playwright and poet William Shakespeare as **the Bard**. *...a new production of the Bard's early tragedy, Richard III.* N-PROPER: *the* N

bare /beəʳ/ **barer, barest; bares, baring, bared** ◆◆◆◇◇

1 If a part of your body is **bare**, it is not covered by any clothing. *She was wearing only a thin robe over a flimsy nightdress, and her feet were bare... She had bare arms and a bare neck.* ADJ

2 A **bare** surface is not covered or decorated with anything. *They would have liked bare wooden floors throughout the house.* ADJ-GRADED: usu ADJ n

3 If a tree or a branch is **bare**, it has no leaves on it. *...an old, twisted tree, its bark shaggy, many of its limbs brittle and bare.* ADJ-GRADED

4 If a room, cupboard, or shelf is **bare**, it is empty. *His fridge was bare apart from three very withered tomatoes... He led me through to a bare, draughty interviewing room.* ADJ-GRADED

5 An area of ground that is **bare** has no plants growing on it. *That's probably the most bare, bleak, barren and inhospitable island I've ever seen.* ADJ-GRADED

6 If someone gives you the **bare** facts or the **barest** details of something, they tell you only the most basic and important things. *Newspaper reporters were given nothing but the bare facts by the Superintendent in charge of the investigation.* ADJ-GRADED: det ADJ =plain ≠detailed

7 If you talk about the **bare** minimum or the **bare** essentials, you mean the very least that is necessary. *The army would try to hold the western desert with a bare minimum of forces... These are the bare essentials you'll need to dress your baby during the first few months.* ADJ-GRADED: det ADJ =absolute

8 **Bare** is used in front of an amount to emphasize how small it is. *Sales are growing for premium wines, but at a bare 2 percent a year.* ADJ: a ADJ amount PRAGMATICS =mere

9 If you **bare** something, you uncover it and show it; used in written English. *Walsh bared his teeth in a grin... He bared his muscular, hairy chest for a women's magazine.* VERB V n

10 ● **the bare bones**: see **bone**.

11 If someone does something **with** their **bare hands**, they do it without using any weapons or tools. *Police believe the killer punched her to death with his bare hands... Rescuers were using their bare hands to reach the trapped miners.* PHRASES PHR after v

12 If you **lay** something **bare**, you uncover it completely so that it can then be seen. *The clearing out of disused workshops laid bare thousands of Italianate glazed tiles.* V inflects =expose

13 If you **lay bare** something or someone, you reveal or expose them. *No one wants to expose themselves, lay their feelings bare.* V inflects

14 If you **bare** your **soul**, you tell someone your most secret thoughts and feelings. *Few men would have bared their soul to a woman as he had.* V inflects, oft PHR *to* n

bareback /beəʳbæk/. If you ride **bareback**, you ride a horse without a saddle. *I mounted my horse and rode bareback to the plantation.* ► Also an adjective. *She had once dreamed of being a bareback rider in a circus.* ADV: ADV after v ADJ: ADJ n

bare-faced; also spelled **barefaced**. You use **bare-faced** to describe someone's behaviour when you want to emphasize that they do not care that they are behaving wrongly; used showing disapproval. *Mr Perry made a mental note of this bare-faced lie... What bare-faced cheek!* ADJ: ADJ n PRAGMATICS =brazen, shameless

barefoot /beəʳfʊt/. Someone who is **barefoot** or **barefooted** is not wearing anything on their feet. *I wore a white dress and was barefoot... Alan came running barefoot through the house. ...barefoot little children.* ◆◇◇◇◇ ADJ: v-link ADJ, ADJ after v, ADJ n

bareheaded /beəʳhedɪd/. Someone who is **bareheaded** is not wearing a hat or any other covering on their head. *He was bareheaded, coatless and soaking wet... I rode bareheaded... One of the police officers was bareheaded, though in uniform.* ADJ: usu v-link ADJ, ADJ after v

barely /beəʳli/ ◆◆◆◇◇

1 You use **barely** to say that something is only just true or only just the case. *Anastasia could barely remember the ride to the hospital... It was 90 degrees and the air conditioning barely cooled the room... His voice was barely audible... She was an elfin-like girl who looked barely 10 years old.* ADV-BRD-NEG: ADV before v, ADV group, oft ADV amount =scarcely

2 If you say that one thing had **barely** happened when something else happened, you mean that the first event was followed immediately by the second. *The water had barely come to a simmer when she cracked four eggs into it... Barely had the bulldozers started when Museum of London archaeologists swooped.* ADV-BRD-NEG: ADV before v =no sooner

barf /bɑːʳf/ **barfs, barfing, barfed.** In American English, if someone **barfs**, they vomit; an informal word which some people find offensive. The usual British word is **puke**. *When I first tasted it I almost barfed.* VERB V

barfly /bɑːʳflaɪ/ **barflies.** A **barfly** is a person who spends a lot of time drinking in bars; an informal word, used mainly in American English. N-COUNT

bargain /bɑːʳgɪn/ **bargains, bargaining, bargained** ◆◆◆◇◇

1 Something that is a **bargain** is good value for money, usually because it has been sold at a lower price than normal. *At this price the wine is a bargain... Fresh salmon is a bargain at the supermarket this week.* N-COUNT

2 A **bargain** is an agreement, especially a formal business agreement, in which two people or groups agree what each of them will do, pay, or receive. *I'll make a bargain with you. I'll play hostess* N-COUNT =deal

if you'll include Matthew in your guest-list... The treaty was based on a bargain between the French and German governments.

3 When people **bargain** with each other, they discuss what each of them will do, pay, or receive. *They prefer to bargain with individual clients, for cash... Shop in small local markets and don't be afraid to bargain.* ♦ **bargainer, bargainers** *A union bargainer said that those jobs have been saved.* ♦ **bargaining** *The government has called for sensible pay bargaining.*
VERB =negotiate V *with* n V
N-COUNT
N-UNCOUNT: oft supp N

4 If people **drive a hard bargain**, they argue with determination in order to achieve a deal which is favourable to themselves. *Ukraine was always going to drive a hard bargain before signing the treaty.*
PHRASES V, ADJ, and N inflect

5 You use **into the bargain** when mentioning an additional quantity, feature, fact, or action, to emphasize the fact that it is also involved. *This machine is designed to save you effort, and keep your work surfaces tidy into the bargain... She is rich. Now you say she is a beauty into the bargain.*
cl PHR PRAGMATICS =as well

6 If you **keep your side of the bargain**, you do what you have promised or arranged to do. *Dealing with this dictator wasn't an option. He wouldn't have kept his side of the bargain.*
V inflects

bargain for. If someone gets something they had not **bargained for** or gets more than they **bargained for**, something happens that they did not expect or something happens to a greater degree than they had expected. *There were lots of expenses I hadn't bargained for... The effects of this policy were more than the government had bargained for.*
PHRASAL VERB usu with brd-neg =anticipate
V P n

bargain basement; also spelled **bargain-basement**. If you refer to something as a **bargain basement** thing, you mean that it is cheap and not very good quality. *...a bargain-basement rock musical.*
ADJ: ADJ n

bargain hunter, bargain hunters; also spelled **bargain-hunter**. A **bargain hunter** is someone who is looking for goods that are value for money, usually because they are on sale at a lower price than normal.
N-COUNT

bargaining chip, bargaining chips; also spelled **bargaining-chip**. In negotiations with other people, a **bargaining chip** is something that you are prepared to give up in order to obtain what you want. *Rubio suggests that oil be used as a bargaining chip in any trade talks.*
N-COUNT =bargaining counter

bargaining counter, bargaining counters; also spelled **bargaining-counter**. A **bargaining counter** is the same as a **bargaining chip**.
N-COUNT

barge /bɑːʳdʒ/ **barges, barging, barged** ◆◆◇◇◇

1 A **barge** is a long, narrow boat with a flat bottom. Barges are used for carrying heavy loads, especially on canals. *Carrying goods by train costs nearly three times more than carrying them by barge.*
N-COUNT: also *by* N =canal boat

2 If you **barge into** a place or **barge through** it, you rush or push into it in a rough and rude way; an informal use. *Students tried to barge into the secretariat buildings... The FBI barged through the gates, demanding to search the plant for evidence.*
VERB =butt in
V *into/through* n

3 If you **barge into** someone or **barge past** them, you bump against them roughly and rudely; an informal use. *He would barge into them and kick them in the shins... He barged past her and sprang at Gillian, knocking her to the floor.*
VERB =shove
V *into/past* n

barge in. If you **barge in** or **barge in** on someone, you rudely interrupt what they are doing or saying; an informal expression. *I'm sorry to barge in like this, but I have a problem I hope you can solve.*
PHRASAL VERB
V P Also V P *on* n

barge pole; also spelled **bargepole**. In British English, if you say that you **wouldn't touch** something **with a barge pole**, you mean that you would not want to have anything to do with it, either because you do not trust it, or because you do not like it; an informal expression.
PHRASE: V inflects

bar graph, bar graphs. A **bar graph** is the same as a **bar chart**; used mainly in American English.
N-COUNT

baritone /bærɪtoun/ **baritones** ◆◇◇◇◇

1 In music, a **baritone** is a man with a fairly deep singing voice that is lower than that of a tenor but higher than that of a bass. *...the young American baritone Monte Pederson.*
N-COUNT

2 If a man has a **baritone** speaking voice, his voice is low and pleasant to listen to. *...a baritone voice... He speaks in a melodious baritone.*
N-SING: oft N n

barium /beəriəm/. **Barium** is a soft, silvery-white metal.
N-UNCOUNT

bark /bɑːʳk/ **barks, barking, barked** ◆◆◇◇◇

1 When a dog **barks**, it makes a short, loud noise, once or several times. *Don't let the dogs bark... A small dog barked at a seagull he was chasing.* ► Also a noun. *The Doberman let out a string of roaring barks.*
VERB V V *at* n
N-COUNT

2 If you **bark** at someone, you shout at them aggressively in a loud, rough voice. *I didn't mean to bark at you... A policeman held his gun in both hands and barked an order.*
VERB V *at* n V n Also V with quote

3 **Bark** is the tough material that covers the outside of a tree.
N-UNCOUNT

4 If you say that someone's **bark is worse than** their **bite**, you mean that they seem much more unpleasant or hostile than they really are; an informal expression. *She was used to Wu's invective. Usually, his bark was far worse than his bite.* ● **be barking up the wrong tree** see **tree**.
PHRASE: V inflects

barker /bɑːʳkəʳ/ **barkers.** A **barker** is a person at a fair, circus, or show who loudly addresses passers-by in order to attract customers.
N-COUNT

barking mad. If you say that someone is **barking mad**, you mean that they are insane or are acting very foolishly; an informal word. *The builder looked at me as though I was barking mad.*
ADJ: v-link ADJ PRAGMATICS =bonkers

barley /bɑːʳli/. **Barley** is a crop that can be recognized by the heads of its stalks which have long spiky hairs surrounding seeds. These seeds are removed and used in the production of food, beer, and whisky. *...fields of ripening wheat and barley... Barley is grown on over four million acres of British soil.*
◆◇◇◇◇ N-UNCOUNT

barley sugar. **Barley sugar** is a sweet made from boiled sugar.
N-UNCOUNT

barley water. **Barley water** is a drink made from barley. It is sometimes flavoured with orange or lemon and is a popular drink in Britain.
N-UNCOUNT

barmaid /bɑːʳmeɪd/ **barmaids.** In British English, a **barmaid** is a woman who serves drinks behind a bar. The American word is **bartender**.
N-COUNT

barman /bɑːʳmən/ **barmen.** A **barman** is a man who serves drinks behind a bar.
◆◇◇◇◇ N-COUNT

bar mitzvah /bɑːʳ mɪtsvə/ **bar mitzvahs.** A **bar mitzvah** is a ceremony and celebration that takes place on the thirteenth birthday of a Jewish boy, after which he has the status, religious duties, and responsibilities of an adult man.
N-COUNT

barmy /bɑːʳmi/ **barmier, barmiest.** In British English, if you say that someone or something is **barmy**, you mean that they are slightly mad or very foolish; an informal word. *Bill used to say I was barmy, and that would really get to me... This policy is absolutely barmy. ...a barmy idea.*
ADJ-GRADED PRAGMATICS =crazy

barn /bɑːʳn/ **barns.** A **barn** is a building on a farm in which crops or animal food can be kept.

N-COUNT

barnacle /bɑːʳnɪkəl/ **barnacles.** **Barnacles** are small shellfish that fix themselves tightly to rocks and the bottoms of boats.
N-COUNT

barn dance, barn dances. A **barn dance** is a social event people go to for country dancing.
N-COUNT

barnstorm /bɑːʳnstɔːʳm/ **barnstorms, barnstorming, barnstormed.** In American English, when people such as politicians, actors, or sports players **barnstorm**, they travel around rural areas making political speeches, putting on shows, or playing matches. *He would ignore the Senate and barnstorm across the nation, rallying the people to the cause. ...the arguments the president will make as he barnstorms the country later this week. ...his barnstorming campaign for the governorship of Louisiana.*
VERB
V prep/adv V n V-ing Also V

barnstorming /bɑːʳnstɔːʳmɪŋ/. In British English, if you describe the performance of an actor, a sports player, or a musician as **barnstorming**,
ADJ: ADJ n PRAGMATICS

you are emphasizing that it is full of energy and very exciting to watch. *...a fabulous version of the classic play, with a barnstorming performance from Gerard Depardieu. ...their barnstorming start to the season.*

barnyard /bɑːʳnjɑːʳd/ **barnyards.** On a farm, the **barnyard** is the area in front of or next to a barn. N-COUNT: usu sing, oft *the* N

barometer /bərɒmɪtəʳ/ **barometers** ◆◇◇◇◇

1 A **barometer** is an instrument that measures air pressure and shows when the weather is changing. N-COUNT

2 If you describe something as a **barometer** of a particular situation, you mean that it indicates how things are changing or how things are likely to develop in a particular situation. *In past presidential elections, Missouri has been a barometer of the rest of the country... Our sleep pattern is a barometer to our psychological well-being.* N-COUNT: with supp, oft N *of* n

barometric pressure /bærəmetrɪk preʃəʳ/ **barometric pressures. Barometric pressure** is atmospheric pressure as indicated on a barometer. *...sensors to measure temperature and barometric pressure.* N-UNCOUNT: also N in pl

baron /bærən/ **barons** ◆◇◇◇◇

1 A **baron** is a man who is a member of the lowest rank of the nobility. *...their stepfather, Baron Michael Distemple.* N-COUNT; N-TITLE

2 You can use **baron** to refer to someone who controls a large amount of a particular industry and who is therefore extremely powerful. *...the battle against the drug barons. ...the British press barons.* N-COUNT: with supp, usu n N

baroness /bærənes/ **baronesses.** A **baroness** is a woman who is a member of the lowest rank of the nobility, or who is the wife of a baron. *...Baroness Blatch.* N-COUNT; N-TITLE

baronet /bærənɪt/ **baronets.** In Britain, a **baronet** is a man who has been given a special honorary knighthood. When a baronet dies, the title is passed on to his son. *Born in 1860, the son of a weaver, Barrie was created a baronet in 1913. ...the fifth baronet, Sir Thomas Grosvenor.* N-COUNT

baronial /bəroʊniəl/

1 If you describe a house or room as **baronial**, you mean that it is large, impressive, and old-fashioned in appearance, and looks as if it belongs to someone from the upper classes. *...baronial manor houses... The rooms have a baronial feel, with oak paneling and leather sofas.* ADJ-GRADED: usu ADJ n

2 **Baronial** means relating to a baron or barons. *...the baronial feuding of the Middle Ages.* ADJ: ADJ n

barony /bærəni/ **baronies.** A **barony** is the rank or position of a baron. N-COUNT

baroque /bərɒk, AM -roʊk/ ◆◇◇◇◇

1 **Baroque** architecture and art is an elaborate style of architecture and art that was popular in Europe in the seventeenth and early eighteenth centuries. *The baroque church of San Leonardo is worth a quick look. ...a collection of treasures dating from the Middle Ages to the Baroque period.* ADJ: ADJ n =rococo ▶ The baroque style and period in art and architecture are sometimes referred to as the **baroque**. *...the seventeenth-century taste for the baroque.* N-SING: *the* N

2 **Baroque** music is a style of European music that was written in the 18th century. *...the German baroque composer Georg Philip Telemann... A more widespread interest in baroque music developed only slowly in the Sixties and Seventies.* ADJ: ADJ n ▶ The baroque style and period in music are sometimes referred to as the **baroque**. *...his argument that Mozart belongs to the end of the baroque and not to the early phase of romantic music.* N-SING: *the* N

3 **Baroque** things are complicated and elaborate. *He was a baroque figure dressed in theatrical, but elegant, clothes. ...Paul Muldoon, who is among the most baroque of contemporary poets.* ADJ-GRADED: usu ADJ n =extravagant

barrack /bærək/ **barracks, barracking, barracked** ◆◆◇◇◇

1 A **barracks** is a building or group of buildings where soldiers or other members of the armed forces live and work. 'Barracks' is the singular and plural form. *...an army barracks in the north of the city. ...the parade grounds of Wellington Barracks.* N-COUNT: oft in names =camp, billet

2 If people in an audience **barrack** public speakers or performers, they interrupt them, for example by making rude remarks; used mainly in British English. *Fans gained more enjoyment barracking him than cheering on the team... President Alan Garcia was barracked by the right wing opposition.* VERB =heckle, jeer V n ♦ **barracking** *He was affected badly by the barracking that he got from the crowd.* N-UNCOUNT =heckling

barracuda /bærəkjuːdə, AM -kuː-/ **barracudas; barracuda** can also be used as the plural form. A **barracuda** is a large tropical sea fish with a protruding lower jaw and sharp teeth. The plural is either 'barracuda' or 'barracudas'. N-COUNT

barrage /bærɑːʒ, AM bərɑːʒ/ **barrages, barraging, barraged.** Pronounced /bɑːrɪdʒ/ for meaning 4 in American English. ◆◇◇◇◇

1 A **barrage** is continuous firing on an area with a large number of artillery weapons such as heavy guns and tanks. *The artillery barrage on the city centre was the heaviest since the ceasefire... The two fighters were driven off by a barrage of anti-aircraft fire.* N-COUNT =bombardment

2 A **barrage** of something such as criticism or complaints is a large number of them directed at someone, often in an aggressive way. *He was faced with a barrage of angry questions from the floor.* N-COUNT: usu sing, oft N *of* n

3 If you **are barraged** by people or things, you have to deal with a great number of people or things you would rather avoid. *Doctors are complaining about being barraged by drug-company salesmen... Hughes was barraged with phone calls from friends who were furious at the indiscreet disclosures.* VB: usu passive =bombarded *be* V-ed *by* n *be* V-ed *with* n

4 A **barrage** is a construction that is built across a river to control the level of the water. *...a hydroelectric tidal barrage.* N-COUNT

barrage balloon, barrage balloons. Barrage balloons are large balloons which are fixed to the ground by strong steel cables. They are used in wartime, when the cables are intended to destroy low-flying enemy aircraft. N-COUNT

barrel /bærəl/ **barrels, barreling, barreled** ◆◆◆◇◇

1 In the oil industry, a **barrel** is a unit of measurement equal to 159 litres. *In 1989, Kuwait was exporting 1.5 million barrels of oil a day... Oil prices were closing at $19.76 a barrel.* N-COUNT: oft N *of* n

2 A **barrel** is a large, round container for liquids or food. In former times, barrels were made of wood and were wider in the middle than at the top and bottom. Nowadays, many barrels are made of metal and have straight sides. *...other red wines which habitually spend time ageing in oak barrels. ...open barrels of pickled fish.* N-COUNT

3 The **barrel** of a gun is the tube through which the bullet moves when the gun is fired. *He pushed the barrel of the gun into the other man's open mouth.* N-COUNT: oft N *of* n, n N

4 If a vehicle or person **is barreling** in a particular direction, they are moving very quickly in that direction; used mainly in American English. *The car was barreling down the street at a crazy speed.* VERB =canon V prep/adv

5 See also **pork barrel**.

6 If you say, for example, that someone moves or buys something **lock, stock, and barrel**, you are emphasizing that they move or buy every part or item of it. *They dug up their New Jersey garden and moved it lock, stock, and barrel back home.* PHRASES PHR after v PRAGMATICS

7 If someone **has** you **over a barrel**, they have put you in a difficult situation where you have little choice but to do what they want you to do; an informal use. V inflects

8 If you say that someone is **scraping the barrel**, or **scraping the bottom of the barrel**, you disapprove of the fact that they are using or doing something of extremely poor quality; an informal use. V inflects PRAGMATICS

-barrelled /-bærəld/; spelled **-barreled** in American English. **-barrelled** combines with adjectives to form adjectives that describe a gun which has a barrel or barrels of the specified type. *...a short-barreled rifle. ...a double-barrelled shotgun.* ● See also **double-barrelled**. COMB in ADJ

barrel organ, barrel organs. A **barrel organ** is a large machine that plays music when you turn the handle on the side. Barrel organs used to be played in the street to entertain passers-by. N-COUNT

barren /bærən/ ◆◇◇◇◇

1 A **barren** landscape is dry and bare, and has very few plants and no trees. *...the by now familiar Tibetan landscape of high barren mountains.* ADJ-GRADED ≠fertile
♦ **barrenness** *...countryside of vast but beautiful barrenness.* N-UNCOUNT

2 **Barren** land consists of soil that is so poor that plants cannot grow in it. *He also wants to use the water to irrigate barren desert land.* ADJ-GRADED =infertile

3 If you describe something such as an activity or a period of your life as **barren**, you mean that you achieve no success during it or that it has no useful results; used in written English. *...an empty exercise barren of utility. ...Ivan Lendl, who ended a 14-month barren spell by winning the Tokyo event in October... As the leaves of autumn wither and fall, so has my own life become barren.* ADJ-GRADED: oft ADJ of n =bereft
♦ **barrenness** *...a film that would force audiences to confront the barrenness of contemporary life.* N-UNCOUNT: oft N of n

4 If you describe a room or a place as **barren**, you do not like it because it has almost no furniture or other objects in it; used in written English. *The room was austere, nearly barren of furniture or decoration... Six stale loaves of brown bread formed a dark blot on the otherwise barren shelves.* ADJ: oft ADJ of n PRAGMATICS

5 A **barren** woman or female animal is unable to have babies; an old-fashioned or technical use. *...the traumas experienced by the maternally inclined woman who finds herself barren. ...a three-year-old barren mare.* ADJ =infertile
♦ **barrenness** *...a ceremony designed to cure women of barrenness.* N-UNCOUNT =infertility

6 A **barren** tree or other plant produces no fruit or flowers. *A beautiful fig tree that had stood in their yard was leafless and barren.* ADJ

barricade /bærɪkeɪd, AM -keɪd/ **barricades, barricading, barricaded** ◆◆◇◇◇

1 A **barricade** is a line of vehicles or other objects placed across a road or open space to stop people getting past, for example during street fighting or as a protest. *Large areas of the city have been closed off by barricades set up by the demonstrators.* N-COUNT =blockade

2 If you **barricade** something such as a road or an entrance, you place a barricade or barrier across it, usually to stop someone getting in. *The rioters barricaded streets with piles of blazing tyres... The doors had been barricaded.* VERB =fortify V n

3 If you **barricade** yourself inside a room or building, you place barriers across the door or entrance so that other people cannot get in. *The students have barricaded themselves into their dormitory building... About forty prisoners are still barricaded inside the wrecked buildings.* VERB V pron-refl prep/adv V-ed

barrier /bæriəʳ/ **barriers** ◆◆◆◇◇

1 A **barrier** is something such as a rule, law, or policy that makes it difficult or impossible for something to happen or be achieved. *Duties and taxes are the most obvious barrier to free trade.* N-COUNT: oft N to/against/between n =obstacle

2 A **barrier** is a problem that prevents two people or groups from agreeing or communicating with each other. *There is no reason why love shouldn't cross the age barrier... She had been waiting for Simon to break down the barrier between them.* N-COUNT: oft supp N, N between pl-n =divide

3 A **barrier** is something such as a fence or wall that is put in place to prevent people from moving easily from one area to another. *The demonstrators broke through heavy police barriers... As each woman reached the barrier one of the men glanced at her papers.* N-COUNT =blockade

4 A **barrier** is an object or layer that physically prevents something from moving from one place to another. *...a severe storm, which destroyed a natural barrier between the house and the lake... The packaging must provide an effective barrier to prevent contamination of the product.* N-COUNT: usu with supp =fortification

5 You can refer to a particular number or amount as a **barrier** when you think it is a significant level, because it is not exceeded very often or easily. *They are fearful that unemployment will soon break the barrier of three million... The Popular Front failed, as expected, to pass the 5 per cent barrier.* N-SING: the N, with supp

6 See also **crash barrier, sound barrier**.

barrier method, barrier methods. Barrier methods of contraception involve the use of condoms, diaphragms, or other devices that physically prevent the sperm from reaching the egg. N-COUNT: usu pl

barring /bɑːrɪŋ/. You use **barring** to indicate that the person, thing, or event that you are mentioning is an exception to your statement. *Barring accidents, I believe they will succeed.* ◆◇◇◇◇ PREP

barrio /bɑːriou/ **barrios**

1 A **barrio** is a mainly Spanish-speaking neighbourhood in an American city; used mainly in American English. *...the barrios of Santa Cruz.* N-COUNT

2 A **barrio** is an urban district in a Spanish-speaking country; used mainly in American English. *...the barrios of Mexico City.* N-COUNT

barrister /bærɪstəʳ/ **barristers.** In England and Wales, a **barrister** is a lawyer who represents clients in the higher courts of law. Compare **solicitor**. ◆◆◇◇◇ N-COUNT

barroom /bɑːʳruːm/ **barrooms;** also spelled **bar-room**. In American English, a **barroom** is a room or building in which alcoholic drinks are served over a counter. *...a barroom brawl.* N-COUNT

barrow /bærou/ **barrows**

1 A **barrow** is the same as a **wheelbarrow**. N-COUNT

2 A **barrow** is a cart from which fruit or other goods are sold in the street; used mainly in British English. *The stolen goods were then sold off barrows in street-markets.* N-COUNT

3 A **barrow** is a mound of earth that prehistoric people used to build over their burial sites. *...the huge barrows built by ancient Norse people.* N-COUNT

barrow boy, barrow boys. In British English, a **barrow boy** is a man or boy who sells fruit or other goods from a barrow in the street. N-COUNT

bartender /bɑːʳtendəʳ/ **bartenders.** In American English, a **bartender** is a person who serves drinks behind a bar. The British word is **barman** or **barmaid**. N-COUNT

barter /bɑːʳtəʳ/ **barters, bartering, bartered.** If you **barter** goods, you exchange them for other goods, rather than selling them for money. *They have been bartering wheat for cotton and timber... The market-place and street were crowded with those who'd come to barter... Traders came to barter horses.* ◆◇◇◇◇ VERB =trade V n for n V V n
► Also a noun. *Overall, barter is a very inefficient means of organizing transactions. ...a barter economy.* N-UNCOUNT: oft N n

basal /beɪsəl/.

1 **Basal** means relating to or forming the base of something; a technical use. *Side shoots should be cut back to one leaf above the basal cluster. ...the basal layer of the skin.* ADJ: ADJ n

2 Your **basal** metabolic rate is the rate at which your body uses energy when it is at rest; a technical use. *Regular exercise can increase your basal metabolic rate... Basal metabolism is much lower for creatures in cold water.* ADJ: ADJ n =basic

basalt /bæsɔːlt, AM bəsɔːlt/ **basalts. Basalt** is a type of black rock that is produced by volcanoes. N-MASS

base /beɪs/ **bases, basing, based; baser, basest** ◆◆◆◆◆

1 The **base** of something is its lowest edge or part. *There was a cycle path running along this side of the wall, right at its base... Line the base and sides of a 20cm deep round cake tin with paper.* N-COUNT: usu the N of n =bottom ≠top

2 The **base** of something is the part at which it is attached to something else. *The surgeon placed catheters through the veins and arteries near the base of the head.* N-COUNT: usu the N of n

3 The **base** of an object such as a box or vase is the lower surface of it that touches the surface it rests on. *Remove from the heat and plunge the base of the pan into a bowl of very cold water.* N-COUNT: usu with poss =bottom, underneath

4 The **base** of an object that has several sections and that rests on a surface is the lower section of it. *The mattress is best on a solid bed base... The clock stands on an oval marble base, enclosed by a glass dome.* N-COUNT: usu with supp, oft n N

5 A **base** is a layer of something which will have another layer added to it. *Spoon the mixture on to the* N-COUNT: usu with supp

biscuit base and cook in a pre-heated oven... On many modern wooden boats, epoxy coatings will have been used as a base for varnishing.

6 A position or thing that is a **base** for something is one from which that thing can be developed or achieved. *The results had given the Conservatives a good base to win the next election... The family base was crucial to my development.* N-COUNT: usu sing, with supp =basis, foundation

7 If you **base** one thing on another thing, the first thing develops from the second thing. *He based his conclusions on the evidence given by the captured prisoners.* ♦ **based** *Three of the new products are based on traditional herbal medicines... The figures are based upon average market prices.* VERB =found V n *on/upon* n; ADJ: v-link ADJ *on* n

8 A military **base** is a place which part of an army, navy, or air force works from. *Gunfire was heard at an army base close to the airport... Lauren Long works in the Air Force motor pool on a massive air base in eastern Saudi Arabia.* N-COUNT: usu supp N

9 Your **base** is the main place where you work, stay, or live. *For most of the spring and early summer her base was her home in Scotland... Between travelling the Ruddles periodically returned to their permanent home base in Sussex.* N-COUNT: usu poss N

10 If a place is a **base** for a certain activity, the activity can be carried out at that place or from that place. *Hong Kong and Taiwan increasingly depend upon mainland China as a base for their exports... The two hotel-restaurants are attractive bases from which to explore southeast Tuscany.* N-COUNT: usu sing, usu N prep

11 The **base** of a substance such as paint or food is the main ingredient of it, to which other substances can be added. *Just before cooking, drain off any excess marinade and use it as a base for a pouring sauce... Oils may be mixed with a base oil and massaged into the skin.* N-COUNT

12 A **base** is a system of counting and expressing numbers. The decimal system uses base 10, and the binary system uses base 2. N-COUNT: also N num

13 A **base** in rounders or baseball is one of the places at each corner of the square on the pitch. N-COUNT

14 **Base** behaviour is behaviour that is immoral or dishonourable; a literary use. *Love has the power to overcome the baser emotions.* ADJ-GRADED

baseball /beɪsbɔːl/ **baseballs** ♦♦♦◇◇

1 **Baseball** is a game played by two teams of nine players. Each player from one team hits a ball with a bat and then tries to run round all four bases before the other team can get the ball back. N-UNCOUNT

2 A **baseball** is a small hard ball which is used in the game of baseball. N-COUNT

based /beɪst/. If you are **based** in a particular place, that is the place where you live or do most of your work. *Both firms are based in Kent... Based on the edge of Lake Matt, Sunbeam Yachts started boatbuilding in 1870.* ► Also after adjectives and nouns referring to places. *...Los Angeles-based writer and poet Wanda Coleman. ...American-based companies.* • See also **base**. ♦♦♦♦♦ ADJ: v-link ADJ =located; COMB in ADJ

-based /-beɪst/

1 **-based** combines with nouns referring to places to mean something positioned or existing mainly in the place mentioned, or operating or organized from that place. *...a Washington-based organization. ...land-based missiles.* COMB: COMB in ADJ

2 **-based** combines with nouns to mean that the thing mentioned is a central part or feature. *...computer-based jobs. ...oil-based sauces.* COMB: COMB in ADJ

3 **-based** combines with adverbs to mean having a particular kind of basis. *There are growing signs of more broadly-based popular unrest.* COMB: COMB in ADJ-GRADED

baseless /beɪsləs/. If you describe an accusation, rumour, or report as **baseless**, you mean that it is not true and is not based on facts. *The government has described reports of a massacre as completely baseless... Baseless allegations have been made and these need to be refuted.* ADJ =unfounded

baseline /beɪslaɪn/ **baselines;** also spelled **base-line.** ♦◇◇◇◇

1 The **baseline** of a tennis or badminton court is one of the lines at each end of the court that mark the limits of play. *Martinez, when she served, usually stayed on the baseline.* N-COUNT: usu sing

2 A **baseline** is a value or starting point on a scale with which other values can be compared. *You'll need such information to use as a baseline for measuring progress.* N-COUNT: usu sing, oft N *for* n/-ing

basement /beɪsmənt/ **basements.** The **basement** of a building is a floor built partly or wholly below ground level. *They bought an old schoolhouse to live in and built a workshop in the basement... They live in a basement flat in Kent.* ♦♦◇◇◇ N-COUNT

base metal, base metals. A **base metal** is a metal such as copper, zinc, tin, or lead that is not a precious metal. N-COUNT ≠precious metal

base rate, base rates. In Britain, the **base rate** is the rate of interest that banks use as a basis when they are calculating the rates that they charge on loans. *Bank base rates of 7 per cent are too high.* ♦◇◇◇◇ N-COUNT

bases. Pronounced /beɪsɪz/ for meaning 1, and /beɪsiːz/ for meaning 2.

1 **Bases** is the plural of **base**.

2 **Bases** is the plural of **basis**.

bash /bæʃ/ **bashes, bashing, bashed** ♦♦◇◇◇

1 A **bash** is a party or celebration, especially a large one held by an official organization or attended by famous people; an informal use. *He threw one of the biggest showbiz bashes of the year as a 36th birthday party for Jerry Hall.* N-COUNT =thrash

2 If someone **bashes** you, they attack you by hitting or punching you hard; an informal use. *If someone tried to bash my best mate they would have to bash me as well... I bashed him on the head and dumped him in the cold, cold water... Two women were hurt and the chef was bashed over the head with a bottle.* VERB V n V n prep/adv *be/get* V-ed prep/adv Also *be/get* V-ed

3 If you **bash** something, you hit it hard in a rough or careless way; an informal use. *Too many golfers try to bash the ball out of sand. That spells disaster... A stand-in drummer bashes on a single snare and a pair of cymbals.* VERB V n prep/adv V prep/adv Also V n

4 If you get a **bash** on a part of your body, somebody or something hits you hard, or you bump into something; an informal use. N-COUNT: usu N *on* n =knock

5 To **bash** someone means to criticize them severely, usually in a public way; used in journalism. *The President could continue to bash Democrats as being soft on crime.* VERB V n

6 If you have a **bash** at something, you try to do it; an informal British use. *He's prepared to have a bash at discussing it intelligently.* N-COUNT: usu sing, N *at* n/-ing

7 See also **-bashing**.

bash in. If someone **bashes** a person's or animal's head **in**, they hit it very hard and cause severe injuries to it. *The butt of a rifle had been used to bash in his skull. ...a dead fox with its head bashed in.* PHRASAL VERB V P n (not pron) V-ed P Also V n P

bash out. If you say that someone **bashes** something **out**, you mean that they produce it quickly or in large quantities, but without much care or thought; an informal use. *Up to then, they'd merrily bashed out albums in between tours... Their ambitions are to bash out good grub with minimal fuss.* PHRASAL VERB V P n

bash up. If someone **bashes** you **up**, they attack you violently and injure you; used in informal British English. *The two sisters apparently bashed each other up when their long overdue reconciliation turned sour... I've been bashed up by people with baseball bats because they said I was thieving on their patch.* PHRASAL VERB =beat up V n P Also V P n (not pron)

-basher /-bæʃəʳ/ **-bashers. -basher** combines with nouns to form nouns referring to someone who is physically violent towards a particular type of person, or who is unfairly critical of a particular type of person; used showing disapproval. *...gay-bashers who go around looking for homosexuals to beat up... These pressures come not from unthinking lawyer-bashers, but from sober legal reformers.* COMB in N-COUNT PRAGMATICS

bashful /bæʃfʊl/. Someone who is **bashful** is shy and easily embarrassed. *Offstage, he is bashful and awkward... In our culture we tend to be bashful about our talents and skills. ...a bashful young* ADJ-GRADED =coy *lady.* ♦ **bashfully** /bæʃfʊli/ *'No,' Wang Fu said bashfully.* ♦ **bashfulness** *Suddenly overcome with bashfulness, he lowered his voice.* ADV-GRADED: ADV with v N-UNCOUNT

-bashing /-bæʃɪŋ/

1 **-bashing** combines with nouns to form nouns or adjectives that refer to strong, public, and often unfair criticism of the specified people or group; used in journalism showing disapproval. *Tory-bashing or Labour-bashing will not be enough to shift bored, suspicious voters.* COMB in N-UNCOUNT, ADJ PRAGMATICS

2 **-bashing** combines with nouns to form nouns or adjectives that refer to the activity of violently attacking the specified people simply because they belong to a particular group or community; an informal use. *...an outburst of violent gay-bashing in New York and other cities.* COMB in N-UNCOUNT, ADJ

3 See also **bash**.

basic /beɪsɪk/ ♦♦♦♦◇

1 You use **basic** to describe things, activities, and principles that are very important or necessary, and on which others depend. *One of the most basic requirements for any form of angling is a sharp hook. ...the basic skills of reading, writing and communicating. ...the basic laws of physics. ...access to justice is a basic right.* ADJ-GRADED: usu ADJ n =fundamental

2 **Basic** goods and services are very simple ones which every human being needs. You can also refer to people's **basic** needs for such goods and services. *...shortages of even the most basic foodstuffs... Hospitals lack even basic drugs for surgical operations. ...the basic needs of food and water.* ADJ-GRADED: usu ADJ n

3 If one thing is **basic** to another, it is absolutely necessary to it, and the second thing cannot exist, succeed, or be imagined without it. *...an oily liquid, basic to the manufacture of a host of other chemical substances... There are certain ethical principles that are basic to all the great religions.* ADJ-GRADED: v-link ADJ *to* n =central

4 You can use **basic** to emphasize that you are referring to what you consider to be the most important aspect of a situation, and that you are not concerned with less important details. *There are three basic types of tea... The basic design changed little from that patented by Edison more than 100 years ago... The basic point is that sanctions cannot be counted on to produce a sure result.* ADJ: ADJ n PRAGMATICS =essential

5 You can use **basic** to describe something that is very simple in style and has only the most necessary features, without any luxuries. *We provide 2-person tents and basic cooking and camping equipment. ...the extremely basic hotel room.* ADJ-GRADED

6 **Basic** research into a subject is concerned with gaining knowledge about the subject itself, rather than with its practical applications. ADJ: ADJ n =pure ≠applied

7 **Basic** is used to describe a price or someone's income when this does not include any additional amounts such as special charges or bonuses. *...an increase of more than twenty per cent on the basic pay of a typical coalface worker... The basic retirement pension will go up by £1.95 a week... The basic price for a 10-minute call is only £2.49.* ADJ: ADJ n

8 The **basic** rate of income tax is the lowest or most common rate, which applies to people who earn average incomes. *All this is to be done without big rises in the basic level of taxation. ...a basic-rate taxpayer.* ADJ: ADJ n

basically /beɪsɪkli/ ♦♦♦◇◇

1 You use **basically** for emphasis when you are stating an opinion, or when you are making an important statement about something. *This gun is designed for one purpose – it's basically to kill people... Basically I think he would be someone who complemented me in terms of character.* ADV: ADV with cl/group PRAGMATICS

2 You use **basically** to show that you are describing a situation in a simple, general way, and that you are not concerned with less important details. *Basically you've got two choices... It's basically a vegan diet... Battery charging systems remain basically the same as those in use half a century ago.* ADV: ADV with cl/group, ADV before v PRAGMATICS

basics /beɪsɪks/ ♦◇◇◇◇

1 The **basics** of something are its simplest, most important elements, ideas, or principles, in contrast to more complicated or detailed ones. *They will concentrate on teaching the basics of reading, writing and arithmetic... A strong community cannot be built until the basics are in place... Let's get down to basics and stop horsing around.* N-PLURAL: usu *the* N, oft N *of* n =fundamentals

2 **Basics** are things such as simple foods, clothes, or equipment that people need in order to live or to deal with a particular situation. *...supplies of basics such as bread and milk... We try to produce items that are the basics of a stylish wardrobe.* N-PLURAL =essentials

3 If you talk about getting **back to basics**, you are suggesting that people have become too concerned with complicated details or new theories, and that they should concentrate on simple, important ideas or activities. *Nurtured carefully, the business can once again get back to basics. ...a new 'back-to-basics' drive to raise standards of literacy in Britain's schools.* PHRASE: usu PHR after v, PHR n

basil /bæzᵊl/. **Basil** is a strong smelling and strong tasting herb that is used in cooking to give food extra flavour. It is often used with tomatoes. ♦◇◇◇◇ N-UNCOUNT

basilica /bəzɪlɪkə/ **basilicas.** A **basilica** is a church which is rectangular in shape and has a rounded end, a central nave, and two or four side aisles. *...Saint Peter's Basilica in Rome.* ♦◇◇◇◇ N-COUNT

basin /beɪsᵊn/ **basins** ♦♦◇◇◇

1 A **basin** is a large or deep bowl that you use for holding liquids, or for mixing or storing food. *Place the eggs and sugar in a large basin. ...a pudding basin.* N-COUNT ► A **basin** of something such as water is an amount of it that is contained in a basin. *We were given a basin of water to wash our hands in.* N-COUNT: N *of* n

2 A **basin** is the same as a **washbasin**. *...a cast-iron bath with a matching basin and wc.* N-COUNT

3 The **basin** of a large river is the area of land around it from which streams run down into it. *...the use of insecticide against malaria-carrying mosquitoes in the Amazon basin.* N-COUNT: with supp, oft in names

4 A **basin** is a particular region of the world where the earth's surface is lower than elsewhere; a technical use in geography. *...countries around the Pacific Basin.* N-COUNT: with supp, oft in names

5 A **basin** is a partially enclosed area of deep water where boats or ships are kept. *The sheltered yacht basin is right in the centre of town.* N-COUNT: usu n N

basis /beɪsɪs/ **bases** /beɪsiːz/ ♦♦♦♦◇

1 If something is done on a particular **basis**, it is done according to that method, system, or principle. *We're going to be meeting there on a regular basis... The tea is prepared on a rota basis by the lady members... They want all groups to be treated on an equal basis... I've always worked on the basis that if I don't know anything technical I shan't be any worse off.* N-SING: with supp, usu *on* N

2 If you say that you are acting **on** the **basis** of something, you are giving that as the reason for your action. *McGregor must remain confined, on the basis of the medical reports we have received... On the basis that recognising the problem is half-way to a solution, Mulcahy's comments yesterday should be well received.* N-SING: *on* N, oft N *of* n, N that PRAGMATICS

3 The **basis** of something is its starting point or an important part of it from which it can be further developed. *All the Cambodian parties had now accepted the plan as a basis for settling the conflict. ...the sub-atomic particles that form the basis of nearly all matter on earth.* N-COUNT: usu sing, usu N *for/of* n =foundation

4 The **basis** for something is a fact or argument that you can use to prove or justify it. *...Japan's attempt to secure the legal basis to send troops overseas... This is a common fallacy which has no basis in fact.* N-COUNT: usu sing

basis point, basis points. A **basis point** is one hundredth of a per cent (.01%); a technical term in finance. ♦◇◇◇◇ N-COUNT: usu pl

bask /bɑːsk, bæsk/ **basks, basking, basked** ♦◇◇◇◇

1 If you **bask** in the sunshine, you lie somewhere sunny and enjoy the warmth. *All through the hot, still days of their holiday Amy basked in the sun... Crocodiles bask on the small sandy beaches.* VERB V in n V

2 If you **bask** in someone's approval, favour, or admiration, you thoroughly enjoy their positive reaction towards you. *He has spent a month basking in* VERB V in n

the adulation of the fans back in Jamaica... Livy smiled and basked in Rachel's approval.

basket /bɑːskɪt, bæs-/ **baskets** ◆◆◇◇◇

1 A **basket** is a container with a fixed shape that is used for carrying or storing objects. Baskets are made from strips of wood, wicker, plastic, or metal woven together. *...big wicker picnic baskets filled with sandwiches... There were a few old dry logs in the basket by the hearth.* N-COUNT ▶ A **basket** of things is a number of things contained in a basket. *...a small basket of fruit and snacks.* N-COUNT: N of n

2 If you talk about a **basket** of currencies or goods, you are referring to the average or total value of a number of different currencies or goods; a technical use in economics. *The pound's value against a basket of currencies hit a new low of 76.9. ...an inflation measure that gauges the price of a fixed basket of goods and services.* N-COUNT: usu sing, N of n

3 In basketball, the **basket** is a net hanging from a ring through which players try to throw the ball in order to score points. N-COUNT

4 See also **bread basket**, **hanging basket**, **wastepaper basket**. • **put all** your **eggs in one basket**: see **egg**.

basketball /bɑːskɪtbɔːl, bæs-/ **basketballs** ◆◆◇◇◇

1 **Basketball** is a game in which two teams of five players each try to score goals by throwing a large ball through a circular net fixed to a metal ring at each end of the court. N-UNCOUNT

2 A **basketball** is a large ball which is used in the game of basketball. N-COUNT

basket case, basket cases

1 If someone describes a country or organization as a **basket case**, they mean that its economy or finances are in a seriously bad state; an informal use. *Ten years ago Latin America was written off as a basket case.* N-COUNT

2 If you describe someone as a **basket case**, you think that they are mad or insane; an informal and offensive use. *You're going to think I'm a basket case when I tell you this.* N-COUNT =nutcase

bas-relief /bɑːrɪliːf, bæs-/ **bas-reliefs**

1 **Bas-relief** is a technique of sculpture in which shapes are carved so that they stand out from the background. *Each piece is hand-decorated in a classic white bas-relief design.* N-UNCOUNT

2 A **bas-relief** is a sculpture carved on a surface so that it stands out from the background. *...a pair of large arches, decorated with bas-reliefs.* N-COUNT

bass, basses. Pronounced /beɪs/ for meanings 1 to 4, and /bæs/ for meaning 5. The plural of the noun in meaning 5 is **bass**. ◆◆◆◇◇

1 A **bass** is a man with a very deep singing voice. *...the great Russian bass Chaliapin.* N-COUNT

2 A **bass** drum, guitar, or other musical instrument is one that produces a very deep sound. *...bass guitarist Dee Murray.* ADJ: ADJ n

3 In popular music, a **bass** is a bass guitar or a **double bass**. *They had a bass and a piano and a sax and percussion. ...Dave Ranson on bass and Kenneth Blevins on drums... Kurt had started out playing bass in a rock band.* N-VAR

4 On a hi-fi or radio, the **bass** is the ability to reproduce the lower musical notes. The **bass** is also the knob which controls this. *...larger models which will then give more bass and a higher fidelity sound.* N-UNCOUNT

5 **Bass** are edible fish that are found in rivers and the sea. There are several types of bass. *They unloaded their catch of cod and bass.* N-VAR ▶ **Bass** is a piece of this fish eaten as food. *...a large fresh fillet of sea bass.* N-UNCOUNT: oft n N

basset hound /bæsɪt haʊnd/ **basset hounds.** A **basset hound** or a **basset** is a dog with short strong legs, a long body, and long, drooping ears. It is kept as a pet or used for hunting. N-COUNT =basset

bassist /beɪsɪst/ **bassists.** A **bassist** is someone who plays the bass guitar or the double bass. ◆◇◇◇◇ N-COUNT

bassoon /bəsuːn/ **bassoons.** A **bassoon** is a wooden orchestral instrument that is shaped like a tube and played by blowing into a curved metal mouthpiece and pressing the keys with your fingers. N-VAR: oft *the* N

bassoonist /bəsuːnɪst/ **bassoonists.** A **bassoonist** is someone who plays the bassoon. N-COUNT

bastard /bɑːstəʳd, bæs-/ **bastards** ◆◆◇◇◇

1 If someone calls a person, usually a man, a **bastard**, they are insulting him, for example because he has behaved very unpleasantly; a rude, offensive use which you should avoid using. N-COUNT PRAGMATICS

2 If someone refers to a person, usually a man, as, for example, a lucky **bastard** or a poor **bastard**, they are expressing strong feelings about him, such as envy or sympathy; an informal use which some people find offensive. N-COUNT: usu adj N PRAGMATICS

3 A **bastard** is a person whose parents were not married to each other at the time that he or she was born; an old-fashioned use. *...King Arthur's bastard son, Mordred. ...a man who fathered an uncountable number of bastards.* N-COUNT: oft N n =illegitimate

4 If someone describes a problem or a situation as a **bastard**, they mean that it is extremely annoying or difficult to deal with; an informal use which some people find offensive. *Life can be a real bastard at times... I had to go early 'cos it's a bastard to get your motor out of the car park.* N-COUNT: usu sing PRAGMATICS

bastardized /bɑːstəʳdaɪzd, bæs-/; also spelled **bastardised**. If you refer to something as a **bastardized** form of something else, you mean that the first thing is similar to or copied from the second thing, but is of much poorer quality; a formal word. ADJ-GRADED: usu ADJ n

baste /beɪst/ **bastes, basting, basted.** If you **baste** meat, you pour hot fat and the juices from the meat itself over it while it is cooking. *Mary stood at the stove basting the roasting chickens... Bake for 15-20 minutes, basting occasionally.* VERB V n V

bastion /bæstiən, AM -tʃən/ **bastions.** If a system or organization is described as a **bastion** of a particular way of life, it is seen as being important and effective in defending that way of life. **Bastion** can be used both when you think that this way of life should be ended and when you think it should be defended. A formal word. *...a town which had been a bastion of white prejudice. ...a bastion of spiritual freedom... The army is still one of the last male bastions.* ◆◇◇◇◇ N-COUNT: with supp, usu N of n =stronghold

bat /bæt/ **bats, batting, batted** ◆◆◆◇◇

1 A **bat** is a specially shaped piece of wood that is used for hitting the ball in cricket, baseball, rounders, or table-tennis. *...a baseball bat.* N-COUNT

2 When you **bat**, you have a turn at hitting the ball with a bat in cricket, baseball, or rounders. *Australia, put in to bat, made a cautious start.* VERB V ♦ **batting** *...his batting average... He's likely to open the batting.* N-UNCOUNT: oft N n, *the* N

3 A **bat** is a small flying animal that looks like a mouse with leathery wings. Bats fly at night. N-COUNT

4 See also **old bat**.

5 In British English, if you say that someone **doesn't bat an eyelid** when something surprising happens or when they do something unpleasant, you are surprised or shocked because they remain calm and unemotional. The usual American expression is **doesn't bat an eye**. *When it comes to naked women on the pages of a glossy magazine, no one seems to bat an eyelid... The conspirators would have killed thousands of people without batting an eyelid.* PHRASES V inflects

6 If you **go to bat for** someone or **go in to bat for** them, you give them your support. *The old judge doesn't like the thought of no one going in to bat for the accused.* V inflects =stand up for

7 If you drive **like a bat out of hell**, you drive extremely fast; an informal expression. *He took off for Helsinki like a bat out of hell.* PHR after v

8 If someone does something **off** their **own bat**, they do it without anyone else suggesting it. *Whatever she did she did off her own bat. Whatever she did was nothing to do with me.* PHR after v

9 If something happens **right off the bat**, it happens immediately; used in American English. *He learned right off the bat that you can't count on anything in this business.* usu PHR after v

batch /bætʃ/ **batches.** A **batch** of things or people is a group of things or people of the same kind, especially a group that is dealt with at the same time or is sent to a particular place at the same time. *...the current batch of trainee priests... She brought a large batch of newspaper cuttings... We're still waiting for the first batch to arrive.* ◆◆◇◇◇ N-COUNT: oft N *of* n

bated /beɪtɪd/. If you wait for something **with bated breath**, you wait anxiously to find out what will happen; a formal expression. *Every Monday the whole office used to wait with bated breath for his report... We would gather round my grandmother and listen with bated breath while she read of Wee Curly's latest adventures.* PHRASE: usu PHR after v

bath /bɑːθ, bæθ/ **baths, bathing, bathed.** When the form **baths** is the plural of the noun it is pronounced /bɑːðz/ or /bæθs/ in British English, and /bæðz/ in American English. When it is used in the present tense of the verb, it is pronounced /bɑːθs/ or /bæθs/. ◆◆◆◇◇

1 In British English, a **bath** is a container, usually a long rectangular one, which you fill with water and sit in while you wash your body. The American word is **bathtub.** *In those days, only quite wealthy families had baths of their own.* N-COUNT

2 When you have or take a **bath**, or when you are in the **bath**, you sit or lie in a bath filled with water in order to wash your body. *...if you have a bath every morning... Take a shower instead of a bath. ...a bath and shower gel.* N-COUNT

3 If you **bath** someone, especially a child, you wash them in a bath; used mainly in British English. *Don't feel you have to bath your child every day.* ► Also a noun. *The midwife gave him a warm bath.* VERB =bathe V n N-COUNT

4 When you **bath**, you have a bath; used mainly in British English. *The three children all bath in the same bath water.* VERB =bathe V prep/adv

5 A **bath** or a **baths** is a public building containing a swimming pool, and sometimes other facilities that people can use to have a wash or a bath. The plural **baths** can be used to refer either to one or to more than one of these places. *One of the most important buildings in this ruined city is a public bath... As well as a Roman amphitheatre and baths, the town has two superb museums.* N-COUNT

6 A **bath** is a container filled with a particular liquid, such as a dye or an acid, in which particular objects are placed, usually as part of a manufacturing or chemical process. *...a developing photograph placed in a bath of fixer.* N-COUNT: usu with supp

7 See also **bloodbath, bubble bath, swimming bath, Turkish bath.**

bathe /beɪð/ **bathes, bathing, bathed** ◆◆◇◇◇

1 If you **bathe** in a sea, river, or lake, you swim, play, or wash yourself in it. Birds and animals can also **bathe**; used mainly in formal British English. *The police have warned the city's inhabitants not to bathe in the polluted river. ...small ponds for the birds to bathe in.* ► Also a noun. *Fifty soldiers were taking an early morning bathe in a nearby lake.* ♦ **bathing** *Nude bathing is not allowed. ...Britain's 440 designated bathing beaches.* VERB V prep/adv Also V N-SING: usu *a* N N-UNCOUNT

2 When you **bathe**, you have a bath; used in American English or formal British English. *At least 60% of us now bathe or shower once a day.* VERB =bath V

3 If you **bathe** someone, especially a child, you wash them in a bath; used in American English or formal British English. *Back home, Shirley plays with, feeds and bathes the baby.* VERB =bath

4 If you **bathe** a part of your body or a wound, you wash it gently or soak it in a liquid. *Bathe the infected area in a salt solution... She paused long enough to bathe her blistered feet.* VERB V n

5 If a place **is bathed** in light, it is covered with light, especially a gentle, pleasant light. *The arena was bathed in warm sunshine... I was led to a small room bathed in soft red light... The lamp behind him seems to bathe him in warmth.* VERB *be* V-ed *in* n V-ed V n *in* n Also V n

6 See also **sunbathe.**

bathed /beɪðd/

1 If someone is **bathed** in sweat, they are sweating a great deal. *Chantal was writhing in pain and bathed in perspiration.* ADJ: v-link ADJ *in* n

2 If someone is **bathed** in a particular emotion such as love, they feel it constantly in a pleasant way; a literary use. *...a physical sensation of being bathed in love. ...a relationship bathed in trust.* ADJ: v-link ADJ *in* n

bather /beɪðəʳ/ **bathers.** A **bather** is a person who is swimming or playing in the sea, a river, or a lake. *The beach was crowded with bathers.* N-COUNT =swimmer

bathing cap /beɪðɪŋ kæp/ **bathing caps.** In American English, a **bathing cap** is a rubber cap which you wear to keep your hair dry when you are swimming. The usual British term is **swimming cap.** N-COUNT

bathing costume /beɪðɪŋ kɒstjuːm, AM -tuːm/ **bathing costumes.** In British English, a **bathing costume** is a piece of clothing that is worn for swimming, especially by women and girls; an old-fashioned word. *She wore a one-piece white bathing costume.* N-COUNT =swimsuit

bathing suit /beɪðɪŋ suːt/ **bathing suits.** A **bathing suit** is a piece of clothing which people wear when they go swimming; used mainly in American English. N-COUNT

bathing trunks /beɪðɪŋ trʌŋks/. **Bathing trunks** are shorts that a man wears when he goes swimming. N-PLURAL =swimming trunks

bathmat /bɑːθmæt, bæθ-/ **bathmats;** also spelled **bath mat.** A **bathmat** is a mat which you stand on while you dry yourself after getting out of the bath. N-COUNT

bathos /beɪθɒs/. **Bathos** is a sudden change in speech or writing from a serious or important subject to a ridiculous or very ordinary one; a technical term in literary criticism. N-UNCOUNT =anticlimax

bathrobe /bɑːθroʊb/ **bathrobes**

1 A **bathrobe** is a loose piece of clothing made of towelling which you wear before or after you have a bath or a swim. N-COUNT

2 In American English, a **bathrobe** is a dressing gown. *He got out of bed and pulled on his bathrobe.* N-COUNT =dressing gown

bathroom /bɑːθruːm, bæθ-/ **bathrooms** ◆◆◆◇◇

1 A **bathroom** is a room in a house that contains a bath or shower, a washbasin, and sometimes a toilet. N-COUNT

2 In American English, a **bathroom** is also a room in a house or public building that contains a toilet. The usual British word is **toilet.** *She had gone in to use the bathroom.* N-SING: usu *the* N =rest room

3 In American English, people say that they **are going to the bathroom** when they want to say that they are going to use the toilet. The British expression is **go to the toilet.** *Although he had been treated with antibiotics, he went to the bathroom repeatedly.* PHRASE: V inflects

bath towel, bath towels. A **bath towel** is a very large towel used for drying your body after you have had a bath. N-COUNT

bathtub /bɑːθtʌb, bæθ-/ **bathtubs.** In American English, a **bathtub** is a long, usually rectangular container which you fill with water and sit in to wash your body. The British word is **bath.** N-COUNT

bath water; also spelled **bathwater.** Your **bath water** is the water in which you sit or lie when you have a bath. *He has to share his bath water with the other three children in the family.* • **to throw the baby out with the bath water:** see **baby.** N-UNCOUNT

batik /bətiːk, bætɪk/ **batiks**

1 **Batik** is a process for printing designs on cloth. Wax is put on those areas of the cloth that you do not want to be coloured by dye. *...a process similar to that used in batik. ...batik bedspreads.* N-UNCOUNT

2 A **batik** is a cloth which has been printed with a batik design. *...a four-poster bed decorated with local batiks. ...batik from Bali.* N-VAR

batman /bætmæn/ **batmen.** In the British armed forces, an officer's **batman** is his personal servant. *...morning tea brought by his batman.* N-COUNT: usu sing, oft poss N

baton /bætɒn, AM bətɑːn/ **batons** ◆◇◇◇◇

1 A **baton** is a short heavy stick which is sometimes N-COUNT

used as a weapon by the police. *Police used batons to beat back two groups of demonstrators.* =truncheon

2 A **baton** is a light, thin stick used by a conductor to conduct an orchestra or a choir. *The conductor raised his baton, waiting for the hall to become silent. ...a gala concert under the baton of the orchestra's music director, Franz Welser-Most.* N-COUNT

3 In athletics, a **baton** is a short stick that is passed from one runner to another in a relay race. *Larry Black almost caught him at the baton pass.* N-COUNT

4 A **baton** is a long stick with a knob on one end that is sometimes carried by a person marching in a parade. The baton is spun round, thrown into the air and caught. *Children watch the marching band and dream of the day when they will be carrying the bass drum or twirling a baton.* N-COUNT

5 If someone **passes the baton** to someone else, they pass responsibility for something to that person. If someone **picks up the baton**, they take over responsibility for something. *Does this mean that the baton of leadership is going to be passed to other nations?* PHRASE: V inflects

baton charge, baton charges, baton charging, baton charged. A **baton charge** is an attacking forward movement made by a large group of policemen carrying batons. *The police made repeated baton charges to disperse the crowds.* ► Also a verb. *A warning was given, then police in riot gear baton-charged the crowd.* N-COUNT; VERB V n

batsman /bætsmən/ **batsmen.** The **batsman** in a game of cricket is the player who is batting. *The batsman rose on his toes and played the rising ball down into the ground... He was the greatest batsman of his generation.* ◆◆◇◇◇ N-COUNT

battalion /bətæljən/ **battalions** ◆◆◇◇◇

1 A **battalion** is a large group of soldiers that consists of three or more companies. *Ten hours later Anthony was ordered to return to his battalion... When war broke out, he joined the second battalion of the Grenadier Guards.* N-COUNT =garrison

2 A **battalion** of people is a large group of them, especially a well-organized, efficient group that has a particular task to do. *There were battalions of highly paid publicists to see that such news didn't make the press.* N-COUNT: N *of* n =horde

batten /bætᵊn/ **battens, battening, battened**

1 A **batten** is a long strip of wood that is fixed to something to strengthen it or to hold it firm; used mainly in British English. *Timber battens can be fixed to the wall so that a decorative wallboard can be attached.* N-COUNT

2 If something **is battened** in place, it is made secure by having battens fixed across it or being closed firmly. *The roof was never securely battened down. ...big pine shutters that could be battened against the noonday sun.* VB: usu passive; be V-ed adv/prep

3 • **batten down the hatches**: see **hatch**.

batten on. If you say that someone **battens on** a particular person or thing, you disapprove of the fact that they become successful by forming a close connection with that person or thing. *...a malicious insurance agent who battens on a Melbourne couple after an accident at home. ...the growth of extremist parties, battening on fears about mass immigration and unemployment.* PHRASAL VERB PRAGMATICS; V P n

batter /bætəʳ/ **batters, battering, battered** ◆◆◇◇◇

1 If a child or a woman is **battered**, they are regularly hit and badly hurt by a member of their own family. *...evidence that the child was being battered. ...boys who witness fathers battering their mothers. ...battered wives.* ♦ **battering** *Leaving the relationship does not mean that the battering will stop.* VERB; be V-ed; V n; V-ed; N-UNCOUNT

2 To **batter** someone means to hit them many times, using fists or a heavy object. *He battered her around the head... A karate expert battered a man to death... He was battered unconscious.* ♦ **battered** *Her battered body was discovered in a field.* VERB; V n prep/adv; V n adj; Also V n; ADJ-GRADED

3 If a place is **battered** by wind, rain, or storms, it has very bad weather for a period of time. This often causes damage to the area. *The country has been battered by winds of between fifty and seventy miles an hour. ...a storm that's been battering the Northeast coastline.* VB: usu passive =pound; be V-ed

4 If you **batter** something, you hit it many times, using your fists or a heavy object. *They were battering the door, they were breaking in... Batter the steaks flat.* VERB; V n; V n adj

5 **Batter** is a mixture of flour, eggs, and milk. You use batter to make things such as pancakes. *Add chocolate chips to the pancake batter. ...fish in batter.* N-VAR

6 In sports such as baseball and cricket, a **batter** is a person who hits the ball with a wooden bat. *...batters and pitchers.* N-COUNT

7 See also **battered, battering**.

batter down. If you **batter** a door **down**, you hit it so hard that it falls to pieces. *He would have to batter the door down... They used lorries to batter down embassy gates.* PHRASAL VERB; V n P; V P n

battered /bætəʳd/. Something that is **battered** is old and in poor condition because it has been used a lot. *He drove up in a battered old car. ...a battered leather suitcase.* ◆◇◇◇◇ ADJ-GRADED

batterer /bætərəʳ/ **batterers.** A **batterer** is someone who regularly hits and injures a member of their own family, especially their wife. *...treatment programs for batterers and shelters for their victims.* N-COUNT

battering /bætərɪŋ/ **batterings.** If something takes a **battering**, it suffers very badly as a result of a particular event or action. *Sterling took a battering yesterday as worries grew about the state of Britain's economy.* N-COUNT =beating

battering ram, battering rams; also spelled **battering-ram.** A **battering ram** is a long heavy piece of wood that is used to knock down the locked doors of buildings. *The battering ram was smashing through the oak door.* N-COUNT

battery /bætəri/ **batteries** ◆◆◇◇◇

1 **Batteries** are small devices that you put in electrical items such as torches and radios. Batteries provide the power to make these items work. *The shavers come complete with batteries. ...a battery-operated cassette player. ...rechargeable batteries.* N-COUNT

2 A car **battery** is a rectangular box containing acid that is found in a car engine. It provides the electricity needed to start the car. *...a car with a flat battery... He turns on a slide machine powered by a car battery.* N-COUNT

3 A **battery** of equipment such as guns, lights, or computers is a large set of it kept together in one place. *They stopped beside a battery of abandoned guns. ...batteries of spotlights set up on rooftops.* N-COUNT: usu N *of* n

4 A **battery** of people or things is a very large number of them. *...a battery of journalists and television cameras... Crack is part of a battery of drugs used by addicts.* N-COUNT: N *of* n =horde

5 A **battery** of tests is a set of tests that is used to assess a number of different aspects of something, such as your health. *We give a battery of tests to each patient... The astronauts are busy conducting a battery of tests.* N-COUNT: usu sing, usu N *of* n

6 In British English, **battery** hens are large numbers of hens kept on farms in very small cages. The eggs they produce are called **battery** eggs. ADJ: ADJ n

7 • to **recharge** your **batteries**: see **recharge**. See also **assault and battery**.

battery farm, battery farms. A **battery farm** is a place where large numbers of hens are bred and used for their meat and their eggs. Each hen is kept in a very small cage where it has very little room to move. N-COUNT

battery farming. **Battery farming** is a system of breeding hens in which large numbers of them are kept in very small cages. The hens are used for their meat and their eggs. N-UNCOUNT

battle /bætᵊl/ **battles, battling, battled** ◆◆◆◆◇

1 A **battle** is a violent fight between groups of people, especially one between military forces during a war. *...the victory of King William III at the Battle of the Boyne. ...after a gun battle between police and drug traffickers. ...men who die in battle.* N-VAR

2 A **battle** is a conflict, quarrel, or contest in which N-COUNT:

different people or groups compete for power or advantage, or try to achieve opposite things. *...a renewed political battle over Britain's attitude to Europe. ...the eternal battle between good and evil in the world. ...a macho battle for supremacy... He was appalled to discover members of the board fighting damaging personal battles.* — usu with supp, oft N prep =struggle

3 You can use **battle** to refer to someone's efforts to achieve something in spite of very difficult circumstances. *...the battle against crime... She has fought a constant battle with her weight... Greg lost his brave battle against cancer two years ago.* — N-COUNT: usu sing, oft N *against* n =fight

4 To **battle** with an opposing group or person means to take part in a fight or contest against them. You can also say that two groups or people **are battling**. In American English, you can also say that one group or person **is battling** another. *In one town thousands of people battled with police and several were reportedly wounded... The sides must battle again for a quarter-final place on December 16... They're also battling the government to win compensation.* — V-RECIP; V *with/against* n; pl-n V; V n; Also pl-n V to-inf

5 To **battle** means to try hard to be successful in spite of very difficult circumstances. In British English, you **battle** against something or with something. In American English, you **battle** something. *Doctors battled throughout the night to save her life. ...a lone yachtsman returning from his months of battling with the elements... In Wyoming, firefighters are still battling the two blazes.* — VERB =fight; V to-inf; V *with/against/through* n; V n

6 See also **pitched battle, running battle**.

7 If one person or group **does battle** with another, they take part in a battle or contest against them. You can also say that two people or groups **do battle**. *...the notorious Montonero guerrilla group who did battle with the army during the dirty war... This March, a British and an American company will do battle in the High Court over the right to press compact discs.* — PHRASES RECIP: V inflects, PHR *with/against* n, pl-n PHR

8 If you say that something is **half the battle**, you mean that it is the most important step towards achieving something. *Choosing the right type of paint for the job is half the battle.* — usu v-link PHR

9 If you say that **the battle lines are drawn** between opposing groups or people, you mean that they are ready to start fighting or arguing, and that it has become clear what the main points of conflict or disagreement will be. *The battle lines were drawn after the government refused to budge from its final offer.* — V inflects

10 If you are **fighting a losing battle**, you are trying to achieve something but are not going to be successful. *The crew fought a losing battle to try to restart the engines. ...on a day when the sun is fighting a losing battle against the lowering clouds.* — V inflects, oft PHR *with/against* n, PHR to-inf

11 If one group or person **battles it out** with another, they take part in a fight or contest against each other until one of them wins or a definite result is reached. You can also say that two groups or people **battle it out**. *In the Cup Final, Leeds battled it out with the old enemy, Manchester United... Barbados could have three new political parties battling it out in the next General Election.* — RECIP: V inflects, PHR *with* n, pl-n PHR

12 If you say that someone may have **lost the battle**, but **won the war**, you mean that, although they have been defeated in a minor conflict, they have won a larger, more important one of which it was a part. If you say that someone has **won the battle** but **lost the war**, you mean that they have won the small conflict but lost the larger one. *The strikers may have won the battle, but they lost the war.* — Vs and *battle* inflect

13 If you refer to a situation as a **battle of wills**, you mean that it involves people who try to defeat each other by refusing to change their oppposing aims or demands and hoping that their opponents will weaken first. *The President offered compromises to parliament to defuse the battle of wills over who should wield power.*

14 If you refer to a situation as a **battle of wits**, you mean that it involves people with opposing aims who compete with each other using their intelligence, rather than force. *With chess you're involved in a battle of wits from start to finish.* — *battle* inflects

battle-axe, battle-axes; also spelled **battleaxe**.
1 If you call a middle-aged or older woman a **battle-axe**, you mean you think she is very difficult and unpleasant because of her fierce and determined attitude; an informal use. *Grandma is something else – a battle axe from the old country who hasn't smiled in decades.* — N-COUNT =dragon
2 A **battle-axe** is a large axe that was used as a weapon. — N-COUNT

battle cruiser, battle cruisers; also spelled **battlecruiser**. A **battle cruiser** is a large fast warship that has lighter armour and is faster and easier to manoeuvre than a battleship. — N-COUNT

battle cry, battle cries; also spelled **battle-cry**.
1 A **battle cry** is a phrase that is used to urge people to take part in activities connected with a cause or campaign. *Their battle-cry will be: 'Sign this petition before they sign away your country.'* — N-COUNT =rallying cry
2 A **battle cry** is a shout that soldiers utter as they go into battle. *He screamed out a battle cry and charged, swinging his sword from side to side.* — N-COUNT

battlefield /bætəlfiːld/ **battlefields** ◆◆◇◇◇
1 A **battlefield** is a place where a battle is fought. *...the battlefields of the Somme.* — N-COUNT =battleground
2 You can refer to an issue or field of activity over which people disagree or compete as a **battlefield**. *...Neil Kinnock's challenge to make education the battlefield for the next election.* — N-COUNT =battleground

battleground /bætəlgraʊnd/ **battlegrounds** ◆◇◇◇◇
1 A **battleground** is the same as a **battlefield**. — N-COUNT
2 You can refer to an issue or field of activity over which people disagree or compete as a **battleground**. *...the battleground of education... Children's literature is an ideological battleground.* — N-COUNT =battlefield

battlements /bætəlmənts/. The **battlements** of a castle or fortress consist of a wall built round the top, with gaps through which guns or arrows can be fired. — N-PLURAL =parapet

battleship /bætəlʃɪp/ **battleships.** A **battleship** is a very large, heavily armoured warship. ◆◇◇◇◇ — N-COUNT

batty /bæti/ **battier, battiest.** If you say that someone is **batty**, you mean that they are rather eccentric or slightly mad; used mainly in informal British English. *Laura's going a bit batty. ...some batty uncle of theirs.* — ADJ-GRADED =barmy

bauble /bɔːbəl/ **baubles.** A **bauble** is a small, cheap ornament or piece of jewellery. *Christmas trees are decorated with candles, fairy lights and coloured baubles.* — N-COUNT =trinket

baulk /bɔːlk, AM bɔːk/. See **balk**.

bauxite /bɔːksaɪt/. **Bauxite** is a clay-like ore from which aluminium is obtained. — N-UNCOUNT

bawdy /bɔːdi/ **bawdier, bawdiest.** A **bawdy** story or joke contains humorous references to sex; an old-fashioned word. *We got arrested once, for singing bawdy songs in a cemetery.* — ADJ-GRADED =lewd

bawl /bɔːl/ **bawls, bawling, bawled** ◆◇◇◇◇
1 If you **bawl**, you shout or sing in a very loud voice, for example because you are angry or you want people to hear you. *When I came back to the hotel Laura and Peter were shouting and bawling at each other... Then a voice bawled: 'Lay off! I'll kill you, you little rascal!'... He tried to direct the video like a fashion show, bawling instructions to the girls.* — VERB =yell; V *at* n; V with quote; V n
► **Bawl out** means the same as **bawl**. *Someone in the audience bawled out 'Not him again!'* — PHRASAL VERB =yell out; V P
2 If you say that a child **is bawling**, you are annoyed because it is crying loudly. *One of the toddlers was bawling, and the other had a runny nose. ...a bawling baby.* — VERB PRAGMATICS; V; V-ing

bawl out. If someone **bawls** you **out**, they shout at you angrily because you have done something wrong; an informal use. *Do you think I'm just going to bawl you out and that'll be an end of it?* ● See also **bawl** 1. — PHRASAL VERB =yell at; V n P; Also V P n (not pron)

bay /beɪ/ **bays, baying, bayed** ◆◆◆◇◇
1 A **bay** is a part of a coastline where the land curves inwards. *...a short ferry ride across the bay. ...the Bay of Bengal. ...the San Francisco Bay area.* — N-COUNT: oft in names
2 A **bay** is a partly enclosed area, inside or outside a — N-COUNT:

building, that is used for a particular purpose. *The animals are herded into a bay, then butchered... The car reversed into the loading bay.* oft supp N

3 On an aircraft or ship, a **bay** is a compartment that is used for carrying cargo or equipment. *...in the cargo bays of aircraft.* N-COUNT: usu n N =hold

4 A **bay** is an area of a room which extends beyond the main walls of a house, especially an area with a large window at the front of a house. N-COUNT

5 A **bay** horse is reddish-brown in colour. ADJ

6 If you say that a number of people **are baying** for something, you mean that they are shouting for something or demanding something angrily, usually that someone should be hurt or punished. *The referee ignored voices baying for a penalty... Opposition politicians have been baying for his blood. ...the baying crowd.* VB: usu cont =clamour V for n V-ing

7 If a dog or wolf **bays**, it makes loud, long cries, often because it is angry or in pain. *A dog suddenly howled, baying at the moon.* VERB V at n Also V

8 See also **sick bay**.

9 If you **keep** something or someone **at bay**, or **hold** them **at bay**, you prevent them from reaching, attacking, or affecting you. *Eating oranges keeps colds at bay... Prisoners armed with baseball bats used the hostages to hold police at bay.* PHRASE: V inflects

bay leaf, bay leaves. A **bay leaf** is a leaf of a small evergreen tree that can be dried and used as a herb in cooking. ◆◇◇◇◇ N-COUNT

bayonet /beɪənət/ **bayonets, bayoneting, bayoneted** ◆◇◇◇◇

1 A **bayonet** is a long, sharp blade that can be fixed to the end of a rifle and used as a weapon. N-COUNT

2 To **bayonet** someone means to stab them with a bayonet. *The soldiers were ordered by their inhuman officers to bayonet every man they could find.* VERB V n

bayou /baɪuː/ **bayous.** A **bayou** is a slow-moving, marshy tributary of a lake or river. N-COUNT

bay window, bay windows. A **bay window** is a window that sticks out from the outside wall of a house. N-COUNT

bazaar /bəzɑːʳ/ **bazaars** ◆◇◇◇◇

1 In areas such as the Middle East and India, a **bazaar** is a place where there are many small shops and stalls. *Kamal was a vendor in Egypt's open-air bazaar.* N-COUNT

2 A **bazaar** is a sale to raise money for charity. *...a church bazaar.* N-COUNT =fete

bazooka /bəzuːkə/ **bazookas.** A **bazooka** is a long, tube-shaped gun that is held on the shoulder and fires rockets. N-COUNT

BBC /biː biː siː/ ◆◆◆◆◇

1 **The BBC** is a British organization which broadcasts programmes on radio and television. **BBC** is an abbreviation for 'British Broadcasting Corporation'. *The concert will be broadcast live by the BBC. ...the BBC correspondent in Tunis.* N-PROPER: the N

2 **BBC** is used to refer to television channels and radio stations that are run by the BBC. *He begins his new series on BBC 2 at 9pm on Thursday. ...BBC Radio Scotland.* N-IN-NAMES

BC /biː siː/. You use **BC** in dates to indicate a number of years or centuries before the year in which Jesus Christ is believed to have been born. *The brooch dates back to the fourth century BC.* ◆◇◇◇◇

be 1 auxiliary verb uses

be /bi, STRONG biː/ **am, are, is, being, was, were, been** ◆◆◆◆◆

In spoken English forms of **be** are often contracted, for example 'I am' is contracted to 'I'm' and 'was not' is contracted to 'wasn't'.

1 You use **be** with a present participle to form the continuous tenses of verbs. *This is happening in every school throughout the country... She didn't always think carefully about what she was doing... Pratt & Whitney has announced that it will be making further job reductions... He had only been trying to help... He's doing better than I am.* • **be going to**: see **going**. AUX AUX-ing AUX

2 You use **be** with a past participle to form the passive voice. *Forensic experts were called in... Her husband was killed in a car crash... The cost of electricity from coal-fired stations is expected to fall... Similar action is being taken by the US government.* AUX AUX-ed

3 You use **be** with an infinitive to indicate that something is planned to happen, that it will definitely happen, or that it must happen. *The talks are to begin tomorrow... It was to be Johnson's first meeting with the board in nearly a month... You must take the whole project more seriously if you are to succeed... You are to answer to Brian, to take your orders from him.* • **be about to**: see **about**. AUX AUX to-inf

4 You use **be** with an infinitive to say or ask what should happen or be done in a particular situation, how it should happen, or who should do it. *What am I to do without him?... Who is to say which of them had more power?... What is to be done?... Professor Hirsch is to be commended for bringing the state of our educational system to public notice.* AUX AUX to-inf

5 You use **was** and **were** with an infinitive to talk about something that happened later than the time you are discussing, and was not planned or certain at that time. *He started something that was to change the face of China... A few hours later he was to prove it.* AUX AUX to-inf

6 You can say that something is **to be** seen, heard, or found in a particular place to mean that people can see it, hear it, or find it in that place. *Little traffic was to be seen on the streets... They are to be found all over the world.* AUX AUX -ed

be 2 other verb uses

be /bi, STRONG biː/ **am, are, is, being, was, were, been** ◆◆◆◆◆

In spoken English forms of **be** are often contracted, for example 'I am' is contracted to 'I'm' and 'was not' is contracted to 'wasn't'.

1 You use **be** to introduce more information about the subject, such as its identity, nature, qualities, or position. *She's my mother... This is Elizabeth Blunt, BBC, West Africa... He is a very attractive man... My grandfather was a butcher... The fact that you were willing to pay in the end is all that matters... He is fifty and has been through two marriages... The sky was black... It is 1,267 feet high... Cheney was in Madrid... His house is next door... Their last major film project was in 1964... 'Is it safe?'—'Well of course it is.'... He's still alive isn't he?... I was home and the children weren't.* V-LINK V n V adj V prep/adv V

2 You use **be**, with 'it' as the subject, in clauses where you are describing something or giving your judgement of a situation. *It was too chilly for swimming... Sometimes it is necessary to say no... It is likely that investors will face losses... It's nice having friends to chat to... It's a good thing I brought lots of handkerchiefs... It's no good just having meetings... It's a good idea to avoid refined food... It's up to us to prove it.* V-LINK it V adj it V adj to-inf it V adj that it V adj -ing it V n that it V n -ing it V n to-inf it V prep to-inf

3 You use **be** with the impersonal pronoun 'there' in expressions like **there is** and **there are** to say that something exists or happens. *Clearly there is a problem here... There are very few cars on this street... There was nothing new in the letter... There were always things to think about when she went walking.* V-LINK there V n

4 You use **be** as a link between a subject and a clause and in certain other clause structures, as exemplified below. *It was me she didn't like, not what I represented... What the media should not do is to exploit people's natural fears... Our greatest problem is convincing them... The question was whether protection could be improved... All she knew was that I'd had a broken marriage... Local residents said it was as if there had been a nuclear explosion.* V-LINK V n V to-inf V -ing V wh V that V as if

5 You use **be** in expressions like **the thing is** and **the point is** to introduce a clause in which you make a statement or give your opinion; used mainly in spoken English. *The fact is, the players gave everything they had... The plan is good; the problem is it doesn't go far enough.* V-LINK PRAGMATICS V cl

6 You use **be** in expressions like **to be fair**, **to be frank**, or **to be serious** to introduce an additional statement or opinion, and to indicate that you are trying to be fair, frank, or serious. *She's always noticed. But then, to be honest, Ghislaine likes being* V-LINK V adj

noticed... It enabled students to devote more time to their studies, or to be more accurate, more time to relaxation.

7 In formal English, the form **'be'** is used occasionally instead of the normal forms of the present tense, especially after 'whether'. *They should then be able to refer you to the appropriate type of practitioner, whether it be your GP, dentist, or optician.* V-LINK be n

8 If something **is**, it exists; used especially in literary or philosophical language. *It hurt so badly he wished to cease to be. ...to be or not to be.* VERB =exist V

9 To **be yourself** means to behave in the way that is right and natural for you and your personality. *She'd learnt to be herself and to stand up for her convictions.* V-LINK V pron-refl

10 If someone or something is, for example, **as** happy **as can be** or **as** quiet **as could be**, they are extremely happy or extremely quiet. PHRASES usu v-link PHR

11 If you talk about what would happen **if it wasn't for** someone or something, you mean that they are the only thing that is preventing it from happening. *I could happily move back into a flat if it wasn't for the fact that I'd miss my garden... If it hadn't been for her your father would be alive today.* V inflects, PHR n

12 You say **'Be that as it may'** when you want to move onto another subject or go further with the discussion, without deciding whether what has just been said is right or wrong. *'Is he still just as fat?'—'I wouldn't know,' continued her mother, ignoring the interruption, 'and be that as it may, he has made a fortune.'* PRAGMATICS

13 If you say that you **are not yourself**, you mean you are not feeling well. *She is not herself. She came near to a breakdown.* V inflects

be- /bɪ-/. **Be-** can be added to a noun followed by an '-ed' suffix to form an adjective that indicates that a person is covered with or wearing the specified thing. *...an elaborately bewigged and bejewelled Elizabeth I. ...a bespectacled librarian.* PREFIX

beach /biːtʃ/ **beaches, beaching, beached** ♦♦♦◇◇

1 A **beach** is an area of sand or pebbles beside the sea. *...a beautiful sandy beach... I just want to lie on the beach in the sun.* N-COUNT =seashore

2 If you **beach** something such as a boat, or if it **is beached**, it is pulled or forced out of the water and onto land. *We beached the canoe, running it right up the bank... The boat beached on a mud flat... Experts are unable to explain why the whales beached themselves.* V-ERG V n V V pron-refl

beach ball, beach balls. A **beach ball** is a large, light ball filled with air, which people play with, especially at the seaside. N-COUNT

beach bum, beach bums. If you refer to someone as a **beach bum**, you mean that they spend a lot of time enjoying themselves on the beach or in the sea. N-COUNT

beachcomber /biːtʃkoʊməʳ/ **beachcombers;** also spelled **beach-comber**. A **beachcomber** is someone who spends their time wandering along beaches looking for usable things, especially objects of value. N-COUNT

beachfront /biːtʃfrʌnt/. A **beachfront** house, cafe, shop, or hotel is situated on or by a beach. ADJ: ADJ n

beachhead /biːtʃhed/ **beachheads;** also spelled **beach-head**. A **beachhead** is an area of land next to the sea or a river where an attacking army has taken control and can prepare to advance further inland. N-COUNT

beacon /biːkən/ **beacons** ♦◇◇◇◇

1 A **beacon** is a light or a fire, usually on a hill or tower, which acts as a signal or a warning. N-COUNT

2 If someone or something acts as a **beacon** to other people, they inspire or encourage people because they are better than anyone else in some way. *Our Parliament has been a beacon of hope to the peoples of Europe... General Rudnicki was a moral beacon for many exiled Poles.* N-COUNT: usu N to/of/for n

bead /biːd/ **beads** ♦◇◇◇◇

1 Beads are small pieces of coloured glass, wood, or plastic with a hole through the middle. Beads are often put together on a piece of string or wire to make necklaces, bracelets, and other jewellery. *...a string of beads. ...a multicoloured bead necklace.* N-COUNT: usu pl

2 A **bead** of liquid or moisture is a small drop of it. *...beads of blood... He wiped away the beads of sweat on his forehead.* N-COUNT: usu N of n

beaded /biːdɪd/

1 A **beaded** dress, cushion, or other object is decorated with beads. ADJ: usu ADJ n

2 If something is **beaded** with a liquid, it is covered in small drops of that liquid. *The man's bald head was beaded with sweat... The cave walls were beaded with moisture.* ADJ: v-link ADJ with n

beading /biːdɪŋ/

1 Beading is a narrow strip of wood that is used for decorating or edging furniture and doors. N-UNCOUNT

2 Beading is an arrangement of beads used for decorating clothes. *...a black velvet bodice with jet black beading.* N-UNCOUNT

beady /biːdi/

1 Beady eyes are small, round, and bright. *Meg felt the old woman's beady eyes on her.* ADJ: usu ADJ n

2 If someone keeps a **beady** eye on a person or organization, they watch them carefully and suspiciously. *A woman concierge sat at a desk and kept a beady eye on people's comings and goings.* ADJ: ADJ n

beagle /biːgᵊl/ **beagles.** A **beagle** is a short-haired black and brown dog with long ears and short legs. It is kept as a pet or used for hunting hares. N-COUNT

beak /biːk/ **beaks** ♦◇◇◇◇

1 A bird's **beak** is the hard curved or pointed part of its mouth. *...a black bird with a yellow beak.* N-COUNT =bill

2 You can use 'the **beak**' to refer to someone in authority, such as a magistrate or a headmaster, who has the power to punish you; an old-fashioned, informal British use. *Take that man before the beak, officer, and throw away the key.* N-COUNT: usu sing, the N

beaker /biːkəʳ/ **beakers**

1 A **beaker** is a plastic cup used for drinking, usually one with no handle. N-COUNT

2 A **beaker** is a glass or plastic jar which is used in chemistry. N-COUNT

be-all and end-all. If something is **the be-all and end-all** to you, it is the only important thing in your life, or the only important feature of a particular activity. *For some people, competing is the be-all and end-all of their running.* PHRASE: v-link PHR, usu PHR of n PRAGMATICS

beam /biːm/ **beams, beaming, beamed** ♦♦◇◇◇

1 If you say that someone **is beaming**, you mean that they have a big smile on their face because they are happy, pleased, or proud about something; used in written English. *Frances beamed at her friend with undisguised admiration... 'Welcome back,' she beamed. ...the beaming face of a 41-year-old man on the brink of achieving his dreams.* VERB V at/with n V with quote V-ing

2 A **beam** is a line of energy, radiation, or particles sent in a particular direction. *...high-energy laser beams. ...a beam of neutrons.* N-COUNT: usu n N, N of n

3 If something such as radio signals or television pictures **are beamed** somewhere, or **beam** somewhere, they are sent there by means of electronic equipment. *The interview was beamed live across America... Soon, CMTV will be beaming into British homes via the Astra satellite. ...a ship which is due to begin beaming radio broadcasts to China.* V-ERG be V-ed prep/adv V prep/adv V n prep/adv

4 A **beam** of light is a line of light that shines from an object such as a torch or the sun. *Once or twice, a beam of light from a motorbike or a car swings past my window.* N-COUNT: usu N of n, n N

5 If something such as the sun or a lamp **beams** down, it sends light to a place and shines on it. *A sharp white spot-light beamed down on a small stage... All you see of the outside world is the sunlight beaming through the cracks in the roof.* VERB V adv/prep

6 A **beam** is a long thick bar of wood, metal, or concrete, especially one used to support the roof of a building. *The ceilings are supported by oak beams.* N-COUNT =plank, girder

7 The **beam** is a piece of gymnastic apparatus that consists of a horizontal wooden bar on which the gymnasts balance and perform movements. *She did a backwards somersault on the beam.* N-SING: usu the N

8 See also **off-beam**.

beam down. In science fiction stories, if someone **is beamed down**, or **beams down**, to a planet, they are transported there by means of special equipment which converts their body into energy or signals which can be transmitted. *They were beamed down from a distant solar system one night when we were asleep... An invisible being from outer space beams down to earth.*
PHRASAL VERB ERG; *be* V-ed P prep/adv; V P prep/adv

beam up. In science fiction stories, if someone **is beamed up**, or **beams up**, from a planet, they are transported away from it by means of special equipment which converts their body into energy or signals which can be transmitted. *It is as though my husband was beamed up into space and an alien came back instead of him.*
PHRASAL VERB ERG; *be* V-ed P prep/adv; Also V P

bean /biːn/ **beans** ◆◆◆◇◇

1 Beans such as green **beans**, french **beans**, or broad **beans** are the seeds of a tall climbing plant or the long thin cases which contain those seeds. N-COUNT: usu pl, usu adj N

2 Beans such as soya **beans** and kidney **beans** are the dried seeds of a bean plant. You soak them in water, then cook them and eat them as a vegetable. N-COUNT: usu pl, usu n N

3 Beans such as coffee **beans** or cocoa **beans** are the seeds of a plant that is used in the production of coffee and chocolate. N-COUNT: usu pl, usu n N

4 **Beans** are **baked beans**. *...sausage and beans.* N-COUNT

5 If someone hasn't got a **bean**, they have no money at all; an informal use. *It's quite incredible to think that he now hasn't got a bean... It doesn't cost a bean.* N-SING =penny

6 If someone is **full of beans**, they are very lively and have a lot of energy and enthusiasm. *Jem was full of beans after a long sleep.* PHRASES v-link PHR

7 If you **spill the beans**, you tell someone something that people have been trying to keep secret. V inflects

bean bag, bean bags; also spelled **beanbag**. A **bean bag** is a large round cushion filled with tiny polystyrene balls or foam rubber. It squashes into a comfortable shape when you sit on it. N-COUNT

bean counter, bean counters; also spelled **bean-counter**. If you disapprove of an accountant or business manager because you think they are only interested in how much money a business makes and spends, you can describe them as **bean counters**. *He believes the reason for their failure is that 'we have bean-counters running our companies.'* N-COUNT PRAGMATICS

beanfeast /biːnfiːst/ **beanfeasts.** In British English, a **beanfeast** is a party or other social event; an informal word. N-COUNT

beanpole /biːnpoul/ **beanpoles.** If you call someone a **beanpole**, you are criticizing them because you think that they are extremely tall and thin; an informal word. N-COUNT PRAGMATICS

bean sprout, bean sprouts; also spelled **beansprout**. **Bean sprouts** are small, long, thin shoots grown from beans. They are frequently used in Chinese cookery. N-COUNT

bear 1 verb uses

bear /beəʳ/ **bears, bearing, bore, borne** ◆◆◆◆◇

1 If you **bear** something somewhere, you carry it there or take it there; a literary use. *They bore the oblong hardwood box into the kitchen and put it on the table.* ♦ **-bearing** *...food-bearing lorries.* VERB =carry V n adv/prep; COMB in ADJ

2 If you **bear** something such as a weapon, you hold it or carry it with you; a formal use. *...the constitutional right to bear arms.* ♦ **-bearing** *...rifle-bearing soldiers. ...hundreds of flag-bearing marchers.* VERB V n; COMB in ADJ

3 If something **bears** the weight of something else, it supports the weight of that thing. *The ice was not thick enough to bear the weight of marching men.* ♦ **-bearing** *...the load-bearing joints of the body.* VERB =support V n; COMB in ADJ

4 If something **bears** a particular mark or characteristic, it has that mark or characteristic. *The houses bear the marks of bullet holes and the streets are practically deserted. ...note paper bearing the Presidential seal. ...a corporation he owned that bore his name... The room bore all the signs of a violent struggle.* VERB V n

5 If you **bear** an unpleasant experience, you accept it because you are unable to do anything about it. *They will have to bear the misery of living in constant fear of war... He bore his sufferings manfully.* VERB =endure V n

6 If you can't **bear** someone or something, you dislike them very much. *I can't bear people who make judgements and label me... I can't bear having to think what I'm going to say... He can't bear to talk about it, even to me.* VB: with neg V n/-ing V to-inf

7 If someone **bears** the cost of something, they pay for it. *Patients should not have to bear the costs of their own treatment.* VERB V n

8 If you **bear** the responsibility for something, you accept responsibility for it. *If a woman makes a decision to have a child alone, she should bear that responsibility alone.* VERB =accept V n

9 If something **bears** no resemblance or no relationship to something else, they are not at all like the second thing. *Their daily menus bore no resemblance whatsoever to what they were actually fed... For many software packages, the price bears little relation to cost.* VB: usu with brd-neg =have V n

10 When a plant or tree **bears** flowers, fruit, or leaves, it produces them. *As the plants grow and start to bear fruit they will need a lot of water.* ♦ **-bearing** *...a strong, fruit-bearing apple tree.* VERB =produce V n; COMB in ADJ

11 If something such as a bank account or an investment **bears** interest, interest is paid on it. *The eight-year bond will bear annual interest of 10.5%.* ♦ **-bearing** *...interest-bearing current accounts.* VERB V n; COMB in ADJ

12 When a woman **bears** a child, she gives birth to it; an old-fashioned use. *Emma bore a son called Karl... She bore him a daughter, Suzanna.* VERB V n V n n

13 If you **bear** someone a feeling such as love or hate, you feel that emotion towards them; a literary use. *She bore no ill will. If people didn't like her, too bad... I have lived with him on the best terms and bear him friendship.* VERB V n V n n

14 If you **bear** yourself in a particular way, you move or behave in that way; a literary use. *There was elegance and simple dignity in the way he bore himself.* VERB =carry V pron-refl adv/prep

15 If you **bear** left or **bear** right when you are driving or walking along, you turn and continue in that direction. *Go left onto the A107 and bear left into Seven Sisters Road.* VERB =veer V adv

16 See also **bore, borne.**

17 If you **bring** something **to bear** on a situation, you use it to deal with that situation. *British Scientists have brought computer science to bear on this problem.* PHRASES V inflects

18 If you **bring** pressure or influence **to bear on** someone, you use it to try and persuade them to do something. *His companions brought pressure to bear on him, urging him to stop wasting money.* V inflects

19 • **bear the brunt of**: see **brunt**. • **bear comparison**: see **comparison**. • **bear fruit**: see **fruit**. • **grin and bear it**: see **grin**. • **bear in mind**: see **mind**. • **bear witness**: see **witness**.

bear down PHRASAL VERB

1 If someone or something **bears down** on you, they move quickly towards you in a threatening way. *A group of half a dozen men entered the pub and bore down on the bar... The girl flashed a dazzling smile at the television crew and cameras bearing down on her.* =advance V P *on* n Also V P

2 To **bear down** on something means to push or press downwards with steady pressure. *The roof support structure had collapsed and the entire weight was bearing down on Adam's plasterwork.* V P *on* n Also V P

bear out. If someone or something **bears** a person **out** or **bears out** what that person is saying, they support what that person is saying. *Recent studies have borne out claims that certain perfumes can bring about profound psychological changes.* PHRASAL VERB =confirm ≠refute V P n (not pron) Also V n P

bear up. If you **bear up** when experiencing problems, you remain cheerful and show courage in spite of them. *How's Mary bearing up?... She was frightened that she would be unable to bear up under the pain of childbirth.* PHRASAL VERB =cope, hold up V P; V P *under* n

bear with. If you ask someone to **bear with** you, you are asking them to be patient. *If you'll bear with me, Frank, just let me try to explain.* PHRASAL VERB V P n

bear 2 noun uses

bear /beə^{r}/ **bears** ◆◇◇◇◇

1 A **bear** is a large, strong wild animal with thick fur and sharp claws. *They were camping in Jasper Country Park, Alberta, when Cherry was attacked by a bear.* N-COUNT

2 On the stock market, **bears** are people who sell shares in expectation of a drop in price, in order to make a profit by buying them back again after a short time. Compare **bull.** N-COUNT: usu pl

3 • **teddy bear**: see **teddy**. See also **polar bear**.

bearable /beərəb^{ə}l/. If something is **bearable**, you feel that you can accept it or deal with it. *A cool breeze made the heat pleasantly bearable.* ADJ-GRADED: usu v-link ADJ =tolerable

beard /bɪə^{r}d/ **beards.** A man's **beard** is the hair that grows on his chin and cheeks. *He's decided to grow a beard. ...Charlie's bushy black beard.* ◆◆◇◇◇ N-COUNT

bearded /bɪə^{r}dɪd/. A **bearded** man has a beard. *...a bearded 40-year-old sociology professor.* ◆◇◇◇◇ ADJ: usu ADJ n

bearer /beərə^{r}/ **bearers** ◆◇◇◇◇

1 The **bearer** of something such as a message is the person who brings it to you. *I hate to be the bearer of bad news.* N-COUNT: usu N *of* n

2 A **bearer** of a particular thing is a person who carries it, especially in a ceremony; a formal use. *...Britain's flag bearer at the Olympic Games opening ceremony... The Speaker is preceded by the mace-bearer upon his entry to the chamber.* N-COUNT: usu n N

3 The **bearer** of something such as a document, a right, or an official position is the person who possesses it or holds it; a formal use. *...the traditional bourgeois notion of the citizen as a bearer of rights... Later he called a meeting of his party's central office bearers... Spanish identity documents state the bearer's profession.* N-COUNT: oft N *of* n, n N =holder

4 The **bearer** of a tradition, idea, or characteristic is someone or something that is particularly associated with it and passes it on to other people or situations; a formal use. *Generally, the lower classes are considered to be the bearers of tradition.* N-COUNT: N *of* n =upholder

5 In former times, especially in India, a **bearer** was a native servant of a European. N-COUNT

6 See also **pallbearer**, **standard bearer**.

bear hug, bear hugs. A **bear hug** is a rather rough, tight, affectionate hug. *He lifted me off the ground with a bear hug.* N-COUNT

bearing /beərɪŋ/ **bearings** ◆◆◆◇◇

1 If something **has a bearing on** a situation or event, it is relevant to it. *Experts generally agree that diet has an important bearing on your general health... My father's achievements really don't have any bearing on what I do.* PHRASE: V inflects =influence

2 Someone's **bearing** is the way in which they move or stand; a literary use. *She later wrote warmly of his bearing and behaviour.* N-SING: usu poss N =manner

3 If you take a **bearing** with a compass, you use it to work out the direction in which a particular place lies or in which something is moving. N-COUNT =reading

4 If you **get** your **bearings** or **find** your **bearings**, you find out where you are or what you should do next. If you **lose** your **bearings**, you do not know where you are or what you should do next. *A sightseeing tour of the city is included to help you get your bearings... How badly the administration had lost its bearings was underlined by what happened yesterday.* PHRASE: V inflects

5 **Bearings** are small metal balls that are placed between moving parts of a machine in order to make them move smoothly and easily over each other. *An oil seal was replaced, along with both front wheel bearings.* • See also **ball bearing**. N-COUNT: usu pl

-bearing /-beərɪŋ/. **-bearing** combines with nouns to form adjectives which describe things that hold the specified substance inside them. *...oil-bearing rocks. ...snow-bearing clouds. ...malaria-bearing mosquitos.* COMB in ADJ =-carrying

bearish /beərɪʃ/. On the stock market, if there is a **bearish** sentiment, prices are expected to fall. Compare **bullish**. *Dealers said investors remain bearish... Many traders forecast a continuation of the market's recent bearish trend.* ADJ-GRADED

bear market, bear markets. A **bear market** is a situation on the stock market when people are selling a lot of shares because they expect that the shares will decrease in value and that they will be able to make a profit by buying them again after a short time. Compare **bull market**. N-COUNT ≠bull market

bearskin /beə^{r}skɪn/ **bearskins**

1 A **bearskin** is a tall fur hat that is worn by some British soldiers on ceremonial occasions. N-COUNT

2 A **bearskin** is the skin and fur of a bear, used for example as a rug or a cover. N-COUNT

beast /biːst/ **beasts** ◆◆◇◇◇

1 You can refer to an animal as a **beast**, especially if it is a large, dangerous, or unusual one; a literary use. *...the threats our ancestors faced from wild beasts. ...a centaur: half man, half beast.* N-COUNT

2 If you refer to a man as a **beast**, you mean that his behaviour, especially his sexual behaviour, is very violent and uncontrolled; used in journalism. *...a sex beast who subjected two sisters to a terrifying ordeal.* N-COUNT: usu with supp

3 If you call someone a **beast**, you strongly disapprove of them because you think that they are behaving in a selfish, cruel, or unpleasant way; an old-fashioned, informal use. *Bully! Hooligan! Beast! Let me go, let go!* N-COUNT; N-VOC PRAGMATICS

4 You can use **beast** to refer to something or someone in a light-hearted way, and to mention that they have a particular quality. *...that rare beast, a sports movie that isn't boring.* N-COUNT: usu adj N =animal

beastly /biːstli/

1 If you describe something as **beastly**, you mean that it is very unpleasant; an old-fashioned, informal use. *The weather was beastly.* ADJ-GRADED =horrible, horrid

2 If you describe someone as **beastly**, you mean that they are unkind, mean, and spiteful; an old-fashioned, informal use. *He must be wondering why everyone is being so beastly to him.* ADJ-GRADED =horrible, horrid

beast of burden, beasts of burden. A **beast of burden** is an animal such as an ox or a donkey that is used for carrying or pulling things. N-COUNT

beat /biːt/ **beats, beating, beaten** The form **beat** is used in the present tense and is also the past tense. ◆◆◆◆◆

1 If you **beat** someone or something, you hit them very hard. *My wife tried to stop them and they beat her... They were beaten to death with baseball bats.* VERB V n, V n *to* n

2 If someone or something **beats** on, at, or against something, or beats something, they hit it hard, usually several times or continuously for a period of time. *There was dead silence but for a fly beating against the glass... Nina managed to free herself and began beating at the flames with a pillow... The rain was beating on the windowpanes.* ▶ Also a noun. *...the rhythmic beat of the surf.* ♦ **beating** *...the silence broken only by the beating of the rain.* VERB =pound; V *against* n, V *at* n, V *on* n, Also V n; N-SING: usu *the* N *of* n; N-SING: usu *the* N *of* n

3 When your heart or pulse **beats**, it continually makes regular rhythmic movements. *I felt my heart beating faster.* ▶ Also a noun. *He could hear the beat of his heart... Most people's pulse rate is more than 70 beats per minute.* ♦ **beating** *I could hear the beating of my heart.* VERB V; N-COUNT: usu with supp; N-SING: usu *the* N *of* n

4 If you **beat** a drum or similar instrument, you hit it in order to make a sound. When a drum **beats**, it makes a sound. *When you beat the drum, you feel good. ...drums beating and pipes playing.* ▶ Also a noun. *...the rhythmical beat of the drum.* V-ERG V n, V; N-SING: usu *the* N *of* n

5 The **beat** of a piece of music is the main rhythm that it has. *...the thumping beat of rock music. ...the dance beats of the last two decades.* N-COUNT: usu sing, *the* N

6 In music, a **beat** is a unit of measurement. The number of beats in a bar of a piece of music is indicated by two numbers at the beginning of the piece. *It's got four beats to a bar.* • See also **upbeat**, **downbeat**. N-COUNT: usu pl

7 If you **beat** eggs, cream, or butter, you mix them thoroughly using a fork or whisk. *Beat the eggs and sugar until they start to thicken.* VERB V n

8 When a bird or insect **beats** its wings or when its wings **beat**, its wings move up and down. *Beating their wings they flew off... Its wings beat slowly.* V-ERG V n, V

9 If you **beat** someone in a competition or election, VERB

you defeat them. *In yesterday's games, Switzerland beat the United States two-one... There are men who simply don't like being beaten by a woman... She was easily beaten into third place.*
V n
V n *into* n

10 If someone **beats** a record or achievement, they do better than it. *He was as eager as his Captain to beat the record.*
VERB
V n

11 If you **beat** something that you are fighting against, for example an organization, a problem, or a disease, you defeat it. *It became clear that the Union was not going to beat the government... They recognise that tough action offers the only hope of beating inflation... Kate Jackson is expecting her first child at 43 – two years after beating breast cancer.*
VERB
=conquer
V n

12 If an attack **is beaten** off or **is beaten** back, it is stopped, often temporarily. *The Croatian state radio claims the attack was beaten back... South Africa's ruling National Party has beaten off a right-wing challenge.*
VB: usu passive
be V-ed adv
V adv n

13 If you say that one thing **beats** another, you mean that it is better than it; an informal use. *Being boss of a software firm beats selling insurance... Nothing quite beats the luxury of soaking in a long, hot bath at the end of a tiring day... For an evening stroll the beach at Dieppe is hard to beat.*
VB: no cont
V n

14 If you say you can't **beat** a particular thing you mean that it is the best thing of its kind. *You can't beat soap and water for cleansing.*
VB: no cont
V n

15 To **beat** a time limit or an event means to achieve something before that time or event. *They were trying to beat the midnight deadline... Those who shop on Sunday to beat the rush are wasting their time.*
VERB
V n

16 A police officer's **beat** is the area for which he or she is responsible. *The team police get to know the people in their patrol areas better than cops who must cover a larger beat.*
N-COUNT

17 You use **beat** in expressions such as 'It beats me' or 'What beats me is' to indicate that you cannot understand or explain something; an informal expression. *'What am I doing wrong, anyway?'—'Beats me, Lewis.'... How you can be so insensitive absolutely beats me.*
PHRASE

18 If you tell someone to **beat it**, you are telling them to go away; an informal expression. *Beat it before it's too late.*
PHRASE
=get lost

19 You can say **Can you beat it?** or **Can you beat that?** to show that you are surprised and perhaps annoyed about something; an informal expression. *Can you beat it; there was Graham Greene in Freetown and there was I on the other side of Africa.*
CONVENTION

20 See also **beaten**, **beaten-up**, **beating**, **beat-up**.

21 If you intend to do something but someone **beats** you **to it**, they do it before you do. *Don't be too long about it or you'll find someone has beaten you to it.*
PHRASES
V inflects

22 **If you can't beat them, join them** means that, if someone is too strong for you to defeat, it is better to be on the same side as them; an informal expression.

23 A police officer **on the beat** is on duty, walking around the area for which he or she is responsible. *The officer on the beat picks up information; hears cries for help; makes people feel safe.*
usu n PHR,
v-link PHR

24 If you **beat time** to a piece of music, you move your hand or foot up and down in time with the music. A conductor **beats time** to show the choir or orchestra how fast they should sing or play the music. *He beats time with hands and feet.*
V inflects
=keep time

25 • to **beat** someone **black and blue**: see **black**. • to **beat** someone's **brains out**: see **brain**. • to **beat** one's **breast**: see **breast**. • to **beat about the bush**: see **bush**. • to **beat the clock**: see **clock**. • to **beat or knock the living daylights out of** someone: see **daylights**. • to **beat the drum for** someone or something: see **drum**. • to **beat** someone **at their own game**: see **game**. • to **beat a path to** someone's **door**: see **path**. • to **beat a retreat**: see **retreat**. • to **beat, kick or knock the shit out of** someone: see **shit**. • **a stick to beat** someone **with**: see **stick**.

beat down
PHRASAL VERB

1 When the sun **beats down**, it is very hot and bright. *The sun was beating down.*
V P

2 When the rain **beats down**, it rains very hard. *Even in the winter with the rain beating down, it's nice and cosy in there.*
V P

3 If you **beat down** a person who is selling you something, you force them to accept a lower price for it than they wanted to get. *A fair employer, when arranging for the pay of a carpenter, does not try to beat him down... Beat down the seller to the price that suits you.*
=barter down
V n P
V P n

beat out
PHRASAL VERB

1 If you **beat out** sounds on a drum or similar instrument, you make the sounds by hitting the instrument. *Drums and cymbals beat out a solemn rhythm.*
=tap out
V P n

2 If you **beat out** a fire, you cause it to go out by hitting it, usually with an object such as a blanket. *His brother beat out the flames with a blanket... She managed to beat the fire out.*
V P n
V n P

3 If you **beat out** someone in a competition, you defeat them; used mainly in American English. *Indianapolis has beat out nearly 100 other cities as the site for a huge United Airlines maintenance center... If we are certain a rival will beat us out, we are wide open to jealousy.*
V P n
V n P

beat up. If someone **beats** a person **up**, they hit or kick the person many times. *Then they actually beat her up as well... The government supporters are beating up anyone they suspect of favouring the demonstrators.* ♦ **beating-up, beatings-up** *There had been no violence, no beatings up until then.*
PHRASAL VERB
V n P
V P n (not pron)
N-COUNT

beat up on. In American English, if someone **beats up on** a person or **beats on** them, they hit or kick the person many times. *He beat up on my brother's kid one time.*
PHRASAL VERB
V P P n
Also V P n

beatable /biːtəbəl/. Someone who is **beatable** can be beaten. *They have a lot of talent, are very aggressive and play tough defence. But they are beatable.*
ADJ-GRADED:
v-link ADJ

beaten /biːtən/ ◆◆◆◇◇

1 **Beaten** earth has been pressed down, often by people's feet, until it is hard. *Before you is a well-worn path of beaten earth.*
ADJ:
ADJ n
=trampled

2 A place that is **off the beaten track** is in an area where not many people live or go. *Tiny secluded beaches can be found off the beaten track.*
PHRASE

beaten-up. A **beaten-up** car or other object is old and in bad condition. *The robber must have mistaken his old, beaten-up black leather jacket for an expensive new one.*
◆◇◇◇◇
ADJ-GRADED:
ADJ n
=battered

beater /biːtər/ **beaters** ◆◇◇◇◇

1 A **beater** is a tool or part of a machine which is used for beating things like eggs and cream. *Whisk the batter with a wire whisk or hand beater until it is smooth and light.*
N-COUNT:
oft n N
=whisk

2 A **beater** is a person who helps hunters by driving animals and birds into the open so that they can be shot. *The beaters began moving forward in a line, smashing at the soft ground with their sticks.*
N-COUNT

3 See also **world beater**.

beatific /biːətɪfɪk/. A **beatific** expression shows or expresses great happiness and calmness; a literary word. *He smiled an almost beatific smile.*
ADJ-GRADED:
usu ADJ n
=blissful

beatify /biætɪfaɪ/ **beatifies, beatifying, beatified.** To **beatify** someone means to declare formally in a church ceremony that someone who is dead is a blessed person, usually as the first step in making them a saint. *In May, Pope John Paul is to beatify Gianna Beretta.* ♦ **beatification** /biætɪfɪkeɪʃən/ *Thousands attended the beatification of Juan Diego.*
VERB
=sanctify
V n
N-UNCOUNT

beating /biːtɪŋ/ **beatings** ◆◆◆◇◇

1 If someone is given a **beating**, they are hit hard many times, especially with something such as a stick. *...the savage beating of a black motorist by white police officers... The team secured pictures of prisoners showing signs of severe beatings.*
N-COUNT

2 If something such as a business, a political party, or a team takes a **beating**, it is defeated by a large
N-SING:
a N

amount in a competition or election. *Our firm has taken a terrible beating in recent years.*

3 If you say that something will **take some beating**, you mean that it is very good and it is unlikely that anything better will be done or made; an informal expression. *For sheer scale and grandeur, Leeds Castle in Kent takes some beating.* PHRASE: V inflects

beatnik /biːtnɪk/ **beatniks.** **Beatniks** were young people in the late 1950's who rejected traditional ways of living, dressing, and behaving. People sometimes use the word beatnik to refer to anyone who lives in an unconventional way. *Rose's mother was a beatnik art student who bought Beatles records and took her children to Bob Marley concerts.* N-COUNT

beat-up. ◆◇◇◇◇ A **beat-up** car or other object is old and in bad condition; an informal word. *...a beat-up old Fiat 131.* ADJ-GRADED: ADJ n =battered

beau /boʊ/ **beaux** or **beaus.** A woman's **beau** is her boyfriend or admirer; an old-fashioned word. *She appeared with her new beau.* N-COUNT: oft poss N =suitor

beaut /bjuːt/ **beauts.** You describe someone or something as a **beaut** when you think they are very good; an informal word, used mainly in Australia and New Zealand. *She was a beaut.* N-COUNT

beauteous /bjuːtiəs/. **Beauteous** means the same as beautiful; a literary word. *...the beauteous Miss Flora Montgomery.* ADJ-GRADED

beautician /bjuːtɪʃᵊn/ **beauticians.** A **beautician** is a person whose job is giving people beauty treatments such as manicuring their nails, treating their skin, and putting on their make-up. N-COUNT

beautiful /bjuːtɪfʊl/ ◆◆◆◆◇

1 A **beautiful** woman or child is very attractive to look at. *She was a very beautiful woman... To me he is the most beautiful child in the world.* ADJ-GRADED ≠ugly

2 If you describe something as **beautiful**, you mean that it is very attractive or pleasing. *New England is beautiful... It was a beautiful morning... He has beautiful manners.* ♦ **beautifully** /bjuːtɪfli/ *The children behaved beautifully. ...a beautifully clear, sunny day.* ADJ-GRADED =delightful; ADV-GRADED: usu ADV after v

3 You can describe something that someone does as **beautiful** when they do it very skilfully. *That's a beautiful shot!* ♦ **beautifully** *Arsenal played beautifully.* ADJ-GRADED; ADV-GRADED: ADV after v, ADV -ed

beautify /bjuːtɪfaɪ/ **beautifies, beautifying, beautified.** If you **beautify** something, you make it look more beautiful; a formal word. *Claire worked to beautify the garden.* VERB =smarten; V n

beauty /bjuːti/ **beauties** ◆◆◆◇◇

1 **Beauty** is the state or quality of being beautiful. *...an area of outstanding natural beauty... Everyone admired her elegance and her beauty.* N-UNCOUNT

2 A **beauty** is a beautiful woman; used in journalism. *She is known as a great beauty.* N-COUNT =belle

3 You can say that something is a **beauty** when you think it is very good; an informal use. *It was the one opportunity in the game – the pass was a real beauty, but the shot was poor.* N-COUNT =peach

4 The **beauties** of something are its attractive qualities or features; a literary use. *He was beginning to enjoy the beauties of nature.* N-COUNT: usu pl, with supp =glories

5 **Beauty** is used to describe people, products, and activities that are concerned with making women look beautiful. *Additional beauty treatments can be booked in advance.* ADJ: ADJ n

6 If you say that a particular feature is the **beauty** of something, you mean that this feature is what makes the thing so good. *There would be no effect on animals – that's the beauty of such water-based materials.* N-COUNT: usu *the* N *of* n =boon

beauty contest, beauty contests. A **beauty contest** is a competition in which young women parade in front of judges who decide which one is the most beautiful. *She was nineteen when she entered the Miss Oregon beauty contest.* N-COUNT

beauty parlour, beauty parlours. A **beauty parlour** is a place where women can go to have treatment to make them look more beautiful, for example to have their nails manicured. N-COUNT =salon

beauty queen, beauty queens. A **beauty queen** is a woman who has won a beauty contest. N-COUNT

beauty salon, beauty salons. A **beauty salon** is the same as a **beauty parlour**. N-COUNT

beauty sleep. If someone goes to bed early saying that they need their **beauty sleep**, they are joking that they need a lot of sleep to help them stay looking young and beautiful. N-UNCOUNT: usu poss N

beauty spot, beauty spots

1 A **beauty spot** is a place in the country that is popular because of its beautiful scenery. *The Valley of Vinales is a lush and fertile valley and one of Cuba's finest beauty spots.* N-COUNT

2 A **beauty spot** is a small, dark spot on the skin which is supposed to add to a woman's beauty. N-COUNT

beaver /biːvəʳ/ **beavers, beavering, beavered** ◆◇◇◇◇

1 A **beaver** is a furry animal like a large rat with a big flat tail. Beavers build dams in streams. N-COUNT

2 **Beaver** is the fur of a beaver, when it is used for making coats, hats, and other clothes. *...elegant moosehide slippers trimmed with beaver.* N-UNCOUNT

beaver away. If you **are beavering away** at something, you are working very hard at it. *They had a team of architects beavering away at a scheme for the rehabilitation of District 6... They are beavering away to get everything ready for us.* PHRASAL VERB: V P *at/on* n, V P

bebop /biːbɒp/. **Bebop** is a form of jazz music with complex harmonies and rhythms. The abbreviation 'bop' is also used. N-UNCOUNT

becalmed /bɪkɑːmd/

1 If a sailing ship is **becalmed**, it is unable to move because there is no wind. *We found ourselves becalmed off Dungeness for several hours.* ADJ: usu v-link ADJ =stranded

2 If something such as the economy, a company, or a series of talks is **becalmed**, it is not progressing at all, although it should be. *Polish industry generally is becalmed. ...the becalmed peace talks.* ADJ =stagnant

became /bɪkeɪm/. **Became** is the past tense of **become**.

because /bɪkʌz, AM bɪkɔːz/ ◆◆◆◆◆

1 You use **because** when stating the reason for something. *He is called Mitch, because his name is Mitchell... Because it is an area of outstanding natural beauty, the number of boats available for hire on the river is limited... Women are doing the job well. This is partly because women are increasingly moving into a man's world... 'Why didn't you tell me, Archie?'—'Because you might have casually mentioned it to somebody else.'* CONJ-SUBORD

2 You use **because** when stating the explanation for a statement you have just made. *Maybe they just didn't want to ask too many questions, because they rented us a room without even asking to see our papers... The President has played a shrewd diplomatic game because from the outset he called for direct talks with the United States... I had a sense of deja vu because I could recognise everything in London.* CONJ-SUBORD PRAGMATICS

3 If an event or situation occurs **because of** something, that thing is the reason or cause. *Many families break up because of a lack of money... Because of the law in Ireland, we had to work out a way of getting her over to Britain.* PHR-PREP

4 You use **just because** in informal spoken English when you want to say that a particular situation should not necessarily make you come to a particular conclusion. *Just because it has a good tune does not mean it is great music... Just because something has always been done a certain way does not make it right.* PHR-CONJ-SUBORD

beck /bek/. If one person is **at** another's **beck and call**, they have to be constantly available and ready to do whatever they ask, and this seems unfair or undesirable. PHRASE: v-link PHR

beckon /bekən/ **beckons, beckoning, beckoned** ◆◇◇◇◇

1 If you **beckon** to someone, you signal to them to come to you. *He beckoned to the waiter... I beckoned her over... Hughes beckoned him to sit down on a sofa.* VERB: V *to* n, V n adv/prep, V n to-inf, Also V

2 If something **beckons**, it is so attractive to some- VERB

one that they feel they must become involved in it. *All the attractions of the peninsula beckon... The bright lights of Hollywood beckon many.* V / V n / Also V *to* n

3 If something **beckons** for someone, it is very likely to happen to them. *The big time beckons for Billy Dodds... Old age beckons.* VERB / V *for* n / V

become /bɪkʌm/ **becomes, becoming, became, become** ◆◆◆◆◆

1 If someone or something **becomes** a particular thing, they start to change and develop into that thing, or start to develop the characteristics mentioned. *I first became interested in Islam while I was doing my nursing training... The cocoa industry dwindled because it became increasingly difficult to cover costs... During the 1980s the world's financial systems became more open... The pilot decided to land, but as we lost altitude the wind became stronger... As she reached the age of thirty she became convinced she would remain single all her life... After leaving school, he became a professional footballer... In 1823 Honduras became a part of the United Provinces of Central America.* V-LINK =get / V adj / V -ed / V n

2 If something **becomes** someone, it makes them look attractive or it seems right for them. *Does Khaki become you?... Don't be crude tonight, Bernard, it doesn't become you.* VB: no passive, no cont =suit / V n

3 If you wonder **what has become of** someone or something, you wonder where they are and what has happened to them. *She thought constantly about her family; she might never know what had become of them... Where will he go to school now he's been thrown out of Eton? What will become of him?* PHRASE: V inflects

becoming /bɪkʌmɪŋ/

1 A piece of clothing, a colour, or a hairstyle that is **becoming** makes the person who is wearing it look attractive; a rather old-fashioned use. *Softer fabrics are much more becoming than stiffer ones.* ADJ-GRADED: usu v-link ADJ =fetching

♦ **becomingly** *Her dress was of blue silk, quite light, and becomingly open at the neck.* ADV

2 Behaviour that is **becoming** is appropriate and proper in the circumstances. *This behaviour is not any more becoming among our politicians than it is among our voters.* ADJ-GRADED: usu v-link ADJ =appropriate

bed /bed/ **beds, bedding, bedded** ◆◆◆◆◇

1 A **bed** is a piece of furniture that you lie on when you sleep. *She went into her bedroom and lay down on the bed... We finally went to bed at about 4am... By the time we got back from dinner, Nona was already in bed... When she had gone Sam and Robina put the children to bed.* N-COUNT: also prep N

2 If a place such as a hospital or a hotel has a particular number of **beds**, it is able to accommodate that number of patients or guests. *The total number of beds for the regular in-patient program was reduced to 14... People are unable to find a bed and the prices are worse than New York.* N-COUNT

3 A **bed** in a garden or park is an area of ground that has been specially prepared so that plants can be grown in it. *The geraniums in the flower bed looked bedraggled from the heavy rain. ...beds of strawberries and rhubarb.* N-COUNT: usu n N, N *of* n

4 A **bed** of shellfish or vegetation is an area in the sea or in a lake where a particular type of shellfish or vegetation is found in large quantities. *Fishermen fear valuable oyster and mussel beds could be decimated... The whole lake was rimmed with thick beds of reeds.* N-COUNT: usu with supp

5 The sea **bed** or a river **bed** is the ground at the bottom of the sea or of a river. *For three weeks a big operation went on to recover the wreckage from the sea bed. ...the bare bed of a dry stream.* N-COUNT: usu sing, usu with supp

6 A **bed** of rock is a layer of rock that is found within a larger area of rock. *Between the white limestone and the greyish pink limestone is a thin bed of clay. ...a sandstone bed.* N-COUNT: usu with supp =stratum

7 If a recipe or a menu says that something is served on a **bed** of a food such as rice or vegetables, it means it is served on a layer of that food. *Heat the curry thoroughly and serve it on a bed of rice.* N-COUNT: usu sing, N *of* n

8 See also **-bedded, bedding**.

9 If someone **gets** someone else **into bed**, they persuade them to have sex with them. *Be careful. He might just try to get you into bed.* PHRASES / V inflects

10 To **go to bed** with someone means to have sex with them. *I'd never go to bed with any man unless I was married to him... Later that evening, Forbes and Rosanna went to bed together for the first time.* RECIP: V inflects, PHR *with* n, pl-n PHR

11 If you say that someone is **in bed** with someone else, you mean that they are having sex in bed. *He found his wife in bed with his best friend.* V-link PHR, PHR after v, usu PHR *with* n

12 You can use **in bed** to refer to sexual activity. For example, if you say that someone is good **in bed**, you mean that they are a skilful lover. *We complement one another perfectly, especially in bed.*

13 If you say that someone **has made** their **bed**, and now they must **lie in it** or **on it**, you mean that since they have chosen to do a particular thing, they must now accept the unpleasant results of their action.

14 When you **make** the **bed**, you neatly arrange the sheets and covers of a bed so that it is ready to sleep in. *Holly Lathan had just finished making the bed when the telephone beside it began to ring... Maria came up to make my bed and do the room.* V and N inflect

15 If you say that someone **got out of bed on the wrong side**, you mean that they have been cross ever since they woke up that morning. V inflects

16 ● **bed of roses**: see **rose**.

bed down. If you **bed down** somewhere, you sleep there for the night, instead of in bed. *On those nights when they could find no monastery or inn to take them in, they bedded down in the fields.* PHRASAL VERB / V P prep/adv

BEd /biː ed/ **BEds.** In Britain, a **BEd** is a degree which qualifies someone to teach in a state school. BEd courses usually last four years. **BEd** is an abbreviation for 'Bachelor of Education.' Compare **PGCE**. N-COUNT

bed and breakfast, bed and breakfasts; also spelled **bed-and-breakfast**. ◆◇◇◇◇

1 In Britain, **bed and breakfast** is a system of accommodation in a hotel or guest house in which you pay for a room for the night and for breakfast the following morning. The abbreviation **B&B** is also used. *Bed and breakfast costs from £20 per person per night. ...a small bed and breakfast hotel near London.* N-UNCOUNT

2 In Britain, a **bed and breakfast** is a guest house that provides bed and breakfast accommodation. The abbreviation **B&B** is also used. *Accommodation can be arranged at local bed and breakfasts.* N-COUNT

bedazzled /bɪdæzəld/. If you are **bedazzled** by someone or something, you are so amazed and impressed by them that you feel confused. *Many people are bedazzled by fame.* ADJ-GRADED: oft ADJ *by* n

bedbug /bedbʌg/ **bedbugs.** A **bedbug** is a small insect with a round body and no wings which lives in dirty houses and feeds by biting people and sucking their blood when they are in bed. N-COUNT =parasite

bedchamber /bedtʃeɪmbəʳ/ **bedchambers;** also spelled **bed-chamber**. A **bedchamber** is a bedroom; a formal word. *...the royal bedchamber.* N-COUNT

bedclothes /bedkloʊðz/. **Bedclothes** are the sheets and covers which you put over yourself when you get into bed. N-PLURAL

-bedded /-bedɪd/. **-bedded** combines with numbers to form adjectives which indicate how many beds a room contains. **-bedded** combines with words such as 'twin' or 'double' to form adjectives which indicate what kind of beds a room contains. *...a four-bedded room. ...twin-bedded cabins.* COMB in ADJ: usu ADJ n

bedding /bedɪŋ/. **Bedding** is sheets, blankets, and covers that are used on beds. ◆◇◇◇◇ N-UNCOUNT

bedding plant, bedding plants. A **bedding plant** is a plant which lasts for one year. It is put in a flower bed before it flowers, and is then removed when it has finished flowering. N-COUNT

bedeck /bɪdek/ **bedecks, bedecking, bedecked.** If flags or other ornaments **bedeck** a place, a lot of them have been hung up to decorate it. *Today, flags bedeck the balcony from which he spoke to the assembled crowd.* VERB / V n

bedecked /bɪdekt/. If a place is **bedecked** with flags or other ornaments, these things have been hung up to decorate it. *On Thanksgiving the American Legation was bedecked with flags.* ► Also a combining form. *...a flower-bedecked stage.* ADJ: v-link ADJ with/in n, adv ADJ; COMB in ADJ

bedevil /bɪdevəl/ **bedevils, bedevilling, bedevilled;** spelled **bedeviling, bedeviled** in American English. If you **are bedevilled** by something unpleasant, it causes you a lot of problems over a period of time; a formal word. *His career was bedevilled by injury... The development has been bedevilled with problems. ...a problem that has bedevilled service industries for decades.* VERB =frustrate; be V-ed; V n

bedfellow /bedfelou/ **bedfellows.** You refer to two things or people as **bedfellows** when they have become associated or related in some way. *It's possible to be bedfellows with someone on one issue, and at odds with them on another... Sex and death are strange bedfellows.* N-COUNT: usu pl

bedhead /bedhed/ **bedheads;** also spelled **bed-head.** A **bedhead** is a board which is fixed to the end of a bed behind your head. N-COUNT

bedlam /bedləm/. **Bedlam** means a great deal of noise and disorder. People often say 'It was bedlam' to mean 'There was bedlam'. *The crowd went absolutely mad. It was bedlam... He is causing bedlam at the hotel.* N-UNCOUNT =chaos

bed linen; also spelled **bed-linen. Bed linen** is sheets and pillowcases. *...crisp white cotton bed linen.* N-UNCOUNT

Bedouin /beduɪn/ **Bedouins. Bedouin** can also be used as the plural form.

1 A **Bedouin** is a member of a particular nomadic Arab tribe. *The Bedouins still mostly live in traditional tents... My parents were Bedouin.* N-COUNT

2 **Bedouin** means relating to the Bedouin people. *...a tent-like roof made of Bedouin carpets.* ADJ

bedpan /bedpæn/ **bedpans;** also spelled **bed-pan.** A **bedpan** is a shallow bowl shaped like a toilet seat, which is used instead of a toilet by people who are too ill to get out of bed. N-COUNT

bedpost /bedpoust/ **bedposts;** also spelled **bed-post.** A **bedpost** is one of the four vertical supports at the corners of a bed with an old-fashioned wooden or iron frame. N-COUNT

bedraggled /bɪdrægəld/. Someone or something that is **bedraggled** looks untidy because they have got wet or dirty. *He looked weary and bedraggled. ...a bedraggled group of journalists.* ADJ-GRADED =scruffy

bedridden /bedrɪdən/. Someone who is **bedridden** is so ill or disabled that they cannot get out of bed. *He had to spend two years bedridden with an injury. ...bedridden patients.* ADJ

bedrock /bedrɒk/ ◆◇◇◇◇

1 The **bedrock** of something is the principles, ideas, or facts on which it is based. *Mutual trust is the bedrock of a relationship... Working-class voters form the bedrock of Labour's support. ...the bedrock principles of British democratic socialism.* N-SING =foundation

2 **Bedrock** is the solid rock in the ground which supports all the soil above it. *It took five years to drill down to bedrock.* N-UNCOUNT

bedroll /bedroul/ **bedrolls;** also spelled **bed-roll.** A **bedroll** is a rolled-up sleeping bag or other form of bedding, which you can carry with you. N-COUNT

bedroom /bedru:m/ **bedrooms.** A **bedroom** is a room used for sleeping in. *...the spare bedroom. ...a two-bedroom apartment.* ◆◆◆◇◇ N-COUNT

-bedroomed /-bedru:md/. **-bedroomed** combines with numbers to form adjectives which indicate how many bedrooms a particular house or flat has. *She moved into a two-bedroomed flat.* COMB in ADJ

bedside /bedsaɪd/ ◆◇◇◇◇

1 Your **bedside** is the area beside your bed. *She put a cup of tea down on the bedside table... He drew a chair up to the bedside and sat down.* N-SING: usu N n

2 If you talk about being at someone's **bedside**, you are talking about being near them when they are ill in bed. *She kept vigil at the bedside of her critically ill son... She was called to her brother's bedside.* N-SING: usu with poss

bedside manner. A doctor's **bedside manner** is the way in which they talk to a patient, and the extent to which this is friendly and reassuring. *Brafman had a good bedside manner and got on well with patients.* N-SING

bedsit /bedsɪt/ **bedsits.** In British English, a **bedsit** is a room you rent which you use for both living in and sleeping in. *He was living alone in a dingy bedsit in London.* N-COUNT =bedsitter

bedsitter /bedsɪtəʳ/ **bedsitters;** also spelled **bed-sitter.** In British English, a **bedsitter** is the same as a **bedsit.** N-COUNT

bedsores /bedsɔːʳz/. **Bedsores** are sore places on a person's skin, caused by having to lie in bed for a long time without changing position. N-PLURAL

bedspread /bedspred/ **bedspreads.** A **bedspread** is a decorative cover which is put over a bed, on top of the sheets and blankets. N-COUNT =coverlet

bedstead /bedsted/ **bedsteads.** A **bedstead** is the metal or wooden frame of an old-fashioned bed. *...an old iron bedstead.* N-COUNT

bedtime /bedtaɪm/. Your **bedtime** is the time when you usually go to bed. *It was eight-thirty, Trevor's bedtime. ...bedtime stories.* ◆◇◇◇◇ N-UNCOUNT

bedwetting /bedwetɪŋ/; also spelled **bed-wetting. Bedwetting** means urinating in bed, usually by small children. N-UNCOUNT

bee /bi:/ **bees** ◆◆◇◇◇

1 A **bee** is an insect with a yellow-and-black striped body that makes a buzzing noise as it flies. Bees make honey, and live in large groups. N-COUNT

2 If you **have a bee in** your **bonnet** about something, you are so enthusiastic or worried about it that you keep mentioning it or thinking about it. *He's got a bee in his bonnet about factory farming.* PHRASE: V and *bee* inflect, oft PHR *about* n

Beeb /bi:b/. The **Beeb** is an informal term for the **BBC.** *He joined the Beeb at 19.* N-PROPER: *the* N

beech /bi:tʃ/ **beeches.** A **beech** or a **beech tree** is a tree with a smooth grey trunk. *...the branch of a huge beech.* ► **Beech** is the wood of this tree. *The worktop is made of solid beech.* ◆◇◇◇◇ N-VAR; N-UNCOUNT

beef /bi:f/ **beefs, beefing, beefed** ◆◆◇◇◇

1 **Beef** is the meat of a cow, bull, or ox. *...roast beef. ...beef stew. ...exports of beef and powdered milk.* • See also **corned beef.** N-UNCOUNT

2 If someone **beefs** about something, they keep complaining about it; an informal use. *Instead of beefing about what Mrs Martin has not done, her critics might take a look at what she is trying to do.* VB: no passive PRAGMATICS =moan

beef up. If you **beef up** something, you increase, strengthen, or improve it. *...a campaign to beef up security... Both sides are still beefing up their military strength. ...a beefed up police presence.* PHRASAL VERB V P n (not pron) V-ed P Also V n P

beefburger /bi:fbɜːʳgəʳ/ **beefburgers;** also spelled **beef burger. Beefburgers** are flat round pieces of minced beef mixed with flour and flavourings. You grill or fry them before eating them. *... beefburgers and chips.* N-COUNT

beefcake /bi:fkeɪk/ **beefcakes.** Attractive men with large muscles can be referred to as **beefcake.** *...the sort of beefcake bodies usually associated with male strippers.* N-VAR: oft N n =hunk

Beefeater /bi:fi:tə/ **Beefeaters. Beefeaters** are guards at the Tower of London. They wear a uniform made in the style of the sixteenth century. N-COUNT

beefsteak /bi:fsteɪk/ **beefsteaks;** also spelled **beef steak. Beefsteak** is **steak.** N-VAR

beefy /bi:fi/ **beefier, beefiest.** Someone, especially a man, who is **beefy** has a big body and large muscles. *...a beefy red-faced Englishman.* ADJ-GRADED: usu ADJ n =brawny

beehive /bi:haɪv/ **beehives**

1 A **beehive** is a structure in which bees are kept, which is designed so that the keeper can collect the honey that they produce. N-COUNT

2 A **beehive** is a hairstyle for women in which the hair is piled up onto the top of the head into a dome shape. *She wore butterfly glasses and had a beehive hairdo.* N-COUNT

beekeeper /bi:ki:pəʳ/ **beekeepers.** A **beekeeper** is a person who owns and takes care of bees. N-COUNT

beekeeping /biːkiːpɪŋ/. **Beekeeping** is the practice of owning and taking care of bees. N-UNCOUNT

beeline /biːlaɪn/; also spelled **bee-line**. If you **make a beeline for** a place, you go to it as quickly and directly as possible; an informal expression. *She made a beeline for the car.* PHRASE: V inflects, PHR n

been /bɪn, biːn/
1 **Been** is the past participle of **be**.
2 If you have **been** to a place, you have gone to it or visited it. *Mr Li has already been to Egypt, Jordan, Iran and Saudi Arabia... I've been there before.* VERB V prep/adv

beep /biːp/ **beeps, beeping, beeped**
1 In British English, a **beep** is a short, loud sound like that made by a car horn or the engaged tone of a telephone. N-COUNT; SOUND
2 If something such as a horn **beeps**, or you beep it, it makes a short, harsh sound. *A cellular telephone beeped... He beeped the horn.* V-ERG V Vn

beeper /biːpəʳ/ **beepers.** A **beeper** is a portable device that makes a beeping noise, usually to tell you to phone someone or to remind you to do something. *His beeper sounded and he picked up the telephone.* N-COUNT =bleeper

beer /bɪəʳ/ **beers. Beer** is a bitter alcoholic drink made from grain. *He sat in the kitchen drinking beer... We have quite a good range of beers.* ◆◆◆◇◇ N-MASS ▸ A glass of beer can be referred to as a **beer**. *Would you like a beer?* N-COUNT

beer belly, beer bellies. If a man has a **beer belly**, he has a fat stomach because of drinking too much beer. *He was short and fat, with a beer belly and a great deal of grey hair.* N-COUNT =paunch

beer gut, beer guts; also spelled **beer-gut**. A **beer gut** is the same as a **beer belly**. N-COUNT

beermat /bɪəʳmæt/ **beermats;** also spelled **beer mat**. A **beermat** is a cardboard mat for resting your glass of beer on in a bar or pub. N-COUNT

beery /bɪəri/. If a person, especially a man, is described as **beery**, they have drunk a lot of beer. *The place was jumping with jolly, beery farmers. ...beery roars of applause.* ADJ-GRADED: usu ADJ n

beeswax /biːzwæks/. **Beeswax** is wax that is made by bees and used especially for making candles and furniture polish. N-UNCOUNT

beet /biːt/ **beets** ◆◇◇◇◇
1 **Beet** is a crop with a thick round root. It is often used to feed animals, especially cows. *...fields of sweet corn and beet.* • See also **sugar beet**. N-UNCOUNT
2 In American English, **beets** are dark purple vegetables that are the roots of a crop. They are often pickled in vinegar. The British word is **beetroot**. *...pickled beets.* N-VAR: usu pl

beetle /biːtəl/ **beetles.** A **beetle** is an insect with a hard covering to its body. ◆◇◇◇◇ N-COUNT

beetroot /biːtruːt/ **beetroots.** In British English, **beetroot** is a dark purple vegetable that is the root of a crop. It is often pickled in vinegar. The American word is **beet**. *Grate the carrots and beetroot.* ◆◇◇◇◇ N-VAR

befall /bɪfɔːl/ **befalls, befalling, befell, befallen.** If something bad or unlucky **befalls** you, it happens to you; a literary word. *...the disaster that befell the island of Flores.* ◆◇◇◇◇ VERB Vn

befit /bɪfɪt/ **befits, befitting, befitted.** If something **befits** a person or thing, it is suitable or appropriate for them. *They offered him a post befitting his seniority and experience... He writes beautifully, as befits a poet.* ◆◇◇◇◇ VERB =become Vn

before /bɪfɔːʳ/ ◆◆◆◆◆
In addition to the uses shown below, **before** is used in the phrasal verbs 'go before' and 'lay before'.
1 If something happens **before** a particular date, time, or event, it happens earlier than that date, time, or event. *Annie was born a few weeks before Christmas... Before World War II, women were not recruited as intelligence officers... My husband rarely comes to bed before 2 or 3am.* PREP ≠after ▸ Also a conjunction. *Stock prices have climbed close to the peak they'd registered before the stock market crashed in 1987.* CONJ-SUBORD
2 If you do something **before** doing something else, you do it earlier then the other thing. *He spent his early life in Sri Lanka before moving to England... Before leaving, he went into his office to fill in the daily timesheet.* PREP: PREP -ing ≠after ▸ Also a conjunction. *He took a cold shower and then towelled off before he put on fresh clothes.* CONJ-SUBORD
3 You use **before** when you are talking about time. For example, if something happened the day **before** or the weekend **before** a particular date or event, it happened during the previous day or during the previous weekend. *The war had ended only a month or so before.* ADV: n ADV ▸ Also a preposition. *It's interesting that he sent me the book twenty days before the deadline for my book.* PREP: n PREP n ▸ Also a conjunction. *Kelman had a book published in the US more than a decade before a British publisher would touch him.* CONJ-SUBORD
4 If you do something **before** someone else can do something, you do it when they have not yet done it. *Before Gallacher could catch up with the ball, Nadlovu had beaten him to it.* CONJ-SUBORD
5 If someone has done something **before**, they have done it on a previous occasion. If someone has not done something **before**, they have never done it. *I've been here before... I had met Professor Lown before... She had never been to Italy before.* ADV: ADV after v
6 If there is a period of time or if several things are done **before** something happens, it takes that amount of time or effort for this thing to happen. *It was some time before the door opened in response to his ring.* CONJ-SUBORD =until
7 If a particular situation has to happen **before** something else happens, this situation must happen or exist in order for the other thing to happen. *There was additional work to be done before all the troops would be ready.* CONJ-SUBORD
8 If someone is **before** something, they are in front of it; a formal use. *They drove through a tall iron gate and stopped before a large white villa.* PREP =in front of
9 If you tell someone that one place is a certain distance **before** another, you mean that they will come to the first place first. *The turn is about two kilometres before the roundabout.* PREP
10 If someone or something appears or comes **before** a person or group, they are there to be heard or considered officially by that person or group. *The Governor will appear before the committee next Tuesday.* PREP =in front of
11 If something happens **before** a particular person or group, it is seen by or happens while this person or this group is present. *The game followed a colourful opening ceremony before a crowd of seventy-four thousand.* PREP =in front of
12 If you have something such as a journey, a task, or a stage of your life **before** you, you must do it or live through it in the future. *Everyone in the room knew it was the single hardest task before them... I saw before me an idyllic life.* PREP: PREP pron =ahead of
13 When you want to say that one person or thing is more important than another, you can say that they come **before** the other person or thing. *Her husband, her children, and the Church came before her needs.* PREP: v PREP n
14 • **before long**: see **long**.

beforehand /bɪfɔːʳhænd/. If you do something **beforehand**, you do it earlier than a particular event. *How could she tell beforehand that I was going to go out?... Saunas can be hazardous if misused. Avoid a big meal beforehand.* ◆◇◇◇◇ ADV: usu ADV after v, also ADV with cl

befriend /bɪfrend/ **befriends, befriending, befriended.** If you **befriend** someone, especially someone who is lonely or far from home, you make friends with them. *The film's about an elderly woman and a young nurse who befriends her... On the aeroplane I was befriended by a delightful German woman.* ◆◇◇◇◇ VERB Vn

befuddle /bɪfʌdəl/ **befuddles, befuddling, befuddled.** If something **befuddles** you, it confuses your mind or thoughts. *Randolph liked to befuddle his readers with at least one unfamiliar word per article.* VERB =muddle Vn ♦ **befuddled** *...his befuddled manner... I was usually befuddled with drink.* ADJ-GRADED

beg /bɛg/ **begs, begging, begged** ◆◆◇◇◇

1 If you **beg** someone to do something, you ask them very anxiously or eagerly to do it. *I begged him to come back to England with me... I begged to be allowed to leave... We are not going to beg for help any more... They dropped to their knees and begged forgiveness.*
VERB =beseech V n to-inf V to-inf-passive V for n V n Also V n with quote

2 If someone who is poor **is begging**, they are asking people to give them food or money. *I was surrounded by people begging for food... There are thousands like him in Los Angeles, begging on the streets and sleeping rough... She was living alone, begging food from neighbors.*
VB: oft cont =panhandle V for n V V n

3 You say '**I beg to differ**' when you are politely emphasizing that you disagree with someone.
PHRASES V inflects PRAGMATICS

4 If you say that something **is going begging**, you mean that it is available but no one is using it or accepting it. *There is other housing going begging in town.*
V inflects

5 If you say that something **begs** a particular **question**, you mean that it makes people want to ask that question; some people consider that this use is incorrect. *Hopewell's success begs the question: why aren't more companies doing the same?*
V and N inflect

6 If you say that something **begs** a particular **question**, you mean that it assumes that the question has already been answered and so does not deal with it; a literary use. *The research begs a number of questions.*
V and N inflect

7 • **I beg your pardon**: see **pardon**.

began /bɪgæn/. **Began** is the past tense of **begin**.

beget /bɪgɛt/ **begets, begetting, begot, begotten**

1 To **beget** something means to cause it to happen or be created; a formal use. *Poverty begets debt... Economic tensions beget political ones.*
VERB V n

2 When a man **begets** a child, he becomes the father of that child; an old-fashioned use. *He wanted to beget an heir.*
VERB =father V n

begetter /bɪgɛtəʳ/ **begetters.** The **begetter** of something has caused this thing to come into existence; a formal word. *...the Centre for Policy Studies, the begetter of Thatcherism.*
N-COUNT: with poss

beggar /bɛgəʳ/ **beggars, beggaring, beggared** ◆◇◇◇◇

1 A **beggar** is someone who lives by asking people for money or food.
N-COUNT =panhandler

2 If something **beggars** a person, country, or organization, it makes them very poor. *He warned that lifting copyright restrictions could beggar the industry.*
VERB V n

3 If something **beggars belief**, it is impossible to believe it. If something **beggars description**, it is impossible to describe it. *The statistics beggar belief... His courage beggars description.*
PHRASE: V inflects

begging bowl, begging bowls. If a country or organization approaches other countries or organizations with a **begging bowl**, it asks them for money. *He said earlier that he is not holding out a begging bowl.*
N-COUNT

begging letter, begging letters. A **begging letter** is a letter from a person or organization in which they ask you to send some money for a particular purpose; used showing disapproval. *He has received sacks of begging letters following reports about his personal fortune.*
N-COUNT PRAGMATICS

begin /bɪgɪn/ **begins, beginning, began, begun** ◆◆◆◆◆

1 When someone or something **begins** to do something, they start doing it. *He stood up and began to move around the room... The weight loss began to look more serious... Snow began falling again.*
VERB =start ≠stop V to-inf V -ing

2 When something **begins** or when you **begin** it, it takes place from a particular time onwards. *The problems began last November... He has just begun his fourth year in hiding... The US is prepared to begin talks immediately.*
V-ERG =start, commence ≠end V V n

3 If someone **begins** with something, or **begins** by doing something, this is the first thing they do. If a person **began** their career as something, this was the first job they had. *Could I begin with a few formalities? ...a businessman who began by selling golf shirts from the boot of his car... He began his career as a sound editor.*
VERB =open, commence ≠conclude V with n V by -ing V n prep

4 You use **begin** to mention the first thing that someone says. *'Professor Theron,' he began, 'I'm very pleased to see you'... He didn't know how to begin.*
VB: no cont ≠conclude V with quote V

5 If one thing **began as** another, it first existed in the form of the second thing. *What began as a local festival has blossomed into an international event.*
VB: no cont =start V as n

6 If you say that a thing or place **begins** somewhere, you are talking about one of its limits or edges. *The fate line begins close to the wrist... Rue Guynemer begins at the front of the Fitzgerald site.*
VB: no cont ≠end V prep/adv

7 If a word **begins with** a particular letter, that is the first letter of that word. *The first word begins with an F.*
VB: no cont =start ≠end V with n

8 If you say that you cannot **begin** to imagine, understand, or explain something, you are emphasizing that it is almost impossible to explain, understand, or imagine. *You can't begin to imagine how much that saddens me.*
VB: no cont, with brd-neg PRAGMATICS V to-inf

9 You use the phrase **to begin with** when you are talking about the first stage of a situation, event, or process. *It was great to begin with but now it's difficult.*
PHRASES PHR with cl =at first

10 You use the phrase **to begin with** to introduce the first of several things that you want to say. *'What do scientists you've spoken with think about that?'— 'Well, to begin with, they doubt it's going to work.'*
PHR with cl PRAGMATICS =firstly

11 • **charity begins at home**: see **charity**. • **begin life**: see **life**.

beginner /bɪgɪnəʳ/ **beginners.** A **beginner** is someone who has just started learning to do something and cannot do it very well yet. *The course is suitable for beginners and advanced students... I am a complete beginner to bird-keeping.*
◆◆◇◇◇ N-COUNT

beginning /bɪgɪnɪŋ/ **beginnings** ◆◆◆◇◇

1 The **beginning** of an event or process is the first part of it. *This was also the beginning of her recording career... Think of this as a new beginning.*
N-COUNT: usu sing =start ≠end

2 The **beginnings** of something are the signs or events which form the first part of it. *I had the beginnings of a headache... The discussions were the beginnings of a dialogue with Moscow.*
N-PLURAL: usu the N, oft N of n

3 The **beginning** of a period of time is the time at which it starts. *The wedding will be at the beginning of March.*
N-SING: the N ≠end

4 The **beginning** of a piece of written material is the first words or sentences of it. *...the question which was raised at the beginning of this chapter.*
N-COUNT: usu sing, oft N of n ≠end

5 If you talk about the **beginnings** of a person, company, or group, you are referring to their backgrounds or origins. *His views come from his own humble beginnings.*
N-PLURAL: usu with supp

6 You use **beginning** to describe someone who is in the early stages of learning to do something. *The people that she had in her classroom were beginning learners.*
ADJ: ADJ n

begonia /bɪgəʊniə/ **begonias.** A **begonia** is a garden plant which has large brightly coloured leaves.
N-COUNT

begot /bɪgɒt/. **Begot** is the past tense of **beget**.

begotten /bɪgɒtᵊn/. **Begotten** is the past participle of **beget**.

begrudge /bɪgrʌdʒ/ **begrudges, begrudging, begrudged**

1 If you say that you do not **begrudge** someone something, you mean that you do not feel angry, upset, or jealous that they have got it. *I certainly don't begrudge him the Nobel Prize.*
VB: usu with brd-neg V n n

2 If you do not **begrudge** something such as time or money, you do not mind giving it up. *I do not begrudge the money I have lost.*
VB: usu with brd-neg V n

begrudgingly /bɪgrʌdʒɪŋli/. If you do something **begrudgingly**, you do it unwillingly. *He agreed to her suggestion begrudgingly.*
ADV: ADV with v =grudgingly

beguile /bɪgaɪl/ **beguiles, beguiling, beguiled**

1 If something **beguiles** you, you are charmed and attracted by it. *His paintings beguiled the Prince of Wales... I was beguiled by the romance and exotic atmosphere of the souks in Marrakech.*
VERB V n

2 If someone or something **beguiles** you **into** doing something, they try to trick you into doing it. *He used his newspapers to beguile the readers into buying shares in his company.* VERB V n *into*-ing

beguiling /bɪga͟ɪlɪŋ/. Something that is **beguiling** is charming and attractive; used in written English. *Mombasa is a town with a beguiling Arabic flavour.* ♦ **beguilingly** *He was beguilingly boyish and attractive.* ADJ-GRADED; ADV-GRADED: ADV adj, ADV with v

begun /bɪgʌ͟n/. **Begun** is the past participle of **begin**.

behalf /bɪhɑ͟ːf, -hæ͟f/ ◆◆◆◇◇

1 If you do something **on** someone's **behalf**, or **on behalf of** someone, you do it for that person as their representative. *She made an emotional public appeal on her son's behalf... Secret Service officer Robin Thompson spoke on behalf of his colleagues.* PHRASE: PHR after v

2 If you feel, for example, embarrassed or angry **on** someone's **behalf**, or **on behalf of** someone, you feel embarrassed or angry for them. *'What do you mean?' I asked, offended on Liddie's behalf.* PHRASE

behave /bɪhe͟ɪv/ **behaves, behaving, behaved** ◆◆◆◇◇

1 The way that you **behave** is the way that you do and say things, and the things that you do and say. *I couldn't believe these people were behaving in this way... He'd behaved badly.* VERB =act V prep/adv

2 If you **behave** or **behave** yourself, you act in the way that people think is correct and proper. *You have to behave... They were expected to behave themselves.* VERB =be good V V pron-refl

3 In science, the way that something **behaves** is the things that it does. *Under certain conditions, electrons can behave like waves rather than particles.* VERB V prep/adv

-behaved /-bɪhe͟ɪvd/. **-behaved** combines with adverbs such as 'well' or 'badly' to form adjectives that describe people's or animals' behaviour. *It is even more important that your horse is well-behaved in traffic... Usually there is a very good reason why they are badly behaved.* COMB in ADJ-GRADED

behaviour /bɪhe͟ɪvjəʳ/ **behaviours;** spelled **behavior** in American English. ◆◆◆◆◇

1 People's or animals' **behaviour** is the way that they behave. *Make sure that good behaviour is rewarded. ...human sexual behaviour.* N-UNCOUNT: with supp =conduct

2 Psychologists refer to a particular way of behaving as a particular **behaviour**. *Was she merely reverting to a learned behavior from force of habit?* N-COUNT: with supp

3 In science, the **behaviour** of something is the way that it behaves. *It will be many years before anyone can predict a hurricane's behavior with much accuracy.* N-UNCOUNT: also N in pl, with poss

4 If someone is **on** their **best behaviour**, they are making a big effort to behave nicely. *After that the two were on their best behaviour.* PHRASE: v-link PHR

behavioural /bɪhe͟ɪvjərəl/ spelled **behavioral** in American English. **Behavioural** means relating to the behaviour of a person or animal, or to the study of their behaviour. *...Emotional and behavioural problems. ...behavioral scientists.* ◆◇◇◇◇ ADJ: ADJ n

behaviourism /bɪhe͟ɪvjərɪzəm/; spelled **behaviorism** in American English. **Behaviourism** is the belief held by some psychologists that the only valid method of studying the psychology of people or animals is to observe how they behave. ♦ **behaviourist, behaviourists** *Even the behaviourists are beginning to question their own theories about this.* N-UNCOUNT; N-COUNT

behead /bɪhe͟d/ **beheads, beheading, beheaded.** If someone **is beheaded**, someone cuts their head off, usually because they have been found guilty of a crime. *Charles I was beheaded by the Cromwellians.* VB: usu passive =decapitate

beheld /bɪhe͟ld/. **Beheld** is the past tense of **behold**.

behemoth /bɪhi͟ːmɒθ, AM -məθ/ **behemoths.** If you call something such as an organization a **behemoth**, you mean that it is extremely large; mainly used in literary English and journalism, and often used to suggest that the thing is unpleasant, inefficient, or difficult to manage. *The city is a sprawling behemoth with no heart. ...his behemoth 1,047 page book about the 1988 race for the White House.* N-COUNT PRAGMATICS =monster

behest /bɪhe͟st/ **behests.** If something is done **at** someone's **behest**, or **at the behest** of someone, it is done because they have ordered or requested it; a formal expression. *In 1970, at his new wife's behest, they moved to Southampton... The policy document was produced at the behest of John Major and other world leaders.* PHRASE: PHR after v

behind 1 preposition and adverb uses

behind /bɪha͟ɪnd/ ◆◆◆◆◆

In addition to the uses shown below, **behind** is also used in a few phrasal verbs, such as 'fall behind' and 'lie behind'.

1 If something is **behind** a thing or person, it is on the other side of them from you, or nearer their back rather than their front. *I put one of the cushions behind his head... They were parked behind the truck... The moon disappeared behind a cloud.* ► Also an adverb. *Rising into the hills behind are 800 acres of parkland... She was attacked from behind.* PREP ≠in front of; ADV: usu n ADV, *from* ADV

2 If you are walking or travelling **behind** someone or something, you are following them. *Keith wandered along behind him... Myra and Sam and the children were driving behind them.* ► Also an adverb. *The troopers followed behind, every muscle tensed for the sudden gunfire.* PREP ≠in front of; ADV: ADV after v

3 If someone is **behind** a desk, counter, or bar, they are on the other side of it from where you are. *The colonel was sitting behind a cheap wooden desk... He could just about see the little man behind the counter.* ● **behind bars**: see **bar**. PREP ≠in front of

4 When you shut a door or gate **behind** you, you shut it after you have gone through it. *I walked out and closed the door behind me... He slammed the gate shut behind him.* PREP: PREP pron

5 The people, reason, or events **behind** a situation are the causes of it or are responsible for it. *It is still not clear who was behind the killing... He is embarrassed about the motives behind his decision.* PREP

6 If something or someone is **behind** you, they support you and help you. *He had the state's judicial power behind him.* PREP: PREP pron

7 If you refer to what is **behind** someone's outside appearance, you are referring to a characteristic which you cannot immediately see or is not obvious, but which you think is there. *What lay behind his anger was really the hurt he felt at Grace's refusal... Behind the smiling eyes lurks the evil that led her to murder the two babies in her care.* PREP

8 If you are **behind** someone, you are less successful than them, or have done less or advanced less. *She finished second behind the American, Ann Cody, in the 800 metres... Food production has already fallen behind the population growth.* ► Also an adverb. *The rapid development of technology means that she is now far behind, and will need retraining... The accounts are more than three months behind.* PREP ≠ahead of; ADV-GRADED: *be* ADV, ADV after v

9 If an experience is **behind** you, it happened in your past and will not happen again, or no longer affects you. *Maureen put the nightmare behind her... He will attempt to put behind him the misery of failing to win a medal in his individual event.* PREP: PREP pron

10 If you have a particular achievement **behind** you, you have managed to reach this achievement, and other people consider it to be important or valuable. *He has 20 years of loyal service to Barclays Bank behind him... Birgit was a popular actress with half a decade of filmmaking behind her.* PREP: *have/with* n PREP pron

11 If something is **behind** schedule, it is not as far advanced as people had planned. If someone is **behind** schedule, they are not progressing as quickly at something as they had planned. *The work is 22 weeks behind schedule... We were two months behind schedule, and already over budget.* PREP: oft n PREP n ≠ahead of

12 If you stay **behind**, you remain in a place after other people have gone. *As women were not permitted in the war zone, Eleanor would have to stay behind... About 1,200 personnel will remain behind to take care of the air base.* ADV: ADV after v

13 If you leave something or someone **behind**, you do not take them with you when you go. *The rebels fled into the mountains, leaving behind their weapons and supplies... He came to Saudi Arabia, leaving behind his wife and their three children.* ADV: ADV after v

14 • **do something behind someone's back**: see **back**. • **behind the scenes**: see **scene**. • **behind the times**: see **time**.

behind 2 noun use

behind /bɪha͟ɪnd/ **behinds.** Your **behind** is the part of your body that you sit on. N-COUNT =bottom

behindhand /bɪha͟ɪndhænd/. If someone is **behindhand**, they have been delayed or have made less progress in their work than they or other people think they should. *Poor Dr Pegler got terribly behindhand with his appointments.* ADJ-GRADED: usu v-link ADJ =behind

behind-the-scenes. See **scene**.

behold /bɪho͟ʊld/ **beholds, beholding, beheld** ◆◇◇◇◇

1 If you **behold** someone or something, you see them; a literary use. *She looked into his eyes and beheld madness... He was a joy to behold.* VERB V n V

2 People used to say or write **'Behold'** to draw people's attention to something. 'Behold' is sometimes used in literary or humourous writing. *Fear Not. Behold The Saviour... Behold a series of thrilling photographs of Felix.* • **lo and behold**: see **lo**. CONVENTION

beholden /bɪho͟ʊldᵊn/. If you are **beholden to** someone, you are in debt to them in some way or you feel that you have a duty to them because they have helped you. *He was made beholden to the Mafia... Americans are beholden to their employers for their health protection.* ADJ: v-link ADJ *to* n

beholder /bɪho͟ʊldəʳ/ **beholders**

1 If you say that something such as beauty or art is **in the eye of the beholder**, you mean that it is a matter of personal opinion. *Beauty is in the eye of the beholder.* PHRASE: v-link PHR

2 The **beholder** of something is the person who is looking at it; an old-fashioned word. *They cannot but inspire wonder in the beholder.* N-COUNT: usu *the* N in sing

behove /bɪho͟ʊv/ **behoves, behoving, behoved;** spelled **behoove** in American English. If **it behoves** you to do something, it is right, necessary, or advantageous for you to do it; a formal word. *I think it behoves us, sir, to get out of here with all speed.* VERB =befit *it* V n to-inf

beige /be͟ɪʒ/. Something that is **beige** is pale brown in colour. *The walls are beige. ...a pair of beige shorts... The living-room had been decorated in muted shades of white and beige.* ◆◇◇◇◇ COLOUR

being /bi͟ːɪŋ/ **beings** ◆◆◆◇◇

1 **Being** is the present participle of **be**.

2 **Being** is used in non-finite clauses where you are giving the reason for something. *It being a Sunday, the old men from the square had the day off... Little boys, being what they are, might decide to play on it... Of course, being young, I did not worry.* V-LINK V n V adj Also V prep

3 You can refer to any real or imaginary creature as a **being**. *People expect a horse to perform like a car, with no thought for its feelings as a living being. ...beings from outer space.* • See also **human being**. N-COUNT

4 **Being** is existence. Something that is **in being** or comes **into being** exists. *Abraham Maslow described psychology as 'the science of being.'... The Kingdom of Italy formally came into being on 17 March 1861. ...the complex process by which the novel is brought into being.* N-UNCOUNT =existence

5 See also **well-being**. • **other things being equal**: see **equal**. • **for the time being**: see **time**.

bejewelled /bɪdʒu͟ːəld/; spelled **bejeweled** in American English. A **bejewelled** person or object is wearing a lot of jewellery or is decorated with jewels. *...bejewelled women. ...a bejewelled gold-en tiara.* ADJ: usu ADJ n

belabour /bɪle͟ɪbəʳ/ **belabours, belabouring, belaboured;** spelled **belabor** in American English. If you **belabour** someone or something, you hit them hard and repeatedly; an old-fashioned word. *Men began to belabour his shoulders, his head, his arms with sticks.* VERB =pummel V n

belated /bɪle͟ɪtɪd/. A **belated** action happens later than it should have done; a formal word. *...the government's belated attempts to alleviate the plight of the poor. ...a belated birthday present.* ♦ **belatedly** *The leaders realized belatedly that the coup would be disastrous for everyone.* ◆◇◇◇◇ ADJ-GRADED =tardy ADV-GRADED: ADV with v

belch /be͟ltʃ/ **belches, belching, belched** ◆◇◇◇◇

1 If someone **belches**, they make a sudden noise in their throat because air has risen up from their stomach. *Garland covered his mouth with his hand and belched discreetly.* ► Also a noun. *He drank and stifled a belch.* VERB =burp V N-COUNT

2 If something **belches** something such as smoke or fire, or if smoke or fire **belches** from something, large amounts of smoke or fire come from it. *Tired old trucks were struggling up the road below us, belching black smoke... Suddenly, clouds of steam started to belch from the engine.* ► **Belch out** means the same as **belch**. *The power-generation plant belched out five tonnes of ash an hour. ...the vast quantities of smoke belching out from the volcano.* V-ERG =emit V n V *from/out of* n PHRASAL VERB ERG V P n (not pron) V P

belch out. See **belch** 2. PHRASAL VERB

beleaguered /bɪli͟ːgəʳd/ ◆◇◇◇◇

1 A **beleaguered** person, organization, or project is experiencing a lot of difficulties, opposition, or criticism; a formal use. *There have been seven coup attempts against the beleaguered government of Mrs Aquino.* ADJ-GRADED: usu ADJ n

2 A **beleaguered** place or army is surrounded by its enemies; a formal use. *The rebels continue their push towards the beleaguered capital.* ADJ =besieged

belfry /be͟lfri/ **belfries.** The **belfry** of a church is the top part of its tower or steeple, where the bells are. N-COUNT

Belgian /be͟ldʒᵊn/ **Belgians. Belgian** means belonging or relating to Belgium or to its people. *...the Belgian capital, Brussels.* ► A **Belgian** is a person who comes from Belgium. ◆◆◆◆◇ ADJ N-COUNT

belie /bɪla͟ɪ/ **belies, belying, belied** ◆◇◇◇◇

1 If one thing **belies** another, it hides the true situation and so creates a false idea or image of someone or something. *Her looks belie her 50 years.* VERB V n

2 If one thing **belies** another, it proves that the other thing is not true or genuine. *The facts of the situation belie his testimony.* VERB =disprove V n

belief /bɪli͟ːf/ **beliefs** ◆◆◆◇◇

1 **Belief** is a feeling of certainty that something exists, is true, or is good. *One billion people throughout the world are Muslims, united by belief in one god. ...a belief in personal liberty.* N-UNCOUNT: usu N *in* n

2 Your religious or political **beliefs** are your views on religious or political matters. *He refuses to compete on Sundays because of his religious beliefs.* N-PLURAL: usu supp N

3 If it is your **belief** that something is the case, it is your strong opinion that it is the case. *It is our belief that improvements in health care will lead to a stronger, more prosperous economy.* N-SING: usu N that

4 You use **beyond belief** to emphasize that something is true to a very great degree or that it happened to a very great degree. *We are devastated, shocked beyond belief... Her son's skin improved beyond belief.* PHRASES adj PHR, PHR after v PRAGMATICS

5 You use the expression **contrary to popular belief** to introduce a statement that is the opposite to what is thought to be true by most ordinary people. *Contrary to popular belief, there is no evidence that what you look like makes much difference to your life.* PHR with cl PRAGMATICS

6 If you do something **in the belief that** something is true or will happen, you do it because you think, usually wrongly, that it is true or will happen. *Civilians had broken into the building, apparently in the belief that it contained food.* PHR after v, PHR cl

believable /bɪli͟ːvəbᵊl/. Something that is **believable** makes you think that it could be true or real. *...believable evidence... This book is full of believable, interesting characters.* ◆◇◇◇◇ ADJ-GRADED ≠unbelievable

believe /bɪli͟ːv/ **believes, believing, believed** ◆◆◆◆◆

1 If you **believe** that something is true, you think that it is true; a formal use. You can say **'I believe'** to indicate that you are not completely sure that VERB =think

what you are saying is accurate or to make a statement sound more factual and less emotional. *Experts believe that the coming drought will be extensive... I believe you have something of mine... The main problem, I believe, lies elsewhere... We believe them to be hidden here in this apartment... 'You've never heard of him?'—'I don't believe so.'* V that V n to-inf V so/not Also V n adj

2 If you **believe** someone or if you **believe** what they say or write, you accept that they are telling the truth. *He did not sound as if he believed her... Never believe anything a married man says about his wife... Don't believe what you read in the papers.* VERB ≠disbelieve V n

3 If you **believe** in fairies, ghosts, or miracles, you are sure that they exist or happen. If you **believe** in a god, you are sure of the existence of that god. *I don't believe in ghosts... Do you believe in magic?* VERB V in n Also V

4 If you **believe in** a way of life or an idea, you are in favour of it because you think it is good or right. *He believed in marital fidelity. ...decent candidates who believed in democracy.* VERB V in n

5 If you **believe in** someone or what they are doing, you have confidence in them and think that they will be successful. *If you believe in yourself you can succeed.* VERB V in n

6 **Believe** is used in expressions such as **I can't believe how** or **it's hard to believe that** in order to express surprise, for example because something bad has happened or something very difficult has been achieved. *It was awful. We couldn't believe what they were doing but we never thought it would make a difference... Many officers I spoke to found it hard to believe what was happening around them... I was a physical and emotional wreck – I still can't believe how I ever got any work done.* VB: with brd-neg PRAGMATICS V wh Also V that

7 If you say that you cannot **believe your eyes** or cannot **believe your ears**, you are emphasizing that you are very surprised about something you have seen or heard. *I could not believe my eyes. She was far more beautiful than I had imagined.* PHRASES V inflects, with brd-neg PRAGMATICS

8 You can use **believe it or not** to emphasize that what you have just said is surprising. *That's normal, believe it or not.* PHR with cl PRAGMATICS

9 If you say **would you believe it**, you are emphasizing your surprise about something. *And would you believe it, he's younger than me!* PHR with cl PRAGMATICS

10 You can use **believe you me** to emphasize that what you are saying is true. *It's absolutely amazing, believe you me.* PHR with cl PRAGMATICS

believer /bɪliːvəʳ/ **believers** ◆◇◇◇◇

1 If you are a great **believer in** something, you think that it is good, right, or beneficial. *Mum was a great believer in herbal medicines.* N-COUNT: N in n, usu adj N ≠opponent

2 A **believer** is someone who is sure that God exists or that their religion is true. *I made no secret of the fact that I was not a believer.* N-COUNT

belittle /bɪlɪtᵊl/ **belittles, belittling, belittled.** ◆◇◇◇◇ If you **belittle** someone or something, you say or imply that they are unimportant or not very good. *We mustn't belittle her outstanding achievement... It makes no sense to belittle the enormity of the disaster.* VERB =demean V n

bell /bel/ **bells** ◆◆◆◇◇

1 A **bell** is a device that makes a ringing sound and is used to give a signal or to attract people's attention. *I had just enough time to finish eating before the bell rang and I was off to my first class... I've been ringing the door bell, there's no answer.* N-COUNT

2 A **bell** is a hollow metal object shaped like a cup which has a piece hanging inside it that hits the sides and makes a sound. *My brother, Neville, was born on a Sunday, when all the church bells were ringing.* N-COUNT

3 If something is **as clear as a bell**, it is very clear indeed. *There are 80 of these pictures and they're all as clear as a bell.* PHRASES usu v-link PHR

4 If you **give someone a bell**, you telephone them; an informal British expression. *I was going to give you a bell tomorrow.* V inflects

5 If you say that something **rings a bell**, you mean that it reminds you of something else, but you cannot remember exactly what it is; an informal expression. *The description of one of the lads is definitely familiar. It rings a bell.* V inflects

6 If something is **as sound as a bell** it is healthy and not damaged in any way. *The horse returned sound as a bell.* v-link PHR

bell-bottoms; the form **bell-bottom** is used as a modifier. **Bell-bottoms** are trousers that are very wide at the bottom of the leg, near your feet. *Flares, loons and bell-bottoms are back... He was clothed in maroon bell-bottom trousers.* N-PLURAL: oft N n =flares

bellboy /belbɔɪ/ **bellboys.** A **bellboy** is a man or boy who works in a hotel, carrying bags or bringing things to the guests' rooms. N-COUNT =bellhop

belle /bel/ **belles.** A **belle** is a beautiful woman, especially the most beautiful woman at a party or in a group; an old-fashioned word. *She was the belle of her Sunday School class.* N-COUNT =beauty

bellicose /belɪkous, -kouz/. You use **bellicose** to refer to aggressive actions or behaviour that are likely to start an argument or a fight; a literary word. *The government is continuing its bellicose statements threatening tough action against illegal strikes.* ADJ-GRADED =belligerent

-bellied /-belid/. **-bellied** can be added to an adjective to describe someone or something that has a stomach of a particular kind. *The fat-bellied officer stood near the door. ...the yellow-bellied sea-snake.* • See also **pot-bellied**. COMB in ADJ

belligerent /bɪlɪdʒərənt/ **belligerents** ◆◇◇◇◇

1 A **belligerent** person is hostile and aggressive. *Mr Gates stressed the danger of belligerent statements by both sides leading to war... He was almost back to his belligerent mood of twelve months ago.* ADJ-GRADED =aggressive

♦ **belligerently** *'Why not?' he asked belligerently.* ADV-GRADED

♦ **belligerence** *He could be accused of passion, but never belligerence.* N-UNCOUNT =aggression

2 The **belligerents** in a war are the countries or groups that are fighting each other; a formal use. *The belligerents were due, once again, to try to settle their differences.* N-COUNT

bellow /belou/ **bellows, bellowing, bellowed** ◆◇◇◇◇

1 If someone **bellows**, they shout angrily in a loud, deep voice. *'I didn't ask to be born!' she bellowed... She prayed she wouldn't come in and find them there, bellowing at each other... He bellowed information into the mouthpiece of his portable telephone.* ► Also a noun. *I was distraught and let out a bellow of tearful rage.* VERB V with quote V at n V n prep Also V N-COUNT

2 When a large animal such as bull or an elephant **bellows**, it roars loudly and deeply. *A heifer bellowed in her stall.* VERB V

3 A **bellows** is or **bellows** are a device used for blowing air into a fire in order to make it burn more fiercely. *...two stone forges, each equipped with bellows.* N-COUNT: also *a pair of* N

bell ringer, bell ringers; also spelled **bell-ringer.** A **bell ringer** is someone who rings church bells as a hobby. N-COUNT

bellwether /belweðəʳ/ **bellwethers.** If you describe something as a **bellwether**, you mean that it is an indication of the way a situation is changing; used mainly in American journalism. *If interest in apartments remains high, it could be a bellwether of another real estate recovery... IBM is considered the bellwether stock on Wall Street.* N-COUNT: usu sing, oft N n

belly /beli/ **bellies** ◆◆◇◇◇

1 The **belly** of a person or animal is their stomach or abdomen; a literary use or, in British English, an informal use. *She laid her hands on her swollen belly. ...a horse with its belly ripped open... You'll eat so much your belly'll be like a barrel.* • See also **beer belly, pot belly**. N-COUNT: with poss =stomach

2 If a company **goes belly up**, it does not have enough money to pay its debts; an informal expression. *I really can't afford to see this company go belly up.* PHRASE: V inflects =go bust

bellyache /belieɪk/ **bellyaches, bellyaching, bellyached;** also spelled **belly-ache**.

1 **Bellyache** is a pain inside your abdomen, especially in your stomach; an informal use. *They may complain of diarrhea or bellyache.* N-VAR =stomach-ache

2 If you say that someone **is bellyaching** you mean VB: usu cont

they complain loudly and frequently about something and you think this is unreasonable or unjustified; an informal use. *Everyone is belly-aching about recession.* =complain V about n Also V

belly button, belly buttons. Your **belly button** is your navel; used mainly by children. N-COUNT

belly dancer, belly dancers; also spelled **belly-dancer**. A **belly dancer** is a woman who performs a Middle Eastern dance in which she moves her hips and abdomen vigorously. N-COUNT

belly laugh, belly laughs; also spelled **belly-laugh**. A **belly laugh** is a very loud, deep laugh. *Each gag was rewarded with a generous belly-laugh.* N-COUNT

belong /bɪlɒŋ, AM -lɔːŋ/ **belongs, belonging, belonged** ◆◆◆◇◇

1 If something **belongs to** you, you own it. *The house had belonged to her family for three or four generations.* VB: no cont V to n

2 You say that something **belongs to** a particular person when you are guessing, discovering, or explaining that it was produced by or is part of that person. *The handwriting belongs to a male... They established that the body belonged to a 15-year-old girl.* VB: no cont V to n

3 If someone **belongs to** a particular group, they are a member of that group. *I used to belong to a youth club.* VB: no cont V to n

4 If something or someone **belongs in** or **to** a particular category, type, or group, they are of that category, type, or group. *The judges could not decide which category it belonged in... I realized that he and I belonged to different worlds.* VB: no cont V in/to n

5 If something **belongs to** a particular time, it comes from that time. *The pictures belong to an era when there was a preoccupation with high society.* VB: no cont V to n

6 If you say that something **belongs to** someone, you mean that person has the right to it. *...but the last word belonged to Rosanne.* VB: no cont V to n

7 If you say that a time **belongs to** a particular system or way of doing something, you mean that that time is or will be characterized by it. *The future belongs to democracy.* VB: no cont V to n

8 If a baby or child **belongs to** a particular adult, that adult is its parent or the person who is looking after it. *He deduced that the two children belonged to the couple.* VB: no cont V to n

9 When lovers say that they **belong** together, they are expressing their closeness or commitment to each other. *I really think that we belong together... He belongs with me.* V-RECIP: no cont V together V with n

10 If a person or thing **belongs** in a particular place or situation, that where they should be. *You don't belong here... This piece really belongs in the concert hall... I'm so glad to see you back where you belong... They need to feel they belong.* ♦ **belonging** *...a man utterly without a sense of belonging.* VB: no cont V adv/prep V N-UNCOUNT

belongings /bɪlɒŋɪŋz, AM -lɔːŋ-/. Your **belongings** are the things that you own, especially things that are small enough to be carried. *I collected my belongings and left... He was identified only by his uniform and personal belongings.* ◆◇◇◇◇ N-PLURAL: usu poss N =possessions

beloved /bɪlʌvɪd/. When the adjective is not followed by a noun it is pronounced /bɪlʌvd/. ◆◆◇◇◇

1 A **beloved** person, thing, or place is one that you feel great affection for. *He lost his beloved wife last year... The rose is the most romantic of flowers, beloved of poets, singers, and artists.* ADJ-GRADED: usu ADJ n, also v-link ADJ of/by n =cherished

2 Your **beloved** is the person that you love; an old-fashioned use. *He takes his beloved into his arms.* N-SING: usu poss N

below /bɪloʊ/ ◆◆◆◆◇

1 If something is **below** something else, it is in a lower position. *He appeared from the apartment directly below Leonard's... The path runs below a long brick wall... The sun had already sunk below the horizon... The boat dipped below the surface of the water.* ► Also an adverb. *We climbed rather perilously down a rope-ladder to the boat below. ...a view to the street below... Spread out below was a great crowd.* PREP ≠above ADV: n ADV, ADV after v

2 If something is **below ground** or **below the ground**, it is in the ground. *They have designed a system which pumps up water from 70m below ground... Coils buried in tunnels below the ground might soon be used to store large amounts of electricity.* PHRASE

3 You use **below** in a piece of writing to refer to something that is mentioned later. *Please write to me at the address below... The BBC Good Food Show is giving away free tickets in a competition. For details, see below.* ADV: n ADV, ADV after v

4 If something is **below** a particular amount, rate, or level, it is less than that amount, rate, or level. *Night temperatures can drop below 15 degrees Celsius... British Telecom agreed to keep overall price increases to 7.5 per cent below inflation... Rainfall has been below average.* ► Also an adverb. *...temperatures at zero or below.* PREP ≠above ADV

5 If someone is **below** you in an organization, they are lower in rank. *Such people often experience less stress than those in the ranks immediately below them. ...pay rises awarded to all white-collar staff below chief officer level.* PREP ≠above

6 ● **below par**: see **par**.

below-the-belt. See **belt**.

belt /belt/ **belts, belting, belted** ◆◆◆◇◇

1 A **belt** is a strip of leather or cloth that you fasten round your waist. *He wore a belt with a large brass buckle.* ● See also **safety belt, seat belt**. N-COUNT

2 A **belt** in a machine is a circular strip of rubber that is used to drive moving parts or to move objects along. *The turning disc is connected by a drive belt to an electric motor.* ● See also **conveyor belt, fan belt**. N-COUNT

3 A **belt** of land or sea is a long, narrow area of it that has some special feature. *Miners in Zambia's northern copper belt have gone on strike... Behind him was a belt of trees, and behind the trees hills and fields.* ● See also **Bible Belt, commuter belt, green belt**. N-COUNT: with supp =strip

4 If someone **belts** you, they hit you very hard; an informal use. *'Is it right she belted old George in the gut?' she asked.* ► Also a noun. *Father would give you a belt over the head with the scrubbing brush.* VERB =thump V n N-COUNT

5 If you **belt** somewhere, you move or travel there very fast; an informal British use. *We belted down Iveagh Parade to where the motor was.* VERB =dash V prep/adv

6 If someone is or has a **belt** of a particular colour in judo or karate, they have reached the standard which that colour represents. *He is a black belt in karate.* N-COUNT: usu adj N

7 See also **belted**.

8 If you do or say something that is **below the belt** or hit someone **below the belt**, you do or say something that is rather cruel and unfair. *Do you think it's a bit below the belt what they're doing? ...this kind of below-the-belt discrimination.* PHRASES

9 If you have to **tighten** your **belt**, you must spend less money and manage without things because you have less money than you used to have. *Clearly, if you are spending more than your income, you'll need to tighten your belt.* V inflects

10 If you have something **under** your **belt**, you have already achieved it or done it. *Clare is now a full-time author with six books, including four novels, under her belt.* have/with n PHR

belt out. If you **belt out** a song, you sing or play it very loudly; an informal expression. *He held a three-hour family Karaoke session in his hotel, belting out Sinatra and Beatles hits.* PHRASAL VERB V P n Also V n P

belt up. If someone tells you to **belt up**, they are telling you in a very impolite way to stop talking; an informal British expression. *Chambers waved his hand. 'Belt up!' he snapped.* PHRASAL VERB PRAGMATICS V P

belted /beltɪd/. If someone's jacket or coat, for example, is **belted**, it has a belt fastened round it. *He wore a belted raincoat that accentuated his portly middle... She wore a brown suede jacket, belted at the waist.* ADJ

belter /beltəʳ/ **belters.** If you describe someone or something as a **belter**, you are emphasizing that they are very good, powerful, or impressive; an informal word. *Shirley's a real belter.* N-COUNT PRAGMATICS

belt-tightening. If you need to do some **belt-tightening**, you must spend less money and manage without things because you have less money than you used to have. *The Bangladeshi government has called for severe belt-tightening.* N-UNCOUNT

bemoan /bɪmoun/ **bemoans, bemoaning, bemoaned.** ◆◇◇◇◇ If you **bemoan** something, you express sorrow or dissatisfaction about it; a formal word. *Universities and other research establishments bemoan their lack of funds.* VERB =lament/mourn V n

bemuse /bɪmjuːz/ **bemuses, bemusing, bemused.** If something **bemuses** you, it puzzles or confuses you. *The sheer quantity of detail would be enough to bemuse any but the most clear-headed author.* VERB =bewilder V n

bemused /bɪmjuːzd/. ◆◇◇◇◇ If you are **bemused**, you are puzzled or confused. *He was rather bemused by children... Mr. Sebastian was looking at the boys with a bemused expression.* ADJ-GRADED =bewildered ♦ **bemusedly** *He was staring bemusedly at the picture of himself.* ADV-GRADED: ADV after v

bench /bentʃ/ **benches** ◆◆◇◇◇

1 A **bench** is a long seat of wood or metal that two or more people can sit on. *He sat down on a park bench.* N-COUNT

2 A **bench** is a long, narrow table in a factory or laboratory. *...the laboratory bench.* N-COUNT

3 In parliament, different groups sit on different **benches**. For example, the government sits on the government **benches**; used in British English. *Mr Shekhar has spent most of his life on the opposition benches.* ● See also **backbencher, backbenches, front bench.** N-PLURAL

4 In a court of law, **the bench** is the judge or magistrates. *The chairman of the bench adjourned the case until October 27.* N-SING-COLL: the N

5 If someone serves on **the bench**, they work as a judge or magistrate. *Allgood served on the bench for more than 50 years.* N-SING: the N

6 If a player is on **the bench** for a particular match, he has been chosen as a substitute for that match; used in sports journalism. *He may gain a place on the bench.* N-SING: the N

benchmark /bentʃmɑːʳk/ **benchmarks;** also spelled **bench mark.** ◆◇◇◇◇ A **benchmark** is something whose quality, quantity, or capability is known and which can therefore be used as a standard with which other things can be compared. *The truck industry is a benchmark for the economy.* N-COUNT: usu sing, oft N for n =yardstick

bend /bend/ **bends, bending, bent** ◆◆◆◇◇

1 When you **bend**, you move the top part of your body downwards and forwards. Other tall upright things also **bend**. *I bent over and kissed her cheek... Turn the pot if the plants show signs of bending towards the light... She bent and picked up a plastic bucket... She was bent over the sink washing the dishes.* VERB V adv/prep V V-ed

2 When you **bend** your head, you move your head forwards and downwards. *Rick appeared, bending his head a little to clear the top of the door.* VERB V n

3 When you **bend** a part of your body such as your arm or leg, or when it **bends**, you change its position so that it is no longer straight. *These cruel devices are designed to stop prisoners bending their legs... As you walk faster, you will find the arms bend naturally and more quickly.* V-ERG V n V ♦ **bent** *Keep your knees slightly bent.* ADJ-GRADED

4 If you **bend** something that is flat or straight, you use force to make it curved or to put an angle in it. *Bend the bar into a horseshoe... She'd cut a jagged hole in the tin, bending a knife in the process.* VERB ≠straighten V n prep V n Also V n with adv ♦ **bent** *...a length of bent wire.* ADJ-GRADED

5 When a road, beam of light, or other long thin thing **bends** or when something **bends** it, it changes direction to form a curve or angle. *The road bent slightly to the right... Glass bends light of different colours by different amounts.* V-ERG V V n

6 A **bend** in a road, pipe, or other long thin object is a curve or angle in it. *The crash occurred on a sharp bend. ...an historic town nestling in a bend of the river.* N-COUNT

7 If someone **bends** to your opinion, or if they **bend** their opinions, they believe or do something different, usually when they are reluctant to. *Congress has to bend to his will... Do you think she's likely to bend on her attitude to Europe?... He would not bend his principles to them.* VERB V to n V V n

8 If you **bend** rules or laws, you interpret them in a way that allows you to do something they would not normally allow you to do. *A minority of officers were prepared to bend the rules.* VERB V n

9 If you **bend** the truth or **bend** the facts, you say something that is not exactly true. *Invariably we are tempted to bend the truth a little in order to spare them the pain of discovering the real facts.* VERB V n

10 See also **bent; hairpin bend.**

11 If you say that someone **is bending over backwards** to be helpful or kind, you are emphasizing that they are trying very hard to be helpful or kind. *People are bending over backwards to please customers.* PHRASES V inflects, usu PHR to-inf PRAGMATICS

12 If you say that someone or something **drives you round the bend**, you mean that you dislike them and they annoy or upset you very much; an informal British expression. *And can you make that tea before your fidgeting drives me completely round the bend.* V inflects PRAGMATICS

13 If you say that someone is **round the bend**, you mean that they do foolish or silly things; an informal British expression. *People thought I was round the bend.* v-link PHR, PHR after v =mad ≠sensible

14 ● to **bend** someone's **ear**: see **ear.**

bended /bendɪd/. If you beg someone for something **on bended knee**, you are kneeling humbly; a formal expression. *I almost begged him on bended knee to let the two accused men be tried in Scotland.* PHRASE: usu PHR after v

bender /bendəʳ/ **benders.** If someone goes on a **bender**, they drink a very large amount of alcohol; an informal word. N-COUNT: usu sing, usu on N

bendy /bendi/ **bendier, bendiest.** A **bendy** object bends easily into a curved or angular shape. *...a bendy toy whose limbs bend in every direction.* ADJ-GRADED: usu ADJ n =flexible

beneath /bɪniːθ/ ◆◆◆◇◇

1 Something that is **beneath** another thing is under the other thing. *She could see the muscles of his shoulders beneath his T-shirt... She found pleasure in sitting beneath the trees... Four storeys of parking beneath the theatre was not enough. ...the frozen grass crunching beneath his feet.* PREP =under ≠above ► Also an adverb. *On a shelf beneath he spotted a photo album. ...aeroplanes roaring above, subways rattling beneath.* ADV: n ADV, ADV after v =below ≠above

2 If you talk about what is **beneath** the surface of something, you are talking about the aspects of it which are hidden or not obvious. *...emotional strains beneath the surface... Somewhere deep beneath the surface lay a caring character... Beneath the festive mood there is an underlying apprehension.* PREP =under

3 If you say that someone or something is **beneath** you, you feel that they are not good enough for you or not suitable for you. *They decided she was marrying beneath her... Many find themselves having to take jobs far beneath them.* PREP

Benedictine /benɪdɪktin, -tiːn/ **Benedictines.** A **Benedictine** is a monk or nun who is a member of a Christian religious community that follows the rule of St. Benedict. *...the famous Benedictine abbey of St Mary.* N-COUNT: oft N n

benediction /benɪdɪkʃən/ **benedictions.** A **benediction** is a prayer or gesture blessing someone; a formal word. *...as the minister pronounced the benediction... I received a parting smile, like a benediction, from Russell... She could only raise her head in a gesture of benediction.* N-VAR =blessing

benefactor /benɪfæktəʳ/ **benefactors.** ◆◇◇◇◇ A **benefactor** is a person who helps a person or organization by giving them money. *In his old age he became a benefactor of the arts.* N-COUNT: oft N of n =patron

beneficent /bɪnefɪsənt/. A **beneficent** person or thing helps people or results in something good; a formal word. *In 1909 nuns were running more than 1,000 beneficent institutions.* ADJ-GRADED: usu ADJ n

beneficial /bɛnɪfɪʃᵊl/. Something that is **beneficial** helps people or improves their lives. ...*vitamins which are beneficial to our health... Using computers has a beneficial effect on children's learning.* ◆◆◇◇◇ ADJ-GRADED: oft ADJ *to* n

beneficiary /bɛnɪfɪʃəri, AM -ʃieri/ **beneficiaries** ◆◇◇◇◇
1 Someone who is a **beneficiary** of something is helped by it. *The main beneficiaries of pension equality so far have been men.* N-COUNT: oft N *of* n =recipient
2 The **beneficiaries** of a will legally receive money or property from someone when they die. N-COUNT

benefit /bɛnɪfɪt/ **benefits, benefiting, benefited;** also spelled **benefitting, benefitted.** ◆◆◆◆◇
1 The **benefit** of something is the help that you get from it or the advantage that results from it. *Each family farms individually and reaps the benefit of its labor... I'm a great believer in the benefits of this form of therapy... For maximum benefit, use your treatment every day.* N-VAR: oft N *of* n =advantage, profit
2 If something is to your **benefit** or is of **benefit** to you, it helps you or improves your life. *This could now work to Albania's benefit... I hope what I have written will be of benefit to someone else who may feel the same way.* N-UNCOUNT: oft with poss, *of* N *to* n =advantage
3 If you **benefit** from something or if it **benefits** you, it helps you or improves your life. *Both sides have benefited from the talks. ...a variety of government programs benefiting children.* V-ERG =profit V *from* n V n Also V
4 If you have the **benefit of** some information, knowledge, or equipment, you are able to use it so that you can achieve something. *Steve didn't have the benefit of a formal college education... With the benefit of hindsight, it is clear we ought to have done more... This remarkable achievement took place without the benefit of our modern telecommunication industry.* N-UNCOUNT: N *of* n =advantage
5 **Benefit** is money that is given by the government to people who are poor, ill, or unemployed. ...*the removal of benefit from school-leavers... I was told that in order to get benefit payments I would have to answer some questions.* N-VAR
6 A **benefit**, or a **benefit** concert or dinner, is an event that is held in order to raise money for a particular charity or person. *I am organising a benefit gig in Bristol to raise these funds.* N-COUNT: oft N n
7 See also **fringe benefit, supplementary benefit, unemployment benefit.**
8 If you give someone **the benefit of the doubt**, you treat them as if they are telling the truth or as if they have behaved properly, even though you are not sure that this is the case. *At first I gave him the benefit of the doubt... Shalford is entitled to the benefit of the doubt.* PHRASES usu PHR after v
9 If you say that someone is doing something **for the benefit of** a particular person, you mean that they are doing it for that person. *You need people working for the benefit of the community... He doesn't have to go through this elaborate display for my benefit!* PHR after v

benevolent /bɪnɛvələnt/ ◆◇◇◇◇
1 If you describe a person in authority as **benevolent**, you mean that they are kind and tolerant. *He has ruled as a benevolent dictator for many years.* ADJ-GRADED
♦ **benevolently** *Thorne nodded his understanding, smiling benevolently.* ADV-GRADED: ADV with v ♦ **benevolence** *A bit of benevolence from people in power is not what we need.* N-UNCOUNT
2 **Benevolent** is used in the names of some organizations that give money and help to people who need it. ...*the Army Benevolent Fund.* ADJ: ADJ n

Bengali /beŋgɔːli/ **Bengalis** ◆◆◆◆◇
1 **Bengali** means belonging or relating to Bengal, or to its people or language. *She married a Bengali doctor.* ADJ ► A **Bengali** is a person who comes from Bangladesh or West Bengal. N-COUNT
2 **Bengali** is the language that is spoken by people who live in Bangladesh and by many people in West Bengal. N-UNCOUNT

benighted /bɪnaɪtɪd/. If you describe people or the place where they live as **benighted**, you mean that you consider them to be unfortunate or ignorant; a literary word. *The terrible circumstances of that benighted country may be too much for anyone to overcome.* ADJ-GRADED: ADJ n PRAGMATICS

benign /bɪnaɪn/ ◆◇◇◇◇
1 You use **benign** to describe someone who is kind, gentle, and harmless. *They are normally a more benign audience... Critics of the scheme take a less benign view.* ADJ-GRADED: usu ADJ n =charitable ♦ **benignly** *I just smiled benignly and stood back.* ADV-GRADED: usu ADV with v
2 A **benign** substance or process does not have any harmful effects. *We're taking relatively benign medicines and we're turning them into poisons.* ADJ-GRADED: usu ADJ n
3 A **benign** tumour will not cause death or serious harm; a medical use. *It wasn't cancer, only a benign tumour.* ADJ: usu ADJ n ≠malignant
4 **Benign** conditions are pleasant or make it easy for something to happen. *They enjoyed an especially benign climate... This plunge came in a time of relatively benign economic conditions.* ADJ-GRADED: usu ADJ n
5 If you describe someone's approach to a problem as one of **benign neglect**, you disapprove of the fact that they are doing nothing and hoping that the problem will solve itself. *America and Japan have settled back into a policy of benign neglect of their currencies.* PHRASE PRAGMATICS

bent /bɛnt/ ◆◆◇◇◇
1 **Bent** is the past tense and past participle of **bend.**
2 If an object is **bent**, it is damaged and no longer has its correct shape. *The trees were all bent and twisted from the wind.* ADJ-GRADED
3 If a person is **bent**, their body has become curved because of old age or disease; used in written English. ...*a bent, frail, old man.* ADJ-GRADED =hunched
4 If someone is **bent on** doing something, especially something destructive, they are determined to do it. *He's bent on suicide.* ADJ-GRADED: v-link ADJ *on/upon* n/-ing PRAGMATICS
5 If you have a **bent** for something, you have a natural ability to do it or a natural interest in it. *His bent for natural history directed him towards his first job.* N-SING: with supp, oft N *for* n =flair
6 If someone is of a particular **bent**, they hold a particular set of beliefs. ...*economists of a socialist bent.* N-SING: adj N =persuasion
7 If you say that someone in a position of responsibility is **bent**, you mean that they are dishonest or do illegal things; used mainly in informal British English. ...*this bent accountant.* ADJ-GRADED
8 In British English, gay people are sometimes described as **bent**; an offensive use. ADJ
9 If someone is **bent double**, the top part of their body is leaning forward towards their legs, usually because they are in great pain or because they are laughing so much. *He left the courtroom on the first day bent double with stomach pain.* PHRASE: oft PHR *with/in* n

benzene /bɛnziːn/. **Benzene** is a clear, colourless liquid which is used in the manufacture of certain plastics and solvents, and is also used as an insecticide. Benzene is poisonous and catches fire very easily. N-UNCOUNT

bequeath /bɪkwiːð/ **bequeaths, bequeathing, bequeathed.** ◆◇◇◇◇
1 If you **bequeath** your money or property to someone, you legally state that they should have it when you die; a formal use. *Fields's will bequeathed his wife Hattie and son Claude the sum of twenty thousand dollars... He bequeathed all his silver to his children.* VERB =leave V n n V n *to* n
2 If you **bequeath** an idea or system, you leave it for other people to use or develop; a formal use. *He bequeaths his successor an economy that is doing quite well... It is true that colonialism did not bequeath much to Africa.* VERB V n n V n *to* n Also V n

bequest /bɪkwɛst/ **bequests.** A **bequest** is money or property which you legally leave to someone when you die. *The church here was left a bequest to hire doctors who would work amongst the poor.* N-COUNT

berate /bɪreɪt/ **berates, berating, berated.** If you **berate** someone, you scold them angrily; a formal word. *Marion berated Joe for the noise he made.* ◆◇◇◇◇ VERB =chide V n *for* n Also V n

Berber /bɜːʳbəʳ/ **Berbers.** **Berber** means belonging or relating to a certain ethnic group of Moslems in North Africa, or to their language or customs. *A Berber rug makes a colourful wall-hanging.* ► A **Berber** is a person from the Berber community.
ADJ
N-COUNT

bereaved /bɪriːvd/. A **bereaved** person is one who has a relative or close friend who has recently died. *Mr Dinkins visited the bereaved family to offer comfort.* ► The **bereaved** are people who are bereaved. *He wanted to show his sympathy for the bereaved.*
◆◇◇◇◇ ADJ: usu ADJ n
N-PLURAL

bereavement /bɪriːvmənt/ **bereavements.** **Bereavement** is the grief you feel or the state you are in when a relative or close friend dies. *When Mary died Anne did not share her brother's sense of bereavement. ...those who have suffered a bereavement.*
◆◇◇◇◇ N-VAR =loss

bereft /bɪreft/. If a person or thing is **bereft** of something, they no longer have it; a formal word. *The place seemed to be utterly bereft of human life.*
◆◇◇◇◇ ADJ-GRADED: usu v-link ADJ, usu ADJ *of* n

beret /bereɪ, AM bəreɪ/ **berets.** A **beret** is a circular, flat hat that is made of soft material and has no brim.
◆◇◇◇◇ N-COUNT

berk /bɜːʳk/ **berks.** If you call someone a **berk**, you mean that you think they are stupid or irritating; an informal and offensive word in British English.
N-COUNT PRAGMATICS

berry /beri/ **berries.** **Berries** are small, round fruit that grow on a bush or a tree. Some berries are edible, for example blackberries and raspberries.
◆◆◇◇◇ N-COUNT

berserk /bəʳzɜːʳk, -sɜːʳk/

1 **Berserk** means crazy and out of control. *He tossed back his head in a howl of berserk laughter.*
ADJ-GRADED =mad

2 If someone or something **goes berserk**, they lose control of themselves and become very angry or violent. *When I saw him I went berserk.*
PHRASE: V inflects =go mad

berth /bɜːʳθ/ **berths, berthing, berthed**
◆◇◇◇◇

1 If you **give** someone or something **a wide berth**, you avoid them because you think they are unpleasant, or dangerous, or simply because you do not like them. *More experienced hands in the Mission had given Miss Pickerstaff a wide berth that morning... She gives showbiz parties a wide berth.*
PHRASE: V inflects

2 A **berth** is a bed on a boat, train, or caravan. *Goldring booked a berth on the first boat he could.*
N-COUNT

3 A **berth** is a space in a harbour where a ship stays for a period of time.
N-COUNT =mooring

4 When a ship **berths**, it sails into harbour and stops at the quay. *As the ship berthed in New York, McClintock was with the first immigration officers aboard.* ♦ **berthed** *There the Gripsholm was berthed next to another ship.*
VERB V
ADJ: usu v-link ADJ, usu ADJ prep

beseech /bɪsiːtʃ/ **beseeches, beseeching, beseeched.** If you **beseech** someone to do something, you ask them very insistently and desperately; a literary word. *She beseeched him to cut his drinking and his smoking... 'How are we going to pay for all those planes we ordered?' they beseeched Mr Ryan.*
VERB =beg
V n to-inf
V with quote
Also V n, V n *for* n

beseeching /bɪsiːtʃɪŋ/. A **beseeching** expression, gesture, or tone of voice suggests that the person who has or makes it very much wants someone to do something; used in written English. *She clung to him and looked up into his face with beseeching eyes.* ♦ **beseechingly** *Hugh looked at his father beseechingly.*
ADJ-GRADED =imploring
ADV-GRADED: ADV after v

beset /bɪset/ **besets, besetting.** The form **beset** is used in the present tense and is the past tense and past participle. If someone or something **is beset** by problems or fears, they have many problems or fears which affect them severely. *The country is beset by severe economic problems... The discussions were beset with difficulties. ...the problems now besetting the country.*
◆◇◇◇◇ VERB
be V-ed *by/with* n
V n

beside /bɪsaɪd/
◆◆◆◇◇

1 Something that is **beside** something else is at the side of it or next to it. *On the table beside an empty plate was a pile of books... I moved from behind my desk to sit beside her.* • See also **besides**.
PREP =next to, by

2 If you are **beside yourself** with anger or excitement, you are extremely angry or excited. *He had shouted down the phone at her, beside himself with anxiety... Cathy was beside herself with excitement.*
PHRASE: v-link PHR, oft PHR *with* n

• **beside the point**: see **point**.

besides /bɪsaɪdz/
◆◆◆◇◇

1 **Besides** something or **beside** something means in addition to it. *I think she has many good qualities besides being very beautiful... There was only one person besides Ford who knew Julia Jameson.* ► Also an adverb. *You get to sample lots of baked things and take home masses of cookies besides.*
PREP: oft PREP -ing =apart from
ADV: cl ADV

2 **Besides** is used to emphasize an additional point that you are making, especially one that you consider to be important. *The house was out of our price range and too big anyway. Besides, I'd grown fond of our little rented house.*
ADV: ADV with cl, not last in cl PRAGMATICS

besiege /bɪsiːdʒ/ **besieges, besieging, besieged**
◆◆◇◇◇

1 If you **are besieged** by people, many people want something from you and continually bother you. *She was besieged by the press and the public.*
VB: usu passive *be* V-ed

2 If soldiers **besiege** a place, they surround it and wait for the people in it to surrender. *The main part of the army moved to Sevastopol to besiege the town... The Afghan air force was using helicopters to supply the besieged town.*
VERB V n V-ed

besmirch /bɪsmɜːʳtʃ/ **besmirches, besmirching, besmirched.** If you **besmirch** someone or their reputation, you say that they are a bad person or that they have done something wrong, usually when this is not true; a literary word. *Lawyers can besmirch reputations and disrupt social harmony.*
VERB =defame
V n

besotted /bɪsɒtɪd/. If you are **besotted** with someone or something, you like them so much that you seem foolish or silly. *He became so besotted with her that even his children were forgotten.*
ADJ-GRADED: usu v-link ADJ, oft ADJ *with* n =infatuated

bespeak /bɪspiːk/ **bespeaks, bespeaking, bespoke, bespoken.** If someone's action or behaviour **bespeaks** a particular quality, feeling, or experience, it indicates that they have that quality, feeling, or experience; an old-fashioned or literary word. *The tone of his text bespeaks a certain tiredness.*
VERB =denote
V n

bespectacled /bɪspektəkəld/. Someone who is **bespectacled** is wearing spectacles; used in written English. *Mr Merrick was a slim, quiet, bespectacled man.*
ADJ: usu ADJ n

bespoke /bɪspoʊk/

1 A **bespoke** craftsman such as a tailor makes or sells things that are specially made for the customer who ordered them; used in formal British English. *Habits made by a bespoke tailor are an expensive item.*
ADJ: ADJ n

2 **Bespoke** things such as clothes have been specially made for the customer who ordered them; used in formal British English. *In the basement fifteen employees are busy making bespoke coats.*
ADJ: ADJ n

best /best/

1 **Best** is the superlative of **good**. *If you want further information the best thing to do is have a word with the driver as you get on the bus... It's not the best place to live if you wish to develop your knowledge and love of mountains.*

2 **Best** is the superlative of **well**. *James Fox is best known as the author of White Mischief, and he is currently working on a new book.*

3 **The best** is used to refer to things of the highest quality or standard. *We offer only the best to our clients... He'll have the best of care.*
N-SING: *the* N ≠worst

4 Someone's **best** is the greatest effort or highest achievement or standard that they are capable of. *Miss Blockey was at her best when she played the piano... One needs to be a first-class driver to get the best out of that sort of machinery.*
N-SING: oft poss N

5 If you say that something **is the best** that can be done or hoped for, you think it is the most pleasant, successful, or beneficial thing that can be done or hoped for. *A draw seems the best they can hope for... The best we can do is try to stay cool and muddle through.*
N-SING: *the* N

6 If you like something **best** or like it **the best**, you prefer it. *The thing I liked best about the show was the music... Mother liked it best when Daniel got money... What was the role you loved the best?* ADV-SUPERL: ADV after v, oft *the* ADV =most

7 Best is used to form the superlative of compound adjectives beginning with 'good' and 'well'. For example, the superlative of 'well-known' is 'best-known'.

8 See also **second best, Sunday best.**

9 You can say **'All the best'** when you are saying goodbye to someone, or at the end of a letter. *Wish him all the best, and tell him we miss him.* PHRASES CONVENTION PRAGMATICS

10 You use **best of all** to indicate that what you are about to mention is the thing that you prefer or that has most advantages out of all the things you have mentioned. *It was comfortable and cheap: best of all, most of the rent was being paid by two American friends.* PHR with cl/group PRAGMATICS

11 If someone does something **as best** they **can**, they do it as well as they can, although it is very difficult. *The older people were left to carry on as best they could.* V inflects, PHR after v

12 You use **at best** to indicate that even if you describe something as favourably as possible or if it performs as well as it possibly can, it is still not very good. *This policy, they say, is at best confused and at worst non-existent... At best they were effective as antidepressants for no more than four months.* PHR with cl/group ≠at worst

13 If you **do** your **best** or **try** your **best** to do something, you try as hard as you can to do it, or do it as well as you can. *I'll do my best to find out... It wasn't her fault, she was trying her best to help... It's a Championship fight—do your best.* V inflects, oft PHR to-inf

14 If you say that something is **for the best**, you mean it is the most desirable or helpful thing that could have happened or could be done, considering all the circumstances. *In the long run, it was for the best... Whatever the circumstances, parents are supposed to know what to do for the best.* PHR after v, v-link PHR

15 If two people are **the best of friends**, they are close friends, especially when they have had a disagreement or fight in the past. *Magda is now married to George Callerby and we are the best of friends.* usu v-link PHR

16 If you say that someone **had best** do something or that they**'d best** do it, you mean they ought to do it. Some people consider this to be non-standard. *You'd best take a look.* MODAL =had better

17 If you say that a particular person **knows best**, you mean that they have a lot of experience and should therefore be trusted to make decisions for other people. *He was convinced that doctors and dentists knew best.* V inflects

18 If you **look your best**, you are looking as smart and attractive as you can. *I made sure I was very clean and looking my best.* V inflects

19 If you **make the best of** something or **make the best of a bad job**, you accept an unsatisfactory situation cheerfully and try to manage as well as you can. *She instilled in the children the virtues of good hard work, and making the best of what you have.* V inflects

20 • **to the best of your ability**: see **ability.** • **the best of the bunch**: see **bunch.** • **to hope for the best**: see **hope.** • **to the best of your knowledge**: see **knowledge.** • **best of luck**: see **luck.** • **the best part**: see **part.** • **at the best of times**: see **time.** • **the best of both worlds**: see **world.**

bestial /bestiəl, AM -stʃəl/. If you describe behaviour or a situation as **bestial**, you mean that it is very unpleasant or disgusting. *A statement on Amman Radio spoke of bestial aggression and a horrible massacre. ...the bestial conditions into which the city has sunk.* ADJ-GRADED =brutish, depraved

bestiality /bestiælɪti, AM -tʃæl-/

1 Bestiality is revolting or disgusting behaviour; a formal use. *It is difficult to believe that humans can behave with such bestiality towards other humans.* N-UNCOUNT

2 Bestiality is sexual activity in which a person has sex with an animal. N-UNCOUNT

best man. The **best man** at a wedding is the man who acts as an attendant to the bridegroom. ◆◇◇◇◇ N-SING

bestow /bɪstou/ **bestows, bestowing, bestowed.** To **bestow** something **on** someone means to give or present it to them; a formal word. *The Queen personally visited his quarters at Windsor to bestow on him his third knighthood.* ◆◇◇◇◇ VERB =confer V *on/upon* n n Also V n *on/upon* n

bestride /bɪstraɪd/ **bestrides, bestriding, bestrode, bestridden.** If someone or something **bestrides** something, they dominate it; a literary word. *IBM bestrode the industry, accounting for 38% of the industry's revenues.* VERB V n

best seller, best sellers; also spelled **bestseller.** A **best seller** is a book of which a great number of copies has been sold. ◆◇◇◇◇ N-COUNT =blockbuster

best-selling; also spelled **bestselling.** ◆◇◇◇◇

1 A **best-selling** product such as a book is very popular and a large quantity of it has been sold. ADJ: ADJ n

2 A **best-selling** author is an author who has sold a very large number of copies of his or her book. ADJ: ADJ n

bet /bet/ **bets, betting.** The form **bet** is used in the present tense and is the past tense and past participle. ◆◆◆◇◇

1 If you **bet** on the result of a horse race, football match, or other event, you give someone a sum of money which they give you back with extra money if the result is what you predicted, or which they keep if it is not. *Jockeys are forbidden to bet on the outcome of races... I bet £10 on a horse called Premonition... He bet them 500 pounds they would lose.* ► Also a noun. *Do you always have a bet on the Grand National?* ♦ **betting** *...his thousand-pound fine for illegal betting. ...betting shops.* VERB V *on* n V n *on* n V n n that N-COUNT N-UNCOUNT

2 A **bet** is a sum of money which you give to someone when you bet. *You can put a bet on almost anything these days.* N-COUNT

3 If someone **is betting** that something will happen, they are hoping or expecting that it will happen; used mainly in journalism. *The big pharmaceutical firms are betting that customers will stick with their own familiar brand names. ...people who were betting on a further easing of credit conditions.* VB: only cont V that V *on* n

4 See also **betting.**

5 If you use informal phrases such as **'I bet', 'I'll bet'**, and **'you can bet'**, you mean that you are sure something is true. *I bet you were good at games when you were at school... I bet you anything you like he's a pimp... I'll bet they'll taste out of this world... You can bet she will be there.* PHRASES PRAGMATICS

6 If you tell someone that something is a **good bet**, you are suggesting that it is the thing or course of action that they should choose. *Textiles are a good bet for a country bent on industrialisation... Your best bet is to choose a guest house.*

7 If you say that it is **a good bet** or **a safe bet** that something is true or will happen, you are saying that is extremely likely to be true or to happen. *It is a safe bet that the current owners will not sell.* usu *it* v-link PHR that

8 If you **hedge your bets**, you follow two courses of action to avoid making a decision between two things because you cannot decide which one is right. *NASA is hedging its bets and adopting both strategies.* V inflects =play safe

9 You use **I bet** or **I'll bet** in reply to a statement to show that you agree with it or that you expected it to be true, usually when you are annoyed or amused by it; an informal expression. *'I'd like to ask you something,' I said. 'I bet you would,' she grinned.* oft PHR that PRAGMATICS

10 You can use **my bet is** or **it's my bet** to give your own personal opinion about something, when you are fairly sure that you are right; an informal expression. *My bet is that next year will be different... It's my bet that he's the guy behind this killing.* PRAGMATICS

11 If you say **don't bet on** something or **I wouldn't bet on** something, you mean that you do not think that something is true or will happen; an informal expression. *'We'll never get a table in there'—'Don't bet on it.'* PRAGMATICS

12 If you reply **'Do you want to bet?'** or **'Want a bet?'** to someone, you mean you are certain that what they have said is wrong; an informal expression. *'Money can't buy happiness'—'Want to bet?'* CONVENTION PRAGMATICS

13 You use **'You bet'** or **'you bet your life'** to say yes PRAGMATICS in an emphatic way or to emphasize a reply or statement. *'It's settled, then?'—'You bet.'... 'Are you afraid of snakes?'—'You bet your life I'm afraid of snakes.'*

beta blocker, /bi͟tə blɒkəʳ, AM be͟ɪtə -/ **beta blockers.** A **beta blocker** is a drug which is used to treat people who have high blood pressure or heart problems. N-COUNT

bete noire /bet nwɑ͟ːʳ/. If you refer to someone or something as your **bete noire**, you mean that you have a particular dislike for them or that they annoy you a great deal. *Our real bete noire is the car boot sale.* N-SING: oft with poss =bugbear

betide /bɪta͟ɪd/. If you say **woe betide** anyone who does a particular thing, you mean that something unpleasant will happen to them if they do it; a formal expression. *Woe betide anyone who got in his way.* PHRASE: PHR n PRAGMATICS

betoken /bɪto͟ʊkən/ **betokens, betokening, betokened.** If something **betokens** something else, it is a sign of this thing; a formal word. *His demeanour betokened embarrassment at his prosperity.* VERB =indicate, signal V n

betray /bɪtre͟ɪ/ **betrays, betraying, betrayed** ◆◆◇◇◇

1 If you **betray** someone who loves or trusts you, your actions hurt and disappoint them. *When I tell someone I will not betray his confidence I keep my word... The President betrayed them when he went back on his promise not to raise taxes.* ♦ **betrayer, betrayers** *She was her friend and now calls her a betrayer.* VERB V n N-COUNT

2 If someone **betrays** their country or their comrades, they give information to an enemy, putting their country's security or their comrades' safety at risk. *They offered me money if I would betray my associates... The group were informers, and they betrayed the plan to the Chinese.* ♦ **betrayer** *'Traitor!' she screamed. 'Betrayer of England!'* VERB V n V n *to* n N-COUNT

3 If you **betray** an ideal or your principles, you say or do something which goes against those beliefs. *We betray the ideals of our country when we support capital punishment.* ♦ **betrayer** *Babearth regarded the middle classes as the betrayers of the Revolution.* VERB =renege on V n N-COUNT

4 If you **betray** a feeling or quality, you show it without intending to. *She studied his face, but it betrayed nothing... He nodded his head instead of saying anything where his voice might betray him.* VERB ≠conceal V n

betrayal /bɪtre͟ɪəl/ **betrayals.** A **betrayal** is an action which betrays someone or something, or the fact of being betrayed. *She felt that what she had done was a betrayal of Patrick... He acknowledged the sense of betrayal by civil rights leaders.* ◆◇◇◇◇ N-VAR: oft N *of* n

betrothal /bɪtro͟ʊðəl/ **betrothals.** A **betrothal** is an engagement to be married; an old-fashioned word. N-VAR

betrothed /bɪtro͟ʊðd/. If you are **betrothed** to someone, you are engaged to be married to them; an old-fashioned word. *She was betrothed to his brother.* ► Your **betrothed** is the person you are betrothed to. *She is here without her betrothed.* ADJ: usu v-link ADJ, oft ADJ *to* n N-SING: usu poss N

better /be͟təʳ/ **betters, bettering, bettered** ◆◆◆◆◆

1 **Better** is the comparative of **good**.

2 **Better** is the comparative of **well**.

3 If you like one thing **better** than another, you like it more. *I like your interpretation better than the one I was taught... I'd like nothing better than to join you girls... They liked it better when it rained.* ADV-COMPAR: ADV after v

4 If you are **better** after an illness or injury, you have recovered from it. If you feel **better**, you no longer feel so ill. *He is much better now, he's fine... The doctors were saying there wasn't much hope of me getting better.* ADJ-GRADED: v-link ADJ

5 You use **had better** or **'d better** when you are advising, warning, or threatening someone, or expressing an opinion about what should happen. *It's half past two. I think we had better go home... You'd better run if you're going to get your ticket... He'd better not try to fool me.* ► In spoken English people sometimes use **better** without 'had' or 'be' before it. It has the same meaning. *Better not say too much aloud... 'I'll call her.'—'You better had.'* PHR-MODAL PRAGMATICS

6 If you say that you expect or deserve **better**, you mean that you expect or deserve a higher standard of achievement, behaviour, or treatment from people than they have shown you. *We expect better of you in the future... Our long-suffering mining communities deserve better than this.* PRON

7 Your **betters** are people who have a higher status or rank than you do; an old-fashioned or humorous use. *Sit down and be quiet in front of your elders and betters.* N-PLURAL: poss N

8 If someone **betters** a high achievement or standard, they achieve something higher. *He recorded a time of 4 minutes 23, bettering the old record of 4-24... As an account of adolescence it could hardly be bettered.* VERB V n

9 If you **better** your situation, you improve your social status or the quality of your life. If you **better** yourself, you improve your social status. *He had dedicated his life to bettering the lot of the oppressed people of South Africa... Our parents chose to come here with the hope of bettering themselves.* VERB V n V pron-refl

10 **Better** is used to form the comparative of compound adjectives beginning with 'good' and 'well.' For example, the comparative of 'well-off' is 'better-off.'

11 You can say that someone **is better** doing one thing than another, or **it is better** doing one thing than another to advise someone about what they should do. *You are better eating just a small snack than hurrying a main meal... Wouldn't it be better putting a time-limit on the task?... Subjects like this are better left alone.* PHRASES V inflects, PHR -ing, PHR -ed PRAGMATICS

12 If something changes **for the better**, it improves. *He dreams of changing the world for the better.* PHR after v

13 If a feeling such as jealousy, curiosity, or anger **gets the better of** you, it becomes too strong for you to conceal or control. *She didn't allow her emotions to get the better of her.* V inflects, PHR n

14 If you **get the better of** someone, you defeat them in a contest, fight, or argument. *He is used to tough defenders, and he usually gets the better of them.* V inflects, PHR n

15 If someone **knows better** or should **know better** than to do something, they have, or ought to have, the experience and maturity to know it is the wrong thing to do. *She knew better than to argue with Adeline... It's bad enough to have anyone joke about such a serious matter but a member of the police force should know better.* V inflects, oft PHR *than* to-inf

16 If you **know better** than someone, you have more information, knowledge, or experience than them. *He thought he knew better than I did, though he was much less experienced... My sister still claims she cheated on us at cards, but I know better.* V inflects, oft PHR *than* n

17 If you say that someone would **be better off** doing something, you are advising them to do it or expressing the opinion that it would benefit them to do it. *If you've got bags you're better off taking a taxi... Their stance seems to be that a baby or child is better off in its country of birth.* PHR -ing/ prep/adv PRAGMATICS

18 If you **go one better**, you do something better than it has been done before or obtain something better than you had before or than someone else has. *Now General Electric have gone one better than nature and made a diamond purer than the best quality natural diamonds.* V inflects, oft PHR *than* n

19 You say **'That's better'** in order to express your approval of what someone has said or done, or to praise or encourage them. *'I came to ask your advice – no, to ask for your help.'—'That's better. And how can I help you?'* CONVENTION PRAGMATICS

20 You can say **'so much the better'** or **'all the better'** to indicate that it is desirable that a particular thing is used, done, or available. *Make sure that you use strong white flour, and if you can get hold of durum wheat flour, then so much the better... If there's good skiing, breathtaking scenery and you don't need to catch a plane, all the better!*

21 You can use expressions like **'The bigger the**

better' or **'The** sooner **the better'** to mean that it will be more beneficial or satisfactory if something is big or happens soon. *The Irish love a party, the bigger the better... The fewer things in the room the better.*

22 If someone does something **the better** to do something else, they do the first thing in order to be able to do the second thing more effectively; a literary expression. *She came on every ride herself, the better to instruct her eager pupils.* PHR to-inf

23 If you intend to do something and then **think better of it**, you decide not to do it because you realize it would not be sensible. *Alberg open his mouth, as if to protest. But he thought better of it.* V inflects

24 If you say that something has happened or been done **for better or worse**, you mean that you are not sure whether the consequences will be good or bad, but they will have to be accepted because the action cannot be changed. *I married you for better or worse, knowing all about these problems.* PHR after v, PHR with cl

25 • **better the devil you know**: see **devil**. • **discretion is the better part of valour**: see **discretion**. • **your better half**: see **half**. • **against your better judgement**: see **judgement**. • **be better than nothing**: see **nothing**. • **the better part**: see **part**.

betterment /betəʳmənt/. The **betterment** of something is the act or process of improving its standard or status; a formal word. *His research is for the betterment of mankind.* N-UNCOUNT: oft N *of* n =improvement

betting /betɪŋ/. If you say **the betting is** that something will happen or is true, you are suggesting that it is very likely to happen or to be true. *The betting is that the experience will make Japan more competitive still.* PHRASE: PHR that

betting shop, betting shops. In Britain, a **betting shop** is a place where people can go to bet on something such as a horse race. ◆◇◇◇◇ N-COUNT =bookie's

between /bɪtwiːn/ ◆◆◆◆◆

In addition to the uses shown below, **between** is used in a few phrasal verbs, such as 'come between'.

1 If something is **between** two things or is **in between** them, it has one of the things on one side of it and the other thing on the other side. *She left the table to stand between the two men... Charlie crossed between the traffic to the far side of the street.* PREP: usu PREP pl-n

2 If people or things travel **between** two places, they travel regularly from one place to the other and back again. *I spent a lot of time in the early Eighties travelling between London and Bradford.* PREP: PREP pl-n

3 A relationship, discussion, or difference **between** two people, groups, or things is one that involves them both or relates to them both. *I think the relationship between patients and doctors has got a lot less personal... There have been intensive discussions between the two governments in recent days... There has always been a difference between community radio and commercial radio.* PREP: PREP pl-n

4 If something stands **between** you and what you want, it prevents you from having it. *His sense of duty often stood between him and the enjoyment of life.* PREP: PREP n *and* n

5 If something is **between** or in **between** two amounts or ages, it is greater or older than the first one and smaller or younger than the second one. *Increase the amount of time you spend exercising by walking between 15 and 20 minutes... Amsterdam is fun – a third of its population is aged between 18 and 30.* PREP: PREP num *and* num

6 If something happens **between** or **in between** two times or events, it happens after the first time or event and before the second one. *The canal was built between 1793 and 1797... Berlin was well known for its good living in between the two world wars.* PREP: PREP pl-n, PREP num *and* num ► Also an adverb. *Henry had to endure a journey by jetfoil, coach and two aircraft, with a four-hour wait in Bangkok in between.* ADV: ADV with cl/group

7 If you must choose **between** two things, you must choose one thing or the other one. *Students will be able to choose between English, French and Russian as their first foreign language.* PREP: PREP pl-n

8 If people or places have a particular amount of something **between** them, this is the total amount that they have. *The three sites employ 12,500 people between them... Between them, they train over fifty horses in Lambourn.* PREP: PREP pron

9 When something is divided or shared **between** people, they each have a share of it. *His company was bought out by Hogg Robinson for £3.5m, divided between five partners... There is only one bathroom shared between eight bedrooms.* PREP: PREP pl-n =amongst

10 When you introduce a statement by saying **'between you and me'** or **'between ourselves'**, you are indicating that you do not want anyone else to know what you are saying. *Between you and me, though, it's been awful for business... Between ourselves, I know he wants to marry her.* PHRASE: PHR with cl

bevelled /bevᵊld/; spelled **beveled** in American English. If a piece of wood, metal, or glass has **bevelled** edges, its edges are cut sloping. *At the bottom of the stairs is a huge mirror with deep bevelled edges.* ADJ: usu ADJ n

beverage /bevərɪdʒ/ **beverages. Beverages** are drinks; a formal word. *Alcoholic beverages are served in the hotel lounge. ...artificially sweetened beverages. ...foods and beverages.* ◆◇◇◇◇ N-COUNT: usu pl, oft adj N =drink

bevvy /bevi/ **bevvies.** If you have a few **bevvies**, you have a few alcoholic drinks; an informal word used in British English. *It was just one of those things that happens after a few bevvies.* N-COUNT: usu pl

bevy /bevi/ **bevies.** A **bevy of** people is a group of people all together in one place. *...a bevy of little girls... He had made it his business to surround himself with a bevy of bright young officers.* N-COUNT: usu sing, N *of* n =group

bewail /bɪweɪl/ **bewails, bewailing, bewailed.** If you **bewail** something, you express great sorrow about it. *All your songs seem to bewail a dissatisfaction in love.* VERB V n

beware /bɪweəʳ/. If you tell someone to **beware** of a person or thing, you are warning them that the person or thing may harm them or be dangerous. *Beware of being too impatient with others... Motorists were warned to beware of slippery conditions... Beware, this recipe is not for slimmers.* ◆◇◇◇◇ VB: only imper and inf; V *of* n/-ing; V

bewilder /bɪwɪldəʳ/ **bewilders, bewildering, bewildered.** If something **bewilders** you, it is so confusing or difficult that you cannot understand it. *The silence from Alex had hurt and bewildered her.* VERB =perplex V n

bewildered /bɪwɪldəʳd/. If you are **bewildered**, you are very confused and cannot understand something or decide what you should do. *Some shoppers looked bewildered by the sheer variety of goods on offer.* ◆◇◇◇◇ ADJ-GRADED =perplexed

bewildering /bɪwɪldərɪŋ/. A **bewildering** thing or situation is very confusing and difficult to understand or to make a decision about. *A glance along his bookshelves reveals a bewildering array of interests... The choice of excursions was bewildering.* ◆◇◇◇◇ ADJ-GRADED =perplexing ♦ **bewilderingly** *The cast of characters in the scandal is bewilderingly large.* ADV-GRADED: usu ADV adj/adv

bewilderment /bɪwɪldəʳmənt/. **Bewilderment** is the feeling of being bewildered. *He shook his head in bewilderment.* ◆◇◇◇◇ N-UNCOUNT: oft *in* N

bewitch /bɪwɪtʃ/ **bewitches, bewitching, bewitched.** If someone or something **bewitches** you, you are so attracted to them that you cannot think about anything else. *She was not moving, as if someone had bewitched her... The doctor is bewitched by Maya's beauty.* VERB V n ♦ **bewitching** *Frank was a quiet young man with bewitching brown eyes.* ADJ-GRADED

beyond /bɪjɒnd/ ◆◆◆◆◇

1 If something is **beyond** a place or barrier, it is on the other side of it. *They heard footsteps in the main room, beyond a door... On his right was a thriving vegetable garden and beyond it a small orchard of apple trees.* PREP ► Also an adverb. *The house had a fabulous view out to the Strait of Georgia and the* ADV: n ADV, *and* ADV

Rockies beyond. ...the need to defend itself against its enemies inside its borders and beyond.

2 If something happens **beyond** a particular time or date, it continues after that time or date has passed. *Few jockeys continue race-riding beyond the age of 40... You may be entitled to Child Benefit if a child continues getting full-time education beyond the date already notified by you.* ► Also an adverb. *The financing of home ownership will continue through the 1990s and beyond.* PREP =past; ADV: and ADV

3 If something extends **beyond** a particular thing, it affects or includes other things. *His interests extended beyond the fine arts to international politics and philosophy.* PREP

4 You use **beyond** to introduce an exception to what you are saying. *He appears to have almost no personal staff, beyond a secretary who can't make coffee... I knew nothing beyond a few random facts.* PREP =apart from

5 If something goes **beyond** a particular point or stage, it progresses or increases so that it passes that point or stage. *Their five-year relationship was strained beyond breaking point... It seems to me he's beyond caring about what anybody does.* PREP: oft PREP -ing

6 If something is, for example, **beyond** understanding or **beyond** belief, it is so extreme in some way that it cannot be understood or believed. *What Jock had done was beyond my comprehension... Sweden is lovely in summer – cold beyond belief in winter... But by the year 2000 business computing will have changed beyond recognition.* PREP

7 If you say that something is **beyond** someone, you mean that they cannot deal with it. *Although he could give her sympathy, any practical help would almost certainly be beyond him... The situation was beyond her control.* PREP =above

8 • **beyond the pale**: see **pale**. • **beyond someone's means**: see **means**. • **beyond your wildest dreams**: see **dream**. • **beyond a joke**: see **joke**.

bi- /baɪ-/

1 **Bi-** is used at the beginning of nouns and adjectives that have 'two' as part of their meaning. *She very much believes that she is living in a bi-cultural society.* PREFIX

2 **Bi-** is used to form adjectives and adverbs indicating that something happens twice in a period of time or that happens once in two consecutive periods of time. *While they are working students meet biweekly as a group to reflect on their experiences... The bimonthly magazine can be bought by subscription.* PREFIX

biannual /baɪænjuəl/. A **biannual** event happens twice a year. *You will need to have a routine biannual examination.* ♦ **biannually** *Only since 1962 has the show been held biannually.* ADJ: usu ADJ n; ADV: ADV after v

bias /baɪəs/ **biases, biasing, biased** ◆◆◇◇◇

1 **Bias** is prejudice against one group and favouritism towards another, which may badly affect someone's judgement of a situation or issue. *Bias against women permeates every level of the judicial system... There were fierce attacks on the BBC for alleged political bias.* N-VAR: usu with supp =prejudice

2 **Bias** is a concern with or interest in one thing more than others. *The Department has a strong bias towards neuroscience.* N-VAR: with supp

3 If something or someone **biases** you or your decision or opinion, they influence your decision or opinion in favour of a particular choice. *We mustn't allow it to bias our teaching.* VERB Vn

4 A dress or skirt that is cut **on the bias** or that is **bias-cut** has been cut diagonally across the material so that it hangs down in a particular way. *The fabric, cut on the bias, hangs as light as a cobweb off a woman's body. ...a bias-cut dress.* PHRASE

biased /baɪəst/ ◆◇◇◇◇

1 If you describe someone or something as **biased**, you believe they show prejudice against one group and favouritism towards another, or are influenced so much by something that any judgement they make is likely to be unfair. *He seemed a bit biased against women in my opinion... The selection of pupils for grammar schools was biased in favour of the middle-class child of a small family from a good area. ...the judge was biased.* ADJ-GRADED: usu v-link ADJ, oft ADJ *against/in favour of* n =prejudiced

2 If something is **biased towards** one thing, it is more concerned with it than with other things. *In Japan firms are biased towards growth rather than profits... University funding was tremendously biased towards scientists.* ADJ-GRADED: v-link ADJ *towards* n

bib /bɪb/ **bibs.** A **bib** is a piece of cloth or plastic which is worn by very young children to protect their clothes while they are eating. N-COUNT

Bible /baɪbᵊl/ **Bibles** ◆◆◇◇◇

1 The **Bible** is the sacred book on which the Jewish and Christian religions are based. N-PROPER: *the* N

2 A **Bible** is a copy of the Bible. N-COUNT

3 If someone describes a book or magazine about their job or interest as their **bible**, they mean that it is the best and most useful book about the subject. *...the photographer's bible – Amateur Photographer.* N-COUNT: poss N

Bible Belt; also spelled **bible belt**. Parts of the southern United States are referred to as **the Bible Belt** because Protestants with strong beliefs have a lot of influence there. N-PROPER: *the* N

biblical /bɪblɪkᵊl/. **Biblical** means contained in or relating to the Bible. *The community, whose links with Syria date back to biblical times, is mainly elderly. ...the biblical story of Noah.* ◆◇◇◇◇ ADJ: usu ADJ n

bibliography /bɪbliɒgrəfi/ **bibliographies** ◆◇◇◇◇

1 A **bibliography** is a list of books on a particular subject. *At the end of the this chapter there is a select bibliography of useful books.* N-COUNT

2 A **bibliography** is a list of the books and articles that are referred to in a particular book. N-COUNT

bicarb /baɪkɑːʳb/. **Bicarb** is an abbreviation for **bicarbonate of soda**; an informal word. N-UNCOUNT

bicarbonate of soda /baɪkɑːʳbəneɪt əv soʊdə/. **Bicarbonate of soda** is a white powder which is used in baking to make cakes rise, and also as a medicine to settle your stomach if you have indigestion. N-UNCOUNT

bicentenary /baɪsentiːnəri, AM -ten-/ **bicentenaries.** A **bicentenary** is the year in which you celebrate something important that happened exactly two hundred years earlier. N-COUNT

bicentennial /baɪsenteniəl/ **bicentennials. Bicentennial** celebrations are held to celebrate a bicentenary. ► Also a noun. *...the American bicentennial in 1976.* ADJ: ADJ n; N-COUNT

biceps /baɪseps/; **biceps** is both the singular and the plural form. Your **biceps** are the large muscles at the front of the upper part of your arms. Some people use 'bicep' as the singular form of 'biceps'. N-COUNT: usu pl

bicker /bɪkəʳ/ **bickers, bickering, bickered.** When people **bicker**, they argue or quarrel about unimportant things. *I went into medicine to care for patients, not to waste time bickering over budgets... The two women bickered constantly. ...as states bicker over territory... He is still bickering with the control tower over admissible approach routes.* ♦ **bickering** *The election will end months of political bickering.* ◆◇◇◇◇ V-RECIP: V *over/about* n (non recip), pl-n V, pl-n V *over/about* n, V *with* n; N-UNCOUNT

bicycle /baɪsɪkᵊl/ **bicycles, bicycling, bicycled** ◆◆◇◇◇

1 A **bicycle** is a vehicle with two wheels which you ride by sitting on it and pushing two pedals with your feet. You steer it by turning a bar that is connected to the front wheel. N-COUNT =bike

2 If you **bicycle** somewhere, you cycle there; an old-fashioned use. *I bicycled on towards the sea.* VERB V adv/prep

bicyclist /baɪsɪklɪst/ **bicyclists.** A **bicyclist** is someone who enjoys bicycling; an old-fashioned word. *The streets were crowded with bicyclists.* N-COUNT =cyclist

bid 1 attempting or offering

bid /bɪd/ **bids, bidding.** The form **bid** is used in the present tense and is the past tense and past participle. ◆◆◆◆◇

1 A **bid** for something or a **bid** to do something is an attempt to obtain it or do it; used in journalism. *...Bill Clinton's successful bid for the US presidency... The Government has already closed down two newspapers in a bid to silence its critics.* N-COUNT: N *for* n, N to-inf =attempt

2 A **bid** is an offer to pay a particular amount of money for something that is being sold. *Hanson made an agreed takeover bid of £351 million.* N-COUNT

3 If you **bid** for something or **bid** to do something, you try to obtain it or do it. *Singapore Airlines is rumoured to be bidding for a management contract to run both airports... I don't think she is bidding to be Prime Minister again.* VERB =try, attempt V for n V to-inf

4 If you **bid** for something that is being sold, you offer to pay a particular amount of money for it. *She wanted to bid for it... The Bank announced its intention to bid... He certainly wasn't going to bid $18 billion for this company.* ♦ **bidding** *The bidding starts at £2 million.* VERB V for n V V n N-UNCOUNT

bid up. If someone **bids up** the value of something, they try to increase it, for example by offering to buy it at a higher price than usual. *...the British passion for bidding up the price of each other's houses... They agreed to bid the picture up to 4,500 francs.* PHRASAL VERB V P n (not pron) V n P

bid 2 saying something

bid /bɪd/ **bids, bidding, bade, bidden** American English sometimes uses the form **bid** for the past tense.

1 If you **bid** someone farewell, you say goodbye to them. If you **bid** them goodnight, you say goodnight to them; a formal use. *She bade farewell to her son... I bade her goodnight.* VERB =wish V n to n V n n

2 If you **bid** someone do something, you ask or invite them to do it; a literary use. *They all smiled at him and bade him eat... I dare say he did as he was bidden.* VERB V n inf be V-ed Also V n to-inf

3 See also **bidding**.

bidden /bɪdᵊn/. **Bidden** is a past participle of **bid**.

bidder /bɪdəʳ/ **bidders** ◆◇◇◇◇

1 A **bidder** is someone who offers to pay a certain amount of money for something that is being sold. If you sell something to the highest **bidder**, you sell it to the person who offers the most money for it. *The sale will be made to the highest bidder subject to a reserve price being attained.* N-COUNT: usu supp N

2 A **bidder** for something is someone who is trying to obtain it or do it. *Vodafone is among successful bidders for two licences to develop cellular telephone systems in Greece.* N-COUNT: usu with supp, oft N for n

bidding /bɪdɪŋ/

1 If you do something **at** someone's **bidding**, you do it because they have asked you to do it; a formal expression. *The Prime Minister was right to reject him, even though it was only at the bidding of his backbenchers.* PHRASE

2 If you say that someone **does** another person's **bidding**, you disapprove of the fact that they do exactly what the other person asks them to do, even when they do not want to; a formal expression. *He dominated her, forcing her to do his bidding.* PHRASE: V inflects PRAGMATICS =obey

3 See also **bid**.

biddy /bɪdi/ **biddies.** If someone describes an elderly woman as an old **biddy**, they are saying in an unkind way that they think she is silly or unpleasant. *We're not just a lot of old biddies going on about jam.* N-COUNT PRAGMATICS

bide /baɪd/ **bides, biding, bided.** If you **bide** your **time**, you wait for a good opportunity before doing something. *He was content to bide his time patiently, waiting for the opportunity to approach her.* PHRASE: V inflects

bidet /biːdeɪ, AM biːdeɪ/ **bidets.** A **bidet** is a low basin in a bathroom which you can fill with water and use to wash your bottom. N-COUNT

biennial /baɪeniəl/ **biennials**

1 A **biennial** event happens or is done once every two years. *...the biennial Commonwealth conference.* ADJ: ADJ n

2 A **biennial** is a plant that lives for two years. It flowers, produces seed, and dies in its second year. N-COUNT

biff /bɪf/ **biffs, biffing, biffed.** If you **biff** someone, you hit them with your fist; an old-fashioned, informal word. *My father biffed him one on the nose.* VERB V n

bifocals /baɪfoʊkᵊlz/; the form **bifocal** is used as a modifier. **Bifocals** are glasses with lenses made in two halves. The top part is for looking at things some distance away, and the bottom part is for reading and looking at things nearby. ► Also an adjective. *Mrs Bierce wears thick bifocal lenses.* N-PLURAL ADJ

big /bɪg/ **bigger, biggest** ◆◆◆◆◆

1 A **big** person or thing is large in physical size. *Australia's a big country... Her husband was a big man... The car was too big to fit into our garage.* ADJ-GRADED =large ≠small

2 Something that is **big** consists of many people or things. *The crowd included a big contingent from Ipswich. ...the big backlog of applications.* ADJ-GRADED =large ≠small

3 If you describe something such as a problem, increase, or change as a **big** one, you mean it is great in degree, extent, or importance. *Her problem was just too big for her to tackle on her own... There could soon be a big increase in unemployment.* ADJ-GRADED =serious ≠small

4 A **big** organization employs many people and has many customers. *Exchange is largely controlled by big banks. ...Formosa Plastics, one of Taiwan's biggest companies.* ADJ-GRADED =large ≠small

5 If you say that someone is **big** in a particular organization, activity, or place, you mean that they have a lot of influence or authority in it; an informal use. *Their father was very big in the army... I'm sure all the big names will come to the club.* ADJ-GRADED: ADJ n, v-link ADJ in n

6 If you call someone a **big** bully or a **big** coward, you are emphasizing your disapproval of them; an informal use. ADJ: ADJ n PRAGMATICS

7 Children often refer to their older brother or sister as their **big** brother or sister. ADJ: ADJ n

8 Capital letters are sometimes referred to as **big** letters; an informal use. *...a big letter J.* ADJ: ADJ n =capital

9 **Big** words are long or rare words which have meanings that are difficult to understand; an informal use. *They use a lot of big words.* ADJ-GRADED: usu ADJ n

10 If you **make it big**, you become successful or famous; an informal expression. *We're not just looking at making it big in the UK, we want to be big internationally.* PHRASES V inflects

11 If you **think big**, you make plans on a large scale, often using a lot of time, effort, or money. *Maybe we're not thinking big enough.* V inflects

12 If something is happening **in a big way**, it is happening on a large scale; an informal expression. *I think boxing will take off in a big way here.* PHR after v

bigamist /bɪgəmɪst/ **bigamists.** A **bigamist** is a person who commits the crime of marrying someone when they are already legally married to someone else. N-COUNT

bigamous /bɪgəməs/. A **bigamous** marriage is one in which one of the partners is already married to someone else. ADJ

bigamy /bɪgəmi/. **Bigamy** is the crime of marrying a person when you are already legally married to someone else. N-UNCOUNT

Big Apple. People sometimes refer to the city of New York as **the Big Apple**; an informal expression. *The main attractions of the Big Apple are well documented.* N-PROPER: the N

big bang theory. **The big bang theory** is a theory in astronomy that suggests that the universe was created as a result of a massive explosion. N-SING: the N

big business ◆◇◇◇◇

1 **Big business** is business or commerce which involves very large companies and very large sums of money. *Big business will never let petty nationalism get in the way of a good deal.* N-UNCOUNT

2 Something that is **big business** is something which people spend a lot of money on, and which has become an important commercial activity. *Britain's railways are big business... Sport has become big business.* N-UNCOUNT

big cat, big cats. **Big cats** are lions, tigers, and other large wild animals in the cat family. N-COUNT

big city. **The big city** is used to refer to a large city which seems attractive to someone because they think there are many exciting things to do there, and many opportunities to earn a lot of ◆◇◇◇◇ N-SING: the N money. ...*a country girl who dreams of the big city and bright lights.*

big deal ◆◇◇◇◇
1 If you say that something is a **big deal**, you mean that it is important or significant in some way; an informal use. *I felt the pressure on me, winning was such a big deal for the whole family... It's no big deal.* N-SING
2 If someone **makes a big deal** out of something, they make a fuss about it or treat it as if it were very important; an informal use. *The Joneses make a big deal out of being 'different'.* PHRASE: V inflects, PHR *out of/of/about* n
3 If you say **'big deal'** to someone, you mean that you are not impressed by something or someone that they consider important or impressive; an informal use. *'You'll miss The Brady Bunch.' 'Big deal.'* CONVENTION PRAGMATICS

big dipper, big dippers. In British English, a **big dipper** is a narrow railway track at a fairground which goes over steep hills and round sharp bends, and on which people can ride for enjoyment and excitement. N-COUNT =roller coaster

big fish; **big fish** is both the singular and the plural form. ◆◇◇◇◇
1 If you describe someone as a **big fish**, you believe that they are powerful or important in some way; an informal use. *The four men arrested were described as really big fish by the U.S. Drug Enforcement Agency.* N-COUNT ≠small fry
2 If you say that someone is a **big fish in a small pond**, you mean that they are powerful or important but only within a small group of people; an informal use; used showing disapproval. *In South Africa, Jani was a big fish in a small pond.* PHRASE: v-link PHR PRAGMATICS

big game. Large wild animals such as lions and elephants that are hunted for sport are often referred to as **big game**. ...*the excitement of hunting big game in Africa.* N-UNCOUNT

biggie /bɪgi/ **biggies.** People sometimes refer to something or someone successful, well-known, or big as a **biggie**; an informal word. *The film is the first of this summer's Hollywood box-office biggies... Patsy Cline is a chart biggie.* N-COUNT

biggish /bɪgɪʃ/. Something that is **biggish** is fairly big; an informal word. *It is a biggish room, comfortable but shabbily decorated.* ADJ

big head, big heads. If you describe someone as a **big head**, you believe that they are arrogant and conceited or that they think they know everything about a subject; an informal expression. N-COUNT =know all

big-headed. If you describe someone as **big-headed**, you disapprove of them because they think they are very clever and know everything. *What an arrogant, big-headed man, thought Gladys.* ADJ-GRADED PRAGMATICS =conceited

big-hearted. If you describe someone as **big-hearted**, you think they are kind and generous to other people, and always willing to help them; used in written English. ...*the bluff big-hearted Irishman.* ADJ-GRADED: usu ADJ n ≠mean

big money. **Big money** is an amount of money that seems very large to you, especially money which you get easily. *They began to make big money during the war.* ◆◇◇◇◇ N-UNCOUNT

big mouth, big mouths. If you say that someone is a **big mouth** or that they have a **big mouth**, you mean that they tell other people things that should have been kept secret; an informal expression. *Why don't you shut your big mouth?* N-COUNT

big name, big names. A **big name** is a person who is successful and famous because of their work. ...*all the big names in rock and pop.* ◆◇◇◇◇ N-COUNT

big noise, big noises. Someone who is a **big noise** has an important position in a group or organization; an informal expression. *He was one of the big noises in founding the Olympic Games in the 1890s.* N-COUNT =big shot

bigot /bɪgət/ **bigots.** If you describe someone as a **bigot**, you mean that they are bigoted. N-COUNT

bigoted /bɪgətɪd/. Someone who is **bigoted** has strong, unreasonable prejudices or opinions and will not change them, even when they are proved to be wrong. *He was bigoted and racist.* ADJ-GRADED

bigotry /bɪgətri/. **Bigotry** is the possession or expression of strong, unreasonable prejudices or opinions. *He deplored religious bigotry.* ◆◇◇◇◇ N-UNCOUNT

big screen. When people talk about **the big screen**, they are referring to films that are made for cinema rather than for television. *She returns to the big screen to play Candy's overbearing mother, Rose.* N-SING: *the* N ≠small screen

big shot, big shots. A **big shot** is an important and powerful person in a group or organization; an informal expression. *He's a big shot in Chilean politics.* N-COUNT

big-ticket. If you describe something as a **big-ticket** item, you mean that it costs a lot of money; used mainly in American English. *A home is a big-ticket item.* ADJ: ADJ n

big time; also spelled **big-time.** ◆◇◇◇◇
1 You can use **big time** to refer to the highest level of an activity or sport where you can achieve the greatest amount of success or importance; an informal use. If you describe a person as **big time**, you mean they are successful and important; an informal use. *He took a long time to settle in to big-time football.* ...*a big-time investment banker.* ADJ: usu ADJ n
2 **The big time** is used to refer to fame or success in a particular area of activity; an informal use. *Matsuoka is the first player from Japan to really hit the tennis big time... He hit the big time with films such as Ghost and Dirty Dancing.* N-SING: *the* N
3 In American English, you can use **big time** if you want to emphasize the importance or extent of something that has happened; an informal use. *Mike Edwards has tasted success big time... They screwed things up big time... America lost big-time.* ADV: ADV after v

big toe, big toes. Your **big toe** is the largest toe on your foot. N-COUNT

big top. The large round tent that a circus uses for its performances is called the **big top**. N-SING

bigwig /bɪgwɪg/ **bigwigs.** If you refer to an important person as a **bigwig**, you are being rather disrespectful; an informal word. *He scandalised most of the local bigwigs.* N-COUNT PRAGMATICS

bijou /biːʒuː/. Small houses are sometimes described as **bijou** houses in order to make them sound attractive or fashionable. ...*a bijou Mayfair flat.* ...*bijou shops and boutiques.* ADJ: ADJ n

bike /baɪk/ **bikes, biking, biked** ◆◆◆◇◇
1 A **bike** is a bicycle or a motorcycle; an informal use. N-COUNT
2 To **bike** somewhere means to go there on a bicycle; an informal use. *I biked home from the beach.* VERB V adv/prep

biker /baɪkəʳ/ **bikers.** **Bikers** are people who ride around on motorbikes, usually in groups. ◆◇◇◇◇ N-COUNT

bikini /bɪkiːni/ **bikinis.** A **bikini** is a two-piece swimming costume worn by women. ◆◇◇◇◇ N-COUNT

bilateral /baɪlætərəl/. **Bilateral** negotiations, meetings, or agreements, involve only the two groups or countries that are directly concerned; a formal word. ...*bilateral talks between Britain and America.* ♦ **bilaterally** *The withdrawal of Soviet troops will be settled bilaterally between Moscow and the Germans.* ◆◆◇◇◇ ADJ: ADJ n; ADV: usu ADV after v, ADV adj

bile /baɪl/ ◆◇◇◇◇
1 **Bile** is a liquid produced by your liver which helps you to digest fat. N-UNCOUNT
2 **Bile** is the bad-smelling liquid that comes out of your mouth when you vomit with no food in your stomach. *She felt sick, bile rising in her throat.* N-UNCOUNT
3 **Bile** is anger or bitterness towards someone or something; a literary use. *He aims his bile at religion, drugs, and politics.* N-UNCOUNT

bilge /bɪldʒ/ **bilges**
1 The **bilge** or the **bilges** are the flat bottom part of a ship or boat. *The oil had been dumped by a ship emptying its bilges.* N-COUNT
2 If you say that something written or spoken is **bilge**, you mean that you think it is untrue or silly; N-UNCOUNT PRAGMATICS =rubbish

an informal use. *I supported us by writing bilge for women's magazines.*

bilingual /baɪlɪŋgwəl/ ◆◇◇◇◇

1 **Bilingual** means involving or using two languages. *...bilingual education. ...the Collins bilingual dictionaries.* ADJ: ADJ n

2 Someone who is **bilingual** can speak two languages extremely fluently, usually because they learnt both languages as a child. *He is bilingual in an Asian language and English.* ADJ: v-link ADJ

bilingualism /baɪlɪŋgwəlɪzəm/. **Bilingualism** is the ability to speak two languages fluently. N-UNCOUNT

bilious /bɪliəs/

1 If someone describes the appearance of something as **bilious**, they mean that they think it looks unpleasant and rather disgusting; used in written English. *...the bilious green overstuffed sofas.* ADJ-GRADED: usu ADJ n PRAGMATICS

2 If you feel **bilious**, you feel sick and have a headache; a literary use. *She appears to be suffering a bilious attack.* ADJ-GRADED

3 **Bilious** is sometimes used in written English to describe the feelings or behaviour of someone who is extremely angry or bad-tempered. *His speech was a bilious, rancorous attack on much of the music of his younger contemporaries.* ADJ-GRADED: usu ADJ n

bilk /bɪlk/ **bilks, bilking, bilked.** To **bilk** someone out of something, especially money, means to cheat them out of it; an informal word, used mainly in American English. *He disappeared in 1980 after being convicted of bilking investors out of $3 million.* VERB =cheat V n out of n Also V n

bill /bɪl/ **bills, billing, billed** ◆◆◆◆◇

1 A **bill** is a written statement of money that you owe for goods or services. *They couldn't afford to pay the bills... He paid his bill for the newspapers promptly. ...phone bills.* N-COUNT

2 If you **bill** someone **for** goods or services you have provided them with, you give or send them a bill stating how much money they owe you for these goods or services. *Are you going to bill me for this?* VB: no cont V n for n Also V n

3 In British English, **the bill** in a restaurant is a piece of paper on which the price of the meal you have just eaten is written and which you are given before you pay. The American word is **check**. N-SING: the N

4 In American English, a **bill** is a piece of paper money. The British word is **note**. *The case contained a large quantity of US dollar bills.* N-COUNT: usu supp N

5 In parliament, a **bill** is a formal statement of a proposed new law that is discussed and then voted on. *This is the toughest crime bill that Congress has passed in a decade... The bill was approved by a large majority.* N-COUNT: usu sing, usu with supp

6 The **bill** of a show or concert is a list of the entertainers who will take part in it. N-SING

7 If someone **is billed** to appear in a particular show, it has been advertised that they are going to be in it. *She was billed to play the Red Queen in Snow White.* ♦ **billing** *...their quarrels over star billing.* VB: usu passive be V-ed to-inf N-UNCOUNT: usu with supp

8 If you **bill** a person or event as a particular thing, you advertise them in a way that makes people think they have particular qualities or abilities. *They bill it as Britain's most exciting museum.* VERB V n as n

9 A bird's **bill** is its beak. N-COUNT

10 See also **Private Member's Bill.**

11 If you say that someone or something **fits the bill** or **fills the bill**, you mean that they are suitable for a particular job or purpose. *If you fit the bill, send a CV to Rebecca Rees.* PHRASES V inflects

12 If you have to **foot the bill** for something, you have to pay for it. *Who is footing the bill for her extravagant holiday?* V inflects

13 If a doctor gives you **a clean bill of health**, they tell you that you are fit and healthy. *President Mitterrand, 75, has been given a clean bill of health by doctors in Paris.* PHR after v

billboard /bɪlbɔːʳd/ **billboards.** A **billboard** is a very large board on which posters are displayed. ◆◇◇◇◇ N-COUNT =hoarding

-billed /-bɪld/. **-billed** combines with adjectives to indicate that a bird has a beak of a particular kind or appearance. *...yellow-billed ducks.* COMB in ADJ

billet /bɪlɪt/ **billets, billeting, billeted**

1 If members of the armed forces **are billeted** in a particular place, that place is provided for them to stay in for a period of time. *The soldiers were billeted in private homes.* VB: usu passive be V-ed adv/prep

2 A **billet** is a house or lodging where a member of the armed forces has been billeted. N-COUNT

billfold /bɪlfoʊld/ **billfolds.** In American English, a **billfold** is a wallet. N-COUNT

billiards /bɪliəʳdz/; the form **billiard** is used as a modifier. **Billiards** is a game played on a large table, in which you use a long stick called a cue to hit small heavy balls against each other or into pockets around the sides of the table. *He enjoyed the occasional game of billiards. ...billiard balls.* N-UNCOUNT

billion /bɪljən/ **billions.** The plural form is **billion** after a number, or after a word or expression referring to a number, such as 'several' or 'a few'. ◆◆◆◆◆

1 A **billion** is a thousand million. *The Ethiopian foreign debt stands at 3 billion dollars... This year, almost a billion birds will be processed in the region.* NUM

2 If you talk about **billions of** people or things, you mean that there is a very large number of them but you do not know or do not want to say exactly how many. *Biological systems have been doing this for billions of years... He urged US executives to invest billions of dollars in his country.* ▶ Also a pronoun. *He thought that it must be worth billions.* QUANT-PL: QUANT of pl-n PRON

billionaire /bɪljəneəʳ/ **billionaires.** A **billionaire** is an extremely rich person who has money or property worth at least a thousand million pounds or dollars. ◆◇◇◇◇ N-COUNT

billionth /bɪljənθ/ **billionths**

1 The **billionth** item in a series is the one you count as number one billion. *Disney will claim its one billionth visitor before the end of the century.* ORD

2 A **billionth** is one of a billion equal parts of something. *...a billionth of a second.* FRACTION

bill of fare, bills of fare. The **bill of fare** at a restaurant is a list of the food for a meal from which you may choose what you want to eat; an old-fashioned expression. N-COUNT =menu

Bill of Rights. A **Bill of Rights** is a written list of citizens' rights which is usually part of the constitution of a country. N-SING

billow /bɪloʊ/ **billows, billowing, billowed** ◆◇◇◇◇

1 When something made of cloth **billows**, it swells out and flaps slowly in the wind. *The curtains billowed in the breeze... Her pink dress billowed out around her. ...the billowing sails.* VERB V V out V-ing

2 When smoke or cloud **billows**, it moves slowly upwards or across the sky. *...thick plumes of smoke billowing from factory chimneys... Steam billowed out from under the bonnet. ...billowing clouds of cigarette smoke.* VERB V prep/adv V-ing

3 A **billow** of smoke or dust is a large mass of it rising slowly into the air. *...smoke stacks belching billows of almost solid black smoke.* N-COUNT: usu N of n =cloud

billy goat /bɪli goʊt/ **billy goats.** A **billy goat** is a male goat. N-COUNT

bimbo /bɪmboʊ/ **bimbos.** If someone calls a young woman a **bimbo**, they think that although she is pretty she is rather stupid, and that the fact that she is pretty is the reason that people like her or that she is successful; an informal word. ◆◇◇◇◇ N-COUNT PRAGMATICS

bimonthly /baɪmʌnθli/. In American English, a **bimonthly** event or publication happens or appears either twice a month or every two months. *...bimonthly assemblies. ...bimonthly newsletters.* ADJ: usu ADJ n

bin /bɪn/ **bins, binning, binned** ◆◆◇◇◇

1 A **bin** is a container that you put rubbish in. *He screwed the paper small and chucked it in the bin.* N-COUNT

2 A **bin** is a container that you keep or store things in. *...a bread bin.* N-COUNT: oft n N

3 If you **bin** something, you throw it away; an informal use. *He decided to bin his paintings.* VERB V n

binary /baɪnəri/ ◆◇◇◇◇

1 The **binary** system expresses numbers using only the two digits 0 and 1. It is used especially in computing. ADJ: usu ADJ n

2 **Binary** is the binary system of expressing numbers. *The machine does the calculations in binary.* N-UNCOUNT

3 **Binary** describes something that has two different parts; a formal use. *...a binary star.* ADJ: ADJ n

bind /baɪnd/ **binds, binding, bound** ◆◆◇◇◇

1 If something **binds** people together, it makes them feel as if they are all part of the same group or have something in common. *It is the memory and threat of persecution that binds them together. ...the social and political ties that bind the USA to Britain. ...a group of people bound together by shared language, culture, and beliefs.* VERB V pl-n *together* V n prep/adv V-ed Also V n

2 If you **are bound** by something such as a rule, agreement, or restriction, you are forced or required to act in a certain way. *The Luxembourg-based satellite service is not bound by the same strict rules as the BBC... The authorities will be legally bound to arrest any suspects... There is a bottom deck though, so you're not bound to sit on top... The treaty binds them to respect their neighbour's independence.* VERB *be* V-ed *by* n *be* V-ed to-inf V n to-inf Also V n ♦ **bound** *The world of advertising is obviously less bound by convention than the world of banking... Few of them feel bound by any enduring loyalties.* ADJ-GRADED: v-link ADJ *by* n

3 If you **bind** something or someone, you tie rope, string, tape, or other material around them so that they are held firmly. *Bind the ends of the cord together with thread. ...the red tape which was used to bind the files... He said there were cases where prisoners were tightly bound, often for several days.* VERB V n adv/prep V n

4 When a book **is bound**, the pages are joined together and the cover is put on. *Each volume is bound in bright-coloured cloth... Their business came from a few big publishers, all of whose books they bound. ...four immaculately bound hardbacks.* VERB *be* V-ed *in* n V n V-ed ♦ **-bound** *...leather-bound stamp albums.* COMB in ADJ

5 If one chemical or particle **is bound** to another, or **binds** to another, it becomes attached to it or reacts with it to form a single particle or substance; a technical use in science. *At present nobody understands why these three quarks which are in the proton are bound together... These may bind to receptor molecules on the surfaces of cells... These compounds bind with genetic material in the liver.* V-ERG *be* V-ed adv/prep V prep

6 In cookery, if you **bind** a mixture of food, you form it into a mass by mixing it with a sticky substance. *Bind the mixture with the raw minced liver and cook for 3 minutes more. ...a divine mixture of vegetarian cheeses bound with egg.* VERB V n *with* n V-ed

7 If you are in **a bind**, you are in a difficult situation, usually because you have to make a decision or a choice and whatever decision or choice you make will have unpleasant consequences; an informal use. *This puts the politicians in a bind as to what course to take... I'll advance you the money for it, here and now, just to help you out of a bind.* N-SING: *a* N

8 In informal British English, if you say that something is **a bind**, you mean that it is unpleasant and boring to do. *It is expensive to buy and a bind to carry home.* N-SING: *a* N

9 See also **binding, bound; double bind**.

bind over. In Britain, if someone **is bound over** by a court or a judge, they are given an order and are legally obliged to do as the order says for a particular period of time; a legal expression. *On many occasions demonstrators were bound over to keep the peace... They put us in a cell, and the next day some bumbling judge bound us over... This imposes a duty on courts to bind over parents when they have no control over their children.* PHRASAL VERB *be* V-ed P to-inf V n P V P n (not pron) Also V P n to-inf

binder /baɪndəʳ/ **binders.** A **binder** is a hard cover with metal rings inside, which is used to hold loose pieces of paper. ◆◇◇◇◇ N-COUNT

binding /baɪndɪŋ/ **bindings** ◆◆◇◇◇

1 A **binding** promise, agreement, or decision must be obeyed or carried out. *...proposals for a legally binding commitment on nations to stabilise emissions of carbon dioxide... The panel's decisions are secret and not binding on the government.* ADJ-GRADED: oft ADJ *on* n

2 The **binding** of a book is its cover. *Its books are noted for the quality of their paper and bindings.* N-VAR: oft with poss

3 **Binding** is a strip of material that you put round the edge of a piece of cloth or other object in order to protect or decorate it. *...the Regency mahogany dining table with satinwood binding.* N-VAR

4 **Binding** is a piece of rope, cloth, tape, or other material that you wrap around something so that it can be gripped firmly or held in place. N-VAR

5 See also **bind**.

binge /bɪndʒ/ **binges, bingeing, binged** ◆◇◇◇◇

1 If you go on a **binge**, you do too much of something, such as drinking alcohol, eating, or spending money; an informal use. *She went on occasional drinking binges.* N-COUNT

2 If you **binge**, you do too much of something, such as drinking alcohol, eating, or spending money; an informal use. *I haven't binged since 1986... I binged on pizzas or milkshakes.* VERB V V *on* n

bingo /bɪŋgoʊ/ ◆◇◇◇◇

1 **Bingo** is a game in which each player has a card with numbers on. Someone calls out numbers and if you are the first person to have all your numbers called out, you win the game. N-UNCOUNT

2 You can say **'bingo!'** when giving an account of something to indicate that something pleasant or something that you hoped for happened, especially in a surprising, unexpected, or sudden way. *I was in a market in Tangier and bingo! I found this.* EXCLAM

bin liner, bin liners. In British English, a **bin liner** is a plastic bag that you put inside a waste bin or dustbin. N-COUNT

binoculars /bɪnɒkjʊləʳz/. **Binoculars** consist of two small telescopes joined together side by side, which you look through in order to look at things that are a long way away. ◆◇◇◇◇ N-PLURAL: also *a pair of* N

bio- /baɪoʊ-, baɪɒ-/. **Bio-** is used at the beginning of nouns and adjectives that refer to life or to the study of living things. *...bio-engineering.* PREFIX

biochemical /baɪoʊkemɪkəl/. **Biochemical** changes, reactions, and mechanisms relate to the chemical processes that happen in living things. ◆◇◇◇◇ ADJ: ADJ n

biochemist /baɪoʊkemɪst/ **biochemists.** A **biochemist** is a scientist or student who studies biochemistry. N-COUNT

biochemistry /baɪoʊkemɪstri/ ◆◇◇◇◇

1 **Biochemistry** is the study of the chemical processes that happen in living things. N-UNCOUNT

2 The **biochemistry** of a living thing or a process it undergoes is the chemical processes that happen in it or are involved in it. N-UNCOUNT

biodegradable /baɪoʊdɪgreɪdəbəl/. Something that is **biodegradable** breaks down or decomposes naturally without any special scientific treatment, and can therefore be thrown away without causing pollution. *...a natural and totally biodegradable plastic.* ADJ-GRADED

biodiversity /baɪoʊdaɪvɜːʳsɪti/. **Biodiversity** is the existence of a wide variety of plant and animal species living in their natural environment. ◆◇◇◇◇ N-UNCOUNT

biographer /baɪɒgrəfəʳ/ **biographers.** Someone's **biographer** is a person who writes an account of their life. ◆◇◇◇◇ N-COUNT: oft with poss

biographical /baɪəgræfɪkəl/. **Biographical** facts, notes, or details are concerned with the events in someone's life. *The book contains few biographical details.* ◆◇◇◇◇ ADJ: usu ADJ n

biography /baɪɒgrəfi/ **biographies** ◆◆◇◇◇

1 A **biography** of someone is an account of their life, written by someone else. N-COUNT: oft with poss

2 **Biography** is the branch of literature which deals with accounts of people's lives. *...a volume of biography and criticism.* N-UNCOUNT

biol. Biol. is a written abbreviation for 'biology' or 'biological'.

biological /baɪəlɒdʒɪkəl/ ◆◆◇◇◇

1 **Biological** is used to describe processes and states that occur in the bodies and cells of living things. *The living organisms somehow concentrated the minerals by biological processes... This is a natural biological response.* ADJ: usu ADJ n ♦ **biologically** /baɪəlɒdʒɪkli/ *Much of our behaviour is biologically determined... Possibly we are accustomed, biologically speaking, to this background radiation.* ADV: ADV with cl/group, ADV with v

2 **Biological** is used to describe activities con- ADJ:

cerned with the study of living things. *...all aspects of biological research associated with leprosy. ...the university's school of biological sciences.* ADJ n

3 Biological weapons and **biological** warfare involve the use of bacteria or other living organisms in order to attack human beings, animals, or plants. *Such a war could result in the use of chemical and biological weapons.* ADJ: usu ADJ n

4 Biological pest control is the use of bacteria or other living organisms in order to destroy other organisms which are harmful to plants or crops. *...Jim Litsinger, a consultant on biological control of agricultural pests.* ADJ: ADJ n

5 A child's **biological** parents are the man and woman who caused him or her to be born, rather than other adults who look after him or her. *...foster parents for young teenagers whose biological parents have rejected them.* ADJ: ADJ n =natural

6 A **biological** washing powder contains enzymes which dissolve dirt. ADJ

biological clock, biological clocks. Your **biological clock** is your body's way of registering time. It does not rely on external events such as day or night, but on more complicated factors such as your habits, your age, and chemical changes taking place in your body. *Whenever we change sleep cycles, our biological clock has to adjust to the new schedule.* N-COUNT: oft poss N

biological diversity. **Biological diversity** is the same as **biodiversity**. N-UNCOUNT

biology /baɪɒlədʒi/ ◆◆◇◇◇

1 Biology is the science which is concerned with the study of living things. ♦ **biologist** /baɪɒlədʒɪst/ **biologists** *...biologists studying the fruit fly.* N-UNCOUNT; N-COUNT

2 The **biology** of a living thing is the way in which its body or cells behave. *The biology of these diseases is terribly complicated. ...human biology.* N-UNCOUNT: the N of n, supp N

3 See also **molecular biology**.

bionic /baɪɒnɪk/. In science fiction books or films, a **bionic** person is someone who has superhuman powers, such as being exceptionally strong or having exceptionally good sight, because parts of their body have been replaced by electronic machinery. *...the Bionic Woman.* ADJ: usu ADJ n

biopic /baɪoʊpɪk/ **biopics.** A **biopic** is a film that tells the story of someone's life. N-COUNT

biopsy /baɪɒpsi/ **biopsies.** A **biopsy** is the removal and examination of fluids or tissue from a patient's body in order to discover why they are ill. N-VAR

biosphere /baɪəsfɪəʳ/. The **biosphere** is the part of the earth's surface and atmosphere which is inhabited by living things; a technical term. ◆◇◇◇◇ N-SING: usu the N

biotech /baɪoʊtek/. **Biotech** means the same as **biotechnology**. *...the biotech industry.* N-UNCOUNT: usu N n

biotechnology /baɪoʊteknɒlədʒi/. **Biotechnology** is the use of living parts such as cells or bacteria in industry and technology; a technical term. ♦ **biotechnologist** /baɪoʊteknɒlədʒɪst/ **biotechnologists** *...biotechnologists turning proteins into pharmaceuticals.* ◆◇◇◇◇ N-UNCOUNT; N-COUNT

bipartisan /baɪpɑːʳtɪzæn, AM baɪpɑːrtɪzᵊn/. **Bipartisan** means concerning or involving two different political parties or groups. *They made an attempt to develop a bipartisan approach to educational reform.* ◆◇◇◇◇ ADJ: usu ADJ n

biped /baɪped/ **bipeds.** A **biped** is a creature with two feet; a technical term in biology. N-COUNT

biplane /baɪpleɪn/ **biplanes.** A **biplane** is an old-fashioned type of aeroplane with two pairs of wings, one above the other. N-COUNT

bipolar /baɪpoʊləʳ/. **Bipolar** systems or situations are dominated by two strong and opposing opinions or elements; a formal word. *...the bipolar world of the Cold War years.* ADJ: usu ADJ n

birch /bɜːʳtʃ/ **birches** ◆◇◇◇◇

1 A **birch** is type of tall tree with thin branches. N-VAR

2 The birch is a punishment in which someone is hit with a wooden cane. N-SING: the N

bird /bɜːʳd/ **birds** ◆◆◆◆◇

1 A **bird** is a creature with feathers and wings. Female birds lay eggs. Most birds can fly. N-COUNT

2 In informal British English, some men refer to young women as **birds**. Most women think that this is insulting. N-COUNT

3 See also **game bird**.

4 If someone says that as a child they were told about **the birds and the bees**, they are referring humorously to being told about sex and sexual reproduction. PHRASES =the facts of life

5 Someone who is **doing bird** is in prison; used in informal British English. *They warned him that next time he'd find himself doing bird.* V inflects =do time

6 If someone is an **early bird**, they usually get up early in the morning. *We've always been early birds, up at 5.30 or 6am.* N inflects, oft v-link PHR =early riser

7 If you say that **the early bird catches the worm** or **gets the worm**, you mean that the person who arrives first in a place is the one who gets what they want. You can refer to someone who arrives first as the **early bird**. *The serious buying happens between six and eight o'clock in the morning and it is very much the case that the early bird catches the worm.* V inflects

8 If you refer to two people as **birds of a feather**, you mean that they have the same interests or are very similar. *She was a drunk, too. Another no-good. Birds of a feather.* v-link PHR

9 If someone who you are looking for has gone somewhere, you can say **'The bird has flown'**. *The bird had flown. By the time they reached the house Pamela had disappeared without trace.* V and N inflect

10 If an entertainer, sportsman, or sportswoman **gets the bird** or if the audience **give** him or her **the bird**, the audience shout loudly in order to show their disappointment or disapproval; an old-fashioned expression used in British English . *He made a couple of mistakes and the crowd immediately gave him the bird.* V inflects

11 If you talk about **a bird in the hand**, you are referring to something that you already have and do not want to risk losing by trying to get something else. *It may not be what you want, but at least it is a bird in the hand.*

12 If you say that a **little bird** told you about something, you mean that someone has told you about it, but you do not want to say who it was.

13 Some people use the phrase **old bird** to refer to someone and say what they are like; an old-fashioned expression. *As usual, Wheeler, a wise old bird, got it right... She was such a decent old bird.* adj PHR

14 If you say that someone or something is a **rare bird**, you mean that they are very unusual. *I was curious about him. He was a rare bird, I felt sure.* N inflects, usu v-link PHR

15 If you say that doing something will **kill two birds with one stone**, you mean that it will enable you to achieve two things that you want to achieve, rather than just one. V inflects

birdcage /bɜːʳdkeɪdʒ/ **birdcages;** also spelled **bird cage**. A **birdcage** is a cage in which birds are kept. N-COUNT

birdie /bɜːʳdi/ **birdies, birdying, birdied** ◆◆◇◇◇

1 In golf, if you get a **birdie**, you get the golf ball into a hole in one stroke fewer than the number of strokes which has been set as the standard for a good player. N-COUNT

2 If a golfer **birdies** a hole, he or she gets a birdie at that hole. *He birdied five of the first seven holes.* VERB V n

birdlife /bɜːʳdlaɪf/; also spelled **bird life**. The **birdlife** in a place is all the birds that live there. N-UNCOUNT

birdlike /bɜːʳdlaɪk/; also spelled **bird-like**. If someone has a **birdlike** manner, they move or look like a bird. *...the birdlike way she darted about.* ADJ

bird of paradise, birds of paradise. A **bird of paradise** is a songbird which is found mainly in New Guinea. The male birds have very brightly coloured feathers. N-COUNT

bird of passage, birds of passage. If you refer to someone as a **bird of passage**, you mean that they are staying in a place for a short time before going to another place. *Most of these emigrants were birds of passage who returned to Spain after a relatively short stay.* N-COUNT

bird of prey, birds of prey. A **bird of prey** is a bird such as an eagle or a hawk that kills and eats other birds and animals. N-COUNT

bird's eye view, bird's eye views. You say that you have a **bird's eye view** of a place when you are looking down at it from a great height, so that you can see a long way but everything looks very small. N-COUNT: usu sing

birdsong /bɜːʳdsɒŋ, AM -sɔːŋ/ **birdsongs;** also spelled **bird song**. **Birdsong** is the sound of a bird or birds calling in a way which sounds musical. *The air is filled with birdsong.* N-UNCOUNT: also N in pl

bird table, bird tables. A **bird table** is a small wooden platform on a pole which some people put in their garden in order to put food for the birds on it. N-COUNT

bird-watcher, bird-watchers; also spelled **birdwatcher**. A **bird-watcher** is a person whose hobby is watching and studying wild birds in their natural surroundings. N-COUNT

bird-watching; also spelled **birdwatching**. **Bird-watching** is the activity of watching and studying wild birds in their natural surroundings. N-UNCOUNT

Biro /baɪəroʊ/ **Biros.** In British English, a **Biro** is a pen with a small metal ball at its tip which transfers the ink onto the paper. **Biro** is a trademark. N-COUNT =ballpoint

birth /bɜːʳθ/ **births** ◆◆◆◇◇

1 When a baby is born, you refer to this event as its **birth**. *It was the birth of his grandchildren which gave him greatest pleasure... She concealed her pregnancy right up to the moment of birth... She weighed 5lb 7oz at birth. ...premature births.* N-VAR

2 You can refer to the beginning or origin of something as its **birth**. *...the birth of popular democracy.* N-UNCOUNT: with poss

3 Some people talk about a person's **birth** when they are referring to the social position of the person's family. *...men of low birth... His birth, background and career show that you can make it in this country on merit alone.* N-UNCOUNT: usu supp N

4 See also **date of birth, home birth**.

5 If, for example, you are French **by birth**, you are French because your parents are French, or because you were born in France. *Sadrudin was an Iranian by birth.* PHRASES adj/n PHR

6 When a woman **gives birth**, she produces a baby from her body. *She's just given birth to a baby girl... She's due to give birth at any moment.* V inflects

7 If something **gives birth to** an idea, situation, or institution, that idea, situation, or institution develops as a result of or in response to that thing. *In 1980, strikes at the Lenin shipyards gave birth to the Solidarity trade union.* V inflects

8 The country, town, or village **of** your **birth** is the place where you were born. n PHR

birth certificate, birth certificates. Your **birth certificate** is an official document which gives details of your birth, such as the date and place of your birth, and the names of your parents. N-COUNT

birth control. **Birth control** means planning whether to have children, and using methods of contraception to prevent having them when they are not wanted. ◆◇◇◇◇ N-UNCOUNT

birthdate /bɜːʳθdeɪt/ **birthdates.** Your **birthdate** is the same as your **date of birth**. N-COUNT

birthday /bɜːʳθdeɪ, -di/ **birthdays.** Your **birthday** is the anniversary of the date on which you were born. ◆◆◆◇◇ N-COUNT

birthday suit, birthday suits. If you are in your **birthday suit**, you are not wearing any clothes; an old-fashioned, informal expression. N-COUNT: poss N

birthing /bɜːʳθɪŋ/. **Birthing** means relating to or used during childbirth. *Some hospitals provide special birthing stools.* ADJ: ADJ n

birthmark /bɜːʳθmɑːʳk/ **birthmarks.** A **birthmark** is a mark on someone's skin that has been there since they were born. N-COUNT

birthplace /bɜːʳθpleɪs/ **birthplaces** ◆◇◇◇◇

1 Your **birthplace** is the place where you were born; used in written English. N-COUNT

2 The **birthplace** of something is the place where it began or originated. *...Athens, the birthplace of the ancient Olympics.* N-COUNT: usu N of n

birth rate, birth rates; also spelled **birth-rate**. The **birth rate** in a place is the number of babies born there for every 1000 people during a particular period of time. *The UK has the highest birth rate among 15 to 19-year-olds in Western Europe. ...a falling birth-rate.* ◆◇◇◇◇ N-COUNT

birthright /bɜːʳθraɪt/ **birthrights.** Something that is your **birthright** is something that you feel you have a basic right to have, simply because you are a human being. *Freedom is the natural birthright of every human.* N-COUNT: usu sing

biscuit /bɪskɪt/ **biscuits** ◆◆◇◇◇

1 In British English, a **biscuit** is a small flat cake that is crisp and usually sweet. The usual American word is **cookie**. N-COUNT

2 In American English, a **biscuit** is a small dry cake that sometimes has dried fruit in it. It can be eaten with butter and jam. N-COUNT

3 If you think someone has done something very stupid, rude, or selfish, you can say that they **take the biscuit** or that what they have done **takes the biscuit**. You say this to emphasize your surprise at how stupid or selfish they have been. *For sheer audacity this takes the biscuit.* PHRASE: V inflects PRAGMATICS

bisect /baɪsekt/ **bisects, bisecting, bisected.** If something long and thin **bisects** an area or line, it divides the area or line in half. *The main street bisects the town from end to end.* VERB V n

bisexual /baɪsekʃuəl/ **bisexuals.** Someone who is **bisexual** is sexually attracted to both men and women. ► Also a noun. *He was an active bisexual.* ♦ **bisexuality** /baɪsekʃuælɪti/ *Lillian opened up to Frank about her bisexuality.* ◆◇◇◇◇ ADJ N-COUNT N-UNCOUNT

bishop /bɪʃəp/ **bishops**

1 A **bishop** is a clergyman of high rank in the Roman Catholic, Anglican, and Orthodox churches. N-COUNT; N-TITLE; N-VOC

2 In chess a **bishop** is a piece that can be moved diagonally across the board on squares that are the same colour. N-COUNT

bishopric /bɪʃəprɪk/ **bishoprics.** A **bishopric** is the area for which a bishop is responsible, or the rank or office of being a bishop. N-COUNT

bison /baɪsᵊn/; **bison** is both the singular and the plural form. A **bison** is a large hairy animal that is a member of the cattle family. Bison have a large head and a humped back. They used to be very common in North America and Europe. N-COUNT =buffalo

bistro /biːstroʊ/ **bistros.** A **bistro** is a small, informal restaurant or a bar where food is served. N-COUNT

bit /bɪt/ **bits** ◆◆◆◆◆

1 **A bit** of something is a small amount of it. *All it required was a bit of work... I got paid a little bit of money.* QUANT: QUANT of n-uncount

2 **A bit** means to a small extent or degree. It is sometimes used to make a statement less extreme. *This girl was a bit strange... I think people feel a bit more confident... She looks a bit like his cousin Maureen... That sounds a bit technical... Isn't that a bit harsh?* PHRASE: PHR adj/adv/prep PRAGMATICS =slightly

3 You can use **a bit of** to make a statement less extreme. For example, the statement 'It's a bit of a nuisance' is less extreme than 'It's a nuisance'. *It's all a bit of a mess... Students have always been portrayed as a bit of a joke... This comes as a bit of a disappointment.* PHRASE: PHR n PRAGMATICS

4 **Quite a bit** means quite a lot. *They're worth quite a bit of money... Things have changed quite a bit... He's quite a bit older than me.* PHRASE: PHR of n, PHR after v, PHR compar

5 You use **a bit** before 'more' or 'less' to mean a small amount more or a small amount less. *I still think I have a bit more to offer... Maybe we'll hear a little bit less noise. ...a bit more than half the total official debt.* PHRASE: PHR *more/less*

6 **A bit** of something is a small part of it; used mainly in British English. *That's the bit of the meeting that I missed... Now comes the really important bit... The best bit was walking along the glacier.* N-COUNT: with supp, oft N of n =part

7 A **bit** of something is a small piece of it; used mainly in British English. *Only a bit of string looped* N-COUNT: usu N of n =piece

round a nail in the doorpost held it shut. ...crumpled bits of paper.

8 You can use **bit** to refer to a particular item or to one of a group or set of things. For example, a **bit** of information is an item of information. *There was one bit of vital evidence which helped win the case... Not one single bit of work has been started towards the repair of this road.* N-COUNT: usu N *of* n

9 You use **bit** in expressions such as **the charity bit** and **the whole marriage bit** when you want to refer to everything that is involved in something, in a dismissive way; an informal use. N-SING: *the* supp N PRAGMATICS =thing

10 In computing, a **bit** is the smallest unit of information that is held in a computer's memory. It is either 1 or 0. Several bits form a byte. N-COUNT

11 A **bit** is a piece of metal that is held in a horse's mouth by the reins and is used to control the horse when you are riding. N-COUNT

12 Bit is the past tense of **bite**.

13 If something happens **bit by bit**, it happens in stages. *Bit by bit I began to understand what they were trying to do.* PHRASES PHR with v

14 If someone **is champing at the bit** or **is chomping at the bit**, they are very impatient to do something, but they are prevented from doing it, usually by circumstances that they have no control over. *I expect you're champing at the bit, so we'll get things going as soon as we can.* V inflects

15 If you **do** your **bit**, you do something that, to a small or limited extent, helps to achieve something. *Marcie always tried to do her bit.* V inflects

16 You say that one thing is **every bit as** good, interesting, or important as another to emphasize that the first thing is just as good, interesting, or important as the second. *My dinner jacket is every bit as good as his.* PHR adj/adv PRAGMATICS =just as

17 In British English, if you do something **for a bit**, you do it for a short period of time; an informal expression. *That should keep you busy for a bit.* PHR with v =while

18 In British English, if you say that something is **a bit much**, you are annoyed because you think someone has behaved in an unreasonable way; an informal expression. *It's a bit much expecting young people to carry the can for lenders' past mistakes.* v-link PHR PRAGMATICS

19 In British English, you use **not a bit** when you want to make a strong negative statement. *I'm really not a bit surprised... 'Are you disappointed?' 'Not a bit.'* PRAGMATICS

20 You say **not a bit of it** to emphasize that something that you might expect to be the case is not the case; used mainly in British English. *Did he give up? Not a bit of it!* PRAGMATICS

21 You can use **bits and pieces** or **bits and bobs** to refer to a collection of different things; an informal expression.

22 If you **get the bit between** your **teeth**, or **take the bit between** your **teeth**, you become very enthusiastic about a job you have to do. V inflects

23 If something is smashed or blown **to bits** it is broken into a number of pieces. If something falls **to bits** it comes apart so that it is in a number of pieces. *She found a pretty yellow jug smashed to bits.* PHR after v

24 • **thrilled to bits**: see **thrilled**.

bitch /bɪtʃ/ **bitches, bitching, bitched** ◆◆◇◇◇

1 If someone calls a woman a **bitch**, they are saying in a very rude way that they think she behaves in a very unpleasant way. You should avoid this use as most people find it offensive. • See also **son of a bitch**. N-COUNT PRAGMATICS

2 If you describe a situation as a **bitch**, you mean that it is very unpleasant or difficult to deal with; an informal use which some people find offensive. N-SING PRAGMATICS

3 If you say that someone **is bitching** about something, you mean that you disapprove of the fact that they are complaining about it in an unpleasant way; an informal use. *They're forever bitching about everybody else.* VB: oft cont PRAGMATICS V *about* n Also V

4 A **bitch** is a female dog. N-COUNT

bitchy /bɪtʃi/ **bitchier, bitchiest.** If you say that someone is being **bitchy** or is making **bitchy** remarks, you mean that you disapprove of the fact that they are saying nasty things about someone else; an informal word. *I'm sorry. I know I was bitchy on the phone... Women are not the only ones who say bitchy things about each other.* ADJ-GRADED PRAGMATICS =catty

♦ **bitchiness** *There's a lot of bitchiness.* N-UNCOUNT

bite /baɪt/ **bites, biting, bit, bitten** ◆◆◆◆◆

1 If you **bite** something, you use your teeth to cut into it, for example in order to eat it or break it. If an animal or person **bites** you, they use their teeth to hurt or injure you. *Both sisters bit their nails as children... He bit into his sandwich... He had bitten the cigarette in two... Every year in this country more than 50,000 children are bitten by dogs... Llamas won't bite or kick.* VERB V n V *into* n V n adv/prep V

2 A **bite** of something, especially food, is the action of biting it. *He took another bite of apple... You cannot eat a bun in one bite.* ► A **bite** is also the amount of food you take into your mouth when you bite it. *Look forward to eating the food and enjoy every bite.* N-COUNT: oft N *of* n N-COUNT

3 If you have **a bite** to eat, you have a small meal or a snack; an informal use. *It was time to go home for a little rest and a bite to eat.* N-SING: *a* N, usu N to-inf

4 If a snake or a small insect **bites** you, it makes a mark or hole in your skin, and often causes the surrounding area of your skin to become painful or itchy. *When an infected mosquito bites a human, spores are injected into the blood... In Indonesia, I was bitten 33 times by mosquitoes.* VERB V n Also V

5 A **bite** is an injury or a mark on your body where an animal, snake, or small insect has bitten you. *Any dog bite, no matter how small, needs immediate medical attention.* N-COUNT: oft n N

6 When an action or policy begins to **bite**, it begins to have a serious or harmful effect. *As the sanctions begin to bite there will be more political difficulties ahead... The recession started biting deeply into British industry in the early eighties.* VERB V V prep/adv

7 If an object **bites** into a surface, it presses hard against it or cuts into it. *There may even be some wire or nylon biting into the flesh... The car's tires bit loudly on the rutted snow in the street.* VERB V prep/adv Also V, V n

8 If you say that a food or drink has **bite**, you like it because it has a strong or sharp taste. *...the addition of tartaric acid to give the wine some bite.* N-UNCOUNT PRAGMATICS

9 If the air or the wind has **a bite**, it feels very cold. *There was a bite in the air, a smell perhaps of snow.* N-SING: *a* N

10 If you say that a performance has **bite**, you mean that it is exciting or effective because it has been inspired by feelings such as anger, resentment, or dislike. *The teams have that extra bite when they are playing against their neighbours.* N-UNCOUNT

11 If a fish **bites** when you are fishing, it takes the hook or bait at the end of your fishing line in its mouth. *After half an hour, the fish stopped biting and we moved on.* ► Also a noun. *If I don't get a bite in a few minutes I lift the rod and twitch the bait.* VERB V N-COUNT

12 A **bite** of something is a small part or amount of it. *...bites of conversation.* N-COUNT: usu N *of* n

13 See also **love bite**, **nail-biting**.

14 If you **bite the hand that feeds** you, you behave badly or ungratefully towards someone who you depend on to give you money or other things that you need. *She may be cynical about the film industry, but ultimately she has no intention of biting the hand that feeds her.* PHRASES Vs inflect

15 If someone speaks or replies to you angrily, and you think they are being unfair or reacting too strongly, you can say that they **bite** your **head off**. *Whenever possible, suggest she talks about it but be aware she may bite your head off for your trouble.* V and N inflect PRAGMATICS

16 If you **bite** your **lip** or your **tongue**, you stop yourself from saying something that you want to say, because it would be the wrong thing to say in the circumstances. *I must learn to bite my lip... He bit his tongue as he found himself on the point of saying 'follow that car'.* V and N inflect

17 If something **takes a bite out of** a sum of money, part of the money is spent or taken away in order to pay for it; used mainly in American English. *Local* V inflects, PHR n

taxes are going to be taking a bigger bite out of people's income than they ever have before.
18 ● **someone's bark is worse than their bite**: see **bark.** ● **bite the bullet**: see **bullet.** ● **bite off more than one can chew**: see **chew.** ● **bite the dust**: see **dust.** ● **once bitten, twice shy**: see **shy.**

bite back PHRASAL VERB
1 If you **bite back** a feeling or something that you were going to say, you stop yourself from expressing it; a literary expression. *Susan bit back the words she would like to have said... A scream rose to her lips again. She had to bite it back.* VPn (not pron) VnP
2 If a person or a group of people who have been defeated, criticized, or insulted **bite back**, they respond strongly or angrily; used by journalists. *The Labour Party should now unite and bite back... Letters: Readers Bite Back.* VP

bite-sized; also spelled **bite-size.**
1 Bite-sized pieces of food are small enough to fit easily in your mouth. *Cut the pumpkin into bite-sized pieces.* ADJ: usu ADJ n
2 If you describe something as **bite-sized**, you like it because it is small enough to be considered or dealt with easily. *...bite-size newspaper items.* ADJ: usu ADJ n PRAGMATICS

biting /baɪtɪŋ/
1 Biting wind or cold is extremely cold. *...a raw, biting northerly wind... Antarctic air brought biting cold to southern Chile on Thursday.* ADJ-GRADED: usu ADJ n =piercing
2 Biting criticism or wit is very harsh or unkind, and is often caused by such feelings as anger, resentment, or dislike. *...a furore caused by the author's biting satire on the Church... This was the most biting criticism made against her.* ADJ-GRADED: usu ADJ n =mordant

bit part, bit parts; also spelled **bit-part.** A **bit part** is a small and unimportant role for an actor in a film or play. N-COUNT

bitten /bɪtᵊn/. **Bitten** is the past participle of **bite.**

bitter /bɪtəʳ/ **bitterest; bitters** ◆◆◆◇◇
1 In a **bitter** argument or conflict, people argue very angrily or fight very fiercely. *...the scene of bitter fighting during the Second World War. ...a bitter attack on the Government's failure to support manufacturing... On the eve of the poll, campaigning was bitter.* ♦ **bitterly** *Any such thing would be bitterly opposed by most of the world's democracies. ...a bitterly fought football match.* ♦ **bitterness** *The rift within the organization reflects the growing bitterness of the dispute.* ADJ-GRADED; ADV-GRADED: usu ADV with v, also ADV adj; N-UNCOUNT
2 If someone is **bitter** after a disappointing experience or after being treated unfairly, they continue to feel angry about it. *She is said to be very bitter about the way she was sacked... His long life was marked by bitter personal and political memories.* ♦ **bitterly** *'And he sure didn't help us,' Grant said bitterly. ...the party bureaucrats who bitterly resented their loss of power.* ♦ **bitterness** *I still feel bitterness and anger towards the person who knocked me down.* ADJ-GRADED; ADV-GRADED: usu ADV with v, also ADV adj; N-UNCOUNT
3 A **bitter** experience makes you feel very disappointed. You can also use **bitter** to emphasize feelings of disappointment. *I think the decision was a bitter blow from which he never quite recovered... A great deal of bitter experience had taught him how to lose gracefully... The statement was greeted with bitter disappointment by many of the other delegates.* ♦ **bitterly** *I was bitterly disappointed to have lost yet another race so near the finish.* ADJ-GRADED: usu ADJ n; ADV-GRADED: ADV adj, ADV with v
4 Bitter weather, or a **bitter** wind, is extremely cold. *Outside, a bitter east wind was accompanied by flurries of snow. ...after spending a night in the bitter cold.* ♦ **bitterly** *It's been bitterly cold here in Moscow.* ADJ-GRADED; ADV: ADV adj
5 A **bitter** taste is sharp, not sweet, and often slightly unpleasant. *The leaves taste rather bitter. ...as the wine ages, losing its bitter harshness, and becoming softer and smoother.* ADJ-GRADED ≠sweet
6 In Britain, **bitter** is a kind of beer that is light brown in colour. *...a pint of bitter.* N-MASS
7 If you say that you will continue doing something **to the bitter end**, especially something difficult or unpleasant, you are emphasizing that you will continue doing it until it is completely finished. *The guerrillas would fight to the bitter end, he said, in order to achieve their main goal.* PHRASES PHR after v PRAGMATICS
8 ● **a bitter pill**: see **pill.**

bitterly /bɪtəʳli/. You use **bitterly** when you describing an attitude which involves strong, unpleasant emotions such as anger, resentment, or dislike. *...a speech bitterly critical of the United States' military build-up in the Gulf. ...Lucy Gannon's fine, bitterly funny play.* ADV-GRADED: ADV adj

bitter-sweet
1 If you describe an experience as **bitter-sweet**, you mean that it has some happy aspects and some sad ones. *He's got bitter-sweet memories of his first appearance for the team.* ADJ
2 A **bitter-sweet** taste seems bitter and sweet at the same time. *...a wine with a bitter-sweet flavour.* ADJ

bitty /bɪti/
1 If you say that something is **bitty**, you mean that it seems to be formed from a lot of different parts which you think do not fit together or go together well; an informal use. *The programme was bitty and absolutely meaningless.* ADJ-GRADED PRAGMATICS
2 In American English, if you describe someone or something as a little **bitty** person or thing, you are emphasizing that they are very small; an informal use. *She's just a little bitty wisp of a girl.* ADJ: ADJ n PRAGMATICS

bitumen /bɪtʃʊmɪn, AM bɪtuːmən/. **Bitumen** is a black sticky substance which is obtained from tar or petrol and is used in making roads. N-UNCOUNT

bivouac /bɪvuæk/ **bivouacs, bivouacking, bivouacked**
1 A **bivouac** is a temporary camp made by soldiers or mountaineers. N-COUNT
2 If you **bivouac** in a particular place, you stop and stay in a bivouac there. *They made us bivouac ten miles out of town.* VERB V prep/adv Also V

biweekly /baɪwiːkli/. In American English, a **biweekly** event or publication happens or appears once every two weeks. The usual British word is **fortnightly.** *He used to see them at the biweekly meetings. ...Jesse Meyers, editor of Beverage Digest, the industry's biweekly newsletter.* ► Also an adverb. *The group meets on a regular basis, usually weekly or biweekly.* ADJ: ADJ n; ADV: ADV with v

biz /bɪz/. **Biz** is sometimes used by journalists to refer to the entertainment business, especially pop music or films; an informal word. *We asked women in the biz for their low-down on film-making. ...a girl in the music biz.* ◆◇◇◇◇ N-SING: oft n N

bizarre /bɪzɑːʳ/. Something that is **bizarre** is very odd and strange. *The game was also notable for the bizarre behaviour of the team's manager... You know, that book you lent me is really bizarre.* ♦ **bizarrely** *She dressed bizarrely... Bizarrely, death is not a disqualification for voting although non-attendance at party meetings is.* ◆◆◇◇◇ ADJ-GRADED =weird; ADV-GRADED: ADV with v, ADV adj, ADV with cl

blab /blæb/ **blabs, blabbing, blabbed.** If someone **blabs** about something secret, they tell people about it; an informal word. *Her mistake was to blab about their affair... No blabbing to your mates!... She'll blab it all over the school.* VERB V about n V to n V n prep Also V

black /blæk/ **blacker, blackest; blacks, blacking, blacked** ◆◆◆◆◆
1 Something that is **black** is of the darkest colour that there is, the colour of the sky at night when there is no light at all. *She was wearing a black coat with a white collar... He had thick black hair... I wear a lot of black... He was dressed all in black.* COLOUR
2 A **black** person belongs to a race of people with dark skins, especially a race from Africa. *He worked for the rights of black people... Sherry is black, tall, slender and soft-spoken. ...the traditions of the black community.* ADJ
3 Black people are sometimes referred to as **blacks**, though some people find this use offensive. *There are about thirty-one million blacks in the US.* N-COUNT: usu pl
4 Black coffee or tea has no milk or cream added to it. *A cup of black tea or black coffee contains no calories... I drink coffee black.* ADJ: ADJ n, v n ADJ
5 If you describe a situation as **black**, you are emphasizing that it is very bad indeed. *It was, he said* ADJ-GRADED PRAGMATICS

later, one of the blackest days of his political career... The future for the industry looks even blacker.

6 If someone is in a **black** mood, they feel very miserable and depressed. *In late 1975, she fell into a black depression... Her mood was blacker than ever.* ADJ-GRADED

7 You use **black** to describe things that you consider to be very cruel or wicked; a literary use. *I think their crime is a blacker one than mere exploitation. ...the blackest laws in the country's history.* ADJ-GRADED PRAGMATICS

8 **Black** humour involves jokes about sad or tragic situations. *'So you can all go over there and get shot,' he said, with the sort of black humour common among British troops here... It's a black comedy of racial prejudice, mistaken identity and thwarted expectations.* ADJ-GRADED: usu ADJ n

9 People who believe in **black** magic believe that it is possible to communicate with evil spirits. *He was also alleged to have conducted black magic ceremonies... The King was unjustly accused of practising the black arts.* ADJ: ADJ n

10 If a group **blacks** particular goods or people, it refuses to handle the goods or to have dealings with the people; used mainly in informal British English. *The Union had blacked containerised goods at the London Docks.* VERB =boycott; V n

11 If someone **blacks** another person's eye, they punch or hit that person in the eye, causing it to bruise and look black. *Her husband blacked her eye... Their mother was trying to hide her two blacked eyes.* • See also **black eye**. VERB; V n; V-ed

12 If you say that someone is **black and blue**, you mean that they are badly bruised. *Whenever she refused, he'd beat her black and blue... Bud's nose was still black and blue.* PHRASES usu PHR after v, v-link PHR

13 If a person or an organization is **in the black**, they do not owe anybody any money. *Remington's operations in Japan are now in the black... Until his finances are in the black I don't want to get married.* v-link PHR, PHR after v

14 If someone gives you a **black look**, they look at you in a way that shows that they are very angry about something. *Passing my stall, she cast black looks at the amount of stuff still unsold.* N inflects, usu PHR after v

black out PHRASAL VERB

1 If you **black out**, you lose consciousness for a short time. *I could feel blood draining from my face. I wondered whether I was about to black out... Samadov said that he felt so ill that he blacked out.* V P

2 If a place **is blacked out**, it is in darkness, usually because it has no electricity supply. *Large parts of Lima and other areas south of the capital were blacked out after electricity pylons was blown up.* be V-ed P

3 If a film or a piece of writing **is blacked out**, it is prevented from being broadcast or published, usually because it contains information which is secret or offensive. *TV pictures of the demonstration were blacked out.* usu passive =censor; be V-ed P

4 If you **black out** a piece of writing, you colour over it in black so that it cannot be seen. *U.S. government specialists went through each page, blacking out any information a foreign intelligence expert could use... Some Welsh activists have started blacking out English language road signs.* =censor; V P n (not pron) Also V n P

5 If you **black out** the memory of something, you try not to remember it because it upsets you. *I tried not to think about it. I blacked it out. It was the easiest way of coping.* • See also **blackout**. V n P Also V P n (not pron)

Black Africa. **Black Africa** is the part of Africa to the south of the Sahara Desert. N-PROPER

black and white; also spelled **black-and-white**. ◆◆◇◇◇

1 In a **black and white** photograph or film, everything is shown in black, white, and grey. *...a black-and-white photo of the two of us together. ...old black and white film footage... The pictures were in black and white.* COLOUR

2 A **black-and-white** television set shows only black-and-white pictures. ADJ: usu ADJ n

3 A **black-and-white** issue or situation is one which involves issues which seem straightforward and simple and therefore easy to make decisions about. *But this isn't a simple black and white affair, Marianne... She saw things in black and white.* ADJ =clear-cut

4 You say that something is **in black and white** when it has been written or printed, and not just said. *He'd seen the proof in black and white... Maybe you don't want to read about Doug's death in black and white.* PHRASE: PHR after v, v-link PHR

blackball /blækbɔːl/ **blackballs, blackballing, blackballed.** If the members of a club **blackball** someone, they vote against that person being allowed to join their club. *Members can blackball candidates in secret ballots.* VERB; V n

black belt, black belts.

1 A **black belt** is worn by someone who has reached a very high standard in judo or karate. *President Collor has a black belt in karate.* N-COUNT

2 You can refer to someone who has a black belt in judo or karate as a **black belt**. *He's a judo black belt and represented England Under 14s.* N-COUNT

blackberry /blækbəri, AM -beri/ **blackberries.** A **blackberry** is a small, soft black or dark purple fruit. ◆◇◇◇◇ N-COUNT

blackbird /blækbɜːʳd/ **blackbirds.** A **blackbird** is a common European bird. The male has black feathers and a yellow beak, and the female has brown feathers. N-COUNT

blackboard /blækbɔːʳd/ **blackboards.** In a classroom, the **blackboard** is a dark-coloured board which teachers write on with chalk. ◆◇◇◇◇ N-COUNT: usu *the* N in sing

black box, black boxes

1 A **black box** is an electronic device in an aircraft which records information about its flights. Black boxes are often used to provide evidence about accidents. N-COUNT

2 You can refer to a system or device as a **black box** when you know that it produces a particular result but you have no understanding of how it works. *They were part of the black box associated with high-flyer management development.* N-COUNT: usu sing

blackcurrant /blækkʌrənt, AM -kɜːrənt/ **blackcurrants. Blackcurrants** are a type of very small, dark purple fruits that grow in bunches. *Place the blackcurrants in a pan. ...a carton of blackcurrant drink.* ◆◇◇◇◇ N-COUNT

black economy. The **black economy** of a country consists of the buying, selling, and producing of goods or services that goes on without the government being informed, so that people can avoid paying tax on it. *...an attempt to clamp down on the black economy.* N-SING

blacken /blækən/ **blackens, blackening, blackened** ◆◇◇◇◇

1 To **blacken** something means to make it black or very dark in colour. *The married women of Shitamachi maintained the custom of blackening their teeth... You need to grill the tomatoes until the skins blacken.* V-ERG; V n; V

2 If someone **blackens** your character, they make other people believe that you are a bad person. *He accused him of knowingly spreading falsehoods in an effort to blacken my character... They're trying to blacken our name.* VERB; V n

black eye, black eyes. If someone has a **black eye**, they have a dark-coloured bruise around their eye. *He punched her in the face at least once giving her a black eye.* N-COUNT: usu sing

blackguard /blægɑːʳd/ **blackguards.** If you describe someone as a **blackguard**, you think that they are wicked and dishonourable; an old-fashioned word. N-COUNT

blackhead /blækhed/ **blackheads. Blackheads** are small, dark spots on someone's skin caused by blocked pores. N-COUNT: usu pl

black hole, black holes ◆◇◇◇◇

1 **Black holes** are areas in space, where gravity is so strong that nothing, not even light, can escape from them. Black holes are thought to be formed by collapsed stars. N-COUNT

2 If you say that something, especially money, has gone into a **black hole**, you mean that it has disappeared and cannot be recovered. *Instead of deposits, there's just a concealed black hole in the accounts.* N-COUNT: usu sing

black ice. Black ice is a thin, transparent layer of ice on a road or path that is very difficult to see. N-SING

blackish /blækɪʃ/. Something that is **blackish** is very dark in colour. *...the water in the well was blackish... The woman was about five feet five, slim, with long blackish hair.* COLOUR

blacklist /blæklɪst/ **blacklists, blacklisting, blacklisted**

1 If someone is on a **blacklist**, they are seen by a government or other organization as being one of a number of people who cannot be trusted or who have done something wrong. *A government official disclosed that they were on a secret blacklist... Most credit agencies run a 15-year blacklist effectively barring bankrupts from receiving credit.* N-COUNT

2 If someone is **blacklisted** by a government or organization, they are put on a blacklist. *He has been blacklisted since being convicted of possessing marijuana in 1969. ...the full list of blacklisted airports.* VB: usu passive; be V-ed; V-ed

♦ **blacklisting** *...a victim of Hollywood's notorious blacklisting.* N-UNCOUNT

blackmail /blækmeɪl/ **blackmails, blackmailing, blackmailed** ◆◇◇◇◇

1 **Blackmail** is the action of threatening to do something unpleasant to someone, such as to reveal a secret about them or to harm them, unless they do something you tell them to do, such as giving you a large sum of money. *It looks like the pictures were being used for blackmail... Opponents accused him of blackmail and extortion.* N-UNCOUNT

2 If you describe an action as emotional or moral **blackmail**, you disapprove of it because someone is using a person's emotions or moral values to persuade them to do something against their will. *The tactics employed can range from overt bullying to subtle emotional blackmail.* N-UNCOUNT PRAGMATICS

3 If one person **blackmails** another person, they use blackmail against them. *He told her their affair would have to stop, because Jack Smith was blackmailing him... The government insisted that it would not be blackmailed by violence... I thought he was trying to blackmail me into saying whatever he wanted.* VERB; V n; V n into -ing/n; Also V n with n

♦ **blackmailer, blackmailers** *The nasty thing about a blackmailer is that his starting point is usually the truth.* N-COUNT

black mark, black marks. A **black mark** against someone is something bad that they have done or a bad quality that they have which affects the way people think about them. *The Commission's verdict was an indelible black mark against me.* N-COUNT

black market, black markets. If something is bought or sold on the **black market**, it is bought or sold illegally. *There is a plentiful supply of arms on the black market. ...black market food prices.* ◆◇◇◇◇ N-COUNT

black marketeer, black marketeers. A **black marketeer** is someone who sells goods on the black market; used in journalism. N-COUNT

blackness /blæknəs/. **Blackness** is the state of being very dark; a literary word. *The twilight had turned to a deep blackness.* ◆◇◇◇◇ N-UNCOUNT

blackout /blækaʊt/ **blackouts;** also spelled **black-out.** ◆◇◇◇◇

1 A **blackout** is a period of time during a war in which towns and buildings are made dark so that they cannot be seen by enemy planes. *The last show had to be over before the blackout began, so people could find their way home... All windows have been fitted with blackout curtains.* N-COUNT: usu sing

2 If a **blackout** is imposed on a particular piece of news, journalists are prevented from broadcasting or publishing it. *...a media blackout imposed by the Imperial Palace... Journalists said there was a virtual news blackout about the rally.* N-COUNT: usu sing, usu n N =embargo

3 If there is a power **blackout**, the electricity supply to a place is temporarily cut off. *There was an electricity black-out in a large area in the north of the country.* N-COUNT: usu sing, usu n N

4 If you have a **blackout**, you temporarily lose consciousness. *I suffered a black-out which lasted for several minutes.* N-COUNT

black pepper. **Black pepper** is pepper which is dark in colour and has been made from the dried berries of the pepper plant, including their black outer casing. ◆◇◇◇◇ N-UNCOUNT

black pudding, black puddings. Black pudding is a thick sausage which has a black skin and is made from pork fat and pig's blood. N-VAR

black sheep. If you describe someone as the **black sheep** of their family or of a group that they are a member of, you mean that they are considered bad or worthless by other people in that family or group. N-COUNT: usu sing, oft the N of n

blacksmith /blæksmɪθ/ **blacksmiths.** A **blacksmith** is a person whose job is making things by hand out of metal that has been heated to a high temperature. ◆◇◇◇◇ N-COUNT

black spot, black spots; also spelled **blackspot.**

1 If you describe a place, time, or part of a situation as a **black spot**, you mean that it is particularly bad or likely to cause problems. *There are recognised black spots in marriages which can lead to trouble... Gainsborough is known as an unemployment blackspot... One black spot in the survey is that firms still expect to cut jobs substantially in the months ahead.* N-COUNT

2 A **black spot** is a place on a road where accidents often happen. *The accident happened on a notorious black spot on the A43.* N-COUNT

black tie; also spelled **black-tie.**

1 A **black tie** event is a formal social event such as a party at which the men wear dinner jackets and bow ties and the women wear evening dresses. *Tonight the college is hosting a black-tie dinner for 100 of its former students.* ADJ: usu ADJ n

2 If a man is dressed in **black tie**, he is wearing formal evening dress, which includes a dinner jacket and a bow tie. *Most of the guests will be wearing black tie.* N-UNCOUNT

blacktop /blæktɒp/. In American English, **blacktop** is a hard black substance which is used as a surface for roads. The usual British word is **tarmac**. *...waves of heat rising from the blacktop.* N-UNCOUNT

bladder /blædəʳ/ **bladders.** Your **bladder** is the part of your body where urine is stored until it leaves your body. See also **gall bladder**. ◆◇◇◇◇ N-COUNT

blade /bleɪd/ **blades** ◆◆◇◇◇

1 The **blade** of a knife, axe, or saw is the edge, which is used for cutting. *Many of them will have sharp blades.* N-COUNT

2 The **blades** of a propeller are the long, flat parts that turn round. N-COUNT: usu pl

3 The **blade** of an oar is the thin flat part that you put into the water. N-COUNT

4 A **blade** of grass is a single piece of grass. N-COUNT

5 • **rotor blade**: see **rotor**. See also **razor blade, shoulder blade.**

blag /blæg/ **blags, blagging, blagged.** If someone **blags** something such as a concert ticket or a record, they get it free, usually by persuading someone to give it to them; used in very informal British English, especially by young people. *She'd heard he was a musician and blagged a tape off a friend of his. ...next time you find yourself unable to blag your way onto the guest list.* VERB; V n; V way prep/adv

blah /blɑː/. You use **blah, blah, blah** to refer to something that is said or written without giving the actual words, because you think that they are boring or unimportant; used in informal English. *...the different challenges of their career, their need to change, to evolve, blah blah blah.* ◆◇◇◇◇ CONVENTION

blame /bleɪm/ **blames, blaming, blamed** ◆◆◆◆◇

1 If you **blame** a person or thing for something bad, you believe or say that they are responsible for it or that they caused it. *The commission is expected to blame the army for many of the atrocities... The police blamed the explosion on terrorists... If it wasn't Sam's fault, why was I blaming him?* ► Also a noun. *Nothing could relieve my terrible sense of blame.* VERB; V n for n; V n on n; V n; N-UNCOUNT

2 The **blame** for something bad that has happened is the responsibility for causing it or letting it happen. *Some of the blame for the miscarriage of justice must be borne by the solicitors... The majority of East Germans put the blame on the previous communist regime.* N-UNCOUNT: oft N *for* n/-ing

3 If you say that you do not **blame** someone for doing something, you mean that you consider it was a reasonable thing to do in the circumstances. *I do not blame them for trying to make some money... He slammed the door and stormed off. I could hardly blame him.* VB: usu with brd-neg; V n *for*-ing; V n

4 If someone or something is **to blame** for something bad that has happened, they are responsible for causing it. *If their forces were not involved, then who is to blame?... The policy is partly to blame for causing the worst unemployment in Europe.* PHRASES; v-link PHR

5 If you say that someone **has only themselves to blame** or **has no-one but themselves to blame**, you are emphasizing that they are responsible for something bad that has happened to them and showing that you have no sympathy for them. *My life is ruined and I suppose I only have myself to blame.* V inflects; PRAGMATICS

blameless /bleɪmləs/. Someone who is **blameless** has not done anything wrong. *He feels he is blameless... The US itself, of course, is not entirely blameless in trading matters. ...a blameless life.* ADJ-GRADED

blanch /blɑːntʃ, blæntʃ/ **blanches, blanching, blanched** ◆◇◇◇◇

1 If you **blanch**, you suddenly become very pale. *Simon Doggett's face blanched as he looked at Sharpe's frayed and blood-drenched uniform... She felt herself blanch at the unpleasant memories.* VERB; V; V *at* n

2 If you say that someone **blanches** at something, you mean that they find it unpleasant and do not want to be involved with it. *Even this government blanched at the thought of investing in the Soviet Union... There are places you can take physically handicapped children where staff don't blanch at the sight of a wheelchair.* VERB; V *at* n

3 If you **blanch** vegetables, fruit, or nuts, you put them into boiling water for a short time, usually in order to remove their skins, or to prepare them for freezing. *Skin the peaches by blanching them.* VERB; V n

blancmange /bləmɒndʒ/ **blancmanges.** In British English, **blancmange** is a cold dessert that is made from milk, sugar, cornflour, and flavouring and looks rather like jelly. N-VAR

bland /blænd/ **blander, blandest** ◆◆◇◇◇

1 If you describe someone or something as **bland**, you mean that they are rather dull and unexciting. *Serle has a blander personality than Howard... It sounds like an advert: easy on the ear but bland and forgettable. ...a bland, 12-storey office block.* ADJ-GRADED
♦ **blandness** *...the blandness of television.* N-UNCOUNT

2 Food that is **bland** has very little flavour. *It tasted bland and insipid, like warmed cardboard.* ADJ-GRADED

blandishments /blændɪʃmənts/. Someone's **blandishments** are pleasant things that they say to someone in order to persuade them to do something; a formal word. *At first Lewis resisted their blandishments.* N-PLURAL: oft with poss; =flattery

blandly /blændli/. If you do something **blandly**, you do it in a calm, quiet, and unexcited way. *'Shouldn't you spend a little more time on it?' Sylvia asked blandly... The nurse smiled blandly.* ADV-GRADED: ADV with v

blank /blæŋk/ **blanks, blanking, blanked** ◆◆◇◇◇

1 Something that is **blank** has nothing on it. *We could put some of the pictures over on that blank wall over there... He tore a blank page from his notebook. ...blank cassettes.* ADJ

2 A **blank** is a space which is left in a piece of writing or on a printed form for you to fill in particular information. *Put a word in each blank to complete the sentence.* N-COUNT

3 If you look **blank**, your face shows no feeling, understanding, or interest. *Abbot looked blank. 'I don't quite follow, sir.'... His daughter gave him a blank look.* ADJ-GRADED
♦ **blankly** *She stared at him blankly.* ADV-GRADED: ADV with v
♦ **blankness** *His eyes have the blankness of someone half-asleep.* N-UNCOUNT

4 If your mind or memory is **a blank**, you cannot think of anything or remember anything. *I'm sorry, but my mind is a blank... I came round in hospital and did not know where I was. Everything was a complete blank.* N-SING: a N

5 **Blanks** are gun cartridges which contain explosive but do not contain a bullet, so that they cause no harm when the gun is fired. *...a starter pistol which only fires blanks.* N-COUNT: usu pl

6 See also **point-blank**.

7 If you **draw a blank** when you are looking for someone or something, you do not succeed in finding them; an informal use. *They drew a blank in their search for the driver.* PHRASES; V inflects

8 If your mind **goes blank**, you are suddenly unable to think of anything appropriate to say, for example in reply to a question. *My mind went totally blank.* V inflects

blank out. If you **blank out** a particular feeling or thought, you do not allow yourself to experience that feeling or to have that thought. *I learned to blank those feelings out... I was trying to blank out previous situations from my mind.* PHRASAL VERB; =block out; V n P; V P n (not pron)

blank cheque, blank cheques; spelled **blank check** in American English.

1 If someone is given a **blank cheque**, they are given the authority to spend as much money as they need or want; used mainly in journalism. *We are not prepared to write a blank cheque for companies that have run into trouble.* N-COUNT

2 If someone is given a **blank cheque**, they are given the authority to do what they think is best in a particular situation; used mainly in journalism. *He has, in a sense, been given a blank cheque to negotiate the new South Africa.* N-COUNT; =carte blanche

blanket /blæŋkɪt/ **blankets, blanketing, blanketed** ◆◆◇◇◇

1 A **blanket** is a large square or rectangular piece of thick cloth, especially one which you put on a bed to keep you warm. N-COUNT

2 A **blanket** of something such as snow is a continuous layer of it which hides what is below or beyond it. *The mud disappeared under a blanket of snow... Cold damp air brought in the new year under a blanket of fog.* N-COUNT: usu sing, N *of* n

3 You can refer to something such as an unpleasant emotion or an undesirable quality that seems to affect every aspect of a particular situation as a **blanket of** that emotion or quality; a literary use. *It seems as if the blanket of depression is in some way necessary to help them blot out the even greater pain of real life... A blanket of silence descended.* N-SING: N *of* n

4 If something such as snow **blankets** an area, it covers it. *More than a foot of snow blanketed parts of Michigan... With a thick mist now blanketing the trees, I got thoroughly lost.* VERB; V n

5 You use **blanket** to describe something when you want to emphasize that it affects or refers to every person or thing in a group, without any exceptions. *There's already a blanket ban on foreign unskilled labour in Japan. ...the blanket coverage of the Barcelona Olympics.* ADJ-GRADED: usu ADJ n; =comprehensive

6 See also **electric blanket, security blanket, wet blanket.**

blank verse. **Blank verse** is poetry that does not rhyme. In English literature it usually consists of lines with five stressed syllables. N-UNCOUNT

blare /bleəʳ/ **blares, blaring, blared.** If something such as a siren or radio **blares**, or if you **blare** it, it makes a loud, unpleasant noise. *The fire engines were just pulling up, sirens blaring... Music blared from the flat behind me... I blared my horn.* ◆◇◇◇◇ V-ERG; V; V n
► Also a noun. *...the blare of a radio through a thin wall.* N-SING: N *of* n
► **Blare out** means the same as **blare**. *Music blares out from every cafe. ...giant loudspeakers which blare out patriotic music and the speeches of their leader.* PHRASAL VERB; ERG; V P; V P n (not pron); Also V n P

blarney /blɑːʳni/. You can use **blarney** to describe the way someone talks when they say a lot of things that are flattering and amusing but probably untrue, and which you think they are N-UNCOUNT; PRAGMATICS only saying in order to please you or to persuade you to do something.

blasé /blɑːzeɪ, AM blɑːzeɪ/; also spelled **blase**. If you describe someone as **blasé**, you mean that they are not easily impressed, excited, or worried by things, usually because they have seen or experienced them before; often used showing disapproval. *The consumer has now become very blasé about the foods he buys and expects to be able to buy fresh strawberries in December. ...his seemingly blasé attitude.* ADJ-GRADED: oft ADJ *about* n PRAGMATICS

blaspheme /blæsfiːm/ **blasphemes, blaspheming, blasphemed.** If someone **blasphemes**, they say rude or disrespectful things about God or religion, or they use God's name as a swear word. *He cursed and blasphemed to his last gasp... The spiritual leader charged that the book blasphemed against Islam.* ♦ **blasphemer, blasphemers** *Such a figure is liable to be attacked as a blasphemer.* VERB; V; V *against* n; N-COUNT

blasphemous /blæsfəməs/. You can describe someone who shows disrespect for God or a religion as **blasphemous**. You can also describe what they are saying or doing as **blasphemous**. *He tried to stop me, saying I was being blasphemous. ...works which they describe as blasphemous or obscene. ...your publication of Sue Phillip's blasphemous comments.* ADJ

blasphemy /blæsfəmi/ **blasphemies.** You can describe something that shows disrespect for God or a religion as **blasphemy**. *He was found guilty of blasphemy and seditious libel and sentenced to three years in jail... The MP described the killings as a blasphemy before God.* ◆◇◇◇◇ N-VAR

blast /blɑːst, blæst/ **blasts, blasting, blasted** ◆◆◆◇◇

1 A **blast** is a big explosion, especially one caused by a bomb. *250 people were killed in the blast.* N-COUNT

2 If something **is blasted** into a particular place or state, an explosion causes it to be in that place or state. If something such as a hole **is blasted** in something, it is created by an explosion. *There is a risk that toxic chemicals might be blasted into the atmosphere. ...a terrible accident in which his left arm was blasted off by some kind of a bomb... Earlier two holes were blasted into the ship's hull to let water out and stabilise the ferry... The explosion which followed blasted out the external supporting wall of her flat.* VERB; *be* V-ed prep/adv; V n with adv; Also V n adj, V n prep

3 If workers **are blasting** rock, they are using explosives to make holes in it or destroy it, for example so that a road or tunnel can be built. *Their work was taken up with boring and blasting rock with gelignite... They're using dynamite to blast away rocks to put a road in.* ♦ **blasting** *Three miles away there was a salvo of blasting in the quarry.* VERB; V n; V n with adv; Also V; N-UNCOUNT

4 To **blast** someone means to shoot them with a gun; used in journalism. *A son blasted his father to death after a life-time of bullying, a court was told yesterday... Alan Barnett, 28, was blasted with a sawn-off shotgun in Oldham on Thursday.* ► Also a noun. *...the man who killed Nigel Davies with a shotgun blast.* VERB; V n *to* n; *be* V-ed *with* n; N-COUNT

5 If someone **blasts** their way somewhere, they get there by shooting at people or causing an explosion. *The police were reported to have blasted their way into the house using explosives... One armoured column attempted to blast a path through a barricade of buses and trucks.* VERB; V *way* prep/adv; V n prep/adv

6 If something **blasts** water or air somewhere, it sends out a sudden, powerful stream of it. *Blasting cold air over it makes the water evaporate... A blizzard was blasting great drifts of snow across the lake.* ► Also a noun. *Blasts of cold air swept down from the mountains.* VERB; V n prep/adv; N-COUNT: usu N *of* n

7 If you **blast** something such as a car horn, or if it **blasts**, it makes a sudden, loud sound. If something **blasts** music, or music **blasts**, the music is very loud. *...drivers who do not blast their horns... The sound of western music blasted as she entered.* ► Also a noun. *The buzzer suddenly responded in a long blast of sound.* V-ERG; V n; V; N-COUNT: usu N *of* n

8 You can say that a sports player **blasts** the ball somewhere if he or she gives it a powerful kick or hit; used in sports journalism. *Ramsay blasted the ball into the back of the net... He may try to blast his way out of trouble, playing attacking shots to balls he would not normally contemplate hitting.* VERB; V n adv/prep; V *way* prep

9 To **blast** someone or something means to criticize them strongly; used in journalism. *Football: Taylor blasts Beck... The Department of Health and a top immunologist have blasted a report in last week's Sunday Times.* ► Also a noun. *Cricket: Blast for Ormrod.* VERB; V n; N-COUNT: usu sing

10 Some people say **'blast'** to show that they are annoyed at something or someone; an informal use. *Blast! I can't do anything with this.* EXCLAM PRAGMATICS

11 If something such as a radio or a heater is on **full blast**, or on **at full blast**, it is producing as much sound or power as it is able to. *In many of those homes the television is on full blast 24 hours a day... You are unlikely to run the heater at full blast for long periods.* PHRASES; PHR after v, v-link PHR

12 You can use **a blast from the past** as a light-hearted way of referring to something such as an old record or fashion that you hear or notice again, and which reminds you of an earlier time; an informal expression.

blast away PHRASAL VERB

1 If a gun, or a person firing a gun, **blasts away**, the gun is fired continuously for a period of time. *Suddenly all the men pull out pistols and begin blasting away.* V P

2 If something such as a radio or a pop group **is blasting away**, it is producing a loud noise. *Clock-radios blast away until you get up.* V P

blast off. When a space rocket **blasts off**, it leaves the ground at the start of its journey. ● See also **blast-off**. PHRASAL VERB

blast out. If something **is blasting out** music or noise, or if music or noise **is blasting out**, loud music or noise is being produced. *...loudspeakers blasting out essential tourist facts in every language known to man... Pop music can be heard 10 miles away blasting out from the huge tented shanty-town.* PHRASAL VERB ERG; V P n (not pron); V P

blasted /blɑːstɪd, blæstɪd/

1 Some people use **blasted** to express anger or annoyance at something or someone; an old-fashioned, informal use. *I couldn't get that blasted door open.* ADJ: ADJ n PRAGMATICS

2 If you describe a landscape as **blasted**, you mean that it has very few plants or trees, and it makes you feel sad or depressed to look at it; a literary use. *The photograph shows the blasted landscape where the battle was fought.* ADJ: usu ADJ n =bleak

blast furnace, blast furnaces. A **blast furnace** is a furnace in which iron ore is heated under pressure so that it melts and the pure iron metal separates out and can be collected. N-COUNT

blast-off. **Blast-off** is the moment when a rocket leaves the ground and rises into the air to begin a journey into space. *The original planned launch was called off four minutes before blast-off.* N-UNCOUNT

blatant /bleɪtᵊnt/. You use **blatant** to describe something bad that is done in an open or very obvious way in order to emphasize your shock or surprise that it is done in such an open or obvious way. *Outsiders will continue to suffer the most blatant discrimination. ...a blatant attempt to spread the blame for the fiasco... The elitism was blatant.* ◆◇◇◇◇ ADJ-GRADED PRAGMATICS

blatantly /bleɪtᵊntli/ ◆◇◇◇◇

1 If, for example, you say that something is **blatantly** untrue, you are saying in a very forceful way that it is clearly untrue. If you say that it is **blatantly** obvious that something bad is going to happen, you are saying in a very forceful way that it is obvious that that thing is going to happen. You only use **blatantly** to describe states or situations which you think are bad. *It became blatantly obvious to me that the band wasn't going to last... For years, blatantly false assertions have gone unchallenged...* ADV-GRADED: usu ADV adj, also ADV with v, ADV with cl PRAGMATICS

This argument is only too blatantly an alibi for domestic repression.

2 You use **blatantly** to describe something bad that is done in an open or very obvious way in order to emphasize your shock or surprise that it is done in such an open or obvious way. *...a blatantly sexist question... They said the song blatantly encouraged the killing of policemen.* ADV-GRADED: ADV adj, ADV with v PRAGMATICS

blather /blæðəʳ/ **blathers, blathering, blathered.** If you say that someone **is blathering** on about something, you mean that they are talking for a long time about something that you consider boring or irrelevant. *The old men love to talk, to blather on and on... Stop blathering... He kept on blathering about police incompetence.* ► Also a noun. *Anyone knows that all this is blather.* VERB V on V V about n N-UNCOUNT

blaze /bleɪz/ **blazes, blazing, blazed** ◆◆◇◇◇

1 When a fire **blazes**, it burns strongly and brightly. *Three people died as wreckage blazed, and rescuers fought to release trapped drivers... The log fire was blazing merrily. ...a blazing fire.* VERB V V-ing

2 A **blaze** is a large fire which is difficult to control and which destroys a lot of things; used in journalism. *Two fireman were hurt in a blaze which swept through a tower block last night.* N-COUNT: usu sing

3 If something **blazes** with light or colour, it is extremely bright; a literary use. *The gardens blazed with colour.* ► Also a noun. *I wanted the front garden to be a blaze of colour.* VERB V with n N-COUNT: usu a N of n

4 If someone's eyes **are blazing** with an emotion, or if an emotion **is blazing** in their eyes, their eyes look very bright because they are feeling that emotion so strongly; a literary use. *He got to his feet and his dark eyes were blazing with anger... Eva stood up and indignation blazed in her eyes... His eyes blazed intently into mine... Miss Turner turned blazing eyes on the victim.* VB: usu cont =burn V with n V V prep V-ing

5 **A blaze of** publicity or attention is a great amount of it. *He was arrested in a blaze of publicity. ...the sporting career that began in a blaze of glory.* N-SING: a N of n

6 If guns **blaze**, or **blaze** away, they fire continuously, making a lot of noise. *Guns were blazing, flares going up and the sky was lit up all around... She took the gun and blazed away with calm and deadly accuracy.* VERB V V away

7 • **with all guns blazing**: see **gun**.

8 If someone **blazes a trail**, they discover or explore something new. *These surgeons have blazed the trail in the treatment of bomb victims.* PHRASE: V inflects =lead the way

blazer /bleɪzəʳ/ **blazers.** A **blazer** is a kind of jacket which is often worn by members of a particular group, especially schoolchildren and members of a sports team. ◆◇◇◇◇ N-COUNT

blazing /bleɪzɪŋ/

1 You use **blazing** or **blazing hot** to describe the weather when it is very hot and sunny. *Quite a few people were eating outside in the blazing sun. ...freezing cold winters and blazing hot summers.* ADJ: ADJ n

2 When people have a **blazing** row, they quarrel in a very noisy and excited way. *My husband has just had a blazing row with his boss.* ADJ: ADJ n

bldg, bldgs. Bldg is a written abbreviation for **building** which is used especially in the names of buildings. *...Old National Bank Bldg.*

bleach /bliːtʃ/ **bleaches, bleaching, bleached** ◆◇◇◇◇

1 If you **bleach** something, you use a chemical to make it white or pale in colour. *These products don't contain peroxide or ammonia, which bleach the hair... Commercial flour is bleached artificially. ...bleached pine tables... Sodium chlorate is used as a bleaching agent.* VERB V n V-ed V-ing

2 If something **bleaches** or if the sun **bleaches** it, its natural colour fades until it is almost white. *The tree's roots are stripped and hung to season and bleach... The sun will bleach the hairs on your face... He has hair which is naturally black but which has been bleached by the sun. ...bleached seaweed.* V-ERG =weather-beaten V V n V-ed

3 **Bleach** is a chemical that is used to make cloth white, or to clean things thoroughly and kill germs. N-MASS

bleachers /bliːtʃəʳz/. In American English, the **bleachers** is an area of seating at an outdoor sports stadium. The bleachers is usually in an uncovered section of the stadium and is the least expensive place where people can sit. N-PLURAL: usu the N

bleak /bliːk/ **bleaker, bleakest** ◆◆◇◇◇

1 If a situation is **bleak**, it is bad, and seems unlikely to improve. *The immediate outlook remains bleak... Many predicted a bleak future.* ♦ **bleakness** *The continued bleakness of the American job market was blamed.* ADJ-GRADED =gloomy ≠bright N-UNCOUNT: usu with supp, oft N of n

2 If you describe a place as **bleak**, you mean that it looks cold, bare, and unattractive. *The island's pretty bleak. ...bleak inner-city streets.* ADJ-GRADED

3 When the weather is **bleak**, it is cold, dull, and unpleasant. *The weather can be quite bleak on the coast.* ADJ-GRADED

4 If someone looks or sounds **bleak**, they look or sound depressed, as if they have no hope or energy. *His face was bleak... Alberg gave him a bleak stare.* ♦ **bleakly** *'There is nothing left,' she says bleakly.* ADJ-GRADED ADV-GRADED: usu ADV with v, also ADV adj

bleary /blɪəri/. If your eyes are **bleary**, they look dull or tired, as if you have not had enough sleep or have drunk too much alcohol. *I arrived bleary-eyed and rumpled... Mona smiled at her through bleary eyes.* ADJ

bleat /bliːt/ **bleats, bleating, bleated**

1 When a sheep or goat **bleats**, it makes the sound that sheep and goats typically make. *From the slope below, the wild goats bleated faintly. ...a small flock of bleating ewes and lambs.* ► Also a noun. *...the faint bleat of a distressed animal.* VERB V V-ing N-COUNT

2 If someone **bleats**, they speak in a weak, high voice; used in written English. *'I don't want it,' Eric bleated.* ► Also a noun. *She wanted to scream, but all that would come out was this faint bleat.* VERB V with quote N-COUNT

3 If you say that someone **bleats** about something, you mean that they complain about it in a way which makes them sound weak and irritating. *They are always bleating about 'unfair' foreign competition... Don't come bleating to me every time something goes wrong.* VERB PRAGMATICS =whinge, whine V about n V prep/adv Also V that

bleat on about. If you say that someone **is bleating on about** something, you mean that they are talking about it a great deal in a way which makes them sound weak and irritating. *It's no good bleating on about it, you ought to do something about it.* PHRASAL VERB PRAGMATICS V P P n

bled /bled/. **Bled** is the past tense and past participle of **bleed**.

bleed /bliːd/ **bleeds, bleeding, bled** ◆◆◇◇◇

1 When you **bleed**, you lose blood from your body as a result of injury or illness. *His head had struck the sink and was bleeding... He was bleeding profusely... She's going to bleed to death!* ♦ **bleeding** *This results in internal bleeding.* VERB V V to n N-UNCOUNT

2 If the colour of one substance **bleeds** into the colour of another substance that it is touching, it goes into the other thing so that its colour changes in an undesirable way. *The colouring pigments from the skins are not allowed to bleed into the grape juice.* VERB V prep

3 If you say that someone **is being bled**, you mean that you disapprove of the fact that someone or something is gradually taking money or other resources away from them. *We have been gradually bled for twelve years... They mean to bleed the British to the utmost.* VERB PRAGMATICS be V-ed V n

4 If you say that someone **is being bled dry** or **is being bled white**, you mean that you disapprove of the fact that someone or something is gradually taking all of their money or other resources away from them. *The war has bled the once-strong Armenian economy dry.* PHRASE: V inflects PRAGMATICS

5 See also **nosebleed**.

bleeding /bliːdɪŋ/. In British English, **bleeding** is a swear word which some people use to emphasize what they are saying, especially when they feel strongly about something or dislike something; an old-fashioned word which some people find offensive. ADJ: ADJ n PRAGMATICS

bleeding-heart; also spelled **bleeding heart**. You use **bleeding-heart** to describe someone when you disapprove of the fact that they are much too sympathetic and kind and they accept ADJ: ADJ n PRAGMATICS other people's weaknesses much too easily as a result. *...a sort of 'soft' option that the bleeding heart liberals will push for.*

bleep /bliːp/ **bleeps, bleeping, bleeped** ◆◇◇◇◇
1 A **bleep** is a short, high-pitched sound, usually one of a series, that is made by an electrical device. N-COUNT =beep
2 If something electronic **bleeps**, it makes a bleep sound. *When we turned the boat about, the signal began to bleep again constantly.* VERB =beep V

bleeper /bliːpəʳ/ **bleepers.** A **bleeper** is the same as a **beeper**; an informal word. N-COUNT

blemish /blemɪʃ/ **blemishes, blemishing, blemished** ◆◇◇◇◇
1 A **blemish** is a small mark on something that spoils its appearance. *Every piece is closely scrutinised, and if there is the slightest blemish on it, it is rejected.* N-COUNT
2 A **blemish** on something is a small fault in it. *This is the one blemish on an otherwise resounding success.* N-COUNT: oft N on n =imperfection
3 If something **blemishes** someone's character or reputation, it spoils it or makes it seem less good than it was in the past. *He wasn't about to blemish that pristine record.* VERB =tarnish V n

blemished /blemɪʃt/. You use **blemished** to describe something such as someone's skin or a piece of fruit when its appearance is spoiled by small marks. *...a skin tonic for oily, blemished complexions.* ADJ-GRADED: usu ADJ n

blend /blend/ **blends, blending, blended** ◆◆◇◇◇
1 If you **blend** substances together or if they **blend**, you mix them together so that they become one substance. *Blend the butter with the sugar and beat until light and creamy... Blend the ingredients until you have a smooth cream... Put the soap and water in a pan and leave to stand until they have blended... Most whiskies are blended whiskies.* V-RECIP-ERG V n with n V pl-n pl-n V V-ed Also V
2 A **blend** of things is a mixture or combination of them that is useful or pleasant. *The public areas offer a subtle blend of traditional charm with modern amenities. ...a blend of wine and sparkling water... He makes up his own blends of flour.* N-COUNT: usu sing, usu N of n
3 When colours, sounds, or styles **blend**, they come together or are combined in a pleasing way. *You could paint the walls and ceilings the same colour so they blend together. ...the picture, furniture and porcelain collections that blend so well with the house itself.* V-RECIP pl-n V V with n
4 If you **blend** ideas, policies, or styles, you use them together in order to achieve something. *His 'cosmic vision' is to blend Christianity with 'the wisdom of all world religions'. ...a band that blended jazz, folk and classical music.* VERB V n with n V n

blend in PHRASAL VERB
1 If something **blends into** the background or **blends in**, it is so similar to the background in appearance or sound that it is difficult to see or hear it separately. *The toad had changed its colour to blend in with its new environment. ...a continuous pale neutral grey, almost blending into the sky... You can blend in so that the voice becomes just another instrument in the band.* V P with n V P n V P
2 If someone **blends into** a particular group or situation, or if they **blend in**, they seem to belong there or are not noticeable, because their appearance or behaviour is similar to that of the other people involved. *It must have reinforced my determination to blend into my surroundings... She felt she would blend in nicely... He blended in with the crowd at the art sale.* V P n V P V P with n

blender /blendəʳ/ **blenders.** A **blender** is an electrical kitchen appliance used for mixing liquids and soft foods together or turning fruit or vegetables into liquid. N-COUNT

bless /bles/ **blesses, blessing, blessed** ◆◆◇◇◇
1 When someone such as a priest **blesses** people or things, he asks for God's favour and protection for them. *...asking for all present to bless this couple and their loving commitment to one another.* VERB V n
2 **Bless** is used in expressions such as 'God bless' or 'bless you' to express affection, thanks, or good wishes; an informal use. *'Bless you, Eva,' he whispered... God bless and thank you all so much.* CONVENTION PRAGMATICS
3 You can say **bless you** to someone who has just sneezed. CONVENTION
4 See also **blessed, blessing.**

blessed. Pronounced /blest/ for meaning 1, and /blesɪd/ for meanings 2 and 3. ◆◇◇◇◇
1 If someone is **blessed with** a particular good quality or skill, they have that good quality or skill. *Both are blessed with uncommon ability to fix things. ...the son of a doctor and well blessed with money.* ADJ-GRADED: v-link ADJ with n
2 You use **blessed** to describe something that you think is wonderful, and that you are thankful for or relieved about. *The final outcome of a live healthy baby is a truly blessed event... Rainy weather brings blessed relief to hay fever victims.* ♦ **blessedly** *Most British election campaigns are blessedly brief.* ADJ: ADJ n PRAGMATICS ADV: usu ADV adj, also ADV with cl
3 Some people use **blessed** to emphasize that they are annoyed about something; used mainly in old-fashioned British English. *No-one knows a blessed thing.* ADJ: ADJ n PRAGMATICS
4 See also **bless.**

blessing /blesɪŋ/ **blessings** ◆◆◇◇◇
1 A **blessing** is something good that you are thankful for. *Rivers are a blessing for an agricultural country. ...the blessings of prosperity.* N-COUNT
2 If something is done with someone's **blessing**, it is done with their approval and support. *With the blessing of the White House, a group of Democrats in Congress is meeting to find additional budget cuts... In April Thai and Indonesian leaders gave their formal blessing to the idea.* N-COUNT: usu sing, with poss =approval
3 A **blessing** is a prayer asking God to look kindly upon the people who are present or the event that is taking place. N-COUNT
4 See also **bless.**
5 If you tell someone to **count** their **blessings**, you are saying that they should think about how lucky they are instead of complaining. *Some would argue this was no burden in fact, and that she should count her blessings.* PHRASES V inflects
6 If you say that something is **a blessing in disguise**, you mean that it causes problems and difficulties at first but later you realize that it was the best thing that could have happened. *The failure to conclude the trade talks last December could prove a blessing in disguise.* usu v-link PHR
7 If you say that a situation is **a mixed blessing**, you mean that it has disadvantages as well as advantages. *For ordinary Italians, Sunday's news probably amounts to a mixed blessing.* usu v-link PHR

blew /bluː/. **Blew** is the past tense of **blow.**

blight /blaɪt/ **blights, blighting, blighted** ◆◇◇◇◇
1 You can refer to something as a **blight** when it causes great difficulties, and damages or spoils other things. *This discriminatory policy has really been a blight on America... Manchester still suffers from urban blight and unacceptable poverty.* N-VAR: usu with supp
2 If something **blights** your life or your hopes, it damages and spoils them. If something **blights** an area, it spoils it and makes it unattractive. *An embarrassing blunder nearly blighted his career before it got off the ground. ...thousands of families whose lives were blighted by unemployment. ...a strategy to redevelop blighted inner-city areas.* VERB V n V-ed
3 **Blight** is a disease which makes plants wither. There are several kinds of blight. N-UNCOUNT: also N in pl

blighter /blaɪtəʳ/ **blighters.** In informal British English, if you refer to someone as a **blighter**, you mean that you do not like them, or that you feel they have done something wrong. It is also sometimes used to express sympathy or mild envy. *He was a nasty little blighter... Lucky blighter, thought King.* N-COUNT PRAGMATICS

Blighty /blaɪti/. In British English, **Blighty** is an old-fashioned, slightly humorous way of referring to England. *See you back in Blighty!* N-PROPER

blimey /blaɪmi/. In informal British English, you can say **blimey** when you are surprised by something or feel strongly about it. *'We walked all the way to Moseley.'—'Blimey!'* EXCLAM PRAGMATICS

blimp /blɪmp/ **blimps.** A **blimp** is the same as an **airship**; used mainly in American English. N-COUNT

blind /blaɪnd/ **blinds, blinding, blinded** ◆◆◆◇◇

1 Someone who is **blind** is unable to see because their eyes are damaged. *I started helping him run the business when he went blind... How would you explain colour to a blind person?* ► **The blind** are people who are blind. *He was a teacher of the blind.* ♦ **blindness** *Early diagnosis and treatment can usually prevent blindness.* ADJ; N-PLURAL: the N; N-UNCOUNT

2 If something **blinds** you, it makes you unable to see, either for a short time or permanently. *The sun hit the windscreen, momentarily blinding him.* VERB; V n

3 If you are **blind** with something such as tears or a bright light, you are unable to see for a short time because of the tears or light. *Her mother groped for the back of the chair, her eyes blind with tears.* ♦ **blindly** *Lettie groped blindly for the glass.* ADJ: v-link ADJ, usu ADJ *with* n; ADV

4 If you say that someone is **blind to** a fact or a situation, you mean that they take no notice of it or are unaware of it, although you think that they should take notice of it or be aware of it. *David's good looks and impeccable manners had always made her blind to his faults... All the time I was blind to your suffering.* ♦ **blindness** *...blindness in government policy to the very existence of the unemployed.* ADJ-GRADED: v-link ADJ *to* n PRAGMATICS; N-UNCOUNT

5 If something **blinds** you to the real situation, it prevents you from realizing that it exists or from understanding it properly. *He never allowed his love of Australia to blind him to his countrymen's faults.* VERB; V n *to* n

6 You can describe someone's beliefs or actions as **blind** when you think that they seem to take no notice of important facts or behave in an unreasonable way. *...her blind faith in the wisdom of the Church... Lesley yelled at him with blind, hating rage.* ADJ-GRADED: usu ADJ n PRAGMATICS

7 A **blind** corner is one that you cannot see round because something is blocking your view. *He tried to overtake three cars on a blind corner and crashed head-on into a lorry.* ADJ: ADJ n

8 A **blind** wall or building is one which has no windows or doors. *I remembered a huddle of stone buildings with blind walls.* ADJ: ADJ n

9 A **blind** is a roll of cloth or paper which you can pull down over a window in order to keep out the light. N-COUNT

10 See also **blinding**, **blindly**; **colour blind**, **Venetian blind**.

11 If you say that someone **is turning a blind eye** to something bad or illegal that is happening, you mean that you think they are pretending not to notice that it is happening so that they will not have to do anything about it. *Teachers are turning a blind eye to pupils smoking at school, a report reveals today... I can't turn a blind eye when someone is being robbed.* PHRASE: V inflects PRAGMATICS

blind alley, blind alleys. If you describe a situation as a **blind alley**, you mean that progress is not possible or that the situation can have no useful results. *We are all now beginning to appreciate that this type of music is a blind alley.* N-COUNT =dead end

blind date, blind dates. A **blind date** is an arrangement made for you to spend a romantic evening with someone you have never met before. N-COUNT

blinder /blaɪndəʳ/ **blinders**

1 In informal British English, if you say that someone such as a sports player or musician has played a **blinder**, you are emphasizing that they have played something very well. N-COUNT: usu sing

2 Blinders are the same as **blinkers**; used mainly in American English. N-PLURAL

blindfold /blaɪndfəʊld/ **blindfolds, blindfolding, blindfolded** ◆◇◇◇◇

1 A **blindfold** is a strip of cloth that is tied over someone's eyes so that they cannot see. N-COUNT

2 If you **blindfold** someone, you tie a blindfold over their eyes. *His abductors blindfolded him and drove him to a flat in southern Beirut... The report says prisoners were often kept blindfolded.* VERB; V n; V-ed

3 If someone does something **blindfold**, they do it while wearing a blindfold. *The Australian chess grandmaster Ian Rogers took on six opponents blindfold and beat five.* ADJ: ADJ after v

4 If you say that you **can** do something **blindfold**, you are emphasizing that you can do it easily, for example because you have done it many times before. *He read the letter again although already he could have recited its contents blindfold.* PHRASE PRAGMATICS

blinding /blaɪndɪŋ/ ◆◇◇◇◇

1 A **blinding** light is extremely bright. *The doctor worked busily beneath the blinding lights of the delivery room.* ADJ: usu ADJ n =dazzling

2 You use **blinding** to emphasize that something is very obvious. *The miseries I went through made me suddenly realise with a blinding flash what life was all about.* ♦ **blindingly** *It is so blindingly obvious that defence must be the responsibility of the state.* ADJ: ADJ n; ADV-GRADED: ADV adj/adv

3 Blinding pain is very strong pain. *There was a pain then, a quick, blinding agony that jumped along Danlo's spine.* ADJ: usu ADJ n

blindly /blaɪndli/. If you say that someone does something **blindly**, you mean that they do it without having enough information, or without thinking about it; used showing disapproval. *Don't just blindly follow what the banker says... Without adequate information, many students choose a college almost blindly. ...the once blindly obedient organ of Soviet government.* • See also **blind.** ADV-GRADED: usu ADV with v, also ADV adj, ADV with cl PRAGMATICS

blind spot, blind spots

1 If you say that someone has a **blind spot** about something, you mean that they seem to be unable to understand it or to see how important it is. *British judges have a complete blind spot when confronted by evidence which indicates police corruption... When I was single I never worried about money - it was a bit of a blind spot.* N-COUNT

2 A **blind spot** is an area in your range of vision that you cannot see properly but which you really should be able to see. For example, when you are driving a car, the area just behind your shoulders is often a blind spot. N-COUNT

blink /blɪŋk/ **blinks, blinking, blinked** ◆◆◇◇◇

1 When you **blink** or when you **blink** your eyes, you shut your eyes and very quickly open them again. *Kathryn blinked and forced a smile... Suddenly, Momma's eyes blinked... She was blinking her eyes rapidly... He blinked at her.* ► Also a noun. *He kept giving quick blinks.* VERB; V; V n; V *at* n; N-COUNT

2 When a light **blinks**, it flashes on and off. *Green and yellow lights blinked on the surface of the harbour... The plane was flying normally for about 15 minutes before a warning light blinked on. ...the blinking lights at the top of the Tutweiler Hotel.* VERB; V; V *on/out/off*; V-ing

3 If you say that something happens in **the blink of an eye**, you mean that it happens very quickly. *It was all over in the blink of an eye.* PHRASES; oft *in* PHR

4 If a machine goes **on the blink**, it stops working properly; an informal expression. *...an old TV that's on the blink.* usu v-link PHR

blinkered /blɪŋkəʳd/. A **blinkered** view, attitude, or approach considers only a narrow point of view and does not take into account other people's opinions. A **blinkered** person has this kind of attitude. Used showing disapproval. *They've got a very blinkered view of life... Haig was limited by his blinkered approach to strategy and tactics... He seems to be so blinkered that he cannot see what is happening around him.* ADJ-GRADED PRAGMATICS =narrow-minded

blinkers /blɪŋkəʳz/

1 In British English, if you describe someone as wearing **blinkers**, you disapprove of them because you think that they are considering only a narrow point of view and are not taking into account other people's opinions. The usual American word is **blinders**. *As far as mathematicians are concerned, there's a certain virtue in wearing intellectual blinkers... At least you have removed your blinkers and can now see the relationship in its true colours.* N-PLURAL PRAGMATICS

2 In British English, **blinkers** are two pieces of leather which are placed at the side of a horse's N-PLURAL eyes so that it can only see straight ahead; the usual American word is **blinders**.

blip /blɪp/ **blips** ◆◇◇◇◇

1 A **blip** is a small spot of light, sometimes occurring with a short, high-pitched sound, which flashes on and off regularly on a piece of equipment such as a radar screen. N-COUNT

2 A **blip** in a straight line, such as the line on a graph, is a point at which the line suddenly makes a sharp change of direction before returning to its original direction. *The blips on the graph are faxed straight back to Tokyo for immediate technical analysis.* N-COUNT

3 A **blip** in a situation is a sudden but temporary change in it. *Interest rates generally have been declining since last spring, despite a few upward blips in recent weeks.* N-COUNT

bliss /blɪs/. **Bliss** is a state of complete happiness. *It was a scene of such domestic bliss.* ◆◇◇◇◇ N-UNCOUNT

blissful /blɪsfʊl/ ◆◇◇◇◇

1 A **blissful** situation or period of time is one in which you are extremely happy. *We spent a blissful week together... There's just nothing more blissful than lying by that pool.* ♦ **blissfully** /blɪsfʊli/ *We're blissfully happy... The summer passed blissfully.* ADJ-GRADED; ADV-GRADED: ADV adj, ADV after v

2 If someone is in **blissful** ignorance of something unpleasant or serious, they are totally unaware of it. *Many country parishes were still living in blissful ignorance of the post-war crime wave.* ♦ **blissfully** *At first, he was blissfully unaware of the conspiracy against him.* ADJ: ADJ n; ADV: usu ADV adj, also ADV before v

blister /blɪstəʳ/ **blisters, blistering, blistered** ◆◇◇◇◇

1 A **blister** is a painful swelling on the surface of your skin. Blisters contain a clear liquid and are usually caused by heat or by something repeatedly rubbing your skin. N-COUNT

2 When your skin **blisters** or when something **blisters** it, blisters appear on it. *The affected skin turns red and may blister... The sap of this plant blisters the skin. ...pausing to bathe their blistered feet.* V-ERG; V; V n; V-ed

blistering /blɪstərɪŋ/ ◆◇◇◇◇

1 **Blistering** heat is very great heat. *...a blistering summer day.* ADJ: usu ADJ n

2 A **blistering** remark expresses great anger or sarcasm. *The president responded to this with a blistering attack on his critics.* ADJ-GRADED: usu ADJ n

3 **Blistering** is used by journalists to describe actions in sport to emphasize that they are done with great speed or force. *Sharon Wild set a blistering pace to take the lead.* ADJ: ADJ n; PRAGMATICS

blithe /blaɪð/ ◆◇◇◇◇

1 You use **blithe** to indicate that something is done casually, without serious or careful thought; used showing disapproval. *It does so with blithe disregard for best scientific practice.* ♦ **blithely** *Your editorial blithely ignores the hard facts... He appears blithely unaware of the disastrous effects of the new system.* ADJ-GRADED: usu ADJ n; PRAGMATICS; ADV: ADV with v, ADV adj

2 Someone who is **blithe** is carefree and cheerful; a literary use. *She said 'hi' with the blithe assurance of someone who knew how much she'd been missed.* ADJ-GRADED

blitz /blɪts/ **blitzes, blitzing, blitzed** ◆◇◇◇◇

1 If a city or building **is blitzed** during a war, it is attacked by bombs dropped by enemy aircraft. *In the autumn of 1940 London was blitzed by an average of two hundred aircraft a night... They blitzed the capital with tanks, artillery, anti-aircraft weapons and machine guns.* VERB; be V-ed; V n

2 The heavy bombing of British cities by German aircraft in 1940 and 1941 is referred to as **the Blitz**. N-PROPER: the N

3 If you have a **blitz** on something, you make a big effort to deal with it or to improve it; an informal use. *Regional accents are still acceptable but there is to be a blitz on incorrect grammar.* N-COUNT: with supp, oft N on n

4 An advertising or publicity **blitz** is a major effort to publicize something. *On December 8 the media blitz began in earnest.* N-COUNT: with supp

blitzkrieg /blɪtskriːg/ **blitzkriegs**

1 A **blitzkrieg** is a fast and intensive military attack that takes the enemy by surprise and is intended to achieve a very quick victory. N-COUNT

2 Journalists sometimes refer to a rapid and powerful attack or campaign in, for example, sport, politics, or advertizing as a **blitzkrieg**; an informal use. *...a blitzkrieg of media hype.* N-COUNT

blizzard /blɪzəʳd/ **blizzards** ◆◇◇◇◇

1 A **blizzard** is a very bad snowstorm with strong winds. N-COUNT

2 You can refer to a large number of things that you do not like or which you think are a nuisance as a **blizzard** of those things; used in written English. *Retailers were hit with a blizzard of new products and brands in all shapes, sizes and colours. ...the annual blizzard of bills and amendments.* N-COUNT: usu sing, usu N of n; PRAGMATICS

bloated /bloʊtɪd/ ◆◇◇◇◇

1 If someone's body or a part of their body is **bloated**, it is much larger than normal, usually because it has a lot of liquid or gas inside it. *...the bloated body of a dead bullock... His face was bloated.* ADJ-GRADED =swollen

2 If you feel **bloated** after eating a large meal, you feel very full and uncomfortable. *Diners do not want to leave the table feeling bloated.* ADJ-GRADED: v-link ADJ

3 If you describe an organization as **bloated**, you mean that it is larger and less efficient than it should be. *...its massive state apparatus and bloated bureaucracy.* ADJ-GRADED: usu ADJ n

bloating /bloʊtɪŋ/. **Bloating** is the swelling of a body or part of a body, usually because it has a lot of gas or liquid in it. *...abdominal bloating and pain.* N-UNCOUNT =swelling

blob /blɒb/ **blobs** ◆◇◇◇◇

1 A **blob** of thick or sticky liquid is a small, often round, amount of it. *...a blob of chocolate mousse... It's only necessary to use just a very small blob.* N-COUNT: usu with supp

2 You can use **blob** to refer to something that you cannot see very clearly, for example because it is in the distance; an informal use. *You could just see vague blobs of faces. ...a blob in the distance.* N-COUNT

bloc /blɒk/ **blocs.** A **bloc** is a group of countries which have similar political aims and interests and that act together over some issues. *...the former Soviet bloc. ...the world's largest trading bloc.* ◆◆◇◇◇ N-COUNT

• See also **en bloc**.

block /blɒk/ **blocks, blocking, blocked** ◆◆◆◆◇

1 A **block** of flats or offices is a large building containing them. *...blocks of council flats. ...a white-painted apartment block.* N-COUNT: usu with supp, oft N of n

2 A **block** in a town is an area of land with streets on all its sides. *She walked four blocks down High Street... He walked around the block three times.* N-COUNT

3 A **block** of a substance is a large rectangular piece of it. *...a block of ice.* N-COUNT: usu N of n

4 To **block** a road, channel, or pipe means to put an object across it or in it so that nothing can pass through it or along it. *Some students today blocked a highway that cuts through the center of the city... When the shrimp farm is built it will block the stream... He can clear blocked drains.* VERB; V n; V-ed

5 If something **blocks** your view, it prevents you from seeing something because it is between you and that thing. *...a row of spruce trees that blocked his view of the long north slope of the mountain.* VERB =obstruct; V n

6 If you **block** someone's way, you prevent them from going somewhere or entering a place by standing in front of them. *I started to move round him, but he blocked my way... Mr Calder tried to leave the shop but the police officer blocked his path.* VERB; V n

7 If you **block** something that is being arranged, you prevent it from being done. *For years the country has tried to block imports of various cheap foreign products... His persistent attempts to complain to his superiors were blocked and ignored.* VERB =prevent; V n

8 A **block** of something such as tickets or shares is a large quantity of them, especially when they are all sold at the same time and are in a particular sequence or order. *Those booking a block of seats get them at reduced rates.* N-COUNT: usu N of n

9 If you have a **mental block** or a **block**, you are temporarily unable to do something that you can normally do which involves using thinking about or remembering something. N-COUNT: usu supp N

10 See also **breeze-block**, **building block**, **road-**

block, stumbling block, tower block, starting block.

11 If someone **lays** their **head on the block**, or **puts** their **head on the block**, they are risking their reputation or position by taking a particular course of action. *The Chancellor, by his unusual statement, has put his head on the block.* PHRASE: V inflects

12 • **a chip off the old block**: see **chip**.

block in. If you **are blocked in**, someone has parked their car in such a way that you cannot drive yours away. *Our cars get blocked in and when we ask the restaurant to move them they don't do it for ages... Oh, is that your car outside? I may have blocked you in.* PHRASAL VERB get V-ed P; V n P; Also V P n (not pron)

block off. When you **block off** a door, window, or passage, you put something across it so that nothing can pass through it. *They had blocked off the fireplaces to stop draughts.* PHRASAL VERB V P n (not pron); Also V n P

block out PHRASAL VERB

1 If someone **blocks out** a thought, they try not to think about it. *She accuses me of having blocked out the past... I had to block the thought out of my mind.* =blank out; V P n (not pron); V n P of n

2 Something that **blocks out** light prevents it from reaching a place. *Thick chipboard across the window frames blocked out the daylight... Those clouds would have cast shadows that would have blocked some sunlight out.* V P n (not pron); V n P

block up. If you **block** something **up** or if it **blocks up**, it is blocked completely so that nothing can get through it. *'Any holes in the kitchen where the mice are getting through?'—'I've blocked them up.'... Powdering a sweaty nose will only block up the pores and make the skin more uncomfortable... With this disease the veins in the liver can block up, and all sorts of damage follows.* PHRASAL VERB ERG; V n P; V P n (not pron); V P

blockade /blɒkeɪd/ **blockades, blockading, blockaded** ◆◆◇◇◇

1 A **blockade** of a place is an action that is taken to prevent goods or people from entering or leaving it. *Striking lorry drivers agreed to lift their blockades of main roads... It's not yet clear who will actually enforce the blockade. ...the economic blockade of Lithuania.* N-COUNT: oft N of n

2 If a group of people **blockade** a place, they take action to prevent goods or people from reaching that place. If they **blockade** a road or a port, they take action to stop people using that road or port to reach a particular place. This is usually done as a protest or as part of a military action. *Truck drivers have blockaded roads to show their anger over new driving regulations... About 50,000 people are trapped in the town, which has been blockaded for more than three months. ...the blockaded Bosnian capital.* VERB V n; V-ed

blockage /blɒkɪdʒ/ **blockages.** A **blockage** in a pipe, tube, or tunnel is an object which blocks it, or the state of being blocked. *The logical treatment is to remove this blockage. ...a total blockage in one of the coronary arteries.* ◆◇◇◇◇ N-COUNT: oft N in/of n

blockbuster /blɒkbʌstəʳ/ **blockbusters.** A **blockbuster** is a film or book that is very popular and successful, usually because of the exciting or sensational events featured in it; an informal word. ◆◇◇◇◇ N-COUNT

blockbusting /blɒkbʌstɪŋ/. A **blockbusting** film or book is one that is very successful, usually because of the exciting or sensational events featured in it; an informal word, used in journalism. *...the blockbusting sci-fi movie 'Suburban Commando'.* ADJ: ADJ n

block capitals. **Block capitals** are simple capital letters that are not decorated in any way. N-PLURAL: usu in N

block letters. **Block letters** are the same as **block capitals**. N-PLURAL: usu in N

block vote, block votes. A **block vote** is a large number of votes that are all cast in the same way by one person on behalf of a group of people. N-COUNT

bloke /bloʊk/ **blokes.** A **bloke** is a man; used in informal British English. *He is a really nice bloke.* ◆◆◇◇◇ N-COUNT

blonde /blɒnd/ **blondes; blonder.** The form **blonde** is usually used to refer to women, and **blond** to refer to men. ◆◆◇◇◇

1 A woman who has **blonde** hair has pale-coloured hair. Blonde hair can be very light brown or light yellow. The form **blond** is used when describing men. *There were two little girls, one Asian and one with blonde hair... The baby had blond curls. ...a darker shade of blonde.* COLOUR

2 Someone who is **blonde** has blonde hair. *She was tall, blonde, and attractive... He was blonder than his brother. ...the striking blond actor.* ADJ-GRADED

3 A **blonde** is a woman who has blonde hair. N-COUNT

blonde bombshell, blonde bombshells. A **blonde bombshell** is a woman with blonde hair who is very sexually attractive; an informal expression, used by journalists. N-COUNT

blood /blʌd/ ◆◆◆◆◇

1 **Blood** is the red liquid that flows inside your body, which you can see if you cut yourself. N-UNCOUNT

2 You can use **blood** to refer to the race or social class of someone's parents or ancestors. *There was Greek blood in his veins: his ancestors originally bore the name Karajannis... He was of noble blood, and an officer.* N-UNCOUNT: usu supp N

3 If you say that there is **bad blood** between people, you mean that they have argued about something and dislike each other. *On this issue there was bad blood between Mrs Thatcher and Sir Geoffrey Howe.* PHRASES oft PHR between pl-n

4 If you say that people **are baying for blood**, you mean that they are demanding that someone should be hurt or punished. *And so what will he say to those who have been baying for his blood?* V inflects

5 If you say that someone has **blue blood**, you mean that they are from a family that has a high social rank. • See also **blue-blooded**.

6 If you say that something **makes** your **blood boil**, you are emphasizing that it makes you very angry. *It makes my blood boil to think two thugs decided to pick on an innocent young girl.* V inflects PRAGMATICS

7 If something violent and cruel is done **in cold blood**, it is done deliberately and in an unemotional way. *The crime had been committed in cold blood.* • See also **cold-blooded**. PHR after v

8 If you say that something **makes** your **blood run cold** or **makes** your **blood freeze**, you mean that it makes you feel very frightened. *The rage in his eyes made her blood run cold... My blood froze as she shouted that all Moslems had to be killed.* V inflects

9 If you say that someone has a person's **blood on** their **hands**, you mean that they are responsible for that person's death. *He has my son's blood on his hands. I hope it haunts him for the rest of his days.*

10 If a quality or talent is **in** your **blood**, it is part of your nature, and other members of your family have it too. *Diplomacy was in his blood: his ancestors had been feudal lords... He has adventure in his blood.* oft v-link PHR

11 You can use the expressions **new blood**, **fresh blood**, or **young blood** to refer to people who are brought into an organization to improve it by thinking of new ideas or new ways of doing things. *There's been a major reshuffle of the cabinet to bring in new blood... The England selectors must start introducing young blood.*

12 If you say that doing something such as getting information or persuading someone to talk to you is like **getting blood out of a stone** or **getting blood from a stone**, you are emphasizing that it is very difficult and that you do not think people are being very helpful. V inflects PRAGMATICS

13 If you say that someone **sweats blood** trying to do something, you are emphasizing that they try very hard to do it. *I had to sweat blood for an M.A.* V inflects PRAGMATICS

14 If you refer to something as involving **blood, sweat, and tears**, you mean that it is a very hard thing to do and requires a lot of effort. *Why do apparently sane people go through all the blood, sweat, tears and heartache involved in getting a PhD?*

15 People say **'blood is thicker than water'** when they mean that their loyalty to their family is greater than their loyalty to anyone else. *Families have their problems and jealousies, but blood is thicker than water.* — V inflects

16 • **flesh and blood**: see **flesh**. • **own flesh and blood**: see **flesh**.

blood and thunder; also spelled **blood-and-thunder**. A **blood and thunder** performer or performance is very loud and emotional. *He was a blood-and-thunder preacher.* — ADJ: ADJ n

blood bank, blood banks. A **blood bank** is a place where blood which has been taken from blood donors is stored until it is needed for blood transfusions. — N-COUNT

bloodbath /blʌdbɑːθ, -bæθ/ **bloodbaths;** also spelled **blood bath**. If you describe an event as a **bloodbath**, you are emphasizing that a lot of people were killed very violently. *The war degenerated into a bloodbath of tribal killings.* — N-COUNT, PRAGMATICS, =massacre

blood brother, blood brothers; also spelled **blood-brother**. A man's **blood brother** is a man he has sworn to treat as a brother, often in a ceremony which involves mixing a small amount of their blood. — N-COUNT

blood count, blood counts. Your **blood count** is the number of blood cells in your bloodstream. A **blood count** can also refer to a medical examination which determines the number of blood cells in your bloodstream. *Her doctors told her that her blood count was normal... We do a blood count to ensure that all is well.* — N-COUNT

blood-curdling; also spelled **bloodcurdling**. A **blood-curdling** sound or story is very frightening and horrible. *Scottish history has its share of blood-curdling tales. ... a bloodcurdling battle cry.* — ADJ-GRADED: usu ADJ n

blood donor, blood donors. A **blood donor** is someone who gives some of their blood so that it can be used for transfusions or operations. — N-COUNT

blood feud, blood feuds. A **blood feud** is a long-lasting, bitter disagreement between two or more groups of people, particularly family groups. Blood feuds often involve members of each group murdering or harming members of the other. — N-COUNT, =vendetta

blood group, blood groups. Someone's **blood group** is the type of blood that they have in their body. There are four main classifications for the different types of blood group: A, B, AB, and O. — N-COUNT: oft poss N, =blood type

blood heat. **Blood heat** is a temperature of 37°C, which is about the same as the normal temperature of the human body. — N-UNCOUNT

bloodhound /blʌdhaʊnd/ **bloodhounds.** A **bloodhound** is a large dog with a very keen sense of smell. Bloodhounds are often used to find people or other animals by following their scent. — N-COUNT

bloodless /blʌdləs/

1 A **bloodless** coup or victory is one in which nobody is killed. *Reports from the area indicate that it was a bloodless coup... The campaign would be short and relatively bloodless.* — ADJ-GRADED ♦ **bloodlessly** *This war had to be fought fast and relatively bloodlessly.* — ADV-GRADED: ADV with v

2 If you describe someone's face or skin as **bloodless**, you mean that it is very pale. *...her face grey and bloodless.* — ADJ, =ashen

blood-letting

1 **Blood-letting** is violence or killing between groups of people, especially between rival armies. *Once again there's been ferocious blood-letting in the township.* — N-UNCOUNT

2 Journalists sometimes refer to a bitter quarrel between two groups of people, usually people from within the same organization, as **blood-letting**, especially when it involves members of each group publicly condemning members of the other. *His comment came as the blood-letting in Conservative ranks over their Eastbourne defeat continued.* — N-UNCOUNT

bloodline /blʌdlaɪn/ **bloodlines.** A person's **bloodline** is their ancestors over many generations, and the characteristics they are believed to have inherited from these ancestors. You can also use **bloodline** to refer to an animal's pedigree. — N-COUNT: usu with supp

blood lust; also spelled **blood-lust**. If you say that someone is driven by a **blood lust**, you mean that they are compelled to act in an extremely violent way because their emotions have been aroused by the events around them. *The mobs became driven by a crazed blood-lust to take the city.* — N-UNCOUNT: also a N

blood money

1 If someone makes a payment of **blood money** to the family of someone who has been killed, they pay that person's family a sum of money as compensation; used showing disapproval. *The families of deceased victims can ask for the death sentence or demand blood money of up to 170,000 rupees.* — N-UNCOUNT, PRAGMATICS

2 **Blood money** is money that is paid to an assassin for murdering someone. — N-UNCOUNT

blood poisoning. **Blood poisoning** is a serious illness resulting from an infection in your blood. — N-UNCOUNT

blood pressure. Your **blood pressure** is the amount of force at which blood flows around your body. *Your doctor will monitor your blood pressure... Prime Minister Pavlov had been taken ill with high blood pressure.* — ◆◆◇◇◇ N-UNCOUNT

blood-red; also spelled **blood red**. Something that is **blood-red** is bright red in colour. *...blood-red cherries.* — COLOUR

blood relation, blood relations; also spelled **blood relative**. A **blood relation** is someone who is related to you by birth rather than by marriage. — N-COUNT

bloodshed /blʌdʃed/. **Bloodshed** is violence in which people are killed or wounded. *The government must increase the pace of reforms to avoid further bloodshed.* — ◆◇◇◇◇ N-UNCOUNT

bloodshot /blʌdʃɒt/. If your eyes are **bloodshot**, the parts that are usually white are red or pink. Your eyes can be bloodshot for a variety of reasons, for example because you are tired or you have drunk too much alcohol. *John's eyes were bloodshot and puffy.* — ADJ-GRADED

blood sport, blood sports; also spelled **bloodsport**. **Blood sports** are sports such as hunting in which animals are killed. — N-COUNT

bloodstain /blʌdsteɪn/ **bloodstains.** A **bloodstain** is a mark on a surface caused by blood. *There were bloodstains on the skirt.* — N-COUNT

bloodstained /blʌdsteɪnd/. Someone or something that is **bloodstained** is covered with blood. *Detectives believe the murderer was heavily bloodstained. ...bloodstained clothing.* — ADJ-GRADED

bloodstock /blʌdstɒk/. Horses that are bred for racing are referred to as **bloodstock**. — N-UNCOUNT: usu N n

bloodstream /blʌdstriːm/ **bloodstreams.** Your **bloodstream** is the blood that flows around your body. *The disease releases toxins into the bloodstream.* — ◆◇◇◇◇ N-COUNT: usu sing, the N, poss N

bloodsucker /blʌdsʌkəʳ/ **bloodsuckers**

1 A **bloodsucker** is any creature that sucks blood from a wound that it has made in an animal or person. — N-COUNT

2 If you call someone a **bloodsucker**, you disapprove of them because you think that they do not make any worthwhile contribution to society but exist by living upon the efforts of other people. *He felt as if he was at last free from the financial bloodsuckers.* — N-COUNT, PRAGMATICS

blood test, blood tests. A **blood test** is a medical examination of a sample of your blood. Blood tests can be carried out for a number of reasons, for example to find out your blood group or to see whether you have an infection of some kind. — ◆◇◇◇◇ N-COUNT

bloodthirsty /blʌdθɜːʳsti/. **Bloodthirsty** people are eager to use violence or display a strong interest in violent things. You can also use **bloodthirsty** to refer to very violent situations. *They were savage and bloodthirsty. ...some of the most tragic scenes witnessed even in this bloodthirsty war.* — ADJ-GRADED

blood transfusion, blood transfusions. A **blood transfusion** is a process in which blood is — N-VAR, =transfusion injected into the body of a person who is badly injured or ill.

blood type, blood types. Someone's **blood type** is the same as their **blood group**. N-COUNT

blood vessel, blood vessels. Blood vessels are the narrow tubes through which your blood flows. ◆◇◇◇◇ N-COUNT: usu pl

bloody /blʌdi/ **bloodier, bloodiest; bloodies, bloodying, bloodied** ◆◆◆◇◇

1 In British English, **bloody** is a swear word. People use 'bloody' to emphasize what they are saying, especially when they are angry. ADJ-GRADED: usu ADJ n PRAGMATICS

2 If you describe a situation or event as **bloody**, you mean that it is very violent and a lot of people are killed. *Forty-three demonstrators were killed in bloody clashes... They came to power in 1975 after a bloody civil war.* ADJ-GRADED: usu ADJ n ♦ **bloodily** *Rebellions in the area were bloodily repressed by pro-government forces.* ADV: ADV with v

3 You can describe someone or something as **bloody** if they are covered in a lot of blood. *He was arrested last October still carrying a bloody knife... Yulka's fingers were bloody and cracked.* ADJ-GRADED: usu ADJ n ♦ **bloodily** *The soldier reeled bloodily away.* ADV: ADV with v

4 If you have **bloodied** part of your body, there is blood on it, usually because you have had an accident or you have been attacked. *One of our children fell and bloodied his knee... She stared at her own bloodied hands, unable to think or move.* VERB V n V-ed

5 If someone or something **is bloodied** by an experience, they are hurt or damaged by it. *She'd been bloodied in love... The reinsurance market has been bloodied by disasters in the U.S.* V-PASSIVE be V-ed

Bloody Mary /blʌdi meəri/ **Bloody Marys;** also spelled **bloody mary.** A **Bloody Mary** is a drink made from vodka and tomato juice. N-COUNT

bloody-minded. In informal British English, if you say that someone is being **bloody-minded**, you are showing that you disapprove of their behaviour because you think they are being deliberately difficult instead of being helpful. *He wouldn't get out of the way. He was just being bloody-minded. He could easily have let the car pass.* ADJ-GRADED PRAGMATICS ♦ **bloody-mindedness** *Maintain a balance between determination and what can amount to bloody-mindedness.* N-UNCOUNT

bloom /bluːm/ **blooms, blooming, bloomed** ◆◆◇◇◇

1 A **bloom** is the flower on a plant; a literary use or a technical use in gardening. *The sweet fragrance of the white blooms makes this climber a favourite... Harry carefully plucked the bloom.* N-COUNT =flower

2 A plant or tree that is **in bloom** has flowers on it. *...a pink climbing rose in full bloom. ...the sweet smell of the blackberry in bloom.* PHRASE =in flower

3 When a plant or tree **blooms**, it produces flowers. When a flower **blooms**, the flower bud opens. *This plant blooms between May and June.* VERB V ♦ **-blooming** *...the scent of night-blooming flowers.* COMB in ADJ

4 If someone or something **blooms**, they develop good, attractive, or successful qualities. *Not many economies bloomed in 1990, least of all gold exporters like Australia... She bloomed into an utterly beautiful creature.* VERB =blossom V V into n

5 If something such as someone's skin has a **bloom**, it has a fresh and healthy appearance. *The skin loses its youthful bloom.* N-UNCOUNT: also a N =glow

6 See also **blooming**.

bloomers /bluːməʳz/. **Bloomers** are an old-fashioned kind of women's underwear which consists of wide, loose trousers gathered at the knees. *Most women in those days wore bloomers which covered up the stocking tops.* N-PLURAL: also a pair of N

blooming /bluːmɪŋ/ ◆◇◇◇◇

1 **Blooming** is a mild swear word used to emphasize what you are saying, especially when you are annoyed; used in British English. *It's a blooming nuisance because it frightens my dog to death.* ADJ: ADJ n PRAGMATICS =bloody ► Also an adverb. *Even though we split up she was blooming marvellous.* ADV: ADV adj

2 Someone who is **blooming** looks attractively healthy and full of energy. *If they were blooming with confidence they wouldn't need me... She's in blooming health.* ADJ

blooper /bluːpəʳ/ **bloopers.** A **blooper** is a silly mistake; an informal word which is used mainly in American English. *...the overwhelming appeal of television bloopers.* N-COUNT

blossom /blɒsəm/ **blossoms, blossoming, blossomed** ◆◆◇◇◇

1 **Blossom** is the flowers that appear on a tree before the fruit. *The cherry blossom came out early in Washington this year. ...the blossoms of plants, shrubs and trees.* N-VAR: oft supp N

2 If someone or something **blossoms**, they develop good, attractive, or successful qualities. *Why do some people take longer than others to blossom?... What began as a local festival has blossomed into an international event. ...the blossoming relationship between Israel and Eastern Europe.* VERB =bloom V V into n V-ing ♦ **blossoming** *...the blossoming of British art, pop and fashion.* N-UNCOUNT: N of n

3 When a tree **blossoms**, it produces blossom. *Rain begins to fall and peach trees blossom.* VERB V

blot /blɒt/ **blots, blotting, blotted** ◆◇◇◇◇

1 If something is a **blot on** a person's or thing's reputation, it spoils their reputation. *...a blot on the reputation of the architectural profession... This drugs scandal is another blot on the Olympics.* N-COUNT: N on n =stain, black mark

2 A **blot** is a drop of liquid that has been spilled on a surface and has dried. *...an ink blot.* N-COUNT

3 If you **blot** a surface, you remove liquid from it by pressing a piece of soft paper or cloth onto it. *Before applying make-up, blot the face with a tissue to remove any excess oils.* VERB V n Also V n adj

4 If you describe something such as a building as a **blot on the landscape**, you mean that you think it is very ugly and spoils an otherwise attractive place. *The developers insist the £80m village will not leave a blot on the landscape.* PHRASE: blot inflects

blot out PHRASAL VERB

1 If one thing **blots out** another thing, it is in front of the other thing and prevents it from being seen. *About the time the three climbers were halfway down, clouds blotted out the sun. ...the victim, whose face was blotted out by a camera blur. ...with mist blotting everything out except the endless black of the spruce on either side.* V P n (not pron) be V-ed P V n P

2 If you try to **blot out** a memory, you try to forget it. If one thought or memory **blots out** other thoughts or memories, it becomes the only one that you can think about. *Are you saying that she's trying to blot out all memory of the incident?... The boy has gaps in his mind about it. He is blotting certain things out... She has suffered an extremely unhappy childhood, but simply blotted it out of her memory.* V P n (not pron) V n P V n P of n

blotch /blɒtʃ/ **blotches.** A **blotch** is a small unpleasant-looking area of colour, for example on someone's skin. *His face was covered in red blotches, seemingly a nasty case of acne.* N-COUNT =mark

blotched /blɒtʃt/. Something that is **blotched** has blotches on it. *Her narrow face is blotched and swollen. ...a dozen cargo planes blotched with camouflage colors.* ADJ: oft ADJ with n =marked

blotchy /blɒtʃi/. Something that is **blotchy** has blotches on it. *Her face had been blotchy and her mascara had run. ...blotchy marks on the leaves.* ADJ-GRADED =spotty

blotter /blɒtəʳ/ **blotters.** A **blotter** is a large sheet of blotting paper kept in a special holder on a desk. N-COUNT

blotting paper. Blotting paper is thick soft paper that you use for soaking up and drying ink on a piece of paper. N-UNCOUNT

blouse /blaʊz, AM blaʊs/ **blouses.** A **blouse** is a kind of shirt worn by a girl or woman. *She was wearing a navy blue skirt and white blouse.* ◆◇◇◇◇ N-COUNT

blow 1 verb uses

blow /bloʊ/ **blows, blowing, blew, blown** ◆◆◆◆◇

1 When a wind or breeze **blows**, the air moves. *A chill wind blew at the top of the hill... We woke to find a gale blowing outside.* VERB V

2 If the wind **blows** something somewhere or if it **blows** there, the wind moves it there. *The wind blew her hair back from her forehead... Strong winds blew away most of the dust... Her cap fell off* V-ERG V n with adv V adv/prep V Also V n prep

in the street and blew away... Sand blew in our eyes... The bushes and trees were blowing in the wind.

3 If you **blow**, you send out a stream of air from your mouth. *Danny rubbed his arms and blew on his fingers to warm them... Take a deep breath and blow.* VERB V prep/adv V

4 If you **blow** something somewhere, you move it by sending out a stream of air from your mouth. *He picked up his mug and blew off the steam.* VERB V n with adv Also V n prep

5 If you **blow** bubbles or smoke rings, you make them by blowing air out of your mouth through liquid or smoke. *He blew a ring of blue smoke.* VERB V n

6 When a whistle or horn **blows** or someone **blows** it, they make a sound by blowing into it. *The whistle blew and the train slid forward... A guard was blowing his whistle.* V-ERG V V n

7 When you **blow** your nose, you force air out of it through your nostrils in order to clear it. *He took out a handkerchief and blew his nose.* VERB V n

8 If someone or something **blows** something out, off, or away, they violently remove or destroy it with an explosion. *The can exploded, wrecking the kitchen and bathroom and blowing out windows... Rival gunmen blew the city to bits.* VERB V n with adv V n prep

9 If you **blow** a large amount of money, you spend it quickly on luxuries; an informal use. *Before you blow it all on a luxury cruise, give a little thought to the future... My brother lent me some money and I went and blew the lot.* VERB V n *on* n V n

10 If you **blow** a chance or attempt to do something, you make a mistake which wastes the chance or causes the attempt to fail; an informal use. *He has almost certainly blown his chance of touring India this winter. ...the high-risk world of real estate, where one careless word could blow a whole deal... Oh you fool! You've blown it!* VERB V n V *it*

11 If a fuse **blows** or if something **blows** it, the fuse melts because too much electricity has been sent through it, and the electrical current is cut off. *The fuse blew as he pressed the button.* V-ERG V Also V n

12 If you **blow** a tyre or if it **blows**, a hole suddenly appears in it and all the air comes out of it. *A lorry blew a tyre and careered into them... The car tyre blew.* ► **Blow out** means the same as **blow**. *A tyre blew out when the coach was on its way.* V-ERG V n V PHRASAL VERB VP

13 See also **full-blown, overblown.** • **to blow away the cobwebs**: see **cobweb.** • **to blow someone's cover**: see **cover.** • **to blow hot and cold**: see **hot.** • **to blow a kiss**: see **kiss.** • **to blow a raspberry**: see **raspberry.** • **to blow your top**: see **top.** • **to blow your own trumpet**: see **trumpet.** • **to blow the whistle**: see **whistle.**

blow out PHRASAL VERB

1 If you **blow out** a flame or a candle, you blow at it so that it stops burning. *I blew out the candle.* V P n (not pron) Also V n P

2 See also **blow** 12, **blow-out.**

blow over. If something such as trouble or an argument **blows over**, it ends without any serious consequences. *Wait, and it'll all blow over.* PHRASAL VERB VP

blow up PHRASAL VERB

1 If someone **blows** something **up** or if it **blows up**, it is destroyed by an explosion. *He was jailed for 45 years for trying to blow up a plane... Their boat blew up as they slept.* ERG V P n (not pron) VP Also V n P

2 If you **blow up** something such as a balloon or a tyre, you fill it with air. *Other than blowing up a tyre I hadn't done any car maintenance.* V P n (not pron) Also V n P

3 If a wind or a storm **blows up**, the weather becomes very windy or stormy. *A storm blew up over the mountains.* VP

4 If you **blow up** at someone, you lose your temper and shout at them; an informal use. *I'm sorry I blew up at you... When Myra told Karp she'd expose his past, he blew up.* =explode VP *at* n VP

5 If someone **blows** an incident **up** or if it **blows up**, it is made to seem more serious or important than it really is. *Newspapers blew up the story... The media may be blowing it up out of proportion... The scandal blew up into a major political furore.* ERG V P n (not pron) V n P V P prep/adv Also V P

6 If a photographic image **is blown up**, a large copy is made of it. *The image is blown up on a large screen. ...two blown up photos of Paddy.* *be* V-ed P V-ed P Also V P n (not pron), V n P

7 See also **blow-up.**

blow 2 noun uses

blow /bloʊ/ **blows** ◆◆◆◇◇

1 If someone receives a **blow**, they are hit with a fist or weapon. *He went off to hospital after a blow to the face.* N-COUNT: oft N *to/on* n

2 If you say that something that happened was a **blow** to someone or something, you mean that it was very upsetting, disappointing, or damaging to them. *When the marriage finally broke up it was obviously a terrible blow to Soames... That ruling comes as a blow to environmentalists... Tourism was dealt a severe blow by Hurricane Andrew.* N-COUNT: oft N *to* n

3 If two people or groups **come to blows**, they start fighting. *The representatives almost came to blows at a meeting.* PHRASES V inflects

4 Something that **softens the blow** or **cushions the blow** makes an unpleasant change or piece of news easier to accept. *The French government is looking for financial compensation from the EC to soften the blow of the agreement.* V inflects

5 If you **strike a blow for** a particular cause or principle, you do something that supports it or makes it more likely to succeed. *The team struck a blow for women's rights by winning the match.* V inflects, PHR n

blow-by-blow. A **blow-by-blow** account of an event describes every stage of it in great detail; an informal expression. *She always demanded a blow-by-blow account of what had happened.* ADJ: usu ADJ n

blow-dry, blow-dries, blow-drying, blow-dried. If you **blow-dry** your hair, you dry it with a hairdryer, often to give it a particular style. *Blow-dry it forwards into a full and classic bob with plenty of volume and spring... The guys have blow-dried hair and the girls still try to look like 'Charlie's Angels'.* ► Also a noun. *The price of a cut and blow dry will vary from £13.95 to £25.* VERB V n V-ed N-SING

blower /bloʊəʳ/. In old-fashioned, informal British English, **the blower** is the telephone. *Anyway, I soon got on the blower to him.* N-SING: *the* N

blowlamp /bloʊlæmp/ **blowlamps;** also spelled **blow lamp**. A **blowlamp** is a device which produces a hot flame; used to heat metal or remove old paint. N-COUNT =blowtorch

blown /bloʊn/. **Blown** is the past participle of **blow.**

blow-out, blow-outs; also spelled **blow out.**

1 A **blow-out** is a large meal, often a celebration with family or friends, at which people may eat too much; an informal use. *Once in a while we had a major blow-out.* N-COUNT =pig-out

2 If you have a **blow-out** while you are driving a car, one of the tyres suddenly bursts. *A lorry travelling south had a blow-out and crashed.* N-COUNT =puncture

blowtorch /bloʊtɔːʳtʃ/ **blowtorches.** A **blowtorch** is the same as a **blowlamp.** N-COUNT

blow-up, blow-ups; also spelled **blowup**. A **blow-up** is an enlargement of a photograph or picture; an informal word. *...a grainy blowup obviously taken with a telephoto lens in bad light. ...yellowing blow-ups of James Dean.* N-COUNT

blub /blʌb/ **blubs, blubbing, blubbed.** In informal British English, if someone **blubs**, they cry because they are unhappy or frightened. *All of a sudden I felt very weak and wanted to blub.* VERB =cry, blubber

blubber /blʌbəʳ/ **blubbers, blubbering, blubbered**

1 **Blubber** is the fat of whales, seals, and similar sea animals. *This enables the baby whale to develop a thick layer of blubber to protect it from the cold sea.* N-UNCOUNT

2 If someone **blubbers**, they cry noisily and in an unattractive way; an informal word. *To their surprise, their mother started to blubber like a child.* VERB V

bludgeon /blʌdʒᵊn/ **bludgeons, bludgeoning, bludgeoned** ◆◇◇◇◇

1 To **bludgeon** someone means to hit them several times with a heavy object. *The guards heard a piercing scream as Martin bludgeoned Tom with the end of his climber's axe... A wealthy businessman has been found bludgeoned to death.* VERB V n V-ed *to* n

2 If someone **bludgeons** you into doing something, they make you do it by bullying or threatening you. *Their approach simply bludgeons you into submission... His relentless aggression bludgeons you into seeing his point.*
VERB =bulldoze
V n *into* n/-ing

blue /bluː/ **bluer, bluest; blues** ◆◆◆◆◆

1 Something that is **blue** is the colour of the sky on a sunny day. *There were swallows in the cloudless blue sky... She fixed her pale blue eyes on her father's. ...colourful blues and reds.*
COLOUR

2 **The blues** is a type of music which was developed by black American musicians in the southern United States. It is characterized by a slow tempo and a strong rhythm. *His singing really does have the depth and the emotional range of the blues. ...the blues bars of Chicago.*
N-PLURAL: *the* N

3 If you have got **the blues**, you feel sad and depressed; an informal use. *Interfering in-laws are the prime sources of the blues.*
N-PLURAL: *the* N

4 If you are feeling **blue**, you are feeling sad or depressed, often when there is no particular reason; an informal use. *There's no earthly reason for me to feel so blue.*
ADJ-GRADED: v-link ADJ =down

5 A Cambridge **blue** or an Oxford **blue** is a man or woman who has played for Cambridge or Oxford University in a particular sport. *Fiona Edmond, the Cambridge blue, has withdrawn from the England side because of injury.*
N-COUNT: usu supp N

6 **Blue** films, stories, or jokes are about sex. *All of us were watching a blue movie.*
ADJ: ADJ n

7 • **bolt from the blue**: see **bolt**. • **blue moon**: see **moon**. • **blue murder**: see **murder**.

blue baby, blue babies. A **blue baby** is a baby who has been born with a heart defect which prevents them from having the correct amount of oxygen in their system. Blue babies have slightly blue skin caused by this lack of oxygen. *Blue baby syndrome is a potentially fatal condition.*
N-COUNT

bluebell /bluːbel/ **bluebells.** **Bluebells** are plants that have blue bell-shaped flowers on thin upright stems. Bluebells flower in the spring. *The woods are full of bluebells.*
◆◇◇◇◇ N-COUNT

blueberry /bluːbəri, AM -beri/ **blueberries.** A **blueberry** is a small dark blue fruit that is found in North America. Blueberries are usually cooked before they are eaten.
N-COUNT

blue-black. Something that is **blue-black** is very dark blue in colour. *...beautiful blue-black hair.*
COLOUR

blue-blooded. A **blue-blooded** person is from a royal or noble family. **Blue-blooded** can also describe something that is associated with royalty. *While not blue-blooded herself, the Duchess married into the most aristocratic family in the British Isles.*
ADJ

blue book, blue books; also spelled **Blue Book**. A **blue book** is an official government report or register of statistics. *The latest figures are contained in the office's 1989 Blue Book.*
N-COUNT

bluebottle /bluːbɒtᵊl/ **bluebottles.** A **bluebottle** is a large fly with a shiny dark-blue body.
N-COUNT

blue chip, blue chips. Blue chip stocks and shares are an investment which are considered relatively safe to invest in while also being profitable. *Blue chip issues were sharply higher, but the rest of the market actually declined slightly by the end of the day.*
◆◇◇◇◇ N-COUNT: oft N n

blue-collar. Blue-collar workers work in industry, doing physical work, rather than in offices. *By 1925, blue-collar workers in manufacturing industry had become the largest occupational group.*
◆◇◇◇◇ ADJ: ADJ n ≠white collar

blue-eyed boy, blue-eyed boys. In British English, someone's **blue-eyed boy** is a young man who they like better than anyone else and who therefore receives better treatment than other people; used showing disapproval. *He was the media's darling, the Government's blue-eyed boy.*
N-COUNT: oft poss N PRAGMATICS =pet, favourite

bluegrass /bluːgrɑːs, -græs/. **Bluegrass** is a style of folk music that originated in the Southern United States. Bluegrass music is characterized by a rapid tempo and strong harmonies.
N-UNCOUNT

blueish /bluːɪʃ/. See **bluish**.

blue jeans. Blue jeans are the same as **jeans**. *...faded blue jeans.*
N-PLURAL: also *a pair of* N

blueprint /bluːprɪnt/ **blueprints** ◆◇◇◇◇

1 A **blueprint** for something is a plan or set of proposals that shows how it is expected to work. *The country's president will offer delegates his blueprint for the country's future... Palestinian groups are drawing up the blueprint of a government for self-rule in the occupied territories.*
N-COUNT: usu N *for* n =scheme

2 A **blueprint** of an architect's building plans or a designer's pattern is a photographic print consisting of white lines on a blue background. Blueprints contain all of the information that is needed to build or make something. *...a blueprint of the whole place, complete with heating ducts and wiring... The documents contain a blueprint for a nuclear device.*
N-COUNT: usu with supp =design

3 A genetic **blueprint** is a pattern which is contained within all living cells. This pattern determines the hereditary characteristics of the organism such as how it develops and what it looks like. *The offspring contain a mixture of the genetic blueprint of each parent... DNA is the genetic material inside every cell that carries the blueprints for everything from hair color to the risk of cancer.*
N-COUNT: usu with supp

blue riband /bluː rɪbənd/ **blue ribands;** also spelled **blue ribband**. If someone or something wins the **blue riband** in a competition, they win first prize. The trophy that they win is sometimes the shape of a blue ribbon. *...the sport's blue riband, the single sculls... Olga did not win the all-round championship, the blue riband event.*
N-COUNT

blue ribbon, blue ribbons. In American English, a **blue ribbon** is the same as a **blue riband**.
N-COUNT

bluestocking /bluːstɒkɪŋ/ **bluestockings;** also spelled **blue-stocking**. If you refer to a woman as a **bluestocking**, you mean that she is more concerned with intellectual ideas than behaving in a traditionally feminine way; often used showing disapproval. *She is a jovial bluestocking and making a bit of a living as a writer.*
N-COUNT PRAGMATICS

bluesy /bluːzi/. If you describe a song or the way it is performed as **bluesy**, you mean that it is performed in a way that is characteristic of the blues. *...bluesy sax-and-strings theme music.*
ADJ: usu ADJ n

blue tit, blue tits. A **blue tit** is a small European bird with a blue head, wings, and tail, and a yellow front.
N-COUNT

bluff /blʌf/ **bluffs, bluffing, bluffed** ◆◇◇◇◇

1 A **bluff** is an attempt to make someone believe that you will do something when you do not really intend to do it. *The letter was a bluff... It is essential to build up the military option and show that this is not a bluff... What we're at here is a game of bluff.* • See also **double bluff**.
N-VAR

2 If you **call** someone's **bluff**, you tell them to do what they have been threatening to do, because you are sure that they will not really do it. *Now that the students have called his bluff, it remains to be seen what Mr Lukanov can do.*
PHRASE: V inflects

3 If you **bluff** or if you **bluff** someone, you make them believe that you will do something when you do not really intend to do it, or that you know something when you do not really know it. *Either side, or both, could be bluffing... In each case the hijackers bluffed the crew using fake grenades... He tried to bluff his way through another test and failed it.*
VERB
V
V n
V *way* prep

4 A **bluff** is a steep cliff or bank, especially by a river or the sea. *...a high bluff over the Congaree River.*
N-COUNT

5 If you describe someone, usually a man, as **bluff**, you mean that they have a very direct way of speaking and behaving. *He comes across as a man with a bluff exterior who, beyond that, is difficult to get to know... He has continued to write with a bluff, vivid humour about Yorkshire life.*
ADJ-GRADED: usu ADJ n

bluish /bluːɪʃ/; also spelled **blueish**. Something that is **bluish** is slightly blue in colour. *...bluish-grey eyes.*
COLOUR

blunder /blʌndəʳ/ **blunders, blundering, blundered** ◆◇◇◇◇

1 A **blunder** is a stupid or careless mistake. *I think he made a tactical blunder by announcing it so far ahead of time.* N-COUNT =gaffe

2 If you **blunder**, you make a stupid or careless mistake. *No doubt I had blundered again... You're a blundering fool.* VERB V V-ing

3 If you **blunder** into a dangerous or difficult situation, you get involved in it by mistake. *People wanted to know how they had blundered into war, and how to avoid it in future.* VERB V *into* n

4 If you **blunder** somewhere, you move there in a clumsy and careless way. *He had blundered into the table, upsetting the flowers.* VERB V prep/adv

blunt /blʌnt/ **blunter, bluntest; blunts, blunting, blunted** ◆◆◇◇◇

1 If you are **blunt**, you say exactly what you think without trying to be polite. *She is blunt about her personal life... His blunt approach to both football and life appeals to the Irish.* ♦ **bluntly** *'I don't believe you!' Jeanne said bluntly... To put it bluntly, he became a pain.* ♦ **bluntness** *His bluntness got him into trouble.* ADJ-GRADED; ADV-GRADED: ADV with v; N-UNCOUNT: oft poss N

2 A **blunt** object has a rounded or flat end rather than a sharp one. *One of them had been struck 13 times over the head with a blunt object.* ADJ: ADJ n ≠pointed

3 A **blunt** knife or blade is no longer sharp and does not cut well. ADJ-GRADED ≠sharp

4 If something **blunts** an emotion, a feeling or a need, it weakens it. *The constant repetition of violence has blunted the human response to it... Our appetite was blunted by the beer.* VERB V n

blur /blɜːʳ/ **blurs, blurring, blurred** ◆◆◇◇◇

1 A **blur** is a shape or area which you cannot see clearly because it has no distinct outline or because it is moving very fast. *Out of the corner of my eye I saw a blur of movement on the other side of the glass... Her face is a blur.* N-COUNT: oft N *of* n

2 When a thing **blurs** or when something **blurs** it, you cannot see it clearly because its edges are no longer distinct. *This creates a spectrum of colours at the edges of objects which blurs the image... If you move your eyes and your head, the picture will blur.* ♦ **blurred** *...blurred black and white photographs.* V-ERG =smudge V n V; ADJ-GRADED

3 If something **blurs** an idea or a distinction between things, that idea or distinction no longer seems clear. *...her belief that scientists are trying to blur the distinction between 'how' and 'why' questions... The evidence is blurred by central banks' reluctance to reveal their blunders.* ♦ **blurred** *The line between fact and fiction is becoming blurred.* VERB =obscure V n; ADJ-GRADED

4 If your vision **blurs**, or if something **blurs** it, you cannot see things clearly. *Her eyes, behind her glasses, began to blur... Sweat ran from his forehead into his eyes, blurring his vision.* ♦ **blurred** *...visual disturbances like eye-strain and blurred vision.* V-ERG V V n; ADJ-GRADED

blurb /blɜːʳb/ **blurbs.** The **blurb** about a new book, film, or exhibition is information about it that is written in order to attract people's interest; an informal word. *The blurb on the cover of the paperback calls it a 'shocking new superthriller'. ...the publisher's blurb.* N-COUNT: usu sing, oft *the* N

blurry /blɜːri/. A **blurry** shape is one that has an unclear outline. *If they ever show a picture of the other side, it's always in black and white and really blurry.* ADJ-GRADED =blurred

blurt /blɜːʳt/ **blurts, blurting, blurted.** If someone **blurts** something, they say it suddenly, after trying hard to keep quiet or to keep it secret; an informal use. *'I was looking for Sally', he blurted, and his eyes filled with tears.* ◆◇◇◇◇ VERB V with quote Also V that

blurt out. If someone **blurts** something **out**, they blurt it; an informal expression. *'You're mad,' the driver blurted out... Over the food, Richard blurted out what was on his mind.* PHRASAL VERB V P with quote V P n (not pron) Also V n P

blush /blʌʃ/ **blushes, blushing, blushed** ◆◇◇◇◇

1 When you **blush**, your face becomes redder than usual because you are ashamed or embarrassed. *'Hello, Maria,' he said, and she blushed again... I blushed scarlet at my stupidity.* ► Also a noun. *'The most important thing is to be honest,' she says, without the trace of a blush.* VERB V V colour; N-COUNT

2 If you **spare** someone's **blushes** or **save** someone's **blushes**, you avoid doing or saying something that will embarrass them; used mainly in journalism. *'We don't want to name the man to spare his blushes,' said a police spokesman.* PHRASE: V inflects

blusher /blʌʃəʳ/ **blushers. Blusher** is a coloured substance that women put on their cheeks. N-MASS

bluster /blʌstəʳ/ **blusters, blustering, blustered.** If you say that someone is **blustering**, you mean that they are speaking aggressively or proudly but without authority, often because they are angry or offended. *'That's lunacy,' he blustered... He was still blustering, but there was panic in his eyes.* ► Also a noun. *...the bluster of the Conservatives' campaign.* ◆◇◇◇◇ VERB V with quote V; N-UNCOUNT

blustery /blʌstəri/. **Blustery** weather is rough, windy, and often rainy, with the wind often changing in strength or direction. *It's a cold night here, with intermittent rain showers and a blustery wind. ...a cool, blustery day.* ADJ-GRADED

Blvd. **Blvd** is a written abbreviation for 'Boulevard'. It is used especially in addresses and on maps or signs. *...1515 Wilson Blvd., Arlington, VA 22209.*

B-movie, B-movies. A **B-movie** is a film which is produced quickly and cheaply and is often considered to have little artistic value. *...some old Hollywood B-movie.* N-COUNT

bn. **bn** is a written abbreviation for **billion**. *...total value, dollars bn 15.6.*

B.O. /biː oʊ/. **B.O.** is an abbreviation for 'body odour'; an unpleasant smell caused by stale sweat on a person's body. N-UNCOUNT

boa /boʊə/ **boas**

1 A **boa** or a **feather boa** is a long soft scarf made of feathers or of short pieces of very light fabric. *She wore a silver sequinned costume with a large pink boa around her neck.* N-COUNT

2 A **boa** is the same as a **boa constrictor**. N-COUNT

boa constrictor, boa constrictors. A **boa constrictor** is a large snake that kills animals by wrapping itself round their bodies and squeezing them to death. Boa constrictors are found mainly in South and Central America and the West Indies. N-COUNT

boar /bɔːʳ/ **boars** ◆◇◇◇◇

1 A **boar** or a **wild boar** is a wild pig. The plural can be 'boar' or 'boars'. *Wild boar are numerous in the valleys.* N-COUNT

2 A **boar** is a male pig. N-COUNT

board /bɔːʳd/ **boards, boarding, boarded** ◆◆◆◆◇

1 A **board** is a flat, thin, rectangular piece of wood or plastic which is used for a particular purpose. *...a chopping board.* N-COUNT: usu n N

2 A **board** is a square piece of wood or stiff cardboard that you use for playing games such as chess. *...a draughts board... Dr Tinsley had five pieces on the board against Chinook's four.* N-COUNT

3 You can refer to a blackboard or a noticeboard as a **board**. *He wrote a few more notes on the board.* N-COUNT

4 **Boards** are long flat pieces of wood which are used, for example, to make floors or walls. *The floor was draughty bare boards.* N-COUNT

5 The **board** of a company or organization is the group of people who control it and direct it. *Arthur has made a recommendation, which he wants her to put before the board at a special meeting scheduled for tomorrow afternoon. ...the agenda for the September 12 board meeting.* N-COUNT: oft *the* N in sing =management

6 **Board** is used in the names of various organizations involved in the promotion or distribution of something. *The Scottish Tourist Board said 33,000 Japanese visited Scotland last year.* N-COUNT: usu *the* n N

7 When you **board** a train, ship, or aircraft, you get on it in order to travel somewhere. *I boarded the plane bound for England.* VERB =get on V n Also V

8 **Board** is the food which is provided when you stay somewhere, for example in a hotel. *Free room and board are provided for all hotel staff.* N-UNCOUNT

9 See also **bulletin board**.

10 An arrangement or deal that is **above board** is legal and is being carried out honestly and openly. *All I knew about were Antony's own financial dealings, which were always above board.* PHRASES usu v-link PHR =honest ≠shady

11 If a policy or a situation applies **across the board**, it affects everything or everyone in a particular group. *There are hefty charges across the board for one-way rental... The President promised across-the-board tax cuts if re-elected.* usu PHR after v, PHR n

12 If something **goes by the board**, it is rejected or ignored, or is no longer possible. *It's a case of not what you know but who you know in this world today and qualifications quite go by the board.* V inflects

13 When you are **on board** a train, ship, or aircraft, you are on it or in it. *They arrived at Gatwick airport on board a plane chartered by the Italian government... A US naval task force with two thousand marines on board is waiting off the coast.* PHR after v, v-link PHR, oft PHR n

14 If someone **sweeps the board** in a competition or election, they win nearly everything that it is possible to win. *Spain swept the board in boys' team competitions.* V inflects

15 If you **take on board** an idea or a problem, you begin to accept it or understand it. *You may have to accept their point of view, but hope that they will take on board some of what you have said.* V inflects

board out. If someone in your care **is boarded out**, they are sent to stay with someone else. *As a child in the care of a local authority he had been boarded out with a farmer in Shropshire.* PHRASAL VERB usu passive be V-ed P

board up. If you **board up** a door or window, you fix pieces of wood over it so that it is covered up. *Shopkeepers have boarded up their windows.* PHRASAL VERB V P n (not pron) Also V n P
♦ **boarded up** *Half the shops are boarded up on the estate's small shopping street. ...the boarded-up houses and the derelict factories of Merseyside.* ADJ

board and lodging. If you are provided with **board and lodging**, you are provided with food and a place to sleep, especially as part of the conditions of a job. *You get a big salary incentive and free board and lodging too.* N-UNCOUNT

boarder /bɔːʳdəʳ/ **boarders.** In British English, a **boarder** is a pupil who lives at school during the term. *Sue started as a boarder at Benenden last September.* N-COUNT

board game, board games; also spelled **board-game**. A **board game** is a game such as chess or snakes-and-ladders, which people play by moving small objects around on a board. *...a new board game played with dice.* N-COUNT

boarding /bɔːʳdɪŋ/
1 **Boarding** is an arrangement by which children live at school during the school term. *They find boarding gives their children roots... Annual boarding fees are £10,350.* N-UNCOUNT
2 **Boarding** is long, flat pieces of wood which can be used to make walls, doors, and fences. *...the white-painted boarding in the sitting room.* N-UNCOUNT

boarding card, boarding cards. A **boarding card** is a card which a passenger must have when boarding a plane or a boat. N-COUNT =boarding pass

boarding house, boarding houses; also spelled **boarding-house**. A **boarding house** is a house which people pay to stay in for a short time. *My parents ran a boarding-house in Scarborough.* N-COUNT =guest-house

boarding school, boarding schools; also spelled **boarding-school**. A **boarding school** is a school which some or all of the pupils live in during the school term. *She sent her son to a boarding school in the East... Of course, now she is away at boarding school.* ◆◇◇◇◇ N-VAR

boardroom /bɔːʳdruːm/ **boardrooms;** also spelled **board room**. The **boardroom** is a room where the board of a company meets. *Everyone had already assembled in the boardroom for the 9:00 a.m. session.* ◆◇◇◇◇ N-COUNT

boardwalk /bɔːʳdwɔːk/ **boardwalks.** In the United States, a **boardwalk** is a footpath made of wooden boards. *A favorite pastime is bicycling up and down the wooden boardwalk along the bay.* N-COUNT

boast /boʊst/ **boasts, boasting, boasted** ◆◆◇◇◇
1 If someone **boasts** about something that they have done or that they own, they talk about it in a way that shows that they are excessively proud of it, and that other people may find irritating or offensive. *Witnesses said Furci boasted that he took part in killing them... Carol boasted about her costume... He's boasted of being involved in the arms theft... We remember our mother's stern instructions not to boast.* ► Also a noun. *It is the charity's proud boast that it has never yet turned anyone away... He was asked about earlier boasts of a quick victory.* VERB PRAGMATICS V that V about/of n/-ing V Also V with quote N-COUNT: oft N that, N prep
2 If someone or something can **boast** a particular achievement or possession, they have achieved or possess that thing. *The houses will boast the latest energy-saving technology... Frommen says his country boasts a healthy economy.* VERB V n

boastful /boʊstfʊl/. If someone is **boastful**, they talk too proudly about something that they have done or that they own; used showing disapproval. *I am not afraid of seeming boastful... The last thing we want to do is make boastful predictions.* ADJ-GRADED PRAGMATICS =bragging

boat /boʊt/ **boats** ◆◆◆◆◇
1 A **boat** is something in which people can travel across water. *One of the best ways to see the area is in a small boat... The island may be reached by boat from the mainland.* N-COUNT: also by N
2 You can refer to a passenger ship as a **boat**. *When the boat reached Cape Town, we said a temporary goodbye.* N-COUNT
3 See also **gravy boat, rowing boat**
4 If you say that someone has **missed the boat**, you mean that they have missed an opportunity and may not get another. PHRASES V inflects
5 If you **push the boat out**, you spend a lot of money on something, especially in order to celebrate. *I earn enough to push the boat out now and again.* V inflects
6 If you say that someone is **rocking the boat**, you mean that they are upsetting a calm situation and causing trouble. *I said I didn't want to rock the boat in any way.* V inflects
7 If two or more people are **in the same boat**, they are in the same unpleasant situation. usu v-link PHR

boatbuilder /boʊtbɪldəʳ/ **boatbuilders;** also spelled **boat builder**. A **boatbuilder** is a person or company that makes boats. N-COUNT

boatbuilding /boʊtbɪldɪŋ/; also spelled **boat-building**. **Boatbuilding** is the craft or industry of making boats. *Sunbeam Yachts started boatbuilding in 1870.* N-UNCOUNT

boater /boʊtəʳ/ **boaters.** A **boater** or a **straw boater** is a hard straw hat with a flat top and brim which is often worn for certain social occasions in the summer. N-COUNT

boathouse /boʊthaʊs/ **boathouses;** also spelled **boat house**. A **boathouse** is a building at the edge of a lake, in which boats are kept. N-COUNT

boating /boʊtɪŋ/. **Boating** is travelling on a lake or river in a small boat for pleasure. *You can go boating or play tennis... They were killed in a boating accident.* ◆◇◇◇◇ N-UNCOUNT: oft N n

boatload /boʊtloʊd/ **boatloads;** also spelled **boat load**. A **boatload** of people or things is a lot of people or things that are, or were, in a boat. *...the latest boatload of refugees... The good news is that a boatload of rice has finally arrived.* N-COUNT: oft N of n

boatman /boʊtmən/ **boatmen.** A **boatman** is a man who is paid by people to take them across an area of water in a small boat, or a man who hires boats out to them for a short time. N-COUNT

boat people. **Boat people** are refugees who left their country in a boat to travel to another country in the hope that they will be able to live there. *...50,000 Vietnamese boat people.* ◆◆◇◇◇ N-PLURAL

boat train, boat trains. A **boat train** is a train that takes you to or from a port. N-COUNT

boatyard /boʊtjɑːʳd/ **boatyards.** A **boatyard** is a place where boats are built and repaired or kept. *The yacht now lies in a boatyard at Lymington.* N-COUNT

bob /bɒb/ **bobs, bobbing, bobbed** ◆◆◇◇◇
1 If something **bobs**, it moves up and down, like VERB

something does when it is floating on water. *Huge balloons bobbed about in the sky above... The raft bobbed along more quietly... People began running along the fence. Torches bobbed.* V prep/adv V

2 If you **bob** somewhere, you move there quickly so that you disappear from view or come into view. *She handed over a form, then bobbed down again behind a typewriter.* VERB V adv/prep

3 When you **bob** your head, you move it quickly up and down once, for example when you greet someone. *A hostess stood at the top of the steps and bobbed her head at each passenger.* ▶ Also a noun. *The young man smiled with a bob of his head.* VERB =nod V n N-COUNT =nod

4 In Britain, people used to refer to a shilling as a **bob**; an informal use. The plural form was also **bob**. *I've only got ten bob on me.* N-COUNT

5 A **bob** is a hair style in which a woman's hair, except for the fringe, is cut to the level of her chin. N-COUNT

6 You can say **Bob's your uncle** after describing an action, to indicate that the result comes easily and quickly; an informal expression. *Load the appropriate MIDI file into your computer, press play, and Bob's your uncle!* EXCLAM

7 **Bits and bobs** are small objects or parts of something; an informal expression. *The microscope contains a few hundred dollars-worth of electronic bits and bobs.* PHRASE =bits and pieces

bobbed /bɒbd/. If a woman's hair is **bobbed**, it is cut in a bob. ADJ

bobbin /bɒbɪn/ **bobbins.** A **bobbin** is a small round object on which thread or wool is wound to hold it, for example on a sewing machine. N-COUNT

bobble /bɒbᵊl/ **bobbles.** In British English, a **bobble** is a small ball of material, usually made of wool, which is used for decorating clothes and soft furnishings. The usual American word is **tassel**. *...the bobble on his nightcap. ...colourful bobble hats.* N-COUNT

bobby /bɒbi/ **bobbies.** A **bobby** is a British policeman, usually of the lowest rank; an old-fashioned, informal word. *These days, the bobby on the beat is a rare sight.* N-COUNT =cop

bobcat /bɒbkæt/ **bobcats.** A **bobcat** is an animal in the cat family which has reddish-brown fur with dark spots or stripes and a short tail. Bobcats live in North America. *Mountain lions and bobcats roam wild in the mountains.* N-COUNT

bobsled /bɒbsled/ **bobsleds.** A **bobsled** is the same as a **bobsleigh**; used mainly in American English. N-COUNT

bobsleigh /bɒbsleɪ/ **bobsleighs.** In British English, a **bobsleigh** is a vehicle with long thin strips of metal fixed to the bottom, which is used for racing downhill on ice. The American word is **bobsled**. N-COUNT

bod /bɒd/ **bods.** In British English, a **bod** is a person; an informal word. *This particular place was run by an ex-Army colonel, a weird old bod called Pryce-Sampson.* N-COUNT: usu supp N =chap

bode /boʊd/ **bodes, boding, boded.** If something **bodes** ill, it makes you think that something bad will happen in the future. If something **bodes** well, it makes you think that something good will happen; a formal word. *She says the way the bill was passed bodes ill for democracy... Grace had dried her eyes. That boded well.* ◆◇◇◇◇ VERB =augur V adv *for* n V adv

bodge /bɒdʒ/ **bodges, bodging, bodged.** In British English, if you **bodge** something, you make it or mend it in a way that is not as good as it should be; an informal word. *He's a craftsman. It hurts him to have to bodge jobs.* VERB =botch V n

bodice /bɒdɪs/ **bodices.** The **bodice** of a dress is the part above the waist. *...a silky green floral cocktail dress with a fitted bodice and circle skirt.* N-COUNT

bodice-ripping. A **bodice-ripping** film or novel is one which has a romantic theme and is set in an earlier century. *...a smoldering seductress in one of those bodice-ripping B-movies.* ADJ: ADJ n

bodily /bɒdɪli/ ◆◇◇◇◇

1 Your **bodily** needs and functions are the needs and functions of your body. *...descriptions of natural bodily functions... There's more to eating than just bodily needs.* ● See also **grievous bodily harm**. ADJ: ADJ n

2 You use **bodily** to indicate that an action involves the whole of someone's body. *I was hurled bodily to the deck.* ADV: ADV with v

body /bɒdi/ **bodies** ◆◆◆◆◆

1 Your **body** is all your physical parts, including your head, arms, and legs. *The largest organ in the body is the liver.* N-COUNT

2 You can also refer to the main part of your body, excluding your arms, head, and legs, as your **body**. *Lying flat on the floor, twist your body on to one hip and cross your upper leg over your body.* N-COUNT =torso, trunk

3 You can refer to a person's dead body as a **body**. *Officials said they had found no traces of violence on the body of the politician.* N-COUNT =corpse

4 A **body** is an organized group of people who deal with something officially. *...the Chairman of the policemen's representative body, the Police Federation. ...the main trade union body, COSATU, Congress of South African Trade Unions.* N-COUNT: usu with supp =organization

5 A **body of** people is a group of people who are together or who are connected in some way. *...that large body of people which teaches other people how to teach.* N-COUNT: N *of* n =group

6 **The body** of something such as a building or a document is the main part of it or the largest part of it. *The main body of the church had been turned into a massive television studio... Give an introduction, followed by the body of the material, then a brief summary.* N-SING: *the* N *of* n =bulk

7 The **body** of a car or aeroplane is the main part of it, not including its engine, wheels, or wings. *The only shade was under the body of the plane.* N-COUNT: usu with supp =shell

8 A **body of** water is a large area of water, such as a lake or a sea. *It is probably the most polluted body of water in the world.* N-COUNT: N *of* n

9 A large **body of** information is a large amount of it. *An increasing body of evidence suggests that all of us have cancer cells in our bodies at times during our lives... It is a cardinal error to an experimenter to deliberately ignore a body of data.* N-COUNT: N *of* n =quantity

10 If you say that an alcoholic drink has **body**, you mean that it has a full and strong flavour. *...a dry wine with good body.* N-UNCOUNT

11 A **body** is the same as a **bodysuit**. N-COUNT

12 See also **foreign body**, **heavenly body**.

13 If someone mentions a possible event and you say **'over my dead body'**, you are emphasizing that you feel very strongly that it should not happen, and that you will do everything you can to prevent it; an informal expression. *'We'll have her over for dinner.'—'Over my dead body!'* PHRASES PRAGMATICS

14 You use **body and soul** to mean every part of you, including your mind and your emotions. *He dedicated himself body and soul to the education of young men... She was now committed to the band, body and soul.* PHR after v

15 If you **keep body and soul together**, you have enough money to provide what you need to live. *He at first kept body and soul together by selling cartoons to the humorous papers.* V inflects =make ends meet

body armour; spelled **body armor** in American English. **Body armour** is special protective clothing which people such as soldiers and police officers sometimes wear when they are in danger of being attacked with guns or other weapons. N-UNCOUNT

body blow, body blows; also spelled **bodyblow**. If you describe something as a **body blow**, you mean that it causes great disappointment and difficulty to someone who is trying to achieve something. *His resignation will be another body blow to the ruling National Liberation Front.* N-COUNT =setback ≠boost

bodybuilder /bɒdibɪldəʳ/ **bodybuilders;** also spelled **body builder**. A **bodybuilder** is a person who does special exercises regularly in order to make his or her muscles grow bigger. N-COUNT

bodybuilding /bɒdibɪldɪŋ/; also spelled **body building**. **Bodybuilding** is the activity of doing special exercises regularly in order to make your muscles grow bigger. *I was always bigger than* N-UNCOUNT *my classmates but I didn't start bodybuilding until I was 26.*

body clock, body clocks. Your **body clock** is the internal biological mechanism which causes your body to automatically behave in particular ways at particular times of the day. *Jet lag is caused because the body clock does not readjust immediately to the time change.* N-COUNT: usu sing

bodyguard /bɒdigɑːʳd/ **bodyguards.** A **bodyguard** is a person or a group of people employed to protect someone. *Three of his bodyguards were injured in the attack... The King had brought his own bodyguard of twenty armed men.* ◆◆◇◇◇ N-COUNT

body language; also spelled **body-language.** Your **body language** is the way in which you show your feelings or thoughts to other people by means of the position or movements of your body, rather than with words. *There was just something in his body language which alerted me to potential danger... Approximately 75 per cent of communication is transmitted through body language.* ◆◇◇◇◇ N-UNCOUNT

body odour; spelled **body odor** in American English. **Body odour** is an unpleasant smell caused by stale sweat on a person's body. *Deodorants combat body odour... Most of us wouldn't dream of mentioning a body odour problem to a partner or colleague.* N-UNCOUNT =B.O.

body politic. The **body politic** is all the people of a nation when they are considered as a complete political group; a formal word. *Unfortunately, this sense of internationalism has yet to spread through the body politic.* N-SING: usu *the* N =state

body search, body searches, body searching, body searched; also spelled **body-search.** If a person **is body searched**, someone such as a police officer searches them while they remain clothed. Compare **strip-search**. *Foreign journalists were body-searched by airport police.* VERB *be* V-ed Also V n ► Also a noun. *Fans may undergo body searches by security guards.* N-COUNT

body stocking, body stockings. A **body stocking** is a piece of clothing that covers the whole of someone's body and fits tightly. Body stockings are often worn by dancers. N-COUNT

bodysuit /bɒdisuːt/ **bodysuits.** A **bodysuit** is a piece of clothing that fits tightly over your body. *...a skintight Lycra bodysuit.* N-COUNT =body

bodywork /bɒdiwɜːʳk/. The **bodywork** of a motor vehicle is the outside part of it. *A second hand car dealer will always look at the bodywork rather than the engine.* N-UNCOUNT

Boer /boʊəʳ, bɔːʳ/ **Boers.** The **Boers** are the descendants of the Dutch people who went to live in South Africa. N-COUNT

boffin /bɒfɪn/ **boffins.** In informal British English, a **boffin** is a scientist, especially one who is doing research. *The boffins of Imperial College in London think they may have found a solution.* N-COUNT =egg-head

bog /bɒg/ **bogs, bogging, bogged** ◆◆◇◇◇

1 A **bog** is an area of land which is very wet and muddy. N-COUNT

2 In informal British English, the **bog** is another name for the toilet. N-COUNT: usu *the* N =toilet

bog down. If a plan or process **bogs down** or if something **bogs** it **down**, it is delayed and no progress is made. *We intended from the very beginning to bog the prosecution down over who did this... The talks have bogged down over the issue of military reform.* ● See also **bogged down**. PHRASAL VERB ERG V n P V P

bogey /boʊgi/ **bogeys** ◆◇◇◇◇

1 A **bogey** is something or someone that people are worried about, perhaps without much cause or reason. *The universal bogey is AIDS... Age is another bogey for actresses.* N-COUNT: usu with supp ► Also an adjective. *Did people still tell their kids imbecilic scare stories about bogey policewomen?* ADJ: ADJ n

2 A **bogey** is a piece of dried mucus that comes from inside your nose; an informal use. N-COUNT

3 In golf, when a player scores a **bogey** at a hole, he or she takes one more shot than the standard that has been fixed for that hole. N-COUNT

bogeyman /boʊgimæn/ **bogeymen;** also spelled **bogey man.**

1 A **bogeyman** is someone whose ideas or actions are disapproved of by some people, and who is described by them as evil or unpleasant in order to make other people afraid; used showing disapproval. *How could he be the left-wing bogeyman that the capitalist media depict him as?* N-COUNT: usu with supp PRAGMATICS =monster

2 A **bogeyman** is an imaginary evil spirit. Some parents tell their children that the bogeyman will catch them if they behave badly. N-COUNT: oft *the* N

bogged down. If you get **bogged down** in something, it prevents you from making progress or getting something done. *But why get bogged down in legal details?... Sometimes this fact is obscured because churches get so bogged down by unimportant rules.* ◆◇◇◇◇ ADJ-GRADED: v-link ADJ, usu ADJ *in* n

boggle /bɒgəl/ **boggles, boggling, boggled.** If you say that the mind **boggles** at something or that something **boggles** the mind, you mean that it is so strange or amazing that it is difficult to imagine or understand. *The mind boggles at the possibilities that could be in store for us... The good grace and humour with which they face the latest privations makes the mind boggle... The management group's decision still boggled his mind.* ● See also **mind-boggling**. ◆◇◇◇◇ V-ERG V *at* n V V n

boggy /bɒgi/. **Boggy** land is very wet and muddy land. ADJ-GRADED

bog-standard. In informal British English, if you describe something as **bog-standard** you mean that is an ordinary example of its kind, with no exciting or interesting features; used showing disapproval. *'The Bodyguard' is a fairly bog-standard thriller.* ADJ-GRADED: usu ADJ n PRAGMATICS =common or garden

bogus /boʊgəs/. If you describe something as **bogus**, you mean that it is not genuine. *...their bogus insurance claim... He said these figures were bogus and totally inaccurate.* ◆◇◇◇◇ ADJ-GRADED =phoney ≠bona fide

bohemian /boʊhiːmiən/ **bohemians.** You can use **bohemian** to describe artistic people who live in an unconventional way. *...a bohemian writer. ...bohemian café society. ...the bohemian lifestyle of the French capital.* ◆◇◇◇◇ ADJ-GRADED: usu ADJ n ► A **bohemian** is someone who lives in a bohemian way. *I am a bohemian. I have no roots.* N-COUNT

Bohemian /bəhiːmiən/. **Bohemian** means belonging or relating to Bohemia or its people. *...the north Bohemian town of Usti Nad Labem.* ADJ

boil /bɔɪl/ **boils, boiling, boiled** ◆◆◆◇◇

1 When a hot liquid **boils** or when you **boil** it, bubbles appear in it and it starts to change into steam or vapour. *I stood in the kitchen, waiting for the water to boil... Boil the water in the saucepan and add the sage... Cook the carrots in a saucepan of boiling water for 3 minutes.* V-ERG V V n V-ing

2 When you **boil** a kettle, or put it on to **boil**, you heat the water inside it until it boils. *He had nothing to do but boil the kettle and make the tea... Marianne put the kettle on to boil.* V-ERG V n V

3 When a kettle **is boiling**, the water inside it has reached boiling point. *Is the kettle boiling?* VB: only cont V

4 When you **boil** food, or when it **boils**, it is cooked in boiling water. *Boil the chick peas, add garlic and lemon juice... I'd peel potatoes and put them on to boil. ...boiled eggs and toast.* V-ERG V n V V-ed

5 If you **are boiling** with anger, you are very angry. *I used to be all sweetness and light on the outside, but inside I would be boiling with rage.* VB: usu cont V *with* n

6 A **boil** is a red, painful swelling on your skin, which contains a thick yellow liquid called pus. N-COUNT =cyst

7 See also **boiling**.

8 When you **bring** a liquid **to the boil**, you heat it until it boils. When it **comes to the boil**, it begins to boil. *Put water, butter and lard into a saucepan and bring slowly to the boil.* ● to **make someone's blood boil**: see **blood**. PHRASE: V inflects

boil away. When you **boil away** a liquid, or when it **boils away**, it is boiled until all of it changes into steam or vapour. *Remove the lid and boil away all the liquid... Check every 20 minutes that the water has not boiled away.* PHRASAL VERB ERG V P n (not pron) V P

boil down. When you **boil down** a liquid or food, or when it **boils down**, it is boiled until there is less of it because some of the water in it has changed into steam or vapour. *He boils down red wine and uses what's left... This may seem a large quantity of mushrooms, but they do boil down considerably.* PHRASAL VERB ERG =reduce V P n (not pron) V P

boil down to. If you say that a situation or problem **boils down to** a particular thing or can **be boiled down to** a particular thing, you mean that this is the most important or the most basic aspect of it. *What they want boils down to just one thing. It is land... For Malcolm work could always be boiled down to one idea: being good in business.* PHRASAL VERB ERG =amount to V P P n be V-ed P P n

boil over PHRASAL VERB

1 When a liquid that is being heated **boils over**, it rises and flows over the edge of the container. *Heat the liquid in a large, wide container rather than a high narrow one, or it can boil over.* V P

2 When someone's feelings **boil over**, they lose their temper or become violent. *Sometimes frustration and anger can boil over into direct and violent action.* =erupt, explode V P

boil up. If you **boil up** a liquid, you heat it until it boils. *I'll put on the kettle for tea. Or boil up some coffee.* PHRASAL VERB V P n (not pron) Also V n P

boiled sweet, boiled sweets. In British English, **boiled sweets** are hard sweets that are made from boiled sugar. N-COUNT

boiler /bɔɪləʳ/ **boilers.** A **boiler** is a device which burns gas, oil, electricity, or coal in order to provide hot water, especially for the central heating in a building. ◆◇◇◇◇ N-COUNT

boiler suit, boiler suits. In British English, a **boiler suit** consists of a single piece of clothing that combines trousers and a jacket. You wear it over your clothes in order to protect them from dirt while you are working. The American word is **overalls**. *...engineers in dirty boiler suits.* N-COUNT =overalls

boiling /bɔɪlɪŋ/ ◆◆◇◇◇

1 Something that is **boiling** or **boiling hot** is very hot. *'It's boiling in here,' complained Miriam... Often the food may be bubbling and boiling hot on the top, but the inside may still be cold.* ADJ =baking

2 If you say that you are **boiling** or **boiling hot**, you mean that you feel very hot, usually unpleasantly hot. *When everybody else is boiling hot, I'm freezing!* ADJ: v-link ADJ

boiling point; also spelled **boiling-point**.

1 The **boiling point** of a liquid is the temperature at which it starts to change into steam or vapour. For example, the boiling point of water is 100° centigrade. *The boiling point of water is 373 K... Heat the cream to boiling point and pour three quarters of it over the chocolate.* N-UNCOUNT

2 If a situation reaches **boiling point**, the people involved have become so angry that they can no longer remain calm and in control of themselves. *The situation is rapidly reaching boiling point, and the army has been put on stand-by... Mal's temper was at boiling point.* N-UNCOUNT

boisterous /bɔɪstərəs/. Someone who is **boisterous** is noisy, lively, and full of energy. *...a boisterous but good-natured crowd... Most of the children were noisy and boisterous.* ♦ **boisterously** *Her friends laughed boisterously, too.* ◆◇◇◇◇ ADJ-GRADED ≠docile ADV-GRADED: ADV with v, ADV adj

bold /bəʊld/ **bolder, boldest** ◆◆◇◇◇

1 Someone who is **bold** is not afraid to do things which involve risk or danger. *Amrita becomes a bold, daring rebel... In 1960 this was a bold move... Poland was already making bold economic reforms.* ♦ **boldly** *You can and must act boldly and confidently.* ♦ **boldness** *Don't forget the boldness of his economic programme.* ADJ-GRADED =brave ≠cautious ADV-GRADED: ADV with v N-UNCOUNT

2 Someone who is **bold** is not shy or embarrassed in the company of other people. *I don't feel I'm being bold, because it's always been natural for me to just speak out about whatever disturbs me.* ♦ **boldly** *'You should do it,' the girl said, boldly.* ADJ-GRADED: usu v-link ADJ =brave ≠timid ADV-GRADED

3 A **bold** colour or pattern is very bright and noticeable. *...bold flowers in various shades of red, blue or white. ...bold, dramatic colours.* ♦ **boldly** *The design is pretty startling and very boldly coloured.* ADJ-GRADED ADV-GRADED

4 **Bold** lines or designs are drawn in a clear, strong way. *Each picture is shown in colour on one page and as a bold outline on the opposite page.* ADJ-GRADED =vivid

5 **Bold** print is thicker and looks blacker than ordinary printed letters; a technical use in printing. N-UNCOUNT: usu N n

bolero, boleros. Pronounced /bɒlərəʊ, AM bəleroʊ/ for meaning 1, and /bəleərəʊ/ for meaning 2.

1 A **bolero** is a very short jacket, sometimes without sleeves. Boleros are worn mainly by women. N-COUNT

2 The **bolero** is a traditional Spanish dance. *They danced a romantic bolero together.* N-COUNT

Bolivian /bəlɪviən/ **Bolivians. Bolivian** means belonging or relating to Bolivia or its people. *...the Bolivian capital of La Paz. ...Bolivian farmers.* ► A **Bolivian** is someone who comes from Bolivia. ◆◆◆◆◇ ADJ N-COUNT

bollard /bɒlɑːʳd/ **bollards**

1 **Bollards** are short thick concrete posts that are used to prevent cars from going on to someone's land or on to part of a road. N-COUNT

2 A **bollard** is a strong wooden or metal post on the side of a river or harbour. **Bollards** are used for mooring boats to. N-COUNT

bollocks /bɒləks/

1 **Bollocks** is a swear word which is used in very informal British English to express disagreement, dislike, or defiance; an offensive use. EXCLAM; N-UNCOUNT PRAGMATICS

2 In very informal British English, a man's **bollocks** are his testicles. N-PLURAL

Bolshevik /bɒlʃɪvɪk/ **Bolsheviks**

1 **Bolshevik** is used to describe the political system and ideas that Lenin and his supporters introduced in Russia after the Russian Revolution of 1917. *Seventy-four years after the Bolshevik Revolution, the Soviet era ended. ...anti-Bolshevik forces.* ADJ

2 A **Bolshevik** was a person who supported Lenin and his political ideas. N-COUNT

Bolshevism /bɒlʃɪvɪzəm/. **Bolshevism** is the political system and ideas that Lenin and his supporters introduced in Russia after the Russian Revolution of 1917. N-UNCOUNT

bolshy /bɒlʃi/; also spelled **bolshie**. In informal British English, if you say that someone is **bolshy**, you mean that they behave in an argumentative and unhelpful way. ADJ-GRADED =stroppy

bolster /bəʊlstəʳ/ **bolsters, bolstering, bolstered** ◆◆◇◇◇

1 If you **bolster** something such as someone's confidence or courage, you increase it. *Hopes of an early cut in interest rates bolstered confidence. ...a number of measures intended to bolster morale.* VERB =boost V n

2 If someone tries to **bolster** their position in a situation, they try to strengthen it. *Britain is free to adopt policies to bolster its economy.* ► **Bolster up** means the same as **bolster**. *...an aid programme to bolster up their troubled economy.* VERB =boost V n PHRASAL VERB V P n (not pron) Also V n P

3 A **bolster** is a firm pillow shaped like a long tube which is sometimes put across a bed under the ordinary pillows. N-COUNT

bolster up. See **bolster** 2. PHRASAL VERB

bolt /bəʊlt/ **bolts, bolting, bolted** ◆◆◇◇◇

1 A **bolt** is a long metal object which screws into a nut and is used to fasten things together. N-COUNT

2 When you **bolt** one thing to another, you fasten them firmly together, using a bolt. *The safety belt is easy to fit as there's no need to bolt it to seat belt anchorage points... Bolt the components together... The doors were bolted on. ...a wooden bench which was bolted to the floor.* VERB V n to n V n with together/on V-ed

3 A **bolt** on a door or window is a metal bar that you can slide across in order to fasten the door or window. *I heard the sound of a bolt being slowly and reluctantly slid open.* N-COUNT

4 When you **bolt** a door or window, you slide the bolt across to fasten it. *He reminded her that he would have to lock and bolt the kitchen door after her... The building is a shell, its masonry rough, the bolted doors opening on dizzy drops.* VERB V n V-ed

5 If a person or animal **bolts**, they suddenly start to VERB

run very fast, often because something has frightened them. *The pig rose squealing and bolted... I made some excuse and bolted for the exit.* =scarper V V prep/adv

6 If you **bolt** your food, you eat it so quickly that you hardly chew it or taste it. *Being under stress can cause you to miss meals, eat on the move, or bolt your food.* ▶ **Bolt down** means the same as **bolt**. *I like to think back to high school, when I could bolt down three or four burgers and a pile of french fries.* VERB V n PHRASAL VERB V P n (not pron) Also V n P

7 A **bolt of** lightning is a flash of lightning that is seen as a white line in the sky. *Suddenly a bolt of lightning crackled through the sky.* N-COUNT: N *of* n

8 A **bolt** of cloth is a long wide piece of it that is wound into a roll round a piece of cardboard. *...bolts of black silk.* N-COUNT: usu N *of* n

9 When vegetables such as lettuces or onions **bolt**, they grow too quickly and produce flowers and seeds, and therefore become less good to eat. *If the soil dries out the plants may bolt.* VERB V

10 If someone **makes a bolt for** somewhere, or **makes a bolt for it**, they make a sudden escape. *His father kept a tight grip on his collar in case he should make a bolt for the door.* PHRASES V inflects, PHR n

11 If a piece of news comes like **a bolt from the blue**, it is completely unexpected and very surprising. *The company decided to appoint a Japanese manager as president of the company. The decision came as a bolt from the blue.*

12 If someone is sitting or standing **bolt upright**, they are sitting or standing very straight. *When I pushed his door open, Trevor was sitting bolt upright in bed.* usu v PHR

13 • **nuts and bolts**: see **nut**. • **close the stable door after the horse has bolted**: see **stable**.

bolt down. See **bolt** 6. PHRASAL VERB

bolt-hole, bolt-holes; also spelled **bolthole**. If you say that someone has a **bolt-hole** to go to, you mean that there is somewhere that they can go when they want to get away from people that they know; used in British English. *The hotel is less than an hour from town and is an ideal bolt-hole for Londoners.* N-COUNT =refuge

bomb /bɒm/ **bombs, bombing, bombed** ◆◆◆◆◇

1 A **bomb** is a device which explodes and damages or destroys a large area. *Bombs went off at two London train stations... It's not known who planted the bomb... Most of the bombs fell in the south... There were two bomb explosions in the city overnight.* N-COUNT

2 Nuclear weapons are sometimes referred to as **the bomb**. *They are generally thought to have the bomb.* N-SING: *the* N

3 When people **bomb** a place, they attack it with bombs. *Airforce jets bombed the airport.* ♦ **bombing, bombings** *Aerial bombing of rebel positions is continuing... There has been a series of car bombings.* VERB V n N-VAR

4 See also **petrol bomb**, **pipe bomb**.

bomb out. If a building or area **is bombed out**, it is destroyed by bombs. If people **are bombed out**, their houses are destroyed by bombs. *London had been bombed out... On 27 October they were bombed out.* • See also **bombed-out**. PHRASAL VERB PASSIVE *be* V-ed P

bombard /bɒmbɑːʳd/ **bombards, bombarding, bombarded** ◆◇◇◇◇

1 If you **bombard** someone with something, you make them face a great deal of it. For example, if you **bombard** them with questions or criticism, you keep asking them a lot of questions or you keep criticizing them. *He bombarded Catherine with questions to which he should have known the answers... The media bombards all of us with images of violence and drugs and sex... I've been bombarded by the press and television since Norway.* VERB =assail V n *with* n *be* V-ed *by* n

2 When soldiers **bombard** a place, they attack it with continuous heavy gunfire or bombs. *Rebel artillery units have regularly bombarded the airport... Several towns were bombarded by the Yugoslav army.* VERB V n

bombardment /bɒmbɑːʳdmənt/ **bombardments** ◆◇◇◇◇

1 A **bombardment** is a strong and continuous attack of gunfire or bombing. *The city has been flattened by heavy artillery bombardments... The capital is still under constant bombardment by the rebel forces.* N-VAR: usu with supp =attack

2 A **bombardment** of ideas, demands, questions, or criticisms is an aggressive and exhausting stream of them. *...the constant bombardment of images urging that work was important.* N-VAR: oft N *of* n =onslaught

bombast /bɒmbæst/. **Bombast** is the use of long, important-sounding words with little meaning in an attempt to impress other people; used showing disapproval. *There were men aboard who could not tolerate his bombast.* N-UNCOUNT PRAGMATICS =pomposity

bombastic /bɒmbæstɪk/. If you describe someone as **bombastic**, you are criticizing them because they use long, important-sounding words with little meaning in an attempt to impress other people. *He was vain and bombastic. ...the bombastic style adopted by his predecessor.* ADJ-GRADED PRAGMATICS =pompous

bomb disposal. **Bomb disposal** is the job of dealing with unexploded bombs by taking out the fuse or by blowing them up in a controlled explosion. *A few hours later bomb disposal experts defused the devices. ...an Army bomb disposal squad.* N-UNCOUNT: usu N n

bombed-out. A **bombed-out** building has been damaged or destroyed by a bomb. *...patients who'd been trapped in a bombed-out hospital.* ADJ: ADJ n

bomber /bɒməʳ/ **bombers** ◆◆◇◇◇

1 A **bomber** is a military aircraft which drops bombs. *...a high speed bomber with twin engines.* N-COUNT

2 **Bombers** are people who cause bombs to explode in public places. *Detectives hunting the London bombers will be keen to interview him.* N-COUNT

bomber jacket, bomber jackets. A **bomber jacket** is a short jacket which is gathered into a band at the waist or hips. *...a black leather bomber jacket.* N-COUNT

bombshell /bɒmʃel/ **bombshells.** A **bombshell** is a sudden piece of bad or unexpected news. *His resignation after thirteen years is a political bombshell... The police told me. It was a bombshell. I had no idea.* • If someone **drops a bombshell**, they give you a sudden piece of bad or unexpected news. *He dropped the bombshell. He told me he was dying.* ◆◇◇◇◇ N-COUNT PHRASE: V and N inflect

bomb site, bomb sites; also spelled **bombsite**. A **bomb site** is an empty area where a bomb has destroyed all the buildings. *In London, where I grew up, we were surrounded by bomb sites.* N-COUNT

bona fide /boʊnə faɪdi/. If something or someone is **bona fide**, they are genuine or real; a formal expression. *We are happy to donate to bona fide charitable causes... We simply cannot believe that a bona fide seller would conduct business on this basis.* ◆◇◇◇◇ ADJ: usu ADJ n =genuine ≠bogus

bona fides /boʊnə faɪdiz/. Someone's **bona fides** are their good or sincere intentions; a formal or legal expression. *Do not hand over money without first establishing the bona fides of the persons you are dealing with.* N-PLURAL: usu with poss

bonanza /bənænzə/ **bonanzas.** You can refer to a sudden great increase in wealth, profitability, success, or luck as a **bonanza**. *The expected sales bonanza hadn't materialised.* ◆◇◇◇◇ N-COUNT =windfall

bonce /bɒns/ **bonces.** In informal British English, your **bonce** is your head. N-COUNT: oft poss N =head

bond /bɒnd/ **bonds, bonding, bonded** ◆◆◆◆◇

1 A **bond** between people is a strong feeling of friendship, love, or shared beliefs and experiences that unites them. *The experience created a very special bond between us. ...the bond that linked them.* N-COUNT: oft N *between* pl-n

2 When people **bond** with each other, they form a relationship based on love or shared beliefs and experiences. You can also say that people **bond** or that something **bonds** them. *Belinda was having difficulty bonding with the baby... They all bonded while writing graffiti together... What had bonded them instantly and so completely was their similar background... The players are bonded by a spirit that is rarely seen in an English team.* ♦ **bonding** *They expect bonding to occur naturally.* V-RECIP-ERG =connect V *with* n pl-n V V pl-n V-ed Also V n *with* n N-UNCOUNT

3 A **bond** between people or groups is a close con- N-COUNT:

nection that they have with each other, for example because they have a special agreement. *...the strong bond between church and nation... There are tangible signs that the republic's successfully breaking its bonds with Moscow.* with supp =union

4 **Bonds** are feelings, duties, or customs that force you to behave in a particular way; a literary use. *Freed from the bonds of convention and the fear of what others may think, the mind responds with new solutions... We must, somehow, find a way to loosen the bonds of tradition.* N-PLURAL: oft N *of* n =ties

5 A **bond** between two things is the way in which they stick to one another or are joined in some way. *If you experience difficulty with the superglue not creating a bond with dry wood, moisten the surfaces with water... The molecule contains four carbon atoms arranged in a ring with a triple bond between two of them.* N-COUNT

6 When one thing **bonds** with another, it sticks to it or becomes joined to it in some way. You can also say that two things **bond** together, or that something **bonds** them together. *Diamond may be strong in itself, but it does not bond well with other materials... In graphite sheets, carbon atoms bond together in rings... Strips of wood are bonded together and moulded by machine.* V-RECIP-ERG =adhere; V *with* n; pl-n V *together*; be V-ed *together*; Also V n *with* n, V pl-n *together*

7 When a government or company issues a **bond**, it borrows money from investors. The certificate which is issued to investors who lend money is also called a **bond**. *Most of it will be financed by government bonds. ...the recent sharp decline in bond prices.* • See also **junk bond, premium bond.** N-COUNT

bondage /bɒndɪdʒ/ ◆◇◇◇◇

1 **Bondage** is the condition of being someone's property and having to work for them; a literary use. *Masters often hired out their slaves and sometimes allowed them to share in earnings and to buy their way out of bondage.* N-UNCOUNT =enslavement

2 **Bondage** is the condition of not being free because you are strongly influenced by something or someone; a formal use. *All people, she said, lived their lives in bondage to hunger, pain and lust.* N-UNCOUNT: oft N *to* n

3 **Bondage** is the practice of being tied up in order to gain sexual pleasure. N-UNCOUNT

bonded /bɒndɪd/. A **bonded** company has entered into a legal agreement which offers its customers some protection if the company does not fulfil its contract with them. *The company is a fully bonded member of the Association of British Travel Agents... The company was not bonded in any way and as such there is no compensation scheme.* ADJ

bondholder /bɒndhoʊldəʳ/ **bondholders;** also spelled **bond holder**. A **bondholder** is a person who owns one or more investment bonds. ◆◇◇◇◇ N-COUNT

bone /boʊn/ **bones, boning, boned** ◆◆◆◇◇

1 Your **bones** are the hard parts inside your body which together form your skeleton. *Many passengers suffered broken bones... Stephen fractured a thigh bone... The body is made up primarily of bone, muscle, and fat... She scooped the chicken bones back into the stewpot.* N-VAR

2 If you **bone** a piece of meat or fish, you remove the bones from it before cooking it. *Make sure that you do not pierce the skin when boning the chicken thighs... The boned fish is so easy to serve.* VERB; V n; V-ed

3 A **bone** tool or ornament is made of bone. *...a small, expensive pocketknife with a bone handle.* ADJ: usu ADJ n

4 See also **marrow bone, T-bone steak.**

5 The **bare bones** of something are the most basic parts or details. *There are not even the bare bones of a garden here – I've got nothing.* PHRASES

6 If something is too **close to the bone**, it makes you feel uncomfortable because it is very close to the truth or to the real nature of something. usu v-link PHR

7 If you say that you feel or know something **in your bones**, you are indicating that you are certain about it, although you cannot explain why. *I've got a feeling in my bones that things are not quite right.* PHR after v

8 If you **make no bones** about something, you talk openly about it, rather than trying to keep it a secret. *Some of them make no bones about their political views.* V inflects, usu PHR *about* n

9 If you **make no bones** about doing something that is unpleasant or difficult or that might upset someone else, you do it without hesitation. *Stafford-Clark made no bones about reapplying for the job when Daldry was standing for it.* V inflects, usu PHR *about* -ing

10 You can say someone is just **skin and bone** when you do not approve of the fact that they are very thin. *He was nothing but skin and bones.* *bone* inflects, v-link PHR PRAGMATICS

11 If something such as costs are cut **to the bone**, they are reduced to an absolute minimum. *It has survived by cutting its costs to the bone... Profit margins have been slashed to the bone in an attempt to keep turnover moving.* PHR after v

12 You use **to the bone** to indicate that you are very deeply affected by something. For example, if you feel chilled **to the bone**, your whole body feels extremely cold, often because you have had a shock. *What I saw chilled me to the bone.* PHR after v

bone up on. If you **bone up on** a subject, you try to find out about it or remind yourself of what you have already learnt about it; an informal expression. *I had spent the last few months boning up on neurology.* PHRASAL VERB; V P P n

bone china. **Bone china** is very fine porcelain that contains powdered bone. N-UNCOUNT

-boned /-boʊnd/. **-boned** combines with adjectives such as 'big' and 'fine' to form adjectives which describe a person as having a particular type of bone structure or build. *He was about seven years old, small and fine-boned like his mother.* COMB in ADJ-GRADED

bone dry; also spelled **bone-dry**. If you say that something is **bone dry**, you are emphasizing that it is very dry indeed. *The lake in the centre of the city is bone dry and cows wander around in it.* ADJ PRAGMATICS

bone marrow. **Bone marrow** is the soft fatty substance inside human or animal bones. *There are 2,000 children worldwide who need a bone marrow transplant.* ◆◇◇◇◇ N-UNCOUNT =marrow

bone meal; also spelled **bonemeal**. **Bone meal** is a substance made from animal bones which is used as a fertilizer. N-UNCOUNT

bone of contention, bones of contention. If a particular matter or issue is a **bone of contention**, it is the subject of a disagreement or argument. *The main bone of contention is the temperature level of the air-conditioners.* N-COUNT

bonfire /bɒnfaɪəʳ/ **bonfires.** A **bonfire** is a fire that is made outdoors, usually to burn rubbish. Bonfires are also sometimes lit as part of a celebration. *With bonfires outlawed in urban areas, gardeners must cart their refuse to a dump... They celebrated the event by holding parades, lighting bonfires and setting off fireworks.* ◆◇◇◇◇ N-COUNT

Bonfire Night; also spelled **bonfire night**. **Bonfire Night** is the popular name for **Guy Fawkes Night.** N-UNCOUNT =Guy Fawkes Night

bong /bɒŋ/ **bongs.** A **bong** is a long, deep sound such as the sound made by a big bell. N-COUNT; SOUND

bongo /bɒŋgoʊ/ **bongos.** A **bongo** is a small drum that you play with your hands. N-COUNT

bonhomie /bɒnəmi/. **Bonhomie** is happy, jolly friendliness; a formal word. *But his soft-spoken bonhomie cannot disguise an artist of the utmost integrity.* N-UNCOUNT

bonk /bɒŋk/ **bonks, bonking, bonked.** In British English, if two people **bonk**, they have sexual intercourse; an informal word. *They are relatively young and healthy and they bonk like crazy... He is bonking most of the female staff.* ♦ **bonking** *Basically, bonking in public is illegal.* V-RECIP; pl-n V; V n (non-recip); N-UNCOUNT

bonkers /bɒŋkəʳz/. If you say that someone is **bonkers**, you mean that they are silly or mad; an informal word. *The man must be bonkers to take such a risk... If the situation was reversed I would go bonkers with frustration.* ADJ: v-link ADJ =barmy, crazy

bon mot /bɒn moʊ/ **bons mots** or **bon mots.** A **bon mot** is a clever, witty remark; used in written English. *He was a genius for dissolving a tense situation with a bon mot.* N-COUNT =witticism

bonnet /bɒnɪt/ **bonnets** ◆◇◇◇◇
1 In British English, the **bonnet** of a car is the metal cover over the engine at the front. The American word is **hood**. *When I eventually stopped and lifted the bonnet, the noise seemed to be coming from the alternator.* N-COUNT
2 A **bonnet** is a hat that has ribbons that are tied under the chin. Nowadays, bonnets are worn by babies. In the past, they were also worn by women. N-COUNT
3 • to **have a bee in** your **bonnet**: see **bee**.

bonny /bɒni/ **bonnier, bonniest.** Someone or something that is **bonny** is attractive and nice to look at; used mainly in Scottish English and some Northern dialects of British English. *Jemima was a bonny Highland lassie of 15.* ADJ-GRADED =lovely

bonsai /bɒnsaɪ/; **bonsai** is both the singular and the plural form.
1 A **bonsai** is a tree or shrub that has been kept very small by growing it in a little pot and trimming it in a special way. *...a beautiful Japanese bonsai tree.* N-COUNT: oft N n
2 **Bonsai** is the art of growing miniature shrubs and trees. N-UNCOUNT

bonus /boʊnəs/ **bonuses** ◆◆◇◇◇
1 A **bonus** is an extra amount of money that is added to someone's pay, usually because they have worked very hard. *Workers in big firms receive a substantial part of their pay in the form of bonuses and overtime. ...a £15 bonus. ...a special bonus payment.* N-COUNT =gratuity
2 A **bonus** is something good that you get in addition to something else, and which you would not usually expect. *We felt we might finish third. Any better would be a bonus... It's made from natural ingredients, but with the added bonus of containing 30 per cent less fat then ordinary cheese.* N-COUNT =plus

bon voyage /bɒn vɔɪɑːʒ/. You say **'bon voyage'** to someone who is going on a journey, as a way of saying goodbye and wishing them good luck. *Goodbye! Bon voyage!* CONVENTION [PRAGMATICS]

bony /boʊni/ ◆◇◇◇◇
1 Someone who has a **bony** face or **bony** hands, for example, has a very thin face or very thin hands, with very little flesh covering their bones; used showing disapproval. *...an old man with a bony face and white hair... He poked a long bony finger in Billy's chest.* ADJ-GRADED: usu ADJ n [PRAGMATICS]
2 The **bony** parts of a person's or animal's body are the parts made of bone. *...the bony ridge of the eye socket.* ADJ: usu ADJ n
3 If you describe fish that you are eating as **bony**, you mean that it has a lot of bones. *...a delicious but extremely bony fish.* ADJ-GRADED

boo /buː/ **boos, booing, booed** ◆◇◇◇◇
1 If you **boo** a speaker or performer, you shout 'boo' or make other loud sounds to indicate that you do not like them, their opinions, or their performance. *People were booing and throwing things at them... Demonstrators booed and jeered him... He was booed off the stage.* ► Also a noun. *She was greeted with boos and hisses.* ♦ **booing** *The fans are entitled to their opinion but booing doesn't help anyone.* VERB V V n be V-ed N-COUNT: usu pl N-UNCOUNT
2 You say **'Boo!'** loudly and suddenly when you want to surprise someone who does not know that you are there. EXCLAM
3 See also **peekaboo**.

boob /buːb/ **boobs, boobing, boobed**
1 A woman's **boobs** are her breasts; an informal use which some people find offensive. N-COUNT: usu pl =breasts
2 In informal British English, if you **boob**, you make a mistake. *Is their timing right, or have they boobed again?* ► Also a noun. *The government once again has made a big boob.* VERB V N-COUNT =mistake

booby prize /buːbi praɪz/ **booby prizes.** The **booby prize** is a prize given as a joke to the person who comes last in a competition. N-COUNT

booby-trap /buːbi træp/ **booby-traps, booby-trapping, booby-trapped;** also spelled **booby trap.**
1 A **booby-trap** is something such as a bomb which is hidden or disguised and which causes death or injury when it is touched. *Police were checking the area for booby traps.* N-COUNT: oft N n
2 If something **is booby-trapped**, a booby-trap is placed in it or on it. *...fears that the area may have been booby trapped... His booby-trapped car exploded.* VB: usu passive be V-ed V-ed

boogie /buːgi/ **boogies, boogying** or **boogieing, boogied.** When you **boogie**, you dance to fast pop music; an old-fashioned, informal word. *At night, a good place to boogie through till sunrise is the Pink Panther Bar.* ◆◇◇◇◇ VERB V

book /bʊk/ **books, booking, booked** ◆◆◆◆◆
1 A **book** is a number of pieces of paper, usually with words printed on them, which are fastened together and fixed inside a cover of stronger paper or cardboard. Books contain information, stories, or poetry, for example. *His eighth book came out earlier this year and was an instant best-seller... 'Robinson Crusoe' is one of the most famous books in the world. ...the author of a book on politics. ...a book about witches. ...a new book by Rosella Brown. ...reference books.* N-COUNT
2 A **book** of something such as stamps, matches, or tickets is a small number of them fastened together between thin cardboard covers. *Can I have a book of first class stamps please?* N-COUNT: usu N of n
3 In British English, when you **book** something such as a hotel room or a ticket, you arrange to have it or use it at a particular time. *British officials have booked hotel rooms for the women and children... Laurie revealed she had booked herself a flight home last night. ...three-star restaurants that are normally booked for months in advance.* VERB =reserve V n V n n V-ed
4 A company's or organization's **books** are its records of money that has been spent and earned or of the names of people who belong to it. *For the most part he left the books to his managers and accountants... Around 12 per cent of the people on our books are in the computing industry.* N-PLURAL =accounts
5 When a football referee **books** a player who has seriously broken the rules of the game, he or she officially records the player's name. If players are booked twice during a game, they are sent off the field. *League referee Keith Cooper booked him in the first half for a tussle with the goalie.* VERB V n
6 When a police officer **books** someone, he or she officially records their name and the offence that they may be charged with; an informal use. *They took him to the station and booked him for assault with a deadly weapon.* VERB =charge V n
7 In a very long written work such as the Bible, a **book** is one of the sections into which it is divided. N-COUNT
8 See also **booking, cheque book, phone book.**
9 If you are **in** someone's **bad books**, they are annoyed with you. If you are **in** their **good books**, they are pleased with you. *Sir John was definitely in the Treasury's bad books for incorrect thinking on economic prospects... Right from my very first day I seemed to be in everyone's good books.* PHRASES v-link PHR
10 If you **bring** someone **to book**, you punish them for an offence or make them explain their behaviour officially. *Police should be asked to investigate so that the guilty can be brought to book soon.* V inflects
11 If you say that someone or something is a **closed book**, you mean that you do not know anything about them. *Frank Spriggs was a very able man but something of a closed book... Economics was a closed book to him.* v-link PHR
12 If a hotel, restaurant, theatre, or transport service is **fully booked**, or **booked solid**, it is **booked up**. *The car ferries from the mainland are often fully booked by February.* v-link PHR
13 **In my book** means 'in my opinion' or 'according to my beliefs'. *The greatest manager there has ever been, or ever will be in my book, is retiring.* PHR with cl =to my mind
14 If someone in authority **throws the book at** someone who has committed an offence, they give the offender the greatest punishment that they are allowed to. V inflects
15 • to **cook the books**: see **cook**. • to **take a leaf out of someone's book**: see **leaf**.

book in or **book into.** In British English, when PHRASAL VERB you **book into** a hotel or when you **book in**, you officially state that you have arrived to stay there, usually by signing your name in a register. The American term is **check in**. *He was happy to book into the Royal Pavilion Hotel... Today Mahoney booked himself into one of the best hotels in Sydney... The three men stayed at two hotels in Nottingham, booking in at one the day before the crime.* VPn VnPn VP Also VnP

bookable /bʊkəbᵊl/

1 If something such as a theatre seat or plane ticket is **bookable**, it can be booked in advance. *Tours leave from Palma and are bookable at some hotels or any travel agency.* ADJ: usu v-link ADJ

2 In sports such as football, a **bookable** offence is a foul for which a player can be officially warned by the referee. *Both men were dismissed for a second bookable offence.* ADJ

bookbinder, /bʊkbaɪndəʳ/ **bookbinders;** also spelled **book-binder**. A **bookbinder** is a person whose job is fastening books together and putting covers on them. N-COUNT

bookbinding /bʊkbaɪndɪŋ/; also spelled **book-binding**. **Bookbinding** is the work of fastening books together and putting covers on them. N-UNCOUNT

bookcase /bʊkkeɪs/ **bookcases.** A **bookcase** is a piece of furniture with shelves that you keep books on. ◆◇◇◇◇ N-COUNT

book club, book clubs. A **book club** is an organization that offers books at reduced prices to its members. N-COUNT

booked up

1 If a hotel, restaurant, theatre, or transport service is **booked up**, it has no rooms, tables, or tickets left for a time or date; used mainly in British English. *St Just seemed pretty booked up, but we managed to find a room at the George.* ADJ-GRADED: v-link ADJ =full

2 If someone is **booked up**, they have made so many arrangements that they have no more time free for any other engagements; used mainly in British English. *Mr Wilson's diary is booked up for months ahead... I'm fully booked up, I couldn't possibly do it now.* ADJ-GRADED: v-link ADJ

bookend /bʊkend/ **bookends;** also spelled **book-end**. **Bookends** are a pair of supports used to hold a row of books in an upright position by placing one at each end of the row. N-COUNT: usu pl

bookie /bʊki/ **bookies.** A **bookie** is the same as a **bookmaker**; an informal word. ◆◇◇◇◇ N-COUNT

booking /bʊkɪŋ/ **bookings.** A **booking** is the arrangement that you make when you book something such as a hotel room, a table at a restaurant, a theatre seat, or a place on public transport. *I suggest you tell him there was a mistake over his late booking.* ◆◆◇◇◇ N-COUNT: usu with supp =reservation

booking clerk, booking clerks. In British English, a **booking clerk** is a person who sells tickets, especially in a railway station. *Mark Reeves is a booking clerk with British Rail.* N-COUNT

booking office, booking offices. A **booking office** is a room where tickets are sold and booked, especially in a theatre or station. N-COUNT =ticket office

bookish /bʊkɪʃ/. Someone who is **bookish** spends a lot of time reading serious books; used showing disapproval. ADJ-GRADED PRAGMATICS =studious

bookkeeper /bʊkkiːpəʳ/ **bookkeepers;** also spelled **book-keeper**. A **bookkeeper** is a person whose job is to keep an accurate record of the money that is spent and received by a business or other organization. N-COUNT

bookkeeping /bʊkkiːpɪŋ/; also spelled **book-keeping**. **Bookkeeping** is the job or activity of keeping an accurate record of the money that is spent and received by a business or other organization. N-UNCOUNT

booklet /bʊklət/ **booklets.** A **booklet** is a small book that has a paper cover and that gives you information about something. ◆◆◇◇◇ N-COUNT =pamphlet

bookmaker /bʊkmeɪkəʳ/ **bookmakers.** A **bookmaker** is a person whose job is to take your money when you bet and to pay you money if you win. ◆◇◇◇◇ N-COUNT

bookmaking /bʊkmeɪkɪŋ/. **Bookmaking** is the activity of taking people's money when they bet and paying them money if they win. *...William Hill, a bookmaking firm.* N-UNCOUNT: oft N n

bookmark /bʊkmɑːʳk/ **bookmarks.** A **bookmark** is a narrow piece of card or leather that you put between the pages of a book so that you can find a particular page easily. N-COUNT

book plate, book plates; also spelled **bookplate**. A **book plate** is a piece of decorated paper which is stuck in the front of a book and on which the owner's name is printed or written. N-COUNT

bookseller /bʊkseləʳ/ **booksellers.** A **bookseller** is a person who sells books. ◆◇◇◇◇ N-COUNT

bookshelf /bʊkʃelf/ **bookshelves.** A **bookshelf** is a shelf on which you keep books. ◆◇◇◇◇ N-COUNT

bookshop /bʊkʃɒp/ **bookshops.** In British English, a **bookshop** is a shop where books are sold. The American word is **bookstore**. ◆◇◇◇◇ N-COUNT

bookstall /bʊkstɔːl/ **bookstalls**

1 A **bookstall** is a long table from which books and magazines are sold, for example at a conference or in a street market. N-COUNT

2 In British English, a **bookstall** is a small shop with an open front where books and magazines are sold. Bookstalls are usually found in railway stations and airports. The usual American word is **newsstand**. N-COUNT =kiosk

bookstore /bʊkstɔːʳ/ **bookstores.** A **bookstore** is a shop where books are sold; used mainly in American English. The usual British word is **bookshop**. ◆◇◇◇◇ N-COUNT

bookworm /bʊkwɜːʳm/ **bookworms.** If you describe someone as a **bookworm**, you mean they are very fond of reading; an informal word. N-COUNT

boom /buːm/ **booms, booming, boomed** ◆◆◆◇◇

1 If there is a **boom** in the economy, there is an increase in economic activity, for example in the amount of things that are being bought and sold. *An economic boom followed, especially in housing and construction... The 1980s were indeed boom years. ...the cycle of boom and bust which has damaged us for 40 years.* N-COUNT: usu sing ≠slump

2 A **boom** in something is an increase in its amount, frequency, or success. *The boom in the sport's popularity has meant more calls for stricter safety regulations... Public transport has not been able to cope adequately with the travel boom.* N-COUNT: usu sing, with supp, oft N *in* n ≠slump

3 If the economy or a business **is booming**, the amount of things being bought or sold is increasing. *By 1988 the economy was booming... Sales are booming... It has a booming tourist industry.* VERB V V-ing

4 On a boat, the **boom** is the long pole which is attached to the bottom of the sail and to the mast and which you move when you want to alter the direction in which you are sailing. N-COUNT: usu sing, *the* N

5 A **boom** is a large floating barrier that is used for stopping an oil spillage from spreading. N-COUNT

6 When something such as someone's voice, a cannon, or a big drum **booms**, it makes a loud, deep, echoing sound. *'Ladies,' boomed Helena, without a microphone, 'we all know why we're here tonight.'... Thunder boomed like battlefield cannons over Crooked Mountain.* ► **Boom out** means the same as **boom**. *Music boomed out from loudspeakers... A megaphone boomed out, 'This is the police.'... He turned his sightless eyes their way and boomed out a greeting.* ► Also a noun. *The stillness of night was broken by the boom of a cannon.* VERB V with quote V prep/adv Also V PHRASAL VERB ERG V P prep/adv V P with quote V P n (not pron) Also V P N-COUNT; SOUND

7 See also **baby boom**.

boom out. See **boom** 6. PHRASAL VERB

boomerang /buːməræŋ/ **boomerangs, boomeranging, boomeranged**

1 A **boomerang** is a curved piece of wood which comes back to you if you throw it in the correct way. Boomerangs were first used by Australian Aborigines as weapons. N-COUNT

2 If a plan **boomerangs**, its result is not the one that was intended and is harmful to the person who made the plan. *The trick boomeranged, though... He risks defeat in the referendum which he called, but which threatens to boomerang against him.* VERB =backfire V V *on/against* n

boom town, boom towns; also spelled **boom-town.** A **boom town** is a town which has become very rich and full of people, usually because industry or business has developed there. *In the eyes of many, Hamburg has become the boom town of Europe.* [N-COUNT ≠ghost town]

boon /bu:n/ **boons.** You can describe something as a **boon** when it makes life better or easier for someone. *It is for this reason that television proves such a boon to so many people... This battery booster is a boon for photographers.* [◆◇◇◇◇ N-COUNT: usu a N to/for n =plus ≠bind]

boor /bʊəʳ/ **boors.** If you refer to someone as a **boor**, you think their behaviour and attitudes are rough, uneducated, and rude. [N-COUNT PRAGMATICS =oaf]

boorish /bʊərɪʃ/. **Boorish** behaviour is rough, uneducated, and rude. *What I did was not just stupid or boorish – my actions were just plain wrong.* [ADJ-GRADED =oafish ≠genteel]

boost /bu:st/ **boosts, boosting, boosted** ◆◆◆◇◇

1 If one thing **boosts** another, it causes it to increase, improve, or be more successful. *It wants the government to take action to boost the economy... The move is designed to boost sales during the peak booking months of January and February.* ► Also a noun. *It would get the economy going and give us the boost that we need... The proposal received a boost on Sunday when The New York Times endorsed it in a leading article.* [VERB V n; N-COUNT: usu sing]

2 If something **boosts** your confidence or morale, it improves it. *We need a big win to boost our confidence... Do what you can to give her confidence and boost her morale.* ► Also a noun. *It did give me a boost to win such a big event.* [VERB =bolster V n; N-COUNT: usu sing]

booster /bu:stəʳ/ **boosters** ◆◇◇◇◇

1 A **booster** is something that increases a positive or desirable quality. *It was amazing what a morale booster her visits proved... Praise is a great confidence booster.* [N-COUNT: usu n N]

2 A **booster** is an extra engine in a machine such as a space rocket, which provides an extra amount of power at certain times. *Ground controllers will then fire the booster, sending the satellite into its proper orbit.* [N-COUNT]

3 A **booster** is a small injection of a drug that you have some time after a larger injection, in order to make sure that the first injection will remain effective. [N-COUNT =jab]

boot /bu:t/ **boots, booting, booted** ◆◆◆◇◇

1 **Boots** are shoes that cover your whole foot and the lower part of your leg. *He sat in a kitchen chair, reached down and pulled off his boots... He was wearing riding pants, high boots, and spurs.* • See also **wellington.** [N-COUNT]

2 **Boots** are strong, heavy shoes which cover your ankle and which have thick soles. You wear them to protect your feet, for example when you are walking or taking part in sport. *The soldiers' boots resounded in the street... Equip yourself with stout walking boots and sticks.* [N-COUNT]

3 If you **boot** something such as a ball, you kick it hard; an informal use. *He booted the ball 40 yards back up field... One guy booted the door down.* [VERB V n adv/prep]

4 In British English, the **boot** of a car is a covered space at the back or front, in which you carry things such as luggage and shopping. The American word is **trunk.** *He opened the boot to put my bags in... Harris got a rope from the car boot.* [N-COUNT]

5 If you **get the boot** or **are given the boot**, you are told that you are not wanted any more, either in your job or by someone you are having a relationship with; an informal expression. *She was a disruptive influence, and after a year or two she got the boot... His girl gave him the boot.* [PHRASES V inflects =get the elbow, get the chop]

6 If someone **puts the boot in**, they attack someone by saying something cruel, often when the person is already feeling weak or upset. [V inflects]

7 You can say **to boot** to emphasize that you have added something else to something or to a list of things that you have just said. *He is making money and receiving free advertising to boot!... They have to be thin, attractive and well-dressed to boot.* [cl/group PHR PRAGMATICS =into the bargain]

boot out. If someone **boots** you **out** of a job, organization, or place, you are forced to leave it; an informal expression. *Schools are booting out record numbers of unruly pupils.* [PHRASAL VERB V P n (not pron) Also V n P]

boot camp, boot camps. In the United States, a **boot camp** is a camp where army, navy, or marine recruits are trained. *Her husband was in boot camp a thousand miles away.* [N-VAR]

bootee /bu:ti:/ **bootees** or **booties**

1 **Bootees** are short woollen socks that babies wear instead of shoes. [N-COUNT: usu pl]

2 **Bootees** are short boots which come to just above the ankle. They are worn especially by women and girls. [N-COUNT]

booth /bu:ð/ **booths** ◆◇◇◇◇

1 A **booth** is a small area separated from a larger public area by screens or thin walls where, for example, people can make a telephone call or vote in secret. *I called her from a public phone booth near the entrance to the bar... In Darlington, queues formed at some polling booths.* [N-COUNT: usu n N =cubicle]

2 In some restaurants, **booths** are small areas that are separated from the rest of the room by low screens so that people can have a meal in private. *They sat in a corner booth, away from other diners.* [N-COUNT]

3 A **booth** is a small tent or stall, usually at a fair, in which you can buy goods or watch some form of entertainment. [N-COUNT]

bootlace /bu:tleɪs/ **bootlaces.** A **bootlace** is a long thin cord which is used to fasten a boot. [N-COUNT: usu pl]

bootleg /bu:tleg/ **bootlegs, bootlegging, bootlegged** ◆◇◇◇◇

1 **Bootleg** is used to describe something that is made secretly and sold illegally. *...a bootleg recording of the band's 1977 tour of Scandinavia.* [ADJ: ADJ n =illegal ≠legal]

2 To **bootleg** something such as a recording means to make and sell it illegally. *He has sued a fan for bootlegging his concerts... Avid Bob Dylan fans treasure bootlegged recordings.* ► Also a noun. *The record was a bootleg.* ♦ **bootlegger, bootleggers** *Bootleggers sold 75 million dollars-worth of copies.* [VERB V n V-ed; N-COUNT; N-COUNT]

bootstraps /bu:tstræps/. If you have **pulled** yourself **up by** your **bootstraps**, you have achieved success by your own efforts, starting from very difficult circumstances and without help from anyone. [PHRASE: V inflects]

booty /bu:ti/. **Booty** is a collection of valuable things stolen from a place, especially by soldiers after a battle. *Troops destroyed the capital and confiscated many works of art as war booty.* [N-UNCOUNT =spoils]

booze /bu:z/ **boozes, boozing, boozed** ◆◇◇◇◇

1 **Booze** is alcoholic drink; an informal use. *...booze and cigarettes. ...empty bottles of booze.* [N-UNCOUNT: also the N]

2 If people **booze**, they drink alcohol; an informal use. *...a load of drunken businessmen who had been boozing all afternoon.* ♦ **boozing** *She had to contend with the boozing and girl-chasing of her husband.* [VERB V; N-UNCOUNT]

boozed /bu:zd/. If someone is **boozed** or **boozed up**, they are drunk; an informal word. *He's half asleep and a bit boozed.* [ADJ-GRADED: usu v-link ADJ]

boozer /bu:zəʳ/ **boozers**

1 In British English, a **boozer** is a pub; an informal use. *She once caught him in a boozer with another woman.* [N-COUNT =pub]

2 A **boozer** is a person who drinks a lot of alcohol; an informal use. *We always thought he was a bit of a boozer.* [N-COUNT]

booze-up, booze-ups. In Britain, a **booze-up** is a party or other social gathering where people drink a lot of alcohol; an informal word. *...a booze-up in the nurses' home.* [N-COUNT =bender]

boozy /bu:zi/. A **boozy** person is someone who drinks a lot of alcohol; an informal word. *...a cheerful, boozy chain-smoker.* [ADJ: usu ADJ n]

bop /bɒp/ **bops, bopping, bopped** ◆◇◇◇◇

1 A **bop** is a dance; an informal use. *People just want a good tune and a good bop.* [N-COUNT =dance]

2 If you **bop**, you dance; an informal use. *He was bopping around, snapping his fingers... Guests bopped and jigged the night away to the disco beat.* [VERB =dance V adv/prep V]

3 See also **bebop.**

bopper /bɒpəʳ/. See **teenybopper**.

borax /bɔːræks/. **Borax** is a white powder used, for example, in the making of glass and as a cleaning chemical. N-UNCOUNT

bordello /bɔːʳdeloʊ/ **bordellos.** A **bordello** is a brothel; a literary word. N-COUNT =bordello

border /bɔːʳdəʳ/ **borders, bordering, bordered** ◆◆◆◆◇

1 The **border** between two countries or regions is the dividing line between them. Sometimes **the border** also refers to the land close to this line. *They fled across the border. ...the isolated jungle area near the Panamanian border... Clifford is enjoying life north of the border. ...the Mexican border town of Tijuana... Soldiers had temporarily closed the border between the two countries.* N-COUNT =frontier

2 A country that **borders** another country, a sea, or a river is next to it. *He spent his time in the countries bordering Iran.* ► **Border on** means the same as **border**. *Both republics border on the Black Sea.* VERB V n; PHRASAL VERB V P n

3 A **border** is a strip or band around the edge of something. *...pillowcases trimmed with a hand-crocheted border.* N-COUNT =hem

4 In a garden, a **border** is a strip of ground planted with flowers along the edge of a lawn. *...a lawn flanked by wide herbaceous borders. ...border plants.* N-COUNT =bed

5 If something **is bordered** by another thing, the other thing forms a line along the edge of it. *...the mile of white sand beach bordered by palm trees and tropical flowers... Caesar marched north into the forests that border the Danube River.* VERB =flank V-ed V n

border on. If you talk about a characteristic or situation **bordering on** something, usually something that you consider bad, you mean that it is almost that thing. *He has never exhibited the self-confidence, bordering on arrogance, of his predecessor... The atmosphere borders on the surreal.* ● See also **border** 2. PHRASAL VERB V P n

borderland /bɔːʳdəʳlænd/ **borderlands**

1 The **borderland** between two things is an area which contains features from both of these things so that it is not possible to say that it belongs to one or the other. *...rather like being on the borderland between sleep and waking.* N-SING: usu with supp

2 The area of land close to the border between two countries or major areas can be called the **borderlands**. *...Lebanon's southern borderlands.* N-COUNT: usu pl

borderline /bɔːʳdəʳlaɪn/ **borderlines** ◆◇◇◇◇

1 The **borderline** between two different or opposite things is the division between them. *...a task which involves exploring the borderline between painting and photography.* N-COUNT: usu N between/of n =borders

2 Something that is **borderline** is only just acceptable as a member of a class or group. *Some were obviously unsuitable and could be ruled out at once. Others were borderline cases.* ADJ-GRADED

bore /bɔːʳ/ **bores, boring, bored** ◆◆◆◇◇

1 If someone or something **bores** you, you find them dull and uninteresting. *Dickie bored him all through the meal with stories of the Navy... I eat very stupidly and only when I'm hungry – it bores me, all that health stuff.* VERB V n with n V n

2 If you say that someone or something **bores** you **to tears**, **bores** you **to death**, or **bores** you **stiff**, you are emphasizing that they bore you very much indeed; an informal expression. *...a handsome engineer who bored me to tears with his tales of motorway maintenance... I dropped out of high school. It bored me to death.* PHRASE: V inflects PRAGMATICS

3 You describe someone as a **bore** when you think that they talk in a very uninteresting way. *There is every reason why I shouldn't enjoy his company – he's a bore and a fool.* N-COUNT =drag

4 You can describe a situation as **a bore** when you find it annoying or a nuisance. *It's a bore to be sick, and the novelty of lying in bed all day wears off quickly.* N-SING: a N =drag

5 If you **bore** a hole in something, you make a deep round hole in it using a special tool. *Get the special drill bit to bore and countersink the correct-size hole for the job.* VERB V n

6 If someone's eyes **bore** into you, they stare intensely at you; used in written English. *His eyes bored into her, paralysing her, robbing her of movement... Her eyes seemed to bore a hole in mine.* VERB V into n V n in n

7 A **bore** is a very large wave that moves quickly up certain river estuaries from the sea at particular times of the year as a result of unusual tides. *One result of this tidal bore is that the actual flow of the river is reversed.* N-COUNT: usu supp N

8 **Bore** is the past tense of **bear**.

9 See also **bored, boring**.

-bore /-bɔːʳ/. **-bore** combines with numbers to form adjectives which indicate the diameter of the barrel of a gun. *He had a 12-bore shotgun.* COMB in ADJ: ADJ n

bored /bɔːʳd/. If you are **bored**, you feel tired and impatient because you have lost interest in something or because you have nothing to do. *I am getting very bored with this entire business.* ◆◆◇◇◇ ADJ-GRADED: usu v-link ADJ, oft ADJ with n/-ing

boredom /bɔːʳdəm/ ◆◇◇◇◇

1 **Boredom** is the state of being bored. *He had given up attending lectures out of sheer boredom... People like to be frightened, believe it or not. It saves them from boredom.* N-UNCOUNT =tedium

2 The **boredom** of a state or situation is the quality that it has which makes it boring. *They often find they begin to chat to relieve the boredom of the flight.* N-UNCOUNT

borehole /bɔːʳhoʊl/ **boreholes.** A **borehole** is a deep round hole made by a special tool or machine, especially one that is made in the ground when searching for oil or water. N-COUNT

boring /bɔːrɪŋ/. Someone or something **boring** is so dull and uninteresting that they make people tired and impatient. *Not only are mothers not paid but also most of their boring or difficult work is unnoticed. ...boring television programmes.* ♦ **boringly** *The meal itself was not so good – everything was boringly brown including the vegetables.* ◆◆◇◇◇ ADJ-GRADED =dull, tedious ≠interesting; ADV-GRADED: usu ADV adj

born /bɔːʳn/ ◆◆◆◆◇

1 When a baby **is born**, it comes out of its mother's body at the beginning of its life. In formal English, if you say that someone **is born** of someone or to someone, you mean that person is their parent. *My mother was 40 when I was born... She was born in London on April 29, 1923... He was born of German parents and lived most of his life abroad... Willie Smith was the second son born to Jean and Stephen.* V-PASSIVE be V-ed be V-ed be V-ed of/to n V-ed

2 If someone **is born** with a particular disease, handicap, or characteristic, they have it from the time they are born. *He was born with only one lung... Some people are born brainy... I think he was born to be editor of a tabloid newspaper... We are all born leaders; we just need the right circumstances in which to flourish.* V-PASSIVE: no cont be V-ed with n be V-ed adj be V-ed to-inf be V-ed n

3 You can use **be born** in front of a particular name to show that a person was given this name at birth, although they may be better known by another name; a formal use. *She was born Jenny Harvey on June 11, 1946.* V-PASSIVE: no cont be V-ed n

4 You use **born** to describe someone who has a natural ability to do a particular activity or job. For example, if you are a **born** cook, you have a natural ability to cook well. *Jack was a born teacher.* ADJ: ADJ n =instinctive

5 When an idea or organization **is born**, it comes into existence. If something **is born** of a particular emotion or activity, it exists as a result of that emotion or activity; a formal use. *The idea for the show was born in his hospital room... Congress passed the National Security Act, and the CIA was born... Energy conservation as a philosophy was born out of the 1973 oil crisis.* V-PASSIVE =conceive be V-ed be V-ed out of/of n

6 See also **-born; first born, newborn**.

7 ● **be born and bred**: see **breed**. ● **be born with a silver spoon in** your **mouth**: see **spoon**.

-born /-bɔːʳn/. **-born** combines with adjectives that relate to countries or with the names of towns and areas to form adjectives that indicate where someone was born; used in journalism. *The German-born photographer was admired by writers such as Oscar Wilde... Lancashire-born Miss Richardson lives alone in London.* COMB in ADJ: usu ADJ n

borne /bɔːʳn/. **Borne** is the past participle of **bear**.

-borne /-bɔːʳn/. **-borne** combines with nouns to form adjectives that describe the method or means by which something is carried or moved. *...water-borne diseases. ...a mosquito-borne infection. ...rocket-borne weapons.*
COMB in ADJ: usu ADJ n

borough /bʌrə, AM bɜːroʊ/ **boroughs.** A **borough** is a town, or a district within a large town, which has its own council. *...the South London borough of Lambeth. ...Kirklees Borough Council.*
◆◆◇◇◇ N-COUNT: oft the N of n, N n

borrow /bɒroʊ/ **borrows, borrowing, borrowed** ◆◆◆◇◇

1 If you **borrow** something that belongs to someone else, you take it or use it for a period of time, usually with their permission. *Can I borrow a pen please?... He wouldn't let me borrow his clothes.*
VERB ≠lend V n

2 If you **borrow** money from someone or from a bank, they give it to you and you agree to pay it back at some time in the future. *Kuwait borrowed $5.5 billion from foreign banks last year... It's so expensive to borrow from finance companies... He borrowed heavily to get the money together.*
VERB V n from n V from n V Also V n

3 If you **borrow** a book from a library, you take it away for a fixed period of time. *I couldn't afford to buy any, so I borrowed them from the library.*
VERB V n from n

4 If you **borrow** something such as a word or an idea from another language or from another person's work, you use it in your own language or work. *I borrowed his words for my book's title... Their engineers are happier borrowing other people's ideas than developing their own.*
VERB V n

5 Someone who **is living on borrowed time** or who **is on borrowed time** has continued to live or to do something for longer than was expected, and is likely to die or be stopped from doing it soon. *Perhaps that illness, diagnosed as fatal, gave him a sense of living on borrowed time.*
PHRASE: V inflects

borrower /bɒroʊəʳ/ **borrowers.** A **borrower** is a person or organization that borrows money.
◆◆◇◇◇ N-COUNT =lender

borrowing /bɒroʊɪŋ/ **borrowings** ◆◆◇◇◇

1 Borrowing is the activity of borrowing money. *We have allowed spending and borrowing to rise in this recession. ...the huge £50 billion public sector borrowing requirement.*
N-UNCOUNT: also N in pl

2 A **borrowing** is something such as a word or an idea that someone has taken from another language or from another person's work and used in their own language or work. *The names are direct borrowings from the Chinese.*
N-COUNT

borstal /bɔːʳstəl/ **borstals.** In Britain, a **borstal** was a kind of prison for young criminals, who were not old enough to be sent to ordinary prisons. *He stayed out of prison apart from a short spell in borstal.*
N-VAR =reform school

bosom /bʊzəm/ **bosoms** ◆◇◇◇◇

1 A woman's breasts are sometimes referred to as her **bosom** or her **bosoms**; an old-fashioned use. *...a large young mother with a baby resting against her ample bosom.*
N-COUNT =chest

2 If you are in **the bosom** of your family or of a community, you are among people who love, accept, and protect you; a literary use. *Joan was delighted to welcome her boyfriend into the bosom of her large, close-knit family.*
N-SING: the N of n

3 A **bosom** friend is a friend who you know very well and like very much indeed. *They were bosom friends... Sakota was her cousin and bosom pal.*
ADJ: ADJ n

4 If you take someone or something **to your bosom**, you accept them and treat or regard them with great affection; a literary expression. *We, at least, have taken her to our bosom.*
PHRASE: PHR after v

boss /bɒs/ **bosses, bossing, bossed** ◆◆◆◆◇

1 Your **boss** is the person in charge of the organization or department where you work. *He cannot stand his boss... Occasionally I have to go and ask the boss for a rise.*
N-COUNT: usu with supp, oft poss N

2 If you are the **boss** in a group or relationship, you are the person who makes all the decisions; an informal use. *He thinks he's the boss.*
N-COUNT: usu the N in sing

3 If you say that someone **bosses** you, you mean that they keep telling you what to do in a way that is irritating. *We cannot boss them into doing more... 'You are not to boss me!' she shouted.* ► **Boss around**, or in British English **boss about**, means the same as **boss**. *He started bossing people around and I didn't like what was happening.*
VERB =order around V n prep/adv V n PHRASAL VERB V n P Also V P n (not pron)

4 If you **are** your **own boss**, you work for yourself or make your own decisions and do not have anyone telling you what to do. *I'm very much my own boss and no one interferes with what I do.*
PHRASE: V inflects

boss around or **boss about.** See **boss** 3.
PHRASAL VERB

bossy /bɒsi/. If you describe someone as **bossy**, you mean that they enjoy telling people what to do; used showing disapproval. *She remembers being a rather bossy little girl.* ♦ **bossiness** *They resent what they see as bossiness.*
ADJ-GRADED PRAGMATICS =overbearing N-UNCOUNT

bosun /boʊsən/ **bosuns.** The **bosun** on a ship is the officer whose job it is to look after the maintenance of the ship and its equipment.
N-COUNT: oft the N

botanic /bətænɪk/. **Botanic** means the same as **botanical**.
ADJ: ADJ n

botanical /bətænɪkəl/ **botanicals** ◆◇◇◇◇

1 Botanical books, research, and activities relate to the scientific study of plants. *The area is of great botanical interest. ...botanical gardens.*
ADJ: ADJ n

2 Botanicals are drugs which are made from plants. *The most effective new botanicals are extracts from cola nut and marine algae.*
N-COUNT

botanist /bɒtənɪst/ **botanists.** A **botanist** is a scientist who studies plants.
◆◇◇◇◇ N-COUNT

botany /bɒtəni/. **Botany** is the scientific study of plants.
N-UNCOUNT

botch /bɒtʃ/ **botches, botching, botched** ◆◇◇◇◇

1 If you **botch** something that you are doing, you do it badly or clumsily; an informal use. *It is a silly idea and he has botched it. ...a botched job.* ► **Botch up** means the same as **botch**. *I hate having builders botch up repairs on my house... Hemingway complained that Nichols had 'botched everything up'.*
VERB =bungle V n V-ed PHRASAL VERB =mess up V P n (not pron) V n P

2 If you make a **botch** of something that you are doing, you botch it; an informal use. *I rather made a botch of that whole thing.*
N-COUNT: usu sing =mess

botch-up, botch-ups. A **botch-up** is the same as a **botch**; an informal word. *Tony Ward described the case as a 'sad botch-up'.*
N-COUNT: usu sing

both /boʊθ/ ◆◆◆◆◆

1 You use **both** when you are referring to two people or things and saying that something is true about each of them. *She cried out in fear and flung both arms up to protect her face... Put both vegetables into a bowl and crush with a potato masher.* ► Also a quantifier. *Both of these women have strong memories of the Vietnam War... We're going to Andreas's Boutique to pick out something original for both of us.* ► Also a pronoun. *Miss Brown and her friend, both from Stoke, were arrested on the 8th of June... Will there be public-works programmes, or community service, or both?* ► Also an emphasizing pronoun. *He visited the Institute of Neurology in Havana where they both worked... 'Well, I'll leave you both, then,' said Gregory.* ► Also a predeterminer. *Both the band's writers are fascinating lyricists... Both the horses were out, tacked up and ready to ride.*
DET: DET pl-n QUANT: QUANT of pl-n PRON PRON-EMPH: n PRON PREDET: PREDET det pl-n

2 You use the structure **both...and** when you are giving two facts or alternatives and emphasizing that each of them is true or possible. *Now women work both before and after having their children... Any such action would have to be approved by both American and Saudi leaders.*
CONJ-COORD

bother /bɒðəʳ/ **bothers, bothering, bothered** ◆◆◆◇◇

1 If you do not **bother** to do something or if you do not **bother** with it, you do not do it, consider it, or use it because you think it is unnecessary or because you are too lazy. *Lots of people don't bother to go through a marriage ceremony these days... Most of the papers didn't even bother reporting it... Nothing I do makes any difference anyway, so why bother? ...and he does not bother with a helmet either.*
VB: with brd-neg V to-inf V -ing V V with/about n

2 Bother means trouble, complication, or difficulty. You can also use **bother** to refer to an activity which causes this, especially when you would pre-
N-UNCOUNT: also a N =trouble

fer not to do it or get involved with it. *I usually buy sliced bread – it's less bother... The courts take too long and going to the police is a bother... Most men hate the bother of shaving.*

3 You use **bother** to refer to serious trouble, usually when you want to make it sound less serious than it really is; an informal use. *Vince is having a spot of bother with the law.* N-UNCOUNT PRAGMATICS

4 If something **bothers** you, or if you **bother** about it, it worries, annoys, or upsets you. *Is something bothering you?... That kind of jealousy doesn't bother me... It bothered me that boys weren't interested in me... Never bother about people's opinions.* V-ERG V n it V n that/when V about n Also it V n to-inf

♦ **bothered** *I was bothered about the blister on my hand... I'm not bothered if he has another child.* ADJ-GRADED: v-link ADJ, oft ADJ about n

5 If someone **bothers** you, they talk to you when you want to be left alone or interrupt you when you are busy. *We are playing a trick on a man who keeps bothering me... I don't know why he bothers me with this kind of rubbish.* VERB V n V n with/about n

6 In British English, some people say **'bother'** or **'bother it'** when they are annoyed about something; an old-fashioned use. PHRASES EXCLAM PRAGMATICS =drat

7 If you say that you **can't be bothered** to do something, you mean that you are not going to do it because you think it is unnecessary or because you are too lazy; an informal expression. *I just can't be bothered to look after the house.* V inflects, usu PHR to-inf

8 If you say **'it's no bother'** after offering to do something for someone, you are emphasizing that you really want to do it and that it will take very little effort. *I'll drive you back to your hotel later. It's no bother.* CONVENTION PRAGMATICS

9 ● **hot and bothered**: see **hot**.

bothersome /bɒðəʳsəm/. Someone or something that is **bothersome** is annoying or irritating; an old-fashioned word. *It's all been very noisy and bothersome in Parliament this week.* ADJ-GRADED =troublesome

bottle /bɒtəl/ **bottles, bottling, bottled** ♦♦♦♦◇

1 A **bottle** is a glass or plastic container in which drinks and other liquids are kept. Bottles are usually round with straight sides and a narrow top. *There were two empty beer bottles on the table... He was pulling the cork from a bottle of wine. ...Victorian scent bottles.* N-COUNT ► A **bottle** of something is an amount of it contained in a bottle. *He had drunk half a bottle of whisky.* N-COUNT: usu N of n

2 To **bottle** a drink or other liquid means to put it into bottles after it has been made. *This is a large truck which has equipment to automatically bottle the wine. ...bottled water.* VERB V n V-ed

3 A **bottle** is a drinking container used by babies. It has a special rubber part at the top through which they can suck their drink. *Gary was holding a bottle to the baby's lips.* N-COUNT: usu with supp ► A **bottle** of milk or other drink is an amount of it contained in a baby's bottle. N-COUNT: with supp

4 To **bottle** fruit means to put it into special jars, in order to preserve it. *Did she do things like bottling fruit or making jam? ...bottled plums.* VERB V n V-ed

5 In British English, **bottle** is used to refer to courage or boldness; an informal use. *But will anyone have the bottle to go through with it?* N-UNCOUNT

6 See also **bottled**; **feeding bottle**, **hot-water bottle**, **water bottle**.

7 If someone **hits the bottle**, they drink a lot of alcohol; an informal expression. *After my mother died my father started hitting the bottle.* PHRASES V inflects

8 In British English, if you say that someone **has bottled it**, you mean that they have lost their courage at the last moment and have not done something they intended to do; an informal expression. *He was scheduled to appear on the Russell Harty Show, but bottled it at the last minute.* V inflects

bottle out. In British English, if you **bottle out**, you lose your courage at the last moment and do not do something you intended to do; an informal expression. *I haven't come all this way to bottle out.* PHRASAL VERB =chicken out VP

bottle up. If you **bottle up** strong feelings, you do not express them or show them, especially when this makes you tense or angry; used showing disapproval. *Tension in the home increases if you bottle things up... Be assertive rather than bottle up your anger.* PHRASAL VERB PRAGMATICS V n P V P n (not pron)

bottle bank, bottle banks. A **bottle bank** is a large container into which people can put empty bottles so that they can be recycled and used again. N-COUNT

bottled /bɒtəld/. **Bottled** gas is kept under pressure in special metal cylinders which can be moved from one place to another. ● See also **bottle**. ADJ: usu ADJ n

bottle-feed, bottle-feeds, bottle-feeding, bottle-fed. If you **bottle-feed** a baby, you give it milk or a liquid like milk in a bottle rather than the baby sucking milk from its mother's breasts. *New fathers love bottle feeding their babies. ...a bottle-fed baby.* VERB ≠breast feed V n V-ed

bottle-green; also spelled **bottle green**. Something that is **bottle-green** is dark green in colour. COLOUR

bottleneck /bɒtəlnek/ **bottlenecks**

1 A **bottleneck** is a place where a road becomes narrow or where there is an important junction that makes the traffic slow down or stop, often causing traffic jams. N-COUNT

2 A **bottleneck** is a situation that stops a process or activity from progressing. *He pushed everyone full speed ahead until production hit a bottleneck.* N-COUNT

bottle-opener, bottle-openers. A **bottle-opener** is a metal device for removing caps or tops from bottles. N-COUNT

bottler /bɒtələʳ/ **bottlers.** A **bottler** is a person or company that puts drinks into bottles. N-COUNT

bottom /bɒtəm/ **bottoms, bottoming, bottomed** ♦♦♦♦◇

1 The **bottom** of something is the lowest or deepest part of it. *He sat at the bottom of the stairs... Answers can be found at the bottom of page 8... They've dug a 400 metre deep bore hole and put a wire right down to the bottom.* N-COUNT: usu the N in sing, oft N of n ≠top

2 The **bottom** of something such as a sea, lake, or valley or ditch is the ground underneath it or at its floor. *...the damp sand of the canyon bottom. ...the bottom of the sea.* N-COUNT: usu the N in sing, usu with supp

3 The **bottom** thing or layer in a series of things or layers is the lowest one. *There's an extra duvet in the bottom drawer of the cupboard.* ADJ: ADJ n ≠top

4 The **bottom** of a hollow object is the flat surface at its lowest point. You can also refer to the inside or outside of this surface as the **bottom**. *Spread the onion slices on the bottom of the dish. ...the bottom of their shoes. ...a suitcase with a false bottom.* N-COUNT: usu the N in sing, usu with supp =base

5 If you say that **the bottom** has dropped or fallen out of a market or industry, you mean that people have stopped buying the products it sells; used mainly in journalism. *The bottom had fallen out of the city's property market.* N-SING: the N

6 **The bottom** of a street, garden, bed, or table is the end of it that is farthest away from where you usually enter it or from where you are. *...the Cathedral at the bottom of the street... Malone sat down on the bottom of the bed.* N-SING: the N, usu N of n =end

7 **The bottom** of an organization or career structure in the lowest level in it, where new employees often start. *He had worked in the theatre for many years, starting at the bottom. ...a contract researcher at the bottom of the pay scale.* N-SING: the N, oft N of n ≠top

8 If someone is **bottom** or at **the bottom** in a survey, test, or league their performance is worse than that of all the other people involved. *He was always bottom of the class... The team is close to bottom of the League.* N-SING: the N, also no det ≠top

9 Your **bottom** is the part of your body that you sit on. *If there was one thing she could change about her body it would be her bottom.* N-COUNT: oft poss N

10 The lower part of a bikini, tracksuit, or pair of pyjamas can be referred to as the **bottoms** or the **bottom**. *She wore blue tracksuit bottoms. ...a skimpy bikini bottom.* N-COUNT: usu pl, oft n N ≠top

11 See also **-bottomed; rock bottom.**

12 You use **at bottom** to emphasize that you are stating what you think is the real nature of something or the real truth about a situation. *The two systems are, at bottom, conceptual models... At bot-* PHRASES PHR with cl

tom, such an attitude is born not of concern for your welfare, but out of fear of losing you.

13 If something is **at the bottom of** a problem or unpleasant situation, it is the real cause of it. *Often I find that anger and resentment are at the bottom of the problem.* PHR n =at the heart of

14 If you say that a country's economy **is bumping along the bottom**, you mean that it has reached its lowest level of performance, and is not getting any better or worse. *The British economy is still bumping along the bottom of recession.* V inflects, oft PHR *of*n

15 You can say that you mean something **from the bottom of** your **heart** to emphasize that you mean it very sincerely. *I'm happy, and I mean that from the bottom of my heart... I want to thank everyone from the bottom of my heart.* *heart* inflects, PHR after v, PHR with cl PRAGMATICS

16 If you want to **get to the bottom of** a problem, you want to solve it by finding out its real cause. *I have to get to the bottom of this mess.* V inflects, PHR n

17 In British English, some people say **bottoms up** to each other just before drinking an alcoholic drink; an informal expression. CONVENTION

18 • to **scrape the bottom of the barrel**: see **barrel**.

bottom out. If a trend such as a fall in prices **bottoms out**, it stops getting worse or decreasing, and remains at a particular level or amount; used mainly in journalism. *He expects the recession to bottom out... House prices have bottomed out.* PHRASAL VERB =level out V P

-bottomed /-bɒtəmd/. **-bottomed** can be added to adjectives or nouns to form adjectives that indicate what kind of bottom an object or person has. *...a loose-bottomed cake tin... You can take a trip in a glass-bottomed boat.* COMB in ADJ

bottomless /bɒtəmləs/

1 If you describe a supply of something as **bottomless**, you mean that it seems so large that it will never run out. *Princess Anne does not have a bottomless purse.* ADJ

2 If you describe something as **bottomless**, you mean that it is so deep that it seems to have no bottom. *His eyes were like bottomless brown pools.* ADJ =unfathomable

3 If you describe something as a **bottomless pit**, you mean that it seems as if you can take things from it and it will never be empty or put things in it and it will never be full. *A gold mine is not a bottomless pit, the gold runs out... The problem is we don't have a bottomless pit of resources... He's a bottomless pit as far as food is concerned.* PHRASE

bottom line, bottom lines ◆◇◇◇◇

1 The **bottom line** in a decision or situation is the most important factor that you have to consider. *The bottom line is that it's not profitable... The bottom line is that it did not get the best out of everybody.* N-COUNT: usu sing, usu *the* N

2 The **bottom line** in a business deal is the least a person is willing to accept. *She says £95,000 is her bottom line.* N-COUNT: usu sing, usu poss N

3 The **bottom line** is the total amount of money that a company has made or lost over a particular period of time. *These small promotions were costly and they did nothing to increase his bottom line. ...to force chief executives to look beyond the next quarter's bottom line.* N-COUNT: oft poss N

botulism /bɒtʃʊlɪzəm/. **Botulism** is a serious form of food poisoning; a medical term. N-UNCOUNT

boudoir /buːdwɑːʳ/ **boudoirs.** A **boudoir** is a woman's bedroom or private sitting room; an old-fashioned word. *Only Mimi's intimates were admitted to her boudoir.* N-COUNT

bouffant /buːfɒn, AM buːfɑːnt/ **bouffants.** A **bouffant** hairstyle is one in which your hair is combed backwards and upwards so that it is high and full. *...blonde bouffant hairdos.* ► Also a noun. *His hair is a honeycomb bouffant.* ADJ: usu ADJ n; N-COUNT

bougainvillaea /buːgənvɪliə/ **bougainvillaeas;** also spelled **bougainvillea**. **Bougainvillaea** is a climbing plant that has thin, red or purple flowers and grows mainly in hot countries. N-VAR

bough /baʊ/ **boughs.** A **bough** is a large branch of a tree; a literary word. *I rested my fishing rod against a pine bough.* N-COUNT

bought /bɔːt/. **Bought** is the past tense and past participle of **buy**.

bouillabaisse /buːjəbes/. **Bouillabaisse** is a rich stew or soup of fish and vegetables. N-UNCOUNT: also *a* N

bouillon /buːjɒn, AM bʊljɑːn/ **bouillons. Bouillon** is a liquid made by boiling meat and bones or vegetables in water and used to make soups and sauces. N-VAR =stock

boulder /boʊldəʳ/ **boulders.** A **boulder** is a large rounded rock. ◆◇◇◇◇ N-COUNT

boules /buːl/. **Boules** is a game in which a small ball is thrown and then the players try to throw balls as close to the first ball as possible. N-UNCOUNT

boulevard /buːləvɑːʳd, AM bʊl-/ **boulevards.** A **boulevard** is a wide street in a city, usually with trees along each side. *...Lenton Boulevard.* ◆◇◇◇◇ N-COUNT: oft in names =avenue

bounce /baʊns/ **bounces, bouncing, bounced** ◆◆◇◇◇

1 When an object such as a ball **bounces** or when you **bounce** it, it moves upwards from a surface or away from it immediately after hitting it. *I bounced a ball against the house... My father would burst into the kitchen bouncing a football. ...a falling pebble, bouncing down the eroded cliff... They watched the dodgem cars bang and bounce.* ► Also a noun. *The wheelchair tennis player is allowed two bounces of the ball.* V-ERG =rebound V n prep V n V prep/adv V Also V n with adv N-COUNT =rebound

2 The **bounce** of a sports pitch is the condition of it, which determines how high a ball will go when it bounces on it. N-UNCOUNT: usu with supp

3 If sound or light **bounces** or **is bounced off** a surface, it reaches the surface and is reflected back. *Your arms and legs need protection from light bouncing off glass... They work by bouncing microwaves off solid objects.* V-ERG V *off*n V n *off*n

4 If something **bounces** or if something **bounces** it, it swings or moves up and down. *Her long black hair bounced as she walked... Then I noticed the car was bouncing up and down as if someone were jumping on it... The wind was bouncing the branches of the big oak trees.* V-ERG =bob V V adv V n

5 If you **bounce** on a soft surface, you jump up and down on it repeatedly. *She lets us do anything, even bounce on our beds.* VERB V prep/adv Also V

6 If you **bounce** a child on your knee, you lift him or her up and down quickly and repeatedly for fun. *Patsy had picked up the baby and was bouncing him on her knee.* VERB V n prep/adv

7 If someone **bounces** somewhere, they move there in an energetic way, because they are feeling happy. *Moira bounced into the office.* VERB =bound V prep/adv

8 If you **bounce** your ideas off someone, you tell them to that person, in order to find out what they think about them. *It was good to bounce ideas off another mind... Let's bounce a few ideas around.* VERB V n *off*n V n *around*

9 If someone **bounces** you **into** doing something you do not really want to do, they make you do it, usually by starting a process which cannot easily be stopped; used mainly in journalism. *Attempts have been made to bounce member states into decisions with major financial implications.* VERB V n *into*n/-ing

10 If a cheque **bounces** or if a bank **bounces** it, the bank refuses to accept it and pay out the money, because the person who wrote it does not have enough money in their account. *Our only complaint would be if the cheque bounced... His bank wrongly bounced cheques worth £75,000.* V-ERG V V n

11 If an email or other electronic message **bounces**, it is returned to the person who sent it because the address was wrong or because of a problem with one of the computers involved in sending it. VERB: V

bounce back. If you **bounce back** after a bad experience, you return very quickly to your previous level of success, enthusiasm, or activity. *We lost two or three early games in the World Cup, but we bounced back... He is young enough to bounce back from this disappointment.* PHRASAL VERB =recover V P V P prep/adv

bouncer /baʊnsəʳ/ **bouncers.** A **bouncer** is a man who stands at the door of a club, prevents unwanted people from coming in, and makes people leave if they cause trouble. ◆◇◇◇◇ N-COUNT

bouncing /baʊnsɪŋ/. If you say that someone is **bouncing** with health, you mean that they are very healthy. You can also refer to a **bouncing** baby. *They are bouncing with health in the good weather... Derek is now the proud father of a bouncing baby girl.* • See also **bounce**. ◆◇◇◇◇ ADJ: v-link ADJ *with* n, ADJ n

bouncy /baʊnsi/ ◆◇◇◇◇
1 Someone or something that is **bouncy** is very lively. *She was bouncy and full of energy. ...good, bouncy pop songs.* ADJ-GRADED
2 A **bouncy** thing can bounce very well or makes other things bounce well. *...a children's paradise filled with bouncy toys. ...a bouncy chair.* ADJ-GRADED: usu ADJ n

bouncy castle, bouncy castles. A **bouncy castle** is a large object filled with air, often in the shape of a castle, which children play on at a funfair or other outdoor event. N-COUNT

bound 1 be bound

bound /baʊnd/ ◆◆◆◇◇
1 **Bound** is the past tense and past participle of **bind**.
2 If you say that something **is bound to** happen, you mean that you are sure it will happen, because it is a natural consequence of something that is already known or exists. *There are bound to be price increases next year... If you are topless in a public place, this sort of thing is bound to happen.* PHR-MODAL =be certain to
3 If you say that something **is bound to** happen or be true, you feel confident and certain of it, although you have no definite knowledge or evidence; used in spoken English. *I'll show it to Benjamin. He's bound to know... We'll have more than one child, and one of them's bound to be a boy.* PHR-MODAL PRAGMATICS =be certain to
4 If one person, thing, or situation is **bound to** another, they are closely associated with each other, and it is difficult for them to be separated or to escape from each other. *We are as tightly bound to the people we dislike as to the people we love... Economic growth is still bound to the issues of poverty, social justice and conservation.* ADJ-GRADED: v-link ADJ *to* n =tied
5 If a vehicle or person is **bound for** a particular place, they are travelling towards it. *The ship was bound for Italy. ...a Russian plane bound for Berlin.* ► Also a combining form. *...a Texas-bound oil freighter. ...homeward-bound commuters.* ADJ: v-link ADJ *for* n COMB in ADJ
6 You can say **'I am bound to say'** to introduce a statement expressing something that you find undesirable or unexpected; a formal expression. *I'm bound to say that it seems to me this is certain to lead to violence.* PHRASES PHR that PRAGMATICS
7 If something is **bound up in** a particular form or place, it is fixed in that form or contained in that place. *The manager of a company does not like having a large chunk of his wealth bound up in its shares... They'd have a lot of hydrogen sulfide gas bound up in their cells.* PHR n =tied up in
8 If one thing is **bound up with** or **in** another, they are closely connected with each other, and it is difficult to consider the two things separately. *My fate was bound up with hers... The story of their exploration is inextricably bound up with the character of the caves themselves... Their interests were completely bound up in their careers.* PHR n, usu v-link PHR =tied up in

bound 2 other uses

bound /baʊnd/ **bounds, bounding, bounded** ◆◆◆◇◇
1 **Bounds** are limits which normally restrict what can happen or what people can do. *Changes in temperature occur slowly and are constrained within relatively tight bounds. ...a forceful personality willing to go beyond the bounds of convention. ...the bounds of good taste.* N-PLURAL: usu *within/beyond* N =restrictions
2 If an area of land **is bounded by** something, that thing is situated around its edge. *Kirgizia is bounded by Uzbekistan, Kazakhstan and Tajikistan. ...the trees that bounded the car park. ...the park, bounded by two busy main roads and a huge housing estate.* VERB be V-ed *by* n V n V-ed
3 If someone's life or situation **is bounded** by certain things, those are its most important aspects and it is limited or restricted by them. *Our lives are bounded by work, family and television.* V-PASSIVE be V-ed *by* n
4 If a person or animal **bounds** in a particular direction, they move quickly with large steps or jumps. *He bounded up the steps and pushed the bell of the door... The dog came bounding back with the stick for Richard to throw again.* VERB =leap V prep/adv
5 A **bound** is a long or high jump. *She leaps in one bound onto her pony's back for a speedy canter around the ring... With one bound Jack was free.* N-COUNT: usu sing
6 If the quantity or performance of something **bounds** ahead, it increases or improves quickly and suddenly. *On March 18th the Hong Kong Stock Market bounded ahead... The economy isn't bounding back as fast as people expected.* VERB V adv
7 If you say that a feeling or quality **knows no bounds**, you are emphasizing that it is very strong or intense. *The passion of Argentinian football fans knows no bounds.* PHRASES V inflects
8 If a place is **out of bounds**, people are not allowed to go there. *For the last few days the area has been out of bounds to foreign journalists.* v-link PHR, PHR after v, oft PHR *to* n
9 If something is **out of bounds**, people are not allowed to do it, use it, see it, or know about it. *American parents may soon be able to rule violent TV programmes out of bounds.* v-link PHR, PHR after v =prohibited, off-limits
10 • **leaps and bounds**: see **leap**.

-bound /-baʊnd/
1 **-bound** combines with nouns to form adjectives which describe a person who finds it impossible or very difficult to leave the specified place. *Andrew has been left wheelchair-bound after the accident... I'm pretty desk-bound, which is very frustrating.* COMB in ADJ
2 **-bound** combines with nouns to form adjectives which describe a place that is greatly affected by the specified type of weather. *Three people were hurt in a 12-car pile up on a fog-bound motorway yesterday. ...a glimmer of sun on a frost-bound field.* COMB in ADJ
3 **-bound** combines with nouns to form adjectives which describe something or someone that is prevented from working properly or is badly affected by the specified situation; used in written English. *...the somewhat tradition-bound officers of the navy. ...a strike-bound factory.* COMB in ADJ-GRADED

boundary /baʊndəri/ **boundaries** ◆◆◇◇◇
1 The **boundary** of an area of land is an imaginary line that separates it from other areas. *The lovely restored bullring marks the western boundary of the town centre... Drug traffickers operate across national boundaries.* N-COUNT: oft N *of/between* n =border
2 The **boundaries** of something such as a subject or activity are the limits that people think that it has. *The boundaries between history and storytelling are always being blurred and muddled. ...extending the boundaries of press freedom.* N-COUNT: usu pl, oft N *of/between* n =perimeters

bounder /baʊndəʳ/ **bounders.** In British English, if you call someone a **bounder**, you mean he behaves in an unkind, deceitful, or selfish way; an old-fashioned word. *The cad! The bounder!* N-COUNT =cad

boundless /baʊndləs/. If you describe something as **boundless**, you mean that there seems to be no end or limit to it. *The work demanded boundless energy and theatrical imagination... His reforming zeal was boundless.* ADJ =infinite, limitless

bountiful /baʊntɪfʊl/
1 A **bountiful** supply or amount of something pleasant is a large one. *That evening's meal was an unusually bountiful one. ...a bountiful harvest of fruits and vegetables.* ADJ-GRADED =plentiful
2 A **bountiful** area or period of time produces or provides large amounts of something, especially food. *The land is bountiful and no one starves.* ADJ-GRADED =rich

bounty /baʊnti/ **bounties** ◆◇◇◇◇
1 You can refer to something that is provided in large amounts as **bounty**; a literary use. *...autumn's bounty of fruits, seeds and berries.* N-VAR: with supp
2 A **bounty** is money that is offered as a reward for doing something, especially for finding or killing a particular person. *A bounty of $50,000 was put on Dr. Alvarez's head... They paid bounties for people to give up their weapons.* N-COUNT

bounty hunter, bounty hunters. A **bounty hunter** is someone who tries to find or kill someone in order to get the reward that has been offered. N-COUNT

bouquet /bouk<u>eɪ</u>, buː-/ **bouquets** ◆◇◇◇◇
1 A **bouquet** is a bunch of flowers which is attractively arranged. *The woman carried a bouquet of dried violets.* N-COUNT: oft N of n
2 The **bouquet** of something, especially wine, is the pleasant smell that it has. *...a Sicilian wine with a light red colour and a bouquet of cloves.* N-VAR =fragrance

bouquet garni /bouk<u>eɪ</u> gɑːʳn<u>iː</u>, buː-/. A **bouquet garni** is a bunch of herbs that are tied together and used in cooking to add flavour to the food. N-SING: also no det

bourbon /b<u>ɜː</u>ʳbən/ **bourbons. Bourbon** is a type of whisky that is made mainly in America. *I poured a little more bourbon into my glass.* ► A **bourbon** is a small glass of bourbon. ◆◇◇◇◇ N-MASS; N-COUNT

bourgeois /b<u>ʊə</u>ʳʒwɑː/ ◆◇◇◇◇
1 If you describe people, their lifestyles, or their attitudes as **bourgeois**, you disapprove of them because you consider them typical of conventional middle-class people. *He's accusing them of having a bourgeois and limited vision.* ADJ-GRADED PRAGMATICS
2 Marxists use **bourgeois** when referring to the capitalist system and to the social class that owns most of the wealth in that system. *...the modern bourgeois society that has sprouted from the ruins of feudal society... His privileged bourgeois family insisted on a good education.* ADJ
3 See also **petit bourgeois.**

bourgeoisie /b<u>ʊə</u>ʳʒwɑːz<u>iː</u>/. In Marxist theory, **the bourgeoisie** are the middle-class people who own most of the wealth in a capitalist system. *...the suppression of the proletariat by the bourgeoisie.* • See also **petit bourgeoisie.** ◆◇◇◇◇ N-SING-COLL: the N

bout /b<u>aʊ</u>t/ **bouts** ◆◆◇◇◇
1 If you have a **bout** of an illness or of an unpleasant feeling, you have it for a short period. *He was recovering from a severe bout of flu... I was suffering with a bout of nerves.* N-COUNT: usu N of n
2 A **bout** of something that is unpleasant is a short time during which it occurs a great deal. *The latest bout of violence has claimed twenty four lives... A half-hour daily walk can be more beneficial than one hard bout of exercise a week.* N-COUNT: usu N of n =spell
3 A **bout** is a boxing or wrestling match. *This will be Eubank's eighth title bout in 19 months.* N-COUNT
4 Some writers use **'bout** or **bout** to represent **about** when the first syllable is not pronounced. *How 'bout some coffee?... I just felt the need to write bout it, I guess.*

boutique /buːt<u>iː</u>k/ **boutiques.** A **boutique** is a small shop that sells fashionable clothes, shoes, or jewellery. ◆◇◇◇◇ N-COUNT

bovine /b<u>oʊ</u>vaɪn/
1 **Bovine** means relating to cattle; a technical term in zoology. ADJ: usu ADJ n
2 If you describe someone's behaviour or appearance as **bovine**, you think that they are stupid or slow-moving. *I'm depressed by the bovine enthusiasm of the crowd's response.* ADJ-GRADED: usu ADJ n PRAGMATICS

bow 1 bending or submitting

bow /b<u>aʊ</u>/ **bows, bowing, bowed** ◆◆◇◇◇
1 When you **bow** to someone, you briefly bend your body towards them as a formal way of greeting them or showing respect. *They bowed low to Louis and hastened out of his way... He bowed slightly before taking her bag.* ► Also a noun. *I gave a theatrical bow and waved.* VERB; V to n; V; N-COUNT: usu sing
2 If you **bow** your head, you bend it downwards so that you are looking towards the ground, for example because you want to show respect or because you are thinking deeply about something. *The Colonel bowed his head and whispered a prayer of thanksgiving... She stood still, head bowed, hands clasped in front of her.* VERB =lower; V n; V-ed
3 If you **bow to** pressure or to someone's wishes, you agree to do what they want you to do. *Some shops are bowing to consumer pressure and stocking organically grown vegetables... Parliament has bowed to the demand for a referendum next year.* VERB; V to n
4 If you **are bowed** by something, you are made unhappy and anxious by it, and lose hope. *George Bush refused to be bowed by the bad poll news.* ► To **be bowed down** means the same as to **be bowed.** *I am bowed down by my sins.* V-PASSIVE be V-ed; PHRASAL VERB PASSIVE be V-ed P
5 If someone **bows to the inevitable** and does something that they do not want to do, they do it, because circumstances force them to do it. *He bowed to the inevitable and announced that he was willing to resume diplomatic relations.* PHRASES V inflects
6 If an actor or entertainer **takes a bow**, he or she shows appreciation of an audience's applause by bowing to them. *They ran to the center of the tent to take their bows.* V and N inflect
7 Journalists sometimes write **Take a bow** in front of a person's name when they want to congratulate that person or show their admiration for them. *Britain tends to breed its sportsmen decent, disciplined and polite (take a bow Seb Coe and Gary Lineker).*

bow down PHRASAL VERB
1 If you **bow down**, you bow very low in order to show great respect. *The Frenchman stood up and bowed down to kiss her hand.* V P
2 If you refuse to **bow down** to another person, you refuse to show them respect or to behave in a way which you think would make you seem weaker or less important than them. *We should not have to bow down to anyone.* oft with brd-neg =kow-tow; V P to n
3 See also **bow** 4.

bow out. If you **bow out** of something, you stop taking part in it; used in written English. *Dr Owen indicated that he would bow out of politics after the next election... He had bowed out gracefully when his successor had been appointed.* PHRASAL VERB; V P of n; V P

bow 2 part of a ship

bow /b<u>aʊ</u>/ **bows.** The front part of a ship is called the **bow** or the **bows**. The plural **bows** can be used to refer either to one or to more than one of these parts. *The waves were about five feet now, and the bow of the boat was leaping up and down. ...the sight of that magnificent ship lit up from bow to stern. ...spray from the ship's bows.* ◆◆◇◇◇ N-COUNT

bow 3 objects

bow /b<u>oʊ</u>/ **bows** ◆◇◇◇◇
1 A **bow** is a knot with two loops and two loose ends that is used in tying shoelaces and ribbons. *Add a length of ribbon tied in a bow.* N-COUNT
2 A **bow** is a weapon for shooting arrows which consists of a long piece of curved wood with a string attached to both its ends. *Some of the raiders were armed with bows and arrows.* N-COUNT
3 The **bow** of a violin or other stringed instrument is a long thin piece of wood with fibres stretched along it, which you move across the strings of the instrument in order to play it. N-COUNT
4 • another **string to** your **bow**: see **string.**

bowdlerize /b<u>aʊ</u>dləraɪz, AM b<u>oʊ</u>d-/ **bowdlerizes, bowdlerizing, bowdlerized;** also spelled **bowdlerise** in British English. To **bowdlerize** a book or film means to take parts of it out before publishing it or showing it; used showing disapproval. *Mark Twain's wife was so prudish she felt it necessary to bowdlerize her husband's prose... We have been reading D.H. Lawrence's masterpiece in a truncated and bowdlerised form.* VERB PRAGMATICS; V n; V-ed

bowed. Pronounced /b<u>oʊ</u>d/ for meaning 1, and /b<u>aʊ</u>d/ for meaning 2.
1 Something that is **bowed** is curved. *...an old lady with bowed legs.* ADJ-GRADED =curved ≠straight
2 If a person's body is **bowed**, it is bent forward. *He walked aimlessly along street after street, head down and shoulders bowed.* ADJ-GRADED =stooped, hunched ≠erect
3 See also **bow.**

bowel /b<u>aʊə</u>l/ **bowels** ◆◆◇◇◇
1 Your **bowels** are the tubes in your body through which digested food passes from your stomach to your anus. N-COUNT
2 You can refer in a polite way to someone defecating by saying that they move, open, or empty their **bowels**. N-PLURAL
3 You can refer to the parts deep inside something such as the earth, a building, or a machine as **the bowels of** that thing; a literary or humorous use. N-PLURAL: the N of n =depths

...deep in the bowels of the earth... Lyn went off into the dark bowels of the building.

bower /baʊəʳ/ **bowers.** A **bower** is a shady, leafy shelter in a garden or wood; a literary word. ◆◇◇◇◇ N-COUNT

bowl /boʊl/ **bowls, bowling, bowled** ◆◆◆◇◇

1 A **bowl** is a round container with a wide uncovered top. You eat and serve food from bowls and use them for mixing ingredients when cooking. *Put all the ingredients into a large bowl... Your dog should have his own bowls for food and water.* N-COUNT

2 The contents of a bowl can be referred to as a **bowl** of something. *He drank three bowls of bitter coffee.* N-COUNT: usu N *of* n

3 A washing-up **bowl** is a large plastic container that you wash dishes in. N-COUNT: oft supp N

4 You can refer to the hollow rounded part of an object as its **bowl**. *He smacked the bowl of his pipe into his hand. ...the toilet bowl.* N-COUNT: usu with supp

5 **Bowls** is a game in which players try to roll large wooden balls as near as possible to a small wooden ball. Bowls is usually played outdoors on grass. N-UNCOUNT

6 A set of **bowls** is a set of round wooden balls that you play bowls with. N-COUNT: usu pl

7 If you **bowl**, you play the game of bowls or the game of bowling. *Everyone wanted to bowl, hence everyone wanted to open a bowling alley.* VERB V

8 In cricket, when a bowler **bowls** a ball, he or she sends it down the pitch towards a batsman. *I can't see the point of bowling a ball like that... He bowled so well that we won two matches.* VERB V n V

9 In cricket, when a batsman **is bowled**, he has to leave the pitch because the bowler has hit the wicket with the ball. *Watkins hit 16 before being bowled by Ambrose.* ► To **bowl** someone **out** means the same as to **bowl** them. *He was bowled out first ball.* VB: usu passive *be* V-ed PHRASE: no cont, usu passive *be* V-ed P

10 If you **bowl** along in a car or on a boat, you move along very quickly, especially when you are enjoying yourself. *Veronica looked at him, smiling, as they bowled along... It felt just like old times, to bowl down Knightsbridge.* VERB V prep/adv

11 A large stadium where sports or concerts take place is sometimes called a **Bowl**. *...the Crystal Palace Bowl.* N-IN-NAMES: *the* n N

12 A competition in which teams compete to see who can win the most American football games can be referred to as a **bowl**. *...the Fiesta college football bowl.* N-COUNT

13 See also **bowling**; **begging bowl**, **fruit bowl**, **mixing bowl**, **punch bowl**, **salad bowl**, **sugar bowl**.

bowl out. In cricket, if a team **is bowled out**, each player in that team has had to stop batting and leave the pitch and there is nobody left to bat. *India were bowled out for 209... Middlesex defeated Derbyshire by bowling out the opposition.* • See also **bowl** 9. PHRASAL VERB no cont *be* V-ed P V P n Also V n P

bowl over PHRASAL VERB

1 To **bowl** someone **over** means to push into them and make them fall to the ground. *The only physical risk I ran was being bowled over by one of the many joggers... Some people had to cling to trees as the flash flood bowled them over.* *be* V-ed P V n P (not pron) Also V P n

2 If you **are bowled over** by something, you are very impressed or surprised by it. *Like any tourist, I was bowled over by India. ...a man who bowled her over with his humour and charm.* *be* V-ed P V n P Also V P n (not pron)

bowler /boʊləʳ/ **bowlers** ◆◆◇◇◇

1 The **bowler** in a game of cricket is the player who is bowling the ball. *He's a rather good fast bowler.* N-COUNT

2 A **bowler** is the same as a **bowler hat.** N-COUNT

bowler hat, bowler hats. A **bowler hat** is a round, hard, black hat with a narrow brim which is worn especially by British businessmen. N-COUNT =bowler

bowlful /boʊlfʊl/ **bowlfuls.** The contents of a bowl can be referred to as a **bowlful** of something. *They ate a large bowlful of cereal... I had a mixed salad - a huge bowlful for £ 1.20.* N-COUNT: usu N *of* n

bowling /boʊlɪŋ/ ◆◆◇◇◇

1 **Bowling** is a game in which you roll a heavy ball down a narrow track towards a group of wooden objects and try to knock down as many of them as possible. *I go bowling for relaxation.* N-UNCOUNT

2 In cricket, **bowling** is the action or activity of bowling the ball towards the batsman. N-UNCOUNT

bowling alley, bowling alleys. A **bowling alley** is a building which contains several tracks for tenpin bowling. N-COUNT

bowling green, bowling greens. A **bowling green** is an area of very smooth, short grass on which the game of bowls is played. N-COUNT

bow tie /boʊ taɪ/ **bow ties;** also spelled **bow-tie.** A **bow tie** is a tie in the form of a bow. Bow ties are worn by men, especially for formal occasions. N-COUNT

box /bɒks/ **boxes, boxing, boxed** ◆◆◆◆◇

1 A **box** is a square or rectangular container with hard or stiff sides. **Boxes** often have lids. *He reached into the cardboard box beside him... They sat on wooden boxes. ...the box of tissues on her desk.* ► A **box** of something is an amount of it contained in a box. *She ate two boxes of liqueurs.* N-COUNT N-COUNT: usu N *of* n

2 You can use **box** to refer to something such as a letter-box or telephone box which has 'box' as the second part of its name, when the thing has already been mentioned or has been indicated by another word. *I begged Tom's telephone number, and called him from the box down the road.* N-COUNT

3 A **box** is a square or rectangle marked by lines, that is printed or drawn on a piece of paper, road, or other surface. *Simply tick the appropriate box.* N-COUNT: usu with supp

4 On a football pitch, **the box** is the **penalty area**. *He scored from the penalty spot after being brought down in the box.* N-SING: *the* N

5 In a theatre or at a sports ground, a **box** is a small area of seats or room overlooking the stage or pitch where a small number of people can sit to watch the performance or game. *They watched the tennis from the royal box.* N-COUNT

6 In British English, television is sometimes referred to as **the box**; an informal use. *Do you watch it live at all or do you watch it on the box?* N-SING: *the* N =telly

7 **Box** is used before a number as a postal address by organizations that receive a lot of mail. *Country Crafts, Box 111, Landisville.* N-COUNT: with supp, usu N num

8 **Box** is a small evergreen tree with dark leaves which is often used to form hedges. *...box hedges.* N-UNCOUNT: oft N n

9 To **box** means to fight someone according to the rules of boxing. *At school I boxed and played rugby... The two fighters had previously boxed a 12-round match.* VERB V V n Also V *as* n

10 See also **boxed, boxing**; **black box, chocolate-box, lunch box, phone box, post office box, post box, sentry box, signal box.**

11 • to **box** someone's **ears**: see **ear**.

box in PHRASAL VERB

1 If you **are boxed in**, you are unable to move from a particular place because you are surrounded by other people or cars. *Armstrong was boxed in with 300 metres to go... The black cabs cut in front of them, trying to box them in.* =hem in, trap V-ed P V n P

2 If something **boxes** you **in**, it puts you in a situation where you have very little choice about what you can do. *The Fed may be boxing itself in, and that's a terrible mistake... The US had unwisely boxed in Saddam... He was too canny to let himself be boxed in.* ♦ **boxed in** *In a way, President Clinton is boxed in - he must choose among a host of unappetizing choices.* V n P V P n (not pron) ADJ-GRADED: usu v-link ADJ

boxed /bɒkst/. A **boxed** set or collection of things is sold in a box. *... a boxed set of six cups and saucers... This boxed collection captures 64 of the greatest modern love songs.* • See also **box**. ADJ: usu ADJ n

boxer /bɒksəʳ/ **boxers** ◆◆◇◇◇

1 A **boxer** is someone who takes part in the sport of boxing. N-COUNT

2 A **boxer** is a dog with short hair and a rather flat face. N-COUNT

boxer shorts. **Boxer shorts** are loose-fitting men's underpants that are shaped like the shorts worn by boxers. N-PLURAL: also *a pair of* N

boxing /bɒksɪŋ/. **Boxing** is a sport in which two people wearing large padded gloves fight accord- ◆◆◇◇◇ N-UNCOUNT ing to special rules. *Some speakers argued that boxing was less dangerous than rugby.*

Boxing Day. In Britain, **Boxing Day** is the 26th of December, the day after Christmas Day. N-UNCOUNT

boxing glove, boxing gloves. Boxing gloves are big padded gloves worn for boxing. N-COUNT

boxing ring, boxing rings. A **boxing ring** is a raised square platform with ropes around it in which boxers fight. N-COUNT

box number, box numbers. A **box number** is a number used as an address, especially one given by a newspaper for replies to a private advertisement. N-COUNT

box office, box offices; also spelled **box-office.** ◆◆◇◇◇

1 The **box office** in a theatre, cinema, or concert hall is the place where the tickets are sold. N-COUNT

2 When people talk about the **box office**, they are referring to the degree of success of a film or play in terms of the number of people who go to watch it or the amount of money it makes. *The film has taken £180 million at the box office... The film was a huge box-office success.* N-SING: usu *the* N, N n

boxwood /bɒkswʊd/. **Boxwood** is a type of wood which is obtained from a box tree. N-UNCOUNT

boxy /bɒksi/. If you describe something as **boxy**, you mean that you do not like it because it is squarish in shape and often lacking in decoration. *...boxy, yellow, apartment buildings.* ADJ-GRADED: usu ADJ n PRAGMATICS

boy /bɔɪ/ **boys** ◆◆◆◆◆

1 A **boy** is a child who will grow up to be a man. *I knew him when he was a little boy... He was still just a boy.* N-COUNT

2 You can refer to a young man as a **boy**, especially when talking about relationships between boys and girls. *...the age when girls get interested in boys.* N-COUNT

3 Someone's **boy** is their son; an informal use. *Eric was my cousin Edward's boy... I have two boys.* N-COUNT: usu poss N

4 You can refer to a man as a **boy**, especially when you are talking about him in an affectionate way; an informal use. *...the local boy who made President... 'Come on boys', he shouted to the sailors.* N-COUNT: with supp PRAGMATICS =lad

5 You can use **boy** when giving instructions to a horse or dog. *Down, boy, down!* N-VOC

6 See also **backroom boy, blue eyed boy, bully boy, head boy, messenger boy, office boy, old boy, stable boy, teddy boy.**

7 The police are sometimes referred to as **the boys in blue**; an old-fashioned use. PHRASES

8 Some people say **boy** or **oh boy** in order to express strong feelings of excitement or admiration; an informal expression used mainly in American English. *Oh Boy! Just think what I could tell him.* EXCLAM

9 If you say **boys will be boys**, for example when a group of men are behaving noisily or aggressively, you are suggesting in a light-hearted way that this is typical male behaviour and will never change.

10 If a man is described as **one of the boys**, he is accepted by a group of male friends who do things that are thought of as typically masculine. *He wants to be accepted as one of the boys.* usu v-link PHR =one of the lads

boycott /bɔɪkɒt/ **boycotts, boycotting, boycotted.** If a country, group, or person **boycotts** a country, organization, or activity, they refuse to be involved with it in any way because they disapprove of it. *The main opposition parties are boycotting the elections.* ► Also a noun. *Opposition leaders had called for a boycott of the vote. ...the lifting of the economic boycott against Israel.* ◆◆◇◇◇ VERB; V n; N-COUNT: oft N *of/against/on* n

boyfriend /bɔɪfrend/ **boyfriends.** Someone's **boyfriend** is a man or boy with whom they are having a romantic or sexual relationship. *...Brenda and her boyfriend Anthony... I don't know if she's got a boyfriend or not.* ◆◆◇◇◇ N-COUNT: oft poss N

boyhood /bɔɪhʊd/. **Boyhood** is the period of a male person's life during which he is a boy. *He has been a Derby County supporter since boyhood.* ◆◇◇◇◇ N-UNCOUNT

boyish /bɔɪɪʃ/ ◆◇◇◇◇

1 If you describe a man as **boyish**, you mean that he is like a boy in his appearance or behaviour, and you find this characteristic quite attractive. *She was relieved to see his face light up with a boyish grin... He loves to learn, and has a boyish enthusiasm for life.* ♦ **boyishly** *John grinned boyishly.* ADJ-GRADED: usu ADJ n PRAGMATICS =youthful; ADV-GRADED

2 If you describe a girl or woman as **boyish**, you mean that she looks like a boy, for example because she has short hair or small breasts. *...her tall, boyish figure.* ADJ-GRADED

boy racer, boy racers. British journalists sometimes refer to young men who drive very fast, especially in expensive and powerful cars, as **boy racers**; used showing disapproval. *Bad driving is not just the preserve of boy racers... Car manufacturers must stop pandering to the boy racers' fantasies about power and speed.* N-COUNT PRAGMATICS

Boy Scout, Boy Scouts; also spelled **boy scout.**

1 **The Boy Scouts** is an organization for boys which teaches them to become disciplined, practical, and self-sufficient. *He's in the Boy Scouts.* N-PROPER-COLL: *the* N =Scouts

2 A **Boy Scout** is a boy who is a member of the Boy Scouts. N-COUNT =Scout

bozo /boʊzoʊ/ **bozos.** If you say that someone is a **bozo**, you mean that you think they are stupid; an informal use. *He makes 'em look like bozos.* N-COUNT PRAGMATICS =idiot

Br. **Br.** is a written abbreviation for **British**. ◆◆◇◇◇

bra /brɑː/ **bras.** A **bra** is a piece of underwear that women wear to support their breasts. ◆◇◇◇◇ N-COUNT =brassiere

brace /breɪs/ **braces, bracing, braced** ◆◆◇◇◇

1 If you **brace** yourself for something unpleasant or difficult, you prepare yourself for it. *He braced himself for the icy plunge into the black water... She braced herself, as if to meet a blow.* VERB; V pron-refl *for* n; V pron-refl

2 If you **brace** yourself **against** something or **brace** part of your body **against** it, you press against something in order to steady your body or to avoid falling. *Elaine braced herself against the dresser and looked in the mirror... He braced his back against the wall.* VERB; V pron-refl *against* n; V n *against* n

3 If you **brace** your shoulders or knees, you keep them stiffly in a particular position. *He braced his shoulders defiantly as another squall of wet snow slashed across his face.* VERB; V n

4 To **brace** something means to strengthen or support it with something else. *Overhead, the lights showed the old timbers, used to brace the roof.* VERB; V n

5 You can refer to two things of the same kind as a **brace** of that thing. The plural form is also **brace**. *Bob Taylor fired his side back to the top of the Division with a brace of goals. ...a few brace of grouse.* N-COUNT: usu N *of* n

6 A **brace** is a device attached to a part of a person's body, for example to a weak leg, in order to strengthen or support it. *He wore leg braces after polio in childhood... She wears a neck brace.* N-COUNT: oft n N =support

7 A **brace** is a metal device that can be fastened to a child's teeth in order to help them grow straight. N-COUNT

8 In British English, **braces** are a pair of straps that pass over your shoulders and fasten to your trousers at the front and back in order to keep them in place. The usual American word is **suspenders**. N-PLURAL

bracelet /breɪslɪt/ **bracelets.** A **bracelet** is a chain or band, usually made of metal, which you wear around your wrist as jewellery. ◆◇◇◇◇ N-COUNT

bracing /breɪsɪŋ/. If you describe something, especially a place, climate, or activity as **bracing**, you mean that it refreshes you and makes you feel full of energy. *...a bracing walk.* ADJ-GRADED =invigorating

bracken /brækən/. **Bracken** is a plant like a large fern that grows on hills and in woods. N-UNCOUNT

bracket /brækɪt/ **brackets, bracketing, bracketed** ◆◇◇◇◇

1 If you say that someone or something is in a particular **bracket**, you mean that they come within a particular range, for example a range of incomes, ages, or prices. *...a 33% top tax rate on everyone in these high-income brackets... Do you fall outside that age bracket?* N-COUNT: usu n N

2 **Brackets** are pieces of metal, wood, or plastic that are fastened to a wall in order to support something such as a shelf. *Fix the beam with the brackets and screws. ...adjustable wall brackets.* N-COUNT

3 If two or more people or things **are bracketed** together, they are considered to be similar or related VERB =categorized

in some way. *The Magi, Bramins, and Druids were bracketed together as men of wisdom... Austrian wine styles are often bracketed with those of northern Germany.* pl-n be V-ed together; be V-ed with n

4 **Brackets** are a pair of written marks such as ( ) that you place round a word, expression, or sentence in order to indicate that you are giving extra information. *The prices in brackets are special rates for the under 18s... My annotations appear in square brackets.* N-COUNT: usu pl, oft *in* N =parenthesis

5 **Brackets** are pair of marks that are placed around a series of symbols in a mathematical expression to indicate that those symbols function as one item within the expression. N-COUNT: usu pl

brackish /brækɪʃ/. **Brackish** water is slightly salty and unpleasant. *...shallow pools of brackish water.* ADJ: usu ADJ n

brag /bræg/ **brags, bragging, bragged.** If you **brag**, you say in a very proud way that you have something or have done something; used showing disapproval. *He's always bragging about his prowess as a cricketer... He'll probably go around bragging to his friends... The chairman never tires of bragging that he and Mr. Bush are old friends.* ◆◇◇◇◇ VERB =boast; V *about* n; V *to* n; V that; Also V with quote, V

Brahman /brɑːmən/ **Brahmans.** A **Brahman** is the same as a **Brahmin**.

Brahmin /brɑːmɪn/ **Brahmins.** A **Brahmin** is a Hindu of the highest caste. N-COUNT

braid /breɪd/ **braids, braiding, braided** ◆◇◇◇◇

1 **Braid** is a narrow piece of decorated cloth or twisted threads, which is used to decorate clothes or curtains. *...a plum-coloured uniform with lots of gold braid.* N-UNCOUNT

2 In American English, if you **braid** hair or a group of threads, you twist three or more lengths of them over and under each other to make one thick length. The usual British word is **plait**. *She had almost finished braiding Louisa's hair... He pictured her with long black braided hair.* VERB; V n; V-ed

3 In American English, a **braid** is a length of hair which has been divided into three or more lengths and then braided. The usual British word is **plait**. *...a tall woman with a braid down to her waist.* N-COUNT

braided /breɪdɪd/. A piece of clothing that is **braided** is decorated with braid. ADJ

Braille /breɪl/. **Braille** is a system of printing for blind people. The letters are printed as groups of raised dots that you can feel with your fingers. N-UNCOUNT

brain /breɪn/ **brains, braining, brained** ◆◆◆◆◇

1 Your **brain** is the organ inside your head that controls your body's activities and enables you to think and to feel things such as heat and pain. *Her father died of a brain tumour.* N-COUNT

2 Your **brain** is your mind and the way that you think. *Once you stop using your brain you soon go stale... Stretch your brain with this puzzle.* N-COUNT: usu poss N =mind, intellect

3 If you say that someone has **brains** or a good **brain**, you mean they have the ability to learn and understand things quickly, to solve problems, and to make good decisions. The plural **brains** can be used when talking about one person or more than one. *They were not the only ones to have brains and ambition... I had a good brain and the teachers liked me.* N-COUNT

4 If you refer to someone as the **brains** behind an idea or an organization, you mean that he or she had that idea or that they make the important decisions about how that organization is managed; an informal use. The plural **brains** can be used to refer to one or to more than one of these people. *Mr White was the brains behind the scheme... Some investigators regarded her as the brains of the gang.* N-COUNT: usu pl, *the* N *behind/of* n

5 To **brain** someone means to hit them forcefully on the head; an informal use. *He had threatened to brain him then and there.* VERB; V n

6 To **beat** someone's **brains out** or **bash** their **brains in** means to hit their head very hard, so that they are badly injured or killed; an informal expression. *They stood over him with clubs raised as if to beat his brains out.* PHRASES; V inflects

7 To **blow** someone's **brains out** means to shoot them in the head, killing them; an informal expression. *Give me all your money or I'll blow your brains out... He blew his brains out with a shotgun.* V inflects

8 If someone **has** something **on the brain**, or **has got** something **on the brain**, they keep thinking about it; an informal expression. *You've had chess on the brain since you were little.* V inflects

9 If you **pick** someone's **brains**, you ask them to help you with a problem because they know more about the subject than you; an informal expression. *Why should a successful company allow another firm to pick its brains?* V inflects

10 ● to **rack** your **brains**: see **rack**.

brainchild /breɪntʃaɪld/; also spelled **brain-child**. Someone's **brainchild** is an idea or invention that they have thought up or created. *The record was the brainchild of rock star Bob Geldof.* ◆◇◇◇◇ N-SING: with poss

brain dead

1 If someone is declared **brain dead**, they have suffered **brain death**. ADJ

2 If you say that someone is **brain dead**, you are saying in a cruel way that you think they are very stupid. ADJ-GRADED PRAGMATICS

brain death. **Brain death** occurs when someone's brain stops functioning, even though their heart may be kept beating using a machine. N-UNCOUNT

brain drain. When people talk about a **brain drain**, they are referring to the movement of a large number of scientists or academics away from their own country to other countries where the conditions and salaries are better. N-SING

-brained /-breɪnd/. You can combine **-brained** with nouns to form adjectives which describe the quality of someone's mind when you consider that person to be rather stupid. *...our refined but slightly feather-brained hostess.* ● See also **hare-brained**. COMB in ADJ-GRADED PRAGMATICS

brainless /breɪnləs/. If you describe someone or something as **brainless**, you mean that you think they are stupid. *I got treated as if I was a bit brainless.* ADJ-GRADED PRAGMATICS =stupid

brainpower /breɪnpaʊəʳ/

1 **Brainpower** is intelligence or the ability to think; used mainly in journalism. *Ginseng boosts your brainpower and makes you feel good.* N-UNCOUNT

2 You can refer to the intelligent people in an organization or country as its **brainpower**; used in journalism. *Scientists are, by definition, the creme de la creme of a country's brainpower.* N-UNCOUNT

brainstorm /breɪnstɔːʳm/ **brainstorms, brainstorming, brainstormed**

1 In British English, if you have a **brainstorm**, you suddenly become forgetful or unable to think clearly. *I can have a brainstorm and be very extravagant.* N-COUNT

2 In American English, if you have a **brainstorm**, you suddenly have a clever idea. The usual British word is **brainwave**. *'Look,' she said, getting a brainstorm, 'Why don't you invite them here?'* N-COUNT =brainwave

3 If a group of people **brainstorm**, they have a meeting in which they all put forward as many ideas and suggestions as they can think of. *The women meet twice a month to brainstorm and set business goals for each other... We can brainstorm a list of the most influential individuals in the company.* ♦ **brainstorming** *Le Shuttle was chosen after hundreds of other ideas had been tried and discarded during two years of brainstorming.* VERB; V; V n; N-UNCOUNT

brain teaser, brain teasers; also spelled **brain-teaser**. A **brain teaser** is a question, problem, or puzzle that is difficult to answer or solve, but is not serious or important. N-COUNT =puzzle, riddle

brainwash /breɪnwɒʃ/ **brainwashes, brainwashing, brainwashed.** If you **brainwash** someone, you force them to believe something by continually telling them that it is true, and preventing them from thinking about it properly. *They brainwash people into giving up all their money... I'd been brainwashed into believing I was worthless... We were brainwashed to believe we were all equal.* VERB; V n *into*-ing; be V-ed to-inf; Also V n

brainwave /breɪnweɪv/ **brainwaves**

1 In British English, if you have a **brainwave**, you N-COUNT

suddenly have a clever idea. The usual American word is **brainstorm.** *In 1980 she had a brainwave that changed her life.*
2 **Brainwaves** are electrical signals produced by the brain which can be recorded and measured. *His brainwaves were constantly monitored.* N-PLURAL

brainy /breɪni/ **brainier, brainiest.** Someone who is **brainy** is clever and good at learning; an informal word. *I don't class myself as being very intelligent or brainy.* ADJ-GRADED =clever

braise /breɪz/ **braises, braising, braised.** When you **braise** meat or a vegetable, you fry it quickly and then cook it slowly in a covered dish with a small amount of liquid. *I braised some beans to accompany a shoulder of lamb. ...braised cabbage.* VERB Vn V-ed

brake /breɪk/ **brakes, braking, braked** ◆◆◇◇◇
1 **Brakes** are devices in a vehicle that make it go slower or stop. *The brakes began locking... A seagull swooped down in front of her car, causing her to slam on the brakes.* N-COUNT
2 When a vehicle or its driver **brakes**, or when a driver **brakes** a vehicle, the driver makes it slow down or stop by using the brakes. *He heard tires squeal as the Roadrunner braked to avoid a collision... She braked sharply to avoid another car... He lit a cigarette and braked the car slightly... She braked to a halt and switched off.* VERB V Vn V to n Also V n to n
3 You can use **brake** in a number of expressions to indicate that something has slowed down or stopped. *Illness had put a brake on his progress... You can take the financial brakes off in June.* N-COUNT

bramble /bræmbᵊl/ **brambles. Brambles** are wild, thorny bushes that produce blackberries. *I became caught in the brambles.* N-COUNT: usu pl

bran /bræn/. The small brown flakes that are left when grain has been used to make flour are known as **bran**. *...oat bran... Fresh fruits and vegetables are important and so is bran.* ◆◇◇◇◇ N-UNCOUNT

branch /brɑːntʃ, bræntʃ/ **branches, branching, branched** ◆◆◆◇◇
1 The **branches** of a tree are the parts that grow out from its trunk and have leaves, flowers, or fruit growing on them. N-COUNT
2 A **branch** of a business or other organization is one of the offices, shops, or groups which belong to it and which are located in different places. *The local branch of Bank of America is handling the accounts... National is Britain's leading autocare service with over 400 branches nationwide.* N-COUNT: oft N of n
3 A **branch** of an organization such as the government or the police force is a department that has a particular function. *Senate employees could take their employment grievances to another branch of government... He had a fascination for submarines and joined this branch of the service. ...the Metropolitan Police Special Branch.* N-COUNT: with supp, oft N of n, adj N
4 A **branch of** a subject is a part or type of it. *Whole branches of science may not receive any grants. ...an experimental branch of naturopathic medicine.* N-COUNT: N of n
5 A **branch** of your family is a group of its members who are descended from one particular person. *This is one of the branches of the Roosevelt family.* N-COUNT: usu N of n

branch off. A road or path that **branches off** from another one starts from it and goes in a slightly different direction. If you **branch off** somewhere, you change the direction in which you are going. *After a few miles, a small road branched off to the right... She branched off down the earth track.* PHRASAL VERB V P prep/adv Also V P, V P n

branch out. If a person or an organization **branches out**, they do something that is different from their normal activities or work. *I continued studying moths, and branched out to other insects... ASEAN has branched out tentatively into the security business.* PHRASAL VERB V P prep/adv Also V P

branch line, branch lines. A **branch line** is a railway line that goes to small towns rather than one that goes between large cities. N-COUNT

brand /brænd/ **brands, branding, branded** ◆◆◆◇◇
1 A **brand** of a product is the version of it that is made by one particular manufacturer. *Winston is a brand of cigarette... I bought one of the leading brands. ...a supermarket's own brand.* N-COUNT: oft N of n, adj N =make
2 A **brand of** something such as a way of thinking or behaving is a particular kind of it. *The British brand of socialism was more interested in reform than revolution.* N-COUNT: N of n =strain
3 If someone **is branded** as something bad, people think they are that thing. *I was instantly branded as a rebel... The company has been branded racist by some of its own staff... The US administration recently branded him a war criminal.* VERB =label be V-ed as n be V-ed adj V n n Also V n as n, V n adj
4 When you **brand** an animal, you put a permanent mark on its skin in order to show who it belongs to, usually by burning a mark onto its skin. *The owner couldn't be bothered to brand the cattle.* VERB Vn
► Also a noun. *A brand was a mark of ownership burned into the hide of an animal with a hot iron.* N-COUNT
5 A **brand** is a permanent mark on the skin of an animal, which shows who it belongs to. N-COUNT

branded /brændɪd/. A **branded** product is one which is made by a well-known manufacturer and has the manufacturer's label on it. *Supermarket lines are often cheaper than branded goods.* ADJ: ADJ n

brandish /brændɪʃ/ **brandishes, brandishing, brandished.** If you **brandish** something, especially a weapon, you hold it in a threatening way. *He appeared in the lounge brandishing a knife.* ◆◇◇◇◇ VERB Vn

brand name, brand names. The **brand name** of a product is the name the manufacturer gives it and under which it is sold. *Drugs can be sold under different brand names throughout the EC... When it comes to soft drinks Coca-Cola is the biggest selling brand name in Britain.* ◆◇◇◇◇ N-COUNT

brand-new. A **brand-new** object is completely new. *Yesterday he went off to buy himself a brand new car.* ◆◆◇◇◇ ADJ

brandy /brændi/ **brandies** ◆◇◇◇◇
1 **Brandy** is a strong alcoholic drink. It is often drunk after a meal. N-MASS
2 A **brandy** is a glass of brandy. *After a couple of brandies Michael started telling me his life story.* N-COUNT

brandy snap, brandy snaps. Brandy snaps are very thin crisp biscuits in the shape of hollow cylinders. They are flavoured with ginger and are often filled with cream. N-COUNT

brash /bræʃ/ **brasher, brashest.** If you describe someone or their behaviour as **brash**, you disapprove of them because you think that they are excessively confident and aggressive. *On stage she seems hard, brash and uncompromising.* ◆◇◇◇◇ ADJ-GRADED PRAGMATICS
♦ **brashly** *I brashly announced to the group that NATO needed to be turned around.* ADV: ADV with v, ADV adj
♦ **brashness** *He was a typical showman with a brashness bordering on arrogance.* N-UNCOUNT

brass /brɑːs, bræs/ **brasses** ◆◆◇◇◇
1 **Brass** is a yellow-coloured metal made from copper and zinc. It is used especially for making ornaments and musical instruments. *The instrument is beautifully made in brass.* N-UNCOUNT
2 The **brass** is the section of an orchestra which consists of brass wind instruments such as trumpets and horns. *He once again raised his baton and brought in the brass.* N-COUNT: usu *the* N in sing
3 **Brasses** are flat pieces of brass with writing or a picture cut into them, which are often found in churches. • See also **brass rubbing**. N-COUNT
4 In informal British English, if you say that someone has the **brass** nerve or the **brass** neck to do something which will shock other people, you mean that they will do it without worrying about what other people think; used showing disapproval. *Jim and Maggie have a brass neck and invariably this will get them into trouble.* ADJ: ADJ n PRAGMATICS
5 If you **get down to brass tacks**, you discuss the basic, most important facts of a situation. *Angola's ruling party was due to get down to brass tacks today with a debate on the party's record.* PHRASE: V inflects

brass band, brass bands. A **brass band** is a band that is made up of brass and percussion instruments. N-COUNT

brasserie /bræsəri, AM -riː/ **brasseries.** A **brasserie** is a small and usually cheap restaurant or bar. ◆◇◇◇◇ N-COUNT

brassica /bræsɪkə/ **brassicas. Brassicas** are vegetables, such as cabbages and turnips, which grow above or just under the soil and which carry their seeds in a seed case that has two sections. N-COUNT: oft N n

brassiere /bræziəʳ, AM brəzɪr/ **brassieres.** A **brassiere** is the same as a **bra**; an old-fashioned word. N-COUNT

brass rubbing, brass rubbings. A **brass rubbing** is a picture made by placing a piece of paper over a brass plate that has writing or a picture on it, and rubbing it with a wax crayon. N-COUNT

brassy /brɑːsi, bræsi/ **brassier, brassiest**

1 **Brassy** music is bold, harsh, and loud. *Musicians blast their brassy jazz from street corners.* ADJ-GRADED

2 If you describe a person's appearance or their behaviour as **brassy**, you think that they do not have good taste, and that they dress or behave in a way that is too bright, daring, harsh, or lively. *...Alec and his brassy blonde wife... Those ladies were brassy and busty, with pudgy fingers and painted eyes.* ADJ-GRADED

3 Something that is **brassy** has a yellow metallic colour and sometimes looks cheap and nasty. *A woman with big brassy ear-rings.* ADJ-GRADED

brat /bræt/ **brats.** If you call someone, especially a child, a **brat**, you mean that he or she behaves badly or annoys you; an informal word. *He's a spoilt brat.* ◆◇◇◇◇ N-COUNT

brat pack, brat packs. A **brat pack** is a group of young people, especially actors or writers, who are popular or successful at the moment; used in journalism. *...the Hollywood Brat Pack.* N-COUNT

bravado /brəvɑːdoʊ/. **Bravado** is an appearance of courage or confidence that someone shows in order to impress other people. *'You won't get away with this,' he said with unexpected bravado.* ◆◇◇◇◇ N-UNCOUNT

brave /breɪv/ **braver, bravest; braves, braving, braved** ◆◆◆◇◇

1 Someone who is **brave** is willing to do things which are dangerous, and does not show fear in difficult or dangerous situations. *He was not brave enough to report the loss of the documents. ...those brave people who dared to challenge the Stalinist regimes.* ADJ-GRADED =courageous ≠cowardly ♦ **bravely** *Our men wiped them out, but the enemy fought bravely and well... Mr Kim bravely stood up to authority.* ADV-GRADED: usu ADV with v, also ADV adj =courageously

2 If you **brave** unpleasant or dangerous conditions, you deliberately expose yourself to them, usually in order to achieve something; used in written English. *Thousands have braved icy rain to demonstrate their support.* VERB V n

3 A **brave** is a young man, especially a warrior, who belongs to a Native American ethic group; an old-fashioned use. N-COUNT

4 If you say that someone **is putting on a brave face** or that they **are putting a brave face on a** difficult situation, you mean they are pretending that they are happy when they are not, or that they can deal with the situation easily when they cannot. *He felt disappointed but he tried to put on a brave face... The White House tried to put a brave face on the job figures.* PHRASE: V inflects

brave new world. If someone refers to a **brave new world**, they are talking about a situation or system that has recently been created and that people think will be successful and fair. *He belonged to a generation that took it for granted that after the war a brave new world was to be ushered in.* N-SING: usu N of n

bravery /breɪvəri/. **Bravery** is brave behaviour or the quality of being brave. *He deserves the highest praise for his bravery.* ◆◇◇◇◇ N-UNCOUNT =courage ≠cowardice

bravo /brɑːvoʊ/. Some people say **'bravo'** to express appreciation when someone has done something well; an old-fashioned word. *'Bravo, Rena! You're right,' the students said.* EXCLAM =well done

bravura /brəvjʊərə, AM -vʊrə/

1 If you say that someone is doing something with **bravura**, you mean that they are using unnecessary extra actions that emphasize their skill or importance; a literary word. *He launched with operatic bravura into what he thought was a live transmission.* N-UNCOUNT

2 A **bravura** performance or piece of work is done with bravura; a literary use. *The scene was stolen by a bravura performance from Durham's scorer, Brian Hunt.* ADJ: usu ADJ n

brawl /brɔːl/ **brawls, brawling, brawled** ◆◇◇◇◇

1 A **brawl** is a rough or violent fight. *He had been in a drunken street brawl.* N-COUNT =punch-up

2 If someone **brawls**, they fight in a very rough or violent way. *He was suspended for a year from University after brawling with police over a speeding ticket... Gangs of neo-Nazis and anarchists brawled in two East German towns this weekend.* V-RECIP V with n pl-n V ♦ **brawling** *The brawling between the England fans and locals last night went on for several hours.* N-UNCOUNT

brawn /brɔːn/

1 **Brawn** is physical strength. *He's got plenty of brains as well as brawn.* N-UNCOUNT =muscle

2 In Britain, **brawn** is a kind of food made from pieces of pork and jelly pressed together so that it is solid and can be sliced. N-UNCOUNT

brawny /brɔːni/. Someone who is **brawny** is strong and muscular. *Oscar turned out to be a brawny young man.* ADJ =strapping

bray /breɪ/ **brays, braying, brayed**

1 When a donkey **brays**, it makes the loud harsh sound that donkeys typically make. *The donkey brayed and tried to bolt.* VERB V

2 If someone **brays**, they make a loud harsh sound or talk in a loud harsh way; used in written English. *Neil brayed with angry laughter... Her voice was shockingly loud. 'Put the chair down,' she brayed... William had a loud, braying voice.* VERB V prep V with quote V-ing ► Also a noun. *She cut him off with a wild bray of laughter.* N-COUNT

brazen /breɪzᵊn/ **brazens, brazening, brazened.** If you describe a person or their behaviour as **brazen**, you mean that they are very bold and do not care what other people think about them or their behaviour. *They're quite brazen about their bisexuality, it doesn't worry them.* ◆◇◇◇◇ ADJ-GRADED =bare-faced ♦ **brazenly** *He was brazenly running a $400,000-a-month drug operation from the prison.* ADV-GRADED: usu ADV with v

brazen out. If you have done something wrong and you **brazen** it **out**, you behave confidently in order not to appear ashamed, even though you probably do feel ashamed. *If you are caught simply argue that 'everyone does it' and brazen it out... Mr Mellor is as determined as ever to brazen out the scandals which threaten to engulf him... Stung by recent publicity, the Home Office now seems to be trying to brazen this issue out.* PHRASAL VERB V it P V P n (not pron) V n P

brazier /breɪziəʳ, AM -ʒər/ **braziers.** A **brazier** is a large metal container in which coal or charcoal is burned to keep people warm when they are outside in cold weather, for example because of their work. N-COUNT

Brazilian /brəzɪliən/ **Brazilians.** ◆◆◆◆◇

1 **Brazilian** means belonging or relating to Brazil, or to its people or culture. *...the beauty of the Brazilian rain forest.* ADJ

2 A **Brazilian** is a person who comes from Brazil. N-COUNT

breach /briːtʃ/ **breaches, breaching, breached** ◆◆◇◇◇

1 If you **breach** an agreement, a law, or a promise, you break it. *The newspaper breached the code of conduct on privacy... The film breached the criminal libel laws.* VERB =violate V n

2 A **breach** of an agreement, a law, or a promise is an act of breaking it. *The Latvian Parliament's declaration of independence is a breach of the Soviet constitution. ...a $1 billion breach of contract suit.* N-VAR =violation

3 A **breach** in a relationship is a serious disagreement which often results in the relationship ending; a formal use. *Their actions threatened a serious breach in relations between the two countries. ...the breach between Tito and Stalin.* N-COUNT: usu N in/between n =rift, rupture

4 If someone or something **breaches** a barrier, they make an opening in it, usually leaving it weakened VERB =rupture

or destroyed; a formal use. *The limestone is sufficiently fissured for tree roots to have breached the roof of the cave... Fire may have breached the cargo tanks and set the oil ablaze.* [V n]

5 If you **breach** someone's security or their defenses, you manage to get through and attack an area that is heavily guarded and protected. *The bomber had breached security by hurling his dynamite from a roof overlooking the building.* [VERB =violate; V n] ► Also a noun. *...widespread breaches of security at Ministry of Defence bases.* [N-COUNT]

6 If you **step into the breach**, you do a job or task which someone else was supposed to do or has done in the past, because they are suddenly unable to do it. *I was persuaded to step into the breach temporarily when they became too ill to continue.* [PHRASE: V inflects]

breach of the peace, breaches of the peace. A **breach of the peace** is noisy or violent behaviour in a public place which is illegal because it disturbs other people; a legal term. *He admitted causing a breach of the peace... Four men were found guilty of breach of the peace.* [N-VAR]

bread /bred/ **breads, breading, breaded** ◆◆◆◇◇

1 Bread is a very common food made from flour, water, and yeast. These ingredients are mixed into a soft dough and baked in an oven. *...a loaf of bread. ...bread and butter... There is more fibre in wholemeal bread than in white bread.* • to **know what side** your **bread is buttered on**: see **butter**. [N-MASS]

2 If you earn your **bread** doing a particular job or activity, you earn your money doing it; an informal use. *There's not a living soul in Colorado who doesn't depend for his bread on silver.* [N-UNCOUNT: usu with poss]

3 If food such as fish or meat is **breaded**, it is covered in breadcrumbs. It can then be fried or grilled. *It is important that food be breaded just minutes before frying.* [VB: usu passive; be V-ed] ► Also an adjective. *...breaded fish.* [ADJ]

bread and butter; also spelled **bread-and-butter**. ◆◇◇◇◇

1 Something that is the **bread and butter** of a person or organization is the activity or work that provides the main part of their income. *The mobile phone business was actually his bread and butter.* [N-UNCOUNT: usu with poss]

2 Bread and butter issues or matters are ones which are important to most people, because they affect them personally. *The opposition gained support by concentrating on bread-and-butter matters.* [ADJ: ADJ n]

bread basket, bread baskets; also spelled **breadbasket**. If an area or region is described as the **bread basket** of a country, it provides a lot of the food for that country because crops grow very easily there. It therefore produces wealth for the country. *The Ukraine is the bread-basket of the Soviet Union.* [N-COUNT: usu with poss]

bread bin, bread bins. In British English, a **bread bin** is a wooden, metal, or plastic container for storing bread. [N-COUNT]

breadboard /bredbɔːʳd/ **breadboards;** also spelled **bread board.** A **breadboard** is a flat piece of wood used for cutting bread on. [N-COUNT]

breadbox /bredbɒks/ **breadboxes;** also spelled **bread box**. In American English, a **breadbox** is a wooden, metal, or plastic container for storing bread. [N-COUNT]

breadcrumb /bredkrʌm/ **breadcrumbs.** ◆◇◇◇◇ **Breadcrumbs** are tiny pieces of dry bread. They are used in cooking. [N-COUNT: usu pl]

breadfruit /bredfruːt/; **breadfruit** is both the singular and the plural form. **Breadfruit** are large round fruit that grow on trees in the Pacific Islands and in tropical parts of America and that, when baked, look and feel like bread. The plural is either 'breadfruit' or 'breadfruits'. [N-VAR]

breadline /bredlaɪn/. Someone who is on or close to the **breadline** is very poor indeed. *We lived on the breadline to get our son through college... They're not exactly on the breadline.* [N-SING: usu on the N]

breadth /bretθ, AM bredθ/ ◆◇◇◇◇

1 The **breadth** of something is the distance between its two sides. *The breadth of the whole camp was 400 paces.* [N-UNCOUNT: oft N of n =width]

2 The **breadth** of something is its quality of consisting of or involving many different things. *Older people have a tremendous breadth of experience... His breadth of knowledge filled me with admiration.* [N-UNCOUNT: oft N of n =range]

3 If you say that someone does something or something happens throughout or across **the length and breadth of** a place, you are emphasizing that it happens everywhere in that place. *The group built their reputation by playing across the length and breadth of North America... She has travelled the length and breadth of Britain.* • See also **hair's breadth.** [PHRASE: PHR n]

breadwinner /bredwɪnəʳ/ **breadwinners;** also spelled **bread-winner**. The **breadwinner** in a family is the person in it who earns the money that the family needs for essential things. *I've always paid the bills and been the breadwinner.* [N-COUNT]

break /breɪk/ **breaks, breaking, broke, broken** ◆◆◆◆◆

1 When an object **breaks** or when you **break** it, it suddenly separates into two or more pieces, often because it has been hit or dropped. *He fell through the window, breaking the glass... The plate broke... Break the cauliflower into florets... The plane broke into three pieces. ...bombed-out buildings, surrounded by broken glass and rubble... The only sound was the crackle of breaking ice.* [V-ERG; V n; V; V n into pl-n; V into pl-n; V-ed; V-ing]

2 If you **break** a part of your body such as your leg, your arm, or your nose, or if a bone **breaks**, you are injured because a bone cracks or splits. *She broke a leg in a skiing accident... Old bones break easily... Several people were treated for broken bones.* [V-ERG; V n; V; V-ed] ► Also a noun. *It has caused a bad break to Gabriella's leg.* [N-COUNT]

3 If a surface, cover, or seal **breaks** or if something **breaks** it, a hole or tear is made in it, so that a substance can pass through. *Once you've broken the seal of a bottle there's no way you can put it back together again... The bandage must be put on when the blister breaks... Do not use the cream on broken skin.* [V-ERG; V n; V; V-ed]

4 When a tool or piece of machinery **breaks** or when you **break** it, it is damaged and no longer works. *When the clutch broke, the car was locked into second gear... Tenants do not have to worry about leaking roofs and broken washing machines.* [V-ERG; V; V-ed; Also V n]

5 If you **break** a rule, promise, or agreement, you do something that you should not do according to that rule, promise, or agreement. *We didn't know we were breaking the law... The company has consistently denied it had knowingly broken arms embargoes. ...broken promises.* [VERB; V n; V-ed]

6 If you **break** free or loose, you free yourself from something or escape from it. *She broke free by thrusting her elbow into his chest. ...his inability to break free of his marriage.* [VERB; V adj]

7 If someone **breaks** something, especially a difficult or unpleasant situation that has existed for some time, they end it or change it. *The Home Secretary aims to break the vicious circle between disadvantage and crime... New proposals have been put forward to break the deadlock among rival factions... The country is heading towards elections which may break the party's long hold on power.* [VERB; V n] ► Also a noun. *Nothing that might lead to a break in the deadlock has been discussed yet.* [N-COUNT: usu sing]

8 If someone **breaks** a silence, they say something or make a noise after a long period of silence, or they talk about something that they have not talked about for a long time. You can also say that a noise **breaks** a silence. *Gary decided to break his silence about his son's suffering yesterday in the hope of helping other families cope with the disease... The unearthly silence was broken by a shrill screaming.* [VERB; V n]

9 If there is a **break** in the cloud or weather, it changes and there is a short period of sunshine or fine weather. *A sudden break in the cloud allowed rescuers to spot Michael Benson.* [N-COUNT]

10 If you **break** with a group of people or a traditional way of doing things, or you **break** your connection with them, you stop being involved with that group or stop doing things in that way. *He was* [VERB; V with n]

once a close adviser to Walesa but broke with him last year... They were determined to break from precedent... Poland and Czechoslovakia were beginning to break their links with communist ideology. ► Also a noun. *Mr Rocard spoke of the need for a break with the past.*
V *from* n / V n *with* n / Also V n / N-COUNT: usu sing

11 If you **break** a habit or if someone **breaks** you of it, you no longer have that habit. *If you continue to smoke, keep trying to break the habit... The professor hoped to break the students of the habit of looking for easy answers.*
VERB / V n / V n *of* n

12 To **break** someone means to destroy their determination and courage, their success, or their career. *He never let his jailers break him... The newspapers and television can make or break you... Ken's wife, Vicki, said: 'He's a broken man.'*
VERB / =destroy / V n / V-ed

13 If someone **breaks** for a short period of time, they rest or change from what they are doing for a short period. *They broke for lunch.*
VERB / V

14 A **break** is a short period of time when you have a rest or a change from what you are doing, especially if you are working or if you are in a boring or unpleasant situation. *They may be able to help with childcare so that you can have a break... I thought a 15 min break from his work would do him good... She rang Moira during a coffee break.* • See also **lunch break, tea break**.
N-COUNT: oft N *from/in* n

15 A **break** is a short holiday. *They are currently taking a short break in Spain.*
N-COUNT

16 To **break** the force of something such as a blow or fall means to weaken its effect, for example by getting in the way of it. *He sustained serious neck injuries after he broke someone's fall.*
VERB / V n

17 When a piece of news **breaks**, people hear about it from the newspapers, television, or radio. *The news broke that the Prime Minister had resigned... He resigned from his post as Bishop when the scandal broke.*
VERB / V

18 When you **break** a piece of bad news to someone, you tell it to them as kindly as you can. *Then Louise broke the news that she was leaving me... I worried for ages and decided that I had better break it to her.*
VERB / V n / V n *to* n

19 A **break** is also a lucky opportunity that someone gets to achieve something; an informal use. *He went into TV and got his first break playing opposite Sid James in the series Citizen James.*
N-COUNT

20 If you **break** a record, you beat the previous record for a particular achievement. *Carl Lewis has broken the world record in the 100 metres... Jurassic Park has broken all box office records.* • See also **record-breaking**.
VERB / V n

21 When day or dawn **breaks**, it starts to grow light after the night has ended. *They continued the search as dawn broke.* • See also **daybreak**.
VERB / V

22 When a wave **breaks**, it passes its highest point and turns downwards, for example when it reaches the shore. *Danny listened to the waves breaking against the shore.*
VERB / V

23 If you **break** a secret code, you work out how to understand it. *It was feared they could break the Allies' codes.*
VERB / =crack / V n

24 If someone's voice **breaks** when they are speaking, it changes its sound or becomes hesitant, for example because they are sad or afraid. *Godfrey's voice broke, and halted.*
VERB / V

25 When a boy's voice **breaks**, usually when he is about fourteen, it becomes deeper and sounds more like a man's voice. *He sings with the strained discomfort of someone whose voice hasn't quite broken.*
VERB / V

26 If the weather **breaks** or a storm **breaks**, it suddenly becomes rainy or stormy after a period of sunshine. *I've been waiting for the weather to break... She hoped she'd be able to reach the hotel before the storm broke.*
VERB / V

27 In tennis, if you **break** your opponent's serve, you win a game in which your opponent is serving. *He broke Mcenroe's serve.* ► Also a noun. *A single break of serve settled the first two sets.*
VERB / V n / N-COUNT

28 See also **broke, broken; heartbreak, heartbreaking, heartbroken, outbreak**.

29 **The break of day** or **the break of dawn** is the time when it begins to grow light after the night; a literary expression. *'I,' he finished poetically, 'will watch over you to the break of day.'*
PHRASES / prep PHR

30 You can say **'give me a break'** to show that you are annoyed by what someone has said or done; an informal expression. *'I'm a real intellectual-type guy, Tracy.' James joked. 'Oh, give me a break,' Tracy moaned.*
CONVENTION / PRAGMATICS

31 If you **make a break** or **make a break for it**, you run to escape from something. *The moment had come to make a break or die... Dan made a break for his car only to find the driver's door locked.*
V inflects / =make a run for

32 • to **break the bank**: see **bank**. • to **break cover**: see **cover**. • to **break even**: see **even**. • to **break new ground**: see **ground**. • to **break someone's heart**: see **heart**. • **all hell breaks loose**: see **hell**. • to **break the ice**: see **ice**. • to **break ranks**: see **rank**. • to **break wind**: see **wind**.

break away
PHRASAL VERB

1 If you **break away** from someone who is trying to hold you or catch you, you free yourself and run away. *I broke away from him and rushed out into the hall... Willie Hamilton broke away early in the race.*
=cut loose / V P *from* n / V P

2 If you **break away** from something or someone that restricts you or controls you, you succeed in freeing yourself from them. *Aboriginal art has finally gained recognition and broken away from being labelled as 'primitive' or 'exotic'... Talabani was once a member of the KDP, but broke away in the 1970s to form his own party.*
V P *from* n/-ing / V P

break down
PHRASAL VERB

1 If a machine or a vehicle **breaks down**, it stops working. *Their car broke down.*
V P

2 If a discussion, relationship, or system **breaks down**, it fails because of a problem or disagreement. *Talks with business leaders broke down last night... Paola's marriage broke down.*
V P

3 To **break down** something such as an idea or statement means to separate it into smaller parts in order to make it easier to understand or deal with. *The report breaks down the results region by region... These rules tell us how a sentence is broken down into phrases.*
V P n (not pron) / *be* V-ed P *into* n / Also V n P *into* n

4 When a substance **breaks down** or when something **breaks** it **down**, a biological or chemical process causes it to separate into the substances which make it up. *Over time, the protein in the eggshell breaks down into its constituent amino acids... The oil is attacked by naturally occurring microbes which break it down.*
ERG / V P / V n P / Also V P n (not pron)

5 If someone **breaks down**, they lose control of themselves and start crying. *Because he was being so kind and concerned, I broke down and cried... The young woman broke down in tears.*
V P

6 If you **break down** a door or barrier, you hit it so hard that it falls to the ground. *An unruly mob broke down police barricades and stormed the courtroom... Firemen were called after his father failed to break the door down.*
V P n (not pron) / V n P

7 To **break down** barriers or prejudices that separate people or restrict their freedom means to change people's attitudes so that the barriers or prejudices no longer exist; used showing approval. *His early experience enabled him to break down barriers between Scottish Catholics and Protestants.*
PRAGMATICS / V P n (not pron) / Also V n P

8 See also **breakdown, broken-down**.

break in
PHRASAL VERB

1 If someone, usually a thief, **breaks in**, they get into a building by force. *Masked robbers broke in and made off with $8,000... The thief had broken in through a first-floor window.* • See also **break-in**.
V P

2 If you **break in** on someone's conversation or activity, you interrupt them. *O'Leary broke in on his thoughts... Mrs Southern listened keenly, occasionally breaking in with pertinent questions... 'She told you to stay here,' Mike broke in.*
V P *on* n / V P / V P with quote

3 If you **break** someone **in**, you get them used to a new job or situation. *The band are breaking in a new backing vocalist.*
V P n (not pron) / Also V n P

4 If you **break in** something new, you gradually use or wear it for longer and longer periods until it is ready to be used or worn all the time. *When breaking in an engine, you probably should refrain from high speed for the first thousand miles... Nathan's new running shoes weren't broken in correctly.* V P n (not pron) Also V n P

break into
PHRASAL VERB

1 If someone **breaks into** a building, they get into it by force. *There was no one nearby who might see him trying to break into the house... In this country a house is broken into every 24 seconds.* V P n

2 If someone **breaks into** something they suddenly start doing it. For example if someone **breaks into** a run they suddenly start running, and if they **break into** song they suddenly start singing. *The moment she was out of sight she broke into a run... Then, breaking into a smile, he said, 'I brought you something.'* V P n

3 If you **break into** a profession or area of business, especially one that is difficult to succeed in, you manage to have some success in it. *She finally broke into films after an acclaimed stage career.* V P n

break off
PHRASAL VERB

1 If part of something **breaks off** or if you **break** it **off**, it comes off or is removed by force. *The two wings of the aircraft broke off on impact... Grace broke off a large piece of the clay... They've torn down wooden fences and broken branches off trees.* ERG V P; V P n (not pron); V n P n; Also V n P

2 If you **break off** when you are doing or saying something, you suddenly stop doing it or saying it. *Llewelyn broke off in mid-sentence... The commander of the German task force radioed that he was breaking off the action.* V P; V P n (not pron); Also V n P

3 If someone **breaks off** a relationship, they end it. *The two West African states had broken off relations two years ago... He doesn't seem to have the courage to break it off with her.* RECIP pl-n V P n (not pron); V *it* P *with* n (non-recip)

break out
PHRASAL VERB

1 If something such as war, fighting, or disease **breaks out**, it begins suddenly. *He was 29 when war broke out... I was in a nightclub in Brixton and a fight broke out.* V P

2 If a prisoner **breaks out** of a prison, they escape from it. *The two men broke out of their cells and cut through a perimeter fence.* • See also **breakout**. V P *of* n; Also V P

3 If you **break out** of a dull situation or routine, you manage to change it or escape from it. *It's taken a long time to break out of my own conventional training... If her marriage becomes too restrictive, she will break out and seek new horizons.* V P *of* n; V P

4 If you **break out** in a rash or a sweat or if it **breaks out** on your body, it appears on your skin. *A person who is allergic to cashews may break out in a rash when he consumes these nuts... A line of sweat broke out on her forehead and she thought she might faint.* V P *in* n; V P

break through
PHRASAL VERB

1 If you **break through** a barrier, you succeed in forcing your way through it. *Protesters tried to break through a police cordon... About fifteen inmates broke through onto the roof.* V P n; V P

2 If you **break through**, you achieve success despite difficulties and obstacles. *There is still scope for new writers to break through... I broke through the poverty barrier and it was education that did it.* V P; V P n

3 When something that was previously hidden or unseen **breaks through**, it appears. *Despite everything, Elizabeth's human side keeps breaking through... Sunlight had broken through the clouds.* V P; V P n

4 See also **breakthrough**.

break up
PHRASAL VERB

1 When something **breaks up** or when you **break** it **up**, it separates or is divided into several smaller parts. *Civil war could come if the country breaks up... There was a danger of the ship breaking up completely... Break up the chocolate and melt it... He broke the bread up into chunks and gave Meer a big one... Tanks are strongly built. It is a complicated and difficult process to break them up.* ERG V P; V P n (not pron); V n P *into* n; V n P

2 If you **break up** with your boyfriend, girlfriend, husband, or wife, your relationship with that person ends. *My girlfriend had broken up with me... He felt appalled by the whole idea of marriage so we broke up.* RECIP =split up; V P *with* n; pl-n V P

3 If a marriage **breaks up** or if someone **breaks** it **up**, the marriage ends and the partners separate. *MPs say they work too hard and that is why so many of their marriages break up... Fred has given me no good reason for wanting to break up our marriage.* ERG V P; V P n (not pron)

4 When a meeting or gathering **breaks up** or when someone **breaks** it **up**, it is brought to an end and the people involved in it leave. *A neighbour asked for the music to be turned down and the party broke up... Police used tear gas to break up a demonstration... He charged into the crowd. 'Break it up,' he shouted.* ERG =disperse; V P; V P n (not pron); V n P

5 When a school or the pupils in it **break up**, the school term ends and the pupils start their holidays; used mainly in British English. *It's the last week before they break up, and they're doing all kinds of Christmas things.* V P

6 See also **break-up**.

breakable /breɪkəbᵊl/ breakables.
Breakable objects are easy to break by accident. *My parents had a remarkable array of breakable objects.* ADJ-GRADED: usu ADJ n

▸ **Breakables** are breakable objects. *Keep any breakables out of reach of very young children.* N-PLURAL

breakage /breɪkɪdʒ/ breakages

1 **Breakage** is the act of breaking something. *Brushing wet hair can cause stretching and breakage... Check that your insurance policy covers breakages and damage during removals.* N-VAR

2 A **breakage** is something that has been broken. *Check that everything is in good repair before moving in, as you have to replace breakages.* N-COUNT: usu pl

breakaway /breɪkəweɪ/.
◆◇◇◇◇ A **breakaway** group is a group of people who have separated from a larger group, for example because of a disagreement. *Sixteen members of Parliament have formed a breakaway group.* ADJ: ADJ n =splinter group

breakdown /breɪkdaʊn/ breakdowns
◆◆◇◇◇

1 The **breakdown** of something such as a relationship, plan, or discussion is its failure or ending. *...the breakdown of trade talks between the US and EC officials. ...the irretrievable breakdown of a marriage... He argues that the breakdown in the legal system has spawned a black market.* N-COUNT: usu sing, oft N *of/in* n =collapse

2 If you have a **breakdown**, you become very depressed, so that you are unable to cope with your life. *My personal life was terrible. My mother had died, and a couple of years later I had a breakdown... They often seem depressed and close to emotional breakdown.* • See also **nervous breakdown**. N-COUNT: usu sing, oft adj N

3 If a car or a piece of machinery has a **breakdown**, it stops working. *Her old car was unreliable, so the trip was plagued by breakdowns... If you stop on the hard shoulder, wait for the police or breakdown service.* N-COUNT

4 A **breakdown** of something is a list of its separate parts. *The organisers were given a breakdown of the costs.* N-COUNT: usu N *of* n =analysis

breaker /breɪkəʳ/ breakers.
◆◇◇◇◇ **Breakers** are big sea waves especially at the point when they just reach the shore. • See also **ice-breaker**, **lawbreaker**, **record-breaker**, **strike-breaker**. N-COUNT

breakfast /brekfəst/ breakfasts, breakfasting, breakfasted
◆◆◆◇◇

1 **Breakfast** is the first meal of the day. It is usually eaten in the early part of the morning. *What's for breakfast?. ...breakfast cereal.* • See also **bed and breakfast**, **continental breakfast**, **English breakfast**. N-VAR

2 A cooked **breakfast** or a hot **breakfast** is a breakfast that consists of cooked food, such as bacon and eggs. N-COUNT: adj N ≠continental

3 When you **breakfast**, you have breakfast; a formal use. *All the ladies breakfasted in their rooms.* VERB V adv/prep

breakfast table, breakfast tables.
You refer to a table as **the breakfast table** when it is being used for breakfast. *...reading the morning papers at the breakfast table.* N-COUNT: usu sing, *the* N

breakfast television.
Breakfast television refers to television programmes which are broad- N-UNCOUNT

cast in the morning at the time when most people are having breakfast.

breakfast time; also spelled **breakfast-time.** N-UNCOUNT: oft prep N **Breakfast time** is the period of the morning when most people have their breakfast. *By breakfast-time he was already at his desk.*

break-in, break-ins. ◆◇◇◇◇ N-COUNT =burglary If there has been a **break-in**, someone has got into a building by force. *The break-in had occurred just before midnight.*

breaking point. N-UNCOUNT: also the/a N If something or someone has reached **breaking point**, they have so many problems or difficulties that they can no longer cope with them, and may soon collapse or be unable to continue. *The report on the riot exposed a prison system stretched to breaking point... Families round here are at breaking point. They have been on half wages since October... The breaking point came when he had to sack his deputy Prime Minister.*

breakneck /breɪknek/. ADJ: ADJ n If you say that something happens or travels at **breakneck** speed, you mean that it happens or travels very fast. *Jack drove to Mayfair at breakneck speed.*

breakout /breɪkaʊt/ **breakouts;** N-COUNT =escape also spelled **break-out.** If there has been a **break-out**, someone has escaped from prison. *A prisoner escaped one day after he was recaptured following a previous break-out... High Point prison had the highest number of breakouts of any jail in Britain.*

breakthrough /breɪkθruː/ **breakthroughs.** ◆◆◇◇◇ N-COUNT: oft N in n A **breakthrough** is an important development or achievement. *The company looks poised to make a significant breakthrough in China... The breakthrough came hours before a UN deadline.*

break-up, break-ups ◆◆◇◇◇

1 The **break-up** of a marriage, relationship, or association is the act of it finishing or coming to an end because the people involved decide that it is not working successfully. N-COUNT: usu N of n, n N =collapse *Since the break-up of his marriage he had not formed any new relationships. ...the acrimonious break-up of the meeting's first session. ...a marital break-up.*

2 The **break-up** of an organization or a country is the act of it separating or dividing into several parts. N-COUNT: usu N of n *...the break-up of British Rail for privatisation... At no time did a majority of Czechoslavakia's citizens support the country's break-up.*

breakwater /breɪkwɔːtəʳ/ **breakwaters.** N-COUNT A **breakwater** is a wooden or stone wall that extends from the shore into the sea and is built in order to protect a harbour or beach from the force of the waves.

breast /brest/ **breasts** ◆◆◆◇◇

1 A woman's **breasts** are the two soft, round pieces of flesh on her chest that can produce milk to feed a baby. N-COUNT: oft poss N *She wears a low-cut dress which reveal her breasts... As my newborn cuddled at my breast, her tiny fingers stroked my skin.* ♦ **-breasted** COMB in ADJ *She was slim and muscular and full-breasted.*

2 A person's **breast** is the upper part of his or her chest; a literary use. N-COUNT: poss N *He struck his breast, asking blessed Mary ever Virgin to pray for him.*

3 The **breast** is often considered to be the part of your body where your emotions are; a literary use. N-COUNT: usu with poss =heart *The verse rose up to fire his breast with inspiration... The battle roared; a sound calculated to arouse the sublimest emotions in the breast of the soldier.*

4 A bird's **breast** is the front part of its body. N-COUNT =chest *The cock's breast is tinged with chestnut and narrowly barred with white.* ♦ **-breasted** COMB in ADJ *...flocks of red-breasted parrots.*

5 **The breast** of a shirt, jacket, or coat is the part which covers the top part of the chest. N-SING: the N *He moved out from beneath an awning, reaching for something inside the breast of his overcoat... He reached into his breast pocket for his cigar case.*

6 A piece of **breast** is a piece of meat that is cut from the front of a bird or lamb. N-VAR *...a chicken breast with vegetables. ...breast of lamb.*

7 see also **double-breasted, single-breasted.**

8 If you say that someone **beats** their **breast**, you are emphasizing that they are very angry or upset about something, or that they are pretending to be very angry or upset about it. PHRASES V inflects PRAGMATICS *The president beat his breast and called that deal a mistake.*

9 If you **make a clean breast of it** or **make a clean breast of** something, you tell someone the truth about yourself or about something wrong that you have done. V inflects =own up *I might as well make a clean breast of it. I have been living as a woman since 1975.*

breastbone /brestboun/ **breastbones;** also spelled **breast bone.** N-COUNT =sternum Your **breastbone** is the long, flat bone which goes from your throat to the bottom of your ribs and to which your ribs are attached.

breast-feed, breast-feeds, breast-feeding, breast-fed; ◆◇◇◇◇ VERB =suckle also spelled **breastfeed** or **breast feed.** When a woman **breast-feeds** her baby, she feeds it with milk from her breasts, rather than from a bottle. V n V-ed Also V *Not all women have the choice whether or not to breast feed their babies... Leading scientists claim breast-fed babies are intellectually brighter.* ♦ **breast-feeding** N-UNCOUNT *There are many advantages to breast feeding.*

breast milk; also spelled **breast-milk.** N-UNCOUNT **Breast milk** is the white liquid produced by women to breast-feed their babies.

breastplate /brestpleɪt/ **breastplates.** N-COUNT A **breastplate** is a piece of armour that covers and protects the chest.

breast pocket, breast pockets. N-COUNT: with poss The **breast pocket** of a man's coat or jacket is a pocket, usually on the inside, next to his chest. *I kept the list in my breast pocket.*

breaststroke /brestrouk/. N-UNCOUNT: also the N **Breaststroke** is a swimming stroke which you do lying on your front, moving your arms and legs horizontally in a circular motion.

breath /breθ/ **breaths** ◆◆◆◇◇

1 Your **breath** is the air that you let out through your mouth when you breathe. If someone has bad **breath** their breath smells unpleasant. N-VAR: oft poss N *I could smell the whisky on his breath... Smoking causes bad breath.*

2 When you take a **breath**, you breathe in once. N-VAR *He took a deep breath, and began to climb the stairs... Gasping for breath, she leaned against the door... He spoke for one and a half hours and barely paused for breath.*

3 If you say that there is not a **breath** of wind or air, you are emphasizing that there is no wind and the air is very still; used in written English. N-SING: usu with brd-neg, usu N of n PRAGMATICS *Not even a breath of wind stirred the pine branches.*

4 A **breath of** something, is a small amount of it; used in written English. N-SING: N of n *It was left to Martina to add a breath of common sense to the proceedings.*

5 If you go outside **for a breath of fresh air** or **for a breath of air**, you go outside because it is stuffy indoors. PHRASES breath inflects

6 If you describe something new or different as **a breath of fresh air**, you mean that it makes a situation or subject more interesting or exciting; used showing approval. usu v-link PHR PRAGMATICS *Her brisk treatment of an almost taboo subject was a breath of fresh air.*

7 In British English, when you **get** your **breath back** after doing something energetic, you start breathing normally again. V inflects =recover *I reached out a hand to steady myself against the house while I got my breath back.*

8 When you **catch** your **breath** while you are doing something energetic, you stop for a short time so that you can start breathing normally again. V and N inflect =recover *He had stopped to catch his breath and make sure of his directions.*

9 If something makes you **catch** your **breath**, it makes you take a short breath of air, usually because it shocks you. V inflects =gasp *Kenny caught his breath as Nikko nearly dropped the bottle.*

10 If you do not have time to **draw breath**, you do not have time to have a break from what you are doing. V inflects, usu with brd-neg

11 If you **hold** your **breath**, you make yourself stop breathing for a few moments, for example because V and N inflect

you are under water. *I held my breath and sank under the water.*

12 If you say that someone **is holding** their **breath**, you mean that they are waiting anxiously or excitedly for something to happen; used in written English. *The whole world holds its breath for this speech.* V and N inflect, oft PHR *for* n

13 If you say that you **won't hold** your **breath**, you mean that you do not expect something to happen even though someone has suggested that it might; an informal expression. *'Next thing you know, I'll be dancing at your wedding,' he cried. 'Don't hold your breath,' my father replied.* V and N inflect

14 When someone takes their **last breath**, they die; a literary expression. *His wife sat with him until he drew his last breath.* usu poss PHR

15 If you are **out of breath**, you are breathing very quickly and with difficulty because you have been doing something energetic. *There she was, slightly out of breath from running.* v-link PHR

16 You can use **in the same breath** or **in the next breath** to indicate that someone says two very different or contradictory things, especially when you are criticizing them. *He hailed this week's arms agreement but in the same breath expressed suspicion about the motivations of the United States.* PHR cl PRAGMATICS

17 If you are **short of breath**, you find it difficult to breathe properly, for example because you are ill. You can also say that someone suffers from **shortness of breath**. *She felt short of breath and flushed... Any exercise that causes undue shortness of breath should be stopped.* usu v-link PHR

18 If you say that something **takes** your **breath away**, you are emphasizing that it is extremely beautiful or surprising. *I heard this song on the radio and it just took my breath away.* V inflects PRAGMATICS =astound

19 If you say something **under** your **breath**, you say it in a very quiet voice, often because you do not want other people to hear what you are saying. *Walsh muttered something under his breath.* PHR after v

20 If someone says you are **wasting** your **breath**, they mean that the person you are talking to will not take any notice and so there is no point saying anything to them. *The tone of her voice told him he was wasting his breath.* V inflects

21 • **with bated breath**: see **bated**. • to **fight for breath**: see **fight**.

breathable /briːðəbᵊl/. A **breathable** fabric allows air to pass through it easily, so that clothing made from it does not become too warm or uncomfortable. ADJ

breathalyze /bre̲θəlaɪz/ **breathalyzes, breathalyzing, breathalyzed;** also spelled **breathalyse**. If the driver of a car **is breathalyzed** by the police, they ask him or her to breathe into a special bag or device in order to test whether he or she has drunk too much alcohol; used mainly in British English. *She was breathalysed and found to be over the limit.* VB: usu passive; *be* V-ed

breathalyzer /bre̲θəlaɪzəʳ/ **breathalyzers;** also spelled **breathalyser**. A **breathalyzer** is a bag or electronic device that the police use to test whether a driver has drunk too much alcohol. N-COUNT

breathe /briːð/ **breathes, breathing, breathed** ◆◆◆◇◇

1 When people or animals **breathe**, they take air into their lungs and let it out again. When they **breathe** smoke or a particular kind of air, they take it into their lungs and let it out again as they breathe. *He stood there breathing deeply and evenly... Always breathe through your nose... No American should have to drive out of town to breathe clean air... A thirteen year old girl is being treated after breathing in smoke.* ♦ **breathing** *Her breathing became slow and heavy... He heard only deep breathing.* VERB =respire; V; V n; V n with *in/out*; N-UNCOUNT: usu with supp

2 If someone **breathes** something, they say it very quietly; a literary use. *'You don't understand,' he breathed.* VERB; V with quote; Also V n

3 If you do not **breathe** a word about something, you say nothing about it, because it is a secret. *He never breathed a word about our conversation.* VB: with brd-neg, no cont; V n

4 If someone **breathes** life, confidence, or excitement **into** something, they improve it by adding this quality; used in written English. *It is the readers who breathe life into a newspaper with their letters.* VERB =instil; V n *into* n

5 If you let wine **breathe**, you open the bottle to allow the air to get in and improve its flavour before you drink it. *Red wines should be allowed to 'breathe' if possible before drinking.* VERB; V

6 When someone **breathes** their **last**, they die; a literary expression. PHRASE: V inflects

7 • to **be breathing down someone's neck**: see **neck**. • to breathe **a sigh of relief**: see **sigh**.

breathe in. When you **breathe in**, you take some air into your lungs. *She breathed in deeply.* PHRASAL VERB; V P

breathe out. When you **breathe out**, you send air out of your lungs through your nose or mouth. *Breathe out and ease your knees in toward your chest.* PHRASAL VERB; V P

breather /briːðəʳ/ **breathers.** If you take a **breather**, you stop what you are doing for a short time and have a rest; an informal word. *Relax and take a breather whenever you feel that you need one.* N-COUNT: usu sing

breathing space, breathing spaces. A **breathing space** is a short period of time between two activities in which you can recover from the first activity and prepare for the second one. *Firms need a breathing space if they are to recover... We hope that it will give us some breathing space.* ◆◇◇◇◇ N-VAR =respite

breathless /bre̲θləs/ ◆◇◇◇◇

1 If you are **breathless**, you have difficulty in breathing properly, for example because you have been running or because you are afraid or excited. *I was a little breathless and my heartbeat was bumpy and fast... We were breathless with anticipation.* ♦ **breathlessly** *'I'll go in,' he said breathlessly.* ♦ **breathlessness** *Asthma causes wheezing and breathlessness.* ADJ-GRADED: usu v-link ADJ; ADV-GRADED: usu ADV with v, also ADV adj; N-UNCOUNT

2 You use **breathless** for emphasis when you are describing feelings of excitement or exciting situations. *Technology has advanced at a breathless pace. ...the breathless excitement of early 1988, when hundreds and thousands of citizens gathered nightly for political meetings.* ♦ **breathlessly** *Nancy waited breathlessly for him to go on.* ADJ: ADJ n PRAGMATICS; ADV: usu ADV with v

breathtaking /bre̲θteɪkɪŋ/; also spelled **breath-taking**. If you say that something is **breathtaking**, you are emphasizing that it is extremely beautiful or amazing. *The house has breathtaking views from every room... Some of their football was breathtaking, a delight to watch... He nevertheless completed the film with breathtaking speed.* ♦ **breathtakingly** *...the most breathtakingly beautiful scenery in Germany. ...a breathtakingly simple gadget from Finland.* ◆◇◇◇◇ ADJ-GRADED PRAGMATICS; ADV-GRADED: usu ADV adj, also ADV after v

breath test, breath tests. A **breath test** is a test carried out by police in which a motorist blows into a piece of equipment to show how much alcohol he or she has drunk. *We do need to do more than simply conduct random breath tests.* N-COUNT

breathy /bre̲θi/. If someone has a **breathy** voice, you can hear their breath when they speak or sing. *Her voice was suddenly breathy.* ADJ

bred /bre̲d/

1 **Bred** is the past tense and past participle of **breed**.

2 See also **ill-bred**, **pure-bred**, **well-bred**.

breech /briːtʃ/ **breeches** /briːtʃɪz/. The **breech** of a gun is the part of the barrel at the back into which you load the bullets. N-COUNT

breeches /brɪtʃɪz/. **Breeches** are trousers which reach as far as your knees; an old-fashioned use. *He wore a tweed jacket and riding breeches.* N-PLURAL: also *a pair of* N

breed /briːd/ **breeds, breeding, bred** ◆◆◆◇◇

1 A **breed** of a pet animal or farm animal is a particular type of it. For example, terriers are a breed of dog. *...rare breeds of cattle... Certain breeds are more dangerous than others.* N-COUNT

2 If you **breed** animals or plants, you keep them for the purpose of producing more animals or plants with particular qualities, in a controlled way. *He* VERB; V n *lived alone, breeding horses and dogs... He used to breed dogs for the police... These dogs are bred to fight.* • See also **cross-bred.** ♦ **breeding** *There is potential for selective breeding for better yields.* V n prep; be V-ed to-inf; N-UNCOUNT

3 When animals **breed**, they mate and produce offspring. *Frogs will usually breed in any convenient pond... The area now attracts over 60 species of breeding birds.* ♦ **breeding** *During the breeding season the birds come ashore.* VERB; V; V-ing; N-UNCOUNT: oft N n

4 If you say that something **breeds** bad feeling or bad behaviour, you mean that it causes bad feeling or bad behaviour to develop. *If they are unemployed it's bound to breed resentment... Reminding all concerned that violence breeds violence, they repeat their appeal for calm and restraint.* VERB =create; V n

5 If you say that someone **has been bred** for a particular lifestyle or **has been bred** to behave in a particular way, you mean that they have been prepared for that lifestyle or behaviour ever since childhood. *...squat, thick-set, gingery women bred for hard labour and childbearing... They have been bred to compete and succeed.* V-PASSIVE; V-ed; be V-ed to-inf

6 You can refer to someone or something as one of a particular **breed** of person or thing when you want to talk about what they are like. *Sue is one of the new breed of British women squash players who are making a real impact... The new breed of walking holidays puts the emphasis on enjoyment, not endurance... I had found that rare breed of man who was not afraid of committing himself.* N-COUNT: usu sing, with supp =strain

7 See also **breeding**; **ill-bred**, **pure-bred**, **well-bred**.

8 Someone who was **born and bred** in a place was born there and spent their childhood there. *I was born and bred in the highlands... Born and bred in this country, he and his wife emigrated to Los Angeles after the war... A Londoner born and bred, she suspected that a month in the country would bore her to distraction.* • **familiarity breeds contempt**: see **familiarity**. PHRASE

breeder /briːdəʳ/ **breeders. Breeders** are people who breed animals or plants. *Her father was a well-known racehorse breeder.* • See also **fast-breeder reactor**. ◆◆◇◇◇ N-COUNT: usu with supp

breeding /briːdɪŋ/. If someone says that a person has **breeding**, they mean that they think the person is from a good social background and has good manners. *It's a sign of good breeding to know the names of all your staff. ...men of low birth and no breeding.* • See also **breed**. N-UNCOUNT

breeding ground, breeding grounds

1 If you refer to a situation or place as a **breeding ground** for something bad such as crime, you mean that this thing can easily develop in that situation or place. *Flaws in the system have created a breeding ground for financial scandals... The current political turbulence represents the ideal breeding ground for this sort of collapse in consumer confidence.* N-COUNT: usu sing, with supp, usu N for n =source

2 The **breeding ground** for a particular type of creature is the place where this creature breeds easily. *Warm milk is the ideal breeding ground for bacteria.* N-COUNT: with supp

breeze /briːz/ **breezes, breezing, breezed** ◆◆◇◇◇

1 A **breeze** is a gentle wind. *...a cool summer breeze.* N-COUNT

2 If you **breeze** into a place or a position, you enter it in a very casual or nonchalant manner. *Mr Collor breezed into office, beguiling the voters with his good looks and grand talk of clean government... He was late, but eventually he breezed in.* VERB; V prep/adv

3 If you **breeze through** something such as a game or test, you cope with it easily. *Jennifer Capriati breezed through her opening match to beat Erika de Lone 6-4, 6-0.* VERB; V through n; Also V through

4 If you say that something is **a breeze**, you mean that it is very easy to do or to achieve; an informal use. *And after being an office manager for 20 people, handling my own tiny staff of three is a breeze!... Making the pastry is a breeze if you have a food processor.* N-SING: a N =cinch

breeze-block, breeze-blocks; also spelled **breeze block**. A **breeze-block** is a large, grey-coloured brick made from ashes and cement. N-COUNT

breezy /briːzi/ ◆◇◇◇◇

1 If you describe someone as **breezy**, you mean that they behave in a brisk, casual, cheerful, and confident manner. *...his bright and breezy personality... Mona tried to sound breezy.* ♦ **breezily** /briːzɪli/ *'Hi,' he said breezily.* ADJ-GRADED; ADV-GRADED: usu ADV with v

2 If you describe something as **breezy**, especially music or clothing, you mean that it is bright, lively, and cheerful; used mainly in journalism. *This album is bright, breezy and playful.* ADJ-GRADED

3 When the weather is **breezy**, there is a fairly strong but pleasant wind blowing. *The day was breezy and warm.* ADJ-GRADED

brethren /breðrɪn/. You can refer to the members of a particular organization or group, especially a religious group, as **brethren**; an old-fashioned word. *We must help our brethren, it is our duty... Sri Lankans share a common ancestry with their Indian brethren.* ◆◇◇◇◇ N-PLURAL: oft with poss

brevity /brevɪti/

1 The **brevity** of something is the fact that it lasts for only a short time; a formal use. *The bonus of this homely soup is the brevity of its cooking time.* N-UNCOUNT: oft N of n

2 **Brevity** is the use of only a few words to say or write something rather than using more; a formal use. *The brevity of the letter concerned me.* N-UNCOUNT

brew /bruː/ **brews, brewing, brewed** ◆◆◇◇◇

1 If you **brew** tea or coffee, you make it by pouring hot water over tea leaves or ground coffee. *I'll get Venner to brew some tea... He brewed a pot of coffee.* VERB; V n

2 A **brew** is a particular kind of tea or coffee. It can also be a particular pot of tea or coffee. *She swallowed a mouthful of the hot strong brew, and wiped her eyes. ...a mild herbal brew.* N-COUNT: usu with supp

3 If a person or company **brews** beer, they make it. *I brew my own beer... The beer is brewed at the Charles Wells Brewery.* ♦ **brewing** *...the brewing of home-made alcohol.* VERB; V n; N-UNCOUNT

4 A **brew** is a particular kind of beer or beer that is produced in a particular place at a particular time. *Britons still consume more than 29 million pints a day, ranging over 1,000 or more different brews. ...low-alcohol brews.* • See also **home-brew**. N-COUNT: usu with supp

5 If a storm **is brewing**, large clouds are beginning to form and the sky is becoming dark because there is going to be a storm. *We'd seen the storm brewing when we were out in the boat.* VB: usu cont; V

6 If an unpleasant or difficult situation **is brewing**, it is starting to develop. *At home a crisis was brewing... There's trouble brewing.* VB: usu cont; V

7 A **brew** of several things is a mixture of those things. *Most cities generate a complex brew of pollutants. ...a potent brew of smooth salesmanship and amateur psychiatry.* N-COUNT: usu sing, N of n

brew up PHRASAL VERB

1 In British English, if someone **brews up** or if they **brew up** some tea, they make tea by pouring hot water over tea leaves; an informal use. *Brew up, Curly. We could all do with a cup of tea.* V P; Also V P n (not pron)

2 If someone is **brewing up** an unpleasant situation or if an unpleasant situation is **brewing up**, it is starting to develop. *I realized the extent of the trouble that Mary Morse was brewing up... There's another security scandal brewing up.* ERG: usu cont; V P n (not pron); V P

brewer /bruːəʳ/ **brewers. Brewers** are people or companies who make beer. ◆◇◇◇◇ N-COUNT

brewery /bruːəri/ **breweries.** A **brewery** is a place where beer is made. *The Muller family have been making specialist beers at their brewery in Munster for 200 years.* ◆◇◇◇◇ N-COUNT

briar /braɪəʳ/ **briars.** A **briar** is a wild rose with long, thorny stems. N-COUNT

bribe /braɪb/ **bribes, bribing, bribed** ◆◆◇◇◇

1 A **bribe** is a sum of money or something valuable that one person offers or gives to another in order to persuade him or her to do something. *He was being investigated for receiving bribes.* N-COUNT

2 If someone **bribes** another person, they give him or her a bribe. *He was accused of bribing a senior* VERB; V n

bank official... The government bribed the workers to be quiet. V n to-inf

bribery /braɪbəri/. **Bribery** is the act of offering money or something valuable to someone in order to persuade them to do something for you. *He was jailed on charges of bribery. ...accusations of bribery and corruption.* ◆◇◇◇◇ N-UNCOUNT

bric-a-brac /brɪkəbræk/. **Bric-a-brac** is an assortment of small ornamental objects of no great value. *The room they entered was crammed with furniture and bric-a-brac.* N-UNCOUNT =knick-knacks

brick /brɪk/ **bricks, bricking, bricked** ◆◆◇◇◇

1 **Bricks** are rectangular blocks of baked clay used for building walls, which are usually red or brown. **Brick** is the material made up of these blocks. *She built bookshelves out of bricks and planks. ...a tiny garden surrounded by high brick walls.* N-VAR

2 If you say that someone is **a brick**, you mean that they have helped you or supported you when you were in a difficult situation; an old-fashioned, informal use. *You were a brick, a real friend in need.* N-SING: a N =pal, mate

3 If you say that you **are banging your head against a brick wall**, you mean that what you are saying or doing is not having any effect although you keep saying or doing it; an informal expression. *I wanted to sort out this problem with him, but it was like banging my head against a brick wall.* PHRASES V inflects, usu cont

4 If someone or something **hits a brick wall** or **comes up against a brick wall**, they are unable to continue or make progress because something stops them; an informal expression. *After that my career just seemed to hit a brick wall... The discussions in Brussels hit a brick wall.* V inflects

5 You can use **bricks and mortar** to refer to houses and other buildings, especially when they are considered as an investment or safeguard for the future. *Paying rent simply helps to line the pockets of landlords. It's far better to put your money into bricks and mortar of your own... As an investment, bricks and mortar are not what they were.*

6 • to **come down on sb like a ton of bricks**: see **ton**.

brick up. If you **brick up** a hole, you close it with a wall of bricks. *We bricked up our windows... All the doors have been bricked up to deter vandals.* PHRASAL VERB V P n (not pron)

brickbat /brɪkbæt/ **brickbats. Brickbats** are very critical or insulting remarks which are made in public about someone or something. *The Sunday Times has been on the receiving end of endless brickbats from the Scottish media.* N-COUNT: usu pl

brickie /brɪki/ **brickies.** In British English, a **brickie** is the same as a **bricklayer**; an informal expression. N-COUNT =bricklayer

bricklayer /brɪkleɪəʳ/ **bricklayers.** A **bricklayer** is a person whose job is to build walls using bricks. N-COUNT

brickwork /brɪkwɜːʳk/. You can refer to the bricks in the walls of a building as the **brickwork**. *There were cracks in the brickwork.* N-UNCOUNT =masonry

bridal /braɪdəl/. **Bridal** is used to describe something that belongs or relates to a bride, or to both a bride and her bridegroom. *She wore a floor length bridal gown. ...the bridal party.* ◆◇◇◇◇ ADJ: ADJ n =wedding

bride /braɪd/ **brides.** A **bride** is a woman who is getting married or who has just got married. ◆◆◇◇◇ N-COUNT

bridegroom /braɪdgruːm/ **bridegrooms.** A **bridegroom** is a man who is getting married. N-COUNT =groom

bridesmaid /braɪdzmeɪd/ **bridesmaids.** A **bridesmaid** is a woman or a girl who helps and accompanies a bride on her wedding day. ◆◇◇◇◇ N-COUNT

bride-to-be, brides-to-be. A **bride-to-be** is a woman who is soon going to be married. N-COUNT

bridge /brɪdʒ/ **bridges, bridging, bridged** ◆◆◆◆◇

1 A **bridge** is a structure that is built over a railway, river, or road so that people or vehicles can cross from one side to the other. *He walked back over the railway bridge. ...the Golden Gate Bridge.* N-COUNT

2 A **bridge** between two places is a piece of land that joins or connects them. *...a land bridge linking Serbian territories.* N-COUNT: usu with supp

3 To **bridge** the gap between two people or things means to make it easier for the differences or disagreements between them to be made smaller or overcome; used showing approval. *It is unlikely that the two sides will be able to bridge their differences.* VERB PRAGMATICS =overcome V n

4 Something that **bridges** the gap between two very different things has some of the qualities of each of these things. *...the singer who bridged the gap between pop music and opera.* VERB V n

5 If something or someone acts as a **bridge** between two people, groups, or things, they make it easier for the differences or disagreements between them to be made smaller or overcome; used showing approval. *We hope this book will act as a bridge between doctor and patient. ...they saw themselves as a bridge to peace.* N-COUNT: usu N prep PRAGMATICS

6 The **bridge** is a structure or cabin on a ship from which it is steered. N-COUNT: usu sing

7 The **bridge** of your nose is the thin top part of it, between your eyes. *On the bridge of his hooked nose was a pair of gold rimless spectacles.* N-COUNT: usu sing, usu N of n

8 The **bridge** of a pair of glasses is the part that rests on your nose. N-COUNT: usu sing

9 The **bridge** of a violin, guitar, or other stringed instrument is the small piece of wood under the strings that holds them up. N-COUNT: usu sing

10 A **bridge** is a piece of metal or plastic that holds false teeth in place by connecting them to natural teeth. N-COUNT

11 **Bridge** is a card game for four players in which the players begin by declaring how many tricks they expect to win. N-UNCOUNT

12 See also **suspension bridge**.

13 If you **burn** your **bridges**, you do something which forces you to continue with a particular course of action, and makes it impossible for you to return to an earlier situation or relationship. PHRASE: V inflects

• **water under the bridge**: see **water**.

bridgehead /brɪdʒhed/ **bridgeheads.** A **bridgehead** is a good position which an army has taken in the enemy's territory and from which it can advance or attack. *A bridgehead was established.* N-COUNT

bridging loan, bridging loans. A **bridging loan** is money that a bank or other company lends you for a short time to cover the period until you get money from somewhere else, for example so that you can buy another house before you have sold the one you already own; used mainly in British English. N-COUNT

bridle /braɪdəl/ **bridles, bridling, bridled** ◆◇◇◇◇

1 A **bridle** is a set of straps that is put around a horse's head and mouth so that the person riding or driving the horse can control it. N-COUNT

2 If you **bridle**, you show that you are angry or displeased by moving your head and body upwards in a proud way; a literary use. *She bridled, then simply shook her head... Alex bridled at the shortness of Pamela's tone.* VERB =bristle V V at n

bridle path, bridle paths; also spelled **bridlepath**. A **bridle path** is the same as a **bridleway**. N-COUNT =bridleway

bridleway /braɪdəlweɪ/ **bridleways.** A **bridleway** is a path intended for people riding horses. N-COUNT =bridle path

Brie /briː/; also spelled **brie**. **Brie** is a type of cheese that comes from France. It is soft and creamy with a hard greyish-white skin. N-UNCOUNT

brief /briːf/ **briefer, briefest; briefs, briefing, briefed** ◆◆◆◆◇

1 Something that is **brief** lasts for only a short time. *She once made a brief appearance on television... This time their visit is brief.* ADJ-GRADED =short ≠lengthy

2 A **brief** speech or piece of writing does not contain too many words or details. *In a brief statement, he concentrated entirely on international affairs... Write a very brief description of a typical problem.* ADJ-GRADED =concise

3 If you are **brief**, you say what you want to say in as few words as possible. *Now please be brief - my time is valuable... I hope to be brief and to the point.* ADJ-GRADED: v-link ADJ =succinct

4 You can describe a period of time as **brief** if you want to emphasize that it is very short. *For a few brief minutes we forgot the anxiety and anguish.* ADJ-GRADED: usu ADJ n PRAGMATICS ≠long

5 Men's or women's underpants can be referred to as **briefs**.
N-PLURAL: also *a pair of* N

6 If someone **briefs** you, especially about a piece of work or a serious matter, they give you information that you need before you do it or consider it. *A Defense Department spokesman briefed reporters... The Prime Minister has been briefed by her parliamentary aides.*
VERB =fill in
V n

7 If someone gives you a **brief**, they officially give you the responsibility for dealing with a particular thing; a formal use. *...customs officials with a brief to stop foreign porn coming into Britain.*
N-COUNT: oft N to-inf =responsibility

8 See also **briefer**, **briefing**.

9 If you refer to something **in brief**, you are referring to a shortened version of it with few details. *...and now sport in brief.*
PHRASES n PHR

10 You can say **in brief** to indicate that you are about to say something in as few words as possible or to summarize what you have just said. *In brief, take no risks.*
PHR with cl =in short ≠in full

briefcase /briːfkeɪs/ **briefcases.** A **briefcase** is a case used for carrying documents in.
◆◇◇◇◇ N-COUNT

briefer /briːfəʳ/ **briefers.** A **briefer** is an official who has the job of giving information about something, for example a war. *Military briefers say the air war has concentrated on disrupting supplies and communications.*
N-COUNT: usu supp N

briefing /briːfɪŋ/ **briefings.** A **briefing** is a meeting at which information or instructions are given to people, especially before they do something. *They're holding a press briefing tomorrow... Security staff did not then receive any briefing before they started each shift.* • See also **brief**.
◆◆◇◇◇ N-VAR

briefly /briːfli/
◆◆◇◇◇

1 Something that happens or is done **briefly** happens or is done for a very short period of time. *He smiled briefly... Guerillas captured and briefly held an important provincial capital.*
ADV-GRADED: ADV with v

2 If you say or write something **briefly**, you use very few words or give very few details. *There are four basic alternatives; they are described briefly below.*
ADV-GRADED: ADV with v =in brief

3 You can say **briefly** to indicate that you are about to say something in as few words as possible. *Briefly, no less than nine of our agents have passed information to us.*
ADV-GRADED: ADV with cl

brig /brɪg/ **brigs.** A **brig** is a type of ship with two masts and square sails.
N-COUNT

Brig. /brɪgədɪəʳ/. **Brig.** is a written abbreviation for **brigadier**. *...Brig. Douglas Erskin Crum.*

brigade /brɪgeɪd/ **brigades**
◆◆◇◇◇

1 A **brigade** is one of the groups which an army is divided into. *...the men of the Seventh Armoured Brigade.* • See also **fire brigade**.
N-COUNT-COLL

2 You can use **brigade** humorously to refer to a group of people who believe strongly in a particular thing or who share a particular characteristic. *...the healthy eating brigade. ...the black T-shirt brigade.*
N-SING: n N

brigadier /brɪgədɪəʳ/ **brigadiers.** A **brigadier** is a senior officer in the armed forces who is in charge of a brigade and has the rank above colonel and below brigadier general.
◆◇◇◇◇ N-COUNT; N-TITLE

brigadier general, brigadier generals; also spelled **brigadier-general.** A **brigadier general** is a senior officer in the US armed forces who is in charge of a brigade and has a rank above colonel and below major general. *...Brigadier General Gary Whipple of the Louisiana National Guard.*
N-COUNT; N-TITLE

brigand /brɪgənd/ **brigands.** A **brigand** is someone who attacks people and steals their property, especially in mountainous areas or forests; a literary word. *He looked like a scruffy brigand caught rustling cattle.*
N-COUNT =bandit

bright /braɪt/ **brighter, brightest**
◆◆◆◆◇

1 A **bright** colour is strong and noticeable, and not dark. *...a bright red dress. ...the bright uniforms of the guards parading at Buckingham Palace.*
ADJ-GRADED: usu ADJ n, ADJ colour
♦ **brightly** *...a display of brightly coloured flowers.*
ADV-GRADED
♦ **brightness** *You'll be impressed with the brightness and the beauty of the colors.*
N-UNCOUNT: oft *the* N *of* n

2 A **bright** light, object, or place is shining strongly or is full of light. *...a bright October day... She leaned forward, her eyes bright with excitement.*
ADJ-GRADED =brilliant ≠dull
♦ **brightly** *...a warm, brightly lit room... The sun shone brightly.*
ADV-GRADED: ADV with v
♦ **brightness** *An astronomer can determine the brightness of each star.*
N-UNCOUNT: oft *the* N *of* n

3 If you describe someone as **bright**, you mean that they are quick at learning things. *I was convinced that he was brighter than average.*
ADJ-GRADED: usu v-link ADJ =clever

4 A **bright** idea is clever and original. *There are lots of books crammed with bright ideas... Ford had the bright idea of paying workers enough to buy cars.*
ADJ-GRADED: usu ADJ n =brilliant

5 If someone looks or sounds **bright**, they look or sound cheerful and lively. *The boy was so bright and animated... 'May I help you?' said a bright American voice over the telephone.*
ADJ-GRADED =cheerful, lively
♦ **brightly** *He smiled brightly as Ben approached.*
ADV-GRADED: ADV with v

6 If the future is **bright**, it is likely to be pleasant or successful. *Both had successful careers and the future looked bright... There are much brighter prospects for a comprehensive settlement than before.*
ADJ-GRADED =promising ≠gloomy

7 If you **look on the bright side**, you try to be cheerful about a bad situation by thinking of some advantages that could result from it, or thinking that it is not as bad as it could have been.
PHRASE: V inflects

brighten /braɪtᵊn/ **brightens, brightening, brightened**
◆◇◇◇◇

1 If someone **brightens** or their face **brightens**, they suddenly look happier. *Seeing him, she seemed to brighten a little... 'Oh, we'd love to!' cried Nancy, her face brightening.*
VERB V
► **Brighten up** means the same as **brighten**. *He brightened up a bit.*
PHRASAL VERB V P

2 If your eyes **brighten**, you suddenly look interested or excited. *His eyes brightened and he laughed... Her tearful eyes brightened with interest.*
VERB V V *with* n

3 If someone or something **brightens** a place, they make it more colourful and attractive. *Tubs planted with wallflowers brightened the area outside the door.*
VERB V n
► **Brighten up** means the same as **brighten**. *David spotted the pink silk lampshade in a shop and thought it would brighten up the room.*
PHRASAL VERB V P n (not pron) Also V n P

4 If someone or something **brightens** a situation or the situation **brightens**, it becomes more pleasant, enjoyable, or favourable. *That does not do much to brighten the prospects of kids in the city... It is undeniable that the economic picture is brightening.*
V-ERG =improve V n V
► **Brighten up** means the same as **brighten**. *His cheerful face brightens up the dullest of days.*
PHRASAL VERB ERG V P n (not pron) Also V P

5 When a light **brightens** a place or when a place **brightens**, it becomes brighter or lighter. *The sky above the ridge of mountains brightened... The late afternoon sun brightened the interior of the church.*
V-ERG V V n

6 If the weather **brightens**, it becomes less cloudy or rainy, and the sun starts to shine. *By early afternoon the weather had brightened.*
VERB V
► **Brighten up** means the same as **brighten**. *Hopefully it will brighten up, or we'll be coming back early.*
PHRASAL VERB *it* V P

bright lights. If someone talks about the **bright lights**, they are referring to life in a big city where you can do a lot of enjoyable and exciting things and be successful. *The bright lights of Hollywood beckon many.*
N-PLURAL: *the* N

bright spark, bright sparks. If you say that some **bright spark** had a particular idea or did something, you mean that their idea or action was clever, or that it seemed clever but was silly in some way; an informal expression. *I should have realised that genius, as some bright spark in the office said, has a lot to do with genes... For some reason, one bright spark thought a samba party was the order of the day.*
N-COUNT

brill /brɪl/. In British English, if you say that something is **brill**, you are very pleased about it or think that it is very good; an informal word. *What a brill idea!*
◆◇◇◇◇ ADJ-GRADED =wonderful, great

brilliant /brɪliənt/
◆◆◆◇◇

1 A **brilliant** person, idea, or performance is extremely clever or skilful. *She had a brilliant mind... It was his brilliant performance in My Left Foot that established his reputation.*
ADJ-GRADED: usu ADJ n
♦ **brilliantly** *It is a very high quality production, brilliantly written and acted.*
ADV-GRADED: usu ADV with v, also ADV adj
♦ **brilliance** *He was a deeply serious musician who had shown his brilliance very early.*
N-UNCOUNT: oft with poss

2 In spoken British English, you can say that some-
ADJ-GRADED

thing is **brilliant** when you are very pleased about it or think that it is very good; an informal use. *If you get a chance to see the show, do go – it's brilliant... My sister's given me this brilliant book.* =great ≠awful
♦ **brilliantly** *It's extremely hard working together but on the whole it works brilliantly and we're still good friends.* ADV-GRADED: ADV with v, ADV adj/adv

3 A **brilliant** career or success is very successful. *He served four years in prison, emerging to find his brilliant career in ruins... The raid was a brilliant success.* ADJ-GRADED: usu ADJ n ♦ **brilliantly** *The strategy worked brilliantly.* ADV-GRADED

4 A **brilliant** colour is extremely bright. *The woman had brilliant green eyes. ...a brilliant white open-necked shirt.* ADJ-GRADED: ADJ n ♦ **brilliantly** *Many of the patterns show brilliantly coloured flowers.* ADV-GRADED: ADV adj/-ed ♦ **brilliance** *...an iridescent blue butterfly in all its brilliance.* N-UNCOUNT

5 You describe light, or something that reflects light, as **brilliant** when it shines very brightly. *The event was held in brilliant sunshine... It was 250 million times more brilliant than the Sun.* ADJ-GRADED ♦ **brilliantly** *It's a brilliantly sunny morning.* ADV-GRADED: ADV adj/-ed, ADV after v ♦ **brilliance** *His eyes became accustomed to the dark after the brilliance of the sun outside.* N-UNCOUNT

brim /brɪm/ **brims, brimming, brimmed** ◆◇◇◇◇

1 The **brim** of a hat is the wide part that sticks outwards at the bottom. *Rain dripped from the brim of his baseball cap. ...a flat black hat with a wide brim.* N-COUNT: oft N of n, adj N ♦ **-brimmed** *She protected her head with a wide-brimmed straw-hat. ...a floppy-brimmed hat.* COMB in ADJ-GRADED: usu ADJ n

2 If you say that someone or something **is brimming with** something, especially a particular quality, you mean that they are full of that thing. *England are brimming with confidence after two straight wins in the tournament.* VB: usu cont V with n ► **Brim over** means the same as **brim**. *I noticed Dorabella was brimming over with excitement... Her heart brimmed over with love and adoration for Charles.* PHRASAL VERB VP with n Also V P

3 When your eyes **are brimming with** tears, they are full of fluid because you are upset, although you are not actually crying. *Michael looked at him imploringly, eyes brimming with tears.* VERB =be full of V with n ► **Brim over** means the same as **brim**. *When she saw me, her eyes brimmed over with tears and she could not speak.* PHRASAL VERB V P with n Also V P

4 If something **brims** with particular things, it is packed full of them. *The flowerbeds brim with a mixture of lilies and roses.* VERB V with n

5 If something, especially a container, **is filled to the brim** or **full to the brim** with something, it is filled right up to the top. *Richard filled her glass right up to the brim... The toilet was full to the brim with insects.* PHRASES V inflects

6 If you are **full to the brim with** a particular emotion, you feel that emotion very strongly, so that it overwhelms all other emotions. *Her heart beat so fast and she was full to the brim with joy.* v-link PHR =be full of

brim over. See **brim** 2 and 3. PHRASAL VERB

brimful /brɪmfʊl/. Someone who is **brimful** of an emotion or quality feels or seems full of it. An object or place that is **brimful** of something is full of it. *I had met Mrs Allen, who is brimful of energy, enthusiasm and Irish charm... The United States is brimful with highly paid doctors.* ADJ: v-link ADJ of/with n =full

brimstone /brɪmstoun/

1 **Brimstone** is the same as **sulphur**; an old-fashioned use. N-UNCOUNT

2 If someone threatens you with **fire and brimstone**, they are referring to hell and emphasizing how people are punished there after death in order to make you behave in a better way; a literary expression. *He does not spare the fire and brimstone.* PHRASE

brine /braɪn/ **brines. Brine** is salty water, especially salty water that is used for preserving food. *Soak the walnuts in brine for four or five days.* N-MASS

bring /brɪŋ/ **brings, bringing, brought** ◆◆◆◆◆

1 If you **bring** someone or something with you when you come to a place, they come with you or you have them with you. *Remember to bring an apron or an old shirt to protect your clothes... Come to my party and bring a girl with you... Someone went upstairs and brought down a huge kettle... My father brought home a book for me.* VERB V n V n with adv V n for n with adv Also V n n with adv, V n prep

2 If you **bring** something somewhere, you move it there. *Reaching into her pocket, she brought out a cigarette... Her mother brought her hands up to her face.* VERB V n with adv Also V n prep

3 If you **bring** something that someone wants or needs, you fetch it for them or carry it to them. *He went and poured a brandy for Dena and brought it to her... The stewardess kindly brought me a blanket.* VERB V n to/for n V n n Also V n

4 To **bring** something or someone to a place or position means to cause them to come to the place or move into that position. *I told you about what brought me here... The shock of her husband's arrival brought her to her feet... Edna Leitch survived a gas blast which brought her home crashing down on top of her.* VERB V n prep/adv V n -ing

5 If you **bring** something new to a place or group of people, you introduce it to that place or cause those people to hear or know about it. *...a brave reporter who had risked death to bring the story to the world. ...the drive to bring art to the public.* VERB V n to n

6 To **bring** someone or something into a particular state or condition means to cause them to be in that state or condition. *He brought the car to a stop in front of the square... His work as a historian brought him into conflict with the Communist establishment... The incident brings the total of people killed to fifteen... They have brought down income taxes.* VERB V n prep V n with adv

7 If something **brings** a particular feeling, situation, or quality, it makes people experience it or have it. *I hope that the election will bring peace to Cambodians... Kinkel said the attacks had brought disgrace on Germany... Banks have brought trouble on themselves by lending rashly... He brought to the job not just considerable experience but passionate enthusiasm... Her three children brought her joy.* VERB V n to/on/from n V to n n V n n

8 If a period of time **brings** a particular thing, it happens during that time. *For Sandro, the new year brought disaster... We don't know what the future will bring.* VERB V n

9 If you **bring** a legal action against someone or **bring** them to trial, you officially accuse them of doing something unlawful. *He campaigned relentlessly to bring charges of corruption against former members of the government... The ship's captain and crew may be brought to trial and even sent to prison.* VERB V n against n be V-ed to n

10 If a television or radio programme **is brought** to you by an organization, they make it, broadcast it, or pay for it to be made or broadcast. *You're listening to Science in Action, brought to you by the BBC World Service... We'll be bringing you all the details of the day's events.* VERB be V-ed to n by n V n n

11 When you are talking, you can say that something **brings** you to a particular point in order to indicate that you have now reached that point and are going to talk about a new subject. *Which brings me to a delicate matter I should like to raise... And that brings us to the end of this special report from Germany.* VERB PRAGMATICS V n to n

12 If you cannot **bring** yourself to do something, you cannot do it because you find it too painful, embarrassing, or disgusting. *It is all very tragic and I am afraid I just cannot bring myself to talk about it at the moment.* VB: with brd-neg =bear V pron-refl to-inf

13 • to **bring something alive**: see **alive**. • to **bring something to bear**: see **bear**. • to **bring the house down**: see **house**. • to **bring up the rear**: see **rear**.

bring about. To **bring** something **about** means to cause it to happen. *The only way they can bring about political change is by putting pressure on the country.* PHRASAL VERB =cause V P n (not pron) Also V n P

bring along. If you **bring** someone or something **along**, you bring them with you when you come to a place. *They brought along Laura Jane in a pram... Dad brought a notebook along to the beach, in case he was seized by sudden inspiration.* PHRASAL VERB V P n (not pron) V n P

bring around. See **bring round**. PHRASAL VERB

bring back PHRASAL VERB

1 Something that **brings back** a memory makes you think about it. *Your article brought back sad* V P n (not pron) *memories for me... Talking about it brought it all back.* V n P

2 When people **bring back** a practice or fashion that existed at an earlier time, they introduce it again. *The House of Commons is to debate once again whether to bring back the death penalty.* =reintroduce V P n (not pron) Also V n P

bring down PHRASAL VERB

1 When people or events **bring down** a government or ruler, they cause the government or ruler to lose power. *They were threatening to bring down the government by withdrawing from the ruling coalition... His challenge to Mrs Thatcher brought her down.* V P n (not pron) V n P

2 If someone or something **brings down** a person or aeroplane, they cause them to fall, usually by shooting them. *Military historians may never know what brought down the jet.* V P n (not pron) Also V n P

bring forward PHRASAL VERB

1 If you **bring forward** a meeting or event, you arrange for it to take place at an earlier date or time than had been planned. *He had to bring forward an 11 o'clock meeting so that he could get to the funeral on time... The election date had to be brought forward by two months.* =put forward ≠put back V P n (not pron) Also V n P

2 If you **bring forward** an argument or proposal, you state it so that people can consider it. *The Government will bring forward several proposals for legislation.* =put forward V P n (not pron) Also V n P

bring in PHRASAL VERB

1 When a government or organization **brings in** a new law or system, they introduce it. *The government brought in a controversial law under which it could take any land it wanted.* =introduce V P n (not pron) Also V n P

2 Someone or something that **brings in** money makes it or earns it. *I have three part-time jobs, which bring in about £6,000 a year.* V P n (not pron) Also V n P

3 If you **bring in** someone from outside a team or organization, you invite them to do a job or participate in an activity or discussion. *The firm decided to bring in a new management team.* V P n (not pron) Also V n P

4 When a jury or inquest **brings in** a verdict, the verdict is officially decided. *The jury took 23 hours to bring in its verdict... The inquest will bring in a verdict of suicide.* V P n (not pron) Also V n P

bring off. If you **bring off** something difficult, you do it successfully. *They were about to bring off an even bigger coup... He thought his book would change society. But he didn't bring it off.* PHRASAL VERB V P n (not pron) V n P

bring on. If something **brings on** an illness, pain, or feeling, especially one that you often suffer from, it causes you to have it. *Severe shock can bring on an attack of acne... Bob died of a heart attack, brought on by his lifestyle.* PHRASAL VERB V P n (not pron) V-ed P Also V n P

bring out PHRASAL VERB

1 When a person or company **brings out** a new product, especially a new book or record, they produce it and put it on sale. *A journalist all his life, he's now brought out a book.* V P n (not pron) Also V n P

2 Something that **brings out** a particular kind of behaviour or feeling in you causes you to show it, especially when it is something you do not normally show. *Sea air seems to bring out the lover in some people... He is totally dedicated and brings out the best in his pupils.* V P n (not pron) Also V n P

bring round or **bring around.** The form **bring round** is mainly used in British English. PHRASAL VERB

1 If you **bring** someone **round** when they are unconscious, you make them become conscious again. *I'd passed out and he'd brought me round.* V n P

2 If you **bring** someone **round**, you cause them to change their opinion about something so that they agree with you. *We will do everything we can to bring parliament round to our point of view.* V n P to n Also V n P

bring to. If you **bring** someone **to** when they are unconscious, you make them become conscious again. PHRASAL VERB V n P =bring round

bring up PHRASAL VERB

1 When someone **brings up** a child, they look after it until it is grown up. If someone has **been brought up** in a certain place or with certain attitudes, they grew up in that place or were taught those attitudes when they were growing up. *She brought up four children... His grandmother and his father brought him up... He was brought up in North Yorkshire... We'd been brought up to think that borrowing money was bad... I was brought up a Methodist.* V P n (not pron) V n P be V-ed P prep/adv be V-ed P to-inf be V-ed P n

2 If you **bring up** a particular subject, you introduce it into a discussion or conversation. *He brought up a subject rarely raised during the course of this campaign... Why are you bringing it up now?* =raise V P n (not pron) V n P

3 If someone **brings up** food or wind, food or air is forced up from their stomach through their mouth. *It's hard for the baby to bring up wind.* V P n (not pron)

bring-and-buy sale, bring-and-buy sales. In British English, a **bring-and-buy sale** is an informal sale to raise money for a charity or other organization. People who come to the sale bring things to be sold and buy things that other people have brought. N-COUNT

bringer /brɪŋəʳ/ **bringers.** A **bringer** of something is someone who brings or provides it; a literary word. *He was the bringer of great glad tidings.* N-COUNT: with supp, usu N of n

brink /brɪŋk/. If you are on the **brink** of something, usually something important, terrible, or exciting, you are just about to do it or experience it. *Their economy is teetering on the brink of collapse... Failure to communicate had brought the two nations to the brink of war.* ◆◆◇◇◇ N-SING: usu on/to/from the N of n =verge

brinkmanship /brɪŋkmənʃɪp/. **Brinkmanship** is a method of behaviour, especially in politics, in which you deliberately get into dangerous situations which could result in disaster but which could also bring success; used mainly in journalism. *A game of political brinkmanship has begun at Westminster with the political careers of some cabinet ministers on the line.* N-UNCOUNT

brioche /briɒʃ/ **brioches. Brioche** is a kind of sweet bread that is often made into small buns. *He sat down before his big cup of milky coffee and a brioche.* N-VAR

brisk /brɪsk/ **brisker, briskest** ◆◆◇◇◇

1 A **brisk** activity or action is done quickly and in an energetic way. *Taking a brisk walk can often induce a feeling of well-being... The horse broke into a brisk trot.* ♦ **briskly** *Eve walked briskly down the corridor to her son's room.* ♦ **briskness** *With determined briskness, Amy stood up and put their cups back on the tray.* ADJ-GRADED: usu ADJ n =energetic ADV-GRADED: ADV with v =energetically N-UNCOUNT

2 If trade or business is **brisk**, things are being sold very quickly and a lot of money is being made. *Vendors were doing a brisk trade in souvenirs... Its sales had been brisk since July.* ♦ **briskly** *A trader said gold sold briskly on the local market.* ADJ-GRADED =good ADV-GRADED: ADV after v

3 If the weather is **brisk**, it is cold and refreshing. *...a typically brisk winter's day on the South Coast... The breeze was cool, brisk and invigorating.* ADJ-GRADED =bracing

4 Someone who is **brisk** behaves in a busy, confident way which shows that they want to get things done quickly. *The Chief summoned me downstairs. He was brisk and businesslike... She is noted for her brisk handling of business.* ♦ **briskly** *'Anyhow,' she added briskly, 'it's none of my business.'* ♦ **briskness** *He felt her familiar briskness, and he knew that it was all over.* ADJ-GRADED =businesslike ADV-GRADED: ADV with v N-UNCOUNT

brisket /brɪskɪt/. **Brisket** is a cut of beef that comes from the breast of the cow. N-UNCOUNT

bristle /brɪsəl/ **bristles, bristling, bristled** ◆◇◇◇◇

1 **Bristles** are the short hairs that grow on a man's chin after he has shaved. The hairs on the top of a man's head can also be called **bristles** when they are cut very short. *...two days' growth of bristles... He rubbed his hands over the soft bristles of his crew cut.* N-COUNT: usu pl =stubble

2 The **bristles** of a brush are the thick hairs or hairlike pieces of plastic which are attached to it. *As soon as the bristles on your toothbrush begin to wear, throw it out.* N-COUNT

3 **Bristles** are thick, strong animal hairs that feel hard and rough. *It has a short stumpy tail covered with bristles.* N-COUNT

4 If the hair on a person's or animal's body **bristles**, it rises away from their skin because they are cold, frightened, or angry. *It makes the hairs at the nape* VERB =stand on end V

of the neck bristle... Cats yowl. My dog's hair bristles in response.
5 If you **bristle** at something, you react to it angrily, and show this in your expression or the way you move. *Ellis bristles at accusations that Berkeley's experiment is ill-conceived... He bristled with indignation at the suggestion that he was racist.* VERB =bridle V *at/with* n Also V
6 If you say that a place or thing **bristles with** people or with other things, you are emphasizing that it contains a great number of them. *The country bristles with armed groups... The idea fairly bristles with controversy... Their vocabulary bristles fashionably with talk of federalism.* VERB PRAGMATICS V *with* n

bristling /brɪslɪŋ/
1 **Bristling** means thick, hairy, and rough. It is used to describe things such as moustaches, beards, or eyebrows. *He was tall, bespectacled, with a bristling white moustache.* ADJ: ADJ n
2 If you describe someone's attitude as **bristling**, you are emphasizing that it is full of energy and enthusiasm. *His bristling determination has become a symbol of England's renaissance. ...bristling, exuberant, rock'n'roll.* ADJ: ADJ n PRAGMATICS

bristly /brɪsli/
1 **Bristly** hair is rough, coarse, and thick. *His bristly red hair was standing on end.* ADJ-GRADED: usu ADJ n =stubbly
2 If a man's chin is **bristly**, it is covered with bristles because he has not shaved recently. *He lifted the beer to his bristly mouth.* ADJ-GRADED

Brit /brɪt/ **Brits.** British people are sometimes referred to as **Brits**; an informal word. *Holiday mad Brits are packing their buckets and spades and heading for the sun.* ◆◆◇◇◇ N-COUNT

British /brɪtɪʃ/ ◆◆◆◆◇
1 **British** means belonging or relating to Great Britain, or to its people or culture. *...the British government. ...traditional British cookery.* ADJ
2 The **British** are the people of Great Britain. N-PLURAL

British Asian, British Asians. A **British Asian** person is someone of Indian, Pakistani, or Bangladeshi origin who has grown up in Britain. *...a British Asian woman. ...the British Asian Business Community.* ► A **British Asian** is someone who is British Asian. *British Asians have begun a campaign calling for an end to discrimination.* ADJ: usu ADJ n =Anglo-Asian N-COUNT =Anglo-Asian

Britisher /brɪtɪʃə/ **Britishers.** British people are sometimes referred to as **Britishers**; an informal word used in American English or old-fashioned British English. N-COUNT

Briton /brɪtᵊn/ **Britons.** A **Briton** is a British citizen, or a person of British origin; a formal word. *The role is played by seventeen-year-old Briton Jane March.* ◆◆◇◇◇ N-COUNT

brittle /brɪtᵊl/ ◆◇◇◇◇
1 An object or substance that is **brittle** is hard but easily broken. *Pine is brittle and breaks. ...the dry, brittle ends of the hair.* ADJ-GRADED
2 If you describe a situation, relationship, or someone's mood as **brittle**, you mean that it is unstable, and may easily change. *...Yugoslavia's brittle peace... The brittle structure of Communist power collapsed quickly in Eastern Europe.* ADJ-GRADED =fragile
3 Someone who is **brittle** seems rather sharp and insensitive and says things which are likely to hurt other people's feelings. *...Noel Coward's brittle comedy of bad manners.* ADJ-GRADED
4 A **brittle** sound is short, loud, and sharp. *Myrtle gave a brittle laugh.* ADJ-GRADED

broach /brəʊtʃ/ **broaches, broaching, broached.** When you **broach** a subject, especially a sensitive one, you mention it in order to start a discussion on it. *Eventually I broached the subject of her early life.* VERB V n

broad /brɔːd/ **broader, broadest; broads** ◆◆◆◆◇
1 Something that is **broad** is wide. *His shoulders were broad and his waist narrow... The hills rise green and sheer above the broad river. ...a broad expanse of green lawn.* ADJ-GRADED ≠narrow
2 A **broad** smile is one in which your mouth is stretched very wide because you are very pleased or amused. *He greeted them with a wave and a broad smile.* ♦ **broadly** *Charles grinned broadly.* ADJ-GRADED: usu ADJ n ADV-GRADED
3 You use **broad** to describe something that includes a large number of different things or people. *A broad range of issues was discussed. ...a broad coalition of workers, peasants, students and middle class professionals.* ♦ **broadly** *This gives children a more broadly based education.* ADJ-GRADED: usu ADJ n =extensive ≠limited ADV-GRADED: ADV with v
4 You use **broad** to describe a word or meaning which covers or refers to a wide range of different things. *The term Wissenschaft has a much broader meaning than the English word 'science'. ...restructuring in the broad sense of the word.* ♦ **broadly** *The new EC code defines sexual harassment very broadly.* ADJ-GRADED: usu ADJ n =general ≠narrow ADV-GRADED: ADV with v
5 You use **broad** to describe a feeling or opinion that is shared by many people, or by people of many different kinds. *The agreement won broad support in the US Congress. ...a film with broad appeal.* ♦ **broadly** *The new law has been broadly welcomed by road safety organisations.* ADJ-GRADED: ADJ n =widespread ≠limited ADV-GRADED: ADV with v
6 A **broad** description or idea is general rather than detailed. *These documents provided a broad outline of the Society's development... In broad terms, this means that the closer you live to a school, the more likely it is that your child will get a place there.* ♦ **broadly** *There are, broadly speaking, three ways in which this is done... Broadly, it makes connections between ideas about healing and how they link to plants.* ADJ-GRADED: usu ADJ n =rough ≠precise ADV-GRADED: ADV with v, ADV with cl/group
7 A **broad** hint is a very obvious hint. *They've been giving broad hints about what to expect.* ♦ **broadly** *He hinted broadly that he would like to come.* ADJ-GRADED: ADJ n ≠subtle ADV
8 A **broad** accent is strong and noticeable. *...a Briton who spoke in a broad Yorkshire accent.* ADJ-GRADED
9 In American English, some men refer to women as **broads**; an offensive use. N-COUNT
10 See also **broadly**.
11 ● **in broad daylight**: see **daylight**.

B-road, B-roads; also spelled **B road**. In Britain, a **B-road** is a minor road. N-COUNT

broad bean, broad beans. **Broad beans** are flat round beans that are light green in colour and are eaten as a vegetable; used mainly in British English. N-COUNT: usu pl

broad-brush; also spelled **broad brush**. A **broad-brush** approach, strategy, or solution deals with a problem in a general way rather than concentrating on details. *Some voters like Perot's broad-brush approach on the economy.* ADJ: usu ADJ n

broadcast /brɔːdkɑːst, -kæst/ **broadcasts, broadcasting.** The form **broadcast** is used in the present tense and is the past tense and past participle of the verb. ◆◆◆◇◇
1 A **broadcast** is a programme, performance, or speech on the radio or on television. *In a broadcast on state radio the government also announced that it was willing to resume peace negotiations.* N-COUNT =programme
2 To **broadcast** a programme means to send it out by radio waves, so that it can be heard on the radio or seen on television. *The concert will be broadcast live on television and radio... CNN also broadcasts in Europe.* VERB =transmit *be* V-ed adv/prep V Also V n

broadcaster /brɔːdkɑːstəʳ, -kæst-/ **broadcasters.** A **broadcaster** is someone who gives talks or takes part in interviews and discussions on radio or television programmes. *...the prominent naturalist and broadcaster, Sir David Attenborough.* ◆◆◇◇◇ N-COUNT

broadcasting /brɔːdkɑːstɪŋ, -kæst-/. **Broadcasting** is the making and sending out of television and radio programmes. *If this happens it will change the face of religious broadcasting. ...the state broadcasting organisation.* ◆◆◆◇◇ N-UNCOUNT

broaden /brɔːdᵊn/ **broadens, broadening, broadened** ◆◇◇◇◇
1 When something **broadens**, it becomes wider. *The trails broadened into roads... The smile broadened to a grin.* VERB =widen V *into/to* n Also V
2 When you **broaden** something such as your experience or popularity or when it **broadens**, the number of things or people that it includes or affects becomes greater. *We must broaden our appeal... I thought you wanted to broaden your horizons... The political spectrum has broadened.* V-ERG V n V

3 If an experience **broadens** your **mind**, it makes you more willing to accept other people's beliefs and customs. *They say that travel broadens the mind.* PHRASE: V inflects

broaden out PHRASAL VERB

1 If something such as a discussion **broadens out** or if someone **broadens** it **out**, the number of things or people that it includes or affects becomes greater. *The debate is broadening out to include questions about the structure of French education... We'll broaden the discussion out in a minute.* ERG; V P; V n P; Also V P n (not pron)

2 When something such as a river or road **broadens out**, it becomes wider. *Here the Nile broadens out between the huge granite boulders.* =widen; V P

broadly /brɔːdli/. You can use **broadly** to indicate that something is generally true. *President Bush broadly got what he wanted out of his meeting... The idea that software is capable of any task is broadly true in theory.* • See also **broad**. ◆◆◇◇◇ ADV-GRADED: ADV with cl =more or less

broadly-based. Something that is **broadly-based** involves many different kinds of things or people. *... a broadly-based political movement for democracy... This gives children a more broadly-based education.* ADJ-GRADED: usu ADJ n

broadminded /brɔːdmaɪndɪd/. If you describe someone as **broadminded**, you approve of them because they are willing to accept types of behaviour which other people consider immoral. *He was always a very fair and broadminded man.* ADJ-GRADED PRAGMATICS ≠narrow minded

broadsheet /brɔːdʃiːt/ **broadsheets.** A **broadsheet** is a newspaper that is printed on large sheets of paper measuring approximately 38 cm by 61 cm. Broadsheets are generally considered to be more serious than other newspapers. Compare **tabloid**. N-COUNT

broadside /brɔːdsaɪd/ **broadsides**

1 A **broadside** is a strong written or spoken attack on a person or institution. *Mr Beregovoy's speech featured a broadside against the IMF and the World Bank.* N-COUNT: oft N *against* n

2 If a ship is **broadside** to something, it has its longest side facing in the direction of that thing; a technical term. *The ship was moored broadside to the pier.* ADV: ADV after v, *be* ADV, oft ADV *on*, ADV *to* n

brocade /brəkeɪd/ **brocades. Brocade** is a thick, expensive material, often made of silk, with a raised pattern on it. *...a cream brocade waistcoat.* N-MASS

broccoli /brɒkəli/. **Broccoli** is a vegetable with green stalks and green or purple flower buds. ◆◇◇◇◇ N-UNCOUNT

brochure /broʊʃəʳ, AM broʊʃʊr/ **brochures.** A **brochure** is a magazine or booklet with pictures that gives you information about a product or service. *...travel brochures.* ◆◆◇◇◇ N-COUNT

brogue /broʊg/ **brogues**

1 If someone has a **brogue**, they speak English with a strong accent, especially Irish or Scots. *Gill speaks in a quiet Irish brogue.* N-SING

2 **Brogues** are thick leather shoes which have an elaborate pattern punched into the leather. N-COUNT: usu pl

broil /brɔɪl/ **broils, broiling, broiled.** In American English, when you **broil** food, you grill it. *I'll broil the lobster. ...broiled chicken.* VERB V n V-ed

broiler /brɔɪləʳ/ **broilers.** A **broiler** is a pan or grill used for broiling food; used mainly in American English. N-COUNT

broiling /brɔɪlɪŋ/. If the weather is **broiling**, it is very hot; an informal word used especially in American English. *...the broiling midday sun.* ADJ =sweltering ≠freezing

broke /broʊk/ ◆◇◇◇◇

1 **Broke** is the past tense of **break**.

2 If you are **broke**, you have no money; an informal use. *What do you mean, I've got enough money? I'm as broke as you are.* ADJ-GRADED: v-link ADJ =skint

3 If a company or person **goes broke**, they lose money and are unable to continue in business or to pay their debts; an informal expression. *Balton went broke twice in his career.* PHRASES V inflects =go bankrupt, go bust

4 If you **go for broke**, you take the most extreme or risky of the possible courses of action in order to try and achieve success; an informal expression. *It was a sharp disagreement about whether to go for broke or whether to compromise.* V inflects ≠play safe

broken /broʊkən/ ◆◇◇◇◇

1 **Broken** is the past participle of **break**.

2 A **broken** line is not continuous but has gaps or spaces in it. *A broken blue line means the course of a waterless valley.* ADJ: ADJ n =dotted

3 You can use **broken** to describe a marriage that has ended in divorce, or a home in which the parents of the family are divorced, when you think this is a sad or bad thing. *She spoke for the first time about the traumas of a broken marriage... Children from broken homes are more likely to leave home before the age of 18.* ADJ: ADJ n PRAGMATICS

4 If someone talks in **broken** English, for example, or in **broken** French, they speak slowly and make a lot of mistakes because they do not know the language very well. *Eric could only respond in broken English.* ADJ: ADJ n ≠fluent, perfect

broken-down. A **broken-down** vehicle or machine no longer works because it has something wrong with it. *...a broken-down car.* ◆◇◇◇◇ ADJ: usu ADJ n

broken-hearted. Someone who is **broken-hearted** is very sad and upset because they have had a serious disappointment. ADJ

broker /broʊkəʳ/ **brokers, brokering, brokered** ◆◆◆◇◇

1 A **broker** is a person whose job is to buy and sell shares, foreign money, or goods for other people. N-COUNT

2 If a country or government **brokers** an agreement, a ceasefire, or a round of talks, they try to negotiate or arrange it. *The United Nations brokered a peace in Mogadishu at the end of March.* VERB =negotiate V n

brokerage /broʊkərɪdʒ/ **brokerages** ◆◇◇◇◇

1 A **brokerage** or a **brokerage** firm is a company of brokers. *...Japan's four biggest brokerages.* N-COUNT: usu N n

2 A **brokerage** fee or commission is the money charged by a broker for his services. N-UNCOUNT: usu N n

brolly /brɒli/ **brollies.** In British English, a **brolly** is the same as an **umbrella**; an informal word. N-COUNT

bromide /broʊmaɪd/ **bromides**

1 **Bromide** is a drug which used to be given to people to calm their nerves when they were worried or upset. *For the first time for months he was able to sleep without bromides.* N-MASS

2 A **bromide** is a comment which is intended to calm someone down when they are angry, but which has been expressed so often that it has become boring and meaningless; a formal use. *The government's actions belie Mr Waldegrave's bromides.* N-COUNT =platitude

bronchial /brɒŋkiəl/. **Bronchial** means affecting or concerned with the bronchial tubes; a medical term. *When he was eight, he got ill with bronchial asthma.* ADJ: ADJ n

bronchial tube, bronchial tubes. Your **bronchial tubes** are the two tubes which connect your windpipe to your lungs; a medical term. N-COUNT: usu pl

bronchitis /brɒŋkaɪtɪs/. **Bronchitis** is an illness like a very bad cough, in which your bronchial tubes become sore and infected. *He was in bed with bronchitis.* N-UNCOUNT

bronco /brɒŋkoʊ/ **broncos.** A **bronco** is a wild horse that cowboys ride in order to try to tame it. *...two cowboys riding bucking broncos.* N-COUNT

brontosaurus /brɒntəsɔːrəs/ **brontosauruses** or **brontosauri.** A **brontosaurus** was a plant-eating dinosaur with a small head, large body, and a long neck and tail. N-COUNT

bronze /brɒnz/ **bronzes** ◆◆◇◇◇

1 **Bronze** is a yellowish-brown metal which is a mixture of copper and tin. *...a bronze statue of Giorgi Dimitrov.* N-UNCOUNT

2 A **bronze** is a statue or sculpture made of bronze. *...a bronze of Napoleon on horseback.* N-COUNT

3 A **bronze** is a **bronze medal**. N-COUNT

4 Something that is **bronze** is yellowish-brown in colour. *Her hair shone bronze and gold. ...huge bronze chrysanthemums.* COLOUR

Bronze Age. The **Bronze Age** was a period of time in pre-history which began when people started making things from bronze about 4,000 - 6,000 years ago. N-PROPER: *the* N

bronzed /brɒnzd/. Someone who is **bronzed** is attractively sun-tanned. *He's bronzed from a short holiday in California.* ADJ-GRADED =tanned

bronze medal, bronze medals. If you win a **bronze medal**, you come third in a competition, especially a sports contest, and are often given a medal made of bronze as a prize. ◆◇◇◇◇ N-COUNT

bronzing /brɒnzɪŋ/. A **bronzing** powder or gel is used to give your skin a healthy, bronze, sun-tanned appearance. ADJ: ADJ n

brooch /brəʊtʃ/ **brooches.** A **brooch** is a small piece of jewellery which has a pin at the back so it can be fastened on a dress, blouse, or coat. N-COUNT

brood /bruːd/ **broods, brooding, brooded** ◆◇◇◇◇

1 A **brood** is a group of baby birds that were born at the same time to the same mother. *They can prove prolific breeders, rearing two or three broods a year.* N-COUNT: usu with supp

2 You can refer to someone's young children as their **brood** when you want to emphasize that there are a lot of them. *...a large brood of children.* N-COUNT: usu sing PRAGMATICS

3 If someone **broods** over something, they think about it a lot, seriously and often unhappily. *I guess everyone broods over things once in a while... She constantly broods about her family... I continued to brood. Would he always be like this?* VERB V over/on/about n V

brooding /bruːdɪŋ/ ◆◇◇◇◇

1 **Brooding** is used in written English to describe an atmosphere or feeling that causes you to feel disturbed or slightly afraid. *The same heavy, brooding silence descended on them.* ADJ-GRADED: usu ADJ n

2 If you describe someone's expression or appearance as **brooding**, you mean that they look as if they are thinking deeply and seriously about something, often something that is making them unhappy; used in written English. *She kissed him and gazed into his dark, brooding eyes.* ADJ-GRADED: usu ADJ n

broody /bruːdi/

1 You say that someone is **broody** when they are thinking a lot about something in an unhappy way. *He became very withdrawn and broody.* ADJ-GRADED

2 A **broody** hen is ready to lay or sit on eggs. ADJ

3 In British English, if you describe a young woman as **broody**, you mean that she wants to have a baby and she keeps thinking about it; an informal use. ADJ-GRADED: usu v-link ADJ

brook /brʊk/ **brooks, brooking, brooked** ◆◇◇◇◇

1 A **brook** is a small stream. N-COUNT

2 If someone in a position of authority is reported as saying that they will **brook** no interference or opposition, they mean that they will not accept any interference or opposition from others. *The Chinese leadership has said it will brook no interference in China's internal affairs... The army will brook no weakening of its power.* VERB =tolerate, allow V n

broom /bruːm/ **brooms** ◆◇◇◇◇

1 A **broom** is a kind of brush with a long handle. You use a broom for sweeping the floor. N-COUNT

2 **Broom** is a wild bush with a lot of tiny yellow flowers which grows on waste ground or sandy ground. N-UNCOUNT

broomstick /bruːmstɪk/ **broomsticks**

1 A **broomstick** is a broom which has a bundle of twigs at the end instead of bristles. N-COUNT

2 A **broomstick** is the handle of a broom. N-COUNT

Bros. Bros. is an abbreviation for **brothers**. It is usually used as part of the name of a company. *...Lazard Bros of New York.* =brothers

broth /brɒθ, AM brɔːθ/ **broths. Broth** is a kind of soup. It usually has vegetables or rice in it. ◆◇◇◇◇ N-VAR

brothel /brɒθᵊl/ **brothels.** A **brothel** is a building where men pay to have sex with prostitutes. *She ran a brothel called the Blue Moon Lodge.* ◆◇◇◇◇ N-COUNT

brother /brʌðəʳ/ **brothers.** The old-fashioned form **brethren** /breðrən/ is still sometimes used as the plural for meanings 2 and 3. ◆◆◆◆◆

1 Your **brother** is a boy or a man who has the same parents as you. *Oh, so you're Peter's younger brother... Have you got any brothers and sisters?* • See also **half-brother, stepbrother**. N-COUNT: oft poss N

2 You might describe as your **brother** a man who belongs to the same race, religion, country, profession, or trade union as you, or who has ideas that are similar to yours. *He told reporters he'd come to be with his Latvian brothers. ...the Cardinal and his brother bishops.* N-COUNT: usu poss N

3 **Brother** is a title given to a man who belongs to a religious community such as a monastery. *...Brother Otto. ...the Christian Brothers community which owns the castle.* N-TITLE; N-COUNT; N-VOC

brotherhood /brʌðəʳhʊd/ **brotherhoods** ◆◇◇◇◇

1 **Brotherhood** is the affection and loyalty that you feel for people who you have something in common with. *People threw flowers into the river between the two countries as a symbolic act of brotherhood... He believed in socialism and the brotherhood of man.* N-UNCOUNT

2 A **brotherhood** is an organization whose members all have the same political aims and beliefs or the same job or profession. *...the Brotherhood of Locomotive Engineers. ...a secret international brotherhood.* N-COUNT: usu with supp

brother-in-law, brothers-in-law. Someone's **brother-in-law** is the brother of their husband or wife, or the man who is married to their sister. ◆◇◇◇◇ N-COUNT: usu poss N

brotherly /brʌðəʳli/. A man's **brotherly** feelings are feelings of love and loyalty which you expect a brother to show. *...family loyalty and brotherly love... He gave her a brief, brotherly kiss.* ADJ-GRADED: usu ADJ n

brought /brɔːt/. **Brought** is the past tense and past participle of **bring**.

brouhaha /bruːhɑːhɑː/. A **brouhaha** is an excited and critical fuss or reaction to something; used mainly in journalism showing disapproval. *...the recent brouhaha over a congressional pay raise.* N-SING: also no det PRAGMATICS

brow /braʊ/ **brows** ◆◇◇◇◇

1 Your **brow** is your forehead. *He wiped his brow with the back of his hand... She wrinkled her brow inquisitively.* • to **knit** your **brow**: see **knit**. N-COUNT: usu poss N =forehead

2 Your **brows** are your eyebrows. *He had thick brown hair and shaggy brows.* N-COUNT: usu pl

3 The **brow** of a hill is the top part of it. *He was on the look-out just below the brow of the hill.* N-COUNT: usu N of n

browbeat /braʊbiːt/ **browbeats, browbeating, browbeaten.** The form **browbeat** is used in the present tense and is also the past tense. If someone tries to **browbeat** you, they try to bully you and force you to do what they want. *...attempts to deceive, con, or browbeat the voters... When I backed out of the 100 metres, an older kid tried to browbeat me into it.* ♦ **browbeaten** *...the browbeaten employees.* VERB V n V n into n ADJ-GRADED

brown /braʊn/ **browner, brownest; browns, browning, browned** ◆◆◆◆◆

1 Something that is **brown** is the colour of earth or of wood. *...her deep brown eyes... The stairs are decorated in golds and earthy browns.* COLOUR

2 You can describe a white-skinned person as **brown** when they have been sitting in the sun until their skin has become darker than usual. *I don't want to be really really brown, just have a nice light golden colour.* ADJ-GRADED: usu v-link ADJ =tanned

3 If someone **browns** in the sun or if the sun **browns** them, they becomes brown in colour. *Her skin was of the fortunate kind that could brown in the sun without burning... There were many gorgeous females busy browning themselves.* V-ERG V V n

4 A **brown** person is someone who belongs to a race of people who have brown-coloured skins. *...a slim brown man with a speckled turban.* ADJ: usu ADJ n

5 When food **browns** or when you **brown** food, you cook it, usually for a short time on a high flame. *Cook for ten minutes until the sugar browns... He browned the chicken in a frying pan.* V-ERG V V n

browned off. If you say that you are **browned off**, you mean that you are annoyed and depressed; used mainly in informal British English. *Far from being content with their lot, these graduates are pretty browned off.* ADJ-GRADED: usu v-link ADJ =fed up

brownie /braʊni/ **brownies;** also spelled **Brownie** for meanings 2, 3, and 4. ◆◇◇◇◇

1 **Brownies** are small flat biscuits or cakes. They are usually chocolate flavoured and have nuts in them. *...chocolate brownies... Michael picked up a tray of brownies in the kitchen.* N-COUNT: oft n N

2 **The Brownies** is a junior version of the Girl Guides for girls between the ages of seven and ten. Members of the Brownies attend a weekly meeting where they play games, sing songs, and learn practical skills. N-PROPER-COLL: *the*N

3 A **brownie** is a girl who is a member of the Brownies. N-COUNT

4 **Brownies** is one of the weekly meetings of the Brownies. *He had to leave at 5pm to pick his daughter up from Brownies.* N-UNCOUNT: usu prep N

brownie point, brownie points. If someone does something to score **brownie points**, they do it because they think they will be recognized or congratulated for it; used showing disapproval. *They're just trying to score brownie points with politicians.* N-COUNT: usu pl PRAGMATICS

brownish /braʊnɪʃ/. Something that is **brownish** is slightly brown in colour. COLOUR

brown nosing. If you say that someone is **brown-nosing**, you are saying in a rather offensive way that you think that they are deliberately flattering or agreeing with someone important in order to gain their support or cooperation; used showing disapproval. *He'd pushed his way to his present moderate eminence by a mixture of hard work, brown-nosing, and ruthless opportunism.* N-UNCOUNT PRAGMATICS

brown rice. **Brown rice** is rice that has not had its outer covering removed. It is cooked and eaten with savoury food. N-UNCOUNT

brownstone /braʊnstoʊn/ **brownstones.** In the United States, a **brownstone** is a type of house which was built during the 19th century. Brownstones have a front that is made from a reddish-brown sandstone. N-COUNT

browse /braʊz/ **browses, browsing, browsed** ◆◇◇◇◇

1 If you **browse** in a shop, you look at things in a fairly casual way, in the hope that you might find something you like. *I stopped in several bookstores to browse... She browsed in an up-market antiques shop... I'm just browsing around.* ► Also a noun. *...a browse around the shops.* ♦ **browser, browsers** *...a casual browser.* VERB; V; V prep/adv; N-COUNT: usu sing; N-COUNT

2 If you **browse** through a book or magazine, you look through it in a fairly casual way. *...sitting on the sofa browsing through the TV pages of the paper... There are plenty of biographies for him to browse over.* VERB; V prep

3 When animals **browse**, they feed on plants. *...the three red deer stags browsing 50 yards from my lodge on the fringes of the forest.* VERB; V; Also V *on*n, V n

bruise /bruːz/ **bruises, bruising, bruised** ◆◆◇◇◇

1 A **bruise** is an injury which appears as a purple mark on your body, although the skin is not broken. *How did you get that bruise on your cheek?... She was treated for cuts and bruises.* N-COUNT

2 If you **bruise** a part of your body, a bruise appears on it, for example because something hits you. If you **bruise** easily, bruises appear when something hits you only slightly. *I had only bruised my knee.* ♦ **bruised** *I escaped with severely bruised legs.* V-ERG; V n; Also V adv/prep; ADJ-GRADED

3 If you **bruise** a fruit, vegetable, or plant, you damage it by handling it roughly, so that there is a mark on the skin and the taste of the fruit is spoilt. If a fruit **bruises** easily, it can be damaged, even if it is not handled roughly. *Choose a warm, dry day to cut them off the plants, being careful not to bruise them. ...bruised tomatoes and cucumbers... Be sure to store them carefully as they bruise easily.* ► Also a noun. *...bruises on the fruit's skin.* V-ERG; V n; V-ed; V adv; Also V; N-COUNT

4 If you **are bruised** by an unpleasant experience, it makes you feel unhappy or emotionally weakened. *The government will be severely bruised by yesterday's events... Their egos are so easily bruised.* ♦ **bruising** *The bruising experience of near-bankruptcy has left him chastened.* VB: usu passive =wound; *be*V-ed; ADJ-GRADED: usu ADJ n

bruiser /bruːzəʳ/ **bruisers.** A **bruiser** is someone who is tough, strong, and aggressive, and enjoys a fight or an argument; used showing disapproval. *Dad was a docker and a bit of a bruiser in his day... Mr Clarke is famed as the best bruiser in the cabinet.* N-COUNT PRAGMATICS

bruising /bruːzɪŋ/ ◆◇◇◇◇

1 If someone has **bruising** on their body, they have bruises on it; a formal use. *She had quite severe bruising and a cut lip.* N-UNCOUNT =bruises, contusions

2 In a **bruising** battle or encounter, people fight or compete with each other in a very aggressive or determined way; used in journalism. *The administration hopes to avoid another bruising battle over civil rights.* ADJ-GRADED: usu ADJ n

Brummie /brʌmi/ **Brummies. Brummie** means belonging to or coming from Birmingham; an informal word. *...a Brummie accent.* ► A **Brummie** is someone who comes from Birmingham. ADJ: usu ADJ n; N-COUNT

brunch /brʌntʃ/ **brunches. Brunch** is a meal that is eaten in the late morning. It is a combination of breakfast and lunch. *I've already invited Mary Ann and Brian to brunch.* N-VAR

brunette /bruːnet/ **brunettes.** A **brunette** is a white-skinned woman or girl with dark brown hair. N-COUNT

brunt /brʌnt/. If someone or something **bears the brunt** or **takes the brunt** of something unpleasant, they suffer the main part or force of it. *Young people are bearing the brunt of unemployment... A child's head tends to take the brunt of any fall.* ◆◇◇◇◇ PHRASE: V inflects, usu PHR *of*n

brush /brʌʃ/ **brushes, brushing, brushed** ◆◆◆◇◇

1 A **brush** is an object which has a large number of bristles fixed to it. You use brushes for painting, for cleaning things, and for tidying your hair. *We gave him paint and brushes... Stains are removed with buckets of soapy water and scrubbing brushes. ...a hair brush.* N-COUNT

2 If you **brush** something or **brush** something such as dirt off it, you clean it or tidy it using a brush. *Have you brushed your teeth?... She brushed the powder out of her hair... Using a small brush, he brushed away the fine sawdust.* ► Also a noun. *I gave it a quick brush with my hairbrush.* VERB; V n; V n prep; V n with adv; N-SING: *a*N

3 If you **brush** something with a liquid, you apply a layer of that liquid using a brush. *Take a sheet of filo pastry and brush it with melted butter.* VERB; V n *with*n

4 If you **brush** something somewhere, you remove it with quick light movements of your hands. *He brushed his hair back with both hands... She brushed away tears as she spoke of him... He brushed the snow off the windshield.* VERB; V n with adv; V n prep

5 If one thing **brushes** against another or if you **brush** one thing against another, the first thing touches the second thing lightly while passing it. *Something brushed against her leg... I felt her dark brown hair brushing the back of my shoulder... She knelt and brushed her lips softly across Michael's cheek.* V-ERG; V prep; V n; V n prep

6 If you **brush** past someone or **brush** by them, you almost touch them as you go past them; used in written English. *My father would burst into the kitchen, brushing past my mother... He brushed by with a perfunctory wave to the crowd.* VERB; V prep/adv

7 If you have a **brush** with someone, you have an argument or disagreement with them. You use **brush** when you want to make an argument or disagreement sound less serious than it really is. *My first brush with a headmaster came six years ago... It is his third brush with the law in less than a year.* N-COUNT: usu N *with*n PRAGMATICS

8 If you have a **brush** with a particular situation, usually an unpleasant one, you almost experience it. *...the trauma of a brush with death... The corporation is fighting to survive its second brush with bankruptcy.* N-COUNT: N *with*n =encounter

9 **Brush** is an area of rough open land covered with small bushes and trees. You also use **brush** to refer to the bushes and trees on this land. *...the brush fire that destroyed nearly 500 acres. ...a meadow of low brush and grass.* N-UNCOUNT =bush

10 See also **broad-brush, nail brush.**

11 ● **tarred with the same brush**: see **tar.**

brush aside or **brush away.** If you **brush aside** or **brush away** an idea, remark, or feeling, you refuse to consider it because you think it is not important or useful, even though it may be. *Perhaps you* PHRASAL VERB =ignore; V n P *shouldn't brush the idea aside too hastily... He brushed away my views on politics.* V P n (not pron)

brush off. If someone **brushes** you **off** when you speak to them, they refuse to talk to you or be nice to you. *When I tried to talk to her about it she just brushed me off.* • See also **brush-off.** PHRASAL VERB V n P Also V P n (not pron)

brush up or **brush up on.** If you **brush up** something or **brush up on** it, you practise it or improve your knowledge of it. *I had hoped to brush up my Spanish... Eleanor spent much of the summer brushing up on her driving.* PHRASAL VERB V P n (not pron) V P P n

brushed /brʌʃt/. **Brushed** cotton, nylon, or other fabric feels soft and furry. ADJ: ADJ n

brush-off. If someone gives you the **brush-off** when you speak to them, they refuse to talk to you or be nice to you; an informal word. *I knew when she said, 'Well, it's not a good time right now,' that I was being given the brush-off.* N-SING

brushstroke /brʌʃstroʊk/ **brushstrokes. Brushstrokes** are the marks made on a surface by a painter with a paintbrush. *He paints with harsh, slashing brushstrokes.* N-COUNT

brushwood /brʌʃwʊd/. **Brushwood** consists of small branches and twigs that have broken off trees and bushes. N-UNCOUNT

brushwork /brʌʃwɜːʳk/. An artist's **brushwork** is their way of using their brush to put paint on a canvas and the effect that this has in the picture. *His colour and brushwork are daring, striving towards a bold effect.* N-UNCOUNT

brusque /brʌsk/. If you describe a person or their behaviour as **brusque**, you mean that they deal with things, or say things, quickly and abruptly and do not show much consideration for other people. *The doctors are brusque and busy... They received a characteristically brusque reply from him.* ♦ **brusquely** *'It's only a sprain,' Paula said brusquely.* ADJ-GRADED =abrupt; ADV-GRADED: ADV with v

brussels sprout /brʌsəlz spraʊt/ **brussels sprouts;** also spelled **Brussels sprout. Brussels sprouts** are vegetables that look like tiny cabbages. N-COUNT: usu pl =sprout

brutal /bruːtəl/ ◆◆◇◇◇

1 A **brutal** act or person is cruel and violent. *He was the victim of a very brutal murder. ...the brutal suppression of anti-government protests... Jensen is a dangerous man, and can be very brutal and reckless.* ♦ **brutally** *Her real parents had been brutally murdered.* ADJ-GRADED =vicious, savage; ADV-GRADED: usu ADV with v

2 If someone expresses something unpleasant with **brutal** honesty or frankness, they express it in a clear and accurate way, without attempting to disguise its unpleasantness. *It was refreshing to talk about themselves and their feelings with brutal honesty... He took an anguished breath. He had to be brutal and say it.* ♦ **brutally** *The talks had been brutally frank... 'Lotte Bruckner is dead.' It came out more brutally than Brand had intended.* ADJ-GRADED; ADV-GRADED: ADV adj, ADV with v

3 **Brutal** is used to describe things that have an unpleasant effect on people, especially when there is no attempt by anyone to reduce their effect. *The dip in prices this summer will be brutal... The afternoon sun had been brutal. ...a brutal adjustment from communism to capitalism.* ♦ **brutally** *The Maastricht referendum has brutally exposed the flaws in France's constitution.* ADJ-GRADED =merciless; ADV-GRADED: usu ADV with v, also ADV adj =mercilessly

brutalise /bruːtəlaɪz/. See **brutalize.**

brutality /bruːtælɪti/ **brutalities. Brutality** is cruel and violent treatment or behaviour. A **brutality** is an instance of cruel and violent treatment or behaviour. *Her experience of men was of domination and brutality. ...police brutality. ...the atrocities and brutalities committed by a former regime.* ◆◇◇◇◇ N-VAR

brutalize /bruːtəlaɪz/ **brutalizes, brutalizing, brutalized;** also spelled **brutalise** in British English.

1 If an unpleasant experience **brutalizes** someone, it makes them cruel, violent, or uncaring. *The occupation brutalized many French men and women... He was selfish, guarded, and brutalized by his Civil War experiences.* VERB V n V-ed

2 If one person **brutalizes** another, they treat them in a cruel or violent way. *The policemen brutalized him and concocted his confessions.* VERB V n

brute /bruːt/ **brutes** ◆◇◇◇◇

1 If you call someone, usually a man, a **brute**, you mean that they are rough, violent, and insensitive. *Custer was an idiot and a brute and he deserved his fate. ...a drunken brute.* N-COUNT

2 When you refer to **brute** strength or force, you are contrasting it with gentler methods or qualities. *He used brute force to take control... Boxing is a test of skill and technique, rather than brute strength.* ADJ: ADJ n

3 **Brute** emotions or facts are basic, unthinking feelings or responses to a situation, or the basic, fundamental facts of this situation. *...brute loyalty to the herd. ...brute historical fact. ...the brute ugliness of nationalism and chauvinism.* ADJ: ADJ n

brutish /bruːtɪʃ/. If you describe a person, their behaviour, or human life as **brutish**, you think that they are brutal and uncivilised. *The man was brutish and coarse. ...brutish bullying. ...the band's view that life is nasty, brutish and short.* ADJ-GRADED

BS /biː es/. ◆◇◇◇◇

1 **BS** is an abbreviation for 'British Standard', a standard that something sold in Britain must reach in a test to prove that it is satisfactory or safe. Each standard has a number for reference. *Does your electric blanket conform to BS 3456?*

2 In American English, a **BS** is the same as a **BSc.**

BSc /biː es siː/ **BScs** ◆◇◇◇◇

1 A **BSc** is a first degree in a science subject. **BSc** is an abbreviation for **Bachelor of Science**. *He completed his BSc in chemistry in 1934.* N-COUNT

2 **BSc** is written after someone's name to indicate that they have a BSc. *...J. Hodgkison BSc.*

BSE /biː es iː/. **BSE** is a fatal disease which affects the nervous system of cattle. It is an abbreviation for 'bovine spongiform encephalopathy'. N-UNCOUNT =mad cow disease

B-side, B-sides. The **B-side** of a pop record has the less important or less popular song on it. *...a compilation of the band's A and B-sides.* N-COUNT

bubble /bʌbəl/ **bubbles, bubbling, bubbled** ◆◆◇◇◇

1 **Bubbles** are small balls of air or gas in a liquid. *Ink particles attach themselves to air bubbles and rise to the surface. ...a bubble of gas trapped under the surface.* N-COUNT

2 A **bubble** is a hollow, delicate ball of soapy liquid that is floating in the air or standing on a surface. *With soap and water, bubbles and boats, children love bathtime.* N-COUNT

3 In a comic or cartoon, a speech **bubble** is the shape which surrounds the words which a character is thinking or saying. N-COUNT

4 When a liquid **bubbles**, bubbles move in it, for example because it is boiling or moving quickly. *Heat the seasoned stock until it is bubbling... The coffeepot bubbled, filling the room with fragrance... The fermenting wine has bubbled up and over the top... Danny looked down at the stream bubbling through the trees nearby.* VERB V V adv/prep

5 If something **bubbles**, it is very active; used in written English. *At the same time, the press bubbles with stories of the sale of Russian arms to Serbia... The show bubbles like pink champagne with pretty sets, exquisite costumes and enchanting dance routines.* VERB V *with* n V

6 A feeling, influence, or activity that **is bubbling** away continues to occur. *...political tensions that have been bubbling away for years... Rumours of financial scandals have come bubbling back to the surface... Retail sales and car sales have been bubbling along, quite nicely, for some months.* VB: usu cont V adv/prep

7 Someone who **is bubbling with** a good feeling is so full of it that they keep expressing the way they feel to everyone around them. *She came to the phone bubbling with excitement... She came back bubbling with ideas.* ► **Bubble over** means the same as **bubble**. *He was quite tireless, bubbling over with vitality.* ► Also a noun. *As she spoke she felt a bubble of optimism rising inside her.* VB: usu cont V *with* n; PHRASAL VERB V P *with* n; N-COUNT: usu N *of* n

8 If you say that **the bubble has burst**, or that **the bubble has been pricked**, you mean that a situa- PHRASE: V inflects

tion or idea which seemed wonderful has ended or has stopped seeming wonderful. *It was only a matter of time before this bubble burst. ...their confidence that they can prick a speculative bubble without hurting the real economy.*

bubble over. See bubble 6. PHRASAL VERB

bubble up. A feeling that **is bubbling up** inside you is growing stronger and stronger. *She could feel the anger growing, bubbling up inside her.* PHRASAL VERB V P

bubble and squeak. In Britain, **bubble and squeak** is a dish made from a mixture of cold cooked cabbage, potato, and sometimes meat. It can be grilled or fried. N-UNCOUNT

bubble bath, bubble baths

1 **Bubble bath** is a liquid that smells nice and makes a lot of foam when you add it to your bath water. *...a bottle of bubble bath.* N-UNCOUNT

2 When you have a **bubble bath**, you lie in a bath of water with bubble bath in it. *...a long, relaxing bubble bath.* N-COUNT

bubble gum; also spelled **bubblegum**. **Bubble gum** is a sweet substance similar to chewing gum. You can blow it out of your mouth so it makes the shape of a bubble. *I got bubblegum on the seat of Nanna's car.* N-UNCOUNT

bubbly /bʌbli/ ◆◇◇◇◇

1 Someone who is **bubbly** is very lively and cheerful and talks a lot; used showing approval. *...a bubbly girl who loves to laugh... She had a bright and bubbly personality.* ADJ-GRADED PRAGMATICS =bouncy

2 Champagne is sometimes called **bubbly**; an informal use. *Guests were presented with glasses of bubbly on arrival.* N-UNCOUNT

3 If something is **bubbly**, it has a lot of bubbles in it. *...a nice hot bubbly bath... Melt the butter over a medium-low heat. When it is melted and bubbly, put in the flour.* ADJ-GRADED

bubonic plague /bjuːbɒnɪk pleɪg, AM buː-/. **Bubonic plague** is an infectious disease spread to people from rats. It causes swellings in the armpit and groin, delirium, and usually death. N-UNCOUNT =plague

buccaneer /bʌkənɪəʳ/ **buccaneers**

1 A **buccaneer** is a pirate, especially one who attacked and stole from Spanish ships in the 17th and 18th centuries. N-COUNT

2 If you describe someone as a **buccaneer**, you mean they are clever and successful, especially in business, but you do not completely trust them. N-COUNT

buccaneering /bʌkənɪərɪŋ/. If you describe someone as **buccaneering**, you mean they enjoy being involved in risky or even dishonest activities, especially in order to make money. *...a buccaneering British businessman.* ADJ-GRADED: ADJ n

buck /bʌk/ **bucks, bucking, bucked** ◆◆◇◇◇

1 A **buck** is a US or Australian dollar; an informal use. *That would probably cost you about fifty bucks... Why can't you spend a few bucks on a coat?... This means big bucks for someone.* N-COUNT =dollar

2 In Southern Africa, a **buck** is the same as an **antelope**. The plural is either 'buck' or 'bucks'. N-COUNT

3 A **buck** is the male of various animals, including the deer and rabbit. N-COUNT

4 In informal American English, a **buck** is a young man. *He'd been a real hell-raiser as a young buck.* N-COUNT

5 If someone has **buck** teeth, their upper front teeth stick forward out of their mouth. ADJ: ADJ n =protruding

6 If a horse **bucks**, it kicks both of its back legs wildly into the air, or jumps into the air wildly with all four feet off the ground. *The stallion bucked as he fought against the reins holding him tightly in. ...cowboys riding bucking broncos.* VERB V V-ing

7 In American English, if someone or something **bucks** against something, they move very suddenly against it. *Fiona bucked against her captor and fought for breath... The revolver bucked violently upwards in his hands.* VERB V prep/adv Also V

8 If someone or something **bucks** the trend or **bucks** the system, they do something to resist it. *While other newspapers are losing circulation, we are bucking the trend... He wants to be the tough rebel who bucks the system... The company believes it is bucking the recession and says orders continue to be satisfactory.* VERB V n

9 If you get more **bang for the buck**, you spend your money wisely and get more for your money than if you spend it in a different way; used mainly in American English. *I think it's very important for those governments to do whatever they can to get a bigger bang for the buck.* PHRASES usu v compar PHR =value for money

10 When someone makes **a fast buck** or makes **a quick buck**, they earn a lot of money quickly and easily, often by doing something which is considered to be dishonest; used in informal English. *His life isn't ruled by looking for a fast buck... They were just in it to make a quick buck.* usu v PHR

11 If you are trying to **make a buck**, you are trying to earn some money; an informal expression. *The owners don't want to overlook any opportunity to make a buck.* V inflects

12 In informal American English, someone who is **buck naked** is not wearing any clothes at all. =stark naked

13 If you **pass the buck**, you refuse to accept responsibility for something, and say that someone else is responsible; an informal expression. *David says the responsibility is Mr Smith's and it's no good trying to pass the buck.* V inflects

14 If you say **'The buck stops here'** or **'The buck stops with** me', you mean that you have to take responsibility for something and will not try to pass the responsibility on to someone else; used in informal English. *The buck stops with him. He is ultimately responsible for every aspect of the broadcast.* V inflects

buck up PHRASAL VERB

1 If you **buck** someone **up** or **buck up** their spirits, you say or do something to make them more cheerful; an informal use. *Anything anybody said to him to try and buck him up wouldn't sink in... The aim, it seemed, was to buck up their spirits in the face of the recession.* =cheer up V n P V P n (not pron)

2 If you tell someone to **buck up** or to **buck up** their ideas, you are telling them to start behaving in a more positive and efficient manner; an informal use. *People are saying if we don't buck up we'll be in trouble... Buck up your ideas or you'll get more of the same treatment.* =pull one's socks up V P V P n (not pron)

bucket /bʌkɪt/ **buckets, bucketing, bucketed** ◆◆◇◇◇

1 A **bucket** is a round metal or plastic container with a handle attached to its sides. Buckets are often used for holding and carrying water. *We drew water in a bucket from the well outside the door... The girls happily played in the sand and sea with buckets and spades.* ► A **bucket** of water is the amount of water contained in a bucket. *She threw a bucket of water over them.* N-COUNT; N-COUNT: usu N of n =bucketful

2 **Buckets** or **bucket-loads** of something means a large amount of it; an informal use. *They obviously have buckets of confidence... They didn't exactly sell bucket-loads of records the first time around.* QUANT: QUANT of n-uncount/pl-n =bucketful

3 If someone cries **buckets**, they cry a great deal because they are very upset. If it rains **buckets**, it rains a great deal; an informal use. *He was weeping buckets... The rain was still coming down in buckets when we went back out.* N-PLURAL

4 If something **buckets** somewhere, it moves there very quickly and unsteadily. *A car came bucketing down the track into the quarry.* VERB V adv/prep Also V

5 If you say that someone **has kicked the bucket**, you mean that they have died; an informal expression which some people find offensive. PHRASE: V inflects

bucket down. If the rain **buckets down**, or if it **buckets down** with rain, it rains very heavily; an informal expression. *As soon as we were inside, the rain began to bucket down... If it hadn't been bucketing down with rain and blowing a gale, I would have had a glorious view.* PHRASAL VERB =pour V P it V P with n

bucketful /bʌkɪtfʊl/ **bucketfuls**

1 A **bucketful** of something is the amount contained in a bucket. *They threw two bucketfuls of seawater on him.* N-COUNT: usu N of n =bucket

2 If you say that someone produces or gets something **by the bucketful**, you mean that they produce or get something in large quantities; an infor- PHRASE: PHR after v

mal expression. *Over the years they have sold records by the bucketful.*

bucket seat, bucket seats. A **bucket seat** is a seat for one person in a car or aeroplane which has rounded sides that partly enclose and support the body. N-COUNT

bucket shop, bucket shops. In Britain, a **bucket shop** is a travel agency that sells airline tickets cheaply in order to fill seats which would otherwise be empty. N-COUNT

buckle /bʌkəl/ **buckles, buckling, buckled** ◆◇◇◇◇
1 A **buckle** is a piece of metal or plastic attached to one end of a belt or strap, which is used to fasten it. *He wore a belt with a large brass buckle.* N-COUNT
2 When you **buckle** a belt or strap, you fasten it. *A door slammed in the house and a man came out buckling his belt.* VERB Vn
3 If an object **buckles** or if something **buckles** it, it becomes bent as a result of very great heat or force. *The door was beginning to buckle from the intense heat... A freak wave had buckled the deck.* V-ERG V Vn
4 If your legs or knees **buckle**, they bend because they have become very weak or tired. *Mcanally's knees buckled and he crumpled down onto the floor... His right leg buckled under him.* VERB V

buckle down. If you **buckle down** to something, you start working seriously at it; an informal expression. *He has buckled down to work in the reserves... I just buckled down and got on with playing.* PHRASAL VERB =knuckle down VP to n VP

buckle under. If you **buckle under** to a person or a situation, you do what they want you to do, even though you do not want to do it. *Protesters accused Wilson of buckling under to right-wing religious groups... If he yelled and screamed, my parents buckled under and gave him whatever he wanted.* PHRASAL VERB VP to n VP

buckle up. When you **buckle up** in a car or a plane, you fasten your seat belt; an informal expression. *A sign just ahead of me said, Buckle Up. It's the Law.* PHRASAL VERB VP

buckled /bʌkəld/. **Buckled** shoes have buckles on them, either to fasten them or as decoration. ADJ: ADJ n

Bucks Fizz; also spelled **Buck's Fizz. Bucks Fizz** is a drink made by mixing champagne or another sparkling white wine with orange juice. N-UNCOUNT

buckshot /bʌkʃɒt/. **Buckshot** consists of large pellets of lead shot used for hunting animals. N-UNCOUNT

buckskin /bʌkskɪn/. **Buckskin** is soft, strong leather made from the skin of a deer or a goat. N-UNCOUNT

buckwheat /bʌkʰwiːt/. **Buckwheat** is a type of small black grain used for feeding animals and making flour. **Buckwheat** also refers to the flour itself. N-UNCOUNT

bucolic /bjuːkɒlɪk/. **Bucolic** means relating to the countryside; a literary word. *...the bucolic surroundings of Chantilly.* ADJ: usu ADJ n =rural

bud /bʌd/ **buds, budding, budded** ◆◆◇◇◇
1 A **bud** is a small pointed lump that appears on a tree or plant and develops into a leaf or flower. *Rosanna's favourite time is early summer, just before the buds open.* N-COUNT
2 When a tree or plant **is budding**, buds are appearing on it or are beginning to open. *The leaves were budding on the trees below.* VB: usu cont
3 In informal American English, some men use **bud** as a way of addressing other men. *You heard what the boss said, bud.* N-VOC =mate
4 See also **budding; cotton bud, taste bud.**
5 When a tree or plant is **in bud** or has come **into bud**, it has buds on it. *The flowers are bronzy in bud and bright yellow when open. ...almond trees that should come into bud soon.* PHRASES
6 If you **nip** something such as bad behaviour **in the bud**, you stop it before it can develop very far; an informal expression. *It is important to recognize jealousy and to nip it in the bud before it gets out of hand.* V inflects

Buddha /bʊdə/ **Buddhas** ◆◇◇◇◇
1 **Buddha** is the title given to Gautama Siddhartha, who was a religious teacher and the founder of Buddhism. N-PROPER: oft the N
2 A **Buddha** is a statue or picture of the Buddha. N-COUNT

Buddhism /bʊdɪzəm/. **Buddhism** is a religion which teaches that the way to end suffering is by overcoming your desires. ◆◇◇◇◇ N-UNCOUNT

Buddhist /bʊdɪst/ **Buddhists** ◆◇◇◇◇
1 A **Buddhist** is a person whose religion is Buddhism. N-COUNT
2 **Buddhist** means relating or referring to Buddhism. *...Buddhist monks. ...Buddhist philosophy.* ADJ: usu ADJ n

budding /bʌdɪŋ/ ◆◇◇◇◇
1 If you describe someone as, for example, a **budding** businessman or a **budding** artist, you mean that they are starting to succeed or become interested in business or art. *The forum is now open to all budding entrepreneurs... Budding linguists can tune in to the activity cassettes in French, German, Spanish and Italian.* ADJ: ADJ n
2 You use **budding** to describe a situation that is just beginning. *Our budding romance was over. ...Russia's budding democracy.* ADJ: ADJ n

buddy /bʌdi/ **buddies** ◆◇◇◇◇
1 A **buddy** is a close friend, usually a male friend of a man; used mainly in American English. *We became great buddies.* N-COUNT =pal
2 In the United States, men sometimes address other men as **buddy**; an informal use. *Hey, no way, buddy.* N-VOC =pal

budge /bʌdʒ/ **budges, budging, budged** ◆◇◇◇◇
1 If someone will not **budge** on a matter, or if nothing **budges** them, they refuse to change their mind or to compromise. *Both sides say they will not budge... The Americans are adamant that they will not budge on this point... No amount of prodding will budge him.* V-ERG: with brd-neg V Vn
2 If someone or something will not **budge**, they will not move. If you cannot **budge** them, you cannot make them move. *Her mother refused to budge from London... The window refused to budge... I got a grip on the boat and pulled but I couldn't budge it.* V-ERG: with brd-neg V Vn

budgerigar /bʌdʒərigɑːʳ/ **budgerigars. Budgerigars** are small, brightly-coloured birds from Australia that people often keep as pets. ◆◇◇◇◇ N-COUNT =budgie

budget /bʌdʒɪt/ **budgets, budgeting, budgeted** ◆◆◆◆◇
1 Your **budget** is the amount of money that you have available to spend. The **budget** for something is the amount of money that a person, organization, or country has available to spend on it. *She will design a fantastic new kitchen for you – and all within your budget... Someone had furnished the place on a tight budget... This year's budget for AIDS prevention probably won't be much higher.* N-COUNT: with supp
2 The **budget** of an organization or country is its financial situation, considered as the difference between the money it receives and the money it spends. *The hospital obviously needs to balance the budget each year. ...his readiness to raise taxes as part of an effort to cut the budget deficit.* N-COUNT
3 In Britain, the **Budget** is the financial plan announced by the government which states how much money they intend to raise through taxation and how they intend to spend it. The **Budget** is also used to refer to the speech in which this plan is announced. *The Chancellor could use the Budget to bring in taxation reforms. ...other indirect tax changes announced in the Budget.* N-PROPER
4 If you **budget** certain amounts of money for particular things, you decide that you can afford to spend those amounts on those things. *The company has budgeted $10 million for advertising... The movie is only budgeted at $10 million... I'm learning how to budget.* ♦ **budgeting** *We have continued to exercise caution in our budgeting for the current year.* VERB V amount for n be V-ed at amount V Also V amount to-inf N-UNCOUNT
5 **Budget** is used in advertising to suggest that something is being sold cheaply. *Cheap flights are available from budget travel agents from £240.* ADJ: ADJ n =economy

budget for. If you **budget for** something, you take account of it when you are deciding how much you can afford to spend on different things. *The authorities had budgeted for some non-* PHRASAL VERB =allow for VP n payment... *The zoo was budgeting for 850,000 visitors this year.*

-budget /-bʌdʒɪt/. **-budget** combines with adjectives such as 'low' and 'big' to form adjectives which indicate how much money has been allocated to something, especially the making of a film. *This obviously low-budget movie offers no attempt to explore the real issues. ...a big-budget adventure movie starring Mel Gibson.* COMB in ADJ-GRADED

budgetary /bʌdʒɪtəri, AM -teri/. A **budgetary** matter or policy is concerned with the amount of money that is available to a country or organization, and how it is to be spent; a formal word. *There are huge budgetary pressures on all governments in Europe to reduce the', armed forces.* ◆◇◇◇◇ ADJ: ADJ n

budgie /bʌdʒi/ **budgies.** A **budgie** is the same as a **budgerigar**; an informal word. N-COUNT =budgerigar

buff /bʌf/ **buffs, buffing, buffed** ◆◇◇◇◇

1 Something that is **buff** is pale brown in colour. *He took a largish buff envelope from his pocket.* COLOUR

2 You use **buff** to describe someone who knows a lot about a particular subject. For example, if you describe someone as a film **buff**, you mean that they know a lot about films; an informal use. *Judge Lanier is a real film buff... Any competent computer buff should be able to do it for you in a few minutes.* N-COUNT: supp N =enthusiast

3 If you **buff** the surface of something, for example your car or your shoes, you rub it with a piece of soft material in order to make it shine. *He was already buffing the car's hubs.* ♦ **buffing** *Regular buffing helps prevent nails from splitting.* VERB =polish V n N-UNCOUNT

buffalo /bʌfəloʊ/ **buffaloes.** The plural can be either **buffaloes** or **buffalo.** ◆◇◇◇◇

1 A **buffalo** is a wild animal like a large cow with horns that curve upwards. Buffalo are usually found in southern and eastern Africa. N-COUNT =bison

2 A **buffalo** is the same as a **water buffalo.** N-COUNT

3 A **buffalo** is the same as a **bison.** N-COUNT

buffer /bʌfəʳ/ **buffers, buffering, buffered** ◆◇◇◇◇

1 A **buffer** is something that prevents something else from being harmed or that prevents two things from harming each other. *Keep savings as a buffer against unexpected cash needs. ...a multinational buffer force between the two sides... Mongolia stands as a buffer between China and the former Soviet Union.* N-COUNT: oft N *against/between* n, N n

2 If something is **buffered**, it is protected from harm. *The company is buffered by long-term contracts with growers.* VERB be V-ed Also V n

3 In British English, the **buffers** on a train or at the end of a railway line are two metal discs on springs that reduce the shock when a train hits them. N-COUNT: usu pl

4 In British English, if you say that someone, usually a man, is an old **buffer**, you mean that you think they are rather foolish. *...a collection of old buffers who meet at the Grosvenor House once a month for lunch.* N-COUNT

buffer state, buffer states. A **buffer state** is a peaceful country situated between two or more larger hostile countries. *Turkey and Greece were buffer states against the Soviet Union.* N-COUNT

buffer zone, buffer zones. A **buffer zone** is a neutral area created to separate opposing forces or groups. N-COUNT

buffet, buffets, buffeting, buffeted. Pronounced /bʊfeɪ, AM bʊfeɪ/ for meanings 1 to 3, and /bʌfɪt/ for meanings 4 and 5. ◆◇◇◇◇

1 A **buffet** is a meal of cold food that is displayed on a long table at a party or public occasion. Guests usually serve themselves from the table. *...a buffet lunch... A cold buffet had been laid out in the dining-room.* N-COUNT: oft N n

2 A **buffet** is a café, usually in a hotel or station. *We sat in the station buffet sipping tea.* N-COUNT: oft n N

3 On a train, the **buffet** or the **buffet car** is the carriage where meals and snacks are sold; used mainly in British English. *There's no heating in the carriages and the buffet's closed.* N-COUNT: usu sing

4 If something **is buffeted** by strong winds or by stormy seas, it is repeatedly struck or blown around by them. *Their plane had been severely buffeted by storms... Storms swept the country, closing roads, buffeting ferries and killing as many as 30 people.* ♦ **buffeting, buffetings** *...the buffetings of the winds.* VERB be V-ed V n N-COUNT

5 If an economy or government **is buffeted** by difficult or unpleasant situations, it experiences many of them. *The whole of Africa had been buffeted by social and political upheavals.* VERB be V-ed

buffoon /bʌfuːn/ **buffoons.** If you call someone a **buffoon**, you mean that they often do foolish things; an old-fashioned word. *...the man once dismissed by the West as a drunken buffoon.* N-COUNT PRAGMATICS =clown

buffoonery /bʌfuːnəri/. **Buffoonery** is foolish behaviour that makes you laugh; an old-fashioned word. *...the music hall buffoonery of Norman Wisdom.* N-UNCOUNT

bug /bʌg/ **bugs, bugging, bugged** ◆◆◇◇◇

1 A **bug** is an insect or similar small creature; an informal use. *We noticed tiny bugs that were all over the walls. ...a bloodsucking bug which infests poor housing.* N-COUNT: usu pl

2 A **bug** is an illness which is caused by small organisms such as bacteria; an informal use. *I think I've got a bit of a stomach bug... There was a bug going around at the club. ...the killer brain bug meningitis.* N-COUNT

3 If there is a **bug** in a computer programme, there is an error in it. *There is a bug in the software.* N-COUNT

4 A **bug** is a tiny hidden microphone which transmits what people are saying. *There was a bug on the phone.* N-COUNT

5 If someone **bugs** a place, they hide tiny microphones in it which transmit what people are saying. *He heard that they were planning to bug his office... I found out my phone was bugged.* ♦ **bugging** *...an electronic bugging device.* VERB =wire, tap V n N-UNCOUNT

6 You can say that someone has been bitten by a particular **bug** when they suddenly become very enthusiastic about something; an informal use. *I've definitely been bitten by the gardening bug... Roundhay Park in Leeds was the place I first got the fishing bug.* N-SING: oft n N

7 If someone or something **bugs** you, they worry or annoy you; an informal use. *I only did it to bug my parents.* VERB V n

bugbear /bʌgbeəʳ/ **bugbears.** Something or someone that is your **bugbear** worries or upsets you. *Money is my biggest bugbear.* N-COUNT

bug-eyed. A **bug-eyed** person or animal has eyes that bulge out. *...bug-eyed monsters... John and Bill and I were bug-eyed in wonderment.* ADJ

bugger /bʌgəʳ/ **buggers, buggering, buggered**

1 In British English, some people describe someone as a **bugger** when that person has done something annoying or stupid. **Bugger** is often used by people pretending to be rude as a joke; an informal use which some people find offensive. N-COUNT: oft adj N PRAGMATICS

2 In British English, some people say that a job or task is a **bugger** when it is difficult to do; an informal use which some people find offensive. N-SING: a N

3 In British English, some people use **bugger** in expressions such as **bugger him** or **bugger the cost** in order to emphasize that they do not care about the person or thing that the word or phrase refers to; an informal use which some people find offensive. VB: only imper, V n PRAGMATICS =blow

4 To **bugger** someone means to have anal intercourse with them, usually in a violent way. *He raped and buggered her then tried to strangle her.* VERB V n

5 In British English, some people say **bugger it** or **bugger** when they are angry that something has gone wrong; an informal expression which some people find offensive. PHRASES EXCLAM PRAGMATICS

6 In British English, some people say **bugger me** to emphasize that they are very surprised about something; an informal expression which some people find offensive. EXCLAM PRAGMATICS

bugger about or **bugger around** PHRASAL VERB

1 In British English, if someone **buggers about** or **buggers around**, they waste time doing unnecessary things; an informal expression which some people find offensive. V P =mess about, mess around

2 In British English, if someone **buggers** you **about** or **buggers** you **around**, they cause you problems; V n P

an informal expression which some people find offensive.

bugger off. In British English, if someone **buggers off**, they go away quickly and suddenly. People often say **bugger off** as a rude way of telling someone to go away; an informal expression which some people find offensive.
PHRASAL VERB V P PRAGMATICS =clear off

bugger up. In British English, if someone **buggers** something **up**, they ruin it or spoil it; an informal expression which some people find offensive.
PHRASAL VERB V n P

bugger all; also spelled **bugger-all.** In British English, if someone says you are doing **bugger all** or that you know **bugger all**, they mean that you are doing nothing or that you know nothing and they are annoyed about this fact; an informal word which some people find offensive.
PRON

buggered /bʌgəʳd/

1 In British English, if someone says that they will be **buggered** if they will do something, they mean that they do not want to do it and they will definitely not do it; an informal use which some people find offensive.
ADJ: v-link ADJ

2 In British English, if someone says that they are **buggered**, they mean that they are very tired; an informal use which some people find offensive.
ADJ: v-link ADJ

3 In British English, if someone says that something is **buggered**, they mean that it is completely ruined or broken; an informal use which some people find offensive.
ADJ: usu v-link ADJ

buggery /bʌgəri/. **Buggery** is anal intercourse.
N-UNCOUNT

buggy /bʌgi/ **buggies**
◆◇◇◇◇

1 A **buggy** is a lightweight, folding pram.
N-COUNT

2 A **buggy** is a small lightweight carriage pulled by one horse. *He helped us into the buggy.*
N-COUNT

bugle /bjuːgəl/ **bugles.** A **bugle** is a simple brass musical instrument that looks like a small trumpet. Bugles are often used in the army to announce when activities such as meals are about to begin.
N-COUNT

bugler /bjuːgləʳ/ **buglers.** A **bugler** is someone who plays the bugle.
N-COUNT

build /bɪld/ **builds, building, built**
◆◆◆◆◆

1 If you **build** something, you make it by joining things together. *Developers are now proposing to build a hotel on the site... The house was built in the early 19th century... Workers at the plant build the F-16 jet fighter.* ♦ **building** *In Japan, the building of Kansai airport continues.* ♦ **built** *Even newly built houses can need repairs... It's a product built for safety. ...structures that are built to last.*
VERB =construct V n; N-UNCOUNT; ADJ: adv ADJ, ADJ for n, ADJ to-inf

2 If you **build** something into a wall or object, you make it in such a way that it is in the wall or object, or is part of it. *If the TV was built into the ceiling, you could lie there while watching your favourite programme.*
VERB be V-ed into n

3 If people **build** an organization, a society, or a relationship, they gradually form it. *He and a partner set up on their own and built a successful fashion company... Their purpose is to build a fair society and a strong economy... I wanted to build a relationship with my team.* ♦ **building** *...the building of the great civilisations of the ancient world.*
VERB V n; N-UNCOUNT: usu the N of n

4 If you **build** an organization, system, or product on something, you base it on it. *We will then have a firmer foundation of fact on which to build theories... The town's nineteenth-century prosperity was built on steel.*
VERB V n prep

5 If you **build** something into a policy, system, or product, you make it part of it. *We have to build computers into the school curriculum... How much delay should we build into the plan?*
VERB =incorporate V n into n

6 If someone or something **builds** someone's confidence or trust, or if their confidence or trust **builds**, that person gradually becomes more confident or trusting. *The encouragement that young boys receive builds a greater self-confidence... Diplomats hope the meetings will build mutual trust... Usually when we're six months or so into a recovery, confidence begins to build.* ► **Build up** means the same as **build**. *The delegations had begun to build up some trust in one another... We will start to see the confidence in the housing market building up again.*
V-ERG V n V; PHRASAL VERB ERG V P n (not pron) V P Also V P to n

7 If you **build** on the success of something, you take advantage of this success in order to make further progress. *Build on the qualities you are satisfied with and work to change those you are unhappy with... The new regime has no successful economic reforms on which to build.*
VERB V on/upon n

8 If pressure, speed, sound, or excitement **builds**, it gradually becomes greater. *The military pressure on Croatia continues to build... The last chords of the suite build to a crescendo.* ► **Build up** means the same as **build**. *We can build up the speed gradually and safely... Economists warn that enormous pressures could build up, forcing people to emigrate westwards.*
VERB V V to/into n; PHRASAL VERB ERG V P n (not pron) V P Also V P to n

9 Someone's **build** is the shape that their bones and muscles give to their body. *He's described as around thirty years old, six feet tall and of medium build... The authority of his voice is undermined by the smallness of his build.*
N-VAR =physique

10 See also **building, built.**

build on. See **build** 7.
PHRASAL VERB

build up
PHRASAL VERB

1 If you **build up** something or if it **builds up**, it gradually becomes bigger, for example because more is added to it. *The regime built up the largest army in Africa... The collection has been built up over the last seventeen years... Slowly a thick layer of fat builds up on the pan's surface.*
ERG V P n (not pron) V P Also V n P, V P to n

2 If you **build** someone **up**, you help them to feel stronger or more confident, especially when they have had a bad experience or have been ill. *Build her up with kindness and a sympathetic ear... Dr. Johnson and I have been trying to build him up physically.*
V n P

3 If you **build** someone or something **up**, you make them seem important or exciting, for example by talking about them a lot. *The media will report on it and the tabloids will build it up... Historians built him up as the champion of parliament... I'd built him up in my head as being the love of my life.*
V n P V n P as n/-ing

4 See also **build** 6 and 8, **build-up, built-up.**

build up to. If you **build up to** something you want to do or say, you try to prepare people for it by starting to do it or introducing the subject gradually. *Other actions we need to take may be more difficult, and we may have to build up to them gradually... Carl was building up to something.*
PHRASAL VERB V P P n

build upon. See **build** 7.
PHRASAL VERB

builder /bɪldəʳ/ **builders.** A **builder** is a person whose job is to build or repair houses and other buildings. *The builders have finished the roof.*
◆◆◇◇◇ N-COUNT

building /bɪldɪŋ/ **buildings.** A **building** is a structure that has a roof and walls, for example a house or a factory. *They were on the upper floor of the building... Crowds gathered around the Parliament building.*
◆◆◆◆◆ N-COUNT

building block, building blocks. If you describe something as a **building block** of something, you mean it is one of the separate parts that combine to make that thing. *...molecules that are the building blocks of all life on earth.*
◆◇◇◇◇ N-COUNT: usu with supp

building site, building sites. A **building site** is an area of land on which a building or a group of buildings is in the process of being built or altered.
◆◇◇◇◇ N-COUNT =construction site

building society, building societies. In Britain, a **building society** is a business which will lend you money when you want to buy a house. You can also invest money in a building society, where it will earn interest.
◆◆◇◇◇ N-COUNT

build-up, build-ups; also spelled **buildup** or **build up.**
◆◆◇◇◇

1 A **build-up** is a gradual increase in something. *There has been a build-up of troops on both sides of the border... The disease can also cause a build up of pressure in the inner ear leading to severe earache.*
N-COUNT: usu sing, oft N of n

2 The **build-up** to an event is the way that journalists, advertisers, or other people talk about it a lot in the period of time immediately before it, and try to make it seem important and exciting. *We should*
N-COUNT: usu sing, oft N to n

wait at least until winter before we start the build-up to Christmas... The exams came, almost an anti-climax after the build-up that the students had given them.

built /bɪlt/ ◆◇◇◇◇
1 **Built** is the past tense and past participle of **build**.
2 If you say that someone is **built** in a particular way, you are describing the kind of body they have. *All the Trollope boys were heavily built and quite tall. ...a strong, powerfully-built man of 60... He was a huge man, built like an oak tree.* ● See also **well-built**. ADJ: adv ADJ, ADJ *like* n, ADJ *for* n/-ing

built-in. **Built-in** devices or features are included in something as a part of it, rather than being separate. *...modern cameras with built-in flash units... We're going to have built-in cupboards in the bedrooms.* ◆◇◇◇◇ ADJ: ADJ n =fitted

built-up. A **built-up** area is an area such as a town or city which has a lot of buildings in it. *A speed limit of 30 mph was introduced in built-up areas.* ADJ-GRADED: usu ADJ n

bulb /bʌlb/ **bulbs** ◆◆◇◇◇
1 A **bulb** is the glass part of an electric lamp, which gives out light when electricity passes through it. *The stairwell was lit by a single bulb.* N-COUNT =light bulb
2 A **bulb** is a root shaped like an onion that grows into a flower or plant. *...tulip bulbs.* N-COUNT

bulbous /bʌlbəs/. Something that is **bulbous** is round and fat in a rather ugly way. *...his bulbous purple nose.* ADJ-GRADED: usu ADJ n

Bulgarian /bʌlgeəriən/ **Bulgarians** ◆◆◆◆◇
1 **Bulgarian** means belonging or relating to Bulgaria, or to its people, language, or culture. *...the Bulgarian capital, Sofia.* ADJ
2 A **Bulgarian** is a Bulgarian citizen, or a person of Bulgarian origin. N-COUNT
3 **Bulgarian** is the main language spoken by people who live in Bulgaria. N-UNCOUNT

bulge /bʌldʒ/ **bulges, bulging, bulged** ◆◇◇◇◇
1 If something such as a person's stomach **bulges**, it sticks out. *Jiro waddled closer, his belly bulging and distended... He bulges out of his black T-shirt... He is 6ft 3ins with bulging muscles.* VERB V V adv/prep V-ing
2 If someone's eyes or veins **are bulging**, they seem to stick out a lot, often because the person is making a strong physical effort or is experiencing a strong emotion. *His eyes seemed to bulge like those of a toad... He shouted at his brother, his neck veins bulging. ...bulging eyes.* VERB =stick out V V-ing
3 If you say that something **is bulging** with things, you are emphasizing that it is full of them. *They returned home with the car bulging with boxes... Wolchak was coming out of the office carrying a bulging briefcase.* VB: oft cont PRAGMATICS V *with* n V-ing Also V
4 **Bulges** are lumps that stick out from a surface which is otherwise flat or smooth. *Why won't those bulges on your hips and thighs go?* N-COUNT =bump
5 If there is a **bulge** in something, there is a sudden large increase in it. *...a bulge in aircraft sales. ...the huge bulge of payments due over the next two years.* N-COUNT: usu sing, with supp, oft N *in/of* n

bulimia /buːlɪmiə/. **Bulimia** or **bulimia nervosa** is an illness in which a person has an overwhelming fear of becoming fat, and so makes themselves vomit after eating. ◆◇◇◇◇ N-UNCOUNT

bulimic /buːlɪmɪk/ **bulimics.** If someone is **bulimic**, they are suffering from bulimia. *...bulimic patients... I was anorexic and bulimic.* ► Also a noun. *...a former bulimic.* ADJ N-COUNT

bulk /bʌlk/ **bulks, bulking, bulked** ◆◆◇◇◇
1 You can refer to something's **bulk** when you want to emphasize that it is very large; used in written English. *The truck pulled out of the lot, its bulk unnerving against the dawn. ...the shadowy bulk of an ancient barn.* N-SING: with supp PRAGMATICS
2 You can refer to a large person's body or to their weight or size as their **bulk**. *Bannol lowered his bulk carefully into the chair... Despite his bulk he moved lightly on his feet.* N-SING: usu poss N
3 The **bulk** of something is most of it. *The bulk of the text is essentially a review of these original documents... The vast bulk of imports and exports are carried by sea.* ► Also a pronoun. *They come from all over the world, though the bulk is from the Indian subcontinent.* QUANT: QUANT *of* def-n =majority PRON
4 If you buy or sell something in **bulk**, you buy or sell it in large quantities. *Buying in bulk is more economical than shopping for small quantities. ...bulk purchasing.* N-UNCOUNT: *in* N, N n =in quantity

bulk up or **bulk out.** To **bulk up** or **bulk out** something or someone means to make them bigger or heavier. You can also say that something or someone **bulks up** or **bulks out**. *Use extra vegetables to bulk up the omelette... Holyfield has bulked up to 15st using weights.* PHRASAL VERB ERG V P n (not pron) V P Also V n P

bulkhead /bʌlkhed/ **bulkheads.** A **bulkhead** is a wall which divides the inside of a ship or aeroplane into separate sections; a technical term. ◆◇◇◇◇ N-COUNT =partition

bulky /bʌlki/ **bulkier, bulkiest.** Something that is **bulky** is large and heavy. **Bulky** things are often difficult to move or deal with. *...bulky items like lawn mowers. ...a bulky man with balding hair.* ◆◇◇◇◇ ADJ-GRADED

bull /bʊl/ **bulls** ◆◆◇◇◇
1 A **bull** is a male animal of the cow family. N-COUNT
2 Some other male animals, including elephants and whales, are called **bulls**. *Suddenly a massive bull elephant with huge tusks charged us.* N-COUNT
3 On the stock market, **bulls** are people who buy shares in expectation of a price rise, in order to make a profit by selling the shares again after a short time. Compare **bear**. N-COUNT
4 In the Roman Catholic church, a papal **bull** is an official statement on a particular subject that is issued by the Pope. N-COUNT =decree
5 If you say that something is **bull** or a load of **bull**, you mean that it is complete nonsense or absolutely untrue; used in informal English. *I think it's a load of bull... The press couldn't deal with that so they made up all this bull.* N-UNCOUNT =rubbish
6 See also **cock-and-bull story, pit bull terrier**.
7 If you say that someone rushes into a situation like **a bull in a china shop**, you are critical of them because they do not stop to think, and are insensitive to other people's feelings; an informal expression. *Still, it'll stop him rampaging all over the place like a bull in a china shop.* PHRASES usu *like* PHR PRAGMATICS
8 You say that someone is like **a bull in a china shop** when they are very clumsy. usu *like* PHR
9 If you **take the bull by the horns**, you do something that you feel you ought to do even though it is difficult, dangerous, or unpleasant. *Now is the time for the Chancellor to take the bull by the horns and announce a two per cent cut in interest rates.* V inflects
10 ● **like a red rag to a bull**: see **rag**.

bulldog /bʊldɒg, AM -dɔːg/ **bulldogs.** A **bulldog** is a small dog with a large square head and short hair. N-COUNT

bulldog clip, bulldog clips. In British English, a **bulldog clip** is a metal clip with a spring lever that opens and closes two flat pieces of metal. It is used for holding papers together. N-COUNT

bulldoze /bʊldoʊz/ **bulldozes, bulldozing, bulldozed**
1 If people **bulldoze** something such as a building, they knock it down using a bulldozer. *She defeated developers who wanted to bulldoze her home to build a supermarket.* VERB
2 If people **bulldoze** earth, stone, or other heavy material, they move it using a bulldozer. *Last week, the department's road builders began to bulldoze a water meadow on Twyford Down.* VERB V n
3 If you say that someone **bulldozes** something through or **bulldozes** someone into doing something, you disapprove of them because they get what they want in an unpleasantly forceful way. *The Red Guards planned to bulldoze through a full socialist programme... Mr Major warned he would be prepared to bulldoze the treaty through the Commons... My parents tried to bulldoze me into going to college.* VERB PRAGMATICS V n with *through* V n *through* n V n *into* n/-ing Also V n

bulldozer /bʊldoʊzəʳ/ **bulldozers.** A **bulldozer** is a large tractor with a broad metal blade at the ◆◇◇◇◇ N-COUNT front, which is used for knocking down buildings or moving large amounts of earth.

bullet /bʊlɪt/ **bullets** ◆◆◇◇◇

1 A **bullet** is a small piece of metal with a pointed or rounded end, which is fired out of a gun. *The bullet hit Joseph right between the eyes... There are three bullet holes in the windscreen.* ● See also **plastic bullet**, **rubber bullet**. N-COUNT

2 If someone **bites the bullet**, they accept that they have to do something unpleasant but necessary; used mainly in journalism. *Tour operators may be forced to bite the bullet and cut prices.* PHRASE: V inflects

bulletin /bʊlɪtɪn/ **bulletins** ◆◆◇◇◇

1 A **bulletin** is a short news report on the radio or television. *...the early morning news bulletin.* N-COUNT

2 A **bulletin** is a short official announcement made publicly to inform people about an important matter. *At 3.30 p.m. a bulletin was released announcing that the president was out of immediate danger.* N-COUNT

3 A **bulletin** is a regular newspaper or leaflet that is produced by an organization or group such as a school or church. N-COUNT

bulletin board, bulletin boards

1 In American English, a **bulletin board** is a board which is usually attached to a wall in order to display notices giving information about something. The usual British word is **noticeboard**. N-COUNT

2 In computing, a **bulletin board** is a system that enables users to send and receive messages of general interest. *Internet is the largest computer bulletin board in the world, and it's growing.* N-COUNT

bullet-proof; also spelled **bulletproof**. Something that is **bullet-proof** is made of a strong material that bullets cannot pass through. *...bullet-proof glass. ...a bullet-proof vest.* ADJ

bullfight /bʊlfaɪt/ **bullfights.** A **bullfight** is a public entertainment in which people make a bull angry by sticking short spears in it before trying to kill it with a sword. Bullfights take place in Spain, Portugal, and Latin America. N-COUNT

bullfighter /bʊlfaɪtəʳ/ **bullfighters.** A **bullfighter** is the person who tries to kill the bull in a bullfight. N-COUNT =matador

bullfighting /bʊlfaɪtɪŋ/. **Bullfighting** is the public entertainment in which people try to kill bulls in bullfights. N-UNCOUNT

bullfinch /bʊlfɪntʃ/ **bullfinches.** A **bullfinch** is a type of small European bird. The male has a black head and a pinkish-red breast. N-COUNT

bullfrog /bʊlfrɒg, AM -frɔːg/ **bullfrogs.** A **bullfrog** is a type of large frog which makes a very loud noise. N-COUNT

bullhorn /bʊlhɔːʳn/ **bullhorns.** In American English, a **bullhorn** is a device for making your voice sound louder in the open air. It is shaped like a hollow cone with open ends. You speak into the small end. The usual British words are **loudhailer** and **megaphone**. N-COUNT

bullion /bʊliən/. **Bullion** is gold or silver in the form of lumps or bars. N-UNCOUNT

bullish /bʊlɪʃ/ ◆◇◇◇◇

1 On the stock market, if there is a **bullish** sentiment, prices are expected to rise. Compare **bearish**. *The market opened in a bullish mood.* ADJ-GRADED

2 If someone is **bullish** about something, they are cheerful and optimistic about it. *Faldo was bullish about his chances of winning a third British Open.* ADJ-GRADED: oft ADJ *about/on* n =optimistic

bull market, bull markets. A **bull market** is a situation on the stock market when people are buying a lot of shares because they expect that the shares will increase in value and that they will be able to make a profit by selling them again after a short time. Compare **bear market**. N-COUNT

bullock /bʊlək/ **bullocks.** A **bullock** is a young bull that has been castrated. N-COUNT

bullring /bʊlrɪŋ/ **bullrings.** A **bullring** is a circular area of ground surrounded by rows of seats where bullfights take place. N-COUNT

bull's-eye, bull's-eyes

1 The **bull's-eye** is the small circular area at the centre of a target. *Five of his bullets had hit the bull's-eye.* N-COUNT: usu *the* N in sing

2 A **bull's-eye** is a shot or throw of a dart that hits the bull's-eye. N-COUNT

3 If something that you do or say hits the **bull's eye**, it has exactly the effect that you intended it to have; an informal expression. N-COUNT

bullshit /bʊlʃɪt/ **bullshits, bullshitting, bullshitted**

1 If you say that something is **bullshit**, you are saying that it is nonsense or completely untrue; an informal use which some people find offensive. *All the rest I said, all that was bullshit.* N-UNCOUNT, also EXCLAM =rubbish

2 If you say that someone **is bullshitting** you, you mean that what they are telling you is nonsense or completely untrue; an informal use which some people find offensive. *Don't bullshit me, Brian!... He's basically bullshitting.* VERB V n V

bull terrier, bull terriers. A **bull terrier** is a breed of strong dog with a short, whitish-coloured coat and a thick neck. ● See also **pit bull terrier**. N-COUNT

bullwhip /bʊlʰwɪp/ **bullwhips.** A **bullwhip** is a very long, heavy whip. N-COUNT

bully /bʊli/ **bullies, bullying, bullied** ◆◆◇◇◇

1 If you describe someone as a **bully**, you mean they use their strength or power to hurt or frighten other people. *I fell victim to the office bully... He's a coward and a bully who confuses physical strength with manhood.* N-COUNT

2 If someone **bullies** you, they use their strength or power to hurt or frighten you. *I wasn't going to let him bully me... I asked her if she was bullied by the other children.* ♦ **bullying** *...schoolchildren who were victims of bullying.* VERB =push around V n; N-UNCOUNT

3 If someone **bullies** you into something, they make you do it by using force or threats. *We think an attempt to bully them into submission would be counterproductive... She used to bully me into doing my schoolwork... The government says it will not be bullied by the press.* VERB V n *into* n/-ing *be* V-ed Also V n

4 If someone says '**Bully for** you', they mean that they are not impressed by what you have told them or by what you have done; an informal expression. *'I'm going out to dinner with Julian,' she said, with some defiance.—'Bully for you.'* PHRASE

bully boy, bully boys; also spelled **bully-boy**.

1 If you describe a man as a **bully boy**, you disapprove of him because he is rough and aggressive. *...bully-boys and murderers.* N-COUNT PRAGMATICS

2 If you say that someone uses **bully-boy** tactics, you disapprove of them because they use rough and aggressive methods; used mainly in journalism. *She was accused of bully-boy tactics in securing an Olympic place.* ADJ: ADJ n PRAGMATICS

bulwark /bʊlwəʳk/ **bulwarks.** Something that is a **bulwark** against something protects you against it. Something that is a **bulwark** of something protects it. *Until recently Pakistan was considered a bulwark against Soviet expansion... The House of Lords is the only bulwark of democracy in this country.* N-COUNT: oft N *against/of* n

bum /bʌm/ **bums, bumming, bummed** ◆◇◇◇◇

1 A **bum** is a person who has no permanent home or job and who gets money by doing occasional work or by begging; an informal use that occurs mainly in American English. N-COUNT =tramp, vagrant

2 If someone refers to another person as a **bum**, they think that person is worthless or irresponsible; an informal use. *You're all a bunch of bums.* N-COUNT PRAGMATICS

3 In British English, someone's **bum** is the part of their body which they sit on; an informal use that some people find offensive. N-COUNT: poss N =bottom

4 Some people use **bum** to describe a situation that they find unpleasant or annoying; an informal use. *He knows you're getting a bum deal.* ADJ: ADJ n

5 If you **bum** something off someone, you ask them for it and they give it to you; an informal use. *Mind if I bum a cigarette?* VERB =cadge V n

6 If you **bum** around, you go from place to place without any particular destination, either for enjoyment or because you have nothing else to do; an informal expression. *I think they're just bumming* VERB V *around*

around at the moment, not doing a lot... She went off to bum round the world with a boyfriend. V round n

7 See also **beach bum**.

8 If you say that the organizers of an event such as a concert want to put **bums on seats**, you disapprove of them because they want a lot of people to attend it but do not really care about the quality of the entertainment; an informal expression. *I know bums on seats are important, but what about the music?* PHRASE PRAGMATICS

bum bag, bum bags. A **bum bag** consists of a pouch attached to a belt which you wear round your waist. You use it to carry things such as money and keys. N-COUNT

bumble /bʌmbᵊl/ **bumbles, bumbling, bumbled**

bumble about or **bumble around.** The form **bumble about** is mainly used in British English. When someone **bumbles about** or **bumbles around**, they behave in a confused, disorganized way, making mistakes and usually not achieving anything. *Most of us are novices on the computer. We bumble about on them and have great fun.* PHRASAL VERB V P

bumblebee /bʌmbᵊlbiː/ **bumblebees;** also spelled **bumble bee**. A **bumblebee** is a large hairy bee. N-COUNT

bumbling /bʌmblɪŋ/. If you describe a person or their behaviour as **bumbling**, you mean that they behave in a confused, disorganized way, making mistakes and usually not achieving anything. *...a clumsy, bumbling, inarticulate figure.* ADJ: ADJ n

bumf /bʌmf/; also spelled **bumph**. **Bumf** consists of documents written for your information which you may not need or find interesting; used in informal British English. *The waste-paper basket was full of bumf, trivial letters and advertising circulars.* N-UNCOUNT

bummer /bʌməʳ/ **bummers.** If you say that something is a **bummer**, you mean that it is unpleasant or annoying; an informal word. *I had a bummer of a day... What a bummer!* N-COUNT: usu sing

bump /bʌmp/ **bumps, bumping, bumped** ◆◆◇◇◇

1 If you **bump** into something or someone, you accidentally hit them while you are moving. *They stopped walking and he almost bumped into them... There was a jerk as the boat bumped against something... He bumped his head on the low beams of the house.* ► Also a noun. *Small children often cry after a minor bump.* VERB V into/against n, V n; N-COUNT

2 A **bump** is the action or the dull sound of two heavy objects hitting each other. *I felt a little bump and I knew instantly what had happened... The child took five steps, and then sat down with a bump.* N-COUNT

3 A **bump** is a minor injury or swelling that you get if you bump into something or if something hits you. *She fell against our coffee table and got a large bump on her forehead.* N-COUNT =lump

4 If you have a **bump** while you are driving a car, you have a minor accident in which you hit something; an informal use. N-COUNT =collision

5 A **bump** on a road is a raised, uneven part. *The truck hit a bump and bounced.* N-COUNT

6 If a vehicle **bumps** over a surface, it travels in a rough, bouncing way because the surface is very uneven. *We left the road, and again bumped over the mountainside... The aircraft bumped along erratically without gathering anything like sufficient speed.* VERB V prep/adv Also V way adv/prep

7 See also **goose bumps**.

8 You use **with a bump** to emphasize that someone suddenly gets into an unpleasant situation or becomes aware of it. For example, if someone comes down to earth **with a bump**, they suddenly start recognizing unpleasant facts after a period of time when they have not been doing this. *Company bosses have come back down to earth with a bump after a period of post-election euphoria.* ● **to bump along the bottom**: see **bottom**. PHRASE: PHR after v PRAGMATICS

bump into. If you **bump into** someone you know, you meet them unexpectedly; an informal expression. *I happened to bump into Mervyn Johns in the hallway.* PHRASAL VERB =run into; V P n

bump off. To **bump** someone **off** means to kill them; an informal expression. *They will probably bump you off anyway! ...the hit man he's hired to bump off his wife.* PHRASAL VERB V n P, V P n (not pron)

bump up. If you **bump up** an amount, you increase it suddenly, usually by a lot; an informal expression. *The extra cost will bump up the price... Add pasta to your salads to bump up your fibre intake.* PHRASAL VERB =boost; V P n (not pron) Also V n P

bumper /bʌmpəʳ/ **bumpers** ◆◇◇◇◇

1 **Bumpers** are bars at the front and back of a vehicle which protect it if it bumps into something. ● If traffic is **bumper to bumper**, the vehicles are so close to one another that they are almost touching and are moving very slowly. *...bumper to bumper traffic jams.* N-COUNT; PHRASE: v-link PHR, PHR n, PHR after v

2 A **bumper** crop or harvest is one that is larger than usual. *...a bumper crop of rice... In the state of Iowa, it's been a bumper year for corn.* ADJ: ADJ n

3 If you say that something is **bumper** size, you mean that it is very large. *...bumper profits. ...a bumper pack of matches.* ADJ: ADJ n

bumper sticker, bumper stickers. A **bumper sticker** is a small piece of paper or plastic with words or pictures on it, designed for sticking onto the back of your car. It usually has a political, religious, or humorous message. *...a bumper sticker that said, 'Happiness Is Being a Grandmother'.* N-COUNT

bumph /bʌmf/. See **bumf**.

bumpkin /bʌmpkɪn/ **bumpkins.** If you refer to someone as a **bumpkin**, you think they are uneducated and stupid because they come from the countryside. *...unsophisticated country bumpkins.* N-COUNT PRAGMATICS =yokel

bumptious /bʌmpʃəs/. If you say that someone is **bumptious**, you disapprove of them because they continually express their own opinions and ideas in a self-important way. *...a bumptious bureaucrat.* ADJ-GRADED PRAGMATICS

bumpy /bʌmpi/ **bumpier, bumpiest** ◆◇◇◇◇

1 A **bumpy** road or path has a lot of bumps on it. *...bumpy cobbled streets.* ADJ-GRADED ≠smooth

2 A **bumpy** journey is uncomfortable and rough, usually because you are travelling over an uneven surface. *...a hot and bumpy ride across the desert... We had a bumpy flight over the centre of Panama.* ADJ-GRADED

bun /bʌn/ **buns** ◆◇◇◇◇

1 **Buns** are small bread rolls. They are sometimes sweet and contain currants or spices. *...a currant bun.* N-COUNT: oft n N

2 In British English, **buns** are small sweet cakes. They often have icing on the top. N-COUNT

3 If a woman has her hair in a **bun**, she has fastened it tightly on top of her head or at the back of her head in the shape of a ball. N-COUNT

bunch /bʌntʃ/ **bunches, bunching, bunched** ◆◆◆◇◇

1 A **bunch** of people is a group of people who share one or more characteristics or who are doing something together; an informal use. *My neighbours are a bunch of busybodies... We were a pretty inexperienced bunch of people really... The players were a great bunch.* N-COUNT: usu sing, oft N of n, adj N =lot

2 A **bunch** of flowers is a number of flowers with their stalks held or tied together. *He had left a huge bunch of flowers in her hotel room.* N-COUNT: usu sing, usu N of n

3 A **bunch** of bananas or grapes is a group of them growing on the same stem. *Lili had fallen asleep clutching a fat bunch of grapes.* N-COUNT: usu sing, usu N of n

4 A **bunch** of keys is a set of keys kept together on a metal ring. *George took out a bunch of keys and went to work on the complicated lock.* N-COUNT: usu sing, usu N of n

5 In American English, a **bunch** of things is a number of things, especially a large number; an informal use. *We did a bunch of songs together.* ► Also a pronoun. *I'd like to adopt a multi-racial child. In fact, I'd love a whole bunch.* QUANT: QUANT of pl-n; PRON

6 If a girl has her hair in **bunches**, it is parted down the middle and tied on each side of her head with something such as a ribbon; a British use. N-PLURAL: usu in N

7 If clothing **bunches** around a part of your body, it VERB

forms a set of creases around it. *She clutches the sides of her skirt until it bunches around her waist.* V around n

8 If you say someone or something is **the best of the bunch** or **the pick of the bunch**, you mean they are the best of a group of people or things; an informal expression. *I watched every game of the World Cup and Craig was the pick of the bunch.* PHRASES usu v-link PHR

bunch up or **bunch together.** If people or things **bunch up** or if you **bunch** them **up**, they move close to each other so that they form a small tight group. **Bunch together** means the same as bunch up. *They were bunching up, almost treading upon each other's heels... People were bunched up at all the exits... If they need to bunch aircraft more closely together to bring in one that is short of fuel, they will do so.* PHRASAL VERB ERG V P V-ed P V n P

bundle /bʌndəl/ **bundles, bundling, bundled** ◆◆◇◇◇

1 A **bundle** of things is a number of them that are tied together or wrapped in a cloth or bag so that they can be carried or stored. *She produced a bundle of notes and proceeded to count out one hundred and ninety-five pounds... He gathered the bundles of clothing into his arms... I have about 20 year's magazines tied up in bundles.* N-COUNT: oft N of n

2 You can refer to a tiny baby as a **bundle**. *They were handed a small bundle wrapped in a shawl... Amy hugged the tiny bundle.* N-COUNT: usu sing

3 If you describe someone as, for example, a **bundle** of fun, you are emphasizing that they are full of fun. If you describe someone as a **bundle** of nerves, you are emphasizing that they are very nervous. *I remember Mickey as a bundle of fun, great to have around... Life at high school wasn't a bundle of laughs, either... He confessed to having been a bundle of nerves.* N-SING: a N of n PRAGMATICS

4 If you refer to a **bundle** of things, you are emphasizing that there is a wide range of them. *The profession offers a bundle of benefits, not least of which is extensive training.* N-COUNT: N of n PRAGMATICS =package

5 If someone or something **is bundled** somewhere, someone pushes them there in a rough and hurried way. *He was bundled into a car and driven 50 miles to a police station... He was bundled in and arrested as soon as he was airborne.* VERB be V-ed prep/adv Also V n prep/adv

6 If you say that something **costs a bundle**, or **costs** someone **a bundle**, you are emphasizing that it is expensive; an informal expression. *You can have it, but it'll cost you a bundle.* PHRASE: V inflects PRAGMATICS =cost a packet

bundle off. If someone **is bundled off** somewhere, they are sent there or taken there in a hurry. *The pair were then bundled off to a neighbour's house by waiting police... We want to bundle them off to bed quickly.* PHRASAL VERB be V-ed P V n P to n Also V n P

bundle up PHRASAL VERB

1 If you **bundle up** a mass of things, you make them into a bundle by gathering or tying them together. *Francis bundled up her clothes again into their small sack... Her mother had bundled all her Forties clothes up and burnt them.* V P n (not pron) V n P

2 If you **bundle up**, you dress in a lot of warm clothes, usually because the weather is very cold. If you **bundle** someone **up**, you dress them in a lot of warm clothes. *After the coffee we bundled up and walked down to the river... The next morning, Franklin and Eleanor bundled up the baby and carried him to New York... I spent much of my time bundled up in sweaters in an effort to keep warm.* =wrap up V P V P n (not pron) V-ed P Also V n P

bung /bʌŋ/ **bungs, bunging, bunged**

1 A **bung** is a round piece of wood, cork, or rubber which you use to close the hole in a container such as a barrel or flask. N-COUNT =stopper

2 If you **bung** something somewhere, you put it there in a quick and careless way; an informal British use. *Pour a whole lot of cold water over the rice, and bung it in the oven.* VERB =stick V n prep/adv

3 If something is **bunged up** it is blocked; an informal British expression. *The sink's bunged up again... My nose is all bunged up.* ADJ: usu v-link ADJ

bungalow /bʌŋgəloʊ/ **bungalows.** A **bungalow** is a house which has only one storey. ◆◇◇◇◇ N-COUNT

bungee jumping /bʌndʒi dʒʌmpɪŋ/. If someone goes **bungee jumping**, they jump from a high place such as a bridge or cliff with a long piece of strong elastic cord tied around their ankle connecting them to the bridge or cliff. N-UNCOUNT

bungle /bʌŋgəl/ **bungles, bungling, bungled.** ◆◇◇◇◇ If you **bungle** something, you fail to do it properly, because you make mistakes or are clumsy. *Two prisoners bungled an escape bid after running either side of a lamp-post while handcuffed. ...the FBI's bungled attempt to end the 51 day siege.* ► Also a noun. *...an appalling administrative bungle.* ♦ **bungling** *...a bungling burglar.* VERB =botch V n V-ed N-COUNT ADJ-GRADED

bungler /bʌŋglər/ **bunglers.** A **bungler** is a person who often fails to do things properly because they make mistakes or are clumsy. N-COUNT

bunion /bʌnjən/ **bunions.** A **bunion** is a large painful lump on the first joint of a person's big toe. N-COUNT

bunk /bʌŋk/ **bunks, bunking, bunked** ◆◇◇◇◇

1 A **bunk** is a bed that is fixed to a wall, especially in a ship or caravan. *He left his bunk and went up on deck again.* N-COUNT

2 If you describe something as **bunk**, you think that it is foolish or untrue; an informal use. *...Henry Ford's opinion that 'history is bunk'.* N-UNCOUNT =nonsense

3 If you **do a bunk**, you suddenly leave a place without telling anyone; used in informal British English. *Imelda's husband vanished, did a bunk.* PHRASE: V inflects

bunk off. If you **bunk off** from school or work, you leave without permission and do something else; used in informal British English. *We thought nothing of bunking off school and travelling 100 miles to find this or that record.* PHRASAL VERB =play truant V P n Also V P

bunk bed, bunk beds. Bunk beds are two beds, one above the other, held in a frame. N-COUNT

bunker /bʌŋkər/ **bunkers, bunkering, bunkered** ◆◆◇◇◇

1 A **bunker** is a place, usually underground, that has been built with strong walls to protect it against heavy gunfire and bombing. *...a Soviet built bunker in the mountains north east of Kabul.* N-COUNT

2 A **bunker** is a container for coal or other fuel. N-COUNT

3 On a golf course, a **bunker** is a large hollow filled with sand, which is deliberately put there as an obstacle that golfers must try and avoid. N-COUNT

4 In golf, if you **bunker** a shot, you hit your ball into the bunker. *She bunkered her second shot.* VERB V n

bunkum /bʌŋkəm/. If you say that something that has been said or written is **bunkum**, you mean that you think it is completely untrue or very stupid; an old-fashioned, informal word. *It's a load of bunkum.* N-UNCOUNT PRAGMATICS =balderdash

bunny /bʌni/ **bunnies.** A **bunny** or **bunny rabbit** is a rabbit; used by children. ◆◇◇◇◇ N-COUNT

bunting /bʌntɪŋ/. **Bunting** consists of rows of small coloured flags that are used to decorate streets and buildings on special occasions. *Red, white and blue bunting hung in the city's renovated train station.* N-UNCOUNT

buoy /bɔɪ, AM buːi/ **buoys, buoying, buoyed** ◆◇◇◇◇

1 A **buoy** is a floating object that is used to show ships and boats where they can go and to warn them of danger. N-COUNT

2 If someone in a difficult situation **is buoyed** by something, it makes them feel more cheerful and optimistic. *Party leaders are buoyed by Clinton's recent rise in the polls... German domestic consumption buoyed the German economy.* ► **buoy up** means the same as **buoy**. *They are buoyed up by a sense of hope... They buoyed me up.* VERB be V-ed by n V n PHRASAL VERB be V-ed P V n P

buoyancy /bɔɪənsi/

1 Buoyancy is the ability that something has to float on a liquid or in the air. *Air can be pumped into the diving suit to increase buoyancy.* N-UNCOUNT

2 Buoyancy is a person's ability to remain cheerful, even in sad or unpleasant situations. *I'll have to take stock, go carefully and regain my buoyancy.* N-UNCOUNT

3 Buoyancy is a feeling of cheerfulness. *...a mood of buoyancy and optimism.* N-UNCOUNT

4 There is economic **buoyancy** when the economy is growing. *The likelihood is that the slump will be followed by a period of buoyancy.* N-UNCOUNT

buoyant /bɔɪənt/ ◆◇◇◇◇
1 If you are in a **buoyant** mood, you feel cheerful and behave in a lively way. *She was in a buoyant mood and they were looking forward to their new life... You will feel more buoyant and optimistic about the future than you have for a long time.* ADJ-GRADED =cheerful
2 A **buoyant** economy is a successful one in which there is a lot of trade and economic activity. *We have a buoyant economy and unemployment is considerably lower than the regional average... High interest rates do not point to a buoyant market this year... Analysts expect the share price to remain buoyant.* ADJ-GRADED
3 A **buoyant** object floats on a liquid. *This was such a small and buoyant boat... While there is still sufficient trapped air within the container to keep it buoyant, it will float.* ADJ-GRADED

burble /bɜːʳbəl/ **burbles, burbling, burbled**
1 If something **burbles**, it makes a low continuous bubbling sound. *The water burbled over gravel... The river gurgled and burbled.* VERB V prep V
2 If you say that someone **is burbling**, you mean that they are talking in a confused way. *He burbled something incomprehensible... Key burbled about the wonderful people who contribute to tourism... He burbles on about freedom.* VERB V n V *about* n V *on about* n Also V that, V with quote

burden /bɜːʳdən/ **burdens, burdening, burdened** ◆◆◆◇◇
1 If you describe a problem or a responsibility as a **burden**, you mean that it causes someone a lot of difficulty, worry, or hard work. *The developing countries bear the burden of an enormous external debt... They don't go around with the burdens of the world on their shoulders the whole time... Her death will be an impossible burden on Paul... The financial burden will be more evenly shared.* N-COUNT: usu with supp, oft N *of/on* n =pressure, strain
2 A **burden** is a heavy load that is difficult to carry; a formal use. N-COUNT
3 If someone **burdens** you with something that is likely to worry you, for example a problem or a difficult decision, they tell you about it. *We decided not to burden him with the news.* VERB =worry V n *with* n Also V n
4 See also **beast of burden**.
5 The **burden of proof** is the task of proving that you are correct, for example when you have accused someone of a crime. *The burden of proof is on the prosecution.* PHRASE

burdened /bɜːʳdənd/ ◆◇◇◇◇
1 If you are **burdened** with something, it causes you a lot of worry or hard work. *Nicaragua was burdened with a foreign debt of $11 billion... They may be burdened by guilt and regret.* ADJ-GRADED: v-link ADJ *with/by* n
2 If you describe someone as **burdened** with a heavy load, you are emphasizing, sometimes in a humorous way, that it is very heavy and that they are holding it or carrying it with difficulty. *...a stocky man who did everything at the run, even when burdened with heavy camera gear... Anna and Rosemary arrived burdened by bags and food baskets.* ADJ-GRADED: v-link ADJ *with/by* n PRAGMATICS =weighed down

burdensome /bɜːʳdənsəm/. If you describe something as **burdensome**, you mean it is worrying or hard to deal with; used in written English. *...a large and burdensome debt... The load was too burdensome.* ADJ-GRADED =onerous

bureau /bjʊərəʊ/. The usual plural in British English is **bureaux**. The usual plural in American English is **bureaus**. ◆◆◇◇◇
1 A **bureau** is an office, organization, or government department that collects and distributes information. *...The National Bureau of Economic Research. ...the Citizen's Advice Bureau.* N-COUNT: oft in names
2 A **bureau** is an office of a company or organization which has its headquarters in another town or country. *...the Wall Street Journal's Washington bureau.* N-COUNT =office
3 In British English, a **bureau** is a writing desk with shelves and drawers and a lid that opens to form the writing surface. N-COUNT =writing desk

bureaucracy /bjʊrɒkrəsi/ **bureaucracies** ◆◆◇◇◇
1 A **bureaucracy** is an administrative system operated by a large number of officials. *State bureaucracies can tend to stifle enterprise and initiative.* N-COUNT: usu pl
2 **Bureaucracy** refers to all the rules and procedures followed by government departments and similar organizations. You refer to bureaucracy especially when you think that the rules and procedures are complicated and cause long delays. *People usually complain about having to deal with too much bureaucracy.* N-UNCOUNT PRAGMATICS =red tape

bureaucrat /bjʊərəkræt/ **bureaucrats. Bureaucrats** are officials who work in a large administrative system. You can refer to officials as bureaucrats especially if you disapprove of them because they seem to follow rules and procedures too strictly. *The economy is still controlled by bureaucrats.* ◆◆◇◇◇ N-COUNT: usu pl PRAGMATICS

bureaucratic /bjʊərəkrætɪk/. **Bureaucratic** means involving complicated rules and procedures which can cause long delays. *Diplomats believe that bureaucratic delays are inevitable... The department has become a bureaucratic nightmare.* ◆◆◇◇◇ ADJ-GRADED: usu ADJ n

bureaux /bjʊərəʊz/. **Bureaux** is a plural form of **bureau**.

burgeon /bɜːʳdʒən/ **burgeons, burgeoning, burgeoned.** If something **burgeons**, it grows or develops rapidly; a literary word. *Plants burgeon from every available space... My confidence began to burgeon later in life. ...Japan's burgeoning satellite-TV industry.* ◆◇◇◇◇ VERB V V-ing

burger /bɜːʳgəʳ/ **burgers.** A **burger** is a flat round mass of minced meat or vegetables, which is fried and often eaten in a bread roll. *...burger and chips. ...vegetable burgers.* ◆◇◇◇◇ N-COUNT

burgher /bɜːʳgəʳ/ **burghers.** The **burghers** of a town or city are the people who live there, especially the richer or more respectable people; an old-fashioned word. *...the burghers of Prato.* N-COUNT: usu pl

burglar /bɜːʳgləʳ/ **burglars.** A **burglar** is a thief who enters a house or other building by force. *Burglars broke into their home.* ◆◇◇◇◇ N-COUNT

burglar alarm, burglar alarms. A **burglar alarm** is an electric device that makes a bell ring loudly if someone tries to enter a building by force. N-COUNT

burglarize /bɜːʳgləraɪz/ **burglarizes, burglarizing, burglarized.** In American English, if a building **is burglarized**, a thief enters it by force and steals things. The usual British word is **burgle**. *Her home was burglarized.* VB: usu passive be V-ed

burglary /bɜːʳgləri/ **burglaries.** If someone commits a **burglary**, they enter a building by force and steal things. **Burglary** is the act of doing this. *An 11-year-old boy committed a burglary... He's been arrested for burglary.* ◆◇◇◇◇ N-VAR

burgle /bɜːʳgəl/ **burgles, burgling, burgled.** In British English, if a building **is burgled**, a thief enters it by force and steals things. The usual American word is **burglarize**. *I found that my flat had been burgled... I thought we had been burgled... Two teenagers burgled the home of Mr Jones's mother.* VERB be V-ed V n

burgundy /bɜːʳgəndi/ **burgundies** ◆◇◇◇◇
1 **Burgundy** is used to describe things that are purplish-red in colour. *He was wearing a burgundy polyester jacket. ...burgundy-coloured armchairs.* COLOUR
2 **Burgundy** is a type of wine. It can be white or red in colour and comes from the region of France called Burgundy. *...a bottle of white burgundy.* N-MASS

burial /beriəl/ **burials.** A **burial** is the act or ceremony of putting a dead body into a grave in the ground. *The priest prepared the body for burial... He can have a decent burial.* ◆◇◇◇◇ N-VAR

burial ground, burial grounds. A **burial ground** is a place where bodies are buried, especially an ancient site. *...an ancient burial ground.* N-COUNT =graveyard

burlap /bɜːʳlæp/. In American English, **burlap** is a thick, rough fabric that is used for making sacks. The usual British word is **hessian**. *...a burlap sack.* N-UNCOUNT

burlesque /bɜːʳlesk/ **burlesques.** A **burlesque** is a performance or a piece of writing that makes N-VAR fun of something by copying it in an exaggerated way. You can also use **burlesque** to refer to a real-life situation that shows this kind of exaggeration. *The book read like a black comic burlesque. ...a trio of burlesque Moscow stereotypes.*

burly /bɜ:ʳli/ **burlier, burliest.** A **burly** man has a broad body and strong muscles. *He was a big, burly man.* ◆◇◇◇◇ ADJ-GRADED: usu ADJ n

Burmese /bɜ:ʳmi:z/. **Burmese** is both the singular and the plural form. ◆◆◆◆◇

1 Burmese means belonging or relating to Burma, or to its people, language, or culture. Burma is now known as Myanmar. *...the Burmese ambassador.* ADJ

2 A **Burmese** is a Burmese citizen or a person of Burmese origin. *...more than 5,200 Burmese.* N-COUNT

3 Burmese is the main language spoken by the people who live in Burma. N-UNCOUNT

burn /bɜ:ʳn/ **burns, burning, burned, burnt** ◆◆◆◆◇
The past tense and past participle is **burned** in American English, and **burned** or **burnt** in British English.

1 If there is a fire or a flame somewhere, you say that there is a fire or flame **burning** there. *Fires were burning out of control in the center of the city... There was a fire burning in the large fireplace... The furnace has a design that allows the flame to burn at a lower temperature.* VERB V

2 If something **is burning**, it is on fire. *When I arrived one of the vehicles was still burning... The building housed 1,500 refugees and it burned for hours... That boy was rescued from a burning house.* ♦ **burning** *When we arrived in our village there was a terrible smell of burning.* VERB V V-ing N-UNCOUNT

3 If you **burn** something, you destroy or damage it with fire. *Protesters set cars on fire and burned a building... Incineration plants should be built to burn household waste... Coal fell out of the fire, and burned the carpet.* ♦ **burning** *The French government has criticized the burning of a US flag outside the American Embassy.* VERB V n N-UNCOUNT

4 If you **burn** a fuel or if it **burns**, it is used to produce heat, light, or energy. *The power stations burn coal from the Ruhr region... Manufacturers are working with new fuels to find one that burns more cleanly than petrol.* V-ERG V n V

5 If you **burn** something that you are cooking or if it **burns**, you spoil it by using too great a heat. *I burnt the toast... Watch them carefully as they finish cooking because they can burn easily.* ♦ **burnt** *...the smell of burnt toast.* V-ERG V n V ADJ-GRADED

6 If you **burn** part of your body, **burn** yourself, or **are burnt**, you are injured by fire or by something very hot. *Take care not to burn your fingers... If you are badly burnt, seek medical attention.* ► Also a noun. *She suffered appalling burns to her back.* VERB V n be V-ed Also V pron-refl N-COUNT

7 If someone **is burnt** or **burnt** to death, they are killed by fire. *Women were burned as witches in the middle ages... At least 80 people were burnt to death when their bus caught fire.* VB: usu passive be V-ed as n be V-ed to n

8 If a light **is burning**, it is shining; a literary use. *The building was darkened except for a single light burning in a third-story window.* VERB V

9 If your face **is burning**, it is red because you are embarrassed or upset. *Liz's face was burning.* VB: usu cont V

10 If you **are burning** with an emotion or **are burning** to do something, you feel that emotion or the desire to do that thing very strongly. *The young boy was burning with a fierce ambition... Dan burned to know what the reason could be.* VERB V with n V to-inf

11 If you **burn** or get **burned** in the sun, the sun makes your skin become red and sore. *Build up your tan slowly and don't allow your skin to burn.* V-ERG V Also V n

12 If a part of your body **burns** or if something **burns** it, it has a painful, hot or stinging feeling. *My eyes burn from staring at the needle... His face was burning with cold. ...delicious Indian recipes which won't burn your throat.* V-ERG V V with n V n

13 If you are **burned** or get **burned**, you lose something as a result of taking a risk, usually in a business deal; an informal expression used mainly in American English. *They always took chances and got burned very badly in past years.* VB: usu passive be/get V-ed

14 See also **burning**.

15 ● to **burn the candle at both ends**: see **candle**. ● to **get your fingers burned**: see **finger**. ● to **burn something to the ground**: see **ground**. ● to **burn the midnight oil**: see **midnight**. ● to **have money to burn**: see **money**.

burn down. If a building **burns down** or if someone **burns** it **down**, it is completely destroyed by fire. *Six months after Bud died, the house burned down... Anarchists burnt down a restaurant.* PHRASAL VERB ERG V P V P n (not pron) Also V n P

burn off PHRASAL VERB

1 If someone **burns off** energy, they use it. *This will improve your performance and help you burn off calories.* V P n (not pron) Also V n P

2 To **burn off** something unwanted means to get rid of it by burning it. *The bushfire actually helped to burn off a lot of dead undergrowth.* V P n (not pron) Also V n P

burn out PHRASAL VERB

1 If a fire **burns** itself **out**, it stops burning because there is nothing left to burn. *Fire officials let the fire burn itself out.* V pron-refl P

2 If you **burn** yourself **out**, you make yourself exhausted or ill by working too hard. *He might burn himself out and go to an early grave.* =wear out V pron-refl P

3 See also **burn-out, burnt-out**.

burn up PHRASAL VERB

1 If something **burns up** or if fire **burns** it **up**, it is completely destroyed by fire or strong heat. *The satellite re-entered the atmosphere and burned up... Fires have burned up 180,000 acres of timber.* ERG V P V P n (not pron) Also V n P

2 If something **burns up** fuel or energy, it uses it. *Brisk walking can burn up more calories than slow jogging.* V P n (not pron) Also V n P

burned-out. See **burnt-out**.

burner /bɜ:ʳnəʳ/ **burners.** A **burner** is a device which produces heat or a flame, especially as part of a cooker or heater. *He put the frying pan on the gas burner.* ● See also **back burner**, **front burner**. ◆◇◇◇◇ N-COUNT

burning /bɜ:ʳnɪŋ/ ◆◆◇◇◇

1 You use **burning** to describe something that is extremely hot. *...the burning desert of Central Asia.* ► Also an adverb. *He touched the boy's forehead. It was burning hot.* ADJ ADV: ADV adj =scorching

2 If you say that someone has **burning** eyes, you mean they look at you in an intense way or have bright eyes because of a strong feeling; a literary use. *She glared at both of them with burning, reproachful eyes.* ADJ: ADJ n

3 If you have a **burning** interest in something or a **burning** desire to do something, you are extremely interested in it or want to do it very much. *I had a burning ambition to become a journalist... She had a burning desire to wreak revenge.* ADJ: ADJ n =passionate

4 A **burning** issue or question is a very important or urgent one that people feel very strongly about. *The burning question in this year's debate over the federal budget is: whose taxes should be raised?* ADJ-GRADED: ADJ n

burnish /bɜ:ʳnɪʃ/ **burnishes, burnishing, burnished.** To **burnish** the image of someone or something means to improve their image; used in journalism. *The European Parliament badly needs a president who can burnish its image.* VERB =improve V n

burnished /bɜ:ʳnɪʃt/. You can describe something as **burnished** when it is bright or smooth; a literary use. *The clouds glowed like burnished gold.* ADJ: usu ADJ n =polished

burn-out. If someone suffers **burn-out**, they exhaust themselves at an early stage in their life or career because they have achieved too much too quickly; an informal expression. N-UNCOUNT

burnt /bɜ:ʳnt/. **Burnt** is a past tense and past participle of **burn**.

burnt-out; also spelled **burned-out**. **Burnt-out** vehicles or buildings have been very badly damaged by fire. *...a burnt-out car.* ◆◇◇◇◇ ADJ: usu ADJ n

burp /bɜ:ʳp/ **burps, burping, burped.** When someone **burps**, they make a noise because air from their stomach has been forced up through their throat. *Charlie burped loudly.* ► Also a noun. *There followed a barely audible burp.* VERB =belch V N-COUNT

burr /bɜːʳ/ **burrs;** also spelled **bur** for meaning one.
1 A **burr** is the part of some plants which contains seeds and which has little hooks on the outside so that it sticks to clothes or fur. N-COUNT
2 If someone has a **burr**, they speak English with a regional accent in which 'r' sounds are pronounced more noticeably than in the standard British way of speaking. *...his warm and amiable West Country burr.* N-COUNT: usu sing

burrow /bʌroʊ, AM bɜː-/ **burrows, burrowing, burrowed** ◆◇◇◇◇
1 A **burrow** is a tunnel or hole in the ground that is dug by an animal such as a rabbit. N-COUNT
2 If an animal **burrows** into the ground or into a surface, it moves through it by making a tunnel or hole. *The larvae burrow into cracks in the floor.* VERB =tunnel V prep/adv
3 If you **burrow** in a container or pile of things, you search there for something using your hands. *He burrowed into the pile of charts feverishly. ...the enthusiasm with which he burrowed through old records in search of facts.* VERB V prep/adv
4 If you **burrow** into something, you move underneath it or press against it, usually in order to feel warmer or safer. *She turned her face away from him, burrowing into her heap of covers.* VERB V prep/adv

bursar /bɜːʳsəʳ/ **bursars.** The **bursar** of a school or college is the person who is in charge of its finance or general administration. N-COUNT =treasurer

bursary /bɜːʳsəri/ **bursaries.** A **bursary** is a sum of money which is given to someone to allow them to study in a college or university; used mainly in British English. N-COUNT =scholarship

burst /bɜːʳst/ **bursts, bursting.** The form **burst** is used in the present tense and is the past tense and past participle. ◆◆◆◇◇
1 When something **bursts** or when you **burst** it, it suddenly breaks open or splits open and the air or other substance inside it comes out. *The driver lost control when a tyre burst... It is not a good idea to burst a blister. ...a flood caused by a burst pipe.* V-ERG V V n V-ed
2 If a dam **bursts**, or if something **bursts** it, it breaks apart because the force of the river is too great. *A dam burst and flooded their villages.* V-ERG V Also V n
3 If a river **bursts** its banks, the banks break apart and water overflows. *Monsoons caused the river to burst its banks.* VERB V n
4 When a door or lid **bursts** open, it opens very suddenly and violently because someone pushes it or there is great pressure behind it. *The door burst open and an angry young nurse appeared.* VERB =fly open V *open/apart*
5 If someone or something **bursts** into or out of a place, they suddenly enter or leave it with a lot of energy or force. *Gunmen burst into his home and opened fire... Rachel burst out as the door was flung open again.* VERB =rush V prep/adv
6 If you say that something **bursts** onto the scene, you mean that it suddenly starts or becomes active, usually after developing quietly for some time; used in written English. *Chinese companies have burst upon the scene with millions of dollars in their pockets.* VERB V *onto/upon* n
7 If you say that someone is about to **burst** with pride, anger, or another emotion, you are emphasizing the intensity of the emotion they are feeling; used in written English. *He almost burst with pride when his son John began to excel at football... He thought his heart would burst with grief.* VERB PRAGMATICS V *with* n Also V
8 When a firework or bomb **bursts** in the air, it explodes. *Hundreds of fireworks burst simultaneously in midair... Every now and then you hear some bombs bursting.* VERB =explode V
9 A **burst** of something is a sudden short period of it. *...a burst of machine-gun fire... It is easier to cope with short bursts of activity than with prolonged exercise... The current flows in little bursts.* N-COUNT: usu N *of* n
10 • to **burst into flames**: see **flame**.

burst into PHRASAL VERB
11 If you **burst into** tears, laughter, or song, you suddenly begin to cry, laugh, or sing. *She burst into tears and ran from the kitchen. ...books that cause adults to burst into helpless laughter.* V P n
12 When plants **burst into** leaf or flower, their leaves or flowers suddenly open; used in written English. *...rows of wallflowers promising to burst into bloom.* =break into V P n
13 If you say that something **bursts into** a particular situation or state, you mean that it suddenly changes into that situation or state. *This weekend's fighting is threatening to burst into full-scale war... The engine burst into life.* =erupt V P n

burst out PHRASAL VERB
14 If someone **bursts out** laughing, crying, or making another noise, they suddenly start making that noise. You can also say that a noise **bursts out**. *The class burst out laughing... Then the applause burst out... Everyone burst out into conversation.* ERG V P -ing V P V P *into/in* n
15 If someone **bursts out** something, they say it suddenly and loudly; used in written English. *'I want to be just like you', she bursts out.* V P with quote
16 If a situation or problem **bursts out**, it suddenly appears. *Malaria is bursting out again all over the world... Then war burst out.* =break out V P prep/adv V P

bursting /bɜːʳstɪŋ/ ◆◇◇◇◇
1 If a place is **bursting** with people or things, it is full of them. *The place appears to be bursting with women directors. ...a terraced vegetable garden, bursting with produce.* ADJ: v-link ADJ, usu ADJ *with* n =teeming
2 If you say that someone is **bursting with** a feeling or quality, you mean that they have a great deal of it. *I was bursting with curiosity. ...a character bursting with energy and vivacity.* ADJ: v-link ADJ *with* n
3 If you are **bursting** to do something, you are very eager to do it; an informal use. *She was bursting to tell everyone... We'll go there bursting to give it our all.* ADJ: v-link ADJ to-inf
4 If someone says they are **bursting**, they are emphasizing that they need to urinate very soon; an informal use. ADJ: v-link ADJ PRAGMATICS
5 If you say that a place is **bursting at the seams** or **full to bursting**, you are emphasizing that it is very full indeed. *The camps are said to be bursting at the seams... The room was full to bursting.* PHRASE PRAGMATICS
6 See also **burst**.

bury /beri/ **buries, burying, buried** ◆◆◆◇◇
1 To **bury** something means to put it into a hole in the ground and cover it up with earth. *They make the charcoal by burying wood in the ground and then slowly burning it. ...squirrels who bury nuts and seeds. ...buried treasure.* VERB V n prep/adv V n V-ed
2 To **bury** a dead person means to put their body into a grave and cover it with earth. *...soldiers who helped to bury the dead in large communal graves... I was horrified that people would think I was dead and bury me alive... More than 9,000 men lie buried here.* VERB =inter V n V n adj V-ed
3 If someone says they **have buried** one of their relatives, they mean that one of their relatives has died. *He had buried his wife some two years before he retired.* VERB V n
4 If you **bury** something under a large quantity of things, you put it there, often in order to hide it. *She buried it under some leaves... I was looking for my handbag, which was buried under a pile of old newspapers.* VERB V n prep/adv
5 If something **buries** a place or person, it falls on top of them so that it completely covers them and often harms them in some way. *Latest reports say that mud slides buried entire villages... Their house was buried by a landslide... He was buried under the debris for several hours.* VERB V n V-ed
6 If you **bury** your head or face in something, you press your head or face against it, often because you are unhappy. *She buried her face in the pillows... He held her closely, burying his head against her shoulder.* VERB =hide V n prep/adv
7 If something **buries** itself somewhere, or if you **bury** it there, it is pushed very deeply in there. *The missile buried itself deep in the grassy hillside... He stood on the sidewalk with his hands buried in the pockets of his dark overcoat.* VERB V pron-refl prep/adv V-ed Also V n prep/adv
8 If you **bury** a feeling, you try not to show it. If you **bury** a memory, you try to forget it; used in written English. *When we feel anger, we bury the emotion* VERB =suppress V n

and feel guilty instead... It is time to bury our past misunderstandings. ...deeply-buried memories. V-ed

9 If you **bury** yourself **in** a place or in an activity such as your work, you spend all your time in that place or doing that activity, usually because you want to forget about things. *His reaction was to withdraw, to bury himself in work. ...the popular image of writers burying themselves in the country in order to write.* VERB V pron-refl *in* n

10 If you **bury** your head in something such as a book or newspaper, or **bury** yourself in it, you look at it closely and concentrate very hard on it. *My father buried his head in his newspaper... He buried himself in his detective story again.* VERB V n *in* n V pron-refl *in* n

11 • to **bury the hatchet**: see **hatchet**.

bus /bʌs/ **buses, busses, bussing, bussed.** ◆◆◆◇◇ **Buses** is the plural of the noun. **Busses** is the third person singular of the verb. American English uses the spellings **buses, busing, bused** for the verb.

1 A **bus** is a large motor vehicle which carries passengers from one place to another. Buses drive along particular routes, and you have to pay to travel in them. *He missed his last bus home... They had to travel everywhere by bus.* N-COUNT: also *by* N

2 When someone is **bussed** to a particular place or when they **bus** there, they travel there on a bus. *On May Day hundreds of thousands used to be bussed in to parade through East Berlin... To get our Colombian visas we bussed back to Medellin... Essential services were provided by Serbian workers bussed in from outside the province.* V-ERG *be* V-ed adv/prep V adv/prep V-ed Also V n adv/prep

3 In the United States, when children are **bused** to school, they are transported by bus to a school in a different area so that children of different races can be educated together. *Many schools were in danger of closing because the children were bused out to other neighborhoods.* ♦ **busing** *The courts ordered busing to desegregate the schools.* VB: usu passive *be* V-ed adv/prep N-UNCOUNT

bush /bʊʃ/ **bushes** ◆◆◇◇◇

1 A **bush** is a large plant which is smaller than a tree and has a lot of branches. *Trees and bushes grew down to the water's edge.* N-COUNT =shrub

2 The wild, uncultivated parts of some hot countries are referred to as the **bush**. *They walked through the dense Mozambican bush for thirty six hours... The jeep was found lying in thick bush.* N-SING: usu *the* N, oft N n

3 If you tell someone not to **beat about the bush**, you mean that you want them to tell you something immediately and quickly, rather than in a complicated, indirect way. *Stop beating about the bush. What's he done?* PHRASE: V inflects, usu with brd-neg PRAGMATICS

bushed /bʊʃt/. If you say that you are **bushed**, you mean that you are extremely tired; an informal word. *I'm bushed. I'm going to bed.* ADJ-GRADED: v-link ADJ =beat

bushel /bʊʃəl/ **bushels.** A **bushel** is a unit of volume that is used for measuring agricultural produce such as corn or beans. A bushel is equivalent in volume to eight gallons. • If you **hide** your **light under a bushel**, you keep your abilities or good qualities hidden from other people. ◆◇◇◇◇ N-COUNT PHRASE: V inflects

Bushman /bʊʃmæn/ **Bushmen.** A **Bushman** is an aboriginal person from the southwestern part of Africa, especially the Kalahari desert region. N-COUNT

bushy /bʊʃi/ **bushier, bushiest** ◆◇◇◇◇

1 Bushy hair or fur is very thick. *...bushy eyebrows. ...a bushy tail.* ADJ-GRADED: usu ADJ n

2 A **bushy** plant has a lot of leaves very close together. *...strong, sturdy, bushy plants.* ADJ-GRADED

busily /bɪzɪli/. If you do something **busily**, you do it in a very active way. *The two saleswomen were busily trying to keep up with the demand.* ◆◇◇◇◇ ADV-GRADED: ADV with v

business /bɪznɪs/ **businesses** ◆◆◆◆◆

1 Business is work relating to the production, buying, and selling of goods or services. *...young people seeking a career in business... Jennifer has an impressive academic and business background. ...Harvard Business School.* N-UNCOUNT

2 Business is used when talking about how many products or services a company is able to sell. If **business** is good, a lot of products or services are being sold and if **business** is bad, few of them are being sold. *They worried that German companies would lose business... Business is booming.* N-UNCOUNT

3 A **business** is an organization which produces and sells goods or which provides a service. *The company was a family business... The majority of small businesses go broke within the first twenty-four months... He was short of cash after the collapse of his business.* N-COUNT =company, firm

4 Business is work or some other activity that you do as part of your job and not for pleasure. *I'm here on business... You can't mix business with pleasure. ...business trips.* N-UNCOUNT: oft *on* N

5 You can use **business** to refer to a particular area of work or activity in which the aim is to make a profit. *May I ask you what business you're in? ...the music business.* N-SING: oft supp N

6 You can use **business** to refer to something that you are doing or concerning yourself with. *...recording Ben as he goes about his business... There was nothing left for the teams to do but get on with the business of racing.* N-SING: with supp

7 You can use **business** to refer to important matters that you have to deal with. *The most important business was left to the last... I've got some unfinished business to attend to.* N-UNCOUNT

8 If you say that something is your **business**, you mean that it concerns you personally and that other people have no right to ask questions about it or disagree with it. *My sex life is my business... If she doesn't want the police involved, that's her business... It's not our business.* N-UNCOUNT: with poss =affair, concern

9 You can use **business** to refer in a general way to an event, situation, or activity. For example, you can say something is 'a wretched business' or you can refer to 'this assassination business'. *We have sorted out this wretched business at last... This whole business is very puzzling.* N-SING: supp N =affair

10 You can use **business** when describing a task that is unpleasant in some way. For example, if you say that doing something is a costly **business**, you mean that it costs a lot; an informal use. *Coastal defence is a costly business... Parenting can be a stressful business.* N-SING: supp N PRAGMATICS =affair

11 See also **big business, show business.**

12 If two people or companies **do business** with each other, one sells goods or services to the other. *I was fascinated by the different people who did business with me.* PHRASES RECIP: V inflects, PHR *with* n, pl-n PHR

13 If you say that someone **has no business** to be in a place or to do something, you mean that they have no right to be there or to do it. *Really I had no business to be there at all.* V inflects, PHR to-inf, PHR -ing

14 A company that is **in business** is currently operating and trading. *You can't stay in business without cash.* v-link PHR

15 If you say you **are in business**, you mean you have everything you need to start something immediately; used in spoken English. *All you need is a microphone, and you're in business.* V inflects, v-link PHR

16 If you say that someone **means business**, you mean they are serious and determined about what they are doing; an informal expression. *Now people are starting to realise that he means business.* V inflects

17 If you say to someone '**mind** your **own business**' or '**it's none of** your **business**', you are rudely telling them not to ask about something that does not concern them; an informal expression. *I asked Laura what was wrong and she told me to mind my own business.* PRAGMATICS

18 If you **make it your business** to do something, you decide to do it, because you are interested in it or because you want to find out something. *She made it her business to find out.* V inflects, PHR to-inf

19 If you say that you **are not in the business of** doing something, you mean that you do not do it, usually when you are annoyed or surprised that someone thinks you do. *We are not in the business of subsidising scroungers.* V inflects, PHR -ing/n PRAGMATICS

20 If a shop or company goes **out of business** or is put **out of business**, it has to stop trading because it is not making enough money. *Thousands of firms could go out of business.* PHR after v

21 If you say that someone or something is **the business**, you mean that they are the best of their kind; an informal expression. *When you watch him in training, you realise that this lad is the business.* v-link PHR PRAGMATICS

22 In a difficult situation, if you say it is **business as usual**, you mean that people will continue doing what they normally do. *The Queen was determined to show it was business as usual.* usu v-link PHR

business card, business cards. A person's **business card** or their **card** is a small card which they give to other people, and which has their name and details of their job and company printed on it. *He handed me his business card.* N-COUNT: oft poss N

business class. On aeroplanes, **business class** accommodation costs less than first-class but more than economy accommodation. *First-class and business class passengers are not returning in anything like previous numbers.* N-UNCOUNT: usu N n

business end. The **business end** of a tool or weapon is the end of it which does the work or causes damage rather than the end that you hold; an informal use. *...the business end of a vacuum cleaner.* N-SING: usu N of n

business hours. **Business hours** are the hours of the day in which a shop or a company is open for business. *All showrooms are staffed during business hours.* N-PLURAL

businesslike /bɪznəslaɪk/. If you describe someone as **businesslike**, you mean that they deal with things in an efficient way without wasting time. *Mr. Penn sounds quite businesslike... This activity was carried on in a businesslike manner.* ◆◇◇◇◇ ADJ-GRADED =efficient

businessman /bɪznɪsmæn/ **businessmen.** A **businessman** is a man who works in business. ◆◆◆◇◇ N-COUNT

business person, business people. **Business people** are people who work in business. *...business people who serve or supply the security forces. ...a self-employed business person.* N-COUNT

businesswoman /bɪznɪswʊmən/ **businesswomen.** A **businesswoman** is a woman who works in business. ◆◇◇◇◇ N-COUNT

busk /bʌsk/ **busks, busking, busked.** People who **busk** play music or sing for money in the streets or other public places; used mainly in British English. *They spent their free time in Glasgow busking in Argyle Street.* ♦ **busking** *Passers-by in the area have been treated to some high-quality busking.* VERB V N-UNCOUNT

busker /bʌskəʳ/ **buskers.** A **busker** is a person who plays music or sings for money in streets and other public places; used mainly in British English. N-COUNT

busload /bʌsloʊd/ **busloads.** A **busload** of people is a large number of passengers on a bus. *...a busload of Japanese tourists.* N-COUNT: usu N of n

busman's holiday /bʌsmənz hɒlɪdeɪ/. If you have a holiday, but spend it doing something similar to your usual work, you can refer to it as a **busman's holiday**. N-SING

bus-shelter, bus-shelters. A **bus-shelter** is a bus stop that has a roof and at least one open side. N-COUNT

bus stop, bus stops. A **bus stop** is a place on a road where buses stop to let passengers on and off. ◆◇◇◇◇ N-COUNT

bust /bʌst/ **busts, busting, busted.** The form **bust** is used as the present tense of the verb, and can also be used as the past tense and past participle. ◆◆◇◇◇

1 If you **bust** something, you break it or damage it so badly that it cannot be used; an informal use. *They will have to bust the door to get him out.* VERB V n

2 If someone **is busted**, the police arrest them; an informal use. *They were busted for possession of cannabis.* VB: usu passive be V-ed

3 If police **bust** a place, they raid it in order to arrest people who are doing something illegal; an informal use. *...police success in busting UK-based drug factories.* ► Also a noun. *...6 tons of cocaine seized last week in Panama's biggest drug bust.* VERB V n N-COUNT

4 A **bust** company or fund has no money left and has been forced to close down; an informal use. *It is taxpayers who will pay most of the bill for bailing out bust banks.* ADJ

5 If a company **goes bust**, it loses so much money that it is forced to close down; an informal expression. *...a Swiss company which went bust last May.* PHRASE: V inflects

6 A **bust** is a statue of the head and shoulders of a person. *...a bronze bust of the Queen.* N-COUNT: oft N of n

7 You can use **bust** to refer to a woman's breasts, especially when you are describing their size. *Good posture also helps your bust look bigger.* N-COUNT

-buster /-bʌstəʳ/ **-busters**

1 **-buster** combines with nouns to form new nouns which refer to someone who breaks a particular law. *The Security Council will consider taking future actions against sanction-busters. ...copyright-busters.* COMB in N-COUNT =-breaker

2 **-buster** combines with nouns to form new nouns which refer to someone or something that fights or overcomes the specified crime or undesirable activity. *Hoover was building his reputation as a crime-buster. ...fraud-busters.* COMB in N-COUNT

bustier /bʌstiəʳ/ **bustiers.** A **bustier** is a type of close-fitting strapless top worn by women. N-COUNT

bustle /bʌsᵊl/ **bustles, bustling, bustled** ◆◇◇◇◇

1 If someone **bustles** somewhere, they move there in a hurried and determined way, often because they are very busy. *My mother bustled around the kitchen... She bustled about, turning on lights, moving pillows around on the sofa.* VERB V prep/adv

2 A place that **is bustling** with people or activity is full of people who are very busy or lively. *The sidewalks are bustling with people... The main attraction was the bustling market.* VERB V with n V-ing

3 **Bustle** is busy, noisy activity. *...the hustle and bustle of modern life... There was a good deal of cheerful bustle.* N-UNCOUNT: oft N of n ≠stillness

bust-up, bust-ups

1 A **bust-up** is a serious quarrel, often resulting in the end of a relationship or partnership; an informal use. *She had had this bust-up with her family.* N-COUNT =row

2 A **bust-up** is a fight; used mainly in informal British English. *...a bust-up which she says left her seriously hurt.* N-COUNT

busty /bʌsti/. If you describe a woman as **busty**, you mean that she has very large breasts; an informal word which some people find offensive. ADJ-GRADED

busy /bɪzi/ **busier, busiest; busies, busying, busied** ◆◆◆◇◇

1 When you are **busy**, you are working hard or concentrating on a task, so that you are not free to do anything else. *What is it? I'm busy... They are busy preparing for a hectic day's activity on Saturday... Rachel said she would be too busy to come... Phil Martin is an exceptionally busy man.* ADJ-GRADED

2 A **busy** time is a period of time during which you have a lot of things to do. *It'll have to wait. This is our busiest time... Even with her busy schedule she finds time to watch TV... I had a busy day and was rather tired.* ADJ-GRADED: usu ADJ n =hectic ≠quiet

3 If you say that someone is **busy** thinking or worrying about something, you mean that it is taking all their attention, often to such an extent that they are unable to think about anything else. *Companies are so busy analysing the financial implications that they overlook the effect on workers... Most people are too busy with their own troubles to give much help.* ADJ-GRADED: v-link ADJ, oft ADJ -ing =preoccupied

4 If you **busy** yourself with something, you occupy yourself by dealing with it. *He busied himself with the camera... She busied herself getting towels ready... For a while Kathryn busied herself in the kitchen.* VERB V pron-refl with n/-ing V pron-refl -ing V pron-refl

5 A **busy** place is full of people who are doing things or moving about. *The Strand is one of London's busiest and most affluent streets... The ward was busy and Amy hardly had time to talk.* ADJ-GRADED

6 When a telephone line is **busy**, you cannot make your call because the line is already being used by someone else; used mainly in American English. *I tried to reach him, but the line was busy.* ADJ: usu v-link ADJ =engaged

7 See also **busily**.

busybody /bɪzibɒdi/ **busybodies.** If you refer to someone as a **busybody**, you disapprove of them because they interfere in other people's affairs; an informal word. *Some busybody tipped off the police, and they arrested someone.* N-COUNT PRAGMATICS

but /bət, STRONG bʌt/ **buts** ◆◆◆◆◆

1 You use **but** to introduce something which contrasts with what you have just said, or to introduce something which adds to what you have just said. *'You said you'd stay till tomorrow.'—'I know, Bel, but I think I would rather go back.'... Place the saucepan over moderate heat until the cider is very hot but not boiling... He not only wants to be taken seriously as a musician, but as a poet too.* CONJ-COORD

2 You also use **but** when you are about to add something further in a discussion or to change the subject. *They need to change the image because they need to recruit more people into the prison service. But another point I'd like to make is that a large proportion of the prisons in this country were built in the nineteenth century.* CONJ-COORD

3 You also use **but** after you have made an excuse or apology for what you are just about to say. *Please excuse me, but there is something I must say... I'm sorry, but it's nothing to do with you... Forgive my asking, but you're not very happy, are you?* CONJ-COORD

4 You use **but** to introduce a reply to someone when you want to indicate surprise, disbelief, refusal, or protest. *'I don't think I should stay in this house.'—'But why?'... 'Somebody wants you on the telephone'—'But no one knows I'm here!'* CONJ-COORD

5 **But** is used to mean 'except'. *Europe will be represented in all but two of the seven races... He didn't speak anything but Greek... The crew of the ship gave them nothing but bread to eat.* PREP: n PREP n

6 **But** is used to mean 'only'; a formal use. *This is but one of the methods used to try and get through to the patients that alcohol, as far as they are concerned, should be a thing of the past. ...Napoleon and Marie Antoinette, to name but two who had stayed in the great state rooms.* ADV: ADV n, ADV num

7 You use **buts** in expressions like **'no buts'** and **'ifs and buts'** to refer to reasons someone gives for not doing something, especially when you do not think that they are good reasons. *'B-b-b-b-but' I stuttered.—'Never mind the buts,' she ranted... There's no ifs or buts. He has to leave Kuwait – he has to obey.* N-PLURAL

8 You use **cannot but**, **could not but**, and **cannot help but** when you want to emphasize that you believe something must be true and that there is no possibility of anything else being the case; a formal use. *The pistol, no larger than the palm of my hand, was positioned where I couldn't help but see it... She could not but congratulate him.* PHRASES PHR inf

9 You use **but for** to introduce the only factor that causes a particular thing not to happen or not to be completely true. *...the small square below, empty but for a delivery van and a clump of palm trees... But for you, they might have given us the slip.* PHR n/-ing =except for

10 You use **but then** or **but then again** before a remark which slightly contradicts what you have just said. *The house is probably unsaleable because the bathroom extension has been built to contravene building regulations. But then again the estate agent thinks that the surveyor is wrong.* PHR cl

11 You use **but then** before a remark which suggests that what you have just said should not be regarded as surprising. *He was a fine young man, but then so had his father been... Sonia might not speak the English language well, but then who did?* PHR cl

12 ● **all but**: see **all.** ● **anything but**: see **anything.**

butane /bjuːteɪn/. **Butane** is a gas that is obtained from petroleum and is used as a fuel. N-UNCOUNT

butch /bʊtʃ/ ◆◇◇◇◇

1 If you describe a woman as **butch**, you mean that you think she behaves or dresses in a masculine way; an offensive use. ADJ-GRADED

2 If you describe a man as **butch**, you mean that he behaves in an exaggeratedly masculine way; an informal use. *... butch northern men.* ADJ-GRADED =macho

butcher /bʊtʃəʳ/ **butchers, butchering, butchered** ◆◇◇◇◇

1 A **butcher** is a shopkeeper who cuts up and sells meat. Some butchers also kill animals for meat and make foods such as sausages and meat pies. *It is best to let the butcher cut up the chicken for you.* N-COUNT

2 A **butcher** or a **butcher's** is a shop where meat is sold. *Mother sent me to the butcher's on a Saturday night to get a nice joint of beef.* N-COUNT: oft *the* N

3 To **butcher** an animal means to kill it and cut it up for meat. *Pigs were butchered, hams were hung to dry from the ceiling.* VERB *be* V-ed

4 You refer to someone as a **butcher** when they have killed a lot of people in a very cruel way, and you want to express your horror and disgust. *Klaus Barbie was known in France as the Butcher of Lyon.* N-COUNT PRAGMATICS

5 You say that someone **has butchered** people when they have killed a lot of people in a very cruel way, and you want to express your horror and disgust. *Guards butchered 1,350 prisoners... Our people are being butchered in their homes.* VERB PRAGMATICS =slaughter V n

butchery /bʊtʃəri/

1 **Butchery** is the cruel killing of a lot of people. *In her view, war is simply a legalised form of butchery.* N-UNCOUNT

2 **Butchery** is the work of cutting up meat and preparing it for sale. *...a carcass hung up for butchery.* N-UNCOUNT

butler /bʌtləʳ/ **butlers.** A **butler** is the most important male servant in a wealthy house. ◆◇◇◇◇ N-COUNT

butt /bʌt/ **butts, butting, butted** ◆◇◇◇◇

1 In American English, someone's **butt** is their bottom; an informal use which some people find offensive. *Frieda grinned, pinching him on the butt.* N-COUNT

2 The **butt** or the **butt end** of a weapon or tool is the thick end of its handle. *Troops used tear gas and rifle butts to break up the protests... Your left hand should be wrapped fairly firmly around the butt-end of the club.* N-COUNT: oft n N, N *of* n

3 The **butt** of a cigarette or cigar is the small part of it that is left when you have finished smoking it. *He dropped his cigarette butt into the street below... He paused to stub out the butt of his cigar.* N-COUNT: oft n N, N *of* n =stub

4 A **butt** is a large barrel used for collecting or storing liquid. *...great butts of wine from the Greek Islands.* N-COUNT: usu with supp

5 If someone or something is the **butt** of jokes or criticism, people often make fun of them or criticize them. *He is still the butt of cruel jokes about his humble origins.* N-SING: usu *the* N *of* n =target

6 If a person or animal **butts** you, they hit you with the top of their head. *Lawrence kept on butting me but the referee did not warn him.* VERB V n Also V n prep

7 See also **head-butt water butt.**

butt in. If you say that someone **is butting in**, you disapprove of the fact that they are joining in a conversation or activity without being asked to. *Sorry, I don't mean to butt in... 'I should think not,' Sarah butted in.* PHRASAL VERB PRAGMATICS =interrupt V P V P with quote Also V P *on* n

butt out. If someone tells you to **butt out**, they are telling you rudely to go away or not to interfere with what they are doing; an informal expression used mainly in American English. *She would have liked to tell him to butt out... The time has come for parents to butt out of the adolescent's daily life.* PHRASAL VERB PRAGMATICS V P V P *of* n

butter /bʌtəʳ/ **butters, buttering, buttered** ◆◆◆◇◇

1 **Butter** is a soft yellow substance made from cream. You spread it on bread or use it in cooking. *...bread and butter... Pour the melted butter into a large mixing bowl.* N-MASS

2 When you **butter** something such as bread or toast, you spread butter on it. *She spread pieces of bread on the counter and began buttering them. ...buttered scones.* VERB V n V-ed

3 See also **bread and butter, peanut butter.**

4 If you say that someone **knows what side their bread is buttered on**, you mean that they know what to do or who to please in order to stay in a good situation or to avoid a bad one. *These chaps know what side their bread's buttered on.* PHRASE: V inflects

butter up. If someone **butters** you **up**, they try to please you because they want you to help or support them; used mainly in informal British English. *He accused Mr Delors of buttering up farmers to* PHRASAL VERB V P n (not pron) V n P *boost his chances of becoming French president... I tried buttering her up. 'I've always admired people with these sorts of talents.'*

butter bean, butter beans. **Butter beans** are the yellowish flat round seeds of a kind of bean plant. They are usually sold dried rather than fresh, and are eaten as a vegetable; used mainly in British English. N-COUNT: usu pl

buttercup /bʌtəʳkʌp/ **buttercups.** A **buttercup** is a small plant with bright yellow flowers. N-COUNT

butterfly /bʌtəʳflaɪ/ **butterflies** ◆◆◇◇◇

1 A **butterfly** is an insect with large colourful wings and a thin body. N-COUNT

2 **Butterfly** is a swimming stroke which you do lying on your front, kicking your legs and bringing your arms over your head together. N-UNCOUNT: also *the* N

3 If you have **butterflies in** your **stomach** or have **butterflies**, you are very nervous or excited about something; an informal use. *An exam, or even an exciting social event may produce butterflies in the stomach.* PHRASE

buttermilk /bʌtəʳmɪlk/. **Buttermilk** is the liquid that remains when fat has been removed from cream when butter is being made. You can drink buttermilk or use it in cooking. N-UNCOUNT

butterscotch /bʌtəʳskɒtʃ/

1 **Butterscotch** is a hard yellowish-brown sweet that tastes similar to toffee. It is made from butter and sugar boiled together. N-UNCOUNT

2 A **butterscotch** flavoured or coloured thing has the flavour or colour of butterscotch. *...butterscotch sauce.* N-UNCOUNT: usu N n

buttery /bʌtəri/. **Buttery** food contains butter or is covered with butter. *...buttery new potatoes. ...the buttery taste of the pastry.* ADJ-GRADED: usu ADJ n

buttock /bʌtək/ **buttocks.** Your **buttocks** are the two rounded fleshy parts of your body that you sit on. ◆◇◇◇◇ N-COUNT

button /bʌtᵊn/ **buttons, buttoning, buttoned** ◆◆◆◇◇

1 **Buttons** are small hard objects sewn on to shirts, coats, or other pieces of clothing. You fasten the clothing by pushing the buttons through holes called buttonholes. *...a coat with brass buttons.* N-COUNT

2 If you **button** a shirt, coat, or other piece of clothing, you fasten it by pushing its buttons through the buttonholes. *Ferguson stood up and buttoned his coat.* ▶ **Button up** means the same as **button.** *I buttoned up my mink coat; it was chilly... The young man slipped on the shirt and buttoned it up... It was freezing out there even in his buttoned-up overcoat.* VERB V n PHRASAL VERB V P n (not pron) V n P V-ed P

3 A **button** is a small object on a machine or electrical device that you press in order to operate the machine or device. *He reached for the remote control and pressed the 'play' button.* N-COUNT

4 In American English, a **button** is a small piece of metal or plastic which you wear in order to show that you support a particular movement, organization, or person. You fasten a button to your clothes with a pin. The British word is **badge**. N-COUNT

5 If you say that someone **presses the right button** or **pushes the right button**, you mean that they get what they want from a particular situation or person in a clever way. *Buchanan pushed all the right buttons, appealing to Maher's loyalty and to his guilt.* PHRASE: V and N inflect

button up. See **button** 2. PHRASAL VERB

button-down. A **button-down** shirt or a shirt with a **button-down** collar has a button under each end of the collar which you can fasten. ADJ: ADJ n

buttoned up; also spelled **buttoned-up**. If you say that someone is **buttoned up**, you mean that they do not usually talk about their thoughts and feelings; an informal expression. *She plays Estella Campion, the rather buttoned-up wife of an English clergyman.* ADJ-GRADED =reserved

buttonhole /bʌtᵊnhoul/ **buttonholes, buttonholing, buttonholed**

1 A **buttonhole** is a hole that you push a button through in order to fasten a shirt, coat, or other piece of clothing. N-COUNT

2 In British English, a **buttonhole** is a flower that you wear on the collar or lapel of your jacket. N-COUNT

3 If you **buttonhole** someone, you stop them and make them listen to you. *Several people buttonholed television reporters to explain to them their reasons for not voting.* VERB =corner V n

button mushroom, button mushrooms. **Button mushrooms** are small mushrooms used in cooking. N-COUNT: usu pl

buttress /bʌtrəs/ **buttresses, buttressing, buttressed** ◆◇◇◇◇

1 **Buttresses** are supports, usually made of stone or brick, that support a wall. N-COUNT

2 To **buttress** an argument, system, or person means to give them support and strength. *He sought to buttress some of his arguments with quotations from Mein Kampf... Yeltsin's tough line is, however, buttressed by a democratic mandate.* VERB V n *with* n V n

butty /bʌti/ **butties.** In British English, a **butty** is a sandwich; an informal word. *It's half past ten and time for a bacon butty.* N-COUNT =sarnie

buxom /bʌksəm/. If you describe a woman as **buxom**, you mean that she looks healthy and attractive and has a rounded body and big breasts. *Melissa was a tall, buxom blonde.* ADJ-GRADED: usu ADJ n

buy /baɪ/ **buys, buying, bought** ◆◆◆◆◆

1 If you **buy** something, you obtain it by paying money for it. *He could not afford to buy a house... They can now be bought fresh in supermarkets... Lizzie bought herself a mountain bike... I'd like to buy him lunch.* VERB V n V pron-refl n V n n

2 If you talk about the quantity or standard of goods an amount of money **buys**, you are referring to the price of the goods or the value of the money. *About £25,000 buys a habitable house... If the pound's value is high, British investors will spend their money abroad because the pound will buy them more.* VERB V n V n n

3 If you **buy** something like time, freedom, or victory, you obtain it but only by offering or giving up something in return. *It was a risky operation, but might buy more time... For them, affluence was bought at the price of less freedom in their work environment.* VERB V n

4 If you say that a person can be **bought**, you mean they can be bribed to give their help or loyalty to someone. *Once he shows he can be bought, they settle down to a regular payment.* VB: usu passive =bribe *be* V-ed

5 If you **buy** an idea or a theory, you believe and accept it; an informal use. *I'm not buying any of that nonsense.* ▶ **Buy into** means the same as **buy.** *I bought into the popular myth that when I got the new car or the next house, I'd finally be happy.* VERB V n PHRASAL VERB V P n

6 If something is a good **buy**, it is of good quality and not very expensive. *This was still a good buy even at the higher price... S & G offers great buys on computer software.* N-COUNT: supp N =bargain

buy into. If you **buy into** a company or an organization, you buy part of it, often in order to gain some control of it. *Other companies could buy into the firm.* ● See also **buy** 5. PHRASAL VERB V P n

buy off. If one person **buys off** another person, the first person bribes the second person not to act against them; used showing disapproval. *...policies designed to buy off the working-class vote... Be careful that in buying your children all these things, you are not in a sense buying them off.* PHRASAL VERB PRAGMATICS V P n (not pron) V n P

buy out PHRASAL VERB

1 If you **buy** someone **out**, you buy their share of something such as a company or piece of property that you previously owned together. *The bank had to pay to buy out most of the 200 former partners... He bought his brother out for $17 million.* ● See also **buyout**. V P n (not pron) V n P

2 If you **buy** someone **out** of the armed forces or another organization, you pay a sum of money so that they can leave before the end of the period they agreed to stay for. *Carling eventually bought himself out of the army.* V n P

buy up. If you **buy up** land, property, or a commodity, you buy large amounts of it, or all that is available. *The mention of price rises sent citizens* PHRASAL VERB V P n (not pron) *out to their shops to buy up as much as they could... The tickets will be on sale from somewhere else because the agencies have bought them up.* V n P

buyer /baɪəʳ/ **buyers** ◆◆◆◇◇
1 A **buyer** is a person who is buying something or who intends to buy it. *Car buyers are more interested in safety and reliability than speed.* N-COUNT ≠seller
2 A **buyer** is a person who works for a large store deciding what goods will be bought from manufacturers to be sold in the store. *I was a buyer for the women's clothing department.* N-COUNT

buyer's market, buyer's markets. When there is a **buyer's market** for a particular product, there are more of the products for sale than there are people who want to buy them, so buyers have a lot of choice and can make prices come down. N-COUNT: usu sing

buyout /baɪaʊt/ **buyouts.** A **buyout** is the buying of a company, especially by its managers or employees. *It is thought that a management buyout is one option.* ◆◇◇◇◇ N-COUNT: oft supp N

buzz /bʌz/ **buzzes, buzzing, buzzed** ◆◆◇◇◇
1 If something **buzzes** or **buzzes** somewhere, it makes a long continuous sound, like that of a bee. *I walk on, furious bees buzzing all around me... The intercom buzzed and he pressed down the appropriate switch... Attack helicopters buzzed across the city.* ▶ Also a noun. *...the irritating buzz of an insect.* ♦ **buzzing** *He switched off the transformer and the buzzing stopped.* VERB V V prep/adv N-COUNT; SOUND N-UNCOUNT
2 If people **are buzzing** around, they are moving around quickly and busily; used in written English. *A few tourists were buzzing about... She was intimidated by the number of businessmen buzzing around the saleroom.* VERB =race V adv/prep
3 If questions or ideas **are buzzing** around your head, or if your head **is buzzing** with questions or ideas, you are thinking about a lot of things, usually in a confused way. *Many more questions were buzzing around my head... Top style consultants will leave you buzzing with new ideas.* VERB V around/about n V with n Also V
4 If a place **is buzzing** with activity or conversation, there is a lot of activity or conversation there, especially because something important or exciting is about to happen. *The rehearsal studio is buzzing with lunchtime activity... The capital is buzzing with rumours of possible demonstrations. ...Hong Kong's buzzing, pulsating atmosphere.* VB: usu cont V with n V-ing Also V, V prep
5 You can use **buzz** to refer to a long continuous sound, usually caused by lots of people talking at once. *A buzz of excitement filled the courtroom as the defendant was led in. ...the excited buzz of conversation.* N-SING: usu N of n
6 If something gives you a **buzz**, it makes you feel very happy or excited for a short time; an informal use. *Performing still gives him a buzz... He got a buzz from creating confrontations.* N-SING
7 You can use **buzz** to refer to a word, idea, or activity which has recently become extremely popular. *...the latest buzz phrase in garden design circles... Sex education in schools was the buzz topic.* ADJ: ADJ n =trendy
8 If you **buzz** someone you call them, usually using an internal telephone line or a buzzer; an informal use. *Later that morning Julie buzzed me.* ▶ Also a noun. *We'll give him a buzz when we get to Maybury Street.* VERB V n N-SING: a N
9 If an aircraft **buzzes** a place, it flies low over it, usually in a threatening way. *American fighter planes buzzed the city.* VERB V n

buzz off. If someone **buzzes off**, they go away. People often say **buzz off** as a rude way of telling someone to go away; used mainly in informal British English. *He buzzed off downstairs... Now be quiet and buzz off.* PHRASAL VERB =clear off V P adv/prep V P

buzzard /bʌzəʳd/ **buzzards**
1 A **buzzard** is a large bird of prey. N-COUNT
2 If you refer to someone as a **buzzard**, you think they are unpleasant or very mean; an informal use. *I'm almost grateful to the old buzzard.* N-COUNT

buzzer /bʌzəʳ/ **buzzers.** A **buzzer** is an electrical device that is used to make a buzzing sound for example, to attract someone's attention. *She rang a buzzer at the information desk.* ◆◇◇◇◇ N-COUNT

buzzword /bʌzwɜːʳd/ **buzzwords;** also spelled **buzz word.** A **buzzword** is a word or expression that has become fashionable in a particular field and is being used a lot by the media. *Biodiversity was the buzzword of the Rio Earth Summit.* N-COUNT

by. The preposition is pronounced /baɪ/. The adverb is pronounced /baɪ/. ◆◆◆◆◆
In addition to the uses shown below, **by** is used in phrasal verbs such as 'abide by', 'put by', and 'stand by'.
1 If something is done **by** a person or thing, that person or thing does it. *The feast was served by his mother and sisters... I was amazed by their discourtesy and lack of professionalism... The town has been under attack by rebel groups for a week now.* PREP
2 If you say that something such as a book, a piece of music, or a painting is **by** a particular person, you mean that this person wrote it or created it. *A painting by Van Gogh has been sold in New York for more than eighty two million dollars... 'Jacob's Ladder', the newest film by Adrian Lyne, is a post-Vietnam horror story.* PREP
3 If you do something **by** a particular means, you do it using that thing. *If you're travelling by car, ask whether there are parking facilities nearby. ...dinners by candlelight.* PREP
4 If you achieve one thing **by** doing another thing, your action enables you to achieve the first thing. *Make the sauce by boiling the cream and stock together in a pan... The all-female yacht crew made history by becoming the first to sail round the world... By using the air ambulance to transport patients between hospitals, he estimates that they can save up to £15,000 per patient.* PREP: PREP -ing
5 You use **by** in phrases such as 'by chance' or 'by accident' to indicate whether or not an event was planned. *I met him by chance out walking yesterday... He opened Ingrid's letter by mistake... Whether by design or accident his timing was perfect.* PREP
6 If someone is a particular type of person **by** nature, **by** profession, or **by** birth, they are that type of person because of their nature, their profession, or the family they were born into. *I am certainly lucky to have a kind wife who is loving by nature... She's a nurse by profession and now runs a counselling service for women... Her parents were in fact American by birth.* PREP: adj/n PREP n
7 If something must be done **by** law, it happens according to the law. If something is the case **by** particular standards, it is the case according to the standards. *Pharmacists are required by law to give the medicine prescribed by the doctor. ...evening wear that was discreet by his standards.* PREP
8 If you say what someone means **by** a particular word or expression, you are saying what they intend the word or expression to refer to. *Stella knew what he meant by 'start again'... 'You're unbelievably lucky'—'What do you mean by that?'* PREP
9 If you hold someone or something **by** a particular part of them, you hold that part. *He caught her by the shoulder and turned her around... She was led by the arm to a small room at the far end of the corridor... He picked up the photocopy by one corner, wiped it clean, and put it in his wallet.* PREP
10 Someone or something that is **by** something else is beside it and close to it. *Judith was sitting in a rocking-chair by the window... Felicity Maxwell stood by the bar and ordered a glass of wine... Emma was by the door.* ▶ Also an adverb. *Large numbers of security police stood by.* PREP ADV: ADV after v
11 When a person or vehicle goes **by** you, they move past you without stopping. *A few cars passed close by me... He kept walking and passed by me on his side of the street.* ▶ Also an adverb. *The bomb went off as a police patrol went by.* PREP: v PREP n ADV: ADV after v
12 If you stop **by** a place, you visit it for a short time. *We had made arrangements to stop by her house in Pacific Grove... Daddy called and asked me to drop by his office.* ▶ Also an adverb. *I'll stop by after dinner and we'll have that talk.* PREP ADV: ADV after v

13 If something happens **by** a particular time, it happens at or before that time. *By eight o'clock he had arrived at my hotel... We all knew by then that the affair was practically over.* PREP

14 If you do something **by** day, you do it during the day. If you do it **by** night, you do it during the night. *By day a woman could safely walk the streets, but at night the pavements became dangerous... She had no wish to hurry alone through the streets of London by night.* PREP

15 In arithmetic, you use **by** before the second number in a multiplication or division sum. *...an apparent annual rate of 22.8 per cent (1.9 multiplied by 12)... 230cm divided by 22cm is 10.45cm.* PREP: PREP num

16 You use **by** to talk about measurements of area. For example, if a room is twenty feet **by** fourteen feet, it measures twenty feet in one direction and fourteen feet in the other direction. *Three prisoners were sharing one small cell 3 metres by 2½ metres.* PREP: PREP num

17 If something increases or decreases **by** a particular amount, that amount is gained or lost. *Violent crime has increased by 10 percent since last year... Their pay has been cut by one-third.* PREP: PREP amount

18 Things that are made or sold **by** the million or **by** the dozen are made or sold in those quantities. *Parcels arrived by the dozen from America... Liberty fabrics, both for furnishing and for dress-making, are sold by the metre.* PREP: PREP *the* n

19 You use **by** in expressions such as 'minute by minute' and 'drop by drop' to talk about things that happen gradually, not all at once. *His father began to lose his memory bit by bit, becoming increasingly forgetful.* PREP: n PREP n

20 If you are **by yourself**, you are alone. *...a dark-haired man sitting by himself in a corner.* PHRASES PHR after v =alone

21 If you do something **by yourself**, you succeed in doing it without anyone helping you. *I didn't know if I could raise a child by myself.* PHR after v =on one's own

bye /baɪ/. **Bye** and **bye-bye** are informal ways of saying goodbye. ◆◆◆◇◇ CONVENTION =cheerio

bye-law. See **bylaw**.

by-election, by-elections. A **by-election** is an election that is held to choose a new member of parliament when a member has resigned or died. ◆◇◇◇◇ N-COUNT

Byelorussian /biəloʊrʌʃᵊn/ **Byelorussians** ◆◆◆◆◇

1 Byelorussian means belonging or relating to Byelorussia or to its people or culture. *The Byelorussian president has announced his resignation.* ADJ

2 A **Byelorussian** is a Byelorussian citizen, or a person or Byelorussian origin. N-COUNT

bygone /baɪgɒn, AM -gɔːn/ **bygones** ◆◇◇◇◇

1 Bygone means happening or existing a very long time ago. *The book recalls other memories of a bygone age. ...bygone generations.* ADJ: ADJ n =past

2 If two people **let bygones be bygones**, they decide to forget about unpleasant things that have happened between them in the past. PHRASE

bylaw /baɪlɔː/ **bylaws;** also spelled **bye-law, by-law.** A **bylaw** is a law which is made by a local authority and which applies only in their area. *The by-law makes it illegal to drink in certain areas.* N-COUNT

by-line, by-lines; also spelled **byline**. A **by-line** is a line at the top of an article in a newspaper or magazine giving the author's name; a technical term in journalism. N-COUNT

bypass /baɪpɑːs, -pæs/ **bypasses, bypassing, bypassed** ◆◆◇◇◇

1 If you **bypass** someone or something that you would normally have to get involved with, you ignore them or do not get involved with them, often because you want to achieve something more quickly. *A growing number of employers are trying to bypass the unions altogether... Regulators worry that controls could easily be bypassed.* VERB =sidestep V n

2 A **bypass** is a surgical operation performed on or near the heart, in which the flow of blood is redirected so that it does not flow through a part of the heart which is diseased or blocked. *...heart bypass surgery.* N-COUNT: oft N n

3 If a surgeon **bypasses** a diseased artery or other part of the body, he or she performs an operation so that blood or other bodily fluids do not flow through it. *Small veins are removed from the leg and used to bypass the blocked up stretch of coronary arteries.* VERB V n

4 A **bypass** is a main road which takes traffic around the edge of a town rather than through its centre. *A new bypass around the city is being built. ...the Hereford bypass.* N-COUNT: oft in names after n

5 If a road **bypasses** a place, it goes around it rather than through it. *...money for new roads to bypass cities.* VERB V n

6 If you **bypass** a place when you are travelling, you avoid going through it. *The rebel forces simply bypassed Zwedru on their way further south.* VERB V n

by-product, by-products ◆◇◇◇◇

1 A **by-product** is something which is produced during the manufacture or processing of another product. *The raw material for the tyre is a by-product of petrol refining.* N-COUNT: oft N *of*n =spin-off

2 Something that is a **by-product** of an event or situation happens as a result of it, although it is usually not expected or planned. *A by-product of their meeting was the release of these fourteen men.* N-COUNT: oft N *of*n =side-effect

byre /baɪəʳ/ **byres.** A **byre** is a cowshed; a literary word. N-COUNT

bystander /baɪstændəʳ/ **bystanders.** A **bystander** is a person who is present when something happens and who sees it but does not take part in it. *It looks like an innocent bystander was killed instead of you.* ◆◇◇◇◇ N-COUNT

byte /baɪt/ **bytes.** In computing, a **byte** is a unit of storage approximately equivalent to one printed character. *...two million bytes of data.* N-COUNT

byway /baɪweɪ/ **byways**

1 A **byway** is a small road which is not used by many cars or people. *...the highways and byways of America. ...the narrow city byways.* N-COUNT: usu pl

2 The **byways** of a subject are the less important or less well known areas of it. *The byways of children's literature mattered to them as much as the mainstream classics.* N-COUNT: usu pl, usu N *of*n

byword /baɪwɜːʳd/ **bywords**

1 Someone or something that is a **byword** for a particular quality is well known for having that quality. *...a region that had become a byword for violence and degeneracy. ...the Rolls-Royce brand name, a byword for quality.* N-COUNT: N *for*n

2 A **byword** is a word or phrase which people often use. *Loyalty, support, and secrecy became the bywords of the day.* N-COUNT

byzantine /bɪzæntaɪn, AM bɪzəntiːn/; also spelled **Byzantine**.

1 Byzantine means related to or connected with the Byzantine Empire. *...Byzantine civilisation... There are also several well-preserved Byzantine frescoes.* ADJ: ADJ n

2 If you describe a system or process as **byzantine**, you disapprove of it because it is complicated or secretive. *...a byzantine system of rules and trading arrangements.* ADJ-GRADED: usu ADJ n PRAGMATICS

C c

C, c /siː/ **C's, c's**
1 **C** is the third letter of the English alphabet. N-VAR
2 In music, **C** is the first note in the scale of C major. N-VAR
3 If you get a **C** as a mark for a piece of work or in an exam, your work is average. N-VAR
4 **c.** is written in front of a date or number to indicate that it is approximate. **c.** is an abbreviation for **circa**. *...the museum's recreation of a New York dining-room (c. 1825-35).*
5 **C** or **c** is used as an abbreviation for words beginning with c, such as 'copyright' or 'Celsius'. *Heat the oven to 180°C.*
6 See also **C-in-C, c/o.**

cab /kæb/ **cabs** ◆◆◇◇◇
1 A **cab** is a taxi. N-COUNT
2 The **cab** of a lorry is the front part in which the driver sits. *A Luton van has additional load space over the driver's cab.* N-COUNT

cabal /kəbæl/ **cabals.** If you refer to a group of politicians or other people as a **cabal**, you disapprove of them because they meet and decide things secretly. *He was accused of being chosen by a cabal of fellow senators. ...a secret government cabal.* N-COUNT: usu with supp PRAGMATICS

cabaret /kæbəreɪ, AM -reɪ/ **cabarets** ◆◇◇◇◇
1 **Cabaret** is live entertainment consisting of dancing, singing, or comedy acts that are performed in the evening in restaurants or nightclubs. *Helen made a successful career in cabaret... He was just starting to become known on the cabaret circuit.* N-UNCOUNT: oft N n
2 A **cabaret** is a show that is performed in a restaurant or nightclub, and that consists of dancing, singing, or comedy acts. *Peter and I also did a cabaret at the Corn Exchange.* N-COUNT
3 A **cabaret** is a restaurant or nightclub where live entertainment such as dancing, singing, or comedy is performed. *He followed her to Paris, where he began singing in bars and cabarets.* N-COUNT

cabbage /kæbɪdʒ/ **cabbages** ◆◆◇◇◇
1 A **Cabbage** is a round vegetable with green leaves that you usually chop up and boil in water before eating. N-VAR
2 If someone refers to a very sick or disabled person as a **cabbage**, they mean that the person is so severely brain-damaged or physically unwell that he or she cannot do anything or enjoy anything; an offensive use. *Although it hurts my wife and I to say this he is little more than a cabbage.* N-COUNT: usu sing =vegetable

cabbie /kæbi/ **cabbies;** also spelled **cabby**. A **cabbie** is a person who drives a taxi; an informal word. ◆◇◇◇◇ N-COUNT =cab driver

caber /keɪbəʳ/ **cabers.** A **caber** is a long, heavy, wooden pole that is thrown into the air as a test of strength in the traditional Scottish Highland sport of tossing the caber. N-COUNT

cabin /kæbɪn/ **cabins** ◆◆◇◇◇
1 A **cabin** is a small room in a ship or boat. *He showed her to a small cabin.* N-COUNT
2 A **cabin** is one of the areas inside a plane. *He sat quietly in the First Class cabin of the British Airways flight looking tired.* N-COUNT
3 A **cabin** is a small wooden house, especially one in an area of forests or mountains. *...a log cabin.* N-COUNT

cabin crew, cabin crews. The **cabin crew** on an aircraft are the people whose job is to look after the passengers. *He was assured by a senior member of the cabin crew that there definitely was not an emergency.* N-COUNT-COLL

cabin cruiser, cabin cruisers. A **cabin cruiser** is a motor boat which has a cabin for people to live or sleep in. N-COUNT

cabinet /kæbɪnɪt/ **cabinets** ◆◆◆◆◇
1 A **cabinet** is a cupboard used for storing things such as medicine or alcoholic drinks or for displaying decorative things in. *The star of my medicine cabinet is the humble aspirin... He looked at the display cabinet with its gleaming sets of glasses.* • See also **filing cabinet.** N-COUNT: usu n N
2 The **Cabinet** is a group of the most senior ministers in a government, who meet regularly to discuss policies. *The announcement came after a three-hour Cabinet meeting in Downing Street. ...a former Cabinet Minister.* N-COUNT: oft N n

cabinet maker, cabinet makers; also spelled **cabinetmaker.** A **cabinet maker** is a person who makes high-quality wooden furniture. N-COUNT

cable /keɪbəl/ **cables, cabling, cabled** ◆◆◆◇◇
1 **Cable** is used to refer to television systems in which the signals are sent along underground wires rather than by radio waves. *They ran commercials on cable systems across the country... The channel is only available on cable.* N-UNCOUNT: oft N n
2 A **cable** is a thick wire, or a bundle of wires inside a rubber or plastic covering, which is used to carry electricity or electronic signals. *...overhead power cables. ...strings of coloured lights with weatherproof cable.* N-VAR
3 A **cable** is a kind of very strong, thick rope, made of wires twisted together. *The miners rode a conveyance attached to a cable made of braided steel wire... Steel cable will be used to replace worn ropes.* N-VAR
4 A **cable** is a message that is sent by means of electricity along a wire over a long distance, often to another country, and is then printed out at the other end. *She sent a cable to her mother... He made up for his absence with a cable which I read to the assembled gathering.* N-COUNT
5 If you **cable** someone, you send them a message in the form of a cable. *'Don't do it again,' Franklin cabled her when he got her letter... She had to decide whether or not to cable the news to Louis. ...a new formula which is being cabled back to capitals for approval.* VERB V n with quote, V n prep/adv, Also V n, V n n, V with quote, V
6 If a country, a city, or someone's home **is cabled**, cables and other equipment are put in place so that the people there can receive cable television. *In France, 27 major cities are soon to be cabled... In the UK, 254,000 homes are cabled.* VB: usu passive; be V-ed; V-ed
7 See also **cabling.**

cable car, cable cars. A **cable car** is a vehicle for taking people up mountains or steep hills. It is pulled by a moving cable. *On the island there is a mountain with a cable car running up to the top.* N-COUNT

cable television. **Cable television** is a television system in which signals are sent along wires rather than by radio waves. ◆◇◇◇◇ N-UNCOUNT

cabling /keɪblɪŋ/. **Cabling** is used to refer to electrical or electronic cables, or to the process of installing them. *...made-to-measure prefabricated offices equipped with computer cabling... Engineers need to find ways to reduce the cabling and wiring.* • See also **cable.** N-UNCOUNT

cache /kæʃ/ **caches.** A **cache** is a quantity of things such as weapons that have been hidden. *A huge arms cache was discovered by police. ...a cache of weapons and explosives.* ◆◇◇◇◇ N-COUNT: with supp =store

cachet /kæʃeɪ, AM kæʃeɪ/. If someone or something has a certain **cachet**, they have a quality which makes people admire them or approve of them; used in written English. *The social cachet* N-SING: with poss *of some form of qualification in India is powerful... A Mercedes carries a certain cachet.*

cack-handed /kæk hændɪd/. If you describe someone as **cack-handed**, you mean that they handle things in an awkward or clumsy way; an informal word, used mainly in British English. *Liz may be good at her job, but she is cack-handed.*
ADJ-GRADED =clumsy

cackle /kækᵊl/ **cackles, cackling, cackled.** If someone **cackles**, they laugh in a loud unpleasant way, often at someone else's misfortune. *The old lady cackled, pleased to have produced so dramatic a reaction... Newington threw his head back and cackled with laughter.* ► Also a noun. *He let out a brief cackle.*
VERB; V; V *with* n; Also V with quote, V *at* n; N-COUNT

cacophonous /kəkɒfənəs/. If you describe a mixture of sounds as **cacophonous**, you mean that they are loud and unpleasant. *...'60s-sounding guitars and cacophonous vocals.*
ADJ-GRADED: usu ADJ n ≠harmonious

cacophony /kəkɒfəni/ **cacophonies.** You can describe a loud, unpleasant mixture of sounds as a **cacophony**. *All around was bubbling a cacophony of voices.*
N-COUNT: usu sing, usu N *of* n

cactus /kæktəs/ **cactuses** or **cacti** /kæktaɪ/. A **cactus** is a thick fleshy plant that grows in deserts. Cacti have no leaves and many of them are covered in spikes.
◆◇◇◇◇ N-COUNT

cad /kæd/ **cads.** If you say that a man is a **cad**, you mean that he treats other people, especially women, badly or unfairly; an old-fashioned word. *He's a scoundrel! A cad!*
N-COUNT ≠gentleman

cadaver /kədævəʳ/ **cadavers.** A **cadaver** is a dead body; a formal use.
N-COUNT =corpse

cadaverous /kədævərəs/. If you describe someone as **cadaverous**, you mean they are extremely thin and pale; used in written English. *The tall, thin man had a long, cadaverous face.*
ADJ-GRADED: usu ADJ n

caddie /kædi/ **caddies, caddying, caddied;** also spelled **caddy**. ◆◇◇◇◇

1 In golf, a **caddie** is a person who carries golf clubs and other equipment for a player.
N-COUNT

2 If you **caddie** for a golfer, you act as their caddie. *Lil caddied for her son.*
VERB; V *for* n; Also V

cadence /keɪdᵊns/ **cadences**

1 The **cadence** of someone's voice is the way their voice gets higher and lower as they speak; a formal use. *He recognized the Polish cadences in her voice... He is not attempting to reproduce the cadence of speech.*
N-COUNT =intonation, lilt

2 A **cadence** is the phrase that ends a section of music or a complete piece of music.
N-COUNT

cadenza /kədenzə/ **cadenzas.** In classical music, a **cadenza** is a long and technically difficult solo passage in a piece for soloist and orchestra. *The players were in the past expected to make up their own cadenzas for concertos.*
N-COUNT

cadet /kədet/ **cadets.** A **cadet** is a young man or woman who is being trained in the army, navy, air force, or police. *...army cadets. ...the Cadet Corps.*
◆◇◇◇◇ N-COUNT

cadge /kædʒ/ **cadges, cadging, cadged.** If someone **cadges** food, money, or help from you, they ask you for it and succeed in getting it; used mainly in informal British English. *Can I cadge a cigarette?... He could cadge a ride from somebody.*
VERB =bum, scrounge; V n; V n *from/off* n

cadmium /kædmiəm/. **Cadmium** is a soft bluish-white metal that is used in the production of nuclear energy.
N-UNCOUNT

cadre /kɑːdəʳ, AM -dreɪ/ **cadres** ◆◇◇◇◇

1 A **cadre** is a small group of people who have been specially chosen, trained, and organized for a particular purpose. *...an elite cadre of Euro-managers.*
N-COUNT: usu with supp

2 In some political parties, especially the Communist Party, a **cadre** is a party worker or official. *It has long ceased to be a grassroots party with cadres in every village.*
N-COUNT: usu with supp

Caesarean /sɪzeəriən/ **Caesareans.** A **Caesarean** or a **Caesarean section** is an operation in which a baby is lifted out of a woman's womb through an opening cut in her abdomen. *My youngest daughter was born by Caesarean... I had to have an emergency Caesarean.*
N-COUNT: also *by* N

café /kæfeɪ, AM kæfeɪ/ **cafés;** also spelled **cafe**. ◆◆◇◇◇

1 A **café** is a place where you can buy drinks, simple meals, and snacks. In Britain cafés do not serve alcoholic drinks.
N-COUNT

2 A street **café** or a pavement **café** is a café which has tables and chairs on the pavement outside it where people can eat and drink. These cafes are common in European cities. *...an Italian street café. ...sidewalk cafes and boutiques.*
N-COUNT: n N

cafeteria /kæfɪtɪəriə/ **cafeterias.** A **cafeteria** is a restaurant where you choose your food from a counter and carry it to your table yourself after paying for it. Cafeterias are usually found in buildings such as hospitals, colleges, and hotels. *...the school cafeteria. ...cafeteria-style catering.*
◆◇◇◇◇ N-COUNT =canteen

caff /kæf/ **caffs.** In British English, a **caff** is a cafe which serves simple British food such as fried eggs, bacon, and sausages; an informal word. *...a transport caff.*
N-COUNT

caffeine /kæfiːn, AM kæfiːn/. **Caffeine** is a chemical substance found in coffee, tea, and cocoa, which affects your brain and body and makes you more active.
◆◇◇◇◇ N-UNCOUNT

caftan /kæftæn/ **caftans;** also spelled **kaftan**. A **caftan** is a long loose garment with long sleeves. Caftans are worn by men in Arab countries, and by women in America and Europe.
N-COUNT

cage /keɪdʒ/ **cages** ◆◆◇◇◇

1 A **cage** is a structure of wire or metal bars in which birds or animals are kept. *I hate to see birds in cages.* ● See also **rib cage**.
N-COUNT

2 If someone **rattles** your **cage**, they do something which is intended to make you feel nervous. *If he's trying to rattle your cage, it's working.*
PHRASE: V and N inflect

caged /keɪdʒd/. A **caged** bird or animal is inside a cage. *Mark was still pacing like a caged animal.*
ADJ

cagey /keɪdʒi/. If you say that someone is being **cagey** about something, you mean that you think they are deliberately not giving you much information or expressing an opinion about it. *He is cagey about what he was paid for the business.* ♦ **cagily** /keɪdʒɪli/ *Smart reacted cagily when Chelsea were mentioned.*
ADJ-GRADED PRAGMATICS =guarded; ADV-GRADED

cahoots /kəhuːts/. If you say that one person is **in cahoots** with another, you do not trust the first person because you think that they are planning something secretly with the other; used showing disapproval. *In his view they were all in cahoots with the police... I am not having you and him in cahoots against me.*
PHRASE: usu v-link PHR, oft PHR *with* n PRAGMATICS

cairn /keəʳn/ **cairns.** A **cairn** is a pile of stones which marks a boundary, a route across rough ground, or the top of a mountain. A cairn is sometimes also built in memory of someone.
N-COUNT

cajole /kədʒoʊl/ **cajoles, cajoling, cajoled.** If you **cajole** someone into doing something, you get them to do it after a persuading them for some time. *It was he who had cajoled Garland into doing the film... He cajoled Mr Izetbegovic to accept the peace plan.*
◆◇◇◇◇ VERB; V n *into* -ing; V n to-inf; Also V n, V

Cajun /keɪdʒən/ **Cajuns**

1 **Cajun** means belonging or relating to a large group of people who originate from Louisiana in the United States, or to their language or culture. *...Cajun fiddler Dewey Balfa... They played some Cajun music. ... a teacher from the Cajun area of Southern Louisiana.*
ADJ: usu ADJ n

2 A **Cajun** is a person of Cajun origin.
N-COUNT

3 **Cajun** is a dialect of French spoken by Cajun people. *...the first book ever written in Cajun.*
N-UNCOUNT

cake /keɪk/ **cakes, caking, caked** ◆◆◆◇◇

1 A **cake** is a sweet food made by baking a mixture of flour, eggs, sugar, and fat in an oven. Cakes may be large and cut into slices or small and intended for one person only. *...a piece of cake... Would you like some chocolate cake? ...little cakes with white icing.*
N-VAR

2 Food that is formed into flat round shapes before it is cooked can be referred to as **cakes**. *...fish cakes. ...home-made potato cakes.*
N-COUNT: usu supp N

3 A **cake** of soap is a small block of it. *...a small cake of lime-scented soap.*
N-COUNT: usu N *of* n

4 If something such as blood or mud **cakes**, it changes from a thick liquid to a dry layer or lump. *The blood had begun to cake and turn brown.* VERB V

5 If you think that someone wants the benefits of doing two things when it is only reasonable to expect the benefits of doing one, you can say that they want to **have their cake and eat it**; used showing disapproval. *What he wants is a switch to a market economy in a way which does not reduce people's standard of living. To many this sounds like wanting to have his cake and eat it.* PHRASES Vs inflect PRAGMATICS

6 If things are **selling like hot cakes**, a lot of people are buying them; an informal expression. *Books on the Royal Family are selling like hot cakes.* V inflects, usu cont

7 If you think something is very easy to do, you can say it is **a piece of cake**. People often say this to stop someone feeling worried about doing something they have to do; an informal expression. *Getting rid of him will be a piece of cake... Just another surveillance job, old chap. Piece of cake to somebody like you.* usu v-link PHR PRAGMATICS

8 • **the icing on the cake**: see **icing**.

caked /keɪkt/. If something is **caked** with mud, blood, or dirt, it is covered with a thick dry layer of it. *Her shoes were caked with mud.* ► Also a combining form. *...blood-caked bandages. ...herds of mud-caked cattle and sheep.* ADJ: usu v-link ADJ *with/in* n =encrusted COMB in ADJ: usu ADJ n =encrusted

cake mix, cake mixes. **Cake mix** is a powder-like substance that you mix with eggs and water or milk, to make a cake. You bake the mixture in the oven. N-VAR

cake tin, cake tins

1 A **cake tin** is a metal container with a lid, which you put a cake into in order to keep it fresh. N-COUNT

2 A **cake tin** is a metal container which you bake a cake in. N-COUNT

cal /kæl/ **cals.** **Cals** are units of measurement for the energy value of food. **Cal** is an abbreviation for **calorie**. *...325 cals per serving.* N-COUNT: usu pl, num N

calamitous /kəlæmɪtəs/. If you describe an event or situation as **calamitous**, you mean it is very unfortunate or serious; a formal word. *...the calamitous state of the country. ...a calamitous air crash.* ADJ-GRADED =disastrous

calamity /kəlæmɪti/ **calamities.** A **calamity** is an event that causes a great deal of damage, destruction, or personal distress; a formal word. *He described drugs as the greatest calamity of the age. ...the calamity of war... It could only end in calamity.* ◆◇◇◇◇ N-VAR =disaster

calcium /kælsiəm/. **Calcium** is a soft white element which is found in bones and teeth, and also in limestone, chalk, and marble. ◆◆◇◇◇ N-UNCOUNT

calculable /kælkjʊləbᵊl/. **Calculable** amounts or consequences can be calculated. ADJ

calculate /kælkjʊleɪt/ **calculates, calculating, calculated** ◆◆◇◇◇

1 If you **calculate** a number or amount, you discover it from information that you already have, by using arithmetic, mathematics, or a special machine. *From this you can calculate the total mass in the Galaxy... We calculate that the average size farm in Lancaster County is 65 acres... A computer calculates by switching currents on or off.* VERB =work out V n V that V Also V wh

2 If you **calculate** the effects of something, especially a possible course of action, you think about them in order to form an opinion or decide what to do. *I believe I am capable of calculating the political consequences accurately... The President is calculating that this will somehow relieve the international pressure on him.* VERB V n V that

calculated /kælkjʊleɪtɪd/ ◆◆◇◇◇

1 If something is **calculated** to have a particular effect, it is specially done or arranged in order to have that effect. *Their movements through the region were calculated to terrify landowners into abandoning their holdings... These tracks were calculated to be controversial and attract attention to the album.* ADJ: v-link ADJ to-inf =designed

2 If you say that something is not **calculated** to have a particular effect, you mean that it is unlikely to have that effect. *German names were not calculated to attract patrons to America's movie theaters in 1941... Such a statement was hardly calculated to deter future immigrants.* ADJ-GRADED: with brd-neg, v-link ADJ to-inf =likely

3 You can describe a clever or dishonest action as **calculated** when is very carefully planned or arranged. *Irene's use of the mop had been a calculated attempt to cover up her crime. ...a calculated and coherent strategy for winning power.* ADJ-GRADED: usu ADJ n

4 If you take a **calculated** risk, you do something which you think might be successful, although you have fully considered the possible bad consequences of your action. *The President took a calculated political risk in throwing his full support behind the rebels.* ADJ: ADJ n

calculating /kælkjʊleɪtɪŋ/. If you describe someone as **calculating**, you disapprove of the fact that they deliberately plan to get what they want, often by hurting or harming other people. *Northbridge is a cool, calculating and clever criminal who could strike again.* ◆◇◇◇◇ ADJ-GRADED =scheming

calculation /kælkjʊleɪʃᵊn/ **calculations** ◆◆◇◇◇

1 A **calculation** is something that you think about and work out mathematically. **Calculation** is the process of working something out mathematically. *Leonard made a rapid calculation: he'd never make it in time. ...the calculation of their assets.* N-VAR: oft N *of* n

2 A **calculation** is something that you think about and arrive at a conclusion on after having considered all the relevant factors. *Mr Mitterrand has two years of power left and he is deep in his calculations.* N-VAR

3 If you describe someone's behaviour as **calculation**, you mean that they think only of themselves and not of other people. *...cold, unspeakably cruel calculation.* N-UNCOUNT

calculator /kælkjʊleɪtəʳ/ **calculators.** A **calculator** is a small electronic device that you use for making mathematical calculations. *...a pocket calculator.* ◆◇◇◇◇ N-COUNT

calculus /kælkjʊləs/. **Calculus** is a branch of advanced mathematics which deals with variable quantities. N-UNCOUNT

caldron /kɔːldrən/. See **cauldron**.

calendar /kælɪndəʳ/ **calendars** ◆◆◇◇◇

1 A **calendar** is a chart or device which displays the date and the day of the week, and often the whole of a particular year divided up into months, weeks, and days. *There was a calendar on the wall above, with large squares around the dates.* N-COUNT

2 A **calendar** is a particular system for dividing time into periods such as years, months, and weeks, often starting from a particular point in history. *The Christian calendar was originally based on the Julian calendar of the Romans.* N-COUNT: usu supp N

3 You can use **calendar** to refer to a series or list of events and activities which take place on particular dates, and which are important for a particular organization, community, or person. *It is one of the British sporting calendar's most prestigious events... Franklin joined her and the children whenever his crowded calendar allowed... They tried to make a calendar of Spain's festivals.* N-COUNT: usu sing, usu with poss =diary

calendar month, calendar months. A **calendar month** is a period of approximately 30 days that is known by a particular name, such as January, May, or September. *The rent is £400 per calendar month.* N-COUNT

calendar year, calendar years. A **calendar year** is a period of 365 or 366 days that begins on January 1st and ends on December 31st. *He predicts the company will sell one million vehicles in the 1990 calendar year.* N-COUNT

calf /kɑːf, AM kæf/ **calves** /kɑːvz, AM kævz/. ◆◇◇◇◇

1 A **calf** is a young cow. N-COUNT

2 Some other young animals, including elephants and whales, are called **calves**. N-COUNT

3 Your **calf** is the thick part at the back of your leg, between your ankle and your knee. *...a calf injury.* N-COUNT

calf-length. **Calf-length** skirts, dresses, and coats come to halfway between your knees and ankles. *...a black, calf-length coat.* ADJ: ADJ n

calfskin /kɑːfskɪn, AM kæf-/. **Calfskin** shoes and clothing are made from the skin of a calf. *...calfskin boots.* [N-UNCOUNT: oft N n]

caliber /kælɪbəʳ/. See **calibre**.

calibrate /kælɪbreɪt/ **calibrates, calibrating, calibrated**

1 If you **calibrate** an instrument or tool, you mark or adjust it so that you can use it to measure something accurately; a technical term. *...instructions on how to calibrate a thermometer. ...a calibrated hypodermic syringe.* [VERB; V n; V-ed] ♦ **calibration, calibrations** [N-VAR] *...to enable effective calibration of the measuring instrument.*

2 If you **calibrate** something, you measure it accurately. *...a way of calibrating the shift of opinion within the Labour Party... Pesticide levels in food are simply too difficult to calibrate.* [VERB; V n] ♦ **calibration** [N-VAR] *...the precise calibration of the achievement level of those observed.*

calibre /kælɪbəʳ/ **calibres**; spelled **caliber** in American English. [◆◇◇◇◇]

1 The **calibre** of a person is the quality or standard of their ability or intelligence, especially when this is high. *I was impressed by the high calibre of the researchers and analysts... It became apparent that we could never get the calibre of people we wanted.* [N-UNCOUNT: with supp, usu adj N, N of n]

2 The **calibre** of something is its quality, especially when it is good. *The quality of his character and the caliber of his accomplishments produced a lasting influence... The calibre of teaching was very high.* [N-UNCOUNT: with supp, oft N of n]

3 The **calibre** of a gun is the width of the inside of its barrel; a technical use. *...a .22 calibre rifle. ...a small-calibre pistol.* [N-COUNT: usu with supp, oft num N, adj N]

calico /kælɪkoʊ/ **calicoes. Calico** is plain white fabric made from cotton. [N-MASS]

caliper /kælɪpəʳ/ **calipers**; also spelled **calliper**.

1 A **caliper** is, or **calipers** are, an instrument consisting of long, thin pieces of metal joined together, which is used to measure the size of things. [N-COUNT: usu pl, also *a pair of* N]

2 Calipers are devices consisting of metal rods held together by straps, which are used to support a person's legs when they cannot walk properly. [N-COUNT: usu pl]

caliph /keɪlɪf/ **caliphs**; also spelled **calif**. A **Caliph** was a Muslim ruler. *...the caliph of Baghdad.* [N-COUNT; N-TITLE]

calisthenics /kælɪsθenɪks/; also spelled **callisthenics. Calisthenics** are simple exercises that you do to keep fit and healthy. [N-PLURAL]

call /kɔːl/ **calls, calling, called** [◆◆◆◆◆]

1 If you **call** someone or something by a particular name or title, you give them that name or title. *I always wanted to call the dog Mufty for some reason... 'Doctor...'—'Sandy, will you please call me Sarah?'... Everybody called each other by their surnames.* [VERB; V n n; V n *by* n] ♦ **called** [ADJ: v-link ADJ] *Klein's most important work is called 'Envy and Gratitude'... There are two Labour politicians called Jim Callaghan. ...a device called an optical amplifier.*

2 If you **call** someone or something a particular thing, you suggest they are that thing or describe them as that thing. *The speech was interrupted by members of the Conservative Party, who called him a traitor... I wouldn't call it a burden; I call it a responsibility... She calls me lazy and selfish... He called it particularly cynical to begin the releases on Christmas Day... Anyone can call themselves a psychotherapist.* [VERB; V n n; V n adj; V *it* adj to-inf; V pron-refl n]

3 If you **call** something, you say it in a loud voice, because you are trying to attract someone's attention. *He could hear the others downstairs in different parts of the house calling his name... 'Boys!' she called again.* [VERB; V n; V with quote] ► **Call out** means the same as **call**. *The butcher's son called out a greeting... The train stopped and a porter called out, 'Middlesbrough!'* [PHRASAL VERB; V P n (not pron); V P with quote; Also V n P]

4 If you **call** someone, you telephone them. *Would you call me as soon as you find out? My number's in the phone book... A friend of mine gave me this number to call... 'May I speak with Mr Coyne, please?'—'May I ask who's calling?'* [VERB =telephone; V n; V]

5 If you **call** someone such as a doctor or the police, you ask them to come to you by telephoning them. *He screamed for his wife to call an ambulance... One night he was called to see a woman with tuberculosis.* [VERB; V n; *be* V-ed to-inf]

6 If you **call** someone, you ask them to come to you by shouting to them. *She called her young son: 'Here, Stephen, come and look at this!'... He called me over the Tannoy.* [VERB; V n; V n prep]

7 When you make a telephone **call**, you telephone someone. *I made a phone call to the United States to talk to a friend... I've had hundreds of calls from other victims... I got a call from him late yesterday evening.* [N-COUNT]

8 If someone in authority **calls** something such as a meeting, rehearsal, or election, they arrange for it to take place at a particular time. *The Committee decided to call a meeting of the All India Congress... The RSC was calling a press conference to announce its closure... The strike was called by the Lebanese Forces militia... A meeting has been called for Monday.* [VERB; V n]

9 If someone **is called** before a court or committee, they are ordered to appear there, usually to give evidence. *The child waited two hours before she was called to give evidence... I was called as an expert witness.* [VB: usu passive =summon; *be* V-ed to-inf; *be* V-ed prep; Also *be* V-ed]

10 If you **call** somewhere, you make a short visit there. *A market researcher called at the house where he was living... Andrew now came almost weekly to call.* [VERB; V prep/adv; V] ► Also a noun. *He decided to pay a call on Tommy Cummings.* [N-COUNT]

11 When a train, bus, or ship **calls** somewhere, it stops there for a short time to allow people to get on or off. *The steamer calls at several palm-fringed ports along the way.* [VERB; V prep/adv]

12 If there is a **call** for something, someone demands that it should happen. *There have been calls for a new kind of security arrangement... Almost all workers heeded a call by the trade unions to stay at home for the duration of the strike.* [N-COUNT: usu N *for* n, N to-inf]

13 If there is little or no **call for** something, very few people want it to be done or provided. *'Have you got just plain chocolate?'—'No, I'm afraid there's not much call for that.'* [N-UNCOUNT: with brd-neg, N *for* n =demand]

14 The **call** of something such as a place is the strong attraction or fascination that it has for you. *You must be feeling exhilarated by the call of the new.* [N-SING: with poss =pull]

15 The **call** of a particular bird or animal is the characteristic sound that it makes. *...the plaintive call of a whale. ...a wide range of animal noises and bird calls.* [N-COUNT]

16 See also **calling**; **so-called**.

17 If you have **first call on** something, you will be asked before anyone else whether you want to buy or use it. *Why should they get first call on the best property?* [PHRASES; PHR after v, PHR n =first refusal on]

18 If you say that **there is no call for** someone to behave in a particular way, you mean that you disapprove of their behaviour, usually because you think it is rude. *There was no call for him to single you out from all the others.* [PHR n to-inf, PHR n; PRAGMATICS; =there is no need for]

19 If someone is **on call**, they are ready to go to work at any time if they are needed, especially when there is an emergency. *In theory I'm on call day and night. ...a doctor on call.* [PHR after v, v-link PHR]

20 If you **call in sick**, you telephone your workplace to tell them you will not be coming to work because you are ill. *'Shouldn't you be at work today?'—'I called in sick.'* [V inflects]

21 • **to call someone's bluff**: see **bluff**. • **to call it a day**: see **day**. • **to call a halt**: see **halt**. • **to call something to mind**: see **mind**. • **call of nature**: see **nature**. • **to call** someone **to order**: see **order**. • **to call** something your **own**: see **own**. • **to call something into question**: see **question**. • **to call it quits**: see **quit**. • **to call a spade a spade**: see **spade**. • **to call the tune**: see **tune**.

call back. If you **call** someone **back**, you telephone them again or in return for a telephone call that they have made to you. *If we're not around she'll take a message and we'll call you back... If you want further advice, you can call back and speak to the same adviser.* [PHRASAL VERB; V n P; V P; Also V P n (not pron)]

call for PHRASAL VERB
1 If you **call for** someone or something, you go to the building where they are to meet them, so that you can go somewhere else together. *I shall be calling for you at seven o'clock.* =pick up; V P n
2 If you **call for** something, you demand that it should happen. *They angrily called for Robinson's resignation... The ceasefire resolution calls for the release of all prisoners of war.* V P n
3 If something **calls for** a particular action or quality, it needs it or makes it necessary. *It's a situation that calls for a blend of delicacy and force.* =demand; V P n

call in PHRASAL VERB
1 If you **call** someone **in**, you ask them to come and help you or do something for you. *Call in an architect or surveyor to oversee the work.* V P n (not pron); Also V n P
2 If you **call in** somewhere, you make a short visit there. *He just calls in occasionally... I got into the habit of calling in on Gloria on my way home.* =drop in; V P; V P *on* n

call off. If you **call off** an event that has been planned, you cancel it. *He has called off the trip... The union threatened a strike but called it off at the last minute.* PHRASAL VERB; V P n (not pron); V n P

call on or **call upon** PHRASAL VERB
1 If you **call on** someone to do something or **call upon** them to do it, you say publicly that you want them to do it. *One of Kenya's leading churchmen has called on the government to resign... Frequently he was called upon to resolve conflicts.* V P n to-inf
2 If you **call on** someone or **call upon** someone, you pay them a short visit. *Sofia was intending to call on Miss Kitts.* V P n

call out. If you **call** someone **out**, you order or request that they come to help, especially in an emergency. *Colombia has called out the army and imposed emergency measures... I called the doctor out... The fire brigade should always be called out to a house fire.* • See also **call** 3. PHRASAL VERB; V P n (not pron); V n P; *be* V-ed P *to* n

call up PHRASAL VERB
1 If you **call** someone **up**, you telephone them; used mainly in American English. *When I'm in Pittsburgh, I call him up... He called up the museum... Sometimes I'd call up at 4 a.m.* =call; V n P; V P n (not pron); V P
2 If someone **is called up**, they are ordered to join the army, navy, or air force, or chosen to play in a sports team. *Youngsters coming up to university were being called up... He is likely to be called up for Thursday's match against Italy... The United States has called up some 150,000 military reservists.* • See also **call-up**. *be* V-ed P; V P n (not pron); Also V n P

call upon. See **call on** 1. PHRASAL VERB

call box, call boxes; also spelled **call-box**. A **call box** is a telephone box; used mainly in British English. N-COUNT =phone box

caller /kɔːlə^{r}/ **callers** ◆◆◇◇◇
1 A **caller** is a person who is making a telephone call. *An anonymous caller told police what had happened.* N-COUNT
2 A **caller** is a person who comes to see you for a short visit. *She ushered her callers into a cluttered living-room.* N-COUNT =visitor

call girl, call girls. A **call girl** is a prostitute who makes appointments by telephone. N-COUNT

calligrapher /kəlɪgrəfə^{r}/ **calligraphers.** A **calligrapher** is a person skilled in the art of calligraphy. *He was a skilled calligrapher and artist.* N-COUNT

calligraphy /kəlɪgrəfi/
1 **Calligraphy** is the art of producing beautiful handwriting using a brush or a special pen. N-UNCOUNT
2 **Calligraphy** is beautiful and artistic handwriting. *Her calligraphy was the clearest I'd ever seen.* N-UNCOUNT

calling /kɔːlɪŋ/ **callings.** A **calling** is a profession or career which someone is strongly attracted to, especially one which involves helping other people. *He was a consultant physician, a serious man dedicated to his calling.* ◆◇◇◇◇ N-COUNT: usu sing =vocation

calling card, calling cards. A **calling card** is a small card with personal information about you on it, such as your name and address, which you can give to people when you go to visit them; used mainly in American English. N-COUNT =card

calliper /kælɪpə^{r}/. See **caliper**.

callisthenics /kælɪsθenɪks/. See **calisthenics**.

callous /kæləs/. A **callous** person or action is very cruel and shows no concern for other people or their feelings. *...his callous disregard for human life.* ♦ **callousness** *...the callousness of Raymond's murder.* ♦ **callously** *He is accused of consistently and callously ill-treating his wife.* ◆◇◇◇◇ ADJ-GRADED =heartless ≠sensitive; N-UNCOUNT; ADV-GRADED: ADV with v

calloused /kæləst/; also spelled **callused**. A foot or hand that is **calloused** is covered in calluses. *...blunt, calloused fingers.* ADJ-GRADED

callow /kæloʊ/. A **callow** young person has very little experience or knowledge of the way they should behave as an adult. *...a callow youth.* ADJ-GRADED: usu ADJ n

call sign, call signs. A **call sign** is the letters and numbers which identify a person, vehicle, or organization that is broadcasting on the radio or sending messages by radio. N-COUNT

call-up, call-ups ◆◇◇◇◇
1 If a person gets their **call-up** papers, they receive an official order to join the army, navy, or air force; used mainly in British English. ADJ: ADJ n
2 A **call-up** is an occasion on which people are ordered to report for service in the armed forces; used mainly in British English. *...the annual call-up for the Soviet forces.* N-COUNT
3 If someone receives a **call-up** to a sports team, such as the national football team, they are chosen to play for that team; used in journalism. N-COUNT

callus /kæləs/ **calluses.** A **callus** is an area of unwanted, unnaturally thick skin, usually on the palms of your hands or the soles of your feet, which has been caused by rubbing. N-COUNT

calm /kɑːm/ **calmer, calmest; calms, calming, calmed** ◆◆◆◇◇
1 A **calm** person does not show or feel any worry, anger, or excitement. *She is usually a calm and diplomatic woman... Try to keep calm and just tell me what happened... She sighed, then continued in a soft, calm voice... Diane felt very calm and unafraid as she saw him off the next morning.* ► Also a noun. *He felt a sudden sense of calm, of contentment.* ♦ **calmly** *Alan looked at him and said calmly, 'I don't believe you.'... Hungary, by contrast, has so far reacted calmly to events in Yugoslavia.* ♦ **calmness** *All those things gave him a feeling of security and calmness.* ADJ-GRADED; N-UNCOUNT: also *a* N; ADV-GRADED: usu ADV with v, also ADV adj; N-UNCOUNT
2 If you **calm** someone, you do something to make them feel less angry, worried, or excited. *The ruling party's veterans know how to calm their critics... Tranquilliser drugs were used to calm the deportees... She was breathing quickly and tried to calm herself... A business lunch helps calm her nerves.* ♦ **calming** *...a fresh, cool fragrance which produces a very calming effect on the mind.* VERB; V n; ADJ-GRADED
3 **Calm** is used to refer to a quiet, still, or peaceful atmosphere in a place. *The house projects an atmosphere of neoclassical calm and order. ...the rural calm of Grand Rapids, Michigan.* N-UNCOUNT =peace
4 If someone says that a place is **calm**, they mean that it is free from fighting or public disorder, when trouble has recently occurred there or had been expected; used in journalism. *The city of Sarajevo appears relatively calm today.* ► Also a noun. *Community and church leaders have appealed for calm and no retaliation... An uneasy calm is reported to be prevailing in the area.* ADJ-GRADED: usu v-link ADJ =peaceful; N-UNCOUNT: also *a* N
5 If someone or something **calms** a situation, they reduce the amount of trouble, violence, or panic there is somewhere. *Officials hoped admitting fewer foreigners would calm the situation... Mr Beazer tried to calm the protests by promising to keep the company's base in Pittsburgh.* VERB; V n
6 If the sea or a lake is **calm**, the water is not moving very much and there are no big waves. *...as we slid into the calm waters of Cowes Harbour.* ADJ-GRADED =still ≠rough
7 **Calm** weather is pleasant weather with little or no wind. *Tuesday was a fine, clear and calm day.* ADJ-GRADED
8 A flat **calm** or a dead **calm** is a condition of the sea or the weather in which there is very little wind or movement of the water; a technical use in sailing. *...during flat calms when the water is crystal* N-COUNT: usu supp N

clear... We had the whole gamut of wind from a dead calm to a force 10 gale.

9 When the sea **calms**, it becomes still because the wind stops blowing strongly. When the wind **calms**, it stops blowing strongly. *Dawn came, the sea calmed but the cold was as bitter as ever.* VERB V

10 To **calm** a pain or an itch means to reduce it or get rid of it. *...more traditional methods of soothing the skin and calming the itch.* VERB =soothe V n

11 You can use **the calm before the storm** to refer to a quiet period in which there is little or no activity, before a period in which there is a lot of trouble or intense activity. PHRASE

calm down PHRASAL VERB

1 If you **calm down** or if someone **calms** you **down**, you become less angry, upset, or excited. *Calm down for a minute and listen to me... I'll try a herbal remedy to calm him down... Do not have a drink or take drugs to calm yourself down.* ERG V P V n P Also V P n (not pron)

2 If things **calm down**, or someone or something **calms** things **down**, the amount of activity, trouble, or panic somewhere is reduced. *We will go back to normal when things calm down... Neil Howorth, director of the academy, tried to calm things down.* ERG =settle down V P V n P

calmly /kɑːmli/. You can use **calmly** to emphasize that someone is behaving in a very controlled or ordinary way in a frightening or unusual situation; used in written English. *She walked up to her lover's wife and calmly shot her in the head.* • See also **calm**. ◆◇◇◇◇ ADV: ADV with v PRAGMATICS

caloric /kəlɔːrɪk/. **Caloric** means relating to calories. *...a daily caloric intake of from 400 to 1200 calories.* ADJ: ADJ n

calorie /kæləri/ **calories. Calories** are units of measurement for the energy value of food. People who are on diets try to eat food that does not contain many calories. *A glass of wine does have quite a lot of calories. ...calorie controlled diets.* • See also **-calorie**. ◆◆◇◇◇ N-COUNT

-calorie /-kæləri/. **-calorie** is used after adjectives such as low or high to indicate that food contains a small or a large number of calories. *...low-calorie margarine. ...reduced-calorie mayonnaise.* COMB in ADJ-GRADED: usu ADJ n

calorific /kælərɪfɪk/. The **calorific** value of something, or its **calorific** content, is the number of calories it contains; a technical term used in science. *...food with a high calorific value. ...highly calorific fats.* ADJ-GRADED: usu ADJ n

calumny /kæləmni/ **calumnies. Calumny** or a **calumny** is an untrue statement made about someone in order to reduce other people's respect and admiration for them; a formal word. *He was the victim of calumny.* N-VAR =slander

calve /kɑːv, AM kæv/ **calves, calving, calved**

1 When a cow **calves**, it gives birth to a calf. *When his cows calve each year he keeps one or two calves for his family.* VERB V

2 Some other female animals, including elephants and whales, are said to **calve** when they give birth to their young. *The whales migrate some 6,000 miles to breed and calve in the warm lagoons.* VERB V

3 **Calves** is the plural of **calf**.

Calvinist /kælvɪnɪst/ **Calvanists**

1 **Calvinist** means belonging or relating to a strict Protestant church founded by John Calvin. *...Calvinist doctrine. ...the Calvinist work ethic.* ADJ: ADJ n

2 A **Calvinist** is a member of the Calvinist church. N-COUNT

calypso /kəlɪpsoʊ/ **calypsos.** A **calypso** is a song about something topical or interesting, sung in a style which comes from the West Indies. N-COUNT

camaraderie /kæmərɑːdəri, AM kɑːm-/. **Camaraderie** is a feeling of trust and friendship among a group of people who have usually known each other for a long time or gone through some kind of experience together. *...the family camaraderie in Italy. ...the cohesiveness and camaraderie of the wartime Army.* N-UNCOUNT

camber /kæmbəʳ/ **cambers.** A **camber** is a gradual downward slope from the centre of a road to each side of it. N-COUNT

camcorder /kæmkɔːʳdəʳ/ **camcorders.** A **camcorder** is a portable video camera which records both picture and sound. ◆◇◇◇◇ N-COUNT

came /keɪm/. **Came** is the past tense of **come**.

camel /kæməl/ **camels.** A **camel** is a large animal that lives in deserts and is used for carrying goods and people. Camels have long necks and one or two humps on their backs. • **the straw that broke the camel's back**: see **straw**. ◆◇◇◇◇ N-COUNT

camel-hair; also spelled **camel hair.** A **camel-hair** coat is made of a kind of soft, thick woollen cloth, usually creamy brown in colour. ADJ: ADJ n

camellia /kəmiːliə/ **camellias.** A **camellia** is a tall plant that has shiny leaves and large white, pink, or red flowers similar to a rose. N-COUNT

Camembert /kæmɒmbeəʳ/ **Camemberts. Camembert** is a type of cheese that comes from Northern France. It is soft and creamy with a hard greyish-white skin. N-VAR

cameo /kæmioʊ/ **cameos** ◆◇◇◇◇

1 A **cameo** is a short description or piece of acting which expresses cleverly and neatly the nature of a situation, event, or person's character. *...a succession of memorable cameos of Scottish history... He played a cameo role, that of a young Aids patient in hospital.* N-COUNT

2 A **cameo** is a piece of jewellery, usually oval in shape, consisting of a raised stone figure or design fixed on to a flat stone of another colour. *...a cameo brooch.* N-COUNT

camera /kæmrə/ **cameras** ◆◆◆◆◇

1 A **camera** is a piece of equipment that is used for taking photographs, making films, or producing television pictures. *Her gran lent her a camera for a school trip to Venice and Egypt. ...a video camera.* N-COUNT

2 If someone or something is **on camera**, they are being filmed. *Fay was so impressive on camera that a special part was written in for her... Just about anything could happen and we'll be there to catch it on camera when it does.* PHRASE: usu PHR after v, v-link PHR

3 If a trial is held **in camera**, the public and the press are not allowed to attend. *This morning's appeal was held in camera... They were sentenced by a military tribunal sitting in camera.* PHRASE: PHR after v

cameraman /kæmrəmæn/ **cameramen.** A **cameraman** is a person who operates a camera for television or film making. ◆◇◇◇◇ N-COUNT

camera-shy. Someone who is **camera-shy** is nervous and uncomfortable about being filmed or about having their photograph taken. ADJ-GRADED

camerawork /kæmrəwɜːʳk/. The **camerawork** in a film or documentary is the technique and style used in filming it, which is noticeable or distinctive in some way. *The director employs sensuous, atmospheric camerawork and deft dramatic touches.* N-UNCOUNT

camisole /kæmɪsoʊl/ **camisoles.** A **camisole** is a piece of clothing that women wear on the top half of their bodies underneath a shirt or blouse, for example. A camisole has shoulder straps and is like a vest. *...silk camisoles.* N-COUNT

camomile /kæməmaɪl/; also spelled **chamomile. Camomile** is a scented plant with daisy-like flowers. It is often used to make herbal tea. ◆◇◇◇◇ N-UNCOUNT

camouflage /kæməflɑːʒ/ **camouflages, camouflaging, camouflaged** ◆◇◇◇◇

1 **Camouflage** consists of things such as leaves, branches, or brown and green paint, which are used to make it difficult for an enemy to see military forces and equipment. *They were dressed in camouflage and carried automatic rifles. ...a camouflage jacket. ...the mottled green camouflage scheme of most military vehicles.* N-UNCOUNT: also a N, oft N n

2 If military buildings or vehicles **are camouflaged**, things such as leaves, branches, or brown and green paint are used to make it difficult for an enemy to see them. *You won't see them from the air. They'd be very well camouflaged... They walked* VB: usu passive be V-ed V-ed

through the trees to a second hut, cunningly camouflaged against air surveillance.
3 If you **camouflage** something such as a feeling or a situation, you hide it or make it appear to be something different. *He has never camouflaged his desire to better himself... This is another clever attempt to camouflage reality.* ▶ Also a noun. *The frenzied merrymaking of her later years was a desperate camouflage for her grief.* VERB =hide V n V n N-UNCOUNT: also a N
4 **Camouflage** is also the way in which some animals are coloured and shaped to blend in with their natural surroundings. *Confident in its camouflage, being the same colour as the rocks, the lizard stands still when it feels danger.* N-UNCOUNT: also a N

camp /kæmp/ **camps, camping, camped** ◆◆◆◆◇
1 A **camp** is a collection of huts and other buildings that is provided for a particular group of people, such as refugees, prisoners, or soldiers, as a place to live or stay. *...a refugee camp... 2,500 foreign prisoners-of-war, including Americans, had been held in camps near Tambov.* N-COUNT: oft n N
2 A **camp** is an outdoor area with buildings, tents, or caravans where people stay on holiday. *They have a 200- or 300-acre summer camp nearby... When she was ten years old, her parents sent her to camp at Huntington Lake.* N-VAR
3 A **camp** is a collection of tents or caravans where people are living or staying, usually temporarily while they are travelling. *...gypsy camps... We'll make camp on that hill ahead.* N-VAR
4 If you **camp** somewhere, you stay or live there for a short time in a tent or caravan, or in the open air. *We camped near the beach. ...the men, who are camping on the pavement in sleeping bags.* ▶ **Camp out** means the same as **camp**. *For six months they camped out in a caravan in a meadow at the back of the house.* ♦ **camping** *They went camping in the wilds. ...a camping trip.* VERB V PHRASAL VERB V P N-UNCOUNT
5 You can refer to a group of people who all support a particular person, policy, or idea as a particular **camp**. *The press release provoked furious protests from the Clinton camp and other top Democrats. ...a close colleague, who had sided with the opposite camp in an office dispute.* N-COUNT: usu supp N
6 If you describe someone's behaviour, performance, or style of dress as **camp**, you mean that it is exaggerated and often amusing in a sexually suggestive way. **Camp** behaviour is sometimes associated with gay people; an informal use. *James Barron turns in a delightfully camp performance as the lovely Lisa's wicked husband.* ▶ Also a noun. *The days of platform-soled high camp are long over.* ADJ-GRADED =campy N-UNCOUNT
7 See also **camped**; **aide-de-camp**, **concentration camp**, **holiday camp**, **labour camp**, **prison camp**, **training camp**.
8 In British English, if a performer **camps it up**, they deliberately perform in an exaggerated and often amusing way; an informal expression. *He camped it up, he told bad taste jokes and endless anecdotes with no point at all.* PHRASE: V inflects

camp out. If you say that people **camp out** somewhere in the open air, you are emphasizing that they stay there for a long time, because they are waiting for something to happen. *...reporters who had camped out in anticipation of her arrival.* • See **camp** 4. PHRASAL VERB PRAGMATICS V P

campaign /kæmpeɪn/ **campaigns, campaigning, campaigned** ◆◆◆◆◆
1 A **campaign** is a planned set of activities that people carry out over a period of time in order to achieve something such as social or political change. *During his election campaign Clinton promised to put the economy back on its feet... Apacs has launched a campaign to improve the training of staff. ...the campaign against public smoking.* N-COUNT: oft N *to-inf*, N *for/against* n
2 If someone **campaigns** for something, they carry out a planned set of activities over a period of time in order to achieve their aim. *We are campaigning for law reform... Mr Burns has actively campaigned against a hostel being set up here... They have been campaigning to improve the legal status of women.* VERB V *for/against* n V to-inf Also V
3 In a war, a **campaign** is a series of planned movements carried out by armed forces. *The allies are intensifying their air campaign. ...a bombing campaign.* N-COUNT: oft n N =operation

campaigner /kæmpeɪnəʳ/ **campaigners.** A **campaigner** is a person who campaigns for social or political change. *...anti-hunting campaigners. ...campaigners for multi-party democracy.* ◆◆◇◇◇ N-COUNT: oft supp N, N *for/against* n

camp bed, camp beds. A **camp bed** is a small bed that you can fold up; used mainly in British English. N-COUNT

camped /kæmpt/. If people are **camped** or **camped out** somewhere in the open air, they are living, staying, or waiting there, often in tents. *Most of the refugees are camped high in the mountains... You will wake to find film crews camped in your backyard... They are camped out in tents on the front lawn.* • See also **camp**. ◆◇◇◇◇ ADJ: v-link ADJ, usu ADJ prep/adv

camper /kæmpəʳ/ **campers** ◆◇◇◇◇
1 A **camper** is someone who is camping somewhere. N-COUNT
2 A **camper** is a van which is equipped with beds and cooking equipment so that you can live, cook, and sleep in it. N-COUNT

camp fire, camp fires; also spelled **camp-fire**. A **camp fire** is a fire that you light out of doors when you are camping. N-COUNT

camp follower, camp followers; also spelled **camp-follower**.
1 If you say that someone is a **camp follower**, you mean that they do not officially belong to a particular group or movement but support it for their own advantage. *...the chief ministers of three important states, who were thought to be camp followers of Mr Devi Lal.* N-COUNT
2 A **camp follower** is a person who travels with a group of people such as an army and sometimes earns money by doing jobs for them. N-COUNT

campground /kæmpgraʊnd/ **campgrounds.** A **campground** is the same as a **campsite**; used mainly in American English. N-COUNT

camphor /kæmfəʳ/. **Camphor** is a strong-smelling white substance used in various medicines, in mothballs and in making plastics. N-UNCOUNT

camping site, camping sites. A **camping site** is the same as a **campsite**. N-COUNT

campsite /kæmpsaɪt/ **campsites.** A **campsite** is a place where people who are on holiday can stay in tents. N-COUNT =camping site

campus /kæmpəs/ **campuses.** A **campus** is the area of land that contains the main buildings of a university. *...during a rally at the campus... Private automobiles are not allowed on campus.* ◆◆◇◇◇ N-COUNT: also prep N

campy /kæmpi/. **Campy** means the same as **camp**. *...a campy spy spoof.* ADJ-GRADED =camp

camshaft /kæmʃɑːft, -ʃæft/ **camshafts.** A **camshaft** is a rod in an engine which works to change circular motion into motion up and down or side to side; a technical term. N-COUNT

can 1 modal uses

can /kən, STRONG kæn/ ◆◆◆◆◆
Can is a modal verb. It is used with the base form of a verb. The form **cannot** is used in negative statements. The usual spoken form of **cannot** is **can't**, pronounced /kɑːnt/.
1 You use **can** when you are mentioning a quality or fact about something which people may make use of if they want to. *Pork is also the most versatile of meats. It can be roasted whole at any stage... Luckily, iron can be reworked and mistakes don't have to be thrown away... A central reservation number operated by the resort can direct you to accommodations that best suit your needs... A selected list of some of those stocking a comprehensive range can be found in Chapter 8. ...the statue which can still be seen in the British Museum.* MODAL
2 You use **can** to indicate that someone has the ability or opportunity to do something. *Don't worry yourself about me, I can take care of myself... I can't give you details because I don't actually have any details... Oh Stephen darling, how can I ever* MODAL

thank you for being so kind?... See if you can find Karlov and tell him we are ready for dinner... 'You're needed here, Livy'—'But what can I do?'... The United States will do whatever it can to help Greece... I cannot describe it, I can't find the words... Customers can choose from sixty hit titles before buying... You can't be with your baby all the time.

3 You use **cannot** to indicate that someone is not able to do something because circumstances make it impossible for them to do it. *People who can't afford to go to the theatre or concerts can afford to go to football matches... We cannot buy food, clothes and pay for rent and utilities on $20 a week... She cannot sleep and the pain is often so bad she wants to scream.* MODAL

4 You use **can** to indicate that something is true sometimes or is true in some circumstances. *...long-term therapy that can last five years or more... A vacant lot or a bombsite can, to the amateur naturalist, produce an extraordinary variety of flora and fauna... I've quite forgotten how closed in London can seem... Exercising alone can be boring... The speed at which we talk can also convey a great deal... Coral can be yellow, and coral can be blue, and coral can be green.* MODAL PRAGMATICS

5 You use **cannot** and **can't** to state that you are certain that something is not the case or will not happen. *From her knowledge of Douglas's habits, she feels sure that that person can't have been Douglas... Things can't be that bad... You can't be serious, Mrs Lorimer?* MODAL PRAGMATICS

6 You use **can** to indicate that someone is allowed to do something. You use **cannot** or **can't** to indicate that someone is not allowed to do something. *You must buy the credit life insurance before you can buy the disability insurance... No-one can set up a waste disposal company unless they can show that they've got enough money and trained staff to do the job properly... Here, can I really have your jeans when you go?... We can't answer any questions, I'm afraid... I can't tell you what he said... You cannot ask for your money back before the agreed date... A teenager who won £588,000 on a fruit machine has been told he cannot keep the money... I'm on tablets and I can't drive.* MODAL

7 You use **cannot** or **can't** to emphasize that you think that it is very important or necessary that something should not happen or that someone should not do something. *It is an intolerable situation and it can't be allowed to go on... The Commission can't demand from Sweden more than it demands from its own members.* MODAL PRAGMATICS =mustn't

8 You use **can**, usually in questions, in order to make suggestions or to offer to do something. *What can I do around here?... This old lady was struggling out of the train and I said, 'Oh, can I help you?'... Hello John. What can we do for you?... You can always try the beer you know – it's usually all right in this bar.* MODAL PRAGMATICS

9 You use **can** in questions in order to make polite requests. You use **can't** in questions in order to request strongly that somebody does something. *Can I have a look at that?... Can you please help?... Can you just lift the table for a second?... Can you fill in some of the details of your career?... Why can't you leave me alone?* MODAL PRAGMATICS

10 In formal spoken English, you use **can** as a polite way of interrupting someone or of introducing what you are going to say next. *Can I interrupt you just for a minute?... But if I can interrupt, Joe, I don't think anybody here is personally blaming you... Can I just ask something 'cos I'm really quite interested in this.* MODAL PRAGMATICS =may

11 In speech and informal written English, you use **can** with verbs such as 'imagine', 'think', and 'believe' in order to emphasize how you feel about a particular situation. *You can imagine he was terribly upset... You can't think how glad I was to see them all go... It's been an appallingly busy morning, I can't tell you... I can't understand why folks complain about false teeth.* MODAL PRAGMATICS

12 In speech you use **can** in questions with 'how' to indicate that you feel strongly about something. *How can you complain about higher taxes?... How can millions of dollars go astray?... How can you say such a thing?... How can you expect me to believe your promises?* MODAL PRAGMATICS

can 2 container

can /kæn/ **cans, canning, canned** ◆◆◇◇◇

1 A **can** is a metal container in which something such as food, drink, or paint is put. The container is usually sealed to keep the contents fresh. *Several young men were kicking a tin can like a football along the middle of the road. ...empty beer cans. ...cans of paint and brushes.* N-COUNT =tin

2 When food or drink **is canned**, it is put into a metal container and sealed so that it will remain fresh. *...fruits and vegetables that will be canned, skinned, diced or otherwise processed... It was always roast lamb and canned peas for Sunday lunch.* VB: usu passive =tin be V-ed V-ed

3 See also **canned**.

4 If you have to **carry the can**, you have to take all the blame for something; used mainly in informal British English. *We are a luxury restaurant and if people have a bad experience, we have to carry the can.* PHRASES V inflects =take the rap

5 If you say that something such as a job that you are doing is **in the can**, you mean that it is completely finished; an informal expression. *With another day's filming in the can, Philip is happy to leave the open countryside and head for his London flat.* v-link PHR

Canadian /kəneɪdiən/ **Canadians** ◆◆◆◆◇

1 **Canadian** means belonging or relating to Canada, or to its people or culture. *...the Canadian government.* ADJ

2 A **Canadian** is a Canadian citizen, or a person of Canadian origin. N-COUNT

canal /kənæl/ **canals** ◆◆◇◇◇

1 A **canal** is a long, narrow stretch of water that has been made for boats to travel along or to bring water to a particular area. *...the Grand Union Canal. ...Venetian canals and bridges.* N-COUNT

2 A **canal** is a narrow tube inside your body for carrying food, air, or other substances. *...delaying its progress through the alimentary canal.* N-COUNT: usu supp N

canal boat, canal boats. A **canal boat** is a long, narrow boat used for travelling on canals. N-COUNT

canapé /kænəpeɪ/ **canapés. Canapés** are small pieces of biscuit or toast with food such as meat, cheese, or paté on top. They are often served with drinks at parties. N-COUNT: usu pl

canard /kænɑːʳd, AM kənɑːrd/ **canards.** A **canard** is an idea or a piece of information that is false. Canards are often made up and spread deliberately in order to discredit someone or their work. *The charge that Harding was a political stooge may be a canard.* N-COUNT =myth

canary /kəneəri/ **canaries. Canaries** are small yellow birds which sing beautifully and are often kept as pets. ◆◇◇◇◇ N-COUNT

canary yellow. Something that is **canary yellow** is a light yellow in colour. *...a canary yellow Porsche.* COLOUR

can-can, can-cans. The **can-can** is a dance in which women kick their legs in the air to fast music. *...the can-can girls in Paris's Moulin Rouge cabaret.* N-COUNT: oft the N

cancel /kænsᵊl/ **cancels, cancelling, cancelled;** spelled **canceling, canceled** in American English. ◆◆◆◇◇

1 If you **cancel** something that has been arranged, you stop it from happening. If you **cancel** an order for goods or services, you tell the person or organization supplying them that you no longer wish to receive them. *The Russian foreign minister yesterday cancelled his visit to Washington... Many trains have been cancelled and a limited service is operating on other lines... The Navy has decided to cancel its contract for the A-12 Stealth attack plane... There is normally no refund should a client choose to cancel.* ♦ **cancellation** /kænsəleɪʃᵊn/ **cancellations** *Outbursts of violence forced the cancellation of Haiti's first free elections in 1987. ...passengers who* VERB V n V N-VAR: oft N of n

suffer delays and cancellations on planes, trains, ferries and buses.

2 If someone in authority **cancels** a document, an insurance policy, or a debt, they officially declare that it is no longer valid or no longer legally exists. *He intends to try to leave the country, in spite of a government order cancelling his passport... She learned her insurance had been canceled by Pacific Mutual Insurance Company... Under the agreement, Germany will cancel seventy 70 million dollars in debts owed by Ethiopia.* ♦ **cancellation** *...a march by groups calling for cancellation of Third World debt.*
VERB
V n
N-UNCOUNT: with supp

3 To **cancel** a stamp or a cheque means to mark it to show that it has already been used and cannot be used again. *The new device can also cancel the check after the transaction is complete. ...cancelled stamps.*
VERB
V n
V-ed

cancel out. If one thing **cancels out** another thing, the two things have opposite effects, so that when they are combined no real effect is produced. *He wonders if the different influences might not cancel each other out... The goal was cancelled out just before half-time by Craig McLurg.*
PHRASAL VERB
V n P
Also V P n (not pron)

cancer /kænsəʳ/ **cancers. Cancer** is a serious disease in which cells in a person's body increase rapidly in an uncontrolled way, producing abnormal growths. *Her mother died of breast cancer when she was six... Jane was just 25 when she learned she had cancer... Ninety per cent of lung cancers are caused by smoking.*
◆◆◆◆◇
N-VAR: oft n N

Cancer, Cancers
◆◆◇◇◇

1 **Cancer** is one of the twelve signs of the zodiac. Its symbol is a crab. People who are born approximately between the 21st of June and the 22nd of July come under this sign.
N-UNCOUNT

2 A **Cancer** is a person whose sign of the zodiac is Cancer.
N-COUNT

cancerous /kænsərəs/. **Cancerous** cells or growths are cells or growths that are the result of cancer. *The production of these cancerous cells suppresses the production of normal white blood cells... Nine out of ten lumps are not cancerous.*
◆◇◇◇◇
ADJ

candelabra /kændəlɑːbrə/ **candelabras.** A **candelabra** is an ornamental holder for two or more candles.
N-COUNT

candelabrum /kændəlɑːbrəm/ **candelabra.** A **candelabrum** is the same as a **candelabra**.
N-COUNT

candid /kændɪd/
◆◇◇◇◇

1 When you are **candid** about something or with someone, you speak honestly. *Nat is candid about the problems she is having with Steve... I haven't been completely candid with him. ...a candid interview.* ♦ **candidly** *He has stopped taking heroin now, but admits candidly that he will always be a drug addict.*
ADJ-GRADED: oft ADJ *about* n, ADJ *with* n
=frank
≠guarded
ADV-GRADED: usu ADV with v, also ADV adj/adv

2 A **candid** photograph of someone is one that was taken when the person did not know they were being photographed.
ADJ: ADJ n

candidacy /kændɪdəsi/ **candidacies.** Someone's **candidacy** is their position of being a candidate in an election. *Today he is formally announcing his candidacy for President.*
◆◇◇◇◇
N-VAR: oft with poss
=candidature

candidate /kændɪdeɪt/ **candidates**
◆◆◆◆◇

1 A **candidate** is someone who is being considered for a position, for example someone standing in an election or applying for a job. *The Democratic candidate is still leading in the polls... He is a candidate for the office of Governor... We all spoke to them and John emerged as the best candidate.*
N-COUNT: oft N for n

2 A **candidate** is someone who is taking an examination. *The papers were taken by more than 150,000 candidates this summer. ...A-level candidates.*
N-COUNT

3 A **candidate** is a person or thing that is regarded as being suitable for a particular purpose or as being likely to do or be a particular thing. *I think Birmingham City are prime candidates for relegation next season... Those who are overweight or indulge in high-salt diets are candidates for hypertension.*
N-COUNT: usu N *for* n

candidature /kændɪtətʃəʳ/ **candidatures.** In British English, someone's **candidature** is their candidacy; a formal word.
N-VAR: usu poss N

candied /kændid/. Food such as **candied** fruit has been covered with sugar or has been cooked in sugar syrup. *Cut up the candied fruit into small pieces.*
ADJ: usu ADJ n

candle /kændəl/ **candles**
◆◆◇◇◇

1 A **candle** is a stick of hard wax with a piece of string called a wick through the middle. You light the wick in order to give a steady flame that provides light. *The bedroom was lit by a single candle.*
N-COUNT

2 If you **burn the candle at both ends**, you try to do too many things in too short a period of time so that you have to stay up very late at night and get up very early in the morning to get them done.
PHRASES
V inflects

3 If one person or thing **can't hold a candle to** another, the first person or thing is not nearly as good as the second. *Girls today can't hold a candle to the beauties of the Fifties.*
V inflects

4 If you say that **the game is not worth the candle**, you mean that something is not worth the trouble or effort needed to achieve or obtain it.
V inflects

candlelight /kændəllaɪt/. **Candlelight** is the light that a candle produces. *They dined by candlelight.*
N-UNCOUNT

candlelit /kændəllɪt/. A **candlelit** room or table is lit by the light of candles. *...a candlelit dinner for two.*
ADJ: usu ADJ n

candlestick /kændəlstɪk/ **candlesticks.** A **candlestick** is a narrow object with a hole at the top which holds a candle.
◆◇◇◇◇
N-COUNT

can-do. If you say that someone has a **can-do** attitude, you are expressing approval of them because they are confident and willing to deal with problems or new tasks, rather than complaining or giving up. *He is known for his optimistic can-do attitude... America is once again being seen as a strong, can-do nation.*
ADJ: ADJ n
PRAGMATICS
=positive, upbeat
≠negative

candour /kændəʳ/; spelled **candor** in American English. **Candour** is the quality of speaking honestly and openly about things. *...a brash, forceful man, noted both for his candour and his quick temper.*
N-UNCOUNT
=frankness
≠guardedness

candy /kændi/ **candies.** In American English, sweet foods such as toffees, chocolates, and mints are referred to as **candy**. The British word is **sweets**. *...a piece of candy... There was a large box of candies on a table nearby.*
◆◇◇◇◇
N-VAR

candy bar, candy bars. In American English, a **candy bar** is a long, thin, sweet biscuit that is often covered in chocolate. Candy bars are individually wrapped and are displayed next to sweets in shops. *Who gave you that candy bar?*
N-COUNT

candyfloss /kændiflɒs, AM -flɔːs/; also spelled **candy-floss.**

1 In British English, **candyfloss** is a large pink or white mass of sugar threads that is eaten from a stick. It is sold at fairs or other outdoor events. The American term is **cotton candy**.
N-UNCOUNT

2 If you think something such as a record or film has no real value, you can say that it is **candyfloss**. *She took to writing candyfloss romances... Most of these songs have not aged well, especially candyfloss like De Do Do Do.*
N-UNCOUNT: oft N n

cane /keɪn/ **canes, caning, caned**
◆◆◇◇◇

1 **Cane** is used to refer to the long, hollow, hard stems of plants such as bamboo. Strips of cane are often used to make furniture, and some types of cane can be crushed and processed to make sugar. *...cane furniture. ...cane sugar... Bamboo produces an annual crop of cane... Dig out and burn infected canes.*
N-VAR: oft N n

2 A **cane** is a specially-shaped stick which you can carry to support yourself when you are walking, or which some people used to carry as a fashion. *He wore a grey suit and leaned heavily on his cane.*
N-COUNT
=walking stick

3 A **cane** is a long, thin, flexible stick which is used to hit people, especially children at school, as a punishment. *Until the 1980s some criminals were still flogged with a rattan cane as a punishment.*
N-COUNT
► **The cane** is used to refer to the punishment of
N-SING: the N

being hit with a cane. *In school, you knew if you misbehaved you would get the cane.*
4 If a child **is caned**, he or she is hit with a cane as a punishment. *In Wales in the same era, boys were caned for speaking Welsh in the playground... I have caned my son when necessary.* VERB *be/get* V-ed *for* -ing/n V n
5 A **cane** is a tall, narrow stick, usually made of bamboo, which is used for supporting plants in gardens. N-COUNT
6 See also **sugar cane**.

canine /keɪnaɪn/ **canines**
1 **Canine** means relating to dogs. *...research into canine diseases.* ADJ: ADJ n
2 **Canine teeth** or **canines** are pointed teeth near the front of the mouth of humans and of some animals. N-COUNT

canister /kænɪstəʳ/ **canisters** ◆◇◇◇◇
1 A **canister** is a strong metal container. It is used to hold gases or chemical substances. *Riot police hurled tear gas canisters and smoke bombs into the crowd. ...canisters of commercial fuel.* N-COUNT: usu n N
2 A **canister** is a metal, plastic, or china container with a lid. It is used for storing food such as sugar and flour. N-COUNT
3 A **canister** is a flat round container. It is usually made of metal and is used to store photographic film. *She bought a travel-bag large enough to contain the film canisters.* N-COUNT: usu with supp

canker /kæŋkəʳ/ **cankers**
1 A **canker** is something evil that spreads and affects things or people; a formal word. *As in Europe, the canker of anti-Semitism is growing again in America.* N-COUNT =cancer
2 **Canker** is a disease which affects the mouth and ears of animals and people, spreading quickly and making the skin sore. N-UNCOUNT
3 **Canker** is a disease which affects the wood of shrubs and trees, making the outer layer peel away to expose the inside of the stem. *In gardens cankers are most prominent on apples and pear trees.* N-VAR

cannabis /kænəbɪs/. **Cannabis** is a drug which some people smoke. Cannabis is illegal in many countries. ◆◇◇◇◇ N-UNCOUNT =dope, pot

canned /kænd/. **Canned** music, laughter, or applause on the television or radio has been recorded beforehand and is added to the programme to make it sound as if there is a live audience. • See also **can**. ADJ: usu ADJ n

cannelloni /kænəloʊni/. Large tube-shaped pieces of pasta that contain a filling of either meat or cheese are referred to as **cannelloni**. N-UNCOUNT

cannery /kænəri/ **canneries.** A **cannery** is a factory where food is canned. N-COUNT

cannibal /kænɪbəl/ **cannibals. Cannibals** are people who eat the flesh of other human beings. *...a tropical island inhabited by cannibals... Cannibal killer Jeffrey Dahmer has been caught trying to hide a razor blade in his cell.* ◆◇◇◇◇ N-COUNT

cannibalism /kænɪbəlɪzəm/. If a group of people practise **cannibalism**, they eat the flesh of other people. *They were forced to practise cannibalism in order to survive.* N-UNCOUNT

cannibalistic /kænɪbəlɪstɪk/. **Cannibalistic** people and practices are connected with cannibalism. *...lurid cannibalistic feasts.* ADJ: usu ADJ n

cannibalize /kænɪbəlaɪz/ **cannibalizes, cannibalizing, cannibalized;** also spelled **cannibalise** in British English.
1 If you **cannibalize** something, you take it to pieces and use it to make something else. *They cannibalized damaged planes for the parts.* VERB V n
2 If one of a company's products **cannibalizes** the company's sales, people buy it instead of any of the company's other products. *Coke then believed that selling a diet soda under the Coke label would cannibalize Coke's sales.* VERB V n

cannon /kænən/ **cannons, cannoning, cannoned** ◆◆◇◇◇
1 A **cannon** is a large gun, usually on wheels, which used to be used in battles. *Their 30mm cannons are also capable of destroying an enemy counterpart up to a mile away.* N-COUNT
2 A **cannon** is a heavy automatic gun, especially one that is fired from an aircraft. N-COUNT
3 If one person or thing **cannons** into another, they bump into them with great force. *One of the reporters cannoned into Arnold... The ball cannoned off the back of a Spartak defender and into the net.* VERB =bump into V prep
4 If you say that someone is a **loose cannon**, you mean that they behave in an independent, headstrong way and nobody can predict what they are going to do. *Max is a loose cannon politically.* • See also **water cannon**. PHRASE: usu v-link PHR

cannonade /kænəneɪd/ **cannonades.** A **cannonade** is an intense continuous attack on something using guns. *...the distant thunder of a cannonade.* N-COUNT =barrage

cannon ball, cannon balls; also spelled **cannon-ball**. A **cannon ball** is a heavy metal ball that is fired from a cannon. N-COUNT

cannon fodder; also spelled **cannon-fodder**. If someone in authority regards people they are in charge of as **cannon fodder**, they do not care if these people are harmed or lost in the course of their work. *...conscripts, who were just fed to the allied forces as cannon fodder... Many cynical managers see employees as cannon fodder.* N-UNCOUNT

cannot /kænɒt, kənɒt/. **Cannot** is the negative form of **can**. and means the same as 'can not'.

canny /kæni/ **cannier, canniest.** A **canny** person is clever and able to think quickly. You can also describe a person's behaviour as **canny**. *He was far too canny to risk giving himself away... A canny investor would need to predict when the dollar will once more start tumbling... Some analysts believe he has made a canny political manoeuvre.* ◆◇◇◇◇ ADJ-GRADED: usu ADJ n =shrewd
♦ **cannily** /kænɪli/ *She built up her fortune by cannily playing the stock market.* ADV-GRADED: usu ADV with v

canoe /kənuː/ **canoes.** A **canoe** is a small, narrow boat that you row using a paddle. ◆◇◇◇◇ N-COUNT

canoeing /kənuːɪŋ/. **Canoeing** is the sport of paddling and racing a canoe. *They went canoeing in the wilds of Canada.* N-UNCOUNT

canoeist /kənuːɪst/ **canoeists.** A **canoeist** is someone who is skilled at racing and performing tests of skill in a canoe. N-COUNT

canon /kænən/ **canons** ◆◇◇◇◇
1 A **canon** is a member of the clergy who is on the staff of a cathedral. N-COUNT
2 A **canon** is a general rule or principle; a formal use. *The very first canon of nursing is to keep the air inside as fresh as the air outside.* N-COUNT =rule

canonical /kənɒnɪkəl/. **Canonical** means allowed by canon law. ADJ: ADJ n

canonize /kænənaɪz/ **canonizes, canonizing, canonized;** also spelled **canonise** in British English. If a dead person **is canonized**, it is officially announced that he or she is a saint; used in the Catholic Church. *Joan of Arc was finally canonized by Pope Benedict XV in 1920.* VB: usu passive *be* V-ed
♦ **canonization** /kænənaɪzeɪʃən, AM -nɪz-/ *...a celebration of the saint's canonization.* N-UNCOUNT

canon law. **Canon law** is the law of the Christian church. It has authority only for that church and its members. *The Church's canon law forbids remarriage of divorced persons.* N-UNCOUNT

canoodle /kənuːdəl/ **canoodles, canoodling, canoodled.** In British English, if two people **are canoodling**, they are kissing and cuddling each other a lot; an informal word. *Inside, freckled girls are canoodling with their boyfriends in dark corners.* V-RECIP V *with* n Also pl-n V

can opener, can openers. A **can opener** is the same as a **tin opener**. N-COUNT

canopied /kænəpid/. A **canopied** building or piece of furniture is covered with a roof or a piece of material supported by poles. *...a canopied Elizabethan bed.* ADJ: usu ADJ n

canopy /kænəpi/ **canopies** ◆◇◇◇◇
1 A **canopy** is a decorated cover, often made of cloth, which is placed above something such as a bed or a throne. N-COUNT =awning
2 A **canopy** is a layer of something that spreads out and covers an area, for example the branches and N-COUNT: usu sing

leaves that spread out at the top of trees in a forest. *The trees formed such a dense canopy that all beneath was a deep carpet of pine-needles.*

cant /kænt/. If you refer to moral or religious statements as **cant**, you disapprove of them because you think the person making them does not really believe what they are saying. *...politicians holding forth with their usual hypocritical cant.* N-UNCOUNT PRAGMATICS

can't /kɑːnt, AM kænt/. **Can't** is the usual spoken form of **cannot**.

cantaloupe /kæntəluːp, AM -loʊp/ **cantaloupes.** A **cantaloupe** is a type of melon. N-COUNT

cantankerous /kæntæŋkərəs/. Someone who is **cantankerous** is always finding things to argue or complain about; used in written English. *...a cantankerous old man.* ADJ-GRADED: usu ADJ n

cantata /kæntɑːtə/ **cantatas.** A **cantata** is a fairly short musical work for singers and orchestral instruments. N-COUNT

canteen /kæntiːn/ **canteens** ◆◇◇◇◇

1 A **canteen** is a place in a factory, shop, or college where meals are served to the people who work or study there. *Rennie had eaten his tea in the canteen. ...a school canteen. ...canteen food.* N-COUNT =cafeteria

2 A **canteen** is a small plastic bottle for carrying water and other drinks. Canteens are used by soldiers. *...a full canteen of water.* N-COUNT =water bottle

3 A **canteen** of cutlery is a set of knives, forks, and spoons in a specially designed box. N-COUNT: usu N *of* n

canter /kæntəʳ/ **canters, cantering, cantered.** ◆◇◇◇◇ When a horse **canters**, it moves at a speed that is slower than a gallop but faster than a trot. *The competitors cantered into the arena to conclude the closing ceremony.* ▶ Also a noun. *Carnac set off at a canter.* VERB V prep/adv Also V; N-COUNT: usu sing

cantilever /kæntɪliːvəʳ/ **cantilevers.** A **cantilever** is a long piece of metal or wood used in a structure such as a bridge. One end is fastened to something and the other end is used to support part of the structure. *...the old steel cantilever bridge.* N-COUNT

cantilevered /kæntɪliːvəʳd/. A **cantilevered** structure is constructed using cantilevers. *...a cantilevered balcony.* ADJ: usu ADJ n

canton /kæntɒn/ **cantons.** A **canton** is a political or administrative region in some countries, for example Switzerland. *...the Swiss canton of Berne.* ◆◇◇◇◇ N-COUNT

Cantonese /kæntəniːz/; **Cantonese** is both the singular and the plural form.

1 **Cantonese** means belonging or relating to the Chinese provinces of Canton and Kwangtung, or to their people or culture, or to the language spoken there. *He settled in Hong Kong and married a Cantonese girl. ...authentic Cantonese food.* ADJ

2 The **Cantonese** are the people who live in or originate from the Chinese provinces of Canton and Kwangtung. *The Cantonese, by contrast, enjoy all of life, including work.* N-COUNT: usu pl

3 **Cantonese** is the language spoken in the Chinese provinces of Canton, Kwangtung, Kwansai, and Hong Kong, as well as in other parts of the world. *Hena grew up speaking Cantonese and Malay.* N-UNCOUNT

cantonment /kæntuːnmənt, AM -toʊn-/ **cantonments.** A **cantonment** is a group of buildings or a camp where soldiers live. N-COUNT

canvas /kænvəs/ **canvases** ◆◆◇◇◇

1 **Canvas** is a strong, heavy cloth usually made of cotton or linen. It is used for making things such as tents, sails, and bags. *...a canvas bag.* N-UNCOUNT

2 A **canvas** is a piece of canvas or similar material on which an oil painting can be done. *Pierre Bonnard often painted on a canvas much larger than he knew the final painting would require.* N-VAR

3 A **canvas** is a painting that has been done on canvas. *The show includes canvases by masters like Carpaccio, Canaletto and Guardi.* N-COUNT =painting, picture

4 If you are living and sleeping **under canvas**, you are living and sleeping in a tent. *Campsites in the New Forest quickly filled up as thousands decided to spend the holiday under canvas.* PHRASE: PHR after v, n PHR

canvass /kænvəs/ **canvasses, canvassing, canvassed** ◆◇◇◇◇

1 If you **canvass** for a particular person or political party, you go round an area trying to persuade people to vote for that person or party. *I'm canvassing for the Conservative Party... She works her way around the room canvassing support for the project.* ♦ **canvasser, canvassers** *...a Conservative canvasser.* VERB V *for* n V n; N-COUNT

2 If you **canvass** public opinion, you find out how people feel about a particular subject. *Members of Parliament are spending the weekend canvassing opinion in their constituencies... The poll canvassed the views of almost eighty economists.* VERB V n

canyon /kænjən/ **canyons.** A **canyon** is a long, narrow valley with very steep sides. *...the Grand Canyon.* ◆◇◇◇◇ N-COUNT: oft in names after n

cap /kæp/ **caps, capping, capped** ◆◆◆◇◇

1 A **cap** is a soft, flat hat with a curved part at the front which is called a peak. Caps are usually worn by men and boys. *...a dark blue baseball cap.* N-COUNT: oft supp N

2 A **cap** is a special hat which is worn as part of a uniform. *...a frontier guard in olive-grey uniform and a peaked cap.* N-COUNT: oft supp N

3 In British English, when a sports player represents their country in a team game such as football, rugby, or cricket, you can say that they have been awarded a **cap**. *Mark Davis will win his first cap for Wales in Sunday's Test match against Australia.* N-COUNT

4 When a sports player **is capped**, they are chosen to represent their country in a team game such as football, rugby, or cricket; used in British English. *Rees, 32, has been capped for England 23 times. ...Underwood, England's most capped rugby union player.* VB: usu passive *be* V-ed V-ed

5 In British English, you can refer to someone who is representing their country for the first time in a team game such as football, rugby, or cricket, as a new **cap**. *The only new cap is Llanelli's 20-year-old left-wing Wayne Proctor.* N-COUNT: adj N

6 If the government **caps** a local authority or council, it limits the amount of money that the authority is allowed to spend. *The Secretary of State for Environment has the power to cap councils which in his opinion plan to spend excessively... Nearly half of all local councils face being capped.* ♦ **capping** *Between 70 and 80 councils face significant spending cuts or capping next year.* VERB V n; N-UNCOUNT

7 The **cap** of a bottle is its lid. *She unscrewed the cap of her water bottle and gave him a drink.* N-COUNT

8 A **cap** is a circular rubber device that a woman places inside her vagina to prevent herself from becoming pregnant. N-COUNT =diaphragm

9 If you **cap** one thing with another, you put the other thing on top. *They had capped the roof with plywood. ...homemade scones capped with cream.* ● See also **snow-capped.** VERB V n *with* n V-ed

10 If someone says that a good or bad event **caps** a series of events, they mean it is the final event in the series, and the other events were also good or bad; used in newspapers and broadcast news. *An epic victory in the rowing finals of the coxed pairs yesterday capped a wonderful weekend for Britain at the Olympic Games... The unrest capped a weekend of right-wing attacks on foreigners.* VERB V n

11 When someone's teeth **are capped**, coverings are fixed over them so that they look better. *He suddenly smiled, revealing teeth that had recently been capped. ...when I had my teeth capped.* VB: usu passive *be* V-ed *have* n V-ed

12 A **cap** is a small amount of explosive that is wrapped in paper. Caps are often used in toy guns. *...a child's cap gun.* N-COUNT

13 See also **ice cap**.

14 If you go **cap in hand** to someone, you go to them very humbly, because you are asking them for something; an informal expression. *He has been given the unenviable task of going round, cap in hand, to various generous companies.* PHRASE: PHR after v

capability /keɪpəbɪlɪti/ **capabilities** ◆◆◇◇◇

1 If someone or something has the **capability** or the **capabilities** to do something, they have the ability or the qualities that are necessary to do it. N-VAR: with supp, oft adj N, N to-inf

People experience differences in physical and mental capability depending on the time of day... The standards set four years ago in Seoul will be far below the athletes' capabilities now. =ability

2 A country's military **capability** is its ability to fight in a war. *Their military capability has gone down because their air force has proved not to be an effective force... They have the capability to destroy the enemy in days rather than weeks.* N-VAR: with supp, usu adj N, N to-inf

capable /keɪpəb^{ə}l/ ◆◆◆◇◇

1 If a person or thing **is capable of** doing something, they have the ability, capacity, or potential to do it. *He appeared hardly capable of conducting a coherent conversation... The kitchen is capable of catering for several hundred people... I had no hesitation in calling the police because I realised he was capable of murder.* ADJ-GRADED: v-link ADJ *of* -ing/n ≠incapable

2 Someone who is **capable** has the skill or qualities necessary to do a particular thing well, or is able to do most things well. *She's a very capable speaker.* ADJ-GRADED =competent, adept

♦ **capably** /keɪpəbli/ *Happily it was all dealt with very capably by the police and security people.* ADV-GRADED: ADV with v =competently

capacious /kəpeɪʃəs/. Something that is **capacious** has a lot of space to put things in; a formal word. *...her capacious handbag.* ADJ-GRADED: usu ADJ n

capacitor /kəpæsɪtə^{r}/ **capacitors.** A **capacitor** is a device for accumulating electric charge. N-COUNT

capacity /kəpæsɪti/ **capacities** ◆◆◆◇◇

1 Your **capacity** for something is your ability to do it, or the amount of it that you are able to do. *Our capacity for giving care, love and attention is limited... Her mental capacity and temperament are as remarkable as his. ...people's creative capacities.* N-VAR: oft with poss, N *for* n/-ing, N to-inf

2 The **capacity** of something such as a factory, industry, or region is the quantity of things that it can produce or deliver with the equipment or resources that are available. *...the amount of spare capacity in the economy... Bread factories are working at full capacity... The region is valued for its coal and vast electricity-generating capacity... Britain must still keep the nuclear and conventional capacity to deal with all conceivable threats.* N-UNCOUNT

3 The **capacity** of a piece of equipment is its size or power, often measured in particular units. *...an aircraft with a bomb-carrying capacity of 454 kg. ...a feature which gave the vehicles a much greater fuel capacity than other trucks.* N-COUNT

4 The **capacity** of a container is its volume, or the amount of liquid it can hold, measured in units such as litres or gallons. *...the fuel tanks, which had a capacity of 140 litres... Grease 6 ramekin dishes of 150 ml (5-6 fl oz) capacity.* N-VAR

5 The **capacity** of a building, place, or vehicle is the number of people or things that it can hold. If a place is filled **to capacity**, it is as full as it can possibly be. *Each stadium had a seating capacity of about 50,000... Toronto hospital maternity wards were filled to capacity.* N-SING: also no det, oft *to* N

6 A **capacity** crowd or audience completely fills a theatre, sports ground, or other place. *A capacity crowd of 76,000 people was at Wembley football stadium for the event.* ADJ: ADJ n

7 If you do something **in** a particular **capacity**, you do it as part of a particular job or duty, or because you are representing a particular organization or person; used in written English. *Mr Haughey is touring European capitals in his capacity as President of the European Community... This article is written in a personal capacity... Since 1928, Major Thomas has served the club in many capacities.* N-COUNT: with supp, *in* N, oft poss N *as* n

cape /keɪp/ **capes** ◆◆◇◇◇

1 A **cape** is a large piece of land that sticks out into the sea from the coast. *In 1978, Naomi James became the first woman to sail solo around the world via Cape Horn.* N-COUNT: oft in names

2 A **cape** is a short cloak. *...a woollen cape.* N-COUNT

caper /keɪpə^{r}/ **capers, capering, capered** ◆◇◇◇◇

1 **Capers** are the small green buds of caper plants. They are usually sold pickled in vinegar. N-COUNT: usu pl

2 If you **caper** about, you run and jump around because you are happy or excited. *They were capering about, shouting and laughing... Painted musicians capered behind gorgeous banners.* VERB =cavort V adv/prep

3 A dishonest or illegal activity can be referred to as a **caper**; an informal use. *She served six months in prison for the helicopter caper.* N-COUNT: usu supp N

4 Activities or behaviour that are not at all serious can be referred to as **capers**; an informal use. *Jack would have nothing to do with such capers... What a mess we were in at the end of this caper – hair, eyes, cheeks and neck covered in treacle.* N-COUNT: usu supp N

capillary /kəpɪləri, AM kæpəleri/ **capillaries.** **Capillaries** are tiny blood vessels in your body. ◆◇◇◇◇ N-COUNT

capital /kæpɪt^{ə}l/ **capitals** ◆◆◆◆◆

1 **Capital** is a large sum of money which you use to start or expand a business, or which you invest in order to make more money. *Companies are having difficulty in raising capital... A large amount of capital is invested in all these branches.* N-UNCOUNT

2 You can use **capital** to refer to buildings or machinery which are necessary to produce goods or to make companies more efficient, but which do not make money directly. *...capital equipment that could have served to increase production... The IDB gave out £78 million in grants, mostly for capital investment.* N-UNCOUNT: usu N n

3 **Capital** is the part of an amount of money borrowed or invested which does not include interest. *With a conventional repayment mortgage, the repayments consist of both capital and interest.* N-UNCOUNT =principal

4 The **capital** of a country is the city or town where its government or parliament meets. *...Kathmandu, the capital of Nepal.* N-COUNT: usu *the* N in sing, oft N *of* n

5 If you say that a place is the **capital** of a particular industry or activity, you mean that it is famous for it, because it happens in that place more than anywhere else. *Colmar has long been considered the capital of the wine trade. ...New York, the fashion capital of the world.* N-COUNT: usu *the* N in sing, with supp

6 **Capitals** or **capital letters** are written or printed letters in the form which is used at the beginning of sentences or names. 'T', 'B', and 'F' are capitals. *The name and address are written in capitals.* N-COUNT

7 A **capital** offence is one that is so serious that the person who commits it can be punished by death. *Espionage is a capital offence in China. ...Americans wrongly convicted of capital crimes.* ADJ: ADJ n

8 A **capital** is the top part of a stone column, which is sometimes decorated with stone leaves or other patterns; a technical use in architecture. N-COUNT ≠base

9 See also **working capital.**

10 If you say that someone **is making capital out of** a situation or **is making capital of** it, you disapprove of them because they are gaining an advantage for themselves through other people's misfortunes or efforts; a formal expression. *He rebuked the President for trying to make political capital out of the hostage situation.* PHRASES V inflects, PHR n PRAGMATICS =cash in on

11 You can use phrases such as 'Life **with a capital** L', to emphasize that a word has a particular significance in the situation you are talking about; an informal expression. *She's not feminist with a capital F but she's fairly controversial.* n PHR n PRAGMATICS

capital gains. **Capital gains** are the profits that you make when you buy something and then sell it again at a higher price. *He called for the reform of capital gains tax.* ◆◆◇◇◇ N-PLURAL

capital goods. **Capital goods** are used to make other products. Compare **consumer goods.** N-PLURAL

capital-intensive. **Capital-intensive** industries and businesses need the investment of large sums of money. Compare **labour-intensive.** ADJ

capitalise /kæpɪtəlaɪz/. See **capitalize.**

capitalism /kæpɪtəlɪzəm/. **Capitalism** is an economic and political system in which property, business, and industry are owned by private individuals and not by the state. *...the two fundamentally opposed social systems, capitalism and socialism.* ◆◆◇◇◇ N-UNCOUNT

capitalist /kæpɪtəlɪst/ **capitalists** ◆◆◇◇◇

1 A **capitalist** country or system supports or is based on the principles of capitalism. *Hong Kong should not attempt to impose its capitalist system* ADJ

and way of life on the mainland. ...capitalist economic theory.

2 A **capitalist** is someone who believes in and supports the principles of capitalism. *Lenin had hoped to even have a working relationship with the capitalists.* N-COUNT

3 A **capitalist** is someone who owns a business which they run in order to make a profit for themselves. *They argue that only private capitalists can remake Poland's economy.* N-COUNT =entrepreneur

capitalistic /kæpɪtəlɪstɪk/. **Capitalistic** means supporting or based on the principles of capitalism. *...the forces of capitalistic greed. ...capitalistic economic growth.* ADJ: ADJ n

capitalize /kæpɪtəlaɪz/ **capitalizes, capitalizing, capitalized;** also spelled **capitalise** in British English. ◆◇◇◇◇

1 If you **capitalize** on a situation, you use it to gain some advantage for yourself. *The rebels seem to be trying to capitalize on the public's discontent with the government.* VERB =take advantage of V *on/upon* n

2 If you **capitalize** something that belongs to you, you sell it in order to make money; a technical use in economics. *Our intention is to capitalize the company by any means we can... The company will be capitalized at £2 million.* ♦ **capitalization** /kæpɪtəlaɪzeɪʃᵊn/ *...a massive capitalization programme.* VERB V n *be* V-ed *at* amount N-UNCOUNT

capital letter, capital letters. Capital letters are the same as **capitals**. N-COUNT

capital punishment. Capital punishment is punishment which involves the legal killing of a person who has committed a serious crime such as murder. *Most democracies have abolished capital punishment.* ◆◇◇◇◇ N-UNCOUNT =the death penalty

capitulate /kəpɪtʃʊleɪt/ **capitulates, capitulating, capitulated.** If you **capitulate**, you stop resisting and do what someone else wants you to do. *The club eventually capitulated and now grants equal rights to women... In less than two hours Cohen capitulated to virtually every demand.* ♦ **capitulation** /kəpɪtʃʊleɪʃᵊn/ *They criticised the government decision as a capitulation to terrorist organisations.* ◆◇◇◇◇ VERB =submit, yield V V *to* n N-UNCOUNT: also *a* N =submission

capon /keɪpən/ **capons.** A **capon** is a male chicken that has had its sex organs removed and has been specially fattened up to be eaten. N-COUNT

cappuccino /kæpətʃiːnoʊ/ **cappuccinos. Cappuccino** is coffee which has hot frothy milk and sometimes powdered chocolate on top. ► A **cappuccino** is a cup of cappuccino. N-UNCOUNT N-COUNT

caprice /kæpriːs/ **caprices.** A **caprice** is an unexpected action or decision which has no strong reason or purpose; a formal word. *Her life was spent in terror of her husband's sudden caprices and moods.* N-VAR =whim, impulse

capricious /kæprɪʃəs/

1 Someone who is **capricious** often changes their mind unexpectedly. *Gerald found that his wife was easily bored, capricious and unpredictable. ...capricious and often brutal leaders.* ♦ **capriciousness** *Lady racehorse owners have a reputation for capriciousness.* ADJ-GRADED =impulsive, mercurial N-UNCOUNT =impulsiveness

2 Something that is **capricious** often changes unexpectedly; a literary use. *Both sides were troubled throughout by a capricious wind. ...a theatre with notoriously capricious acoustics.* ♦ **capriciousness** *Pat stuck it out, despite the capriciousness and inhospitality of the English weather.* ADJ-GRADED =unpredictable ≠dependable N-UNCOUNT: usu N *of* n =unpredictability

Capricorn /kæprɪkɔːʳn/ **Capricorns** ◆◆◇◇◇

1 **Capricorn** is one of the twelve signs of the zodiac. Its symbol is a goat. People who are born approximately between the 22nd of December and the 19th of January come under this sign. N-UNCOUNT

2 A **Capricorn** is a person whose sign of the zodiac is Capricorn. N-COUNT

capsicum /kæpsɪkəm/ **capsicums. Capsicums** are mild tasting vegetables that look similar to peppers. N-VAR

capsize /kæpsaɪz, AM kæpsaɪz/ **capsizes, capsizing, capsized.** If you **capsize** a boat or if it **capsizes**, it turns upside down in the water. *The sea got very rough and the boat capsized... I didn't count on his capsizing the raft.* ◆◇◇◇◇ V-ERG =overturn V V n

capstan /kæpstən/ **capstans.** A **capstan** is a machine consisting of a drum that turns round and pulls in a heavy rope or something attached to a rope, for example an anchor. N-COUNT

capsule /kæpsjuːl, AM kæpsᵊl/ **capsules** ◆◇◇◇◇

1 A **capsule** is a very small tube containing powdered or liquid medicine, which you swallow. *...cod liver oil capsules... You can also take red ginseng in convenient tablet or capsule form.* N-COUNT

2 A **capsule** is a small container with a drug or other substance inside it, which is used for medical or scientific purposes. *They first implanted capsules into the animals' brains... The clear capsules start dissolving as soon as they are immersed in the lake.* N-COUNT

3 In some plants, a **capsule** is a part which forms a case or container for seeds, fruit, or spores; a technical use. *...a large shiny brown nut, enclosed in a large spiny seed capsule.* N-COUNT: oft n N =case

4 A space **capsule** is the part of a spacecraft in which people travel, and which often separates from the main rocket. *A Russian space capsule is currently orbiting the Earth.* N-COUNT

Capt. Capt. is a written abbreviation for captain. *Capt. Hunt asked which engine was on fire.* ◆◆◇◇◇ N-TITLE

captain /kæptɪn/ **captains, captaining, captained** ◆◆◆◆◇

1 In the army, navy, and some other armed forces, a **captain** is an officer of middle rank. *...Captain Mark Phillips. ...a captain in the British army... Are all your MC-130s in place, Captain?* N-TITLE; N-COUNT; N-VOC

2 The **captain** of a sports team is the player in charge of it. *...Mickey Thomas, the captain of Wrexham football club. ...Bob Willis, the former England cricket captain.* N-COUNT: oft N *of* n, n N =skipper

3 The **captain** of a ship is the sailor in charge of it. *...the captain of an excursion boat. ...a beefy German sea captain.* N-COUNT: oft N *of* n =skipper

4 The **captain** of an aeroplane is the pilot in charge of it. N-COUNT; N-TITLE

5 In the United States and some other countries, a **captain** is a police officer of fairly senior rank. N-COUNT; N-TITLE

6 If you **captain** a team or a ship, you are the captain of it. *...Bobby Moore, who captained England's World-Cup-winning soccer team in 1966... I did once dream of becoming the first woman to captain an ocean liner.* VERB =skipper V n

captaincy /kæptɪnsi/. The **captaincy** of a team is the position of being captain. *His captaincy of the team was ended by mild eye trouble.* ◆◇◇◇◇ N-UNCOUNT: oft *the* N, poss N

captain of industry, captains of industry. You can refer to the owners or senior managers of industrial companies as **captains of industry**. N-COUNT

caption /kæpʃᵊn/ **captions, captioning, captioned** ◆◆◆◆◇

1 A **caption** is the words printed underneath a picture or cartoon which explain what it is about. *The local paper featured me standing on a stepladder with a caption, 'Wendy climbs the ladder to success.'* N-COUNT

2 When someone **captions** a picture or cartoon, they put a caption under it. *The Sun had captioned a picture of Princess Diana 'Princess of Veils'... The photograph is captioned 'People Power'... The book is well written, properly illustrated and excellently captioned.* VERB V n quote V-ed

captivate /kæptɪveɪt/ **captivates, captivating, captivated.** If you **are captivated** by someone or something, you find them fascinating and attractive. *I was captivated by her brilliant mind... For 40 years she has captivated the world with her radiant looks.* ◆◇◇◇◇ VERB *be* V-ed V n

captivating /kæptɪveɪtɪŋ/. Someone or something that is **captivating** fascinates or attracts you. *...her captivating smile and alluring looks.* ADJ-GRADED =fascinating

captive /kæptɪv/ **captives** ◆◆◇◇◇

1 A **captive** person or animal is being kept imprisoned or enclosed; a literary use. *Her heart had begun to pound inside her chest like a captive animal.* ► A **captive** is someone who is captive. *He de-* ADJ N-COUNT =prisoner

scribed the difficulties of surviving for four months as a captive.

2 A **captive** audience or market is a group of people who are not free to leave a certain place and so have to watch or listen to someone or have to buy things from a particular person or company. *We all performed action songs, sketches and dances before a captive audience of parents and patrons... Airlines consider business travellers a captive market.* ADJ: ADJ n

3 If you **take** someone **captive** or **hold** someone **captive**, you take or keep them as a prisoner. *Richard was finally released on February 4, one year and six weeks after he'd been taken captive... Rebels in Liberia have released four foreigners after holding them captive for a week.* PHRASE: V inflects

captivity /kæptɪvɪti/. **Captivity** is the state of being kept imprisoned or enclosed. *The great majority of barn owls are reared in captivity... An American missionary was released today after more than two months of captivity... He had been kept in a small room, bound and blindfolded for much of his captivity.* ◆◇◇◇◇ N-UNCOUNT: oft *in/of* N

captor /kæptəʳ/ **captors.** You can refer to the person who has captured a person or animal as their **captor**. *They did not know what their captors planned for them.* ◆◇◇◇◇ N-COUNT: usu poss N

capture /kæptʃəʳ/ **captures, capturing, captured** ◆◆◆◇◇

1 If you **capture** someone or something, you catch them or take possession of them, especially in a war, or after a struggle or chase. *The guerrillas shot down one aeroplane and captured the pilot... The whole town celebrated when two tanks were captured... King Arthur himself captures the beast and cuts off its head... The federal army now appears ready to capture more territory from Croatia. ...the murders of fifteen thousand captured Polish soldiers.* ► Also a noun. *...the final battles which led to the army's capture of the town... The shooting happened while the man was trying to evade capture by the security forces.* VERB; V n; V n *from* n; V-ed; N-UNCOUNT: oft with poss

2 If something or someone **captures** a particular quality, feeling, or atmosphere, they represent or express it successfully. *Chef Idris Caldora offers an inspired menu that captures the spirit of the Mediterranean... Their mood was captured by one who said, 'Students here don't know or care about campus issues.'* VB: no cont =encapsulate; V n

3 If something **captures** your attention or imagination, you begin to be interested or excited by it. If someone or something **captures** your heart, you begin to love them or like them very much. *...the great names of the Tory party who usually capture the historian's attention. ...the issue that has captured the imagination of nearly the whole nation. ...one man's undying love for the woman who captured his heart.* VERB; V n

4 If an event **is captured** in a photograph or on film, it is photographed or filmed. *The incident was captured on videotape... The images were captured by TV crews filming outside the base. ...photographers who captured the traumatic scene.* VERB; *be* V-ed *on/in* n; *be* V-ed; V n; Also V n *on/in* n

5 If you **capture** something that you are trying to obtain in competition with other people, you succeed in obtaining it. *In 1987, McDonald's captured 19 percent of all fast-food sales... Mr Ion Iliescu has captured eighty-five per cent of the vote in the three-way presidential race.* VERB =win, secure; V n

car /kɑːʳ/ **cars** ◆◆◆◆◆

1 A **car** is a motor vehicle with room for a small number of passengers. *He had left his tickets in his car... They arrived by car.* N-COUNT: also *by* N

2 In American English, a **car** is one of the separate sections of a train. *Tour buses have replaced railway cars.* N-COUNT

3 In British English, railway carriages are called **cars** when they are used for a particular purpose. *He made his way into the dining car for breakfast.* N-COUNT: usu supp N

4 See also **cable car**.

carafe /kəræf/ **carafes.** A **carafe** is a glass container in which you serve water or wine. *He ordered a carafe of wine.* ► A **carafe** of something is the amount of it contained in a carafe. *At dinner, share a half carafe of agreeable wine with an agreeable companion.* N-COUNT: oft N *of* n; N-COUNT

caramel /kærəmel/ **caramels** ◆◇◇◇◇

1 A **caramel** is a chewy sweet made from sugar, butter, and milk. N-VAR

2 **Caramel** is burnt sugar used for colouring and flavouring food. *Stir constantly until the caramel is completely dissolved and the sauce is smooth.* N-UNCOUNT, also *a* N

caramelize /kærəməlaɪz/ **caramelizes, caramelizing, caramelized;** also spelled **caramelise** in British English.

1 If sugar **caramelizes**, it turns to caramel. *Place pan over a high heat until the butter and sugar start to caramelize.* VERB; V

2 If you **caramelize** something such as fruit, you cook it with sugar so that it is coated with caramel. *I decided to caramelize the onion, and use it to bring some sweetness to the dish. ...caramelised apples and pears.* VERB; V n; V-ed

carapace /kærəpeɪs/ **carapaces**

1 A **carapace** is the protective shell on the back of some animals such as tortoises or crabs; a formal word. N-COUNT

2 You can refer to an attitude that someone has in order to protect themselves as their **carapace**; a literary use. *The arrogance became his protective carapace.* N-COUNT: usu with supp

carat /kærət/ **carats** ◆◇◇◇◇

1 A **carat** is a unit for measuring the weight of diamonds and other precious stones. It is equal to 0.2 grams. *The gemstone is 28.6 millimetres high and weighs 139.43 carats. ...a huge eight-carat diamond.* N-COUNT: usu num N

2 **Carat** is used after a number to indicate the purity of gold. The purest gold is 24-carat gold. *...a 14-carat gold fountain pen.* COMB in ADJ

caravan /kærəvæn/ **caravans** ◆◇◇◇◇

1 A **caravan** is a vehicle with beds and other equipment inside, in which people live or spend their holidays. Caravans are usually pulled by a car. This word is mainly used in British English; the usual American word is **trailer**. *The Becketts spend their holidays in a caravan in France.* N-COUNT

2 A **caravan** is a group of people and animals or vehicles who travel together. *The caravan was resting. ...the old caravan routes from Central Asia to China.* N-COUNT

caravanning /kærəvænɪŋ/. **Caravanning** is the activity of having a holiday in a caravan; used in British English. *He was on a caravanning holiday.* N-UNCOUNT

caraway /kærəweɪ/. **Caraway** is a plant with strong-tasting seeds that are used in cooking. Caraway seeds are often used to flavour bread and cakes. N-UNCOUNT: oft N n

carbine /kɑːʳbaɪn, AM -biːn/ **carbines.** A **carbine** is a light automatic rifle. N-COUNT

carbohydrate /kɑːʳboʊhaɪdreɪt/ **carbohydrates.** **Carbohydrates** are substances, found in certain kinds of food, that provide you with energy. The foods that contain these substances, for example sugar and bread, can also be referred to as **carbohydrates**. *Food is made up of carbohydrates, proteins and fats. ...carbohydrates such as bread, pasta or chips.* ◆◆◇◇◇ N-VAR: usu pl

carbolic acid /kɑːʳbɒlɪk æsɪd/. **Carbolic acid** or **carbolic** is a liquid that is used as a disinfectant and antiseptic. *Carbolic acid is usually used in chiropody and for cleaning... She was ordered to scrub herself with carbolic soap in cold water.* N-UNCOUNT

carbon /kɑːʳbən/ **carbons** ◆◆◆◇◇

1 **Carbon** is a chemical element that diamonds and coal are made up of. N-UNCOUNT

2 A **carbon** is a sheet of carbon paper. *He inserted the paper and two carbons.* N-COUNT

carbonate /kɑːʳbəneɪt/ **carbonates.** **Carbonate** is used in the names of some substances that are formed from carbonic acid, which is a compound of carbon dioxide and water; a technical use in chemistry. *...1,500 milligrams of calcium carbonate. ...carbonate of ammonia solution.* N-VAR: oft N n, N *of* n

carbonated /kɑːʳbəneɪtɪd/. **Carbonated** drinks are drinks that contain small bubbles of carbon dioxide. *...colas and other carbonated soft drinks.* ADJ: usu ADJ n =fizzy

carbon copy, carbon copies
1 If you say that one person or thing is a **carbon copy** of another, you mean that they look or behave exactly like them. *She's a carbon copy of her mother... Theresa's first marriage was almost a carbon copy of her parents'.* N-COUNT: usu N of n =replica
2 A **carbon copy** is a copy of a piece of writing that is made using carbon paper. N-COUNT

carbon dating. **Carbon dating** is the system of calculating the age of a very old object by measuring the amount of radioactive carbon it contains. *Carbon dating techniques can only be used for dating things less than 40,000 years old.* N-UNCOUNT

carbon dioxide. **Carbon dioxide** is a gas. It is produced by animals and people breathing out, and by chemical reactions. ◆◆◇◇◇ N-UNCOUNT

carbon monoxide. **Carbon monoxide** is a poisonous gas that is produced especially by the engines of vehicles. *The limit for carbon monoxide is 4.5 per cent of the exhaust gas.* ◆◇◇◇◇ N-UNCOUNT

carbon paper. **Carbon paper** is thin paper with a dark substance on one side. You use it to make copies of letters, bills, and other papers. *The drawing is transferred onto the wood by means of carbon paper.* N-UNCOUNT

car boot sale, car boot sales. In Britain, a **car boot sale** is a sale where people sell things they own and do not want from a little stall or from the back of their car. *She discovered the magazine as she rummaged through boxes at a car boot sale.* N-COUNT

carbuncle /kɑːʳbʌŋkəl/ **carbuncles.** A **carbuncle** is a large swelling under the skin. N-COUNT =boil

carburettor /kɑːʳbəretəʳ, AM -reɪtəʳ/ **carburettors;** spelled **carburetor** in American English. A **carburettor** is the part of an engine, usually in a car, in which air and petrol are mixed together. N-COUNT

carcass /kɑːʳkəs/ **carcasses;** also spelled **carcase.** ◆◇◇◇◇
1 A **carcass** is the body of a dead animal. *A cluster of vultures crouched on the carcass of a dead buffalo... Prepare the chicken stock using the carcases, the diced vegetables and herbs.* N-COUNT
2 The **carcass** of a vehicle or building is its remains after most of it has decayed or been destroyed. *...the carcass of a rusted tractor.* N-COUNT: oft N of n =remains

carcinogen /kɑːʳsɪnədʒən, kɑːʳsɪnədʒen/ **carcinogens.** A **carcinogen** is a substance which can cause cancer; a medical term. N-COUNT

carcinogenic /kɑːʳsɪnədʒenɪk/. A substance that is **carcinogenic** is likely to cause cancer; a medical term. ADJ-GRADED

carcinoma /kɑːʳsɪnoʊmə/ **carcinomas**
1 **Carcinoma** is cancer; a medical term. N-UNCOUNT
2 **Carcinomas** are malignant tumours; a medical term. N-COUNT

card /kɑːʳd/ **cards** ◆◆◆◆◇
1 A **card** is a piece of stiff paper or thin cardboard on which something is written or printed. *Check the numbers below against the numbers on your card.* N-COUNT
2 A **card** is a piece of cardboard or plastic, or a small document, which shows information about you and which you carry with you, for example to prove your identity. *...they check my bag and press card. ...her membership card... The authorities have begun to issue ration cards.* N-COUNT: with supp, usu n N
3 A **card** is a rectangular piece of plastic, issued by a bank, company, or shop, which you can use to buy things or obtain money. *He paid the whole bill with an American Express card... Holidaymakers should beware of using plastic cards in foreign cash dispensers.* N-COUNT: oft n-proper N
4 A **card** is a folded piece of stiff paper with a picture and sometimes a message printed on it, which you send to someone on a special occasion. *She sends me a card on my birthday. ...millions of get-well cards.* N-COUNT: oft supp N
5 A **card** is the same as a **postcard**. *Send your details on a card to the following address.* N-COUNT
6 A **card** is a piece of thin cardboard carried by someone such as a business person in order to give to other people. A card shows the name, address, telephone number, and other details of the person who carries it. *Here's my card. You may need me.* N-COUNT: oft poss N =business card
7 **Cards** are thin pieces of cardboard with numbers or pictures printed on them which are used to play various games. *...a pack of cards... Kurt picked up his hand and fanned out the cards one by one.* N-COUNT: usu pl =playing card
8 If you are playing **cards**, you are playing a game using cards. *They enjoy themselves drinking wine, smoking and playing cards.* N-UNCOUNT
9 You can use **card** to refer to something that gives you an advantage in a particular situation. If you play a particular **card**, you use that advantage. *This permitted Western manufacturers to play their strong cards: capital and technology... The country's sporting prowess was the strongest card in the hand of its Communist leader.* N-COUNT
10 **Card** is strong, stiff paper or thin cardboard. *She put the pieces of card in her pocket.* N-UNCOUNT
11 You can use **card** to refer to a series of races or matches at a particular sporting event. *Paradise Boy and the Galloping General have clear chances in the opening two events on the card... He will now fight Kevin Ford on the five-bout card.* N-COUNT: oft on N
12 See also **bank card, business card, calling card, cash card, cheque card, Christmas card, identity card, index card, payment card, place card, playing card, report card, smart card, wild card.**
13 In British English, If you say that something is **on the cards**, you mean that it is very likely to happen. The American expression is **in the cards**. *Last summer she began telling friends that a New Year marriage was on the cards.* PHRASES usu v-link PHR =likely ≠unlikely
14 If you say that someone will achieve success if they **play** their **cards right**, you mean that they will achieve success if they act skilfully and use the advantages that they have. *He could even be the next manager of the England team if he plays his cards right.* V inflects
15 If you **put** or **lay your cards on the table**, you deal with a situation by speaking openly about your feelings, ideas, or plans. *Put your cards on the table and be very clear about your complaints.* V inflects

cardamom /kɑːʳdəməm/ **cardamoms;** also spelled **cardamon**. **Cardamom** is a spice. It comes from the seeds of a plant grown in Asia. N-VAR

cardboard /kɑːʳdbɔːʳd/. **Cardboard** is thick, stiff paper that is used for example to make boxes and models. *...a cardboard box. ...life-size cardboard cut-outs of men wielding shotguns.* ◆◇◇◇◇ N-UNCOUNT: oft N n

card-carrying. A person who is a **card-carrying** member of an organization, especially a political party, is an official, fully committed member. *Card-carrying members of the British Communist Party seldom stood for election.* ADJ: usu ADJ n

card game, card games. A **card game** is a game that is played using a set of playing cards. *Blackjack is far and away the most popular card game in U.S. casinos.* N-COUNT

cardholder /kɑːʳdhoʊldəʳ/ **cardholders.** A **cardholder** is someone who has a bank card or credit card. *The average cardholder today carries three to four bank cards.* N-COUNT

cardiac /kɑːʳdiæk/. **Cardiac** means relating to the heart; a medical term. *The king was suffering from cardiac weakness.* ◆◇◇◇◇ ADJ: ADJ n

cardiac arrest, cardiac arrests. A **cardiac arrest** is a heart attack; a medical term. N-VAR =heart attack

cardie /kɑːʳdi/ **cardies.** A **cardie** is the same as a **cardigan**; an informal word. N-COUNT

cardigan /kɑːʳdɪgən/ **cardigans.** A **cardigan** is a knitted woollen jumper that you can fasten at the front with buttons or a zip. ◆◇◇◇◇ N-COUNT

cardinal /kɑːʳdnəl/ **cardinals** ◆◆◇◇◇
1 A **cardinal** is a high-ranking priest in the Catholic church. *In 1448, Nicholas was appointed a cardinal... They were encouraged by a promise from Cardinal Hume.* N-COUNT; N-TITLE

2 A **cardinal** rule or quality is the one that is considered to be the most important; a formal use. *As a salesman, your cardinal rule is to bend over backwards to satisfy a customer... Harmony, balance and order are cardinal virtues to the French.* ADJ: ADJ n =chief, principal

cardinal number, cardinal numbers. A **cardinal number** is a number such as 'one', 'three', and 'ten' that tells you how many things there are in a group but not what order they are in. Compare **ordinal number**. N-COUNT

cardinal point, cardinal points. The **cardinal points** are the four main points of the compass, north, south, east, and west. N-COUNT

cardinal sin, cardinal sins. If you describe an action as a **cardinal sin**, you are indicating in a humorous way that some people strongly disapprove of it. *I committed the physician's cardinal sin: I got involved with my patients.* N-COUNT

card index, card indexes. A **card index** is a number of cards with information written on them which are arranged in a particular order, usually alphabetical, so that you can find the information you want easily. N-COUNT

cardiologist /kɑːʳdiɒlədʒɪst/ **cardiologists.** A **cardiologist** is a doctor who specializes in the heart and its diseases. N-COUNT

cardiology /kɑːʳdiɒlədʒi/. **Cardiology** is the study of the heart and its diseases. N-UNCOUNT

cardiovascular /kɑːʳdioʊvæskjʊləʳ/. **Cardiovascular** means relating to the heart and blood vessels; a medical term. *Smoking places you in serious jeopardy of cardiovascular and respiratory disease.* ◆◇◇◇◇ ADJ: ADJ n

card table, card tables; also spelled **card-table.** A **card table** is a small light table which can be folded up and which is sometimes used for playing games of cards on. N-COUNT

care /keəʳ/ **cares, caring, cared** ◆◆◆◆◆

1 If you **care** about something, you feel that it is important and are concerned about it. *...a company that cares about the environment. ...young men who did not care whether they lived or died... Does anybody know we're here, does anybody care?* VB: no cont; V *about* n; V wh; V

2 If you **care** for someone, you feel a lot of affection for them. *He wanted me to know that he still cared for me. ...people who are your friends, who care about you.* ♦ **caring** *...the 'feminine' traits of caring and compassion.* VB: no cont; V *for/about* n; Also V; N-UNCOUNT

3 If you **care** for someone or something, you look after them and keep them in a good state or condition. *They hired a nurse to care for her. ...these distinctive cars, lovingly cared for by private owners. ...well-cared-for homes.* ► Also a noun. *Most of the staff specialise in the care of children. ...sensitive teeth which need special care... She denied the murder of four children who were in her care.* VERB =look after ≠neglect; V *for* n; V-ed; N-UNCOUNT: usu with supp ≠neglect

4 Children who are in **care** are looked after by the state because their parents are dead or unable to look after them properly. *...a home for children in care... She was taken into care as a baby.* N-UNCOUNT: oft *in* N

5 If you say that you do not **care** for something or someone, you mean that you do not like them; an old-fashioned use. *She had met both sons and did not care for either.* VB: no cont, with brd-neg; V *for* n

6 If you say that someone does something when they **care** to do it, you mean that they do it, although they should do it more willingly or more often. *The woman tells anyone who cares to listen that she's going through hell... Experts reveal only as much as they care to.* VB: no cont =choose; V to-inf

7 If someone asks you if you would **care** for something, or if you would **care** to do something, they are asking you politely if you would like to have something or if you would like to do something. *Would you care for some orange juice?... He said he was off to the beach and would we care to join him.* VB: no cont PRAGMATICS =like; V *for* n; V to-inf

8 If you do something with **care**, you do it in a detailed or attentive way because you do not want to make any mistakes or cause any damage. *Condoms are an effective method of birth control if used with care... We'd taken enormous care in choosing the location.* N-UNCOUNT: oft *with* N =carefully

9 Your **cares** are your worries, anxieties, or fears. *Lean back in a hot bath and forget all the cares of the day... Johnson seemed without a care in the world.* N-COUNT =worries

10 See also **caring; after-care, day care, intensive care.**

11 You can use **for all I care** to emphasize that it does not matter at all to you what someone does. *You can go right now for all I care.* PHRASES V inflects, PHR with cl PRAGMATICS

12 If you say that you **couldn't care less** about someone or something, you are emphasizing that you are not interested in them or worried about them. *I couldn't care less about the bloody woman... Personally, I couldn't have cared less whether the ice-cream came from Italy or Ilfracombe.* V inflects, oft PHR *about* n PRAGMATICS

13 If someone sends you a letter or parcel **care of** a particular person or place, they send it to that person or place, and it is then passed on to you. *Please write to me care of the publishers.* PHR n

14 If you **take care of** someone or something, you look after them and prevent them from being harmed or damaged. *There was no one else to take care of their children... You have to learn to take care of your possessions.* V inflects, PHR n =look after

15 You can say **'Take care'** when saying goodbye to someone. CONVENTION PRAGMATICS

16 If you **take care** to do something, you make sure that you do it. *Foley followed Albert through the gate, taking care to close the latch.* V inflects, usu PHR to-inf

17 To **take care of** a problem, task, or situation means to deal with it. *They leave it to the system to try and take care of the problem... 'Do you need clean sheets?' 'No. Mrs. May took care of that.'* V inflects, PHR n =deal with

18 You can say **'Who cares?'** to emphasize that something does not matter to you at all. *Who cares about some stupid vacation... 'But we might ruin the stove.'—'Who cares?'* oft PHR *about* n PRAGMATICS

careen /kəriːn/ **careens, careening, careened.** If someone or something **careens** somewhere, they rush forward in an uncontrollable way; used mainly in American English. *He stood to one side as they careened past him... The truck sways wildly, careening down narrow mountain roads.* VERB =career, hurtle; V prep/adv

career /kərɪəʳ/ **careers, careering, careered** ◆◆◆◆◇

1 A **career** is the job or profession that someone does for a long period of their life. *She is now concentrating on a career as a fashion designer... Dennis had recently begun a successful career conducting opera. ...a career in journalism. ...a political career.* N-COUNT

2 Your **career** is the part of your life that you spend working. *During his career, he wrote more than fifty plays... She began her career as a teacher.* N-COUNT

3 **Careers** advice or guidance consists of information about different jobs and help with deciding what kind of job you want to do. *She received very little careers guidance when young... Get hold of the company list from your careers advisory service.* ADJ: ADJ n

4 If a person or vehicle **careers** somewhere, they move fast and in an uncontrolled way. *His car careered into a river... He went careering off down the track.* VB: oft cont =hurtle; V prep/adv

career girl, career girls. A **career girl** is the same as a **career woman**. Some women do not like to be referred to as 'career girls', as they think it is patronising. N-COUNT

careerist /kərɪərɪst/ **careerists. Careerist** people are ambitious and think that their career is more important than anything else. *...careerist politicians.* ► Also a noun. *...a singleminded careerist with few friends.* ADJ: usu ADJ n; N-COUNT

career woman, career women. A **career woman** is a woman with a career who is interested in working and progressing in her job, rather than staying at home doing housework and looking after children. N-COUNT

carefree /keəʳfriː/. A **carefree** person or period of time doesn't have or involve any problems, worries, or responsibilities. *They certainly gave the impression of a carefree couple who delighted* ◆◇◇◇◇ ADJ-GRADED: usu ADJ n *in each other's company... Chantal remembered carefree past summers at the beach.*

careful /keəʳfʊl/ ◆◆◆◆◇

1 If you are **careful**, you give serious attention to what you are doing, in order to avoid harm, damage, or mistakes. If you are **careful** to do something, you make sure that you do it. *Be very careful with this stuff, it can be dangerous if it isn't handled properly... Careful on those stairs!... We had to be very careful not to be seen... Pupils will need careful guidance on their choice of options.* ♦ **carefully** *Have a nice time, dear, and drive carefully... He had chosen his words carefully in declaring that the murderers were madmen.*

ADJ-GRADED: usu v-link ADJ, oft ADJ *about/with/of*n, ADJ to-inf ≠careless
ADV-GRADED: ADV with v ≠carelessly

2 **Careful** work, thought, or examination is thorough and shows a concern for details. *He has decided to prosecute her after careful consideration of all the relevant facts... What we now know about the disease was learned by careful study of diseased organs.* ♦ **carefully** *...a vast series of deliberate and carefully planned thefts... He explained very carefully what he was doing.*

ADJ-GRADED: usu ADJ n =painstaking
ADV-GRADED: ADV with v

3 If you tell someone to be **careful about** doing something, you think that what they intend to do is probably wrong, and that they should think seriously before they do it. *I think you should be careful about talking of the rebels as heroes... It is important, I think, for everyone to be careful about claiming victory.* ♦ **carefully** *He should think carefully about actions like this which play into the hands of his opponents.*

ADJ-GRADED: v link ADJ *about/of*-ing PRAGMATICS =cautious, circumspect
ADV: ADV after v

4 If you are **careful** with something such as money or resources, you use or spend only what is necessary. *You will have to make a special effort to train your child to be careful with her pocket-money... It would force industries to be more careful with natural resources.*

ADJ-GRADED: usu v-link ADJ *with* n =prudent

5 You can say **'You can't be too careful'** as a way of advising someone to take precautions, even when these seem unnecessary; used in spoken English. *You can't be too careful when a young child is near water.*

PHRASE PRAGMATICS

care giver care givers; also spelled **care-giver**. A **care giver** is someone who is responsible for looking after another person, for example, a person who is disabled, ill, or very young. *She is the primary care giver of the family... It is nearly always women who are the primary care givers.*

N-COUNT

careless /keəʳləs/ ◆◇◇◇◇

1 If you are **careless**, you do not pay enough attention to what you are doing, and so you make mistakes, or cause harm or damage. *I'm sorry. How careless of me... Some parents are accused of being careless with their children's health... Mr Clarke had pleaded guilty to causing death by careless driving.* ♦ **carelessly** *She was fined £100 for driving carelessly... The fire is believed to have been started by a carelessly discarded cigarette.* ♦ **carelessness** *The defence conceded stupid goals through sheer carelessness.*

ADJ-GRADED: oft ADJ *with* n ≠careful
ADV-GRADED: ADV with v ≠carefully
N-UNCOUNT

2 If you say that someone is **careless** of something such as their health or appearance, you mean that they do not seem to be concerned about it, or do nothing to keep it in a good condition. *He had shown himself careless of personal safety where the life of his colleagues might be at risk... She's careless about her hygiene... That shows a fairly careless attitude to clothes, doesn't it?*

ADJ-GRADED: oft ADJ *of/about* n

3 If you describe someone's movements as **careless**, you mean that they are relaxed or confident, and do not seem to require much effort or thought; a literary use. *With a careless flip of his wrists, he sent the ball quickly on its way.*

ADJ-GRADED: usu ADJ n =casual

carelessly /keəʳləsli/. If someone does something **carelessly**, they do it without much thought or effort; used in written English. *Houston carelessly tossed the notebooks on the bed... 'Oh,' he said carelessly. 'I'm in no hurry to get back.'* ● See also **careless**.

ADV-GRADED: ADV with v =casually

carer /keərəʳ/ **carers.** A **carer** is someone who looks after another person, especially a child who cannot live with his or her parents, or an old person. *We are looking for foster carers who can care for a child for a few days... Women are more likely than men to be carers of elderly dependent relatives.*

◆◇◇◇◇ N-COUNT

caress /kəres/ **caresses, caressing, caressed.** If you **caress** someone, you stroke them gently and affectionately; used in written English. *He was gently caressing her golden hair.* ► Also a noun. *Margaret took me to one side, holding my arm in a gentle caress.*

◆◇◇◇◇ VERB =stroke V n
N-COUNT

caretaker /keəʳteɪkəʳ/ **caretakers** ◆◇◇◇◇

1 In British English, a **caretaker** is a person whose job is to look after a large building such as a school or a block of flats and deal with small repairs to it.

N-COUNT =janitor

2 A **caretaker** government or leader is in charge temporarily until a new government or leader is appointed. *The military intends to hand over power to a caretaker government and hold elections within six months.*

ADJ: ADJ n =acting ≠permanent

3 A **caretaker** is someone who is responsible for looking after another person, for example, a person who is disabled, ill, or very young; used mainly in American English.

N-COUNT =care giver

care worker, care workers. A **care worker** is a person whose work involves helping and looking after people who cannot look after themselves, especially people who are in residential care such as children, the mentally ill, or the elderly.

N-COUNT

careworn /keəʳwɔːʳn/. A person who looks **careworn** looks worried, tired, and unhappy. *In recent years his face had become craggy, somewhat careworn.*

ADJ-GRADED

cargo /kɑːʳgoʊ/ **cargoes.** The **cargo** of a ship or plane is the goods that it is carrying. *The boat calls at the main port to load its regular cargo of bananas. ...cargo planes.*

◆◆◇◇◇ N-VAR: oft N *of* n =consignment

Caribbean /kærəbiːən, AM kərɪbiən/ **Caribbeans** ◆◆◆◇◇

1 The **Caribbean** is the sea which is between the West Indies, Central America and the north coast of South America.

N-PROPER: *the* N

2 **Caribbean** means belonging or relating to the Caribbean Sea and its islands, or to its people. *...the Caribbean island of St Thomas.* ► A **Caribbean** is a person from a Caribbean island. *Caribbeans settled in Sheffield in the early '50s.* ● See also **Afro-Caribbean.**

ADJ
N-COUNT

caribou /kærɪbuː/; **caribou** is both the singular and the plural form. A **caribou** is a large north American deer.

N-COUNT

caricature /kærɪkətʃʊəʳ, AM -tʃəʳ/ **caricatures, caricaturing, caricatured** ◆◇◇◇◇

1 A **caricature** of someone is a drawing or description of them that exaggerates their appearance or behaviour in a humorous or satirical way. *The poster showed a caricature of Hitler with a devil's horns and tail... The Spanish Steps were crowded with the sellers of grotesque caricatures.*

N-COUNT: oft N *of* n =cartoon

2 If you **caricature** someone, you draw or describe them in an exaggerated way in order to be humorous or satirical. *He started to talk to her as if he wanted to caricature a fatherly tone... He was caricatured as a turnip.*

VERB V n *be* V-ed *as* n Also V n *as* n

3 If you describe something as a **caricature** of an event or situation, you mean that it is a very exaggerated account of it. *Hall is angry at what he sees as a caricature of the training offered to modern-day social workers.*

N-COUNT: usu N *of* n

caricaturist /kærɪkətʃʊərɪst/ **caricaturists.** A **caricaturist** is a person who portrays other people in an exaggerated way, especially in drawings or cartoons.

N-COUNT =cartoonist

caries /keəriz/. **Caries** is decay in teeth; a technical term in dentistry. *Fluoride in drinking water can help prevent dental caries in the teeth of growing children.*

N-UNCOUNT =decay

caring /keərɪŋ/ ◆◆◆◇◇

1 If someone is **caring**, they are affectionate, helpful, and sympathetic. *He is a lovely boy, very gentle and caring. ...a loving, caring husband.*

ADJ-GRADED =loving

2 The **caring** professions are those such as nursing and social work that are involved with looking after

ADJ: ADJ n

people who are ill or who need help in coping with their lives. *The course is also suitable for those in the caring professions. ...the caring services.*

car-jacker, car-jackers. A **car-jacker** is someone who attacks and steals from people in their own cars; used mainly in journalism. N-COUNT

carjacking /kɑːrdʒækɪŋ/ **carjackings.** A **carjacking** is an attack on a person in their own car during which they may be robbed or harmed physically; used mainly in journalism. *The crime of carjacking has claimed numerous lives in America.* N-VAR

carload /kɑːrloud/ **carloads.** A **carload** of people or things is as many people or things as a car can carry. *Wherever he goes, a carload of soldiers goes with him.* N-COUNT: usu N *of* n

carmine /kɑːrmaɪn, -mɪn/. **Carmine** is a deep bright red colour; a literary word. *...a tulip with carmine petals.* COLOUR

carnage /kɑːrnɪdʒ/. **Carnage** is the violent killing of large numbers of people, especially in a war; a literary word. *...his strategy for stopping the carnage in Bosnia. ...the carnage of motorway accidents.* ◆◇◇◇◇ N-UNCOUNT =slaughter

carnal /kɑːrnəl/. If you describe feelings and desires as **carnal**, you mean that they are purely sexual and sensual; a formal word. *Their ruling passion is that of carnal love.* ADJ: usu ADJ n =sexual

carnal knowledge. **Carnal knowledge** is sexual intercourse; a formal or legal expression. N-UNCOUNT

carnation /kɑːrneɪʃən/ **carnations.** A **carnation** is a plant with white, pink, or red flowers. ◆◇◇◇◇ N-COUNT

carnival /kɑːrnɪvəl/ **carnivals** ◆◆◇◇◇

1 A **carnival** is a public festival during which people play music and sometimes dance in the streets. N-COUNT

2 A **carnival** of something such as colours or sounds is a bright or exciting mixture of them; a literary use. *The avenues lined with jacaranda trees burst into a carnival of purple.* N-COUNT: N *of* n

carnivore /kɑːrnɪvɔːr/ **carnivores**

1 A **carnivore** is an animal that eats meat; a technical use in biology. N-COUNT

2 If someone describes a person as a **carnivore**, they are saying, especially in a humorous way, that the person is not a vegetarian. *This is a vegetarian dish that carnivores love.* N-COUNT =meat-eater ≠vegetarian

carnivorous /kɑːrnɪvərəs/

1 **Carnivorous** animals eat meat; a technical use in biology. *Snakes are carnivorous, mainly eating small animals such as rats and frogs.* ADJ

2 **Carnivorous** can be used, especially humorously, to describe someone who is not a vegetarian. ADJ =meat-eating

carob /kærəb/ **carobs**

1 A **carob** or **carob tree** is a Mediterranean tree that stays green all year round. It has dark brown fruit that you can eat. *Every square metre of soil was used, mainly for olives, oranges and carobs.* N-COUNT

2 The dark brown fruit of the carob tree can be referred to as **carob**. It is often made into powder and used instead of cocoa in health food. *If you do yearn for chocolate, try a carob bar instead.* N-UNCOUNT: oft N n

carol /kærəl/ **carols.** **Carols** are Christian religious songs that are sung at Christmas. *The singing of Christmas carols is a custom derived from early dance routines of pagan origin... There are presents to wrap, a Christmas tree to decorate and carol singers at the door.* ◆◇◇◇◇ N-COUNT

carotid artery /kərɒtɪd ɑːrtəri/ **carotid arteries.** A **carotid artery** is one of the two arteries in the neck that supply the head with blood; a medical term. N-COUNT

carouse /kəraʊz/ **carouses, carousing, caroused.** If you say that people **are carousing**, you mean that they are behaving very noisily and drinking a lot of alcohol as they enjoy themselves. *They told him to stay home with his wife instead of going out and carousing with friends.* VERB V
♦ **carousing** *The singing and carousing did not end until after midnight.* N-UNCOUNT

carousel /kærəsel/ **carousels**

1 A **carousel** at a funfair is a large circular mechanical device with seats, often in the shape of animals or cars, on which children sit and go round and round; used mainly in American English. The usual British word is **merry-go-round** or **roundabout.** N-COUNT

2 At an airport, a **carousel** is a belt that moves round from which passengers can collect their luggage. N-COUNT

carp /kɑːrp/ **carps, carping, carped.** **Carp** can also be used as the plural form for meaning 1. ◆◆◇◇◇

1 A **carp** is a kind of fish that lives in lakes and rivers. N-VAR

2 If you **carp**, you keep criticizing or complaining about someone or something. *He cannot understand why she's constantly carping at him... This was the man whom other trainers love to carp about.* VERB V *at/about* n Also V
♦ **carping** *She was in no mood to put up with Blanche's carping.* N-UNCOUNT

car park, car parks; also spelled **carpark.** In British English, a **car park** is an area or building where people can leave their cars. The usual American term is **parking lot.** ◆◆◇◇◇ N-COUNT

carpenter /kɑːrpɪntər/ **carpenters.** A **carpenter** is a person whose job is making and repairing wooden things. ◆◇◇◇◇ N-COUNT

carpentry /kɑːrpɪntri/. **Carpentry** is the activity of making and repairing wooden things. N-UNCOUNT

carpet /kɑːrpɪt/ **carpets, carpeting, carpeted** ◆◆◇◇◇

1 A **carpet** is a thick covering of soft material which is laid over a floor or a staircase. *They put down wooden boards, and laid new carpets on top. ...the stain on our living-room carpet.* N-VAR

2 If a floor or a room **is carpeted**, a carpet is laid on the floor. *The room had been carpeted and the windows glazed with coloured glass... The main gaming room was thickly carpeted.* VB: usu passive *be* V-ed V-ed

3 A **carpet** of something such as leaves or plants is a layer of them which covers the ground; a literary use. *The carpet of leaves in my yard became more and more noticeable.* N-COUNT: usu sing, usu N *of* n =layer

4 If the ground **is carpeted** with something such as leaves or plants, it is completely covered by them; a literary use. *The ground was thickly carpeted with pine needles.* VB: usu passive =cover *be* V-ed *with* n

5 See also **carpeting; red carpet.** ● to **sweep** something **under the carpet**: see **sweep.**

carpetbagger /kɑːrpɪtbægər/ **carpetbaggers.** In American English, if you call someone a **carpetbagger**, you disapprove of them because they are trying to become a politician in an area which is not their home, simply because they think they are more likely to succeed there. *He had come to Washington, not as a common carpetbagger, but a man well known.* N-COUNT PRAGMATICS

carpet bombing. **Carpet bombing** is heavy bombing from aircraft, with the intention of hitting as many places as possible in a particular area. N-UNCOUNT

carpeting /kɑːrpɪtɪŋ/. You use **carpeting** to refer to a carpet, or to the type of material that is used to make carpets. *...the long lovely lounge with its wall-to-wall carpeting... Carpeting is about the cheapest covering one can put on a floor.* ● See also **carpet.** N-UNCOUNT

carpet slipper, carpet slippers. **Carpet slippers** are soft, comfortable slippers. N-COUNT

car pool, car pools. A **car pool** is a number of cars that are owned by a company or organization for the use of its employees or members. N-COUNT

car port, car ports; also spelled **carport.** A **car port** is a shelter for one or two cars which is attached to a house and consists of a flat roof supported on pillars. N-COUNT

carriage /kærɪdʒ/ **carriages** ◆◆◇◇◇

1 A **carriage** is an old-fashioned vehicle, usually for a small number of passengers, which is pulled by horses. *The President-elect followed in an open carriage drawn by six beautiful gray horses.* N-COUNT: also *by* N

2 In British English, a **carriage** is one of the separate, long sections of a train that carries passengers. The usual American word is **car.** *Don't sit too close to a woman on her own in a railway carriage.* N-COUNT =coach

3 In American English, a **carriage** is the same as a **baby carriage.** N-COUNT

4 Carriage is the cost or action of transporting or delivering goods; a formal use. *It costs £10.86 for one litre including carriage... If the Government introduces a carbon tax on road haulage, then carriage by water will become more attractive.* N-UNCOUNT

5 Your **carriage** is the way you hold your body and head when you are walking, standing, or sitting; a literary use. *Her legs were long and fine, her hips slender, her carriage erect.* N-UNCOUNT: usu with poss =deportment

carriageway /kærɪdʒweɪ/ **carriageways.** In British English, a **carriageway** is one of the two sides of a motorway or dual carriageway. Each carriageway may have two or more lanes. *There had been a serious multiple accident and both carriageways were blocked.* ◆◇◇◇◇ N-COUNT

carrier /kæriəʳ/ **carriers** ◆◆◆◇◇

1 A **carrier** is a vehicle that is used for carrying people, especially soldiers, or things. *There were armoured personnel carriers and tanks on the streets... Deliveries are made by common carrier or van line.* • See also **aircraft carrier.** N-COUNT

2 A **carrier** is a passenger airline. *Switzerland's national carrier, Swissair, has been having a hard time recently.* N-COUNT

3 A **carrier** is a person or an animal that is infected with a disease and so can make other people or animals ill. *...an AIDS carrier... Harsh Arctic climates killed off the carriers of disease such as mosquitoes and worms.* N-COUNT: usu n N, N *of* n

carrier bag, carrier bags. In British English, a **carrier bag** is a bag made of paper or plastic which you carry shopping in. N-COUNT

carrion /kæriən/. **Carrion** is the decaying flesh of dead animals. *Crows circled overhead, looking for carrion.* N-UNCOUNT

carrot /kærət/ **carrots** ◆◆◇◇◇

1 Carrots are long, thin, orange-coloured vegetables. They grow under the ground, and have green shoots above the ground. N-VAR

2 Something that is offered to people in order to persuade them to do something can be referred to as a **carrot**. A punishment or disincentive can be referred to in the same sentence as a 'stick'. *They will be set targets, with a carrot of extra cash and pay if they achieve them... Why the new emphasis on sticks instead of diplomatic carrots?* • See also **carrot and stick.** N-COUNT =incentive

carrot and stick. If an organization has a **carrot and stick** approach or policy, they offer people things in order to persuade them to do something and punish them if they refuse to do it. *Congress also wants to use a carrot and stick approach to force both sides to negotiate an end to the war.* ADJ: ADJ n

carry /kæri/ **carries, carrying, carried** ◆◆◆◆◆

1 If you **carry** something, you take it with you, holding it so that it does not touch the ground. *He was carrying a briefcase... He carried the plate through to the dining-room... She carried her son to the car... If your job involves a lot of paperwork, you're going to need something to carry it all in.* VERB V n V n prep/adv

2 If you **carry** something, you have it with you wherever you go. *You have to carry a bleeper so that they can call you in at any time.* VERB V n

3 If something **carries** a person or thing somewhere, it takes them there. *Flowers are designed to attract insects which then carry the pollen from plant to plant... The delegation was carrying a message of thanks to President Mubarak... The ship could carry seventy passengers.* VERB =transport V n adv/prep V n

4 If a person or animal is **carrying** a disease, they are infected with it and can pass it on to other people or animals. *The official number of people carrying the AIDS virus is low... Frogs eat pests which destroy crops and carry diseases.* VERB V n

5 If an action or situation has a particular quality or consequence, you can say that it **carries** it. *Check that any medication you're taking carries no risk for your developing baby... Individualism, and the breakdown of social harmony, had a constructive purpose. But they also carried a price.* VB: no passive, no cont V n

6 If a quality or advantage **carries** someone into a particular position or through a difficult situation, it helps them to achieve that position or deal with that situation. *He had the ruthless streak necessary to carry him into the Cabinet... The warmth and strength of their relationship carried them through difficult times.* VERB V n prep/adv

7 If you **carry** an idea or a method to a particular extent, you use or develop it to that extent. *It's not such a new idea, but I carried it to extremes... We could carry that one step further by taking the same genes and putting them into another crop.* VERB =take V n prep/adv

8 If a newspaper or poster **carries** a picture or a piece of writing, it contains it or displays it. *Several papers carry the photograph of Mr Anderson.* VERB V n

9 In a debate, if a proposal or motion **is carried**, a majority of people vote in favour of it. *A motion backing its economic policy was carried by 322 votes to 296.* VB: usu passive *be* V-ed

10 If a crime **carries** a particular punishment, a person who is found guilty of that crime will receive that punishment. *It was a crime of espionage and carried the death penalty.* VB: no cont V n

11 If a sound **carries**, it can be heard a long way away. *Even in this stillness Leaphorn doubted if the sound would carry far.* VERB V adv Also V

12 In American English, if a candidate or party **carries** a state or area, they win the election in that state or area. The usual British word is **take**. *George Bush carried the state with 56 percent of the vote.* VB: no passive V n

13 If you **carry** yourself in a particular way, you walk and move in that way. *They carried themselves with great pride and dignity.* VERB V pron-refl prep/adv

14 If a woman **is carrying** a child, she is pregnant. *There are many theories that claim to be able to predict whether you're carrying a boy or a girl.* VB: usu cont V n

15 If you **get carried away** or **are carried away**, you are so eager or excited about something that you do something hasty or foolish. *I got completely carried away and almost cried.* PHRASES V inflects =lose control ≠keep control

16 If a person or team **carries all before them**, they succeed very easily. *In the formative years their alliance carried all before it.* V inflects

17 • to **carry the can**: see **can.** • to **carry conviction**: see **conviction.** • to **carry the day**: see **day.** • to **carry weight**: see **weight.**

carry off PHRASAL VERB

1 If you **carry** something **off**, you do it successfully. *He's got the experience and the authority to carry it off.* V n P Also V P n (not pron)

2 If you **carry off** a prize or a trophy, you win it. *It carried off the Evening Standard drama award for best play.* V P n (not pron) Also V n P

carry on PHRASAL VERB

1 If you **carry on** doing something, you continue to do it. *The assistant carried on talking... Rachael Carr intends to carry on teaching... Her bravery has given him the will to carry on with his life and his work... His eldest son Joseph carried on his father's traditions... 'Do you mind if I just start with the few formal questions please?'—'Carry on.'* =continue V P -ing V P *with* n V P n V P

2 If you **carry on** an activity, you do it or take part in it for a period of time. *The consulate will carry on a political dialogue with the Soviet Union... He carried on a passionate affair with Mrs Gilbert.* =conduct V P n (not pron)

3 If you say that someone **is carrying on**, you are irritated with them because they are talking very excitedly and saying a lot of unnecessary things; an informal expression. *She was yelling and screaming and carrying on... He was carrying on about some stupid television series.* PRAGMATICS =make a fuss V P V P *about* n

4 If you say that someone **is carrying on** with someone else, you mean that they are having a sexual relationship and you do not approve of this, usually because one of them is married; an informal expression. *Every week a fresh scandal emerges about ministers carrying on with film actresses and call girls.* usu cont PRAGMATICS =have an affair V P *with* n Also V P

carry out. If you **carry out** a threat, task, or instruction, you do it or act according to it. *The Social Democrats could still carry out their threat to leave the government... Police say they believe the attacks were carried out by nationalists... Commitments* PHRASAL VERB V P n (not pron) V n P

have been made with very little intention of carrying them out.

carry over. If something **carries over** or **is carried over** from one situation to another, it continues to exist or apply in the new situation. *Priestley's rational outlook in science carried over to religion... Springs and wells were decorated, a custom which was carried over into Christian times in Europe.*
PHRASAL VERB ERG; V P *into/to* n; be V-ed P *into/to* n

carry through. If you **carry** something **through**, you do it or complete it, often in spite of difficulties. *We don't have the confidence that the UN will carry through a sustained program... The state announced a clear-cut policy and set out to carry it through.*
PHRASAL VERB; V P n (not pron); V n P

carrycot /kærikɒt/ **carrycots.** In British English, a **carrycot** is a cot for small babies which has handles so it can be carried.
N-COUNT

cart /kɑːʳt/ **carts, carting, carted** ◆◆◇◇◇

1 A **cart** is an old-fashioned wooden vehicle that is used for transporting goods or people. Some carts are pulled by animals. *...a country where horse-drawn carts far outnumber cars.*
N-COUNT =wagon

2 If you **cart** things or people somewhere, you carry them or transport them there, often with difficulty; an informal use. *After both their parents died, one of their father's relatives carted off the entire contents of the house... One of them protests loudly, and the Americans cart him away in plastic handcuffs... I've been trying to cut down on the stuff that I cart around with me.*
VERB; V n with adv; Also V n prep

3 In American English, a **cart** is a small motorized vehicle. *Cars are prohibited, so transportation is by electric cart or by horse and buggy.*
N-COUNT

4 In American English, a **cart** or a **shopping cart** is a large metal basket on wheels which is provided by shops such as supermarkets for customers to use while they are in the shop.
N-COUNT

5 If you say that someone **is putting the cart before the horse**, you mean that they are doing things in the wrong order; an informal expression. *This puts the cart before the horse; elections should follow, not precede, agreement on a constitution.*
PHRASE: V inflects

carte blanche /kɑːʳt blɒnʃ/. If someone gives you **carte blanche**, they give you the authority to do whatever you think is right. *She gave the children carte blanche to do what they liked... She was given carte blanche with the redecoration.*
N-UNCOUNT: oft N to-inf

cartel /kɑːʳtel/ **cartels.** A **cartel** is an association of similar companies or businesses that have grouped together in order to prevent competition and to control prices. *...a drug cartel... Ecuador says it's planning to drop out of OPEC, becoming the oil cartel's first member to do so.*
◆◆◇◇◇ N-COUNT

carthorse /kɑːʳthɔːʳs/ **carthorses;** also spelled **cart-horse.** A **carthorse** is a large, powerful horse that is used to pull carts or farm machinery. *Where we use tractors, obviously they used carthorses in those days.*
N-COUNT

cartilage /kɑːʳtɪlɪdʒ/ **cartilages. Cartilage** is a strong, flexible substance in your body, especially around your joints and in your nose. *Andre Agassi has pulled out of next week's Grand Slam Cup after tearing a cartilage in his chest.*
◆◇◇◇◇ N-VAR

cartographer /kɑːʳtɒgrəfəʳ/ **cartographers.** A **cartographer** is a person whose job is drawing maps.
N-COUNT

cartography /kɑːʳtɒgrəfi/. **Cartography** is the art or activity of drawing maps and geographical charts.
N-UNCOUNT

carton /kɑːʳtən/ **cartons** ◆◇◇◇◇

1 A **carton** is a plastic or cardboard container in which food or drink is sold. *A two-pint carton of milk comes cheaper than two single pints.*
N-COUNT: oft N *of* n

2 In American English, a **carton** is a large, strong cardboard box in which goods are packed for storage and transport.
N-COUNT

cartoon /kɑːʳtuːn/ **cartoons** ◆◆◇◇◇

1 A **cartoon** is a humorous drawing or series of drawings in a newspaper or magazine. *One of Britain's best-loved cartoon characters, Rupert the Bear, celebrates his seventieth birthday today.* • See also **strip cartoon.**
N-COUNT

2 A **cartoon** is a film in which all the characters and scenes are drawn rather than being real people or objects. *...a TV set blares out a cartoon comedy.*
N-COUNT

cartoonist /kɑːʳtuːnɪst/ **cartoonists.** A **cartoonist** is a person whose job is to draw cartoons for newspapers and magazines.
◆◇◇◇◇ N-COUNT

cartridge /kɑːʳtrɪdʒ/ **cartridges** ◆◇◇◇◇

1 A **cartridge** is a metal or cardboard tube containing a bullet and an explosive substance. Cartridges are used in guns.
N-COUNT

2 A **cartridge** is part of a machine or device that can be easily removed and replaced when it is worn out or empty. *Change the filter cartridge as often as instructed by the manufacturer.*
N-COUNT

cartwheel /kɑːʳtʰwiːl/ **cartwheels, cartwheeling, cartwheeled**

1 If you do a **cartwheel**, you do a fast, circular movement with your body. You fall sideways, put your hands on the ground, swing your legs over, and return to a standing position. *Their four children turn cartwheels in the grass as we talk.*
N-COUNT

2 If a person or something such as a vehicle **cartwheels** down or across something in an uncontrollable way, they turn over and over. *Suddenly I was cartwheeling down the slope, all orientation gone... The two cars cartwheeled horrifyingly into the sand trap at the first corner.*
VERB =roll; V prep/adv; Also V

carve /kɑːʳv/ **carves, carving, carved** ◆◆◇◇◇

1 If you **carve** an object, you make it by cutting it out of a substance such as wood or stone. If you **carve** something such as wood or stone into an object, you make the object by cutting it out. *One of the prisoners has carved a beautiful wooden chess set... He carves his figures from white pine... I picked up a piece of wood and started carving. ...carved stone figures.* • See also **carving.**
VERB =sculpt; V n; V n prep; V; V-ed

2 If you **carve** writing or a design on an object, you cut it into the surface of the object. *He carved his name on his desk... The ornately carved doors were made in the seventeenth century.*
VERB; V n *in/on* n; V-ed

3 If you **carve** a piece of cooked meat, you cut slices from it so that you can eat it. *Andrew began to carve the chicken... Carve the beef into slices.*
VERB; V n; V n *into* n

4 If you **carve** a career or a niche for yourself, you succeed in getting the career or the position that you want by your own efforts. *She has carved a niche for herself as a comic actor... They may be loyally standing by their men, but they are also carving their own careers... The girl from nowhere clearly means to carve herself a place in history.* ► **Carve out** means the same as **carve.** *He is hoping to carve out a much greater role for himself... Wood has not had much luck in carving out a career.*
VB: no passive; V n *for* pron-refl; V n; V pron-refl n; PHRASAL VERB: no passive; V P n *for* pron-refl; V P n

5 If a road **is carved** through a place, it is built so that it goes through that place. *Two three-lane roads will be carved through countryside.*
VB: usu passive; *be* V-ed prep

carve out See **carve** 4.
PHRASAL VERB

carve up
PHRASAL VERB

1 If you say that someone **carves** something **up**, you disapprove of the way they have divided it into small parts. *He has set about carving up the company which Hammer created from almost nothing... They have begun carving the country up like a pie.*
PRAGMATICS; V P n (not pron); V n P

2 In informal English, to **carve** someone **up** means to hurt them badly using a knife. *He wanted to go into the street and carve someone's face up.*
V n P; Also V P n

carver /kɑːʳvəʳ/ **carvers.** A **carver** is a person who carves wood or stone, as a job or as a hobby. *The ivory industry employed about a thousand carvers.*
◆◇◇◇◇ N-COUNT: oft n N

carving /kɑːʳvɪŋ/ **carvings** ◆◇◇◇◇

1 A **carving** is an object or a design that has been cut out of a material such as stone or wood. *...a wood carving of a human hand.*
N-COUNT: oft n N

2 **Carving** is the art of carving objects, or of carving designs or writing on objects. *I found wood carving satisfying and painting fun.*
N-UNCOUNT: usu n N

carving knife, carving knives. A **carving knife** is a long sharp knife that is used to cut cooked meat.
N-COUNT

cascade /kæskeɪd/ **cascades, cascading, cascaded** ◆◇◇◇◇

1 If you refer to a **cascade** of something, you mean that there is a large amount of it; a literary use. *The women have lustrous cascades of black hair... A cascade of mail arrived from friends.* N-COUNT: usu N *of* n =lots

2 A **cascade** is a waterfall; a literary use. N-COUNT

3 When water **cascades** somewhere, it pours or flows downwards very fast and in large quantities. *She hung on as the freezing, rushing water cascaded past her... A waterfall cascades down the cliff from the hills behind.* VERB V adv/prep Also V

4 If one thing **cascades** over another, it falls or hangs over it; a literary use. *Vivid red and pink geraniums cascade over my balcony... From her tiny waist a crinolined skirt cascaded in three deep tiers.* VERB V prep V

case 1 instances and other abstract meanings

case /keɪs/ **cases** ◆◆◆◆◆

1 A particular **case** is a particular situation or incident, especially one that you are using as an individual example or instance of something. *Surgical training takes at least nine years, or 11 in the case of obstetrics... Suffering can have beneficial results and certainly I know that was true in my case... In extreme cases, insurance companies can prosecute for fraud... The Honduran press published reports of eighteen cases of alleged baby snatching.* N-COUNT: oft *in* N, N *of* n

2 A **case** is a person or their particular problem that a doctor, social worker, or other professional is dealing with. *Dr Thomas Bracken describes the case of a 45-year-old Catholic priest much given to prayer whose left knee became painful... Some cases of arthritis respond to a gluten-free diet... Child protection workers were meeting to discuss her case.* N-COUNT

3 If you say that someone is a sad **case** or a hopeless **case**, you mean that they are in a sad situation or a hopeless situation. *I knew I was going to make it – that I wasn't a hopeless case.* ● See also **basket case, nut case**. N-COUNT: adj N

4 A **case** is a crime or mystery that the police are investigating. *The police have several suspects in the case of five murders committed in Gainesville, Florida... Mr. Hitchens said you have solved some very unusual cases.* N-COUNT

5 In an argument or debate, the **case** for or against a plan or idea consists of the facts and reasons used to support it or oppose it. *He sat there while I made the case for his dismissal... Both these facts strengthen the case against hanging... She argued her case.* N-COUNT: usu sing, oft N *for/against* n

6 In law, a **case** is a trial or other legal inquiry. *It can be difficult for public figures to win a libel case... The case was brought by his family, who say their reputation has been damaged by allegations about him.* ● See also **test case**. N-COUNT

7 You say **in any case** when you are adding something which is more important than what you have just said, but which supports or corrects it. *The concert was booked out, and in any case, most of the people gathered in the square could not afford the price of a ticket.* PHRASES PHR with cl PRAGMATICS =anyway, besides

8 You say **in any case** after talking about things that you are not sure about, to emphasize that your next statement is the most important thing or the thing that you are sure about. *Either he escaped, or he came to grief. In any case, he was never seen again.* PHR with cl PRAGMATICS =at any rate

9 If you do something or have something **in case** or **just in case** a particular thing happens or is true, you do it or have it because that thing might happen or might be true. *In case anyone was following me, I made an elaborate detour... Extra boiling water should be kept at hand just in case it is needed.* CONJ-SUBORD

10 If you do something or have something **in case of** a particular thing, you do it or have it because that thing might happen or be true. *Many shops along the route have been boarded up in case of trouble.* PREP: PHR n

11 You use **in case** in expressions like 'in case you didn't know' or 'in case you've forgotten' in a rather irritated way, when you are telling someone something that you think is either obvious or none of their business. *She's nervous about something, in case you didn't notice... 'I'm waiting for Mary Ann,' she said, 'in case you're wondering.'* PHR with cl PRAGMATICS

12 You say **in that case** or **in which case** to indicate that what you are going to say is true if the possible situation that has just been mentioned actually exists. *Perhaps you've some doubts about the attack. In that case it may interest you to know that Miss Woods witnessed it... Members are concerned that a merger might mean higher costs, in which case they would oppose it.* PHR with cl

13 You can say that you are doing something **just in case** to refer vaguely to the possibility that a thing might happen or be true, without saying exactly what it is. *I guess we've already talked about this but I'll ask you again just in case.* PHR with cl

14 You say **as the case may be** or **whatever the case may be** to indicate that the statement you are making applies equally to the two or more alternatives that you have mentioned. *They know how everything works – or doesn't work, as the case may be.*

15 If you say that a task or situation is **a case of** a particular thing, you mean that it consists of that thing or can be described as that thing. *It's a case of relaxing, then playing... It's not a case of whether anyone would notice or not.* =a matter of

16 If you say that something is **a case in point**, you mean that it is a good example of something you have just mentioned. *In many cases religious persecution is at the root of mass flights. A case in point is colonial India.*

17 If you say that something **is the case**, you mean that it is true or correct. *You'll probably notice her having difficulty swallowing. If this is the case, give her plenty of liquids... Consumers had hoped the higher prices would mean more goods in stores. But that was not the case.* V inflects

case 2 containers

case /keɪs/ **cases** ◆◆◇◇◇

1 A **case** is a container that is specially designed to hold or protect something. *...a black case for his spectacles. ...a 10-foot-long stuffed alligator in a glass case.* ● See also **attaché case, bookcase, briefcase, packing case, pillowcase, showcase.** N-COUNT: oft n N

2 A **case** is a suitcase. N-COUNT

3 A **case** of wine or other alcoholic drink is a box containing several bottles, usually twelve, which is sold as a single unit. *...a case of champagne.* N-COUNT: oft N *of* n

case 3 grammar term

case /keɪs/ **cases**

1 In the grammar of many languages, the **case** of a group such as a noun group or adjective group is the form it has which shows its relationship to other groups in the sentence. See also **accusative, nominative**. N-COUNT

2 See also **lower case, upper case.**

casebook /keɪsbʊk/ **casebooks.** A **casebook** is a written record of the cases dealt with by someone such as a doctor, social worker, or police officer. N-COUNT

case history, case histories. A person's **case history** is the record of past events or problems that have affected them, especially their medical history. *I took her to a homoeopath, who started by taking a very long and detailed case history.* N-COUNT

case law. **Case law** is law that has been established by following decisions made by judges in earlier cases; a legal term. N-UNCOUNT

caseload /keɪsloʊd/ **caseloads.** The **caseload** of someone such as a doctor, social worker, or lawyer is the number of cases that they have to deal with. *His caseload of 200 active files increased to 350 as waves of new clients arrived.* N-COUNT: oft with poss

casement /keɪsmənt/ **casements.** A **casement** or a **casement window** is a window that opens by means of hinges, usually at the side; used in written English. N-COUNT

case study, case studies. A **case study** is a written account that gives detailed information about a person, group, or thing and their development over a period of time. *...a large case study of malaria in West African children.* ◆◇◇◇◇ N-COUNT

casework /keɪswɜːʳk/. **Casework** is social work that involves actually dealing or working with the people who need help. N-UNCOUNT

caseworker /keɪswɜːʳkəʳ/ **caseworkers.** A **caseworker** is someone who does casework. N-COUNT

cash /kæʃ/ **cashes, cashing, cashed** ◆◆◆◆◇

1 **Cash** is money in the form of notes and coins rather than cheques. *...two thousand pounds in cash.* N-UNCOUNT

● See also **hard cash, petty cash.**

2 In informal English, **cash** means the same as money, especially money which is immediately available. *...a state-owned financial-services group with plenty of cash.* N-UNCOUNT =money

3 If you **cash** a cheque, you exchange it at a bank for the amount of money that it is worth. *There are similar charges if you want to cash a cheque or withdraw money at a branch other than your own.* VERB V n

cash in PHRASAL VERB

1 If you say that someone **cashes in** on a situation, you disapprove of them for using it to gain an advantage, often in an unfair or dishonest way. *Residents said local gang leaders had cashed in on the violence to seize valuable land... He said that public servants should use government to serve and not to cash in.* PRAGMATICS V P on n V P

2 If you **cash in** something such as an insurance policy, you exchange it for money. *Avoid cashing in a policy early as you could lose out heavily... He did not cash in his shares.* V P n (not pron) Also V n P

cash-and-carry, cash-and-carries. A **cash-and-carry** is a large shop where you can buy goods in large quantities at a lower price than in ordinary shops. Cash-and-carries are not only open to the general public, but usually to people in business who buy goods for their shops or companies. N-COUNT =wholesaler's

cash card, cash cards; also spelled **cashcard.** A **cash card** is a card that banks give to their customers so that they can get money out of a cashpoint. N-COUNT =cashpoint card

cash cow, cash cows. In business, a **cash cow** is a product or investment that steadily continues to be profitable. *The business was such a cash cow that the managers just milked its sales and grew lazy at manufacturing.* N-COUNT

cash crop, cash crops. A **cash crop** is a crop that is grown in order to be sold. *Cranberries have become a major cash crop.* N-COUNT

cash desk, cash desks. A **cash desk** is a place in a large shop where you pay for the things you want to buy. *She took the tracksuit to the cash desk and paid.* N-COUNT =counter

cash dispenser, cash dispensers. A **cash dispenser** is a machine built into the wall of a bank or other building, which allows people to take out money from their bank account by using a special card. N-COUNT

cashew /kæʃuː, kæʃuː/ **cashews.** A **cashew** or a **cashew nut** is a curved nut that you can eat. N-COUNT

cash flow; also spelled **cashflow.** The **cash flow** of a firm or business is the movement of money into and out of it. *A French-based pharmaceuticals company ran into cash-flow problems and faced liquidation.* ◆◇◇◇◇ N-UNCOUNT

cashier /kæʃɪəʳ/ **cashiers, cashiering, cashiered** ◆◇◇◇◇

1 A **cashier** is a person that customers pay money to or get money from in a shop, garage, or bank. N-COUNT

2 If a person in the armed forces **is cashiered,** he or she is forced to leave because they have done something seriously wrong. *The government had to recall many officers who had been cashiered on political grounds. ...a cashiered army colonel.* VB: usu passive be V-ed V-ed

cashmere /kæʃmɪəʳ, AM kæʒmɪr/. **Cashmere** is a kind of very fine, soft wool. *...a big soft cashmere sweater.* ◆◇◇◇◇ N-UNCOUNT: oft N n

cashpoint /kæʃpɔɪnt/ **cashpoints.** In British English, a **cashpoint** is the same as a **cash dispenser. Cashpoint** is a trademark. The usual American word is **ATM.** N-COUNT

cash register, cash registers. A **cash register** is a machine in a shop, pub, or restaurant that is used to add up and record how much money people pay, and in which the money is kept. N-COUNT =till

cash-starved. A **cash-starved** company or organization does not have enough money to operate properly, usually because another organization, such as the government, is not giving them the money that they need; used in journalism. *We are heading for a crisis, with cash-starved councils forced to cut back on vital community services.* ADJ: usu ADJ n

cash-strapped. If journalists describe a person or organization as **cash-strapped,** they mean that they do not have enough money to buy or pay for the things they want or need. *Union leaders say the wage package is the best they believe the cash-strapped government will offer.* ADJ: usu ADJ n

casing /keɪsɪŋ/ **casings.** A **casing** is a substance or object that covers something and protects it. *...the outer casings of missiles.* N-COUNT: oft supp N

casino /kəsiːnoʊ/ **casinos.** A **casino** is a building or room where people play gambling games such as roulette. ◆◆◇◇◇ N-COUNT

cask /kɑːsk, kæsk/ **casks.** A **cask** is a wooden barrel that is used for storing things, especially alcoholic drink. *The casks of sherry are stored horizontally one on top of the other.* N-COUNT =barrel

casket /kɑːskɪt, kæsk-/ **caskets**

1 A **casket** is a small box in which you keep valuable things; a literary use. *He reached sideways and picked up a bronze casket which stood on his desk.* N-COUNT

2 A **casket** is a coffin; used mainly in American English. N-COUNT

cassava /kəsɑːvə/

1 **Cassava** is a South American plant with thick roots. It is grown for food. N-UNCOUNT =manioc

2 **Cassava** is a substance that comes from the root of the cassava plant and is used to make flour. N-UNCOUNT

casserole /kæsəroʊl/ **casseroles, casseroling, casseroled** ◆◇◇◇◇

1 A **casserole** is a dish made of meat and vegetables that have been cooked slowly in a liquid. *...a huge beef casserole, full of herbs, vegetables and wine.* N-COUNT: oft n N

2 A **casserole** or a **casserole dish** is a large heavy container with a lid. You cook casseroles and other dishes in it. *Place all the chopped vegetables into a casserole dish. ...a flameproof casserole.* N-COUNT

3 If you **casserole** meat and vegetables, you cook them slowly in a liquid. *If you casserole chicken pieces, take the skin off first. ...casseroled chicken.* VERB V n V-ed

cassette /kəset/ **cassettes.** A **cassette** is a small, flat, rectangular plastic container with magnetic tape inside which is used for recording and playing back sounds. *His two albums released on cassette have sold more than 10 million copies.* ◆◆◇◇◇ N-COUNT: also on N =tape

cassette player, cassette players. A **cassette player** is a machine that is used for playing cassettes and sometimes also recording them. N-COUNT

cassette recorder, cassette recorders. A **cassette recorder** is a machine that is used for recording and listening to cassettes. N-COUNT =tape recorder

cassock /kæsək/ **cassocks.** A **cassock** is a long robe, often black, that is worn by members of the clergy in some churches. *Over his long black cassock he had donned the white surplice he normally wore only in church.* N-COUNT

cast /kɑːst, kæst/ **casts, casting.** The form **cast** is used in the present tense and is the past tense and past participle. ◆◆◆◆◇

1 The **cast** of a play or film is all the people who act in it. *The show is very amusing and the cast are very good.* N-COUNT-COLL

2 To **cast** an actor in a play or film means to choose them to act a particular role in it. *The world premiere of Harold Pinter's new play casts Ian Holm in the lead role... He was cast as a college professor... He had no trouble casting the movie.* ♦ **casting** *The film could have done without the casting of the director's daughter in a central role. ...the casting director of Ealing film studios.* VERB V n in/as n V n N-UNCOUNT: oft N of n, N n

3 To **cast** someone in a particular way or as a particular thing means to describe them in that way or VERB

suggest they are that thing. *Democrats have been worried about being cast as the party of the poor... Holland would never dare cast himself as a virtuoso pianist.* V n *as/in* n; V pron-refl *as/in* n

4 If you **cast** your eyes or **cast** a look in a particular direction, you look quickly in that direction; used in written English. *He cast a stern glance at the two men... I cast my eyes down briefly... The maid, casting black looks, hurried out.* VERB; V n prep/adv; V n; Also V n n

5 If something **casts** a light or shadow somewhere, it causes it to appear there; used in written English. *The moon cast a bright light over the yard... They flew in over the beach, casting a huge shadow.* VERB; V n prep; V n

6 To **cast** doubt on something means to cause people to be unsure about it. *Last night a top criminal psychologist cast doubt on the theory.* VERB; V n *on* n

7 When you **cast** your vote in an election, you vote. *About ninety-five per cent of those who cast their votes approve the new constitution... Gaviria had been widely expected to obtain well over half the votes cast.* VERB; V n; V-ed

8 To **cast** something or someone somewhere means to throw them there; a literary use. *Any true lover casting a pin into the fountain and gazing into it will see his or her future partner... John had Maude and her son cast into a dungeon.* VERB; V n prep; *have* n V-ed prep

9 When someone **casts** a fishing line or **casts**, they throw one end of the fishing line into the water. *Some way from them, the fisherman cast his line.* VERB; V n; Also V

10 To **cast** an object means to make it by pouring a liquid such as hot metal into a specially shaped container and leaving it there until it becomes hard. *The stair grips, cast in either brass or bronze, resemble exotic sea shells.* VERB; V-ed *in* n; Also V n *in* n, V n

11 A **cast** is a model that has been made by pouring a liquid such as plaster or hot metal onto something or into something, so that when it hardens it has the same shape as that thing. *An orthodontist took a cast of the inside of Billy's mouth to make a dental plate.* N-COUNT: oft N *of* n; =casting

12 A **cast** is the same as a **plaster cast**. *She had one arm in a cast and a bandage over her forehead.* N-COUNT

13 If someone has a particular **cast** of mind or **cast** of thought, they have that kind of character or way of thinking of things. *The Social Democratic Party was full of people of an academic cast of mind... Hers was an essentially sunny cast of mind.* N-COUNT

14 See also **casting**.

15 • to **cast anchor**: see **anchor**. • to **cast aspersions**: see **aspersions**. • **the die is cast**: see **die**. • to **cast lots**: see **lot**. • to **cast your mind back**: see **mind**. • to **cast your net wide**: see **net**. • to **cast pearls before swine**: see **pearl**.

cast around for; the form **cast about for** is also used, mainly in British English. If you **cast around for** something or **cast about for** it, you try to find it or think of it. *She had been casting around for a good excuse to go to New York.* PHRASAL VERB; V P P n

cast aside. If you **cast aside** someone or something, you get rid of them because they are no longer necessary or useful to you. *Sweden needs to cast aside outdated policies and thinking... The Princess was cruelly cast aside when she failed to produce an heir... Now that Fantina is old, she has cast her aside like some useless object.* PHRASAL VERB =reject; V P n (not pron); V n P

cast down. If someone **is cast down** by something, they are sad or worried because of it; a literary expression. *I am not cast down by it because I believe in the fundamental strength of the business... Ever since I saw the diary excerpts I've been cast down.* PHRASAL VERB PASSIVE =depressed; *be* V-ed P; V-ed P

cast off PHRASAL VERB

1 If you **cast off** something, you get rid of it because it is no longer necessary or useful to you, or because it is harmful to you; a literary expression. *The essay exhorts women to cast off their servitude to husbands and priests... There was an extraordinary feeling of hope and relief, as if a great burden had been cast off.* • See also **cast-off**. V P n (not pron); Also V n P

2 If you are on a boat and you **cast off**, you untie the rope that is keeping the boat in a fixed position. *He cast off, heading out to the bay.* V P

cast out. To **cast out** something or someone means to get rid of them because you do not like or need them, or do not want to take responsibility for them. *One of the roles which science plays is that of casting out superstition... To be cast out from civilization was the worst fate that could possibly befall me.* PHRASAL VERB =throw out; V P n (not pron); Also V n P

castanets /kæstənets/. **Castanets** are a Spanish musical instrument consisting of two small round pieces of wood or plastic held together by a cord. You hold the castanets in your hand and knock the pieces together with your fingers. N-PLURAL: also *a pair of* N

castaway /kɑːstəweɪ, kæst-/ **castaways.** A **castaway** is a person who has managed to swim or float to a lonely island or shore after their boat has been wrecked. N-COUNT

caste /kɑːst, kæst/ **castes** ◆◆◇◇◇

1 A **caste** is one of the traditional social classes into which people are divided in a Hindu society. *Most of the upper castes worship the Goddess Kali.* N-COUNT =class

2 **Caste** is the system of dividing people in a society into different social classes. *Caste is defined primarily by social honour attained through personal life-style... The caste system shapes nearly every facet of Indian life.* N-UNCOUNT =class

castellated /kæstəleɪtɪd/. A **castellated** wall or building has turrets and battlements like a castle; a technical term in architecture. *...a castellated hotel styled from local honey-coloured sandstone.* ADJ: usu ADJ n

caster /kɑːstəʳ, kæstəʳ/. See **castor**.

caster sugar; also spelled **castor sugar.** In Britain, **caster sugar** is white sugar that has been very finely ground. It is used in cooking. ◆◇◇◇◇ N-UNCOUNT

castigate /kæstɪgeɪt/ **castigates, castigating, castigated.** If you **castigate** someone or something, you scold them or criticize them severely; a formal word. *Marx never lost an opportunity to castigate colonialism... She castigated him for having no intellectual interests.* ♦ **castigation** /kæstɪgeɪʃᵊn/ *Helen's merciless castigation of Michelle was prompted by her daughter's year-long deception.* ◆◇◇◇◇ VERB =chastise; V n; V n *for* n/-ing; N-UNCOUNT

casting /kɑːstɪŋ, kæst-/ **castings.** A **casting** is an object or piece of machinery which has been made by pouring a liquid such as hot metal into a container, so that when it hardens it has the required shape. *...stainless steel castings for Waterloo Station.* • See also **cast**. ◆◇◇◇◇ N-COUNT =cast

casting vote, casting votes. When a committee has given an equal number of votes for and against a proposal, the chairperson can give a **casting vote**. This vote decides whether or not the proposal will be passed. *The vote was tied and a local union leader used his casting vote in favour of the return to work.* N-COUNT: usu sing

cast iron ◆◇◇◇◇

1 **Cast iron** is iron which contains a small amount of carbon. It is hard and cannot be bent so it has to be made into objects by casting. *Made from cast iron, it is finished in graphite enamel. ...the cast-iron chair legs.* N-UNCOUNT

2 A **cast-iron** guarantee or alibi is one that is absolutely certain to be effective and will not fail you. *They would have to offer cast-iron guarantees to invest in long-term projects.* ADJ: usu ADJ n

castle /kɑːsᵊl, kæsᵊl/ **castles** ◆◆◆◇◇

1 A **castle** is a large building with thick, high walls. Castles were built by important people, such as kings, in former times, especially for protection during wars and battles. • See also **sand castle**. N-COUNT

2 In chess, a **castle** is a piece that can be moved forwards, backwards, or sideways. N-COUNT =rook

cast-off, cast-offs; also spelled **castoff. Cast-off** things, especially clothes, are ones which you no longer use because they are old or unfashionable, and which you give to someone else or throw away. *Alexandra looked plump and awkward in her cast-off clothing.* ► Also a noun. *I never had anything new to wear as a child, only a cousin's cast-offs.* ◆◇◇◇◇ ADJ: ADJ n; N-COUNT: usu pl

castor /kɑːstəʳ, kæst-/ **castors;** also spelled **caster.** **Castors** are small wheels fitted to a piece of furniture so that it can be moved more easily. N-COUNT

castor oil. **Castor oil** is a thick yellow oil that is obtained from the seeds of the castor oil plant. It has a very unpleasant taste and in former times was used as a medicine. *She has gone to bed and had a dose of castor oil.* N-UNCOUNT

castor sugar. See **caster sugar.**

castrate /kæstreɪt, AM kæstreɪt/ **castrates, castrating, castrated.** To **castrate** a male animal means to remove its testicles so that it cannot reproduce. *In the ancient world, it was probably rare to castrate a dog or cat. ...a castrated male horse.* ♦ **castration** /kæstreɪʃᵊn/ **castrations** *...the castration of male farm animals.* ◆◇◇◇◇ VERB; V n; V-ed; N-VAR

casual /kæʒuəl/ ◆◆◇◇◇

1 If you are **casual**, you are, or you pretend to be, relaxed and not very concerned about what is happening or what you are doing. *It's difficult for me to be casual about anything... He's an easy-going, friendly young man with a casual sort of attitude towards money.* ♦ **casually** *'No need to hurry,' Ben said casually.* ♦ **casualness** *Bayldon asked the question with studied casualness.* ADJ-GRADED =unconcerned; ADV-GRADED: ADV with v; N-UNCOUNT

2 A **casual** event or situation happens by chance or without planning. *What you mean as a casual remark could be misinterpreted... Even a casual observer could hardly have failed to notice the heightening of an already tense atmosphere.* ADJ: ADJ n

3 **Casual** clothes are ones that you normally wear at home or on holiday, and not on formal occasions. *I also bought some casual clothes for the weekend.* ♦ **casually** *They were smartly but casually dressed.* ADJ-GRADED: ADJ n ≠formal; ADV-GRADED: ADV -ed, ADV after v

4 **Casual** work is done for short periods and not on a permanent or regular basis. *...establishments which employ people on a casual basis, such as pubs and restaurants... It became increasingly expensive to hire casual workers.* ADJ: ADJ n =temporary ≠permanent

casualty /kæʒuəlti/ **casualties** ◆◆◆◇◇

1 A **casualty** is a person who is injured or killed in a war or in an accident. *Troops fired on demonstrators near the Royal Palace causing many casualties.* N-COUNT

2 A **casualty** of a particular event or situation is a person or a thing that has suffered badly as a result of the event or situation. *Fiat has been one of the greatest casualties of the recession.* N-COUNT: usu N *of* n =victim

3 In British English, **casualty** is the ward or department of a hospital where people who have severe injuries or sudden illness are taken for emergency treatment. The usual American expression is **emergency room.** *I was taken to casualty at St Thomas's Hospital.* N-UNCOUNT

casuistry /kæzjuɪstri, AM kæʒu-/. **Casuistry** is reasoning that is extremely subtle and designed to mislead other people; a formal word. N-UNCOUNT

cat /kæt/ **cats** ◆◆◆◇◇

1 A **cat** is a small, furry animal with a tail, whiskers, and sharp claws. Cats are often kept as pets. N-COUNT

2 **Cats** are lions, tigers, and other wild animals in the same family. N-COUNT

3 See also **Cheshire cat, fat cat, wildcat.**

4 If you **let the cat out of the bag**, you tell people about something that was being kept secret. You often do this by mistake. PHRASES V inflects

5 You say **'Curiosity killed the cat'** in order to tell someone that they should not be curious about something which does not concern them. *'All right, I've been reading it. So what?'—'Curiosity killed the cat, that's what.'* PRAGMATICS

6 If you **look like something the cat dragged in** or **brought in**, you are very untidy or dirty. *I must look like something the cat dragged in.* Vs inflect

7 In a fight or contest, if the stronger person or group plays **cat and mouse**, or a **game of cat and mouse**, with the other, they choose to defeat their opponent slowly, using skill and deceit, rather than force or violence. *After three hours of playing cat and mouse, they threatened to open fire on our vessel, so we stopped... It's a cat-and-mouse game to him, and I'm the bloody mouse.* usu v PHR, PHR n

8 If you **put the cat among the pigeons** or **set the cat among the pigeons**, you cause argument or controversy by doing or saying something. *The bank is poised to put the cat among the pigeons this morning by slashing the cost of borrowing.* V inflects

9 If you say **'There's no room to swing a cat'** or **'You can't swing a cat'**, you mean that the place you are talking about is very small or crowded. *It was described as a large, luxury mobile home, but there was barely room to swing a cat.* with brd-neg, usu v-link PHR

cataclysm /kætəklɪzəm/ **cataclysms.** A **cataclysm** is an event that causes great change or harm; a formal word. N-COUNT

cataclysmic /kætəklɪzmɪk/. A **cataclysmic** event is one that changes a situation or society very greatly, especially in an unpleasant way; a formal word. *...the cataclysmic events that were destroying his faith in humanity... Few had expected that change to be as cataclysmic as it turned out to be.* ADJ-GRADED

catacomb /kætəkuːm, AM -koʊm/ **catacombs.** **Catacombs** are a series of ancient underground passages and rooms, especially under a city. They used to be used for burial. N-COUNT: usu pl

Catalan /kætəlæn/ ◆◇◇◇◇

1 Something that is **Catalan** belongs or relates to Catalonia, its people, or its language. Catalonia is a region of Spain. *...the Catalan language, flag and anthem.* ADJ: usu ADJ n

2 **Catalan** is one of the languages spoken in Catalonia. *The publication of books in Catalan was permitted once again in the mid-1940s.* N-UNCOUNT

catalogue /kætəlɒg/ **catalogues, cataloguing, catalogued;** spelled **catalog** in American English. ◆◆◇◇◇

1 A **catalogue** is a list of things such as the goods you can buy from a particular company, the objects in a museum, or the books in a library. *...the world's biggest seed catalogue.* N-COUNT =list

2 To **catalogue** things means to make a list of them. *The Royal Greenwich Observatory was founded to observe and catalogue the stars.* VERB =list V n

3 A **catalogue** of similar things, especially bad things, is a number of them considered or discussed one after another. *His story is a catalogue of misfortune. ...a catalogue of nuclear disasters.* N-COUNT: N *of* n

4 If you **catalogue** a series of similar events or qualities, you list them. *Speaker after speaker lined up to catalogue a series of failures under his leadership.* VERB =list V n

catalyse /kætəlaɪz/ **catalyses, catalysing, catalysed;** spelled **catalyze** in American English.

1 If something **catalyses** a thing or a situation, it makes it active. *Any unexpected circumstance that arises may catalyze a sudden escalation of violence.* VERB V n

2 If something **catalyses** a reaction or event, it causes it to happen; a technical use in chemistry. *It had been known for some time that chemical reactions can be catalyzed by materials with large surface areas... The wires do not have a large enough surface to catalyse a big explosion.* VERB *be* V-ed V n

catalysis /kətælɪsɪs/. **Catalysis** is the speeding up of a chemical reaction by adding a catalyst to it; a technical term in chemistry. N-UNCOUNT

catalyst /kætəlɪst/ **catalysts** ◆◇◇◇◇

1 You can describe a person or thing that causes a change or event to happen as a **catalyst**. *I very much hope that this case will prove to be a catalyst for change... He said he saw the bank's role as a catalyst to encourage foreign direct investment.* N-COUNT: oft N *for* n

2 A **catalyst** is a substance that causes a chemical reaction to take place more quickly. N-COUNT

catalytic /kætəlɪtɪk/ ◆◇◇◇◇

1 A **catalytic** substance or a substance with **catalytic** properties is a substance which increases the speed of a chemical reaction; a technical use in chemistry. *...carbon molecules with unusual chemical and catalytic properties.* ADJ: ADJ n

2 If you describe a person or thing as having a **catalytic** effect, you mean that they cause things to happen or they increase the speed at which things happen. *Governments do, however, have a vital catalytic role in orchestrating rescue operations.* ADJ-GRADED: usu ADJ n

catalytic converter, catalytic converters. A **catalytic converter** is a device which is fitted to a car's exhaust to reduce the amount of pollutants coming from the exhaust. N-COUNT

catamaran /kætəmərən/ **catamarans.** A **catamaran** is a sailing boat with two parallel hulls that are held in place by a single deck. N-COUNT

catapult /kætəpʌlt/ **catapults, catapulting, catapulted** ◆◇◇◇◇

1 In British English, a **catapult** is a device for shooting small stones. It is made of a Y-shaped stick with a piece of elastic tied between the two top parts. The usual American word is **slingshot.** N-COUNT

2 A **catapult** is a device that is used to launch aircraft from an aircraft carrier. N-COUNT

3 If someone or something **catapults** or **is catapulted** through the air, they are thrown very suddenly, quickly, and violently through it. *Mr. Jensen practically catapulted out of the jeep and ran towards Pete... The car catapulted out of the pits and headed for the first bend... He was catapulted into the side of the van.* V-ERG V prep be V-ed prep/adv Also V n prep/adv

4 If something **catapults** you into a particular state or situation, or if you **catapult** there, you are suddenly and unexpectedly caused to be in that state or situation. *'Basic Instinct' catapulted her to top status among Hollywood's glamour goddesses... Suddenly she was catapulted into his jet-set lifestyle.* V-ERG V n prep/adv Also V to n

cataract /kætərækt/ **cataracts** ◆◇◇◇◇

1 **Cataracts** are layers over a person's eyes that prevent them from seeing properly. Cataracts usually develop because of old age or illness. *In one study, light smokers were more than twice as likely to get cataracts as non-smokers... Age is not a factor in cataract surgery.* N-COUNT: usu pl, N n

2 A **cataract** is a large waterfall; a literary use. *The peaks, wreathed in mists and split by cataracts, are twisted and gnarled.* N-COUNT

catarrh /kətɑːʳ/. **Catarrh** is a medical condition in which a lot of mucus is produced in your nose and throat. You may get catarrh when you have a cold. *Hay-fever is characterized by red, itchy eyes, sneezing and catarrh.* N-UNCOUNT

catastrophe /kətæstrəfi/ **catastrophes.** A **catastrophe** is an unexpected event that causes great suffering or damage. *From all points of view, war would be a catastrophe... If the world is to avoid environmental catastrophe, advanced economies must undergo a profound transition.* ◆◆◇◇◇ N-COUNT =disaster

catastrophic /kætəstrɒfɪk/ ◆◇◇◇◇

1 Something that is **catastrophic** involves or causes a sudden terrible disaster. *A tidal wave caused by the earthquake hit the coast causing catastrophic damage... The water shortage in this country is potentially catastrophic... The Chinese minister warned that if war broke out, it would be catastrophic for the whole world.* ♦ **catastrophically** /kætəstrɒfɪkli/ *The faulty left-hand engine failed catastrophically as the aircraft approached the airport.* ADJ-GRADED =disastrous ADV-GRADED: usu ADV after v, also ADV adj/-ed/adv

2 If you describe something as **catastrophic**, you mean that it is very bad or unsuccessful. *...another catastrophic attempt to arrest control from a rival Christian militia... His mother's untimely death had a catastrophic effect on him.* ADJ-GRADED =disastrous

♦ **catastrophically** *By the time we had to sell, prices had fallen catastrophically.* ADV-GRADED: usu ADV after v

catatonic /kætətɒnɪk/. If you describe someone as being in a **catatonic** state, you mean that they are not moving or responding at all, usually as a result of illness, shock, or drug abuse. *...and the traumatised heroine sinks into a catatonic trance.* ADJ-GRADED

catbird seat /kætbɜːʳd siːt/. In informal American English, if you say that someone is **in the catbird seat**, you think that their situation is very good. *If he had not been hurt I think his team would be sitting in the catbird seat.* PHRASE: v-link PHR

cat burglar, cat burglars. A **cat burglar** is a thief who steals from houses or other buildings by climbing up walls and entering through windows or through the roof. N-COUNT

catcall /kætkɔːl/ **catcalls. Catcalls** are loud noises that people make to show that they disapprove of something they are watching or listening to. *The crowd is already restive, greeting the hapless opening act with boos and catcalls.* N-COUNT: usu pl =jeer ≠cheer

catch /kætʃ/ **catches, catching, caught** ◆◆◆◆◇

1 If you **catch** a person or animal, you capture them after pursuing them, or by using a trap, net, or other device. *Police say they are confident of catching the gunman... Where did you catch the fish?... I wondered if it was an animal caught in a trap.* VERB =capture V n V-ed

2 If you **catch** an object that is moving through the air, you seize it with your hands. *I jumped up to catch a ball and fell over.* ► Also a noun. *He missed the catch and the match was lost.* VERB V n N-COUNT

3 If you **catch** a part of someone's body, you take or seize it with your hand, often in order to stop them going somewhere. *Liz caught his arm... He knelt beside her and caught her hand in both of his... Garrido caught her by the wrist.* VERB =seize V n V n prep

4 If something **catches** something else, it hits it accidentally or manages to hit it. *The stinging slap almost caught his face... I may have caught him with my elbow but it was just an accident... He caught her on the side of her head with his other fist.* VERB V n V n *with* n V n *on* n

5 If something **catches** on or in an object or **is caught** on or in it, it accidentally becomes attached to the object or becomes trapped. *When she tried to follow, her heel caught on a rusty bedspring... A man caught his foot in the lawnmower.* V-ERG V prep V n prep

6 When you **catch** a bus, train, or plane, you get on it in order to travel somewhere. *We were in plenty of time for Anthony to catch the ferry... He caught a taxi to Harrods.* VERB =get ≠miss V n V n prep

7 If you **catch** someone doing something wrong, you see or find them doing it. *He caught a youth breaking into a car... I don't want to catch you pushing yourself into the picture to get some personal publicity... Three years ago my wife and I divorced. I caught her with her boss.* VERB V n -ing V n prep

8 If you **catch** yourself doing something, especially something surprising, you suddenly become aware that you are doing it. *I caught myself feeling almost sorry for poor Mr Laurence.* VERB =find V pron-refl -ing

9 If you **catch** something or **catch** a glimpse of it, you notice it or manage to see it briefly. *As she turned back she caught the puzzled look on her mother's face... He caught a glimpse of the man's face in a shop window.* VERB ≠miss V n

10 If you **catch** something that someone has said, you manage to hear it. *His ears caught a faint cry... I do not believe I caught your name... The men out in the corridor were trying to catch what they said.* VERB ≠miss V n V wh

11 If you **catch** a TV or radio programme or an event, you manage to see or listen to it. *Bill turns on the radio to catch the local news... The exhibition is on at Droitwich until May 24. You can also catch it at Leominster from June 5.* VERB ≠miss V n

12 If you **catch** someone, you manage to contact or meet them to talk to them, especially when they are just about to go somewhere else. *I dialled Elizabeth's number thinking I might catch her before she left for work... Hello, Dolph. Glad I caught you.* VERB ≠miss V n

13 If something or someone **catches** you by surprise or at a bad time, you were not expecting them or do not feel ready or able to deal with them. *She looked as if the photographer had caught her by surprise... I'm sorry but I just cannot say anything. You've caught me at a bad time... The sheer number of spectators has caught everyone unprepared.* VERB V n prep V n adj

14 If something **catches** your attention or your eye, you notice it or become interested in it. *My shoes caught his attention... A quick movement across the aisle caught his eye.* VERB V n

15 If someone or something **catches** a mood or an atmosphere, they successfully represent it or reflect it. *There's no doubt Mr Yeltsin's speech caught the mood of most deputies.* VERB =capture V n

16 If you **are caught** in a storm or other unpleasant situation, it happens when you cannot avoid its V-PASSIVE

effects. *When he was fishing off the island he was caught in a storm and almost drowned... Visitors to the area were caught between police and the rioters.* be/get V-ed prep

17 If you **are caught between** two alternatives or two people, you do not know which one to choose or follow. *The Jordanian leader is caught between both sides in the dispute... She was caught between envy and admiration.* V-PASSIVE be V-ed *between* pl-n

18 If you **catch** a cold or a disease, you become ill with it. *The more stress you are under, the more likely you are to catch a cold.* VERB =contract V n

19 To **catch** liquids or small pieces that fall from somewhere means to collect them in a container. *The fish is laid out on a large serving plate to catch the juices. ...a specially designed breadboard with a tray to catch the crumbs.* VERB =collect V n

20 If something **catches** the light or if the light **catches** it, it reflects the light and looks bright or shiny. *They saw the ship's guns, catching the light of the moon... Often a fox goes across the road in front of me and I just catch it in the headlights.* VERB V n V n *in* n

21 If the wind or water **catches** something, it carries or pushes it along. *A gust of wind caught the parachute.* VERB V n

22 A **catch** on a window, door, or container is a device that fastens it. *She fiddled with the catch of her bag... Fit windows with safety locks or catches.* N-COUNT

23 A **catch** is a hidden problem or difficulty in a plan or an offer that seems surprisingly good. *The catch is that you work for your supper, and the food and accommodation can be very basic... 'It's your money. You deserve it.'—'What's the catch?'* N-COUNT: usu sing =snag

24 When people have been fishing, their **catch** is the total number of fish that they have caught. *The catch included one fish over 18 pounds.* N-COUNT

25 If you describe someone as a good **catch**, you mean that they have lots of good qualities and you think their partner or employer is very lucky to have found them; an informal use. *I was so in love with him and all my friends said what a good catch he was.* N-SING

26 **Catch** is a game in which children throw a ball to each other. N-UNCOUNT

27 **Catch** is a game in which one child chases other children and tries to touch or catch one of them. N-UNCOUNT =tag

28 See also **catching**.

29 You can say things such as '**You wouldn't catch me doing that**' to emphasize that you would never do something; an informal expression. *You won't catch me giving him a bad review!... You wouldn't catch me in there, I can tell you.* PHRASES PHR -ing, PHR prep/adv PRAGMATICS

30 If someone **is caught with their trousers down** or **caught with their pants down**, something happens that they are unprepared for and that reveals something embarrassing or shocking about them, for example that they are having an affair. *It makes soldiers happy to know that somebody right at the top has been caught with his trousers down... I think we caught them with their pants down. They're a bit confused.* V inflects

31 • to **catch your breath**: see **breath**. • to **catch fire**: see **fire**. • to **catch hold of something**: see **hold**. • to **be caught between a rock and a hard place**: see **rock**. • to **be caught short**: see **short**. • to **catch sight of something**: see **sight**.

catch on PHRASAL VERB

1 When you **catch on** to something, you understand it, or realize that it is happening. *He got what he could out of me before I caught on to the kind of person he'd turned into... Wait a minute! I'm beginning to catch on.* V P *to* n V P

2 If something **catches on**, it becomes popular. *The idea has been around for ages without catching on.* V P

catch out. To **catch** someone **out** means to cause them to make a mistake that reveals that they are lying about something, do not know something, or cannot do something; used mainly in British English. *Detectives followed him for months hoping to catch him out in some deception... He did not like to be caught out on details... The government has been caught out by the speed of events.* PHRASAL VERB V n P prep Also V n P, V P n (not pron)

catch up PHRASAL VERB

1 If you **catch up** with someone who is in front of you, you reach them by walking faster than they are walking. *I stopped and waited for her to catch up... We caught up with the nuns.* V P V P *with* n

2 To **catch up** with someone means to reach the same standard, stage, or level that they have reached. *Most late developers will catch up with their friends... John began the season better than me but I have fought to catch up... During the evenings, the school is used by kids who want to catch up on English and mathematics.* V P *with* n V P V P *on/in* n

3 If you **catch up** on an activity that you have not had much time to do, you spend time doing it. *I was catching up on a bit of reading.* V P *on/with* n

4 If you **catch up** on friends who you have not seen for some time or on their lives, you talk to them and find out what has happened in their lives since you last talked together. *The ladies spent some time catching up on each other's health and families... She plans to return to Dublin to catch up with the relatives she has not seen since she married.* V P *on* n V P *with* n

5 If you **are caught up** in something, you are involved in it, usually unwillingly. *The people themselves weren't part of the conflict; they were just caught up in it... Many African women, for reasons of poverty, get caught up in the drug trade.* PASSIVE =involved be V-ed P *in* n get V-ed P *in* n Also be/get V-ed P

catch up with PHRASAL VERB

1 When people **catch up with** someone who has done something wrong, they succeed in finding them in order to arrest or punish them. *The law caught up with him yesterday.* V P P n

2 If something **catches up with** you, you are forced to deal with something unpleasant that happened or that you did in the past, which you have been able to avoid until now. *Although he subsequently became a successful businessman, his criminal past caught up with him.* V P P n

Catch 22 /kætʃ twenti tuː/. If you describe something as a **Catch 22** or a **Catch 22** situation, you mean it is an impossible situation because you cannot do one thing until you do another thing, but you cannot do the second thing until you do the first thing. *It's a Catch 22 situation here. Nobody wants to support you until you're successful, but without the support how can you ever be successful?* N-SING: oft N n

catch-all, catch-alls. A **catch-all** is a term or category which includes many different things. *The charge of 'gross indecency', is a catch-all that covers many things... To him, women's issues, that nebulous, catch-all term, most importantly means sexual equality.* N-COUNT

catcher /kætʃəʳ/ **catchers** ◆◇◇◇◇

1 In baseball, the **catcher** is the player who stands behind the batter. The catcher has a special glove for catching the ball. N-COUNT

2 You can refer to someone who catches something as a **catcher**. *...the catcher of the largest fish. ...a rat-catcher.* N-COUNT: usu with supp

catching /kætʃɪŋ/ ◆◇◇◇◇

1 If an illness or a disease is **catching**, it is easily passed on or given to someone else; an informal use. *There are those who think eczema is catching.* ADJ-GRADED: v-link ADJ =infectious

2 If a feeling or emotion is **catching**, it has a strong influence on other people and spreads quickly, for example through a crowd. *Enthusiasm is very catching.* ADJ-GRADED: v-link ADJ =infectious

catchment /kætʃmənt/ **catchments.** The **catchment** of a river is the area of land from which water flows into the river; a technical term in geography. *...land use in the catchment and floodplains of this vital river.* N-COUNT

catchment area, catchment areas. The **catchment area** of a school, hospital, or other service is the area that it serves; used mainly in British English. *...the catchment areas of the district general hospitals.* N-COUNT: oft N *of* n

catch-phrase, catch-phrases; also spelled **catch phrase**. A **catch-phrase** is a sentence or phrase which becomes popular or well-known, often because it is frequently used by a famous N-COUNT person. *Mr Bresslaw, whose catch phrase was 'I only asked', died in hospital last night.*

catchy /kætʃi/ **catchier, catchiest.** ◆◇◇◇◇ ADJ-GRADED If you describe a tune, name, or advertisement as **catchy**, you mean that it is attractive and easy to remember. *The songs were both catchy and cutting... The initiative has been given the supposedly catchy title of the 'Citizen's Charter'.*

catechism /kætɪkɪzəm/ **catechisms.** N-COUNT: usu sing In a Catholic or Orthodox Church, the **catechism** is a series of questions and answers about religious beliefs, which has to be learned by people before they can become full members of that Church.

categoric /kætɪgɒrɪk, AM -gɔːr-/. ADJ **Categoric** means the same as **categorical**; an informal word.

categorical /kætɪgɒrɪkəl, AM -gɔːr-/. ◆◇◇◇◇ ADJ-GRADED =definite If you are **categorical** about something, you state your views with certainty and firmness; a formal word. *...his categorical denial of the charges of sexual harassment... He is quite categorical that the UN should only help the innocent civilian population.*
♦ **categorically** /kætɪgɒrɪkli, AM -gɔːr-/ ADV-GRADED: ADV with v =definitely *They totally and categorically deny the charges... He stated categorically that this would be his last season in Formula One.*

categorize /kætɪgəraɪz/ **categorizes, categorizing, categorized;** ◆◇◇◇◇ VERB =classify also spelled **categorise** in British English. If you **categorize** people or things, you divide them into sets or you say which set they belong to. *Lindsay, like his films, is hard to categorise...* V n *Make a list of your child's toys and then categorise them as sociable or anti-social...* V n as n *These statements perpetuate the labeling, categorizing and discrimination of people.* V-ing
♦ **categorization** /kætɪgəraɪzeɪʃən/ **categorizations** N-VAR =classification *Her first novel, defies easy categorisation. ...the categorisation of new types of missiles.*

category /kætɪgri, AM -gɔːri/ **categories.** ◆◆◆◇◇ N-COUNT =class If people or things are divided into **categories**, they are divided into groups in such a way that the members of each group are similar to each other in some way. *This book clearly falls into the category of fictionalised autobiography... The tables were organised into six different categories... Designer wedding dresses make wedding fashion a separate category from mainstream fashion.*

cater /keɪtəʳ/ **caters, catering, catered** ◆◆◇◇◇

1 VERB In British English, to **cater** for a group of people means to provide all the things that they need or want. In American English, you **cater** to a person or group of people. *Minorca is the sort of place that caters for families...* V for n *We cater to an exclusive clientele.* V to n

2 VERB In British English, to **cater** for something means to take it into account. In American English, you **cater** to something. *We have to cater for demand.* V for n *...shops that cater for the needs of men... Exercise classes cater to all levels of fitness.* V to n

3 VERB If a person or company **caters** for an occasion such as a wedding or a party, they provide food and drink for all the people there. *Nunsmere Hall can cater for receptions of up to 300 people...* V for n *The chef is pleased to cater for vegetarian diets... Does he cater parties too?* V n ● See also **catering, self-catering**.

caterer /keɪtərəʳ/ **caterers.** ◆◇◇◇◇ N-COUNT **Caterers** are people or companies that provide food and drink for a place such as an office or for special occasions such as weddings and parties. *The caterers were already laying out the tables for lunch. ...food brought in from outside caterers.*

catering /keɪtərɪŋ/. ◆◆◇◇◇ N-UNCOUNT: also the N, oft N n **Catering** is the activity of providing food and drink for a large number of people, for example at weddings and parties. *His catering business made him a millionaire at 41... He recently did the catering for a presidential reception.*

caterpillar /kætəʳpɪləʳ/ **caterpillars.** ◆◇◇◇◇ N-COUNT A **caterpillar** is a small, worm-like animal that feeds on plants and eventually develops into a butterfly or moth.

caterwaul /kætəʳwɔːl/ **caterwauls, caterwauling, caterwauled.** VERB =wail If a person or animal **caterwauls**, they make an unpleasant noise by wailing or howling loudly. *At the water's edge they resumed caterwauling and waving their crosses.* V
► Also a noun. N-COUNT *People muffled their ears against the bird's blood-curdling caterwauls.*
♦ **caterwauling** N-UNCOUNT =wailing *There came from within the walls the highest-pitched moaning and caterwauling that I had ever heard.*

catfish /kætfɪʃ/; **catfish** is both the singular and plural form. N-VAR **Catfish** are fish with long thin spines that look like whiskers around their mouth.

catharsis /kəθɑːʳsɪs/. N-UNCOUNT **Catharsis** is the getting rid of unhappy memories or strong emotions such as anger or sadness by expressing them in some way. *He wrote out his rage and bewilderment, which gradually became a form of catharsis leading to understanding.*

cathartic /kəθɑːʳtɪk/. ADJ-GRADED Something that is **cathartic** has the effect of catharsis; a formal word. *His laughter was cathartic, an animal yelp that brought tears to his eyes. ...a liberating and cathartic experience.*

cathedral /kəθiːdrəl/ **cathedrals.** ◆◆◇◇◇ N-COUNT A **cathedral** is a very large and important church which has a bishop in charge of it. *...St. Paul's Cathedral. ...the cathedral city of Canterbury.*

catherine wheel /kæθərɪn ʰwiːl/ **catherine wheels.** N-COUNT A **catherine wheel** is a firework in the shape of a circle which spins round and round.

catheter /kæθɪtəʳ/ **catheters.** N-COUNT A **catheter** is a tube which is used to introduce liquids into a human body or to withdraw liquids from it; a medical term.

cathode-ray tube, cathode-ray tubes. N-COUNT A **cathode-ray tube** is a device used in televisions and computer terminals which sends an image onto the screen; a technical term in electronics.

Catholic /kæθlɪk/ **Catholics** ◆◆◆◇◇

1 ADJ: usu ADJ n The **Catholic** Church is the branch of the Christian Church that accepts the Pope as its leader and that is based in the Vatican in Rome. *...the Catholic Church. ...Catholic priests. ...the Catholic faith.* ● See also **Anglo-Catholic**.

2 N-COUNT A **Catholic** is a member of the Catholic Church. *At least nine out of ten Mexicans are baptised Catholics.*

3 ADJ-GRADED PRAGMATICS =varied If you describe a collection of things or people as **catholic**, you are emphasizing that they are very varied. *He was a man of catholic tastes, a lover of grand opera, history and the fine arts.*

Catholicism /kəθɒlɪsɪzəm/. ◆◇◇◇◇ N-UNCOUNT **Catholicism** is the traditions, the behaviour, and the set of Christian beliefs that are held by Catholics. *...her conversion to Catholicism.*

catkin /kætkɪn/ **catkins.** N-COUNT A **catkin** is a long, thin, soft flower that hangs on some trees, for example birch trees and hazel trees.

catnap /kætnæp/ **catnaps;** N-COUNT =doze, nap also spelled **cat-nap**. A **catnap** is a short sleep, usually one which you have during the day; an informal word.

catsuit /kætsuːt/ **catsuits.** N-COUNT A **catsuit** is a piece of women's clothing that is made in one piece and fits tightly over the body and legs.

catsup /kætsəp/. N-UNCOUNT In American English, **catsup** is a thick cold sauce made from tomatoes. The British word is **ketchup**. *...scrambled eggs smothered with catsup.*

cattery /kætəri/ **catteries.** N-COUNT A **cattery** is a place where you can leave your cat when you go on holiday.

cattle /kætəl/. ◆◆◇◇◇ N-PLURAL **Cattle** are cows and bulls. *...the finest herd of beef cattle for two hundred miles.*

cattle grid, cattle grids. N-COUNT A **cattle grid** is a set of metal bars in the surface of a road which prevents cattle and sheep from walking along the road, but allows people and vehicles to pass.

cattleman /kætəlmæn/ **cattlemen.** N-COUNT =rancher A **cattleman** is a man who looks after or owns cattle, especially in North America or Australia.

cattle market, cattle markets
1 A **cattle market** is a market where cattle are bought and sold. N-COUNT
2 If you refer to an event such as a disco or a beauty contest as a **cattle market**, you disapprove of it because it is an event where women are considered only in terms of their sexual attractiveness or availability. N-COUNT PRAGMATICS

cattle prod, cattle prods. A **cattle prod** is an object shaped like a long stick. Farmers make cattle move in a particular direction by pushing the cattle prod against the bodies of the animals. *...an electric cattle-prod.* N-COUNT

catty /kæti/ **cattier, cattiest.** If you say that someone, especially a woman or girl, is being **catty**, you mean that they are being unpleasant and spiteful; an informal word. *His mother was catty, status-conscious and loud. ...catty remarks.* ADJ-GRADED =bitchy

catwalk /kætwɔːk/ **catwalks** ◆◇◇◇◇
1 At a fashion show, the **catwalk** is a narrow platform that models walk along to display clothes. *She's been called the queen of the catwalk.* N-COUNT: usu sing
2 A **catwalk** is a narrow bridge high in the air between two parts of a tall building or on the outside of a large structure. N-COUNT

Caucasian /kɔːkeɪʒən/ **Caucasians** ◆◇◇◇◇
1 A **Caucasian** person is a white person; a formal word. *...a 25-year-old Caucasian male.* ► A **Caucasian** is someone who is Caucasian. *Ann Hamilton was a Caucasian from New England.* ADJ =white N-COUNT
2 Anthropologists use **Caucasian** to refer to someone from a racial grouping coming from Europe, North Africa and western Asia; a technical term in anthropology. *...blue eyes and Caucasian features.* ► A **Caucasian** is someone who is Caucasian. ADJ: usu ADJ n N-COUNT

caucus /kɔːkəs/ **caucuses.** A **caucus** is a group of people within an organization who share similar aims and interests or who have a lot of influence; a formal word. *...the Black Caucus of minority congressmen.* ◆◇◇◇◇ N-COUNT

caught /kɔːt/. **Caught** is the past tense and past participle of **catch**.

cauldron /kɔːldrən/ **cauldrons** ◆◇◇◇◇
1 A **cauldron** is a very large, round metal pot used for cooking over a fire; a literary word. N-COUNT
2 If you describe a situation as a **cauldron**, you mean that it is unstable or dangerous; used mainly in journalism. *A thin veneer of law and order barely keeps the seething, bubbling cauldron of chaos and anarchy in check.* N-COUNT: usu sing, oft N of n

cauliflower /kɒliflaʊəʳ, AM kɔː-/ **cauliflowers.** **Cauliflower** is a hard, roundish, white vegetable that is surrounded by green leaves. ◆◇◇◇◇ N-VAR

causal /kɔːzəl/. If there is a **causal** relationship between two things, one thing is responsible for causing the other thing; a formal word. *Rawlins stresses that it is impossible to prove a causal link between the drug and the deaths... He would dearly love to show a causal relationship between culture and imperialism, but cannot.* ADJ: usu ADJ n

causality /kɔːzælɪti/. **Causality** is the relationship of cause and effect; a formal word. *An explanation of an earthquake is a description of the chain of causality that produces it.* N-UNCOUNT

causation /kɔːzeɪʃən/
1 The **causation** of something, usually something bad, is the factors that have caused it; a formal use. *Therefore it is clear that the gene is only part of the causation of illness.* N-UNCOUNT =cause
2 **Causation** is a study of the factors involved in causing something; a formal use. *...an unexamined set of assumptions concerning social causation.* N-UNCOUNT

causative /kɔːzətɪv/. **Causative** factors are ones which are responsible for causing something; a formal word. *Both nicotine and carbon monoxide inhaled with cigarette smoking have been incriminated as causative factors. ...the prime causative agent of AIDS.* ADJ: ADJ n

cause /kɔːz/ **causes, causing, caused** ◆◆◆◆◆
1 The **cause** of an event, usually a bad event, is the thing that makes it happen. *Smoking is the biggest preventable cause of death and disease... The causes are a complex blend of local and national tensions.* N-COUNT: oft N of n ≠effect
2 To **cause** something, usually something bad, means to make it happen. *Attempts to limit family size among some minorities are likely to cause problems... This was a genuine mistake, but it did cause me some worry. ...a protein that gets into animal cells and attacks other proteins, causing disease to spread. ...the damage to Romanian democracy caused by events of the past few days.* VERB V n V n n V n to-inf V-ed
3 If you have **cause** for a particular feeling or action, you have good reasons for feeling it or doing it. *Only a few people can find any cause for celebration... Both had much cause to be grateful for the secretiveness of government in Britain.* N-UNCOUNT: N for n, N to-inf =reason
4 A **cause** is an aim or principle which a group of people supports or is fighting for. *Refusing to have one leader has not helped the cause either.* • See also **lost cause**. N-COUNT
5 If one group of people **makes common cause with** another, they act together in order to achieve a particular aim even though their aims and beliefs are normally very different; used mainly in journalism. *They make common cause for a few purposes, but for the most part, they pursue their own interests.* PHRASES V inflects
6 If you say that something is **in a good cause**, or **for a good cause**, you mean that it is worth doing or contributing to because it will help other people, for example by raising money for charity. *The Raleigh International Bike Ride is open to anyone who wants to raise money for a good cause.*

cause célèbre /koʊz seɪlebrə/ **causes célèbres;** also spelled **cause celebre**. A **cause célèbre** is a controversial issue, person, or criminal trial that has attracted a lot of public attention; a formal word. *The Kravchenko trial became a cause celebre in Paris and internationally.* N-COUNT

causeway /kɔːzweɪ/ **causeways.** A **causeway** is a raised path or road that crosses water or marshland. ◆◇◇◇◇ N-COUNT

caustic /kɔːstɪk/ ◆◇◇◇◇
1 **Caustic** chemical substances are very powerful and can dissolve other substances. *...caustic cleaning agents... Remember that this is caustic; use gloves or a spoon.* ADJ-GRADED =corrosive
2 A **caustic** remark is extremely critical, cruel, or bitter; a formal use. *His abrasive wit and caustic comments were an interviewer's nightmare... He was often caustic and mocking, or flew into rages.* ADJ-GRADED =bitter, acid
♦ **caustically** /kɔːstɪkli/ *She was caustically brilliant, yet totally loyal, unpretentious, human and tolerant.* ADV-GRADED: ADV with v, ADV adj

caustic soda. **Caustic soda** is a powerful chemical substance used to make strong soaps and drain cleaners. N-UNCOUNT

cauterize /kɔːtəraɪz/ **cauterizes, cauterizing, cauterized;** also spelled **cauterise** in British English. If a doctor **cauterizes** a wound, he or she burns it with heat or with a chemical in order to close it up and prevent it from becoming infected. *He dug out the bullet and cauterized the wound with a piece of red-hot iron.* VERB V n

caution /kɔːʃən/ **cautions, cautioning, cautioned** ◆◆◇◇◇
1 **Caution** is great care which you take in order to avoid possible danger. *Extreme caution should be exercised when buying part-worn tyres... Michael Heseltine is a man of caution.* N-UNCOUNT =prudence
2 If someone **cautions** you, they warn you about problems or danger. *Tony cautioned against misrepresenting the situation... The statement clearly was intended to caution Seoul against attempting to block the council's action again... He cautioned that opposition attacks on the Communist Party would not further political co-operation.* ► Also a noun. *There was a note of caution for the Treasury in the figures.* VERB V against n/-ing V n against/about n/-ing V that Also V n that, V n to-inf N-UNCOUNT =warning
3 If someone who has broken the law **is cautioned** by the police, they are warned that if they break the law again official action will be taken against them; used in British English. *The two men were cau-* VB: usu passive be V-ed

tioned but police say they will not be charged... Tapp was eventually cautioned for wasting police time. ► Also a noun. *In November 1987 Paula escaped with a caution. In October 1988 she was fined.* N-COUNT

4 If someone who has been arrested **is cautioned**, the police warn them that anything that they say may be used as evidence in a trial. *Nobody was cautioned after arrest. Nobody was given their rights.* VB: usu passive; *be* V-ed

5 If you **throw caution to the wind**, you behave in a way that is not considered sensible or prudent. *I threw caution to the wind and rode flat out for every point.* ● to **err on the side of caution**: see **err**. PHRASE: V inflects

cautionary /kɔːʃənri, AM -neri/. A **cautionary** story or a **cautionary** note to a story is one that is intended to give a warning to people. *Barely fifteen months later, it has become a cautionary tale of the pitfalls of international mergers and acquisitions... An editorial in The Times sounds a cautionary note.* ◆◇◇◇◇ ADJ-GRADED: usu ADJ n

cautious /kɔːʃəs/ ◆◆◆◇◇

1 Someone who is **cautious** acts very carefully in order to avoid possible danger. *The scientists are cautious about using enzyme therapy on humans... He is a very cautious man.* ♦ **cautiously** *David moved cautiously forward and looked over the edge... Cautiously, he moved himself into an upright position.* ADJ-GRADED: oft ADJ *about* n/-ing =careful ≠rash; ADV-GRADED: usu ADV with v, also ADV adj

2 If you describe someone's attitude or reaction as **cautious**, you mean that it is limited or careful; used mainly by journalists. *He has been seen as a champion of a more cautious approach to economic reform.* ♦ **cautiously** *I am cautiously optimistic that a new government will be concerned and aware about the environment... Rebel sources have so far reacted cautiously to the threat.* ADJ-GRADED =careful ≠rash, foolhardy; ADV-GRADED: usu ADV adj, also ADV with v =carefully ≠rashly

cavalcade /kævəlkeɪd/ **cavalcades.** A **cavalcade** is a procession of people on horses or in cars or carriages. *...a cavalcade of limousines and police motorcycles.* N-COUNT: oft N *of* n

cavalier /kævəlɪəʳ/. If you describe a person or their behaviour as **cavalier**, you disapprove of them because you think that they do not consider other people's feelings or take account of the seriousness of a situation. *The Editor takes a cavalier attitude to the concept of fact checking.* ADJ-GRADED [PRAGMATICS] =casual

cavalry /kævəlri/ ◆◆◇◇◇

1 The **cavalry** is the part of an army that uses fast armoured vehicles for fighting. *The Cavalry were exercising on Salisbury Plain. ...the US Army's 1st Cavalry Division.* N-SING

2 The **cavalry** is the group of soldiers in an army who ride horses. *...a young cavalry officer.* N-SING

cavalryman /kævəlrimæn/ **cavalrymen.** A **cavalryman** is a soldier who is in the cavalry, especially one who rides a horse. N-COUNT

cave /keɪv/ **caves, caving, caved.** A **cave** is a large hole in the side of a cliff or hill, or one that is under the ground. *Outside the cave mouth the blackness of night was like a curtain.* ◆◆◆◇◇ N-COUNT

cave in PHRASAL VERB

1 If something such as a roof or a ceiling **caves in**, it collapses inwards. *Part of the roof has caved in... The wall caved in to reveal a blocked-up Victorian fireplace... I had a nervous breakdown, everything just seemed to cave in on top of me.* ● see also **cave-in**. =collapse; V P

2 If you **cave in**, you suddenly stop arguing or resisting, especially when people put pressure on you to stop. *After a ruinous strike, the union caved in... The Prime Minister has caved in to backbench pressure... He's caved in on capital punishment.* =give in; V P; V P *to* n; V P *on* n

caveat /kæviæt, AM keɪv-/ **caveats.** A **caveat** is a warning of a specific limitation of something such as information or an agreement; a formal word. *With the caveat that almost every figure in this survey is suspect, it can at least be said that the world travel and tourism industry is huge... There was one caveat: he was not to enter into a merger or otherwise dilute the Roche family's control of the firm.* N-COUNT: oft N that

caveat emptor /kæviæt emptɔːʳ, AM keɪv-/. **Caveat emptor** means 'buyer beware', and is a warning for someone buying something that it is their responsibility to identify and accept any faults in it; a formal expression. *Auction house catalogues all carry a disclaimer on condition, so if you buy at auction it is caveat emptor.* CONVENTION [PRAGMATICS]

cave-in, cave-ins. A **cave-in** is the sudden collapse of the roof of a cave or mine. ◆◇◇◇◇ N-COUNT

caveman /keɪvmæn/ **cavemen.** **Cavemen** were people in prehistoric times who lived mainly in caves. N-COUNT

caver /keɪvəʳ/ **cavers.** A **caver** is someone who explores caves as a sport. N-COUNT

cavern /kævəʳn/ **caverns** ◆◇◇◇◇

1 A **cavern** is a large deep cave. N-COUNT

2 If you describe the inside of a building or a room as a **cavern**, you mean that it is very large and, usually, dark or without much furniture. *The kitchen now is a dark cavern, with an antiquated black stove in a corner.* N-COUNT

cavernous /kævəʳnəs/. A **cavernous** room or building is very large inside, and so it reminds you of a cave. *Climbing steep stairs to the choir gallery you peer into a cavernous interior.* ◆◇◇◇◇ ADJ-GRADED

caviar /kæviɑːʳ/ **caviars;** also spelled **caviare.** The salted eggs of a fish called sturgeon are referred to as **caviar**. Caviar is a very expensive food and is considered to be a luxury. ◆◇◇◇◇ N-MASS

cavil /kævəl/ **cavils, cavilling, cavilled;** spelled **caviling, caviled** in American English. If you say that someone **cavils** at something, you mean that they make unimportant and often unnecessary objections about it; a formal word, used showing disapproval. *Since the government has insisted that cash will be shifted into this area, the opposition can hardly cavil... Historians tend to cavil at suggestions that this event marked the start of the Civil War.* ► Also a noun. *These cavils aside, most of the essays are very good indeed.* VB: no passive [PRAGMATICS] =quibble; V; V *at* n; N-COUNT

cavity /kævɪti/ **cavities** ◆◇◇◇◇

1 A **cavity** is a space or hole in something such as a solid object or a person's body; a rather formal word. N-COUNT

2 In dentistry, a **cavity** is a hole in a tooth, caused by decay. N-COUNT

cavity wall, cavity walls. A **cavity wall** is a wall that consists of two separate walls with a space between them. Cavity walls help to keep out noise and cold. *...cavity wall insulation.* N-COUNT: oft N n

cavort /kəvɔːʳt/ **cavorts, cavorting, cavorted.** When people **cavort**, they leap about in a noisy, excited and, often, sexual way. *You can enjoy a quick snack while your children cavort in the sand... It was claimed she cavorted with a police sergeant in a jacuzzi but she denies this.* VERB =romp; V; V *with* n

caw /kɔː/ **caws, cawing, cawed.** When a bird such as a crow or a rook **caws**, it makes a loud harsh sound. *Outside, a raven cawed again and then there was silence... The rooks had begun their evening cawing.* VERB; V; V-ing

cayenne pepper /kaɪen pepəʳ/. **Cayenne pepper** or **cayenne** is a hot-tasting red powder made from dried peppers. It is used to flavour and add colour to food. *Season with salt, pepper and a pinch of cayenne.* N-UNCOUNT

CB /siː biː/. **CB**, an abbreviation for 'Citizens' Band', is a range of radio waves which the general public is allowed to use to send messages to each other. N-UNCOUNT

cc /siː siː/

1 **cc** is an abbreviation for 'cubic centimetres'. You use 'cc' when referring to the volume or capacity of something such as the size of a car engine. *...1,500 cc sports cars.*

2 **cc** is used at the end of a business letter to indicate that a copy is being sent to another person. *...cc J. Chater, S. Cooper.*

CD /siː diː/ **CDs.** **CD** is an abbreviation for 'compact disc'. CDs are shiny discs on which sound, especially music, is recorded. *The Beatles' Red* ◆◆◆◇◇ N-COUNT *and Blue compilations are issued on CD for the first time next month.*

CD player **CD players.** A **CD player** is a machine on which you can play the music or other sounds recorded on a CD. ◆◇◇◇◇ N-COUNT

Cdr. **Cdr** is the written abbreviation for 'Commander' when it is used as a title. *...Cdr A.C. Moore.* N-TITLE

CD-ROM /siː diː rɒm/ **CD-ROMs.** A **CD-ROM** is a shiny disc on which a very large amount of data, such as text, images, and sound, is stored. You can get the information on a CD-ROM by using a CD-ROM drive with a computer. CD-ROM is an abbreviation for 'compact disc read-only memory'. *A single CD-ROM can hold more than 500 megabytes of data... The collected Austen novels on CD-ROM will cost £35.* ◆◇◇◇◇ N-COUNT

CD-ROM drive /siː diː rɒm draɪv/ **CD-ROM drives.** A **CD-ROM drive** is the machine, or part of the machine, you use with a computer to access CD-ROMs. N-COUNT

cease /siːs/ **ceases, ceasing, ceased** ◆◆◆◇◇

1 If something **ceases**, it stops happening or existing; a formal use. *At one o'clock the rain had ceased.* VERB =stop V

2 If someone or something **ceases** to do something, they stop doing it; a formal use. *He never ceases to amaze me... The secrecy about the President's condition had ceased to matter... A small number of firms have ceased trading.* VERB V to-inf V -ing

3 If you **cease** something, you stop it happening or working; a formal use. *The Tundra Times, a weekly newspaper in Alaska, ceased publication this week.* VERB =stop V n

ceasefire /siːsfaɪəʳ/ **ceasefires;** also spelled **cease-fire**. A **ceasefire** is an arrangement in which countries or groups of people that are fighting each other agree to stop fighting. *They have agreed to a ceasefire after three years of conflict... UN officials are expressing cautious optimism that the latest cease-fire is holding.* ◆◆◆◇◇ N-COUNT =truce

ceaseless /siːsləs/. If something, often something unpleasant, is **ceaseless**, it continues for a long time without stopping or changing; a rather formal word. *There is a ceaseless struggle from noon to night.* ♦ **ceaselessly** *The characters complain ceaselessly about food queues, prices and corruption.* ADJ-GRADED =endless ADV: usu ADV with v =endlessly

cedar /siːdəʳ/ **cedars.** A **cedar** is a large evergreen tree with wide branches and small leaves shaped like needles. ► **Cedar** is the wood of this tree. *The yacht is built of cedar strip planking.* ◆◇◇◇◇ N-COUNT N-UNCOUNT: oft N n

cede /siːd/ **cedes, ceding, ceded.** If someone in a position of authority **cedes** land or power to someone else, they let them have the land or power, often as a result of military or political pressure; a formal word. *Only a short campaign took place in Puerto Rico, but after the war Spain ceded the island to America... The General had promised to cede power by January.* ◆◇◇◇◇ VERB =concede V n to n V n

cedilla /sɪdɪlə/ **cedillas.** A **cedilla** is a symbol that is written under the letter 'c' in French, Portuguese, and some other languages to show that you pronounce it like a letter 's' rather than like a letter 'k'. It is written ç. N-COUNT

ceilidh /keɪli/ **ceilidhs.** A **ceilidh** is an informal entertainment, especially in Scotland or Ireland, at which there is folk music, singing, and dancing. N-COUNT

ceiling /siːlɪŋ/ **ceilings** ◆◆◇◇◇

1 A **ceiling** is the horizontal surface that forms the top part or roof inside a room. *The rooms were spacious, with tall windows and high ceilings... The study was lined from floor to ceiling on every wall with bookcases.* N-COUNT

2 A **ceiling** on something such as prices or wages is an official upper limit that has been put on it and that cannot be exceeded. *...an informal agreement to put a ceiling on salaries... The agreement sets the ceiling of twenty-two-point-five million barrels a day on OPEC production.* N-COUNT: oft N *of* n =limit

3 A **ceiling** is the greatest height at which a particular aircraft can fly safely; a technical use. N-COUNT

celeb /sɪleb/ **celebs. Celeb** means the same as **celebrity**; an informal word which is used mainly by journalists. *In fact, celeb-spotters were rather thicker on the ground than celebs.* N-COUNT

celebrant /selɪbrənt/ **celebrants.** A **celebrant** is a person who performs or takes part in a religious ceremony; a formal word. N-COUNT

celebrate /selɪbreɪt/ **celebrates, celebrating, celebrated** ◆◆◆◇◇

1 If you **celebrate** or if you **celebrate** something, you do something enjoyable because of a special occasion or to honour someone's success. *I was in a mood to celebrate... Tom celebrated his 24th birthday two days ago.* VERB V V n

2 If an organization or country **is celebrating** an anniversary, it has existed for that length of time and is doing something special because of it. *The British Boomerang Society is celebrating its tenth anniversary this year.* VERB V n

3 When priests **celebrate** Holy Communion or Mass, they officially perform the actions and ceremonies that are involved. *Pope John Paul celebrated mass today in a city in central Poland.* VERB V n

celebrated /selɪbreɪtɪd/. A **celebrated** person or thing is famous and much admired. *He was soon one of the most celebrated young painters in England... Dean died three days before the opening of Rebel Without Cause, his most celebrated film.* ◆◆◇◇◇ ADJ-GRADED: usu ADJ n =renowned

celebration /selɪbreɪʃᵊn/ **celebrations** ◆◆◆◇◇

1 A **celebration** is a special enjoyable event that people organize because something pleasant has happened or because it is someone's birthday or anniversary. *I can tell you, there was a celebration in our house that night. ...his eightieth birthday celebrations.* N-COUNT

2 The **celebration** of something is praise and appreciation which is given to it. *This was not a memorial service but a celebration of life... He sees the poem as a celebration of human love.* N-SING: usu N *of* n

celebratory /seləbreɪtəri, AM selɪbrətɔːri/. A **celebratory** meal, drink, or other activity takes place to celebrate something such as a birthday, anniversary, or victory. *That night she, Nicholson and the crew had a celebratory dinner.* ADJ: usu ADJ n

celebrity /sɪlebrɪti/ **celebrities.** A **celebrity** is someone who is famous, especially in areas of entertainment such as films, music, writing, or sport. *In 1944, at the age of 30, Hersey suddenly became a celebrity. ...a host of celebrities.* ◆◆◇◇◇ N-COUNT =star

celery /seləri/. **Celery** is a vegetable with long pale green stalks. It is eaten raw in salads. *...a stick of celery.* ◆◇◇◇◇ N-UNCOUNT

celestial /sɪlestiəl/ ◆◇◇◇◇

1 **Celestial** is used to describe things relating to heaven or to the sky; a literary word. *...the clusters of celestial bodies in the ever-expanding universe... In the process of their careful watching and recording the celestial movements the Chinese provided valuable and interesting information for succeeding generations.* ADJ

2 If you describe something as **celestial**, you mean that it is wonderful. *...a chocolate cake with an apricot filling and celestial effect on the taste buds.* ADJ-GRADED =heavenly

celibacy /selɪbəsi/

1 If you are in a state of **celibacy**, you have not had sex with anyone for a long time or for a particular period of your life. *They have claimed that it is celibacy, rather than sex, which frees the individual.* N-UNCOUNT =chastity

2 If you are in a state of **celibacy**, you have stayed unmarried, usually because of your religious beliefs. *...young men who wish to take a vow of celibacy for life and study for the priesthood.* N-UNCOUNT

celibate /selɪbət/ **celibates**

1 Someone who is **celibate** does not marry or have sex, because of their religious beliefs. *The Pope bluntly told the world's priests yesterday to stay celibate.* ► A **celibate** is someone who is celibate. ADJ N-COUNT

2 Someone who is **celibate** does not have sex during a particular period of their life. *I was celibate for two years.* ADJ: usu v-link ADJ

cell /sel/ **cells** ◆◆◆◆◇

1 A **cell** is the smallest part of an animal or plant that is able to function independently. Every animal or plant is made up of millions of cells. *Those cells divide and give many other different types of cells. ...blood cells... Soap destroys the cell walls of bacteria.* N-COUNT

2 A **cell** is a small room in which a prisoner is locked. A **cell** is also a small room in which a monk or nun lives. N-COUNT

3 You can refer to a small group of people within a larger organization as a **cell**. *...Communist Party cells.* N-COUNT: usu n N

cellar /selə^r/ **cellars** ◆◇◇◇◇

1 A **cellar** is a room underneath a building, which is often used for storing things in. *The box of papers had been stored in a cellar at the family home.* N-COUNT

2 A person's or restaurant's **cellar** is the collection of different wines that they have. *Choose a superb wine to complement your meal from our extensive wine cellar.* N-COUNT: usu sing

cellist /tʃelɪst/ **cellists.** A **cellist** is someone who plays the cello. N-COUNT

cellmate /selmeɪt/ **cellmates;** also spelled **cell-mate.** In a prison, someone's **cellmate** is the person they share their cell with. N-COUNT: usu with poss

cello /tʃeloʊ/ **cellos.** A **cello** is a musical instrument with four strings that looks like a large violin. You play the cello with a bow while sitting down and holding it upright between your legs. ◆◇◇◇◇ N-VAR: oft *the* N

cellophane /seləfeɪn/. **Cellophane** is a thin, transparent material that is used to wrap things such as cigarette packets or boxes of chocolates. *She tore off the cellophane, pulled out a cigarette, and lit it. ...the cellophane wrapper.* N-UNCOUNT

cellphone /selfoʊn/ **cellphones;** also spelled **cell-phone.** A **cellphone** is the same as a **cellular phone**; an informal word. N-COUNT =cellular phone

cellular /seljʊlə^r/. **Cellular** means relating to the cells of animals or plants. *Many toxic effects can be studied at the cellular level.* ◆◇◇◇◇ ADJ: usu ADJ n

cellular phone, cellular phones. A **cellular phone** or **cellular telephone** is a type of telephone which does not need wires to connect it to a telephone system. N-COUNT =cellphone

cellulite /seljʊlaɪt/. **Cellulite** is lumpy fat which people may get under their skin, especially on their thighs. *Does massage get rid of cellulite?* ◆◇◇◇◇ N-UNCOUNT

celluloid /seljʊlɔɪd/. You can use **celluloid** to refer to films and the cinema. *King's works seem to lack something on celluloid.* N-UNCOUNT: oft N n

cellulose /seljʊloʊs/. **Cellulose** is a substance that exists in the cell walls of plants and is used to make paper, plastic, and various textiles and fibres. *...the cellulose in fruit skins.* N-UNCOUNT

Celsius /selsiəs/. **Celsius** is a scale for measuring temperature, in which water freezes at 0 degrees and boils at 100 degrees. It is represented by the symbol C. *Highest temperatures 11° Celsius, that's 52° Fahrenheit.* ◆◇◇◇◇ ADJ: n/num ADJ =centigrade ► Also a noun. *The thermometer shows the temperature in Celsius and Fahrenheit.* N-UNCOUNT

Celt /kelt, selt/ **Celts.** If you describe someone as a **Celt**, you mean that they are part of the racial group which comes from Scotland, Wales, Ireland, and some other areas such as Brittany. ◆◇◇◇◇ N-COUNT

Celtic /keltɪk, sel-/. If you describe something as **Celtic**, you mean that it is connected with the people and the culture of Scotland, Wales, Ireland, and some other areas such as Brittany. *...important figures in Celtic tradition.* ◆◆◇◇◇ ADJ: usu ADJ n

cement /sɪment/ **cements, cementing, cemented** ◆◆◇◇◇

1 **Cement** is a grey powder which is mixed with sand and water in order to make concrete. *Builders have trouble getting the right amount of cement into their concrete.* N-UNCOUNT

2 **Cement** is the same as **concrete**. *...the hard cold cement floor.* N-UNCOUNT =concrete

3 Glue that is made for sticking particular substances together is sometimes called **cement**. *Stick the pieces on with tile cement.* N-UNCOUNT: usu n N

4 Something that **cements** a relationship or agreement makes it stronger. *Nothing cements a friendship between countries so much as trade.* VERB V n

5 **Cement** is something that makes a relationship or agreement stronger and more long-lasting. *...the power of the party, once the cement that held the Soviet Union together... In the old days, television was the cement of society.* N-UNCOUNT: usu with supp

6 If things **are cemented** together, they are stuck or fastened together. *Most artificial joints are cemented into place.* VB: usu passive *be* V-ed prep/adv

cement mixer, cement mixers. A **cement mixer** is a machine with a large revolving container into which builders put cement, sand, and water in order to make concrete. N-COUNT

cemetery /semətri, AM -teri/ **cemeteries.** A **cemetery** is a place where dead people's bodies or their ashes are buried. ◆◆◇◇◇ N-COUNT =graveyard

cenotaph /senətɑːf, -tæf/ **cenotaphs.** A **cenotaph** is a monument that is built in honour of soldiers who died in a war. *Poppies and red carnations were laid at the Cenotaph in memory of those who died.* N-COUNT

censor /sensə^r/ **censors, censoring, censored** ◆◇◇◇◇

1 If someone in authority **censors** letters or the media, they officially examine them and cut out any information that is regarded as secret. *The military-backed government has heavily censored the news.* VERB V n

2 A **censor** is a person who has been officially appointed to examine letters or the media and to cut out any parts that are regarded as secret. *The report was cleared by the American military censors.* N-COUNT

3 If someone in authority **censors** a book, play, or film, they officially examine it and cut out any parts that are considered to be immoral or inappropriate. *The Late Show censored the band's live version of 'Bullet In The Head'... ITV companies tend to censor bad language in feature films.* VERB V n

4 A **censor** is a person who has been officially appointed to examine plays, films, and books and to cut out any parts that are considered to be immoral. *...the British Board of Film Censors.* N-COUNT

censorious /sensɔːriəs/. Someone who is **censorious** strongly disapproves of and criticizes someone else's behaviour; a formal word, used showing disapproval. *Despite strong principles he was never censorious.* ADJ-GRADED PRAGMATICS =critical

censorship /sensə^rʃɪp/. **Censorship** is the censoring of books, plays, films, or reports, especially by government officials, because they are considered immoral or secret in some way. *The government today announced that press censorship was being lifted.* ◆◇◇◇◇ N-UNCOUNT

censure /senʃə^r/ **censures, censuring, censured.** If you **censure** someone for something that they have done, you tell them that you strongly disapprove of it; a formal word. *The ethics committee may take a decision to admonish him or to censure him... I would not presume to censure Osborne for hating his mother.* ◆◇◇◇◇ VERB =condemn V n V n *for*-ing/n ► Also a noun. *It is a controversial policy which has attracted international censure.* N-UNCOUNT

census /sensəs/ **censuses.** A **census** is an official survey of the population of a country that is carried out in order to find out how many people live there and to obtain details of such things as people's ages and occupations. *For the most recent period the 1982 population census provides a considerable amount of detail.* ◆◆◇◇◇ N-COUNT

cent /sent/ **cents.** A **cent** is a small unit of money worth one hundredth of the main unit of money in many countries, for example the United States or Australia. *A cup of rice which cost thirty cents a few weeks ago is now being sold for up to one dollar... We haven't got a cent.* • See also **per cent.** ◆◆◇◇◇ N-COUNT: usu num N

centaur /sentɔː^r/ **centaurs.** In classical mythology, a **centaur** is a creature with the head, arms, and body of a man, and the body and legs of a horse. N-COUNT

centenarian /sentɪneəriən/ **centenarians.** A **centenarian** is someone who is a hundred years old or older. *Japan has more than 4,000 centenarians.* N-COUNT

centenary /senti:nəri, AM -ten-/ **centenaries.** The **centenary** of an event such as someone's birth is the 100th anniversary of that event; used mainly in British English. *This week is the centenary of the death of the world-famous Dutch painter, Vincent Van Gogh.* ◆◇◇◇◇ N-COUNT: oft N *of* n

centennial /senteniəl/. A **centennial** is the same as a **centenary**; used mainly in American English or in formal British English. *The centennial Olympics will be in Atlanta, Georgia.* ◆◇◇◇◇ N-SING: oft N n

center /sentəʳ/. See **centre**.

centigrade /sentɪgreɪd/. **Centigrade** is a scale for measuring temperature, in which water freezes at 0 degrees and boils at 100 degrees. It is represented by the symbol C. *...daytime temperatures of up to forty degrees centigrade.* ► Also a noun. *The number at the bottom is the recommended water temperature in Centigrade.* ADJ: usu n/num ADJ =Celsius; N-UNCOUNT

centilitre /sentɪli:təʳ/ **centilitres;** spelled **centiliter** in American English. A **centilitre** is a unit of volume in the metric system equal to ten millilitres or one-hundredth of a litre. N-COUNT

centimetre /sentɪmi:təʳ/ **centimetres;** spelled **centimeter** in American English. A **centimetre** is a unit of length in the metric system equal to ten millimetres or one-hundredth of a metre. *...a tiny fossil plant, only a few centimetres high.* ◆◇◇◇◇ N-COUNT

centipede /sentɪpi:d/ **centipedes.** A **centipede** is a long, thin creature with a lot of legs. N-COUNT

central /sentrəl/ ◆◆◆◆◆

1 A **central** group or organization makes all the important decisions that are followed throughout a larger organization or a country. *There is a lack of trust towards the central government in Rome. ...the central committee of the Cuban communist party.* ♦ **centrally** *This is a centrally planned economy.* ADJ: ADJ n; ADV: ADV -ed, ADV after v

2 Something that is **central** is in the middle of a place or area. *...Central America's Caribbean coast... The disruption has now spread and is affecting a large part of central Liberia. ...a rich woman living in central London.* ♦ **centrally** *The main cabin has its full-sized double bed centrally placed with plenty of room around it.* ADJ; ADV: ADV -ed, ADV after v

3 A place that is **central** is easy to reach because it is in the centre of a city. *...a central location in the capital.* ♦ **centrally** *...this centrally located hotel, situated on the banks of the Marne Canal.* ADJ-GRADED; ADV-GRADED: ADV -ed, ADV after v

4 The **central** person or thing in a particular situation is the most important one. *Black dance music has been central to mainstream pop since the early '60s. ...a central part of their culture.* ♦ **centrality** *The centrality of the German economy to the welfare of Europe must be recognised.* ♦ **centrally** *In her memoirs Naomi is quick to acknowledge that her grandmother was centrally important in her venture as a writer.* ADJ-GRADED: oft ADJ *to* n; N-UNCOUNT: usu N *of* n; ADV-GRADED: ADV with cl/group, ADV after v

central government, central governments. A **central government** is the government of a whole country, when this is in contrast to smaller organizations which govern local areas. *Some countries, such as Britain and France, have strong central government.* ◆◆◇◇◇ N-VAR

central heating. **Central heating** is a heating system for buildings. Air or water is heated in one main tank and travels round a building through pipes and radiators. ◆◇◇◇◇ N-UNCOUNT

centralise /sentrəlaɪz/. See **centralize.**

centralism /sentrəlɪzəm/. **Centralism** is a way of governing a country, or organizing something such as industry, education, or politics, which involves having one central group of people who give instructions to all the other regional groups. *Rigid centralism was built into the BBC from the outset.* N-UNCOUNT ≠focus

centralist /sentrəlɪst/ **centralists. Centralist** organizations govern a country or organize things using one central group of people who control and instruct other regional groups. *...a strong centralist state.* ► A **centralist** is someone with centralist views. ADJ: usu ADJ n; N-COUNT

centralize /sentrəlaɪz/ **centralizes, centralizing, centralized;** also spelled **centralise** in British English. To **centralize** a country, state, or organization means to create a system in which one central group of people gives instructions to regional groups. *In the mass production era multinational firms tended to centralize their operations... The economy of the times made it difficult to support centralized rule.* ♦ **centralization** /sentrəlaɪzeɪʃᵊn/ *Nowhere in Britain has bureaucratic centralization proceeded with more pace than in Scotland.* ◆◇◇◇◇ VERB; V n; V-ed; N-UNCOUNT

centrally heated. A **centrally heated** building or room has central heating. *Most centrally heated houses and offices tend to have too dry an atmosphere.* ADJ: usu ADJ n

central nervous system, central nervous systems. Your **central nervous system** is the part of your nervous system that consists of the brain and spinal cord. N-COUNT

central reservation, central reservations. In British English, the **central reservation** is the strip of ground, often covered with grass, that separates the two sides of a motorway or dual carriageway. *The lorry crashed through the central reservation.* N-COUNT

centre /sentəʳ/ **centres, centring, centred;** spelled **center** in American English. ◆◆◆◆◆

1 A **centre** is a building where people have meetings, take part in a particular activity, or get help of some kind. *We went to a party at the leisure centre... She now also does pottery classes at a community centre. ...the National Exhibition Centre.* N-COUNT: usu with supp, oft in names after n

2 If an area or town is a **centre** for an industry or activity, that industry or activity is very important there. *London is also the major international insurance centre.* N-COUNT: with supp

3 The **centre** of something is the middle of it. *A large wooden table dominates the centre of the room... Bake until light golden and crisp around the edges and slightly soft in the centre.* N-COUNT: usu sing

4 The **centre** of a town or city is the part where there are the most shops and businesses and where a lot of people come from other areas to work or shop. *...the city centre.* N-COUNT: usu sing

5 If something or someone is at the **centre** of a situation or someone's work, they are the most important thing or person involved. *...the man at the centre of the controversy... At the centre of the heated row was the question: Who leaked little Jennifer's name?* N-COUNT: usu sing, usu N *of* n

6 If someone or something is the **centre** of attention or interest, people are giving them a lot of attention. *The rest of the cast was used to her being the centre of attention... The centre of attraction was Pierre Auguste Renoir's oil painting.* N-COUNT: usu sing, N *of* n =focus

7 In politics, **the centre** refers to groups, such as liberals and social democrats, and their beliefs, which are considered to be neither left-wing nor right-wing. *The Democrats have become a party of the centre. ...the centre parties.* N-SING: *the* N, oft N n

8 If you **centre** something, you move it so that it is at the centre of something else. *Centre the design on the cloth before you start.* VERB; V n *on* n; Also V n

9 If something **centres** or **is centred** on a particular thing or person, that thing or person is the main feature or subject of attention. *...talks in Jakarta which centred on the Cambodia problem... All his concerns were centred around himself rather than Rachel... When working with patients, my efforts are centred on helping them to overcome illness and debility.* ♦ **-centred** *...a child-centred approach to teaching. ...patient-centred care.* V-ERG; V *on/around* n; *be* V-ed *on/around* n; Also V n *on/around* n; COMB in ADJ-GRADED

10 If an industry or event **is centred** in a place, or if it **centres** there, it takes place to the greatest extent there. *The fighting has been centred around the town of Vucovar... The disturbances have centred round the two main university areas... Between 100 and 150 travellers' vehicles were scattered around* V-ERG; *be* V-ed prep; V prep; V-ed

the county, with the largest gathering centred on Ampfield.

11 See also **community centre, detention centre, garden centre, health centre, job centre, left-of-centre, nerve centre, reception centre, remand centre, right-of-centre, shopping centre.**

centred /sentəʳd/; spelled **centered** in American English. If an industry or event is **centred** in a place, it takes place to the greatest extent there. *...the silk industry, which was centered in Valencia. ...the tremor, which was centred on the Carpathian Mountains.* ◆◆◇◇◇ ADJ: v-link ADJ prep

-centred /-sentəʳd/; spelled **-centered** in American English. **-centred** can be added to adjectives and nouns to indicate what kind of a centre something has. *...lemon-centered white chocolates.* • See also **self-centred.** COMB in ADJ

centrefold /sentəʳfould/ **centrefolds;** spelled **centerfold** in American English. A **centrefold** is a picture that covers the two central pages of a magazine, especially a photograph of a naked or semi-naked woman in a pornographic magazine. N-COUNT =pin-up

centre-forward, centre-forwards. A **centre-forward** in a team sport such as football or hockey is the player or position in the middle of the front row of attackers. ◆◇◇◇◇ N-COUNT

centre of gravity, centres of gravity. The **centre of gravity** of an object is a point in it. If this point is above the base of the object, it stays stable, rather than falling over. N-COUNT

centrepiece /sentəʳpi:s/ **centrepieces;** spelled **centerpiece** in American English. ◆◇◇◇◇

1 The **centrepiece** of a number of things is something that you show as the best one among them or as the biggest attraction. *This year the centrepiece of the Festival will be its presentation of two rarely performed operas.* N-COUNT: usu N *of* n

2 A **centrepiece** is an ornament which you put in the middle of something, especially a dinner table. N-COUNT

centre stage; also spelled **centre-stage**, and spelled **center stage** in American English. If something or someone takes **centre stage**, they become very prominent or noticeable. *Britain will take centre stage in Europe as Mr Major takes the Community presidency for six months... Nuclear proliferation has returned to centre stage in international affairs.* ◆◇◇◇◇ N-UNCOUNT: also *the* N

centrifugal force /sentrɪfjʊgəl fɔːʳs/. **Centrifugal force** is the force that makes objects move outwards when they are spinning around something or travelling in a curve; a technical term in physics. *The juice is extracted by centrifugal force.* N-UNCOUNT

centrifuge /sentrɪfju:dʒ/ **centrifuges.** A **centrifuge** is a machine that spins mixtures of different substances around very quickly so that they separate by centrifugal force. N-COUNT

centrist /sentrɪst/ **centrists. Centrist** policies and parties are moderate rather than extreme. *He had left the movement because it had abandoned its centrist policies.* ► A **centrist** is someone with centrist views. ◆◇◇◇◇ ADJ-GRADED: usu ADJ n; N-COUNT

centurion /sentjʊəriən, AM -tʊr-/ **centurions.** A **centurion** was an officer in the Roman army. N-COUNT

century /sentʃəri/ **centuries** ◆◆◆◆◆

1 A **century** is a period of a hundred years that is used when stating a date. For example, the 19th century was the period from 1801 to 1900. *The material position of the Church had been declining since the late eighteenth century. ...a 17th-century merchant's house.* N-COUNT: usu ord N

2 A **century** is any period of a hundred years. *The drought there is the worst in a century.* N-COUNT

3 In cricket, a **century** is a score of one hundred runs or more by one batsman. N-COUNT

ceramic /sɪræmɪk/ **ceramics** ◆◆◇◇◇

1 **Ceramic** is clay that has been heated to a very high temperature so that it becomes hard. *...ceramic tiles. ...items made from hand-painted ceramic.* N-MASS: usu N n

2 **Ceramics** are ceramic ornaments or objects. *...a collection of Chinese ceramics.* N-COUNT: usu pl

3 **Ceramics** is the art of making artistic objects out of clay. N-UNCOUNT

cereal /sɪəriəl/ **cereals** ◆◆◇◇◇

1 **Cereal** or **breakfast cereal** is a food made from grain. In Britain, it is mixed with milk and eaten for breakfast. *I have a glass of fruit juice and a bowl of cereal every morning.* N-MASS

2 **Cereals** are plants such as wheat, maize, or rice that produce grain. *...the rich cereal-growing districts of the Paris Basin.* N-COUNT

cerebral /serɪbrəl/ ◆◇◇◇◇

1 If you describe someone or something as **cerebral**, you mean that they are intellectual and rational rather than emotional; a formal use. *Washington struck me as a precarious place from which to publish such a cerebral newspaper.* ADJ-GRADED =intellectual

2 **Cerebral** means relating to the brain; a medical use. *My father died suddenly and unexpectedly of a cerebral haemorrhage.* ADJ: ADJ n

cerebral palsy. Cerebral palsy is an illness caused by damage to a baby's brain before it is born, which makes its limbs and muscles permanently weak. N-UNCOUNT

ceremonial /serɪmouniəl/ **ceremonials** ◆◇◇◇◇

1 Something that is **ceremonial** relates to a ceremony or is used in a ceremony. *He represented the nation on ceremonial occasions... Feathers of various kinds are used by Native Americans for ceremonial purposes.* ♦ **ceremonially** *Corporal Andrew Satchell ceremonially rolled up the flag of the Royal Regiment of Fusiliers.* ADJ: ADJ n; ADV: ADV with v

2 A position, function, or event that is **ceremonial** is considered to be representative of an institution, but has very little authority or influence. *Up to now the post of president has been largely ceremonial.* ADJ

3 **Ceremonial** consists of all the impressive things that are done, said, and worn on very formal occasions. *...papal ceremonial. ...the ceremonials leading up to the young Emperor's wedding.* N-VAR

4 A **ceremonial** is a ceremony. *...a religious ceremonial.* N-COUNT =ceremony

ceremoniously /serɪmouniəsli/. If someone does something **ceremoniously**, they do it in an extremely formal way; used in written English. *The waiter ceremoniously lifted rolls from a basket with a pair of silver tongs... Edith greeted them ceremoniously.* ADV: ADV with v

ceremony /serɪməni, AM -mouni/ **ceremonies** ◆◆◆◇◇

1 A **ceremony** is a formal event such as a wedding or a coronation. *...his grandmother's funeral, a private ceremony attended only by the family... Today's award ceremony took place at the British Embassy in Tokyo.* N-COUNT

2 **Ceremony** consists of the special things that are said and done on very formal occasions. *The Republic was proclaimed in public with great ceremony. ...the pomp and ceremony of the Pope's visit.* N-UNCOUNT: usu *with* N

3 If you do something **without ceremony**, you do it quickly and in a casual way. *'Is Hilton here?' she asked without ceremony.* N-UNCOUNT: *without* N

4 See also **master of ceremonies.**

cerise /səri:s/. Something that is **cerise** is a bright pinkish red. *She is wearing a cerise suit.* COLOUR

cert /sɜːʳt/ **certs.** If you say that someone or something is a **cert**, you mean that you are certain they will succeed; used in informal British English. *There's no such things as a cert in horse racing... Anthony was a dead cert for promotion.* N-COUNT

cert., certs. Cert. is a written abbreviation for **certificate**, especially when it is referring to a film classification certificate. ◆◇◇◇◇

certain 1 being sure

certain /sɜːʳtən/ ◆◆◆◇◇

1 If you are **certain** about something, you firmly believe it is true and have no doubt about it. If you are not **certain** about something, you do not have definite knowledge about it. *She's absolutely certain she's going to make it in the world... We are not certain whether the appendix had already burst or not... It wasn't a balloon – I'm certain of that.* ADJ-GRADED: v-link ADJ, oft ADJ that/wh, ADJ *of/about* n =sure

2 If you say that something is **certain** to happen, you mean that it will definitely happen. *However,* ADJ-GRADED: oft ADJ to-inf, *it* v-link ADJ

the scheme is certain to meet opposition from fishermen's leaders... It's not certain they'll accept the Front's candidate if he wins... Brazil need to beat Uruguay to be certain of a place in the finals... The Prime Minister is heading for certain defeat if he forces a vote... Victory looked certain.
that/wh, ADJ *of*n/-ing

3 If you say that something is **certain**, you firmly believe that it is true, or have definite knowledge about it. *One thing is certain, both have the utmost respect for each other... It is certain that Rodney arrived the previous day..*
ADJ: v-link ADJ, oft *it* v-link ADJ that/wh

4 If you have **certain** knowledge, you know that a particular thing is true. *He had been there four times to my certain knowledge.*
ADJ-GRADED: ADJ n

5 If you know something **for certain**, you have no doubt at all about it. *She couldn't know what time he'd go, or even for certain that he'd go at all... Hill had to find out for certain.*
PHRASES PHR with cl (not first in cl) =for sure

6 If you **make certain** that something is the way you want or expect it to be, you take action to ensure that it is. *Firstly, they must make certain that their pension needs are adequately catered for... To make extra certain, a police helicopter kept watch from the skies.*
V inflects =make sure

certain 2 referring and indicating amount

certain /sɜːʳtᵊn/ ◆◆◆◆◇

1 You use **certain** to indicate that you are referring to one particular thing, person, or group, although you are not saying exactly which it is. *There will be certain people who'll say 'I told you so!'... You owe a certain person a sum of money... Leaflets have been air dropped telling people to leave certain areas.*
ADJ: det ADJ, ADJ n

2 When you refer to **certain** of a group of people or things, you are referring to some particular members of that group; a formal use. *They'll have to give up completely on certain of their studies.*
QUANT: QUANT *of* def-pl-n =some

3 You can use **a certain** before the name of a person in order to indicate that you do not know the person or anything else about them. *She managed to arrange for them to be hidden in the house of a certain Father Boduen.*
ADJ: *a* ADJ n-proper

4 You use **a certain** to indicate that something such as a quality or condition exists, and often to suggest that it is not great in amount or degree. *That was the very reason why he felt a certain bitterness... There is a certain impatience among some of the soldiers... I received a certain amount of sympathy immediately after the attack.*
ADJ: *a* ADJ sing-n/ n-uncount =some

certainly /sɜːʳtᵊnli/ ◆◆◆◆◇

1 You use **certainly** to emphasize what you are saying when you are making a statement. *The public is certainly getting tired of hearing about it... The bombs are almost certainly part of a much bigger conspiracy... Today's inflation figure is certainly too high... Certainly, pets can help children develop friendship skills.*
ADV-GRADED: ADV with cl/ group PRAGMATICS =undoubtedly

2 You use **certainly** when you are agreeing with what someone has said. *'In any case you remained friends.'—'Certainly.'... 'You keep out of their way don't you?'—'I certainly do.'*
ADV as reply PRAGMATICS

3 You say **certainly not** when you want to say 'no' in a strong way. *'Perhaps it would be better if I withdrew altogether.'—'Certainly not!'*
ADV as reply PRAGMATICS =absolutely not

certainty /sɜːʳtᵊnti/ **certainties** ◆◆◇◇◇

1 **Certainty** is the state of being definite or of having no doubts at all about something. *I have told them with absolute certainty there'll be no change of policy... There is too little certainty about the present state of the German economy.*
N-UNCOUNT: oft *with* N, N that

2 **Certainty** is the fact that something is certain to happen. *A general election became a certainty three weeks ago. ...the certainty of more violence and bloodshed... I began to realize the certainty of freezing to death if I remained where I was.*
N-UNCOUNT: also *a* N =inevitability

3 **Certainties** are things that nobody has any doubts about. *There are no certainties in modern Europe... The old certainties of socialism and feminism are dead.*
N-COUNT: usu pl

certifiable /sɜːʳtɪfaɪəbᵊl/.

1 If you describe someone as **certifiable**, you think that their behaviour is extremely unreasonable or foolish. *By the time we left he must have considered that all film crews were certifiable.*
ADJ-GRADED PRAGMATICS =crazy

2 Someone who is **certifiable** is mentally ill and can be declared insane.
ADJ

certificate /səʳtɪfɪkət/ **certificates** ◆◆◇◇◇

1 A **certificate** is an official document stating that particular facts are true. *Some parents hold on to their children's birth certificates. ...share certificates.*
N-COUNT: usu with supp

2 A **certificate** is an official document that you receive when you have completed a course of study or training. The qualification that you receive after a course of study or training is sometimes also called a **certificate**. *...to the right of the fireplace are various framed certificates. ...the Post-Graduate Certificate of Education.*
N-COUNT: with supp

certificated /səʳtɪfɪkeɪtɪd/. A **certificated** person has been awarded a certificate to prove that they have achieved a certain level or standard. *He was not a mere surgeon but a genuine certificated physician.*
ADJ: usu ADJ n =certified

certify /sɜːʳtɪfaɪ/ **certifies, certifying, certified** ◆◇◇◇◇

1 If someone in an official position **certifies** something, they officially state that it is true. *...if the president certified that the project would receive at least $650m from overseas sources... The National Election Council is supposed to certify the results of the election... It has been certified as genuine... Mrs Simpson was certified dead.* ♦ **certification** /səʳtɪfɪkeɪʃᵊn/ **certifications** *An employer can demand written certification that the relative is really ill.*
VERB V that V n *be* V-ed *as* adj *be* V-ed adj Also V n adj, V n *as* adj
N-VAR

2 If someone **is certified** as a particular kind of worker, they are given a certificate stating that they have successfully completed a course of training in their profession. *They wanted to get certified as divers. ...a certified accountant... All three doctors are certified as addictions specialists.* ♦ **certification** *Pupils would be offered on-the-job training leading to the certification of their skill in a particular field.*
VB: usu passive *get* V-ed *as* n V-ed
N-UNCOUNT: oft N *of*n

certitude /sɜːʳtɪtjuːd, AM -tuːd/ **certitudes.** **Certitude** is the same as **certainty**; a formal word. *We have this definite certitude that Cicippio will be freed.*
N-UNCOUNT: also N in pl, oft N that

cervical /sɜːʳvɪkᵊl, səʳvaɪkᵊl/ ◆◇◇◇◇

1 **Cervical** means relating to the cervix; a medical use. *Doctors aim to cut the number of women dying from cervical cancer by half this decade.*
ADJ: ADJ n

2 **Cervical** means relating to the neck; a medical use. *Making a circle so your head leans back could damage the cervical spine.*
ADJ: ADJ n

cervix /sɜːʳvɪks/ **cervixes** or **cervices** /səʳvaɪsiːz/. The **cervix** is the entrance to the womb; a medical term.
◆◇◇◇◇ N-COUNT

cessation /seseɪʃᵊn/. The **cessation** of something is the stopping of it; a formal word. *He would not agree to a cessation of hostilities.*
◆◇◇◇◇ N-UNCOUNT: also *a* N, usu with supp

cesspit /sespɪt/ **cesspits.** A **cesspit** is a hole or tank in the ground into which waste water and sewage flow.
N-COUNT =cesspool

cesspool /sespuːl/ **cesspools.** A **cesspool** is the same as a **cesspit**.
N-COUNT

cetacean /sɪteɪʃᵊn/ **cetaceans.** Whales, dolphins, and porpoises belong to the family of creatures known as **cetaceans**.
N-COUNT: usu pl

cetera. See **etcetera**.

cf. **Cf.** is used in writing to introduce something that should be considered in connection with the subject you are discussing. *For the more salient remarks on the matter, cf. Isis Unveiled, Vol. I.*
◆◇◇◇◇ =compare

CFC /siː ef siː/ **CFCs.** **CFCs** are chemicals that are used in aerosols, refrigerators, and cooling systems, and in the manufacture of various plastics. CFCs can cause damage to the ozone layer. CFC is an abbreviation for 'chlorofluorocarbon'.
◆◇◇◇◇ N-COUNT =chlorofluorocarbon

ch., ch. Ch. is a written abbreviation for **chapter**.
N-VAR num

cha-cha /tʃɑː tʃɑː/ **cha-chas.** A **cha-cha** is a Latin American dance with small fast steps.
N-COUNT: oft *the* N

chafe /tʃeɪf/ **chafes, chafing, chafed**

1 If your skin **chafes** or **is chafed** by something, it becomes sore as a result of something rubbing
V-ERG =rub

against it. *The shorts were chafing my thighs, as was the T-shirt my arms... She turned him in the bed so that the sheets wouldn't chafe his skin into sores... His wrists began to chafe against the cloth strips binding them... The messenger bent and scratched at his knee where the strapping chafed.* V n / V against n / V

2 If you **chafe** at something such as a restriction, you feel annoyed about it; a formal use. *He had chafed at having to take orders from another... He was chafing under the company's new ownership.* VB: no passive / V at/under/against n/-ing

chaff /tʃɑːf, tʃæf/

1 **Chaff** is the outer part of grain such as wheat. It is removed before the grain is used as food. N-UNCOUNT

2 If you **separate the wheat from the chaff** or **sort the wheat from the chaff**, you decide which people or things in a group are good or important and which are bad or unimportant. *Another problem is sorting the wheat from the chaff as a huge amount of information floods in.* PHRASE: V inflects

chaffinch /tʃæfɪntʃ/ **chaffinches.** A **chaffinch** is a small European songbird. Male chaffinches have reddish-brown fronts and grey heads. N-COUNT

chagrin /ʃægrɪn, AM ʃəgrɪn/. **Chagrin** is a feeling of annoyance or disappointment; a formal word. *One of the first things we did when we moved in, to the chagrin of the architect, was to replace the leaded windows.* N-UNCOUNT: usu with poss

chagrined /ʃægrɪnd, AM ʃəgrɪnd/. If you are **chagrined** by something, it annoys or disappoints you. *The chair of the committee did not appear chagrined by the compromises and delays.* ADJ-GRADED: usu v-link ADJ

chain /tʃeɪn/ **chains, chaining, chained** ◆◆◆◇◇

1 A **chain** consists of metal rings connected together in a line. *His open shirt revealed a fat gold chain... The dogs were leaping and growling at the full stretch of their chains.* N-COUNT

2 If prisoners are **in chains**, they have thick rings of metal round their wrists or ankles to prevent them from escaping. *He'd spent four and a half years in windowless cells, much of the time in chains.* N-PLURAL: in N

3 You can refer to feelings and duties which prevent you from doing what you want to do as **chains**; a literary use. *He had to break right now the chains of habit that bound him to the present.* N-PLURAL: oft N of n =fetters

4 If a person or thing **is chained** to something, they are fastened to it with a chain. *The dog was chained to the leg of the one solid garden seat... She chained her bike to the railings... Some demonstrators chained themselves to railings inside the court building... We were sitting together in our cell, chained to the wall.* ► **Chain up** means the same as **chain**. *I'll lock the doors and chain you up... They kept me chained up every night and released me each day... All the rowing boats were chained up.* VERB =tie / be V-ed to n / V n to n / V-ed / Also V n adv/prep / PHRASAL VERB / V n P / V-ed P / Also V P n (not pron)

5 A **chain of** things is a group of them existing or arranged in a line. *...a chain of islands known as the Windward Islands... Students tried to form a human chain around the parliament.* N-COUNT: N of n

6 A **chain** of shops, hotels, or other businesses is a number of them owned by the same person or company. *...a large supermarket chain. ...Italy's leading chain of cinemas.* N-COUNT: with supp

7 A **chain of** events is a series of them happening one after another. *...the bizarre chain of events that led to his departure in January 1938.* N-SING: N of n =series

8 See also **food chain**.

chain up. See **chain** 4. PHRASAL VERB

chained /tʃeɪnd/. If you say that someone is **chained to** a person or a situation, you are emphasizing that there are reasons why they cannot leave that person or situation, even though you think they might like to. *Surely modern women want to be informed of world current affairs; we are no longer chained to the kitchen sink!... In the bad old days women used to be chained to unhappy marriages for financial or social reasons.* ◆◇◇◇◇ ADJ: v-link ADJ to n PRAGMATICS

chain gang, chain gangs. In the United States, a **chain gang** was a group of prisoners who were chained together to do work outside their prison. N-COUNT

chain letter, chain letters. A **chain letter** is a letter, often with a promise of money, that is sent to several people who send copies on to several more people. Chain letters are illegal in some countries. N-COUNT

chain mail. **Chain mail** is armour made from small metal rings joined together so that they are like a piece of cloth. N-UNCOUNT

chain reaction, chain reactions ◆◇◇◇◇

1 A **chain reaction** is a series of chemical changes, each of which causes the next. N-COUNT

2 A **chain reaction** is a series of events, each of which causes the next. *Whenever recession strikes, a chain reaction is set into motion... The powder immediately ignited and set off a chain reaction of explosions.* N-COUNT

chain saw, chain saws; also spelled **chainsaw**. A **chain saw** is a big saw with teeth fixed in a chain that is driven round by a motor. N-COUNT

chain-smoke, chain-smokes, chain-smoking, chain-smoked. Someone who **chain-smokes** smokes cigarettes or cigars continuously. *Melissa had chain-smoked all evening while she waited for a phone call from Tom.* VERB / V / Also V n

chain-smoker, chain-smokers; also spelled **chain smoker**. A **chain-smoker** is a person who chain-smokes. N-COUNT

chain store, chain stores; also spelled **chain-store**. A **chain store** is one of several similar shops that are owned by the same person or company, especially one that sells a variety of things. N-COUNT

chair /tʃeəʳ/ **chairs, chairing, chaired** ◆◆◆◆◇

1 A **chair** is a piece of furniture for one person to sit on, with a back and four legs. *He rose from his chair and walked to the window.* N-COUNT

2 At a university, a **chair** is the post of professor. *He has been appointed to the chair of sociology at Southampton University... He gave London University £600,000 to establish a chair in Islamic art.* N-COUNT: usu sing, oft N of/in n =professorship

3 The person who is the **chair** of a committee or meeting is the person in charge of it. *She is the chair of the Defense Advisory Committee on Women in the Military.* N-COUNT: usu sing, oft N of n =chairperson

4 If you **chair** a meeting or a committee, you are the person in charge of it. *He was about to chair a meeting in Venice of EC foreign ministers... The declaration was drafted by a committee chaired by Dr Robert Song.* VERB / V n

5 If you **are in the chair** or **take the chair** at a meeting, you are the person in charge of it. *In the chair was Morien Morgan... Wheeler took the chair of this sub-committee. ...Britain's turn in the EC chair.* PHRASE: V inflects

chair lift, chair lifts; also spelled **chairlift**. A **chair lift** is a line of chairs that hang from a moving cable and carry people up and down a mountain or ski slope. N-COUNT

chairman /tʃeəʳmən/ **chairmen** ◆◆◆◆◇

1 The **chairman** of a committee, organization, or company is the head of it. *Glyn Ford is chairman of the Committee which produced the report... I had done business with the company's chairman.* N-COUNT: oft with poss

2 The **chairman** of a meeting or debate is the person in charge, who decides when each person is allowed to speak. *The chairman declared the meeting open... I hear you, Mr. Chairman.* N-COUNT; N-VOC: Mr/Madam N

chairmanship /tʃeəʳmənʃɪp/ **chairmanships.** The **chairmanship** of a committee or organization is the fact of being its chairman. Someone's **chairmanship** can also mean the period during which they are chairman. *The Government has set up a committee under the chairmanship of Professor Roy Goode.* ◆◇◇◇◇ N-VAR: usu with supp

chairperson /tʃeəʳpɜːʳsən/ **chairpersons.** The **chairperson** of a meeting, committee, or organization is the person in charge of it. *She's the chairperson of the safety committee.* N-COUNT

chairwoman /tʃeəʳwʊmən/ **chairwomen.** The **chairwoman** of a meeting, committee, or organization is the woman in charge of it. *Primakov was in Japan meeting with the chairwoman of the Socialist Party there.* N-COUNT

chaise longue /ʃeɪz lɒŋ/ **chaises longues;** the singular and the plural are both pronounced in the same way. A **chaise longue** is a couch with N-COUNT only one arm and usually a back along half its length.

chalet /ʃæleɪ, AM ʃæleɪ/ **chalets.** A **chalet** is a small wooden house, especially in a mountain area or a holiday camp. ◆◇◇◇◇ N-COUNT

chalice /tʃælɪs/ **chalices**

1 A **chalice** is a large gold or silver cup with a stem. Chalices are used to hold wine in the Christian service of Holy Communion. N-COUNT

2 If you refer to a job or an opportunity as a **poisoned chalice**, you mean that it seems to be very attractive but you believe it will lead to failure. *He does not regard his new job as a poisoned chalice... Some people even claimed that he appointed his political rival only in the belief that he was giving him a poisoned chalice and that he would not last more than a year.* PHRASE: usu v-link PHR, PHR after v

chalk /tʃɔːk/ **chalks, chalking, chalked** ◆◇◇◇◇

1 **Chalk** is a type of soft white rock. You can use small pieces of it for writing or drawing with. *...the highest chalk cliffs in Britain... Her skin was chalk white and dry-looking.* N-UNCOUNT: oft N n

2 **Chalk** is small sticks of chalk, or a substance similar to chalk, used for writing or drawing with. *...somebody writing with a piece of chalk. ...drawing a small picture with coloured chalks.* N-UNCOUNT: also N in pl

3 If you **chalk** something, you draw or write it using a piece of chalk. *He chalked the message on the blackboard... There was a blackboard with seven names chalked on it.* VERB V n V-ed

4 If you say that two people or things are as different as **chalk and cheese**, you are emphasizing that they are completely different from each other. *The two places, he insists, are as different as chalk and cheese... We are very aware of our differences, we accept that we are chalk and cheese.* PHRASES PRAGMATICS

5 In British English, you can use **by a long chalk** to add emphasis to something you are saying. *The rest of us hadn't finished our drinks, not by a long chalk.* oft with brd-neg, PHR with cl PRAGMATICS

chalk up. If you **chalk up** a success, a victory, or a number of points in a game, you achieve it. *For almost 11 months, the Bosnian army chalked up one victory after another... Andy Wilkinson chalked up his first win of the season.* PHRASAL VERB V P n (not pron) Also V n P

chalkboard /tʃɔːkbɔːʳd/ **chalkboards.** In a classroom, the **chalkboard** is a board which teachers write on with chalk; used especially in American English. N-COUNT: usu sing, usu *the* N =blackboard

chalky /tʃɔːki/

1 Something that is **chalky** contains chalk or is covered with chalk. *The chalky soil around Saumur produces the famous Anjou wines.* ADJ-GRADED

2 Something that is **chalky** is a pale dull colour or has a powdery texture. *Her face became a chalky white.* ADJ-GRADED

challenge /tʃælɪndʒ/ **challenges, challenging, challenged** ◆◆◆◆◇

1 A **challenge** is something new and difficult which requires great effort and determination. *I like a big challenge and they don't come much bigger than this... The new government's first challenge is the economy.* N-VAR

2 If someone **rises to the challenge**, they act in response to a difficult situation which is new to them and are successful. *The new Germany must rise to the challenge of its enhanced responsibilities... They rose to the challenge of entertaining 80 schoolchildren for an afternoon.* PHRASE: V inflects

3 A **challenge** to something is a questioning of its truth or value. A **challenge** to someone is a questioning of their authority. *The demonstrators have now made a direct challenge to the authority of the government.* N-VAR: oft N *to* n

4 If you **challenge** ideas or people, you question their truth, value, or authority. *Democratic leaders have challenged the president to sign the bill... The move was immediately challenged by two of the republics... I challenged him on the hypocrisy of his political attitudes.* VERB V n to-inf *be* V-ed V n *on/about* n Also V with quote, V n

5 If you **challenge** someone, you invite them to fight or compete with you in some way. *Marsyas thought he could play the flute better than Apollo and challenged the god to a contest... He left a note at the scene of the crime, challenging detectives to catch him... We challenged a team who called themselves 'College Athletes'.* ▶ Also a noun. *A third presidential candidate emerged to mount a serious challenge and throw the campaign wide open.* VERB V n *to* n V n to-inf V n N-COUNT

6 If someone **is challenged** by a guard, they are ordered to stop and say who they are or why they are there. *The men apparently opened fire after they were challenged by a patrol.* VERB *be* V-ed

7 See also **challenged, challenging.**

challenged /tʃælɪndʒd/. If you say that someone is **challenged** in a particular way, you mean that they have a disability in that area. **Challenged** is often combined with inappropriate words for humorous effect. *...terms like 'vertically-challenged' – meaning short... She ran off with intellectually challenged ski instructor.* ◆◆◇◇◇ ADJ: adv ADJ

challenger /tʃælɪndʒəʳ/ **challengers.** A **challenger** is someone who competes with you for a position or title that you already have, for example being a sports champion or a political leader. *Draskovic has emerged as the strongest challenger to the leader of the Serbian government... The One Australia syndicate is to become the sixth challenger for the 1995 Americas Cup.* ◆◆◇◇◇ N-COUNT: oft N *to/for* n

challenging /tʃælɪndʒɪŋ/ ◆◆◇◇◇

1 A **challenging** task or job requires great effort and determination. *Mike found a challenging job as a computer programmer... I'm ready to do all those things which are more challenging.* ADJ-GRADED =demanding ≠unchallenging, undemanding

2 If you do something in a **challenging** way, you seem to be inviting people to argue with you or compete against you in some way. *Mona gave him a challenging look.* ADJ-GRADED: usu ADJ n =defiant

chamber /tʃeɪmbəʳ/ **chambers** ◆◆◆◇◇

1 A **chamber** is a large room, especially one that is used for formal meetings. *We are going to be in the council chamber every time he speaks.* N-COUNT: usu supp N

2 You can refer to a country's parliament or to one section of it as a **chamber**. *More than 80 parties are contesting seats in the two-chamber parliament... Signor Amato's government has only a 16-seat majority in the Chamber of Deputies.* N-COUNT =house

3 A **chamber** is a room designed and equipped for a particular purpose. *For many, the dentist's surgery remains a torture chamber.* ● See also **gas chamber.** N-COUNT: with supp

4 A **chamber** is a hollow place inside the body of a person or animal, or inside a plant. N-COUNT

5 The offices used by judges and barristers are referred to as **chambers.** N-PLURAL

chamberlain /tʃeɪmbəʳlɪn/ **chamberlains.** A **chamberlain** is the person who is in charge of the household affairs of a king, queen, or person of high social rank. N-COUNT

chambermaid /tʃeɪmbəʳmeɪd/ **chambermaids.** A **chambermaid** is a woman who cleans and tidies the bedrooms in a hotel. N-COUNT

chamber music. **Chamber music** is classical music written for a small number of instruments. N-UNCOUNT

chamber of commerce, chambers of commerce. A **chamber of commerce** is an organization of businessmen that promotes local commercial interests. ◆◇◇◇◇ N-COUNT

chamber orchestra, chamber orchestras. A **chamber orchestra** is a small orchestra which plays classical music. N-COUNT

chamber pot, chamber pots. A **chamber pot** is a round container shaped like a very large cup. Chamber pots used to be kept in bedrooms so that people could urinate in them instead of having to leave their room during the night. N-COUNT

chameleon /kəmiːliən/ **chameleons.** A **chameleon** is a lizard whose skin changes colour to match the colour of its surroundings. N-COUNT

chamois. **Chamois** is both the singular and the plural form; it is pronounced /ʃæmwɑː/ for meaning 1 in British English, and /ʃæmi/ for both meanings in American English, and for meaning 2 in British English.

1 **Chamois** are small goat-like antelope that live in the mountains of Europe and South West Asia. N-COUNT

2 A **chamois** or a **chamois leather** is a soft leather cloth used for cleaning and polishing. N-COUNT =chammy

chamomile /kæməmaɪl/. See **camomile.**

champ /tʃæmp/ **champs.** In informal English, a **champ** is the same as a champion. *...boxing champ Mike Tyson... He had been, he said modestly, swimming champ at high school.* ◆◇◇◇◇ N-COUNT: oft n N

champagne /ʃæmpeɪn/ **champagnes** ◆◆◇◇◇

1 **Champagne** is an expensive French sparkling white wine. It is often drunk to celebrate something that has happened. N-MASS

2 If you talk about **champagne corks popping**, you are talking about people celebrating something that has happened. *Champagne corks will be popping tonight.* PHRASE: V inflects

champers /ʃæmpəʳz/. **Champers** is champagne; used mainly in informal British English. N-UNCOUNT =bubbly

champion /tʃæmpiən/ **champions, championing, championed** ◆◆◆◆◇

1 A **champion** is someone who has won the first prize in a competition, contest, or fight. *...a former Olympic champion... Kasparov became world champion. ...champion boxer Lennox Lewis.* N-COUNT: usu with supp

2 If you are a **champion** of a person, a cause, or a principle, you support or defend them. *He received acclaim as a champion of the oppressed... He was once known as a champion of social reform.* N-COUNT: with supp, usu N *of* n =defender

3 If you **champion** a person, a cause, or a principle, you support or defend them. *He passionately championed the poor... The amendments had been championed by pro-democracy activists.* VERB =defend V n

championship /tʃæmpiənʃɪp/ **championships** ◆◆◆◆◇

1 A **championship** is a competition to find the best player or team in a particular sport. *...the world chess championship.* N-COUNT: usu supp N

2 **The championship** refers to the title or status of being a sports champion. *He went on to take the championship... This season I expect us to retain the championship and win the European Cup.* N-SING: *the* N

chance /tʃɑːns, tʃæns/ **chances, chancing, chanced** ◆◆◆◆◆

1 If there is a **chance** of something happening, it is possible that it will happen. *Do you think they have a chance of beating Australia?... This partnership has a good chance of success... The specialist who carried out the brain scan thought Tim's chances of survival were still slim... There was really very little chance that Ben would ever have led a normal life.* N-VAR: oft N *of*-ing/n, N that

2 If you have a **chance** to do something, you have the opportunity to do it. *The electoral council announced that all eligible people would get a chance to vote... Most refugee doctors never get the chance to practice medicine in British hospitals... I felt I had to give him a chance.* N-SING: usu N to-inf, N *for* n to-inf

3 A **chance** meeting or event is one that is not planned or expected. *...a chance meeting.* ► Also a noun. *...a victim of chance and circumstance.* ADJ: ADJ n N-UNCOUNT

4 If you **chance** to do something or **chance** on something, you do it or find it although you had not planned or tried to; a formal use. *A man I chanced to meet proved to be a most unusual character... It was just then that I chanced to look round. ...Christopher Columbus, who chanced upon the Dominican Republic nearly 500 years ago.* VERB =happen to V to-inf V *upon/on/across* n

5 If you **chance** something, you do it even though there is a risk that you may not succeed or that something bad may happen. *Andy knew the risks. I cannot believe he would have chanced it... He decided no assassin would chance a shot from amongst that crowd.* VERB =risk V it V n

6 See also **off-chance.**

7 Something that happens **by chance** was not planned by anyone. *He had met Mr Heseltine by chance.* PHRASES PHR after v, PHR with cl =by accident

8 You can use **by any chance** when you are asking questions in order to find out whether something that you think might be true is actually true. *Are they by any chance related?* PHR with cl (not first in cl) PRAGMATICS =perhaps

9 If you say that someone **stands a chance** of achieving something, you mean that they are likely to achieve it. If you say that someone doesn't **stand a chance** of achieving something, you mean that they cannot possibly achieve it. *Being very good at science subjects, I stood a good chance of gaining high grades... Neither is seen as standing any chance of snatching the leadership from him.* V inflects, usu PHR *of*-ing

10 When you **take a chance**, you try to do something although there is a large risk of danger or failure. *You take a chance on the weather if you holiday in the UK... From then on, the Chinese were taking no chances... Dennis was not a man to take chances.* V and N inflect =take a risk

chancel /tʃɑːnsəl, tʃænsəl/ **chancels.** The **chancel** is the part of a church containing the altar, where the clergy and the choir usually sit. N-COUNT

chancellery /tʃɑːnsələri, tʃæns-/ **chancelleries**

1 A **chancellery** is the building where a chancellor has his offices. N-COUNT

2 The **chancellery** is the officials who work in a chancellor's office. *Mr Brandt is in close touch with the Foreign Ministry and the Chancellery.* N-SING: usu *the* N

Chancellor /tʃɑːnsləʳ, tʃæns-/ **Chancellors** ◆◆◆◆◇

1 **Chancellor** is the title of the head of government in Germany and Austria. *...Chancellor Helmut Kohl of Germany. ...as the Chancellor arrived.* N-TITLE; N-COUNT: usu *the* N

2 In Britain, the **Chancellor** is the Chancellor of the Exchequer. N-COUNT: usu *the* N

3 The **Chancellor** of a British university is the official head of the university. The Chancellor does not run the university as this is an honorary position. *In 1980 he became Chancellor of Bath University.* N-COUNT: usu *the* N

4 The head of some American universities is called the **Chancellor.** N-COUNT: usu *the* N

5 See also **vice-chancellor.**

Chancellor of the Exchequer, Chancellors of the Exchequer. The **Chancellor of the Exchequer** is the minister in the British government who makes decisions about finance and taxes. ◆◇◇◇◇ N-COUNT

chancellorship /tʃɑːnsləʳʃɪp, tʃæns-/. The **chancellorship** is the position of chancellor. Someone's **chancellorship** is the period of time when they are chancellor. *Austria prospered under Kreisky's chancellorship.* N-SING: usu *the* N

Chancery /tʃɑːnsəri, tʃæns-/. In Britain, the **Chancery** or **Chancery Division** is the Lord Chancellor's court, which is a division of the High Court of Justice. N-SING: also *in* N

chancy /tʃɑːnsi, tʃænsi/. Something that is **chancy** involves a lot of risk or uncertainty; an informal word. *Producing the grapes suitable for fine wine is always a chancy business.* ADJ-GRADED =risky

chandelier /ʃændəlɪəʳ/ **chandeliers.** A **chandelier** is a large, decorative frame which holds light bulbs or candles and hangs from the ceiling. ◆◇◇◇◇ N-COUNT

change /tʃeɪndʒ/ **changes, changing, changed** ◆◆◆◆◆

1 If there is a **change** in something, it becomes different. *The Bosnian leader appealed for a change in US policy... What is needed is a change of attitude on the part of architects... There are going to have to be some drastic changes... In Zaire political change is on its way... 1988 was an important year for everyone: a time of change.* • See also **sea change.** N-VAR: usu with supp

2 If you say that something is a **change** or makes a **change**, you mean that it is enjoyable because it is different from what you are used to; used showing approval. *It is a complex system, but it certainly makes a change... You're feeling the call of the new and could do with a change.* N-SING PRAGMATICS

3 When something **changes** or when you **change** it, it becomes different. *We are trying to detect and understand how the climates change... In the union office, the mood gradually changed from resignation to rage... She has now changed into a happy, self-confident woman... They should change the law to make it illegal to own replica weapons... Trees are changing colour earlier than last year... He is a changed man since you left... A changing world has put pressures on the corporation.* V-ERG =alter V V *from* n *to* n V *into* n V n V-ed V-ing Also V n *into* n

4 To **change** something means to replace it with something new or different. *I paid £80 to have my* VERB V n

car radio fixed and I bet all they did was change a fuse... If you want to change your doctor there are two ways of doing it.* ▶ Also a noun. *A change of leadership alone will not be enough.* (N-COUNT: oft a N of n)

5 When you **change** your clothes or **change**, you take some or all of your clothes off and put on different ones. *Ben had merely changed his shirt... They had allowed her to shower and change... I changed into a tracksuit... I've got to get changed first. I've got to put my uniform on.* (VERB; V n; V; V into/out of n; get V-ed)

6 A **change of** clothes is an extra set of clothes that you take with you when you go to stay somewhere or to participate in an activity. *He stuffed a bag with a few changes of clothing.* (N-COUNT: N of n)

7 When you **change** a bed or **change** the sheets, you take off the dirty sheets and put on clean ones. *After changing the bed, I would fall asleep quickly... I changed the sheets on your bed today.* (VERB; V n)

8 When you **change** a baby or **change** its nappy, you take off its dirty nappy and put on a clean one. *She criticizes me for the way I feed or change him... He needs his nappy changed.* (VERB; V n; V-ed)

9 When you **change** buses, trains, or planes or **change**, you get off one bus, train, or plane and get on to another in order to continue your journey. *At Glasgow I changed trains for Greenock... We were turned off the train at Hanover, where we had to change.* (VERB; V n; V)

10 In British English, when you **change** gear or **change** into another gear, you move the gear lever on a car, bicycle, or other vehicle in order to use a different gear. In American English, you **shift** gears. *There were other sounds: a dog barking, a lorry changing gear... He looked up into the mirror as he changed through his gears.* (VERB; V n; V prep)

11 Your **change** is the money that you receive when you pay for something with more money than it costs because you do not have exactly the right amount of money. *'There's your change.'—'Thanks very much.'... They told the shopkeeper to keep the change.* (N-UNCOUNT)

12 Change is coins, rather than notes. *Thieves ransacked the office, taking a sack of loose change... The man in the store won't give him change for the phone unless he buys something.* • See also **small change**. (N-UNCOUNT)

13 If you have **change** for a note or a large coin, you have the same amount of money in smaller notes or coins, which you can give to someone in exchange. *The courier had change for a £10 note.* (N-UNCOUNT: usu N for n)

14 When you **change** money, you exchange it for the same amount of money in a different currency, or in smaller coins or notes. *You can expect to pay the bank a fee of around 1% to 2% every time you change money... If you travel frequently, find an agency that will change one foreign currency directly into another.* (VERB; V n; V n into n)

15 If you say that you are doing something or something is happening **for a change**, you mean that you do not usually do it or it does not usually happen, and you are glad to be doing it or that it is happening. *Now let me ask you a question, for a change... Liz settled back in her seat, comfortably relaxed, enjoying being driven for a change.* (PHRASE: PHR with cl; PRAGMATICS; =for once)

16 • to **change for the better**: see **better**. • to **change hands**: see **hand**. • **a change of heart**: see **heart**. • to **change your mind**: see **mind**. • to **change places**: see **place**. • to **ring the changes**: see **ring**. • to **change the subject**: see **subject**. • to **change tack**: see **tack**. • to **change your tune**: see **tune**. • to **change for the worse**: see **worse**.

change down. In British English, when you **change down**, you move the gear lever in the vehicle you are driving in order to use a lower gear. In American English, you **shift down**. *Changing down, he turned into the drive... I braked at the second corner and changed down to third.* (PHRASAL VERB; VP; VP to n)

change over. If you **change over** from one thing to another, you stop doing one thing and start doing the other. *We are gradually changing over to a completely metric system... The two men swapped places, always extinguishing the light when they changed over.* • See also **changeover**. (PHRASAL VERB =switch over; VP from/to n; VP)

change up. In British English, when you **change up**, you move the gear lever in the vehicle you are driving in order to use a higher gear. In American English, you **shift up**. *I accelerated and changed up.* (PHRASAL VERB; VP)

changeable /tʃeɪndʒəbəl/. Someone or something that is **changeable** is likely to change many times. *The forecast is for changeable weather.* (ADJ-GRADED =unsettled)

changeling /tʃeɪndʒlɪŋ/ **changelings.** A **changeling** is a child who was substituted for another child when they were both very young babies. In stories changelings were often taken or left by fairies; a literary word. *I have always felt like a changeling born into the wrong family.* (N-COUNT)

change of life. **The change of life** is the menopause. (N-SING: the N)

changeover /tʃeɪndʒoʊvər/ **changeovers.** A **changeover** is a change from one activity or system to another. *He again called for a faster changeover to a market economy... Right now we are in the changeover period between autumn and winter.* (N-COUNT)

changing room, changing rooms. A **changing room** is a room where you can change your clothes and usually have a shower, for example at a sports centre. (N-COUNT)

channel /tʃænəl/ **channels, channelling, channelled;** spelled **channeling**, **channeled** in American English. ◆◆◆◆◇

1 A **channel** is a wavelength on which television programmes or radio messages are broadcast. *...the only serious current affairs programme on either channel. ...the proliferating number of television channels in America. ...Mr John Willis, director of Channel 4 programmes.* (N-COUNT: oft in names =station)

2 If you do something through a particular **channel**, or particular **channels**, that is the system or organization that you use to achieve your aims or to communicate. *The government will surely use the diplomatic channels available... The Americans recognise that the UN can be the channel for greater diplomatic activity... Moscow and the Baltic republics are re-opening channels of communication.* (N-COUNT: with supp, oft adj N, N for/of n)

3 If you **channel** money or resources into something, you arrange for them to be used for that thing, rather than for a wider range of things. *Jacques Delors wants a system set up to channel funds to the poor countries... Revenues from 'green taxes' could then be channelled back into energy efficiency.* (VERB; V n prep)

4 If you **channel** your energies or emotions into something, you concentrate on or do that one thing, rather than a range of things. *Stephen is channelling his energies into a novel called Blue.* (VERB; V n into n; Also V n adv)

5 A **channel** is a passage along which water flows. *Keep the drainage channel clear.* (N-COUNT)

6 A **channel** is a route used by boats. *When the boat was following a channel close to the shore, you could hear the forest's noises.* (N-COUNT)

7 The Channel or **the English Channel** is the narrow area of water between England and France. (N-PROPER: the N)

channel-hopping. In British English, **channel-hopping** means switching quickly between different television channels because you are looking for something interesting to watch. The usual American term is **channel-surfing**. (N-UNCOUNT)

channel-surfing. **Channel-surfing** is the same as **channel-hopping**; used mainly in American English. (N-UNCOUNT)

chant /tʃɑːnt, tʃænt/ **chants, chanting, chanted** ◆◆◇◇◇

1 A **chant** is a word or group of words that is repeated over and over again. *He was greeted by the chant of 'Judas! Judas!'.* (N-COUNT: oft N of n)

2 A **chant** is a religious song or prayer that is sung on only a few notes. *...a Gregorian chant. ...a Buddhist chant.* (N-COUNT: usu adj N)

3 If you **chant** something or if you **chant**, you repeat the same words over and over again. *Demonstrators chanted slogans... The crowd chanted 'We are with you.'... Several thousand people chanted* (VERB; V n; V with quote; V; Also V that) *and demonstrated outside the building.* ♦ **chanting** *A lot of the chanting was in support of the deputy Prime Minister.* N-UNCOUNT

4 If you **chant** or if you **chant** something, you sing a religious song or prayer. *Muslims chanted and prayed... Mr Sharma lit incense and chanted Sanskrit mantras.* ♦ **chanting** *The chanting inside the temple stopped.* VERB V V n N-UNCOUNT

Chanukah /hɑːnəkə/. **Chanukah** is the same as **Hanukkah**. N-UNCOUNT =Hanukkah

chaos /keɪɒs/. **Chaos** is a state of complete disorder and confusion. *The world's first transatlantic balloon race ended in chaos last night... It is impossible to establish democracy amid economic chaos.* ◆◆◆◇◇ N-UNCOUNT

chaotic /keɪɒtɪk/. Something that is **chaotic** is in a state of complete disorder and confusion. *My own house feels as filthy and chaotic as a bus terminal... Mullins began to rummage among the chaotic mess of papers on his desk.* ♦ **chaotically** *Everything breakable had been broken and scattered chaotically about the room.* ◆◇◇◇◇ ADJ-GRADED ADV: ADV after v, ADV -ed/adj

chap /tʃæp/ **chaps** ◆◆◇◇◇

1 A **chap** is a man or boy; an informal use. *'I am a very lucky chap,' he commented. 'The doctors were surprised that I was not paralysed.'* N-COUNT =bloke, guy

2 Some people use **chap** when they are talking in a patronizing way to a man who they think is less important than themselves. *Just hold this, would you, there's a good chap?* N-COUNT PRAGMATICS

3 See also **chapped**.

chap., chaps. Chap. is a written abbreviation for **chapter**. *Today the best tests are performed in the hospital (see chap. 17).* N-VAR num

chapel /tʃæpəl/ **chapels** ◆◆◇◇◇

1 A **chapel** is a part of a church which has its own altar and which is used for private prayer. *...the chapel of the Virgin Mary.* N-COUNT: oft *the* N *of* n

2 A **chapel** is a small church attached to a hospital, school, or prison. *We married in the chapel of Charing Cross Hospital in London.* N-COUNT

3 A **chapel** is a building used for worship by members of some Christian churches. **Chapel** refers to the religious services that take place there. *...a Methodist chapel... On Sundays, the family went three times to chapel.* N-VAR

chaperone /ʃæpəroʊn/ **chaperones, chaperoning, chaperoned;** also spelled **chaperon**.

1 A **chaperone** is someone who accompanies another person somewhere in order to make sure that they do not come to any harm. N-COUNT

2 If you **are chaperoned** by someone, they act as your chaperone. *We were chaperoned by a tall red-haired girl.* VB: usu passive *be* V-ed

chaplain /tʃæplɪn/ **chaplains.** A **chaplain** is a member of the Christian clergy who does religious work in a place such as a hospital, school, prison, or in the army. *He joined the 40th Division as an army chaplain.* ◆◇◇◇◇ N-COUNT: oft n N

chaplaincy /tʃæplɪnsi/ **chaplaincies**

1 A **chaplaincy** is the building or office in which a chaplain works. N-COUNT

2 A **chaplaincy** is the position or work of a chaplain. *...the chaplaincy of the Royal Hospital.* N-COUNT

chapped /tʃæpt/. If your skin is **chapped**, it is dry, cracked, and sore. *...chapped hands... Her skin felt chapped.* ADJ-GRADED

chappy /tʃæpi/ **chappies.** A **chappy** is the same as a chap; an informal word. *I'm no longer the apparently eternally cheerful chappy he remembers... Robin Cousins exploits his brash, cheeky chappy personality.* N-COUNT

chapter /tʃæptəʳ/ **chapters** ◆◆◆◆◇

1 A **chapter** is one of the parts that a book is divided into. Each chapter has a number, and sometimes a title. *Chromium supplements were used successfully in the treatment of diabetes (see Chapter 4)... I took the title of this chapter from one of my favorite books.* N-COUNT: also N num

2 A **chapter** in someone's life or in history is a period of time during which a major event or series of related events takes place; used in written English. *This had been a particularly difficult chapter in Lebanon's recent history. ...one of the most dramatic chapters of recent British politics.* N-COUNT: supp N, oft N *in* n, adj N

3 A **chapter** is a group of Christian clergy who work in or who are connected with a cathedral. *The Archbishop began his address, thanking the Dean and Chapter of Westminster for inviting him to the Abbey.* N-COUNT-COLL

4 A **chapter** is a branch of a society or club. *This chapter of the AWGB has 75 members.* N-COUNT

5 If you say that someone gives you **chapter and verse** on a particular subject, you are emphasizing that they tell you every detail about it. *In the course of the evening he gave me chapter and verse on the mosses of the Islay peat bogs.* PHRASE: PHR after v PRAGMATICS

chapter house, chapter houses. A **chapter house** is the building or set of rooms in the grounds of a cathedral where the members of the clergy hold their meetings. N-COUNT

char /tʃɑːʳ/ **chars, charring, charred** ◆◇◇◇◇

1 If food **chars** or if you **char** it, it burns slightly and turns black as it is cooking. *Toast hazelnuts on a baking sheet until the skins char... Halve the peppers and char the skins under a hot grill.* ♦ **charring** *The chops should be cooked over moderate heat to prevent excessive charring.* V-ERG V V n N-UNCOUNT

2 If a woman **chars** for someone, she works as their cleaner; used in old-fashioned British English. *I'm calling round at the Rodings to ask if Mrs Higgins will char for you... My mother worked hard for us, charring at people's houses.* ♦ **charring** *There was very little work for women other than charring.* VERB V *for* n V N-UNCOUNT

3 Tea that you drink can be referred to as **char**; an old-fashioned, informal British use. *Is there any char going?* N-UNCOUNT

4 See also **charred**.

charabanc /ʃærəbæŋ/ **charabancs.** In British English, a **charabanc** is a large old-fashioned coach with several rows of seats. Charabancs were used especially for taking people sightseeing or on holiday. N-COUNT

character /kærɪktəʳ/ **characters** ◆◆◆◆◇

1 The **character** of a person or place consists of all the qualities they have that make them distinct from other people or places. *Perhaps there is a negative side to his character that you haven't seen yet... The character of this country has been formed by immigration.* N-COUNT: usu with supp =nature

2 If something has a particular **character**, it has a particular quality. *The financial concessions granted to British Aerospace were, he said, of a precarious character... The state farms were semi-military in character.* N-SING: usu supp N, also *in* N =nature

3 You can use the word **character** to refer to the qualities that people from a particular place are believed to have. *Individuality is a valued and inherent part of the British character.* N-SING: supp N =psyche

4 You use **character** to say what kind of person someone is. For example, if you say that someone is a strange **character**, you mean they are strange. *It's that kind of courage and determination that makes him such a remarkable character... What a sad character that Nigel is.* N-COUNT: usu adj N

5 Someone's **character** is their personality, usually considered in relation to how reliable and honest they are. If someone is of good **character**, they are reliable and honest. If they are of bad **character**, they are unreliable and dishonest. *He's begun a series of personal attacks on my character... Mr Bartman was a man of good character.* N-VAR: usu supp N

6 If you say that someone has **character**, you mean that they have the ability to deal effectively with difficult, unpleasant, or dangerous situations; used showing approval. *She showed real character in her attempts to win over the crowd... I didn't know Ron had that much strength of character.* N-UNCOUNT PRAGMATICS

7 If you say that a place has **character**, you mean that it has an interesting or unusual quality which makes you notice it and like it; used showing approval. *A soulless shopping centre stands across from one of one the few buildings with character, the Town Hall.* N-UNCOUNT PRAGMATICS

8 The **characters** in a film, book, or play are the people that it is about. *The film is autobiographical and the central character is played by Collard himself... He's made the characters believable.*
N-COUNT

9 If you say that someone is a **character**, you mean that they are interesting, unusual, or amusing; an informal use. *He'll be sadly missed. He was a real character.*
N-COUNT =eccentric

10 A **character** is a letter, number, or other symbol that is written or printed.
N-COUNT

11 If you say that someone's actions are **in character**, you mean they are what you would expect them to do, knowing what kind of person they are. If their actions are **out of character**, they are not what you would expect them to do. *It was entirely in character for Rachel to put her baby first... What else could make him behave so out of character?*
PHRASE: usu v-link PHR

character actor, character actors. A **character actor** is an actor who specializes in playing unusual or eccentric people.
N-COUNT

character assassination, character assassinations. A **character assassination** is a deliberate attempt to destroy someone's reputation, especially by criticizing them in an unfair and dishonest way when they are not present. *A full-scale character assassination of the dead woman got underway in the tabloid press.*
N-VAR

characterful /kærɪktəʳfʊl/. If you describe something as **characterful**, you mean that it is pleasant and interesting; used mainly in journalism. *One of the most characterful places to eat early evening is Mon Plaisir.*
ADJ-GRADED: usu ADJ n ≠characterless

characteristic /kærɪktərɪstɪk/ **characteristics** ◆◆◆◇◇

1 The **characteristics** of a person or thing are the qualities or features that belong to them and make them recognizable. *Genes determine the characteristics of every living thing. ...their physical characteristics.*
N-COUNT: usu pl, usu with supp =features, traits

2 A quality or feature that is **characteristic** of someone or something is one which is often seen in them and seems typical of them. *...the absence of strife between the generations that was so characteristic of such societies... Windmills are a characteristic feature of the Mallorcan landscape... Nehru responded with characteristic generosity.*
ADJ-GRADED: oft ADJ *of* n =typical ≠uncharacteristic

♦ **characteristically** /kærɪktərɪstɪkli/ *He replied in characteristically robust style... MacMillan's music characteristically makes a dramatic impact... Characteristically, he worked hard at the assignment.*
ADV-GRADED: usu ADV adj, also ADV with v, ADV with cl

characterization /kærɪktəraɪzeɪʃᵊn/ **characterizations;** also spelled **characterisation** in British English. **Characterization** is the way an author or an actor portrays a character. *As a writer I am interested in characterization. ...Chaucer's characterization of Criseyde.* ● See also **characterize**.
◆◇◇◇◇ N-VAR

characterize /kærɪktəraɪz/ **characterizes, characterizing, characterized;** also spelled **characterise** in British English. ◆◆◇◇◇

1 If something **is characterized** by a particular feature or quality, that feature or quality is very evident in it; a formal use. *This election campaign has been characterized by violence... A bold use of colour characterizes the bedroom.*
VERB =typify
be V-ed *by* n
V n

2 If you **characterize** someone or something **as** a particular thing, you describe them as that thing; a formal use. *Both companies have characterized the relationship as friendly... This play is characterized as a comedy.* ♦ **characterization, characterizations** *I don't fully agree with that characterization of the welfare system.*
VERB =describe
V n *as* adj/n
N-VAR: usu N *of* n

characterless /kærɪktəʳləs/. If you describe something as **characterless**, you mean that it is dull and uninteresting. *They felt the back garden was boring and characterless... We have too many pasteurised, bland and characterless cheeses in this country.*
ADJ-GRADED ≠characterful

charade /ʃərɑːd, AM -reɪd/ **charades** ◆◇◇◇◇

1 If you describe someone's actions as a **charade**, you mean that their actions are a pretence that is so obvious that it does not convince anyone; used showing disapproval. *I wondered why he had gone through the elaborate charade... The UN at the moment is still trying to maintain the charade of neutrality.*
N-COUNT: usu sing PRAGMATICS

2 **Charades** is a game for teams of players in which one team mimes a word or phrase, syllable by syllable, until other players guess the whole word or phrase. *She and her three brothers played charades.*
N-UNCOUNT

charcoal /tʃɑːʳkoʊl/. **Charcoal** is a black substance obtained by burning wood without much air. It can be burned as a fuel, and small sticks of it are used for drawing with.
◆◇◇◇◇ N-UNCOUNT

chard /tʃɑːʳd/. **Chard** is a plant with a round root, large leaves, and a thick stalk.
N-UNCOUNT

charge /tʃɑːʳdʒ/ **charges, charging, charged** ◆◆◆◆◆

1 If you **charge** someone an amount of money, you ask them to pay that amount for something that you have sold to them or done for them. *Even local nurseries charge £100 a week... The majority of stalls charged a fair price... Some banks charge if you access your account to determine your balance. ...the architect who charged us a fee of seven hundred and fifty pounds.*
VERB
V n
V
V n n

2 If you **charge** something **to** a person or organization, you tell the people providing it to send the bill to that person or organization. If you **charge** something **to** someone's account, you add it to their account so they do not have to pay for it immediately. *Go out and buy a pair of glasses, and charge it to us... All transactions have been charged to your account.*
VERB =bill
V n *to* n

3 A **charge** is an amount of money that you have to pay for a service. *We can arrange this for a small charge... Customers who arrange overdrafts will face a monthly charge of £5.*
N-COUNT

4 A **charge** is a formal accusation that someone has committed a crime. *He may still face criminal charges... They appeared at court yesterday to deny charges of murder.*
N-COUNT =indictment

5 When the police **charge** someone, they formally accuse them of having done something illegal. *They have the evidence to charge him... Police have charged Mr Bell with murder.*
VERB
V n
V n *with* n

6 If you **charge** someone **with** doing something wrong or unpleasant, you publicly say that they have done it; used in written English. *He charged the minister with lying about the economy.*
VERB =accuse
V n *with*-ing/n

7 If you take **charge** of someone or something, you make yourself responsible for them and take control over them. If someone or something is in your **charge**, you are responsible for them. *A few years ago Bacryl took charge of the company... I have been given charge of this class... They would never forget their time in his charge.*
N-UNCOUNT: usu N *of* n

8 If you are **in charge** in a particular situation, you are the most senior person and have control over something or someone. *Who's in charge here? ...the Swiss governess in charge of the smaller children.*
PHRASE: v-link PHR, oft PHR *of* n

9 If you describe someone as your **charge**, they have been given to you to be looked after and you are responsible for them. *The coach tried to get his charges motivated.*
N-COUNT: usu pl, poss N

10 If you **charge** towards someone or something, you move quickly and aggressively towards them. *He charged through the door to my mother's office... He ordered us to charge. ...a charging bull.* ► Also a noun. *...a bayonet charge.*
VERB
V prep/adv
V
V-ing
N-COUNT

11 To **charge** a battery means to pass an electrical current through it in order to make it more powerful or to make it last longer. *Alex had forgotten to charge the battery.* ► **Charge up** means the same as **charge**. *There was nothing in the brochure about having to drive it every day to charge up the battery.*
VERB
V n
PHRASAL VERB
V P n (not pron)
Also V n P

12 An electrical **charge** is an amount of electricity that is held in or carried by something.
N-COUNT: usu sing

13 The **charge** in a cartridge or shell is the explosive inside it. You can also refer to the cartridge or shell itself as a **charge**.
N-COUNT

14 See also **charged; baton charge, cover charge, depth charge, service charge**.

15 If something is **free of charge**, it does not cost
PHRASES

anything. *The leaflet is available free of charge from post offices.* =free

charge up See **charge** 8. PHRASAL VERB

chargeable /tʃɑːʳdʒəbᵊl/

1 If something is **chargeable**, you have to pay a sum of money for it; a formal use. *The day of discharge is not chargeable if rooms are vacated by 12.00 noon.* ADJ: usu v-link ADJ

2 If something is **chargeable**, you have to pay tax on it; a formal use. *...the taxpayer's chargeable gain.* ADJ

charge card, charge cards; also spelled **chargecard.**

1 In British English, a **charge card** is a plastic card that you use to buy goods on credit from a particular store or group of stores. At the end of each month you are supposed to pay off the full balance of what you have spent. Compare **credit card**. N-COUNT

2 In American English, a **charge card** is the same as a **credit card**. N-COUNT

charged /tʃɑːʳdʒd/ ◆◇◇◇◇

1 If a situation is **charged**, it is filled with emotion and therefore very tense or exciting. *There was a highly charged atmosphere... A wedding is an emotionally charged situation.* ADJ-GRADED: usu adv ADJ

2 **Charged** particles carry an electrical charge. *...negatively charged ions.* ADJ: oft adv ADJ

chargé d'affaires /ʃɑːʳʒeɪ dæfeəʳ/ **chargés d'affaires**

1 A **chargé d'affaires** is a person appointed to act as head of a diplomatic mission in a foreign country while the ambassador is away. N-COUNT

2 A **chargé d'affaires** is the head of a minor diplomatic mission in a foreign country. N-COUNT

charge nurse, charge nurses. In Britain, a **charge nurse** is a nurse who is in charge of a hospital ward. N-COUNT

charger /tʃɑːʳdʒəʳ/ **chargers** ◆◇◇◇◇

1 A **charger** is a device used for charging or recharging batteries. N-COUNT

2 A **charger** was a strong horse that a knight in the Middle Ages used to ride in battle. N-COUNT

charge sheet, charge sheets; also spelled **charge-sheet.** A **charge sheet** is the official form which is used by the police when they write down legal charges against a person; used mainly in British English. N-COUNT

char-grilled; also spelled **chargrilled. Chargrilled** meat or fish has been cooked so that it burns slightly and turns black. ADJ: usu ADJ n

chariot /tʃæriət/ **chariots.** In ancient times, **chariots** were fast-moving vehicles with two wheels that were pulled by horses. ◆◇◇◇◇ N-COUNT

charioteer /tʃæriətɪəʳ/ **charioteers.** In ancient times, a **charioteer** was a chariot driver. N-COUNT

charisma /kərɪzmə/. You say that someone has **charisma** when they can attract, influence, and inspire people by their personal qualities. *He has neither the policies nor the personal charisma to inspire people.* ◆◇◇◇◇ N-UNCOUNT =magnetism

charismatic /kærɪzmætɪk/ ◆◇◇◇◇

1 A **charismatic** person attracts, influences, and inspires people by their personal qualities. *With her striking looks and charismatic personality, she was noticed far and wide.* ADJ-GRADED: usu ADJ n =magnetic

2 The **charismatic** church is the part of the Christian Church that believes that people can obtain special supernatural gifts from God, for example prophecy, healing, and speaking in tongues. ADJ: usu ADJ n

charitable /tʃærɪtəbᵊl/ ◆◆◇◇◇

1 A **charitable** organization or activity helps and supports people who are ill, handicapped, or very poor. *...charitable work for the handicapped.* ADJ: ADJ n

2 Someone who is **charitable** to people is kind or tolerant towards them. *I am inclined to be charitable to politicians.* ♦ **charitably** /tʃærɪtəbli/ *Still, he reflected charitably, it was hardly her fault.* ADJ-GRADED: usu v-link ADJ; ADV-GRADED: ADV with v

charity /tʃærɪti/ **charities** ◆◆◆◇◇

1 A **charity** is an organization which raises money in order to help people who are ill, handicapped, or very poor. *The National Trust is a registered charity. ...an Aids charity.* N-COUNT: oft supp N

2 If you give money to **charity**, you give it to one or more charitable organizations. If you do something for **charity**, you do it in order to raise money for one or more charitable organizations. *He made substantial donations to charity... Gooch will be raising money for charity. ...a charity event.* N-UNCOUNT

3 People who live on **charity** live on money or goods which other people give them because they are poor. *She was very proud was my mum. She wouldn't accept charity... Her husband is unemployed and the family depends on charity.* N-UNCOUNT

4 **Charity** is kindness and tolerance towards other people; a formal use. N-UNCOUNT

5 If you say **charity begins at home**, you mean that people should deal with the needs of people close to them before they think about helping others. PHRASE: V inflects

charity shop, charity shops. In British English, a **charity shop** is a shop that sells second-hand goods cheaply and gives its profits to a charity. The usual American expression is **thrift shop**. N-COUNT

charlatan /ʃɑːʳlətᵊn/ **charlatans.** If you describe someone as a **charlatan**, you mean that they pretend to have skills or knowledge that he or she does not really possess; a formal word. *He was exposed as a charlatan.* N-COUNT =imposter

charleston /tʃɑːʳlstən/. The **charleston** is a lively dance that was popular in the 1920s. N-SING: usu *the* N

charm /tʃɑːʳm/ **charms, charming, charmed** ◆◆◇◇◇

1 **Charm** is the quality of being pleasant or attractive. *'Snow White and the Seven Dwarves', the 1937 Disney classic, has lost none of its original charm... The house had its charms, not the least of which was the furniture that came with it.* N-VAR

2 Someone who has **charm** behaves in a friendly, pleasant way that makes people like them. *He was a man of great charm and distinction.* N-UNCOUNT

3 If you **charm** someone, you please them, especially by using your charm. *He even charmed Mrs Prichard, carrying her shopping and flirting with her, though she's 83... The Indians, in turn, were charmed by the famous author's cultured and civilised outlook... You can't force – or even charm – him into behaving differently if he doesn't want to.* VERB V n V n *into* -ing

4 If you **charm** your **way** into or out of a place or situation, you use your charm to get into or out of that place or situation. *...charming his way into the British Embassy in Teheran... He charmed his way out of trouble.* VERB V *way* prep

5 If you say that someone **charmed** something **out of** you or **from** you, you mean that they used their charm to persuade you to give it to them; used showing disapproval. *He is good at charming money out of companies.* VERB PRAGMATICS V n *from/out of* n

6 A **charm** is a small ornament that is fixed to a bracelet or necklace. N-COUNT

7 A **charm** is an act, saying, or object that is believed to have magic powers. *They cross their fingers and spit over their shoulders as charms against the evil eye. ...a good luck charm.* N-COUNT

8 If you say that someone **turned on the charm**, you mean that they behaved in a way that seemed very friendly but which you think was insincere, sometimes in order to obtain something or deceive someone; used mainly in British English. *He figured out that you're lonely, like most widows, and he turned on the charm.* PHRASES V inflects PRAGMATICS

9 If you say that something **worked like a charm**, you mean that it was very effective or successful. *Economically, the policy worked like a charm.* V inflects

charmed /tʃɑːʳmd/ ◆◇◇◇◇

1 A **charmed** place, time, or situation is one that is very beautiful or pleasant, and seems slightly separate from the real world or real life; a literary word. *...the charmed atmosphere of Oxford in the late Twenties.* ADJ: ADJ n

2 If you say that someone **leads** or **has a charmed life**, you mean that they always seem to be lucky, as if they are protected or helped by magic; used mainly in British English. PHRASE: V and N inflect

charmed circle. If you refer to a group of people as a **charmed circle**, you disapprove of the fact that they have unfair power or influence and N-SING PRAGMATICS rarely allow anyone else to join their group; used mainly in written English. *...the immense role played by this very small charmed circle of critics.*

charmer /tʃɑːʳməʳ/ **charmers.** If you refer to someone, especially a man, as a **charmer**, you think that they behave in a very charming but rather insincere way; used showing disapproval. *...an immaculately groomed charmer.* • See also **snake charmer**. N-COUNT PRAGMATICS

charming /tʃɑːʳmɪŋ/ ◆◆◇◇◇

1 If you say that something is **charming**, you mean that it is very pleasant or attractive. *...a charming little fishing village. ...the charming custom of wearing a rose on that day.* ♦ **charmingly** *There's something charmingly old-fashioned about his brand of entertainment.* ADJ-GRADED PRAGMATICS ≠charmless; ADV-GRADED: ADV adj, ADV after v =delightfully

2 If you describe someone as **charming**, you mean they behave in a friendly, pleasant way that makes people like them. *...a charming young man... He found her as smart and beautiful as she is charming... He can be charming to his friends.* ♦ **charmingly** *Calder smiled charmingly and put out his hand. 'A pleasure, Mrs Talbot.'* ADJ-GRADED; ADV-GRADED: ADV after v

3 You can say **'Charming!'** to indicate your disapproval when someone has just been rude to you or told you about someone's bad behaviour. *'I'm glad I'm not going with you, that's for sure.'—'Oh, charming!'... 'They wanted to stop my dole money for those days.'—'Charming!'* CONVENTION PRAGMATICS

charmless /tʃɑːʳmləs/. If you say that something or someone is **charmless**, you mean that they are unattractive or uninteresting; used in written English. *...flat, charmless countryside. ...a charmless bully.* ADJ-GRADED ≠charming

charm offensive. If you say that someone has launched a **charm offensive**, you disapprove of the fact that they are being very friendly to their opponents or people who are causing problems for them; used mainly in journalism. *He launched what was called a charm offensive against MPs who might not support the Government.* N-SING PRAGMATICS

charnel house /tʃɑːʳnəl haʊs/ **charnel houses.** A **charnel house** is a place where the bodies and bones of dead people are stored. N-COUNT

charred /tʃɑːʳd/. **Charred** plants, buildings, or vehicles have been badly burnt and have become black because of fire. *...the charred remains of a tank.* ◆◇◇◇◇ ADJ-GRADED: usu ADJ n =burnt

chart /tʃɑːʳt/ **charts, charting, charted** ◆◆◆◇◇

1 A **chart** is a diagram, picture, or graph which is intended to make information easier to understand. *Male unemployment was 14.2%, compared with 5.8% for women (see chart on next page)... The chart below shows our top 10 choices.* • See also **bar chart, flow chart, pie chart.** N-COUNT =diagram

2 A **chart** is a map of the sea or stars. *...charts of Greek waters.* N-COUNT

3 If you **chart** an area of land, sea, or sky, or a feature in that area, you make a map of the area or show the feature in it. *Portuguese explorers had charted the west coast of Africa as far as Sierra Leone... Ptolemy charted more than 1000 stars in 48 constellations... These seas have been well charted.* VERB =map; V n

4 The **charts** are the official lists that show which pop records have sold the most copies each week. *This album confirmed The Orb's status as national stars, going straight to Number One in the charts... They topped both the US singles and album charts at the same time.* N-COUNT: usu pl =hit parade

5 If a musical performer or one of their records **charts**, their record sells enough copies to be in the list of best-selling records for a particular week; used in journalism. *The Temptations' album has already charted.* VERB; V

6 If you **chart** the development or progress of something, you observe and record it carefully. You can also say that a report or graph **charts** the development or progress of something. *One GP has charted a dramatic rise in local childhood asthma since the M25 was built nearby... Bulletin boards charted each executive's progress.* VERB =monitor; V n

7 If a person or plan **charts** a course of action, they describe what should be done in order to achieve something or to make progress in the future; a formal use. *We've charted a possible way forward... NATO had charted a new course for stability and cooperation in Europe... Your future is already neatly planned and charted.* VERB =outline; V n

charter /tʃɑːʳtəʳ/ **charters, chartering, chartered** ◆◆◆◇◇

1 A **charter** is a formal document describing the rights, aims, or principles of an organization or group of people. *...Article 50 of the United Nations Charter. ...the EC's Social Charter of workers' rights.* N-COUNT: with supp

2 A **charter** plane or boat is one which is hired for use by a particular person or group and which is not part of a regular service. *...the last charter plane carrying out foreign nationals. ...frequent charter flights to Spain, the most popular package-holiday destination.* ADJ: ADJ n

3 If a person or organization **charters** a plane, boat, or other vehicle, they hire it for their own use. *He chartered a jet to fly her home from California to Switzerland... Yesterday, a cargo ship chartered by the UN arrived in the capital carrying 1,550 tons of rice.* VERB; V n; V-ed

4 If you describe a decision or policy as **a charter for** a group or activity you disapprove of, you mean that the decision or policy is likely to help that group or increase that activity. *They described the Home Office scheme as a 'charter for cheats'... They condemned the white paper as a charter for centralisation and selective education.* PHRASE PRAGMATICS

chartered /tʃɑːʳtəʳd/. In British English, a **chartered** accountant or **chartered** surveyor is an accountant or surveyor who has formally qualified in their profession. ◆◆◇◇◇ ADJ: ADJ n

charwoman /tʃɑːʳwʊmən/ **charwomen.** A **charwoman** is a woman who is employed to clean houses or offices; used in old-fashioned British English. N-COUNT =cleaner

chary /tʃeəri/. If you are **chary** of doing something, you are fairly cautious about doing it. *I am rather chary of making too many idiotic mistakes.* ADJ-GRADED: v-link ADJ, usu ADJ *of/about*-ing/n

chase /tʃeɪs/ **chases, chasing, chased** ◆◆◆◇◇

1 If you **chase** someone, or **chase** after them, you run after them or follow them quickly in order to catch or reach them. *She chased the thief for 100 yards... He said nothing to waiting journalists, who chased after him as he left.* ► Also a noun. *He was reluctant to give up the chase... Police said he was arrested without a struggle after a car chase through the streets of Biarritz.* VERB =pursue; V n; V after n; N-COUNT =pursuit

2 If you **are chasing** something you want, such as work or money, you are trying hard to get it. *In Wales, 14 people are chasing every job... There are too many schools chasing too few pupils. ...publishers and booksellers chasing after profits from high-volume sales.* ► Also a noun. *They took an invincible lead in the chase for the championship.* VERB; V n; V after n; N-SING: N *for* n

3 If someone **chases** someone that they are attracted to, or **chases** after them, they try hard to persuade them to have a sexual relationship with them. *Women also have another reason for not chasing men too hard, of course... 'I was always chasing after men who just couldn't handle intimacy,' she says.* ► Also a noun. *The chase is always much more exciting than the conquest anyway.* VERB; V n; V after n; N-SING: *the* N

4 If someone **chases** you from a place, they force you to leave by using threats or violence. *Many farmers will then chase you off their land quite aggressively... Angry demonstrators chased him away.* VERB; V n *from/out of/off* n; V n *away/off/out*

5 If someone or something **chases** a person or group from a job or a powerful position, they force that person or group to leave that job or position. *His single-minded pursuit of European union helped chase Mrs Thatcher from power.* VERB; V n *from/out of* n

6 If you **chase** somewhere, you run or rush there. *They chased down the stairs into the narrow, dirty street. ...chasing about late at night in search of life's necessities.* VERB =run, rush, dash; V prep/adv

7 **The chase** is the activity of hunting animals; an N-SING:

old-fashioned use. *...bear robes, mountain lion hides, and other trophies of the chase.* theN

8 In British English, **Chase** is often used in the name of important horse races in which the horses have to jump over fences, ditches, or bushes. *...the Champion Hunter Chase.* N-IN-NAMES =steeplechase

9 See also **wild goose chase**.

10 If you **give chase**, you run after someone or follow them quickly in order to catch them. *Other officers gave chase but the killers escaped.* PHRASES V inflects

11 If you talk about **the thrill of the chase**, you are referring to the excitement that people feel when they are trying hard to get something. *People who adore the thrill of the chase know that prizes, like diamonds, are worth striving for.*

chase away. If someone or something **chases away** worries, fears, or other bad feelings, they cause those feelings to change and become happier; used mainly in written English. *Ellery's return will help to chase away some of the gloom... The rise in industrial production helped chase away lingering fears that the economy is slipping into a new recession.* PHRASAL VERB =get rid of V P n (not pron)

chase down PHRASAL VERB

1 If you **chase** someone **down**, you run after them or follow them quickly and catch them; used mainly in American English. *Ness chased the thief down and held him until police arrived... For thousands of years chasing down game was the main activity in which humans were involved.* V n P V P n (not pron)

2 If you **chase** someone or something **down**, you manage to find them after searching for them. *That's when I chased her down to be the singer in my band... Bank officials argued that it is not their job to chase down every asset of every bank debtor.* =track down V n P V P n (not pron)

chase up PHRASAL VERB

1 If you **chase up** something that is needed or needs dealing with, you find it or find out what is being done about it. *When I didn't hear from the suppliers or receive a refund, I chased the matter up... The authority can chase up the source of the pollution and demand that the owner clean it up.* V n P V P n (not pron)

2 If you **chase** someone **up**, you look for them and find them because you want them to do something or give you something. *...the story of a man who comes to Hollywood to chase up a client who has defaulted on a debt.* V P n (not pron) Also V n P

chaser /tʃeɪsəʳ/ **chasers.** A **chaser** is an alcoholic drink that you have after you have drunk a stronger or weaker alcoholic drink. *...whiskey with beer chasers.* ◆◇◇◇◇ N-COUNT: oft n N

chasm /kæzəm/ **chasms** ◆◇◇◇◇

1 A **chasm** is a very deep crack in rock, earth, or ice. N-COUNT

2 If you say that there is a **chasm** between two things or between two groups of people, you mean that there is a very large difference between them. *...the chasm that divides the worlds of university and industry... The chasm between rich and poor in America is too wide.* N-COUNT: usu with supp, oft N *between* pl-n =gulf, gap

3 A **chasm** of an emotion or problem such as loneliness or poverty is a large and apparently endless amount of this emotion or problem. *Beneath Morisot at twenty-one yawned the chasm of despair and aimlessness.* N-COUNT: usu N *of*n =abyss

chassis /ʃæsi/; **chassis** /ʃæsiz/ can also be used as the plural form. A **chassis** is the framework that a vehicle is built on. ◆◇◇◇◇ N-COUNT

chaste /tʃeɪst/

1 If you describe a person or their behaviour as **chaste**, you mean that they do not have sex with anyone, or they only have sex with their husband or wife; an old-fashioned word. *He remained chaste... Abramov did not live a chaste life.* ADJ-GRADED

2 Something that is **chaste** is very simple in style, without very much decoration. *...chaste clothes.* ADJ: ADJ n

chasten /tʃeɪsᵊn/ **chastens, chastening, chastened.** If you **are chastened** by something, it makes you feel sorry that you have behaved badly or foolishly; a formal word. *He has clearly not been chastened by his thirteen days in detention... A chastened Agassi flew home for a period of deep contemplation.* ♦ **chastened** *The President now seems a more chastened and less confident politician than when he set out a week ago.* VB: usu passive be V-ed *by*n V-ed Also *be* V-ed *into*n/-ing ADJ-GRADED

chastening /tʃeɪsənɪŋ/. A **chastening** experience makes you regret that you have behaved foolishly or badly. *From this chastening experience he learnt some useful lessons.* ADJ-GRADED

chastise /tʃæstaɪz/ **chastises, chastising, chastised.** If you **chastise** someone, you scold or punish them for something wrong that they have done; a formal word. *Thomas Rane chastised Peters for his cruelty... The Securities Commission chastised the firm but imposed no fine... I just don't want you to chastise yourself.* VERB =reprimand V n V pron-refl

chastisement /tʃæstaɪzmənt/. **Chastisement** is the same as punishment; an old-fashioned word. N-UNCOUNT: also *a* N

chastity /tʃæstɪti/. **Chastity** is the state of not having sex with anyone, or of only having sex with your husband or wife; an old-fashioned word. *He took a vow of chastity and celibacy.* N-UNCOUNT

chat /tʃæt/ **chats, chatting, chatted.** When people **chat**, they talk to each other in an informal and friendly way. *The women were chatting... I was chatting to him the other day... He's chatting with his dad... We chatted about old times.* ▸ Also a noun. *I had a chat with John.* ◆◆◆◇◇ V-RECIP =natter pl-n V V *to/with*n V *about*n N-COUNT =natter

chat up. In British English, if you **chat** someone **up**, usually someone you do not know very well, you talk to them in a friendly way because you are sexually attracted to them; an informal expression. *He'd spent most of that evening chatting up one of my friends... She was chatting one of the guys up.* PHRASAL VERB V P n (not pron) V n P

château /ʃætoʊ/ **châteaux** /ʃætoʊz/; also spelled **chateau**. A **château** is a large country house or castle in France. ◆◇◇◇◇ N-COUNT

chatelaine /ʃætəleɪn/ **chatelaines.** A **chatelaine** is the female owner, or the wife of the owner, of a castle or large country house. N-COUNT

chatline /tʃætlaɪn/ **chatlines;** also spelled **chat line**. People phone in to **chatlines** to have conversations with other people who have also phoned in. *She started using chat lines basically for someone to talk to.* N-COUNT

chat show, chat shows. In British English, a **chat show** is a television or radio show in which an interviewer and his or her guests talk in a friendly, informal way about different topics; the usual American expression is **talk show**. ◆◇◇◇◇ N-COUNT =talk show

chattel /tʃætᵊl/ **chattels. Chattels** are things that belong to you; an old-fashioned word. *They were slaves, to be bought and sold as chattels.* N-VAR

chatter /tʃætəʳ/ **chatters, chattering, chattered** ◆◇◇◇◇

1 If you **chatter**, you talk quickly and continuously, usually about things which are not important. *Everyone's chattering away in different languages... Erica was friendly and chattered about Andrew's children... He listened to chattering maids as they passed by.* ▸ Also a noun. *...idle chatter... Lila kept up a steady stream of chatter.* VERB V adv/prep V *about*n V-ing Also V N-UNCOUNT

2 If your teeth **chatter**, they click together repeatedly because you are very cold or very nervous. *She was so cold her teeth chattered.* VERB V

3 If objects **chatter**, they make repeated rattling sounds. *The telex chattered all day and night with news bulletins.* ▸ Also a noun. *...the mountains where the chatter of the chairlift cable over the pulley wheel is the loudest noise.* VERB =rattle V N-UNCOUNT: usu *the* N *of*n

4 When birds or animals **chatter**, they make high-pitched noises; a literary use. *Birds were chattering somewhere, and occasionally he could hear a vehicle pass by.* ▸ Also a noun. *...almond trees vibrating with the chatter of crickets.* VERB V N-UNCOUNT: usu *the* N *of*n

chatterbox /tʃætəʳbɒks/ **chatterboxes.** A **chatterbox** is someone who talks a lot; an informal word. *I was a chatterbox at school.* N-COUNT =chatterer

chatterer /tʃætərəʳ/ **chatterers.** A **chatterer** is the same as a **chatterbox**. N-COUNT

chattering classes. The **chattering classes** is a term used by journalists to describe people such as other journalists or broadcasters who comment on events but have little or no influence over them; used showing disapproval. *Radi-* N-PLURAL: usu *the* N PRAGMATICS *cal feminism is currently the fashionable topic among the chattering classes.*

chatty /tʃæti/

1 Someone who is **chatty** talks a lot in a friendly, informal way. *She's quite a chatty person.* ADJ-GRADED =talkative

2 A **chatty** style of writing or talking is friendly and informal. *He wrote a chatty letter to his wife.* ADJ-GRADED

chat-up line, chat-up lines. A **chat-up line** is a remark that someone makes in order to start a conversation with a person who they do not know but who they find sexually attractive. Chat-up lines often seem silly or insincere. *...locals with chat-up lines like 'Hello, my name's Adam, you must be Eve'.* N-COUNT

chauffeur /ʃoʊfəʳ, ʃoʊfɜːʳ/ **chauffeurs, chauffeuring, chauffeured** ◆◇◇◇◇

1 The **chauffeur** of a rich or important person is the man or woman who is employed to look after their car and drive them around in it. N-COUNT

2 If you **chauffeur** someone somewhere, you drive them there in a car, usually as part of your job. *It was certainly useful to have her there to chauffeur him around... Caroline had a chauffeured car waiting to take her to London.* VERB V n adv/prep V-ed Also V n

chauvinism /ʃoʊvɪnɪzəm/. **Chauvinism** is a strong, unreasonable belief that your own country is more important and morally better than other people's. *...it may also appeal to the latent chauvinism of many ordinary people.* • See also **male chauvinism.** ♦ **chauvinist, chauvinists** *Antwerpers are so convinced that their city is best that other Belgians think them chauvinists.* ◆◇◇◇◇ N-UNCOUNT PRAGMATICS N-COUNT

chauvinistic /ʃoʊvɪnɪstɪk/

1 If you describe someone as **chauvinistic**, you believe that they think their own country is more important and morally better than any other. *...national narrow-mindedness and chauvinistic arrogance. ...the highly chauvinistic coverage of the war.* ADJ-GRADED: usu ADJ n PRAGMATICS

2 If you describe a man or his behaviour as **chauvinistic**, you disapprove of the fact that he believes that men are naturally better and more important than women. *My ex-boyfriend Anthony was very chauvinistic.* ADJ-GRADED PRAGMATICS

cheap /tʃiːp/ **cheaper, cheapest** ◆◆◆◆◇

1 Goods or services that are **cheap** cost less money than usual or than you expected. *I'm going to live off campus if I can find somewhere cheap enough... Smoke detectors are cheap and easy to put up... Running costs are coming down because of cheaper fuel... They served breakfast all day and sold it cheap.* ♦ **cheaply** *It will produce electricity more cheaply than a nuclear plant.* ♦ **cheapness** *The cheapness and simplicity of the design makes it ideal for our task.* ADJ-GRADED: v-link ADJ, ADJ n, v n ADJ ≠expensive, dear ADV-GRADED: ADV after v N-UNCOUNT

2 If you describe goods as **cheap**, you mean they cost less money than similar products but their quality is poor. *Don't resort to cheap copies; save up for the real thing. ...a tight suit made of some cheap material.* ADJ: ADJ n =shoddy

3 If you describe the cost of someone's work as **cheap**, you disapprove of the way people are taking advantage of a situation to pay someone less than they should for the work that they do. *...unscrupulous employers who treat children as a cheap source of labour.* ADJ: ADJ n PRAGMATICS

4 If you describe someone's remarks or actions as **cheap**, you mean that they are unkindly or insincerely using a situation to benefit themselves or to harm someone else; used showing disapproval. *These tests will inevitably be used by politicians to make cheap political points.* ADJ: ADJ n PRAGMATICS

5 If you say that **life is cheap** or **life has become cheap**, you mean that a situation such as a war has made it normal for large numbers of people to die unnecessarily and often violently without anyone caring. *We will end up living in a society where life is cheap.* PHRASES V inflects

6 If you say that someone does or buys something **on the cheap**, you mean they spend less money on it than is required because they are more concerned with what it costs than its quality; an informal expression, often used showing disapproval. *Most modern housing estates are terrible and inevitably done on the cheap.* PHR after v

cheapen /tʃiːpən/ **cheapens, cheapening, cheapened.** If something **cheapens** a person or thing, it lowers their reputation or dignity. *When America boycotted the Moscow Olympics it cheapened the medals won... Love is a word cheapened by overuse.* VERB V n

cheapo /tʃiːpoʊ/. **Cheapo** things are very inexpensive and probably of poor quality; an informal word. *Cheese also features in my favourite cheapo meal. ...cheapo deals on wobbly airlines.* ADJ: ADJ n

cheap shot, cheap shots. A **cheap shot** is a comment someone makes which you think is unfair or unkind. *He always throws out the tacky comment and the cheap shot. He has no class.* N-COUNT PRAGMATICS

cheapskate /tʃiːpskeɪt/ **cheapskates.** If you say that someone is a **cheapskate**, you think that they are mean and very reluctant to spend money. *Tell your husband not to be a cheapskate. ...cheapskate employers.* N-COUNT PRAGMATICS =skinflint

cheat /tʃiːt/ **cheats, cheating, cheated** ◆◆◇◇◇

1 When someone **cheats**, they do not obey a set of rules which they should be obeying, for example in a game or exam. *Students may be tempted to cheat in order to get into top schools.* ♦ **cheating** *In an election in 1988, he was accused of cheating by his opponent.* VERB V N-UNCOUNT

2 Someone who is a **cheat** does not obey a set of rules which they should be obeying. *Cheats will be disqualified.* N-COUNT

3 If someone **cheats** you out of something, they get it from you by behaving dishonestly. *The company engaged in a deliberate effort to cheat them out of their pensions... Many brokers were charged with cheating customers in commodity trades.* VERB V n *out of/of* n V n

4 If you say that someone **cheats death**, you mean they narrowly avoid being killed; used in journalism. *He cheated death when he was rescued from the roof of his blazing cottage.* PHRASES V inflects

5 If you **feel cheated**, you feel that you have been let down or treated unfairly. *The storyline is fatally compromised by an ending that leaves you feeling horribly cheated.* V inflects

cheat on PHRASAL VERB

1 If someone **cheats on** their husband, wife, or partner, they have a sexual relationship with another person; an informal expression. *I'd found Philippe was cheating on me and I was angry and hurt.* =be unfaithful to V P n

2 If someone **cheats on** something such as an agreement or their taxes, they do not do what they should do under a set of rules; used especially in American English. *Their job is to check that none of the signatory countries is cheating on the agreement.* V P n

cheater /tʃiːtəʳ/ **cheaters.** A **cheater** is someone who cheats; used mainly in American English. N-COUNT

check /tʃek/ **checks, checking, checked** ◆◆◆◆◇

1 If you **check** something such as information or a document, you make sure that it is correct or satisfactory. *Check the accuracy of everything in your CV... It's worth checking each item for obvious flaws... I think there is an age limit, but I'd have to check... She hadn't checked whether she had a clean ironed shirt... He checked that he had his room key... I shall need to check with the duty officer.* • See also **cross-check.** ► Also a noun. *He is being constantly monitored with regular checks on his blood pressure. ...a security check.* VERB V n V V wh V that V *with* n N-COUNT: usu with supp

2 If you **check on** someone or something, you make sure they are in a safe or satisfactory condition. *Stephen checked on her several times during the night... He decided to check on things at the warehouse.* VERB V *on* n

3 To **check** something, usually something bad, means to stop it from spreading or continuing. *Sex education is also expected to help check the spread of AIDS. ...free press that will check corruption by ensuring total transparency in government.* VERB =curb V n

4 If you **check** yourself or if something **checks** you, VERB

you suddenly stop what you are doing or saying. *He was about to lose his temper but checked himself in time... I held up one finger to check him.* V pron-refl V n

5 When you **check** your luggage at an airport, you give it to an official so that it can be taken aboard the plane you will be travelling on. *We arrived at the airport, checked our baggage and wandered around the gift shops... You can check you baggage right through to its final destination.* ▶ To **check in** your luggage means the same as to **check** it. *They checked in their luggage and found seats in the departure lounge.* VERB V n V n prep/adv PHRASAL VERB V P n (not pron) Also V n P

6 The **check** in a restaurant is a piece of paper on which the price of your meal is written and which you are given before you pay; used mainly in American English. N-COUNT =bill

7 In a game of chess, you say **check** when you are attacking your opponent's king. CONVENTION

8 A pattern of squares, usually of two colours, can be referred to as **checks** or a **check**. *Styles include stripes and checks. ...a red and white check dress.* N-COUNT: oft N n

9 If something or someone **is held in check** or **is kept in check**, they are controlled and prevented from becoming too great or powerful. *Life on Earth will become unsustainable unless population growth is held in check... He's found someone with a bit of fight to keep him in check.* PHRASE: V inflects

10 See also **cheque**, **double-check**, **rain check**, **spot check**.

check in PHRASAL VERB

1 When you **check in** or **check into** a hotel or clinic, or if someone **checks** you **in**, you arrive and go through the necessary procedures before you stay there. *I'll ring the hotel. I'll tell them we'll check in tomorrow... He has checked into an alcohol treatment centre... Check us in at the hotel and wait for my call.* ERG =register ≠check out V P V P n V n P Also V n P n

2 When you **check in** at an airport, you arrive and show your ticket before going on a flight. *He had checked in at Amsterdam's Schiphol airport for a flight to Manchester.* • See also **check-in**, **check** 5. V P

check off. When you **check** things **off**, you check or count them while referring to a list of them, to make sure you have considered all of them. *Once you've checked off the items you ordered, put this record in your file... I haven't checked them off but I would say that's about the number.* PHRASAL VERB =tick off V P n (not pron) V n P

check out PHRASAL VERB

1 When you **check out** of a hotel or clinic where you have been staying, or is someone **checks** you **out**, you pay the bill and leave. *They packed and checked out of the hotel... I was disappointed to miss Bryan, who had just checked out... I'd like to check him out of here the day after tomorrow.* ERG ≠check in V P *of* n V P V n P *of* n Also V P n (not pron), V n P

2 If you **check out** something or someone, you find out information about them to make sure that everything is correct or satisfactory. *Maybe we ought to go down to the library and check it out... We ought to check him out on the computer... The police had to check out the call.* =investigate V n P V P n

3 See also **checkout**.

check up PHRASAL VERB

1 If you **check up** on something, you find out information about it. *It is certainly worth checking up on your benefit entitlements... The Government employs tax inspectors to check up and make sure people pay all their tax.* • See also **check-up**. V P *on* n V P

2 If you **check up** on someone, you obtain information about them, usually secretly. *I'm sure he knew I was checking up on him.* V P *on* n

checkbook /tʃekbʊk/. See **cheque book**.

checked /tʃekt/. Something that is **checked** has a pattern of small squares, usually of two colours. *He was wearing blue jeans and checked shirt.* ◆◆◇◇◇ ADJ =check

checker /tʃekər/ **checkers**

1 In American English, **checkers** is a game for two people, played with 24 round pieces on a board. The British word is **draughts**. N-UNCOUNT

2 A **checker** is a person or machine that has the job of checking something. *Janie worked as a checker at the A&P... Modern word processors usually have spelling checkers and even grammar checkers.* N-COUNT

checkerboard /tʃekərbɔːrd/ **checkerboards;** also spelled **chequerboard** in British English.

1 In American English, a **checkerboard** is a special board that is used to play chess or draughts on. The surface of a checkerboard is covered by alternate, equal-sized, black and white squares. The usual British word is **chessboard**. N-COUNT

2 A **checkerboard** pattern is made up of equal-sized squares of two different colours, usually black and white. ADJ: ADJ n

checkered /tʃekərd/. See **chequered**.

check-in, check-ins. At an airport, a **check-in** counter or desk is the place where you check in. ◆◇◇◇◇ N-COUNT

checking account, checking accounts. In American English, a **checking account** is a personal bank account which you can take money out of at any time using your cheque book or cash card. The usual British expression is **current account**. N-COUNT

checklist /tʃeklɪst/ **checklists.** A **checklist** is a list of all the things that you need to do, information that you want to find out, or things that you need to take somewhere, which you make in order to ensure that you do not forget anything. *Make a checklist of the tools and materials you will need for each part of the job.* ◆◇◇◇◇ N-COUNT: usu with supp, oft N *of* n =list

checkmate /tʃekmeɪt/. In chess, **checkmate** is a situation in which you cannot stop your king being captured and so you lose the game. N-UNCOUNT =mate

checkout /tʃekaʊt/ **checkouts;** also spelled **check-out**. In a supermarket, a **checkout** is a counter where you pay for things you are buying. *...queuing at the checkout in Sainsbury's.* ◆◇◇◇◇ N-COUNT

checkpoint /tʃekpɔɪnt/ **checkpoints.** A **checkpoint** is a place where traffic is stopped so that it can be checked. ◆◇◇◇◇ N-COUNT

check-up, check-ups. A **check-up** is a medical examination by your doctor or dentist to make sure that there is nothing wrong with your health. *The disease was detected during a routine check-up. ...a regular check-up at the dentist.* ◆◇◇◇◇ N-COUNT

cheddar /tʃedər/ **cheddars. Cheddar** is a type of hard yellow cheese, usually made in Britain. ◆◇◇◇◇ N-MASS

cheek /tʃiːk/ **cheeks.** ◆◆◇◇◇

1 Your **cheeks** are the sides of your face below your eyes. *Tears were running down her cheeks... She kissed him lightly on both cheeks.* ♦ **-cheeked** *...rosy-cheeked children. ...a fat, chubby-cheeked fellow.* N-COUNT COMB in ADJ

2 You say that someone has a **cheek** when you are annoyed or shocked at something unreasonable that they have done; an informal use. *I'm amazed they had the cheek to ask in the first place... I still think it's a bit of a cheek sending a voucher rather than a refund... The cheek of it, lying to me like that!* N-SING: also no det, oft *the* N to-inf

3 If you **turn the other cheek** when someone harms or insults you, you do not harm or insult them in return. PHRASE: V inflects

4 • **cheek by jowl**: see **jowl**.

cheekbone /tʃiːkboʊn/ **cheekbones.** Your **cheekbones** are the two bones in your face just below your eyes. *She was very beautiful, with high cheekbones.* ◆◇◇◇◇ N-COUNT: usu pl

cheeky /tʃiːki/ **cheekier, cheekiest.** If you describe a person or their behaviour as **cheeky**, you think that they are slightly rude or disrespectful but in a charming or amusing way. *The boy was cheeky and casual... Martin gave her a cheeky grin.* ♦ **cheekily** /tʃiːkɪli/ *He strolled cheekily past the commissionaires for a free wash in the gentlemen's cloakroom.* ◆◇◇◇◇ ADJ-GRADED =saucy ADV-GRADED: usu ADV with v, also ADV with cl

cheer /tʃɪər/ **cheers, cheering, cheered** ◆◆◆◇◇

1 When people **cheer**, they shout loudly to show their approval of something or to encourage someone who is doing something such as taking part in a game. *A picture of the President was set on fire as the crowd cheered and sang... Swiss fans cheered Jakob Hlasek during yesterday's match with Courier... Cheering crowds lined the route.* ▶ Also a VERB ≠boo, jeer V V n V-ing N-COUNT noun. *The colonel was rewarded with a resounding cheer from the men.*

2 If you **are cheered** by something, it makes you happier or less worried. *Stephen noticed that the people around him looked cheered by his presence... The weather was perfect for a picnic, he told himself, but the thought did nothing to cheer him.* VERB =hearten ≠sadden *be* V-ed V n
♦ **cheering** *...very cheering news... It is cheering to see that customers are to benefit from a rebate on their electricity bills.* ADJ-GRADED =heartening ≠saddening

3 **Cheer** is a feeling of cheerfulness and well-being. *They were impressed by his steadfast good cheer... A timely bingo win brought some cheer to Juliet Little's family yesterday.* N-UNCOUNT

4 People sometimes say **'Cheers'** to each other just before they drink an alcoholic drink. CONVENTION PRAGMATICS

5 In British English, some people say **'Cheers'** as an informal way of saying 'thank you'. CONVENTION PRAGMATICS

6 In British English, some people say **'Cheers'** as an informal way of saying goodbye. CONVENTION PRAGMATICS

cheer on. When you **cheer** someone **on**, you shout loudly in order to encourage them, for example when they are taking part in a game. *A thousand supporters packed into the stadium to cheer them on... Most will probably be cheering on their favourite players.* PHRASAL VERB V n P V P n (not pron)

cheer up. When you **cheer up** or when something **cheers** you **up**, you stop feeling depressed and become more cheerful. *I think he misses her terribly. You might cheer him up... I wrote that song just to cheer myself up... Cheer up, better times may be ahead.* PHRASAL VERB ERG V n P V pron-refl P V P Also V P n (not pron)

cheerful /tʃɪəʳfʊl/ ◆◆◇◇◇

1 Someone who is **cheerful** is happy and joyful and shows this in their behaviour. *They are both very cheerful in spite of their colds... Jack sounded quite cheerful about the idea.* ♦ **cheerfully** *'We've come with good news,' Pat said cheerfully... She greeted him cheerfully.* ♦ **cheerfulness** *I remember this extraordinary man with particular affection for his unfailing cheerfulness.* ADJ-GRADED =cheery; ADV-GRADED: ADV with v; N-UNCOUNT: oft adj N

2 Something that is **cheerful** is pleasant and makes you feel happy. *The nursery is bright and cheerful, with plenty of toys.* ADJ-GRADED

3 If you describe someone's attitude as **cheerful**, you mean they are not worried about something, and you think that they should be. *There is little evidence to support many of Mr Will's cheerful assumptions.* ♦ **cheerfully** *...cheerfully ignoring medical advice which could have prolonged his life.* ADJ-GRADED: usu ADJ n =optimistic; ADV: ADV before v

cheerio /tʃɪəriəʊ/. In British English, people sometimes say **'Cheerio'** as an informal way of saying goodbye. CONVENTION =bye

cheerleader /tʃɪəʳliːdəʳ/ **cheerleaders** ◆◇◇◇◇

1 A **cheerleader** is one of the people who leads the crowd in cheering at a large public event, especially a sports event. N-COUNT

2 If you say that someone is a **cheerleader** for a particular cause or an individual politician, you mean that they are one of the chief supporters of this cause or politician and work hard to raise support for them. *Chancellor Helmut Kohl was the leading cheerleader for German unification.* N-COUNT

cheerless /tʃɪəʳləs/. A place that is **cheerless** is gloomy and depressing. *The kitchen was dank and cheerless. ...a bleak, cheerless dawn with driving rain clouds.* ADJ-GRADED =gloomy

cheery /tʃɪəri/ **cheerier, cheeriest.** If you describe a person or their behaviour as **cheery**, you mean that they are cheerful and happy. *She was cheery and talked to them about their problems.* ◆◇◇◇◇ ADJ-GRADED =cheerful
♦ **cheerily** *'Come on in,' she said cheerily.* ADV-GRADED

cheese /tʃiːz/ **cheeses** ◆◆◆◇◇

1 **Cheese** is a solid food made from milk. It is usually white or yellow. *...bread and cheese. ...cheese sauce... He cut the mould off a piece of cheese. ...delicious French cheeses.* • See also **cottage cheese, cream cheese, goat cheese, macaroni cheese.** N-MASS

2 Someone who has a very important job or position can be referred to as a **big cheese**; an informal expression. *He is a big cheese in the Art Fraud Squad. ...big cheeses from the State Department.* PHRASES N inflects

3 If someone tells you to **say 'cheese'** when they are taking your photograph, they are indicating that they want you to smile. V inflects

4 • **as different as chalk and cheese**: see **chalk.**

cheeseboard /tʃiːzbɔːʳd/ **cheeseboards;** also spelled **cheese board.** A **cheeseboard** is a wooden or plastic board from which a selection of cheeses are served at a meal. *The desserts on the trolley looked tempting but instead I chose the cheese board.* N-COUNT: usu sing

cheeseburger /tʃiːzbɜːʳgəʳ/ **cheeseburgers.** A **cheeseburger** is a flat piece of cooked meat with a layer of cheese, served in a bread bun. N-COUNT

cheesecake /tʃiːzkeɪk/ **cheesecakes. Cheesecake** is a dessert that consists of a base made from crumbled biscuits covered with a soft mixture containing cream cheese. N-VAR

cheesecloth /tʃiːzklɒθ, AM -klɔːθ/. **Cheesecloth** is cotton cloth that is very thin and light. There are tiny holes between the threads of the cloth. *...cheesecloth shirts... Strain the mixture through a double thickness of muslin or cheesecloth.* N-UNCOUNT

cheesed off /tʃiːzd ɒf/. If you are **cheesed off**, you are annoyed, bored, or disappointed; used in informal British English. *Jean was thoroughly cheesed off by the whole affair... I did get a bit cheesed off with the movie's rather plodding pace.* ADJ-GRADED: v-link ADJ

cheesy /tʃiːzi/ **cheesier, cheesiest**

1 **Cheesy** food is food that tastes or smells of cheese. *...cheesy biscuits... The sauce was too runny and not cheesy enough.* ADJ-GRADED: usu ADJ n

2 In informal American English, something that is **cheesy** is considered to be cheap, unpleasant, or insincere. *...a cheesy Baghdad hotel... The King's Road was getting increasingly cheesy... Politicians persist in imagining that 'the people' warm to their cheesy slogans.* ADJ-GRADED

cheetah /tʃiːtə/ **cheetahs.** A **cheetah** is a wild animal that looks like a large cat with black spots on its body. Cheetahs can run very fast. N-COUNT

chef /ʃef/ **chefs.** A **chef** is a cook in a restaurant or hotel. ◆◆◇◇◇ N-COUNT

chemical /kemɪkəl/ **chemicals** ◆◆◆◆◇

1 **Chemical** means involving or resulting from a reaction between two or more substances, or relating to the substances that something consists of. *...chemical reactions that cause ozone destruction. ...the chemical composition of the ocean. ...chemical weapons.* ♦ **chemically** /kemɪkli/ *...chemically treated foods... The medicine chemically affects your physiology.* ADJ: ADJ n; ADV: ADV with v, ADV adj

2 **Chemicals** are substances that are used in a chemical process or made by a chemical process. *The whole food chain is affected by the over-use of chemicals in agriculture. ...a chemicals company. ...the chemical industry.* N-COUNT: usu pl

chemical engineer, chemical engineers. A **chemical engineer** is a person who designs and constructs the machines needed for industrial chemical processes. N-COUNT

chemical engineering. Chemical engineering is the designing and constructing of machines that are needed for industrial chemical processes. N-UNCOUNT

chemise /ʃəmiːz/ **chemises.** A **chemise** is a full-length, loose undergarment worn by women in former times. N-COUNT

chemist /kemɪst/ **chemists** ◆◆◇◇◇

1 In Britain, a **chemist** or a **chemist's** is a shop where drugs and medicines are sold or given out, and where you can buy cosmetics and some household goods. *There are many creams available from the chemist which should clear the infection... She went into a chemist's and bought some aspirin.* N-COUNT: oft *the* N =pharmacy

2 In British English, a **chemist** is someone who works in a chemist's shop and is qualified to prepare and sell medicines prescribed by a doctor. The American word is **druggist** or **pharmacist**. *The chemist will be only too pleased to help teach you* N-COUNT =pharmacist

how to read your thermometer... It is often better to consult your chemist than your doctor.
3 A **chemist** is a person who does research connected with chemistry or who studies chemistry. *She worked as a research chemist.* N-COUNT

chemistry /kemɪstri/ ◆◆◇◇◇
1 Chemistry is the scientific study of the characteristics and composition of substances and of the way that they react with other substances. N-UNCOUNT
2 If you talk about the **chemistry** of an organism or a material, you are referring to the chemical substances that make it up and the chemical reactions that go on inside it. *We have literally altered the chemistry of our planet's atmosphere... If the supply of vitamins and minerals in the diet is inadequate, this will result in changes in body chemistry.* N-UNCOUNT: usu with supp
3 If you say that there is **chemistry** between two people, you mean that is obvious they are attracted to each other or like each other very much. *...the extraordinary chemistry between Ingrid and Bogart... Janis and I became friends but we were never close. The chemistry wasn't there.* N-UNCOUNT

chemotherapy /kiːmoʊθerəpi/. **Chemotherapy** is the treatment of disease using chemicals. It is often used in treating cancer. ◆◇◇◇◇ N-UNCOUNT

chenille /ʃəniːl/. **Chenille** is cloth or clothing made from thick, furry **chenille** yarn. *...an old chenille bathrobe.* N-UNCOUNT

cheque /tʃek/ **cheques;** spelled **check** in American English. A **cheque** is a printed form on which you write an amount of money and who it is to be paid to. Your bank then pays the money to that person from your account. *He wrote them a cheque for £10,000... I'd like to pay by cheque.* ● See also **blank cheque, traveller's cheque**. ◆◆◇◇◇ N-COUNT: also by N

cheque book, cheque books; also spelled **chequebook**. Spelled **checkbook** in American English. A **cheque book** is a book of blank cheques which your bank gives you so that you can pay for things by cheque. *Leave your cheque book and credit cards at home unless you know you will need them.* N-COUNT

cheque-book journalism; spelled **checkbook journalism** in American English. **Cheque-book journalism** is the practice of getting material for newspaper articles by paying people large sums of money for exclusive information or interviews; used showing disapproval. N-UNCOUNT PRAGMATICS

cheque card, cheque cards. In Britain, a **cheque card** or a **cheque guarantee card** is a small plastic card given to you by your bank and which you have to show when you are paying for something by cheque or when you are cashing a cheque at another bank. *As the girl copied the cheque card number onto the back of his cheque, Jarvis saw Dr Pont go past the shop-window.* N-COUNT =banker's card

chequerboard /tʃekəʳbɔːʳd/. See **checkerboard**.

chequered /tʃekəʳd/; spelled **checkered** in American English.
1 If a person or organization has had a **chequered** career or history, they have had a varied past with both good and bad periods. *He had a chequered political career spanning nearly forty years... Alan had led a very chequered past and had been to prison lots of times.* ADJ-GRADED: usu ADJ n
2 Something that is **chequered** has a pattern with squares of two or more different colours. *...red chequered tablecloths.* ADJ: ADJ n =checked

cherish /tʃerɪʃ/ **cherishes, cherishing, cherished** ◆◇◇◇◇
1 If you **cherish** something such as a hope or a pleasant memory, you keep it in your mind for a long period of time. *The president will cherish the memory of this visit to Ohio... It was a wonderful occasion which we will cherish for many years to come.* ♦ **cherished** *...the cherished dream of a world without wars.* VERB =treasure V n; ADJ-GRADED: ADJ n
2 If you **cherish** someone or something, you take good care of them because you love them. *He genuinely loved and cherished her... The previous owners had cherished the house.* ♦ **cherished** *He described the picture as his most cherished possession.* VERB V n; ADJ-GRADED: ADJ n
3 If you **cherish** a right, a privilege, or a principle, you regard it as important and try hard to keep it. *Chinese people cherish their independence and sovereignty.* ♦ **cherished** *Freud called into question some deeply cherished beliefs.* VERB V n; ADJ-GRADED: ADJ n

cheroot /ʃəruːt/ **cheroots.** A **cheroot** is a cigar with both ends cut flat. N-COUNT

cherry /tʃeri/ **cherries** ◆◆◇◇◇
1 Cherries are small, round fruit with red skins. N-COUNT
2 A **cherry** or a **cherry tree** is a tree that cherries grow on. N-COUNT

cherub /tʃerəb/ **cherubs.** A **cherub** is an angel that is represented in art as a plump naked child with wings. *...in the bedroom a mural depicts a pair of chubby cherubs.* N-COUNT =angel

cherubic /tʃəruːbɪk/. If you say that someone looks **cherubic**, you mean that they look plump, sweet, and innocent like a cherub; a literary word. *I was born cherubic and chubby. ...her beaming, cherubic face.* ADJ

chervil /tʃɜːʳvɪl/. **Chervil** is a herb that tastes of aniseed. N-UNCOUNT

Cheshire cat /tʃeʃəʳ kæt/. If you say that someone is grinning **like a Cheshire cat** or **like the Cheshire cat**, you mean that they are smiling very widely. *He had a grin on his face like a Cheshire Cat. ...a Cheshire Cat smile.* PHRASE

chess /tʃes/. **Chess** is a game for two people, played on a chessboard. Each player has 16 pieces, including a king. Your aim is to move your pieces so that your opponent's king cannot escape being taken. *...the world chess championships.* ◆◆◇◇◇ N-UNCOUNT

chessboard /tʃesbɔːʳd/ **chessboards.** A **chessboard** is a square board that you play chess on. It is divided into 64 black and white squares. N-COUNT

chest /tʃest/ **chests** ◆◆◆◇◇
1 Your **chest** is the top part of the front of your body where your ribs, lungs, and heart are. *He crossed his arms over his chest... He was shot in the chest... He complained of chest pain.* ♦ **-chested** *He was bare-chested and barefoot... I'm 15 and completely flat-chested.* N-COUNT: oft poss N; COMB in ADJ
2 A **chest** is a large, heavy box used for storing things. *At the very bottom of the chest were his carving tools. ...a treasure chest. ...a medicine chest.* N-COUNT =trunk
3 If you **get** something **off** your **chest**, you talk about something that has been worrying you. *I feel it's done me good to get it off my chest.* PHRASE: V inflects ≠bottle up

chestnut /tʃesnʌt/ **chestnuts** ◆◇◇◇◇
1 A **chestnut** or **chestnut tree** is a tall tree with broad leaves. ● See also **horse chestnut**. N-COUNT
2 Chestnuts are the reddish-brown nuts that grow on chestnut trees. You can eat chestnuts. N-COUNT
3 Something that is **chestnut** is dark reddish-brown in colour. *...a woman with chestnut hair. ...a chestnut mare.* COLOUR
4 If you refer to a statement, a story, or a joke as an **old chestnut** or a **hoary chestnut**, you mean that it has been repeated so often that it is no longer interesting. *...that old chestnut, the war between man and machines.* PHRASE: N inflects

chest of drawers, chests of drawers. A **chest of drawers** is a low, flat piece of furniture with drawers in which you keep clothes and other things. N-COUNT

chesty /tʃesti/. If you have a **chesty** cough, you have a lot of catarrh in your lungs; used mainly in British English. ADJ: ADJ n

chevron /ʃevrɒn/ **chevrons** ◆◇◇◇◇
1 A **chevron** is a V shape. *The chevron or arrow road sign indicates a sharp bend to the left or right.* N-COUNT
2 A **chevron** is one of a number of V shapes worn on the sleeve by someone in the armed forces or in the police force. It shows his or her rank. *He wore shoulderstrap rank slides with sergeant's chevrons.* N-COUNT

chew /tʃuː/ **chews, chewing, chewed** ◆◆◇◇◇
1 When you **chew** food, you use your teeth to break it up in your mouth so that it becomes easier to swallow. *Be certain to eat slowly and chew your* VERB V n

food extremely well... Daniel leaned back on the sofa, still chewing on his apple. ...the sound of his mother chewing and swallowing. V *at/on* n V

2 If you **chew** gum or tobacco, you keep biting it and moving it around your mouth to taste the flavour of it. You do not swallow it. *One girl was chewing gum... He chews tobacco constantly.* VERB V n

3 If you **chew** your lips or your fingernails, you keep biting them because you are nervous. *He chewed his lower lip nervously.* VERB V n

4 If a person or animal **chews** an object, they bite it with their teeth. *They pause and chew their pencils... One owner left his pet under the stairs where the animal chewed through electric cables.* VERB =bite V n V prep

5 In British English, a **chew** is a sweet that you have to chew very hard before it becomes soft. *...a selection of penny chews.* N-COUNT

6 If you say that someone **has bitten off more than** they **can chew**, you mean that they are trying to do something which is too difficult for them. *Micky is used to handling dodgy deals but this time fears he may have bitten off more than he can chew.* PHRASES *bite* inflects

7 If people **chew the fat**, they talk or gossip; an informal expression. *We'd been lounging around, chewing the fat for a couple of hours.* RECIP: V inflects, pl-n PHR, PHR *with* n

8 • **to chew the cud**: see **cud**.

chew out. If you **chew** someone **out**, you tell them off in a very angry way; an informal expression. *He chewed out the player, who apologized the next time I saw him... When Tom got back to Dallas, Perot called him over and chewed him out.* PHRASAL VERB V P n (not pron) V n P

chew over. If you **chew** something **over**, you keep thinking about it. *He tends to chew things over too much in his mind... Goldstone chewed over the idea further.* PHRASAL VERB V n P V P n (not pron)

chew up PHRASAL VERB

1 If you **chew** food **up**, you chew it until it is completely crushed or softened. *I took one of the pills and chewed it up.* V n P Also V P n (not pron)

2 If something **is chewed up**, it has been destroyed or damaged in some way; an informal expression. *Every spring the ozone is chewed up, and the hole appears. ...rebels who are now chewing up Croatian territory... This town is notorious for chewing people up and spitting them out.* *be* V-ed P V P n (not pron) V n P

chewing gum. **Chewing gum** is a kind of sweet that you can chew for a long time. You do not swallow it. *...a stick of chewing gum.* N-UNCOUNT =gum

chewy /tʃu:i/ **chewier, chewiest.** If food is **chewy**, it needs to be chewed a lot before it becomes soft enough to swallow. *The meat was too chewy. ...chewy chocolate cookies.* ADJ-GRADED

chiaroscuro /kiærəskʊərou/. **Chiaroscuro** is the use of light and shade in a picture or place. *...the natural chiaroscuro of the place.* N-UNCOUNT

chic /ʃi:k/ ◆◇◇◇◇

1 Something or someone that is **chic** is fashionable and sophisticated. *Her gown was very French and very chic.* ADJ-GRADED =elegant

2 **Chic** is used to refer to a particular style or to the quality of being chic. *...French designer chic... He radiates charm and chic.* N-UNCOUNT

chicanery /ʃɪkeɪnəri/ **chicaneries.** **Chicanery** is trickery and double-dealing; a formal word. *...the tycoon's commercial chicanery.* N-UNCOUNT: also N in pl =trickery

chicano /tʃɪkeɪnou/ **chicanos.** In America, a **chicano** is an American citizen, whose family originally came from Mexico. *Gary Soto is a Chicano poet and a professor of Chicano and Latino literature.* N-COUNT

chick /tʃɪk/ **chicks** ◆◆◇◇◇

1 A **chick** is a baby bird. N-COUNT

2 Some men refer to women as **chicks**; a very informal term which some women find quite offensive. *Dad married a chick young enough to be his daughter.* N-COUNT

chicken /tʃɪkɪn/ **chickens, chickening, chickened** ◆◆◆◇◇

1 **Chickens** are birds which are kept on a farm for their eggs and for their meat. *Lionel built a coop so that they could raise chickens and have a supply of fresh eggs. ...free-range chickens.* ► **Chicken** is the flesh of this bird eaten as food. *...roast chicken with wild mushrooms. ...chicken soup.* N-COUNT =hen N-UNCOUNT

2 If someone calls you a **chicken**, they mean that you are afraid to do something; an informal use. *I'm scared of the dark. I'm a big chicken.* ► Also an adjective. *Why are you so chicken, Gregory?* N-COUNT PRAGMATICS =coward ADJ-GRADED: v-link ADJ

3 If you say that someone **is counting their chickens**, you mean that they are assuming that they will be successful or get something, when this is not certain. PHRASES V inflects

4 If you describe a situation as a **chicken and egg** situation, you mean that it is impossible to decide which of two things caused the other one. *It's a chicken and egg situation. Does the deficiency lead to the eczema or has the eczema led to certain deficiencies?* PHR n

5 If you say that someone is **running round like a headless chicken** or **rushing around like a headless chicken**, you think they are doing unnecessary tasks very quickly when they should be thinking more carefully about what needs to be done. *Instead of running round like a headless chicken use your efforts in a more productive way.* V and N inflect PRAGMATICS

6 • **chickens come home to roost**: see **roost**.

chicken out. If someone **chickens out** of something they were intending to do, they decide not to do it because they are afraid; an informal expression. *His mother complains that he makes excuses to chicken out of family occasions such as weddings... I had never ridden on a motor-cycle before. But it was too late to chicken out.* PHRASAL VERB V P *of* n V P

chicken feed; also spelled **chickenfeed.** If you think that an amount of money is so small it is hardly worth having or considering, you can say that it is **chicken feed.** *I was making a million a year, but that's chicken feed in the pop business.* N-UNCOUNT =peanuts

chickenpox /tʃɪkɪnpɒks/; also spelled **chicken pox.** **Chickenpox** is a disease which gives you a high temperature and red spots that itch. N-UNCOUNT

chicken wire. **Chicken wire** is a type of thin wire netting. N-UNCOUNT

chick pea, chick peas; also spelled **chickpea.** **Chick peas** are hard round seeds that look like pale brown peas. They can be cooked and eaten. N-COUNT: usu pl

chickweed /tʃɪkwi:d/. **Chickweed** is a plant with small leaves and white flowers which grows close to the ground. It is regarded as a weed. N-UNCOUNT

chicory /tʃɪkəri/. **Chicory** is a plant with crunchy bitter tasting leaves. It is eaten in salads. N-UNCOUNT

chide /tʃaɪd/ **chides, chiding, chided.** If you **chide** someone, you scold them because they have done something wicked or foolish; an old-fashioned word. *Cross chided himself for worrying... He gently chided the two women.* ◆◇◇◇◇ VERB =scold V n *for/about* -ing/n V n

chief /tʃi:f/ **chiefs** ◆◆◆◆◆

1 The **chief** of an organization is the person who is in charge of it. *...a commission appointed by the police chief. ...Gorbachev's chief of security.* N-COUNT: with supp

2 The **chief** of a tribe is its leader. *...Sitting Bull, chief of the Sioux tribes of the Great Plains.* N-COUNT; N-TITLE

3 **Chief** is used in the job titles of the most senior worker or workers of a particular kind in an organization. *...the chief test pilot.* ADJ: ADJ n =head

4 The **chief** cause, part, or member of something is the most important one. *Financial stress is well established as a chief reason for divorce... The job went to one of his chief rivals.* ADJ: ADJ n =main, principal

Chief Constable, Chief Constables. A **Chief Constable** is the officer who is in charge of the police force in a particular county or area in Britain. *...the Chief Constable of Greater Manchester.* ◆◇◇◇◇ N-COUNT; N-TITLE

Chief Justice, Chief Justices. A **Chief Justice** is the most important judge of a court of law, especially a supreme court. *...Chief Justice Marshall.* ◆◇◇◇◇ N-COUNT; N-TITLE

chiefly /tʃi:fli/. You use **chiefly** to indicate that a particular reason, emotion, method, or feature is the main or most important one. *He joined the consular service in China, chiefly because this was one of the few job vacancies... His response to attacks on his work was chiefly bewilderment.* ◆◇◇◇◇ ADV: ADV with cl/group, ADV with v =mainly, primarily

Chief of Staff, Chiefs of Staff. The **Chiefs of Staff** are the highest-ranking officers of each service of the armed forces. *...General Carl Vano, the chief of staff of the Army.* ◆◆◇◇◇ N-COUNT

chieftain /tʃiːftən/ **chieftains.** A **chieftain** is the leader of a tribe. *...the legendary British chieftain, King Arthur.* N-COUNT

chiffon /ʃɪfɒn, AM ʃɪfɑːn/ **chiffons. Chiffon** is a kind of very thin silk or nylon cloth that you can see through. *...floaty chiffon skirts.* ◆◇◇◇◇ N-MASS

chignon /ʃiːnjɒn, AM ʃiːnjɑːn/ **chignons.** A **chignon** is a knot of hair worn at the back of a woman's head. N-COUNT =bun

chihuahua /tʃɪwɑːwɑː/ **chihuahuas.** A **chihuahua** is a very small short-haired dog. N-COUNT

chilblain /tʃɪlbleɪn/ **chilblains. Chilblains** are painful red swellings which people sometimes get on their fingers or toes in cold weather. N-COUNT: usu pl

child /tʃaɪld/ **children.** ◆◆◆◆◆

1 A **child** is a human being who is not yet an adult. *When I was a child I lived in a country village... He's just a child. ...a child of six... It was only suitable for children.* N-COUNT

2 Someone's **children** are their sons and daughters of any age. *How are the children?... His children have left home... The young couple decided to have a child.* N-COUNT

childbearing /tʃaɪldbeərɪŋ/

1 **Childbearing** is the process of giving birth to babies. N-UNCOUNT

2 A woman of **childbearing** age is of an age when women are normally able to give birth to children. ADJ: ADJ n

child benefit. In Britain, **child benefit** is an allowance paid weekly by the state to families for each of their children. ◆◇◇◇◇ N-UNCOUNT

childbirth /tʃaɪldbɜːʳθ/. **Childbirth** is the act of giving birth to a child. *She died in childbirth.* ◆◇◇◇◇ N-UNCOUNT =labour

childcare /tʃaɪldkeəʳ/. **Childcare** refers to looking after children, and to the facilities which help parents to do so. *...both partners shared childcare... Britain has one of the worst records for state-run pre-school childcare in Western Europe.* ◆◇◇◇◇ N-UNCOUNT

childhood /tʃaɪldhʊd/ **childhoods.** A person's **childhood** is the period of their life when they are a child. *She had a happy childhood... He was remembering a story heard in childhood. ...childhood illnesses.* ◆◆◆◇◇ N-VAR: oft poss N, N n

childish /tʃaɪldɪʃ/ ◆◇◇◇◇

1 **Childish** means relating to or typical of a child. *...childish enthusiasm.* ADJ: usu ADJ n

2 If you describe someone, especially an adult, as **childish**, you disapprove of them because they behave in an immature way. *...Penny's selfish and childish behaviour... Don't be so childish.* ♦ **childishly** *He hit back angrily, saying such remarks were childishly simplistic... He knew that he had behaved childishly.* ♦ **childishness** *...regressing into childishness.* ADJ-GRADED PRAGMATICS =immature; ADV-GRADED: ADV adj, ADV with v; N-UNCOUNT

childless /tʃaɪldləs/. Someone who is **childless** has no children. *...childless couples.* ◆◇◇◇◇ ADJ

childlike /tʃaɪldlaɪk/. You describe someone as **childlike** when they seem like a child in their character, appearance, or behaviour. *His most enduring quality is his childlike innocence... Her behaviour was childlike and dependent.* ◆◇◇◇◇ ADJ-GRADED

childminder /tʃaɪldmaɪndəʳ/ **childminders.** A **childminder** is someone whose job is to look after children when the children's parents are away or are at work. Childminders usually work in their own homes. *...a registered childminder.* N-COUNT =minder

childminding /tʃaɪldmaɪndɪŋ/; also spelled **child-minding. Childminding** is the supervision and care given to children by a childminder or by a local government authority. N-UNCOUNT

child prodigy, child prodigies. A **child prodigy** is a child with a very great talent. *She was a child prodigy, giving concerts before she was a teenager.* N-COUNT

childproof /tʃaɪldpruːf/; also spelled **child proof.** Something that is **childproof** is designed in a way which ensures that children cannot harm it or be harmed by it. *A medicine chest should be secure and childproof.* ADJ

children /tʃɪldrən/. **Children** is the plural of **child.**

chili /tʃɪli/. See **chilli.**

chill /tʃɪl/ **chills, chilling, chilled.** ◆◆◇◇◇

1 When you **chill** something or when it **chills**, you lower its temperature so that it becomes colder but does not freeze. *Chill the fruit salad until serving time... These doughs can be rolled out while you wait for the pastry to chill. ...a glass of chilled champagne.* V-ERG ≠heat; V n; V; V-ed

2 When cold weather or something cold **chills** a person or a place, it makes that person or that place feel very cold. *The marble floor was beginning to chill me... An exposed garden may be chilled by cold winds... Wade placed his chilled hands on the radiator and warmed them... The boulder sheltered them from the chilling wind.* VERB =freeze; V n; V-ed; V-ing

3 If you say that something you see, hear, or feel **chills** you, you mean that it frightens you; used in written English. *There was a coldness in her that chilled him... Some films chill you to the marrow of your bones.* VERB; V n; V n *to* n

4 If something sends a **chill** through you, it gives you a sudden feeling of fear or anxiety. *The violence used against the students sent a chill through Czechoslovakia... He smiled, an odd, dreamy smile that sent chills up my back.* N-COUNT =shiver

5 A **chill** is a mild illness which can give you a slight fever and headache. *He caught a chill while performing at a rain-soaked open-air venue.* N-COUNT

6 **Chill** weather is cold and unpleasant. *...chill winds, rain and choppy seas.* ► Also a noun. *September is here, bringing with it a chill in the mornings. ...the cold chill of the night.* ADJ: ADJ n; N-SING

chill out. To **chill out** means to relax after you have done something tiring or stressful; an informal expression used by young people. *After raves, we used to chill out in each others' bedrooms.* PHRASAL VERB =relax; V P

chiller /tʃɪləʳ/ **chillers.** A **chiller** is a very frightening film. *'Witchcraft' is a two-part chiller set in rural Oxfordshire.* N-COUNT

chilli /tʃɪli/ **chillies;** also spelled **chili.** ◆◆◇◇◇

1 **Chillies** are small red or green seed pods. They have a hot spicy taste and are used in cooking. N-VAR

2 **Chilli** or **chilli con carne** is a dish made from minced meat, vegetables, and powdered or fresh chillies. N-UNCOUNT

chilli con carne /tʃɪli kɒn kɑːʳni/. **Chilli con carne** is the same as **chilli.** N-UNCOUNT

chilling /tʃɪlɪŋ/. If you describe something as **chilling**, you mean it is frightening. *The report gives a chilling account of how the plane disintegrated after the explosion.* ♦ **chillingly** *...since the murder of a London teenager in chillingly similar circumstances in February.* ◆◇◇◇◇ ADJ-GRADED: usu ADJ n; ADV-GRADED: usu ADV adj

chilli powder; also spelled **chili powder. Chilli powder** is a very strong-tasting powder made from dried chillies. It is used for flavouring food. N-UNCOUNT

chill-out. Chill-out places or things are intended to help you relax after you have done something tiring or stressful; an informal word used by young people. *He shuffled off to one of the chill-out rooms to collect his thoughts. ...some summer chill-out music.* ADJ: ADJ n

chilly /tʃɪli/ **chillier, chilliest** ◆◇◇◇◇

1 Something that is **chilly** is uncomfortably cold. *It was a chilly afternoon... The rooms had grown chilly.* ADJ-GRADED: oft *it* v-link ADJ

2 If you feel **chilly**, you feel rather cold. *I'm a bit chilly.* ADJ-GRADED: v-link ADJ

3 You say that relations between people are **chilly** or that a person's response is **chilly** when they are not friendly, welcoming, or enthusiastic. *I was slightly afraid of their chilly distant politeness.* ADJ-GRADED

chime /tʃaɪm/ **chimes, chiming, chimed** ◆◇◇◇◇

1 When a bell or a clock **chimes**, it makes ringing sounds. *He heard the front doorbell chime. ...as the Guildhall clock chimed three o'clock. ...a mahogany chiming clock.* VERB; V; V n; V-ing

2 A **chime** is a ringing sound made by a bell, espe- N-COUNT

cially when it is part of a clock. *At that moment a chime sounded from the front of the house... The ceremony started as the chimes of midnight struck.*
3 **Chimes** are a set of small objects which make a ringing sound when they are blown by the wind. *...the haunting sound of the wind chimes.* N-PLURAL: usu supp N

chime in. If someone **chimes in**, they say something just after someone else has spoken. *'Why?' Pete asked impatiently.—'Yes, why?' Bob chimed in. 'It seems like a good idea to me.'... At this, some of the others chime in with memories of prewar deprivations.* PHRASAL VERB V P with quote V P with n Also V P

chime in with or **chime with.** If one thing **chimes in with** another thing or **chimes with** it, the two things are similar or consistent with each other. *He has managed to find a response to each new political development that chimes in with most Germans' instinct... The president's remarks do not entirely chime with those coming from American and British politicians.* PHRASAL VERB V P P n V P n

chimera /kaɪmɪərə/ **chimeras**
1 A **chimera** is an unrealistic idea that you have about something or a hope that you have that is unlikely to be fulfilled; a formal use. *Religious unity remained as much a chimera as ever.* N-COUNT =illusion
2 In Greek mythology, a **chimera** is a monster with the head of a lion, the body of a goat, and the tail of a snake. N-COUNT

chimney /tʃɪmni/ **chimneys.** A **chimney** is a pipe through which smoke goes up into the air, usually through the roof of a building. *Thick, yellow smoke pours constantly out of the chimneys at the steelworks in Katowice.* ◆◇◇◇◇ N-COUNT

chimney breast, chimney breasts; also spelled **chimney-breast**. In British English, a **chimney breast** is the part of a wall in a room which is built out round a chimney. N-COUNT

chimneypiece /tʃɪmnipiːs/ **chimneypieces;** also spelled **chimney-piece**. In British English, a **chimneypiece** is the same as a **mantlepiece**. *...the William IV marble chimneypiece, acquired specially for the room.* N-COUNT =mantlepiece

chimney pot, chimney pots; also spelled **chimney-pot**. A **chimney pot** is a short pipe which is fixed on top of a chimney. N-COUNT

chimney stack, chimney stacks; also spelled **chimney-stack**. In British English, a **chimney stack** is the brick or stone part of a chimney that is above the roof of a building. N-COUNT

chimney sweep, chimney sweeps; also spelled **chimney-sweep**. A **chimney sweep** is a person whose job is to clean the soot out of chimneys. N-COUNT

chimp /tʃɪmp/ **chimps.** A **chimp** is the same as a **chimpanzee**; an informal word. N-COUNT

chimpanzee /tʃɪmpænziː/ **chimpanzees.** A **chimpanzee** is a kind of small African ape. ◆◇◇◇◇ N-COUNT

chin /tʃɪn/ **chins** ◆◆◇◇◇
1 Your **chin** is the part of your face that is below your mouth and above your neck. *...a double chin... He rubbed the gray stubble on his chin.* N-COUNT
2 If you say that someone **took** something **on the chin**, you mean that they accepted an unpleasant or difficult situation bravely and without making a lot of fuss about it; an informal expression. *When the police arrived he took it on the chin and apologised for the trouble he'd caused them.* PHRASE: V inflects

china /tʃaɪnə/ ◆◆◇◇◇
1 **China** is a kind of very thin clay from which cups, saucers, plates, and ornaments are made. *...a small boat made of china. ...china cups.* ● See also **bone china**. N-UNCOUNT: oft N n
2 Cups, saucers, plates, and ornaments made of china are referred to as **china**. *Judy collects blue and white china.* N-UNCOUNT
3 ● **a bull in a china shop**: see **bull**.

China tea. **China tea** is tea made from large dark green or reddish-brown tea leaves. It is usually drunk without milk or sugar. N-UNCOUNT

Chinatown /tʃaɪnətaʊn/. **Chinatown** is the name given to the area in a city where there are many Chinese shops and restaurants, and which is a social centre for the Chinese community in the city. N-UNCOUNT

Chinese /tʃaɪniːz/. **Chinese** is both the singular and the plural form. ◆◆◆◆◇
1 Something that is **Chinese** relates or belongs to China or its languages or people. *...the Chinese government. ...Chinese women.* ▸ The **Chinese** are the people who come from China. *The British and the Chinese are at last talking about constitutional matters... She married a Chinese.* ADJ N-COUNT: usu pl
2 The languages that are spoken in China, especially Mandarin, are often referred to as **Chinese**. *The education provided was given in Chinese.* N-UNCOUNT

chink /tʃɪŋk/ **chinks, chinking, chinked**
1 A **chink** in a surface is a very narrow crack or opening in it. *...a chink in the wall... He peered through a chink in the curtains.* N-COUNT: usu N in n
2 A **chink of** light is a small patch of light that shines through a small opening in something. *I noticed a chink of light at the end of the corridor.* N-COUNT: N of n
3 When objects **chink**, or you **chink** them, they touch each other, making a small ringing sound. *...cutlery chinking in the silence... They poured out the rest of the wine and she chinked his mug.* V-ERG =clink V V n
4 If you say that someone has a **chink in** their **armour**, you mean that they have a small weakness in their character or in their ideas which makes it easy to harm them. PHRASE: *chink* inflects =Achilles heel

chinos /tʃiːnoʊz/. **Chinos** are casual, loose trousers made from cotton. N-PLURAL: also *a pair of* N

chintz /tʃɪnts/ **chintzes.** **Chintz** is a cotton fabric decorated with flowery patterns. *...chintz curtains.* N-MASS

chintzy /tʃɪntsi/. Something that is **chintzy** is decorated or covered with chintz; used mainly in British English. *...huge great sofas and chintzy armchairs.* ADJ-GRADED

chip /tʃɪp/ **chips, chipping, chipped** ◆◆◆◇◇
1 In British English, **chips** are long, thin pieces of potato fried in oil or fat and eaten hot, usually with a meal. The American expression is **French fries**. *I had fish and chips in a cafe... Frank Browne shook more sauce over his chips.* N-COUNT: usu pl
2 In American English, potato **chips** are very thin slices of potato fried until they are hard and crunchy and eaten cold as a snack. The British word is **crisps**. *...a package of onion-flavored potato chips.* N-COUNT: usu pl
3 A silicon **chip** is a very small piece of silicon with electronic circuits on it which is part of a computer or other piece of machinery. *...the chips that control 'intelligent' machines such as televisions.* N-COUNT
4 A **chip** is a small piece of something or a small piece which has been broken off something. *It contains real chocolate chips... He was burning wood chips to make charcoal... Teichler's eyes gleamed like chips of blue glass.* N-COUNT: oft supp N
5 A **chip** in a piece of crockery or furniture is a mark where a small piece has been broken off it. *The washbasin had a small chip.* N-COUNT
6 If you **chip** something or if it **chips**, a small piece is broken off it. *The blow chipped the woman's tooth... Steel baths are lighter but chip easily.* ♦ **chipped** *The wagon's paint was badly chipped on the outside... They drank out of chipped mugs.* V-ERG V n V ADJ-GRADED
7 **Chips** are plastic counters used in gambling to represent money. *He put the pile of chips in the center of the table and drew a card.* N-COUNT: usu pl
8 In discussions between people or governments, a **chip** or a **bargaining chip** is something of value which one side holds, which can be exchanged for something they want from the other side. *The information could be used as a bargaining chip to extract some parallel information from Britain... He was not expected to be released because he was considered a valuable chip in this game.* N-COUNT
9 See also **blue chip**.
10 If you describe someone as **a chip off the old block**, you mean that they are just like one of their parents in character or behaviour. *Her fifth child was born, a son who Sally at first thought was another chip off the old block.* PHRASES usu v-link PHR

11 If you say that something happens **when the chips are down**, you mean it happens when a situation gets very difficult; an informal expression. *When the chips are down, she's very tough.*

12 If you say that someone has **a chip on** their **shoulder**, you think that they feel inferior or that they believe they have been treated unfairly; an informal expression. *He had this chip on his shoulder about my mum and dad thinking that they're better than him.* — Ns inflect, usu *have/with* PHR; PRAGMATICS

chip away at — PHRASAL VERB

1 If you **chip away at** something such as an idea, a feeling, or a system, you gradually make it weaker or less likely to succeed by repeated efforts. *Instead of an outright coup attempt, the rebels want to chip away at her authority.* — =erode; V P P n

2 If you **chip away at** a debt or an amount of money, you gradually reduce it. *The group had hoped to chip away at its debts by selling assets.* — V P P n

chip in — PHRASAL VERB

1 When a number of people **chip in**, each person gives some money so that they can pay for something together; an informal expression. *They chip in for the petrol and food... The brothers chip in a certain amount of money each month to hire a home health aide.* — =contribute; V P; V P n (not pron); Also V P *with* n

2 If someone **chips in** during a conversation, they interrupt it in order to say something; an informal expression. *'That's true,' chipped in Quaver... He chipped in before Clements could answer.* — V P with quote; V P

chipboard /tʃɪpbɔːʳd/. **Chipboard** is a hard material made out of wood chips which have been pressed together. It is often used for making doors and furniture. — N-UNCOUNT

chipmunk /tʃɪpmʌŋk/ **chipmunks.** A **chipmunk** is a small animal which looks like a squirrel but which has a striped back. — N-COUNT

Chippendale /tʃɪpəndeɪl/. **Chippendale** is a style of furniture that dates from the eighteenth century. *...a pair of Chippendale chairs.* — ADJ: ADJ n

chipper /tʃɪpəʳ/. **Chipper** means cheerful and lively; an old-fashioned word. *He looked unusually chipper this morning.* — ADJ-GRADED; =bright

chippings /tʃɪpɪŋz/. Wood **chippings** or stone **chippings** are small pieces of wood or stone which are used, for example, to cover surfaces such as paths or roads. *Paths of bark chippings will help to give the impression of a woodland walkway.* — N-PLURAL: usu n N

chippy /tʃɪpi/ **chippies;** also spelled **chippie.** In Britain, a **chippy** is the same as a **chip shop**; an informal word. *For years he's visited the chippy at least once a week.* — N-COUNT

chip shop, chip shops. In Britain, a **chip shop** is a shop which sells hot food such as fish and chips, fried chicken, sausages, and meat pies. The food is cooked in the shop and people take it away to eat at home or in the street. — N-COUNT; =fish and chip shop

chiropodist /kɪrɒpədɪst/ **chiropodists.** A **chiropodist** is a person whose job is to treat and care for people's feet. — N-COUNT; =podiatrist

chiropody /kɪrɒpədi/. **Chiropody** is the professional treatment and care of people's feet. — N-UNCOUNT; =podiatry

chiropractic /kaɪərəpræktɪk/. **Chiropractic** is the treatment of diseases by the manipulation of people's joints, especially the backbone. — N-UNCOUNT

chiropractor /kaɪərəpræktəʳ/ **chiropractors.** A **chiropractor** is a person who treats diseases by manipulating people's joints, especially the backbone. — N-COUNT

chirp /tʃɜːʳp/ **chirps, chirping, chirped**

1 When a bird or an insect such as a cricket or grasshopper **chirps**, it makes short high-pitched sounds. *The crickets chirped faster and louder.* — VERB; =chirrup; V
► Also a noun. *The chirps of the small garden birds sounded distant.* — N-COUNT
♦ **chirping** *...the chirping of birds.* — N-UNCOUNT

2 You say that a person **chirps** when they say something in a cheerful, high-pitched voice; used in written English. *'See you soon, I hope!' chirped my mother.* — VERB; V with quote

chirpy /tʃɜːʳpi/ **chirpier, chirpiest.** If you describe a person or their behaviour as **chirpy**, you mean they are very cheerful and lively; an informal word. *Hutson is a small, chirpy bloke... She sounded quite chirpy, all she needs is rest.* — ADJ-GRADED; =cheerful

chirrup /tʃɪrəp, AM tʃɜːrəp/ **chirrups, chirruping, chirruped.** If a person or bird **chirrups**, they make short high-pitched sounds. *'My gosh,' she chirruped... I woke up to the sound of larks chirruping.* — VERB; =chirp; V with quote; V; Also V n

chisel /tʃɪzᵊl/ **chisels, chiselling, chiselled;** spelled **chiseling, chiseled** in American English. ◆◇◇◇◇

1 A **chisel** is a tool that has a long metal blade with a sharp edge at the end. It is used for cutting and shaping wood and stone. *...a hammer and chisel.* — N-COUNT

2 If you **chisel** wood or stone, you cut and shape it using a chisel. *He set out to chisel a dog out of sandstone.* — VERB; V n

chiselled /tʃɪzᵊld/; spelled **chiseled** in American English. If you say that someone, usually a man, has **chiselled** features you mean that their face has a strong, well-defined bone structure. *Women find his chiselled features irresistible. ...a chiselled jaw.* — ADJ: usu ADJ n

chit /tʃɪt/ **chits.** A **chit** is a short official note, such as a receipt, an order, or a memo, usually signed by someone in authority. *Schrader initialled the chit for the barman.* — N-COUNT

chit-chat; also spelled **chitchat. Chit-chat** is informal talk about things that are not very important. *Not being a mother, I found the chit-chat exceedingly dull.* — N-UNCOUNT

chivalric /ʃɪvælrɪk/. **Chivalric** means relating to or connected with the system of chivalry that was believed in and followed by medieval knights. *...chivalric ideals.* — ADJ: ADJ n

chivalrous /ʃɪvəlrəs/. A **chivalrous** man is polite, kind, and unselfish, especially towards women. *He was handsome, upright and chivalrous.* — ADJ-GRADED

chivalry /ʃɪvəlri/

1 **Chivalry** is polite, kind, and unselfish behaviour, especially by men towards women. *Marie seemed to revel in his old-fashioned chivalry.* — N-UNCOUNT; =gallantry

2 In the Middle Ages, **chivalry** was the set of rules and conventions which knights had to follow. *...the age of chivalry.* — N-UNCOUNT

chives /tʃaɪvz/. **Chives** are the long thin hollow green leaves of a herb with purple flowers. Chives are cut into small pieces and added to food to give it a flavour similar to onions. — ◆◇◇◇◇ N-PLURAL

chivvy /tʃɪvi/ **chivvies, chivvying, chivvied.** If you **chivvy** someone, you keep urging them to do something that they do not want to do; used mainly in British English. *There, the health care authority chivvies doctors into doing more preventive medicine... They maintained control by sending their representatives to the front to chivvy army commanders along.* — VERB; =badger; V n *into*-ing/n; V n with adv; Also V n to-inf, V n, V n prep

chloride /klɔːraɪd/ **chlorides. Chloride** is a chemical compound of chlorine and another substance. *The scientific name for common salt is sodium chloride.* — ◆◇◇◇◇ N-MASS: oft n N

chlorinated /klɔːrɪneɪtɪd/. **Chlorinated** water, for example drinking water or water in a swimming pool, has been disinfected by adding chlorine to it. *Tell your hairdresser if you regularly swim in a chlorinated pool.* — ADJ: usu ADJ n

chlorine /klɔːriːn/. **Chlorine** is a strong-smelling gas that is used to disinfect water and to make cleaning products. — ◆◇◇◇◇ N-UNCOUNT

chlorofluorocarbon /klɔːroʊflʊəroʊkɑːʳbən/ **chlorofluorocarbons. Chlorofluorocarbons** are the same as **CFCs**. — N-COUNT; =CFC

chloroform /klɒrəfɔːʳm, AM klɔːr-/. **Chloroform** is a colourless liquid with a strong sweet smell, which makes you unconscious if you breathe its vapour. — N-UNCOUNT

chlorophyll /klɒrəfɪl, AM klɔːr-/. **Chlorophyll** is a green substance in plants which enables them to use the energy from sunlight in order to grow. — N-UNCOUNT

choc-ice /tʃɒk aɪs, AM tʃɔːk -/ **choc-ices;** also spelled **choc ice. Choc-ices** are small blocks of ice-cream covered in chocolate. — N-COUNT

chock-a-block /tʃɒk ə blɒk/. A place that is **chock-a-block** is very full of people, things, or vehicles; an informal word. *The small roads are chock-a-block with traffic.* ADJ: v-link ADJ, oft ADJ *with* n =packed

chock-full /tʃɒk fʊl/. Something that is **chock-full** is completely full; an informal word. *The 32-page catalog is chock-full of things that add fun to festive occasions.* ADJ: v-link ADJ, usu ADJ *of* n =bursting

chocoholic /tʃɒkəhɒlɪk, AM tʃɔːkəhɔːlɪk/ **chocoholics.** If you say that someone is a **chocoholic**, you mean that they eat a great deal of chocolate and find it hard to stop themselves eating it. *Many chocoholics get rid of their cravings by having a cup of chocolate-flavored coffee.* N-COUNT

chocolate /tʃɒklɪt, AM tʃɔːk-/ **chocolates** ◆◆◆◇◇

1 **Chocolate** is a sweet hard food made from cocoa beans. It is usually brown in colour and is eaten as a sweet. *...a bar of chocolate... I like nibbling things like crisps and chocolate. ...rich chocolate cake.* ● See also **milk chocolate**, **plain chocolate**. N-MASS

2 **Chocolate** or **hot chocolate** is a drink made from a powder containing chocolate. It is usually made with hot milk. *...a small cafeteria where the visitors can buy tea, coffee and chocolate... I sipped the hot chocolate she had made.* N-UNCOUNT =drinking chocolate ► A cup of chocolate can be referred to as a **chocolate**. *I'll have a hot chocolate please.* N-COUNT

3 **Chocolates** are small sweets or nuts covered with a layer of chocolate. They are usually sold in a box. *...a box of chocolates... Here, have a chocolate.* N-COUNT

4 **Chocolate** is used to describe things that are dark brown in colour. *The curtains and the coverlet of the bed were chocolate velvet... She placed the chocolate-colored coat beside the case.* COLOUR

chocolate-box; also spelled **chocolate box.** When people talk about **chocolate-box** places or images, they mean that the places or images are very pretty but in a boring or conventional way; used showing disapproval. *...a village of chocolate-box timbered houses.* ADJ-GRADED: ADJ n PRAGMATICS

choice /tʃɔɪs/ **choices; choicer, choicest** ◆◆◆◆◇

1 If there is a **choice** of things, there are several of them and you can choose the one you want. *It's available in a choice of colours... At lunchtime, there's a choice between the buffet or the set menu... Club Sportif offer a wide choice of holidays.* N-COUNT =selection

2 Your **choice** is someone or something that you choose from a range of things. *Although he was only grumbling, his choice of words made Rodney angry.* N-COUNT: usu poss N =selection

3 **Choice** means of very high quality; a formal use. *...Fortnum and Mason's choicest chocolates.* ADJ-GRADED: ADJ n =select

4 If you **have no choice** but to do something or **have little choice** but to do it, you cannot avoid doing it. *They had little choice but to agree to what he suggested.* PHRASES V inflects

5 The thing or person **of** your **choice** is the one that you choose. *...tickets to see the football team of your choice... In many societies children still marry someone of their parents' choice.* n PHR

choir /kwaɪəʳ/ **choirs** ◆◆◇◇◇

1 A **choir** is a group of people who sing together, for example in a church or school. *He has been singing in his church choir since he was six.* N-COUNT

2 In a church building, the **choir** is the area in front of the altar where the choir sits. *...the impressive frescoes above the choir.* N-COUNT: usu sing

choirboy /kwaɪəʳbɔɪ/ **choirboys.** A **choirboy** is a boy who sings in a church choir. N-COUNT

choirmaster /kwaɪəʳmɑːstəʳ, -mæst-/ **choirmasters.** A **choirmaster** is a person whose job is to train a choir. N-COUNT

choke /tʃoʊk/ **chokes, choking, choked** ◆◆◇◇◇

1 When you **choke** or when something **chokes** you, you cannot breathe properly or get enough air into your lungs. *The coffee was almost too hot to swallow and made him choke for a moment... A small child could choke on the doll's hair... Dense smoke swirled and billowed, its rank fumes choking her... The girl choked to death after breathing in smoke.* V-ERG V V *on* n V n V *to* n

2 To **choke** someone means to squeeze their neck until they are dead. *The men pushed him into the entrance of a nearby building where they choked him with his tie.* VERB =strangle V n

3 If a place **is choked** with things or people, it is full of them and they prevent movement in it. *The village's roads are choked with traffic... His pond has been choked by the fast-growing weed.* VB: usu passive be V-ed *with* n be V-ed *by* n

4 The **choke** in a car, lorry, or other vehicle is a device that reduces the amount of air going into the engine and makes it easier to start. N-COUNT: usu sing, usu *the* N

choke back. If you **choke back** tears or a strong emotion, you force yourself not to show your emotion. *Choking back tears, he said Mary died in his arms.* PHRASAL VERB =suppress V P n (not pron)

choke off. If someone or something **chokes off** financial growth, they do something to restrict or control the rate at which a country's economy can grow. *They warned the Chancellor that raising taxes in the Budget could choke off the recovery.* PHRASAL VERB V P n (not pron)

choked /tʃoʊkt/

1 If you say something in a **choked** voice or if your voice is **choked with** emotion, your voice does not have its full sound, because you are upset or frightened. *'Why did Ben do that?' she asked, in a choked voice... One young conscript rose with a message of thanks, his voice choked with emotion.* ADJ: ADJ n, v-link ADJ *with* n

2 If you feel **choked** about something, you are very angry or upset about it. *I still feel choked about him leaving.* ADJ-GRADED: v-link ADJ

choker /tʃoʊkəʳ/ **chokers.** A **choker** is a necklace or band of material that fits very closely round a woman's neck. *...a pearl choker.* N-COUNT

cholera /kɒlərə/. **Cholera** is a serious, often fatal disease that affects people's digestive organs. It is caused by drinking infected water or by eating infected food. *...a cholera epidemic.* ◆◇◇◇◇ N-UNCOUNT

choleric /kɒlərɪk/. A **choleric** person gets angry very easily. You can also use **choleric** to describe a person who is very angry; a formal word. *...his choleric disposition... Most choleric of all were those who suspected the BBC of foul play.* ADJ-GRADED =fiery

cholesterol /kəlestərɒl, AM -rɔːl/. **Cholesterol** is a substance that exists in the fat, tissues, and blood of all animals. Too much cholesterol in a person's blood can cause heart disease. *...a dangerously high cholesterol level.* ◆◆◇◇◇ N-UNCOUNT

chomp /tʃɒmp/ **chomps, chomping, chomped.** If a person or animal **chomps** their way through food or **chomps** on food, they chew it noisily; an informal use. *On the diet I would chomp my way through breakfast, even though I'm never hungry in the morning... I chomped hungrily through the large steak... I lost a tooth while chomping on a French baguette!* ● to **chomp at the bit**: see **bit**. VERB =munch V *way through* n V prep/adv Also V n

choose /tʃuːz/ **chooses, choosing, chose, chosen** ◆◆◆◆◇

1 If you **choose** someone or something from several people or things that are available, you decide which person or thing you want to have. *They will be able to choose their own leaders in democratic elections... This week he has chosen Clarence Thomas to replace Thurgood Marshall... There are several patchwork cushions to choose from... Houston was chosen as the site for the convention... He did well in his chosen profession.* VERB =select V n V n to-inf V *from* n be V-ed *as* n V-ed Also V n *as* n, V

2 If you **choose** to do something, you do it because you want to or because you feel that it is right. *The NRDC chose to inform the public about the risks posed by pesticides in foods... You can just take out the interest each year, if you choose.* VERB V to-inf V

3 If there is **little to choose between** people or things or **nothing to choose between** them, it is difficult to decide which is better or more suitable. *There is very little to choose between the world's top tennis players.* PHRASES v-link PHR

4 If you refer to a group of people as the **chosen few**, you mean they are a select group who are treated differently from other people or who are more privileged than other people, and you are sometimes implying that this is unfair. *Learning should no longer be an elitist pastime for the chosen few.* =elite

5 • to **pick and choose**: see **pick**.

choosy /tʃuːzi/. Someone who is **choosy** is difficult to please because they will only accept something if it is exactly what they want or if it is of very high quality. *Skiers should be particularly choosy about the insurance policy they buy.* ADJ-GRADED: usu v-link ADJ, oft ADJ *about* n/wh =selective, exacting

chop /tʃɒp/ **chops, chopping, chopped** ◆◆◆◇◇

1 If you **chop** something, you cut it into pieces with strong downward movements of a knife or an axe. *Chop the butter into small pieces... Chop the onions very finely... Visitors were set to work chopping wood. ...chopped tomatoes.* VERB V n *into* n V n V-ed

2 A **chop** is a small piece of meat cut from the ribs of a sheep or pig. *...grilled lamb chops.* N-COUNT: usu n N

3 When people **chop and change**, they keep changing their minds about what to do or how to act; an informal expression used mainly in British English. *Don't ask me why they have chopped and changed so much.* PHRASES Vs inflect

4 If something is **for the chop** or is going to **get the chop**, it is going to be stopped or closed. If someone is **for the chop**, they are going to lose their job or position; an informal expression used in British English. *He won't say which programmes are for the chop... I was both disappointed and amazed when I got the chop from the Wales team.* =get the boot

chop down. If you **chop down** a tree, you cut through its trunk with an axe so that it falls to the ground. *Sometimes they have to chop down a tree for firewood.* PHRASAL VERB =cut down V P n (not pron) Also V n P

chop off. To **chop off** something such as a part of someone's body means to cut it off. *She chopped off her golden, waist-length hair... They dragged him to the village square and chopped his head off.* PHRASAL VERB =cut off V P n (not pron) V n P

chop up. If you **chop** something **up**, you chop it into small pieces. *Chop up three firm tomatoes. ...chopped up banana.* PHRASAL VERB =cut up V P n (not pron) V-ed P

chopper /tʃɒpəʳ/ **choppers.** A **chopper** is a helicopter; an informal word. *Overhead, the chopper roared and the big blades churned the air.* ◆◇◇◇◇ N-COUNT =helicopter

chopping board, chopping boards. A **chopping board** is a wooden or plastic board that you chop meat and vegetables on. N-COUNT

choppy /tʃɒpi/ **choppier, choppiest.** When water is **choppy**, there are a lot of small waves on it because there is a wind blowing. *A gale was blowing and the sea was choppy.* ADJ-GRADED =rough

chopstick /tʃɒpstɪk/ **chopsticks. Chopsticks** are a pair of thin sticks which people in China and the Far East use to eat their food with. N-COUNT: usu pl

chop suey /tʃɒp suːi/. **Chop suey** is a Chinese-style dish that consists of meat and vegetables that have been stewed together. N-UNCOUNT

choral /kɔːrəl/. **Choral** music is sung by a choir. *His collection of choral music from around the world is called 'Voices'.* ◆◇◇◇◇ ADJ: usu ADJ n

chorale /kɔːrɑːl, -ræl/ **chorales.** A **chorale** is a piece of music sung as part of a church service. *...a Bach chorale.* N-COUNT

chord /kɔːʳd/ **chords** ◆◆◇◇◇

1 A **chord** is a number of musical notes played or sung at the same time with a pleasing effect. *...the opening chords of 'Stairway to Heaven'.* • See also **vocal cords.** N-COUNT

2 If something **strikes a chord** with you, it makes you feel sympathy or enthusiasm. *Mr Jenkins' arguments for stability struck a chord with Europe's two most powerful politicians... Burke's sentiments undoubtedly struck a responsive chord in Parliament.* PHRASE: V inflects

chore /tʃɔːʳ/ **chores** ◆◇◇◇◇

1 A **chore** is a task that you must do but that you find unpleasant or boring. *She sees exercise primarily as an unavoidable chore... Making pasta by hand with a rolling pin can be a real chore.* N-COUNT: usu sing =burden

2 Chores are tasks such as cleaning, washing, and ironing that have to be done regularly at home. *My husband and I both go out to work so we share the household chores.* N-COUNT: usu pl =housework

choreograph /kɒriəgrɑːf, AM kɔːriəgræf/ **choreographs, choreographing, choreographed.** When someone **choreographs** a ballet or other dance, they invent the steps and movements and tell the dancers how to perform them. *Achim had choreographed the dance in Act II himself... She has danced, choreographed, lectured and taught all over the world.* VERB V n V

choreographed /kɒriəgrɑːft, AM kɔːriəgræft/. You describe an activity involving several people as **choreographed** when it is arranged but is intended to appear natural. *Political conventions are more choreographed and less spontaneous than they used to be.* ADJ-GRADED

choreographer /kɒriɒgrəfəʳ, AM kɔː-/ **choreographers.** A **choreographer** is someone who invents the movements for a ballet or other dance and tells the dancers how to perform them. *Balanchine was the choreographer for a company called Ballet Russe de Monte Carlo.* ◆◇◇◇◇ N-COUNT

choreographic /kɒriəgræfɪk, AM kɔː-/. **Choreographic** means relating to or connected with choreography. *...his choreographic work for The Birmingham Royal Ballet.* ADJ: usu ADJ n

choreography /kɒriɒgrəfi, AM kɔː-/. **Choreography** is the inventing of steps and movements for ballets and other dances. *The choreography of Eric Hawkins is considered radical by ballet audiences.* ◆◇◇◇◇ N-UNCOUNT

chorister /kɒrɪstəʳ, AM kɔː-/ **choristers.** A **chorister** is a singer in a church choir. N-COUNT

chortle /tʃɔːʳtᵊl/ **chortles, chortling, chortled.** When you **chortle**, you laugh loudly, producing a sound that is halfway between a laugh and a snort. *There was silence for a moment, then Larry began chortling like an idiot.* ► Also a noun. *He gave a chortle.* VERB V N-COUNT

chorus /kɔːrəs/ **choruses, chorusing, chorused** ◆◆◇◇◇

1 A **chorus** is a part of a song which is repeated after each verse. *Caroline sang two verses and the chorus of her song... Everyone joined in the chorus.* N-COUNT =refrain

2 A **chorus** is a large group of people who sing together. *The chorus was singing 'The Ode to Joy'.* N-COUNT =choir

3 A **chorus** is a piece of music written to be sung by a large group of people. *...the Hallelujah Chorus.* N-COUNT

4 A **chorus** is a group of singers or dancers who perform together in a show, in contrast to the soloists. *Students played the lesser parts and sang in the chorus.* N-COUNT

5 When there is a **chorus** of criticism, disapproval, or praise, that attitude is expressed by a lot of people at the same time. *The government is defending its economic policies against a growing chorus of criticism.* N-COUNT: usu sing, oft N *of* n

6 When people **chorus** something, they say it or sing it together. *'Hi,' they chorused.* ► Also a noun. *He was greeted with a rousing chorus of Happy Birthday... 'All the best,' called the other typists in chorus.* VERB V with quote N-COUNT: with supp, also *in* N

7 See also **dawn chorus.**

chorus girl, chorus girls; also spelled **chorusgirl**. A **chorus girl** is a young woman who sings or dances in the chorus of a show or film. N-COUNT

chose /tʃoʊz/. **Chose** is the past tense of **choose.**

chosen /tʃoʊzᵊn/. **Chosen** is the past participle of **choose.**

chow /tʃaʊ/ **chows**

1 In informal American English, food can be referred to as **chow.** *Help yourself to some chow.* N-UNCOUNT

2 A **chow** is a kind of dog that has a thick coat and a curled tail. Chows originally came from China. N-COUNT

chowder /tʃaʊdəʳ/ **chowders. Chowder** is a thick soup containing pieces of fish. N-MASS: usu n N

chow mein /tʃaʊ meɪn, - miːn/. **Chow mein** is a Chinese-style dish that consists of fried noodles, cooked meat, and vegetables. *...chicken chow mein.* N-UNCOUNT

Christ /kraɪst/ ◆◆◇◇◇

1 Christ is one of the names of Jesus, whom Christians believe to be the son of God and whose teachings are the basis of Christianity. *...the teachings of Christ.* N-PROPER

2 Some people say **'Christ!'** when they are sur- EXCLAM prised, shocked, or annoyed, or in order to emphasize what they are saying; an informal use which some people find offensive. *He looked at her watch. 'Christ! We have three minutes!'* PRAGMATICS

christen /krɪsᵊn/ **christens, christening, christened** ◆◇◇◇◇

1 When a baby **is christened**, he or she is given a name during the Christian ceremony of baptism. *She was born in March and christened in June.: She was christened Susan.* VB: usu passive, be V-ed, be V-ed n-proper

2 You say that you **christen** a person, place, or object something if you choose a name for them and start calling them by that name; an informal use. *My housemaster christened me The Agitator!... We had a tiny little room which was christened Hades.* VERB, V n n

3 You say that you **christen** something new when you use it for the first time, especially if you do something special to mark the occasion; an informal use. *To christen the new hall, a number of great orchestras have been invited to play.* VERB, V n

Christendom /krɪsᵊndəm/. All the Christian people and countries in the world can be referred to as **Christendom**; an old-fashioned word. N-PROPER

christening /krɪsᵊnɪŋ/ **christenings.** A **christening** is a Christian ceremony in which a baby is made a member of the Christian church and is officially given his or her name. *...my granddaughter's christening. ...a christening robe.* ◆◇◇◇◇ N-COUNT

Christian /krɪstʃən/ **Christians** ◆◆◆◆◇

1 A **Christian** is someone who follows the teachings of Jesus Christ. *He was a devout Christian... Last week there were clashes during protests by Christians and Muslims.* N-COUNT

2 **Christian** means relating to Christianity or Christians. *...the Christian Church. ...the Christian faith. ...Christian areas of Beirut... Most of my friends are Christian.* ADJ: usu ADJ n

Christianity /krɪstiænɪti/. **Christianity** is a religion that is based on the teachings of Jesus Christ and the belief that he was the son of God. *He converted to Christianity that day.* ◆◆◇◇◇ N-UNCOUNT

Christian name, Christian names. Some people refer to their first names as their **Christian names**. *Despite my attempts to get him to call me by my Christian name he insisted on addressing me as 'Mr Kennedy'.* N-COUNT =given name, forename

Christian Science. **Christian Science** is a type of Christianity which emphasizes the use of prayer to cure illness. *...members of the Christian Science Church.* ♦ **Christian Scientist, Christian Scientists** *She was brought up in a family of Christian Scientists.* N-UNCOUNT: oft N n; N-COUNT

Christmas /krɪsməs/ **Christmases** ◆◆◆◆◇

1 **Christmas** is a Christian festival when the birth of Jesus Christ is celebrated. Christmas is celebrated on the 25th of December. *The day after Christmas is generally a busy one for retailers... Merry Christmas, Mom.* N-VAR: oft N n

2 **Christmas** is the period of several days around and including Christmas Day. *During the Christmas holidays there's a tremendous amount of traffic between the Northeast and Florida... He'll be in the hospital over Christmas, so we'll be spending our Christmas Day there.* N-VAR: oft N n

Christmas cake, Christmas cakes. A **Christmas cake** is a special cake that is eaten at Christmas. It is a rich, dark, heavy cake which contains a lot of dried fruit and which is usually covered with marzipan and icing. N-VAR

Christmas card, Christmas cards. **Christmas cards** are greetings cards which people send to friends and family at Christmas. *He still writes to her sometimes and sends her a Christmas card every year.* ◆◇◇◇◇ N-COUNT

Christmas Day. **Christmas Day** is the 25th of December, when Christmas is celebrated. ◆◇◇◇◇ N-UNCOUNT

Christmas Eve. **Christmas Eve** is the 24th of December, the day before Christmas Day. ◆◇◇◇◇ N-UNCOUNT

Christmas pudding, Christmas puddings. **Christmas pudding** is a special pudding that is eaten at Christmas. It is a rich, dark, heavy pudding containing dried fruit, spices, and suet; used mainly in British English. N-VAR =plum pudding

Christmas stocking, Christmas stockings. A **Christmas stocking** is a long sock which children hang by their bed or by the fireplace on Christmas Eve. During the night, parents fill the stocking with fruit, sweets, and small presents, which children believe have been put there by Father Christmas. N-COUNT =stocking

Christmassy /krɪsməsi/. Something that is **Christmassy** is typical of or suitable for Christmas; an informal word. *It was the last week of school and they were doing all kinds of Christmassy things.* ADJ-GRADED

Christmas tree, Christmas trees. A **Christmas tree** is a fir tree, or an artificial tree that looks like a fir tree, which people put in their houses at Christmas and decorate with coloured lights and ornaments. ◆◇◇◇◇ N-COUNT

chrome /kroʊm/. **Chrome** is metal plated with chromium. *...old-fashioned chrome taps.* ◆◇◇◇◇ N-UNCOUNT: oft N n

chromium /kroʊmiəm/. **Chromium** is a hard, shiny metallic element, used to make steel alloys and to coat other metals. *...chromium-plated fire accessories.* ◆◇◇◇◇ N-UNCOUNT

chromosomal /kroʊməsoʊmᵊl/. **Chromosomal** means relating to or connected with chromosomes. *More than half of all miscarriages are caused by chromosomal abnormalities.* ADJ: ADJ n

chromosome /kroʊməsoʊm/ **chromosomes.** A **chromosome** is a part of a cell in an animal or plant. It contains genes which determine what characteristics the animal or plant will have. *Each cell of our bodies contains 46 chromosomes.* ◆◇◇◇◇ N-COUNT

chronic /krɒnɪk/ ◆◆◇◇◇

1 A **chronic** illness or disability lasts for a very long time. Compare **acute**. *...chronic back pain.* ♦ **chronically** /krɒnɪkli/ *Most of them were chronically ill.* ADJ: usu ADJ n =persistent; ADV: ADV adj/-ed

2 You can describe someone's bad habits or behaviour as **chronic** when they have behaved like that for a long time and do not seem to be able to stop themselves. *Anyone who does not believe that smoking is an addiction has never been a chronic smoker. ...a chronic worrier.* ADJ: ADJ n =habitual, inveterate

3 A **chronic** situation or problem is very severe and unpleasant. *One cause of the artist's suicide seems to have been chronic poverty... There is a chronic shortage of patrol cars in this police district.* ♦ **chronically** *Research and technology are said to be chronically underfunded.* ADJ: usu ADJ n =severe; ADV: ADV adj/-ed

chronicle /krɒnɪkᵊl/ **chronicles, chronicling, chronicled** ◆◇◇◇◇

1 To **chronicle** a series of events means to write about them or show them in broadcasts in the order in which they happened. *The series chronicles the everyday adventures of two eternal bachelors.* ♦ **chronicler, chroniclers** *...the chronicler of the English civil war.* VERB =recount, V n, Also V wh; N-COUNT

2 A **chronicle** is an account or record of a series of events. *...this vast chronicle of Napoleonic times.* N-COUNT: usu N of n

3 The word **Chronicle** is sometimes used as part of the name of a newspaper. *...the San Francisco Chronicle.* N-IN-NAMES

chronological /krɒnəlɒdʒɪkᵊl/ ◆◇◇◇◇

1 If things are described or shown in **chronological** order, they are described or shown in the order in which they happened. *I have arranged these stories in chronological order.* ♦ **chronologically** *The exhibition is organised chronologically.* ADJ: usu ADJ n =sequential; ADV: ADV after v, ADV -ed/adj

2 If you refer to someone's **chronological** age, you are referring to the number of years they have lived, in contrast to their mental age or the stage they have reached in their physical or emotional development; a formal use. ADJ: ADJ n

chronology /krənɒlədʒi/ **chronologies**

1 The **chronology** of a series of past events is the times at which they happened in the order in which they happened. *She gave him a factual account of the chronology of her brief liaison.* N-UNCOUNT: oft N of n

2 A **chronology** is an account or record of the times and the order in which a series of past events took N-COUNT: oft N of n =account

place. *The second part of Duffy's book is a detailed chronology of the Reformation.*

chronometer /krɒnɒmɪtə^r^/ **chronometers.** A **chronometer** is an extremely accurate clock that is used especially by sailors at sea. [N-COUNT]

chrysalis /krɪsəlɪs/ **chrysalises**
1 A **chrysalis** is a butterfly or moth in the stage between being a larva and an adult. [N-COUNT]
2 A **chrysalis** is the hard, protective covering that a chrysalis has. *...a butterfly emerging from its chrysalis.* [N-COUNT]

chrysanthemum /krɪzænθəməm/ **chrysanthemums.** A **chrysanthemum** is a large garden flower with many long, thin petals. [◆◇◇◇◇ N-COUNT]

chubby /tʃʌbi/ **chubbier, chubbiest.** A **chubby** person is rather fat. *Do you think I'm too chubby? ...his chubby hands.* [ADJ-GRADED =tubby ≠skinny]

chuck /tʃʌk/ **chucks, chucking, chucked** [◆◆◇◇◇]
1 When you **chuck** something somewhere, you throw it there in a casual or careless way; an informal use. *I took a great dislike to the clock, so I chucked it in the dustbin... That second night, Sid Vicious chucked a bottle at the stage.* [VERB =throw; V n prep/adv; Also V n, V n n]
2 If you **chuck** your job or some other activity, you stop doing it; an informal use. *Last summer, he chucked his 10-year career as a London stockbroker and headed for the mountains.* ▶ **Chuck in** and **chuck up** mean the same as **chuck.** *Almost half the British public think about chucking in their jobs and doing their own thing at least once a month.* [VERB; V n; PHRASAL VERB; V P n (not pron); Also V n P]
• If someone **chucks it all, chucks it all up,** or **chucks it all in,** they stop doing their job, and usually move somewhere else, before starting to do something less well-paid or less secure. *Then I met my husband, and I chucked it all up for him... Sometimes I'd like to chuck it all and go fishing.* [PHRASE: V inflects]
3 If your girlfriend or boyfriend **chucks** you, they end the relationship; an informal use. *There wasn't a great hoo-ha when I chucked her.* [VERB; V n]
4 A **chuck** is a device for holding a tool in a machine such as a drill. [N-COUNT]

chuck away. If you **chuck** something **away,** you throw it away or waste it; an informal expression. *You cannot chuck money away on little luxuries like that.* [PHRASAL VERB; V n P]

chuck in. See **chuck** 2. [PHRASAL VERB]

chuck out [PHRASAL VERB]
1 If you **chuck** something **out,** you throw it away, because you do not need it or cannot use it; an informal use. *Many companies have struggled valiantly to use less energy and chuck out less rubbish.* [=throw away; V P n (not pron); Also V n P]
2 If a person **is chucked out** of a job, a place, or their home, they are forced by other people to leave; an informal use. *Any head teacher who made errors like this would be chucked out... I was chucked out of my London flat in 1960... Her parents are going to chuck her out on the street.* [be V-ed P; be V-ed P of n; V n P]

chuck up. See **chuck** 2. [PHRASAL VERB]

chuckle /tʃʌk^ə^l/ **chuckles, chuckling, chuckled.** When you **chuckle,** you laugh quietly. *The banker chuckled and said, 'Of course not.'... He chuckled at her forthrightness.* ▶ Also a noun. *He gave a little chuckle.* [◆◇◇◇◇ VERB; V; V at/over n; Also V with quote; N-COUNT]

chuffed /tʃʌft/. If you are **chuffed** about something, you are very pleased about it; an informal word in British English. *She had just moved into a new house and was pretty chuffed about that... I'm chuffed that the boss is staying... Naturally I wasn't chuffed. Who would be?* [ADJ-GRADED: v-link ADJ, oft ADJ about/with n, ADJ to-inf, ADJ that]

chug /tʃʌg/ **chugs, chugging, chugged.** When a vehicle **chugs** somewhere, it goes there slowly with its engine making short thudding sounds. *The train chugs down the track.* ▶ Also a noun. *In the distance I could hear the chug of farm machinery.* [◆◇◇◇◇ VERB; V prep/adv; N-SING]

chum /tʃʌm/ **chums.** Your **chum** is your friend; an old-fashioned informal word. *...his old chum Anthony.* [◆◇◇◇◇ N-COUNT: usu with poss =pal]

chummy /tʃʌmi/ **chummier, chummiest.** If people or social events are **chummy,** they are pleasant and friendly; an old-fashioned, informal word. *Following the performances there were chummy gatherings in the drawing room.* [ADJ-GRADED =friendly]
♦ **chumminess** /tʃʌminəs/ *He distrusted his wife's escalating chumminess with the Halcyon-Wilsons.* [N-UNCOUNT]

chump /tʃʌmp/ **chumps.** If you call someone who you like a **chump,** you are telling them that they have done something rather stupid or foolish, or that they are always doing stupid things; an informal word. *The guy's a chump. I could do a better job myself.* [N-COUNT PRAGMATICS =idiot]

chunk /tʃʌŋk/ **chunks** [◆◆◇◇◇]
1 **Chunks** of something are thick solid pieces of it. *They had to be careful of floating chunks of ice. ...a chunk of meat... Cut the melon into chunks.* [N-COUNT: oft N of n =lump]
2 A **chunk** of something is a large amount or large part of it; an informal use. *The company owns a chunk of farmland near Gatwick Airport.* [N-COUNT: usu N of n]

chunky /tʃʌŋki/ **chunkier, chunkiest** [◆◇◇◇◇]
1 A **chunky** person is broad and heavy. *The soprano was a chunky girl from California.* [ADJ-GRADED: usu ADJ n]
2 A **chunky** object is large and thick. *Her taste in fiction was for chunky historical romances. ...a chunky sweater. ...chunky jewellery.* [ADJ-GRADED: usu ADJ n]

church /tʃɜː^r^tʃ/ **churches** [◆◆◆◆◇]
1 A **church** is a building in which Christians worship. You usually refer to this place as **church** when you are talking about the time that people spend there. *...one of Britain's most historic churches. ...St Helen's Church... I didn't see you in church on Sunday.* [N-VAR]
2 A **Church** is one of the groups of people within the Christian religion, for example Catholics or Methodists, that have their own beliefs, clergy, and forms of worship. *...co-operation with the Catholic Church... Church leaders said he was welcome to return. ...the separation of church and state.* [N-COUNT: usu with supp, oft adj N, N of n]
3 You can refer to an organization, group, or area of activity as a **broad church** when it includes a wide range of opinions, beliefs, or styles. *By 1990 the Communist Party was a broad church, including social democrats, free market liberals and rightwing nationalists... It rapidly became apparent that rock'n'roll was a very broad church indeed.* [PHRASE: oft v-link PHR]

churchgoer /tʃɜː^r^tʃgoʊə^r^/ **churchgoers;** also spelled **church-goer.** A **churchgoer** is a person who goes to church regularly. [N-COUNT]

churchman /tʃɜː^r^tʃmən/ **churchmen.** A **churchman** is the same as a clergyman; a formal word. [◆◇◇◇◇ N-COUNT]

Church of England. **The Church of England** is the main church in England. It has the Queen as its head and it does not recognize the authority of the Pope. [◆◇◇◇◇ N-PROPER: the N]

church school, church schools. A **church school** is a school which has a special relationship with a particular branch of the Christian church, and where there is strong emphasis on worship and the teaching of religion. [N-COUNT]

churchwarden /tʃɜː^r^tʃwɔː^r^d^ə^n/ **churchwardens.** In the Anglican Church, a **churchwarden** is the person who has been chosen by a congregation to help the vicar of a parish with administration and other duties. [N-COUNT]

churchyard /tʃɜː^r^tʃjɑː^r^d/ **churchyards.** A **churchyard** is an area of land around a church where dead people are buried. [◆◇◇◇◇ N-COUNT]

churlish /tʃɜː^r^lɪʃ/. Someone who is **churlish** is unfriendly, bad-tempered, or impolite. *She would think him churlish if he refused... The room was so lovely it seemed churlish to argue.* [ADJ-GRADED: oft it v-link ADJ to-inf]

churn /tʃɜː^r^n/ **churns, churning, churned** [◆◇◇◇◇]
1 A **churn** is a container which is used for making butter. [N-COUNT: oft n N]
2 If something **churns** water, mud, or dust, it moves it about violently. *Ferries churn the waters of Howe Sound from Langdale to Horseshoe Bay. ...unsurfaced roads now churned into mud by the annual rains.* ▶ **Churn up** means the same as **churn.** *The recent rain had churned up the waterfall into a muddy whirlpool... Occasionally they slap the water with their tails or churn it up in play. ...muddy, churned-up ground.* [VERB; V n; V-ed; PHRASAL VERB; V P n (not pron); V n P; V-ed P]

3 If you say that your stomach **is churning**, you mean that you feel sick. You can also say that something **churns** your stomach. *My stomach churned as I stood up... I don't enjoy having a churning stomach but if you are going to win tournaments, you must go through it.* — V-ERG =heave; V; V-ing; Also V n

churn out. To **churn out** something means to produce large quantities of it very quickly; an informal expression. *He began to churn out literary compositions in English.* — PHRASAL VERB =turn out; V P n (not pron); Also V n P

churn up. See **churn** 2. — PHRASAL VERB

churning /tʃɜːʳnɪŋ/. **Churning** water is moving about violently; a literary word. *...anything to take our minds off that gap and the brown, churning water below.* — ADJ: ADJ n =swirling

chute /ʃuːt/ **chutes**

1 A **chute** is a steep, narrow slope down which people or things can slide. *Passengers escaped from the plane's front four exits by sliding down emergency chutes.* — N-COUNT: oft n N

2 A **chute** is a parachute; an informal use. *You can release the chute with either hand, but it is easier to do it with the left.* — N-COUNT =parachute

chutney /tʃʌtni/ **chutneys. Chutney** is a cold sauce made from fruit, vinegar, sugar, and spices. It is sold in jars and you eat it with meat or cheese. *...mango chutney.* — N-MASS

chutzpah /hʊtspə/. If you say that someone has **chutzpah**, you mean that you admire the fact that they are not afraid or embarrassed to do or say things that shock, surprise, or annoy other people; an informal word, used mainly in American English. *Such was his chutzpah that he even persuaded the general to pose in front of a rocket for a snapshot.* — N-UNCOUNT PRAGMATICS =cheek, nerve

CIA /siː aɪ eɪ/. **The CIA** is the agency in the United States that tries to obtain secret information about the political and military activities of individuals or governments in other countries. **CIA** is an abbreviation for 'Central Intelligence Agency'. — ◆◆◇◇◇ N-PROPER: the N

ciabatta /tʃəbætə/. **Ciabatta** or **ciabatta bread** is a type of flattish white bread that is made with olive oil and that has a crisp crust. It is traditionally made in Italy. — N-UNCOUNT

ciao /tʃaʊ/. Some people say **'Ciao'** as an informal way of saying goodbye to someone who they expect to see again soon. — CONVENTION PRAGMATICS =see you

cicada /sɪkɑːdə, AM -keɪdə/ **cicadas.** A **cicada** is a large insect that lives in hot countries and makes a loud high-pitched noise. — N-COUNT

CID /siː aɪ diː/. The **CID** is the branch of the police force in Britain concerned with finding out who has committed crimes. **CID** is an abbreviation for 'Criminal Investigation Department'. — ◆◇◇◇◇ N-PROPER: oft the N

cider /saɪdəʳ/ **ciders. Cider** is a drink made from apples. In Britain, cider is alcoholic. In the United States, cider is usually non-alcoholic. ► A glass of cider can be referred to as a **cider**. *Inside, he ordered a cider, the alcoholic English variety.* — ◆◇◇◇◇ N-MASS; N-COUNT

cigar /sɪgɑːʳ/ **cigars. Cigars** are rolls of dried tobacco leaves which people smoke. *He was sitting alone smoking a big cigar.* — ◆◇◇◇◇ N-COUNT

cigarette /sɪgəret/ **cigarettes. Cigarettes** are small tubes of paper containing tobacco which people smoke. *He went out to buy a packet of cigarettes.* — ◆◆◆◇◇ N-COUNT

cigarette end, cigarette ends. A **cigarette end** is the part of a cigarette that you throw away when you have finished smoking. *The floor below his chair was strewn with cigarette ends.* — N-COUNT =butt, stub

cigarette holder, cigarette holders; also spelled **cigarette-holder**. A **cigarette holder** is a narrow tube that you can put a cigarette into in order to hold it while you smoke it. *He puffed constantly through an elegant cigarette holder.* — N-COUNT

cigarette lighter, cigarette lighters. A **cigarette lighter** is a device which produces a small flame when you flick a switch and which you use to light a cigarette or cigar. — N-COUNT =lighter

ciggy /sɪgi/ **ciggies;** also spelled **ciggie**. In informal British English, a **ciggy** is a cigarette. — N-COUNT

C-in-C. A **C-in-C** is the same as a **commander-in-chief.** — N-SING

cinch /sɪntʃ/. If you say that something is **a cinch**, you mean that you think it is very easy to do; an informal expression. *It sounds difficult, but compared to full-time work it was a cinch.* — N-SING: a N =doddle

cinder block /sɪndəʳ blɒk/ **cinder blocks;** also spelled **cinderblock**. In American English, a **cinder block** is a large, grey-coloured brick made from coal cinders and cement which is used for building. The British word is **breeze-block**. — N-COUNT: oft N n

Cinderella /sɪndərelə/ **Cinderellas.** If you describe a person or organization as a **Cinderella**, you mean that they receive very little attention and that they deserve to receive more. *It is a Cinderella among charities, and still needs more help.* — N-COUNT: usu sing, oft N n

cinders /sɪndəʳz/. **Cinders** are the pieces of blackened material that are left after something such as wood or coal has burned. *The wind sent sparks and cinders flying.* — N-PLURAL =embers

cine /sɪni/. **Cine** is used to refer to things that are used in or connected with the making or showing of films. *Transferring cine film or slides to video should be a doddle. ...a cine camera. ...a cine projector.* — ADJ: ADJ n

cinema /sɪnɪmɑː/ **cinemas** — ◆◆◆◇◇

1 In British English, a **cinema** is a place where people go to watch films for entertainment. The American term is **movie theater** or **movie house**. *Madonna's new film is so erotic it may be banned from many cinemas.* — N-COUNT

2 In British English, you can talk about **the cinema** when you are talking about seeing a film in a cinema. The American term is **the movies**. *I can't remember the last time we went to the cinema... They decided to spend an evening at the cinema.* — N-SING: the N

3 **Cinema** is the business and art of making films. *Contemporary African cinema has much to offer in its vitality and freshness. ...in the early days of cinema.* — N-UNCOUNT =film

cinematic /sɪnɪmætɪk/. **Cinematic** means relating to films made for the cinema. *...a genuine cinematic masterpiece.* — ◆◇◇◇◇ ADJ: usu ADJ n

cinematographer /sɪnɪmətɒgrəfəʳ/ **cinematographers.** A **cinematographer** is a person who decides what filming techniques should be used during the shooting of a film. — N-COUNT

cinematography /sɪnɪmətɒgrəfi/. **Cinematography** is the technique of making films for the cinema. *...an admirer of Arthur Jafa's breathtaking cinematography.* — N-UNCOUNT

cinnamon /sɪnəmən/. **Cinnamon** is a spice used for flavouring sweet food. — ◆◇◇◇◇ N-UNCOUNT

cipher /saɪfəʳ/ **ciphers;** also spelled **cypher**.

1 A **cipher** is a secret system of writing that you use to send messages. *They cracked the cipher. ...a cipher clerk.* — N-COUNT =code

2 If you describe someone as a **cipher**, you mean that they have no power and are used by other people to achieve a particular purpose. *He was little more than a cipher who faithfully carried out the Fuehrer's commands.* — N-COUNT =nobody

circa /sɜːʳkə/. **Circa** is used in front of a particular year to say that this is the approximate date when something happened or was made; a formal word. *The story tells of a runaway slave girl in Louisiana, circa 1850.* — ◆◇◇◇◇ PREP =around

circle /sɜːʳkəl/ **circles, circling, circled** — ◆◆◆◆◇

1 A **circle** is a shape consisting of a curved line completely surrounding an area. Every part of the line is the same distance from the centre of the area. *The flag was red, with a large white circle in the center... I wrote down the number 46 and drew a circle around it.* — N-COUNT =ring

2 A **circle** of something is a round flat piece or area of it. *Cut out 4 circles of pastry. ...a circle of yellow light.* — N-COUNT: usu N of n =ring

3 A **circle** of objects or people is a group of them arranged in the shape of a circle. *The monument consists of a circle of gigantic stones... We stood in a circle holding hands.* — N-COUNT: oft N of n =ring

4 If something **circles** an object or place, or **circles** around it, it forms a circle around it. *This is the ring road that circles the city. ...the long curving driveway that circled around the vast clipped lawn.* VERB =encircle V n V around/round n

5 If an aircraft or a bird **circles** or **circles** something, it moves round in a circle in the air. *The plane circled, awaiting permission to land... There were two helicopters circling around. ...like a hawk circling prey.* VERB V V adv/prep V n

6 To **circle** around someone or something, or to **circle** them, means to move around them. *Emily kept circling around her mother... The silent wolves would track and circle them.* VERB =go round V around/round n V n

7 If you **circle** something on a piece of paper, you draw a circle around it. *Circle the correct answers on the coupon below.* VERB =ring V n

8 You can refer to a group of people as a **circle** when they meet each other regularly because they are friends or because they belong to the same profession or share the same interests. *He has a small circle of friends... Alton has made himself fiercely unpopular in certain circles.* N-COUNT: with supp

9 In a theatre or cinema, **the circle** is an area of seats on the upper floor. N-SING: the N

10 See also **Arctic Circle**, **dress circle**, **inner circle**, **vicious circle**, **virtuous circle**.

11 If you say that you **have come full circle** or **have turned full circle**, you mean that after a long series of events or changes the same situation that you started with still exists. *We've come full circle and dark-blue jeans are once again the height of style.* PHRASES V inflects

12 In British English, if you say that someone **is going round in circles**, you mean that they are not achieving anything because they keep coming back to the same point or problem. V inflects ≠progress

circuit /sɜːʳkɪt/ **circuits** ◆◆◆◇◇

1 An electrical **circuit** is a complete route which an electric current can flow around. *Any attempts to cut through the cabling will break the electrical circuit.* • See also **closed circuit**, **short-circuit**. N-COUNT

2 A **circuit** is a series of places that are visited regularly by a person or group, especially as a part of their job. *He joined the professional circuit... It's a common problem, the one I'm asked about most when I'm on the lecture circuit.* N-COUNT: usu supp N

3 A racing **circuit** is a track on which cars, motorbikes, or cycles race; used mainly in British English. N-COUNT

4 A **circuit** of a place or area is a journey all the way round it; a formal use. *She made a slow circuit of the room.* N-COUNT: usu N of n

circuit breaker, circuit breakers; also spelled **circuit-breaker**. A **circuit breaker** is a device which can stop the flow of electricity around a circuit by switching itself off if anything goes wrong. *There is an internal circuit breaker to protect the instrument from overload.* N-COUNT

circuitous /səʳkjuːɪtəs/. A **circuitous** route is long and complicated rather than simple and direct; a formal word. *They were taken on a circuitous route, from mainland China through Hong Kong to Europe and then to Panama... Stuart came into film-making via a circuitous route.* ADJ-GRADED: usu ADJ n =roundabout

circuitry /sɜːʳkɪtri/. **Circuitry** is a system of electric circuits. *The computer's entire circuitry was on a single board.* N-UNCOUNT

circuit training. **Circuit training** is a type of fitness training in which you do a series of different exercises, each for a few minutes. *I do circuit training once a week.* N-UNCOUNT

circular /sɜːʳkjʊləʳ/ **circulars** ◆◆◇◇◇

1 Something that is **circular** is shaped like a circle. *...a circular hole twelve feet wide and two feet deep... Place your hands on your shoulders and move your elbows up, back, and down, in a circular motion.* • See also **semi-circular**. ADJ: usu ADJ n

2 A **circular** journey or route is one in which you go to a place and return by a different route. *Both sides of the river can be explored on this circular walk.* ADJ: usu ADJ n

3 A **circular** argument or theory is not valid because it uses a statement to prove something which is then used to prove the statement. ADJ-GRADED

4 A **circular** is an official letter or advertisement that is sent to a large number of people at the same time. *The proposal has been widely publicised in BBC-TV press information circulars sent to 1,800 newspapers.* N-COUNT

circular saw, circular saws. A **circular saw** is a rotating metal disk with a sharp serrated edge. It is powered by an electric motor and is used for cutting wood and other materials. N-COUNT

circulate /sɜːʳkjʊleɪt/ **circulates, circulating, circulated** ◆◆◇◇◇

1 If a piece of writing **circulates** or **is circulated**, copies of it are passed round among a group of people. *The document was previously circulated in New York at the United Nations... Public employees, teachers and liberals are circulating a petition for his recall... This year anonymous leaflets have been circulating in Peking.* ♦ **circulation** /sɜːʳkjʊleɪʃᵊn/ *...an inquiry into the circulation of 'unacceptable literature'.* V-ERG be V-ed V n V N-UNCOUNT: usu the N of n

2 If something such as a rumour **circulates** or **is circulated**, the people in a place tell it to each other. *Rumours were already beginning to circulate that the project might have to be abandoned... I deeply resented those sort of rumours being circulated at a time of deeply personal grief.* V-ERG =spread V be V-ed Also V n

3 When something **circulates**, it moves easily and freely within a closed place or system. *...a virus which circulates via the bloodstream and causes ill health in a variety of organs... Cooking odors can circulate throughout the entire house.* ♦ **circulation** *The north pole is warmer than the south and the circulation of air around it is less well contained. ...the principle of free circulation of goods.* VERB V Also V prep N-UNCOUNT

4 If you **circulate** at a party, you move among the guests and talk to different people. *Let me get you something to drink, then I must circulate.* VERB V

circulation /sɜːʳkjʊleɪʃᵊn/ **circulations** ◆◆◇◇◇

1 The **circulation** of a newspaper or magazine is the number of copies that are sold each time it is produced. *The Daily News once had the highest circulation of any daily in the country... The paper has proved unable to maintain its circulation figures.* N-COUNT: with supp

2 Your **circulation** is the movement of blood through your body. *Anyone with heart, lung or circulation problems should seek medical advice before flying. ...cold spots in the fingers caused by poor circulation.* N-UNCOUNT

3 See also **circulate**.

4 If something such as money is **in circulation**, it is being used by the public. If something is **out of circulation** or has been **withdrawn from circulation**, it is no longer available for use by the public. *The supply of money in circulation was drastically reduced overnight. ...a society like America, with perhaps 180 million guns in circulation. ...the decision to take 50 and 100 ruble bills out of circulation.* PHRASES

5 If someone is **out of circulation**, they do not appear in public or at social gatherings for a period of time. You can also say that someone is **out of circulation** when they are in prison. *Political trials were being used to keep prominent activists out of circulation... I had been out of circulation for a month and knew that many friends would be there.*

circulatory /sɜːʳkjʊleɪtəri, AM -lətɔːri/. **Circulatory** means relating to the circulation of blood in the body; a medical term. *...the human circulatory system.* ADJ: ADJ n

circumcise /sɜːʳkəmsaɪz/ **circumcises, circumcising, circumcised** ◆◇◇◇◇

1 If a boy or man **is circumcised**, the loose skin at the end of his penis is cut off, usually for religious, cultural, or health reasons. *He had been circumcised within eight days of birth as required by Jewish law.* ♦ **circumcision** /sɜːʳkəmsɪʒᵊn/ *Jews and Moslems practise circumcision for religious reasons.* VB: usu passive be V-ed N-UNCOUNT: also a N

2 In some cultures, if a girl or woman **is circumcised**, parts of her genitals are slit or cut out. *An estimated number of 90 to 100 million women around the world living today have been circum-* VB: usu passive be V-ed

cised. ♦ **circumcision** *...a campaigner against female circumcision.* N-UNCOUNT

circumference /səʳkʌmfrəns/

1 The **circumference** of a circle, place, or round object is the distance around its edge. *...a scientist calculating the earth's circumference... The island is 3.5 km in circumference.* N-UNCOUNT

2 The **circumference** of a circle, place, or round object is its edge. *Cut the salmon into long strips and wrap it round the circumference of the bread.* N-UNCOUNT

circumflex /sɜːʳkəmfleks/ **circumflexes.** A **circumflex** or a **circumflex accent** is a symbol written over a vowel in French and other languages, usually to indicate that it should be pronounced longer than usual. It is used for example in the word 'rôle'. N-COUNT

circumlocution /sɜːʳkəmloʊkjuːʃᵊn/ **circumlocutions.** A **circumlocution** is a way of saying or writing something using more words than are necessary instead of being clear and direct; a formal word. *It was always when you most wanted a direct answer that Greenfield came up with a circumlocution.* N-VAR

circumnavigate /sɜːʳkəmnævɪgeɪt/ **circumnavigates, circumnavigating, circumnavigated.** If someone **circumnavigates** the world or an island, they sail all the way around it; a formal word. *For this year at least, our race to circumnavigate the globe in less than 80 days is over.* VERB; V n
♦ **circumnavigation** /sɜːʳkəmnævɪgeɪʃᵊn/ **circumnavigations** *He married in Fiji during a two-year circumnavigation of the globe in his yacht, Surma.* N-VAR: oft N *of* n

circumscribe /sɜːʳkəmskraɪb/ **circumscribes, circumscribing, circumscribed.** If someone's power or freedom **is circumscribed**, it is limited or restricted; a formal word. *The army evidently fears that, under him, its activities would be severely circumscribed... There are laws circumscribing the right of individual citizens to cause bodily harm to others.* VERB =limit; be V-ed; V n

circumspect /sɜːʳkəmspekt/. If you are **circumspect**, you are cautious in what you do and say and do not take risks; a formal word. *The banks should have been more circumspect in their dealings... You seem to be implying, in your usual circumspect manner, that perhaps it might not be a wonderful idea.* ADJ-GRADED =cautious, careful ≠reckless ♦ **circumspectly** *I would suggest that for the time being you behave as circumspectly as possible in political matters.* ADV-GRADED: ADV after v =cautiously ≠recklessly

circumspection /sɜːʳkəmspekʃᵊn/. **Circumspection** is cautious behaviour and a refusal to take risks; a formal word. *The angry man would have to be handled with circumspection.* N-UNCOUNT: oft *with* N =caution, care

circumstance /sɜːʳkəmstæns/ **circumstances** ♦♦♦◇◇

1 The **circumstances** of a particular situation are the conditions which affect what happens. *Recent opinion polls show that 60 percent favor abortion under certain circumstances... The strategy was too dangerous in the explosive circumstances of the times... I wish we could have met under happier circumstances.* N-COUNT: usu pl, with supp

2 The **circumstances** of an event are the way it happened or the causes of it. *I'm making inquiries about the circumstances of Mary Dean's murder... Hundreds of people had died there in terrible circumstances during and after the revolution.* N-PLURAL: with supp, oft *the* N *of* n

3 Your **circumstances** are the conditions of your life, especially the amount of money that you have. *...help and support for the single mother, whatever her circumstances... I wouldn't have expected to find you in such comfortable circumstances.* N-PLURAL: usu with poss =situation

4 Events and situations which cannot be controlled are sometimes referred to as **circumstance**. *There are those, you know, who, by circumstance, end up homeless... You might say that we've been victims of circumstance.* N-UNCOUNT

5 You can emphasize that something must not or will not happen by saying that it must not or will not happen **under any circumstances**. *Racism is wholly unacceptable under any circumstances... She made it clear that under no circumstances would she cancel the trip.* PHRASES; PHR with cl; PRAGMATICS

6 You can use **in the circumstances** or **under the circumstances** before or after a statement to indicate that you have considered the conditions affecting the situation before making the statement. *Under the circumstances, a crash was unavoidable... In the circumstances, Paisley's plans looked highly appropriate.* PHR with cl; PRAGMATICS

circumstantial /sɜːʳkəmstænʃᵊl/

1 **Circumstantial** evidence is evidence that makes it seem likely that something happened, but does not prove it; a formal use. *Fast work by the police in Birmingham had started producing circumstantial evidence.* ADJ: usu ADJ n

2 Something that is **circumstantial** is related to a particular circumstance; a formal use. *The reasons for the project collapsing were circumstantial.* ADJ

circumvent /sɜːʳkəmvent/ **circumvents, circumventing, circumvented** ♦◇◇◇◇

1 If someone **circumvents** a rule or restriction, they avoid having to obey the rule or restriction, in a clever and perhaps dishonest way; a formal use. *Military planners tried to circumvent the treaty.* VERB =get round; V n
♦ **circumvention** /sɜːʳkəmvenʃᵊn/ *America won't countenance any such circumvention of the sanctions.* N-UNCOUNT: usu N *of* n

2 If you **circumvent** someone, you cleverly prevent them from achieving something, especially when they are trying to harm you; a formal use. *Roosevelt occasionally attempted to circumvent him.* VERB =outwit; V n

circus /sɜːʳkəs/ **circuses** ♦♦◇◇◇

1 A **circus** is a group that consists of clowns, acrobats, and animals which travels around to different places and performs shows. *My real ambition was to work in a circus. ...circus performers.* N-COUNT ► **The circus** is the show performed by these people. *My dad took me to the circus.* N-SING: *the* N

2 If you describe a group of people or an event as a **circus**, you disapprove of them because they attract a lot of attention but do not achieve anything useful. *It could well turn into some kind of a media circus. ...the travelling circus of political journalists.* N-SING; PRAGMATICS

3 In Britain, **Circus** is sometimes used as part of the name of a street which goes in a circle. *...Piccadilly Circus.* N-IN-NAMES: n N

cirrhosis /sɪroʊsɪs/. **Cirrhosis** or **cirrhosis of the liver** is a disease which destroys a person's liver and which can kill them. It is often caused by drinking too much alcohol. N-UNCOUNT

cissy /sɪsi/. See **sissy**.

cistern /sɪstəʳn/ **cisterns.** A **cistern** is a container which holds water, for example to flush a toilet or to store the water supply for a building. N-COUNT =tank

citadel /sɪtədᵊl/ **citadels** ♦◇◇◇◇

1 In the past, a **citadel** was a strongly fortified building in or near a city, where people could shelter for safety. *The citadel at Besançon towered above the river.* N-COUNT =fortress

2 If you describe a system or organization as a **citadel** of a particular way of life, usually one you disapprove of, you mean that it is powerful and effective in defending that way of life; a formal use. *Even the communist party, the citadel of Soviet power, was threatened with disintegration and falling membership.* N-COUNT: usu N *of* n; PRAGMATICS =bastion, stronghold

citation /saɪteɪʃᵊn/ **citations** ♦◇◇◇◇

1 A **citation** is an official document or speech which praises a person for something brave or special that they have done. *His citation says he showed outstanding and exemplary courage.* N-COUNT

2 A **citation** from a book or other piece of writing is a passage or phrase from it. N-COUNT =quotation

3 In American English, a **citation** is an official order to appear in a court of law. The usual British word is **summons**. *The court could issue a citation and fine Ms. Robbins.* N-COUNT

cite /saɪt/ **cites, citing, cited** ♦♦♦◇◇

1 If you **cite** something, you quote it or mention it, especially as an example or proof of what you are saying; a formal use. *She cites a favourite poem by George Herbert... He cites just one example... I am* VERB; V n; V n *as* adj/n

merely citing his reaction as typical of British industry... Spain was cited as the most popular holiday destination.

2 In a legal case, to **cite** a person means to officially name them. To **cite** a reason or cause means to state it as the official justification for your case. *They cited Alex's refusal to return to the marital home... Three admirals and a top Navy civilian will be cited for failing to act on reports of sexual assaults.*
VERB
V n

citizen /sɪtɪz³n/ **citizens** ◆◆◆◆◇

1 Someone who is a **citizen** of a particular country is legally accepted as belonging to that country. *...American citizens... The life of ordinary citizens began to change.*
N-COUNT: usu with supp

2 The **citizens** of a town or city are the people who live there. *...the citizens of Buenos Aires.*
N-COUNT: usu N of n

3 See also **senior citizen.**

citizenry /sɪtɪz³nri/. The people living in a country, state, or city can be referred to as the **citizenry**; used in American English and in formal British English. *He used the medium of radio when he wanted to enlist public support or reassure the citizenry... I think we lack a citizenry that is adequately willing to take responsibility.*
N-SING-COLL

Citizens' Band. **Citizens' Band** is a range of radio waves which the general public is allowed to use to send messages to each other. It is used especially by lorry drivers and other motorists who use radio sets in their vehicles. *...citizens' band radios.*
N-PROPER: oft N n =CB

citizenship /sɪtɪz³nʃɪp/ ◆◇◇◇◇

1 If you have **citizenship** of a country, you are legally accepted as belonging to it. *After 15 years in the USA, he has finally decided to apply for American citizenship... Only people who can trace their family history in Kuwait back before 1920 are entitled to citizenship.*
N-UNCOUNT: oft adj N

2 **Citizenship** is the fact of belonging to a community because you live in it, and the duties and responsibilities that this brings. *Their German peers had a more developed sense of citizenship.*
N-UNCOUNT

citric acid /sɪtrɪk æsɪd/. **Citric acid** is a weak acid found in many kinds of fruit, especially citrus fruit such as oranges and lemons.
N-UNCOUNT

citrus /sɪtrəs/. A **citrus** fruit is a juicy, sharp-tasting fruit such as an orange, lemon, or grapefruit. *...citrus groves.*
◆◇◇◇◇ ADJ: ADJ n

city /sɪti/ **cities.** A **city** is a large town. *...the city of Bologna. ...a busy city centre.*
◆◆◆◆◆ N-COUNT

City. **The City** is the part of London where many important financial institutions have their main offices. People often refer to these financial institutions as **the City**. *...a foreign bank in the City... The City fears that profits could fall.*
◆◆◆◆◇ N-PROPER: the N

city fathers; also spelled **City Fathers**. You can refer to the members of a city council as the **city fathers**. *The city fathers in Birmingham would say we have no future in the twenty-first century as a major metal manufacturer.*
N-PLURAL

city hall, city halls; also spelled **City Hall**. The **city hall** is the building which a city council uses as its main offices. *There were speeches outside the City Hall. ...at Sheffield City Hall.*
◆◇◇◇◇ N-COUNT; N-PROPER

civic /sɪvɪk/ ◆◆◇◇◇

1 You use **civic** to describe people or things that have an official status in a town or city. *...the businessmen and civic leaders of Manchester. ...Bromley Civic Centre.*
ADJ: ADJ n =municipal

2 You use **civic** to describe the duties or feelings that people have because they belong to a particular community. *...a sense of civic pride.*
ADJ: ADJ n

civics /sɪvɪks/. **Civics** is the study of the rights and duties of the citizens of a society. *...my high-school civics class.*
N-UNCOUNT: oft N n

civil /sɪv³l/ ◆◆◆◆◇

1 You use **civil** to describe events that happen within a country and that involve the different groups of people in it. *...civil unrest.*
ADJ: ADJ n

2 You use **civil** to describe people or things in a country that are not connected with its armed forces. *...the US civil aviation industry.*
ADJ: usu ADJ n ≠military

3 You use **civil** to describe things that are connected with the state rather than with a religion. *They were married on August 9 in a civil ceremony in Venice. ...Jewish civil and religious law.*
ADJ: ADJ n ≠religious

4 You use **civil** to describe the rights that people have within a society. *...a United Nations covenant on civil and political rights.*
ADJ: ADJ n

5 Someone who is **civil** is polite in a formal way, but not particularly friendly; a formal use. *As visitors, the least we can do is be civil to the people in their own land.* ♦ **civilly** *The man nodded civilly to Sharpe, then consulted a notebook.* ♦ **civility** /sɪvɪlɪti/ *...civility to underlings.*
ADJ-GRADED =polite
ADV-GRADED
N-UNCOUNT

civil defence; spelled **civil defense** in American English. **Civil defence** is the organization and training of the ordinary people in a country so that they can help the armed forces, medical services, or police force, for example if the country is attacked by an enemy. *...a series of civil defence exercises.*
◆◇◇◇◇ N-UNCOUNT: oft N n

civil disobedience. **Civil disobedience** is the refusal by ordinary people in a country to obey laws or pay taxes, usually as a protest. *The opposition threatened a campaign of civil disobedience.*
N-UNCOUNT

civil engineer, civil engineers. A **civil engineer** is a person who plans, designs, and constructs roads, bridges, harbours, and public buildings.
N-COUNT

civil engineering. **Civil engineering** is the planning, design, and construction of roads, bridges, harbours, and public buildings. *The Channel Tunnel project is the biggest civil engineering project in Europe.*
N-UNCOUNT

civilian /sɪvɪliən/ **civilians** ◆◆◆◇◇

1 In a military situation, a **civilian** is anyone who is not a member of the armed forces. *The safety of civilians caught up in the fighting must be guaranteed.*
N-COUNT

2 In a military situation, **civilian** is used to describe people or things that are not military. *...the country's civilian population. ...civilian casualties. ...a soldier in civilian clothes.*
ADJ: usu ADJ n ≠military

civilisation /sɪvɪlaɪzeɪʃ³n/. See **civilization.**

civilise /sɪvɪlaɪz/. See **civilize.**

civility /sɪvɪlɪti/. See **civil.**

civilization /sɪvɪlaɪzeɪʃ³n/ **civilizations;** also spelled **civilisation** in British English. ◆◆◇◇◇

1 A **civilization** is a human society with its own social organization and culture. *The ancient civilizations of Central and Latin America were founded upon corn... It seemed to him that western civilization was in grave economic and cultural danger.*
N-VAR

2 **Civilization** is the state of having an advanced level of social organization and a comfortable way of life. *...our advanced state of civilisation.*
N-UNCOUNT

3 You can refer to a place where you can enjoy the comforts that you consider to be necessary as **civilization**. *...when I returned to civilization.*
N-UNCOUNT

civilize /sɪvɪlaɪz/ **civilizes, civilizing, civilized;** also spelled **civilise** in British English. To **civilize** a person or society means to educate them and improve their way of life. *...a comedy about a man who tries to civilise a woman – but she ends up civilising him... It exerts a civilizing influence on mankind.*
◆◇◇◇◇ VERB
V n
V-ing

civilized /sɪvɪlaɪzd/; also spelled **civilised** in British English. ◆◇◇◇◇

1 If you describe a society as **civilized**, you mean that it is advanced and has sensible laws and customs. *I believed that in civilized countries, torture had ended long ago.*
ADJ-GRADED ≠barbaric

2 If you describe a person or their behaviour as **civilized**, you mean that they are polite and reasonable. *I wrote to my ex-wife. She was very civilised about it.*
ADJ-GRADED

civil law. **Civil law** is the part of a country's set of laws which is concerned with the private affairs of citizens, for example marriage and property ownership, rather than with crime.
N-UNCOUNT: oft the N ≠criminal law

civil liberties; the form **civil liberty** is used as a modifier. A person's **civil liberties** are the
◆◇◇◇◇ N-PLURAL =human rights

rights they have to say, think, and do what they want as long as they respect other people's rights. *...his commitment to human rights and civil liberties. ...civil liberty campaigners.*

Civil List. In Britain, **the Civil List** is money paid by the state every year to members of the Royal Family to cover their living expenses. *She gets £230,000 from the Civil List.* N-PROPER: *the*N

civil rights. ◆◆◇◇◇ **Civil rights** are the rights that people have in a society to equal treatment and equal opportunities, whatever their race, sex, or religion. *...the civil rights movement. ...violations of civil rights.* N-PLURAL: oft N n

civil servant, civil servants. ◆◆◇◇◇ A **civil servant** is a person who works in the Civil Service in Britain and some other countries, or for the local, state, or federal government in the United States. *...two senior civil servants.* N-COUNT

Civil Service. ◆◇◇◇◇ The **Civil Service** of a country consists of all the government departments and all the people who work in them. *...a job in the Civil Service.* N-SING: usu *the*N

civil war, civil wars. ◆◆◆◇◇ A **civil war** is a war which is fought between different groups of people who live in the same country. *...the Spanish Civil War.* N-COUNT

civvies /sɪviz/. People in the armed forces use **civvies** to refer to ordinary clothes that are not part of a uniform; an informal word. *They might have been soldiers in civvies.* N-PLURAL: oft *in*N

civvy street /sɪvi striːt/. People in the armed forces use **civvy street** to refer to life and work which is not connected with the armed forces; used in informal British English. *If they were in civvy street they would be compensated anyway.* N-UNCOUNT: usu prep N

cl. **cl** is a written abbreviation for **centilitre**. *...two 75cl bottles of quality wine.*

clack /klæk/ **clacks, clacking, clacked.** If things **clack** or if you **clack** them, they make a short loud noise, especially when they hit each other. *The windshield wipers clacked back and forth... Once, he clacked one ski hard against the other and almost tripped.* ► Also a noun. *...listening to the clack of her shoes on the stairs... Her bracelets were going clack-clack-clack, she was shaking so hard.* V-ERG; V; V n; N-SING; SOUND

clad /klæd/ ◆◇◇◇◇

1 If you are **clad** in particular clothes, you are wearing them; a literary use. *...the figure of a woman, clad in black... Johnson was clad casually in slacks and a light blue golf shirt. ...posters of scantily-clad women.* ► Also a combining form. *...the leather-clad biker.* ADJ: v-link ADJ *in* n, adv ADJ; COMB in ADJ

2 A building, part of a building, or mountain that is **clad** with something is covered by that thing; a literary use. *The walls and floors are clad with ceramic tiles.* ► Also a combining form. *...the distant shapes of snow-clad mountains. ...the ivy-clad house.* ADJ: v-link ADJ *in/with* n; COMB in ADJ

cladding /klædɪŋ/

1 **Cladding** is a covering of tiles, wooden boards, or other material that is fixed to the outside of a building to protect it against bad weather or to make it look more attractive. *...aluminium double-glazing and stone cladding on Victorian terraced houses.* N-UNCOUNT: oft n N =facing

2 **Cladding** is a layer of metal which is put round fuel rods in a nuclear reactor. N-UNCOUNT

claim /kleɪm/ **claims, claiming, claimed** ◆◆◆◆◆

1 If you say that someone **claims** that something is true, you mean they say that it is true but you are not sure whether or not they are telling the truth. *He claimed that it was all a conspiracy against him... A man claiming to be a journalist threatened to reveal details about her private life... 'I had never received one single complaint against me,' claimed the humiliated doctor... He claims a 70 to 80 per cent success rate.* VERB =maintain; V that; V to-inf; V with quote; V n

2 A **claim** is something which someone says which they cannot prove and which may be false. *He repeated his claim that the people of Trinidad and Tobago backed his action... He rejected claims that he had affairs with six women.* N-COUNT: usu with supp, oft N that

3 If you say that someone **claims** responsibility or credit for something, you mean they say that they are responsible for it, but you are not sure whether or not they are telling the truth. *An underground organisation has claimed responsibility for the bomb explosion... He was too modest to claim the credit.* VERB; V n

4 If you **claim** something, you try to get it because you think you have a right to it. *Now they are returning to claim what was theirs.* VERB; V n

5 A **claim** is a demand for something that you think you have a right to. *Rival claims to Macedonian territory caused conflict in the Balkans.* N-COUNT: oft N *to* n

6 If someone **claims** a record, title, or prize, they gain or win it; used in journalism. *Zhuang claimed the record in 54.64 seconds... Steffi Graf claimed a fourth Wimbledon title in 1992.* VERB; V n

7 If you have a **claim on** someone or their attention, you have the right to demand things from them or to demand their attention. *She'd no claims on him now... He was surrounded by people, all with claims on his attention.* N-COUNT: N *on* n

8 If something or someone **claims** your attention, they need you to spend your time and effort on them. *There is already a long list of people claiming her attention.* VERB; V n

9 If you **claim** money from the government, an insurance company, or another organization, you officially apply to them for it, because you think you are entitled to it according to their rules. *Some 25 per cent of the people who are entitled to claim State benefits do not do so... John had taken out redundancy insurance but when he tried to claim, he was refused payment... They intend to claim for damages against the three doctors.* ► Also a noun. *...the office which has been dealing with their claim for benefit... Last time we made a claim on our insurance they paid up really quickly.* VERB; V n; V; V *for* n; N-COUNT: oft N *for* n

10 If you **claim** money or other benefits from your employers, you demand them because you think you deserve or need them. *The National Union of Teachers claimed a pay rise worth four times the rate of inflation.* ► Also a noun. *They are making substantial claims for improved working conditions... Electricity workers have voted for industrial action in pursuit of a pay claim.* VERB; V n; N-COUNT: oft N *for* n

11 If you say that a war, disease, or accident **claims** someone's life, you mean that they are killed in it or by it; a formal use. *The war in Bosnia claimed the life of a U.N. interpreter yesterday... Heart disease is the biggest killer, claiming 180,000 lives a year.* VERB =take; V n

12 See also **no claims**.

13 Someone's **claim to fame** is something quite important or interesting that they have done or that is connected with them. *Barbara Follett's greatest claim to fame is that she taught Labour MPs how to look good on television.* PHRASES *claim* inflects, oft poss PHR

14 If you **lay claim to** something you do not have, you say that it belongs to you; a formal expression. *Five Asian countries lay claim to the islands.* V inflects, PHR n

15 ● to **stake a claim**: see **stake**.

claimant /kleɪmənt/ **claimants** ◆◇◇◇◇

1 A **claimant** is someone who is receiving money from the state because they are unemployed or unable to work because of sickness; used mainly in British English. *...benefit claimants.* N-COUNT

2 A **claimant** is someone who asks to be given something which they think they are entitled to. *The claimants allege that manufacturers failed to warn doctors that their drugs should only be used only in limited circumstances. ...Louis-Alphonso, the rival claimant to the French throne.* N-COUNT

clairvoyant /kleəʳvɔɪənt/ **clairvoyants.**

1 Someone who is believed to be **clairvoyant** is believed to know about future events or to be able to communicate with dead people. *...clairvoyant powers.* ♦ **clairvoyance** *...his well-attested powers of telepathy and clairvoyance.* ADJ; N-UNCOUNT

2 A **clairvoyant** is someone who claims to be clairvoyant. *You did not have to be a clairvoyant to see that the war would go on.* N-COUNT

clam /klæm/ **clams, clamming, clammed.** ◆◇◇◇◇ **Clams** are a kind of shellfish which can be eaten. N-COUNT

clam up. If someone **clams up**, they stop talking, often because they are shy or to avoid giving away secrets; an informal expression. *As soon as I told her my name, she clammed up.* PHRASAL VERB VP

clamber /klæmbəʳ/ **clambers, clambering, clambered.** If you **clamber** somewhere, you climb there with difficulty, usually using your hands as well as your feet. *They clambered up the stone walls of a steeply terraced olive grove... Clambering over sackfuls of lemons, Boris tried to find a way out.* ◆◇◇◇◇ VERB =scramble V prep/adv

clammy /klæmi/. Something that is **clammy** is unpleasantly damp or sticky. *Think of the clammy hands you get when you visit the dentist!... My shirt was clammy with sweat.* ADJ-GRADED

clamorous /klæmərəs/. If you describe people or their voices as **clamorous**, you mean they are talking loudly or shouting; a literary word. *...the crowded, clamorous streets filled with Irish, German, Italian, Jewish, and Chinese children.* ADJ-GRADED: usu ADJ n

clamour /klæməʳ/ **clamours, clamouring, clamoured;** spelled **clamor** in American English. ◆◇◇◇◇
1 If people **are clamouring** for something, they are demanding it in a desperate, noisy, or angry way; used mainly in journalism. *...competing parties clamouring for the attention of the voter... At breakfast next morning my two grandsons were clamouring to go swimming.* ► Also a noun. *...the clamour for his resignation.* VERB V for n V to-inf N-SING: oft N for n
2 **Clamour** is used to describe the loud noise of a large group of people talking or shouting together. *Kathryn's quiet voice stilled the clamour... She could hear a clamour in the road outside.* N-SING =uproar

clamp /klæmp/ **clamps, clamping, clamped** ◆◆◇◇◇
1 A **clamp** is a device that holds two things firmly together. N-COUNT
2 When you **clamp** one thing **to** another, you fasten the two things together with a clamp. *Somebody forgot to bring along the U-bolts to clamp the microphones to the pole.* VERB V n to n
3 To **clamp** something in a particular place means to put it or hold it there firmly and tightly. *Simon finished dialing and clamped the phone to his ear... He clamped his lips together... You entreat him to try just one spoonful, and he clamps his mouth shut... Peter jumped to his feet with his hand clamped to his neck.* VERB V n prep V n together V n adj V-ed
4 A **clamp** is a large metal device which is fitted to the wheel of an illegally parked car or other vehicle in order to prevent it from being driven away. The motorist has to pay to have the clamp removed. N-COUNT =wheel clamp
5 To **clamp** a car means to fit a clamp to one of its wheels so that it cannot be driven away. *Courts in Scotland have ruled it illegal to clamp a car parked on private ground and then to demand a fine.* ♦ **clamping** *The Automobile Association yesterday called for laws to regulate clamping firms.* ♦ **clamper, clampers** *Private clampers demanded £57 to release her van.* VERB V n N-UNCOUNT N-COUNT

clamp down. To **clamp down** on people or activities means to take strong official action to stop or control them; used in journalism. *If the government clamps down on the movement, that will only serve to strengthen it in the long run... They may not have informed banking regulators, who failed to clamp down until earlier this month.* PHRASAL VERB VP on n VP

clampdown /klæmpdaʊn/ **clampdowns;** also spelled **clamp-down.** A **clampdown** is a sudden restriction on a particular activity by a government or other authority; used in journalism. *...a clampdown on the employment of illegal immigrants... Ironically, the latest clampdown has just led to renewed international criticism.* ◆◇◇◇◇ N-COUNT: oft N on n

clan /klæn/ **clans** ◆◆◇◇◇
1 A **clan** is a group which consists of families that are related to each other. *...rival clans.* N-COUNT
2 You can refer to a group of people with the same interests as a **clan**; an informal use. *...a powerful clan of industrialists from Monterrey.* N-COUNT

clandestine /klændestɪn/. Something that is **clandestine** is hidden or kept secret, often because it is illegal; a formal word. *...their clandestine meetings.* ♦ **clandestinely** *He left the country clandestinely.* ◆◇◇◇◇ ADJ: usu ADJ n =secret ADV: ADV with v

clang /klæŋ/ **clangs, clanging, clanged.** When a large metal object **clangs**, it makes a loud noise. *A little later the church bell clanged... The door clanged shut behind them.* ► Also a noun. *He pulled the gates to with a clang... In the older part of the city, the clang and bang of the builders goes on all day.* ♦ **clanging** *...the clanging of the cell doors.* VERB V N-VAR N-UNCOUNT

clanger /klæŋəʳ/ **clangers.** In informal British English, you can refer to something stupid or embarrassing that someone does or says as a **clanger**. *Despite his clanger, Martyn won the sympathy of his manager Steve Coppell.* • If you say that you have **dropped a clanger**, you mean that you have done or said something stupid or embarrassing. N-COUNT PHRASE: V and N inflect

clank /klæŋk/ **clanks, clanking, clanked.** When metal objects **clank**, they make a noise because they are banging together or banging against something hard. *A pan rattled and clanked... 'Here we are now,' Beth said, as the train clanked into a tiny station. ...the clanking noise of the ferry.* ► Also a noun. *...the clank and rattle of human activity.* VERB V V prep V-ing N-VAR

clannish /klænɪʃ/. If you describe a group of people as **clannish**, you mean that they often spend time together and may seem unfriendly to other people who are not in the group; an informal word. *...a Liverpool nightclub run by and for the clannish Irish community.* ADJ-GRADED =cliquey

clansman /klænzmən/ **clansmen. Clansmen** are people who are members of the same clan. *He was still known as a lord to his clansmen.* N-COUNT: usu pl

clap /klæp/ **claps, clapping, clapped** ◆◇◇◇◇
1 When you **clap**, you hit your hands together to express appreciation or attract attention. *The men danced and the women clapped... Midge clapped her hands, calling them back to order... Londoners came out on to the pavement to wave and clap the marchers.* ► Also a noun. *As long as the crowd give them a clap, they're quite happy.* VERB V V n N-SING: a N
2 If you **clap** your hand or an object onto something, you put it there quickly and firmly. *I clapped a hand over her mouth.* VERB V n prep
3 If you **clap** someone **on** the back or on the shoulder, you hit their back or shoulder with your hand in a friendly way. *While Onassis might clap a friend on the back, Niarchos would extend a businesslike hand.* VERB =slap V n on n
4 A **clap of thunder** is a sudden and loud noise of thunder. N-COUNT: N of n
5 • to **clap eyes on** someone: see **eye**.

clapboard /klæpbɔːʳd, klæbəʳd/. A **clapboard** building has walls which are covered with long narrow pieces of wood, usually painted white. ADJ: ADJ n

clapped-out; also spelled **clapped out**. In informal British English, if you describe a person or a machine as **clapped-out**, you mean that they are old and no longer able to work properly. *...his clapped-out old car. ...clapped out comedians.* ADJ-GRADED: usu ADJ n

clapperboard /klæpəʳbɔːʳd/ **clapperboards;** also spelled **clapper-board**. A **clapperboard** consists of two pieces of wood that are connected by a hinge and banged together before each scene when making a film, to make it easier to match the sound and pictures of different scenes. N-COUNT

claptrap /klæptræp/. If you describe something that someone says as **claptrap**, you mean that it is stupid or foolish although it may sound important; an informal word. *This is the claptrap that politicians have peddled many times before.* N-UNCOUNT PRAGMATICS =drivel

claret /klærət/ **clarets** ◆◇◇◇◇
1 **Claret** is a type of French red wine. N-MASS
2 Something that is **claret** is purplish-red in colour; a literary use. COLOUR

clarify /klærɪfaɪ/ **clarifies, clarifying, clarified** ◆◆◇◇◇
1 To **clarify** something means to make it easier to understand, usually by explaining it in more detail; a formal use. *Thank you for writing and allowing me to clarify the present position... A bank spokes-* VERB V n

man was unable to clarify the situation. ♦ **clarification** /klærɪfɪkeɪʃᵊn/ **clarifications** *The union has written to Zurich asking for clarification of the situation.* N-VAR

2 To **clarify** something such as a liquid or butter means to make it clearer, usually by taking away impurities which are in it. *In the 17th century they started straining off the liquid and clarifying it for soups... Melt the clarified butter in a pan.* VERB V n V-ed

clarinet /klærɪnet/ **clarinets.** A **clarinet** is a musical instrument of the woodwind family in the shape of a pipe with a single reed. You play the clarinet by blowing into it and covering and uncovering the holes with your fingers. ◆◇◇◇◇ N-VAR: oft *the* N

clarinettist /klærɪnetɪst/ **clarinettists;** also spelled **clarinetist**. A **clarinettist** is someone who plays the clarinet. N-COUNT

clarion call, clarion calls. A **clarion call** is a strong and emotional appeal to people to do something; a literary expression. *This is a clarion call for our country to face the challenges of the end of the Cold War.* N-COUNT

clarity /klærɪti/ ◆◇◇◇◇

1 The **clarity** of something such as a book or argument is its quality of being well explained and easy to understand. *...the ease and clarity with which the author explains difficult technical and scientific subjects.* N-UNCOUNT =lucidity

2 **Clarity** is the ability to think clearly. *In business circles he is noted for his flair and clarity of vision.* N-UNCOUNT: oft N *of* n

3 **Clarity** is the quality of being clear in outline or sound. *This remarkable technology provides far greater clarity than conventional x-rays.* N-UNCOUNT =precision

4 The **clarity** of a liquid, of glass, or of the air is the degree to which it is clear and free from impurities. *The first thing to strike me was the amazing clarity of the water.* N-UNCOUNT

clash /klæʃ/ **clashes, clashing, clashed** ◆◆◆◇◇

1 When people **clash**, they fight, argue, or disagree with each other; used mainly in journalism. *A group of 400 demonstrators ripped down the state Parliament's front gate and clashed with police... Behind the scenes, Parsons clashed with almost everyone on the show... The United States and Israel clashed over demands for a UN investigation into the killings.* ► Also a noun. *There have been a number of clashes between police in riot gear and demonstrators.* V-RECIP V *with* n pl-n V N-COUNT: oft N *between/with* n

2 Beliefs, ideas, or qualities that **clash** with each other are very different from each other and therefore are opposed. *Don't make any policy decisions which clash with official company thinking... Here, morality and good sentiments clash headlong.* ► Also a noun. *Inside government, there was a clash of views.* V-RECIP V *with* n pl-n V N-COUNT: N *of* n

3 If one event **clashes with** another, the two events happen at the same time so that you cannot attend both of them. *The detective changed his holiday dates when his flight was brought forward and it now clashed with the trial.* VERB V *with* n

4 If one colour or style **clashes** with another, the colours or styles look ugly together. You can also say that two colours or styles **clash**. *The red door clashed with the soft, natural tones of the stone walls... So what if the colours clashed?* V-RECIP ≠match V *with* n pl-n V

5 Sports journalists sometimes say that two individuals or teams who compete against each other **clash**, especially when a lot of feeling is involved. *Lewis has recently recovered his fitness and will clash with Christie in the 4x100m relay... The two sides will clash there only if Chelsea beat Sunderland in their quarter-final replay.* ► Also a noun. *Australia's rugby union team for the return clash with New Zealand is weakened by injury.* V-RECIP V *with* n pl-n V N-COUNT: oft N *between/with* n

6 When metal objects **clash**, they make a lot of noise by being hit together; a literary use. *The golden bangles on her arms clashed and jingled.* ► Also a noun. *...a noise like the clash of cymbals.* VERB pl-n V N-COUNT

clasp /klɑːsp, klæsp/ **clasps, clasping, clasped** ◆◇◇◇◇

1 If you **clasp** someone or something, you hold them tightly in your hands or arms. *She clasped the children to her... He paced the corridor, hands clasped behind his back.* ► Also a noun. *With one last clasp of his hand, she left him and went to her usual chair.* VERB V n V-ed N-COUNT: usu sing

2 A **clasp** is a small device that fastens something. *...the clasp of her handbag... There was even a new clasp in her hair.* N-COUNT: usu with supp

class /klɑːs, klæs/ **classes, classing, classed** ◆◆◆◆◆

1 A **class** is a group of pupils or students who are taught together. *He had to spend about six months in a class with younger students... Reducing class sizes should be a top priority.* N-COUNT

2 A **class** is a course of teaching in a particular subject. *He acquired a law degree by taking classes at night... I go to dance classes here in New York.* N-COUNT: oft n N =lesson

3 If you do something **in class**, you do it during a lesson in school. *There is lots of reading in class.* N-UNCOUNT: *in* N

4 The students in a school or university who finish their course in a particular year are often referred to as the **class of** that year. *These two members of Yale's Class of '57 never miss a reunion.* N-SING: N *of* date

5 **Class** refers to the division of people in a society into groups according to their social status. *...the relationship between social classes... What it will do is create a whole new ruling class. ...the characteristics of the British class structure.* • See also **chattering classes**, **middle class**, **upper class**, **working class**. N-VAR

6 A **class** of things is a group of them with similar characteristics. *Harbour staff noticed that measurements given for the same class of boats often varied. ...the division of the stars into six classes of brightness.* N-COUNT: usu N *of* n

7 If someone or something **is classed as** a particular thing, they are regarded as belonging to that group of things. *Since they can and do successfully inter-breed they cannot be classed as different species... I class myself as an ordinary working person... I would class my garden as medium in size... Malaysia wants to send back refugees classed as economic migrants.* VERB be V-ed *as* n/adj V pron-refl *as* n V n *as* adj/n V-ed

8 If you say that someone or something has **class**, you mean that they are elegant and sophisticated. *He's got the same style off the pitch as he has on it – sheer class.* N-UNCOUNT

9 If you describe someone or something as a **class** person or thing, you mean that they are very good; an informal use, used mainly in journalism. *Kite is undoubtedly a class player.* ADJ: ADJ n

10 See also **business class**, **first-class**, **second-class**, **third-class**, **top-class**, **world-class**.

11 If you say that someone such as a sports player or a performer is a **class act**, you mean that they are very good at what they do; an informal expression, used mainly in journalism. PHRASES N inflects

12 If you say that someone is **in a class of** their **own**, you mean that they have more of a particular skill or quality than anyone else. If you say that something is **in a class of its own**, you mean that it is better than any other similar thing. *As a player, he was in a class of his own.* usu v-link PHR

class-conscious. Someone who is **class-conscious** is very aware of the differences between the various classes of people in society, and often has a strong feeling of belonging to a particular class. *I think the Americans are even more class-conscious than we are.* ♦ **class-consciousness** *There was very little snobbery or class-consciousness in the wartime navy.* ADJ-GRADED N-UNCOUNT

classic /klæsɪk/ **classics** ◆◆◆◆◇

1 A **classic** example of a thing or situation has all the features which you expect such a thing or situation to have. *The debate in the mainstream press has been a classic example of British hypocrisy... His first two goals were classic cases of being in the right place at the right time.* ► Also a noun. *It was a classic of interrogation: first the bully, then the kind one who offers sympathy.* ADJ: usu ADJ n =typical N-COUNT: oft N *of* n

2 A **classic** film, piece of writing, or piece of music is of very high quality and has become a standard against which similar things are judged. *...the classic children's film Huckleberry Finn. ...a classic* ADJ: ADJ n

study of the American penal system. ► Also a noun. *The record won a gold award and remains one of the classics of modern popular music. ...a film classic.* — N-COUNT: usu with supp

3 A **classic** is a book which is well-known and considered to be of a very high literary standard. *As I grow older, I like to reread the classics regularly.* — N-COUNT

4 **Classic** style is simple and traditional and is not affected by changes in fashion. *Wear classic clothes which feel good and look good... These are classic designs which will fit in well anywhere.* — ADJ-GRADED: usu ADJ n

5 **Classics** is the study of the ancient Greek and Roman civilizations, especially their languages, literature, and philosophy. *...a Classics degree.* — N-UNCOUNT

classical /klæsɪkəl/ ◆◆◆◇◇

1 You use **classical** to describe something that is traditional in form, style, or content. *Fokine did not change the steps of classical ballet; instead he found new ways of using them. ...the scientific attitude of Smith and earlier classical economists.* — ADJ: usu ADJ n ≠modern

2 **Classical** music is music that is considered to be serious and of lasting value. — ADJ: usu ADJ n

3 **Classical** is used to describe things which relate to the ancient Greek or Roman civilizations. *...the healers of ancient Egypt and classical Greece... It's a technological achievement that is unrivalled in the classical world. ...classical architecture.* — ADJ: usu ADJ n

4 A **classical** language is a form of a language that was used in ancient times and is now no longer used, or only used in formal writing. *...a line of classical Arabic poetry.* — ADJ: ADJ n

classically /klæsɪkli/

1 Someone who has been **classically** trained in something such as art, music, or ballet has learned the traditional skills and methods of that subject. *Peter is a classically trained pianist.* — ADV: ADV -ed

2 **Classically** is used to indicate that something is based on or reminds people of the culture of ancient Greece and Rome. *...the classically inspired church of S. Francesco.* — ADV: ADV adj/-ed

3 Something that is **classically** designed is traditional, and beautiful in a simple way. *...five classically shaped vases... Older women look best in classically elegant styles.* — ADV: ADV adj/-ed

4 You use **classically** to indicate that you are saying what usually happens in the case of a particular type of thing. *Classically, overweight people underestimate the volume of food that they consume.* — ADV: ADV with cl, ADV with v =typically

classicism /klæsɪsɪzəm/. **Classicism** is a style of art practised especially in the 18th century in Europe. It has simple regular forms and the artist does not attempt to express strong emotions. — N-UNCOUNT

classicist /klæsɪsɪst/ **classicists**

1 A **classicist** is someone who studies the ancient Greek and Roman civilizations, especially their languages, literature, and philosophy. — N-COUNT

2 In the arts, especially in architecture, a **classicist** is someone who follows the principles of classicism in their work. — N-COUNT

classification /klæsɪfɪkeɪʃən/ **classifications.** ◆◇◇◇◇ A **classification** is a division or category in a classifying system. *Bottom of the league come engineering companies, a classification that includes the car companies.* • See also **classify**. — N-COUNT

classified /klæsɪfaɪd/. ◆◇◇◇◇ **Classified** information or documents are officially secret. *He has a security clearance that allows him access to classified information... The document was highly classified and circulated to a very limited group of people.* — ADJ

classified ad, classified ads. Classified ads or **classified advertisements** are small advertisements in a newspaper or magazine which are ordered in categories according to their subject. They are usually from a person or a small company to individual people. — N-COUNT

classifieds /klæsɪfaɪdz/. The **classifieds** are the same as **classified ads**. *Your best hope of obtaining a copy is to place an advert in the classifieds.* — N-PLURAL: usu *the* N

classify /klæsɪfaɪ/ **classifies, classifying, classified.** ◆◆◇◇◇ To **classify** things means to divide them into groups or types so that things with similar characteristics are in the same group. *It is necessary initially to classify the headaches into certain types... Rocks can be classified according to their mode of origin... The coroner immediately classified his death as a suicide.* — VERB =categorize; V n; V n as n ♦ **classification** /klæsɪfɪkeɪʃən/ **classifications** *...the arbitrary classification of knowledge into fields of study. ...the British Board of Film Classification.* — N-VAR

classless /klɑːsləs, klæs-/. ◆◇◇◇◇ When politicians talk about a **classless** society, they mean a society in which everyone has the same social and economic status; used showing approval. *...the new Prime Minister's vision of a classless society.* — ADJ-GRADED: usu ADJ n PRAGMATICS ♦ **classlessness** *...the myth of classlessness.* — N-UNCOUNT

classmate /klɑːsmeɪt, klæs-/ **classmates.** ◆◇◇◇◇ Your **classmates** are students who are in the same class as you at school or college. — N-COUNT: oft poss N

classroom /klɑːsruːm, klæs-/ **classrooms.** ◆◆◇◇◇ A **classroom** is a room in a school where lessons take place. — N-COUNT

classy /klɑːsi, klæsi/ **classier, classiest.** ◆◇◇◇◇ If you describe someone or something as **classy**, you mean they are stylish and sophisticated; an informal word. *The German star put in a classy performance... Both GM and Ford believe they need classier brand names to sell upmarket cars.* — ADJ-GRADED

clatter /klætəʳ/ **clatters, clattering, clattered** ◆◇◇◇◇

1 If you say that people or things **clatter** somewhere, you mean that they move there noisily. *He turned and clattered down the stairs.* — VERB; V prep/adv

2 If something hard **clatters**, it makes repeated short noises as it hits against another hard thing; a literary use. *His hobnail boots clattered on the stone floor... She set her cup down, and it clattered against the saucer.* — VERB; V prep ► Also a noun. *From somewhere distant he heard the clatter of a typewriter.* — N-SING: usu with supp

clause /klɔːz/ **clauses** ◆◆◇◇◇

1 A **clause** is a section of a legal document. *He has a clause in his contract which entitles him to a percentage of the profits. ...a compromise document sprinkled with escape clauses. ...a complaint alleging a breach of clause 4 of the code.* — N-COUNT: oft N num

2 In grammar, a **clause** is a group of words containing a verb. Sentences contain one or more clauses. There are finite clauses and non-finite clauses. • See also **main clause**, **relative clause**, **subordinate clause**. — N-COUNT

claustrophobia /klɔːstrəfoʊbiə/

1 Someone who suffers from **claustrophobia** feels very uncomfortable or anxious when they are in small or enclosed places. — N-UNCOUNT

2 If you talk about the **claustrophobia** of a place or situation, you mean it makes you feel uncomfortable or unhappy because you are enclosed or restricted. *In the claustrophobia of her parents' house she had no stimulus for creativity.* — N-UNCOUNT: oft *the* N *of* n

claustrophobic /klɔːstrəfoʊbɪk/ ◆◇◇◇◇

1 You describe a place or situation as **claustrophobic** when it makes you feel uncomfortable and unhappy because you are enclosed or restricted. *They lived in an unhealthily claustrophobic atmosphere... The house felt too claustrophobic.* — ADJ-GRADED

2 If you feel **claustrophobic**, you feel very uncomfortable or anxious when you are in a small, crowded, or enclosed place. *The churning, pressing crowds made her feel claustrophobic.* — ADJ-GRADED: usu v-link ADJ

clavichord /klævɪkɔːʳd/ **clavichords.** A **clavichord** is a musical instrument rather like a small piano. When you press the keys, small pieces of metal come up and hit the strings. Clavichords were especially popular during the eighteenth century. — N-VAR: oft *the* N

clavicle /klævɪkəl/ **clavicles.** Your **clavicles** are your collar bones; a medical term. — N-COUNT

claw /klɔː/ **claws, clawing, clawed** ◆◇◇◇◇

1 The **claws** of a bird or animal are the thin, hard, curved nails at the end of its feet. *The cat tried to cling to the edge by its claws.* — N-COUNT: usu pl

2 The **claws** of a lobster, crab, or scorpion are the two pointed parts at the end of its legs which are used for grasping things. — N-COUNT: usu pl

3 If an animal **claws** something, it scratches or — VERB damages it with its claws. *The wolf clawed at the tree and howled the whole night.* V n

4 When people or animals **claw** at something, they try to get hold of it or damage it by using their nails or claws. *His fingers clawed at Blake's wrist... He stumbled, clawed wildly at the air and fell backwards into the water.* VERB; V at n; Also V n

5 If you **claw** your **way** somewhere, you move there with great difficulty, trying desperately to find things to hold on to. *From the flooded depths of the ship some did manage to claw their way up iron ladders to the safety of the upper deck.* VERB; V *way* prep/adv

6 If someone **claws** their **way** to a successful position, they achieve it with great determination in spite of many difficulties. *Gino clawed his way out of underworld obscurity to become a millionaire hotelier.* VERB; V *way* prep/adv

7 If someone gets their **claws** into another person, they start doing or saying things, especially unpleasant things, which affect that person. *She should take her claws out of Tom and let him get on with his life.* N-PLURAL: poss N

claw back PHRASAL VERB

1 If someone **claws back** some of the money or power which they had lost, they get some of it again. *They will eventually be able to claw back all or most of the debt... In the meantime his generals will want to claw back some of their old influence.* V P n (not pron); Also V n P

2 When a government **claws back** money, it finds a way of taking money back from people that it gave money to in another way. For example, it may raise indirect taxes in order to recover money that has been paid in state benefits; a technical term in economics. *The Chancellor will try to claw back £3.5 billion in next year's Budget.* V P n (not pron); Also V n P

clawback /klɔːbæk/ **clawbacks.** A **clawback** is a measure by which an organization takes back money from people it gave money to; a technical term in economics, used in British English. N-VAR

clay /kleɪ/ **clays** ◆◆◇◇◇

1 Clay is a kind of earth that is soft when it is wet and hard when it is dry. Clay is shaped and baked to make things such as pots and bricks. *...the heavy clay soils of Cambridgeshire... As the wheel turned, the potter shaped and squeezed the lump of clay into a graceful shape. ...a little clay pot.* N-MASS: oft N n

2 In tennis, matches played on **clay** are played on courts whose surface is covered with finely crushed stones or brick. *Most tennis is played on hard courts, but a substantial amount is played on clay... Agassi was equally impressive in beating Frana, a clay court specialist.* N-UNCOUNT: oft *on* N, N n

3 If you say that a person who is respected or admired has **feet of clay** or has **clay feet**, you mean that they have serious faults which you or other people did not know about before; a formal expression. *When those idols are found to have feet of clay, the pain of disenchantment can be profound.* PHRASE

clay pigeon, clay pigeons. Clay pigeons are discs of baked clay which are thrown into the air by a machine as targets for gun shooting practice. *...hunting and clay-pigeon shooting.* N-COUNT: usu N n

clean /kliːn/ **cleaner, cleanest; cleans, cleaning, cleaned** ◆◆◆◆◇

1 Something that is **clean** is free from dirt or unwanted marks. *He wore his cleanest slacks, a clean shirt and a navy blazer... Disease has not been a problem because clean water is available... The metro is efficient and spotlessly clean... Tiled kitchen floors are easy to keep clean.* ADJ-GRADED ≠dirty

2 You say that people or animals are **clean** when they keep themselves or their surroundings clean. ADJ-GRADED ≠dirty

3 A **clean** fuel or chemical process does not create many harmful or polluting substances. *Fans of electric cars say they are clean, quiet and economical.* ♦ **cleanly** *Manufacturers are working with new fuels to find one that burns more cleanly than petrol.* ADJ-GRADED ≠dirty; ADV-GRADED: ADV after v

4 If you **clean** something or **clean** dirt off it, you make it free from dirt and unwanted marks, for example by washing or wiping it. If something **cleans** easily, it is easy to clean. *Her father cleaned his glasses with a paper napkin... It took half an hour to clean the orange powder off the bath... He cleaned the flakes away with his coat sleeve... Wood flooring not only cleans easily, but it's environmentally friendly into the bargain.* ▶ Also a noun. *Give the cooker a good clean.* V-ERG; V n; V n prep/adv; V adv; N-SING

5 If you **clean** a room or house, you make the inside of it and the furniture in it free from dirt and dust. *With them also lived Mary Burinda, who cooked and cleaned... She got up early and cleaned the flat.* ♦ **cleaning** *I do the cleaning myself.* VERB; V; V n; N-UNCOUNT

6 If you describe something such as a book, joke, or lifestyle as **clean**, you think that they are not sexually immoral or offensive; used showing approval. *They're trying to show clean, wholesome, decent movies... Flirting is good clean fun... He became a model of clean living and Bible Belt virtues.* ADJ-GRADED; PRAGMATICS; ≠dirty

7 If someone has a **clean** reputation or record, they have never done anything illegal or wrong. *Accusations of tax evasion have tarnished his clean image... You can hire these from most car hire firms, provided you have a clean driving licence.* ADJ-GRADED

8 A **clean** game or fight is carried out fairly, according to the rules. *He called for a clean fight in the election and an end to 'negative campaigning'... It was a clean match, well refereed.* ♦ **cleanly** *The game had been cleanly fought.* ADJ-GRADED: usu ADJ n =fair ≠dirty; ADV: ADV after v, ADV -ed

9 If you describe a flavour, smell, or colour as **clean**, you like it because it is light and fresh. *...the fresh, clean smell of the sea... Soft tones of blue and grey create a clean, bright look.* ADJ-GRADED; PRAGMATICS

10 A **clean** sheet of paper has no writing or drawing on it. *Take a clean sheet of paper and down the left-hand side make a list.* ADJ: usu ADJ n =blank

11 If you make a **clean** break or start, you end a situation completely and start again in a different way. *Voters have chosen to make a clean break with the communist past.* ADJ: ADJ n

12 Clean is used to emphasize that something was done completely; an informal use. *It burned clean through the seat of my overalls... The thief got clean away with the money... I clean forgot everything I had prepared.* ADV: usu ADV prep/adv, also ADV before v; PRAGMATICS

13 A **clean** shape is simple and regular, with definite, smooth edges. *He admires the clean lines of Shaker furniture... The drill should be slowly rotated to ensure a clean hole.* ♦ **cleanly** *Cut horizontally and cleanly through the stem.* ADJ-GRADED: usu ADJ n ≠ragged; ADV-GRADED: ADV with v

14 You can describe an action as **clean** to indicate that it is carried out simply and quickly without mistakes. *They were more concerned about the dogs' welfare than a clean getaway... Paul had arrested countless men like this one before and was expecting a clean, quick job.* ♦ **cleanly** *I struck the ball cleanly and my shot was on target.* ADJ-GRADED: usu ADJ n ≠messy; ADV-GRADED: ADV after v, ADV -ed

15 If you **come clean** about something that you have been keeping secret, you admit it or tell people about it; an informal expression. *It would be better if you come clean about it and let her know what kind of man she is seeing.* PHRASE: V inflects, oft PHR *about/on* n

16 • to **clean up** your **act**: see **act.** • **a clean bill of health**: see **bill.** • to **make a clean breast of it**: see **breast.** • to **keep** your **nose clean**: see **nose.** • **a clean slate, to wipe the slate clean**: see **slate.** • **a clean sweep**: see **sweep.** • **clean as a whistle**: see **whistle.**

clean out PHRASAL VERB

1 If you **clean out** something such as a cupboard, room, or container, you take everything out of it and clean the inside of it thoroughly. *Mr. Wall asked if I would help him clean out the bins... If you are using the same pan, clean it out.* V P n (not pron); V n P

2 In informal English, if someone **cleans** you **out**, they take all the money and valuables you have. If they **clean out** a place, they take everything of value that is in it. *I'm sure the burglars waited until my insurance claim was through and came back to clean me out again... When they first captured the port, they virtually cleaned out its warehouses.* V n P; V P n (not pron)

clean up PHRASAL VERB

1 If you **clean up** a mess or **clean up** a place where there is a mess, you make things tidy and free of dirt again. *Police in the city have been cleaning up the debris left by a day of violent confrontation... Nina and Mary were in the kitchen, cleaning up after dinner.* V P n (not pron) / V P / Also V n P

2 To **clean up** something such as the environment or an industrial process means to make it free from substances or processes that cause pollution. *Under pressure from the public, many regional governments cleaned up their beaches.* V P n (not pron) / Also V n P

3 If the police or authorities **clean up** a place or area of activity, they make it free from crime, corruption, and other unacceptable forms of behaviour. *After years of neglect and decline the city was cleaning itself up... Since then, the authorities have tried to clean up the sport.* V n P / V P n (not pron)

clean up after. If you **clean up after** someone, you clean or tidy a place that they have made dirty or untidy. *At the end, he nursed Lilly and cleaned up after her without minding.* PHRASAL VERB / V P P n

clean-cut. Someone, especially a boy or man, who is **clean-cut** has a neat, tidy appearance. *...his clean-cut good looks.* ADJ-GRADED

cleaner /kliːnər/ **cleaners** ◆◆◇◇◇

1 A **cleaner** is someone who is employed to clean the rooms and furniture inside a building. N-COUNT

2 A **cleaner** is someone whose job is to clean a particular type of thing. *He was a window cleaner.* N-COUNT: n N

3 A **cleaner** is a substance used for cleaning things. *...oven cleaner. ...abrasive cleaners.* N-MASS: usu n N

4 A **cleaner** is a device used for cleaning things. *...an air cleaner.* • See also **pipe cleaner, vacuum cleaner**. N-COUNT: usu n N

5 A **cleaner** or a **cleaner's** is a shop where things such as clothes are dry-cleaned. N-COUNT: oft *the* N

6 If someone **takes** you **to the cleaners**, they unfairly take a lot of your money, for example in a business deal or in gambling; an informal expression, used in British English. PHRASE: V inflects

cleaning lady, cleaning ladies. A **cleaning lady** is a woman who is employed to clean the rooms and furniture inside a building. N-COUNT =cleaner

cleaning woman, cleaning women. A **cleaning woman** is the same as a **cleaning lady**. N-COUNT

cleanliness /klenlɪnəs/. **Cleanliness** is the degree to which people keep themselves and their surroundings clean. *Many of Britain's beaches fail to meet minimum standards of cleanliness. ...the importance of personal cleanliness.* ◆◇◇◇◇ N-UNCOUNT

cleanse /klenz/ **cleanses, cleansing, cleansed** ◆◆◇◇◇

1 To **cleanse** a place, person, or organization of something dirty, unpleasant, or evil means to make them free from it. *Straight after your last cigarette your body will begin to cleanse itself of tobacco toxins... It urged the party to cleanse its own ranks of those found guilty of human rights violations... Garlic helps to cleanse the system and stimulate immune resistance.* • See also **ethnic cleansing**. VERB / V n *of* n / V n

2 If you **cleanse** your skin or a wound, you clean it. *Catherine demonstrated the proper way to cleanse the face. ...cleansing lotions.* VERB / V n / V-ing

3 If a person or their soul **is cleansed**, they are made pure or free from sin. *I had the sensation that I was being cleansed... Confession cleanses the soul.* VERB / *be* V-ed / V n

cleanser /klenzər/ **cleansers.** A **cleanser** is a liquid or cream that you use for cleaning something, especially your skin. ◆◇◇◇◇ N-MASS

clean-shaven. If a man is **clean-shaven**, he does not have a beard or a moustache; used mainly in written English. ADJ

clean-up, clean-ups; spelled **cleanup** in American English. A **clean-up** is the removing of dirt, pollution, crime, or corruption from somewhere. *...the need for a clean-up of Italian institutions... The Governor has now called in the National Guard to assist the cleanup operation.* ◆◆◇◇◇ N-COUNT

clear /klɪər/ **clearer, clearest; clears, clearing, cleared** ◆◆◆◆◆

1 Something that is **clear** is easy to understand, see, or hear. *The book is clear, readable and adequately illustrated... The space telescope has taken the clearest pictures ever of Pluto... He repeated his answer, this time in a clear, firm tone of voice.* ADJ-GRADED ≠unclear, confusing ♦ **clearly** *Whales journey up the coast of Africa, clearly visible from the beach... It was important for children to learn to express themselves clearly.* ADV-GRADED: usu ADV -ed/adj, also ADV after v

2 Something that is **clear** is obvious and impossible to be mistaken about. *It was a clear case of homicide... The clear message of the scientific reports is that there should be a drastic cut in car use... A spokesman said the British government's position is perfectly clear... It became clear that I hadn't been able to convince Mike... It's not clear whether the incident was an accident or deliberate.* ADJ-GRADED: oft *it* v-link ADJ that/wh =obvious, plain ≠unclear ♦ **clearly** *Clearly, the police cannot break the law in order to enforce it... He clearly believes that India should have de-valued its currency.* ADV-GRADED: ADV with cl/group =obviously

3 If you are **clear** about something, you understand it completely. *It is important to be clear about what Chomsky is doing here... He is not entirely clear on how he will go about it... People use scientific terms with no clear idea of their meaning.* ADJ-GRADED: usu v-link ADJ *about/on* n/wh

4 If your mind or your way of thinking is **clear**, you are able to think sensibly, reasonably, and logically, and you are not affected by confusion or by a drug such as alcohol. *She needed a clear head to carry out her instructions.* ADJ-GRADED ♦ **clearly** *The only time I can think clearly is when I'm alone.* ADV-GRADED: ADV after v

5 To **clear** your mind or your head means to free it from confused thoughts or from the effects of a drug such as alcohol. *He walked up Fifth Avenue to clear his head... Our therapists will show you how to clear your mind of worries.* VERB / V n / V n *of* n

6 A **clear** substance is one which you can see through and which has no colour, like clean water. *...a clear glass panel. ...a clear gel... The water is clear and plenty of fish are visible.* ADJ: usu ADJ n =transparent

7 A **clear** colour is bright and strong. *Ladybird pupae vary in colour from brown to clear orange.* ADJ-GRADED: usu ADJ n

8 If a surface, place, or view is **clear**, it is free of obstructions or unwanted objects. *The runway is clear – go ahead and land... All exits must be kept clear in case of fire or a bomb scare... Caroline prefers her worktops to be clear of clutter... The windows will allow a clear view of the beach.* ADJ: usu v-link ADJ

9 When you **clear** an area or place or **clear** something from it, you remove things from it that you do not want to be there. *To clear the land and harvest the bananas they decided they needed a male workforce... Stewart was trying to clear a path for the stretcher... Workers could not clear the tunnels of smoke... Firemen were still clearing rubble from apartments damaged at the scene of the attack.* VERB / V n / V n *of* n / V n *from/off* n / Also V n with adv

10 If something or someone **clears** the way or the path **for** something to happen, they make it possible. *The Prime Minister resigned today, clearing the way for the formation of a new government... A court in Berlin has dropped the charges against him, clearing the way for him to leave Germany.* VERB / V n *for* n / V n *for* n to-inf

11 If it is a **clear** day or if the sky is **clear**, there is no mist, rain, or cloud. *On a clear day you can see the French coast... The winter sky was clear.* ADJ-GRADED

12 When fog or mist **clears**, it gradually disappears. *The early morning mist had cleared.* VERB / V

13 **Clear** eyes look healthy, attractive, and shining. *...clear blue eyes... Her eyes were clear and steady.* ADJ-GRADED

14 If your skin is **clear**, it is healthy and free from spots. ADJ-GRADED

15 If you say that your conscience is **clear**, you mean you do not think you have done anything wrong. *Mr Garcia said his conscience was clear over the jail incidents... I can look back on things with a clear conscience. I did everything I could.* ADJ

16 If something or someone is **clear** of something else, it is not touching it or is a safe distance away from it. *As soon as he was clear of the terminal building he looked round... She placed a towel on a cluster of rocks just clear of the tidemark... He lifted him clear of the deck with one arm.* ADJ: v-link ADJ *of* n, v n ADJ

17 If an animal or person **clears** an object or **clears** a certain height, they jump over the object, or over something that height, without touching it. VERB / V n

Sotomayor, the Cuban holder of the world high jump record, cleared 2.36 metres.

18 When a bank **clears** a cheque or when a cheque **clears**, the bank agrees to pay the sum of money mentioned on it. *Polish banks can still take two or three weeks to clear a cheque... Allow time for the cheque to clear.* V-ERG V n V

19 If a course of action **is cleared**, people in authority give permission for it to happen. *Linda Gradstein has this report from Jerusalem, which was cleared by an Israeli censor... Within an hour, the helicopter was cleared for take-off... The hormone, developed by US drug companies, is expected to be cleared for use in the US soon.* VB: usu passive *be* V-ed *be* V-ed *for* n Also *be* V-ed to-inf

20 If someone **is cleared**, they are proved to be not guilty of a crime or mistake. *She was cleared of murder and jailed for just five years for manslaughter... In a final effort to clear her name, Eunice has written a book.* VERB *be* V-ed *of* n/-ing V n

21 See also **clearing**; **crystal clear**.

22 You can say **'Is that clear?'** or **'Do I make myself clear?'** after you have told someone your wishes or instructions, to make sure that they have understood you, and to emphasize your authority. *We're only going for half an hour, and you're not going to buy anything. Is that clear?* PHRASES CONVENTION PRAGMATICS

23 If someone is **in the clear**, they are free from blame, suspicion, or danger. *The Audit Commission said that the ministry was in the clear.* v-link PHR, PHR after v

24 If you **make** something **clear**, you say something in a way that makes it impossible for there to be any doubt about your meaning, wishes, or intentions. *Mr O'Friel made it clear that further insults of this kind would not be tolerated... The far-right has now made its intentions clear.* V inflects, oft PHR that

25 In British English, if something or someone is a certain amount **clear of** a competitor, they are that amount ahead of them in a competition or race. *Kevin Keegan's team are now seven points clear of West Ham... He crossed the line three seconds clear of Tom Snape.* PREP: amount PREP n

26 If you **steer clear** or **stay clear** of someone or something, you avoid them. *The rabbis try to steer clear of political questions.* V inflects, oft PHR *of* n =avoid

27 • to **clear the air**: see **air**. • **the coast is clear**: see **coast**. • to **clear the decks**: see **deck**. • **loud and clear**: see **loud**. • to **clear** your **throat**: see **throat**.

clear away. When you **clear** things **away** or **clear away**, you put away the things that you have been using, especially for eating or cooking. *The waitress had cleared away the plates and brought coffee... Tania cooked, served, and cleared away.* PHRASAL VERB V P n (not pron) V P Also V n P

clear off. If you tell someone to **clear off**, you are telling them rather rudely to go away; an informal expression. *They looked at me as if I was nuts and told me to clear off.* PHRASAL VERB PRAGMATICS =push off V P

clear out PHRASAL VERB

1 If you tell someone to **clear out** of a place or to **clear out**, you are telling them rather rudely to leave the place; an informal expression. *She turned to the others in the room. 'The rest of you clear out of here.'... 'Clear out!' he bawled. 'Private property!'* PRAGMATICS =get out V P *of* n V P

2 If you **clear out** a container, room, or house, you tidy it and throw away the things in it that you no longer want. *I took the precaution of clearing out my desk before I left.* • See also **clear-out**. V P n (not pron) Also V n P

clear up PHRASAL VERB

1 When you **clear up** or **clear** a place **up**, you tidy things and put them away. *After breakfast they played while I cleared up... I cleared up my room.* V P V P n (not pron) Also V n P

2 To **clear up** a problem, misunderstanding, or mystery means to settle it or find a satisfactory explanation for it. *There should be someone to whom you can turn for any advice or to clear up any problems... During dinner the confusion was cleared up: they had mistaken me for Kenny.* • See also **clear-up**. V P n (not pron) Also V n P

3 To **clear up** a medical problem, infection, or disease means to cure it or get rid of it. If a medical problem **clears up**, it goes away. *Antibiotics should be used to clear up the infection... Acne often clears up after the first three months of pregnancy.* ERG V P n (not pron) V P Also V n P

4 When the weather **clears up**, it stops raining or being cloudy. *It all depends on the weather clearing up.* V P

clearance /klɪərəns/ **clearances** ◆◇◇◇◇

1 **Clearance** is the removal of old buildings, trees, or other things that are not wanted from an area. *...a slum clearance operation in Nairobi... The UN pledged to help supervise the clearance of mines. ...widespread clearance of jungle land.* N-VAR

2 If you get **clearance** to do or have something, you get official approval or permission to do or have it. *Thai Airways said the plane had been given clearance to land... He has a security clearance that allows him access to classified information.* N-VAR =authorization

3 The **clearance** of a bridge is the distance between the lowest point of the bridge and the road or the water under the bridge. *The lowest fixed bridge has 12.8m clearance.* N-VAR

clearance sale, clearance sales. A **clearance sale** is a sale in which the goods in a shop are sold at reduced prices, because the shopkeeper wants to get rid of them quickly or because the shop is closing down. N-COUNT

clear-cut. Something that is **clear-cut** is easy to recognize and quite distinct. *This was a clear-cut case of the original land owner being in the right... The issue is not so clear cut.* ◆◇◇◇◇ ADJ-GRADED =cut-and-dried

clear-headed. If you describe someone as **clear-headed**, you mean that they are sensible and think clearly, especially in difficult situations. *...his clear-headed grasp of the laws of economics.* ADJ-GRADED

clearing /klɪərɪŋ/ **clearings.** A **clearing** is a small area in a forest where there are no trees or bushes. *A helicopter landed in a clearing in the dense jungle.* ◆◆◇◇◇ N-COUNT

clearing bank, clearing banks. The **clearing banks** are the major banking organizations in Britain. Clearing banks use the central clearing house in London to deal with all their transactions with other banks. N-COUNT

clearing house, clearing houses; also spelled **clearing-house.**

1 If an organization acts as a **clearing house**, it collects, sorts, and distributes specialized information. *The centre will act as a clearing house for research projects for former nuclear scientists.* N-COUNT

2 A **clearing house** is a central bank which deals with all the transactions between the banks that use its services. N-COUNT

clear-out, clear-outs. When you have a **clear-out**, you collect together all the things that you do not want and throw them away; an informal word used in British English. N-COUNT: usu sing

clear-sighted. If you describe someone as **clear-sighted**, you admire them because they are able to understand situations well and to make sensible judgements and decisions about them. *He was clear-sighted enough to keep a sense of perspective... The best way to travel to success is to have a clear-sighted view of your objective.* ADJ-GRADED PRAGMATICS

clear-up. The **clear-up** rate for a crime or in an area is the percentage of criminals caught by the police, compared to the total number of crimes reported. *The clear-up rate for murders remains high... The Metropolitan Police say clear-up figures were improved.* ◆◇◇◇◇ ADJ: ADJ n

cleat /kliːt/ **cleats.** A **cleat** is a kind of double hook which is used for securing rope, especially on sailing boats. N-COUNT

cleavage /kliːvɪdʒ/ **cleavages** ◆◇◇◇◇

1 A woman's **cleavage** is the space between her breasts, especially the top part which you see if she is wearing a low-cut dress. N-COUNT

2 A **cleavage** between two people or things is a division or disagreement between them; a formal use. *...the economic cleavages between the two regions.* N-COUNT =division

cleave /kliːv/ **cleaves, cleaving.** The past tense can be either **cleaved** or **clove**; the past participle can be **cleaved, cloven,** or **cleft** for meaning 1, and is **cleaved** for meaning 2.

1 When you **cleave** something, you split or divide it into two separate parts, often violently; a literary use. *...the shovel with which Wendy is about to cleave his cranium.* VERB =split; V n

2 If someone **cleaves to** something or **to** someone else, they begin or continue to have strong feelings of loyalty towards them or have a link with them; a formal use. *Inevitably, as Morisot and Manet cleaved to each other, previous bonds weakened... He still clove to this ideal.* VERB; V *to* n

cleaver /kliːvəʳ/ **cleavers.** A **cleaver** is a knife with a large square blade, used for chopping meat or vegetables. *...a meat cleaver.* N-COUNT

clef /klef/ **clefs.** A **clef** is a symbol at the beginning of a line of music that indicates the pitch of the written notes. N-COUNT

cleft /kleft/ **clefts**

1 A **cleft** in a rock or in the ground is a narrow opening in it. *...a narrow cleft in the rocks too small for humans to enter.* N-COUNT =fissure

2 If someone has a **cleft** in their chin, their chin has a shallow vertical indentation in the middle. N-COUNT

3 If someone has a **cleft** chin, they have a cleft in their chin. ADJ: ADJ n

4 If you say that a person or organization is **in a cleft stick**, you mean that they are in a difficult situation that will bring them problems and harm whatever they decide to do. PHRASE: v-link PHR, PHR after v

5 **Cleft** is a past participle of **cleave**.

cleft palate, cleft palates. If someone has a **cleft palate**, they were born with a narrow opening along the roof of their mouth which makes it difficult for them to speak properly. N-VAR

clematis /klemətɪs/ **clematises;** the plural form can be **clematis** or **clematises**. A **clematis** is a type of flowering shrub which can be grown to climb up walls or fences. There are many different varieties of clematis. ◆◇◇◇◇ N-VAR

clemency /klemənsi/. If someone is granted **clemency**, they receive merciful treatment from a person who has the authority to punish them; a formal word. *Seventeen prisoners held on death row are to be executed after their pleas for clemency were turned down.* N-UNCOUNT

clement /klemənt/. **Clement** weather is pleasantly mild and dry; a formal word. ADJ-GRADED: usu ADJ n ≠inclement

clementine /kleməntaɪn/ **clementines.** A **clementine** is a fruit that looks like a small orange. N-COUNT

clench /klentʃ/ **clenches, clenching, clenched** ◆◇◇◇◇

1 When you **clench** your fist or your fist **clenches**, you curl your fingers up tightly, usually because you are very angry. *Alex clenched her fists and gritted her teeth... She pulled at his sleeve and he turned on her, fists clenching again before he saw who it was. ...angry protestors with clenched fists.* V-ERG; V n; V; V-ed

2 When you **clench** your teeth or they **clench**, you squeeze your teeth together firmly, usually because you are angry or upset. *Patsy had to clench her jaw to suppress her anger... Slowly, he released his breath through clenched teeth.* VERB =grit; V n; V-ed; Also V

3 If you **clench** something in your hand or in your teeth, you hold it tightly with your hand or your teeth. *I clenched the arms of my chair.* VERB =grip; V n

clergy /klɜːʳdʒi/. The **clergy** are the officially appointed leaders of the religious activities of a particular group of believers. *Stalin deported Catholic clergy to Siberia.* ◆◇◇◇◇ N-PLURAL

clergyman /klɜːʳdʒimən/ **clergymen.** A **clergyman** is a male member of the clergy. ◆◇◇◇◇ N-COUNT

cleric /klerɪk/ **clerics.** A **cleric** is a member of the clergy. *His grandfather was a Muslim cleric.* ◆◇◇◇◇ N-COUNT

clerical /klerɪkᵊl/ ◆◇◇◇◇

1 **Clerical** jobs, skills, and workers are concerned with work that is done in an office. *...a strike by clerical staff in all government departments... The hospital blamed the mix-up on a clerical error.* ADJ: ADJ n =administrative

2 **Clerical** means relating to the clergy. *...a bearded man in a dark suit and clerical collar. ...Iran's clerical leadership.* ADJ: ADJ n

clerk /klɑːʳk, AM klɜːrk/ **clerks clerking clerked** ◆◆◇◇◇

1 A **clerk** is a person who works in an office, bank, or law court and whose job is to look after the records or accounts. *She was offered a job as an accounts clerk with a travel firm.* N-COUNT

2 A **clerk** is a receptionist; used mainly in American English. *...a hotel clerk.* N-COUNT

3 To **clerk** means to work as a clerk; used mainly in American English. *Gene clerked at the auction... He clerked for the chief justice of the Supreme Court.* VERB; V; V *for* n

clever /klevəʳ/ **cleverer, cleverest** ◆◆◆◇◇

1 Someone who is **clever** is intelligent and able to understand things easily or plan things well. *He's a very clever man... My sister was always a lot cleverer than I was... Her mother was clever at many things.* ♦ **cleverly** *She would cleverly pick up on what I said.* ♦ **cleverness** *Her cleverness seems to get in the way of her emotions.* ADJ-GRADED; ADV-GRADED; N-UNCOUNT

2 A **clever** idea, book, or invention is extremely effective and shows the skill of the people involved. *It is a clever and gripping novel, yet something is missing from its heart... A colleague of mine in Milan devised the following very clever little experiment. ...this clever new gadget.* ♦ **cleverly** *...a cleverly designed swimsuit.* ADJ-GRADED: usu ADJ n =ingenious; ADV-GRADED: ADV -ed

3 If you say that someone is **too clever by half**, you disapprove of them because they are very clever and they show their cleverness in a way that annoys other people. *His many admirers describe him as clever: his enemies as too clever by half.* PHRASE PRAGMATICS

cliché /kliːʃeɪ, AM kliːʃeɪ/ **clichés;** also spelled **cliche**. A **cliché** is an idea or phrase which has been used so much that it is no longer interesting or effective or no longer has much meaning; used showing disapproval. *I've learned that the cliche about life not being fair is true... It has become a cliche to describe Asia-Pacific as the world's most dynamic economic area.* ◆◇◇◇◇ N-COUNT PRAGMATICS

clichéd /kliːʃeɪd, AM kliːʃeɪd/; also spelled **cliched**. If you describe something as **clichéd**, you mean that it has been said, done, or used many times before, and is boring or untrue; used showing disapproval. *The dialogue and acting in Indecent Proposal are tired, cliched and corny. ...the cliched image of the professional footballer.* ADJ-GRADED PRAGMATICS

click /klɪk/ **clicks, clicking, clicked** ◆◆◇◇◇

1 If something **clicks** or if you **click** it, it makes a short, sharp sound. *The applause rose to a crescendo and cameras clicked... He clicked off the radio... Blake clicked his fingers at a passing waiter, who hurried across to them.* ► Also a noun. *A click of a button on the mouse controlled the computer's functions.* V-ERG; V; V n with *off/on*; V n; N-COUNT

2 When you suddenly understand something, you can say that it **clicks**; an informal use. *When I saw the television report it all clicked... It suddenly clicked that this was fantastic fun.* VERB; V; it V that

3 If you **click** with someone, you like each other and become friendly as soon as you meet. You can also say that two people **click**. An informal use. *They clicked immediately. They loved the same things. ...the man who clicks with the world's most beautiful women.* V-RECIP; pl-n V; V *with* n

4 • to **click** your **heels**: see **heel**. • to **click into place**: see **place**.

client /klaɪənt/ **clients.** A **client** of a professional person or organization is a person or company that receives a service from them in return for payment. *...a solicitor and his client... The company required clients to pay substantial fees in advance.* ◆◆◆◇◇ N-COUNT

clientele /kliːɒntel, klaɪən-/. The **clientele** of a place or organization are its customers or clients. *This pub had a mixed clientele... I have built up a loyal satisfied clientele for both African and European clothes.* ◆◇◇◇◇ N-SING-COLL

client state, client states. A **client state** is a country which is controlled or influenced by another larger and more powerful state, or which is dependent on this state for support and protection. *...the Soviet Union and its former East European client states.*

cliff /klɪf/ **cliffs.** A **cliff** is a high area of land with a very steep side, especially one next to the sea. *The car rolled over the edge of a cliff.* ◆◆◇◇◇ N-COUNT

cliff-hanger, cliff-hangers. A **cliff-hanger** is a situation or part of a play or film that is very exciting or frightening because you are left for a long time not knowing what will happen next. *Wednesday's election is likely to be a cliff-hanger... The series always had a cliff-hanger ending.* N-COUNT

clifftop /klɪftɒp/ **clifftops.** A **clifftop** is the area of land around the top of a cliff. *I have this beautiful house on a clifftop. ...25 acres of spectacular clifftop scenery.* N-COUNT

climactic /klaɪmæktɪk/. A **climactic** moment in a story or a series of events is one in which a very exciting or important event occurs; a formal word. *...the film's climactic scene.* ADJ-GRADED: ADJ n

climate /klaɪmət/ **climates** ◆◆◆◇◇

1 The **climate** of a place is the general weather conditions that are typical of it. *...the hot and humid climate of Cyprus.* N-VAR

2 You can use **climate** to refer to the general atmosphere or situation somewhere. *The economic climate remains uncertain. ...the existing climate of violence and intimidation... A major change of political climate is not in prospect.* N-COUNT: usu with supp

climatic /klaɪmætɪk/. **Climatic** conditions, changes, and effects relate to the general weather conditions of a place. *...the threat of rising sea levels and climatic change from overheating of the atmosphere.* ◆◇◇◇◇ ADJ: ADJ n

climatologist /klaɪmətɒlədʒɪst/ **climatologists.** A **climatologist** is someone who studies climates. N-COUNT

climax /klaɪmæks/ **climaxes, climaxing, climaxed** ◆◆◇◇◇

1 The **climax** of something is the most exciting or important moment in it, usually near the end. *For Pritchard, reaching an Olympics was the climax of her career... It was the climax to 24 hours of growing anxiety... The last golf tournament of the European season is building up to a dramatic climax.* N-COUNT: oft N *of/to* n

2 The event that **climaxes** a sequence of events is an exciting or important event that comes at the end. You can also say that a sequence of events **climaxes** with a particular event. Used in journalism. *The demonstration climaxed two weeks of strikes... They've just finished a sell-out UK tour that climaxed with a three-night stint at Brixton Academy.* V-ERG V n V *with* n Also V

3 A **climax** is an orgasm. N-VAR

4 When someone **climaxes**, they have an orgasm. *Often, a man can enjoy making love but may not be sufficiently aroused to climax.* VERB V

climb /klaɪm/ **climbs, climbing, climbed** ◆◆◆◇◇

1 If you **climb** something such as a tree, mountain, or ladder, or **climb** up it, you move towards the top of it. If you climb **down** it, you move towards the bottom of it. *Climbing the first hill took half an hour... He picked up his suitcase and climbed the stairs... I told her about him climbing up the drainpipe... Kelly climbed down the ladder into the water... Children love to climb.* ▶ Also a noun. *...an hour's leisurely climb through olive groves and vineyards.* VERB V n V *up* n V *down* n V Also V *up/down* N-COUNT: oft N prep

2 If you **climb** somewhere, you move there carefully, and sometimes awkwardly, for example because you are moving into a small space or trying to avoid falling. *The girls hurried outside, climbed into the car, and drove off... He must have climbed out of his cot... He climbed down from the cab.* VERB V prep/adv

3 When something such as an aeroplane **climbs**, it moves upwards to a higher position. When the sun **climbs**, it moves higher in the sky. *The plane took off for LA, lost an engine as it climbed, and crashed just off the runway.* VERB =rise V Also V prep

4 When something **climbs**, it increases in value or amount. *The nation's unemployment rate has been climbing steadily since last June... Prices have climbed by 21% since the beginning of the year... The FA Cup Final's audience climbed to 12.3 million... Jaguar shares climbed 43 pence to 510 pence.* VERB V V *by* amount V *to/from* amount V amount

5 See also **climbing.** ● **a mountain to climb**: see **mountain**.

climb down. If you **climb down** in an argument or dispute, you admit that you are wrong, or change your intentions or demands. *If Lafontaine is forced to climb down, he may wish to reconsider his position... He has climbed down on pledges to reduce capital gains tax.* PHRASAL VERB V P V P *on/over* n

climb-down, climb-downs; also spelled **climbdown**. A **climb-down** in an argument or dispute is the act of admitting that you are wrong or of changing your intentions or demands. *This week's climb-down by the Department of Transport is thought to be the first time a road has been halted on environmental grounds.* N-COUNT

climber /klaɪməʳ/ **climbers** ◆◇◇◇◇

1 A **climber** is someone who climbs rocks or mountains as a sport or a hobby. N-COUNT

2 A **climber** is a plant that grows upwards by attaching itself to other plants or objects. N-COUNT

climbing /klaɪmɪŋ/. **Climbing** is the activity of climbing rocks or mountains. ● See also **climb**, **rock climbing**, **social climbing**. ◆◆◇◇◇ N-UNCOUNT

climbing frame, climbing frames. A **climbing frame** is a structure that is made for children to climb and play on. It consists of metal or wooden bars joined together. N-COUNT

clime /klaɪm/ **climes.** You use **clime** in expressions such as **warmer climes** and **foreign climes** to refer to a place that has a particular kind of climate; a literary word. *He left Britain for the sunnier climes of Southern France... We always take our holidays in foreign climes.* N-COUNT: usu pl, usu adj N

clinch /klɪntʃ/ **clinches, clinching, clinched** ◆◆◇◇◇

1 If you **clinch** something you are trying to achieve, such as a business deal or victory in a contest, you succeed in obtaining it. *Dynamo Kiev clinched their 13th Soviet League title when they beat CSKA Moscow 4-1... This has fuelled speculation that he is about to clinch a deal with an American engine manufacturer.* VERB =secure V n V n *with* n

2 The thing that **clinches** an uncertain matter settles it or provides a definite answer. *Evidently this information clinched the matter... That was the clue which clinched it for us.* VERB V n V *it*

3 A **clinch** is a romantic embrace; used mainly in journalism. *They were caught in a clinch when their parents returned home unexpectedly.* N-COUNT

clincher /klɪntʃəʳ/ **clinchers.** A **clincher** is something that finally proves something, settles an argument or decision, or helps someone achieve a victory; an informal word. *DNA fingerprinting has proved the clincher in many criminal and other forensic identifications... The clincher was Haig's assurance that he could withstand any German attack for at least eighteen days.* N-COUNT

cling /klɪŋ/ **clings, clinging, clung** ◆◆◇◇◇

1 If you **cling** to someone or something, you hold onto them tightly. *Another man was rescued as he clung to the riverbank... She had to cling onto the doorhandle until the pain passed... They hugged each other, clinging together under the lights.* VERB V *to/onto* n V *together*

2 If someone **clings** to a position or a possession they have, they do everything they can to keep it even though this may be very difficult. *Instead, he appears determined to cling to power... Another minister clung on with a majority of only 18... Japan's productivity has overtaken America in some industries, but elsewhere the United States has clung on to its lead.* VERB V *to/onto* n V *on* V *on to* n

3 Clothes that **cling to** you stay pressed against your body when you move. *His sodden trousers were clinging to his shins.* ♦ **clinging** *...clinging black garments.* VERB V *to* n ADJ-GRADED: usu ADJ n

4 Something that **is clinging to** something else is stuck on it or just attached to it. *Her glass had bits of orange clinging to the rim.* VERB V *to* n

5 If someone **clings to** someone they are fond of, they do not allow that person to have enough free- VERB PRAGMATICS

dom or independence; used showing disapproval. *I was terrified he would leave me, so I was clinging to him.* ♦ **clinging** *She was anxious not to appear clinging.* — V *to* n; ADJ-GRADED

6 If you **cling to** an idea or way of behaving, you continue to believe in its value or importance, even though it may no longer be valid or useful. *They know scholars reject their legend, but they still cling to their belief... They're clinging to the past.* — VERB; V *to* n

clingfilm /klɪŋfɪlm/; also spelled **cling film. Clingfilm** is a thin, clear, stretchy plastic which you use to cover food to keep it fresh. — N-UNCOUNT

clingy /klɪŋi/
1 If you describe someone as **clingy**, you mean that they become very attached to people and too dependent on them; used showing disapproval. *A very clingy child can drive a parent to distraction.* — ADJ-GRADED PRAGMATICS =clinging
2 Clingy clothes fit tightly round your body. *...long clingy skirts.* — ADJ-GRADED =clinging

clinic /klɪnɪk/ **clinics.** A **clinic** is a building where people go to receive medical advice or treatment. *...a family planning clinic.* — ◆◆◆◇◇ N-COUNT

clinical /klɪnɪkᵊl/ — ◆◆◇◇◇
1 Clinical means involving or relating to the direct medical treatment or testing of patients; a medical use. *The first clinical trials were expected to begin next year. ...a clinical psychologist.* ♦ **clinically** /klɪnɪkli/ *She was diagnosed as being clinically depressed... It has been clinically proved that it is better to stretch the tight muscles first.* — ADJ: ADJ n; ADV: usu ADV adj/-ed
2 You use **clinical** to describe thought or behaviour which is very logical and detached and does not involve any emotion; used showing disapproval. *All this questioning is so analytical and clinical – it kills romance.* — ADJ-GRADED PRAGMATICS =impersonal

clinician /klɪnɪʃᵊn/ **clinicians.** A **clinician** is a doctor who specializes in clinical work. — ◆◇◇◇◇ N-COUNT

clink /klɪŋk/ **clinks, clinking, clinked.** When objects made of glass, pottery, or metal **clink** or when you **clink** them, they touch each other and make a short, light sound. People sometimes clink glasses when drinking together, especially when they are celebrating something. *She clinked her glass against his... They clinked glasses... The empty whisky bottle clinked against the seat... Their glasses clinked, their eyes met.* ► Also a noun. *...the clink of a spoon in a cup.* — V-RECIP-ERG; V n *against/with* n; V pl-n; V *against* n; pl-n V; N-COUNT; SOUND

clip /klɪp/ **clips, clipping, clipped** — ◆◆◇◇◇
1 A **clip** is a small device, usually made of metal or plastic, that is specially shaped for holding things together. *She took the clip out of her hair.* — N-COUNT
2 When you **clip** something to something else, you fasten it to that thing by means of one or more clips. You can also say that something **clips** to something else. *He clipped his safety belt to a fitting on the deck... He clipped his cufflinks neatly in place. ...an electronic pen which clips to the casing... His flashlight was still clipped to his belt.* — V-ERG; V n *to/on* n; V n prep/adv; V *to* n; V-ed
3 A **clip** from a film or a radio or television programme is a short piece of it that is broadcast separately. *...an historical film clip of Lenin speaking. ...a clip from the movie 'Shane'.* — N-COUNT: oft n N, N *from/of* n
4 If you **clip** something, you cut small pieces from it, especially in order to shape it. *I saw an old man out clipping his hedge... He had already clipped his hair close to the skull.* ► Also a noun. *Give hedges a last clip.* — VERB; V n; N-SING
5 If you **clip** something out of a newspaper or magazine, you cut it out. *Kids in his neighborhood clipped his picture from the newspaper and carried it around.* — VERB; V n *from/out of* n
6 If something **clips** something else, it hits it accidentally at an angle before moving off in a different direction. *The lorry clipped the rear of a tanker and then crashed into a second truck.* — VERB; V n
7 If you give someone a **clip** round the ear, you hit their head fairly lightly with the palm of your hand, usually as a punishment. *The boy was later given a clip round the ear by his father.* — N-COUNT
8 If you **clip** a small amount off the time taken to do something, you reduce it by that amount. *Boardman finished in 1hr 43mins, clipping 49 seconds from his own course record.* — VERB; V amount *off/from* n
9 An ammunition **clip** is a metal container on an automatic weapon which holds ammunition. — N-COUNT: oft n N
10 See also **clipping, clipped; bulldog clip, paper clip.**
11 If something moves or happens **at a** fast **clip**, it moves or happens quickly; an informal expression. *They moved out from the airport at a brisk clip... Studios are releasing movies at a fast clip.* • to **clip** someone's **wings**: see **wing**. — PHRASE: PHR after v

clipboard /klɪpbɔːʳd/ **clipboards.** A **clipboard** is a board with a clip at the top. It is used to hold together pieces of paper that you need to carry around, and provides a firm base for writing. — N-COUNT

clip-on. A **clip-on** object is designed to be fastened to something by means of a clip. *...a clip-on tie. ...a clip-on light.* — ADJ: ADJ n

clipped /klɪpt/ — ◆◇◇◇◇
1 Clipped means neatly trimmed. *...a quiet street of clipped hedges and flowering gardens. ...a dapper man with a clipped moustache.* — ADJ: usu ADJ n
2 If you say that someone has a **clipped** way of speaking, you mean they speak with quick, short sounds, and usually that they sound upper-class. *The Chief Constable's clipped tones crackled over the telephone line.* — ADJ

clipper /klɪpəʳ/ **clippers** — ◆◇◇◇◇
1 Clippers are a tool used for cutting small amounts from something, especially from someone's hair or nails, or from a hedge. — N-PLURAL: also *a pair of* N
2 In former times, a **clipper** was a fast sailing ship. — N-COUNT

clipping /klɪpɪŋ/ **clippings** — ◆◇◇◇◇
1 A **clipping** is an article, picture, or advertisement that has been cut from a newspaper or magazine. *...bulletin boards crowded with newspaper clippings.* — N-COUNT: oft n N
2 Clippings are small pieces of something that have been cut from something larger. *Having mown the lawn, there are all those grass clippings to get rid of. ...nail clippings.* — N-COUNT: usu pl, oft n N

clique /kliːk/ **cliques.** If you describe a group of people as a **clique**, you mean that they spend a lot of time together and seem unfriendly towards people who are not in the group; used showing disapproval. *Anna Ford recently hit out at the male clique which she believes holds back women in television.* — ◆◇◇◇◇ N-COUNT PRAGMATICS

cliquey /kliːki/. If you describe a group of people or their behaviour as **cliquey**, you mean they spend their time only with other members of the group and seem unfriendly towards people who are not in the group; used showing disapproval. *...cliquey gossip.* — ADJ-GRADED PRAGMATICS

clitoral /klɪtərəl/. **Clitoral** means concerned with or relating to the clitoris. *...clitoral stimulation.* — ADJ: ADJ n

clitoris /klɪtərɪs/ **clitorises.** A woman's **clitoris** is the small sensitive lump above her vagina which, when touched, causes pleasant sexual feelings that can lead to an orgasm. — N-COUNT

Cllr. Cllr is a written abbreviation for **Councillor.** *...Cllr Ned Dewitt.*

cloak /kloʊk/ **cloaks, cloaking, cloaked** — ◆◇◇◇◇
1 A **cloak** is a loose, sleeveless piece of clothing which someone wears over their other clothes when they go out. Cloaks are not often worn nowadays. — N-COUNT
2 A **cloak of** something such as mist or snow completely covers and hides something. *Today most of England will be under a cloak of thick mist.* — N-SING: N *of* n =blanket
3 If you refer to something as a **cloak**, you mean that it is intended to hide the truth about something. *Preparations for the wedding were made under a cloak of secrecy... Moderation was held to be a cloak for unmanliness.* — N-SING: N *of/for* n
4 To **cloak** something means to cover it or hide it; used in written English. *...the decision to cloak major tourist attractions in unsightly hoardings... A fire could have been deliberately started to cloak small coordinated troop movements... The beautiful sweeping coastline was cloaked in mist.* — VERB; V n *in* n; V n; V-ed

cloak-and-dagger; also spelled **cloak and dagger**. A **cloak-and-dagger** activity is one which involves mystery and secrecy. *She was released from prison in a cloak and dagger operation yesterday... They met in classic cloak-and-dagger style beside the lake in St James's Park.* ADJ: usu ADJ n

cloakroom /kloʊkru:m/ **cloakrooms**
1 In a public building, the **cloakroom** is the place where people can leave their coats, umbrellas, and so on. *...a cloakroom attendant.* N-COUNT
2 In British English, a **cloakroom** is a room in a public building containing toilets and washbasins, or a downstairs room in someone's house containing a toilet. N-COUNT

clobber /klɒbəʳ/ **clobbers, clobbering, clobbered** ◆◇◇◇◇
1 You can refer to someone's belongings, especially their clothes, as their **clobber**; used in informal British English. *He nipped down to Mr Byrite on Oxford Street for some new clobber.* N-UNCOUNT
2 If you **clobber** someone, you hit them; an informal use. *Hillary clobbered him with a vase.* VERB V n
3 If a person or company **is clobbered** by something, they are very badly affected by it; an informal use. *The construction industry was clobbered by recession... Sticky weather in May and June clobbered sales of Thorntons' chocolates.* VERB be V-ed V n

cloche /klɒʃ/ **cloches**
1 A **cloche** is a long, low cover made of glass or clear plastic that is put over young plants to protect them from the cold. N-COUNT
2 A **cloche** or a **cloche hat** is a tight-fitting woman's hat shaped like a bell. Cloche hats were popular in the 1920s. N-COUNT

clock /klɒk/ **clocks, clocking, clocked** ◆◆◆◇◇
1 A **clock** is an instrument, for example in a room or on the outside of a building, that shows what time of day it is. *He was conscious of a clock ticking... He also repairs clocks and watches... The hands of the clock on the wall moved with a slight click. ...a digital clock.* N-COUNT
2 A time **clock** in a factory or office is a device that is used to record the hours that people work. Each worker puts a special card into the device when they arrive and leave, and the times are recorded on the card. *Government workers were made to punch time clocks morning, noon and night.* N-COUNT: oft n N
3 In a car, the **clock** is an instrument that shows the speed of the car or the distance it has travelled. *The car had 160,000 miles on the clock... At 240 mph the needle went off the clock.* N-COUNT: usu sing, the N
4 To **clock** a particular time or speed in a race means to reach that time or speed. *Elliott clocked the fastest time this year for the 800 metres... The yacht swayed in 40-knot winds, clocking speeds of 17 knots at times.* VERB =reach V n
5 If something or someone **is clocked** at a particular time or speed, their time or speed is measured at that level. *He has been clocked at 11 seconds for 100 metres... 170-mile-an-hour winds were clocked on a mountaintop in North Carolina.* VB: usu passive be V-ed at amount be V-ed
6 In informal British English, if you **clock** something, you notice or see it. *If there was any scandal in that company, you can be sure that Bobby will have clocked it.* VERB V n
7 See also **alarm clock, biological clock, body clock, cuckoo clock, grandfather clock, o'clock.**
8 If you are doing something **against the clock**, you are doing it in a great hurry, because there is very little time. *The emergency services were working against the clock as the tide began to rise... It's now become a race against the clock.* PHRASES PHR after v, n PHR
9 If someone **beats the clock**, they finish doing something or succeed in doing something before the time allowed for doing it has ended. V inflects
10 If something is done **round the clock** or **around the clock**, it is done all day and all night without stopping. *Rescue services have been working round the clock to free stranded motorists... We can't afford to give you around-the-clock protection.* PHR with v, PHR n
11 If you want to **turn the clock back** or **put the clock back**, you want to return to a situation that used to exist, usually because the present situation is unpleasant. *In some ways we wish we could turn the clock back... We cannot put back the clock.* V inflects
12 If you **are watching the clock**, you keep looking to see what time it is, usually because you are bored by something and want it to end as soon as possible; an informal expression. *I started to watch the clock about halfway through the class.* V inflects

clock in. When you **clock in** at work, you arrive there or put a special card into a device to show what time you arrived. *I have to clock in by eight.* PHRASAL VERB ≠clock off V P

clock in at. If something such as a record or film **clocks in at** a particular amount of time, it is that amount of time long. *There are four more songs, each clocking in at around 12 minutes.* PHRASAL VERB V P P amount

clock off. When you **clock off** at work, you leave work or put a special card into a device to show what time you left. *The Night Duty Officer was ready to clock off... They clocked off duty and left at ten to three.* PHRASAL VERB ≠clock in V P V P n

clock on. When workers **clock on** at a factory or office, they put a special card into a device to show what time they arrived. *They arrived to clock on and found the factory gates locked.* PHRASAL VERB =clock in V P

clock out. Clock out means the same as **clock off**. *She had clocked out of her bank at 5.02pm using her plastic card.* PHRASAL VERB V P of n Also V P

clock up. If you **clock up** a large number or total of things, you reach that number or total. *In two years, he clocked up over 100 victories... Rude taxi drivers clocked up a total of 239 offences in 1990.* PHRASAL VERB =chalk up V P n (not pron)

clock tower, clock towers. A **clock tower** is a tall, narrow building with a clock at the top. N-COUNT

clockwise /klɒkwaɪz/. When something is moving **clockwise**, it is moving in a circle in the same direction as the hands on a clock. *He told the children to start moving clockwise around the room.* ► Also an adjective. *Water usually escapes down the plughole in a clockwise direction.* ◆◇◇◇◇ ADV: ADV after v ≠anti-clockwise ADJ: ADJ n

clockwork /klɒkwɜ:ʳk/ ◆◇◇◇◇
1 A **clockwork** toy or device has machinery inside it which makes it move or operate when it is wound up with a key. *...a clockwork train-set.* ADJ: ADJ n
2 If you say that something happens **like clockwork**, you mean that it happens without any problems or delays, or happens regularly. *The Queen's holiday is arranged to go like clockwork, everything pre-planned to the minute... He reorganized Standard Brands twice a year, like clockwork.* PHRASE: PHR after v

clod /klɒd/ **clods.** A **clod** of earth is a large lump of earth. N-COUNT: oft N of n

clog /klɒg/ **clogs, clogging, clogged** ◆◇◇◇◇
1 When something **clogs** a hole or place, it blocks it so that nothing can pass through. *Excess sebum clogs the pores, which develop blackheads and spots... The traffic clogged the Thames bridges.* VERB =block V n
♦ **clogged** *...a clogged drain... The streets were clogged with people.* ADJ-GRADED
2 **Clogs** are heavy leather or wooden shoes with thick wooden soles. N-COUNT: usu pl
3 If you say that someone has **popped** their **clogs**, you mean that they have died; an informal expression, used in British English. PHRASE: V inflects

clog up. When something **clogs up** a hole or a place, or when a hole or place **clogs up**, the hole or place becomes blocked so that nothing can pass through. *...with 22,000 tourists clogging up the pavements... The result is that the lungs clog up with a thick mucus.* PHRASAL VERB ERG V P n (not pron) V P
♦ **clogged up** *The drains are badly clogged up.* ADJ-GRADED

cloister /klɔɪstəʳ/ **cloisters.** A **cloister** is a paved and covered area round a square in a monastery or a cathedral. *The thirteenth-century cloisters are amongst the most beautiful in central Italy.* N-COUNT

cloistered /klɔɪstəʳd/. If you have a **cloistered** way of life, you live quietly and are not involved in the normal busy life of the world around you. *...the cloistered world of royalty.* ADJ-GRADED: usu ADJ n =sheltered

clone /kloʊn/ **clones, cloning, cloned** ◆◇◇◇◇
1 If you say that someone is a **clone** of someone else, you disapprove of them because they try to copy this person and have no individuality of their N-COUNT: usu with supp PRAGMATICS

own. *Tom was in some ways a younger clone of his handsome father... Designers are mistaken if they believe we all want to be supermodel clones.*

2 A **clone** is an animal or plant that has been produced artificially, for example in a laboratory, from the cells of another animal or plant. A clone is identical to the original animal or plant. N-COUNT

3 To **clone** an animal or plant means to produce it as a clone. *The idea of cloning extinct life forms still belongs to science fiction.* VERB V n

4 A **clone** of a computer, usually an IBM, is a cheaper close copy of it. N-COUNT

close 1 shutting or completing

close /klouz/ **closes, closing, closed** ◆◆◆◆◆

1 When you **close** something such as a door or lid or when it **closes**, it moves so that a hole, gap, or opening is covered. *If you are cold, close the window... Zacharias heard the door close... Keep the curtains closed.* V-ERG =shut ≠open V n V V-ed

2 When you **close** something such as an open book or umbrella, you move the different parts of it together. *Slowly he closed the book.* VERB V n

3 When you **close** your eyes or your eyes **close**, your eyelids move downwards, so that you can no longer see. *Bess closed her eyes and fell asleep.* V-ERG V n Also V

4 When a shop or other public place **closes** or **is closed**, work or activity stops there for a short period, for example during the night or at lunchtime. *Shops close only on Christmas Day and New Year's Day... It was Saturday; they could close the office early... The Croatian authorities closed the airport... The restaurant was closed for the night.* V-ERG =shut ≠open V V n V-ed

5 If a place such as a factory, shop, or school **closes**, or if it **is closed**, all work or activity stops there permanently. *Many enterprises will be forced to close... If they do close the local college I'll have to go to Worcester.* ► **Close down** means the same as **close**. *Minford closed down the business and went into politics... Many of the smaller stores have closed down.* ♦ **closing** *...since the closing of the steelworks in nearby Duquesne in 1984.* V-ERG V V n PHRASAL VERB ERG V P n (not pron) V P Also V n P N-SING =closure

6 To **close** a road or border means to block it in order to prevent people from using it. *They were cut off from the West in 1948 when their government closed that border crossing.* VERB V n

7 To **close** a conversation, event, or matter means to bring it to an end or to complete it. *Judge Isabel Oliva said last night: 'I have closed the case. There was no foul play.'... He needs another $30,000 to close the deal... The Prime Minister is said to now consider the matter closed. ...the closing ceremony of the National Political Conference.* VERB V n V-ed V-ing

8 If you **close** a bank account, you take all your money out of it and inform the bank that you will no longer be using the account. *He had closed his account with the bank five years earlier.* VERB ≠open V n

9 On the stock market or the currency markets, if a share price or a currency **closes** at a particular value, that is its value at the end of the day's business. *Dawson shares closed at 219p, up 5p... The US dollar closed higher in Tokyo today.* VERB ≠open V prep/adv V adj-compar

10 The **close** of a period of time or an activity is the end of it. To bring or draw something to a **close** means to end it. *By the close of business last night, most of the big firms were hailing yesterday's actions as a success... Brian's retirement brings to a close a glorious chapter in British football history... As 1992 draws to a close, the story is changing.* N-SING: oft *the* N *of* n, *to a* N =end

11 See also **closed, closing.** ● to **close the door on** something: see **door.** ● to **close your eyes to** something: see **eye.** ● to **close ranks**: see **rank.**

close down. See close 5 PHRASAL VERB

close off. To **close** something **off** means to separate it from other things or people so that they do not have access to it. *Police closed off about 12 blocks of a major San Francisco thoroughfare for today's march... The old guard of leaders are closed off behind walls built of yesterday's ideology.* PHRASAL VERB V P n (not pron) Also V n P

close up PHRASAL VERB

1 If someone **closes up** a building, they shut it completely and securely, often because they are going away. *Just close up the shop... The summer house had been closed up all year.* =shut up, lock up V P n (not pron) V-ed P

2 If an opening, gap, or something hollow **closes up**, or if you **close it up**, it becomes closed or covered. *Don't use cold water as it shocks the blood vessels into closing up.* ERG V P Also V n P

close 2 nearness; adjective uses

close /klous/ **closer, closest** ◆◆◆◆◆

1 If one thing or person is **close** to another, there is only a very small distance between them. *Her lips were close to his head and her breath tickled his ear... The whales were too close; this posed an immediate problem for my photography... The man moved closer, lowering his voice... The tables were pushed close together so diners could talk across the aisles.* ♦ **closely** *They crowded more closely around the stretcher... Wherever they went they were closely followed by security men.* ADJ-GRADED: v-link ADJ, ADJ after v, oft ADJ prep/adv =near ≠far ADV-GRADED: ADV after v, ADV -ed

2 You say that people are **close** to each other when they like each other very much and know each other very well. *She and Linda became very close... As a little girl, Karan was closest to her sister Gail... I shared a house with a close friend from school... I had a close relationship with my grandfather.* ♦ **closeness** *I asked whether her closeness to her mother ever posed any problems.* ADJ-GRADED: oft ADJ *to* n =intimate N-UNCOUNT

3 Your **close** relatives are the members of your family who are most directly related to you, for example your parents and your brothers or sisters. *...large changes such as the birth of a child or death of a close relative.* ADJ-GRADED: ADJ n ≠distant

4 A **close** ally or partner of someone knows them well and is very involved in their work. *He was once regarded as one of Mr Gorbachev's closest political advisers... A senior source close to Mr Major told us: 'Our position has not changed.'* ADJ-GRADED: usu ADJ n, also v-link ADJ *to* n

5 **Close** contact or co-operation involves seeing or communicating with someone often. *Both nations are seeking closer links with the West... He lived alone, keeping close contact with his three grown-up sons.* ♦ **closely** *We work closely with the careers officers in schools.* ADJ-GRADED: ADJ n ADV-GRADED: ADV after v

6 If there is a **close** connection or resemblance between two things, they are strongly connected or are very similar. *There is a close connection between pain and tension... Clare's close resemblance to his elder sister invoked a deep dislike in him.* ♦ **closely** *...a pattern closely resembling a cross. ...fruits closely related to the orange.* ADJ-GRADED: usu ADJ n =strong ADV-GRADED: ADV before v, ADV -ed

7 **Close** inspection or observation of something is careful and thorough. *He discovered, on closer inspection, that the rocks contained gold... All these definitions, while sounding impressive, do not stand up under close scrutiny... Let's have a closer look.* ♦ **closely** *If you look closely at many of the problems in society, you'll see evidence of racial discrimination.* ADJ-GRADED =thorough ADV-GRADED: ADV with v

8 A **close** competition or election is won or seems likely to be won by only a small amount. *It is still a close contest between two leading opposition parties... It's going to be very close.* ♦ **closely** *This will be a closely fought race.* ADJ-GRADED ADV-GRADED: usu ADV -ed

9 If you are **close** to something or if it is **close**, it is likely to happen or come soon. If you are **close** to doing something, you are likely to do it soon. *She sounded close to tears... Drought has left more than two million people in Kenya and Somalia close to starvation... A senior White House official said the agreement is close... He's close to signing a contract.* ADJ-GRADED: v-link ADJ, usu ADJ *to* n/-ing =near

10 If something is **close** or comes **close** to something else, it almost is, does, or experiences that thing. *There is a simplicity about the interior which comes close to blandness... An airliner came close to disaster while approaching Heathrow Airport... Her desire was closer to passion than love.* ADJ-GRADED: v-link ADJ, usu ADJ *to* n =near

11 If the atmosphere somewhere is **close**, it is uncomfortably warm with not enough air. ADJ-GRADED

12 Something that is **close by** or **close at hand** is near to you. *Did a new hairdressing shop open close by?... His wife remains behind in Germany, but Jason, his 18-year-old son, is closer at hand.* PHRASES usu v-link PHR, PHR after v =near by

13 If you describe an event as a **close shave**, a **close**

thing, or a **close call**, you mean that an accident or a disaster very nearly happened. *You had a close shave, but you knew when you accepted this job that there would be risks.*

14 If you **keep a close eye** on someone or something or **keep a close watch** on them, you observe them carefully to make sure they are progressing as you want them to. *President Clinton and his foreign policy team are keeping a close eye on events.* V inflects, usu PHR on n

15 Close to or **close on** a particular amount or distance means slightly less than that amount or distance. *Sisulu spent close to 30 years in prison... Close to 50,000 people took part... Catering may now account for close on a quarter of pub turnover.* PREP: PREP amount =almost, nearly

16 If you look at something **close up** or **close to**, you look at it when you are very near to it. *They always look smaller close up.* • See also **close-up**. usu PHR after v, v-link PHR

17 • **at close quarters**: see **quarter**. • **at close range**: see **range**.

close 3 nearness; verb uses

close /kl<u>oʊ</u>z/ **closes, closing, closed.** If you **are closing** on someone or something that you are following, you are getting nearer and nearer to them. *I was within 15 seconds of the guy in second place and closing on him.* ◆◆◆◇◇ VERB; V on n; Also V

close in PHRASAL VERB

1 If a group of people **close in** on a person or place, they come nearer and nearer to them and gradually surround them. *Hitler himself committed suicide as Soviet forces were closing in on Berlin... As Parretti walked across the tarmac, fraud officers closed in.* =move in; V P on n; V P

2 When winter or darkness **closes in**, it arrives. *The dark nights and cold weather are closing in.* =descend; V P

close 4 used as a road name

Close /kl<u>oʊ</u>s/ **Closes. Close** is used in the names of some streets in Britain. *...116 Dendridge Close.* N-IN-NAMES: n N

close-cropped /kl<u>oʊ</u>s kr<u>ɒ</u>pt/. **Close-cropped** hair or grass is cut very short. ADJ-GRADED: usu ADJ n

closed /kl<u>oʊ</u>zd/ ◆◆◇◇◇

1 A **closed** group of people does not welcome new people or ideas from outside. *They said that the EC had never been a closed circle... It is a closed society in the sense that they've not been exposed to many things.* ADJ-GRADED: usu ADJ n ≠open

2 See also **close**. • **a closed book**: see **book**. • **behind closed doors**: see **door**.

cl<u>o</u>sed c<u>i</u>rcuit. A **closed circuit** television or video system is one that operates within a limited area such as a building. *There's a closed-circuit television camera in the reception area.* ADJ: ADJ n

cl<u>o</u>sed sh<u>o</u>p, closed shops. If a factory, shop, or other business is a **closed shop**, the employees must be members of a particular trade union. *...the trade union which they are required to join under the closed shop agreement.* N-COUNT

close-fitting /kl<u>oʊ</u>s fɪtɪŋ/. **Close-fitting** clothes fit tightly and show the shape of your body. ADJ-GRADED: usu ADJ n

close-knit /kl<u>oʊ</u>s nɪt/. A **close-knit** group of people are closely linked, do things together, and take an interest in each other. *We're a very close-knit family... Events over the last year have created a close-knit community.* ADJ-GRADED: usu ADJ n

close-run /kl<u>oʊ</u>s rʌn/. If you describe something such as a race or contest as a **close-run** thing, you mean that it is only won by a very small margin. *It was a close run thing before Spain beat Poland 3-2... In such a close-run race as this election, the campaign becomes all important.* ADJ-GRADED: ADJ n

close season /kl<u>oʊ</u>s siːzən/ ◆◇◇◇◇

1 In football and some other sports, the **close season** is the period of the year when the sport is not played professionally. *Roberts joined the club in the close season on a free transfer from West Bromwich.* N-SING

2 In Britain, the **close season** in hunting, fishing, and shooting is the time in the year when you are not allowed to kill particular birds, animals, or fish. N-SING

closet /kl<u>ɒ</u>zɪt/ **closets** ◆◇◇◇◇

1 In American English, a **closet** is a piece of furniture with doors at the front and shelves inside, which is used for storing things. The usual British word is **cupboard**. N-COUNT

2 A **closet** is a very small storage room, especially one without windows; used mainly in American English or old-fashioned British English. N-COUNT

3 Closet is used to describe a person who has beliefs, habits, or feelings which they keep secret, often because they are embarrassed about them. **Closet** is also used of their beliefs, habits, or feelings. *He is a closet Fascist. ...closet misogyny.* ADJ: ADJ n

4 If someone **comes out of the closet**, they reveal a belief or habit they have which they had previously kept secret, often because they were embarrassed about it. You can also say that an issue **comes out of the closet** when it starts to be publicly discussed. PHRASE: V inflects

5 See also **closeted**. • **a skeleton in the closet**: see **skeleton**.

closeted /kl<u>ɒ</u>zɪtɪd/. If you are **closeted** with someone, you are talking privately to them. *The prime minister has been closeted with his finance ministers for the past 12 hours... Charles and I were closeted in his study for the briefing session.* ADJ: v-link ADJ, usu ADJ with/in n

close-up /kl<u>oʊ</u>s ʌp/ **close-ups.** A **close-up** is a photograph or a picture in a film that shows a lot of detail because it is taken very near to the subject. *...a close-up of Harvey's face.* • If you see something **in close-up**, you see it in great detail in a photograph or piece of film which has been taken very near to the subject. *Hughes stared up at him in close-up from the photograph.* ◆◇◇◇◇ N-COUNT; PHRASE

closing /kl<u>oʊ</u>zɪŋ/. The **closing** part of an activity or period of time is the final part of it. *He entered RAF service in the closing stages of the war... In the closing minutes of the match, Boca's captain was fouled... The north cannot achieve sustained economic development without the south, he added in his closing remarks.* • See also **close**. ◆◇◇◇◇ ADJ: ADJ n

cl<u>o</u>sing price, closing prices. On the Stock Exchange, the **closing price** of a share is its price at the end of a day's business. *The price is slightly above yesterday's closing price.* N-COUNT

cl<u>o</u>sing time, closing times. Closing time is the time when something such as a shop, library, or pub closes and people have to leave. *He met his brother John and some friends in a pub and they stayed until closing time.* N-VAR

closure /kl<u>oʊ</u>ʒə^r/ **closures** ◆◆◇◇◇

1 The **closure** of a place such as a business or factory is the permanent ending of the work or activity there. *...the closure of the Ravenscraig steelworks. ...British Coal's proposed pit closures... Almost three in four clinics say they face closure by the end of the year.* N-VAR

2 The **closure** of a road or border is the blocking of it in order to prevent people from using it. N-COUNT: usu with supp

clot /kl<u>ɒ</u>t/ **clots, clotting, clotted** ◆◇◇◇◇

1 A **clot** is a sticky lump that forms when blood dries up or thickens. *He needed emergency surgery to remove a blood clot from his brain.* N-COUNT

2 When blood **clots**, it thickens and forms a lump. *The patient's blood refused to clot... Aspirin apparently thins the blood and inhibits clotting. ...dark clotted blood.* VERB; V; V-ing; V-ed

cloth /kl<u>ɒ</u>θ, AM kl<u>ɔː</u>θ/ **cloths** ◆◆◇◇◇

1 Cloth is fabric which is made by weaving or knitting a substance such as cotton, wool, silk, or nylon. Cloth is used especially for making clothes. *She began cleaning the wound with a piece of cloth.* N-MASS =fabric, material

2 A **cloth** is a piece of cloth which you use for a particular purpose, such as cleaning something or covering something. *Clean the surface with a damp cloth. ...a tray covered with a cloth.* N-COUNT

3 The cloth is sometimes used to refer to Christian priests and ministers. *I've got as much respect for the cloth as the next man. ...a man of the cloth.* N-SING: the N =clergy ≠laity

cl<u>o</u>th c<u>a</u>p, cloth caps. A **cloth cap** is a soft flat cap with a stiff, curved part at the front called a peak. Cloth caps are usually worn by men. N-COUNT

clothe /kl<u>oʊ</u>ð/ **clothes, clothing, clothed.** To **clothe** someone means to provide them with clothes to wear. *She was on her own with two kids to feed and clothe.* • See also **clothed**, **clothes**, **clothing**. VERB; V n

clothed /kloʊðd/ ◆◇◇◇◇

1 If you are **clothed** in a certain way, you are dressed in that way. *He lay down on the bed fully clothed... She was clothed in a flowered dress. ...women clothed in black.* ADJ: adv ADJ, v-link ADJ *in* n =dressed

2 If a place or thing is **clothed in** something, it is covered in that thing; a literary use. *The south side of the gorge is now clothed in trees.* ADJ: v-link ADJ *in* n =covered

clothes /kloʊðz/. **Clothes** are the things that people wear, such as shirts, coats, trousers, and dresses. *Moira walked upstairs to change her clothes... He dressed quickly in casual clothes.* ● See also **plain-clothes**. ◆◆◆◆◇ N-PLURAL

clothes horse, clothes horses

1 A **clothes horse** is a folding frame used inside someone's house to hang washing on while it dries. N-COUNT

2 If you describe someone, especially a woman, as a **clothes horse**, you mean that they are fashionable and think a lot about their clothes, but have little intelligence or no other abilities; used showing disapproval. N-COUNT PRAGMATICS

clothesline /kloʊðzlaɪn/ **clotheslines;** also spelled **clothes line.** A **clothesline** is a thin rope on which you hang washing so that it can dry. *He hung his clothes out to dry on the clothesline across the doorway.* N-COUNT =washing line

clothes peg, clothes pegs. In British English, a **clothes peg** is a small device which you use to fasten clothes to a washing line. The American word is **clothespin.** N-COUNT

clothespin /kloʊðzpɪn/ **clothespins.** In American English, a **clothespin** is a small device which you use to fasten clothes to a washing line. The British expression is **clothes peg.** N-COUNT

clothing /kloʊðɪŋ/. **Clothing** is the things that people wear. *Some locals offered food and clothing to the refugees... What is your favourite item of clothing?... Wear protective clothing. ...the clothing industry.* ◆◆◆◇◇ N-UNCOUNT

clotted cream. **Clotted cream** is very thick cream made by heating milk gently and taking the cream off the top. It is made and eaten mainly in the south west of England. N-UNCOUNT

cloud /klaʊd/ **clouds, clouding, clouded** ◆◆◆◇◇

1 A **cloud** is a mass of water vapour that floats in the sky. Clouds are usually white or grey in colour. *...the varied shapes of the clouds... The sky was almost entirely obscured by cloud. ...the risks inherent in flying through cloud.* N-VAR

2 A **cloud** of something such as smoke or dust is a mass of it floating in the air. *The hens darted away on all sides, raising a cloud of dust.* N-COUNT: usu N *of* n

3 If you say that something **clouds** your view of a situation, you mean that it makes you unable to understand the situation or judge it properly. *Perhaps anger had clouded his vision, perhaps his judgement had been faulty... In his latter years religious mania clouded his mind.* VERB V n

4 If you say that something **clouds** a situation, you mean that it makes it unpleasant. *Poor job prospects have clouded the outlook for the economy... The atmosphere has already been clouded by the BJP's anger at the media.* VERB V n

5 If your eyes or face **cloud** or if sadness or anger **clouds** them, your eyes or your face suddenly show sadness or anger; a literary use. *Trish's face clouded with disappointment... As he looked at Katherine, great sorrow clouded his eyes.* ► **Cloud over** means the same as **cloud.** *I saw Sean's face cloud over at this blatant lie.* V-ERG V *with* n V n Also V PHRASAL VERB V P

6 If glass **clouds** or if moisture **clouds** it, tiny drops of water cover the glass, making it difficult to see through. *The mirror clouded beside her cheek... I run the water very hot, clouding the mirror.* V-ERG =mist V V n

7 If you say that someone **has** their **head in the clouds**, you are criticizing them because they are ignoring or are unaware of the problems associated with a situation; an informal expression. PHRASES V and N inflect PRAGMATICS

8 If you say that someone is **on cloud nine**, you are emphasizing that they are very happy; an informal expression. *When Michael was born I was on cloud nine.* usu v-link PHR PRAGMATICS

9 If someone is **under a cloud**, people have a poor opinion of them because of something they have done. *The military are under a cloud for killing civilians while breaking up a demonstration.* v-link PHR, PHR after v =in disgrace

10 ● **every cloud has a silver lining**: see **silver lining.**

cloud over. If the sky **clouds over**, it becomes covered with clouds. *After a fine day, the sky had clouded over and suddenly rain lashed against the windows.* ● See also **cloud** 5. PHRASAL VERB V P

cloudburst /klaʊdbɜːʳst/ **cloudbursts.** A **cloudburst** is a sudden, very heavy fall of rain. N-COUNT

cloud-cuckoo-land. If you say that someone is living in **cloud-cuckoo-land**, you are criticizing them because they think there are no problems and that things will happen exactly as they want them to, when this is obviously not the case; an informal word. *A Labour Party spokesman said the government was living in cloud-cuckoo-land if it believed such findings.* N-UNCOUNT: also *a* N PRAGMATICS

cloudless /klaʊdləs/. If the sky is **cloudless**, there are no clouds in it. ADJ ≠cloudy

cloudy /klaʊdi/ **cloudier, cloudiest** ◆◇◇◇◇

1 If it is **cloudy**, there are a lot of clouds in the sky. *...a windy, cloudy day.* ADJ-GRADED ≠cloudless

2 A **cloudy** liquid is less clear than it should be. ADJ-GRADED

3 Ideas, opinions, or issues that are **cloudy** are confused or uncertain. *...an absurdly cloudy political debate... The legal position is very cloudy.* ADJ-GRADED =indistinct

clout /klaʊt/ **clouts, clouting, clouted** ◆◇◇◇◇

1 If you **clout** someone, you hit them; an informal use. *Rachel clouted him... The officer clouted her on the head.* ► Also a noun. *I was half tempted to give one of them a clout myself.* VERB V n V n *on* n N-COUNT

2 A person or institution that has **clout** has influence and power; an informal use. *Mr Sutherland may have the clout needed to push the two trading giants into a deal... The two firms wield enormous clout in financial markets.* N-UNCOUNT =weight

clove /kloʊv/ **cloves** ◆◇◇◇◇

1 **Cloves** are small dried flower buds which are used as a spice. *...chicken soup with cloves.* N-VAR

2 A **clove** of garlic is one of the sections of a garlic bulb. N-COUNT: usu N *of* n

3 **Clove** is a past tense of **cleave.**

cloven hoof /kloʊvᵊn huːf/ **cloven hooves** or **cloven hoofs.** Animals that have **cloven hooves** have feet that are divided into two parts. Cows, sheep, and goats have cloven hooves. N-COUNT

clover /kloʊvəʳ/ **clovers**

1 **Clover** is a small plant with pink or white ball-shaped flowers. *...a four leaf clover.* N-VAR

2 If you say that someone is **in clover**, you mean that they are living a luxurious and comfortable life. *...a contract that Ford hoped would keep him in clover for the rest of his life.* PHRASE: v-link PHR, PHR after v

clown /klaʊn/ **clowns, clowning, clowned** ◆◇◇◇◇

1 A **clown** is a performer in a circus who wears funny clothes and bright make-up, and does silly things in order to make people laugh. N-COUNT

2 If you **clown**, you do silly things in order to make people laugh. *He clowned with John Belushi and Bill Murray in National Lampoon shows.* ► **Clown around** and **clown about** mean the same as **clown.** *Bev made her laugh, the way she was always clowning around.* ♦ **clowning** *She senses that behind the clowning there is a terrible sense of anguish.* VERB =mess around V PHRASAL VERB V P N-UNCOUNT

3 If you say that someone is a **clown**, you mean that they say funny things or do silly things to amuse people. *He was laughing, the clown of the twosome, there always is one.* N-COUNT =joker

4 If you describe someone as a **clown**, you disapprove of them and have no respect for them; an informal use. *I still think I could do a better job than those clowns in Washington.* N-COUNT PRAGMATICS =idiot, fool

clownish /klaʊnɪʃ/. If you describe a person's appearance or behaviour as **clownish**, you mean that they look or behave rather like a clown, and often that they appear rather foolish. *He had a* ADJ-GRADED *clownish sense of humour. ...their clownish stupidity.*

cloying /klɔɪɪŋ/. You use **cloying** to describe something that you find unpleasant because it is excessively sweet and sickly, or too sentimental. *Her cheap, cloying scent enveloped him... Most TV kids are so cloying.* ♦ **cloyingly** *The film is too cloyingly sentimental.*
ADJ-GRADED =nauseating
ADV GRADED: ADV adj/adv

cloze /kloʊz/ **clozes.** In language teaching, a **cloze** test is a test in which words are removed from a text and replaced with spaces. The task of the learner is to fill each space with the missing word or a suitable word.
N-COUNT: usu N n =gap-fill

club /klʌb/ **clubs, clubbing, clubbed** ◆◆◆◆◆

1 A **club** is an organization of people interested in a particular activity or subject who usually meet on a regular basis. *...the Chorlton Conservative Club. ...a youth club... He was club secretary.*
N-COUNT

2 A **club** is a place where the members of a club meet. *I stopped in at the club for a drink.*
N-COUNT: oft poss N

3 A **club** is a team which competes in professional or amateur sporting competitions. *...the New York Yankees baseball club. ...Liverpool football club.*
N-COUNT

4 A **club** is the same as a **nightclub**. *It's a big dance hit in the clubs. ...the London club scene.*
N-COUNT

5 A **club** is a long, thin, metal stick with a piece of wood or metal at one end that you use to hit the ball in golf. *...a six-iron club.*
N-COUNT =golf club

6 A **club** is a thick heavy stick that can be used as a weapon. *Men armed with knives and clubs attacked his home.*
N-COUNT

7 To **club** a person or animal means to hit them hard with a thick heavy stick or a similar weapon. *Two thugs clubbed him with baseball bats... Clubbing baby seals to death for their pelts is wrong.*
VERB V n V n to n

8 **Clubs** is one of the four suits in a pack of playing cards. Each card in the suit is marked with one or more black symbols: ♣. *...the ace of clubs.* ► A **club** is a playing card of this suit. *The next player discarded a club.*
N-UNCOUNT-COLL
N-COUNT

9 A **club** is one of the thirteen playing cards in the suit of clubs.
N-COUNT

club together. In British English, if people **club together** to do something, they all give money towards the cost of it. *For my thirtieth birthday, my friends clubbed together and bought me a watch.*
PHRASAL VERB V P

clubbable /klʌbəbᵊl/. If you describe someone as **clubbable**, you mean they have an outgoing personality and like to socialize, which makes them good members of social club. *He is a clubbable chap.*
ADJ-GRADED PRAGMATICS

clubber /klʌbəʳ/ **clubbers.** A **clubber** is someone who regularly goes to nightclubs.
N-COUNT

clubbing /klʌbɪŋ/. **Clubbing** is the activity of going to night clubs. *It was going to be a long night of clubbing.*
N-UNCOUNT

clubby /klʌbi/. If you describe an institution or a group of people as **clubby**, you mean that all the people in it are friendly with each other and do not welcome other people in; an informal word. *Politics is clubby, careerist, and cynical... The British media is in the hands of clubby men.*
ADJ-GRADED =cliquey

club foot, club feet; also spelled **clubfoot**. If someone is born with a **club foot**, their foot is twisted and deformed.
N-COUNT

clubhouse /klʌbhaʊs/ **clubhouses;** also spelled **club-house**. A **clubhouse** is the place where the members of a sports club meet. *They stopped for a soft drink at the clubhouse.*
◆◇◇◇◇ N-COUNT

clubland /klʌblænd/

1 A city's **clubland** is the area that contains all the best nightclubs; used mainly in British English. *...a drugs and guns tale set in London's clubland.*
N-UNCOUNT

2 In British English, **Clubland** refers to the most popular nightclubs and the people that go to them. *He was telling his tales of conquest in clubland. ...a contemporary clubland sound.*
N-UNCOUNT: oft N n

cluck /klʌk/ **clucks, clucking, clucked**

1 When a hen **clucks**, it makes short, abrupt noises. *The hens were already roosting high above my head, clucking softly into their feathers.*
VERB V

2 If you say that someone **clucks** over someone or something, you are showing your disapproval of the fact that they behave in a fussy or protective way. *I've never been one to cluck over babies of either sex... The seamstresses cluck around a dummy, discussing a tuck here and there.*
VERB PRAGMATICS V over/around n

3 If you say that someone **clucks** at someone or something, you are indicating that you do not like the fact that they make disapproving noises or say things in a disapproving way. *Superintendent Fairbairn was still clucking at the photographers, warning them he'd be speaking to their editor... He clucks in disapproval... Teddy clucked his tongue like a disapproving English matron.*
VERB PRAGMATICS V at n V V n

clue /kluː/ **clues** ◆◆◇◇◇

1 A **clue** to a problem or mystery is something that helps you to find the answer to it. *Geneticists in Canada have discovered a clue to the puzzle of why our cells get old and die... How a man shaves may be a telling clue to his age.*
N-COUNT: oft N to n

2 A **clue** is an object or piece of information that helps the police or a detective to solve a crime. *The vital clue to the killer's identity was his nickname, Peanuts.*
N-COUNT: oft N to n

3 A **clue** is a short piece of writing in a crossword or game, giving information which helps you to work out the answer to a question.
N-COUNT

4 If you **haven't a clue** about something, you do not know anything about it or you have no idea what to do about it; an informal expression. *I haven't a clue what I'll give Carl for his birthday next year.*
PHRASE: usu PHR wh

clued-up; also spelled **clued up**. If you say that someone is **clued-up** on a particular subject, you are showing your approval of the fact that they have a great deal of detailed knowledge and information about it; an informal word. *I've always found him clued-up on whatever he was talking about... I'm quite clued up on America.*
ADJ-GRADED: usu v-link ADJ, oft ADJ on n/wh PRAGMATICS

clueless /kluːləs/. If you describe someone as **clueless**, you are showing your disapproval of the fact that they do not know anything about a particular subject or that they are incapable of doing a particular thing properly; an informal word. *I came into adult life clueless about a lot of things that most people take for granted... We have found some drivers clueless as to the law.*
ADJ-GRADED: oft ADJ about n PRAGMATICS

clump /klʌmp/ **clumps, clumping, clumped** ◆◇◇◇◇

1 A **clump** of things such as trees or plants is a small group of them growing together. *...a clump of trees bordering a side road. ...a sweetly scented perennial that grows in clumps.*
N-COUNT: oft N of n, in N in pl =cluster

2 A **clump** of people or things such as wires or hair is a group of them collected together in one place. *The only signs of life are occasional clumps of men, some armed, some not... I was combing my hair and it was just falling out in clumps.*
N-COUNT: oft N of n, in N in pl

3 If someone **clumps** somewhere, they walk there with heavy, clumsy footsteps. *They went clumping up the stairs... Men in big construction boots were clumping in and out with plans in their hands.*
VERB =stomp V prep/adv

4 If things **clump together**, they gather together and form small groups or lumps. *Brown rice takes longer to cook but it doesn't clump together as easily as white rice.*
VERB V together

clumpy /klʌmpi/ **clumpier, clumpiest. Clumpy** means big and clumsy. *...clumpy shoes.*
ADJ-GRADED

clumsy /klʌmzi/ **clumsier, clumsiest** ◆◇◇◇◇

1 A **clumsy** person moves or handles things in a careless, awkward way, often so that things are knocked over or broken. *I'd never seen a clumsier, less coordinated boxer... Unfortunately, I was still very clumsy behind the wheel of the jeep.* ♦ **clumsily** /klʌmzɪli/ *The rooks flew clumsily towards their nests.* ♦ **clumsiness** *His clumsiness and ineptitude with the wooden sticks did not embarrass him.*
ADJ-GRADED =awkward ≠coordinated
ADV-GRADED: ADV with v
N-UNCOUNT

2 A **clumsy** action or statement is not skilful or is tactless and likely to upset people. *The action seemed a clumsy attempt to topple the Janata Dal government... He denied the announcement was clumsy and insensitive.* ♦ **clumsily** *If the matter were handled clumsily, it could cost Miriam her life.*
ADJ-GRADED ≠sensitive
ADV-GRADED: usu ADV with v

♦ **clumsiness** *I was ashamed at my clumsiness and insensitivity.* [N-UNCOUNT ≠sensitivity]

3 An object that is **clumsy** is not neat in design or appearance, and is often awkward to use. *The keyboard is a large and clumsy instrument as far as portable computers are concerned... It was a clumsy looking aeroplane.* [ADJ-GRADED =ungainly ≠elegant]

clung /klʌŋ/. **Clung** is the past tense and past participle of **cling**.

clunk /klʌŋk/ **clunks, clunking, clunked**

1 A **clunk** is a sound made by a heavy object hitting something hard. *Something fell to the floor with a clunk.* [N-COUNT: usu sing; SOUND]

2 If a heavy object **clunks** on or against something, it hits it and makes a dull sound. *His feet clunked on the wooden steps. ...a slight clunking noise.* [VERB; V prep; V-ing]

clunker /klʌŋkəʳ/ **clunkers.** In American English, if you describe an machine, especially a car, as a **clunker**, you mean that it is very old and almost falling apart. [N-COUNT =banger]

clunky /klʌŋki/. If you describe something as **clunky**, you mean that it is solid, heavy, and rather awkward. *...a clunky piece of architecture.* [ADJ-GRADED: usu ADJ n]

cluster /klʌstəʳ/ **clusters, clustering, clustered** ◆◆◇◇◇

1 A **cluster** of people or things is a small group of them close together. *...clusters of men in formal clothes... There's no town here, just a cluster of shops, cabins and motels at the side of the highway.* [N-COUNT: oft N of n]

2 If people **cluster** together, they gather together in a small group. *The passengers clustered together in small groups... The children clustered around me.* [VERB; V together; V around/round n; Also V prep]

• See also **clustered**.

cluster bomb, cluster bombs. A **cluster bomb** is a type of bomb which is dropped from an aircraft. It contains a large number of smaller bombs that spread out before they hit the ground. [N-COUNT]

clustered /klʌstəʳd/. If people or things are **clustered** somewhere, there is a group of them close together there. *Officials were clustered at every open office door, talking excitedly... We pass villages clustered around wet rice fields.* ◆◇◇◇◇ [ADJ: v-link ADJ prep/adv]

clutch /klʌtʃ/ **clutches, clutching, clutched** ◆◆◇◇◇

1 If you **clutch** at something or **clutch** something, you hold it tightly, usually because you are afraid or anxious. *I staggered and had to clutch at a chair for support... She was clutching a photograph, pressing it to her breast.* [VERB =grasp, grip; V at n; V n]

2 If someone is in another person's **clutches**, that person has captured them or has power over them. *Tony fell into the clutches of an attractive American who introduced him to drugs... Stojanovic escaped their clutches by jumping from a moving vehicle.* [N-PLURAL: usu with poss =grasp]

3 In a vehicle, the **clutch** is the mechanism which enables power from the engine to be disconnected from the drive shaft in order to allow you to change gear. You can also refer to the pedal that you press before you change gear as the **clutch**. *Laura let out the clutch and pulled slowly away down the drive.* [N-COUNT]

4 A **clutch** of eggs is a number of eggs laid by a bird at one time. *...the second clutch of eggs.* [N-COUNT: oft N of n]

5 A **clutch** of people or things is a small group of them; used in written English. *The party has attracted a clutch of young southern liberals. ...a clutch of songs about adolescent experiences.* [N-COUNT: N of n]

6 • to **clutch at straws**: see **straw**.

clutter /klʌtəʳ/ **clutters, cluttering, cluttered** ◆◇◇◇◇

1 **Clutter** is a lot of things in an untidy state, especially things that are not useful or necessary. *Caroline prefers her worktops to be clear of clutter.* [N-UNCOUNT]

2 If things or people **clutter** a place, they fill it untidily. *Empty soft-drink cans lie everywhere. They clutter the desks and are strewn across the floor... The roads were cluttered with cars and vans.* [VERB; V n; be V-ed with n]

► **Clutter up** means the same as **clutter**. *The vehicles cluttered up the car park... This room is so impressive it would be a shame to clutter it up.* [PHRASAL VERB; V P n (not pron); V n P; Also V n P with n]

♦ **cluttered** *...a sad, dirty, cluttered room filled with the evidence of a sloppy man.* [ADJ-GRADED]

cm. **cm** is the written abbreviation for **centimetre**. *His height had increased by 2.5 cm.* ◆◆◇◇◇

Cmdr. **Cmdr** is a written abbreviation for **Commander**. *...Cmdr Richard Mason.* [=commander]

c/o. You write **c/o** before an address on an envelope when you are sending it to someone who is staying or working at that address, often for only a short time. **c/o** is an abbreviation for 'care of'. *...Mr A D Bright, c/o Sherman Ltd, 62 Burton Road, Bristol 8.* ◆◇◇◇◇

co- /koʊ-/

1 **co-** is used to form verbs or nouns that refer to people sharing things or doing things together. *...commercial co-operation between the two countries... He co-produced the album with Bowie.* [PREFIX]

2 **co-** is used to form nouns that refer to people who share a job or task with someone else. *His co-workers hated him... Quincy Barnes is co-partner of a San Antonio firm that organizes trade shows.* [PREFIX]

Co. ◆◆◆◆◇

1 **Co.** is used as an abbreviation for **company** when it is part of the name of an organization. *...the Blue Star Amusement Co.* [=company]

2 **Co.** is used as a written abbreviation for **county** before the names of some counties, especially in Ireland. *...Co. Waterford.*

3 You use **and co.** after someone's name to mean the group of people associated with that person; an informal expression. *Wayne Hussey and co. will be playing two live sets each evening.* [PHRASE: n-proper PHR]

C.O. /siː oʊ/ **C.O.s.** A soldier's **C.O.** is his or her **commanding officer**. [N-COUNT]

coach /koʊtʃ/ **coaches, coaching, coached** ◆◆◆◆◇

1 A **coach** is someone who trains a person or team of people in a particular sport. *Tony Woodcock has joined German amateur team SC Brueck as coach.* [N-COUNT =trainer]

2 When a trainer **coaches** a person or a team, he or she helps them to become better at a particular sport. *Beckenbauer coached the West Germans to success in the World Cup final in Italy... He was an educated man who coached the roughest gang of football players ever.* [VERB =train; V n to n; V n]

3 A **coach** is someone who gives people special teaching in a particular subject, especially in order to prepare them for an examination. *What you need is a drama coach.* [N-COUNT: oft n N =teacher]

4 If you **coach** someone, you give them special teaching in a particular subject, especially in order to prepare them for an examination. *He gently coached me in French.* [VERB; V n]

5 A **coach** is a large, comfortable bus that carries passengers on long journeys; used mainly in British English. *As we headed back to Calais, the coach was badly delayed by roadworks... I hate travelling by coach.* [N-COUNT: also by N]

6 A **coach** is one of the separate sections of a train that carries passengers; used mainly in British English. *The train was an elaborate affair of sixteen coaches.* [N-COUNT =car]

7 A **coach** is an enclosed four-wheeled vehicle pulled by horses, in which people used to travel. Coaches are still used for ceremonial events. [N-COUNT]

coachload /koʊtʃloʊd/ **coachloads;** also spelled **coach-load.** A **coachload** of people is a group of people who are travelling somewhere together in a coach. *Dorset is as yet unspoilt by coachloads of tourists.* [N-COUNT: usu N of n]

coachman /koʊtʃmən/ **coachmen.** A **coachman** was a man who drove a horse-drawn coach; an old-fashioned word. [N-COUNT]

coach station, coach stations. In British English, a **coach station** is an area or building which coaches leave from or arrive at on regular journeys. [N-COUNT]

coagulate /koʊægjʊleɪt/ **coagulates, coagulating, coagulated.** When a liquid **coagulates**, it becomes very thick. *As the egg whites cook, they coagulate and rise to the surface... The blood coagulates to stop wounds bleeding.* [VERB =congeal; V]

♦ **coagulation** /koʊægjʊleɪʃən/ *Blood becomes stickier to help coagulation in case of a cut.* [N-UNCOUNT]

coal /koʊl/ **coals** 

1 **Coal** is a hard black substance that is extracted from the ground and burned as fuel. *Gas-fired elec-* [N-UNCOUNT]

tricity is cheaper than coal... Today, oil and natural gas have replaced coal and wood in most areas.

2 **Coals** are burning pieces of coal. *The iron teakettle was hissing splendidly over live coals... When grilling on charcoal, it is important to get the coals white-hot before you start.* N-PLURAL

3 If a person in authority **hauls** or **drags** someone **over the coals**, they speak to them severely about something foolish or wrong that they have done. *I heard later that Uncle Jim had been hauled over the coals for not letting anyone know where we were... The museum's P.R. man was going to be dragged over the coals for sure.* PHRASES V inflects, oft PHR *for* n/-ing =reprimand

4 If you say that someone is selling or taking **coals to Newcastle**, you mean that they are trying to supply someone with something that they already have plenty of. *Taking a gun to the United States would be like taking coals to Newcastle.* usu v PHR

coalesce /koʊəles/ **coalesces, coalescing, coalesced.** If two or more things **coalesce**, they come together and form a larger group or system; a formal word. *Cities, if unrestricted, tend to coalesce into bigger and bigger conurbations... His sporting and political interests coalesced admirably in his writing about climbing.* VERB =amalgamate V prep V

coalface /koʊlfeɪs/ **coalfaces.** In a coal mine, the **coalface** is the part where the coal is being cut out of the rock. N-COUNT

coalfield /koʊlfiːld/ **coalfields.** A **coalfield** is a region where there is coal under the ground. *The park lies on top of a coalfield.* N-COUNT

coalition /koʊəlɪʃən/ **coalitions** ◆◆◆◇◇

1 A **coalition** is a government consisting of people from two or more political parties. *Since June the country has had a coalition government... It took five months for the coalition to agree on and publish a medium-term economic programme.* N-COUNT: oft N n

2 A **coalition** is a group consisting of people from different political or social groups who are cooperating to achieve a particular aim. *He had been opposed by a coalition of about 50 civil rights, women's and Latino organizations.* N-COUNT: oft N *of* n =alliance

coal mine, coal mines; also spelled **coalmine.** A **coal mine** is a place where coal is dug out of the ground. ◆◇◇◇◇ N-COUNT

coal miner, coal miners; also spelled **coalminer.** A **coal miner** is a person whose job is mining coal. N-COUNT

coal scuttle, coal scuttles. A **coal scuttle** is a special kind of bucket for keeping coal in. N-COUNT

coal tar; also spelled **coal-tar. Coal tar** is a thick black liquid made from coal which is used for making drugs and chemical products. *...coal tar dyes.* N-UNCOUNT

coarse /kɔːʳs/ **coarser, coarsest** ◆◆◇◇◇

1 **Coarse** things have a rough texture because they consist of thick strands or large pieces. *...a jacket made of very coarse cloth. ...a beach of coarse sand.* ADJ-GRADED =rough ≠fine ♦ **coarsely** *...coarsely ground black pepper.* ADV

2 If you describe someone as **coarse**, you mean that he or she talks and behaves in a rude and offensive way. *The soldiers did not bother to moderate their coarse humour in her presence.* ADJ-GRADED =vulgar, crude ♦ **coarsely** *The women laughed coarsely at some vulgar joke.* ADV-GRADED: ADV with v =rudely ♦ **coarseness** *The coarseness of her cursing amazed the workmen.* N-UNCOUNT

coarsen /kɔːʳsən/ **coarsens, coarsening, coarsened**

1 If something **coarsens** or **is coarsened**, it becomes thicker or rougher in texture. *Skin thickens, dries and coarsens after sun exposure. ...his gnarled, coarsened features.* V-ERG V V-ed Also V n

2 If someone's behaviour or speech **coarsens** or if they **coarsen** it, they become less polite or they begin to speak in a less pleasant way. *Her voice has deepened and coarsened with the years... He had coarsened his voice to an approximation of Cockney.* V-ERG V V n

coast /koʊst/ **coasts, coasting, coasted** ◆◆◆◆◇

1 The **coast** is an area of land that is next to the sea. *Camp sites are usually situated along the coast, close to beaches. ...the west coast of Scotland.* N-COUNT: oft adj N, N *of* n

2 If a vehicle **coasts** somewhere, it continues to move there with the motor switched off, or without being pushed or pedalled. *My gearbox broke with a crunch and I coasted into the pits to retire... They picked up momentum, then slipped into neutral and coasted quietly down the slope.* VERB =freewheel V prep/adv Also V

3 If a person or a team **is coasting**, they are doing something easily, especially winning a competitive contest. *Ivan Lendl coasted to a 6-3, 6-2, 6-3 victory over Roger Rasheed... The company was coasting on the enormous success of its early products.* VERB =cruise V *to* n V Also V adv

4 If you say that someone **is coasting**, you are emphasizing that they are not putting enough effort into what they are doing. *There was a time when Charles was coasting at school and I should have told him to buckle down.* ► **Coast along** means the same as **coast**. *Matthew had no drive. He coasted along on his good looks.* VERB PRAGMATICS V Also V prep PHRASAL VERB V P

5 If you say that **the coast is clear**, you mean that there is nobody around to see you or catch you. *You can come out now,' he called. 'The coast is clear. She's gone.'* PHRASE: V inflects

coastal /koʊstəl/. **Coastal** is used to refer to things that are in the sea or on the land near a coast. *Local radio stations serving coastal areas often broadcast forecasts for yachtsmen... The fish are on sale from our own coastal waters.* ◆◆◇◇◇ ADJ: ADJ n

coaster /koʊstəʳ/ **coasters** ◆◇◇◇◇

1 A **coaster** is a small mat that you put underneath a glass or mug to protect the surface of a table. *She placed the glass mug on a coaster.* N-COUNT

2 In British English, a **coaster** is a ship that sails along the coast taking goods to ports. N-COUNT

3 see also **roller-coaster.**

coastguard /koʊstgɑːʳd/ **coastguards** ◆◇◇◇◇

1 A **coastguard** is an official who watches the sea near a coast in order to get help for sailors when they need it and to prevent smuggling. N-COUNT

2 The **coastguard** is the organization to which coastguards belong. *The survivors were lifted off by two helicopters, one from the Coastguard and one from the RAF. ...the American coastguard picked up 28 Cubans on rafts.* N-SING: *the* N

coastline /koʊstlaɪn/ **coastlines.** A country's **coastline** is the outline of its coast. *This is some of the most exposed coastline in the world... Thousands of volunteers gave up part of their weekend to clean up the California coastline.* ◆◇◇◇◇ N-VAR: oft supp N

coat /koʊt/ **coats, coating, coated** ◆◆◆◇◇

1 A **coat** is a piece of clothing with long sleeves which you wear over your other clothes when you go outside. *He turned off the television, put on his coat and walked out.* N-COUNT

2 An animal's **coat** is the fur or hair on its body. *Vitamin B6 is great for improving the condition of dogs' and horses' coats.* N-COUNT: usu with poss

3 If you **coat** something **with** a substance or **in** a substance, you cover it with a thin layer of the substance. *Coat the fish with seasoned flour.* ♦ **coated** *TV pictures showed a dying bird coated with oil... Dip the pieces of squid in this mixture so that they are completely coated.* VERB V n *with/in* n ADJ: v-link ADJ, ADJ *with/in* n, adv ADJ

4 A **coat** of paint or varnish is a thin layer of it on a surface. *The front door needs a new coat of paint... You will need to apply three coats of varnish.* N-COUNT: oft N *of* n

-coated /koʊtɪd/

1 **-coated** combines with colour adjectives such as 'white' and 'red', or words for types of coat like 'fur', to form adjectives that describe someone as wearing a certain sort of coat. *At the top of the stairs stood the white-coated doctors.* COMB in ADJ: ADJ n

2 **-coated** combines with names of substances such as 'sugar' and 'plastic' to form adjectives that describe something as being covered with a thin layer of that substance. *...chocolate-coated sweets. ...plastic-coated wire.* COMB in ADJ

coat hanger, coat hangers; also spelled **coathanger.** A **coat hanger** is a curved piece of wood, metal, or plastic that you hang a piece of clothing on. N-COUNT

coating /koʊtɪŋ/ **coatings.** A **coating** of a substance is a thin layer of it spread over a surface. ◆◇◇◇◇ N-COUNT: usu with supp

Under the coating of dust and cobwebs, he discovered a fine French Louis XVI clock. ...fluffy chocolate mousse, topped off with a crisp chocolate coating.

coat of arms, coats of arms. The **coat of arms** of a family, town, or organization is a design in the form of a shield that they use as an emblem. *There was a stained-glass window with the family coat of arms.* N-COUNT: usu with supp =crest

coat-tails; also spelled **coattails.**
1 A man's **coat-tails** are the two long pieces at the back of a formal coat. N-PLURAL: oft poss N
2 If someone does something **on the coat-tails of** someone else, they are able to do it because of the other person's success, and not because of their own efforts. *Then, he was largely unknown and could ride on the coat-tails of Reagan.* PHRASE: usu PHR after v

co-author, co-authors, co-authoring, co-authored ◆◇◇◇◇
1 The **co-authors** of a book, play, or report are the people who have written it together. *He is co-author, with Andrew Blowers, of 'The International Politics of Nuclear Waste'.* N-COUNT: oft N *of* n
2 If two or more people **co-author** a book, play, or report, they write it together. *He's co-authored a book on Policy for Tourism... Karen Matthews co-authored the study with Lewis Kullers.* VERB V n V n *with* n

coax /koʊks/ **coaxes, coaxing, coaxed** ◆◇◇◇◇
1 If you **coax** someone into doing something, you gently try to persuade them to do it. *After lunch, she watched, listened and coaxed Bobby into talking about himself... The government coaxed them to give up their strike by promising them temporary residence permits.* VERB =cajole V n prep V n to-inf Also V n
2 If you **coax** something such as information out of someone, you gently persuade them to give it to you. *The WPC talked yesterday of her role in trying to coax vital information from the young victim... It took Louis until Easter to coax a grudging consent from the French King.* VERB =wheedle V n *out of/from* n
3 If you **coax** a machine or device into doing something, you make it work by operating it very slowly and gently. *He would stride on stage then proceed to coax the sweetest possible sounds out of his violin... He was delighted to coax the monoplane to 330 m.p.h.* VERB V n prep

cob /kɒb/ **cobs** ◆◇◇◇◇
1 In British English, a **cob** is a small round loaf of bread. N-COUNT =roll
2 A **cob** is a heavily-built type of horse or pony. N-COUNT
3 See also **corn on the cob.**

cobalt /koʊbɔːlt/ ◆◇◇◇◇
1 **Cobalt** is a hard silvery-white metal which is used in hardening steel and for producing a blue dye. *...a country rich in copper, cobalt and diamonds.* N-UNCOUNT
2 **Cobalt** or **cobalt blue** is a deep blue colour. *They walked past stalls selling huge sprays of crimson, saffron and cobalt flowers. ...a woman in a soft cobalt blue dress.* COLOUR

cobble /kɒbəl/ **cobbles, cobbling, cobbled.** **Cobbles** are the same as **cobblestones.** *They found Trish sitting on the cobbles of the stable yard.* N-COUNT: usu pl

cobble together. If you say that someone has **cobbled** something **together**, you mean that they have made or produced it roughly or quickly; used showing disapproval. *The group had cobbled together a few decent songs... You can cobble it together from any old combination of garments.* PHRASAL VERB PRAGMATICS V P n (not pron) V n P

cobbled /kɒbəld/. A **cobbled** street has a surface made of cobblestones. *Cottrell strode out across the cobbled courtyard.* ◆◇◇◇◇ ADJ: usu ADJ n

cobbler /kɒbləʳ/ **cobblers**
1 A **cobbler** is a person whose job is to make or mend shoes; an old-fashioned use. N-COUNT
2 In British English, if you describe something that someone has just said as **cobblers**, you mean that you think it is nonsense; an informal use. *The idea that greens are good for you is a load of cobblers... These guys talk an awful load of old cobblers.* N-UNCOUNT =codswallop

cobblestone /kɒbəlstoʊn/ **cobblestones.** **Cobblestones** are stones with a rounded upper surface which were once used for making streets. *...the narrow, cobblestone streets of the Left Bank.* N-COUNT: usu pl

cobra /koʊbrə/ **cobras.** A **cobra** is a kind of poisonous snake that can make the skin on the back of its neck into a hood. N-COUNT

cobweb /kɒbweb/ **cobwebs**
1 A **cobweb** is the net which a spider makes for catching insects. *The cobwebs on the ceiling fluttered in the heat from the stove.* N-COUNT
2 If something **blows** or **clears away the cobwebs**, it makes you feel more mentally alert and lively when you had previously been feeling tired. *...a walk on the South Downs to blow away the cobwebs.* PHRASE: V inflects

cobwebbed /kɒbwebd/. A **cobwebbed** surface is covered with cobwebs. *There are tall, cobwebbed racks of musty clothing and piles of junk all over.* ADJ: usu ADJ n

cocaine /koʊkeɪn/. **Cocaine** is a powerful drug which some people take for pleasure, but which they can become addicted to. In most countries it is illegal to take cocaine. ◆◆◇◇◇ N-UNCOUNT

coccyx /kɒksɪks/ **coccyxes.** The **coccyx** is the small triangular bone at the lower end of the spine in human beings and some apes. N-COUNT

cochineal /kɒtʃɪniːl/. **Cochineal** is a red substance that is used for colouring food. N-UNCOUNT

cochlea /kɒkliə/ **cochleae.** The **cochlea** is the spiral shaped part of the inner ear. N-COUNT

cock /kɒk/ **cocks, cocking, cocked** ◆◆◇◇◇
1 In British English, a **cock** is an adult male chicken. The usual American word is **rooster.** *The cock was announcing the start of a new day.* N-COUNT =rooster
2 You refer to a male bird, especially a male game bird, as a **cock** when you want to distinguish it from a female bird. *...a cock pheasant.* N-COUNT: oft N n
3 A man's **cock** is his penis; an informal use which some people find offensive. N-COUNT
4 If you **cock** a part of your body in a particular direction, you lift it or point it in that direction. *He paused and cocked his head as if listening... The Brigadier thought about this for a moment, head cocked to one side.* VERB V n V-ed
5 If someone **cocks** their ear, they try very hard to hear something from a particular direction. *He suddenly cocked an ear and listened... All ears were cocked for the footsteps on the stairs.* VERB V n
6 When someone **cocks** a gun, they set a small device in the gun so that it is ready to fire. *His hands were too weak to cock his revolver.* VERB V n
7 See also **stopcock.**
8 • to **cock a snook at** someone: see **snook.**

cock up. In British English, if you **cock** something **up**, you ruin it by doing something wrong; an informal expression which some people find offensive. *'Seems like I've cocked it up,' Egan said... They've cocked up the address.* • See also **cock-up.** PHRASAL VERB V n P V P n (not pron)

cock-a-hoop. If you are **cock-a-hoop**, you are extremely pleased about something that you have done; an old-fashioned, informal expression. ADJ: usu v-link ADJ

cock-and-bull story, cock-and-bull stories. If you describe something that someone tells you as a **cock-and-bull story**, you mean that you do not believe it is true; an informal expression. *Was it him who made you come to us with this cock-and-bull story?* N-COUNT

cockatoo /kɒkətuː, AM -tuː/ **cockatoos.** A **cockatoo** is a kind of parrot from Australia or New Guinea which has a crest on its head. N-COUNT

cocked hat, cocked hats
1 A **cocked hat** is a hat with three corners that used to be worn with some uniforms. N-COUNT
2 If you say that one thing **knocks** another thing **into a cocked hat**, you mean that it is much better or much more significant than the other thing. *I bet his IQ would knock Kane's into a cocked hat.* PHRASE: V inflects

cockerel /kɒkərəl/ **cockerels.** A **cockerel** is a young male chicken. N-COUNT

cocker spaniel /kɒkəʳ spænjəl/ **cocker spaniels.** A **cocker spaniel** is a breed of small dog with silky hair and long ears. N-COUNT

cockeyed /kɒkaɪd, AM -aɪd/; also spelled **cock-eyed.**

1 If you say that an idea or scheme is **cockeyed,** you mean that you think it is very unlikely to succeed. *Maybe she has some cockeyed delusions about becoming a big coal baroness.* ADJ-GRADED =absurd

2 If something is **cockeyed,** it looks wrong because it is not in a level or straight position. *...dusty photographs hanging at cockeyed angles on the walls.* ADJ-GRADED

cockle /kɒkᵊl/ **cockles. Cockles** are small edible shellfish. N-COUNT: usu pl

cockney /kɒkni/ **cockneys** ◆◇◇◇◇

1 A **cockney** is a person who was born in the East End of London. *...a Cockney cab driver... Pomeroy was a cockney barrow-boy at heart.* N-COUNT: oft N n

2 **Cockney** is the dialect and accent of the East End of London. *The man spoke with a Cockney accent.* N-UNCOUNT

cockpit /kɒkpɪt/ **cockpits.** In an aeroplane or racing car, the **cockpit** is the part where the pilot sits. ◆◆◇◇◇ N-COUNT

cockroach /kɒkroʊtʃ/ **cockroaches.** A **cockroach** is a large brown insect that is sometimes found in warm places or where food is kept. ◆◇◇◇◇ N-COUNT

cocksure /kɒkʃʊəʳ/. Someone who is **cocksure** is very self-confident and rather cheeky; an old-fashioned word. ADJ-GRADED

cocktail /kɒkteɪl/ **cocktails** ◆◆◇◇◇

1 A **cocktail** is an alcoholic drink which contains several ingredients. *On arrival, guests are offered wine or a champagne cocktail... A cocktail party was thrown at the British Officers Club. ...an expert at mixing cocktails.* N-COUNT

2 A **cocktail** is a mixture of a number of different things, especially ones that do not go together well. *The court was told she had taken a cocktail of drugs and alcohol... Children and guns are a potentially lethal cocktail.* N-COUNT: oft N of n

3 see also **fruit cocktail, prawn cocktail, Molotov cocktail.**

cocktail dress, cocktail dresses. A **cocktail dress** is a dress that is suitable for formal social occasions. *At his side stood his wife Olivia, dark-haired and exquisite, in a white cocktail dress.* N-COUNT

cocktail lounge, cocktail lounges. A **cocktail lounge** is a room in a hotel, restaurant, or club where you can buy alcoholic drinks. *We could go for a drink in the cocktail lounge of the Hilton, if you like.* N-COUNT

cock-up, cock-ups. In British English, if you make a **cock-up** of something, you ruin it by doing something wrong; an informal word which some people find offensive. *He was in danger of making a real cock-up of this... This was just an administrative cock-up.* N-COUNT

cocky /kɒki/ **cockier, cockiest.** Someone who is **cocky** is very self-confident and rather cheeky; an informal word used showing disapproval. *He was a little bit cocky when he was about 11 because he was winning everything.* ◆◇◇◇◇ ADJ-GRADED PRAGMATICS ♦ **cockiness** *The pair of them were both blinded by their own cockiness.* N-UNCOUNT

cocoa /koʊkoʊ/ ◆◇◇◇◇

1 **Cocoa** is a brown powder made from the seeds of a tropical tree. It is used in making chocolate. *The Ivory Coast became the world's leading cocoa producer. ...cocoa beans.* N-UNCOUNT

2 **Cocoa** is a hot drink made from cocoa powder and milk or water. *My wife was tucked up in bed with her cup of cocoa.* N-UNCOUNT

coconut /koʊkənʌt/ **coconuts** ◆◇◇◇◇

1 A **coconut** is a very large nut with a hairy shell, which has white flesh and milky juice inside it. *...the smell of roasted meats mingled with spices, coconut oil and ripe tropical fruits.* N-COUNT

2 **Coconut** is the white flesh of a coconut. *Desiccated coconut is used by confectioners and cake makers for its flavour.* N-UNCOUNT

coconut milk. Coconut milk is the milky juice inside coconuts. N-UNCOUNT

coconut palm, coconut palms. A **coconut palm** is a tall tree on which coconuts grow. N-COUNT

cocoon /kəkuːn/ **cocoons, cocooning, cocooned**

1 A **cocoon** is a covering of silky threads that the larvae of moths and other insects make for themselves before they grow into adults. *The pictures featured here show the pupa bursting out of the cocoon and climbing up a twig.* N-COUNT

2 If you are in a **cocoon** of something, you are wrapped up in it or surrounded by it. *He stood there in a cocoon of golden light.* N-COUNT: usu N of n

3 If you are living in a **cocoon,** you are in an environment in which you feel protected and safe, and sometimes isolated from everyday life. *...her innocent desire to envelop her beloved in a cocoon of love... Even though we're living together we walk around in this cocoon of silence... You cannot live in a cocoon and overlook these facts.* N-COUNT: usu N of n

4 If something **cocoons** you from something, it protects you or isolates you from it. *There is nowhere to hide when things go wrong, no organisation to cocoon you from blame... The playwright cocooned himself in a world of pretence.* VERB V n from/in n V pron-refl in n

cocooned /kəkuːnd/

1 If someone is **cocooned** in blankets or clothes, they are completely wrapped in them. *She is comfortably cocooned in pillows and only half awake... In each cot, a small tightly cocooned figure lay on its side.* ADJ: usu v-link ADJ, oft ADJ in n

2 If you say that someone is **cocooned,** you mean that they are isolated and protected from everyday life and problems. *White was cocooned in a private world of concentration... For so long they have been cocooned from the experience of illness.* ADJ-GRADED: oft ADJ in/from n =cloistered

cod /kɒd/. ◆◇◇◇◇

1 **Cod** are a type of large edible fish. The form 'cod' is also used as the plural. ► **Cod** is this fish eaten as food. *A Catalan speciality is to serve salt cod cold.* N-VAR N-UNCOUNT

2 In informal British English, you use **cod** to describe something which is not genuine and which is intended to deceive or amuse people by looking or sounding like the real thing. *...a cod documentary on what animals think of living in a zoo.* ADJ: ADJ n =fake

coda /koʊdə/ **codas**

1 A **coda** is a separate passage at the end of something such as a book or a speech that finishes it off. N-COUNT

2 In music, a **coda** is the final part of a fairly long piece of music which is added in order to finish it off in a pleasing way. N-COUNT

coddle /kɒdᵊl/ **coddles, coddling, coddled.** If you say that someone **coddles** another person, you are showing your disapproval of the fact that they treat the person too kindly or protect them too much. *She coddled her youngest son madly... The warders' union has been denouncing the government for coddling prisoners.* VERB PRAGMATICS V n

code /koʊd/ **codes** ◆◆◆◇◇

1 A **code** is a set of rules about how people should behave or about how something must be done. *...Article 159 of the Turkish penal code. ...local building codes.* N-COUNT: oft n N, N of n

2 A **code** is a system of replacing the words in a message with other words or symbols, so that nobody can understand it unless they know the system. *They used elaborate secret codes, as when the names of trees stood for letters... If you can't remember your number, write it in code in a diary.* N-COUNT: also in N

3 A **code** is a group of numbers or letters which is used to identify something, such as a postal address or part of a telephone system. *Callers dialing the wrong area code will not get through.* N-COUNT

4 A **code** is any system of signs or symbols that has a meaning. *It will need other chips to reconvert the digital code back into normal TV signals.* N-COUNT

5 Computer **code** is a system or language for expressing information and instructions in a form which can be understood by a computer; a technical term in computing. N-UNCOUNT =programme

6 See also **bar code, Highway Code, machine code, morse code, postcode, zip code.**

coded /koʊdɪd/ ◆◇◇◇◇

1 **Coded** messages have words or symbols which represent other words, so that the message is se- ADJ: usu ADJ n

cret unless you know the system behind the code. *In a coded telephone warning, Scotland Yard were told four bombs had been planted in the area.*

2 If you say that someone is using **coded** language, you mean that they are expressing their opinion in an indirect or obscure way, usually because that opinion is likely to offend people. *They have sent barely coded messages to the Education Secretary endorsing this criticism... It's widely assumed that his lyrics were coded references to homosexuality.* ADJ: usu ADJ n

3 **Coded** electronic signals use a binary system of digits which can be decoded by an appropriate machine; a technical use. *The coded signal is received by satellite dish aerials.* ADJ: ADJ n

codeine /koʊdiːn/. **Codeine** is a drug which is used to relieve pain, especially headaches, and the symptoms of a cold. N-UNCOUNT

code name, code names, code naming, code named; also spelled **codename, codename.**

1 A **code name** is a name used for someone or something in order to keep their identity secret. *One of their informers was working under the code name Czerny... The operation was given the code name Dynamo.* N-COUNT: usu N n

2 If a military or police operation **is code-named** something, it is given a name which only the people involved in it know. *The operation was code-named Moonlight Sonata... The French have a two-thousand strong military contingent, code-named Sparrowhawk.* VB: usu passive; *be* V-ed n; V-ed

code of conduct, codes of conduct. The **code of conduct** for a group or organization is a voluntary agreement on rules of behaviour for the members of that group or organization. *Doctors in Britain say a new code of conduct is urgently needed to protect the doctor-patient relationship.* ◆◇◇◇◇ N-COUNT

code of practice, codes of practice. A **code of practice** is a set of written rules which explains how people working in a particular profession should behave. *The auctioneers are violating a code of practice by dealing in stolen goods.* ◆◇◇◇◇ N-COUNT

code word, code words; also spelled **codeword** or **code-word.**

1 A **code word** is a word or phrase that has a special meaning, different from its normal meaning, for the people who have agreed to use it in this way. *Their instructions were to volunteer for a special mission when we gave them a code-word.* N-COUNT

2 A **code word** is a word or phrase that someone, especially a public figure, uses in order to avoid saying something else. *I think nationalism is just a code word for racism... 'Tired and emotional' is a code word for being drunk.* N-COUNT: usu N *for* n

codex /koʊdeks/ **codices.** A **codex** is an ancient book which was written by hand, not printed. N-COUNT

codger /kɒdʒəʳ/ **codgers.** If you refer to an old man as an old **codger**, you are referring to him in a disrespectful way. *I sidled over to the snug bar, where three old codgers were huddled over half-pints of milk stout.* N-COUNT: usu adj N; PRAGMATICS

codices /koʊdɪsiːz/. **Codices** is the plural of **codex.**

codicil /koʊdɪsɪl, AM kɑːd-/ **codicils.** A **codicil** is an instruction that is added to a will after the main part of it has been written; a legal term. N-COUNT

codify /koʊdɪfaɪ, AM kɑːd-/ **codifies, codifying, codified.** If you **codify** a set of rules, you define them or present them in a clear and ordered way. *The latest draft of the agreement codifies the panel's decision.* ♦ **codification** /koʊdɪfɪkeɪʃᵊn, AM kɑːd-/ *The codification of the laws began in the 1840s.* VERB; V n; N-UNCOUNT: usu N *of* n

coding /koʊdɪŋ/. **Coding** is a method of making something recognizable or distinct, for example by colouring it or by giving it a unique feature. *...a colour coding that will ensure easy reference for potential users.* ◆◇◇◇◇ N-UNCOUNT: usu adj N

cod-liver oil; also spelled **cod liver oil. Cod liver oil** is a thick yellow oil which is given as a medicine, especially to children, because it is full of vitamins A and D. N-UNCOUNT

codpiece /kɒdpiːs/ **codpieces.** A **codpiece** was a piece of material worn by men in the 15th and 16th centuries to cover their genitals. N-COUNT

codswallop /kɒdzwɒləp/. In British English, if you describe something that someone has just said as **codswallop**, you mean that you think it is nonsense; an informal word. *It's a load of old codswallop. I never did anything.* N-UNCOUNT; PRAGMATICS; =cobblers

co-ed, co-eds; also spelled **coed.**

1 A **co-ed** school or college is the same as a co-educational school or college. *He was educated at Ecclesbourne School, a co-ed comprehensive school.* ADJ; =mixed; ≠single-sex

2 In American English, a **co-ed** is a female student at a co-educational college or university; an informal use. *...two University of Florida coeds.* N-COUNT

3 In American English, a **co-ed** sports facility or sporting activity is one that both males and females use or take part in at the same time. The usual British word is **mixed**. *You have a choice of co-ed or single-sex swimming exercise classes.* ADJ: ADJ n; ≠single-sex

co-educational. A **co-educational** school, college, or university is attended by both boys and girls. *The college has been co-educational since 1971.* ADJ

coefficient /koʊɪfɪʃənt/ **coefficients.** A **coefficient** is a number that expresses a measurement of a particular quality of a substance or object under specified conditions; a technical term in science. *...production coefficients... A coefficient of one means the markets move perfectly in step.* N-COUNT: usu with supp

coerce /koʊɜːʳs/ **coerces, coercing, coerced.** If you **coerce** someone into doing something, you make them do it, although they do not want to; a formal word. *Potter had argued that the government coerced him into pleading guilty... Clark had somehow been able to coerce Jenny into doing whatever he told her to do.* ◆◇◇◇◇ VERB; =pressurize; V n *into*-ing/n; Also V n to-inf

coercion /koʊɜːʳʃᵊn/. **Coercion** is the act or process of persuading someone forcefully to do something that they did not want to do. *It was vital that the elections should be free of coercion or intimidation.* ◆◇◇◇◇ N-UNCOUNT

coercive /koʊɜːʳsɪv/. **Coercive** measures are intended to force people to do something that they do not want to do. *...increasingly coercive measures on the part of the state... The eighteenth-century Admiralty had few coercive powers over its officers.* ◆◇◇◇◇ ADJ-GRADED: usu ADJ n

coexist /koʊɪgzɪst/ **coexists, coexisting, coexisted;** also spelled **co-exist.** If one thing **coexists** with another, they exist together at the same time or in the same place. You can also say that two things **coexist**. *Pockets of affluence coexist with poverty... Bankers and clockmakers have coexisted in the City for hundreds of years.* V-RECIP; V *with* n; pl-n V

coexistence /koʊɪgzɪstᵊns/; also spelled **co-existence.** The **coexistence** of one thing with another is the fact that they exist together at the same time or in the same place. *He also believed in coexistence with the West.* N-UNCOUNT: oft N *of/with/between* n

C of E. C of E is an abbreviation for **Church of England.** *Mrs Steele was head of Didcot's C of E primary school.*

coffee /kɒfi, AM kɔːfi/ **coffees** ◆◆◆◇◇

1 **Coffee** is a hot brown drink that you make by pouring boiling water onto coffee beans that have been roasted and ground or onto instant coffee powder. *Would you like some coffee?... Newman poured more black coffee and lit a cigarette.* ► A **coffee** is a cup of coffee. *I made a coffee.* N-UNCOUNT; N-COUNT

2 **Coffee** is the roasted seeds or powder from which the drink is made. *Brazil harvested 28m bags of coffee in 1991, the biggest crop for four years. ...superior quality coffee.* N-MASS

coffee bar, coffee bars. A **coffee bar** is a small café where non-alcoholic drinks and snacks are sold. N-COUNT

coffee bean, coffee beans. Coffee beans are small dark brown beans that are roasted and N-COUNT: usu pl ground to make coffee. They are the seeds of the coffee plant.

coffee break, coffee breaks. A **coffee break** is a short period of time, usually in the morning or afternoon, when you stop working and have a cup of coffee. *It looks like she'll be too busy to stop for a coffee break.* N-COUNT

coffee cup, coffee cups; also spelled **coffee-cup**. A **coffee** cup is a cup in which coffee is served. Coffee cups are usually smaller than tea cups. N-COUNT

coffee grinder, coffee grinders. A **coffee grinder** is a machine for grinding coffee beans. N-COUNT

coffee house, coffee houses; also spelled **coffee-house**. A **coffee house** is a kind of bar where people sit to drink coffee and talk. Coffee houses were especially popular in Britain in the 18th century. N-COUNT

coffee morning, coffee mornings. A **coffee morning** is a social event that takes place in the morning in someone's house, and is usually intended to raise money for charity. N-COUNT

coffee pot, coffee pots; also spelled **coffeepot**. A **coffee pot** is a tall narrow pot with a spout and a lid, in which coffee is made or served. N-COUNT

coffee shop, coffee shops; also spelled **coffee-shop**. A **coffee shop** is a kind of restaurant that sells coffee, tea, cakes, and sometimes sandwiches and light meals. ◆◇◇◇◇ N-COUNT =cafe

coffee table, coffee tables; also spelled **coffee-table**. A **coffee table** is a small low table in a living-room. ◆◇◇◇◇ N-COUNT

coffee-table book, coffee-table books. A **coffee-table book** is a large expensive book with a lot of pictures, which is designed to be looked at rather than to be read properly, and is usually placed where people can see it easily. N-COUNT

coffer /kɒfəʳ/ **coffers** ◆◇◇◇◇

1 A **coffer** is a large strong chest used for storing valuable objects such as money or gold and silver; an old-fashioned use. N-COUNT

2 The **coffers** of an organization consist of the money that it has to spend, imagined as being collected together in one place. *The proceeds from the lottery go towards sports and recreation, as well as swelling the coffers of the government... Large public and private companies have long been contributors to Tory party coffers.* N-PLURAL: with supp, oft N *of*n, n N

coffin /kɒfɪn, AM kɔːfɪn/ **coffins** ◆◆◇◇◇

1 A **coffin** is a box in which a dead body is buried or cremated. N-COUNT

2 If you say that one thing is **a nail in the coffin** of another thing, you mean that it will help bring about its end or failure. *A fine would be the final nail in the coffin of the airline.* PHRASE: oft PHR *of*n

cog /kɒg/ **cogs**

1 A **cog** is a wheel with square or triangular teeth around the edge, which is used in a machine to turn another wheel or part. N-COUNT

2 If you describe someone as **a cog in a machine** or **wheel**, you mean that they are a small part of a large organization or group. *Mr Lake was an important cog in the Republican campaign machine.* PHRASE: v-link PHR

cogent /koʊdʒənt/. A **cogent** reason, argument, or example is strong and convincing; a formal word. *There were perfectly cogent reasons why Julian Cavendish should be told of the Major's impending return.* ♦ **cogency** *The film makes its points with cogency and force.* ♦ **cogently** *The authors argue cogently that it is high time the church lost its obsession with the subject.* ADJ-GRADED =convincing; N-UNCOUNT; ADV-GRADED: ADV with v =convincingly

cogitate /kɒdʒɪteɪt/ **cogitates, cogitating, cogitated.** If you **are cogitating**, you are thinking deeply about something; a formal word. *You're listening and cogitating are you?... Frido cogitated on the term.* ♦ **cogitation** /kɒdʒɪteɪʃən/ *On retirement, and after much cogitation, Pat and I decided to live in the Isle of Wight.* VERB; V; V *on/about*n; N-UNCOUNT

cognac /kɒnjæk, AM koʊn-/ **cognacs;** also spelled **Cognac**. **Cognac** is a type of brandy made in the south west of France. *...a bottle of Cognac. ...one of the world's finest cognacs.* ► A **cognac** is a glass of cognac. *Phillips ordered a cognac.* ◆◇◇◇◇ N-MASS; N-COUNT

cognate /kɒgneɪt/. **Cognate** things are related to each other; a formal word. *...cognate words.* ADJ: oft ADJ *with*n

cognisance /kɒgnɪzəns/. See **cognizance**.

cognisant /kɒgnɪzənt/. See **cognizant**.

cognition /kɒgnɪʃən/. **Cognition** is the mental process involved in knowing, learning, and understanding things; a formal word. *...processes of perception and cognition.* N-UNCOUNT

cognitive /kɒgnɪtɪv/. **Cognitive** means relating to the mental process involved in knowing, learning, and understanding things; a formal or technical word. *As children grow older, their cognitive processes become sharper. ...Vygotsky's theory of cognitive development.* ◆◇◇◇◇ ADJ: ADJ n

cognizance /kɒgnɪzəns/; also spelled **cognisance**.

1 If you **take cognizance of** something, you take notice of it or acknowledge it; a formal use. *The government has in the past not taken cognisance of any protest unless there has been some show of violence.* PHRASE: V inflects =acknowledge

2 **Cognizance** is knowledge or understanding; a formal use. *...the teacher's developing cognizance of the child's intellectual activity.* N-UNCOUNT: oft N *of*n

cognizant /kɒgnɪzənt/; also spelled **cognisant**. If someone is **cognizant** of something, they are aware of it or understand it; a formal word. *Walter was cognizant of the limitations of his argument.* ADJ-GRADED: v-link ADJ, usu ADJ *of*n =conscious

cognoscenti /kɒnjəʃenti/. The **cognoscenti** are the people who know a lot about a particular subject; a formal word. *She has an international reputation among film cognoscenti.* N-PLURAL: oft n N =connoisseurs

cohabit /koʊhæbɪt/ **cohabits, cohabiting, cohabited.** If two people **are cohabiting**, they are living together and have a sexual relationship, but are not married; a formal word. *In Italy people hardly ever cohabit... The dentist left his wife of 15 years and openly cohabited with his receptionist... Any solicitor will tell you, if you're cohabiting and the man leaves you, you haven't got a leg to stand on.* ♦ **cohabitation** /koʊhæbɪteɪʃən/ *The decline in marriage has been offset by a rise in cohabitation.* ◆◇◇◇◇ V-RECIP; pl-n V; V *with*n; V (non-recip); N-UNCOUNT

cohere /koʊhɪəʳ/ **coheres, cohering, cohered.** If the different elements of a piece of writing, a piece of music, or a set of ideas **cohere**, they fit together well so that they form a united whole. *Opposed cultures, indigenous and imported, had no hope of cohering... We make sense of particular beliefs only as they cohere with other beliefs... It failed to cohere as a single work.* V-RECIP =hang together; pl-n V; V *with*n; V (non-recip)

coherence /koʊhɪərəns/. **Coherence** is a state or situation in which all the parts or ideas fit together well so that they form a united whole. *The anthology has a surprising sense of coherence.* ◆◇◇◇◇ N-UNCOUNT

coherent /koʊhɪərənt/ ◆◇◇◇◇

1 If something is **coherent**, it is well planned, so that it is clear and sensible and all its parts go well with each other. *He has failed to work out a coherent strategy for modernising the service... The President's policy is perfectly coherent.* ♦ **coherence** *The campaign was widely criticised for making tactical mistakes and for a lack of coherence.* ♦ **coherently** *The government has to convince voters it is proceeding coherently toward its goals.* ADJ-GRADED ≠muddled; N-UNCOUNT; ADV: ADV with v, ADV adj

2 If someone is **coherent**, they express their thoughts in a clear and calm way, so that other people can understand what they are saying. *He's so calm when he answers questions in interviews. I wish I could be that coherent.* ♦ **coherence** *This was debated eagerly at first, but with diminishing coherence as the champagne took hold.* ♦ **coherently** *He talked coherently.* ADJ-GRADED: v-link ADJ ≠incoherent; N-UNCOUNT; ADV-GRADED

cohesion /koʊhiːʒən/. If there is **cohesion** within a society, organization, or group, the different members fit together well and form a united whole. *By 1990, it was clear that the cohesion of the armed forces was rapidly breaking down...* ◆◇◇◇◇ N-UNCOUNT =cohesiveness

The group's teaching and methods threatened social cohesion.

cohesive /koʊhiːsɪv/. Something that is **cohesive** consists of parts that fit together well and form a united whole. *'Daring Adventures from '86' is a far more cohesive and successful album... Huston had assembled a remarkably cohesive and sympathetic cast.* ♦ **cohesiveness** *They had no group cohesiveness. They were in competition with each other all the time.* ♦◇◇◇◇ ADJ-GRADED N-UNCOUNT

cohort /koʊhɔːʳt/ **cohorts** ♦◇◇◇◇

1 A person's **cohorts** are their companions, supporters, or associates; used showing disapproval. *Drake and his cohorts were not pleased with my appointment.* N-COUNT: usu poss N PRAGMATICS

2 A **cohort** of people is a group who have something in common. **Cohort** is used especially when a group is being looked at as a whole for statistical purposes. *Tests were carried out by teachers on the entire cohort of eight to nine year-olds in their third year at primary school... She speaks for a whole cohort of young Japanese writers.* N-COUNT: usu with supp

coiffed /kwɑːft/. If someone has neatly **coiffed** hair, their hair is very carefully arranged; a formal word. *Her hair was perfectly coiffed.* ADJ: usu adv ADJ

coiffure /kwɑːfjʊəʳ/ **coiffures.** A person's **coiffure** is their hairstyle; a formal word. *...her immaculate golden coiffure.* N-COUNT

coiffured /kwɑːfjʊəʳd/. **Coiffured** means the same as **coiffed**; a formal word. ADJ: usu adv ADJ

coil /kɔɪl/ **coils, coiling, coiled** ♦◇◇◇◇

1 A **coil** of rope or wire is a length of it that has been wound into a series of loops. *Tod shook his head angrily and slung the coil of rope over his shoulder... The steel arrives at the factory in coils.* N-COUNT: oft N *of* n

2 A **coil** is one loop in a series of loops. *Pythons kill by tightening their coils so that their victim cannot breathe.* N-COUNT

3 A **coil** is a thick spiral of wire through which an electrical current passes. N-COUNT

4 In a vehicle, the **coil** is the part on a petrol engine that sends electricity to the spark plugs. N-COUNT

5 The **coil** is a contraceptive device used by women. It is fitted inside a woman's womb, usually for several months or years. N-COUNT: usu *the* N in sing =IUD

6 If you **coil** something, you wind it into a series of loops or into the shape of a ring. If it **coils** around something, it forms loops or a ring. *He turned off the water and began to coil the hose... Louisa was dancing, spinning by herself, her skirt flying out and coiling around her feet... A huge rattlesnake lay coiled on the blanket.* ► **Coil up** means the same as **coil**. *Once we have the wire, we can coil it up into the shape of a spring... Her hair was coiled up on top of her head.* V-ERG V n V prep/adv V-ed PHRASAL VERB V n P V-ed P Also V P n (not pron)

coiled /kɔɪld/. **Coiled** means in the form of a series of loops. *...a heavy coiled spring. ...special coiled kettle flexes.* ADJ: ADJ n

coin /kɔɪn/ **coins, coining, coined** ♦♦◇◇◇

1 A **coin** is a small piece of metal which is used as money. *...50 pence coins. ...Frederick's gold coin collection.* N-COUNT

2 If you **coin** a word or a phrase, you are the first person to say it. *Jaron Lanier coined the term 'virtual reality' and pioneered its early development... The word 'lunatic' was coined to describe people who went mad at the full moon.* VERB V n

3 If you say that someone **is coining** it or **is coining** money, you are emphasizing that they are making a lot of money very quickly, often without really earning it; an informal use. *Many private colleges are coining it... One wine shop is coining money selling Wembley-label champagne.* ► **Coining in** means the same as **coining**. *She's coining it in with a $10 million contract with Revlon.* VB: usu cont PRAGMATICS V *it* V n PHRASAL VERB V *it* P

4 You say **'to coin a phrase'** to show that you realize you are making a pun or using a cliché. *Fifty local musicians have, to coin a phrase, banded together to form the Jazz Umbrella.* PHRASES PRAGMATICS

5 If you talk about **the other side of the coin,** you are talking about a different, often contradictory, aspect of a situation. *It's short, but the other side of the coin is that it's very light.* PHR with cl PRAGMATICS

6 If you say that two things are **two sides of the same coin**, you mean that they are different ways of looking at or dealing with the same situation. *The minister reportedly stressed that economic and political reforms were two sides of the same coin.* usu v-link PHR

coinage /kɔɪnɪdʒ/

1 **Coinage** is the coins which are used in a country. *The city produced its own coinage from 1325 to 1864. ...the world's finest collection of medieval European coinage.* N-UNCOUNT

2 **Coinage** is the system of money used in a country. *It took four years for Britain just to decimalise its own coinage.* N-UNCOUNT

coincide /koʊɪnsaɪd/ **coincides, coinciding, coincided** ♦♦◇◇◇

1 If one event **coincides** with another, they happen at the same time. *The exhibition coincides with the 50th anniversary of his death... Although his mental illness had coincided with his war service it had not been caused by it... The beginning of the solar and lunar years coincided every 13 years.* V-RECIP V *with* n pl-n V

2 If the ideas or interests of two or more people **coincide**, they are the same. *The kids' views on life don't always coincide, but they're not afraid of voicing their opinions. ...a case in which public and private interests coincide... He gave great encouragement to his students, especially if their passions happened to coincide with his own.* V-RECIP pl-n V V *with* n

coincidence /koʊɪnsɪdəns/ **coincidences.** A **coincidence** is when two or more similar or related events occur at the same time by chance and without any planning. *Mr. Berry said the timing was a coincidence and that his decision was unrelated to Mr. Roman's departure. ...a string of amazing coincidences... The premises of Chabert and Sons were situated by the river and, by coincidence, not too far away from where Eric Talbot had met his death.* ♦♦◇◇◇ N-VAR

coincident /koʊɪnsɪdənt/

1 **Coincident** events happen at the same time; a formal use. *...coincident birth times... Coincident with her marriage to Ambassador Davies and his posting to Moscow, she began buying Russian art.* ADJ: oft v-link ADJ *with* N

2 **Coincident** opinions, ideas, or policies are the same or are very similar to each other; a formal use. *The purposes and goals of the US are coincident with the purposes and goals of the UN Security Council. ...the coincident views between the British development economists D. Seers and P. Streeten.* ADJ-GRADED: oft v-link ADJ *with* N

coincidental /koʊɪnsɪdentəl/. Something that is **coincidental** is the result of a coincidence and has not been deliberately arranged. *Any resemblance to actual persons, places or events is purely coincidental... I think that it is not coincidental that we now have arguably the best bookshops in the world.* ADJ: usu v-link ADJ, oft *it* v-link ADJ that

coincidentally /koʊɪnsɪdentli/. You use **coincidentally** when you want to draw attention to a coincidence. *Coincidentally, I had once found myself in a similar situation... They immediately got in touch with Dr Ting who was, purely coincidentally, also in California... Two Manchester City fans, Geoff Watts and Howard Davies, coincidentally wrote similar letters to the club.* ♦◇◇◇◇ ADV: usu ADV with cl/group, also ADV before v

coir /kɔɪəʳ/. **Coir** is a rough material made from coconut shells which is used to make ropes and mats. N-UNCOUNT

coital /koʊɪtəl/. **Coital** means connected with or relating to sexual intercourse; a technical term. *Many women say that this is the only coital position in which they can achieve an orgasm. ...coital techniques.* ADJ: ADJ n

coitus /koʊɪtəs/. **Coitus** is sexual intercourse; a technical term. N-UNCOUNT

coke /koʊk/ ♦◇◇◇◇

1 **Coke** is a solid black substance that is produced from coal and is burned as a fuel. *...a coke-burning stove.* N-UNCOUNT

2 **Coke** is the same as cocaine; an informal use. N-UNCOUNT

col., cols. **col.** is a written abbreviation for 'column' and 'colour'.

Col. **Col.** is a written abbreviation for 'Colonel' when 'Colonel' is being used as a title in front of someone's name. *Col Frank Weldon was a truly outstanding horseman.* ◆◇◇◇◇ N-TITLE

cola /koʊlə/ **colas.** **Cola** is a sweet brown non-alcoholic fizzy drink. *...a can of cola.* ◆◆◇◇◇ N-MASS

colada /kɒlɑːdə/ **coladas.** See **pina colada.**

colander /kɒləndə, kʌl-/ **colanders.** A **colander** is a bowl-shaped container with holes in it which you wash or drain food in. N-COUNT

cold /koʊld/ **colder, coldest; colds** ◆◆◆◆◇

1 Something that is **cold** has a very low temperature or a lower temperature than is normal or acceptable. *Rinse the vegetables under cold running water... He likes his tea neither too hot nor too cold... Your dinner's getting cold.* ♦ **coldness** *She complained about the coldness of his hands.* ADJ-GRADED ≠hot, warm; N-UNCOUNT ≠warmth

2 If it is **cold**, or if a place is **cold**, the temperature of the air is very low. *It was bitterly cold... The house is cold because I can't afford to turn the heat on... This is the coldest winter I can remember.* ♦ **coldness** *Within quarter of an hour the coldness of the night had gone.* ADJ-GRADED: oft *it* v-link ADJ ≠hot, warm; N-UNCOUNT: usu with supp

3 Cold weather or low temperatures can be referred to as the **cold**. *He must have come inside to get out of the cold... His feet were blue with cold.* N-UNCOUNT: also *the* N ≠heat

4 If you are **cold**, your body is at an unpleasantly low temperature. *I was freezing cold... I'm hungry, I'm cold and I've nowhere to sleep.* ADJ-GRADED: usu v-link ADJ

5 **Cold** food, such as salad or meat that has been cooked and cooled, is not intended to be eaten hot. *A wide variety of hot and cold snacks will be available. ...cold meats.* ADJ: usu ADJ n ≠hot

6 **Cold** colours or **cold** light give an impression of coldness. *Generally, warm colours advance in painting and cold colours recede. ...the cold blue light from a streetlamp.* ADJ-GRADED ≠warm

7 If you say that someone is **cold**, you mean that they do not show much emotion, especially affection, and therefore seem unfriendly and unsympathetic. If you say that someone's voice is **cold**, you mean that they speak in an unfriendly unsympathetic way. *What a cold, unfeeling woman she was... 'Send her away,' Eve said in a cold, hard voice.* ♦ **coldly** *'I'll see you in the morning,' Hugh said coldly.* ♦ **coldness** *His coldness angered her.* ADJ-GRADED =unfeeling ≠warm; ADV-GRADED; N-UNCOUNT

8 A **cold** trail or scent is one which is old and therefore difficult to follow. *He could follow a cold trail over hard ground and even over stones.* ADJ-GRADED ≠fresh

9 If you say that someone is **cold** when they are trying to guess the answer to a question or puzzle, you mean that they are thinking about it in the wrong way and are going to give a wrong answer. ADJ-GRADED: v-link ADJ ≠close, warm

10 If you have a **cold**, you have a mild, very common illness which makes you sneeze a lot and gives you a sore throat or a cough. N-COUNT

11 See also **common cold**.

12 If you **catch cold**, or **catch a cold**, you become ill with a cold. *Let's dry our hair so's we don't catch cold.* PHRASES V inflects

13 If something **leaves** you **cold**, it fails to excite or interest you. *Lawrence is one of those writers who either excite you enormously or leave you cold.* V inflects

14 If someone is **out cold**, they are unconscious or sleeping very heavily. *She was out cold but still breathing.* v-link PHR

15 If you say that a person, group, or country has been left **out in the cold**, you mean that they have been ignored by others rather than being invited to take part in some activity with them. *Developing countries might be left out in the cold in current world trade talks.* PHR after v, v-link PHR

16 • **in cold blood**: see **blood.** • to **get cold feet**: see **foot.** • to **blow hot and cold**: see **hot.** • to **pour cold water on** something: see **water.**

cold-blooded

1 Someone who is **cold-blooded** does not show any pity or emotion; used showing disapproval. *...a cold-blooded murderer... This was a brutal and cold-blooded killing.* ♦ **cold-bloodedly** *He hated whites from the age of six, when they cold-bloodedly murdered his father.* ADJ-GRADED PRAGMATICS; ADV-GRADED: usu ADV with v

2 **Cold-blooded** animals have a body temperature that changes according to the surrounding temperature. Reptiles, for example, are cold-blooded; a technical use in biology. ADJ

cold comfort. If you say that a slightly encouraging fact or event is **cold comfort** to someone, you mean that it gives them little or no comfort because their situation is so difficult or unpleasant. *These figures may look good on paper but are cold comfort to the islanders themselves.* N-UNCOUNT: oft N *to/for* n

cold cream. **Cold cream** is a cream that people use for softening and cleaning their skin, especially skin on their face. N-UNCOUNT

cold cuts. In American English, **cold cuts** are thin slices of cooked meat which are served cold. N-PLURAL

cold fish. If you say that someone is a **cold fish**, you mean that you think that they are unfriendly and unemotional; used showing disapproval. N-SING PRAGMATICS

cold frame, cold frames. A **cold frame** is a wooden frame with a glass top in which you grow small plants to protect them from cold weather. N-COUNT

cold-hearted. A **cold-hearted** person does not feel any affection or compassion for other people; used showing disapproval. *That Harriet is a cold-hearted bitch.* ADJ-GRADED: usu ADJ n PRAGMATICS ≠warm-hearted

cold-shoulder, cold-shoulders, cold-shouldering, cold-shouldered

1 If one person gives another the **cold-shoulder**, they behave towards them in an unfriendly way, to show them that they do not care about them or that they want them to go away. *But when Gough looked to Haig for support, he was given the cold shoulder.* N-SING: usu *the* N

2 If one person **cold-shoulders** another, they give them the cold-shoulder. *Even her own party considered her shrewish and nagging, and cold-shouldered her in the corridors.* VERB V n

cold snap, cold snaps. A **cold snap** is a short period of cold and frosty weather. *...plants damaged during last week's cold snap.* N-COUNT: usu sing

cold sore, cold sores. **Cold sores** are small sore spots that sometimes appear on or near someone's lips and nose when they have a cold. N-COUNT

cold storage

1 If something such as food is put in **cold storage**, it is kept in an artificially cooled place in order to preserve it. *The strawberries are picked before they are ripe and kept in cold storage to prevent them spoiling during transportation.* N-UNCOUNT

2 If you put an idea or plan **into cold storage** or **in cold storage**, you postpone it for a while rather than acting on it as you originally intended. *A few years ago I was asked by a publisher to consider writing a novel, and the idea has been in cold storage ever since.* PHRASE: v-link PHR, PHR after v

cold store, cold stores. A **cold store** is a building or room which is artificially cooled so that food can be preserved in it. N-COUNT

cold sweat, cold sweats. If you are in a **cold sweat**, you are sweating and feel cold, usually because you are very afraid or nervous. *He awoke from his sleep in a cold sweat.* N-COUNT: usu sing, usu *in/into* N

cold turkey. **Cold turkey** is the unpleasant physical reaction that people experience when they suddenly stop taking a drug that they have become addicted to; an informal use. *We'd go through three days of cold turkey and then she would do the run to London to buy more.* N-UNCOUNT

Cold War; also spelled **cold war.** When people refer to **the Cold War**, they are referring to the situation of extreme political hostility and tension which existed between the Soviet bloc and the United States together with its allies in the period after the Second World War and before Perestroika. *...the end of the cold war and the collapse of communism. ...the first major crisis of the post-Cold War era.* ◆◆◇◇◇ N-PROPER: *the* N

coleslaw /koʊlslɔː/. **Coleslaw** is a salad of chopped cabbage, carrots, onions, and other vegetables, mixed together in mayonnaise. N-UNCOUNT

colic /kɒlɪk/. **Colic** is an illness in which you get severe pains in your stomach and bowels. Babies especially suffer from colic. *The doctor said it was colic and that she would grow out of it.* N-UNCOUNT

colicky /kɒlɪki/. If someone, especially a baby, is **colicky**, they are suffering from colic. ADJ-GRADED

colitis /kəlaɪtɪs/. **Colitis** is an illness in which your colon becomes inflamed. N-UNCOUNT

collaborate /kəlæbəreɪt/ **collaborates, collaborating, collaborated** ◆◇◇◇◇

1 When one person or group **collaborates** with another, they work together, especially on a book or on some research. *Much later he collaborated with his son Michael on the English translation of a text on food production... The government is prodding Japan's aircraft firms to collaborate with more foreigners... He turned his country house into a place where professionals and amateurs collaborated in the making of music... The two men met and agreed to collaborate.* V-RECIP; V *with* n *on/in* n/-ing; V *with* n; pl-n V *on/in* n/-ing; pl-n V; Also pl-n V to-inf, V *with* n to-inf

2 If someone **collaborates** with the enemy during the war, he or she helps them; used showing disapproval. *He was accused of having collaborated with the Communist secret police.* VERB; PRAGMATICS; V *with* n; Also V

collaboration /kəlæbəreɪʃən/ **collaborations** ◆◆◇◇◇

1 **Collaboration** is the act of working together to produce a piece of work, especially a book or some research. *There is substantial collaboration with neighbouring departments... Close collaboration between the Bank and the Fund is not merely desirable, it is essential. ...scientific collaborations... Drummond was working on a book in collaboration with Zodiac Mindwarp.* N-VAR: oft N *with* n, N *between* pl-n, *in* N

2 A **collaboration** is a piece of work that has been produced as the result of people or groups working together. *He was also a writer of beautiful stories, some of which are collaborations with his fiancee.* N-COUNT: usu N *between* pl-n, N *with* n

3 **Collaboration** is the act of helping the enemy during the war; used showing disapproval. *...rumors of his collaboration with the occupying forces during the war.* N-UNCOUNT: usu with supp, oft N *with* n; PRAGMATICS

collaborationist /kəlæbəreɪʃənɪst/. A **collaborationist** government or individual is one that helps or gives support to the enemy during the war; used showing disapproval. *Quinn continued to head the collaborationist government for the duration of the war.* ADJ: usu ADJ n; PRAGMATICS

collaborative /kəlæbərətɪv, AM -reɪt-/. A **collaborative** piece of work is done by two or more people or groups working together; a formal word. *...a collaborative research project... 'The First Day' is their first collaborative album.* ◆◇◇◇◇ ADJ: ADJ n
♦ **collaboratively** *He was not the kind of artist who worked collaboratively.* ADV: ADV with v

collaborator /kəlæbəreɪtəʳ/ **collaborators** ◆◇◇◇◇

1 A **collaborator** is someone that you work with to produce a piece of work, especially a book or some research. *The Irvine group and their collaborators are testing whether lasers do the job better.* N-COUNT: oft poss N

2 A **collaborator** is someone who helps the enemy during the war; used showing disapproval. *Two alleged collaborators were shot dead by masked activists.* N-COUNT; PRAGMATICS

collage /kɒlɑːʒ, AM kəlɑːʒ/ **collages** ◆◇◇◇◇

1 A **collage** is a picture that has been made by sticking pieces of coloured paper and cloth onto paper. N-COUNT

2 **Collage** is the method of making pictures by sticking pieces of coloured paper and cloth onto paper. N-UNCOUNT

3 You can refer to something that has been made by combining a number of very different things as a **collage** of a particular kind. *Rego's work is a rich collage of 20th-century painting styles.* N-COUNT: usu N *of* n

collagen /kɒlədʒən/. **Collagen** is a protein that is found in the bodies of people and animals. It is often used as an ingredient in cosmetics or is injected into the face in cosmetic surgery, in order to make the skin look younger. *The collagen that is included in face creams comes from animal skin. ...collagen injections.* ◆◇◇◇◇ N-UNCOUNT

collapse /kəlæps/ **collapses, collapsing, collapsed** ◆◆◆◆◇

1 If a building or other structure **collapses**, it falls down very suddenly. *A section of the Bay Bridge had collapsed... The roof collapsed in a roar of rock and rubble... Most of the deaths were caused by landslides and collapsing buildings.* VERB; V; V-ing
▶ Also a noun. *Governor Deukmejian called for an inquiry into the freeway's collapse.* N-UNCOUNT

2 If something, for example a system or institution, **collapses**, it fails or comes to an end completely and suddenly. *His business empire collapsed under a massive burden of debt... Communism has collapsed in Eastern Europe... The rural people have been impoverished by a collapsing economy.* VERB; V; V-ing
▶ Also a noun. *The coup's collapse has speeded up the drive to independence... Their economy is teetering on the brink of collapse.* N-UNCOUNT

3 If you **collapse**, you suddenly faint or fall down because you are very ill or weak. *He collapsed following a vigorous exercise session at his home... It's commonplace to see people collapsing from hunger in the streets.* VERB; V
▶ Also a noun. *A few days after his collapse he was sitting up in bed.* N-UNCOUNT

4 If you **collapse** onto something, you sit or lie down suddenly because you are very tired. *She arrived home exhausted and barely capable of showering before collapsing on her bed.* VERB; V prep; Also V

5 If something with air inside **collapses**, it falls inwards and becomes smaller or flatter. *He plunged 300ft to the ground when his parachute collapsed... He was rushed to hospital last week after suffering a collapsed lung.* VERB; V; V-ed

collapsible /kəlæpsɪbəl/. A **collapsible** object is designed to be folded flat when it is not being used. *...a collapsible chair.* ADJ: usu ADJ n =folding

collar /kɒləʳ/ **collars, collaring, collared** ◆◆◇◇◇

1 The **collar** of a shirt or coat is the part which fits round the neck and is usually folded over. *His tie was pulled loose and his collar hung open. ...a coat with a huge fake fur collar.* ● See also **blue-collar**, **dog-collar**, **white-collar**. N-COUNT

2 A **collar** is a band of leather or plastic which is put round the neck of a dog or cat. N-COUNT

3 If you **collar** someone who has done something wrong or who is running away, you catch them and hold them so that they cannot escape; an informal use. *As Kerr fled towards the exit, Boycott collared him at the ticket barrier.* VERB =grab; V n

4 If you **collar** someone, you stop them and make them listen to you; an informal use. *Beattie managed to collar Atkins in a hallway... Bernard was once collared by an aggressive stranger in Soho.* VERB; V n

5 If someone **gets hot under the collar** about something, they get very annoyed, angry, or excited about it; an informal expression. *Some of you were getting very hot under the collar about Royals.* PHRASE: V inflects, oft PHR *about* n

collar bone, collar bones; also spelled **collarbone**. Your **collar bones** are the two long bones which run from the base of your neck to your shoulders. *Harold had a broken collarbone.* N-COUNT

collarless /kɒləʳləs/. A **collarless** shirt or jacket has no collar. ADJ: ADJ n

collate /kəleɪt/ **collates, collating, collated.** When you **collate** pieces of information, you gather them all together and examine them. *Roberts has spent much of his working life collating the data on which the study was based... They have begun to collate their own statistics on racial abuse.* ◆◇◇◇◇ VERB; V n
♦ **collation** /kəleɪʃən/ *Many countries have no laws governing the collation of personal information.* N-UNCOUNT: oft N *of* n

collateral /kəlætərəl/. **Collateral** is money or property which is used as a guarantee that someone will repay a loan; a formal word. *Many people use personal assets as collateral for small business loans... Most people here cannot borrow from banks because they lack collateral.* ◆◇◇◇◇ N-UNCOUNT: oft *as* N =security

collateral damage. **Collateral damage** is unintentional injury to civilians or damage to civil- N-UNCOUNT ian buildings which occurs during a military operation; a euphemistic expression. *To minimize collateral damage maximum precision in bombing was required.*

colleague /kɒliːg/ **colleagues.** Your **colleagues** are the people you work with, especially in a professional job. *Without consulting his colleagues he flew from Lisbon to Split... A colleague urged him to see a psychiatrist, but Faulkner refused.* ◆◆◆◆◇ N-COUNT: oft with poss

collect /kəlekt/ **collects, collecting, collected.** The pronunciation /kɒlɪkt/ is used for the noun. ◆◆◆◆◇

1 If you **collect** a number of things, you bring them together from several places or from several people. *Two young girls were collecting firewood... Elizabeth had been collecting snails for a school project... 1.5 million signatures have been collected.* VERB =gather; V n

2 If you **collect** things, such as stamps or books, as a hobby, you get a large number of them over a period of time because they interest you. *I used to collect stamps... One of Tony's hobbies was collecting rare birds.* ♦ **collecting** *...hobbies like stamp collecting and fishing.* VERB; V n; N-UNCOUNT: with supp, oft n N

3 When you **collect** someone or something, you go and get them from a place where they are waiting for you or have been left for you. *David always collects Alistair from school on Wednesdays... She had just collected her pension from the post office... After collecting the cash, the kidnapper made his escape down the disused railway line.* VERB =pick up; V n *from* n; V n

4 If a substance **collects** somewhere, or something **collects** it, it keeps arriving over a period of time and is held in that place or thing. *Methane gas does collect in the mines around here. ...water tanks which collect rainwater from the house roof.* V-ERG; V prep/adv; V n; Also V

5 If something **collects** light, energy, or heat, it attracts it. *Like a telescope it has a curved mirror to collect the sunlight.* VERB; V n

6 If you **collect** for a charity or for a present for someone, you ask people to give you money for it. *Are you collecting for charity?... They collected donations for a fund to help military families.* VERB; V *for* n; V n *for* n; Also V n

7 If you **collect** yourself or **collect** your thoughts, you make an effort to calm yourself or prepare yourself mentally. *She paused for a moment to collect herself... He was grateful for a chance to relax and collect his thoughts.* VERB =compose; V pron-refl; V n

8 In American English, a **collect call** is a telephone call that is paid for by the person receiving it, not the person making it. *She received a collect phone call from Alaska.* ● In American English, if you **call collect** when you make a telephone call, the person who you are phoning pays the cost of the call and not you. The usual British term is to **reverse the charges**. *Should you lose your ticket call collect on STA's helpline.* ADJ: ADJ n; PHRASE: V inflects

collect up. If you **collect up** things, you bring them all together, usually when you have finished using them. *Would you go and collect up the dishes?... Harold had all the copies collected up and burned.* PHRASAL VERB; V P n (not pron); Also V n P

collectable /kəlektəbᵊl/ **collectables;** also spelled **collectible**. A **collectable** object is one which is valued very highly by collectors because it is rare or beautiful. *Visitors will be impressed with the enormous range of collectable objets d'art on offer... Many of these cushions have survived and are very collectible.* ► **Collectables** are collectable objects. *Jane Pollock Antiques deals in silver and small collectables.* ADJ-GRADED; N-COUNT: usu pl

collected /kəlektɪd/ ◆◆◇◇◇

1 An author's **collected** works or letters are all their works or letters published in one book or in a set of books. *...the collected works of Rudyard Kipling... His collected poems have just been published.* ADJ: ADJ n =complete

2 If you say that someone is **collected**, you mean that they are very calm and self-controlled, especially when they are in a difficult or serious situation. *Police say she was cool and collected during her interrogation.* ADJ-GRADED: usu v-link ADJ

3 See also **collect**.

collectible /kəlektɪbᵊl/ **collectibles.** See **collectable**.

collecting /kəlektɪŋ/. A **collecting** tin or box is one that is used to collect money for charity. *Volunteers with collecting tins will be on street corners everywhere.* ● See also **collect**. ADJ: ADJ n

collection /kəlekʃᵊn/ **collections** ◆◆◆◆◇

1 A **collection** of things is a group of similar things that you have deliberately acquired, usually over a period of time. *Robert's collection of prints and paintings has been bought over the years... The Art Gallery of Ontario has the world's largest collection of sculptures by Henry Moore... He made the mistake of leaving his valuable record collection with a former sweetheart.* N-COUNT: oft N *of* n

2 A **collection** of stories, poems, or articles is a number of them published in one book. *Two years ago he published a collection of short stories called 'Facing The Music'... The Brookings Institution has assembled a collection of essays from foreign affairs experts.* N-COUNT: oft N *of* n

3 A **collection** of things is a group of things. *Wye Lea is a collection of farm buildings that have been converted into an attractive complex.* N-COUNT: usu N *of* n

4 A fashion designer's new **collection** consists of the new clothes they have designed for the next season. *Neither Armani nor Valentino's new collections will be available here for a while.* N-COUNT

5 **Collection** is the act of collecting something from a place or from people. *Money can be sent to any one of 22,000 agents worldwide for collection. ...computer systems to speed up collection of information. ...public services including mail delivery and garbage collection.* N-UNCOUNT

6 If you organize a **collection** for charity, you collect money from people to give to charity. *I asked my headmaster if he could arrange a collection for a refugee charity.* N-COUNT

7 A **collection** is money that is given by people in church during some Christian services. N-COUNT

collective /kəlektɪv/ **collectives** ◆◆◆◇◇

1 **Collective** actions, situations, or feelings involve or are shared by every member of a group of people. *It was a collective decision... The country's politicians are already heaving a collective sigh of relief.* ♦ **collectively** *They collectively decided to recognize the changed situation... The Cabinet is collectively responsible for policy.* ADJ: ADJ n =joint; ADV: oft ADV with cl

2 A **collective** amount of something is the total obtained by adding together the amounts that each person or thing in a group has. *Their collective volume wasn't very large.* ♦ **collectively** *In 1968 the states collectively spent $2 billion on it.* ADJ: ADJ n =combined; ADV: ADV with v

3 The **collective** term for two or more types of thing is a general word or expression which refers to all of them. *Social science is a collective name, covering a series of individual sciences.* ♦ **collectively** *...other sorts of cells (known collectively as white corpuscles).* ADJ: ADJ n; ADV: ADV with v

4 A **collective** is a business or farm which is run, and often owned, by a group of people. *He will see that he is participating in all the decisions of the collective.* N-COUNT =co-operative

collective bargaining. When a trade union engages in **collective bargaining**, it has talks with an employer about its members' pay and working conditions. N-UNCOUNT

collective noun, collective nouns. A **collective noun** is a noun such as 'family' or 'team' that refers to a group of people or things. When it is used in the singular, the noun can take a singular or plural verb. Many collective nouns are followed by 'of', as in 'a swarm of bees' or 'a flock of sheep'. There is often a restriction on which collective noun you can use when referring to a particular type of animal, person, or thing. N-COUNT

collective unconscious. The **collective unconscious** is the basic ideas and images that some psychologists believe that people share because they have inherited them. N-SING: usu *the* N

collectivise /kəlektɪvaɪz/. See **collectivize**.

collectivism /kəlektɪvɪzəm/. **Collectivism** is the political belief that a country's industries and services should be owned and controlled by the state or by all the people in a country. Socialism and communism are both forms of collectivism. N-UNCOUNT

collectivist /kəlektɪvɪst/. **Collectivist** means relating to collectivism. *...collectivist ideals. ...anti-collectivist groups.* ADJ: usu ADJ n

collectivize /kəlektɪvaɪz/ **collectivizes, collectivizing, collectivized;** also spelled **collectivise** in British English. If farms or factories are **collectivized**, they are brought under state ownership and control, usually by combining a number of small farms or factories into one large one. *Virtually all of the largest businesses were collectivized in the first couple of months of the war... He forced the country to collectivize agriculture and industrialize. ...large collectivised farms.* VERB be V-ed V n V-ed

♦ **collectivization** /kəlektɪvaɪzeɪʃən/ *In the late 20s he oversaw the forced collectivisation of agriculture. ...opponents of collectivization.* N-UNCOUNT: oft N of n

collector /kəlektəʳ/ **collectors** ◆◆◇◇◇

1 A **collector** is a person who collects things of a particular type as a hobby. *...a stamp-collector. ...a respected collector of Indian art... His work is much sought after by collectors.* N-COUNT: oft n N, N of n

2 You can use **collector** to refer to someone whose job is to take something such as money, tickets, or rubbish from people. For example, a rent **collector** collects rent from tenants. *He earned his living as a tax collector. ...a garbage collector.* N-COUNT: with supp, usu n N

collector's item, collector's items. A **collector's item** is an object which is highly valued by collectors because it is rare or beautiful. *Someone once told me that this camera was rare and possibly a collector's item.* N-COUNT

college /kɒlɪdʒ/ **colleges** ◆◆◆◆◇

1 A **college** is an institution where students study after they have left school. *Their daughter Joanna is doing business studies at a local college... Stephanie took up making jewellery after leaving art college this summer... He is now a professor of economics at Western New England College in Springfield, Massachussetts.* N-VAR: oft in names

2 A **college** is one of the institutions which some British universities are divided into. *He was educated at Balliol College, Oxford.* N-COUNT: oft in names after n

3 **College** is used in Britain in the names of some secondary schools which charge fees. *In 1854, Cheltenham Ladies College became the first girls' public school.* N-IN-NAMES

4 A **college** of a particular kind is an organized group of people who have special duties and powers; a formal use. *He is a member of the Royal College of Physicians... There is a college of international supervisors working together.* N-COUNT: with supp, oft in names

collegiate /kəliːdʒiət/. **Collegiate** means belonging or relating to a college or to college students; used mainly in American English. *The 1933 national collegiate football championship was won by Michigan. ...collegiate life.* ◆◇◇◇◇ ADJ: ADJ n =college

collide /kəlaɪd/ **collides, colliding, collided** ◆◇◇◇◇

1 If two or more moving people or objects **collide**, they crash into one another. If a moving person or object **collides** with a stationary person or object, they crash into them. *Two trains collided head-on in north-eastern Germany early this morning... Racing up the stairs, he almost collided with Daisy... He collided with a pine tree near the North Gate.* V-RECIP pl-n V V with n V with n (non-recip)

2 If the aims, opinions, or interests of one person or group **collide** with those of another person or group, they are very different from each other and are therefore opposed. *The aims of the negotiators in New York again seem likely to collide with the aims of the warriors in the field... In the next two years, Nasser regularly collided with the different Western powers, who refused to arm him... What happens when the two interests collide will make a fascinating spectacle.* V-RECIP =clash V with n pl-n V

collie /kɒli/ **collies.** A **collie** or a **collie dog** is a dog with long hair and a long, narrow muzzle. N-COUNT

colliery /kɒljəri/ **collieries.** In British English, a **colliery** is a coal mine and all the buildings and equipment which are connected with it. ◆◇◇◇◇ N-COUNT =pit

collision /kəlɪʒən/ **collisions** ◆◆◇◇◇

1 A **collision** occurs when a moving object crashes into something. *They were on their way to the Shropshire Union Canal when their van was involved in a collision with a car... I saw a head-on collision between two aeroplanes.* N-VAR: oft N with/between n =crash

2 A **collision** of cultures or ideas occurs when two very different cultures or people meet and conflict. *It's the collision of disparate ideas that alters one's perspective... The play represents the collision of three generations.* N-COUNT: oft N of/between/with n =clash

collision course

1 If two or more people or things are on a **collision course**, there is likely to be a sudden and violent disagreement between them. *The two communities are now on a collision course... Britain's universities are set on a collision course with the government.* N-SING: usu on a N, oft N with n

2 If two or more people or things are on a **collision course**, they are likely to meet and crash into each other violently. *There is an asteroid on a collision course with the Earth.* N-SING: usu on a N, oft N with n

collocate, collocates, collocating, collocated. The noun is pronounced /kɒləkət/. The verb is pronounced /kɒləkeɪt/.

1 A **collocate** of a particular word is another word which often occurs with that word; a technical term in linguistics. N-COUNT

2 If one word **collocates** with another, they often occur together; a technical term in linguistics. *'Detached' collocates with 'house'.* V-RECIP V with n Also pl-n V

collocation /kɒləkeɪʃən/ **collocations. Collocation** is the way that some words occur regularly whenever another word is used; a technical term in linguistics. *...the basic notion of collocation.* N-VAR

colloquial /kəloʊkwiəl/. **Colloquial** words and phrases are informal and are used mainly in conversation. *...a colloquial expression... His stumbling attempts at colloquial Russian amused her.* ADJ-GRADED

♦ **colloquially** *The people who write parking tickets in New York are known colloquially as 'brownies'.* ADV-GRADED: ADV with v

colloquialism /kəloʊkwiəlɪzəm/ **colloquialisms.** A **colloquialism** is a colloquial word or phrase. N-COUNT

colloquium /kəloʊkwiəm/ **colloquiums** or **colloquia** /kəloʊkwiə/. A **colloquium** is a large academic seminar; a formal word. N-COUNT

colloquy /kɒləkwi/ **colloquies.** A **colloquy** is a conversation or meeting; a formal word. *An observer would have thought he was witnessing a warm colloquy between lovers.* N-COUNT

collude /kəluːd/ **colludes, colluding, colluded.** If one person **colludes** with another, they cooperate with them secretly or illegally; used showing disapproval. *Several local officials are in jail on charges of colluding with the Mafia... My mother colluded in the myth of him as the swanky businessman... The store's 'no refunds' policy makes it harder for dishonest cashiers and customers to collude.* V-RECIP PRAGMATICS V with n V in n/-ing pl-n V Also pl-n V to-inf

collusion /kəluːʒən/. **Collusion** is secret or illegal cooperation, especially between countries or organizations; a formal word used showing disapproval. *He found no evidence of collusion between record companies and retailers... Some stockbrokers, in collusion with bank officials, obtained large sums of money for speculation.* ◆◇◇◇◇ N-UNCOUNT: usu N between pl-n, N with n, in N PRAGMATICS

collusive /kəluːsɪv/. **Collusive** behaviour involves secret or illegal cooperation, especially between countries or organizations; a formal word used showing disapproval. *Any evidence of collusive behaviour by the banks could be sent to the Office of Fair Trading. ...collusive business practices.* ADJ-GRADED: usu ADJ n PRAGMATICS

cologne /kəloun/ **colognes. Cologne** is a kind of weak perfume or aftershave. *She smelled of cologne and shampoo, clean and fresh.* ◆◇◇◇◇ N-MASS

Colombian /kəlʌmbiən/ **Colombians** ◆◆◆◆◇

1 **Colombian** means belonging or relating to Colombia or its people or culture. *...the Colombian coast. ...Colombian farmers.* ADJ

2 A **Colombian** is a Colombian citizen, or a person of Colombian origin. N-COUNT

colon /koulən/ **colons** ◆◇◇◇◇

1 A **colon** is a punctuation mark (:), which you can use in several ways. For example, you can put it before a list of things or before reported speech. N-COUNT

2 Your **colon** is the part of your intestine above your rectum. *In the US, there are 60,000 deaths a year from cancer of the colon.* N-COUNT

colonel /kɜːʳnəl/ **colonels.** A **colonel** is a senior officer in an army or air force. *This particular place was run by an ex-Army colonel. ...Colonel Edward Staley.* ◆◆◆◇◇ N-COUNT; N-TITLE; N-VOC

colonial /kəlouniəl/ **colonials** ◆◆◇◇◇

1 **Colonial** means relating to countries that are colonies, or to colonialism. *...the 31st anniversary of Jamaica's independence from British colonial rule. ...the colonial civil service.* ADJ: ADJ n

2 People who have lived for a long time in a colony but who belong to the colonizing country are sometimes referred to as **colonials**. *...a group of ex-colonials.* N-COUNT: usu pl

3 A **Colonial** building or piece of furniture was built or made in a style that was popular in America in the 17th and 18th centuries; used mainly in American English. *...the white colonial houses on the north side of the campus... I sat on the Colonial bench that was just to the left of the office doorway.* ADJ: usu ADJ n

colonialism /kəlouniəlɪzəm/. **Colonialism** is the practice by which a powerful country directly controls less powerful countries and uses their resources to increase its own power and wealth. *...the bitter oppression of slavery and colonialism... It is interesting to reflect why European colonialism ended.* ◆◇◇◇◇ N-UNCOUNT

colonialist /kəlouniəlɪst/ **colonialists**

1 **Colonialist** means relating to colonialism. *Earlier, the Cuban government had accused the Spanish Foreign Minister of colonialist attitudes. ...the European colonialist powers.* ADJ

2 A **colonialist** is a person who believes in colonialism or helps their country to get colonies. *The colonialists built economic, administrative, legal and social structures for the domination and exploitation of the people.* N-COUNT

colonist /kɒlənɪst/ **colonists. Colonists** are people who start a colony or who are among the first settlers to live in a colony. *The apple was brought over here by the colonists when they came. ...the early American colonists.* ◆◇◇◇◇ N-COUNT

colonize /kɒlənaɪz/ **colonizes, colonizing, colonized;** also spelled **colonise** in British English. ◆◇◇◇◇

1 If people **colonize** a foreign country, they go to live there and take control of it. *The first British attempt to colonize Ireland was in the twelfth century... Liberia was never colonised by the European powers... For more than 400 years, we were a colonized people.* ♦ **colonizer, colonizers** *To the former Belgian colonizers, Rwanda was a paradise.* ♦ **colonization** /kɒlənaɪzeɪʃən/ *...the European colonization of America.* VERB V n V-ed; N-COUNT: usu pl; N-UNCOUNT: usu with supp

2 When large numbers of animals **colonize** a place, they go to live there and make it their home. *Toads are colonising the whole place.* VERB V n

3 When an area **is colonized** by a type of plant, the plant grows there in large amounts. *The area was then colonized by scrub.* VB: usu passive be V-ed by n

colonnade /kɒləneɪd/ **colonnades.** A **colonnade** is a row of evenly spaced columns. *...a colonnade with stone pillars.* N-COUNT

colonnaded /kɒləneɪdɪd/. A **colonnaded** building has evenly spaced columns. ADJ: ADJ n

colony /kɒləni/ **colonies** ◆◆◇◇◇

1 A **colony** is a country which is controlled by a more powerful country. *In France's former North African colonies, anti-French feeling is growing... Puerto Rico, though it calls itself a Commonwealth, is really a self-governing American colony.* N-COUNT: usu supp N

2 You can refer to a place where a particular group of people lives as a particular kind of **colony**. *In 1932, he established a school and artists' colony in Stone City, Iowa. ...a penal colony. ...industrial colonies.* N-COUNT: usu with supp =settlement

3 In old-fashioned British English, **the colonies** means all the countries that used to be British colonies. *Many of our troops and officers were scattered around the world in the service of His Majesty in the colonies.* N-PLURAL: the N

4 A **colony** of birds, insects, or animals is a group of them that live together. *The Shetlands are famed for their colonies of sea birds... The caterpillars feed in large colonies.* N-COUNT: oft N of n

color /kʌləʳ/. See **colour**.

coloration /kʌləreɪʃən/. The **coloration** of an animal or a plant is the colours and patterns on it. *...plants with yellow or red coloration.* N-UNCOUNT

coloratura /kɒlərətʊərə, AM kʌl-/ **coloraturas**

1 **Coloratura** is very complicated and difficult music for a solo singer, especially in opera; a technical use. *She needs coloratura for her opening aria.* N-UNCOUNT

2 A **coloratura** is a singer, usually a woman, who is skilled at singing coloratura; a technical use. *...the world's leading coloratura soprano.* N-COUNT: oft N n

colorization /kʌləraɪzeɪʃən/; also spelled **colorisation** in British English. **Colorization** is a technique used to add colour to old black and white films. *...the colorization of old film classics.* N-UNCOUNT

colorized /kʌləraɪzd/. A **colorized** film is an old black and white film which has had colour added to it using a special technique. *The film is available in a colorized version.* ADJ: usu ADJ n

color line. If a black person breaks the **color line**, they take part in an activity or go to a place which is usually only for white people; used in American English. *Jackie Robinson will always be remembered as the man who broke the color line in baseball.* • See also **colour bar**. N-SING

colossal /kəlɒsəl/. If you describe something as **colossal**, you are emphasizing that it is very large. *There has been a colossal waste of public money... The task they face is colossal.* ♦ **colossally** *Their policies have been colossally destructive.* ◆◇◇◇◇ ADJ-GRADED PRAGMATICS =enormous, immense; ADV: ADV adj

colossus /kəlɒsəs/ **colossi** /kəlɒsaɪ/

1 If you describe someone or something as a **colossus**, you think that they are extremely important and great in ability or size; used mainly in journalism. *He was a colossus, a legend. ...saxophone colossus Sonny Rollins... He became a colossus of the labour movement.* N-COUNT: usu sing: oft N of n PRAGMATICS =giant

2 A **colossus** is an extremely large statue. N-COUNT

colostomy /kəlɒstəmi/ **colostomies.** A **colostomy** is a surgical operation in which a permanent opening from the colon is made; a medical term. N-COUNT

colour /kʌləʳ/ **colours, colouring, coloured;** spelled **color** in American English. ◆◆◆◆◆

1 The **colour** of something is the appearance that it has as a result of the way in which it reflects light. Red, blue, and green are colours. *'What colour is the car?' – 'Red.'... Her silk dress was sky-blue, the colour of her eyes... Judi's favourite colour is pink... The badges come in twenty different colours and shapes.* N-COUNT: usu with supp

2 A **colour** is a substance you use to give something a particular colour. Dyes and make-up are sometimes referred to as **colours**. *...The Body Shop Herbal Hair Colour... It is better to avoid all food colours. ...the latest lip and eye colours.* N-VAR

3 If you **colour** something, you use dyes, paint, or crayons to change its colour. *Many women begin colouring their hair in their mid-30s... We'd been making cakes and colouring the posters... The petals can be cooked with rice to colour it yellow.* ♦ **colouring** *They could not afford to spoil those maps by careless colouring.* VERB V n V n adj; N-UNCOUNT

4 If someone **colours**, their face becomes redder VERB

than it normally is, usually because they are embarrassed. *Andrew couldn't help noticing that she coloured slightly.* =blush V

5 Someone's **colour** is the colour of their skin. People often use **colour** in this way to refer to a person's race. *I don't care what colour she is... He acknowledged that Mr Taylor's colour and ethnic origins were utterly irrelevant in the circumstances.* N-COUNT: usu sing, oft poss N

6 A **colour** television, photograph, or picture is one that shows things in all their colours, and not just in black, white, and grey. *In Japan 99 per cent of all households now have a colour television set.* ADJ: usu ADJ n

7 **Colour** is a quality that makes something especially interesting or exciting. *She had resumed the travel necessary to add depth and colour to her novels.* • See also **local colour**. N-UNCOUNT

8 If something **colours** your opinion, it affects the way that you think about something. *All too often it is only the negative images of Ireland that are portrayed, colouring opinions and hiding the true nature of the country... The attitude of the parents toward the usefulness of what is learned must colour the way children approach school.* VERB =affect V n

9 A country's national **colours** are the colours of its national flag. *The Opera House is decorated with the Hungarian national colours: green, red and white.* N-PLURAL

10 People sometimes refer to a particular country's flag as that country's **colours**; a literary use. *Kuwaiti troops raised the country's colors in a special ceremony. ...the battalion's colours.* N-PLURAL: poss N

11 A sports team's **colours** are the colours of the clothes they wear when they play. *I was wearing the team's colours.* N-PLURAL

12 See also **coloured**, **colouring**.

13 If you pass a test **with flying colours**, you have done very well in the test. *So far McAllister seemed to have passed all the tests with flying colors.* PHRASES PHR after v

14 If a film or television programme is **in colour**, it has been made so that you see the picture in all its colours, and not just in black, white, or grey. *Was he going to show the film? Was it in colour?... You can go home afterwards and watch Inspector Morse in colour.* v-link PHR, PHR after v

15 If someone **nails** their **colours to the mast**, they say what they really think about something. *I shall nail my colours firmly to the mast on this subject—as a feminist I find movies like this offensive.* V inflects

16 If you **nail your colours to** someone's **mast**, or if you **nail your colours to** a particular **mast**, you show that you support a particular person or issue. *He has nailed his colours firmly to Mr Gorbachev's mast... Mr Major had at last nailed his colours to the European mast.* V inflects

17 If you say that you want to **see the colour of** someone's **money**, you mean that you are not prepared to sell them something or do something for them until they have proved that they have the money to pay for it. *He made a mental note never to enter into conversation with a customer until he'd at least seen the colour of his money.* V inflects

18 People **of colour** are people who belong to a race with dark skins. *Black communities spoke up to defend the rights of all people of color.* n PHR

19 If you see someone **in** their **true colours** or if they **show** their **true colours**, you realize what they are really like. *The children are seeing him in his true colours for the first time now... Here, the organization has had time to show its true colours, to show its inefficiency and its bungling.* PHR after v

colour in. If you **colour in** a drawing, you give it different colours using crayons or paints. *Someone had coloured in all the black and white pictures... Draw simple shapes for your child to colour in.* PHRASAL VERB V P n (not pron) Also V n P

colourant /kʌlərənt/ **colourants;** spelled **colorant** in American English. A **colourant** is a substance that is used to give something a particular colour. *...a new range of hair colourants.* N-COUNT

colour bar; spelled **color bar** in American English. A **colour bar** is a social system which does not allow black people to take part in the same activities or go to the same places as white people. *I understand you are operating a colour bar here.* • See also **color line**. N-SING

colour blind; spelled **color-blind** in American English.

1 Someone who is **colour blind** cannot see the difference between colours, especially between red and green. *Sixteen times as many men are colour blind as women.* ♦ **colour-blindness** *What exactly is colour-blindness and how do you find out if you have it?* ADJ: usu v-link ADJ; N-UNCOUNT

2 A **colour blind** system or organization does not discriminate against people because of their race or nationality. *...the introduction of more colour blind anti-poverty programmes... He said he wanted a color-blind government where everybody's treated the same.* ADJ

colour-coded; spelled **color-coded** in American English. Things that are **colour-coded** use colours to represent different features or functions. *The map is colour-coded and easy to follow... The contents are emptied into color-coded buckets.* ADJ

coloured /kʌləʳd/ **coloureds;** spelled **colored** in American English. ◆◆◆◇◇

1 Something that is **coloured** a particular colour is that colour. *The illustration shows a cluster of five roses coloured apricot orange. ...a cheap gold-coloured bracelet.* ADJ

2 Something that is **coloured** is a particular colour or combination of colours, rather than being just white, black, or the colour that it is naturally. *You can often choose between plain white or coloured and patterned scarves. ...brightly coloured silks laid out on market stalls.* ADJ

3 A **coloured** person belongs to a race of people with dark skins; an old-fashioned use which many people find offensive. ADJ: usu ADJ n

4 People whose skin is dark are sometimes referred to as **coloureds**; an old-fashioned use which many people find offensive. N-COUNT

colour fast; spelled **color fast** in American English. A fabric that is **colour fast** has a colour that will not fade when the fabric is washed or worn. ADJ

colourful /kʌləʳfʊl/; spelled **colorful** in American English. ◆◆◇◇◇

1 Something that is **colourful** has bright colours or a lot of different colours. *The flowers were colourful and the scenery magnificent... People wore colorful clothes and seemed to be having a good time.* ♦ **colourfully** *...the sight of dozens of colourfully dressed people.* ADJ-GRADED; ADV-GRADED

2 A **colourful** story is full of exciting details. *The story she told was certainly colourful, and extended over her life in England, Germany and Spain. ...the country's colourful and often violent history.* ADJ-GRADED

3 A **colourful** character is a person who behaves in an interesting and amusing way. *Casey Stengel was probably the most colorful character in baseball.* ADJ-GRADED: usu ADJ n

4 If someone has had a **colourful** past or a **colourful** career, they have been involved in exciting but often slightly shocking things. *More details surfaced of her colourful past as the story developed. ...a well-known City business man with a rather colourful background.* ADJ-GRADED: usu ADJ n

5 **Colourful** language is rude or offensive language. *Bryant is alleged to have used colourful language.* ADJ-GRADED: usu ADJ n =bad

colouring /kʌlərɪŋ/ also spelled **coloring**. ◆◇◇◇◇

1 The **colouring** of something is the colour or colours that it is. *Other countries vary the coloring of their bank notes as well as their size. ...the scenery was losing its bright colouring.* N-UNCOUNT: usu with poss

2 Someone's **colouring** is the colour of their hair, skin, and eyes. *None of them had their father's dark colouring... Choose shades which tone in with your natural colouring.* N-UNCOUNT: usu with poss

3 **Colouring** is a substance that is used to give colour to food. *A few drops of green food coloring were added.* N-UNCOUNT

4 See also **colour**.

colouring book, colouring books; spelled **coloring book** in American English. A **colouring book** is a book of simple drawings which children can colour in. N-COUNT

colourist /kʌlərɪst/ **colourists;** spelled **colorist** in American English.

1 A **colourist** is someone such as an artist or a fashion designer who uses colours in an interesting and original way. N-COUNT

2 A **colourist** is a hairdresser who specializes in colouring people's hair. N-COUNT

colourless /kʌlə'ləs/; spelled **colorless** in American English.

1 Something that is **colourless** has no colour at all. *A colourless, almost odourless liquid with a sharp, sweetish taste.* ADJ

2 If someone's face is **colourless**, it is very pale, usually because they are frightened, shocked, or ill. *Her face was colourless, and she was shaking... His complexion was colorless and he hadn't shaved.* ADJ: usu v-link ADJ

3 **Colourless** people or places are dull and uninteresting. *...the much more experienced but colourless General... We hurried through the colourless little town set on the fast-flowing Nyakchu.* ADJ-GRADED: usu ADJ n

colour scheme, colour schemes; spelled **color scheme** in American English. In a room or house, the **colour scheme** is the way in which colours have been used to decorate it. *I was so pleased with the yellow colour scheme that I chose a similar colour for the walls of the nursery.* ◆◇◇◇◇ N-COUNT

colour supplement, colour supplements. In British English, a **colour supplement** is a colour magazine which is one of the sections of a newspaper, especially at weekends. N-COUNT

colt /koʊlt/ **colts.** A **colt** is a young male horse. N-COUNT

coltish /koʊltɪʃ/. A young person or animal that is **coltish** is full of energy but clumsy or awkward, because they lack physical skill or control. *We're surrounded by teenagers with flat stomachs, coltish legs and manes of sunkissed hair.* ADJ-GRADED

column /kɒləm/ **columns** ◆◆◆◇◇

1 A **column** is a tall, often decorated cylinder of stone which is built as a monument or forms part of a building. *...a London landmark, Nelson's Column in Trafalgar Square.* N-COUNT =pillar

2 A **column** is something that has a tall narrow shape. *The explosion sent a column of smoke thousands of feet into the air.* N-COUNT: usu N *of* n

3 A **column** is a group of people or animals which moves in a long line. *There were reports of columns of military vehicles appearing on the streets.* N-COUNT: usu N *of* n

4 On a printed page such as a page of a dictionary, newspaper, or printed chart, a **column** is one of several vertical sections which are read downwards. *We had stupidly been looking at the wrong column of figures... In The Dictionary of Quotations, there are no fewer than one and a half columns devoted to 'kiss'.* N-COUNT

5 In a newspaper or magazine, a **column** is a section that is always written by the same person or is always about the same topic. *His name features frequently in the social columns of the tabloid newspapers... She also writes a regular column for the Times Educational Supplement.* N-COUNT: usu supp N

6 See also **agony column**, **gossip column**, **personal column**, **spinal column**, **steering column**.

columnist /kɒləmɪst/ **columnists.** A **columnist** is a journalist who regularly writes a particular kind of article in a newspaper or magazine. *Clarence Page is a columnist for the Chicago Tribune. ...the gossip columnists' favourite target.* ◆◆◇◇◇ N-COUNT: oft N *for* n

coma /koʊmə/ **comas.** Someone who is in a **coma** is in a state of deep unconsciousness. *She was in a coma for seven weeks... She had slipped into a coma by the time she reached hospital.* ◆◇◇◇◇ N-COUNT: usu *in/into* N

comatose /koʊmətoʊs/

1 A person who is **comatose** is in a coma; a medical use. *The right side of my brain had been so severely bruised that I was comatose for a month.* ADJ =unconscious

2 A person who is **comatose** is in a deep sleep, usually because they are tired or have drunk too much alcohol; an informal use. *Grandpa lies comatose on the sofa.* ADJ: oft ADJ after v

comb /koʊm/ **combs, combing, combed** ◆◇◇◇◇

1 A **comb** is a flat piece of plastic or metal with narrow pointed teeth along one side, which you use to tidy your hair. N-COUNT

2 When you **comb** your hair, you tidy it using a comb. *Salvatore combed his hair carefully... Her reddish hair was cut short and neatly combed.* VERB V n V-ed

3 If you **comb** a place, you search everywhere in it in order to find someone or something. *Officers combed the woods for the murder weapon... They fanned out and carefully combed the temple grounds.* VERB V n *for* n V n

4 If you **comb** through information, you look at it very carefully in order to find something. *Eight policemen then spent two years combing through the evidence.* VERB V *through* n

5 See also **fine-tooth comb**.

combat, combats, combating or **combatting, combated** or **combatted.** The noun is pronounced /kɒmbæt/. The verb is pronounced /kəmbæt/. ◆◆◆◇◇

1 **Combat** is fighting that takes place in a war. *Over 16 million men had died in combat... Yesterday saw hand-to-hand combat in the city. ...combat aircraft.* N-UNCOUNT

2 A **combat** is a battle, or a fight between two people. *It was the end of a long combat.* N-COUNT

3 If people in authority **combat** something, they try to stop it happening. *Congress has criticised new government measures to combat crime.* VERB V n

combatant /kɒmbətᵊnt, AM kəmbæt-/ **combatants.** A **combatant** is a person, group, or country that takes part in the fighting in a war. *I have never suggested that UN forces could physically separate the combatants in Bosnia... They come from the combatant nations.* ◆◇◇◇◇ N-COUNT: usu pl

combative /kɒmbətɪv, AM kəmbætɪv/. A person who is **combative** is aggressive and eager to fight or argue. *He conducted the meeting in his usual combative style, refusing to admit any mistakes.* ◆◇◇◇◇ ADJ-GRADED =antagonistic

♦ **combativeness** *They quickly developed a reputation for combativeness.* N-UNCOUNT

combination /kɒmbɪneɪʃᵊn/ **combinations.** A **combination** of things is a mixture of them. *...a fantastic combination of colours. ...the combination of science and art.* ◆◆◆◇◇ N-COUNT: usu N *of* n

combination lock, combination locks. A **combination lock** is a lock which can only be opened by turning a dial or a number of dials according to a particular series of letters or numbers. *...a black leather suitcase with combination locks.* N-COUNT

combine, combines, combining, combined. The verb is pronounced /kəmbaɪn/. The noun is pronounced /kɒmbaɪn/. ◆◆◆◇◇

1 If you **combine** two or more things or if they **combine**, they exist together. *The Church has something to say on how to combine freedom with responsibility... If improved education is combined with other factors dramatic results can be achieved... Relief workers say it's worse than ever as disease and starvation combine to kill thousands... This suits China's aim of gradual industrial reform combined with fast economic growth.* V-RECIP-ERG V n *with* n pl-n V V-ed Also V *with* n, V pl-n

2 If you **combine** two or more things or if they **combine**, they join together to make a single thing. *David Jacobs was given the job of combining the data from these 19 studies into one giant study... Combine the flour with 3 tablespoons water to make a paste... Carbon, hydrogen and oxygen combine chemically to form carbohydrates and fats... Combined with other compounds, they created a massive dynamite-type bomb.* V-RECIP-ERG V pl-n V n *with* n pl-n V V-ed Also V *with* n

3 If someone or something **combines** two qualities or features, they have both those qualities or features at the same time. *Their system seems to combine the two ideals of strong government and proportional representation. ...a clever, far-sighted lawyer who combines legal expertise with social concern... Her tale has a consciously youthful tone and storyline, combined with a sly humour.* VERB V pl-n V n *with* n V-ed

4 If someone **combines** two activities, they do them both at the same time. *It is possible to com-* VERB V n *with* n/-ing

bine a career with being a mother... *He will combine the two jobs over the next three years.* V n with n/-ing V pl-n

5 If two or more groups or organizations **combine** or if someone **combines** them, they join to form a single group or organization. *...an announcement by Steetley and Tarmac of a joint venture that would combine their brick, tile and concrete operations... Different states or groups can combine to enlarge their markets.* V-RECIP-ERG =amalgamate V pl-n pl-n V Also V with n, V n with n

6 A **combine** is a group of people or organizations that are working or acting together. *...Veba, an energy-and-chemicals combine that is Germany's fourth-biggest company.* N-COUNT

combined /kəmbaɪnd/ ◆◆◇◇◇

1 A **combined** effort or attack is made by two or more groups of people at the same time. *These refugees are looked after by the combined efforts of the host countries and non-governmental organisations.* ADJ: ADJ n =joint

2 The **combined** size or quantity of two or more things is the total of their sizes or quantities added together. *Banco Central and Banco Hispano Americano will have combined assets worth 8.8 trillion pesetas.* ADJ: ADJ n =total

combine harvester, combine harvesters. A **combine harvester** is a large machine which is used on farms to cut, sort, and clean grain. N-COUNT

combining form, combining forms. A **combining form** is a word that is used, or used with a particular meaning, only when joined to another word. For example, '-legged' as in 'four-legged' and '-fold' as in 'fivefold' are combining forms. N-COUNT

combo /kɒmboʊ/ **combos.** A **combo** is a small group of musicians who play jazz, dance, or popular music; an informal word. *...a new-wave rock combo.* N-COUNT =band

combustible /kəmbʌstɪbəl/

1 A **combustible** material or gas catches fire and burns easily; a formal use. *The ability of coal to release a combustible gas has long been known.* ADJ-GRADED: usu ADJ n =inflammable

2 A **combustible** situation is likely to result in conflict or trouble. *I was desperate to change the subject, and we moved to less combustible talk about her future plans.* ADJ-GRADED: usu ADJ n =sensitive

combustion /kəmbʌstʃən/. **Combustion** is the act of burning something or the process of burning; a technical term. *The energy is released by combustion on the application of a match... The two principal combustion products are water vapor and carbon dioxide.* • See also **internal combustion engine.** ◆◇◇◇◇ N-UNCOUNT: oft N n

come /kʌm/ **comes, coming, came.** The form **come** is used in the present tense and is the past participle. ◆◆◆◆◆

1 When a person or thing **comes** to a particular place, especially to a place where you are, they move there. *Two police officers came into the hall... Come here, Tom... You'll have to come with us... We want you to come to lunch... I came over from Ireland to start a new life after my divorce... We heard the train coming... Can I come too?... The impact blew out some of the windows and the sea came rushing in.* VERB V prep/adv V V -ing prep/adv

2 When someone **comes** to do something, they move to the place where someone else is in order to do it, and they do it. In British English, someone can also **come and** do something. In American English, someone can also **come** do something, but you say that someone **came and** did something. *Eleanor had come to visit her... Come and meet Roger... A lot of our friends came and saw me... I want you to come visit me.* VERB V to-inf V and v V inf

3 When you **come to** a place, you reach it. *He came to a door that led into a passageway.* VERB V to n

4 If something **comes up** to a particular point or **down** to it, it is tall enough, deep enough, or long enough to reach that point. *...two elderly gentlemen whose trouser waistbands come up to their armpits... I wore a large shirt of Jamie's which came down over my hips.* VERB V up/down prep

5 If something **comes apart** or **comes to pieces**, it breaks into pieces. If something **comes off** or **comes away**, it becomes detached from something else. *The pistol had to be dismantleable. It had to come to pieces, easily and quickly... The door knobs came off in our hands.* VERB V adv/prep

6 You use **come** in expressions such as **come to an end** or **come into operation** to indicate that someone or something enters or reaches a particular state or situation. *The summer came to an end... The Communists came to power in 1944... I came into contact with very bright Harvard and Yale students. ...new taxes which come into force next month... Their worst fears may be coming true.* V-LINK V to n V into n V adj

7 If someone **comes** to do something, they do it at the end of a long process or period of time. *She said it so many times that she came to believe it... Although it was a secret wedding, the press did eventually come to hear about it.* VERB V to-inf

8 You can ask how something **came** to happen when you want to know what caused it to happen or made it possible. *How did you come to meet him?* VERB V to-inf

9 When a particular event or time **comes**, it arrives or happens. *The announcement came after a meeting at the Home Office... The time has come for us to move on... There will come a time when the crisis will occur.* ♦ **coming** *Most of my patients welcome the coming of summer.* VERB V prep/adv V there V n N-SING: usu the N of n

10 You can use **come** before a date, time, or event to mean when that date, time, or event arrives. For example, you can say **come the spring** to mean 'when the spring arrives'. *Come the election on the 20th of May, we will have to decide... He's going to be up there again come Sunday.* PREP

11 If a thought, idea, or memory **comes to** you, you suddenly think of it or remember it. *He was about to shut the door when an idea came to him... Then it came to me that perhaps he did understand.* VERB =strike V to n it V to n that

12 If money or property is going to **come to** you, you are going to inherit or receive it. *The fortune will come to you... He did have pension money coming to him when the factory shut down.* VERB V to n

13 If a case **comes before** a court or tribunal or **comes to** court, it is presented there so that the court or tribunal can examine it. *The membership application came before the Council of Ministers in September... President Cristiani expected the case to come to court within ninety days.* VERB V before n V to n

14 If something **comes to** a particular number or amount, it adds up to it. *Lunch came to $80.* VERB V to amount

15 If someone or something **comes from** a particular place or thing, that place or thing is their origin, source, or starting point. *Nearly half the students come from abroad... Chocolate comes from the cacao tree... The term 'claret', used to describe Bordeaux wines, may come from the French word 'clairet'.* VERB V from n

16 Something that **comes from** something else or **comes of** it is the result of it. *There is a feeling of power that comes from driving fast... Some good might come of all this gloomy business... He asked to be transferred there some years ago, but nothing came of it.* VERB V from n/-ing V of n/-ing

17 If someone **comes of** a particular family or type of family, they are descended from them; a formal use. *She comes of a very good family.* VERB V of n

18 If someone or something **comes** first, next, or last, they are first, next, or last in a series, list, or competition. *The two countries have been unable to agree which step should come next... The alphabet might be more rational if all the vowels came first... The horse had already won at Lincolnshire and come second at Lowesby.* VERB V ord

19 If a type of thing **comes** in a particular range of colours, forms, styles, or sizes, it can have any of those colours, forms, styles, or sizes. *Bikes come in all shapes and sizes... The wallpaper comes in black and white only.* VERB V in n

20 You use **come** in expressions such as **it came as a surprise** when indicating a person's reaction to something that happens. *Major's reply came as a complete surprise to the House of Commons... The arrest has come as a terrible shock.* VERB V as n to n V as n

21 The next subject in a discussion that you **come to** is the one that you talk about next. *Finally in the programme, we come to the news that the American composer and conductor, Leonard Bernstein, has died... That is another matter altogether. And we shall come to that next.* VERB V to n

22 People say **'Come'** to encourage, reassure, or comfort someone; an old-fashioned expression. *'Come, eat!' the old woman urged.* CONVENTION PRAGMATICS =come on

23 To **come** means to have an orgasm; an informal use. VERB: V

24 See also **coming, comings and goings.**

25 Some people say **'Come again?'** when they want you to repeat what you have just said. PHRASES CONVENTION PRAGMATICS

26 If you say that someone is, for example, **as** good **as they come**, or **as** stupid **as they come**, you are emphasizing that they are extremely good or extremely stupid. *The new finance minister was educated at Oxford and is as financially orthodox as they come.* PRAGMATICS

27 People say **'Come, come'** to indicate that they disapprove of or disagree with what someone has just said or done; an old-fashioned expression. *'You hope for something in Mrs Zuckerman's will?'—'Come, come, Mr Trethowan. Of course not.'* CONVENTION PRAGMATICS =come on

28 You can use the expression **when it comes down to it** or **when you come down to it** for emphasis, when you are giving a general statement or conclusion. *When you come down to it, however, the basic problems of life have not changed... Few people, when it comes down to it, are so selfless.* PHR with cl PRAGMATICS =basically

29 In informal English, if you say that someone **has it coming to** them, you mean that they deserve everything bad that is going to happen to them, because they have done something wrong or are a bad person. If you say that someone **got what was coming to** them, you mean that they deserved the punishment or bad experience that they have had. *He was pleased that Brady was dead because he probably had it coming to him.* V inflects

30 You use the expression **come to think of it** to indicate that you have suddenly realized something, often something obvious. *He was his distant relative, as was everyone else on the island, come to think of it... You know, when you come to think of it, this is very odd.* PHR with cl PRAGMATICS

31 When you refer to a time or an event **to come** or one that is still **to come**, you are referring to a future time or event. *The War will remain a heated topic of debate for some time to come... I hope in years to come he will reflect on his decision... The worst of the storm is yet to come.* usu n PHR, also v-link PHR

32 You can use the expression **when it comes to** or **when it comes down to** in order to introduce a new topic or a new aspect of a topic that you are talking about. *Most of us know we should cut down on fat. But knowing such things isn't much help when it comes to shopping and eating... However, when it comes down to somebody that they know, they have a different feeling.* PHR n/-ing PRAGMATICS

33 Come is used in a large number of expressions which are explained under other words in this dictionary. For example, the expression 'to come to terms with something' is explained at 'term'.

come about. When you say how or when something **came about**, you say how or when it happened. *Any possible solution to the Irish question can only come about through dialogue... That came about when we went to Glastonbury last year... Thus it came about that, after many years as an interior designer and antiques dealer, he combined both businesses.* PHRASAL VERB V P *through* n V P *it* V P that

come across PHRASAL VERB

1 If you **come across** something or someone, you find them or meet them by chance. *He came across the jawbone of a 4.5 million-year-old marsupial... We like to identify and celebrate women's success whenever we come across it.* =encounter V P n

2 If someone or what they are saying **comes across** in a particular way, they make that impression on people who meet them or are listening to them. *When sober he can come across as an extremely pleasant and charming young man... He came across very, very well. And his composure continued even under cross examination.* =come over V P *as* n V P adv

come along PHRASAL VERB

1 You tell someone to **come along** to encourage them in a friendly way to do something, especially to attend something. *There's a big press launch today and you're most welcome to come along.* PRAGMATICS V P

2 You say **'come along'** to someone to encourage them to hurry up, usually when you are rather annoyed with them. *Come along, Osmond. No sense in your standing around.* CONVENTION PRAGMATICS

3 When something or someone **comes along**, they occur or arrive by chance. *I waited a long time until a script came along that I thought was genuinely funny... It was lucky you came along.* V P

4 If something **is coming along**, it is developing or making progress. *Pentagon spokesman Williams says those talks are coming along quite well... How's Ferguson coming along?* V P adv V P

come around or **come round** PHRASAL VERB

1 If someone **comes around** or **comes round** to your house, they call there to see you. *Beryl came round this morning to apologize... Quite a lot of people came round to the house.* V P V P *to* n

2 If you **come around** or **come round** to an idea, you eventually change your mind and accept it or agree with it. *It looks like they're coming around to our way of thinking... She will eventually come round.* V P *to* n V P

3 When something **comes around** or **comes round**, it happens as a regular or predictable event. *I hope still to be in the side when the World Cup comes around next year.* V P

4 When someone who is unconscious **comes around** or **comes round**, they recover consciousness. *When I came round I was on the kitchen floor.* =come to V P

come at. If a person or animal **comes at** you, they move towards you in a threatening way and try to attack you. *He maintained that he was protecting himself from Mr Cox, who came at him with an axe.* PHRASAL VERB V P n *with* n Also V P n

come back PHRASAL VERB

1 If something that you had forgotten **comes back** to you, you remember it. *He was also an MP – I'll think of his name in a moment when it comes back to me... When I thought about it, it all came back.* V P *to* n V P

2 When something **comes back**, it becomes fashionable again. *I'm glad hats are coming back.* V P

3 See also **comeback.**

come back to. If you **come back** to a topic or point, you talk about it again later. *'What does that mean please?'—'I'm coming back to that. Just write it down for the minute.'* PHRASAL VERB V P P n

come between. If someone or something **comes between** two people, or **comes between** a person and a thing, they make the relationship or connection between them less close or happy. *It's difficult to imagine anything – even Houston's marriage – coming between them... He's coming between you and your work.* PHRASAL VERB no passive V P pl-n

come by. To **come by** something means to obtain it or find it. *How did you come by that cheque?... In rural France, English language magazines are rather hard to come by.* PHRASAL VERB =get hold of V P n

come down PHRASAL VERB

1 If the cost, level, or amount of something **comes down**, it becomes less than it was before. *Interest rates should come down... If you buy three bottles, the bottle price comes down to £2.42... The price of petrol is coming down by four pence a gallon.* V P V P *to/from* n V P *by* n

2 If something **comes down**, it falls to the ground. *The cold rain came down... The curtain came down after the first act... A Boeing 737 came down on the M1 motorway.* V P

3 See also **come-down.**

come down on PHRASAL VERB

1 If you **come down on** one side of an argument, you declare that you support that side. *He clearly and decisively came down on the side of President Rafsanjani.* V P P n

2 If you **come down on** someone, you criticize

them severely or treat them strictly. *If Douglas came down hard enough on him, Dale would rebel.* VPPn

come down to. If a problem, decision, or question **comes down to** a particular thing, that thing is the most important factor involved. *Walter Crowley says the problem comes down to money... I think that it comes down to the fact that people do feel very dependent on their automobile... What it comes down to is, there are bad people out there, and somebody has to deal with them.* PHRASAL VERB VPPn *it*VPPn

come down with. If you **come down with** an illness, you get it. *Thomas came down with chickenpox at the weekend.* PHRASAL VERB VPPn

come for. If people such as soldiers or police **come for** you, they come to find you, usually in order to harm you or take you away, for example to prison. *Lotte was getting ready to fight if they came for her.* PHRASAL VERB VPn

come forward. If someone **comes forward**, they offer to do something or to give some information in response to a request for help. *A vital witness came forward to say that she saw Tanner wearing the boots.* PHRASAL VERB VP

come in PHRASAL VERB

1 If information, a report, or a telephone call **comes in**, it is received. *Reports are now coming in of trouble at yet another jail.* VP

2 If you have some money **coming in**, you receive it regularly as your income. *She had no money coming in and no funds.* usu cont VP

3 If someone **comes in** on a discussion, arrangement, or task, they join it. *Can I come in here too, on both points?... He had a designer come in and redesign the uniforms.* VP *on*n VP

4 When a new idea, fashion, or product **comes in**, it becomes popular or available. *It was just when geography was really beginning to change and lots of new ideas were coming in... I wouldn't be sorry to see proportional representation and I think it's a thing which will gradually come in.* VP

5 If you ask where something or someone **comes in**, you are asking what their role is in a particular matter. *Rose asked again, 'But where do we come in, Henry?'... Finally, he could do no more, which is where Jacques came in.* VP

6 When the tide **comes in**, the water in the sea gradually moves so that it covers more of the land. VP

come in for. If someone or something **comes in for** criticism or blame, they receive it. *The plans have already come in for fierce criticism in many quarters of the country.* PHRASAL VERB VPPn

come into PHRASAL VERB

1 If someone **comes into** some money, some property, or a title, they inherit it. *My father has just come into a fortune in diamonds.* no passive =inherit VPn

2 If someone or something **comes into** a situation, they have a role in it. *We don't really know where Hortense comes into all this, Inspector... It's an unrestricted journey, and rules of any sort don't come into it.* no passive VPn

come off PHRASAL VERB

1 If something **comes off**, it is successful or effective. *It was a good try but it didn't quite come off... Slovo said it was a great occasion which he hoped would come off in an orderly and peaceful way.* VP

2 If someone **comes off** worst in a contest or conflict, they are in the worst position after it. If they **come off** best, they are in the best position. *Some Democrats still have bitter memories of how, against all odds, they came off worst during the Iran-contra inquiry... In these circumstances, it is the managers who come off best.* VPadv

3 If you **come off** a drug or medication, you stop taking it. *...people trying to come off tranquillizers.* no passive VPn

4 You say **'come off it'** to someone to show them that you think what they are saying is untrue or wrong; an informal expression. CONVENTION PRAGMATICS

come on PHRASAL VERB

1 You say **'Come on'** to someone to encourage them to do something they do not much want to do. *Come on Doreen, let's dance.* CONVENTION PRAGMATICS

2 You say **'Come on'** to someone to encourage them to hurry up. CONVENTION PRAGMATICS

3 You say **'Come on'** to someone when you think that what they are saying is silly or unreasonable. *'Have you said all this to the police?'—'Aw, come on!'... Come on, Sue, that was two years ago.* CONVENTION PRAGMATICS

4 If you have an illness or a headache **coming on**, you can feel it starting. *Tiredness and fever are much more likely to be a sign of flu coming on.* usu cont VP

5 If something or someone **is coming on** well, they are developing well or making good progress. *Lee is coming on very well now and it's a matter of deciding how to fit him into the team... The knee's coming on fine, I'm walking comfortably already.* usu cont =come along VPadv

6 When something such as a machine or system **comes on**, it starts working or functioning. *The central heating was coming on and the ancient wooden boards creaked.* VP

7 If a new season or type of weather **is coming on**, it is starting to arrive. *Winter was coming on again... I had two miles to go and it was just coming on to rain.* usu cont VP *it*VP to-inf

come on to PHRASAL VERB

1 When you **come on to** a particular topic, you start discussing it. *We're now looking at a smaller system but I'll come on to that later.* VPPn

2 If someone **comes on to** you, they show that they are interested in starting a sexual relationship with you; an informal expression used mainly in American English. *I don't think that a woman, by using make-up, is trying to come on to a man.* VPPn

come out PHRASAL VERB

1 When a new product such as a book or record **comes out**, it becomes available to the public. *The book comes out this week... Christian Slater has a new movie coming out next month in which he plays a vigilante.* VP

2 If a fact **comes out**, it becomes known to people. *The truth is beginning to come out about what happened... It will come out that she has covertly donated considerable sums to the IRA.* VP *it*VP that

3 When a gay person **comes out**, they let people know that they are gay. *...the few gay men there who dare to come out... I came out as a lesbian when I was still in my teens.* VP VP *as*n/adj

4 To **come out** in a particular way means to be in the position or state described at the end of a process or event. *In this grim little episode of recent American history, few people come out well... So what makes a good marriage? Faithfulness comes out top of the list... Julian ought to have resigned, then he'd have come out of it with some credit.* VPadv/prep VPadj VP*of*n adv/prep

5 If you **come out** for something, you declare that you support it. If you **come out** against something, you declare that you do not support it. *Helmut Kohl and Francois Mitterrand have come out in favour of direct financial aid... Its members had come out virtually unanimously against the tests.* VPprep/adv

6 When a group of workers **comes out** on strike, they go on strike. *On September 18 the dockers again came out on strike.* VPprep

7 If a photograph does not **come out**, it is blank or unclear when it is developed and printed. *None of her snaps came out.* VP

8 When the sun, moon, or stars **come out**, they appear in the sky. *Oh, look. The sun's come out.* VP

come out in. If you **come out in** spots, you become covered with them. *When I changed to a new soap I came out in a terrible rash.* PHRASAL VERB no passive =break out in VPPn

come out with. If you **come out with** a remark, especially a surprising one, you make it. *Everyone who heard it just burst out laughing when he came out with it... What was that marvellous quote that she came out with?* PHRASAL VERB no passive VPn

come over PHRASAL VERB

1 If a feeling or urge **comes over** you, especially a strange or surprising one, it affects you strongly. *As I entered the corridor which led to my room that eerie feeling came over me... I'm sorry, I don't know what came over me.* no passive VPn

2 If someone **comes over** all dizzy or shy, for example, they suddenly start feeling or acting in that LINK

way. *When Connie pours her troubles out to him, Joe comes over all sensitive... Now you are coming over all puritanical about nothing.* VP adj

3 If someone or what they are saying **comes over** in a particular way, they make that impression on people who meet them or are listening to them. *You come over as a capable and amusing companion... He came over well – perhaps a little pompous, but nevertheless honest and straightforward.* =come across; VP as n; VP adv

come round. See **come around.** PHRASAL VERB

come through PHRASAL VERB

1 To **come through** a dangerous or difficult situation means to survive it and recover from it. *The city had faced racial crisis and come through it... He's too old to come through a fall like that.* no passive; VP n

2 If a feeling or message **comes through**, it is clearly shown in what is said or done. *I hope my love for the material came through, because it is a great script... Their talk is often hard to fathom but their exuberance still comes through.* VP

3 If something **comes through**, it arrives, especially after some procedure has been carried out. *The father of the baby was waiting for his divorce to come through... The news came through at about five o'clock on election day.* VP

4 If you **come through** with what is expected or needed from you, you succeed in doing or providing it. *He puts his administration at risk if he doesn't come through on these promises for reform... We found that we were totally helpless, and our women came through for us.* VP on/with n; VP for n

come to. When someone who is unconscious **comes to**, they recover consciousness. *When he came to and raised his head he saw Barney.* PHRASAL VERB; =come around; VP

come under PHRASAL VERB

1 If you **come under** attack or pressure, for example, people attack you or put pressure on you. *The police came under attack from angry crowds... In parliament last week the Finance Minister came under heavy pressure to resign... His relationship with the KGB came under scrutiny.* no passive; VP n

2 If something **comes under** a particular authority, it is managed or controlled by that authority. *They were neglected before because they did not come under the Ministry of Defence.* no passive; VP n

3 If something **comes under** a particular heading, it is in the category mentioned. *There was more news about Britain, but it came under the heading of human interest.* no passive; VP n

come up PHRASAL VERB

1 If someone **comes up** or **comes up** to you, they approach you until they are standing close to you. *Her cat came up and rubbed itself against their legs... He came up to me and said: 'Come on, John.'* VP; VP to n

2 If something **comes up** in a conversation or meeting, it is mentioned or discussed. *The subject came up at a news conference in Peking today... Jeane Kirkpatrick's name has come up a lot.* VP

3 If something **is coming up**, it is about to happen or take place. *Plan your activities so that you are rested and refreshed when something important is coming up... We do have elections coming up.* VP

4 If something **comes up**, it happens unexpectedly. *I was delayed – something came up at home... Other projects came up and the emphasis of my work altered.* VP

5 If a job **comes up** or if something **comes up** for sale, it becomes available. *A research fellowship came up at Girton and I applied for it and got it... The house came up for sale and the couple realised they could just about afford it.* VP; VP for n

6 When the sun or moon **comes up**, it rises. *It will be so great watching the sun come up.* VP

7 In law, when a case **comes up**, it is heard in a court of law. *He is one of the reservists who will plead not guilty when their cases come up.* VP

come up against. If you **come up against** a problem or difficulty, you are faced with it and have to deal with it. *We came up against a great deal of resistance in dealing with the case.* PHRASAL VERB; VPP n

come up for. When someone or something **comes up** for consideration or action of some kind, the time arrives when they have to be considered or dealt with. *The TV rights contract came up for renegotiation in 1988... These three clubs could come under close scrutiny when their licenses come up for renewal.* PHRASAL VERB; VP for n

come upon PHRASAL VERB

1 If you **come upon** someone or something, you meet them or find them by chance. *I came upon a irresistible item at a yard sale.* =come across; VP n

2 If an attitude or feeling **comes upon** you, it begins to affect you; a literary expression. *A sense of impending doom came upon all of us.* VP n

come up to. To **be coming up to** a time or state means to be getting near to it. *It's just coming up to ten minutes past eleven now.* PHRASAL VERB; usu cont; VPP n

come up with PHRASAL VERB

1 If you **come up with** a plan or idea, you think of it and suggest it. *Several of the members have come up with suggestions of their own... 30 years ago, scientists came up with the theory that protons and neutrons are composed of three smaller particles.* VPP n

2 If you **come up with** a sum of money, you manage to produce it when it is needed. *If Warren can come up with the $15 million, we'll go to London.* VPP n

comeback /kʌmbæk/ **comebacks** ◆◆◇◇◇

1 If someone such as an entertainer or sports personality makes a **comeback**, they return to their profession or sport after a period of absence. *Sixties singing star Petula Clark is making a comeback.* N-COUNT

2 If something makes a **comeback**, it becomes fashionable again. *Tight fitting T-shirts are making a comeback.* N-COUNT

3 If you have no **comeback** when someone has done something wrong to you, there is nothing you can do to have them punished or held responsible, for example because the law or a rule prevents it. N-UNCOUNT: with brd-neg; =redress

comedian /kəmiːdiən/ **comedians.** A **comedian** is an entertainer whose job is to make people laugh, by telling jokes or funny stories. ◆◆◇◇◇ N-COUNT; =comic

comedic /kəmiːdɪk/. **Comedic** means relating to comedy; a formal word. *She brings an unsuspected comedic touch to her role.* ADJ: usu ADJ n; ≠tragic

comedienne /kəmiːdien/ **comediennes.** A **comedienne** is a female entertainer whose job is to make people laugh, by telling them jokes and funny stories. N-COUNT; =comic

come-down; also spelled **comedown.** If you say that something is **a come-down**, you think that it is not as good as something else that you have just done or had. *After getting your degree and being on a high, it's quite a comedown to experience constant rejection.* ◆◆◇◇◇ N-SING: a N; =let-down

comedy /kɒmədi/ **comedies** ◆◆◆◇◇

1 Comedy consists of types of entertainment, such as plays and films, or particular scenes in them, that are intended to make people laugh. *Actor Dom Deluise talks about his career in comedy. ...a TV comedy series.* N-UNCOUNT

2 A **comedy** is a play, film, or television programme that is intended to make people laugh. N-COUNT; ≠tragedy

3 The **comedy** of a situation are those aspects of it that make you laugh. *Jackie sees the comedy in her millionaire husband's thrifty habits.* N-UNCOUNT; =humour

4 See also **situation comedy**.

comely /kʌmli/ **comelier, comeliest.** A **comely** woman is attractive; an old-fashioned word. ADJ-GRADED: usu ADJ n

come-on, come-ons. A **come-on** is a gesture or remark which someone, especially a woman, makes in order to encourage another person to make sexual advances to them; an informal use. *The image Sue projected was both a come-on and a challenge to every man in the club that night... He ignores come-ons from the many women who seem to find him attractive.* N-COUNT

comer /kʌmər/ **comers** ◆◇◇◇◇

1 You can use **comers** to refer to people who arrive at a particular place. *The house of God should be open to all comers... The first comer was the Sultan himself.* • See also **latecomer, newcomer**. N-COUNT: usu pl, supp N

2 If a contest or sporting event is open to **all comers**, anyone is allowed to take part in it or challenge PHRASE the champion. *She has made it clear she is ready for all comers.*

comet /kɒmɪt/ **comets.** A **comet** is an object that travels around the sun leaving a bright trail behind it. *Halley's Comet is going to come back in 2061.*
◆◆◇◇◇ N-COUNT

comeuppance /kʌmʌpəns/; also spelled **come-uppance.** If you say that someone has got their **comeuppance**, you approve of the fact that they have been punished or have suffered for something wrong that they have done; an informal word. *The central character is a bad man who shoots people and gets his comeuppance.*
N-SING: usu poss N PRAGMATICS =just deserts

comfort /kʌmfərt/ **comforts, comforting, comforted**
◆◆◆◇◇

1 If you are doing something in **comfort**, you are physically relaxed and contented, and are not feeling any pain or other unpleasant sensations. *This will enable the audience to sit in comfort while watching the shows... The shoe has padding around the collar, heel and tongue for added comfort.*
N-UNCOUNT: oft *in/for* N ≠discomfort

2 **Comfort** is a style of life in which you have enough money to have everything you need. *Surely there is some way of ordering our busy lives so that we can live in comfort and find spiritual harmony too.*
N-UNCOUNT: oft *in* N

3 **Comfort** is a feeling of relief from worries or unhappiness. *He welcomed the truce, but pointed out it was of little comfort to families spending Christmas without a loved one... He will be able to take some comfort from inflation figures due on Friday... He found comfort in Eva's blind faith in him.* • See also **cold comfort**.
N-UNCOUNT

4 If you refer to a person, thing, or idea as a **comfort**, you mean that it helps you to stop worrying or makes you feel less unhappy. *At least he has given her a child who will be a great comfort to her in the years ahead... It's a comfort talking to you... Being able to afford a drink would be a comfort in these tough times.*
N-COUNT: usu sing, oft N *to* n, *it* v-link N to-inf/-ing

5 If you **comfort** someone, you make them feel less worried, unhappy, or upset, for example by saying kind things to them. *Ned put his arm around her, trying to comfort her.*
VERB =console
V n

6 **Comforts** are things which make your life easier and more pleasant, such as electrical devices you have in your home. *She enjoys the material comforts married life has brought her... Electricity provides us with warmth and light and all our modern home comforts... I do like my comforts.* • See also **creature comforts**.
N-COUNT: usu pl

7 If you say that something is, for example, **too** close **for comfort**, you mean you are worried because it is closer than you would like it to be. *The bombs fell in the sea, many too close for comfort... Although crimes against visitors were falling, the levels of crime were still too high for comfort.*
PHRASE: PHR after v, v-link PHR

comfortable /kʌmftəbəl/
◆◆◆◇◇

1 If a piece of furniture or an item of clothing is **comfortable**, it makes you feel physically relaxed when you use it, for example because it is soft. *...a comfortable fireside chair... Trainers are so comfortable to wear.*
ADJ-GRADED ≠uncomfortable

2 If a building or room is **comfortable**, it makes you feel physically relaxed when you spend time in it, for example because it is warm and has nice furniture. *A home should be comfortable and friendly. ...somewhere warm and comfortable.*
ADJ-GRADED

♦ **comfortably** /kʌmftəbli/ *...the comfortably furnished living-room.*
ADV-GRADED: usu ADV -ed

3 If you are **comfortable**, you are physically relaxed and at ease because of the place or position you are sitting or lying in. *Lie down on your bed and make yourself comfortable... She tried to maneuver her body into a more comfortable position.*
ADJ-GRADED ≠uncomfortable

♦ **comfortably** *Are you sitting comfortably?... He would be tucked comfortably into bed.*
ADV-GRADED: ADV with v

4 If you say that someone is **comfortable**, you mean that they have enough money to be able to live without financial problems. *'Is he rich?'—'He's comfortable.'... She came from a stable, comfortable, middle-class family.* ♦ **comfortably** *Cayton describes himself as comfortably well-off.*
ADJ-GRADED
ADV-GRADED

5 In a race, competition, or election, if you are in a **comfortable** position or if you have a **comfortable** lead, you are likely to win it easily. If you gain a **comfortable** victory or majority, you win it easily. *By half distance we held a comfortable two-lap lead... He appeared to be heading for a comfortable victory.* ♦ **comfortably** *...the Los Angeles Raiders, who comfortably beat the Bears earlier in the season.*
ADJ-GRADED: ADJ n
ADV-GRADED: ADV with v =easily

6 If you feel **comfortable** with a particular situation or person, you feel confident and relaxed with them. *Nervous politicians might well feel more comfortable with a step-by-step approach... He liked me and I felt comfortable with him... I'll talk to them, but I won't feel comfortable about it.* ♦ **comfortably** *They talked comfortably of their plans.*
ADJ-GRADED: v-link ADJ, oft ADJ prep
ADV-GRADED: ADV after v

7 When a sick or injured person is said to be **comfortable**, they are in a stable physical condition. *He was described as comfortable in hospital last night.*
ADJ

8 A **comfortable** life, job, or situation does not cause you any problems or worries. *...a comfortable teaching job at a university... Kohl's future looks far from comfortable.*
ADJ-GRADED

comfortably /kʌmfərtəbli/. If someone or something **comfortably** does something, they do it easily. *Only take upon yourself those things that you know you can manage comfortably... Three of the six have comfortably exceeded their normal life expectancy.* • See also **comfortable**.
◆◇◇◇◇ ADV-GRADED: ADV with v

comfortably off. If someone is **comfortably off**, they have enough money to be able to live without financial problems. *He had no plans to retire even though he is now very comfortably off.*
ADJ-GRADED: usu v-link ADJ

comforter /kʌmfərtər/ **comforters**

1 A **comforter** is a person or thing that comforts you. *He became Vivien Leigh's devoted friend and comforter.*
N-COUNT

2 In American English, a **comforter** is a quilted bedcover. The usual British word is **quilt**.
N-COUNT

comforting /kʌmfərtɪŋ/. If you say that something is **comforting**, you mean it makes you feel less worried or unhappy. *My mother had just died and I found the book very comforting... In the midst of his feelings of impotence, a comforting thought arrived.* ♦ **comfortingly** *'Everything's under control here,' her mother said comfortingly. 'You've nothing to worry about.'*
◆◇◇◇◇ ADJ-GRADED
ADV-GRADED: usu ADV with v, ADV adj, also ADV with cl

comfrey /kʌmfri/. **Comfrey** is a herb that is used to make drinks and medicines.
N-UNCOUNT

comfy /kʌmfi/ **comfier, comfiest.** A **comfy** item of clothing, piece of furniture, room, or position is a comfortable one; an informal word. *Loose-fitting shirts are comfy. ...a comfy chair.*
ADJ-GRADED

comic /kɒmɪk/ **comics**
◆◆◇◇◇

1 If you describe something as **comic**, you mean that it makes you laugh, and is often intended to make you laugh. *The novel is comic and tragic... Most of these trips had exciting or comic moments.*
ADJ-GRADED

2 **Comic** is used to describe comedy as a form of entertainment, and the actors and entertainers who perform it. *Grodin is a fine comic actor. ...a comic opera.*
ADJ: ADJ n

3 A **comic** is an entertainer who tells jokes in order to make people laugh.
N-COUNT =comedian

4 A **comic** is a magazine that contains stories told in pictures; used mainly in British English. The usual American term is **comic book**. *Joe loved to read 'Superman' comics.*
N-COUNT =comic book

comical /kɒmɪkəl/. If you describe something as **comical**, you mean that it makes you want to laugh because it seems funny or silly. *Her expression is almost comical... Events took a comical turn.* ♦ **comically** /kɒmɪkli/ *She raised her eyebrows comically... The display of prehistoric monsters is comically naive.*
◆◇◇◇◇ ADJ-GRADED =funny
ADV-GRADED: ADV with v, ADV adj

comic book, comic books. A **comic book** is a magazine that contains stories told in pictures; used mainly in American English. The usual British word is **comic**.
◆◇◇◇◇ N-COUNT =comic

comic strip, comic strips. A **comic strip** is a series of drawings that tell a story. N-COUNT

coming /kʌmɪŋ/. A **coming** event or time is an event or time that will happen soon. *This obviously depends on the weather in the coming months... They talk of the coming battle.* • See also **come**. ◆◆◆◆◆ ADJ: ADJ n

coming of age
1 When something reaches an important stage of development and is accepted by a large number of people, you can refer to this as its **coming of age**. *...postwar Germany's final coming-of-age as an independent sovereign state.* N-SING: with supp
2 Someone's **coming of age** is the time when they become legally an adult. *...traditional coming-of-age ceremonies.* N-SING: with poss

comings and goings. The **comings and goings** of people are their arrivals and departures at a particular place. *Crowds of Somalis gather to watch the comings and goings of the journalists... She had to report her comings and goings to Sister Giuseppe.* N-PLURAL: with poss

comma /kɒmə/ **commas.** A **comma** is the punctuation mark (,) which is used to separate parts of a sentence or items in a list. N-COUNT

command /kəmɑːnd, -mænd/ **commands, commanding, commanded** ◆◆◆◇◇
1 If someone in authority **commands** you to do something, they tell you that you must do it. *He commanded his troops to attack... 'Get in your car and follow me,' he commanded... He commanded that roads be built to link castles across the land... 'Don't panic,' I commanded myself.* ► Also a noun. *The tanker failed to respond to a command to stop... I closed my eyes at his command. ...the note of command in his voice.* VERB =instruct, order V n to-inf V with quote V that V n with quote Also V n N-VAR =instruction
2 If you **command** something such as respect or obedience, you obtain it because you are popular, famous, or important. *...an excellent physician who commanded the respect of all his colleagues... There is no limit to what can be achieved here because of the fantastic support we command.* VB: no cont V n
3 If an army or country **commands** a place, they have total control over it. *The Royal Navy would command the seas... Yemen commands the strait at the southern end of the Red Sea.* ► Also a noun. *...the struggle for command of the air.* VERB =rule V n N-UNCOUNT: usu N of n
4 An officer who **commands** part of an army, navy, or air force is responsible for controlling and organizing it. *...the French general who commands the UN troops in Bosnia... He didn't just command. He personally fought in several heavy battles.* ► Also a noun. *...a small garrison under the command of Major James Craig... In 1942 he took command of 108 Squadron.* VERB V n V N-UNCOUNT =charge
5 In the armed forces, a **command** is a group of officers who are responsible for organizing and controlling part of an army, navy, or air force. *He had authorisation from the military command to retaliate... The army's supreme command has said the army will withdraw, provided the other side does so also.* N-COUNT-COLL: usu supp N
6 In the armed forces, a **command** is a group of soldiers that a particular officer is in charge of. *There would continue to be a joint command of US and Saudi forces operating within Saudi borders. ...the Strategic Air Command.* N-COUNT-COLL: oft in names after n
7 In computing, a **command** is an instruction that you give to a computer. N-COUNT
8 If someone has **command** of a situation, they have control of it because they have, or seem to have, power or authority. *Whoever was waiting for them there had command of the situation... Mr Baker would take command of the campaign... In times of currency crisis interest rates can raised as a sign that a government is in command.* N-UNCOUNT
9 Your **command of** something, such as a foreign language, is your knowledge of it and your ability to use this knowledge. *His command of English was excellent. ...a singer with a natural command of melody.* N-UNCOUNT: N of n =grasp
10 If a place **commands** a view, especially an impressive one, you can see the view clearly from that place. If a person **commands** a view of something, they can see it clearly from where they are; a formal use. *The house commanded some splendid views of Delaware Bay. ...a point of rock, from which we could command a view of the loch.* VB: no cont PRAGMATICS V n
11 See also **high command**, **second-in-command**.
12 If you have a particular skill or particular resources **at** your **command**, you have them and can use them fully; a formal use. *He came from the Sudan without a word of English at his command... The country should have the right to defend itself with all legal means at its command.* PHRASES
13 If you are **in command** or **in command of** yourself, you are relaxed and able to react and behave in the way that you want to. *Nixon looked comfortable and in command... The man appeared to be in complete command of himself.* usu v-link PHR =in control

commandant /kɒməndænt/ **commandants.** A **commandant** is an army officer in charge of a particular place or group of people. ◆◇◇◇◇ N-COUNT; N-TITLE

command economy, command economies. In a **command economy**, business activities and the allocation of resources are determined by the government, and not by market forces. *...Czechoslovakia's transition from a command economy to a market system.* N-COUNT =planned economy

commandeer /kɒməndɪəʳ/ **commandeers, commandeering, commandeered**
1 If the armed forces **commandeer** a vehicle or building owned by someone else, they officially take charge of it so that they can use it. *The soldiers commandeered vehicles in the capital and occupied the television station... They drove in convoy round the city in commandeered cars.* VERB =requisition V n V-ed
2 If someone **commandeers** something owned by someone else, they take charge of it so that they can use it; used showing disapproval. *He decides to commandeer their room... The hijacker commandeered the plane on a domestic flight.* VERB PRAGMATICS =usurp V n

commander /kəmɑːndəʳ, -mænd-/ **commanders** ◆◆◆◇◇
1 A **commander** is an officer in charge of a military operation or organization. *The commander and some of the men had been released. ...according to Commander Bob Marks.* N-COUNT; N-TITLE; N-VOC
2 A **commander** is an officer in the Royal Navy. *Many of its officers followed their commander's example and left the navy.* N-COUNT; N-TITLE; N-VOC

commander-in-chief, commanders-in-chief. A **commander-in-chief** is an officer in charge of all the forces in a particular area. *He was to be the commander-in-chief of the armed forces.* ◆◇◇◇◇ N-COUNT; N-TITLE

commanding /kəmɑːndɪŋ, -mænd-/ ◆◇◇◇◇
1 If you are in a **commanding** position or situation, you are in a strong or powerful position or situation. *Right now you're in a more commanding position than you have been for ages... The French vessel has a commanding lead.* ADJ-GRADED: usu ADJ n
2 If you describe someone as **commanding**, you mean that they are powerful and confident; used showing approval. *Lovett was a tall, commanding man with a waxed gray mustache... The voice at the other end of the line was serious and commanding.* ADJ-GRADED PRAGMATICS =authoritative
3 If a building has a **commanding** position, it is high up and has good views of the surrounding area. *The size of the castle and its commanding position still impress the visitor today... What other home offers such a commanding view of the capital?* ADJ-GRADED
4 See also **command.**

commanding officer, commanding officers. A **commanding officer** is an officer who is in charge of a military unit. *He got permission from his commanding officer to join me.* ◆◇◇◇◇ N-COUNT

commandment /kəmɑːndmənt, -mænd-/ **commandments.** The Ten **Commandments** are the ten rules of behaviour which, according to the Old Testament of the Bible, people should obey. *The eighth commandment is 'Thou shalt not steal'.* N-COUNT

commando /kəmɑːndoʊ, -mænd-/ **commandos** or **commandoes** ◆◇◇◇◇
1 A **commando** is a group of soldiers who have been specially trained to carry out raids. *...a small commando of marines... The hostages were freed in the commando raid.* N-COUNT: oft N n
2 A **commando** is a soldier who is a member of a commando. *Captain David Clement and 150 commandos stormed the port this morning.* N-COUNT

command performance, command performances. A **command performance** is a special performance of a play or show which is given for a head of state. *He had given a command performance for Queen Victoria.* N-COUNT

command post, command posts. A **command post** is a place from which a commander in the army controls and organizes his forces. *Inside the command post there was complete silence.* N-COUNT

commemorate /kəmeməreɪt/ **commemorates, commemorating, commemorated.** To **commemorate** an important event or person means to remember them by means of a special action, ceremony, or specially created object. *One room contained a gallery of paintings commemorating great moments in baseball history... The 200th anniversary of Mozart's death is being commemorated around the world with concerts featuring his work.* ◆◆◇◇◇ VERB =celebrate V n
♦ **commemoration** /kəmeməreɪʃən/ **commemorations** *...the 50th Anniversary Commemoration of the Warsaw Ghetto Uprising. ...a service of commemoration. ...a march in commemoration of Malcolm X.* N-VAR: usu with supp

commemorative /kəmemərətɪv/. A **commemorative** object or event is intended to make people remember a particular event or person. *The Queen unveiled a commemorative plaque.* ◆◇◇◇◇ ADJ: ADJ n

commence /kəmens/ **commences, commencing, commenced.** When something **commences** or you **commence** it, it begins; a formal word. *The academic year commences at the beginning of October... They commenced a systematic search... The hunter knelt beside the animal carcass and commenced to skin it.* ◆◇◇◇◇ V-ERG =start V V n/-ing V to-inf

commencement /kəmensmənt/
1 The **commencement** of something is its beginning; a formal use. *All applicants should be at least 16 years of age at the commencement of this course.* N-UNCOUNT: usu *the* N *of* n
2 In the United States, **commencement** is a ceremony at a university in which graduates formally receive their degrees. *Hillary Rodham Clinton gave the commencement address at the University of Pennsylvania in Philadelphia.* N-SING: usu N n

commend /kəmend/ **commends, commending, commended** ◆◇◇◇◇
1 If you **commend** someone or something, you praise them formally. *I commended her for that action... I commend Ms. Orth on writing such an informative article... The book was widely commended for its candour... The reports commend her bravery... His actions were commended by the Jury.* VERB V n *for/on* n/-ing V n
♦ **commendation** /kɒmendeɪʃən/ **commendations** *The Company received a commendation from the Royal Society of Arts.* N-COUNT
2 If someone **commends** something or someone **to** you, they tell you that you will find them good or useful. *I can commend it to him as a realistic course of action.* VERB =recommend V n *to* n
3 If something **commends** itself **to** you, you approve of it. *The Rousseau model commended itself to a lot of early socialists.* VERB =recommend V pron-refl *to* n
4 If you say that something has **much to commend** it, you approve of it. If you say that something has **little to commend** it, you disapprove of it; a formal expression. *The Prime Minister's initiative has much to commend it.* PHRASE: usu v PHR pron

commendable /kəmendəbəl/. If you describe someone's behaviour as **commendable**, you approve of it or are praising it; a formal word. *Mr Sparrow has acted with commendable speed... The tone of Mr Kinnock's speech was commendable.* ◆◇◇◇◇ ADJ-GRADED PRAGMATICS =admirable
♦ **commendably** /kəmendəbli/. *Her manner was commendably restrained... They all behaved very commendably... Exercise classes, commendably, are limited to groups of 5.* ADV-GRADED: ADV adj/adv, ADV with v, ADV with cl

commensurate /kəmensərət/. If the level of one thing is **commensurate** with another, the first level is in proportion to the second; a formal word. *Employees are paid salaries commensurate with those of teachers... Managers saw a commensurate fall in their revenues.* ADJ: v-link ADJ *with/to* n, ADJ n
♦ **commensurately** *Japanese real wages have not yet increased commensurately with the wealth of Japan... The gain will be commensurately modest.* ADV: usu ADV after v, ADV adj/-ed

comment /kɒment/ **comments, commenting, commented** ◆◆◆◆◇
1 If you **comment** on something, you give your opinion about it or you give an explanation for it. *So far, Mr Clinton has not commented on these reports... Stratford police refuse to comment on whether anyone has been arrested... You really can't comment till you know the facts... 'I'm always happy with new developments,' he commented... Stuart commented that this was very true.* VERB V *on* n/wh V V with quote V that
2 A **comment** is something that you say which expresses your opinion of something or which gives an explanation of it. *He made his comments at a news conference in Baghdad... I was wondering whether you had any comments about that?... There's been no comment so far from police about the allegations... Lady Thatcher, who is abroad, was not available for comment.* N-VAR
3 If you say that an event or situation is a **comment** on something, you mean that it reveals something, usually something bad, about that thing. *He argues that family problems are typically a comment on some unresolved issues in the family.* N-SING: usu *a* N *on* n =reflection
4 People say **'no comment'** as a way of refusing to answer a question, usually when it is asked by a journalist. *No comment. I don't know anything.* CONVENTION

commentary /kɒməntri, AM -teri/ **commentaries** ◆◆◇◇◇
1 A **commentary** is a description of an event that is broadcast on radio or television while the event is taking place. *He gave the listening crowd a running commentary... That programme will include live commentary on the England-Ireland game.* N-VAR
2 A **commentary** is an article or book which explains or discusses something. *Mr Rich will be writing a twice-weekly commentary on American society and culture.* N-COUNT
3 **Commentary** is discussion or criticism of something. *The show mixed comedy with social commentary... When I was able to elicit only a gentle smile, I thought perhaps this was a commentary on my humor.* N-UNCOUNT: also *a* N, with supp =comment

commentate /kɒmənteɪt/ **commentates, commentating, commentated.** To **commentate** means to give a radio or television commentary on an event. *They are in Sweden to commentate on the European Championships... He commentates for the BBC.* ◆◇◇◇◇ VERB V *on* n V

commentator /kɒmənteɪtər/ **commentators** ◆◆◆◇◇
1 A **commentator** is a broadcaster who gives a radio or television commentary on an event. *...a sports commentator.* N-COUNT: usu with supp
2 A **commentator** is also someone who often writes or broadcasts about a particular subject. *...a political commentator... A. M. Babu is a commentator on African affairs.* N-COUNT: usu with supp

commerce /kɒmɜːrs/. **Commerce** is the activities and procedures involved in buying and selling things. *They have made their fortunes from industry and commerce.* ● See also **chamber of commerce.** ◆◆◆◇◇ N-UNCOUNT

commercial /kəmɜːrʃəl/ **commercials** ◆◆◆◆◇
1 **Commercial** means involving or relating to the buying and selling of goods. *Docklands in its heyday was a major centre of industrial and commercial activity... Attacks were reported on police, vehicles and commercial premises.* ADJ: usu ADJ n
2 **Commercial** organizations and activities are concerned with making money or profits, rather than, for example, with scientific research or pro- ADJ-GRADED

viding a public service. *British Rail has indeed become more commercial over the past decade... Conservationists in Chile are concerned over the effect of commercial exploitation of forests... Whether the project will be a commercial success in the long term is still extremely uncertain.*

♦ **commercially** *British Aerospace reckon that the plane will be commercially viable if 400 can be sold... Insulin is produced commercially from animals... Designers are becoming more commercially minded.* ADV-GRADED: usu ADV adj, ADV with v, also ADV with cl

3 A **commercial** product is made to be sold to the public. *They are the leading manufacturer in both defence and commercial products.* ADJ: ADJ n

♦ **commercially** *It was the first commercially available machine to employ artificial intelligence.* ADV: usu ADV adj, also ADV with v

4 A **commercial** vehicle is a vehicle used for carrying goods, or passengers who pay. *Commercial vehicles, coaches and lorries are required by law to be fitted with tachographs. ...the fastest crossing of the Atlantic by a commercial passenger vessel.* ADJ: usu ADJ n

5 **Commercial** television and radio are paid for by the broadcasting of advertisements, rather than by the government. *...Classic FM, the first national commercial radio station.* ADJ: usu ADJ n ≠public

6 If you use **commercial** to describe something such as a film or a type of music, you mean that it is intended to be popular with the public, and does not have much originality or artistic merit. *There's a feeling among a lot of people that music has become too commercial.* ADJ-GRADED

7 A **commercial** is an advertisement that is broadcast on television or radio. *The government has launched a campaign of television commercials and leaflets.* N-COUNT

commercial bank, commercial banks. A **commercial bank** is a bank which makes short-term loans using money from current accounts. ♦◇◇◇◇ N-COUNT

commercialism /kəmɜːʳʃəlɪzəm/. **Commercialism** is the practice of making a lot of money from things without caring about their quality; used showing disapproval. *Koons has engrossed himself in a world of commercialism that most modern artists disdain.* N-UNCOUNT PRAGMATICS

commercialize /kəmɜːʳʃəlaɪz/ **commercializes, commercializing, commercialized;** also spelled **commercialise** in British English. If something **is commercialized**, it is used or changed in such a way that it makes money or profits, often in a way that people disapprove of. *It seems such a pity that a distinguished and honored name should be commercialized in such a manner... Federal agencies should commercialize research.* VERB be V-ed V n

♦ **commercialized** *Rock'n'roll has become so commercialised and safe since punk.* ADJ-GRADED

♦ **commercialization** /kəmɜːʳʃəlaɪzeɪʃən/ *...the commercialization of Christmas.* N-UNCOUNT: oft N of n

commie /kɒmi/ **commies.** A **commie** is someone who believes in communism; an offensive word, used mainly in American English. N-COUNT

commiserate /kəmɪzəreɪt/ **commiserates, commiserating, commiserated.** If you **commiserate with** someone, you show them pity or sympathy when something unpleasant has happened to them. *When I lost, he commiserated with me.* VERB V with n

♦ **commiseration** /kəmɪzəreɪʃən/ **commiserations** *After half an hour's commiseration, we turned to more practical matters... We have sent the team our commiserations.* N-UNCOUNT: also N in pl

commissariat /kɒmɪseəriət/ **commissariats.** A **commissariat** is a military department that is in charge of food supplies. N-COUNT

commissary /kɒmɪsəri, AM -seri/ **commissaries.** In American English, a **commissary** is a shop that provides food and equipment in a place such as a military camp or a prison. N-COUNT

commission /kəmɪʃən/ **commissions, commissioning, commissioned** ♦♦♦♦◇

1 If you **commission** something or **commission** someone to do something, you formally arrange for someone to do a piece of work for you. *The Ministry of Agriculture commissioned a study into low-input farming... You can commission them to paint something especially for you. ...specially commissioned reports.* VERB V n V n to-inf V-ed ▶ Also a noun. *Our china can be bought off the shelf or by commission... He approached John Wexley with a commission to write the screenplay of the film.* N-VAR ♦ **-commissioned** *...Government-commissioned research.* COMB in ADJ

2 A **commission** is a piece of work that someone is asked to do and is paid for. *Just a few days ago, I finished a commission.* N-COUNT

3 **Commission** is a sum of money paid to a salesperson for every sale that he or she makes. If a salesperson is paid on **commission**, the amount they receive depends on the amount they sell. *The salesmen, who work on commission only, are given a harsh debriefing by bosses if they fail to make a sale... He also got a commission for bringing in new clients.* N-VAR: oft on N

4 If a bank or other company charges **commission**, they charge a fee for a providing a service, for example for exchanging money or issuing an insurance policy. *Travel agents charge 1 per cent commission on sterling cheques... Sellers pay a fixed commission fee.* N-UNCOUNT

5 A **commission** is a group of people who have been appointed to find out about something or to control something. *The authorities have been asked to set up a commission to investigate the murders. ...the Press Complaints Commission.* N-COUNT-COLL

6 The **commission** of a crime is the act of committing a crime; a formal use. *...an organisation which is actively engaged in the commission of criminal terrorist acts.* N-UNCOUNT

7 If a member of the armed forces receives a **commission**, he or she becomes an officer. *He accepted a commission as a naval officer.* N-COUNT

8 If a member of the armed forces **is commissioned**, he or she is made an officer. *He was commissioned as second lieutenant in the Air Force... Only commissioned officers qualify for the Military Cross.* VB: usu passive be V-ed as n V-ed Also be V-ed

9 If something, for example a ship or a piece of equipment, is **out of commission**, it is broken and cannot be used until it is repaired. *The operator expects the ship to be out of commission until the end of September.* PHRASE: v-link PHR, PHR after v

10 See also **High Commission**.

commissioner /kəmɪʃənəʳ/ **commissioners;** also spelled **Commissioner**. A **commissioner** is an important official in a government department or other organization. *...the European Commissioner for External Affairs. ...police commissioner.* • See also **High Commissioner**. ♦♦♦◇◇ N-COUNT: usu with supp

commit /kəmɪt/ **commits, committing, committed** ♦♦♦♦◇

1 If someone **commits** a crime or a sin, they do something illegal or bad. *I have never committed any crime... This is a man who has committed murder. ...the temptation to commit adultery.* VERB V n

2 If someone **commits** suicide, they deliberately kill themselves. *There are unconfirmed reports he tried to commit suicide. ...Japanese warriors committing hara-kiri.* VERB V n

3 If you **commit** money or resources to something, you decide to use them for a particular purpose. *They called on Western nations to commit more money to the poorest nations... The government had committed billions of pounds for a programme to reduce acid rain... He should not commit American troops without the full consent of Congress.* VERB V n to/for n/-ing V n

4 If you **commit** yourself to a course of action or way of life, you definitely decide that you will do it or have it. If you **commit** yourself to a person, you definitely decide that your relationship will be a long term one. *I would advise people to think very carefully about committing themselves to working Sundays... I'd like a friendship that might lead to something deeper, but I wouldn't want to commit myself too soon... You don't have to commit to anything over the phone.* VERB V pron-refl to -ing/n V pron-refl V to n Also V n to n

♦ **committed** *He said the government remained committed to peace. ...a committed socialist.* ADJ-GRADED: oft ADJ to n/-ing

5 If you do not want to **commit** yourself on something, you do not want to say what you really think about it or what you are going to do. *It isn't their diplomatic style to commit themselves on such a delicate issue... She didn't want to commit herself one way or the other.* VB: with brd neg; V pron-refl *on* n; V pron-refl

6 If someone **is committed** to a hospital, prison, or other institution, they are officially sent there for a period of time. *Arthur's drinking caused him to be committed to a psychiatric hospital.* VB: usu passive =admit; *be* V-ed *to* n; Also *be* V-ed

7 In the British legal system, if someone **is committed for trial**, they are sent by magistrates to stand trial in a crown court. *He is expected to be committed for trial at Liverpool Crown Court.* VB: usu passive; *be* V-ed *for* n

8 If you **commit** something **to** paper or to writing, you record it by writing it down. If you **commit** something to memory, you memorize it. *She had not committed anything to paper about it... I'll repeat that so you can commit it to memory.* VERB; V n *to* n

commitment /kəmɪtmənt/ **commitments** ◆◆◆◆◇

1 **Commitment** is a strong belief in an idea or system. *...commitment to the ideals of Bolshevism.* N-UNCOUNT: oft N *to* n

2 A **commitment** is something which regularly takes up some of your time because of an agreement you have made or because of responsibilities that you have. *I've got a lot of commitments... Work commitments forced her to uproot herself and her son from Reykjavik.* N-COUNT

3 If you make a **commitment** to do something, you promise faithfully that you will do it; a formal use. *We made a commitment to keep working together... They made a commitment to peace.* N-COUNT: usu N to-inf, N *to* n

committal /kəmɪtəl/ **committals. Committal** is the process of officially sending someone to prison or to hospital. *...his committal to prison. ...committal proceedings.* N-VAR

committee /kəmɪti/ **committees.** A **committee** is a group of people who meet to make decisions or plans for a larger group or organization that they represent. *...a committee of ministers. ...an elected Management Committee who serve the Association on a voluntary basis. ...the Committee for Safety in Medicine... My reasons were stated in writing and circulated to all committee members.* ◆◆◆◆◆ N-COUNT-COLL: usu with supp

commode /kəmoud/ **commodes.** A **commode** is a movable piece of furniture shaped like a chair or a stool, which has a large pot below or inside it. It is used as a toilet, especially by people who are too ill to be able to walk to the toilet easily. N-COUNT

commodious /kəmoudiəs/. A **commodious** room or house is large and has a lot of space; used in written English. ADJ-GRADED: usu ADJ n

commodity /kəmɒdɪti/ **commodities.** A **commodity** is something that is sold for money; a technical term in economics. *The government increased prices on several basic commodities like bread and meat.* ◆◆◇◇◇ N-COUNT =goods

commodore /kɒmədɔːr/ **commodores.** A **commodore** is an officer of senior rank in the navy or air force. ◆◇◇◇◇ N-COUNT; N-TITLE

common /kɒmən/ **commoner commonest; commons** ◆◆◆◆◆

1 If something is **common**, it is found in large numbers or it happens often. *His name was Hansen, a common name in Norway... Oil pollution is the commonest cause of death for seabirds... Earthquakes are not common in this part of the world... It was common practice for prisoners to carve objects from animal bones to pass the time.* ♦ **commonly** *Parsley is probably the most commonly used of all herbs.* ADJ-GRADED ≠rare; ADV-GRADED: ADV with v

2 If something is **common** to two or more people or groups, it is done, possessed, or used by them all. *Moldavians and Romanians share a common language... Such behaviour is common to all young people.* ADJ: oft ADJ *to* n

3 When there are more animals or plants of a particular species than there are of related species, then the first species is called **common**. *...the common house fly.* ADJ: ADJ n

4 **Common** is used to indicate that someone or something is of the ordinary kind and not special in any way. *Democracy might elevate the common man to a position of political superiority... Common salt is made up of 40% sodium and 60% chloride.* ADJ: ADJ n

5 If you talk about **common** decency or **common** courtesy, you are referring to the decency or courtesy which most people have. You usually say this when someone has not shown these characteristics in their behaviour to show your disapproval of them. *No one had the common decency to inform our Association of any such bursary. ...if he'd had the common courtesy to ask permission.* ADJ: oft with brd-neg, ADJ n PRAGMATICS

6 You can use the word **common** to describe knowledge, an opinion, or a feeling that is shared by people in general. *It is common knowledge that swimming is one of the best forms of exercise. ...the common view that acupuncture is only a fringe area of medicine.* ♦ **commonly** *A little adolescent rebellion is commonly believed to be healthy.* ADJ: ADJ n; ADV: ADV -ed

7 If you describe someone as **common**, you mean that they behave in a way that shows lack of taste, education, and good manners. If you describe someone's behaviour, dress, or name as **common**, you mean that it implies lack of taste, education, and good manners. Used showing disapproval. *She might be a little common at times, but she was certainly not boring.* ADJ-GRADED PRAGMATICS =ill-bred ≠refined

8 A **common** is an area of grassy land, usually in or near a village or small town, where the public is allowed to go. *We are warning women not to go out on to the common alone. ...Wimbledon Common.* N-COUNT: oft in names after n

9 **The Commons** is the same as the **House of Commons**. The members of the House of Commons can also be referred to as **the Commons**. *The Prime Minister is to make a statement in the Commons this afternoon... The Commons has spent over three months on the bill.* N-PROPER-COLL

10 See also **lowest common denominator**.

11 If two or more things have something **in common**, they have the same characteristic or feature. *The oboe and the clarinet have got certain features in common... In common with most Italian lakes, access to the shores of Orta is restricted.* PHRASES oft PHR *with* n

12 If two or more people have something **in common**, they share the same interests or experiences. *He had very little in common with his sister.* usu *have* n PHR, oft PHR *with* n

13 • to **make common cause with** someone: see **cause.** • **the common good**: see **good.** • **common ground**: see **ground.** • **the common touch**: see **touch.**

commonality /kɒmənælɪti/ **commonalities. Commonality** is used to refer to a feature or purpose that is shared by two or more people or things; a formal word. *We don't have the same commonality of interest... I'm going to look at some of the differences and also some of the commonalities.* N-VAR: oft N *of* n

common cold, common colds. The **common cold** is a mild illness. If you have it, your nose is blocked, you sneeze a lot, and you have a sore throat or a cough. N-COUNT: usu sing, *the* N =cold

common currency. If you say that an idea or belief has become **common currency**, you mean it is widely used and accepted. *The story that she was trapped in a loveless marriage became common currency.* N-UNCOUNT

common denominator, common denominators

1 A **common denominator** is a number which can be divided exactly by all the denominators in a group of fractions; a technical use in mathematics. N-COUNT

2 A **common denominator** is a characteristic or attitude that is shared by all members of a group of people. *Narcissism is the common denominator for our customers.* N-COUNT

commoner /kɒmənər/ **commoners.** In countries which have a nobility, **commoners** are the people who are not members of the nobility. *It's only the second time a potential heir to the throne has married a commoner.* ◆◇◇◇◇ N-COUNT

common land, common lands. **Common land** is land which everyone is allowed to go on. N-UNCOUNT: also N in pl

common law; also spelled **common-law.** ◆◇◇◇◇

1 **Common law** is the system of law which is based on judges' decisions and on custom rather than on written laws. *Canadian libel law is based on English common law.* N-UNCOUNT

2 A **common law** relationship is regarded as a marriage because it has lasted a long time, although no official marriage contract has been signed. *...his common law wife.* ADJ: ADJ n

common market, common markets ◆◇◇◇◇

1 A **common market** is an organization of countries who have agreed to trade freely with each other and make common decisions about industry and agriculture. *...the Central American Common Market.* N-COUNT

2 **The Common Market** is the former name of the **European Union**. Some people still refer to the European Union as the **Common Market**. *Spain and Portugal are joining the Common Market.* N-PROPER: the N

common noun, common nouns. A **common noun** is a noun such as 'tree', 'water', or 'beauty' that is not the name of one particular person or thing. Compare **proper noun**. N-COUNT

common-or-garden; also spelled **common or garden**. You can use **common-or-garden** to describe something you think is ordinary and not special in any way; used mainly in British English. *These crumbs were grated on a common-or-garden cheese grater.* ADJ: ADJ n

commonplace /kɒmənpleɪs/ **commonplaces** ◆◇◇◇◇

1 If something is **commonplace**, it happens often or is often found, and is therefore not surprising. *Foreign vacations have become commonplace... It is commonplace for snipers to open fire on aid convoys.* ADJ-GRADED: usu v-link ADJ

2 A **commonplace** is something that happens often or is often found. *It's become a commonplace to see people collapsing from hunger in the streets.* N-COUNT: usu sing, oft N to-inf/that

3 A **commonplace** is a remark or opinion that is often expressed and is therefore not original or interesting. *It is a commonplace to say that Northern Ireland is a backwater in the modern Europe.* N-COUNT: usu sing

common room, common rooms; also spelled **common-room**. A **common room** is a room in a university or school where people can sit, talk, and relax. N-COUNT

common sense; also spelled **commonsense**. Your **common sense** is your natural ability to make good judgements and to behave in a practical and sensible way. *Use your common sense... She always had a lot of common sense. ...a common-sense approach.* ◆◆◇◇◇ N-UNCOUNT

commonwealth /kɒmənwelθ/ **commonwealths** ◆◆◇◇◇

1 **The Commonwealth** is a voluntary association of independent countries, consisting of the United Kingdom and most of the countries that were formerly under its rule. *...Pakistan's decision to rejoin the Commonwealth. ...Commonwealth countries.* N-PROPER: the N

2 **Commonwealth** is used in the official names of some countries, groups of countries, or parts of countries. *...the Commonwealth of Australia. ...the Commonwealth of Independent States, which replaced the Soviet Union.* N-IN-NAMES: the N of n

3 If you refer to a **commonwealth** of nations, you are referring to a group of countries who are friendly towards each other and have something in common; a formal use. *...a commonwealth of nations without economic borders.* N-SING: usu N of n

commotion /kəmoʊʃᵊn/ **commotions.** A **commotion** is a lot of noise, confusion, and excitement. *He heard a commotion outside... Sounds of voices and commotion could be heard downstairs now.* ◆◇◇◇◇ N-VAR

communal /kɒmjʊnᵊl, AM kəmjuːnᵊl/ ◆◆◇◇◇

1 **Communal** means relating to particular groups in a country or society. *Communal violence broke out in different parts of the country. ...intercommunal relations.* ADJ: ADJ n

2 You use **communal** to describe something that is shared by a group of people. *The inmates ate in a communal dining room. ...communal ownership.* ADJ: usu ADJ n

♦ **communally** *Meals are taken communally in the dining room.* ADV: usu ADV after v

commune, communes, communing, communed. The noun is pronounced /kɒmjuːn/. The verb is pronounced /kəmjuːn/. ◆◇◇◇◇

1 A **commune** is a group of people who live together and share everything. *Mack lived in a commune.* N-COUNT

2 In France and some other countries, a **commune** is a town, village, or area which has its own council. N-COUNT

3 If you say that someone **is communing with** an animal or spirit, or **with** nature, you mean that they appear to be communicating with it; a literary use. *He was so happy communing with the dolphin in Dingle Bay... She would happily trot behind him as he set off from the lodge to commune with nature.* VERB V with n

communicable /kəmjuːnɪkəbᵊl/. A **communicable** disease is one that can be passed on to another person; a medical term. ADJ: usu ADJ n =infectious

communicant /kəmjuːnɪkənt/ **communicants.** A **communicant** is a person in the Christian church who receives communion; a formal word. N-COUNT

communicate /kəmjuːnɪkeɪt/ **communicates, communicating, communicated** ◆◆◆◇◇

1 If you **communicate** with someone, you share or exchange information with them, for example by speaking, writing, or using equipment. You can also say that two people **communicate**. *My natural mother has never communicated with me... Officials of the CIA depend heavily on electronic mail to communicate with each other... They communicated in sign language.* V-RECIP V with n pl-n V with pron-recip pl-n V

♦ **communication** *Lithuania hasn't had any direct communication with Moscow. ...use of the radio telephone for communication between controllers and pilots... We were in communication with each other.* N-UNCOUNT: oft N with/between n

2 If you **communicate** information, a feeling, or an idea to someone, you let them know about it. *They successfully communicate their knowledge to others... The results will be communicated to parents... People must communicate their feelings.* VERB V n to n V n

3 If one person **communicates** with another, they successfully make each other aware of their feelings and ideas. You can also say that two people **communicate**. *He was never good at communicating with the players... Family therapy showed us how to communicate with each other. ...considerate individuals who can communicate and work in a team.* V-RECIP V with n pl-n V with pron-recip pl-n V

♦ **communication** *There was a tremendous lack of communication between us... Good communication with people around you could prove difficult. ...communication skills.* N-UNCOUNT: oft N with/between n

♦ **communicator, communicators** *She's a good communicator.* N-COUNT

communication /kəmjuːnɪkeɪʃᵊn/ **communications** ◆◆◆◇◇

1 **Communications** are the systems and processes that are used to communicate or broadcast information, especially by means of electricity or radio waves. *...a communications satellite. ...communications equipment.* N-PLURAL: oft N n

2 A **communication** is a message that is sent to someone by, for example, making a telephone call, or sending a letter or fax; a formal use. *The ambassador has brought with him a communication from the President.* N-COUNT

communicative /kəmjuːnɪkətɪv/

1 Someone who is **communicative** talks to people, for example about their feelings, and tells people things. *She has become a lot more tolerant and communicative.* ADJ-GRADED =open

2 **Communicative** means relating to the ability to communicate. *...the notion of communicative competence... We have a very communicative approach to teaching languages.* ADJ-GRADED: usu ADJ n

communion /kəmjuːnjən/ **communions** ◆◇◇◇◇

1 **Communion** with nature or some other power or spirit, or **communion** with a person is the feeling that you are sharing thoughts or feelings with them. *...communion with nature. ...a communion of souls.* N-UNCOUNT: also a N, oft N with n

2 **Communion** is the Christian ceremony in which N-UNCOUNT:

people eat bread and drink wine in memory of Christ's death. *Most villagers took communion only at Easter. ...the Communion service.* also N in pl

communiqué /kəmjuːnɪkeɪ, AM -keɪ/ **communiqués.** A **communiqué** is an official statement or announcement; a formal word. *Representatives of Jordan, Syria, and Lebanon issued a joint communiqué today after a two-day meeting in Amman.* ◆◇◇◇◇ N-COUNT

communism /kɒmjʊnɪzəm/; also spelled **Communism. Communism** is the political belief that all people are equal and that workers should control the means of producing things. *...the collapse of communism in Eastern Europe.* ◆◆◇◇◇ N-UNCOUNT ≠capitalism

communist /kɒmjʊnɪst/ **communists** ◆◆◆◆◇

1 A **communist** is someone who believes in communism. N-COUNT

2 **Communist** means relating to communism. *...the Communist Party.* ADJ: usu ADJ n

community /kəmjuːnɪti/ **communities** ◆◆◆◆◆

1 The **community** is all the people who live in a particular area or place. *He's well liked by people in the community... 'The community are getting impatient,' said a representative of the Residents' Association... The growth of such vigilante gangs has worried community leaders, police and politicians.* N-SING-COLL: usu *the* N

2 A particular **community** is a group of people who are alike in some way. *The police haven't really done anything for the black community in particular. ...the business community.* N-COUNT-COLL: usu supp N

3 **Community** is friendship between different people or groups, and a sense of having something in common. *A supportive house for eight to ten older people, each with his or her own room, provides privacy and a sense of community... Two of our greatest strengths are diversity and community.* N-UNCOUNT

community centre, community centres. A **community centre** is a place that is specially provided for the people, groups, and organizations in a particular area, where they can go in order to meet one another and do things. ◆◇◇◇◇ N-COUNT

community charge. In Britain in the early 1990s, the **community charge** was a tax that people paid to their local authority in order to pay for local services. Within each area most adults had to pay the same amount of community charge. ◆◇◇◇◇ N-UNCOUNT: also *the* N =poll tax

community policing. Community policing is a system in which policemen work only in one particular area of the community, so that everyone knows them. N-UNCOUNT

community service. Community service is unpaid work that criminals sometimes do as a punishment instead of being sent to prison. *He was sentenced to 140 hours community service.* ◆◇◇◇◇ N-UNCOUNT

commute /kəmjuːt/ **commutes, commuting, commuted** ◆◆◇◇◇

1 If you **commute**, you travel a long distance every day between your home and your place of work. *Mike commutes to London every day... McLaren began commuting between Paris and London... He's going to commute.* ♦ **commuter, commuters** *The number of commuters to London has dropped by 100,000. ...a commuter train.* VERB V *to/from* n V *between* n *and* n V N-COUNT

2 In American English, a **commute** is the journey that you make when you commute. *The average Los Angeles commute is over 60 miles a day.* N-COUNT

3 If a death sentence or prison sentence **is commuted** to a less serious punishment, it is changed to that punishment. *His death sentence was commuted to life imprisonment... Prison sentences have been commuted.* VB: usu passive *be* V-ed *to* n *be* V-ed

commuter belt, commuter belts. A **commuter belt** is the area surrounding a large city, where many people who work in the city live. *...people who live in the commuter belt around the capital. ...a commuter-belt town.* N-COUNT

compact, compacts, compacting, compacted. The adjective and verb are pronounced /kəmpækt/. The noun is pronounced /kɒmpækt/. ◆◆◇◇◇

1 If you describe something as **compact**, you mean it is small or takes up very little space, and you think this is a good quality. *...my compact office in Washington. ...the new, more compact Czechoslovak government.* ♦ **compactness** *The very compactness of the cottage made it all the more snug and appealing.* ADJ-GRADED: usu ADJ n PRAGMATICS N-UNCOUNT

2 If you describe someone's physical appearance as **compact**, you mean that they are small and well-proportioned. *He was compact, probably no taller than me... He looked physically very powerful, athletic in a compact way.* ADJ

3 A **compact** cassette, camera, or car is a small type of cassette, camera, or car. ADJ: ADJ n

4 To **compact** something means to press it so that it becomes more dense; a formal use. *The Smith boy was compacting the trash... The soil settles and is compacted by the winter rain.* ♦ **compacted** *...a pile of compacted earth.* ♦ **compaction** /kəmpækʃᵊn/ *Regular forking of beds and borders relieves the compaction caused by rain.* VERB =compress V n ADJ-GRADED N-UNCOUNT

5 A **compact** is a small, flat case that contains face-powder and a mirror. N-COUNT

compact disc, compact discs. Compact discs are small shiny records which are played on special machines which use lasers to read their signals and convert the signals into sound of a very high quality. The abbreviation 'CD' is also used. *The soundtrack of 'Highlander II' will be released on compact disc at Easter.* ◆◇◇◇◇ N-COUNT: also *on* N

companion /kəmpænjən/ **companions.** A **companion** is someone who you spend time with or who you are travelling with. *Fred had been her constant companion for the last six years of her life... I asked my travelling companion what he thought of the situation in Algeria.* ◆◆◇◇◇ N-COUNT

companionable /kəmpænjənəbᵊl/

1 If you describe a person as **companionable**, you mean they are friendly and pleasant to be with; used in written English. ♦ **companionably** /kəmpænjənəbli/ *They walked companionably back to the house in the sunshine.* ADJ-GRADED =affable ADV-GRADED: ADV with v

2 When two people are enjoying being together but are not talking, you can say that they are sitting or walking **in companionable silence**; used in written British English. *They ate an early dinner in companionable silence.* PHRASE: PHR after v

companionship /kəmpænjənʃɪp/. **Companionship** is having someone you know and like with you, rather than being on your own. *I depended on his companionship and on his judgement... The majority of people own a dog for companionship.* ◆◇◇◇◇ N-UNCOUNT =company

companionway /kəmpænjənweɪ/ **companionways.** A **companionway** is a stairway or ladder that leads from one deck to another on a ship. N-COUNT

company /kʌmpəni/ **companies** ◆◆◆◆◆

1 A **company** is a business organization that makes money by selling goods or services. *Sheila found some work as a secretary in an insurance company. ...the Ford Motor Company.* N-COUNT-COLL: oft in names after n =business

2 A **company** is a group of opera singers, dancers, or actors who work together. *...the Phoenix Dance Company.* N-COUNT-COLL: oft in names after n

3 A **company** is a group of soldiers that is usually part of a battalion or regiment, and that is divided into two or more platoons. *The division will consist of two tank companies and one infantry company... C Company's sentries were just ahead.* N-COUNT: oft in names after n

4 **Company** is the state of having another person or other people with you, usually when this is pleasant or stops you feeling lonely. *'I won't stay long.'—'No, please. I need the company'... Ross had always enjoyed the company of women... She would be grateful for their company on the drive back... I'm not in the mood for company.* N-UNCOUNT

5 See also **joint-stock company, public company.**

6 You can say **and company** after mentioning a person's name, to refer also to the people who are associated with that person; an informal expression. *Keegan and company approached the game with understandable caution.* PHRASES n-proper PHR

7 If you say that someone **is in good company**, you mean that they should not be ashamed of a mis- V inflects

take or opinion, because some important or respected people have made the same mistake or have the same opinion. *Mr Koo is in good company. The prime minister made a similar slip a couple of years back.*

8 If you **have company**, you have a visitor or friend with you. *He didn't say he had had company.* V inflects

9 When you are **in company**, you are with a person or group of people. *When they were in company she always seemed to dominate the conversation... I feel awkward and shy in company.* v-link PHR, PHR after v ≠alone

10 If you feel, believe, or know something **in company with** someone else, you both feel, believe, or know it; a formal expression. *Saudi Arabia, in company with some other Gulf oil states, is concerned to avoid any repetition of the two oil price shocks of the 1970s.* PREP: PHR n

11 If you **keep** someone **company**, you spend time with them and stop them feeling lonely or bored. *Why don't you stay here and keep Emma company?* V inflects

12 If you **keep company with** a person or with a particular kind of person, you spend a lot of time with them. *He keeps company with all sorts of lazy characters.* V inflects

13 If two or more people **part company**, they go in different directions after going in the same direction together; used in written English. *The three of them parted company at the bus stop.* RECIP: V inflects, pl-n PHR, PHR *with* n

14 If you **part company** with someone, you end your association with them, often because of a disagreement; a formal expression. *Boris Becker has parted company with his Austrian trainer... We have agreed to part company after differences of opinion.* RECIP: V inflects, PHR *with* n, pl-n PHR

15 If you **part company** with someone on a particular subject, you disagree with them on it; a formal expression. *Where I part company with him, however, is over the link he forges between science and liberalism.* V inflects, oft PHR *with* n

16 If you are making a general, unfavourable comment about a particular type of person, and you are with people of that type, you can say **'present company excepted'** as a way of making your comment sound more polite. PHR with cl PRAGMATICS

company car, company cars. A **company car** is a car which is owned or leased by a company but which is given to an employee to use as their own, usually as a benefit of having a particular job. ◆◇◇◇◇ N-COUNT

company secretary, company secretaries. In business, a **company secretary** is a high-ranking official within a company who is responsible for keeping the legal affairs, accounts, and administration in order. N-COUNT

comparable /kɒmpərəbəl/ ◆◆◇◇◇

1 Something that is **comparable** to something else is roughly similar, for example in amount or importance. *...paying the same wages to men and women for work of comparable value... Farmers were meant to get an income comparable to that of townspeople... The risk it poses is comparable with smoking just one cigarette every year.* ADJ: oft ADJ *to/with* n =equal

♦ **comparably** /kɒmpərəbli/ *...to assess a number of comparably qualified students.* ADV: ADV adj/-ed

♦ **comparability** /kɒmpərəbɪlɪti/ *The rises are the result of a comparability study.* N-UNCOUNT

2 If two or more things are **comparable**, they are of the same kind or are in the same situation, and so they can reasonably be compared. *In other comparable countries real wages increased much more rapidly... By contrast, the comparable figure for the Netherlands is 16 per cent... Published rates are not always directly comparable.* ♦ **comparability** *The result is a lack of comparability between the accounts of similar companies.* ADJ =equivalent; N-UNCOUNT

comparative /kəmpærətɪv/ **comparatives** ◆◆◇◇◇

1 You use **comparative** to indicate that you are judging something against what has previously been the case, or judging it against something else. For example, **comparative** calm is a situation which is calmer than before or calmer than the situation in other places. *...those who manage to reach the comparative safety of Fendel... The task was accomplished with comparative ease.* ADJ: ADJ n =relative

♦ **comparatively** *...a comparatively small nation. ...children who find it comparatively easy to make and keep friends.* ADV: ADV adj/adv

2 A **comparative** study is a study that involves the comparison of two or more things of the same kind. *...a comparative study of the dietary practices of people from various regions of India. ...a professor of English and comparative literature.* ADJ: ADJ n

3 In grammar, the **comparative** form of an adjective or adverb is the form that indicates that something has more of a quality than it used to have or than something else has. For example, 'bigger' is the comparative form of 'big', and 'more quickly' is the comparative form of 'quickly'. Compare **superlative.** ► Also a noun. *The comparative of 'pretty' is 'prettier'.* ADJ: ADJ n; N-COUNT: oft *the* N

compare /kəmpeəʳ/ **compares, comparing, compared** ◆◆◆◇◇

1 When you **compare** things, you consider them and discover the differences or similarities between them. *Compare the two illustrations in Fig 60... Was it fair to compare independent schools with state schools?... Note how smooth the skin of the upper arm is, then compare it to the skin on the elbow.* ● to **compare notes**: see **note**. VERB V pl-n V n *with* n V n *to* n

2 If you **compare** one person or thing to another, you say that they are like the other person or thing. *Some commentators compared his work to that of James Joyce... I can only compare the experience to falling in love.* VERB =liken V n *to/with* n/-ing

3 If one thing **compares** favourably with another, it is better than the other thing. If it **compares** unfavourably, it is worse than the other thing. *Our road safety record compares favourably with that of other European countries... How do the two techniques compare in terms of application?* V-RECIP V adv *with* n V adv

4 If you say that something does not **compare with** something else, you mean that it is much worse. *The flowers here do not compare with those at home... The more recent conifer plantations cannot yet compare with the old woodlands.* VB: usu with neg V *with* n

5 If you describe something as **beyond compare**, you mean that it is extremely good or extremely great; a literary expression. *She was a storyteller beyond compare. ...riches beyond compare.* PHRASE: n/adj PHR, v-link PHR

6 See also **compared**.

compared /kəmpeəʳd/ ◆◆◆◆◇

1 If you say, for example, that one thing is large or small **compared with** another or **compared to** another, you mean that it is larger or smaller than the other thing. *The room was light and lofty compared with our Tudor ones... Columbia was a young city compared to venerable Charleston.* PHR-PREP

2 You talk about one situation or thing **compared with** another or **compared to** another when contrasting the two situations or things. *Women are smoking two extra cigarettes a week, compared with four years ago... In 1800 Ireland's population was nine million, compared to Britain's 16 million.* PHR-PREP

comparison /kəmpærɪsən/ **comparisons** ◆◆◆◇◇

1 When you make a **comparison**, you consider two or more things and discover the differences between them. *...a comparison of the British and German economies... Its recommendations are based on detailed comparisons between the public and private sectors... There are no previous statistics for comparison.* N-VAR: oft N *of/between* pl-n

2 When you make a **comparison**, you say that one thing is like another in some way. *It is demonstrably an unfair comparison... He finds the comparison of insect wings with a sailing boat useful up to a point... The comparison of her life to a sea voyage simplifies her experience.* N-COUNT

3 If you say, for example, that something is large or small **in comparison** with, **in comparison** to, or **by comparison** with something else, you mean that it is larger or smaller than the other thing. *Is the human heart weak in comparison with the other organs?... The amount of carbon dioxide released by human activities such as burning coal and oil is* PHRASES oft PHR *with/to* n =compared with *small in comparison... Those places are modern by comparison with Tresillian.*

4 If you say **there is no comparison** between one thing and another, you mean that you think the first thing is much better than the second, or very different from it. *There is no comparison between the knowledge and skill of such a player and the ordinary casual participant.*
oft PHR *between* pl-n

5 If you say that someone or something **stands** or **bears comparison with** someone or something else, you mean that they are as good, or almost as good; a formal expression. *...the only post-war French intellectual who stands comparison with De Tocqueville.*

compartment /kəmpɑːʳtmənt/ **compartments** ◆◇◇◇◇

1 A **compartment** is one of the separate spaces into which a railway carriage is divided. *On the way home we shared our first class compartment with a group of businessmen.*
N-COUNT

2 A **compartment** is one of the separate parts of an object that is used for keeping things in. *I put a bottle of Sainsbury's champagne in the freezer compartment. ...the secret compartment of my jewel box.* • See also **glove compartment.**
N-COUNT

compartmentalize /kɒmpɑːʳtmentəlaɪz/ **compartmentalizes, compartmentalizing, compartmentalized;** also spelled **compartmentalise** in British English. To **compartmentalize** something means to divide it into separate sections. *Traditionally men have compartmentalized their lives, never letting their personal lives encroach upon their professional lives.*
VERB
V n
Also V n *into* n

♦ **compartmentalized** *...the compartmentalised world of Japanese finance.*
ADJ-GRADED

compass /kʌmpəs/ **compasses** ◆◇◇◇◇

1 A **compass** is an instrument that you use for finding directions. It has a dial and a magnetic needle that always points to the north. *We had to rely on a compass and a lot of luck to get here.*
N-COUNT

2 **Compasses** are a hinged V-shaped instrument that you use for drawing circles.
N-PLURAL: also *a pair of* N

3 Something that is within the **compass** of something or someone is within their limits or their possible range of action or operation; a formal use. *Within the compass of a normal sized book such a comprehensive survey was not practicable... 36 holes a day would be within the compass of most players.*
N-COUNT: usu sing, with supp

compassion /kəmpæʃᵊn/. **Compassion** is a feeling of pity, sympathy, and understanding for someone who is suffering. *Elderly people need time and compassion from their physicians.* ◆◆◇◇◇
N-UNCOUNT

compassionate /kəmpæʃᵊnət/. If you describe someone or something as **compassionate**, you mean that they feel or show pity, sympathy, and understanding for people who are suffering. *My father was a deeply compassionate man... She has a wise, compassionate face... Robert Tanitch describes the film as 'deeply compassionate'.* ◆◇◇◇◇
ADJ-GRADED: usu ADJ n

♦ **compassionately** *He smiled compassionately at her.*
ADV-GRADED: ADV with v

compassionate leave. **Compassionate leave** is time away from your work that your employer allows you for personal reasons, especially when a member of your family dies or is seriously ill.
N-UNCOUNT

compass point, compass points. A **compass point** is one of the 32 marks on the dial of a compass that show direction, for example north, south, east, and west.
N-COUNT

compatible /kəmpætɪbᵊl/ ◆◆◇◇◇

1 If things, for example systems, ideas, and beliefs, are **compatible**, they work well together or can exist together successfully. *Free enterprise, he argued, was compatible with Russian values and traditions... Marriage and the life I live just don't seem compatible.*
ADJ-GRADED: oft ADJ *with* n ≠incompatible

♦ **compatibility** /kəmpætɪbɪlɪti/ *National courts can freeze any law while its compatibility with European Community legislation is being tested.*
N-UNCOUNT: oft N *with/of/between* n ≠incompatibility

2 If you say that you are **compatible** with someone, you mean that you have a good relationship with them because you have similar opinions and interests. *Mildred and I are very compatible. She's interested in the things that interest me... In a large city you're almost certain to find a physician with whom you are compatible and feel comfortable.*
ADJ-GRADED: oft ADJ *with* n ≠incompatible

♦ **compatibility** *As a result of their compatibility, Haig and Fraser were able to bring about wide-ranging reforms.*
N-UNCOUNT ≠incompatibility

3 If one brand of computer or computer equipment is **compatible** with another brand, especially an IBM, they can be used together and can use the same software.
ADJ: oft ADJ *with* n

compatriot /kəmpætriət, AM -peɪt-/ **compatriots.** Your **compatriots** are people from your own country. *Chris Robertson of Australia beat his compatriot Chris Dittmar in the final.* ◆◇◇◇◇
N-COUNT: usu poss N =countryman

compel /kəmpel/ **compels, compelling, compelled** ◆◆◇◇◇

1 If a situation, a rule, or a person **compels** you to do something, they force you to do it. *...the introduction of legislation to compel cyclists to wear a helmet... Leonie's mother was compelled to take in washing to help support her family... Local housing authorities have been compelled by the housing crisis to make offers of sub-standard accommodation.*
VERB
V n to-inf
Also V n

2 If you **feel compelled** to do something, you feel that you must do it, because it is the right thing to do. *Dickens felt compelled to return to the stage for a final good-bye... I felt morally compelled to help.*
PHRASE: V inflects, PHR to-inf

compelling /kəmpelɪŋ/ ◆◆◇◇◇

1 A **compelling** argument or reason is one that convinces you that something is true or that something should be done. *Factual and forensic evidence makes a suicide verdict the most compelling answer to the mystery of his death... My second and more compelling reason for going to Dearborn was to see the Henry Ford Museum.*
ADJ-GRADED: usu ADJ n

2 If you describe something such as a film or book, or someone's appearance, as **compelling**, you mean you want to keep looking at it or reading it because you find it so interesting. *...a frighteningly violent yet compelling film... Her eyes were her best feature, wide-set and compelling.*
ADJ-GRADED

♦ **compellingly** *She wrote compellingly, with great zest.*
ADV-GRADED: ADV with v, ADV adj

compendium /kəmpendiəm/ **compendiums.** A **compendium** is a short but detailed collection of information, usually in a book. *The Roman Catholic Church has issued a compendium of its teachings.*
N-COUNT

compensate /kɒmpənseɪt/ **compensates, compensating, compensated** ◆◆◇◇◇

1 To **compensate** someone for money or things that they have lost means to pay them money or give them something to replace that money or those things. *The official promise to compensate people for the price rise clearly hadn't been worked out properly... To ease financial difficulties, farmers could be compensated for their loss of subsidies.*
VERB
V n *for* n
Also V n

2 If you **compensate** for a lack of something or for something you have done wrong, you do something to make the situation better. *The company agreed to keep up high levels of output in order to compensate for supplies lost... She would then feel guilt for her anger and compensate by doing even more for the children.*
VERB =make up
V *for* n
V

3 Something that **compensates for** something else balances it or counteracts its effects. *MPs say it is crucial that a mechanism is found to compensate for inflation... The pluses more than compensated for the inconveniences involved in making the trip.*
VERB
V *for* n

4 If you try to **compensate** for something that is wrong or missing in your life, you try to do something that removes or reduces the harmful effects. *People who sense that they are inferior have to compensate, and often over-compensate by way of outward achievement.*
VERB
V
Also V *for* n

compensation /kɒmpənseɪʃᵊn/ **compensations** ◆◆◆◇◇

1 **Compensation** is money that someone who has undergone loss or suffering claims from the person or organization responsible, or from a state fund. *He received one year's salary as compensation for loss of office... There should be compensation for*
N-UNCOUNT =damages

British farmers hit by the slump in demand... The Court ordered Dr Williams to pay £300 compensation and £100 costs after admitting assault.

2 If something is some **compensation** for something bad that has happened, it makes you feel better. *Helen gained some compensation for her earlier defeat by winning the final open class... Despite a reduction in earnings there are compensations in moving to the north-east where the quality of life is excellent... The toy glider she left him as a Christmas present was no compensation for her absence.* N-VAR: oft N *for* n/-ing

compensatory /kɒmpənseɪtəri/

1 **Compensatory** payments involve money paid as compensation; a formal use. *The jury awarded $11.2 million in compensatory damages.* ADJ: usu ADJ n

2 **Compensatory** measures are designed to help people who have special problems or disabilities; a formal use. *Money should be spent on compensatory programmes for deprived pre-school and infant-school children.* ADJ: usu ADJ n

compere /kɒmpeəʳ/ **comperes, compering, compered**

1 In British English, a **compere** is the person who introduces the performers or contestants on a radio or television show or at a live show; the usual American word is **emcee**. N-COUNT =host

2 In British English, the person who **comperes** a show introduces the performers or contestants. *Sarita Sagharwal from TV Asia compered the programme... They wanted Ben Elton to compere.* VERB =host V n V

compete /kəmpiːt/ **competes, competing, competed** ◆◆◆◇◇

1 When one firm or country **competes** with another, it tries to get people to buy its own goods in preference to those of the other firm or country. You can also say that two firms or countries **compete**. *The banks have long competed with American Express's charge cards and various store cards... The stores will inevitably end up competing with each other in their push for increased market shares... Banks and building societies are competing fiercely for business... The American economy, and its ability to compete abroad, was slowing down according to the report.* V-RECIP V *with* n pl-n V *with* pron-recip pl-n V *for* n V (non-recip) Also pl-n V

2 If you **compete** with someone for something, you try to get it for yourself and stop the other person getting it. You can also say that two people **compete** for something. *Kangaroos compete with sheep and cattle for sparse supplies of food and water... Schools should not compete with each other or attempt to poach pupils... More than 2300 candidates from 93 political parties are competing for 486 seats.* V-RECIP V *with* n *for* n pl-n V *with* pron-recip pl-n V *for* n

3 If you **compete** in a contest or a game, you take part in it. *He will be competing in the London-Calais-London race... Dubbed foreign language films will not be allowed to compete for best film... It is essential for all players who wish to compete that they earn computer ranking points.* VERB V prep V

4 See also **competing**.

competence /kɒmpɪtəns/. **Competence** is the ability to do something well or effectively. *His competence as an economist had been reinforced by his successful fight against inflation... We've always regarded him as a man of integrity and high professional competence.* ◆◇◇◇◇ N-UNCOUNT

competency /kɒmpɪtənsi/. **Competency** means the same as **competence**. *...managerial competency.* N-UNCOUNT

competent /kɒmpɪtənt/ ◆◆◇◇◇

1 Someone who is **competent** is efficient and effective. *He was a loyal, distinguished and very competent civil servant. ...a competent performance.* ADJ-GRADED ♦ **competently** *The government performed competently in the face of multiple challenges.* ADV-GRADED: ADV with v, ADV adj

2 If you are **competent** to do something, you have the skills, abilities, or experience necessary to do it well. *Most adults do not feel competent to deal with a medical emergency involving a child.* ADJ-GRADED: oft ADJ to-inf =able

competing /kəmpiːtɪŋ/. **Competing** ideas, requirements, or interests cannot all be right or satisfied at the same time. *They talked about the competing theories of the origin of life. ...the competing interests of beach development and sea turtle protection. ...the competing demands of work and family.* ● See also **compete**. ◆◆◇◇◇ ADJ: ADJ n =conflicting

competition /kɒmpɪtɪʃən/ **competitions** ◆◆◆◆◇

1 **Competition** is a situation in which two or more people or groups are trying to get something which not everyone can have. *There's been some fierce competition for the title... It was in these studios that young painters found the support and stimulating competition of peers.* N-UNCOUNT: usu with supp, oft adj N, N prep

2 The **competition** is the person or people you are competing with. *I have to change my approach, the competition is too good now.* N-SING: usu *the* N

3 **Competition** is an activity involving two or more firms, in which each firm tries to get people to buy its own goods in preference to the other firms' goods. *The deal would have reduced competition in the commuter-aircraft market... The farmers have been seeking higher prices as better protection from foreign competition... Clothing stores also face heavy competition from factory outlets.* N-UNCOUNT: usu with supp, oft adj N, N prep

4 The **competition** is the goods that a rival organization is selling. *The American aerospace industry has been challenged by some stiff competition.* N-UNCOUNT

5 A **competition** is an event in which many people take part in order to find out who is best at a particular activity. *...a surfing competition... The council has organised a series of events and competitions for school children in the area... He will be banned from international competition for four years.* N-VAR

competitive /kəmpetɪtɪv/ ◆◆◆◇◇

1 **Competitive** is used to describe situations or activities in which people or firms compete with each other. *Only by keeping down costs will America maintain its competitive advantage over other countries... Japan is a highly competitive market system... Universities are very competitive for the best students.* ADJ-GRADED ♦ **competitively** *He's now back up on the slopes again, skiing competitively in events for the disabled.* ADV: ADV after v

2 A **competitive** person is eager to be more successful than other people. *He has always been ambitious and fiercely competitive... I'm a very competitive person and I was determined not be beaten.* ADJ-GRADED =ambitious ♦ **competitively** *They worked hard together, competitively and under pressure.* ADV-GRADED: ADV after v =ambitiously ♦ **competitiveness** *I can't stand the pace, I suppose, and the competitiveness, and the unfriendliness.* N-UNCOUNT =ambition

3 Goods or services that are at a **competitive** price or rate are likely to be bought, because they are less expensive than other goods of the same kind. *Only those homes offered for sale at competitive prices will secure interest from serious purchasers. ...a travel company specialising in amazingly competitive rates for flights.* ADJ-GRADED ♦ **competitively** *...a number of early Martin and Gibson guitars, which were competitively priced.* ADV-GRADED: ADV -ed, ADV after v ♦ **competitiveness** *It is only on the world market that we can prove the competitiveness and quality of our goods.* N-UNCOUNT

competitor /kəmpetɪtəʳ/ **competitors** ◆◆◆◇◇

1 A company's **competitors** are companies who are trying to sell similar goods or services to the same people. *The bank isn't performing as well as some of its competitors.* N-COUNT: oft poss N =rival

2 A **competitor** is a person who takes part in a competition or contest. *Herbert Blocker of Germany, one of the oldest competitors, won the individual silver medal.* N-COUNT

compilation /kɒmpɪleɪʃən/ **compilations.** A **compilation** is a book, record, or programme that contains many different items that have been gathered together, usually ones which have already appeared elsewhere. *His latest album release is a compilation of his jazz works over the past decade.* ● See also **compile**. ◆◇◇◇◇ N-COUNT =collection

compile /kəmpaɪl/ **compiles, compiling, compiled.** When you **compile** something such as a report, book, or programme, you produce it by collecting and putting together many pieces of information. *Councils were required to compile a register of all adults living in their areas... The* ◆◆◇◇◇ VERB V n V-ed *book took 10 years to compile... A report compiled by the Fed's Philadelphia branch described the economy as weak.* ♦ **compilation** /kɒmpɪleɪʃən/ *There have been enormous advances in the compilation of data on suspected terrorists.* N-UNCOUNT

compiler /kəmpaɪləʳ/ **compilers**

1 A **compiler** is someone who compiles books, reports, or lists of information. *...the compilers of dictionaries and grammars.* N-COUNT: oft N *of* n

2 A **compiler** is a computer program which converts language that people can use into a code that the computer can understand; a technical use. N-COUNT

complacency /kəmpleɪsənsi/. **Complacency** is the state of being complacent about a situation. *...a worrying level of complacency about the risks of infection from AIDS... She warned that there was no room for complacency on inflation.* ♦◇◇◇◇ N-UNCOUNT PRAGMATICS

complacent /kəmpleɪsənt/. If you say that someone is **complacent**, you are critical of them because they are very pleased with themselves or feel that they do not need to worry or do anything about a situation, even though the situation may be uncertain or dangerous. *We cannot afford to be complacent about our health. ...the Chancellor's complacent attitude towards the far-right's activities.* ♦ **complacently** *He sat back, smiling complacently at his own cleverness.* ♦◇◇◇◇ ADJ-GRADED PRAGMATICS; ADV-GRADED: usu ADV with v

complain /kəmpleɪn/ **complains, complaining, complained** ♦♦♦♦◇

1 If you **complain** about a situation, you say that you are not satisfied with it. *Miners have complained bitterly that the government did not fulfill their promises... The American couple complained about the high cost of visiting Europe... For my own part, I have nothing to complain of... They are liable to face more mistreatment if they complain to the police... People should complain when they consider an advert offensive... 'I do everything you ask of me,' he complained, 'but still you act as if you're suffering.'* VERB V that V *about/of* n V *to* n V V with quote

2 If you **complain of** pain or illness, you say that you are feeling pain or feeling ill. *He complained of a headache.* VERB V *of* n

complainant /kəmpleɪnənt/ **complainants.** A **complainant** is a person who starts a court case in a court of law; a legal term. N-COUNT ≠respondent

complainer /kəmpleɪnəʳ/ **complainers.** If you say that someone is a **complainer**, you are critical of them because they complain a lot about their problems or about things that they don't like. *He was a terrible complainer and used to make a great deal of his illness.* N-COUNT PRAGMATICS

complaint /kəmpleɪnt/ **complaints** ♦♦♦◇◇

1 A **complaint** is a statement in which you express your dissatisfaction with a particular situation. *There's been a record number of complaints about the standard of service on Britain's railways... People have been reluctant to make formal complaints to the police... If you feel you have any cause for complaint about the service you should write to the Hospital Administrator.* N-VAR: oft N *about* n

2 A **complaint** is a reason for complaining. *If you have a complaint about shoes bought from a shop covered by the Footwear Code, there are several ways of putting the matter right... I've got no complaints about them... My main complaint is that we can't go out on the racecourse anymore.* N-COUNT

3 You can refer to an illness as a **complaint**, especially if it is not very serious. *Eczema is a common skin complaint which often runs in families.* N-COUNT =ailment

complaisant /kəmpleɪzənt/. If you are **complaisant**, you are willing to accept what other people are doing without complaining; an old-fashioned word. *...his pretty and complaisant wife.* ADJ-GRADED

complement, complements, complementing, complemented. The verb is pronounced /kɒmplɪment/. The noun is pronounced /kɒmplɪmənt/. ♦♦◇◇◇

1 If one thing **complements** another, it goes well with the other thing and makes its good qualities more noticeable. *Nutmeg, parsley and cider all complement the flavour of these beans well.* VERB =set off V n

2 If people or things **complement** each other, they are different or do something different, which makes them a good combination. *There will be a written examination to complement the practical test... We complement one another perfectly.* VERB V n

3 Something that is a **complement** to something else complements it. *The green wallpaper is the perfect complement to the old pine of the dresser... Political knowledge is a necessary complement to science in approaching solutions to these problems.* N-COUNT: usu sing, oft N *to* n

4 The **complement** of things or people that something has is the number of things or people that it normally has, which enable it to function properly; a formal use. *Each ship had a complement of around a dozen officers and 250 men... Not one house on the Close still had its full complement of windows.* N-COUNT: usu sing, oft N *of* n

5 In grammar, the **complement** of a link verb is an adjective group or noun group which comes after the verb and describes or identifies the subject. For example, in the sentence 'They felt very tired', 'very tired' is the complement. In 'They were students', 'students' is the complement. Some verbs can have a complement after their object which describes the object. For example, in 'It made him angry', 'angry' is the object complement. N-COUNT

complementary /kɒmplɪmentri/ ♦◇◇◇◇

1 **Complementary** things are different from each other but make a good combination; a formal use. *To improve the quality of life through work, two complementary strategies are necessary... Many plain tiles and complementary borders are also available... He has done experiments complementary to those of Eigen.* ♦ **complementarity** /kɒmplɪmentærɪti/ *...the complementarity between public and private authorities.* ADJ: usu ADJ n, also v-link ADJ *to* n; N-UNCOUNT

2 **Complementary** medicine means ways of treating patients which are different from the ones used by most Western doctors. Examples are acupuncture and homoeopathy. *...combining orthodox treatment with a wide range of complementary therapies.* ADJ: ADJ n ≠orthodox, conventional

complementation /kɒmplɪmenteɪʃən/. A **complementation** pattern of a verb, noun, or adjective is a combination of word classes that typically follows it. N-UNCOUNT: usu N n

complete /kəmpliːt/ **completes, completing, completed** ♦♦♦♦♦

1 You use **complete** to emphasize that something is as great in extent, degree, or amount as it possibly can be. *The rebels had taken complete control... It shows a complete lack of understanding by management... The resignation came as a complete surprise... He was the complete opposite of Raymond.* ♦ **completely** *Dozens of flats had been completely destroyed... Make sure that you defrost it completely. ...something completely different.* ADJ: usu ADJ n PRAGMATICS =total, absolute ≠partial; ADV: ADV with v, ADV adj/adv =totally

2 You can use **complete** to emphasize that you are referring to the whole of something and not just part of it. *A complete tenement block was burnt to the ground... The job sheets eventually filled a complete book.* ADJ: ADJ n PRAGMATICS =entire, whole

3 If something is **complete**, it contains all the parts that it should contain. *The list may not be complete. ...a complete dinner service... No garden is complete without a bed of rose bushes.* ADJ

♦ **completeness** *...the accuracy and completeness of the information obtained.* N-UNCOUNT

4 To **complete** a set or group means to provide the last item that is needed to make it a full set or group. *Children don't complete their set of 20 baby teeth until they are two to three years old. ...the stickers needed to complete the collection.* VB: no cont V n

5 The **complete** works of an author or poet are all their books or poems published together in one book or as a set of books. *...the Complete Works of William Shakespeare.* ADJ: ADJ n =collected

6 If one thing comes **complete with** another, it has that thing as an extra or additional part. *The diary comes complete with a gold-coloured ballpoint pen.* PHR-PREP: PREP n

7 If something is **complete**, it has been finished. ADJ:

The work of restoring the farmhouse is complete... It'll be two years before the process is complete. v-link ADJ ≠incomplete

8 If you **complete** something, you finish doing, making, or producing it. *Peter Mayle has just completed his first novel. ...the rush to get the stadiums completed on time.* VERB V n get n V-ed
♦ **completion** /kəmpliːʃən/ **completions** *The project is nearing completion... House completions for the year should be up from 1,841 to 2,200.* N-VAR

9 If you **complete** something, you do all of it. *She completed her degree in two years... This book took years to complete.* VB: no cont =finish V n

10 If you **complete** a form or questionnaire, you write the answers or information asked for in it. *Simply complete the coupon below... We ask candidates to complete a psychometric questionnaire... Use the enclosed envelope to return your completed survey.* VERB =fill in V n V-ed

11 You can use **complete** to emphasize that someone is skilled at all aspects of a particular activity and is therefore the best example of that kind of person. *He was the complete all-round journalist.* ADJ: ADJ n PRAGMATICS

complex /kɒmpleks/ **complexes.** The adjective is pronounced /kəmpleks/ in American English. ◆◆◆◆◇

1 Something that is **complex** has many different parts, and is therefore often difficult to understand. *...in-depth coverage of today's complex issues. ...a complex system of voting. ...her complex personality. ...complex machines.* ADJ-GRADED =complicated ≠simple

2 In grammar, a **complex** sentence contains one or more subordinate clauses as well as a main clause. Compare **compound**. ADJ: ADJ n

3 A **complex** is a group of buildings designed for a particular purpose, or one large building divided into several smaller areas. *...plans for constructing a new stadium and leisure complex. ...a complex of offices and flats.* N-COUNT: usu with supp

4 A **complex** of things is a group or system of things that are connected with each other in a complicated way. *...the complex of clans which occupied the land. ...the military-industrial complex.* N-COUNT: with supp =network

5 If someone has a **complex** about something, they have a mental or emotional problem relating to it, often because of an unpleasant experience in the past. *I have never had a complex about my height. ...a deranged attacker, driven by a persecution complex.* • See also **guilt complex, inferiority complex.** N-COUNT

complexion /kəmplekʃən/ **complexions** ◆◇◇◇◇

1 When you refer to someone's **complexion**, you are referring the natural colour or condition of the skin on their face. *She had short brown hair and a pale complexion. ...those with acne or oily complexions. ...her flawless complexion.* N-COUNT: oft adj N

2 The **complexion** of something is its general nature or character; a formal use. *Every time the political complexion of the government changed, so did the defence policy... But surely this puts a different complexion on things.* N-COUNT: with supp

complexities /kəmpleksɪtiz/. The **complexities** of something are the many complicated factors involved in it. *...those who find it hardest to cope with the complexities of modern life... The issue is surrounded by legal complexities.* ◆◇◇◇◇ N-PLURAL: usu with supp

complexity /kəmpleksɪti/. **Complexity** is the state of having many different parts connected or related to each other in a complicated way. *...a diplomatic tangle of great complexity. ...the increasing complexity of modern weapon systems.* ◆◆◇◇◇ N-UNCOUNT: usu with supp ≠simplicity

compliance /kəmplaɪəns/. **Compliance** with something, for example a law, treaty, or agreement means doing what you are required or expected to do. *Inspectors were sent to visit nuclear sites and verify compliance with the treaty... The company says it is in full compliance with US labor laws... The Security Council aim to ensure compliance by all sides, once an agreement is signed.* ◆◇◇◇◇ N-UNCOUNT: oft N *with* n

compliant /kəmplaɪənt/. If you say that someone is **compliant**, you mean they willingly do what they are asked to do; a formal word. *She was much naughtier than her compliant brother. ...a docile and compliant workforce.* ADJ-GRADED =pliant, pliable

complicate /kɒmplɪkeɪt/ **complicates, complicating, complicated.** To **complicate** something means to make it more difficult to understand or deal with. *What complicates the issue is the burden of history... The day's events, he said, would only complicate the task of the peacekeeping forces... To complicate matters further, everybody's vitamin requirements vary... Bad weather continues to complicate efforts to deal with oil spilling from the tanker.* ◆◇◇◇◇ VERB V n

complicated /kɒmplɪkeɪtɪd/. If you say that something is **complicated**, you mean it has so many parts or aspects that it is difficult to understand or deal with. *The situation in Lebanon is very complicated. ...a very complicated voting system.* ◆◆◆◇◇ ADJ-GRADED =complex ≠uncomplicated, simple

complication /kɒmplɪkeɪʃən/ **complications** ◆◆◇◇◇

1 A **complication** is a problem or difficulty that makes a situation harder to deal with. *The age difference was a complication to the relationship... An added complication is the growing concern for the environment.* N-COUNT

2 A **complication** is a medical problem that occurs as a result of another illness or disease. *Blindness is a common complication of diabetes... He died of complications from a heart attack.* N-COUNT

complicity /kəmplɪsɪti/. **Complicity** is involvement with other people in an illegal activity or plan; a formal word. *Recently a number of policemen were sentenced to death for their complicity in the murder. ...evidence of complicity with international terrorists.* ◆◇◇◇◇ N-UNCOUNT: oft N *in* n =collusion

compliment, compliments, complimenting, complimented. The verb is pronounced /kɒmplɪment/. The noun is pronounced /kɒmplɪmənt/. ◆◆◇◇◇

1 A **compliment** is a polite remark that you say to someone to show that you like their appearance, appreciate their qualities, or approve of what they have done. *You can do no harm by paying a woman compliments... 'Well done, Cassandra,' Crook said. She blushed, but accepted the compliment with good grace.* N-COUNT

2 If you **compliment** someone, you pay them a compliment. *They complimented me on the way I looked each time they saw me... Firstly I compliment you on most of your excellent Spring issue of 'Triangle'.* VERB V n *on* n Also V n

3 If you consider something that a person says or does as a **compliment**, it convinces you of your own good qualities, or that that person appreciates them. *We consider it a compliment to be called 'conservative'... It's obvious he's worried about us and I'm taking it as a compliment.* N-COUNT

4 You can refer to your **compliments** when you want to formally express thanks, good wishes, or respect to someone. *My compliments to the chef... Give my compliments to your lovely wife when you write home.* N-PLURAL: usu poss N, oft N *to* n PRAGMATICS

5 If you say that someone **returns the compliment**, you mean that they do the same thing to someone else as that person has done to them. *The actors have entertained us so splendidly during this weekend, I think it's time we returned the compliment.* PHRASES V inflects

6 If you say that you are giving someone something **with** your **compliments**, you are saying in a polite and fairly formal way that you are giving it to them, especially as a gift or a favour. *Please give this to your boss with my compliments... On my bedside table awaited, with the compliments of the management, an appetizing breakfast.* PHR after v PRAGMATICS

complimentary /kɒmplɪmentəri/ ◆◇◇◇◇

1 If you are **complimentary** about something, you express admiration for it. *The staff have been very complimentary, and so have the customers... We often get complimentary remarks regarding the cleanliness of our patio.* ADJ-GRADED: usu v-link ADJ =flattering

2 A **complimentary** seat, ticket, or book is given to you free. *He had complimentary tickets to take his* ADJ: usu ADJ n *wife to see the movie. ...a complimentary copy of Dr Sherwood's recently published book.*

comply /kəmplaɪ/ **complies, complying, complied.** ◆◆◇◇◇ VERB If you **comply** with an order or set of rules, you do what you are required or expected to do. *The commander said that the army would comply with the ceasefire...* V with n *Children of whatever background have to comply with the tests as they are compulsory...* V *There are calls for his resignation, but there is no sign yet that he will comply.* Also V to n

component /kəmpoʊnənt/ **components** ◆◆◆◇◇

1 The **components** of something are the parts that it is made of. N-COUNT *Enriched uranium is a key component of a nuclear weapon... The management plan has four main components... They were automotive component suppliers to motor manufacturers.*

2 The **component** parts of something are the parts that make it up. ADJ: ADJ n *President Gorbachev has finalised the Union Treaty which, he hopes, will keep the component parts of the Soviet Union together... Polish workers will now be making component parts for Boeing 757s.*

comport /kəmpɔːʳt/ **comports, comporting, comported.** VERB If you **comport** yourself in a particular way, you behave in that way; a formal word. *He comports himself with modesty... They should be able to comport themselves as they want.* V pron-refl prep/adv

compose /kəmpoʊz/ **composes, composing, composed** ◆◆◇◇◇

1 The things that something **is composed** of are its parts or members. The separate things that **compose** something are the parts or members that form it. VERB =make up *The force would be composed of troops from NATO countries...* be V-ed of n *Protein molecules compose all the complex working parts of living cells...* V n *They agreed to form a council composed of leaders of the rival factions.* V-ed

2 When someone **composes** a piece of music, they write it. VERB *Vivaldi composed a large number of very fine concertos...* V n *Cale also uses electronic keyboards to compose.* V

3 If you **compose** something such as a letter, poem, or speech, you write it, often using a lot of concentration or skill; a formal use. VERB *He started at once to compose a reply to Anna...* V n *The document composed in Philadelphia transformed the confederation of sovereign states into a national government.* V-ed

4 If you **compose** a picture or image, you arrange it in an attractive and artistic way; a technical use. VERB *Anthony dismounted with his camera and walked away from the walls to compose a shot...* V n *The drawing is beautifully composed.* V-ed

5 If you **compose** yourself or if you **compose** your features, you succeed in becoming calm after you have been angry, excited, or upset. VERB *She quickly composed herself as the car started off...* V pron-refl *Then he composed his features, took Godwin's hand awkwardly and began to usher him from the office.* V n

composed /kəmpoʊzd/. ADJ-GRADED: usu v-link ADJ If someone is **composed**, they are calm and able to control their feelings. *Laura was standing beside him, very calm and composed... It wasn't the peaceful, composed experience I had expected.*

composer /kəmpoʊzəʳ/ **composers.** ◆◆◇◇◇ N-COUNT A **composer** is a person who writes music, especially classical music.

composite /kɒmpəzɪt, AM kəmpɑːzɪt/ **composites.** ◆◆◇◇◇ ADJ: usu ADJ n A **composite** object or item is made up of several different things, parts, or substances. *Galton devised a method of creating composite pictures in which the features of different faces were superimposed over one another.* ► Also a noun. N-COUNT: usu sing, oft N of n *Spain is a composite of diverse traditions and people.*

composition /kɒmpəzɪʃᵊn/ **compositions** ◆◆◇◇◇

1 When you talk about the **composition** of something, you are referring to the way in which its various parts are put together and arranged. N-UNCOUNT: usu with supp, oft N of n =make-up *Television has transformed the size and social composition of the audience at great sporting occasions... Forests vary greatly in composition from one part of the country to another.*

2 The **compositions** of a composer, painter, or other artist are the works of art that they have produced. N-COUNT =creation *Mozart's compositions are undoubtedly amongst the world's greatest.*

3 A **composition** is a piece of written work that children write at school. N-COUNT =essay

4 **Composition** is the technique or skill involved in creating a work of art. N-UNCOUNT *He taught the piano, organ and composition... The course is designed to help students with colour and composition.*

5 **Composition** is the act of composing something such as a piece of music or a poem. N-UNCOUNT *These plays are arranged in their order of composition.*

compositional /kɒmpəzɪʃənᵊl/. ADJ: ADJ n **Compositional** refers to the way composers and artists use their skills or techniques in their work. *...a study of Olivier Messiaen's compositional style.*

compositor /kəmpɒzɪtəʳ/ **compositors.** N-COUNT A **compositor** is a person who arranges the text and illustrations of a book, magazine, or newspaper before it is printed.

compost /kɒmpɒst, AM -poʊst/ **composts, composting, composted** ◆◆◇◇◇

1 **Compost** is a mixture of decaying plants and manure, which is added to the soil to help plants grow. N-UNCOUNT *...a small compost heap.*

2 **Compost** is a specially treated soil or peat mixed with fertilizer that you buy and use to grow seeds and plants in pots. N-MASS

3 When someone **composts** things such as unwanted bits of plants, they make them into compost. VERB *Cut down and compost spent cucumbers, tomatoes and other crops...* V n *All garden waste should be composted and returned to the garden.*
♦ **composting** N-UNCOUNT *Composting is the ideal way of getting rid of vegetable, garden and organic waste.*

composure /kəmpoʊʒəʳ/. ◆◇◇◇◇ N-UNCOUNT Someone's **composure** is their appearance or feeling of calmness and their control of their feelings; a formal word. *For once Dimbleby lost his composure. It was all he could do to stop tears of mirth falling down his cheeks... Stopping only briefly to regain her composure, she described her agonising ordeal.*

compote /kɒmpoʊt/ **compotes.** N-VAR **Compote** is fruit stewed with sugar or in syrup.

compound, compounds, compounding, compounded. ◆◆◇◇◇ The noun is pronounced /kɒmpaʊnd/. The verb is pronounced /kəmpaʊnd/.

1 A **compound** is an enclosed area of land that is used for a particular purpose. N-COUNT =enclosure *Police fired on them as they fled into the embassy compound. ...a military compound.*

2 In chemistry, a **compound** is a substance that consists of two or more elements. N-COUNT *Organic compounds contain carbon in their molecules.*

3 If something is a **compound** of different things, it consists of those things; a formal use. N-COUNT: usu sing, usu N of n =mixture *Honey is basically a compound of water, two types of sugar, vitamins and enzymes.*

4 **Compound** is used to indicate that something consists of two or more parts or things. ADJ: ADJ n =composite ≠simple *...a tall shrub with shiny compound leaves. ...the compound microscope.*

5 In grammar, a **compound** noun, adjective, or verb is one that is made up of two or more words, for example 'fire engine', 'bottle-green', and 'force-feed'. ADJ: ADJ n

6 In grammar, a **compound** sentence is one that is made up of two or more main clauses. Compare **complex**. ADJ: ADJ n

7 To **compound** a problem, difficulty, or mistake means to make it worse by adding to it; a formal use. VERB =add to *Additional bloodshed and loss of life will only compound the tragedy...* V n *The problem is compounded by the medical system here.*

compounded /kɒmpaʊndɪd/. ◆◇◇◇◇ ADJ: v-link ADJ of n =composed of If something is **compounded of** different things, it is a mixture of those things; a formal word. *An emotion oddly* *compounded of pleasure and bitterness flooded over me.*

compound fracture, compound fractures. A **compound fracture** is a fracture in which the broken bone sticks through the skin. N-COUNT

compound interest. **Compound interest** is interest that is calculated both on an original sum of money and on interest which has previously been added to the sum. N-UNCOUNT

comprehend /kɒmprɪhend/ **comprehends, comprehending, comprehended.** If you cannot **comprehend** something, you cannot understand it; a formal word. *I just cannot comprehend your attitude... Whenever she failed to comprehend she invariably laughed.* ◆◇◇◇◇ VB: with brd-neg =understand V n V

comprehensible /kɒmprɪhensɪbᵊl/. Something that is **comprehensible** can be understood; a formal word. *He spoke abruptly, in barely comprehensible Arabic.* ADJ-GRADED ≠incomprehensible

comprehension /kɒmprɪhenʃᵊn/ **comprehensions** ◆◇◇◇◇

1 **Comprehension** is the ability to understand something; a formal use. *This was utterly beyond her comprehension.* N-UNCOUNT =understanding

2 **Comprehension** is full knowledge and understanding of the meaning of something; a formal use. *They turned to one another with the same expression of dawning comprehension, surprise, and relief.* N-UNCOUNT =realisation

3 When pupils do **comprehension**, they do an exercise to find out how well they understand a piece of spoken or written language. *The course also features creative writing exercises and listening comprehension.* N-VAR

comprehensive /kɒmprɪhensɪv/ **comprehensives** ◆◆◆◇◇

1 Something that is **comprehensive** includes everything that is needed or relevant. *The Rough Guide to Nepal is a comprehensive guide to the region.* ADJ-GRADED =complete ≠partial

2 In Britain, a **comprehensive** is a state school in which children of all abilities are taught together. *...Birmingham's inner-city comprehensives... She taught French at Cheam Comprehensive in South London.* ► Also an adjective. *He left comprehensive school at the age of 16. ...Rushcliffe Comprehensive School.* N-COUNT: oft in names after n; ADJ: ADJ n

comprehensively /kɒmprɪhensɪvli/. Something that is done **comprehensively** is done thoroughly. *She was comprehensively outplayed by Coetzer.* ADV-GRADED: usu ADV with v

compress, compresses, compressing, compressed. The verb is pronounced /kəmpres/. The noun is pronounced /kɒmpres/. ◆◇◇◇◇

1 When you **compress** something or when it **compresses**, it is pressed or squeezed so that it takes up less space. *Poor posture, sitting or walking slouched over, compresses the body's organs... Air will compress but the brake fluid won't.* ♦ **compression** /kəmpreʃᵊn/ *The compression of the wood is easily achieved.* V-ERG V n V; N-UNCOUNT

2 If you **compress** something such as a piece of writing or a description, you make it shorter. *He never understood how to organize or compress large masses of material... All those three books are compacted and compressed into one book.* VERB =condense V n

3 If an event **is compressed** into a short space of time, it is given less time to happen than normal or previously. *The four debates will be compressed into an unprecedentedly short eight-day period... Some courses such as engineering had to be compressed.* VB: usu passive; be V-ed into n; be V-ed

4 A **compress** is a pad of wet or dry cloth pressed on part of a patient's body to reduce fever. *Sore throats may be relieved by cold compresses.* N-COUNT

compressed /kəmprest/. **Compressed** air or gas is squeezed into a small space or container and is therefore at a higher pressure than normal. It is used especially as a source of power for machines. ADJ: usu ADJ n =pressurized

compressor /kəmpresəʳ/ **compressors.** A **compressor** is a machine or part of a machine that squeezes gas or air and makes it take up less space. N-COUNT

comprise /kəmpraɪz/ **comprises, comprising, comprised** ◆◆◇◇◇

1 If you say that something **comprises** or **is comprised of** a number of things or people, you mean it has them as its parts or members; a formal use. *The special cabinet committee comprises Mr Lamont, Mr Portillo, and Tony Newton... The exhibition comprises 50 oils and watercolours... The task force is comprised of congressional leaders, cabinet heads and administration officials... A crowd comprised of the wives and children of scientists staged a demonstration.* VERB V n; be V-ed of n; V-ed

2 The things or people that **comprise** something are the parts or members that form it; a formal use. *...the multitude of ideas, ambitions and regrets that comprises the culture of Russia today... Women comprise 44% of hospital medical staff.* VERB =form, make up V n

compromise /kɒmprəmaɪz/ **compromises, compromising, compromised** ◆◆◆◇◇

1 A **compromise** is a situation in which people accept something slightly different from what they really want, because of circumstances or because they are considering the wishes of other people. *Encourage your child to reach a compromise between what he wants and what you want... Be ready and willing to make compromises between your needs and those of your partner... The government's policy of compromise is not universally popular.* N-VAR

2 If you **compromise** with someone, you reach an agreement with them in which you both give up something that you originally wanted. You can also say that two people or groups **compromise**. *The government has compromised with its critics over monetary policies... 'Nine,' said I. 'Nine thirty,' tried he. We compromised on 9.15... Israel had originally wanted $1 billion in aid, but compromised on the $650 million.* V-RECIP; V with n over n; pl-n V on n; V on n (non-recip); Also pl-n V, V (non-recip)

3 If someone **compromises** themselves or their beliefs, they do something which causes people to doubt their honesty, loyalty, or moral principles; used showing disapproval. *...members of the government who have compromised themselves by co-operating with the emergency committee... He would rather shoot himself than compromise his principles.* VERB PRAGMATICS; V pron-refl; V n

compromising /kɒmprəmaɪzɪŋ/. If you describe information or a situation as **compromising**, you mean that it reveals an embarrassing or guilty secret about someone. *How had this compromising picture come into the possession of the press?* ◆◇◇◇◇ ADJ-GRADED: usu ADJ n

comptroller /kəntroʊləʳ/ **comptrollers.** A **comptroller** is someone who is in charge of the accounts of a business or a government department. *...Robert Clarke, US Comptroller of the Currency.* ◆◇◇◇◇ N-COUNT: oft N of n

compulsion /kəmpʌlʃᵊn/ **compulsions** ◆◇◇◇◇

1 A **compulsion** is a strong desire to do something, which you find difficult to control. *He felt a sudden compulsion to drop the bucket and run... It's a compulsion to write, more than talent, that makes a writer.* N-COUNT: oft N to-inf =urge

2 If someone uses **compulsion** in order to get you to do something, they force you to do it, for example by threatening to punish you if you do not do it. *Many universities argued that students learned more when they were in classes out of choice rather than compulsion... There is already an element of compulsion in existing government schemes for the unemployed.* N-UNCOUNT =coercion

compulsive /kəmpʌlsɪv/ ◆◇◇◇◇

1 You use **compulsive** to describe people or their behaviour when they cannot stop doing something wrong, harmful, or unnecessary. *...a compulsive liar... He was a compulsive gambler and often heavily in debt. ...women with compulsive eating problems.* ♦ **compulsively** *John is compulsively neat and clean, he's terrified of germs.* ADJ: ADJ n; ADV

2 If a book or television programme is **compulsive**, it is so interesting that you do not want to stop ADJ-GRADED

reading or watching it. *The BBC series Hot Chefs is compulsive viewing... These chilling heroines make Hart's books compulsive reading.* ♦ **compulsively** *...a series of compulsively readable novels.* ADV-GRADED: ADV adj

compulsory /kəmpʌlsəri/. If something is **compulsory**, you must do it or accept it, because it is the law or because someone in a position of authority says you must. *In East Germany learning Russian was compulsory... Many young men are trying to get away from compulsory military conscription.* ♦ **compulsorily** /kəmpʌlsərɪli/ *Five of the company's senior managers have been made compulsorily redundant.* ◆◆◇◇◇ ADJ =mandatory; ADV: ADV with v, ADV adj

compunction /kəmpʌŋkʃən/. If you say that someone has no **compunction** about doing something, you mean that they do it without feeling ashamed or guilty; used showing disapproval. *Although tears well up, he has no compunction about relating how he killed his father.* N-UNCOUNT PRAGMATICS

computation /kɒmpjʊteɪʃən/ **computations.** **Computation** is mathematical calculation. *The discrepancies resulted from different methods of computation... He took a few notes and made computations.* N-VAR =calculation

computational /kɒmpjʊteɪʃənəl/. **Computational** means using computers. *Students may pursue research in any aspect of computational linguistics. ...the limits of the computational methods available 50 years ago.* ADJ: usu ADJ n

compute /kəmpjuːt/ **computes, computing, computed.** To **compute** a quantity or number means to calculate it. *I tried to compute the cash value of the ponies and horse boxes.* ◆◇◇◇◇ VERB =calculate V n

computer /kəmpjuːtəʳ/ **computers.** A **computer** is an electronic machine that can quickly make calculations, store, rearrange, and retrieve information, or control another machine. *The data are then fed into a computer... The company installed a $650,000 computer system... It's done on a computer?... The car was designed by computer for the driver of the 1990s.* ● See also **personal computer**. ◆◆◆◆◇ N-COUNT: also *by/on* N

computerate /kəmpjuːtərət/. If someone is **computerate**, they have enough skill and knowledge to be able to use a computer. ADJ-GRADED =computer-literate

computer game, computer games. A **computer game** is a game that you play on a computer or on a small portable piece of electronic equipment. ◆◇◇◇◇ N-COUNT

computerize /kəmpjuːtəraɪz/ **computerizes, computerizing, computerized;** also spelled **computerise** in British English. To **computerize** a system, process, or type of work means to arrange for a lot of the work to be done by computer. *I'm trying to make a spreadsheet up to computerize everything that's done by hand at the moment... Many hospitals say they simply can't afford to computerize.* ♦ **computerization** /kəmpjuːtəraɪzeɪʃən/ *...the benefits of computerization.* ◆◆◇◇◇ VERB V n V; N-UNCOUNT

computerized /kəmpjuːtəraɪzd/; also spelled **computerised.** ◆◇◇◇◇

1 A **computerized** system, process, or business is one in which the work is done by computer. *The National Cancer Institute now has a computerized system that can quickly provide information. ...the most highly computerized businesses.* ADJ-GRADED: usu ADJ n

2 **Computerized** information is stored on a computer. *Computerized data bases are proliferating fast... The public registry in Panama City keeps computerized records of all companies.* ADJ: usu ADJ n

computer-literate. If someone is **computer-literate**, they have enough skill and knowledge to be able to use a computer. *We look for applicants who are numerate, computer-literate and energetic self-starters.* ADJ-GRADED =computerate

computing /kəmpjuːtɪŋ/ ◆◆◇◇◇

1 **Computing** is the activity of using a computer and writing programs for it. *Courses range from cookery to computing.* N-UNCOUNT

2 **Computing** means relating to computers and their use. *Many graduates are employed in the electronics and computing industries.* ADJ: ADJ n

comrade /kɒmreɪd, AM -ræd/ **comrades** ◆◇◇◇◇

1 Someone's **comrades** are their friends or companions; a literary use. *Unlike so many of his comrades he survived the war.* N-COUNT: usu poss N

2 Socialists or communists sometimes call each other **comrade**, especially in meetings. *...Comrade Stalin... The Party's authority, comrades, will be put to a serious test. ...the remarks made by the comrades in the Central Committee.* N-TITLE; N-VOC; N-COUNT PRAGMATICS

comrade-in-arms, comrades-in-arms; also spelled **comrade in arms.** A **comrade-in-arms** is someone who has worked for the same cause or purpose as you and has shared the same difficulties and dangers. *...Deng Xiaoping, Mao's long-time comrade-in-arms.* N-COUNT: oft poss N

comradely /kɒmreɪdli, AM -ræd-/. If you do something in a **comradely** way, you are being pleasant and friendly to other people; a formal word. *They worked in comradely silence.* ADJ-GRADED: usu ADJ n =friendly

comradeship /kɒmreɪdʃɪp, AM -ræd-/. **Comradeship** is friendship between a number of people who are doing the same work or who share the same difficulties or dangers. *...the comradeship of his fellow soldiers.* N-UNCOUNT

con /kɒn/ **cons, conning, conned** ◆◆◇◇◇

1 If someone **cons** you, they persuade you to do something or believe something by telling you things that are not true; an informal use. *He claimed that the businessman had conned him of £10,000... White conned his way into a job as a warehouseman with Dutch airline, KLM... The British motorist has been conned by the government.* VERB =cheat, trick V n *of/out of/into* n/-ing V *way into* n *be* V-ed Also V n

2 A **con** is a trick in which someone deceives you by telling you something that is not true; an informal use. *Slimming snacks that offer miraculous weight loss are a con... She is the victim of a big con trick.* N-COUNT =confidence trick

3 A **con** is the same as a **convict**; an informal use. N-COUNT

4 See also **mod cons.** ● **pros and cons**: see **pro**.

Con ◆◇◇◇◇

1 **Con** is the written abbreviation for 'constable', when it is part of a policeman's title. *...Det Con Terence Woodwiss.*

2 In Britain, **Con** is the written abbreviation for **Conservative**. *...Philip Goodhart MP for Beckenham (Con).*

conc. **Conc.** is used when mentioning a concessionary fare or price that is charged to pensioners, students, and the unemployed. *The guided tours cost £4 (conc £3.50).*

concatenation /kɒnkætəneɪʃən/. A **concatenation** of things or events is their occurrence one after another, because they are linked; a formal word. *...the concatenation of crisis conditions in seventeenth-century Europe.* N-UNCOUNT: usu N *of* n

concave /kɒnkeɪv, kɒnkeɪv/. A surface that is **concave** curves inwards in the middle. *...a concave stomach. ...the concave bottom of an empty hair spray container.* ADJ-GRADED ≠convex

conceal /kənsiːl/ **conceals, concealing, concealed** ◆◆◇◇◇

1 If you **conceal** something, you cover it or hide it carefully. *Frances decided to conceal the machine behind a hinged panel... Five people were arrested for carrying concealed weapons.* VERB V n V-ed

2 If you **conceal** a piece of information or a feeling, you do not let other people know about it. *Robert could not conceal his relief... She knew at once that he was concealing something from her.* VERB ≠reveal V n V n *from* n

3 If something **conceals** something else, it covers it and prevents it from being seen. *...a pair of carved Indian doors which conceal a built-in cupboard... The hat concealed her hair.* VERB V n

concealment /kənsiːlmənt/

1 **Concealment** is the state of being hidden or the act of hiding something. *The criminals vainly sought concealment from the searchlight. ...the concealment of weapons.* N-UNCOUNT

2 The **concealment** of information or a feeling involves keeping it secret. *His concealment of his true* N-UNCOUNT: oft N *of* n

motives was masterly... I think there was deliberate concealment of relevant documents.

concede /kənsiːd/ **concedes, conceding, conceded** ◆◆◆◇◇

1 If you **concede** something, you admit, often unwillingly, that it is true or correct. *Bess finally conceded that Nancy was right... 'Well,' he conceded, 'I do sometimes mumble a bit.'... Mr. Chapman conceded the need for Nomura's U.S. unit to improve its trading skills.*
VERB V that V with quote V n Also V n n

2 If you **concede** something to someone, you allow them to have it as a right or privilege. *Poland's Communist government conceded the right to establish independent trade unions... Facing total defeat in Vietnam, the French subsequently conceded full independence to Laos.*
VERB =allow V n V n to n Also V n n

3 If you **concede** something you give it to the person who has been trying to get it from you. *A strike by some ten thousand bank employees has ended after the government conceded some of their demands.*
VERB V n

4 In sport, if you **concede** goals or points, you are unable to prevent your opponent from scoring them. *They conceded four goals to Leeds United... Luton conceded a free kick on the edge of the penalty area.*
VERB V n to n V n

5 If you **concede** a game, contest, or argument, you end it by admitting that you can no longer win. *Reiner, 56, has all but conceded the race to his rival... Alain Prost finished third and virtually conceded the world championship.*
VERB V n to n V n

6 If you **concede** defeat, you accept that you have lost a struggle. *Airtours conceded defeat in its attempt to take control of holiday industry rival Owners Abroad.*
VERB =admit V n

conceit /kənsiːt/ **conceits** ◆◇◇◇◇

1 Conceit is very great pride in your abilities or achievements that other people feel is undeserved. *He knew, without conceit, he was considered a genius... Pamela knew she was a good student, and that was not just a conceit.*
N-UNCOUNT: also a N =arrogance

2 A **conceit** is a clever or unusual metaphor or comparison; a literary use. *Critics may complain that the novel's central conceit is rather simplistic.*
N-COUNT

conceited /kənsiːtɪd/. If you say that someone is **conceited**, you are showing your disapproval of the fact that they are far too proud of their abilities or achievements. *I thought him conceited and arrogant... You conceited idiot.*
ADJ-GRADED PRAGMATICS =vain

conceivable /kənsiːvəbəl/. If something is **conceivable**, you can imagine it or believe it. *Without their support the project would not have been conceivable... It is just conceivable that a single survivor might be found... Through the centuries, flowers have been used for cooking in every conceivable way.* ♦ **conceivably** /kənsiːvəbli/ *The mission could conceivably be accomplished within a week.*
◆◇◇◇◇ ADJ: oft it v-link ADJ that ≠inconceivable
ADV: usu ADV before v

conceive /kənsiːv/ **conceives, conceiving, conceived** ◆◆◇◇◇

1 If you cannot **conceive** of something, you cannot imagine it or believe it. *I just can't even conceive of that quantity of money... He was immensely ambitious but unable to conceive of winning power for himself.*
VB: usu with brd-neg V of n/-ing Also V that

2 If you **conceive** something as a particular thing, you consider it to be that thing. *The ancients conceived the earth as afloat in water... We conceive of the family as being in a constant state of change... Elvis conceived of himself as a ballad singer.*
VERB V n as n/-ing V of n as n/-ing

3 If you **conceive** a plan or idea, you think of it and work out how it can be done. *She had conceived the idea of a series of novels, each of which would reveal some aspect of Chinese life... He conceived of the first truly portable computer in 1968.*
VERB V n V of n

4 When a woman **conceives**, she becomes pregnant. *Women, he says, should give up alcohol before they plan to conceive... About one in six couples has difficulty conceiving... A mother who already has non-identical twins is more likely to conceive another set of twins.*
VERB V V n

concentrate /kɒnsəntreɪt/ **concentrates, concentrating, concentrated** ◆◆◆◇◇

1 If you **concentrate** on something, or **concentrate** your mind on it, you give all your attention to it. *It was up to him to concentrate on his studies and make something of himself... Water companies should concentrate on reducing waste instead of building new reservoirs... At work you need to be able to concentrate... This helps you to be aware of time and concentrates your mind on the immediate task.*
VERB V on n/-ing V V n on n

2 If something **is concentrated** in an area, it is all there rather than being spread around. *Italy's industrial districts are concentrated in its north-central and north-eastern regions... Most development has been concentrated in and around cities.*
VB: usu passive be V-ed in n Also be V-ed adv

3 Concentrate is a liquid or substance from which unnecessary substances such as water have been removed in order to increase its strength and power or to decrease its bulk and make it easier to transport. *...orange juice made from concentrate.*
N-MASS

4 If you say that an unpleasant fact or situation **concentrates** someone's **mind**, you mean that it makes them think clearly, because they are aware of the serious consequences if they do not. *A term in prison will concentrate his mind wonderfully.*
PHRASE: V and N inflect

concentrated /kɒnsəntreɪtɪd/ ◆◆◇◇◇

1 A **concentrated** liquid has been increased in strength by having water removed from it. *Sweeten dishes sparingly with honey, or concentrated apple or pear juice.*
ADJ-GRADED ≠diluted

2 A **concentrated** activity is directed with great intensity in one place. *...a more concentrated effort to reach out to troubled kids.*
ADJ-GRADED: usu ADJ n =concerted ≠half-hearted

concentration /kɒnsəntreɪʃən/ **concentrations** ◆◆◆◇◇

1 Concentration on something involves giving all your attention to it. *Neal kept interrupting, breaking my concentration... We lacked concentration and it cost us the goal and the game.*
N-UNCOUNT

2 A **concentration** of something is a large amount of it or large numbers of it in a small area. *The area has one of the world's greatest concentrations of wildlife... There's been too much concentration of power in the hands of central authorities.*
N-VAR: usu N of n

3 The **concentration** of a substance is the proportion of essential ingredients or substances in it. *pH is a measure of the concentration of free hydrogen atoms in a solution... The latest data showed that global ozone concentrations had dropped several per cent over the last decade.*
N-VAR: with supp, oft N of n, n N

concentration camp, concentration camps. A **concentration camp** is a prison in which large numbers of non-military prisoners are kept in very bad conditions, usually in wartime. The term is used especially to refer to the prisons which were run by the Nazis during the Second World War.
◆◇◇◇◇ N-COUNT

concentric /kənsentrɪk/. **Concentric** circles or rings have the same centre. *Stonehenge is an ancient collection of enormous standing stones, mysteriously arranged in two concentric circles.*
ADJ: ADJ n

concept /kɒnsept/ **concepts.** A **concept** is an idea or abstract principle. *She added that the concept of arranged marriages is misunderstood in the west. ...basic legal concepts.*
◆◆◆◇◇ N-COUNT: oft N of n =notion

conception /kənsepʃən/ **conceptions** 

1 A **conception** of something is an idea that you have of it in your mind. *My conception of a garden was based on gardens I had visited in England... I see him as someone with not the slightest conception of teamwork.*
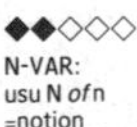
N-VAR: usu N of n =notion

2 Conception is the forming of an idea for something in your mind. *The symphony is admirable in conception... The other fundamental consideration in the conception of a plan is function.*
N-UNCOUNT

3 Conception is the process in which the egg in a woman is fertilized and she becomes pregnant. *Six weeks after conception your baby is the size of your little fingernail... Teenage conceptions have risen steadily in the last ten years.*
N-VAR

conceptual /kənseptʃuəl/. **Conceptual** means related to ideas and concepts formed in the
◆◇◇◇◇ ADJ: ADJ n

mind. *NATO requires a better intellectual and conceptual framework to guide its thinking.* ♦ **conceptually** *The monograph is conceptually confused, unclear in its structure and weak in its methodology.*
ADV: usu ADV with v, ADV adj, also ADV with cl

conceptualize /kənseptʃuəlaɪz/ **conceptualizes, conceptualizing, conceptualized;** also spelled **conceptualise** in British English. If you **conceptualize** something, you form an idea of it in your mind. *How we conceptualize things has a lot to do with what we feel... It is nowadays better to conceptualize religion as a cultural resource than as a social institution.* ♦ **conceptualization** /kənseptʃuəlaɪzeɪʃən/ **conceptualizations** *...the existing conceptualization of women's liberation.*
VERB
V n
V n *as* n
N-VAR: oft N *of* n

concern /kənsɜːʳn/ **concerns, concerning, concerned** ◆◆◆◆◆

1 **Concern** is worry about a situation. *The European Community has expressed concern about reports of political violence in Africa... The move follows growing public concern over the spread of the disease... As the militants gather, there is concern that the protest might again run out of control... There is no cause for concern.*
N-UNCOUNT: oft N prep, N that

2 If something **concerns** you, it worries you. *The growing number of people seeking refuge in Thailand is beginning to concern Western aid agencies... It concerned her that Bess was developing a crush on Max.* ♦ **concerned** *I've been concerned about you lately... We're naturally concerned for our daughter's safety... We are deeply concerned that terrorists appear to be targeting roads. ...a phone call from a concerned neighbor.*
VB: no cont
V n
it V n that
ADJ-GRADED: usu v-link ADJ, oft ADJ *about/for* n, ADJ that

3 A **concern** is a fact or situation that worries you. *His concern was that people would know that he was responsible... Unemployment was the electorate's main concern.*
N-COUNT: usu with poss =worry

4 Someone's **concern** with something is their feeling that it is important. *...a story that illustrates how dangerous excessive concern with safety can be.*
N-VAR: oft N *with* n

5 Someone's **concerns** are the things that they consider to be important. *Feminism must address issues beyond the concerns of middle-class whites.*
N-COUNT: usu with poss

6 A person's **concern** for someone is a feeling that they want them to be happy, safe, and well. If you do something out of **concern** for someone, you do it because you want them to be happy, safe, and well. *Without her care and concern, he had no chance at all... He had only gone along out of concern for his two grandsons.*
N-VAR: oft poss N

7 If you **concern** yourself with something, you give it attention because you think that it is important. *I didn't concern myself with politics... He would concern himself solely with the plight of the hostages.* ♦ **concerned** *The agency is more concerned with making arty ads than understanding its clients' businesses.*
VERB
V pron-refl *with* n
ADJ-GRADED: v-link ADJ *with* n

8 If something such as a book or a piece of information **concerns** a particular subject, it is about that subject. *The bulk of the book concerns Sandy's two middle-aged children... Chapter 2 concerns itself with the methodological difficulties.* ♦ **concerned** *Randolph's work was exclusively concerned with the effects of pollution on health.*
VB: no cont =be about
V n
V pron-refl *with* n
ADJ: v-link ADJ *with* n

9 If a situation, event, or activity **concerns** you, it affects or involves you. *It was just a little unfinished business from my past, and it doesn't concern you at all.* ♦ **concerned** *It's a very stressful situation for everyone concerned... I believe he was concerned in all those matters you mention.*
VB: no cont
V n
ADJ: n ADJ, v-link ADJ *in/with* n

10 If a situation or problem is your **concern**, it is something that you have a duty or responsibility to be involved with. *The technical aspects were the concern of the Army... I would be glad to get rid of them myself. But that is not our concern.*
N-SING: with poss =affair, business

11 You can refer to a company or business as a **concern**, usually when you are describing what type of company or business it is; a formal use. *If not a large concern, Queensbury Nursery was at least a successful one.*
N-COUNT: oft supp N

12 You can say **'as far as** I'm **concerned'** to indicate that you are giving your own opinion. *As far as I'm concerned the officials incited the fight.*
PHRASES
PHR with cl
PRAGMATICS

13 You can say **as far as** something **is concerned** to indicate the subject that you are talking about. *As far as starting a family is concerned, the trend is for women having their children later in life.*
PHR with cl
PRAGMATICS

14 If a company is a **going concern**, it is actually doing business, rather than having stopped trading or not yet having started trading. *The receivers will always prefer to sell a business as a going concern.*
N inflects, oft *as* PHR, v-link PHR

15 If something is **of concern** to someone, they find it worrying and unsatisfactory. *Any injury to a child is a cause of great concern to us... The survey's findings are a matter of great concern.*
oft PHR *to* n

16 If something is **of concern** to you, it is important to you. *How they are paid should be of little concern to the bank as long as they are paid.*
oft PHR *to* n

concerned /kənsɜːʳnd/ ◆◆◆◇◇

1 See **concern**.

2 If you are **concerned** to do something, you want to do it because you think it is important. *We were very concerned to keep the staff informed about what we were doing.*
ADJ-GRADED: v-link ADJ to-inf

concerning /kənsɜːʳnɪŋ/. You use **concerning** to indicate what a question or piece of information is about; a formal word. *For more information concerning the club contact I. Coldwell. ...various questions concerning pollution and the environment.*
◆◆◇◇◇
PREP: oft n PREP n =about

concert /kɒnsəʳt/ **concerts** ◆◆◆◇◇

1 A **concert** is a performance of music. *...a short concert of piano music... I've been to plenty of live rock concerts. ...a new concert hall.*
N-COUNT

2 If a musician or group of musicians appears **in concert**, they are giving a live performance. *I want people to remember Elvis in concert.*
PHRASES
PHR after v

3 If a number of people do something **in concert**, they do it together; a formal use. *He wants to act in concert with other nations.*
PHR after v

concerted /kənsɜːʳtɪd/ ◆◇◇◇◇

1 A **concerted** action is done by several people or groups working together. *Martin Parry, author of the report, says it's time for concerted action by world leaders.*
ADJ-GRADED: ADJ n

2 If you make a **concerted** effort to do something, you try very hard to do it. *He made a concerted effort to win me away from my steady, sweet but boring boyfriend.*
ADJ-GRADED: ADJ n =concentrated

concertgoer /kɒnsəʳtgoʊəʳ/ **concertgoers;** also spelled **concert-goer**. A **concertgoer** is someone who goes to concerts regularly.
N-COUNT

concertina /kɒnsəʳtiːnə/ **concertinas, concertinaing concertinaed**

1 A **concertina** is a musical instrument consisting of two end-pieces, with stiff paper or cloth that folds up between them. You play the concertina by pressing the buttons on the end-pieces while moving them together and apart.
N-VAR: oft *the* N

2 If something **concertinas** or **is concertinaed**, it becomes more compressed. *What should be several separate items have concertinaed together. ...the cramped feel of a widescreen film that has been concertinaed for television.*
V-ERG: no cont
V
be V-ed

concerto /kəntʃeəʳtoʊ/ **concertos.** A **concerto** is a piece of music written for one or more solo instruments and an orchestra. *...Tchaikovsky's First Piano Concerto. ...a wonderful concerto for two violins and string orchestra.*
◆◇◇◇◇
N-COUNT: usu with supp

concession /kənseʃən/ **concessions** ◆◆◆◇◇

1 If you make a **concession** to someone, you agree to let them do or have something, especially in order to end an argument or conflict. *It appears that Britain has made sweeping concessions to China in order to reach a settlement.*
N-COUNT: oft N *to/from* n

2 A **concession** is a special right or privilege that is given to someone. *The government has granted concessions to three private telephone companies. ...tax concessions for mothers who chose to stay at home with their children.*
N-COUNT

3 A **concession** is a special fare or price which is lower than the usual fare or price and which is
N-COUNT

often given to pensioners, students, and the unemployed. *Open daily; admission £1.10 with concessions for children and oaps.*

concessionaire /kənseʃəneəʳ/ **concessionaires.** A **concessionaire** is a person or company that has been given special rights or privileges, for example to sell a particular product or to run a business on the premises of another business or in a public place; used mainly in American English. N-COUNT

concessionary /kənseʃənri/. A **concessionary** fare or price is a special fare or price which is lower than the normal one and which is often given to pensioners, students, and the unemployed. *There are concessionary rates for OAP's and students.* ADJ: ADJ n

concessive clause /kənsesɪv klɔːz/ **concessive clauses.** A **concessive clause** is a subordinate clause which refers to a situation that contrasts with the one described in the main clause. For example, in the sentence 'Although he was tired, he couldn't get to sleep', the first clause is a concessive clause. N-COUNT

conch /kɒntʃ, kɒŋk/ **conches.** A **conch** is a shellfish with a large shell rather like a snail's. A **conch** or a **conch shell** is the shell of this creature. N-COUNT

concierge /kɒnsieəʳʒ/ **concierges.** A **concierge** is a person, especially in France, who looks after a block of flats and checks people entering and leaving the building. N-COUNT

conciliate /kənsɪlieɪt/ **conciliates, conciliating, conciliated.** If you **conciliate** someone, you try to end a disagreement with them; a formal word. *His duty was to conciliate the people, not to provoke them... The President has a strong political urge to conciliate... He spoke in a low, nervous, conciliating voice.* ♦ **conciliator, conciliators** *Douglas Hurd is widely seen as a conciliator, occupying the central ground of Conservative politics.* VERB V n V V-ing N-COUNT

conciliation /kənsɪlieɪʃən/. **Conciliation** is willingness to end a disagreement or the process of ending a disagreement. *Resolving the dispute will require a mood of conciliation on both sides... The experience has left him sceptical about peace talks and efforts at conciliation.* ◆◇◇◇◇ N-UNCOUNT

conciliatory /kənsɪliətri, AM -tɔːri/. When you are **conciliatory** in your actions or behaviour, you show that you are willing to end a disagreement with someone. *The next time he spoke he used a more conciliatory tone... The President's speech was hailed as a conciliatory gesture toward business.* ◆◇◇◇◇ ADJ-GRADED

concise /kənsaɪs/ ◆◇◇◇◇

1 Something that is **concise** says everything that is necessary without using any unnecessary words. *Burton's text is concise and informative... Whatever you are writing make sure you are clear, concise, and accurate.* ♦ **concisely** *He'd delivered his report clearly and concisely.* ADJ-GRADED =succinct ≠verbose ADV-GRADED: ADV with v

2 A **concise** edition of a book, especially a dictionary, is shorter than the original edition. *...Sotheby's Concise Encyclopedia of Porcelain.* ADJ: ADJ n

conclave /kɒŋkleɪv/ **conclaves.** A **conclave** is a meeting at which people keep what happens secret. The meeting of cardinals held to elect a new Pope is called a conclave. N-COUNT

conclude /kənkluːd/ **concludes, concluding, concluded** ◆◆◆◇◇

1 If you **conclude** that something is true, you decide that it is true using the facts you know as a basis. *Larry had concluded that he had no choice but to accept Paul's words as the truth... So what can we conclude from this debate?... 'The situation in the inner cities is bad and getting worse,' she concluded.* VERB V that V with quote

2 When you **conclude**, you say the last thing that you are going to say; formal when used in spoken English. *'It's a waste of time,' he concluded... I would like to conclude by saying that I do enjoy your magazine.* ♦ **concluding** *On the radio I caught Mrs Thatcher's concluding remarks at the Bournemouth conference.* VERB ≠begin V with quote V ADJ: ADJ n

3 When something **concludes**, or when you **conclude** it, you end it; a formal use. *The evening concluded with dinner and speeches... The Group of Seven major industrial countries concluded its annual summit meeting today.* V-ERG =end ≠begin V adv/prep V n

4 If one person or group **concludes** an agreement, such as a treaty or business deal, with another, they arrange it or agree it. You can also say that two people or groups **conclude** an agreement; a formal use. *Mexico and the Philippines have both concluded agreements with their commercial bank creditors... If the clubs cannot conclude a deal, an independent tribunal will decide.* V-RECIP =settle V n *with* n pl-n V n

conclusion /kənkluːʒən/ **conclusions** ◆◆◆◇◇

1 When you come to a **conclusion** you decide that something is true after you have thought about it carefully and have considered all the relevant facts. *Over the years I've come to the conclusion that she's a very great musician... I have tried to give some idea of how I feel – other people will no doubt draw their own conclusions.* N-COUNT: oft N that

2 The **conclusion** of something is its ending. *At the conclusion of the programme, I asked the children if they had any questions they wanted to ask me.* N-SING: also no det, usu with supp =end

3 The **conclusion** of a treaty or a business deal is the act of arranging it or agreeing it. *...the expected conclusion of a free-trade agreement between Mexico and the United States.* N-SING: usu with supp

4 You can refer to something that seems certain to happen as **a foregone conclusion.** *It was a foregone conclusion that I would end up in the same business as him... The championship result was almost a foregone conclusion.* PHRASES oft *it* v-link PHR that =certainty

5 You say **'in conclusion'** to indicate that what you are about to say is the last thing that you want to say. *In conclusion, walking is a cheap, safe, enjoyable and readily available form of exercise.* PHR with cl PRAGMATICS =to finish

6 If you say that someone **jumps to a conclusion,** you are critical of them because they decide too quickly that something is true, when they do not know all the facts. *I didn't want her to jump to the conclusion that the divorce was in any way her fault... Forgive me. I shouldn't be jumping to conclusions.* V and N inflect, oft PHR that PRAGMATICS

conclusive /kənkluːsɪv/. **Conclusive** evidence shows with certainty that something is true. *Her attorneys claim there is no conclusive evidence that any murders took place... Research on the matter is far from conclusive.* ♦ **conclusively** *A new study proved conclusively that smokers die younger than non-smokers.* ◆◇◇◇◇ ADJ-GRADED ADV-GRADED: ADV with v

concoct /kənkɒkt/ **concocts, concocting, concocted** ◆◇◇◇◇

1 If you **concoct** an excuse or explanation, you invent one that is not true. *Mr Ferguson said the prisoner concocted the story to get a lighter sentence.* VERB V n

2 If you **concoct** something, especially something unusual, you make it by mixing several things together. *Eugene was concocting Rossini Cocktails from champagne and pureed raspberries. ...a specially concocted massage oil.* VERB V n V-ed

concoction /kənkɒkʃən/ **concoctions.** A **concoction** is something that has been made out of several things mixed together. *...a concoction of honey, yogurt, oats, and apples.* ◆◇◇◇◇ N-COUNT: oft N *of* n

concomitant /kənkɒmɪtənt/ **concomitants**

1 **Concomitant** is used to describe something that happens at the same time as another thing and is connected with it; a formal use. *New methods had to be learnt, with concomitant delays in successful production... This approach was concomitant with the move away from relying on officially recorded crime as a data source.* ADJ: ADJ n, v-link ADJ *with* n

2 A **concomitant** of something is another thing that happens at the same time and is connected with it; a formal use. *The right to deliberately alter quotations is not a concomitant of a free press.* N-COUNT: oft N *of* n

concord /kɒŋkɔːʳd/

1 **Concord** is a state of peaceful agreement; a formal use. *They expressed the hope that he would* N-UNCOUNT =harmony ≠discord

pursue a neutral and balanced policy for the sake of national concord.

2 In grammar, **concord** refers to the way that a word has a form appropriate to the number or gender of the noun or pronoun it relates to. For example, in 'He hates it', there is concord between the singular form of the verb and the singular pronoun 'he'. N-UNCOUNT =agreement

concordance /kənkɔːʳdᵊns/ **concordances**

1 If there is **concordance** between two things, they are similar to each other or consistent with each other; a formal use. *...a partial concordance between theoretical expectations and empirical evidence.* N-VAR

2 A **concordance** is a list of the words in a text or group of texts, with information about where in the text each word occurs and how often it occurs. The sentences each word occurs in are often given. N-COUNT

concourse /kɒŋkɔːʳs/ **concourses**

1 A **concourse** is a wide hall in a public building, for example a hotel, airport, or station. N-COUNT

2 A **concourse** is a large group of people gathered together; a formal use. *The great concourse of people seemed to have been similarly impressed.* N-COUNT: oft N *of* n =assembly

concrete /kɒŋkriːt/ **concretes, concreting, concreted** ◆◆◆◇◇

1 **Concrete** is a substance used for building which is made by mixing together cement, sand, small stones, and water. *The posts have to be set in concrete... They had lain on sleeping bags on the concrete floor. ...concrete barriers.* N-UNCOUNT: oft N n

2 When you **concrete** something such as a path, you cover it with concrete. *He merely cleared and concreted the floors.* VERB V n

3 You use **concrete** to indicate that something is definite and specific. *He had no concrete evidence... There were no concrete proposals on the table... I must have something to tell him. Something concrete.* ♦ **concretely** *...by way of making their point more concretely.* ADJ-GRADED: usu ADJ n; ADV-GRADED: oft ADV with cl

4 A **concrete** object is a real, physical object. *...using concrete objects to teach addition and subtraction.* ADJ: usu ADJ n

5 A **concrete** noun is a noun that refers to a physical object rather than to a quality or idea. ADJ: ADJ n ≠abstract

6 If a plan or idea is **set in concrete** or **embedded in concrete**, it is fixed and cannot be changed. *As Mr Hurd emphasised, nothing is yet set in concrete.* PHRASE: v-link PHR

concrete jungle, concrete jungles. If you refer to a city or area as a **concrete jungle**, you mean that it has a lot of modern buildings and you think it is ugly or unpleasant to live in. N-COUNT PRAGMATICS

concubine /kɒŋkjʊbaɪn/ **concubines.** In former times, a wealthy man's **concubine** was a woman with whom he had a sexual relationship. The woman was not his wife, and the man may also have had a wife. The man usually gave the woman financial support and had authority over her. N-COUNT

concur /kənkɜːʳ/ **concurs, concurring, concurred.** If one person **concurs** with another person, the two people agree. You can also say that two people **concur**. This is a formal word. *Local feeling does not necessarily concur with the press... Daniels and Franklin concurred in an investigator's suggestion that the police be commended... Butler and Stone concur that the war threw people's lives into a moral relief... Four other judges concurred... After looking at the jug, Faulkner concurred that it was late Roman, third or fourth century... 'It's not an agreeable state of affairs,' concurs Heitham.* ◆◇◇◇◇ V-RECIP =agree; V *with* n; V *in* n; pl-n V that; pl-n V; NON-RECIP: V that; V with quote; Also V

concurrence /kənkʌrəns, AM -kɜːr-/ **concurrences**

1 Someone's **concurrence** is their agreement to something; a formal use. *Any change ought not to be made without full discussion and the general concurrence of all concerned.* N-VAR: oft with poss =agreement

2 If there is a **concurrence** of two or more things, they happen at the same time. *The concurrence of their disappearances had to be more than coincidental.* N-VAR

concurrent /kənkʌrənt, AM -kɜːr-/. **Concurrent** events or situations happen at the same time. *Galerie St. Etienne is holding three concurrent exhibitions... He will actually be serving three concurrent five-year sentences... Concurrent with her acting career, Bron has managed to write two books of her own.* ♦ **concurrently** *He was jailed for 33 months to run concurrently with a sentence he is already serving for burglary.* ◆◇◇◇◇ ADJ: usu ADJ n, also v-link ADJ *with* n, v-link ADJ; ADV: ADV with v

concussed /kənkʌst/. If someone is **concussed**, they lose consciousness or feel sick or confused because they have been hit hard on the head. *My left arm is badly bruised and I was slightly concussed... He was badly winded and concussed.* ADJ-GRADED: usu v-link ADJ

concussion /kənkʌʃᵊn/ **concussions.** If you suffer **concussion** after a blow to your head, you lose consciousness or feel sick or confused. *Nicky was rushed to hospital with concussion... She fell off a horse and suffered a concussion.* N-VAR

condemn /kəndem/ **condemns, condemning, condemned** ◆◆◆◇◇

1 If you **condemn** something, you say that it is very bad and unacceptable. *Political leaders united yesterday to condemn the latest wave of violence... Graham was right to condemn his players for lack of ability, attitude and application. ...a document that condemns sexism as a moral and social evil.* VERB =denounce ≠endorse, praise; V n; V n *for* n; V n *as* n; Also V pron-refl

2 If someone **is condemned** to a punishment, they are given this punishment. *He was condemned to life imprisonment. ...appeals by prisoners condemned to death.* VB: usu passive =sentence; *be* V-ed *to* n; V-ed

3 If circumstances **condemn** you to an unpleasant situation, they make it certain that you will suffer in that way. *Their lack of qualifications condemned them to a lifetime of boring, usually poorly-paid, work... He felt condemned to being alone... Mark was condemned to do most of the work.* VERB =doom; V n *to* n/-ing; *be* V-ed to-inf; Also V n to-inf

4 If authorities **condemn** a building, they officially decide that it is not safe and must be pulled down. *State officials said the court's ruling clears the way for proceedings to condemn buildings in the area.* VERB V n

5 See also **condemned**.

condemnation /kɒndemneɪʃᵊn/ **condemnations. Condemnation** is the act of saying that something or someone is very bad and unacceptable. *There was widespread condemnation of Saturday's killings... The raids have drawn a strong condemnation from the United Nations Security Council.* ◆◆◇◇◇ N-VAR: with supp, usu N *of* n

condemnatory /kɒndemneɪtəri, kəndemnətɔːri/. **Condemnatory** means expressing strong disapproval. *He was justified in some of his condemnatory outbursts.* ADJ-GRADED

condemned /kəndemd/ ◆◇◇◇◇

1 A **condemned** man or woman is going to be executed. *...prison officers who had sat with the condemned man during his last days.* ADJ

2 A **condemned** building is in such a bad condition that it is not safe to live in and is due to be demolished. *They took over a condemned 1960s tower block last year for one night.* ADJ

condemned cell, condemned cells. A **condemned cell** is a prison cell for someone who is going to be executed. N-COUNT

condensation /kɒndenseɪʃᵊn/. **Condensation** consists of small drops of water which form when warm water vapour or steam touches a cold surface such as a window. *He used his sleeve to wipe the condensation off the glass.* N-UNCOUNT

condense /kəndens/ **condenses, condensing, condensed** ◆◇◇◇◇

1 If you **condense** something, especially a piece of writing or speech, you make it shorter, usually by including only the most important parts. *We have learnt how to condense serious messages into short, self-contained sentences... The English translation may have been condensed into a single more readable book.* VERB V n *into* n; Also V n

2 When a gas or vapour **condenses**, or **is condensed** it changes into a liquid. *Water vapour condenses to form clouds... The compressed gas is* V-ERG V; V *into/out of* n; Also V n

cooled and condenses into a liquid... As the air rises it becomes colder and moisture condenses out of it.

condensed /kəndenst/

1 A **condensed** book, explanation, or piece of information has been made shorter, usually by including only the most important parts. *The Council was merely given a condensed version of what had already been disclosed in Washington.* ADJ-GRADED: usu ADJ n

2 **Condensed** liquids have been thickened by removing some of the water in them. *...condensed mushroom soup.* ADJ-GRADED: usu ADJ n =concentrated

condensed milk. **Condensed milk** is very thick sweetened milk that is sold in tins. N-UNCOUNT

condenser /kəndensəʳ/ **condensers**

1 A **condenser** is a device that cools gases into liquids. N-COUNT

2 A **condenser** is a device for accumulating electric charge. N-COUNT =capacitor

condescend /kɒndɪsend/ **condescends, condescending, condescended**

1 If you say that someone **condescends** to do something, you are showing your disapproval of the fact that they agree to do it, but in a way which shows that they think they are superior to other people and should not have to do it. *When he condescended to speak, he contradicted himself three or four times in the space of half an hour.* VERB PRAGMATICS V to-inf

2 If you say that someone **condescends** to other people, you are showing your disapproval of the fact that they behave in a way which shows that they think they are superior to other people. *Don't condescend to me.* VERB PRAGMATICS V *to* n Also V

condescending /kɒndɪsendɪŋ/. If you say that someone is **condescending**, you are showing your disapproval of the fact that they talk or behave in a way which shows that they think they are superior to other people. *I'm fed up with your money and your whole condescending attitude... They can be a bit condescending.* ADJ-GRADED PRAGMATICS

♦ **condescendingly** *'The practical work you did for us in Brazil was of great value,' he went on condescendingly.* ADV-GRADED: ADV after v

condescension /kɒndɪsenʃᵊn/. **Condescension** is condescending behaviour. *There was a tinge of condescension in the way the girl received me.* N-UNCOUNT PRAGMATICS

condiment /kɒndɪmənt/ **condiments.** A **condiment** is a substance such as salt, pepper, or mustard that you add to food when you eat it in order to improve the flavour. N-COUNT

condition /kəndɪʃᵊn/ **conditions, conditioning, conditioned** ◆◆◆◆◆

1 If you talk about the **condition** of a person or thing, you are talking about the state that they are in, especially how good or bad their physical state is. *He remains in a critical condition in a California hospital... I received several compliments on the condition of my skin... The two-bedroom chalet is in good condition... You can't drive in that condition.* N-SING: also no det, with supp

2 The **conditions** under which something is done or happens are all the factors or circumstances which directly affect it. *This change has been timed under laboratory conditions... In ideal conditions, a devaluation will work by putting up the prices of imported goods while boosting exports... The conditions are ripe for the spread of disease.* N-PLURAL: usu with supp

3 The **conditions** in which people live or work are the factors which affect their comfort, safety, or health. *People are living in appalling conditions... He could not work in these conditions any longer... The conditions in the camp are just awful.* N-PLURAL: usu with supp

4 If you talk about the **condition** of a group of people, you are talking about their situation in life, especially with regard to the difficulties or hardship they have; a formal use. *The condition of the people could be elevated by a programme of social reform... The government has encouraged its people to better their condition. ...the human condition.* N-SING: with supp

5 A **condition** is something which must happen or be done in order for something else to be possible, especially when this is written into a contract or law. *Argentina failed to hit the economic targets set as a condition for loan payments. ...terms and conditions of employment... Egypt had agreed to a summit subject to certain conditions.* N-COUNT: with supp =requirement

6 If someone has a particular **condition**, they have an illness or other medical problem. *Doctors suspect he may have a heart condition. ...a rare condition that causes degeneration of the brain tissue.* N-COUNT: usu with supp =complaint

7 If someone **is conditioned** by their upbringing or environment, they are influenced by it over a period of time so that they do certain things or think in a particular way. *We are all conditioned by early impressions and experiences... You have been conditioned to believe that it is weak to be scared... I just feel women are conditioned into doing housework. ...a conditioned response.* ♦ **conditioning** *Because of social conditioning, men don't expect themselves to be managed by women.* VB: usu passive *be* V-ed *be* V-ed to-inf *be* V-ed *into* -ing/n V-ed N-UNCOUNT

8 To **condition** your hair or skin means to put something on it which will keep it in good condition. *...a protein which is excellent for conditioning dry and damaged hair.* VERB V n

9 If you say that someone is **in no condition** to do something, you mean that they are too ill, upset, or drunk to do it. *She was clearly in no condition to see anyone.* PHRASES v-link PHR, usu PHR to-inf =unfit

10 When you agree to do something **on condition that** something else happens, you mean that you will only do it if this other thing also happens. *He spoke to reporters on condition that he was not identified.* CONJ-SUBORD

11 If someone is **out of condition**, they are unhealthy and unfit, because they have stopped exercising regularly. *He was too out of condition to clamber over the top.* usu v-link PHR =unfit

12 • **in mint condition**: see **mint**.

conditional /kəndɪʃənᵊl/ ◆◇◇◇◇

1 If a situation or agreement is **conditional** on something, it will only happen or continue if this thing happens. *Their support is conditional on his proposals meeting their approval. ...a conditional offer. ...a conditional ceasefire.* ♦ **conditionally** /kəndɪʃᵊnəli/ *Mr Smith has conditionally agreed to buy a shareholding in the club.* ADJ: oft ADJ *on* n/-ing ADV: ADV with v

2 In grammar, a **conditional** clause is a subordinate clause which refers to a situation which may exist or whose possible consequences you are considering. Most conditional clauses begin with 'if' or 'unless', as in 'If that happens, we'll be in big trouble' and 'You don't have to come unless you want to'. ADJ: ADJ n

conditional discharge, conditional discharges. In Britain, if someone who is convicted of an offence is given a **conditional discharge** by a court, they are not punished unless they later commit a further offence. N-COUNT: usu sing

conditioner /kəndɪʃənəʳ/ **conditioners** ◆◇◇◇◇

1 A **conditioner** is a substance which you can put on your hair after shampooing and rinsing it in order to make your hair softer and easier to comb. N-MASS

2 A **conditioner** is a thick liquid which you can use when you wash clothes in order to make them feel softer. *Using a fabric conditioner will make clothes easier to handle and iron.* N-MASS: oft n N

3 See also **air-conditioner**.

condo /kɒndoʊ/ **condos. Condo** is an abbreviation for **condominium.** N-COUNT

condolence /kəndoʊləns/ **condolences** ◆◇◇◇◇

1 A message of **condolence** is a message in which you express your sympathy for someone because one of their friends or relatives has died recently. *Neil sent him a letter of condolence.* N-UNCOUNT

2 When you offer or express your **condolences** to someone, you express your sympathy for them because one of their friends or relatives has died recently. *He expressed his condolences to the families of the people who died in the incident.* N-PLURAL

condom /kɒndɒm/ **condoms.** A **condom** is a covering made of rubber which a man can wear on his penis as a contraceptive or as protection against disease during sexual intercourse. ◆◆◇◇◇ N-COUNT

condominium /kɒndəmɪniəm/ **condominiums** ◆◇◇◇◇

1 In American English, a **condominium** is a block N-COUNT

of flats in which each flat is owned by the person who lives there.
2 In American English, a **condominium** is one of the privately owned flats in a condominium. N-COUNT
condone /kəndoun/ **condones, condoning, condoned.** If someone **condones** behaviour that is morally wrong, they accept it and allow it to happen. *I have never encouraged nor condoned violence... I couldn't condone what she was doing.* ◆◇◇◇◇ VB: oft with brd-neg ≠condemn V n
condor /kɒndɔːʳ/ **condors.** A **condor** is a large South American bird that eats the meat of dead animals. ◆◇◇◇◇ N-COUNT
conducive /kəndjuːsɪv, AM -duːsɪv/. If one thing is **conducive** to another thing, it makes the other thing likely to happen. *Make your bedroom as conducive to sleep as possible... Sometimes the home environment just isn't conducive to reading.* ◆◇◇◇◇ ADJ-GRADED: usu v-link ADJ, usu ADJ *to* n/-ing
conduct, conducts, conducting, conducted. ◆◆◆◆◇
The verb is pronounced /kəndʌkt/. The noun is pronounced /kɒndʌkt/.
1 When you **conduct** an activity or task, you organize it and carry it out. *I decided to conduct an experiment... He said they were conducting a campaign against democrats across the country... The council conducted a survey of the uses to which farm buildings are put.* VERB =carry out V n
2 The **conduct** of a task or activity is the way in which it is organized and carried out. *Also up for discussion will be the conduct of free and fair elections... The Conservative Party did not in the main disagree with Bevin's conduct of foreign policy.* N-SING: with supp
3 If you **conduct** yourself in a particular way, you behave in that way. *The way he conducts himself reflects on the party and will increase criticisms against him... Most people believe they conduct their private and public lives in accordance with Christian morality.* VERB V pron-refl V n
4 Someone's **conduct** is the way they behave in particular situations. *For Europeans, the law is a statement of basic principles of civilised conduct... He has trouble understanding that other people judge him by his social skills and his conduct.* N-UNCOUNT: with supp =behaviour
5 When someone **conducts** an orchestra or choir, they stand in front of it and direct its performance. *Dennis had recently begun a successful career conducting opera in Europe... Solti will continue to conduct here and abroad... At the Curtis Institute he studied conducting with Fritz Reiner.* VERB V n V V-ing
6 If something **conducts** heat or electricity, it allows heat or electricity to pass through it or along it. *Water conducts heat faster than air.* VB: no cont V n
7 If you **conduct** someone to a place, you go there with them; a formal use. *He asked if he might conduct us to the ball which was to bring the proceedings to an end.* • See also **safe-conduct.** VERB V n
conducted tour, conducted tours. A **conducted tour** is a visit to a building, town, or area during which someone goes with you and explains everything to you. N-COUNT =guided tour
conduction /kəndʌkʃᵊn/. **Conduction** is the process by which heat or electricity passes through or along something; a technical term in science. *Temperature becomes uniform by heat conduction until finally a permanent state is reached.* N-UNCOUNT: usu with supp
conductive /kəndʌktɪv/. A **conductive** substance is able to conduct things such as heat and electricity; a technical term in science. *Salt water is much more conductive than fresh water is.* ADJ-GRADED
♦ **conductivity** /kɒndʌktɪvɪti/ *...a device which monitors the electrical conductivity of the skin.* N-UNCOUNT
conductor /kəndʌktəʳ/ **conductors** ◆◆◇◇◇
1 A **conductor** is a person who stands in front of an orchestra or choir and directs its performance. N-COUNT
2 On a bus or train, the **conductor** is a person who sells tickets for a journey. N-COUNT
3 A **conductor** is a substance that heat or electricity can pass through or along. • See also **lightning conductor, semiconductor.** N-COUNT
conduit /kɒndjuɪt, AM -duɪt/ **conduits** ◆◇◇◇◇
1 A **conduit** is a small tunnel, pipe, or channel through which water or electrical wires go. N-COUNT =pipe
2 A **conduit** is a person or country that carries information or goods between two or more other people or countries. *Mr Gorbachev could still act as a conduit for aid from the West.* N-COUNT: oft N *for/to* n
cone /koun/ **cones** ◆◇◇◇◇
1 A **cone** is a shape with a circular base and smooth curved sides ending in a point at the top. *He had bought her sweets, brilliantly coloured, in a twisted cone of paper.* N-COUNT
2 A **cone** is the fruit of a tree such as a pine or fir. It consists of a cluster of woody scales containing seeds. *...a bowl of fir cones.* N-COUNT
3 A **cone** is a cone-shaped wafer that is used for holding ice cream. You can also refer to an ice cream that you eat in this way as a **cone**. *She stopped by the ice-cream shop and had a chocolate cone.* N-COUNT =cornet
4 See also **pine cone, traffic cone.**
confection /kənfekʃᵊn/ **confections**
1 A **confection** is an elaborately decorated cake or some other sweet food; used in written English. *...a confection made with honey and nuts.* N-COUNT
2 A **confection** is something that is elaborately made or built; used in written English. *He found himself staring at an extraordinary architectural confection of old and new.* N-COUNT: oft N *of* n
confectioner /kənfekʃənəʳ/ **confectioners.** A **confectioner** is a person whose job is making or selling sweets and chocolates. N-COUNT
confectioners' sugar. In American English, **confectioners' sugar** is very fine white sugar that is used for making icing and sweets. The British term is **icing sugar**. N-UNCOUNT
confectionery /kənfekʃənri, AM -neri/. **Confectionery** is sweets and chocolates; used in written English. *...hand-made confectionery.* N-UNCOUNT =sweets
confederacy /kənfedərəsi/ **confederacies.** A **confederacy** is a union of states or people who are trying to achieve the same thing. *They've entered this new confederacy because the central government's been unable to control the collapsing economy.* N-COUNT
confederate /kənfedərət/ **confederates.** Someone's **confederates** are the people they are working with in a secret activity. ◆◇◇◇◇ N-COUNT =accomplice
confederation /kənfedəreɪʃᵊn/ **confederations.** A **confederation** is an organization or alliance consisting of smaller groups or states, especially one that exists for business or political purposes. *...the Confederation of Indian Industry. ...plans to partition the republic into a confederation of mini-states.* ◆◆◇◇◇ N-COUNT: oft in names, oft N *of* n
confer /kənfɜːʳ/ **confers, conferring, conferred** ◆◇◇◇◇
1 When you **confer** with someone, you discuss something with them in order to make a decision. You can also say that two people **confer**. *He conferred with Hill and the others in his office... His doctors conferred by telephone and agreed that he must get away from his family for a time.* V-RECIP V *with* n pl-n V
2 If someone or something **confers** something such as power or an honour on you, they give it to you; a formal use. *The constitution also confers large powers on Brazil's 25 constituent states... An honorary doctorate of law was conferred on him by Newcastle University in 1976... Never imagine that rank confers genuine authority.* VERB V n *on* n V n
conference /kɒnfrəns/ **conferences** ◆◆◆◆◆
1 A **conference** is a meeting, often lasting a few days, which is organized on a particular subject or to bring together people who have a common interest. *George Bush took the unprecedented step of summoning all the state governors to a conference on education. ...the Conservative Party conference... Last weekend the Roman Catholic Church in Scotland held a conference, attended by 450 delegates.* N-COUNT
2 A **conference** is a meeting at which formal discussions take place. *They sat down at the dinner table, as they always did, before the meal, for a conference... Her employer was in conference with two lawyers and did not want to be interrupted.* N-COUNT: also *in* N
3 See also **press conference.**

confess /kənfes/ **confesses, confessing, confessed** ◆◆◇◇◇

1 If someone **confesses** to doing something wrong or something that they are ashamed of, they admit that they did it. *He had confessed to seventeen murders... Her husband confessed to having had an affair... I had expected her to confess that she only wrote these books for the money... Most rape victims confess a feeling of helplessness... Ray changed his mind, claiming that he had been forced into confessing... 'I played a very bad match,' he confessed.* — VERB =admit ≠deny; V to n/-ing; V that; V n; V; V with quote; Also V wh, V pron-refl adj/n

2 If someone **confesses** or **confesses** their sins, they tell God or a priest about their sins so that they can be forgiven. *You just go to the church and confess your sins... Once we have confessed our failures and mistakes to God, we should stop feeling guilty.* — VERB; V n; V n to n; Also V, V to n

3 You use expressions like **'I confess'**, **'I must confess'**, or **'I have to confess'** to apologize slightly for admitting something you are ashamed of or that you think might offend or annoy someone. *I confess it's got me baffled... I must confess I'm not a great enthusiast for long political programmes.* — PHRASE: PHR with cl; PRAGMATICS; =admit

confessed /kənfest/. You use **confessed** to describe someone who openly admits that they have a particular fault or have done something wrong. *James Earl Ray Jr has become notorious as the confessed killer of Martin Luther King.* — ◆◇◇◇◇ ADJ: ADJ n =self-confessed

confession /kənfeʃən/ **confessions** ◆◆◇◇◇

1 A **confession** is a signed statement by someone in which they admit that they have committed a particular crime. *They forced him to sign a confession.* — N-COUNT

2 **Confession** is the act of admitting that you have done something that you are ashamed of or embarrassed about. *The diaries are a mixture of confession and observation... I have a confession to make.* — N-VAR

3 If you make a **confession** of your beliefs or feelings, you publicly tell people that this is what you believe or feel. *...Tatyana's confession of love.* — N-VAR: usu N of n =declaration

4 In the Catholic church and in some other churches, if you go to **confession**, you privately tell a priest about your sins and ask for forgiveness. *He never went to Father Porter for confession again.* — N-VAR

5 **Confessions** is used in the titles of some books and films which claim to tell you sensational things about a particular lifestyle or job. *...The Confessions of a Tabloid Journalist.* — N-PLURAL

confessional /kənfeʃənəl/ **confessionals** ◆◇◇◇◇

1 A **confessional** is the small room in a church where Christians, especially Roman Catholics, go to confess their sins. — N-COUNT

2 A **confessional** speech or letter is one in which you confess something. *The convictions rest solely on disputed witness and confessional statements... Their first album was painfully frank to the point of being confessional.* — ADJ-GRADED

3 A **confessional** is a statement or meeting in which a person or people confess things. *In regular group confessionals, the worst performers have to explain themselves to their peers.* — N-COUNT

confessor /kənfesəʳ/ **confessors**

1 A **confessor** is a priest who hears a person's confession. — N-COUNT

2 If you describe someone as your **confessor**, you mean that they are the person you can talk to about your secrets or problems. *He had listened in his role of father confessor, increasingly concerned as he sensed her pain.* — N-COUNT

confetti /kənfeti/. **Confetti** is small pieces of coloured paper that people throw over the bride and groom at a wedding. — N-UNCOUNT

confidant /kɒnfɪdænt, -dænt/ **confidants.** Someone's **confidant** is a man who they are able to discuss their private problems with. *...a close confidant of the president.* — N-COUNT: usu with poss

confidante /kɒnfɪdænt, -dænt/ **confidantes.** Someone's **confidante** is a woman who they are able to discuss their private problems with. *You are her closest friend and confidante.* — N-COUNT: usu with poss

confide /kənfaɪd/ **confides, confiding, confided.** If you **confide** in someone, you tell them a secret. *I knew she had some fundamental problems in her marriage because she had confided in me a year earlier... He confided to me that he felt like he was being punished... On New Year's Eve he confided that he had suffered rather troubling chest pains... I confided my worries to Michael.* — ◆◇◇◇◇ VERB; V in n; V to n that; V that; V n to n; Also V with quote

♦ **confiding** *Ford's letters to her are fond and confiding.* — ADJ-GRADED

confidence /kɒnfɪdəns/ **confidences** ◆◆◆◆◇

1 If you have **confidence** in someone, you feel that you can trust them. *I have every confidence in you... This has contributed to the lack of confidence in the police... His record on ceasefires inspires no confidence.* — N-UNCOUNT: usu N in n =faith

2 If you have **confidence**, you feel sure about your abilities, qualities, or ideas. *The band is on excellent form and brimming with confidence... I always thought the worst of myself and had no confidence whatsoever.* — N-UNCOUNT =self-assurance

3 If you can say something with **confidence**, you feel certain it is correct. *I can say with confidence that such rumors were totally groundless.* — N-UNCOUNT: usu with N

4 If you tell someone something in **confidence**, you tell them a secret. *We told you all these things in confidence... Even telling Lois seemed a betrayal of confidence.* — N-UNCOUNT: usu in N

● If you **take** someone **into** your **confidence**, you tell them a secret. *If your daughter takes you into her confidence, don't rush off to tell your husband.* — PHRASE: V inflects =confide in

5 A **confidence** is a secret that you tell someone. *Gregory shared confidences with Carmen.* — N-COUNT

6 See also **vote of no confidence**.

confidence trick, confidence tricks. A **confidence trick** is a trick in which someone deceives you by telling you something that is not true. — N-COUNT

confident /kɒnfɪdənt/ ◆◆◆◇◇

1 If you are **confident** about something, you are certain that it will happen in the way you want it to. *I am confident that everything will come out right in time... Mr Ryan is confident of success... Management is confident about the way business is progressing.* — ADJ-GRADED: usu v-link ADJ, oft ADJ that, ADJ prep ≠sceptical

♦ **confidently** *I can confidently promise that this year is going to be very different.* — ADV-GRADED: ADV with v

2 If a person or their manner is **confident**, they feel sure about their own abilities, qualities, or ideas. *In time he became more confident and relaxed... She is a confident woman who is certain of her views.* — ADJ-GRADED =assured

♦ **confidently** *She walked confidently across the hall.* — ADV-GRADED: usu ADV with v

3 If you are **confident** that something is true, you are sure that it is true. A **confident** statement is one that the speaker is sure is true. *She is confident that everybody is on her side... 'Bet you I can', comes the confident reply.* — ADJ-GRADED: oft ADJ that

♦ **confidently** *I can confidently say that none of them were or are racist.* — ADV-GRADED: ADV with v

confidential /kɒnfɪdenʃəl/ ◆◆◇◇◇

1 Information that is **confidential** is meant to be kept secret or private. *She accused them of leaking confidential information about her private life... We'll take good care and keep what you've told us strictly confidential, Mr. Lane.* — ADJ-GRADED ≠public

♦ **confidentially** *People can phone in the knowledge that any information they give will be treated confidentially.* — ADV-GRADED: ADV with v =privately

♦ **confidentiality** /kɒnfɪdenʃiælɪti/ *...the confidentiality of the client-solicitor relationship.* — N-UNCOUNT

2 If you talk to someone in a **confidential** way, you talk to them quietly because what you are saying is secret or private. *'Look,' he said in a confidential tone, 'I want you to know that me and Joey are cops.'... His face suddenly turned solemn, his voice confidential.* — ADJ-GRADED: usu ADJ n

♦ **confidentially** *Nash hadn't raised his voice, still spoke rather softly, confidentially.* — ADV-GRADED: ADV after v

confidentially /kɒnfɪdenʃəli/. **Confidentially** is used to say that what you are telling someone is a secret and should not be discussed with anyone else. *Confidentially, I am not sure that it wasn't above their heads.* ● See also **confidential**. — ADV: ADV with cl =between us

configuration /kənfɪgʊreɪʃən, AM -fɪgjə-/ **configurations.** A **configuration** is an arrangement of a group of things; a formal word. *...Stonehenge, in south-western England, an ancient configuration of giant stones.* — ◆◇◇◇◇ N-COUNT

confine, confines, confining, confined. The verb is pronounced /kənfaɪn/. The noun **confines** is pronounced /kɒnfaɪnz/. ◆◆◇◇◇

1 To **confine** something to a particular place or group means to prevent it from spreading beyond that place or group. *Health officials have successfully confined the epidemic to the Tabatinga area... The US will soon be taking steps to confine the conflict.* VERB =restrict V n to n V n

2 If you **confine** yourself or your activities **to** something, you do only that thing and are involved with nothing else. *He did not confine himself to the one language... Yoko had largely confined her activities to the world of big business... His genius was not confined to the decoration of buildings.* VERB =limit, restrict V n to n V-ed

3 If someone **is confined to** a mental institution, prison, or other place, they are sent there and are not allowed to leave for a period of time. *The woman will be confined to a mental institution... He announced that the army and police had been confined to barracks.* VB: usu passive be V-ed to n

4 Something that is within the **confines** of an area or place is within the boundaries enclosing it; a formal use. *The movie is set entirely within the confines of the abandoned factory. ...the wild grass and weeds that grew in the confines of the grandstand.* N-PLURAL: usu prep *the* N of n

5 The **confines** of a situation, system, or activity are the limitations or restrictions it involves. *...away from the confines of the British class system... I can't stand the confines of this marriage.* N-PLURAL: usu *the* N of n =constraint

confined /kənfaɪnd/ ◆◆◇◇◇

1 If something is **confined to** a particular place, it exists only in that place. If it is **confined** to a particular group, only members of that group have it. *The problem is not confined to Germany... These dangers are not confined to smokers.* ADJ: v-link ADJ to n =restricted

2 A **confined** space or area is small and enclosed by walls. *His long legs bent up in the confined space.* ADJ-GRADED: usu ADJ n

3 If someone is **confined to** a wheelchair, bed, or house, they have to stay there, because they are disabled or ill. *He had been confined to a wheelchair since childhood.* ADJ: v-link ADJ to n

confinement /kənfaɪnmənt/ **confinements** ◆◇◇◇◇

1 **Confinement** is the state of being forced to stay in a prison or another place which you cannot leave. *She had been held in solitary confinement for four months... He'd obviously kept himself fit despite his years of confinement.* N-UNCOUNT

2 A woman's **confinement** is the period of time just before and during which she gives birth to a child; a formal use. *There has been a movement to support women seeking home confinement.* N-VAR =labour

confirm /kənfɜːʳm/ **confirms, confirming, confirmed** ◆◆◆◆◇

1 If something **confirms** what you believe, suspect, or fear, it shows that it is definitely true. *X-rays have confirmed that he has not broken any bones... These new statistics confirm our worst fears about the depth of the recession... This confirms what I suspected all along.* VB: no cont =affirm V that V n ♦ **confirmation** /kɒnfəʳmeɪʃən/ *They took her resignation from Bendix as confirmation of their suspicions.* N-UNCOUNT =affirmation

2 If you **confirm** something that has been stated or suggested, you say that it is true because you know about it. *The spokesman confirmed that the area was now in rebel hands... He confirmed what had long been feared... Can you confirm this?* VERB V that V n ♦ **confirmation** *She glanced over at James for confirmation.* N-UNCOUNT

3 If you **confirm** an arrangement or appointment, you say that it is definite, usually in a letter or on the telephone. *You make the reservation, and I'll confirm it in writing.* VERB V n ♦ **confirmation** *Travel arrangements are subject to confirmation by State Tourist Organisations.* N-UNCOUNT

4 If someone **is confirmed**, they are formally accepted as a member of a Christian church during a ceremony in which they say they believe what the church teaches. *He was confirmed as a member of the Church of England.* VB: usu passive be V-ed ♦ **confirmation, confirmations** *...when I was being prepared for Confirmation... Flu prevented her from attending her daughter's confirmation.* N-VAR

5 If something **confirms** you **in** your decision, belief, or opinion, it makes you think that you are definitely right. *It has confirmed me in my decision not to become a nun.* VB: no cont =strengthen V n in n

6 If a person or organization **confirms** their position, role, or power, they do something to make their power, position, or role stronger or more definite. *Edberg has confirmed his position as the world's number one tennis player.* VERB V n

7 If something **confirms** you **as** something, it shows that you definitely deserve a name, role, or position. *His new role could confirm him as one of our leading actors.* VERB V n as n

confirmed /kənfɜːʳmd/. You use **confirmed** to describe someone who has a particular habit or belief that they are very unlikely to change. *I'm a confirmed bachelor... Leonard, a confirmed atheist, simply could not understand.* ◆◇◇◇◇ ADJ: ADJ n

confiscate /kɒnfɪskeɪt/ **confiscates, confiscating, confiscated.** If you **confiscate** something from someone, you take it away from them, usually as a punishment. *There is concern that police use the law to confiscate assets from people who have committed minor offences... They confiscated weapons, ammunition and propaganda material.* ◆◇◇◇◇ VERB =seize V n from n V n ♦ **confiscation** /kɒnfɪskeɪʃən/ **confiscations** *The new laws allow the confiscation of assets purchased with proceeds of the drugs trade.* N-VAR: oft N of n =seizure

conflagration /kɒnfləgreɪʃən/ **conflagrations.** A **conflagration** is a fire that burns over a large area and destroys property. N-COUNT =blaze

conflate /kənfleɪt/ **conflates, conflating, conflated.** If you **conflate** two or more descriptions or ideas, or if they **conflate**, you combine them in order to produce a single one; a formal word. *Her letters conflate past and present... Unfortunately the public conflated fiction with reality and made her into a saint... The two meanings conflated.* V-RECIP-ERG V pl-n V n with n pl-n V ♦ **conflation** /kənfleɪʃən/ **conflations** *The story was a conflation of Greek myths.* N-VAR: usu N of n

conflict, conflicts, conflicting, conflicted. The noun is pronounced /kɒnflɪkt/. The verb is pronounced /kənflɪkt/. ◆◆◆◆◇

1 **Conflict** is serious disagreement and argument about something important. If two people or groups are in **conflict**, they have had a serious disagreement or argument and have not yet reached agreement. *Try to keep any conflict between you and your ex-partner to a minimum... Employees already are in conflict with management over job cuts... The two companies came into conflict.* N-UNCOUNT: oft *in/into* N

2 **Conflict** is a state of mind in which you find it impossible to make a decision. *...the anguish of his own inner conflict.* N-UNCOUNT =turmoil

3 **Conflict** is fighting between countries or groups of people; used in journalism and written English. *...talks aimed at ending four decades of conflict... The National Security Council has met to discuss ways of preventing a military conflict.* N-VAR

4 A **conflict** is a serious difference between two or more beliefs, ideas, or interests. If two beliefs, ideas, or interests are in **conflict**, they are very different. *There is a conflict between what they are doing and what you want... Do you feel any conflict of loyalties?... The two objectives are in conflict.* N-VAR: oft N *between* pl-n

5 If ideas, beliefs, or accounts **conflict**, they are very different from each other and it seems impossible for them to exist together or to each be true. *Personal ethics and professional ethics sometimes conflict... He held firm opinions which usually conflicted with my own... There are conflicting reports about the identity of the hostage. ...three powers with conflicting interests.* V-RECIP =clash pl-n V V with n V-ing

confluence /kɒnfluəns/ **confluences**

1 The **confluence** of two rivers is the place where they join and become one larger river. *The 160-metre falls mark the dramatic confluence of the rivers Nera and Velino.* N-SING: oft N of n

2 If there is a **confluence** of two things, they join, N-COUNT:

combine, or come together; a formal use. *Like most cases of extreme weather, its severity was due to an unusual confluence of events. ...the confluence of African and Portuguese cultures in Brazil.* oft N *of* n

conform /kənfɔːʳm/ **conforms, conforming, conformed** ◆◆◇◇◇

1 If something **conforms** to a law or regulation or to someone's wishes, it is of the type or quality that is required or desired. *The Night Rider lamp has been designed to conform to new British Standard safety requirements... The meat market can continue only if it is radically overhauled to conform with strict EC standards.* VERB; V *to/with* n

2 If you **conform**, you behave in the way that you are expected or supposed to behave. *Many children who can't or don't conform are often bullied... He did not feel obliged to conform to the rules that applied to ordinary men... We conformed with social and family expectations.* VERB ≠rebel; V; V *to/with* n

3 If someone or something **conforms to** a pattern or type, they are very similar to it. *I am well aware that we all conform to one stereotype or another... Like most 'peacetime wars' it did not conform to preconceived ideas.* VERB; V *to* n

conformist /kənfɔːʳmɪst/ **conformists.** Someone who is **conformist** behaves or thinks like everyone else rather than doing things that are original. *He may have to become more conformist if he is to prosper again... Mr Gordon now feels forced into an ever more conformist way of running his practice.* ► A **conformist** is someone who is conformist. ADJ-GRADED; N-COUNT

conformity /kənfɔːʳmɪti/ ◆◇◇◇◇

1 If something happens in **conformity** with a law or regulation or with someone's wishes, it happens as the law or regulation says it should happen, or as the person wants it to happen. *The prime minister is, in conformity with the constitution, chosen by the president.* N-UNCOUNT: oft *in* N *with* n

2 **Conformity** means behaving in the same way as most other people. *Excessive conformity is usually caused by fear of disapproval... Pressure appears to be mounting for conformity in how people speak English.* N-UNCOUNT

confound /kənfaʊnd/ **confounds, confounding, confounded.** If someone or something **confounds** you, they make you feel surprised or confused, often by showing you that your opinions or expectations of them were wrong. *He momentarily confounded his critics by his cool handling of the Gulf crisis... The choice of Governor may confound us all.* ◆◇◇◇◇ VERB; V n

confront /kənfrʌnt/ **confronts, confronting, confronted** ◆◆◆◇◇

1 If you **are confronted** with a problem, task, or difficulty, you have to deal with it. *She was confronted with severe money problems... Ministers underestimated the magnitude of the task confronting them.* VERB =face; *be* V-ed *with/by* n; V n

2 If you **confront** a difficult situation or issue, you accept the fact that it exists and try to deal with it. *We are learning how to confront death... NATO countries have been forced to confront fundamental moral questions.* VERB =face; V n

3 If you **are confronted** by something that you find threatening or difficult to deal with, it is there in front of you. *I was confronted with an array of knobs, levers, and switches.* VB: usu passive =face; *be* V-ed *with/by* n

4 If you **confront** someone, you stand or sit in front of them, especially when you are going to fight, argue, or compete with them. *She pushed her way through the mob and confronted him face to face... They don't hesitate to open fire when confronted by police... The candidates confronted each other during a televised debate.* VERB; V n

5 If you **confront** someone with something, you present facts or evidence to them in order to accuse them of something. *She had decided to confront Kathryn with what she had learnt... I could not bring myself to confront him about it... His confronting me forced me to search for the answers.* VERB; V n *with* n; V n *about* n; V n

confrontation /kɒnfrʌnteɪʃən/ **confrontations.** A **confrontation** is a dispute, fight, or battle between two groups of people. *The issue has caused great tension between the two countries and could lead to a military confrontation... The commission remains so weak that it will continue to avoid confrontation with governments.* ◆◆◆◇◇ N-VAR: oft N *with/between* n

confrontational /kɒnfrʌnteɪʃənəl/. If you describe the way that someone behaves as **confrontational**, you are showing your disapproval of the fact that they are aggressive and likely to cause an argument or dispute. *The committee's confrontational style of campaigning has made it unpopular... Riot police are on hand but have not been confrontational.*  ADJ-GRADED PRAGMATICS

confuse /kənfjuːz/ **confuses, confusing, confused** ◆◆◇◇◇

1 If you **confuse** two things, you get them mixed up, so that you think one of them is the other one. *Great care is taken to avoid confusing the two types of projects... I can't see how anyone could confuse you with another!* ♦ **confusion** /kənfjuːʒən/ *Use different colours of felt pen on your sketch to avoid confusion.* VERB; V pl-n; V n *with* n; N-UNCOUNT

2 To **confuse** someone means to make it difficult for them to know exactly what is happening or what to do. *German politics surprised and confused him.* VERB =bewilder; V n

3 To **confuse** a situation means to make it complicated or difficult to understand. *To further confuse the issue, there is an enormous variation in the amount of sleep people feel happy with.* VERB; V n

confused /kənfjuːzd/ ◆◆◇◇◇

1 If you are **confused**, you do not know exactly what is happening or what to do. *A survey showed people were confused about what they should eat to stay healthy... Things were happening much too quickly and Brian was confused.* ♦ **confusedly** /kənfjuːzɪdli/ *He shook his head confusedly.* ADJ-GRADED: oft ADJ *about/by* n =bewildered; ADV-GRADED: ADV with v

2 Something that is **confused** does not have any order or pattern and is difficult to understand. *The situation remains confused as both sides claim success. ...a modern society in which values have become increasingly confused.* ADJ-GRADED

confusing /kənfjuːzɪŋ/. Something that is **confusing** makes it difficult for people to know exactly what is happening or what to do. *The statement is highly confusing... The uncertainty created by this situation must be confusing for you.* ♦ **confusingly** *Confusingly, blind people also respond to the light.* ◆◆◇◇◇ ADJ-GRADED ≠clear; ADV-GRADED: usu ADV with cl

confusion /kənfjuːʒən/ **confusions** ◆◆◇◇◇

1 If there is **confusion** about something, it is not clear what the true situation is, especially because people believe different things. *There's still confusion about the number of casualties... Omissions in my recent article must have caused confusion.* N-VAR

2 **Confusion** is a situation in which everything is in disorder, especially because there are lots of things happening at the same time. *There was confusion when a man fired shots... The rebel leader appears to have escaped in the confusion.* N-UNCOUNT

3 If your mind is in a state of **confusion**, you do not know what to believe or what you should do. *We always left his office in a state of confusion. ...the pressures and confusions of puberty.* N-VAR

4 See also **confuse**.

conga /kɒŋgə/ **congas.** If a group of people dance a **conga**, they dance in a long winding line, with each person holding on to the back of the person in front. N-COUNT

congeal /kəndʒiːl/ **congeals, congealing, congealed.** When a liquid **congeals**, it becomes very thick and sticky and almost solid. *The blood had started to congeal. ...spilled wine mingled with congealed soup.* VERB; V; V-ed

congenial /kəndʒiːniəl/. A **congenial** person, place, or environment is pleasant; a formal word. *He is back in more congenial company.* ◆◇◇◇◇ ADJ-GRADED: usu ADJ n =agreeable

congenital /kəndʒenɪtəl/

1 A **congenital** disease or medical condition is one that a person has had from birth, but is not inherit- ADJ: usu ADJ n

ed; a medical use. *When John was 17, he died of congenital heart disease.* ♦ **congenitally** ...*congenitally handicapped children.* ADV: ADV adj/-ed

2 A **congenital** characteristic or feature in a person is so strong that you cannot imagine it ever changing, although there may be no apparent reason for it. *He was a congenital liar and usually in debt.* ADJ: usu ADJ n =incorrigible
♦ **congenitally** *I admit to being congenitally lazy.* ADV

conger /kɒŋgəʳ/ **congers.** A **conger** or a **conger eel** is a large snake-like sea eel. ◆◇◇◇◇ N-VAR

congested /kəndʒestɪd/ ◆◇◇◇◇

1 A **congested** road or area is extremely crowded and blocked with traffic or people. *He first promised two weeks ago to clear Britain's congested roads... Some areas are congested with both cars and people.* ADJ-GRADED =blocked

2 If a part of the body is **congested**, it is blocked; a formal use. *The arteries in his neck had become fatally congested.* ADJ-GRADED =blocked

congestion /kəndʒestʃᵊn/ ◆◇◇◇◇

1 If there is **congestion** in a place, the place is extremely crowded and blocked with traffic or people. *The problems of traffic congestion will not disappear in a hurry... Energy consumption, congestion and pollution have increased.* N-UNCOUNT: usu with supp, oft adj N

2 **Congestion** in a part of the body is a medical condition in which the part becomes blocked; a formal use. ...*nasal congestion.* N-UNCOUNT: usu with supp, oft adj N

congestive /kəndʒestɪv/. A **congestive** disease is a medical condition where a part of the body becomes blocked; a medical term. ...*congestive heart failure.* ADJ: ADJ n

conglomerate /kənglɒmərət/ **conglomerates.** A **conglomerate** is a large business firm consisting of several different companies. *Fiat is Italy's largest industrial conglomerate.* ◆◇◇◇◇ N-COUNT: oft adj N

conglomeration /kənglɒmәreɪʃᵊn/ **conglomerations.** A **conglomeration** of things is a group of many different things, gathered together; a formal word. ...*a conglomeration of buildings, all tightly packed together.* ...*a conglomeration of peoples speaking different languages.* N-COUNT: usu N *of* n

congratulate /kəngrætʃʊleɪt/ **congratulates, congratulating, congratulated** ◆◆◇◇◇

1 If you **congratulate** someone, you say something that indicates you are pleased something special or nice has happened to them. *She congratulated him on the birth of his son... I was absolutely astonished by the reaction to our engagement. Everyone started congratulating us.* ♦ **congratulation** /kəngrætʃʊleɪʃᵊn/ *We have received many letters of congratulation.* VERB V n *on/for* n/-ing V n N-UNCOUNT

2 If you **congratulate** someone, you praise them for something admirable that they have done. *I really must congratulate the organisers for a well run and enjoyable event... We specifically wanted to congratulate certain players.* VERB V n *for/on* n/-ing V n

3 If you **congratulate** yourself, you are pleased about something that you have done or that has happened to you. *Waterstone has every reason to congratulate himself... Journalists have been congratulating themselves on the role the press has played in the investigations.* VERB V pron-refl V pron-refl *on/for*-ing/n

congratulations /kəngrætʃʊleɪʃᵊnz/ ◆◇◇◇◇

1 You say **'Congratulations'** to someone in order to congratulate them on something nice that has happened to them or something admirable that they have done. *Congratulations, you have a healthy baby boy... Congratulations on your interesting article... Congratulations to everybody who sent in their ideas.* CONVENTION PRAGMATICS

2 If you offer someone your **congratulations**, you congratulate them on something nice that has happened to them or on something admirable that they have done. *The club also offers its congratulations to D. Brown on his appointment as president.* N-PLURAL

congratulatory /kəngrætʃʊleɪtəri, AM -lətɔːri/. A **congratulatory** message expresses congratulations. *He sent Kim a congratulatory letter.* ADJ

congregant /kɒŋgrɪgənt/ **congregants. Congregants** are members of a congregation; used mainly in American English. N-COUNT

congregate /kɒŋgrɪgeɪt/ **congregates, congregating, congregated.** When people **congregate**, they gather together and form a group. *Youngsters love to congregate here in the evenings outside cinemas showing American films... Visitors congregated on Sunday afternoons to view public exhibitions.* ◆◇◇◇◇ VERB V

congregation /kɒŋgrɪgeɪʃᵊn/ **congregations.** The people who are attending a church service or who regularly attend a church service are referred to as the **congregation**. *Most members of the congregation begin arriving a few minutes before services.* ◆◇◇◇◇ N-COUNT-COLL

congress /kɒŋgres/ **congresses.** A **congress** is a large meeting that is held to discuss ideas and policies. *A lot has changed after the party congress.* ...*a congress of coal miners.* ◆◆◇◇◇ N-COUNT-COLL: usu with supp

Congress. **Congress** is the elected group of politicians that is responsible for making the law in the USA. It consists of two parts: the House of Representatives and the Senate. *We want to cooperate with both the administration and Congress.* ◆◆◆◆◇ N-PROPER-COLL

congressional /kəngreʃənᵊl/. A **congressional** policy, action, or person relates to the US Congress. *The president explained his plans to congressional leaders.* ...*a congressional report published on September 5th.* ◆◆◆◇◇ ADJ: ADJ n

congressman /kɒŋgrɪsmən/ **congressmen.** A **congressman** is a male member of the US Congress, especially of the House of Representatives. ◆◆◇◇◇ N-COUNT; N-TITLE

congressperson /kɒŋgrɪspɜːʳsᵊn/ **congresspeople.** A **congressperson** is a member of the US Congress, especially of the House of Representatives. N-COUNT

congresswoman /kɒŋgrɪswʊmən/ **congresswomen.** A **congresswoman** is a female member of the US Congress, especially of the House of Representatives. *The meeting was organised by Congresswoman Maxine Waters.* N-COUNT; N-TITLE

congruence /kɒŋgruəns/. **Congruence** is similarity or correspondence between two or more things; a formal word. ...*a necessary congruence between political, cultural and economic forces.* N-UNCOUNT: also *a* N, usu N *between* pl-n

congruent /kɒŋgruənt/. If one thing is **congruent** with another thing, there is a similarity or correspondence between them; a formal word. *The interests of landowners were by no means congruent with those of industrial capitalists.* ADJ: usu v-link ADJ, usu ADJ *with* n

conical /kɒnɪkᵊl/. A **conical** object is shaped like a cone. *We were soon aware of a great conical shape to the north-east.* ADJ: usu ADJ n

conifer /kɒnɪfəʳ/ **conifers. Conifers** are a group of trees and shrubs that grow in cooler areas of the world. They have needle-like leaves which they do not normally lose in winter, and often produce cones. ◆◇◇◇◇ N-COUNT

coniferous /kənɪfərəs, AM koʊ-/. A **coniferous** forest or woodland is made up of conifers. ADJ: usu ADJ n

conjectural /kəndʒektʃərəl/. A statement that is **conjectural** is based on incomplete or doubtful information; a formal word. *There is something undeniably conjectural about such claims.* ADJ-GRADED =hypothetical

conjecture /kəndʒektʃəʳ/ **conjectures, conjecturing, conjectured** ◆◇◇◇◇

1 If you say that a conclusion is a **conjecture**, you mean that it is a guess based on incomplete or doubtful information and you do not know for certain that it is true; a formal use. *That was a conjecture, not a fact... There are several conjectures... The attitudes of others were matters of conjecture although there were plenty of rumours about how individuals had behaved.* N-VAR =surmise

2 When you **conjecture**, you form an opinion or reach a conclusion on the basis of incomplete or doubtful information; a formal use. *He conjectured that some individuals may be able to detect major calamities... This may be true or partly true; we are all conjecturing here.* VERB =surmise V that V Also V wh, V n

conjoin /kəndʒɔɪn/ **conjoins, conjoining, conjoined.** If two or more things **conjoin** or if you **conjoin** them, they are united and joined togeth- V-RECIP-ERG er; a formal word. *If only time and place hadn't conjoined then and there... America's rise in rates was conjoined with higher rates elsewhere. ...if we conjoin the two responses.* pl-n V; be V-ed with n; V pl-n; Also V n with n, V with n

conjugal /kɒndʒʊgəl/. **Conjugal** means relating to marriage and the relationship between a husband and wife, especially their sexual relationship; a formal word. *...a man deprived of his conjugal rights.* ADJ: ADJ n

conjugate /kɒndʒʊgeɪt/ **conjugates, conjugating, conjugated.** When pupils or teachers **conjugate** a verb, they give its different forms in a particular order. *...a child who can read at one and is conjugating Latin verbs at four.* VERB; V n

conjunction /kəndʒʌŋkʃən/ **conjunctions** ◆◆◇◇◇

1 A **conjunction** of two or more things is the occurrence of them at the same time or place; a formal use. *...the conjunction of two events. ...a conjunction of religious and social factors.* N-COUNT: usu N of n

2 In grammar, a **conjunction** is a word or group of words that joins together words, groups, or clauses. In English, there are co-ordinating conjunctions such as 'and' and 'but', and subordinating conjunctions such as 'although', 'because', and 'when'. N-COUNT

3 If one thing is done or used **in conjunction** with another, the two things are done or used together; a formal expression. *The army should have operated in conjunction with the fleet to raid the enemy's coast... Since iron destroys vitamin E, these two nutrients should not be taken in conjunction.* PHRASE: usu PHR with n =together

conjunctivitis /kəndʒʌŋktɪvaɪtɪs/. **Conjunctivitis** is an eye infection which causes the thin skin that covers the eyeball to become inflamed; a medical term. N-UNCOUNT

conjure /kʌndʒəʳ, AM kɑːn-/ **conjures, conjuring, conjured** ◆◇◇◇◇

1 If you **conjure** something out of nothing, you make it appear as if by magic. *Thirteen years ago she found herself having to conjure a career from thin air... They managed to conjure a victory.* ► **Conjure up** means the same as **conjure**. *Every day a different chef will be conjuring up delicious dishes in the restaurant... He conjured up a smile and reached out to squeeze her hand.* VERB =conjure up; V n from/out of n; V n; PHRASAL VERB; V P n (not pron); Also V n P

2 If you say that the name of a particular person or organization is a **name to conjure with**, you mean that that person or organization is very important and influential in the field you are discussing. *By 1920, Fox and Universal were already names to conjure with.* PHRASE: N inflects, v-link PHR

conjure up PHRASAL VERB

1 If you **conjure up** a memory, picture, or idea, you create it in your mind. *When he closed his eyes, he could conjure up in exact colour almost every event of his life... When we think of adventurers, many of us conjure up images of larger-than-life characters trekking to the North Pole.* V P n (not pron); Also V n P

2 If something such as a word or sound **conjures up** particular images or ideas, it makes you think of them. *Jimmy Buffett's music conjures up a warm night in the tropics... What does the word 'feminist' conjure up for you?* =evoke; V P n (not pron)

3 See **conjure** 1

conjurer /kʌndʒərəʳ, AM kɑːn-/ **conjurers;** also spelled **conjuror**. A **conjurer** is a person who entertains people by doing magic tricks. N-COUNT

conjuring trick, conjuring tricks. A **conjuring trick** is a trick in which something is made to appear or disappear as if by magic. N-COUNT =magician

conjuror /kʌndʒərəʳ, AM kɑːn-/. See **conjurer**.

conk /kɒŋk/ **conks, conking, conked**

conk out. If something such as a machine or a vehicle **conks out**, it stops working or breaks down; an informal expression. *Sometimes the dynamo which provided the electricity conked out and the castle was plunged into darkness.* PHRASAL VERB; V P

conker /kɒŋkəʳ/ **conkers**

1 **Conkers** are round brown nuts which come from horse chestnut trees; used in British English. N-COUNT

2 In Britain, **conkers** is a children's game in which you tie a conker to a piece of string and try to break your opponent's conker by hitting it as hard as you can with your own. N-UNCOUNT

con man, con men; also spelled **conman**. A **con man** is a man who persuades people to give him their money or property by lying to them. *A few years ago she was the victim of a con man.* N-COUNT

connect /kənekt/ **connects, connecting, connected** ◆◆◇◇◇

1 If something or someone **connects** one thing to another, or if one thing **connects** to another, the two things are joined together. *You can connect the machine to your hi-fi... The traditional method is to enter the exchanges at night and connect the wires... Two cables connect to each corner of the plate. ...a television camera connected to the radio telescope.* V-RECIP-ERG =attach ≠disconnect; V n to n; V pl-n; V to n; V-ed; Also pl-n V

2 If a piece of equipment or a place **is connected** to a source of power or water, it is joined to that source so that it has power or water. *These appliances should not be connected to power supplies... Ischia was now connected to the mainland water supply.* ► **Connect up** means the same as **connect**. *The shower is easy to install – it needs only to be connected up to the hot and cold water supply... They turned the barricade into a potential death trap by connecting it up to the mains.* VERB; be V-ed to n; V-ed; Also V n to n; PHRASAL VERB; be V-ed P to n; V n P to n; Also V P n (not pron) to n

3 If a telephone operator **connects** you, he or she enables you to speak to another person by telephone. *To call the police, an ambulance or the fire brigade dial 999 and the operator will connect you... He asked to be connected to the central switchboard.* VERB =put through; V n; be V-ed to n; Also V n to n

4 If two things or places **connect** or if something **connects** them, they are joined and people or things can pass between them. *...the long hallway that connects the rooms... The fallopian tubes connect the ovaries with the uterus... His workshop connected with a small building in the garden... The two rooms have connecting doors.* V-RECIP-ERG; V pl-n; V n with n; V with n; V-ing; Also pl-n V

5 If one train or plane, for example, **connects** with another, it arrives at a time which allows passengers to change to the other one in order to continue their journey. *...a train connecting with a ferry to Ireland... My connecting plane didn't depart for another six hours.* V-RECIP =link up; V with/to n; V-ing; Also pl-n V

6 If you **connect** to a particular plane or train, or if another plane or train **connects** you to it, you change to that plane or train from another one in order to continue your journey. *...business travellers wanting to connect to a long-haul flight... That will connect you with time to spare for the seven o'clock Concorde.* V-ERG; V to n; V n; Also V n to n

7 If you **connect** a person or thing with something, you realize that there is a link or relationship between them. *I hoped he would not connect me with that now-embarrassing review I'd written seven years earlier... I wouldn't have connected the two things.* VERB =associate; V n with/to n; V pl-n

8 Something that **connects** a person or thing with something else shows or provides a link or relationship between them. *A search of Brady's house revealed nothing that could connect him with the robberies... What connects them?* VERB =link; V n with/to n; V pl-n

9 If a person or their ideas **connect** with you, you feel a sense of agreement and familiarity with them because you have the same kind of ideas. You can also say that two people **connect**. *If you stand on stage and share your view of the world, people will connect with you. ...no matter how magically two people connect.* V-RECIP; V with n; pl-n V

connect up. See **connect** 2. PHRASAL VERB

connected /kənektɪd/. If one thing is **connected** with another, there is a link or relationship between them. *Have you ever had any skin problems connected with exposure to the sun?... The dispute is not directly connected to the negotiations... She was born at Ambala, India, her family being closely connected with the Indian army.* • See also **connect, well-connected.** ◆◆◇◇◇ ADJ: usu v-link ADJ, oft ADJ with/to n

connection /kənekʃən/ **connections;** also spelled **connexion** in British English. ◆◆◆◇◇

1 A **connection** is a relationship between two things, people, or groups. *There was no evidence of* N-VAR: usu N prep =association,

a connection between BSE and the brain diseases recently confirmed in cats... The police say he had no connection with the security forces... He has denied any connection to the bombing. =link

2 A **connection** is a joint where two wires or pipes are joined together. *Check all radiators for small leaks, especially round pipework connections.* N-COUNT

3 If a place has good road, rail, or air **connections**, many places can be directly reached from there by car, train, or plane. *Fukuoka has excellent air and rail connections to the rest of the country.* N-COUNT: usu n N

4 If you get a **connection** at a station or airport, you catch a train, bus, or plane, after getting off another train, bus, or plane, in order to continue your journey. *My flight was late and I missed the connection.* N-COUNT: usu sing

5 Your **connections** are the people who you know or are related to, especially when they are in a position to help you. *She used her connections to full advantage.* N-PLURAL

6 If you write or talk to someone **in connection with** something, you write or talk to them about that thing; a formal expression. *I am writing in connection with Michael Shower's letter... 13 men have been questioned in connection with the murder.* PHRASES PREP

7 You say **in this connection** or **in that connection** to indicate that what you are talking about is related to what you have just mentioned; a formal expression. *It is the 100th anniversary of his death. We here are having very great celebrations in this connection.* PHR with cl PRAGMATICS

connective /kənektɪv/ **connectives.** A **connective** is the same as a **conjunction**. N-COUNT

connective tissue. Connective tissue is the substance in the bodies of animals and people which fills in the spaces between organs and connects muscles and bones; a technical term in biology. N-UNCOUNT

connector /kənektəʳ/ **connectors.** A **connector** is a device that joins two pieces of equipment, wire, or piping together. N-COUNT

connexion /kənekʃᵊn/. See **connection**.

connivance /kənaɪvᵊns/. **Connivance** is a willingness to allow or assist something to happen even though you know it is wrong; used showing disapproval. *It was stolen by Odysseus, with the connivance of Helen... The murder had been carried out with police connivance.* N-UNCOUNT: usu with supp, oft *with the* N *of* n PRAGMATICS

connive /kənaɪv/ **connives, conniving, connived**

1 If you say that one person **connives** with another to do something, you are critical of them because they secretly try to achieve something which is to their common advantage. *He accused ministers of conniving with foreign companies to tear up employment rights... Senior politicians connived to ensure that he was not released. ...local authorities suspected of conniving with the Mafia.* V-RECIP PRAGMATICS =conspire; V *with* n to-inf; pl-n V to-inf; V *with* n

2 If you say that someone **connives** at something or **connives** in something, you are critical of them because they allow or assist it to happen even though they know that it is wrong and that they ought to prevent it. *He suspected elements within the South African government were conniving at the disturbances to try to weaken the ANC... To buy things cheaply from a poor country is to connive in its poverty.* VERB PRAGMATICS; V *at/in* n/-ing

conniving /kənaɪvɪŋ/. If you describe someone as **conniving**, you mean you dislike them because they make secret plans in order to get things for themselves or harm other people. *Edith was seen as a conniving, greedy woman.* ADJ: usu ADJ n PRAGMATICS =scheming

connoisseur /kɒnəsɜːʳ/ **connoisseurs.** A **connoisseur** is someone who knows a lot about the arts, food, drink, or some other subject. *Sarah tells me you're something of an art connoisseur. ...connoisseurs of good food.* ◆◇◇◇◇ N-COUNT: oft n N, N *of* n

connotation /kɒnəteɪʃᵊn/ **connotations.** The **connotations** of a particular word or name are the ideas or qualities which it makes you think of. *It's just one of those words that's got so many negative connotations... 'Urchin', with its connotation of mischievousness, may not be a particularly apt word.* ◆◇◇◇◇ N-COUNT: usu with supp, oft N *of* n =association

connote /kənoʊt/ **connotes, connoting, connoted.** If a word or name **connotes** something, it makes you think of a particular idea or quality; a formal word. *The term 'ladies' connotes females who are simultaneously put on a pedestal and patronised.* VERB =suggest, imply; V n

conquer /kɒŋkəʳ/ **conquers, conquering, conquered** ◆◆◇◇◇

1 If one country or group of people **conquers** another, they take complete control of their land. *During 1936, Mussolini conquered Abyssinia... Early in the eleventh century the whole of England was again conquered by the Vikings.* VERB V n

2 If you **conquer** something such as a problem, you succeed in ending it or dealing with it successfully. *I was certain that love was quite enough to conquer our differences... He has never conquered his addiction to smoking. ...the first man in history to conquer Everest.* VERB V n

conqueror /kɒŋkərəʳ/ **conquerors** ◆◇◇◇◇

1 The **conquerors** of a country or group of people are the people who have taken complete control of that country or group's land. *The people of an oppressed country obey their conquerors because they want to go on living.* N-COUNT: usu pl

2 The **conqueror** of a person or team is the person or team that beats them in a game or contest; used in journalism. *He easily overcame 24-year-old Matsuoka, Saturday's conqueror of Stefan Edberg... Her conqueror, Senator Pete Wilson, is a diffident, moderate man.* N-COUNT: usu with poss

conquest /kɒŋkwest/ **conquests** ◆◇◇◇◇

1 Conquest is the act of conquering a country or group of people. *He had led the conquest of southern Poland in 1939... After the Norman Conquest the forest became a royal hunting preserve... Jerusalem has seen endless conquests and occupations.* N-UNCOUNT: also N in pl, oft N *of* n

2 Conquests are lands that have been conquered in war. *He had realized that Britain could not have peace unless she returned at least some of her former conquests.* N-COUNT: usu pl

3 If someone makes a **conquest**, they succeed in attracting and usually sleeping with another person. You usually use **conquest** when you want to indicate that this relationship is not important to the person concerned. *Despite his conquests, he remains lonely and isolated. ...men who boast about their sexual conquests to all their friends.* N-COUNT: usu poss N

4 You can refer to the person that someone has succeeded in attracting as their **conquest**. *Pushkin was a womaniser whose conquests included everyone from prostitutes to princesses.* N-COUNT: oft poss N

5 The **conquest** of something such as a problem is success in ending it or dealing with it. *The conquest of inflation has been the Government's overriding economic priority for nearly 15 years. ...the conquest of cancer.* N-SING: usu *the* N *of* n =defeat

conquistador /kɒnkwɪstədɔːʳ/ **conquistadors** or **conquistadores.** The **conquistadors** were the sixteenth century Spanish conquerors of Central and South America. N-COUNT

conscience /kɒnʃᵊns/ **consciences** ◆◆◇◇◇

1 Your **conscience** is the part of your mind that tells you whether what you are doing is right or wrong. If you have a **guilty conscience**, you feel guilty about something because you know it was wrong. If you have a **clear conscience**, you do not feel guilty because you know you have done nothing wrong. *I have battled with my conscience over whether I should actually send this letter... What if he got a guilty conscience and brought it back?... I could go away again with a clear conscience.* N-COUNT: usu sing, with supp, oft poss N, adj N

2 Conscience is doing what you believe is right even though it might be unpopular, difficult, or dangerous. *He refused for reasons of conscience to sign a new law legalising abortion. ...the law on freedom of conscience and religious organizations.* N-UNCOUNT

● See also **prisoner of conscience**.

3 Conscience is a feeling of guilt because you know you have done something that is wrong. *I'm so glad* N-UNCOUNT =guilt *he had a pang of conscience... They have shown a ruthless lack of conscience.*

4 If you say that you cannot do something **in all conscience**, you mean that you cannot do it because you think it is wrong; used mainly in British English. In American English, the usual expression is **in good conscience**. *She could not, in good conscience, back out on her deal with him.* PHRASES PHR with cl

5 If you have something **on** your **conscience**, you feel guilty because you know you have done something wrong. *Now the murderer has two deaths on his conscience.* PHR after v, v-link PHR

conscientious /kɒnʃienʃəs/. Someone who is **conscientious** is very careful to do their work properly. *We are generally very conscientious about our work... Virginia was still struggling to be a conscientious and dedicated mother.* ◆◇◇◇◇ ADJ-GRADED
♦ **conscientiously** *He studied conscientiously and enthusiastically.* ADV-GRADED: usu ADV with v

conscientious objector, conscientious objectors. A **conscientious objector** is a person who refuses to join the armed forces because they think that it is morally wrong to do so. N-COUNT

conscious /kɒnʃəs/ ◆◆◆◇◇

1 If you are **conscious** of something, you notice it or realize that it is happening. *He was conscious of the faint, musky aroma of aftershave... She was very conscious of Max studying her... Conscious that he was becoming light-headed again, he went over to the window.* ADJ-GRADED: v-link ADJ *of* n/-ing, v-link ADJ that =aware

2 If you are **conscious** of something, you think about it a lot, especially because you are unhappy about it or because you think it is important. *I'm very conscious of my weight... He is acutely conscious that this transition will bring with it the risk of social unrest.* ADJ-GRADED: v-link ADJ *of* n/-ing, v-link ADJ that =aware

3 A **conscious** decision or action is made or done deliberately with you giving your full attention to it. *I don't think we ever made a conscious decision to have a big family... Make a conscious effort to relax your muscles.* ADJ: usu ADJ n =deliberate ♦ **consciously** *Sophie was not consciously seeking a replacement after her father died.* ADV: ADV with v

4 Someone who is **conscious** is awake rather than asleep or unconscious. *She was fully conscious all the time and knew what was going on.* ADJ: usu v-link ADJ ≠unconscious

5 **Conscious** memories or thoughts are ones that you are aware of. *He had no conscious memory of his four-week stay in hospital... Beneath the conscious mind there are many levels of the unconscious.* ADJ: ADJ n ≠subconscious ♦ **consciously** *Most people cannot consciously remember much before the ages of 5 to 7 years... Sometimes we are not consciously aware of these feelings.* ADV: ADV with v, ADV adj

-conscious /kɒnʃəs/. **-conscious** combines with words such as 'health', 'fashion', 'politically', and 'environmentally' to form adjectives which describe someone who believes that the aspect of life indicated is important. *We're all becoming increasingly health-conscious these days... Environmentally conscious West Germans are worried about the pollution the car produces.* COMB in ADJ-GRADED =aware

consciousness /kɒnʃəsnəs/ **consciousnesses** ◆◆◆◇◇

1 Your **consciousness** is your mind and your thoughts. *That idea has been creeping into our consciousness for some time.* N-COUNT: usu sing, usu poss N =awareness

2 The **consciousness** of a group of people is their set of ideas, attitudes, and beliefs. *The Greens were the catalysts of a necessary change in the European consciousness.* N-UNCOUNT: with supp =awareness

3 You use **consciousness** to refer to an interest in and knowledge of a particular subject or idea. *Her political consciousness sprang from her upbringing when her father's illness left the family short of money.* N-UNCOUNT: supp N =awareness

4 **Consciousness** is the state of being awake rather than being asleep or unconscious. If someone **loses consciousness**, they become unconscious, and if they **regain consciousness**, they become conscious after being unconscious. *She banged her head and lost consciousness... He drifted in and out of consciousness.* N-UNCOUNT

5 See also **stream of consciousness**.

consciousness raising. **Consciousness raising** is the process of developing awareness of an unfair situation, with the aim of making people want to help in changing it. *...consciousness-raising groups.* N-UNCOUNT: oft N n

conscript, conscripts, conscripting, conscripted. The noun is pronounced /kɒnskrɪpt/. The verb is pronounced /kənskrɪpt/. ◆◇◇◇◇

1 A **conscript** is a person who has been made to join the armed forces of a country. N-COUNT ≠volunteer

2 If someone **is conscripted**, they are officially made to join the armed forces of a country. *He was conscripted into the German army... Peter was conscripted like every other young man.* VB: usu passive *be* V-ed *into* n, *be* V-ed

conscription /kənskrɪpʃᵊn/. **Conscription** is officially making people in a particular country join the armed forces. *All adult males will be liable for conscription.* ◆◇◇◇◇ N-UNCOUNT

consecrate /kɒnsɪkreɪt/ **consecrates, consecrating, consecrated.** When a building, place, or object **is consecrated**, it is officially declared to be holy. When a person **is consecrated**, they are officially declared to be a bishop. *The church was consecrated in 1234... He defied Pope John Paul II by consecrating four bishops without his approval.* ◆◇◇◇◇ VERB *be* V-ed, V n ♦ **consecration** /kɒnsɪkreɪʃᵊn/ *...the consecration of Barbara Harris as a Bishop.* N-UNCOUNT

consecutive /kənsekjʊtɪv/. **Consecutive** periods of time or events happen one after the other without interruption. *The AIAW basketball championship was won for the third consecutive year by Delta State... Photographs taken at the same time on two consecutive sunny days can be quite different from one another.* ◆◆◇◇◇ ADJ: usu ADJ n =successive ♦ **consecutively** *...a CD player which plays six CDs consecutively.* ADV: ADV after v

consensual /kənsenʃuəl/

1 A **consensual** approach, view, or decision is one that is based on general agreement amongst all the members of a group. *What I did argue for was a less abrasive, more consensual approach to policy.* ADJ-GRADED: usu ADJ n

2 If sexual activity is **consensual**, both partners willingly take part in it; a legal use. *Consensual sexual contact between two males can be a criminal activity.* ADJ

consensus /kənsensəs/. A **consensus** is general agreement amongst a group of people. *The consensus amongst the world's scientists is that the world is likely to warm up over the next few decades... The question of when the troops should leave would be decided by consensus.* ◆◆◇◇◇ N-SING: also no det

consent /kənsent/ **consents, consenting, consented** ◆◆◇◇◇

1 If you give your **consent** to something, you give someone permission to do it; a formal use. *At approximately 11:30 p.m., Pollard finally gave his consent to the search... Can my child be medically examined without my consent?* N-UNCOUNT: usu with poss

2 If you **consent** to something, you agree to do it or to allow it to be done; a formal use. *He finally consented to go... He asked Ginny if she would consent to a small celebration after the christening... I was a little surprised when she consented.* VERB =agree V to-inf, V *to*n/-ing, V

3 See also **age of consent**.

4 If something happens **by common consent** or **by mutual consent**, it happens as the result of an agreement between the people or groups involved. *By common consent their talk avoided the reason for their being there at all... He left the company by mutual consent last September.* PHRASES PHR with v

5 You can use **by general consent** or **by common consent** to indicate that most people agree that something is true. *By common consent this election constituted a historic step on the road to democracy.* PHR with cl

consenting /kənsentɪŋ/. A **consenting** adult is a person who is considered to be old enough to make their own decisions about who they have sex with. *What consenting adults do in private is their own business.* ADJ: ADJ n

consequence /kɒnsɪkwens/ **consequences** 

1 The **consequences** of something are the results or effects of it. *Her lawyer said she understood the* N-COUNT: usu with supp, oft N *of*n

consequences of her actions and was prepared to go to jail. ...people who are suffering and dying as a consequence of cigarette smoking... An economic crisis may have tremendous consequences for our global security.

2 If one thing happens and then another thing happens **in consequence**, the second thing happens as a result of the first. *His death was totally unexpected and, in consequence, no plans had been made for his replacement... Maternity services were to be reduced in consequence of falling birth rates.*
PHRASE: PHR with cl/group PRAGMATICS =consequently

3 Something or someone **of consequence** is important or valuable. If something or someone is **of** no **consequence**, or **of** little **consequence**, they are not important or valuable. A formal use. *As a post-office overseer in Banagher, aged 26, he suddenly found himself a person of consequence... The religious affiliation of those they choose to marry is of no consequence to anyone but the individuals concerned.*
PHRASE: oft with brd-neg, n PHR, v-link PHR =importance

4 If you tell someone that they must **take the consequences** or **face the consequences**, you warn them that something unpleasant will happen to them if they do not stop behaving in a particular way. *These pilots must now face the consequences of their actions and be brought to trial... If climate changes continue, we will suffer the consequences.*
PHRASE: V inflects

consequent /kɒnsɪkwənt/. **Consequent** means happening as a direct result of an event or situation; a formal word. *The warming of the Earth and the consequent climatic changes affect us all... The changes in social work consequent upon reorganization have been considerable.*
◆◇◇◇◇ ADJ: usu ADJ n, also n ADJ *upon/on* n =consequential

consequential /kɒnsɪkwenʃᵊl/

1 **Consequential** means the same as **consequent**; a formal use. *The actual estimate for extra staff and consequential costs such as accommodation was an annual £9.18m.*
ADJ: ADJ n =consequent

2 Something that is **consequential** is important or significant; a formal use. *This new transformation is at least as consequential as that one was... From a medical standpoint a week is usually not a consequential delay.*
ADJ-GRADED =significant ≠inconsequential

consequently /kɒnsɪkwentli/. **Consequently** means as a result; a formal word. *Grandfather Dingsdale had sustained a broken back while working in the mines. Consequently, he spent the rest of his life in a wheelchair... Relations between the two companies had, consequently, never been close.*
◆◆◇◇◇ ADV: ADV with cl PRAGMATICS =as a result

conservancy /kənsɜːʳvənsi/. **Conservancy** is used in the names of organizations that work for the preservation and protection of the environment. *...the Nature Conservancy Council.*
N-UNCOUNT: usu N n =conservation

conservation /kɒnsəʳveɪʃᵊn/
◆◆◇◇◇

1 **Conservation** is the preservation and protection of the environment. *...a four-nation regional meeting on elephant conservation. ...tree-planting and other conservation projects.*
N-UNCOUNT: usu with supp

2 **Conservation** is the preservation and protection of historical objects or works of art such as paintings, sculptures, or buildings. *Then he began his most famous work, the conservation and rebinding of the Book of Kells... You probably won't need to apply for planning permission unless you live in a listed building or conservation area.*
N-UNCOUNT

3 The **conservation** of a supply of something is the careful use of it so that it lasts for a long time. *...projects aimed at promoting energy conservation. ...rules concerning the conservation of fishery resources.*
N-UNCOUNT: usu with supp

conservationist /kɒnsəʳveɪʃənɪst/ **conservationists.** A **conservationist** is a someone who cares greatly about the conservation of the environment and who works and campaigns for its protection.
◆◇◇◇◇ N-COUNT =environmentalist

conservatism /kənsɜːʳvətɪzəm/; also spelled **Conservatism** for meaning 1.
◆◇◇◇◇

1 **Conservatism** is a political philosophy which believes that if changes need to be made to society, they should be made gradually. You can also refer to the political beliefs of a conservative party in a particular country as **Conservatism**. *...the philosophy of modern Conservatism.*
N-UNCOUNT

2 **Conservatism** is unwillingness to accept changes and new ideas. *The conservatism of the literary establishment in this country is astounding... He began his professional life as an accountant, the very model of respectability and conservatism.*
N-UNCOUNT

conservative /kənsɜːʳvətɪv/ **conservatives;** also spelled **Conservative** for meaning 1.
◆◆◆◆◇

1 A **Conservative** politician or voter is a member of or votes for the Conservative Party. *Most Conservative MPs appear happy with the government's reassurances. ...disenchanted Conservative voters.*
► Also a noun. *In 1951 the Conservatives were returned to power.*
ADJ =Tory; N-COUNT

2 Someone who is **conservative** has right-wing views. *...counties whose citizens invariably support the most conservative candidate in any election.*
► Also a noun. *The new judge is 50-year-old David Suitor who's regarded as a conservative.*
ADJ-GRADED =right-wing; N-COUNT

3 Someone who is **conservative** or has **conservative** ideas is unwilling to accept changes and new ideas. *People tend to be more aggressive when they're young and more conservative as they get older... It is essentially a narrow and conservative approach to child care.*
ADJ-GRADED =traditionalist

4 If someone dresses in a **conservative** way, their clothes are conventional in style. *The girl was well dressed, as usual, though in a more conservative style.* ♦ **conservatively** *She was always very conservatively dressed when we went out.*
ADJ-GRADED; ADV-GRADED: ADV with v

5 A **conservative** estimate or guess is one in which you are cautious and estimate or guess a low amount which is probably less that the real amount. *A conservative estimate of the bill, so far, is about £22,000... This guess is probably on the conservative side.* ♦ **conservatively** *The bequest is conservatively estimated at £30 million.*
ADJ-GRADED: usu ADJ n; ADV-GRADED: ADV with v

Conservative Party. The **Conservative Party** is the main right of centre party in the United Kingdom. It is committed to free enterprise, low personal taxation, and the maintenance of the United Kingdom in its present form.
◆◆◇◇◇ N-PROPER: usu *the* N

conservatoire /kənsɜːʳvətwɑːʳ/ **conservatoires.** A **conservatoire** is an institution where musicians are trained. *...the Paris Conservatoire.*
N-COUNT: oft in names =conservatory

conservator /kənsɜːʳvətəʳ/ **conservators.** A **conservator** is someone whose job is to maintain and restore historical objects or works of art.
N-COUNT

conservatory /kənsɜːʳvətri, AM -tɔːri/ **conservatories**
◆◇◇◇◇

1 A **conservatory** is a room with glass walls and a glass roof, which is attached to a house. Plants are often grown in a conservatory.
N-COUNT

2 A **conservatory** is an institution where musicians are trained. *...the New England Conservatory of Music.*
N-COUNT: oft in names =conservatoire

conserve, conserves, conserving, conserved. The verb is pronounced /kənsɜːʳv/. The noun is pronounced /kɒnsɜːʳv/.
◆◇◇◇◇

1 If you **conserve** a supply of something, you use it carefully so that it lasts for a long time. *The republic's factories have closed for the weekend to conserve energy.*
VERB =save V n

2 To **conserve** something means to protect it from harm, loss, or change. *...a big increase in US aid to help developing countries conserve their forests. ...the Government-funded body responsible for conserving historic buildings.*
VERB =preserve V n

3 **Conserve** is jam containing a large proportion of fruit, usually in whole pieces.
N-MASS

4 See also **conservation.**

consider /kənsɪdəʳ/ **considers, considering, considered**
◆◆◆◆◆

1 If you **consider** a person or thing to be something, you have the opinion that this is what they are. *We don't consider our customers to be mere consumers; we consider them to be our friends... I had always considered myself a strong, competent woman... The paper does not explain why foreign ownership should be considered bad... I consider activities such as jogging and weightlifting as un-*
VERB =think V n to-inf V n n/adj V n *as* adj/n V that

natural... Barbara considers that pet shops which sell customers these birds are very unfair.

2 If you **consider** something, you think about it carefully. *The government is being asked to consider a plan to fix the date of the Easter break... You do have to consider the feelings of those around you... Consider how much you can afford to pay for a course, and what is your upper limit.*
VERB =think about V n V wh

3 If you **are considering** doing something, you intend to do it, but have not yet made a final decision whether to do it. *I had seriously considered telling the story from the point of view of the wives... Watersports enthusiasts should consider hiring a wetsuit as well as a lifejacket... They are considering the launch of their own political party.*
VERB =think about V -ing V n

4 You say **all things considered** to indicate that you are making a judgement after taking all the facts into account. *All things considered, I think you have behaved marvellously in coming here.*
PHRASE: PHR with cl PRAGMATICS =all in all

5 See also **considered**, **considering**.

considerable /kənsɪdərəbᵊl/. **Considerable** means great in amount or degree; a formal word. *To be without Pearce would be a considerable blow... Doing it properly makes considerable demands on our time... Vets' fees can be considerable, even for routine visits.* ♦ **considerably** *Children vary considerably in the rate at which they learn these lessons... Their dinner parties had become considerably less formal.*
◆◆◆◆◇ ADJ-GRADED: usu ADJ n =substantial
ADV-GRADED: ADV with v, ADV compar =significantly

considerate /kənsɪdərət/. Someone who is **considerate** pays attention to the needs, wishes, or feelings of other people. *I think he's the most charming, most considerate man I've ever known... I've always understood one should try and be considerate of other people.*
◆◇◇◇◇ ADJ-GRADED: oft ADJ *of* n ≠inconsiderate

♦ **considerately** *He treats everyone equally and considerately.*
ADV-GRADED: ADV with v

consideration /kənsɪdəreɪʃᵊn/ **considerations**
◆◆◆◇◇

1 **Consideration** is careful thought about something. *He said there should be careful consideration of the future role of the BBC.*
N-UNCOUNT

2 If something is **under consideration**, it is being discussed. *Several proposals are under consideration by the state assembly.*
N-UNCOUNT: *under* N

3 If you show **consideration**, you pay attention to the needs, wishes, or feelings of other people. *Show consideration for other rail travellers... Really, her tone said, some people have absolutely no consideration.*
N-UNCOUNT: oft N *for* n

4 A **consideration** is something that should be thought about, especially when you are planning or deciding something. *They should not allow partisan political considerations or interests to cloud their judgement... Price has become a more important consideration for shoppers in choosing which store to visit than it was before the recession.*
N-COUNT: usu supp N

5 If you **take** something **into consideration**, you think about it because it is relevant to what you are doing. *The whole affair is bound to be taken into consideration when the Indian side is picked... Safe driving is good driving because it takes into consideration the lives of other people.*
PHRASE: V inflects =take into account

considered /kənsɪdəʳd/. A **considered** opinion or act is the result of careful thought. *Obviously it was Anne's considered opinion that Mavis was a bold-faced liar... We would hope to be able to give a considered response to the unions' proposals by the end of the year.* ● See also **consider**.
◆◇◇◇◇ ADJ-GRADED: ADJ n

considering /kənsɪdərɪŋ/
◆◆◆◇◇

1 You use **considering** to indicate that you are thinking about a particular fact when making a judgement or giving an opinion. *He must be hoping, but considering the situation in June he may hoping for too much too soon... The former hostage is in remarkably good shape considering his ordeal.*
PREP

2 You use **considering that** to indicate that you are thinking about a particular fact when making a judgement or giving an opinion. *Considering that you are no longer involved with this man, your response is a little extreme.*
CONJ-SUBORD PRAGMATICS

3 When you are giving an opinion or making a judgement, you can use **considering** to suggest that you have thought about all the circumstances, and often that something has succeeded in spite of these circumstances; used in spoken English. *I think you're pretty safe, considering.*
ADV: cl ADV PRAGMATICS =all things considered

consign /kənsaɪn/ **consigns, consigning, consigned.** To **consign** something or someone **to** a place where they will be forgotten about, or to an unpleasant situation or place, means to put them there. *For decades, many of Malevich's works were consigned to the basements of Soviet museums... It was time to consign his bat and glove to the cupboard... In less than a year, the old hard-line Communist state of East Germany had been consigned to history.*
◆◇◇◇◇ VERB =relegate V n *to* n

consignment /kənsaɪnmənt/ **consignments.** A **consignment** of goods is a load that is being delivered to a place or person. *The first consignment of food has already left Bologna.*
◆◇◇◇◇ N-COUNT: oft N *of* n =batch

consist /kənsɪst/ **consists, consisting, consisted**
◆◆◆◇◇

1 Something that **consists of** particular things or people is formed from them. *My diet consisted almost exclusively of chocolate-covered biscuits and glasses of milk... Her crew consisted of children from Devon and Cornwall.*
VERB =be made up of V *of* n/-ing

2 Something that **consists in** something else has that thing as its main or only part. *His work as a consultant consisted in advising foreign companies on the siting of new factories. ...Baudelaire's idea that genius consists in the ability to summon up childhood.*
VERB V *in* n/-ing

consistency /kənsɪstənsi/
◆◇◇◇◇

1 **Consistency** is the quality or condition of being consistent. *He scores goals with remarkable consistency... There's always a lack of consistency in matters of foreign policy.*
N-UNCOUNT

2 The **consistency** of a substance is its degree of thickness or smoothness. *Dilute the paint with water until it is the consistency of milk... I added a little milk to mix the dough to the right consistency.*
N-UNCOUNT: usu with supp

consistent /kənsɪstənt/
◆◆◆◇◇

1 Someone who is **consistent** always behaves in the same way, has the same attitudes towards people or things, or achieves the same level of success in something. *Becker has never been the most consistent of players anyway. ...his consistent support of free trade.* ♦ **consistently** *It's something I have consistently denied... Jones and Armstrong maintain a consistently high standard.*
ADJ-GRADED
ADV-GRADED: ADV with v, ADV adj/adv

2 If one fact or idea is **consistent** with another, they do not contradict each other. *This result is consistent with the findings of Garnett & Tobin... New goals are not always consistent with the existing policies.*
ADJ: v-link ADJ, usu ADJ *with* n

3 An argument or set of ideas that is **consistent** is one in which no part contradicts or conflicts with any other part. *A theory should be internally consistent.*
ADJ =coherent

consolation prize, consolation prizes

1 A **consolation prize** is a small prize which is given to a person who fails to win a competition.
N-COUNT

2 A **consolation prize** is something that happens or is given to a person to cheer them up when they have failed to achieve something better. *Her appointment was seen as a consolation prize after she had failed to win a seat in the Senate.*
N-COUNT

console, consoles, consoling, consoled. The verb is pronounced /kənsoʊl/. The noun is pronounced /kɒnsoʊl/.
◆◆◇◇◇

1 If you **console** someone who is unhappy about something, you try to make them feel more cheerful. *'Never mind, Ned,' he consoled me... Often they cry, and I have to play the role of a mother, consoling them... He will have to console himself by reading about the success of his compatriots... I can console myself with the fact that I'm not alone... He consoled himself that Emmanuel looked like a nice boy, who could be a good playmate for his daughter.*
VERB =comfort V with quote V n V pron-refl V pron-refl *with/for* n V pron-refl that Also V n *with/for* n, V n that

♦ **consoling** *It is not a consoling thought to Germans to see that Americans have the same kind of problem, too.* ♦ **consolation** /kɒnsəleɪʃᵊn/ **consolations** *The only consolation for the Scottish thea-*
ADJ-GRADED =cheering
N-VAR =comfort

tre community is that they look likely to get another chance... He knew then he was right, but it was no consolation.

2 A **console** is a panel with a number of switches or knobs that is used to operate a machine. N-COUNT

consolidate /kənsɒlɪdeɪt/ **consolidates, consolidating, consolidated** ◆◆◇◇◇

1 If you **consolidate** something that you have, for example power or success, you strengthen it so that it becomes more effective or secure. *The question is: will the junta consolidate its power by force?... Brydon's team-mate Martin Williamson consolidated his lead in the National League when he won the latest round.* VERB; V n ♦ **consolidation** /kənsɒlɪdeɪʃən/ *But change brought about the growth and consolidation of the working class... Even if not total, the Romans' hold was sufficient for them to begin the task of consolidation.* N-UNCOUNT: oft N *of* n

2 To **consolidate** a number of small groups or firms means to make them into one large organization. *Judge Charles Schwartz is giving the state 60 days to disband and consolidate Louisiana's four higher education boards... IBM, which consolidated some operations last summer, has made clear that it needs to continue to streamline them.* VERB; V n ♦ **consolidation, consolidations** *This consolidation meant having to reduce the numerical strength of the Army... Further consolidations in the industry could follow.* N-VAR

consommé /kɒnsɒmeɪ, AM kɒnsəmeɪ/ **consommés.** **Consommé** is a thin, clear soup, usually made from meat juices. *The chicken consommé was watery.* N-MASS: oft n N

consonant /kɒnsənənt/ **consonants**

1 A **consonant** is a sound such as 'p', 'f', 'n', or 't' which you pronounce by stopping the air flowing freely through your mouth. Compare **vowel**. N-COUNT

2 Something that is **consonant with** something else fits or agrees with it very well; a formal use. *I found their work very much consonant with this way of thinking.* ADJ-GRADED: v-link ADJ *with* n

consort, consorts, consorting, consorted. ◆◇◇◇◇ The verb is pronounced /kənsɔːʳt/. The noun is pronounced /kɒnsɔːʳt/.

1 If you say that someone **consorts with** a particular person or group, you mean that they spend a lot of time with them, and usually that you do not think this is a good thing; a formal use. *He regularly consorted with known drug-dealers.* VERB PRAGMATICS =associate; V *with* n

2 The ruling monarch's wife or husband is called their **consort**. *At tea-time, Victoria sang duets with her Consort, Prince Albert... She was surely the most distinguished queen consort we have had.* N-COUNT; N-TITLE: oft n N

3 A **consort** of musicians or instruments is a group of them. *The Sinfonietta shares the stage with a consort of viols.* N-COUNT

consortium /kənsɔːʳtiəm/ **consortia** /kənsɔːʳtiə/ or **consortiums.** A **consortium** is a group of people or firms who have agreed to work in cooperation with each other. *The consortium includes some of the biggest building contractors in Britain.* ◆◆◇◇◇ N-COUNT-COLL

conspicuous /kənspɪkjuəs/ ◆◇◇◇◇

1 If someone or something is **conspicuous**, people can see or notice them very easily. *The most conspicuous way in which the old politics is changing is in the growing use of referendums... You may feel tearful in situations where you feel conspicuous.* ADJ-GRADED ≠inconspicuous ♦ **conspicuously** *Britain continues to follow US policy in this and other areas where American policies have most conspicuously failed... Johnston's name was conspicuously absent from the list.* ADV-GRADED: ADV with v, ADV adj

2 If you say that someone or something is **conspicuous by** their **absence**, you are drawing attention to the fact that they are not in a place or situation where you think they should be. *He played no part in the game and was conspicuous by his absence in the post-match celebrations.* PHRASE

conspicuous consumption. **Conspicuous consumption** means spending your money in such a way that other people can see how wealthy you are. *It was an age of conspicuous consumption – those who had money liked to display it.* N-UNCOUNT

conspiracy /kənspɪrəsi/ **conspiracies** ◆◆◇◇◇

1 **Conspiracy** is the secret planning by a group of people to do something illegal. *Seven men, all from Bristol, admitted conspiracy to commit arson... He believes there probably was a conspiracy to kill President Kennedy in 1963.* N-VAR: oft N to-inf =plot

2 A **conspiracy** is an agreement between a group of people which other people think is wrong or is likely to be harmful. *It's all part of a conspiracy to dispense with the town centre all together and move everything out to Meadowhall... It was like some kind of conspiracy against men.* N-COUNT: oft N to-inf

3 If there is a **conspiracy of silence** about something, people who know about it have agreed that they will not talk publicly about it, although it would probably be a good thing if people in general knew about it. *Detectives have run into a conspiracy of silence in the tight-knit communities of the peninsula.* PHRASE

conspiracy theory conspiracy theories. If you say that someone has a **conspiracy theory**, you mean that they think that a group of people are secretly trying to harm someone or achieve something. You are usually implying that you think this is unlikely. *Did you ever swallow the conspiracy theory about Kennedy?* N-COUNT

conspirator /kənspɪrətəʳ/ **conspirators.** A **conspirator** is a person who joins a conspiracy. ◆◇◇◇◇ N-COUNT

conspiratorial /kənspɪrətɔːriəl/

1 If someone does something such as speak, smile, or wink in a **conspiratorial** way, they do it in a way that suggests they are sharing a secret with someone. *His voice had sunk to a conspiratorial whisper... When I went to collect the car, Bill met me with a conspiratorial grin.* ADJ-GRADED: usu ADJ n ♦ **conspiratorially** *The officer leaned forward conspiratorially and said: 'I shouldn't worry about it, mate.'* ADV-GRADED: ADV after v

2 Something that is **conspiratorial** is secret and illegal, often with a political purpose. *There is nothing sinister or conspiratorial about the export licensing system. ...a secret and supposedly conspiratorial Communist party meeting.* ADJ

conspire /kənspaɪəʳ/ **conspires, conspiring, conspired** ◆◇◇◇◇

1 If two or more people or groups **conspire** to do something illegal or harmful, they make a secret agreement to do it. *They'd conspired to overthrow the government... Mr Farmer and Mrs Jones both admitted conspiring to murder her husband. ...a defendant convicted of conspiring with his brother to commit robberies... I had a persecution complex and thought people were conspiring against me.* V-RECIP =plot; pl-n V to-inf; V *with* n to-inf; pl-n V *against* n; Also V *with* n

2 If events **conspire** to produce a particular result, they seem to work together to cause this result; a literary use. *History and geography have conspired to bring Greece to a moment of decision... But fateful forces beyond the band's control were to conspire against them.* VERB =combine; V to-inf; V *against* n

constable /kʌnstəbəl, kɒn-/ **constables.** In Britain and some other countries, a **constable** is a police officer of the lowest rank. *He was a constable at Sutton police station. ...Constable Stuart Clark... Thanks for your help, Constable.* ● See also **Chief Constable**. ◆◆◇◇◇ N-COUNT; N-TITLE; N-VOC

constabulary /kənstæbjʊləri, AM -leri/ **constabularies.** In Britain and some other countries, a **constabulary** is the police force of a particular area. *...the Chief Constable of the Nottinghamshire Constabulary.* ◆◇◇◇◇ N-COUNT

constancy /kɒnstənsi/

1 **Constancy** is the quality of staying the same even though other things change. *Climate reflects a basic struggle between constancy and change... We live in a world without constancy.* N-UNCOUNT

2 **Constancy** is faithfulness and loyalty to a particular person or belief even when you are in difficulty or danger; used showing approval. *Even before they were married, she had fretted over his constancy.* N-UNCOUNT PRAGMATICS =fidelity

constant /kɒnstənt/ **constants** ◆◆◆◆◇

1 You use **constant** to describe something that happens all the time or is always there. *She suggests that women are under constant pressure to be abnormally thin... Inflation is a constant threat... He has been her constant companion for the last four months.* ♦ **constantly** *The direction of the wind is constantly changing... We are constantly being reminded to cut down our fat intake.*
ADJ: usu ADJ n =continual
ADV-GRADED: usu ADV with v, also ADV adv/adj

2 If an amount or level is **constant**, it stays the same over a particular period of time. *The body feels hot and the temperature remains more or less constant at the new elevated level.*
ADJ-GRADED =stable

3 A **constant** is a thing or value that always stays the same. *In the world of fashion it sometimes seems that the only constant is ceaseless change... Two significant constants have been found in a number of research studies.*
N-COUNT ≠variable

constellation /kɒnstəleɪʃən/ **constellations** ◆◇◇◇◇

1 A **constellation** is a group of stars which form a pattern and have a name. *...a planet orbiting a star in the constellation of Cepheus.*
N-COUNT

2 A **constellation** of similar things is a group of them; a formal use. *Most patients have a constellation of diseases, with few clear-cut distinctions between them... The largest gallery contains at its centre a constellation of photographs called My Wishes.*
N-COUNT: with supp, usu N of n

consternation /kɒnstəʳneɪʃən/. **Consternation** is a feeling of anxiety or fear; a formal word. *His decision caused consternation in the art photography community... Sam stared at him in consternation.*
◆◇◇◇◇ N-UNCOUNT =alarm, dismay

constipated /kɒnstɪpeɪtɪd/. Someone who is **constipated** has difficulty in defecating.
ADJ-GRADED: usu v-link ADJ

constipation /kɒnstɪpeɪʃən/. **Constipation** is a medical condition which causes people to have difficulty defecating.
◆◇◇◇◇ N-UNCOUNT

constituency /kənstɪtʃuənsi/ **constituencies** ◆◆◇◇◇

1 A **constituency** is an area for which someone is elected as the representative in a parliament.
N-COUNT

2 A particular **constituency** is a section of society that may give political support to a particular party or politician. *Mr Jackson had a natural constituency among American blacks... In France, farmers are a powerful political constituency.*
N-COUNT: usu with supp

constituent /kənstɪtʃuənt/ **constituents** ◆◆◇◇◇

1 A **constituent** is someone who lives in a particular constituency, especially someone who is able to vote in an election.
N-COUNT

2 A **constituent** of a mixture, substance, or system is one of the things from which it is formed. *Caffeine is the active constituent of drinks such as tea and coffee.*
N-COUNT: usu N of n

3 The **constituent** parts of something are the things from which it is formed; a formal use. *...a plan to split the company into its constituent parts and sell them separately. ...the leaders of Russia's constituent republics.*
ADJ: ADJ n

constituent assembly, constituent assemblies. A **constituent assembly** is a body of representatives that is elected to create or revise their country's constitution.
◆◇◇◇◇ N-COUNT

constitute /kɒnstɪtjuːt, AM -tuːt/ **constitutes, constituting, constituted** ◆◆◇◇◇

1 If something **constitutes** a particular thing, it can be regarded as being that thing. *Testing patients without their consent would constitute a professional and legal offence... The vote hardly constitutes a victory... What constitutes abuse?*
V-LINK: no cont
V n

2 If a number of things or people **constitute** something, they are the parts or members that form it. *China's ethnic minorities constitute less than 7 per cent of its total population. ...the four companies constituting the Aramco partnership.*
V-LINK: no cont =comprise
V n

3 When something such as a committee or government **is constituted**, it is formally established and given authority to operate; a formal use. *On 6 July a Peoples' Revolutionary Government was constituted... The accused will appear before a specially constituted military tribunal.*
VB: usu passive =set up
be V-ed
V-ed

constitution /kɒnstɪtjuːʃən, AM -tuː-/ **constitutions** ◆◆◆◇◇

1 The **constitution** of a country or organization is the system of laws which formally states people's rights and duties. *The king was forced to adopt a new constitution which reduced his powers. ...the American Constitution... The club's constitution prevented women from becoming full members.*
N-COUNT

2 Your **constitution** is your health. *He must have an extremely strong constitution... I've always had the constitution of an ox.*
N-COUNT: usu sing

constitutional /kɒnstɪtjuːʃənəl, AM -tuː-/. **Constitutional** means relating to the constitution of a particular country or organization. *Political leaders are making no progress in their efforts to resolve the country's constitutional crisis... We have a constitutional right to demonstrate... A Romanian judge has asked for a Constitutional Court ruling on the law.* ♦ **constitutionally** *...a nationwide conspiracy to deprive women of their constitutionally protected rights.*
◆◆◆◇◇ ADJ: usu ADJ n
ADV

constitutionality /kɒnstɪtjuːʃənælɪti, AM -tuː-/. In a particular political system, the **constitutionality** of a law or action is the fact that it is allowed by the constitution; a formal word. *They plan to challenge the constitutionality of the law.*
N-UNCOUNT: usu the N of n

constrain /kənstreɪn/ **constrains, constraining, constrained** ◆◇◇◇◇

1 To **constrain** someone or something means to limit their development or force them to behave in a particular way; a formal use. *Women are too often constrained by family commitments and by low expectations... How can we produce top-class engineers when universities are constrained to offer salaries that can only attract mediocre staff?... It's the capacity of those roads which is going to constrain the amount of travel by car that can take place.* ♦ **constrained** *These will be very constrained budgets designed to get the deficit down.*
VERB
be V-ed
be V-ed to-inf
V n
ADJ-GRADED

2 If you **feel constrained** to do something, you feel that you must do it, even though you would prefer not to. *For some reason he felt constrained to lower his voice.*
PHRASE: V inflects, PHR to-inf

constraint /kənstreɪnt/ **constraints** ◆◆◇◇◇

1 A **constraint** is something that limits or controls what you can do. *Their decision to abandon the trip was made because of financial constraints... Water shortages in the area will be the main constraint on development.*
N-COUNT: oft adj N, N on n

2 **Constraint** is control over the way you behave which prevents you from doing what you want to do.
N-UNCOUNT =restraint

constrict /kənstrɪkt/ **constricts, constricting, constricted** ◆◇◇◇◇

1 If a part of your body, especially your throat, **is constricted** or if it **constricts**, something causes it to become narrower. *Severe migraine can be treated with a drug which constricts the blood vessels... My throat constricted, so that I had to concentrate on breathing.* ♦ **constricted** *His throat began to feel swollen and constricted.* ♦ **constriction** /kənstrɪkʃən/ *The pain is produced by constriction of the blood vessels.*
V-ERG
V n
V
ADJ-GRADED
N-UNCOUNT

2 If something **constricts** you, it limits your actions so that you cannot do what you want to do. *She objects to the tests the Government's advisers have devised because they constrict her teaching style... Men and women alike have been constricted by traditional sexual roles.* ♦ **constricted** *Many of the women I spoke to left because they felt constricted.* ♦ **constricting** *I find the office environment too rigid and constricting... The bill is filled with constricting amendments.* ♦ **constriction** *A general anxiousness developed and increased, leading to a constriction of her normal activities.*
VERB =limit
V n
ADJ-GRADED =restricted
ADJ-GRADED =limiting
N-UNCOUNT

constriction /kənstrɪkʃən/ **constrictions.** **Constrictions** are rules or factors which limit what you can do and prevent you from doing what you want to do. *I remember my fury at the constrictions placed upon me as a child.* ● See also **constrict**.
N-COUNT: usu pl =restriction

construct, constructs, constructing, constructed. ◆◆◇◇◇ The verb is pronounced /kənstrʌkt/. The noun is pronounced /kɒnstrʌkt/.

1 If you **construct** something such as a building, road, or machine, you build it or make it. *The French constructed a series of fortresses from Dunkirk on the Channel coast to Douai... The boxes should be constructed from rough-sawn timber... They thought he had escaped through a specially constructed tunnel.*
VERB =build V n be V-ed from/of/out of n V-ed

2 If you **construct** something such as an idea, piece of writing, or system, you create it by putting different parts together. *You will find it difficult to construct a spending plan without first recording your spending... He eventually constructed a business empire which ran to Thailand, Taiwan, Singapore and Hong Kong... The novel is constructed from a series of on-the-spot reports. ...using carefully constructed tests.*
VERB =create V n be V-ed from/out of n V-ed

3 A **construct** is a complex idea; a formal use. *...the underlying constructs (beliefs, philosophy, etc.) which influence action and behaviour... It was a re-enactment of the same mental construct under which slavery was justified.*
N-COUNT =concept

4 A **construct** is something that is built, made, or created; a formal use. *As the flimsy constructs soared, the men paid out twine until the kites reached three or four thousand feet... The country was an artificial construct held together by force and intimidation for more than 70 years.*
N-COUNT =creation

construction /kənstrʌkʃən/ **constructions** ◆◆◆◇◇

1 **Construction** is the building of things such as houses, factories, roads, and bridges. *He'd already started construction on a hunting lodge. ...the only nuclear power station under construction in Britain. ...the downturn in the construction industry... Quincy wants a job in construction.*
N-UNCOUNT =building ≠demolition

2 The **construction** of something such as a vehicle or machine is the making of it. *...companies who have long experience in the construction of those types of equipment... With the exception of teak, this is the finest wood for boat construction.*
N-UNCOUNT: with supp

3 The **construction** of something such as a system is the creation of it. *...the construction of a just system of criminal justice.*
N-UNCOUNT: with poss =creation

4 You can refer to an object that has been built or made as a **construction**. *The British pavilion is an impressive steel and glass construction the size of Westminster Abbey.*
N-COUNT: usu supp N =structure

5 You use **construction** to refer to the structure of something and the way it has been built or made. *The Shakers believed that furniture should be plain, simple, useful, practical and of sound construction... The chairs were light in construction yet extremely strong.*
N-UNCOUNT: usu with supp =structure

6 The **construction** that you put on what someone says or does is your interpretation of what it means. *The denial was limited to rejecting the construction put on his remarks... He put the wrong construction on what he saw.*
N-COUNT: usu sing =interpretation

7 A grammatical **construction** is a particular arrangement of words in a sentence, clause, or phrase. *Avoid complex verbal constructions.*
N-COUNT =structure

constructive /kənstrʌktɪv/. ◆◆◇◇◇ A **constructive** discussion, comment, or approach is useful and helpful rather than negative and unhelpful. *She welcomes constructive criticism... After their meeting, both men described the talks as frank, friendly and constructive... The Prime Minister has promised that Israel will play a constructive role... At least I'm doing something constructive.*
ADJ-GRADED =positive ≠negative

♦ **constructively** *We are prepared to sit down and talk constructively with our European partners... Use the time constructively.*
ADV-GRADED: ADV with v

constructor /kənstrʌktəʳ/ **constructors.** A racing car **constructor** or aircraft **constructor** is a company that builds cars or aircraft.
N-COUNT

construe /kənstruː/ **construes, construing, construed.** ◆◇◇◇◇ If something **is construed** in a particular way, its nature or meaning is interpreted in that way; a formal word. *What may seem helpful behaviour to you can be construed as interference by others... He may construe the approach as a hostile act... We are taught to construe these terms in a particular way.*
VERB be V-ed as n V n as n V n prep/adv

consul /kɒnsəl/ **consuls.** ◆◇◇◇◇ A **consul** is an official who is sent by his or her government to live in a foreign city in order to look after all the people there that belong to his or her own country. *The British Consul in Zurich has confirmed that a British man was among the people killed.*
N-COUNT: oft supp N; N-TITLE

consular /kɒnsjʊləʳ, AM -sə-/. ◆◇◇◇◇ **Consular** means involving or relating to a consul or the work of a consul. *If you need to return to the UK quickly, British Consular officials may be able to arrange it.*
ADJ: ADJ n

consulate /kɒnsjʊlət, AM -sə-/ **consulates.** ◆◇◇◇◇ A **consulate** is the place where a consul works. *They managed to make contact with the British consulate in Lyons.*
N-COUNT: oft supp N

consult /kənsʌlt/ **consults, consulting, consulted** ◆◆◆◇◇

1 If you **consult** an expert or someone senior to you or **consult** with them, you ask them for their opinion and advice about what you should do or their permission to do something. *Consult your doctor about how much exercise you should attempt... He needed to consult with an attorney... If you are in any doubt, consult a financial adviser.*
VERB V n prep wh/wh-to-inf V with n V n

2 If a person or group of people **consults** with other people or **consults** them, they talk and exchange ideas and opinions about what they might decide to do. *After consulting with her daughter and manager she decided to take on the part, on her terms... The two countries will have to consult their allies... The umpires consulted quickly.*
V-RECIP V with n V n pl-n V

3 If you **consult** a book or a map, you look in it or look at it in order to find some information. *Consult the chart on page 44 for the correct cooking times... He had to consult a pocket dictionary.*
VERB V n

consultancy /kənsʌltənsi/ **consultancies** ◆◇◇◇◇

1 A **consultancy** is a company that gives expert advice on a particular subject. *A survey of 57 hospitals by Newchurch, a consultancy, reveals striking improvements. ...a management consultancy from Switzerland.*
N-COUNT

2 **Consultancy** is expert advice on a particular subject which a person or group is paid to provide to a company or organization. *He is acting on a consultancy basis... The project provides both consultancy and training.*
N-UNCOUNT: oft N n

consultant /kənsʌltənt/ **consultants** ◆◆◆◇◇

1 A **consultant** is an experienced doctor who specializes in one area of medicine; used mainly in British English. *Shirley's brother is now a consultant heart surgeon in Sweden.*
N-COUNT: oft N n

2 A **consultant** is a person who gives expert advice to a person or organization on a particular subject. *He was a consultant to the Swedish government. ...a team of management consultants sent in to reorganise the department.*
N-COUNT: oft N to n, supp N

consultation /kɒnsəlteɪʃən/ **consultations** ◆◆◇◇◇

1 A **consultation** is a meeting which is held to discuss something. **Consultation** is discussion about something. *Next week he'll be in Florida for consultations with President Mitterrand... The plans were drawn up in consultation with the World Health Organisation... The strike was called in protest at the government's lack of consultation with the unions.*
N-VAR

2 A **consultation** with a doctor or other expert is a meeting with them to discuss a particular problem and get their advice. **Consultation** is the process of getting advice from a doctor or other expert. *A personal diet plan is devised after a consultation with a nutritionist. ...fees paid for consultation and advice in tax matters.*
N-VAR

3 **Consultation** of a book or other source of information is looking at it in order to find out certain facts. *With such excellent studies available for consultation, it should be easy to avoid the pitfalls.*
N-UNCOUNT

4 A **consultation** paper or document is a document containing ideas for changes in the law. The document is published by the government or by a
ADJ: ADJ n

committee or organization, so that people can discuss it and give their opinions on it. *The Government proposed a common retirement age of 63 in a consultation paper published yesterday.*

consultative /kənsʌltətɪv/. A **consultative** committee or document gives advice or makes proposals about a particular problem or subject. *...the consultative committee on local government finance.* ◆◇◇◇◇ ADJ: usu ADJ n =advisory

consulting room, consulting rooms. A doctor's or therapist's **consulting room** is the room in which they see their patients. N-COUNT

consumable /kənsjuːməbᵊl, AM -suː-/ **consumables. Consumable** goods are items which are intended to be bought, used, and then replaced; a formal word. *...demand for consumable articles.* ADJ: usu ADJ n
▶ Also a noun. *...low-margin consumables like health and beauty aids.* N-COUNT: usu pl

consume /kənsjuːm, AM -suːm/ **consumes, consuming, consumed** ◆◆◇◇◇

1 If you **consume** something, you eat or drink it; a formal use. *Martha would consume nearly a pound of cheese per day. ...serving chocolate ice-creams for the children to consume in the kitchen.* VERB Vn

2 To **consume** an amount of fuel, energy, or time means to use it up. *Some of the most efficient refrigerators consume 70 percent less electricity than traditional models. ...plans which will consume hours of time and deplete your cash reserves.* VERB =use up Vn
♦ **-consuming** *...oil-consuming countries... It is very space-consuming.* COMB in ADJ

3 If a fire **consumes** a building, it completely destroys it. *...the fire which consumed the dwelling.* VERB Vn

4 If a feeling or idea **consumes** you, it affects you very strongly indeed; a literary use. *The memories consumed him.* VERB Vn

5 See also **consumed, consuming**.

consumed /kənsjuːmd, AM -suːmd/. If you are **consumed** with a feeling or idea, it affects you very strongly indeed; a literary use. *They are consumed with envy and jealousy at what has happened to their sister.* ADJ-GRADED: v-link ADJ *with/by*n =eaten up

consumer /kənsjuːməʳ, AM -suː-/ **consumers.** A **consumer** is a person who buys things or uses services. *...claims that tobacco companies failed to warn consumers about the dangers of smoking. ...improving public services and consumer rights.* ◆◆◆◆◇ N-COUNT: oft N n

consumer durable, consumer durables. Consumer durables are goods which are expected to last a long time, and are bought infrequently. *Consumer durables such as refrigerators, television sets, bicycles and so on were produced in large quantities.* N-COUNT: usu pl

consumer goods. Consumer goods are items bought by people for their own use, rather than by businesses. *The choice of consumer goods available in local shops is small.* ◆◇◇◇◇ N-PLURAL

consumerism /kənsjuːmərɪzəm, AM -suː-/

1 **Consumerism** is the belief that it is good to buy and use a lot of goods; sometimes used showing disapproval. *They have clearly embraced Western consumerism.* N-UNCOUNT: oft supp N

2 **Consumerism** is the protection of the rights and interests of consumers. N-UNCOUNT

consumerist /kənsjuːmərɪst, AM -suː-/. **Consumerist** economies are ones which encourage the consumption of a lot of goods; sometimes used showing disapproval. *...our consumerist society.* ADJ: usu ADJ n

consuming /kənsjuːmɪŋ, AM -suː-/. A **consuming** passion or interest is more important to you than anything else. *He has developed a consuming passion for chess.* ● See also **consume, time-consuming.** ◆◇◇◇◇ ADJ: usu ADJ n

consummate, consummates, consummating, consummated. The adjective is pronounced /kənsʌmət/. The verb is pronounced /kɒnsəmeɪt/. ◆◇◇◇◇

1 You use **consummate** to describe someone who is extremely skilful; a formal use. *He acted the part with consummate skill... Those familiar with Sanders call him a consummate politician.* ADJ-GRADED: usu ADJ n
♦ **consummately** *The film is a well made, atmospheric, consummately acted piece.* ADV-GRADED

2 If two people **consummate** a marriage or relationship, they make it complete by having sex. *They consummated their passion only after many hesitations and delays.* VERB Vn
♦ **consummation** /kɒnsəmeɪʃᵊn/ *...the morning after the consummation of their marriage.* N-UNCOUNT

3 To **consummate** an agreement means to complete it; a formal use. *There have been several close calls, but no one has been able to consummate a deal.* VERB Vn

consumption /kənsʌmpʃᵊn/ ◆◆◇◇◇

1 The **consumption** of fuel or natural resources is the amount of them that is used or the act of using them. *The laws have led to a reduction in fuel consumption in the US. ...a tax on the consumption of non-renewable energy resources.* N-UNCOUNT: with supp

2 The **consumption** of food or drink is the act of eating or drinking something, or the amount that is eaten or drunk; a formal use. *Most of the wine was unfit for human consumption... The average daily consumption of fruit and vegetables is around 200 grams... Excessive alcohol consumption is clearly bad.* N-UNCOUNT: usu with supp

3 **Consumption** is the act of buying and using things; a technical use in economics. *They were prepared to put people out of work and reduce consumption by strangling the whole economy... The production and consumption of goods and services is the ultimate aim of all economic endeavour.* N-UNCOUNT

4 If you do or say something **for** a particular person's or group's **consumption**, you intend it to be seen or heard by that person or group, although your private thoughts or plans may be very different. *The hard-line speech appears to be mostly for domestic consumption... The report was obviously designed for the consumption of members of the War Committee.* PHRASE: usu v-link PHR, PHR after v

5 See also **conspicuous consumption.**

consumptive /kənsʌmptɪv/. A **consumptive** person suffers from tuberculosis; an old-fashioned use. *He took her on tour of Europe, but the travel only hastened her consumptive decline and death.* ADJ: usu ADJ n

cont. Cont. is an abbreviation for 'continued', which is used at the bottom of a page to indicate that a letter or text continues on another page.

contact /kɒntækt/ **contacts, contacting, contacted** ◆◆◆◆◇

1 **Contact** involves meeting or communicating with someone, especially regularly. *Opposition leaders are denying any contact with the government in Kabul... He forbade contacts between directors and executives outside his presence.* N-UNCOUNT: also N in pl, oft N *with/between*n

2 If you are **in contact** with someone, you regularly meet them or communicate with them. *He was in direct contact with the kidnappers... We do keep in contact.* PHRASE: usu v-link PHR, oft PHR *with*n =in touch

3 If you **contact** someone, you telephone them, write to them, or go to see them in order to tell or ask them something. *Contact the Tourist Information Bureau for further details... When she first contacted me Frances was upset.* VERB =get in touch with Vn

4 If you come **into contact with** someone or something, you meet that person or thing in the course of your work or other activities. *Doctors I came into contact with voiced their concern... The college has brought me into contact with western ideas.* N-UNCOUNT: *into*N *with*n

5 If you **make contact** with someone, you find out where they are and talk or write to them. *How did you make contact with the terrorists?* PHR-RECIP: V inflects, PHR *with*n, pl-n V

6 If you **lose contact** with someone who you have been friendly with, you no longer see them, speak to them, or write to them. *Though they all live nearby, I lost contact with them really quickly... Mother and son lost contact when Nicholas was in his early twenties.* PHR-RECIP: V inflects, PHR *with*n, pl-n V =lose touch

7 When people or things are in **contact**, they are touching each other. *They compared how these organisms behaved when left in contact with different materials... The cry occurs when air is brought into* N-UNCOUNT: oft *in/into*N *with*n

contact with the baby's larynx... There was no physical contact, nor did I want any... This shows where the foot and shoe are in contact.

8 Radio **contact** is communication by means of radio. *He failed to make radio contact. ...a technical problem reported by the pilot moments before he lost contact with the control tower.* N-UNCOUNT

9 A **contact** is someone you know in an organization or profession who helps you or gives you information. *Their contact in the United States Embassy was called Phil.* N-COUNT

10 • to **make eye contact**: see **eye**.

contact lens, contact lenses. **Contact lenses** are small plastic lenses that you put on the surface of your eyes to help you see better, instead of wearing glasses. ◆◇◇◇◇ N-COUNT: usu pl

contagion /kənteɪdʒᵊn/ **contagions**

1 **Contagion** is the spreading of a particular disease by someone touching another person who is already affected by the disease. *They have been reluctant to admit AIDS patients, in part because of unfounded fears of contagion... I'm a blood donor; I can't risk any contagion.* N-UNCOUNT

2 You can use **contagion** to refer to the spreading of ideas, or attitudes, or feelings that you consider to be bad or unacceptable from one group of people to another. *...to continue to insulate his country from the contagion of foreign ideas.* N-SING: oft N of n PRAGMATICS

3 A **contagion** is a contagious disease; an old-fashioned use. N-COUNT

contagious /kənteɪdʒəs/ ◆◇◇◇◇

1 A disease that is **contagious** can be caught by touching people or things that are infected with it. *...a highly contagious disease of the lungs.* ADJ-GRADED =catching

2 A feeling or attitude that is **contagious** spreads quickly among a group of people. *Laughing is contagious... Antonio has a contagious enthusiasm for the beautiful aspect of food.* ADJ-GRADED: usu v-link ADJ =infectious

contain /kənteɪn/ **contains, containing, contained** ◆◆◆◆◇

1 If something such as a box, bag, room, or place **contains** things, those things are inside it. *The bag contained a Christmas card... Factory shops contain a wide range of cheap furnishings... The 77,000-acre estate contains five of the highest peaks in Scotland.* VB: no cont V n

2 If a substance **contains** something, that thing is a part of it. *Greek yogurt contains much less fat than double cream... Many cars run on petrol which contains lead.* VB: no cont V n

3 If writing, speech, or film **contains** particular information, ideas, or images, it includes them. *This sheet contained a list of problems a patient might like to raise with the doctor... The two discs also contain two of Britten's lesser-known song-cycles.* VB: no cont V n

4 If a group or organization **contains** a certain number of people, those are the people that are in it. *The committee contains 11 Democrats and nine Republicans.* VB: no cont V n

5 If you **contain** something, you control it and prevent it from spreading or increasing. *More than a hundred firemen are still trying to contain the fire at the plant... The city authorities said the curfew had contained the violence.* VERB =control V n

6 If you cannot **contain** a feeling such as excitement or anger, or if you cannot **contain** yourself, you cannot prevent yourself from showing your feelings. *But he was bursting with curiosity, and one day he just couldn't contain himself. 'What are you going to do?' he asked... Evans could barely contain his delight: 'I'm so proud of her,' he said.* VERB V pron-refl V n

7 See also **self-contained**.

container /kənteɪnəʳ/ **containers** ◆◆◇◇◇

1 A **container** is something such as a box or bottle that is used to hold or store things in. *...the plastic containers in which fish are stored and sold. ...stainless steel or glass containers.* N-COUNT: usu supp N =receptacle

2 A **container** is a very large metal or wooden box used for transporting goods so that they can be loaded easily onto ships and lorries. N-COUNT: usu N of n

container ship, container ships. A **container ship** is a ship that is designed for carrying goods that are packed in large metal or wooden boxes. N-COUNT

containment /kənteɪnmənt/ ◆◇◇◇◇

1 **Containment** is the action or policy of keeping another country's power or area of control within acceptable limits or boundaries. N-UNCOUNT

2 The **containment** of something dangerous or unpleasant is the act or process of keeping it under control within a particular area or place. *Fire crews are hoping they can achieve full containment of the fire before the winds pick up. ...containment of the disease. ...a national health board to oversee cost containment and health-care reform.* N-UNCOUNT: usu N of n =control

contaminant /kəntæmɪnənt/ **contaminants.** A **contaminant** is something that contaminates a substance such as water or food; a formal word. *Contaminants found in poultry will also be found in their eggs... We are exposed to an overwhelming number of chemical contaminants every day in our air, water and food.* N-COUNT: usu pl

contaminate /kəntæmɪneɪt/ **contaminates, contaminating, contaminated.** If something **is contaminated** by dirt, chemicals, or radiation, it becomes polluted by them and is then impure or harmful. *Have any fish been contaminated in the Arctic Ocean? ...vast tracts of empty land, much of it contaminated by years of army activity.* ◆◆◇◇◇ VERB be V-ed V-ed Also V n

♦ **contaminated** *Nuclear weapons plants across the country are heavily contaminated with toxic wastes... More than 100,000 people could fall ill after drinking contaminated water.* ADJ-GRADED

♦ **contamination** /kəntæmɪneɪʃᵊn/ *The contamination of the sea around Capri may be just the beginning.* N-UNCOUNT: usu with supp

contemplate /kɒntəmpleɪt/ **contemplates, contemplating, contemplated** ◆◆◇◇◇

1 If you **contemplate** an action, you think about whether to do it or not. *For a time he contemplated a career as an army medical doctor... She contemplates leaving for the sake of the kids.* VERB =consider V n/-ing

2 If you **contemplate** an idea or subject, you think about it carefully for a long time. *As he lay in his hospital bed that night, he cried as he contemplated his future... That makes it difficult to contemplate the idea that the present policy may not be sustainable.* ♦ **contemplation** /kɒntəmpleɪʃᵊn/ *It is a place of quiet contemplation.* VERB V n N-UNCOUNT

3 If you **contemplate** something or someone, you look at them for a long time. *He contemplated his hands, still frowning.* ♦ **contemplation** *He was lost in the contemplation of the landscape for a while.* VERB V n N-UNCOUNT: oft N of n

contemplative /kəntemplətɪv/. Someone who is **contemplative** thinks deeply, or is thinking in a serious and calm way. *Martin is a quiet, contemplative sort of chap... I went for long, contemplative walks by the river... Life there is slow and contemplative.* ADJ-GRADED

contemporaneous /kəntempəreɪniəs/. If two events or situations are **contemporaneous**, they happen or exist during the same period of time; a formal word. *Militant nationalism and militant revolutionism seem to be contemporaneous.* ADJ

♦ **contemporaneously** *The confession was not a precise record taken down contemporaneously during the interview.* ADV: ADV with v

contemporary /kəntempərəri, AM -pəreri/ **contemporaries** ◆◆◆◇◇

1 **Contemporary** things are modern and relate to the present time. *She writes a lot of contemporary music for people like Whitney Houston... Perhaps he should have a more updated look, a more contemporary style... Only the names are ancient; the characters are modern and contemporary.* ADJ-GRADED: usu ADJ n =modern

2 **Contemporary** people or things were alive or happened at the same time as something else you are talking about. *...drawing upon official records and the reports of contemporary witnesses.* ADJ: usu ADJ n

3 Someone's **contemporary** is a person who is or was alive at the same time as them. *Like most of my contemporaries, I grew up in a vastly different* N-COUNT: usu pl, poss N

world. ...a glossary of musical terms found in Shakespeare and his contemporaries.

contempt /kəntempt/ ◆◆◇◇◇

1 If you have **contempt** for someone or something, you have no respect for them or think that they are unimportant. *He has contempt for those beyond his immediate family circle... I hope voters will treat his advice with the contempt it deserves.*
N-UNCOUNT: oft N *for* n ≠respect

2 **Contempt** means the same as **contempt of court**. *Mr. Kelly was sentenced to six months in prison for contempt.*
N-UNCOUNT =contempt of court

3 If you **hold** someone or something **in contempt**, you feel contempt for them. *Small wonder that many voters hold their politicians in contempt.*
PHRASE: V inflects

• **familiarity breeds contempt**: see **familiarity**.

contemptible /kəntemptɪbᵊl/. If you feel that someone or something is **contemptible**, you feel strong dislike and disrespect for them; a formal word. *Catherine was ready to explode. 'I think you're contemptible!'... It was an even more contemptible performance than Butler's.*
ADJ-GRADED =despicable

contempt of court. **Contempt of court** is the criminal offence of disobeying an instruction from a judge or a court of law; a legal term. *He faced imprisonment for contempt of court.*
N-UNCOUNT =contempt

contemptuous /kəntemptʃuəs/. If you are **contemptuous** of someone or something, you do not like or respect them at all. *He was contemptuous of private farmers... He's openly contemptuous of all the major political parties... She gave a contemptuous little laugh.* ♦ **contemptuously** *'A deal!' she said contemptuously, 'I hate all deals.'*
◆◇◇◇◇ ADJ-GRADED: usu v-link ADJ, oft ADJ *of* n ≠respectful; ADV-GRADED: ADV with v

contend /kəntend/ **contends, contending, contended** ◆◆◇◇◇

1 If you have to **contend with** a problem or difficulty, you have to deal with it or overcome it. *It is time, once again, to contend with racism... American businesses could soon have a new kind of lawsuit to contend with.*
VERB V *with* n

2 If you **contend** that something is true, you state or argue that it is true; a formal use. *The government contends that he is fundamentalist... 'You were just looking,' contends Samantha. 'I was the one doing all the work.'*
VERB V that; V with quote

3 If you **contend** with someone for something such as power, you compete with them to try to get it. *...the two main groups contending for power. ...with 10 UK construction yards contending with rivals from Norway, Holland, Italy and Spain. ...a binding political settlement between the contending parties.*
V-RECIP pl-n V *for* n; V *with* n; V-ing

contender /kəntendəʳ/ **contenders**. A **contender** is someone who takes part in a competition; used in journalism. *Sally Gunnell said yesterday that she would be a strong contender for an Olympic gold medal in the 400 metres hurdles next week... Our British Affairs correspondent reports on how the three contenders reacted to the news of the resignation.*
◆◆◇◇◇ N-COUNT: usu with supp, oft N *for/in* n

content 1 noun uses

content /kɒntent/ **contents** ◆◆◆◇◇

1 The **contents** of a container such as a bottle, box, or room are the things that are inside it. *Empty the contents of the pan into the sieve... I emptied the contents of the fridge into carrier bags... Sandon Hall and its contents will be auctioned by Sotheby's on October 6.*
N-PLURAL: usu with supp, oft N *of* n

2 If you refer to the **content** or **contents** of something such as a book, speech, or television programme, you are referring to the subject that it deals with, the story that it tells, or the ideas that it expresses. *She is reluctant to discuss the content of the play... Stricter controls were placed on the content of video films... The letter's contents were not disclosed.*
N-UNCOUNT: also N in pl, usu N *of* n

3 The **contents** of a book are its different chapters and sections, usually shown in a list at the beginning of the book. *There is no initial list of contents.*
N-PLURAL

4 The **content** of something such as an educational course or a programme of action is the elements that it consists of. *Previous students have had nothing but praise for the course content and staff... This is how we see our tasks, and the substance and content of our work for the forthcoming period.*
N-UNCOUNT: usu with supp, oft N *of* n

5 You can use **content** to refer to the amount or proportion of something that a substance contains. *Sunflower margarine has the same fat content as butter... He was astonished at the high gold content in the 340 million-year-old rock.*
N-SING: n N

content 2 adjective and verb uses

content /kəntent/ **contents, contenting, contented** ◆◆◇◇◇

1 If you are **content** to do something or if you are **content with** something, you are willing to do, have, or accept that thing, rather than wanting something more or something better. *I am content to admire the mountains from below... I'm perfectly content with the way the campaign has gone... Not content with rescuing one theatre, Sally Green has taken on another.*
ADJ-GRADED: v-link ADJ, ADJ to-inf, ADJ *with* n/-ing

2 If you are **content**, you are fairly happy or satisfied. *He says his daughter is quite content.*
ADJ-GRADED: v-link ADJ

3 If you **content** yourself with something, you accept it and do not try to do or have other things. *He wisely contented himself with his family and his love of nature... Most manufacturers content themselves with updating existing models.*
VERB V pron-refl *with* n; V pron-refl *with/by* -ing

4 • **to your heart's content**: see **heart**.

contented /kəntentɪd/. If you are **contented**, you are satisfied with your life or the situation you are in. *Whenever he returns to this place he is happy and contented... She was gazing at him with a soft, contented smile on her face.* ♦ **contentedly** *The landlady sighed contentedly.*
◆◇◇◇◇ ADJ-GRADED ≠discontented; ADV-GRADED

contention /kəntenʃᵊn/ **contentions** ◆◆◇◇◇

1 Someone's **contention** is the idea or opinion that they are expressing in an argument or discussion. *It is my contention that death and murder always lurk as potentials in violent relationships... Sufficient research evidence exists to support this contention.*
N-COUNT: usu poss N =belief

2 If something is a cause of **contention**, it is a cause of disagreement or argument. *They generally tried to avoid subjects of contention between them... A particular source of contention are plans to privatise state-run companies.* • See also **bone of contention**.
N-UNCOUNT: usu n *of* N

3 If you are **in contention** in a contest, you have a chance of winning it. *He was in contention for a place in the European championship squad.*
PHRASE: v-link PHR

contentious /kəntenʃəs/ ◆◇◇◇◇

1 A **contentious** issue causes a lot of disagreement or arguments; a formal use. *Sanctions are expected to be among the most contentious issues. ...a country where land prices are politically contentious.* ♦ **contentiously** *This time he was contentiously omitted from the team.*
ADJ-GRADED =controversial; ADV-GRADED

2 A **contentious** person seems to like arguing and disagreeing with other people; a formal use. *Rodney was a cheerful, elegant and gregarious if rather contentious man.*
ADJ-GRADED =argumentative

contentment /kəntentmənt/. **Contentment** is a feeling of quiet happiness and satisfaction. *I cannot describe the feeling of contentment that was with me at that time.*
◆◇◇◇◇ N-UNCOUNT =happiness ≠discontent

contest, contests, contesting, contested. ◆◆◆◇◇
The noun is pronounced /kɒntest/. The verb is pronounced /kəntest/.

1 A **contest** is a competition or game in which people try to win. *Few contests in the recent history of British boxing have been as thrilling. ...a writing contest.* • See also **beauty contest**.
N-COUNT

2 A **contest** is a struggle to win power or control. *The state election due in November will be the last such ballot before next year's presidential contest... The contest between capitalism and socialism is over.*
N-COUNT

3 If someone **contests** an election or competition, they take part in it and try to win it. *He quickly won his party's nomination to contest the elections. ...a closely contested regional flower show.*
VERB V n; V-ed

4 If you **contest** a statement or decision, you object to it formally because you think it is wrong or unreasonable. *Your former employer has to reply*
VERB =dispute; V n

within 14 days in order to contest the case... Gender discrimination is a hotly contested issue. V-ed

contestant /kəntestənt/ **contestants.** A **contestant** in a competition or quiz is a person who takes part in it. ◆◇◇◇◇ N-COUNT =competitor

context /kɒntekst/ **contexts** ◆◆◆◇◇

1 The **context** of an idea or event is the general situation that relates to it, and which helps it to be understood. *We are doing this work in the context of reforms in the economic, social and cultural spheres. ...the historical context in which Chaucer wrote... This is the context in which President Bill Clinton must decide his policy.* N-VAR: usu with supp, oft adj N, N of n

2 The **context** of a word, sentence, or text consists of the words, sentences, or text before and after it which help to make its meaning clear. *Without a context, I would have assumed it was written by a man.* N-VAR

3 If something is seen **in context** or if it is put **into context**, it is considered together with all the factors that relate to it. *Taxation is not popular in principle, merely acceptable in context... It is important that we put Jesus into the context of history.* PHRASES ≠out of context

4 If a statement or remark is quoted **out of context**, the circumstances in which it was said are not correctly reported, so that it seems to mean something different from the meaning that was intended. *Thomas says that he has been taken out of context on the issue... Quotes can be manipulated and used out of context.* ≠in context

contextual /kəntekstʃuəl/. A **contextual** issue or account relates to the context of something; a formal word. *The writer builds up a clever contextual picture of upper class life.* ADJ: usu ADJ n

contiguous /kəntɪgjuəs/. Things that are **contiguous** are next to each other or touch each other; a formal word. *Its vineyards are virtually contiguous with those of Ausone. ...two years of travel throughout the 48 contiguous states.* ADJ: oft ADJ *to/with* n =adjacent, adjoining

continent /kɒntɪnənt/ **continents** ◆◆◆◇◇

1 A **continent** is a very large area of land, such as Africa or Asia, that consists of several countries. *She loved the African continent... Dinosaurs evolved when most continents were joined in a single land mass.* N-COUNT

2 In Britain, the mainland of Europe is sometimes referred to as **the Continent**. *Its shops are among the most stylish on the Continent.* N-PROPER: *the* N

continental /kɒntɪnentəl/ **continentals** ◆◆◇◇◇

1 In British English, **continental** means situated on or belonging to the mainland of Europe, especially central and southern Europe. *He sees no signs of improvement in the UK and continental economy.* ADJ: ADJ n

2 In informal British English, a **continental** is someone who comes from the mainland of Europe, especially central or southern Europe. N-COUNT: usu pl

3 In informal British English, if you describe someone or something as **continental**, you think that they are typical of central or southern Europe. *He's very continental... Torquay is undeniably continental.* ADJ-GRADED: usu v-link ADJ

4 **Continental** is used to refer to something that belongs to or relates to a continent. *Since these substances are not licensed, they cannot be sold in the continental United States.* ADJ: ADJ n

continental breakfast, continental breakfasts. A **continental breakfast** is breakfast that consists of food such as bread, butter, jam, and a hot drink. There is no cooked food. N-COUNT

continental drift. **Continental drift** is the slow movement of the Earth's continents towards and away from each other. N-UNCOUNT

continental shelf. The **continental shelf** is the area which forms the edge of a continent, ending in a steep slope to the depths of the ocean; a technical term in geography. *...the deep water off the Continental Shelf.* N-UNCOUNT

contingency /kəntɪndʒənsi/ **contingencies** ◆◇◇◇◇

1 A **contingency** is something that might happen in the future; a formal use. *I need to examine all possible contingencies.* N-VAR =possibility, eventuality

2 A **contingency** plan or measure is one that is intended to be used if a possible future situation actually arises; a formal use. *We have contingency plans.* ADJ: ADJ n

contingent /kəntɪndʒənt/ **contingents** ◆◆◇◇◇

1 A **contingent** of police, soldiers, or military vehicles is a group of them; a formal use. *Nigeria provided a large contingent of troops to the West African Peacekeeping Force... There were contingents from the navies of virtually all EC countries.* N-COUNT: usu with supp, oft N *of* n

2 A **contingent** is a group of people representing a country or organization at a meeting or other event; a formal use. *The strong British contingent suffered mixed fortunes... The whistles from the large contingent of England fans away to our left are deafening.* N-COUNT: usu with supp, oft adj N

3 If something is **contingent** on something else, the first thing depends on the second in order to happen or exist; a formal use. *In effect, growth is contingent on improved incomes for the mass of the low-income population.* ADJ: usu ADJ *on/upon* n/-ing =dependent

continual /kəntɪnjuəl/ ◆◆◇◇◇

1 A **continual** process or situation happens or exists without stopping. *The school has been in continual use since 1883... They felt continual pressure to perform well... Despite continual pain, he refused all drugs.* ♦ **continually** *She cried almost continually and threw temper tantrums... The large rotating fans whirred continually.* ADJ: ADJ n =continuous; ADV: usu ADV with v =continuously

2 **Continual** events happen again and again. *...the government's continual demands for cash to finance its chronic deficit... She suffered continual police harassment.* ♦ **continually** *Malcolm was continually changing his mind... I had been writing him continually, trying to get him to call me.* ADJ: ADJ n; ADV: usu ADV with v

continuance /kəntɪnjuəns/. The **continuance** of something is its continuation; a formal word. *...thus ensuring the continuance of the human species.* N-UNCOUNT: usu with poss =continuation

continuation /kəntɪnjueɪʃən/ **continuations** ◆◇◇◇◇

1 The **continuation** of something is the fact that it continues, rather than stopping. *It's the coalition forces who are to blame for the continuation of the war... What we'll see in the future is, in fact, a continuation of that trend.* N-VAR: usu with poss

2 Something that is a **continuation of** something else is closely connected with it or forms part of it. *...since this chapter is a continuation of Chapter 8... It would just be a continuation of previous visits he has made to Israel.* N-COUNT: usu sing, N *of* n

continue /kəntɪnjuː/ **continues, continuing, continued** ◆◆◆◆◆

1 If someone or something **continues** to do something, they keep doing it and do not stop. *I hope they continue to fight for equal justice after I'm gone... Interest rates on long-term housing continue to fall... Diana and Roy Jarvis are determined to continue working when they reach retirement age... If you are pregnant, there is no reason why you should not start exercising, or continue with any sport or activity you already enjoy.* VERB V to-inf V -ing V *with* n

2 If something **continues** or if you **continue** it, it does not stop happening. *He insisted that the conflict would continue until conditions were met for a ceasefire... But as the investigation continued, the plot began to thicken... Outside the building people continue their vigil, huddling around bonfires. ...the continued existence of a species.* V-ERG V V n V-ed

3 If you **continue** with something, you start doing it again after a break or interruption. *I went up to my room to continue with my packing... She looked up for a moment, then continued drawing.* VERB =carry on V *with* n V -ing

4 If something **continues** or if you **continue** it, it starts again after a break or interruption. *He denies 18 charges. The trial continues today... Once, he did dive for cover but he soon reappeared and continued his activities.* V-ERG V V n

5 If you **continue**, you begin speaking again after a pause or interruption. *'You have no right to intimidate this man,' Alison continued... Tony drank some coffee before he continued... Please continue.* VERB V with quote V

6 If you **continue** as something or **continue** in a particular state, you remain in a particular job or VERB

state. *He had hoped to continue as a full-time career officer... For ten days I continued in this state.* V as n / V prep

7 If you **continue** in a particular direction, you keep walking or travelling in that direction. *He continued rapidly up the path, not pausing until he neared the Chapter House.* VERB / V prep/adv

8 If a road or path **continues** somewhere, it goes there after the place you have mentioned. *The main road continues towards Viterbo before turning right to Bolsena.* VERB / V prep/adv

continuing education. **Continuing education** is education for adults in a variety of subjects, most of which are practical, not academic. *But those lacking a family tradition of continuing education still face difficulties.* N-UNCOUNT

continuity /kɒntɪnjuːɪti, AM -nuː-/ **continuities** ◆◇◇◇◇

1 **Continuity** is the fact that something continues to happen or exist, with no great changes or interruptions; used showing approval. *An historical awareness also imparts a sense of continuity. ...a tank designed to ensure continuity of fuel supply during aerobatics. ...the problems of trying to maintain continuity between your youthful past and your middle-aged present... He said he stood for continuity rather than change.* N-VAR / PRAGMATICS / ≠discontinuity

2 In film-making, **continuity** is the way that things filmed at different times look as if they were filmed at the same time or in the right sequence. *Walt and I referred to a video cassette of the original footage to check continuity and lighting.* N-UNCOUNT

continuity announcer, continuity announcers. A **continuity announcer** is someone who introduces the next programme on a radio or television station. N-COUNT

continuous /kəntɪnjuəs/ ◆◆◇◇◇

1 A **continuous** process or event continues for a period of time without stopping. *Residents report that they heard continuous gunfire. ...all employees who had a record of five years' continuous employment with the firm... There is a continuous stream of phone calls.* ♦ **continuously** *The civil war has raged almost continuously since 1976... It is the oldest continuously inhabited city in America.* ADJ: usu ADJ n / =unbroken / ≠spasmodic; ADV: usu ADV with v

2 A **continuous** line or surface has no gaps or holes in it. *...a continuous line of boats. ...the continuous frieze of sculpted figures.* ADJ: usu ADJ n / =unbroken

3 In English grammar, **continuous** verb groups are formed using the auxiliary 'be' and the present participle of a verb, as in 'I'm feeling a bit tired' and 'She had been watching them for some time'. Continuous verb groups are used especially when you are focusing on a particular moment. Compare **simple**. ADJ / =progressive

continuous assessment. If pupils or students undergo **continuous assessment**, they get qualifications partly or entirely because of work they do during the year, rather than because of exam results. N-UNCOUNT

continuum /kəntɪnjuəm/ **continua** /kəntɪnjuə/ or **continuums** ◆◇◇◇◇

1 A **continuum** is a set of things on a scale, which have a particular characteristic to different degrees; a formal use. *These various complaints are part of a continuum of ill-health... It is at one end of the cost continuum.* N-COUNT: usu sing

2 A **continuum** is a continuous series of closely-connected events; a formal use. *The medical professional bodies reply that development from fertilisation onwards is a continuum.* N-COUNT: usu sing

contort /kəntɔːʳt/ **contorts, contorting, contorted.** If someone's face or body **contorts** or **is contorted**, it moves into an unnatural and unattractive shape or position. *His face contorts as he screams out the lyrics... The gentlest of her caresses would contort his already tense body... Brenner was breathing hard, his face contorted with pain. ...their contorted bodies.* V-ERG / V / V n / V-ed

contortion /kəntɔːʳʃᵊn/ **contortions.** **Contortions** are movements of your body or face into unusual shapes or positions. *I cannot but admire the contortions of the gymnasts.* N-COUNT

contortionist /kəntɔːʳʃənɪst/ **contortionists.** A **contortionist** is someone who twists their body into strange and unnatural shapes and positions in order to entertain other people, for example in a circus. N-COUNT

contour /kɒntʊəʳ/ **contours** ◆◇◇◇◇

1 You can refer to the general shape or outline of an object as its **contours**; a literary use. *...the texture and colour of the skin, the contours of the body... I cradled my video camera nervously on my lap, but its cold contours did nothing to comfort me.* N-COUNT: usu pl, usu with supp, oft N of n

2 A **contour** on a map is a line joining points of equal height and indicating hills, valleys, and the steepness of slopes. *There were three moderate climbs to just below the 450 feet contour. ...a contour map showing two hills and this large mountain in the middle.* N-COUNT

contoured /kɒntʊəʳd/. A **contoured** surface has curves and slopes on it, rather than being flat. *...the lush fairways and contoured greens of the course... Sophia settled into her comfortably contoured seat.* ADJ: ADJ n

contraband /kɒntrəbænd/. **Contraband** refers to goods that are taken into or out of a country illegally. *The ship was found not to be carrying any contraband... Most of the city markets were flooded with contraband goods.* N-UNCOUNT: oft N n

contraception /kɒntrəsepʃᵊn/. **Contraception** refers to methods of preventing pregnancy. *Use a reliable method of contraception.* ◆◇◇◇◇ N-UNCOUNT =birth control

contraceptive /kɒntrəseptɪv/ **contraceptives** ◆◇◇◇◇

1 A **contraceptive** method or device is a method or a device which a woman uses to prevent herself from becoming pregnant. *...a demand for a greater choice of effective contraceptive methods... It was at that time she started taking the contraceptive pill.* ADJ: ADJ n

2 A **contraceptive** is a device or pill that prevents a woman from becoming pregnant. *...those who are taking oral contraceptives... The service covers contraceptive advice and health checks, and is available free.* N-COUNT

contract, contracts, contracting, contracted. The noun is pronounced /kɒntrækt/. The verb is pronounced /kəntrækt/. ◆◆◆◆◇

1 A **contract** is a legal agreement, usually between two companies or between an employer and employee, which involves doing work for a stated sum of money. *The company won a prestigious contract for work on Europe's tallest building... He was given a seven-year contract with an annual salary of $150,000.* N-COUNT

2 If you **contract** with someone to do something, you legally agree to do it for them or for them to do it for you; a formal use. *You can contract with us to deliver your cargo... The Boston Museum of Fine Arts has already contracted to lease part of its collection to a museum in Japan.* VERB / V *with* n to-inf / V to-inf

3 When something **contracts** or when something **contracts** it, it becomes smaller or shorter. *Blood is only expelled from the heart when it contracts... New research shows that an excess of meat and salt can contract muscles.* ♦ **contraction** /kəntrækʃᵊn/ **contractions** *...the contraction and expansion of blood vessels... Foods and fluids are mixed in the stomach by its muscular contractions.* V-ERG / V / V n; N-VAR

4 When something **contracts**, it becomes smaller. *As a casting cools, it contracts... The manufacturing economy contracted in October for the sixth consecutive month.* VERB / V / V

5 If you **contract** a serious illness, you become ill with it; a formal use. *He contracted AIDS from a blood transfusion... Ovarian cancer is the sixth most common cancer contracted by women.* VB: no cont / V n / V-ed

6 If you **contract** a marriage, alliance, or other relationship with someone, you arrange to have that relationship with them; a formal use. *She contracted a formal marriage to a British ex-serviceman.* VERB / =enter into / V n

7 If you are **under contract** to someone, you have signed a contract agreeing to work for them, and for no-one else, during a fixed period of time. *The director wanted Olivia de Havilland, then under contract to Warner Brothers.* PHRASE: oft PHR *to* n

contract out PHRASAL VERB
1 If a company **contracts out** work, they employ other companies to do it. *Firms can contract out work to one another... When Barclays Bank contracted out its cleaning, the new company was cheaper. ...the trend of contracting services out rather than performing them in-house.*
V P n (not pron) *to* n; V P n (not pron); V n P; Also V n P *to* n, V P
2 If a person or group **contracts out** of a system or scheme, they formally say that they do not want to take part in it; used mainly in British English. *Employees can contract out of their employer's occupational pension scheme. ...a free deal which automatically converts into a pay as-you-go service unless you contract out.*
V P *of* n; V P

contraction /kəntrækʃən/ **contractions** ◆◇◇◇◇
1 When a woman who is about to give birth has **contractions**, she experiences a very strong, painful tightening of the muscles of her uterus. N-COUNT
2 A **contraction** is a shortened form of a word or words. *'It's' (with an apostrophe) should be used only as a contraction for 'it is'.* N-COUNT
3 See also **contract.**

contractor /kɒntræktəʳ, kəntræk-/ **contractors.** ◆◆◇◇◇ N-COUNT: oft n N
A **contractor** is a person or company that does work for other people or organizations. *We told the building contractor that we wanted a garage big enough for two cars. ...a major US defense contractor.*

contractual /kəntræktʃuəl/. ◆◇◇◇◇ ADJ: usu ADJ n
A **contractual** arrangement or relationship involves a legal agreement between people; a formal word. *The company has not fulfilled certain contractual obligations... This will be done by contractual arrangement.* ♦ **contractually** *Rank was contractually obliged to hand him a cheque for $30 million.* ADV: usu ADV after v

contradict /kɒntrədɪkt/ **contradicts, contradicting, contradicted** ◆◇◇◇◇
1 If you **contradict** someone, you say that what they have just said is wrong, or suggest that it is wrong by saying something different. *She dared not contradict him... A month later, Alan Clark, then defence minister, appeared to contradict Mr Bevan... He often talks in circles, frequently contradicting himself and often ends up saying nothing.* VERB; V n; V pron-refl
2 If one statement or piece of evidence **contradicts** another, the first one makes the second one appear to be wrong. *Her version contradicted the Government's claim that they were shot after being challenged... The result seems to contradict a major U.S. study reported last November.* VERB; V n
3 If one policy or situation **contradicts** another, there is a conflict between them, and they cannot both exist or be successful. *Mr Grant feels that the cut-backs contradict the Government's commitment to better educational standards.* VERB; V n

contradiction /kɒntrədɪkʃən/ **contradictions** ◆◆◇◇◇
1 If you describe an aspect of a situation as a **contradiction**, you mean that it is completely different from other aspects, and so makes the situation confused or difficult to understand. *...the contradictions between her private life and the public persona... The performance seemed to me unpardonable, a contradiction of all that the Olympics is supposed to be... The militants see no contradiction in using violence to bring about a religious state.* N-COUNT: oft N *between* pl-n, N *of* n
2 If you say that something is a **contradiction in terms**, you mean that it is described as having a quality that it cannot have. *A public service run for profit – a contradiction in terms if there ever was one.* PHRASE: *contradiction* inflects

contradictory /kɒntrədɪktəri, AM -tɔːri/. ◆◇◇◇◇ ADJ-GRADED
If two or more facts, ideas, or statements are **contradictory**, they state or imply that opposite things are true. *Customs officials have made a series of contradictory statements about the equipment... The public are capable of holding a number of apparently contradictory attitudes. ...advice that sometimes is contradictory and confusing.*

contraflow /kɒntrəfləʊ/ **contraflows.** N-COUNT
When there are repairs on a major road, a **contraflow** is a situation in which vehicles travelling in one direction have to use lanes that are normally used by traffic travelling in the opposite direction; used in British English. *The M5 has got a contraflow between junctions eleven and twelve near to Gloucester.*

contraindication /kɒntrəɪndɪkeɪʃən/ **contraindications;** also spelled **contra-indication.** N-COUNT: usu pl
Contraindications are specific medical reasons for not using a particular treatment for a medical condition in the usual way; a medical term. *Contraindications for this drug include liver or kidney impairment.*

contralto /kəntræltəʊ/ **contraltos.** N-COUNT: oft N n
A **contralto** is a woman with a low singing voice. *The score calls for a contralto... I had a very low contralto voice.*

contraption /kəntræpʃən/ **contraptions.** N-COUNT =gadget
You can refer to a device or machine as a **contraption**, especially when it looks strange or you do not know what it is used for. *...a strange contraption called the General Gordon Gas Bath.*

contrarian /kəntreəriən/ **contrarians.** N-COUNT: oft N n
A **contrarian** is a person who deliberately behaves in a way that is different from the people around them; a formal word. *He is by nature a contrarian. ...the young contrarian intellectual.*

contrary /kɒntrəri, AM -treri/ ◆◆◇◇◇
1 Ideas, attitudes, or reactions that are **contrary** to each other are completely different from each other. *This view is contrary to the aims of critical social research for a number of reasons... Several of those present, including Weinberger, had contrary information.* ADJ: usu v-link ADJ *to* n
2 If you say that something is true **contrary to** other people's beliefs or opinions, you are emphasizing that it is true and that they are wrong. *Contrary to popular belief, moderate exercise actually decreases your appetite... Contrary to what you might think, neither man was offended.* PHRASES; PREP
3 You use **on the contrary** when you have just said or implied that something is not true and are going to say that the opposite is true. *It is not an idea around which the Community can unite. On the contrary, I see it as one that will divide us.* PHR with cl; PRAGMATICS
4 You can use **on the contrary** when you are disagreeing emphatically with something that has just been said or implied, or are making a strong negative reply. *'People just don't do things like that.'—'On the contrary, they do them all the time.'* PRAGMATICS
5 You can use **quite the contrary** to emphasize a previous negative statement, or when you are making a strong negative reply. *I'm not a feminist, quite the contrary... 'Are there any signs that he may quit soon?'—'Quite the contrary.'* PHR with cl; PRAGMATICS; =quite the opposite
6 When a particular idea is being considered, evidence or statements **to the contrary** suggest that this idea is not true or that the opposite is true. *That does not automatically mean, however, that the money supply has been curbed, and there is considerable evidence to the contrary... Despite repeated assurances to the contrary, Pakistan has not ended its nuclear programme.* n PHR

contrast, contrasts, contrasting, contrasted. ◆◆◆◇◇
The noun is pronounced /kɒntrɑːst, -træst/. The verb is pronounced /kəntrɑːst, -træst/.
1 A **contrast** is a great difference between two or more things which is clear when you compare them. *...the contrast between town and country... The two visitors provided a startling contrast in appearance... Silk was used with wool for contrast.* N-VAR: oft N *between* pl-n
2 You say **by contrast** or **in contrast**, or **in contrast to** something, to show that you are mentioning a very different situation from the one you have just mentioned. *The private sector, by contrast, has plenty of money to spend... In contrast, the lives of girls in well-to-do families were often very sheltered... In contrast to similar services in France and Germany, British Rail's Intercity rolling stock is very rarely idle.* PHRASE: PHR with cl; PRAGMATICS
3 If one thing is **in contrast** to another, it is very different from it. *His public statements have always been in marked contrast to those of his son... That is* PHRASE: v-link PHR, usu PHR *to* n

in stark contrast to the situation during the 1970 oil crisis.

4 If one thing is a **contrast** to another, it is very different from it. *The boy's room is a complete contrast to the guest room. ...a country of great contrasts.* [N-COUNT: oft N *to/with* n]

5 If you **contrast** one thing with another, you point out or consider the differences between those things. *She contrasted the situation then with the present crisis... Contrast that approach with what goes on in most organizations... In this section we contrast four possible broad approaches.* [VERB; V n *with* n; V pl-n]

6 If one thing **contrasts** with another, it is very different from it. *Johnson's easy charm contrasted sharply with the prickliness of his boss... Paint the wall in a contrasting colour.* [V-RECIP; V *with* n; V-ing; Also pl-n V]

7 **Contrast** is the degree of difference between the darker and lighter parts of a photograph or television picture. *...a television with brighter colours, better contrast, and digital sound.* [N-UNCOUNT]

contravene /kɒntrəviːn/ **contravenes, contravening, contravened.** To **contravene** a law or rule means to do something that is forbidden by the law or rule; a formal word. *The Board has banned the film on the grounds that it contravenes criminal libel laws... He said the article did not contravene the industry's code of conduct.* ♦ **contravention** /kɒntrəvenʃən/ **contraventions** *The government has lent millions of pounds to debt-ridden banks in contravention of local banking laws.* [◆◇◇◇◇; VERB =break; V n; N-VAR: oft *in* N *of* n]

contretemps /kɒntrətɒm/; **contretemps** is both the singular and the plural form. A **contretemps** is a small disagreement that is rather embarrassing; a literary word. *There had been a slight contretemps between Mr. and Mrs. Keely over who was to drive.* [N-COUNT: usu sing =clash]

contribute /kəntrɪbjuːt/ **contributes, contributing, contributed** [◆◆◆◇◇]

1 If you **contribute** to something, you say or do things to help to make it successful. *The three sons also contribute to the family business... I believe that each of us can contribute to the future of the world... He believes he has something to contribute to a discussion concerning the uprising.* [VERB; V *to* n; V n *to* n; Also V]

2 If a person, organization, or country **contributes** money or resources to something, they give money or resources to help pay for something or to help achieve a particular purpose. *The US is contributing $4 billion in loans, credits and grants... They say they would like to contribute more to charity, but money is tight this year... NATO officials agreed to contribute troops and equipment to such an operation if the UN Security Council asked for it.* ♦ **contributor** /kəntrɪbjʊtəʳ/ **contributors** *...the largest net contributors to EC funds.* [VERB =donate; V n; V n *to/towards* n; Also V; N-COUNT]

3 If something **contributes** to an event or situation, it is one of the causes of it. *The report says design faults in both the vessels contributed to the tragedy... Stress, both human and mechanical, may also be a contributing factor.* [VERB; V *to* n; V-ing]

4 If you **contribute** to a magazine or book, you write things that are published in it. *I was asked to contribute to a newspaper article making predictions for the new year... Frank Deford is a contributing editor for Vanity Fair magazine.* ♦ **contributor** *Reporter Alan Nearn covers Central America and is a regular contributor to The New Yorker.* [VERB; V *to* n; V-ing; N-COUNT]

contribution /kɒntrɪbjuːʃən/ **contributions** [◆◆◆◇◇]

1 If you make a **contribution** to something, you do something to help make it successful or to produce it. *American economists have made important contributions to the field of financial and corporate economics... He was awarded a prize for his contribution to world peace.* [N-COUNT: oft N *to* n]

2 A **contribution** is a sum of money that you give in order to help pay for something. *This list ranked companies that make charitable contributions of a half million dollars or more.* [N-COUNT: oft N *of* n =donation]

3 A **contribution** to a book or magazine is something that you write to be published in it. [N-COUNT]

contributor /kəntrɪbjʊtəʳ/ **contributors.** You can use **contributor** to refer to one of the causes of an event or situation, especially if that event or situation is an unpleasant one. *Old buses are major contributors to pollution in British cities... All this can lead to divisive family arguments to which guilt is a major contributor.* ● See also **contribute**. [◆◆◇◇◇; N-COUNT: oft N *to* n]

contributory /kəntrɪbjʊtəri, AM -tɔːri/. A **contributory** factor of a problem or accident is one of the things which caused it to exist or happen; a formal word. *We now know that repressing anger is a contributory factor in many physical illnesses. ...an allegation of contributory negligence.* [ADJ: usu ADJ n]

contrite /kəntraɪt, kɒntraɪt/. If you are **contrite**, you are very sorry because you have done something wrong; a formal word. *She was instantly contrite. 'Oh, I am sorry! You must forgive me.'* ♦ **contrition** /kəntrɪʃən/ *The next day he'd be full of contrition, weeping and begging forgiveness.* [ADJ-GRADED: usu v-link ADJ =sorry; N-UNCOUNT =remorse]

contrivance /kəntraɪvəns/ **contrivances**

1 If you describe something as a **contrivance**, you disapprove of it because it is unnecessary and artificial; a formal use. *The thing that they all have in common is that they wear simple clothes and shun modern contrivances. ...works which reflect intellectual or 'arty' contrivance for the sake of fame, grants or ephemeral fashion.* [N-VAR; PRAGMATICS]

2 A **contrivance** is an unfair or dishonest scheme or trick to gain an advantage for yourself. *...some contrivance to raise prices.* [N-COUNT =ploy]

contrive /kəntraɪv/ **contrives, contriving, contrived** [◆◇◇◇◇]

1 If you **contrive** an event or situation, you succeed in making it happen, often by tricking someone; a formal use. *The oil companies were accused of contriving a shortage of gasoline to justify price increases.* [VERB; V n]

2 If you **contrive** something such as a device or piece of equipment, you invent and construct it in a clever or unusual way. *We therefore had to contrive a very large black-out curtain.* [VERB =engineer; V n]

3 If you **contrive** to do something difficult, you succeed in doing it; a formal use. *The orchestra contrived to produce some of its best playing for years.* [VERB; V to-inf]

4 You can say that someone **has contrived to** do something when they have done something stupid. *They somehow contrived to lose tens of thousands of applications.* [VERB; PRAGMATICS =manage; V to-inf]

contrived /kəntraɪvd/ [◆◇◇◇◇]

1 If you say that something someone says or does is **contrived**, you think it is false and deliberate, rather than spontaneous and natural; used showing disapproval. *There was nothing contrived or calculated about what he said... It mustn't sound like a contrived compliment.* [ADJ-GRADED; PRAGMATICS =artificial ≠spontaneous]

2 If you say that the plot of a play, film, or novel is **contrived**, you mean that it is unlikely and unconvincing; used showing disapproval. *The plot seems cumbersomely contrived.* [ADJ-GRADED; PRAGMATICS]

control /kəntroʊl/ **controls, controlling, controlled** [◆◆◆◆◆]

1 **Control** of an organization, place, or system is the power to make all the important decisions about the way that it is run. *The restructuring involves Mr Ronson giving up control of the company... The first aim of his government would be to establish control over the republic's territory.* ● If you are **in control** of something, you have the power to make all the important decisions about the way it is run. *Nobody knows who is in control of the club... In the West, people feel more in control of their own lives.* ● If something is **under** your **control**, you have the power to make all the important decisions about the way that it is run. *All the newspapers were taken under government control.* [N-UNCOUNT: oft N *of/over* n; PHRASE: usu v-link PHR, usu PHR *of* n; PHRASE: PHR after v, v-link PHR]

2 If you have **control** of something or someone, you are able to make them do what you want them to do. *He lost control of his car... Some teachers have more control over pupils than their parents have.* [N-UNCOUNT: oft N *of/over* n]

3 If you show **control**, you prevent yourself behaving in an angry or emotional way. *He had a terrible temper, and sometimes he would completely lose* [N-UNCOUNT; PRAGMATICS]

control... He was working hard to keep control of himself.

4 The people who **control** an organization or place have the power to take all the important decisions about the way that it is run. *He now controls the largest retail development empire in southern California... Almost all of the countries in Latin America were controlled by dictators... Minebea ended up selling its controlling interest in both firms.* VERB V n V-ing

♦ **-controlled** *AGA Gas is Swedish-controlled. ...the state-controlled media.* COMB in ADJ

5 To **control** a piece of equipment, process, or system means to make it work in the way that you want it to work. *...a computerised system to control the gates... Scientists would soon be able to manipulate human genes to control the ageing process. ...the controlled production of energy from sugar by a cell.* VERB V n V-ed ♦ **-controlled** *...computer-controlled traffic lights.* COMB in ADJ

6 When a government **controls** prices, wages, or the activity of a particular group, it uses its power to restrict them. *The federal government tried to control rising health-care costs. ...measures to control illegal mining.* VERB V n ▶ Also a noun. *Control of inflation remains the government's absolute priority.* N-UNCOUNT: with supp

7 If you **control** yourself, or if you **control** your feelings, voice, or expression, you make yourself behave calmly even though you are feeling angry, excited, or upset. *Jo was advised to learn to control herself... I just couldn't control my temper.* VERB =restrain V pron-refl V n ♦ **controlled** *Her manner was quiet and very controlled.* ADJ-GRADED =restrained

8 To **control** something dangerous means to prevent it from becoming worse or from spreading. *...the need to control environmental pollution... One of the biggest tasks will be to control the spread of malaria.* VERB V n

9 A **control** is a device such as a switch or lever which you use in order to operate a machine or other piece of equipment. *I practised operating the controls. ...the control box.* N-COUNT ● If someone is at the **controls** of a machine or other piece of equipment, they are operating it. *He died of a heart attack while at the controls of the plane.* PHRASE

10 **Controls** are the methods that a government uses to restrict increases, for example in prices, wages, or weapons. *Critics question whether price controls would do any good... Their talks are expected to focus on arms control... They have very strict gun control in Sweden.* N-VAR

11 The word **control** is used to refer to a place where your documents or luggage are officially checked when you enter a foreign country. *He went straight through Passport Control without incident. ...an agreement to abolish border controls.* N-VAR: n N

12 See also **air-traffic control**, **birth control**, **quality control**, **remote control**, **stock control**.

13 If something is **out of control**, no-one has any power over it. *The fire is burning out of control... I'm dealing with customers all the time who have let their debts get out of control.* PHRASES usu v PHR, v-link PHR PRAGMATICS

14 If something harmful is **under control**, it is being dealt with successfully and is unlikely to cause any more harm. *The situation is under control... If the current violence is to be brought under control, the government needs to act.* v-link PHR, PHR after v PRAGMATICS

control freak, control freaks. If you say that someone is a **control freak**, you mean that they want to be in control of every situation they find themselves in; an informal expression, used showing disapproval. N-COUNT PRAGMATICS

controllable /kəntrəʊləbəl/. If something is **controllable** you are able to control or influence it. *They introduced fins for surfboards, making them more controllable. ...controllable aspects of life.* ADJ-GRADED

controller /kəntrəʊləʳ/ **controllers.** A **controller** is a person who has responsibility for a particular organization or for a particular part of an organization. *...the job of controller of BBC 1. ...The financial controller of W H Smith.* ● See also **air traffic controller**. ◆◆◇◇◇ N-COUNT: oft N *of* n

control tower, control towers. A **control tower** is a building at an airport from which instructions are given to aircraft when they are taking off or landing. You can also refer to the people who work in a control tower as the **control tower**. *The pilot told the control tower that he'd run into technical trouble.* N-COUNT

controversial /kɒntrəvɜːʳʃəl/. If you describe something or someone as **controversial**, you mean that they are the subject of intense public argument, disagreement, or disapproval. *Immigration is a controversial issue in many countries. ...the controversial new book, 'Diana, Her True Story.'... The changes are bound to be controversial. ...the controversial 19th century politician Charles Parnell.* ◆◆◆◇◇ ADJ-GRADED ♦ **controversially** *More controversially, he claims that these higher profits cover the cost of finding fresh talent... David Hirst was controversially sent off on his European debut for Sheffield Wednesday last night.* ADV-GRADED: usu ADV with cl, also ADV with v

controversy /kɒntrəvɜːʳsi, kəntrɒvəʳsi/ **controversies. Controversy** is a lot of discussion and argument about something, often involving strong feelings of anger or disapproval. *The proposed cuts have caused considerable controversy. ...a fierce political controversy over human rights abuses.* ◆◆◆◇◇ N-VAR: oft N *over/about* n

contusion /kəntjuːʒən, AM -tuː-/ **contusions.** A **contusion** is a bruise; a medical term. N-COUNT

conundrum /kənʌndrəm/ **conundrums.** A **conundrum** is a problem or puzzle which is difficult or impossible to solve; a formal word. *...this theological conundrum of the existence of evil and suffering in a world created by a good God.* ◆◇◇◇◇ N-COUNT

conurbation /kɒnəʳbeɪʃən/ **conurbations.** In British English, a **conurbation** consists of a large city together with the smaller towns around it; a formal word. *...London and all the other major conurbations.* N-COUNT

convalesce /kɒnvəles/ **convalesces, convalescing, convalesced.** If you **are convalescing**, you are resting and regaining your health after an illness or operation; a formal word. *After two weeks, I was allowed home, where I convalesced for three months. ...those convalescing from illness or surgery.* VERB =recuperate V V *from* n

convalescence /kɒnvəlesəns/. **Convalescence** is the period or process of becoming healthy and well again after an illness or operation; a formal word. N-UNCOUNT =recuperation

convalescent /kɒnvəlesənt/. **Convalescent** means relating to convalescence; a formal word. *...an officers' convalescent home.* ADJ: usu ADJ n

convection /kənvekʃən/. **Convection** is the process by which heat travels through air, water, and other gases and liquids; a scientific term. *...clouds which lift warm, moist air by convection high into the atmosphere. ...convection currents.* N-UNCOUNT

convector heater, convector heaters. A **convector heater** is a heater that heats a room by means of hot air. N-COUNT

convene /kənviːn/ **convenes, convening, convened.** If someone **convenes** a meeting or conference, they arrange for it to take place; a formal use. You can also say that people **convene** or that a meeting **convenes**. *Last August he convened a meeting of his closest advisers at Camp David... Senior officials convened in October 1991 in London. ...the convening of an international peace conference.* ◆◆◇◇◇ V-ERG V n V V-ing

convener /kənviːnəʳ/. See **convenor**.

convenience /kənviːniəns/ **conveniences** ◆◇◇◇◇

1 If something is done for your **convenience**, it is done in a way that is useful or suitable for you. *He was happy to make a detour for her convenience. ...the need to put the rights of citizens above the convenience of elected officials.* N-UNCOUNT: with poss ● If something is arranged to happen **at your convenience**, it happens at a time which is most suitable for you; a formal expression. *Delivery times are arranged at your convenience.* PHRASE: PHR with v

2 If you describe something as a **convenience**, you N-COUNT

mean that it is very useful. *Mail order is a convenience for buyers who are too busy to shop.*
3 **Conveniences** are pieces of equipment designed to make your life easier. *Some TVRs have power steering and conveniences such as central locking and powered windows. ...an apartment with all the modern conveniences.* N-COUNT: usu pl
4 In British English, a public **convenience** is a building containing toilets which is provided in a public place for anyone to use; a formal use. *...the cubicles of a public convenience.* N-COUNT: usu supp N
5 See also **convenient**.

convenience food. **Convenience food** is frozen, dried, or tinned food that can be heated and prepared very quickly and easily. *Today we tend to rely on fast-food and convenience food.* N-UNCOUNT

convenience store, convenience stores. A **convenience store** is a shop in a residential area which sells mainly groceries and which is usually open until late at night. Convenience stores are mainly found in the United States. N-COUNT

convenient /kənviːniənt/ ◆◆◇◇◇
1 If a way of doing something is **convenient**, it is easy, or very useful or suitable for a particular purpose. *...a flexible and convenient way of paying for business expenses... The family thought it was more convenient to eat in the kitchen.* ADJ-GRADED: oft *it* v-link ADJ to-inf ≠inconvenient ♦ **convenience** *They may use a credit card for convenience. ...the convenience of a fast non-stop flight.* N-UNCOUNT
♦ **conveniently** *The body spray slips conveniently into your sports bag for freshening up after a game.* ADV-GRADED: usu ADV with v, also ADV with cl
2 If you describe a place as **convenient**, you are pleased because it is near to where you are, or because you can reach another place from there quickly and easily. *The town is well placed for easy access of London and convenient for Heathrow Airport... Martin drove along until he found a convenient parking place.* ADJ-GRADED: oft ADJ *for* n PRAGMATICS =handy ♦ **conveniently** *It was very conveniently situated just across the road from the City Reference Library... He chose Simi Valley in Ventura County mainly because it was conveniently close to Los Angeles. ...two conveniently placed push-buttons.* ADV-GRADED: usu ADV adj/-ed, also ADV after v, ADV with cl ≠inconveniently
3 A **convenient** time to do something, for example to meet someone, is a time when you are free to do it or would like to do it. *She will try to arrange a mutually convenient time and place for an interview... Would this evening be convenient for you?* ADJ-GRADED ≠inconvenient
4 If you describe someone's attitudes or actions as **convenient**, you disapprove of them because you think that they are only adopting those attitudes or performing those actions in order to avoid dealing with a difficult or serious matter. *We cannot make this minority a convenient excuse to turn our backs. ...a convenient scapegoat... It does seem a bit convenient, doesn't it?* ADJ-GRADED PRAGMATICS ♦ **conveniently** *They've conveniently forgotten the risk of heart disease... Conveniently, he had developed amnesia about that part of his life.* ADV-GRADED: usu ADV before v, also ADV with cl

convenor /kənviːnəʳ/ **convenors;** also spelled **convener.**
1 A **convenor** is a trade union official who organizes the shop stewards at a particular factory; used in British English. N-COUNT
2 A **convenor** is someone who convenes a meeting. N-COUNT

convent /kɒnvᵊnt/ **convents** ◆◇◇◇◇
1 A **convent** is a building in which a community of nuns live. N-COUNT
2 A **convent** is the same as a **convent school**. N-COUNT

convention /kənvenʃᵊn/ **conventions** ◆◆◆◇◇
1 A **convention** is a way of behaving that is considered to be correct or polite by most people in a society. *It's just a social convention that men don't wear skirts. ...the chains of custom and convention.* N-VAR =custom
2 In art, literature, or the theatre, a **convention** is a traditional method or style. *We go offstage and come back for the convention of the encore. ...the conventions of Western art.* N-COUNT
3 A **convention** is an official agreement between countries or groups of people. *...the UN convention on climate change. ...the Geneva convention.* N-COUNT: oft n N
4 A **convention** is a large meeting of an organization or political group. *...the annual convention of the Society of Professional Journalists. ...the Republican convention.* N-COUNT =assembly

conventional /kənvenʃənᵊl/ ◆◆◆◇◇
1 Someone who is **conventional** has behaviour or opinions that are ordinary and normal. *...a respectable married woman with conventional opinions.* ADJ-GRADED ≠unconventional ♦ **conventionally** *People still wore their hair short and dressed conventionally.* ADV-GRADED: usu ADV with v
2 A **conventional** method or product is one that is usually used or that has been in use for a long time. *...the risks and drawbacks of conventional family planning methods... These discs hold more than 400 times as much information as a conventional computer floppy disk.* ADJ: usu ADJ n =traditional ♦ **conventionally** *Organically grown produce does not differ greatly in appearance from conventionally grown crops.* ADV: ADV with v
3 **Conventional** weapons and wars do not involve nuclear explosives. *We must reduce the danger of war by controlling nuclear, chemical and conventional arms.* ADJ: usu ADJ n
4 ● **conventional wisdom**: see **wisdom**.

conventioneer /kənvenʃənɪəʳ/ **conventioneers.** **Conventioneers** are people who are attending a convention; used mainly in American English. N-COUNT: usu pl

convent school, convent schools. A **convent school** is a school where many of the teachers are nuns. N-COUNT

converge /kənvɜːʳdʒ/ **converges, converging, converged** ◆◇◇◇◇
1 If people or vehicles **converge on** a place, they move towards it from different directions. *Competitors from more than a hundred countries have converged on Sheffield for the Games... Hundreds of coaches will converge on the capital.* VERB V *on* n
2 If roads or lines **converge**, they meet or join at a particular place; a formal use. *As they flow south, the five rivers converge.* VERB ≠diverge pl-n V
3 If different ideas or societies **converge**, they stop being different and become similar to each other. *Speeches delivered yesterday by Mr Gorbachev and Mr Yeltsin indicated their views were converging... The views of the richest householders converged with those of the poorest and created a new consensus.* V-RECIP ≠diverge pl-n V V *with* n

convergence /kənvɜːʳdʒᵊns/ **convergences.** The **convergence** of different ideas, groups, or societies is the process by which they stop being different and become more alike; a formal word. *...the need to move towards greater economic convergence... There is a convergence between capitalist firms and co-operatives in terms of business strategy.* ◆◇◇◇◇ N-VAR ≠divergence

conversant /kənvɜːʳsᵊnt/. If you are **conversant** with something, you are familiar with it and able to deal with it; a formal word. *Those in business are not, on the whole, conversant with basic scientific principles.* ADJ-GRADED: v-link ADJ, usu ADJ *with* n

conversation /kɒnvəʳseɪʃᵊn/ **conversations** ◆◆◆◇◇
1 If you have a **conversation** with someone, you talk with them, usually in an informal situation. *He's a talkative guy, and I struck up a conversation with him... I waited for her to finish a telephone conversation.* N-COUNT
2 If you say that people are **in conversation**, you mean that they are talking together. *When I arrived I found her in conversation with Mrs Williams.* PHRASE: v-link PHR
3 If you **make conversation**, you talk to someone in order to be polite and not because you really want to. *He had been trying to make conversation.* PHRASE: V inflects

conversational /kɒnvəʳseɪʃənᵊl/. **Conversational** means relating to, or similar to, casual and informal talk. *What is refreshing is the author's easy, conversational style... His father wanted him to learn conversational German.* ◆◇◇◇◇ ADJ-GRADED: usu ADJ n
♦ **conversationally** *Lyrics are written almost conversationally, yet sung with passion.* ADV-GRADED: usu ADV after v

conversationalist /kɒnvəʳseɪʃənəlɪst/ **conversationalists.** A good **conversationalist** is someone who talks about interesting things when they have conversations. *Joan is a brilliant conversa-* N-COUNT: usu adj N *tionalist... He hadn't seemed much of a conversationalist.*

converse, converses, conversing, conversed. The verb is pronounced /kənvɜːʳs/. The noun is pronounced /kɒnvɜːʳs/. ◆◇◇◇◇

1 If you **converse** with someone, you talk to them; a formal use. *Luke sat directly behind the pilot and conversed with him... They were conversing in German, their only common language.* V-RECIP V with n pl-n V

2 **The converse** of a statement is its opposite or reverse; a formal use. *What you do for a living is critical to where you settle and how you live - and the converse is also true.* N-SING: the N =opposite

conversely /kɒnvɜːʳsli, kənvɜːʳsli/. You say **conversely** to indicate that the situation you are about to describe is the opposite or reverse of the one you have just described; a formal word. *Malaysia and Indonesia rely on open markets for forest and fishery products. Conversely, some Asian countries are highly protectionist.* ◆◇◇◇◇ ADV: ADV with cl PRAGMATICS

conversion /kənvɜːʳʃᵊn/ **conversions** ◆◆◇◇◇

1 **Conversion** is the act or process of changing something into a different state or form. *...the conversion of disused rail lines into cycle routes... A loft conversion can add considerably to the value of a house.* N-VAR: usu with supp

2 If someone changes their religion or beliefs, you can refer to their **conversion** to their new religion or beliefs. *...his conversion to Christianity... It's hard to trust the President's conversion.* N-VAR: usu with supp, oft with poss

3 In rugby, if a player makes or kicks a **conversion**, he scores points by kicking the ball over the crossbar just after a try has been scored. N-COUNT

convert, converts, converting, converted. The verb is pronounced /kənvɜːʳt/. The noun is pronounced /kɒnvɜːʳt/. ◆◆◆◇◇

1 If one thing **is converted** or **converts** into another, it is changed into a different form. *The signal will be converted into digital code. ...naturally occurring substances which the body can convert into vitamins. ...a table that converts into an ironing board.* V-ERG be V-ed into/to n V n into/to n V into/to n

2 If someone **converts** a room or building, they alter it in order to use it for a different purpose. *By converting the loft, they were able to have two extra bedrooms. ...the entrepreneur who wants to convert County Hall into an hotel... He is living in a converted barn.* VERB V n V n into n V-ed

3 If you **convert** a vehicle or piece of equipment, you change it so that it can use a different fuel. *Save money by converting your car to unleaded... The programme to convert every gas burner in Britain took 10 years.* VERB V n to/into n V n

4 If you **convert** a quantity from one system of measurement to another, you calculate what the quantity is in the second system. *Converting metric measurements to U.S. equivalents is easy.* VERB V n prep Also V n

5 If someone **converts** you, they persuade you to change your religious or political beliefs. You can also say that someone **converts** to a different religion. *If you try to convert him, you could find he just walks away... He was a major influence in converting Godwin to political radicalism... He converted to Catholicism in 1917.* V-ERG V n V n to n V to n

6 A **convert** is someone who has changed their religious or political beliefs. *She, too, was a convert to Roman Catholicism. ...a Muslim convert now known as Yusuf Islam.* N-COUNT: oft N to n

7 If someone **converts** you to something, they make you very enthusiastic about it. *He quickly converted me to the joys of cross-country skiing.* VERB V n to n Also V n

8 If you describe someone as a **convert** to something, you mean that they have recently become very enthusiastic about it. *As recent converts to vegetarianism and animal rights, they now live with a menagerie of stray animals.* N-COUNT: usu N to n

9 ● to **preach to the converted**: see **preach**.

converter /kənvɜːʳtəʳ/ **converters.** A **converter** is a device that changes something into a different form. ● See also **catalytic converter**. ◆◇◇◇◇ N-COUNT

convertible /kənvɜːʳtɪbᵊl/ **convertibles** ◆◆◇◇◇

1 A **convertible** is a car with a soft roof that can be folded down or removed. *Her own car is a convertible Golf.* N-COUNT =soft top

2 **Convertible** investments or money can be easily exchanged for other forms of investments or money; a technical use in economics. *...the introduction of a convertible currency.* ♦ **convertibility** /kənvɜːʳtɪbɪlɪti/ *...the convertibility of the rouble. ...rapid export growth based on currency convertibility.* ADJ N-UNCOUNT

convex /kɒnveks/. **Convex** is used to describe something that curves outwards. *...the large convex mirror above the fireplace.* ADJ-GRADED ≠concave

convey /kənveɪ/ **conveys, conveying, conveyed** ◆◆◇◇◇

1 To **convey** information or feelings means to cause them to be known or understood by someone. *When I returned home, I tried to convey the wonder of this machine to my husband... In every one of her pictures she conveys a sense of immediacy... Mr Boucher said the Americans had conveyed their views to the Romanian government.* VERB =communicate V n

2 To **convey** someone or something to a place means to carry or transport them there; a formal use. *The railway company extended a branch line to Brightlingsea to convey fish direct to Billingsgate.* VERB =transport V n

conveyance /kənveɪəns/ **conveyances**

1 A **conveyance** is a vehicle; a literary use. *Mahoney had never seen such a conveyance before.* N-COUNT =vehicle

2 The **conveyance** of something is the process of carrying or transporting it from one place to another; a formal use. *...the conveyance of bicycles on Regional Railways trains.* N-UNCOUNT: with supp =transport

conveyancing /kənveɪənsɪŋ/. **Conveyancing** is the process of transferring the legal ownership of property; a legal term used in British English. N-UNCOUNT

conveyor belt /kənveɪəʳ belt/ **conveyor belts.**

1 A **conveyor belt** or a **conveyor** is a continuously moving strip of rubber or metal which is used in factories for moving objects along so that they can be dealt with as quickly as possible. *The damp bricks went along a conveyor belt into another shed to dry.* N-COUNT

2 If you describe a situation as a **conveyor belt**, you dislike it because it produces things or people which are all the same or always deals with things or people in the same way. *They feel scared and powerless in conveyor-belt hospital wards.* N-COUNT PRAGMATICS

convict, convicts, convicting, convicted. The verb is pronounced /kənvɪkt/. The noun is pronounced /kɒnvɪkt/. ◆◆◆◇◇

1 If someone **is convicted** of a crime, they are found guilty of that crime in a law court. *In 1977 he was convicted of murder and sentenced to life imprisonment... There was insufficient evidence to convict him. ...a convicted drug dealer.* VERB be V-ed of n/-ing V n V-ed Also V n of n

2 A **convict** is someone who is in prison; used mainly in journalism. N-COUNT =prisoner

conviction /kənvɪkʃᵊn/ **convictions** ◆◆◆◇◇

1 A **conviction** is a strong belief or opinion. *It is our firm conviction that a step forward has been taken... Their religious convictions prevented them from taking up arms.* N-COUNT: usu N that =belief

2 If you have **conviction**, you have great confidence in your beliefs or opinions. *'We shall, sir,' said Thorne, with conviction.* N-UNCOUNT

3 If something **carries conviction**, it is likely to be true or likely to be believed. *Nor did his denial carry conviction.* PHRASE: V inflects

4 If someone has a **conviction**, they have been found guilty of a crime in a court of law. *He will appeal against his conviction... The man was known to the police because of previous convictions.* N-COUNT

convince /kənvɪns/ **convinces, convincing, convinced** ◆◆◆◇◇

1 If someone or something **convinces** you of something, they make you believe that it is true or that it exists. *Although I soon convinced him of my innocence, I think he still has serious doubts about my sanity... The waste disposal industry is finding it difficult to convince the public that its operations are safe.* VERB V n of n V n that Also V n

2 If someone or something **convinces** you to do VERB

something, they persuade you to do it; used mainly in American English. *That weekend in Plattsburgh, he convinced her to go ahead and marry Bud.* =persuade V n to-inf Also V n

convinced /kənvɪnst/. If you are **convinced** that something is true, you feel sure that it is true. *He was convinced that I was part of the problem... He became convinced of the need for cheap editions of good quality writing... I'm not convinced... He was a convinced Communist.* ◆◆◆◇◇ ADJ: usu v-link ADJ, usu ADJ that, ADJ of n

convincing /kənvɪnsɪŋ/. If you describe someone or something as **convincing**, you mean that they cause you to believe that something is true, correct, or genuine. *Scientists say there is no convincing evidence that power lines have anything to do with cancer... He sounded very convincing.* ◆◆◇◇◇ ADJ-GRADED =plausible ≠unconvincing
♦ **convincingly** *He argued forcefully and convincingly that they were likely to bankrupt the budget... Benito Garozzo won convincingly.* ADV-GRADED: usu ADV with v, also ADV adj ≠unconvincingly

convivial /kənvɪviəl/. **Convivial** people or occasions are pleasant, friendly, and relaxed; a formal word. *...looking forward to a convivial evening... The atmosphere was quite convivial.* ADJ-GRADED
♦ **conviviality** /kənvɪviælɪti/ *...the conviviality of the restaurant.* N-UNCOUNT

convocation /kɒnvəkeɪʃən/ **convocations.** A **convocation** is a meeting or ceremony attended by a large number of people; a formal word. *...a convocation of the American Youth Congress.* N-COUNT

convoluted /kɒnvəluːtɪd/. If you describe a sentence, idea, or system as **convoluted**, you mean that it is complicated and difficult to understand; a formal word, used showing disapproval. *Despite its length and convoluted plot, 'Asta's Book' is a rich and rewarding read... The policy is so convoluted even college presidents are confused.* ADJ-GRADED PRAGMATICS =complicated ≠straightforward

convolution /kɒnvəluːʃən/ **convolutions**
1 **Convolutions** are curves on an object or design that has a lot of curves; a literary use. N-COUNT: usu pl
2 You can use **convolutions** to refer to a situation that is very complicated; a literary use. *...the thorny convolutions of love.* N-VAR: oft N of n

convoy /kɒnvɔɪ/ **convoys, convoying, convoyed** ◆◆◇◇◇
1 A **convoy** is a group of vehicles or ships travelling together. *...a U.N. convoy carrying food and medical supplies. ...humanitarian relief convoys... They travel in convoy with armed guards.* N-COUNT: also in N
2 To **convoy** goods or people somewhere means to move them there in a convoy. *He ordered the combined fleet to convoy troops to Naples.* VERB V n prep/adv Also V n

convulse /kənvʌls/ **convulses, convulsing, convulsed.** If someone **convulses** or if they **are convulsed** by something, their body moves suddenly in an uncontrolled way. *Olivia's face convulsed in a series of twitches... He let out a cry that convulsed his bulky frame and jerked his arm.* ► Also an adjective. *The opposing team were so convulsed with laughter that they almost forgot to hit the ball.* V-ERG V V n ADJ-GRADED: v-link ADJ with/by n

convulsion /kənvʌlʃən/ **convulsions** ◆◇◇◇◇
1 If someone has **convulsions**, they suffer uncontrollable movements of their muscles. N-COUNT
2 If there are **convulsions** in a country, system, or organization, there are major unexpected changes in it. *...the political convulsions that led to de Gaulle's return to power in May 1958. ...the great convulsion of the eighteenth century.* N-COUNT

convulsive /kənvʌlsɪv/. A **convulsive** movement or action is sudden and cannot be controlled; a formal word. *She thought she could never stop until convulsive sobs racked her even more.* ♦ **convulsively** *His arms and legs jerked convulsively.* ADJ: usu ADJ n ADV: ADV with v

coo /kuː/ **coos, cooing, cooed** ◆◇◇◇◇
1 When a dove or pigeon **coos**, it makes the soft sounds that doves and pigeons typically make. *Pigeons fluttered in and out, cooing gently.* VERB V
2 When someone **coos**, they speak in a very soft, quiet voice which is intended to sound attractive. *She paused to coo at the baby... 'Isn't this marvelous?' she cooed.* VERB V at/over n V with quote

cook /kʊk/ **cooks, cooking, cooked** ◆◆◆◆◇
1 When you **cook** a meal, you prepare food for eating and then heat it, for example in a saucepan. *I have to go and cook the dinner... Chefs at the St James Court restaurant have cooked for the Queen... We'll cook them a nice Italian meal.* VERB V n V V n n
♦ **cooking** *Her hobbies include music, dancing, sport and cooking.* N-UNCOUNT
2 When you **cook** food, or when food **cooks**, it is heated until it is ready to be eaten. *...some basic instructions on how to cook a turkey... Let the vegetables cook gently for about 10 minutes... Drain the pasta as soon as it is cooked.* V-ERG V n V V-ed
3 A **cook** is a person whose job is to prepare and cook food, especially in someone's home or in an institution. *They had a butler, a cook, and a maid.* N-COUNT =chef
4 If you say that someone is a good **cook**, you mean they are good at preparing and cooking food. N-COUNT: adj N
5 If you say that someone has **cooked the books**, you mean that they have changed figures or a written record in order to deceive people; an informal expression. PHRASE: V inflects
6 See also **cooking**.

cook up PHRASAL VERB
1 If someone **cooks up** a dishonest scheme, they plan it; an informal expression. *He must have cooked up his scheme on the spur of the moment.* V P n (not pron) Also V n P
2 If someone **cooks up** an explanation or a story, they make it up; an informal expression. *She'll cook up a convincing explanation.* V P n (not pron) Also V n P
3 If you **cook up** a quantity of food, especially a large quantity, you heat it until it is ready to be eaten. *Hot food is available, though the prisoners have to cook it up themselves... He used to cook up great cauldrons of pasta.* V n P V P n (not pron)

cookbook /kʊkbʊk/ **cookbooks;** also spelled **cook-book**. A **cookbook** is a book that contains recipes for preparing food. ◆◇◇◇◇ N-COUNT =cookery book

cooker /kʊkəʳ/ **cookers.** In British English, a **cooker** is a large metal device for cooking food using gas or electricity. A cooker usually consists of a grill, an oven, and some gas or electric rings. The usual American word is **range**. *...a gas cooker.* • See also **pressure cooker**. ◆◇◇◇◇ N-COUNT

cookery /kʊkəri/. **Cookery** is the activity of preparing and cooking food. *The school runs cookery courses throughout the year.* ◆◇◇◇◇ N-UNCOUNT

cookery book, cookery books. In British English, a **cookery book** is the same as a **cookbook**. N-COUNT

cookie /kʊki/ **cookies.** ◆◇◇◇◇
1 A **cookie** is a sweet biscuit; used mainly in American English. N-COUNT
2 If you say that someone is a **tough cookie**, you mean that they have a strong and determined character; an informal expression. PHRASE: N inflects

cooking /kʊkɪŋ/ ◆◆◆◇◇
1 **Cooking** is food which has been cooked. *The menu is based on classic French cooking. ...Mom's home cooking.* N-UNCOUNT: usu supp N
2 **Cooking** ingredients or utensils are ones which are used in cookery. *Finely slice the cooking apples. ...cooking chocolate.* ADJ: ADJ n
3 See also **cook**.

cookout /kʊkaʊt/ **cookouts.** In American English, a **cookout** is the same as a **barbecue**. N-COUNT

cookware /kʊkweəʳ/. **Cookware** is the range of pans and pots which are used in cooking. *...several lines of popular cookware and utensils.* N-UNCOUNT

cool /kuːl/ **cooler, coolest; cools, cooling, cooled** ◆◆◆◆◇
1 Something that is **cool** has a temperature which is low but not very low. *I felt a current of cool air... The water was slightly cooler than a child's bath... The vaccines were kept cool in refrigerators.* ADJ-GRADED ≠warm
♦ **coolness** *His knees felt the coolness of the tiled floor.* N-UNCOUNT: oft N of n
2 If it is **cool**, or if a place is **cool**, the temperature of the air is low but not very low. *Thank goodness it's cool in here... Store grains and cereals in a cool, dry place. ...a cool November evening.* ► Also a noun. *She walked into the cool of the hallway.* ADJ-GRADED: oft it v-link ADJ ≠warm N-SING: the N, oft N of n

♦ **coolness** *Soon we left the coolness of the olive groves.* N-UNCOUNT: oft N *of*n

3 Clothing that is **cool** is made of thin material so that you do not become too hot in hot weather. *In warm weather, you should wear clothing that is cool and comfortable.* ADJ-GRADED ≠warm

4 Cool colours are light colours which give an impression of coolness. *Choose a cool colour such as cream... The drawing-room was a cool silver green.* ADJ-GRADED: ADJ n ≠warm

5 When something **cools** or when you **cool** it, it becomes lower in temperature. *Drain the meat and allow it to cool... Huge fans will have to cool the concrete floor to keep it below 150 degrees. ...a cooling breeze.* ► To **cool down** means the same as to **cool**. *Avoid putting your car away until the engine has cooled down... The other main way the body cools itself down is by panting.* ♦ **cooling** *Being immobile in a cold room leads to a cooling of the body temperature.* V-ERG V V n V-ing PHRASAL VERB ERG V P V n P Also V P n (not pron) N-UNCOUNT: usu N *of*n

6 When a feeling or emotion **cools**, or when you **cool** it, it becomes less powerful. *Within a few minutes tempers had cooled... His weird behaviour had cooled her passion.* V-ERG V V n

7 If you say that a person or their behaviour is **cool**, you mean that they are calm and unemotional, especially in a difficult situation; used showing approval. *He was marvelously cool again, smiling as if nothing had happened... At that, Reno lost her cool composure.* ♦ **coolly** *Everyone must think this situation through calmly and coolly. ...coolly 'objective' professionals.* ♦ **coolness** *Detectives praised him for his coolness.* ADJ-GRADED PRAGMATICS =calm ADV-GRADED N-UNCOUNT: usu with supp

8 If you say that a person or their behaviour is **cool**, you mean that they are unfriendly or unenthusiastic. *I didn't like him at all. I thought he was cool, aloof, and arrogant... The idea met with a cool response... He was given a cool reception.* ♦ **coolly** *'It's your choice, Nina,' David said coolly.* ♦ **coolness** *She seemed quite unaware of the sudden coolness of her friend's manner.* ADJ-GRADED ADV-GRADED: usu ADV with v, also ADV adj N-UNCOUNT: usu with supp

9 If you say that a person or their behaviour is **cool**, you mean that they are fashionable and attractive; an informal use. *He was trying to be really cool and trendy. ...some 15-year-old kid who thinks it's cool to do heroin.* ADJ-GRADED PRAGMATICS

10 In informal English, if you say that someone is **cool** about something, you mean that they accept it and are not angry or upset about it; used showing approval. *Bev was really cool about it all.* ADJ-GRADED: v-link ADJ, oft ADJ *about* n PRAGMATICS

11 If you say that something is **cool**, you think it is very good; an informal use. *Kathleen gave me a really cool dress.* ADJ-GRADED =great

12 You can use **cool** to emphasize that an amount or figure is very large, especially when it has been obtained easily; an informal use. *Columbia recently re-signed the band for a cool $30 million.* ADJ-GRADED: ADJ n PRAGMATICS

13 If you tell someone to **cool it**, you want them to stop being angry and aggressive and to behave more calmly; used in spoken English. *Can't you guys just cool it?* PHRASES =calm down

14 If you **keep** your **cool** in a difficult situation, you manage to remain calm. If you **lose** your **cool**, you get angry or upset. *She kept her cool and managed to get herself out of the ordeal... The big Irishman was on the verge of losing his cool.* V inflects

15 If you **play it cool**, you deliberately behave in a calm, unemotional way because you do not want people to know you are enthusiastic or angry about something; an informal expression. *It's ridiculous to play it cool if someone you're mad about is mad about you too.* V inflects

16 • **as cool as a cucumber**: see **cucumber**. • **to cool** your **heels**: see **heel**.

cool down PHRASAL VERB

1 See **cool** 5.

2 If someone **cools down** or if you **cool** them **down**, they become less angry than they were. *He has had time to cool down and look at what happened more objectively... First McNeil had to cool down the volatile Australian 20-year old.* ERG =calm down V P V P n (not pron)

cool off. If someone or something **cools off**, or if you **cool** them **off**, they become cooler after having been hot. *Maybe he's trying to cool off out there in the rain... She made a fanning motion, pretending to cool herself off... Cool off the carrots quickly.* PHRASAL VERB ERG V P V n P V P n (not pron)

coolant /kuːlənt/ **coolants. Coolant** is a liquid used to keep a machine or engine cool while it is operating. N-MASS

cooler /kuːləʳ/ **coolers.** A **cooler** is a container for keeping things cool, especially drinks. • See also **cool**. ◆◇◇◇◇ N-COUNT =cool box

cool-headed. If you describe someone as **cool-headed**, you mean that they stay calm in difficult situations; used showing approval. *A good chef is cool-headed and very observant. ...a cool-headed, responsible statesman.* ADJ-GRADED PRAGMATICS =calm

coolie /kuːli/ **coolies.** In former times, unskilled workers in China or other parts of Asia were sometimes referred to as **coolies**; an offensive word. N-COUNT

cooling-off period, cooling-off periods. A **cooling-off period** is an agreed period of time during which two sides with opposing views try to resolve a dispute before taking any serious action. *There should be a seven-day cooling-off period between a strike ballot and industrial action. ...a one-year cooling-off period before couples were granted a divorce.* N-COUNT

cooling tower, cooling towers. A **cooling tower** is a very large, round, high building which is used to cool water from factories or power stations. *...landscapes dominated by coal tips, cooling towers and tall factory chimneys.* N-COUNT

coon /kuːn/ **coons. Coon** is an extremely offensive word for a black person. N-COUNT

coop /kuːp/ **coops**

1 A **coop** is a cage where you keep small animals or birds such as chickens and rabbits. N-COUNT

2 If you say that someone **has flown the coop**, you mean that they have left a place or situation that limits their freedom. *...a family whose children have grown up and flown the coop... She graduates to senior stylist and then flies the coop to set up in a salon of her own.* PHRASE: V inflects

co-op, co-ops. A **co-op** is a co-operative; an informal word. *The co-op sells the art work at exhibitions.* N-COUNT

cooped up /kuːpt ʌp/. If you say that someone is **cooped up**, you mean that they live or are kept in a place which is too small, or which does not allow them much freedom. *He is cooped up in a cramped cell with 10 other inmates... It isn't good for her to be cooped up all the time.* ADJ: v-link ADJ

cooper /kuːpəʳ/ **coopers.** A **cooper** is a person who makes barrels; an old-fashioned word. N-COUNT

co-operate, co-operates, co-operating, co-operated; also spelled **cooperate**. ◆◆◆◇◇

1 If you **co-operate** with someone, you work with them or help them for a particular purpose. You can also say that two people **co-operate**. *The UN had been co-operating with the State Department on a plan to find countries willing to take the refugees... The couple spoke about how they would co-operate in the raising of their child... The French and British are co-operating more closely than they have for years.* ♦ **co-operation** *A deal with Japan could indeed open the door to economic co-operation with East Asia.* V-RECIP V *with* n pl-n V Also V (non-recip) N-UNCOUNT

2 If you **co-operate**, you do what someone has asked or told you to do. *He agreed to co-operate with the police investigation... The plan failed because the soldiers refused to co-operate.* ♦ **co-operation** *The police underlined the importance of the public's co-operation in the hunt for the bombers.* VERB V *with* n V N-UNCOUNT =assistance

co-operative, co-operatives; also spelled **co-operative**. ◆◇◇◇◇

1 A **co-operative** is a business or organization run by the people who work for it, who share its benefits and profits. *They decided a housing co-operative was the way to regenerate Ormiston Crescent... The restaurant is run as a co-operative.* N-COUNT =collective

2 A **co-operative** activity is done by people working together. *He was transferred to FBI custody in a* ADJ: usu ADJ n *smooth co-operative effort between Egyptian and US authorities... The President said the visit would develop friendly and co-operative relations between the two countries.* ♦ **co-operatively** *They agreed to work co-operatively to ease tensions wherever possible.* ADV-GRADED: ADV after v

3 If you say that someone is **co-operative**, you mean that they do what you ask them to without complaining or arguing. *I made every effort to be co-operative.* ADJ-GRADED =obliging

co-operative society, co-operative societies. In Britain, a **co-operative society** is a commercial organization with several shops in a particular district. Customers can join this organization and get a share of its profits. N-COUNT =co-op

co-opt, co-opts, co-opting, co-opted

1 If you **co-opt** someone, you persuade them to help or support you. *Mr Rao tries to co-opt rather than defeat his critics... Sofia Petrovna co-opted Natasha as her assistant.* VERB V n

2 If someone **is co-opted** into a group, they are asked by that group to become a member, rather than joining or being elected in the normal way. *He was co-opted into the Labour Government of 1964... He's been authorised to co-opt anyone he wants to join him.* VERB be V-ed into/onto n V n

3 If a group or political party **co-opts** a slogan or policy, they take it, often from another group or political party, and use it themselves. *He co-opted many nationalist slogans and cultivated a populist image.* VERB V n

co-ordinate, co-ordinates, co-ordinating, co-ordinated; also spelled **coordinate**. The verb is pronounced /koʊɔːʳdɪneɪt/. The noun is pronounced /koʊɔːʳdɪnət/. ♦♦◇◇◇

1 If you **co-ordinate** an activity, you organize the various people and things involved in it. *Government officials visited the earthquake zone on Thursday morning to co-ordinate the relief effort. ...the setting up of an advisory committee to co-ordinate police work.* ♦ **co-ordinated** *...a rapid and well co-ordinated international rescue operation.* ♦ **co-ordinator, co-ordinators** *...the party's campaign co-ordinator, Mr Jack Cunningham.* VERB V n; ADJ-GRADED; N-COUNT: usu with supp

2 If you **co-ordinate** clothes or furnishings that are used together, or if they **co-ordinate**, they are similar in some way and look nice together. *She'll show you how to co-ordinate pattern and colours... Tie it with fabric bows that co-ordinate with other furnishings... Colours and looks must fit the themes of the seasons so that the shops co-ordinate well. ...curtains and co-ordinating bed covers.* V-RECIP-ERG V pl-n V with n pl-n V V-ing

3 **Co-ordinates** are pieces of clothing or soft furnishings which are similar and which are intended to be worn or used together. *...new lingerie co-ordinates.* N-PLURAL

4 If you **co-ordinate** the different parts of your body, you make them work together efficiently to perform particular movements. *They spend several weeks each year undergoing intensive treatment which enables them to coordinate their limbs better.* VERB V n

5 The **co-ordinates** of a point on a map or graph are the two sets of numbers or letters that you need in order to find that point; a technical use in mathematics and geography. *Can you give me your co-ordinates? ...the latitude and longitude co-ordinates of any location in the world.* N-COUNT: usu pl

co-ordinating conjunction, co-ordinating conjunctions. A **co-ordinating conjunction** is a word such as 'and', 'or', or 'but' which joins two or more words, groups, or clauses of equal status, for example two main clauses. Compare **subordinating conjunction.** N-COUNT

co-ordination ♦◇◇◇◇

1 **Co-ordination** means organizing the activities of two or more groups so that they work together efficiently and know what the others are doing. *...the lack of co-ordination between the civilian and military authorities. ...the co-ordination of EC economic policy.* • If you do something **in co-ordination with** someone else, you both organize your activities so that you work together efficiently. *...operating either in coordination with federal troops or alone.* N-UNCOUNT: oft N between/of n; PHR-PREP

2 **Co-ordination** is the ability to use the different parts of your body together efficiently. *...clumsiness and lack of co-ordination... To improve hand-eye co-ordination, practise throwing and catching balls.* N-UNCOUNT

coot /kuːt/ **coots.** A **coot** is a water bird with black feathers and a white patch on its forehead. N-COUNT

cop /kɒp/ **cops, copping, copped** ♦♦◇◇◇

1 A **cop** is a policeman or policewoman; an informal use. *Frank didn't like having the cops know where to find him.* N-COUNT

2 If you **cop it**, you are punished or scolded by someone for doing something wrong; used mainly in informal British English. *Motel owners and restaurant managers copped it for neglecting their clients.* PHRASES V inflects

3 If you say that something is **not much cop**, you mean that it is not very good, and is disappointing; used in informal British English. *The Jane's 'Triple X Album' came out in 1986, and wasn't much cop actually.* v-link PHR

cop out. If you say that someone **is copping out**, you mean they are avoiding doing something they should do; an informal expression used showing disapproval. *'Will you call the board to alert them that I feel I should resign?'—'I'll do it. But I think you're copping out.'* • See also **cop-out.** PHRASAL VERB PRAGMATICS V P

cope /koʊp/ **copes, coping, coped** ♦♦♦◇◇

1 If you **cope** with a problem or task, you deal with it successfully. *It was amazing how my mother coped with bringing up three children on less than three pounds a week... The problems were an annoyance, but we managed to cope.* VERB =manage V with n/-ing V

2 If you have to **cope with** an unpleasant situation, you have to accept it or endure it. *Never before has the industry had to cope with war and recession at the same time... She has had to cope with losing all her previous status and money.* VERB =contend V with n/-ing

3 If a machine or a system can **cope** with something, it is large enough or complex enough to deal with it satisfactorily. *New blades have been designed to cope with the effects of dead insects... The country's prisons are filled with drug-takers, and cannot cope with the numbers... The speed of economic change has been so great that the tax-collecting system has been unable to cope.* VERB V with n V

4 A **cope** is a long cloak worn by some Christian priests on special occasions. N-COUNT

copier /kɒpiəʳ/ **copiers.** A **copier** is a machine which makes exact copies of writing or pictures on paper, usually by a photographic process. N-COUNT =photocopier

co-pilot, co-pilots. The **co-pilot** of an aircraft is a pilot who assists the chief pilot. *The pilot was seriously injured and the co-pilot, took over.* N-COUNT

copious /koʊpiəs/. A **copious** amount of something is a large amount of it. *I went out for a meal last night and drank copious amounts of red wine... He attended his lectures and took copious notes.* ♦ **copiously** *The victims were bleeding copiously.* ♦◇◇◇◇ ADJ-GRADED: usu ADJ n =abundant; ADV-GRADED: ADV after v, ADV -ed

cop-out, cop-outs. If you refer to something as a **cop-out**, you think that it is a way for someone to avoid doing something that they should do; an informal word used showing disapproval. *Wallowing in guilt about the past is a cop-out that prevents you from taking responsibility for yourself now... The film's ending is an unsatisfactory cop-out.* N-COUNT: usu sing PRAGMATICS

copper /kɒpəʳ/ **coppers** ♦♦◇◇◇

1 **Copper** is reddish brown metal that is used to make things such as coins and electrical wires. *Chile is the world's largest producer of copper. ...a copper mine.* N-UNCOUNT

2 **Copper** is sometimes used to describe things that are reddish-brown in colour; a literary use. *His hair has reverted back to its original copper hue.* ADJ: usu ADJ n

3 In British English, **coppers** are brown metal coins of low value; an informal use. N-COUNT

4 In British English, a **copper** is a policeman or a N-COUNT

policewoman; an informal use. *...your friendly, neighbourhood copper.*

copper beech, copper beeches. A **copper beech** is type of a tree with reddish-brown leaves. N-VAR

copper-bottomed. If you describe something as **copper-bottomed**, you believe that it is certain to be successful; used mainly in British English. *The combination of sex and treachery proved a copper-bottomed circulation booster... Their copper-bottomed scheme went badly wrong.* ADJ: usu ADJ n

coppery /kɒpəri/. A **coppery** colour is red-brown like copper. *...pale coppery leaves.* ADJ: usu ADJ n

coppice /kɒpɪs/ **coppices, coppicing, coppiced**

1 A **coppice** is a small group of trees growing very close to each other. *...coppices of willow. ...the mixed coppice is an ideal habitat for nesting birds.* N-COUNT =copse

2 To **coppice** trees or bushes means to cut off parts of them, in order to make them look more attractive or to make it easier to obtain wood from them; a technical use. *The villagers have common rights to gather timber and coppice trees from their local woods. ...extensive oak woods with coppiced hazel and sweet chestnut. ...areas where coppicing of hawthorn and hazel occurs.* VERB V n V-ed V-ing

cops-and-robbers. A **cops-and-robbers** film, television programme, or book is one whose story involves the police trying to catch criminals. ADJ: ADJ n

copse /kɒps/ **copses.** A **copse** is a small group of trees growing very close to each other. *...a little copse of fir trees.* N-COUNT =coppice

copter /kɒptəʳ/ **copters.** A **copter** is a helicopter; an informal word. N-COUNT =helicopter

Coptic /kɒptɪk/. **Coptic** means belonging or relating to a part of the Christian Church which was founded in Egypt. *The Coptic Church is among the oldest churches of Christianity.* ADJ: ADJ n

copula /kɒpjʊlə/ **copulas.** A **copula** is the same as a **link verb.** N-COUNT

copulate /kɒpjʊleɪt/ **copulates, copulating, copulated.** If one animal or person **copulates** with another, they have sex. You can also say that two animals or people copulate. A technical term in biology. *During the time she is paired to a male, the female allows no other males to copulate with her... Whales take twenty-four hours to copulate.* ♦ **copulation** /kɒpjʊleɪʃən/ **copulations** *...acts of copulation.* V-RECIP V with n pl-n V N-VAR

copy /kɒpi/ **copies, copying, copied** ◆◆◆◆◇

1 If you make a **copy** of something, you produce something that looks like the original thing. *The reporter apparently obtained a copy of Steve's resignation letter... Always keep a copy of everything in your own files.* N-COUNT: usu N of n =duplicate

2 If you **copy** something, you produce something that looks like the original thing. *She never participated in obtaining or copying any classified documents for anyone. ...lawsuits against companies who have unlawfully copied computer programs. ...top designers, whose work has been widely copied... Firmicus relates that he copied the chart from a book by Aesculapius.* VERB V n V n from n

3 If you **copy** a piece of writing, you write it again exactly. *He would allow John slyly to copy his answers to impossibly difficult algebra questions... He copied the data into a notebook... We're copying from textbooks because we don't have enough textbooks.* ▶ **Copy out** means the same as **copy.** *He wrote the title on the blackboard, then copied out the text sentence by sentence... 'Did he leave a phone number?'—'Oh, yes.' She copied it out for him.* VERB V n V n into n V from n PHRASAL VERB V P n (not pron) V n P

4 If you **copy** a person or what they do, you try to do what they do or try to be like them, usually because you admire them or what they have done. *Children can be seen to copy the behaviour of others whom they admire or identify with... He can claim to have been defeated by opponents copying his own tactics. ...the coquettish gestures she had copied from actresses in soap operas.* ♦ **copying** *Children learn by copying.* VERB =imitate V n V n from n N-UNCOUNT

5 A **copy** of a book, newspaper, or record is one of the many identical ones that have been printed or produced. *I bought a copy of 'USA Today' from a street-corner machine... You can obtain a copy for $2 from New York Central Art Supply.* N-COUNT: oft N of n

6 In journalism, **copy** is written material that is ready to be printed or read in a broadcast; a technical use. *...his ability to write the most lyrical copy in the history of sports television. ...advertising copy.* N-UNCOUNT

7 In journalism, **copy** is news or information that can be used in an article in a newspaper; a technical use. *...journalists looking for good copy.* N-UNCOUNT

8 See also **back copy, carbon copy, hard copy.**

copy down. If you **copy down** something that someone has said or written, you write it down exactly. *Instructors read slowly and students copied down what was said... I copied it down the way my lawyer read it to me this morning.* PHRASAL VERB V P n (not pron) V n P

copy out. See **copy** 3. PHRASAL VERB

copybook /kɒpibʊk/

1 A **copybook** action is done perfectly, according to established rules. *Yuri gave a copybook display.* ADJ: usu ADJ n

2 If you **blot** your **copybook**, you spoil your good reputation by doing something wrong. *Alec blotted his copybook—got sent home for bad behaviour.* PHRASE: V inflects

copycat /kɒpikæt/ **copycats;** also spelled **copy-cat.**

1 A **copycat** crime is committed by someone who is copying someone else. *...a series of copycat attacks by hooligan gangs.* ADJ: ADJ n

2 If you call someone a **copycat**, you are accusing them of copying your behaviour, dress, or ideas; used showing disapproval. *The Beatles have copycats all over the world.* N-COUNT PRAGMATICS

copyist /kɒpiɪst/ **copyists.** A **copyist** copies other people's music or paintings, or makes handwritten copies of documents. *She copies the true artist's signature as part of a paining, as do most copyists.* N-COUNT

copyright /kɒpiraɪt/ **copyrights.** If someone has **copyright** on a piece of writing or music, it is illegal to reproduce or perform it without their permission. *To order a book one first had to get permission from the monastery that held the copyright... She threatened legal action against the Sun for breach of copyright.* ◆◆◇◇◇ N-VAR

copyrighted /kɒpiraɪtɪd/. **Copyrighted** material is protected by a copyright. *Lawyers say the play used copyrighted music without permission.* ADJ

copywriter /kɒpiraɪtəʳ/ **copywriters.** A **copywriter** is a person whose job is to write the words for advertisements. N-COUNT

coquette /kɒket, AM koʊ-/ **coquettes.** A **coquette** is a woman who behaves in a coquettish way. N-COUNT =flirt

coquettish /kɒketɪʃ, AM koʊ-/. If you describe a woman as **coquettish**, you mean she acts in a playful way that is intended to make men find her attractive. *She gave him a coquettish glance.* ADJ-GRADED =flirtatious

cor /kɔːʳ/. You can say **cor** when you are surprised or impressed; an informal word used mainly in British English. *Cor, look, Annie.* EXCLAM PRAGMATICS

coracle /kɒrəkəl, AM kɔː-/ **coracles.** In former times, a **coracle** was a simple round rowing boat made of woven sticks covered with animal skins. N-COUNT

coral /kɒrəl, AM kɔː-/ **corals** ◆◇◇◇◇

1 **Coral** is a hard substance formed from the skeletons of very small sea animals. It is often used to make jewellery. *The women have elaborate necklaces of turquoise and pink coral.* N-VAR

2 **Corals** are very small sea animals. N-COUNT

3 Something that is **coral** is dark orangey-pink in colour. *...coral lipstick. ...the coral-colored flower buds.* COLOUR

coral reef, coral reefs. A **coral reef** is a ridge of coral and other substances, the top of which is usually just above or just below the surface of the sea. *An unspoilt coral reef encloses the bay.* N-COUNT

cord /kɔːʳd/ **cords** ◆◆◇◇◇

1 **Cord** is strong, thick string. *The door had been tied shut with a length of nylon cord. ...gilded cords and tassels.* N-VAR

2 **Cord** is wire covered in rubber or plastic which N-VAR

connects electrical equipment to an electricity supply. ...*electrical cord... We used so many lights that we needed four extension cords.* =cable, flex
3 **Cords** are trousers made of corduroy. *He had bare feet, a T-shirt and cords on.* N-PLURAL: also *a pair of* N
4 **Cord** means made of corduroy. ...*a pair of cord trousers.* ADJ: ADJ n
5 See also **spinal cord, umbilical cord, vocal cords.**

cordial /kɔːʳdiəl, AM -dʒəl/ **cordials** ◆◇◇◇◇
1 **Cordial** means friendly; a formal use. *He had never known him to be so chatty and cordial... He said the two countries had close and cordial relations.* ♦ **cordially** *They all greeted me very cordially and were eager to talk about the new project.* ♦ **cordiality** /kɔːʳdiælɪti, AM -dʒæl-/ *Egypt wants to solve the problem in an atmosphere of cordiality.* ADJ-GRADED ≠hostile; ADV-GRADED: ADV with v; N-UNCOUNT =friendliness ≠hostility
2 In British English, **cordial** is a sweet non-alcoholic drink made from fruit juice. ...*fruit cordials.* N-MASS

cordite /kɔːʳdaɪt/. **Cordite** is an explosive substance used in guns and bombs. N-UNCOUNT

cordless /kɔːʳdləs/. A **cordless** telephone or piece of electric equipment is operated by a battery fitted inside it and is not connected to the electricity mains. *The waitress approached Picone with a cordless phone. ...the cordless drill.* ADJ: usu ADJ n

cordon /kɔːʳdᵊn/ **cordons, cordoning, cordoned.** A **cordon** is a line or ring of police, soldiers, or vehicles preventing people from entering or leaving an area. *Police formed a cordon between the two crowds.* ◆◇◇◇◇ N-COUNT

cordon off. If police or soldiers **cordon off** an area, they prevent people from entering or leaving it, usually by forming a line or ring. *Police cordoned off part of the city centre... The police cordoned everything off.* PHRASAL VERB V P n (not pron) V n P

cordon bleu /kɔːʳdɒn blɜː/. **Cordon bleu** is used to describe cookery or cooks of the highest standard. *I took a cordon bleu cookery course.* ADJ: ADJ n

corduroy /kɔːʳdərɔɪ/ **corduroys**
1 **Corduroy** is thick cotton cloth with parallel raised lines on the outside. ...*a corduroy jacket.* N-UNCOUNT
2 **Corduroys** are trousers made out of corduroy or needle cord; an old-fashioned word. N-PLURAL

core /kɔːʳ/ **cores, coring, cored** ◆◆◆◇◇
1 The **core** of a fruit is the central part of it. It contains seeds or pips. *Someone threw an apple core... Peel the pears and remove the cores.* N-COUNT: oft n N
2 If you **core** a fruit, you remove its core. ...*machines for peeling and coring apples.* VERB V n
3 The **core** of an object, building, or city is the central part of it. ...*the earth's core... The core of the city is a series of ancient squares.* N-COUNT: usu with poss =centre
4 **The core** of something such as a problem or an issue is the part of it that has to be understood or accepted before the whole thing can be understood or dealt with. ...*the ability to get straight to the core of a problem... The notion that blacks comprise a problem is at the core of racist reasoning.* N-SING: *the* N, usu N *of* n =heart
5 A **core** team or a **core** group is a group of people who do the main part of a job or piece of work. Other people may also help, but only for limited periods of time. *We already have our core team in place... A core of about six staff would continue with the project.* N-SING: N n, N *of* n
6 In a school or college, **core** subjects are a group of subjects that have to be studied. *The core subjects are English, mathematics and science... I'm not opposed to a core curriculum in principle, but I think requiring a foreign language is unrealistic. ...a core of nine academic subjects.* N-SING: usu N n
7 The **core** businesses or the **core** activities of a company or organization are their most important ones. *The core activities of local authorities were reorganised... The group plans to concentrate on six core businesses... However, the main core of the company performed outstandingly.* N-SING: usu N n
8 See also **hard core.**
9 You can use **to the core** when you are describing someone who is a very strong supporter of someone or something and will never change their views. For example, you can say that someone is Republican **to the core**. *The villagers are royalist to the core.* PHRASES adj/n PHR =through and through
10 If someone is shaken **to the core** or shocked **to the core**, they are extremely shaken or shocked. *Leonard was shaken to the core; he'd never seen or read anything like it.* usu -ed PHR

co-religionist, co-religionists. A person's **co-religionists** are people who are followers of the same religion; a formal word. *They will turn for help to their co-religionists in the Middle East.* N-COUNT: usu pl, oft poss N =fellow-believers

corgi /kɔːʳgi/ **corgis.** A **corgi** is a type of small dog with short, stumpy legs and a pointed nose. N-COUNT

coriander /kɒriændəʳ, AM kɔː-/. **Coriander** is a plant with seeds that are used as a spice and leaves that are used as a herb. ◆◇◇◇◇ N-UNCOUNT

cork /kɔːʳk/ **corks, corking, corked** ◆◇◇◇◇
1 **Cork** is a soft, light substance which forms the bark of a type of Mediterranean tree. ...*cork floors. ...cork-soled clogs.* N-UNCOUNT
2 A **cork** is a piece of cork or plastic that is pushed into the opening of a bottle to close it. N-COUNT
3 To **cork** a bottle means to seal it by putting a cork in it. *He righted the bottle and corked it. ...corked frosted-glass oil and vinegar bottles.* VERB V n V-ed

corker /kɔːʳkəʳ/ **corkers.** If you say that someone or something is a **corker**, you mean that they are very good; an old-fashioned, informal word. *Howard Wilkinson has come up with an absolute corker of an idea.* N-COUNT

corkscrew /kɔːʳkskruː/ **corkscrews.** A **corkscrew** is a device for pulling corks out of bottles. It has a spiral-shaped metal rod with a point that you push into the cork and a handle which you pull to remove the cork. N-COUNT

cormorant /kɔːʳmərənt/ **cormorants.** A **cormorant** is a type of dark-coloured bird with a long neck. Cormorants nest near coastal areas and catch fish by diving into the sea. N-COUNT

corn /kɔːʳn/ **corns** ◆◆◇◇◇
1 In British English, **corn** is used to refer to crops such as wheat and barley. It can also be used to refer to the seeds from these plants. The American word is **grain**. ...*fields of corn... He filled the barn to the roof with corn.* N-UNCOUNT
2 **Corn** is the same as maize; used mainly in American English. ...*rows of corn in an Iowa field.* N-UNCOUNT
3 **Corns** are small, painful areas of hard skin which can form on your foot, especially near your toes. They are often formed by wearing badly fitting shoes. N-COUNT: usu pl

cornbread /kɔːʳnbred/; also spelled **corn bread**. **Cornbread** is bread made from ground maize. It is popular in the United States. N-UNCOUNT

corn cob, corn cobs; also spelled **corncob**. **Corn cobs** are the long rounded parts of the maize plant on which small yellow seeds grow. N-COUNT: usu pl

cornea /kɔːʳniə/ **corneas.** The **cornea** is the transparent skin covering the outside of your eye. N-COUNT

corneal /kɔːʳniəl/. **Corneal** means relating to the cornea of the eye. ...*corneal scars.* ADJ: ADJ n

corned beef /kɔːʳnd biːf/. **Corned beef** is beef which has been cooked and preserved in salt water. N-UNCOUNT

corner /kɔːʳnəʳ/ **corners, cornering, cornered** ◆◆◆◆◇
1 A **corner** is a point or an area where two or more edges, sides, or surfaces of something join. *He saw the corner of a magazine sticking out from under the blanket... Write 'By Airmail' in the top left hand corner.* N-COUNT: usu with supp
2 The **corner** of a room, box, or other square-shaped space is the area inside it, near the place where two or three of its edges or walls meet. ...*a card table in the corner of the living room... The ball hurtled into the far corner of the net... Finally I spotted it, in a dark corner over by the piano.* N-COUNT
3 The **corner** of your mouth or eye is the side of it. *She flicked a crumb off the corner of her mouth... Out of the corner of her eye she saw that a car had stopped.* N-COUNT: usu sing, oft N *of* n
4 The **corner** of a street is the place where it joins N-COUNT:

another street. *She would spend the day hanging round street corners... We can't have police officers on every corner... He waited until the man had turned a corner.* usu with supp

5 A **corner** is a right-angled bend in a road. *...a sharp corner... The road is a succession of hairpin bends, hills, and blind corners.* N-COUNT =bend

6 If you talk about the **corners** of the world, a country, or some other place, you are referring to places that are far away or difficult to get to; used in written English. *Buyers came from all corners of the world... The group has been living in a remote corner of the Cambodian jungle.* N-COUNT: with supp, usu N *of* n

7 In football, hockey, and some other sports, a **corner** is a free shot or kick taken from the corner of the pitch. N-COUNT

8 If you **corner** a person or animal, you force them into a place they cannot escape from. *A police motor-cycle chased his car twelve miles, and cornered him near Rome... He was still sitting huddled like a cornered animal.* VERB V n V-ed

9 If you **corner** someone, you force them to speak to you when they have been trying to avoid you. *Golan managed to corner the young producer-director for an interview.* VERB V n

10 If a company or place **corners** an area of trade, they gain control over it so that no one else can have any success in that area. *This restaurant has cornered the Madrid market for specialist paellas... Zurich's affluence came initially from cornering a sizeable chunk of the 14th Century silk trade.* VERB =monopolize V n

11 If a car, or the person driving it, **corners** in a particular way, the car goes round bends in roads in this way. *Peter drove jerkily, cornering too fast and fumbling the gears.* VERB V adv/prep

12 If you say that something is **around the corner** or **round the corner**, you mean that it will happen very soon. *The Chancellor of the Exchequer says that economic recovery is just around the corner.* PHRASES usu v-link PHR =imminent

13 If you say that something is **around the corner** or **round the corner**, you mean that it is very near; an informal expression. *My new place is just around the corner.* v-link PHR, PHR after v

14 If you **cut corners**, you do something quickly by doing it in a less thorough way than you should; used showing disapproval. *Take your time, don't cut corners and follow instructions to the letter.* V inflects PRAGMATICS

15 You can use expressions such as **the four corners of the world** to refer to places that are a long way from each other; used in written English. *They've combed the four corners of the world for the best accessories... Young people came from the four corners of the nation.* PHR n

16 If you are **in a corner** or **in a tight corner**, you are in a situation which is difficult to deal with and get out of. *The government is in a corner on interest rates... He appears to have backed himself into a tight corner.* N inflects, v-link PHR, PHR after v =tight spot

corner shop, corner shops; also spelled **corner-shop**. In British English, a **corner shop** is a small shop, usually on the corner of a street, that sells mainly food and household goods. The American term is **corner store**. N-COUNT

cornerstone /kɔːʳnəʳstoun/ **cornerstones;** also spelled **corner-stone**. The **cornerstone** of something is the basic part of it on which its existence, success, or truth depends; a formal word. *Research is the cornerstone of the profession.* ◆◇◇◇◇ N-COUNT: oft N *of* n =keystone

corner store, corner stores. In American English, a **corner store** is a small shop, usually on the corner of a street, that sells mainly food and household goods. The British term is **corner shop**. N-COUNT

cornet /kɔːʳnɪt, AM kɔːʳnet/ **cornets**

1 A **cornet** is a musical instrument that looks like a small trumpet. *I've been learning to play the cornet.* N-VAR: oft *the* N

2 In British English, an ice cream **cornet** is a soft thin biscuit shaped like a cone with ice cream in it. N-COUNT =cone

corn exchange, corn exchanges; also spelled **Corn Exchange**. A **corn exchange** is a large building where corn used to be bought and sold. N-COUNT

cornfield /kɔːʳnfiːld/ **cornfields;** also spelled **corn field**. A **cornfield** is a field in which corn is being grown. N-COUNT

cornflake /kɔːʳnfleɪk/ **cornflakes. Cornflakes** are small dry flakes made from maize that are eaten with milk as a breakfast cereal. They are popular in Britain and the United States. N-COUNT: usu pl

cornflour /kɔːʳnflauəʳ/; also spelled **corn flour**. In British English, **cornflour** is a fine white powder made from maize which is used to thicken sauces, gravy, and soup. The American word is **cornstarch**. N-UNCOUNT

cornflower /kɔːʳnflauəʳ/ **cornflowers. Cornflowers** are small plants with bright flowers. The flowers are usually blue. *Her eyes were a bright, cornflower blue.* N-VAR

cornice /kɔːʳnɪs/ **cornices.** A **cornice** is a strip of plaster, wood, or stone which goes along the top of a wall or building. N-COUNT

Cornish /kɔːʳnɪʃ/ ◆◇◇◇◇

1 Cornish means belonging or relating to the English county of Cornwall. *...the rugged Cornish coast. ...Cornish fishermen.* ADJ

2 The Cornish are the people of Cornwall. *The Cornish are up in arms.* N-PLURAL: *the* N

3 Cornish is a language that used to be spoken by the people of Cornwall. It is now only spoken by a very small number of people. N-UNCOUNT

Cornish pasty, Cornish pasties; also spelled **cornish pasty**. **Cornish pasties** are flat semi-circular pies with meat and vegetables inside. N-COUNT

cornmeal /kɔːʳnmiːl/; also spelled **corn meal**. **Cornmeal** is a coarse powder made from maize. It is used in cooking. N-UNCOUNT

corn on the cob, corn on the cobs; also spelled **corn-on-the-cob**. **Corn on the cob** is the long rounded part of the maize plant on which small yellow seeds grow. N-VAR

corn silk; also spelled **cornsilk**. The silky strands that lie under the leaves of a corn cob are referred to as **corn silk**. *...a baby with hair the colour of corn silk.* N-UNCOUNT

cornstarch /kɔːʳnstɑːʳtʃ/; also spelled **corn starch**. In American English, **cornstarch** is a fine white powder made from maize which is used to thicken sauces, gravy, and soup. The British word is **cornflour**. N-UNCOUNT

cornucopia /kɔːʳnjʊkoupiə/. A **cornucopia** of things is a large number of different things; used in written English. *...a cornucopia of fruits... The success of business has opened up a cornucopia of career options.* N-SING =abundance

corny /kɔːʳni/ **cornier, corniest.** If you describe something as **corny**, you mean that it is obvious or sentimental and not at all original. *I know it sounds corny, but I'm really not motivated by money. ...corny jokes.* ADJ-GRADED

corollary /kərɒləri, AM kɔːrəleri/ **corollaries.** A **corollary** of something is an idea, argument, or fact that results directly from it; a formal word. *The number of prisoners increased as a corollary of the government's determination to combat violent crime.* N-COUNT: oft with poss =consequence

corona /kərounə/. The sun's **corona** is its outer atmosphere; a technical term. N-SING

coronary /kɒrənri, AM kɔːrəneri/ **coronaries** ◆◇◇◇◇

1 Coronary means belonging or relating to the heart; a medical use. *If all the coronary arteries are free of significant obstructions, all parts of the heart will receive equal amounts of oxygen.* ADJ: ADJ n

2 If someone has a **coronary**, the flow of blood to their heart is blocked by a large blood clot. *He had a coronary on the way to work.* N-COUNT =heart attack

coronary thrombosis, coronary thromboses. A **coronary thrombosis** is the same as a **coronary**; a medical term. *The cause of death was coronary thrombosis.* N-VAR

coronation /kɒrəneɪʃən, AM kɔːr-/ **coronations.** A **coronation** is the ceremony at which a king or queen is crowned. *...the coronation of Her Majesty Queen Elizabeth II.* ◆◇◇◇◇ N-COUNT

coroner /kɒrənəʳ, AM kɔːr-/ **coroners.** ◆◇◇◇◇ N-COUNT A **coroner** is an official who is responsible for investigating the deaths of people who have died in a sudden, violent, or unusual way. *The coroner recorded a verdict of accidental death.*

coronet /kɒrənət, AM kɔːrənet/ **coronets.** N-COUNT A **coronet** is a small crown.

Corp. ◆◆◆◆◇ **Corp.** is a written abbreviation for 'corporation'. *...Sony Corp. of Japan.*

corpora /kɔːʳpərə/. **Corpora** is a plural of **corpus.**

corporal /kɔːʳprəl/ **corporals.** ◆◇◇◇◇ N-COUNT; N-TITLE A **corporal** is a non-commissioned officer in the army. *The corporal shouted an order at the men. ...Corporal Devereux.*

corporal punishment. N-UNCOUNT **Corporal punishment** is the punishment of people by beating them. *My father was against corporal punishment.*

corporate /kɔːʳprət/. ◆◆◆◇◇ ADJ: ADJ n **Corporate** means relating to business corporations or to a particular business corporation. *...top US corporate executives. ...the UK corporate sector. ...a corporate lawyer... This established a strong corporate image.*

corporate raider, corporate raiders. N-COUNT A **corporate raider** is a person or organization that tries to take control of a company by buying a large number of its shares.

corporation /kɔːʳpəreɪʃən/ **corporations** ◆◆◆◇◇

1 N-COUNT: oft in names after n A **corporation** is a large business or company. *...multi-national corporations. ...the Seiko Corporation.*

2 N-COUNT =local authority In some large British cities, the **corporation** is the local authority that is responsible for providing public services. *...the corporation's task of regenerating 900 acres of the inner city.*

corporation tax. N-UNCOUNT **Corporation tax** is a tax that companies have to pay on the profits they make.

corporatism /kɔːʳprətɪzəm/. N-UNCOUNT PRAGMATICS **Corporatism** is the organization and control of a country by groups who share a common interest or profession; used showing disapproval. *'The age of corporatism must be put firmly behind us,' he proclaimed.*

corporatist /kɔːʳprətɪst/ **corporatists**

1 ADJ-GRADED: usu ADJ n PRAGMATICS You use **corporatist** to describe organizations, ideas, or systems which follow the principles of corporatism; used showing disapproval. *... a corporatist political system... They did show decidedly corporatist tendencies.*

2 N-COUNT PRAGMATICS A **corporatist** is someone who believes in the principles of corporatism; used showing disapproval. *The defeat of the corporatists is easy to understand.*

corporeal /kɔːʳpɔːriəl/. ADJ-GRADED: usu ADJ n =physical **Corporeal** means involving or relating to the physical world rather than the spiritual world; a formal word. *...man's corporeal existence.*

corps /kɔːʳ/; **corps** is both the singular and the plural form. ◆◆◇◇◇

1 N-COUNT: oft in names after n A **corps** is a part of the army which has special duties. *...the Army Medical Corps. ...the Russian Officer Corps.*

2 N-COUNT: supp N A **corps** is a small group of people who do a special job. *...the diplomatic corps. ...the foreign press corps.*

corps de ballet /kɔːʳ də bæleɪ, AM - bæleɪ/. N-SING The **corps de ballet** is the group of dancers who dance together in a ballet, in contrast to the principal dancers.

corpse /kɔːʳps/ **corpses.** ◆◆◇◇◇ N-COUNT =body A **corpse** is a dead body, especially the body of a human being.

corpulent /kɔːʳpjʊlənt/. ADJ-GRADED If you describe someone as **corpulent**, you mean they are fat; a literary word. *...a rather corpulent farmer.*

corpus /kɔːʳpəs/ **corpora** /kɔːʳpərə/ or **corpuses** ◆◇◇◇◇

1 N-COUNT: usu with supp A **corpus** is a large collection of written or spoken texts that is used for language research; a technical use. *...a corpus of two hundred million words of general English.*

2 See **habeas corpus.**

corpuscle /kɔːʳpʌsəl, AM -pəsəl/ **corpuscles.** N-COUNT: usu pl **Corpuscles** are red or white blood cells. *Deficiency of red corpuscles is caused by a lack of iron.*

corral /kərɑːl, AM -ræl/ **corrals.** N-COUNT In the United States, a **corral** is a space surrounded by a fence where cattle or horses are kept, for example on a ranch or farm.

correct /kərekt/ **corrects, correcting, corrected** ◆◆◆◆◇

1 ADJ =right ≠incorrect If something is **correct**, it is in accordance with the facts and has no mistakes; a formal use. *The correct answers can be found at the bottom of page 8... The following information was correct at time of going to press... Doctors examine their patients thoroughly in order to make a correct diagnosis.* ♦ **correctly** ADV: ADV with v *Did I pronounce your name correctly?... You have to correctly answer each question.* ♦ **correctness** N-UNCOUNT =accuracy *Ask the investor to check the correctness of what he has written.*

2 ADJ: v-link ADJ =right ≠wrong If someone is **correct**, what they have said or thought is true; a formal use. *You are absolutely correct. The leaves are from a bay tree... If Casey is correct, the total cost of the cleanup would come to $110 billion.*

3 ADJ: ADJ n =right The **correct** thing or method is the thing or method that is required or is most suitable in a particular situation. *The use of the correct materials was crucial... White was in no doubt the referee made the correct decision. ...the correct way to produce a crop of tomato plants.* ♦ **correctly** ADV: ADV with v =properly *If correctly executed, this shot will give them a better chance of getting the ball close to the hole.*

4 ADJ: usu ADJ *in* -ing/n PRAGMATICS =right If you say that someone is **correct** in doing something, you approve of their action. *You are perfectly correct in trying to steer your mother towards increased independence... I think the president was correct to reject the offer.* ♦ **correctly** ADV: ADV with cl *When an accident happens, quite correctly questions are asked.*

5 VERB =rectify V n If you **correct** a problem, mistake, or fault, you do something which puts it right. *He may need surgery to correct the problem... He has criticised the government for inefficiency and delays in correcting past mistakes.* ♦ **correction** /kərekʃən/ **corrections** N-VAR =amendment *...legislation to require the correction of factual errors... We will then make the necessary corrections.*

6 VERB V n with quote V n Also V with quote If you **correct** someone, you say something which you think is more accurate or appropriate than what they have just said. *'Actually, that isn't what happened,' George corrects me... I must correct him on a minor point.*

7 VERB V n When someone **corrects** a piece of writing, they look at it and mark the mistakes in it. *It took an extraordinary effort to focus on preparing his classes or correcting his students' work.*

8 ADJ-GRADED =proper If a person or their behaviour is **correct**, their behaviour is in accordance with social or other rules. *I think English men are very polite and very correct... We were rather surprised by their sporting and correct behaviour.* ♦ **correctly** ADV-GRADED: ADV with v *The High Court of Parliament began very correctly with a prayer for the Queen.* ♦ **correctness** N-UNCOUNT *...his stiff-legged gait and formal correctness.*

9 CONVENTION PRAGMATICS You say '**correct me if I'm wrong**' to indicate that you are not entirely sure that what you are about to say is true. *As I recall, but correct me if I am wrong, it was in a car park in Carmarthen.*

correction /kərekʃən/ **corrections** ◆◆◇◇◇

1 N-COUNT: usu pl **Corrections** are marks or comments made on a piece of work, especially school work, which indicate where there are mistakes and what are the right answers.

2 N-UNCOUNT: oft N n **Correction** is the improvement, usually by punishment, of the behaviour of offenders; used mainly in American English. *...jails and other parts of the correction system. ...the Department of Correction.*

3 See also **correct.**

correctional /kərekʃənəl/. ADJ: ADJ n **Correctional** institutions, services, or staff are concerned with improving the behaviour of offenders, usually by punishing them; used mainly in American English. *He is currently being held in a metropolitan correctional center. ...a jail correctional officer.*

corrective /kərektɪv/ **correctives** ◆◇◇◇◇

1 **Corrective** measures or techniques are intended to put right something that is wrong. *Scientific institutions have been reluctant to take corrective action... He has received extensive corrective surgery to his skull.* ADJ: usu ADJ n =remedial

2 If something is a **corrective** to a particular view or account, it gives a more accurate or fairer picture than there would have been without it; a formal use. *...a useful corrective to the mistaken view that all psychologists are behaviourists.* N-COUNT: oft N *to* n

correlate /kɒrəleɪt, AM kɔːr-/ **correlates, correlating, correlated** ◆◇◇◇◇

1 If one thing **correlates** or **is correlated** with another, there is a close similarity or connection between them, often because one thing causes the other. You can also say that two things **correlate** or **are correlated**; a formal use. *Obesity correlates with increased risk for hypertension and stroke... The political opinions of spouses correlate more closely than their heights... The loss of respect for British science is correlated to reduced funding... At the highest executive levels earnings and performance aren't always correlated.* V-RECIP-ERG; V *with/to* n; pl-n V; be V-ed *with/to* n; be V-ed

2 If you **correlate** things, you work out the way in which they are connected or the way they influence each other; a formal use. *Attempts to correlate specific language functions with particular parts of the brain have not advanced very far... Lieutenant Ryan closed his eyes, first mentally viewing the different crime scenes, then correlating the data.* VERB; V n *with* n; V n

correlation /kɒrəleɪʃən, AM kɔːr-/ **correlations.** A **correlation** between things is a connection or link between them; a formal word. *...the correlation between smoking and disease.* ◆◇◇◇◇ N-COUNT: oft N *between* pl-n

correlative /kɒrelətɪv/ **correlatives.** If one thing is a **correlative** of another, the first thing is caused by the second thing, or occurs together with it; a formal word. *Man has rights only in so far as they are a correlative of duty.* N-COUNT: oft N *of* n

correspond /kɒrɪspɒnd, AM kɔːr-/ **corresponds, corresponding, corresponded** ◆◆◇◇◇

1 If one thing **corresponds** to another, there is a close similarity or connection between them. You can also say that two things **correspond**. *Racegoers will be given a number which will correspond to a horse running in a race... A 22 per cent increase in car travel corresponds with a 19 per cent drop in cycle mileage per person... The two maps of London correspond closely... Her expression is concerned but her body-language does not correspond.* V-RECIP; V *to/with* n; pl-n V; V (non-recip)
♦ **corresponding** *March and April sales this year were up 8 per cent on the corresponding period in 1992. ...the inexorable rise in Britain's fortunes and the corresponding decline of France as an international power.* ADJ: ADJ n

2 If you **correspond** with someone, you write letters to them. You can also say that two people **correspond**. *She still corresponds with American friends she met in Majorca nine years ago... We corresponded regularly.* V-RECIP; V *with* n; pl-n V

correspondence /kɒrɪspɒndəns, AM kɔːr-/ **correspondences** ◆◆◇◇◇

1 **Correspondence** is the act of writing letters to someone. *The judges' decision is final and no correspondence will be entered into... His interest in writing came from a long correspondence with a close college friend.* N-UNCOUNT: also *a* N, oft N *with* n

2 Someone's **correspondence** is the letters that they receive or send. *He always replied to his correspondence... She virtually never mentions him in her correspondence or notebooks.* N-UNCOUNT

3 If there is a **correspondence** between two things, there is a close similarity or connection between them. *In African languages there is a close correspondence between sounds and letters. ...correspondences between Eastern religions and Christianity.* N-COUNT: oft N *between* pl-n

correspondence course, correspondence courses. A **correspondence course** is a course in which you study at home, receiving your work by post and sending it back by post. *I took a correspondence course in computing.* N-COUNT

correspondent /kɒrɪspɒndənt, AM kɔːr-/ **correspondents.** A **correspondent** is a newspaper or television reporter, especially one who specializes in a particular type of news. *As our Diplomatic Correspondent Mark Brayne reports, the president was given a sympathetic hearing.* ◆◆◆◆◇ N-COUNT =reporter

correspondingly /kɒrɪspɒndɪŋli, AM kɔːr-/. You use **correspondingly** when describing a situation which is closely connected with one you have just mentioned or is similar to it. *As his political stature has shrunk, he has grown correspondingly more dependent on the army.* ADV: ADV with v, ADV adj/adv

corridor /kɒrɪdɔːʳ, AM kɔːrɪdər/ **corridors** ◆◆◇◇◇

1 A **corridor** is a long passage in a building or train, with doors and rooms on one or both sides. N-COUNT

2 A **corridor** is a strip of land that connects one country to another or gives it a route to the sea through another country. *East Prussia and the rest of Germany were separated, in 1919, by the Polish corridor.* N-COUNT

corroborate /kərɒbəreɪt/ **corroborates, corroborating, corroborated.** To **corroborate** something that has been said or reported means to provide evidence or information that supports it; a formal word. *I had access to a wide range of documents which corroborated the story... Alice corroborated what Blair had said.* ◆◇◇◇◇ VERB =confirm; V n
♦ **corroboration** /kərɒbəreɪʃən/ *He could not get a single witness to establish independent corroboration of his version of the accident.* N-UNCOUNT =confirmation

corroborative /kərɒbərətɪv, AM -reɪtɪv/. **Corroborative** evidence or information supports an idea, account, or argument; a formal word. *The police did not have enough corroborative evidence for a probable conviction.* ADJ: ADJ n

corrode /kəroʊd/ **corrodes, corroding, corroded**

1 If metal or stone **corrodes**, or **is corroded**, it is gradually destroyed by a chemical or by rust. *He has devised a process for making gold wires which neither corrode nor oxidise... Engineers found the structure had been corroded by moisture... Acid rain destroys trees and corrodes buildings.* V-ERG; V; be V-ed; V n
♦ **corroded** *The investigators found that the underground pipes were badly corroded.* ADJ-GRADED

2 To **corrode** something means to gradually weaken, worsen, or harm it; a literary use. *Suffering was easier to bear than the bitterness he felt corroding his spirit... He warns that corruption is corroding Russia.* VERB =corrupt; V n

corrosion /kəroʊʒən/. **Corrosion** is the damage that is caused when something is corroded. *Zinc is used to protect other metals from corrosion.* ◆◇◇◇◇ N-UNCOUNT

corrosive /kəroʊsɪv/

1 A **corrosive** substance is able to destroy solid materials by a chemical reaction. *Sodium and sulphur are highly corrosive.* ADJ-GRADED

2 If you say that something has a **corrosive** effect, you mean that it gradually causes serious harm; a formal use. *...the corrosive effects of inflation.* ADJ-GRADED =damaging

corrugated /kɒrəgeɪtɪd, AM kɔːr-/. **Corrugated** metal or cardboard has been folded into a series of small parallel folds to make it stronger. *...a hut with a corrugated iron roof.* ◆◇◇◇◇ ADJ: usu ADJ n

corrupt /kərʌpt/ **corrupts, corrupting, corrupted** ◆◆◇◇◇

1 Someone who is **corrupt** behaves in a way that is morally wrong, especially by doing dishonest or illegal things in return for money or power. *...to save the nation from corrupt politicians of both parties. ...corrupt police officers... He had accused three opposition members of corrupt practices.* ADJ-GRADED ≠fair, honest, just
♦ **corruptly** *...several government officials charged with acting corruptly.* ADV-GRADED: ADV with v

2 If someone **is corrupted** by something, it causes them to become dishonest and unjust and unable to be trusted. *It's sad to see a man so corrupted by the desire for money and power.* VB: usu passive; be V-ed

3 To **corrupt** someone means to cause them to VERB

stop caring about moral standards. *...warning that television will corrupt us all... Cruelty depraves and corrupts.* V n V

4 If something **is corrupted**, it becomes damaged or spoiled in some way. *Some of the finer type-faces are corrupted by cheap, popular computer printers... They can ensure that traditional cuisines are not totally corrupted by commercial practices. ...corrupted data.* VB: usu passive be V-ed V-ed

corruption /kərʌpʃᵊn/ **corruptions** ◆◆◆◇◇

1 **Corruption** is dishonesty and illegal behaviour by people in positions of authority or power. *The President faces 54 charges of corruption and tax evasion... Distribution of food throughout the country is being hampered by inefficiency and corruption. ...bribery and corruption.* N-UNCOUNT

2 A **corruption** is a word that is derived from an earlier word, but which has become changed in some way; a technical use in linguistics. *'Morris' is an English corruption of 'Moorish', meaning North African.* N-COUNT: usu N of n

corsage /kɔːʳsɑːʒ/ **corsages.** A **corsage** is a very small bunch of flowers that is fastened to a woman's dress below the shoulder. N-COUNT

corset /kɔːʳsɪt/ **corsets.** A **corset** is a stiff piece of underwear worn by some women. It fits tightly around their hips and waist and makes them appear slimmer. N-COUNT

corseted /kɔːʳsɪtɪd/. A woman who is **corseted** is wearing a corset. ADJ

cortege /kɔːʳteɪʒ, AM -teʒ/ **corteges.** A **cortege** is a procession of people who are walking or riding in cars to a funeral. N-COUNT-COLL

cortex /kɔːʳteks/ **cortices** /kɔːʳtɪsiːz/. The **cortex** of the brain or of another organ is its outer layer; a medical term. *...the cerebral cortex.* ◆◇◇◇◇ N-COUNT: usu sing, oft the N

cortisone /kɔːʳtɪzoʊn/. **Cortisone** is a hormone used in the treatment of arthritis, allergies, and some skin diseases. N-UNCOUNT

coruscating /kɒrəskeɪtɪŋ, AM kɔːr-/. A **coruscating** speech or performance is lively, intelligent, and impressive; used in literary English. *...an unstoppable flow of coruscating humour.* ADJ: usu ADJ n =dazzling, brilliant

corvette /kɔːʳvet/ **corvettes.** A **corvette** is a small fast warship that is used to protect other ships from attack. N-COUNT

'cos /kəz/; also spelled **cos. 'Cos** means the same as **because**; an informal word. *It was absolutely horrible going up the hills 'cos they were really, really steep.* ◆◆◆◆◇ CONJ-SUBORD

cosh /kɒʃ/ **coshes, coshing, coshed**

1 A **cosh** is a heavy piece of rubber or metal which is used as a weapon; used mainly in British English. N-COUNT

2 To **cosh** someone means to hit them hard on the head with a cosh or some other blunt weapon; used mainly in British English. *When the couple said they did not have a safe the masked men punched Tom and coshed Helen.* VERB V n

cosmetic /kɒzmetɪk/ **cosmetics** ◆◆◇◇◇

1 **Cosmetics** are substances such as lipstick or powder, which people put on their face to make themselves look more attractive. N-COUNT: usu pl =make-up

2 If you describe measures or changes as **cosmetic**, you mean they improve the appearance of a situation or thing but do not change its basic nature, and you are usually implying that they are inadequate. *It is a cosmetic measure which will do nothing to help the situation long term... In general, the students view these changes as merely cosmetic.* ADJ PRAGMATICS =superficial

cosmetic surgery. **Cosmetic surgery** is surgery done to make a person look more attractive. N-UNCOUNT

cosmic /kɒzmɪk/ ◆◇◇◇◇

1 **Cosmic** means occurring in, or coming from, the part of space that lies outside earth and its atmosphere. *...cosmic radiation. ...cosmic debris.* ADJ: usu ADJ n

2 **Cosmic** means belonging or relating to the universe. *...the cosmic laws governing our world. ...humanity's place in the cosmic order of things.* ADJ: usu ADJ n

cosmic rays. **Cosmic rays** are rays that reach earth from outer space and that consist of atomic nuclei. N-PLURAL

cosmology /kɒzmɒlədʒi/ **cosmologies**

1 A **cosmology** is a theory about the origin and nature of the universe. *...the ideas implicit in Big Bang cosmology.* N-VAR

2 **Cosmology** is the study of the origin and nature of the universe. ♦ **cosmologist, cosmologists** *...astronomers and cosmologists.* ♦ **cosmological** /kɒzməlɒdʒɪkᵊl/ *...cosmological sciences. ...John Outram, the cosmological theorist.* N-UNCOUNT N-COUNT ADJ: ADJ n

cosmonaut /kɒzmənɔːt/ **cosmonauts.** A **cosmonaut** is an astronaut from the former Soviet Union. N-COUNT

cosmopolitan /kɒzməpɒlɪtən/ ◆◇◇◇◇

1 A **cosmopolitan** place or society is full of people from many different countries and cultures; used showing approval. *London has always been a cosmopolitan city.* ADJ-GRADED PRAGMATICS ≠insular

2 Someone who is **cosmopolitan** has had a lot of contact with people and things from many different countries and as a result is very open to different ideas and ways of doing things; used showing approval. *The family are rich, and extremely sophisticated and cosmopolitan.* ADJ-GRADED PRAGMATICS =insular

cosmos /kɒzmɒs, AM -məs/. **The cosmos** is the universe; a literary word. *...the natural laws of the cosmos.* ◆◇◇◇◇ N-SING: the N =universe

cosset /kɒsɪt/ **cossets, cosseting, cosseted;** also spelled **cossetting, cossetted.** If someone **is cosseted**, everything possible is done for them and they are protected from anything unpleasant. *Our kind of travel is definitely not suitable for people who expect to be cosseted.* ♦ **cosseted** *I don't want to be treated like a cosseted movie queen.* VB: usu passive =pamper be V-ed ADJ-GRADED

cost /kɒst, AM kɔːst/ **costs, costing.** The form **cost** is used in the present tense, and is also the past tense and participle, except for meaning 4, where the form **costed** is used. ◆◆◆◆◆

1 The **cost** of something is the amount of money that is needed in order to buy, do, or make it. *The cost of a loaf of bread has increased five-fold... In 1989 the price of coffee fell so low that in many countries it did not even cover the cost of production... Badges are also available at a cost of £2.50.* N-COUNT: usu sing, oft N of n

2 If something **costs** a particular amount of money, you can buy, do, or make it for that amount. *This course is limited to 12 people and costs £50... Painted walls look much more interesting and doesn't cost much... It's going to cost me over $100,000 to buy new trucks.* VERB V amount V n amount

3 Your **costs** are the total amount of money that you must spend on running your home or business. *Costs have been cut by 30 to 50 per cent... The company admits its costs are still too high.* N-PLURAL =expenses

4 When something that you plan to do or make **is costed**, the amount of money you need is calculated in advance. *Everything that goes into making a programme, staff, rent, lighting, is now costed. ...seventy apartments, shops, offices, a restaurant and hotel, costed at around 10 million pounds.* VB: usu passive be V-ed V-ed

► **Cost out** means the same as **cost**. *...training days for charity staff on how to draw up contracts and cost out proposals... It is always worth having a loft conversion costed out.* PHRASAL VERB V P n (not pron) have n V-ed P Also V n P

5 In law, if someone who has been convicted of a crime is ordered by the court to pay **costs**, they have to pay a sum of money towards the expenses of their court case. *He was jailed for 18 months and ordered to pay £550 costs.* N-PLURAL

6 If something is sold at **cost**, it is sold without any profit, for the same price as it cost the manufacturer to produce it or the seller to buy it. *...a store that provided cigarettes and candy bars at cost. ...a practice known as dumping – that is, selling below cost to drive competition out of business.* N-UNCOUNT: prep N =cost price

7 The **cost** of something is the loss, damage, or injury that is involved in trying to achieve it. *In March Mr Salinas shut down the city's oil refinery at a cost of $500 million and 5,000 jobs. ...being so afraid of something that you feel you have to avoid it whatever the cost to your lifestyle.* N-SING: oft N of n

8 If an event or mistake **costs** you something, you VERB lose that thing as the result of it. *...a six-year-old boy whose life was saved by an operation that cost him his sight... The increase will hurt small business and cost many thousands of jobs.* V n n / V n

9 If you say that something must be avoided **at all costs**, you are emphasizing that it must not be allowed to happen under any circumstances. *They told EC president Jacques Delors a disastrous world trade war must be avoided at all costs.* PHRASES PHR after v PRAGMATICS

10 If you say that something must be done **at any cost**, you are emphasizing that it must be done, even if this requires a lot of effort or money. *This book is of such importance that it must be published at any cost... He ordered the army to recapture the camp at any cost.* PHR after v PRAGMATICS

11 If someone **counts the cost** of something that has happened or will happen, they consider how the consequences of that action or event affect them. *Several countries in eastern Europe are counting the cost of yesterday's earthquake... Many people act on impulse without counting the cost.* V inflects

12 If you say that something **costs money**, you mean that it has to be paid for, and perhaps cannot be afforded. *Well-designed clothes cost money.* V inflects

13 If you know something **to** your **cost**, you know it because of an unpleasant experience that you have had. *Kathryn knows to her cost the effect of having served a jail sentence... There are very few people he can talk to in total confidence, as he has discovered to his cost.* PHR after v

14 • to **cost** someone **dear**: see **dear**.

cost out. See **cost** 4. PHRASAL VERB

cost accounting. Cost accounting is the recording and analysis of all the various costs of running a business. N-UNCOUNT

co-star, co-stars, co-starring, co-starred ◆◇◇◇◇

1 An actor's or actress's **co-stars** are the other actors or actresses who also have one of the main parts in a particular film. *During the filming, Curtis fell in love with his co-star, Christine Kaufmann.* N-COUNT: usu poss N

2 If an actor or actress **co-stars** with another actor or actress, the two of them have the main parts in a particular film. *This fall she co-stars in a film with the acclaimed British actor Kenneth Branagh... Wright and Penn met when they co-starred in the movie State Of Grace... Cosby had originally selected her to co-star in his movie 'Leonard Part 6'.* V-RECIP V *with* n pl-n V *in* n V *in* n (non-recip)

3 If a film **co-stars** particular actors, they have the main parts in it. *Produced by Oliver Stone, 'Wild Palms' co-stars Dana Delaney, Jim Belushi and Angie Dickinson.* VERB V n

cost-effective. Something that is **cost-effective** saves or makes a lot of money in comparison with the costs involved. *The bank must be run in a cost-effective way.* ♦ **cost-effectively** *The management tries to produce the magazine as cost-effectively as possible.* ♦ **cost-effectiveness** *A Home Office report has raised doubts about the cost-effectiveness of the proposals.* ◆◇◇◇◇ ADJ-GRADED =economical; ADV-GRADED: ADV after v; N-UNCOUNT

costing /kɒstɪŋ, AM kɔːst-/ **costings.** A **costing** is an estimation of all the costs involved in something such as a project or a business venture. *We'll put together a proposal, including detailed costings, free of charge.* ◆◆◇◇◇ N-VAR =estimate

costly /kɒstli, AM kɔːst-/ **costlier, costliest** ◆◆◇◇◇

1 If you say that something is **costly**, you mean that it costs a lot of money, often more than you would want to pay. *Having professionally made curtains can be costly, so why not make your own?* ADJ-GRADED =expensive ≠cheap

2 If you describe someone's action or mistake as **costly**, you mean that it results in a serious disadvantage for them, for example the loss of a large amount of money or the loss of their reputation. *Psychometric tests can save organizations from grim and costly mistakes... This sort of scandal in international banking has been politically costly.* ADJ-GRADED

cost of living. The **cost of living** is the average amount of money that people in a particular place need in order to be able to afford basic food, housing, and clothing. *The cost of living has increased dramatically... Companies are moving jobs to towns with a lower cost of living.* ◆◇◇◇◇ N-SING

cost-plus. A **cost-plus** basis for a contract about work to be done is one in which the buyer agrees to pay the seller or contractor all the cost plus a profit. *All vessels were to be built on a cost-plus basis. ...cost-plus contracts.* ADJ: ADJ n

cost price, cost prices. If something is sold at **cost price**, it is sold without any profit, for the same price as it cost the manufacturer to produce it or the seller to buy it. *...a factory shop where you can buy very fashionable shoes at cost price... The shop claims to have sold computers below the manufacturer's cost price for three years.* N-VAR: oft *at* N =cost

costume /kɒstjuːm, AM -tuːm/ **costumes** ◆◆◇◇◇

1 An actor's or performer's **costume** is the set of clothes they wear while they are performing. *Even from a distance the effect of his fox costume was stunning... The performers, in costume and make-up, were walking up and down backstage... In all, she has eight costume changes.* N-VAR =outfit

2 The clothes worn by people at a particular time in history, or in a particular country, are referred to as a particular type of **costume**. *...men and women in eighteenth-century costume... In the colourful markets at Chincero and Pisac, women still wear their traditional costume.* N-UNCOUNT: supp N =dress

3 A **costume** play or drama is one which is set in the past and in which the actors wear the type of clothes that were worn in that period. *...a lavish costume drama set in Ireland and the US in the 1890s.* ADJ: ADJ n

costume jewellery. Costume jewellery is jewellery made from cheap materials. N-UNCOUNT

costumier /kɒstjuːmiəʳ, AM -tuː-/ **costumiers.** A **costumier** is a person or company that makes or supplies theatrical or fancy dress costumes. *...a theatrical costumier.* N-COUNT

cosy /kouzi/ **cosies; cosier, cosiest;** spelled **cozy** in American English. ◆◆◇◇◇

1 A house or room that is **cosy** is comfortable and warm. *Downstairs there's a breakfast room and guests can relax in the cosy bar.* ♦ **cosily** /kouzɪli/ *We took time to relax in the cosily decorated drawing room.* ♦ **cosiness** *In the evening a log fire would provide cosiness.* ADJ-GRADED =homely; ADV-GRADED; N-UNCOUNT

2 If you are **cosy**, you are comfortable and warm. *They like to make sure their guests are comfortable and cosy.* ♦ **cosily** *He was settled cosily in the corner with an arm round Lynda.* ADJ-GRADED: v-link ADJ; ADV-GRADED: ADV after v

3 You use **cosy** to describe activities that are pleasant and friendly, and involve people who know each other well. *...a cosy chat between friends... My mood this year is for a cosy, nice and thoroughly wholesome Christmas.* ♦ **cosily** *...chatting cosily with friends over coffee.* ♦ **cosiness** *...the cosiness and solidity of family life.* ADJ-GRADED =intimate; ADV-GRADED: ADV with v; N-UNCOUNT

4 A **cosy** is a soft cover which you put over a teapot or a boiled egg to keep it warm. N-COUNT

cot /kɒt/ **cots** ◆◇◇◇◇

1 In British English, a **cot** is a bed for a baby, with bars or panels round it so that the baby cannot fall out. The American word is **crib**. N-COUNT

2 In American English, a **cot** is a narrow bed, usually made of canvas fitted over a frame which can be folded up. The British term is **camp bed**. N-COUNT

cot death, cot deaths. In British English, **cot death** is the sudden death of a baby while it is asleep, although the baby had not previously been ill. The usual American term is **crib death**. *In developed countries, cot death is the main cause of death between the ages of one week and one year... Doctors still aren't sure what causes cot deaths.* N-VAR

coterie /koutəri/ **coteries.** A **coterie** of a particular kind is a small group of people who are close friends or have a common interest, and who do not want other people to join them; a formal word. *The songs he recorded were written by a small coterie of dedicated writers.* N-COUNT-COLL: usu with supp =circle, set

cottage /kɒtɪdʒ/ **cottages.** A **cottage** is a small house, usually in the country. *They used to have a cottage in N.W. Scotland... My sister Yvonne also came to live at Ockenden Cottage with me.* ◆◆◆◇◇ N-COUNT: oft in names after n

cottage cheese. **Cottage cheese** is a soft, white, lumpy cheese made from sour milk. N-UNCOUNT

cottage industry, cottage industries. A **cottage industry** is a small business that is run from someone's home, especially one that involves a craft such as knitting or pottery. *Bookbinding is largely a cottage industry.* N-COUNT

cottage loaf, cottage loaves. In Britain, a **cottage loaf** is a loaf of bread which has a smaller round part on top of a larger round part. N-COUNT

cottage pie, cottage pies. In Britain, **cottage pie** is a dish which consists of minced meat in gravy with mashed potato on top. N-VAR =shepherd's pie

cottager /kɒtɪdʒəʳ/ **cottagers.** A **cottager** is a person who lives in a cottage; an old-fashioned word. N-COUNT

cottaging /kɒtɪdʒɪŋ/. In British English, **cottaging** is homosexual activity between men in public toilets; an informal word. N-UNCOUNT

cotton /kɒtᵊn/ **cottons, cottoning, cottoned** ◆◆◆◇◇

1 **Cotton** is a type of cloth made from soft fibres from a particular plant. *...a cotton shirt.* N-MASS: oft N n

2 **Cotton** is a plant which is grown in warm countries and which produces soft fibres used in making cotton cloth. *...a large cotton plantation in Tennessee.* N-UNCOUNT

3 **Cotton** is thread that is used for sewing, especially thread that is made from cotton; used mainly in British English. *There's a needle and cotton there.* N-MASS

4 In American English, **cotton** is soft, fluffy cotton, used especially for applying liquids or creams to your skin. The British term is **cotton wool**. N-UNCOUNT

cotton on. In British English, if you **cotton on** to something, you understand it or realize it, especially without people telling you about it; an informal expression. *She had already cottoned on to the fact that the nanny was not all she appeared... It wasn't until he started laughing that they cottoned on!* PHRASAL VERB =catch on; V P to n; V P

cotton bud, cotton buds. A **cotton bud** is a small stick with a ball of cotton wool at each end, which people use, for example, for cleaning their ears or applying make-up. N-COUNT

cotton candy. In American English, **cotton candy** is a large pink or white mass of sugar threads that is eaten from a stick. It is sold at fairs or other outdoor events. The British word is **candyfloss**. N-UNCOUNT

cottonwood /kɒtᵊnwʊd/ **cottonwoods.** A **cottonwood** or a **cottonwood tree** is a kind of poplar that grows in North America and has seeds that are covered with cotton-like hairs. N-COUNT

cotton wool. In British English, **cotton wool** is soft, fluffy cotton, used especially for applying liquids or creams to your skin. The American word is **cotton**. ◆◇◇◇◇ N-UNCOUNT

couch /kaʊtʃ/ **couches, couching, couched** ◆◆◇◇◇

1 A **couch** is a long, comfortable seat for two or three people. *She was sitting beside her grandmother on the living room couch.* N-COUNT =sofa, settee

2 A **couch** is a bed in a doctor's or psychiatrist's consulting room, which patients lie on while they are being examined or treated. People sometimes talk about **the psychiatrist's couch** as a way of referring to psychotherapy. *Marina Cantacuzino interviews three men who've sought help on the therapist's couch.* N-COUNT

3 If a statement **is couched** in a particular style of language, it is expressed in that style of language; used in written English. *The new centre-right government's radical objectives are often couched in moderate terms... This time the proposal was couched as an ultimatum.* VB: usu passive =phrase; be V-ed in/as n

couchette /kuːʃet/ **couchettes.** A **couchette** is a bed in a railway carriage or on a ferry boat which is either folded against the wall or used as an ordinary seat during the day; used mainly in British English. N-COUNT

couch potato, couch potatoes. If you describe someone as a **couch potato**, you disapprove of them because they spend most of their time sitting at home watching television and do not exercise or have any interesting hobbies; an informal expression. *...couch potatoes flicking through endless satellite TV channels.* N-COUNT PRAGMATICS

cougar /kuːgəʳ/ **cougars.** A **cougar** is a wild animal that is a member of the cat family. Cougars have brownish-grey fur and live in mountain regions of North and South America. N-COUNT

cough /kɒf, AM kɔːf/ **coughs, coughing, coughed** ◆◆◆◇◇

1 When you **cough**, you force air out of your throat with a sudden, harsh noise. You often cough when you are ill, or when you are nervous or want to attract someone's attention. *Graham began to cough violently... He coughed. 'Excuse me, Mrs Allsworthy, could I have a word?'* ► Also a noun. *Coughs and sneezes spread infections much faster in a warm atmosphere... They were interrupted by an apologetic cough.* ♦ **coughing** *He was then overcome by a terrible fit of coughing.* VERB; V; N-COUNT; N-UNCOUNT

2 A **cough** is an illness in which you cough often and your chest or throat hurts. *...if you have a persistent cough for over a month.* N-COUNT

3 If you **cough** blood or phlegm, it comes up out of your throat or mouth when you cough. *I started coughing blood so they transferred me to a hospital.* ► **Cough up** means the same as **cough**. *On the chilly seas, Keats became feverish, continually coughing up blood.* VERB; V n; PHRASAL VERB; V P n (not pron); Also V n P

4 If an engine or other machine **coughs**, it makes a sudden, harsh noise. *Then suddenly, the engine coughed, spluttered and died.* VERB; V

cough up. If you **cough up** an amount of money, you pay or spend that amount, usually when you would prefer not to; an informal expression. *I'll have to cough up $10,000 a year for tuition... Will this be enough to persuade Congress to cough up?* • See also **cough** 3. PHRASAL VERB =fork out; V P n for n; V P; Also V P n, V P for n

cough mixture, cough mixtures. Cough mixture is liquid medicine that you take when you have a cough. N-MASS

could /kəd, STRONG kʊd/ ◆◆◆◆◆

Could is a modal verb. It is used with the base form of a verb. **Could** is sometimes considered to be the past form of **can**, but in this dictionary the two words are dealt with separately.

1 You use **could** to indicate that someone had the ability to do something. You use **could not** or **couldn't** to say that someone was unable to do something. *For my return journey, I felt I could afford the extra and travel first class... I could see that something was terribly wrong... He could not resist telling her the truth... When I left school at 16, I couldn't read or write... There was no way she could have coped with a baby around.* MODAL

2 You use **could** to indicate that something sometimes happened. *Though he had a temper and could be nasty, it never lasted... He could be very pleasant when he wanted to.* MODAL

3 You use **could have** to indicate that something was a possibility in the past, although it did not actually happen. *He could have made a fortune as a lawyer... You could have been killed!... He did not regret saying what he did but felt that he could have expressed it differently.* MODAL

4 You use **could** to indicate that something is possibly true, or that it may possibly happen. *Doctors told him the disease could have been caused by years of working in smokey clubs... An improvement in living standards could be years away... He was jailed in February 1992 and could be released next year.* MODAL =might

5 You use **could not** or **couldn't** to indicate that it is not possible that something is true. *They argued all the time and thought it couldn't be good for the baby... Anne couldn't be expected to understand the situation... He couldn't have been more than fourteen years old.* MODAL

6 You use **could** to talk about a possibility, ability, MODAL

or opportunity that is dependent on other conditions. *Their hope was that a new and better East Germany could be born... I knew that if I spoke to Myra, I could get her to call my father.*

7 You use **could** when you are saying that one thing or situation resembles another. *The charming characters she draws look like they could have walked out of the 1920s.* MODAL

8 You use **could**, or **couldn't** in questions, when you are making offers and suggestions. *I could call the local doctor... We need money right? We could go around and ask if people need odd jobs done or something... 'It's boring to walk all alone.'—'Couldn't you go for walks with your friends?'... You could look for a career abroad where environmental jobs are better paid and more secure... It would be a good idea if you could do this exercise twice or three times on separate days.* MODAL PRAGMATICS

9 You use **could** in questions when you are making a polite request or asking for permission to do something. Speakers sometimes use **couldn't** instead of 'could' to show that they realize that their request may be refused. *Could I stay tonight?... Could I speak to you in private a moment, John?... I wonder if some time I could have a word with you... Sir, could you please come to the commanding officer's office?... Could we go outside just for a second?... He asked if he could have a cup of coffee... Couldn't I watch you do it?* MODAL PRAGMATICS

10 In formal spoken English, speakers sometimes use structures with **if I could** or **could I** as polite ways of interrupting someone or of introducing what they are going to say next. *Well, if I could just interject... Could I stop you there?... Could I ask you if there have been any further problems?... First of all, could I begin with an apology for a mistake I made last week?* MODAL PRAGMATICS =may

11 You use **could** to say emphatically that someone ought to do the thing mentioned, especially when you are annoyed because they have not done it. You use **why couldn't** in questions to express your surprise or annoyance that someone has not done something. *We've come to see you, so you could at least stand and greet us properly... Idiot! You could have told me!... He could have written... Why couldn't she have said something?... But why couldn't he tell me straight out?* MODAL PRAGMATICS

12 You use **could** when you are expressing strong feelings about something by saying that you feel as if you want to do the thing mentioned, although you do not do it. *I could kill you! I swear I could!... 'Welcome back' was all they said. I could have kissed them!... She could have screamed with tension.* MODAL PRAGMATICS

13 You use **could** after 'if' when talking about something that you do not have the ability or opportunity to do, but which you are imagining in order to consider what the likely consequences might be. *If I could afford it I'd have four television sets... If only I could get some sleep, I would be able to cope.* MODAL

14 You use **could not** or **couldn't** with comparatives to emphasize that someone or something has as much as is possible of a particular quality. For example, if you say **I couldn't be happier**, you mean that you are very happy indeed. *The rest of the players are a great bunch of lads and I couldn't be happier... Darling Neville, I couldn't be more pleased for you... The news couldn't have come at a better time.* MODAL PRAGMATICS

15 In speech, you use **how could** in questions to emphasize that you feel strongly about something bad that has happened. *How could you allow him to do something like that?... How could I have been so stupid?... How could she do this to me?... How could you have lied to us all these years?* MODAL PRAGMATICS

16 You say **'I couldn't'** as an informal way of refusing an offer of more food or drink. *'More cake?'—'Oh no, I couldn't.'* CONVENTION PRAGMATICS

17 • **could do with**: see **do**.

couldn't /kʊdᵊnt/. **Couldn't** is the usual spoken form of **could not**.

could've /kʊdəv/. **Could've** is the usual spoken form of **could have**, when 'have' is an auxiliary verb.

council /kaʊnsᵊl/ **councils** ◆◆◆◆◆

1 A **council** is a group of people who are elected to govern a local area such as a city or a county. *...Cheshire County Council... The city council has voted almost unanimously in favour. ...David Ward, one of just two Liberal Democrats on the council. ...reports of local council meetings.* N-COUNT-COLL: oft in names after n =local authority

2 In British English, **council** houses or flats are owned by the local council, and people pay rent to live in them. *There is a shortage of council housing... Council tenants around the country are planning a mass lobby of Parliament.* ADJ: ADJ n

3 **Council** is used in the names of some advisory or administrative groups. *...the National Council for Civil Liberties. ...the Arts Council. ...community health councils.* N-COUNT-COLL: usu in names

4 In some organizations, the **council** is the group of people that controls or governs it. *The permanent council of the Organization of American States meets today here in Washington. ...the Bundesbank's central council.* N-COUNT-COLL: usu sing, usu with supp

5 A **council** is a specially organized, formal meeting that is attended by a particular group of people. *President Najibullah said he would call a grand council of all Afghans... The president also meets ministers at inter-ministerial councils held at the Elysée Palace.* N-COUNT =assembly

councillor /kaʊnsələʳ/ **councillors;** spelled **councilor** in American English. A **councillor** is a member of a local council. *...the first black New York City councillor, Benjamin Davis Jr. ...Councillor Michael Poulter.* ◆◆◇◇◇ N-COUNT; N-TITLE

councilman /kaʊnsᵊlmən/ **councilmen.** In American English, a **councilman** is a man who is a member of a local council. The British word is **councillor**. *...a city councilman. ...Councilman Simpkins.* N-COUNT; N-TITLE

council of war, councils of war. A **council of war** is a meeting that is held in order to decide how a particular threat or emergency should be dealt with; a formal expression. N-COUNT

council tax. In Britain, the **council tax** is a tax that you pay to your local authority in order to pay for local services such as schools, libraries, and rubbish collection. The amount of council tax that you pay depends on the value of the house or flat where you live. ◆◇◇◇◇ N-UNCOUNT: also *the* N

councilwoman /kaʊnsᵊlwʊmən/ **councilwomen.** In American English, a **councilwoman** is a woman who is a member of a local council. The British word is **councillor**. *...a well-known Los Angeles City councilwoman. ...Councilwoman Johnson.* N-COUNT; N-TITLE

counsel /kaʊnsᵊl/ **counsels, counselling, counselled;** spelled **counseling**, **counselled** in American English. ◆◆◆◇◇

1 **Counsel** is advice; a formal use. *He had always been able to count on her wise counsel... His parishioners sought his counsel and loved him.* N-UNCOUNT =advice

2 If you **counsel** someone to take a course of action or if you **counsel** a course of action, you advise that course of action; a formal use. *My advisers counselled me to do nothing... The prime minister was right to counsel caution about military intervention.* VERB =advise V n to-inf V n Also V with quote

3 If you **counsel** people, you give them advice about their problems. *...a psychologist who counsels people with eating disorders... Crawford counsels her on all aspects of her career.* VERB V n V n *on* n Also V *on* n

4 Someone's **counsel** is the lawyer who gives them advice on a legal case and speaks on their behalf in court. *Singleton's counsel said after the trial that he would appeal... The defence counsel warned that the judge should stop the trial.* N-COUNT: oft supp N

5 If you **keep** your **own counsel**, you keep quiet about your opinions or intentions. *Guscott rarely speaks out, preferring to keep his own counsel.* PHRASE: V inflects

counselling /kaʊnsəlɪŋ/; spelled **counseling** in American English. **Counselling** is advice which a ◆◆◇◇◇ N-UNCOUNT therapist or other expert gives to someone about a particular problem. *She will need medical help and counselling to overcome the tragedy... She brought her husband in for marriage counseling.*

counsellor /kaʊnsələr/ **counsellors;** spelled **counselor** in American English. A **counsellor** is a person whose job is to give advice to people who need it, especially advice on their personal problems. *Children who have suffered like this should see a counsellor experienced in bereavement... They sought the help of a marriage counsellor.*
◆◆◇◇◇ N-COUNT

count /kaʊnt/ **counts, counting, counted** ◆◆◆◆◇

1 When you **count**, you say all the numbers one after another up to a particular number. *He was counting slowly under his breath... Brian counted to twenty and lifted his binoculars.*
VERB; V; V *to* num

2 If you **count** all the things in a group, you add them up in order to find how many there are. *At the last family wedding, George's wife counted the total number in the family... I counted the money. It was more than five hundred pounds... I counted 34 wild goats grazing... With more than 90 percent of the votes counted, the Liberals should win nearly a third of the seats.* ▶ **Count up** means the same as **count**. *Couldn't we just count up our ballots and bring them to the courthouse?* ♦ **counting** *The counting of votes is proceeding smoothly.*
VERB; V n; V num; V-ed; Also V; PHRASAL VERB; V P n (not pron); Also V n P; N-UNCOUNT: usu *the* N *of* n

3 A **count** is the action of counting a particular set of things, or the number that you get when you have counted them. *The final count in last month's referendum on the Maastricht treaty showed 56.7 per cent in favour... At the last count the police in the Rimini area had 247 people in custody.*
N-COUNT: usu supp N

4 You use **count** when referring to the level or amount of something that someone or something has; a scientific term. *A glass or two of wine will not significantly add to the calorie count... My husband had a very low sperm count.* ● See also **blood count, pollen count.**
N-COUNT: n N

5 You use **count** in expressions such as **a count of three** or **a count of ten** when you are measuring a length of time by counting slowly up to a certain number. *Hold your breath for a count of five, then slowly breathe out... The fight ended when Mendoza landed a hard right to the chin of Palacios, who went down for a count of eight.*
N-SING: N *of* num

6 If something or someone **counts** for something or **counts**, they are important or valuable. *Surely it doesn't matter where charities get their money from: what counts is what they do with it... It's as if your opinions, your likes and dislikes just don't count... When I first came to college I realised that brainpower didn't count for much... Experience counts for a lot in poker.*
VERB; =matter; V; V *for* amount

7 If something **counts** or **is counted** as a particular thing, it is regarded as being that thing, especially in particular circumstances or under particular rules. *You must remember that a conservatory counts as an extension... Any word that's not legible will be counted as wrong... Two of the trucks were stopped because they had tents in them, and under the commanders' definition of humanitarian aid, that didn't count... It can be counted a success, in that it has built up substantial sales.*
V-ERG; V *as* n/-ing/adj; *be* V-ed *as* n/-ing/adj; V; *be* V-ed n/adj; Also V n n/adj, V n *as* n/-ing/adj

8 If you **count** something when you are making a calculation, you include it in that calculation. *It's under 7 percent only because statistics don't count the people who aren't qualified to be in the work force... The years before their arrival in prison are not counted as part of their sentence.*
VERB; =include; V n; *be* V-ed *as* n; Also V n *as* n

9 You can use **count** to refer to one or more points that you are considering. For example, if someone is wrong **on two counts**, they are wrong in two ways. *'You drink Scotch,' she said. 'All Republicans drink Scotch.'—'Wrong on both counts. I'm a Democrat, and I drink bourbon.'*
N-COUNT: *on* supp N

10 In law, a **count** is one of a number of charges brought against someone in court. *He was indicted by a grand jury on two counts of murder.*
N-COUNT: usu N *of* n

11 If you **keep count** of a number of things, you note or keep a record of how many have occurred. If you **lose count** of a number of things, you cannot remember how many have occurred. *The authorities say they are not able to keep count of the bodies still being found as bulldozers clear the rubble... She'd lost count of the interviews she'd been called for.*
PHRASES; V inflects, oft PHR *of* n

12 If someone is **out for the count**, they are unconscious or very deeply asleep; an informal expression.
v-link PHR

13 If you say that someone should **stand up and be counted**, you mean that they should make public their opinion about something or their involvement in something, and not hide it or be ashamed of it. *Those involved and benefiting from it must be prepared to stand up and be counted.*

14 ● to **count** your **blessings**: see **blessing**.

count against. If something **counts against** you, it may cause you to be rejected or punished, or cause people to have a lower opinion of you. *He is highly regarded, but his youth might count against him.*
PHRASAL VERB; V P n

count in. If you tell someone to **count** you **in**, you mean that you want to be included in an activity. *'Count me in!' said a wiry Scotsman.*
PHRASAL VERB; usu imper; PRAGMATICS; V n P

count on or **count upon**
PHRASAL VERB

1 If you **count on** something or **count upon** it, you expect it to happen and include it in your plans. *The Communists thought they could count on the support of the trades unions... I'll be back. You can count on it... He is counting on winning seats and perhaps a share in the new government.*
=rely on; V P n/-ing

2 If you **count on** someone or **count upon** them, you rely on them to support you or help you. *Don't count on Lillian... I can always count on you to cheer me up... Diana seemed a strong young girl who could be counted upon to produce an heir.*
=rely on; V P n; V P n to-inf

count out
PHRASAL VERB

1 If you **count out** a sum of money, you count the notes or coins as you put them in a pile one by one. *Mr. Rohmbauer counted out the money and put it in an envelope.*
V P n (not pron); Also V n P

2 If you tell someone to **count** you **out**, you mean that you do not want to be included in an activity. *If this is the standard to which I have to drop to gain membership, then count me out!*
usu imper; PRAGMATICS; =exclude; V n P

count towards or **count toward.** If something **counts towards** or **counts toward** an achievement or entitlement, it is included as one of the things that give you the right to it. *In many courses, work from the second year onwards can count towards the final degree.*
PHRASAL VERB; V P n

count up. See **count** 2.
PHRASAL VERB

count upon. See **count on**.
PHRASAL VERB

Count /kaʊnt/ **Counts.** A **Count** is a European nobleman with the same rank as an English earl. *Her father was a Polish Count. ...Count Otto Lambsdorff, leader of the Free Democratic Party.*
◆◇◇◇◇ N-COUNT; N-TITLE; N-VOC

countable noun /kaʊntəbəl naʊn/ **countable nouns.** A **countable noun** is the same as a **count noun**.
N-COUNT

countdown /kaʊntdaʊn/. A **countdown** is the counting aloud of numbers in reverse order before something happens, especially before a spacecraft is launched. *The countdown has begun for the launch later today of the American space shuttle... There were three more things to do before countdown.*
◆◇◇◇◇ N-SING: also no det

countenance /kaʊntɪnəns/ **countenances, countenancing, countenanced** ◆◇◇◇◇

1 If someone will not **countenance** something, they do not agree with it and will not allow it to happen; a formal use. *Jake would not countenance Janis's marrying while still a student. ...the military men who refused to countenance the overthrow of the president.*
VB: usu with brd-neg; =tolerate; V n

2 Someone's **countenance** is their face; a literary use. *He met each inquiry with an impassive countenance.*
N-COUNT

counter /kaʊntər/ **counters, countering, countered** ◆◆◆◇◇

1 In a place such as a shop or café, a **counter** is a long narrow table or flat surface at which customers are served. *...those fellows we see working be-*
N-COUNT

hind the counter at our local video rental store. ...the cosmetics counter... We were sitting on stools at the counter having coffee.

2 If you do something to **counter** a particular action or process, you do something which has an opposite effect to it or makes it less effective. *The leadership discussed a plan of economic measures to counter the effects of such a blockade... Congestion could be countered by persuading more drivers to get on their bikes... Sears then countered by filing an antitrust lawsuit.* VERB V n V *by*-ing

3 Something that is **a counter to** something else has an opposite effect to it or makes it less effective. *...NATO's traditional role as a counter to the military might of the Warsaw pact.* N-SING: a N *to* n

4 If you **counter** something that someone has said, you say something which shows that you disagree with them or which proves that they are wrong. *Both of them had to counter fierce criticism by the Moscow intellectuals... The union countered with letters rebutting the company's claims... The Prime Minister countered by stating that he had grave misgivings about the advice he had been given... 'But Peter, it's not that simple,' Goldstone countered in a firm voice.* VERB V n V *with* n V *by*-ing V with quote Also V that

5 A **counter** is a mechanical or electronic device which keeps a count of something and displays the total. *...an answerphone with one-touch playback and LED display call counter.* N-COUNT: usu supp N

6 A **counter** is a small, flat, round object used in board games. N-COUNT

7 See also **bargaining counter**, **bean counter**, **Geiger counter**, **rev counter**.

8 If a medicine can be bought **over the counter**, you do not need a prescription to buy it. *Are you taking any other medicines (whether on prescription or bought over the counter)? ...basic over-the-counter remedies.* PHRASES

9 If one thing **runs counter to** another, or if one thing **is counter to** another, the first thing is the opposite of the second thing or conflicts with it; a formal expression. *Much of the plan runs counter to European Community agriculture and environmental policy... The finding ran counter to all expectations. ...the introduction of social legislation in Europe, which is counter to American practice.* V inflects, PHR *to* n

10 If someone buys or sells goods **under the counter**, they buy or sell them secretly and illegally. *The smugglers allegedly sold the gold under the counter, cheating the VAT man out of £5 million.* PHR after v

counter- /kaʊntəʳ-/. **Counter-** is used to form words which refer to actions or activities that are intended to prevent other actions or activities or that respond to them. *Intelligence activities will now be limited to counter-espionage. ...various counter-revolutionary activities. ...a counter-demonstration by anti-war protesters... In recent weeks, Abrams has counterattacked.* PREFIX

counteract /kaʊntərækt/ **counteracts, counteracting, counteracted.** To **counteract** something means to reduce its effect by doing something that produces an opposite effect. *My husband has to take several pills to counteract high blood pressure... This event will counteract such trends.* ◆◇◇◇◇ VERB V n

counter-argument, counter-arguments. A **counter-argument** is an argument that makes an opposing point to another argument; a formal word. *But the counter-argument to that is that political reform must go hand-in-hand with economic reform.* N-COUNT ≠argument

counter-attack, counter-attacks, counter-attacking, counter-attacked; also spelled **counterattack**. If you **counter-attack**, you attack someone who has attacked you. *The security forces counter-attacked the following day and quelled the unrest... Marion's father counter-attacked by saying that Blaze's claims were cruel and untrue.* ▶ Also a noun. *The army began its counter-attack this morning.* ◆◇◇◇◇ VERB =retaliate V Also V n N-COUNT

counterbalance /kaʊntəʳbæləns/ **counterbalances, counterbalancing, counterbalanced;** also spelled **counter-balance.**

1 To **counterbalance** something means to balance or correct it with something that has an equal but opposite effect. *Add honey to counterbalance the acidity... His patriarchal generosity is counterbalanced by his ruthlessness.* VERB =offset V n

2 Something that is a **counterbalance** to something else counterbalances that thing. *...organisations set up as a counterbalance to groups allied to the ANC.* N-COUNT: oft N *to* n

counterblast /kaʊntəʳblɑːst, -blæst/ **counterblasts;** also spelled **counter-blast**. A **counterblast** is a strong angry reply to something that has been said, written, or done; used in journalism. *Last week experts in Britain delivered a strong counter-blast to the Professor's claims.* N-COUNT: oft N *to* n

counterclockwise /kaʊntəʳklɒkwaɪz/; also spelled **counter-clockwise**. In American English, if something is moving **counterclockwise**, it is moving in the opposite direction to the direction in which the hands of a clock move. The British word is **anticlockwise**. *Rotate the head clockwise and counterclockwise.* ▶ Also an adjective. *The dance moves in a counter-clockwise direction.* ADV: ADV after v ≠clockwise ADJ: ADJ n ≠clockwise

counter-culture, counter-cultures; also spelled **counterculture**.

1 Counter-culture is a set of values, ideas, and ways of behaving that are completely different from those of the rest of society. *...a history of British counter-culture.* N-VAR

2 A **counter-culture** is a group in society whose values, ideas, and ways of behaving are completely different from those of the rest of society. *Not everyone joined the counterculture, not everyone demonstrated, dropped out, took drugs, or dodged the draft.* N-COUNT

counter-espionage; also spelled **counter espionage**. **Counter-espionage** consists of the measures that a country takes in order to find out whether another country is spying on it and to prevent it from doing so. N-UNCOUNT

counterfeit /kaʊntəʳfɪt/ **counterfeits, counterfeiting, counterfeited** ◆◇◇◇◇

1 Counterfeit money, goods, or documents are not genuine, but have been made to look exactly like genuine ones in order to deceive people. *He admitted possessing and delivering counterfeit currency.* ▶ Also a noun. *Levi Strauss says counterfeits of the company's jeans are flooding Europe.* ADJ: usu ADJ n =fake N-COUNT =fake

2 If someone **counterfeits** something, they make a version of it that is not genuine but has been made to look genuine in order to deceive people. *...the coins Davies is alleged to have counterfeited.* ♦ **counterfeiting** *The business of counterfeiting appears to be expanding.* ♦ **counterfeiter, counterfeiters** *...a gang of counterfeiters.* VERB V n N-UNCOUNT N-COUNT: usu pl

counterfoil /kaʊntəʳfɔɪl/ **counterfoils.** A **counterfoil** is the part of a cheque, ticket, or other document that you keep when you give the other part to someone else. N-COUNT

countermand /kaʊntəʳmɑːnd, -mænd/ **countermands, countermanding, countermanded.** If you **countermand** an order, you cancel it, usually by giving a different order; a formal word. *I can't countermand an order Winger's given.* VERB =reverse V n

counter-measure, counter-measures; also spelled **countermeasure**. A **counter-measure** is an action that you take in order to weaken the effect of another action or a situation, or to make it harmless. *Because the threat never developed, we didn't need to take any real countermeasures.* N-COUNT

counterpane /kaʊntəʳpeɪn/ **counterpanes.** A **counterpane** is a decorative cover on a bed; an old-fashioned word. N-COUNT

counterpart /kaʊntəʳpɑːʳt/ **counterparts.** Someone's or something's **counterpart** is another person or thing that has a similar function or position in a different place. *As soon as he heard what was afoot, the Foreign Secretary telephoned his German and Italian counterparts to protest...* ◆◆◆◇◇ N-COUNT: with supp, usu poss N =equivalent

The Finnish organization was very different from that of its counterparts in the rest of the Nordic region.

counterpoint /kaʊntəʳpɔɪnt/ **counterpoints, counterpointing, counterpointed**

1 Something that is a **counterpoint** to something else contrasts with it in a satisfying way; used mainly in journalism. *Paris is just a short train journey away, providing the perfect counterpoint to the peace and quiet of Reims.* N-COUNT: usu sing, oft N to n =complement

2 If one thing **counterpoints** another, it contrasts with it in a satisfying way; used in journalism. *A good sharp dressing counterpointed the sweetness of the dried fruit.* VERB V n

3 In music, **counterpoint** is a technique in which two or more different tunes are played together at the same time. *...lessons in counterpoint and harmony.* N-UNCOUNT

counter-productive; also spelled **counterproductive**. Something that is **counter-productive** achieves the opposite result from the one that you want to achieve. *In practice, however, such an attitude is counter-productive... It is counter-productive to address an interviewee in patronizing tones.* ◆◇◇◇◇ ADJ-GRADED: usu v-link ADJ

counter-revolution, counter-revolutions

1 A **counter-revolution** is a revolution that is intended to reverse the effects of a previous revolution. *The consequences of the counter-revolution have been extremely bloody.* N-COUNT

2 You can refer to activities that are intended to reverse the effects of a previous revolution as **counter-revolution**. *Such actions would be regarded as counter-revolution – a crime punishable by death.* N-UNCOUNT

counter-revolutionary, counter-revolutionaries

1 **Counter-revolutionary** activities are activities intended to reverse the effects of a previous revolution. *...counter-revolutionary propaganda.* ADJ

2 A **counter-revolutionary** is a person who is trying to reverse the effects of a previous revolution. N-COUNT

countersign /kaʊntəʳsaɪn/ **countersigns, countersigning, countersigned.** If you **countersign** a document, you sign it after someone else has signed it. *The President has so far refused to countersign the Prime Minister's desperate decree... Dolores, please come in and countersign a cheque.* VERB V n

countertenor /kaʊntəʳtenəʳ/ **countertenors;** also spelled **counter-tenor**. A **countertenor** is a man who sings with a high voice that is similar to a low female singing voice. N-COUNT =alto

countervailing /kaʊntəʳveɪlɪŋ/. A **countervailing** force, power, or opinion is one which is of equal strength to another one but is its opposite or opposes it. *Their strategy is expansionist and imperialist, and it is greatest in effect, of course, when there is no countervailing power... There were two central and countervailing forces in the life of Nikola Tesla.* ADJ: ADJ n

counterweight /kaʊntəʳweɪt/ **counterweights, counterweighting, counterweighted**

1 A **counterweight** is an action or proposal that is intended to balance or counter other actions or proposals. *His no-inflation bill serves as a useful counterweight to proposals less acceptable to the Committee.* N-COUNT: oft N n

2 If one action or proposal is intended to **counterweight** another, it is intended to balance or counter the other action or proposal. *This will be used to counterweight the capital gains argument.* VERB =counter V n

countess /kaʊntɪs/ **countesses.** A **countess** is a woman who has the same rank as a count or earl, or who is married to a count or earl. *...the Countess of Lichfield.* ◆◇◇◇◇ N-COUNT; N-TITLE; N-VOC

counting /kaʊntɪŋ/ ◆◇◇◇◇

1 **Not counting** a particular thing means not including that thing. **Counting** a particular thing means including that thing. *...an average operating profit of 15% to 16% of sales, not counting administrative expenses.* PREP =including

2 If you say **and counting** after a number or an amount of something, you mean that the number or amount is continuing to increase. *There is a 1,700-year-old tea tree still living in southern China which is more than 100-feet tall and counting.* PHRASE: amount PHR

countless /kaʊntləs/. **Countless** means very many. *She brought joy to countless people through her music... There are countless small ski areas dotted about the province.* ◆◆◇◇◇ ADJ: ADJ n =innumerable

count noun, count nouns. A **count noun** is a noun such as 'bird', 'chair', or 'year' which has a singular and a plural form and is always used after a determiner in the singular. N-COUNT =countable noun

countrified /kʌntrɪfaɪd/

1 You use **countrified** to describe something that seems or looks like something in the country, rather than in a town. *The house was so handsome, with a lovely countrified garden.* ADJ-GRADED: usu ADJ n

2 **Countrified** is used to describe pop music that sounds similar to country and western; used in journalism. *The sound veers between jazz and countrified blues.* ADJ-GRADED: usu ADJ n

country /kʌntri/ **countries** ◆◆◆◆◆

1 A **country** is one of the political units which the world is divided into, covering a particular area of land. *Indonesia is the fifth most populous country in the world. ...that disputed boundary between the two countries... Young people do move around the country quite a bit these days.* N-COUNT

2 The people who live in a particular country can be referred to as the **country**. *The country had confounded the pundits by electing a fourth-term Tory government... Seventy per cent of this country is opposed to blood sports.* N-SING: usu the N

3 **The country** consists of places such as farms, open fields, and villages which are away from towns and cities. *...a healthy life in the country... She was cycling along a country road near Compiegne... I was a simple country boy from Norfolk.* N-SING: the N =countryside

4 A particular kind of **country** is an area of land which has particular characteristics or is connected with a particular well-known person. *Varese Ligure is a small town in mountainous country east of Genoa. ...some of the best walking country in the Sierras... The Japanese visitors set off in search of Brontë country.* N-UNCOUNT: supp N

5 **Country** music is the same as country and western music. *For a long time I just wanted to play country music. ...a famous country singer named Katie Cocker.* N-UNCOUNT: usu N n

6 If you travel **across country**, you travel through country areas, avoiding major roads and towns. *From here we walked across country to Covington.* PHRASES v PHR

7 If you travel **across country**, you travel a long distance, from one part of a country to another. *We've just moved all the way across country to begin a new life.* v PHR

8 In British English, if a head of government or a government **goes to the country**, they hold a general election. *The Prime Minister does not have to go to the country for another year.* V inflects

country and western; also spelled **country-and-western. Country and western** is popular music in the style of white people's folk music of the southern United States. *...a successful country and western singer.* N-UNCOUNT: oft N n

country club, country clubs. A **country club** is a club in the country where you can play sports and attend social events. ◆◇◇◇◇ N-COUNT

country cousin, country cousins. If you refer to someone who comes from the country as a **country cousin**, you despise them slightly because they are unsophisticated and are inexperienced in city ways. N-COUNT PRAGMATICS

country dancing. Country dancing is traditional dancing in which people dance in rows or circles. N-UNCOUNT

country house, country houses. A **country house** is a large attractive house in the country, usually one that is or was owned by a rich or noble family. ◆◇◇◇◇ N-COUNT

countryman /kʌntrimən/ **countrymen** ◆◇◇◇◇
1 Your **countrymen** are people from your own country. *He beat his fellow countryman, Andre Agassi, 6-4, 6-3, 6-2.* N-COUNT: usu poss N =compatriot
2 A **countryman** is a person who lives in the country rather than in a city or a town. *He had the red face of a countryman.* N-COUNT

country seat, country seats. A **country seat** is a large house and estate in the country which is owned by someone who also owns a house in a town. *His family have a country seat in Oxfordshire.* N-COUNT

countryside /kʌntrisaɪd/. The **countryside** is land which is away from towns and cities. *I've always loved the English countryside... We are surrounded by lots of beautiful countryside.* ◆◆◆◇◇ N-UNCOUNT: oft *the* N

countrywide /kʌntriwaɪd/. Something that happens or exists **countrywide** happens or exists throughout the whole of a particular country. *Armed robbery and abduction have been on the increase countrywide... They sent out questionnaires to 100 schools countrywide.* ADV: ADV after v, n ADV ► Also an adjective. *...a countrywide network of volunteers.* ADJ: ADJ n

countrywoman /kʌntriwʊmən/ **countrywomen**
1 A **countrywoman** is a woman who lives in the country rather than in a city or a town. *She had the slow, soft voice of a countrywoman.* N-COUNT
2 Your **countrywomen** are women from your own country. *Britain's Martine Le Moignan defeated her countrywoman Suzanne Horner in four games.* N-COUNT: usu poss N =compatriot

county /kaʊnti/ **counties.** A **county** is a region of Britain, Ireland, or the USA which has its own local government. *He is living now in his mother's home county of Oxfordshire... Over 50 events are planned throughout the county.* ◆◆◆◆◇ N-COUNT

county council, county councils. A **county council** is an organization which administers local government in a county in Britain. *...Devon County Council.* ◆◇◇◇◇ N-COUNT: oft in names after n

county seat, county seats. In American English, a **county seat** is the most important town in a county, from which the county is administered. The British term is **county town**. *...Glasgow, the county seat of Barren County, Kentucky.* N-COUNT

county town, county towns. In British English, a **county town** is the most important town in a county, from which the county is administered. The American term is **county seat**. *We met in Dorchester, Dorset's bustling county town.* N-COUNT

coup /kuː/ **coups** ◆◆◆◇◇
1 When there is a **coup**, a group of people seize power in a country. *...a military coup... They were sentenced to death for their part in April's coup attempt.* N-COUNT =coup d'état
2 A **coup** is an achievement which is thought to be especially brilliant because it was very difficult. *The sale is a big coup for the auction house... Regency Opera have scored something of a coup by persuading her to undertake the role.* N-COUNT

coup de grace /kuː də grɑːs/. A **coup de grace** is an action or event which finally destroys something, for example an institution, which has been gradually growing weaker; a formal expression. *He has alienated almost all his colleagues and may have given the coup de grace to the party itself.* N-SING =deathblow

coup d'état /kuː deɪtɑː/ **coups d'état.** When there is a **coup d'état**, a group of people seize power in a country. ◆◇◇◇◇ N-COUNT =coup

coupé /kuːpeɪ, AM kuːp/ **coupés.** A **coupé** is a car with a fixed roof, a sloping back, two doors, and seats for four people. ◆◇◇◇◇ N-COUNT

couple /kʌpᵊl/ **couples, coupling, coupled** ◆◆◆◆◇
1 If you refer to **a couple of** people or things, you mean two or approximately two of them, although the exact number is not important or you are not sure of it; an informal use. *Across the street from me there are a couple of police officers standing guard... I think the trouble will clear up in a couple of days. ...a small working-class town in Massachusetts, a couple of hundred miles from New York City.* QUANT: QUANT *of* pl-n ► Also a determiner in spoken American English, and before 'more' and 'less'. *...a couple weeks before the election... I think I can play maybe for a couple more years.* DET ► Also a pronoun. *I've got a couple that don't look too bad.* PRON
2 A **couple** is two people who are married, living together, or having a sexual relationship. *The couple have no children. ...after burglars ransacked an elderly couple's home. ...an isolated spot popular with courting couples.* N-COUNT-COLL
3 A **couple** is two people that you see together on a particular occasion or that have some association. *...as the four couples began the opening dance... They were an odd couple.* N-COUNT-COLL
4 If you say that one thing produces a particular effect when it **is coupled with** another, you mean that the two things combine to produce that effect. *...a problem that is coupled with lower demand for the machines themselves... Over-use of those drugs, coupled with poor diet, leads to physical degeneration... This, coupled with the fact that flying machines remained universally a subject for jeers and derision, made the brothers secretive.* VB: usu passive =combine *be* V-ed *with* n V-ed
5 If one piece of equipment **is coupled** to another, it is joined to it so that the two pieces of equipment work together. *Its engine is coupled to a semiautomatic gearbox... The various elementary detector systems are coupled together in complex arrays.* VB: usu passive *be* V-ed *to* n *be* V-ed *together*
♦ **coupling** *The technique requires the coupling of a particle accelerator and a mass spectrometer.* N-SING: usu *the* N *of* n
6 See also **coupling**.

couplet /kʌplɪt/ **couplets.** A **couplet** is two lines of poetry which come next to each other, especially two lines that rhyme with each other and are the same length. *...rhyming couplets.* N-COUNT

coupling /kʌplɪŋ/ **couplings** ◆◇◇◇◇
1 A **coupling** is a device which is used to join two vehicles or pieces of equipment together. *Before driving away, re-check the trailer coupling.* N-COUNT: oft supp N
2 When two different things, ideas, or activities are combined, or when two people work together, you can refer to this combination as a **coupling**; used in written English. *Anton the chef concocts a sensual coupling of lobster and asparagus... The uneasy coupling of fascism and conservatism spawned a new kind of political regime... Morrissey and Prince: the unlikeliest musical coupling of the year.* N-COUNT: usu sing, usu N *of* pl-n =combination, union
3 An act of sexual intercourse is sometimes referred to as a **coupling**; a formal use. *...sexual couplings.* N-COUNT
4 See also **couple**.

coupon /kuːpɒn/ **coupons** ◆◆◇◇◇
1 A **coupon** is a piece of printed paper which is issued by the maker or supplier of a product and which allows you to pay less money than usual for it. *Bring the coupon below to any Tecno store and pay just £10.99. ...a 50p money-off coupon.* N-COUNT =voucher
2 A **coupon** is a small form, for example in a newspaper or magazine, which you send off to ask for information, to order something, or to enter a competition. *Send the coupon with a cheque for £18.50, made payable to 'Good Housekeeping'... He was filling in his pools coupon.* N-COUNT
3 A **coupon** is a piece of printed paper issued by the government that gives you the right to buy a product that is rationed. *...ration coupons.* N-COUNT

courage /kʌrɪdʒ, AM kɜːr-/ ◆◆◆◇◇
1 **Courage** is the quality shown by someone who decides to do something difficult or dangerous, even though they may be afraid. *General Lewis Mackenzie has impressed everyone with his authority and personal courage... They do not have the courage to apologise for their actions.* • See also **Dutch courage**. N-UNCOUNT =bravery
2 If you have **the courage of** your **convictions**, you have the confidence to do what you believe is right, even though other people may not agree or approve. *Developers should have the courage of their convictions and stick to what they do best.* • to **pluck up the courage**: see **pluck**. PHRASE: PHR after v

courageous /kəreɪdʒəs/. Someone who is **courageous** shows courage. *It was a very frightening* ◆◇◇◇◇ ADJ-GRADED =brave *experience and they were very courageous... It was a courageous decision, and one that everybody admired.* ♦ **courageously.** *If Coetzer fights as courageously as he did against Bowe, it could be an interesting night.* ADV-GRADED: ADV with v

courgette /kʊəʳʒet/ **courgettes.** In British English, **courgettes** are long thin green vegetables of the marrow family. The usual American word is **zucchini**. ◆◇◇◇◇ N-VAR

courier /kʊriəʳ/ **couriers** ◆◆◇◇◇

1 A **courier** is a person who is paid to take letters and parcels direct from one place to another. *He worked as a motorcycle courier... The cheques were delivered to the bank by a private courier firm.* N-COUNT

2 A **courier** is a person employed by a travel company to look after people who are on holiday. N-COUNT =rep

course /kɔːʳs/ **courses, coursing, coursed** ◆◆◆◆◆

1 Course is often used in the expression 'of course', or instead of 'of course' in informal spoken English. See **of course**. =of course

2 The **course** of a vehicle, especially a ship or aircraft, is the route along which it is travelling. *Aircraft can avoid each other by going up and down, as well as by altering course to left or right... The tug was seaward of the Hakai Passage on a course that diverged from the Calvert Island coastline.* N-UNCOUNT: also a N

3 A **course** of action is an action or a series of actions that you can do in a particular situation. *My best course of action was to help Gill by being loyal, loving and endlessly sympathetic... He must fall on his sword. That's the only course left open to him... Vietnam is trying to decide on its course for the future.* N-COUNT: usu sing

4 You can refer to the way that events develop as, for example, **the course of history** or **the course of events**. *...a series of decisive naval battles which altered the course of history... In the natural course of events cows would wish to be milked more than twice a day... His adult life mirrored the downward course of his father's life.* N-SING: the N of n

5 A **course** is a series of lessons or lectures on a particular subject. *...a course in business administration... I'm shortly to begin a course on the modern novel.* • See also **access course**, **correspondence course**, **refresher course**, **sandwich course**. N-COUNT: oft N in/on n

6 A **course of** medical treatment is a series of treatments that a doctor gives someone. *Treatment is supplemented with a course of antibiotics to kill the bacterium... She went to her doctor, who offered to put her on a course of tranquillizers.* N-COUNT: N of n

7 A **course** is one part of a meal. *The lunch was excellent, especially the first course. ...a three-course dinner.* N-COUNT: usu supp N

8 In sport, a **course** is an area of land where races are held or golf is played, or the land over which a race takes place. *Only 12 seconds separated the first three riders on the Bickerstaffe course... In July comes the Tour de France, when 200 cyclists cover a course of 2,000 miles.* N-COUNT: usu with supp

9 The **course** of a river is the channel along which it flows. *Romantic chateaux and castles overlook the river's twisting course.* N-COUNT

10 If a liquid **courses** somewhere, it flows quickly; a literary use. *The tears coursed down his cheeks... When you're sitting still, you need less blood coursing through your arteries.* VERB =run V prep/adv

11 If something happens **in the course of** a particular period of time, it happens during that period of time. *In the course of the 1930s steel production in Britain approximately doubled... We struck up a conversation, in the course of which it emerged that he was a sailing man.* PHRASES PREP =during

12 If you do something **as a matter of course**, you do it as part of your normal work or way of life. *If police are carrying arms as a matter of course then doesn't it encourage criminals to carry them?* PHR after v

13 If a ship or aircraft is **on course**, it is travelling along the correct route. If it is **off course**, it is no longer travelling along the correct route. *The ill fated ship was sent off course into shallow waters and rammed by another vessel.* PHR after v, v-link PHR

14 If you are **on course for** something, you are likely to achieve it. *England are well on course for a place at the 1998 World Cup Finals... The company is on course for profits of £20m in 1992.* PREP: usu v-link PREP

15 If something **runs its course** or **takes its course**, it develops naturally and comes to a natural end. *They estimated that between 17,000 and 20,000 cows would die before the epidemic had run its course... As for the imprisoned leaders, he asserted that justice would have to take its course.* V inflects

16 If you **stay the course**, you finish something that you have started, even though it has become very difficult. *The oldest president in American history had stayed the course for two terms.* V inflects

17 If something changes or becomes true **in the course of time**, it changes or becomes true over a long period of time. *In the course of time, many of their myths become entangled.* PHR with cl

18 • **in due course**: see **due**.

course book, course books; also spelled **coursebook**. A **course book** is a textbook that students and teachers use as the basis of a course. N-COUNT

course work; also spelled **coursework**. **Course work** is work that students do during the year, rather than in exams, especially work that counts towards a student's final grade. *Some 20 per cent of marks are awarded for coursework.* N-UNCOUNT

coursing /kɔːʳsɪŋ/. **Coursing** is a sport in which rabbits or hares are hunted with dogs. N-UNCOUNT

court 1 noun uses

court /kɔːʳt/ **courts** ◆◆◆◆◆

1 A **court** is a place where legal matters are decided by a judge and jury or by a magistrate. *At this rate, we could find ourselves in the divorce courts! ...a county court judge... He was deported on a court order following a conviction for armed robbery... The 28-year-old striker was in court last week for breaking a rival player's jaw.* N-COUNT: oft n N, N n, also in/at N

2 You can refer to the people in a court, especially the judge, jury, or magistrates, as a **court**. *A court at Tampa, Florida has convicted five officials on charges of handling millions of dollars earned from illegal drugs deals.* N-COUNT

3 A **court** is an area in which you play a game such as tennis, badminton, or squash. *The hotel has several tennis and squash courts... Graf watched a few of the games while waiting to go on court against Tauziat.* N-COUNT: usu supp N, also on/off N

4 The **court** of a king or queen is the place where he or she lives and carries out ceremonial or administrative duties. *She came to visit England, where she was presented at the court of James I... Their family was certainly well regarded at court.* N-COUNT: oft with poss, also at N

5 In Britain, **Court** is used in the names of large houses and blocks of flats. *...7 Ivebury Court, Latimer Rd, London W10 6RA.* N-IN-NAMES: n N

6 See also **Crown Court**, **High Court**, **kangaroo court**.

7 If you **go to court** or **take** someone **to court**, you take legal action against them. *They have received at least twenty thousand pounds each but had gone to court to demand more. ...members of trade associations who want to take bad debtors to court.* PHRASES V inflects

8 If someone **holds court** in a place, they are surrounded by a lot of people who are paying them a lot of attention because they are interesting or famous. *...in the days when Marlene Dietrich and Ernest Hemingway held court in the famous El Floridita club.* V inflects

9 If you **laugh** someone **out of court**, you say that their opinions or ideas are so ridiculous that they are not worth considering. *It's easy for a younger generation of critics to laugh Limon out of court... Polytechnic lecturers have asked for 12.5 per cent, a claim sure to be laughed out of court.* V inflects

10 If a legal matter is decided or settled **out of court**, it is decided without legal action being taken in a court of law. *The Government is anxious to keep the whole case out of court. ...a payment of two million pounds in an out of court settlement to a fifteen-year-old Scottish boy.* PHR after v, PHR n

court 2 verb uses

court /kɔːʳt/ **courts, courting, courted** ◆◆◇◇◇

1 If you **are courting** someone of the opposite sex, you spend a lot of time with them, because you are intending to get married. You can also say that a man and a woman **are courting**. An old-fashioned use. *I was courting Billy at 19 and married him when I was 21... Derek criticised every aspect of Pauline's behaviour, something he had never done when they were courting. ...an isolated spot popular with courting couples.*
V-RECIP: usu cont; V n; pl-n V; V-ing

2 To **court** a particular person, group, or country means to try to please them or improve your relations with them, often so that they will do something that you want them to do; used in journalism. *Both Democratic and Republican parties are courting former supporters of Ross Perot... Stars are courted by manufacturers who value their influence on style-conscious fans.*
VERB =cultivate; V n

3 If you **court** something such as publicity or popularity, you try to attract it. *Having spent a lifetime avidly courting publicity, Paul has suddenly become secretive. ...his ability to get things done, usually by manipulating, courting favour or cleverly finding a way around opponents.*
VERB; V n

4 If you **court** something unpleasant such as disaster or unpopularity, you act in a way that makes it likely to happen. *If he thinks he can remain in power by force he is courting disaster... They argue that the commission should risk courting unpopularity and push on with its legislative programmes.*
VERB =invite; V n

courteous /kɜːʳtiəs/. Someone who is **courteous** is polite, respectful, and considerate. *He was a kind and courteous man... My friend's reply was courteous but firm.* ♦ **courteously** *Then he nodded courteously to me and walked off to perform his unpleasant duty.*
◆◇◇◇◇ ADJ-GRADED =polite ≠rude; ADV-GRADED: usu ADV with v, also ADV adj

courtesan /kɔːʳtɪzæn, AM -zən/ **courtesans.** In former times, a woman who was looked after by the rich and important men that she had sexual relationships with was referred to a **courtesan**.
N-COUNT

courtesy /kɜːʳtɪsi/ **courtesies** ◆◆◇◇◇

1 **Courtesy** is politeness, respect, and consideration for others; a formal use. *...a gentleman who behaves with the utmost courtesy towards ladies... He did not even have the courtesy to reply to my fax.*
N-UNCOUNT =politeness ≠rudeness

2 If you refer to the **courtesy** of doing something, you are referring to a polite action; a formal use. *By extending the courtesy of a phone call to my clients, I was building a personal relationship with them... At least if they're arguing, they're doing you the courtesy of being interested.*
N-SING: usu *the* N *of* -ing/n

3 **Courtesies** are polite, conventional things that people say in formal situations; a formal use. *Hugh and John were exchanging barbed courtesies.*
N-COUNT: usu pl =formalities

4 **Courtesy** is used to describe services that are provided free of charge by an organization to its customers, or to the general public. *A courtesy shuttle bus operates between the hotel and the town. ...a courtesy phone.*
ADJ: ADJ n

5 A **courtesy** call or a **courtesy** visit is a formal visit that you pay someone as a way of showing them politeness or respect. *Mr Havel also met President Francesco Cossiga, and paid a courtesy call on Pope John Paul.*
ADJ: ADJ n

6 A **courtesy** title is a title that someone is allowed to use, although it has no legal or official status. *Both were accorded the courtesy title of Lady... My title, by courtesy only, is the Honourable Amalia Lovell.*
N-UNCOUNT: N n, *by* N

7 If you say that something is provided **courtesy of** someone or **by courtesy of** someone, you are saying that they provided it, and often thanking them for it or suggesting that it was provided as a favour. *The waitress brings over some congratulatory glasses of champagne, courtesy of the restaurant... Illustrations by courtesy of the National Gallery.*
PHRASES PREP PRAGMATICS

8 If you say that one thing happens **courtesy of** another or **by courtesy of** another, you mean that the second thing causes or is responsible for the first thing. *The air was fresh, courtesy of three holes in the roof... As millions will have seen, by courtesy of the slow motion re-runs, the referee made a mistake.*
PREP

courthouse /kɔːʳthaʊs/ **courthouses.** A **courthouse** is a building in which a court of law meets; used mainly in American English. The usual British word is **court**.
◆◇◇◇◇ N-COUNT

courtier /kɔːʳtiəʳ/ **courtiers. Courtiers** were noblemen and women who spent a lot of time at the court of a king or queen.
◆◇◇◇◇ N-COUNT

courtly /kɔːʳtli/. You use **courtly** to describe someone whose behaviour is very polite and well-mannered, often in a rather old-fashioned way; a literary word. *Brian was courtly and reserved... The waiter made a courtly bow.*
ADJ-GRADED =gracious

court-martial, court-martials, court-martialling, court-martialled; spelled **court-martialing, court-martialed** in American English. ◆◇◇◇◇

1 A **court-martial** is a trial in a military court of a member of the armed forces who is charged with breaking a military law. *He is due to face a court martial on drugs charges... He was arrested, tried by court martial and shot.*
N-VAR

2 If a member of the armed forces **is court-martialled**, he or she is tried in a military court. *I was court-martialled and sentenced to six months in a military prison.*
VB: usu passive *be* V-ed

court of appeal, courts of appeal. A **court of appeal** is a court which deals with appeals against legal judgements. *The case is being referred to the Court of Appeal.*
◆◇◇◇◇ N-COUNT

court of inquiry, courts of inquiry

1 A **court of inquiry** is a group of people who are officially appointed to investigate a serious accident or incident. *On January 17, Daniels appointed a court of inquiry to look into the Newport scandal.*
N-COUNT

2 A **court of inquiry** is an official investigation into a serious accident or incident. *Isherwood was at the court of inquiry to hear the evidence.*
N-COUNT

court of law, courts of law. When you refer to a **court of law**, you are referring to a legal court, especially when talking about the evidence that might be given in a trial. *We have a witness who would swear to it in a court of law.*
N-COUNT

courtroom /kɔːʳtruːm/ **courtrooms.** A **courtroom** is a room in which a legal court meets.
◆◇◇◇◇ N-COUNT

courtship /kɔːʳtʃɪp/ **courtships** ◆◇◇◇◇

1 **Courtship** is the activity of courting or the time during which a man and a woman are courting; an old-fashioned use. *They were more interested in courtship and cars than in school... After a short courtship, she accepted his marriage proposal.*
N-VAR

2 The **courtship** of male and female animals is their behaviour before they mate. *Courtship is somewhat vocal with a lot of displaying by the male. ...elaborate courtship dances.*
N-UNCOUNT

court shoe, court shoes. In British English, **court shoes** are ladies' shoes that do not cover the top part of the foot and are usually made of plain leather with no design; the usual American word is **pumps**.
N-COUNT

courtyard /kɔːʳtjɑːʳd/ **courtyards.** A **courtyard** is an open area of ground, often paved, which is surrounded by buildings or walls. *They walked through the arch and into the cobbled courtyard.*
◆◇◇◇◇ N-COUNT

couscous /kuːskuːs/. **Couscous** is a type of food that is made from crushed steamed semolina, or a dish consisting of this food served with a spicy stew. It is traditionally eaten in North Africa.
N-UNCOUNT

cousin /kʌzᵊn/ **cousins** ◆◆◆◆◇

1 Your **cousin** is the child of your uncle or aunt. *My cousin Mark helped me... We are cousins.* • See also **second cousin**.
N-COUNT: oft with poss =first cousin

2 If you refer to two things or groups of people as **cousins**, you mean that they are equivalents or that there is a connection between them. *Whereas West Germans drink wine, their Eastern cousins prefer Schnapps... The average European kitchen is smaller than its American cousin. ...misanthropy and its cousin racism.* • See also **country cousin**.
N-COUNT

couture /kuːtjʊəʳ, AM -tʊr/. **Couture** refers to the designing and making of high-quality fashion
◆◇◇◇◇ N-UNCOUNT: oft N n

clothes, or to the clothes themselves; a formal word. ...*Christian Lacroix's first Paris couture collection.* =haute couture

couturier /kuːtʊəriei, AM kuːturieɪ/ **couturiers.** A **couturier** is a person who designs, makes, and sells expensive, high-quality fashion clothes for women. *The Paris couturiers showed their collections for winter last week.* N-COUNT =designer

cove /koʊv/ **coves.** A **cove** is a small bay on the coast. *He knew a little cove where hardly anyone went. ...a hillside overlooking Fairview Cove.* ◆◇◇◇◇ N-COUNT: oft in names after n

coven /kʌvən/ **covens.** A **coven** is a group of witches that meet together. N-COUNT-COLL

covenant /kʌvənənt/ **covenants** ◆◇◇◇◇

1 A **covenant** is a formal written agreement between two or more people or groups of people which is recognized in law. *...the International Covenant on Civil and Political Rights.* N-COUNT

2 A **covenant** is a formal written promise to pay a sum of money each year for a fixed period, especially to a charity. *If you make regular gifts through a covenant we can reclaim the income tax which you have already paid on this money.* N-COUNT: also *by* N

Coventry /kɒvəntri, AM kʌvɪntri/. If people **send** you **to Coventry**, they avoid speaking to you whenever they meet you, as a way of punishing you for something that you have done; a British expression. PHRASE: V inflects =ostracize

cover /kʌvəʳ/ **covers, covering, covered** ◆◆◆◆◆

1 If you **cover** something, you place something else over it in order to protect it, hide it, or close it. *Cover the casserole with a tight-fitting lid... He whimpered and covered his face... Keep what's left in a covered container in the fridge.* VERB V n *with* n V n V-ed

2 If something **covers** something else, it has been placed over it in order to protect it, hide it, or close it. *His finger went up to touch the black patch which covered his left eye... His head was covered with a khaki turban.* VERB V n

3 If something **covers** something else, it forms a layer over its surface. *The clouds had spread and nearly covered the entire sky... Two oil slicks are covering a total area of seven square miles... The desk was covered with papers... I looked in the mirror and saw that my face was covered in blood.* ♦ **-covered** *...chocolate-covered biscuits.* VERB V n be V-ed *with/in* n COMB in ADJ

4 To **cover** something **with** or **in** something else means to put a layer of the second thing over its surface. *The trees in your garden may have covered the ground with apples, pears or plums... She covered the walls with the signs of the zodiac.* VERB V n *with/in* n

5 If you **cover** a particular distance, you travel that distance. *It would not be easy to cover ten miles on that amount of petrol... It covered the distance in 28 hours compared with the train's six days.* VERB V n

6 To **cover** someone or something means to protect them from attack, for example by pointing a gun in the direction of people who may attack them, ready to fire the gun if necessary. *You go first. I'll cover you.* VERB V n

7 Cover is protection from enemy attack that is provided for troops or ships carrying out a particular operation, for example by aircraft. *They said they could not provide adequate air cover for ground operations.* N-UNCOUNT =protection

8 Cover is trees, rocks, or other places where you shelter from the weather or from an attack, or hide from someone. *Charles lit the fuses and they ran for cover. ...barren wastes of field with no trees and no cover.* N-UNCOUNT =shelter

9 An insurance policy that **covers** a person or thing guarantees that money will be paid by the insurance company in relation to that person or thing. *Their insurer paid the £900 bill, even though the policy did not strictly cover it... These items are not covered by your medical insurance... You should take out travel insurance covering you and your family against theft.* VERB V n V n *against* n

10 Insurance **cover** is a guarantee from an insurance company that money will be paid by them if it is needed. *Make sure that the firm's insurance cover is adequate.* N-UNCOUNT =protection

11 If a law **covers** a particular set of people, things, or situations, it applies to them. *The law covers four categories of experiments... Like any other commodity, pedigree dogs are covered by the Sale of Goods Act.* VERB =deal with V n

12 If you **cover** a particular topic, you discuss it in a lecture, course, or book. *The Oxford Chemistry Primers aim to cover important topics in organic chemistry... Other subjects covered included nerves and how to overcome them.* VERB =deal with V n V-ed

13 If reporters, newspapers, or television companies **cover** an event, they report on it. *Robinson was sent to Italy to cover the 1990 World Cup... The US news media will cover the trial closely.* VERB V n

14 If a sum of money **covers** something, it is enough to pay for it. *Send it to the address given with £1.50 to cover postage and administration... Those figures might not even cover the cost of breakages.* VERB =pay for V n

15 A **cover** is something which is put over an object, usually in order to protect it. *...a family room with washable covers on the furniture. ...a duvet cover.* N-COUNT: oft n N

16 The **covers** on your bed are the sheet, blankets, and bedspread that you have on top of you. *She set her glass down and slid farther under the covers.* N-PLURAL: usu *the* N =bedclothes

17 The **cover** of a book or a magazine is the outside part of it. *A few years ago, David Byrne was on the cover of Time magazine. ...a small spiral-bound booklet with a green cover... I used to read every issue from cover to cover.* N-COUNT

18 Something that is a **cover** for secret or illegal activities seems respectable or normal, and is intended to hide the activities. *They set up a spurious temple that was a cover for sexual debauchery... As a cover story he generally tells people he is a freelance photographer.* N-COUNT: usu sing =front

19 If you **cover for** someone who is doing something secret or illegal, you give false information or do not give all the information you have, in order to protect them. *Why would she cover for someone who was trying to kill her?* VERB V *for* n

20 If you **cover for** someone who is ill or away, you do their work for them while they are absent. *She did not have enough nurses to cover for those who went ill or took holiday.* VERB V *for* n

21 To **cover** a song originally performed by someone else means to record a new version of it. *He must make a decent living from other artists covering his songs.* VERB V n

22 A **cover** is the same as a **cover version**. *The single is a cover of an old Rolling Stones song.* N-COUNT: usu N *of* n

23 See also **covered, covering**.

24 To **blow** someone's **cover** means to cause their true identity or the true nature of their work to be revealed. *Asking those kind of questions could blow my cover... The young man looked embarrassed, as if he were a spy whose cover had been blown.* PHRASES V inflects

25 If you **break cover**, you leave a place where you have been hiding or sheltering from attack, usually in order to run to another place. *They began running again, broke cover and dashed towards the road.* V inflects

26 If you **take cover**, you shelter from gunfire, bombs, or the weather. *Shoppers took cover behind cars as police marksmen returned fire.* V inflects, oft PHR prep =shelter

27 If you are **under cover**, you are under something that protects you from gunfire, bombs, or the weather. *'Get under cover!' shouted Billy, and we darted once more for the tables.* PHR after v, v-link PHR

28 If you do something **under cover of** a particular situation, you are able to do it without being noticed because of that situation. *They move under cover of darkness.* PREP

cover up PHRASAL VERB

1 If you **cover** something or someone **up**, you put something over them in order to protect or hide them. *He fell asleep in the front room so I covered him up with a duvet.* V n P Also V P n (not pron)

2 If you **cover up** something that you do not want people to know about, you conceal the truth about it. *He suspects there's a conspiracy to cover up the* V P n (not pron) *crime... They knew they had done something terribly wrong and lied to cover it up... How do we know you're not just covering up for your friend?* • See also **cover-up**. V n P; V P *for* n

coverage /kʌvərɪdʒ/. The **coverage** of something in the news is the reporting of it. *Now a special TV network gives live coverage of most races... Most media coverage disapproves of the travellers' lifestyle and values.* ◆◆◆◇◇ N-UNCOUNT

cover charge, cover charges. A **cover charge** is a sum of money that you must pay in some restaurants and nightclubs in addition to the money that you pay there for your food and drink. N-COUNT: usu sing

covered /kʌvəʳd/. A **covered** area is an area that has a roof. *There are 40 shops, cafes and restaurants in a covered mall.* ◆◇◇◇◇ ADJ: ADJ n

covered wagon, covered wagons. A **covered wagon** is a horse-drawn wagon with an arched canvas roof. Covered wagons were used by the early American settlers as they travelled across the country. N-COUNT

cover girl, cover girls. A **cover girl** is an attractive woman whose photograph appears on the front of a magazine. N-COUNT

covering /kʌvərɪŋ/ **coverings.** A **covering** is a layer of something that protects or hides something else. *Leave a thin covering of fat... Sawdust was used as a hygienic floor covering.* ◆◆◇◇◇ N-COUNT

covering letter, covering letters. A **covering letter** is a letter that you send with a parcel or with another letter in order to provide extra information. N-COUNT

coverlet /kʌvəʳlɪt/ **coverlets.** A **coverlet** is the same as a **bedspread**; an old-fashioned word. N-COUNT

covert /kʌvəʳt, koʊvɜːʳt/ **coverts** ◆◇◇◇◇

1 **Covert** activities or situations are secret or hidden; a formal use. *They have been supplying covert military aid to the rebels... The depth of covert racism in my own profession frightens me.* ♦ **covertly** *They covertly observed Lauren, who was sitting between Ned and Algie at a nearby table.* ADJ-GRADED: usu ADJ n ≠overt; ADV-GRADED: usu ADV with v ≠overtly

2 A **covert** is a group of small trees or bushes very close to each other where small animals or game birds can hide. N-COUNT

cover-up, cover-ups. A **cover-up** is an attempt to hide a crime or mistake. *General Schwarzkopf denied there'd be any cover-up.* ◆◇◇◇◇ N-COUNT =whitewash

cover version, cover versions. A **cover version** of a song is a version of it recorded by a singer or band who did not originally perform the song. *...a new album of Cole Porter cover versions.* ◆◇◇◇◇ N-COUNT: oft N *of* n =cover

covet /kʌvɪt/ **covets, coveting, coveted.** If you **covet** something, you strongly want to have it for yourself; a formal word. *She coveted his job so openly that conversations between them were tense.* VERB =desire; V n

coveted /kʌvɪtɪd/. You use **coveted** to describe something that very many people would like to have. *Allan Little from Radio 4 took the coveted title of reporter of the year. ...one of sport's most coveted trophies. ...a supply of highly coveted hard currency.* ◆◇◇◇◇ ADJ-GRADED: usu ADJ n

covetous /kʌvɪtəs/. Someone who is **covetous** has a strong desire to possess something, especially something that belongs to another person; a formal word, used showing disapproval. *Even here a red Lamborghini Diablo sports car attracts covetous stares.* ADJ-GRADED PRAGMATICS

covey /kʌvi/ **coveys.** A **covey** of grouse or partridges is a small group of them. N-COUNT: oft N *of* n

cow /kaʊ/ **cows, cowing, cowed** ◆◆◆◇◇

1 A **cow** is a large female animal that is kept on farms for its milk. People sometimes refer to male and female animals of this species as **cows**. *He kept a few dairy cows... Dad went out to milk the cows. ...a herd of cows.* • See also **cattle**. N-COUNT

2 Some female animals, including elephants and whales, are called **cows**. *...a cow elephant.* N-COUNT: oft N n

3 If someone describes a woman as a **cow**, they dislike her and think that she is unpleasant or stupid; an offensive use. N-COUNT PRAGMATICS

4 If someone **is cowed**, they are made afraid, or made to behave in a particular way because they have been frightened or oppressed; a formal use. *The government, far from being cowed by these threats, has vowed to continue its policy. ...cowing them into submission.* ♦ **cowed** *By this time she was so cowed by the beatings that she meekly obeyed.* VERB =intimidate; *be* V-ed; V n *into* n/-ing; ADJ-GRADED: oft ADJ *by* n

5 If you say that someone can do something **until the cows come home**, but it will have no effect, you are emphasizing that it will have no effect even if they do it for a very long time; an informal expression. *You can initiate policies until the cows come home, but unless they're monitored at a senior level, you won't get results.* PHRASE: PHR after v PRAGMATICS

6 See also **mad cow disease, sacred cow**.

coward /kaʊəʳd/ **cowards.** If you call someone a **coward**, you disapprove of them because they are easily frightened and avoid dangerous or difficult situations. *She accused her husband of being a coward.* ◆◇◇◇◇ N-COUNT PRAGMATICS

cowardice /kaʊəʳdɪs/. **Cowardice** is cowardly behaviour. *He openly accused his opponents of cowardice.* N-UNCOUNT ≠bravery, courage

cowardly /kaʊəʳdli/. If you describe someone as **cowardly**, you disapprove of them because they are easily frightened and avoid doing dangerous and difficult things. *I was too cowardly to complain. ...a cowardly act of violence.* ◆◇◇◇◇ ADJ-GRADED PRAGMATICS ≠brave, courageous

cowbell /kaʊbel/ **cowbells.** A **cowbell** is a small bell that is hung around a cow's neck so that the ringing sound makes it possible to find the cow. N-COUNT

cowboy /kaʊbɔɪ/ **cowboys** ◆◆◇◇◇

1 A **cowboy** is a man employed to look after cattle in the United States, especially in former times. N-COUNT

2 A **cowboy** is a male character in a western. *Boys used to play at cowboys and Indians. ...cowboy films.* N-COUNT

3 In British English, you can refer to someone who runs a business as a **cowboy** if they run it dishonestly or are not experienced, skilful, or careful in their work. *We don't want to look like a bunch of cowboys... Fortunately, such cowboy firms are becoming rarer.* N-COUNT: oft N n PRAGMATICS ≠professional

cower /kaʊəʳ/ **cowers, cowering, cowered.** If you **cower**, you bend forward and downwards because you are very frightened. *The hostages cowered in their seats.* VERB; V

cowhide /kaʊhaɪd/. **Cowhide** is leather made from the skin of a cow. *...cowhide boots.* N-UNCOUNT: oft N n

cowl /kaʊl/ **cowls.** A **cowl** is a large loose hood covering a person's head, or their head and shoulders. Cowls are worn especially by monks. N-COUNT

cowling /kaʊlɪŋ/ **cowlings.** A **cowling** is a removable metal covering for an engine, especially on an aircraft. N-COUNT

cowpat /kaʊpæt/ **cowpats;** also spelled **cow pat**. A **cowpat** is a pile of faeces from a cow. N-COUNT

cowshed /kaʊʃed/ **cowsheds.** A **cowshed** is a building where cows are kept or milked. N-COUNT

cowslip /kaʊslɪp/ **cowslips.** A **cowslip** is a small wild plant with yellow, sweet-smelling flowers. N-COUNT

cox /kɒks/ **coxes.** In a rowing boat, the **cox** is the person who tells the rowers which direction to row in. N-COUNT

coxswain /kɒksᵊn/ **coxswains.** The **coxswain** of a lifeboat or other small boat is the person who steers the boat. N-COUNT

coy /kɔɪ/ ◆◇◇◇◇

1 If you describe someone, especially a woman, as **coy**, you find them irritating because they are shy, or pretend to be shy, about matters of love and sex. *She is modest without being coy... I was sickened by the way Carol charmed all the men by turning coy.* ♦ **coyly** *She smiled coyly at Algie as he took her hand and raised it to his lips.* ♦ **coyness** *The public may once have liked her, but her coyness and flirting now interfere with her interviews.* ADJ-GRADED PRAGMATICS =demure; ADV-GRADED: ADV with v; N-UNCOUNT

2 If someone is being **coy**, they are unwilling to talk about something that they feel guilty or embar- ADJ-GRADED: usu v-link ADJ, oft ADJ *about* n rassed about. *The hotel are understandably coy about the incident... Mr Alexander is not the slightest bit coy about his ambitions.* =reticent ♦ **coyly** *The administration coyly refused to put a firm figure on the war's costs.* ADV-GRADED: ADV with v ♦ **coyness** *...their coyness about financial aid.* N-UNCOUNT =reticence

coyote /kaɪoʊti/ **coyotes.** A **coyote** is a small wolf which lives in the plains of North America. N-COUNT

coypu /kɔɪpuː/ **coypus.** A **coypu** is a large South American rodent which lives near water. N-COUNT

cozy /koʊzi/. See **cosy**.

Cpl. **Cpl.** is the written abbreviation for 'corporal' when it is used as a title. *...Cpl. G. Walker.* N-TITLE

CPU /siː piː juː/ **CPUs.** In a computer, the **CPU** is the part that processes all the data and makes the computer work. **CPU** is an abbreviation for 'central processing unit'. N-COUNT

crab /kræb/ **crabs.** A **crab** is a sea creature with a flat round body covered by a shell, and five pairs of legs with large claws on the front pair. Crabs usually move sideways. ◆◇◇◇◇ N-COUNT ► **Crab** is the flesh of this creature eaten as food. N-UNCOUNT

crab apple, crab apples. A **crab apple** is a tree like an apple tree that produces small sour fruit. N-COUNT

crabbed /kræbɪd/.
1 **Crabbed** means the same as **crabby**; used in written English. ADJ-GRADED: usu ADJ n
2 If you describe something, especially handwriting, as **crabbed**, you mean it does not take up as much room as it should; used in written English. ADJ-GRADED

crabby /kræbi/. Someone who is **crabby** is bad-tempered and unpleasant to people; an informal word. ADJ-GRADED

crabmeat /kræbmiːt/; also spelled **crab meat**. **Crabmeat** is the part of a crab that you eat. N-UNCOUNT

crack 1 verb uses

crack /kræk/ **cracks, cracking, cracked** ◆◆◆◇◇
1 If something hard **cracks** or if you **crack** it, it becomes slightly damaged, with lines appearing on its surface. *A gas main had cracked under my neighbour's garage and gas had seeped into our homes... Remove the dish from the oven, crack the salt crust and you will find the skin just peels off the fish.* V-ERG V Vn
2 If something **cracks** or if you **crack** it, it makes a sharp sound like the sound of a piece of wood breaking. *Thunder cracked in the sky... He cracked his fingers nervously.* V-ERG V Vn
3 If you **crack** a hard part of your body, such as your knee or your head, you hurt it by accidentally hitting it hard against something. *He cracked his head on the pavement and was knocked cold.* VERB =bang, bash Vn
4 When you **crack** something that has a shell, such as an egg or a nut, you break the shell in order to reach the inside part. *Crack the eggs into a bowl.* VERB =break Vn
5 If you **crack** a problem or a code, you solve it, especially after a lot of thought. *He has finally cracked the system after years of painstaking research.* VERB Vn
6 If someone **cracks**, they lose control of their emotions or actions because they are under a lot of pressure. *She's calm and strong, and she is just not going to crack... I had the conviction Larkin's nerve would crack and he'd squeeze the trigger in a reflex action... European Community countries are showing signs of cracking under intense pressure from the United States.* VERB V
7 If your voice **cracks** when you are speaking or singing, it changes in pitch because you are feeling a strong emotion. *Her voice cracked and she began to cry.* VERB V
8 If you **crack** a joke, you tell it. *He drove a Volkswagen, cracked jokes, and talked about beer and girls.* VERB Vn
9 See also **cracked, cracking**.
10 If you say that something is **not all it's cracked up to be**, you mean that it is not as good as other people have said it is; an informal expression. *Package holidays are not always all they're cracked up to be.* PHRASE: V inflects

crack down. If people in authority **crack down** on a group of people, they become stricter in making the group obey rules or laws. *The government has cracked down hard on those campaigning for greater democracy... There has been a lot of drinking. We are cracking down now. Anyone who gets caught is fired.* PHRASAL VERB =clamp down VP on n VP ● See also **crackdown**.

crack up. If someone **cracks up**, they are under such a lot of emotional strain that they become mentally ill; an informal expression. *She would have cracked up if she hadn't allowed herself some fun.* PHRASAL VERB =go to pieces VP

crack 2 noun and adjective uses

crack /kræk/ **cracks** ◆◆◇◇◇
1 A **crack** is a very narrow gap between two things, or between two parts of a thing. *Kathryn had seen him through a crack in the curtains.* N-COUNT =chink
2 If you open something such as a door, window, or curtain **a crack**, you open it only a small amount. *He went to the door, opened it a crack, and listened.* N-SING
3 A **crack** is a line that appears on the surface of something when it is slightly damaged. *The plate had a crack in it... Hundreds of office buildings and homes developed large cracks in walls and ceilings.* N-COUNT
4 A **crack** is a sharp sound, like the sound of a piece of wood breaking. *Suddenly there was a loud crack and glass flew into the car... 'Crack!' – The first shot rang out, dropping Paolo.* N-COUNT; SOUND
5 If you have a **crack at** something, you make an attempt to do or achieve something; an informal expression. *I should love to have a crack at the Olympia title in my last year... She decided to head for the dormitory to take another crack at locating Blanche.* N-SING: N at n/-ing =go, shot
6 A **crack** is a slightly rude or cruel joke. *When Paul made the crack about the 'famous girl detective', I began to suspect that he had it in for you.* N-COUNT =jibe
7 You can refer to a situation where people are chatting and having a good time as **the crack**; an informal use. *What they most enjoyed about foreign driving was the crack.* N-SING: the N
8 **Crack** is a form of the drug cocaine which has been purified and made into crystals. N-UNCOUNT
9 A **crack** soldier or sportsman is highly trained and very skilful. *...a crack undercover police officer... He is said to be a crack shot, despite weak vision in one eye.* ADJ-GRADED: ADJ n
10 If you say that someone does something **at the crack of dawn**, you are emphasizing that they do it very early in the morning. *I often start work at the crack of dawn when there is a big order to get out.* PHRASES PHR after v PRAGMATICS
11 If you **paper over the cracks**, you try to hide all the things that are wrong with something. *The meeting was stormy, and the two sides managed only to paper over the cracks on some issues.* V inflects
12 If you get **a fair crack of the whip**, you are allowed a reasonable opportunity to succeed at something; an informal expression in British English. *None of them is expecting any favours, just a fair crack of the whip.* PHR after v

crackdown /krækdaʊn/ **crackdowns.** A **crackdown** is strong official action that is taken to punish people who break laws. *...anti-government unrest that ended with the violent army crackdown.* ◆◆◇◇◇ N-COUNT =clampdown

cracked /krækt/ ◆◇◇◇◇
1 An object that is **cracked** has lines on its surface because it is damaged. *The ceiling was grey and cracked. ...a cracked mirror.* ADJ-GRADED
2 A **cracked** voice or a **cracked** musical note sounds rough and unsteady. *When he spoke, his voice was hoarse and cracked.* ADJ-GRADED
3 If you say that someone is **cracked**, you think that their behaviour or ideas are very strange; an informal and offensive use. ADJ-GRADED =crazy

cracker /krækəʳ/ **crackers** ◆◇◇◇◇
1 A **cracker** is a thin, crisp biscuit which is often eaten with cheese. N-COUNT
2 In British English, if you say that someone or something is a **cracker**, you like and admire them very much; an informal use. *She's a cracker... 'Dude' is a cracker of an album.* N-COUNT: oft N of n
3 A **cracker** is a hollow cardboard tube covered with coloured paper. Crackers make a bang when N-COUNT

they are pulled apart and usually contain a small toy, a joke, and a paper hat. They are used mainly at children's parties and Christmas meals. *...a Christmas cracker.*

4 If you say that someone is **crackers**, you think they are mad or are behaving as if they are mad; an informal and offensive use in British English. *They looked at her as though she was crackers.* ADJ: v-link ADJ =mad, nuts

crack house, crack houses; also spelled **crackhouse**. A **crack house** is a place where crack cocaine is available. N-COUNT

cracking /krækɪŋ/ ◆◇◇◇◇

1 In informal British English, you use **cracking** to describe something you think is very good or exciting. *It's a cracking novel... The way Liverpool play, and the way we play, I think it will be a cracking game.* ADJ: usu ADJ n =great, brilliant

2 If you tell someone to **get cracking**, you are telling them to start doing something immediately; used mainly in informal British English. *Mark, you'd better get cracking, the sooner the better... Vouchers must be redeemed before September 14th so you'd better get cracking to cash in.* PHRASES *get* inflects

3 In informal British English, if you say that someone or something is moving **at a cracking pace**, you mean that they are moving very quickly. *She set off at a cracking pace to Mr Ramzan's Superstore... The film belts along at a cracking pace.* PHR after v

crackle /krækᵊl/ **crackles, crackling, crackled.** If something **crackles**, it makes a rapid series of short, harsh noises. *The radio crackled again. ...a crackling fire.* ► Also a noun. *...the crackle of flames and gunfire.* ◆◇◇◇◇ VERB V V-ing N-COUNT

crackly /krækᵊli/. Something that is **crackly**, especially a recording or broadcast, has or makes a lot of short, harsh noises. *...the crackly sound of a wind-up gramophone. ...a crackly phone line.* ADJ-GRADED

crackpot /krækpɒt/ **crackpots.** If you describe someone or their ideas as **crackpot**, you disapprove of them because you think that their ideas are strange and crazy; an informal word. *...a crackpot millionaire. ...crackpot schemes.* ► A **crackpot** is a crackpot person. *She was no more a crackpot than the rest of us.* ADJ: ADJ n PRAGMATICS N-COUNT =nutter

cradle /kreɪdᵊl/ **cradles, cradling, cradled** ◆◇◇◇◇

1 A **cradle** is a baby's bed with high sides. Cradles often have curved bases so that they rock. N-COUNT =crib

2 The **cradle** is the part of a telephone on which the receiver rests while it is not being used. *I dropped the receiver back in the cradle.* N-COUNT

3 A **cradle** is a frame which supports or protects something. *He fixed the towing cradle round the hull.* N-COUNT

4 A place that is referred to as **the cradle of** something is the place where it began. *Mali is the cradle of some of Africa's richest civilizations. ...New York, the cradle of capitalism.* N-COUNT: usu sing, *the* N *of* n

5 If you **cradle** someone or something in your arms or hands, you hold them carefully and protectively. *I cradled her in my arms... He was sitting at the big table cradling a large bowl of milky coffee.* VERB V n *in* n V n

6 If something affects you **from the cradle to the grave**, it affects you throughout your life. *The bond of brotherhood was one to last from the cradle to the grave.* PHRASE: PHR after v

craft /krɑːft, kræft/ **crafts, crafting, crafted; craft** is both the singular and the plural form for meaning 1. ◆◆◆◇◇

1 You can refer to a boat, a spacecraft, or an aircraft as a **craft**. *With great difficulty, the fisherman manoeuvred his small craft close to the reef... The troops are reported to have advanced nearly four miles since they were landed from naval craft on Sunday evening.* ● See also **landing craft**. N-COUNT

2 A **craft** is an activity such as weaving, carving, or pottery that involves making things skilfully with your hands. *...the arts and crafts of the North American Indians... All kinds of traditional craft industries are preserved here.* N-COUNT

3 You can use **craft** to refer to any activity or job that involves doing something skilfully. *...the craft of writing... Maurice Murphy, one of the country's leading classical trumpeters, learnt his craft with the Black Dyke Mills band.* N-COUNT

4 If something **is crafted**, it is made skilfully. *The windows would probably have been crafted in the latter part of the Middle Ages... Many delegates were willing to craft a compromise... The author extracts the maximum from every carefully-crafted scene in this witty tale. ...original, hand-crafted bags at affordable prices.* VERB *be* V-ed V n V-ed

craft fair, craft fairs. A **craft fair** is an event at which people sell hand-made goods. N-COUNT

craftily /krɑːftɪli, kræft-/. See **crafty**.

craftsman /krɑːftsmən, kræft-/ **craftsmen.** A **craftsman** is a man who makes things skilfully with his hands. *The table in the kitchen was made by a local craftsman.* ◆◇◇◇◇ N-COUNT

craftsmanship /krɑːftsmənʃɪp, kræft-/ ◆◇◇◇◇

1 Craftsmanship is the skill that someone uses when they make beautiful things with their hands. *It is easy to appreciate the craftsmanship of Armani.* N-UNCOUNT

2 Craftsmanship is the quality that something has when it is beautiful and has been very carefully made. *His canoes are known for their style, fine detail and craftsmanship.* N-UNCOUNT

craftspeople /krɑːftspiːpᵊl, kræft-/. **Craftspeople** are people who make things skilfully with their hands. *...highly skilled craftspeople.* N-PLURAL

craftswoman /krɑːftswʊmən, kræfts-/ **craftswomen.** A **craftswoman** is a woman who makes things skilfully with her hands. N-COUNT

crafty /krɑːfti, kræfti/ **craftier, craftiest.** If you describe someone as **crafty**, you mean that they achieve what they want in a clever way, often by deceiving people. *...a crafty, lying character who enjoys plotting against others... A crafty look came to his eyes... That was my crafty little plan.* ◆◇◇◇◇ ADJ-GRADED =cunning

♦ **craftily** *The government has craftily put up all the hidden taxes.* ADV-GRADED: usu ADV with v

crag /kræg/ **crags.** A **crag** is a steep rocky cliff or part of a mountain. N-COUNT

craggy /krægi/

1 A **craggy** cliff or mountain is steep and rocky. *...tiny villages on craggy cliffs.* ADJ-GRADED: usu ADJ n

2 A **craggy** face has large features and deep lines. *He's a very small man with a lined, craggy face.* ADJ-GRADED: usu ADJ n

cram /kræm/ **crams, cramming, crammed** ◆◇◇◇◇

1 If you **cram** things or people into a container or place, you put them into it, although there is hardly enough room for them. *While nobody was looking, she squashed her school hat and crammed it into a wastebasket... I crammed my bag full of swimsuits and T-shirts and caught the sleeper down to Beziers... She crammed her mouth with caviar.* VERB =stuff V n prep/adv V n *full of* n V n *with* n

2 If people **cram** into a place or vehicle or **cram** a place or vehicle, so many of them enter it at one time that it is completely full. *We crammed into my car and set off... Friends and admirers crammed the chapel at the small Los Angeles cemetery where Monroe is buried.* VERB =pack V prep V n

3 If you **cram** a tightly-fitting hat on, you put it on, especially in a hurry. *I crammed on my cap again, helped the Duke up and tried to dust him off.* VERB V n with *on* Also V n *on* n

4 If you **are cramming for** an examination, you are learning as much as possible in a short time just before you take the examination. *She was cramming for her Economics exam... It would take two or three months of cramming to prepare for Vermont's bar exam.* VERB V *for* n V-ing

crammed /kræmd/ ◆◇◇◇◇

1 If a place is **crammed** with things or people, it is full of them, so that there is hardly room for anything or anyone else. *The house is crammed with priceless furniture and works of art... Living in a divided city crammed with foreign soldiers is not a matter we joke about.* ADJ: usu v-link ADJ, usu ADJ *with/full of* n =bursting, packed

2 If people or things are **crammed** into a place or vehicle, it is full of them. *Between two and three thousand refugees were crammed into the church buildings.* ADJ: v-link ADJ prep/adv =packed

crammer /kræməʳ/ **crammers.** A **crammer** is a school, teacher, or book which prepares students for an exam quickly and intensively. *Robert was* N-COUNT *about to go to a crammer to improve his A-level maths.*

cramp /kræmp/ **cramps, cramping, cramped** ◆◇◇◇◇
1 **Cramp** is a sudden strong pain caused by a muscle suddenly contracting. You sometimes get cramp in a muscle after you have been making a physical effort over a long period of time. *Hillsden was complaining of cramp in his calf muscles. ...muscle cramp... She started getting stomach cramps this morning.* [N-UNCOUNT: also N in pl]
2 If someone or something **cramps** your **style**, their presence or existence restricts your behaviour in some way; an informal expression. *Like more and more women, she believes wedlock would cramp her style.* [PHRASE: V inflects]

cramped /kræmpt/. A **cramped** room or building is not big enough for the people or things in it. *There are hundreds of families living in cramped conditions on the floor of the airport lounge... In later years he lived in a rather cramped little flat in Bristol.* ◆◇◇◇◇ [ADJ-GRADED =confined ≠spacious]

crampon /kræmpɒn/ **crampons.** **Crampons** are metal plates with spikes underneath which mountain climbers fasten to the bottom of their boots, especially when there is snow or ice, in order to make climbing easier. [N-COUNT: usu pl]

cranberry /krænbəri, AM -beri/ **cranberries.** **Cranberries** are red berries with a sour taste. They are often used to make a sauce or jelly that you eat with poultry. ◆◇◇◇◇ [N-COUNT: usu pl, oft N n]

crane /kreɪn/ **cranes, craning, craned** ◆◆◇◇◇
1 A **crane** is a large machine that moves heavy things by lifting them in the air. *The little prefabricated hut was lifted away by a huge crane.* [N-COUNT]
2 A **crane** is a kind of large bird with a long neck and long legs. [N-COUNT]
3 If you **crane** your neck or head, you stretch your neck in a particular direction in order to see or hear something better. *She craned her neck to get a better view... Children craned to get close to him... She craned forward to look at me.* [VERB] [V n] [V to-inf] [V adv/prep]

cranefly /kreɪnflaɪ/ **craneflies;** also spelled **crane fly.** A **cranefly** is a harmless flying insect with long legs. [N-COUNT =daddy longlegs]

cranial /kreɪniəl/. **Cranial** means relating to your cranium; a technical term in biology. *...cranial bleeding.* [ADJ: ADJ n]

cranium /kreɪniəm/ **craniums** or **crania** /kreɪniə/. Your **cranium** is the round part of your skull that contains your brain; a technical term in biology. [N-COUNT]

crank /kræŋk/ **cranks, cranking, cranked** ◆◇◇◇◇
1 If you call someone a **crank**, you think they have peculiar ideas or behaviour; an informal use. *The Labour leader called the Prime Minister 'a crank'... He looked like a crank.* [N-COUNT] [PRAGMATICS] [=nutter, crackpot]
2 A **crank** is a device that you turn in order to make something move. [N-COUNT]
3 If you **crank** an engine or machine, you make it move or function, especially by turning a handle. *The chauffeur got out to crank the motor.* [VERB] [V n]

crank up [PHRASAL VERB]
1 If you **crank up** a machine or device, you make it function harder or at a greater level. *Just crank up your hearing aid a peg or two. ...May's warm weather, which caused Americans to crank up their air conditioners.* [V P n (not pron)] [Also V n P]
2 If you **crank up** the volume of something, you turn it up until it is very loud; an informal use. *Someone cranked up the volume of the public address system... Crank it up... By about six, they're cranking the music up loud again.* [=turn up] [V P n (not pron)] [V n P] [V n P adj]
3 To **crank** something **up** means to increase it or make it more intense; an informal use. *The incident that cranked up the fear was the murder of Brian Smith... The legal authorities cranked up the investigation.* [V P n (not pron)] [Also V n P]

crank out. If you say that a company or person **cranks out** a quantity of similar things, you mean they produce them quickly, in the same way, and are usually implying that the things are unoriginal or of poor quality; an informal expression. *In 1933 the studio cranked out fifty-five feature films... The writer must have cranked it out in his lunch-hour.* [PHRASAL VERB] [PRAGMATICS] [=turn out] [V P n (not pron)] [V n P]

crankshaft /kræŋkʃɑːft, -ʃæft/ **crankshafts.** A **crankshaft** is the main shaft of an internal combustion engine. *The engine had a broken crankshaft.* [N-COUNT]

cranky /kræŋki/
1 If you describe ideas or ways of behaving as **cranky**, you disapprove of them because you think they are strange; an informal use. *Vegetarianism has shed its cranky image... The Front has often been dismissed as a cranky fringe group.* [ADJ-GRADED] [PRAGMATICS] [=eccentric]
2 In American English, **cranky** means bad-tempered; an informal use. *It was a long trek, and Jack and I both started to get cranky after about ten minutes.* [ADJ-GRADED =ratty]

cranny /kræni/ **crannies.** **Crannies** are very narrow openings or spaces in something. *They fled like lizards into crannies in the rocks.* • **every nook and cranny**: see **nook**. [N-COUNT: usu pl =crevice]

crap /kræp/ **craps, crapping, crapped** ◆◆◇◇◇
1 If you describe something as **crap**, you think that it is wrong or of very poor quality; an offensive use. [ADJ-GRADED] ▶ Also a noun. *It is a tedious, humourless load of crap.* [N-UNCOUNT =rubbish]
2 **Crap** is sometimes used to refer to faeces; an offensive use. [N-UNCOUNT]
3 To **crap** means to get rid of faeces from your body; an offensive use. [VERB: V]
4 **Craps** or **crap** is a gambling game, played mainly in the United States, in which you throw two dice and bet on the total score. *I'll shoot some craps or play some blackjack.* [N-UNCOUNT]

crappy /kræpi/ **crappier, crappiest.** If you describe something as **crappy**, you think it is of very poor quality; an informal word which some people find offensive. *She read for a while, a crappy detective novel.* [ADJ-GRADED: usu ADJ n]

crash /kræʃ/ **crashes, crashing, crashed** ◆◆◆◆◇
1 A **crash** is an accident in which a moving vehicle hits something and is damaged or destroyed. *His elder son was killed in a car crash a few years ago. ...a plane crash.* [N-COUNT: oft n N =accident]
2 If a moving vehicle **crashes** or if the driver **crashes** it, it hits something and is damaged or destroyed. *The plane crashed mysteriously near the island of Ustica. ...when his car crashed into the rear of a van... Even his death, after crashing his motorcycle on a bridge in New Orleans, was spectacular... Her body was found near a crashed car.* [V-ERG] [V] [V *into* n] [V n] [V-ed]
3 If something **crashes** somewhere, it moves and hits something else violently, making a loud noise. *The door swung inwards to crash against a chest of drawers behind it... My words were lost as the walls above us crashed down, filling the cellar with brick dust... I heard them coming, crashing through the undergrowth, before I saw them.* [VERB] [V prep/adv]
4 A **crash** is a sudden, loud noise. *Two people in the flat recalled hearing a loud crash about 1.30 a.m.* [N-COUNT]
5 If a business or financial system **crashes**, it fails suddenly, often with serious effects. *When the market crashed, they assumed the deal would be cancelled.* ▶ Also a noun. *He predicted correctly that there was going to be a stock market crash.* [VERB] [V] [N-COUNT]
6 If a computer or a computer program **crashes**, it fails suddenly. *...after the computer crashed for the second time in 10 days.* [VERB] [V]

crash out. If someone **crashes out** somewhere, they fall asleep where they are because they are very tired or drunk; an informal expression. *I just want to crash out on the sofa... The band are crashed out on the floor.* [PHRASAL VERB] [V P] [V-ed P]

crash barrier, crash barriers. In British English, a **crash barrier** is a strong low fence built along the side of a road at a dangerous corner or between the two halves of a motorway in order to prevent accidents. The usual American word is **guardrail**. [N-COUNT]

crash course, crash courses. A **crash course** in a particular subject is a short course in which you are taught basic facts or skills, for example [N-COUNT: usu with supp, oft N *in* n] before you start a new job. *I did a 15-week crash course in typing.*

crash helmet, crash helmets. A **crash helmet** is a helmet that motorcyclists wear in order to protect their heads if they have an accident. N-COUNT

crash-land, crash-lands, crash-landing, crash-landed; also spelled **crash land.** If a pilot **crash-lands** an aircraft or if it **crash-lands**, the pilot lands the aircraft in an abnormal and dangerous way, for example when it has developed a fault and cannot land normally. *He arrives in his biplane and crash lands it in a tree... A light aircraft crash-landed on a putting green yesterday.* V-ERG; V n; V
♦ **crash-landing, crash-landings** *His plane made a crash-landing during a sandstorm yesterday.* N-COUNT

crass /kræs/ **crasser, crassest. Crass** behaviour is stupid and insensitive. *The government has behaved with crass insensitivity... Pop records can be crass and cynical.* ◆◇◇◇◇ ADJ-GRADED
♦ **crassly** *...one of the most crassly stupid political acts of modern times... These teachings can be crassly misinterpreted.* ADV-GRADED: ADV adj, ADV with v
♦ **crassness** *...the crassness of his conversation.* N-UNCOUNT

crate /kreɪt/ **crates, crating, crated** ◆◇◇◇◇

1 A **crate** is a large box used for transporting or storing things. *...a pile of wooden crates... A crane was already unloading crates and pallets.* N-COUNT

2 If something **is crated**, it is packed in a crate so that it can be transported or stored somewhere safely. *The much repaired plane was crated for the return journey.* VB: usu passive; be V-ed

3 A **crate** is a plastic or wire tray divided into sections which is used for carrying bottles. *Two young lads were loading a dozen bottles into a plastic milk crate.* N-COUNT ► A **crate** of something is the amount of it that is contained in a crate. *We've also got a bonus quiz with crates of beer as prizes!* N-COUNT: usu N of n

crater /kreɪtəʳ/ **craters.** A **crater** is a very large hole in the ground, which has been caused by something hitting it or by an explosion. ◆◇◇◇◇ N-COUNT

cratered /kreɪtəʳd/. If the surface of something is **cratered**, it has many craters in it. *The Sun blazes down on its barren, cratered landscape.* ADJ-GRADED: usu ADJ n

cravat /krəvæt/ **cravats.** A **cravat** is a piece of cloth which a man wears wrapped around his neck and tucked inside the collar of his shirt. N-COUNT

crave /kreɪv/ **craves, craving, craved.** If you **crave** something, you want to have it very much. *There may be certain times of day when smokers crave their cigarette... You may be craving for some fresh air.* ◆◇◇◇◇ VERB; V n; V for n; Also V to-inf
♦ **craving, cravings** *...a craving for sugar. ...her craving to be loved.* N-COUNT: usu with supp

craven /kreɪvᵊn/. If you describe someone as **craven**, you disapprove of them because they are cowardly; used in written English. *The craven attackers pounced on the boy and stabbed him before fleeing. ...his craven obedience to his employers.* ADJ-GRADED; PRAGMATICS; =cowardly; ≠brave

crawl /krɔːl/ **crawls, crawling, crawled** ◆◆◇◇◇

1 When you **crawl**, you move forward on your hands and knees. *Don't worry if your baby seems a little reluctant to crawl or walk... I began to crawl on my hands and knees towards the door... As he tried to crawl away, he was hit in the shoulder.* VERB; V; V prep/adv

2 When an insect **crawls** somewhere, it moves there quite slowly. *I watched the moth crawl up the outside of the lampshade.* VERB; V prep

3 If someone or something **crawls** somewhere, they move or progress slowly or with great difficulty. *I crawled out of bed at nine-thirty... The Polish economy is crawling out of the mess it was in when communist rule ended... Hairpin turns force the car to crawl at 10 miles an hour in some places.* VERB; V prep/adv; V ► Also a noun. *The traffic on the approach road slowed to a crawl.* N-SING: a N

4 If you say that a place **is crawling with** people or animals, you are emphasizing that it is full of them; an informal use. *This place is crawling with police. ...rock-hard earth littered with rubbish and crawling with vermin.* VB: only cont; PRAGMATICS; V with n

5 **The crawl** is a kind of swimming stroke which you do lying on your front, swinging one arm over your head, and then the other arm. N-SING: the N

6 If something **makes** your **skin crawl** or **makes** your **flesh crawl**, it makes you feel horrified or revolted. *I hated this man, his very touch made my skin crawl.* PHRASE: V inflects

7 See also **kerb crawling, pub crawl.**

crayfish /kreɪfɪʃ/; **crayfish** is both the singular and the plural form. A **crayfish** is a small shellfish with five pairs of legs which lives in rivers and ponds. Some types of crayfish are edible. N-COUNT

crayon /kreɪɒn/ **crayons.** A **crayon** is a pencil containing coloured wax or clay, or a rod of coloured wax used for drawing. ◆◇◇◇◇ N-COUNT

craze /kreɪz/ **crazes.** If there is a **craze** for something, it is very popular for a short time. *...the craze for Mutant Ninja Turtles... Walking is the latest fitness craze.* ◆◇◇◇◇ N-COUNT: usu with supp =fad

crazed /kreɪzd/. **Crazed** people are wild and uncontrolled, and perhaps insane; used mainly in written English. *A crazed gunman slaughtered five people last night. ...a crazed act of revenge.* ◆◇◇◇◇ ADJ: usu ADJ n =crazy

-crazed /-kreɪzd/. **-crazed** combines with nouns to form adjectives that describe people whose behaviour is wild and uncontrolled because of the thing the noun refers to. *...a drug-crazed killer. ...a power-crazed TV executive.* COMB in ADJ

crazily /kreɪzɪli/. If something moves **crazily**, it moves in a way or in a direction that you do not expect; used in written English. *The three of us set off, our wheels skidding crazily under that drenching rain... The ball bounced crazily over his shoulder into the net.* • See also **crazy.** ADV: ADV after v =wildly

crazy /kreɪzi/ **crazier, craziest; crazies.** ◆◆◆◇◇

1 If you describe someone or something as **crazy**, you think they are very foolish or strange; an informal use. *People thought they were all crazy to try to make money from manufacturing... That's why he's got so caught up with this crazy idea about Mr. Trancas. ...that crazy, mixed-up world out there.* ADJ-GRADED; PRAGMATICS; =mad
♦ **crazily** *The teenagers shook their long, black hair and gesticulated crazily... Our policies are crazily extravagant and very destructive.* ADV: ADV after v, ADV adj
♦ **craziness** *We had to have a sense of humour because of the craziness of it all.* N-UNCOUNT

2 Someone who is **crazy** is insane; an informal use. *If I sat home and worried about all this stuff, I'd go crazy... He strides around the room beaming like a crazy man.* ADJ-GRADED =mad ► Also a noun. *Outside, mumbling, was one of New York's ever-present crazies.* N-COUNT =loony

3 If you are **crazy about** something, you are very enthusiastic about it. If you are not **crazy** about something, you do not like it; an informal use. *He's still crazy about both his work and his hobbies... I'm also not crazy about the initial terms of the deal.* ADJ-GRADED: v-link ADJ about n =mad ► Also a combining form. *Every football-crazy schoolboy in Europe dreams of one day being involved in the championships.* COMB in ADJ

4 If you are **crazy about** someone, you are deeply in love with them; an informal use. *None of that matters, because we're crazy about each other.* ADJ-GRADED: v-link ADJ about n =mad

5 If something or someone makes you **crazy** or drives you **crazy**, it makes you extremely annoyed or upset; an informal use. *This sitting around is driving me crazy... When Jock woke up and found you gone he went crazy.* ADJ-GRADED: v-link ADJ =mad

6 You use **like crazy** to emphasize that something happens to a great degree; an informal expression. *The stuff was selling like crazy... Some people can diet like crazy and not lose weight.* PHRASE: PHR after v; PRAGMATICS; =like mad

crazy paving. Crazy paving is paving that consists of slabs of irregular shapes. N-UNCOUNT

creak /kriːk/ **creaks, creaking, creaked.** If something **creaks**, it makes a short, high-pitched sound when it moves. *The bed-springs creaked... The door creaked open... The steps creaked beneath his feet. ...the creaking stairs.* ◆◇◇◇◇ VERB; V; V prep; V-ing ► Also a noun. *The door was pulled open with a creak.* N-COUNT

creaky /kriːki/.

1 A **creaky** object creaks when it moves. *She pushed open a creaky door.* ADJ-GRADED

2 If you describe something as **creaky**, you think it ADJ-GRADED

is bad in some way because it is old or old-fashioned. *...its creaky and corrupt political system. ...this creaky old British thriller.*

cream /kriːm/ **creams, creaming, creamed** ◆◆◆◇◇

1 Cream is a thick yellowish-white liquid taken from milk. You can use it in cooking or put it on fruit or puddings. *...strawberries and cream.* ● See also **clotted cream, double cream, single cream, sour cream, whipping cream.** N-UNCOUNT

2 Cream is used in the names of soups that contain cream or milk. *...cream of mushroom soup.* N-UNCOUNT: N *of* n

3 A **cream** is a substance that you rub into your skin, for example to keep it soft or to heal or protect it. *Gently apply the cream to the affected areas. ...sun protection creams.* ● See also **face cream.** N-VAR

4 Something that is **cream** is yellowish-white in colour. *...cream silk stockings. ...a cream-coloured Persian cat.* COLOUR

5 Cream is used in expressions such as **the cream of society** and **the cream of British athletes** to refer to the best people or things of a particular kind. *The Ball was attended by the cream of Hollywood society. ...the cream of Chicago's 200 jazz and blues clubs.* N-SING-COLL: *the* N *of* n =best ● You can refer to the best people or things of a particular kind as **the cream of the crop.** PHRASE

6 See also **ice cream, peaches and cream, salad cream, shaving cream.**

cream off PHRASAL VERB

1 To **cream off** part of a group of people means to take them away and treat them in a special way, because they are better than the others. *The private schools cream off many of the best pupils.* PRAGMATICS V P n (not pron)

2 If a person or organization **creams off** a large amount of money, they take it and use it for themselves; an informal use showing disapproval. *This means smaller banks can cream off big profits during lending booms... Funds raised through selling these magazines are creamed off to support armed violence.* PRAGMATICS V P n (not pron)

cream cheese. Cream cheese is a very rich, soft white cheese. N-UNCOUNT

cream cracker, cream crackers. In British English, **cream crackers** are crisp, dry, unsweetened biscuits which are eaten with cheese. N-COUNT =cracker

creamer /kriːməʳ/ **creamers**

1 Creamer is a white powder that is used in tea and coffee instead of milk. *...coffee whitened with a non-dairy creamer.* N-MASS

2 In American English, a **creamer** is a small jug used for pouring cream or milk. The British term is **milk jug.** N-COUNT

creamery /kriːməri/ **creameries.** A **creamery** is a place where milk and cream are made into butter and cheese. N-COUNT =dairy

cream of tartar. Cream of tartar is a white powder used in baking. N-UNCOUNT

cream tea, cream teas. In Britain, a **cream tea** is an afternoon meal that consists of tea to drink and scones with jam and clotted cream to eat. Cream teas are served in places such as tea shops. N-COUNT

creamy /kriːmi/ **creamier, creamiest** ◆◇◇◇◇

1 Food or drink that is **creamy** contains a lot of cream or milk. *...rich, creamy coffee. ...a creamy chocolate and nut candy bar.* ADJ-GRADED

2 Food that is **creamy** has a soft smooth texture and appearance. *...creamy mashed potato... Whisk the mixture until it is smooth and creamy. ...a delicious soft blue cheese with a creamy texture.* ADJ-GRADED

crease /kriːs/ **creases, creasing, creased** ◆◇◇◇◇

1 Creases are lines that are made in cloth or paper when it is crushed or folded. *She stood up, frowning at the creases in her silk dress... Papa flattened the creases of the map with his broad hands. ...cream coloured trousers with sharp creases.* N-COUNT: usu pl

2 If cloth or paper **creases** or if you **crease** it, lines form in it when it is crushed or folded. *Most outfits crease a bit when you are travelling... Liz sat down on the bed, lowering herself carefully not to crease her skirt.* V-ERG =crumple V V n ♦ **creased** *His clothes were creased, as if he had slept in them.* ADJ-GRADED

3 If your face **creases** or if an expression **creases** it, lines appear on it because you are frowning or smiling; used in written English. *His ruddy face still routinely creases with mirth... For just the second time a look of emotion creases his face.* V-ERG =wrinkle V V n

4 Creases in someone's skin are lines which form where their skin folds when they move. *...the tiny creases at the corners of his eyes... When Crevecoeur smiled, the creases in his face deepened.* N-COUNT =wrinkle ♦ **creased** *...Jock's creased drunken face.* ADJ GRADED

5 In cricket, the **crease** is a line on the playing surface near the wicket where the batsman stands. *Haynes was still at the crease, unbeaten on 84.* N-SING: *the* N, poss N

crease up. If someone or something makes you **crease up** or **creases** you **up**, they make you laugh a lot; an informal British expression. *I do make him laugh. Don't ask me why, but I'll be saying something and he'll just crease up... He's trying to say hello in Italian and he says goodbye in Spanish, it creases me up every time.* PHRASAL VERB ERG V P V n P

create /krieɪt/ **creates, creating, created** ◆◆◆◆◆

1 To **create** something means to cause it to happen or exist. *We set business free to create more jobs in Britain... She could create a fight out of anything... The lights create such a glare it's next to impossible to see anything behind them... Criticizing will only destroy a relationship and create feelings of failure.* VERB =produce ≠destroy V n ♦ **creation** /krieɪʃən/ *These businesses stimulate the creation of local jobs... The creation of large parks and forests is of lower priority than some twenty years ago.* N-UNCOUNT: usu N *of* n

2 When someone **creates** a new product or process, they invent it or design it. *It is really great for a radio producer to create a show like this... He's creating a whole new language of painting.* VERB =invent V n

creation /krieɪʃən/ **creations** ◆◆◇◇◇

1 In many religions, **creation** is the making of the universe, earth, and creatures by God. *...the Creation of the universe as told in Genesis Chapter One... For the first time since creation, the survival of the Earth is entirely in our hands.* N-UNCOUNT: also *the* N

2 People sometimes refer to the entire universe as **creation**; a literary use. *In primitive times both gods and goddesses were seen to manifest their energies throughout the whole of creation.* N-UNCOUNT

3 You can refer to something that someone has made as a **creation**, especially if it shows skill, imagination, or artistic ability. *The bathroom is entirely my own creation... Featured are both his classics and his latest creations... You'll be amazed at the culinary creations possible in a Dutch oven.* N-COUNT: usu with supp

4 See also **create.**

creative /krieɪtɪv/ ◆◆◆◇◇

1 A **creative** person has the ability to invent and develop original ideas, especially in the arts. *Like so many creative people he was never satisfied. ...her obvious creative talents.* ADJ-GRADED: usu ADJ n ♦ **creativity** /kriːeɪtɪvɪti/ *American art reached a peak of creativity in the '50s and 60s.* N-UNCOUNT

2 Creative activities involve the inventing and making of new kinds of things. *...creative writing. ...creative arts... Cooking is creative.* ADJ: usu ADJ n

3 If you use something in a **creative** way, you use it in a new way that produces interesting and unusual results. *...his creative use of words.* ADJ-GRADED: usu ADJ n ♦ **creatively** *Genet teaches you to think creatively.* ADV-GRADED

creative accounting. If you say that a company or other organization practises **creative accounting**, you are saying in a polite way that they present or organize their accounts in such a way that they gain money for themselves or give a false impression of their profits. *Much of the apparent growth in profits that occurred in the 1980s was the result of creative accounting.* N-UNCOUNT PRAGMATICS

creator /krieɪtəʳ/ **creators** ◆◆◇◇◇

1 The **creator** of something is the person who made it or invented it. *...Ian Fleming, the creator of James Bond... I have always believed that a garden dies with its creator.* N-COUNT: usu with poss

2 God is sometimes referred to as **the Creator**. *This was the first object placed in the heavens by the Creator.* N-PROPER: *the* N

creature /kriːtʃəʳ/ **creatures** ◆◆◇◇◇

1 You can refer to any living thing that is not a plant as a **creature**, especially when it is of an unknown or unfamiliar kind. People also refer to imaginary animals and beings as **creatures**. *Alaskan Eskimos believe that every living creature possesses a spirit... The garden is surrounded by a hedge in which many small creatures can live... They have been visited by creatures from outer space.* N-COUNT =animal

2 If you say that someone is a particular type of **creature**, you are focusing on a particular quality they have. *She's charming, a sweet creature... I am not a vain creature... She was a creature of the emotions, rather than reason.* ● **a creature of habit**: see **habit**. N-COUNT: with supp PRAGMATICS

3 If you describe someone as someone else's **creature**, you mean that they are controlled by or depend on that person; used showing disapproval. *We are not creatures of the Conservative government.* N-COUNT: with poss PRAGMATICS

creature comforts. Creature comforts are the things that you need to feel comfortable in a place, for example good food and modern equipment. *They appreciate all the creature comforts of home.* N-PLURAL

crèche /kreʃ/ **crèches;** also spelled **creche**. A **crèche** is a place where small children can be left and looked after while their parents are working or doing something else; used mainly in British English. ◆◇◇◇◇ N-COUNT =nursery

cred /kred/. **Cred** is the same as **street cred**. N-UNCOUNT

credence /kriːdəns/ ◆◇◇◇◇

1 If something lends or gives **credence** to a theory or story, it makes it easier to believe; a formal use. *Good studies are needed to lend credence to the notion that genuine progress can be made in this important field.* N-UNCOUNT =credibility

2 If you give **credence** to a theory or story, you believe it; a formal use. *You're surely not giving any credence to this story of Hythe's?* N-UNCOUNT

credentials /krɪdenʃəlz/ ◆◇◇◇◇

1 Someone's **credentials** are their previous achievements, training, and general background, which indicate that they are qualified to do something. *...Mr Clinton's credentials as a new Democrat... I can testify to the credentials of the clientele.* N-PLURAL: with supp

2 Someone's **credentials** are a letter or certificate that proves their identity or qualifications. *Britain's new ambassador to Lebanon, Mr David Tatham, has presented his credentials to President Hrawi.* N-PLURAL: usu poss N

credibility /kredɪbɪlɪti/. If someone or something has **credibility**, people believe in them and trust them. *The police have lost their credibility... The president will have to work hard to restore his credibility.* ◆◆◇◇◇ N-UNCOUNT

credibility gap. A **credibility gap** is the difference between what a person says or promises and what they actually think or do. *British economic policy has had a credibility gap since the ERM suspension.* N-SING

credible /kredɪbəl/. ◆◆◇◇◇

1 **Credible** means able to be trusted or believed. *...a credible threat of terrorist action... Mrs Thatcher's claims seem credible to many.* ♦ **credibly** /kredɪbli/ *Ministers can equally credibly claim that the opposition is to blame.* ADJ-GRADED =convincing ≠unconvincing ADV-GRADED: usu ADV with v

2 A **credible** candidate, policy, or system, for example, is one that appears to have a chance of being successful. *Mr Delors would be a credible candidate... The challenge before the opposition is to offer credible alternative policies for the future.* ♦ **credibly** *He was the only figure who could credibly run the country.* ADJ-GRADED ADV-GRADED: ADV with v

credit /kredɪt/ **credits, crediting, credited** ◆◆◆◆◇

1 If you are allowed **credit**, you are allowed to pay for goods or services several weeks or months after you have received them. *The group can't get credit to buy farming machinery... You can ask a dealer for a discount whether you pay cash or buy on credit.* N-UNCOUNT: oft *on* N

2 If someone or their bank account is **in credit**, their bank account has money in it. *The idea that I could be charged when I'm in credit makes me very angry... I made sure the account stayed in credit... Interest is payable on credit balances.* N-UNCOUNT: *in* N, N n

3 When a sum of money **is credited** to an account, the bank adds that sum of money to the total in the account. *She noticed that only $80,000 had been credited to her account... Midland decided to change the way it credited payments to accounts... Interest is calculated daily and credited once a year, on 1 April.* VERB ≠debit *be* V-ed *to* n V n *to* n *be* V-ed Also V n

4 A **credit** is a sum of money which is added to an account; a technical term in finance. *The statement of total debits and credits is known as a balance.* N-COUNT ≠debit

5 A **credit** is an entitlement to have a particular amount of money; a technical term in finance. *Senator Bill Bradley outlined his own tax cut, giving families $350 in tax credits per child... Japan has provided about $2.5 billion in credits to Russia and about $50 million in direct aid.* N-COUNT =allowance

6 If you get the **credit** for something good, people praise you because you are responsible for it, or are thought to be responsible for it. *We don't mind who gets the credit so long as we don't get the blame... It would be wrong for us to take all the credit... Some of the credit for her relaxed manner must go to Andy.* N-UNCOUNT: oft *the* N *for* n/-ing ≠blame

7 If people **credit** someone **with** an achievement or if it **is credited to** them, people say or believe that they were responsible for it. *The staff are crediting him with having saved Hythe's life... The 74-year-old mayor is credited with helping make Los Angeles the financial capital of the West Coast... The screenplay for 'Gabriel Over the White House' is credited to Carey Wilson.* VERB V n *with* -ing/n *be* V-ed *to* n Also V n *to* n

8 If you **credit** someone **with** a quality, you believe or say that they have it. *I wonder why you can't credit him with the same generosity of spirit... They are crediting science with power it doesn't possess.* VERB V n *with* n

9 If you say that someone is, for example, **a credit to their profession** or **a credit to their parents**, you are praising them and saying that their qualities or achievements will make people have a better opinion of the group or person mentioned. *He is one of the greatest British players of recent times and is a credit to his profession.* N-SING: *a* N *to* n =disgrace

10 If you cannot **credit** something, you cannot believe that it is true. *Roosevelt either did not learn of the scandal or refused to credit what he heard... It seems hard to credit that such things went on among senior Directors.* VB: no cont, with brd-neg =believe V n V that

11 The list of people who helped to make a film, a record, or a television programme is called the **credits**. *The star Marlon Brando wants his name removed from the credits. ...a moviegoer who remains in his seat until the credits are over.* N-COUNT: usu pl

12 A **credit** is the successful completion of a part of a higher education course. At some universities and colleges you need a certain number of credits to be awarded a degree. N-COUNT

13 If you say that something **does** someone **credit**, you mean that they should be praised or admired because of it. *You're a nice girl, Lettie, and your kind heart does you credit.* PHRASES V inflects

14 If you say **'credit where credit's due'**, you are admitting that you ought to praise someone for something that they have done or for a good quality that they possess. *His gift was an extremely kind gesture. Credit where credit's due.*

15 To **give** someone **credit for** a good quality means to believe that they have it. *Bruno had more ability than the media gives him credit for.* V inflects, PHR n

16 You say **on the credit side** in order to introduce one or more good things about a situation or person, usually when you have already mentioned the bad things about them. *On the credit side, he's always been wonderful with his mother.* PHR with cl PRAGMATICS

17 If you say that, **to** someone's **credit**, they did something or do something, you mean that they deserve praise for it. *She had managed to pull herself together and, to her credit, continued to look upon life as a positive experience... Although the of-* PHR with cl, *it* v-link PHR that PRAGMATICS

fences were horrific it was to her credit that she had owned up.

18 If you already have one or more achievements **to** your **credit**, you have achieved them. *I have twenty novels, a score of successful plays, and countless magazine stories to my credit.*

creditable /kreditəbəl/. ◆◇◇◇◇

1 A **creditable** performance or achievement is of a reasonably high standard. *They turned out a quite creditable performance... Gazza finished a creditable third.* ♦ **creditably** /kreditəbli/ *British riders performed creditably... She puts in a creditably spirited performance.* ADJ-GRADED =respectable; ADV-GRADED: usu ADV with v, also ADV adj/adv

2 If you describe someone's actions or aims as **creditable**, you mean that they are morally good or admirable. *Not a very creditable attitude, I'm afraid.* ADJ-GRADED

credit card, credit cards. A **credit card** is a plastic card that you use to buy goods on credit. ◆◆◇◇◇ N-COUNT

credit note, credit notes. A **credit note** is a piece of paper that a shop gives you when you return goods that you have bought from them. It states that you are entitled to take goods of the same value without paying for them. N-COUNT

creditor /kreditər/ **creditors.** Your **creditors** are the people who you owe money to. *The company said it would pay in full all its creditors except Credit Suisse.* ◆◆◇◇◇ N-COUNT: usu pl ≠debtor

credit rating. Your **credit rating** is a judgement of how likely you are to pay money back if you borrow it or buy things on credit. ◆◇◇◇◇ N-SING

credit transfer, credit transfers. A **credit transfer** is a direct payment of money from one bank account to another. N-COUNT: also *by* N

creditworthy /kreditwɜːrði/; also spelled **credit-worthy.** A **creditworthy** person or organization is one who can safely be lent money or allowed to have goods on credit, for example because in the past they have always paid back what they owe. *Building societies make loans to creditworthy customers.* ♦ **creditworthiness** *They now take extra steps to verify the creditworthiness of customers.* ADJ-GRADED; N-UNCOUNT

credo /kriːdoʊ, kreɪ-/ **credos.** A **credo** is a set of beliefs, principles, or opinions that strongly influence the way a person lives or works; a formal word. *Lord Clarendon's liberal credo was one of the foundations of his political conduct.* N-COUNT =creed

credulity /krɪdjuːlɪti, AM -duː-/. **Credulity** is a willingness to believe that something is real or true; used in written English. *The plot does stretch credulity.* N-UNCOUNT

credulous /kredʒʊləs/. If you describe someone as **credulous**, you have a low opinion of them because they are too ready to believe what people tell them and are easily deceived. *...quack doctors charming money out of the pockets of credulous health-hungry citizens.* ADJ-GRADED PRAGMATICS =gullible

creed /kriːd/ **creeds** ◆◇◇◇◇

1 A **creed** is a set of beliefs, principles, or opinions that strongly influence the way people live or work; a formal use. *...their devotion to their creed of self-help.* N-COUNT =credo

2 A **creed** is a religion; a formal use. *The centre is open to all, no matter what race or creed.* N-COUNT =religion

creek /kriːk/ **creeks** ◆◇◇◇◇

1 In British English, a **creek** is a narrow inlet where the sea comes a long way into the land. N-COUNT: oft in names

2 In American English, a **creek** is a small stream or river. *Follow Austin Creek for a few miles.* N-COUNT: oft in names

3 If you say that someone or something is **up the creek**, you mean they are in a bad or difficult situation, or are wrong in some way. You can also say that someone in a bad situation is **up the creek without a paddle**. PHRASE: v-link PHR

creep /kriːp/ **creeps, creeping, crept** ◆◆◇◇◇

1 When people or animals **creep** somewhere, they move quietly and slowly. *Back I go to the hotel and creep up to my room... The rabbit creeps away and hides in a hole.* VERB V adv/prep

2 If something **creeps** somewhere, it moves very slowly. *Mist had crept in again from the sea.* VERB V adv/prep

3 If something **creeps** in or **creeps** back, it begins to occur or becomes part of something without people realising or without them necessarily wanting it. *Insecurity might creep in... An increasing ratio of mistakes, perhaps induced by tiredness, crept into her game. ...a proposal that crept through unnoticed at the National Council in December... Now his other major works are creeping back into concert programmes... Their organisation has been subjected to creeping privatisation since 1981.* VERB V in; V into n; V adv/prep; V-ing

4 If a rate or number **creeps** up to a higher level, it gradually reaches that level. *The inflation rate has been creeping up to 9.5 per cent... The average number of students in each class is creeping up from three to four.* VERB V up to n; V up; Also V adj-compar

5 If you describe someone as a **creep**, you mean that you dislike them a great deal, especially because they are insincere and flatter people; an informal use. N-COUNT PRAGMATICS

6 If someone or something **gives** you **the creeps**, they make you feel very uneasy or frightened; an informal expression. *I always hated that statue. It gave me the creeps.* PHRASE: V inflects

7 ● to **make** someone's **flesh creep**: see **flesh**.

creep up on PHRASAL VERB

1 If you **creep up on** someone, you move slowly closer to them without being seen by them. *They'll creep up on you while you're asleep.* V P P n

2 If a feeling or state **creeps up on** you, you hardly notice that it is beginning to affect you or happen to you. *The desire to be a mother may creep up on you unexpectedly.* V P P n

creeper /kriːpər/ **creepers. Creepers** are plants with long stems that wind themselves around objects. N-COUNT

creepy /kriːpi/ **creepier, creepiest.** If you say that something or someone is **creepy**, you mean they make you feel very uneasy or frightened; an informal word. *There were certain places that were really creepy at night... Was she still married to that creepy guy, Dennis?* ◆◇◇◇◇ ADJ-GRADED =weird

creepy-crawly /kriːpi krɔːli/ **creepy-crawlies.** You refer to insects as **creepy-crawlies** when they give you a feeling of fear or disgust; an informal British word used especially by children. N-COUNT: usu pl PRAGMATICS

cremate /krɪmeɪt, AM kriːmeɪt/ **cremates, cremating, cremated.** When someone **is cremated**, their dead body is burned, usually as part of a funeral service. *She wants Chris to be cremated.* ♦ **cremation** /krɪmeɪʃən/ **cremations** *At Miss Garbo's request there was a cremation after a private ceremony... Half of California's deceased opt for cremation.* ◆◇◇◇◇ VB: usu passive *be* V-ed; N-VAR

crematorium /kremətɔːriəm/ **crematoria** /kremətɔːriə/ or **crematoriums.** A **crematorium** is a building in which the bodies of dead people are burned. N-COUNT

crème de la crème /krem də lɑː krem/. If you refer to someone or something as **the crème de la crème**, you mean they are the very best person or thing of their kind; used mainly in journalism. *Scientists are the crème de la crème of a country's brainpower.* N-SING: *the* N =best

crenellated /krenəleɪtɪd/. A **crenellated** wall has gaps in the top or openings through which to fire at attackers; a technical term in architecture. *...crenellated turrets.* ADJ: usu ADJ n

creole /kriːoʊl/ **creoles;** also spelled **Creole.** ◆◇◇◇◇

1 A **creole** is a language that has developed from a mixture of different languages and has become the main language in a particular place. *She begins speaking in the Creole of Haiti. ...French Creole.* N-VAR =patois

2 A **Creole** is a person of mixed African and European race, who lives in the West Indies and speaks a creole language. N-COUNT

3 A **Creole** is a person descended from the Europeans who first colonized the West Indies or the southern United States of America. N-COUNT

4 Creole means belonging to or relating to the Creole community. *Coconut Rice Balls is a creole dish. ...Creole culture.* ADJ: usu ADJ n

creosote /kriːəsoʊt/. **Creosote** is a thick dark liquid made from coal tar which is used to prevent wood from rotting. N-UNCOUNT

crepe /kreɪp/ **crepes.**

1 Crepe is a thin fabric made of cotton, silk, or wool with an uneven, ridged surface. *Use a crepe bandage to support the affected area.* N-UNCOUNT: oft N n

2 A **crepe** is a thin pancake. *...chicken-filled crepes.* N-COUNT

3 Crepe is a type of rubber with a rough surface. *...a pair of crepe-soled ankle-boots.* N-UNCOUNT: oft N n

crepe paper. Crepe paper is stretchy paper with an uneven, ridged surface. Coloured crepe paper is often used for making decorations. N-UNCOUNT

crept /krept/. **Crept** is the past tense and past participle of **creep**.

crepuscular /krɪpʌskjʊləʳ/. **Crepuscular** means relating to twilight; a literary word. *They merged together in the crepuscular light.* ADJ: ADJ n

crescendo /krɪʃendoʊ/ **crescendos**

1 A **crescendo** is a noise that gets louder and louder. Some people also use **crescendo** to refer to the point when a noise is at its loudest. *She spoke in a crescendo: 'You are a bad girl! You are a wicked girl! You are evil!'... The crescendo of noise was continuous... The applause rose to a crescendo and cameras clicked.* N-COUNT: usu sing, oft N *of* n

2 People sometimes describe an increase in the intensity of something, or its most intense point, as a **crescendo**; used mainly in journalism. *There was a crescendo of parliamentary and press criticism... And now the story reaches a crescendo.* N-COUNT: usu sing

3 In music, a **crescendo** is a section of a piece of music in which the music gradually gets louder and louder. N-COUNT: usu sing

crescent /kresᵊnt, krez-/ **crescents** ◆◇◇◇◇

1 A **crescent** is a curved shape that is wider in the middle than at its ends, like the shape of the moon during its first and last quarters. It is the most important symbol of the Islamic faith. *A glittering Islamic crescent tops the mosque. ...a narrow crescent of sand dunes. ...a crescent moon.* N-COUNT

2 In Britain, **Crescent** is sometimes used as part of the name of a street or row of houses that is built in a curve. *...44 Colville Crescent.* N-IN-NAMES

cress /kres/. **Cress** is a plant with small, strong-tasting green leaves that are used in salads or as a garnish for food. N-UNCOUNT

crest /krest/ **crests cresting crested** ◆◇◇◇◇

1 The **crest** of a hill or a wave is the top of it. *Burns was clear over the crest of the hill.* N-COUNT ● If you say that you are **on the crest of a wave**, you mean that you are feeling very happy and confident because things are going well for you. *The band are riding on the crest of a wave with the worldwide success of their number one selling single.* PHRASE: v-link PHR, PHR after v

2 When someone **crests** a hill, they reach the top of it; used in written English. *...as the first wave of marchers crested the hill.* VERB V n

3 A bird's **crest** is a tuft of feathers on the top of its head. *Both birds had a dark blue crest.* N-COUNT

4 A **crest** is a design that is the symbol of a noble family, a town, or an organization. *On the wall is the family crest.* N-COUNT

crested /krestɪd/

1 A **crested** bird is a bird that has a tuft of feathers on its head. *...crested hawks.* ADJ: ADJ n

2 Crested objects have on them the crest of a noble family, a town, or an organization. *...crested china. ...crested writing paper.* ADJ: usu ADJ n

crestfallen /krestfɔːlən/. If you look **crestfallen**, you look sad and disappointed about something. ADJ-GRADED: usu v-link ADJ

cretin /kretɪn, AM kriːtᵊn/ **cretins.** If you call someone a **cretin**, you think they are very stupid; an offensive word. N-COUNT PRAGMATICS =moron

cretinous /kretɪnəs, AM kriːtənəs/. If you describe someone as **cretinous**, you think they are very stupid; an offensive word. ADJ-GRADED PRAGMATICS

crevasse /krɪvæs/ **crevasses.** A **crevasse** is a large, deep crack in thick ice or rock. *He fell down a crevasse.* N-COUNT

crevice /krevɪs/ **crevices.** A **crevice** is a narrow crack or gap, especially in a rock. *...a huge boulder with rare ferns growing in every crevice.* N-COUNT =fissure

crew /kruː/ **crews, crewing, crewed** ◆◆◆◇◇

1 The **crew** of a ship, an aircraft, or a spacecraft is the people who work on and operate it. *The mission for the crew of the space shuttle Endeavour is essentially over... Despite their size, these vessels carry small crews, usually of around twenty men... The surviving crew members were ferried ashore.* N-COUNT-COLL

2 A **crew** is a group of people with special technical skills who work together on a task or project. *...a two-man film crew making a documentary... A paramedic ambulance crew went to the accident scene but were unable to save Mrs Wilson.* N-COUNT: usu with supp

3 If you **crew** a boat, you work on it as part of the crew. *She was already a keen and experienced sailor, having crewed in both Merlin and Grayling... There were to be five teams of three crewing the boat. ...a fully crewed yacht.* VERB V V n V-ed

4 You can use **crew** to refer to a group of people you disapprove of; an informal use. *...the motley crew of failed and aspiring actors who comprised the 'distinguished guests'... This crew of killers and life-wreckers are headed by the mad but cunning Nino Brown.* N-SING-COLL: oft N *of* n PRAGMATICS =rabble, gang

crew cut, crew cuts; also spelled **crewcut**. A **crew cut** is a man's hairstyle in which his hair is cut very short. N-COUNT

crewman /kruːmæn/ **crewmen.** A **crewman** is a member of a crew. ◆◇◇◇◇ N-COUNT

crew neck, crew necks; also spelled **crewneck**. A **crew neck** or a **crew neck** sweater is a sweater with a round neck. N-COUNT

crib /krɪb/ **cribs, cribbing, cribbed** ◆◇◇◇◇

1 A **crib** is a baby's cot. N-COUNT

2 If you **crib**, you copy something that someone else has written and pretend that it is your own work; an old-fashioned use. *You have been cribbing from Bennett... He had been caught cribbing in an exam.* VERB =copy V *from* n V Also V n *from* n

crib death, crib deaths. In American English, **crib death** is the sudden death of a baby while it is asleep, although the baby had not previously been ill. The usual British term is **cot death**. N-VAR

crick /krɪk/ **cricks.** If you have a **crick** in your neck or in your back, you have a pain there caused by muscles becoming stiff. N-COUNT

cricket /krɪkɪt/ **crickets** ◆◆◆◇◇

1 Cricket is an outdoor game played between two teams. Players try to score points, called runs, by hitting a ball with a wooden bat. *During the summer term we would play cricket at the village ground. ...the Yorkshire County Cricket Club.* N-UNCOUNT

2 If you say that someone's behaviour is **not cricket**, you mean that they have not behaved in a fair or honourable way; an old-fashioned expression. *Their treatment of staff is definitely not cricket.* PHRASE: v-link PHR

3 A **cricket** is a small jumping insect that produces short, loud sounds by rubbing its wings together. N-COUNT

cricketer /krɪkɪtəʳ/ **cricketers.** A **cricketer** is a person who plays cricket. ◆◇◇◇◇ N-COUNT

cricketing /krɪkɪtɪŋ/. **Cricketing** means relating to or taking part in cricket. *...England's cricketing heroes. ...his brief cricketing career.* ◆◇◇◇◇ ADJ: ADJ n

crier /kraɪəʳ/. See **town crier**.

crikey /kraɪki/. Some people say **crikey** in order to express surprise, especially at something unpleasant; an informal expression. EXCLAM PRAGMATICS =blimey

crime /kraɪm/ **crimes** ◆◆◆◆◇

1 A **crime** is an illegal action or activity for which a person can be punished by law. *He and Lieutenant Cassidy were checking the scene of the crime... Mr Steele has committed no crime and poses no danger to the public... Endangering their lives will be regarded as a crime against humanity. ...the growing problem of organised crime... We need a positive programme of crime prevention.* N-VAR

2 If you say that doing something is a **crime**, you think it is very wrong or a serious mistake. *A language is a finely tuned instrument which it is a* N-COUNT: usu sing, oft *it* v-link N to-inf *crime to damage... It would be a crime to travel all the way to Australia and not stop in Sydney.* PRAGMATICS =sin

crime wave; also spelled **crimewave**. When more crimes than usual are committed in a particular place, you can refer to this as a **crime wave**. *The police blame much of the recent crime wave on rival gangs.* N-SING

criminal /krɪmɪnᵊl/ **criminals** ◆◆◆◆◇

1 A **criminal** is a person who has committed a crime. *A group of gunmen attacked a prison and set free nine criminals in Moroto.* N-COUNT =offender

2 **Criminal** means connected with crime. *Her husband faces various criminal charges... At 17, he had a criminal record for petty theft... Doug was found guilty of criminal assault and sentenced to six months in jail.* ♦ **criminality** /krɪmɪnælɪti/ *Between 1960 and 1985 we had a tenfold increase of criminality.* ♦ **criminally** *...a hospital for the criminally insane.* ADJ: usu ADJ n; N-UNCOUNT; ADV: usu ADV adj/-ed

3 If you describe an action as **criminal**, you think it is very wrong or a serious mistake. *He said a full-scale dispute involving strikes would be criminal.* ♦ **criminally** *It was, he said, criminally irresponsible for any party to say it would never raise personal taxation.* ADJ: usu v-link ADJ PRAGMATICS; ADV: ADV adj

criminalize /krɪmɪnəlaɪz/ **criminalizes, criminalizing, criminalized;** also spelled **criminalise** in British English. If a government **criminalizes** an action or person, it officially declares that the action or the person's behaviour is illegal. *There is no move to criminalise alcohol. ...a deliberate campaign to criminalise members of the former Communist leadership.* VERB; V n

criminology /krɪmɪnɒlədʒi/. **Criminology** is the scientific study of crime and criminals. ♦ **criminologist** /krɪmɪnɒlədʒɪst/ **criminologists** *...a criminologist at the University of Montreal.* ◆◇◇◇◇ N-UNCOUNT; N-COUNT

crimp /krɪmp/ **crimps, crimping, crimped**

1 If you **crimp** something such as a piece of fabric or pastry, you make small folds in it. *Crimp the edges to seal them tightly.* VERB; V n

2 In American English, to **crimp** something means to restrict or reduce it. *The dollar's recent strength is crimping overseas sales and profits.* VERB; V n

crimplene /krɪmpliːn/. **Crimplene** is a man-made fabric used for making clothes which does not crease easily. **Crimplene** is a trademark. N-UNCOUNT: oft N n

crimson /krɪmzᵊn/ **crimsons** ◆◇◇◇◇

1 Something that is **crimson** is deep red in colour. *...a mass of crimson flowers. ...the lurid, crimson glow of the blast furnaces.* COLOUR

2 If a person goes **crimson**, their face becomes red because they are angry or embarrassed. *I used to refuse invitations to parties because I knew I'd go crimson every time someone talked to me.* ADJ: usu v-link ADJ

cringe /krɪndʒ/ **cringes, cringing, cringed.** If you **cringe** at something, you feel embarrassed or disgusted, and perhaps show this feeling in your expression or by making a slight movement. *Molly had cringed when Ann started picking up the guitar... Chris had cringed at the thought of using her own family for publicity... I cringed in horror.* ◆◇◇◇◇ VERB =recoil; V; V at n; V in n

crinkle /krɪŋkᵊl/ **crinkles, crinkling, crinkled**

1 If something **crinkles** or if you **crinkle** it, it becomes slightly creased or folded. *He shrugged whimsically, his eyes crinkling behind his glasses... When she laughs, she crinkles her perfectly-formed nose... If a plant has spotted or crinkled leaves, do not use it for propagation.* V-ERG; V; V n; V-ed

2 **Crinkles** are small creases or folds. *His mouth had a permanent crinkle of irony.* N-COUNT

crinkly /krɪŋkli/. A **crinkly** object has many small creases or folds in it. *...her big crinkly face... He was a tall man with a low forehead and crinkly black hair.* ADJ-GRADED: usu ADJ n

crinoline /krɪnəlɪn/ **crinolines.** A **crinoline** is a frame of hoops worn as an undergarment by women in the 19th century to make their skirts very full. N-COUNT

cripple /krɪpᵊl/ **cripples, crippling, crippled** ◆◆◇◇◇

1 A person with a physical disability or a serious permanent injury is sometimes referred to as a **cripple**; a use which some people find offensive. *She has gone from being a healthy, fit, and sporty young woman to being a cripple.* N-COUNT

2 If someone **is crippled** by an injury, it is so serious that they can never move their body properly again. *Mr Easton was seriously crippled in an accident and had to leave his job... He had been warned that another bad fall could cripple him for life... He heaved his crippled leg into an easier position.* VERB; be V-ed; V n; V-ed

3 If you describe someone as an emotional **cripple**, you mean that they have a particular psychological or emotional problem which prevents them from living a normal life. N-COUNT

4 If something **cripples** a person, it causes them severe psychological or emotional problems. *Howard wanted to be a popular singer, but stage fright crippled him... I'm not perfect but I'm also not emotionally crippled or lonely.* VERB; V n; V-ed

5 To **cripple** a machine, organization, or system means to damage it severely or prevent it from working properly. *Let's try to cripple their communications... A total cut-off of supplies would cripple Jordan's economy... The pilot was able to maneuver the crippled aircraft out of the hostile area.* VERB; V n; V-ed

crippling /krɪplɪŋ/ ◆◇◇◇◇

1 A **crippling** illness or disability is one that severely damages your health or your body. *Arthritis and rheumatism are prominent crippling diseases... They both suffered from crippling pains in their hips.* ADJ: ADJ n

2 If you say that an action, policy, or situation has a **crippling** effect on something, you mean it has a very serious, harmful effect. *The high cost of capital has a crippling effect on many small American high-tech firms... The American military presence on the islands had suffered a crippling blow.* ♦ **cripplingly** *...cripplingly high interest rates.* ADJ: usu ADJ n; ADV

crisis /kraɪsɪs/ **crises** /kraɪsiːz/. A **crisis** is a situation in which something or someone is affected by one or more very serious problems. *Natural disasters have obviously contributed to the continent's economic crisis... The Italian political system has been judged to be in terminal crisis for decades. ...children's illnesses or other family crises... He's having a mid-life crisis. ...someone to turn to in moments of crisis.* ◆◆◆◆◇ N-VAR: oft supp N

crisp /krɪsp/ **crisper, crispest; crisps, crisping, crisped.** ◆◆◇◇◇

1 Food that is **crisp** is pleasantly hard and crunchy, or has a pleasantly hard and crunchy surface. *Bake the potatoes for 15 minutes, till they're nice and crisp. ...crisp bacon. ...crisp lettuce.* ♦ **crispness** *The pizza base retains its crispness without becoming brittle.* ♦ **crisply** *...crisply fried onion rings.* ADJ-GRADED ≠soggy; N-UNCOUNT; ADV-GRADED

2 If food **crisps** or if you **crisp** it, it becomes pleasantly hard, for example because you have heated it at a high temperature. *Cook the bacon until it begins to crisp... Spread breadcrumbs on a dry baking sheet and crisp them in the oven.* V-ERG; V; V n

3 In British English, **crisps** are very thin slices of potato that have been fried until they are hard, dry, and crispy. The American word is **chips** or **potato chips**. *...a packet of crisps. ...onion-flavoured potato crisps.* N-COUNT: usu pl

4 Weather that is pleasantly fresh, cold, and dry can be described as **crisp**. *...a crisp autumn day.* ADJ-GRADED PRAGMATICS

5 **Crisp** cloth or paper is clean and has no creases in it. *He wore a panama hat and a crisp white suit... I slipped between the crisp clean sheets. ...crisp banknotes.* ♦ **crisply** *...his crisply pressed suit.* ADJ-GRADED: usu ADJ n; ADV-GRADED

6 Leaves or snow that make a crunching noise when you walk on them can be described as **crisp**. *...crisp autumn leaves... He crunched through the crisp snow.* ADJ-GRADED

7 If you describe someone's writing or speech as **crisp**, you mean they write or speak very clearly, without mentioning unnecessary details. This may make them seem unfriendly. *'Very well,' I said, adopting a crisp authoritative tone.* ♦ **crisply** *'I'm not a journalist,' said Mary Ann crisply.* ADJ-GRADED; ADV-GRADED: usu ADV after v

8 If something **is burnt to a crisp**, it is completely burnt; an informal expression. PHRASE: V inflects

crispbread /krɪspbred/ **crispbreads. Crispbread** is thin dry biscuits made from wheat or rye. It is often eaten instead of bread by people who want to lose weight. N-VAR

crispy /krɪspi/ **crispier, crispiest.** Food that is **crispy** is pleasantly hard and crunchy, or has a pleasantly hard and crunchy surface. *...crispy fried onions. ...crispy bread rolls.* ADJ-GRADED PRAGMATICS =crisp

criss-cross /krɪs krɒs, AM - krɔːs/ **criss-crosses, criss-crossing, criss-crossed;** also spelled **crisscross.** ◆◇◇◇◇

1 If a person or thing **criss-crosses** an area, they travel from one side to the other and back again many times, following different routes. If a number of things **criss-cross** an area, they cross it, and cross over each other. *They criss-crossed the country by bus... Telephone wires criss-cross the street.* VERB V n

2 If two sets of lines or things **criss-cross**, they cross over each other. *Wires criss-cross between the tops of the poles, forming a grid... The roads here are quite a maze, criss-crossing one another in a fashion that at times defies logic. ...a complicated labyrinth of criss-crossing paths... Support rows of beans with criss-crossed canes.* V-RECIP pl-n V V pron-recip V-ing V-ed Also V n

3 A **criss-cross** pattern or design consists of lines crossing each other. *Slash the tops of the loaves with a sharp serrated knife in a criss-cross pattern.* ADJ: ADJ n

criterion /kraɪtɪəriən/ **criteria** /kraɪtɪəriə/. A **criterion** is a factor on which you judge or decide something. *The most important criterion for entry is that applicants must design and make their own work... British defence policy had to meet three criteria if it was to succeed.* ◆◆◇◇◇ N-COUNT: oft N for n/-ing

critic /krɪtɪk/ **critics** ◆◆◆◆◇

1 A **critic** is a person who writes reviews and expresses opinions about things such as books, films, music, and art. *Mather was film critic on the Daily Telegraph for many years... The New York critics had praised her performance.* N-COUNT: oft n N =reviewer

2 Someone who is a **critic** of a person or system disapproves of them and criticizes them publicly. *The newspaper has been the most consistent critic of the government... He became a fierce critic of the tobacco industry... Her critics accused her of caring only about success.* N-COUNT: usu with poss

critical /krɪtɪkəl/ ◆◆◆◆◇

1 A **critical** time, factor, or situation is extremely important. *The incident happened at a critical point in the campaign... Environmentalists say a critical factor in the city's pollution is its population... He says setting priorities is of critical importance... How you finance a business is critical to the success of your venture.* ♦ **critically** /krɪtɪkli/ *Economic prosperity depends critically on an open world trading system... It was a critically important moment in his career.* ADJ-GRADED =crucial ADV-GRADED: ADV with v, ADV adj

2 A **critical** situation is very serious and dangerous. *The German authorities are considering an airlift if the situation becomes critical... Its day-to-day finances are in a critical state.* ♦ **critically** *Moscow is running critically low on food supplies.* ADJ ADV: usu ADV adj

3 If a person is **critical** or in a **critical** condition in hospital, they are seriously ill. *Ten of the injured are said to be in critical condition.* ♦ **critically** *She was critically ill... A youth was killed and another critically injured.* ADJ ADV: usu ADV adj, also ADV with v

4 To be **critical** of someone or something means to criticize them. *His report is highly critical of the trial judge. ...a few dozen intellectuals who've been critical of the regime... He has apologised for critical remarks he made about the referee.* ♦ **critically** *She spoke critically of Lara.* ADJ-GRADED: oft ADJ of n ADV-GRADED

5 A **critical** approach to something involves examining and judging it carefully. *We need to become critical text-readers... Marx's work was more than a critical study of capitalist production. ...the critical analysis of political ideas.* ♦ **critically** *Wyman watched them critically.* ADJ: ADJ n =analytical ADV-GRADED

6 If something or someone receives **critical** acclaim, critics say that it is very good. *The film met with considerable critical and public acclaim... The show was also a resounding critical success.* ADJ: ADJ n

critical mass.

1 The **critical mass** of a substance is the minimum amount of it that is needed for a nuclear chain reaction; a technical use in physics. N-SING: also no det

2 A **critical mass** of something is an amount of it that makes it possible for something to happen or continue. *Only in this way can the critical mass of participation be reached.* N-SING: also no det

criticise /krɪtɪsaɪz/. See **criticize.**

criticism /krɪtɪsɪzəm/ **criticisms** ◆◆◆◆◇

1 **Criticism** is the action of expressing disapproval of something or someone. A **criticism** is a statement that expresses disapproval. *This policy had repeatedly come under strong criticism on Capitol Hill... The criticism that the English do not truly care about their children was often voiced.* N-VAR: oft N of n, N that ≠praise

2 **Criticism** is a serious examination and judgement of something such as a book or play. *She has published more than 20 books including novels, poetry and literary criticism.* N-UNCOUNT =analysis, review

criticize /krɪtɪsaɪz/ **criticizes, criticizing, criticized;** also spelled **criticise** in British English. If you **criticize** someone or something, you express your disapproval of them by saying what you think is wrong with them. *His mother had rarely criticized him or any of her children... The minister criticised the police for failing to come up with any leads... The regime has been harshly criticized for serious human rights violations.* ◆◆◆◇◇ VERB ≠praise V n V n for n/-ing

critique /krɪtiːk/ **critiques.** A **critique** is a written examination and judgement of a situation or of a person's work or ideas; a formal word. *She had brought a book, a feminist critique of Victorian lady novelists. ...the Marxist critique of capitalism.* ◆◇◇◇◇ N-COUNT: oft N of n =evaluation

critter /krɪtəʳ/ **critters.** In American English, a **critter** is a living creature; an informal word. *...little furry critters.* N-COUNT

croak /kroʊk/ **croaks, croaking, croaked**

1 When a frog or bird **croaks**, it makes a harsh, low sound. *Thousands of frogs croaked in the reeds by the riverbank.* ► Also a noun. *...the guttural croak of the frogs.* VERB V N-COUNT

2 If someone **croaks** something, they say it in a hoarse, rough voice. *Tiller moaned and managed to croak, 'Help me.'... She croaked something unintelligible.* ► Also a noun. *His voice was just a croak.* VERB V with quote V n N-COUNT

croaky /kroʊki/. If someone's voice is **croaky**, it is hoarse and rough. ADJ-GRADED

crochet /kroʊʃeɪ, AM kroʊʃeɪ/ **crochets, crocheting, crocheted**

1 **Crochet** is a way of making cloth out of cotton or wool by using a needle with a small hook at the end. *...a black crochet waistcoat.* N-UNCOUNT

2 If you **crochet**, you make cloth by using a needle with a small hook at the end. *She offered to teach me to crochet... Ma and I crocheted new quilts. ...crocheted rugs.* VERB V V n V-ed

crock /krɒk/ **crocks**

1 A **crock** is an earthenware pot or jar; an old-fashioned use. *...an earthenware bread crock.* N-COUNT

2 In British English, if you describe someone as an old **crock**, you mean that they are old and weak; an informal old-fashioned use. *But you don't want some old crock like me.* N-COUNT

3 • **a crock of gold**: see **gold.**

crockery /krɒkəri/. **Crockery** is the plates, cups, saucers, and dishes that you use at mealtimes; used mainly in British English. *We had no fridge, cooker, cutlery or crockery.* N-UNCOUNT

crocodile /krɒkədaɪl/ **crocodiles** ◆◇◇◇◇

1 A **crocodile** is a large reptile with a long body and strong jaws. Crocodiles live in rivers and eat meat. N-COUNT

2 A **crocodile** of people, especially school children, or vehicles is a long line of them, moving together; used mainly in British English. *The children walk in crocodiles from the schoolhouse to the dining-room for lunch. ...a long crocodile of coaches.* N-COUNT: oft N of n, also in N

crocodile tears. If you say that someone is crying **crocodile tears**, you mean that their tears N-PLURAL and other expressions of grief are not genuine or sincere. *The sight of George shedding crocodile tears made me sick.*

crocus /kroʊkəs/ **crocuses. Crocuses** are small white, yellow, or purple flowers that are grown in parks and gardens in the early spring. N-COUNT

croft /krɒft, AM krɔːft/ **crofts.** In Scotland, a **croft** is a small piece of land which is owned and farmed by one family and which provides them with food. *...a remote croft near Loch Nevis.* N-COUNT

crofter /krɒftəʳ, AM krɔːft-/ **crofters.** In Scotland, a **crofter** is the owner or tenant of a croft or small farm. N-COUNT

crofting /krɒftɪŋ, AM krɔːft-/. In Scotland, **crofting** is the activity of farming on small pieces of land. *...isolated crofting communities.* N-UNCOUNT: oft N n

croissant /kwæsɒn, AM kwɑːsɑːn/ **croissants. Croissants** are small crescent-shaped pieces of sweetened bread that are eaten for breakfast. They are very popular in France. *...coffee and croissants.* N-VAR

crone /kroʊn/ **crones**

1 A **crone** is an old woman; a literary use. *The shabby old crone took off her shoes.* N-COUNT

2 If you refer to a woman as a **crone**, you mean that she is old and ugly; an offensive use. N-COUNT PRAGMATICS

crony /kroʊni/ **cronies.** Your **cronies** are the friends who you spend a lot of time with; an informal word. *Daily he returned, tired and maudlin from lunchtime drinking sessions with his business cronies.* ◆◇◇◇◇ N-COUNT: usu poss N

cronyism /kroʊniɪzəm/. If you accuse someone in authority of **cronyism**, you mean that they use their power or authority to get jobs for their friends; used in journalism. N-UNCOUNT PRAGMATICS

crook /krʊk/ **crooks, crooking, crooked** ◆◆◇◇◇

1 A **crook** is a dishonest person or a criminal; an informal use. *The man is a crook and a liar... Donaldson was a petty crook with a string of previous offences.* N-COUNT

2 The crook of your arm or leg is the soft inside part where you bend your elbow or knee. *She hid her face in the crook of her arm.* N-COUNT: usu sing, the N of n

3 If you **crook** your arm or finger, you bend it. *He crooked his finger: 'Come forward,' he said.* VERB V n

4 A **crook** is a long pole with a large hook at the end. A crook is carried by a bishop in religious ceremonies, or by a shepherd. *...a shepherd's crook.* N-COUNT

5 If someone says they will do something **by hook or by crook**, they are determined to do it, even if they have to make a great effort or use dishonest means. *They intend to get their way, by hook or by crook.* PHRASE: PHR with cl, PHR with v

crooked /krʊkɪd/ ◆◇◇◇◇

1 If you describe something as **crooked**, especially something that is usually straight, you mean that it is bent or twisted. *...the crooked line of his broken nose. ...a crooked little tree.* ADJ-GRADED ≠straight

2 A **crooked** smile is uneven and bigger on one side than the other. *Polly gave her a crooked grin.* ADJ-GRADED =lopsided ♦ **crookedly** *Nick was smiling crookedly at her.* ADV

3 If you describe a person or an activity as **crooked**, you mean that they are dishonest or criminal; an informal use. *...a crooked cop... She might expose his crooked business deals to her tax inspector brother.* ADJ =bent ≠straight

croon /kruːn/ **croons, crooning, crooned** ◆◇◇◇◇

1 If you **croon**, you sing or hum quietly and gently. *He would much rather have been crooning in a smoky bar... Later in the evening, Lewis began to croon another Springsteen song.* VERB V V n

2 If one person talks to another in a soft gentle voice, you can describe them as **crooning**, especially if you think they are being sentimental or insincere. *'Dear boy,' she crooned, hugging him heartily... The man was crooning soft words of encouragement to his wife.* VERB V with quote V n Also V

crooner /kruːnəʳ/ **crooners.** A **crooner** is a male singer who sings sentimental songs, especially the love songs of the 1930s and 1940s. N-COUNT

crop /krɒp/ **crops, cropping, cropped** ◆◆◆◇◇

1 Crops are plants such as wheat and potatoes that are grown in large quantities for food. *Rice farmers here still plant and harvest their crops by hand... The main crop is wheat and this is grown even on the very steep slopes.* • See also **cash crop**. N-COUNT

2 The plants or fruits that are collected at harvest time are referred to as a **crop**. *Each year it produces a fine crop of fruit... The US government says that this year's corn crop should be about 8 percent more than last year... In the Middle Ages, years of crop failure were always followed by terrible disease.* N-COUNT: usu with supp =harvest

3 You can refer to a group of people or things that have appeared together as a **crop of** people or things; an informal use. *The present crop of books and documentaries about Marilyn Monroe exploit the thirtieth anniversary of her death... Next year's crop of undergraduates opting to take physics represents just 2 per cent of all undergraduates.* N-SING: N of n =batch

4 When a plant **crops**, it produces fruits or parts which people want. *Although these vegetables adapt well to our temperate climate, they tend to crop poorly.* VERB V

5 When you **crop** something that you have planted, you collect the fruits or parts that you want from it. *I started cropping my beans in July.* VERB V n

6 When an animal such as a cow or horse **crops** leaves or plants, it eats them. *I let the horse drop his head to crop the spring grass.* VERB V n

7 To **crop** someone's hair means to cut it short. *She cropped her hair and dyed it blonde.* ♦ **cropped** *She had cropped grey hair.* VERB V n ADJ

8 A **crop** is a short hairstyle. *She had her long hair cut into a boyish crop.* N-COUNT: usu sing

9 If you **crop** a photograph, you cut part of it off, in order to get rid of part of the picture or to be able to frame it. *I decided to crop the picture just above the water line... Her husband was cropped from the photograph.* VERB V n be V-ed from n Also V n from n

10 • **the cream of the crop**: see **cream**.

crop up. If something **crops up**, it appears or happens, usually unexpectedly. *Gillian Shephard's name has cropped up several times in reports about who should take Mr Ryder's place... Problems will crop up and hit you before you are ready.* PHRASAL VERB V P

cropped /krɒpt/. **Cropped** items of clothing are shorter than normal. *Women athletes wear cropped tops and tight shorts.* • See also **crop**. ◆◇◇◇◇ ADJ: usu ADJ n

cropper /krɒpəʳ/. If you say that someone **has come a cropper**, you mean that they have had an unexpected and embarrassing failure; an informal expression. *Several companies that made use of elastic accounting practices have since come a cropper.* PHRASE: V inflects

croquet /kroʊkeɪ, AM kroʊkeɪ/. **Croquet** is a game in which the players use long-handled wooden mallets to hit balls through metal arches stuck in a lawn. N-UNCOUNT

croquette /kroʊket/ **croquettes. Croquettes** are small amounts of mashed potato or meat rolled in breadcrumbs and fried. N-COUNT

cross 1 verb and noun uses

cross /krɒs, AM krɔːs/ **crosses, crossing, crossed** ◆◆◆◆◇

1 If you **cross** something such as a room, a road, or an area of land or water, you move or travel to the other side of it. If you **cross** to a place, you move or travel over a room, road, or area of land or water in order to reach that place. *She was partly to blame for failing to look as she crossed the road... Nine Albanians have crossed the border into Greece and asked for political asylum... In 1838 the first iron sailing vessel crossed the Atlantic... Egan crossed to the drinks cabinet and poured a Scotch.* VERB =go across V n V to/into n Also V adv/prep

2 A road, railway, or bridge that **crosses** an area of land or water passes over it. *The Defford to Eckington road crosses the river half a mile outside Eckington.* VERB V n

3 Lines or roads that **cross** meet and go across each other. *...the intersection where Main and Centre streets cross... It is near where the pilgrimage route crosses the road to Quimper.* V-RECIP pl-n V V n

4 If someone or something **crosses** a limit or boundary, for example the limit of acceptable be- VERB

haviour, they go beyond it. *I normally never write into magazines but Mr Stubbs has finally crossed the line... No party is entitled to a seat in the new parliament unless it gets at least 5 per cent of the vote. Many will fail to cross that threshold.*
V n

5 If an expression **crosses** someone's face, it appears briefly on their face; used in written English. *Berg tilts his head and a mischievous look crosses his face... A faint smile crossed his lips.*
VERB
V n

6 A **cross** is a shape that consists of a vertical line or piece with a shorter horizontal line or piece across it. It is the most important Christian symbol. *Round her neck was a cross on a silver chain... He solemnly made the sign of the cross... Christ died on the cross.*
N-COUNT

7 If Christians **cross** themselves, they make the sign of a cross by moving their hand across the top half of their body. *'Holy Mother of God!' Marco crossed himself.*
VERB
V pron-refl

8 If you describe something as a **cross** that someone has to bear, you mean it is a problem or disadvantage which they have to deal with or endure. *My wife is much cleverer than me; it is a cross I have to bear.*
N-COUNT
=burden

9 A **cross** is a written mark in the shape of an X. You can use it, for example, to indicate that an answer to a question is wrong, to mark the position of something on a map, or to indicate your vote on a ballot paper. *Put a tick next to those activities you like and a cross next to those you dislike.*
N-COUNT

10 In Britain, if a cheque **is crossed**, two parallel lines are drawn across it to indicate that it must be paid into a bank account and cannot be cashed. *Cheques/postal orders should be crossed and made payable to Newmarket Promotions. ...a crossed cheque.*
VB: usu passive
be V-ed
V-ed

11 If you **cross** your arms, legs, or fingers, you put one of them on top of the other. *Jill crossed her legs and rested her chin on one fist, as if lost in deep thought... Pop crossed his arms over his chest and watched us... He was sitting there in the living room with his legs crossed.*
VERB
V n
V-ed

12 If you dare to **cross** someone who is likely to get angry, you dare to oppose them or refuse to do what they want. *If you ever cross him, forget it, you're finished.*
VERB
V n

13 Something that is **a cross between** two things is neither one thing nor the other, but a mixture of both. *'Ha!' It was a cross between a laugh and a bark... It was a lovely dog. It was a cross between a collie and a golden retriever.*
N-SING:
a N between pl-n

14 In some team sports such as football and hockey, a **cross** is the passing of the ball from the side of the field to a player in the centre, usually in front of the goal. *Le Tissier hit an accurate cross to Groves.*
N-COUNT

15 See also **crossing.** • to **cross** your **fingers**: see **finger.** • **cross** my **heart**: see **heart.** • to **cross** your **mind**: see **mind.** • people's **paths cross**: see **path.** • to **cross the Rubicon**: see **Rubicon.** • to **cross swords**: see **sword.**

cross off. If you **cross off** words on a list, you decide that they no longer belong on the list, and often you draw a line through them to indicate this. *I checked the chart and found I had crossed off the wrong thing... They have enough trouble finding nutritious food without crossing meat off their shopping lists.*
PHRASAL VERB
V P n (not pron)
V n P
Also V n P

cross out. If you **cross out** words on a page, you draw a line through them, because they are wrong or because you want to change them. *He crossed out 'fellow subjects', and instead inserted 'fellow citizens'.*
PHRASAL VERB
=delete
V P n (not pron)
Also V n P

cross 2 adjective use

cross /krɒs, AM krɔːs/ **crosser, crossest.** Someone who is **cross** is rather angry or irritated. *The women are cross and bored... I'm terribly cross with him... She was rather cross about having to trail across London.* ♦ **crossly** *'No, no, no,' Morris said crossly.*
◆◆◇◇◇
ADJ-GRADED:
usu v-link ADJ
=annoyed
ADV-GRADED:
ADV with v

crossbar /krɒsbɑːʳ, AM krɔːs-/ **crossbars**

1 A **crossbar** is a horizontal piece of wood attached to two upright pieces, for example the top part of the goal in football.
N-COUNT

2 The **crossbar** of a man's or boy's bicycle is the horizontal metal bar between the handlebars and the saddle.
N-COUNT

crossbones /krɒsbəʊnz, AM krɔːs-/. See **skull and crossbones.**

cross-border.
◆◇◇◇◇

1 **Cross-border** trade occurs between companies in different countries. *Currency-conversion costs remain one of the biggest obstacles to cross-border trade... The stock market is convinced more cross-border deals will take place.*
ADJ:
ADJ n
=overseas
≠domestic

2 **Cross-border** attacks involve people crossing a border and going a short way into another country. *...a cross-border raid into Zambian territory.*
ADJ:
ADJ n

crossbow /krɒsbəʊ, AM krɔːs-/ **crossbows.** A **crossbow** is a weapon consisting of a small bow that is fixed across a piece of wood, which releases an arrow with great power when you press a trigger.
N-COUNT

cross-breed, cross-breeds, cross-breeding, cross-bred; also spelled **crossbreed.**

1 If one species of animal or plant **cross-breeds** or **is cross-bred** with another, they reproduce, and new or different animals or plants are produced. *By cross breeding with our native red deer, the skia deer have affected the gene pool... Unfortunately attempts to cross breed it with other potatoes have been unsuccessful... Dr Russel is creating an elite herd by cross-breeding goats from around the globe. ...a cross-bred labrador.* ♦ **cross-breeding** *...centuries of crossbreeding.*
V-RECIP-ERG
V with n
V n with n
V pl-n
V-ed
Also pl-n V
N-UNCOUNT

2 A **cross-breed** is an animal that is the result of cross-breeding.
N-COUNT

cross-Channel; also spelled **cross-channel.** **Cross-Channel** travel is travel across the English Channel, especially by boat. *I was awaiting the cross-channel ferry from Ostend to Dover... Dieppe has plenty to attract cross-Channel visitors.*
ADJ:
ADJ n

cross-check, cross-checks, cross-checking, cross-checked. If you **cross-check** information, you check that it is correct using a different method or source from the one originally used to obtain it. *You have to scrupulously check and cross-check everything you hear... His version will later be cross-checked against that of the university... They want to ensure such claims are justified by cross-checking with other records.*
VERB
V n
be V-ed against n
V with n
Also V,
V n with n

cross-country.
◆◆◇◇◇

1 **Cross-country** is the sport of running, riding, or skiing across open countryside rather than along roads or around a running track. *She finished third in the world cross-country championships in Antwerp.*
N-UNCOUNT:
oft N n

2 A **cross-country** journey involves less important roads or railway lines, or takes you from one side of a country to the other. *...cross-country rail services... The group made a 13-concert cross-country tour, including a stop in New York.* ► Also an adverb. *I drove cross-country in his van.*
ADJ:
ADJ n
ADV:
ADV after v

cross-cultural. **Cross-cultural** means involving two or more different cultures. *Minority cultures within the United States often raised issues of cross-cultural conflict.*
ADJ:
ADJ n

cross-current, cross-currents

1 A **cross-current** is a current in a river or sea that flows across another current. *Cross-currents wait just offshore to sweep the strongest swimmer helplessly away.*
N-COUNT:
usu pl

2 You can refer to conflicting ideas or traditions as **cross-currents.** *...the cross-currents within the Conservative Party.*
N-COUNT:
usu pl,
usu with supp

cross-dress, cross-dresses, cross-dressing, cross-dressed. If someone **cross-dresses**, they wear the clothes of the opposite sex, especially for sexual pleasure. *Gerald started to cross-dress at 14 when he tried on some of his mother's underwear.* ♦ **cross-dresser, cross-dressers** *Now that I have met other cross-dressers I feel tremendous relief.* ♦ **cross-dressing** *Myra tolerated*
VERB
V
N-COUNT
=transvestite
N-UNCOUNT

Clive's cross-dressing until he joined a club for transvestites. =transvestism

cross-examine, cross-examines, cross-examining, cross-examined. ◆◇◇◇◇ VERB When a lawyer **cross-examines** someone during a trial or hearing, he or she questions them about the evidence that they have already given. *The accused's lawyers will get a chance to cross-examine him... You know you are liable to be cross-examined mercilessly about the assault.* V n; be V-ed about n; Also V n about n ♦ **cross-examination** /krɒs ɪgzæmɪneɪʃən/ **cross-examinations** N-VAR *...during the cross-examination of a witness in a murder case... Under cross-examination, he admitted the state troopers used more destructive ammunition than usual.*

cross-eyed. Someone who is **cross-eyed** has eyes that seem to look towards each other. ADJ

crossfire /krɒsfaɪəʳ, AM krɔːs-/; also spelled **cross-fire**.

1 **Crossfire** is gunfire, for example in a battle, that comes from two or more different directions and passes through the same area. N-UNCOUNT

2 If you are **caught in the crossfire**, you become involved in an unpleasant situation in which people are arguing with each other, although you do not want to be involved or say which person you agree with. *They say they are caught in the crossfire between the education establishment and the government.* PHRASE: v-link PHR

crossing /krɒsɪŋ, AM krɔːs-/ **crossings** ◆◆◇◇◇

1 A **crossing** is a journey by boat or ship to a place on the other side of a sea. *He made the crossing from Cape Town to Sydney in just over twenty-six days... The vessel docked in Swansea after a ten-hour crossing.* N-COUNT

2 A **crossing** is the same as a **pedestrian crossing**. *A car hit her on a crossing.* ● See also **pelican crossing, zebra crossing**. N-COUNT

3 A **crossing** is the same as a **level crossing**. N-COUNT

cross-legged. If someone is sitting **cross-legged**, they are sitting on the floor with their legs bent so that their knees point outwards. *He sat cross-legged on the floor.* ADV: ADV after v ► Also an adjective. *The cross-legged deity exudes wisdom and composure.* ADJ: usu ADJ n

crossover /krɒsoʊvəʳ, AM krɔːs-/ **crossovers** ◆◇◇◇◇

1 A **crossover** of one style and another, especially in music or fashion, is a combination of the two different styles. *This LP has to be one of the most curious and successful crossovers of recent times. ...the contemporary crossover of pop, jazz and funk. ...dance/rock crossover bands.* N-VAR: oft N n

2 In music or fashion, if someone makes a **crossover** from one style to another, they become successful outside the style they were originally known for. *I told her the crossover from actress to singer is easier than singer to actress.* N-SING: usu N from/to n

cross-purposes; also spelled **cross purposes**. If people are **at cross-purposes**, there is a misunderstanding between them because they are working towards or talking about different things without realizing it. *The two friends find themselves at cross-purposes with the officials.* PHRASE: PHR after v, v-link PHR, oft PHR with n

cross-question, cross-questions, cross-questioning, cross-questioned. VERB If you **cross-question** someone, you ask them a lot of questions about something. *The police came back and cross-questioned Des again.* V n

cross-reference, cross-references, cross-referencing, cross-referenced

1 A **cross-reference** is a note in a book which tells you that there is relevant or more detailed information in another part of the book. N-COUNT

2 If something such as a book **is cross-referenced**, cross-references are put in it. *Nearly 2,300 plant lists have been checked and cross-referenced. ...an index of products and services which is cross-referenced to the supplying companies.* VB: usu passive; be V-ed; V-ed

crossroads /krɒsroʊdz, AM krɔːs-/; **crossroads** is both the singular and the plural form. ◆◇◇◇◇

1 A **crossroads** is a place where two roads meet and cross each other. *Turn right at the first crossroads.* N-COUNT

2 If you say that something is at a **crossroads**, you mean that it has reached a very important stage in its development where it could go one way or another. *The company was clearly at a crossroads... They had reached a crossroads in their relationship.* N-SING: oft at a N

cross-section, cross-sections ◆◇◇◇◇

1 If you refer to a **cross-section** of particular things or people, you mean a group of them that you think is typical or representative of all of them. *I was surprised at the cross-section of people there... It is good that there is a wide cross-section of sport on television.* N-COUNT: usu N of n

2 A **cross-section** of an object is what you would see if you could cut straight through the middle of it. *...a cross-section of an airplane... The hall is square in cross-section.* N-COUNT: also in N

cross-stitch; also spelled **cross stitch**. **Cross-stitch** is a type of decorative sewing where one stitch crosses another. N-UNCOUNT

crosswalk /krɒswɔːk, AM krɔːs-/ **crosswalks.** In American English, a **crosswalk** is a place where pedestrians can cross a street and where motorists must stop to let them cross. The usual British word is **pedestrian crossing**. N-COUNT

crosswind /krɒswɪnd, AM krɔːs-/ **crosswinds;** also spelled **cross-wind**. A **crosswind** is a strong wind that blows across the direction that vehicles, boats, or aircraft are travelling in, and that makes it difficult for them to keep moving steadily forward. N-COUNT

crosswise /krɒswaɪz, AM krɔːs-/. **Crosswise** means diagonally across something. *Rinse and slice the courgettes crosswise.* ADV: ADV after v =diagonally

crossword /krɒswɜːʳd, AM krɔːs-/ **crosswords.** ◆◇◇◇◇ N-COUNT A **crossword** or **crossword puzzle** is a word game in which you work out the answers to clues, and write the answers in the white squares of a pattern of small black and white squares.

crotch /krɒtʃ/ **crotches**

1 Your **crotch** is the part of your body between the tops of your legs. *Glover kicked him hard in the crotch.* N-COUNT

2 The **crotch** of a pair of trousers or pants is the part that covers the area between the tops of your legs. *They were too long in the crotch.* N-COUNT

crotchet /krɒtʃɪt/ **crotchets.** A **crotchet** is a musical note that has a time value equal to two quavers; used mainly in British English. N-COUNT

crotchety /krɒtʃɪti/. A **crotchety** person is bad-tempered and easily irritated; an informal word. *...a crotchety old man.* ADJ-GRADED: usu ADJ n =grumpy

crouch /kraʊtʃ/ **crouches, crouching, crouched** ◆◆◇◇◇

1 If you **are crouching**, your legs are bent under you so that you are close to the ground and leaning forward slightly. *We were crouching in the bushes... I crouched on the ground... The man was crouched behind the Mercedes.* VERB =squat; V prep/adv; V-ed ► Also a noun. *They walked in a crouch, each bent over close to the ground.* N-SING ► **Crouch down** means the same as **crouch**. *He crouched down and reached under the mattress... He crouched down beside him.* PHRASAL VERB V P; V P prep/adv

2 If you **crouch** over something, you bend over it so that you are very near to it. *Meantime, here I crouch over a cup of tea in my unheated study. ...sitting crouched over the steering wheel.* VERB V prep/adv; V-ed

croup /kruːp/. **Croup** is a disease which children sometimes suffer from that makes it difficult for them to breathe and causes them to cough a lot. N-UNCOUNT: also the N

croupier /kruːpieɪ, AM -iər/ **croupiers.** A **croupier** is the person in charge of a gambling table in a casino, who collects the bets and pays money to the people who have won. N-COUNT

crouton /kruːtɒn/ **croutons. Croutons** are small pieces of toasted or fried bread that are added to soup just before you eat it. *...French onion soup with cheese croutons.* N-COUNT: usu pl

crow /kroʊ/ **crows, crowing, crowed** ◆◇◇◇◇

1 A **crow** is a large black bird which makes a loud, harsh noise. N-COUNT

2 When a cock **crows**, it utters a loud sound, often VERB

early in the morning. *The cock crows and the dawn chorus begins.* V

3 If you say that someone **is crowing** about something they have achieved or are pleased about, you disapprove of them because they keep telling people proudly about it; an informal use. *Edwards is already crowing about his assured victory... We've seen them all crowing that socialism's dead.* VERB PRAGMATICS =boast V *about/over* n V that

4 If someone **crows**, they make happy sounds or say something happily. *She was crowing with delight... 'I'm not sure I've ever driven a better lap,' crowed a delighted Mansell.* VERB V *with* n V with quote

5 If you say that a place is a particular distance away **as the crow flies**, you mean that it is that distance away measured in a straight line. *I live at Mesa, Washington, about 10 miles as the crow flies from Hanford.* PHRASE: oft amount PHR

crowbar /kroʊbɑːʳ/ **crowbars.** A **crowbar** is a heavy iron bar which is used as a lever. *Neighbours eventually levered open the door with a crowbar.* N-COUNT

crowd /kraʊd/ **crowds, crowding, crowded** ◆◆◆◆◇

1 A **crowd** is a large group of people who have gathered together, for example to watch or listen to something interesting, or to protest about something. *A huge crowd gathered in a square outside the Kremlin walls... It took some two hours before the crowd was fully dispersed... The crowd were enormously enthusiastic... The explosions took place in shopping centres as crowds of people were shopping for Mothers' Day.* N-COUNT-COLL: oft N *of* n =throng

2 A particular **crowd** is a group of friends, or a set of people who share the same interests or occupation; an informal use. *All the old crowd have come out for this occasion.* N-COUNT: usu supp N

3 When people **crowd** around someone or something, they gather closely together around them. *The hungry refugees crowded around the tractors... Police blocked off the road as hotel staff and guests crowded around.* VERB =cluster V *round/around* n V *round/around*

4 If people **crowd** into a place or **are crowded** into a place, large numbers of them enter it so that it becomes very full. *Hundreds of thousands of people have crowded into the center of the Lithuanian capital, Vilnius... One group of journalists were crowded into a minibus... 'Bravo, bravo,' chanted party workers crowded in the main hall.* V-ERG =pack, cram V *into* n *be* V-ed *into* n V-ed Also V n *into*

5 If a group of people **crowd** a place, there are so many of them there that it is full. *Thousands of demonstrators crowded the streets shouting slogans.* VERB =pack V n

6 If people **crowd** you, they stand very closely around you trying to see or speak to you, so that you feel uncomfortable. *It had been a tense, restless day with people crowding her all the time.* VERB V n

crowd in. If problems or thoughts **crowd in** on you, a lot of them happen to you or affect you at the same time, so that they occupy all your attention and make you feel unable to escape. *Everything is crowding in on me... She tried to sleep, but thoughts crowded in and images flashed into her mind.* PHRASAL VERB V P *on* n V P

crowd out. If one thing **crowds out** another, it is so successful or widespread that the other thing does not have the opportunity to be successful or exist. *In the 1980s American exports crowded out European films.* PHRASAL VERB =push out V P n (not pron) Also V n P

crowded /kraʊdɪd/ ◆◆◇◇◇

1 If a place is **crowded**, it is full of people. *He peered slowly around the small crowded room... The street was crowded and noisy... The old town square was crowded with people.* ADJ-GRADED: oft ADJ *with* n ≠empty, deserted

2 If a place is **crowded**, a lot of people live there. *...a crowded city of 2 million... The best housing they could afford was crowded and filthy.* ADJ-GRADED =overpopulated

3 If your timetable, your life, or your mind is **crowded**, it is full of events, activities, or thoughts. *Never before has a European Community summit had such a crowded agenda. ...a long life crowded with incident... She slept fitfully, her mind crowded with confusing dreams.* ADJ-GRADED: oft ADJ *with* n =packed

crowd-pleaser, crowd-pleasers; also spelled **crowd pleaser**. If you describe a performer, politician, or sports player as a **crowd-pleaser**, you mean they always please their audience. You can also describe an action or event as a **crowd-pleaser**. *He gets spectacular goals and is a real crowd pleaser.* N-COUNT

crowd-puller, crowd-pullers; also spelled **crowd puller**. If you describe a performer or event as a **crowd-puller**, you mean that they attract a large audience. *The exhibition is hardly a crowd-puller.* N-COUNT

crown /kraʊn/ **crowns, crowning, crowned** ◆◆◆◇◇

1 A **crown** is a circular ornament, usually made of gold and jewels, which a king or queen wears at official ceremonies. You can also use **crown** to refer to anything circular that is used to adorn someone's head. *...colour pictures of the Queen with her crown on. ...a crown of thorns.* N-COUNT

2 The monarchy of a particular country is referred to as **the Crown** when it is regarded as an institution rather than as an individual person. The prosecutor in British criminal cases is **the Crown**. *She says the sovereignty of the Crown must be preserved. ...a Minister of the Crown. ...chief witness for the Crown.* N-PROPER: *the* N

3 When a king or queen **is crowned**, a crown is placed on their head as part of a ceremony in which they are officially made king or queen. *Elizabeth was crowned in Westminster Abbey on 2 June 1953... Two days later, Juan Carlos was crowned king. ...the newly crowned King.* VB: usu passive *be* V-ed *be* V-ed n V-ed

4 If one thing **crowns** another, it is on top of it; a literary use. *Here another rugged castle crowns the cliffs and crags. ...a very striking face, crowned by an abundance of hair.* VERB V n V-ed

5 Your **crown** is the top part of your head, at the back. *He laid his hand gently on the crown of her head.* N-COUNT: usu sing, usu with supp

6 The **crown** of a hat is the part which covers the top of your head. N-COUNT: usu sing

7 A **crown** was a British coin worth five shillings. N-COUNT

8 A **crown** is an artificial top piece fixed over a broken or decayed tooth. N-COUNT

9 In sport, a **crown** is a title or championship. *...his dream of a fourth Wimbledon crown.* N-COUNT: oft n N

10 An achievement or event that **crowns** something makes it perfect, successful, or complete. *It is an important moment, crowning the efforts of the Cup organisers... The summit was crowned by the signing of the historic START treaty. ...the crowning achievement of his career.* VERB V n V-ing

11 If you **crown** your career with a success or achievement, you have a final success or achievement which is greater than all the others you have had. *He went on to crown a distinguished career in radio and television with his book 'The Price of Victory'.* VERB V n *with* n Also V n *by*-ing

Crown Court, Crown Courts. In England and Wales, a **Crown Court** is a court in which criminal cases are tried by a judge and jury rather than by a magistrate. *He appeared at Manchester Crown Court on Thursday on a drink-driving charge.* ◆◆◇◇◇ N-COUNT: usu sing, oft in names

crown jewel, crown jewels

1 **The Crown Jewels** are the crown, sceptre, and other precious objects which are used on important official occasions by the King or Queen. N-PLURAL: *the* N

2 If you describe something as someone's **crown jewel**, you mean it is the most important or valuable thing they have. *The company is also willing to sell 20% of its crown jewel, its credit-card business.* N-COUNT: usu poss N

Crown Prince, Crown Princes. A **Crown Prince** is a prince who will be king of his country when the present king or queen dies. *...the crown prince's palace. ...Sultan Mahmood's son, Crown Prince Ibrahim Mahmood.* ◆◇◇◇◇ N-COUNT: usu *the* N in sing; N-TITLE

Crown Princess, Crown Princesses. A **Crown Princess** is a princess who is the wife of a Crown Prince, or will be queen of her country when the present king or queen dies. *...his second wife, Crown Princess Catherine.* N-COUNT: usu *the* N in sing; N-TITLE

crow's feet. **Crow's feet** are wrinkles which some older people have at the outside corners of their eyes. N-PLURAL

crow's nest. On a ship, the **crow's nest** is a small platform high up on the mast, where a person can go to look in all directions. N-SING

crucial /kruːʃəl/. If you describe something as **crucial**, you mean it is extremely important. *He had administrators under him but took the crucial decisions himself. ...the most crucial election campaign for years... Improved consumer confidence is crucial to an economic recovery.* ◆◆◆◇◇ ADJ-GRADED: oft ADJ *to* n =critical
♦ **crucially** *Chewing properly is crucially important... Crucially, though, it failed to secure the backing of the banks.* ADV-GRADED

crucible /kruːsɪbəl/ **crucibles**
1 A **crucible** is a pot in which metals or other substances can be melted or heated up to very high temperatures. N-COUNT
2 **Crucible** is used to refer to a situation in which something is tested or a conflict takes place, often one which produces something new; a literary use. *...a system in which ideas are tested in the crucible of party contention... The regime served as a crucible for the forging of right-wing ideas and values.* N-SING: oft N *of* n

crucifix /kruːsɪfɪks/ **crucifixes.** A **crucifix** is a cross with a figure of Christ on it. N-COUNT

crucifixion /kruːsɪfɪkʃən/ **crucifixions** ◆◇◇◇◇
1 **Crucifixion** is a way of killing people which was common in the Roman Empire, in which they were tied or nailed to a cross and left to die. *...her historical novel about the crucifixion of Christians in Rome.* N-VAR
2 **The Crucifixion** is the crucifixion of Christ. *...the central message of the Crucifixion.* N-PROPER: *the* N

cruciform /kruːsɪfɔːʳm/. A **cruciform** building or object is shaped like a cross; a formal word. *...a cruciform tower.* ADJ: usu ADJ n

crucify /kruːsɪfaɪ/ **crucifies, crucifying, crucified** ◆◇◇◇◇
1 If someone **is crucified**, they are killed by being tied or nailed to a cross and left to die. *...the day that Christ was crucified.* VB: usu passive *be* V-ed
2 To **crucify** someone means to criticize or punish them severely; an informal use. *She'll crucify me if she finds you still here... She was crucified by the critics for her performance.* VERB V n

crude /kruːd/ **cruder, crudest; crudes** ◆◆◇◇◇
1 A **crude** method or measurement is not exact or detailed, but may be useful or correct in a rough, general way. *Standard measurements of blood pressure are an important but crude way of assessing the risk of heart disease or strokes... Birthplace data are only the crudest indicator of actual migration paths.* ADJ-GRADED ≠rough
♦ **crudely** *The donors can be split – a little crudely – into two groups... Put crudely, the liberationists favour extending a number of rights to children.* ADV-GRADED: usu ADV with v, also ADV adj
2 If you describe an object that someone has made as **crude**, you mean that it has been made in a very simple way or from very simple parts. *...crude wooden boxes.* ADJ-GRADED
♦ **crudely** *...a crudely carved wooden form... In some places maps are scarce, and are often crudely produced.* ADV-GRADED: usu ADV -ed
3 If you describe someone as **crude**, you disapprove of them because they speak or behave in a rude, offensive, or unsophisticated way. *Nev! Must you be quite so crude? ...crude language. ...crude sexual jokes.* ADJ-GRADED PRAGMATICS =coarse
♦ **crudely** *He hated it when she spoke so crudely... To put it crudely, nobody really gives a toss about this any more.* ADV-GRADED: usu ADV with v, also ADV adj
♦ **crudity** /kruːdɪti/ *He had not expected such crudity from so sophisticated a minister.* N-UNCOUNT
♦ **crudeness** *Crudeness is on the rise in all fields of entertainment.* N-UNCOUNT
4 **Crude** substances are in a natural or unrefined state, and have not yet been used in manufacturing processes. *...8.5 million tonnes of crude steel.* ADJ: ADJ n =raw ≠refined
5 **Crude** is the same as **crude oil.** N-MASS

crude oil. **Crude oil** is oil in its natural state before it has been processed or refined. *A thousand tons of crude oil has spilled into the sea from an oil tanker.* ◆◇◇◇◇ N-UNCOUNT

crudites /kruːdɪteɪ, AM -teɪ/. **Crudites** are pieces of raw vegetable, often served before a meal with a dip. N-PLURAL

cruel /kruːəl/ **crueller, cruellest** ◆◆◇◇◇
1 Someone who is **cruel** deliberately causes pain or distress to people or animals. *Children can be so cruel... Don't you think it's cruel to cage a creature up?* ADJ-GRADED: oft *it* v-link ADJ to-inf ≠kind
♦ **cruelly** *Douglas was often cruelly tormented by jealous siblings.* ADV-GRADED: ADV with v
2 A situation or event that is **cruel** is very harsh and causes people distress. *...struggling to survive in a cruel world with which they cannot cope... By a cruel irony, his horse came down on a flat part of the course.* ADJ-GRADED
♦ **cruelly** *His life has been cruelly shattered by an event not of his own making.* ADV-GRADED: usu ADV with v

cruelty /kruːəlti/ **cruelties.** **Cruelty** is behaviour that deliberately causes pain or distress to people or animals. *Britain had laws against cruelty to animals but none to protect children... He had been unable to escape the cruelties of war.* ◆◆◇◇◇ N-VAR: usu with supp, oft N *to* n ≠kindness

cruet /kruːɪt/ **cruets.** A **cruet** is a small container, or set of containers, for salt, pepper, or mustard which you use at mealtimes. *...a cruet set.* N-COUNT

cruise /kruːz/ **cruises, cruising, cruised** ◆◆◆◇◇
1 A **cruise** is a holiday during which you travel on a ship or boat and visit a number of places. *He and his wife were planning to go on a world cruise... The next stop on this cruise is likely to be in Cornwall.* N-COUNT
2 If you **cruise** a sea, river, or canal, you travel around it or along it on a cruise. *She wants to cruise the canals of France in a barge... During their summer holidays they cruised further afield to Normandy and Brittany.* VERB V n V prep/adv
♦ **cruising** *...a 51ft cruising yacht.* N-UNCOUNT
3 If a car, ship, or aircraft **cruises** somewhere, it moves at a constant speed that is comfortable and unhurried. *A black and white police car cruised past.* VERB V prep/adv
4 If a team or sports player **cruises to** victory, they win easily; used in journalism. *Graf looked in awesome form as she cruised to an easy 6-2, 6-1 victory.* VERB V *to* n
5 If someone, especially a gay man, **is cruising**, they are searching in public places for a sexual partner. *...gay men cruising on Clapham Common.* VERB V

cruise missile, cruise missiles. A **cruise missile** is a missile which carries a nuclear warhead and which is guided by a computer. ◆◇◇◇◇ N-COUNT

cruiser /kruːzəʳ/ **cruisers** ◆◇◇◇◇
1 A **cruiser** is a motor boat which has a cabin for people to live or sleep in. *...a motor cruiser.* N-COUNT: oft n N
2 A **cruiser** is a large fast warship. *Italy had lost three cruisers and two destroyers.* N-COUNT

cruiserweight /kruːzəʳweɪt/ **cruiserweights.** A **cruiserweight** is a professional boxer who weighs between 160 and 175 pounds, or an amateur boxer who weighs between 165 and 179 pounds. N-COUNT

crumb /krʌm/ **crumbs** ◆◇◇◇◇
1 **Crumbs** are tiny pieces that fall from bread, biscuits, or cake when you cut it or eat it. *I stood up, brushing crumbs from my trousers.* N-COUNT: usu pl
2 A **crumb** of something, for example information, is a very small amount of it. *At last Andrew gave them a crumb of information... The government were able to draw a few crumbs of comfort from today's unemployment figures.* N-COUNT: usu N *of* n

crumble /krʌmbəl/ **crumbles, crumbling, crumbled** ◆◆◇◇◇
1 If something soft or brittle **crumbles**, or if you **crumble** it, it breaks into a lot of small pieces. *Under the pressure, the flint crumbled into fragments... Roughly crumble the cheese into a bowl.* V-ERG V V n
2 If an old building or piece of land **is crumbling**, parts of it keep breaking off. *The high and low-rise apartment blocks built in the 1960s are crumbling... The cliffs were estimated to be crumbling into the sea at the rate of 10ft an hour.* VERB =disintegrate V V prep/adv
► **Crumble away** means the same as **crumble**. *Britain's coastline stretches 4000 kilometres and much of it is crumbling away.* PHRASAL VERB V P
3 If something such as a system, relationship, or hope **crumbles**, it comes to an end. *Their economy crumbled under the weight of United Nations sanctions... The traditional marriage is crumbling fast... It only takes a minute for the football hopes of an entire country to crumble.* VERB =fall apart V
► **Crumble away** means PHRASAL VERB

the same as **crumble**. *Opposition more or less crumbled away.*

4 If someone **crumbles**, they stop resisting or trying to win, or become unable to cope. *Brighton have too many experienced players to crumble just because we are in town... He is a skilled and ruthless leader who isn't likely to crumble under pressure.* VERB V

5 In British English, a **crumble** is a baked pudding made with fruit covered in a crumbly mixture of flour, butter, and sugar. *...apple crumble.* N-VAR: usu n N

crumble away. See **crumble** 2 and 3. PHRASAL VERB

crumbly /krʌmbli/ **crumblier, crumbliest.** Something that is **crumbly** is easily broken into a lot of little pieces. *...crumbly cheese.* ADJ-GRADED

crummy /krʌmi/ **crummier, crummiest.** If you describe something as **crummy**, you mean it is of very poor quality; an informal word. *Here I am at a crummy hotel, with no clean clothes.* ADJ-GRADED: usu ADJ n =grotty

crumpet /krʌmpɪt/ **crumpets**

1 In Britain, **crumpets** are round, flat pieces of a substance like bread or batter with small holes in them. You toast them and eat them with butter. N-COUNT

2 In British English, some men refer to attractive women as **crumpet**; an informal, offensive use. N-UNCOUNT

crumple /krʌmpᵊl/ **crumples, crumpling, crumpled** ◆◇◇◇◇

1 If you **crumple** something such as paper or cloth, or if it **crumples**, it is squashed and becomes full of untidy creases and folds. *She crumpled the paper in her hand... The front and rear of the car will crumple during a collision.* ► **Crumple up** means the same as **crumple**. *She crumpled up her coffee cup... Nancy looked at the note angrily, then crumpled it up and threw it in a nearby wastepaper basket.* ♦ **crumpled** *His uniform was crumpled, untidy, splashed with mud.* V-ERG V n V PHRASAL VERB ERG V P n (not pron) V n P ADJ-GRADED

2 If someone **crumples**, they collapse in an untidy and helpless way, for example when they have received a shock; used in written English. *His body crumpled... He immediately crumpled to the floor... Chance McAllister lay crumpled on the floor.* VERB V V prep V-ed

3 If someone's face **crumples**, they suddenly look very disappointed or as if they want to cry; used in written English. *She faltered, and then her face crumpled once more.* VERB V

4 See **crumple** 1.

crunch /krʌntʃ/ **crunches, crunching, crunched** ◆◆◇◇◇

1 If you **crunch** something hard, such as a sweet, you crush it noisily between your teeth. *She sucked an ice cube into her mouth, and crunched it loudly... Richard crunched into the apple.* VERB V n V *into/on* n

2 If something **crunches** or if you **crunch** it, it makes a breaking or crushing noise, for example when you step on it. *A piece of china crunched under my foot... He crunched the sheets of paper in his hands.* ► Also a noun. *She heard the crunch of tires on the gravel driveway.* V-ERG =scrunch V V n N-COUNT; SOUND

3 If you **crunch** across a surface made of very small stones, you move across it causing it to make a crunching noise. *I crunched across the gravel. ...wheels crunching over a stony surface.* VERB V prep/adv

4 You can refer to a crucial time or event, for example when an important decision has to be made, as the **crunch**. *Tomorrow, though, is the crunch... He can rely on my support when the crunch comes... Mr Major is expected to call a crunch meeting on Monday.* • If you say that something will happen **if** or **when it comes to the crunch**, you mean that it will happen if or when the time comes when something has to be done. *If it comes to the crunch, I'll resign over this.* N-SING: usu *the* N, oft N n PHRASE: V inflects

5 To **crunch** numbers means to do a lot of calculations using a calculator or computer. *I pored over the books with great enthusiasm, often crunching the numbers until 1:00 a.m.* VERB V n

6 A situation in which a business or economy has very little money can be referred to as a **crunch**. *The UN is facing a cash crunch. ...a financial crunch that could threaten the company's future.* N-COUNT: usu supp N =crisis

crunchy /krʌntʃi/ **crunchier, crunchiest.** Food that is **crunchy** is pleasantly hard or crisp so that it makes a noise when you eat it. *...fresh, crunchy vegetables... Bake the mixture for 30 minutes until the top is golden and crunchy.* ADJ-GRADED PRAGMATICS =crisp

crusade /kruːseɪd/ **crusades, crusading, crusaded** ◆◇◇◇◇

1 A **crusade** is a long and determined attempt to achieve something for a cause that you feel strongly about. *Footballers launched an unprecedented crusade against racism on the terraces... He made it his crusade to teach children to love books.* N-COUNT: oft N *against/for* n, N to-inf =campaign

2 If you **crusade** for a particular cause, you make a long and determined effort to achieve something for it. *...a newspaper that has crusaded against the country's cocaine traffickers. ...an adopted boy whose cause is taken up by a crusading lawyer.* VERB =campaign V *against/for* n V-ing

3 **The Crusades** were the holy wars that were fought by Christians in Palestine against the Muslims during the eleventh, twelfth, and thirteenth centuries. N-PROPER-PLURAL: *the* N

crusader /kruːseɪdəʳ/ **crusaders** ◆◇◇◇◇

1 A **crusader** for a cause is someone who does a lot in support of it. *He has set himself up as a crusader for higher press and broadcasting standards.* N-COUNT: with supp

2 A **Crusader** was a knight who fought in the Crusades. N-COUNT

crush /krʌʃ/ **crushes, crushing, crushed** ◆◆◇◇◇

1 To **crush** something means to press it very hard so that its shape is destroyed or so that it breaks into pieces. *Andrew crushed his empty can... Their vehicle was crushed by an army tank... Peel and crush the garlic. ...crushed ice.* VERB V n V-ed

2 To **crush** a protest or movement, or a group of opponents, means to defeat it completely, usually by force. *The military operation was the first step in a plan to crush the uprising. ...in his bid to crush the rebels.* ♦ **crushing** *...the violent crushing of anti-government demonstrations.* VERB V n N-UNCOUNT: usu N *of* n

3 If you **are crushed** by something, it upsets you a great deal. *Listen to criticism but don't be crushed by it.* VB: usu passive =devastate *be* V-ed

4 If you **are crushed** against someone or something, you are pushed or pressed against them. *We were at the front, crushed against the stage.* VB: usu passive *be* V-ed prep

5 A **crush** is a closely-packed crowd of people, in which it is difficult to move. *His thirteen-year-old son somehow got separated in the crush... Everywhere he went he was mobbed by a crush of fans.* N-COUNT: usu sing

6 If you have a **crush** on someone, you are in love with them but do not have a relationship with them; an informal use. *She had a crush on you, you know... I'd got over my schoolgirl crush.* N-COUNT: usu N *on* n

crusher /krʌʃəʳ/ **crushers.** A **crusher** is a piece of equipment used for crushing things. *Squeeze the peeled ginger in a garlic crusher. ...a 40-ton stone crusher.* N-COUNT: usu n N

crushing /krʌʃɪŋ/. A **crushing** defeat, burden, or disappointment is a very great or severe one. *...since their crushing defeat in the local elections. ...a crushing burden of debt... Mr Tambo's death comes as a crushing blow to the ANC.* ◆◇◇◇◇ ADJ: ADJ n

crushingly /krʌʃɪŋli/. You can use **crushingly** to emphasize the degree of a negative quality. *...a collection of crushingly bad jokes... The band's approach tends to be crushingly tedious.* ADV-GRADED: ADV adj PRAGMATICS =extremely

crust /krʌst/ **crusts** ◆◇◇◇◇

1 The **crust** on a loaf of bread is the outside part. N-COUNT

2 A pie's **crust** is the cooked pastry on top. N-COUNT

3 A **crust** is a hardened layer of something, especially on top of a softer or wetter substance. *As the water evaporates, a crust of salt is left on the surface of the soil.* N-COUNT

4 The earth's **crust** is its outer layer. *Earthquakes leave scars in the earth's crust.* N-COUNT: with supp

5 If you **earn a crust**, you earn enough money to live on, especially by doing work you would prefer not to do; used mainly in British English. *In his early days, he would do almost anything to earn a crust from the sport.* PHRASE: V inflects

6 See also **upper crust**.

crustacean /krʌsteɪʃᵊn/ **crustaceans.** A **crustacean** is an animal with a hard shell and several N-COUNT pairs of legs, which usually lives in water. Crabs, lobsters, and shrimps are crustaceans.

crusted /krʌstɪd/. If something is **crusted** with a substance, it is covered with a hard or thick layer of that substance; a literary word. *...flat grey stones crusted with lichen... He moved all the caked and crusted dishes into the kitchen.* ► Also a combining form. *He sat down on the shabby brown sofa to remove his mud-crusted boots.*
ADJ: oft ADJ *with* n =encrusted — COMB in ADJ

crusty /krʌsti/ **crustier, crustiest** ◆◇◇◇◇
1 **Crusty** bread has a hard, crisp outside. *...crusty French loaves.* ADJ-GRADED: usu ADJ n
2 If you describe someone, especially an old man, as **crusty**, you mean they are impatient and easily irritated. *...a crusty old colonel.* ADJ-GRADED: usu ADJ n =grumpy

crutch /krʌtʃ/ **crutches** ◆◇◇◇◇
1 A **crutch** is a stick whose top fits round or under the user's arm, which someone with an injured foot or leg uses to support their weight when walking. *I can walk without the aid of crutches... I was on crutches for a while.* N-COUNT: usu pl, oft *on* N
2 If you refer to someone or something as a **crutch**, you mean that they give you help or support. *The calculator is a tool, not a crutch; yet it is increasingly being used as a crutch by many children... He gave up the crutch of alcohol.* N-SING
3 Your **crutch** is the same as your **crotch**. *He kicked him in the crutch.* N-COUNT

crux /krʌks/. **The crux** of a problem or argument is the most important or difficult part of it which affects everything else. *He said the crux of the matter was economic policy.* N-SING: *the* N, usu N *of* n

cry /kraɪ/ **cries, crying, cried** ◆◆◆◆◇
1 When you **cry**, tears come from your eyes, usually because you are unhappy or hurt. *I hung up the phone and started to cry... Please don't cry... He cried with anger and frustration. ...a crying baby.* ► Also a noun. *A nurse patted me on the shoulder and said, 'You have a good cry, dear.'* ♦ **crying** *She had been unable to sleep for three days because of her 13-week-old son's crying.* VERB V V *with* n V-ing N-SING N-UNCOUNT: usu with poss
2 If you **cry** something, you shout it or say it loudly. *'Nancy Drew,' she cried, 'you're under arrest!'... I cried: 'It's wonderful news!'* ► **Cry out** means the same as **cry**. *'You're wrong, quite wrong!' Henry cried out, suddenly excited... According to the legend, she cried out that no storm was going to stop her from finishing her ride.* VERB V with quote Also V that PHRASAL VERB V P with quote V P that Also V P n
3 A **cry** is a loud, high sound that you make when you feel a strong emotion such as fear, pain, or pleasure. *A cry of horror broke from me... Her brother gave a cry of recognition... With a cry, she rushed forward.* N-COUNT: oft N *of* n
4 A **cry** is a shouted word or phrase, usually one that is intended to attract someone's attention. *Thousands of Ukrainians burst into cries of 'bravo' on the steps of the parliament... Passers-by heard his cries for help.* ● See also **battle cry, rallying cry**. N-COUNT: oft N *of/for* n =shout
5 You can refer to a public protest about something or appeal for something as a **cry** of some kind; used mainly in journalism. *There have been cries of outrage about this expenditure... Many other countries have turned a deaf ear to their cries for help.* N-COUNT: usu N *of/for* n
6 A bird's or animal's **cry** is the loud, high sound that it makes. *...the cry of a seagull.* N-COUNT =call
7 See also **crying**.
8 Something that is **a far cry from** something else is very different from it. *Their lives are a far cry from his own poor childhood.* PHRASES v-link PHR, PHR n
9 When someone is **in full cry**, they are expressing their views very strongly or are very active. *The main opposition party is already in full cry over this mishandling of security.* v-link PHR
10 In informal speech, you can use the expression **for crying out loud** in order to express annoyance or impatience, or to add force to a question or request. *I mean, what's he ever done in his life, for crying out loud?* EXCLAM, PHR with cl PRAGMATICS
11 ● to **cry** your **eyes out**: see **eye**. ● **a shoulder to cry on**: see **shoulder**.

cry off. If you **cry off**, you tell someone that you cannot do something that you have agreed or arranged to do. *Barron invited her to the races and she agreed, but she caught flu and had to cry off at the last minute.* PHRASAL VERB =cancel VP

cry out. If you **cry out**, you call out loudly because you are frightened, unhappy, or in pain. *He was crying out in pain on the ground when the ambulance arrived... Hart cried out as his head struck rock.* ● See also **cry** 2. PHRASAL VERB V P *in* n V P

cry out for. If you say that something **cries out for** a particular thing or action, you mean that it needs that thing or action very much. *This is a disgraceful state of affairs and cries out for a thorough investigation.* PHRASAL VERB V P P n

cry-baby, cry-babies. If someone calls a child a **cry-baby**, they mean that the child cries a lot for no good reason; an informal word used showing disapproval. N-COUNT PRAGMATICS

crying /kraɪɪŋ/
1 If you say that there is **a crying need for** something, you mean that there is a very great need for it. *There is a crying need for more magistrates from the ethnic minority communities.* PHRASES v-link PHR, PHR n =pressing
2 If you say that something is **a crying shame**, you are emphasizing what a great shame it is, often when you are annoyed about it. *It's a crying shame that police have to put up with these mindless attacks.* v-link PHR, oft *it* v-link PHR that PRAGMATICS
3 ● See also **cry**.

cryogenics /kraɪoʊdʒenɪks/; the form **cryogenic** is used as a modifier. **Cryogenics** is a branch of physics that studies what happens to things at extremely low temperatures. N-PLURAL

crypt /krɪpt/ **crypts.** A **crypt** is an underground room beneath a church or cathedral. *...people buried in the crypt of an old London church.* ◆◇◇◇◇ N-COUNT

cryptic /krɪptɪk/. A **cryptic** remark or message contains a hidden meaning or is difficult to understand. *He has issued a short, cryptic statement denying the spying charges... My father's notes are more cryptic here.* ♦ **cryptically** *'Not necessarily,' she says cryptically.* ◆◇◇◇◇ ADJ-GRADED ADV-GRADED: ADV with v

crypto- /krɪptoʊ-/. **Crypto-** is added to adjectives and nouns to form other adjectives and nouns which refer to people who have hidden beliefs and principles. *He has been accused of being a crypto-fascist.* COMB in ADJ and N

crystal /krɪstəl/ **crystals** ◆◆◆◇◇
1 A **crystal** is a small piece of a substance that has formed naturally into a regular symmetrical shape. *...salt crystals. ...ice crystals. ...a single crystal of silicon.* ● See also **liquid crystal, liquid crystal display**. N-COUNT: oft n N
2 **Crystal** is a transparent rock that is used to make jewellery and ornaments. *...a strand of crystal beads.* N-VAR
3 **Crystal** is a high quality glass, usually with patterns cut into its surface. *Some of the finest drinking glasses are made from lead crystal. ...crystal glasses. ...an immense crystal chandelier.* N-UNCOUNT
4 Glasses and other containers made of crystal are referred to as **crystal**. *Get out your best china and crystal.* N-UNCOUNT

crystal ball, crystal balls. If you talk about someone, especially an expert, looking into a **crystal ball**, you mean they are trying to predict the future. Crystal balls are traditionally used by fortune-tellers. *Local economists have looked into their crystal balls and seen something rather nasty... Remember that these are only guidelines: I don't have a crystal ball.* N-COUNT

crystal clear ◆◇◇◇◇
1 Water that is **crystal clear** is absolutely clear and transparent like glass. *The cliffs, lapped by a crystal-clear sea, remind her of Capri.* ADJ
2 If you say that a message or statement is **crystal clear**, you are emphasizing that it is very easy to understand. *The message is crystal clear – if you lose weight, you will have a happier, healthier, better life... We are not going to devalue the pound. I have made that crystal clear.* ADJ: usu v-link ADJ PRAGMATICS

crystalline /krɪstəlaɪn/
1 A **crystalline** substance is in the form of crystals ADJ:

or contains crystals; a technical term in chemistry. *Diamond is the crystalline form of the element carbon. ...hard, crystalline rock.* usu ADJ n
2 **Crystalline** means clear or bright; a literary use. *...a huge plain, crisscrossed by rivers and dotted with crystalline lakes.* ADJ: usu ADJ n
crystallize /krɪstəlaɪz/ **crystallizes, crystallizing, crystallized;** also spelled **crystallise** in British English. ◆◇◇◇◇
1 If you **crystallize** an opinion or idea, or if it **crystallizes**, it becomes fixed and definite in someone's mind. *He has managed to crystallise the feelings of millions of ordinary Russians... Now my thoughts really began to crystallise.* V-ERG V n V
♦ **crystallization** /krɪstəlaɪzeɪʃən/ *...encouraging the crystallization of new values.* N-UNCOUNT: usu N *of* n
2 If a substance **crystallizes**, or something **crystallizes** it, it turns into crystals. *Don't stir or the sugar will crystallise. ...a 19th century technique that actually crystallizes the tin.* ♦ **crystallization** *...experiments on the crystallisation of glass.* V-ERG V V n N-UNCOUNT
crystallized /krɪstəlaɪzd/. **Crystallized** fruits and sweets are covered in sugar which has been melted and then allowed to go hard. ADJ: usu ADJ n
CSE /siː es iː/ **CSEs. CSEs** are British educational qualifications which schoolchildren used to take at the age of fifteen or sixteen. In 1988, CSEs and O Levels were replaced by GCSEs. **CSE** is an abbreviation for 'Certificate of Secondary Education'. *He left school at 16 with seven CSEs.* N-VAR
CS gas. **CS gas** is a gas which causes you to cry and makes breathing painful. It is sometimes used by the army in war or to control a crowd which is rioting; used mainly in British English. N-UNCOUNT
cub /kʌb/ **cubs;** also spelled **Cub** for meanings 2, 3, and 4. ◆◇◇◇◇
1 A **cub** is a young wild animal such as a lion, wolf, or bear. *...three five-week-old lion cubs.* N-COUNT: oft n N
2 **The Cubs** or **the Cub Scouts** is a junior version of the Scouts for boys between the ages of eight and ten. Members of the Cubs attend a weekly meeting where they play games, sing songs, and learn practical skills. N-PROPER-COLL: *the* N
3 A **cub** or a **cub scout** is a boy who is a member of the Cubs. N-COUNT
4 **Cubs** is one of the weekly meetings of the Cubs. *He was on his way to Cubs.* N-UNCOUNT: usu prep N
Cuban /kjuːbən/ **Cubans** ◆◆◆◆◇
1 **Cuban** means belonging or relating to Cuba, or to its people or culture. *...the Cuban capital, Havana.* ADJ
2 A **Cuban** is a Cuban citizen, or a person of Cuban origin. *...easing the restrictions on foreign travel for young Cubans.* N-COUNT
cubby-hole /kʌbi hoʊl/ **cubby-holes.** A **cubby-hole** is a very small room or space for storing things. *This is my office, my little cubbyhole... It's in the cubby hole under the stairs.* N-COUNT
cube /kjuːb/ **cubes, cubing, cubed** ◆◆◇◇◇
1 A **cube** is a solid object with six square surfaces which are all the same size. *...cold water with ice cubes in it. ...a box of sugar cubes... The cabinet comes with locks and key and is shaped like a cube.* N-COUNT: usu with supp
2 When you **cube** food, you cut it into cube-shaped pieces. *Remove the seeds and stones and cube the flesh... Serve with cubed bread.* VERB V n V-ed
3 The **cube** of a number is another number that is produced by multiplying the first number by itself twice. For example, the cube of 2 is 8. N-COUNT: usu sing, usu *the* N *of* n
cube root, cube roots. The **cube root** of a number is another number that makes the first number when it is multiplied by itself twice. For example, the cube root of 8 is 2. N-COUNT: usu sing, *the* N *of* n
cubic /kjuːbɪk/. **Cubic** is used in front of units of length to form units of volume such as **cubic metre** and **cubic foot.** *...3 billion cubic metres of soil.* ◆◇◇◇◇ ADJ: ADJ n
cubicle /kjuːbɪkəl/ **cubicles.** A **cubicle** is a very small enclosed area, for example one where you can have a shower or change your clothes. *...a separate shower cubicle... He made his way to the nearest toilet and locked himself in a cubicle.* ◆◇◇◇◇ N-COUNT
cubism /kjuːbɪzəm/. **Cubism** is a style of art, begun in the early twentieth century, in which objects are represented as if they could be seen from several different positions at the same time, using many lines and geometrical shapes. N-UNCOUNT
Cubist /kjuːbɪst/ **Cubists**
1 A **Cubist** is an artist who painted in the style of Cubism. *The Cubists raised questions concerning the nature of reality itself.* N-COUNT
2 **Cubist** art is art in the style of Cubism. *...Picasso's seminal Cubist painting, 'The Poet'.* ADJ: ADJ n
cub reporter, cub reporters. A **cub reporter** is a young newspaper reporter who is still being trained. *He had been a cub reporter for the Kansas City Star.* N-COUNT
cub scout. See **cub**.
cuckold /kʌkoʊld/ **cuckolds, cuckolding, cuckolded**
1 A **cuckold** is a man whose wife is having an affair with another man; a literary use. *Arthur himself has been portrayed as a weak cuckold.* N-COUNT
2 If a married woman is having an affair, she and her lover **are cuckolding** her husband; a literary use. *His wife had cuckolded him.* VERB V n
cuckoo /kʊkuː/ **cuckoos.** A **cuckoo** is a bird that has an easily recognizable call of two quick notes, and that lays its eggs in other birds' nests. ◆◇◇◇◇ N-COUNT
cuckoo clock, cuckoo clocks. A **cuckoo clock** is a clock with a door from which a toy cuckoo comes out and makes noises like a cuckoo every hour or half hour. N-COUNT
cucumber /kjuːkʌmbəʳ/ **cucumbers** ◆◇◇◇◇
1 A **cucumber** is a long thin vegetable with a hard green skin and wet transparent flesh. It is eaten raw in salads. N-VAR
2 If you say that someone is **as cool as a cucumber**, you are emphasizing that they are very calm and relaxed, especially when you would not expect them to be. *You can hardly be held responsible for Darrow waltzing in, cool as a cucumber, and demanding thousands of pounds.* PHRASE PRAGMATICS
cud /kʌd/. When animals such as cows or sheep **chew the cud**, they slowly chew their partly digested food over and over again in their mouth before finally swallowing it. PHRASE: V inflects =ruminate
cuddle /kʌdəl/ **cuddles, cuddling, cuddled.** If you **cuddle** someone, you put your arms round them and hold them close as a way of showing your affection. *He cuddled the newborn girl... They used to kiss and cuddle in front of everyone.* ► Also a noun. *It would have been nice to give him a cuddle and a kiss but there wasn't time.* ◆◇◇◇◇ V-RECIP =hug V n (non-recip) pl-n V N-COUNT =hug
cuddle up. If you **cuddle up** to someone, you sit or lie as near to them as possible. *'Yes,' he laughs, cuddling up to Debbie... Then we'd go home and cuddle up together to watch TV.* PHRASAL VERB RECIP V P *to* n V P *together* Also V P
cuddly /kʌdəli/ **cuddlier, cuddliest** ◆◇◇◇◇
1 If you describe a person or animal as **cuddly**, you find them attractive because they are plump or soft and look nice to cuddle. *He is a small, cuddly man with spectacles. ...these cuddly creatures from South East Asia.* ADJ-GRADED PRAGMATICS
2 **Cuddly** toys are toys that look like animals. They are made of soft material and stuffed. ADJ: ADJ n
cudgel /kʌdʒəl/ **cudgels**
1 A **cudgel** is a thick, short stick that is used as a weapon. N-COUNT
2 If you **take up the cudgels** for someone or something, you speak or fight in support of them. *The trade unions took up the cudgels for the 367 staff made redundant.* PHRASE: V inflects, oft PHR *for/against* n
cue /kjuː/ **cues, cueing, cued** ◆◆◆◇◇
1 In the theatre or in a musical performance, a performer's **cue** is something another performer says or does that is a signal for them to begin speaking, playing, or doing something. *The actors not performing sit at the side of the stage in full view, waiting for their cues... I had never known him miss a cue.* N-COUNT: oft with poss
2 If one performer **cues** another, they say or do something which is a signal for the second per- VERB

former to begin speaking, playing, or doing something. *He read the scene, with Seaton cueing him.* V n

3 If you say that something that happens is a **cue** for an action, you mean that people start doing that action when it happens. *Mr Clinton's excitement was the cue for a vigorous lobbying campaign... That was Nicholas's cue to ask for another chocolate chip cookie.* N-COUNT: oft N *for* n, N to-inf

4 A **cue** is a long, thin wooden stick that is used to hit the ball in games such as snooker, billiards, and pool. *Their youngest brother was nine when he picked up a cue for the first time.* N-COUNT

5 If you say that something happened **on cue** or **as if on cue**, you mean that it happened just when it was expected to happen, or just at the right time. *Kevin arrived right on cue to care for Harry... 'It's almost eight o'clock.' As if on cue the bell in the chapel began to toll for Matins.* PHRASES

6 If you **take** your **cue** from someone or something, you do something similar in a particular situation. *Taking his cue from his companion, he apologized for his earlier display of temper.* V inflects, usu PHR *from* n

cuff /kʌf/ **cuffs, cuffing, cuffed** ◆◇◇◇◇

1 The **cuffs** of a shirt or dress are the parts at the ends of the sleeves, which are thicker than the rest of the sleeve. *...a pale blue shirt with white collar and cuffs.* N-COUNT: usu pl

2 In American English, the **cuffs** on a pair of pants or trousers are the parts at the ends of the legs, which are folded up. The British term is **turn-up**. *...the cuffs of his jeans.* N-COUNT: usu pl

3 If you **cuff** someone, you hit them quickly and lightly with your hand, usually on their head or their ear. *Brodie cuffed him on the side of the head.* ► Also a noun. *He gave the dog a cuff.* VERB; V n; N-COUNT

4 If the police **cuff** someone, they put handcuffs on them; an informal use. *She hoped they wouldn't cuff her hands behind her back.* VERB; V n

5 An **off-the-cuff** remark is made without being prepared or thought about in advance. *I didn't mean any offence. It was a flippant, off-the-cuff remark... Mr Baker was speaking off the cuff when he made those suggestions.* PHRASE: PHR n, PHR after v

cufflink /kʌflɪŋk/ **cufflinks. Cufflinks** are small decorative objects used for holding together shirt cuffs around the wrist. *...a pair of gold cufflinks.* N-COUNT: usu pl

cuisine /kwɪziːn/ **cuisines** ◆◇◇◇◇

1 The **cuisine** of a country or district is the style of cooking that is characteristic of that place. *The cuisine of Japan is low in fat. ...traditional French cuisine.* N-VAR: usu with supp =cooking

2 The **cuisine** of a restaurant is the range of food that is served in it. *The dining room has lakeside views and offers excellent cuisine... Establishing a new hotel and its cuisine takes time.* N-VAR: usu supp N

3 The skill or profession of cooking unusual or interesting food can be referred to as **cuisine**. *...residential courses in gourmet cuisine.* N-UNCOUNT

cul-de-sac /kʌl dɪ sæk, AM - sæk/ **cul-de-sacs.** A **cul-de-sac** is a short road which is closed at one end. *We have a four-bedroom detached house in a quiet cul-de-sac near Chelmsford.* N-COUNT: usu sing =close

culinary /kʌlɪnəri, AM kjuːləneri/. **Culinary** means concerned with cooking. *She was keen to acquire more advanced culinary skills... A three course dinner completes the culinary delights.* ◆◇◇◇◇ ADJ: ADJ n

cull /kʌl/ **culls, culling, culled** ◆◇◇◇◇

1 If items or ideas **are culled from** a particular source or number of sources, they are taken and gathered together. *All this, needless to say, had been culled second-hand from radio reports... Laura was passing around photographs she'd culled from the albums at home. ...information culled from movies he had seen on television.* VERB; *be* V-ed *from* n; V n *from* n; V-ed

2 To **cull** animals means to kill the weaker animals in a group in order to reduce their numbers. *To save remaining herds and habitat, the national parks department is planning to cull 2000 elephants.* ► Also a noun. *In the reserves of Zimbabwe and South Africa, annual culls are already routine.* ♦ **culling** *The culling of seal cubs has led to an outcry from environmental groups.* VERB; V n; N-COUNT; N-UNCOUNT: usu with supp

culminate /kʌlmɪneɪt/ **culminates, culminating, culminated.** If you say that an activity, process, or series of events **culminates in** or **with** a particular event, you mean that event happens at the end of it. *They had an argument, which culminated in Tom getting drunk... The celebration of the centenary will culminate with a dinner on November 20.* ◆◇◇◇◇ VERB =end; V *in/with* n

culmination /kʌlmɪneɪʃən/. Something, especially something important, that is the **culmination** of an activity, process, or series of events happens at the end of it. *Their arrest was the culmination of an operation in which 120 other people were detained.* ◆◇◇◇◇ N-SING: usu *the* N *of* n

culottes /kjuːlɒts, AM kuː-/. **Culottes** are knee-length women's trousers that look like a skirt. N-PLURAL: also *a pair of* N

culpable /kʌlpəbəl/. If someone or their conduct is **culpable**, they are responsible for something wrong or bad that has happened; a formal word. *Their decision to do nothing makes them culpable. ...manslaughter resulting from culpable negligence.* ♦ **culpability** /kʌlpəbɪlɪti/ *He added there was clear culpability on the part of the government.* ADJ-GRADED; N-UNCOUNT

culprit /kʌlprɪt/ **culprits** ◆◇◇◇◇

1 When you are talking about a crime or something wrong that has been done, you can refer to the person who did it as the **culprit**. *All the men were being deported even though the real culprits in the fight have not been identified.* N-COUNT: usu *the* N =offender

2 When you are talking about a problem or bad situation, you can refer to its cause as the **culprit**. *About 10% of Japanese teenagers are overweight. Nutritionists say the main culprit is increasing reliance on Western fast food.* N-COUNT

cult /kʌlt/ **cults** ◆◆◇◇◇

1 A **cult** is fairly small religious group, especially one which is considered strange. *The teenager may have been abducted by a religious cult... The cult of Isis was carried from Egypt into Greece and Rome.* N-COUNT: usu sing, oft N *of* n

2 Someone or something that is, for example, a **cult** figure or a **cult** hit is very popular or fashionable among a particular group of people. You can also say that someone or something has a **cult** following. *Since her death, she has become a cult figure... The film is destined to become a cult classic... The Osaka-based group is popular home in Japan and has developed a cult following in the United States.* ADJ: ADJ n

3 Someone or something that is a **cult** has become very popular or fashionable among a particular group of people. *Ludlam was responsible for making Ridiculous Theatre something of a cult... The bra has gone from being a fashion classic to a fashion cult.* N-SING

4 The **cult** of something is a situation in which people regard that thing as very important or special; used showing disapproval. *...the cult of youth that recently gripped publishing... Society is entitled and bound to protect itself against a cult of violence... Meanwhile the personality cult around this campaigner grew.* N-COUNT: usu *the* N *of* n

PRAGMATICS

cultivate /kʌltɪveɪt/ **cultivates, cultivating, cultivated** ◆◆◇◇◇

1 If you **cultivate** land or crops, you prepare land and grow crops on it. *She also cultivated a small garden of her own. ...the few patches of cultivated land.* ♦ **cultivation** /kʌltɪveɪʃən/ *...the cultivation of fruits and vegetables... Farmers with many acres under cultivation profited.* VERB; V n; V-ed; N-UNCOUNT: usu with supp, prep N

2 If you **cultivate** an attitude, image, or skill, you try hard to develop it and make it stronger or better. *He has written eight books and has cultivated the image of an elder statesman... Cultivating a positive mental attitude towards yourself can reap tremendous benefits.* ♦ **cultivation** *...the cultivation of a positive approach to life and health.* VERB; V n; N-UNCOUNT: usu N *of* n

3 If you **cultivate** someone or **cultivate** a friendship with them, you try hard to develop a friendship with them. *Howe carefully cultivated Daniel C. Roper, the Assistant Postmaster General... Estonia* VERB; V n *has done much to cultivate the friendship of western European countries.*

cultivated /kʌltɪveɪtɪd/ ◆◇◇◇◇

1 If you describe someone as **cultivated**, you mean they are well-educated and have good manners; a formal use. *His mother was an elegant, cultivated woman.* ADJ-GRADED =refined

2 **Cultivated** plants have been developed for growing on farms or in gardens. *...a mixture of wild and cultivated varieties.* ADJ: ADJ n ≠wild

cultivator /kʌltɪveɪtəʳ/ **cultivators**

1 A **cultivator** is a tool or machine which is used to break up the earth or to remove weeds, for example in a garden or field. N-COUNT

2 A **cultivator** is someone who prepares the ground and grows crops in it; a formal use. N-COUNT

cultural /kʌltʃərəl/ ◆◆◆◇◇

1 **Cultural** means relating to a particular society and its ideas, customs, and art. *...a deep sense of personal honor which was part of his cultural heritage. ...the Rajiv Gandhi Foundation which promotes cultural and educational exchanges between Britain and India.* ♦ **culturally** *...an informed guide to culturally and historically significant sites... Culturally, they have much in common with their neighbours just across the border.* ADJ: usu ADJ n; ADV: ADV adj, ADV with cl

2 **Cultural** means involving or concerning the arts. *...the sponsorship of sports and cultural events by tobacco companies.* ♦ **culturally** *...one of our better-governed, culturally active regional centres – Manchester or Birmingham, say.* ADJ: ADJ n; ADV: ADV adj, ADV with cl

culture /kʌltʃəʳ/ **cultures, culturing, cultured** ◆◆◆◆◇

1 **Culture** consists of activities such as the arts and philosophy, which are considered to be important for the development of civilization and of people's minds. *There is just not enough fun and frivolity in culture today. ...aspects of popular culture. ...France's Minister of Culture and Education.* N-UNCOUNT

2 A **culture** is a particular society or civilization, especially considered in relation to its beliefs, way of life, or art. *...people from different cultures... I was brought up in a culture that said you must put back into the society what you have taken out.* N-COUNT

3 The **culture** of a particular organization or group consists of the habits of the people in it and the way they generally behave. *But social workers say that this has created a culture of dependency, particularly in urban areas... The institutions have realised they need to change their culture to improve efficiency and service.* N-COUNT: usu with supp

4 In science, a **culture** is a group of bacteria or cells which are grown, usually in a laboratory as part of an experiment. *...a culture of human cells. ...a number of tissue culture experiments.* N-COUNT

5 In science, to **culture** a group of bacteria or cells means to grow them, usually in a laboratory as part of an experiment. *To confirm the diagnosis, the hospital laboratory must culture a colony of bacteria. ...cultured human blood cells.* VERB V n V-ed

cultured /kʌltʃəʳd/. If you describe someone as **cultured**, you mean that they have good manners, are well educated, and know a lot about the arts. *He is a cultured man with a wide circle of friends.* ◆◇◇◇◇ ADJ-GRADED

cultured pearl, cultured pearls. A **cultured pearl** is a pearl that is created by putting sand or grit into an oyster. N-COUNT

culture shock. **Culture shock** is a feeling of anxiety, loneliness, and confusion that people sometimes experience when they first arrive in another country. *...Callum, recently arrived in Glasgow, jobless, homeless, friendless, and suffering from culture shock.* N-UNCOUNT: also a N

culvert /kʌlvəʳt/ **culverts.** A **culvert** is a water pipe or sewer that crosses under a road or railway. N-COUNT

-cum- /-kʌm-/. **-cum-** is put between two nouns to form a noun referring to something or someone that is partly one thing and partly another. *...a dining-room-cum-study. She was a sort of policewoman-cum-prosecutor.* COMB in N-COUNT

cumbersome /kʌmbəʳsəm/ ◆◇◇◇◇

1 Something that is **cumbersome** is large and heavy and therefore difficult to carry, wear, or handle. *Although the machine looks cumbersome, it is actually easy to use. ...muffled up in thick and cumbersome clothing.* ADJ-GRADED =unwieldy ≠delicate

2 A **cumbersome** system or process is very complicated and inefficient. *...an old and cumbersome computer system... The proposed regulations are ill-defined and cumbersome and could be unnecessarily costly.* ADJ-GRADED =clumsy

cumin /kʌmɪn/. **Cumin** is a sweet-smelling spice used to flavour meat dishes. It is popular in Indian cooking. N-UNCOUNT

cummerbund /kʌməʳbʌnd/ **cummerbunds.** A **cummerbund** is a wide sash worn round the waist as part of a man's evening dress. N-COUNT

cumulative /kjuːmjʊlətɪv/. If a series of events have a **cumulative** effect, each event makes the effect greater. *It is simple pleasures, such as a walk on a sunny day, which have a cumulative effect on our mood... The benefits from eating fish are cumulative.* ♦ **cumulatively** *His administration was plagued by one petty scandal after another, cumulatively very damaging.* ◆◇◇◇◇ ADJ; ADV

cumulus /kjuːmjʊləs/ **cumuli** /kjuːmjʊlaɪ/. **Cumulus** is a type of thick, fluffy, white cloud formed when hot air rises very quickly. *...huge cumulus clouds.* N-VAR

cunnilingus /kʌnɪlɪŋgəs/. **Cunnilingus** is oral sex which involves someone using their mouth to stimulate a woman's genitals. N-UNCOUNT

cunning /kʌnɪŋ/ ◆◇◇◇◇

1 Someone who is **cunning** has the ability to achieve things in a clever way, often by deceiving other people. *These disturbed kids can be cunning. ...Mr Major's cunning plan.* ♦ **cunningly** *They were cunningly disguised in golf clothes.* ADJ-GRADED =crafty; ADV-GRADED: usu ADV with v

2 **Cunning** is the ability to achieve things in a clever way, often by deceiving other people. *...one more example of the cunning of today's art thieves... He tackled the job with a great deal of imagination, skill and cunning.* N-UNCOUNT

cunt /kʌnt/ **cunts.**

Cunt is a rude and offensive word which you should avoid using.

1 **Cunt** is a word that some people use to refer to a woman's vagina. N-COUNT

2 If someone calls another person a **cunt**, they are expressing contempt for that person. N-COUNT PRAGMATICS

cup /kʌp/ **cups, cupping, cupped** ◆◆◆◆◆

1 A **cup** is a small round container that you drink from. Cups usually have handles and are made from china or plastic. *...cups and saucers.* ► A **cup** of something is the amount of something contained in a cup. *Mix about four cups of white flour with a pinch of salt.* N-COUNT; N-COUNT: usu N of n

2 Things, or parts of things, that are small, round, and hollow in shape can be referred to as **cups**. *...the brass cups of the small chandelier.* N-COUNT: oft N of n

3 A **cup** is a large two-handled metal cup on a stem that is given to the person or team that wins a game or competition. *We had a pretty good chance of winning one of the cups.* N-COUNT =trophy

4 **Cup** is used in the names of some sports competitions in which the prize is a cup. *Sri Lanka's cricket team will play India in the final of the Asia Cup. ...after his fateful injury in the 1991 FA Cup final.* N-COUNT: usu the n N

5 If you **cup** your **hands**, you make them into a curved dish-like shape. *He cupped his hands around his mouth and called out for Diane... David knelt, cupped his hands and splashed river water on to his face... She held it in her cupped hands for us to see.* VERB V n prep V n V-ed

6 If you **cup** something in your hands, you make your hands into a curved dish-like shape and support it or hold it gently. *He cupped her chin in the palm of his hand... He cradled the baby in his arms, his hands cupping her tiny skull.* VERB V n prep V n

7 If someone is **in** their **cups**, they are drunk; an old-fashioned, informal expression. *He talked too* PHRASE: usu v-link PHR

freely when, as was too often the case, he was in his cups. ● **not** your **cup of tea**: see **tea**.

cupboard /kʌbəʳd/ **cupboards.** A **cupboard** is a piece of furniture which has one or two doors at the front and usually shelves inside it, and which is used for storage. You also use **cupboard** to refer to a very small storage room, especially one without windows. *The kitchen cupboard was stocked with tins of soup and food.* ● **a skeleton in the cupboard**: see **skeleton**. ◆◆◇◇◇ N-COUNT

cupcake /kʌpkeɪk/ **cupcakes.** **Cupcakes** are small iced cakes for one person. N-COUNT

cupful /kʌpfʊl/ **cupfuls.** A **cupful** of something is the amount of something a cup can contain. *...a cupful of warm milk.* N-COUNT: usu N *of* n

cupid /kjuːpɪd/ **cupids;** also spelled **Cupid.**

1 **Cupid** is the Roman god of love. He is usually drawn as a baby boy with wings and a bow and arrow. People, especially journalists, refer to him when talking about people starting a romantic relationship. *...the aristocrat who played Cupid to the Duke and Duchess of York.* N-PROPER

2 A **cupid** is a picture or statue of a pretty little boy with wings, often holding a bow and arrow. *I would like my wedding cake decorated with cupids.* N-COUNT

cupidity /kjuːpɪdɪti/. **Cupidity** is a greedy desire for money and possessions; a formal word. *His eyes gave him away, shining with cupidity.* N-UNCOUNT =avarice

cupola /kjuːpələ/ **cupolas.** A **cupola** is a roof or part of a roof that is shaped like a bowl turned upside-down; a formal word. N-COUNT =dome

cuppa /kʌpə/ **cuppas.** In British English, a **cuppa** is a cup of tea; an informal word. *Have you time for a cuppa?* N-COUNT

cup tie, cup ties; also spelled **cup-tie.** In sport, especially football, a **cup tie** is a match between two teams who are competing in a competition in which the prize is a cup. ◆◇◇◇◇ N-COUNT

cur /kɜːʳ/ **curs.** A **cur** is a vicious dog, especially a mongrel; an old-fashioned word. N-COUNT

curable /kjʊərəbᵊl/. If a disease or illness is **curable**, it can be cured. *Most skin cancers are completely curable if detected in the early stages.* ADJ ≠incurable

curate, curates, curating, curated. The noun is pronounced /kjʊərət/. The verb is pronounced /kjʊreɪt/. ◆◇◇◇◇

1 A **curate** is a clergyman in the Church of England who helps the vicar or rector of a parish. N-COUNT

2 If an exhibition **is curated** by someone, they organize it. *The Hayward exhibition has been curated by the artist Bernard Luthi.* VB: usu passive *be* V-ed

curative /kjʊərətɪv/. Something that has **curative** properties can cure people's illnesses; a formal word. *Ancient civilizations believed in the curative powers of fresh air and sunlight. ...curative herbs.* ADJ =healing

curator /kjʊreɪtəʳ/ **curators.** A **curator** is someone who is in charge of the objects or works of art in a museum or art gallery. *Peter Forey is curator of fossil fishes at the Natural History Museum.* ◆◇◇◇◇ N-COUNT

curatorial /kjʊrətɔːriəl/. **Curatorial** means relating to curators and their work; a formal word. *...the museum's curatorial team. ...valuable curatorial expertise.* ADJ: ADJ n

curb /kɜːʳb/ **curbs, curbing, curbed** ◆◆◇◇◇

1 If you **curb** something, you control it and keep it within limits. *Yeltsin needs to curb inflation in Russia. ...advertisements aimed at curbing the spread of Aids.* ► Also a noun. *He called for much stricter curbs on immigration.* VERB =check, restrain V n; N-COUNT: oft N *on* n

2 If you **curb** an emotion or your behaviour, you keep it under control. *He curbed his temper... You must curb your extravagant tastes.* VERB =check, restrain V n

3 See **kerb**.

curd /kɜːʳd/ **curds.** The thick white substance which is formed when milk turns sour can be referred to as **curds**. N-VAR: usu pl

curdle /kɜːʳdᵊl/ **curdles, curdling, curdled.** If milk or eggs **curdle** or if you **curdle** them, they separate into different bits. *The sauce should not boil or the egg yolk will curdle... The herb has been used for centuries to curdle milk.* V-ERG V; V n

cure /kjʊəʳ/ **cures, curing, cured** ◆◆◆◇◇

1 If doctors or medical treatments **cure** an illness or injury, they cause it to end or disappear. *An operation finally cured his shin injury... Her cancer can only be controlled, not cured.* VERB V n

2 If doctors or medical treatments **cure** a person, they make the person well again after an illness or injury. *MDT is an effective treatment and could cure all the leprosy sufferers worldwide... Almost overnight I was cured... Now doctors believe they have cured him of the disease.* VERB =heal V n; V n *of* n

3 A **cure** for an illness is a medicine or other treatment that cures the illness. *There is still no cure for a cold... Atkinson has been told rest is the only cure for his ankle injury.* N-COUNT: oft N *for* n

4 If someone or something **cures** a problem, they bring it to an end. *Private firms are willing to make large scale investments to help cure the Soviet Union's economic troubles... We need to cure our environmental problems.* VERB V n

5 A **cure** for a problem is something that will bring it to an end. *Punishment can never be an effective cure for acute social problems... The magic cure for inflation does not exist.* N-COUNT: usu with supp, oft N *for* n =solution

6 If an action or event **cures** someone of a habit or an attitude, it makes them stop having it. *The experience was a detestable ordeal, and it cured him of any ambitions to direct again... He went to a clinic to cure his drinking and overeating.* VERB V n *of* n; V n

7 When food, tobacco, or animal skin **is cured**, it is dried, smoked, or salted so that it will last for a long time. *Legs of pork were cured and smoked over the fire. ...sliced cured ham.* VB: usu passive *be* V-ed; V-ed

cure-all, cure-alls. Something that is believed to be a **cure-all** is believed, usually wrongly, to be able to solve all the problems someone or something has, or to cure a wide range of illnesses. *Gorbachev said the introduction of market discipline to the Soviet economy was not a magic cure-all for its problems... Broussais was the first physician to use leeches as a cure-all.* N-COUNT: oft N *for* n =panacea

curfew /kɜːʳfjuː/ **curfews.** A **curfew** is a law stating that people must stay inside their houses after a particular time at night, for example during a war. *The village was placed under curfew... In Lucknow crowds of people defied the curfew to celebrate on the streets.* ◆◆◇◇◇ N-VAR

curio /kjʊəriəʊ/ **curios.** A **curio** is an object such as a small ornament which is unusual and fairly rare. *...Oriental curios. ...antique and curio shops.* N-COUNT

curiosity /kjʊəriɒsɪti/ **curiosities** ◆◆◇◇◇

1 **Curiosity** is a desire to know about something. *Ryle accepted more out of curiosity than anything else. ...an enthusiasm and genuine curiosity about the past... To satisfy our own curiosity we traveled to Baltimore.* N-UNCOUNT =inquisitiveness

2 A **curiosity** is something that is unusual, interesting, and fairly rare. *There is much to see in the way of castles, curiosities, and museums... Reed International is a curiosity in the international world of publishing.* N-COUNT

3 ● **curiosity killed the cat**: see **cat**.

curious /kjʊəriəs/ ◆◆◆◇◇

1 If you are **curious** about something, you are interested in it and want to know more about it. *Steve was intensely curious about the world I came from... Children are naturally curious. ...a group of curious villagers.* ♦ **curiously** *The woman in the shop had looked at them curiously... 'Is that how you got that scar on your face?' Bess asked curiously.* ADJ-GRADED: usu v-link ADJ, oft ADJ *about* n =inquisitive; ADV-GRADED: ADV after v

2 If you describe something as **curious**, you mean that it is unusual or difficult to understand. *There is a curious thing about her writings in this period... The pageant promises to be a curious mixture of the ancient and modern... The naval high command's response to these developments is rather curious.* ♦ **curiously** *Harry was curiously silent through all this... Curiously, the struggle to survive has greatly improved her health.* ADJ-GRADED =odd, peculiar, funny; ADV-GRADED: ADV adj, ADV with cl

curl /kɜːʳl/ **curls, curling, curled** ◆◆◇◇◇

1 If you have **curls**, your hair is in the form of tight curves and spirals. *...the little girl with blonde curls... A curl of black hair fell loosely across his forehead.* N-COUNT

2 If your hair has **curl**, it is full of curls. *Dry curly hair naturally for maximum curl and shine.* N-UNCOUNT

3 If your hair **curls** or if you **curl** it, it is full of curls. *She has hair that refuses to curl... Maria had curled her hair for the event... Afro hair is short and tightly curled.* V-ERG V V n V-ed

4 A **curl** of something is a piece or quantity of it that is curved or spiral in shape. *A thin curl of smoke rose from a rusty stove. ...curls of lemon peel.* N-COUNT: usu with supp, oft N *of* n

5 If your toes, fingers, or other parts of your body **curl**, or if you **curl** them, they form a curved or round shape. *His fingers curled gently round her wrist... Raise one foot, curl the toes and point the foot downwards... She sat with her legs curled under her.* V-ERG =bend V prep/adv V n V-ed Also V, V n prep/adv

6 If something **curls** somewhere, or if you **curl** it there, it moves there in a spiral or curve. *Smoke was curling up the chimney... He curled the ball into the net.* V-ERG V prep/adv V n prep/adv

7 If a person or animal **curls into** a ball, they move into a position in which their body makes a rounded shape. *He wanted to curl into a tiny ball... The kitten was curled on a cushion on the sofa.* ▶ **Curl up** means the same as **curl**. *In colder weather, your cat will curl up into a tight, heat-conserving ball... She curled up next to him... He was asleep there, curled up in the fetal position.* VERB V *into* n V-ed PHRASAL VERB V P *into* n V P V-ed P

8 When a leaf, a piece of paper, or another flat object **curls**, its edges bend towards the centre. *The rose leaves have curled because of an attack by grubs.* ▶ **Curl up** means the same as **curl**. *The corners of the lino were curling up.* VERB V PHRASAL VERB V P

9 If you **curl** your lip, or if your lip **curls**, you move your upper lip slightly at one side, as a way of showing anger, contempt, or scorn. *He curled his upper lip in a show of scepticism... She had a small, mean mouth that curled disapprovingly each time her husband wrote something in his diary.* V-ERG V n V

curl up. See **curl** 7 and 8. PHRASAL VERB

curler /kɜːʳləʳ/ **curlers. Curlers** are small plastic or metal tubes that women roll their hair round in order to make it curly. *...a woman in a flowered apron with her hair in curlers.* N-COUNT =roller

curlew /kɜːʳljuː/ **curlews.** A **curlew** is a large brown bird with long legs and a long curved beak. Curlews live near water and have a very distinctive cry. N-COUNT

curlicue /kɜːʳlɪkjuː/ **curlicues. Curlicues** are decorative twists and curls, usually carved or made with a pen; a literary word. *Her stern was embellished with curlicues of gold.* N-COUNT: usu pl

curly /kɜːʳli/ **curlier, curliest** ◆◇◇◇◇

1 **Curly** hair is full of curls. *I've got naturally curly hair... Her hair was dark and curly.* ADJ-GRADED ≠straight

2 **Curly** is sometimes used to describe things that are curved or spiral in shape. *...cauliflowers with extra long curly leaves. ...dragons with curly tails. ...spectacular curly water slides.* ADJ-GRADED: usu ADJ n =straight

curmudgeon /kəʳmʌdʒən/ **curmudgeons.** If you call someone a **curmudgeon**, you do not like them because they are mean or bad-tempered; an old-fashioned word. *...such a terrible old curmudgeon.* N-COUNT PRAGMATICS

curmudgeonly /kəʳmʌdʒənli/. If you describe someone as **curmudgeonly**, you do not like them because they are mean or bad-tempered; an old-fashioned word. *...her curmudgeonly cynic of a boss... He displayed a curmudgeonly unwillingness to accept the voters' verdict.* ADJ-GRADED PRAGMATICS =churlish

currant /kʌrənt, AM kɜːr-/ **currants**

1 **Currants** are small dried black grapes, used especially in cakes. N-COUNT

2 **Currants** are bushes which produce edible red, black, or white berries. The berries are also called **currants.** N-COUNT

currency /kʌrənsi, AM kɜːr-/ **currencies** ◆◆◆◇◇

1 The money used in a particular country is referred to as its **currency**. *Tourism is the country's top earner of foreign currency... More people favour a single European currency than oppose it. ...Western currencies.* N-VAR

2 If a custom, idea, or word has **currency**, it is used and accepted by a lot of people at a particular time; a formal use. *His theory of the social contract had wide currency in America... 'Loop' is one of those computer words that has gained currency in society.* N-UNCOUNT =acceptance

3 See also **common currency.**

current /kʌrənt, AM kɜːr-/ **currents** ◆◆◆◆◆

1 A **current** is a steady and continuous flowing movement of some of the water in a river, lake, or sea. *Under normal conditions, the ocean currents of the tropical Pacific travel from east to west... The couple were swept away by the strong current.* N-COUNT

2 A **current** is a steady flowing movement of air. *I felt a current of cool air blowing in my face.* N-COUNT: usu with supp

3 An electric **current** is a flow of electricity through a wire or circuit. *A powerful electric current is passed through a piece of graphite.* N-COUNT

4 A particular **current** is a particular feeling, idea, or quality that exists within a group of people. *Each party represents a distinct current of thought... A strong current of nationalism runs through ideology and politics in the Arab world.* N-COUNT: with supp, oft N *of* n

5 **Current** means happening, being used, or being done at the present time. *The current situation is very different to that in 1990... He plans to repeal a number of current policies... When asked for your views about your current job, on no account must you be negative.* ♦ **currently** *Twelve potential AIDS vaccines are currently being tested on human volunteers... He currently has no strong rivals for power.* ADJ: usu ADJ n ADV: ADV before v

6 Ideas and customs that are **current** are generally accepted and used by most people. *Current thinking suggests that toxins only have a small part to play in the build up of cellulite... This custom was still current in the late 1960s.* ADJ

7 See also **alternating current, direct current.**

current account, current accounts ◆◇◇◇◇

1 In British English, a **current account** is a personal bank account which you can take money out of at any time using your cheque book or cash card. The American term is **checking account**. *His current account was seriously overdrawn.* N-COUNT

2 A country's **current account** is the difference in value between its exports and imports over a particular period of time; a technical use in economics. *Portugal will probably have a small current-account surplus for 1992.* N-COUNT: usu sing, oft N n

current affairs. If you refer to **current affairs**, you are referring to political events and problems in society which are discussed in newspapers, and on television and radio. *I am ill-informed on current affairs. ...the BBC's current affairs programme 'Panorama'.* ◆◇◇◇◇ N-PLURAL

curriculum /kərɪkjʊləm/ **curriculums** or **curricula** /kərɪkjʊlə/ ◆◆◇◇◇

1 A **curriculum** is all the different courses of study that are taught in a school, college, or university. *There should be a broader curriculum in schools for post-16-year-old pupils... Russian is the one compulsory foreign language on the school curriculum.* • See also **National Curriculum.** N-COUNT

2 A particular **curriculum** is one particular course of study that is taught in a school, college, or university. *...the history curriculum.* N-COUNT: usu n N =syllabus

curriculum vitae /kərɪkjʊləm viːtaɪ, AM -ti/. A **curriculum vitae** is the same as a **CV**; used mainly in British English. The usual American word is **résumé**. N-SING

curried /kʌrid, AM kɜːrid/. **Curried** meat or vegetables have been flavoured with hot spices. ADJ: ADJ

curry /kʌri, AM kɜːri/ **curries, currying, curried** ◆◇◇◇◇

1 **Curry** is a dish composed of meat and vegetables, or just vegetables, in a sauce containing hot spices. It is usually eaten with rice and is one of the main dishes of India. *...vegetable curry... I went for a curry last night.* N-VAR

2 If one person tries to **curry favour** with another, they do things in order to try to gain their support or cooperation. *Politicians are eager to promote their 'happy family' image to curry favour with voters.* PHRASE: V inflects, oft PHR *with* n

curry powder, curry powders. Curry powder is a powder made from a mixture of spices. It is used in cooking, especially when making curry. N-MASS

curse /kɜːʳs/ **curses, cursing, cursed** ◆◆◇◇◇

1 If you **curse**, you use rude or offensive language, usually because you are angry about something; used in written English. *I cursed and hobbled to my feet.* ▶ Also a noun. *He shot her an angry look and a curse.* VERB =swear V N-COUNT

2 If you **curse** someone, you say insulting things to them because you are angry with them. *Grandma protested, but he cursed her and rudely pushed her aside... He cursed himself for having been so careless.* VERB V n V pron-refl

3 If you **curse** something, you complain angrily about it, especially using rude language. *So we set off again, cursing the delay, towards the west... She silently cursed her own stupidity.* VERB V n

4 If you say that there is a **curse** on someone, you mean that there seems to be a supernatural power causing unpleasant things to happen to them. *Maybe there is a curse on my family... He's been the object of a voodoo curse.* N-COUNT: oft N *on/upon* n

5 You can refer to something that causes a great deal of trouble or harm as a **curse**. *Apathy is the long-standing curse of British local democracy... Summer colds are a terrible curse.* N-COUNT: usu sing, oft N *of* n =plague

cursed /kɜːʳst/. The pronunciation /kɜːʳsɪd/ is used for meaning 3. ◆◇◇◇◇

1 If you are **cursed with** something, you are very unlucky in having it. *Bulman was cursed with a poor memory for names.* ADJ: v-link ADJ *with* n

2 Someone or something that is **cursed** is suffering as the result of a curse. *The whole family seemed cursed... The ground was cursed because of him.* ADJ: usu v-link ADJ

3 **Cursed** is a mild swear word used to describe something you are angry about; an old-fashioned use. *I wish this cursed place was burned.* ADJ: ADJ n PRAGMATICS

cursor /kɜːʳsəʳ/ **cursors.** On a computer screen, the **cursor** is a small, movable shape which indicates where anything that is typed by the user will appear. N-COUNT

cursory /kɜːʳsəri/. A **cursory** glance or examination is a brief one in which you do not pay much attention to detail. *Burke cast a cursory glance at the menu, then flapped it shut... I gave the letter a fairly cursory reading.* ADJ-GRADED: ADJ n =perfunctory

curt /kɜːʳt/. If you say describe someone as **curt**, you mean that they speak or reply in a brief and rather rude way. *Her tone of voice was curt... 'The matter is closed,' was the curt reply.* ♦ **curtly** *'I'm leaving,' she said curtly.* ◆◇◇◇◇ ADJ-GRADED =abrupt, brusque ADV-GRADED: ADV with v

curtail /kɜːʳteɪl/ **curtails, curtailing, curtailed.** If you **curtail** something, you reduce or limit it; a formal word. *The US plans to curtail the number of troops being sent to Somalia... I told Louie that old age would curtail her activities in time... His powers will be severely curtailed.* ◆◇◇◇◇ VERB =limit V n

curtailment /kɜːʳteɪlmənt/. The **curtailment** of something is the act of reducing or limiting it; a formal word. *...a considerable curtailment of military spending. ...the curtailment of presidential power.* N-SING: usu N *of* n

curtain /kɜːʳtən/ **curtains** ◆◆◆◇◇

1 In British English, **curtains** are large pieces of material which you hang from the top of a window. You pull them across the window when you want to keep light out or prevent people from seeing in. The usual American word is **drapes.** *Her bedroom curtains were drawn.* N-COUNT

2 In American English, **curtains** are pieces of very thin material which you hang in front of windows in order to prevent people from seeing in. The usual British word is **net curtains.** N-COUNT

3 In a theatre, **the curtain** is the large piece of material that hangs in front of the stage until a performance begins. *The curtain rises toward the end of the Prelude.* N-SING: *the* N

4 You can refer to something as a **curtain** when it is thick and difficult to see through or get past; a literary use. *...a curtain of cigarette smoke... He saw something dark disappear behind the curtain of leaves.* ● See also **Iron Curtain.** N-SING: usu N *of* n

5 If something **brings down the curtain on** an event or state of affairs, or **brings the curtain down on** an event or state of affairs, it causes or marks the end of the event or state of affairs. *Management changes are under way that will finally bring down the curtain on Lord Forte's extraordinary working life.* PHRASE: V inflects, PHR n =end

curtain call, curtain calls; also spelled **curtain-call.** In a theatre, when actors or performers take a **curtain call**, they come forward to the front of the stage after a performance in order to receive the applause of the audience. *The first time they danced together, there were 23 curtain calls.* N-COUNT

curtained /kɜːʳtənd/. A **curtained** window, door, or other opening has a curtain hanging across it. *He could make out no light from behind the curtained windows.* ADJ: usu ADJ n

curtain-raiser, curtain-raisers. A **curtain-raiser** is an event, especially a sporting event or a performance, that takes place before a more important one, or starts off a series of events; used in journalism. *The three-race series will be a curtain-raiser to the Monaco Grand Prix in May... The President's address tonight from the Oval Office is a curtain-raiser for the economic policy message set for delivery to Congress on Wednesday.* N-COUNT: usu sing

curtsy /kɜːʳtsi/ **curtsies, curtsying, curtsied;** also spelled **curtsey.** If a woman or a girl **curtsies**, she lowers her body briefly, bending her knees and sometimes holding her skirt with both hands, as a way of showing respect for an important person. *We were taught how to curtsy to the Queen... Ingrid shook the Duchess's hand and curtsied.* ▶ Also a noun. *She gave a curtsy.* VERB V *to* n V N-COUNT

curvaceous /kɜːʳveɪʃəs/. If someone describes a woman as **curvaceous**, they think she is attractive because of the curves of her body; a journalistic word which some women find offensive. *...a curvaceous blonde.* ADJ-GRADED PRAGMATICS =curvy ≠skinny

curvature /kɜːʳvətʃəʳ/. The **curvature** of something is its curved shape, especially when this shape is part of the circumference of a circle; a technical word. *...the curvature of the earth... He suffered from curvature of the spine.* N-UNCOUNT: oft N *of* n

curve /kɜːʳv/ **curves, curving, curved** ◆◆◇◇◇

1 A **curve** is a smooth, gradually bending line, for example part of the edge of a circle. *...the curve of his lips. ...a curve in the road.* N-COUNT: usu with supp

2 If something **curves**, or if someone or something **curves** it, it has the shape of a curve. *Her spine curved... The track curved away below him. ...a knife with a slightly curving blade... A small, unobtrusive smile curved the cook's thin lips.* V-ERG V V adv/prep V-ing V n

3 If something **curves**, it moves in a curve, for example through the air. *The ball curved strangely in the air.* VERB V

4 You can refer to a change in something as a particular **curve**, especially when it is represented on a graph. *Each firm will face a downward-sloping demand curve... Was it just a temporary blip on an otherwise healthy growth curve?* ● See also **learning curve.** N-COUNT: usu with supp

curved /kɜːʳvd/. A **curved** object has the shape of a curve or has a smoothly bending surface. *...a small, curved staircase. ...the curved lines of the chairs.* ◆◇◇◇◇ ADJ-GRADED

curvy /kɜːʳvi/. If someone describes a woman as **curvy**, they think she is attractive because of the curves of her body; an informal word which some women find offensive. ADJ-GRADED PRAGMATICS =curvaceous ≠skinny

cushion /kʊʃən/ **cushions, cushioning, cushioned** ◆◆◇◇◇

1 A **cushion** is a fabric case filled with soft material, N-COUNT

which you put on a seat to make it more comfortable. *...a velvet cushion.*

2 A **cushion** is a soft pad or barrier, especially one that protects something from impacts. *The company provides a styrofoam cushion to protect the tablets during shipping.* N-COUNT

3 Something that **cushions** an object when it hits something protects it by reducing the force of the impact. *There is also a new steering wheel with an energy absorbing rim to cushion the driver's head in the worst impacts... The suspension is designed to cushion passengers from the effects of riding over rough roads.* VERB V n V n *from* n

4 To **cushion** the effect of something unpleasant means to reduce it. *They said Western aid was needed to cushion the blows of vital reform... The price rises will be cushioned by welfare benefits... The subsidies are designed to cushion farmers against unpredictable weather.* VERB V n V n *against* n

5 Something that is a **cushion** against something unpleasant reduces its effect. *Housing benefit provides a cushion against hardship.* N-COUNT: usu sing, usu with supp

cushioning /kʊʃənɪŋ/. **Cushioning** is something soft that protects an object when it hits something by reducing the force of the impact. *Walkers need cushioning under the ball of the foot.* N-UNCOUNT

cushy /kʊʃi/ **cushier, cushiest.** If you describe someone's job or situation as **cushy**, you think it is pleasant for them because it does not involve much work or effort, and you are envious or resentful of them; an informal word. *...a cushy job in the civil service... He had a fairly cushy upbringing.* ADJ-GRADED: usu ADJ n PRAGMATICS

cusp /kʌsp/. If you say that someone or something is **on the cusp**, you mean they are between two states, or are about to be in a particular state. *I am sitting on the cusp of middle age... Prague is on the cusp between communism and capitalism.* PHRASE: PHR after v, v-link PHR

cuss /kʌs/ **cusses, cussing, cussed.** If someone **cusses**, they swear at someone or use bad language; an old-fashioned, informal word. *Tosh was known to be a man who would cuss and shout... He rails and cusses at those pop stars.* VERB =curse V V *at* n Also V n

cussed /kʌsɪd/. If you describe someone as **cussed**, you mean that they are stubborn and refuse to do what other people want or expect them to do; an old-fashioned word. *The older she got the more cussed she became.* ♦ **cussedness** *...his self-admitted cussedness.* ADJ-GRADED =pig-headed N-UNCOUNT

custard /kʌstəʳd/ **custards. Custard** is a sweet yellow sauce made from milk and eggs or from milk and a powder. It is eaten with fruit and puddings. *...bananas and custard.* ◆◇◇◇◇ N-MASS

custard pie, custard pies. Custard pies are fake pies which clowns and comedians sometimes throw at each other. *...a custard pie fight.* N-COUNT

custodial /kʌstoʊdiəl/

1 **Custodial** means relating to keeping people in prison; a formal use. *If he is caught again he will be given a custodial sentence.* ADJ: ADJ n

2 If a child's parents are divorced or separated, the **custodial** parent is the parent who has custody of the child; a legal use. ADJ: ADJ n

custodian /kʌstoʊdiən/ **custodians.** The **custodian** of an official building, a companies' assets, or something else valuable is the person who is officially in charge of it. *...the custodian of the holy shrines in Mecca and Medina.* ◆◇◇◇◇ N-COUNT

custody /kʌstədi/ ◆◆◇◇◇

1 **Custody** is the legal right to keep and look after a child, especially the right given to a child's mother or father when they get divorced. *I'm going to go to court to get custody of the children... Child custody is normally granted to the mother. ...a bitter custody battle.* N-UNCOUNT: oft N *of* n

2 Someone who is **in custody** or has been taken **into custody** has been arrested and is being kept in prison until they can be tried in a court. *Three people appeared in court and two of them were remanded in custody... She was taken into custody later that day.* PHRASE: PHR after v

3 If someone is being held in a particular type of **custody**, they are being kept in a place that is similar to a prison. *The youngster got nine months' youth custody... Barrett was taken into protective custody.* N-UNCOUNT: usu with supp

custom /kʌstəm/ **customs** ◆◆◇◇◇

1 A **custom** is an activity, a way of behaving, or an event which is usual or traditional in a particular society or in particular circumstances. *The custom of lighting the Olympic flame goes back centuries... Chung has tried to adapt to local customs.* N-VAR: usu with supp, oft N *of* -ing

2 If it is your **custom** to do something, you usually do it in particular circumstances. *It was his custom to approach every problem cautiously... As is the custom, police forensic experts carried out a painstaking search of the debris.* N-SING: oft with poss

3 If a shop has your **custom**, you regularly buy things there; a formal use, mainly in British English. *You have the right to withhold your custom if you so wish... Providing discounts is not the only way to win custom.* N-UNCOUNT: usu with poss

4 If you use **custom** to describe something such as a vehicle or a piece of clothing, you mean that it has been designed for one particular customer. *Her one-of-a-kind custom garments are priced from one hundred dollars to more than a thousand dollars.* ADJ: ADJ n

5 See also **customs.**

customary /kʌstəmri, AM -meri/ ◆◇◇◇◇

1 **Customary** is used to describe things that people usually do in a particular society or in particular circumstances; a formal use. *It is customary to offer a drink or a snack to guests... At Christmas it was customary for the children to perform bits of poetry... They interrupted the customary one minute's silence with jeers and shouts.* ♦ **customarily** /kʌstəmrəli, AM -eərɪli/ *Marriages in medieval Europe were customarily arranged by the families.* ADJ: oft *it* v-link ADJ to-inf =usual ADV

2 **Customary** is used to describe something that a particular person usually does or has. *The king carried himself with his customary elegance... Yvonne took her customary seat behind her desk.* ADJ: ADJ n =usual

custom-built. If something **is custom-built**, it is built according to someone's special requirements. *The machine was custom-built by Steve Roberts... The couple ordered a custom-built kitchen.* V-PASSIVE =custom-made *be* V-ed V-ed

customer /kʌstəməʳ/ **customers** ◆◆◆◆◇

1 A **customer** is someone who buys goods or services, especially from a shop. *Our customers have very tight budgets. ...a satisfied customer. ...the quality of customer service... We also improved our customer satisfaction levels.* N-COUNT

2 In informal British English, you can use **customer** in expressions such as **a cool customer** or **a tough customer** to indicate what someone's behaviour or character is like. *She's a real cool customer. ...two pretty awkward customers.* N-COUNT: adj N

customize /kʌstəmaɪz/ **customizes, customizing, customized;** also spelled **customise** in British English. If you **customize** something, you change its appearance or features to suit your tastes or needs. *...a control that allows photographers to customise the camera's basic settings. ...customized software.* ◆◇◇◇◇ VERB V n V-ed

custom-made. If something **is custom-made**, it is made according to someone's special requirements. *Furniture can also be custom-made to suit your own requirements. ...a custom-made suit.* V-PASSIVE *be* V-ed V-ed

customs /kʌstəmz/ ◆◆◇◇◇

1 **Customs** is the official organization responsible for collecting taxes on goods coming into a country and preventing illegal goods from being brought in. *...components similar to those seized by British customs. ...customs officers.* N-PROPER: oft N n

2 **Customs** is the place where people arriving from a foreign country have to declare goods that they bring with them. *He walked through customs.* N-UNCOUNT

3 **Customs** duties are taxes that people pay for importing and exporting goods. ADJ: ADJ n

4 See also **custom.**

Customs and Excise. **Customs and Excise** is a British government department which is responsible for collecting taxes on imported goods and on some goods produced in Britain. N-PROPER

cut /kʌt/ **cuts, cutting.** The form **cut** is used in the present tense and is the past tense and past participle. ◆◆◆◆◆

1 If you **cut** something, you use a knife or a similar tool to divide it into pieces, or to mark it or damage it. If you **cut** a shape or a hole in something, you make the shape or hole by using a knife or similar tool. *Mrs. Haines stood nearby, holding scissors to cut a ribbon... She tried to cut her wrists... Cut the tomatoes in half vertically... The thieves cut a hole in the fence... Then cut shapes out of felt scraps for eyes, nose, ears, and mouth... Mr. Long was now cutting himself a piece of the pink cake. ...thinly cut cucumber sandwiches.* ▶ Also a noun. *The operation involves making several cuts in the cornea.*
VERB; V n; V n prep/adv; V n n; V-ed; N-COUNT

2 If you **cut** yourself or **cut** a part of your body, you accidentally injure yourself on a sharp object so that you bleed. *Johnson cut himself shaving... I started to cry because I cut my finger... Zoe was badly cut as she scrambled down rocks to reach him... Blood from his cut lip trickled over his chin.* ▶ Also a noun. *He had sustained a cut on his left eyebrow... All I got was assorted cuts and bruises.*
VERB; V pron-refl; V n; V-ed; N-COUNT

3 If you **cut** something such as grass, your hair, or your fingernails, you shorten them using scissors or another tool. *The most recent tenants hadn't even cut the grass... You have to learn not to cut your toenails in the living room... You've had your hair cut, it looks great... She had dark red hair, cut short.* ▶ Also a noun. *Prices vary from salon to salon, starting at £17 for a cut and blow-dry.*
VERB; V n; *have* n V-ed; V-ed; N-SING

4 The way that clothes **are cut** is the way they are designed and made. *It was cut high up the thigh to make her legs look longer. ...badly cut blue suits.*
VB: usu passive; *be* V-ed; V-ed

5 To **cut through** something means to move or pass through it easily. *I could see long canoes cutting through the waves.*
VERB; V *through* n

6 If you **cut across** or **through** a place, you go through it because it is the shortest route to another place. *He decided to cut across the Heath, through Greenwich Park.* ● See also **short cut**.
VERB; V *across/through* n

7 If you **cut** something, you reduce it. *The first priority is to cut costs. ...an agreement to cut farm subsidies by 30 per cent... The UN force is to be cut by 90%. ...a deal to cut 50 billion dollars from the federal deficit.* ▶ Also a noun. *The economy needs an immediate 2 per cent cut in interest rates. ...the government's plans for tax cuts.* ▶ **Cut down** means the same as **cut**. *We'd like politicians to get together and agree ways to cut down atmospheric pollution... We've cut it down to just five years.*
VERB =reduce; V n; V n *by* amount; V amount *from/off* n; N-COUNT: with supp, oft N *in* n; PHRASAL VERB; V P n (not pron); V n P *to* n; Also V n P

8 If you **cut** a text, broadcast, or performance, you shorten it. If you **cut** a part of a text, broadcast, or performance, you do not publish, broadcast, or perform that part. *Branagh has cut the play judiciously... The audience wants more music and less drama, so we've cut some scenes.* ▶ Also a noun. *It has been found necessary to make some cuts in the text.*
VERB; V n; N-COUNT

9 To **cut** a supply of something means to stop providing it or stop it being provided. *They used pressure tactics to force them to return, including cutting food and water supplies.* ▶ Also a noun. *The strike had already led to cuts in electricity and water supplies in many areas.*
VERB; V n; N-COUNT: with supp, usu N *in* n

10 If you **cut** a pack of playing cards, you divide it into two. *Place the cards face down on the table and cut them.*
VERB; V n

11 When the director of a film says **'cut'**, they want the actors and the camera crew to stop filming.
CONVENTION

12 When a singer or band **cuts** a record, they make a recording of their music. *She eventually cut her own album.*
VERB; V n

13 When a child **cuts** a tooth, a new tooth starts to grow through the gum. *Many infants do not cut their first tooth until they are a year old.*
VERB; V n

14 If a child **cuts** classes or **cuts** school, they do not go to classes or to school when they are supposed to; used mainly in American English. *Cutting school more than once in three months is a sign of trouble.*
VERB =miss; V n

15 If you tell someone to **cut** something, you are telling them in an irritated way to stop it; an informal use, mainly in American English. *'Cut the euphemisms, Daniel,' Brenda snapped... Why don't you just cut the crap and open the door.*
VERB; PRAGMATICS; V n

16 A **cut** of meat is a piece or type of meat which is cut in a particular way from the animal, or from a particular part of it. *Use a cheap cut such as spare rib chops.*
N-COUNT: with supp

17 Someone's **cut** of the profits or winnings from something, especially ones that have been obtained dishonestly, is their share; an informal use. *The lawyers, of course, take their cut of the little guy's winnings.*
N-SING: oft poss N =share

18 See also **cutting**.

19 If you say that someone or something is **a cut above** other people or things of the same kind, you mean they are better than the others; an informal expression. *Joan Smith's detective stories are a cut above the rest.*
PHRASES; v-link PHR n

20 If you see someone you know and **cut** them **dead**, you ignore them.
V inflects

21 If you say that a situation or solution is **cut and dried**, you mean that it is clear and definite. *Unfortunately, things cannot be as cut and dried as many people would like... We are aiming for guidelines, not cut-and-dried answers.*
v-link PHR, PHR n =clear-cut

22 If a person or an organization **cuts loose** or **is cut loose**, they become free from the influence or authority of other people. *He's cut loose from this business except, possibly, where James is concerned... It's about to be cut loose from the state on which it has so long depended.*
V inflects

23 If you say that someone **cuts and runs** in a difficult situation, you disapprove of the fact that they try to escape from it quickly and gain the most advantage for themselves, rather than deal with the situation in a responsible way; an informal expression. *...his cowardly decision to cut and run.*
Vs inflect; PRAGMATICS

24 If you say that something **cuts both ways**, you mean that it can have two opposite effects, or can have both good and bad effects. *This publicity cuts both ways. It focuses on us as well as on them.*
V inflects

25 ● to **cut** something **to the bone**: see **bone**. ● to **cut corners**: see **corner**. ● to **cut a** particular **figure**: see **figure**. ● to **cut the mustard**: see **mustard**. ● to **cut** someone **to the quick**: see **quick**. ● to **cut** someone **down to size**: see **size**. ● to **cut a long story short**: see **story**. ● to **cut your teeth on** something: see **tooth**.

cut across. If an issue or problem **cuts across** the division between two or more groups of people, it affects or matters to people in all the groups. *The problem cuts across all socioeconomic lines and affects all age groups... School crime and violence cuts across urban, rural and suburban areas.*
PHRASAL VERB; V P n

cut back. If you **cut back** something such as expenditure or **cut back** on it, you reduce it. *They will be concerned to cut back expenditure on unnecessary items... The Government has cut back on defence spending... We have been cutting back a bit: we did have thirteen horses, but now it's nine.* ● See also **cutback**.
PHRASAL VERB; V P n (not pron); V P *on* n; V P; Also V n P

cut down
PHRASAL VERB

1 If you **cut down** on something or **cut down** something, you consume or do less of it. *He cut down on coffee and cigarettes, and ate a balanced diet... Car owners were asked to cut down travel... If you spend more than your income, can you try to cut down?*
V P *on* n; V P n (not pron); V P; Also V n P

2 If you **cut down** a tree, you cut through its trunk so that it falls to the ground. *A vandal with a chainsaw cut down a tree.*
V P n (not pron); Also V n P

3 See **cut** 7.

cut in. If you **cut in** on someone, you interrupt them when they are speaking. *Immediately, Daniel cut in on Joanne's attempts at reassurance... 'Not true,' the Duchess cut in.*
PHRASAL VERB =interrupt; V P *on* n; V P with quote; Also V P

cut off
PHRASAL VERB

1 If you **cut** something **off**, you remove it with a

knife or a similar tool. *Mrs Kreutz cut off a generous piece of the meat... He cut me off a slice... He threatened to cut my hair off.* V P n (not pron) V n P n (not pron) V n P
2 To **cut** someone or something **off** means to separate them from things that they are normally connected with. *One of the goals of the campaign is to cut off the elite Republican Guard from its supplies... The exiles had been cut off from all contact with their homeland... The storm has cut us off.* =isolate V P n (not pron) from n V n P
♦ **cut off** *Without a car we still felt very cut off.* ADJ-GRADED
3 To **cut off** a supply of something means to stop providing it or stop it being provided. *The rebels have cut off electricity from the capital... His company is preparing to shut down in the event that their water supply is cut off... Our phone's been cut off... Why cut the money off?* V P n (not pron) V n P
4 If you get **cut off** when you are on the telephone, the line is suddenly disconnected and you can no longer speak to the other person. *When you do get through, you've got to say your piece quickly before you get cut off... I'm going to cut you off now because we've got lots of callers waiting.* =disconnect get/be V-ed P V n P Also V P n (not pron)
5 If you **cut** someone **off** when they are speaking, you interrupt them and stop them from speaking. *'But, sir, I'm under orders to – ' Clark cut him off. 'Don't argue with me.'* V n P Also V P n (not pron)
6 See also **cut-off**. ● to **cut off** your **nose to spite** your **face**: see **spite**.

cut out PHRASAL VERB
1 If you **cut** something **out**, you remove or separate it from what surrounds it using scissors or a knife. *Cut out the coupon and send those cheques off today... I cut it out and pinned it to my studio wall.* V P n (not pron) V n P
2 If you **cut out** a part of a text, you do not print, publish, or broadcast that part, because to include it would make the text too long or unacceptable. *I listened to the programme and found they'd cut out all the interesting stuff... Her editors wanted her to cut out the poetry from her novel... Several extraneous prefaces were cut out of the prayer book at the beginning of the eleventh century.* =cut, omit V P n (not pron) V P n (not pron) from/of n Also V n P
3 To **cut out** something unnecessary or unwanted means to remove it completely from a situation. For example, if you **cut out** a particular type of food, you stop eating it, usually because it is bad for you. *I've simply cut egg yolks out entirely... We will be pressing ahead with our policies on privatisation, deregulation and cutting out waste... A guilty plea cuts out the need for a long trial.* =eliminate V n P V P n (not pron)
4 If you tell someone to **cut** something **out**, you are telling them in an irritated way to stop it; an informal expression. *Do yourself a favour, and cut that behaviour out... 'Cut it out, Chip,' I said... He had better cut out the nonsense.* PRAGMATICS =stop V n P V it P V P n (not pron)
5 If you **cut** someone **out** of an activity or inheritance, you do not allow them to be involved in it or to share in it. *Environmentalists say this would cut them out of the debate over what to do with public lands... 'Cut her out of your will,' urged his nephew... He felt that he was being cut out.* =exclude ≠include V n P of n be V-ed P Also V P n (not pron)
6 If an object **cuts out** the light, it is between you and the light so that you are in the dark. *The curtains were half drawn to cut out the sunlight.* V P n (not pron) Also V n P
7 If an engine **cuts out**, it suddenly stops working. *The helicopter crash landed when one of its two engines cut out.* V P
8 See also **cut-out**, **cut out**. ● to **have** your **work cut out**: see **work**.

cut up PHRASAL VERB
1 If you **cut** something **up**, you cut it into several pieces. *He sits in his apartment cutting up magazines... Halve the tomatoes, then cut them up coarsely.* ● See also **cut up**. V P n (not pron) V n P
2 If one driver **cuts** another **up**, the first driver goes too close in front of the second one, for example after overtaking them. *They were crossing from lane to lane, cutting everyone up.* V n P

cut and dried. See **cut**.

cutaway /kʌtəweɪ/ **cutaways;** also spelled **cut-away**.
1 In a film or video, a **cutaway** or a **cutaway shot** is a picture that shows something different from the main thing that is being shown. *...a few sardonic cutaways of military bands and fighter planes.* N-COUNT
2 In American English, a **cutaway** or a **cutaway** coat or jacket is one which is cut diagonally from the front to the back, so that the back is longer. The usual British word is **tailcoat**. *They were all in top hats and cutaways despite the growing heat.* N-COUNT
3 A **cutaway** picture shows what something such as a machine looks like inside. ADJ: ADJ n

cutback /kʌtbæk/ **cutbacks;** also spelled **cut-back**. A **cutback** is a reduction that is made in something. *London Underground said it may have to axe 500 signalling jobs because of government cutbacks in its investment. ...the 200-person staff cutback announced yesterday.* ◆◇◇◇◇ N-COUNT: oft N in n =reduction

cute /kjuːt/ **cuter, cutest** ◆◇◇◇◇
1 If you describe something or someone as **cute**, you mean that they are very pretty or attractive, or that they are intended to appear pretty or attractive; an informal use. *Oh, look at that dog! He's so cute. ...a cute little house. ...a cute little baby.* ADJ-GRADED =sweet
2 In American English, if you describe someone as **cute**, you think they are sexually attractive; an informal use. *There was this girl, and I thought she was really cute.* ADJ-GRADED
3 If you describe someone as **cute**, you mean that they deal with things cleverly; used mainly in American English. *After all, he had merely taken up the silver baton and been cute enough not to drop it... That's a cute trick.* ADJ-GRADED =clever

cutesy /kjuːtsi/. If you describe someone or something as **cutesy**, you dislike them because you think they are unpleasantly pretty and sentimental; an informal word. *Macaulay Culkin receives his first screen kiss from cutesy 11-year-old Anna Chlumsky. ...cutesy paintings of owls.* ADJ-GRADED: usu ADJ n PRAGMATICS

cut glass; also spelled **cut-glass**. **Cut glass** is glass that has patterns cut into its surface. *...a cut-glass bowl.* N-UNCOUNT: oft N n

cuticle /kjuːtɪkᵊl/ **cuticles.** Your **cuticles** are the skin at the base of your fingernails and toenails. N-COUNT

cutlass /kʌtləs/ **cutlasses.** A **cutlass** is a short sword that used to be used by sailors. N-COUNT

cutlery /kʌtləri/. The knives, forks, and spoons that you eat your food with are referred to as **cutlery**; used mainly in British English. *She arranged plates and cutlery on a small table.* ◆◇◇◇◇ N-UNCOUNT

cutlet /kʌtlət/ **cutlets.** A **cutlet** is a small piece of meat which is usually fried or grilled. *...grilled lamb cutlets.* N-COUNT

cut-off, cut-offs; also spelled **cutoff**. ◆◆◇◇◇
1 A **cut-off** or a **cut-off** point is the level or limit at which you decide that something should stop happening. *The cut-off point depends on age and length of employment... The cut-off date for registering is yet to be announced... On young girls it can look really great, but there is a definite age cut-off on this.* N-COUNT: usu sing, oft N n
2 The **cut-off** of a supply or service is the complete stopping of the supply or service. *A total cut-off of supplies would cripple the country's economy... The United States resisted an arms cutoff.* N-COUNT: usu sing

cut out. If you are not **cut out** for a particular type of work, you do not have the qualities that are needed to be able to do it well. *I left medicine anyway. I wasn't really cut out for it... He doesn't feel he is cut out to be a leader.* ADJ: usu with brd-neg, v-link ADJ, ADJ for n, ADJ to-inf

cut-out, cut-outs
1 A **cut-out** is a device that turns off a machine automatically in particular circumstances. *Use a kettle with an automatic cut-out so it doesn't boil for longer than necessary... Engine cut-out devices and steering wheel locks do not protect the car's contents.* N-COUNT: oft N n
2 A cardboard **cut-out** is a shape that has been cut from thick card. *You'd swear he was a cardboard cut-out except that he'd moved his rifle... You can have your picture taken with a cutout of George Bush.* N-COUNT

cut-price. **Cut-price** goods or services are available at a cheaper price than usual. *...a shop* ◆◇◇◇◇ ADJ: ADJ n *selling cut-price videos and CDs in Oxford Street.* =cut-rate *...cut-price tickets.*

cut-rate. **Cut-rate** means the same as **cut-price**. ADJ: ADJ n *...cut-rate auto insurance.*

cutter /kʌtəʳ/ **cutters.** ◆◇◇◇◇

1 A **cutter** is a tool that you use for cutting through something. *...a pastry cutter. ...wire cutters.* N-COUNT: usu n N

2 A **cutter** is a person who cuts or reduces something. *...a glass cutter... He has been using every opportunity to boost his credibility as a budget cutter.* N-COUNT: with supp

3 A **cutter** is a type of boat. N-COUNT

cut-throat. If you describe a situation as **cut-throat**, you mean that the people or companies involved all want success and do not care if they harm each other in getting it. *...the cut-throat competition in personal computers. ...the cut-throat world of international finance.* ADJ-GRADED: usu ADJ n =ruthless

cutting /kʌtɪŋ/ **cuttings** ◆◆◆◇◇

1 A **cutting** is a piece of writing which has been cut from a newspaper or magazine; used mainly in British English. The usual American word is **clipping**. *...a stack of old photographs and newspaper cuttings... Here are the press cuttings and reviews.* N-COUNT =clipping

2 A **cutting** from a plant is a part of the plant that you have cut off so that you can grow a new plant from it. *Take cuttings from it in July or August.* N-COUNT

3 A railway **cutting** is a narrow valley cut through a hill so that a railway line can pass through. N-COUNT

4 A **cutting** remark is unkind and likely to hurt someone's feelings. *People make cutting remarks to help themselves feel superior or powerful.* ADJ-GRADED

cutting edge ◆◇◇◇◇

1 If you are at the **cutting edge** of a particular field of activity, you are involved in its most important or most exciting developments. *This shipyard is at the cutting edge of world shipbuilding technology.* N-SING: usu *at/on the* N *of*n =forefront

2 If someone or something gives you a **cutting edge**, they give you motivation and energy, and an advantage over your competitors. *If Pearce had been fit, we would have won. We missed the cutting edge he would have given us.* N-SING

cutting room. The **cutting room** in a film production company is the place where the film is edited. *Her scene ended up on the cutting room floor.* N-SING: usu *the* N

cuttlefish /kʌtəlfɪʃ/; **cuttlefish** is both the singular and the plural form. A **cuttlefish** is a sea animal with a soft body, tentacles, and a hard internal shell. Cuttlefish live close to the bottom of the sea near a coast. N-COUNT

cut up. If you are **cut up** about something that has happened, you are very unhappy because of it; used mainly in informal British English. *Terry was very cut up about Jim's death.* ◆◇◇◇◇ ADJ-GRADED: v-link ADJ

CV /siː viː/ **CVs.** Your **CV** is a brief written account of your personal details, your education, and the jobs you have had. You are often asked to send a CV when you are applying for a job. **CV** is an abbreviation for 'curriculum vitae'. *Send them a copy of your CV.* ◆◇◇◇◇ N-COUNT

cwt. **cwt** is a written abbreviation for **hundredweight**.

-cy /-si/ **-cies**

1 **-cy** replaces '-te', '-t', and '-tic' at the end of some adjectives to form nouns referring to the state or quality described by the adjective. *...the emotional intimacy of a family... They were sworn to secrecy.* SUFFIX

2 **-cy** is added to some nouns referring to people with a particular rank or post in order to form nouns that refer to this rank or post. *He is likely to retain the England captaincy. ...the chaplain of the university chaplaincy.* SUFFIX

cyanide /saɪənaɪd/. **Cyanide** is a highly poisonous substance. *Someone had fed him a lethal dose of cyanide... The police say he swallowed a cyanide capsule to avoid arrest.* ◆◇◇◇◇ N-UNCOUNT

cybernetics. /saɪbəʳnetɪks/. **Cybernetics** is a branch of science which involves studying the way electronic machines and human brains work, and developing machines that do things or think rather like people. N-UNCOUNT

cyberpunk /saɪbəʳpʌŋk/. **Cyberpunk** is a type of science fiction. The stories are set in a threatening future society dominated by computer technology. N-UNCOUNT

cyberspace /saɪbəʳspeɪs/. In computer technology, **cyberspace** refers to data banks and networks, considered as a space. N-UNCOUNT

cyborg /saɪbɔːʳg/ **cyborgs.** In science fiction, a **cyborg** is a being that is part human and part robot, or a robot that looks like a human being. N-COUNT

cyclamen /sɪkləmən/; **cyclamen** is both the singular and the plural form. A **cyclamen** is a plant with white, pink, or red flowers. N-COUNT

cycle /saɪkəl/ **cycles, cycling, cycled** ◆◆◆◇◇

1 If you **cycle**, you ride a bicycle. *He cycled to Ingwold... Britain could save £4.6 billion a year in road transport costs if more people cycled... Over 1000 riders cycled 100 miles around the Vale of York.* ♦ **cycling** *The quiet country roads are ideal for cycling.* VERB V prep/adv V V n N-UNCOUNT

2 A **cycle** is a bicycle. *...an eight-mile cycle ride.* N-COUNT

3 In American English, a **cycle** is a motorcycle. N-COUNT

4 A **cycle** is a series of events or processes that is repeated again and again, always in the same order. *...the life cycle of the plant... The figures marked the final low point of the present economic cycle... They must break out of the cycle of violence.* N-COUNT: usu with supp, oft N *of*n

5 A **cycle** is a single complete series of movements in an electrical, electronic, or mechanical process. *...10 cycles per second.* N-COUNT: usu pl

6 A **cycle** is a series of songs or poems that are intended to be performed or read one after the other. *...Wagner's Ring cycle.* N-COUNT: usu with supp

cycleway /saɪkəlweɪ/ **cycleways.** A **cycleway** is a special road, route, or path intended for use by cyclists. N-COUNT

cyclic /sɪklɪk, saɪk-/. **Cyclic** means the same as **cyclical**. ADJ

cyclical /sɪklɪkəl, saɪk-/. A **cyclical** process is one in which a series of events happen again and again in the same order. *...the cyclical nature of the airline business.* ◆◇◇◇◇ ADJ =cyclic

cyclist /saɪklɪst/ **cyclists.** A **cyclist** is someone who rides a bicycle, or is riding a bicycle. ◆◇◇◇◇ N-COUNT

cyclone /saɪkloʊn/ **cyclones.** A **cyclone** is a violent tropical storm in which the air goes round and round. *A cyclone in the Bay of Bengal is threatening the eastern Indian states.* ◆◇◇◇◇ N-COUNT

cygnet /sɪgnɪt/ **cygnets.** A **cygnet** is a young swan. N-COUNT

cylinder /sɪlɪndəʳ/ **cylinders** ◆◆◇◇◇

1 A **cylinder** is an object with flat circular ends and long straight sides. *...a cylinder of foam... It was recorded on a wax cylinder.* N-COUNT

2 A gas **cylinder** is a cylinder-shaped container in which gas is kept under pressure. *...oxygen cylinders.* N-COUNT: usu with supp

3 In an engine, a **cylinder** is a cylinder-shaped part in which a piston moves backwards and forwards. *...a 2.5 litre, four-cylinder engine.* N-COUNT

cylindrical /sɪlɪndrɪkəl/. Something that is **cylindrical** is in the shape of a cylinder. *...a cylindrical aluminium container... It is cylindrical in shape.* ADJ

cymbal /sɪmbəl/ **cymbals.** A **cymbal** is a flat circular brass object that is used as a musical instrument. You hit it with a stick or hit two cymbals together, making a loud noise. N-COUNT

cynic /sɪnɪk/ **cynics** ◆◇◇◇◇

1 If you describe someone as a **cynic**, you mean they believe that people always act selfishly. *I have come to be very much of a cynic in these matters.* N-COUNT

2 If journalists say what **cynics** might say about something, they are indirectly putting forward a suggestion that there is a selfish or bad reason for it. *Cynics might sneer that box-office success mattered more than artistic merit when the awards were handed out.* N-COUNT

cynical /sɪnɪkəl/ ◆◆◇◇◇

1 If you describe someone as **cynical**, you mean they believe that people always act selfishly. *...his cynical view of the world.* ♦ **cynically** *As a back-* ADJ-GRADED ≠idealistic ADV-GRADED:

packer said cynically, 'He's probably pocketed the difference!' ADV with v

2 If you are **cynical** about something, you do not believe that it can be successful or that the people involved are honourable. *It's hard not to be cynical about reform... It has also made me more cynical about relationships.* ADJ-GRADED: usu v-link ADJ, usu ADJ *about* n

cynically /sɪnɪkli/. If you say that someone is **cynically** doing something, you mean they are doing it to benefit themselves and they do not care that they are deceiving, harming, or exploiting people; used showing disapproval. *The people who publish this magazine are cynically using sex as a circulation ploy... I firmly believe our strategy is being deliberately, cynically manipulated.* • See also **cynical**. ADV-GRADED: usu ADV before v PRAGMATICS

cynicism /sɪnɪsɪzəm/ ◆◇◇◇◇

1 **Cynicism** is the belief that people always act selfishly. *I found Ben's cynicism wearing at times.* N-UNCOUNT ≠idealism

2 **Cynicism** about something is the belief that it cannot be successful or that the people involved are not honourable. *This talk betrays a certain cynicism about free trade.* N-UNCOUNT

cypher /saɪfəʳ/. See **cipher**.

cypress /saɪprəs/ **cypresses.** A **cypress** is a type of conifer. ◆◇◇◇◇ N-COUNT

Cypriot /sɪpriət/ **Cypriots** ◆◆◆◆◇

1 **Cypriot** means belonging or relating to Cyprus, or to its people or culture. *...the two Cypriot communities.* ADJ

2 A **Cypriot** is a Cypriot citizen, or a person of Cypriot origin. N-COUNT

cyrillic /sɪrɪlɪk/

1 The **cyrillic** alphabet is the alphabet that is used to write some Slavonic languages, such as Russian and Bulgarian. ADJ: ADJ n

2 **Cyrillic** is the cyrillic alphabet. *...signs written in Cyrillic.* N-UNCOUNT

cyst /sɪst/ **cysts.** A **cyst** is a growth containing liquid that appears inside your body or under your skin. *He had a minor operation to remove a cyst.* ◆◇◇◇◇ N-COUNT

cystic fibrosis /sɪstɪk faɪbroʊsɪs/. **Cystic fibrosis** is a rare hereditary disease of the glands which usually develops during early childhood. ◆◇◇◇◇ N-UNCOUNT

cystitis /sɪstaɪtɪs/. **Cystitis** is a bladder infection; a medical term. *...an attack of cystitis.* N-UNCOUNT

czar /zɑːʳ/. See **tsar**.

czarina /zɑːriːnə/. See **tsarina**.

czarist /zɑːrɪst/. See **tsarist**.

Czech /tʃek/ **Czechs** ◆◆◆◆◇

1 **Czech** means belonging or relating to the Czech Republic, or to its people, language, or culture. *...Czech industry. ...Czech novels.* ADJ

2 A **Czech** is a Czech citizen, or a person of Czech origin. N-COUNT

3 **Czech** is the language spoken in the Czech Republic. N-UNCOUNT

Czechoslovak /tʃekəsloʊvæk/ **Czechoslovaks** ◆◆◆◆◇

1 **Czechoslovak** means belonging or relating to the former state of Czechoslovakia. *...the Czechoslovak capital, Prague.* ADJ: usu ADJ n

2 A **Czechoslovak** was a Czechoslovak citizen, or a person of Czechoslovak origin. N-COUNT

Czechoslovakian /tʃekəsləvækiən/ **Czechoslovakians** ◆◆◆◆◇

1 **Czechoslovakian** means the same as **Czechoslovak**. *...the Czechoslovakian government.* ADJ

2 A **Czechoslovakian** was a Czechoslovak citizen, or a person of Czechoslovak origin. N-COUNT

D d

D, d /diː/ **D's, d's**

1 **D** is the fourth letter of the English alphabet. N-VAR

2 In music, **D** is the second note in the scale of C major. N-VAR

3 If you get a **D** as a mark for a piece of work or in an exam, your work is below average or poor. *I got a D+.* N-VAR

4 **d.** is an abbreviation for **died** when it is written in front of dates, for example on memorials or in reference books.

5 **d.** was a written abbreviation for **penny** or **pence** in Britain before decimal currency was introduced in 1971.

6 **D** or **d** is used as an abbreviation for words beginning with d, such as 'day', 'defeated', or 'district'.

'd. Pronounced /-d/ after a vowel sound and /-əd/ after a consonant sound.

1 **'d** is a short form of **had**, especially when it is an auxiliary verb; used in spoken English. *She said she'd met you in England.*

2 **'d** is a short form of **would**; used in spoken English. *I'd like a word with you.*

d' /d-/. See **d'you**.

D.A. /diː eɪ/ **D.A.s.** In the United States, a **D.A.** is a **District Attorney**. ◆◇◇◇◇ N-COUNT

dab /dæb/ **dabs, dabbing, dabbed** ◆◇◇◇◇

1 If you **dab** something, you touch it several times using quick, light movements. If you **dab** a substance onto a surface, you put it there using quick, light movements. *She arrived weeping, dabbing her eyes with a tissue... She spread the icing over the cake, dabbing it with a knife... She dabbed iodine on the cuts on her forehead... He dabbed at his lips with the napkin.* VERB V n V n prep/adv V *at* n Also V

2 A **dab of** something is a small amount of it that is put onto a surface; an informal use. *She wore no make-up, not even a dab of lipstick. ...a dab of glue.* N-COUNT: N *of* n

3 A **dab** is a small flat fish with rough scales. N-VAR

dabble /dæbᵊl/ **dabbles, dabbling, dabbled.** If you **dabble** in something, you take part in it but not very seriously. *He dabbled in business... She dabbled with drugs... Magicians do not dabble, they work hard.* ◆◇◇◇◇ VERB V *in/with/at* n V

dab hand, dab hands. In British English, if you are a **dab hand** at something, you are very good at doing it; an informal expression. *She was a dab hand at solving difficult crossword puzzles.* N-COUNT: usu N *at* n/-ing

dace /deɪs/; **dace** is both the singular and the plural form. A **dace** is a type of freshwater fish. ◆◇◇◇◇ N-VAR

dacha /dætʃə, AM dɑːtʃə/ **dachas.** A **dacha** is a country house in Russia. N-COUNT

dachshund /dækshʊnd, AM dɑːksʊnt/ **dachshunds.** A **dachshund** is a small dog that has very short legs, a long body, and long ears. N-COUNT

Dacron /dækrɒn/. **Dacron** is a synthetic polyester fibre or fabric. **Dacron** is a trademark. N-UNCOUNT

dad /dæd/ **dads.** Your **dad** is your father; an informal word. *How do you feel, Dad?... I talked to Dad... He's living with his mum and dad.* ◆◆◆◇◇ N-FAMILY

daddy /dædi/ **daddies.** Children often call their father **daddy**; an informal word. *Look at me, Daddy!... I wrote a letter to Daddy... She wanted her mummy and daddy.* ◆◆◇◇◇ N-FAMILY

daddy longlegs /dædi lɒŋlegz, AM - lɔːŋ-/; **daddy longlegs** is both the singular and the plural form. A **daddy longlegs** is a flying insect with very long legs. N-COUNT =cranefly

dado /deɪdoʊ/ **dados.** In some rooms, a **dado** is a layer of wood that is fixed to the lower part of a wall, and usually painted a different colour. N-COUNT

daffodil /dæfədɪl/ **daffodils.** A **daffodil** is a yellow trumpet-shaped flower with a long stem that blooms in the spring. ◆◇◇◇◇ N-COUNT

daffy /dæfi/. If you describe a person or thing as **daffy**, you mean that they are strange or foolish, but in a rather attractive way; an informal word. *The assumption is that small women are sweet and daffy. ...a daffy storyline.* ADJ-GRADED PRAGMATICS

daft /dɑːft, dæft/ **dafter, daftest.** In British English, if you describe a person or their behaviour as **daft**, you think that they are stupid, impractical, or rather strange; an informal word. *He's not so daft as to listen to rumours... I can lose a few pounds without resorting to daft diets... Don't be daft!* ◆◇◇◇◇ ADJ-GRADED PRAGMATICS =barmy

dagger /dægəʳ/ **daggers** ◆◇◇◇◇

1 A **dagger** is a weapon like a knife with two sharp edges. N-COUNT

2 In British English, if you say that two people are **at daggers drawn**, you mean they are having an argument and are still very angry with each other. *She and her mother were at daggers drawn.* PHRASE

dahlia /deɪliə/ **dahlias.** A **dahlia** is a garden flower with a lot of brightly coloured petals. ◆◇◇◇◇ N-COUNT

daily /deɪli/ **dailies** ◆◆◆◆◇

1 If something happens **daily**, it happens every day. *Cathay Pacific flies daily non-stop to Hong Kong from Heathrow... The Visitor Centre is open daily Mon – Fri 8.30 a.m. – 4.30 p.m.* ► Also an adjective. *They held daily press briefings.* ADV: ADV after v; ADJ: ADJ n

2 **Daily** quantities or rates relate to a period of one day. *...a diet containing adequate daily amounts of fresh fruit... Baghdad exported more than half of its daily oil production.* ADJ: ADJ n

3 A **daily** is a newspaper that is published every day of the week except Sunday. *Copies of the local daily had been scattered on a table.* ► Also an adjective. *He studied the daily papers.* N-COUNT; ADJ: ADJ n

4 Your **daily life** is the things that you do every day as part of your normal life. *All of us in our daily life react favourably to people who take us and our views seriously.* PHRASE: N inflects

dainty /deɪnti/ **daintier, daintiest.** If you describe a movement, person, or object as **dainty**, you mean that they are small, delicate, and pretty. *The girls were dainty and feminine. ...dainty pink flowers.* ♦ **daintily** *She walked daintily down the steps.* ◆◇◇◇◇ ADJ-GRADED; ADV-GRADED: ADV with v, ADV adj

daiquiri /daɪkɪri, dæk-/ **daiquiris.** A **daiquiri** is a drink made with rum, lime juice, sugar, and ice. N-COUNT

dairy /deəri/ **dairies** ◆◆◇◇◇

1 A **dairy** is a shop or company that sells milk and food made from milk, such as butter, cream, and cheese. N-COUNT

2 On a farm, the **dairy** is the building where milk is kept or where cream, butter, and cheese are made. N-COUNT

3 **Dairy** is used to refer to foods such as butter and cheese that are made from milk. *...dairy produce. ...vitamins found in eggs, meat and dairy products.* ADJ: ADJ n

4 **Dairy** is used to refer to the use of cattle to produce milk rather than meat. *...a small vegetable and dairy farm. ...the feeding of dairy cows.* ADJ: ADJ n

dais /deɪɪs/ **daises.** A **dais** is a raised platform in a hall. N-COUNT

daisy /deɪzi/ **daisies.** A **daisy** is a small wild flower with a yellow centre and white petals. ◆◇◇◇◇ N-COUNT

daisy chain, daisy chains; also spelled **daisy-chain**. A **daisy chain** is a string of daisies that have been joined together by their stems to make a necklace; used in British English. N-COUNT

daisy wheel, daisy wheels; also spelled **daisy-wheel**. A **daisy wheel** is a small flat disc which has letters on thin stalks around its edge and which is the part of an electric typewriter or word processor that prints the letters. It is also a printer or typewriter which has this kind of printing device. N-COUNT

dale /deɪl/ **dales.** In old-fashioned British English, a **dale** is a valley. N-COUNT =vale

dalliance /dæliəns/ **dalliances**

1 When two people have a brief romantic relationship, you can say that they have a **dalliance** with each other; an old-fashioned use. *...my dalliance with a certain footballer. ...sexual dalliances.* N-VAR: oft N with n

2 Someone's **dalliance** with something is a brief involvement with it; an old-fashioned use. *...my brief dalliance with higher education.* N-COUNT: oft poss N, N with n

dally /dæli/ **dallies, dallying, dallied**

1 If you **dally**, you act or move very slowly, wasting time; an old-fashioned use. *The bureaucrats dallied too long... He did not dally over the choice of a suitable partner.* VERB V; V over n/-ing; Also V with n

2 If someone **dallies** with you, they have a romantic, but not serious, relationship with you; an old-fashioned use. *In his social and sexual life he dallied with actresses and lady novelists.* VERB V with n

Dalmatian /dælmeɪʃᵊn/ **Dalmatians.** A **Dalmatian** is a large dog with short, smooth, white hair and black or dark brown spots. N-COUNT

dam /dæm/ **dams, damming, dammed** ◆◆◇◇◇

1 A **dam** is a wall that is built across a river in order to stop the water flowing and to make a lake. *They went ahead with plans to build a dam on the Danube River. ...the Aswan Dam.* N-COUNT

2 To **dam** a river means to build a dam across it. *...plans to dam the nearby Delaware River... This reservoir was formed by damming the River Blith.* VERB V n

3 An animal's **dam** is its mother; a technical use in livestock breeding. N-COUNT: usu with poss

damage /dæmɪdʒ/ **damages, damaging, damaged** ◆◆◆◆◇

1 To **damage** an object means to break it, spoil it physically, or stop it from working properly. *He maliciously damaged a car with a baseball bat... Lemon juice has the potential to damage hair, rendering it dry and brittle.* VERB =harm V n

2 To **damage** something means to cause it to become less good, pleasant, or successful. *Jackson doesn't want to damage his reputation as a political personality... He warned that the action was damaging the economy.* ♦ **damaging** *Many observers believe the resignation will be very damaging to the Soviet leader.* VERB =harm ≠boost V n; ADJ-GRADED =harmful

3 **Damage** is physical harm that is caused to an object. *The blast had serious effects with quite extensive damage to the house... Many professional boxers end their careers with eye and brain damage.* N-UNCOUNT: oft N to n

4 **Damage** consists of the unpleasant effects that something has on a person, situation, or type of activity. *He believes the scandal stories are doing lasting damage to the Duchess and to her children... Adhering to the new rules meant inflicting serious damage on motor racing.* N-UNCOUNT: oft N to n

5 If a court of law awards **damages** to someone, it orders money to be paid to them by a person who has damaged their reputation or property, or who has injured them. *He was vindicated in court and damages were awarded.* N-PLURAL

6 If you say **'the damage is done'**, you mean that it is too late now to prevent the harmful effects of something that has already happened. *Once the damage is done, even modern surgery can't undo it entirely.* PHRASE

damask /dæməsk/ **damasks. Damask** is a type of heavy cloth with a pattern woven into it. N-MASS

dame /deɪm/ **dames** ◆◆◇◇◇

1 In old-fashioned American English, a **dame** is a woman. *Who does that dame think she is?* N-COUNT =broad

2 In Britain, **Dame** is a title given to a woman as a special honour because of important service or work that she has done. *...Dame Joan Sutherland.* N-TITLE

dammit /dæmɪt/. See **damn**.

damn /dæm/ **damns, damning, damned** ◆◆◇◇◇

1 **Damn, damn it**, and **dammit** are swear words which some people use to express anger or frustration. *Don't be flippant, damn it! This is serious.* EXCLAM

2 **Damn** is a swear word which some people use to emphasize what they are saying. *There's not a damn thing you can do about it now.* ► Also an adverb. *As it turned out, I was damn right... Let's have a damn good party... Frankly, they can call me anything they damn well please.* ADJ: ADJ n PRAGMATICS; ADV: ADV adj/adv

3 If you say that a person or a news report **damns** something such as a policy or action, you mean VERB =slam

that they are very critical of it. *...a sensational book in which she damns the ultra-right party. ...a report damning the chocolate advertising people for targeting women in their campaigns.*
V n

4 See also **damned, damning.**

5 If you say that someone **does not give a damn** about something, you mean that they do not care about it at all; an informal expression.
PHRASES
V inflects

6 People use **damn near** to emphasize that what they are saying is not actually true, but is very close to being true; an informal expression. *I damn near went crazy... That's a question damn near every woman who ever lived has had to answer for herself.*
PHR before v, PHR n/adj
PRAGMATICS

7 Some people say **as near as damn it** or **as near as dammit** to emphasize that what they have said is almost exactly accurate, but not quite; an informal expression. *I have been leading as near as damn it a normal life this past five or six weeks... The stadium will be as near as dammit empty.*
usu PHR n
PRAGMATICS

damnable /dæmnəbᵊl/. You use **damnable** to emphasize that you dislike or disapprove of something a great deal; an old-fashioned word. *What a damnable climate we have!... The charge of rape was a damnable lie.*
ADJ:
ADJ n
PRAGMATICS

♦ **damnably** /dæmnəbli/ *It was damnably unfair that he should suffer so much.*
ADV:
ADV adj

damnation /dæmneɪʃᵊn/

1 According to some religions, if someone suffers **damnation**, they are condemned to stay in hell for ever after their death because of their sin. *She has a healthy fear of hellfire and eternal damnation.*
N-UNCOUNT

2 Some people say **damnation!** as a swear word to express anger or frustration.
EXCLAM

damned /dæmd/
◆◆◇◇◇

1 **Damned** is a swear word that some people use, especially when they are angry or frustrated, to emphasize what they are saying. *The damned meeting seemed endless... They're a damned nuisance most of the time.*
ADJ:
ADJ n
PRAGMATICS

► Also an adverb. *We are making a damned good profit, I tell you that.*
ADV:
ADV adj/adv

2 According to some religions, **the damned** are people who have been condemned to stay in hell for ever after they have died.
N-PLURAL:
the N

3 If someone says '**I'm damned if I'm** going to do it' or '**I'll be damned if I'll** do it', they are emphasizing that they do not intend to do it and think it is unreasonable for anyone to expect them to do it; an informal expression.
PHRASE:
V inflects
PRAGMATICS

4 Some people say '**I'll be damned!**' when they are expressing surprise at something; an informal expression.
PHRASE

damnedest /dæmdɪst/

1 If you say that you will **do** your **damnedest** to achieve something, you mean that you will try as hard as you can to do it, even though you think that it will take a lot of effort; an informal expression. *I did my damnedest to persuade her.*
PHRASE:
V inflects,
usu PHR to-inf

2 If you say that something is the **damnedest** thing, you are emphasizing that it is surprising or odd; an informal expression. *Today I heard somebody say the damnedest thing about Cross... You pick the damnedest places to eat!*
ADJ-SUPERL:
ADJ n

damn fool. **Damn fool** is a mild swear word meaning 'very stupid'; an old-fashioned expression. *What a damn fool thing to do!*
ADJ-GRADED:
ADJ n
PRAGMATICS

damning /dæmɪŋ/. If you describe evidence or a report as **damning**, you mean that it suggests very strongly that someone is guilty of a crime or error. *...a damning report into the government's handling of the salmonella affair... He was most damning in his comments about the army.*
◆◇◇◇◇
ADJ-GRADED

Damocles /dæməkliːz/. If you say that someone has the **Sword of Damocles** hanging over their head, you mean that they are in a situation in which something very bad could happen to them at any time. *As a Grand Prix driver, you have the Sword of Damocles hanging over your head at every moment.*
PHRASE

damp /dæmp/ **damper, dampest; damps, damping, damped**
◆◆◇◇◇

1 Something that is **damp** is slightly wet. *Her hair was still damp. ...the damp, cold air... She wiped the table with a damp cloth.*
ADJ-GRADED
=moist

2 **Damp** is moisture that is found on the inside walls of a house or in the air. *There was damp everywhere and the entire building was in need of rewiring.* • See also **rising damp.**
N-UNCOUNT

3 If you **damp** something, you make it slightly wet. *Hillsden damped a hand towel and laid it across her forehead.*
VERB
=dampen
V n

damp down. To **damp down** something such as a strong emotion, an argument, or a crisis means to make it calmer or less intense. *His hand moved to his mouth as he tried to damp down the panic... Mr Major tried to damp down the row yesterday.*
PHRASAL VERB
=calm
V P n (not pron)

damp course, damp courses. In Britain, a **damp course** is a layer of waterproof material which is put into the bottom of the outside wall of a building to prevent moisture from rising.
N-COUNT

dampen /dæmpən/ **dampens, dampening, dampened**
◆◇◇◇◇

1 To **dampen** something such as someone's enthusiasm or excitement means to make it less lively or intense. *Nothing seems to dampen his perpetual enthusiasm... I hate to dampen your spirits but aren't you overlooking a couple of minor points.*
VERB
V n

► To **dampen** something **down** means the same as to **dampen** it. *Although unemployment rose last month, this is unlikely to dampen down wage demands... After the boom, the economy overheated and the Government resorted to interest rates to dampen it down.*
PHRASAL VERB
V P n (not pron)
V n P

2 If you **dampen** something, you make it slightly wet. *She took the time to dampen a washcloth and do her face.*
VERB
V n

dampener /dæmpnəʳ/. To **put a dampener on** something means the same as to **put a damper on** it. *Boy, did this woman know how to put a dampener on your day.*
PHRASE:
V inflects,
PHR n

damper /dæmpəʳ/ **dampers**

1 A **damper** is a small sheet of metal in a fire, boiler, or furnace that can be moved to increase or reduce the amount of air that enters.
N-COUNT

2 A **damper** is a device in a piano or similar musical instrument which makes the sound less loud by restricting the movement of the strings.
N-COUNT

3 If someone or something **puts a damper on** something, they have an effect on it which stops it being as enjoyable or as successful as it should be; an informal expression. *Unseasonably cool weather has put a damper on many plans for the day... That would put a damper on the future growth of U.S. steel exports.*
PHRASE:
V inflects,
PHR n

dampness /dæmpnəs/

1 **Dampness** is moisture in the air, or on the surface of something. *I could see big circles of dampness under each arm... The tins had to be kept away from dampness, soot and cooking fumes.*
N-UNCOUNT
=moisture

2 **Dampness** is the quality of being damp. *The dampness of the forest did not agree with him physically.*
N-UNCOUNT

damp-proof course, damp-proof courses. A **damp-proof course** is the same as a **damp course.**
N-COUNT

damsel /dæmzᵊl/ **damsels.** A **damsel** is a young, unmarried woman; an old-fashioned, literary word.
◆◇◇◇◇
N-COUNT
=maiden

damson /dæmzᵊn/ **damsons.** A **damson** is a small, sour, purple plum.
N-COUNT

dance /dɑːns, dæns/ **dances, dancing, danced**
◆◆◆◆◇

1 When you **dance**, you move your body and feet in a way which follows a rhythm, usually in time to music. *Polly had never learned to dance... I like to dance to the music on the radio.*
VERB
V
V to n

2 A **dance** is a particular series of rhythmic movements of your body and feet, which you usually do in time to music. *Sometimes the people doing this dance hold brightly colored scarves... She describes the tango as a very sexy dance.*
N-COUNT

3 When you **dance** with someone, the two of you take part in a dance together, as partners. You can also say that two people **dance.** *It's a terrible thing when nobody wants to dance with you... Shall we*
V-RECIP
V with n
pl-n V
V (non-recip)

dance?... He asked her to dance. ► Also a noun. *Come and have a dance with me.* N-COUNT

4 A **dance** is a social event where people dance with each other. *She often went to parties and dances at Littlecote... At the school dance he sat and talked to her all evening.* N-COUNT

5 **Dance** is the activity of performing dances, as a public entertainment or an art form. *Their contribution to international dance, drama and music is inestimable... No show prior to 'On The Town' had told so much of its story through dance... She no longer has the time or energy for her dance classes.* N-UNCOUNT

6 If you **dance** a particular kind of dance, you do it or perform it. *Then we put the music on, and we all danced the Charleston... They will dance two performances of Ashton's 'Romeo and Juliet'.* VERB V n

7 If you **dance** somewhere, you move there lightly and quickly, usually because you are happy or excited. *Kicking me sharply in the shins, he danced off down the road... Amy went and kissed him, and then danced out of his reach.* VERB V adv/prep

8 If you say that something **dances**, you mean that it moves about, or seems to move about, lightly and quickly. *Patterns of light, reflected by the river, dance along the base of the cliffs... She tried to read it more slowly and carefully, but the words danced and dissolved before her eyes.* VERB V adv/prep

9 If someone **leads** you **a merry dance**, they make you do things over a long period of time which cause you problems and do not benefit you in any way; used in British English. PHRASE: V inflects

10 • to **dance to** someone's **tune**: see **tune**. • to **make a song and dance about** something: see **song and dance**.

dance floor, dance floors; also spelled **dancefloor**. In a restaurant or night club, the **dance floor** is the area where people can dance. ◆◇◇◇◇ N-COUNT

dance hall, dance halls. Dance halls were large rooms or buildings where people paid to go and dance, usually in the evening. Most dance halls closed down when disco dancing became popular. N-COUNT

dancer /dɑːnsəʳ, dæns-/ **dancers** ◆◆◇◇◇

1 A **dancer** is a person who earns money by dancing, or a person who is dancing. *His previous girlfriend was a dancer with the Royal Ballet... The dancers began to walk away from the floor.* N-COUNT

2 If you say that someone is a good **dancer** or a bad **dancer**, you are saying how well or badly they can dance. *He was the best dancer in LA.* N-COUNT: adj N

dance studio, dance studios. A **dance studio** is a place where people pay to learn how to dance. N-COUNT

dancing /dɑːnsɪŋ, dæns-/. When people dance for enjoyment or to entertain others, you can refer to this activity as **dancing**. *All the schools have music and dancing as part of the curriculum... Let's go dancing tonight. ...dancing shoes.* ◆◆◆◇◇ N-UNCOUNT

dandelion /dændɪlaɪən/ **dandelions.** A **dandelion** is a wild plant which has yellow flowers with lots of thin petals. When the petals drop off, they leave fluffy balls of seeds. ◆◇◇◇◇ N-COUNT

dandruff /dændrʌf/. **Dandruff** is small white pieces of dead skin in someone's hair, or fallen from someone's hair. *He has very bad dandruff.* N-UNCOUNT

dandy /dændi/ **dandies** ◆◇◇◇◇

1 A **dandy** is a man who thinks a great deal about his appearance and always dresses in smart clothes. *He was handsome and a dandy.* N-COUNT

2 If you say that something is **dandy**, you mean it is good or just right; an informal word, used mainly in old-fashioned American English. *There's a zoo round here? That's dandy for my kids.* ADJ =fine

Dane /deɪn/ **Danes.** A **Dane** is a person who comes from Denmark. *The Danes dismissed the allegation as nonsense.* ◆◇◇◇◇ N-COUNT

danger /deɪndʒəʳ/ **dangers** ◆◆◆◆◇

1 **Danger** is the possibility that someone may be harmed or killed. *My friends endured tremendous danger in order to help me... Please Vanya, your life is in danger here. Do what Tenzin says.* N-UNCOUNT ≠safety

2 A **danger** is something or someone that can hurt or harm you. *...the dangers of smoking. ...the danger of open conflict... Britain's roads are a danger to cyclists... Public health physicians say there are other dangers, too.* N-COUNT: usu N of-ing/n, N to n =threat

3 If there is a **danger** that something unpleasant will happen, it is possible that it will happen. *There is a real danger that some people will no longer be able to afford insurance... There was no danger that any of these groups would be elected to power... If there is a danger of famine, we should help.* N-SING: also no det, N that, N of n/-ing

4 If someone who has been seriously ill is **out of danger**, they are still ill, but they are not expected to die. PHRASE: v-link PHR

dangerous /deɪndʒərəs/. If something is **dangerous**, it is able or likely to hurt or harm you. *It's a dangerous stretch of road. ...dangerous drugs... It's dangerous to jump to early conclusions.* ◆◆◆◆◇ ADJ-GRADED: oft it v-link ADJ to-inf =unsafe

♦ **dangerously** *He is dangerously ill... He rushed downstairs dangerously fast... The coach rocked dangerously.* ADV-GRADED: usu ADV adj/adv/-ed, also ADV after v

dangle /dæŋgəl/ **dangles, dangling, dangled** ◆◇◇◇◇

1 If something **dangles** from somewhere or if you **dangle** it somewhere, it hangs or swings loosely. *A gold bracelet dangled from his left wrist... Crystal chandeliers dangled from every ceiling... He and I were sitting out on his jetty dangling our legs in the water.* V-ERG V prep/adv V n prep/adv Also V, V n

2 If you say that someone **is dangling** something attractive before you, you mean they are offering it to you in order to try and persuade you to do something or buy something. *Ever since, when they've dangled rich rewards before me, I've taken fright... Foreign currency mortgages that dangle the carrot of interest rates of 10 per cent or less should be resisted at all costs.* VERB V n before/in front of n V n

Danish /deɪnɪʃ/ ◆◆◆◆◇

1 **Danish** means belonging or relating to Denmark, its people, its language, or culture. *...the Danish coast... He was the son of a Danish father and a Venezuelan mother.* ADJ: usu ADJ n

2 **Danish** is the language spoken in Denmark. N-UNCOUNT

Danish pastry, Danish pastries. Danish pastries are cakes made from sweet pastry. They often have fillings such as apple or almond paste. N-COUNT

dank /dæŋk/. A **dank** place, especially an underground place such as a cave or cellar, is unpleasantly damp and cold. *The kitchen was dank and cheerless.* ADJ

dapper /dæpəʳ/. A man who is **dapper** has a very neat and clean appearance, and is small and slim. *The bartender, a dapper little man named Al, was beaming at him.* ADJ-GRADED

dappled /dæpəld/. You use **dappled** to describe something that has dark or light patches on it, or that is made up of patches of light and shade. *...a dappled horse... Sometimes I carry a book out under the pear trees and sit in the dappled shade... The path was dappled with sunlight.* ADJ: ADJ n, v-link ADJ with/by/in n

dare /deəʳ/ **dares, daring, dared** ◆◆◆◇◇

Dare sometimes behaves like an ordinary verb, for example 'He dared to speak' and 'He doesn't dare to speak' and sometimes like a modal, for example 'He daren't speak'.

1 If you do not **dare** to do something, you do not have enough courage to do it, or you do not want to do it because you fear the consequences. If you **dare** to do something, you do something which requires a lot of courage. *Since he was stuck in a lift a year ago he hasn't dared to get back into one... Most people hate Harry but they don't dare to say so... He has also dared to take unpopular, but principled stands at times... We have had problems in our family that I didn't dare tell Uncle.* ► Also a modal. *Dare she risk staying where she was?... The yen is weakening. But Tokyo dare not raise its interest rates again... 'Are you coming with me?'—'I can't, Alice. I daren't.'.* VB: oft with brd-neg V to-inf V inf MODAL

2 If you **dare** someone to do something, you challenge them to prove that they are not frightened of doing it. *Over coffee, she lit a cigarette, her eyes daring him to comment... I dare you to sit through forty-five minutes with someone like Vincent!* VERB V n to-inf

3 A **dare** is a challenge which one person gives to another to do something dangerous or frightening. *He'd do pretty much anything on a dare... When found, the children said they'd run away for a dare.* N-COUNT: usu sing, usu *as/for/on a* N

4 If you say to someone **'don't you dare'** do something, you are telling someone not to do it and letting them know that you are angry. *Don't speak to me like that. Don't you dare... Allen, don't you dare go anywhere else, you hear?* PHRASES oft PHR inf

5 You say **'how dare you'** when you are very shocked and angry about something that someone has done. *How dare you pick up the phone and listen in on my conversations!... Suddenly the peace was destroyed by someone shouting, 'Get back! Go away! How dare you!'* usu PHR inf

6 You use **'dare I say it'** when you know that what you are going to say will disappoint or annoy someone. *Politicians usually attract younger women, dare I say it, because of the status they have in society.* PHR with cl

7 You can use **'I dare say'** or **'I daresay'** before or after a statement to indicate that you believe it is probably true; used in spoken English. *I dare say that the computer would provide a clear answer to that... People always think I'm a fool, and I dare say they're right... Luke badly wanted a pass mark. Still does, I daresay.* PHR that, cl PHR =I suppose

daredevil /deəʳdevəl/ **daredevils**

1 **Daredevil** people enjoy doing physically dangerous things. *A daredevil parachutist jumped from the top of Tower Bridge today.* ► Also a noun. *He was a daredevil when young.* ADJ: ADJ n; N-COUNT

2 You use **daredevil** to describe actions that are physically dangerous and require courage. *The show's full of daredevil feats by cowboys and Indians with horses, buffalos and stagecoaches.* ADJ: ADJ n

daren't /deəʳnt/. In informal English, 'dare not' is usually said or written as **daren't**.

daresay /deəʳseɪ/. See **dare**.

daring /deərɪŋ/ ◆◆◇◇◇

1 People who are **daring** are willing to do or say things which are new or which might shock or anger other people. *Bergit was probably more daring than I was... He realized this to be a very daring thing to ask. ...one of the most daring political theatres in Prague.* ♦ **daringly** *'Cheers,' he said and winked daringly at her. ...a daringly low-cut dress.* ADJ-GRADED =bold; ADV-GRADED: ADV with v, ADV adj

2 A **daring** person is willing to do things that might be dangerous. *...the heroic and daring Charlie Pierce... His daring rescue saved the lives of the youngsters.* ADJ-GRADED: usu ADJ n =bold

3 **Daring** is the courage to do things which might be dangerous or which might shock or anger other people. *His daring may have cost him his life.* N-UNCOUNT =bravery, boldness ≠cowardice

dark /dɑːʳk/ **darker, darkest** ◆◆◆◆◇

1 When it is **dark**, there is not enough light to see properly, for example because it is night. *When she awoke it was evening and already dark... It was too dark inside to see much... People usually draw the curtains once it gets dark... She snapped off the light and made her way back through the dark kitchen and up the stairs.* ♦ **darkness** *The light went out, and the room was plunged into darkness.* ♦ **darkly** *In a darkly lit, seedy dance hall, hundreds of men lounge around small tables.* ADJ-GRADED ≠light; N-UNCOUNT; ADV: ADV -ed

2 **The dark** is the lack of light in a place. *Her mother was sitting in the dark by the stove in her rocking chair... I've always been afraid of the dark.* N-SING: *the* N =darkness ≠light

3 If you describe something as **dark**, you mean that it is black in colour, or a shade that is close to black. *He wore a dark suit and carried a black attaché case... The heavy dark table is inlaid with lighter wood.* ♦ **darkly** *The freckles on Joanne's face suddenly stood out darkly against her pale skin... The tea was darkly amber, the way he liked it.* ADJ-GRADED ≠light; ADV: ADV after v, ADV adj/-ed

4 When you use **dark** to describe a colour, you are referring to a shade of that colour which is close to black, or seems to have some black in it. *She was wearing a dark blue dress.* COMB in COLOUR ≠light

5 If someone has **dark** hair, eyes, or skin, they have brown or black hair, eyes, or skin. *He had dark, curly hair... Leo went on, his dark eyes wide with pity and concern.* ADJ-GRADED

6 If you describe a white person as **dark**, you mean that they have brown or black hair, and often a brownish skin. *Carol is a tall, dark, Latin type of woman... The driver was very dark. Maltese, maybe.* ♦ **darkly** *He was a slim, solemn, darkly handsome young man who prided himself on his level-headedness.* ADJ-GRADED ≠fair; ADV: ADV adj

7 A **dark** period of time is unpleasant or frightening. *Once again there's talk of very dark days ahead... This was the darkest period of the war.* ADJ-GRADED: usu ADJ n =black ≠happy

8 A **dark** place or area is mysterious and not fully known about. *The spacecraft is set to throw new light on to a dark corner of the solar system. ...the dark recesses of the mind.* ADJ-GRADED: ADJ n

9 **Dark** thoughts are sad, and show that you are expecting something unpleasant to happen; a literary use. *Troy's endless happy chatter kept me from thinking dark thoughts.* ♦ **darkly** *Her thoughts circled darkly round Bernard's strange behaviour.* ADJ-GRADED: usu ADJ n =gloomy; ADV-GRADED: ADV with v

10 **Dark** looks or remarks make you think that the person giving them wants to harm you or that something horrible is going to happen. *Garin shot him a dark glance, as if in warning. ...dark threats.* ♦ **darkly** *'Something's wrong here,' she said darkly... They shake their heads and mutter darkly.* ADJ-GRADED: usu ADJ n =sinister; ADV-GRADED: ADV with v

11 If you describe something as **dark**, you mean that it is related to things that are serious or unpleasant, rather than light-hearted. *He smiled when he talked about their dark humor that never failed to astound him and that few adults understand... Nina took a kind of dark pleasure in being the focus of the tension between her father and her brother.* ♦ **darkly** *The atmosphere after Wednesday's debut was as darkly comic as the film itself... Von Otter was superb both in the darkly dramatic songs, and in the lighter ones.* ADJ-GRADED: usu ADJ n; ADV-GRADED: ADV adj

12 See also **pitch-dark**.

13 If you do something **after dark**, you do it when night has begun. *They avoid going out alone after dark.* PHRASES

14 If you do something **before dark**, you do it before the sun sets and night begins. *They'll be back well before dark.*

15 If you are **in the dark** about something, you do not know anything about it. *The investigators admit that they are completely in the dark about the killing... I managed to keep my parents in the dark about this... I'm as much in the dark as you.* v-link PHR, PHR after v, oft PHR *about* n

16 If you describe something someone says or does as **a shot in the dark** or a **stab in the dark**, you mean they are guessing that what they say is correct or that what they do will be successful. *Every single one of those inspired guesses had been shots in the dark.* *shot* inflects

17 • **leap in the dark**: see **leap**.

dark age, dark ages; also spelled **Dark Age**.

1 If you refer to a period in the history of a society as a **dark age**, you think that it is characterized by ignorance and a lack of progress; used in written English. *The Education Secretary accuses teachers of wanting to return to a dark age.* N-COUNT PRAGMATICS

2 **The Dark Ages** are the period of European history between about 500 A.D. and about 1000 A.D. N-PROPER: *the* N

darken /dɑːʳkən/ **darkens, darkening, darkened** ◆◇◇◇◇

1 If something **darkens** or if someone or something **darkens** it, it becomes darker; used in written English. *The sky darkened abruptly... She had put on her make-up and darkened her eyelashes.* V-ERG ≠lighten; V; V n

2 If someone's mood **darkens** or if something **darkens** their mood, they suddenly become rather unhappy; used in written English. *My sunny mood suddenly darkened... Nothing was going to darken his mood today.* V-ERG; V; V n

3 If someone's face **darkens**, they suddenly look angry; used in written English. *Rawley's face darkened again.* VERB; V

darkened /dɑːʳkənd/. A **darkened** building or room has no lights on inside it. *He drove past darkened houses.* ◆◇◇◇◇ ADJ: ADJ n

dark glasses. Dark glasses are glasses which have dark-coloured lenses to protect your eyes in the sunshine. N-PLURAL: also *a pair of* N =sunglasses

dark horse, dark horses. If you describe someone as a **dark horse**, you mean that people know very little about them, although they may have recently had success or may be about to have success. *Until recently A. S. Byatt was a dark horse, known only by those steeped in literature.* N-COUNT

darkroom /dɑːʳkruːm/ **darkrooms.** A **darkroom** is a room which has been sealed off from natural daylight and is lit only by red light. It is used for developing photographs. ◆◇◇◇◇ N-COUNT

darling /dɑːʳlɪŋ/ **darlings** ◆◆◇◇◇

1 You call someone **darling** if you love them or like them very much. *Thank you, darling... Oh darling, I love you.* N-VOC PRAGMATICS

2 In some parts of Britain, people call other people **darling** as a sign of friendliness. N-VOC PRAGMATICS

3 Some people use **darling** to describe someone or something that they love or like very much. *To have a darling baby boy was the greatest gift I could imagine... What a darling film – everyone adored it.* ADJ: ADJ n

4 If you describe someone as a **darling**, you are fond of them and think that they are nice. *He's such a darling, and of course Flora, she's so ravishing.* N-COUNT

5 The **darling** of a group of people is someone who is especially liked by that group. *Rajneesh was the darling of a prosperous family.* N-COUNT: with poss

darn /dɑːʳn/ **darns, darning, darned** ◆◇◇◇◇

1 When you **darn** something knitted or made of cloth, you mend a hole in it by sewing stitches across the hole and then weaving stitches in and out of them. *Aunt Emilie darned old socks... Mari refolded the darned pullover and socks.* ♦ **darning** *...chores such as sewing and darning.* VERB V n V-ed N-UNCOUNT

2 A **darn** is a part of a piece of clothing that has been darned. N-COUNT

3 People sometimes use **darn** or **darned** to emphasize what they are saying, often when they are annoyed; an informal use. *There's not a darn thing he can do about it... You invariably leave your health club a darned sight less healthy than when you went in.* ► Also an adverb. *...the desire to be free to do just as we darn well please... We start working pretty darn early.* ADJ: ADJ n =damn, damned ADV: ADV adj/adv

4 You can say **darn it** to show that you are very annoyed about something; an informal expression used in American English. *OK, I admit it, it was me. But darn it, I was right!* PHRASES EXCLAM PRAGMATICS

5 You can say **I'll be darned** to show that you are very surprised about something; an informal expression used in American English. *'Pepsi-Cola!' he exclaimed. 'Well, I'll be darned.'* PRAGMATICS

dart /dɑːʳt/ **darts, darting, darted** ◆◆◇◇◇

1 If a person or animal **darts** somewhere, they move there suddenly and quickly; used in written English. *Ingrid darted across the deserted street... The girl turned and darted away through the trees.* VERB V prep/adv

2 If you **dart** a glance at someone or something, or if your eyes **dart** to them, you look at them very quickly; used in written English. *She darted a sly sideways glance at Bramwell... The conductor's eyes darted to Wilfred, then fixed on Michael again.* VERB V n *at* n V prep/adv

3 A **dart** is a small, narrow object with a sharp point which can be thrown or shot. *Markov died after being struck by a poison dart.* N-COUNT

4 Darts is a game in which you throw darts at a round board which has numbers on it. N-UNCOUNT

dartboard /dɑːʳtbɔːʳd/ **dartboards.** A **dartboard** is a circular board with numbers on it which is used as the target in a game of darts. N-COUNT

dash /dæʃ/ **dashes, dashing, dashed** ◆◆◇◇◇

1 If you **dash** somewhere, you run or go there quickly and suddenly. *Suddenly she dashed down to the cellar... She dashed in from the garden.* ► Also a noun. *...a 160-mile dash to hospital.* VERB V adv/prep N-SING

2 If you say that you have to **dash**, you mean that you are in a hurry and have to leave immediately; an informal use. *Oh, Tim! I'm sorry but I have to dash... See you tomorrow night. Must dash now.* VB: no cont =rush V

3 A **dash** of something is a small quantity of it which you add when you are preparing food or mixing a drink. *Pour over olive oil and a dash of balsamic vinegar to accentuate the sweetness.* N-COUNT: usu N *of* n

4 A **dash** of a quality is a small amount of it that is found in something and often makes it more interesting or distinctive. *...a story with a dash of mystery thrown in. ...entrepreneurs who brought that vital dash of financial ambition to Hong Kong.* N-COUNT: usu N *of* n

5 If you **dash** something somewhere, you throw or push it violently, often so hard that it breaks. *She seized the doll and dashed it against the stone wall with tremendous force.* VERB V n *against* n Also V n prep

6 If an event or person **dashes** someone's hopes or expectations, it destroys them by making it impossible that the thing that is hoped for or expected will ever happen. *The Bank of England dashed hopes yesterday of a rush to economic recovery by warning that Britain's upturn will be slow... The participants will experience having their hopes and expectations raised and then dashed.* VERB V n *have* n V-ed

7 If you do something in a **dash**, you do it very quickly, perhaps with disastrous results. *He's in a dash to get Russia back into Europe. ...the euphoric consensus that supported a dash to the free market is fading.* N-SING =rush

8 In American English, a **dash** is a short fast race. *This isn't a hundred yard dash, it's a marathon.* N-COUNT =sprint

9 A **dash** is a straight, horizontal line (—) used in writing, for example to separate two main clauses whose meanings are closely connected. N-COUNT

10 You can say **dash** or **dash it** or **dash it all** when you are rather annoyed about something; an old-fashioned, informal expression. *Dash it all. It's just not playing the game, is it?* EXCLAM

11 The **dash** of a car is its dashboard. *A screen mounted on the dash displays a colourful road map.* N-COUNT

12 Dash is a mixture of stylishness, enthusiasm, and courage; an old-fashioned use. *The Prince was driving with great fire and dash.* N-UNCOUNT =panache, verve

13 If you say that someone **cuts a dash**, you mean that they have an attractively stylish appearance or a rather bold manner; an old-fashioned expression. *She cut a dash at a public engagement in Derbyshire by clashing her titian locks with a red double breasted jacket.* PHRASES V inflects

14 If you **make a dash for** a place, you run there very quickly, for example to escape from someone or something. *I made a dash for the front door but he got there before me... Hand clamped over his mouth, he made a dash for the bathroom.* V inflects, PHR n

dash off PHRASAL VERB

1 If you **dash off** to a place, you go there very quickly. *He dashed off to lunch at the Hard Rock Cafe... They dashed off to Paris for a couple of days.* V P *to* n

2 If you **dash off** a piece of writing, you write or compose it very quickly, without thinking about it very much. *He dashed off a couple of novels.* V P n (not pron)

dashboard /dæʃbɔːʳd/ **dashboards.** The **dashboard** in a car is the panel facing the driver's seat where most of the instruments and switches are. ◆◇◇◇◇ N-COUNT

dashing /dæʃɪŋ/. A **dashing** person or thing is very stylish and attractive; an old-fashioned word. *He was the very model of the dashing RAF pilot... Two elegant Scotsmen travelling together wore dashing kilts at dinner.* ◆◇◇◇◇ ADJ-GRADED: usu ADJ n

dastardly /dæstəʳdli/

1 If you describe an action as **dastardly**, you mean it is wicked and planned to hurt someone; an old-fashioned use. *He described the killing as a dastardly act. ...a dastardly attack on the queen.* ADJ-GRADED: ADJ n

2 If you describe a person as **dastardly**, you mean they are wicked; an old-fashioned use. *...the heiress who is badly treated by her dastardly uncle.* ADJ-GRADED: ADJ n

DAT /dæt/. **DAT** is an abbreviation for **digital audio tape**. ◆◇◇◇◇ N-UNCOUNT

data /deɪtə/. The form **data** can be used as a singular or plural. Some people use the form **datum** for the singular. **Data** is information, usually in the form of facts or statistics that you can analyse. *The study was based on data from 2,100 women. ...the latest year for which data is avail-* ◆◆◆◆◇ N-UNCOUNT *able.* ► In formal and technical English, **data** is sometimes a plural noun. *To cope with these data, hospitals bought large mainframe computers.* N-PLURAL

data bank, data banks; also spelled **databank.** A **data bank** is the same as a **database.** N-COUNT

database /deɪtəbeɪs/ **databases;** also spelled **data base.** A **database** is a collection of data that is stored in a computer and that can easily be used and added to. *They maintain a database of hotels that cater for businesswomen.* ◆◇◇◇◇ N-COUNT

data processing; also spelled **data-processing. Data processing** is the series of operations that are carried out on data, especially by computers, in order to present, interpret, or obtain information. *Taylor's company makes data-processing systems.* N-UNCOUNT

date /deɪt/ **dates, dating, dated** ◆◆◆◆◇

1 A **date** is a specific time that can be named, for example a particular day or a particular year. *What's the date today?... You will need to give the dates you wish to stay and the number of rooms you require.* N-COUNT

2 When you **date** something, you give or discover the date when it was made or when it began. *You cannot date the carving and it is difficult to date the stone itself... I think we can date the decline of Western Civilization quite precisely... Archaeologists have dated the fort to the reign of Emperor Antoninus Pius.* VERB V n V n *to* n

3 When you **date** something such as a letter or a cheque, you write that day's date on it. *Once the decision is reached, he can date and sign the sheet... The letter is dated 2 July 1993.* VERB V n V-ed

4 If you want to refer to a future or past event without saying exactly when it will happen or when it happened, you can say that it will happen or happened **at** some **date** in the future or past. *Retain copies of all correspondence, since you may need them at a later date... He did leave open the possibility of direct American aid at some unspecified date in the future... At some date in the 1990s British oil production will probably tail off.* N-SING: with supp, *at* N

5 To date means up until the present time. *'Dottie' is by far his best novel to date... She is without question the craziest person I've met to date... To date we have spent eight thousand pounds between us.* PHRASE: PHR with cl =so far

6 If something **dates**, it goes out of fashion and becomes unacceptable to modern tastes. *Blue and white is the classic colour combination for bathrooms. It always looks smart and will never date... This album has hardly dated at all.* VERB V

7 If your ideas, what you say, or the things that you like or can remember **date** you, they show that you are quite old or older than the people you are with. *It's going to date me now. I attended that school in nineteen-sixty-nine to nineteen-seventy-two.* VERB V n

8 A **date** is an appointment to meet someone or go out with them, especially someone with whom you are having, or may soon have, a romantic relationship. *I have a date with Bob... He had made a date with a girl he had met the day before... I think we should make a date to go and see Gwendolen soon.* N-COUNT

9 When you have a date with someone with whom you are having, or may soon have, a romantic relationship, you can refer to that person as your **date**; used mainly in American English. *He lied to Essie, saying his date was one of the girls in the show.* N-COUNT: usu poss N

10 If you **are dating** someone, you go out with them regularly because you are having, or may soon have, a romantic relationship with them. You can also say that two people **are dating**; used mainly in American English. *For a year I dated a woman who was a research assistant... They've been dating for three months... In high school, he did not date very much.* V-RECIP V n pl-n V V (non-recip)

11 A **date** is a small, dark-brown, sticky fruit with a stone inside. Dates grow on palm trees in hot countries. N-COUNT

12 See also **blind date, carbon dating, dated, out of date, up to date.**

date back. If something **dates back** to a particular time, it started or was made at that time. *The Royal Palace, which dates back to the 16th century, is undergoing extensive restoration... This tradition dates back over 200 years.* PHRASAL VERB V P *to* n V P amount

date from. If something **dates from** a particular time, it started or was made at that time. *All the cupboards and appliances dated from the 1950s... The present controversy dates from 1986.* PHRASAL VERB V P n

dated /deɪtɪd/. **Dated** things seem old-fashioned, although they may once have been fashionable or modern. *...people in dated dinner-jackets.* ADJ-GRADED

date of birth, dates of birth. Your **date of birth** is the exact date on which you were born, including the year. *The registration form showed his date of birth as August 2, 1979.* N-COUNT: oft poss N

date palm, date palms. A **date palm** is a palm tree on which dates grow. N-COUNT

date rape. Date rape is when a man rapes a woman after having spent the evening socially with her. N-UNCOUNT

dative /deɪtɪv/. In the grammar of some languages, for example Latin, **the dative**, or the **dative** case, is the case used for a noun when it is the indirect object of a verb, or when it comes after some prepositions. N-SING: *the* N

datum /deɪtəm, dɑːtəm/. See **data.**

daub /dɔːb/ **daubs, daubing, daubed.** When you **daub** a substance such as mud or paint on something, you spread it on that thing in a rough or careless way. *The make-up woman had been daubing mock blood on Jeremy Fox when last he'd seen her... They sent death threats and daubed his home with slogans... Children, many with their faces daubed with paint, ran among the vehicles.* VERB V n prep/adv V n *with* n V-ed

daughter /dɔːtəʳ/ **daughters.** Someone's **daughter** is their female child. *...Flora and her daughter Catherine. ...the daughter of a university professor... I have two daughters.* ◆◆◆◆◆ N-COUNT: oft with poss

daughter-in-law, daughters-in-law ◆◇◇◇◇ Someone's **daughter-in-law** is the wife of their son. N-COUNT: usu poss N

daunt /dɔːnt/ **daunts, daunting, daunted.** If something **daunts** you, it makes you feel slightly afraid or worried about dealing with it. *...a gruelling journey that would have daunted a woman half her age... I'm somewhat daunted by the size of the task.* VERB V n ♦ **daunted** *It is hard to pick up such a book and not to feel a little daunted.* ADJ-GRADED: v-link ADJ

daunting /dɔːntɪŋ/. Something that is **daunting** makes you feel slightly afraid or worried about dealing with it. *He and his wife Jane were faced with the daunting task of restoring the gardens to their former splendour... The move to Prague was a daunting prospect for the bishop... Occasionally I find the commitment and responsibility daunting.* ◆◇◇◇◇ ADJ-GRADED =intimidating ♦ **dauntingly** *She is dauntingly articulate.* ADV-GRADED

dauntless /dɔːntləs/. A **dauntless** person is brave and not easily frightened or discouraged; a formal word. *Perseverance and dauntless courage brought them to their goal.* ADJ =resolute

dauphin /dɔːfɪn, doʊfæn/; also spelled **Dauphin.** In former times, the king of France's eldest son was called **the dauphin.** N-SING: *the* N

dawdle /dɔːdᵊl/ **dawdles, dawdling, dawdled**

1 If you **dawdle**, you spend more time than is necessary going somewhere. *Eleanor will be back any moment, if she doesn't dawdle... They dawdled arm in arm past the shopfronts.* VERB V

2 If you **dawdle** over something, you spend more time than is necessary doing something. *He got fed up as bank staff dawdled over cashing him a cheque... She downed two glasses of white wine while I dawdled over a draught beer.* VERB V *over* n/-ing

dawn /dɔːn/ **dawns, dawning, dawned** ◆◆◇◇◇

1 Dawn is the time of day when light first appears in the sky, before the sun rises. *Nancy woke at dawn.* N-VAR =sunrise, daybreak

2 The **dawn** of a period of time or a situation is the beginning of it; a literary use. *We can only guess what went through the mind of a man who could* N-SING: usu *the* N *of* n *look back to the dawn of powered flight. ...the dawn of the radio age.*

3 If something **is dawning**, it is beginning to develop or come into existence; used in written English. *Throughout Europe a new railway age, that of the high-speed train, has dawned... A new era seemed to be about to dawn for the coach and his young team... Now there is a dawning realisation that drastic action is necessary.* ♦ **dawning** *...the dawning of the space age... Tettlinger uncovered his eyes in the first dawning of hope.* VERB V V-ing N-SING: oft *the* N *of* n

4 When you say that a particular day **dawned**, you mean it arrived or began, when it became light; used in written English. *When the great day dawned, the inevitable first concern was the weather... The next day dawned sombre and gloomy.* VERB V V adj

5 ● **at the crack of dawn**: see **crack**.

dawn on or **dawn upon.** If a fact or idea **dawns on** you, you realize it. *It gradually dawned on me that I still had talent and ought to run again... Then the chilling truth dawned on Captain Gary Snavely.* PHRASAL VERB *it* V P n that V P n

dawn chorus. In British English, the **dawn chorus** is the singing of birds at dawn. N-SING

day /deɪ/ **days** ◆◆◆◆◆

1 A **day** is one of the seven twenty-four hour periods of time in a week. N-COUNT

2 **Day** is the time when it is light, or the time when you are awake and doing things. *The weather did not help; hot by day, cold at night... 27 million working days are lost each year due to work accidents and sickness... He arranged for me to go down to London one day a week... The snack bar is open during the day.* N-VAR ≠night

3 You can refer to a particular period in history as a particular **day** or as particular **days**. *He began to talk about the Ukraine of his uncle's day... Did you learn anything in your day, as a student? ...his early days of struggle and deep poverty... She is doing just fine these days.* N-COUNT: with supp

4 If something happens **day after day**, it happens every day without stopping. *The newspaper job had me doing the same thing day after day.* PHRASES

5 **In this day and age** means in modern times. *Even in this day and age the old attitudes persist.*

6 If you say that something **has seen better days**, you mean that it is old and in poor condition. *The tweed jacket she wore had seen better days.* V inflects

7 If you **call it a day**, you decide to stop what you are doing because you are tired with it or because it is not successful. *Faced with mounting debts, the decision to call it a day was inevitable... I want Alan Whicker's job when he calls it a day.* V inflects

8 If you **carry the day**, you are the winner in contest such as a battle, debate, or sporting competition. *For the time being, those in favour of the liberalisation measures seem to have carried the day.* V inflects

9 If you say that something **has had** its **day**, you mean that the period during which it was most successful has now passed. *Popular music may finally have had its day... Interior decoration by careful co-ordination seems to have had its day.* V inflects

10 If something **makes** your **day**, it makes you feel very happy; an informal use. *The chairman of the opposition said Mrs Thatcher's resignation had made his day... You've made my day Simon.* V inflects

11 If something happens **day and night** or **night and day**, it happens all the time without stopping. *Chantal kept a fire burning night and day... He would have a nurse in constant attendance day and night.*

12 **One day** or **some day** or **one of these days** means at some time in the future. *I too dreamed of living in London one day... I hope some day you will find the woman who will make you happy... One of these days we will get lucky.* PHR with cl

13 If you say that something happened **the other day**, you mean that it happened a few days ago. *I phoned your office the other day... We had lunch the other day at our favorite restaurant.* PHR with cl =a few days ago

14 If someone or something **saves the day** in a situation which seems likely to fail, they manage to make it successful. *...this story about how he saved the day at his daughter's birthday party... A last moment election can save the day.* V inflects

15 If something happens **from day to day** or **day by day**, it happens each day. *Your needs can differ from day to day... I live for the moment, day by day, not for the past.*

16 If it is a month or a year **to the day** since a particular thing happened, it is exactly a month or a year since it happened. *It was January 19, a year to the day since he had arrived in Singapore... Twenty-five years ago, to the day, England reached the sport's pinnacle by winning the World Cup.* amount PHR

17 **To this day** means up until and including today. *To this day young Zulu boys practise fighting.* PHR with cl

18 If a particular person, group, or thing **wins the day**, they win a battle, struggle, or competition. If they **lose the day**, they are defeated. *His determination, his refusal to back down, and possibly his sincerity had won the day... Few in Westminster doubt that the government will win the day.* V inflects

19 If you say that a task is **all in a day's work** for someone, you mean that they do not mind doing it although it may be difficult, because it is part of their job or because they often do it. *For war reporters, dodging snipers' bullets is all in a day's work... I said: 'How can I ever thank you?' but he waved the question aside. 'It's all in a day's work.'* usu v-link PHR, oft PHR *for* n

20 ● **it's early days yet**: see **early**. ● **at the end of the day**: see **end**. ● **late in the day**: see **late**. ● **see the light of day**: see **light**. ● **someone's days are numbered**: see **number**. ● **the good old days**: see **old**. ● **pass the time of day**: see **time**.

-day /-deɪ/. You use **-day** with a number to indicate how long something lasts. *The Sudanese leader has left for a two-day visit to Zambia.* COMB in ADJ

daybreak /deɪbreɪk/. **Daybreak** is the time in the morning when light first appears. *It was six-thirty, almost daybreak... Pedro got up every morning before daybreak.* N-UNCOUNT =dawn

day care. **Day care** is care that is provided during the day for people who cannot look after themselves, such as small children, old people, or people who are ill. Day care is provided by paid workers. *Day care enables women to get involved in other activities. ...a day-care centre for elderly people.* ◆◇◇◇◇ N-UNCOUNT: oft N n

daydream /deɪdriːm/ **daydreams, daydreaming, daydreamed;** also spelled **day-dream.** ◆◇◇◇◇

1 When you **daydream**, you think about pleasant things for a period of time, usually about things that you would like to happen. *Do you work hard for success rather than daydream about it?... He daydreams of being a famous journalist... I am inclined to daydream.* VERB V *about* n V *of* n/-ing V

2 A **daydream** is a series of pleasant thoughts, usually about things that you would like to happen. *He learnt to escape into daydreams of handsome men and beautiful women... The idea for the story came to him in a daydream.* N-COUNT

Day-glo /deɪ gloʊ/; also spelled **Dayglo**. **Day-glo** colours are shades of orange, pink, green, and yellow which are so bright that they seem to glow. **Day-glo** is a trademark. N-UNCOUNT: usu N n

day job. If someone tells you **not to give up the day job**, they are saying in a humorous way that they think you should continue doing what you are good at, rather than trying something new which they think you will fail at. *It's a kind way of telling aspiring novelists, 'Don't give up the day job'.* PHRASE: V inflects

daylight /deɪlaɪt/ ◆◆◇◇◇

1 **Daylight** is the natural light that there is during the day, before it gets dark. *It was still daylight but all the cars had their headlights on... Lack of daylight can make people feel depressed.* N-UNCOUNT ≠night

2 **Daylight** is the time of day when it begins to get light. *Quinn returned shortly after daylight yesterday morning.* N-UNCOUNT =dawn

3 If you say that a crime is committed **in broad daylight**, you are expressing your surprise that it is done during the day when people can see it, rather than at night. *A girl was attacked on a train in* PHRASE: PHR after v PRAGMATICS

broad daylight... *The recent murder happened in broad daylight in a supposedly 'safe' part of London.*

daylight robbery. If someone charges you a great deal of money for something and you think this is unfair or unreasonable, you can refer to this as **daylight robbery**; an informal British expression. *'Daylight robbery – that's what it is,' she would declare.* N-UNCOUNT PRAGMATICS

daylights /deɪlaɪts/
1 If you **knock the living daylights out of** someone, or **beat the living daylights out of** them, you hit them very hard many times; an informal use. *Go on lads, beat the living daylights out of them!* PHRASE: V inflects
2 If someone or something **scares the living daylights out of** you, they make you feel extremely scared; an informal use. PHRASE: V inflects

daylight saving time. In American English, **daylight saving time** is a period of time in the summer during which the clocks are set one hour forward, so that people can have extra daylight in the evening. The British word is **summer time**. *Most Americans will get an extra hour of sleep tonight as the nation switches from daylight-saving time to standard time.* N-UNCOUNT

day nursery, day nurseries. A **day nursery** is a place where children who are too young to go to school can be left all day while their parents are at work. N-COUNT =crèche

day off, days off. A **day off** is a day when you do not go to work, even though it is usually a working day. *It was Mrs Dearden's day off, and Paul was on duty in her place.* ◆◇◇◇◇ N-COUNT

day of reckoning. If someone talks about the **day of reckoning**, they mean a day or time in the future when people will be forced to deal with an unpleasant situation which they have avoided until now. *You can't ignore the day of reckoning – these issues have to be dealt with.* N-SING: usu *the* N

day pupil, day pupils; also spelled **day-pupil**. A **day pupil** is a pupil who goes to a boarding school but lives at home. N-COUNT ≠boarder

day release; also spelled **day-release**. In Britain, **day release** is a system in which workers spend one day each week at a college in order to study a subject connected with their work. *This course can be taken either on a full-time basis over one year or on a day-release basis (one day a week) over two years.* N-UNCOUNT

day return, day returns. In Britain, a **day return** is a train or bus ticket which allows you to go somewhere and come back on the same day for a lower price than an ordinary return ticket. N-COUNT

day room, day rooms. A **day room** is a room in a hospital where patients can sit and relax during the day. *She had made a friend of one of the other patients, and they sat in the day room together.* N-COUNT

day school, day schools. A **day school** is a school where the pupils go home every evening and do not live at the school. Compare **boarding school**. N-COUNT

daytime /deɪtaɪm/. The **daytime** is the part of a day between the time when it gets light and the time when it gets dark. *In the daytime he stayed up in his room, sleeping, or listening to music... Please give a daytime telephone number, if possible... Even at the end of the war, German factories mainly operated only in daytime.* ◆◇◇◇◇ N-SING: *the* N, also no det ≠night-time

day-to-day. **Day-to-day** things or activities exist or happen every day as part of ordinary life. *I am a vegetarian and use a lot of lentils in my day-to-day cooking.* ◆◆◇◇◇ ADJ: ADJ n

day trip, day trips; also spelled **day-trip**. A **day trip** is a journey for pleasure to a place and back again on the same day. ◆◇◇◇◇ N-COUNT

day-tripper, day-trippers; also spelled **day tripper**. A **day-tripper** is someone who makes a day trip. N-COUNT

daze /deɪz/. If someone is in a **daze**, they are feeling confused and unable to think clearly, often because they have had a shock or surprise. *For 35 minutes I was walking around in a daze.* N-SING: oft *in a* N

dazed /deɪzd/. If someone is **dazed**, they are confused and unable to think clearly, often because of shock or a blow to the head. *At the end of the interview I was dazed and exhausted.* ◆◇◇◇◇ ADJ-GRADED =confused

dazzle /dæzᵊl/ **dazzles, dazzling, dazzled** ◆◇◇◇◇
1 If someone or something **dazzles** you, you are extremely impressed by their skill, qualities, or beauty. *George dazzled her with his knowledge of the world... Historical novels tend to dazzle in a way that appeals particularly to women.* VERB V n with n V Also V n
2 The **dazzle** of something is a quality it has, such as beauty or skill, which is impressive and attractive. *The dazzle of stardom and status attracts them.* N-SING: with poss
3 If a bright light **dazzles** you, it makes you unable to see properly for a short time. *The sun, glinting from the pool, dazzled me... Kelly was dazzled by the lights.* VERB V n
4 The **dazzle** of a light is its brightness, which makes it impossible for you to see properly for a short time. *The sun's dazzle on the water hurts my eyes. ...a filter that can cut dazzle.* N-UNCOUNT: also *a* N
5 See also **razzle-dazzle**.

dazzling /dæzlɪŋ/ ◆◇◇◇◇
1 Something that is **dazzling** is very impressive or beautiful. *He gave Alberg a dazzling smile.* ADJ-GRADED =stunning ♦ **dazzlingly** *The view was dazzlingly beautiful.* ADV-GRADED
2 A **dazzling** light is very bright and makes you unable to see properly for a short time. *He shielded his eyes against the dazzling declining sun.* ADJ ♦ **dazzlingly** *The loading bay seemed dazzlingly bright.* ADV-GRADED: ADV adj

DC /diː siː/. **DC** is used to refer to an electric current that always flows in the same direction. **DC** is an abbreviation for 'direct current'. ◆◇◇◇◇ N-UNCOUNT

D-day You can use **D-day** to refer to the day that is chosen for the beginning of an important activity. *D-day for my departure was set for 29th June.* N-UNCOUNT

DDT /diː diː tiː/. **DDT** is a poisonous substance which is used for killing insects. N-UNCOUNT

de- /diː-/
1 **De-** is added to a verb in order to change the meaning of the verb to its opposite. *The jury may have become desensitized to the video and its brutality after seeing it dozens of times... The need to cleanse herself, to somehow decontaminate her body was compulsive.* PREFIX
2 **De-** is added to a noun in order to make it a verb referring to the removal of the thing described by the noun. *I've defrosted the freezer... The fires are likely to permanently deforest the land.* PREFIX

deacon /diːkən/ **deacons** ◆◇◇◇◇
1 A **deacon** is a member of the clergy, for example in the Church of England, who is lower in rank than a priest. N-COUNT
2 A **deacon** is a person who is not ordained but who assists the minister in some Protestant churches. N-COUNT

deactivate /diæktɪveɪt/ **deactivates, deactivating, deactivated.** If someone **deactivates** an explosive device or an alarm, they make it harmless or unable to operate. *Russia is deactivating some of its deadliest missiles.* VERB =disable V n

dead /ded/ ◆◆◆◆◇
1 A person, animal, or plant that is **dead** is no longer living. *'You're a widow?'—'Yes. My husband's been dead a year now.'... The group had shot dead another hostage. ...their dead brother. ...old newspapers and dead flowers.* ► **The dead** are people who are dead. *The dead included six people attending a religious ceremony. ...the annual festival when Chinese traditionally honour the dead.* ADJ ≠alive N-PLURAL: *the* N
2 Land or water that is **dead** contains no living things. *...charred land, mountainsides of dead earth and stumps of trees... But this water seems dead: it's polluted and horribly stagnant.* ADJ
3 If you describe a place or a period of time as **dead**, you mean that there is very little activity taking place in it. *...some dead little town where the liveliest thing is the flies... This made that holiday week a particularly dead period.* ADJ-GRADED =quiet

4 Something that is **dead** is no longer being used or is finished. *The dead cigarette was still between his fingers... This bottle's dead. But we've got another one.*
ADJ =finished

5 If you say that an idea, plan, or subject is **dead**, you mean that people are no longer interested in it or willing to develop it any further. *It's a dead issue, Baxter... But that doesn't mean this brand of politics is dead or dying... The deal with Chelsea may not, however, be dead.*
ADJ

6 A **dead** language is no longer spoken or written as a means of communication, although it may still be studied. *We used to grumble that we were wasting time learning a dead language.*
ADJ: usu ADJ n

7 A telephone or piece of electrical equipment that is **dead** is no longer functioning, for example because it no longer has any electrical power. *On another occasion the Duke answered the phone and the line went dead.*
ADJ: usu v-link ADJ

8 In sport, when a ball is **dead**, it has gone outside the playing area, or a situation has occurred in which the game has to be temporarily stopped, and none of the players can score points or gain an advantage.
ADJ

9 A **dead** sound or colour is dull rather than lively or bright. *'That is correct, Meg,' he answered in his cold, dead voice... Then he heard a piercing scream echoing down the deep well, ending in a dull, dead thud.* ▶ Also a combining form. *The blood drained from his face, leaving the skin dead white.*
ADJ-GRADED; COMB in COLOUR

10 Dead is used to mean complete or absolute, especially with the words 'centre', 'silence', and 'stop'. *He adjusted each chesspiece so that it stood dead centre in its square... They hurried about in dead silence, with anxious faces... Lila's boat came to a dead stop.*
ADJ: ADJ n

11 Dead means precisely or exactly. *Mars was visible, dead in the centre of the telescope... Their arrows are dead on target... A fishing boat came out of nowhere, dead ahead.*
ADV: ADV prep/adv/adj

12 Dead is sometimes used to mean very; used mainly in informal spoken British English. *Meadowhall is also dead easy for people to get to... His poems sound dead boring, actually... I am dead against the legalisation of drugs.*
ADV: ADV adj/adv/prep

13 If you reply **'Over my dead body'** when a plan or action has been suggested, you are saying emphatically that you dislike it, and will do everything you can to prevent it; an informal expression. *'Let's invite her to dinner.'—'Over my dead body!'*
PHRASES CONVENTION PRAGMATICS

14 If you say that something such as an idea or situation is **dead and buried**, you are emphasizing that you think that it is completely finished or past, and cannot happen or exist again in the future. *I thought the whole business was dead and buried... In two years, the British coal industry will be dead and buried.*
v-link PHR PRAGMATICS

15 If you say that a person or animal **dropped dead** or **dropped down dead**, you mean that they died very suddenly and unexpectedly. *He dropped dead on the quayside.*
V inflects PRAGMATICS

16 If you tell someone to **drop dead**, you are insulting them, rudely disagreeing with them or refusing to do something, or telling them to stop bothering you. *75% of the firms he called were hostile and told him to 'drop dead.'* • See also **drop-dead**.
PRAGMATICS

17 If you say that someone is **dead and gone**, you are emphasizing that they are dead, and thinking about what happened or will happen after their death. *Often a genius is recognized only after he is dead and gone.*
v-link PHR PRAGMATICS

18 If you say that you **feel dead** or **are half dead**, you mean that you feel very tired or ill and very weak. *I thought you looked half dead at dinner, and who could blame you after that journey... I feel pretty dead right now.*
v-link PHR PRAGMATICS

19 If something happens **in the dead of night, at dead of night**, or **in the dead of winter**, it happens in the middle part of the night or the winter, when it is darkest or coldest; a literary expression. *I couldn't fly illegally into a country in the dead of night... We buried it in the garden at dead of night... Early one Thursday morning in the dead of winter I awoke to a blizzard.*

20 When Christians say that Jesus Christ **rose from the dead** or **raised** someone **from the dead**, they mean that Jesus came back to life after he had died, or brought a dead person back to life.
V inflects

21 If you say that someone or something **rises** or **comes back from the dead**, you mean that they become active or successful again after being inactive or unsuccessful for a while. *This was a company that, by all appearances, had risen from the dead... Faldo came back from the dead to win his third Open golf championship.*
V inflects

22 If you say that you wouldn't **be seen dead** or **be caught dead** in particular clothes, places, or situations, you are expressing strong dislike or disapproval for them; an informal expression. *I wouldn't be seen dead in a straw hat. ...men who wouldn't be seen dead pushing a pram... I wouldn't be caught dead in such an old-fashioned place.*
PHR prep, PHR -ing PRAGMATICS

23 To **stop dead** means to suddenly stop happening, moving, or doing something. To **stop** someone or something **dead** means to cause them to suddenly stop happening, moving, or doing something. *We all stopped dead and looked at it... She had meant to make a discreet entrance, but conversation stopped dead... The sight of it stopped them dead.*
V inflects

24 If you say that someone or something is **dead in the water**, you are emphasizing that they have failed, and that there is little hope of them being successful in the future. *A 'no' vote would have left the treaty dead in the water.*
v-link PHR PRAGMATICS

25 • to **flog a dead horse**: see **flog**. • **a dead loss**: see **loss**. • **a dead ringer**: see **ringer**. • to **stop dead in** your **tracks**: see **track**.

deadbeat /dedbiːt/ **deadbeats.** If you refer to someone as a **deadbeat**, you think they are lazy and do not want to be part of ordinary society; used in informal American English, showing disapproval. *He and a collection of fellow hustlers and deadbeats live in an abandoned hotel.*
N-COUNT PRAGMATICS

dead-beat; also spelled **dead beat**. If you are **dead-beat**, you are very tired and have no energy left; an informal word.
ADJ-GRADED: v-link ADJ =shattered

dead duck, dead ducks. If you describe someone or something as a **dead duck**, you mean that you think they have absolutely no chance of succeeding in something; an informal expression. *The government is a dead duck.*
N-COUNT PRAGMATICS =no-hoper

deaden /dedən/ **deadens, deadening, deadened.** If something **deadens** a feeling or a sound, it makes it less strong or loud. *He needs morphine to deaden the pain in his chest... They managed to deaden the sound on TV every time the alleged victim's name was spoken.*
VERB =reduce; V n

dead end, dead ends ◆◇◇◇◇

1 If a street is a **dead end**, there is no way out at one end of it.
N-COUNT =cul-de-sac

2 A **dead end** job or course of action does not lead to further developments or progression. *Waitressing was a dead-end job.*
N-COUNT: oft N n

deadening /dedənɪŋ/. A **deadening** situation destroys people's enthusiasm and creativity. *She soon became bored with what she felt was the deadening routine of her life.*
ADJ: usu ADJ n

dead hand. You can refer to something which has a discouraging or depressing influence on a particular situation as a **dead hand**. *...removing the dead hand of the state from economic life.*
N-SING: usu *the* N *of* n

dead-head, dead-heads, dead-heading, dead-headed; also spelled **dead head**. To **dead-head** a plant which produces flowers means to remove all the dead flowers from it. *Dead-head roses as the blooms fade.*
VERB; V n

dead heat, dead heats. If a race or contest is a **dead heat**, two or more competitors are joint winners, or are both winning at a particular moment in the race or contest. In American English, you can say that a race or contest is in a **dead heat**. *The French St Leger ended in a dead heat between two English horses at Longchamp... A na-*
N-COUNT

tional poll shows the presidential race in a dead heat.

dead letter, dead letters. If you say that a law or agreement is a **dead letter**, you mean that it still exists but people ignore it. *No one does anything about it and the law becomes a dead letter.* N-COUNT

deadline /dedlaɪn/ **deadlines.** A **deadline** is a time or date before which a particular task must be finished or a particular thing must be done. *We were not able to meet the deadline because of manufacturing delays... The deadline for submissions to the competition will be Easter 1994... The remaining 'New Age' travellers left Kerry just 30 minutes before the deadline set for their eviction.* ◆◆◆◇◇ N-COUNT: oft N *for* n/-ing

deadlock /dedlɒk/ **deadlocks.** If a dispute or series of negotiations reaches **deadlock**, neither side is willing to give in at all and no agreement can be made. *They called for a compromise on all sides to break the deadlock in the world trade talks... Peace talks between the two sides ended in deadlock last month.* ◆◇◇◇◇ N-VAR =impasse

deadlocked /dedlɒkt/. If a dispute or series of negotiations is **deadlocked**, no agreement can be reached because neither side will give in at all. You can also say that the people involved are **deadlocked**. *The peace talks have been deadlocked over the issue of human rights since August... But after nearly a week of deliberations, the jury remained deadlocked.* ◆◇◇◇◇ ADJ: v-link ADJ, oft ADJ *over* n

deadly /dedli/ **deadlier, deadliest** ◆◆◇◇◇

1 If something is **deadly**, it is likely or able to cause someone's death, or has already caused someone's death. *He was acquitted on charges of assault with a deadly weapon. ...a deadly disease currently affecting dolphins... Passive smoking can be deadly too... The authorities are looking into last week's deadly gas explosions.* ADJ-GRADED =lethal, fatal

2 If you describe a person or their behaviour as **deadly**, you mean that they will do or say anything to get what they want, without caring about other people. *His mother's voice was one he knew; ice cold and deadly... The Duchess levelled a deadly look at Nikko.* ADJ-GRADED =menacing

3 If you describe someone or something as **deadly**, you mean that they are very dull and boring; an informal use. *She finds these parties deadly.* ADJ =boring

4 You can use **deadly** to emphasize an unpleasant or undesirable quality. *Broadcast news was accurate and reliable but deadly dull... The north wind was bitter and deadly cold... The United States had been deadly serious in its threat of military action.* ADV: ADV adj PRAGMATICS =dreadfully

5 A **deadly** situation has unpleasant or dangerous consequences. *...the deadly combination of low expectations and low achievement... It is here that most students fall into a subtle and deadly trap.* ADJ-GRADED: usu ADJ n

6 **Deadly** enemies or rivals fight or compete with each other in a very aggressive way. *The two became deadly enemies... That would make the competition between rival suppliers even deadlier.* ADJ-GRADED =implacable

7 In sport, **deadly** players and actions are extremely skilful and successful; used in journalism. *Agassi played with deadly accuracy to beat Becker in straight sets. ...the fastest and deadliest bowlers in world cricket today.* ADJ-GRADED

dead meat. If you say that someone is **dead meat**, you mean that they are in very serious trouble that may result in them being hurt or injured in some way; an informal expression. N-UNCOUNT

deadpan /dedpæn/. **Deadpan** humour is when you appear to be serious and are hiding the fact that you are joking or teasing someone. *...her natural capacity for irony and deadpan humour... She put the letter on the desk in front of me, her face deadpan, not a flicker of a smile.* ADJ-GRADED

dead weight, dead weights

1 A **dead weight** is a load which is surprisingly heavy and difficult to lift. *He hoisted the dead weight over his shoulder.* N-COUNT

2 You can refer to something that makes change or progress difficult as a **dead weight**. *...the dead weight of post-modernist tradition.* N-COUNT: usu sing

dead wood. People or things that have been used for a very long time and that are no longer useful can be referred to as **dead wood**. *...the idea that historical linguistics is so much dead wood.* N-UNCOUNT PRAGMATICS

deaf /def/ **deafer, deafest** ◆◆◇◇◇

1 Someone who is **deaf** is unable to hear anything or is unable to hear very well. *She is now profoundly deaf.* ▶ **The deaf** are people who are deaf. *Many regular TV programs are captioned for the deaf.* ♦ **deafness** *Because of her deafness she was hard to make conversation with.* ADJ-GRADED / N-PLURAL: *the* N / N-UNCOUNT

2 If you say that someone is **deaf to** people's pleas, arguments, or criticisms, you disapprove of them because they refuse to pay attention to them. *The provincial assembly were deaf to all pleas for financial help.* ADJ: v-link ADJ *to* n PRAGMATICS =impervious

3 • to **fall on deaf ears**: see **ear.** • to **turn a deaf ear**: see **ear.**

deafen /defən/ **deafens, deafening, deafened** ◆◇◇◇◇

1 If a noise **deafens** you, it is so loud that you cannot hear anything else at the same time. *The noise of the typewriters deafened her.* VERB V n

2 If you **are deafened** by something, you are made deaf by it, or are unable to hear for some time. *He was deafened by the noise from the gun.* VB: usu passive *be* V-ed

3 See also **deafening.**

deafening /defənɪŋ/ ◆◇◇◇◇

1 A **deafening** noise is a very loud noise. *...the deafening roar of fighter jets taking off.* ADJ-GRADED

2 If you say there was a **deafening** silence, you are emphasizing that there was no reaction or response to something that was said or done. *What was truly despicable was the deafening silence maintained by the candidates concerning the riots.* ADJ PRAGMATICS

deaf-mute, deaf-mutes. A **deaf-mute** is someone who cannot hear or speak. Some people find this word offensive. N-COUNT

deal 1 quantifier uses

deal /diːl/ ◆◆◆◇◇

1 **A great deal of** or **a good deal of** something is a lot of it. *...a great deal of money... I am in a position to save you a good deal of time.* ▶ Also an adverb. *As a relationship becomes more established, it also becomes a good deal more complex... He depended a great deal on his wife for support.* ▶ Also a pronoun. *Although he had never met Geoffrey Hardcastle, he knew a good deal about him.* QUANT: QUANT *of* n-uncount/def-n / ADV: ADV compar, ADV after v / PRON

2 A **deal of** something is a lot of it; an old-fashioned use. *He had a deal of work to do.* QUANT: QUANT *of* n-uncount

deal 2 verb and noun uses

deal /diːl/ **deals, dealing, dealt** ◆◆◆◆◆

1 If you make a **deal** or do a **deal**, you complete an agreement or an arrangement, especially in business. *Japan will have to do a deal with America on rice imports... Mr Bush and John Major said that they wanted a deal by mid-January... He was involved in shady business deals... You're not going to get out of here unless we make a deal.* N-COUNT

2 If a person, company, or shop **deals in** a particular type of goods, their business involves buying or selling those goods. *They deal in antiques... The Soviet government is giving all its citizens the right to deal in hard currency.* VERB V *in* n

3 If someone **deals** illegal drugs, they sell them. *I certainly don't deal drugs.* ♦ **dealing** *...his involvement in drug dealing and illegal money laundering.* VERB V n / N-UNCOUNT: oft n N

4 If someone has had a **bad deal**, they have been unfortunate or have been treated unfairly. *The people of Liverpool have had a bad deal for many, many years.* • **a raw deal**: see **raw.** N-COUNT: adj N

5 When you **deal** playing cards, you give them out to the players in a game of cards. *The croupier dealt each player a card, face down... He once dealt cards in an illegal gambling joint.* ▶ **Deal out** means the same as **deal.** *Dalton dealt out five cards to each player.* VERB V n n / V n / PHRASAL VERB V P n (not pron)

6 If an event **deals a blow** a blow to something or someone, it causes them great difficulties or makes failure more likely; used in journalism. *The demise of communism in the Soviet Union has dealt a severe blow to the world's remaining communist re-* PHRASE: V inflects

gimes... The French were dealt another blow yesterday when Serge Viars withdrew from the squad.*
7 See also **dealings**; **wheel and deal**.

deal out. If someone **deals out** a punishment or harmful action, they punish or harm someone; used in written English. *...a failure by the governments of established states to deal out effective punishment to aggressors. ...the tale of a shy, pregnant woman who refuses to accept the injustice dealt out to her husband.* • See also **deal** 5. PHRASAL VERB; V P n (not pron) *to* n; V-ed P; Also V P n (not pron), V n P

deal with PHRASAL VERB
1 When you **deal with** something or someone that needs attention, you give your attention to them, and often solve a problem or make a decision concerning them. *...the way that building societies deal with complaints... In dealing with suicidal youngsters, our aims should be twofold... The President said the agreement would allow other vital problems to be dealt with.* V P n
2 If you **deal with** an unpleasant emotion or an emotionally difficult situation, you recognize it, and remain calm and in control of yourself in spite of it. *She saw a psychiatrist who used hypnotism to help her deal with her fear... He was able to deal with his captivity by maintaining a high degree of anger about the unfairness of his capture.* PRAGMATICS; =cope with; V P n
3 If a book, speech, or film **deals with** a particular thing, it has that thing as its subject or is concerned with it. *...the parts of his book which deal with contemporary Paris.* V P n
4 If you **deal with** a particular person or organization, you have business relations with them. *When I worked in Florida I dealt with British people all the time... He's a hard man to deal with.* V P n

dealer /diːləʳ/ **dealers.** A **dealer** is a person whose business involves buying and selling things. *...an antique dealer. ...dealers in commodities and financial securities.* • See also **wheeler-dealer**. ◆◆◆◇◇ N-COUNT

dealership /diːləʳʃɪp/ **dealerships.** A **dealership** is a company that sells cars, usually for one car company. *...a car dealership. ...a Chevrolet dealership in San Francisco.* ◆◇◇◇◇ N-COUNT

dealings /diːlɪŋz/. Someone's **dealings** with a person or organization are the relations that they have with them or the business that they do with them. *He has learnt little in his dealings with the international community. ...her family's business dealings.* ◆◆◇◇◇ N-PLURAL: usu with supp, oft N *with* n

dealt /delt/. **Dealt** is the past tense and past participle of **deal**.

dean /diːn/ **deans** ◆◇◇◇◇
1 A **dean** is an important administrator at a university or college. *She is currently Dean of the faculty of International Studies at Sophia University.* N-COUNT
2 A **dean** is a priest who is the main administrator of a large church. *...Alan Webster, former Dean of St Paul's.* N-COUNT

dear /dɪəʳ/ **dearer, dearest; dears** ◆◆◆◇◇
1 You use **dear** to describe someone or something that you feel affection for. *Mrs Cavendish is a dear friend of mine... At last I am back at my dear little desk.* ADJ: ADJ n
2 If something is **dear to** you or **dear to** your heart, you care deeply about it. *His family life was very dear to him... This is a subject very dear to the hearts of academics up and down the country.* ADJ-GRADED: v-link ADJ *to* n
3 You use **dear** in expressions such as '**my dear fellow**', '**dear girl**', or '**my dear Richard**' when you are addressing someone whom you know and are fond of. You can also use expressions like this in an arrogant way that indicates that you think you are superior to the person you are addressing. *Of course, Toby, my dear fellow, of course... Take as long as you like, dear boy.* ADJ: ADJ n; PRAGMATICS
4 **Dear** is written at the beginning of a letter, followed by the name or title of the person you are writing to. *Dear Peter, I have been thinking about you so much during the past few days... 'Dear sir,' she began.* ADJ: ADJ n
5 You can call someone **dear** as a sign of affection. *You're a lot like me, dear... 'Good night, my dears,' she called to us as we closed her door behind us.* N-VOC; PRAGMATICS
6 You can use **dear** in expressions such as '**oh dear**', '**dear me**', and '**dear, dear**' when you are sad, disappointed, or surprised about something. *'Oh dear, oh dear.' McKinnon sighed. 'You, too.'... Outside, Bruce glanced at his watch: 'Dear me, nearly one o'clock.'* EXCLAM; PRAGMATICS
7 You can call someone a **dear** when you are fond of them and think that they are nice. *He's such a dear.* N-COUNT
8 If you say that something is **dear**, you mean that it costs a lot of money, usually more than you can afford or more than you think it should cost. *It's getting dearer now but it used to be pretty reasonable to buy... They're too dear.* ADJ-GRADED: usu v-link ADJ; PRAGMATICS; =expensive; ≠cheap
9 If something that someone does **costs** them **dear**, they suffer a lot as a result of it. *Such complacency is costing the company dear.* PHRASE: V inflects

dearest /dɪərɪst/ ◆◇◇◇◇
1 You can call someone **dearest** when you are very fond of them; an old fashioned use. *What's wrong, my dearest? You look tired.* N-VOC
2 When you are writing to someone you are very fond of, you can use **dearest** at the beginning of the letter before the person's name or the word you are using to address them. *Dearest Maria, Aren't I terrible, not coming back like I promised?.* ADJ-SUPERL: ADJ n
3 Your **dearest** wishes or hopes are things that you hope very much will happen; an old-fashioned use. *It is my dearest hope that one day she will find the happiness she truly deserves.* ADJ-SUPERL: ADJ n
4 • **nearest and dearest**: see **near**.

dearie /dɪəri/. Some people use **dearie** as a friendly or sometimes condescending way of addressing someone; an informal word, used mainly in British English. N-VOC; PRAGMATICS; =dear

dearly /dɪəʳli/ ◆◇◇◇◇
1 If you love someone **dearly**, you love them very much; a formal use. *She loved her father dearly.* ADV-GRADED: ADV with v
2 If you would **dearly** like to do or have something, you would very much like to do it or have it; a formal use. *I would dearly love to marry.* ADV-GRADED: ADV before v
3 If you **pay dearly** for doing something or it **costs** you **dearly**, you suffer a lot as a result; a formal use. *He drank too much and is paying dearly for the pleasure... The Republican candidate's admissions about his failure to pay taxes cost him dearly.* PHRASE: V inflects

dearth /dɜːʳθ/. If there is a **dearth** of something, there is not enough of it. *...the dearth of good fiction by English authors.* N-SING: usu N *of* n; =lack

death /deθ/ **deaths** ◆◆◆◆◇
1 **Death** is the permanent end of the life of a person or animal. *1.5 million people are in immediate danger of death from starvation. ...the thirtieth anniversary of her death... The report mentions the death of 18 people in suspicious circumstances... They were told only that there had been a death in the family.* N-VAR; ≠birth, life
2 A particular kind of **death** is a particular way of dying. *They made sure that he died a horrible death... He would rather have a decent death which served some purpose than a meaningless death.* N-COUNT: with supp; =end
3 The **death** of something is the permanent end of it. *It meant the death of everything he had ever been or ever hoped to be. ...the death of pop music.* N-SING: usu *the* N *of* n; =end
4 If you say that someone is **at death's door**, you mean they are very ill indeed; an informal expression. *He told his boss a tale about his mother being at death's door... My dad was the same. He could be at death's door but wouldn't say a word.* PHRASES; v-link PHR
5 If you say that you will **fight to the death** for something, you are emphasizing that you will do anything to achieve or preserve it, even if you suffer as a consequence. *He said they did not want war - but if attacked they would fight to the death... She'd have fought to the death for that child.* V inflects; PRAGMATICS
6 If you refer to a fight or contest as **a fight to the death**, you are emphasizing that it will not stop until the death or total victory of one of the opponents. *...an eleven-hour fight to the death between a* PRAGMATICS

baboon and leopard... He now faces a fight to the death to reach the quarter-finals.

7 If you say that something is a matter of **life and death**, you are emphasizing that it is extremely important, often because someone may die if people do not act immediately. *Well, never mind, John, it's not a matter of life and death... We're dealing with a life-and-death situation here... It is only a hobby, not a life or death struggle.* n of PHR, PHR n PRAGMATICS

8 If someone **is put to death** they are executed. *America's first female serial killer broke down in tears yesterday after a jury recommended she be put to death in the electric chair... Those put to death by firing squad included three generals.* V inflects

9 You use **to death** to indicate that a particular action or process results in someone's death. *He was stabbed to death. ...relief missions to try to keep the country's population from starving to death... He almost bled to death after the bullet severed an artery.* PHR after v

10 You use **to death** after an adjective or a verb to emphasize the action, state, or feeling mentioned. For example, if you are **frightened to death** or **bored to death**, you are very frightened or bored. *He scares teams to death with his pace and power... Whereas 10 years ago I would have worried myself to death about it, now I accept it is part of the game... I went out last night, but not for very long. I was bored to death.* adj PHR, PHR after v PRAGMATICS

11 If you **work** someone **to death**, you make them work very hard indeed. *They worked themselves to death but never lost their humour.* V inflects

deathbed /deθbed/ **deathbeds.** If someone is on their **deathbed**, they are in a bed and about to die. *He promised his mother on her deathbed that he would never marry. ...after the man who murdered him nearly 40 years ago made a deathbed confession.* N-COUNT: usu sing, usu with poss, oft *on* N

death blow; also spelled **death-blow**. If you say that an event or action deals a **death blow** to something such as a plan or hope, or is a **death blow** to something, you mean that it puts an end to it; used mainly in journalism. *The deportations would be a death blow to the peace process... The people of Hatfield went into shock as they learned their town had been dealt a death blow.* N-SING: oft N *to* n

death certificate, death certificates. A **death certificate** is an official certificate signed by a doctor which states the cause of a person's death. N-COUNT

death duties. In British English, **death duties** were a tax which had to be paid on the money and property of someone who had died. This tax is now called 'inheritance tax'. The usual American term is 'death taxes'. N-PLURAL

death knell; also spelled **death-knell**. If you say that something sounds the **death knell** for something else, you mean that, because the first thing happens, the other thing will end soon. *The tax increase sounded the death knell for the business... It's going to be the death knell of the red deer.* N-SING: usu *the* N *for/of* n

deathly /deθli/

1 If you say that someone is **deathly** pale or **deathly** still, you are emphasizing that they are as pale or still as a dead person; used in written English. *Bernadette turned deathly pale... She lay deathly still.* ADV: ADV adj

2 If you say that someone is **deathly** afraid, you are emphasizing that they are very afraid. You can also say that someone or something is **deathly** silent, dull, boring, cold, or tired. *He is deathly afraid of black crows... I took a deathly dull job.* ADV-GRADED: ADV adj PRAGMATICS

3 If you say that there is a **deathly** silence or a **deathly** hush, you are emphasizing that it is very quiet; used in written English. *A deathly silence hung over the square.* ADJ: ADJ n PRAGMATICS

death mask, death masks; also spelled **death-mask**. A **death mask** is a model of someone's face, which is made from a mould that was taken of their face soon after they died. N-COUNT

death penalty. The **death penalty** is the punishment of death used in some countries for people who have committed very serious crimes. *If convicted for murder, both youngsters could face the death penalty.* ◆◇◇◇◇ N-SING: usu *the* N

death rate, death rates. The **death rate** is the number of people per thousand who die in a particular area during a particular period of time. *By the turn of the century, Pittsburgh had the highest death rate in the United States.* ◆◇◇◇◇ N-COUNT

death rattle; also spelled **death-rattle**. If you say that something is the **death rattle** of something else, you mean that it is a sign that very soon that thing will come to an end; used mainly in journalism. *Sir Geoffrey Howe's resignation is the death-rattle of the Thatcher dynasty.* N-SING

death row /deθ rou/. In American English, if someone is on **death row**, they are in the part of a prison which contains the cells for criminals who have been sentenced to death. *He has been on Death Row for 11 years... Most death row inmates avoid execution for many years by filing several appeals.* ◆◇◇◇◇ N-UNCOUNT: oft *on* N

death sentence, death sentences. A **death sentence** is a punishment of death given by a judge to someone who has been found guilty of a serious crime such as murder. *His original death sentence was commuted to life in prison.* ◆◇◇◇◇ N-COUNT

death squad, death squads. Death squads are groups of people who operate illegally and carry out the execution of people such as their political opponents or criminals. ◆◇◇◇◇ N-COUNT

death throes; also spelled **death-throes**.

1 The **death throes** of something are its final stages, just before it fails completely or ends. *Their work is a despairing metaphor for a society in its death throes... The dead tycoon's sons will remain in their plush offices overseeing the death throes of the family empire.* N-PLURAL: usu with poss

2 If a person or animal is in their **death throes**, they are dying and making violent, uncontrolled movements, usually because they are suffering great pain. N-PLURAL: oft *in* poss N

death toll, death tolls; also spelled **death-tolls**. The **death toll** of an accident, disaster, or war is the number of people who die in it. ◆◇◇◇◇ N-COUNT

death trap, death traps; also spelled **death-trap**. If you say that a place or vehicle is a **death trap**, you mean it is in such bad condition that it might cause someone's death; an informal expression. *Badly-built kit cars can be death traps.* N-COUNT

death warrant, death warrants; also spelled **death-warrant**.

1 A **death warrant** is an official document which orders that someone is to be executed as a punishment for a crime. N-COUNT

2 If you say that someone **is signing their own death warrant**, you mean that they are behaving in a way which will cause their ruin or death. *The day that he accused a reigning King of murder was the day he signed his own death warrant, and he knew it.* PHRASE: V inflects

death wish; also spelled **death-wish**. A **death wish** is a conscious or unconscious desire to die or be killed. N-SING

deb /deb/ **debs.** A **deb** is the same as a **debutante**. N-COUNT

debacle /deɪbɑːkəl, AM dɪb-/ **debacles;** also spelled **débâcle**. A **debacle** is an event or attempt that is a complete failure. *People believed it was a privilege to die for your country, but after the debacle of the war they never felt the same again... The convention was a debacle.* ◆◇◇◇◇ N-COUNT =fiasco

debar /dɪbɑːʳ, diː-/ **debars, debarring, debarred.** If you **are debarred** from doing something, you are prevented from doing it by a law or regulation; a formal word. *If found guilty, she could be debarred from politics for seven years... Convictions for criminal offences might lead to the persons concerned being debarred from entering the teaching profession.* VB: usu passive =ban *be* V-ed *from* n/-ing

debase /dɪbeɪs/ **debases, debasing, debased.** To **debase** something means to reduce its value or quality; a formal word. *The popular debate about environmental issues has debased the meaning of the word ecology... He said parliament and the process of democracy had been debased.* ♦ **debased** *Debased versions of this gypsy dance are sometimes performed for tourists.*
VERB =degrade; V n; ADJ-GRADED

debasement /dɪbeɪsmənt/. **Debasement** is the action of reducing the value or quality of something; a formal word. *...the debasement of popular culture and the triumph of vulgarity.*
N-UNCOUNT: oft N *of* n

debatable /dɪbeɪtəbᵊl/. If you say that something is **debatable**, you mean that it is not certain. *Whether they would have actually used their submarines to attack shipping is highly debatable... It is debatable whether or not the shareholders were ever properly compensated... Whether older women miscarry more often or whether they report more miscarriages is a debatable point.*
◆◇◇◇◇ ADJ-GRADED: usu v-link ADJ, oft *it* v-link ADJ wh; PRAGMATICS; =arguable

debate /dɪbeɪt/ **debates, debating, debated** ◆◆◆◆◇

1 A **debate** is a discussion about a subject on which people have different views. *An intense debate is going on within the Israeli government... There has been a lot of debate among scholars about this.*
N-VAR: oft N *on/over/about* n =discussion

2 A **debate** is a formal discussion, for example in a parliament, in which people express different opinions about a particular subject and then vote on it. *Mr Hamilton was speaking on the second day of a debate on defence spending.*
N-COUNT: oft N *on/about* n

3 If people **debate** a topic, they discuss it fairly formally, putting forward different views. You can also say that one person **debates** a topic with another person. *The United Nations Security Council will debate the issue today... The causes of anorexia are much debated... Scholars have debated whether or not Yagenta became a convert... He is a bulky and belligerent newspaperman who debates issues with his friends.* ♦ **debating** *It is an excellent idea to encourage them to join a school debating society. ...debating skills.*
V-RECIP; pl-n V n; pl-n V wh; V n *with* n; Also V *with* n; N-UNCOUNT: oft N n

4 If you **debate** whether to do something or what to do, you think or talk about possible courses of action before deciding exactly what you are going to do. *Taggart debated whether to have yet another double vodka... At the moment we are debating what furniture to buy for the house... I debated going back inside, but weariness won out and I started the car and drove off.*
VERB =deliberate; V wh; V -ing

5 If you say that a matter is **open to debate**, you mean that people have different opinions about it, or it has not yet been firmly decided. *The Government is committed to enforcing some of the recommendations, but others will be open to debate.*
PHRASE: v-link PHR =debatable

debater /dɪbeɪtəʳ/ **debaters.** A **debater** is someone who takes part in debates. *Both men are lawyers and skilled debaters.*
N-COUNT: oft adj N

debauched /dɪbɔːtʃt/. If you describe someone as **debauched**, you mean they behave in a way that is socially unacceptable, for example because they drink a lot of alcohol or are sexually promiscuous; an old-fashioned word. *...a debt-ridden and debauched lifestyle.*
ADJ-GRADED

debauchery /dɪbɔːtʃəri/. You use **debauchery** to refer to drunkenness or sexual activity when you disapprove of it or regard it as excessive. *The police were called in to quell scenes of drunken violence and debauchery.*
N-UNCOUNT PRAGMATICS

debenture /dɪbentʃəʳ/ **debentures.** A **debenture** is a type of savings bond which offers a fixed rate of interest over a long period. Debentures are usually issued by a company or a government agency.
N-COUNT

debilitate /dɪbɪlɪteɪt/ **debilitates, debilitating, debilitated** ◆◇◇◇◇

1 If you **are debilitated** by something such as an illness, it causes your body or mind to become gradually weaker; a formal use. *Stewart took over yesterday when Russell was debilitated by a stomach virus.* ♦ **debilitating** *A debilitating illness has been the cause of Tim Gould's current loss of form.* ♦ **debilitated** *Occasionally a patient is so debilitated that he must be fed intravenously.*
VB: usu passive; *be* V-ed *by* n; ADJ-GRADED; ADJ-GRADED

2 To **debilitate** an organization, society, or government means to gradually make it weaker; a formal use. *...their efforts to debilitate the political will of the Western alliance.* ♦ **debilitating** *...people exhausted by years of debilitating economic crisis.* ♦ **debilitated** *...an engineered takeover, designed to keep a debilitated communist party in power.*
VERB; V n; ADJ-GRADED; ADJ-GRADED

debility /dɪbɪlɪti/ **debilities. Debility** is a weakness of a person's body or mind, especially one caused by an illness; a formal word. *Anxiety or general debility can play a part in food intolerance or allergy.*
N-VAR =weakness, infirmity

debit /debɪt/ **debits, debiting, debited** ◆◇◇◇◇

1 When your bank **debits** your account, money is taken from it and paid to someone else. *We will always confirm the revised amount to you in writing before debiting your account.*
VERB; V n

2 A **debit** is a record of the money taken from your bank account, for example when you write a cheque. *The total of debits must balance the total of credits.*
N-COUNT

3 See also **direct debit**.

debonair /debəneəʳ/. A man who is **debonair** is confident, charming, and well-dressed; used showing approval. *He was a handsome, debonair, death-defying racing-driver.*
ADJ-GRADED PRAGMATICS =suave

debrief /diːbriːf/ **debriefs, debriefing, debriefed.** When someone such as a soldier, diplomat, or astronaut **is debriefed**, they are asked to give a report on a mission or task that they have just completed. *The men have been debriefed by British and Saudi officials... He went to Rio after the CIA had debriefed him.*
VERB; *be* V-ed; V n

debriefing /diːbriːfɪŋ/ **debriefings.** A **debriefing** is a meeting where someone such as a soldier, diplomat, or astronaut is asked to give a report on a mission or task that they have just completed. *A debriefing would follow this operation, to determine where it went wrong... He is here for medical check-ups and debriefing by State Department officials.*
N-VAR

debris /deɪbri, AM deɪbriː/. **Debris** is pieces from something that has been destroyed or pieces of rubbish or unwanted material which are strewn around. *I stood at the foot of the collapsed tower and watched the rescue workers sifting through the debris... A number of people were killed by flying debris... Clear away stones and debris to protect the mower blades from damage.*
◆◆◇◇◇ N-UNCOUNT

debt /det/ **debts** ◆◆◆◆◇

1 A **debt** is a sum of money that you owe someone. *Three years later, he is still paying off his debts... Shrinking economies mean falling tax revenues and more government debt. ...reducing the country's $18 billion foreign debt.* • See also **bad debt**.
N-VAR

2 **Debt** is the state of owing money. *Stress is a main reason for debt.* • If you are **in debt** or **get into debt**, you owe money. If you are **out of debt** or **get out of debt**, you succeed in paying all the money that you owe. *He was already deeply in debt through gambling losses... How can I accumulate enough cash to get out of debt?*
N-UNCOUNT; PHRASE

3 You use **debt** in expressions such as **I owe you a debt** or **I am in your debt** when you are expressing gratitude for something that someone has done for you; a formal use. *He was so good to me that I can never repay the debt I owe him... I owe a debt of thanks to Joyce Thompson, whose careful and able research was of great help... I know I shall feel for ever in her debt.*
N-COUNT: usu sing, oft *in* poss N; PRAGMATICS

debtor /detəʳ/ **debtors.** A **debtor** is a country, organization, or person who owes money. *...important improvements in the situation of debtor countries.*
◆◇◇◇◇ N-COUNT: oft N n

debug /diːbʌg/ **debugs, debugging, debugged.** When someone **debugs** a computer program, they look for the faults in it and correct them so that it will run properly. *The production*
VERB; V n

lines ground to a halt for hours while technicians tried to debug software.

debunk /diːbʌŋk/ **debunks, debunking, debunked.** If you **debunk** a widely held belief, you show that it is false. If you **debunk** something that is widely admired, you show that it is not as good as people think it is. *Historian Michael Beschloss debunks a few myths. ...the Frenchmen of the enlightenment who debunked the church and the crown.*
VERB =expose; V n

debut /deɪbjuː, AM deɪbjuː/ **debuts.** The **debut** of a performer or sports player is their first public performance, appearance, or recording. *Dundee United's Dave Bowman makes his international debut. ...her debut album 'Sugar Time'.*
◆◆◆◇◇ N-COUNT: oft with poss

debutante /debjʊtɑːnt/ **debutantes.** A **debutante** is a young woman from the upper classes who has started going to social events with other young people; an old-fashioned word. *She dazzled London society as the most beautiful debutante of her generation.*
N-COUNT

Dec. Dec. is a written abbreviation for **December.**
◆◆◇◇◇

decade /dekeɪd/ **decades.** A **decade** is a period of ten years, especially one that begins with a year ending in 0, for example 1980 to 1989. *...the last decade of the nineteenth century.*
◆◆◆◆◇ N-COUNT

decadent /dekədənt/. If you say that a person or society is **decadent**, you mean that they have low standards, especially low moral standards. *...restrictions on the number of decadent western films that were allowed to be shown. ...the excesses and stresses of their decadent rock 'n' roll lifestyles.* ♦ **decadence** *The empire had for years been falling into decadence.*
◆◇◇◇◇ ADJ-GRADED PRAGMATICS; N-UNCOUNT

decaf /diːkæf/ **decafs;** also spelled **decaff. Decaf** is decaffeinated coffee; an informal word. *He only drinks decaf.*
N-MASS

decaffeinated /diːkæfɪneɪtɪd/. **Decaffeinated** coffee has had most of the caffeine removed from it.
ADJ: usu ADJ n

decamp /dɪkæmp/ **decamps, decamping, decamped.** If you **decamp**, you go away from somewhere secretly or suddenly. *Bugsy decided to decamp to Hollywood from New York.*
VERB; V

decant /dɪkænt/ **decants, decanting, decanted.** If you **decant** a liquid into another container, you put it into another container; a formal word. *She always used to decant the milk into a jug... Vintage ports must be decanted to remove natural sediments.*
VERB; V n *into* n; *be* V-ed; Also V n

decanter /dɪkæntəʳ/ **decanters.** A **decanter** is a glass bottle or jug that you use for serving wine, sherry, or port.
N-COUNT

decapitate /dɪkæpɪteɪt/ **decapitates, decapitating, decapitated.** If someone **is decapitated**, their head is cut off; a formal word. *A worker was decapitated when a lift plummeted down the shaft on top of him... He recently decapitated a tramp on the London Underground. ...a pile of freshly decapitated chickens.* ♦ **decapitation** /dɪkæpɪteɪʃən/ **decapitations** *In the space of 16 months I saw 700 executions by decapitation.*
VERB; *be* V-ed; V n; V-ed; N-VAR

decathlon /dɪkæθlɒn/ **decathlons.** The **decathlon** is a competition in which athletes compete in 10 different sporting events.
N-COUNT: oft *the* N

decay /dɪkeɪ/ **decays, decaying, decayed**
◆◆◇◇◇

1 When something such as a body, a dead plant, or a tooth **decays**, it becomes rotten. *The bodies buried in the fine ash slowly decayed... The ground was scattered with decaying leaves.* ► Also a noun. *When not removed, plaque causes tooth decay and gum disease.* ♦ **decayed** *Even young children have teeth so decayed they need to be pulled.*
VERB =rot; V; V-ing; N-UNCOUNT; ADJ-GRADED =rotten

2 If something such as a society, system, or institution **decays**, it gradually becomes weaker or its condition gets worse. *In practice, the agency system has decayed. Most 'agents' now sell only to themselves or their immediate family... Congress has tried dozens of approaches to revitalize decaying urban and rural areas.* ► Also a noun. *There are problems of urban decay and gang violence.*
VERB; V; V-ing; N-UNCOUNT

deceased /dɪsiːst/; **deceased** is both the singular and the plural form.
◆◇◇◇◇

1 **The deceased** is used to refer to a particular person or to particular people who have recently died; a legal use. *The Navy is notifying next of kin now that the identities of the deceased have been determined.*
N-COUNT: *the* N

2 A **deceased** person is one who has recently died; a formal use. *...his recently deceased mother.*
ADJ =dead

deceit /dɪsiːt/ **deceits. Deceit** is behaviour that is deliberately intended to make people believe something which is not true. *It's just like before. The same lies and half lies. The same deceits.*
◆◇◇◇◇ N-VAR =deception

deceitful /dɪsiːtfʊl/. If you say that someone is **deceitful**, you mean that they behave in a dishonest way by making other people believe something that is not true. *They claimed the government had been deceitful... The ambassador called the report deceitful and misleading.*
ADJ-GRADED

deceive /dɪsiːv/ **deceives, deceiving, deceived**
◆◇◇◇◇

1 If you **deceive** someone, you make them believe something that is not true, usually in order to get some advantage for yourself. *He has deceived and disillusioned us all... If you can make the last 10 seconds exciting, you can deceive your audience into thinking it's been like that all along.*
VERB; V n; V n *into* -ing

2 If you **deceive** yourself, you do not admit to yourself something that you know is true. *Alcoholics are notorious for their ability to deceive themselves about the extent of their problem.*
VERB; V pron-refl

3 If something **deceives** you, it gives you a wrong impression and makes you believe something that is not true. *The alacrity with which he'd agreed did not deceive Joanna; she knew that he had no intention of abandoning his harebrained plan... The boys, if my eyes did not deceive me, were praying.*
VERB =mislead; V n

decelerate /diːseləreɪt/ **decelerates, decelerating, decelerated**

1 When a vehicle or machine **decelerates** or when someone in a vehicle **decelerates**, the speed of the vehicle or machine is reduced. *The chauffeur kept accelerating and decelerating between 60 and 90 mph.* ♦ **deceleration** /diːseləreɪʃən/ *The hydraulic system ensures that the harder the brake pedal is pressed, the greater the car's deceleration.*
VERB ≠accelerate; V; N-UNCOUNT ≠acceleration

2 When the rate of something such as inflation or economic growth **decelerates**, it slows down. *Inflation has decelerated remarkably over the past two years.* ♦ **deceleration** *This is a significant deceleration from the 4.2% annual rate of growth between April and June.*
VERB ≠accelerate; V; N-UNCOUNT ≠acceleration

December /dɪsembəʳ/ **Decembers. December** is the twelfth and last month of the year in the Western calendar. *...a bright morning in mid-December... Just before Christmas, on 17th December, Joanna had a baby girl... The talks are due to be concluded this December.*
◆◆◆◆◇ N-VAR

decency /diːsənsi/
◆◇◇◇◇

1 **Decency** is the quality of following accepted moral standards. *Unfortunately, on Friday night he showed neither decency nor dignity... His sense of decency forced him to resign. ...the threat of rampant materialism to common decency and enlightened values.*
N-UNCOUNT =integrity

2 If you say that someone did not **have the decency** to do something, you mean that there was a particular action which they did not do but which you believe they ought to have done. *Somebody should have had the decency to inform myself and John Prescott of what was planned.*
PHRASE: oft with brd-neg, V inflects, PHR to-inf PRAGMATICS

decent /diːsənt/
◆◆◇◇◇

1 **Decent** is used to describe something which is considered to be of an acceptable standard or quality. *Nearby is a village with a decent pub... He didn't get a decent explanation... The lack of a decent education did not defeat Rey.* ♦ **decently** *The allies say they will treat their prisoners decently... This year's festival can boast a decently long list of sponsors.*
ADJ: usu ADJ n =reasonable; ADV-GRADED: usu ADV with v, also ADV adj =reasonably

2 **Decent** is used to describe something which is morally correct or acceptable. *But, after a decent*
ADJ: usu ADJ n =respectable

interval, trade relations began to return to normal... She watched his face, as the coffin was lowered into the ground. As soon as it was decent, he plunged through the crowd towards the cars. ♦ **decently** ADV-GRADED: usu ADV with v, also ADV adj =respectably *There were at least four hours before he could decently go to the pub... And can't you dress more decently – people will think you're a tramp.*

3 **Decent** people are honest and behave in a way that most people approve of. ADJ-GRADED: usu ADJ n =upright *The majority of people around here are decent people... The jury will see what a decent guy he is.*

4 If you say that someone should **do the decent thing**, you mean that they should do something which they do not really want to do, but which you think they are morally obliged to do; an old-fashioned expression. PHRASE: V inflects PRAGMATICS *He should do the decent thing and resign.*

decentralize /diːsentrəlaɪz/ **decentralizes, decentralizing, decentralized;** also spelled **decentralise** in British English. ◆◇◇◇◇ VERB To **decentralize** government or a large organization means to move some departments or branches away from the main administrative area, or to give more power to local departments or branches. V n V V-ed *They have at last persuaded the bureaucracy to decentralise the company, slim it down and make it more entrepreneurial. ...the need to decentralize and devolve power to regional governments... The German constitution is an excellent model of decentralised government.* ♦ **decentralization** N-UNCOUNT /diːsentrəlaɪzeɪʃᵊn/ *He seems set against the idea of increased decentralisation and greater powers for regional authorities.*

deception /dɪsepʃᵊn/ **deceptions. Deception** ◆◇◇◇◇ N-VAR is the act of deceiving someone or the state of being deceived by someone. *He admitted conspiring to obtain property by deception... You've been the victim of a rather cruel deception.*

deceptive /dɪseptɪv/. If something is **deceptive**, it encourages you to believe something which is not true. ◆◇◇◇◇ ADJ-GRADED =misleading *Johnston isn't tired of London yet, it seems, but appearances can be deceptive.* ♦ **deceptively** *The storyline is deceptively simple.* ADV

decibel /desɪbel/ **decibels.** A **decibel** is a unit of measurement which is used to indicate how loud a sound is. N-COUNT: oft num N *Continuous exposure to sound above 80 decibels could be harmful.*

decide /dɪsaɪd/ **decides, deciding, decided** ◆◆◆◆◆

1 If you **decide** to do something, you choose to do it, usually after you have thought carefully about the other possibilities. VERB =make up one's mind V to-inf V that V *against/in favour of* n/-ing V wh V *She decided to do a secretarial course... He has decided that he doesn't want to embarrass the movement and will therefore step down... The house needed totally rebuilding, so we decided against buying it... I had a cold and couldn't decide whether to go to work or not... Think about it very carefully before you decide.*

2 If a person or group of people **decides** something, they choose what something should be like or how a particular problem should be solved. VERB V n *She was still young, he said, and that would be taken into account when deciding her sentence... This is an issue that should be decided by local and metropolitan government.*

3 If an event or fact **decides** something, it makes it certain that a particular choice will be made or that there will be a particular result. VERB =settle V n V wh V-ing *The goal that decided the match came just before the interval... The results will decide if he will win a place at a good university... Luck is certainly not the only deciding factor, but it does play an exceptionally large role.*

4 If you **decide** that something is true, you form that opinion about it after considering the facts. VERB V that V wh *He decided Franklin must be suffering from a bad cold... For a long time I couldn't decide whether the original settlers were insane or just stupid.*

5 If something **decides** you to do something, it is the reason that causes you to choose to do it. VERB V n to-inf V n Also V n that, V n *against/in favour of* n/-ing *The banning of his English play decided him to write something about censorship... What decided him was a cynical question: 'If I fail, I'll be no worse off than I am now, will I?'*

decide on. If you **decide on** something or **decide upon** something, you choose it from two or more possibilities. PHRASAL VERB =settle for V P n *After leaving university, Therese decided on a career in publishing.*

decided /dɪsaɪdɪd/. **Decided** means clear and definite. ADJ-GRADED: ADJ n =definite *Support from the outgoing party of government is expected to help Mr Fujimori to a decided advantage in many parts of the interior... He's a man of very decided opinions.*

decidedly /dɪsaɪdɪdli/. **Decidedly** means to a great extent and in a way that is very obvious. ◆◇◇◇◇ ADV-GRADED: ADV group *He admits there will be moments when he's decidedly uncomfortable at what he sees on the screen... Representatives of the other branches adopted a decidedly different view... It soon became clear that authors were decidedly in the majority.*

decider /dɪsaɪdəʳ/ **deciders**

1 In sport, a **decider** is one of the games in a series of games, which establishes which player or team wins the series; used in British English. N-COUNT *He won the decider which completed England's 3-2 victory over Austria.*

2 In games such as football or hockey, the **decider** is the last goal to be scored in a match that is won by a margin of only one goal; used in British English. N-COUNT *McGrath scored the decider in Villa's 2-1 home win over Forest.*

deciduous /dɪsɪdʒuəs/. A **deciduous** tree or bush is one that loses its leaves in the autumn every year. ADJ: usu ADJ n ≠evergreen

decimal /desɪmᵊl/ **decimals**

1 A **decimal** system involves counting in units of ten. ADJ: ADJ n *...the decimal system of metric weights and measures... In 1971, the 1p and 2p decimal coins were introduced in Britain.*

2 A **decimal** is a fraction that is written in the form of a dot followed by one or more numbers which represent tenths, hundredths, and so on: for example .5, .51, .517. N-COUNT *...simple math concepts, such as decimals and fractions.*

decimal point, decimal points. A **decimal point** is the dot in front of a decimal fraction. N-COUNT

decimate /desɪmeɪt/ **decimates, decimating, decimated** ◆◇◇◇◇

1 To **decimate** something such as a group of people or animals means to destroy a very large number of them. VERB V n *The pollution could decimate the river's thriving population of kingfishers... British forces in the Caribbean were being decimated by disease.* ♦ **decimation** /desɪmeɪʃᵊn/ N-UNCOUNT: usu N *of* n *...the decimation of the great rain forests.*

2 To **decimate** a system or organization means to reduce its size and effectiveness greatly. VERB V n *...a recession which decimated the nation's manufacturing industry.* ♦ **decimation** N-UNCOUNT: usu N *of* n *Government policies have resulted in a decimation of essential services used by the poor.*

decipher /dɪsaɪfəʳ/ **deciphers, deciphering, deciphered.** If you **decipher** a piece of writing or a message, you work out what it says, even though it is very difficult to read or understand. ◆◇◇◇◇ VERB V n *I'm still no closer to deciphering the code.*

decision /dɪsɪʒᵊn/ **decisions** ◆◆◆◆◆

1 When you make a **decision**, you choose what should be done or which is the best of various possible actions. N-COUNT: oft N to-inf, N *on* n/wh *The decision to discipline Marshall was taken by the party chairman with the support of the Prime Minister... The president said he'd made no firm decision on whether he would run for a second term in office... I don't want to make the wrong decision and regret it later... Who makes the financial decisions in your household?*

2 **Decision** is the act of deciding something or the need to decide something. N-UNCOUNT *The growing pressures of the crisis may mean that the moment of decision can't be too long delayed... This was a matter for decision by the individual.*

3 **Decision** is the ability to decide quickly and definitely what to do. N-UNCOUNT =decisiveness *He is very quick-thinking and very much a man of decision and action.*

decision-making. Decision-making is the process of reaching decisions, especially in a ◆◆◇◇◇ N-UNCOUNT large organization or in government. *She wants to see more women involved in decision making... Shortening the decision-making process would provide one solution.*

decisive /dɪsaɪsɪv/ ◆◆◇◇◇

1 If a fact, action, or event is **decisive**, it makes it certain that there will be a particular result. *...his decisive victory in the presidential elections... The election campaign has now entered its final, decisive phase... The meeting between Molotov, Bidault and Bevin was decisive.* ADJ-GRADED ♦ **decisively** *The plan was decisively rejected by Congress three weeks ago.* ADV: usu ADV with v

2 If someone is **decisive**, they have or show an ability to make quick decisions in a difficult or complicated situation. *He should give way to a younger, more decisive leader.* ADJ-GRADED ♦ **decisively** *'I'll call for you at half ten,' she said decisively.* ADV-GRADED ♦ **decisiveness** *His supporters admire his decisiveness.* N-UNCOUNT

deck /dek/ **decks, decking, decked** ◆◆◆◇◇

1 A **deck** on a bus, ship, or train is a downstairs or upstairs area on it. *...sitting on the top deck of the number 13 bus. ...a luxury liner with five passenger decks.* • See also **flight deck**. N-COUNT: oft supp N

2 The **deck** of a ship is the top part of it that forms a floor in the open air which you can walk on. *She stood on the deck and waved her hand to them as the steamer moved off.* N-COUNT: also *on* N

3 A tape **deck** or record **deck** is a piece of equipment on which you play tapes or records. *...the tape deck in my car... I stuck a tape in the deck.* N-COUNT: oft n N

4 A **deck** of cards is a complete set of playing cards; used mainly in American English. The usual British word is **pack**. *Matt picked up the cards and shuffled the deck.* N-COUNT

5 If something **is decked** with pretty things, it is decorated with them; used in written English. *Villagers decked the streets with bunting... The house was decked with flowers.* VERB · V n *with* n · V-ed

6 If someone or something is **below decks**, they are inside a ship in the part of it that is underneath the deck. *The crew of the trawler were gathered below decks.* PHRASES

7 If you **clear the decks**, you get ready to start something new by finishing any work that has to be done or getting rid of any problems that are in the way. *The hostage release could clear the decks for war. ...the classic situation of a new management taking over a troubled firm and wishing to clear the decks.* V inflects

8 If someone or something **hits the deck**, they fall to the ground; an informal expression. *Andover's body hit the deck.* V inflects

deck out. If someone or something **is decked out** with or in something, they are decorated with it or wearing it, usually for a special occasion. *The cab was decked out with multi-coloured lights... She had decked him out from head to foot in expensive clothes.* PHRASAL VERB · *be* V-ed P · V n P · Also V P n (not pron)

deckchair /dektʃeəʳ/ **deckchairs.** A **deckchair** is a simple chair with a folding frame and a piece of canvas forming the seat and back. Deckchairs are usually used at the seaside, on a ship, or in the garden. N-COUNT

-decker /-dekəʳ/. **-decker** is used after adjectives like 'double' and 'single' to indicate how many levels or layers something has. *...a red double-decker bus full of tourists. ...a triple-decker peanut butter and jelly sandwich.* COMB in ADJ: ADJ n

deckhand /dekhænd/ **deckhands.** A **deckhand** is a person who does the cleaning and other work on the deck of a ship. N-COUNT

declaim /dɪkleɪm/ **declaims, declaiming, declaimed.** If you **declaim**, you speak dramatically, as if you were acting in a theatre; used in written English. *He raised his right fist and declaimed: 'Liar and cheat!'... I can remember the way he used to declaim French verse to us with this immense energy.* VERB · V with quote · V n · Also V, V that

declamatory /dɪklæmətri, AM -tɔːri/. A **declamatory** phrase, statement, or way of speaking is dramatic and confident; a formal word. *Rebels like Katharine Hamnett have made a name for bold, declamatory statements.* ADJ-GRADED

declaration /dekləreɪʃᵊn/ **declarations** ◆◆◆◇◇

1 A **declaration** is an official announcement or statement. *They will sign the declaration tomorrow... The opening speeches sounded more like declarations of war than offerings of peace. ...the issues arising from their declaration of independence.* N-COUNT: oft N *of* n

2 A **declaration** is a firm, emphatic statement which shows that you have no doubts about what you are saying. *She needed time to adjust to Clive's declaration. ...declarations of undying love.* N-COUNT

3 A **declaration** is a written statement about something which you have signed and which can be used as evidence in a court of law. *On the customs declaration, the sender labeled the freight as agricultural machinery... They will ask you to sign a declaration allowing your doctor to disclose your medical details.* N-COUNT

declare /dɪkleəʳ/ **declares, declaring, declared** ◆◆◆◆◇

1 If you **declare** that something is true, you say that it is true in a firm, deliberate way. You can also **declare** an attitude or intention. This use occurs in written English. *Speaking outside Ten Downing Street, she declared that she would fight on... 'I'm absolutely thrilled to have done what I've done,' he declared... He declared his intention to become the best golfer in the world... Glasses of Madeira wine were brought to us. We declared it delicious... He turned up in northern Cyprus, declaring himself happy to be home.* VERB · =announce · V that · V with quote · V n · V n adj · V pron-refl adj/prep · Also V n n, V n to-inf

2 If you **declare** something, you state officially and formally that it exists or is the case. *The government is ready to declare a permanent ceasefire... His lawyers are confident that the judges will declare Mr Ashwell innocent... The U.N. has declared it to be a safe zone... On striking his sword on the stone, he declared himself Lord of the City... Yeltsin declared that a vote for him would be a vote for a new constitution.* VERB · V n · V n adj · V n to-inf · V n n · V that

3 If you **declare** goods that you have bought abroad or money that you have earned, you say how much you have bought or earned so that you can pay tax on it. *Declaring the wrong income by mistake will no longer lead to an automatic fine... She had nothing to declare, and was starting to go through the 'Green' channel when she was stopped.* VERB · V n

declare for. If you **declare for** something or someone, you say that you are in favour of them. *The Catalans declared for Charles and a civil war erupted in Valencia and Aragon... Only a month earlier, Mr. Stenholm had declared for the tax cut.* PHRASAL VERB · V P n

declassify /diːklæsɪfaɪ/ **declassifies, declassifying, declassified.** If secret documents or records **are declassified**, it is officially stated that they are no longer secret. *The existence of these reports only became known when some of them were declassified in 1985.* VB: usu passive · *be* V-ed

decline /dɪklaɪn/ **declines, declining, declined** ◆◆◆◆◇

1 If something **declines**, it becomes less in quantity, importance, or strength. *The number of staff has declined from 217,000 to 114,000... Hourly output by workers declined 1.3% in the first quarter... Union membership and union power are declining fast. ...a declining birth rate.* VERB · V *from/to/by* amount · V amount · V · V-ing

2 If you **decline** something or **decline** to do something, you politely refuse to accept it or do it; a formal use. *He declined their invitation... The band declined to comment on the story... He offered the boys some coffee. They declined politely.* VERB · V n · V to-inf · V

3 If there is a **decline** in something, it becomes less in quantity, importance, or quality. *There wasn't such a big decline in enrollments after all. ...Rome's decline in the fifth century... The first signs of economic decline became visible.* N-VAR: oft N with poss, N *in* n

4 If something is **in decline** or **on the decline**, it is gradually decreasing in importance, quality, or power. *Thankfully the smoking of cigarettes is on the decline... He is still one of the world's most popular golfers, but his game is in decline.* PHRASES · v-link PHR

5 If something goes or falls **into decline**, it begins to gradually decrease in importance, quality, or power. *Libraries are an investment for the future and they should not be allowed to fall into decline.*

decode /diːkoʊd/ **decodes, decoding, decoded**

1 If you **decode** a message that has been written or spoken in a code, you change it into ordinary language. *All he had to do was decode it and pass it over... The secret documents were intercepted and decoded.* VERB =decipher V n

2 If you **decode** something such as a play or a work of art, or someone's behaviour, you manage to understand its meaning or implications, although they are not obvious. *You don't need a Ph.D to decode their work, but they do try to challenge audiences with unconventional material.* VERB V n

3 A device that **decodes** a broadcast signal changes it into a form that can be displayed on a television screen. *About 60,000 subscribers have special adapters to receive and decode the signals.* VERB V n

decoder /diːkoʊdəʳ/ **decoders.** A **decoder** is a device used to decode messages or signals sent in code, for example the television signals from a satellite. N-COUNT

decolonization /diːkɒlənaɪzeɪʃən/; also spelled **decolonisation. Decolonization** means giving a country that was formerly a colony political independence. *Between 1775 and 1825 there was a wave of decolonization in the Americas.* N-UNCOUNT ≠colonization

decommission /diːkəmɪʃən/ **decommissions, decommissioning, decommissioned.** When something such as a nuclear reactor or a large machine **is decommissioned**, it is taken to pieces because it is no longer going to be used. *A spokesman said HMS Warspite would be decommissioned as part of the defence cuts announced earlier this year. ...a decommissioned power plant in Colorado.* VERB be V-ed V-ed Also V n

decompose /diːkəmpoʊz/ **decomposes, decomposing, decomposed.** When things such as dead plants or animals **decompose**, or something **decomposes** them, they change chemically and begin to rot. *...a dead body found decomposing in a wood... The debris slowly decomposes into compost... The mixture heated up to more than 150 degrees as various strains of furiously procreating bacteria decomposed and digested the garbage.* ♦ **decomposed** *The body was too badly decomposed to be identified at once.* ◆◇◇◇◇ V-ERG =rot, decay V V into n V n ADJ-GRADED

decomposition /diːkɒmpəzɪʃən/. **Decomposition** is the process of rotting that takes place when a living thing dies and changes chemically; a formal word. N-UNCOUNT

decompression /diːkəmpreʃən/

1 **Decompression** is the reduction of the force on something that is caused by the weight of the air. *Decompression blew out a window in the plane.* N-UNCOUNT

2 **Decompression** is the process of bringing someone back to the normal pressure of the air after they have been deep underwater. *...after spending a short while in the decompression chamber.* N-UNCOUNT: usu N n

decongestant /diːkəndʒestənt/ **decongestants.** A **decongestant** is a medicine which helps someone who has a cold to breathe more easily. N-MASS

deconstruct /diːkənstrʌkt/ **deconstructs, deconstructing, deconstructed.** To **deconstruct** an idea or text means to show the contradictions in its meaning, and to show how it does not fully explain what it claims to explain; a technical term in philosophy and literary criticism. *She sets up a rigorous intellectual framework to deconstruct various categories of film.* ◆◇◇◇◇ VERB V n

♦ **deconstruction** /diːkənstrʌkʃən/ *...the deconstruction of the macho psyche.* N-UNCOUNT

decontaminate /diːkəntæmɪneɪt/ **decontaminates, decontaminating, decontaminated.** To **decontaminate** something means to remove all radioactivity, germs, or dangerous substances from it. *...procedures for decontaminating pilots hit by chemical weapons.* ♦ **decontamination** /diːkəntæmɪneɪʃən/ *The land will require public money for decontamination.* VERB V n N-UNCOUNT

decontrol /diːkəntroʊl/ **decontrols, decontrolling, decontrolled.** When governments **decontrol** an activity, they remove controls from it so that companies or organizations have more freedom; used mainly in American English. *The Russian government chose not to decontrol oil and gas prices last January.* ► Also a noun. *...continuing decontrol of banking institutions.* VERB =deregulate V n N-VAR: oft n N, N of n

decor /deɪkɔːʳ/. The **decor** of a house or room is its style of furnishing and decoration. *The decor is simple – black lacquer panels on white walls.* ◆◇◇◇◇ N-UNCOUNT

decorate /dekəreɪt/ **decorates, decorating, decorated** ◆◆◆◇◇

1 If you **decorate** something, you make it more attractive by adding things to it. *He decorated his room with pictures of all his favorite sports figures... Simply collect shells and then experiment by using them to decorate boxes, trays, mirrors or even pots.* VERB V n with n V n

2 If you **decorate** a building or room, you put new paint or wallpaper on the walls and ceiling, and paint the woodwork. *When they came to decorate the rear bedroom, it was Jemma who had the final say... The boys are planning to decorate when they get the time... I had the flat decorated quickly so that Philippa could move in. ...a small, badly decorated office.* ♦ **decorating** *I did a lot of the decorating myself.* ♦ **decoration** *From start to finish, the renovation process and decoration took four months.* VERB V n V have n V-ed V-ed N-UNCOUNT N-UNCOUNT

3 If something **decorates** a place or an object, it makes it look more attractive; used in written English. *Constable posters decorate the walls.* VERB =adorn V n

4 If someone **is decorated**, they are given a medal or other honour as an official reward for something that they have done. *Kramar was decorated for his services to the Communist Party.* VB: usu passive be V-ed

decoration /dekəreɪʃən/ **decorations** ◆◆◇◇◇

1 The **decoration** of a room is its furniture, wallpaper, and ornaments. *The decoration and furnishings had to be practical enough for a family home... With its simple decoration, the main bedroom is a peaceful haven.* N-UNCOUNT: oft with poss =decor

2 **Decorations** are features that are added to something in order to make it look more attractive. *The only wall decorations are candles and a single mirror... The planting of winter and spring-flowering bulbs will supply colourful decoration at a time when most gardens are looking fairly desolate.* N-VAR

3 **Decorations** are brightly coloured objects such as pieces of paper and balloons, which you put up in a room on special occasions to make it look more attractive. *Colorful streamers and festive paper decorations had been hung from the ceiling.* N-COUNT: usu pl

4 A **decoration** is an official title or honour which is given to someone, usually in the form of a medal, as a reward for military bravery or public service. *He was awarded several military decorations by grateful Allied governments.* N-COUNT =award

decorative /dekərətɪv/. Something that is **decorative** is intended to look pretty or attractive. *The curtains are for purely decorative purposes and do not open or close. ...highly decorative iron brackets.* ◆◆◇◇◇ ADJ-GRADED

decorator /dekəreɪtəʳ/ **decorators.** In British English, a **decorator** is a person whose job is to paint houses or put wallpaper up. • See also **interior decorator**. ◆◇◇◇◇ N-COUNT

decorous /dekərəs/. **Decorous** behaviour is very respectable, calm, and polite; a formal word. *They go for decorous walks every day in parks with their nanny.* ♦ **decorously** *He sipped his drink decorously.* ADJ-GRADED =seemly, proper ADV-GRADED

decorum /dɪkɔːrəm/. **Decorum** is behaviour that people consider to be correct, polite, and respectable; a formal word. *I was treated with decorum and respect throughout the investigation.* N-UNCOUNT =propriety

decouple /diːkʌpəl/ **decouples, decoupling, decoupled.** If two countries, organizations, or ideas that were connected in some way **are decoupled**, the connection between them is ended; a formal word. *This is exemplified in Trudeau's* VERB V pl-n *conception which decouples culture and politics... The issue threatened to decouple Europe from the United States... Other forms of discourse have successfully been decoupled from politics.* V n from n

decoy /diːkɔɪ/ **decoys** ♦◇◇◇◇

1 If you refer to something or someone as a **decoy**, you mean that they are intended to attract people's attention and deceive them, for example by leading them into a trap or away from a particular place. *The owner disguises himself as Napoleon as a decoy to fool the French... A plane was waiting at the airport with its engines running but this was just one of the decoys.* N-COUNT

2 A **decoy** is a model of a bird that is used to attract wild birds towards it so that people can study them or shoot them. N-COUNT

decrease, decreases, decreasing, decreased. The verb is pronounced /dɪkriːs/. The noun is pronounced /diːkriːs/. ♦♦◇◇◇

1 When something **decreases** or when you **decrease** it, it becomes less in quantity, size, or intensity. *Population growth is decreasing by 1.4% each year... The number of independent firms decreased from 198 to 96... Raw-steel production by the nation's mills decreased 2.1% last week... Since 1945 air forces have decreased in size... Gradually decrease the amount of vitamin C you are taking when you begin to feel better... We've got stable labor, decreasing interest rates, low oil prices.* V-ERG; V by amount; V from/to amount; V amount; V in n; V n; V-ing

2 A **decrease** is a reduction in the quantity, size, or intensity of something. *In Spain and Portugal there has been a decrease in the number of young people out of work... Bank base rates have fallen from 10 per cent to 6 per cent - a decrease of 40 per cent.* N-COUNT: oft N in/of n

decree /dɪkriː/ **decrees, decreeing, decreed** ♦♦◇◇◇

1 A **decree** is an official order or decision, especially one made by the ruler of a country. *In July he issued a decree ordering all unofficial armed groups in the country to disband... He is prepared to use his recently-acquired powers to introduce reform by presidential decree.* N-COUNT: also by N

2 If someone in authority **decrees** that something must happen, they decide or state this officially. *The government decreed that all who wanted to live and work in Kenya must hold Kenyan passports... Within 48 hours the king got the two deputies off the hook by decreeing a general amnesty.* VERB; V that; V n

3 A **decree** is a judgement made by a law court; used mainly in American English. *Men do not always get their own way, as court decrees on custody show.* N-COUNT

decree absolute, decrees absolute. A **decree absolute** is the final order made by a court in a divorce case which ends a marriage completely. N-COUNT: usu sing

decree nisi /dɪkriː naɪsaɪ/ **decrees nisi.** A **decree nisi** is an order made by a court which states that a divorce must take place at a certain time in the future unless a good reason is produced to prevent this. N-COUNT: usu sing

decrepit /dɪkrepɪt/. Something that is **decrepit** is old and in bad condition. Someone who is **decrepit** is old and weak. *The film had been shot in a decrepit old police station. ...a decrepit old man.* ADJ-GRADED

decrepitude /dɪkrepɪtjuːd, AM -tuːd/. **Decrepitude** is the state of being very old and in poor condition; a formal word. *Even opposite the Presidential residence there was a general air of decrepitude and neglect.* N-UNCOUNT

decriminalize /diːkrɪmɪnəlaɪz/ **decriminalizes, decriminalizing, decriminalized;** also spelled **decriminalise** in British English. When a criminal offence **is decriminalized**, the law changes so that it is no longer a criminal offence. *An important question to consider is whether prostitution should be decriminalized in this country.* VERB; be V-ed; Also V n
♦ **decriminalization** /diːkrɪmɪnəlaɪzeɪʃᵊn/ *...the decriminalisation of homosexuality in the Isle of Man.* N-UNCOUNT: oft N of n

decry /dɪkraɪ/ **decries, decrying, decried.** If someone **decries** an idea or action, they criticize it strongly; a formal word, used showing disapproval. *He is impatient with those who decry the scheme... Anyone who decries this as a waste of money should consider how much has been spent repairing motorways in the last 25 years.* VERB; PRAGMATICS; =condemn; V n; V n as n

dedicate /dedɪkeɪt/ **dedicates, dedicating, dedicated** ♦♦◇◇◇

1 If you say that someone **has dedicated** themselves to something, you approve of the fact that they have decided to give a lot of time and effort to it because they think that it is important. *Back on the island, he dedicated himself to politics... Bessie has dedicated her life to caring for others.* VERB; PRAGMATICS; =devote; V pron-refl to n/-ing; V n to n/-ing
♦ **dedicated** *He's quite dedicated to his students. ...a company staffed by capable and dedicated people.* ADJ-GRADED: oft ADJ to n ♦ **dedication** *We admire her courage, compassion and dedication to the cause of humanity, justice and peace... To be successful takes hard work and dedication.* N-UNCOUNT: oft N to n

2 If someone **dedicates** something such as a book, play, or piece of music to you, they mention your name, for example in the front of a book or when a piece of music is performed, as a way of showing affection or respect for you. *She dedicated her first album to Woody Allen, whom she says understands her obsession... This book is dedicated to the memory of my mother.* VERB; V n to n

3 If a monument, building, or church **is dedicated** to someone, a formal ceremony is held to show that the building will always be associated with them. *The other day, in a little church near Brighton, a window was dedicated to the memory of the Revd. Michael Scott... The church is dedicated to St Mary of Bec.* VB: usu passive; be V-ed to n; V-ed to n ♦ **dedication** *...the dedication of the Holocaust Museum... Some 250 guests attended the dedication ceremony.* N-UNCOUNT: oft N of n

dedicated /dedɪkeɪtɪd/ ♦♦◇◇◇

1 You use **dedicated** to describe someone who enjoys a particular activity very much and spends a lot of time doing it. *Her great-grandfather had clearly been a dedicated and stoical traveller. ...dedicated followers of classical music.* ADJ-GRADED: usu ADJ n

2 You use **dedicated** to describe something that is made, built, or designed for one particular purpose or thing. *Such areas should also be served by dedicated cycle routes. ...the world's first museum dedicated to ecology.* ADJ: oft ADJ to n

dedication /dedɪkeɪʃᵊn/ **dedications.** A **dedication** is a message which is written at the beginning of a book, or a short announcement which is sometimes made before a play or piece of music is performed, as a sign of affection or respect for someone. • See also **dedicate**. N-COUNT

deduce /dɪdjuːs, AM -duːs/ **deduces, deducing, deduced.** If you **deduce** something or **deduce** that something is true, you reach that conclusion because of other things that you know to be true. *Alison had got to work and cleverly deduced that I was the author of the letter... The date of the document can be deduced from references to the Civil War. ...hoping he hadn't deduced the reason for her visit.* ♦◇◇◇◇ VERB; =infer; V that; be V-ed from n; V n; Also V n from n, V with quote

deduct /dɪdʌkt/ **deducts, deducting, deducted.** When you **deduct** an amount from a total, you subtract it from the total. *The company deducted this payment from his compensation... Up to 5% of marks in the exams will be deducted for spelling mistakes.* ♦♦◇◇◇ VERB; V n from n; be V-ed; Also V n

deduction /dɪdʌkʃᵊn/ **deductions** ♦♦◇◇◇

1 A **deduction** is a conclusion that you have reached about something because of other things that you know to be true. *It was a pretty astute deduction... Lady Starmouth had consequently made her own shrewd deductions about what was going on in my marriage.* N-COUNT: oft N about n

2 **Deduction** is the process of reaching a conclusion about something because of other things that you know to be true. *Miss Allan beamed at him. 'You are clever to guess. I'm sure I don't know how you did it.'—'Deduction,' James said.* N-UNCOUNT

3 A **deduction** is an amount that has been subtracted from a total. *...your gross income (before tax and National Insurance deductions)... After deduc-* N-COUNT *tions for war reparations, the balance would be used to buy food and humanitarian supplies.*

4 **Deduction** is the act or process of subtracting an amount of money from a total amount. *The profit figure was struck after the deduction of a £56,000 'golden handshake' for Harold Stonefield who retired as purchasing director in March.* N-UNCOUNT

deductive /dɪdʌktɪv/. **Deductive** reasoning involves deducing conclusions logically from other things that are already known; a formal word. *She didn't seem at all impressed by his deductive powers.* ADJ: usu ADJ n

deed /diːd/ **deeds** ◆◇◇◇◇

1 A **deed** is something that is done, especially something that is very good or very bad; a literary use. *His heroic deeds were celebrated in every corner of India. ...the warm feeling one gets from doing a good deed... The perpetrators of this evil deed must be brought to justice.* N-COUNT =act

2 A **deed** is a document containing the terms of an agreement, especially an agreement concerning the ownership of land or a building; a legal use. *He asked if I had the deeds to his father's property.* N-COUNT

deed poll. In Britain, if you change your name **by deed poll**, you change it officially and legally. PHRASE: PHR after v

deem /diːm/ **deems, deeming, deemed.** If something **is deemed** to have a particular quality or to do a particular thing, it is considered to have that quality or do that thing; a formal word. *French and German were deemed essential... He says he would support the use of force if the UN deemed it necessary... I was deemed to be a competent shorthand typist.* ◆◆◇◇◇ VERB =judge *be*V-ed adj/n V n adj/n *be*V-ed to-inf Also V n to-inf

deep /diːp/ **deeper, deepest** ◆◆◆◆◇

1 If something is **deep**, it extends a long way down from the ground or from the top surface of something. *The water is very deep and mysterious-looking... Den had dug a deep hole in the centre of the garden... Kelly swore quietly, looking at the deep cut on his left hand. ...a deep ravine.* ADJ-GRADED ≠shallow ► Also an adverb. *Deep in the earth's crust the rock may be subjected to temperatures high enough to melt it... Gingerly, she put her hand in deeper, to the bottom.* ADV-GRADED: ADV prep/adv, ADV after v ♦ **deeply** *There isn't time to dig deeply and put in manure or compost... It removes deeply embedded dirt and grease so allowing your horse's skin to breathe more easily.* ADV-GRADED: ADV after v, ADV adj/-ed

2 A **deep** container, such as a wardrobe or cupboard, extends or measures a long distance from front to back. *The wardrobe was very deep.* ADJ-GRADED

3 You use **deep** to talk or ask about how much something measures from the surface to the bottom, or from front to back. *I found myself in water only three feet deep... The mud is ankle deep around Shush Square... How deep did the snow get?* ► Also a combining form. *...an inch-deep stab wound. ...one of the many points on the river where the water runs thigh-deep.* ADJ-GRADED: amount ADJ, n ADJ, *how* ADJ, *as* ADJ *as*, ADJ-compar *than* COMB in ADJ

4 **Deep** in an area means a long way inside it. *Picking up his bag the giant strode off deep into the forest. ...deep inside the country... The first goal originated from a free-kick deep inside Everton's half.* ADV-GRADED: ADV prep/adv, ADV after v

5 In sports such as football and tennis, a **deep** shot is one that sends the ball a long way towards the end of the pitch or court. *...Steve Staunton's deep cross. ...a deep volley.* ADJ-GRADED ≠short

6 If you say that things or people are two, three, or four **deep**, you mean that there are two, three, or four rows or layers of them there. *A crowd three deep seemed paralysed by the images on these monitors... The rest of the space was taken up by cardboard boxes piled right to the ceiling, ten deep.* ADV: num ADV

7 You use **deep** to emphasize the seriousness, strength, importance, or degree of something. *I had a deep admiration for Sartre. ...a period of deep personal crisis... This attitude was in deep contrast with popular feeling in the rest of Italy... He wants to express his deep sympathy to the family.* ADJ-GRADED: usu ADJ n PRAGMATICS =profound ♦ **deeply** *Our meetings and conversations left me deeply depressed... He loved his brother deeply.* ADV-GRADED =profoundly

8 If you experience or feel something **deep** inside you or **deep** down, you feel it very strongly even though you do not necessarily show it. *I kept reassuring them but deep in my heart I knew we had no hope... Deep down, she supported her husband's involvement in the organization.* ADV-GRADED: ADV prep/adv, ADV with cl =inwardly

9 If you are in a **deep** sleep, you are sleeping peacefully and it is difficult to wake you. *Una soon fell into a deep sleep.* ADJ-GRADED: ADJ n ≠light ♦ **deeply** *She slept deeply but woke early.* ADV-GRADED: ADV after v

10 If you are **deep in** thought or **deep in** conversation, you are concentrating very hard on what you are thinking or saying and are not aware of the things that are happening around you. *Abby had been so deep in thought that she had walked past her aunt's car without even seeing it... Before long, we were deep in conversation.* ADJ-GRADED: v-link ADJ *in* n =engrossed

11 A **deep** gaze or look seems to see right into your mind. *Peter gave him a long deep look.* ADJ: ADJ n ► Also an adverb. *He paused, staring deep into Mary's eyes.* ADV-GRADED ♦ **deeply** *That's when he turned to me, looked deeply into my eyes and said, 'Something's happening and we both feel it, don't we?'* ADV-GRADED: ADV after v, ADV prep

12 A **deep** breath or sigh uses or fills the whole of your lungs. *Caz took a long, deep breath, struggling to control his own emotions... At last he gave a deep sigh.* ADJ-GRADED: ADJ n ♦ **deeply** *She sighed deeply and covered her face with her hands.* ADV-GRADED: ADV after v

13 You use **deep** to describe colours that are strong and fairly dark. *The sky was peach-colored in the east, deep blue and starry in the west... The tree has gnarled red branches and deep green leaves.* COMB in COLOUR ≠pale ► Also an adjective. *These Amish cushions in traditional deep colours are available in two sizes.* ADJ-GRADED: usu ADJ n ≠pale

14 A **deep** sound is low in pitch. *His voice was deep and mellow... They heard a deep, distant roar.* ADJ-GRADED ≠high

15 If you describe someone as **deep**, you mean that they are quiet and reserved in a way that makes you think that they have good qualities such as intelligence or determination. *James is a very deep individual... That expressionless face had seemed deep and mysterious.* ADJ-GRADED ≠shallow

16 If you describe something such as a problem or a piece of writing as **deep**, you mean that it is important, serious, or complicated. *This is a very deep question... They're written as adventure stories. They're not intended to be deep.* ADJ-GRADED

17 If you are **deep** in debt, you have a lot of debts. *He is so deep in debt and desperate for money that he's apparently willing to say anything... The company is sliding even deeper into the red.* ADV-GRADED: ADV *in/into* n ♦ **deeply** *Because of her medical and her legal bills, she is now penniless and deeply in debt.* ADV-GRADED: ADV *in/into* n

18 **The deep** means the sea; a literary use. *...a vast unfrequented pool, traversed by whales and creatures of the deep.* N-SING: *the* N

19 If you say that you **took a deep breath** before doing something dangerous or frightening, you mean that you tried to make yourself feel strong and confident. *I took a deep breath and went in.* PHRASES V inflects

20 If you say that something **goes deep** or **runs deep**, you mean that it is very serious or strong and is hard to change. *His anger and anguish clearly went deep... The problems went deeper than mere teething difficulties.* V inflects

21 • **in at the deep end**: see **end.** • **in deep water**: see **water.**

deepen /diːpən/ **deepens, deepening, deepened** ◆◆◇◇◇

1 If a situation or emotion **deepens** or if something **deepens** it, it becomes stronger and more intense. *If this is not stopped, the financial crisis will deepen... If anything, Sloan's uneasiness deepened... My marriage was rough, but it deepened my emotions, it made me think about life.* V-ERG V V n

2 If you **deepen** your knowledge or understanding of a subject, you learn more about it and become more interested in it. *The course is an exciting opportunity for anyone wishing to deepen their understanding of themselves and other people.* VERB =extend V n

3 When light or a colour **deepens** or **is deepened**, it becomes darker; a literary use. *Dusk was deepening as they drove back to the lights of Shillingham...* V-ERG V V n

This spice is used particularly in poultry feed to deepen the colour of egg yolks.

4 When a sound **deepens** or **is deepened**, it becomes lower in tone. *Her voice has deepened and coarsened with the years... The music room had been made to reflect and deepen sounds.* V-ERG V Vn

5 When your breathing **deepens**, or you **deepen** it, you take more air into your lungs when you breathe. *He heard her breathing deepen... When you are ready to finish the exercise, gradually deepen your breathing.* V-ERG V Vn

6 If people **deepen** something, they increase its depth by digging out its lower surface. *A major project has now begun to deepen the main approach channel to a depth of between 12.5m and 13.0m... The tunnels have been widened and deepened.* VERB Vn

7 Something such as a river or a sea **deepens** where the bottom begins to slope downwards. *As we drew nearer to it the water gradually deepened.* VERB V

deep freeze, deep freezes; also spelled **deep-freeze.** A **deep freeze** is the same as a **freezer**. N-COUNT

deep-fry, deep-fries, deep-frying, deep-fried. If you **deep-fry** food, you fry it in a large amount of fat or oil. *Heat the oil and deep fry the fish fillets. ...deep-fried chicken and chips.* VERB Vn V-ed

deep-rooted. **Deep-rooted** means the same as **deep-seated**. *...long-term solutions to a deep-rooted problem. ...the deep-rooted divisions and suspicions between the two superpowers.* ADJ-GRADED: usu ADJ n =deep-seated

deep-sea. **Deep-sea** activities take place in the areas of the sea that are a long way from the coast. *...deep-sea diving. ...a deep-sea fisherman.* ADJ: ADJ n

deep-seated. A **deep-seated** problem, feeling, or belief is difficult to change because its causes have been there for a long time. *The country is still suffering from deep-seated economic problems. ...our morbid and deep-seated fear of death.* ◆◇◇◇◇ ADJ-GRADED: usu ADJ n =deep-rooted, ingrained

deep-set. **Deep-set** eyes have deep sockets; used mainly in written English. *He had black hair and deep-set brown eyes.* ADJ: usu ADJ n

deer /dɪəʳ/; **deer** is both the singular and the plural form. A **deer** is a large wild animal that eats grass and leaves. A male deer usually has large, branching horns. ◆◆◇◇◇ N-COUNT

deface /dɪfeɪs/ **defaces, defacing, defaced.** If someone **defaces** something such as a wall or a notice, they spoil it by writing or drawing things on it. *It's illegal to deface banknotes.* VERB Vn

de facto /deɪ fæktoʊ/. **De facto** is used to indicate that something is a particular thing, although it was not specifically planned or intended to be that thing; a formal expression. *This might be interpreted as a de facto recognition of the republic's independence.* ► Also an adverb. *German unity has now de facto replaced the signing of such a treaty.* ◆◇◇◇◇ ADJ: ADJ n ≠de jure ADV: ADV with cl

defamation /defəmeɪʃᵊn/. **Defamation** is the damaging of someone's good reputation by saying something bad and untrue about them; a formal word. *He was considering suing for defamation.* N-UNCOUNT =slander

defamatory /dɪfæmətri, AM -tɔːri/. Speech or writing that is **defamatory** is likely to damage someone's good reputation by saying something bad and untrue about them; a formal word. *The article was highly defamatory.* ADJ-GRADED =slanderous

defame /dɪfeɪm/ **defames, defaming, defamed.** If you **defame** someone or something, you say something bad and untrue about them; a formal word. *Sgt Norwood complained that the article defamed him.* VERB Vn

default /dɪfɔːlt/ **defaults, defaulting, defaulted.** Pronounced /diːfɔːlt/ for meaning 2. ◆◆◇◇◇

1 If a person, company, or country **defaults on** something that they have legally agreed to do, such as paying some money or doing a piece of work before a particular time, they fail to do it; a legal term. *The credit card business is down, and more borrowers are defaulting on loans... The first warning signals came in March when the company defaulted on its initial payment of £40 million.* ► Also a noun. *The corporation may be charged with default on its contract with the government... The creditors haven't declared them in default.* VERB V on n N-UNCOUNT: oft N prep, in N

2 A **default** situation is what exists or happens unless someone or something changes it. *Sometimes he simply keyed in default passwords installed on commercial machines and left unaltered by buyers... Death, not life, is the default state of cells.* ADJ: ADJ n

3 If something happens **by default**, it happens only because something else which might have prevented it or changed it has not happened; a formal expression. *Spassky won the first game, and was awarded by the second by default, when Fischer failed to put in an appearance... I would rather pay the individuals than let the money go to the State by default.* PHRASES PHR after v, PHR with cl

4 If something happens **in default of** something else, it happens because that other thing does not happen or proves to be impossible; a formal expression. *Mr Horsforth, having demonstrated his authority over his dog, in default of being able to do it over Mary, smiled thinly... Malvolio becomes, in default of competition, the play's moral centre.* PREP: PREP n/-ing

defaulter /dɪfɔːltəʳ/ **defaulters.** A **defaulter** is someone who does not do something that they are legally supposed to do, such as make a payment at a particular time, or appear in a court of law. N-COUNT

defeat /dɪfiːt/ **defeats, defeating, defeated** ◆◆◆◆◇

1 If you **defeat** someone, you win a victory over them in a battle, game, or contest. *His guerrillas defeated the colonial army in 1954... The NHL Stanley Cup was won by the Montreal Canadiens, who defeated the Boston Bruins four games to one.* VERB =beat ≠lose to Vn

2 If a proposal or motion in a debate **is defeated**, more people vote against it than for it. *In 1972 a proposal to knock down the 18th-century cloth market was defeated by just one vote.* VB: usu passive =beat be V-ed

3 If a task or a problem **defeats** you, it is so difficult that you cannot do it or solve it. *There were times when the structural challenges of constructing such a huge novel almost defeated her.* VERB Vn

4 To **defeat** an action or plan means to cause it to fail. *The navy played a limited but significant role in defeating the rebellion... He swore to defeat Odin's plan.* VERB =thwart Vn

5 **Defeat** is the experience of being beaten in a battle, game, or contest, or of failing to achieve what you wanted to. *The most important thing is not to admit defeat until you really have to... The vote is seen as something of a defeat for the anti-abortion lobby... A 2-1 defeat by Sweden left them bottom of Group One.* N-VAR

defeatism /dɪfiːtɪzəm/. **Defeatism** is a way of thinking or talking which suggests that you expect to be unsuccessful. *...the mood of economic defeatism.* N-UNCOUNT

defeatist /dɪfiːtɪst/ **defeatists.** A **defeatist** is someone who thinks or talks in a way that suggests that they expect to be unsuccessful. ► Also an adjective. *There is no point going out there with a defeatist attitude.* N-COUNT ADJ-GRADED

defecate /defəkeɪt/ **defecates, defecating, defecated.** When people and animals **defecate**, they get rid of waste matter from their body through their anus; a formal word. *Animals defecate after every meal.* ♦ **defecation** /defəkeɪʃᵊn/ *The drug has side-effects including sweating, vomiting and involuntary defecation.* VERB V N-UNCOUNT

defect, defects, defecting, defected. The noun is pronounced /diːfekt/. The verb is pronounced /dɪfekt/. ◆◆◇◇◇

1 A **defect** is a fault or imperfection in a person or thing. *He was born with a hearing defect. ...a defect in the aircraft caused the crash... A report has pointed out the defects of the present system.* N-COUNT: usu with supp =imperfection

2 If you **defect**, you leave your country, political party, or other group, and join an opposing country, party, or group. *He tried to defect to the West last year... He defected from the party in the late 1970s. ...a KGB officer who defected in 1963.* ♦ **defection** /dɪfekʃᵊn/ **defections** *...the defection of at least sixteen Parliamentary deputies.* VERB V to/from n V N-VAR

defective /dɪfektɪv/. If something is **defective**, there is something wrong with it and it does not work properly. *Her sight was becoming defective... Retailers can return defective merchandise.* ◆◇◇◇◇ ADJ-GRADED

defector /dɪfektəʳ/ **defectors.** A **defector** is someone who leaves their country, political party, or other group, and joins an opposing country, party, or group. ◆◇◇◇◇ N-COUNT: usu with supp

defence /dɪfens/ **defences;** spelled **defense** in American English. Pronounced /diːfens/ for meaning 8 in American English. ◆◆◆◆◇

1 Defence is action that is taken to protect someone or something against attack. *The land was flat, giving no scope for defence... By wielding a knife in defence you run the risk of having it used against you.* N-UNCOUNT

2 Defence is the organization of a country's armies and weapons, and their use to protect the country or its interests. *Twenty eight percent of the federal budget is spent on defense. ...the French defence minister. ...a five per cent cut in defence spending.* N-UNCOUNT: oft N n

3 The **defences** of a country or region are all its armed forces and weapons. *He emphasised the need to maintain Britain's defences at a level sufficient to deal with the unexpected.* N-PLURAL

4 A **defence** is something that people or animals can use or do to protect themselves. *Despite anything the science of medicine may have achieved, the immune system is our main defence against disease... The boy could have felt sorry for himself and become depressed, or he could have adopted hardened cynicism as a defense.* N-COUNT: oft N *against* n =protection

5 A **defence** is something that you say or write which supports ideas or actions that have been criticized or questioned. *Chomsky's defence of his approach goes further... Peking yesterday published a 37,000-word defence of its rule of Tibet... 'I've never used my Nigerian name, even before I was Chrystal Rose,' she said in defence.* N-COUNT: oft N *of* n, also *in* N =justification ≠attack

6 In a court of law, an accused person's **defence** is the process of presenting evidence in their favour. *He has insisted on conducting his own defence.* N-COUNT: oft with poss

7 The **defence** is the case that is presented by a lawyer in a trial for the person who has been accused of a crime. You can also refer to this person's lawyers as the **defence**. *The defence was that the records of the interviews were fabricated by the police... The defence pleaded insanity, but the defendant was found guilty and sentenced. ...defence lawyers.* N-SING: usu *the* N

8 In games such as football or hockey, the **defence** is the group of players in a team who try to stop the opposing players scoring a goal or a point. *Their defence, so strong last season, has now conceded 12 goals in six games... I still prefer to play in defence.* N-SING-COLL: oft poss N, also *in* N ≠attack

9 If you come **to** someone's **defence**, you help them by doing or saying something to protect them. *He realized none of his schoolmates would come to his defense... Tony sprang to the defence of the 21-year-old, saying he was not to blame.* PHRASE: PHR after v

defenceless /dɪfensləs/; spelled **defenseless** in American English. If someone or something is **defenceless**, they are weak and unable to defend themselves properly. *...a savage attack on a defenceless young girl. ...the kind of leader who would leave the country isolated and defenceless.* ADJ-GRADED =vulnerable

defence mechanism, defence mechanisms. A **defence mechanism** is a way of behaving or thinking which is not conscious or deliberate and is an automatic reaction to unpleasant experiences or feelings such as anxiety or fear. N-COUNT

defend /dɪfend/ **defends, defending, defended** ◆◆◆◆◇

1 If you **defend** someone or something, you take action in order to protect them. *Every man who could fight was now committed to defend the ridge... His courage in defending religious and civil rights inspired many outside the church... They would have killed him if he had not defended himself... In 1991 he and his friends defended themselves against some white racist thugs who set upon them for no other reason than their skin colour.* VERB V n; V pron-refl; V pron-refl *against* n; Also V n *against* n

2 If you **defend** someone or something when they have been criticized, you argue in support of them. *Clarence's move was unpopular, but Matt had to defend it, like he defended all of Clarence's decisions, right or wrong... The author defends herself against charges of racism by noting that blacks are only one of her targets... Police chiefs strongly defended police conduct against a wave of criticism.* VERB V n; V pron-refl *against* n; V n *against* n; Also V pron-refl

3 When a lawyer **defends** a person who has been accused of something, the lawyer argues on their behalf in a court of law that the charges are not true. *He was a lawyer who defended dissidents in the former Communist state... He has hired a lawyer to defend him against the allegations... Guy Powell, defending, told London's Marlborough Street magistrates: 'It's a sad and disturbing case.'* VERB V n; V n *against* n; V

4 When a sports player plays in the tournament which they won the previous time it was held, you can say that they **are defending** their title or championship. *Torrence expects to defend her title successfully in the next Olympics... India had to struggle to beat defending champions South Korea 2-0.* VERB V n; V-ing

defendant /dɪfendənt/ **defendants.** A **defendant** is a person who has been accused of breaking the law and is being tried in court. ◆◆◇◇◇ N-COUNT

defender /dɪfendəʳ/ **defenders** ◆◆◇◇◇

1 If someone is a **defender** of a particular thing or person that has been criticized or attacked, they argue or act in support of that thing or person. *...the most ardent defenders of conventional family values. ...a strong defender of human rights or religious freedom.* N-COUNT: usu N *of* n

2 A **defender** in a game such as football or hockey is a player whose main task is to try and stop the other side scoring. N-COUNT

defense /dɪfens/. See **defence**.

defensible /dɪfensɪbᵊl/. An opinion, system, or action that is **defensible** is one that people can argue is right or good. *Her reasons for acting are morally defensible.* ADJ-GRADED ≠indefensible

defensive /dɪfensɪv/ ◆◆◇◇◇

1 You use **defensive** to describe things that are intended to protect someone or something. *The Government hastily organized defensive measures, deploying searchlights and anti-aircraft guns around the target cities... The union leaders were pushed into a more defensive position by the return of a Republican Congress in November.* ADJ: usu ADJ n

2 Someone who is **defensive** is behaving in a way that shows they feel unsure or threatened. *Clary is defensive about his pet project... She heard the blustering, defensive note in his voice and knew that he was ashamed.* ADJ-GRADED ♦ **defensively** *'Oh, I know, I know,' said Kate, defensively.* ADV-GRADED ♦ **defensiveness** *It's just our national defensiveness. We're always worried about what people will think of us.* N-UNCOUNT

3 If someone is **on the defensive**, they are trying to protect themselves or their interests because they feel unsure or threatened. *The civil service is on the defensive, scorned by zealots impatient of red tape and regulations... He smiled, not wanting to put the man on the defensive.* PHRASE: usu v-link PHR, PHR after v

4 In sport, **defensive** play is play that is intended to prevent your opponent from scoring goals or points against you. *I'd always played a defensive game, waiting for my opponent to make a mistake.* ADJ-GRADED: usu ADJ n ≠attacking ♦ **defensively** *Mexico did it not by playing defensively. They did it with exciting, flowing, attacking football.* ADV-GRADED: ADV after v

defer /dɪfɜːʳ/ **defers, deferring, deferred** ◆◇◇◇◇

1 If you **defer** an event or action, you arrange for it to happen at a later date, rather than immediately or at the previously planned time. *Customers often defer payment for as long as possible... I'm not going to defer decisions just because they are not immediately politically popular.* VERB =postpone V n/-ing

2 If you **defer to** someone, you accept their opinion or do what they want you to do, even when you do not agree with it yourself, because you respect them or their authority. *Doctors are encouraged to defer to experts.* VERB =yield V *to* n

deference /defrəns/. **Deference** is a polite and respectful attitude towards someone, especially ◆◇◇◇◇ N-UNCOUNT: oft N *to* n because they have an important position. *The old sense of deference and restraint in royal reporting has vanished... Out of deference to him, I lowered my head as he prayed.*

deferential /dɛfərɛnʃəl/. Someone who is **deferential** is polite and respectful towards someone else. *They like five-star hotels and deferential treatment. ...the traditional requirement for Asian women to be submissive and deferential to men.* ADJ-GRADED: oft ADJ *to* n
♦ **deferentially** *The Spaniards stood back deferentially to let the others take their places.* ADV-GRADED: ADV with v

deferment /dɪfɜːʳmənt/ **deferments** N-VAR =postponement
Deferment means arranging for something to happen at a later date; a formal word. *...conflicts over the deferment of national service for lycée students.*

deferral /dɪfɜːrəl/ **deferrals. Deferral** means the same as **deferment**. N-VAR

defiance /dɪfaɪəns/ ◆◆◇◇◇
1 **Defiance** is behaviour or an attitude which shows that you are not willing to obey someone. *...his courageous defiance of the government.* N-UNCOUNT: oft N *of* n
2 If you do something **in defiance of** a person, rule, or law, you do it even though you know that you are not allowed to do it. *Thousands of people have taken to the streets in defiance of the curfew.* PHRASE: PHR n

defiant /dɪfaɪənt/. If you say that someone is **defiant**, you mean they show aggression or independence by refusing to obey someone. *The players are in defiant mood as they prepare for tomorrow's game... Despite the risk of suspension, he remained defiant.* ◆◆◇◇◇ ADJ-GRADED
♦ **defiantly** *They defiantly rejected any talk of a compromise.* ADV-GRADED: usu ADV with v

deficiency /dɪfɪʃənsi/ **deficiencies** ◆◆◇◇◇
1 **Deficiency** in something, especially something that your body needs, is a lack or shortage of it; a formal use. *They did blood tests on him for signs of vitamin deficiency... There are serious deficiencies in the numbers of suitable aircraft.* N-VAR: with supp
2 A **deficiency** that someone or something has is a weakness or imperfection in them; a formal use. *The most serious deficiency in Nato's air defence is the lack of an identification system to distinguish friend from foe.* N-VAR: with supp

deficient /dɪfɪʃənt/ ◆◇◇◇◇
1 If someone or something is **deficient** in a particular thing, they do not have the full amount of it that they need in order to function normally or work properly; a formal use. *...a diet deficient in vitamin B.* ▶ Also a combining form. *Vegetarians too can become iron-deficient.* ADJ: usu v-link ADJ, usu ADJ *in* n =lacking; COMB in ADJ
2 Someone or something that is **deficient** is not good enough for a particular purpose; a formal use. *...deficient landing systems.* ADJ-GRADED =inadequate

deficit /dɛfəsɪt/ **deficits.** A **deficit** is the amount by which something is less than what is required or expected, especially the amount by which the total money received is less than the total money spent. *They're ready to cut the federal budget deficit for the next fiscal year. ...a deficit of 3.275 billion francs.* ◆◆◆◆◇ N-COUNT: oft n N
• If an account or organization is **in deficit**, more money has been spent than has been received. *The current account of the balance of payments is in deficit.* PHRASE: usu v-link PHR

defile /dɪfaɪl/ **defiles, defiling, defiled.**
1 If someone **defiles** something that people think is important or holy, they do something to it or say something about it which is offensive; a literary use. *He had defiled the sacred name of the Holy Prophet.* VERB; V n
2 A **defile** is a very narrow valley or passage, usually through mountains; a formal use. N-COUNT =pass

definable /dɪfaɪnəbəl/. Something that is **definable** can be described or identified. *Fifteen percent of the adult population suffered from a definable alcohol, drug, or mental disorder. ...groups broadly definable as conservative.* ADJ-GRADED

define /dɪfaɪn/ **defines, defining, defined** ◆◆◆◇◇
1 If you **define** something, you show, describe, or state clearly what it is and what its limits are, or what it is like. *The Supreme Court decision could define how far Congress can go in trying to determine the outcome of court cases... I tried to define my own attitude: I found Rosie repulsive, but I didn't hate her.* VERB; V wh; V n
♦ **defined** *...a party with a clearly defined programme and strict rules of membership.* ADJ-GRADED: usu adv ADJ =delineated
2 If you **define** a word or expression, you explain its meaning, for example in a dictionary. *When people are asked 'What is intelligence?' they tend to reply: 'I don't know how to define it, but I can certainly recognize it when I see it.'... Collins English Dictionary defines a workaholic as 'a person obsessively addicted to work'.* VERB; V n; V n *as* n

defined /dɪfaɪnd/. If something is clearly **defined** or strongly **defined**, its outline is clear or strong. *A clearly defined track now leads down to the valley... Here the path is less defined... She had a strongly defined chin, a high forehead, and light grey eyes.* ◆◇◇◇◇ ADJ-GRADED: usu adv ADJ

definite /dɛfɪnɪt/ ◆◆◇◇◇
1 If something such as a decision or an arrangement is **definite**, it is firm and clear, and unlikely to be changed. *It's too soon to give a definite answer... Her Royal Highness has definite views about most things... She made no definite plans for her future.* ADJ-GRADED
2 **Definite** evidence or information is true, rather than being someone's opinion or guess. *We didn't have any definite proof... If you have any definite news of my husband, please let me know... The police had nothing definite against her.* ADJ: usu ADJ n
3 You use **definite** to emphasize the strength of your opinion or belief. *There has already been a definite improvement... That's a very definite possibility.* ADJ-GRADED: ADJ n PRAGMATICS =real
4 Someone who is **definite** behaves or talks in a firm, confident way. *Mary is very definite about this.* ADJ-GRADED
5 A **definite** shape or colour is clear and noticeable. *Studying his face in the bathroom mirror he wished he had more definite features.* ADJ-GRADED: usu ADJ n

definite article, definite articles. The word 'the' is sometimes called the **definite article**; a technical term in linguistics. N-COUNT: usu *the* N

definitely /dɛfɪnɪtli/ ◆◆◆◇◇
1 You use **definitely** to emphasize that something is the case, or to emphasize the strength of your intention or opinion. *I'm definitely going to get in touch with these people... Something should definitely be done about that... 'I think the earlier ones are a lot better.'—'Mm, definitely.'* ADV-GRADED: ADV before v, ADV with cl/group PRAGMATICS
2 If something has been **definitely** decided, the decision will not be changed. *He told them that no venue had yet been definitely decided.* ADV: ADV before v

definition /dɛfɪnɪʃən/ **definitions** ◆◆◆◇◇
1 A **definition** is a statement giving the meaning of a word or expression, especially in a dictionary. *There is no general agreement on a standard definition of intelligence... My definition of a good hospice is one where some of the patients start feeling too good to die.* N-COUNT: oft N *of* n
• If you say that something has a particular quality **by definition**, you mean that it has this quality simply because of what it is. *Human perception is highly imperfect and by definition subjective.* PHRASE: PHR with cl PRAGMATICS =per se
2 **Definition** is the quality of being clear and distinct. *Give your brows extra definition with Outdoor Girl's Eyebrow Pencil in Brown... The first speakers at the conference criticised his new programme for lack of definition.* N-UNCOUNT

definitive /dɪfɪnɪtɪv/ ◆◆◇◇◇
1 Something that is **definitive** provides a firm conclusion that cannot be questioned. *No one has come up with a definitive answer as to why this should be so... There is no definitive test as yet for the condition.* ADJ-GRADED: usu ADJ n
♦ **definitively** *The Constitution did not definitively rule out divorce.* ADV
2 A **definitive** book or performance is thought to be the best of its kind that has ever been done or that will ever be done. *His 'An Orkney Tapestry' is still the definitive book on the islands.* ADJ-GRADED: usu ADJ n

deflate /dɪfleɪt/ **deflates, deflating, deflated** ◆◇◇◇◇
1 If you **deflate** someone or something, you take away their confidence or make them seem less important. *Like any actor he can be self-centred but I* VERB; V n

think I've worked out how to deflate him... Britain's other hopes of medals were deflated earlier in the day. ♦ **deflated** *When she refused I felt deflated.* ADJ-GRADED

2 When something such as a tyre or balloon **deflates**, or when you **deflate** it, all the air comes out of it. *When it returns to shore, the life-jacket will deflate and revert to a harness. ...a deflated dinghy.* V-ERG ≠inflate V V-ed Also V n

deflation /diːfleɪʃᵊn, dɪf-/. **Deflation** is a reduction in economic activity that leads to lower levels of industrial output, employment, investment, trade, profits, and prices. *Deflation is beginning to take hold in the clothing industry.* N-UNCOUNT ≠inflation

deflationary /diːfleɪʃənri, AM -neri/. A **deflationary** economic policy or measure is one that is intended to or likely to cause deflation. *...the government's refusal to implement deflationary measures.* ADJ: usu ADJ n

deflect /dɪflekt/ **deflects, deflecting, deflected** ◆◇◇◇◇

1 If you **deflect** something such as criticism or attention, you act in a way that prevents it from being directed towards you or affecting you. *Cage changed his name to deflect accusations of nepotism... I think maybe it's a maneuver just to deflect the attention of the people from what is really happening.* VERB V n V n *from* n

2 If something or someone **deflects** you from a course of action you have started or decided on, they make you decide not to do it or continue with it by putting pressure on you or by offering you something desirable. *The war did not deflect him from the path he had long ago taken... Never let a little problem deflect you.* VERB =sidetrack V n *from* n/-ing V n

3 If you **deflect** something that is moving, you make it go in a slightly different direction, for example by hitting or blocking it. *He stuck out his boot and deflected the shot over the bar seconds before the final whistle... My forearm deflected most of the first punch.* VERB V n prep V n

deflection /dɪflekʃᵊn/ **deflections**

1 The **deflection** of something means making it change direction; a technical use. *...the deflection of light as it passes through the regularly spaced slits in the grating.* N-VAR

2 In sport, you talk about the **deflection** of a ball, kick, or shot when the ball hits an object and starts moving in a different direction. N-COUNT

deflower /diːflaʊəʳ/ **deflowers, deflowering, deflowered.** When a woman **is deflowered**, she has sexual intercourse with a man for the first time; a literary word. *Nora was deflowered by a man who worked in a soda-water factory.* VERB *be* V-ed Also V n

defoliant /diːfoʊliənt/ **defoliants.** A **defoliant** is a chemical used on trees and plants which makes all their leaves fall off. Defoliants are especially used in warfare to remove protection from an enemy. N-MASS

defoliate /diːfoʊlieɪt/ **defoliates, defoliating, defoliated.** To **defoliate** an area or the plants in it means to cause the leaves on the plants to fall off or be destroyed, especially in warfare. *Dioxin was the ingredient in Agent Orange, used to defoliate Vietnam.* ♦ **defoliation** /diːfoʊlieɪʃᵊn/ *...preventing defoliation of trees by caterpillars.* VERB V n N-UNCOUNT

deforest /diːfɒrɪst, AM -fɔːr-/ **deforests, deforesting, deforested.** If an area **is deforested**, all the trees there are cut down or destroyed. *...the 400,000 square kilometres of the Amazon basin that have already been deforested.* ◆◇◇◇◇ VB: usu passive *be* V-ed

♦ **deforestation** /diːfɒrɪsteɪʃᵊn, AM -fɔːr-/ *One percent of Brazil's total forest cover is being lost every year to deforestation.* N-UNCOUNT

deform /dɪfɔːʳm/ **deforms, deforming, deformed.** If something **deforms** a person's body or something else, it causes it to have an unnatural shape. In technical English, you can also say that the second thing **deforms**. *Bad rheumatoid arthritis deforms limbs... What makes any metal useful is its ability to deform to a new shape without cracking.* ♦ **deformed** *He was born with a deformed right leg.* ♦ **deformation** /diːfɔːʳmeɪʃᵊn/ *...deformations Changing stresses bring about more cracking and rock deformation.* ◆◇◇◇◇ V-ERG V n V ADJ-GRADED =malformed N-VAR

deformity /dɪfɔːʳmɪti/ **deformities**

1 A **deformity** is a part of someone's body which is not the normal shape because of injury or illness, or because they were born this way. *...facial deformities in babies.* N-COUNT

2 **Deformity** is the condition of having a deformity. *The bones begin to grind against each other, leading to pain and deformity.* N-UNCOUNT

defraud /dɪfrɔːd/ **defrauds, defrauding, defrauded.** If someone **defrauds** you, they take something away from you or stop you from getting something that belongs to you by means of tricks and lies. *He pleaded guilty to charges of conspiracy to defraud the government... They conspired to defraud the federal government of millions of dollars in income taxes.* ◆◇◇◇◇ VERB V n V n *of/out of* n

defray /dɪfreɪ/ **defrays, defraying, defrayed.** If you **defray** someone's costs or expenses, you give them money which represents the amount that they have spent, for example while they have been doing something for you or acting on your behalf; a formal word. *The government has committed billions toward defraying the costs of the war.* VERB =repay V n

defrost /diːfrɒst, AM -frɔːst/ **defrosts, defrosting, defrosted**

1 When you **defrost** frozen food or when it **defrosts**, you allow or cause it to become unfrozen so that you can eat it or cook it. *She has a microwave, but uses it mainly for defrosting bread... Once the turkey has defrosted, remove the giblets.* V-ERG ≠freeze V n V

2 When you **defrost** a fridge or freezer, you switch it off or press a special switch so that the ice inside it can melt. You can also say that a fridge or freezer **is defrosting**. *Defrost the fridge regularly so that it works at maximum efficiency.* V-ERG V n Also V

deft /deft/ **defter, deftest.** A **deft** action is skilful and often quick; used in written English. *With a deft flick of his foot, Mr Worth tripped one of the raiders up.* ♦ **deftly** *One of the waiting servants deftly caught him as he fell.* ♦ **deftness** *...Dr Holly's surgical deftness and experience.* ◆◇◇◇◇ ADJ-GRADED ADV-GRADED N-UNCOUNT

defunct /dɪfʌŋkt/. If something is **defunct**, it no longer exists or has stopped functioning or operating. *...the leader of the now defunct Social Democratic Party... They bought all their equipment from a defunct brewery in Manhattan.* ◆◇◇◇◇ ADJ

defuse /diːfjuːz/ **defuses, defusing, defused** ◆◇◇◇◇

1 If you **defuse** a dangerous or tense situation, you calm it. *Police administrators credited the organization with helping defuse potentially violent situations... Officials will hold four days of talks aimed at defusing tensions over trade.* VERB V n

2 If someone **defuses** a bomb, they remove the fuse from it so that it cannot explode. *Police have defused a bomb found in a building in London.* VERB V n

defy /dɪfaɪ/ **defies, defying, defied** ◆◆◇◇◇

1 If you **defy** someone or something that is trying to make you behave in a particular way, you refuse to obey them and behave in that way. *This was the first (and last) time that I dared to defy my mother... Nearly eleven-thousand people have been arrested for defying the ban on street trading.* VERB V n

2 If you **defy** someone to do something, you challenge them to do it when you think that they will be unable to do it or too frightened to do it. *I defy you to come up with one major accomplishment of the current Prime Minister... He looked at me as if he was defying me to argue.* VERB =dare V n to-inf

3 If something **defies** description or understanding, it is so strange, extreme, or surprising that it is almost impossible to understand or explain. *When the flowers open in spring they fill the night air with a fragrance that defies description... It's a devastating and barbaric act that defies all comprehension.* VB: no passive, no cont V n

4 If you say that someone **defies their age**, or **defies the years**, you mean that their appearance or behaviour suggests that they are younger than they really are. *The singer continues to defy her age by wearing the scantiest of outfits.* PHRASE: V inflects

degeneracy /dɪdʒenərəsi/. If you refer to the behaviour of a group of people as **degeneracy**, you mean that you think it is shocking, immoral, or disgusting. *...the moral degeneracy of society.* N-UNCOUNT =depravity

degenerate, degenerates, degenerating, degenerated. The verb is pronounced /dɪdʒenəreɪt/. The adjective and noun are pronounced /dɪdʒenərət/. ◆◇◇◇◇

1 If you say that someone or something **degenerates**, you mean that they become worse in some way, for example weaker, lower in quality, or more dangerous. *Inactivity can make your joints stiff, and the bones may begin to degenerate... From then on the whole tone of the campaign began to degenerate. ...a very serious humanitarian crisis which could degenerate into a catastrophe.* VERB =deteriorate V V into n

♦ **degeneration** /dɪdʒenəreɪʃən/ *...various forms of physical and mental degeneration. ...the degeneration of our political system.* N-UNCOUNT

2 You describe a person or their behaviour as **degenerate** when you disapprove of them because you think they have low standards of behaviour or morality. *...a group of degenerate computer hackers. ...the degenerate attitudes he found among some of his fellow officers.* ADJ-GRADED PRAGMATICS =dissolute

3 You refer to someone as a **degenerate** when you disapprove of them because you think they have low standards of behaviour or morality. N-COUNT PRAGMATICS

degenerative /dɪdʒenərətɪv/. A **degenerative** disease or condition is one that gets worse as time progresses. *...degenerative diseases of the brain, like Alzheimer's.* ADJ: usu ADJ n

degradation /degrədeɪʃən/ **degradations** ◆◇◇◇◇

1 You use **degradation** to refer to a situation, condition, or experience which you consider humiliating and disgusting, especially one which involves poverty, dirtiness, or immorality. *They were sickened by the scenes of misery and degradation they found. ...she described the degradations she had been forced to suffer.* N-VAR

2 Degradation is the action or process of something becoming worse or weaker, or being made worse or weaker. *As in the past, to the degradation of democracy, the debate again turned into a screaming match.* N-UNCOUNT: with supp

3 The **degradation** of land or of the environment is the process of its becoming damaged and poorer, for example because of the effects of pollution, industry, and modern agricultural methods. *There are serious problems of land degradation in some arid zones. ...the accelerating degradation of our planet's natural environment.* N-UNCOUNT: usu with supp

4 The **degradation** of a substance is the process of its breaking down into its separate components or elements; a technical term in science. *...the degradation of salicylic acid in plants.* N-UNCOUNT: usu with poss

degrade /dɪgreɪd/ **degrades, degrading, degraded** ◆◇◇◇◇

1 Something that **degrades** someone causes people to have less respect for them. *...the notion that pornography degrades women... When I asked him if he had ever been to a prostitute he said he wouldn't degrade himself like that.* VERB V n V pron-refl ♦ **degrading** *Mr Porter was subjected to a degrading strip-search.* ADJ-GRADED =humiliating

2 To **degrade** something means to cause it to deteriorate; a formal use. *...the ability to meet human needs indefinitely without degrading the environment.* VERB V n

3 If a substance **degrades** or if something **degrades** it, it changes chemically and decays or separates into different substances; a technical use in science. *This substance degrades rapidly in the soil. ...the ability of these enzymes to degrade cellulose.* V-ERG =break down V V n

degree /dɪgriː/ **degrees** ◆◆◆◆◇

1 You use **degree** to indicate the extent to which something happens or is the case, or the amount which something is felt. *These man-made barriers will ensure a very high degree of protection for several hundred years... Recent presidents have used television, as well as radio, with varying degrees of success.* ● If something has **a degree of** a particular quality, it has a small but significant amount of that quality. *Their wages do, however, allow them a degree of independence... A degree of cautious optimism is justified.* N-COUNT: with supp, usu N of n PRAGMATICS PHRASE: PHR n PRAGMATICS =a measure of

2 You use **degree** in expressions such as **a matter of degree** and **different in degree** to indicate that you are talking about the comparative quantity, scale, or extent of something, rather than other factors. *The first change is a matter of degree, the second is a fundamental shift... Generally, the programs of the president and the proposals of the governor appear to differ in degree and emphasis rather than ideology.* N-UNCOUNT: of/in N PRAGMATICS

3 A **degree** is a unit of measurement that is used to measure temperatures. It is often written as '°', for example 23°. *It's over 80 degrees outside... Pure water sometimes does not freeze until it reaches minus 40 degrees Celsius.* N-COUNT: usu num N

4 A **degree** is a unit of measurement that is used to measure angles, and also longitude and latitude. It is often written as '°', for example 23°. *It was pointing outward at an angle of 45 degrees. ...McMurdo Station in Antarctica, which is at 78 degrees South.* N-COUNT: usu num N

5 A **degree** at a university or college is a course of study that you take there, or the qualification that you get when you have passed the course. *It was two years later that he returned to take a master's degree in economics at Yale. ...an engineering degree. ...the first year of a degree course.* N-COUNT: usu with supp

6 See also **third-degree**.

7 If something happens **by degrees**, it happens slowly and gradually. *The crowd in Robinson's Coffee-House was thinning, but only by degrees.* PHRASES =gradually

8 You use expressions such as **to some degree, to a large degree**, or **to a certain degree** in order to indicate that something is partly true, but not entirely true. *These statements are, to some degree, all correct.* PHR with cl PRAGMATICS =to some extent

9 You use expressions such as **to what degree** and **to the degree that** when you are discussing how true a statement is, or in what ways it is true. *To what degree would you say you had control over things that went on?... He believes in himself to such a degree that he abuses his friends.* PRAGMATICS =to what extent, to the extent that

10 ● **to the nth degree**: see **nth**.

dehumanize /diːhjuːmənaɪz/ **dehumanizes, dehumanizing, dehumanized;** also spelled **dehumanise** in British English. If you say that something **dehumanizes** people, you mean it takes away from them good human qualities such as kindness and individuality. *The years of civil war have dehumanized all of us.* VERB =brutalize V n ♦ **dehumanizing** *...the brutal, dehumanising experience of slavery.* ADJ-GRADED ♦ **dehumanization** /diːhjuːmənaɪzeɪʃən/ *She was horrified at the dehumanisation involved in much of the imagery.* N-UNCOUNT

dehydrate /diːhaɪdreɪt, -haɪdreɪt/ **dehydrates, dehydrating, dehydrated** ◆◇◇◇◇

1 When something such as food **is dehydrated**, all the water is removed from it, often in order to preserve it. *Normally specimens have to be dehydrated.* VB: usu passive be V-ed ♦ **dehydrated** *Dehydrated meals, soups and sauces contain a lot of salt.* ADJ

2 If you **dehydrate** or if something **dehydrates** you, you lose too much water from your body so that you feel weak or ill. *People can dehydrate in weather like this... Alcohol quickly dehydrates your body.* V-ERG V V n ♦ **dehydrated** *Drink lots of water to avoid becoming dehydrated.* ADJ-GRADED ♦ **dehydration** /diːhaɪdreɪʃən/ *...a child who's got diarrhoea and is suffering from dehydration.* N-UNCOUNT

deification /deɪɪfɪkeɪʃən, AM diː-/. If you talk about the **deification** of someone or something, you mean that they are regarded with very great respect and are not criticized at all; a formal word. *...the deification of science in the 1940s.* N-UNCOUNT: usu with supp

deify /deɪɪfaɪ, AM diː-/ **deifies, deifying, deified.** If someone **is deified**, they are considered to be a god or are regarded with very great respect; a formal word. *Odin was deified after his death.* VB: usu passive be V-ed

deign /deɪn/ **deigns, deigning, deigned.** If you say that someone **deigned** to do something, you are expressing your disapproval of the fact that they did it reluctantly, because they thought they were too important to do it; a formal word. *At last, Harper deigned to speak... Weatherby didn't deign to reply.* VERB PRAGMATICS V to-inf

deity /deɪɪti, AM diː-/ **deities.** A **deity** is a god or goddess; a formal word. ◆◇◇◇◇ N-COUNT: usu with supp

déjà vu /deɪʒɑː vuː/. **Déjà vu** is the feeling that you have already experienced the things that are happening to you now. *The sense of déjà vu was overwhelming.* N-UNCOUNT

dejected /dɪdʒektɪd/. If you are **dejected**, you feel miserable or unhappy, especially because you have just been disappointed by something. *Everyone has days when they feel dejected or down.* ♦ **dejectedly** *Passengers queued dejectedly for the increasingly dirty toilets.* ADJ-GRADED =despondent ADV-GRADED: ADV with v

dejection /dɪdʒekʃən/. **Dejection** is a feeling of sadness that you get, for example, when you have just been disappointed by something. *There was a slight air of dejection about her.* N-UNCOUNT =despondency

de jure /deɪ dʒʊəreɪ, AM diː dʒʊri/. **De jure** is used to indicate that something legally exists or is a particular thing; a legal term. *...politicians and kings, de jure leaders of men.* ► Also an adverb. *Finland had recognised Soviet annexation de facto, but not de jure.* ADJ: ADJ n ≠de facto ADV: ADV with cl ≠de facto

delay /dɪleɪ/ **delays, delaying, delayed** ◆◆◆◆◇

1 If you **delay** doing something, you do not do it immediately or at the planned or expected time, but you leave it until later. *For sentimental reasons I wanted to delay my departure until June 1980... They had delayed having children, for the usual reason, to establish their careers... So don't delay, write in now for your chance of a free gift.* VERB =postpone ≠bring forward V n/-ing V

2 To **delay** someone or something means to make them late or to slow them down. *Can you delay him in some way?... Various set-backs and problems delayed production... The passengers were delayed for an hour.* VERB =hold up V n

3 If you **delay**, you deliberately take longer than necessary to do something. *If he delayed any longer, the sun would be up.* VERB =hang on V

4 If there is a **delay**, something does not happen until later than planned or expected. *They claimed that such a delay wouldn't hurt anyone... Although the tests have caused some delay, flights should be back to normal this morning.* N-VAR =hold-up

5 **Delay** is a failure to do something immediately or in the required or usual time. *There is no time left for delay... We'll send you a quote without delay.* N-UNCOUNT

delectable /dɪlektəbəl/

1 If you describe something, especially food or drink, as **delectable**, you mean that it is very pleasant. *...delectable wine.* ADJ-GRADED =delightful

2 If you describe someone as **delectable**, you think that they are very attractive; a literary use. *He didn't seem to notice the delectable Miss Campbell.* ADJ-GRADED: usu ADJ n

delectation /diːlekteɪʃən/. If you do something **for** someone**'s delectation**, you do it to give them enjoyment or pleasure; a formal expression. *She rushes about cooking pasties and scones for the delectation of visitors.* PHRASE: PHR with poss

delegate, delegates, delegating, delegated. ◆◆◆◇◇ The noun is pronounced /delɪgət/. The verb is pronounced /delɪgeɪt/.

1 A **delegate** is a person who is chosen to vote or make decisions on behalf of a group of other people, especially at a conference or a meeting. N-COUNT =representative

2 If you **delegate** duties, responsibilities, or power to someone, you give them those duties, those responsibilities, or that power so that they can act on your behalf. *He talks of travelling less, and delegating more authority to his deputies in Britain and Australia... How many of their activities can be safely and effectively delegated to less trained staff?... Many employers find it hard to delegate.* ♦ **delegation** *A key factor in running a business is the delegation of responsibility.* VERB V n to n V Also V n N-UNCOUNT: usu with supp

3 If you **are delegated** to do something, you are given the duty of acting on someone else's behalf by making decisions, voting, or doing some particular work. *Officials have now been delegated to start work on a draft settlement.* VB: usu passive =appoint be V-ed to-inf

delegation /delɪgeɪʃən/ **delegations.** A **delegation** is a group of people who have been sent somewhere to have talks with other people on behalf of a larger group of people. *...a delegation from Somaliland. ...the first Soviet trade delegation to visit South Africa for more than thirty years.* • See also **delegate.** ◆◆◆◇◇ N-COUNT

delete /dɪliːt/ **deletes, deleting, deleted.** If you **delete** something that has been written down or stored in a computer, you cross it out or remove it. *He also deleted files from the computer system... The word 'exploded' had been deleted.* ♦ **deletion** /dɪliːʃən/ **deletions** *This involved the deletion of a great deal of irrelevant material... David wanted to make several deletions and additions to the text.* ◆◇◇◇◇ VERB =erase V n N-VAR

deleterious /delɪtɪəriəs/. Something that has a **deleterious** effect on something has a harmful effect on it; a formal word. *The fear of crime is having a deleterious effect on community life.* ADJ-GRADED =destructive, detrimental

deliberate, deliberates, deliberating, deliberated. The adjective is pronounced /dɪlɪbərət/. The verb is pronounced /dɪlɪbəreɪt/. ◆◆◆◇◇

1 If you do something that is **deliberate**, you planned or decided to do it beforehand, and so it happens intentionally rather than by chance. *It has a deliberate policy to introduce world art to Britain... Witnesses say the firing was deliberate and sustained.* ♦ **deliberately** *It looks as if the blaze was started deliberately... Mr Christopher's answer was deliberately vague.* ADJ-GRADED =intentional ADV-GRADED: ADV with v, ADV adj

2 If a movement or action is **deliberate**, it is done slowly and carefully. *His movements were gentle and deliberate. ...stepping with deliberate slowness up the steep paths.* ♦ **deliberately** *The Japanese have acted calmly and deliberately.* ADJ-GRADED =measured ADV-GRADED: ADV after v

3 If you **deliberate**, you think about something carefully, especially before making a very important decision. *She deliberated over the decision for a good few years before she finally made up her mind... The six-person jury deliberated about two hours before returning with the verdict... The Court of Criminal Appeals has been deliberating his case for almost two weeks.* VERB =ponder V prep V V n

deliberation /dɪlɪbəreɪʃən/ **deliberations** ◆◇◇◇◇

1 **Deliberation** is careful and often lengthy consideration of a subject. *In this house nothing is there by chance: it is always the result of great deliberation... After five minutes of deliberation, he was found guilty of murdering the president.* N-UNCOUNT

2 **Deliberations** are formal discussions where an issue is considered carefully. *...the outcome of the deliberations... Their deliberations were rather inconclusive.* N-PLURAL =debate

3 If you say or do something with **deliberation**, you do it slowly and carefully. *Fred spoke with deliberation... My mother folded her coat across the back of the chair with careful deliberation.* N-UNCOUNT: usu *with* N

delicacy /delɪkəsi/ **delicacies** ◆◇◇◇◇

1 **Delicacy** is the quality of being fragile, in an attractive or graceful way. *...the delicacy of a rose. ...a country where the feminine ideal is delicacy, slimness and grace.* N-UNCOUNT

2 If you say that a situation or problem is of some **delicacy**, you mean that it is difficult to handle and needs careful and tactful treatment. *There was a matter of some delicacy on which he would be grateful for her advice... He sensed the delicacy of the situation.* N-UNCOUNT: usu with supp

3 If someone handles a difficult situation with **delicacy**, they handle it very carefully, making sure that nobody is offended. *Both countries are behaving with rare delicacy... He's shown considerable delicacy and tact in feeling the public mood.* N-UNCOUNT: oft *with* N =sensitivity, tact

4 A **delicacy** is a rare or expensive food that is considered especially nice to eat. *Yak meat is quite a delicacy for Tibetans... We were served course after course of mouthwatering local delicacies.* N-COUNT

delicate /delɪkət/ ◆◆◇◇◇
1 Something that is **delicate** is small and beautifully shaped. *He had delicate hands. ...an evergreen tree with large flame-coloured leaves and delicate blossom.* ♦ **delicately** *She was a shy, delicately pretty girl with enormous blue eyes.*
ADJ-GRADED: usu ADJ n =dainty; ADV-GRADED: ADV adj/-ed =daintily
2 Something that is **delicate** has a colour, taste, or smell which is pleasant and not strong or intense. *Young haricot beans have a tender texture and a delicate, subtle flavour... The colours are delicate and shimmering.* ♦ **delicately** *...a soup delicately flavoured with nutmeg.*
ADJ-GRADED =subtle ≠strong; ADV-GRADED: ADV -ed/adj
3 If something is **delicate**, it is easy to harm, damage, or break, and needs to be handled or treated carefully. *Although the coral looks hard, it is very delicate. ...a washing machine catering for every fabric - even the most delicate.*
ADJ-GRADED =fragile ≠robust
4 Someone who is **delicate** is not healthy and strong, and becomes ill easily. *She was physically delicate and psychologically unstable.*
ADJ-GRADED: usu v-link ADJ =frail, sickly
5 You use **delicate** to describe a situation, problem, matter, or discussion that needs to be dealt with carefully and tactfully in order to avoid upsetting things or offending people. *The European members are afraid of upsetting the delicate balance of political interests... This sensitive book tackles the delicate issue of adoption with care and simplicity... She turned to Mary Ann. 'This is kind of delicate. Would you excuse us for a moment?'* ♦ **delicately** *The president has tried to reject the Soviet proposal as delicately as possible. ...his delicately worded assessment of the course.*
ADJ-GRADED; ADV-GRADED: ADV with v
6 A **delicate** task, movement, action, or product needs or shows great skill and attention to detail. *...a long and delicate operation carried out at a hospital in Florence... Each motion must be delicate and precise, involving tiny movements.* ♦ **delicately** *She picked her way delicately over the rocks. ...the delicately embroidered sheets.*
ADJ-GRADED; ADV-GRADED: ADV with v

delicatessen /delɪkətesᵊn/ **delicatessens.** A **delicatessen** is a shop that sells high quality foods such as cheeses and cold meats that have been imported from other countries.
N-COUNT

delicious /dɪlɪʃəs/ ◆◆◇◇◇
1 Food that is **delicious** has a very pleasant taste. *There's always a wide selection of delicious meals to choose from... Pecan nuts are delicious both raw and cooked.* ♦ **deliciously** *This yoghurt has a deliciously creamy flavour.*
ADJ-GRADED =tasty; ADV: ADV adj/-ed
2 If you describe something as **delicious**, you mean that it is very pleasant. *There is a delicious irony in all this. ...that delicious feeling of surprise.* ♦ **deliciously** *It leaves your hair smelling deliciously fresh and fragrant.*
ADJ-GRADED: usu ADJ n; ADV: ADV adj/-ed

delight /dɪlaɪt/ **delights, delighting, delighted** ◆◆◆◇◇
1 **Delight** is a feeling of very great pleasure. *Throughout the house, the views are a constant source of surprise and delight... Andrew roared with delight when he heard Rachel's nickname for the baby... To my great delight, it worked perfectly.*
N-UNCOUNT
2 If someone **takes delight** or **takes a delight** in something, they get a lot of pleasure from it. *Haig took obvious delight in proving his critics wrong... I enjoy seeing your parents take such a delight in the boys.*
PHRASE: V inflects, usu PHR *in* -ing/n
3 You can refer to someone or something that gives you great pleasure or enjoyment as a **delight**. *Isn't she a delight?... The aircraft was a delight to fly... Sampling the local cuisine is one of the delights of a holiday abroad.*
N-COUNT: oft N *of* n/-ing, N to-inf PRAGMATICS =joy
4 If something **delights** you, it gives you a lot of pleasure. *She has created a style of music that has delighted audiences all over the world... The report has delighted environmentalists.*
VERB ≠disappoint V n
5 If you **delight** in something, you get a lot of pleasure from it. *Generations of adults and children have delighted in the story... He delighted in sharing his love of birds with children.*
VERB V *in* n/-ing

delighted /dɪlaɪtɪd/ ◆◆◆◇◇
1 If you are **delighted**, you are extremely pleased and excited about something. *I know Frank will be delighted to see you... He said that he was delighted with the public response.* ♦ **delightedly** *'There!' Jackson exclaimed delightedly.*
ADJ-GRADED: usu v-link ADJ, oft ADJ to-inf, ADJ *with* n =thrilled; ADV: ADV with v
2 If someone invites or asks you to do something, you can say that you would be **delighted** to do it, as a way of showing that you are very willing to do it. *'You must come to Tinsley's graduation party.'—'I'd be delighted.'*
ADJ: v-link ADJ, oft ADJ to-inf PRAGMATICS

delightful /dɪlaɪtfʊl/. If you describe something or someone as **delightful**, you mean they are very pleasant. *It was the most delightful garden I had ever seen... She remembered Lucy as beautiful, charming and absolutely delightful.* ♦ **delightfully** *This delightfully refreshing cologne can be splashed on liberally. ...fine cheese and delightfully packaged foie gras.*
◆◆◇◇◇ ADJ-GRADED =agreeable; ADV-GRADED: ADV adj/-ed

delimit /dɪlɪmɪt/ **delimits, delimiting, delimited.** If you **delimit** something, you fix or establish its limits; a formal word. *This is not meant to delimit what approaches social researchers can adopt.*
VERB =determine V n

delineate /dɪlɪnieɪt/ **delineates, delineating, delineated**
1 If you **delineate** something such as an idea or situation, you describe it or define it, often in a lot of detail; a formal use. *Biography must to some extent delineate characters... The relationship between Church and State was delineated in a formal agreement.* ♦ **delineation** /dɪlɪnieɪʃᵊn/ *...his razor-sharp delineation of ordinary life.*
VERB V n; N-UNCOUNT
2 If you **delineate** a border, you say exactly where it is going to be; a formal use. *We needed a peace settlement in order to determine and delineate the border.* ♦ **delineation** *...differences in the delineation of the provincial borders.*
VERB V n; N-UNCOUNT

delinquency /dɪlɪŋkwənsi/ **delinquencies**
1 **Delinquency** is criminal behaviour, especially that of young people. *He had no history of delinquency. ...a whole range of crimes and delinquencies.* ● See also **juvenile delinquency**.
N-UNCOUNT: also N in pl
2 In American English, **delinquency** is failure to pay a debt or tax; a technical use in finance. *Not all delinquencies lead to foreclosure. ...increases in mortgage delinquency rates.*
N-UNCOUNT: also N in pl

delinquent /dɪlɪŋkwənt/ **delinquents** ◆◇◇◇◇
1 Someone, usually a young person, who is **delinquent** repeatedly commits minor crimes. *...remand homes for delinquent children.* ▶ Also a noun. *...a nine-year-old delinquent.* ● See also **juvenile delinquent**.
ADJ; N-COUNT
2 In American English, a **delinquent** debtor or taxpayer is someone who has failed to pay their debts or taxes; a technical use in finance. *...a delinquent borrower.*
ADJ: ADJ n

delirious /dɪlɪəriəs/ ◆◇◇◇◇
1 Someone who is **delirious** is unable to think or speak in a rational way, usually because they are very ill and have a fever. *I was delirious and blacked out several times.*
ADJ: usu v-link ADJ
2 Someone who is **delirious** is extremely excited and happy. *His tax-cutting pledge brought a delirious crowd to their feet... I was delirious with joy.* ♦ **deliriously** *Dora returned from her honeymoon deliriously happy... Barking deliriously, the dog bounded towards his mistress.*
ADJ-GRADED: oft ADJ *with* n =ecstatic; ADV: usu ADV adj, also ADV after v

delirium /dɪlɪəriəm/. If someone is suffering from **delirium**, they are not able to think or speak in a rational way because they are very ill and have a fever. *In her delirium, she had fallen to the floor several times.*
N-UNCOUNT

deliver /dɪlɪvəʳ/ **delivers, delivering, delivered** ◆◆◆◆◇
1 If you **deliver** something somewhere, you take it there. *The Canadians plan to deliver more food to southern Somalia... The spy returned to deliver a second batch of classified documents... We were told the pizza would be delivered in 20 minutes.*
VERB V n *to* n, V n, Also V
2 When you **deliver** something that you have promised to do or make, you do it or make it. *They have yet to show that they can really deliver working technologies... His track record so far as prime minister shows that he can't deliver.*
VERB V n, V
3 If you **deliver** someone or something into some-
VERB

one else's care, you give them responsibility for it; a formal use. *Mrs Parish was delivered into Mr Hinchcliffe's care... David delivered Holly gratefully into the woman's outstretched arms... He was led in in handcuffs and delivered over to me.* =hand over be V-ed into/to n V n into/to n be V-ed over

4 If you **deliver** a lecture or speech, you give it in public. *The president will deliver a speech about schools... It is shocking that only one woman has delivered the lecture in 44 years.* VERB =make V n

5 When someone **delivers** a baby, they help the woman who is giving birth to the baby. *Although we'd planned to have our baby at home, we never expected to deliver her ourselves!* VERB V n

6 If someone **delivers** a blow to someone else, they hit them; used in written English. *Those blows to the head could have been delivered by a woman.* VERB be V-ed Also V n

7 If someone **delivers** you from something, they rescue or save you from it; an old-fashioned use. *I have given thanks to God for delivering me from that pain.* VERB V n from n

8 • **deliver the goods**: see **goods**.

deliverance /dɪlɪvərəns/. **Deliverance** is rescue from captivity, danger, or evil; a literary word. *The opening scene shows them celebrating their sudden deliverance from war... She prayed to God for deliverance.* N-UNCOUNT: oft N from n =salvation

delivery /dɪlɪvəri/ **deliveries** ◆◆◆◇◇

1 **Delivery** or a **delivery** is the bringing of letters, parcels, or other goods to someone's house or to another place where they want them. *Please allow 28 days for delivery... It is available at £108, including VAT and delivery. ...the delivery of goods and resources.* N-VAR: oft N of n

2 A **delivery** of something is the goods that are delivered. *I got a delivery of fresh eggs this morning.* N-COUNT: usu with supp

3 You talk about someone's **delivery** when you are referring to the way in which they give a speech or lecture. *His speeches were magnificently written but his delivery was hopeless.* N-UNCOUNT: usu poss N

4 **Delivery** is the process of giving birth to a baby. *In the end, it was an easy delivery: a fine baby boy... Premature birth is three times more likely for twins, and delivery at 36 to 38 weeks is normal.* N-VAR =birth

dell /del/ **dells.** A **dell** is a small valley which has trees growing in it; a literary word. N-COUNT

delphinium /delfɪniəm/ **delphiniums.** A **delphinium** is a garden plant which has a tall stem with blue flowers growing up it. N-COUNT

delta /deltə/ **deltas.** A **delta** is an area of low, flat land shaped like a triangle, where a river splits and spreads out into several branches before entering the sea. *...the Mississippi delta.* ◆◇◇◇◇ N-COUNT: oft n N

delude /dɪluːd/ **deludes, deluding, deluded**

1 If you **delude** yourself, you let yourself believe that something is true, even though it is not true. *The President was deluding himself if he thought he was safe from such action... We delude ourselves that we are in control... I had deluded myself into believing that it would all come right in the end.* VERB V pron-refl V pron-refl that V pron-refl into -ing

2 If something or someone **deludes** you into thinking something, they make you believe something that is not true. *Television deludes you into thinking you have experienced reality, when you haven't... He had been unwittingly deluded by their mystical nonsense.* VERB =deceive V n into -ing be V-ed Also V n

deluded /dɪluːdɪd/. Someone who is **deluded** believes something that is not true. *But those planning to put the new invention to good use were sadly deluded... You poor deluded fool!* ADJ-GRADED =misguided

deluge /deljuːdʒ/ **deluges, deluging, deluged** ◆◇◇◇◇

1 A **deluge** of things is a large number of them which arrive or happen at the same time. *A deluge of manuscripts began to arrive in the post... This has brought a deluge of criticism.* N-COUNT: usu sing, usu N of n =flood

2 If a place or person **is deluged** with things, a large number of them arrive or happen at the same time. *During 1933, Papen's office was deluged with complaints.* VB: usu passive be V-ed with/by n

3 A **deluge** is a sudden, very heavy fall of rain. *About a dozen homes were damaged in the deluge.* N-COUNT =downpour

4 If rain **deluges** a place, it falls very heavily there, sometimes causing floods; used in written English. *At least 150 people are believed to have died after two days of torrential rain deluged the capital.* VERB =flood V n

delusion /dɪluːʒᵊn/ **delusions** ◆◇◇◇◇

1 A **delusion** is a false idea. *I was under the delusion that he intended to marry me. ...mansions built by men with delusions of grandeur.* N-COUNT: usu with supp

2 **Delusion** is the state of believing things that are not true. *Insinuations about her mental state, about her capacity for delusion were being made.* N-UNCOUNT

deluxe /dɪ lʌks/; also spelled **de luxe** in British English. **Deluxe** goods or services are better in quality and more expensive than ordinary ones. *...a rare, highly prized deluxe wine. ...exclusive fashion de luxe for the businesswoman.* ◆◇◇◇◇ ADJ: ADJ n, n ADJ =luxury

delve /delv/ **delves, delving, delved** ◆◇◇◇◇

1 If you **delve** into something, you try to discover new information about it. *Tormented by her ignorance, Jenny delves into her mother's past... When you delve a bit deeper, you discover that what makes you leave things to the last minute is fear of failure.* VERB =dig, probe V into n V adv

2 If you **delve** inside something such as a cupboard or a bag, you search inside it. *She delved into her rucksack and pulled out a folder.* VERB V prep/adv

demagogic /deməgɒdʒɪk/. If you say that someone is **demagogic**, you mean that what they say is typical of a demagogue; a formal word, used showing disapproval. *...a demagogic populist.* ADJ-GRADED PRAGMATICS

demagogue /deməgɒg, AM -gɔːg/ **demagogues.** A **demagogue** is a political leader who tries to win support by appealing to people's emotions rather than by rational arguments; used showing disapproval. N-COUNT: oft adj N PRAGMATICS =agitator

demagogy /deməgɒdʒi/. **Demagogy** is a method of political rule which involves appealing to people's emotions rather than using rational arguments; used showing disapproval. N-UNCOUNT PRAGMATICS

demand /dɪmɑːnd, -mænd/ **demands, demanding, demanded** ◆◆◆◆◆

1 If you **demand** something such as information or action, you ask for it in a very forceful way. *The Labour Party has demanded an explanation from the government... Russia demanded that Unita send a delegation to the peace talks... The hijackers are demanding to speak to representatives of both governments... 'What did you expect me to do about it?' she demanded.* VERB V n from/for n V that V to-inf V with quote

2 If one thing **demands** another, the first needs the second in order to happen or be dealt with successfully. *He said the task of reconstruction would demand much patience, hard work and sacrifice... There would be fewer international crises demanding his attention... But he could also turn on the style when the occasion demanded.* VERB =require V n V

3 A **demand** is a firm request for something. *There have been demands for services from tenants up there... They consistently rejected the demand to remove US troops... He grew ever more fierce in his demands.* N-COUNT: usu with supp

4 If you refer to **demand**, or to the **demand** for something, you are referring to how many people want to have it, do it, or buy it. *Another flight would be arranged on Saturday if sufficient demand arose... Demand for coal is down and so are prices... The demand to see her work is much greater than expected... Because of the slump in domestic demand, production has stopped.* N-UNCOUNT =call ≠supply

5 The **demands** of something or its **demands** on you are the things which it needs or the things which you have to do for it. *Researchers wrongly assumed that people were quite clear about the demands of the task. ...the demands and challenges of a new job... There were too many other demands on his loyalty now.* N-PLURAL: usu N of n, N on n =requirements

6 If someone or something is **in demand** or **in great demand**, they are very popular and a lot of people want them. *He was much in demand as a lecturer in the US, as well as at universities all over Europe.* PHRASES v-link PHR =sought after

7 If someone or something **makes demands** on you, they require you to do things which need a lot V inflects, usu PHR on n

of time, energy, or money. *I had no right to make demands on his time.*

8 If something is available or happens **on demand**, you can have it or it happens whenever you want it or ask for it. *...a national commitment to providing treatment on demand for drug abusers.*

demanding /dɪmɑːndɪŋ, -mænd-/ ◆◇◇◇◇

1 A **demanding** job or task requires a lot of your time, energy, or attention. *He tried to return to work, but found he could no longer cope with his demanding job... It is a demanding role and she needs to work hard at it.* ADJ-GRADED: usu ADJ n

2 People who are **demanding** are not easily satisfied or pleased. *Ricky was a very demanding child... Her boss was very demanding but appreciative of Christina's talents.* ADJ-GRADED

demarcate /diːmɑːʳkeɪt, AM dɪmɑːrk-/ **demarcates, demarcating, demarcated.** If you **demarcate** something, you establish its boundaries or limits; a formal word. *A special UN commission was formed to demarcate the border.* VERB =delimit; V n

demarcation /diːmɑːʳkeɪʃᵊn/. **Demarcation** is the establishment of boundaries or limits separating two areas, groups, or things; a formal word. *...the demarcation line between Indian and Pakistani Kashmir... Talks were continuing about the demarcation of the border between the two countries.* N-UNCOUNT: oft N n

demean /dɪmiːn/ **demeans, demeaning, demeaned**

1 If you **demean** yourself, you do something which makes people have less respect for you. *I wasn't going to demean myself by acting like a suspicious wife.* VERB; V pron-refl

2 To **demean** someone or something means to make people have less respect for them. *Some groups say that pornography demeans women and incites rape.* VERB =degrade; V n

demeaning /dɪmiːnɪŋ/. Something that is **demeaning** makes people have less respect for the person who is treated in that way, or who does that thing. *...making demeaning sexist comments... Aid, however it is obtained, is demeaning to the recipients.* ADJ-GRADED: oft ADJ *to* n =degrading

demeanour /dɪmiːnəʳ/; spelled **demeanor** in American English. Your **demeanour** is the way you behave, which gives people an impression of your character and feelings; a formal word. *From his general demeanour I didn't get the impression that he was being ironical. ...her calm and cheerful demeanour.* ◆◇◇◇◇ N-UNCOUNT: usu poss N =manner

demented /dɪmentɪd/ ◆◇◇◇◇

1 Someone who is **demented** has a severe mental illness, especially Alzheimer's disease; an old-fashioned or medical term. *At what point does it become necessary to place a demented person in a nursing home?* ADJ-GRADED

2 If you describe someone as **demented**, you think that their actions are strange, foolish, or uncontrolled; an informal use. *He had been granted his own TV show by some demented executive. ...as Sid broke into demented laughter.* ADJ-GRADED PRAGMATICS =crazy

dementia /dɪmenʃə/ **dementias. Dementia** is a serious illness of the mind; a medical term. ◆◇◇◇◇ N-VAR

demerara sugar /deməreərə ʃʊgəʳ/. **Demerara sugar** is a type of brown sugar. It is made from sugar cane that is grown in the West Indies. N-UNCOUNT

demerge /diːmɜːʳdʒ/ **demerges, demerging, demerged.** In Britain, if a large company **is demerged** or **demerges**, it is broken down into several smaller companies. *Zeneca was at last demerged from its parent firm, ICI... Several informed observers believe his ultimate aim is to demerge the group... Have you ever wondered why so many companies merge and so few demerge?* V-ERG ≠merge; be V-ed *from* n; V n; V; Also V n *from* n

demerger /diːmɜːʳdʒəʳ/ **demergers.** In Britain, a **demerger** is the separation of a large company into several smaller companies. N-COUNT ≠merger

demerit /diːmerɪt/ **demerits.** The **demerits** of something or someone are their faults or disadvantages; a formal word. *...editorials and leading articles debating the merits and demerits of the three candidates.* N-COUNT: usu pl, usu with poss ≠merit

demigod /demigɒd/ **demigods**

1 In mythology, a **demigod** is a less important god, especially one who is half god and half human. N-COUNT

2 If you describe a famous or important person such as a politician, writer, or rock-musician as a **demigod**, you mean that you disapprove of the way in which they are admired or treated by people as if they were divine. N-COUNT PRAGMATICS

demilitarize /diːmɪlɪtəraɪz/ **demilitarizes, demilitarizing, demilitarized;** also spelled **demilitarise** in British English. To **demilitarize** an area means to ensure that all military forces are removed from it. *He said the UN had made remarkable progress in demilitarizing the region... The area could be turned into a demilitarized zone.* ◆◇◇◇◇ VERB; V n; V-ed

♦ **demilitarization** /diːmɪlɪtəraɪzeɪʃᵊn/ *He said demilitarization of the country was out of the question.* N-UNCOUNT

demise /dɪmaɪz/. The **demise** of something or someone is their end or death; a formal word. *...the demise of communism in Eastern Europe... Smoking, rather than genetics, was the cause of his early demise.* ◆◆◇◇◇ N-SING: usu with poss

demo /demoʊ/ **demos** ◆◇◇◇◇

1 In British English, a **demo** is a demonstration by a group of people to show their opposition to something or their support for something; an informal use. *...an anti-racist demo.* N-COUNT

2 A **demo** is a record or tape with a sample of someone's music recorded on it; an informal use. *He listened to one of my demo tapes and said he was keen to work with me... Send us a demo with one or two of your best songs.* N-COUNT: oft N n

demob /diːmɒb/. Someone's **demob** is their release from the armed forces; an informal word used in British English. *I didn't get back to Brussels until after my demob... Didn't they give you a demob suit?* N-UNCOUNT

demobbed /diːmɒbd/. When soldiers **are demobbed**, they are released from the armed forces; an informal word used in British English. *I'm still in the air force, though I'll be demobbed in a couple of months. ...housing and retraining demobbed soldiers.* V-PASSIVE; be V-ed; V-ed

demobilize /diːmoʊbɪlaɪz/ **demobilizes, demobilizing, demobilized;** also spelled **demobilise** in British English. If a country or armed force **demobilizes** its troops, or if its troops **demobilize**, its troops are released from service and go home. *Dos Santos has demanded that UNITA sign a cease-fire and demobilize its troops... It is highly unlikely that the rebels will agree to give up their weapons and demobilise.* ◆◇◇◇◇ V-ERG; V n; V

♦ **demobilization** /diːmoʊbɪlaɪzeɪʃᵊn/ *The government had previously been opposed to the demobilisation of its 100,000 strong army.* N-UNCOUNT: usu with supp

democracy /dɪmɒkrəsi/ **democracies** 

1 Democracy is a system of government in which people choose their rulers by voting for them in elections. *The spread of democracy in Eastern Europe appears to have had negative as well as positive consequences. ...the pro-democracy movement.* N-UNCOUNT

2 A **democracy** is a country in which the people choose their government by voting for it. *The new democracies face tough challenges.* N-COUNT: usu supp N

3 Democracy is a system of running organizations, businesses, and groups in which each member is entitled to vote and participate in decisions. *...the union's emphasis on industrial democracy.* N-UNCOUNT: usu supp N

democrat /deməkræt/ **democrats** 

1 A **Democrat** is a member or supporter of a particular political party which has the word 'democrat' or 'democratic' in its title, for example the Democratic Party in the United States. *...a senior Christian Democrat... Congressman Tom Downey is a Democrat from New York.* N-COUNT: oft supp N 

2 A **democrat** is a person who believes in the ideals of democracy, personal freedom, and equality. *This is the time for democrats and not dictators.* N-COUNT

democratic /demәkrætɪk/ ◆◆◆◆◇
1 A **democratic** country, government, or political system is governed by representatives who are elected by the people. *Bolivia returned to democratic rule in 1982, after a series of military governments. ...the country's first democratic elections.* ADJ: usu ADJ n
♦ **democratically** /demәkrætɪkli/ *That June, Yeltsin became Russia's first democratically elected President.* ADV: ADV adj, ADV with v
2 Something that is **democratic** is based on the idea that everyone should have equal rights and should be involved in making important decisions. *Education is the basis of a democratic society... He called for widespread changes to make the armed forces more democratic and less expensive.* ADJ-GRADED =egalitarian
♦ **democratically** *This committee will enable decisions to be made democratically.* ADV-GRADED
3 **Democratic** is used in the titles of some political parties. *...the Social Democratic Party. ...the People's Democratic Party of Afghanistan... Maxine Waters is a Democratic Congresswoman, representing South Central Los Angeles.* ADJ: ADJ n

democratize /dɪmɒkrәtaɪz/ **democratizes, democratizing, democratized;** also spelled **democratise** in British English. If a country or a system **is democratized**, it is made democratic; used mainly in journalism. *...a further need to democratize the life of society as a whole... When he left his native country, he said he would not return until it had been fully democratised.* VERB V n
♦ **democratization** /dɪmɒkrәtaɪzeɪʃәn/ *...the democratisation of Eastern Europe. ...the democratization process.* N-UNCOUNT: oft *the* N *of* n

demographic /demәgræfɪk/. **Demographic** means relating to or concerning demography. ◆◇◇◇◇ ADJ: ADJ n

demography /dɪmɒgrәfi/. **Demography** is the study of the changes in numbers of births, deaths, marriages, and cases of disease in a community over a period of time. N-UNCOUNT

demolish /dɪmɒlɪʃ/ **demolishes, demolishing, demolished** ◆◇◇◇◇
1 To **demolish** something such as a building means to destroy it completely. *A storm moved directly over the island, demolishing buildings and flooding streets... The building is now being demolished to make way for a motorway.* VERB V n
2 If you **demolish** someone's ideas or arguments, you prove that they are wrong or invalid. *Our intention was quite the opposite – to demolish rumours that have surrounded him since he took office... The myth that Japan is not open to concerns from outside has, I think, been demolished at a stroke.* VERB V n
3 If a person or team **demolishes** their opponents, they defeat them by a great amount; used in journalism. *Millwall demolished Notts County 6-0 on Saturday.* VERB =annihilate V n

demolition /demәlɪʃәn/ **demolitions** ◆◇◇◇◇
1 The **demolition** of a building is the act of deliberately destroying it, often in order to build something else in its place. *The project required the total demolition of the old bridge... The High Court has granted permission for the demolition work to continue.* N-VAR
2 The **demolition** of a team or opponent is their defeat by a great amount; used in journalism. *...Lazio's impressive 3-1 demolition of Inter Milan.* N-UNCOUNT =annihilation

demon /diːmәn/ **demons;** also spelled **daemon** in British English. ◆◇◇◇◇
1 A **demon** is an evil spirit. *...a woman possessed by demons.* N-COUNT
2 Sources of worry or conflict which torment a person or group of people are sometimes referred to as **demons**. *His private demons drove him to drink excessively for many years. ...the demons of hatred, violence and ethnic fanaticism.* N-COUNT: usu pl
3 If you approve of someone because they are very skilled at what they do or that they do it energetically, you can say that they do it like a **demon**. *He played like a demon... He is a demon organizer.* N-COUNT PRAGMATICS
4 If you refer to a powerful person such as a politician as a **demon**, you mean that you believe they are bad and might be dangerous. *She was a dictator and a demon... He was seen as a demon, determined to hand the country over to Communists.* N-COUNT

demonic /dɪmɒnɪk/; also spelled **daemonic**.
1 **Demonic** means coming from or belonging to a demon or being demon-like. *...demonic forces. ...a demonic grin.* ADJ: usu ADJ n
2 If someone has **demonic** energy, drive, or abilities, they are more energetic, determined, or clever than most people. *...a demonic drive to succeed.* ADJ: ADJ n

demonize /diːmәnaɪz/ **demonizes, demonizing, demonized;** also spelled **demonise** in British English. If people **demonize** someone, they convince themselves that that person is evil. *Each side began to demonize the other.* VERB V n

demonology /diːmәnɒlәdʒi/. **Demonology** is a set of beliefs which says that a particular situation or group of people is evil or unacceptable. *In popular demonology, the administration looms as large in France as the trades unions used to do in Britain.* N-UNCOUNT

demonstrable /dɪmɒnstrәbәl/. A **demonstrable** fact or quality can be shown to be true or to exist; a formal word. *An additive is permitted in food only where there is a genuine demonstrable need for it... Despite its demonstrable speed and safety, the boat failed to become popular.* ADJ: usu ADJ n
♦ **demonstrably** /dɪmɒnstrәbli/. *...demonstrably false statements.* ADV

demonstrate /demәnstreɪt/ **demonstrates, demonstrating, demonstrated** ◆◆◆◇◇
1 To **demonstrate** a fact means to make it clear to people. *The study also demonstrated a direct link between obesity and mortality... You have to demonstrate that you are reliable... They are anxious to demonstrate to the voters that they have practical policies... He's demonstrated how a campaign based on domestic issues can move votes.* VERB =show, prove V n V that V *to* n that V wh
2 If you **demonstrate** a particular skill, quality, or feeling, you show by your actions that you have it. *Have they, for example, demonstrated a commitment to democracy?... The government's going to great lengths to demonstrate its military might.* VERB =show, display V n
3 When people **demonstrate**, they march or gather somewhere to show their opposition to something or their support for something. *Some 30,000 angry farmers arrived in Brussels yesterday to demonstrate against possible cuts in subsidies... In the cities vast crowds have been demonstrating for change... Thousands of people have been demonstrating outside the parliament building in Sofia.* VERB =protest V *against* n V *for* n V
4 If you **demonstrate** something, you show people how it works or how to do it. *The BBC has just successfully demonstrated a new digital radio transmission system... He flew the prototype to West Raynham to demonstrate it to a group of senior officers... They prepare them with a detailed manual, then demonstrate how to do the job.* VERB V n V n *to* n V how

demonstration /demәnstreɪʃәn/ **demonstrations** ◆◆◆◇◇
1 A **demonstration** is a march or gathering which people take part in to show their opposition to something or their support for something. *Riot police used teargas and truncheons this afternoon to break up a demonstration by students. ...mass demonstrations.* N-COUNT
2 A **demonstration** of something is a talk by someone who shows you how to do it or how it works. *...a cookery demonstration. ...demonstrations of new products.* N-COUNT: usu with supp
3 A **demonstration** of a fact or situation is a clear proof of it. *It was an unprecedented demonstration of people power by the citizens of Moscow... This was a very practical demonstration of why the Army trained people to be disciplined.* N-COUNT: usu N *of* n
4 A **demonstration of** a quality or feeling is an expression of it. *There's been no public demonstration of opposition to the President. ...physical demonstrations of affection.* N-COUNT: N *of* n =display

demonstrative /dɪmɒnstrәtɪv/ **demonstratives**
1 Someone who is **demonstrative** shows affection ADJ-GRADED

freely and openly. *Richard was not normally demonstrative, but he came forward quickly and gave her a hug.* ♦ **demonstratively** *Some children respond more demonstratively than others.* ≠reserved ADV-GRADED

2 The words 'this', 'that', 'these', and 'those' are sometimes called **demonstratives**; a technical use in linguistics. N-COUNT

demonstrator /demənstreɪtəʳ/ **demonstrators** ◆◆◆◇◇

1 **Demonstrators** are people who are marching or gathering somewhere to show their opposition to something or their support for something. *I saw the police using tear gas to try and break up a crowd of demonstrators.* N-COUNT: usu pl

2 A **demonstrator** is someone who shows people how something works or how to do something. N-COUNT

demoralize /dɪmɒrəlaɪz, AM -mɔːr-/ **demoralizes, demoralizing, demoralized;** also spelled **demoralise** in British English. If something **demoralizes** someone, it makes them lose so much confidence in what they are doing that they want to give up. *Clearly, one of the objectives is to demoralize the enemy troops in any way they can.* ◆◇◇◇◇ VERB =dishearten V n

♦ **demoralized** *The Bismarck could now move only at a crawl and her crew were exhausted, hopeless and utterly demoralized. ...legitimate grievances raised by a demoralized police force.* ADJ-GRADED =dispirited

♦ **demoralization** /dɪmɒrəlaɪzeɪʃən, AM -mɔːr-/ *...the lingering demoralization that followed defeat in World War I.* N-UNCOUNT

demoralizing /dɪmɒrəlaɪzɪŋ, AM -mɔːr-/; also spelled **demoralising** in British English. If something is **demoralizing**, it makes you lose so much confidence in what you are doing that you want to give up. *Redundancy can be a demoralising prospect... Persistent disapproval or criticism can be highly demoralizing.* ADJ-GRADED =disheartening

demote /dɪmoʊt/ **demotes, demoting, demoted** ◆◇◇◇◇

1 If someone **demotes** you, they give you a lower rank or a less important position than you already have, often as a punishment. *It's very difficult to demote somebody who has been standing in during maternity leave... If they prove ineffective they should be demoted or asked to retire.* ♦ **demotion** /dɪmoʊʃən/ **demotions** *He is seeking redress for what he alleges was an unfair demotion.* VERB ≠promote V n N-VAR ≠promotion

2 If a team in a sports league **is demoted**, that team is ordered by the sport's ruling body to play in a lower division, as a punishment. *Swindon Town were demoted two divisions after the club admitted thirty-six breaches of the Football League's rules.* VB: usu passive ≠promote be V-ed

♦ **demotion** *The demotion was imposed as a punishment for infringing the rules governing irregular payments to players.* N-VAR ≠promotion

demotic /dɪmɒtɪk/

1 **Demotic** language is the type of informal language used by ordinary people; a formal use. *...television's demotic style of language.* ADJ =colloquial

2 **Demotic** is used to describe something or someone that is typical of ordinary people; a formal use. *Maria Fyfe, MP for Glasgow Maryhill, will impart a demotic flavour to the rarefied inner circle of power.* ADJ: usu ADJ n

demur /dɪmɜːʳ/ **demurs, demurring, demurred**

1 If you **demur**, you say that you do not agree with something or will not do something that you have been asked to do; a formal word. *Hunt wanted to know, would I be prepared to take over the whole operation and supervise it? At first I demurred... The doctor demurred, but Piercey was insistent.* VERB V

2 If you do something **without demur**, you do it immediately and without making any objection; a formal expression. *When Scobie opened the door and stood aside for her to enter she did so without demur.* PHRASE: PHR after v

demure /dɪmjʊəʳ/

1 If you describe someone, usually a young woman, as **demure**, you mean they are quiet and rather shy, and behave very correctly. *She's very demure and sweet... The luscious Miss Wharton gave me a demure but knowing smile.* ♦ **demurely** *She smiled demurely.* ADJ-GRADED =reserved ADV-GRADED: usu ADV with v

2 **Demure** clothes do not reveal your body and they give the impression that you are shy and behave correctly; used in written English. *...a demure high-necked white blouse.* ♦ **demurely** *...she was demurely dressed in a black woollen suit.* ADJ-GRADED: usu ADJ n ADV-GRADED: ADV -ed, ADV after v

demystify /diːmɪstɪfaɪ/ **demystifies, demystifying, demystified.** If you **demystify** something, you make it easier to understand by giving a clear explanation of it. *To enter the consumer market, it was necessary to demystify the computer... We urge colleges and universities to demystify the selection process.* VERB V n

den /den/ **dens** ◆◇◇◇◇

1 A **den** is the home of certain types of wild animals such as lions or foxes. N-COUNT =lair

2 In American English, your **den** is a quiet room in your house where you can go to study, work, or carry on a hobby without being disturbed. *He would shut himself up alone in the den to watch wrestling on television.* N-COUNT

3 A **den** is a secret place where people meet, usually for a dishonest purpose. *I could provide you with the addresses of at least three illegal drinking dens. ...the crack dens of urban America.* N-COUNT: usu supp N

4 If you describe a place as a **den of** a particular vice, you mean that a lot of that vice goes on there. *...the one-bedroomed flat that was to become his den of savage debauchery. ...a den of greed.* N-COUNT: N of n

denationalize /diːnæʃənəlaɪz/ **denationalizes, denationalizing, denationalized;** also spelled **denationalise** in British English. To **denationalize** an industry or business means to transfer it into private ownership so that it is no longer owned and controlled by the state; an old-fashioned word. *The Korean government started to denationalize the financial institutions in the early 1980s... Eventually Sunderland Shipbuilders was denationalised.* ♦ **denationalization** /diːnæʃənəlaɪzeɪʃən/ *He made it clear that the party was not against the denationalisation of industry.* VERB =privatize ≠nationalize V n N-UNCOUNT =privatization

denial /dɪnaɪəl/ **denials** ◆◆◇◇◇

1 A **denial** of something is a statement that it is not true, does not exist, or did not happen. *It seems clear that despite official denials, differences of opinion lay behind the Ambassador's decision to quit... Denial of the Mafia's existence is nothing new.* N-VAR: oft N of n

2 The **denial** of something to someone is the act of refusing to let them have it; a formal use. *...the denial of visas to international relief workers... This does not justify the denial of constitutional protection.* N-UNCOUNT: usu N of n

3 In psychology, **denial** is a person's refusal, perhaps subconscious, to accept an unpleasant truth. *With major life traumas, like losing a loved one, for instance, the mind's first reaction is denial.* N-UNCOUNT

denier /deniəʳ/. **Denier** is used when indicating the thickness of stockings and tights. *...fifteen-denier stockings.* N-UNCOUNT: num N

denigrate /denɪgreɪt/ **denigrates, denigrating, denigrated.** If you **denigrate** someone or something, you criticize them unfairly or insult them. *The amendment prohibits obscene or indecent materials which denigrate the objects or beliefs of a particular religion... The Canadian Supreme Court ruled that the State can ban pornographic images which 'denigrate women'.* ◆◇◇◇◇ VERB =degrade V n

♦ **denigration** /denɪgreɪʃən/ *...the denigration of minorities in this country.* N-UNCOUNT: usu N of n

denim /denɪm/. **Denim** is a thick cotton cloth, usually blue, which is used to make clothes. Jeans are made from denim. *...a light blue denim jacket... Dennis was dressed in denim.* ◆◇◇◇◇ N-UNCOUNT: oft N n

denims /denɪmz/. **Denims** are casual trousers made of denim. *She was dressed in blue denims.* N-PLURAL: also *a pair of* N =jeans

denizen /denɪzən/ **denizens.** A **denizen** of a particular place is a person, animal, or plant that lives or grows in this place; a formal word. *Gannets are denizens of the open ocean. ...the denizens of Her Majesty's House of Commons.* N-COUNT: usu N of n

denomination /dɪnɒmɪneɪʃən/ **denominations** ◆◇◇◇◇

1 A particular **denomination** is a particular religious group which has slightly different beliefs N-COUNT

from other groups within the same faith. *Acceptance of women preachers varies greatly from denomination to denomination.*

2 The **denomination** of a banknote or coin is its official value. N-COUNT *...a pile of bank notes, mostly in small denominations.*

denominational /dɪnɒmɪneɪʃənəl/. **Denominational** means relating to or organized by a particular religious denomination. ADJ: ADJ n *The Black church community has sought to bring together Christians from different denominational backgrounds... A multi-denominational group of religious leaders led the mourners in prayer.*

denominator /dɪnɒmɪneɪtəʳ/ **denominators.** In mathematics, the **denominator** is the number which appears under the line in a fraction. N-COUNT ● See also **common denominator**, **lowest common denominator**.

denote /dɪnoʊt/ **denotes, denoting, denoted** ◆◇◇◇◇

1 If one thing **denotes** another, it is a sign or indication of it; a formal use. VERB =indicate *Red eyes denote strain and fatigue...* V n *Yet there had been a message waiting on the blackboard, denoting that someone had been here ahead of her.* V that

2 What a symbol **denotes** is what it represents; a formal use. VERB =represent *In figure 24 'Dt' denotes quantity demanded in the current period and 'St' denotes quantity supplied.* V n

3 What a word or name **denotes** is what it means or refers to; a formal use. VERB *In the Middle Ages the term 'drab' denoted a very simple type of woollen cloth which was used by peasants to make their clothes.* V n

denouement /deɪnuːmɒn/ **denouements;** also spelled **dénouement**. In a book, play, or series of events, the **denouement** is the sequence of events at the end, when things come to a conclusion. N-COUNT: usu sing *The book's sentimental denouement is pure Hollywood. ...an unexpected denouement.*

denounce /dɪnaʊns/ **denounces, denouncing, denounced** ◆◆◇◇◇

1 If you **denounce** a person or an action, you criticize them severely and publicly because you feel strongly that they are wrong or evil. VERB *The letter called for trade union freedom and civil rights, but did not openly denounce the regime...* V n *German leaders all took the opportunity to denounce the attacks and plead for tolerance... Some 25,000 demonstrators denounced him as a traitor.* V n *as* n/adj

2 If you **denounce** someone who has broken a rule or law, you report them to the authorities. VERB *They were at the mercy of informers who might at any moment denounce them.* V n Also V n *to* n

dense /dens/ **denser, densest** ◆◆◇◇◇

1 Something that is **dense** contains a lot of things or people in a small area. ADJ-GRADED ≠sparse, thin *Where Bucharest now stands, there once was a large, dense forest... Its fur is short, dense and silky... They went out on to the pavement, thrusting their way again through the dense crowd.* ♦ **densely** ADV-GRADED: usu ADV -ed ≠sparsely *Java is a densely populated island... The fire struck a densely wooded area of Oakland.*

2 Dense fog or smoke is difficult to see through because it is very heavy and dark. ADJ-GRADED =thick ≠thin *A dense column of smoke rose several miles into the air.*

3 A **dense** substance is very heavy in relation to its volume; a technical use in science. ADJ-GRADED *...a small dense star.*

4 If you describe writing or a film as **dense**, you mean that it is difficult to understand because it contains a lot of information and ideas. ADJ-GRADED PRAGMATICS =tightly-packed *His prose is vigorous and dense, occasionally to the point of obscurity.*

5 If you say that someone is **dense**, you mean that they are stupid and that they take a long time to understand simple things; an informal use. ADJ-GRADED: v-link ADJ PRAGMATICS =thick *He's not a bad man, just a bit dense.*

density /densɪti/ **densities** ◆◇◇◇◇

1 Density is the extent to which something is filled or covered with people or things. N-VAR: usu with supp, oft N *of* n *The law which restricts the density of housing in the Balearics was changed recently... Taiwan has a very high population density. ...areas with high densities of immigrant populations.*

2 The **density** of a substance or object is the relation of its mass or weight to its volume; a technical use in science. N-VAR: usu with supp, oft with poss *Jupiter's moon Io, whose density is 3.5 grams per cubic centimetre, is all rock.*

dent /dent/ **dents, denting, dented** ◆◇◇◇◇

1 If you **dent** the surface of something, you make a hollow dip in it by hitting or pressing it. VERB *A great chunk of loose kerbing smashed into my left-front wheel, bursting the tyre and denting the rim... Its brass feet dented the carpet's thick pile.* V n ♦ **dented** ADJ-GRADED *Watch out for bargains, but never buy dented cans.*

2 A **dent** is a hollow in the surface of something which has been caused by hitting or pressing it. N-COUNT *I was convinced there was a dent in the bonnet which hadn't been there before.*

3 If something **dents** your ideas or your pride, it makes you realize that your ideas are wrong, or that you are not as good or successful as you thought. VERB *This has not dented the City's enthusiasm for the company... After a while that sort of thing dents your confidence.* V n

4 If one thing makes a **dent** in another, it reduces it considerably. N-COUNT: usu N *in* n *The commission had barely begun to make a dent in the problem... I hated to put any dents in his enthusiasm, but I was trying to be realistic.*

dental /dentəl/. **Dental** is used to describe things that relate to teeth or to the care and treatment of teeth. ◆◆◇◇◇ ADJ: ADJ n *You can get free prescriptions and dental treatment while you are pregnant. ...the dental profession.*

dentist /dentɪst/ **dentists.** A **dentist** is a person who is qualified to examine and treat people's teeth. ◆◆◇◇◇ N-COUNT *Visit your dentist twice a year for a check-up.* ► **The dentist** or **the dentist's** is used to refer to the surgery or clinic where a dentist works. N-SING: *the* N *It's worse than being at the dentist's.*

dentistry /dentɪstri/. **Dentistry** is the work done by a dentist. ◆◇◇◇◇ N-UNCOUNT

dentures /dentʃəʳz/; the form **denture** is used as a modifier. **Dentures** are artificial teeth worn by people who no longer have all their own teeth. N-PLURAL =false teeth

denude /dɪnjuːd, AM -nuːd/ **denudes, denuding, denuded**

1 To **denude** an area means to destroy the plants in it; a formal use. VERB *Migrants from teeming Brazilian cities were denuding Amazonia to open private farmsteads... Many hillsides had been denuded of trees.* V n *be* V-ed *of* n Also V n *of* n

2 To **denude** something or someone of something means to take that thing away from them; a formal use. VERB =divest *Mrs Thatcher had claimed that a single European currency would denude Parliament of economic powers... In such areas we see villages denuded of young people.* V n *of* n V-ed

denunciation /dɪnʌnsieɪʃən/ **denunciations** ◆◇◇◇◇

1 Denunciation of someone or something is severe public criticism of them. N-VAR: oft N *of* n =condemnation *On September 24, he wrote a stinging denunciation of his critics... He has been scathing in his denunciation of corrupt and incompetent politicians.*

2 Denunciation is the act of reporting someone who has broken a rule or law to the authorities. N-VAR *...memories of the denunciation of French Jews to the Nazis during the Second World War.*

deny /dɪnaɪ/ **denies, denying, denied** ◆◆◆◆◇

1 When you **deny** something, you state that it is not true. VERB PRAGMATICS =repudiate ≠admit *She denied both accusations... The government has denied that the authorities have uncovered a plot to assassinate the president... They all denied ever having seen her.* V n V that V -ing

2 If you **deny** someone or something, you say that they have no connection with you or do not belong to you; a formal use. VERB =repudiate *I denied my father because I wanted to become someone else.* V n

3 If you **deny** someone something that they need or want, you refuse to let them have it. VERB =refuse *If he is unlucky, he may find that his ex-partner denies him access to his children... If you regularly take snacks instead of eating properly, you will deny yourself the* V n n V pron-refl n V pron-refl *important nutrients that your body requires... My mother denied herself for us.*

deodorant /dioʊdərənt/ **deodorants. Deodorant** is a substance that you can use to hide or prevent the smell of perspiration on your body. ◆◇◇◇◇ N-MASS =anti-perspirant

deodorize /dioʊdəraɪz/ **deodorizes, deodorizing, deodorized;** also spelled **deodorise** in British English. If you **deodorize** something, you hide or remove unpleasant smells from it; a formal word. *The machine uses minute quantities of ozone to sterilise and deodorise refrigerated food vehicles. ...a deodorising foot spray.* VERB V n V-ing

depart /dɪpɑːʳt/ **departs, departing, departed** ◆◆◇◇◇

1 When something or someone **departs** from a place, they leave it and start a journey to another place. *Our tour departs from Heathrow Airport on 31 March and returns 16 April... Mr. Bush departed for Camp David... The coach departs Potsdam in the morning for the drive to Leipzig.* VERB V from n V for n V n Also V

2 If you **depart** from a traditional, accepted, or agreed way of doing something, you do it in a different or unexpected way. *Why is it in this country that we have departed from good educational sense?... The Prime Minister gave a press conference which departed from the agreed text.* VERB =deviate V from n

3 If someone **departs** from a job, they resign from it or leave it. In American English, you can say that someone **departs** a job. *Prime Minister Margaret Thatcher departed from office, after over eleven years in power. ...a number of staff departed during his reign as rector of the Royal College of Art... He had the good fortune to depart baseball in the '60s at just about that moment when it was becoming tarnished.* VERB =leave V from n V V n

4 When somebody **departs** this life, or **departs** this earth, they die. *He departed this world with a sense of having fulfilled his destiny.* VERB V n

departed /dɪpɑːʳtɪd/. **Departed** friends or relatives are people who have died; a formal word. *Departed friends can no longer be replaced at my age.* ► **The departed** are people who have died. *We held services for the departed at our church last Thursday.* ADJ: usu ADJ n N-PLURAL: the N =deceased

department /dɪpɑːʳtmənt/ **departments** ◆◆◆◆◆

1 A **department** is one of the sections in an organization such as a government, business, or university. A department is also one of the sections in a large shop. *...the U.S. Department of Health, Education and Welfare... He moved to the sales department. ...the geography department of Moscow University. ...the jewelry department.* N-COUNT: usu with supp

2 If you say that a task or area of knowledge **is not** your **department**, you mean that you are not responsible for it or do not know much about it. *'I'm afraid the name means nothing to me,' he said. 'That's not my department.'* PHRASE: V inflects

departmental /diːpɑːʳtmentᵊl/. **Departmental** is used to describe the activities, responsibilities, or possessions of a department in a government, company, or other organization. *The Secretary of State for Education is right to seek a bigger departmental budget.* ◆◇◇◇◇ ADJ: ADJ n

department store, department stores. A **department store** is a large shop which sells many different kinds of goods. ◆◆◇◇◇ N-COUNT

departure /dɪpɑːʳtʃəʳ/ **departures** ◆◆◆◇◇

1 **Departure** or a **departure** is the act of going away from somewhere. *...the President's departure for Helsinki... They hoped this would lead to the departure of all foreign forces from the country... The airline has more than 90 scheduled departures from here every day.* N-VAR: oft with poss ≠arrival

2 The **departure** of a person from a job, or a member from an organization, is their act of leaving it or being forced to leave it; a formal use. *This would inevitably involve his departure from the post of Prime Minister. ...the republic's departure from the Yugoslav federation.* N-VAR: with poss, oft N from n

3 If someone does something different or unusual, you can refer to their action as a **departure**. *Taylor announced another departure from practice in that England will train at Wembley... Now she's written a novel which is not a mystery and is a considerable departure from her previous work.* N-COUNT: oft N from n =deviation

depend /dɪpend/ **depends, depending, depended** ◆◆◆◆◇

1 If you say that one thing **depends** on another, you mean that the first thing will be affected or determined by the second. *The cooking time needed depends on the size of the potato... What happened later would depend on his talk with De Solina... How much it costs depends upon how much you buy.* VERB V on/upon n V on/upon wh

2 If you **depend** on someone or something, you need them in order to be able to survive physically, financially, or emotionally. *They may hate what he does but their survival depends on him... He depended on his writing for his income... Nora grew accustomed to depending on her husband... Choosing the right account depends on working out your likely average balance.* VERB =rely V on/upon n/-ing

3 If you can **depend** on a person, organization, or law, you know that they will support you or help you when you need them. *'You can depend on me,' Cross assured him.* VERB =rely V on/upon n

4 You use **depend** in expressions such as **it depends** to indicate that you cannot give a clear answer to a question because the answer will be affected or determined by other factors. *'But how long can you stay in the house?'—'I don't know. It depends.'... It all depends on your definition of punk, doesn't it?* VERB it/that V it V on n/wh

5 You use **depending on** when you are saying that something varies according to the circumstances mentioned. *I tend to have a different answer, depending on the family... People in the rest of the country celebrated independence even later, depending on when the news of Congress's action reached them.* PHR-PREP: PREP n/wh

dependable /dɪpendəbᵊl/. If you say that someone or something is **dependable**, you mean you can be sure that they will always act consistently or sensibly, or do what you need or expect them to do; used showing approval. *He was a good friend, a dependable companion.* ◆◇◇◇◇ ADJ-GRADED PRAGMATICS =reliable

dependant /dɪpendənt/ **dependants;** also spelled **dependent**. Your **dependants** are the people you support financially, such as your children; a formal word. *The British Legion raises funds to help ex-service personnel and their dependants... He said he thought the compensation would be minimal because Mr Ryan was a single man with no dependants.* ◆◇◇◇◇ N-COUNT

dependence /dɪpendəns/ ◆◇◇◇◇

1 Your **dependence** on something or someone is your need for them in order to succeed or be able to survive. *...Vietnam's past dependence on the Soviet Union for economic aid... Do you look forward to old age, or do you dread frailty, loss of memory and dependence on others?* N-UNCOUNT: usu N on n =reliance ≠independence

2 If you talk about drug **dependence** or alcohol **dependence**, you are referring to a situation where someone is addicted to drugs or is an alcoholic. *French doctors tend to regard drug dependence as a form of deep-rooted psychological disorder.* N-UNCOUNT: usu n N =addiction

3 You talk about the **dependence** of one thing on another when the first thing will be affected or determined by the second. *...the dependence of circulation on production.* N-UNCOUNT: usu with supp ≠independence

dependency /dɪpendənsi/ **dependencies** ◆◇◇◇◇

1 A **dependency** is a country which is controlled by another country. *...the tiny British dependency of Montserrat in the eastern Caribbean.* N-COUNT

2 You talk about someone's **dependency** when they have a deep emotional, physical, or financial need for a particular person or thing, especially one that you consider excessive or undesirable. *We saw his dependency on his mother and worried that he might not survive long if anything happened to her... Ukraine is handicapped by its near-total dependency on Russian oil.* N-UNCOUNT: oft N on n ≠independence

3 If you talk about alcohol **dependency** or chemical **dependency**, you are referring to a situation where someone is an alcoholic or is addicted to N-VAR: usu n N =addiction

drugs; used mainly in American English. *In 1985, he began to show signs of alcohol and drug dependency... In 1979 she quit her teaching job because her dependency had affected her work.*

dependent /dɪpendənt/ ◆◆◇◇◇

1 To be **dependent** on something or someone means to need them in order to succeed or be able to survive. *The local economy is overwhelmingly dependent on oil and gas extraction... Up to two million people there are dependent on food aid... Britain became increasingly dependent upon American technology... In his own way, he was dependent on her... Just 26 per cent of households are married couples with dependent children.* ADJ-GRADED: oft ADJ *on/upon* n =reliant ≠independent

2 If one thing is **dependent** on another, the first thing will be affected or determined by the second. *The results you get from weight training are largely dependent upon how you use those weights and what type of exercise programme you follow. ...companies whose earnings are largely dependent on the performance of the Chinese economy.* ADJ: v-link ADJ *on/upon* n =contingent ≠independent

3 See also **dependant**.

depersonalize /diːpɜːʳsənəlaɪz/ **depersonalizes, depersonalizing, depersonalized;** also spelled **depersonalise** in British English.

1 To **depersonalize** a system or a situation means to treat it as if it did not really involve people, or to treat it as if the people involved were not really important. *It is true that modern weaponry depersonalised war.* VERB; V n

2 To **depersonalize** someone means to treat them as if they do not matter because their individual feelings and thoughts are not important. *She does not feel that the book depersonalises women.* VERB; V n

depict /dɪpɪkt/ **depicts, depicting, depicted** ◆◆◇◇◇

1 To **depict** someone or something means to show or represent them in a work of art such as a drawing or painting. *...a gallery of pictures depicting Nelson's most famous battles.* VERB; V n

2 To **depict** someone or something means to describe them or give an impression of them in writing. *Margaret Atwood's novel depicts a gloomy, futuristic America... Children's books often depict farmyard animals as gentle, lovable creatures.* VERB =portray; V n; V n *as* n

depiction /dɪpɪkʃᵊn/ **depictions.** A **depiction** of something is a picture or a written description of it. *The lecture will trace the depiction of horses from earliest times to the present day. ...the depiction of socialists as Utopian dreamers.* ◆◇◇◇◇ N-VAR =portrayal

depilatory /dɪpɪlətəri, AM -tɔːri/ **depilatories**

1 **Depilatory** substances and processes remove unwanted hair from your body. *...a depilatory cream.* ADJ: ADJ n

2 A **depilatory** is a depilatory substance. N-COUNT

deplete /dɪpliːt/ **depletes, depleting, depleted.** To **deplete** a stock or amount of something means to reduce it; a formal word. *...substances that deplete the ozone layer... They fired in long bursts, which depleted their ammunition... Most native mammal species have been severely depleted.* ◆◆◇◇◇ VERB; V n ♦ **depleted** *...Robert E. Lee's worn and depleted army.* ADJ-GRADED ♦ **depletion** /dɪpliːʃᵊn/ *...the problem of ozone depletion. ...the depletion of underground water supplies.* N-UNCOUNT: usu with supp

deplorable /dɪplɔːrəbᵊl/. If you say that something is **deplorable**, you mean it is very bad and unacceptable, and you disapprove of it; a formal word. *Many of them live under deplorable conditions... The Chief Constable said that sexual harassment was deplorable.* ◆◇◇◇◇ ADJ-GRADED PRAGMATICS ♦ **deplorably** *The spokesman said American reporters travelling with the President behaved deplorably.* ADV-GRADED: ADV after v, ADV adj

deplore /dɪplɔːʳ/ **deplores, deploring, deplored.** If you say that you **deplore** something, you mean that you disapprove of it and think it is wrong or immoral; a formal word. *He's a judo black belt but he says he deplores violence... He deplored the fact that the Foreign Secretary was driven into resignation... I deplore what has happened.* ◆◇◇◇◇ VERB PRAGMATICS; V n

deploy /dɪplɔɪ/ **deploys, deploying, deployed.** To **deploy** troops or military resources means to organize or position them so that they are ready to be used. *The president said he had no intention of deploying ground troops. ...the US-made Patriot anti-missile system which was deployed in the Gulf war.* ◆◆◇◇◇ VERB; V n

deployment /dɪplɔɪmənt/ **deployments.** The **deployment** of troops, resources, or equipment is the organization and positioning of them so that they are ready for immediate action. *...the deployment of troops into townships.* ◆◆◇◇◇ N-VAR: oft N *of* n

depopulate /diːpɒpjʊleɪt/ **depopulates, depopulating, depopulated.** To **depopulate** an area means to greatly reduce the number of people living there. *The famine endured for generations, threatening at times to depopulate the continent.* VERB; V n ♦ **depopulated** *...a small, rural, and depopulated part of the south-west.* ADJ-GRADED ♦ **depopulation** /diːpɒpjʊleɪʃᵊn/ *Falling church attendances have been made more acute by rural depopulation.* N-UNCOUNT

deport /dɪpɔːʳt/ **deports, deporting, deported.** If a government **deports** someone, usually someone who is not a citizen of that country, it sends them out of the country because they have committed a crime or because it believes they do not have the right to be there. *...a government decision earlier this month to deport all illegal immigrants... More than 240 England football fans are being deported from Italy following riots last night.* ◆◆◇◇◇ VERB =expel; V n; be V-ed *from/to* n; Also V n *from/to* n ♦ **deportation** /diːpɔːʳteɪʃᵊn/ **deportations** *...thousands of Albanian migrants facing deportation... Civil rights lawyers tried to halt the deportations.* N-VAR

deportee /diːpɔːʳtiː/ **deportees.** A **deportee** is someone who is being deported. N-COUNT

deportment /dɪpɔːʳtmənt/. Your **deportment** is the way you behave, especially the way you walk and move; a formal word. *Deportment and poise were as important as good marks for young ladies.* N-UNCOUNT =manner

depose /dɪpoʊz/ **deposes, deposing, deposed.** If a ruler or political leader **is deposed**, they are forced to give up their position. *Mr Ben Bella was deposed in a coup in 1965... Ferdinand Marcos fled to Hawaii in 1986 after being deposed as president of the Philippines. ...Nicolae Ceausescu, Romania's deposed Communist dictator.* ◆◇◇◇◇ VB: usu passive =oust; be V-ed; be V-ed *as* n; V-ed

deposit /dɪpɒzɪt/ **deposits, depositing, deposited** ◆◆◆◇◇

1 A **deposit** is a sum of money which is part of the full price of something, and which you pay when you agree to buy it. *A £50 deposit is required when ordering, and the balance is due upon delivery.* N-COUNT: usu sing =down payment

2 A **deposit** is a sum of money which you pay when you start renting something. The money is returned to you if you do not damage what you have rented. *It is common to ask for the equivalent of a month's rent as a deposit.* N-COUNT: usu sing

3 A **deposit** is a sum of money which is in a bank account or other savings account, especially a sum which will be left there for some time. N-COUNT

4 In Britain, a **deposit** is a sum of money which you have to pay if you want to be a candidate in a parliamentary or European election. The money is returned to you if you receive more than a certain percentage of the votes. *The Tory candidate lost his deposit.* N-COUNT: oft poss N

5 A **deposit** is an amount of a substance that has been left somewhere as a result of a chemical or geological process. *After 10 minutes the surplus material is washed away and any remaining deposit examined with ultra violet light. ...underground deposits of gold and diamonds. ...mineral deposits.* N-COUNT: usu with supp

6 To **deposit** someone or something somewhere means to put them or leave them there. *Just before the explosion someone was seen running from the scene after apparently depositing the packet... Fritz was on his way out, having just deposited a glass and two bottles of beer in front of Wolfe... Imagine if you were suddenly swept up and deposited in* VERB =plant, drop; V n; V n prep/adv

Morocco. How well could you cope with the language, the weather, the people, and so on?

7 When you **deposit** something somewhere, you put it where it will be safe until it is needed again. *You are advised to deposit valuables in the hotel safe.*
VERB
V n prep/adv

8 When you **deposit** a sum of money, you pay it into a bank account or other savings account. *The drawbacks here are that the customer has to deposit a minimum of £100 monthly.*
VERB
=pay in
≠withdraw
V n

9 If a substance **is deposited** somewhere, it is left there as a result of a chemical or geological process. *The phosphate was deposited by the decay of marine microorganisms.*
VB: usu passive
be V-ed

deposit account, deposit accounts. A **deposit account** is a type of bank account in which the money earns interest.
N-COUNT

deposition /depəzɪʃᵊn/ **depositions** ◆◇◇◇◇

1 A **deposition** is a formal written statement, made for example by a witness to a crime, which can be used in a court of law if the witness cannot be present. *The material would be checked against the depositions from other witnesses.*
N-COUNT

2 **Deposition** is a process in which layers of a substance are formed inside something or on its surface over a period of time. *Continued deposition of silt along the coast is crucial in counteracting the rise in sea level... This leads to calcium deposition in the blood-vessels.*
N-UNCOUNT: usu with supp
≠erosion

3 The **deposition** of a political leader is the removal of him or her from office. *It was this issue which led to the deposition of the king.*
N-UNCOUNT: usu with poss

depositor /dɪpɒzɪtəʳ/ **depositors.** A bank's **depositors** are the people who have accounts with that bank. ◆◇◇◇◇
N-COUNT

depository /dɪpɒzɪtəri/ **depositories.** A **depository** is a place where objects can be stored safely. *They have 2,500 tons of paper stored in their depository.*
N-COUNT

depot /depoʊ, AM diː-/ **depots** ◆◇◇◇◇

1 A **depot** is a place where large amounts of raw materials, equipment, or other supplies are kept until they are needed. *...food depots. ...a government arms depot.*
N-COUNT
=warehouse

2 A **depot** is a large building or yard where buses or railway engines are kept when they are not being used.
N-COUNT

3 A **depot** is a bus station or railway station; used mainly in American English. *She was reunited with her boyfriend in the bus depot of Ozark, Alabama.*
N-COUNT

deprave /dɪpreɪv/ **depraves, depraving, depraved.** Something that **depraves** someone makes them morally bad or evil; a formal word. *It is a crime to publish or show material likely to deprave or corrupt those who see, hear or read it.*
VERB
=corrupt
V n

depraved /dɪpreɪvd/. **Depraved** actions, things, or people are morally bad or evil. *It has been condemned as the most disturbing and depraved film of its kind... She described it as the work of depraved and evil criminals.*
ADJ-GRADED
=immoral, degenerate

depravity /dɪprævɪti/. **Depravity** is moral corruption; a formal word. *I have seen the absolute depravity that can exist in times of war. ...the righteous struggle between decency and depravity.*
N-UNCOUNT
=immorality

deprecate /deprɪkeɪt/ **deprecates, deprecating, deprecated.** If you **deprecate** something, you speak critically about it; a formal word. *As time went on he also deprecated the low quality of entrants to the profession... As a lawyer, I would deprecate any sort of legal control on gene therapy at this stage.*
VERB
V n

deprecating /deprɪkeɪtɪŋ/. A **deprecating** attitude, gesture, or remark shows that you think that something is not very good, especially something associated with yourself; used in written English. *Erica responded by making a little deprecating shrug.* ♦ **deprecatingly** *He speaks deprecatingly of his father as a lonely man.*
ADJ-GRADED
ADV: ADV after v

depreciate /dɪpriːʃieɪt/ **depreciates, depreciating, depreciated.** If something such as a currency **depreciates** or if something **depreciates** it, it loses some of its original value. *Inflation is rising rapidly; the yuan is depreciating... The demand for foreign currency depreciates the real value of local currencies... In the five years to September 1986, inflation dropped from 16% to 3% while the pound depreciated by a quarter... We think lower German interest rates in due course will allow European currencies to depreciate against the dollar bloc.* ♦ **depreciation** /dɪpriːʃieɪʃᵊn/ **depreciations** *...miscellaneous costs, including machinery depreciation and wages... A depreciation of a currency's value makes imports more expensive and exports cheaper.*
◆◇◇◇◇
V-ERG
V
V n
V *by* amount
V *against* n
N-VAR

depredation /deprɪdeɪʃᵊn/ **depredations.** The **depredations** of a person, animal, or force are their harmful actions, which usually involve taking or damaging something; a formal word. *Crops can be all too easily decimated by unchecked depredations by deer... Much of the region's environmental depredation is a result of poor planning.*
N-VAR: usu with supp

depress /dɪpres/ **depresses, depressing, depressed** ◆◇◇◇◇

1 If someone or something **depresses** you, they make you feel sad and disappointed. *I must admit the state of the country depresses me ... I know he is too optimistic but I don't want to depress him.*
VERB
V n

2 If something **depresses** prices, wages, or figures, it causes them to become less. *The stronger U.S. dollar depressed sales.*
VERB
V n

depressed /dɪprest/ ◆◆◇◇◇

1 If you are **depressed**, you are sad and feel that you cannot enjoy anything, because your situation is so difficult and unpleasant. *He seemed somewhat depressed... She's been very depressed and upset about this whole situation.*
ADJ-GRADED: usu v-link ADJ
=despondent

2 A **depressed** place or industry does not have enough business or employment to be prosperous. *Many states already have Enterprise Zones and legislation that encourage investment in depressed areas... The construction industry is no longer as depressed as it was.*
ADJ-GRADED
=run-down
≠thriving

3 A **depressed** point on a surface is lower than the parts around it. *Acupressure is manual pressure applied to a specific slightly depressed point on the body.*
ADJ-GRADED

depressing /dɪpresɪŋ/. Something that is **depressing** makes you feel sad and disappointed. *Yesterday's unemployment figures were as depressing as those of the previous 22 months... I'm rather keen to go in February because I think it's a very dismal, depressing month.* ♦ **depressingly** *It all sounded depressingly familiar to Haig.*
◆◆◇◇◇
ADJ-GRADED
ADV-GRADED: usu ADV adj

depression /dɪpreʃᵊn/ **depressions** ◆◆◆◇◇

1 **Depression** is a mental state in which you are sad and feel that you cannot enjoy anything, because your situation is so difficult and unpleasant. *Mr Thomas was suffering from depression... I slid into a depression and became morbidly fascinated with death.*
N-VAR
=despondency
≠euphoria

2 A **depression** is a time when there is very little economic activity, which causes a lot of unemployment and poverty. *He never forgot the hardships he witnessed during the Great Depression of the 1930s.*
N-COUNT
=slump

3 A **depression** in a surface is an area which is lower than the parts surrounding it. *...an area pockmarked by rainfilled depressions.*
N-COUNT
=hollow
≠mound

4 A **depression** is a mass of air that has a low pressure and that often causes rain; a technical term. *The storm started as a typical mid-Atlantic depression in an area to the west of Spain.*
N-COUNT

depressive /dɪpresɪv/ **depressives**

1 **Depressive** means relating to depression or to being depressed. *He's no longer a depressive character. ...a severe depressive disorder.*
ADJ: usu ADJ n

2 A **depressive** is someone who suffers from depression. *He was a bit of a depressive and ended up dying very young... The clinic has a reputation for treating depressives who feel they can no longer cope.* ● See also **manic-depressive**.
N-UNCOUNT

deprivation /deprɪveɪʃ°n/ **deprivations.** If you suffer **deprivation**, you do not have or are prevented from having something that you want or need. *...long-term patients who face a life of deprivation... Millions more suffer from serious sleep deprivation caused by long work hours. ...the effects of social deprivations on families.* ◆◇◇◇◇ N-VAR: oft supp N

deprive /dɪpraɪv/ **deprives, depriving, deprived.** If you **deprive** someone **of** something that they want or need, you take it away from them, or you prevent them from having it. *The disintegration of the Soviet Union deprived western intelligence agencies of their main enemies... They've been deprived of the fuel necessary to heat their homes.* ◆◆◇◇◇ VERB; V n of n

deprived /dɪpraɪvd/. **Deprived** people or people from **deprived** areas do not have the things that people consider to be essential in life, for example acceptable living conditions or education. *...probably the most severely deprived children in the country. ...the problems associated with life in a deprived inner city area.* ◆◇◇◇◇ ADJ-GRADED: usu ADJ n =underprivileged

dept, depts. Dept is used as a written abbreviation for 'department', usually in the name of a department. *...the Internal Affairs Dept.* ◆◇◇◇◇

depth /depθ/ **depths** ◆◆◆◇◇

1 The **depth** of something such as a river or hole is the distance downwards from its top surface, or between its upper and lower surfaces. *The smaller lake ranges from five to fourteen feet in depth... The depth of the shaft is 520 yards... Pour the vegetable oil into a frying pan to a depth of about 1cm... They were detected at depths of more than a kilometre in the Mediterranean Sea, Black Sea and North Sea.* N-VAR: oft amount in N, with poss, N of amount

2 The **depth** of something such as a cupboard or drawer is the distance between its front surface and its back. N-VAR: oft amount in N, with poss, N of amount

3 If an emotion is very strongly or intensely felt, you can talk about its **depth**. *I am well aware of the depth of feeling that exists in Londonderry... 'Tough, isn't it?' was all she said, but Amy felt the depth of her unspoken sympathy.* N-VAR: usu N of n =strength

4 The **depth** of a situation is its extent and seriousness. *The country's leadership had underestimated the depth of the crisis.* N-UNCOUNT: usu N of n =severity

5 The **depth** of someone's knowledge is the great amount that they know. *We felt at home with her and were impressed with the depth of her knowledge... It makes invaluable reading for anyone who wants to acquire a greater depth of understanding of the subject.* N-UNCOUNT: usu N of n =profundity

6 The **depth** of a colour is its quality of richness and strength. *White wines tend to gain depth of colour with age... The blue base gives the red paint more depth.* N-UNCOUNT =intensity

7 In photography and art, you say that a picture has **depth** or **depth of field** when you mean that it appears three-dimensional rather than flat; a technical term. *All the paintings are startlingly dramatic as a result of their depth of field and colour.* N-UNCOUNT: oft N of n ≠shallowness

8 If you say that someone or something has **depth**, you mean that they have serious and interesting qualities which are not immediately obvious and which you have to think about carefully before you can fully understand them. *His music lacks depth... There are hidden depths in all of us.* N-UNCOUNT: also N in pl =profundity ≠shallowness

9 **The depths** are places that are a long way below the surface of the sea or earth; a literary use. *Leaves, brown with long immersion, rose to the surface and vanished back into the depths.* N-PLURAL: the N

10 If you talk about **the depths of** an area, you mean the parts of it which are very remote. *...the depths of the countryside... Somewhere in the depths of the pine forest an identical sound reverberated.* N-PLURAL: the N of n

11 If you are in **the depths of** an unpleasant emotion, you feel that emotion very strongly. *I was in the depths of despair when the baby was terribly sick every day, and was losing weight.* N-PLURAL: the N of n

12 If something happens in **the depths of** a difficult or unpleasant period of time, it happens in the middle and most severe or intense part of it. *The country is in the depths of a recession. ...the depths of winter.* N-PLURAL: the N of n

PHRASES

13 If you deal with a subject **in depth**, you deal with it very thoroughly and consider all the aspects of it. *We will discuss these three areas in depth... Their achievements have already been analysed in depth and do not require further discussion.* PHR after v =in detail, thoroughly

14 If you say that someone is **out of** their **depth**, you mean that they are in a situation that is much too difficult for them to be able to cope with it. *Mr Gibson is clearly intellectually out of his depth... I'd always struggled at school. I hated it and felt out of my depth.* usu v-link PHR

15 If you are **out of** your **depth**, you are in water that is deeper than you are tall, with the result that you cannot stand up with your head above water. v-link PHR

16 • to **plumb new depths**: see **plumb**. • to **plumb the depths**: see **plumb**.

depth charge, depth charges. A **depth charge** is a type of bomb which explodes under water and which is used especially to destroy enemy submarines. N-COUNT

deputation /depjʊteɪʃ°n/ **deputations.** A **deputation** is a small group of people who have been asked to speak to someone on behalf of a larger group of people, especially in order to make a complaint. *A deputation of elders from the village arrived headed by its chief.* N-COUNT =delegation

depute /dɪpjuːt/ **deputes, deputing, deputed.** If you **are deputed** to do something, someone instructs or authorizes you to do it on their behalf; a formal word. *The Dalai Lama was deputed to lead the Tibetan delegation.* VB: usu passive; be V-ed to-inf

deputize /depjʊtaɪz/ **deputizes, deputizing, deputized;** also spelled **deputise** in British English. If you **deputize** for someone, you do something on their behalf, for example attend a meeting. *It was some time before I became skilful enough to deputise for him in the kitchen... Herr Schulmann apologizes that he cannot be here to welcome you and he has asked me to deputize.* VERB; V for n; V

deputy /depjʊti/ **deputies** ◆◆◆◆◇

1 A **deputy** is the second most important person in an organization such as a business or government department. Someone's deputy often acts on their behalf when they are absent. *...Jack Lang, France's minister for culture, and his deputy, Catherine Tasca. ...the academy's deputy director, Vladimir Kudryatsev.* N-COUNT: oft N n

2 In some parliaments, the elected members are called **deputies**. *The president appealed to deputies to approve the plan quickly.* N-COUNT

derail /diːreɪl/ **derails, derailing, derailed** ◆◇◇◇◇

1 If someone or something **derails** something such as a plan or a series of negotiations, they prevent it from continuing as planned. *The present wave of political killings is the work of people trying to derail peace talks. ...a fear that any reform could be derailed by hard-line Communists.* VERB =wreck; V n

2 If a train **is derailed** or if it **derails**, it comes off the track on which it is running. *At least six people were killed and about twenty injured when a train was derailed in an isolated mountain region... No-one knows why the train derailed.* V-ERG; be V-ed; V; Also V n

derailment /diːreɪlmənt/ **derailments.** A **derailment** is an accident in which a train comes off the track on which it is running. N-VAR

deranged /dɪreɪndʒd/. Someone who is **deranged** behaves in a wild and uncontrolled way, often as a result of mental illness. *Three years ago today a deranged man shot and killed 14 people in the main square.* ◆◇◇◇◇ ADJ-GRADED =demented

derangement /dɪreɪndʒmənt/. **Derangement** is the state of being mentally ill and unable to think or act in a controlled way; an old-fashioned word. *...serious evidence of mental derangement.* N-UNCOUNT

derby /dɑːʳbi, AM dɜːrbi/ **derbies** ◆◇◇◇◇

1 **The Derby** is a famous English horse race which takes place every year. N-PROPER: the N

2 A **derby** is a sporting event between teams from the same area or city. *...a North London derby between Arsenal and Tottenham.* N-COUNT

deregulate /diːregjʊleɪt/ **deregulates, deregulating, deregulated.** To **deregulate** something means to remove controls and regulations from it. *...the need to deregulate the US airline industry... Once wholesale prices are deregulated, consumer prices will also rise.*
◆◇◇◇◇ VERB; V n

deregulation /diːregjʊleɪʃᵊn/. **Deregulation** is the removal of controls and restrictions in a particular area of business or trade. *Since deregulation, banks are permitted to set their own interest rates.*
◆◇◇◇◇ N-UNCOUNT

derelict /derɪlɪkt/ **derelicts**
◆◇◇◇◇

1 A place or building that is **derelict** is empty and in a bad state of repair because it has not been used or lived in for a long time. *Her body was found dumped in a derelict warehouse less than a mile from her home.*
ADJ-GRADED

2 A **derelict** is a person who has no home or job and who has to live on the streets; a formal use.
N-COUNT =vagrant

dereliction /derɪlɪkʃᵊn/. If a building or a piece of land is in a state of **dereliction**, it is deserted or abandoned. *The previous owners had rescued the building from dereliction.*
N-UNCOUNT

dereliction of duty. **Dereliction of duty** is deliberate or accidental failure to do what you should do as part of your job; a formal expression. *Sergeant Slater pleaded guilty to wilful dereliction of duty and lying in a sworn statement.*
N-UNCOUNT =negligence

deride /dɪraɪd/ **derides, deriding, derided.** If you **deride** someone or something, you say that they are stupid or have no value; a formal word. *Opposition MPs derided the Government's response to the crisis... This theory is widely derided by conventional scientists.*
◆◇◇◇◇ VERB =ridicule; V n

de rigueur /də rɪgɜːʳ/. If you say that a possession or habit is **de rigueur**, you mean that it is fashionable and therefore necessary for anyone who wants to avoid being considered old-fashioned or unusual. *T-shirts now seem almost de rigueur in the West End.*
ADJ: v-link ADJ

derision /dɪrɪʒᵊn/. If you treat someone or something with **derision**, you express contempt for them. *He tried to calm them, but was greeted with shouts of derision.*
N-UNCOUNT =disdain

derisive /dɪraɪsɪv/. A **derisive** noise, expression, or remark expresses contempt. *There was a short, derisive laugh.* ♦ **derisively** *Phil's tormentor snorted derisively.*
ADJ-GRADED =contemptuous; ADV-GRADED: ADV with v

derisory /dɪraɪzəri/

1 If you describe something such as an amount of money as **derisory**, you are emphasizing that it is so small or inadequate that it seems silly or not worth considering. *She was being paid what I considered a derisory amount of money... Were the contracts that were offered to the players as derisory as we have been led to believe?*
ADJ-GRADED PRAGMATICS =laughable

2 **Derisory** means the same as **derisive**. *...derisory remarks about the police.*
ADJ-GRADED: usu ADJ n

derivation /derɪveɪʃᵊn/ **derivations.** The **derivation** of something, especially a word, is its origin or source. *The derivation of its name is obscure... The word is of old French derivation.*
N-VAR: oft N *of* n, *of* adj N

derivative /dɪrɪvətɪv/ **derivatives**
◆◇◇◇◇

1 A **derivative** is something which has been developed or obtained from something else. *...a poppy-seed derivative similar to heroin... This isn't an entirely new car, but a new derivative of the Citroen XM.*
N-COUNT

2 If you say that something is **derivative**, you are criticizing it because it is not new or original but has been developed from something else. *...their dull, derivative debut album... A lot of what you see in stand-up comedy today is very derivative.*
ADJ-GRADED PRAGMATICS

derive /dɪraɪv/ **derives, deriving, derived**
◆◆◇◇◇

1 If you **derive** something such as pleasure or benefit **from** someone or something, you get it from them; a formal use. *Mr Ying is one of those happy people who derive pleasure from helping others.*
VERB; V n *from* n/-ing

2 If you say that something such as a word or feeling **derives** or **is derived from** something else, you mean that it comes from that thing. *The name Anastasia is derived from a Greek word meaning 'of the resurrection'. ...defensive behaviour patterns which derive from our subconscious fears.*
V-ERG =stem from; *be* V-ed *from* n; V *from* n; Also V n *from* n

dermatitis /dɜːʳmətaɪtɪs/. **Dermatitis** is a medical condition which makes your skin red and painful.
N-UNCOUNT

dermatologist /dɜːʳmətɒlədʒɪst/ **dermatologists.** A **dermatologist** is a doctor who specializes in the study of skin and the treatment of skin diseases.
◆◇◇◇◇ N-COUNT

derogatory /dɪrɒgətri, AM -tɔːri/. If you make a **derogatory** remark or comment about someone or something, you express your low opinion of them. *He refused to withdraw derogatory remarks made about his boss.*
ADJ-GRADED: usu ADJ n

derrick /derɪk/ **derricks**

1 A **derrick** is a simple crane that is used to move cargo on a ship.
N-COUNT

2 A **derrick** is a tower built over an oil well which is used to raise and lower the drill.
N-COUNT

derring-do /derɪŋ duː/. **Derring-do** is the quality of being bold and daring, often in a rather showy or foolish way; an old-fashioned word.
N-UNCOUNT

dervish /dɜːʳvɪʃ/ **dervishes.** A **dervish** is a member of a Moslem religious group which has a very active and lively dance as part of its worship. If you say that someone is like a **dervish**, you mean that they are turning round and round, waving their arms about, or working very quickly. *In the heart of the Anatolian steppe, dervishes still whirl on festive occasions in mystic union with God... Brian was whirling like a dervish, slapping at the mosquitoes and moaning.*
N-COUNT

desalination /diːsælɪneɪʃᵊn/. **Desalination** is the process of removing salt from sea water so that it can be used for drinking, or for watering crops.
N-UNCOUNT

descant /deskænt/ **descants.** A **descant** is a tune which is played or sung above the main tune in a piece of music. *An elderly woman, arms crossed, sang the descant.*
N-COUNT

descend /dɪsend/ **descends, descending, descended**
◆◆◇◇◇

1 If you **descend** or if you **descend** a staircase, you move downwards from a higher to a lower level; a formal use. *Things are cooler and more damp as we descend to the cellar... She walked over to the carpeted stairs at the end of the corridor and descended one flight.*
VERB =go down ≠rise; V prep; V n; Also V

2 When a mood or atmosphere **descends** on a place or on the people there, it affects them by spreading among them; a literary use. *An uneasy calm descended on the area... A reverent hush descended on the multitude.*
VERB =fall; V *on/upon/over* n; Also V

3 If a large group of people arrive to see you, especially if their visit is unexpected or causes you a lot of work, you can say that they **have descended** on you. *Some 3,000 city officials will descend on Capitol Hill on Tuesday to lobby for more money... Curious tourists and reporters from around the globe are descending upon the peaceful villages.*
VERB =invade; V *on/upon* n

4 When night, dusk, or darkness **descends**, it starts to get dark; a literary use. *Darkness has now descended and the moon and stars shine hazily in the clear sky.*
VERB =fall; V

5 If you say that someone **descends to** something which you consider unacceptable or unworthy of them, you are expressing your disapproval of the fact that they do it. *We're not going to descend to such methods... She's got too much dignity to descend to writing anonymous letters.*
VERB PRAGMATICS =stoop, sink; V *to* n/-ing

6 When you want to emphasize that the situation that someone is entering is very bad, you can say that they **are descending into** that situation. *He was ultimately overthrown and the country descended into chaos.*
VERB PRAGMATICS =fall, slide; V *into* n

descendant /dɪsendənt/ **descendants**
◆◇◇◇◇

1 Someone's **descendants** are the people in later generations who are related to them. *They are descendants of the original English and Scottish settlers. ...Lord Cochrane and his descendants.*
N-COUNT: usu pl, usu with poss ≠ancestor

2 Something modern which evolved or developed from an older thing can be called a **descendant** of
N-COUNT: usu N *of* n ≠ancestor

it. *His design was a descendant of a 1956 device... They are the descendants of plants imported by the early settlers.*

descended /dɪse̲ndɪd/ ◆◇◇◇◇

1 A person who is **descended from** someone who lived a long time ago is directly related to them. *She used to tell us that she was descended from some Scottish Lord but we thought she was bragging.* ADJ: v-link ADJ *from* n

2 An animal that is **descended from** another sort of animal has developed from the original sort. *Domestic chickens are descended from jungle fowl of Southeast Asia.* ADJ: v-link ADJ *from* n

descending /dɪse̲ndɪŋ/. When a group of things is listed or arranged in **descending** order, each thing is smaller or less important than the thing before it. *All the other ingredients, including water, have to be listed in descending order by weight.* ADJ: ADJ n

descent /dɪse̲nt/ **descents** ◆◇◇◇◇

1 A **descent** is a movement from a higher to a lower level or position. *Sixteen of the youngsters set off for help, but during the descent three collapsed in the cold and rain. ...the crash of an Airbus A300 on its descent into Kathmandu airport.* N-VAR

2 A **descent** is a surface that slopes downwards, for example the side of a steep hill. *On the descents, cyclists spin past cars, freewheeling downhill at tremendous speed.* N-COUNT

3 When you want to emphasize that a situation becomes very bad, you can talk about someone's or something's **descent** into that situation. *The only lasting solution lies in a political settlement. Without it, their descent into chaos will be guaranteed. ...his swift descent from respected academic to struggling small businessman.* N-SING: usu poss N *into/from/to* n PRAGMATICS =decline

4 You use **descent** to talk about a person's family background, for example their nationality or social status; a formal use. *All the contributors were of African descent.* N-UNCOUNT: usu *of* adj N =origin, ancestry

describe /dɪskra̲ɪb/ **describes, describing, described** ◆◆◆◆◆

1 If you **describe** a person, object, event, or situation, you say what they are like or what happened. *We asked her to describe what kind of things she did in her spare time... She broke down describing how she was arrested for refusing a breath test... She read a poem by Carver which describes their life together... The myth of Narcissus is described in Ovid's work... Just before his death he described seeing their son in a beautiful garden.* VERB V wh V n V -ing

2 If a person **describes** someone or something **as** a particular thing, he or she believes that they are that thing and says so. *He described it as an extraordinarily tangled and complicated tale... One of them was a man described by police as a leading terrorist... Hume describes her as a large, bony and masculine woman... Even his closest allies describe him as forceful, aggressive and determined... The President has described the meeting as marking a new stage between the military super-powers.* VERB PRAGMATICS V n *as* n V n *as* adj V n *as* -ing

3 If something **describes** a particular shape, it forms that shape or makes a movement that follows the line of that shape; a formal use. *His pass described a perfect arc through the leaden sky.* VB: no passive V n

description /dɪskrɪ̲pʃᵊn/ **descriptions** ◆◆◆◇◇

1 A **description** of someone or something is an account which explains what they are or what they look like. *Police have issued a description of the man who was aged between fifty and sixty. ...a detailed description of the movements and battle plans of Italy's fleet... He has a real gift for vivid description.* N-VAR: oft N *of* n

2 If something is **of** a particular **description**, it belongs to the general class of items that are mentioned. *...the oldest Catholic church of any description in England... Events of this description occurred daily.* N-SING: *of* N =kind, type

3 You say that something is beyond **description**, or that it defies **description** to emphasize that it is very unusual, impressive, dreadful, or extreme. *His face is weary beyond description... We were in a disaster situation that defies description.* N-UNCOUNT: oft *beyond* N PRAGMATICS

descriptive /dɪskrɪ̲ptɪv/. **Descriptive** language or writing indicates what someone or something is like. *The Group adopted the simpler, more descriptive title of Angina Support Group.* ◆◇◇◇◇ ADJ-GRADED

desecrate /de̲sɪkreɪt/ **desecrates, desecrating, desecrated.** If someone **desecrates** something which is considered to be sacred or very special, they deliberately damage or insult it. *She shouldn't have desecrated the picture of a religious leader... The earth is to be honoured; it is not to be desecrated.* ♦ **desecration** /de̲sɪkre̲ɪʃᵊn/ *The whole area has been shocked by the desecration of the cemetery.* ◆◇◇◇◇ VERB =defile V n N-UNCOUNT: oft N *of* n

deseed /di̲ːsi̲ːd/ **deseeds, deseeding, deseeded;** also spelled **de-seed.** In British English, to **deseed** a fruit or vegetable means to remove all the seeds from it. *Halve and deseed the peppers.* VERB V n

desegregate /diːse̲grɪgeɪt/ **desegregates, desegregating, desegregated.** To **desegregate** something such as a place, institution, or service means to officially cease keeping the people who use it in separate groups, especially groups defined by race. *...efforts to desegregate sport... The school system itself is not totally desegregated.* ♦ **desegregation** /di̲ːsegrəge̲ɪʃᵊn/ *Desegregation may be harder to enforce in rural areas.* VERB =integrate ≠segregate V n V-ed N-UNCOUNT

desensitize /di̲ːse̲nsɪtaɪz/ **desensitizes, desensitizing, desensitized;** also spelled **desensitise** in British English. To **desensitize** someone means to cause them to react less strongly to things such as pain, anxiety, or other people's suffering. *...the language that is used to desensitize us to the terrible reality of war... Your immune system has been desensitized because it has become used to the substance.* VERB V n *to* n *be* V-ed Also V n

desert, deserts, deserting, deserted. The noun is pronounced /de̲zəʳt/. The pronunciation /dɪzɜ̲ːʳt/ is used for the verb and for meaning 8. ◆◆◆◇◇

1 A **desert** is a large area of land, usually in a hot region, where there is almost no water, rain, trees, or plants. *...the Sahara Desert. ...the burning desert sun... The vehicles have been modified to suit conditions in the desert.* N-VAR: oft in names after n

2 If you refer to a place or situation as a **desert**, you think it is bad for people because it is not interesting, exciting, or useful in any way. *They live in 12 high-rise apartment buildings that sit in a desert of concrete... Pubs are a cultural desert.* N-COUNT: with supp PRAGMATICS

3 If people or animals **desert** a place, they leave it and it becomes empty. *Poor farmers are deserting their parched farm fields and coming here looking for jobs... After the show, the audience deserts the Blackpool streets.* ♦ **deserted** *They went off to swim in the pool, which was now deserted... She led them into a deserted sidestreet.* VERB V n ADJ-GRADED =empty

4 If someone **deserts** you, they go away and leave you, and no longer help or support you. *Mrs Roding's husband deserted her years ago... He has been deserted by most of his advisers.* ♦ **desertion** /dɪzɜ̲ːʳʃᵊn/ **desertions** *It was a long time since she'd referred to her father's desertion.* VERB V n N-VAR

5 If you **desert** something that you support, use, or are involved with, you stop supporting it, using it, or being involved with it. *The paper's new price rise, putting it up to 27p, will encourage readers to desert in even greater droves... He was pained to see many youngsters deserting kibbutz life... Spaniards are worried about German investors deserting Spain for Eastern Europe.* ♦ **desertion** *They blamed his proposal for much of the mass desertion by the Socialist electorate. ...possible further desertions from the party at its conference.* VERB V V n V n *for* n N-VAR

6 If a quality or skill that you normally have **deserts** you, you suddenly find that you do not have it when you need it or want it. *Even when he appeared to be depressed, a dry sense of humour never deserted him... She lost the next five games, and the set, as her touch abruptly deserted her.* VERB =leave V n

7 If someone **deserts**, or **deserts** a job, especially a job in the armed forces, they leave that job without permission. *He was a second-lieutenant in the* VERB V *army until he deserted... He deserted from army intelligence last month... Young workers are more willing to desert jobs they don't like.* ♦ **desertion** *The high rate of desertion has added to the army's woes... There were a growing number of desertions from the federal army.* V from n / V n / N-VAR

8 If you say that someone has got their **just deserts**, you mean that they deserved the unpleasant things that have happened to them, because they did something bad. *At the end of the book the child's true identity is discovered, and the bad guys get their just deserts.* PHRASE PRAGMATICS

deserter /dɪzɜːʳtəʳ/ **deserters.** A **deserter** is someone who leaves their job in the armed forces without permission. ◆◇◇◇◇ N-COUNT

desertification /dɪzɜːʳtɪfɪkeɪʃᵊn/. **Desertification** is the process by which a piece of land becomes dry, bare, and unsuitable for growing trees or crops on. *A third of Africa is under threat of desertification.* N-UNCOUNT

desert island /dezəʳt aɪlənd/ **desert islands.** A **desert island** is a small tropical island, where nobody lives. ◆◇◇◇◇ N-COUNT

deserve /dɪzɜːʳv/ **deserves, deserving, deserved** ◆◆◆◇◇

1 If you say that someone or something **deserves** something, you mean that they should have it or receive it because of their qualities or actions. *Government officials clearly deserve some of the blame as well... They know the sport inside out, and we treat them with the respect they deserve... These people deserve to make more than the minimum wage... His children's books are classics that deserve to be much better known... By the time I left he'd become pretty hostile. I felt I deserved better than that... The Park Hotel has been in business since 1834 and has a well-deserved reputation.* VERB / V n / V to-inf / V compar / V-ed

2 If you say that someone **got what they deserved**, you mean that they deserved the bad thing that happened to them, and you have no sympathy for them. *One of them said the two dead joy riders got what they deserved.* PHRASE PRAGMATICS

deservedly /dɪzɜːʳvɪdli/. You use **deservedly** to indicate that someone deserved what happened to them, especially when it was something good. *He deservedly won the Player of the Year award... You will have to book well in advance for this deservedly popular hotel... He was highly praised, and deservedly so, by the Asian Times.* ADV: ADV with v, ADV adj/adv, ADV with cl PRAGMATICS

deserving /dɪzɜːʳvɪŋ/ ◆◇◇◇◇

1 If you describe a person, organization, or cause as **deserving**, you mean that you think they should be helped; a formal use. *The money saved could be used for more deserving causes.* ADJ-GRADED

2 If someone is **deserving of** something, they have qualities or have done something which makes it right that they should receive it. *...artists deserving of public subsidy.* ADJ-GRADED: v-link ADJ of n

desiccated /desɪkeɪtɪd/

1 **Desiccated** things have lost all the moisture that was in them; a formal use. *...desiccated flowers and leaves.* ADJ: usu ADJ n =dehydrated

2 **Desiccated** food has been dried in order to preserve it. *...desiccated coconut.* ADJ: ADJ n

desiccation /desɪkeɪʃᵊn/. **Desiccation** is the process of becoming completely dried out; a formal word. *...the disastrous consequences of the desiccation of the wetland.* N-UNCOUNT

design /dɪzaɪn/ **designs, designing, designed** ◆◆◆◆◆

1 When someone **designs** a garment, building, machine, or other object, they plan it and make a detailed drawing of it from which it can be built or made. *They wanted to design a machine that was both attractive and practical. ...men wearing specially designed boots.* VERB / V n / V-ed

2 When someone **designs** a survey, policy, or system, they plan and prepare it, and decide on all the details of it. *We may be able to design a course to suit your particular needs... Computer security systems will be designed by independent technicians... A number of very well designed studies have been undertaken.* VERB / V n / V-ed

3 **Design** is the process and art of planning and making detailed drawings of something. *He was a born mechanic with a flair for design... Most mobile robots are still in the design stage... She came to London in 1960 to study fashion design.* N-UNCOUNT

4 The **design** of something is the way in which it has been planned and made. *These machines are constantly updated by improving the design of the computers. ...a new design of clock... The shoes were of good design and good quality... BMW is recalling 8,000 cars because of a design fault.* N-UNCOUNT: usu with supp

5 A **design** is a drawing which someone produces to show how they would like something to be built or made. *When Bernardello asked them to build him a home, they drew up the design in a week.* N-COUNT =plan

6 A **design** is a pattern of lines, flowers, or shapes which is used to decorate something. *Their range of tableware is decorated with a blackberry design... Many pictures have been based on simple geometric designs.* N-COUNT =motif

7 A **design** is an overall plan or intention that someone has in their mind when they are doing something. *Is there some design in having him in the middle?... The intelligence service conceived a grand design to assassinate the War Minister.* N-COUNT

8 If something **is designed** for a purpose, it is intended for that purpose. *This project is designed to help landless people... It's not designed for anyone under age eighteen.* V-PASSIVE =intended / be V-ed to-inf / be V-ed for n

9 If something happens or is done **by design**, someone does it deliberately, rather than by accident. *The pair met often - at first by chance but later by design.* PHRASES =on purpose

10 If someone **has designs on** something, they want it and are planning to get it, often in a dishonest way. *His colonel had designs on his wife... Greece has always stressed that it had no designs on the territory.* V inflects

designate, designates, designating, designated. The verb is pronounced /dezɪgneɪt/. The adjective is pronounced /dezɪgnət/. ◆◆◇◇◇

1 When you **designate** someone or something, you formally give them a particular description or name. *...a man interviewed in one of our studies whom we shall designate as E... There are efforts under way to designate the bridge a historic landmark... I live in Exmoor, which is designated as a national park.* VERB / V n as n / V n n / V-ed

2 If something **is designated** for a particular purpose, it is set aside for that purpose. *Some of the rooms were designated as offices. ...scholarships designated for minorities... Smoking is allowed in designated areas.* VB: usu passive / be V-ed as/for n / V-ed

3 When you **designate** someone as something, you formally choose them to do that particular job. *Designate someone as the spokesperson... The President's designated successor is his son.* VERB / V n as n / V-ed

4 **Designate** is used to describe someone who has been formally chosen to do a particular job, but has not yet started doing it. *Japan's Prime Minister-designate is completing his Cabinet today.* ADJ: n ADJ

designation /dezɪgneɪʃᵊn/ **designations.** A **designation** is a description, name, or title that is given to someone or something. **Designation** is the fact of giving that description, name, or title. *...a level four alert, a designation reserved for very serious incidents. ...the designation of Madrid as European City of Culture 1992.* ◆◇◇◇◇ N-VAR

designer /dɪzaɪnəʳ/ **designers** ◆◆◆◇◇

1 A **designer** is a person whose job is to design things by making drawings of them. *Carolyne is a fashion designer.* N-COUNT

2 **Designer** clothes or **designer** labels are expensive, fashionable clothes made by a famous designer, rather than mass-produced in a factory. *He wears designer clothes and drives an antique car... People want to buy designer labels for snob value.* ADJ: ADJ n

3 You can use **designer** to describe things that are worn or bought because they are fashionable; an informal use. *Tousled hair and designer stubble are chic... Designer beers and trendy wines have replaced the good old British pint.* ADJ: ADJ n

desirable /dɪza͟ɪərəbəl/ ◆◆◇◇◇
1 Something that is **desirable** is worth having or doing because it is useful, necessary, or popular. *Prolonged negotiation was not desirable... The crowd moved indoors for what were deemed the most desirable items.* ADJ-GRADED ♦ **desirability** /dɪza͟ɪərəbɪ̱lɪti/ *...the desirability of democratic reform. ...the debate on the desirability of banning the ivory trade.* N-UNCOUNT: usu *the* N *of* n/-ing
2 Someone who is **desirable** is considered to be sexually attractive. *...the young women of his own age whom his classmates thought most desirable.* ADJ-GRADED ♦ **desirability** *He had not at all overrated Veronica's desirability.* N-UNCOUNT: usu poss N

desire /dɪza͟ɪəʳ/ **desires, desiring, desired** ◆◆◆◆◇
1 A **desire** is a strong wish to do or have something. *I had a strong desire to help and care for people... They seem to have lost their desire for life.* N-COUNT: oft N to-inf, N *for* n
2 If you **desire** something, you want it; a formal use. *She had remarried and desired a child with her new husband... But Fred was bored and desired to go home... He desired me to inform her that he had made his peace with God.* VB: no cont; V n; V to-inf; V n to-inf ♦ **desired** *You may find that just threatening this course of action will produce the desired effect... His warnings have provoked the desired response.* ADJ-GRADED: ADJ n
3 **Desire** for someone is a strong feeling of wanting to have sex with them. *Teenage sex, for instance, may come not out of genuine desire but from a need to get love.* N-UNCOUNT
4 If you **desire** someone, you want to have sex with them. *It never occurred to him that she might not desire him.* VB: no cont; V n
5 **If desired** is used in instructions in written English to indicate that the course of action mentioned is optional. *Additional courses may be taken if desired... Transfer this sauce to a separate saucepan, if desired.* PHRASES
6 If you say that someone or something is your **heart's desire**, you mean that you want that person or thing very much; a literary expression. *He was extremely devious in his efforts to achieve his heart's desire.* Ns inflect, usu poss PHR
7 If you say that something **leaves** a lot **to be desired**, you mean that it is not as good as it should be. *The selection of TV programmes, especially at the weekend, leaves a lot to be desired... Food seems to have been available, even if the quality left much to be desired... It is just possible that the accuracy of the information provided might leave something to be desired.* V inflects

desirous /dɪza͟ɪərəs/. If you are **desirous of** doing something or **desirous of** something, you want to do it very much or want it very much; a formal word. *Desirous of knowing something about the operations, I stood and watched the spectacle... The enemy is so desirous of peace that he will agree to any terms.* ADJ-GRADED: v-link ADJ *of* -ing/n

desist /dɪzɪ̱st/ **desists, desisting, desisted.** If you **desist** from doing something, you stop doing it; a formal word. *Ford never desisted from trying to persuade him to return to America... The magazine will desist from such language after receiving complaints... She rubbed her arms, but they hurt and she desisted.* VERB; V *from* -ing/n; V

desk /de̱sk/ **desks** ◆◆◆◆◇
1 A **desk** is a table, often with drawers, which you sit at to write or work. N-COUNT
2 The place in a hotel, hospital, airport, or other building where you check in or obtain information is referred to as a particular **desk**. *I told the girl on the reception desk that I was terribly sorry, but I was half an hour late... A map and a bird-watchers' field checklist are available at the front desk. ...the main information desk.* N-SING: usu supp N
3 A particular department of a broadcasting company, or a newspaper or magazine company, can be referred to as a particular **desk**. *Let our news desk know as quickly as possible on 414 3926... Over now to Simon Ingram at the sports desk.* N-SING: supp N

de̱sk clerk, desk clerks. In American English, a **desk clerk** is a receptionist in a hotel. N-COUNT

desktop /de̱sktɒp/ **desktops;** also spelled **desk-top.**
1 **Desktop** computers are a convenient size for using on a desk or table, but are not designed to be portable. *When launched, the Macintosh was the smallest desktop computer ever produced.* ADJ: ADJ n
2 A **desktop** is a desktop computer. N-COUNT

de̱sktop pu̱blishing; also spelled **desk-top publishing. Desktop publishing** is the production of printed materials such as newspapers and magazines using a desktop computer and a laser printer, rather than using conventional printing methods. N-UNCOUNT

desolate, desolates, desolating, desolated. ◆◇◇◇◇
The adjective is pronounced /de̱sələt/. The verb is pronounced /de̱səleɪt/.
1 A **desolate** place is empty of people and lacking in comfort. *...a desolate landscape of flat green fields broken by marsh... Half-ruined, hardly a building untouched, it's a desolate place.* ADJ-GRADED =bleak
2 If someone is **desolate**, they feel very sad, lonely, and without hope. *He was desolate without her.* ADJ-GRADED: usu v-link ADJ
3 If something **desolates** you, it upsets you and makes you very unhappy; used mainly in literary English. *Their inclination to wait and demand more resources desolated President Lincoln.* VERB =devastate; V n ♦ **desolated** *I saw them walk away and felt absolutely desolated.* ADJ ♦ **desolating** *They have maintained their optimism in the face of desolating subjugation.* ADJ-GRADED

desolation /de̱səle͟ɪʃən/
1 **Desolation** is a feeling of great unhappiness and despair. *Kozelek expresses his sense of desolation absolutely without self-pity.* N-UNCOUNT =misery
2 If you refer to **desolation** in a place, you mean that it is empty and frightening, for example because it has been destroyed by a violent force or army. *We looked out upon a scene of desolation and ruin... She says the army left desolation and death through the whole of northern Morazan.* N-UNCOUNT PRAGMATICS =devastation

despair /dɪspe͟əʳ/ **despairs, despairing, despaired** ◆◆◇◇◇
1 **Despair** is the feeling that everything is wrong and that nothing will improve. *I looked at my wife in despair... There is always someone to whom you can admit feelings of despair or inadequacy.* N-UNCOUNT: also N in pl
2 If you **despair**, you feel that everything is wrong and that nothing will improve. *'Oh, I despair sometimes,' he says in mock sorrow... He does despair at much of the press criticism.* VERB; V; V *at* n
3 If you **despair of** something, you feel that there is no hope that it will happen or improve. If you **despair of** someone, you feel that there is no hope that they will improve. *He wished to earn a living through writing but despaired of doing so. ...efforts to find homes for people despairing of ever having a roof over their heads... There are signs that many voters have already despaired of politicians.* VERB; V *of* -ing/n

despatch /dɪspæ̱tʃ/. See **dispatch**.

desperado /de̱spərɑ͟ːdoʊ/ **desperadoes** or **desperados.** A **desperado** is someone who does illegal, violent things without worrying about the danger; an old-fashioned word. N-COUNT

desperate /de̱spərət/ ◆◆◆◇◇
1 If you are **desperate**, you are in such a bad situation that you are willing to try anything to change it. *Troops are needed to help get food into parts of Bosnia where people are in desperate need... Desperate with anxiety, Bob and Hans searched the whole house... A family from Siberia made a desperate attempt to hijack a plane to the West.* ADJ-GRADED ♦ **desperately** *Thousands are desperately trying to leave their battered homes and villages.* ADV-GRADED: ADV with v
2 If you are **desperate** for something or **desperate** to do something, you want or need it very much indeed. *They'd been married nearly four years and June was desperate to start a family... People are desperate for him to do something.* ADJ-GRADED: v-link ADJ, usu ADJ to-inf, ADJ *for* n ♦ **desperately** *He was a boy who desperately needed affection.* ADV-GRADED: ADV with v
3 A **desperate** situation is very difficult, serious, or dangerous. *They said the situation in Kuwait was becoming desperate, with supplies of food running* ADJ-GRADED =dire

low... I decided not to abandon John when he was in such a desperate position.

desperation /dɛ̱spəre͟ɪʃᵊn/. **Desperation** is the feeling that you have when you are in such a bad situation that you will try anything to change it. *This feeling of desperation and helplessness was common to most of the refugees... In desperation I joined a physical exercise class.* ◆◇◇◇◇ N-UNCOUNT

despicable /dɪspɪ̱kəbᵊl, AM dɛ̱spɪk-/. If you say that a person or action is **despicable**, you are emphasizing that they are extremely nasty, cruel, or evil. *The Minister, who visited the scene a few hours after the explosion, said it was a despicable crime.* ADJ-GRADED PRAGMATICS =contemptible, vile

despise /dɪspa͟ɪz/ **despises, despising, despised.** If you **despise** something or someone, you dislike them and have a very low opinion of them. *I can never, ever forgive him. I despise him... She secretly despises his work... How I despised myself for my cowardice!* ◆◇◇◇◇ VERB; V n; V pron-refl *for* n/-ing

despite /dɪspa͟ɪt/ ◆◆◆◆◇

1 You use **despite** to introduce a fact which makes the other part of the sentence surprising. *Despite a thorough investigation, no trace of Dr Southwell has been found... The National Health Service has visibly deteriorated, despite increased spending... He was obviously distressed despite being unconscious.* PREP: PREP n/-ing =in spite of

2 If you do something **despite** yourself you do it although you did not really intend or expect to. *Despite myself, Harry's remarks had caused me to stop and reflect.* PREP: PREP pron-refl =in spite of

3 You use **despite** to introduce an idea that appears to contradict your main statement, without suggesting that this idea is true or that you believe it. *She told friends she will stand by husband, despite reports that he sent another woman love notes... Despite rumours of a fondness for alcohol, he is revealed as a man who never swears.* PREP =in spite of

despoil /dɪspɔ͟ɪl/ **despoils, despoiling, despoiled.** To **despoil** a place means to make it less attractive, valuable, or important by taking things away from it or by destroying it; a formal word. *People picking mushrooms are sometimes stopped by passers-by and ticked off for despoiling the countryside. ...a landscape despoiled by coal-mining and heavy industry.* VERB; V n; V-ed

despondency /dɪspɒ̱ndənsi/. **Despondency** is a strong feeling of unhappiness caused by difficulties which you feel you cannot overcome. *There's a mood of gloom and despondency in the country.* N-UNCOUNT =dejection

despondent /dɪspɒ̱ndənt/. If you are **despondent**, you are very unhappy because you have been experiencing difficulties that you think you will not be able to overcome. *John often felt despondent after dragging his portfolio around various agencies.* ♦ **despondently** *Despondently, I went back and told Bill the news.* ADJ-GRADED =depressed; ADV-GRADED: ADV with v

despot /dɛ̱spɒt, AM -pət/ **despots.** A **despot** is a ruler or other person who has a lot of power and who uses it unfairly or cruelly. N-COUNT =tyrant, dictator

despotic /dɪspɒ̱tɪk/. If you say that someone is **despotic**, you are emphasizing that they use their power over other people in a very unfair or cruel way. *The country was ruled by a despotic tyrant.* ADJ-GRADED PRAGMATICS =tyrannical

despotism /dɛ̱spətɪzəm/. **Despotism** is cruel and unfair government by a ruler or rulers who have a lot of power. N-UNCOUNT =tyranny

dessert /dɪzɜ͟ːʳt/ **desserts. Dessert** is something sweet, such as fruit or a pudding, that you eat at the end of a meal. *She had homemade ice cream for dessert... I am partial to desserts that combine fresh fruit with fine pastry.* ◆◆◇◇◇ N-MASS =sweet, pudding

dessertspoon /dɪzɜ͟ːʳtspuːn/ **dessertspoons;** also spelled **dessert spoon.**

1 A **dessertspoon** is a spoon which is midway between the size of a teaspoon and a tablespoon. You use it to eat desserts. N-COUNT

2 A **dessertspoon** of a food or liquid is the amount of it that a dessertspoon will hold. *...a rounded dessertspoon of flour.* N-COUNT: oft N *of* n =dessertspoonful

dessertspoonful /dɪzɜ͟ːʳtspuːnfʊl/ **dessertspoonfuls** or **dessertspoonsful.** A **dessertspoonful** of a food or liquid is the amount of it that a dessertspoon will hold. *...a dessertspoonful of olive oil.* N-COUNT: oft N *of* n =dessertspoon

dessert wine, dessert wines. A **dessert wine** is a sweet wine, usually a white wine, that is served with dessert. N-MASS

destabilize /diːste͟ɪbəlaɪz/ **destabilizes, destabilizing, destabilized;** also spelled **destabilise** in British English. To **destabilize** something such as a country or government means to create a situation which reduces its power or influence. *Their sole aim is to destabilize the Indian government.* ♦ **destabilization** /diːste͟ɪbᵊlaɪze͟ɪʃᵊn/ *He said that these events had provoked the destabilization of the country.* ◆◇◇◇◇ VERB; V n; N-UNCOUNT

destination /dɛ̱stɪne͟ɪʃᵊn/ **destinations.** The **destination** of someone or something is the place to which they are going or being sent. *Spain is still our most popular holiday destination... Only half of the emergency supplies have reached their destination.* ◆◆◇◇◇ N-COUNT

destined /dɛ̱stɪnd/ ◆◆◇◇◇

1 If something is **destined** to happen or if someone is **destined** to do something, that thing is planned or will definitely happen. *He feels that he was destined to become a musician... London seems destined to lose more than 2,000 hospital beds... Everyone knew that Muriel was destined for great things.* ADJ: v-link ADJ, ADJ to-inf, ADJ *for* n

2 If someone is **destined for** a particular place, or if goods are **destined for** a particular place, they are travelling towards that place or will be sent to that place. *...products destined for Saudi Arabia.* ADJ: v-link ADJ *for* n =bound for

destiny /dɛ̱stɪni/ **destinies** ◆◆◇◇◇

1 A person's **destiny** is everything that happens to them during their life, including what will happen in the future, especially when it is considered to be controlled by someone or something else. *We are masters of our own destiny... It is my destiny one day to be king.* N-COUNT: usu sing, usu with poss =fate

2 **Destiny** is the force which some people believe controls the things that happen to you in your life. *Is it destiny that brings people together, or is it accident?* N-UNCOUNT =fate

destitute /dɛ̱stɪtjuːt, AM -tuːt/. Someone who is **destitute** has no money or possessions; a formal word. *...destitute children who live on the streets.* ◆◇◇◇◇ ADJ-GRADED

destitution /dɛ̱stɪtju͟ːʃᵊn, AM -tu͟ː-/. **Destitution** is the state of having no money or possessions; a formal word. N-UNCOUNT

destroy /dɪstrɔ͟ɪ/ **destroys, destroying, destroyed** ◆◆◆◆◇

1 To **destroy** something means to cause so much damage to it that it is completely ruined or does not exist any more. *That's a sure recipe for destroying the economy and creating chaos... No one was injured in the explosion, but the building was completely destroyed... Even the most gifted can have confidence destroyed by the wrong instructor.* VERB =wreck; V n

2 To **destroy** someone means to ruin their life or to make their situation unbearable. *If I was younger or more naive, the criticism would have destroyed me.* VERB; V n

3 If an animal **is destroyed**, it is killed, either because it is ill or because it is dangerous. *Lindsay was unhurt but the horse had to be destroyed.* VB: usu passive =be put down; *be* V-ed

4 See also **soul-destroying**.

destroyer /dɪstrɔ͟ɪəʳ/ **destroyers** ◆◇◇◇◇

1 A **destroyer** is a small, heavily armed warship. N-COUNT

2 Something or someone that is described as a **destroyer** destroys things or people. *The company is the world's largest destroyer of tropical forests.* N-COUNT: with poss, usu N *of* n

destruction /dɪstrʌ̱kʃᵊn/. **Destruction** is the act of destroying something, or the state of being destroyed. *...an international agreement aimed at halting the destruction of the ozone layer. ...weapons of mass destruction.* ◆◆◆◇◇ N-UNCOUNT

destructive /dɪstrʌ̱ktɪv/. Something that is **destructive** causes or is capable of causing great damage, harm, or injury. *...the awesome destruc-* ◆◆◇◇◇ ADJ-GRADED

tive power of nuclear weapons... Guilt can be very destructive. ♦ **destructiveness** *...the size of armies and the destructiveness of their weapons.* N-UNCOUNT
♦ **destructively** *Power can be used creatively or destructively.* ADV-GRADED

desultory /desəltri, AM -tɔːri/. Something that is **desultory** is done in an unplanned and disorganized way, and without enthusiasm; a formal word. *The constables made a desultory attempt to keep them away from the barn.* ADJ-GRADED ♦ **desultorily** /desəltrɪli, AM -tɔːrɪli/ *The man continued talking. She answered him desultorily.* ADV-GRADED: ADV with v

detach /dɪtætʃ/ **detaches, detaching, detached** ◆◇◇◇◇
1 If you **detach** one thing from another that it is fixed to, you remove it. If one thing **detaches** from another, it becomes separated from it; a formal use. *Detach the white part of the application form and keep it for reference only... Detach the currants from the stems by simply running a fork down the length of the stem... Stale eggs are instantly detectable as the white detaches almost completely from the yolk.* V-ERG; V n; V n *from* n; V *from* n; Also V
2 If you **detach** yourself from something, you become less involved in it or less concerned about it than you used to. *It helps them detach themselves from their problems and become more objective.* VERB; V pron-refl *from* n
3 If you **detach** yourself from a person or place, you leave them; a formal use. *Alexis saw his father detach himself from the group and walk away down the hill by himself.* VERB; V pron-refl *from* n

detachable /dɪtætʃəbᵊl/. If a part of an object is **detachable**, it has been made so that it can be removed from the object. *...a cake tin with a detachable base.* ADJ =removable

detached /dɪtætʃt/ ◆◇◇◇◇
1 Someone who is **detached** is not personally involved in something or has no emotional interest in it. *He tries to remain emotionally detached from the prisoners, but fails... It is written in a detached, precise style.* ADJ-GRADED
2 A **detached** house is one that is not joined to any other house. • See also **semi-detached**. ADJ

detachment /dɪtætʃmənt/ **detachments** ◆◇◇◇◇
1 **Detachment** is the feeling that you have of not being personally involved in something or of having no emotional interest in it. *She did not care for the idea of socialising with her clients. It would detract from her professional detachment... Ridley viewed his work with a cynical detachment.* N-UNCOUNT
2 A **detachment** is a group of soldiers who are sent away from the main group to do a special job. *...a detachment of marines.* N-COUNT: oft N *of* n

detail /diːteɪl/ **details, detailing, detailed.** The pronunciation /dɪteɪl/ is also used in American English. ◆◆◆◆◇
1 The **details** of something are its individual features or elements. *...a meeting in Jakarta called to discuss the details of a peace agreement for Cambodia... No details of the discussions have been given... I recall every detail of the party.* N-COUNT: usu with supp, oft N *of* n
2 **Details** about someone or something are facts or pieces of information about them. *See the bottom of this page for details of how to apply for this exciting offer... Full details will be announced soon.* N-PLURAL: oft N *of* n/wh, adj N
3 A **detail** is a minor point or aspect of something, as opposed to the central ones. *Only minor details now remain to be settled.* N-COUNT: oft adj N
4 You can refer to the small features of something which are often not noticed as **detail**. *We like his attention to detail and his enthusiasm.* N-UNCOUNT
5 A **detail** of a picture is a small part of it that is printed separately and perhaps enlarged, so that the smaller features can be clearly seen. N-COUNT
6 If you **detail** things, you list them or give information about them. *The report detailed the human rights abuses committed during the war.* VERB; V n; Also V how
7 If someone **is detailed** to do a task or job, they are officially ordered to do it. *He detailed a constable to take it to the Incident Room.* VERB; V n to-inf; Also V n *to* n
8 If someone does not **go into details** about a subject, or does not **go into the detail**, they mention it without explaining it fully or properly. *He said he had been in various parts of Britain but did not go into details... Neither of them were prepared to go into the detail of their talks.* PHRASES; V inflects
9 If you examine or discuss something **in detail**, you do it thoroughly and carefully. *Mr Gorbachev described in detail the events of Monday.*

detailed /diːteɪld, AM dɪteɪld/. A **detailed** report or plan contains a lot of details. *Yesterday's letter contains a detailed account of the decisions... I started drawing up more detailed budgets.* ◆◆◆◇◇ ADJ-GRADED: usu ADJ n

detain /dɪteɪn/ **detains, detaining, detained** ◆◆◇◇◇
1 When people such as the police **detain** someone, they keep them in a place under their control; a formal use. *The act allows police to detain a suspect for up to 48 hours... He was arrested and detained for questioning.* VERB; V n
2 To **detain** someone means to delay them, for example by talking to them; a formal use. *Millson stood up. 'Thank you. We won't detain you any further, Mrs Stebbing.'* VERB; V n

detainee /diːteɪniː/ **detainees.** A **detainee** is someone who is held prisoner by a government because of his or her political views or activities. ◆◇◇◇◇ N-COUNT

detect /dɪtekt/ **detects, detecting, detected** ◆◆◇◇◇
1 To **detect** something means to find it or discover that it is present somewhere by using equipment or making an investigation. *...a sensitive piece of equipment used to detect radiation... Most skin cancers can be cured if detected and treated early... Doctors have developed a device which can detect who is more at risk from sudden death following a mild heart attack.* VERB; V n; V wh
2 If you **detect** something, you notice it or sense it, even though it is not very obvious. *Arnold could detect a certain sadness in the old man's face.* VERB =sense; V n

detectable /dɪtektəbᵊl/. Something that is **detectable** can be noticed or discovered. *Doctors say the disease is probably inherited but not detectable at birth.* ADJ-GRADED

detection /dɪtekʃᵊn/ ◆◇◇◇◇
1 **Detection** is the act of noticing or sensing something. *...the early detection of breast cancer.* N-UNCOUNT: oft N *of* n
2 **Detection** is the discovery of something which is supposed to be hidden. *They are cheating but are sophisticated enough to avoid detection.* N-UNCOUNT: oft N *of* n
3 **Detection** is the work of investigating a crime in order to find out what has happened and who committed it. *The detection rate for motor vehicle theft that year was just 11.7 per cent... The most important deterrent for most criminals is the likelihood of detection and arrest.* N-UNCOUNT

detective /dɪtektɪv/ **detectives.** A **detective** is someone whose job is to discover what has happened in a crime or other situation and to find the people involved. Some detectives work in the police force and others work privately. *Now detectives are appealing for witnesses who may have seen anything suspicious last night. ...Detective Inspector Ian Mosley.* ◆◆◆◇◇ N-COUNT ► Also a title in American English. *...Detective Nardosa of the New York City Police Department.* N-TITLE; N-VOC

detector /dɪtektəʳ/ **detectors.** A **detector** is an instrument which is used to discover that something is present somewhere, or to measure how much of something there is. *...a metal detector. ...fire alarms, smoke detectors, and other warning systems.* ◆◇◇◇◇ N-COUNT: oft n N

detente /deɪtɒnt/; also spelled **détente**. **Detente** is a state of friendly relations between two countries when previously there had been problems between them; a formal word. *...their desire to pursue a policy of detente... They have made the first move towards a detente.* 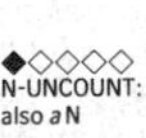 N-UNCOUNT: also *a* N

detention /dɪtenʃᵊn/ **detentions** 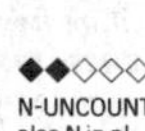
1 **Detention** is the arrest or imprisonment of someone, especially for political reasons. *...the detention without trial of government critics... They have been held in detention since the end of June... The government says the detentions are necessary on national security grounds.* N-UNCOUNT: also N in pl
2 **Detention** is a punishment for naughty N-VAR

schoolchildren, who are made to stay at school after the other children have gone home. *The teacher kept the boys in detention after school.*

detention centre, detention centres; spelled **detention center** in American English. A **detention centre** is a sort of prison, for example a place where illegal immigrants are kept whilst a decision is made about what to do with them. N-COUNT

deter /dɪtɜːʳ/ **deters, deterring, deterred.** To **deter** someone from doing something means to make them not want to do it or continue doing it. *Supporters of the death penalty argue that it would deter criminals from carrying guns... Arrests and jail sentences have done nothing to deter the protesters... Jeremy was not deterred by this criticism.* ◆◆◇◇◇ VERB =discourage V n *from* -ing V n

detergent /dɪtɜːʳdʒᵊnt/ **detergents. Detergent** is a chemical substance, usually in the form of a powder or liquid, which is used for washing things such as clothes or dishes. ◆◇◇◇◇ N-MASS

deteriorate /dɪtɪəriəreɪt/ **deteriorates, deteriorating, deteriorated.** If something **deteriorates**, it becomes worse in some way. *There are fears that the situation might deteriorate into full-scale war... The weather conditions are deteriorating... Grant's health steadily deteriorated.* ◆◆◇◇◇ VERB ≠improve V
♦ **deterioration** /dɪtɪəriəreɪʃᵊn/ *...concern about the rapid deterioration in relations between the two countries. ...the slow steady deterioration of a patient with Alzheimer's disease.* N-UNCOUNT ≠improvement

determinant /dɪtɜːʳmɪnənt/ **determinants.** A **determinant** of something causes it to be of a particular kind or to happen in a particular way; a formal word. *The windows and the views beyond them are major determinants of a room's character. ...the types of determinants that are likely to influence trade in a specific industry.* ◆◇◇◇◇ N-COUNT: usu with supp

determinate /dɪtɜːʳmɪneɪt/. **Determinate** means fixed and definite; a formal word. *...a contract for the exclusive possession of land for some determinate period.* ADJ: usu ADJ n ≠indeterminate

determination /dɪtɜːʳmɪneɪʃᵊn/. **Determination** is the quality that you show when you have decided to do something and you will not let anything stop you. *Everyone concerned acted with great courage and determination... He reaffirmed their determination to tackle inflation... His cooking reflects a determination to acknowledge his northern roots... There was an expression of fierce determination on her face.* ◆◆◇◇◇ N-UNCOUNT: oft N to-inf

determine /dɪtɜːʳmɪn/ **determines, determining, determined** ◆◆◆◆◇

1 If a particular factor **determines** the nature of a thing or event, it causes it to be of a particular kind. *The size of the chicken pieces will determine the cooking time... Social status is largely determined by the occupation of the main breadwinner... What determines whether you are a career success or a failure?* ♦ **determination** *...the gene which is responsible for male sex determination.* VERB V n V wh N-UNCOUNT: with supp

2 To **determine** a fact means to discover it as a result of investigation. *The investigation will determine what really happened... Experts say testing needs to be done on each contaminant to determine the long-term effects on humans... The best science can do is determine that a risk is so small that it's not worth worrying about.* VERB V wh V n V that Also V wh

3 If you **determine** something, you decide it or settle it. *The Baltic people have a right to determine their own future... The final wording had not yet been determined... My aim was first of all to determine what I should do next.* ♦ **determination, determinations** *We must take into our own hands the determination of our future.* VERB V n V wh-to-inf Also V that N-COUNT: usu sing, usu *the* N *of* n

4 If you **determine** to do something, you make a firm decision to do it; a formal use. *He determined to rescue his two countrymen... I determined that I would ask him outright.* VERB V to-inf V that

determined /dɪtɜːʳmɪnd/. If you are **determined** to do something, you have made a firm decision to do it and will not let anything stop you. *His enemies are determined to ruin him... She is a remarkably adroit and determined politician... He made determined efforts to overcome the scandal.* ♦ **determinedly** *She shook her head, determinedly.* ◆◆◆◇◇ ADJ-GRADED: oft ADJ to-inf ADV-GRADED =resolutely

determiner /dɪtɜːʳmɪnəʳ/ **determiners.** A **determiner** is a word which is used at the beginning of a noun group to indicate, for example, which thing you are referring to or whether you are referring to one thing or several. Common English determiners are 'a', 'the', 'some', 'this', and 'each'. N-COUNT

determinism /dɪtɜːʳmɪnɪzəm/. **Determinism** is the belief that all actions and events result from other actions, events, or situations, so people cannot in fact choose what to do; a formal word. *I don't believe in historical determinism.* N-UNCOUNT: oft adj N

determinist /dɪtɜːʳmɪnɪst/ **determinists**

1 A **determinist** is someone who believes in determinism; a formal use. N-COUNT

2 **Determinist** ideas are based on determinism; a formal use. *The determinist doctrines in question maintained that certain people were born to be slaves, by their very nature.* ADJ

deterministic /dɪtɜːʳmɪnɪstɪk/

1 **Deterministic** ideas or explanations are based on determinism; a formal use. *...a deterministic view of human progress.* ADJ-GRADED

2 **Deterministic** forces and factors cause things to happen in a way that cannot be changed; a formal use. *The rise or decline of the United States is not a function of deterministic forces.* ADJ

deterrence /dɪterəns, AM -tɜːr-/. **Deterrence** is the prevention of something, especially war or crime, by having something such as weapons or punishment to use as a threat. *...policies of nuclear deterrence.* ◆◇◇◇◇ N-UNCOUNT

deterrent /dɪterənt, AM -tɜːr-/ **deterrents** ◆◇◇◇◇

1 A **deterrent** is something that prevents people from doing something by making them afraid of what will happen to them if they do it. *They seriously believe that capital punishment is a deterrent... The tough new law should act as a deterrent.* N-COUNT

2 A **deterrent** is a weapon or set of weapons designed to prevent potential enemies from attacking by making them afraid to do so. *The idea of building a nuclear deterrent is completely off the political agenda.* N-COUNT

3 If something has a **deterrent** effect, it has the effect of discouraging people from doing certain things. *Hopefully, that will have a deterrent effect on drug syndicates in the future. ...his belief in the deterrent value of capital punishment.* ADJ: ADJ n

detest /dɪtest/ **detests, detesting, detested.** If you **detest** someone or something, you dislike them very much. *My mother detested him... Jean detested being photographed.* ♦ **detestation** /diːtesteɪʃᵊn/ *They were united in their detestation of the government.* ◆◇◇◇◇ VERB =loathe V n/-ing N-UNCOUNT: oft N *of* n

detestable /dɪtestəbᵊl/. If you say that someone or something is **detestable**, you mean you dislike them very much; a formal word. *I find their views detestable.* ADJ-GRADED =despicable, repugnant

dethrone /diːθroʊn/ **dethrones, dethroning, dethroned.** If a king, queen, or other powerful person **is dethroned**, they are removed from their position of power. *He was dethroned and went into exile.* VB: usu passive =depose *be* V-ed

detonate /detəneɪt/ **detonates, detonating, detonated.** If someone **detonates** a device such as a bomb, or if it **detonates**, it explodes. *...the terrorists who planted and detonated the bomb... An explosive device detonated on the roof of the building late last night.* ◆◇◇◇◇ V-ERG V n V

detonation /detəneɪʃᵊn/ **detonations**

1 A **detonation** is a large or powerful explosion; a formal use. N-COUNT

2 **Detonation** is the action of causing a device such as a bomb to explode; a formal use. *...accidental detonation of nuclear weapons.* N-UNCOUNT

detonator /detəneɪtəʳ/ **detonators.** A **detonator** is a small amount of explosive or a piece of elec- N-COUNT trical or electronic equipment which is used to explode a bomb or other explosive device.

detour /di̲ːtʊəʳ/ **detours, detouring, detoured** ◆◇◇◇◇

1 If you make a **detour** on a journey, you go by a route which is not the shortest way, because you want to avoid something such as a traffic jam, or because there is something you want to do on the way. *He did not take the direct route to his home, but made a detour around the outskirts of the city.* N-COUNT

2 If you **detour**, you make a detour. *On the way back, Jarvis detoured to check the time of services at the church.* VERB V Also V prep

detox /di̲ːtɒks/. **Detox** is the same as **detoxification**. *Each patient sees a detox therapist who does the initial assessment.* N-UNCOUNT: oft N n

detoxification /diːtɒksɪfɪke̲ɪʃᵊn/. **Detoxification** is treatment given to people who are addicted to drugs or alcohol in order to stop them being addicted. N-UNCOUNT

detoxify /diːtɒ̲ksɪfaɪ/ **detoxifies, detoxifying, detoxified**

1 To **detoxify** something means to remove all the poisonous or harmful substances from it. *Seaweed baths can help to detoxify the body.* VERB V n

2 To **detoxify** a poisonous substance means to change it chemically so that it is no longer poisonous. *Vitamin C helps to detoxify pollutants in the body.* VERB V n

detract /dɪtræ̲kt/ **detracts, detracting, detracted.** If one thing **detracts** from another, it makes it seem less good or impressive. *They feared that the publicity surrounding him would detract from their own election campaigns.* ◆◇◇◇◇ VERB V *from* n Also V n *from* n

detractor /dɪtræ̲ktəʳ/ **detractors.** The **detractors** of a person or thing are people who criticize that person or thing; used mainly in journalism. *This performance will silence many of his detractors... The news will have delighted detractors of the scheme.* ◆◇◇◇◇ N-COUNT: usu pl, usu with poss =critic

detriment /de̲trɪmənt/ ◆◇◇◇◇

1 If something happens **to the detriment of** something or **to** someone's **detriment**, it causes harm or damage to them. *These tests will give too much importance to written exams to the detriment of other skills.* PHRASES usu PHR after v, v-link PHR

2 If something happens **without detriment to** someone or something, it does not harm or damage them. *These difficulties have been overcome without detriment to performance.* PHR n

detrimental /de̲trɪme̲ntᵊl/. Something that is **detrimental** to something else has a harmful or damaging effect on it. *Many foods are suspected of being detrimental to health because of the chemicals and additives they contain... The government's policy of high interest rates is having a detrimental effect on industry.* ◆◇◇◇◇ ADJ-GRADED: oft ADJ *to* n

detritus /dɪtra̲ɪtəs/. **Detritus** is the small pieces of rubbish that remain after an event has finished or when something has been used; a formal word. *...burnt-out buildings, littered with the detritus of war.* N-UNCOUNT: with supp

deuce /dju̲ːs, AM du̲ːs/ **deuces. Deuce** is the score in a game of tennis when both players have forty points. One player has to win two points in succession to win the game. N-UNCOUNT: also N in pl

devalue /diːvæ̲ljuː/ **devalues, devaluing, devalued** ◆◆◇◇◇

1 To **devalue** something means to cause it to be thought less impressive or worthy of respect. *They spread tales about her in an attempt to devalue her work... Wabel's victory was in no way devalued by the absence of series leader Tom Fisher.* ♦ **devalued** *Selling tickets for a devalued championship is becoming increasingly difficult... The child will be able to accept punishment without feeling devalued and worthless.* VERB V n *be* V-ed; ADJ-GRADED: usu ADJ n

2 To **devalue** the currency of a country means to reduce its value in relation to other currencies; a technical term in economics. *India has devalued the Rupee by about eleven per cent... The Pound would be devalued, we were told... Economic theory suggests that the devalued pound will boost the economy.* ♦ **devaluation** /diːvæljue̲ɪʃᵊn/ **devaluations** *It will lead to devaluation of a number of European currencies... There were massive devaluations of several currencies.* VERB V n *by* amount *be* V-ed V-ed Also V n; N-VAR

devastate /de̲vəsteɪt/ **devastates, devastating, devastated.** If something **devastates** an area or a place, it damages it very badly or destroys it totally. *A few days before, a fire had devastated large parts of Windsor Castle.* ◆◇◇◇◇ VERB =ravage, wreck V n

devastated /de̲vəsteɪtɪd/. If you are **devastated** by something, you are very shocked and upset by it. *Bishop Daly said he was devastated by news of the Cardinal's death... Teresa was devastated, her dreams shattered.* ◆◇◇◇◇ ADJ-GRADED: v-link ADJ

devastating /de̲vəsteɪtɪŋ/ ◆◆◇◇◇

1 If you describe something as **devastating**, you mean that it is very destructive or damaging. *The city of Ormac took the full force of the winds and devastating floods... Affairs do have a devastating effect on marriages.* ADJ-GRADED: usu ADJ n

2 You can use **devastating** to emphasize that something is very shocking, upsetting, or terrible. *The diagnosis was devastating. She had cancer.* ADJ-GRADED PRAGMATICS

3 You can use **devastating** to emphasize that something or someone is very impressive. *He returned to his best with a devastating display of galloping and jumping... I was devastating, if I do say so myself.* ♦ **devastatingly** *Its advertising is devastatingly successful... She was charming and devastatingly beautiful too.* ADJ PRAGMATICS; ADV-GRADED: usu ADV adj/-ed

devastation /de̲vəste̲ɪʃᵊn/. **Devastation** is severe and widespread destruction or damage. *A huge bomb blast brought chaos and devastation to the centre of Belfast yesterday.* ◆◇◇◇◇ N-UNCOUNT

develop /dɪve̲ləp/ **develops, developing, developed** ◆◆◆◆◆

1 When something **develops**, it grows or changes over a period of time and usually becomes more advanced, complete, or severe. *As children develop, some of the most important things they learn have to do with their sense of self... It's hard to say at this stage how the market will develop... These clashes could develop into open warfare. ...as society begins to have an impact on the developing child.* ♦ **developed** *Their bodies were well-developed and super fit.* VERB V V *into* n V-ing; ADJ-GRADED

2 If a problem or difficulty **develops**, it begins to occur. *A huge row has developed about the pollution emanating from a chemical plant.* VERB =arise V

3 If you say that a country **develops**, you mean that it changes from being a poor agricultural country to being a rich industrial country. *All countries, it was predicted, would develop and develop fast.* VERB =progress V

4 If you **develop** a business or industry, or if it **develops**, it becomes bigger and more successful. *An amateur hat-maker has won a scholarship to pursue her dreams of developing her own business... Over the last few years tourism has developed considerably on the attractive neighbouring beaches.* ♦ **developed** *Housing finance is less developed and less competitive in continental Europe.* V-ERG =build, expand V n V; ADJ-GRADED

5 If a person or company **develops** land or property, they make it more useful or profitable, by building houses or factories or by improving the existing buildings. *European entrepreneurs developed fashionable restaurants, bars and discotheques in the area. ...the cost of acquiring or developing property.* ♦ **developed** *Developed land was to grow from 5.3% to 6.9%.* VERB =improve V n Also V; ADJ-GRADED

6 If you **develop** a habit, reputation, or belief, you start to have it and it then becomes stronger or more noticeable. *She later developed a taste for expensive nightclubs... Mr Baker has developed the reputation of a master strategist.* VERB =acquire V n

7 If you **develop** a skill, quality, or relationship, or if it **develops**, it becomes better or stronger. *Now you have a good opportunity to develop a greater understanding of each other. ...weekly workshops that are designed to develop acting and theatre skills... We must develop closer ties with Germany... Their friendship developed through their shared interest* V-ERG V n V

in the Arts. ♦ **developed** *...a highly developed instinct for self-preservation.* ADJ-GRADED

8 If you **develop** an illness, or if it **develops**, you become affected by it. *The test should identify which smokers are most prone to develop lung cancer... A sharp ache developed in her back muscles.* V-ERG V n V

9 If a piece of equipment **develops** a fault, it starts to have the fault. *The aircraft made an unscheduled landing at Gatwick after developing an electrical fault.* VERB V n

10 If someone **develops** a new product, they design it and produce it. *He claims that several countries have developed nuclear weapons secretly. ...a computer system specially developed for the Coastguard service.* VERB V n V-ed

11 If you **develop** an idea, theory, story, or theme, or if it **develops**, it gradually becomes more detailed, advanced, or complex. *I would like to thank them for allowing me to develop their original idea... This point is developed further at the end of this chapter... My question was why theory develops, and why theories of a particular type develop when they do.* V-ERG V n V

12 To **develop** photographs means to make negatives or prints from a photographic film. *...after developing one roll of film.* VERB V n

developed /dɪvelǝpt/. If you talk about **developed** countries or the **developed** world, you mean the countries or the parts of the world that are wealthy and have many industries; a technical term in economics and politics. *The developed nations have to recognize the growing gap between rich and poor around the world... This scarcity is inevitable in less developed countries.* ♦♦◇◇◇ ADJ-GRADED

developer /dɪvelǝpǝʳ/ **developers** ♦♦◇◇◇

1 A **developer** is a person or a company that buys land and builds houses, offices, shops, or factories on it, or buys existing buildings and modernizes them. *...common land which would have a high commercial value if sold to developers. ...a corrupt, self-made property developer.* N-COUNT

2 A **developer** is someone who develops something such as an idea, a design, or a product. *John Bardeen was also co-developer of the theory of superconductivity. ...a software developer.* N-COUNT: with supp

3 **Developer** is a chemical used for developing photographs or films; a technical term in photography. *The time the film is left in the developer is also a crucial factor.* N-UNCOUNT

developing /dɪvelǝpɪŋ/. If you talk about **developing** countries or the **developing** world, you mean the countries or the parts of the world that are poor and have few industries; a technical term in economics and politics. *In the developing world cigarette consumption is increasing.* ♦♦◇◇◇ ADJ: ADJ n

development /dɪvelǝpmǝnt/ **developments** ♦♦♦♦♦

1 **Development** is the gradual growth or formation of something. *...an ideal system for studying the development of the embryo... The development of scientific concepts and attitudes are taken as central to the children's education... First he surveys Islam's development.* N-UNCOUNT: with supp, oft N *of* n

2 **Development** is the growth or expansion of something such as a firm or an industry. *We want Britain to play a leading part in the further political, economic and monetary development of the European Community... What are your plans for the development of your company?* N-UNCOUNT: with supp, oft N *of* n

3 **Development** is the process or result of making a basic design gradually better and more advanced. *It is spending $850m on research and development to get to the market place as soon as possible with faster microprocessors. ...the development of new and innovative telephone services.* N-VAR

4 **Development** is the process of making an area of land or water more useful or profitable. *...the fostering of development in the rural areas... He'd discussed with Mr Major setting up a bank for the development and reconstruction of Kurdish areas.* N-UNCOUNT: with supp

5 A **development** is an event or incident which has recently happened and is likely to have an effect on the present situation. *The police spokesman said: 'We believe there has been a significant development in the case.' ...the latest developments in Moscow... What do you think today's developments will mean for him?* N-COUNT

6 A **development** is an area of houses or buildings which have been built by property developers. N-COUNT

developmental /dɪvelǝpmentᵊl/. **Developmental** means relating to the development of someone or something. *...the emotional, educational, and developmental needs of the child.* ♦◇◇◇◇ ADJ: usu ADJ n

deviant /diːviǝnt/ **deviants** ♦◇◇◇◇

1 **Deviant** behaviour or thinking is different from what people normally consider to be acceptable. *...the social reactions to deviant and criminal behaviour... Of course, not all alcoholics and drug abusers produce deviant offspring.* ♦ **deviance** /diːviǝns/ *...sexual deviance, including the abuse of children.* ADJ-GRADED N-UNCOUNT

2 A **deviant** is someone whose behaviour or beliefs are different from what people normally consider to be acceptable. N-COUNT

deviate /diːvieɪt/ **deviates, deviating, deviated.** To **deviate** from something means to start doing something different or something that was not planned. *They stopped you as soon as you deviated from the script... He planned his schedule far in advance, and he didn't deviate from it... From very early on he believed a military revolution was necessary and he has never deviated from that ideological path.* VERB V *from* n Also V

deviation /diːvieɪʃᵊn/ **deviations** ♦◇◇◇◇

1 **Deviation** means doing something that is different from what people consider to be normal or acceptable. *Deviation from the norm is not tolerated. ...sexual deviation... To abstain from meat was a serious deviation.* N-VAR: oft N *from* n

2 **Deviation** is the difference between the value of one number in a series of numbers and the average value of all the numbers in the series; a technical term in statistics. *A 10 to 15 percent deviation is considered acceptable.* N-VAR

device /dɪvaɪs/ **devices** ♦♦♦◇◇

1 A **device** is an object that has been invented for a particular purpose, for example for recording or measuring something. *...the electronic device that tells the starter when an athlete has moved from his blocks prematurely. ...a device that could measure minute quantities of matter... We believe that an explosive device had been left inside a container.* N-COUNT: usu with supp

2 A **device** is a method of achieving something. *They claim that military spending is used as a device for managing the economy. ...the literary device of the metaphor.* N-COUNT

3 If you **leave** someone **to** their **own devices**, you leave them alone to do as they wish. *Left to his own devices, Osborn is a fluent – and often original – guitarist.* PHRASE: V inflects

devil /devᵊl/ **devils** ♦♦◇◇◇

1 In Judaism, Christianity, and Islam, **the Devil** is the most powerful and important evil spirit. *There are two forces at work, God and the devil.* N-PROPER: *the* N =Satan

2 A **devil** is an evil spirit. *...the idea of angels with wings and devils with horns and hoofs.* N-COUNT =demon

3 You can use **devil** to emphasize the way you feel about someone. For example, if you call someone a poor **devil**, you are saying that you feel sorry for them. You can call someone you are fond of an old **devil** or a little **devil**; an informal use. *I felt sorry for Blake, poor devil... Manfred, you're a suspicious old devil... He's an aggravating little devil.* N-COUNT PRAGMATICS

4 If you refer to someone as a **devil**, you mean that they do not behave very well but you like them and are not angry with them; an informal use. *'I think he was a bit of a devil,' Constance said.* N-COUNT PRAGMATICS

5 **Devil** can be used to emphasize what you think about someone or something. For example, if you say that someone is **a devil of a** nuisance, you are saying that you think they are very annoying. If you say that something is **a devil of a** problem, you think it is a very difficult problem. *He was always a devil of a nuisance... It's a devil of a tricky problem, isn't it?* PHRASES v-link PHR n PRAGMATICS =a hell of a

6 If you say **better the devil you know** or **better the devil you know than the devil you don't know**, you mean that you would prefer to have contact with or do business with a person you already know, even though you don't like them, than with a person you don't know. PRAGMATICS

7 If you say that you **had the devil's own job** to do something or that you **had a devil of a job** doing something, you are emphasizing that it was difficult to do it. *We had the devil's own job to persuade him to take part.* V inflects, PHR to-inf, PHR -ing PRAGMATICS

8 If you say that someone does something **like the devil**, you are emphasizing that they put a lot of effort into it. If you say that someone goes or drives **like the devil**, you are emphasizing that they go or drive very fast. *He drives himself on, working like the devil from seven in the morning until midnight... He must have driven like the devil.* PRAGMATICS

9 You can say **the devil take the hindmost** to describe or comment on a situation in which people do only what is best for themselves without thinking about other people; used expressing disapproval. *Every one for himself and the devil take the hindmost.* PRAGMATICS

10 If you say that you are **between the devil and the deep blue sea**, you mean that you are in a difficult situation where you have to choose between two equally unpleasant courses of action. v-link PHR

11 If you say that someone has **sold** their **soul to the devil**, you mean that you disapprove of them because they have done something that you think is not right in order to get what they want. V inflects PRAGMATICS

12 People say **talk of the devil** or **speak of the devil** if someone they have just been talking about arrives unexpectedly. *Well, talk of the devil!*

13 When you want to emphasize how annoyed or surprised you are, you can use an expression such as **what the devil**, **how the devil**, or **why the devil**; an informal expression. *'What the devil's the matter?'... Tim wondered how the devil they had managed it... 'Why the devil did you do that?'* PRAGMATICS

devilish /devəlɪʃ/

1 A **devilish** idea or action is cruel or unpleasant. *The Gulf war showed the devilish destructiveness of modern conventional weapons.* ADJ-GRADED: usu ADJ n =atrocious

2 You can use **devilish** to emphasize how extreme or difficult something is. *...a devilish puzzle.* ► Also an adverb. *I'd been devilish lucky.* ♦ **devilishly** *It is devilishly painful.* ADJ-GRADED: usu ADJ n PRAGMATICS ADV ADV-GRADED

devil-may-care. If you say that someone has a **devil-may-care** attitude, you mean that you approve of them because they seem relaxed and unconcerned about the consequences of their actions. *I love Italian food and wine and the devil-may-care attitude of the people.* ADJ: usu ADJ n PRAGMATICS

devil's advocate. If you say that you are playing **devil's advocate** in a discussion or debate, you mean that you are expressing an opinion which you do not agree with in order to make the argument more interesting. If you say that someone else is playing **devil's advocate**, you mean that you disapprove of them because they are pretending to hold an unpopular opinion in order to make an argument more interesting. N-UNCOUNT: also with det PRAGMATICS

devious /diːviəs/ ◆◇◇◇◇

1 **Devious** people are dishonest and secretive, often in a complicated way. *The Government was very devious by incorporating the two acts together... By devious means she tracked down the other woman.* ♦ **deviousness** *...the deviousness of drug traffickers in their attempts to conceal illegal substances.* ADJ-GRADED N-UNCOUNT

2 A **devious** route or path to a place involves many changes in direction, rather than being as straight and direct as possible. *He followed a devious route.* ADJ-GRADED: usu ADJ n =circuitous

devise /dɪvaɪz/ **devises, devising, devised.** If you **devise** a plan, system, or machine, you have the idea for it and design it. *We devised a scheme to help him... New long-range objectives must be devised.* ◆◆◇◇◇ VERB V n

devoid /dɪvɔɪd/. If you say that someone or something is **devoid of** a quality or thing, you are emphasizing that they have none of it; a formal word. *I have never looked on a face that was so devoid of feeling... The skies are virtually devoid of birdlife.* ◆◇◇◇◇ ADJ-GRADED: v-link ADJ of n PRAGMATICS =bereft of

devolution /diːvəluːʃən, dev-/. **Devolution** is the transfer of some authority or power from a central organization or government to smaller organizations or government departments. *...the devolution of power to the regions... We are talking about devolution for Scotland.* ◆◇◇◇◇ N-UNCOUNT: oft N of n

devolve /dɪvɒlv/ **devolves, devolving, devolved.** If you **devolve** power, authority, or responsibility to a less important or powerful person or group, or if it **devolves** upon them, it is transferred to them. *...the need to decentralize and devolve power to regional governments... The best companies are those that devolve responsibility as far as they can... A larger portion of this cost devolves upon the patient than for most other medical treatments.* ◆◇◇◇◇ V-ERG V n to n V n V upon/on n

devote /dɪvoʊt/ **devotes, devoting, devoted** ◆◆◇◇◇

1 If you **devote** yourself, your time, or your energy to something, you spend all or most of your time or energy on it. *He decided to devote the rest of his life to scientific investigation... Considerable resources have been devoted to proving him a liar... She gladly gave up her part-time job to devote herself entirely to her art.* VERB =dedicate V n to n/-ing V pron-refl to n/-ing

2 If you **devote** a particular proportion of a piece of writing or a speech to a particular subject, you deal with the subject in that amount of space or time. *He devoted a major section of his massive report to an analysis of US aircraft design... Page upon page is devoted to the chain of events leading to the Prime Minister's resignation.* VERB V n to n

devoted /dɪvoʊtɪd/ ◆◆◇◇◇

1 Someone who is **devoted** to a person loves that person very much. *...a loving and devoted husband... Today, 50 years on and three children later, the couple are still devoted to one another.* ADJ-GRADED: ADJ n, v-link ADJ to n

2 If you are **devoted** to something, you care about it a lot and are very enthusiastic about it. *I have personally been devoted to this cause for many years... Horace is so devoted to his garden that he hasn't been away for 10 years... Joyce Bryt is a devoted Star Trek fan.* ADJ-GRADED: v-link ADJ to n, ADJ n

3 Something that is **devoted to** a particular thing deals only with that thing or contains only that thing. *...a major touring exhibition devoted to the work of disabled artists. ...the original Jane Churchill shop, now devoted to a new range of accessories.* ADJ: v-link ADJ to n

devotee /devətiː/ **devotees** ◆◇◇◇◇

1 Someone who is a **devotee** of a subject or activity is very enthusiastic about it. *Mr Carpenter is obviously a devotee of Britten's music.* N-COUNT: with supp, oft N of n =fan

2 A **devotee** is a member of a religious group. *Monks shave their heads, as do devotees of the Hare Krishna movement.* N-COUNT

devotion /dɪvoʊʃən/ ◆◇◇◇◇

1 **Devotion** is great love, affection, or admiration for someone. *At first she was flattered by his devotion.* N-UNCOUNT: oft poss N

2 **Devotion** is commitment to a particular activity. *...devotion to the cause of the people and to socialism... I don't mean to keep criticising his devotion to his job.* N-UNCOUNT: oft N to n =dedication

3 **Devotion** is religious worship or strong religious feeling. *He was kneeling by his bed in an attitude of devotion.* N-UNCOUNT

devotional /dɪvoʊʃənəl/. **Devotional** activities, writings, or objects relate to religious worship. *...a domestic altar stacked with devotional pictures and sacred objects.* ADJ: ADJ n

devotions /dɪvoʊʃənz/. Someone's **devotions** are the prayers that they say. *Normally he performs his devotions twice a day.* N-PLURAL: oft poss N

devour /dɪvaʊəʳ/ **devours, devouring, devoured** ◆◇◇◇◇

1 If a person or animal **devours** something, they eat it quickly and eagerly. *A medium-sized dog will devour at least one can of food plus biscuits per* VERB V n

day... She drank two glasses of tequila and devoured half an apple pie.

2 If you **devour** a book or magazine, for example, you read it quickly and with great eagerness. *She began buying and devouring newspapers when she was only 12.* VERB Vn

devout /dɪvaʊt/ ◆◇◇◇◇

1 A **devout** person has deep religious beliefs. *She was a devout Christian... His devout Catholicism appeals to ordinary people.* ADJ-GRADED ▸ **The devout** are people who are devout. *...priests instructing the devout.* N-PLURAL: the N

2 If you describe someone as a **devout** supporter or a **devout** opponent of something, you mean that they support it enthusiastically or oppose it strongly. *Devout Marxists believed fascism was the 'last stand of the bourgeoisie'.* ADJ-GRADED: ADJ n =passionate, committed

devoutly /dɪvaʊtli/

1 Devoutly is used to emphasize how sincerely or deeply you hope for something or believe in something; a formal use. *He devoutly hoped it was true.* ADV-GRADED: ADV with v PRAGMATICS

2 Devoutly is used to emphasize how deep someone's religious beliefs are, or to indicate that something is done in a devout way. *...in this devoutly Buddhist country.* ADV: ADV adj, ADV with v PRAGMATICS

dew /djuː, AM duː/. **Dew** is small drops of water that form on the ground and other surfaces outdoors during the night. *The dew gathered on the leaves.* N-UNCOUNT

dewy /djuːi, AM duːi/

1 Something that is **dewy** is wet with dew; a literary use. *The satin slippers tread daintily through the dewy grass.* ADJ-GRADED

2 If your skin looks **dewy**, it looks soft and glows healthily. ADJ-GRADED

dewy-eyed. If you say that someone is **dewy-eyed**, you mean that they are unrealistic and think events and situations are better than they really are; used showing disapproval. *I can never understand why people become dewy-eyed and sentimental about the past.* ADJ-GRADED PRAGMATICS

dexterity /dekster*ɪ*ti/. **Dexterity** is skill in using your hands, or sometimes your mind. *...Reid's dexterity on the guitar. ...the wit and verbal dexterity of the script.* N-UNCOUNT

dexterous /dekstrəs/; also spelled **dextrous**. Someone who is **dexterous** is very skilful and clever with their hands. *As people grow older they generally become less dexterous and physically slower. ...a dextrous blues pianist.* ADJ-GRADED

dextrose /dekstroʊz, AM -roʊs/. **Dextrose** is a natural form of sugar that is found in fruits, honey, and in the blood of animals. N-UNCOUNT

diabetes /daɪəbiːtiːz, AM -t*ɪ*s/. **Diabetes** is a medical condition in which someone has too much sugar in their blood. ◆◆◇◇◇ N-UNCOUNT

diabetic /daɪəbetɪk/ **diabetics** ◆◇◇◇◇

1 A **diabetic** is a person who suffers from diabetes. *...an insulin-dependent diabetic.* N-COUNT ▸ Also an adjective. *...diabetic patients.* ADJ

2 Diabetic means relating to diabetes. *He found her in a diabetic coma.* ADJ: ADJ n

3 Diabetic foods are suitable for diabetics. *...diabetic jams and marmalades.* ADJ: ADJ n

diabolic /daɪəbɒlɪk/. **Diabolic** is used to describe things that people think are caused by or belong to the Devil; a formal word. *...the diabolic forces which lurk in all violence.* ADJ: ADJ n

diabolical /daɪəbɒlɪkᵊl/

1 If you describe something as **diabolical**, you are emphasizing that it is very bad, extreme, or unpleasant; an informal use. *It was a diabolical error, a schoolboy error... The pain was diabolical.* ADJ-GRADED PRAGMATICS =appalling
♦ **diabolically** /daɪəbɒlɪkli/ *...diabolically difficult clues.* ADV

2 Diabolical is used to emphasize how evil something is. *...sins committed in a spirit of diabolical enjoyment... One speaker today called the plan diabolical and sinister.* ADJ: usu ADJ n PRAGMATICS

diadem /daɪədem/ **diadems.** A **diadem** is a small crown with precious stones in it. N-COUNT

diagnose /daɪəgnoʊz, AM -noʊs/ **diagnoses, diagnosing, diagnosed.** If someone or something **is diagnosed** as having a particular illness or problem, their illness or problem is identified. If an illness or problem **is diagnosed**, it is identified. *The soldiers were diagnosed as having flu... Susan had a mental breakdown and was diagnosed with schizophrenia... In 1894 her illness was diagnosed as cancer... He could diagnose an engine problem simply by listening... This disorder is easily diagnosed but not so easily treated.* ◆◆◇◇◇ VERB be V-ed as -ing/adj, be V-ed with n, be V-ed as n, Vn, Also be V-ed adj

diagnosis /daɪəgnoʊsɪs/ **diagnoses. Diagnosis** is the discovery and identification of what is wrong with someone who is ill or with something that is not working properly. *I need to have a second test to confirm the diagnosis... Symptoms may not appear for some weeks, so diagnosis can be difficult.* ◆◆◇◇◇ N-VAR

diagnostic /daɪəgnɒstɪk/. **Diagnostic** equipment, methods, or systems are used for discovering what is wrong with people who are ill or with things that do not work properly. *...X-rays and other diagnostic tools.* ◆◇◇◇◇ ADJ: ADJ n

diagonal /daɪægənᵊl/ **diagonals** ◆◇◇◇◇

1 A **diagonal** line or movement goes in a slanting direction. *...a pattern of diagonal lines.* ADJ: usu ADJ n
♦ **diagonally** *Vaulting the stile, he headed diagonally across the paddock... In a moment he was seated, diagonally opposite her, brow furrowed.* ADV: ADV with v, oft ADV prep

2 A **diagonal** is a line that goes in a slanting direction. *The bedlinen is patterned in stylish checks, stripes, diagonals and triangles.* N-COUNT

3 A **diagonal** is a straight line that joins two opposite corners in a flat four-sided shape such as a square; a technical term in geometry. *Mark five points an equal distance apart along the diagonals.* N-COUNT

diagram /daɪəgræm/ **diagrams.** A **diagram** is a simple drawing consisting mainly of lines that is used, for example, to explain how a machine works. *...a circuit diagram... Can you reduce some long explanations to simple charts or diagrams?* ◆◇◇◇◇ N-COUNT: usu with supp

diagrammatic /daɪəgrəmætɪk/. Something that is in **diagrammatic** form is arranged or drawn as a diagram. *This is the virus in very crude simple diagrammatic form.* ADJ: usu ADJ n

dial /daɪəl/ **dials, dialling, dialled;** spelled **dialing, dialled** in American English. ◆◆◇◇◇

1 A **dial** is an indicator on a clock, meter, or other instrument which shows you the time or a measurement that has been recorded. *The luminous dial on the clock showed five minutes to seven... The dials of most barometers are inscribed with weather terms.* N-COUNT

2 A **dial** is a control on a device or piece of equipment, which you move in order to adjust the setting, for example to select or change the frequency on a radio or the temperature of a cooker. *He turned the dial on the radio... The heat dial was set at 150 degrees.* N-COUNT

3 A **dial** on some models of telephone is a circular disc that you rotate according to the number that you want to call. The disc has holes in it, and numbers or letters behind the holes. *...turning the dial on the phone.* N-COUNT

4 If you **dial** or if you **dial** a number, you turn the dial or press the buttons on a telephone in order to phone someone. *He lifted the phone and dialled her number... He dialled, and spoke briefly to the duty officer.* VERB Vn, V

dialect /daɪəlekt/ **dialects.** A **dialect** is a form of a language that is spoken in a particular area. *Azerbaijan is a predominantly Islamic country and the majority of its people speak a dialect of Turkish... They began to speak rapidly in dialect.* ◆◇◇◇◇ N-COUNT: also in N

dialectic /daɪəlektɪk/ **dialectics**

1 In formal English, people refer to the **dialectic** or **dialectics** of a situation when they are referring to the way in which two very different forces or factors interact with each other, and the way in which their differences are resolved. *...the intricate dialectic of these two contrasting concepts. ...the dia-* N-COUNT: with supp, oft the N of/between n *lectics of class struggle and of socio-economic change.*

2 In philosophy, **dialectics** is a method of reasoning and reaching conclusions by considering theories and ideas together with ones that contradict them. N-UNCOUNT

dialectical /daɪəlektɪkəl/. **Dialectical** is used to describe situations, theories, and methods which depend on resolving opposing factors; a technical word in philosophy. *The essence of dialectical thought is division.* ADJ: usu ADJ n

dialling code, dialling codes; spelled **dialing code** in American English. A **dialling code** is a telephone number which you dial before someone's personal number in order to be connected to the right area, town, or village. N-COUNT

dialling tone, dialling tones. In British English, the **dialling tone** is the noise which you hear when you pick up a telephone receiver and which means that you can dial the number you want. The usual American term is **dial tone**. N-COUNT

dialogue /daɪəlɒg, AM -lɔːg/ **dialogues;** also spelled **dialog** in American English. ◆◆◆◇◇

1 **Dialogue** is communication or discussion between people or groups of people such as governments or political parties. *People of all social standings should be given equal opportunities for dialogue... They have begun dialogues to promote better understanding between both communities... She came back and tried to start a dialogue with the man.* N-VAR

2 A **dialogue** is a conversation between two people in a book, film, or play. *Although the dialogue is sharp, the actors move rather too awkwardly around the stage... He is a very deft novelist too, with a superb ear for dialogue. ...Shakespeare's dialogues.* N-VAR

dial tone, dial tones. In American English, the **dial tone** is the noise which you hear when you pick up a telephone receiver and which means that you can dial the number you want. The usual British term is **dialling tone**. N-COUNT

dialysis /daɪælɪsɪs/. **Dialysis** or **kidney dialysis** is a method of treating kidney failure by using a machine to remove waste material from the kidneys. *I was on dialysis for seven years before my first transplant.* N-UNCOUNT

diamante /daɪəmænti, AM diːəmɑːnteɪ/. **Diamante** jewellery is made from small pieces of cut glass which look like diamonds. *...diamante earrings.* N-UNCOUNT: oft N n

diameter /daɪæmɪtəʳ/ **diameters.** The **diameter** of a round object is the length of a straight line that can be drawn across it, passing through the middle of it. *...a tube less than a fifth of the diameter of a human hair. ...a length of 22-mm diameter steel pipe. ...a tiny capsule, between 1 and 3 millimetres in diameter.* ◆◆◇◇◇ N-COUNT: also *in* N

diametrically /daɪəmetrɪkli/. If you say that two things are **diametrically** opposed, you are emphasizing that they are completely different from each other. *They came to conclusions diametrically opposed to ours... The economic crisis was interpreted in diametrically opposing ways.* ADV: ADV adj PRAGMATICS

diamond /daɪəmənd/ **diamonds** ◆◆◇◇◇

1 A **diamond** is a hard, bright, precious stone which is clear and colourless. Diamonds are used in jewellery and for cutting very hard substances. *...a pair of diamond earrings. ...a sphere made of diamond without impurity or flaw.* N-VAR

2 **Diamonds** are jewellery such as necklaces and bracelets which have diamonds set into them. *Nicole loves wearing her diamonds, even with jeans and a white T-shirt.* N-PLURAL

3 A **diamond** is a shape with four straight sides of equal length: ♦. *...forming his hands into the shape of a diamond.* N-COUNT

4 **Diamonds** is one of the four suits of cards in a pack of playing cards. Each card in the suit is marked with one or more red symbols in the shape of a diamond. *He drew the seven of diamonds.* ► A **diamond** is a playing card of this suit. N-UNCOUNT-COLL N-COUNT

diamond jubilee, diamond jubilees. A **diamond jubilee** is the sixtieth anniversary of an important event. N-COUNT

diaper /daɪəpəʳ/ **diapers.** In American English, a **diaper** is a piece of soft towel or absorbent paper, which you put round a baby's bottom in order to soak up its urine and faeces. The British word is **nappy**. *He never changed her diapers, never bathed her.* ◆◇◇◇◇ N-COUNT

diaphanous /daɪæfənəs/. **Diaphanous** cloth is very thin and almost transparent; a literary word. *...a diaphanous dress of pale gold.* ADJ: usu ADJ n

diaphragm /daɪəfræm/ **diaphragms** ◆◇◇◇◇

1 Your **diaphragm** is a muscle between your lungs and your stomach. It is used especially when you breathe deeply. N-COUNT

2 A **diaphragm** is a circular contraceptive device that a woman places inside her vagina. N-COUNT

diarist /daɪərɪst/ **diarists.** A **diarist** is a person who records things in a diary which is later published. N-COUNT

diarrhoea /daɪəriːə/; spelled **diarrhea** in American English. If someone has **diarrhoea**, a lot of liquid faeces comes out of their body at frequent intervals, because they are ill. ◆◇◇◇◇ N-UNCOUNT

diary /daɪəri/ **diaries.** A **diary** is a book which has a separate space for each day of the year. You use a diary to write down things you plan to do, or to record what happens in your life day by day. ◆◆◆◇◇ N-COUNT

diaspora /daɪæspərə/. People who come from a particular nation, or whose ancestors came from it, but who now live in many different parts of the world are sometimes referred to as the **diaspora**; a formal word. *...the history of peoples from the African diaspora. ...the Jews of the diaspora.* N-SING: usu *the* N

diatribe /daɪətraɪb/ **diatribes.** A **diatribe** is an angry speech or article which is extremely critical of someone's ideas or activities. *The last chapter of this book is an extended diatribe against the academic left.* N-COUNT: usu with supp =tirade

dibber /dɪbəʳ/ **dibbers.** In British English, a **dibber** is a small tool used by gardeners to make a hole in the soil where they want to put a seed or small plant. N-COUNT

dice /daɪs/ **dices, dicing, diced** ◆◇◇◇◇

1 A **dice** is a small cube which has one to six spots or numbers on its sides, and which is used in games to provide random numbers. In old-fashioned English, 'dice' was used only as a plural form, and the singular was **die**, but now 'dice' is used as both the singular and the plural form. N-COUNT

2 **Dice** is a game which is played using dice. N-UNCOUNT

3 When you **dice** food, you cut it into small cubes. *Dice the onion and boil in the water for about fifteen minutes... Add the crushed garlic and remaining diced vegetables.* VERB V n V-ed

dicey /daɪsi/ **dicier, diciest.** Something that is **dicey** is slightly dangerous or uncertain; used mainly in informal British English. *There was a dicey moment as one of our party made a risky climb up the cliff wall.* ADJ-GRADED

dichotomy /daɪkɒtəmi/ **dichotomies.** If there is a **dichotomy** between two things, there is a very great difference or opposition between them; a formal word. *There is a dichotomy between the academic world and the industrial world.* N-COUNT: usu sing, oft N *between* pl-n

dick /dɪk/ **dicks.** A man's **dick** is his penis; an informal word which some people find offensive. ◆◇◇◇◇ N-COUNT

dicker /dɪkəʳ/ **dickers, dickering, dickered.** If you say that people **are dickering** about something, you mean that they are arguing or disagreeing about it, often in a way that you think is foolish or unnecessary; used mainly in British English. *Management and labor are dickering over pay, benefits and working conditions... He may be expecting us to dicker. Don't.* V-RECIP =haggle pl-n V *over/about* n V (non-recip) Also pl-n V

dictate, dictates, dictating, dictated. The verb is pronounced /dɪkteɪt, AM dɪkteɪt/. The noun is pronounced /dɪkteɪt/. ◆◆◇◇◇

1 If you **dictate** something, you say or read it aloud for someone else to write down. *Sheldon writes* VERB V n

every day of the week, dictating his novels in the morning... Everything he dictated was signed and sent out the same day. Also V

2 If someone **dictates** to someone else, they tell them what they should do or can do. *He had warned the West against trying to dictate to the Soviet Union... What right has one country to dictate the environmental standards of another?... He cannot be allowed to dictate what can and cannot be inspected... What gives them the right to dictate to us what we should eat?... The officers were more or less able to dictate terms to successive governments... The rules of court dictate that a defendant is entitled to all evidence which may help his case.* VERB V *to* n V n V wh V *to* n wh V n *to* n V that

3 If one thing **dictates** another, the first thing causes or influences the second thing. *The film's budget dictated a tough schedule... The way in which they dress is dictated by very rigid fashion rules... Of course, a number of factors will dictate how long an apple tree can survive... Circumstances dictated that they played a defensive rather than attacking game.* VERB V n V wh V that

4 You say that reason or common sense **dictates** that a particular thing is the case when you believe strongly that it is the case and that reason or common sense will cause other people to agree. *Commonsense now dictates that it would be wise to sell a few shares.* VERB V that

5 A **dictate** is an order which you have to obey. *Its officers work alongside commanders at all levels to ensure that the dictates of the Party are followed.* N-COUNT: usu with supp, oft N *of* n

6 **Dictates** are principles or rules which you consider to be extremely important. *We have followed the dictates of our consciences and have done our duty.* N-COUNT: usu pl, with supp, usu N *of* n

dictation /dɪkteɪʃən/

1 **Dictation** is the speaking or reading aloud of words for someone else to write down. *...taking dictation from the dean of the Faculty... He had had an arm amputated and relied on her to take down his books from dictation.* N-UNCOUNT

2 **Dictation** is the giving of orders in a forceful and commanding way. *The Europeans, while keen for partnership with the US, would not accept dictation.* N-UNCOUNT

dictator /dɪkteɪtəʳ, AM dɪkteɪt-/ **dictators.** A **dictator** is a ruler who has complete power in a country, especially power which was obtained by force; used showing disapproval. ◆◆◇◇◇ N-COUNT PRAGMATICS

dictatorial /dɪktətɔːriəl/ ◆◇◇◇◇

1 **Dictatorial** means controlled or used by a dictator. *He suspended the constitution and assumed dictatorial powers.* ADJ-GRADED

2 If you describe someone's behaviour as **dictatorial**, you mean that they tell people what to do in a forceful and unfair way; used showing disapproval. *If you are too strict with them, your children will see you as dictatorial. ...his dictatorial management style.* ADJ-GRADED PRAGMATICS =domineering, overbearing

dictatorship /dɪkteɪtəʳʃɪp/ **dictatorships** ◆◆◇◇◇

1 **Dictatorship** is government by a dictator. *...a new era of democracy after a long period of military dictatorship in the country. ...countries which are ruled by dictatorships.* N-VAR

2 A **dictatorship** is a country which is ruled by a dictator or by a very authoritarian government. *Every country in the region was a communist dictatorship.* N-COUNT =tyrant

diction /dɪkʃən/. Someone's **diction** is how clearly they speak or sing. *His diction wasn't very good and the accent was extraordinary... Clear diction is important.* N-UNCOUNT

dictionary /dɪkʃənri, AM -neri/ **dictionaries** ◆◆◇◇◇

1 A **dictionary** is a book in which the words and phrases of a language are listed alphabetically, together with their meanings or their translations in another language. *...a Welsh-English dictionary.* N-COUNT

2 A **dictionary** is an alphabetically ordered reference book on one particular subject or limited group of subjects. *...the Dictionary of National Biography.* N-COUNT: with supp, oft N *of* n

dictum /dɪktəm/ **dictums** or **dicta**

1 A **dictum** is a saying that describes an aspect of life in an interesting or wise way. *...the dictum that it is preferable to be roughly right than precisely wrong... She reminded us of Barnum's dictum: You could sell anything to anybody if you marketed it right.* N-COUNT: oft N that =saying

2 A **dictum** is a formal statement made by someone who has authority. *...Disraeli's dictum that the first priority of the government must be the health of the people.* N-COUNT: oft N that

did /dɪd/. **Did** is the past tense of **do**.

didactic /daɪdæktɪk/

1 Something that is **didactic** is intended to teach people something, especially a moral lesson; a formal use. *In totalitarian societies, art exists for didactic purposes.* ADJ-GRADED

2 Someone who is **didactic** tells people things rather than letting them find things out or discussing things; a formal use. *He is much more didactic in his approach and sees the teacher's role as extremely important in the learning process.* ADJ-GRADED

diddle /dɪdəl/ **diddles, diddling, diddled.** If someone **diddles** you, they take money from you dishonestly or unfairly; an informal word, used mainly in British English. *They diddled their insurance company by making a false claim.* VERB =con V n

didn't /dɪdənt/. **Didn't** is the usual spoken form of **did not**. ◆◆◆◆◆

die /daɪ/ **dies, dying, died** ◆◆◆◆◆

1 When people, animals, and plants **die**, they stop living. *A year later my dog died and I went to pieces... Sadly, both he and my mother died of cancer... I would die a very happy person if I could stay in music my whole life... Reynolds says he is haunted by the ghosts of friends who died young.* VB: no passive V V *of/from* n V n V adj

2 If a person, animal, or plant **is dying**, they are so ill or so badly injured that they will not live very much longer. *The elm trees are all dying... Every working day I treat people who are dying from lung diseases caused by smoking.* VB: only cont ≠recover V V *of/from* n

3 If someone **dies** a violent, unnatural, or painful death, they die in a violent, unnatural, or painful way. *Watching helplessly as his mother died an agonizing death permanently altered Billy... I'm no expert, but I don't think Tracy died a natural death.* VB: no passive V n

4 When a machine or device **dies**, it stops completely, especially after a period of functioning more and more slowly or ineffectively. *Then suddenly, the engine coughed, spluttered and died.* VERB =break down V

5 When a fire or light **dies**, it stops burning or shining. *Her cigarette glowed brightly, then died.* VERB V

6 When an emotion or facial expression **dies**, it disappears completely, usually after a period of gradually becoming weaker and less noticeable. *My love for you will never die... Kathryn looked down at the floor and the smile died on her lips.* VERB V

7 In informal English, you say that you **are dying of** thirst, hunger, boredom, or curiosity to emphasize that you are very thirsty, hungry, bored, or curious. *Order me a pot of tea, I'm dying of thirst.* VB: only cont PRAGMATICS V *of* n

8 In informal English, you say that you **are dying for** something or **are dying** to do something to emphasize that you very much want to have it or do it. *I'm dying for a breath of fresh air... She was dying to talk to Frank.* VB: only cont PRAGMATICS V *for* n V to-inf

9 In informal English, you use **die** in expressions such as **I almost died** or **I'd die if anything happened** where you are emphasizing your feelings about a situation, for example to say that it is very shocking, upsetting, embarrassing, or amusing. *I nearly died when I learned where I was ending up... I nearly died of shame... I thought I'd die laughing.* VERB PRAGMATICS V V *of* n V -ing

10 A **die** is a specially shaped or patterned block of metal which is used to press or cut other metal into a particular shape. N-COUNT

11 See also **dying**.

12 You say that **the die is cast** to draw attention to the importance of an event or decision which is going to affect your future and which cannot be changed or avoided. *It was too late and too urgent to turn back. The die was cast.* PHRASES V inflects

13 If you say that habits or attitudes **die hard**, you mean that they take a very long time to disappear or change, so that it may not be possible to get rid of them completely. *Old habits die hard... Such prejudices die hard.*
V inflects

die away. If a sound **dies away**, it gradually becomes weaker or fainter and finally disappears altogether. *The firing finally began to die away in the late afternoon... The sound died away and silence reigned.*
PHRASAL VERB =fade away
V P

die back. When a plant **dies back**, its leaves die but its roots remain alive. *They often take a long time to die back after flowering.*
PHRASAL VERB
V P

die down. If something **dies down**, it becomes very much quieter or less intense. *The rain remained steady though the wind had died down... The controversy is unlikely to die down.*
PHRASAL VERB
V P

die out. If something **dies out**, it becomes less and less common and eventually disappears completely. *How did the dinosaurs die out?... We used to believe that capitalism would soon die out.*
PHRASAL VERB
V P

diehard /daɪhɑːʳd/ **diehards;** also spelled **die-hard.** A **diehard** is someone who is very strongly opposed to change and new ideas, or who is a very strong supporter of someone or something. *The president hopes the diehards will resign over the reform proposals... Not even their diehard supporters can pretend that this was a great game.*
N-COUNT: oft N n

diesel /diːzəl/ **diesels** ◆◆◇◇◇

1 Diesel or **diesel oil** is the heavy oil used in a diesel engine.
N-MASS

2 A **diesel** is a vehicle which has a diesel engine.
N-COUNT

diesel engine, diesel engines. A **diesel engine** is an internal combustion engine in which oil is burnt by very hot air. Diesel engines are used in buses and lorries, and in some trains and cars.
N-COUNT

diet /daɪət/ **diets, dieting, dieted** ◆◆◆◆◇

1 Your **diet** is the type and range of food that you regularly eat. *It's never too late to improve your diet. ...a healthy diet rich in fruit and vegetables... Poor diet and excess smoking will seriously damage the health of your hair.*
N-VAR

2 If a doctor puts someone on a **diet**, he or she makes them eat a special type or range of foods in order to improve their health. *He was put on a diet of milky food. ...a special diet for children with high cholesterol.*
N-COUNT: usu with supp

3 If you are on a **diet**, you eat special kinds of food or you eat less food than usual because you are trying to lose weight. *Have you been on a diet? You've lost a lot of weight... Diet and exercise will alter your shape... I've only lost sixteen pounds since I started this diet.*
N-VAR

4 If you **are dieting**, you eat special kinds of food or you eat less food than usual because you are trying to lose weight. *I've been dieting ever since the birth of my fourth child... Most of us have dieted at some time in our lives.* ♦ **dieting** *She has already lost around two stone through dieting.*
VERB
V
N-UNCOUNT

5 Diet drinks or foods have been specially produced so that they do not contain many calories. *...sugar-free diet drinks. ...diet margarine.*
ADJ: ADJ n

6 If someone is fed on a **diet** of something, especially something unpleasant or of poor quality, they receive or experience a very large amount of it. *The radio had fed him a diet of pop songs... People are rejecting this constant diet of despair.*
N-COUNT: usu N of n
PRAGMATICS

dietary /daɪətri, AM -teri/ ◆◇◇◇◇

1 You can use the word **dietary** to describe anything that concerns a person's diet. *Dr Susan Hankinson has studied the dietary habits of more than 50,000 women... As with all dietary changes, reducing salt should be done gradually.*
ADJ: usu ADJ n

2 You can use the word **dietary** to describe substances such as fibre and fat that are found in food. *Wheat bran is the commonest source of dietary fibre.*
ADJ: ADJ n

dieter /daɪətəʳ/ **dieters.** A **dieter** is someone who is on a diet or who regularly goes on diets. ◆◇◇◇◇
N-COUNT =slimmer

dietetic /daɪətetɪk/. In formal American English, **dietetic** food or drink is food or drink that has been specially produced so that it does not contain many calories. *All dietetic meals are low in sugar.*
ADJ: ADJ n =diet, low-calorie

dietician /daɪətɪʃən/ **dieticians;** also spelled **dietitian.** A **dietician** is a person whose job is to give people advice about the kind of food they should eat. Dieticians often work in hospitals.
N-COUNT

differ /dɪfəʳ/ **differs, differing, differed** ◆◆◇◇◇

1 If two or more things **differ**, they are unlike each other in some way. *The story he told police differed from the one he told his mother... Management styles differ.*
V-RECIP
V from n
pl-n V

2 If people **differ** about something, they do not agree with each other about it. *The two leaders had differed on the issue of sanctions... That is where we differ... Since his retirement, Crowe has differed with the President on several issues.*
V-RECIP
pl-n V prep
pl-n V
V with n

3 ● **'I beg to differ'**: see **beg.**

4 ● **agree to differ**: see **agree.**

difference /dɪfrəns/ **differences** ◆◆◆◆◇

1 The **difference** between two things is the way in which they are unlike each other. *That is the fundamental difference between the two societies... There is no difference between the sexes. ...the vast difference in size... We do have social problems here. The difference is the people know each other and try to help each other.*
N-COUNT: usu N prep

2 A **difference** between two quantities is the amount by which one quantity is less than the other. *The difference is 8532.*
N-SING

3 If people have their **differences** about something, they disagree about it. *The two communities are learning how to resolve their differences.*
N-COUNT: usu pl, oft poss N

4 If something **makes** a **difference** or **makes** a lot of **difference**, it affects you and helps you in what you are doing. If something **makes** no **difference**, it does not have any effect on what you are doing. *Where you live can make such a difference to the way you feel... Exercise makes all the difference... It is sad to see him go but it won't make any difference to the way we conduct our affairs.*
PHRASES
V inflects

5 If you **split the difference** with someone, you agree on an amount or price which is halfway between two suggested amounts or prices. *Shall we split the difference and say $7,500?*
V inflects

6 If you describe a job or holiday, for example, as a job **with a difference** or a holiday **with a difference**, you mean that the job or holiday is very interesting and unusual; an informal expression. *When she starts work on Monday it will be in a job with a difference – she'll be her own boss. ...a politician with a difference.*
n PHR

7 If there is a **difference of opinion** between two or more people or groups, they disagree about something. *Was there a difference of opinion over what to do with the Nobel Prize money?*
difference inflects

different /dɪfrənt/ ◆◆◆◆◆

1 If two people or things are **different**, they are not like each other in one or more ways. *London was different from most European capitals... If he'd attended music school, how might things have been different?... We have totally different views.* ► In British English, people sometimes say that one thing is **different to** another. Some people consider this use to be incorrect. *My approach is totally different to his.* ► People sometimes say that one thing is **different than** another. This use is often considered incorrect in British English, but it is acceptable in American English. *We're not really any different than they are. ...a style of advertising that's different than the rest of the country.* ♦ **differently** *Every individual learns differently... They still get treated differently from almost every other contemporary British band... The skeleton consists of differently shaped bones held together by ligaments.*
ADJ-GRADED: oft ADJ from n
ADJ-GRADED: v-link ADJ to n
ADJ-GRADED: v-link ADJ than n/cl
ADV-GRADED: ADV after v, ADV -ed, oft ADV from n

2 You use **different** to indicate that you are talking about two or more separate and distinct things of the same kind. *Different countries specialised in different products... The number of calories in different brands of drinks varies enormously.*
ADJ: ADJ n =discrete ≠identical

3 You can describe something as **different** when it is unusual and not like others of the same kind. *The*
ADJ-GRADED: v-link ADJ =distinctive

result is interesting and different, but do not attempt the recipe if time is short.

differential /dɪfərenʃəl/ **differentials** ◆◇◇◇◇

1 A **differential** is a difference between two values in a scale; a technical term in mathematics and economics. *Germany and France pledged to maintain the differential between their two currencies.* N-COUNT

2 In British English, a **differential** is a difference between rates of pay for different types of work, especially work done by people in the same industry or company. *During the Second World War, industrial wage differentials in Britain widened.* N-COUNT

3 **Differential** means relating to or using a difference between groups or things; a formal use. *Sweden may at some stage also be forced to eliminate differential voting rights.* ADJ: ADJ n

differentiate /dɪfərenʃieɪt/ **differentiates, differentiating, differentiated** ◆◆◇◇◇

1 If you **differentiate** between things or you **differentiate** one thing from another, you recognize or show the difference between them. *A child may not differentiate between his imagination and the real world... At this age your baby cannot differentiate one person from another.* VERB =distinguish V *between* pl-n V n *from* n

2 A quality or feature that **differentiates** one thing from another makes the two things different. *...distinctive policies that differentiate them from the other parties.* VERB =distinguish V n *from* n ♦ **differentiation** /dɪfərenʃieɪʃən/ *Their marketing director claims the differentiation between the two ranges will increase.* N-UNCOUNT

difficult /dɪfɪkəlt/ ◆◆◆◆◆

1 Something that is **difficult** is not easy to do, understand, or deal with. *Hobart found it difficult to get her first book published... The lack of childcare provisions made it difficult for single mothers to get jobs... It was a very difficult decision to make... We're living in difficult times... It's very difficult being a woman in motor racing.* ADJ-GRADED: oft *it* v-link ADJ to-inf, *it* v-link ADJ -ing ≠easy

2 Someone who is **difficult** behaves in an unreasonable and unhelpful way. *I had a feeling you were going to be difficult about this.* ADJ-GRADED =awkward

difficulty /dɪfɪkəlti/ **difficulties** ◆◆◆◆◇

1 A **difficulty** is a problem. *...the difficulty of getting accurate information... The country is facing great economic difficulties.* N-COUNT

2 If you have **difficulty** doing something, you are not able to do it easily. *Do you have difficulty getting up?... The injured man mounted his horse with difficulty.* N-UNCOUNT

3 If you are **in difficulty** or **in difficulties**, you are having a lot of problems. *You have to admit that you are, in fact, in difficulties... Rumours spread about banks being in difficulty.* PHRASE: v-link PHR

diffident /dɪfɪdənt/. Someone who is **diffident** is rather shy and does not enjoy talking about themselves or being noticed by other people. *John was as bouncy and ebullient as Helen was diffident and reserved.* ◆◇◇◇◇ ADJ-GRADED ♦ **diffidence** /dɪfɪdəns/ *He tapped on the door, opened it and entered with a certain diffidence.* N-UNCOUNT ♦ **diffidently** *'Would you,' he asked diffidently, 'like to talk to me about it?'* ADV-GRADED: ADV with v

diffuse, diffuses, diffusing, diffused. The verb is pronounced /dɪfjuːz/. The adjective is pronounced /dɪfjuːs/. ◆◇◇◇◇

1 If something such as knowledge or information **is diffused**, or if it **diffuses** somewhere, it is made known or becomes available over a wide area or to a lot of people. *Over time, however, the technology is diffused and adopted by other countries. ...to diffuse new ideas obtained from elsewhere... As agriculture developed, was it the ideas of agriculture that diffused across Europe? Or the people that moved with their ideas?* V-ERG =spread *be* V-ed V n V prep ♦ **diffusion** /dɪfjuːʒən/ *...the development and diffusion of ideas.* N-UNCOUNT: with supp

2 To **diffuse** a feeling, especially an undesirable one, means to cause it to weaken and lose its power to affect people. *The arrival of letters from the Pope did nothing to diffuse the tension.* VERB =dissipate V n

3 When something **diffuses** light, it causes the light to spread faintly and in a lot of directions; a technical use in science. *Diffusing a light also reduces its power... The sun slid behind trees, its last light diffused by wintry branches.* VERB ≠focus V n

4 To **diffuse** or **be diffused** through something means to move and spread through it. *It allows nicotine to diffuse slowly and steadily into the bloodstream... It created a glowing centre of warmth that quickly diffused through my limbs... The moisture present in all foods absorbs the flavour of the smoke and eventually diffuses that flavour into its interior.* V-ERG =permeate V prep V n prep Also V, V n ♦ **diffusion** *There are data on the rates of diffusion of molecules.* N-UNCOUNT: with supp

5 Something that is **diffuse** is not directed towards one place or concentrated in one place but spread out over a large area. *...a diffuse community... A cold, diffuse light filtered in through the skylight.* ADJ-GRADED

6 If you describe something as **diffuse**, you mean that it is vague and difficult to understand or explain. *His writing is so diffuse, obscure, and overwrought that it is difficult to make out what it is he is trying to say.* ADJ-GRADED

dig /dɪg/ **digs, digging, dug** ◆◆◆◇◇

1 When people or animals **dig**, they make a hole in the ground or in a pile of earth, stones, or debris. *They tried digging in a patch just below the cave... Dig a largish hole and bang the stake in first... Rescue workers are digging through the rubble in search of other victims. ...digging for shellfish at the Battery at low tide... Two men were standing by the freshly dug grave.* VERB V V n V *through* n V *for* n V-ed

2 If you **dig** into something such as a deep container, you put your hand in it to search for something. *He dug into his coat pocket for his keys.* VERB =delve V *into/in* n

3 If you **dig** one thing into another or if one thing **digs** into another, the first thing is pushed hard into the second, or presses hard into it. *She digs the serving spoon into the moussaka... I grab George's arm and dig my nails into his flesh... He could feel the beads digging into his palm... Graham was standing there, his hands dug into the pockets of his baggy white trousers.* V-ERG V n *into* n V *into* n V-ed

4 If you **dig into** a subject or a store of information, you study it very carefully in order to discover or check facts. *...as a special congressional enquiry digs deeper into the alleged financial misdeeds of his government... He has been digging into the local archives.* VERB =probe V *into* n

5 If you say that you **dig** something, you mean that you like it and understand it; an old-fashioned, informal use. *'They play classic rock'n'roll,' states her boyfriend, 'My dad digs them too.'... I can dig it. I don't expect a band always to be innovative.* VERB V n V *it*

6 A **dig** is an organized activity in which people dig into the ground in order to discover ancient historical objects; an informal use. *He's an archaeologist and has been on a dig in Crete for the past year.* N-COUNT: oft *on* N =excavation

7 If you have a **dig** at someone or something, you say something which is intended to make fun of them or upset them; an informal use. *Americans are always quick to have a dig at the British... She couldn't resist a dig at Dave after his unfortunate performance.* N-COUNT: usu N *at* n =gibe

8 If you give someone a **dig** in a part of their body, you poke them with your finger or your elbow, usually as a warning or as a joke, or to remind them about a secret that you both know. *Cassandra silenced him with a sharp dig in the small of the back.* N-COUNT

9 If you live in **digs**, you live in a room in someone else's house and pay them rent; an old-fashioned, informal use in British English. *He went to London to do his articles and lived in digs in Gloucester Road... I called for Charles at his digs.* N-PLURAL: oft *in* N =lodgings

10 If you **dig deep**, you do a very thorough investigation into something. *I want you to dig deep. Find out who the hell she is, and where she came from.* PHRASES V inflects

11 If someone **digs into** their **pocket** or **digs into** their **purse**, they manage after some difficulty to find the money to pay for something. *Holidaymakers are digging deep into their pockets to book late summer breaks.* V and N inflect

12 • to **dig one's heels in**: see **heel**.

dig around PHRASAL VERB

1 If you **dig around** in a place or container, you =rummage

search for something in every part of it. *I went home to dig around in my closets for some old tapes.* around VP inn Also VP

2 If you **dig around**, you try to find information about someone or something. *They said, after digging around, the photo was a phoney.* VP

dig in PHRASAL VERB

1 If you **dig** a substance **in**, or **dig** it **into** the soil, you mix it into the soil by digging. *I usually dig in a small barrow load of compost in late summer... To dig calcium into the soil, he warned, does not help the plant.* VPn (not pron) VnPn

2 When soldiers **dig in** or **dig** themselves **in**, they dig trenches and prepare themselves for an attack by the enemy. *The Canadian battalion arrived this morning and went directly to the airport to begin digging in... The enemy must be digging themselves in now ready for the attack... Our forces are dug in along the river.* VP V pron-refl P V-ed P

3 If you say that someone **is digging in**, you mean that they are not changing their mind or weakening their efforts, although they are losing a contest or facing difficult problems. *A yawning North-South gulf has opened up with both sides digging in... When his game is a fraction off and things are not flowing, he can dig in, and impose mind over matter.* =entrench VP

4 If someone **digs in**, or **digs into** some food, they start eating eagerly. If you tell someone to **dig in**, you are inviting them to start eating, and encouraging them to eat as much as they want; an informal expression. *'Listen,' said Daisy, digging into her oatmeal... Pull up a chair and dig in!* =tuck in VPn VP

dig out PHRASAL VERB

1 If you **dig** someone or something **out** of a place, you get them out by digging or by forcing them from the things surrounding them. *...digging minerals out of the Earth... Rescue crews have been digging people out of collapsed buildings. ...trying to dig out a trombone from under four saxophones.* =extract VnP ofn VPn (not pron) Also VnP

2 If you **dig** something **out**, you find it after it has been stored, hidden, or forgotten for a long time; an informal use. *Recently, I dug out Barstow's novel and read it again... We'll try and dig the number out for you if you want it.* =search out VPn (not pron) VnP

dig over. If you **dig over** an area of soil, you dig it thoroughly, so that the soil becomes looser and free from lumps. *Dig over any ground that is clear of crops and plants... Dig the soil over thoroughly.* PHRASAL VERB VPn (not pron) VnP

dig up PHRASAL VERB

1 If you **dig up** something, you remove it from the ground where it has been buried or planted. *You would have to dig up the plant yourself... More bodies have been dug up at the site... He dug it up and Doris took one look and said: 'That's not my dog.'* VPn (not pron) VnP

2 If you **dig up** an area of land, you dig holes in it. *Yesterday they continued the search, digging up the back yard of a police station.* VPn (not pron) Also VnP

3 If you **dig up** information or facts, you discover something that has not previously been widely known. *Managers are too expensive and important to spend time digging up market information... His description fits perfectly the evidence dug up by Clyde.* =unearth VPn (not pron) V-ed P Also VnP

digest, digests, digesting, digested. The verb is pronounced /daɪdʒest/. The noun is pronounced /daɪdʒest/. ◆◆◇◇◇

1 When food **digests** or when you **digest** it, it passes through your body to your stomach. Your stomach removes the substances that your body needs and gets rid of the rest. *Do not undertake strenuous exercise for a few hours after a meal to allow food to digest... She couldn't digest food properly... Nutrients from the digested food can be absorbed into the blood.* V-ERG V Vn V-ed

2 If you **digest** information, you think about it carefully so that you understand it. *They learn well but seem to need time to digest information... She read everything, digesting every fragment of news.* VERB Vn

3 If you **digest** some unpleasant news, you think about it until you are able to accept it and know how to deal with it. *All this has upset me. I need time to digest it all.* VERB Vn

4 A **digest** is a collection of pieces of writing. They are published together in a shorter form than they were originally published. *The organization publishes a regular digest of environmental statistics. ...the Middle East Economic Digest.* N-COUNT

digestible /daɪdʒestɪbəl/

1 **Digestible** food is food that is easy to digest. *Bananas are easily digestible and make a satisfying and filling snack at any time of day.* ♦ **digestibility** /daɪdʒestɪbɪlɪti/ *Processing and refining can alter digestibility.* ADJ-GRADED: oft adv ADJ N-UNCOUNT

2 Food that is **digestible** is pleasant to eat. *Fish is inexpensive, easy to cook and very digestible.* ADJ-GRADED: usu v-link ADJ

3 If a theory or idea is **digestible**, it is easy to understand. *The book was launched five years ago in the hope of making economic theory more digestible.* ADJ-GRADED =accessible

digestion /daɪdʒestʃən/ **digestions** ◆◇◇◇◇

1 **Digestion** is the process of digesting food. *No liquids are served with meals because they interfere with digestion. ...the digestion of fats.* N-UNCOUNT

2 Your **digestion** is the system in your body which digests your food. *My digestion ain't so hot these days, either.* N-COUNT: usu poss N

digestive /daɪdʒestɪv/ **digestives** ◆◇◇◇◇

1 You can describe things that are related to the digestion of food as **digestive**. *...digestive juices that normally work on breaking down our food... Peppermint oil is very good for regulating digestive disorders.* ADJ: ADJ n

2 In Britain, a **digestive** or a **digestive biscuit** is a type of biscuit made from wholemeal flour. **Digestive** is a trademark. *...a packet of chocolate digestives.* N-COUNT

digestive system, digestive systems. Your **digestive system** is the set of organs in your body that digest the food you eat. N-COUNT: usu poss N

digger /dɪgəʳ/ **diggers.** A **digger** is a machine that is used for digging. *...a mechanical digger.* ◆◇◇◇◇ N-COUNT

digit /dɪdʒɪt/ **digits** ◆◇◇◇◇

1 A **digit** is a written symbol for any of the ten numbers from 0 to 9. *Her telephone number differs from mine by one digit.* N-COUNT

2 A **digit** is a finger, thumb, or toe; a formal use. *Many animals have five digits.* N-COUNT

digital /dɪdʒɪtəl/ ◆◆◇◇◇

1 **Digital** systems record or transmit information in the form of thousands of very small signals. Compare **analogue**. *The new digital technology would allow a rapid expansion in the number of TV channels.* ♦ **digitally** *...digitally recorded sound.* ADJ ADV

2 **Digital** devices such as watches or clocks give information by displaying numbers rather than by having a pointer which moves round a dial. Compare **analogue**. *...a digital display.* ADJ: ADJ n

digital audio tape. **Digital audio tape** is a type of magnetic tape used to make very high quality recordings of sound by recording it in digital form. N-UNCOUNT =DAT

digital recording, digital recordings

1 **Digital recording** is the process of converting sound or images into numbers. N-UNCOUNT

2 A **digital recording** is a recording made by converting sound or images into numbers. N-COUNT

digitize /dɪdʒɪtaɪz/ **digitizes, digitizing, digitized;** also spelled **digitise** in British English. To **digitize** information means to turn it into a form that can be read easily by a computer. *It also digitizes the letters, so the information can be stored in a computer... The picture is digitised by a scanner.* VERB Vn

dignified /dɪgnɪfaɪd/. If you say that someone or something is **dignified**, you mean they are calmly impressive and worthy of respect. *He seemed a very dignified and charming man... Mr Smith is maintaining a dignified silence.* ◆◇◇◇◇ ADJ-GRADED

dignify /dɪgnɪfaɪ/ **dignifies, dignifying, dignified**

1 To **dignify** something means to make it impressive; a literary use. *It is the function of tragic literature to dignify sorrow and disaster... The gatepost* VERB Vn

was dignified by the weathered brass plate of Dr Harcourt Sibley.
2 If you say that a particular reaction or description **dignifies** something you have a low opinion of, you mean that it makes it appear acceptable. *We see no point in dignifying this kind of speculation with a comment... It was a technique later dignified by the term 'info-tainment'.* VERB PRAGMATICS V n

dignitary /dɪgnɪtri, AM -teri/ **dignitaries. Dignitaries** are people who are considered to be important because they have a high rank in government or in the Church. ◆◇◇◇◇ N-COUNT: usu pl

dignity /dɪgnɪti/ ◆◆◇◇◇
1 If someone behaves or moves with **dignity**, they are calm, controlled, and admirable. *...her extraordinary dignity and composure.* N-UNCOUNT =self-possession
2 If you talk about the **dignity** of people or their lives or activities, you mean that they are valuable and worthy of respect. *...the sense of human dignity. ...the integrity and the dignity of our lives and feelings.* N-UNCOUNT: usu with supp
3 Your **dignity** is the sense that you have of your own importance and value, and other people's respect for you. *If you were wrong, admit it. You won't lose dignity, but will gain respect... She still has her pearls and her dignity.* N-UNCOUNT =self-respect

digress /daɪgres/ **digresses, digressing, digressed.** If you **digress**, you move away from the subject you are talking or writing about and talk or write about something different for a while. *I've digressed a little to explain the situation so far, so let me now recap.... She digressed from her prepared speech to pay tribute to the President.* ♦ **digression** /daɪgreʃᵊn/ **digressions** *The text is dotted with digressions.* VERB V V from n N-VAR

dike /daɪk/. See **dyke**.

diktat /dɪktæt, AM dɪktɑːt/ **diktats.** You use **diktat** to refer to something such as a law or government which is imposed upon people without their consent; used showing disapproval. N-VAR PRAGMATICS

dilapidated /dɪlæpɪdeɪtɪd/. A building that is **dilapidated** is old and in a generally bad condition. ◆◇◇◇◇ ADJ-GRADED =run-down

dilate /daɪleɪt/ **dilates, dilating, dilated.** When things such as blood vessels or the pupils of your eyes **dilate** or when something **dilates** them, they become wider or bigger. *At night, the pupils dilate to allow in more light... Exercise dilates blood vessels on the surface of the brain.* ♦ **dilated** *His eyes seemed slightly dilated.* ◆◇◇◇◇ V-ERG =enlarge V V n ADJ-GRADED

dilatory /dɪlətri, AM -tɔːri/. Someone or something that is **dilatory** is slow and causes delay; a formal word. *You might expect politicians to smooth things out when civil servants are being dilatory.* ADJ-GRADED

dildo /dɪldoʊ/. **dildos.** A **dildo** is an object which is used as a substitute for an erect penis. N-COUNT

dilemma /daɪlemə, AM dɪl-/ **dilemmas.** A **dilemma** is a difficult situation in which you have to choose between two or more alternatives. *He was faced with the dilemma of whether or not to return to his country... The issue raises a moral dilemma.* • **on the horns of a dilemma**: see **horn**. ◆◆◇◇◇ N-COUNT

dilettante /dɪlətænti, AM -tɑːnt/ **dilettantes** or **dilettanti.** A **dilettante** is someone who seems interested in a subject, especially in art, but who does not really know very much about it; a formal word, used showing disapproval. N-COUNT PRAGMATICS

diligent /dɪlɪdʒᵊnt/. Someone who is **diligent** works hard in a careful and conscientious way. *Meyers is a diligent and prolific worker... The historical research was impressively diligent.* ♦ **diligence** /dɪlɪdʒᵊns/ *The police are pursuing their inquiries with great diligence.* ♦ **diligently** *The two sides are now working diligently to resolve their differences.* ◆◇◇◇◇ ADJ-GRADED N-UNCOUNT ADV-GRADED: ADV with v

dill /dɪl/. **Dill** is a herb with yellow flowers and a strong sweet smell. ◆◇◇◇◇ N-UNCOUNT

dilute /daɪluːt/ **dilutes, diluting, diluted** ◆◆◇◇◇
1 If a liquid **is diluted** or **dilutes**, it is added to or mixes with water or another liquid, and becomes weaker. *If you give your baby juice, dilute it well with cooled, boiled water... The liquid is then diluted... The poisons seeping from Hanford's contaminated land quickly dilute in the water.* ♦ **dilution** *...ditches dug for flood protection, drinking-water supply and sewage dilution.* V-ERG V n prep be V-ed V Also V n N-UNCOUNT
2 A **dilute** liquid is very thin and weak, usually because it has had water added to it. *...a dilute solution of bleach.* ADJ-GRADED: usu ADJ n
3 If someone or something **dilutes** a belief, quality, or value, they make it weaker and less effective. *There was a clear intention to dilute black voting power... Serious attention is being given to diluting the value of personal tax allowances.* ♦ **dilution** *The result was a potentially devastating dilution of earnings per share.* VERB V n N-UNCOUNT: oft N of n

dilution /daɪluːʃᵊn/ **dilutions.** A **dilution** is a liquid that has been diluted with water or another liquid, so that it becomes weaker. *'Aromatherapy oils' are not pure essential oils but dilutions.* N-COUNT

dim /dɪm/ **dimmer, dimmest; dims, dimming, dimmed** ◆◆◇◇◇
1 **Dim** light is not bright. *She stood waiting, in the dim light... Below decks, the lights were dim.* ♦ **dimly** *Two lamps burned dimly... He followed her into a dimly lit kitchen.* ♦ **dimness** *...the dimness of an early September evening.* ADJ-GRADED ADV-GRADED: ADV after v, ADV -ed N-UNCOUNT
2 A **dim** place is rather dark because there is not much light in it. *The room was dim and cool and quiet.* ♦ **dimness** *I stood just inside the doorway, squinting to adjust my eyes to the dimness.* ADJ-GRADED N-UNCOUNT
3 A **dim** figure or object is not very easy to see, either because it is in shadow or darkness, or because it is far away. *Pete's torch picked out the dim figures of Bob and Chang.* ♦ **dimly** *The shoreline could be dimly seen.* ADJ-GRADED =faint ADV-GRADED: usu ADV with v
4 If you have a **dim** memory or awareness of something, it is difficult to remember or unclear in your mind. *It seems that the '60s era of social activism is all but a dim memory.* ♦ **dimly** *Christina dimly recalled the procedure... I was dimly aware that dozens of curious people were looking at us.* ADJ-GRADED: usu ADJ n =hazy ADV-GRADED: ADV with v, ADV adj
5 If the prospects for something are **dim**, you have no reason to feel hopeful or optimistic about them. *The prospects for a peaceful solution are dim.* ADJ-GRADED ≠hopeful, promising
6 If you describe someone as **dim**, you think that they are stupid; an informal use. ADJ-GRADED PRAGMATICS
7 If you **dim** a light or if it **dims**, it becomes less bright. *Dim the lighting – it is unpleasant to lie with a bright light shining in your eyes... The houselights dimmed.* V-ERG V n V
8 If your prospects, hopes, or emotions **dim** or if something **dims** them, they become less good or less strong. *Their economic prospects have dimmed... Forty eight years of marriage have not dimmed the passion between Bill and Helen.* V-ERG V V n
9 If your eyes **dim** or **are dimmed** by something, they become weaker or unable to see clearly. *Her eyes dimmed with sorrow... The twinkle in his eyes was dimmed by tears.* V-ERG V be V-ed
10 If your memories **dim** or if something **dims** them, they become less clear in your mind. *Their memory of what happened has dimmed... Not even the distance of twenty years has dimmed a memory so fraught with horror.* V-ERG V V n
11 • **take a dim view**: see **view**.

dime /daɪm/ **dimes.** A **dime** is an American coin worth ten cents. ◆◇◇◇◇ N-COUNT

dimension /daɪmenʃᵊn, dɪm-/ **dimensions** ◆◆◇◇◇
1 A particular **dimension** of something is a particular aspect of it. *There is a political dimension to the accusations... This adds a new dimension to our work.* N-COUNT: usu with supp
2 If you talk about the **dimensions** of a situation or problem, you are talking about its extent and size. *He considers the dimensions of the problem... The dimensions of the market collapse, in terms of turnover and price, were certainly not anticipated.* N-PLURAL: usu with supp
3 A **dimension** is a measurement such as length, width, or height. If you talk about the **dimensions** of an object or place, you are referring to its size and proportions. *Drilling will continue on the site* N-COUNT: usu pl, usu N of n

to assess the dimensions of the new oilfield... I don't think it would spoil the dimensions of the room. ...the grandiose dimensions of the building.

4 In mathematics and science, **dimension** is used in describing spatial concepts such as points, lines, and solids. *The three dimensions of space are constant only when measured within the same frame of reference.*
N-COUNT

5 See also **fourth dimension**.

dimensional /daɪmenʃənəl, AM dɪm-/. See **two-dimensional, three-dimensional**.

diminish /dɪmɪnɪʃ/ **diminishes, diminishing, diminished** ◆◆◇◇◇

1 When something **diminishes**, or when something **diminishes** it, it becomes reduced in size, importance, or intensity. *The threat of nuclear war has diminished... Federalism is intended to diminish the power of the central state... Universities are facing grave problems because of diminishing resources... This could mean diminished public support for the war.*
V-ERG ≠increase V V n V-ing V-ed

2 If you **diminish** someone or something, you talk about them or treat them in a way that makes them appear less important than they really are. *He never put her down or diminished her... He could no longer cope; he relied on me, and felt diminished by it.*
VERB =belittle V n V-ed

diminution /dɪmɪnjuːʃᵊn, AM -nuː-/. A **diminution** of something is its reduction in size, importance, or intensity; a formal word. *The president has accepted a diminution of the powers he originally wanted. ...despite a slight diminution in asset value.*
N-UNCOUNT: usu N *of/in* n =reduction

diminutive /dɪmɪnjʊtɪv/ **diminutives** ◆◇◇◇◇

1 A **diminutive** person or object is very small. *Her eyes scanned the room until they came to rest on a diminutive figure standing at the entrance.*
ADJ-GRADED: usu ADJ n =tiny

2 A **diminutive** is an informal form of a name. For example, 'Jim' and 'Jimmy' are diminutives of 'James'.
N-COUNT

3 A **diminutive** is a suffix which is added to a word to show affection or to indicate that something is small. For example, '-ie' and '-ette' are diminutives, as in 'doggie' and 'statuette'.
N-COUNT

dimmer /dɪməʳ/ **dimmers.** A **dimmer** or a **dimmer switch** is a switch that allows you to gradually change the brightness of an electric light.
N-COUNT

dimple /dɪmpᵊl/ **dimples.** A **dimple** is a small hollow in someone's cheek or chin, often one that you can see when they smile. *Bess spoke up, smiling so that her dimples showed.*
N-COUNT

dimpled /dɪmpᵊld/. Something that is **dimpled** has small hollows in it. *...a pleasant faced man with silvery hair and a dimpled chin.*
ADJ

dimwit /dɪmwɪt/ **dimwits.** If you say that someone is a **dimwit**, you mean that they are ignorant and stupid; an informal word.
N-COUNT PRAGMATICS =idiot

dim-witted; also spelled **dimwitted**. If you describe someone as **dim-witted**, you are saying in quite an unkind way that you do not think they are very clever; an informal word.
ADJ-GRADED =stupid

din /dɪn/. A **din** is a very loud and unpleasant noise that lasts for some time. *They tried to make themselves heard over the din of the crowd.*
◆◇◇◇◇ N-SING =racket

dine /daɪn/ **dines, dining, dined.** When you **dine**, you have dinner; a formal use. *He dines alone most nights... That night the two men dined at Wilson's club... They used to enjoy going out to dine.* • to **wine and dine**: see **wine**.
◆◆◇◇◇ VB: no passive V adv/prep V

dine on. If you **dine on** a particular sort of food, you have it for dinner; used in written English. *My daughters could dine on caviar and champagne for the rest of their lives.*
PHRASAL VERB V P n

dine out. If you **dine out**, you have dinner away from your home, usually at a restaurant. *She does not enjoy parties or dining out.*
PHRASAL VERB V P

diner /daɪnəʳ/ **diners** ◆◇◇◇◇

1 In American English, a **diner** is a small cheap restaurant that is open all day.
N-COUNT

2 The people who are having dinner in a restaurant can be referred to as **diners**. *They sat in a corner, away from other diners.*
N-COUNT

ding-dong /dɪŋ dɒŋ, AM - dɔːŋ/

1 **Ding-dong** is used in writing to represent the sound made by a bell. *'Ding-dong,' went the doorbell.*
SOUND

2 In informal British English, a **ding-dong** is a lively quarrel or fight. *My two daughters had a ding-dong.*
N-SING

dinghy /dɪŋgi/ **dinghies.** A **dinghy** is a small open boat that you sail or row.
◆◇◇◇◇ N-COUNT

dingo /dɪŋgoʊ/ **dingoes.** A **dingo** is a Australian wild dog.
N-COUNT

dingy /dɪndʒi/ **dingier, dingiest**

1 A **dingy** building or place is rather dark and depressing, and perhaps dirty. *Shaw took me to his rather dingy office.*
ADJ-GRADED

2 **Dingy** clothes, curtains, or furnishings look dirty or dull. *...wallpaper with stripes of dingy yellow.*
ADJ-GRADED: usu ADJ n

dining car, dining cars. A **dining car** is a carriage on a train where passengers can have a meal.
N-COUNT

dining room, dining rooms; also spelled **dining-room**. The **dining room** is the room in a house where people have their meals, or a room in a hotel where meals are served.
◆◆◇◇◇ N-COUNT: usu *the* N

dining table, dining tables; also spelled **dining-table**. A **dining table** is a table that is used for having meals on.
◆◇◇◇◇ N-COUNT

dinky /dɪŋki/. In informal British English, if you describe something as **dinky**, you mean that you find it attractive and appealing, usually because it is quite small and well-designed. *Darby drove a dinky old Fiat sports car.*
ADJ-GRADED =natty

dinner /dɪnəʳ/ **dinners** ◆◆◆◆◇

1 **Dinner** is the main meal of the day, usually served in the early part of the evening. *She invited us to her house for dinner... Would you like to stay and have dinner?... Enjoy your dinner. ...four-course dinners.* • See also **TV dinner**.
N-VAR

2 In British English, any meal you eat in the middle of the day can be referred to as **dinner**.
N-VAR

3 A **dinner** is a formal social event at which a meal is served. It is held in the evening. *...a series of official lunches and dinners... The Professional Cricketers' Association held its annual dinner in London.*
N-COUNT

dinner dance, dinner dances; also spelled **dinner-dance**. In British English, a **dinner dance** is a social event where a large number of people come to have dinner and to dance. Dinner dances are held in the evening at hotels, restaurants, and social clubs.
N-COUNT

dinner jacket, dinner jackets; also spelled **dinner-jacket**. A **dinner jacket** is a jacket, usually black, worn by men for formal social events; used mainly in British English. The usual American word is **tuxedo**.
N-COUNT

dinner party, dinner parties. A **dinner party** is a social event where a small group of people are invited to have dinner and spend the evening at someone's house.
◆◇◇◇◇ N-COUNT

dinner service, dinner services. A **dinner service** is a set of plates and dishes from which meals are eaten and served. It may also include cups and saucers. *...a 60-piece dinner service.*
N-COUNT

dinner table, dinner tables; also spelled **dinner-table**. In British English, you refer to a table as the **dinner table** when it is being used for dinner. *Sam was left at the dinner table with Peg.*
◆◇◇◇◇ N-COUNT: usu sing, usu *the*/poss N

dinnertime /dɪnəʳtaɪm/; also spelled **dinner time. Dinnertime** is the period of the day when most people have their dinner. *The telephone call came shortly before dinnertime. ...Sunday dinnertime.*
N-UNCOUNT: oft prep N

dinosaur /daɪnəsɔːʳ/ **dinosaurs. Dinosaurs** were large reptiles which lived in prehistoric times.
◆◆◇◇◇ N-COUNT

dint /dɪnt/. If you achieve a result **by dint of** something, you achieve it by means of that thing; used in written English. *He succeeds by dint of sheer hard work... He has acquired, by dint of threatening to resign, a directorate-general with about 150 officials.*
PHR-PREP =by means of

diocesan /daɪɒsɪsən/. **Diocesan** means belonging or relating to a diocese. *The church commissioners are cutting their contributions to diocesan funds. ...the diocesan synod.* ADJ: ADJ n

diocese /daɪəsɪs/ **dioceses.** A **diocese** is the area over which a bishop has control. ◆◇◇◇◇ N-COUNT

dioxide /daɪɒksaɪd/. See **carbon dioxide**.

dioxin /daɪɒksɪn/ **dioxins. Dioxins** are poisonous chemicals which occur as a by-product of the manufacture of certain weed-killers and disinfectants. N-VAR

dip /dɪp/ **dips, dipping, dipped** ◆◆◇◇◇

1 If you **dip** something into a liquid, you put it into the liquid for a short time, so that only part of it is covered, and take it out again. *They dip the food into the sauce... Quickly dip the base in and out of cold water.* ► Also a noun. *One dip into the bottle should do an entire nail.* VERB =dunk; V n into/in n; N-COUNT

2 If you **dip** your hand into a container or **dip** into the container, you put your hand into it in order to take something out of it. *She dipped a hand into the jar of sweets and pulled one out... Watch your fingers as you dip into the pot... Ask the children to guess what's in each container by dipping their hands in.* VERB; V n into n; V into n; V n with *in*

3 If something **dips**, it makes a downward movement, usually quite quickly. *Blake jumped in expertly; the boat dipped slightly under his weight... The sun dipped below the horizon.* ► Also a noun. *I noticed little things, a dip of the head, a twitch in the shoulder.* VERB; V; V prep; N-COUNT

4 If an area of land, a road, or a path **dips**, it goes down quite suddenly to a lower level. *The road dipped and rose again as it neared the top of Parker Mountain. ...a path which suddenly dips down into a tunnel.* ► Also a noun. *Where the road makes a dip, soon after a small vineyard on the right, turn right.* VERB; V; V adv/prep; N-COUNT

5 When farmers **dip** sheep or other farm animals, they put them into a container of liquid with chemicals in it, in order to kill harmful insects which live on the animals' bodies. *Their father was helping to dip the sheep.* ♦ **dipping** *He digs potatoes and helps with the sheep dipping.* VERB; V n; N-UNCOUNT

6 **Dip** is a liquid with chemicals in it which animals or objects can be dipped in to disinfect or clean them. *...sheep dip.* N-UNCOUNT: also N in pl, usu supp N

7 If the amount or level of something **dips**, it becomes smaller or lower, usually only for a short period of time. *Unemployment dipped to 6.9 per cent last month... The president became more cautious as his popularity dipped.* ► Also a noun. *...the current dip in farm spending.* VERB =decrease, fall; V prep/adv; V; N-COUNT: oft N in n

8 A **dip** is a thick creamy sauce. You dip pieces of raw vegetable or biscuits into the sauce and then eat them. *Maybe we could just buy some dips. ...fresh asparagus with lemon and sunflower dip.* N-VAR

9 If you have or take a **dip**, you go for a quick swim in the sea, a river, or a swimming pool. *She flicked through a romantic paperback between occasional dips in the pool.* N-COUNT =swim

10 If you are driving a car and **dip** your headlights, you operate a switch that makes them shine downwards, so that they do not shine directly into the eyes of other drivers; used mainly in British English. *He dipped his headlights as they came up behind a slow-moving van... This picture shows the view from a car using normal dipped lights.* VERB; V n; V-ed

11 If you **dip into** a book, you have a brief look at it without reading or studying it seriously. *...a chance to dip into a wide selection of books on Tibetan Buddhism.* VERB; V into n

12 If you **dip into** a sum of money that you had intended to save, you use some of it to buy something or pay for something. *Just when she was ready to dip into her savings, Greg hastened to her rescue.* VERB; V into n

13 See also **lucky dip.** ● to **dip** your **toes** into something: see **toe**.

Dip. Dip. is a written abbreviation for **diploma**.

diphtheria /dɪfθɪəriə, dɪp-/. **Diphtheria** is a dangerous infectious disease which causes fever and difficulty in breathing and swallowing. N-UNCOUNT

diphthong /dɪfθɒŋ, dɪp-/ **diphthongs.** A **diphthong** is a vowel in which the speaker's tongue changes position while it is being pronounced, so that the vowel sounds like a combination of two other vowels. The vowel sound in 'tail' is a diphthong. N-COUNT

diploma /dɪpləʊmə/ **diplomas.** A **diploma** is a qualification which a student may be awarded by a university or college. *...a new two-year course leading to a diploma in social work.* ◆◇◇◇◇ N-COUNT

diplomacy /dɪpləʊməsi/ ◆◆◇◇◇

1 **Diplomacy** is the activity or profession of managing relations between the governments of different countries. *Today's Security Council resolution will be a significant success for American diplomacy... The real advantage Russia enjoyed in Tibet derived partly from the shrewd diplomacy of Dorjieff.* ● See also **shuttle diplomacy**. N-UNCOUNT

2 **Diplomacy** is the skill of being tactful and saying or doing things without offending people. *He stormed off in a fury, and it took all Minnelli's powers of diplomacy to get him to return.* N-UNCOUNT

diplomat /dɪpləmæt/ **diplomats.** A **diplomat** is a senior official who negotiates with another country on behalf of his or her own country, usually working as a member of an embassy. ◆◆◆◇◇ N-COUNT

diplomatic /dɪpləmætɪk/ ◆◆◆◇◇

1 **Diplomatic** means relating to diplomacy and diplomats. *...before the two countries resume full diplomatic relations... Efforts are being made to avert war and find a diplomatic solution... These diplomatic skills led to her appointment as the President of the United Nations General Assembly.* ADJ: usu ADJ n

♦ **diplomatically** /dɪpləmætɪkli/ *...a growing sense of doubt that the conflict can be resolved diplomatically... The President made it clear he did not want to see China diplomatically isolated.* ADV: ADV with v, ADV adj

2 Someone who is **diplomatic** is able to be tactful and say or do things without offending people. *She is very direct. I tend to be more diplomatic, I suppose.* ♦ **diplomatically** *'I really like their sound, although I'm not crazy about their lyrics,' he says, diplomatically.* ADJ-GRADED; ADV-GRADED: ADV with v

diplomatic bag, diplomatic bags. A **diplomatic bag** is a bag or container in which mail is sent to and from foreign embassies. Diplomatic bags are protected by law, and so they are not opened by anyone except the official or embassy they are addressed to; used mainly in British English. N-COUNT

diplomatic corps; diplomatic corps is both the singular and the plural form. The **diplomatic corps** is the group of all the diplomats who work in one city or country. N-COUNT-COLL: usu *the* N

diplomatic immunity. Diplomatic immunity is the freedom from legal action and from paying taxes that a diplomat has in the country in which he or she is working. *He was arrested along with an embassy official who claimed diplomatic immunity and was later released.* N-UNCOUNT

diplomatic service. The diplomatic service is the government department that employs diplomats to work in foreign countries. N-PROPER: *the* N

dippy /dɪpi/. If you describe someone as **dippy**, you mean that they are slightly odd or unusual, but in a way that you find charming and likeable; an informal word. ADJ-GRADED

dipstick /dɪpstɪk/ **dipsticks.** A **dipstick** is a metal rod with notches along one end. It is used to measure the amount of liquid in a container, especially the amount of oil in a car engine. N-COUNT

dire /daɪəʳ/ ◆◇◇◇◇

1 **Dire** is used to emphasize how serious or terrible a situation or event is. *The government looked as if it would split apart, with dire consequences for domestic peace... He was in dire need of hospital treatment. ...dire poverty.* ADJ-GRADED: usu ADJ n PRAGMATICS =awful

2 If you describe something as **dire**, you are emphasizing that it is of very low quality; an informal ADJ-GRADED: usu v-link ADJ PRAGMATICS

use. ...*a book of children's verse, which ranged from the barely tolerable to the utterly dire.*

direct /daɪre̲kt, dɪ-/ **directs, directing, directed** ◆◆◆◆◆

1 Direct means moving towards a place or object, without changing direction and without stopping, for example in a journey. *They'd come on a direct flight from the Soviet Union. ...the direct route from Amman to Bombay.* ► Also an adverb. *You can fly direct to Amsterdam from most British airports.* ADJ-GRADED: usu ADJ n ≠indirect ADV: ADV after v
♦ **directly** *The jumbo jet is due to fly the hostages directly back to London.* ADV: ADV after v

2 If something is in **direct** heat or light, it is strongly affected by the heat or light, because there is nothing between it and the source of heat or light to protect it. *All medicines should be stored away from moisture, direct sunlight and heat... Direct illumination is harsh and unflattering.* ADJ: ADJ n

3 You use **direct** to describe an experience, activity, or system which only involves the people, actions, or things that are necessary to make it happen. *He has direct experience of the process of privatisation... He seemed to be in direct contact with the Boss... He is expected to extend direct rule by the central government for another six months.* ► Also an adverb. *I can deal direct with your Inspector Kimble... Write to us direct with details of your clubs.* ♦ **directly** *We cannot measure pain directly. It can only be estimated... The British could do nothing directly to help the Austrians.* ADJ-GRADED: usu ADJ n ADV: ADV after v ADV-GRADED: ADV with v

4 You use **direct** to emphasize the closeness of a connection between two things. *They were unable to prove that the unfortunate lady had died as a direct result of his injection... His visit is direct evidence of the improvement in their relationship... The minister denied there was a direct connection between the two issues.* ADJ-GRADED: usu ADJ n PRAGMATICS ≠indirect

5 If you describe a person or their behaviour as **direct**, you mean that they are honest and open, and say exactly what they mean. *He avoided giving a direct answer... The new songs are more direct... No direct reference was made to the call by the Foreign Office minister.* ♦ **directly** *At your first meeting, explain simply and directly what you hope to achieve... But he then went on to refer very directly to the argument.* ♦ **directness** *Using 'I' ensures clarity and directness, and it adds warmth to a piece of writing... 'I like Rupert enormously,' she said, with a directness which made Pat flush.* ADJ-GRADED ≠indirect ADV-GRADED: ADV after v N-UNCOUNT

6 If you **direct** something at a particular thing, you aim or point it at that thing. *I reached the cockpit and directed the extinguisher at the fire without effect... He directed the tiny beam of light at the roof.* VERB =aim V n *at/towards/on* n

7 If your attention, emotions, or actions **are directed** at a particular person or thing, you are focusing them on that person or thing. *The learner's attention needs to be directed to the significant features... Do not be surprised if, initially, she directs her anger at you... One assassination attempt was directed against the country's top three government leaders.* VERB =focus be V-ed *to/towards* n/-ing V n *at* n be V-ed *against* n Also V n *to* n/-ing

8 If a remark or look **is directed** at you, someone says something to you or looks at you. *She could hardly believe the question was directed towards her... The abuse was directed at the TV crews... Arnold directed a meaningful look at Irma.* VERB be V-ed *towards* n be V-ed *at* n V n *at* n

9 If you **direct** someone somewhere, you tell them how to get there. *Could you direct them to Dr Lamont's office, please... Inside, a guard directed them to the right.* VERB V n *to* n Also V n adv/prep

10 When someone **directs** a project or a group of people, they are responsible for organizing the people and activities that are involved. *Christopher will direct day-to-day operations. ...his coolness in directing the rescue of nine hostages.* ♦ **direction** /daɪre̲kʃᵊn, dɪr-/ *Organizations need clear direction, set priorities and performance standards, and clear controls... The house was built under the direction of John's partner.* VERB =oversee V n N-UNCOUNT

11 When someone **directs** a film, play, or television programme, they are responsible for the way in which it is performed and for telling the actors and assistants what to do. *He directed various TV shows... The film was directed by Howard Hawks. ...Miss Birkin's long-held ambition to direct as well as act.* VERB V n V

12 If you **are directed** to do something, someone in authority tells you to do it; a formal use. *They have been directed to give special attention to the problem of poverty... The Bishop directed the faithful to stay at home.* VERB be V-ed to-inf V n to-inf

13 If you are a **direct** descendant of someone, you are related to them through your parents and their parents and so on. *She is a direct descendant of Queen Victoria.* ADJ: ADJ n

14 See also **direction, directly**.

dire̲ct a̲ction. **Direct action** involves doing something such as going on strike or demonstrating in order to put pressure on an employer or government to do what you want, instead of relying on persuasion. *Only with mass direct action will we obtain such change.* N-UNCOUNT

dire̲ct cu̲rrent, direct currents. A **direct current** is an electric current that always flows in the same direction. The abbreviation 'DC' is also used. *Some kinds of batteries can be recharged by connecting them to a source of direct current.* N-VAR

direct de̲bit, direct debits. If you pay a bill by **direct debit**, you give permission for the company who is owed money to transfer the correct amount from your bank account into theirs. *Switch to paying your mortgage by direct debit – you don't have to keep notifying the bank to alter your repayments.* N-VAR

dire̲ct hi̲t, direct hits. If a place suffers a **direct hit**, a bomb, bullet, or other missile that has been aimed at it lands exactly in that place, rather than some distance away. *The dug-outs were secure from everything but a direct hit.* N-COUNT

direction /daɪre̲kʃᵊn/ **directions** ◆◆◆◆◇

1 A **direction** is the general line that someone or something is moving or pointing in. *St Andrews was ten miles in the opposite direction... He got into Margie's car and swung out onto the road in the direction of Larry's shop... Civilians were fleeing in all directions as soldiers yelled at them to get off the streets... The instruments will register every change of direction or height.* N-VAR: usu with supp

2 A **direction** is the general way in which something develops or progresses. *They threatened to lead a mass walk-out if the party did not sharply change direction... I've never done any sustained writing, but that might be one of my next directions.* N-VAR: usu with supp

3 Directions are instructions that tell you what to do, how to do something, or how to get somewhere. *I should know by now not to throw away the directions until we've finished cooking... He proceeded to give Dan directions to the computer room.* N-PLURAL: with supp

4 The **direction** of a film, play, or television programme is the work that the director does while it is being made. *His failures underline the difference between theatre and film direction.* N-UNCOUNT

5 See also **direct**.

directional /daɪre̲kʃənᵊl, dɪr-/

1 If something such as a radio aerial, microphone, or loudspeaker is **directional**, it works most effectively in one direction, rather than equally in all directions at once; a technical use. *Dish aerials are highly directional... The directional microphone trained on Foresters Cottage could pick up every word uttered inside at several hundred yards.* ADJ-GRADED

2 Directional means relating to the direction in which something is pointing or going; a technical use. *Jets of compressed air gave the aircraft lateral and directional stability.* ADJ: usu ADJ n

directionless /daɪre̲kʃᵊnləs, dɪr-/. If you describe an activity or an organization as **directionless**, you mean that it does not seem to have any point or purpose. If you describe a person as **directionless**, you mean that they do not seem to have any plans or ideas. *...his seemingly disorganized and directionless campaign... I was still fairly directionless, and went into secretarial temping for British Gas.* ADJ-GRADED =aimless

directive /daɪre̲ktɪv, dɪr-/ **directives.** A **directive** is an official instruction that is given by someone in authority. *Thanks to a new EC directive, insecticide labelling will be more specific.*  N-COUNT =ruling

directly /daɪre̲ktli, dɪr-/ ◆◇◇◇◇

1 If something is **directly** above something, below something, or in front of something, it is in exactly that position. *The second rainbow will be bigger than the first, and directly above it... There, directly below me, was a guy holding the ball... The naked bulb was directly over his head... They are sleeping in the carpenter's shop directly above.* ADV: ADV prep/adv =exactly, right

2 If you do one action **directly** after another, you do the second action as soon as the first one is finished. *Directly after the meeting, a senior cabinet minister spoke to the BBC... Directly after lunch we were packed and ready to go... Directly following this treatment, he had a hollow, empty feeling in his stomach.* ADV: ADV prep/adv =immediately

3 If something happens **directly**, it happens without any delay; used mainly in old-fashioned British English. *He will be there directly.* ADV: ADV after v

4 See also **direct**.

dire̲ct ma̲il; also spelled **direct-mail. Direct mail** is a method of marketing which involves companies sending advertising material directly to people who they think may be interested in their products. *...efforts to solicit new customers by direct mail and television advertising... Direct mail advertising is of course a huge business.* N-UNCOUNT: oft N n

dire̲ct ma̲rketing. Direct marketing is the same as **direct mail**. *The direct marketing industry has become adept at packaging special offers.* N-UNCOUNT: oft N n

dire̲ct o̲bject, direct objects. The **direct object** of a transitive verb is the noun group which is used to refer to someone or something directly affected by or involved in the action performed by the subject. For example, in 'I saw him yesterday', 'him' is the direct object. Compare **indirect object**. N-COUNT =object

director /daɪre̲ktəʳ, dɪr-/ **directors** ◆◆◆◆◆

1 The **director** of a play, film, or television programme is the person who decides how it will appear on stage or screen, and who tells the actors and technical staff what to do. N-COUNT

2 In some organizations and public authorities, the person in charge is referred to as the **director**. *...the director of the intensive care unit at Guy's Hospital. ...the Director of Public Prosecutions.* N-COUNT: oft *the* N

3 The **directors** of a company are its most senior managers, who meet regularly to make important decisions about how it will be run. *He served on the board of directors of a local bank. ...Karl Uggerholt, the financial director of Braun UK.* N-COUNT

directorate /daɪre̲ktərət, dɪr-/ **directorates** ◆◇◇◇◇

1 A **directorate** is a board of directors in a company or organization. *The European Central Bank would be managed by a directorate of around five professional bankers.* N-COUNT

2 A **directorate** is a part of a government department which is responsible for one particular thing. *...the Health and Safety Directorate of the EC.* N-COUNT: with supp

dire̲ctor ge̲neral, directors general; also spelled **director-general**. The **director general** of a large organization such as the BBC is the person who is in charge of it. ◆◆◇◇◇ N-COUNT: usu sing

directorial /daɪrektɔ̲ːriəl, dɪr-/. **Directorial** means relating to the job of being a film or theatre director. *In the later stages of his directorial career, Orson Welles began work on several ambitious films. ...Nora Ephron's directorial debut.* ADJ: ADJ n

directorship /daɪre̲ktəʳʃɪp, dɪr-/ **directorships.** A **directorship** is the job or position of a company director. *Barry resigned his directorship in December 1973.* N-COUNT

directory /daɪre̲ktəri, dɪr-/ **directories.** A **directory** is a book which gives lists of facts, for example people's names, addresses, and telephone numbers, or the names and addresses of business companies, usually arranged in alphabetical order. *...a telephone directory.* ◆◆◇◇◇ N-COUNT: oft N *of* n, n N

dire̲ctory enqu̲iries. In Britain, **directory enquiries** is a service which you can telephone to find out someone's telephone number. The usual term in American English is **information** or **directory assistance**. *He dialled directory enquiries.* N-UNCOUNT

dire̲ct ru̲le. Direct rule is a system in which a central government rules a province which has had its own parliament or law-making organization in the past. N-UNCOUNT

di̲rect speech. In grammar, **direct speech** is speech which is reported by using the exact words that the speaker used. N-UNCOUNT

dire̲ct ta̲x, direct taxes. A **direct tax** is a tax which a person or organization pays directly to the government, for example income tax. N-COUNT

dire̲ct taxa̲tion. Direct taxation is a system in which a government raises money by means of direct taxes. N-UNCOUNT

dirge /dɜ̲ːʳdʒ/ **dirges.** A **dirge** is a slow, sad song or piece of music. **Dirges** are sometimes performed at funerals. *...the mournful dirge, 'Erin's Lament'.* N-COUNT: usu sing

dirt /dɜ̲ːʳt/ ◆◆◇◇◇

1 If there is **dirt** on something, there is dust, mud, or a stain on it. *I started to scrub off the dirt.* N-UNCOUNT =grime

2 You can refer to the earth on the ground as **dirt**, especially when it is muddy or dusty. *They all sit on the dirt in the dappled shade of a tree.* N-UNCOUNT =earth

3 A **dirt** road or track is made from earth, without any gravel or tarmac laid on it. A **dirt** floor is made from earth without any cement, stone, or wood laid on it. *I drove along the dirt road... The rooster chased me across the dirt floor of the barn.* ADJ: ADJ n

4 If you say that you have **dirt** on someone, you mean that you have information that could harm their reputation or career; an informal use. *Steve was mad keen to get all the dirt he could on the Langenbach woman... Both parties use computers to dig up dirt on their opponents.* N-SING: oft *the* N, N *on* n

5 In informal British English, if you say that someone **dishes the dirt** on someone else, you disapprove of them because they tell people things about that person without worrying if they will hurt that person's feelings. *He dishes the dirt on his buddies.* PHRASES V inflects, oft PHR *on* n PRAGMATICS

6 If you say that someone **treats** you **like dirt**, you are angry with them because you think that they treat you unfairly and with no respect. *People think they can treat me like dirt!* V inflects

di̲rt-che̲ap. If you say that something is **dirt-cheap**, you are emphasizing that it is very cheap indeed; used in informal English. *They're always selling off stuff like that dirt cheap... He got me a bass dirt cheap.* ADJ PRAGMATICS

dirty /dɜ̲ːʳti/ **dirtier, dirtiest; dirties, dirtying, dirtied** ◆◆◆◇◇

1 If something is **dirty**, it is marked or covered with stains, spots, or mud, and needs to be cleaned. *She still did not like the woman who had dirty fingernails... The dress had been brightly coloured, but it was stained and dirty now.* ADJ-GRADED =grubby ≠clean

2 To **dirty** something means to cause it to become dirty. *He was afraid the dog's hairs might dirty the seats... With poor quality tapes you could also risk dirtying the heads on your video recorder.* VERB V n

3 If you describe an action as **dirty**, you disapprove of it and consider it unfair, immoral, or dishonest. *The gunman had been hired by a rival Mafia family to do the dirty deed.* ► Also an adverb. *Jim Browne is the kind of fellow who can fight dirty, but make you like it.* ADJ-GRADED: usu ADJ n PRAGMATICS; ADV: ADV after v

4 If you describe something such as a joke, a book, or someone's language as **dirty**, you mean that it refers to sex in a way that some people find offensive. *He laughed at their dirty jokes and sang their raucous ballads... Of course lots of kids read dirty books in their rooms and hide them under the mattress.* ► Also an adverb. *I'm often asked whether the men talk dirty to me. The answer is no.* ADJ-GRADED: usu ADJ n PRAGMATICS =smutty; ADV: ADV after v

5 **Dirty** is used informally before words of criticism to emphasize that you do not approve of someone ADJ: ADJ n PRAGMATICS

or something. *You dirty liar, don't try to be funny with me. I made you what you are.*

6 In British English, if you say that someone **washes** their **dirty linen in public**, you disapprove of them discussing or arguing about unpleasant or private things in front of other people. The usual American expression is **wash** your **dirty laundry in public**. *The spectacle of the former naval officers washing their dirty linen in public was distinctly embarrassing... We shouldn't wash our dirty laundry in public and if I was in his position, I'd say nothing at all.*

PHRASES V inflects PRAGMATICS

7 If someone gives you a **dirty look**, they look at you in a way which shows that they are angry with you; an informal use. *Jack was being a real pain. Michael gave him a dirty look and walked out.*

N inflects, PHR after v

8 **Dirty old man** is an expression some people use to describe an older man who they think shows an unnatural interest in sex; used showing disapproval. *He was always trying it on. But now he's 71, it's causing problems. He's just like a dirty old man.*

N inflects, usu v-link PHR PRAGMATICS

9 To **do** someone's **dirty work** means to do a task for them that is dishonest or unpleasant and which they do not want to do themselves. *As a member of an elite army hit squad, the army would send us out to do their dirty work for them.*

V inflects

10 A **dirty weekend** is a weekend during which two people go away together in order to have sex; an informal expression.

N inflects

11 If you say that an expression is **a dirty word** in a particular group of people, you mean it refers to an idea that they strongly dislike or disagree with. *Marketing became a dirty word at the company.*

v-link PHR

dirty trick, dirty tricks. You describe the actions of an organization or political group as **dirty tricks** when you think they are using illegal methods to harm the reputation or effectiveness of their rivals. *He claimed he was the victim of a dirty tricks campaign in the run-up to last year's general election.*

◆◇◇◇◇ N-COUNT: usu pl

dis- /dɪs-/. **Dis-** is added to some words that describe processes, qualities, or states, in order to form words describing the opposite processes, qualities, or states. For example, if you do not agree with someone, you disagree with them; if one thing is not similar to something else, it is dissimilar to it.

PREFIX

disability /dɪsəbɪlɪti/ **disabilities**

◆◆◇◇◇

1 A **disability** is a permanent injury, illness, or physical or mental condition that tends to restrict the way that someone can live their life. *Facilities for people with disabilities are still insufficient. ...athletes who have overcome a physical disability to reach the top of their sport.*

N-COUNT =handicap

2 **Disability** is the state of being disabled. *Disability can make extra demands on financial resources because the disabled need extra care.*

N-UNCOUNT

disable /dɪseɪbᵊl/ **disables, disabling, disabled**

◆◇◇◇◇

1 If an injury or illness **disables** someone, it affects them so badly that it restricts the way that they can live their life. *She did all this tendon damage and it really disabled her... Although disabled by polio during the Second World War, Proctor was also a first-rate helmsman.* ♦ **disabling** *The result is skin ulcers which, although not life-threatening, are disfiguring and sometimes disabling.*

VERB =handicap V n V-ed ADJ-GRADED

2 If someone or something **disables** a system or mechanism, they stop it working, usually temporarily. *...if you need to disable a car alarm.*

VERB V n

disabled /dɪseɪbᵊld/. Someone who is **disabled** has an illness, injury, or condition that tends to restrict the way that they can live their life, especially by making it difficult for them to move about. *...an insight into the practical problems encountered by disabled people in the workplace.* ► People who are disabled are sometimes referred to as **the disabled**. *There are toilet facilities for the disabled.*

◆◆◇◇◇ ADJ-GRADED =handicapped N-PLURAL: the N

disablement /dɪseɪbᵊlmənt/. **Disablement** is the state of being disabled or the experience of becoming disabled; a formal word. *...permanent total disablement resulting in inability to work.*

N-UNCOUNT

disabuse /dɪsəbjuːz/ **disabuses, disabusing, disabused.** If you **disabuse** someone of something, you tell them or persuade them that what they believe is in fact untrue; a formal word. *Their view of country people was that they like to please strangers. I did not disabuse them of this notion.*

VERB V n *of* n Also V n

disadvantage /dɪsədvɑːntɪdʒ, -væn-/ **disadvantages**

◆◆◇◇◇

1 A **disadvantage** is a factor which makes something or someone less useful or acceptable than other people or things, or less likely to be successful. *His two main rivals suffer the disadvantage of having been long-term political exiles... Military commanders had been weighing up the advantages and disadvantages of allowing their soldiers to marry.*

N-COUNT: oft N *of* n ≠advantage

2 If you are **at a disadvantage**, you have a problem or difficulty that many other people do not have, which makes it harder for you to be successful. *The children from poor families were at a distinct disadvantage... England's players would be left at a disadvantage against those of the rest of the world.*

PHRASES v-link PHR

3 If something is **to** your **disadvantage** or works **to** your **disadvantage**, it creates difficulties for you. *...an opposition attempt to prevent a snap election which would be to their disadvantage... Depression is the third thing that works to my patients' disadvantage.*

v-link PHR, PHR after v =to your detriment

disadvantaged /dɪsədvɑːntɪdʒd, -væn-/. People who are **disadvantaged** or live in **disadvantaged** areas live in bad conditions and tend not to get a good education or have a reasonable standard of living. *...the educational problems of disadvantaged children... The centre aims to help disadvantaged areas of Europe, mainly by fostering new businesses.* ► **The disadvantaged** are people who are disadvantaged. *...people who claim to be champions of the poor, the disadvantaged, and the helpless.*

◆◇◇◇◇ ADJ-GRADED =deprived N-PLURAL: the N

disadvantageous /dɪsædvənteɪdʒəs/. Something that is **disadvantageous** to you puts you in a worse position than other people. *The Second World War started in the most disadvantageous possible way for the western powers.*

ADJ-GRADED: oft ADJ *to/for* n =unfavourable

disaffected /dɪsəfektɪd/. **Disaffected** people no longer fully support something such as an organization or political ideal which they previously supported. *He attracts disaffected voters... Environmental issues provided a rallying point for people disaffected with the government.*

◆◇◇◇◇ ADJ-GRADED

disaffection /dɪsəfekʃᵊn/. **Disaffection** is the attitude that people have when they stop supporting something such as an organization or political ideal. *The media were eager to find evidence of the Cuban people's disaffection with their country and its leaders.*

N-UNCOUNT: oft N *with* n

disagree /dɪsəgriː/ **disagrees, disagreeing, disagreed**

◆◆◇◇◇

1 If you **disagree** with someone or **disagree** with what they say, you do not accept that what they say is true or correct. You can also say that two people **disagree**. *You must continue to see them no matter how much you may disagree with them... They can communicate even when they strongly disagree... 'I think it is inappropriate to put up a statue.' 'Well, I disagree. We've got a statue for Churchill and Nelson.'... The two men had disagreed about reincarnation.*

V-RECIP ≠agree V *with* n pl-n V V (non-recip) pl-n V prep Also V *with* n prep

2 If you **disagree** with a particular action or proposal, you disapprove of it and believe that it is wrong; used mainly in British English. *I respect the president but I disagree with his decision... I disagree with drug laws in general.*

VERB =oppose V *with* n

3 If a particular food or drink **disagrees** with you, it makes you feel unwell; used mainly in informal British English. *Orange juice seems to disagree with some babies.*

VERB V *with* n

disagreeable /dɪsəgriːəbᵊl/

1 Something that is **disagreeable** is rather unpleas-

ADJ-GRADED

ant. *...a disagreeable odour. ...a comfort kit designed to make flying an altogether less disagreeable experience.* ♦ **disagreeably** /dɪsəgriːəbli/ *The taste is bitter and disagreeably pungent.* ADV: usu ADV adj, also ADV with v

2 Someone who is **disagreeable** is unfriendly or unhelpful. *He's a shallow, disagreeable man, for all his business acumen.* ADJ-GRADED: usu ADJ n =nasty

disagreement /dɪsəgriːmənt/ **disagreements** ♦♦◇◇◇

1 **Disagreement** means objecting to something such as a proposal. *Britain and France have expressed some disagreement with the proposal.* N-UNCOUNT: usu N prep =objection

2 When there is **disagreement** about something, people disagree or argue about what should be done. *The United States Congress and the President are still locked in disagreement over proposals to reduce the massive budget deficit... Plans for a peace conference failed due to disagreement on who should be allowed to attend... Disagreements among the twelve EC countries prevented them from taking any concerted action... My instructor and I had a brief disagreement.* N-VAR: usu with supp, oft *in* N =dispute

disallow /dɪsəlaʊ/ **disallows, disallowing, disallowed.** If something **is disallowed**, it is not allowed or accepted officially, because it has not been done correctly. *England scored again, but the whistle had gone and the goal was disallowed... The Internal Revenue Service sought to disallow the payments... It was a shock to hear him rule that my testimony would be disallowed.* ♦◇◇◇◇ VERB *be* V-ed V n

disappear /dɪsəpɪəʳ/ **disappears, disappearing, disappeared** ♦♦♦◇◇

1 If you say that someone or something **disappears**, you mean that you can no longer see them, usually because you or they have changed position. *The black car drove away from them and disappeared... Clive disappeared into a room by himself... The airliner disappeared off their radar.* VERB =vanish V V prep

2 If someone or something **disappears**, they go away or are taken away somewhere where nobody can find them. *...a Japanese woman who disappeared thirteen years ago... Janet's husband and sister noticed that small kitchen objects were disappearing with increasing regularity.* VERB V

3 If something **disappears**, it stops existing or happening. *The immediate threat of the past has disappeared and the security situation in Europe has significantly improved.* VERB V

disappearance /dɪsəpɪərəns/ **disappearances** ♦◇◇◇◇

1 If you refer to someone's **disappearance**, you are referring to the fact that nobody knows where they have gone. *Her disappearance has baffled police... They say the government is not doing enough to investigate tens of thousands of killings and disappearances over the past few years.* N-VAR: oft with poss

2 If you refer to the **disappearance** of an object, you are referring to the fact that it has been lost or stolen. *Police are investigating the disappearance from council offices of confidential files.* N-COUNT: usu sing, usu with poss, oft N *from* n =loss

3 The **disappearance** of a type of thing, person, or animal is a process in which it becomes less common and finally no longer exists. *...the virtual disappearance of common dolphins from the western Mediterranean in recent years.* N-UNCOUNT: usu with supp, oft N *of* n

disappoint /dɪsəpɔɪnt/ **disappoints, disappointing, disappointed.** If things or people **disappoint** you, they are not as good as you had hoped, or do not do what you hoped they would do. *She would do anything she could to please him, but she knew that she was fated to disappoint him... A spokesman for UNHCR said he was surprised and disappointed by the decision.* ♦◇◇◇◇ VERB =let down V n

disappointed /dɪsəpɔɪntɪd/ ♦♦♦◇◇

1 If you are **disappointed**, you are rather sad because something has not happened or because something is not as good as you had hoped. *Castle-hunters won't be disappointed with the Isle of Man... I was disappointed that Kluge was not there... I was disappointed to see the lack of coverage afforded to this event.* ADJ-GRADED: oft ADJ prep, ADJ that, ADJ to-inf

2 If you are **disappointed in** someone, you are rather sad because they have not behaved as well as you expected them to. *You should have accepted that. I'm disappointed in you.* ADJ-GRADED: v-link ADJ *in* n

disappointing /dɪsəpɔɪntɪŋ/. Something that is **disappointing** is not as good or as large as you hoped it would be. *The wine was excellent, but the meat was overdone and the vegetables disappointing... The recession is largely blamed for the disappointing response to the appeal.* ♦♦◇◇◇ ADJ-GRADED =unsatisfactory

♦ **disappointingly** *Progress is disappointingly slow... Disappointingly, this show is only on view for a week.* ADV: ADV adj, ADV with cl

disappointment /dɪsəpɔɪntmənt/ **disappointments** ♦♦◇◇◇

1 **Disappointment** is the state of feeling disappointed. *Despite winning the title, their last campaign ended in great disappointment... Book early to avoid disappointment.* N-UNCOUNT =dissatisfaction

2 Something or someone that is a **disappointment** is not as good as you had hoped. *For many, their long-awaited homecoming was a bitter disappointment. ...this ne'er-do-well brother who was such a disappointment to his family.* N-COUNT =let down

disapproval /dɪsəpruːvᵊl/. If you feel or show **disapproval** of something or someone, you feel or show that you do not approve of them. *His action had been greeted with almost universal disapproval. ...a society that registered its disapproval of alcohol by banning it.* ♦◇◇◇◇ N-UNCOUNT: oft N *of* n

disapprove /dɪsəpruːv/ **disapproves, disapproving, disapproved.** If you **disapprove** of something or someone, you feel or show that you do not like them or do not approve of them. *Most people disapprove of such violent tactics... Her mother disapproved of her working in a pub... The Prime Minister did not publicly denounce him, but went as far as hinting that he disapproved.* ♦◇◇◇◇ VERB ≠approve V *of* n/-ing V

disapproving /dɪsəpruːvɪŋ/. A **disapproving** action or expression shows that you do not approve of something or someone. *Janet gave him a disapproving look.* ♦ **disapprovingly** *Antonio looked at him disapprovingly.* ADJ-GRADED ADV-GRADED: ADV after v

disarm /dɪsɑːʳm/ **disarms, disarming, disarmed** ♦◇◇◇◇

1 To **disarm** a person or group means to take away all their weapons. *We will agree to disarming troops and leaving their weapons at military positions.* VERB V n

2 If a country or group **disarms**, it gives up the use of weapons, especially nuclear weapons. *There has also been a suggestion that the forces in Lebanon should disarm... We're not ready to disarm ourselves in order to make it easier for them to kill us.* VERB V V pron-refl

3 If a person or their behaviour **disarms** you, they cause you to feel less angry, hostile, or critical towards them. *His unease disarmed her... She did her best to disarm her critics.* VERB =win over V n

disarmament /dɪsɑːʳməmənt/. **Disarmament** is the act of reducing the number of weapons, especially nuclear weapons, that a country has. *The goal would be to increase political stability in the region and accelerate the pace of nuclear disarmament. ...unilateral disarmament.* ♦◇◇◇◇ N-UNCOUNT

disarming /dɪsɑːʳmɪŋ/. If someone or something is **disarming**, they make you feel less angry or hostile. *Leonard approached with a disarming smile... When you meet him, he is disarming as he talks about himself.* ♦ **disarmingly** *He is, as ever, business-like, and disarmingly honest... She looked at him directly and occasionally smiled disarmingly at him.* ADJ-GRADED =charming ADV: usu ADV adj, also ADV with v

disarray /dɪsəreɪ/ ♦◇◇◇◇

1 If people or things are in **disarray**, they are disorganized and confused. *The nation is in disarray following rioting led by the military... 12,000 crossed the border in one day alone, throwing evacuation plans into disarray... This would add to the disarray in world markets.* N-UNCOUNT: oft *in* N =disorder

2 If things or places are in **disarray**, they are in a very untidy state. *She was left lying on her side and her clothes were in disarray... He found the room in disarray, with food dumped on the floor and drawers pulled open.* N-UNCOUNT: oft *in* N =mess

disassemble /dɪsəsembəl/ **disassembles, disassembling, disassembled.** To **disassemble** something means to take it to pieces; a formal word. *Dennet disassembled the cabin and packed it away.*
VERB =dismantle V n

disassociate /dɪsəsoʊʃieɪt/ **disassociates, disassociating, disassociated**
1 If you **disassociate** yourself from something or someone, you say or show that you are not connected with them, usually in order to avoid trouble or blame. *I wish to disassociate myself from this very sad decision... He proposed that the Council should disassociate itself from such behaviour.*
VERB =distance ≠associate V pron-refl *from* n
2 If you **disassociate** one group or thing from another, you separate them. *...an attempt by the president to disassociate the military from politics.*
VERB V n *from* n

disaster /dɪzɑːstəʳ, -zæs-/ **disasters** ◆◆◆◇◇
1 A **disaster** is a very bad accident such as an earthquake or a plane crash, especially one in which a lot of people are killed. *It was the second air disaster in the region in less than two months... Many had lost all in the disaster and were destitute.*
N-COUNT =tragedy
2 If you refer to something as a **disaster**, you are emphasizing that you think it is extremely bad or unacceptable. *The whole production was just a disaster!... It would be a disaster for them not to reach the semi-finals... 'This tax is a disaster waiting to happen,' said an angry Tory backbencher.*
N-COUNT PRAGMATICS =catastrophe
3 **Disaster** is something which has very bad consequences for you. *He warned that war in the Gulf would be an ecological catastrophe and an economic disaster... For some the best way of coping with disaster is not to confront it directly.*
N-UNCOUNT =catastrophe
4 If you say that something is **a recipe for disaster**, you mean that it is very likely to have unpleasant consequences.
PHRASE: v-link PHR

disaster area, disaster areas
1 A **disaster area** is a part of a country or the world which has been very seriously affected by a disaster such as an earthquake or flood. *President Bush today declared parts of Kentucky disaster areas because of flooding last month.*
N-COUNT
2 If you describe a place, person, or situation as a **disaster area**, you mean that they are in a state of great disorder or failure; an informal use. *His office was a disaster area of papers and full ashtrays... He's a nice old rascal but a disaster area as a politician.*
N-COUNT: usu sing

disastrous /dɪzɑːstrəs, -zæs-/ ◆◆◇◇◇
1 A **disastrous** event has extremely bad consequences and effects. *...the recent, disastrous earthquake... The effect on coffee prices has been disastrous for the producers.*
ADJ-GRADED =terrible
♦ **disastrously** *The vegetable harvest is disastrously behind schedule... Their scheme went disastrously wrong.*
ADV-GRADED: ADV adj/prep, ADV with v
2 If you describe something as **disastrous**, you mean that it was very unsuccessful. *England's cricketers have had another disastrous day. ...after their disastrous performance in the general election of 1906.*
ADJ-GRADED
♦ **disastrously** *...debts resulting from the company's disastrously timed venture into property development.*
ADV-GRADED: ADV adj, ADV with v

disavow /dɪsəvaʊ/ **disavows, disavowing, disavowed.** If you **disavow** something, you say that you are not connected with it or responsible for it; a formal word. *Dr. Samuels immediately disavowed the newspaper story.*
VERB =disown, repudiate V n

disavowal /dɪsəvaʊəl/ **disavowals.** A **disavowal** of something is a statement that you are not connected with it or responsible for it, or that you no longer agree with or believe in it; a formal word. *...a public disavowal of his beliefs.*
N-COUNT: oft N *of* n =repudation

disband /dɪsbænd/ **disbands, disbanding, disbanded.** If someone **disbands** a group of people, or if the group **disbands**, it stops operating as a single unit. *All the armed groups will be disbanded... The rebels were to have fully disbanded by June the tenth.*
◆◇◇◇◇ V-ERG =break up *be* V-ed V Also V n

disbelief /dɪsbɪliːf/. **Disbelief** is not believing that something is true or real. *She looked at him in disbelief.*
◆◇◇◇◇ N-UNCOUNT: oft *in* N

disbelieve /dɪsbɪliːv/ **disbelieves, disbelieving, disbelieved**
1 If you **disbelieve** someone or **disbelieve** something that they say, you do not believe that what they say is true. *There is no reason to disbelieve him... He had never been able to disbelieve it completely.*
VERB ≠believe V n Also V that
2 If you **disbelieve** in something, you do not believe that it exists or that it works. *Frank disbelieved in astrology.*
VERB V *in* n

disburse /dɪsbɜːʳs/ **disburses, disbursing, disbursed.** To **disburse** an amount of money means to pay it out, usually from a fund which has been collected for a particular purpose; a formal word. *The aid will not be disbursed until next year... The bank has disbursed over $350m for the project.*
VERB *be* V-ed V n

disbursement /dɪsbɜːʳsmənt/ **disbursements**
1 **Disbursement** is the paying out of a sum of money, especially from a fund; a formal use.
N-UNCOUNT =payment
2 A **disbursement** is a sum of money that is paid out; a formal use.
N-COUNT =payment

disc /dɪsk/ **discs;** spelled **disk** in American English. ◆◆◇◇◇
1 A **disc** is a flat, circular shape or object. *Most shredding machines are based on a revolving disc fitted with replaceable blades.*
N-COUNT
2 A **disc** is one of the thin, circular pieces of cartilage which separates the bones in your back. *I had slipped a disc and was frozen in a spasm of pain.*
N-COUNT
3 A **disc** is a gramophone record; an old-fashioned use. *This disc includes the piano sonata in C minor.*
N-COUNT
4 See also **disk, compact disc, slipped disc.**

discard /dɪskɑːʳd/ **discards, discarding, discarded.** If you **discard** something, you get rid of it because you no longer want it or need it. *Read the manufacturer's guidelines before discarding the box. ...looking for discarded cigarette butts.*
◆◆◇◇◇ VERB =dispose of V n V-ed

discern /dɪsɜːʳn/ **discerns, discerning, discerned** ◆◇◇◇◇
1 If you can **discern** something, you are aware of it and know what it is; a formal use. *You need a long series of data to be able to discern such a trend... It was hard to discern why this was happening.*
VERB V n V wh Also V that
2 If you can **discern** something, you can just see it, but not clearly; a formal use. *Below the bridge we could just discern a narrow, weedy ditch.*
VERB V n

discernible /dɪsɜːʳnəbəl/. If something is **discernible**, you can see it or recognize that it exists. *Far away the outline of the island is just discernible... There has been no discernible overall trend since 1975.*
◆◇◇◇◇ ADJ-GRADED =apparent

discerning /dɪsɜːʳnɪŋ/. If you describe someone as **discerning**, you mean that they are able to judge which things of a particular kind are good and which are bad; used showing approval. *...tailor-made holidays to suit the more discerning traveller... Her childhood passion for collecting has not dimmed, but now she is more discerning.*
◆◇◇◇◇ ADJ-GRADED PRAGMATICS =discriminating

discernment /dɪsɜːʳnmənt/. **Discernment** is the ability to judge which things of a particular kind are good and which are bad. *...their lack of discernment and acceptance of inferior quality.*
N-UNCOUNT =judgement

discharge, discharges, discharging, discharged. The verb is pronounced /dɪstʃɑːʳdʒ/. The noun is pronounced /dɪstʃɑːʳdʒ/. ◆◆◇◇◇
1 When someone **is discharged** from hospital, prison, or one of the armed services, they are officially allowed to leave, or told that they must leave. *He has a broken nose but may be discharged today... You are being discharged on medical grounds. ...the regulation that gay people should be discharged from the military... Five days later Mansell discharged himself from hospital.*
VERB *be* V-ed V n
► Also a noun. *He was given a conditional discharge and ordered to pay Miss Smith £100 compensation.*
N-VAR
2 If someone **discharges** their duties or responsibilities, they do everything that needs to be done in order to complete them. If they **discharge** a debt, they pay all the money that needs to be paid; a formal use. *...the quiet competence with which he discharged his many college duties... The goods will*
VERB V n

be sold for a fraction of their value in order to discharge the debt.

3 If something **is discharged** from inside a place, it comes out; a formal use. *The resulting salty water will be discharged at sea... The bird had trouble breathing and was discharging blood from the nostrils.*
VERB
be V-ed prep
V n prep

4 When there is a **discharge** of a substance, the substance comes out from inside somewhere; a formal use. *They develop a fever and a watery discharge from their eyes... All discharges and disposals of radioactive waste from Springfields were within relevant limits.*
N-VAR: usu with supp
=emission

5 If someone **discharges** a gun, they fire it; an old-fashioned use. *Lewis was tried for unlawfully and dangerously discharging a weapon.*
VERB
V n

disciple /dɪsaɪpəl/ **disciples.** If you are someone's **disciple**, you are influenced by their teachings and try to follow their example. *...a major intellectual figure with disciples throughout Europe. ...one of the disciples of Christ.*
◆◇◇◇◇
N-COUNT: oft with poss
=follower

disciplinarian /dɪsɪplɪneəriən/ **disciplinarians.** If you describe someone as a **disciplinarian**, you mean that they believe in imposing strict rules of behaviour and in punishing severely anyone who disobeys the rules. *He has a reputation for being a strict disciplinarian.*
N-COUNT
=authoritarian

disciplinary /dɪsɪplɪnəri, AM -neri/. **Disciplinary** bodies or actions are concerned with making sure that people obey rules or regulations and that they are suitably punished if they do not. *He will now face a disciplinary hearing for having an affair... He was unhappy that no disciplinary action was being taken.*
◆◆◇◇◇
ADJ: ADJ n

discipline /dɪsɪplɪn/ **disciplines, disciplining, disciplined**
◆◆◆◇◇

1 Discipline is the practice of making people obey rules or standards of behaviour, and punishing them when they do not. *Order and discipline have been placed in the hands of headmasters and governing bodies. ...discipline problems in the classroom.*
N-UNCOUNT

2 Discipline is the quality of being able to behave and work in a controlled way which involves obeying particular rules or standards. *It was that image of calm, control and discipline that appealed to millions of voters.*
N-UNCOUNT
=self-control

3 If you refer to an activity or situation as a **discipline**, you mean that, in order to be successful in it, you need to behave in a strictly controlled way and obey particular rules or standards. *...inner disciplines like transcendental meditation... The discipline of studying music can help children develop good work habits and improve self-esteem.*
N-VAR
PRAGMATICS

4 If someone **is disciplined** for something that they have done wrong, they are punished for it. *The workman was disciplined by his company but not dismissed... Her husband had at last taken a share in disciplining the boy.*
VERB
be V-ed
V n

5 If you **discipline** yourself to do something, you train yourself to behave and work in a strictly controlled and regular way. *Out on the course you must discipline yourself to let go of detailed theory... I'm very good at disciplining myself.*
VERB
=punish
V pron-refl to-inf
V pron-refl

6 A **discipline** is a particular area of study, especially a subject of study in a college or university; a formal use. *You've got to make sure that people work together across disciplines... We're looking for people from a wide range of disciplines.*
N-COUNT
=subject

7 See also **self-discipline**.

disciplined /dɪsɪplɪnd/. Someone who is **disciplined** behaves or works in a controlled way. *For me it meant being very disciplined about how I run my life... Soldiers are disciplined people.*
◆◇◇◇◇
ADJ-GRADED

disc jockey, disc jockeys. A **disc jockey** is someone who plays and introduces pop records on the radio or at a disco.
N-COUNT

disclaim /dɪskleɪm/ **disclaims, disclaiming, disclaimed.** If you **disclaim** knowledge of something or **disclaim** responsibility for something, you say that you did not know about it or are not responsible for it; a formal word. *Mrs Lee disclaims any knowledge of her husband's business concerns... The government has disclaimed responsibility for the deaths of six people.*
VERB
=deny
V n

disclaimer /dɪskleɪmər/ **disclaimers.** A **disclaimer** is a statement in which someone says that they did not know about something or that they are not responsible for something; a formal word. *The company asserts in a disclaimer that it won't be held responsible for the accuracy of information.*
N-COUNT

disclose /dɪsklouz/ **discloses, disclosing, disclosed.** If you **disclose** new or secret information, you tell people about it. *Neither side would disclose details of the transaction... The company disclosed that its chairman will step down in May.*
◆◆◇◇◇
VERB
=reveal
V n
V that
Also V wh

disclosure /dɪsklouʒər/ **disclosures. Disclosure** is the act of giving people new or secret information. *...insufficient disclosure of negative information about the company. ...unauthorised newspaper disclosures.*
◆◆◇◇◇
N-VAR
=revelation

disco /dɪskou/ **discos.** A **disco** is a place or event at which people dance to pop music, which is usually played by a disc jockey. *Fridays and Saturdays are regular disco nights.*
◆◆◇◇◇
N-COUNT

discography /dɪskɒgrəfi/ **discographies.** A **discography** is a list of all the recordings made by a particular artist or group.
N-COUNT

discolour /dɪskʌlər/ **discolours, discolouring, discoloured;** spelled **discolor** in American English. If something **discolours** or if it **is discoloured** by something else, its original colour changes, so that it looks unattractive. *A tooth which has been hit hard may discolour... Some oil had seeped out, discolouring the grass.*
V-ERG
V
V n

♦ **discoloured** *Some of the prints were badly discoloured around the edges.*
ADJ-GRADED

♦ **discoloration** /dɪskʌləreɪʃən/ *...the discoloration of the soil from acid spills.*
N-UNCOUNT

discomfit /dɪskʌmfɪt/ **discomfits, discomfiting, discomfited.** If you **are discomfited** by something, it causes you to feel slightly embarrassed or confused; used in written English. *He will be particularly discomfited by the minister's dismissal of his plan... The opposition leader has regularly discomfited him in parliament.*
VERB
be V-ed
V n

♦ **discomfited** *Will wanted to do likewise, but felt too discomfited.*
ADJ-GRADED: usu v-link ADJ

discomfiture /dɪskʌmfɪtʃər/. **Discomfiture** is a feeling of slight embarrassment or confusion; used in written English.
N-UNCOUNT
=unease

discomfort /dɪskʌmfərt/ **discomforts**
◆◆◇◇◇

1 Discomfort is a painful feeling in part of your body when you have been hurt slightly or when you have been uncomfortable for a long time. *She carried her left arm at an awkward angle, as if it were causing her discomfort... Steve had some discomfort, but no real pain.*
N-UNCOUNT
=soreness

2 Discomfort is a feeling of worry caused by shame or embarrassment. *He sniffed, fidgeting in discomfort, uneasy at the suggestion... She hears the discomfort in his voice.*
N-UNCOUNT
=uneasiness

3 Discomforts are conditions which cause you to feel physically uncomfortable. *...the discomforts of camping. ...reducing the physical discomforts and difficulties faced by women.*
N-COUNT: with supp

disconcert /dɪskənsɜːrt/ **disconcerts, disconcerting, disconcerted.** If something **disconcerts** you, it makes you feel uneasy, confused, or embarrassed. *Antony's wry smile disconcerted Sutcliffe... The ambassador was clearly disconcerted by the British reaction.*
VERB
=unsettle
V n

♦ **disconcerted** *He was disconcerted to find his fellow diners already seated.*
ADJ-GRADED: usu v-link ADJ, oft ADJ to-inf

disconcerting /dɪskənsɜːrtɪŋ/. If you say that something is **disconcerting**, you mean that it makes you feel uneasy, confused, or embarrassed. *The reception desk is not at street level, which is a little disconcerting.*
◆◇◇◇◇
ADJ-GRADED
=disturbing

♦ **disconcertingly** *She looks disconcertingly like a familiar aunt or grandmother... At times she could be almost disconcertingly absent-minded.*
ADV-GRADED: usu ADV adj/-ed/prep

disconnect /dɪskənekt/ **disconnects, disconnecting, disconnected** ◆◇◇◇◇

1 If you **disconnect** a piece of equipment, you detach it from its source of power. *The device automatically disconnects the ignition when the engine is switched off... Vicky Brown arrived home to find the men disconnecting her microwave.* VERB ≠connect V n

2 If you **are disconnected** by a gas, electricity, water, or telephone company, they turn off the connection to your house, usually because you have not paid the bill. *You are likely to be given almost three months – until the time of your next bill – before you are disconnected.* VB: usu passive ≠connect *be* V-ed

3 If you **disconnect** something from something else, you separate the two things. *He disconnected the IV bottle from the overhead hook and carried it beside the moving cart.* VERB ≠connect V n *from* n

disconnected /dɪskənektɪd/. **Disconnected** things are not linked in any way. *...sequences of utterly disconnected events... His ability to absorb bits of disconnected information was astonishing.* ADJ-GRADED: usu ADJ n =disjointed

disconnection /dɪskənekʃᵊn/ **disconnections**

1 The **disconnection** of a gas, water, or electricity supply, or of a telephone, is the act of disconnecting it so that it cannot be used. *The rate of disconnections following non-payment of water charges is rising. ...the disconnection of his phone.* N-VAR: oft *the* N *of* n

2 The **disconnection** of two things is the act or process of separating them so that the are no longer connected or linked in any way. *He hopes for a gradual disconnection from the federation.* N-UNCOUNT

disconsolate /dɪskɒnsələt/. Someone who is **disconsolate** is very unhappy and depressed; used in written English. *He did not have much success, but tried to keep from getting too disconsolate.* ♦ **disconsolately** *Disconsolately, he walked back down the course.* ADJ-GRADED =dejected; ADV-GRADED: ADV with v

discontent /dɪskəntent/ **discontents. Discontent** is the feeling that you have when you are not satisfied with your situation. *There are reports of widespread discontent in the capital.* ◆◇◇◇◇ N-UNCOUNT: also N in pl =dissatisfaction

discontented /dɪskəntentɪd/. If you are **discontented**, you are not satisfied with your situation. *The government tried to appease discontented workers. ...farmers discontented with low prices for their produce.* ADJ-GRADED: oft ADJ *with* n =dissatisfied

discontinue /dɪskəntɪnjuː/ **discontinues, discontinuing, discontinued** ◆◇◇◇◇

1 If you **discontinue** something that you have been doing regularly, you stop doing it; a formal use. *Do not discontinue the treatment without consulting your doctor.* VERB V n Also V -ing

2 If a product **is discontinued**, the manufacturer stops making it. *The Leica M2 was discontinued in 1967... They have a huge selection of discontinued cookers.* VB: usu passive *be* V-ed V-ed

discontinuity /dɪskɒntɪnjuːɪti, AM -nuː-/ **discontinuities. Discontinuity** in a process is a lack of smooth or continuous development; a formal word. *The text is good in parts, but suffers from discontinuity... There may appear to be discontinuities between broadcasts.* N-VAR =disjointedness ≠coherence

discontinuous /dɪskəntɪnjuəs/. A process that is **discontinuous** happens in stages with intervals between them, rather than continuously. ADJ =intermittent

discord /dɪskɔːʳd/. **Discord** is disagreement and argument between people; a literary word. ◆◇◇◇◇ N-UNCOUNT =conflict

discordant /dɪskɔːʳdᵊnt/

1 Something that is **discordant** is strange or unpleasant because it does not fit in with other things. *His agenda is discordant and out of time with ours.* ADJ-GRADED =incongruous

2 A **discordant** sound or musical effect is unpleasant to hear. ADJ-GRADED

discotheque /dɪskətek/ **discotheques.** A **discotheque** is the same as a **disco**. N-COUNT

discount, discounts, discounting, discounted. Pronounced /dɪskaʊnt/ for meanings 1 and 2, and /dɪskaʊnt/ for meaning 3. ◆◆◆◇◇

1 A **discount** is a reduction in the usual price of something. *They are often available at a discount... All full-time staff get a 20 per cent discount on goods up to £1,000 each year. ...discontinued ranges of tiles at discount prices.* N-COUNT

2 If a shop or company **discounts** an amount or percentage from something that they are selling, they deduct the amount or percentage from the usual price. *This has forced airlines to discount fares heavily in order to spur demand... Tour prices are being discounted as much as 33%.* VERB V n

3 If you **discount** an idea, fact, or theory, you consider that it is not true, not important, or not relevant. *However, traders tended to discount the rumor... This theory has now been discounted.* VERB =disregard V n

discounter /dɪskaʊntəʳ/ **discounters.** A **discounter** is a shop or organization which specializes in selling things very cheaply. Discounters usually sell things in large quantities, or offer only a very limited range of goods. N-COUNT

discourage /dɪskʌrɪdʒ, AM -kɜːr-/ **discourages, discouraging, discouraged** ◆◆◇◇◇

1 If someone or something **discourages** you, they cause you to lose your enthusiasm about doing something. *It may be difficult to do at first. Don't let this discourage you.* ♦ **discouraged** *She was determined not to be too discouraged.* ♦ **discouraging** *Today's report is rather more discouraging for the economy.* VERB =dishearten V n; ADJ-GRADED: usu v-link ADJ; ADJ-GRADED: usu v-link ADJ

2 To **discourage** an action or to **discourage** someone from doing it means to make them not want to do it. *...typhoons that discouraged shopping and leisure activities. ...a campaign to discourage children from smoking.* VERB =deter V n/-ing V n *from* -ing

discouragement /dɪskʌrɪdʒmənt, AM -kɜːr-/ **discouragements**

1 **Discouragement** is the act of trying to make someone not want to do something. *He persevered in the face of active discouragement from those around him.* N-UNCOUNT

2 A **discouragement** is something that makes you unwilling to do something because you are afraid of the consequences. *Uncertainty is one of the many discouragements to investment.* N-COUNT =deterrent

discourse, discourses, discoursing, discoursed. The noun is pronounced /dɪskɔːʳs/. The verb is pronounced /dɪskɔːʳs/. ◆◇◇◇◇

1 **Discourse** is spoken or written communication between people, especially serious discussion of a particular subject. *...a tradition of political discourse.* N-UNCOUNT: usu with supp

2 A **discourse** is a serious talk or piece of writing which is intended to teach or explain something; a formal use. *Gates responds with a lengthy discourse on deployment strategy.* N-COUNT

3 If someone **discourses** on something, they talk for a long time about it in an authoritative way; a formal use. *He discoursed for several hours on French and English prose.* VERB V prep Also V

4 In linguistics, **discourse** is natural spoken or written language in context, especially when complete texts are being considered. *The Centre has a strong record of research in discourse analysis. ...our work on discourse and the way people talk to each other.* N-UNCOUNT: oft N n

discourteous /dɪskɜːʳtiəs/. If you say that someone is **discourteous**, you mean that they are rude and have no consideration for the feelings of other people; a formal word. *Staff are often discourteous and sometimes downright rude.* ADJ-GRADED: usu v-link ADJ, oft ADJ *to* n =ill-mannered ≠polite

discourtesy /dɪskɜːʳtɪsi/ **discourtesies. Discourtesy** is rude and ill-mannered behaviour; a formal word. N-VAR =rudeness

discover /dɪskʌvəʳ/ **discovers, discovering, discovered** ◆◆◆◆◇

1 If you **discover** something that you did not know about before, you become aware of it or learn of it. *She discovered that they'd escaped... I discovered I was pregnant... As he discovered, she had a brilliant mind... It was difficult for the inspectors to discover which documents were important and which were not... Haskell did not live to discover the deception... It was discovered that the tapes were missing.* VERB =find out about V that V wh V n *it be* V-ed that Also *be* V-ed to-inf

2 If someone or something **is discovered**, someone finds them, either by accident or because they VERB =find

have been looking for them. *A few days later his badly beaten body was discovered on a roadside outside the city.* — be V-ed; Also V n

3 When someone **discovers** a new place, substance, scientific fact, or scientific technique, they are the first person to find it or become aware of it. *...the first European to discover America... In the 19th century, gold was discovered in California... They discovered how to form the image in a thin layer on the surface.* ♦ **discoverer, discoverers** *...the myth of Columbus as the heroic discoverer of the Americas 500 years ago.* — VERB; V n; V wh; Also V that; N-COUNT: oft N of n

4 If you say that someone **has discovered** a particular activity or subject, you mean that they have tried doing it or studying it for the first time and that they enjoyed it. *I wish I'd discovered photography when I was younger... Discover the delights and luxury of a private yacht.* — VERB; V n

5 When a actor, musician, or other performer who is not well-known **is discovered**, someone recognizes that they have talent and helps them in their career. *The Beatles were discovered in the early 1960's.* — VB: usu passive; be V-ed

discovery /dɪskʌvəri/ **discoveries** ◆◆◆◇◇

1 If someone makes a **discovery**, they become aware of something or learn of something that they did not know about before. *I felt I'd made an incredible discovery. ...the discovery that both his wife and son are HIV positive.* — N-VAR: usu with supp

2 If someone makes a **discovery**, they are the first person to find or become aware of a place, substance, or scientific fact that no one knew about before. *In that year, two momentous discoveries were made. ...the discovery of the ozone hole over the South Pole... The fascination of discovery has never left him.* — N-VAR: usu with supp

3 If someone makes a **discovery**, they recognize that an actor, musician, or other performer who is not well-known has talent. *He prides himself on the discovery and promotion of artists who will become the future masters.* — N-VAR: usu with supp

4 When the **discovery** of people or objects happens, someone finds them, either by accident or as a result of looking for them. *...the discovery and destruction by soldiers of millions of marijuana plants.* — N-VAR: usu with supp

discredit /dɪskredɪt/ **discredits, discrediting, discredited** ◆◆◇◇◇

1 To **discredit** someone or something means to cause them to lose people's respect or trust. *...a secret unit within the company that had been set up to discredit its major rival... He says his accusers are trying to discredit government foreign-aid policies... He said such methods discredited the communist fight worldwide.* ♦ **discredited** *The old Communist parties are, by now, thoroughly discredited. ...the old, discredited regimes.* — VERB; PRAGMATICS; V n; ADJ-GRADED

2 If someone or something **discredits** an idea or evidence, they make the idea or evidence appear false or doubtful. *They realized there would be difficulties in discrediting the evidence.* — VERB; V n

discreditable /dɪskredɪtəbəl/. **Discreditable** behaviour is not acceptable because people consider it to be shameful and wrong; a formal word. *She had been suspended from her job for discreditable behaviour.* — ADJ-GRADED; =improper

discreet /dɪskriːt/ ◆◆◇◇◇

1 If you are **discreet**, you are polite and careful in what you do or say, because you want to avoid embarrassing or offending someone. *They were gossipy and not always discreet... He followed at a discreet distance.* ♦ **discreetly** *I took the phone, and she went discreetly into the living room.* — ADJ-GRADED; ADV-GRADED: usu ADV with v

2 If you are **discreet** about something you are doing, you do not tell other people about it, in order to avoid being embarrassed or to gain an advantage. *We were very discreet about the romance... She's making a few discreet inquiries with her mother's friends.* ♦ **discreetly** *Everyone worked to make him welcome, and, more discreetly, to find out about him.* — ADJ-GRADED: oft ADJ about n; ADV-GRADED: usu ADV with v, also ADV with cl

3 If you describe something as **discreet**, you approve of it because it is small in size or degree, or not easily noticed. *She is wearing a noticeably stylish, feminine dress, plus discreet jewellery.* ♦ **discreetly** *...stately houses, discreetly hidden behind great avenues of sturdy trees... The two rooms were relatively small and discreetly lit.* — ADJ-GRADED; PRAGMATICS; ADV-GRADED: ADV -ed/adj

discrepancy /dɪskrepənsi/ **discrepancies.** ◆◇◇◇◇ If there is a **discrepancy** between two things that ought to be the same, there is a noticeable difference between them. *...the discrepancy between press and radio reports. ...major discrepancies in payments made to claimants in similar circumstances.* — N-VAR: usu with supp, oft N between pl-n, N in n; =inconsistency

discrete /dɪskriːt/. **Discrete** ideas or things are separate and distinct from each other; a formal word. *...instruction manuals that break down jobs into scores of discrete steps.* — ADJ: usu ADJ n; =separate

discretion /dɪskreʃən/ ◆◆◇◇◇

1 **Discretion** is the quality of behaving in a quiet and controlled way without drawing attention to yourself or giving away personal or private information; a formal use. *Larsson sometimes joined in the fun, but with more discretion... He appreciated his discretion and his fidelity.* — N-UNCOUNT

2 If someone in a position of authority uses their **discretion** or has the **discretion** to do something in a particular situation, they have the freedom and authority to decide what to do; a formal use. *This committee may want to exercise its discretion to look into those charges... School governors have the discretion to allow parents to withdraw pupils in exceptional circumstances.* — N-UNCOUNT

3 If something happens **at** someone's **discretion,** it can happen only if they decide to do it or give their permission; a formal expression. *We may vary the limit at our discretion and will notify you of any change... Where there are no service charges added to the bill, tip at your discretion... Visits are at the discretion of the owners.* — PHRASES; usu PHR after v, v-link PHR

4 If you say **discretion is the better part of valour,** you mean that avoiding a dangerous or unpleasant situation is sometimes the most sensible thing to do. — V inflects

discretionary /dɪskreʃənri, AM -neri/. **Discretionary** things are not fixed by rules but are decided on by people in authority, who consider each individual case. *Magistrates were given wider discretionary powers... Check whether you are entitled to a discretionary grant for your course.* — ◆◇◇◇◇ ADJ: usu ADJ n

discriminate /dɪskrɪmɪneɪt/ **discriminates, discriminating, discriminated** ◆◇◇◇◇

1 If you can **discriminate** between two things, you can recognize that they are different. *He is incapable of discriminating between a good idea and a terrible one... The device can discriminate between the cancerous and the normal cells.* — VERB; V between pl-n

2 To **discriminate** against a group of people or in favour of a group of people means to unfairly treat them worse or better than other groups. *They believe the law discriminates against women. ...legislation which would discriminate in favour of racial minorities... The Commission for Racial Equality teaches organisations not to discriminate.* — VERB; ≠favour; V against n; V in favour of n; V

discriminating /dɪskrɪmɪneɪtɪŋ/. Someone who is **discriminating** has the ability to recognize things that are of good quality; used showing approval. *The more discriminating visitor is often inclined nowadays to shun the area.* — ADJ-GRADED; PRAGMATICS; =discerning

discrimination /dɪskrɪmɪneɪʃən/ ◆◆◇◇◇

1 **Discrimination** is the practice of treating one person or group of people less fairly or less well than other people or groups. *She is exempt from sex discrimination laws. ...discrimination against immigrants. ...measures to counteract racial discrimination.* — N-UNCOUNT: usu with supp

2 **Discrimination** is awareness of what is good or of high quality. *They cooked without skill and ate without discrimination.* — N-UNCOUNT; =taste

3 **Discrimination** is the ability to recognize and understand the differences between two things. *We will then have an objective measure of how colour discrimination and visual acuity develop at the* — N-UNCOUNT: usu with supp

level of the brain. ...the system that allows a mother to make the discrimination between her own and alien lambs.

discriminatory /dɪskrɪmɪnətri, AM -tɔːri/. **Discriminatory** laws or practices are unfair because they treat one group of people worse than other groups. *These reforms will abolish racially discriminatory laws.* ◆◇◇◇◇ ADJ =biased

discursive /dɪskɜːˈsɪv/. If a style of writing is **discursive**, it includes a lot of facts or opinions that are not necessarily relevant; a formal word. *...a livelier, more candid and more discursive treatment of the subject.* ADJ-GRADED

discus /dɪskəs/ **discuses**

1 A **discus** is a heavy circular object which athletes try to throw as far as they can as a sport. N-COUNT

2 **The discus** is the competitive event of throwing a discus. *He won the discus at the Montreal Olympics.* N-SING: *the* N

discuss /dɪskʌs/ **discusses, discussing, discussed** ◆◆◆◆◇

1 If people **discuss** something, they talk about it, often in order to reach a decision. *I will be discussing the situation with colleagues tomorrow... The cabinet met today to discuss how to respond to the ultimatum.* VERB V n V wh-to-inf Also V wh

2 If you **discuss** something, you write or talk about it in detail. *I will discuss the role of diet in cancer prevention in Chapter 7... Coming up after the news, Dan Schorr discusses the state of the presidential campaign.* VERB V n

discussion /dɪskʌʃən/ **discussions** ◆◆◆◆◇

1 If there is **discussion** about something, people talk about it, often in order to reach a decision. *There was a lot of discussion about the wording of the report... Council members are due to have informal discussions later on today... The whole question of school curriculum is up for discussion... The plan may well be over-ambitious, and is clearly open to discussion.* N-VAR: oft N *of/about/on* n • If something is **under discussion**, it is still being talked about and a final decision has not yet been reached. *'The proposals are still under discussion,' she said.* PHRASE: v-link PHR

2 A **discussion** of a subject is a piece of writing or a lecture in which someone talks about it in detail. *For a discussion of biology and sexual politics, see chapter 4.* N-COUNT: usu N *of* n

disdain /dɪsdeɪn/ **disdains, disdaining, disdained** ◆◇◇◇◇

1 If you feel **disdain** for someone or something, you dislike them because you think that they are inferior or unimportant. *Janet looked at him with disdain... She shared her daughter's disdain for her fellow countrymen.* N-UNCOUNT: oft N *for* n =contempt, scorn

2 If you **disdain** someone or something, you regard them with disdain. *Jackie disdained the servants that her millions could buy.* VERB V n

3 If you **disdain** to do something, you do not do it, because you feel that you are too important, superior, or dignified to do it. *Franklin told Sara that he had himself disdained to take the job.* VERB =scorn V to-inf

disdainful /dɪsdeɪnfʊl/. If someone is **disdainful**, they dislike something or someone because they think that thing or person is inferior or unimportant. *He is highly disdainful of anything to do with the literary establishment... Edgar cast a disdainful look at his twin.* ADJ-GRADED: oft ADJ *of* n =scornful, contemptuous ♦ **disdainfully** *'You're thorough,' Yvonne said disdainfully, 'but clearly not thorough enough.'* ADV-GRADED: ADV with v

disease /dɪziːz/ **diseases** ◆◆◆◆◇

1 A **disease** is an illness which affects people, animals, or plants, for example one which is caused by bacteria or infection. *...the rapid spread of disease in the area. ...illnesses such as heart disease... Doctors believe they have cured him of the disease.* N-VAR

2 You can refer to a bad attitude or habit, usually one that a group of people have, as a **disease**; a literary use. *...the wretched disease of racism eating away at the core of our society.* N-COUNT: with supp =blight

diseased /dɪziːzd/ ◆◇◇◇◇

1 Something that is **diseased** is affected by a disease. *The arteries are diseased and a transplant is the only hope... Clear away dead or diseased plants.* ADJ ≠healthy

2 If you say that someone's mind is **diseased**, you are emphasizing that you think it is not normal or balanced. *Gardner describes the book as 'the product of a diseased and evil mind'.* ADJ: usu ADJ n PRAGMATICS

disembark /dɪsɪmbɑːˈk/ **disembarks, disembarking, disembarked.** When passengers **disembark** from a ship, aeroplane, or bus, they leave it at the end of their journey; a formal word. *I looked towards the plane. Six passengers had already disembarked.* VERB =get off V Also V *from* n ♦ **disembarkation** /dɪsembɑːˈkeɪʃən/ *Disembarkation is at 7.30am.* N-UNCOUNT

disembodied /dɪsɪmbɒdid/

1 **Disembodied** means seeming not to be attached to or to come from anyone. *A disembodied voice sounded from the back of the cabin.* ADJ: usu ADJ n

2 **Disembodied** means separated from or existing without a body. *...a disembodied head.* ADJ: usu ADJ n

disembowel /dɪsɪmbaʊəl/ **disembowels, disembowelling, disembowelled;** spelled **disemboweling, disemboweled** in American English.

1 To **disembowel** a person or animal means to remove their internal organs, especially their stomach, intestines, and bowels. *...a psychopath who hangs and disembowels his prey... It shows a fox being disembowelled by a pack of hounds.* VERB =gut V n

2 To **disembowel** something means to take out the inside of it, especially in a such a way that it is destroyed or made completely useless; a literary use. *Next, she disembowelled a melon with a quiet fury... The interiors were disembowelled and rebuilt.* VERB V n

disenchanted /dɪsɪntʃɑːntɪd, -tʃænt-/. If you are **disenchanted** with something, you are disappointed with it and no longer believe that it is good or worthwhile. *I'm disenchanted with the state of British theatre at the moment.* ◆◇◇◇◇ ADJ-GRADED: oft ADJ *with* n =disillusioned

disenchantment /dɪsɪntʃɑːntmənt, -tʃænt-/. **Disenchantment** is the feeling of being disappointed with something, and no longer believing that it is good or worthwhile. *There's growing disenchantment with the Government.* N-UNCOUNT: oft N *with* n =disillusionment

disenfranchise /dɪsɪnfræntʃaɪz/ **disenfranchises, disenfranchising, disenfranchised.** To **disenfranchise** a group of people means to take away their right to vote, or their right to vote for what they really want. *...fears of an organized attempt to disenfranchise supporters of Father Aristide. ...the helplessness of disenfranchised minorities.* VERB V n V-ed

disengage /dɪsɪngeɪdʒ/ **disengages, disengaging, disengaged**

1 If you **disengage** something, you separate it from something which it has become attached to. If something **disengages**, it separates from something which it is attached to. *She disengaged the film advance mechanism on the camera... John gently disengaged himself from his sister's tearful embrace... When his front brake cable disengaged, he was forced to brake with his foot.* V-ERG V n V pron-refl *from* n V Also V n *from* n

2 If an army **disengages** from an area, it withdraws from that area. *...the evident desire of both superpowers to disengage from Afghanistan... More vigorous action is needed to force the federal army to disengage.* VERB V *from* n V

disengaged /dɪsɪngeɪdʒd/. If someone is **disengaged** from something, they are not as involved with it as you would expect. *The film has the feel of a man curiously disengaged from his material.* ADJ-GRADED: oft ADJ *from* n =detached

disengagement /dɪsɪngeɪdʒmənt/. **Disengagement** is a process by which people gradually stop being involved in a conflict, activity, or organization. *This policy of disengagement from the European war had its critics.* N-UNCOUNT: oft N *from* n =withdrawal

disentangle /dɪsɪntæŋgəl/ **disentangles, disentangling, disentangled**

1 If you **disentangle** a complicated or confused situation, you make it easier to understand or manage to understand it, by clearly recognizing each separate element. *In this new book, Harrison* VERB V n

brilliantly disentangles complex debates... It's impossible to disentangle the myth from reality. V n *from* n

2 If you **disentangle** something from an undesirable thing or situation, you separate it from that thing or remove it from that situation. *They are looking at ways to disentangle him from this major policy decision... The first thing they must do is disentangle themselves from the past.* VERB =distance V n *from* n

3 If you **disentangle** something, you separate it from things that are twisted around it, or things that it is twisted or knotted around. *She clawed at the bushes to disentangle herself... The rope could not be disentangled and had to be cut.* VERB =unsnarl V n Also V n *from* n

disequilibrium /dɪsiːkwɪlɪbriəm/. **Disequilibrium** is a state in which things are not stable or certain, but are likely to change suddenly; a formal word. *There may be a period of disequilibrium as family members adjust to the new baby.* N-UNCOUNT: also *a* N

disestablish /dɪsɪstæblɪʃ/ **disestablishes, disestablishing, disestablished.** To **disestablish** a church or religion means to take away its official status, so that it is no longer recognized as a national institution; a formal word. *For several reasons, it would be right to disestablish the church.* VERB V n
♦ **disestablishment** /dɪsɪstæblɪʃmənt/ *His clergyman father was a victim of Welsh Anglican disestablishment.* N-UNCOUNT

disfavour /dɪsfeɪvəʳ/; spelled **disfavor** in American English.

1 If someone or something is in **disfavour**, people dislike or disapprove of them. If someone or something falls into **disfavour**, people start to dislike or disapprove of them; a formal use. *He had escaped from Russia because his boss was in disfavour with the communist party... He fell into disfavor as the president fell in the polls.* N-UNCOUNT: usu *in/into* N

2 If you look at someone or something with **disfavour**, the expression on your face shows that you dislike or disapprove of them; a formal use. *She eyed his unruly collar-length hair with disfavour.* N-UNCOUNT: usu *with* N =distaste

disfigure /dɪsfɪgəʳ, AM -gjər/ **disfigures, disfiguring, disfigured** ◆◇◇◇◇

1 If someone **is disfigured**, their appearance is spoiled. *Many of the wounded had been badly disfigured.* ♦ **disfigured** *She tried not to look at the scarred, disfigured face... Two dogs attacked him, leaving him horribly disfigured.* VB: usu passive *be* V-ed ADJ-GRADED

2 To **disfigure** an object or a place means to spoil its appearance. *Wind turbines are large and noisy and they disfigure the landscape.* VERB V n

disfigurement /dɪsfɪgəʳmənt, AM -gjər-/ **disfigurements.** A **disfigurement** is something, for example a scar, that spoils a person's appearance. *He had surgery to correct a facial disfigurement.* N-VAR: oft supp N =blemish

disgorge /dɪsgɔːʳdʒ/ **disgorges, disgorging, disgorged**

1 If something **disgorges** its contents, it empties them out; used in written English. *The ground had opened to disgorge a boiling stream of molten lava.* VERB V n

2 If you say that a vehicle or building **disgorges** people, especially a lot of people, you mean that the people leave the vehicle or building; used in written English. *The bus drew up in the village square and disgorged its passengers.* VERB V n

3 If an animal **disgorges** something it has swallowed, it produces it again from its mouth. *They pursue other birds, forcing them to disgorge the fish they have caught.* VERB V n

disgrace /dɪsgreɪs/ **disgraces, disgracing, disgraced** ◆◇◇◇◇

1 If you say that someone is in **disgrace**, you are emphasizing that other people disapprove of them and do not respect them because of something that they have done. *His vice president also had to resign in disgrace... She has brought disgrace upon womankind.* N-UNCOUNT: oft *in* N PRAGMATICS =dishonour

2 If you say that something is **a disgrace**, you are emphasizing that it is very bad or wrong, and that you find it completely unacceptable. *The way the sales were handled was a complete disgrace... The national airline is a disgrace.* N-SING: *a* N PRAGMATICS =scandal

3 You say that someone is **a disgrace** to someone else when you want to emphasize that their behaviour causes the other person to feel ashamed. *GOP leaders called him a disgrace to the party... What went on was a scandal. It was a disgrace to Britain.* N-SING: *a* N, usu N *to* n PRAGMATICS =scandal

4 If you say that someone **disgraces** someone else, you are emphasizing that their behaviour causes the other person to feel ashamed. *I have disgraced my family's name... I've disgraced myself by the actions I've taken.* VERB PRAGMATICS V n V pron-refl

disgraced /dɪsgreɪst/. You use **disgraced** to describe someone whose bad behaviour has caused them to lose the approval and respect of the public or of people in authority. *...the disgraced leader of the coup.* ◆◇◇◇◇ ADJ-GRADED: usu ADJ n =discredited

disgraceful /dɪsgreɪsfʊl/. If you say that something such as behaviour or a situation is **disgraceful**, you disapprove of it strongly, and feel that the person or people responsible should be ashamed of it. *It's disgraceful that they have detained for him so long... I complained about his disgraceful behaviour... I think what's happening is disgraceful.* ♦ **disgracefully** *He felt that his brother had behaved disgracefully.* ◆◇◇◇◇ ADJ-GRADED: oft *it* v-link ADJ that =shocking, scandalous ADV-GRADED: ADV after v

disgruntled /dɪsgrʌntəld/. If you are **disgruntled**, you are cross and dissatisfied because things have not happened the way that you wanted them to happen. *Disgruntled employees recently called for his resignation... Party members are disgruntled at the way the campaign is being handled.* ◆◇◇◇◇ ADJ-GRADED: oft ADJ *by/at/over* n =discontented

disguise /dɪsgaɪz/ **disguises, disguising, disguised** ◆◆◇◇◇

1 If you are in **disguise**, you are not wearing your usual clothes or you have altered your appearance in other ways, so that people will not recognize you. *You'll have to travel in disguise... He was wearing that ridiculous disguise... She's adopted so many disguises her own mother wouldn't recognize her.* N-VAR: oft *in* N

2 If you **disguise** yourself, you put on clothes which make you look like someone else or alter your appearance in other ways, so that people will not recognize you. *She disguised herself as a man so she could fight on the battlefield.* ♦ **disguised** *The extremists entered the building disguised as medical workers... I was heavily disguised.* VERB V pron-refl *as* n Also V pron-refl ADJ-GRADED: usu v-link ADJ, oft ADJ *as* n

3 To **disguise** something means to hide it or make it appear different so that people will not know about it or will not recognize it. *He made no attempt to disguise his agitation... Their healthy image disguises the fact that they are highly processed foods... I played along, and disguised my voice.* ♦ **disguised** *The proposal is a thinly disguised effort to revive the price controls of the 1970s.* VERB V n ADJ-GRADED

4 ● a **blessing in disguise**: see **blessing**.

disgust /dɪsgʌst/ **disgusts, disgusting, disgusted** ◆◆◇◇◇

1 Disgust is a feeling of very strong dislike or disapproval. *He spoke of his disgust at the incident... A look of disgust came over his face... I threw the book aside in disgust.* N-UNCOUNT =revulsion

2 To **disgust** someone means to make them feel a strong sense of dislike and disapproval. *He disgusted many with his boorish behaviour.* VERB V n

disgusted /dɪsgʌstɪd/. If you are **disgusted**, you feel a strong sense of dislike and disapproval at something. *I'm disgusted with the way that he was treated... He was disgusted that a British minister could have behaved so disgracefully.* ♦ **disgustedly** *'It's a little late for that,' Ritter said disgustedly.* ◆◇◇◇◇ ADJ-GRADED: oft ADJ *with/by/at* n, ADJ that =appalled ADV: ADV with v

disgusting /dɪsgʌstɪŋ/ ◆◇◇◇◇

1 If you say that something is **disgusting**, you are criticizing it because it is extremely unpleasant. *It tasted disgusting... Smoking is a disgusting habit.* ADJ-GRADED =revolting

2 If you say that something is **disgusting**, you mean that you find it completely unacceptable. *It's disgusting that the taxpayer is subsidising this project.* ADJ-GRADED: oft *it* v-link ADJ that =disgraceful

dish /dɪʃ/ **dishes, dishing, dished** ◆◆◆◇◇

1 A **dish** is a shallow container with a wide uncovered top. You eat and serve food from dishes and N-COUNT

cook food in them. *...plastic bowls and dishes... Pile potatoes into a warm serving dish.*
2 The contents of a dish can be referred to as a **dish** of something. *Nicholas ate a dish of spaghetti.* N-COUNT: usu N *of* n
3 Food that is prepared in a particular style or combination can be referred to as a **dish**. *This dish is best served cold... There are plenty of vegetarian dishes to choose from. ...a delicious fish dish.* N-COUNT
4 All the objects that have been used to cook, serve, and eat a meal can be referred to as the **dishes**. *There were dirty dishes in the sink... He'd cooked dinner and washed the dishes.* N-PLURAL
5 You can use the word **dish** to refer to anything that is round and hollow in shape with a wide uncovered top. *...a dish used to receive satellite broadcasts.* N-COUNT: usu with supp
6 See also **satellite dish, side dish.**
7 If you **do the dishes**, you wash the dishes. *I hate doing the dishes.* ● to **dish the dirt**: see **dirt**. PHRASE: V inflects

dish out PHRASAL VERB
1 If you **dish out** something, you distribute it among a number of people; an informal use. *Doctors, not pharmacists, are responsible for dishing out drugs... The GCC wants to dish the money out to specific projects.* V P n (not pron) V n P
2 If someone **dishes out** criticism or punishment, they give it to someone. *Do you usually dish out criticism to someone who's doing you a favour?.* V P n (not pron) Also V n P
3 If you **dish out** food, you serve it to people at the beginning of each course of a meal. *Here in the dining hall the cooks dish out chicken à la king.* V P n

dish up. If you **dish up** food, you serve it to people at the beginning of each course of a meal. *They dished up a superb meal... I'll dish up and you can grate the Parmesan.* PHRASAL VERB V P n (not pron) V P Also V n P

disharmony /dɪshɑːʳməni/. When there is **disharmony**, people disagree about important things and this causes an unpleasant atmosphere; a formal word. *...the root causes of racial disharmony.* N-UNCOUNT =conflict ≠harmony

dishcloth /dɪʃklɒθ, AM -klɔːθ/ **dishcloths.**
1 A **dishcloth** is a cloth used to dry dishes after they have been washed. N-COUNT =tea-towel
2 A **dishcloth** is a cloth used for washing dishes, pans, and cutlery. N-COUNT

disheartened /dɪshɑːʳtənd/. If you are **disheartened**, you feel disappointed about something and have less confidence or less hope about it than you did before. *He was disheartened by their hostile reaction.* ADJ-GRADED: usu v-link ADJ, oft ADJ *by* n =dejected

disheartening /dɪshɑːʳtənɪŋ/. If something is **disheartening**, it makes you feel disappointed and less confident or less hopeful. ADJ-GRADED =depressing

dishevelled /dɪʃevəld/; spelled **disheveled** in American English. If you describe someone's hair, clothes, or appearance as **dishevelled**, you mean that it is very untidy. *She arrived flushed and dishevelled.* ADJ-GRADED =unkempt

dishonest /dɪsɒnɪst/. If you say that someone or their behaviour is **dishonest**, you mean that they are not truthful or honest, and that you cannot trust them. *You have been dishonest with me... It would be dishonest to mislead people and not to present the data as fairly as possible.* ◆◇◇◇◇ ADJ-GRADED: oft *it* v-link ADJ to-inf
♦ **dishonestly** *The key issue was whether the four defendants acted dishonestly.* ADV-GRADED: usu ADV with v

dishonesty /dɪsɒnɪsti/. **Dishonesty** is dishonest behaviour. *She accused the government of dishonesty and incompetence.* ◆◇◇◇◇ N-UNCOUNT

dishonour /dɪsɒnəʳ/ **dishonours, dishonouring, dishonoured;** spelled **dishonor** in American English.
1 If you **dishonour** someone, you behave in a way that damages their good reputation; a formal use. *It would dishonour my family if I didn't wear the veil.* VERB V n
2 **Dishonour** is a state in which people disapprove of you and lose their respect for you; a formal use. *This time it is not a question of choosing between death and dishonour... She refuses to see her beloved boy die in such dishonor.* N-UNCOUNT =disgrace
3 If someone **dishonours** an agreement or transaction, they refuse to act according to its conditions. *We found that the bank had dishonoured some of our cheques. ...the dishonoured pledges to British manufacturing.* VERB V n V-ed

dishonourable /dɪsɒnərəbəl/; spelled **dishonorable** in American English. Someone who is **dishonourable** is not honest and does things which you consider to be morally unacceptable. *Mark had done nothing dishonourable... He was not a dishonourable man, he was merely a professional.* ADJ-GRADED =disreputable
♦ **dishonourably** /dɪsɒnərəbli/ *He will not be seen to act dishonourably. He could not live with that.* ADV-GRADED: ADV after v, ADV -ed

dish towel, dish towels. In American English, a **dish towel** is a cloth used to dry dishes after they have been washed. The British word is **tea towel.** N-COUNT

dishwasher /dɪʃwɒʃəʳ/ **dishwashers.** A **dishwasher** is an electrically operated machine that washes and dries kitchen and eating utensils such as plates, saucepans, and cutlery. ◆◇◇◇◇ N-COUNT

dishwater /dɪʃwɔːtəʳ/. **Dishwater** is water that dishes, pans, and cutlery have been washed in. N-UNCOUNT

dishy /dɪʃi/. In British English, if someone describes someone else as **dishy**, they mean they think that person is very good looking and attractive; an informal word, used especially by women about men. ADJ-GRADED

disillusion /dɪsɪluːʒən/ **disillusions, disillusioning, disillusioned** ◆◇◇◇◇
1 If something or someone **disillusions** you, they make you realize that something is not as good as you thought. *I'd hate to be the one to disillusion him... He said he had been bitterly disillusioned by his country's failure to change into a democracy.* VERB V n
2 **Disillusion** is the same as **disillusionment**. *There is disillusion with established political parties.* N-UNCOUNT: also N in pl

disillusioned /dɪsɪluːʒənd/. If you are **disillusioned** with something, you are disappointed, because it is not as good as you had expected or thought. *I've become very disillusioned with politics... He had become disillusioned because he could not find a job.* ◆◇◇◇◇ ADJ-GRADED: oft ADJ *with* n =disenchanted

disillusionment /dɪsɪluːʒənmənt/. **Disillusionment** is the disappointment that you feel when you discover that something is not as good as you had expected or thought. *There is evidence of a general sense of disillusionment with the government. ...the pain, disillusionment and despair we experience when someone we idolized has betrayed our trust.* ◆◇◇◇◇ N-UNCOUNT: oft N *with* n =disenchantment

disincentive /dɪsɪnsentɪv/ **disincentives.** A **disincentive** is something which discourages people from behaving or acting in a particular way; a formal word. *High marginal tax rates may act as a disincentive to working longer hours.* N-VAR: oft N *to* n/-ing, N to-inf =deterrent

disinclination /dɪsɪnklɪneɪʃən/. A **disinclination** to do something is a feeling that you do not want to do it; a formal word. *They are showing a marked disinclination to pursue these opportunities.* N-SING: usu N to-inf =reluctance

disinclined /dɪsɪnklaɪnd/. If you are **disinclined** to do something, you do not want to do it; a formal word. *He was disinclined to talk about himself, especially to his students... They are disinclined to use violence because it is against their Buddhist faith.* ADJ: v-link ADJ, usu ADJ to-inf =reluctant, unwilling

disinfect /dɪsɪnfekt/ **disinfects, disinfecting, disinfected.** If you **disinfect** something, you clean it using a substance that kills germs. *Chlorine is used to disinfect water... Make sure the draining board, sink and plug hole are regularly disinfected.* VERB =sterilize V n

disinfectant /dɪsɪnfektənt/ **disinfectants. Disinfectant** is a substance that kills germs. It is used, for example, for cleaning kitchens and bathrooms. *Effluent from the sedimentation tank is dosed with disinfectant to kill any harmful organisms... Salt is a natural disinfectant.* N-MASS =antiseptic

disinflation /dɪsɪnfleɪʃən/. **Disinflation** is a reduction in the rate of inflation, especially as a result of government policies. N-UNCOUNT ≠inflation

disinformation /dɪsɪnfəʳmeɪʃᵊn/. If you accuse someone of spreading **disinformation**, you are accusing them of spreading false information in order to deceive people. *They spread scandal and disinformation in order to discredit certain politicians... The government has been involved in a disinformation campaign, deliberately misleading and harassing its citizens.* N-UNCOUNT

disingenuous /dɪsɪndʒenjuəs/. Someone who is **disingenuous** is slightly dishonest and insincere in what they say; a formal word. *It is certainly an interesting colour, but it would be disingenuous to claim that this is a work of great beauty.* ADJ-GRADED: oft *it* v-link ADJ to-inf
♦ **disingenuously** *He disingenuously remarked that 'he did not understand about strategy and tactics'.* ADV-GRADED: usu ADV with v, also ADV adj

disinherit /dɪsɪnherɪt/ **disinherits, disinheriting, disinherited.** If you **disinherit** someone such as your son or daughter, you arrange that they will not become the owner of your money and property after your death, usually because they have done something that you do not approve of. *He resorted to financial blackmail, threatening to disinherit her if she refused to end her relationship with Pierre.* VERB; V n

disinherited /dɪsɪnherɪtɪd/. You say that people are **disinherited** when they have lost their cultural or social traditions; a formal word. ADJ

disintegrate /dɪsɪntɪgreɪt/ **disintegrates, disintegrating, disintegrated** ◆◆◇◇◇
1 If something **disintegrates**, it becomes seriously weakened, and is divided or destroyed. *During October 1918 the Austro-Hungarian Empire began to disintegrate.* ♦ **disintegration** /dɪsɪntɪgreɪʃᵊn/ *...the violent disintegration of Yugoslavia. ...the disintegration of an ordinary marriage.* VERB; V; N-UNCOUNT: oft N *of* n
2 If an object or substance **disintegrates**, it breaks into many small pieces or parts and is destroyed. *At 420 mph the windscreen disintegrated.* VERB; V
♦ **disintegration** *The report describes the catastrophic disintegration of the aircraft after the explosion.* N-UNCOUNT

disinter /dɪsɪntɜːʳ/ **disinters, disinterring, disinterred**
1 If you **disinter** something, you start using it again after it has not been used for a long time; often used humorously. *...the trend for disinterring sixties soul classics for TV commercials.* VERB; V n
2 When a dead body **is disinterred**, it is dug up from out of the ground. *The bones were disinterred and moved to a burial site.* VB: usu passive; *be* V-ed

disinterest /dɪsɪntrəst/. If there is **disinterest** in something, people are not interested in it. *The fact Liberia has no oil seems to explain foreign disinterest in its internal affairs... We have had to contend with the disinterest of much of the medical profession about this topic.* N-UNCOUNT: oft N *in* n

disinterested /dɪsɪntrəstɪd/
1 Someone who is **disinterested** is not involved in a particular situation or not likely to benefit from it and is therefore able to act in a fair and unselfish way. *The current sole superpower is far from being a disinterested observer... Scientists, of course, can be expected to be impartial and disinterested... Such benevolence, however, was not completely disinterested.* ADJ-GRADED =impartial
2 If you are **disinterested** in something, you are not interested in it. Some users of English believe that it is not correct to use **disinterested** with this meaning. *We had both become jaded, disinterested, and disillusioned... Lili had clearly regained her appetite but Doran was disinterested in food.* ADJ-GRADED: oft ADJ *in* n

disjointed /dɪsdʒɔɪntɪd/
1 **Disjointed** words, thoughts, or ideas are not presented in a smooth or logical way and are therefore difficult to understand. *Sally was used to hearing his complaints, usually in the form of disjointed, drunken ramblings.* ADJ-GRADED =confused
2 **Disjointed** societies, systems, and activities are ones in which the different parts or elements are not as closely connected as they should be or as they used to be. *...something which can help to give cohesion and roots to our increasingly fragmented and disjointed society.* ADJ-GRADED =divided

disk /dɪsk/ **disks.** In a computer, the **disk** is the part where information is stored. *The program takes up 2.5 megabytes of disk space and can be run on a standard personal computer.* ● See also **disc, disk drive, floppy disk, hard disk.** ◆◇◇◇◇ N-COUNT: also *on/to* N

disk drive, disk drives; also spelled **disc drive** in British English. The **disk drive** on a computer is the part that contains the disk or into which a disk can be inserted. The disk drive allows you to read information from the disk and store information on the disk. N-COUNT

diskette /dɪsket/ **diskettes.** A **diskette** is the same as a **floppy disk**. N-COUNT =floppy disk

dislike /dɪslaɪk/ **dislikes, disliking, disliked** ◆◆◇◇◇
1 If you **dislike** someone or something, you consider them to be unpleasant and do not like them. *Liver is a great favourite of his and we don't serve it often because so many people dislike it... David began to dislike all his television heroes who smoked.* VERB; V n
2 **Dislike** is the feeling that you do not like someone or something. *My dislike of thunder and even small earthquakes was due to Mother... Years of dislike boiled over and blows were exchanged.* N-UNCOUNT =loathing
3 Your **dislikes** are the things that you do not like. *Consider what your likes and dislikes are about your job... Strong irrational dislikes of other people can easily be picked up from others.* N-COUNT: usu pl
4 If you **take a dislike** to someone or something, you decide that you do not like them. *I took a violent dislike to him... He may suddenly take a dislike to foods that he's previously enjoyed.* PHRASE: V inflects

dislocate /dɪsləkeɪt/ **dislocates, dislocating, dislocated** ◆◇◇◇◇
1 If you **dislocate** a bone or joint in your body, or someone else's body, it moves out of its proper position in relation to other bones, usually in an accident. *Harrison dislocated a finger... He suffered a dislocated shoulder, cuts and bruises.* VERB; V n; V-ed
2 To **dislocate** something such as a system, process, or way of life means to disturb it greatly or prevent it from continuing as normal. *It would help to end illiteracy and disease, but it would also dislocate a traditional way of life... The strike at the financial nerve centre was designed to dislocate the economy. ...America's chronicler of dislocated lives.* VERB =disrupt; V n; V-ed

dislocation /dɪsləkeɪʃᵊn/ **dislocations. Dislocation** is a situation in which something such as a system, process, or way of life is greatly disturbed or prevented from continuing as normal. *Millions of refugees have suffered a total dislocation of their lives.* ◆◇◇◇◇ N-VAR: oft N *of* n =disruption

dislodge /dɪslɒdʒ/ **dislodges, dislodging, dislodged.** To **dislodge** something or someone from a particular place or position means to cause them to leave that place or position, although they were fixed, held, or established there. *Rainfall from a tropical storm dislodged the debris from the slopes of the volcano... He may challenge the Prime Minister even if he decides he cannot dislodge her this time... In the exertion Tompkins' hat had become dislodged.* ◆◇◇◇◇ VERB =displace; V n *from* n; V n; V-ed

disloyal /dɪslɔɪəl/. Someone who is **disloyal** to their friends, family, colleagues, or country does not support them or does things that could harm them. *She was so disloyal to her deputy she made his position untenable... Brian sided with his sister, which led his mother to accuse him of being disloyal.* ADJ-GRADED: oft ADJ *to* n ≠loyal

disloyalty /dɪslɔɪəlti/. **Disloyalty** is disloyal behaviour. *Charges had already been made against certain communists suspected of disloyalty to Moscow.* N-UNCOUNT: oft N *to* n =faithlessness

dismal /dɪzmᵊl/ ◆◇◇◇◇
1 Something that is **dismal** is depressingly bad. *...Israel's dismal record in the Olympics... My prospects of returning to a suitable job are dismal... It was a dismal failure.* ♦ **dismally** *He failed dismally in his opening match.* ADJ-GRADED =terrible; ADV
2 Something that is **dismal** is bleak, sad, and depressing, especially in appearance. *The main part* ADJ-GRADED =dreary

of the hospital is pretty dismal but the children's ward is really lively. ...a dark dismal day with rain falling steadily... You can't occupy yourself with dismal thoughts all the time.

dismantle /dɪsmæntᵊl/ **dismantles, dismantling, dismantled** ◆◆◇◇◇

1 If you **dismantle** a machine or structure, you carefully separate it into its different parts. *He asked for immediate help from the United States to dismantle the warheads.*
VERB
V n

2 To **dismantle** an organization or system means to cause it to stop functioning by gradually reducing its power or purpose. *...opposition to the president's policy of dismantling apartheid... Public services of all kinds are being dismantled.*
VERB
V n

dismay /dɪsmeɪ/ **dismays, dismaying, dismayed** ◆◆◇◇◇

1 **Dismay** is a strong feeling of fear, worry, or sadness that is caused by something unpleasant and unexpected; a formal use. *Local councillors have reacted with dismay and indignation... Lucy discovered to her dismay that she was pregnant... The ministers expressed dismay at the continued practice of ethnic cleansing... Meg looked up at her in dismay.*
N-UNCOUNT: oft *to* N with poss

2 If you **are dismayed** by something, it makes you feel afraid, worried, or sad; a formal use. *The committee was dismayed by what it had been told... McKee suddenly realized she was crying and the thought dismayed him.* ♦ **dismayed** *He was dismayed at the cynicism of the youngsters... He was dismayed to find that his hands were shaking.*
VERB
be V-ed
V n
ADJ-GRADED: usu v-link ADJ, oft ADJ *at* n, ADJ to-inf/that

dismember /dɪsmembəʳ/ **dismembers, dismembering, dismembered** ◆◇◇◇◇

1 To **dismember** the body of a dead person or animal means to cut or pull it into pieces. *He then dismembered her, hiding parts of her body in the cellar... His dismembered body was found in a rubbish bin.*
VERB
V n
V-ed

2 To **dismember** a country or organization means to break it up into smaller parts. *...Hitler's plans to occupy and dismember Czechoslovakia... Many investors must be hoping that he will be dethroned, his publishing empire dismembered.*
VERB
V n

dismemberment /dɪsmembəʳmənt/

1 **Dismemberment** is the cutting or pulling into pieces of a body. *They found a scene of unbelievable horror involving bodies in various states of decay and dismemberment.*
N-UNCOUNT

2 **Dismemberment** is the breaking up into smaller parts of a country or organization. *...the dismemberment of Pakistan and the creation of Bangladesh in 1971. ...the case for dismemberment or even abolition of the BBC.*
N-UNCOUNT: oft N *of* n =division

dismiss /dɪsmɪs/ **dismisses, dismissing, dismissed** ◆◆◆◇◇

1 If you **dismiss** something, you decide or say that it is not important enough for you to think about or consider. *Mr Wakeham dismissed the reports as speculation... I would certainly dismiss any allegations of impropriety by the Labour Party... I wouldn't dismiss it out of hand.*
VERB =discount
V n *as* n
V n

2 If you **dismiss** something from your mind, you stop thinking about it. *I dismissed him from my mind... 'It's been a lovely day,' she said, dismissing the episode.*
VERB =banish
V n *from* n
V n

3 When an employer **dismisses** an employee, the employer tells the employee that they are no longer needed to do the job that they have been doing. *...the power to dismiss civil servants who refuse to work... The military commander has been dismissed.*
VERB =sack, fire
V n

4 If you **are dismissed** by someone in authority, they tell you that you can go away from them. *Two more witnesses were called, heard and dismissed... The hired carriage was dismissed.*
VERB =sent away
be V-ed
Also V n

5 When a judge **dismisses** a case against someone, he or she formally states that there is no need for a trial, usually because there is not enough evidence for the case to proceed. *An American judge yesterday dismissed murder charges against Dr Jack Kevorkian. ...their attempt to have the case against them dismissed.*
VERB
V n
have n V-ed

dismissal /dɪsmɪsᵊl/ **dismissals** ◆◆◇◇◇

1 When an employee is dismissed from their job, you can refer to their **dismissal**. *...Mr Low's dismissal from his post at the head of the commission.*
N-VAR: oft with poss

2 **Dismissal** of something means deciding or saying that it is not important. *...bureaucratic indifference to people's rights and needs, and high-handed dismissal of public opinion.*
N-UNCOUNT: usu N *of* n

dismissive /dɪsmɪsɪv/. If you are **dismissive** of someone or something, you say or show that you think they are not important or have no value. *Mr Jones was dismissive of the report, saying it was riddled with inaccuracies. ...the dismissive attitude scientists often take in regard to questions such as telepathy or homeopathic medicine.* ♦ **dismissively** *'Critical acclaim from people who don't know what they're talking about is meaningless,' he claims dismissively.*
◆◇◇◇◇
ADJ-GRADED: oft ADJ *of* n
ADV-GRADED: usu ADV with v, also ADV adj

dismount /dɪsmaʊnt/ **dismounts, dismounting, dismounted.** If you **dismount** from a horse or a bicycle, you get down from it; a formal word. *Emma dismounted and took her horse's bridle.*
VERB
V

disobedience /dɪsəbiːdiəns/. **Disobedience** is deliberately not doing what someone tells you to do, or what a rule or law says that you should do.
◆◇◇◇◇
N-UNCOUNT

disobedient /dɪsəbiːdiənt/. If you are **disobedient**, you deliberately do not do what someone in authority tells you to do, or what a rule or law says that you should do. *Her tone was that of a parent ordering a disobedient child to behave itself.*
ADJ-GRADED

disobey /dɪsəbeɪ/ **disobeys, disobeying, disobeyed.** When someone **disobeys** a person or an order, they deliberately do not do what they have been told to do. *...a naughty boy who often disobeyed his mother and father... He urged Russian soldiers to disobey orders if asked to fire on civilian targets... They were threatened with punishment for themselves and their families if they disobeyed.*
VERB =defy
V n
V

disorder /dɪsɔːʳdəʳ/ **disorders** ◆◆◇◇◇

1 A **disorder** is a problem or illness which affects someone's mind or body. *...a rare nerve disorder that can cause paralysis of the arms. ...a psychiatrist who specialises in eating disorders... He appeared to be suffering from a severe mental disorder and had served a term in prison.*
N-VAR: usu with supp =complaint

2 **Disorder** is a state of being untidy, badly prepared, or badly organized. *The emergency room was in disorder... Inside all was disorder: drawers fallen out, shoes and boots scattered.*
N-UNCOUNT: oft *in* N =confusion

3 **Disorder** is violence or rioting in public. *The government issued a decree calling on the authorities to uphold the law and stop public disorder... There are other forms of civil disorder – most notably, football hooliganism.*
N-VAR: usu supp N =unrest

disordered /dɪsɔːʳdəʳd/

1 If you describe something as **disordered**, you mean it is untidy and is not neatly arranged. *Moretti ran a hand through his disordered red hair. ...a disordered heap of mossy branches.*
ADJ-GRADED =messy

2 Someone who is mentally **disordered** or who has a **disordered** mind is mentally ill. *...agencies working with mentally disordered offenders. ...events that crystallized into a conspiracy in one disordered mind.*
ADJ-GRADED =disturbed

disorderly /dɪsɔːʳdəʳli/

1 If you describe something as **disorderly**, you mean that it is untidy, irregular, or disorganized; a formal use. *There were young men and women working away at tables all over the large and disorderly room.*
ADJ-GRADED =chaotic

2 If you describe someone as **disorderly**, you mean that they are behaving in a noisy, rude, or violent way in public. You can also describe a place or event as **disorderly** if the people there behave in this way; a formal use. *He pleaded guilty to being disorderly on licensed premises... In most of the residence halls we visited, rules prohibit disorderly conduct... Football matches are disorderly events.*
ADJ-GRADED =rowdy

3 If someone is charged with being **drunk and disorderly**, they are accused of being drunk and behaving in a noisy, offensive, or violent way in public; a legal expression.
PHRASE: v-link PHR

disorganization /dɪsɔ͟ːʳgənaɪzeɪ͟ʃᵊn/; also spelled **disorganisation** in British English. If something is in a state of **disorganization**, it is disorganized.
N-UNCOUNT =disarray

disorganized /dɪsɔ͟ːʳgənaɪzd/; also spelled **disorganised** in British English. ◆◇◇◇◇

1 Something that is **disorganized** is in a confused state or is badly planned or managed. *A report by the state prosecutor described the police action as confused and disorganised... He has helped to transform the party from a disorganised, demoralised rabble into a force which must again be taken seriously.*
ADJ-GRADED ≠organized

2 Someone who is **disorganized** is very bad at organizing things in their life. *My boss is completely disorganised and leaves the most important items until very late.*
ADJ-GRADED ≠organized

disorient /dɪsɔ͟ːrient/ **disorients, disorienting, disoriented.** British English also uses the form **disorientate**. If something **disorients** you, you lose your sense of direction, or you generally feel lost and uncertain, for example because you are in an unfamiliar environment. *An overnight stay at a friend's house disorients me... They were disorientated by the smoke and were firing blindly into it.* ♦ **disoriented** *I feel dizzy and disoriented.* ♦ **disorienting** *An abrupt change of location can be disorienting.* ♦ **disorientation** /dɪsɔ͟ːriənteɪ͟ʃᵊn/ *Morris was so stunned by this that he experienced a moment of total disorientation. ...side-effects including disorientation, dizziness and poor coordination.*
◆◇◇◇◇ VERB =confuse; V n; ADJ-GRADED: usu v-link ADJ; ADJ-GRADED; N-UNCOUNT

disorientate /dɪsɔ͟ːriənteɪt/ **disorientates, disorientating, disorientated.** See **disorient**.

disown /dɪsoʊ͟n/ **disowns, disowning, disowned.** If you **disown** someone or something, you say or show that you no longer want to have any connection with them or any responsibility for them. *The man who murdered the girl is no son of mine. I disown him... Those comments were later disowned by an official army spokesman.*
VERB; V n

disparage /dɪspæ͟rɪdʒ/ **disparages, disparaging, disparaged.** If you **disparage** someone or something, you speak about them in a way which shows that you do not have a good opinion of them; a formal word. *...Larkin's tendency to disparage literature... The tax cut is widely disparaged by senators from both parties as a budget gimmick.*
VERB =denigrate; V n

disparagement /dɪspæ͟rɪdʒmənt/. **Disparagement** is the act of speaking about someone or something in a way which shows that you do not have a good opinion of them; a formal word. *Reviewers have been almost unanimous in their disparagement of this book.*
N-UNCOUNT: oft N *of* n =criticism

disparaging /dɪspæ͟rɪdʒɪŋ/. If you are **disparaging** about someone or something, or make **disparaging** comments about them, you say things which show that you do not have a good opinion of them. *He was critical of the people, disparaging of their crude manners... The Minister was alleged to have made disparaging remarks about the rest of the Cabinet.* ♦ **disparagingly** *Do not talk disparagingly about your company in public. ...what businessmen disparagingly call 'cut-throat competition'.*
ADJ-GRADED: oft ADJ *about/of* n =derisive; ADV-GRADED: ADV with v

disparate /dɪspərət/ ◆◇◇◇◇

1 **Disparate** things are clearly different from each other in quality or type; a formal use. *Scientists are trying to pull together disparate ideas in astronomy... The nine republics are immensely disparate in size, culture and wealth.*
ADJ-GRADED: usu ADJ n =contrasting

2 A **disparate** thing is made up of very different elements; a formal use. *...a very disparate nation, with enormous regional differences. ...their disparate coalition of Southern conservatives and liberals.*
ADJ-GRADED: usu ADJ n =diverse

disparity /dɪspæ͟rɪti/ **disparities.** If there is a **disparity** between two or more things, there is a noticeable difference between them; a formal word. *...the economic disparities between East and West Berlin. ...the great disparity of wealth between rich and poor countries.*
◆◇◇◇◇ N-VAR: oft N *between/in* pl-n =difference

dispassionate /dɪspæ͟ʃənət/. Someone who is **dispassionate** is calm and reasonable, and not affected by emotions. *We, as prosecutors, try to be dispassionate about the cases we bring... He spoke in the flat, dispassionate tone of a lecturer.* ♦ **dispassionately** *He sets out the facts coolly and dispassionately.*
ADJ-GRADED =detached ≠involved; ADV-GRADED: ADV with v

dispatch /dɪspæ͟tʃ/ **dispatches, dispatching, dispatched;** also spelled **despatch** in British English. ◆◆◇◇◇

1 If you **dispatch** someone to a place, you send them there for a particular reason; a formal use. *He had been continually dispatching scouts ahead... The Italian government was preparing to dispatch 4,000 soldiers to search the island.* ► Also a noun. *The despatch of the task force is purely a contingency measure.*
VERB =send; V n adv/prep; V n to-inf; N-UNCOUNT: usu N *of* n

2 If you **dispatch** a message, letter, or parcel, you send it to a particular person or destination; a formal use. *The victory inspired him to dispatch a gleeful telegram to Roosevelt... Free gifts are dispatched separately so please allow 28 days for delivery.* ► Also a noun. *We have 125 cases ready for dispatch.*
VERB =send; V n prep/adv; *be* V-ed; Also V n; N-UNCOUNT

3 A **dispatch** is a special report that is sent to a newspaper or broadcasting organization by a journalist who is in a different town or country. *...this despatch from our West Africa correspondent.*
N-COUNT =bulletin

4 A **dispatch** is a message or report that is sent, for example, by army officers or government officials to their headquarters. *I was carrying dispatches from the ambassador.* • If a soldier **is mentioned in dispatches**, he or she is considered to have been extremely brave in a battle, and is recommended for a medal. *He was hailed as a hero, mentioned in dispatches and finally given a medal.*
N-COUNT =communication; PHRASE: V inflects

5 To **dispatch** a person or an animal means to kill them; an old-fashioned use. *The fox takes his chance with a pack of hounds which may catch him and despatch him immediately.*
VERB; V n

6 To **dispatch** a job or task means to finish it quickly and efficiently without wasting time; an old-fashioned use. *Amy sat outside in the sun while Gerald despatched his business.*
VERB =conclude; V n

7 If you do something **with dispatch**, you do it very quickly; an old-fashioned use. *He feels we should act with despatch.*
N-UNCOUNT: *with* N

dispel /dɪspe͟l/ **dispels, dispelling, dispelled.** To **dispel** an idea or feeling that people have means to stop them having it. *The President is attempting to dispel the notion that he has neglected the economy.*
◆◇◇◇◇ VERB =banish; V n

dispensable /dɪspe͟nsəbᵊl/. If someone or something is **dispensable** they are not really needed. *All those people in the middle are dispensable.*
ADJ-GRADED: usu v-link ADJ ≠essential

dispensary /dɪspe͟nsəri/ **dispensaries.** A **dispensary** is a place, for example in a hospital, where medicines are prepared and given out.
N-COUNT

dispensation /dɪspe nseɪ͟ʃᵊn/ **dispensations**

1 A **dispensation** is special permission to do something that is normally not allowed. *A special dispensation may by obtained from the domestic union concerned... They were promised dispensation from military service... The committee was not prepared to use its discretion and grant special dispensation.*
N-VAR

2 **Dispensation of** something is the issuing of it, especially from a position of authority; a formal use. *...our application of consistent standards in the dispensation of justice.*
N-UNCOUNT: N *of* n

3 A **dispensation** is a religious or political system that has authority at a particular time. *The new dispensation proved a success, certainly with the business community.*
N-COUNT: usu supp N

dispense /dɪspe͟ns/ **dispenses, dispensing, dispensed** ◆◇◇◇◇

1 If someone **dispenses** something that they possess or control, they give, provide, or administer it
VERB =give out

to a number of people; a formal use. *The Union had already dispensed £400 in grants... The local welfare office is where government dispenses many of its services... I thought of myself as a patriarch, dispensing words of wisdom to all my children.* Vn / Vn *to* n

2 If you obtain a product by getting it out of a machine, you can say that the machine **dispenses** the product. *For two weeks, the cash machine spewed out receipts apologising for its inability to dispense money... The lotion is dispensed by a handy pump action spray.* VERB / Vn

3 When a chemist **dispenses** medicine, he or she prepares it, and gives or sells it to the patient or customer. *Some shops gave wrong or inadequate advice when dispensing homeopathic medicines... Four out of five prescriptions are dispensed free to people who are exempt... The government would like doctors to confine themselves to prescribing rather than dispensing.* VERB / Vn / *be* V-ed *to* n / V / Also V n *to* n

dispense with. If you **dispense with** something, you stop using it or get rid of it altogether, especially because you no longer need it. *Many households have dispensed with their old-fashioned vinyl turntable.* PHRASAL VERB / V P n

dispenser /dɪspensəʳ/ **dispensers.** A **dispenser** is a machine or container designed so that you can get an item or quantity of something from it in an easy and convenient way. *...cash dispensers. ...a fridge with a drinks dispenser.* ◆◇◇◇◇ N-COUNT: oft n N

dispersal /dɪspɜːʳsəl/

1 **Dispersal** is the spreading of things over a wide area. *Plants have different mechanisms of dispersal for their spores.* N-UNCOUNT =distribution

2 The **dispersal** of a crowd involves splitting it up and making the people leave in different directions. *The police ordered the dispersal of the crowds gathered round the building.* N-UNCOUNT: oft N *of* n

disperse /dɪspɜːʳs/ **disperses, dispersing, dispersed** ◆◆◇◇◇

1 When something **disperses** or when you **disperse** it, it spreads over a wide area. *The oil appeared to be dispersing... The intense currents disperse the sewage... Because the town sits in a valley, air pollution is not easily dispersed.* V-ERG / V / Vn

2 When a group of people **disperses** or when someone **disperses** them, the group splits up and the people leave in different directions. *Police fired shots and used teargas to disperse the demonstrators... The crowd dispersed peacefully after prayers.* V-ERG =scatter / Vn / V

dispersed /dɪspɜːʳst/. Things that are **dispersed** are situated in many different places, a long way apart from each other. *...his widely dispersed businesses... They live high in the Andes, in small and dispersed groups.* ◆◇◇◇◇ ADJ-GRADED =scattered

dispersion /dɪspɜːʳʃən/. **Dispersion** is the spreading of people or things over a wide area; a formal word. *The threat complicates military planning, forcing greater dispersion of their forces.* N-UNCOUNT: oft N *of* n

dispirited /dɪspɪrɪtɪd/. If you are **dispirited**, you have lost your enthusiasm and excitement. *I left eventually at six o'clock feeling utterly dispirited and depressed.* ADJ-GRADED =dejected

dispiriting /dɪspɪrɪtɪŋ/. Something that is **dispiriting** causes you to lose your enthusiasm and excitement. *It's very dispiriting for anyone to be out of a job.* ADJ-GRADED =disheartening

displace /dɪspleɪs/ **displaces, displacing, displaced** ◆◆◇◇◇

1 If one thing **displaces** another, it forces the other thing out of its place, position, or role, and then occupies that place, position, or role itself. *These factories have displaced tourism as the country's largest source of foreign exchange... Coal is to be displaced by natural gas and nuclear power.* VERB / Vn

2 If a person or group of people **is displaced**, they are forced to moved away from the area where they live. *In Europe alone thirty million people were displaced... Most of the civilians displaced by the war will be unable to return to their homes. ...the task of resettling refugees and displaced persons.* VB: usu passive / *be* V-ed / V-ed

displacement /dɪspleɪsmənt/ ◆◇◇◇◇

1 **Displacement** is the removal of something from its usual place or position by something which then occupies that place or position; a formal use. *No barrier prevents our gradual, purposeful displacement of tradition. ...too much resistance to the displacement of your reason by your emotions.* N-UNCOUNT

2 **Displacement** is the forcing of people away from the area or country where they live. *...the gradual displacement of the American Indian.* N-UNCOUNT

3 **Displacement** is the weight or volume of a liquid that is displaced by an object submerged or floating in it, for example the weight of water displaced by a ship floating in it; a technical use. N-UNCOUNT

display /dɪspleɪ/ **displays, displaying, displayed** ◆◆◆◆◇

1 If you **display** something that you want people to see, you put it in a particular place, so that people can see it easily. *Among the protesters and war veterans proudly displaying their medals was Aubrey Rose... The cabinets display seventeenth-century blue-and-white porcelain.* ► Also a noun. *Most of the other artists whose work is on display were his pupils or colleagues.* VERB =exhibit / Vn / N-UNCOUNT: oft *on* N

2 If you **display** something, you show it to people. *She displayed her wound to the twelve gentlemen of the jury... The chart can then display the links connecting these groups.* VERB =show / V n *to* n / Vn

3 If you **display** a characteristic, quality, or emotion, you behave in a way which shows that you have it. *It was unlike Gordon to display his feelings... Clinton, too, displayed remarkable courage.* ► Also a noun. *Normally, such an outward display of affection is reserved for his mother..* VERB =show / Vn / N-VAR: oft N *of* n =show

4 When a computer **displays** information, it shows it on a screen. *They started out by looking at the computer screens which display the images... Using the option to display only text speeds things up a lot.* VERB / Vn

5 A **display** is an arrangement of things that have been put in a particular place, so that people can see them easily. *...a display of your work... She was leaning against a display case of prints of Paris.* N-COUNT: oft N *of* n

6 A **display** is a public performance or other event which is intended to entertain people. *...the firework display. ...gymnastic displays. ...the Royal Air Force Red Arrows display team.* N-COUNT: with supp =show

7 The **display** on a computer screen is the information that is shown there. The screen itself can also be referred to as the **display**. *A hard copy of the screen display can also be obtained from a printer. ...obscure error messages appearing on the display.* N-COUNT: usu sing =screen

● See also **liquid crystal display**.

displease /dɪspliːz/ **displeases, displeasing, displeased.** If something or someone **displeases** you, they make you annoyed or rather angry. *Not wishing to displease her, he avoided answering the question.* VERB / Vn

displeased /dɪspliːzd/. If you are **displeased** with something, you are annoyed or rather angry about it. *Businessmen are displeased with erratic economic policy-making... He was not displeased at the way he had handled the meeting.* ADJ-GRADED: v-link ADJ, oft ADJ *with/at* n, ADJ to-inf

displeasure /dɪspleʒəʳ/. Someone's **displeasure** is a feeling of annoyance that they have about something that has happened. *The population has already begun to show its displeasure at the slow pace of change.* ◆◇◇◇◇ N-UNCOUNT: oft poss N, N *with/at* n

disport /dɪspɔːʳt/ **disports, disporting, disported.** If you **disport** yourself somewhere, you amuse yourself there in a happy and energetic way; an old-fashioned word, now used humorously. *...the rich and famous disporting themselves in glamorous places.* VERB =divert / V pron-refl prep/adv

disposable /dɪspoʊzəbəl/ ◆◇◇◇◇

1 A **disposable** product is designed to be thrown away after it has been used. *...disposable nappies suitable for babies up to 8lb... He shaved himself with a disposable razor.* ► Disposable products can be referred to as **disposables**. *It's estimated that around 80 per cent of babies wear disposables.* ADJ: usu ADJ n / N-COUNT: usu pl

2 Your **disposable** income is the amount of income you have left after you have paid income tax and ADJ: ADJ n

social security contributions. *Gerald had little disposable income... The nation's disposable earnings in 1987 amounted to £586 billion.*

disposal /dɪspoʊzəl/ ◆◆◇◇◇

1 If you have something **at** your **disposal**, you are able to use it whenever you want, and for whatever purpose you want. If you say that you are **at** someone's **disposal**, you mean that you are willing to help them in any way you can. *Do you have this information at your disposal?... He has said he will use all the weapons at his disposal... If I can be of service, I am at your disposal.*
PHRASE: usu PHR after v, v-link PHR

2 **Disposal** is the act of getting rid of something that is no longer wanted or needed. *...methods for the permanent disposal of radioactive wastes. ...waste disposal sites.*
N-UNCOUNT: oft n N, N *of* n

dispose /dɪspoʊz/ **disposes, disposing, disposed** ◆◆◇◇◇

dispose of
PHRASAL VERB

1 If you **dispose of** something that you no longer want or need, you throw it away. *Just fold up the nappy and dispose of it in the normal manner. ...the safest means of disposing of nuclear waste... Engine oil cannot be disposed of down drains.*
=discard
V P n

2 If you **dispose of** a problem, task, or question, you deal with it. *You did us a great favour by the manner in which you disposed of that problem... The justices have been arguing about how the case should be disposed of.*
=settle
V P n

3 To **dispose of** a person or an animal means to kill them; a formal use. *He alleged that they had hired an assassin to dispose of him.*
V P n

disposed /dɪspoʊzd/ ◆◇◇◇◇

1 If you are **disposed** to do something, you are willing or eager to do it; a formal use. *We passed one or two dwellings, but were not disposed to stop... I might have been disposed to like him in other circumstances... He is then more generously disposed to admit the validity of opposing views.*
ADJ-GRADED: v-link ADJ to-inf
=inclined

2 You can use **disposed** when you are talking about someone's general attitude or opinion about someone or something. For example, if you are well or favourably **disposed** to someone or something, you like them or approve of them; a formal use. *I saw that the publishers were well disposed towards my book... Every government is ill-disposed to the press, all or some of the time... I think they want kids to be favorably disposed to this company and see them in a more positive light.*
ADJ-GRADED: adv ADJ, usu v-link ADJ, usu ADJ *to/towards* n

3 If things are **disposed** in a particular way, they are arranged in that way; a formal use. *Anyone seeking to paint 18th-century rooms needs to be familiar with the way colour was disposed within a room.*
ADJ: v-link ADJ

disposition /dɪspəzɪʃən/ **dispositions** ◆◇◇◇◇

1 Someone's **disposition** is the way that they tend to behave or feel. *The rides are unsuitable for people of a nervous disposition... He was a man of decisive action and an adventurous disposition. ...his friendly and cheerful disposition.*
N-COUNT: usu supp N
=character

2 A **disposition** to do something is a willingness to do it; a formal use. *This has given him a disposition to consider our traditions critically... They show no disposition to improvise or to take risks.*
N-SING: usu N to-inf
=inclination

3 If you refer to **the disposition of** a number of objects, you mean the pattern in which they are arranged or their positions in relation to each other; a formal use. *...to understand the buildings from the disposition of walls and entrances.*
N-SING: *the* N *of* n

4 The **disposition of** money or property is the act of giving or distributing it to a number of people; a legal use. *...Judge John Stacks, appointed to oversee the disposition of funds.*
N-COUNT: N *of* n
=distribution

dispossess /dɪspəzes/ **dispossesses, dispossessing, dispossessed.** If you **are dispossessed** of something that you own, especially land or buildings, it is taken away from you. *...people who were dispossessed of their land under apartheid... They settled the land, dispossessing many of its original inhabitants... Droves of dispossessed people emigrated to Canada.* ► **The dispossessed** are people who are dispossessed. *...the plight of the poor and the dispossessed.*
VERB
be V-ed *of* n
V n
V-ed
Also V n *of/from* n
N-PLURAL: *the* N

disproportion /dɪsprəpɔːʳʃən/ **disproportions.** A **disproportion** is a state in which two things are unequal; a formal word. *There does seem a striking disproportion in the legal resources available to the two sides.*
N-VAR
=imbalance

disproportionate /dɪsprəpɔːʳʃənət/. Something that is **disproportionate** is surprising or unreasonable in amount or size, compared with something else. *A disproportionate amount of time was devoted to one topic... This sentence is totally disproportionate to the alleged offence.* ♦ **disproportionately** *There is a disproportionately high suicide rate among prisoners facing very long sentences.*
◆◇◇◇◇
ADJ-GRADED: oft ADJ *to* n
=excessive
ADV: ADV group, ADV with v

disprove /dɪspruːv/ **disproves, disproving, disproved, disproven.** To **disprove** an idea, belief, or theory means to show that it is not true. *The statistics to prove or disprove his hypothesis will take years to collect.*
◆◇◇◇◇
VERB
=refute
V n

disputation /dɪspjʊteɪʃən/ **disputations. Disputation** is discussion on a subject which people cannot agree about; a formal word. *After much legal disputation our right to resign was established.*
N-VAR
=debate

dispute /dɪspjuːt/ **disputes, disputing, disputed.** ◆◆◆◆◇

1 A **dispute** is an argument or disagreement between people or groups. *They have won previous pay disputes with the government... Negotiators failed to resolve the bitter dispute between the European Community and the United States over cutting subsides to farmers.*
N-VAR: usu with supp, oft N *with/over* n, N *between* pl-n

2 If you **dispute** a fact, statement, or theory, you say that it is incorrect or untrue. *He disputed the allegations... Nobody disputed that Davey was clever... Some economists disputed whether consumer spending is as strong as the figures suggest.*
VERB
V n
V that
V wh

3 When people or animals **dispute** something, they fight for control or ownership of it. You can also say that one group of people **dispute** something with another group. *Russia and Ukraine have been disputing the ownership of the fleet... Fishermen from Bristol disputed fishing rights with the Danes. ...a disputed border region.*
V-RECIP
pl-n V n
V n *with* n
V-ed
Also V n (non-recip)

4 If two or more people or groups are **in dispute**, they are arguing or disagreeing about something. *The two countries are in dispute over the boundaries of their coastal waters... It is currently in dispute with the government over price fixing.*
PHRASES
RECIP: v-link PHR, oft PHR *with* n, PHR *over* n

5 If something is **in dispute**, people are questioning it or arguing about it. *All those matters are in dispute and it is not for me to decide them.*
v-link PHR

disqualify /dɪskwɒlɪfaɪ/ **disqualifies, disqualifying, disqualified.** When someone **is disqualified**, they are officially stopped from taking part in a particular event, activity, or competition, usually because they have done something wrong. *He was convicted of corruption, and will be disqualified from office for seven years... The stewards conferred and eventually decided to disqualify us.* ♦ **disqualification** /dɪskwɒlɪfɪkeɪʃən/ **disqualifications** *Livingston faces a four-year disqualification from athletics.*
◆◇◇◇◇
VERB
=debar
be V-ed *from* n
V n
Also V n *from* n
N-VAR: oft with poss

disquiet /dɪskwaɪət/ **disquiets, disquieting, disquieted** ◆◇◇◇◇

1 **Disquiet** is a feeling of worry or anxiety; a formal use. *There is growing public disquiet about the cost of such policing.*
N-UNCOUNT
=uneasiness

2 If something **disquiets** you, it makes you feel anxious; a formal use. *She had been favored with some inside information and this disquieted him.* ♦ **disquieting** *He found her letter disquieting.*
VERB
V n
ADJ-GRADED

disquisition /dɪskwɪzɪʃən/ **disquisitions.** A **disquisition** is a detailed explanation of a particular subject; a formal word. *Amanda launched into an authoritative disquisition about contracts.*
N-VAR

disregard /dɪsrɪgɑːʳd/ **disregards, disregarding, disregarded.** If you **disregard** something, you ignore it or do not take account of it. *He disregarded the advice of his executives... Critics say he allowed the police and security forces to disregard human rights.* ► Also a noun. *Whoever*
◆◇◇◇◇
VERB
V n
N-UNCOUNT

planted the bomb showed a total disregard for the safety of the public.

disrepair /dɪsrɪpeə^r/. If something is **in disrepair** or is **in a state of disrepair**, it is broken or in bad condition. *The house was unoccupied and in a bad state of disrepair... Many of the older buildings had fallen into disrepair.*
PHRASE: usu v-link PHR

disreputable /dɪsrepjʊtəb^əl/. If you say that someone or something is **disreputable**, you are critical of them because they are not respectable or trustworthy. *He was found to have been enjoying the company of disreputable women. ...the noisiest and most disreputable bars.*
ADJ-GRADED PRAGMATICS

disrepute /dɪsrɪpjuːt/. If something is brought **into disrepute** or falls **into disrepute**, it loses its good reputation, because it is connected with activities that people do not approve of. *It is a disgrace that such people should bring our profession into disrepute.*
◆◇◇◇◇ PHRASE: PHR after v, v-link PHR

disrespect /dɪsrɪspekt/

1 If someone shows **disrespect**, they speak or behave in a way that shows lack of respect for a person, law, or custom. *...young people with attitudes and complete disrespect for authority.*
N-UNCOUNT: also *a* N, oft N *for* n ≠respect

2 You can say '**no disrespect** to someone or something' when you are just about to criticize them, in order to indicate that you are not hostile towards them or admire them for other things. *No disrespect to John Beck, but the club has been happier since he left.*
PHRASE: usu PHR *to* n PRAGMATICS

disrespectful /dɪsrɪspektfʊl/. If you are **disrespectful**, you show no respect in the way that you speak or behave to someone. *...accusations that he had been disrespectful to the Queen... They shouldn't treat their mother in this disrespectful way.* ♦ **disrespectfully** *They get angry if they think they are being treated disrespectfully.*
ADJ-GRADED: oft ADJ *to/of* n
ADV-GRADED: ADV with v

disrobe /dɪsroʊb/ **disrobes, disrobing, disrobed.** When someone **disrobes**, they remove their clothes; a formal word. *She stood up and began to disrobe, folding each garment neatly.*
VERB =undress
V

disrupt /dɪsrʌpt/ **disrupts, disrupting, disrupted.** If someone or something **disrupts** an event, system, or process, they cause difficulties that prevent it from continuing or operating in a normal way. *Anti-war protesters disrupted the debate... The drought has severely disrupted agricultural production.*
◆◆◇◇◇ VERB =disturb
V n

disruption /dɪsrʌpʃ^ən/ **disruptions.** When there is **disruption** of an event, system, or process, it is prevented from continuing or operating in a normal way. *The strike is expected to cause delays and disruption to flights from Britain... The rail strike is causing major disruptions at the country's ports.*
◆◇◇◇◇ N-VAR

disruptive /dɪsrʌptɪv/. If someone or something is **disruptive**, they prevent something from continuing or operating in a normal way. *Alcohol can produce violent, disruptive behavior... The process of implementing these changes can be very disruptive to a small company.*
◆◇◇◇◇ ADJ-GRADED

dissatisfaction /dɪssætɪsfækʃ^ən/ **dissatisfactions.** If you feel **dissatisfaction** with something, you are not contented or pleased with it. *She has already expressed her dissatisfaction with this aspect of the policy... Low pay is the main cause of job dissatisfaction among teachers.*
◆◇◇◇◇ N-VAR: oft N *with* n ≠satisfaction

dissatisfied /dɪssætɪsfaɪd/. If you are **dissatisfied** with something, you are not contented or pleased with it. *82% of voters are dissatisfied with the way their country is being governed... Dissatisfied customers can return the product for a full refund... He felt restless and dissatisfied as he drove home.*
◆◇◇◇◇ ADJ-GRADED: oft ADJ *with* n =discontented

dissect /daɪsekt, dɪ-/ **dissects, dissecting, dissected**
◆◇◇◇◇

1 If someone **dissects** the body of a dead person or animal, they carefully cut it up in order to examine it scientifically. *We dissected a frog in biology class.* ♦ **dissection** /daɪsekʃ^ən, dɪ-/ **dissections** *Researchers need a growing supply of corpses for dissection.*
VERB
V n
N-VAR

2 If someone **dissects** something such as a theory, a situation, or a piece of writing, they consider and talk about each detail of it. *People want to dissect his work and question his motives.* ♦ **dissection, dissections** *...her calm, condescending dissection of my proposals.*
VERB =scrutinize
V n
N-VAR: usu N *of* n

dissemble /dɪsemb^əl/ **dissembles, dissembling, dissembled.** When people **dissemble**, they hide their real motives or emotions; a literary word. *Henry was not slow to dissemble when it served his purposes.*
VERB
V
Also V n

disseminate /dɪsemɪneɪt/ **disseminates, disseminating, disseminated.** To **disseminate** information or knowledge means to distribute it so that it reaches many people or organizations. *It took years to disseminate information about Aids in Africa... They disseminated anti-French propaganda.* ♦ **dissemination** /dɪsemɪneɪʃ^ən/ *He actively promoted the dissemination of scientific ideas about matters such as morality.*
◆◇◇◇◇ VERB =circulate
V n
N-UNCOUNT: usu N *of* n

dissension /dɪsenʃ^ən/ **dissensions. Dissension** is disagreement and argument; a formal word. *The tax cut issue has caused dissension among administration officials.*
N-UNCOUNT: also N in pl =discord

dissent /dɪsent/ **dissents, dissenting, dissented**
◆◆◇◇◇

1 **Dissent** is strong disagreement or dissatisfaction with a decision or opinion, especially a decision or opinion that is supported by most people or by people in authority. *He is the toughest military ruler yet and has responded harshly to any dissent... Political dissent would no longer be tolerated... I made a gesture of dissent.*
N-UNCOUNT =opposition

2 If you **dissent**, you express disagreement with a decision or opinion, especially one that is supported by most people or by people in authority; a formal use. *Just one of the 10 members dissented... No one dissents from the decision to unify... There are likely to be many dissenting voices.*
VERB
V
V *from* n
V-ing

dissenter /dɪsentə^r/ **dissenters. Dissenters** are people who say that they do not agree with something that other people agree with or that is official policy. *The Party does not tolerate dissenters in its ranks.*
N-COUNT

dissertation /dɪsə^rteɪʃ^ən/ **dissertations.** A **dissertation** is a long formal piece of writing on a particular subject, especially for a university degree. *He is currently writing a dissertation on the Somali civil war.*
◆◇◇◇◇ N-COUNT: oft N *on* n

disservice /dɪssɜː^rvɪs/. If you do someone or something a **disservice**, you do something that harms them; a formal word. *He said the protesters were doing a disservice to the nation... You could do yourself a grave disservice by revealing all to a potential rival.*
N-SING: oft N *to* n

dissident /dɪsɪdənt/ **dissidents**
◆◆◇◇◇

1 **Dissidents** are people who disagree with and criticize their government, which is totalitarian or repressive. *...political dissidents. ...former Soviet dissident Natan Schransky.*
N-COUNT

2 **Dissident** people disagree with or criticize their government or a powerful organization they belong to. *...a dissident Chinese novelist... She was suspected of having links with a dissident group. ...dissident shareholders.*
ADJ: ADJ n

dissimilar /dɪsɪmɪlə^r/. If one thing is **dissimilar** to another, or if two things are **dissimilar**, they are very different from each other. *His methods were not dissimilar to those used by Freud... It would be difficult to find two men who were more dissimilar... The identical treatment of such dissimilar items is totally illogical.* ♦ **dissimilarity** /dɪsɪmɪlærɪti/ **dissimilarities** *One of his main themes is the dissimilarity between parents and children.*
ADJ-GRADED: oft ADJ *to* n =unlike
N-VAR: oft N *between* pl-n

dissimulate /dɪsɪmjʊleɪt/ **dissimulates, dissimulating, dissimulated.** When people **dissimulate**, they hide their true feelings, motives, or nature; a formal word. *This man was too injured to dissimulate well... They were decked out in tracksuits, seemingly to dissimulate their true function.*
VERB =dissemble
V
V n

dissipate /dɪsɪpeɪt/ **dissipates, dissipating, dissipated** ◆◇◇◇◇

1 When something **dissipates** or when you **dissipate** it, it becomes less or becomes less strong until it disappears or goes away completely; a formal use. *The tension in the room had dissipated... He wound down the windows to dissipate the heat.* V-ERG =dispel V Vn

♦ **dissipation** *...heat dissipation.* N-UNCOUNT

2 When someone **dissipates** money, time, or effort, they waste it in a foolish way; a formal use. *He needs someone who can keep him from dissipating his time and energy on too many different things... Her father had dissipated her inheritance.* VERB Vn

♦ **dissipation** *...the dissipation of my wealth.* N-UNCOUNT

dissipated /dɪsɪpeɪtɪd/. If you describe someone as **dissipated**, you disapprove of them because they spend a lot of time drinking alcohol and enjoying other physical pleasures, and are probably unhealthy because of this. *Flynn was a charming fellow, still handsome though dissipated, and always eager to have a good time.* ADJ-GRADED PRAGMATICS =dissolute

dissipation /dɪsɪpeɪʃᵊn/. If someone leads a dissipated life, you can also say that they lead a life of **dissipation**; a literary word. *Her face was a revelation of age and dissipation.* N-UNCOUNT =debauchery

dissociate /dɪsoʊʃieɪt/ **dissociates, dissociating, dissociated**

1 If you **dissociate** yourself from something or someone, you say or show that you are not connected with them, usually in order to avoid trouble or blame. *It seems harder and harder for the president to dissociate himself from the scandals that surround Mr Galdos.* VERB =disassociate V pron-refl *from* n

2 If you **dissociate** one thing from another, you consider the two things as separate from each other, or you separate them; a formal use. *Almost the first lesson they learn is how to dissociate emotion from reason.* ♦ **dissociation** /dɪsoʊsieɪʃᵊn/ *There is a war between the sexes but this should not result in their complete dissociation from one another.* VERB =divorce V n *from* n N-UNCOUNT: oft N *from* n

dissolute /dɪsəluːt/. Someone who is **dissolute** does not care at all about morals and lives in a way that is considered to be wicked and immoral; used showing disapproval. ADJ-GRADED =degenerate

dissolution /dɪsəluːʃᵊn/ ◆◇◇◇◇

1 **Dissolution** is the act of breaking up officially an organization or institution, or of formally ending a parliament. *He stayed on until the dissolution of the firm in 1948... Politicians say it could lead to a dissolution of parliament.* N-UNCOUNT: also *a* N, oft N *of* n

2 **Dissolution** is the act of officially ending a formal agreement, for example a marriage or a business arrangement. *...the statutory requirement for granting dissolution of a marriage.* N-UNCOUNT: also *a* N, oft N *of* n =termination

3 **Dissolution** is a process in which something becomes weaker and then disappears ; a formal use. *...the dissolution of traditional family life.* N-UNCOUNT: also *a* N, oft N *of* n

dissolve /dɪzɒlv/ **dissolves, dissolving, dissolved** ◆◆◇◇◇

1 If a substance **dissolves** in liquid or if you **dissolve** it, it becomes mixed with the liquid and disappears. *Heat gently until the sugar dissolves... Dissolve the salt in a little boiled water.* V-ERG V Vn

2 When an organization or institution **is dissolved**, it is officially ended or broken up. *The committee has been dissolved... The King agreed to dissolve the present commission.* VERB *be* V-ed Vn

3 When a parliament **is dissolved**, it is formally ended, so that elections for a new parliament can be held. *The present assembly will be dissolved on April 30th... Kaifu threatened to dissolve the Parliament and call an election.* VERB *be* V-ed Vn

4 When a marriage or business arrangement **is dissolved**, it is officially ended. *The marriage was dissolved in 1976.* VB: usu passive *be* V-ed

5 If something such as a problem or feeling **dissolves** or **is dissolved**, it becomes weaker and disappears. *His new-found optimism dissolved... Lenny still could not dissolve the nagging lump of tension in his chest.* V-ERG =dissipate V Vn

dissolve into. If you **dissolve into** or **dissolve in** tears or laughter, you begin to cry or laugh, because you cannot control yourself. *She dissolved into tears at the mention of Munya's name.* PHRASAL VERB V P n (not pron)

dissonance /dɪsənəns/. **Dissonance** is a lack of agreement or harmony between things; a formal word. N-UNCOUNT =discord

dissuade /dɪsweɪd/ **dissuades, dissuading, dissuaded.** If you **dissuade** someone from doing or believing something, you persuade them not to do or believe it; a formal word. *Doctors had tried to dissuade patients from smoking... She steadfastly maintained that her grandsons were innocent, and nothing could dissuade her from that belief... He considered emigrating, but his family managed to dissuade him.* ◆◇◇◇◇ VERB V n *from* -ing/n Vn

distance /dɪstəns/ **distances, distancing, distanced** ◆◆◆◆◇

1 The **distance** between two points or places is the amount of space between them. *...the distance between the island and the nearby shore... Everything is within walking distance... Geographical distance is also a factor.* N-VAR: with supp, oft N *between* pl-n

2 When two things are very far apart, you talk about the **distance** between them. *The distance wouldn't be a problem.* N-UNCOUNT

3 When you want to emphasize that two people or things do not have a close relationship or are not the same, you can refer to the **distance** between them. *...the emotional distance between them... There was a vast distance between psychological clues and concrete proof... Mr Hurd was careful to put some distance between the government and Mr Heath's mission.* N-UNCOUNT; usu N *between* pl-n PRAGMATICS ≠closeness

4 If you can see something **in the distance**, you can see it, far away from you. *We suddenly saw her in the distance... Mr. Dambar found himself gazing into the distance for a moment or two.* N-SING: *in/into the* N

5 **Distance** is detachment and remoteness in the way that someone behaves so that they do not seem friendly; a formal use. *There were periods of sulking, of pronounced distance, of coldness.* N-UNCOUNT: usu with supp =aloofness ≠warmth

6 If you **distance** yourself from someone or something or if something **distances** you from them, you feel less friendly or positive towards them, or become less involved with them. *The author distanced himself from some of the comments in his book... Television may actually be distancing the public from the war.* ♦ **distanced** *Clough felt he'd become too distanced from his fans.* VERB V pron-refl *from* n V n *from* n ADJ-GRADED: v-link ADJ

7 If you are **at a distance** from something or if you see it or remember it **from a distance**, you are a long way away from it in space or time. *The only way I can cope with my mother is at a distance. ...now that I can look back on the whole tragedy from a distance of nearly forty years.* PHRASES PHR after v, v-link PHR

8 If you **go the distance** in a race or sports competition, you continue running or playing until the end of the race or match; an informal expression. *More riders than ever are now determined to go the distance.* V inflects

9 If you **keep** your **distance** from someone or something or **keep** them **at a distance**, you do not become involved with them. *Jay had always tended to keep his girlfriends at a distance.* V inflects

10 If you **keep** your **distance** from someone or something, you do not get physically close to them; an old-fashioned expression. *He walked towards the doorway, careful to keep his distance.* V inflects

distant /dɪstənt/ ◆◆◇◇◇

1 **Distant** means very far away. *The mountains rolled away to a distant horizon. ...the war in that distant land.* ADJ-GRADED: usu ADJ n =faraway ≠nearby

2 You use **distant** to describe a time or event that is very far away in the future or in the past. *There is little doubt, however, that things will improve in the not too distant future... Last summer's drought is a distant memory.* ADJ-GRADED: usu ADJ n =faraway ≠near

3 A **distant** relative is one who you are not closely related to. *He's a distant relative of the mayor... They were distant cousins.* ♦ **distantly** *His father's distantly related to the Royal family.* ADJ-GRADED: usu ADJ n ≠close ADV-GRADED: usu ADV -ed

4 If you describe someone as **distant**, you mean that you find them cold and emotionally detached. ADJ-GRADED: v-link ADJ =aloof

He found her cold, ice-like and distant... He is direct and courteous but distant. ≠approachable

5 If you describe someone as **distant**, you mean that they are not concentrating on what they are doing because they are thinking about other things. *There was a distant look in her eyes from time to time, her thoughts elsewhere, dwelling on something.* ADJ-GRADED =detached

distantly /dɪstəntli/

1 **Distantly** means very far away; a literary use. *They were too distantly seated for any conversation... Distantly, to her right, she could make out the town of Chiffa.* ADV-GRADED: ADV -ed, ADV with cl =faraway ≠nearby

2 If you are **distantly** aware of something or if you **distantly** remember it, you are aware of it or remember it, but not very strongly. *She became distantly aware that the light had grown strangely brighter and was flickering gently... They distantly remember that the islands were the only part of Britain occupied during the war.* ADV-GRADED: ADV adj, ADV with v =vaguely ≠distinctly

3 If you do or say something **distantly**, you do it without showing much emotion or involvement, for example because you are thinking about something else or because you do not care. *'Do you like this colour, Victor?' she asked. 'It is fine,' said Vincent distantly.* ADV-GRADED: ADV after v

4 See also **distant**.

distaste /dɪsteɪst/. If you feel **distaste** for someone or something, you dislike them and consider them to be unpleasant, disgusting, or immoral. *Roger looked at her with distaste... He professed a violent distaste for everything related to commerce, production, and money.* ◆◇◇◇◇ N-UNCOUNT: oft N *for* n =aversion

distasteful /dɪsteɪstfʊl/. If something is **distasteful** to you, you think it is unpleasant, disgusting, or immoral. *He found it distasteful to be offered a cold buffet and drinks before witnessing the execution.* ◆◇◇◇◇ ADJ-GRADED: oft ADJ *to* n =repugnant

distemper /dɪstempəʳ/

1 **Distemper** is a dangerous and infectious disease that can be caught by animals, especially dogs. N-UNCOUNT

2 **Distemper** is a kind of paint sometimes used for painting walls. N-UNCOUNT

distend /dɪstend/ **distends, distending, distended.** If a part of your body **is distended** or if it **distends**, it becomes swollen and unnaturally large; a formal or medical term. *Through this incision, the abdominal cavity is distended with carbon dioxide gas... The colon, or large intestine, distends and fills with gas.* ♦ **distended** *...an infant with a distended belly.* V-ERG =bloat *be* V-ed V Also V n; ADJ-GRADED

distension /dɪstenʃən/; also spelled **distention**. **Distension** is abnormal swelling or bloating in a person's or animal's body; a medical term. N-UNCOUNT

distil /dɪstɪl/ **distils, distilling, distilled;** spelled **distill** in American English. ◆◇◇◇◇

1 If a liquid such as whisky or water **is distilled**, it is heated until it evaporates and then cooled until it becomes liquid again. This is usually done in order to purify it. *The whisky had been distilled in 1926 and sat quietly maturing until 1987... You can't actually drink the water from the marshland. But you can distil it... When water is used this must be distilled water or spring water; never tap water.* ♦ **distillation** /dɪstɪleɪʃən/ *Any faults in the original cider stood out sharply after distillation.* VERB *be* V-ed V n V-ed; N-UNCOUNT

2 If an oil or liquid **is distilled** from a plant, it is produced by a process which extracts the main part or essence of the plant. To **distil** a plant means to produce an oil or liquid from it by this process. *The oil is distilled from the berries of this small tree. ...the art of distilling rose petals... A skin lotion distilled from the root is a marvellous cure for sore rashes and spots.* ♦ **distillation** *The distillation of rose petals to produce rosewater almost certainly originated in Ancient Persia.* VERB *be* V-ed *from* n V n V-ed Also V n *from* n; N-UNCOUNT: usu N *of* n

3 If a thought or idea **is distilled** from previous thoughts, ideas, or experiences, it is derived from them. If it **is distilled** into something, it becomes part of that thing. *Reviews are distilled from articles previously published in the main column... Eventually passion was distilled into the natural beauty of a balmy night... Roy distills these messages into something powerful... The advice is based on the distilled wisdom of a panel of heart specialists.* ♦ **distillation** *The material below is a distillation of his work.* VERB *be* V-ed *from* n *be* V-ed *into* n V n *into* n V-ed; N-SING: usu N *of* n

distiller /dɪstɪləʳ/ **distillers.** A **distiller** is a person or a company that makes whisky or a similar strong alcoholic drink by a process of distilling. N-COUNT

distillery /dɪstɪləri/ **distilleries.** A **distillery** is a place where whisky or a similar strong alcoholic drink is made by a process of distilling. ◆◇◇◇◇ N-COUNT

distinct /dɪstɪŋkt/ ◆◆◇◇◇

1 If something is **distinct** from something else of the same type, it is recognizably different or separate from it. *Engineering and technology are disciplines distinct from one another and from science... This book is divided into two distinct parts.* ♦ **distinctly** *...a banking industry with two distinctly different sectors.* ADJ-GRADED: oft ADJ *from* n; ADV-GRADED: ADV adj

2 If something is **distinct**, you can hear, see, or taste it clearly. *...to impart a distinct flavor with a minimum of cooking fat.* ♦ **distinctly** *I distinctly heard the loudspeaker calling passengers for the Turin-Amsterdam flight.* ADJ-GRADED; ADV-GRADED: ADV with v

3 If an idea, thought, or intention is **distinct**, it is clear and definite. *Now that Tony was no longer present, there was a distinct change in her attitude... I have distinct memories of him in his last years.* ♦ **distinctly** *I distinctly remember wishing I had not got involved.* ADJ-GRADED: usu ADJ n; ADV-GRADED: ADV with v

4 You can use **distinct** to emphasize that something is great enough in amount or degree to be noticeable or important. *Being 6ft 3in tall has some distinct disadvantages!... Another Cup marathon between the two sides is now a distinct possibility.* ♦ **distinctly** *His government is looking distinctly shaky.* ADJ-GRADED: ADJ n PRAGMATICS =definite; ADV-GRADED: ADV adj/-ed

5 If you say that you are talking about one thing **as distinct from** another, you are indicating exactly which thing you mean. *There's a lot of evidence that oily fish, as distinct from fatty meat, has a beneficial effect.* PHR-PREP

distinction /dɪstɪŋkʃən/ **distinctions** ◆◆◇◇◇

1 A **distinction** is a difference between similar things. *There are obvious distinctions between the two wine-making areas... The distinction between craft and fine art is more controversial.* ● If you **draw a distinction** or **make a distinction**, you say that two things are different. *I did not yet make a distinction between the pleasures of reading and of writing fiction... He draws a distinction between art and culture.* N-COUNT: usu N *between* pl-n; PHRASE: V inflects, usu PHR *between* pl-n

2 **Distinction** is the quality of excellence, superiority, and merit; a formal use. *Lewis emerges as a composer of distinction and sensitivity. ...pieces of furniture of distinction.* N-UNCOUNT

3 A **distinction** is a special award or honour that is given to someone as a recognition of their very high level of achievement. *The order was created in 1902 as a special distinction for eminent men and women... I did an M.A. at Liverpool University in Latin American Studies and got a distinction.* N-COUNT =honour

4 If you say that someone or something has the **distinction** of being something, you are drawing attention to the fact that they have the special or unique quality of being that thing. **Distinction** is normally used to refer to good qualities, but can sometimes also be used to refer to bad qualities. *He has the distinction of being regarded as the Federal Republic's greatest living writer.* N-SING: oft *the* N *of* n/-ing PRAGMATICS

distinctive /dɪstɪŋktɪv/. Something that is **distinctive** has a special quality or feature which makes it easily recognizable and different from other things of the same type. *...the distinctive odour of chlorine. ...a distinctive blue and yellow flag... His voice was very distinctive.* ♦ **distinctively** *...the distinctively fragrant taste of elderflowers... Each room is distinctively decorated with light, bright colors and floral prints.* ♦ **distinctiveness** *His own distinctiveness was always evident at school.* ◆◆◇◇◇ ADJ-GRADED; ADV-GRADED: ADV adj/-ed; N-UNCOUNT: oft with poss

distinguish /dɪstɪŋgwɪʃ/ **distinguishes, distinguishing, distinguished** ◆◆◇◇◇
1 If you can **distinguish** one thing from another, you can see or understand the difference between them. *Could he distinguish right from wrong?... Research suggests that babies learn to see by distinguishing between areas of light and dark... It is necessary to distinguish the policies of two successive governments.* VERB =tell apart V n *from* n V *between* pl-n V pl-n
2 A feature or quality that **distinguishes** one thing from another causes the two things to be regarded as different, because only the first thing has the feature or quality. *There is something about music that distinguishes it from all other art forms... The bird has no distinguishing features.* VERB =set apart V n *from* n V-ing
3 If you can **distinguish** something, you can see, hear, or taste it although it is very difficult to detect; a formal use. *There were cries, calls. He could distinguish voices.* VERB =make out V n
4 If you **distinguish** yourself, you do something that makes you famous or important. *Over the next few years he distinguished himself as a leading constitutional scholar... They distinguished themselves at the Battle of Assaye.* VERB V pron-refl *as* n V pron-refl

distinguishable /dɪstɪŋgwɪʃəbəl/
1 If something is **distinguishable** from other things, it has a quality or feature which makes it possible for you to recognize it and see that it is different. *...features that make their products distinguishable from those of their rivals... This is vintage port, and it is distinguishable by its deep red colour.* ADJ-GRADED: usu v-link ADJ, oft ADJ *from* n
2 If something is **distinguishable**, you can see or hear it in conditions when it is difficult to see or hear anything. *He put his ear to the floor and heard angry shouts, but no words were distinguishable... It would be getting light soon now. Already shapes were more distinguishable.* ADJ-GRADED: v-link ADJ =discernible

distinguished /dɪstɪŋgwɪʃt/ ◆◆◇◇◇
1 If you describe a person or their work as **distinguished**, you mean they have been very successful in their career and have a good reputation. *...a distinguished academic family. ...a distinguished career.* ADJ-GRADED =illustrious
2 If you describe someone as **distinguished**, you mean that they look very noble and dignified. *His suit was immaculately cut and he looked very distinguished. ...a distinguished gentleman.* ADJ-GRADED

distort /dɪstɔːʳt/ **distorts, distorting, distorted** ◆◆◇◇◇
1 If you **distort** a statement, fact, or idea, you report or represent it in an untrue way. *The media distorts reality; categorises people as all good or all bad... The minister has said his remarks at the weekend have been distorted.* ♦ **distorted** *These figures give a distorted view of the significance for the local economy.* VERB V n ADJ-GRADED
2 If something you can see or hear **is distorted** or **distorts**, its appearance or sound is changed or twisted so that it seems strange or unclear. *A painter may exaggerate or distort shapes and forms... His size was persistently distorted by the cartoonists... His face was beginning to distort, and there was a strange tone to his voice.* ♦ **distorted** *Sound was becoming more and more distorted through the use of hearing aids.* V-ERG V n V ADJ-GRADED

distortion /dɪstɔːʳʃən/ **distortions** ◆◇◇◇◇
1 **Distortion** is the changing of something into something that is not true or not acceptable; used showing disapproval. *I think it would be a gross distortion of reality to say that they were motivated by self-interest... He later accused reporters of wilful distortion and bias.* N-VAR: usu with supp PRAGMATICS
2 **Distortion** is the changing of the appearance or sound of something in a way that makes it seem strange or unclear. *He demonstrated how audio signals could be transmitted along cables without distortion.* N-VAR

distract /dɪstrækt/ **distracts, distracting, distracted.** If something **distracts** you or your attention from something, it takes your attention away from it. *Tom admits that playing video games sometimes distracts him from his homework... Don't let yourself be distracted by fashionable theories... A disturbance in the street distracted my attention.* ◆◇◇◇◇ VERB =sidetrack V n *from* n *be* V-ed V n

distracted /dɪstræktɪd/. If you are **distracted**, you are not concentrating on something because you are worried or are thinking about something else. *She had seemed curiously distracted... She seemed less like a poetess than a distracted housewife.* ♦ **distractedly** *He looked up distractedly. 'Be with you in a second.'* ◆◇◇◇◇ ADJ-GRADED ADV: ADV with v

distracting /dɪstræktɪŋ/. If you say that something is **distracting**, you mean that it makes it difficult for you to concentrate properly on what you are doing. *I find it slightly distracting to have someone watching me while I work.* ADJ-GRADED =off-putting

distraction /dɪstrækʃən/ **distractions** ◆◇◇◇◇
1 A **distraction** is something that turns your attention away from something you want to concentrate on. *I feel this is getting to be a distraction from what I really want to do... Total concentration is required with no distractions.* N-VAR: oft N *from* n
2 A **distraction** is an activity which is intended to entertain and amuse you. *...every conceivable distraction from show jumping to bouncy castles... Their national distraction is going to the disco.* N-COUNT =diversion
3 If you say that something or someone **drives** you **to distraction**, you are emphasizing that they annoy you a great deal. *A very clingy child can drive a parent to distraction.* PHRASE: V inflects PRAGMATICS

distraught /dɪstrɔːt/. If someone is **distraught**, they are so upset and worried that they cannot think clearly. *Mr Barker's distraught parents were last night being comforted by relatives.* ◆◇◇◇◇ ADJ-GRADED =distressed

distress /dɪstres/ **distresses, distressing, distressed** ◆◆◇◇◇
1 **Distress** is a state of extreme sorrow, suffering, or pain. *Jealousy causes distress and painful emotions... Her mouth grew stiff with pain and distress.* N-UNCOUNT =suffering
2 **Distress** is the state of being in extreme danger and needing urgent help. *He expressed concern that the ship might be in distress... The constable received a distress call, and saw two youths attacking his colleague.* N-UNCOUNT: oft *in* N
3 If someone or something **distresses** you, they cause you to be upset or worried. *The idea of Toni being in danger distresses him enormously... I did not want to frighten or distress the horse.* VERB V n

distribute /dɪstrɪbjuːt/ **distributes, distributing, distributed** ◆◆◇◇◇
1 If you **distribute** things, you hand them or deliver them to a number of people. *Students shouted slogans and distributed leaflets... Thousands of soldiers are working to distribute food and blankets to the refugees... In the move most of the furniture was left to the neighbours or distributed among friends.* VERB V n V n *to* n *be* V-ed *among* n
2 When a company **distributes** goods, it supplies them to the shops or businesses that sell them. *We didn't understand how difficult it was to distribute a national paper.* VERB V n
3 If you **distribute** things among the members of a group, you share them among those members. *Immediately after his election he began to distribute major offices among his friends and supporters.* VERB V n *among* n Also V n
4 To **distribute** a substance **over** something means to scatter it over it; a formal use. *Distribute the topping evenly over the fruit.* VERB V n *over* n
5 See also **distributed**.

distributed /dɪstrɪbjuːtɪd/. If things are **distributed** throughout an area, object, or group, they exist throughout it. *These cells are widely distributed throughout the body... Galactic surveys show that distant galaxies are not as evenly distributed in space as theory predicts.* ◆◆◇◇◇ ADJ: usu v-link ADJ prep/adv, adv ADJ

distribution /dɪstrɪbjuːʃən/ **distributions** ◆◆◆◇◇
1 The **distribution** of things involves giving or delivering them to a number of people or places. *...the council which controls the distribution of foreign aid... He admitted there had been distribution problems. ...emergency food distribution.* N-UNCOUNT: usu with supp =dispersal
2 The **distribution** of something is how much of it there is in each place or at each time, or how much of it each person has. *Mr Roh's economic planners sought to achieve a more equitable distribution of* N-VAR: usu with supp

wealth... One of the side effects may be to change the geographical distribution of parasitic diseases such as malaria.

distributional /dɪstrɪbjuːʃənəl/

1 **Distributional** means relating to the distribution of goods. *What they're doing is setting up distributional networks.* ADJ: ADJ n

2 **Distributional** effects and policies relate to the share of a country's wealth that different groups of people have; a formal use. *...the distributional effects of free markets, which lead to inequalities in income.* ADJ: ADJ n

distributive /dɪstrɪbjuːtɪv/. **Distributive** means relating to the distribution of goods. *It is abundantly clear that a reorganization is necessary on the distributive side of this industry.* ADJ: ADJ n

distributor /dɪstrɪbjʊtəʳ/ **distributors** ◆◆◇◇◇

1 A **distributor** is a company that supplies goods to shops or other businesses. *...Spain's largest distributor of petroleum products... Bulmer is the UK distributor for Perrier and the Jamaican lager Red Stripe... Theater owners lease films from film distributors.* N-COUNT: usu with supp

2 The **distributor** in a car or other motor vehicle is a device that sends electric current to the spark plugs in the engine. N-COUNT: usu sing

distributorship /dɪstrɪbjʊtəʳ/ **distributorships.** N-COUNT A **distributorship** is a company that supplies goods to shops or other businesses, or the right to supply goods to shops and businesses. *...the general manager of an automobile distributorship.*

district /dɪstrɪkt/ **districts** ◆◆◆◆◇

1 A **district** is a particular area of a town or country. *I drove around the business district. ...Nashville's shopping district. ...a summer holiday hike in the Lake District... Varieties of these crops have been collected from all around the district.* N-COUNT: usu supp N

2 A **district** is an area of a town or country which has been given official boundaries for the purpose of administration. *...the home of the governor of the district. ...the continuing support of Glasgow District Council. ...the district health authority.* N-COUNT: with supp, oft N n

District Attorney, District Attorneys. In the United States, a **District Attorney** is a lawyer who works for the State, and who prosecutes people who are accused of crimes. The abbreviation **D.A.** is also used. ◆◇◇◇◇ N-COUNT

district nurse, district nurses. In Britain, a **district nurse** is a nurse who goes to people's houses to give them medical treatment and advice. N-COUNT

distrust /dɪstrʌst/ **distrusts, distrusting, distrusted** ◆◇◇◇◇

1 If you **distrust** someone or something, you think they are not honest, reliable, or safe. *I don't have any particular reason to distrust them.* VERB ≠mistrust V n

2 **Distrust** is the feeling of suspicion that you have towards someone or something you distrust. *What he saw there left him with a profound distrust of all political authority. ...a decision that should help to dispel much of the atmosphere of distrust.* N-UNCOUNT: also a N, oft N *of* n

distrustful /dɪstrʌstfʊl/. If you are **distrustful** of someone or something, you think that they are not honest, reliable, or safe. *Voters are deeply distrustful of all politicians... The older you get the more distrustful you become.* ADJ-GRADED: usu v-link ADJ, oft ADJ *of* n

disturb /dɪstɜːʳb/ **disturbs, disturbing, disturbed** ◆◆◇◇◇

1 If you **disturb** someone, you interrupt what they are doing and cause them inconvenience. *Did you sleep well? I didn't want to disturb you. You looked so peaceful... Find a quiet, warm, comfortable room where you won't be disturbed.* VERB =interrupt V n

2 If something **disturbs** you, it makes you feel upset or worried. *I dream about him, dreams so vivid that they disturb me for days... He had been disturbed by the news of the attack on Hector Coyne.* VERB =worry V n

3 If something **is disturbed**, its position or shape is changed. *He'd placed his notes in the brown envelope. They hadn't been disturbed... The old woman put her arm gently around Mona's shoulders, taking care not to disturb the costume.* VERB be V-ed V n

4 If something **disturbs** a situation or atmosphere, it spoils or unsettles it. *Neither Baker nor Levy seemed eager to disturb the cordial atmosphere by discussing more sensitive issues.... What could possibly disturb such tranquility?* VERB V n

5 If someone is accused of **disturbing the peace**, they are accused of behaving in a noisy and offensive way in public; a legal expression. PHRASE: V inflects

disturbance /dɪstɜːʳbəns/ **disturbances** ◆◆◇◇◇

1 A **disturbance** is an incident in which people behave violently in public. *During the disturbance which followed, three Englishmen were hurt. ...the worst of last September's disturbances.* N-COUNT

2 **Disturbance** means upsetting or disrupting something which was previously in a calm and well-ordered state. *The home would cause less disturbance to local residents than a school... The animals are very sensitive to disturbance and have never bred in captivity.* N-UNCOUNT: usu with supp

3 You can use **disturbance** to refer to a medical or psychological problem, when someone's body or mind is not working in the normal way. *Poor educational performance is related to emotional disturbance. ...the treatment of certain heart rhythm disturbances.* N-VAR: with supp

disturbed /dɪstɜːʳbd/ ◆◆◇◇◇

1 A **disturbed** person is very upset emotionally, and often needs special care or treatment. *...working with severely emotionally disturbed children... The murderer was apparently mentally disturbed.* ADJ-GRADED

2 You can say that someone is **disturbed** when they are very worried or anxious. *Doctors were disturbed that less than 30 percent of the patients were women... I was disturbed to hear that the selection committee originally decided not to send a British team to this year's Championships.* ADJ-GRADED: usu v-link ADJ, oft ADJ that, ADJ to-inf =troubled

3 If you describe a situation or period of time as **disturbed**, you mean that it is unhappy and full of problems. *...these disturbed times. ...women from disturbed backgrounds.* ADJ-GRADED: usu ADJ n =troubled

disturbing /dɪstɜːʳbɪŋ/. Something that is **disturbing** makes you feel worried or upset. *There was something about him she found disturbing... There are disturbing reports of killings at the two centres.* ◆◆◇◇◇ ADJ-GRADED ♦ **disturbingly** *The Government has itself recognised the disturbingly high frequency of racial attacks.* ADV-GRADED: usu ADV adj, ADV with v

disunited /dɪsjʊnaɪtɪd/. If a group of people are **disunited**, there is disagreement and division among them. *...an increasingly disunited Communist Party.* ADJ-GRADED

disunity /dɪsjuːnɪti/. **Disunity** is lack of agreement among people which prevents them from working together effectively. *He had been accused of promoting disunity within the armed forces.* N-UNCOUNT

disuse /dɪsjuːs/. If something falls into **disuse**, people stop using it. If something becomes worse as a result of **disuse**, it becomes worse because no one uses it. *...a church which has fallen into disuse... The wheel had long since rusted from years of disuse.* N-UNCOUNT: oft *into* N

disused /dɪsjuːzd/. A **disused** place or building is empty and is no longer used. *...a disused airfield near Maidenhead.* ◆◇◇◇◇ ADJ: usu ADJ n

ditch /dɪtʃ/ **ditches, ditching, ditched** ◆◆◇◇◇

1 A **ditch** is a long narrow channel cut into the ground at the side of a road or field. N-COUNT

2 If you **ditch** something that you have or are responsible for, you abandon it or get rid of it, because you no longer want it; an informal use. *I decided to ditch the sofa bed... Unpopular policies such as unilateral disarmament were ditched.* VERB =dump V n

3 If someone **ditches** someone, they end a relationship with that person; an informal use. *I can't bring myself to ditch him and start again.* VERB =dump V n

4 If a pilot **ditches** an aircraft or if it **ditches**, the pilot makes an emergency landing. *One American pilot was forced to ditch his jet in the Gulf... A survivor was knocked unconscious when the helicopter ditched.* V-ERG =crash-land V n V

5 See also **last-ditch**.

dither /dɪðəʳ/ **dithers, dithering, dithered.** [◆◇◇◇◇] [VERB] When someone **dithers**, they hesitate because they are unable to make a quick decision about something. *We have been living together for five years, and we're still dithering over whether to marry... If you have been dithering about buying shares, now could be the time to do it.* [V over wh/n] [V about -ing/wh/n] [Also V]

ditto /dɪtoʊ/. [PRAGMATICS] In informal English, you can use **ditto** to represent a word or phrase that you have just used in order to avoid repeating it. In written lists, **ditto** can be represented by ditto marks (the symbol ") underneath the word that you want to repeat. *Lister's dead. Ditto three Miami drug dealers and a lady.*

ditty /dɪti/ **ditties.** [N-COUNT] A **ditty** is a short or light-hearted song or poem; used in written English.

diuretic /daɪəretɪk/ **diuretics.** [◆◇◇◇◇] [N-COUNT] A **diuretic** is a substance which makes your body increase its production of waste fluids, with the result that you need to urinate more often than usual; a technical term. *Like caffeine, alcohol acts as a diuretic, making you even more dehydrated.* ▶ Also an adjective. [ADJ] *Many remedies effective in joint disease are primarily diuretic.*

diurnal /daɪɜːʳnəl/. [ADJ: usu ADJ n ≠nocturnal] **Diurnal** means happening or active during the daytime; a formal word. *Kangaroos are diurnal animals.*

diva /diːvə/ **divas.** [◆◇◇◇◇] [N-COUNT] You can refer to a successful and famous female opera singer as a **diva**.

divan /dɪvæn/ **divans**

1 In British English, a **divan** or **divan bed** is a bed that has a thick base under the mattress. [N-COUNT]

2 A **divan** is a long soft seat that has no back or arms. [N-COUNT]

dive /daɪv/ **dives, diving, dived;** American English sometimes uses the form **dove** for the past tense. [◆◆◇◇◇]

1 If you **dive** into some water, you jump in head-first with your arms held straight above your head. [VERB] [V into n] *He tried to escape by diving into a river... She was standing by a pool, about to dive in... Joanne had just learnt to dive.* [V in] [V] ▶ Also a noun. [N-COUNT] *Pat had earlier made a dive of 80 feet from the Chasm Bridge.*

2 If you **dive**, you go under the surface of the sea or a lake, using special breathing equipment. [VERB] *Bezanik is diving to collect marine organisms.* [V] ▶ Also a noun. [N-COUNT] *This sighting occurred during my dive to a sunken wreck off Sardinia.*

3 When birds and animals **dive**, they go quickly downwards, head-first, through the air or through water. [VERB] *...a pelican which had just dived for a fish... The shark dived down and swam under the boat.* [V] [V adv/prep]

4 If an aeroplane **dives**, it flies or drops down quickly and suddenly. [VERB] *He was killed when his monoplane stalled and dived into the ground.* [V prep/adv] [Also V] ▶ Also a noun. [N-COUNT] *Witnesses said the plane failed to pull out of a dive and smashed down in a field.*

5 If you **dive** in a particular direction or into a particular place, you jump or move there quickly. [VERB =leap] [V prep/adv] *They dived into a taxi... The cashier dived for cover when a gunman opened fire... He would dive under one obstacle, round another, and lightly step over a third.* ▶ Also a noun. [N-COUNT] *He made a sudden dive for Uncle Jim's legs to try to trip him up.*

6 If you **dive** into a bag or container, you put your hands into it quickly in order to get something out. [VERB] [V into n] *She dived into her bag and brought out a folded piece of paper.*

7 If shares, profits, or figures **dive**, their value falls suddenly and dramatically; used in journalism. [VERB] *If we cut interest rates, the pound would dive... Profits have dived from £7.7m to £7.1m... The shares dived 22p to 338p.* [V] [V from/to/by amount] [V amount] ▶ Also a noun. [N-COUNT] *Stock prices took a dive.*

8 If you describe a bar or club as a **dive**, you mean it is dirty and dark, and not very respectable; an informal use. [N-COUNT] [PRAGMATICS] *We've played in all the little pubs and dives around Liverpool.*

dive-bomb, dive-bombs, dive-bombing, dive-bombed. [VERB] If a plane **dive-bombs** an area, it suddenly flies down low over it to drop bombs onto it. *The Russians had to dive-bomb the cities to regain control.* [V n] [Also V]

dive-bomber, dive-bombers. [N-COUNT] You can refer to a plane that flies down low over a place in order to drop bombs on it as a **dive-bomber**. *The port had been attacked by German dive bombers for the past five days.*

diver /daɪvəʳ/ **divers.** [◆◇◇◇◇] [N-COUNT] A **diver** is a person who swims under water using special breathing equipment. *Police divers have recovered the body of a sixteen year old boy.*

diverge /daɪvɜːʳdʒ, AM dɪ-/ **diverges, diverging, diverged** [◆◇◇◇◇]

1 If one thing **diverges** from another similar thing, the first thing becomes different from the second or develops differently from it. You can also say that two things **diverge**. [V-RECIP] *His interests increasingly diverged from those of his colleagues... Scientists believe that man diverged from the apes between 5 and 7 million years ago... When the aims of the partners begin to diverge, there's trouble.* [V from n] [pl-n V]

2 If one opinion or idea **diverges** from another, they contradict each other or are different. You can also say that two opinions or ideas **diverge**. [V-RECIP: no cont] *The view of the Estonian government does not diverge that far from Lipmaa's thinking... Needless to say, theory and practice sometimes diverged. ...the widely diverging ideologies of the two states.* [V from n] [pl-n V] [V-ing]

3 If one road, path, or route **diverges** from another, they lead in different directions after starting from the same place. You can also say that roads, paths, or routes **diverge**. [V-RECIP =part] *...a course that diverged from the Calvert Island coastline... Where three roads diverge take the middle branch.* [V from n] [pl-n V]

divergence /daɪvɜːʳdʒəns, AM dɪ-/ **divergences.** [N-VAR: usu with supp] A **divergence** is a difference between two or more things, attitudes, or opinions; a formal word. *There's a substantial divergence of opinion within the party... This overall figure conceals wide divergences between the main industrial countries... The tenor of the opening remarks reflects the divergence in the priorities of the two sides.*

divergent /daɪvɜːʳdʒənt, AM dɪ-/. [ADJ-GRADED: usu ADJ n] **Divergent** things are different from each other; a formal word. *Two people who have divergent views on this question are George Watt and Bob Marr... Similar customs were known in widely divergent cultures such as Ancient Egypt and Scandinavia.*

diverse /daɪvɜːʳs, AM dɪ-/ [◆◆◇◇◇]

1 If a group or range of things is **diverse**, it is made up of a wide variety of things. [ADJ-GRADED =varied] *...shops selling a diverse range of gifts... Society is now much more diverse than ever before.*

2 **Diverse** people or things are very different from each other. [ADJ-GRADED] *Albert Jones' new style will inevitably put him in touch with a much more diverse and perhaps younger audience.*

diversify /daɪvɜːʳsɪfaɪ, AM dɪ-/ **diversifies, diversifying, diversified.** [◆◆◇◇◇] [VERB =branch out] When an organization or person **diversifies** into other things, or **diversifies** their range of something, they increase the variety of things that they do or make. *The company's troubles started only when it diversified into new products... As demand has increased, so manufacturers have been encouraged to diversify and improve quality... These firms have been given a tough lesson in the need to diversify their markets.* [V into n/-ing] [V] [V n] ♦ **diversification** /daɪvɜːʳsɪfɪkeɪʃən, AM dɪ-/ **diversifications** [N-VAR] *The seminar was to discuss diversification of agriculture... These strange diversifications could have damaged or even sunk the entire company.*

diversion /daɪvɜːʳʃən, AM dɪvɜːrʒən/ **diversions** [◆◇◇◇◇]

1 A **diversion** is an action or event that attracts your attention away from what you are doing or concentrating on. [N-COUNT] *...armed robbers who escaped after throwing smoke bombs to create a diversion... The whole argument is a diversion.*

2 A **diversion** is an activity that you do for pleasure; a formal use. [N-COUNT =amusement] *Finger painting is very messy but an excellent diversion.*

3 A **diversion** is a special route arranged for traffic to follow when the normal route cannot be used; used in British English. *They turned back because of traffic diversions.*
N-COUNT

4 **The diversion of** something involves changing its course or destination. *...the illegal diversion of profits from secret arms sales. ...the diversion of a ship to Lebanon with $8m worth of aluminium on board.*
N-UNCOUNT: theN ofn

diversionary /daɪvɜːʳʃənri, AM dɪvɜːrʒəneri/. A **diversionary** activity is one intended to attract people's attention away from something which you do not want them to think about, know about, or deal with. *It's thought the fires were started by the prisoners as a diversionary tactic... They asked the British to launch a diversionary attack on the north coast.*
ADJ: usu ADJ n

diversity /daɪvɜːʳsɪti, AM dɪ-/ **diversities** ◆◆◇◇◇

1 The **diversity** of something is the fact that it contains many very different elements. *...the cultural diversity of British society. ...to introduce more choice and diversity into the education system.*
N-VAR: usu with supp =variety

2 A **diversity of** things is a range of things which are very different from each other. *Forslan's object is to gather as great a diversity of genetic material as possible.*
N-SING: N ofn

divert /daɪvɜːʳt, AM dɪ-/ **diverts, diverting, diverted** ◆◆◇◇◇

1 To **divert** vehicles or travellers means to make them follow a different route or go to a different destination than they originally intended. You can also say that someone or something **diverts** from a particular route or to a particular place. *...Rainham Marshes, east London, where a new bypass will divert traffic from the A13... During the strike, ambulances will be diverted to private hospitals... We diverted a plane to rescue 100 passengers... She insists on diverting to a village close to the airport... The capital remained jammed with diverted traffic.*
V-ERG; V n from/to n; V n; V from/to n; V-ed

2 To **divert** money or resources means to cause them to be used for a different purpose. *The government is trying to divert more public funds from west to east. ...government departments involved in diverting resources into community care.*
VERB; V n prep/adv; Also V n

3 To **divert** a phone call means to send it to a different number or place from the one that was dialled by the person making the call. *He instructed switchboard staff to divert all Laura's calls to him... Customers will only incur additional call charges if the call is diverted outside the UK.*
VERB; V n prep/adv; Also V n

4 If you say that someone **diverts** your attention from something important or serious, you disapprove of them doing something which stops you thinking about it. *They want to divert the attention of the people from the real issues... The President needed to divert attention away from his own economic record.*
VERB; PRAGMATICS; =distract; V n prep/adv; Also V n

diverting /daɪvɜːʳtɪŋ, AM dɪ-/. If you describe something as **diverting**, you mean that it is amusing or entertaining; an old-fashioned word. *It was a witty and diverting programme.*
◆◇◇◇◇ ADJ-GRADED =enjoyable

divest /daɪvest, AM dɪ-/ **divests, divesting, divested**

1 If you **divest** yourself of something that you own or are responsible for, you get rid of it or stop being responsible for it; a formal use. *The company divested itself of its oil interests.*
VERB; V pron-refl ofn

2 If something or someone **is divested** of a particular quality, they lose that quality or it is taken away from them; a formal use. *...in the 1960s, when sexual love had been divested of sin... They have divested rituals of their original meaning... Divested of the hype surrounding its launch, the show can now emerge as a full-fledged classic.*
VERB; beV-ed ofn; V n ofn; V-ed

3 If you **divest** someone of something that they are wearing or carrying, you take it off them or away from them; an old-fashioned use. *...the formalities of divesting her of her coat. ...detectors installed at the entrances to make youngsters divest themselves of guns and knives.*
VERB; V n ofn; V pron-refl ofn; Also V n

divide /dɪvaɪd/ **divides, dividing, divided** ◆◆◆◆◇

1 When people or things **are divided** or **divide** into smaller groups or parts, they become separated into smaller parts. *The physical benefits of exercise can be divided into three factors... It will be easiest if we divide them into groups... Divide the pastry in half and roll out each piece... We divide into pairs and each pair takes a region... Bacteria reproduce by dividing and making copies of themselves.*
V-ERG =split; beV-ed intopl-n; V n intopl-n; V n infraction; V intopl-n; V; Also V n

2 If you **divide** something among people or things, you separate it into several parts or portions which you distribute to the people or things. *Paul divides most of his spare time between the study and his bedroom... Divide the sauce among 4 bowls.*
VERB; V n between/amongpl-n; Also V n

3 If you **divide** a larger number by a smaller number or **divide** a smaller number into a larger number, you calculate how many times the smaller number can fit exactly into the larger number. *Measure the floor area of the greenhouse and divide it by six.*
VERB; V n by/into num

4 If a border or line **divides** two areas or **divides** an area into two, it keeps the two areas separate from each other. *...remote border areas dividing Tamil and Muslim settlements. ...the artificial line that divides the city. ...the long frontier dividing Mexico from the United States.*
VERB =separate; V n; V n fromn; Also V n into pl-n

5 If people **divide** over something or if something **divides** them, it causes strong disagreement between them. *She has done more to divide the Conservatives than anyone else... The democrats are divided over whether to admit him into their group... The party is as likely to divide along national lines as along ideological lines.*
V-ERG ≠unite; V n; V; V prep; Also V n prep

6 A **divide** is a significant distinction between two groups, often one that causes conflict. *...a deliberate attempt to create a Hindu-Muslim divide in India.*
N-COUNT: usu sing, usu with supp =gulf, rift

7 A **divide** is a moment in time or a point in a process when there is a complete change from one situation to another. *The time had come to cross the great divide between formality and truth.*
N-COUNT: usu sing, usu with supp =watershed

8 In American English, a **divide** is a line of high ground between areas that are drained by different rivers. The usual British word is **watershed**.
N-COUNT

9 You use **divide and rule** to refer to a policy which is intended to keep someone in a position of power by causing disagreements between people who might otherwise unite against them. *The government's policies of divide and rule have only contributed to the volatility of the region.*
PHRASE

divide off. If something **divides** an area **off**, it forms a barrier that keeps it separate from another area. *...a bamboo partition dividing off another room for the girls.*
PHRASAL VERB; V P n (not pron); Also V n P

divide up
PHRASAL VERB

1 If you **divide** something **up**, you separate it into smaller or more useful groups. *The idea is to divide up the country into four sectors... The National Trust needs a new Act of Parliament, to divide it up into smaller bodies and permit some of its properties to revert to private ownership.*
V P n (not pron) intopl-n; V n P intopl-n; Also V n P

2 If you **divide** something **up**, you share it out among a number of people or groups in approximately equal parts. *The aim was to divide up state property, give everyone an equal start in the race to capitalism.*
V P n (not pron); Also V n P

divided highway, divided highways. In the United States, a **divided highway** is a road which has two lanes of traffic travelling in each direction with a strip of grass or concrete down the middle to separate the two lots of traffic. The British expression is **dual carriageway**.
N-COUNT

dividend /dɪvɪdend/ **dividends** ◆◆◆◇◇

1 A **dividend** is the part of a company's profits which is paid to people who have shares in the company. *The first quarter dividend has been increased by nearly 4 per cent.*
N-COUNT

2 If something **pays dividends**, it brings advantages at a later date. *Steps taken now to maximise your health will pay dividends later on.*
PHRASE: V inflects

3 See also **peace dividend**.

divider /dɪvaɪdəʳ/ **dividers**

1 A **divider** is something which forms a barrier between two areas or sets of things. *A curtain acted as*
N-COUNT: usu with supp

a divider between this class and another. ...room dividers.

2 **Dividers** are an instrument used for measuring lines and for marking points along them. Dividers consist of two pointed arms joined with a hinge. N-PLURAL: also a pair of N

dividing line, dividing lines

1 A **dividing line** is a distinction or set of distinctions which marks the difference between two types of thing or two groups. *There's a very thin dividing line between joviality and hysteria.* N-COUNT: usu sing, oft N *between* pl-n

2 The **dividing line** between two areas is the boundary between them. *...people on both sides of the dividing line between Israel and the occupied territories.* N-SING: oft N *between* pl-n

divination /dɪvɪneɪʃᵊn/. **Divination** is the art or practice of discovering what will happen in the future using supernatural means; a formal word. N-UNCOUNT

divine /dɪvaɪn/ **divines, divining, divined** ◆◆◇◇◇

1 You use **divine** to describe something that is provided by or relates to a god or goddess. *He suggested that the civil war had been a divine punishment. ...divine inspiration.* ♦ **divinely** *The law was divinely ordained.* ADJ: usu ADJ n; ADV: usu ADV -ed

2 A **divine** is a priest who specializes in the study of theology; an old-fashioned use. N-COUNT

3 In old-fashioned informal English, people use **divine** to express their pleasure or enjoyment of something. *'Isn't it divine?' she said. 'I wish I had the right sort of brooch to lend you for it.'... Darling how lovely to see you, you look simply divine.* ♦ **divinely** *...divinely glamorous singer Jeffrey McDonald.* ADJ-GRADED PRAGMATICS =heavenly; ADV-GRADED: usu ADV adj

4 If you **divine** something, you discover or learn it by guessing; a literary use. *The child developed an unconscious ability to intuit or divine the needs of the parents and respond to them... We may divine that kings did not sleep any better than peasants.* VERB V n V that Also V wh

5 If you **divine**, you try to find underground supplies of water or minerals, using a special rod or pair of rods. *The only reason I was divining for water was because of the drought. ...a divining rod.* VERB =dowse V *for* n V-ing Also V

diving /daɪvɪŋ/ ◆◇◇◇◇

1 **Diving** is the activity of working or exploring underwater, using special breathing equipment. *...equipment and accessories for diving.* N-UNCOUNT

2 **Diving** is the sport or activity in which you jump into water head first with your arms held straight above your head, usually from a diving board. *Weight is crucial in diving because the aim is to cause the smallest splash possible.* N-UNCOUNT

diving bell, diving bells. A **diving bell** is a container shaped like a bell, in which people can breathe air while they work under water. N-COUNT

diving board, diving boards. A **diving board** is a board high above a swimming pool from which people can dive into the water. N-COUNT

divinity /dɪvɪnɪti/ **divinities** ◆◇◇◇◇

1 **Divinity** is the study of religion. *He entered Otago University to study arts and divinity.* N-UNCOUNT =theology

2 **Divinity** is the quality of being divine. *...a lasting faith in the divinity of Christ's word.* N-UNCOUNT: oft with poss

3 A **divinity** is a god or goddess. *The three statues above are probably Roman divinities.* N-COUNT

divisible /dɪvɪzɪbᵊl/. If one number is **divisible** by another number, the second number can be divided into the first exactly, with no remainder. *Twenty-eight is divisible by seven.* ADJ: v-link ADJ *by* num

division /dɪvɪʒᵊn/ **divisions** ◆◆◆◆◇

1 The **division** of a large unit into two or more distinct parts is the act of separating them into these parts. *...the unification of Germany, after its division into two states at the end of World War Two.* N-UNCOUNT: oft with poss, oft N *into* pl-n =split

2 The **division** of something among people or things is its separation into parts which are distributed among the people or things. *The current division of labor between workers and management will alter.* N-UNCOUNT: oft N *of* n *among/between* pl-n

3 **Division** is the arithmetical process of dividing one number into another number. *I taught my daughter how to do division at the age of six.* N-UNCOUNT ≠multiplication

4 A **division** is a significant distinction or argument between two groups, which causes the two groups to be considered as very different and separate. *The division between the prosperous west and the impoverished east remains.* N-VAR: oft N *between/among* pl-n =split

5 In a large organization, a **division** is a group of departments whose work is done in the same geographical area or is connected with similar tasks. *...the bank's Latin American division. ...the sales division.* N-COUNT: usu supp N =group

6 A **division** is a group of military units which fight as a single unit. *Several armoured divisions are being moved from Germany.* N-COUNT: usu supp N

7 In the British Parliament, a **division** is a vote where the MPs go into separate rooms in order to record their vote. N-COUNT

8 In football and some other sports, a **division** is one of the groups of teams which make up a league. The teams in each division are considered approximately the same standard, and they all play against each other during the season. *Villa had just been relegated from the First Division. ...the Scottish Premier Division leaders, Dundee United.* N-COUNT: usu supp N

divisional /dɪvɪʒənᵊl/. **Divisional** means relating to a division of a large organization or group. *The team won the divisional championship... An alarm links the police station to the divisional headquarters.* ◆◇◇◇◇ ADJ: ADJ n

division sign, division signs. A **division sign** is the symbol ÷ used between two numbers to show that the first number has to be divided by the second. N-COUNT

divisive /dɪvaɪsɪv/. Something that is **divisive** causes hostility and argument between people. *Abortion has always been a divisive issue... A referendum would be divisive.* ♦ **divisiveness** *...the divisiveness that has separated Miami's black and Latino communities.* ◆◇◇◇◇ ADJ-GRADED; N-UNCOUNT

divorce /dɪvɔːʳs/ **divorces, divorcing, divorced** ◆◆◆◇◇

1 A **divorce** is the formal ending of a marriage by law. *Numerous marriages now end in divorce... Their divorce became final this weekend... The divorce proceedings have accelerated.* N-VAR

2 If a man and woman **divorce** or if one of them **divorces** the other, their marriage is legally ended. *My parents divorced when I was very young... He and Lillian had got divorced... I am absolutely furious that he divorced me to marry her... Mr Gold is divorcing for the second time... I got divorced when I was about 31.* V-RECIP pl-n V pl-n *get* V-ed V n NON-RECIP: V *get* V-ed

3 A **divorce** between two things is a separation between them which is permanent or is likely to be permanent. *...this divorce of Christian culture from the roots of faith... This process is, in no sense, a divorce between the Labour Party and the trade union movement.* N-SING: usu N *of* n *from* n, N *between* pl-n

4 If you say that one thing cannot **be divorced from** another, you mean that the two things cannot be considered as different and separate things. *Good management in the police cannot be divorced from accountability... We have been able to divorce sex from reproduction.* VERB =dissociate *be* V-ed *from* n V n *from* n

divorced /dɪvɔːʳst/ ◆◆◇◇◇

1 Someone who is **divorced** from their former husband or wife has separated from them and is no longer legally married to them. *Princess Margaret is divorced from Lord Snowdon... He is divorced, with a young son.* ADJ: oft ADJ *from* n

2 If you say that one thing **is divorced from** another, you mean that the two things are very different and separate from each other. *...speculative theories divorced from political reality.* ADJ-GRADED: v-link ADJ *from* n =unconnected

3 If you say that someone **is divorced from** a situation, you mean that they act as if they are completely unaffected by it. *This just shows how divorced from reality she's become.* ADJ-GRADED: v-link ADJ *from* n

divorcee /dɪvɔːʳsiː/ **divorcees.** A **divorcee** is a person, especially a woman, who is divorced. N-COUNT

divot /dɪvət/ **divots.** A **divot** is a small piece of grass and earth which is dug out accidentally, for example by a golf club. N-COUNT

divulge /daɪvʌldʒ, AM dɪ-/ **divulges, divulging, divulged.** If you **divulge** a piece of secret or pri- ◆◇◇◇◇ VERB =reveal vate information, you tell it to someone; a formal word. *Officials refuse to divulge details of the negotiations... He was charged with divulging state secrets... I do not want to divulge where the village is.* V n V wh Also V n to n, V that

divvy /dɪvi/ **divvies, divvying, divvied.** If you call someone a **divvy**, you are saying in a humorous way that you think they are rather foolish; used in informal British English. N-COUNT PRAGMATICS

divvy up. If you **divvy up** something such as money or food, you share it out; an informal expression. *Johnson was free to divvy up his share of the money as he chose.* PHRASAL VERB =divide V P n (not pron) Also V n P

Diwali /dɪwɑːli/; also spelled **Divali**. **Diwali** is a Hindu festival held in honour of Lakshmi, the goddess of wealth. It is celebrated in October or November with the lighting of lamps in homes and temples, and with prayers to Lakshmi. N-UNCOUNT

DIY /diː aɪ waɪ/ ◆◇◇◇◇

1 In British English, **DIY** is the activity of making or repairing things yourself, especially in your home. **DIY** is an abbreviation for 'do-it-yourself'. *He's useless at DIY. He won't even put up a shelf.* N-UNCOUNT

2 A **DIY** shop is one that sells tools, paint, and other equipment needed for DIY; used in British English. *You can get kits to do this from DIY stores.* ADJ: ADJ n =do-it-yourself

3 **DIY** things are things that you make or do yourself, rather than buying them ready-made or paying someone else to do them; used in British English. *They sell materials for DIY mosaics and ready-made panels.* ADJ: ADJ n =do-it-yourself

dizzy /dɪzi/ **dizzier, dizziest; dizzies, dizzying, dizzied** ◆◆◇◇◇

1 If you feel **dizzy**, you feel that you are losing your balance and are about to fall. *Her head still hurt, and she felt slightly dizzy and disoriented... He began to get dizzy spells.* ♦ **dizzily** /dɪzɪli/ *Her head spins dizzily as soon as she sits up.* ♦ **dizziness** *His complaint causes dizziness and nausea.* ADJ-GRADED ADV-GRADED: usu ADV with v N-UNCOUNT

2 You can use **dizzy** to describe a woman who is careless and forgetful, but likeable. *She is famed for playing dizzy blondes. ...a charmingly dizzy great-grandmother.* ADJ-GRADED: usu ADJ n

3 If something **dizzies** you, it causes you to feel unsteady or confused. *The sudden height dizzied her and she clung tightly.* ♦ **dizzying** *We're descending now at dizzying speed.* VERB V n ADJ-GRADED: usu ADJ n

4 If you say that someone has reached the **dizzy heights** of something, you are emphasizing that they have reached a very high level by achieving it; often used humorously. *I escalated to the dizzy heights of director's secretary.* PHRASE: usu PHR after v, oft PHR of n PRAGMATICS

DJ /diː dʒeɪ/ **DJs;** also spelled **dj**. ◆◆◇◇◇

1 A **DJ** is the dame as a **disc jockey**. N-COUNT

2 A **DJ** is the same as a **dinner jacket**. N-COUNT

DNA /diː en eɪ/. **DNA** is an acid in the chromosomes in the centre of the cells of living things. DNA determines the particular structure and functions of every cell and is responsible for characteristics being passed on from parents to their children. **DNA** is an abbreviation for 'deoxyribonucleic acid'. ◆◆◇◇◇ N-UNCOUNT

DNA fingerprinting DNA **fingerprinting** is the same as **genetic fingerprinting**. N-UNCOUNT

do 1 auxiliary verb uses

do /də, STRONG duː/ **does, doing, did, done** ◆◆◆◆◆

Do is used as an auxiliary with the simple present tense. **Did** is used as an auxiliary with the simple past tense. In spoken English negative forms of **do** are often contracted, for example **do not** is contracted to **don't** and **did not** is contracted to **didn't**.

1 **Do** is used to form the negative of main verbs, by putting 'not' after 'do' and before the main verb in its infinitive form (without 'to'). *They don't want to work... I did not know Jamie had a knife... It doesn't matter if you win or lose.* AUX AUX neg inf

2 **Do** is used to form questions, by putting the subject after 'do' and before the main verb in its infinitive form (without 'to'). *Do you like music?... What did he say?... Where does she live?* AUX AUX n v

3 **Do** is used in question tags. *You know about Andy, don't you?... I'm sure they had some of the same questions last year didn't they?.* AUX cl AUX n

4 You use **do** when you are confirming or contradicting a statement containing 'do', or giving a negative or positive answer to a question. *'Did he think there was anything suspicious going on?'—'Yes, he did.'... 'Do you have a metal detector?'—'No, I don't.'... They say they don't care, but they do.* AUX AUX

5 **Do** is used with a negative to tell someone not to behave in a certain way. *Don't be silly... Don't touch that!* AUX: only imper AUX neg inf

6 **Do** is used to give emphasis to the main verb when there is no other auxiliary. *Veronica, I do understand... You did have a tape recorder with you.* AUX AUX inf

7 **Do** is used as a polite way of inviting or trying to persuade someone to do something. *Do sit down... Do help yourself to another drink.* AUX: only imper PRAGMATICS AUX inf

8 **Do** can be used to refer back to another verbal group when you are comparing or contrasting two things, or saying that they are the same. *I make more money than he does... One day she will walk out, just as her own mother did... I had fantasies, as do all mothers, about how life would be when my girls were grown... Girls receive less health care and less education in the developing world than do boys.* VERB PRAGMATICS V as V n than V n

9 You use **do** after 'so' and 'nor' to say that the same statement is true for two people or groups. *You know that's true, and so do I... We don't forget that. Nor does he... Her actions and thoughts became distorted. So did her behavior.* VERB PRAGMATICS V n

do 2 other verb uses

do /duː/ **does, doing, did, done** ◆◆◆◆◆

1 When you **do** something, you take some action or perform an activity or task. **Do** is often used instead of a more specific verb, to talk about a common action involving a particular thing. For example you can say 'do your teeth' instead of 'brush your teeth'. *I was trying to do some work... After lunch Elizabeth and I did the washing up... Dad does the garden... Let me do your hair.* VERB V n

2 **Do** can be used to stand for any verbal group, or to refer back to another verbal group, including one that was in a previous sentence. *What are you doing?... So tell me what this molecule does that makes it special... Think twice before doing anything... A lot of people got arrested for looting so they will think before they do it again... After the meal I said I would go up to bed. I often did this because they would drink port wine and stay up very late... The first thing is to get some more food. When we've done that we ought to start again... Brian counted to twenty and lifted his binoculars. Elena did the same... He turned towards the open front door but, as he did so, she pushed past him.* VERB PRAGMATICS V n V pron-indef V it V this V that V the same V so

3 You can use **do** in a clause at the beginning of a sentence after words like 'what' and 'all', to give special emphasis to the information that comes at the end of the sentence. *All she does is complain... What I should do is go and see her... The best that can be done is to make things as difficult as possible.* VERB PRAGMATICS V n

4 If you **do** a particular thing with something, you use it in that particular way. *I was allowed to do whatever I wanted with my life... What did he do with the thirty pounds?... The technology was good, but you couldn't do much with it.* VERB V n with n V amount with n

5 If you **do** something about a problem, you take action to try to solve it. *They refuse to do anything about the real cause of crime: poverty... Well, what are you going to do about it?... Sexual harassment, that's against the law. Something should be done about it... In an ordinary aircraft, if an engine packs in, like, there's not much the engineer can do about it until the plane is back on the ground.* VERB V n about n V amount about n

6 If an action or event **does** a particular thing, such as harm or good, it has that result or effect. *A few bombs can do a lot of damage... It'll do you good to take a rest... The publicity did her career no harm.* VERB V n V n n

7 You can use **do** to talk about the degree to which a person, action, or event affects or improves a particular situation. *The current reforms will do much* VERB V amount to-inf *to create these conditions... Such incidents do nothing for live music's reputation... They did everything they could to help us... Mr de Klerk must do everything possible to free political prisoners... I'd just tried to do what I could for Lou.* V amount for n / V n to-inf / V n for n

8 You can talk about what someone or something **does** to someone to mean that they have a very harmful effect on them. *I saw what the liquor was doing to her... You overlook the pressure you're under and what it does to you.* VERB / V to n

9 If you ask someone what they **do**, you want to know what their job or profession is. *'What does your father do?'—'Well, he's a civil servant.'... He knew what he wanted to do from the age of 14.* VERB / V n

10 If you **are doing** something, you are busy or active in some way, or have planned an activity for some time in the future. *Are you doing anything tomorrow night?... 'What are you doing for Christmas?' Ella asked. 'We're going to Aunt Molly's.'... Once the novelty of watching TV and videos all day has worn off, there is nothing to do.* VERB / V n

11 If you say that someone or something **does** well or badly, you are talking about how successful or unsuccessful they are. *Connie did well at school and graduated with honours... Out-of-town superstores are doing well... How did I do?* VERB / V adv

12 If a person or organization **does** a particular service or product, they provide that service or sell that product. *They provide design services and do printing and packaging... They do a good range of herbal tea.* VERB / V n

13 You can use **do** when referring to the speed or rate that something or someone achieves or is able to achieve. *They were doing 70 miles an hour... His catamaran will do 37 knots.* VERB / V amount

14 If you **do** a subject, author, or book, you study them at school or college; used in spoken English. *I'd like to do maths at university... 'So you did "Macbeth" in the first year?'—'No, in the first year we did "Julius Caesar".'* VERB / V n

15 If you **do** a particular person, accent, or role, you mimic that person or accent or act that role. *Gina does accents extremely well.* VERB / V n

16 If you say that something will **do** or will **do** you, you mean that it is sufficient in quantity or quality to meet your requirements or to satisfy you. *Anything to create a scene and attract attention will do... We need a win – a draw won't do at all... 'I don't know what you like to eat,' she said, smiling.—'Anything'll do me, Eva.'* VERB / V / V n

17 If you say that you **could do with** something, you mean that you need it or would benefit from it. *I could do with a cup of tea... The range could do with being extended.* PHRASES / V inflects, PHR n/-ing

18 You can ask someone **what** they **did with** something as another way of asking them where they put it. *What did you do with that notebook?* V inflects, PHR n

19 If you ask **what** someone or something **is doing** in a particular place, you are asking why they are there. *'Dr Campbell,' he said, clearly surprised. 'What are you doing here?'... What was he doing in Hyde Park at that time of the morning?* PHR adv/prep

20 If you say **that will do** to a child, you are telling them to stop behaving in the way that they are. CONVENTION / PRAGMATICS

21 If you say that one thing **has** something **to do with** or **is** something **to do with** another thing, you mean that the two things are connected or that the first thing is about the second thing. *Mr Forlani denies having anything to do with the episode... They were shouting at each other. It was something to do with money... That's none of your business, it has nothing to do with you... A lot of this has to do with power and greed.* have/be inflects, PHR n

22 **do** is used in a large number of expressions which are explained under other words in the dictionary. For example, the expression 'easier said than done' is explained at 'easy'.

do away with. To **do away with** something means to remove it completely or abolish it. *The long-range goal must be to do away with nuclear weapons altogether.* PHRASAL VERB / V P P n

do down. If someone **does** you **down**, they try to make other people think that you are unpleasant or unsuccessful by criticizing you; used in informal British English. *Glover thinks that Smith did him down, perhaps out of envy.* PHRASAL VERB / =run down / V n P / Also V P n

do for. If you say that you **are done for**, you mean that you are in a disastrous and hopeless situation; an informal expression. *The police have only got to start thinking along those lines and I'm done for.* PHRASAL VERB / usu passive / be V-ed P

do in. To **do** someone **in** means to kill them; an informal expression. *Whoever did him in removed a man who was brave as well as ruthless.* PHRASAL VERB / V n P / Also V P n

do out. If a room or building is **done out** in a particular way, it is decorated and furnished in that way; used in British English. *...a room newly done out in country-house style.* PHRASAL VERB / usu passive / be V-ed P prep/adv

do out of. If you **do** someone **out of** something, you unfairly cause them not to have or get something that they were expecting to have; an informal expression. *He complains that the others have done him out of his share.* PHRASAL VERB / V n P P n

do over PHRASAL VERB

1 In American English, if you **do** a task **over**, you perform it again from the beginning; an informal expression. *Braun said if she had the chance to do it over, she would have hired a press secretary.* V n P

2 In British English, if someone **does** a place **over**, they rob it or search it and leave it very untidy; an informal expression. *The door was open. They had done the place over.* V n P / Also V P n

3 In British English, to **do** someone **over** means to hurt them badly, for example by hitting or kicking them; an informal expression. *We could get someone to do him over, couldn't we?* =beat up / V n P / Also V P n

do up PHRASAL VERB

1 If you **do** something **up**, you fasten it. *Mari did up the buttons... Keep your scarf on, do your coat up.* V P n (not pron) / V n P

2 If you **do up** an old building, you decorate and repair it so that it is in a better condition; used mainly in British English. *Nicholas has bought a barn in Provence and is spending August doing it up.* V n P / Also V P n (not pron)

3 If you say that a person or room **is done up** in a particular way, you mean they are dressed or decorated in that way, often a way that is rather ridiculous or extreme. *...Beatrice, usually done up like the fairy on the Christmas tree... She's had her blond hair done up exactly like Jackie's.* usu passive / be V-ed prep/adv / have n V-ed P

do without PHRASAL VERB

1 If you **do without** something you need, want, or usually have, you are able to survive, continue, or succeed although you do not have it. *We can't do without the help of your organisation... We've had a bit more money and that, and the baby doesn't do without.* V P n / V P

2 If you say that you could **do without** something, you mean that you would prefer not to have it or it is of no benefit to you; an informal expression. *He could do without her rhetorical questions at five o'clock in the morning. ...those who love France but can do without the natives... Like all teenagers there's one thing she'd rather do without – spots.* V P n

do 3 noun uses

do /duː/ **dos**

1 A **do** is a party, dinner party, or other social event; used in informal British English. *A friend of his is having a do in Stoke... They always have all-night dos there.* N-COUNT

2 If someone tells you the **dos and don'ts** of a particular situation, they advise you what you should and should not do in that situation. *Please advise me on the most suitable colour print film and some dos and don'ts.* PHRASE

do. **do.** is an old-fashioned written abbreviation for **ditto**.

d.o.b. **d.o.b.** is used as a written abbreviation for 'date of birth', especially on official forms.

doberman /doʊbəʳmən/ **dobermans.** A **doberman** is a type of large dog with short dark fur. N-COUNT

doc /dɒk/ **docs.** In American English, some people call a doctor **doc**; an informal word. N-VOC; N-COUNT

docile /doʊsaɪl, AM dɑːsᵊl/. A person or animal that is **docile** is quiet, not aggressive, and easily controlled. *...docile, obedient children... They* ◆◇◇◇◇ ADJ-GRADED =amenable *wanted a low-cost, docile workforce.* ♦ **docility** /dɒsɪlɪti/ *She was a quiet, placid baby, and her docility had surprised him.* ♦ **docilely** *She stands, hands behind her, as if docilely awaiting my decision.* N-UNCOUNT; ADV-GRADED: ADV with v

dock /dɒk/ **docks, docking, docked** ◆◆◇◇◇

1 A **dock** is an enclosed area in a harbour where ships go to be loaded, unloaded, and repaired. *...the loading dock... She headed for the docks, thinking that Ricardo might be hiding in one of the boats... What other ships are in dock here?* N-COUNT: also *in/into* N

2 When a ship **docks** or **is docked**, it is brought into a dock. *The vessel docked at Liverpool in April 1811... Russian commanders docked a huge aircraft carrier in a Russian port... The aircraft carrier has been docked there since last month.* V-ERG; V; V n; V-ed

3 When one spacecraft **docks** or **is docked** with another, the two crafts join together in space. *The space shuttle Atlantis is scheduled to dock with Russia's Mir space station... They have docked a robot module alongside the orbiting space station... American astronauts spent 44 hours docked with the Soviet-built spacecraft.* V-ERG-RECIP; V *with* n; V n prep; V-ed

4 In American English, a **dock** is a platform for loading vehicles or trains. *The truck left the loading dock with hoses still attached.* N-COUNT

5 In American English, a **dock** is a small structure at the edge of water where boats can tie up, especially one that is privately owned. *He had a house there and a dock and a little aluminum boat.* N-COUNT =jetty

6 In a law court, the **dock** is the place where the person accused of a crime stands or sits; used in British English. *What about the odd chance that you do put an innocent man in the dock?* N-SING: usu *in the* N

7 In British English, if you **dock** someone's wages or money, you take some of the money away. If you **dock** their points in a contest, you take away some of the points that they have. *He threatens to dock her fee... To dock points would be wrong.* VERB; V n; Also V n n

8 A **dock** is a plant with large leaves which grows wild in Britain and some other northern countries. Dock leaves are supposed to soothe nettle stings. N-VAR

9 See also **dry dock**.

docker /dɒkəʳ/ **dockers.** In British English, a **docker** is a person who works in the docks, loading and unloading ships. The usual American word is **longshoreman**. N-COUNT

docket /dɒkɪt/ **dockets**

1 A **docket** is a certificate or ticket which shows the contents of something such as a parcel or cargo, and proves who the goods belong to; used mainly in British English. *The clerk asked me to sign the docket.* N-COUNT

2 A **docket** is a list of cases awaiting trial in a law court; used mainly in American English. *The Court has about 1,400 appeals on its docket.* N-COUNT

dockland /dɒklænd/ **docklands.** In British English, the **dockland** or **docklands** of a town or city is the area around the docks. ◆◇◇◇◇ N-VAR

dock worker, dock workers. A **dock worker** is a person who works in the docks, loading and unloading ships. N-COUNT

dockyard /dɒkjɑːʳd/ **dockyards.** A **dockyard** is a place where ships are built, maintained, and repaired. N-COUNT

doctor /dɒktəʳ/ **doctors, doctoring, doctored** ◆◆◆◆◇

1 A **doctor** is someone who is qualified in medicine and treats people who are ill. *Do not discontinue the treatment without consulting your doctor... Doctor Paige will be here right after lunch to see her.* N-COUNT; N-TITLE; N-VOC

2 The **doctor's** is used to refer to the surgery or clinic where a doctor works. *I have an appointment at the doctors.* N-COUNT: usu sing, *the* N

3 A **doctor** is someone who has been awarded the highest academic or honorary degree by a university. *He is a doctor of philosophy.* N-COUNT; N-TITLE

4 If someone **doctors** something, they change it in order to deceive people. *They doctored the prints, deepening the lines to make her look as awful as possible. ...a cleverly doctored photograph.* VERB =tamper with; V n; V-ed

♦ **doctoring** *The doctoring of the document has become a live political issue.* N-UNCOUNT

5 If someone **doctors** food or drink, they add a poison or drug to it; used mainly in written English. *She had no doubt that it was he who had doctored her milk. ...doctored wine.* VERB; V n; V-ed

doctoral /dɒktərəl/. A **doctoral** thesis or piece of research is written or done in order to obtain a doctor's degree. ADJ: ADJ n

doctorate /dɒktərət/ **doctorates.** A **doctorate** is the highest degree awarded by a university. *Professor Lanphier obtained his doctorate in Social Psychology from the University of Michigan.* ◆◇◇◇◇ N-COUNT

doctrinaire /dɒktrɪneəʳ/. If you say that someone is **doctrinaire** or has a **doctrinaire** attitude, you disapprove of them because they have fixed principles which they try to impose on other people; a formal word. *He is firm but not doctrinaire.* ADJ-GRADED PRAGMATICS =dogmatic

doctrinal /dɒktraɪnəl, AM dɑːktrɪnəl/. **Doctrinal** means relating to doctrines; a formal word. *Doctrinal differences were vigorously debated among religious leaders.* ADJ: usu ADJ n

doctrine /dɒktrɪn/ **doctrines** ◆◆◇◇◇

1 A **doctrine** is a set of principles or beliefs, especially religious ones. *...the Marxist doctrine of perpetual revolution... I disagree with the doctrine that the writer's life and intention have no bearing on his texts.* N-VAR: usu with supp, oft N *of* n

2 In American English, a **doctrine** is a statement of official government policy, especially foreign policy. *Following World War II, the first U.S. commitment to Europe came in the form of the 1947 Truman Doctrine.* N-COUNT

docudrama /dʌkjʊdrɑːmə/ **docudramas;** also spelled **docu-drama**. A **docudrama** is a film based on events that really happened. Docudramas are usually shown on television rather than in a cinema. N-VAR

document, documents, documenting, documented. The noun is pronounced /dɒkjəmənt/. The verb is pronounced /dɒkjəment/. ◆◆◆◆◇

1 A **document** is one or more official pieces of paper with writing on them. *The foreign ministers of the two countries signed the documents today. ...a policy document for the Labour Party conference... The policeman wanted to see all our documents.* N-COUNT =paper

2 If you **document** something, you make a detailed record of it in writing or on film or tape. *He wrote a book documenting his prison experiences... The effects of smoking have been well documented.* VERB; V n; *be* V-ed

documentary /dɒkjəmentri/ **documentaries** ◆◆◇◇◇

1 A **documentary** is a television or radio programme, or a film, which shows real events or provides factual information about a particular subject. *...a TV documentary on homelessness.* N-COUNT

2 **Documentary** evidence consists of things that are written down. *The government says it has documentary evidence that the two countries were planning military action.* ADJ: ADJ n

documentation /dɒkjəmenteɪʃən/. **Documentation** consists of documents which provide proof or evidence of something, or are a record of something. *Passengers must carry proper documentation.* ◆◇◇◇◇ N-UNCOUNT

doddering /dɒdərɪŋ/. If you refer to someone as a **doddering** old man or woman, you are saying in a disrespectful way that they are old and not strong. *...a doddering old man making his will before he's too senile.* ADJ: usu ADJ n PRAGMATICS =decrepit

doddery /dɒdəri/. Someone who is **doddery** walks in an unsteady and shaky way, especially because of old age. ADJ-GRADED

doddle /dɒdəl/. In informal British English, if you say that something is **a doddle**, you mean that it is very easy to do. N-SING: *a* N ≠difficult

dodge /dɒdʒ/ **dodges, dodging, dodged** ◆◆◇◇◇

1 If you **dodge**, you move suddenly, often to avoid being hit, caught, or seen. *He dodged amongst the seething crowds of men... We dodged behind a pillar out of sight of the tourists.* VERB; V prep/adv

2 If you **dodge** something, you avoid it by quickly moving aside or out of reach so that it cannot hit or VERB =sidestep

reach you. *He desperately dodged a speeding car trying to run him down.* Vn

3 If you **dodge** something, you deliberately avoid thinking about it or dealing with it, often by being deceitful. *He boasts of dodging military service by feigning illness... Many struggling firms are ready to break the law by dodging tax.* ▶ Also a noun. *This was not just a tax dodge.* VERB =evade Vn N-COUNT: usu supp N

dodgem /dɒdʒəm/ **dodgems.** In British English, a **dodgem** or **dodgem car** is a small electric car with a wide rubber bumper all round. People drive dodgems around a special enclosure at a fairground and sometimes crash into each other for fun. **Dodgem** is a trademark. N-COUNT: usu pl

dodger /dɒdʒəʳ/ **dodgers.** A **dodger** is someone who avoids an obligation or duty, such as paying taxes or train fares. *...tax dodgers who hide their interest earnings. ...a crackdown on fare dodgers.* ◆◇◇◇◇ N-COUNT: usu n N =evader

• See also **draft dodger.**

dodgy /dɒdʒi/ **dodgier, dodgiest** ◆◇◇◇◇

1 If you describe someone or something as **dodgy**, you disapprove of them because they seem rather dishonest and unreliable; used in informal British English. *He was a bit of a dodgy character. ...cash made in dodgy underworld deals.* ADJ-GRADED PRAGMATICS =suspect

2 If you say that something is **dodgy**, you mean that it seems rather risky, dangerous, or unreliable; used in informal British English. *Predicting voting trends from economic forecasts is a dodgy business.* ADJ-GRADED =chancy

3 If you say that someone has a **dodgy** heart or knee, for example, you mean that that part of their body is not very strong or healthy; used in informal British English. *My heart's a bit dodgy with all those years of painkillers.* ADJ-GRADED

dodo /doʊdoʊ/ **dodos** or **dodoes**

1 A **dodo** was a very large bird that was unable to fly. Dodos are now extinct. N-COUNT

2 If you refer to someone as a **dodo**, you think they are foolish or silly; an informal use. *Any dodo could put this together.* N-COUNT PRAGMATICS

doe /doʊ/ **does.** A **doe** is an adult female rabbit, hare, or deer. N-COUNT

doer /duːəʳ/ **doers.** If you refer to someone as a **doer**, you mean that they do jobs promptly and efficiently, without spending a lot of time thinking about them. *Robertson was a doer, not a thinker.* N-COUNT

does /dəz, STRONG dʌz/. **Does** is the third person singular in the present tense of **do**.

doesn't /dʌzᵊnt/. **Doesn't** is the usual spoken form of **does not**. ◆◆◆◆◆

doff /dɒf, AM dɔːf/ **doffs, doffing, doffed.** If you **doff** your hat or coat, you take it off; an old fashioned word. *The peasants doff their hats.* VERB Vn

dog /dɒg, AM dɔːg/ **dogs, dogging, dogged** ◆◆◆◆◇

1 A **dog** is a very common four-legged animal that is often kept by people as a pet or to guard or hunt. There are many different breeds of dog. *Outside, a dog was barking... The dog growled again... The British are renowned as a nation of dog lovers.* N-COUNT

2 You use **dog** to refer to a male dog, or to the male of some related species such as wolves or foxes. *Is this a dog or a bitch? ...a dog fox.* N-COUNT ≠bitch

3 In informal English, if someone calls a man a **dog**, they mean that they dislike him and strongly disapprove of him. *The men in these films are just dogs.* N-COUNT PRAGMATICS =villain

4 In informal American English, people use **dog** to refer to something that they consider unsatisfactory or of poor quality. *It's a real dog.* N-COUNT PRAGMATICS

5 If problems or injuries **dog** you, they are with you all the time. *The problems that have dogged him all year are just a temporary setback... His career has been dogged by bad luck.* VERB Vn

6 In informal British English, people refer to a sports meeting where dogs, especially greyhounds, race and people bet on which dog will win as **the dogs**. N-PLURAL: theN

7 See also **dogged**; **guide dog**, **prairie dog**, **sniffer dog**.

8 In informal British English, you describe something as a **dog's breakfast** in order to express your disapproval of it, for example because it is very untidy, badly organized, or badly done. *The whole place was a bit of a dog's dinner, really... Our own Board are going to make a dog's breakfast out of it if we aren't careful.* PHRASES v-link PHR, PHR after v PRAGMATICS =mess

9 You use **dog eat dog** to express your disapproval of a situation where everyone wants to succeed and is willing to harm other people in order to do so. *It is very much dog eat dog out there... The TV business today is a dog-eat-dog business.* v-link PHR, PHR n PRAGMATICS =cut-throat

10 If you say that something **is going to the dogs**, you mean that it is becoming weaker and worse in quality. *They sit in impotent opposition while the country goes to the dogs.* V inflects PRAGMATICS

11 If someone tells you to **let sleeping dogs lie**, they are warning you not to disturb or interfere with a situation, because you are likely to cause trouble and problems. *Why can't she let sleeping dogs lie?* *let* inflects

12 If you say **'You can't teach an old dog new tricks'**, you are suggesting that someone is unwilling to try new ways of doing things. *dog* inflects

dog-collar, dog-collars; also spelled **dog collar.**

1 A **dog-collar** is a stiff, round, white collar that fastens at the back and that is worn by Christian priests and ministers; an informal use. N-COUNT =clerical collar

2 A **dog-collar** is a collar worn by a dog. N-COUNT

dog-eared. A book or piece of paper that is **dog-eared** has been used so much that the corners of the pages are turned down or torn. *...dog-eared copies of ancient history books.* ADJ-GRADED

dogfight /dɒgfaɪt, AM dɔːg-/ **dogfights;** also spelled **dog fight.**

1 A **dogfight** is a fight between fighter planes, in which they fly close to one another and manoeuvre very fast. N-COUNT

2 If you say that organizations or people are involved in a **dogfight**, you mean they are struggling very hard against each other in order to succeed. *The airline emerged from its dogfight with recession yesterday looking distinctly the worse for wear.* N-COUNT: usu with supp

dogfish /dɒgfɪʃ, AM dɔːg-/; **dogfish** is both the singular and the plural form. A **dogfish** is a small shark. There are several kinds of dogfish. ◆◇◇◇◇ N-COUNT

dogged /dɒgɪd, AM dɔː-/. If you describe someone's actions as **dogged**, you mean that they are determined to continue with something even if it becomes difficult or dangerous. *They have, through sheer dogged determination, slowly gained respect for their efforts. ...his dogged insistence on their rights.* ◆◇◇◇◇ ADJ-GRADED: ADJ n =resolute, persistent

♦ **doggedly** *She would fight doggedly for her rights as the children's mother.* ADV-GRADED: usu ADV with v

♦ **doggedness** *Most of my accomplishments came as the result of sheer doggedness rather than talent.* N-UNCOUNT

doggerel /dɒgərᵊl, AM dɔː-/. If you refer to a poem as **doggerel**, you are emphasizing that you think it is very bad poetry. *...fragments of meaningless doggerel.* N-UNCOUNT PRAGMATICS

doggie /dɒgi, AM dɔː-/ **doggies. Doggie** is a child's word for a dog. N-COUNT

doggy /dɒgi, AM dɔː-/ **doggies.** See **doggie**.

doghouse /dɒghaʊs, AM dɔːg-/ **doghouses;** also spelled **dog-house.**

1 If you are **in the doghouse**, you are in disgrace and people are annoyed with you; an informal expression. *Her husband was in the doghouse for leaving her to cope on her own.* PHRASE: v-link PHR

2 In American English, a **doghouse** is a small building made especially for a dog to sleep in. The usual British word is **kennel**. N-COUNT

dogleg /dɒgleg, AM dɔːg-/ **doglegs.** A **dogleg** is a sharp bend, especially one in a road. N-COUNT

dogma /dɒgmə, AM dɔːg-/ **dogmas.** If you refer to a belief or a system of beliefs as a **dogma**, you are criticizing it for expecting people to accept that it is true, without questioning it. *Their political dogma has blinded them to the real needs of the country... He stands for freeing the country from the grip of dogma.* ◆◇◇◇◇ N-VAR: usu with supp PRAGMATICS

dogmatic /dɒgmætɪk, AM dɔːg-/. If you say that someone is **dogmatic**, you are critical of them because they are convinced that they are right, and refuse to consider that other opinions might also be justified. *Many writers at this time held rigidly dogmatic views... The regime is dogmatic, and no one dares to express personal opinions.* ◆◇◇◇◇ ADJ-GRADED PRAGMATICS =dictatorial
♦ **dogmatically** /dɒgmætɪkli, AM dɔːg-/. *Bennett had wanted this list of books to be dogmatically imposed on the nation's universities.* ADV-GRADED: ADV with v

dogmatism /dɒgmətɪzəm, AM dɔːg-/. If you refer to an opinion as **dogmatism**, you are criticizing it for being strongly asserted without consideration of all the relevant facts or other people's opinions. *We cannot allow dogmatism to stand in the way of progress.* N-UNCOUNT PRAGMATICS ♦ **dogmatist, dogmatists** *Intellectuals are becoming unhappy with dogmatists in the party leadership.* N-COUNT

do-gooder, do-gooders. If you describe someone as a **do-gooder**, you mean that they do things which they think will help other people, although you think that they are interfering. N-COUNT PRAGMATICS

dogsbody /dɒgzbɒdi, AM dɔːgz-/ **dogsbodies.** In British English, a **dogsbody** is a person who has to do all the boring jobs that nobody else wants to do; an informal word. *I thought it would be glamorous but I just turned out to be a general dogsbody.* N-COUNT =gofer

dog tag, dog tags. Dog tags are metal identification tag that are worn on a chain around the neck by members of the United States armed forces. N-COUNT: usu pl

dog-tired. If you say that you are **dog-tired**, you are emphasizing that you are extremely tired; an informal word. *By dusk we were dog-tired and heading for home.* ADJ: v-link ADJ PRAGMATICS

doily /dɔɪli/ **doilies.** A **doily** is a small, round piece of paper or cloth that has a pattern of tiny holes in it. Doilies are put on plates under cakes and sandwiches. N-COUNT

doings /duːɪŋz/. Someone's **doings** are their activities at a particular time. *The film chronicles the everyday doings of a group of London schoolchildren.* N-PLURAL: usu with poss

do-it-yourself ◆◇◇◇◇
1 **Do-it-yourself** is the same as **DIY**. N-UNCOUNT
2 A **do-it-yourself** shop is one that sells tools, paint, and other equipment needed for DIY. *You can buy all these tools at a do-it-yourself store.* ADJ: ADJ n =DIY
3 **Do-it-yourself** things are things that you make or do yourself, rather than buying them ready-made or paying someone else to make them or do them. *...do-it-yourself shelving.* ADJ: ADJ n =DIY

Dolby /dɒlbi/. **Dolby** is a system which reduces the background noise on electronic cassette players. **Dolby** is a trademark. *...a cassette deck equipped with Dolby noise reduction.* N-UNCOUNT: oft N n

doldrums /dɒldrəmz/. If an activity or situation is **in the doldrums**, it is very quiet and nothing new or exciting is happening. *The economy is in the doldrums.* ◆◇◇◇◇ PHRASE: usu v-link PHR

dole /dəʊl/ **doles, doling, doled** ◆◆◇◇◇
1 In British English, the **dole** is money that is given regularly by the government to people who are unemployed. The usual American word is **welfare**. N-UNCOUNT: also *the* N =benefit
2 In British English, someone who is **on the dole** is registered as unemployed and receives money to live on from the government. The usual American expression is **on welfare**. *It's not easy living on the dole.* PHRASE: PHR after v, v-link PHR
dole out. If you **dole** something **out**, you give a certain amount of it to each member of a group. *I got out my wallet and began to dole out the money.* PHRASAL VERB V P n (not pron) Also V n P

doleful /dəʊlfʊl/. A **doleful** expression, manner, or voice is depressing and miserable. *He stared over his glasses with a long, doleful look of disbelief.* ADJ-GRADED =mournful ♦ **dolefully** *'I don't know why they left,' he said dolefully.* ADV-GRADED: ADV with v

dole queue, dole queues. In British English, when people talk about the **dole queue**, they are talking about the state of being unemployed, especially when saying how many people are unemployed. The usual American expression is **unemployment line**. *Another 29,100 people have joined the dole queue. ...a backdrop of lengthening dole queues.* N-COUNT

doll /dɒl/ **dolls, dolling, dolled.** A **doll** is a child's toy which looks like a small person or baby. ◆◆◇◇◇ N-COUNT
doll up. If a woman **dolls** herself **up**, she puts on smart or fashionable clothes in order to try and look attractive for a particular occasion; used in informal English. *We used to doll ourselves up and go into town.* PHRASAL VERB V pron-refl P ♦ **dolled up** *She was dolled up for the occasion.* ADJ-GRADED: usu v-link ADJ

dollar /dɒləʳ/ **dollars.** The **dollar** is the unit of money used in the USA, Canada, and some other countries. It is represented by the symbol $. A dollar is divided into one hundred smaller units called cents. *She gets paid seven dollars an hour... The government is spending billions of dollars on new urban rail projects.* ◆◆◆◆◆ N-COUNT: usu num N ► The **dollar** is also used to refer to the American currency system. *In early trading in Tokyo, the dollar fell sharply against the yen.* N-SING: the N

dollop /dɒləp/ **dollops.** A **dollop** of soft or sticky food is a large scoop of it served in a casual way; an informal word. *...a dollop of cream.* N-COUNT: usu N *of* n

doll's house, doll's houses; the form **dollhouse** is used in American English. A **doll's house** or **dollhouse** is a toy in the form of a small house, which children can use when they are playing with dolls. N-COUNT

dolly /dɒli/ **dollies.** A **dolly** is a child's word for a doll. ◆◇◇◇◇ N-COUNT

dolphin /dɒlfɪn/ **dolphins.** A **dolphin** is a mammal which lives in the sea and looks like a large fish with a pointed mouth. ◆◆◇◇◇ N-COUNT

dolt /dəʊlt/ **dolts.** If you call someone a **dolt**, you think they are stupid, or have done something stupid; an informal word. *He's a first-class dolt who insists on doing things his way.* N-COUNT PRAGMATICS =idiot

domain /dəʊmeɪn/ **domains** ◆◇◇◇◇
1 A **domain** is a particular field of thought, activity, or interest, especially one over which someone has control, influence, or rights; a formal use. *...the great experimenters in the domain of art... This information should be in the public domain.* N-COUNT: usu with supp
2 Someone's **domain** is the area they own or have control over; a literary use. *...the mighty king's domain.* N-COUNT: usu with poss

dome /dəʊm/ **domes** ◆◆◇◇◇
1 A **dome** is a round roof. *...the dome of St Paul's cathedral.* N-COUNT
2 A **dome** is any object that has a similar shape to a dome. *...the dome of the hill.* N-COUNT

domed /dəʊmd/. Something that is **domed** is in the shape of a dome. *...the great hall with its domed ceiling.* ADJ

domestic /dəmestɪk/ **domestics** ◆◆◆◆◇
1 **Domestic** political activities, events, and situations happen or exist within one particular country. *...over 100 domestic flights a day to 15 UK destinations. ...sales in the domestic market.* ● See also **gross domestic product.** ADJ: usu ADJ n =home ≠foreign ♦ **domestically** /dəmestɪkli/ *Opportunities will improve as the company expands domestically and internationally... Domestically, he's going to make some compromises that he doesn't want to make.* ADV: ADV after v, ADV -ed/adj, ADV with cl
2 **Domestic** duties and activities are concerned with the running of a home and family. *...a plan for sharing domestic chores.* ADJ: ADJ n =household
3 **Domestic** items and services are intended to be used in people's homes rather than in factories or offices. *...domestic appliances.* ADJ: ADJ n =household ≠industrial
4 A **domestic** situation or atmosphere is one which involves a family and their home. *It was a scene of such domestic bliss... I was called out to attend a domestic dispute.* ADJ: usu ADJ n
5 Someone who is **domestic** enjoys being at home and running a family. *She was kind and domestic and put her family before her part-time job.* ADJ-GRADED
6 A **domestic** animal is one that is not wild and is ADJ

kept either on a farm to produce food or in someone's home as a pet. *...a domestic cat.* ≠wild

7 A **domestic**, a **domestic help**, or a **domestic worker** is a person who is paid to come to help with the work that has to be done in a house such as the cleaning, washing, and ironing. N-COUNT

domesticate /dəmestɪkeɪt/ **domesticates, domesticating, domesticated.** When people **domesticate** wild animals or plants, they bring them under control and use them to produce food or as pets. *Presumably, we domesticated the dog to help us with our hunting. ...sheep, cattle, horses, and other domesticated animals.* ◆◇◇◇◇ VERB =tame V n V-ed

♦ **domestication** /dəmestɪkeɪʃən/ *Sheep are particularly well suited for domestication.* N-UNCOUNT

domesticated /dəmestɪkeɪtɪd/. Someone who is **domesticated** willingly does household tasks such as cleaning. *I'm very domesticated and organised in a way that Mum definitely isn't.* ADJ-GRADED

domesticity /doʊmestɪsɪti/. **Domesticity** is the state of being at home with your family. *...a small rebellion against routine and cosy domesticity.* N-UNCOUNT

domestic science. In British schools, **domestic science** was the name used to refer to the subject which involved the teaching of cookery, needlework, and other household skills. The subject is now referred to as **home economics**, which is also the usual American term. N-UNCOUNT

domicile /dɒmɪsaɪl/ **domiciles.** Your **domicile** is the place where you live; a formal word. N-COUNT: oft with poss

domiciled /dɒmɪsaɪld/. If you are **domiciled** in a particular place, you live there; a formal word. *Frank is currently domiciled in Berlin.* ADJ: usu v-link ADJ, oft ADJ *in* n

dominance /dɒmɪnəns/. The **dominance** of a particular person or thing is the fact that it is more powerful, successful, or prominent than other people or things. *The latest fighting appears to be an attempt by each group to establish dominance over the other... These economies will no doubt maintain their dominance of financial markets... Legislation is the only route to ending the car's dominance as a form of transport.* ◆◇◇◇◇ N-UNCOUNT: oft N *of/over* n =supremacy

dominant /dɒmɪnənt/ ◆◆◇◇◇

1 Someone or something that is **dominant** is more powerful, successful, influential, or noticeable than other people or things. *...a change which would maintain his party's dominant position in Scotland... She was a dominant figure in the French film industry.* ADJ-GRADED =pre-eminent

2 A **dominant** gene is one that produces a particular characteristic regardless of whether a person has only one of these genes from one parent, or two of them, one from each parent; a technical term in biology. Compare **recessive**. *Because it is carried by a dominant gene, an affected individual can expect about half of his or her children to inherit the illness.* ADJ-UNGRADED: usu ADJ n

dominate /dɒmɪneɪt/ **dominates, dominating, dominated** ◆◆◆◆◇

1 To **dominate** a situation means to be the most powerful or important person or thing in it. *The book is expected to dominate the best-seller lists. ...countries where life is dominated by war... No single factor appears to dominate.* ♦ **domination** /dɒmɪneɪʃən/ *...the domination of the market by a small number of organizations.* VERB V n V N-UNCOUNT

2 If one country or person **dominates** another, it has power over it. *He denied that his country wants to dominate Europe... Women are no longer dominated by the men in their relationships... The countries of Eastern Europe immediately started to dominate.* ♦ **domination** *They had five centuries of domination by the Romans.* VERB V n V N-UNCOUNT

3 If a building, mountain, or other object **dominates** an area, it is so large or impressive that you cannot avoid seeing it. *It's one of the biggest buildings in this area, and it really dominates this whole place. ...its skyline dominated by the central mosque.* VERB =overshadow V n

dominating /dɒmɪneɪtɪŋ/. A **dominating** person has a very strong personality and influences the people around them. *She certainly was a dominating figure, a leader who gave her name to a political philosophy... The boy was brought up by his mother, who was a dominating influence in his life.* ADJ-GRADED: usu ADJ n =commanding

domineering /dɒmɪnɪərɪŋ/. If you say that someone is **domineering**, you disapprove of them because you feel that they try to control other people without any consideration for their feelings or opinions. *Mick was stubborn and domineering with a very bad temper... She is not a domineering mother.* ADJ-GRADED PRAGMATICS =overbearing

dominion /dəmɪnjən/ **dominions** ◆◇◇◇◇

1 **Dominion** is control or authority; a formal use. *They truly believe they have dominion over us.* N-UNCOUNT: oft N *over* n

2 A **dominion** is an area of land that is controlled by a ruler. *The Republic is a dominion of the Brazilian people.* N-COUNT: oft with poss

3 The **Dominions** were the nations which in the past were part of the British Empire but which had their own government. N-COUNT

domino /dɒmɪnoʊ/ **dominoes** ◆◇◇◇◇

1 **Dominoes** are small rectangular blocks marked with two groups of spots on one side. They are used for playing various games. N-COUNT

2 **Dominoes** is a game in which players put dominoes onto a table in turn. N-UNCOUNT

domino effect. If one event causes another similar event, which in turn causes another event, and so on, you can refer to this as a **domino effect**. *What really underlies Mr Gorbachev's actions is fear of the domino effect. If one republic leaves the Soviet Union with impunity, others will follow.* N-SING =knock on effect

don /dɒn/ **dons, donning, donned**

1 If you **don** clothing, you put it on; used in written English. *The crowd threw petrol bombs at the police, who responded by donning riot gear.* VERB V n

2 A **don** is a lecturer at Oxford or Cambridge University in England. In some British newspapers, lecturers from any university are referred to as **dons**. N-COUNT

donate /doʊneɪt/ **donates, donating, donated** ◆◆◇◇◇

1 If you **donate** something to a charity or other organization, you give it to them. *He frequently donates large sums to charity... Others donated secondhand clothes... The silver trophy was donated by a Leicester businessman.* ♦ **donation** /doʊneɪʃən/ *...the donation of his collection to the art gallery.* VERB V n *to* n V n N-UNCOUNT: usu N *of* n

2 If you **donate** your blood or a part of your body, you allow doctors to use it to help somebody who is ill. *...people who are willing to donate their organs for use after death... All donated blood is screened for HIV.* ♦ **donation** *...measures aimed at encouraging organ donation.* VERB V n V-ed N-UNCOUNT: usu with supp

donation /doʊneɪʃən/ **donations.** A **donation** is something which someone gives to a charity or other organization. *Employees make regular donations to charity... Charities appealed for donations of food and clothing for victims of the hurricane.* • See also **donate**. ◆◆◇◇◇ N-COUNT: oft N *to/of/from* n =gift

done /dʌn/ ◆◆◆◇◇

1 **Done** is the past participle of **do**.

2 A task or activity that is **done** has been completed successfully. *When her deal is done, the client emerges with her purchase.* ADJ: v-link ADJ

3 When something that you are cooking is **done**, it has been cooked long enough and is ready. *As soon as the cake is done, remove it from the oven.* ADJ: v-link ADJ

4 You say **'Done'** when you are accepting a deal, arrangement, or bet that someone has offered to make with you. *'You lead and we'll look for it.'—'Done.'* CONVENTION PRAGMATICS

5 If you say that something is **over and done with**, you mean that it is completely finished and you do not have to think about it any more; used in spoken English. *Once this is all over and done with she's to go into the clinic for a complete rest.* PHRASE: v-link PHR, PHR after v

Don Juan /dɒn dʒuːən/ **Don Juans.** If you describe a man as a **Don Juan**, you mean he has seduced many women. N-COUNT

donkey /dɒŋki/ **donkeys** ◆◇◇◇◇
1 A **donkey** is an animal which is like a horse but which is smaller and has longer ears. N-COUNT
2 In informal British English, if you say that something has been happening or has been the case for **donkey's years**, you are emphasizing that it has been happening or has been the case for a very long time. *I've been a vegetarian for donkey's years. ...old iron mines that haven't been used in donkey's years.* PHRASE: prep PHR PRAGMATICS =ages

donkey jacket, donkey jackets. A **donkey jacket** is a thick, warm jacket worn by workmen; used mainly in British English. N-COUNT

donkey work. In British English, if you do the **donkey work**, you do the hard work or the less interesting part of the work that needs to be done; an informal expression. N-SING: usu *the* N

donnish /dɒnɪʃ/. If you describe a man as **donnish**, you think he is rather serious and intellectual; used mainly in British English. *He is precise and mildly donnish in manner.* ADJ-GRADED

donor /doʊnəʳ/ **donors** ◆◆◇◇◇
1 A **donor** is someone who gives a part of their body or some of their blood to be used by doctors to help a person who is ill. *Doctors removed the healthy kidney from the donor.* N-COUNT: oft n N
2 **Donor** organs or parts are organs or parts of the body which people allow doctors to use to help people who are ill. ADJ: ADJ n
3 A **donor** is a person or organization who gives something, especially money, to a charity, organization, or country that needs it. *Donor countries are becoming more choosy about which countries they are prepared to help.* N-COUNT

donor card, donor cards. A **donor card** is a card which people carry in order to make sure that, when they die, their organs are be used by doctors to help people who are ill. N-COUNT

don't /doʊnt/. **Don't** is the usual spoken form of **do not**. ◆◆◆◆◆

donut /doʊnʌt/ **donuts.** See **doughnut**.

doodad /duːdæd/ **doodads.** A **doodad** is the same as a **doodah**; an informal word, used in American English. N-COUNT

doodah /duːdɑː/ **doodahs.** In informal British English, you can refer to something, especially an electronic gadget, as a **doodah** when you do not know exactly what is called. *The car has all the latest electronic doodahs.* N-COUNT

doodle /duːdᵊl/ **doodles, doodling, doodled**
1 A **doodle** is a pattern or picture that you draw when you are bored or thinking about something else. N-COUNT
2 When someone **doodles**, they draw doodles. *He looked across at Jackson, doodling on his notebook.* VERB V Also V n

doom /duːm/ **dooms, dooming, doomed** ◆◇◇◇◇
1 **Doom** is a terrible future state or event which you cannot prevent. *...his warnings of impending doom. ...a wicked mermaid who lured sailors to their doom.* N-UNCOUNT =fate
2 If you have a sense or feeling of **doom**, you feel that things are going very badly and are likely to get even worse. *Why are people so full of gloom and doom?... Attendance figures had been steadily dropping, creating a mood of doom and discouragement among theatre directors.* N-UNCOUNT
3 If a fact or event **dooms** someone or something to a particular fate, it makes certain that something unpleasant or unwanted is going to happen to them. *That argument was the turning point for their marriage, and the one which doomed it to failure.* VERB =condemn V n to n Also V n to-inf

doomed /duːmd/ ◆◆◇◇◇
1 If something **is doomed** to happen, or if you **are doomed** to a particular state, something unpleasant is certain to happen, and you can do nothing to prevent it. *Their plans seemed doomed to failure... He knew that if he lived, he would be doomed to spend the war as a prisoner.* ADJ: v-link ADJ, ADJ *to* n, ADJ to-inf
2 Someone or something that is **doomed** is certain to fail or be destroyed. *Fireman battled through the smoke in a doomed attempt to rescue the children... I used to pour time and energy into projects that were doomed from the start.* ADJ =hopeless

doomsday /duːmzdeɪ/
1 **Doomsday** is a day or time when you expect something terrible or unpleasant is going to happen. *...the doomsday scenario of civil war between the two factions.* N-UNCOUNT
2 In the Christian religion, **Doomsday** is the last day of the world, on which God will judge everyone. N-PROPER

door /dɔːʳ/ **doors** ◆◆◆◆◆
1 A **door** is a movable piece of wood, glass, or metal, which is used to open and close the entrance to a building, room, cupboard, or vehicle. *I was knocking at the front door there was no answer... The policeman opened the door and looked in... I heard a door slamming.* N-COUNT
2 A **door** is the space in a wall when a door is open. *She looked through the door of the kitchen. Her daughter was at the stove.* N-COUNT =doorway
3 The **door** is the entrance to a large building such as a shop, hotel, or theatre. *He entered Harrods by the main door... The queues at the door wound around the building.* N-COUNT =entrance
4 In informal English, you use **doors** in expressions such as **a few doors down** or **three doors up** when you are referring to a place that is a particular number of buildings away from where you are. *Mrs Cade's house was only a few doors down from her daughter's apartment.* N-PLURAL: amount N *down/up*
5 See also **next door**.
6 When you **answer the door**, you go and open the door because a visitor has knocked on it or rung the bell. *Carol answered the door as soon as I knocked.* PHRASES V inflects
7 If you say that someone gets something or does something **by the back door** or **through the back door**, you are criticizing them for doing it secretly and unofficially. *The government would not allow anyone to sneak in by the back door and seize power by force... They claim the Government is privatising dentistry through the back door.* PHR after v PRAGMATICS =sneakily
8 If someone **closes the door on** something, they stop thinking about it or dealing with it. *We never close the door on a successful series.* V inflects: PHR n
9 If people have talks and discussions **behind closed doors**, they have them in private because they want them to be kept secret. *...decisions taken in secret behind closed doors.* PHR after v, PHR n =in private
10 If someone goes **from door to door** or goes **door to door**, they go along a street calling at each house in turn, for example selling something. *They are going from door to door collecting money from civilians. ...a door-to-door salesman... Police immediately started door-to-door inquiries.* PHR after v, PHR n
11 If you talk about a distance or journey **from door to door** or **door to door**, you are talking about the distance from the place where the journey starts to the place where it finishes. *...tickets covering the whole journey from door to door... Flying out on Friday from Gatwick it took seven hours door-to-door.*
12 If you say that something helps someone to get their **foot in the door** or their **toe in the door**, you mean that it gives them an opportunity to start doing something such as trading in a new market which they have put a lot of effort into getting. *The bondholding may help the firm get its foot in the door to win the business... The Philips deal also gives Sparc a foot in the door of a new market-consumer electronics.* N inflects, PHR after v
13 If someone **shuts the door in** your **face** or **slams the door in** your **face**, they refuse to talk to you or give you any information. *Did you say anything to him or just shut the door in his face?* V inflects
14 If you **lay** something **at** someone's **door**, you blame them for something unpleasant that has happened. *I'm not sure his death can be laid at medicine's door alone... The blame is generally laid at the door of the government.* V inflects
15 If someone or something **opens the door** to a good new idea or situation, they introduce it or V and N inflect, oft PHR *to* n

make it possible. *This book opens the door to some of the most exciting findings in solid-state physics... Researchers are pushing back the frontiers and opening doors to reveal why things happen and how things work.*

16 When you are **out of doors**, you are not inside a building, but in the open air. *The weather was fine enough for working out of doors.* PHR after v, v-link PHR =outdoors

17 If you **see** someone **to the door**, you go to the door with a visitor when they leave. V inflects

18 If someone **shows** you **the door**, they ask you to leave because they are angry with you. *Would they forgive and forget – or show him the door?* V inflects

19 • **at death's door**: see **death**.

doorbell /dɔːʳbel/ **doorbells.** A **doorbell** is a bell on the outside of a house which you can ring so that the people inside know that you want to see them. ◆◇◇◇◇ N-COUNT

doorkeeper /dɔːʳkiːpəʳ/ **doorkeepers.** A **doorkeeper** is a person whose job is to stand at the door of a building such as a hotel and help people who are going in or out. N-COUNT

doorknob /dɔːʳnɒb/ **doorknobs.** A **doorknob** is a round handle on a door. N-COUNT

doorman /dɔːʳmən/ **doormen.** A **doorman** is a person whose job is to stay by the main entrance of a large building, and help people visiting the building. N-COUNT

doormat /dɔːʳmæt/ **doormats**

1 A **doormat** is a mat by a door which people can wipe their shoes on when they enter a house or building. N-COUNT

2 If you say that someone is a **doormat**, you are criticizing them because they let other people treat them badly, and do not complain or defend themselves when they are being treated unfairly; an informal word. *If you always give in to others you will end up feeling like a doormat.* N-COUNT PRAGMATICS

doorstep /dɔːʳstep/ **doorsteps, doorstepping, doorstepped** ◆◇◇◇◇

1 A **doorstep** is a step in front of a door on the outside of a building. N-COUNT

2 In British English, when journalists **doorstep** someone, they go to their home and try to get an interview or photographs, even when the person does not want to talk to them; used showing disapproval. *The newspaper contacted his grandmother to trace his present address, and later doorstepped him at his home.* VERB PRAGMATICS V n

3 If a place is **on** your **doorstep**, it is very near to where you live. If something happens **on** your **doorstep**, it happens very close to where you live. *It is all too easy to lose sight of what is happening on our own doorstep... They have to put up with a giant oil refinery right on their doorstep.* PHRASE: v-link PHR, PHR after v ≠far off

doorstop /dɔːʳstɒp/ **doorstops.** A **doorstop** is a heavy object that you use to keep a door open. N-COUNT

door-to-door. See **door**.

doorway /dɔːʳweɪ/ **doorways** ◆◆◇◇◇

1 A **doorway** is a space in a wall where a door opens and closes. *Hannah looked up to see David and another man standing in the doorway... We were escorted through a low doorway.* N-COUNT

2 A **doorway** is a covered space just outside the door of a building. *...homeless people sleeping in shop doorways.* N-COUNT

dope /doʊp/ **dopes, doping, doped** ◆◇◇◇◇

1 **Dope** is a drug, usually an illegal drug such as cannabis or cocaine; used in informal English. *A man asked them if they wanted to buy some dope... He has failed a dope test for cocaine... You got dope dealers on every corner.* N-UNCOUNT =drug

2 If someone **dopes** a person or animal or **dopes** their food or drink, they put drugs into their food or drink, or force them to take drugs. *Anyone could have got in and doped the wine... I'd been doped with Somnolin... They've got him doped to the eyeballs. ...recent cases of horse doping.* VERB =drug V n be V-ed with n V-ed V-ing Also V n with n

3 If someone calls a person a **dope**, they think that the person is stupid; an informal use. *I'm more comfortable with them. I don't feel I'm such a dope.* N-COUNT PRAGMATICS =idiot

4 **Dope** is information which you have been given illegally or secretly; an informal use. *The government had plenty of dope on him.* N-UNCOUNT =lowdown

doped up. If someone is **doped up**, they are in a state where they cannot think clearly because they are under the influence of drugs; an informal use. *'How do you feel.'—'A bit doped-up, but okay.'... The girl lay on an army cot, all doped up with Valium.* ADJ-GRADED: usu v-link ADJ

dopey /doʊpi/

1 Someone who is **dopey** is sleepy, as though they have been drugged. *The medicine always made him feel dopey and unable to concentrate.* ADJ-GRADED =groggy

2 If you describe someone as **dopey**, you mean that they are rather stupid; an informal use. ADJ-GRADED =dozy

dork /dɔːʳk/ **dorks.** If you say that someone is a **dork**, you think they dress badly in old-fashioned clothes and behave very awkwardly in social situations; used in informal American English. *...their unshakeable conviction that family holidays were strictly for dorks.* N-COUNT =nerd

dorm /dɔːʳm/ **dorms.** A **dorm** is the same as a **dormitory**; an informal word. N-COUNT

dormant /dɔːʳmənt/. Something that is **dormant** is not active, growing, or being used at the present time but is capable of becoming active later on. *...when the long dormant volcano of Mount St Helens erupted in 1980... The virus remains dormant in nerve tissue until activated... The United Nations is resuming a diplomatic effort that has lain dormant for almost two decades.* ♦ **dormancy** /dɔːʳmənsi/ *During dormancy the plants must be kept very dry.* ◆◇◇◇◇ ADJ N-UNCOUNT

dormer /dɔːʳməʳ/ **dormers.** A **dormer** or **dormer window** is a window that is built upright in a sloping roof. N-COUNT

dormitory /dɔːʳmɪtri, AM -tɔːri/ **dormitories** ◆◇◇◇◇

1 A **dormitory** is a large bedroom where several people sleep, for example in a boarding school. *...the boys' dormitory... The latest refugees were housed in makeshift dormitories.* N-COUNT

2 In American English, a **dormitory** is a building in a college or university where students live. The usual British term is **hall of residence**. *She lived in a college dormitory.* N-COUNT

3 In British English, if you refer to a place as a **dormitory** suburb or town, you mean that most of the people who live there travel to work in another, larger town nearby. *It had become almost a dormitory suburb of the city.* ADJ: ADJ n

dormouse /dɔːʳmaʊs/ **dormice** /dɔːʳmaɪs/. A **dormouse** is a small rodent that looks like a mouse. It is found in southern England and Wales. N-COUNT

dorsal /dɔːʳsᵊl/. **Dorsal** means relating to the back of a fish or animal; a technical word. *...a dolphin's dorsal fin.* ADJ: ADJ n

dosage /doʊsɪdʒ/ **dosages.** A **dosage** is the amount of a medicine or drug that someone takes or should take. *He was put on a high dosage of vitamin C.* ◆◇◇◇◇ N-COUNT

dose /doʊs/ **doses, dosing, dosed** ◆◆◇◇◇

1 A **dose** of medicine or a drug is a measured amount of it which is intended to be taken at one time. *One dose of penicillin can wipe out the infection.* N-COUNT: oft N of n

2 You can refer to an amount of something as a **dose** of that thing, especially when you want to emphasize that there is a great deal of it. *She was born with a healthy dose of self-confidence... The West is getting a heavy dose of snow and rain today.* N-COUNT: usu adj N of n PRAGMATICS

3 If you **dose** a person or animal with medicinal drug, you give them an amount of it. *The doctor fixed the rib, dosed him heavily with drugs, and said he would probably get better... I dosed myself with quinine.* ► **Dose up** means the same as **dose**. *I dosed him up with Valium.* VERB V n with n V pron-refl with n PHRASAL VERB V n P with n

doss /dɒs/ **dosses, dossing, dossed.** If someone **dosses** somewhere, they sleep in a place which is uncomfortable, usually because they have nowhere else to live; an informal word, used in British English. *Increasing numbers of young people dossing in the streets of our great* VERB V prep/adv *cities also bears witness to much grave family distress.* ► **Doss down** means the same as **doss.** *When we had eaten, we dossed down in the lounge.* PHRASAL VERB V P prep/adv

dosser /dɒsəʳ/ **dossers.** In British English, a **dosser** is a city person who does not have a permanent home and sleeps in the streets or in hostels: an informal word which some people find offensive. N-COUNT

doss-house, doss-houses; also spelled **doss house.** A **doss-house** is a kind of cheap hotel in a city for people who have no home and very little money; an informal word, used in British English. N-COUNT

dossier /dɒsieɪ, -iəʳ/ **dossiers.** A **dossier** is a collection of papers containing information on a particular event, or on a person such as a criminal or a spy. *The company is compiling a dossier of evidence to back its allegations... The government kept dossiers on thousands of its citizens.* ◆◇◇◇◇ N-COUNT: oft N *of/on* n

dost /dʌst/. **Dost** is an old-fashioned way of saying or writing the second person singular form of the verb 'do'.

dot /dɒt/ **dots, dotting, dotted** ◆◆◇◇◇

1 A **dot** is a very small round mark, for example one that is used as the top part of the letter 'i', as a full stop, or as a decimal point. N-COUNT

2 You can refer to something that you can see in the distance and that looks like a small round mark as a **dot.** *Soon they were only dots above the hard line of the horizon.* N-COUNT =speck, spot

3 When things **dot** a place or an area, they are scattered or spread all over it. *Small coastal towns dot the landscape.* VERB V n

4 See also **dotted, polka dots.**

5 If you arrive somewhere or do something **on the dot**, you arrive there or do it at exactly the time that you were supposed to. *They appeared on the dot of 9.50 pm as always... At nine o' clock on the dot, they have breakfast.* PHRASES =punctually

6 If you say that someone **dots the i's and crosses the t's**, you mean that they pay great attention to every small detail in a task; often used to express your annoyance because such detailed work seems unnecessary and takes a very long time. Vs inflect PRAGMATICS

7 **The year dot** is used in informal English to mean a very long time ago. *You've wanted to be a barrister since the year dot.*

dotage /doʊtɪdʒ/. If someone is in their **dotage**, they are very old and becoming weak. *Even in his dotage, the Professor still sits on the committee. ...spending his dotage in a riverside cottage.* N-UNCOUNT: usu poss N

dote /doʊt/ **dotes, doting, doted.** If you say that someone **dotes** on a person or a thing, you mean that they love or care about them very much and ignore any faults they may have. *He dotes on his nine-year-old son.* VERB =adore V *on/upon* n

doth /dʌθ/. **Doth** is an old-fashioned way of saying or writing the third person singular form of the verb 'do'.

doting /doʊtɪŋ/. If you say that someone is, for example, a **doting** mother, husband, or friend, you mean that they show a lot of love for someone. *His doting parents bought him his first racing bike at 13.* ADJ-GRADED: usu ADJ n =adoring

dot matrix printer, dot matrix printers. A **dot matrix printer** is a computer printer using a device with a series of dots or pins stamped onto it to produce words and numbers. N-COUNT

dotted /dɒtɪd/ ◆◇◇◇◇

1 A **dotted** line is a line which is made of a row of dots. *Cut along the dotted line.* • If you **sign on the dotted line**, you formally agree to something by signing an official document. *Once you sign on the dotted line you are committed to that property.* ADJ: usu ADJ n PHRASE: V inflects

2 You use **dotted** to describe something that is covered with large dots. *...a dotted bow tie.* ADJ: usu ADJ n

3 If a place or object **is dotted with** things, it has many of those things scattered over its surface. *The maps were dotted with the names of small towns. ...a pond that's dotted with water lilies.* ADJ: v-link ADJ *with* n

4 If things are **dotted** around a place, they can be found in many different parts of that place. *Many pieces of sculpture are dotted around the house.* ADJ: v-link ADJ prep =scattered

5 See also **dot.**

dotty /dɒti/ **dottier, dottiest.** If you say that someone is **dotty**, you mean that they are slightly mad or likely to do strange things; used in informal British English. *She was obviously going a bit dotty.* ADJ-GRADED PRAGMATICS =eccentric

double /dʌbᵊl/ **doubles, doubling, doubled** ◆◆◆◆◇

1 You use **double** to indicate that something includes or is made of two things of the same kind. *...a pair of double doors into the room from the new entrance hall. ...a lone skier gliding along smooth double tracks. ...three varieties: double toffee, double chocolate, and vanilla.* ADJ: ADJ n

2 You use **double** before a singular noun to refer to two things of the same type that occur together, or that are connected in some way. *...an extremely nasty double murder... The government committed a double blunder... It was to have been a double wedding.* ADJ: ADJ n

3 If something is **double** the amount or size of another thing, it is twice as large. *The offer was to start a new research laboratory at double the salary he was then getting... Leeds Prison is reported to have almost double the number of prisoners it's designed to accommodate. ...tropical Queensland, more than double the size of Texas.* ► Also a pronoun. *On average doctors write just over seven prescriptions each year per patient; in Germany it is double.* PREDET: PREDET *the* n =twice ≠half PRON

4 You use **double** to describe something which is twice the normal size or twice the normal capacity. *...a double helping of ice cream. ...a large double garage... Allow the loaves to rise until just about double in size.* ADJ

5 A **double** room is a room intended for two people, usually a couple, to stay or live in. *...bed and breakfast for £180 for two people in a double room.* ► Also a noun. *The Great Western Hotel is ideal, costing around £40 a night for a double.* ADJ: usu ADJ n N-COUNT

6 A **double** bed is a bed that is wide enough for two people to sleep in. ADJ: ADJ n

7 You use **double** to describe a drink that is twice the normal measure. *He was drinking his double whiskey too fast and scowling.* ► Also a noun. *'Give me a whisky,' Debilly said to Francis. 'Make it a double.'* ADJ: ADJ n N-COUNT

8 **Double** is used when you are spelling a word or telling someone a number to show that a letter or digit is repeated. *Ring four two double two double two if you'd like to speak to our financial adviser.* ADJ: ADJ n

9 When something **doubles** or when you **double** it, it becomes twice as great in number, amount, or size. *The number of managers must double to 100 within 3 years... The program will double the amount of money available to help pay for child care.* V-ERG V V n

10 If you refer to someone as a person's **double**, you mean that they look exactly like them. *Your mother sees you as her double.* N-COUNT: poss N

11 If a person or thing **doubles** as someone or something else, they have a second job or purpose as well as their main one. *...a farmer who doubles as a night nurse... Lots of homes in town double as businesses.* ► **Double up** means the same as **double.** *The lids of the casserole dishes are designed to double up as baking dishes.* VERB V *as* n PHRASAL VERB V P *as* n

12 In tennis or badminton, when people play **doubles**, two teams consisting of two players on each team play against each other on the same court. N-UNCOUNT

13 If you do something **at the double** or **on the double**, you do it very quickly or immediately; an informal expression. *Two soldiers entered at the double and saluted... Come to my office, please, at the double.* PHRASES usu PHR after v =immediately

14 When you **bend double**, you bend the top half of your body downwards a long way. *There wasn't room to stand up and he had to bend double.* V inflects

15 If you are **bent double**, the top half of your body is bent downwards so that your head is close to your knees. *Before sunrise pickers are bent double, plucking each flower with lightning speed.* v-link PHR

16 If you **are seeing double**, there is something wrong with your eyes, and you can see two images instead of one. *For 35 minutes I was walking around in a daze. I was dizzy, seeing double.* V inflects

17 • **in double figures**: see **figure**.

double back. If you **double back** you go back in the direction that you came from. *Double back perhaps 50 yards on Route 64 and there is a sign for Brunswick Road.* PHRASAL VERB VP

double up. If something **doubles** you **up**, or if you **double up**, you bend your body quickly or violently, for example because you are laughing a lot or because you are feeling a lot of pain. **Double over** means the same as **double up**. *...a savage blow in the crutch which doubled him up... Some people laugh so hard that stomach contractions cause them to double up with laughter... Everyone was doubled over in laughter.* PHRASAL VERB ERG VnP VP with/in n V-ed P Also VP

double act, double acts; also spelled **double-act**. Two comedians or entertainers who perform together are referred to as a **double act**. Their performance can also be called a **double act**. *...a famous comedy double act... I met a pal of mine later and he suggested that we do a double act.* N-COUNT

double agent, double agents. A **double agent** is someone who works as a spy for a particular country or organization, but who also works for its enemies. N-COUNT

double-barrelled; spelled **double-barreled** in American English.

1 A **double-barrelled** gun has two barrels. *...a double-barrelled shotgun.* ADJ: ADJ n

2 In British English, a **double-barrelled** surname has two parts which are joined by a hyphen, for example 'Miss J. Heydon-Smith'. ADJ: ADJ n

3 Double-barrelled is used by journalists to describe something such as a plan which has two main parts. *The company announced a double-barreled investment and management-compensation plan.* ADJ: ADJ n

double bass /dʌbəl beɪs/ **double basses;** also spelled **double-bass**. A **double bass** is the largest instrument in the violin family. N-VAR: oft *the* N

double bill, double bills; also spelled **double-bill**. A **double bill** is a theatre or cinema performance in which there are two shows on the programme. N-COUNT: oft N *of* n

double bind, double binds. If you are in a **double bind**, you are in a very difficult situation, usually because any decision you make will work against you achieving your aims. *Women are caught in a double bind, marginalised in the community if they are not wives and mothers, under excessive pressure to be perfect if they are.* N-COUNT: usu sing =catch 22

double bluff, double bluffs. A **double bluff** is an attempt to deceive someone by saying exactly what you intend to do when you know that they will assume you are lying. *They suspected this was a double bluff on the part of Cairo Intelligence. ...a continual round of bluff and double bluff.* N-VAR

double-breasted. A **double-breasted** jacket or suit has two very wide sections at the front of the jacket which overlap when you button them up. ADJ: usu ADJ n

double-check, double-checks, double-checking, double-checked. If you **double-check** something, you examine or test it a second time to make sure that it is completely correct or safe. *Check and double-check spelling and punctuation... Double-check that the ladder is secure... Don't believe what you are told; double-check with an independent source.* VERB Vn V that V *with* n Also V

double chin, double chins. If someone has a **double chin**, they have a fold of fat under their chin, making them look as if they have two chins. N-COUNT: usu sing

double cream. In British English, **double cream** is very thick cream. The usual American expression is **heavy cream**. ◆◇◇◇◇ N-UNCOUNT

double-cross, double-crosses, double-crossing, double-crossed. If someone you trust **double-crosses** you, they do something which harms you instead of doing something they had promised to do; an informal word. *Don't try and double-cross me, Taylor, because I'll kill you... They were frightened of being double-crossed.* ► Also a noun. *...a novel about double-crosses, blackmail and intrigue.* VERB =betray Vn N-COUNT

double-dealing. **Double-dealing** is behaviour which is deliberately deceitful. *He had seen marriages broken, friends estranged, lives ruined by the revelation of double-dealing and betrayal.* N-UNCOUNT =betrayal, duplicity

double-decker, double-deckers

1 A **double-decker** or a **double-decker bus** is a bus that has two levels, so passengers can sit upstairs or downstairs. N-COUNT ≠single-decker

2 Double-decker items or structures have two layers or levels instead of one. *...a double-decker sandwich. ...a double-decker pleasure boat.* ADJ: ADJ n

double-edged

1 If you say that a comment is **double-edged**, you mean that it has two meanings, so that you are not sure whether the person who said it is being critical or is giving praise. *Even his praise is double-edged.* ADJ

2 If you say that something is **double-edged**, you mean that its positive effects are balanced or outweighed by its negative effects. *But tourism is double-edged, for although it's boosting the country's economy, the Reef could be damaged... Riley's early celebrity proved to be double-edged.* • **a double-edged sword**: see **sword**. ADJ-GRADED: usu v-link ADJ

double entendre /duːbəl ɒntɒndrə/ **double entendres.** A **double entendre** is a word or phrase that has two meanings, one of which is rude and often sexual. *He is a master of the pun and the double entendre... He has a fondness for outrageous double entendre.* N-VAR =play on words

double-glaze, double-glazes, double-glazing, double-glazed. If someone **double-glazes** a house or its windows, they fit the windows with a second layer of glass which keeps the inside of the house warmer and quieter. *The company is now offering to double-glaze the windows for £3,900... We recently had our house double-glazed.* ♦ **double-glazed** *Make sure double-glazed windows can be opened easily in an emergency.* VERB Vn *have* n V-ed ADJ

double-glazing. If someone has **double-glazing** in their house, their windows are fitted with two layers of glass. People install double-glazing in order to keep buildings warmer or more quiet. N-UNCOUNT

double-header double-headers; also spelled **doubleheader** in American English. In North America, a **doubleheader** is a sporting contest between two teams, usually baseball teams, that involves two separate games being played one after the other on the same match programme. N-COUNT

double life, double lives. If you say that someone is living a **double life**, you mean that they lead two separate and very different lives, and they appear to be a different person in each. *She threatened to publicly expose his double life if he left her.* N-COUNT: usu sing

double-park, double-parks, double-parking, double-parked. If someone **double-parks** their car or their car **double parks**, they park in a road by the side of another parked car. *Murray double-parked his car... The car pulled in and double-parked in front of the town hall.* V-ERG Vn V

double-quick. If you say that you will do something **double-quick**, you are emphasizing that you will do it very quickly; an informal word. *Don't worry. We'll have you out of here double-quick.* • **In double quick time** means the same as **double-quick**. *I was over the fence in double-quick time.* ADV: ADV after v PRAGMATICS PHRASE: PHR after v

doublespeak /dʌbəlspiːk/. If you refer to what someone says as **doublespeak**, you are criticizing them for presenting things in a way that is intended to mislead people and hide the truth. *...the doublespeak so fluently used by governments and their press offices.* ◆◇◇◇◇ N-UNCOUNT PRAGMATICS

double standard, double standards. If you accuse a person or institution of applying **double** ◆◇◇◇◇ N-COUNT PRAGMATICS

standards in their treatment of different groups of people, you mean that they unfairly allow more freedom of behaviour to one group than to another. *Mrs Starky accused the local police of operating double standards... We cannot have a double standard where we say everybody else must play by the rules, but we do not need to.*

doublet /dʌblɪt/ **doublets.** A **doublet** was a short, tight-fitting jacket that was worn by men in the fifteenth, sixteenth, and early seventeenth centuries. [N-COUNT]

double-take, double-takes. If you do a **double-take** when you see or hear something strange or surprising, you hesitate for a moment before reacting to it because you wonder if you really saw or heard what you thought you saw or heard. *I did a double-take when I saw her. I wasn't even sure it was a woman, dressed as she was in biker's gear.* [N-COUNT]

double-talk; also spelled **double talk**. If you refer to something someone says as **double-talk**, you mean that it can deceive people or is difficult to understand because it has two possible meanings. [N-UNCOUNT]

double vision. If someone is suffering from **double vision**, they see a single object as two objects, for example because they are ill or have drunk too much alcohol. [N-UNCOUNT]

doubly /dʌbli/ ◆◇◇◇◇

1 You use **doubly** to indicate that there are two aspects or features that are having an influence on a particular situation. *She now felt doubly guilty; she had embarrassed Franklin and she had cost her partner money... Employees choosing to move with a relocating company benefit doubly from employer-related housing assistance and lower house prices.* [ADV: ADV group, ADV with v]

2 You use **doubly** to emphasize that something exists or happens to a greater degree than usual. *Mr. Bush's task is made doubly difficult by his election pledge of 'no new taxes'... Secretly he was afraid; doubly so.* [ADV: ADV adj/adv]

doubt /daʊt/ **doubts, doubting, doubted** ◆◆◆◆◇

1 If you have **doubt** or **doubts** about something, you feel uncertain about it and do not know whether it is true or possible. If you say you have no **doubt** about it, you mean that you are certain it is true. *This raises doubts about the point of advertising... I had my doubts when she started, but she's getting really good... They were troubled and full of doubt... There can be little doubt that bombing Serbia would drive thousands more to take up arms... Local inhabitants haven't the slightest doubt as to who is the rightful owner.* [N-VAR: oft N *about/as to* n, N that =uncertainty]

2 If you **doubt** whether something is true or possible, you believe that it is probably not true or possible. *Others doubted whether that would happen... He doubted if he would learn anything new from Marie... She doubted that the accident could have been avoided.* [VERB ≠believe; V whether, V if, V that]

3 If you **doubt** something, you believe that it might not be true or genuine. *No one doubted his ability... Nobody that I spoke to doubted his sincerity as a politician.* [VERB; V n]

4 If you **doubt** someone or **doubt** their word, you think that they may not be telling the truth. *No one directly involved with the case doubted him... I still have no reason to doubt his word.* [VERB ≠trust; V n]

5 You say that something is **beyond doubt** or **beyond reasonable doubt** when you are certain that it is true and it cannot be contradicted or disproved. *A referendum showed beyond doubt that voters wanted independence... His ability is beyond any doubt.* [PHRASES; PHR after v, v-link PHR; PRAGMATICS]

6 If you are **in doubt** about something, you feel unsure or uncertain about it. *He is in no doubt as to what is needed... When in doubt, call the doctor.* [v-link PHR, oft PHR *about/as to* n]

7 You say **I doubt it** as a response to a question or statement about something that you think is untrue or unlikely. *'Somebody would have seen her.'—'I doubt it, not on Monday.'* [CONVENTION; PRAGMATICS]

8 If you say that something is **in doubt** or **open to doubt**, you consider it to be uncertain or unreliable. *The outcome was still in doubt... That claim is increasingly open to doubt.* [v-link PHR =uncertain]

9 You use **no doubt** to emphasize that something seems certain or very likely to you. *The contract for this will no doubt be widely advertised... She's a very sweet woman, as you no doubt know by now.* [PHR with cl; PRAGMATICS =undoubtedly]

10 You use **no doubt** to indicate that you accept the truth of a particular point, but that you do not consider it is important or contradicts the rest of what you are saying. *No doubt I'm biased, but it was the most cruel, evil human face I ever set eyes on... No doubt many will regard these as harsh words, but regrettably they are true.* [PHR with cl; PRAGMATICS]

11 If you say that something is true **without doubt** or **without a doubt**, you are emphasizing that it is definitely true. *Without doubt this has become the most important relationship I've developed while at college... The refugees, without a doubt, are the most vulnerable.* [PHR with cl; PRAGMATICS =undoubtedly]

12 • **the benefit of the doubt**: see **benefit.** • **a shadow of a doubt**: see **shadow**.

doubter /daʊtəʳ/ **doubters.** If you refer to people as **doubters**, you mean that they have doubts about something, especially their religious or political system. *Some doubters fear this may not be quite the good news it appears to be.* [N-COUNT: usu pl ≠believer]

doubtful /daʊtfʊl/ ◆◆◇◇◇

1 If it is **doubtful** that something will happen, it seems unlikely to happen or you are uncertain whether it will happen. *For a time it seemed doubtful that he would move at all... It is doubtful whether Tweed, even with his fluent French, passed for one of the locals... Whether the authorities will allow inspection is highly doubtful.* [ADJ-GRADED: usu v-link ADJ, oft *it* v-link ADJ that/wh; PRAGMATICS =debatable]

2 If you are **doubtful** about something, you feel unsure or uncertain about it. *I was still very doubtful about the chances for success... Why did he sound so doubtful?* ♦ **doubtfully** *Keeton shook his head doubtfully.* [ADJ-GRADED: usu v-link ADJ, oft ADJ *about* n =dubious; ADV-GRADED: ADV after v =dubiously]

3 If you say that something is of **doubtful** quality or value, you mean that it is of low quality or value. *...selling something that is overpriced or of doubtful quality... They also seemed of very doubtful value. ...information that he described as having doubtful reliability.* [ADJ-GRADED: usu ADJ n; PRAGMATICS =dubious]

4 If a sports player is **doubtful** for a match or event, he or she seems unlikely to play, usually because of injury; used in journalism. *Forsyth is doubtful for tonight's game with a badly bruised leg.* [ADJ-GRADED: oft ADJ *for* n]

Doubting Thomas /daʊtɪŋ tɒməs/ **Doubting Thomases.** If you describe someone as a **Doubting Thomas**, you mean they refuse to believe something until they see definite proof or evidence of it. [N-COUNT]

doubtless /daʊtləs/. If you say that something is **doubtless** the case, you mean that you think it is probably or almost certainly the case. *He will doubtless try and persuade his colleagues to change their minds... Doubtless he was justified in some of his criticism of the media... She took off her shoes, doubtless because her feet hurt.* ◆◇◇◇◇ [ADV: ADV with cl/group; PRAGMATICS =no doubt]

douche /duːʃ/ **douches, douching, douched**

1 A **douche** is a method of washing the vagina using a jet of water. You also refer to the object which you use to wash the vagina in this way as a **douche**. [N-COUNT]

2 To **douche** means to wash the vagina using a jet of water. *Never douche if you are pregnant.* [VERB; V]

dough /doʊ/ **dough** ◆◇◇◇◇

1 **Dough** is a fairly firm mixture of flour, water, and sometimes also fat and sugar. It can be cooked to make bread, pastry, and biscuits. *Roll out the dough into one large circle... Work the flour and yeast mixture together until you have a sticky dough.* [N-MASS]

2 You can refer to money as **dough**; an old-fashioned informal use. *He worked hard for his dough.* [N-UNCOUNT]

doughnut /doʊnʌt/ **doughnuts;** also spelled **donut**. A **doughnut** is a bread-like cake made ◆◇◇◇◇ [N-COUNT] from sweet dough that has been cooked in hot fat.

doughty /daʊti/. If you describe someone as a **doughty** fighter or campaigner, you mean they are brave, determined, and not easily defeated; an old-fashioned word. *His doughty campaigns for the underprivileged have earned him national respect.* ADJ-GRADED: ADJ n PRAGMATICS

doughy /doʊi/. If you describe something as **doughy**, you mean that it has a fairly soft texture like dough. *Add water and mix with a knife to a doughy consistency.* ADJ-GRADED

dour /dʊəʳ, daʊəʳ/. If you describe someone as **dour**, you mean that they have a rather severe and unfriendly manner. *...a dour, taciturn man... No wonder he looked so dour.* ◆◇◇◇◇ ADJ-GRADED ♦ **dourly** *'They criticized it for being jingoistic,' he says dourly.* ADV-GRADED: usu ADV with v, also ADV adj

douse /daʊs/ **douses, dousing, doused;** also spelled **dowse.** ◆◇◇◇◇

1 If you **douse** a fire, you stop it burning by pouring a lot of water over it. *The pumps were started and the crew began to douse the fire with water.* VERB V n

2 If you **douse** someone or something with a liquid, you throw a lot of that liquid over them. *They hurled abuse at their victim as they doused him with petrol.* VERB V n *with/in* n

3 If you **douse** a light, you turn it off. *I doused the headlights and got out.* VERB V n

dove, doves; pronounced /dʌv/ for meanings 1 and 2, and /doʊv/ for meaning 3. ◆◇◇◇◇

1 A **dove** is a bird that looks like pigeon but is smaller and lighter in colour. Doves are often used as a symbol of peace. • See also **turtle dove**. N-COUNT

2 In politics, you can refer to people who support the use of peaceful methods to solve difficult situations as **doves**. Compare **hawk**. *A clear split over tactics appears to be emerging between doves and hawks in the party.* N-COUNT

3 In American English, **dove** is sometimes used as the past tense of **dive**.

dovecote /dʌvkɒt, -koʊt/ **dovecotes;** also spelled **dovecot**. A **dovecote** is a small building or a container for pigeons or doves to live in. N-COUNT

dovetail /dʌvteɪl/ **dovetails, dovetailing, dovetailed**

1 If two ideas or things **dovetail** or if one idea or thing **dovetails** with another, the two ideas or things fit together neatly or have some common characteristics. *I'm following up a few things that might dovetail. ...an attempt to look for areas where U.S. interests can dovetail with Japanese concerns... It is important that we dovetail our respective interests... The management of local affairs should dovetail regional interests with those of the country as a whole.* V-RECIP-ERG pl-n V, V *with* n, V pl-n, V n *with* n

2 A **dovetail** or a **dovetail joint** is a wedge-shaped joint used in carpentry for fitting two pieces of wood tightly together. N-COUNT

dovish /dʌvɪʃ/; also spelled **doveish**. Journalists use **dovish** to describe politicians or governments who are in favour of using peaceful and diplomatic methods to achieve something, rather than using force and violence. *It must be said that the defence minister is a little bit more dovish than other people in the ruling elite.* ADJ-GRADED ≠hawkish

dowager /daʊədʒəʳ/ **dowagers**

1 You use **dowager** to refer to the widow of a duke, emperor, or other high-ranking man. *...the Dowager Countess Spencer... Nobody was allowed to eat in the Empress Dowager's presence.* ▶ Also a noun. ADJ: ADJ n, n ADJ; N-COUNT

2 If you describe a woman as a **dowager**, you mean that she is old and rich or grand-looking; a literary use. *...like stately dowagers on a traipse to the water's edge.* N-COUNT

dowdy /daʊdi/ **dowdier, dowdiest.** If you describe someone or their clothes as **dowdy**, you mean their clothes are dull and unfashionable; used showing disapproval. *...playing hostess to a lot of officials and their dowdy wives... Her clothes were clean but dowdy.* ADJ-GRADED PRAGMATICS =drab, frumpish

dowel /daʊəl/ **dowels.** A **dowel** is a short thin piece of wood or metal which is used for joining larger pieces of wood or metal together. N-COUNT

down 1 preposition and adverb uses

down /daʊn/ ◆◆◆◆◆

Down is often used with verbs of movement, such as 'fall' and 'pull', and also in phrasal verbs such as 'bring down' and 'calm down'.

1 If someone or something goes **down** something such as a slope or a pipe, they go towards the ground or to a lower level. *We're going down a mountain... A man came down the stairs to meet them... The tears began flooding down her cheeks.* ▶ Also an adverb. *She went down to the kitchen again... She sat on the window seat until they climbed down from the roof... I saw her push the boulder down on you... Any unauthorized war planes flying in the area are to be shot down.* PREP ≠up; ADV: ADV after v

2 If you are a particular distance **down** something, you are that distance below the top or surface of it. *He managed to cling on to a ledge 40ft down the rock face... The union leader was last night staging a protest vigil 400 yards down a mineshaft.* ▶ Also an adverb. *For the last 18 months miners have cut a face to develop a new shaft 400 metres down.* PREP: amount PREP n; ADV: amount ADV

3 You use **down** to say that you are looking or facing in a direction that is towards the ground or towards a lower level. *She was still looking down at her papers... She put her head down, her hands over her face... He bent down and picked up a rock from the rubble.* ADV: ADV after v ≠up

4 If you put something **down**, you put it onto a surface. *Danny put down his glass... After two rings I put down the phone... He laid his knife down.* ADV: ADV after v

5 If you go or look **down** something such as a road or river, you go or look along it. If you are **down** a road or river, you are somewhere along it. *They set off at a jog up one street and down another... Karl looked down the street... She lives a few miles down the road at Burnham. ...sailing down the river on a barge.* PREP: oft amount PREP n ≠up

6 If you are travelling to a particular place, you can say that you are going **down** to that place, especially if you are going towards the south or to a lower level of land. **Down** can also suggest that your journey is casual or unhurried; used in spoken English. *I went down to L.A. all the way from Seattle... I have seen him walking down to the shops a mile or so away... I'll take you back down to the valley. ...holidaymakers coming down here in the summer.* ADV: ADV after v

7 If you are **down** a place, you are at that place. If you go **down** a place, you go to that place; an informal use, which some people believe is incorrect. *People are down the pub, getting drunk... We got in the car and went down the supermarket and started buying food.* PREP: v-link PREP n, v PREP n

8 If an amount of something goes **down**, it decreases. If an amount of something is **down**, it has decreased and is at a lower level than it was. *Interest rates came down today... Inflation will be down to three percent... My weight went down to seventy pounds... My department had a healthy interest in keeping expenses down... The Dow Jones industrial average is down 5 points at 2,913. ...with hotel occupation down by around half.* ADV: ADV after v, *be* ADV, oft ADV *to/from/by* amount ≠up

9 If you say that there are a number of things **down** and a number **to go**, you are saying how many of the things have already been dealt with and how many remain to be dealt with. *Thirteen months down, twenty-four years to go.* PHRASE: PHR with amount

10 **Down to** a particular detail means including everything, even that detail. **Down to** a particular person means including everyone, even that person. *I was a soldier down to my shoelaces. ...from the chairman right down to the tea ladies.* PHR-PREP

11 If you are **down to** a certain amount of something, you have only that amount left. *The poor man's down to his last £3.* PHR-PREP: PREP amount

12 If a situation is **down to** a particular person or thing, it has been caused by that person or thing. *Any mistakes are entirely down to us... That's down to pure hard work.* PHR-PREP

13 If someone or something is **down for** something, it has been arranged that they will do that thing, or that thing will happen. *Mark had told me that he was down for an interview. ...derelict houses that were down for demolition.* PHR-PREP

14 If you are **down with** an illness, you have that illness; an informal use. *One of the office girls was down with the flu. ...a little girl down with that nasty bout of measles.* • See also **come down with.** PHR-PREP

15 If people shout **'down with'** something or someone, they are saying that they dislike them and want to get rid of them. *Demonstrators chanted 'down with communism'.* PHRASE: PHR n PRAGMATICS

16 • **up and down**: see **up.** • **ups and downs**: see **up.** • **down in the dumps**: see **dump.**

down 2 adjective uses

down /daʊn/

1 If you are feeling **down**, you are feeling unhappy or depressed; an informal use. *I have been down since the injury happened... Try to support each other when one of you is feeling down... The old man sounded really down.* ADJ-GRADED: v-link ADJ =depressed

2 If something is **down** on paper, it has been written on the paper. *That date wasn't down on our news sheet.* ADJ: v-link ADJ, usu ADJ *on* n

3 If a piece of equipment, especially a computer system, is **down**, it is temporarily not working because of a fault. *The computer's down again.* ADJ: v-link ADJ ≠operational

down 3 verb uses

down /daʊn/ **downs, downing, downed** ◆◆◇◇◇

1 If you say that someone **downs** food or a drink, you mean that they eat or drink it; used in written English. *We downed bottles of local wine.* VERB =consume V n

2 If something or someone **is downed**, they fall to the ground because they have been hurt or damaged in some way; used in journalism. *A couple of jet fighters were downed during the five-week rebellion... A bank guard shot him in the leg and downed him.* ♦ **downing** *...the downing of an airliner, which killed 107 people.* VERB be V-ed V n V-ed N-UNCOUNT

3 • to **down tools**: see **tool.**

down 4 noun uses

down /daʊn/

1 **Down** consists of the small, soft feathers on young birds. Down is used to make pillows or quilts. *...goose down.* N-UNCOUNT

2 **Down** is very fine hair. *The whole plant is covered with fine down.* • See also **downs.** N-UNCOUNT

down-and-out, down-and-outs; also spelled **down and out.** If you describe someone as **down-and-out**, you mean that they have no job and nowhere to live, and they have no real hope of improving their situation. *...a short story about a down-and-out advertising copywriter... He looked unshaven, shabby, and down-and-out.* ► Also a noun in British English. *...some poor down-and-out in need of a meal... They are both down-and-outs, sleeping under the city's oldest bridge.* ADJ-GRADED: usu ADJ n; N-COUNT =tramp

down-at-heel; also spelled **down at heel.** Something that is **down-at-heel** is in a in bad condition because it has been used too much or has not been looked after properly. If you say that someone is **down-at-heel**, you mean that they are wearing old, worn clothes because they have little money. *...a down-at-heel disco in central East Berlin. ...a down-at-heel waitress in a greasy New York diner.* ADJ-GRADED: usu ADJ n =shabby

downbeat /daʊnbiːt/ **downbeats**

1 If people or their opinions are **downbeat**, they are deliberately casual and restrained about a situation; an informal use. *Its headlines were suitably downbeat and don't scream out. ...a downbeat assessment of 1992's economic prospects.* ADJ-GRADED: usu ADJ n ≠upbeat

2 If you are feeling **downbeat**, you are feeling depressed and pessimistic. *They found him in gloomy, downbeat mood.* ADJ-GRADED ≠optimistic

3 In music, the **downbeat** is the downward movement of the conductor's hand, indicating the first beat of the bar. N-COUNT ≠upbeat

downcast /daʊnkɑːst, -kæst/

1 If you are **downcast**, you are feeling sad and pessimistic. *After his defeat Mr Rabin looked downcast. ...a glum, downcast expression.* ADJ-GRADED: usu v-link ADJ =dejected

2 If your eyes are **downcast**, you are looking towards the ground, usually because you are feeling sad or embarrassed. *Eve remained seated, eyes modestly downcast... She was silent, her eyes downcast.* ADJ: usu v-link ADJ

downer /daʊnəʳ/ **downers**

1 **Downers** are drugs, such as barbiturates, that make you feel sleepy or very calm; an informal use. *She was taking uppers and downers at the time.* N-COUNT ≠upper

2 If you describe a situation as a **downer**, you think that it is very depressing; an informal use. *For divorced people, Christmas can be a downer.* • If you are **on a downer**, you are feeling depressed and pessimistic; an informal use. *We've been on a bit of a downer since the Liverpool game.* N-COUNT: usu sing, a N; PHRASE: v-link PHR

downfall /daʊnfɔːl/ ◆◇◇◇◇

1 The **downfall** of a successful or powerful person or institution is their loss of success or power. *His lack of experience had led to his downfall. ...people wishing to see the downfall of the government.* N-UNCOUNT: also N in pl, usu with poss ≠rise

2 The thing that was a person's **downfall** caused them to fail or lose power. *His honesty had been his downfall... Alan's downfall was women.* N-UNCOUNT: usu with poss =undoing

downgrade /daʊngreɪd/ **downgrades, downgrading, downgraded** ◆◇◇◇◇

1 If something **is downgraded**, it is given less importance than it used to have or than you think it should have. *The boy's condition has been downgraded from critical to serious... The female role has been downgraded altogether in the drive for greater equality.* VB: usu passive ≠upgrade be V-ed

2 If someone **is downgraded**, their job or status is changed so that they become less important or receive less money. *There was no criticism of her work until after she was downgraded... His superiors suspended him, and then downgraded him.* VERB =demote ≠upgrade be V-ed V n

downhearted /daʊnhɑːʳtɪd/. If you are **downhearted**, you are feeling sad and discouraged. *Max sighed, sounding even more downhearted... Don't be too downhearted. There's always a way.* ADJ-GRADED: usu v-link ADJ =dejected

downhill /daʊnhɪl/ ◆◇◇◇◇

1 If something or someone is moving **downhill** or is **downhill**, they are moving down a slope or are located towards the bottom of a hill. *He headed downhill towards the river... The lake itself lies only a few hundred yards off to your right and slightly downhill... It was a clearing just downhill from a peak of eight thousand feet.* ► Also an adjective. *Bessie was on the downhill path. ...downhill ski runs... We began a steady downhill run.* ADV: ADV after v, be ADV, ADV *from* n ≠uphill; ADJ: ADJ n

2 If you say that something is going **downhill**, you mean that it is becoming worse or less successful. *Since I started to work longer hours things have gone steadily downhill... For the movie business, it was all downhill from there... His career was heading downhill fast.* ADV: ADV after v, be ADV

3 If you say that a task or situation is **downhill** after a particular stage or time, you mean that it is easy to deal with after that stage or time. *Well, I guess it's all downhill from here.* ADJ: v-link ADJ

Downing Street /daʊnɪŋ striːt/. **Downing Street** is the street in London in which the Prime Minister and the Chancellor of the Exchequer live. You can also use **Downing Street** to refer to the Prime Minister and his or her officials. *The Prime Minister arrived back at Downing Street from Paris this morning... Downing Street is taking the French opinion polls very seriously indeed.* ◆◆◇◇◇ N-PROPER

download /daʊnloud/ **downloads, downloading, downloaded.** To **download** data means to transfer it to or from a computer along a line such as a telephone line, a radio link, or a computer network. *Users can download their material to a desktop PC back in the office... The machine automatically downloads the required information to his or her fax.* VERB V n

downmarket /daʊnmɑːʳkɪt/; also spelled **down-market.** If you describe a product or service as **downmarket**, you think that they are cheap and are not very good in quality. *...downmarket tele-* ADJ-GRADED: usu ADJ n ≠upmarket

vision drama... It is a downmarket eating house, seating about 60. ► Also an adverb. *Why is the company going downmarket and developing smaller machines?*
ADV: ADV after v ≠upmarket

down payment, down payments; also spelled **downpayment**. If you make a **down payment** on something, you pay only a percentage of the total cost when you buy it. You pay the remaining amount later, usually in instalments. *If you're borrowing money for the down payment, provide a copy of the entire loan agreement... Celeste asked for the money as a down payment on an old farmhouse.*
◆◇◇◇◇ N-COUNT

downplay /daʊnpleɪ/ **downplays, downplaying, downplayed.** If you **downplay** a fact or feature, you try to make people think that it is less important or serious than it really is. *The government and the press are trying to downplay the violence which broke out yesterday. ...to downplay the dangers of nuclear accidents.*
◆◇◇◇◇ VERB =play down; V n

downpour /daʊnpɔːʳ/ **downpours.** A **downpour** is a sudden and unexpected heavy fall of rain. *...sheltering from a sudden downpour of rain.*
◆◇◇◇◇ N-COUNT =cloudburst

downright /daʊnraɪt/. You use **downright** to emphasize unpleasant or bad qualities or behaviour. *...ideas that would have been downright dangerous if put into practice... She was often downright rude to him.* ► Also an adjective. *...suspicion and downright hostility. ...downright bad manners.*
◆◇◇◇◇ ADV: ADV adj PRAGMATICS =positively; ADJ: ADJ n =out-and-out

down-river; also spelled **downriver**. Something that is moving **down-river** is moving towards the mouth of a river, from a point further up the river. Something that is **down-river** is towards the mouth of a river. *By 09.30 we had cast off and were heading down river. ...a big tourist hotel a few hundred yards down-river... Cologne is not so very far down-river from Mainz.* ► Also an adjective. *...downriver factories dispensing billows of smoke.*
ADV: ADV after v, *be* ADV, n ADV, oft ADV *from* n ≠up-river; ADJ: ADJ n ≠up-river

downs /daʊnz/. In British English, **downs** are areas of gentle hills with few trees. *Walking across the downs now reminds me of my favourite childhood memories. ...the Wiltshire downs.*
N-PLURAL: oft in names, usu *the* N

downside /daʊnsaɪd/. The **downside** of a situation is the aspect of it which is less positive, pleasant, or useful than its other aspects. *The downside of this approach is a lack of clear leadership... There is a downside to it: the more she remembers, the more bitter she feels about what has happened.*
◆◇◇◇◇ N-SING: oft *the* N *of* n

downsize /daʊnsaɪz/ **downsizes, downsizing, downsized.** To **downsize** something such as a business or industry means to make it smaller; used in American English. *American manufacturing organizations have been downsizing their factories. ...Soviet plans to downsize its nuclear arsenal. ...today's downsized economy.*
VERB =reduce; V n; V-ed

♦ **downsizing** *...a trend toward downsizing in the personal computer market.*
N-UNCOUNT

downspout /daʊnspaʊt/ **downspouts.** In American English a **downspout** is a pipe attached to the side of building, through which water flows from the roof into a drain. The British word is **drainpipe**. *He installed rain gutters and downspouts.*
N-COUNT =drainpipe

Down's syndrome. American English usually uses the form **Down syndrome. Down's syndrome** is a genetic disorder in which a person is born with a flat forehead and sloping eyes and lower than average intelligence.
N-UNCOUNT =mongolism

downstage /daʊnsteɪdʒ/. When an actor is **downstage** or moves **downstage**, he or she is or moves towards the front part of the stage; a technical word. *Krishna stands downstage in the open area.* ► Also an adjective. *...downstage members of the cast.*
ADV: ADV after v, *be* ADV ≠upstage; ADJ: ADJ n

downstairs /daʊnsteəʳz/ ◆◆◇◇◇

1 If you go **downstairs** in a building, you go down a staircase towards the ground floor. *Denise went downstairs and made some tea.*
ADV: ADV after v ≠upstairs

2 If something or someone is **downstairs** in a building, they are on the ground floor or on a lower floor than you. *The telephone was downstairs in the entrance hall... Everybody was downstairs watching a movie. ...the woman who lives in the flat downstairs.*
ADV: *be* ADV, n ADV ≠upstairs

3 **Downstairs** means situated on the ground floor of a building or on a lower floor than you are. *She repainted the downstairs rooms and closed off the second floor.*
ADJ: ADJ n ≠upstairs

4 **The downstairs** of a building is its lower floor or floors. *The downstairs of the two little houses had been entirely refashioned.*
N-SING: *the* N ≠upstairs

downstream /daʊnstriːm/. Something that is moving **downstream** is moving towards the mouth of a river, from a point further up the river. Something that is **downstream** is further towards the mouth of a river than where you are. *We had drifted downstream. ...a district called Lupitu, which in fact was downstream of the dam... Communities downstream have been alerted.* ► Also an adjective. *They will destroy dams in the Kurdistan mountains, flooding Baghdad and other downstream cities.*
◆◇◇◇◇ ADV: ADV after v, *be* ADV, n ADV, oft ADV *of/from* n ≠upstream; ADJ: ADJ n ≠upstream

downswing /daʊnswɪŋ/ **downswings.** A **downswing** is a sudden decline in something such as an economy, that had previously been improving. *Industry may disappear if the manufacturing economy remains on a downswing. ...inflation and the threat of an economic downswing.*
N-COUNT: usu sing ≠upswing

downtime /daʊntaɪm/. In industry, **downtime** is the time during which machinery or equipment is not operating. *On the production line, downtime has been reduced from 55% per cent to 26%.*
N-UNCOUNT

down-to-earth. If you say that someone is **down-to-earth**, you approve of the fact that they concern themselves with practical things and actions, rather than with abstract theories. *Gloria is probably the most down to earth person I've ever met. ...her sincerity and her down-to-earth common sense... Their ideas seem to be far more down to earth and sensible.*
◆◇◇◇◇ ADJ-GRADED PRAGMATICS =practical

downtown /daʊntaʊn/. In American English, **downtown** places are in or towards the centre of a large town or city, where the shops and places of business are. *...an office in downtown Chicago.* ► Also an adverb. *By day he worked downtown for American Standard... You have to be downtown in a hurry.*
◆◆◇◇◇ ADJ: ADJ n ≠uptown; ADV: ADV after v, *be* ADV ≠uptown

downtrend /daʊntrend/. A **downtrend** is a general decline in something such as a company's profits or the economy. *The increase slowed to 0.4 percent, possibly indicating the start of a downtrend.*
N-SING ≠uptrend

downtrodden /daʊntrɒdᵊn/. People who are **downtrodden** are treated very badly by people with power, and do not have the ability or the energy to rebel. *The owner is making huge profits at the expense of downtrodden peasants... His mother was old, badly dressed and obviously downtrodden.* ► **The downtrodden** are people who are downtrodden. *...support for the downtrodden and underprivileged.*
ADJ =oppressed; N-PLURAL: *the* N =oppressed

downturn /daʊntɜːʳn/ **downturns.** If there is a **downturn** in the economy or in a company or industry, it becomes worse or less successful than it had been. *They predicted a severe economic downturn. ...unchanged profits for 1990 due to a sharp downturn in the industry.*
◆◇◇◇◇ N-COUNT: oft N *in* n ≠upturn

down under. In British English, you can refer to Australia and New Zealand as **down under**; an informal expression. *For summer skiing down under, there is no better place than New Zealand.*
◆◇◇◇◇ PHRASE: prep PHR, PHR after v

downward /daʊnwəʳd/ ◆◇◇◇◇

1 A **downward** movement or look is directed towards a lower place or a lower level. *...a firm downward movement of the hands.* ● See also **downwards.**
ADJ: ADJ n ≠upward

2 If you refer to a **downward** trend, you mean that something is decreasing or that a situation is getting worse. *The downward trend in home ownership is likely to continue. ...a decline*
ADJ: ADJ n

in the economy, resulting in a general downward spiral.

downwards /daʊnwəʳdz/; the form **downward** is also used. ♦◇◇◇◇

1 If you move or look **downwards**, you move or look towards the ground or a lower level. *Benedict pointed downwards again with his stick... She gazed downwards... The child lay face downwards.* ADV: ADV after v, n ADV ≠upwards

2 If an amount or rate moves **downwards**, it decreases. *Inflation is moving firmly downwards.* ADV: ADV after v

3 If you want to emphasize that a statement applies to everyone in an organization, you can say that it applies from its leader **downwards**. *...from the Prime Minister downwards.* ADV: from n ADV PRAGMATICS

downwind /daʊnwɪnd/. If something moves **downwind**, it moves in the same direction as the wind. If something is **downwind**, the wind is blowing towards it. *He attempted to return downwind to the airfield. ...people who are living downwind of Nevada nuclear test sites.* ▶ Also an adjective. *...the downwind end of the field.* ADV: ADV after v, be ADV, oft ADV of n ≠upwind; ADJ: ADJ n

downy /daʊni/ **downier, downiest**

1 Something that is **downy** is filled or covered with small soft feathers. *...the warm downy quilt. ...the white downy bodies of two chicks.* ADJ-GRADED: usu ADJ n

2 Something that is **downy** is covered with very fine hairs. *...tiny toes and fingers, his downy head and beautiful skin. ...leaves that are often downy underneath.* ADJ-GRADED =velvety

dowry /daʊəri/ **dowries.** A woman's **dowry** is the money and goods which, in some cultures, her family gives to the man that she marries. *The money from her dowry was invested in her mother's store.* N-COUNT

dowse /daʊs/ **dowses, dowsing, dowsed.** If someone **dowses** for underground water, minerals, or some other substance, they search for it with the aid of a special rod or a pendulum. *He said that dowsing for water is complete nonsense... Terry Ross dowses oil and ore in South America for big companies. ...a dowsing rod.* • See also **douse**. ♦◇◇◇◇ VERB V for n V n V-ing Also V

doyen /dɔɪən, dɔɪen/ **doyens.** If you refer to a man as the **doyen** of a group or profession, you mean that he is the oldest and most experienced and respected member of it; a formal word, used showing approval. *Sir Robin Day is widely regarded as the doyen of political interviewers.* N-COUNT: usu sing, usu the N of n PRAGMATICS

doyenne /dɔɪen/ **doyennes.** If you refer to a woman as the **doyenne** of a group or profession, you mean that she is the oldest and most experienced and respected woman in it; a formal word, used showing approval. *Jean Muir has often been described as the doyenne of British fashion.* N-COUNT: usu sing, usu the N of n PRAGMATICS

doze /doʊz/ **dozes, dozing, dozed.** When you **doze**, you sleep lightly or for a short period, especially during the daytime. *For a while she dozed fitfully.* ▶ Also a noun. *After lunch I had a doze.* ♦◇◇◇◇ VERB =nap V; N-SING: a N

doze off. If you **doze off** you fall into a light sleep, especially during the daytime. *I closed my eyes for a minute and must have dozed off.* PHRASAL VERB V P

dozen /dʌzᵊn/ **dozens.** The plural form is **dozen** after a number, or after a word or expression referring to a number, such as 'several' or 'a few'. ♦♦♦♦◇

1 If you have a **dozen** things, you have twelve of them. *...a dozen eggs... You will be able to take ten dozen bottles free of duty through customs... He ordered a dozen of their best red roses... His chicken eggs sell for $22 a dozen.* NUM: usu a/num NUM

2 You can refer to a group of approximately twelve things or people as a **dozen** things or people. You can refer to a group of approximately six things or people as **half a dozen** things or people. *I was sitting only a dozen feet away... In half a dozen words, he had explained the bond that linked them... The riot left four people dead and several dozen injured.* NUM: usu a/num NUM

3 If you refer to **dozens of** things or people, you are emphasizing that there are very many of them. *...a storm which destroyed dozens of homes and buildings.* ▶ Also a pronoun. *Just as revealing are Mr Johnson's portraits, of which there are dozens.* QUANT: QUANT of pl-n PRAGMATICS =loads of; PRON

dozy /doʊzi/ **dozier, doziest**

1 If you are **dozy**, you are feeling sleepy and not very alert. *Maybe I eat too much and that's what makes me dozy.* ADJ-GRADED =drowsy

2 In informal British English, if you describe someone as **dozy**, you mean they are rather stupid and slow to understand things. ADJ-GRADED PRAGMATICS

Dr, Drs; this abbreviation is usually followed by a full stop in American English. ♦♦♦♦◇

1 **Dr** is a written abbreviation for **Doctor**. *...Dr John Hardy of St Mary's Medical School in London.*

2 **Dr** is used as a written abbreviation for **Drive** when it is part of a street name. *...6 Queen's Dr.*

drab /dræb/ **drabber, drabbest** ♦◇◇◇◇

1 If you describe something as **drab**, you think that it is dull and boring to look at or experience. *Mary was wearing the same drab grey dress. ...his drab little office... The rest of the day's activities often seemed drab or depressing.* ♦ **drabness** *...the dusty drabness of nearby villages.* ADJ-GRADED =dreary; N-UNCOUNT

2 See also **dribs and drabs**.

drachma /drækmə/ **drachmas.** The **drachma** is the unit of money that is used in Greece. ▶ The **drachma** is also used to refer to the Greek currency system. *In April 1992 the Greek drachma was the only Community currency not yet part of the EMS exchange-rate mechanism.* N-COUNT: num N; N-SING: the N

draconian /drəkoʊniən/. **Draconian** laws or measures are extremely harsh and severe; a formal word. *...indications that there would be no draconian measures to lower US healthcare costs. ...draconian censorship laws.* ♦◇◇◇◇ ADJ-GRADED: usu ADJ n

draft /drɑːft, dræft/ **drafts, drafting, drafted** ♦♦♦◇◇

1 A **draft** is an early version of a letter, book, or speech. *I rewrote his rough draft, which was published under my name... I faxed a first draft of this article to him.* N-COUNT: usu with supp

2 When you **draft** a letter, book, or speech, you write the first version of it. *He drafted a standard letter to the editors... The legislation was drafted by House Democrats.* VERB V n

3 If you **are drafted**, you are ordered to serve in the armed forces. *During the Second World War, he was drafted into the US Army... He wasn't drafted for the war; he volunteered for the Navy.* VB: usu passive =conscript be V-ed into n be V-ed

4 If people **are drafted** into a place, they are moved there to do a particular job. *Extra police have been drafted into the town after the violence... The manager will make a special plea to draft the player into his squad as a replacement.* VERB be V-ed in/into n V n in/into n Also be V-ed

5 **The draft** is the practice of ordering people to serve in the armed forces, usually for a limited period of time. *...his effort to avoid the draft.* N-SING: the N =conscription

6 A **draft** is a written order for payment of money by a bank, especially from one bank to another. *The money was payable by a draft drawn by the home... Ten days later Carmen received a bank draft for a plane ticket.* N-COUNT: oft by N

7 See also **draught**.

draft dodger, draft dodgers. A **draft dodger** is someone who avoids joining the armed forces when normally they would be obliged to join; used showing disapproval. N-COUNT PRAGMATICS

draftee /drɑːftiː, dræft-/ **draftees.** In American English, a **draftee** is the same as a **conscript**. N-COUNT

draftsman, draftsmen /drɑːftsmən, dræfts-/. See **draughtsman**.

drafty /drɑːfti, dræfti/. See **draughty**.

drag /dræg/ **drags, dragging, dragged** ♦♦♦◇◇

1 If you **drag** something, you pull it along the ground, often with difficulty. *He got up and dragged his chair towards the table.* VERB V n prep/adv

2 If someone **drags** you somewhere, they pull you there, or force you to go there by physically threatening you. *The vigilantes dragged the men out of the vehicles... There were no signs she'd been dragged across the grass.* VERB V n prep/adv

3 If someone **drags** you somewhere you do not want to go, they make you go there. *When you can drag him away from his work, he can also be a devoted father... I've been dragged back from Australia for no sufficient reason.* VERB V n adv/prep

4 If you say that you **drag** yourself somewhere, you are emphasizing that you have to make a very strong effort to go there. *I find it really hard to drag myself out and exercise regularly. ...if you manage to drag yourself away from the luxury of the hotel.* VERB PRAGMATICS V pron-refl adv/prep

5 If you **drag** your foot or your leg behind you, you walk with great difficulty because you foot or leg is injured in some way. *He was barely able to drag his poisoned leg behind him... He drags his leg, and he can hardly lift his arm.* VERB V n prep V n

6 If the police **drag** a river or lake, they pull nets or hooks across the bottom of it in order to look for something. *Yesterday police frogmen dragged a small pond on the Common.* VERB V n

7 If a period of time or an event **drags**, it is very boring and seems to last a long time. *The minutes dragged past... The pacing was uneven, and the early second act dragged.* VERB V adv V

8 If something is **a drag on** the development or progress of something, it slows it down or makes it more difficult. *The satellite acts as a drag on the shuttle... Spending cuts will put a drag on growth.* N-SING: *a* N *on* n

9 If you say that something is **a drag**, you mean that it is a nuisance or is very dull; an informal use. *As far as shopping for clothes goes, it's a drag... A dry sandwich is a drag to eat.* N-SING: *a* N, oft N to-inf PRAGMATICS

10 If you take a **drag** on a cigarette or pipe that you are smoking, you take in air through it; an informal use. *He took a drag on his cigarette, and exhaled the smoke.* N-COUNT: oft N *on* n

11 Drag is also the resistance to the movement that is experienced by something that is moving through air or through a fluid; a technical term in science. *The drag of those extra air molecules brought the satellite crashing to Earth.* N-UNCOUNT: oft *the* N *of* n

12 Drag is the wearing of women's clothes by a male entertainer. *Entertainment is laid on too, in the form of drag on Wednesdays and strippers on Sundays... The neighborhood is given over to performers, stilt walkers and drag queens.* N-UNCOUNT: oft N n ● If a man is **in drag**, he is wearing women's clothes. *The band dressed up in drag.* PHRASE: PHR after v, v-link PHR

13 If you **drag** your **feet** or **drag** your **heels**, you delay doing something or do it very slowly because you do not want to do it. *The government, he claimed, was dragging its feet, and this was definitely threatening moves towards peace.* PHRASE: V inflects =hold back

drag down PHRASAL VERB

1 To **drag** someone **down** means to reduce them to an inferior social status or to lower standards of behaviour. *She dragged him down with her... There were fears he would be dragged down by the scandal.* V n P (not pron) *be* V-ed P *by* n

2 Something that **drags** you **down** makes you feel weak or depressed. *I have had really bad bouts of flu that have really dragged me down.* V n P

drag in. When you are talking, if you **drag in** a subject, you mention something that is not relevant and that other people do not want to discuss. *They disapproved of my dragging in his wealth... We were able to stick to the main issue without incidental grievances being dragged in.* PHRASAL VERB =bring in V P n Also V n P

drag into. To **drag** something or someone **into** an event or situation means to involve them in it when it is not necessary or not desirable. *Why should Carmela have dragged him into the argument?... We may find ourselves dragged into new wars and new threats of wars.* PHRASAL VERB =involve V n P n

drag on. You say that an event or process **drags on** when you disapprove of the fact that it lasts for longer than necessary. *The conflict with James has dragged on for two years.* PHRASAL VERB PRAGMATICS V P

drag out PHRASAL VERB

1 If you **drag** something **out**, you make it last for longer than is necessary. *...a company that was willing and able to drag out the proceedings for years... Let's get it over with as soon as possible, rather than drag it out.* V P n (not pron) V n P

2 If you **drag** something **out** of someone, you persuade them to tell you something that they do not want to tell you. *The families soon discovered that every piece of information had to be dragged out of the authorities.* V n P *of* n

drag up. If someone **drags up** an unpleasant event or an old story from the past, they mention it when people do not want to be reminded of it. *I don't want to go back there and drag up that anger again... Painful memories were dragged up for Tina during the filming.* PHRASAL VERB V P n (not pron) Also V n P

dragnet /drægnet/. A **dragnet** is a method used by police to catch suspected criminals. A large number of police officers search a specific area, in the hope that they will eventually find the person they are looking for. *...a massive police dragnet for two suspected IRA killers.* N-SING: oft n N

dragon /drægən/ **dragons** ◆◆◇◇◇

1 In stories and legends, a **dragon** is an animal like a big lizard. It has wings and claws, and breathes out fire. N-COUNT

2 If someone calls a woman a **dragon**, they mean that she is fierce and unpleasant; an offensive use. N-COUNT

dragonfly /drægənflaɪ/ **dragonflies. Dragonflies** are brightly-coloured insects with long, thin bodies and two sets of wings. **Dragonflies** are often found near slow-moving water. N-COUNT

dragoon /drəguːn/ **dragoons, dragooning, dragooned** ◆◇◇◇◇

1 A **dragoon** was a soldier in old European armies. Dragoons usually fought on horseback. N-COUNT

2 If someone **dragoons** you into doing something that you do not want to do, they persuade you to do it even though you try hard not to agree. *...the history professor who had dragooned me into taking the exam... Her husband had also been dragooned into the excursion.* VERB PRAGMATICS V n *into* -ing/n

drain /dreɪn/ **drains, draining, drained** ◆◆◆◇◇

1 If you **drain** a liquid from a place or object, you remove the liquid by causing it to flow somewhere else. If a liquid **drains** somewhere, it flows there. *Miners built the tunnel to drain water out of the mines... Now the focus is on draining the water... Springs and rivers that drain into lakes carry dissolved nitrates and phosphates... The water slowly drained away, down through the porous soil.* V-ERG V n adv/prep V n V prep/adv

2 If you **drain** a place or object, you dry it by causing water to flow out of it. If a place or object **drains**, water flows out of it until it is dry. *The authorities have mobilised vast numbers of people to drain flooded land and build or repair dykes... The soil drains freely and slugs aren't a problem.* V-ERG V n V

3 If you **drain** food or if food **drains**, you remove the liquid that it has been in, especially after it has been cooked or soaked in water. *Drain the pasta well, arrange on four plates and pour over the sauce... Wash the leeks thoroughly and allow them to drain.* V-ERG V n V

4 A **drain** is a pipe that carries water or sewage away from a place, or an opening in a surface that leads to the pipe. *Tony built his own house and laid his own drains. ...storm drains.* N-COUNT

5 If someone **drains** a glass, they empty it by drinking what is in it; a literary use. *Pamela drained her glass and refilled it.* VERB V n

6 If the colour or the blood **drains** or **is drained** from someone's face, they become very pale; a literary use. You can also say that someone's face **drains** or **is drained** of colour. *Harry felt the colour drain from his face... The blood had drained from his face and his eyes were half shut... Thacker's face drained of colour... Jock's face had been suddenly drained of all colour... His usually florid complexion seemed drained of colour.* VERB V *from* n V *of* n *be* V-ed *of* n V-ed Also V n *from* n

7 If a feeling **drains** or **is drained** out of you, it gradually becomes less strong until you no longer feel it. *And then, suddenly, the euphoria began to drain away... She felt the tension drain out of her... The happiness and the excitement had been drained completely from her voice.* V-ERG V adv/prep *be* V-ed *from* n

8 If something **drains** you, it leaves you feeling physically and emotionally exhausted. *My emotional turmoil had drained me.* ♦ **drained** *As United stalked off, stunned and drained, Liverpool looked as though they had won already!* ♦ **draining** VERB V n ADJ-GRADED ADJ-GRADED

This work is physically exhausting and emotionally draining.

9 If energy **drains** or **is drained** from you, you lose all energy and become very tired. *As his energy drained away, his despair and worry grew... I can help resolve conflicts that drain energy.* ► Also an adjective. *He could rest only when he was too drained of energy to fret further.*
V-ERG
V adv/prep
V n
ADJ-GRADED: usu v-link ADJ, usu ADJ *of* n

10 If you say that something is a **drain** on an organization's finances or resources, you mean that it costs the organization a large amount of money, and you do not consider that it is worth it. *...an ultra-modern printing plant, which has been a big drain on resources... Fraud trials are often complex and have become an expensive drain on the public purse.* ● See also **brain drain**.
N-SING: usu adj N, N *on* n

11 If you say that a country's or a company's resources or finances **are drained**, you mean that they are used or spent completely. *The state's finances have been drained by drought and civil disorder... The company has steadily drained its cash reserves.*
VERB
be V-ed
V n

12 If you say that something is going **down the drain**, you mean that it is being destroyed or wasted; an informal expression. *They were aware that their public image was rapidly going down the drain... He lamented that four years of his life had gone down the drain because of an injury to his groin.*
PHRASES
usu PHR after v

13 If you say that a business is going **down the drain**, you mean that it is failing financially; an informal expression.. *The department stores are going down the drain, victims of inner-city blight and the rush for suburbia.*
usu PHR after v

drainage /dreɪnɪdʒ/. **Drainage** is the system or process by which water or other liquids are drained from a place. *Line the pots with pebbles to ensure good drainage... The drainage system has collapsed because of too much rain.*
◆◇◇◇◇
N-UNCOUNT

draining board, draining boards. The **draining board** is the place on a sink unit where things such as cups, plates, and cutlery are put to drain after they have been washed.
N-COUNT: usu *the* N in sing

drainpipe /dreɪnpaɪp/ **drainpipes.** A **drainpipe** is a pipe attached to the side of a building, through which rainwater flows from the roof into a drain. *He evaded police by climbing through a window and shinning down a drainpipe.*
N-COUNT

drake /dreɪk/ **drakes.** A **drake** is a male duck.
N-COUNT

dram /dræm/ **drams.** A **dram** is a small measure of whisky; used especially in Scottish English. *...a dram of whisky... Would you care for a dram?*
N-COUNT: oft N *of* n

drama /drɑːmə/ **dramas**
◆◆◆◇◇

1 A **drama** is a serious play for the theatre, television, or radio. *He acted in radio dramas.*
N-COUNT

2 You use **drama** to refer to plays in general or to work that is connected with plays and the theatre, such as acting or producing. *He knew nothing of Greek drama... She met him when she was at drama school.*
N-UNCOUNT

3 You can refer to a real situation which is exciting or distressing as **drama**. *There was none of the drama and relief of a hostage release... For all its drama, the event was not unexpected.*
N-VAR

dramatic /drəmætɪk/
◆◆◆◆◇

1 A **dramatic** change or event happens suddenly and is very noticeable and surprising. *A fifth year of drought is expected to have dramatic effects on the California economy... This policy has led to a dramatic increase in our prison populations.* ♦ **dramatically** /drəmætɪkli/ *At speeds above 50mph, serious injuries dramatically increase.*
ADJ-GRADED: usu ADJ n =striking
ADV-GRADED: usu ADV with v, also ADV adj

2 A **dramatic** action, event, or situation is exciting and impressive. *He witnessed many dramatic escapes as people jumped from as high as the fourth floor... Their arrival was dramatic and exciting.* ♦ **dramatically** *He tipped his head to one side and sighed dramatically.*
ADJ-GRADED
ADV-GRADED: usu ADV with v, also ADV adj

3 You use **dramatic** to describe things connected with or relating to the theatre, drama, or plays. *...a dramatic arts major in college... I had no thoughts of making a dramatic film. I was working in documentary.*
ADJ: ADJ n

dramatics /drəmætɪks/

1 You use **dramatics** to refer to activities connected with the theatre and drama, such as acting in plays or producing them, usually as an amateur. *Angela says she longs to join an amateur dramatics class. ...the university dramatics society.*
N-UNCOUNT: usu with supp

2 You talk about **dramatics** to express your disapproval of behaviour which seems to show too much emotion, and which you think is done deliberately in order to impress people. *...another wearisome outbreak of Nancy's dramatics.*
N-PLURAL
PRAGMATICS

dramatis personae /dræmətɪs pəʳsoʊnaɪ/. In formal English, the characters in a play are sometimes referred to as **the dramatis personae**.
N-PLURAL: *the* N

dramatist /dræmətɪst/ **dramatists.** A **dramatist** is someone who writes plays.
◆◇◇◇◇
N-COUNT

dramatize /dræmətaɪz/ **dramatizes, dramatizing, dramatized;** also spelled **dramatise** in British English.
◆◇◇◇◇

1 If a book or story **is dramatized**, it is written or presented as a play, film, or television drama. *...an incident later dramatized in the movie 'The Right Stuff'. ...a dramatised version of the novel.* ♦ **dramatization** /dræmətaɪzeɪʃᵊn/ **dramatizations** *...a dramatisation of D H Lawrence's novel, 'Lady Chatterley's Lover.'*
VB: usu passive
be V-ed
V-ed
N-COUNT: with supp

2 If you say that someone **dramatizes** a situation or event, you mean that they try to make it seem more serious, more important, or more exciting than it really is; used showing disapproval. *They have a tendency to show off, to dramatize almost every situation.*
VERB
PRAGMATICS
=exaggerate
V n
Also V

3 If something that happens or is done **dramatizes** a situation, it focuses people's attention on the situation in a dramatic way; used mainly in American English. *More than 400 exiles were on a dawn-to-dusk hunger strike to dramatize their plight... The need for change has been dramatized by plummeting bank profits.*
VERB
=highlight
V n

drank /dræŋk/. **Drank** is the past tense of **drink**.

drape /dreɪp/ **drapes, draping, draped**
◆◇◇◇◇

1 If you **drape** a piece of cloth somewhere, you place it there so that it hangs down in a casual and graceful way. *Natasha took the coat and draped it over her shoulders... A soft white robe had been draped over a chair for Joanna's use... She had a towel draped around her neck.*
VERB
=hang
V n prep
V-ed prep

2 If someone or something **is draped** in a piece of cloth, they are loosely covered by it. *The coffin had been draped in a Union Jack... He draped himself in the Canadian flag and went round the track... She opened her front door draped in a towel.*
VERB
be V-ed *in/with* n
V n *in/with* n
V-ed

3 If you **drape** a part of your body somewhere, you lay it there in a relaxed and graceful way. *Nicola slowly draped herself across the couch... He draped his arm over Daniels' shoulder... They sprawl at ease across the sofa, arms draped over the back.*
VERB
V pron-refl prep
V n prep
V-ed prep

4 In American English, **drapes** are pieces of heavy fabric you hang across a window that you can close to keep the light out or stop people looking in. The British word is **curtains**. *He pulled the drapes shut, locked the door behind him.*
N-COUNT: usu pl

draper /dreɪpəʳ/ **drapers**
◆◇◇◇◇

1 In British English, a **draper** is a shopkeeper who sells cloth.
N-COUNT

2 In British English, a **draper** or a **draper's** is a shop where cloth is sold.
N-COUNT: oft *the* N

drapery /dreɪpəri/ **draperies**

1 You can refer to cloth, curtains, or clothing hanging in folds as **drapery** or **draperies**. *In the dining-room the draperies create an atmosphere of elegance and luxury.*
N-UNCOUNT: also N in pl

2 In British English, **drapery** is cloth that you buy in a shop. *My mother ran a couple of drapery shops.*
N-UNCOUNT: oft N n

drastic /dræstɪk/
◆◆◇◇◇

1 If you have to take **drastic** action in order to solve a problem, you have to do something extreme, severe, and radical to solve it. *Drastic measures are needed to clean up the profession... He's not going to do anything drastic about economic policy.*
ADJ-GRADED
=radical

2 A **drastic** change is a very great change. *Elderly people are not in a position to make drastic changes at this stage of their life... Foreign food aid has led to a drastic reduction in the numbers of people dying of starvation.* ♦ **drastically** *As a result, services have been drastically reduced.*
ADJ-GRADED; ADV: ADV with v

draught /drɑːft, dræft/ **draughts;** spelled **draft** in American English. ◆◆◇◇◇

1 A **draught** is a current of air that comes into a place in an undesirable way. *Block draughts around doors and windows... On a cold day there can be quite a draught from the letterbox.*
N-COUNT

2 Draught beer is beer which is kept in barrels rather than bottles. *Draught beer is available too.*
ADJ: usu ADJ n

• Beer that is **on draught** is kept in and served from a barrel rather than a bottle. *They drink bitter on draught in the local bar.*
PHRASE: PHR after v, v-link PHR

3 A **draught** of liquid is a large amount that you swallow. *He took a draught of beer... Having added more fruit juice on top, drink it down in one draught.*
N-COUNT: with supp, oft N *of* n

4 In British English, **draughts** is a game for two people, played with 24 round pieces on a board. The usual American word is **checkers**. *He was in the study playing draughts by the fire with Albert.*
N-UNCOUNT

5 In British English, a **draught** is also one of the round pieces which are used in the game of draughts. The usual American word is **checker**.
N-COUNT

6 A **draught** animal is one which pulls heavy loads, for example on a farm. *...an Irish draught mare.*
ADJ: ADJ n

7 A **draught** is a medicine in the form of a liquid which you drink; an old-fashioned use. *One of the night-duty nuns gave her a sleeping draught.*
N-COUNT: usu supp N

draughtsman /drɑːftsmən, dræfts-/ **draughtsmen;** spelled **draftsman** in American English.

1 A **draughtsman** is someone whose job is to prepare very detailed drawings of machinery, equipment, or buildings.
N-COUNT

2 If someone is a good **draughtsman**, they are very skilled at drawing. *This is a great drawing by one of the 19th century's finest draughtsmen.*
N-COUNT: usu adj N

draughtsmanship /drɑːftsmənʃɪp, dræfts-/; spelled **draftsmanship** in American English. **Draughtsmanship** is the ability to draw well or the art of drawing.
N-UNCOUNT

draughty /drɑːfti, dræfti/ **draughtier, draughtiest;** spelled **drafty** in American English. A **draughty** room or building has currents of cold air blowing through it, usually because the windows and doors do not fit very well.
ADJ-GRADED

draw /drɔː/ **draws, drawing, drew, drawn** ◆◆◆◆◆

1 When you **draw** or when you **draw** something, you use a pencil, pen, or crayon to produce a picture, pattern, or diagram. *She would sit there drawing with the pencil stub... Draw a rough design for a logo... He starts a painting by quickly drawing simplified shapes.* ♦ **drawing** *I like dancing, singing and drawing.*
VERB =sketch; V; V n; N-UNCOUNT

2 When a vehicle **draws** somewhere, it moves there smoothly and steadily. *Claire had seen the taxi drawing away... A carriage door struck him as a train drew into Basildon station.*
VERB; V adv/prep

3 If you **draw** somewhere, you move there slowly; used in written English. *She drew away and did not smile... When we drew level, he neither slowed down nor accelerated.*
VERB; V adv/prep; V adj

4 If you **draw** something or someone in a particular direction, you move them in that direction, usually by pulling them gently; used in written English. *He drew his chair nearer the fire... He put his arm around Caroline's shoulders and drew her close to him... Wilson drew me aside after an interview.*
VERB =pull; V n prep; V n adj; V n with adv

5 When you **draw** a curtain or blind, you pull it across a window, either to cover or to uncover it. *After drawing the curtains, she lit a candle... Mother was lying on her bed, with the blinds drawn.*
VERB; V n; V-ed

6 If someone **draws** a gun, knife, or other weapon, they pull it out of its holder and threaten you with it. *He drew his dagger and turned to face his pursuers.*
VERB =take out; V n

7 If an animal or vehicle **draws** something such as a cart, carriage, or trailer, it pulls it along. *...a slow-moving tractor, drawing a trailer. ...a chariot drawn by six black mules.*
VERB; V n; V-ed

8 If you **draw** a deep breath, you breathe in deeply once. *He paused, drawing a deep breath.*
VERB; V n

9 If you **draw** on a cigarette, you breathe the smoke from it into your mouth or lungs. *He drew on an American cigarette... Her cheeks hollowed as she drew smoke into her lungs.*
VERB; V on n; V n *into* n; Also V n with *in*

10 To **draw** something such as water or energy **from** a particular source means to take it from that source. *Villagers still have to draw their water from wells.*
VERB; V n *from* n

11 If something that hits you or presses part of your body **draws** blood, it cuts your skin so that it bleeds. *Any practice that draws blood could increase the risk of getting the virus.*
VERB; V n

12 If you **draw** money out of a bank, building society, or savings account, you get it from the account so that you can use it. *She was drawing out cash from a cash machine... Companies could not draw money from bank accounts as cash.*
VERB; V n with *out*; V n *from* n; Also V n

13 If you **draw** a salary or a sum of money, you receive a sum of money regularly. *For the first few years I didn't draw any salary at all... He is moving ever closer to drawing his pension.*
VERB; V n

14 To **draw** something means to choose it or to be given it at random, as part of a competition, game, or lottery. *We delved through a sackful of letters to draw the winning name... Aston Villa have drawn a Czech team in the first round of the UEFA Cup.* ► Also a noun. *The draw for the quarter-finals is made at Lord's this morning.*
VERB; V n; N-COUNT

15 A **draw** is a competition where people pay money for numbered or named tickets, then some of those tickets are chosen at random, and the owners are given prizes.
N-COUNT

16 To **draw** something **from** a particular thing or place means to take or get it from that thing or place. *I draw strength from the millions of women who have faced this challenge successfully... The students are drawn from a cross-section of backgrounds.*
VERB; V n *from* n

17 If you **draw** a particular conclusion, you decide that that conclusion is true. *He draws two conclusions from this... He says he cannot yet draw any conclusions about the murders.*
VERB; V n *from* n; V n

18 If you **draw** a comparison, parallel, or distinction, you compare or contrast two different ideas, systems, or other things. *He draws a comparison between what's going on in Yugoslavia now and what happened in Germany fifty years ago... Interesting distinctions can be drawn between the two populations.*
VERB; V n; Also V n *with* n

19 If you **draw** someone's attention to something, you make them aware of it or make them think about it. *He was waving his arms to draw their attention... He just wants to draw attention to the plight of the unemployed.*
VERB; V n; V n *to* n

20 If someone or something **draws** a particular reaction, people react to it in that way. *Such a policy would inevitably draw fierce resistance from farmers. ...an official tour to South Africa which drew angry political reactions.*
VERB; V n *from* n; V n

21 If something such as a film or an event **draws** a lot of people, it is so interesting or entertaining that a lot of people go to it. *The game is currently drawing huge crowds.*
VERB PRAGMATICS; V n

22 If someone or something **draws** you, it attracts you very strongly. *In no sense did he draw and enthral her as Alex had done... What drew him to the area was its proximity to central London.*
VERB; V n; V n *to* n

23 If someone will not **be drawn** or refuses to **be drawn**, they will not reply to questions in the way that you want them to, or will not reveal information or their opinion. *The ambassador would not be drawn on questions of a political nature... 'Did he say why?'—'No, he refuses to be drawn.'*
VB: with brd-neg, usu passive; be V-ed *on* n; be V-ed

24 In a game or competition, if one person or team **draws** with another one, or if two people or teams **draw**, they have the same number of points at the end of the game. *Holland and the Republic of Ireland drew one-one... We drew with Ireland in the*
V-RECIP =tie; pl-n V num; V *with/against* n

first game... Egypt drew two of their matches in Italy. ► Also a noun. *We were happy to come away with a draw against Sweden.* V n (non-recip) Also pl-n V, V (non-recip) N-COUNT

25 See also **drawing**.

26 When an event or period of time **draws to a close** or **draws to an end**, it finishes; a formal expression. *Another celebration had drawn to its close.* PHRASES V inflects

27 If an event or period of time **is drawing closer** or **is drawing nearer**, it is approaching. *And all the time next spring's elections are drawing closer... As the day set for departure drew near, I told my wife that I could not accompany them.* V inflects

28 • **to draw a blank**: see **blank**. • **to draw breath**: see **breath**. • **to draw** someone's **fire**: see **fire**. • **to draw the line**: see **line**. • **to draw lots**: see **lot**. • **the luck of the draw**: see **luck**.

draw in PHRASAL VERB

1 In British English, if you say that the nights, evenings, or days **are drawing in**, you mean that it is becoming dark at an earlier time in the evening, because autumn or winter is approaching. *The days draw in and the mornings get darker.* V P

2 If you **draw** someone **in** or **draw** them **into** something you are involved with, you cause them to become involved with it. *It won't be easy for you to draw him in... You gradually fall under the spell and get drawn in deeper and deeper... Don't let him draw you into his strategy.* V n P V n P n Also V P n (not pron)

3 If you **draw in** your breath, you breathe in deeply. If you **draw in** air, you take it into your lungs as you breathe in. *Rose drew her breath in sharply... Roll the wine around in your mouth, drawing in air at the same time.* V n P V P n (not pron)

draw into. See **draw in** 2. PHRASAL VERB

draw off. If a quantity of liquid **is drawn off** from a larger quantity, it is taken from it, usually by means of a syringe or pipe. *The fluid can be drawn off with a syringe... He allowed the doctors to open a vein of his arm and draw off a pint of blood.* PHRASAL VERB *be* V-ed P V P n (not pron) Also V n P

draw on PHRASAL VERB

1 If you **draw on** or **draw upon** something such as your skills or experience, you make use of it in order to do something. *He drew on his experience as a yachtsman to make a documentary programme.* V P n

2 As a period of time **draws on**, it passes and the end of it gets closer. *As the afternoon drew on we were joined by more of the regulars.* V P

draw out PHRASAL VERB

1 If you **draw out** a sound or a word, you make it last longer than usual. *Liz drew the word out carefully.* V n P Also V P n (not pron)

2 If you **draw** someone **out**, you make them feel less nervous and more willing to talk. *Her mother tried every approach to draw her out.* V n P

draw up PHRASAL VERB

1 If you **draw up** a document, list, or plan, you prepare it and write it out. *They agreed to establish a working party to draw up a formal agreement... He wants his ministers to concentrate on implementing policy, not on drawing it up.* V P n (not pron) V n P

2 If you **draw up** a chair, you move it nearer to a person or place, for example so that you can watch something or join in with something. *He drew up a chair and sat down.* V P n (not pron) Also V n P

3 If you **draw** yourself **up**, you make your back very straight, rather than stooping. *He drew himself up to his full height... 'Well!', said the innkeeper, drawing herself up indignantly.* V pron-refl P *to* n V pron-refl P

draw upon. See **draw on** 1. PHRASAL VERB

drawback /drɔːbæk/ **drawbacks.** A **drawback** is an aspect of something or someone that makes them less acceptable than they would otherwise be. *He felt the apartment's only drawback was that it was too small.* ◆◇◇◇◇ N-COUNT =disadvantage

drawbridge /drɔːbrɪdʒ/ **drawbridges.** A **drawbridge** is a bridge that can be pulled up, for example to prevent people from getting into a castle or to allow ships to pass underneath it. N-COUNT

drawer /drɔːəʳ/ **drawers** ◆◆◇◇◇

1 A **drawer** is part of a desk, chest, or other piece of furniture that is shaped like a box and is designed for putting things in. You pull it towards you to open it. *He opened a drawer in his writing-table and brought out a sheet of notepaper.* N-COUNT

2 Drawers are knickers or underpants; an old-fashioned use. N-PLURAL: also *a pair of* N

3 See also **chest of drawers**.

drawing /drɔːɪŋ/ **drawings.** A **drawing** is a picture made with a pencil, pen, or crayon. *She did a drawing of me.* • See also **draw**. ◆◆◇◇◇ N-COUNT: oft N *of* n

drawing board, drawing boards; also spelled **drawing-board**. ◆◇◇◇◇

1 A **drawing board** is a large flat board, often fixed to a metal frame so that it looks like a desk, on which you place your paper when you are drawing or designing something. N-COUNT

2 If you say that you will have to go **back to the drawing board**, you mean that something which you have done has not been successful and that you will have to start again or try another idea. PHRASE: PHR after v

drawing pin, drawing pins; also spelled **drawing-pin**. In British English, a **drawing pin** is a short pin with a broad, flat top which is used for fastening papers or pictures to a board, wall, or other surface. The usual American term is **thumbtack**. N-COUNT

drawing room, drawing rooms. A **drawing room** is a room, especially a large room in a large house, where people sit and relax, or entertain guests; a formal word. ◆◇◇◇◇ N-COUNT

drawl /drɔːl/ **drawls, drawling, drawled.** If someone **drawls**, they speak slowly and not very clearly, with long vowel sounds. *'I guess you guys don't mind if I smoke?' he drawled. He has a deep voice and he drawls slightly.* ► Also a noun. *Jack's southern drawl had become more pronounced as they'd traveled southward.* ◆◇◇◇◇ VERB V with quote V N-COUNT: with supp

drawn /drɔːn/ ◆◇◇◇◇

1 Drawn is the past participle of **draw**.

2 If someone or their face looks **drawn**, their face is thin and they look very tired, ill, worried, or unhappy. *She looked drawn and tired when she turned towards me.* ADJ-GRADED PRAGMATICS

drawn-out. You can describe something as **drawn-out** when it lasts or takes longer than you would like it to. *Pulling out of a recession is a lengthy and drawn-out process... The road to peace will be long and drawn-out.* ◆◇◇◇◇ ADJ-GRADED =protracted

drawstring /drɔːstrɪŋ/ **drawstrings;** also spelled **draw-string**. A **drawstring** is a cord that goes through a seam round an opening, for example at the top of a bag or a pair of trousers. When the cord is pulled tighter, the opening gets smaller. *...a velvet bag with a drawstring.* N-COUNT: usu sing, oft N n

dray /dreɪ/ **drays.** A **dray** is a large flat cart with four wheels which is pulled by horses. N-COUNT

dread /dred/ **dreads, dreading, dreaded** ◆◆◇◇◇

1 If you **dread** something which may happen, you feel very anxious and unhappy about it because you think it will be unpleasant or upsetting. *I'm dreading Christmas this year... I dreaded coming back, to be honest... I suffer badly from cold sores and dread them appearing on my wedding day... I'd been dreading that the birth would take a long time.* VERB ≠look forward to V n/-ing V n -ing V that Also V to-inf

2 Dread is a feeling of great anxiety and fear about something that may happen. *She thought with dread of the cold winters to come.* N-UNCOUNT =apprehension

3 Dread means terrible and greatly feared; a literary use. *...a more effective national policy to combat this dread disease.* ADJ: usu ADJ n =dreaded

4 In informal English, you can use **dread** to describe something that you find annoying, inconvenient, or undesirable, when you expect others to understand and agree or sympathize with you. *...the dread phrase 'politically correct'.* ADJ: ADJ n PRAGMATICS =dreaded

5 See also **dreaded**.

6 If you say that you **dread to think** what might happen, you mean that you are anxious about it because it is likely to be very unpleasant. *I dread to think what will happen in the case of a major emergency... I dread to think what Hollywood is planning to do with this interesting little story.* PHRASE: V inflects, usu PHR wh

dreaded /drɛ̲dɪd/ ◆◇◇◇◇
1 **Dreaded** means terrible and greatly feared. *No one knew how to treat this dreaded disease.* ADJ-GRADED: ADJ n
2 In informal English, you can use **dreaded** to describe something that you find annoying, inconvenient, or undesirable, when you expect others to understand and agree or sympathize with you. *She's a victim of the dreaded hay fever... Team orders on the final day were to avoid the dreaded blank at all costs.* ADJ: ADJ n PRAGMATICS =dread

dreadful /drɛ̲dfʊl/ ◆◆◇◇◇
1 If you say that something is **dreadful**, you mean that it is very bad or unpleasant, or very poor in quality. *They told us the dreadful news... My financial situation is dreadful.* ♦ **dreadfully** *You behaved dreadfully... They treated him dreadfully.* ADJ-GRADED =awful, appalling ADV-GRADED: ADV with v
2 **Dreadful** is used to emphasize the degree or extent of something bad. *We've made a dreadful mistake... I had a dreadful headache.* ADJ: ADJ n PRAGMATICS
3 If someone **looks** or **feels dreadful**, they look or feel very ill, tired, or upset. *Are you all right? You look dreadful... I feel absolutely dreadful about what has happened.* ADJ-GRADED: feel/look ADJ

dreadfully /drɛ̲dfʊli/. You use **dreadfully** to emphasize the degree or intensity of something, especially something bad or unpleasant; an informal word. *He looks dreadfully ill... His mother must be dreadfully worried... I miss him dreadfully.* ● See also **dreadful**. ADV: ADV adj, ADV after v PRAGMATICS =awfully, terribly

dreadlocks /drɛ̲dlɒks/. If someone has **dreadlocks**, their hair is divided into a large number of short, tight pigtails. **Dreadlocks** are worn especially by men who are Rastafarians. *He was turned down for a driving job when he refused to cut his dreadlocks.* N-PLURAL

dream /driː̲m/ **dreams, dreaming, dreamed, dreamt** ◆◆◆◆◇
1 A **dream** is an imaginary series of events that you experience in your mind while you are asleep. *He had a dream about Claire... I had a dream that I was in an old study, surrounded by leather books.* N-COUNT
2 When you **dream**, you experience imaginary events in your mind while you are asleep. *Ivor dreamed that he was on a bus... She dreamed about her baby.* VERB V that V about/of n Also V
3 You can refer to a situation or event as a **dream** if you often think about it because you would like it to happen. *He had finally accomplished his dream of becoming a full pilot... My dream is to have a house in the country... You can make that dream come true.* N-COUNT: usu with supp =ambition
4 If you often think about something that you would very much like to happen or have, you can say that you **dream** of it. *As a schoolgirl, she had dreamed of becoming an actress... For most of us, a brand new designer kitchen is something we can only dream about... I dream that my son will attend college and find a good job.* VERB V of/about n/-ing V that
5 You can use **dream** to describe something that you think is ideal or perfect, especially if it is something that you thought you would never be able to have or experience. *He had his dream house built on the banks of the river Bure. ...a dream holiday to Jamaica.* ADJ: ADJ n
6 If you describe something as a particular person's **dream**, you think that it would be ideal for that person and that he or she would like it very much. *Greece is said to be a botanist's dream... He's every girl's dream!* N-SING: poss N
7 If you say that something is **a dream**, you mean that it is wonderful; an informal use. N-SING: a N
8 You can refer to a situation or event that does not seem real as a **dream**, especially if it is very strange or unpleasant. *When the right woman comes along, this bad dream will be over.* N-COUNT: usu sing, with supp
9 If you say that you would not **dream of** doing something, you are emphasizing that you would never do it because you think it is wrong or is not possible or suitable for you. *I wouldn't dream of making fun of you... My sons would never dream of expecting their clothes to be ironed.* VB: with neg PRAGMATICS V of-ing/n
10 If you say that you never **dreamed** that something would happen, you are emphasizing that you did not think that it would happen because it seemed very unlikely. *I never dreamed that I would be able to afford a home here... Who could ever dream of a disaster like this?... I find life more charming and more astonishing than I'd ever dreamed.* VB: with brd-neg PRAGMATICS V that V of n V
11 See also **pipe dream**. See also **wet dream**.
12 If you say that you are **in a dream**, you mean that you do not concentrate properly on what you are doing because you are thinking about other things. *All day long I moved in a dream, my body performing its duties automatically.* PHRASES PHR after v, v-link PHR
13 If you say that someone does something **like a dream**, you think that they do it very well. If you say that something happens **like a dream**, you mean that it happens successfully without any problems. *She cooked like a dream... His ship had sailed like a dream.* PHR after v
14 If you describe someone or something as the person or thing **of** your **dreams**, you mean that you consider them to be ideal or perfect. *This could be the man of my dreams.* n PHR
15 If you say that you could not imagine a particular thing **in** your **wildest dreams**, you are emphasizing that you think it is extremely strange or unlikely. *Never in my wildest dreams could I imagine there would be this kind of money in the game.* with brd-neg, PHR with cl PRAGMATICS
16 If you describe something as being **beyond** your **wildest dreams**, you are emphasizing that it is better than you could have imagined or hoped for. *She had already achieved success beyond her wildest dreams.* n PHR, PHR after v, v-link PHR PRAGMATICS

dream up. If you **dream up** a plan or idea, you work it out or create it in your mind. *I dreamed up a plan to solve both problems at once... The event was dreamed up by Mick Jagger... His son hadn't dreamed it up.* PHRASAL VERB V P n (not pron) V n P

dreamer /driː̲məʳ/ **dreamers.** If you describe someone as a **dreamer**, you mean that they spend a lot of time thinking about and planning for things that they would like to happen but which are improbable or impractical. *Far from being a dreamer, she's a level-headed pragmatist.* ◆◇◇◇◇ N-COUNT

dreamily /driː̲mɪli/. If you say or do something **dreamily**, you say or do it in a way that shows your mind is occupied with pleasant, relaxing thoughts. *'They were divine,' she sighs, dreamily... She stared dreamily out of the small window at the blue horizon.* ADV: usu ADV with v, also ADV adj

dreamland /driː̲mlænd/
1 If you describe a place as a **dreamland**, you mean that it is so beautiful it is hard to believe that it is real. *...a dreamland of snowy moonlit peaks and twinkling lights.* N-SING
2 If you refer to a situation as **dreamland**, you mean that it represents what someone would like to happen, but that it is completely unrealistic; used mainly in British English. *In dreamland we play them in the final.* N-UNCOUNT: also a N

dreamless /driː̲mləs/. A **dreamless** sleep is very deep and peaceful, and without dreams. *He fell into a deep dreamless sleep the moment he got into bed.* ADJ: usu ADJ n

dreamlike /driː̲mlaɪk/. If you describe something as **dreamlike**, you mean it seems strange and unreal. *Her paintings have a naive, dreamlike quality.* ADJ-GRADED =surreal

dreamt /drɛ̲mt/. **Dreamt** is a past tense and past participle of **dream**.

dream ticket. When journalists refer to a particular person or small group of people as a **dream ticket**, they mean that they think the people will be extremely successful in a particular situation. *His deputy Roy Hattersley, elected as part of the dream ticket to succeed Michael Foot in 1983, will also resign.* N-SING

dreamy /driː̲mi/ **dreamier, dreamiest** ◆◇◇◇◇
1 If you say that someone has a **dreamy** expression, you mean that they are not paying attention to things around them and look as if they are think- ADJ-GRADED

ing about something pleasant. *His face assumed a sort of dreamy expression.*

2 If you describe something as **dreamy**, you mean that you like it and that it seems gentle and soft, like something in a dream. *...dreamy shots of beautiful sunsets. ...a dreamy, delicate song.* [ADJ-GRADED: usu ADJ n] [PRAGMATICS]

3 If you describe a person or an idea as **dreamy**, you mean that they are not very practical. *He's like some dreamy kid playing on his own... The changes would move the party away from the dreamy leftism that alienated many Japanese.* [ADJ-GRADED: usu ADJ n]

4 See also **dreamily**.

dreary /drɪəri/ **drearier, dreariest.** If you describe something as **dreary**, you mean that it is dull and depressing. *...a dreary little town in the Midwest... They live such dreary lives.* ♦ **drearily** *...a drearily familiar scenario.* [◆◇◇◇◇] [ADJ-GRADED =dismal] [ADV-GRADED: ADV adj, ADV with v]

dredge /dredʒ/ **dredges, dredging, dredged.** When people **dredge** a harbour, river, or other area of water, they remove mud and unwanted material from the bottom with a special machine in order to make it deeper or to look for something. *Police have spent weeks dredging the lake but have not found his body.* [◆◇◇◇◇] [VERB] [V n]

dredge up [PHRASAL VERB]

1 If someone **dredges up** a piece of information they learnt a long time ago or if they **dredge up** a distant memory, they manage to remember it. *...an American trying to dredge up some French or German learned in high school... The fragments of memory she dredges up do not fit together.* [=rake up] [V P n (not pron)] [Also V n P]

2 If someone **dredges up** a damaging or upsetting fact about your past, they remind you of it or tell other people about it. *She dredges up a minor misdemeanour: 'You didn't give me money for the school trip.'... It's the media who keep dredging it up.* [V P n (not pron)] [V n P]

dredger /dredʒəʳ/ **dredgers.** A **dredger** is a boat which is fitted with a special machine that is used to enlarge waterways, such as harbours, rivers, and canals. [N-COUNT]

dregs /dregz/

1 The **dregs** of a liquid are the last drops left at the bottom of a container, together with any solid bits that have sunk to the bottom. *Colum drained the dregs from his cup.* [N-PLURAL: usu *the* N]

2 If you talk about the **dregs** of a society or community, you mean the people in it who you consider to be the most worthless and bad; used showing disapproval. *It sees the dissidents as anti-social elements and the dregs of society.* [N-PLURAL: usu *the* N *of* n] [PRAGMATICS] [=scum]

drench /drentʃ/ **drenches, drenching, drenched.** To **drench** something or someone means to make them completely wet. *They turned fire hoses on the people and drenched them. ...the idea of spending two whole days hanging on to a raft and getting drenched by icy water... We were completely drenched and cold... I reached Kilmarnock in the early morning in drenching rain.* ♦ **-drenched** *...the rain-drenched streets of the capital.* [◆◇◇◇◇] [VERB =soak] [V n] [*get* V-ed] [V-ed] [V-ing] [COMB in ADJ]

dress /dres/ **dresses, dressing, dressed** [◆◆◆◆◇]

1 A **dress** is a piece of clothing worn by a woman or girl. It covers her body and extends down over her legs. *She was wearing a black dress.* [N-COUNT]

2 You can refer to clothes worn by men or women as **dress**. *He's usually smart in his dress. ...hundreds of Cambodians in traditional dress.* ● See also **evening dress, fancy dress, full dress, morning dress**. [N-UNCOUNT]

3 When you **dress** or **dress** yourself, you put on clothes. *He told Sarah to wait while he dressed... Sue had dressed herself neatly for work.* [VERB] [V] [V n]

4 If you **dress** someone, for example a child, you put clothes on them. *She bathed her and dressed her in clean clothes.* [VERB] [V n]

5 If someone **dresses** in a particular way, they wear clothes of a particular style or colour. *He dresses in a way that lets everyone know he's got authority... She used to dress in jeans.* [VERB] [V *in* n]

6 If you **dress** for something, you put on special clothes for it. *We don't dress for dinner here.* [VERB] [V *for* n]

7 When someone **dresses** a wound, they clean it and cover it. *The poor child never cried or protested when I was dressing her wounds.* [VERB] [V n]

8 If you **dress** a salad, you cover it with a sort of sauce made from oil, vinegar, and herbs or flavourings. *Scatter the tomato over, then dress the salad. ...a bowl of dressed salad.* [VERB] [V n] [V-ed]

9 To **dress** meat, poultry, or fish means to prepare it for cooking by cleaning it and removing bits that you cannot eat. *Her mother dressed the meat. ...dressed crab.* [VERB] [V n] [V-ed]

10 See also **dressing, dressed**.

dress down [PHRASAL VERB]

1 If you **dress down**, you wear clothes that are less smart than usual. *She dresses down in dark glasses and baggy clothes to avoid hordes of admirers.* [V P]

2 If you **dress** someone **down**, you speak angrily to them because they have done something bad or foolish. *Campbell dressed them down in public.* ● See also **dressing-down**. [=tell off] [V n P] [Also V P n (not pron)]

dress up [PHRASAL VERB]

1 If you **dress up** or **dress** yourself **up**, you put on different clothes, in order to make yourself look smarter than usual or to disguise yourself. *You do not need to dress up for dinner... I just love the fun of dressing up in another era's clothing... Little girls dress up as angels for fiestas.* [V P] [V P *in/as* n] [Also V n P]

2 If you **dress** someone **up**, you give them special clothes to wear, in order to make them look smarter or to disguise them. *Mother loved to dress me up.* [V n P] [Also V P n (not pron)]

3 If you **dress** something **up**, you try to make it seem more attractive, acceptable, or interesting than it really is. *Politicians are happier to dress up their ruthless ambition as a necessary pursuit of the public good... However you dress it up, a bank only exists to lend money.* [V P n (not pron)] [V n P]

4 See also **dressed up, dressing-up**.

dressage /dresɑːʒ/. **Dressage** is a competition in which horse riders have to make their horse perform controlled movements. [◆◆◇◇◇] [N-UNCOUNT]

dress circle. The **dress circle** is the lowest balcony in a theatre. [N-SING]

dressed /drest/ [◆◆◆◇◇]

1 If you are **dressed**, you are wearing clothes rather than being naked or wearing your night clothes. If you get **dressed**, you put on your clothes. *He was fully dressed, including shoes... He went into his bedroom to get dressed.* [ADJ: usu v-link ADJ]

2 If you are **dressed** in a particular way, you are wearing clothes of a particular colour or kind. *...a tall thin woman dressed in black. ...a tall, elegantly dressed man.* ● See also **well-dressed**. [ADJ: v-link ADJ *in/as* n, adv ADJ]

3 If someone is **dressed to kill**, they are wearing very smart or glamorous clothes because they want people to notice them and think they are attractive; an informal expression. *...a solitary blonde, beautiful, haughty and dressed to kill.* [PHRASE]

dressed up [◆◇◇◇◇]

1 If someone is **dressed up**, they are wearing special clothes, in order to look smarter than usual or in order to disguise themselves. *You're all dressed up. Are you going somewhere?... You don't have to get dressed up for this party.* [ADJ-GRADED: usu v-link ADJ]

2 If you say that something is **dressed up** as something else, you mean that someone has tried to make it more acceptable or attractive by making it seem like that other thing, and you disapprove of this fact. *He tried to organise things so that the trip would be dressed up as a UN mission.* [ADJ: v-link ADJ *as/in* n] [PRAGMATICS]

3 ● **dressed up to the nines**: see **nine**.

dresser /dresəʳ/ **dressers** [◆◇◇◇◇]

1 In American English, a **dresser** is a chest of drawers, usually with a mirror on the top. [N-COUNT]

2 In British English, a **dresser** is a piece of furniture which has cupboards or drawers in the lower part and shelves in the top part, and which is usually used for storing china. [N-COUNT]

3 A **dresser** is someone who works in a theatre and helps the actors and actresses to dress. *'Tell them to hold all my calls, Theresa,' she instructed her dresser.* [N-COUNT: oft poss N]

4 You can use **dresser** to refer to the kind of clothes that a person wears. For example, if you say that [N-COUNT: adj N] someone is a **smart dresser**, you mean that they wear smart clothes. *She had always been a smart dresser and had on one of her linen frocks. ...a legendary beauty and unconventional dresser who only once bought 'normal' clothes.*

dressing /dresɪŋ/ **dressings** ◆◇◇◇◇

1 A salad **dressing** is a mixture of oil, vinegar, and herbs or flavourings, which you pour over a salad. *Mix the ingredients for the dressing in a bowl.*
N-MASS: oft supp N

2 A **dressing** is a covering that is put on a wound to protect it while it heals. *Miss Finkelstein will put a dressing on your thumb.*
N-COUNT

dressing-down. If someone gives you a **dressing-down**, they speak angrily to you because you have done something bad or foolish; an informal expression. *I gave him a good dressing-down.*
N-SING =telling off

dressing gown, dressing gowns; also spelled **dressing-gown**. A **dressing gown** is a long, loose garment which you wear over pyjamas or a nightdress when you are not in bed.
◆◇◇◇◇ *N-COUNT*

dressing room, dressing rooms; also spelled **dressing-room**. A **dressing room** is a room in a theatre or sports stadium where performers or players can get dressed and ready for their performance or game.
◆◇◇◇◇ *N-COUNT*

dressing table, dressing tables; also spelled **dressing-table**. A **dressing table** is a small table in a bedroom. It has drawers underneath and a mirror on top.
◆◇◇◇◇ *N-COUNT*

dressing-up; also spelled **dressing up**. When children play at **dressing-up**, they put on special or different clothes and pretend to be different people.
◆◇◇◇◇ *N-UNCOUNT*

dressmaker /dresmeɪkəʳ/ **dressmakers.** A **dressmaker** is a person who makes women's or children's clothes.
N-COUNT

dressmaking /dresmeɪkɪŋ/. **Dressmaking** is the activity or job of making clothes for women or girls.
N-UNCOUNT

dress rehearsal, dress rehearsals

1 The **dress rehearsal** of a play, opera, or show is the final rehearsal before it is performed, in which the performers wear their costumes and the lights and scenery are all used as they will be in the performance.
N-COUNT

2 You can describe an event as a **dress rehearsal** for a later, more important event when it indicates how the later event will be. *These elections, you could almost say, are a dress rehearsal for the real elections.*
N-COUNT

dress shirt, dress shirts. A **dress shirt** is a special shirt which men wear on formal occasions. It is worn with a dinner jacket and bow tie.
N-COUNT

dressy /dresi/ **dressier, dressiest.** **Dressy** clothes are smart clothes which you wear when you want to look elegant or formal.
ADJ-GRADED

drew /druː/. **Drew** is the past tense of **draw**.

dribble /drɪbəl/ **dribbles, dribbling, dribbled** ◆◇◇◇◇

1 If a liquid **dribbles** somewhere, or if you **dribble** it, it drips down slowly or flows in a thin stream. *Sweat dribbled down Hart's face... Dribble the hot mixture slowly into the blender.*
V-ERG =trickle; V prep/adv; V n prep/adv

2 A **dribble of** a liquid is a very small amount of it. *Apply a dribble of baby shampoo. ...lettuce with dribbles of vinaigrette.*
N-COUNT: N of n =drop

3 When players **dribble** the ball in a game such as football, they kick it or tap it several times in quick succession in order to keep it moving. *He dribbled the ball towards Ferris... He dribbled past four defenders... Her dribbling skills look second to none.*
VERB; V n; V; V-ing

4 If a person **dribbles**, saliva trickles from their mouth. *...to protect cot sheets when the baby dribbles... She's dribbling on her collar.*
VERB =drool; V

5 **Dribble** is saliva that has trickled from someone's mouth. *His top is soaked in dribble and he needs his nose wiping quite frequently.*
N-UNCOUNT =drool

6 If people or things **dribble** somewhere, they move there slowly and in small numbers. *...as the workers dribbled away from city square.*
VERB =trickle; V prep/adv

dribs and drabs /drɪbz ən dræbz/. If people or things arrive **in dribs and drabs**, they arrive in small numbers over a period of time rather than arriving all together; an informal expression. *It was a couple of months before I got any clients and then they only came in dribs and drabs.*
PHRASE: PHR after v

dried /draɪd/. **Dried** food or milk has had all the water removed from it so that it will last for a long time. *...an infusion which may be prepared from the fresh plant or the dried herb... Thirty-six trucks were loaded with some 100 tons of dried milk and bandages.* • See also **dry**.
◆◆◇◇◇ *ADJ: ADJ n =dehydrated*

dried fruit, dried fruits. **Dried fruit** is fruit that has been preserved by being dried; used especially to refer to currants, raisins, or sultanas, which are kinds of dried grapes.
N-VAR

dried-up. If you describe someone as **dried-up**, you are saying rudely that they are old and dull, and not worth paying attention to; an informal use. *She has no intention of becoming a dried-up old prune tossed out on a heap and forgotten.* • See also **dry up**.
ADJ-GRADED: usu ADJ n PRAGMATICS ≠vibrant

drier /draɪəʳ/. See **dry, dryer**.

drift /drɪft/ **drifts, drifting, drifted** ◆◆◆◇◇

1 When something **drifts** somewhere, it is carried there by the movement of wind or water. *We proceeded to drift on up the river... The waves became rougher as they drifted.*
VERB; V adv/prep; V

2 If someone or something **drifts** into a situation, they get into that situation in a way that is not planned or controlled. *We need to offer young people drifting into crime an alternative set of values... She and her husband drifted apart and, eventually, they divorced... There is a general sense that the country and economy alike are drifting.*
VERB; V prep/adv; V

3 If you say that someone **drifts** around, you mean that they travel from place to place without a plan or settled way of life; used showing disapproval. *You've been drifting from job to job without any real commitment... You drift around the streets.*
VERB PRAGMATICS; V prep/adv; Also V

4 A **drift** is a movement away from somewhere or something, or a movement towards somewhere or something different. *...the drift towards the cities.*
N-COUNT: usu N prep

5 To **drift** somewhere means to move there slowly or gradually. *As rural factories shed labour, people drift towards the cities... The climbing balloon drifted silently over the countryside.*
VERB; V prep

6 If sounds **drift** somewhere, they can be heard but they are not very loud. *Cool summer dance sounds are drifting from the stereo indoors.*
VERB; V prep/adv

7 If snow **drifts**, it builds up into piles as a result of the movement of the wind. *The snow, except where it drifted, was only calf-deep... The storm caused severe drifting. ...the white and drifted snow.*
VERB; V; V-ing; V-ed

8 A **drift** is a mass of snow that has built up into a pile as a result of the movement of wind. *A nine-year-old boy was trapped in a snow drift.*
N-COUNT

9 A **drift** of something is an amount of it that has been created by the movement of wind or water. *There was a drift of smoke above the trees.*
N-COUNT: with supp, usu N of n

10 The **drift of** an argument or speech is the general point that is being made in it. *Grace was beginning to get his drift... Anybody who's listening will get the drift of what he was saying... I follow the drift of her conversation.*
N-SING: poss N, N of n =gist

drift off. If you **drift off** to sleep, you gradually fall asleep. *It was only when he finally drifted off to sleep that the headaches eased.*
PHRASAL VERB; V P to n; Also V P

drifter /drɪftəʳ/ **drifters.** If you describe someone as a **drifter**, you mean that they do not stay in one place or in one job for very long; used showing disapproval.
N-COUNT PRAGMATICS

driftwood /drɪftwʊd/. **Driftwood** is wood which has been carried onto the shore by the motion of the sea or a river, or which is still floating on the water.
N-UNCOUNT

drill /drɪl/ **drills, drilling, drilled** ◆◆◇◇◇

1 A **drill** is a tool or machine that you use for making holes. *...pneumatic drills. ...a dentist's drill.*
N-COUNT

2 When you **drill** into something or **drill** a hole in something, you make a hole in it using a drill. *He drilled into the wall of Lili's bedroom... I drilled five holes at equal distance.*
VERB; V prep; V n

3 When people **drill** for oil or water, they search for
VERB

it by drilling deep holes in the ground or in the bottom of the sea. *There have been proposals to drill for more oil... The team is still drilling.* ♦ **drilling** *Drilling is due to start early next year.*
V for n; V; N-UNCOUNT

4 A **drill** is a way that teachers teach their students something by making them repeat it many times. *The teacher runs them through a drill – the days of the week, the weather and some counting.*
N-COUNT

5 If you **drill** people, you teach them to do something by making them repeat it many times. *He drills the choir to a high standard.* ♦ **drilling** *...stimulation rather than repetitive drilling.*
VERB; V n; N-UNCOUNT

6 A **drill** is repeated training for a group of people, especially soldiers, so that they can do something quickly and efficiently. *The Marines carried out landing exercises in a drill that includes 18 ships and 90 aircraft... His hands were clasped behind him like a drill sergeant.*
N-VAR: oft N n

7 A **drill** is a routine exercise or activity, in which people practise what they should do in dangerous situations. *...a fire drill. ...air-raid drills.*
N-COUNT: oft n N

8 Drill is thick cotton material which is used for making uniforms and trousers. *...cotton drill.*
N-UNCOUNT: oft n N, N n

9 A **drill** is a long line in the earth, a few centimetres deep, which a farmer or gardener makes to plant seeds in. *Sow the seeds in drills about 1/2in. deep and 12in. apart.*
N-COUNT

drily /draɪli/. See **dry**.

drink /drɪŋk/ **drinks, drinking, drank, drunk** ◆◆◆◆◇

1 When you **drink** a liquid, you take it into your mouth and swallow it. *He drank his cup of tea... They'd stopped drinking beer and started on tequila... He drank thirstily from the pool under the rock.*
VERB; V n; V

2 To **drink** means to drink alcohol. *By his own admission, he was smoking and drinking too much... Never accept a ride with people who have been drinking.* ♦ **drinking** *She had left him because of his drinking... They patched up their differences by spending an evening of heavy drinking together.*
VERB; V; N-UNCOUNT

3 A **drink** is an amount of a liquid which you drink. *I'll get you a drink of water.*
N-COUNT: oft N *of* n

4 A **drink** is an alcoholic drink. *She felt like a drink after a hard day.*
N-COUNT

5 Drink is alcohol, such as beer, wine, or whisky. *Too much drink is bad for your health.*
N-UNCOUNT

6 See also **drinking**.

7 If you **drink** yourself **into a stupor** or **drink** yourself **into oblivion**, you drink so much alcohol that you lose consciousness or fall deeply asleep. *We drank ourselves into a stupor on cheap wine.*
PHRASES; V inflects

8 If someone **drinks** you **under the table**, they drink more alcohol than you are able to on a particular occasion. *At sixteen he could drink me under the table.*
V inflects

9 If someone **takes to drink**, they start to drink a lot of alcohol regularly, usually because they are depressed or worried about something. *He took to drink after his wife died.*
V inflects

10 People say '**I'll drink to that**' to show that they agree with and approve of something that someone has just said; an informal expression.
CONVENTION; PRAGMATICS

11 • to **drink** someone's **health**: see **health**.

drink in. If you **drink in** something that you see or hear, you pay a lot of attention to it and enjoy it. *She stood drinking in the glittering view.*
PHRASAL VERB; V P n (not pron); Also V n P

drink to. When people **drink to** someone or something, they refer to them and raise their glasses before drinking, as a way of celebrating something or showing that they want something to happen. *Let's drink to his memory, eh?.*
PHRASAL VERB; V P n

drink up. When you **drink up** an amount of liquid, you finish it completely. *Drink up your sherry and we'll go... Drink up, there's time for another.*
PHRASAL VERB; V P n (not pron); V P

drinkable /drɪŋkəbᵊl/

1 Water that is **drinkable** is clean and safe for drinking.
ADJ

2 If you say that a particular wine, beer, or other drink is **drinkable**, you mean that it tastes quite pleasant. *The food was good and the wine drinkable. ...a very drinkable plonk.*
ADJ-GRADED

drinker /drɪŋkəʳ/ **drinkers** ◆◇◇◇◇

1 If someone is a tea **drinker** or a beer **drinker**, for example, they regularly drink tea or beer. *Sherry drinkers far outnumber wine drinkers or whisky drinkers.*
N-COUNT: supp N

2 If you describe someone as a **drinker**, you mean that they drink alcohol, especially in large quantities. *You don't need to be a smoker or a drinker to risk heart disease... I'm not a heavy drinker.*
N-COUNT

drinking /drɪŋkɪŋ/. Someone's **drinking** friends or companions are people they regularly drink alcohol with. • See also **drink**.
ADJ: ADJ n

drinking fountain, drinking fountains. A **drinking fountain** is a device which supplies water for people to drink in places such as streets, parks, or schools.
N-COUNT

drinking water. **Drinking water** is water which it is safe to drink. ◆◇◇◇◇
N-UNCOUNT

drip /drɪp/ **drips, dripping, dripped** ◆◆◇◇◇

1 When liquid **drips** somewhere, or you **drip** it somewhere, it falls in individual small drops. *Sit your child forward and let the blood drip into a tissue or on to the floor... Amid the trees the sea mist was dripping and moisture formed on Tom's glasses. ...harassed parents trying to stop their children from dripping Coke on the carpets.*
V-ERG; V prep/adv; V; V n prep/adv

2 When something **drips**, drops of liquid fall from it. *A tap in the kitchen was dripping... Lou was dripping with perspiration... He was holding a cloth that dripped pink drops upon the floor.*
VERB; V; V *with* n; V n

3 A **drip** is a small individual drop of a liquid. *Drips of water rolled down the trousers of his uniform.*
N-COUNT

4 A **drip** is a piece of medical equipment by which a liquid is slowly passed through a tube into a patient's bloodstream. *I had a bad attack of pneumonia and spent two days in hospital on a drip.*
N-COUNT

5 If you say that something **is dripping with** a particular thing, you mean that it contains a lot of that thing; a literary use. *They were dazed by window displays dripping with diamonds and furs... His voice was dripping with sarcasm.*
VB: usu cont; V *with* n

6 If you call someone a **drip**, you mean that they are rather stupid and lacking in enthusiasm or energy; an informal use.
N-COUNT; PRAGMATICS

7 See also **drip-dry**, **dripping**.

drip-dry. **Drip-dry** clothes or sheets are made of a fabric that dries free of creases when it is hung up wet. *...drip-dry shirts.*
ADJ

dripping /drɪpɪŋ/

1 Dripping is the fat which comes out of meat when it is fried or roasted, and which can be used for frying food.
N-UNCOUNT

2 If you are **dripping wet**, you are so wet that water is dripping from you. *We were dripping wet from the spray.*
PHRASE: usu v-link PHR =sopping

3 See also **drip**.

drippy /drɪpi/. If you describe someone as **drippy**, you mean that they are rather stupid and weak. If you describe something such as a book or a type of music as **drippy**, you mean that you think it is rather stupid, dull, and sentimental; an informal word. *These men look a bit drippy. ...drippy infantile ideas.*
ADJ-GRADED; PRAGMATICS; =wet

drive /draɪv/ **drives, driving, drove, driven** ◆◆◆◆◆

1 When you **drive** somewhere, you operate a car or other vehicle and control its movement and direction. *I drove into town and went to a restaurant for dinner... He put the bags in the car and drove off... She never learned to drive... Mrs Glick drove her own car and the girls went in Nancy's convertible.* ♦ **driving** *It was an outrageous piece of dangerous driving.*
VERB; V prep/adv; V; V n; Also V n prep/adv; N-UNCOUNT

2 If you **drive** someone somewhere, you take them there in a car or other vehicle. *His daughter Carly drove him to the train station.*
VERB; V n prep/adv; Also V n

3 A **drive** is a journey in a car or other vehicle. *I thought we might go for a drive on Sunday.*
N-COUNT

4 A **drive** is a wide piece of hard ground, or sometimes a private road, that leads from the road to a person's house.
N-COUNT =driveway

5 If something **drives** a machine, it supplies the
VERB

power that makes it work. *The current flows into electric motors that drive the wheels.* V n

6 Drive is the power supplied by the engine to particular wheels in a car or other vehicle to make the vehicle move. *He put the jeep in four-wheel drive and splashed up the slope.* N-UNCOUNT: usu n N

7 You use **drive** to refer to the mechanical part of a computer which reads the data on disks and tapes, or writes data onto them. *The firm specialised in supplying pieces of equipment, such as terminals, tape drives or printers.* • See also **disk drive.** N-COUNT: usu supp N

8 If you **drive** something such as a nail into something else, you push it in or hammer it in using a lot of effort. *I had to use our sledgehammer to drive the pegs into the side of the path... We managed to hold a strip of lead along it long enough for me to drive in a nail.* VERB; V n prep; V n with adv

9 In games such as cricket, golf, or football, if a player **drives** a ball somewhere, they kick or hit it there with a lot of force. *The clearance fell to Armstrong, who drove the ball into the roof of the Liverpool net.* VERB; V n prep/adv; Also V n

10 In golf, a **drive** is the first stroke a player makes from the tee. *Woosnam sliced his drive into the bushes.* N-COUNT

11 If the wind, rain, or snow **drives** in a particular direction, it moves with great force in that direction. *Rain drove against the window.* ♦ **driving** *He crashed into a tree in driving rain. ...rescuers battling through driving snow.* VERB; V prep/adv; ADJ: ADJ n

12 If you **drive** people or animals somewhere, you make them go to or from that place. *The last offensive drove thousands of people into Thailand... Every summer the shepherds drive the sheep up to pasture... The smoke also drove mosquitoes away.* VERB; V n prep; V n with adv

13 To **drive** someone into a particular state or situation means to force them into that state or situation. *The recession and hospital bills drove them into bankruptcy... He nearly drove Elsie mad with his fussing.* VERB; V n *into/to* n; V n adj

14 The desire or feeling that **drives** someone to do something, especially something extreme, is the desire or feeling that causes them to do it. *More than once, depression drove him to attempt suicide... Jealousy drives people to murder... If we are driven by guilt, resentment and anxiety, our children will absorb these feelings and express them too. ...a man driven by a pathological need to win.* VERB; V n to-inf; V n *to* n; *be* V-ed; V-ed; Also V n

15 If you say that someone has **drive**, you mean they have energy and determination. *John will be best remembered for his drive and enthusiasm.* N-UNCOUNT

16 A **drive** is a very strong need or desire in human beings that makes them act in particular ways. *...compelling, dynamic sex drives.* N-COUNT =campaign

17 A **drive** is a special effort made by a group of people for a particular purpose. *The ANC is about to launch a nationwide recruitment drive... The Church in Haiti has played an important role in the drive towards democracy.* N-SING: with supp

18 Drive is used in the names of some streets. *...23 Queen's Drive, Malvern, Worcestershire.* N-IN-NAMES

19 See also **driving.**

20 If you ask someone **what** they **are driving at**, you are asking what they are trying to say or what they are saying indirectly. *It was clear Cohen didn't understand what Millard was driving at.* PHRASE: V inflects

21 • to **drive a hard bargain**: see **bargain.** • to **drive a point home**: see **home.**

drive away. To **drive** people **away** means to make them want to go away or stay away. *Patrick's boorish rudeness soon drove Monica's friends away... Increased crime in the Fifth Ward is driving away customers.* PHRASAL VERB; V n P; V P n (not pron)

drive off. If you **drive** someone or something **off**, you force them to go away and to stop attacking you or threatening you. *The government said it drove the guerrillas off with infantry and air strikes... Men drove off the dogs with stones.* PHRASAL VERB; V n P; V P n (not pron)

drive out. To **drive out** something means to make it disappear or stop operating. *Herbert offered whisky 'to drive out the chill'... He cut his rates to drive out rivals.* PHRASAL VERB; V P n (not pron)

drive-in, drive-ins. A **drive-in** is a restaurant, cinema, or other commercial place which is specially designed so that customers can use the services provided while staying in their cars. *...a small neat town, uncluttered by stores, gas stations or fast food drive-ins.* ► Also an adjective. *...a drive-in movie theater.* ◆◇◇◇◇ N-COUNT; ADJ: ADJ n

drivel /drɪvᵊl/. If you describe something that is written or said as **drivel**, you are critical of it because you think it is very silly; an informal word. *What absolute drivel!... She is still writing mindless drivel.* N-UNCOUNT PRAGMATICS =nonsense

driven /drɪvᵊn/. **Driven** is the past participle of **drive.**

driver /draɪvəʳ/ **drivers.** The **driver** of a vehicle is the person who is driving it. *The driver got out of his van. ...a taxi driver.* • See also **back-seat driver.** ◆◆◆◆◇ N-COUNT

driver's license, driver's licenses. In American English, a **driver's license** is a card showing that you are qualified to drive because you have passed a driving test. The usual British term is **driving licence.** N-COUNT

driver's seat

1 In a vehicle such as a car or a bus, the **driver's seat** is the seat where the person who is driving sits. N-SING: usu *the* N

2 If you say that someone **is in the driver's seat**, you mean that they are in control in a situation. *Now he knows he's in the driver's seat and can wait for a better deal.* PHRASE: v-link PHR, PHR after v

drive shaft, drive shafts. A **drive shaft** is a shaft in a car or other vehicle that transfers power from the gear box to the wheels. N-COUNT

driveway /draɪvweɪ/ **driveways.** A **driveway** is a piece of hard ground that leads from the road to a person's garage or front door. ◆◇◇◇◇ N-COUNT =drive

driving /draɪvɪŋ/. The **driving** force, idea, or motive behind something that happens or is done is the main thing that has a strong effect on it and makes it happen or be done in a particular way. *Consumer spending was the driving force behind the economic growth in the summer... Bruce Rioch's driving ambition is the main reason behind their new-found success.* • See also **drive.** ◆◇◇◇◇ ADJ: ADJ n

driving licence, driving licences; also spelled **driving license** in American English. In British English, a **driving licence** is a card showing that you are qualified to drive because you have passed a driving test. The usual American term is **driver's license.** ◆◇◇◇◇ N-COUNT =driver's licence

driving school, driving schools. A **driving school** is a business that employs instructors who give people lessons in how to drive a car. N-COUNT

driving seat

1 In a vehicle such as a car or a bus, the **driving seat** is the seat where the person who is driving the vehicle sits. *He got into the driving seat and started the engine.* N-SING: usu *the* N =driver's seat

2 If you say that someone is **in the driving seat**, you mean that they are in control in a situation. *At 69 he is as firmly in the driving seat of the company as ever.* PHRASE: usu v-link PHR, PHR after v

drizzle /drɪzᵊl/ **drizzles, drizzling, drizzled** ◆◇◇◇◇

1 Drizzle is light rain falling in fine drops. *The drizzle had now stopped and the sun was breaking through.* N-UNCOUNT: also *a* N

2 If it **is drizzling**, it is raining very lightly. *Clouds had come down and it was starting to drizzle... I walked home in the drizzling rain.* VERB; *it* V; V-ing

3 If you **drizzle** a liquid over food or **drizzle** food with a liquid, you pour a small quantity of the liquid all over the food. *Drizzle the remaining dressing over the duck and salad... Drizzle them with warmed extra virgin olive oil.* VERB; V n *over* n; V n *with* n; Also V n with *over*

drizzly /drɪzəli/. When the weather is **drizzly**, the sky is dull and grey and it is raining softly and steadily. *...a dull, drizzly afternoon... It was dull and slightly drizzly as we left.* ADJ-GRADED: oft *it* v-link ADJ

droll /droʊl/. Something or someone that is **droll** is amusing or witty, sometimes in an unexpected way; used in written English. *The band have a droll sense of humour.* ADJ-GRADED

drone /droun/ **drones, droning, droned** ◆◇◇◇◇

1 If something **drones**, it makes a low, continuous humming noise. *Above him an invisible plane droned through the night sky. ...a virtually non-stop droning noise in the background.* ▸ Also a noun. *...the constant drone of the motorways.* ♦ **droning** *...the droning of a plane far overhead.*
VERB; V; V-ing; N-SING: usu N *of* n; N-SING: usu N *of* n

2 If you say that someone **drones**, you mean that they keep talking about something in a boring way. *Chambers' voice droned, maddening as an insect around his head... The droning murmur of the doctor's voice in the bedroom had ceased.* ▸ Also a noun. *The minister's voice was a relentless drone.* ▸ **Drone on** means the same as **drone**. *Aunt Maimie's voice droned on... Daniel just drones on about American policy.*
VERB; PRAGMATICS; V; V-ing; N-SING; PHRASAL VERB; V P; V P *about* n

3 People who do not contribute anything to society or to an organization are sometimes described as **drones**. *A few are dim-witted drones, but most are talented, frustrated, wasted people.*
N-COUNT: usu pl; PRAGMATICS

4 A **drone** is a male bee.
N-COUNT

drone on. See **drone** 2.
PHRASAL VERB

drool /dru:l/ **drools, drooling, drooled**

1 If you say that someone **is drooling** over someone or something, you mean that they are looking at them with great pleasure, perhaps in an exaggerated or ridiculous way; used showing disapproval. *Fashion editors drooled over every item... Advertisers are already drooling at reports that this might bring 20 million dollars. ...his wife's constant drooling over a poodle.*
VERB; PRAGMATICS; V *over* n; V prep; V-ing; Also V

2 If a person or animal **drools**, saliva trickles from their mouth. *My dog Jacques is drooling on my shoulder.*
VERB; =slobber; V

droop /dru:p/ **droops, drooping, drooped.** ◆◇◇◇◇ If something **droops**, it hangs or leans downwards with no strength or firmness. *Crook's eyelids drooped and he yawned... Pale wilting roses drooped from a blue vase. ...a young man with a drooping moustache.* ▸ Also a noun. *...the droop of his shoulders.*
VERB; V; V prep; V-ing; N-SING: usu N *of* n

droopy /dru:pi/ **droopier, droopiest.** If you describe something as **droopy**, you mean that it hangs down limply with no strength or firmness. *...a tall man with a droopy moustache.*
ADJ-GRADED

drop /drɒp/ **drops, dropping, dropped** ◆◆◆◆◇

1 If a level or amount **drops** or if someone or something **drops** it, it quickly becomes less. *Temperatures can drop to freezing at night... Once the rate rises it never drops back to its previous level... His blood pressure had dropped severely... He had dropped the price of his London home by £1.25m.* ▸ Also a noun. *He was prepared to take a drop in wages... The poll indicates a drop in support for the Conservatives.*
V-ERG; V prep/adv; V; V n; N-COUNT: usu sing, oft N *in* n

2 If you **drop** something, you accidentally let it fall. *I dropped my glasses and broke them.*
VERB; V n

3 If something **drops** onto something else, it falls onto that thing. If something **drops** from somewhere, it falls from that place. *He felt hot tears dropping onto his fingers... Burning embers started dropping from the ceiling... His toupee dropped off, revealing his bald head.*
VERB; V prep/adv

4 If you **drop** something somewhere or if it **drops** there, you deliberately let it fall there. *Drop the noodles into the water... He dropped his plate into the sink. ...shaped pots that simply drop into their own container... Bombs drop round us and the floor shudders.* ♦ **dropping** *...the anniversary of the dropping of the first atomic bomb.*
V-ERG; V n prep/adv; V prep/adv; V; N-UNCOUNT: usu N *of* n

5 If a person or a part of their body **drops** to a lower position, or if they **drop** a part of their body to a lower position, they move to that position, often in a tired and lifeless way. *Nancy dropped into a nearby chair... She let her head drop... He dropped his hands on to his wasted, motionless legs.*
V-ERG; V prep/adv; V; V n prep/adv

6 To **drop** is used in expressions such as **to be about to drop** and **to dance until you drop** to emphasize that you are exhausted and can no longer continue doing something. *She looked about to drop... You have to run until you drop.*
VB: no cont; PRAGMATICS; V

7 If a man **drops** his trousers or pants, he pulls them down, usually as a joke and to be rude. *A couple of boozy revellers dropped their trousers.*
VERB; V n

8 If your voice **drops** or if you **drop** your voice, you speak more quietly. *Her voice will drop to a dismissive whisper... He dropped his voice and glanced round at the door.*
V-ERG; V *to* n; V n; Also V, V n *to* n

9 If you **drop** someone or something somewhere, you take them somewhere and leave them there, usually in a car or other vehicle. *He dropped me outside the hotel... Many children had been dropped at the stadium by their parents... Tim had dropped the letter in earlier.* ▸ **Drop off** means the same as **drop**. *Just drop me off at the airport... He was dropping off a late birthday present.*
VERB; V n prep/adv; PHRASAL VERB; V n P prep/adv; V P n (not pron)

10 If you **drop** an idea, course of action, or habit, you do not continue with it. *He was told to drop the idea... The prosecution was forced to drop the case... Many nations still had not dropped sanctions against South Africa.* ♦ **dropping** *This was one of the factors that led to President Suharto's dropping of his previous objections.*
VERB; =give up; V n; N-UNCOUNT: N *of* n

11 If someone **is dropped** by a sports team or organization, they are no longer included in that team or employed by that organization. *The country's captain was dropped from the tour party to England.*
VB: usu passive; *be* V-ed

12 If you **drop** a game or part of a game in a sports competition, you lose it. *Oremans, who has yet to drop a set, is on course for a match with Jana Novotna.*
VERB; V n

13 If you **drop** to a lower position in a sports competition, you move to that position. *Britain has dropped from second to third place in the league.*
VERB; V prep/adv

14 A **drop** of a liquid is a very small amount of it shaped like a little ball. In informal English, you can also use **drop** when you are referring to a very small amount of something such as a drink. *...a drop of blue ink... Add the cream a few drops at a time... I'll have another drop of that Italian milk.*
N-COUNT: oft N *of* n

15 **Drops** are a kind of medicine which you put drop by drop into your ears, eyes, or nose.
N-PLURAL: oft n N

16 Fruit or chocolate **drops** are small round sweets with a fruit or chocolate flavour.
N-COUNT: usu pl, n N

17 You use **drop** to talk about vertical distances. For example, a thirty-foot **drop** is a distance of thirty feet between the top of a cliff or wall and the bottom of it. *There was a sheer drop just outside my window... It's only a four-foot drop.*
N-COUNT: usu with supp

18 If you **drop a hint**, you give a hint or say something in a casual way. *If I drop a few hints he might give me a cutting.*
PHRASE: V inflects

19 If you want someone to **drop the subject**, **drop it**, or **let it drop**, you want them to stop talking about something, often because you are annoyed that they keep talking about it. *Mary Ann wished he would just drop it... Does that mean you're going to drop the subject?*
PHRASE: V inflects

20 See also **air-drop**. ● to **drop dead**: see **dead**. ● **at the drop of a hat**: see **hat**. ● to **drop** someone **a line**: see **line**. ● **a drop in the ocean**: see **ocean**.

drop away. If land or ground **drops away**, it slopes down so that it is at a lower level to where you are or from a particular point that has been mentioned. *To the south the hills dropped away to farmland... From the house, the garden drops away, surrounded by a rural scene of woodland.*
PHRASAL VERB; V P prep; V P

drop by. If you **drop by**, you visit someone informally; used mainly in American English. *She and Danny will drop by later... He tried to drop by the office of the guy in charge of marketing.*
PHRASAL VERB; V P; V P n

drop in. If you **drop in** on someone, you visit them informally, usually without having arranged it. *Whenever I'm up there I always drop in... Why not drop in for a chat?... She spent most of the day dropping in on friends in Edinburgh.*
PHRASAL VERB; =call in; V P; V P *on* n

drop off
PHRASAL VERB

1 See **drop** 9.

2 If you **drop off** to sleep, you go to sleep; an informal expression. *I must have dropped off to sleep... Just as I was dropping off, a strange thought crossed my mind.*
V P *to sleep*; V P

3 If the level of something **drops off**, it becomes
=decrease

less. *Sales to the British forces are expected to drop off... The daily toll of casualties has dropped off sharply.* VP

drop out PHRASAL VERB

1 If someone **drops out** of college or a race, for example, they leave it without finishing what they started. *He'd dropped out of high school at the age of 16... She dropped out after 20 kilometres with stomach trouble.* VP of n; VP

2 If someone **drops out**, they reject the accepted ways of society and live outside the usual system; often used showing disapproval. *She encourages people to keep their jobs rather than dropping out to live in a commune.* ● See also **drop-out**. VP

drop-dead. If you describe someone as, for example, **drop-dead** gorgeous, you mean that they are so gorgeous that people cannot fail to notice them; an informal expression. *She said that she sat next to Campbell-Black at dinner and that he was drop-dead gorgeous... The effect is soft and pretty rather than drop-dead sexy.* ▶ Also an adjective. *...the drop-dead glamour of the designer decade.* ADV: ADV adj; ADJ: ADJ n

droplet /drɒplət/ **droplets.** A **droplet** is a very small drop of liquid. *Droplets of sweat were welling up on his forehead. ...water droplets.* ◆◇◇◇◇ N-COUNT: oft N of n, n N

drop-out, drop-outs; also spelled **dropout.** ◆◇◇◇◇

1 If you describe someone as a **drop-out**, you disapprove of the fact that they have rejected the accepted ways of society, for example by not having a regular job. N-COUNT

2 A **drop-out** is someone who has left school or college before they have finished their studies. *...high-school drop-outs.* N-COUNT

3 If you refer to the **drop-out** rate, you are referring to the number of people who leave a school or college early, or leave a course or other activity before they have finished it. *The drop-out rate among students is currently one in three.* ADJ: ADJ n

dropper /drɒpəʳ/ **droppers.** A **dropper** is a small glass tube with a hollow rubber part on one end which you use for drawing up and dropping small amounts of liquid. N-COUNT

droppings /drɒpɪŋz/. **Droppings** are the faeces of birds and small animals. *...pigeon droppings.* ◆◇◇◇◇ N-PLURAL

dross /drɒs, AM drɔːs/. If you describe something as **dross**, you mean that it is of very poor quality or has no value; a literary word. *I go through phases where I can't write anything for two or three months and what I do write is just dross.* N-UNCOUNT =rubbish

drought /draʊt/ **droughts.** A **drought** is a long period of time during which no rain falls. *...a country where drought and famines have killed up to two million people during the last eighteen years... He told a press conference that Spain was suffering one of the worst droughts of the century.* ◆◆◇◇◇ N-VAR

drove /droʊv/. **Drove** is the past tense of **drive**.

drover /droʊvəʳ/ **drovers.** A **drover** is someone whose job is to make herds of sheep or cattle walk from one place to another. N-COUNT

droves /droʊvz/. If you say that people are going somewhere or doing something **in droves**, you are emphasizing that there is a very large number of them. *Scientists are leaving the country in droves... In the warm petrol-scented night, droves of young men and girls were strolling along the quays and packing the bars.* ◆◇◇◇◇ N-PLURAL: usu *in* N, *in* poss N, N *of* n PRAGMATICS

drown /draʊn/ **drowns, drowning, drowned** ◆◆◇◇◇

1 When someone **drowns** or **is drowned**, they die because they have gone or been pushed under water and cannot breathe. *Forty-eight people have drowned after their boat capsized during a storm... A child can drown in only a few inches of water... Last night a boy was drowned in the river... He walked into the sea and drowned himself... Dolphins have sometimes been known to save drowning swimmers.* V-ERG; V; *be* V-ed; V pron-refl; V-ing; Also V n

2 If you say that someone or something **is drowning** in something, you are emphasizing that they have a very large amount of it, or are completely covered in it. *We were drowning in data but starved of information. ...people who gradually find themselves drowning in debt... The potatoes were drowned in chilli.* VERB PRAGMATICS =inundate; V *in* n; *be* V-ed

3 If something **drowns** a sound, it is so loud that you cannot hear that sound properly. *Clapping drowned the speaker's words for a moment... The conversation was drowned by the arrival of the taxi.* VERB; V n

▶ **Drown out** means the same as **drown**. *Their cheers drowned out the protests of demonstrators... Her voice was drowned out by a loud crash.* PHRASAL VERB; V P n (not pron); Also V n P

4 If you say that someone **is drowning** their **sorrows**, you mean that they are drinking alcohol in order to forget something sad or upsetting that has happened to them. PHRASE: V inflects

drowse /draʊz/ **drowses, drowsing, drowsed.** If you **drowse**, you are almost asleep or just asleep. *Nina drowsed for a while.* VERB; V

drowsy /draʊzi/ **drowsier, drowsiest.** If you feel **drowsy**, you feel sleepy and cannot think clearly. *He felt pleasantly drowsy and had to fight off the urge to sleep.* ♦ **drowsiness** *Big meals during the day cause drowsiness.* ♦ **drowsily** /draʊzɪli/ *'Mm,' she answered drowsily.* ◆◇◇◇◇ ADJ-GRADED; N-UNCOUNT; ADV-GRADED: ADV with v

drudge /drʌdʒ/ **drudges.** If you describe someone as a **drudge**, you mean they have to work hard at a job which is not very important or interesting. N-COUNT

drudgery /drʌdʒəri/. You use **drudgery** to refer to jobs and tasks which are boring or unpleasant but which must be done. *People want to get away from the drudgery of their everyday lives.* N-UNCOUNT

drug /drʌg/ **drugs, drugging, drugged** ◆◆◆◆◆

1 A **drug** is a chemical which is given to people in order to treat or prevent an illness or disease. *The drug will be useful to hundreds of thousands of infected people. ...the drug companies.* N-COUNT

2 Drugs are also substances that some people smoke or inject into their blood because of their stimulating or pleasurable effects. In most countries, these uses of drugs are illegal. *His mother was on drugs, on cocaine... She was sure Leo was taking drugs... The problem of drug abuse and drug traffic continues to grow.* N-COUNT

3 If you **drug** a person or animal, you give them a chemical substance in order to make them sleepy or unconscious. *They drugged the guard dog with doped meatballs... She was drugged and robbed... He grew tired, and drifted off into a drugged sleep.* VERB; V n; V-ed

4 If food or drink **is drugged**, a chemical substance is added to it in order to make someone sleepy or unconscious when they eat or drink it. *I wonder now if that drink had been drugged... Anyone who knew you would drink that wine could have drugged it... A tourist was robbed after being given a drugged orange.* VERB; *be* V-ed; V n; V-ed

druggie /drʌgi/ **druggies;** also spelled **druggy.** If you refer to someone as a **druggie** you mean they are involved with or addicted to illegal drugs; an informal word. N-COUNT PRAGMATICS

druggist /drʌgɪst/ **druggists**

1 In American English, a **druggist** is someone who is qualified to sell medicines and drugs prescribed by a doctor. The British word is **chemist**. N-COUNT

2 In American English, a **druggist** or a **druggist's** is a shop where medicines and drugs prescribed by a doctor are sold. The British word is **chemist**. N-COUNT: oft *the* N

drugstore /drʌgstɔːʳ/ **drugstores.** In America, a **drugstore** is a shop where drugs and medicines are sold or given out, and where you can buy cosmetics, some household goods, and also drinks and snacks. ◆◇◇◇◇ N-COUNT: oft *the* N

Druid /druːɪd/ **Druids;** also spelled **druid.** A **Druid** is a priest of the Celtic religion. ◆◇◇◇◇ N-COUNT

drum /drʌm/ **drums, drumming, drummed** ◆◆◆◇◇

1 A **drum** is a musical instrument consisting of a skin stretched tightly over a round frame. You play a drum by beating it rhythmically with sticks or with your hands. N-COUNT: oft *the* N

2 A **drum** is also a large cylindrical container which is used to store fuel or other substances. *...an oil drum. ...a drum of chemical waste.* N-COUNT: usu with supp

3 A **drum** is also a hollow cylindrical structure N-COUNT which is part of a machine, for example a washing machine.

4 A **drum** is also a circular object on which wire or rope is wound and kept. *He had found a drum of electric cable.* N-COUNT

5 People sometimes refer to the eardrum as the **drum**. *Zara had been clutching her ear and when I examined it, I found that the drum was bright red and inflamed.* N-COUNT: usu *the* N in sing

6 If something **drums** on a surface, it hits it regularly, making a continuous beating sound. *He drummed his fingers on the leather top of his desk... Rain drummed on the roof of the car.* VERB V n *on/against* n V *on* n

7 See also **drumming**.

8 If someone **beats the drum** or **bangs the drum** for something, they support it strongly. *The trade secretary disagreed but promised to 'bang the drum for industry'.* PHRASE: V inflects

drum into. If you **drum** something **into** someone, you keep saying it to them until they understand it or remember it. *All through school we had it drummed into us that you need a degree to get a job... Standard examples were drummed into students' heads... They drummed it into her that you were not to know she was working for them.* PHRASAL VERB usu passive *have it* V-ed P n that *be* V-ed P n V *it* P n that Also V P n that

drum out. If someone **is drummed out of** an organization such as the armed forces or a club, they are forced to leave it in disgrace. *Sailors caught in a drugs scandal are to be drummed out of the service.* PHRASAL VERB usu passive *be* V-ed P P n

drum up. If you **drum up** support or business, you try to get it. *Kuwait is sending a delegation to drum up international support... It is to be hoped that he is merely drumming up business.* PHRASAL VERB V P n (not pron)

drumbeat /drʌmbiːt/ **drumbeats**

1 A **drumbeat** is the sound of a beat on a drum. N-COUNT

2 People sometimes describe a series of warnings or continuous pressure on someone to do something as a **drumbeat**; used mainly in American journalism. *All the while, the interventionists kept up the steady drumbeat of pressure to force the President into open conflict with Nazi Germany.* N-COUNT: oft N *of* n

drum kit, drum kits. A **drum kit** is a set of drums and cymbals. N-COUNT

drum major, drum majors. A **drum major** is a sergeant in the army who is in charge of the drummers in a military band, or who leads the band when they are marching. N-COUNT

drum majorette, drum majorettes. A **drum majorette** is a girl or young woman who marches in front of a band in a procession. Drum majorettes wear uniforms and carry sticks which at intervals they throw into the air and catch. N-COUNT

drummer /drʌməʳ/ **drummers.** A **drummer** is a person who plays a drum or drums in a band or group. ◆◆◇◇◇ N-COUNT

drumming /drʌmɪŋ/ ◆◇◇◇◇

1 **Drumming** is the action of playing the drums. N-UNCOUNT

2 **Drumming** is the sound or feeling of continuous beating. *He pointed up to the roof, through which the steady drumming of rain could be heard... His mouth was dry and he felt a drumming in his temples.* N-UNCOUNT: also *a* N, oft N *of* n

drum roll, drum rolls; also spelled **drumroll.** A **drum roll** is a series of drumbeats that follow each other so quickly that they make a continuous sound. A drum roll is often used to show that someone important is arriving, or to introduce someone. *A long drum roll introduced the trapeze artists.* N-COUNT

drumstick /drʌmstɪk/ **drumsticks**

1 A **drumstick** is the lower part of the leg of a bird such as a chicken which is cooked and eaten. N-COUNT: usu pl

2 **Drumsticks** are sticks used for beating a drum. N-COUNT

drunk /drʌŋk/ **drunks** ◆◆◇◇◇

1 Someone who is **drunk** has drunk so much alcohol that they cannot speak clearly or behave sensibly. *Stewart could not remember exactly why he had done it because he was so drunk... I got drunk and had to be carried home... He was arrested on suspicion of drunk driving.* ADJ-GRADED =inebriated

2 A **drunk** is someone who is drunk or frequently gets drunk. *A drunk lay in the alley.* N-COUNT =drunkard

3 If you are **drunk** with a strong emotion or an experience, you are in a state of great excitement because of it. *They are currently drunk with success... I felt drunk with the excitement of life.* ADJ-GRADED: v-link ADJ, usu ADJ *with* n

4 **Drunk** is the past participle of **drink**.

drunkard /drʌŋkəʳd/ **drunkards.** A **drunkard** is someone who frequently gets drunk. N-COUNT

drunken /drʌŋkən/ ◆◇◇◇◇

1 **Drunken** is used to describe events and situations that involve people who are drunk. *The pain roused him from his drunken stupor... He hit her with a frying pan during a drunken brawl.* ADJ-GRADED: ADJ n

2 A **drunken** person is drunk or is frequently drunk; used showing disapproval. *Groups of drunken hooligans smashed shop windows and threw stones.* ♦ **drunkenly** *One night Bob stormed drunkenly into her house and smashed some chairs.* ♦ **drunkenness** *He was arrested for drunkenness on his way to the football ground.* ADJ-GRADED: ADJ n PRAGMATICS ADV-GRADED: ADV with v N-UNCOUNT

dry /draɪ/ **drier** or **dryer, driest; dries, drying, dried** ◆◆◆◆◇

1 If something is **dry**, there is no water or moisture on it or in it. *Clean the metal with a soft dry cloth... Pat it dry with a soft towel... Once the paint is dry, apply a coat of the red ochre emulsion paint... The path was dry and slithery from the drought.* ♦ **dryness** *...the parched dryness of the air.* ADJ-GRADED ≠wet, damp N-UNCOUNT

2 When something **dries** or when you **dry** it, it becomes dry. *The washing might dry outside today, the sun's shining... Leave your hair to dry naturally whenever possible... Wash and dry the lettuce... Liz laughed again, got up from the water and began to dry herself.* V-ERG V V n

3 When you **dry** the dishes after a meal, you wipe the water off the plates, cups, knives, pans, and other things when they have been washed, using a cloth. *Mrs. Madrigal picked up a towel and began drying dishes next to her daughter.* ▶ **Dry up** means the same as **dry**; used in British English. *He got up and stood beside Julie, drying up the dishes while she washed.* VERB =wipe V n Also V PHRASAL VERB V P n (not pron) Also V P

4 If you say that your skin or hair is **dry**, you mean that it is less moist, oily, or soft than average or than normal. *Nothing looks worse than dry, cracked lips... Dry hair can be damaged by washing it too frequently... My skin's been getting a little dry recently.* ♦ **dryness** *Dryness of the skin can also be caused by living in centrally heated homes and offices.* ADJ-GRADED ≠greasy N-UNCOUNT

5 If the weather or a period of time is **dry**, there is no rain or there is much less rain than average. *Exceptionally dry weather over the past year had cut agricultural production... The spring had been unusually dry and we received only two tenths of an inch of rain during the entire month of June.* ADJ-GRADED ≠wet

6 A **dry** place or climate is one that gets very little rainfall. *It was one of the driest and dustiest places in Africa. ...a hot, dry climate where the sun is shining all the time.* ♦ **dryness** *He was advised to spend time in the warmth and dryness of Italy.* ADJ-GRADED: usu ADJ n =arid ≠wet N-UNCOUNT

7 In **the dry** means in a place or at a time that is not damp, wet, or rainy; used mainly in British English. *Such cars, however, do grip the road well, even in the dry.* N-SING: *the* N, usu *in* N ≠wet

8 If a river, lake, or well is **dry**, it is empty of water, usually because of hot weather and lack of rain. *The aquifer which had once fed the wells was pronounced dry... The single-engine plane landed at a dry lake in western Arizona... In the end the Volga's waters will run dry.* ADJ-GRADED

9 If an oil well is **dry**, it is no longer producing any oil. *To harvest oil and gas profitably from the North Sea, it must focus on the exploitation of small reserves as the big wells run dry.* ADJ: usu v-link ADJ =exhausted ≠productive

10 If you are **dry**, you are thirsty and need to drink something; an informal use. *She was suddenly thirsty and dry.* ADJ-GRADED: v-link ADJ =parched

11 If your mouth or throat is **dry**, it has little or no saliva in it, and so feels very unpleasant, perhaps because you are tense or ill. *His mouth was still dry, he would certainly be glad of a drink... My throat* ADJ-GRADED: usu v-link ADJ

was dry. I was at a loss for words. ♦ **dryness** *Symptoms included frequent dryness in the mouth.* N-UNCOUNT: usu with supp

12 A **dry** cough is one that does not produce any phlegm. ADJ: ADJ n

13 If someone has **dry** eyes, there are no tears in their eyes; often used with negatives or in contexts where you are expressing surprise that they are not crying. *There were few dry eyes in the house when I finished... She didn't wince and her eyes were dry. Talk about brave. She was unbelievable.* ADJ ≠moist

14 If a country, state, or city is **dry**, it has laws or rules which forbid anyone to drink, sell, or buy alcoholic drink; an informal use. *Gujrat has been a totally dry state for the past thirty years.* ADJ =teetotal

15 If you say that someone is sucking something **dry** or milking it **dry**, you are criticizing them for taking all the good things from it until there is nothing left. *...a shady rip-off industry that sucks its talent dry then discards it... He's just milking the company dry.* ADJ: v n ADJ PRAGMATICS

16 **Dry** humour is very amusing, but in a subtle and clever way; used expressing approval. *Though the pressure Fulton is under must be considerable, he has retained his dry humour... Mr Brooke is renowned for his dry wit.* ADJ-GRADED: usu ADJ n PRAGMATICS =witty ♦ **drily** *As Rossini drily observed, 'Wagner has lovely moments but awful quarters of an hour.' ...a frank and drily witty woman.* ADV: ADV with v, ADV adj ♦ **dryness** *The song has a wry dryness you won't recognise.* N-UNCOUNT

17 If you describe a voice as **dry**, you mean that it is cold or dull, and does not express any emotions; mainly used in written English. *When he crept back to his desk, he heard the dry voice of Father Laurence.* ADJ-GRADED =thin ≠rich ♦ **drily** *'Possible,' I said drily, 'but not likely'.* ADV: ADV with v

18 If you describe something such as a book, play, or activity as **dry**, you mean that it is dull and uninteresting. *My eyelids were drooping over the dry, academic phrases... A lot of the work was very dry and boring in Westminster.* ADJ-GRADED =dull, boring

19 **Dry** bread or toast is plain and not covered with butter or jam. *For breakfast, they had dry bread and tea.* ADJ: ADJ n =unbuttered

20 **Dry** sherry or wine does not have a sweet taste. *...a glass of chilled, dry white wine.* ADJ ≠sweet

21 If an actor or actress **dries**, he or she forgets his or her lines in a play; used mainly in British English. *My opening was fair, the second spot fair and I dried completely in the 4th.* VERB V

22 • **high and dry**: see **high**. • **home and dry**: see **home**.

dry off. If something **dries off** or if you **dry** it **off**, the moisture on its surface disappears or is removed. *They are then scrubbed with clean water and left to dry off for an hour or two in a warm room... When the bath water started to cool I got out, dried myself off, and dressed.* PHRASAL VERB ERG V P V n P Also V P n (not pron)

dry out PHRASAL VERB

1 If something **dries out** or **is dried out**, it loses all the moisture that was in it and becomes hard. *If the soil is allowed to dry out the tree could die... The cold winds dry out your skin very quickly.* ERG V P V P n (not pron) Also V n P

2 If someone **dries out** or **is dried out**, they are cured of alcoholism; an informal use. *He checked into Cedars Sinai Hospital to dry out... I approved the doctor's order to keep him in the room till he was dried out.* ERG V P V-ed P

dry up PHRASAL VERB

1 If something **dries up** or if something **dries** it **up**, it loses all its moisture and becomes completely dry and shrivelled or hard. *As the day goes on, the pollen dries up and becomes hard... Warm breezes from the South dried up the streets.* ERG V P V P n (not pron) Also V n P ♦ **dried-up** *...a tuft or two of dried-up grass.* ADJ =dessicated

2 If a river, lake, or well **dries up**, it becomes empty of water, usually because of hot weather and a lack of rain. *Reservoirs are drying up and farmers have begun to leave their land in search of water... The fountain is reputed never to dry up.* V P ♦ **dried-up** *...a dried-up river bed.* ADJ =dry

3 If a supply of something **dries up**, it stops. *The main source of income and employment, tourism, is expected to dry up completely this summer... Credit from foreign banks is drying up... New orders have dried up and some existing ones look dodgy.* =disappear V P

4 If you **dry up** when you are speaking, you stop in the middle of what you were saying, because you cannot think what to say next. *If you ask a woman what she is good at she will dry up after two minutes, but if you ask what she is not good at she will talk for two hours.* V P

5 See **dry** 3.

6 See also **dried-up**, **drying-up**.

dry-clean, dry-cleans, dry-cleaning, dry-cleaned. When things such as clothes **are dry-cleaned**, they are cleaned with a liquid chemical rather than with water. *Natural-filled duvets must be dry-cleaned by a professional.* VB: usu passive be V-ed

dry cleaner, dry cleaners

1 A **dry cleaner** is someone who has a shop where things can be dry-cleaned. N-COUNT

2 A **dry cleaner** or a **dry cleaner's** is a shop where things can be dry-cleaned. N-COUNT

dry-cleaning; also spelled **dry cleaning**.

1 **Dry-cleaning** is the action or work of dry-cleaning things such as clothes. *He owns a dry-cleaning business.* N-UNCOUNT

2 **Dry-cleaning** is things that have been dry-cleaned, or that are going to be dry-cleaned. N-UNCOUNT

dry dock, dry docks. A **dry dock** is a dock from which water can be removed so that ships, boats, or barges can be repaired or finished. N-COUNT

dryer /draɪəʳ/ **dryers;** also spelled **drier**. A **dryer** is a machine for drying things. There are different kinds of dryer, for examples ones designed for drying clothes, crops, or people's hair or hands. *If you buy a drier, look for one with a sensor which switches off when clothes are dry. ...hot air electric hand dryers.* • See also **dry**, **tumble-dryer**. ◆◇◇◇◇ N-COUNT: oft n N

dry-eyed. If you say that someone is **dry-eyed**, you mean that although they are in a very sad situation they are not actually crying. *At the funeral he held her hand, but she was dry-eyed, composed, for tears achieved nothing.* ADJ ≠tearful

dry goods. In American English, **dry goods** are cloth, thread, and other things that are sold at a draper's shop. N-PLURAL

drying up. When you do the **drying up**, you dry things such as plates, pans, knives, and cups after they have been washed. N-UNCOUNT: also *the* N

dry land. If you talk about **dry land**, you are referring to land, in contrast to the sea or the air. *We were glad to be on dry land again.* N-UNCOUNT: oft *on* N

dry rot. **Dry rot** is a serious disease of wood. It is caused by a fungus and causes wood to decay. *The house was riddled with dry rot.* N-UNCOUNT

dry-stone wall, dry-stone walls. American English uses the form **dry wall**. A **dry-stone wall** is a wall that has been built by fitting stones together without using any mortar. N-COUNT

DT's /diː tiːz/. When alcoholics have **the DT's**, the alcohol they have drunk causes their bodies to shake uncontrollably, and makes them unable to think clearly. N-PLURAL: *the* N

dual /djuːəl, AM duː-/. **Dual** means having two parts, functions, or aspects. *...his dual role as head of the party and head of state... Rob may be entitled to dual nationality.* ◆◆◇◇◇ ADJ: ADJ n

dual carriageway, dual carriageways; also spelled **dual-carriageway**. In Britain, a **dual carriageway** is a road which has two lanes of traffic travelling in each direction with a strip of grass or concrete down the middle to separate the two lots of traffic. The American expression is **divided highway**. N-VAR

dualism /djuːəlɪzəm, AM duː-/. **Dualism** is the state of having two main parts or aspects, or the belief that something has two main parts or aspects; a formal word. *He ignores the traditional Christian dualism between body and soul. ...the Gnostic dualism of good and evil struggling for supremacy.* N-UNCOUNT

duality /djuːælɪti, AM duː-/ **dualities.** A **duality** is a situation in which two contradictory ideas or feelings exist at the same time; a formal word. *We live in a world of duality, day and night, positive and negative, male and female, etc.* N-VAR

dub /dʌb/ **dubs, dubbing, dubbed** ◆◆◇◇◇
1 If someone or something **is dubbed** a particular thing, they are given that description or nickname. *...the man whom the Labour opposition dubbed as the 'no change Prime Minister'... At the height of her career, Orson Welles dubbed her 'the most exciting woman in the world'.* VERB V n *as* n V n n
2 If a film or soundtrack **is dubbed**, a different soundtrack is added with actors speaking a translation of the dialogue. *It was dubbed into Spanish for Mexican audiences. ...a badly dubbed foreign film.* VB: usu passive *be* V-ed *into* n V-ed Also *be* V-ed

dubious /djuːbiəs, AM duː-/ ◆◆◇◇◇
1 If you describe something as **dubious**, you mean that you do not consider it to be completely honest, safe, or reliable. *This claim seems to us to be rather dubious... Soho was still a highly dubious area... Those figures alone are a dubious basis for such a conclusion.* ♦ **dubiously** *Carter was dubiously convicted of shooting three white men in a bar.* ADJ-GRADED =questionable ADV-GRADED: ADV after v, ADV adj/-ed
2 If you are **dubious** about something, you are not completely sure about it and have not yet made up your mind about it. *My parents were a bit dubious about it all at first but we soon convinced them.* ♦ **dubiously** *He eyed Coyne dubiously.* ADJ-GRADED: v-link ADJ, oft ADJ *about* n =uncertain ADV
3 If you say that someone has the **dubious** honour or the **dubious** pleasure of doing something, you are indicating that what they are doing is not an honour or pleasure at all, but is, in fact, unpleasant or bad. *Nagy has the dubious honour of being the first athlete to be banned in this way... El Salvador has earned the dubious distinction of having the worst soil erosion in continental America.* ADJ-GRADED: ADJ n PRAGMATICS

ducal /djuːkᵊl, AM duː-/. **Ducal** places or things belong to or are connected with a duke; a formal word. ADJ: ADJ n

duchess /dʌtʃɪs/ **duchesses.** A **duchess** is a woman who has the same rank as a duke, or who is a duke's wife or widow. *...the Duchess of York.* ◆◇◇◇◇ N-COUNT: oft *the* N *of* n

duchy /dʌtʃi/ **duchies.** A **duchy** is an area of land that is owned or ruled by a duke. *...the Duchy of Cornwall.* ◆◇◇◇◇ N-COUNT: oft *the* N *of* n

duck /dʌk/ **ducks, ducking, ducked** ◆◆◇◇◇
1 A **duck** is a very common water bird with short legs, webbed feet, a short neck, and a large flat beak. *Chickens and ducks scratch around the outbuildings.* ► **Duck** is the flesh of this bird when it is eaten as food. *...honey roasted duck.* N-VAR N-UNCOUNT
2 A **duck** is a female duck. The male is called a drake. *I brought in one drake and three ducks.* N-COUNT
3 If you **duck**, you move your head or the top half of your body quickly downwards to avoid something that might hit you, or to avoid being seen. *He ducked in time to save his head from a blow from the poker... He ducked his head to hide his admiration... I wanted to duck down and slip past but they saw me.* VERB V V n V adv/prep
4 If you **duck** something such as a blow, you avoid it by moving your head or body quickly downwards. *Hans deftly ducked their blows.* VERB =dodge V n
5 If you **duck** into a place, you move there quickly, often in an attempt to avoid danger or to avoid being seen. *Matt ducked into his office... He ducked through the door and looked about frantically.* VERB =dart V prep/adv
6 You say that someone **ducks** a duty or responsibility when you disapprove of the fact that they avoid it. *The Opposition reckons the Health Secretary has ducked all the difficult decisions... He had ducked the confrontation with United Nations inspectors last summer.* VERB PRAGMATICS =shirk V n
7 If someone **ducks** someone else, they force them or their head under water for a short time. *She splashed around in the pool with Mark, rowdily trying to duck him.* VERB V n
8 See also **lame duck, sitting duck.**
9 In British English, some people call other people **duck** or **ducks** as a sign of affection. *Oh, I am glad to see you, duck.* N-VOC PRAGMATICS
10 You say that criticism is **like water off a duck's back** or **water off a duck's back** to emphasize that it is not having any effect on the person being criticized. *All the criticism is water off a duck's back to me.* PHRASES v-link PHR PRAGMATICS
11 If you **take to** something **like a duck to water**, you discover that you are naturally good at it or that you find it very easy to do. *Some mothers take to breastfeeding like a duck to water, while others find they need some help to get started.* V inflects

duck out. If you **duck out** of something that you are supposed to do, you avoid doing it. *George ducked out of his forced marriage to a cousin... You can't duck out once you've taken on a responsibility.* PHRASAL VERB V P *of* n V P

duckling /dʌklɪŋ/ **ducklings.** A **duckling** is a young duck. • See also **ugly duckling.** N-COUNT

duct /dʌkt/ **ducts** ◆◇◇◇◇
1 A **duct** is a pipe, tube, or channel which carries a liquid or gas. *...a big air duct in the ceiling.* N-COUNT: usu with supp
2 A **duct** is a tube in your body which carries a liquid such as tears or bile. *...tear ducts.* N-COUNT: with supp

dud /dʌd/ **duds. Dud** means not working properly or not successful; an informal word. *He replaced a dud valve.* ► Also a noun. *The mine was a dud.* ◆◇◇◇◇ ADJ: ADJ n N-COUNT

dude /djuːd, AM duːd/ **dudes.** A **dude** is a man; an informal word, used mainly in American English. *My doctor is a real cool dude.* ◆◇◇◇◇ N-COUNT

dude ranch, dude ranches. A **dude ranch** is an American ranch where people can have holidays during which they can do activities such as riding or camping. N-COUNT

dudgeon /dʌdʒᵊn/. If you say that someone is **in high dudgeon**, you are emphasizing that they are very angry or resentful about something. *Washington businesses are in high dudgeon over the plan.* PHRASE: v-link PHR PRAGMATICS

due /djuː, AM duː/ **dues** ◆◆◆◆◇
1 If an event is **due to** something, it happens or exists as a direct result of that thing. *The country's economic problems are largely due to the weakness of the recovery... If the trip is a success, a lot of this will be due to Mr Green's efforts.* PHR-PREP: v-link PREP n =because of
2 You can say **due to** to introduce the reason for something happening. Some speakers of English believe that it is not correct to use **due to** in this way. *Due to the large volume of letters he receives Dave regrets he is unable to answer queries personally... Jobs could be lost in the defence industry due to political changes sweeping Europe.* PHR-PREP =owing to
3 If something is **due** at a particular time, it is expected to happen, be done, or arrive at that time. *The results are due at the end of the month... The first price increases are due to come into force in July... Jason is currently in Britain to finish recording his second album which is due out in May... Mr Carter is due in London on Monday. ...customers who paid later than twenty days after the due date.* ADJ: usu v-link ADJ, oft ADJ to-inf, ADJ prep/adv =expected
4 **Due** attention and consideration is the proper, reasonable, or deserved amount of it under the circumstances. *After due consideration it was decided to send him away to live with foster parents... I do hope that people will make use of footpaths and treat them with due attention that is needed.* ADJ: ADJ n =proper
5 Something that is **due**, or that is **due** to someone, is owed to them, either as a debt or because they have a right to it. *I was sent a cheque for £1,525 and advised that no further pension was due... I've got some leave due to me and I was going to Tasmania for a fortnight.* ► Also a preposition. *He had not taken a summer holiday that year but had accumulated the leave due him.* ADJ: v-link ADJ, oft ADJ *to* n PREP: oft n PREP n
6 If someone is **due for** something, that thing is planned to happen or be given to them now, or very soon, often after they have been waiting for it for a long time. *The deputy chief inspector rang me up and said, 'Miss Smith, you know you are due for a move?'... Although not due for release until 2001, he was let out of his low-security prison to spend a* ADJ: v-link ADJ *for* n

weekend with his wife. ► Also a preposition. *I reckon I'm due one of my travels.* PREP

7 **Dues** are sums of money that you give regularly to an organization that you belong to, for example a social club or trade union, in order to pay for your membership. *Only 18 of the UN's 180 members had paid their dues by the January deadline.* N-PLURAL: oft poss N

8 **Due** is used before the words 'north', 'south', 'east', or 'west' to indicate that something is in exactly the direction mentioned. *They headed due north... The Thames flows due south from Oxford, through the market town of Abingdon. ...a mining town 40 miles due east of Los Angeles.* ADV: ADV adv/adj

9 If you say that something will happen or take place **in due course**, you mean that you cannot make it happen any quicker and it will happen when the time is right for it. *In due course the baby was born... The arrangements will be published in due course.* PHRASES PHR with cl

10 You can say **'to give** him his **due'**, or **'giving** him his **due'** when you are admitting that there are some good things about someone, even though there are things that you do not like about them. *To give Linda her due, she had tried to encourage John in his school work.* PRAGMATICS =to be fair

11 You can say **'with due respect'** when you are about to disagree politely with someone. *With all due respect I submit to you that you're asking the wrong question.* PHR cl PRAGMATICS

duel /djuːəl, AM duː-/ **duels, duelling, duelled;** spelled **dueling, dueled** in American English. ◆◇◇◇◇

1 A **duel** is a formal fight between two people in which they use guns or swords in order to settle a quarrel. *He killed a man in one duel and was himself wounded in another.* N-COUNT

2 You can refer to a conflict between two people or groups as a **duel**. *The area has been the scene of sporadic artillery duels over the last six weeks.* N-COUNT

3 To **duel** means to fight a duel or be involved in a conflict. *We duelled for two years and Peterson made the most of it, playing us off against each other. ...two silver French duelling pistols.* V-RECIP pl-n V V-ing Also V *with* n, V (non-recip)

duet /djuːet, AM duː-/ **duets.** A **duet** is a piece of music sung or played by two people. ◆◇◇◇◇ N-COUNT

duff /dʌf/ **duffs, duffing, duffed.** In informal British English, if you describe something as **duff**, you mean it is useless, broken, or of poor quality. *Most of us have had to take a duff job sometime in our lives when opportunities were scarce.* ◆◇◇◇◇ ADJ-GRADED

duff up. To **duff** someone **up** means to hit them many times and injure them; used in informal British English. *She began telling us about some fight on a bus in which our kids had duffed up the bus conductor.* PHRASAL VERB =beat up V P n (not pron) Also V n P

duffel /dʌfᵊl/ **duffels**

1 A **duffel** is the same as a **duffel coat**. N-COUNT

2 A **duffel** is the same as a **duffel bag**. N-COUNT

duffel bag /dʌfᵊl bæg/ **duffel bags;** also spelled **duffle bag**. A **duffel bag** is a bag shaped like a cylinder and made of strong fabric such as canvas. A duffel bag has a string at one end that is used to close the bag and to carry it with. N-COUNT

duffel coat /dʌfᵊl kout/ **duffel coats;** also spelled **duffle coat**. A **duffel coat** is a heavy coat with a hood and long buttons that fasten with loops. N-COUNT

duffer /dʌfəʳ/ **duffers.** If you describe someone as a **duffer**, you mean that they are very bad at doing something; an old-fashioned, informal word, used mainly in British English. *Waugh was a duffer at cricket.* N-COUNT PRAGMATICS

duffle /dʌfᵊl/. See **duffel bag, duffel coat.**

dug /dʌg/. **Dug** is the past tense and past participle of **dig**.

dugout /dʌgaʊt/ **dugouts**

1 A **dugout** is a canoe that is made by hollowing out a log. N-COUNT

2 A **dugout** is a shelter made by digging a hole in the ground and then covering it or tunnelling so that the shelter has a roof over it. N-COUNT

duke /djuːk, AM duːk/ **dukes.** A **duke** is a nobleman of high rank. *...the Queen and the Duke of Edinburgh.* ◆◇◇◇◇ N-COUNT: oft *the* N *of* n

dukedom /djuːkdəm, AM duːk-/ **dukedoms**

1 A **dukedom** is the rank or title of a duke. *...the present heir to the dukedom.* N-COUNT

2 A **dukedom** is the land owned by a duke. N-COUNT

dulcet /dʌlsɪt/

1 A **dulcet** voice is one that is gentle and pleasant to listen to; a literary word. *Quickly, in her dulcet voice, Tamara told him what had happened.* ADJ: ADJ n

2 People often use the expression **dulcet tones** to refer humorously to someone's voice. *You hear his dulcet tones on the Radio 1 trailers in the morning.* PHRASE: with poss

dull /dʌl/ **duller, dullest; dulls, dulling, dulled** ◆◆◇◇◇

1 If you describe someone or something as **dull**, you mean they are not interesting or exciting. *They are both nice people but can be rather dull... I felt she found me boring and dull... The documentary lasts for more than two-and-a-half hours, and there is scarcely a dull minute.* ♦ **dullness** *They enjoy anything that breaks the dullness of their routine life.* ADJ-GRADED PRAGMATICS =boring ≠lively N-UNCOUNT

2 Someone or something that is **dull** is not very lively or energetic. *The body's natural rhythms mean we all feel dull and sleepy between 1 and 3pm.* ♦ **dully** *His giant face had a rough growth of stubble, his eyes looked dully ahead.* ♦ **dullness** *Did you notice any unusual depression or dullness of mind?* ADJ-GRADED =sluggish ADV: ADV after v N-UNCOUNT

3 A **dull** colour or light is not bright. *The stamp was a dark, dull blue colour with a heavy black postmark.* ♦ **dully** *The street lamps gleamed dully through the night's mist.* ADJ-GRADED: usu ADJ n =sombre ADV: ADV with v

4 You say the weather is **dull** when it is very cloudy. *It's always dull and raining.* ADJ-GRADED ≠sunny

5 **Dull** sounds are not very clear or loud. *The long whining whistle of a shell was followed by the dull boom of the explosion... The coffin closed with a dull thud.* ♦ **dully** *He heard his heart thump dully but more quickly.* ADJ-GRADED: usu ADJ n ≠sharp ADV: ADV after v

6 **Dull** feelings are weak and not intense. *The pain, usually a dull ache, gets worse with exercise... I realized with a kind of dull shock that I didn't recognize a single name.* ♦ **dully** *His arm throbbed dully.* ADJ-GRADED: ADJ n ≠sharp ADV

7 If a knife or blade is **dull**, it is not sharp; a fairly old-fashioned use. ADJ-GRADED =blunt

8 If something **dulls** or if it **is dulled**, it becomes less intense, bright, or lively. *Her eyes dulled and she gazed blankly... He can dull your senses with facts and figures... Share prices and trading have been dulled by worries over the war.* V-ERG ≠enliven V V n

dullard /dʌləʳd/ **dullards.** If you say that someone is a **dullard**, you mean that they are rather slow-witted and unimaginative; an old-fashioned word, used mainly in American English. N-COUNT

duly /djuːli, AM duː-/ ◆◇◇◇◇

1 If you say that something **duly** happened or was done, you mean that it was expected to happen or was requested, and it did happen or it was done. *It was the beginning of the end and Watson duly went on to win his fourth Open Golf Championship... Westcott appealed to Waite for an apology, which he duly received.* ADV: ADV before v

2 If something is **duly** done, it is done in the correct way; a formal use. *He is a duly elected president of the country and we're going to be giving him all the support we can.* ADV: ADV before v

dumb /dʌm/ **dumber, dumbest** ◆◇◇◇◇

1 Someone who is **dumb** is completely unable to speak. *...a young deaf and dumb man.* ADJ =mute

2 If someone is **dumb** on a particular occasion, they cannot speak because they are angry, shocked, or surprised; a literary use. *We were all struck dumb for a minute.* ♦ **dumbly** *I shook my head dumbly, not believing him.* ADJ: v-link ADJ =mute ADV: ADV with v

3 In informal English, if you call a person **dumb**, you mean that they are stupid or foolish. *I've met a lot of dumb people... The questions were set up to make her look dumb.* ADJ-GRADED PRAGMATICS

4 If you say that something is **dumb**, you think that it is silly and annoying; an informal use, used ADJ-GRADED =stupid mainly in American English. *I came up with this dumb idea... It's the media that's dumb.*

5 Something that is **dumb** is done or expressed without words; a literary use. *An expression of dumb recognition wiggled across her features.* ADJ: ADJ n =mute ≠eloquent

dumb-bell /dʌmbel/ **dumb-bells;** also spelled **dumbbell**. A **dumb-bell** is a short bar with weights on either side which people use for physical exercise to strengthen their arm and shoulder muscles. N-COUNT

dumbfound /dʌmfaʊnd/ **dumbfounds, dumbfounding, dumbfounded.** If someone or something **dumbfounds** you, they surprise you very much. *This suggestion dumbfounded Joe.* VERB =astonish V n

dumbfounded /dʌmfaʊndɪd/. If you are **dumbfounded**, you are extremely surprised by something. *I stood there dumbfounded, scarcely able to believe the evidence of my senses.* ADJ-GRADED: usu v-link ADJ =astonished

dumbstruck /dʌmstrʌk/. If you are **dumbstruck**, you are so shocked or surprised that you cannot speak. *We were dumbstruck. We just couldn't believe our eyes when she appeared.* ADJ-GRADED: usu v-link ADJ PRAGMATICS =speechless

dumb waiter, dumb waiters; also spelled **dumbwaiter**. A **dumb waiter** is a lift used to carry food and dishes from one floor of a building to another. N-COUNT

dum-dum /dʌm dʌm/ **dum-dums.** A **dum-dum** or a **dum-dum bullet** is a bullet that is very soft or hollow at the front. Dum-dum bullets cause large and serious wounds because they break into small pieces and spread out when they hit someone. N-COUNT

dummy /dʌmi/ **dummies** ◆◇◇◇◇

1 A **dummy** is a model of a person, often used to display clothes. *...the bottom half of a shop-window dummy. ...the ventriloquist's dummy.* N-COUNT

2 You can use **dummy** to refer to things that are not real, but have been made to look or behave as if they are real. *Dummy patrol cars will be set up beside motorways to frighten speeding motorists... They asked her to put together a dummy for a new magazine... Soldiers were still using dummy weapons because real guns were not yet available.* N-COUNT: oft N n =fake, false

3 In British English, a baby's **dummy** is a rubber or plastic object that you give the baby to suck so that it feels comforted. The usual American word is **pacifier**. N-COUNT

4 If you call someone a **dummy**, you mean that you think they are stupid; an informal use. *'You're a dummy, Mack,' she yelled.* N-COUNT PRAGMATICS =numbskull

5 A **dummy** or **dummy hand** is a hand of cards in a game of bridge or whist which is placed on the table so all the players can see it. N-COUNT

dummy run, dummy runs. A **dummy run** is a trial or test procedure which is carried out in order to see if a plan or process works properly; used in British English. *Before we started we did a dummy run, checking out all the streets and offices we would use, and planning our escape route.* N-COUNT =test run

dump /dʌmp/ **dumps, dumping, dumped** ◆◆◆◇◇

1 If you **dump** something somewhere, you put it or unload it there quickly and carelessly; an informal use. *We dumped our bags at the nearby Grand Hotel and hurried towards the market... He got my haversack from the cab and dumped it at my feet.* VERB V n prep/adv

2 If something **is dumped** somewhere, it is put or left there because it is no longer wanted or needed; an informal use. *The getaway car was dumped near a motorway tunnel... A million tonnes of untreated sewage is dumped into the sea... The government declared that it did not dump radioactive waste at sea.* ♦ **dumping** *German law forbids the dumping of hazardous waste on German soil.* VERB =get rid of be V-ed V n; N-UNCOUNT

3 A **dump** is a place where rubbish is left, for example on open ground outside a town. *...companies that bring their rubbish straight to the dump... The walled garden was used as a dump.* N-COUNT =tip

4 If you say that a place is a **dump**, you think it is ugly and unpleasant to live in or visit; an informal use. *'What a dump!' Christabel said, standing in the doorway of the youth hostel.* N-COUNT PRAGMATICS

5 A **dump** is a place where an army stores food, weapons, or ammunition temporarily while it is stationed in a particular place. N-COUNT: usu n N

6 To **dump** something such as an idea, policy, or practice means to stop supporting or using it; an informal use. *Ministers believed it was vital to dump the poll tax before the election.* VERB =ditch V n

7 If a firm or company **dumps** goods, it sells large quantities of them at prices far below their real value, usually in another country, in order to gain a bigger market share or to keep prices high in the home market. *It produces more than it needs, then dumps its surplus onto the world market.* VERB V n

8 If you **dump** someone, you end your relationship with them; an informal use. *My heart sank because I thought he was going to dump me for another girl... She was dumped by her long-term lover after five years... I suggested that we not only dump the two companies, but that we also should ditch any other business not involved in soft drinks.* VERB =ditch V n

9 If you say that a parent **dumps** a child with someone, you are criticizing the parent for leaving the child to be looked after by that person; an informal use. *I was sometimes dumped with my grandmother or left with highly unsuitable au pairs... He can't cope and dumps his two teenage boys on them to be looked after.* VERB PRAGMATICS be V-ed with n V n on n

10 To **dump** computer data or memory means to copy it from one storage system onto another, such as from disk to magnetic tape; a technical term in computing. *It can take a couple of hours to dump a thousand telephone numbers into a 128k EPROM pack... All the data is then dumped into the main computer.* VERB V n into n

11 If someone **dumps on** you, they treat you very badly and unfairly; an informal use. *He was a nice guy, Mona. He didn't dump on me.* VERB V on n

12 If you are **down in the dumps**, you are feeling very depressed and miserable; an informal expression. *She's feeling a bit down in the dumps and needs cheering up.* PHRASE: v-link PHR

dumper truck, dumper trucks. A **dumper truck** is the same as a **dump truck**; used in British English. N-COUNT

dumping ground, dumping grounds. If you say that a place is a **dumping ground** for something, usually something unwanted, you mean that people leave or send large quantities of that thing there, and you disapprove of their action. *Eastern Europe is rapidly becoming a dumping-ground for radioactive residues.* N-COUNT: usu N for n, supp N PRAGMATICS

dumpling /dʌmplɪŋ/ **dumplings. Dumplings** are small lumps of dough that are cooked and eaten, either with meat and vegetables or as part of a sweet pudding. N-VAR

Dumpster /dʌmpstəʳ/ **Dumpsters.** In American English, a **Dumpster** is a large metal container for holding rubbish or things for recycling. **Dumpster** is a trademark. The usual British word is **skip**. N-COUNT

dump truck, dump trucks. A **dump truck** is a truck whose carrying part can be tipped backwards so that the load falls out. N-COUNT

dumpy /dʌmpi/. If you describe someone as **dumpy**, you mean they are short and fat, and are usually implying they are unattractive. ADJ-GRADED PRAGMATICS

dun /dʌn/. Something that is **dun** is a dull grey-brown colour. *...her dun mare.* COLOUR

dunce /dʌns/ **dunces.** If you say that someone is a **dunce**, you think they are rather stupid because they find it difficult or impossible to learn what someone is trying to teach them. *Michael may have been a dunce at mathematics, but he was gifted at languages.* N-COUNT PRAGMATICS

dune /djuːn, AM duːn/ **dunes.** A **dune** is a hill of sand near the sea or in a desert. ◆◇◇◇◇ N-COUNT

dung /dʌŋ/. **Dung** is faeces from animals, especially from large animals such as cattle and horses. ◆◇◇◇◇ N-UNCOUNT

dungarees /dʌŋgəriːz/. **Dungarees** are a one-piece garment consisting of trousers, a piece of cloth which covers your chest, and straps which N-PLURAL: also a pair of N go over your shoulders. In American English, **dungarees** can also refer to jeans.

dungeon /dʌndʒən/ **dungeons.** A **dungeon** is a dark underground prison in a castle. N-COUNT

dunk /dʌŋk/ **dunks, dunking, dunked**

1 If you **dunk** something such as a biscuit or a piece of bread **in** a drink or **in** soup, you dip it into the drink or soup before eating it. *Many people dunk their foods in coffee, tea or milk.* VERB =dip V n in n

2 If you **dunk** something **in** a liquid, you put it in the liquid, especially for a particular purpose and for a short time. *Dunk new plants in a bucket of water for an hour or so before planting.* VERB =steep V n in n

dunno /dənoʊ/. **Dunno** is sometimes used in written English to represent an informal way of saying 'don't know'. *'How on earth did she get it?'—'I dunno.'* ◆◇◇◇◇

duo /djuːoʊ, AM duː-/ **duos** ◆◇◇◇◇

1 A **duo** is two musicians, singers, or other performers who perform together as a pair. *...a famous dancing and singing duo.* N-COUNT

2 You can refer to two people together as a **duo**, especially when they have something in common; used especially in newspapers. *...Britain's golden Olympic duo of Linford Christie and Sally Gunnell.* N-COUNT

duodenal /djuːoʊdiːnəl, AM duː-/. **Duodenal** means relating to or contained in the duodenum; a medical term. *...duodenal ulcers.* ADJ: ADJ n

duodenum /djuːoʊdiːnəm, AM duː-/ **duodenums.** Your **duodenum** is the part of your small intestine that is just below your stomach; a medical term. N-COUNT

duopoly /djuːɒpəli/ **duopolies**

1 If two companies or people have a **duopoly** on something such as an industry, they share complete control over it and it is impossible for others to become involved in it. N-VAR

2 A **duopoly** is a group of two companies which are the only providers of a particular product or service, and which therefore have complete control over an industry. N-COUNT

dupe /djuːp, AM duːp/ **dupes, duping, duped** ◆◇◇◇◇

1 If someone **dupes** you, they trick you into doing something, or into believing something which is not true. *...a plot to dupe stamp collectors into buying fake rarities... We know some sex offenders dupe the psychologists who assess them.* VERB V n into -ing V n

2 A **dupe** is someone who is tricked by someone else. *He was accused of being a dupe of the communists.* N-COUNT

duplex /djuːpleks, AM duː-/ **duplexes**

1 In North America, a **duplex** is a house which has been divided into two separate units for two different families or groups of people. N-COUNT

2 In North America, a **duplex** or a **duplex apartment** is a flat which has rooms on two floors. N-COUNT

duplicate, duplicates, duplicating, duplicated. The verb is pronounced /djuːplɪkeɪt, AM duː-/. The noun and adjective are pronounced /djuːplɪkət, AM duː-/. ◆◇◇◇◇

1 If you **duplicate** something that has already been done, you repeat or copy it. *His task will be to duplicate his success overseas here at home... Scientists hope the work done in collaboration with other researchers may be duplicated elsewhere.* ► Also a noun. *He was organising a duplicate of Operation Gladio to be activated if the left gained power.* VERB V n N-COUNT

2 To **duplicate** something which has been written, drawn, or recorded onto tape means to make exact copies of it. *She found Ned alone in the photocopy room, duplicating some articles. ...a business which duplicates video and cinema tapes for the movie makers.* ► Also a noun. *I'm on my way to Switzerland, but I've lost my card. I've got to get a duplicate.* VERB V n N-COUNT: also in N

3 **Duplicate** is used to describe things that have been made as an exact copy of other things, usually in order to serve the same purpose. *He let himself in with a duplicate key. ...a duplicate copy of the loan contract.* ADJ: ADJ n

4 See also **duplication**.

duplication /djuːplɪkeɪʃən, AM duː-/. If you say that there has been **duplication** of something, you mean that someone has done a task unnecessarily because it has already been done before. *There could be a serious loss of efficiency through unnecessary duplication of resources.* N-UNCOUNT PRAGMATICS

duplicity /djuːplɪsɪti, AM duː-/. If you accuse someone of **duplicity**, you mean that they are deceitful; a formal word. *Malcolm believed his former mentor was guilty of duplicity in his private dealings.* N-UNCOUNT =deceit

durable /djʊərəbəl, AM dʊr-/. Something that is **durable** is strong and lasts a long time without breaking or becoming weaker. *Fine bone china is eminently practical, since it is strong and durable.* ◆◆◇◇◇ ADJ-GRADED =hard-wearing

♦ **durability** /djʊərəbɪlɪti, AM dʊr-/ *Airlines recommend hard-sided cases for durability.* N-UNCOUNT

duration /djʊreɪʃən, AM dʊr-/ ◆◆◇◇◇

1 The **duration** of an event or state is the time during which it happens or exists. *He was given the task of protecting her for the duration of the trial... Courses are of two years' duration.* N-UNCOUNT: oft the N of n

2 If you say that something will happen **for the duration**, you mean that it will happen for as long as a particular situation continues. *His wounds knocked him out of combat for the duration.* PHRASE: PHR after v

duress /djʊəres, AM dʊr-/. If someone does something under **duress**, they do it because someone forces them to do it or threatens them; a formal word. *The diplomat would not comment on whether he thought her confession had been made under duress.* N-UNCOUNT: usu under N

Durex /djʊəreks, AM dʊreks/. **Durex** is both the singular and the plural form. In Britain, a **Durex** is a type of contraceptive sheath. **Durex** is a trademark. N-COUNT =condom

during /djʊərɪŋ, AM dʊrɪŋ/ ◆◆◆◆◆

1 If something happens **during** a period of time or an event, it happens continuously, or happens several times between the beginning and end of that period or event. *Sandstorms are common during the Saudi Arabian winter... Plants need to be looked after and protected during bad weather.* PREP

2 If something develops **during** a period of time, it develops gradually from the beginning to the end of that period. *Wages have fallen by more than twenty percent during the past two months... American business in Britain during the 1950s grew much faster than British business.* PREP

3 An event that happens **during** a period of time happens at some point or moment in that period. *The attack is believed to have been carried out during the early morning hours... During his visit, the Pope will also bless the new hospital.* PREP

dusk /dʌsk/ ◆◇◇◇◇

1 **Dusk** is the time just before night when the daylight has almost gone but when it is not completely dark. *We arrived home at dusk.* N-UNCOUNT

2 The **dusk** is the dim, rather shadowy light there is at dusk; a literary use. *She turned and disappeared into the dusk.* N-UNCOUNT: also the N

dusky /dʌski/

1 **Dusky** means rather dark; a literary use. *Heavy gold earrings gleamed against her dusky cheeks... He was walking down the road one dusky Friday evening.* ADJ-GRADED

2 A **dusky** colour is soft rather than bright; a literary use. *...dusky pink carpet.* COMB in COLOUR

dust /dʌst/ **dusts, dusting, dusted** ◆◆◆◇◇

1 **Dust** is very small dry particles of earth or sand. *Tanks raise huge trails of dust when they move... He reversed into the stockade in a cloud of dust.* N-UNCOUNT

2 **Dust** is the very small pieces of dirt which you find inside buildings, for example on furniture, floors, or lights. *I could see a thick layer of dust on the stairs... The rooms were empty of furniture and dust lay everywhere.* N-UNCOUNT

3 **Dust** is a fine powder which consists of very small particles of a substance such as gold, wood, or coal. *The air is so black with diesel fumes and coal dust, I can barely see.* N-UNCOUNT: oft n N

4 When you **dust** something such as furniture, you remove dust from it, usually using a cloth. *I vacuumed and dusted and polished the living* VERB V n V

room... She dusted, she cleaned, and she did the washing-up. ♦ **dusting** *I'm very fortunate in that I don't have to do the washing-up or the dusting.* N-UNCOUNT

5 If you **dust** something with a fine substance such as powder or if you **dust** a fine substance onto something, you cover it lightly with that substance. *Lightly dust the fish with flour... Dust and blend blusher on the apples of your cheeks... Dry your feet well and then dust between the toes with baby powder.* VERB V n prep/adv V adv/prep

6 If you say that something **has bitten the dust**, you are emphasizing that it no longer exists or that it has failed; an informal and humorous expression. *In the last 30 years many cherished values have bitten the dust... The allegation has caused one lecturer's career to bite the dust.* PHRASES V inflects PRAGMATICS

7 In informal English, if you say that something will happen when **the dust settles**, you mean that a situation will be clearer after it has calmed down. If you let **the dust settle** before doing something, you let a situation calm down before you try to do anything else. *Once the dust had settled Beck defended his decision... I think we need to let the dust settle and see what's going to happen after that.* V inflects

8 If you say that something **is gathering dust**, you mean that it has been left somewhere and nobody is using it or doing anything with it. *Many of the machines are gathering dust in basements... The album is finally being released in October after gathering dust for over a year.* V inflects

dust down or **dust off** PHRASAL VERB

1 If you say that someone **dusts** something **down** or **dusts** it **off**, you mean they are reusing something such as an idea which is old rather than trying something new. *Critics were busy dusting down the same superlatives they had applied to their first three films... Long-mothballed projects like widening the Suez Canal are being dusted off.* V P n (not pron) Also V n P

2 If you say that someone has **dusted** himself or herself **down** or **dusted** themselves **off**, you mean that they have managed to recover from a severe setback which has affected their lives. *Tina Turner dusted herself down, got rid of Ike and became the greatest show on earth... When we are rejected, although we have been hurt we can pick ourselves up, dust ourselves off and start again.* V pron-refl P

3 If someone **dusts down** something or **dusts** dirt **off** something, they remove dirt or dust from it. *He stood and dusted down his suit and folded the letter away... Use loose powder to set your makeup, dusting the excess off with a brush.* V P n (not pron) V n P

dustbin /dʌstbɪn/ **dustbins.** In British English, a **dustbin** is a large round container with a lid which people put their rubbish in and which is usually kept outside their house. The usual American term is **garbage can.** ◆◇◇◇◇ N-COUNT

dustcart /dʌstkɑːʳt/ **dustcarts.** In British English, a **dustcart** is a lorry which collects the rubbish from the dustbins outside people's houses. The usual American term is **garbage truck**. N-COUNT

duster /dʌstəʳ/ **dusters.** A **duster** is a cloth which you use for removing dust from furniture, ornaments, or other objects. • See also **feather duster.** N-COUNT

dust jacket, dust jackets; also spelled **dust-jacket.** A **dust jacket** is a loose paper cover which is put on a book to protect it. It often contains information about the book and its author. N-COUNT =dust cover

dustman /dʌstmən/ **dustmen.** In British English, a **dustman** is a person whose job is to empty the rubbish from people's dustbins and take it away to be disposed of. The usual American term is **garbage man.** N-COUNT

dustpan /dʌstpæn/ **dustpans.** A **dustpan** is a small flat container made of metal or plastic. You hold it flat on the floor and sweep dirt and dust into it. N-COUNT

dust sheet, dust sheets; also spelled **dust-sheet.** A **dust sheet** is a large cloth which is used to cover objects such as furniture in order to protect them from dust. N-COUNT

dust-up, dust-ups. A **dust-up** is a quarrel that often involves some fighting; an informal word. *He's now facing suspension after a dust-up with the referee.* N-COUNT =scrap

dusty /dʌsti/ **dustier, dustiest** ◆◇◇◇◇

1 If places, roads, or other things outside are **dusty**, they are covered with tiny bits of earth or sand, usually because it has not rained for a long time. *They started strolling down the dusty road in the moonlight. ...a dusty old car.* ADJ-GRADED: usu ADJ n

2 If a room, house, or object is **dusty**, it is covered with very small pieces of dirt. *...a dusty attic... The books looked faded, dusty and unused.* ADJ-GRADED

Dutch /dʌtʃ/ ◆◆◆◆◇

1 Dutch means belonging or relating to the Netherlands, or to its people, language, or culture. *...the Dutch prime minister.* ADJ

2 The Dutch are the people of the Netherlands. *The Dutch developed a custom by which children put out shoes which Saint Nicholas would fill with gifts when he came visiting.* N-PLURAL: the N

3 Dutch is the language that is spoken by the people who live in the Netherlands. N-UNCOUNT

4 If two or more people **go Dutch**, each of them pays their own bill, for example in a restaurant; an informal expression. *We went dutch on the cheap Chinese in Shaftesbury Avenue.* PHRASE: V inflects

Dutch courage. **Dutch courage** is the courage that you get by drinking alcoholic drinks; an informal expression. N-UNCOUNT

Dutchman /dʌtʃmən/ **Dutchmen.** A **Dutchman** is a man who is a native of the Netherlands. ◆◇◇◇◇ N-COUNT

dutiful /djuːtɪfʊl, AM duː-/. If you say that someone is **dutiful**, you mean that they do everything that they are expected to do. *The days of the dutiful wife, who sacrifices her career for her husband, are over.* ♦ **dutifully** *The inspector dutifully recorded the date in a large red book.* ◆◇◇◇◇ ADJ-GRADED ADV: ADV with v

duty /djuːti, AM duːti/ **duties** ◆◆◆◆◇

1 Duty is work that you have to do for your job. *Staff must report for duty at their normal place of work... My duty is to look after the animals.* N-UNCOUNT

2 Your **duties** are tasks which you have to do because they are part of your job. *I carried out my duties conscientiously... He was relieved of his duties as presidential adviser.* N-PLURAL

3 If you say that something is your **duty**, you believe that you ought to do it because it is your responsibility. *I consider it my duty to write to you and thank you.* N-SING: oft with poss

4 Duties are taxes which you pay to the government on goods that you buy. *Import duties still average 30%. ...customs duties... They are pressing the Chancellor to reduce excise duty on beer.* N-VAR

5 If someone such as a policeman or a nurse is **off duty**, they are not working. If someone is **on duty**, they are working. *I'm off duty... Four officers were told to go off duty and rest at home... There were 2,250 policemen on duty in and around the stadium... Extra staff had been put on duty.* PHRASES PHR after v, v-link PHR

duty-bound; also spelled **duty bound**. If you say you are **duty-bound** to do something, you are emphasizing that you feel it is your duty to do it; a formal word. *'I didn't want to work on it but felt duty bound to help,' Wilson said.* ADJ: v-link ADJ to-inf PRAGMATICS

duty-free. **Duty-free** goods are sold at airports or on planes or ships at a cheaper price than usual because you do not have to pay import tax on them. *...duty-free cigarettes.* ◆◇◇◇◇ ADJ

duty-free shop, duty-free shops. A **duty-free shop** is a shop, for example at an airport, where you can buy goods at a cheaper price than usual, because no tax is paid on them. N-COUNT

duvet /duːveɪ, AM duːveɪ/ **duvets.** A **duvet** is a large cover filled with feathers or similar material which you put over yourself in bed instead of a sheet and blankets; used mainly in British English. ◆◇◇◇◇ N-COUNT =quilt

dwarf /dwɔːʳf/ **dwarves, dwarfs, dwarfing, dwarfed** ◆◆◇◇◇

1 If one person or thing **is dwarfed** by another, the second is so much bigger than the first that it VERB makes them look very small. *His figure is dwarfed by the huge red McDonald's sign... The US air travel market dwarfs that of Britain.* be V-ed V n

2 **Dwarf** is used to describe a particular kind of star which is relatively small and not very bright. *...a white dwarf star. ...a red dwarf.* N-COUNT: with supp

3 **Dwarf** is used to describe varieties or species of plants and animals which are much smaller than the usual size for their kind. *...dwarf shrubs.* ADJ: ADJ n

4 In children's stories, a **dwarf** is an imaginary creature that is like a small man. **Dwarfs** often have magical powers. N-COUNT

5 In former times, people who were much smaller than normal were called **dwarfs**; an old-fashioned use which is now considered offensive. N-COUNT

dweeb /dwiːb/ **dweebs.** If you call someone, especially a man or a boy, a **dweeb**, you are saying in a rather unkind way that you think they are stupid and weak; an informal word; used mainly in American English by young people. N-COUNT PRAGMATICS =drip, nerd

dwell /dwel/ **dwells, dwelling, dwelt** or **dwelled** ◆◇◇◇◇

1 If you **dwell** on something, especially something unpleasant, you think, speak, or write about it a lot or for quite a long time. *'I'd rather not dwell on the past,' he told me.* VERB V on/upon n

2 If you **dwell** somewhere, you live there; a formal use. *They are concerned for the fate of the forest and the Indians who dwell in it... Shiva is a dark god; he dwells in the mountains and deserts.* VERB V prep/adv

3 See also **dwelling**.

dweller /dweləʳ/ **dwellers.** A city **dweller** or slum **dweller**, for example, is a person who lives in the kind of place or house indicated. *The number of city dwellers is growing... But in some respects cave dwellers were far cleverer than us.* ◆◇◇◇◇ N-COUNT: supp N

dwelling /dwelɪŋ/ **dwellings.** A **dwelling** or a **dwelling place** is a place where someone lives; a formal word. *Some 3500 new dwellings are planned for the area... We hiked the Grand Canyon, exploring Indian cliff dwellings.* ◆◇◇◇◇ N-COUNT

dwelt /dwelt/. **Dwelt** is the past tense and past participle of **dwell**.

dwindle /dwɪndəl/ **dwindles, dwindling, dwindled.** If something **dwindles**, it becomes smaller, weaker, or less in number. *The factory's workforce has dwindled from over 4,000 to a few hundred... Exports are dwindling and the trade deficit is swelling... He is struggling to come to terms with his dwindling authority.* ◆◇◇◇◇ VERB V V-ing

dye /daɪ/ **dyes, dyeing, dyed** ◆◆◇◇◇

1 If you **dye** something such as hair or cloth, you change its colour by soaking it in a special liquid. *The women prepared, spun and dyed the wool... She had dyed black hair.* VERB V n V-ed

2 **Dye** is a substance made from plants or chemicals which is mixed into a liquid and used to change the colour of something such as cloth or hair. *...bottles of hair dye.* N-MASS

dyed-in-the-wool. If you use **dyed-in-the-wool** to describe someone or their beliefs, you are saying that they have very strong, rigid opinions about something which they refuse to change. *He was a dyed-in-the-wool conservative.* ADJ-GRADED: ADJ n

dying /daɪɪŋ/ ◆◆◇◇◇

1 **Dying** is the present participle of **die**.

2 A **dying** person or animal is very ill and likely to die soon. *...a dying man.* ► **The dying** are people who are dying. *By the time our officers arrived, the dead and the dying were everywhere.* ADJ: ADJ n N-PLURAL: the N

3 You use **dying** to describe something which happens at the time when someone dies, or is connected with that time. *It'll stay in my mind till my dying day... She was compelled to fulfil the dying wishes of her mother.* ADJ: ADJ n

4 The **dying** days or **dying** minutes of a state of affairs or an activity are its last days or minutes. *The islands were seized by the Soviet army in the dying days of the second world war... A penalty by Thierry Lacroix broke the deadlock in the dying minutes of the game.* ADJ: ADJ n =final

5 A **dying** tradition or industry is becoming less important and is likely to finish altogether. *Shipbuilding is a dying business.* ADJ: ADJ n

6 A **dying** fire is no longer hot and bright and will not burn for much longer. ADJ: ADJ n

dyke /daɪk/ **dykes;** also spelled **dike**. ◆◇◇◇◇

1 A **dyke** is a thick wall that is built to stop water flooding onto very low-lying land from a river or from the sea. N-COUNT

2 A **dyke** is a lesbian; an informal use which is considered offensive. N-COUNT

dynamic /daɪnæmɪk/ **dynamics** ◆◆◇◇◇

1 If you describe someone as **dynamic**, you approve of them because they are full of energy or full of new and exciting ideas. *He seemed a dynamic and energetic leader... Marcus was handsome, dynamic and ambitious.* ♦ **dynamically** /daɪnæmɪkli/ *He's one of the most dynamically imaginative jazz pianists still functioning.* ADJ-GRADED PRAGMATICS ADV-GRADED: ADV adj/-ed, ADV after v

2 If you describe something as **dynamic**, you approve of it because it is very active and energetic. *South Asia continues to be the most dynamic economic region in the world. ...90 minutes of dynamic Indian folk dance.* ADJ-GRADED PRAGMATICS

3 A **dynamic** process is one that constantly changes and progresses. *...a dynamic, evolving worldwide epidemic... Political debate is dynamic.* ♦ **dynamically** *Germany has a dynamically growing market at home.* ADJ ≠static ADV: usu ADV adj/-ed

4 The **dynamic** of a system or process is the force that causes it to change or progress. *The dynamic of the market demands constant change and adjustment... Politics has its own dynamic.* N-COUNT: usu with supp

5 The **dynamics** of a situation or group of people are the opposing forces within it that cause it to change. *What is needed is insight into the dynamics of the social system... The interchange of ideas aids an understanding of family dynamics.* N-PLURAL: usu with supp

6 **Dynamics** are forces which produce power or movement; a technical term in science. *Scientists observe the same dynamics in fluids.* N-UNCOUNT

7 **Dynamics** is the scientific study of motion, energy, and forces. *His idea was to apply geometry to dynamics.* N-UNCOUNT

dynamism /daɪnəmɪzəm/ ◆◇◇◇◇

1 If you say that someone or something has **dynamism**, you are expressing approval of the fact that they are full of energy or full of new and exciting ideas. *...a situation that calls for dynamism and new thinking.* N-UNCOUNT PRAGMATICS =energy

2 If you refer to the **dynamism** of a situation or system, you are referring to the fact that it is changing in an exciting and dramatic way. *Such changes are also indicators of economic dynamism and demographic expansion.* N-UNCOUNT ≠stasis

dynamite /daɪnəmaɪt/ **dynamites, dynamiting, dynamited** ◆◇◇◇◇

1 **Dynamite** is a type of explosive that contains nitroglycerin. *Fifty yards of track was blown up with dynamite.* N-UNCOUNT

2 If someone **dynamites** something, they blow it up by using dynamite. *The rebels dynamited power lines... The slum is to be dynamited.* VERB V n

3 If you describe a piece of information as **dynamite**, you think that people will react violently to it; an informal use. *The book is dynamite, and if she publishes it, there will be no hiding place for her.* N-UNCOUNT

4 If you describe someone or something as **dynamite**, you think that they are exciting and stimulating; an informal use. *Carmen was pure dynamite... The first kiss is dynamite.* N-UNCOUNT PRAGMATICS

dynamo /daɪnəmoʊ/ **dynamos** ◆◇◇◇◇

1 A **dynamo** is a device that uses the movement of a machine or vehicle to produce electricity. N-COUNT

2 If you describe someone as a **dynamo**, you mean that they are very energetic and are always busy and active. *Myles is a human dynamo.* N-COUNT

dynastic /daɪnæstɪk/. **Dynastic** means typical of or relating to a dynasty. *The country's democratic rulers were trying to revive dynastic rule.* ADJ: usu ADJ n

dynasty /dɪnəsti, AM daɪn-/ **dynasties** ◆◇◇◇◇

1 A **dynasty** is a series of rulers of a country who all N-COUNT belong to the same family. *The Seljuk dynasty of Syria was founded in 1094.*

2 A **dynasty** is a period of time during which a country is ruled by members of the same family. *...carvings dating back to the Ming dynasty.* N-COUNT: with supp

3 A **dynasty** is a family which has members from two or more generations who are important in a particular field of activity, for example in business or politics. *This is a family-owned company – the current president is the fourth in this dynasty.* N-COUNT

d'you /dju:, dʒu:/. **d'you** is a short form of **do you** or **did you**, used in writing to represent informal spoken English. *What d'you say?*

dysentery /dɪsəntri, AM -teri/. **Dysentery** is an infection in a person's intestines that causes severe diarrhoea, in which blood and mucus are mixed with the person's faeces. N-UNCOUNT

dysfunction /dɪsfʌŋkʃən/ **dysfunctions**

1 If you refer to a **dysfunction** in something such as a relationship or someone's behaviour, you mean that it is different from what is considered to be normal; a formal use. *...his severe emotional dysfunction was very clearly apparent.* N-COUNT

2 If someone has a physical **dysfunction**, part of their body is not working properly; a medical use. *...kidney and liver dysfunction.* N-VAR

dysfunctional /dɪsfʌŋkʃənəl/. **Dysfunctional** is used to describe relationships or behaviour which are different from what is considered to be normal; a formal term. *...the characteristics that typically occur in a dysfunctional family.* ADJ-GRADED: usu ADJ n

dyslexia /dɪsleksiə/. If someone suffers from **dyslexia**, they have difficulty with reading because of a slight disorder of their brain; a technical term in psychology and education. N-UNCOUNT

dyslexic /dɪsleksɪk/. If someone is **dyslexic**, they have difficulty with reading because of a slight disorder of their brain; a technical term in psychology and education. *He was diagnosed as severely dyslexic but extraordinarily bright.* ADJ-GRADED

dyspepsia /dɪspepsiə, AM -ʃə/. **Dyspepsia** is the same as **indigestion**; a medical term. N-UNCOUNT

dystrophy /dɪstrəfi/. See **muscular dystrophy**.

E e

E, e /iː/ **E's, e's**

1 **E** is the fifth letter of the English alphabet. N-VAR

2 In music, **E** is the third note in the scale of C major. N-VAR

3 **E** or **e** is an abbreviation for words beginning with e, such as 'English', 'east', and 'eastern'.

each /iːtʃ/ ◆◆◆◆◆

1 If you refer to **each** thing or **each** person in a group, you are referring to every member of the group and considering them as individuals. *Each book is beautifully illustrated... Each year, hundreds of animals are killed in this way... Blend in the eggs, one at a time, beating well after each one.* DET: DET sing-n
► Also a pronoun. *...two bedrooms, each with three beds... She began to consult doctors, and each had a different diagnosis.* PRON
► Also an emphasizing pronoun. *We each have different needs and interests.* PRON-EMPH
► Also an adverb. *The children were given one each, handed to them or placed on their plates... They were selling tickets at six pounds each.* ADV: amount ADV
► Also a quantifier. *He handed each of them a page of photos... Each of these exercises takes one or two minutes to do... The machines, each of which is perhaps five feet in diameter, are far from the largest devices in the room.* QUANT: QUANT of def-pl-n

2 If you refer to **each one** of the members of a group, you are referring in a slightly emphatic way to each of them. *He picked up forty of these publications and read each one of them.* QUANT: QUANT of def-pl-n PRAGMATICS

3 You can refer to **each and every** member of a group to emphasize that you mean all the members of that group. *My goal was that each and every person responsible for Yankel's murder be brought to justice... They can't destroy truth without destroying each and every one of us.* PHRASE: PHR n, PHR of n PRAGMATICS

4 You use **each other** when you are saying that each member of a group does something to the others or has a particular connection with the others. *We looked at each other in silence, each equally shocked... Both sides are willing to make allowances for each other's political sensitivities... Uncle Paul and I hardly know each other.* PRON-RECIP: v PRON, prep PRON =one another

eager /iːgər/ ◆◆◆◇◇

1 If you are **eager** to do or have something, you want to do or have it very much. *Robert was eager to talk about life in the Army... When my own son was five years old, I became eager for another baby... The low prices still pull in crowds of eager buyers.* ADJ-GRADED: usu v-link ADJ, ADJ to-inf, ADJ for n =keen
♦ **eagerness** *...an eagerness to learn.* N-UNCOUNT

2 If you look or sound **eager**, you look or sound as if you expect something interesting or enjoyable to happen. *Arty sneered at the crowd of eager faces around him... Her voice was girlish and eager.* ADJ-GRADED =impatient
♦ **eagerly** *'So what do you think will happen?' he asked eagerly.* ADV-GRADED
♦ **eagerness** *It was the voice of a woman speaking with breathless eagerness.* N-UNCOUNT =enthusiasm

eagle /iːgəl/ **eagles** ◆◇◇◇◇

1 An **eagle** is a large bird that lives by eating small animals. N-COUNT

2 If you talk about someone's **eagle eye**, you mean that they are watching someone or something carefully or are very good at noticing things. *He did the work under the eagle eye of his teacher... The Captain's eagle eye swept the room and came to rest on the bed.* PHRASE: usu with poss

eagle-eyed. If you describe someone as **eagle-eyed**, you mean that they watch things very carefully and seem to notice everything. *Three cannabis plants were found by eagle-eyed police officers.* ADJ

ear /ɪər/ **ears** ◆◆◆◇◇

1 Your **ears** are the two parts of your body, one on each side of your head, with which you hear sounds. *He whispered something in her ear... I'm having my ears pierced.* N-COUNT

2 If you have an **ear** for music or language, you are able to hear its sounds accurately and to interpret them or reproduce them well. *Moby certainly has a fine ear for a tune... An ear for foreign languages is advantageous.* N-SING: with supp, usu N for n

3 The word **ear** is often used to refer to people's willingness to listen to what someone is saying. *What would cause the masses to give him a far more sympathetic ear?... They insisted on shutting their eyes and ears to everything that had been improved in South Africa.* N-COUNT: oft adj N

4 The **ears** of a cereal plant such as wheat or barley are the parts at the top of the stem, which contain the seeds or grains. N-COUNT: usu pl

5 If someone says that they are **all ears**, they mean that they are ready and eager to listen; an informal expression. PHRASES usu v-link PHR

6 If you say that someone **is bending** your **ear** about something, you mean that they keep talking to you about it because they think it is important; used especially when you are irritated by this. *He was fed up with people bending his ear about staying on at school.* V inflects

7 If someone **boxes** a child's **ears**, they punch or V inflects

slap them on the side of their head as a punishment; an old-fashioned expression.
8 If a request **falls on deaf ears** or if the person to whom the request is made **turns a deaf ear** to it, they take no notice of it. *I hope that our appeals will not fall on deaf ears... He has turned a resolutely deaf ear to American demands for action.* V inflects
9 If you **keep** or **have** your **ear to the ground**, you make sure that you find out about the things that people are doing or saying. *Jobs in manufacturing are relatively scarce but I keep my ear to the ground.* V inflects
10 If you listen to something or someone **with only half an ear**, you do not give your full attention to what is being said. PHR after v
11 If you **lend an ear** to someone or their problems, you listen to them carefully and sympathetically. *They are always willing to lend an ear and offer what advice they can.* V inflects
12 If you say that something goes **in one ear and out the other**, you mean that someone pays no attention to it, or forgets about it immediately. *That rubbish goes in one ear and out the other.* V inflects
13 If someone says that you will be **out on** your **ear**, they mean that you will be thrown out or dismissed suddenly and unpleasantly. *We never objected. We'd have been out on our ears looking for another job if we had.* N inflects, v-link PHR
14 If you **play by ear** or **play** a piece of music **by ear**, you play music by relying on your sense of tune and harmony or on your memory, rather than by reading printed music. *Neil sat at the piano and began playing, by ear, the music he'd heard his older sister practicing.* V inflects
15 If you **play it by ear**, you decide what to say or do in a situation by responding to events rather than by following a plan which you have decided on in advance. V inflects
16 If you are **up to** your **ears** in something, it is taking up all of your time, attention, or resources. *'Why don't you come with me?'—'I can't. I'm up to my ears in reports.'... He was desperate. He was in debt up to his ears.* v-link PHR, oft PHR *in* n
17 • to **make a pig's ear of** something: see **pig**. • **music to** your **ears**: see **music**. • **wet behind the ears**: see **wet**.

earache /ɪəreɪk/ **earaches. Earache** is a pain in the inside part of your ear. *He complained of an earache... Blowing your nose too hard can cause earache.* N-VAR

eardrum /ɪəʳdrʌm/ **eardrums;** also spelled **ear drum**. Your **eardrums** are the thin pieces of tightly stretched skin inside each ear, which vibrate when sound waves reach them. N-COUNT

earful /ɪəʳfʊl/. If you say that you got **an earful**, you mean that someone spoke angrily to you for quite an long time; an informal word. *I bet Sue gave you an earful when you got home.* N-SING: a N

earl /ɜːʳl/ **earls.** An **earl** is a British nobleman. *He became the fourth earl on the death of his father earlier this year. ...the first Earl of Birkenhead.* ◆◇◇◇◇ N-COUNT: oft N *of* n

earldom /ɜːʳldəm/ **earldoms.** An **earldom** is the rank or title of an earl. N-COUNT

earlier /ɜːʳliəʳ/ ◆◆◆◆◇
1 **Earlier** is the comparative of **early**.
2 **Earlier** is used to refer to a point or period in time before the present or before the one you are talking about. *As mentioned earlier, the University supplements this information with an interview... Earlier, it had been hoped to use the indoor track. ...political reforms announced by the President earlier this year... Many years earlier, Grundy had been the first presenter to give The Beatles their first television break.* ► Also an adjective. *Earlier reports of gunshots have not been substantiated.* ADV-COMPAR: ADV with v, ADV with cl, oft amount ADV; ADJ-COMPAR: ADJ n

earliest /ɜːʳliɪst/ ◆◆◇◇◇
1 **Earliest** is the superlative of **early**.
2 **At the earliest** means not before the date or time mentioned. *The first official results are not expected until Tuesday at the earliest.* PHRASE: cl PHR

earlobe /ɪəʳloʊb/ **earlobes;** also spelled **ear lobe**. Your **earlobes** are the soft parts at the bottom of your ears. N-COUNT

early /ɜːʳli/ **earlier, earliest** ◆◆◆◆◆
1 **Early** means before the usual time that a particular event or activity happens. *I knew I had to get up early... Why do we have to go to bed so early?* ► Also an adjective. *I decided that I was going to take early retirement... I planned an early night.* ADV-GRADED: ADV after v ≠late; ADJ-GRADED: ADJ n
2 **Early** means near the beginning of a day, week, year, or other period of time. *...in the 1970s and the early 1980s. ...a few weeks in early summer... She was in her early teens. ...the early hours of Saturday morning.* ► Also an adverb. *We'll hope to see you some time early next week. ...early in the season.* ADJ-GRADED: ADJ n ≠late; ADV-GRADED: ADV with cl, ADV n/prep
3 **Early** means before the time that was arranged or expected. *She arrived early to secure a place at the front... The first snow came a month earlier than usual.* ► Also an adjective. *I'm always early.* ADV-GRADED: ADV after v ≠late; ADJ-GRADED
4 **Early** means near the beginning of a period in history, or in the history of something such as the world, a society, or an activity. *...the early stages of pregnancy. ...Fassbinder's early films. ...the early days of the occupation... It's too early to declare his efforts a success.* ADJ-GRADED: ADJ n
5 **Early** means near the beginning of something such as a piece of work or a process. *...the book's early chapters.* ► Also an adverb. *...an incident which occurred much earlier in the game.* ADJ-GRADED: ADJ n; ADV-GRADED: ADV with cl, ADV prep
6 **Early** refers to plants which flower or crop before or at the beginning of the main season. *...these early cabbages and cauliflowers.* ► Also an adverb. *This early flowering gladiolus is not very hardy.* ADJ-GRADED: ADJ n; ADV-GRADED: ADV with v
7 **Early** reports or indications of something are the first reports or indications about it; a formal use. *The early indications look encouraging... Earlier reports that troops opened fire are now being denied.* ADJ-GRADED: ADJ n
8 You can use **as early as** to emphasize that a particular time or period is surprisingly early. *Inflation could fall back into single figures as early as this month. ...as early as 1838.* PHRASE: PHR n PRAGMATICS
9 If you say about something that might be true that **it is early days**, you mean that it is too soon for you to be completely sure about it; an informal use. *The chances of Francis eventually becoming manager of England are perhaps higher. It is early days, of course, and he has yet to win anything.* PHRASE: V inflects

early-warning. An **early-warning** system is a system which gives a warning at the earliest possible moment that something bad is likely to happen, for example that a machine is about to stop working, or an enemy has launched missiles against your country. ◆◇◇◇◇ ADJ: ADJ n

earmark /ɪəʳmɑːʳk/ **earmarks, earmarking, earmarked** ◆◇◇◇◇
1 If resources such as money **are earmarked** for a particular purpose, they are reserved for that purpose. *...the extra money being earmarked for the new projects... China has earmarked more than $20bn for oil exploration... Some of the money has been earmarked to pay for the re-settlement of people from contaminated areas. ...money earmarked for environmental purposes.* VERB =set aside; *be* V-ed *for* n; V n *for* n; *be* V-ed to-inf; V-ed
2 If something **has been earmarked** for closure or disposal, for example, people have decided that it will be closed or disposed of. *Their support meant that he was not forced to sell the business which was earmarked for disposal last year... The pit was one of the 31 earmarked for closure by the Trade and Industry Secretary.* VB: usu passive =mark out; *be* V-ed *for* n; V-ed

earmuffs /ɪəʳmʌfs/; also spelled **ear muffs**. **Earmuffs** consist of two thick soft pieces of cloth joined by a band, which you wear over your ears to protect them from the cold or from loud noise. N-PLURAL: also *a pair of* N

earn /ɜːʳn/ **earns, earning, earned** ◆◆◆◆◇
1 If you **earn** money, you receive money in return for work that you do. *Charlie was earning eight pounds, I was earning five... What a lovely way to earn a living... The dancers can earn anything between £50 and £100 for each session... She was always out earning.* VERB: V n; V

2 If something **earns** money, it produces money as profit or interest. *...a current account which earns little or no interest... We buy everything abroad with the money earned from oil imports.* VERB V n

3 If you **earn** something such as praise, you get it because you deserve it. *Companies must earn a reputation for honesty... I think that's earned him very high admiration.* VERB V n V n n

4 • **earn a crust**: see **crust**.

earner /ɜːʳnəʳ/ **earners** ◆◇◇◇◇

1 An **earner** is someone or something that earns money or produces profit. *...a typical wage earner... Sugar is Fiji's second biggest export earner.* N-COUNT: usu supp N

2 In British English, if you describe something as a **nice little earner**, you mean that it is something that you can make money from easily; an informal expression. *T-shirts are a nice little earner and it's better than the dole.* PHRASE: N inflects, usu v-link PHR, PHR after v

earnest /ɜːʳnɪst/ ◆◆◇◇◇

1 If something is done or happens **in earnest**, it happens to a much greater extent and more seriously than before. *Campaigning will begin in earnest tomorrow... The two countries can finally start negotiating in earnest about issues of mutual concern.* PHRASE: PHR after v =seriously

2 **Earnest** people are very serious and sincere in what they say or do, because they think that their actions and beliefs are important. *Ella was a pious, earnest woman... His expression is as earnest when he smiles as when he is arguing... Despite their earnest efforts, they still struggle to win support.* ADJ-GRADED =sincere ♦ **earnestness** *He was admired by many for his earnestness.* N-UNCOUNT =sincerity

3 If you are **in earnest**, you are sincere in what you are doing and saying. *It presented in satirical terms points made in earnest by Catholic writers... No one could tell whether he was in earnest or in jest.* PHRASE: usu v PHR, v-link PHR

earnestly /ɜːʳnɪstli/ ◆◇◇◇◇

1 If you say something **earnestly**, you say it very seriously, often because you believe that it is important or you are trying to persuade someone else to believe it. *'Did you?' she asked earnestly... In 1990, we were all earnestly assured that property values could only go up.* ADV-GRADED: ADV with v

2 If you do something **earnestly**, you do it in a thorough and serious way, intending to succeed. *She always listened earnestly as if this might help her to understand.* ADV-GRADED: usu ADV with v, also ADV adj

3 If you **earnestly** hope or wish for something, you hope or wish strongly and sincerely for it. *I earnestly hope what I learned will serve me well in my new job.* ADV-GRADED: ADV before v

earnings /ɜːʳnɪŋz/. Your **earnings** are the sums of money that you earn by working. *Average weekly earnings rose by 1.5% in July... He was satisfied with his earnings as an accountant.* ◆◆◆◇◇ N-PLURAL =pay, income

earnings-related. An **earnings-related** payment or benefit provides higher or lower payments according to the amount a person was earning while working. *...the Government's State Earnings Related Pension Scheme.* ADJ: usu ADJ n

earphone /ɪəʳfoʊn/ **earphones. Earphones** are a small piece of equipment which you wear over or inside your ears so that you can listen to a radio or cassette recorder without anybody else hearing. N-COUNT: usu pl

earpiece /ɪəʳpiːs/ **earpieces**

1 The **earpiece** of a telephone receiver, hearing aid, or other device is the part that is held up to or put into your ear. N-COUNT

2 The **earpieces** of a pair of glasses are the parts which fit over your ears to keep the glasses on. N-COUNT

earplug /ɪəʳplʌg/ **earplugs;** also spelled **ear plug**. **Earplugs** are small pieces of a soft material which you put into your ears to keep out noise, water, or cold air. N-COUNT: usu pl

earring /ɪərɪŋ/ **earrings. Earrings** are pieces of jewellery which you attach to your earlobes. ◆◇◇◇◇ N-COUNT

earshot /ɪəʳʃɒt/. If you are **within earshot** of someone or something, you are close enough to be able to hear them. If you are **out of earshot**, you are too far away to hear them. *The waiter continued to hover within earshot... Mark was out of earshot, walking ahead of them.* PHRASE: PHR after v, v-link PHR, oft PHR of n

ear-splitting. An **ear-splitting** noise is very loud. *The little boy emitted a torrent of ear-splitting screams.* ADJ: usu ADJ n

earth /ɜːʳθ/ **earths** ◆◆◆◆◇

1 **Earth** or **the Earth** is the planet on which we live. People usually say **Earth** when they are referring to the planet as part of the universe, and **the Earth** when they are talking about the planet as the place where we live. *The space shuttle Atlantis returned safely to earth today... Shifting plates of the Earth's crust push against each other, triggering volcanic eruptions and earthquakes.* N-PROPER: oft *the* N

2 **The earth** is the land surface on which we live and move about. *The earth shook and swayed and the walls of neighbouring houses fell around them.* N-SING: *the* N =ground

3 **Earth** is the substance on the land surface of the earth, for example clay or sand, in which plants grow. *The road winds for miles through parched earth, scrub and cactus... They will revert to tilling the earth in an old-fashioned way.* N-UNCOUNT =soil

4 An **earth** is a hole in the ground in which an animal such as a fox lives. N-COUNT

5 The **earth** in an electric plug or piece of electrical equipment is the wire in it through which electricity can pass into the ground, which makes the equipment safe even if something goes wrong with it. *The earth wire was not connected.* N-SING ♦ **earthed** *Light fittings with metal parts should always be earthed.* ADJ: usu v-link ADJ

6 See also **down-to-earth**.

7 **On earth** is used for emphasis in questions that begin with words such as 'how', 'why', 'what', or 'where'. It is often used to suggest that there is no obvious or easy answer to the question being asked. *How on earth did that happen?... What on earth had Luke done?... Why on earth would he want to go to such a place?* PHRASES quest PHR PRAGMATICS =in the world

8 **On earth** is used for emphasis after some negative noun groups, for example 'no reason'. *There was no reason on earth why she couldn't have moved in with us... There is no feeling on earth like winning for the first time.* with neg, n PHR PRAGMATICS =in the world

9 **On earth** is used for emphasis after a noun group that contains a superlative adjective. *He wanted to be the fastest man on earth. ...the site of the worst ecological disaster on earth.* adj-superl n PHR PRAGMATICS =in the world

10 If you come **down to earth** or **back to earth**, you have to face the reality of everyday life after a period of great excitement. *When he came down to earth after his win he admitted: 'It was an amazing feeling'... I was shocked, brought down to earth by this revelation.* PHR after v

11 If you **run** someone or something **to earth,** you find them after searching for them for a long time; used mainly in British English. *She ran him to earth in the pub at five to one.* V inflects =track down

12 If you say that something **cost the earth** or that you **paid the earth** for it, you are emphasizing that it cost a very large amount of money; an informal expression. *It must have cost the earth.* V inflects PRAGMATICS

13 • **hell on earth**: see **hell.** • to **move heaven and earth**: see **heaven.** • **salt of the earth**: see **salt**.

earthbound /ɜːʳθbaʊnd/

1 If something is **earthbound**, it is unable to fly, or is on the ground rather than in the air or in space. *The Hubble telescope is producing images much sharper than those of earthbound telescopes... The earthbound larvae from which they develop are less pretty, but just as predatory.* ADJ

2 If you describe someone or something as **earthbound**, you mean that they do not have very much imagination. *...the daughter of a stolid, earthbound salesman and a wild actress.* ADJ-GRADED

earthen /ɜːʳðən/

1 **Earthen** containers and objects are made of clay that is baked so that it becomes hard. *...an earthen jar.* ADJ: ADJ n

2 An **earthen** floor, bank, or mound is made of earth pressed together. *Despite the mud outside, the earthen floor was clean.* ADJ: ADJ n

earthenware /ɜːʳðənweəʳ/
1 **Earthenware** bowls, pots, or other objects are made of clay that is baked so that it becomes hard. *The dresser is laden with earthenware pots.* ADJ: ADJ n
2 Earthenware objects are referred to as **earthenware.** *...colourful Italian china and earthenware.* N-UNCOUNT

earthling /ɜːʳθlɪŋ/ **earthlings.** Some science-fiction writers use **earthlings** to refer to human beings who live on the planet Earth. N-COUNT: usu pl

earthly /ɜːʳθli/ ◆◇◇◇◇
1 **Earthly** means happening in the material world of our life on earth and not in any spiritual life or life after death. *...the need to confront evil during the earthly life... They lived in an earthly paradise.* ADJ: ADJ n
2 **Earthly** is used for emphasis in phrases such as **no earthly reason**. If you say that there is **no earthly reason** why something should happen, you are emphasizing that there is no reason at all why it should happen. *There is no earthly reason why they should ever change... What earthly reason would they have for lying?... There's no earthly use saying it isn't true.* ADJ: ADJ n PRAGMATICS

earthquake /ɜːʳθkweɪk/ **earthquakes.** An **earthquake** is a shaking of the ground caused by movement of the earth's crust. ◆◆◇◇◇ N-COUNT

earth-shattering. Something that is **earth-shattering** is very surprising or shocking. *...earth-shattering news.* ADJ-GRADED

earthwork /ɜːʳθwɜːʳk/ **earthworks. Earthworks** are large mounds of earth that have been built for defence, especially mounds which were built a very long time ago. *...Europe's biggest Stone Age earthworks at Silbury Hill in Wiltshire.* N-COUNT: usu pl

earthworm /ɜːʳθwɜːʳm/ **earthworms.** An **earthworm** is a kind of worm which lives in the ground. N-COUNT

earthy /ɜːʳθi/ **earthier, earthiest** ◆◇◇◇◇
1 If you describe someone as **earthy**, you mean that they are open and direct, and talk about subjects which other people avoid or feel ashamed about. *She is a very physical young woman, earthy, and very intense. ...his extremely earthy humour.* ADJ-GRADED
♦ **earthiness** *Dede grinned at her companion, delighting in her earthiness.* N-UNCOUNT
2 If you describe something as **earthy**, you mean it looks, smells, or feels like earth. *I'm attracted to warm, earthy colours... The rooms had the clean earthy smell of wet clay.* ADJ-GRADED: usu ADJ n

earwig /ɪəʳwɪɡ/ **earwigs.** An **earwig** is a small, thin brown insect that has a pair of pincers at the back end of its body. N-COUNT

ease /iːz/ **eases, easing, eased** ◆◆◆◇◇
1 If you do something **with ease**, you do it easily, without difficulty or effort. *Anne was intelligent and capable of passing her exams with ease. ...the ease with which young people could find work.* PHRASE: PHR after V ≠difficulty
2 If you talk about the **ease of** a particular activity, you are referring to the way that it has been made easier to do, or to the fact that it is already easy to do. *For ease of reference, only the relevant extracts of the regulations are included. ...the camera's ease of use in manual mode.* N-UNCOUNT: N of n
3 **Ease** is the state of being very comfortable and able to live as you want, without any worries or problems. *She lived a life of ease.* N-UNCOUNT =comfort
4 If something unpleasant **eases** or if you **ease** it, it is reduced in degree, speed, or intensity. *Tensions had eased... The heavily falling snow had eased... I gave him some brandy to ease the pain.* ♦ **easing** *...editorials calling for the easing of sanctions.* V-ERG; V; V n; N-UNCOUNT: usu N of n
5 If you **ease** your way somewhere or **ease** somewhere, you move there slowly, carefully, and gently. If you **ease** something somewhere, you move it there slowly, carefully, and gently. *I eased my way towards the door... She eased back into the chair and nodded... He eased his foot off the accelerator... Leaphorn eased himself silently upward... I eased open the door.* VERB; V way prep/adv; V prep/adv; V n prep/adv; V pron-refl adv/prep; V n with adj
6 If you are **at ease**, you are feeling confident and relaxed, and are able to talk to people without feeling nervous or anxious. If you put someone **at** their **ease**, you make them feel at ease. *It is essential to feel at ease with your therapist... Both men were unwelcoming, making little attempt to put Kathryn or her companions at their ease.* PHRASES: v-link PHR, PHR after v
7 **'At ease'** or **'Stand at ease'** is an order given to a group of soldiers to stand with their feet apart and their hands behind their backs. *At ease, Sergeant. This is completely informal.* PRAGMATICS
8 If you are **ill at ease**, you feel rather uncomfortable, anxious, or worried. *He appeared embarrassed and ill at ease with the sustained applause that greeted him.* usu v-link PHR, PHR after v, oft PHR with n

ease off. If something **eases off**, or someone or something **eases** it **off**, it is reduced in degree, speed, or intensity. *These days, the pressure has eased off... The rain had eased off... Kelly eased off his pace as they reached the elevator.* PHRASAL VERB: ERG; V P; V P n (not pron); Also V n P

ease up PHRASAL VERB
1 If something **eases up** it is reduced in degree, speed, or intensity. *The rain had eased up... New figures indicate the recession may be easing up.* V P
2 If you **ease up**, you start to make less effort. *He told supporters not to ease up even though he's leading in the presidential race... Christie was easing up over the last 10m to finish third.* V P
3 If you **ease up** on someone or something, your behaviour or attitude towards them becomes less severe or strict; an informal expression. *The manager does not intend to ease up on his players for some time... Officials have eased up on the press restrictions.* V P on n

easel /iːzəl/ **easels.** An **easel** is a wooden frame that supports a picture which an artist is painting or drawing. N-COUNT

easily /iːzɪli/ ◆◆◆◇◇
1 You use **easily** to emphasize that something is very likely to happen, or is very likely to be true. *It could easily be another year before the economy starts to show some improvement. ...an ancient barn that is easily the length of two tennis courts.* ADV-GRADED: usu ADV before v, also ADV n/adj PRAGMATICS
2 You use **easily** to say that something happens more quickly or more often than is usual or normal. *He had always cried very easily... They have nightmares, they startle easily.* ADV-GRADED: ADV after v
3 See also **easy**.

east /iːst/; also spelled **East**. ◆◆◆◆◆
1 The **east** is the direction where the sun rises. *...the vast swamps which lie to the east of the River Nile... The principal range runs east to west.* N-UNCOUNT: also the N
2 The **east** of a place, country, or region is the part which is in the east. *...a village in the east of the country... They are said to control large parts of the east and south of the country.* N-SING: usu the N, oft N of n
3 If you go **east**, you travel towards the east. *To drive, go east on Route 9.* ADV: ADV after v
4 Something that is **east** of a place is positioned to the east of it. *...just east of the center of town.* ADV: usu ADV of n
5 The **east** edge, corner, or part of a place or country is the part which is towards the east. *...a low line of hills running along the east coast.* ADJ: ADJ n
6 **East** is used in the names of some countries, states, and regions in the east of a larger area. *He had been on safari in East Africa with his son.* ADJ: ADJ n
7 An **east** wind is a wind that blows from the east. ADJ
8 **The East** is used to refer to the southern and eastern part of Asia, including India, China, and Japan. *Every so often, a new martial art arrives from the East.* N-SING: the N
9 See also **Middle East, Far East.**

eastbound /iːstbaʊnd/. **Eastbound** roads, cars, trains, or flights lead to or are travelling towards the east; a formal word. *He caught an eastbound train to Tottenham Court Road.* ADJ: ADJ n

Easter /iːstəʳ/ **Easters** ◆◆◇◇◇
1 **Easter** is a Christian festival when the resurrection of Jesus Christ is celebrated. It is celebrated on a Sunday in March or April. *'Happy Easter,' he yelled. ...the first Easter morning.* N-VAR: oft N n
2 **Easter** is the period of several days around and including Easter Sunday. *They usually have a walking holiday at Easter... She spends her Easter holidays taking groups of children to France... The* N-VAR: oft N n

government declared Easter Monday a public holiday.

Easter egg, Easter eggs. An **Easter egg** is an egg made of chocolate that is given as a present at Easter. N-COUNT

easterly /iːstərli/

1 An **easterly** point, area, or direction is to the east or towards the east. *He progressed slowly along the coast in an easterly direction.* ADJ-GRADED: usu ADJ n

2 An **easterly** wind is a wind that blows from the east. *...the cold easterly winds from Scandinavia.* ADJ: usu ADJ n

eastern /iːstərn/ ◆◆◆◆◇

1 Eastern means in or from the east of a region or country. *...Eastern Europe. ...Pakistan's eastern city of Lahore. ...France's eastern border with Germany.* ADJ: ADJ n

2 Eastern means coming from or associated with the people or countries of the East, such as India, China, or Japan. *In many Eastern countries massage was and is a part of everyday life.* ● See also **Middle Eastern**. ADJ: ADJ n

easterner /iːstərnər/ **easterners.** An **easterner** is a person who was born in or who lives in the eastern part of a place or country, especially an American from the East Coast of the USA; used mainly in American English. N-COUNT

easternmost /iːstərnmoust/. The **easternmost** part of an area is the one that is farthest towards the east; a formal word. *...Irian Jaya, the easternmost province of Indonesia.* ADJ-SUPERL: ADJ n

Easter Sunday. **Easter Sunday** is the Sunday in March or April when Easter is celebrated. N-UNCOUNT

East German, East Germans ◆◆◆◆◇

1 East German is used to describe things that belonged or related to the former German Democratic Republic. *...the former East German leader Erich Honecker.* ADJ

2 The **East Germans** were the people from the German Democratic Republic. The people who come from the part of Germany which was the German Democratic Republic are referred to as **east Germans**. *At elections in March 1990, East Germans chose a non-communist government... More than 30% of east Germans are either unemployed or working on short-time.* N-COUNT

eastward /iːstwərd/. The form **eastwards** is also used. **Eastward** or **eastwards** means towards the east. *A powerful snow storm is moving eastward... They were pressing on eastwards towards the city's small airfield.* ► Also an adjective. *...the eastward expansion of the City of London.* ADV: ADV after v =east; ADJ

easy /iːzi/ **easier, easiest** ◆◆◆◆◆

1 If a job or action is **easy**, you can do it without difficulty or effort, because it is not complicated and causes no problems. *The shower is easy to install... It's easy to get a seat at the best shows in town... This is not an easy task... The home is situated within easy access of shops and other facilities.* ♦ **easily** *Dress your child in layers of clothes you can remove easily.* ADJ-GRADED: oft *it* v-link ADJ to-inf, ADJ to-inf =simple ≠difficult; ADV-GRADED: usu ADV with v =simply

2 If you describe an action or activity as **easy**, you mean that it is done in a confident, relaxed way, without any anxiety or emotional tension. If someone is **easy** about something, they feel relaxed and confident about it. *She is laughing and joking and making easy conversation with people she has never met before... He was an easy person to talk to... Once you are both feeling a little easier about the break up of your relationship, you'll find that you can be more flexible.* ♦ **easily** *They talked amiably and easily about a range of topics.* ADJ-GRADED: oft ADJ *about* n ≠tense; ADV-GRADED: ADV with v

3 If you say that someone has an **easy** life, you mean that they live comfortably without any problems or worries. *She has not had an easy life.* ADJ-GRADED: usu ADJ n =simple

4 If you say that something is **easy** or too **easy**, you are criticizing someone because you believe that they have simply accepted or done the most obvious or least difficult thing, and have not considered the situation carefully enough. *That's easy for you to say... It was all too easy to believe it.* ADJ-GRADED: v-link ADJ, oft *it* v-link ADJ to-inf, ADJ to-inf PRAGMATICS

5 You use **easy** in expressions such as **easy on the ear** or **easy on the eye** when you are describing things that are pleasant and that do not need much effort to be enjoyed or done; an informal use. *The music sounds like an advert – easy on the ear but bland and forgettable... The layout should be clear and easy on the eye. ...a low-impact form of aerobic exercise that's easy on the joints.* ADJ-GRADED: v-link ADJ *on the* n =gentle, undemanding

6 If you describe someone or something as **easy prey** or as an **easy target**, you mean that they can easily be attacked or criticized. *Tourists have become easy prey... The World Bank, with its poor environmental record, is an easy target for blame.* ADJ-GRADED: ADJ n =soft

7 See also **easily**.

8 You use the expression **easy come, easy go** to indicate that the person you are talking about does not care much about money and possessions; an informal expression. *My attitude to money is slightly easy come, easy go.* PHRASES

9 If you say **'Easy does it'**, you are telling someone to be careful and not to use too much effort, especially when they are moving something large and awkward; used in spoken English. CONVENTION

10 If you tell someone to **go easy on** something, you are telling them to use only a small amount of it; an informal expression. *Go easy on the alcohol.* V inflects, PHR n PRAGMATICS

11 If you tell someone to **go easy on**, or **be easy on**, a particular person, you are telling them not to punish or treat that person very severely; an informal expression. *'Go easy on him,' Sam repeated, opening the door... Be a little easier on yourself and enjoy yourself more... This agency has been far too easy on the timber industry over the years.* V and ADJ inflect, PHR n PRAGMATICS

12 If you say that something is **easier said than done**, you are emphasizing that although it sounds like a good idea in theory, you think it would be difficult to actually do it. *Avoiding mosquito bites is easier said than done.* v-link PHR PRAGMATICS

13 If someone tells you to **take it easy** or **take things easy**, they mean that you should relax and not do very much at all; an informal expression. *It is best to take things easy for a week or two.* V and ADJ inflect PRAGMATICS

easy chair, easy chairs. An **easy chair** is a large, comfortable padded chair. N-COUNT

easy-going. If you describe someone as **easy-going**, you mean that they are not easily annoyed, worried, or upset, and you think this is a good quality. *He was easy-going and good-natured... Athenians have a very easy-going attitude to life.* ◆◇◇◇◇ ADJ-GRADED PRAGMATICS

eat /iːt/ **eats, eating, ate, eaten** ◆◆◆◆◇

1 When you **eat** something, you put it into your mouth, chew it, and swallow it. *She was eating a sandwich... The bananas should be eaten within two days... We took our time and ate slowly.* VERB V n V

2 If you **eat** sensibly or healthily, you eat food that is good for you. *...a campaign to persuade people to eat more healthily.* VERB V adv

3 If you **eat**, you have a meal. *Let's go out to eat... We ate lunch together a few times.* VERB V V n

4 If something **is eating** you, it is annoying or worrying you; an informal use. *'What the hell's eating you?' he demanded.* VB: only cont V n

5 If you say that someone **will be eaten alive**, you mean that they will find it very difficult to deal with a group of people because they lack experience or confidence. *Sid would be eaten alive by the hardened criminals at the jail... The press would eat him alive.* PHRASES V inflects

6 If you have someone **eating out of** your **hand**, they are completely under your control. *No-one can handle the press as she can and she usually has them eating out of her hand by the time they leave.* V and N inflect

7 If someone **is eating** their **heart out**, they are very sad or jealous because they cannot have something that someone else has. People often use expressions like 'eat your heart out Mozart' when they are doing something that they think the person named would be jealous of. *A limousine was sent to pick me up and deliver me to the set. Eat your heart out, Tom Selleck!... I want everyone back in Cleveland to be eating their crummy little hearts out.* V and N inflect

8 If you **eat** someone **out of house and home**, you eat a lot of their food, especially when you are V inflects living with them; an informal expression. *Is Karen still eating you out of house and home?*

9 ● to **have** your **cake and eat it**: see **cake.** ● **dog eat dog**: see **dog.** ● to **eat humble pie**: see **humble.**

eat away. If one thing **eats away** another or **eats away** at another, it gradually destroys or uses it up. *Water pours through the roof, encouraging rot to eat away the interior of the house... The recession is eating away at their revenues.* — PHRASAL VERB; V P n (not pron); V P *at* n; Also V n P

eat into — PHRASAL VERB

1 If something **eats into** your time or your resources, it uses them, when they should be used for other things. *Responsibilities at home and work eat into his time... Wages were rising faster than productivity and this was eating into profits.* — V P n

2 If a substance such as acid or rust **eats into** something, it destroys or damages its surface. *Ulcers occur when the stomach's natural acids eat into the lining of the stomach.* — V P n

eat up — PHRASAL VERB

1 When you **eat up** your food, you eat all of it. *Eat up your lunch... Some seed fell along the footpath; and the birds came and ate it up.* — V P n (not pron); V n P

2 If something **eats up** money, time, or resources, it uses them or consumes them in great quantities. *Health insurance costs are eating up his income.* — V P n (not pron)

eaten /iːtᵊn/. **Eaten** is the past participle of **eat.**

eaten up. If someone is **eaten up with** jealousy, curiosity, or desire, they feel it very intensely; an informal word. *Don't waste your time being eaten up with envy.* — ADJ: v-link ADJ *with* n

eater /iːtəʳ/ **eaters.** You use the word **eater** to refer to someone who eats in a particular way or who eats particular kinds of food. *I've never been a fussy eater... Vegetarians have a significantly lower blood pressure than meat eaters.* — ◆◇◇◇◇ N-COUNT: supp N

eatery /iːtəri/ **eateries.** An **eatery** is a place where you can buy and eat food. *...one of the most elegant old eateries in town.* — N-COUNT

eating apple, eating apples. An **eating apple** is an ordinary apple that is usually eaten raw rather than cooked. — N-COUNT ≠cooking apple

eau de cologne /oʊ də kəloʊn/. **Eau de cologne** is a fairly weak, sweet-smelling perfume. People often refer to it as **cologne**, especially in American English. — N-UNCOUNT

eaves /iːvz/. The **eaves** of a house are the lower edges of its roof. *There were icicles hanging from the eaves.* — N-PLURAL

eavesdrop /iːvzdrɒp/ **eavesdrops, eavesdropping, eavesdropped.** If you **eavesdrop** on someone, you listen secretly to what they are saying. *The government illegally eavesdropped on his telephone conversations... The housemaid eavesdropped from behind the kitchen door.* ♦ **eavesdropping** *Eavesdropping is a pastime for the nosy.* ♦ **eavesdropper, eavesdroppers** *Modern technology enables eavesdroppers to pick up conversations through windows or walls.* — ◆◇◇◇◇ VERB =listen in; V *on* n; V; N-UNCOUNT; N-COUNT

ebb /eb/ **ebbs, ebbing, ebbed** — ◆◇◇◇◇

1 When the tide or the sea **ebbs**, its level gradually falls. *As the tide ebbs, an ominous swell begins to run in.* — VERB; V

2 The **ebb** or the **ebb** tide is one of the regular periods, usually two per day, when the sea gradually falls to a lower level as the tide moves away from the land. *...the spring ebb tide... We decided to leave on the ebb at six o'clock next morning.* — N-COUNT: usu *the* N

3 If someone's life, support, or feeling **ebbs**, it becomes weaker and gradually disappears; a formal use. *...as a man's physical strength ebbs... Were there occasions when enthusiasm ebbed?* ► **Ebb away** means the same as **ebb**. *His little girl's life ebbed away... They suspect that their popular support is ebbing away.* — VERB; V; PHRASAL VERB; V P

4 If someone or something is **at a low ebb** or **at** their **lowest ebb**, they are not being very successful or profitable. *...a time when everyone is tired and at a low ebb... The Government's popularity is at its lowest ebb.* — PHRASE: v-link PHR

5 You can use **ebb and flow** to describe the way that something repeatedly increases and decreases or rises and falls. *...the ebb and flow of feeling and moods.* — PHRASE: usu PHR *of* n

ebony /ebəni/

1 **Ebony** is a very hard, heavy, dark-coloured wood. *...a small ebony cabinet.* — N-UNCOUNT: oft N n

2 Something that is **ebony** is a very deep black colour; a literary use. *He had rich, soft ebony hair.* — ADJ

ebullient /ɪbʌliənt, -bʊl-/. If you describe someone as **ebullient**, you mean that they are lively and full of enthusiasm or excitement about something; a formal word. *...the ebullient Russian President.* ♦ **ebullience** /ɪbʌliəns, -bʊl-/ *His natural ebullience began to return.* — ◆◇◇◇◇ ADJ-GRADED =exhilarated; N-UNCOUNT

eccentric /ɪkse̲ntrɪk/ **eccentrics.** If you say that someone is **eccentric**, you mean that they behave in a strange way, and have habits or opinions that are different from those of most people; often used showing disapproval. *He is an eccentric character who likes wearing a beret and dark glasses. ...Mr Thomas, a businessman with eccentric views.* ► An **eccentric** is a eccentric person. ♦ **eccentrically** /ɪkse̲ntrɪkli/ *...painters, eccentrically dressed and already half drunk.* —  ADJ-GRADED PRAGMATICS =odd; N-COUNT; ADV-GRADED

eccentricity /e̲ksentrɪsɪti/ **eccentricities** — ◆◇◇◇◇

1 **Eccentricity** is unusual behaviour that other people consider strange and peculiar; often used showing disapproval. *He was known as Mad Shelley partly because of his eccentricity and partly because of his violent temper... She is unusual to the point of eccentricity.* — N-UNCOUNT PRAGMATICS =oddness

2 **Eccentricities** are ways of behaving that people think are strange, or habits or opinions that are different from those of most people. *We all have our eccentricities. ...the eccentricities of British life.* — N-COUNT: usu pl, oft with poss =peculiarity

ecclesiastic /ɪkli̲ːziæstɪk/ **ecclesiastics.** An **ecclesiastic** is a priest or clergyman in the Christian Church; a formal word. — N-COUNT

ecclesiastical /ɪkli̲ːziæ̲stɪkᵊl/. **Ecclesiastical** means belonging to or connected with the Christian Church. *My ambition was to travel upwards in the ecclesiastical hierarchy.* — ◆◇◇◇◇ ADJ: usu ADJ n

ECG, ECGs /iː siː dʒiː/. **ECG** is an abbreviation for **electrocardiogram.** — N-VAR

echelon /eʃəlɒn/ **echelons** — ◆◇◇◇◇

1 An **echelon** in an organization or society is a level or rank in it; a formal word. *...the lower echelons of society.* — N-COUNT: usu adj N, oft N *of* n

2 An **echelon** is a military formation in which soldiers, vehicles, ships, or aircraft follow each other but are spaced out sideways so that they can see ahead. — N-COUNT: usu supp N

echo /ekoʊ/ **echoes, echoing, echoed** — ◆◆◆◇◇

1 An **echo** is a sound which is caused by a noise being reflected off a surface such as a wall. *He listened and heard nothing but the echoes of his own voice dying in the cave.* — N-COUNT: oft N *of* n

2 If a sound **echoes**, it is a reflected off a surface and can be heard again after the original sound has stopped. *His feet echoed on the bare board floor... The bang came suddenly, echoing across the buildings, shattering glass.* — VERB =reverberate; V; V prep/adv

3 In a place that **echoes**, a sound is reflected off a surface, and is repeated after the original sound has stopped. *The room echoed... The corridor echoed with the barking of a dozen dogs. ...the bare stone floors and the echoing hall.* — VERB; V; V *with*/*in* n; V-ing

4 If you **echo** someone's words, you repeat them or express agreement with their attitude or opinion. *Many phrases in the last two chapters echo earlier passages... Their views often echo each other... 'That was a truly delicious piece of pork,' he said. 'Yes, wasn't it?' echoed Penelope.* — VERB; V n; V with quote

5 An **echo** is an expression of an attitude, opinion, or statement which has already been expressed. *I hear an echo of the thinking that got us into this mess in the first place... Political attacks work only if they find an echo with voters.* — N-COUNT: usu with supp

6 A detail or feature which reminds you of something else can be referred to as an **echo**. *The accident has echoes of past disasters.* — N-COUNT: usu N *of* n =reminder

7 If one thing **echoes** another, the first is a copy of a — VERB

particular detail or feature of the other. *Pinks and beiges were chosen to echo the colours of the ceiling.* =imitate V n

8 To **echo** means to continue to be discussed and be important or influential in a particular situation or amongst a particular group of people. *The old fable continues to echo down the centuries.* VERB =resound V prep

éclair /ɪkle͟əʳ, AM eɪk-/ **éclairs;** also spelled **eclair.** An **éclair** is a long thin cake made of very light pastry, which is filled with cream and usually has chocolate on top. N-COUNT

eclectic /ɪkle͟ktɪk/. If you describe a collection of objects, ideas, or beliefs as **eclectic**, you mean that they are wide-ranging and come from many different sources; a formal word. *...an eclectic collection of paintings, drawings, and prints.* ◆◇◇◇◇ ADJ-GRADED =diverse

eclecticism /ɪkle͟ktɪsɪzəm/. **Eclecticism** is the principle or practice of choosing or involving objects, ideas, and beliefs from many different sources; a formal word. *The eclecticism of the designs means it is difficult to define one overall look. ...her cultural eclecticism.* N-UNCOUNT: usu with supp

eclipse /ɪklɪ͟ps/ **eclipses, eclipsing, eclipsed** ◆◇◇◇◇

1 An **eclipse** of the sun is an occasion when the moon is between the earth and the sun, so that for a short time you cannot see part or all of the sun. An **eclipse** of the moon is an occasion when the earth is between the sun and the moon, so that for a short time you cannot see part or all of the moon. *...the solar eclipse on May 21st. ...the total lunar eclipse. ...an eclipse of the sun.* N-COUNT: usu with supp, oft adj N, N *of* n

2 If one thing **is eclipsed** by a second thing that is bigger, newer, or more important than it, the first thing is no longer noticed because the second thing gets all the attention. *Only recently has the gramophone been eclipsed by new technology such as the compact disc... Of course, nothing is going to eclipse winning the Olympic title.* VERB =overshadow *be* V-ed V n

eco- /i͟ːkoʊ-/. **Eco-** combines with nouns and adjectives to form other nouns and adjectives which describe something as being related to ecology. *...the eco-friendly image of cycling. ...the eco-horror of the North Sea oil spill.* PREFIX

ecological /i͟ːkəlɒ͟dʒɪkəl/ ◆◆◇◇◇

1 Ecological means involved with or concerning ecology. *Large dams have harmed Siberia's delicate ecological balance. ...ecological disasters, such as the destruction of rainforest.* ADJ: ADJ n ♦ **ecologically** /i͟ːkəlɒ͟dʒɪkli/ *It is economical to run and ecologically sound.* ADV

2 Ecological groups, movements, and people are concerned with the preservation of the environment and natural resources, and with improving the quality of life. *Ecological groups say that nothing is being done to tackle the problem.* ADJ: ADJ n

ecologist /ɪkɒ͟lədʒɪst/ **ecologists** ◆◇◇◇◇

1 An **ecologist** is a person who studies ecology. *Ecologists argue that the benefits of treating sewage with disinfectants are doubtful.* N-COUNT

2 An **ecologist** is a person who believes that the environment and natural resources should be preserved and used in a sensible way, rather than exploited wastefully. *In the opinion polls the ecologists reached 20 per cent alongside the Socialists earlier in the year.* N-COUNT

ecology /ɪkɒ͟lədʒi/ **ecologies** ◆◇◇◇◇

1 Ecology is the study of the relationships between plants, animals, people, and their environment, and the balances between these relationships. *...a senior lecturer in ecology.* N-UNCOUNT

2 When you talk about the **ecology** of a place, you are referring to the pattern and balance of relationships between plants, animals, people, and the environment in that place. *...the ecology of the rocky Negev desert in Israel. ...the extinction of the marshes' unique ecology... Global ecological efforts can easily be at odds with local ecologies.* N-VAR: usu with supp

economic /i͟ːkənɒ͟mɪk, e͟k-/ ◆◆◆◆◆

1 Economic means concerned with the organization of the money, industry, and trade of a country, region, or society. *...Poland's radical economic reforms... The pace of economic growth is picking up.* ADJ: usu ADJ n ♦ **economically** /i͟ːkənɒ͟mɪkli, e͟k-/ *...an economically depressed area... How will Croatia do economically after independence?... Economically and politically, this affair couldn't come at a worse time.* ADV-GRADED: ADV adj/-ed, ADV after v, ADV with cl

2 If something is **economic**, it produces a profit. *Critics say that the new system may be more economic but will lead to a decline in programme quality.* ADJ-GRADED =profitable

economical /i͟ːkənɒ͟mɪkəl, e͟k-/ ◆◇◇◇◇

1 Something that is **economical** does not require a lot of money to operate. For example a car that only uses a small amount of petrol is **economical**. *...plans to trade in their car for something smaller and more economical... It is more economical to wash a full load.* ADJ-GRADED: oft ADJ to-inf, *it* v-link ADJ to-inf ♦ **economically** *Services could be operated more efficiently and economically.* ADV-GRADED: ADV after v

2 Someone who is **economical** spends money sensibly and does not want to waste it on things that are unnecessary. A way of life that is **economical** does not need a lot of money. *...ideas for economical housekeeping.* ADJ-GRADED =prudent, thrifty

3 Economical means using the minimum amount of time, effort, or language that is necessary. *His gestures were economical, his words generally mild.* ADJ-GRADED: usu v-link ADJ ♦ **economically** *Burn's novel, vividly and economically written, is a sombre reflection on fame and its cost.* ADV-GRADED: ADV -ed

economics /i͟ːkənɒ͟mɪks, e͟k-/ ◆◆◆◇◇

1 Economics is the study of the way in which money, industry, and trade are organized in a society. *He gained a first class Honours degree in economics.* ● See also **home economics.** N-UNCOUNT

2 The **economics** of a society or industry is the system of organizing money and trade in it. *He is regarded as a committed supporter of a radical free-market economics policy. ...the economics of the third world.* N-UNCOUNT

economist /ɪkɒ͟nəmɪst/ **economists.** An **economist** is a person who studies, teaches, or writes about economics. ◆◆◇◇◇ N-COUNT

economize /ɪkɒ͟nəmaɪz/ **economizes, economizing, economized;** also spelled **economise** in British English. If you **economize**, you save money by spending it very carefully. *We're going to have to economize from now on... Hollywood has been talking about economizing on movie budgets.* VERB =cut costs V V *on* n

economy /ɪkɒ͟nəmi/ **economies** ◆◆◆◆◆

1 An **economy** is the system according to which the money, industry, and trade of a country or region are organized. *Zimbabwe boasts Africa's most industrialised economy.* N-COUNT

2 A country's **economy** is the wealth that it gets from business and industry. *The Japanese economy grew at an annual rate of more than 10 per cent.* N-COUNT: usu *the* N in sing

3 Economy is the use of the minimum amount of money, time, or other resources needed to achieve something, so that nothing is wasted. *...improvements in the fuel economy of cars... There was mostly silence. I have never known such economy with words.* N-UNCOUNT: with supp

4 If you make **economies**, you try to save money by not spending money on unnecessary things. *They will make economies by hiring fewer part-time workers.* N-COUNT: usu pl =savings

5 Economy services such as travel are cheap and have no luxuries or extras. *Travelling economy class costs 200 marks.* ADJ: ADJ n

6 Economy can be used to describe large-size packages of goods which are cheaper than the normal-sized packages on sale. *...an economy pack containing 150 assorted screws.* ADJ: ADJ n

7 If you describe an attempt to save money as **a false economy**, you mean that you have not saved any money as you will have to spend a lot more later. *A cheap bed can be a false economy, so spend as much as you can afford... It seems a false economy to me to cut down on libraries.* PHRASE: v-link PHR

ecosystem /i͟ːkoʊsɪstəm, AM e͟kə-/ **ecosystems.** An **ecosystem** is all the plants and animals that live in a particular area together with the complex relationship that exists between them and their environment; a technical word. ◆◇◇◇◇ N-COUNT

Madagascar's ecosystems range from rainforest to semi-desert. ...the forest ecosystem.

ecru /eɪkruː/. Something that is **ecru** is pale, creamy white in colour, like the colour of string or unbleached cloth. *...cuffs of ecru lace.* COLOUR

ecstasy /ekstəsi/ **ecstasies** ◆◇◇◇◇

1 Ecstasy is a feeling of very great happiness. *...a state of almost religious ecstasy. ...the agony and ecstasy of holiday romance.* N-VAR

2 Ecstasy is an illegal drug which acts as a stimulant and can cause hallucinations. N-UNCOUNT

3 If you are **in ecstasy** about something, you are very excited about it. If you go **into ecstasies**, you become very excited. *My father was in ecstasy when I won my scholarship... She went into ecstasies over actors.* PHRASE: N inflects

ecstatic /ekstætɪk/ ◆◇◇◇◇

1 If you are **ecstatic**, you feel very happy and full of excitement. *His wife gave birth to their first child, and he was ecstatic about it... They were greeted by the cheers of an ecstatic crowd.* ♦ **ecstatically** /ekstætɪkli/ *We are both ecstatically happy.* ADJ-GRADED =delirious; ADV-GRADED

2 You can use **ecstatic** to describe reactions that are very enthusiastic and excited. For example, if someone receives an **ecstatic** reception or an **ecstatic** welcome, they are greeted with great enthusiasm and excitement. *They gave an ecstatic reception to the speech... The production received ecstatic reviews and had audiences weeping.* ADJ-GRADED: ADJ n =rapturous

ecu /eɪkjuː/ **ecus.** The **ecu** is a unit of money used for accounting purposes by the European Union's financial institutions, although it is not yet used as currency in any country. **Ecu** is an abbreviation for 'European Currency Unit'. *Barring unforeseen disasters, EC citizens are likely to have ecus in their pockets in 1997, or, at the latest, in 1999.* ◆◆◇◇◇ N-COUNT

ecumenical /iːkjuːmenɪkəl, ek-/. **Ecumenical** activities, ideas, and movements try to unite different Christian Churches; a formal word. *...ecumenical church services... He was deeply involved in the ecumenical movement.* ADJ: usu ADJ n

ecumenism /ɪkjuːmenɪzəm/. **Ecumenism** is used to refer to the belief that the different Christian Churches should be as united as possible, and to actions based on this belief; a formal word. N-UNCOUNT

eczema /eksmə, AM ɪgziːmə/. If you suffer from **eczema**, you have an uncomfortable skin disease which makes your skin itch and become sore, rough, and broken. ◆◇◇◇◇ N-UNCOUNT

-ed. Pronounced /-ɪd/ after /t/ or /d/, and /-t/ after one of the following sounds: /p, f, θ, s, tʃ, ʃ, k/. In other cases, it is pronounced /-d/.

1 -ed is added to verbs to form their past tense or their past participle. If the verb ends in e, one of the e's is dropped. If the verb ends in y, the y is usually changed to i. *I posted the letter... He danced well... 'I quite understand,' he replied.* SUFFIX

2 -ed is added to nouns to form adjectives that describe someone or something as having a particular feature or features. *...a fat, bearded man. ...coloured flags.* SUFFIX

3 -ed is added to nouns or verbs combined with other words, to form compound adjectives. *He rolled a scrap of paper into a cone-shaped container... He wore green-tinted glasses.* SUFFIX

ed., eds. ed. is a written abbreviation for **editor**. ◆◆◇◇◇

eddy /edi/ **eddies, eddying, eddied**

1 An **eddy** is a movement in water or in the air which goes round and round instead of flowing in one continuous direction. N-COUNT

2 To **eddy** means to move round and round, or to move in a disorganized way; a literary use. *The dust whirled and eddied in the sunlight... The crowds were eddying into the road.* VERB V V prep/adv

edge /edʒ/ **edges, edging, edged** ◆◆◆◆◇

1 The **edge** of something is the place or line where it stops, or the part of it that is furthest from the middle. *We were on a hill, right on the edge of town... She was standing at the water's edge... Daniel stepped in front of her desk and sat down on its edge.* N-COUNT: usu with supp

2 The **edge** of something sharp such as a knife or an axe is its sharp or narrow side. *...the sharp edge of the sword.* N-COUNT: usu with supp

3 If someone or something **edges** somewhere, they move very slowly in that direction. *He edged closer to the telephone, ready to grab it... He is edging ahead in the opinion polls.* VERB V prep/adv

4 The **edge** of something, especially something bad, is the point at which it may start to happen. *They have driven the rhino to the edge of extinction... She was on the edge of tears.* N-SING: usu *the* N *of* n =verge, brink

5 If someone or something has an **edge**, they have an advantage that makes them stronger or more likely to be successful than another thing or person. *The three days France have to prepare could give them the edge over England... Through superior production techniques they were able to gain the competitive edge.* N-SING: oft N *over* n, N *in* n/-ing =upper hand

6 If you say that someone or something has **an edge**, you mean that they have a powerful quality. *Featuring new bands gives the show an edge... Greene's stories had an edge of realism.* N-SING: *a* N

7 An **edge** to someone's voice is a quality of sharpness, bitterness, or controlled emotion in it. *But underneath the humour is an edge of bitterness... There was a nervous edge to his voice.* N-SING: oft N *of* n, N *to* n

8 See also **cutting edge, knife-edge, leading edge.**

9 If you or your nerves are **on edge**, you are tense, nervous, and unable to relax. *My nerves were constantly on edge.* PHRASES usu v-link PHR

10 If you say that someone is **on the edge of** their **seat** or **chair**, you mean that they are very interested in what is happening or what is going to happen. *Most of the time the audience is on the edge of its seat.* N inflects, usu v-link PHR, v PHR

11 If you say that a person or a piece of entertainment has **rough edges**, you mean that they have some small faults, although generally you approve of them. *The show, despite some rough edges, was an instant success.*

12 If something **takes the edge off** a situation, usually an unpleasant one, it weakens its effect or intensity. *A spell of poor health took the edge off her performance.* V inflects, PHR n

13 ● to **set** your **teeth on edge**: see **tooth.**

edge out. If someone **edges out** someone else, they just manage to beat them or get in front of them in a game, race, or contest. *In the second race, Germany and France edged out the British team by less than a second... McGregor's effort was enough to edge Johnson out of the top spot.* PHRASAL VERB V P n (not pron) V n P *of* n Also V n P

edged /edʒd/. If something is **edged** with a particular thing, that thing forms a border around it. *...a large lawn edged with flowers and shrubs. ...blank pages edged in black.* ► Also a combining form. *...clutching a lace-edged handkerchief.* ◆◆◇◇◇ ADJ: v-link ADJ *with/in* n COMB in ADJ

-edged /-edʒd/. **-edged** combines with words such as 'sharp', 'razor', 'raw', and 'dark' to form adjectives which indicate how powerful, critical, or unsentimental something such as a play or a style is. *...a sharp-edged satire that puts the Hollywood system under the microscope. ...the raw-edged vitality and daring of these works.* ● See also **edge, edged, hard-edged.** COMB in ADJ-GRADED

edgeways /edʒweɪz/. The form **edgewise**, /edʒwaɪz/, is also used, especially in American English. If you say that you **cannot get a word in edgeways**, you are complaining that you do not have the opportunity to speak because someone else is talking so much; an informal expression. *He spent all the time talking and they could not get a word in edgeways.* PHRASE: V inflects PRAGMATICS

edging /edʒɪŋ/ **edgings. Edging** is something that is put along the borders or sides of something else, usually to make it look attractive. *...the satin edging on Randall's blanket.* N-VAR

edgy /edʒi/ **edgier, edgiest.** If someone is **edgy**, they are nervous and anxious, and seem likely to lose control of themselves; an informal word. *She was nervous and edgy, still chain-smoking.* ◆◇◇◇◇ ADJ-GRADED =uptight, tense

edible /e̲dɪbəl/. If something is **edible**, it is safe to eat and not poisonous. *...edible fungi.* ◆◇◇◇◇ ADJ ≠inedible

edict /i̲ːdɪkt/ **edicts.** An **edict** is a command or instruction given by someone in authority; a formal word. *In 1741 Catherine the Great issued an edict of toleration for Buddhism... He issued an edict that none of his writings be destroyed.* ◆◇◇◇◇ N-COUNT: oft N that, N *against* n =order

edification /e̲dɪfɪke̲ɪʃən/. If something is done for your **edification**, it is done to benefit you in some way, for example by teaching you about something; a formal word. *No further information was provided for the edification of policy makers on the implications of this omission.* N-UNCOUNT: oft with poss

edifice /e̲dɪfɪs/ **edifices** ◆◇◇◇◇

1 An **edifice** is a large and impressive building; a formal use. *The taxi-driver reeled off a list of historic edifices they must not fail to visit.* N-COUNT

2 You can describe a system of beliefs or a traditional institution as an **edifice**; a formal use. *...an edifice of British constitutional tradition.* N-COUNT: usu with supp

edifying /e̲dɪfaɪɪŋ/

1 If you describe something as **edifying**, you mean that it benefits you in some way, for example by teaching you about something; a formal use. *In the 18th century art was seen, along with music and poetry, as something edifying.* ADJ-GRADED =instructive

2 You say that something is not very **edifying** when you want to express your disapproval or dislike of it, or to suggest that there is something unpleasant or unacceptable about it. *It all brought back memories of a not very edifying past.* ADJ-GRADED: with brd-neg PRAGMATICS

edit /e̲dɪt/ **edits, editing, edited** ◆◆◆◇◇

1 If you **edit** a text such as an article or a book, you correct and adapt it so that it is suitable for publishing. *The majority of contracts give the publisher the right to edit a book after it's done. ...an edited version of the speech.* ♦ **editing** *Throughout the editing of this book, we have had much support and encouragement.* VERB V n V-ed N-UNCOUNT

2 If you **edit** a book or a series of books, you collect several pieces of writing by different authors and prepare them for publishing. *This collection of essays is edited by Ellen Knight... She has edited the media studies quarterly, Screen. ...the Real Sandwich Book, edited by Miriam Polunin.* ♦ **editing** *He was certainly not cut out to combine the jobs of editing and writing as a journalist.* VERB *be* V-ed *by* n V n V-ed N-UNCOUNT

3 If you **edit** a film or a television or radio programme, you choose some of what has been filmed or recorded and arrange it in a particular order. *He taught me to edit and splice film... He is editing together excerpts of some of his films.* ♦ **editing** *He sat in on much of the filming and early editing.* VERB V n V n with *together* N-UNCOUNT

4 Someone who **edits** a newspaper, magazine, or journal is in charge of it. *I used to edit the college paper in the old days.* VERB V n

5 An **edit** is the process of examining and correcting a text so that it is suitable for publishing; a technical term in publishing. *The purpose of the edit is fairly simple – to chop out the boring bits from the original.* N-COUNT

edit out. If you **edit** something **out** of a book or film, you remove it, often because it might be offensive to some people. *His voice will be edited out of the final film... She edited that line out again.* PHRASAL VERB =cut V P n (not pron) V n P

edition /ɪdɪ̲ʃən/ **editions** ◆◆◆◆◇

1 An **edition** is a particular version of a book, magazine, or newspaper that is printed at one time. *A paperback edition is now available at bookshops.* N-COUNT: usu supp N =version

2 An **edition** is the total number of copies of a particular book or newspaper that are printed at one time. *The second edition was published only in America.* N-COUNT: usu supp N

3 An **edition** is a single television or radio programme that is one of a series about a particular subject. *They appeared on an edition of BBC2's Arena.* N-COUNT: with supp =episode

editor /e̲dɪtəʳ/ **editors** ◆◆◆◆◇

1 An **editor** is the person who is in charge of a newspaper or magazine and who decides what will be published in each edition of it. *Tarmu Tammerk is the editor of the Baltic Independent.* N-COUNT

2 An **editor** is a journalist who is responsible for a particular section of a newspaper or magazine. *Cookery Editor Moyra Fraser takes you behind the scenes. ...by Alan Travis, Home Affairs Editor.* N-COUNT: supp N

3 An **editor** is a person who checks and corrects texts before they are published. *Your role as editor is important, for you can look at a piece of writing objectively.* N-COUNT

4 An **editor** is a radio or television journalist who reports on a particular type of news. *As our economics editor, Dominic Harrod, reports, trade and investment are important issues on the agenda.* N-COUNT: supp N

5 An **editor** is a person who prepares a film, or a radio or television programme, by selecting some of what has been filmed or recorded and putting it in a particular order. *A few years earlier, she had worked at 20th Century Fox as a film editor.* N-COUNT

6 An **editor** is a person who collects pieces of writing by different authors and prepares them for publication in a book or a series of books. *Michael Rosen is the editor of the anthology.* N-COUNT

7 An **editor** is a computer program that enables you to make alterations and corrections to stored data. N-COUNT

editorial /e̲dɪtɔ̲ːriəl/ **editorials** ◆◆◆◇◇

1 **Editorial** means involved in preparing a newspaper, magazine, or book for publication. *He has been on the editorial staff of 'Private Eye' since 1963... I went to the editorial board meetings when I had the time.* ♦ **editorially** *Rosie Boycott was not involved editorially with Virago.* ADJ: ADJ n ADV

2 **Editorial** means involving the attitudes, opinions, and contents of something such as a newspaper, magazine, or television programme. *We are not about to change our editorial policy.* ♦ **editorially** *Editorially, they never really became a unique distinct product.* ADJ: ADJ n ADV: usu ADV after v, ADV with cl

3 An **editorial** is an article in a newspaper which gives the opinion of the editor or publisher on a topic or item of news. *In an editorial, The Independent suggests the victory could turn nasty.* N-COUNT

editorialize /e̲dɪtɔ̲ːriəlaɪz/ **editorializes, editorializing, editorialized;** also spelled **editorialise** in British English. If someone **editorializes,** they express their opinion about something rather than just stating facts; mainly used in contexts where you are talking about journalists and newspapers. *Other papers have editorialized, criticizing the Czech government for rushing to judgment on this individual.* VERB V

editorship /e̲dɪtəʳʃɪp/ **editorships.** The **editorship** of a newspaper or magazine is the position of its editor, or his or her work as its editor. *Under his editorship, the Economist has introduced regular sports coverage.* N-VAR: oft poss N, N *of* n

educate /e̲dʒʊkeɪt/ **educates, educating, educated** ◆◆◇◇◇

1 When someone, especially a child, **is educated**, he or she is taught at a school or college. *He was educated at Haslingden Grammar School.* VB: usu passive *be* V-ed

2 To **educate** people means to teach them better ways of doing something or a better way of living. *Drinkwise Day is mainly designed to educate people about the destructive effects of alcohol abuse.* VERB =inform V n

educated /e̲dʒʊkeɪtɪd/. Someone who is **educated** has a high standard of learning. *The general secretary of the TUC is an educated, amiable and decent man.* ◆◆◇◇◇ ADJ-GRADED =learned

-educated /-e̲dʒʊkeɪtɪd/

1 **-educated** combines with nouns and adjectives to form adjectives indicating where someone was educated. *...the Oxford-educated son of a Liverpool merchant. ...an American-educated lawyer.* COMB in ADJ

2 **-educated** combines with adverbs to form adjectives indicating how much education someone has had and how good it was. *Many of the immigrants are well-educated. ...impoverished, undernourished, and ill-educated workers.* COMB in ADJ-GRADED

e̲ducated gu̲ess, educated guesses. An **educated guess** is a guess which is based on a N-COUNT certain amount of knowledge and is therefore likely to be correct. *Estimating the right cooking time will always be an educated guess.*

education /ed͟ʒʊke͟ɪʃᵊn/ **educations** ◆◆◆◆◇
1 Education involves teaching people various subjects, usually at a school or college, or being taught. *They're cutting funds for education... Paul prolonged his education with six years of advanced study in English. ...a man with little education.* N-VAR
2 Education of a particular kind involves teaching the public about a particular issue. *...better health education.* N-UNCOUNT: usu with supp
3 See also **adult education, further education, higher education.**

educational /ed͟ʒʊke͟ɪʃənᵊl/ ◆◆◆◇◇
1 Educational matters or establishments are concerned with or relate to education. *...the British educational system. ...pupils with special educational needs.* ♦ **educationally** *By far the largest category of pupils requiring special education are the educationally sub-normal.* ADJ: usu ADJ n; ADV
2 An **educational** experience teaches you something. *The staff should make sure the kids have an enjoyable and educational day.* ADJ-GRADED =instructive

educationalist /ed͟ʒʊke͟ɪʃənəlɪst/ **educationalists.** An **educationalist** is a specialist in the theories and methods of education; used mainly in British English. The usual American word is **educator**. *British educationalists are divided about how best to teach reading.* N-COUNT

educationist /edʒʊke͟ɪʃənɪst/ **educationists.** An **educationist** is the same as an **educationalist**; used mainly in British English. N-COUNT

educative /ed͟ʒʊkətɪv, AM -keɪt-/. Something that has an **educative** role teaches you something; a formal word. *...the educative value of allowing broadcasters into their courts.* ADJ-GRADED =instructive

educator /ed͟ʒʊkeɪtəʳ/ **educators.** ◆◇◇◇◇
1 An **educator** is a person who educates people; used mainly in formal British English. N-COUNT =teacher
2 An **educator** is a specialist in the theories and methods of education; used mainly in American English. The usual British word is **educationalist**. N-COUNT

edutainment /ed͟ʒʊte͟ɪnmənt/. People use **edutainment** to refer to things such as computer games which are designed to be entertaining and educational at the same time. *...the increased demand for edutainment software.* N-UNCOUNT

Edwardian /edwɔ͟ːʳdiən/. **Edwardian** means belonging to, connected with, or typical of Britain in the first decade of the 20th century, when Edward VII was King. *...the Edwardian era. ...his old Edwardian office. ...a baggy Edwardian suit.* ◆◇◇◇◇ ADJ: usu ADJ n

eel /i͟ːl/ **eels.** An **eel** is a long, thin fish that looks like a snake. ► **Eel** is the flesh of this fish which is eaten as food. *...smoked eel.* ◆◆◇◇◇ N-VAR; N-UNCOUNT

eerie /ɪ͟əri/ **eerier, eeriest.** If you describe something as **eerie**, you mean that it seems strange and frightening, and makes you feel nervous. *I walked down the eerie dark path. ...an eerie calm.* ♦ **eerily** /ɪ͟ərɪli/ *Monrovia after the fighting is eerily quiet.* ◆◇◇◇◇ ADJ-GRADED; ADV-GRADED

efface /ɪfe͟ɪs/ **effaces, effacing, effaced.** If someone or something **effaces** something, they destroy or remove it so that it cannot be seen; a formal word. *...an event that has helped efface the country's traditional image... The name of the ship had been effaced from the menus.* ● See also **self-effacing.** VERB; V n

effect /ɪfe͟kt/ **effects, effecting, effected** ◆◆◆◆◆
1 The **effect** of one thing on another is the change that the first thing causes in the second thing. *Parents worry about the effect of music on their adolescent's behavior... The austerity measures will have little immediate adverse effect on the average Moroccan... Even minor head injuries can cause long-lasting psychological effects... Maybe talent does have a knock-on effect, inspiring and creating more talent... At fourteen he still had no grasp of cause and effect.* N-VAR: oft N *of/on* n, N *of*-ing, adj N
2 An **effect** is an impression that a speaker, artist, or designer deliberately creates by their style. *The whole effect is cool, light and airy.* N-COUNT =impression
3 A person's **effects** are the things that they have with them at a particular time, for example when they are arrested or admitted to hospital, or the things that they owned when they died; a formal use. *His daughters were collecting his effects.* N-PLURAL: with poss =belongings
4 The **effects** in a film are the specially created sounds and scenery. N-PLURAL
5 If you **effect** something that you are trying to achieve, you succeed in causing it to happen; a formal use. *Prospects for effecting real political change seemed to have taken a major step backwards.* VERB; V n
6 See also **greenhouse effect, placebo effect, ripple effect, side-effect, sound effect, special effect.**
7 If you say that someone is doing something **for effect**, you mean that they are doing it in order to impress people and to draw attention to themselves. *Jock paused for effect, his eyes glinting over his glass as he took another drink... The Cockney accent was put on for effect.* PHRASES; PHR after v
8 You add **in effect** to a statement or opinion that is not precisely accurate, but which you feel is a reasonable description or summary of a particular situation. *That deal would create, in effect, the world's biggest airline.* PHR with cl; PRAGMATICS; =effectively
9 If you **put, bring,** or **carry** a plan or idea **into effect**, you cause it to happen in practice. *These and other such measures ought to have been put into effect in 1985. ...a decree bringing into effect the political reforms adopted last month.* V inflects =implement
10 If a law or policy **takes effect** or **comes into effect** at a particular time, it officially begins to apply or be valid from that time. If it **remains in effect**, it still applies or is still valid. *...the ban on new logging permits which will take effect from July... The decision was taken yesterday and will remain in effect until further government instructions.* V inflects
11 You can say that something **takes effect** when it starts to produce the results that are intended. *The second injection should only have been given once the first drug had taken effect... International sanctions were beginning to take effect.* V inflects =work
12 You use **effect** in expressions such as **to good effect** and **to no effect** in order to indicate how successful or impressive an action is. *Mr Morris feels the museum is using advertising to good effect... Mr Charles complained, to no effect.* PHR after v
13 You use **to this effect, to that effect,** or **to the effect that** to indicate that you have given or are giving a summary of something that was said or written, and not the actual words used. *I understand that a circular to this effect will be issued in the next few weeks... Legislation to that effect created fierce controversy both in Parliament and outside... He cited a Chinese proverb to the effect that you should never wish ill on your neighbour.* n PHR; PRAGMATICS
14 If you say that something will happen **with immediate effect** or **with effect** from a particular time, you mean that it will begin to act, apply, or be valid immediately or from the stated time; used mainly in formal British English. *We are now resuming relations with Syria with immediate effect... The price of the Saturday edition is going up with effect from 3 November.* PHR after v

effective /ɪfe͟ktɪv/ ◆◆◆◆◇
1 Something that is **effective** works well and produces the results that were intended. *The project looks at how we could be more effective in encouraging students to enter teacher training... Simple antibiotics are effective against this organism... Such conditions would make an effective public transport system possible.* ♦ **effectively** *...the team roles which you believe to be necessary for the team to function effectively... Services need to be more effectively organised than they are at present.* ♦ **effectiveness** *...the effectiveness of computers as an educational tool.* ADJ-GRADED: oft ADJ *in*-ing, ADJ *against* n; ADV-GRADED: usu ADV after v, also ADV -ed; N-UNCOUNT: oft N *of* n
2 Effective means having a particular role or result in practice, though not officially or in theory. *They have had effective control of the area since the security forces left. ...a restructuring that would have* ADJ: ADJ n =actual

resulted in an effective increase on one of their most popular excursion fares.

3 When something such as a law or an agreement becomes **effective**, it begins officially to apply or be valid. *The new rules will become effective in the next few days.* ADJ: v-link ADJ

effectively /ɪfektɪvli/. You use **effectively** with a statement or opinion to indicate that it is not accurate in every detail, but that you feel it is a reasonable description or summary of a particular situation. *This effectively means that the government does not agree with the proposals... The region was effectively independent.* ◆◆◇◇◇ ADV: usu ADV before v, also ADV adj PRAGMATICS =in effect

effectual /ɪfektʃuəl/. If an action or plan is **effectual**, it succeeds in producing the results that were intended; a formal word. *This is the only effectual way to secure our present and future happiness.* ADJ-GRADED =effective ≠ineffectual

effeminate /ɪfemɪnət/. If you describe a man or boy as **effeminate**, you think he behaves, looks, or sounds like a woman or girl; often used to express disapproval of him. *...a skinny, effeminate guy in lipstick and earrings... His voice was curiously high-pitched, reedy, almost effeminate.* ADJ-GRADED ≠manly

effervescent /efərvesənt/

1 An **effervescent** liquid is one that contains or releases bubbles of gas. *...an effervescent mineral water.* ADJ

2 If you describe someone as **effervescent**, you mean that they are lively, entertaining, enthusiastic, and exciting; usually used showing approval. *...an effervescent blonde actress... America is the most intellectually, artistically and politically effervescent of nations.* ♦ **effervescence** *...writing about Gillespie's effervescence, magnetism and commitment.* ADJ-GRADED PRAGMATICS =bubbly, vivacious; N-UNCOUNT

effete /ɪfiːt/. If you describe someone as **effete**, you are criticizing them for being weak, powerless, and ineffective; a fairly formal word. *...the charming but effete Russian gentry of the 1840s and 1850s.* ADJ-GRADED PRAGMATICS

efficacious /efɪkeɪʃəs/. If you say that something is **efficacious**, you mean that it is effective and succeeds at doing what it is supposed to; a formal word. *The nasal spray was new on the market and highly efficacious.* ADJ-GRADED =effective

efficacy /efɪkəsi/. If you talk about the **efficacy** of something, you are talking about its effectiveness and its ability to do what it is supposed to; a formal word. *Recent medical studies confirm the efficacy of a healthier lifestyle.* ◆◇◇◇◇ N-UNCOUNT: usu with poss

efficiency /ɪfɪʃənsi/ ◆◆◇◇◇

1 **Efficiency** is the quality of being able to do a task successfully, without wasting time or energy. *There are many ways to increase agricultural efficiency in the poorer areas of the world. ...energy efficiency.* N-UNCOUNT

2 **Efficiency** is the difference between the amount of energy a machine needs to make it work, and the amount it produces; a technical term in physics and engineering. N-UNCOUNT; also N in pl

efficient /ɪfɪʃənt/. If something or someone is **efficient**, they are able to do tasks successfully, without wasting time or energy. *With today's more efficient contraception women can plan their families and careers.* ♦ **efficiently** *I work very efficiently and am decisive, and accurate in my judgement.* ◆◆◆◇◇ ADJ-GRADED; ADV-GRADED

effigy /efɪdʒi/ **effigies**

1 An **effigy** is a quickly and roughly made figure, often ugly or funny, that represents someone you hate or despise. N-COUNT

2 An **effigy** is a statue or carving of a famous person; a formal use. N-COUNT

effing /efɪŋ/. In British English, some people use **effing** to emphasize a word or phrase, especially when they are feeling angry or annoyed; an offensive word which you should avoid using. ADJ: ADJ n PRAGMATICS

effluent /efluənt/ **effluents.** **Effluent** is liquid waste material that comes out of factories or sewage works; a formal word. *The effluent from the factory was dumped into the river... All industrial chemical plants produce waste effluents.* N-MASS =waste

effort /efərt/ **efforts** ◆◆◆◆◆

1 If you make an **effort** to do something, you try very hard to do it. *He made no effort to hide his disappointment... Finding a cure requires considerable time and effort... His efforts to reform and revitalise Italian research have won wide praise... Despite the efforts of the United Nations, the problem of drug abuse and drug traffic continues to grow... But a concerted effort has begun to improve the quality of the urban air.* N-VAR: oft N to-inf

2 If you say that someone did something with **effort** or with **an effort**, you mean it was difficult for them to do; used in written English. *She took a deep breath and sat up slowly and with great effort... With an effort she contained her irritation.* N-UNCOUNT: usu with N, also a N =difficulty ≠ease

3 An **effort** is a particular series of activities that is organized by a group of people in order to achieve something. *...a famine relief effort in Angola.* N-COUNT: usu supp N

4 If you say that something is **an effort**, you mean that an unusual amount of physical or mental energy is needed to do it. *Even carrying the camcorder while hiking in the forest was an effort.* N-SING: a N =strain, struggle

5 If you **make the effort** to do something, you do it, even though you need extra energy to do it or you do not really want to. *I don't get lonely now because I make the effort to see people.* PHRASES V inflects, oft PHR to-inf

6 If you do something difficult or painful by **an effort of will**, you manage to make yourself do it. *It was only by a supreme effort of will and courage that he was able to pull himself together.*

7 If you say that something is **worth the effort**, you mean that it will justify the energy that you have spent or will spend on it. *Fortunately, the chore of leaf sweeping is well worth the effort.* v-link PHR

effortless /efərtləs/ ◆◇◇◇◇

1 If you describe something as **effortless**, you mean that it has been achieved or accomplished easily and has been done well. *In a single effortless motion, he scooped Frannie into his arms. ...effortless and elegant Italian cooking.* ♦ **effortlessly** *Her son Peter adapted effortlessly to his new surroundings.* ADJ-GRADED: usu ADJ n =easy; ADV-GRADED

2 You use **effortless** to describe a quality that someone has naturally and does not have to learn. *She liked him above all for his effortless charm.* ADJ-GRADED: usu ADJ n

effrontery /ɪfrʌntəri/. If you accuse someone of **effrontery**, you are accusing them of bold, rude, or cheeky behaviour; a formal word. *One could only gasp at the sheer effrontery of the man.* N-UNCOUNT PRAGMATICS

effusion /ɪfjuːʒən/ **effusions.** If someone expresses their emotions or ideas with **effusion**, they express them with more enthusiasm and for longer than is usual or expected. *His employer greeted him with an effusion of relief... I did not embarrass her with my effusions.* N-VAR

effusive /ɪfjuːsɪv/. If you describe someone as **effusive**, you mean that they express pleasure, gratitude, or approval in a very enthusiastic way. *He was effusive in his praise for the general... She was very gushing and very effusive.* ♦ **effusively** *She greeted them effusively.* ADJ-GRADED =unreserved; ADV-GRADED

EFL /iː ef el/. **EFL** is the teaching of English to people whose first language is not English. **EFL** is an abbreviation for 'English as a Foreign Language'. *...an EFL teacher.* N-UNCOUNT: oft N n

e.g. /iː dʒiː/. **e.g.** is an abbreviation that means 'for example'. It is used before a noun, or to introduce another sentence. *We need helpers of all types, engineers, scientists (e.g. geologists) and teachers... Or consider how you can acquire these skills, e.g. by taking extra courses.* ◆◆◇◇◇ =for instance

egalitarian /ɪgælɪteəriən/. **Egalitarian** means supporting or following the idea that all people are equal and should have the same rights and opportunities. *I still believe in the notion of an egalitarian society.* ◆◇◇◇◇ ADJ-GRADED

egalitarianism /ɪgælɪteəriənɪzəm/. **Egalitarianism** is used to refer to the belief that all people are equal and should have the same rights and opportunities, and to actions that are based on this belief. N-UNCOUNT

egg /eg/ **eggs, egging, egged** ◆◆◆◆◇
1 An **egg** is a small round or oval object produced by a female bird from which a baby bird later emerges. Reptiles, fish, and insects also lay eggs. *...a baby bird hatching from its egg. ...ant eggs.* N-COUNT
2 In Western countries, **eggs** often means hen's eggs, eaten as food. *Break the eggs into a shallow bowl and beat them lightly. ...bacon and eggs.* N-VAR
3 **Egg** is used to refer to an object in the shape of a hen's egg. *...a chocolate egg.* N-COUNT: usu supp N
4 An **egg** is a cell that is produced in the bodies of female animals and humans. If it is fertilized by a male reproductive cell, a baby develops from it. *It only takes one sperm to fertilize an egg.* N-COUNT
5 See also **Easter egg, nest egg, Scotch egg.**
6 If someone puts **all** their **eggs in one basket**, they put all their effort or resources into doing one thing so that, if it fails, they have no alternatives left. *The key word here is diversify; don't put all your eggs in one basket.* PHRASES usu v PHR
7 If someone has **egg on** their **face** or has **egg all over** their **face**, they have been made to look foolish. *If they take this game lightly they could end up with egg on their faces.* *face* inflects, *have/with* PHR
8 • **a chicken and egg situation**: see **chicken.** • **the goose that lay the golden egg**: see **goose.**
egg on. If you **egg** someone **on**, you encourage them to do something, especially something daring or foolish. *He was lifting up handfuls of leaves and throwing them at her. She was laughing and egging him on... They egged each other on to argue and to fight.* PHRASAL VERB V n P V n P to-inf Also V P n (not pron)

egg cup, egg cups; also spelled **eggcup.** An **egg cup** is a small container in which you put a boiled egg while you eat it. N-COUNT

egghead /eghed/ **eggheads.** If you think someone is more interested in ideas and theories than in practical actions you can say they are an **egghead**; an informal word. *The Government was dominated by self-important eggheads.* N-COUNT PRAGMATICS =boffin

eggnog /egnɒg/; also spelled **egg nog. Eggnog** is a drink made from egg, milk, sugar, spices, and alcohol such as rum or brandy. N-UNCOUNT

eggplant /egplɑːnt, -plænt/ **eggplants.** An **eggplant** is the same as an **aubergine**; used especially in American English. N-VAR

eggshell /egʃel/ **eggshells;** also spelled **egg shell** for meaning 1.
1 An **eggshell** is the hard covering on the outside of an egg. N-VAR
2 **Eggshell** paint makes surfaces dull, not shiny, when it is painted on them. *The walls had been painted an eggshell white.* ADJ: usu ADJ n

egg timer, egg timers; also spelled **egg-timer.** An **egg timer** is a device that measures the time needed to boil an egg. N-COUNT

egg whisk, egg whisks. An **egg whisk** is a piece of kitchen equipment used for mixing the different parts of an egg together. N-COUNT

ego /iːgoʊ, egoʊ/ **egos.** You refer to someone's **ego** when you are referring to their sense of their own self and their worth. For example, if you say that they have a large **ego**, you mean that they think they are very important and valuable. *He had a massive ego, never would he admit he was wrong.* • See also **alter ego, super-ego.** ◆◆◇◇◇ N-VAR

egocentric /iːgoʊsentrɪk, eg-/. If you describe someone as **egocentric**, you are criticizing them for thinking only of themselves and their own wants, and not considering other people. *He was egocentric, a man of impulse who expected those around him to serve him.* ADJ-GRADED PRAGMATICS =self-centred, selfish

egoism /iːgoʊɪzəm, eg-/. **Egoism** is the same as **egotism.** N-UNCOUNT

egoist /iːgoʊɪst, eg-/ **egoists.** An **egoist** is the same as an **egotist.** N-COUNT

egoistic /iːgoʊɪstɪk, eg-/. **Egoistic** means the same as **egotistic.** ADJ-GRADED

egomania /iːgoʊmeɪniə, eg-/. If you accuse someone of **egomania**, you are criticizing them for thinking only of themselves and not caring if they harm other people in order to get what they want. *United Artists was bankrupted by the egomania of a single film maker who spent more than 40 million dollars on a film.* N-UNCOUNT PRAGMATICS =selfishness

egomaniac /iːgoʊmeɪniæk, eg-/ **egomaniacs.** If you describe someone as an **egomaniac**, you are criticizing them for thinking only of themselves and not caring if they harm other people in order to get what they want. *Adam is clever enough, but he's also something of an egomaniac.* N-COUNT PRAGMATICS

egotism /iːgətɪzəm, eg-/. If you accuse someone of **egotism**, you are criticizing them for behaving selfishly and believing themselves to be more important than other people. *With an actress's born egotism, she imagines herself as the center of a hundred glamorous fantasies.* N-UNCOUNT PRAGMATICS =selfishness

egotist /iːgətɪst, eg-/ **egotists.** If you describe someone as an **egotist**, you are criticizing them for behaving selfishly and believing themselves to be more important than other people. *Wilf was an egotist taken up with his own self importance.* N-COUNT PRAGMATICS

egotistic /iːgətɪstɪk, eg-/. The form **egotistical** is also used. If you describe someone as **egotistic** or **egotistical**, you are criticizing them for behaving selfishly and believing themselves to be more important than other people. *Susan and Deborah share an intensely selfish, egotistic streak.* ADJ-GRADED PRAGMATICS =self-centred

ego trip, ego trips. If you say that someone is on an **ego trip**, you are criticizing them for doing something for their own satisfaction and enjoyment, often to show that they think they are more important than other people. *He's on one a big ego trip.* N-COUNT PRAGMATICS

egregious /ɪgriːdʒəs/. **Egregious** means very bad indeed; a formal word. *...the most egregious abuses of human rights.* ADJ-GRADED: usu ADJ n =grievous

Egyptian /ɪdʒɪpʃən/ **Egyptians** ◆◆◆◆◇
1 **Egyptian** means belonging or relating to Egypt or its people. *The Egyptian president arrived in Baghdad.* ADJ
2 The **Egyptians** are the people who come from Egypt. N-COUNT
3 **Egyptian** means related to or connected with ancient Egypt. *...the Egyptian pharaoh.* ADJ
4 The **Egyptians** were the people who lived in ancient Egypt. *The Babylonians and the Egyptians were responsible for the building of the great civilisations of the ancient world.* N-COUNT

eh /eɪ/. **Eh** is used in writing to represent a noise that people make as a response in conversation, for example to express agreement or to ask for something to be explained or repeated. *Let's talk all about it outside, eh?... 'He's um ill in bed.'—'Eh?'—'He's ill in bed.'* ◆◆◇◇◇ CONVENTION

eiderdown /aɪdərdaʊn/ **eiderdowns.** An **eiderdown** is a bed covering, placed on top of sheets and blankets, that is filled with small soft feathers or warm material. The usual American word is **comforter.** N-COUNT =quilt

eight /eɪt/ **eights. Eight** is the number 8. *So far eight workers have been killed.* ◆◆◆◆◆ NUM

eighteen /eɪtiːn/. **Eighteen** is the number 18. *He was employed by them for eighteen years.* ◆◆◆◆◆ NUM

eighteenth /eɪtiːnθ/. The **eighteenth** item in a series is the one that you count as number eighteen. *The siege is now in its eighteenth day.* ◆◆◆◆◇ ORD

eighth /eɪtθ/ **eighths** ◆◆◆◆◇
1 The **eighth** item in a series is the one that you count as number eight. *...the eighth prime minister of India.* ORD
2 An **eighth** is one of eight equal parts of something. *The Kuban produces an eighth of Russia's grain, meat and milk.* FRACTION

eightieth /eɪtiəθ/. The **eightieth** item in a series is the one that you count as number eighty. *Mr Stevens recently celebrated his eightieth birthday.* ◆◆◆◆◇ ORD

eighty /eɪti/ **eighties.** ◆◆◆◆◆
1 **Eighty** is the number 80. *Eighty horses trotted up.* NUM
2 When you talk about the **eighties**, you are referring to numbers between 80 and 89. For example, if you are **in your eighties**, you are aged between 80 and 89. If the temperature is **in the eighties**, the N-PLURAL

temperature is between 80 and 89 degrees. *He was in his late eighties and had become the country's most respected elder statesman.*

3 **The eighties** is the decade between 1980 and 1989. *He ran a property development business in the eighties.* N-PLURAL: *the* N

eisteddfod /aɪstedfɒd, AM -vɑːd/ **eisteddfods.** An **eisteddfod** is a Welsh festival at which competitions are held in music, poetry, drama, and art. N-COUNT

either /aɪðəʳ, iːðəʳ/ ◆◆◆◆◆

1 You use **either** in front of the first of two or more alternatives, when you are stating the only possibilities or choices that there are. The other alternatives are introduced by 'or'. *They gave money to the Conservative Party either personally or through their companies... Sightseeing is best done either by tour bus or by bicycles... The former President was demanding that he should be either put on trial or set free... Either she goes or I go.* CONJ-COORD PRAGMATICS

2 You use **either** in a negative statement in front of the first of two alternatives to indicate that the negative statement refers to both the alternatives. *...music that fails to be either funny or funky... There had been no indication of either breathlessness or any loss of mental faculties right until his death.* CONJ-COORD PRAGMATICS

3 You can use **either** to refer to one of two things, people, or situations, when you want to say that they are both possible and it does not matter which one is chosen or considered. *There were glasses of iced champagne and cigars. Unfortunately not many of either were consumed... If either were killed, delicate negotiations would be seriously disrupted.* PRON ► Also a quantifier. *They are able to talk openly to one another whenever either of them feels hurt... Do either of you smoke or drink heavily?* QUANT: QUANT *of* def-pl-n ► Also a determiner. *...a special Indian drug police that would have the authority to pursue suspects into either country.* DET: DET sing-n

4 You use **either** in a negative statement to refer to each of two things, people, or situations to indicate that the negative statement includes both of them. *She warned me that I'd never marry or have children.—'I don't want either.'* PRON: with brd-neg PRAGMATICS ► Also a quantifier. *There are no simple answers to either of those questions.* QUANT ► Also a determiner. *He sometimes couldn't remember either man's name.* DET

5 You use **either** by itself in negative statements to indicate that there is a similarity or connection with a person or thing that you have just mentioned. *He did not even say anything to her, and she did not speak to him either... 'I'm afraid I've never been there.'—'Well, of course, I haven't myself either.'* ADV: ADV after v, with brd-neg

6 When one negative statement follows another, you can use **either** at the end of the second one to indicate that you are adding an extra piece of information, and to emphasize that both are equally important. *Don't agree, but don't argue either... I can't manage that by myself and I don't see why it should be expected of me either.* ADV: ADV after v PRAGMATICS

7 You can use **either** to introduce a noun that refers to each of two things when you are talking about both of them. *The basketball nets hung down from the ceiling at either end of the gymnasium... I suddenly realized that I didn't have a single intelligent thing to say about either team.* DET: DET sing-n

ejaculate /ɪdʒækjʊleɪt/ **ejaculates, ejaculating, ejaculated** ◆◇◇◇◇

1 When a man **ejaculates**, sperm comes out through his penis. *... a tendency to ejaculate quickly.* VERB V ♦ **ejaculation** /ɪdʒækjʊleɪʃən/ **ejaculations** *Each male ejaculation will contain up to 300 million sperm.* N-VAR

2 If you **ejaculate**, you suddenly say or shout something, for example because you are very surprised; an old-fashioned, literary use. *'What?' Catherine ejaculated.* VERB =exclaim V with quote Also V n

eject /ɪdʒekt/ **ejects, ejecting, ejected** ◆◇◇◇◇

1 If you **eject** someone from a place, you force them to leave. *Officials used guard dogs to eject the protesters... He was ejected from a restaurant.* VERB V n V n *from* n ♦ **ejection** /ɪdʒekʃən/ **ejections** *...the ejection and manhandling of hecklers at the meeting.* N-VAR =expulsion

2 To **eject** something means to remove it or push it out forcefully. *He aimed his rifle, fired a single shot, then ejected the spent cartridge.* VERB =expel V n

3 When pilots **eject** from their aircraft, they leave the aircraft rapidly by means of ejector seats, usually because the plane is about to crash. *The pilot ejected from the plane and escaped injury.* VERB =bail out V *from* n Also V

ejector seat, ejector seats. An **ejector seat** is a special seat which can throw the pilot out of a fast military aircraft in an emergency. N-COUNT

eke /iːk/ **ekes, eking, eked.** If you **eke a living** or **eke out an existence**, you manage to survive with very little money. *That forced peasant farmers to try to eke a living off steep hillsides ... He ekes out a living with a market stall... He was eking out an existence on a few francs a day.* PHRASE: V inflects

eke out. If you **eke out** something, you make your supply of it last as long as possible. *Many workers can only eke out their redundancy money for about 10 weeks.* PHRASAL VERB V P n (not pron) Also V n P

elaborate, elaborates, elaborating, elaborated. The adjective is pronounced /ɪlæbərət/. The verb is pronounced /ɪlæbəreɪt/. ◆◆◇◇◇

1 You use **elaborate** to describe something that is very complex because it has a lot of different parts. *...an elaborate research project. ...an elaborate ceremony that lasts for eight days.* ADJ-GRADED: usu ADJ n =complicated

2 **Elaborate** plans, systems, and procedures are complicated because they have been planned in very great detail, sometimes too much detail. *...elaborate efforts at the highest level to conceal the problem... The company has worked out an elaborate management training scheme for graduates.* ADJ-GRADED: usu ADJ n =complicated ♦ **elaborately** *It was clearly an elaborately planned operation.* ADV-GRADED

3 **Elaborate** clothing or material is made with a lot of detailed artistic designs. *He is known for his elaborate costumes.* ADJ-GRADED: usu ADJ n ♦ **elaborately** *...elaborately costumed dolls.* ADV-GRADED

4 If you **elaborate** a plan or theory, you develop it by making it more complicated and more effective. *His task was to elaborate policies which would make a market economy compatible with a clean environment. ...the plan elaborated by the five permanent members of the UN Security Council.* VERB V n ♦ **elaboration** /ɪlæbəreɪʃən/ *...the elaboration of specific policies and mechanisms.* N-UNCOUNT: oft N *of* n

élan /eɪlɑːn/; also spelled **elan**. If you say that someone does something with **élan**, you mean that they do it in an energetic and confident way; a literary word. *This small part was taken with elan by a promising young tenor.* N-UNCOUNT =panache

elapse /ɪlæps/ **elapses, elapsing, elapsed.** When time **elapses**, it passes; a formal word. *Forty-eight hours have elapsed since his arrest.*  VERB V

elastic /ɪlæstɪk/ 

1 **Elastic** is a rubber material that stretches when you pull it and returns to its original size and shape when you let it go. Elastic is often used in clothes to make them fit tightly, for example round the waist. *...a piece of elastic. ...my plaid Bermuda shorts with the elastic waist.* N-UNCOUNT

2 Something that is **elastic** is able to stretch easily and then return to its original size and shape. *Beat it until the dough is slightly elastic. ...an elastic rope.* ADJ-GRADED =stretchy

3 If you describe people's ideas, plans, or policies as **elastic**, you mean that they change in order to suit new circumstances or conditions as they arise. *...an elastic interpretation of the rules of boxing... If export and import demand is elastic then the change in trade volumes will operate to remove the surplus.* ADJ-GRADED =adaptable

elasticated /ɪlæstɪkeɪtɪd/. If a piece of clothing or part of a piece of clothing is **elasticated**, elastic has been sewn or woven into it to make it fit better and to help it keep its shape; used mainly in British English. *...a pink silk jacket with an elasticated waist.* ADJ

elastic band, elastic bands. An **elastic band** is a thin circle of very stretchy rubber that you can put around bundles of things such as papers in order to hold them together; used mainly in British English. The usual American term is **rubber band.** N-COUNT =rubber band

elasticity /iːlæstɪsɪti, ɪlæst-/ **elasticities** ◆◇◇◇◇

1 The **elasticity** of a material or substance is its ability to return to its original shape, size, and condition after it has been stretched. *Daily facial exercises help her to retain the skin's elasticity... Gluten develops elasticity in a dough.* N-UNCOUNT =stretchiness

2 The **elasticity** of something, especially the demand for a product, is the degree to which it changes in response to changes in circumstances; a technical use in economics. *The elasticity of demand for a single newspaper is bound to be higher than the figure for newspapers as a whole.* N-UNCOUNT: also N in pl, with supp, oft N of n, n N

elated /ɪleɪtɪd/. If you are **elated**, you are extremely happy and excited because of something that has happened. *We are elated that democracy has come to Czechoslovakia... 'That was one of the best races of my life,' said an elated Mansell.* ◆◇◇◇◇ ADJ-GRADED: usu v-link ADJ =exhilarated

elation /ɪleɪʃᵊn/. **Elation** is a feeling of great happiness and excitement about something that has happened. *His supporters have reacted to the news with elation.* N-UNCOUNT =delight

elbow /elbou/ **elbows, elbowing, elbowed** ◆◆◇◇◇

1 Your **elbow** is the part of your arm where the upper and lower halves of the arm are joined. *He slipped and fell, badly bruising an elbow.* N-COUNT

2 If you **elbow** someone aside or to one side, you push them out of the way, using your elbows. *They also claim that the security team elbowed aside a steward... In the school lunchroom we girls elbow one another out of the way... Mr Smith elbowed me in the face... She elbowed and shoved, now she was pushing with all the strength of her body.* VERB =jostle V n with *aside* V n *out of* n V n *in* n V

3 If you **elbow** your way somewhere, you move there by pushing other people out of the way, using your elbows. *Brand elbowed his way to the centre of the group of bystanders.* VERB V *way* prep/adv

4 If you say that someone or something **elbows** its way somewhere, or **elbows** other people or things out of the way, you mean that they achieve success by being aggressive and ruthless. *Non-state firms gradually elbow aside the inefficient state-owned ones... With the survival of the whole planet in mind, environmental concerns will elbow their way right to the top of the agenda.* VERB V n with *aside/out* V *way* prep Also V n prep, V n

elbow grease. People use the expression **elbow grease** to refer to the strength and energy that you use when doing physical work like rubbing or polishing; an informal expression. *It took a considerable amount of polish and elbow grease before the brass shone like new.* N-UNCOUNT

elbow room

1 **Elbow room** is the freedom to do what you want to do or need to do in a particular situation; an informal use. *His speech won a standing ovation – but it was also designed to give himself more political elbow room.* N-UNCOUNT =leeway

2 If there is enough **elbow room** in a place or vehicle, it is not too small or too crowded; an informal use. *There was not much elbow room in the cockpit of a Snipe.* N-UNCOUNT =space

elder /eldəʳ/ **elders** ◆◆◇◇◇

1 The **elder** of two people is the one who was born first. *...his elder brother. ...the elder of her two daughters.* ADJ-COMPAR: ADJ n, *the* ADJ, *the* ADJ *of* n

2 A person's **elder** is someone who is older than them, especially someone quite a lot older; a formal use. *The young have no respect for their elders.* N-COUNT: poss N

3 In some societies, an **elder** is one of the respected older people who have influence and authority. *...a meeting of political figures and tribal elders.* N-COUNT

4 In some Christian churches, an **elder** is one of the people who hold a position of responsibility, but not usually an ordained minister. *He is now an elder of the village church.* N-COUNT

5 An **elder** is a bush or small tree which has groups of small white flowers and red or black berries. N-COUNT

elderberry /eldəʳberi/ **elderberries**

1 **Elderberries** are the edible red or black berries that grow on an elder bush or tree. N-COUNT: usu pl

2 An **elderberry** is an elder bush or tree. N-VAR

elderly /eldəʳli/ ◆◆◆◇◇

1 You use **elderly** as a polite way of saying that someone is old. *There was an elderly couple on the terrace... Many of those most affected are elderly.* ADJ-GRADED

► The **elderly** are people who are old. *The elderly are a formidable force in any election.* N-PLURAL: usu *the* N

2 If you describe an object as **elderly**, you are referring, often in a humorous way, to the fact that it is rather old or old-fashioned and not as good or efficient as a new one would be. *Some of those artillery pieces look a little elderly.* ADJ-GRADED

elder statesman, elder statesmen

1 An **elder statesman** is an old and respected politician or former politician who still has influence because of his or her experience. N-COUNT

2 An experienced and respected member of an organization or profession is sometimes referred to as an **elder statesman.** N-COUNT: usu with supp

eldest /eldɪst/. The **eldest** person in a group is the one who was born before all the others. *The eldest child was a daughter called Fiona... David was the eldest of three boys... The two eldest are already doing well at Kings Wood.* ◆◇◇◇◇ ADJ-SUPERL

elect /ɪlekt/ **elects, electing, elected** ◆◆◆◆◇

1 When people **elect** someone, they choose that person to represent them, by voting for them. *The people of the Philippines have voted to elect a new president... Manchester College elected him Principal in 1956... The country is about to take a radical departure by electing a woman as its new president.* VERB V n V n n V n *as* n

♦ **elected** *...the country's democratically elected president.* ADJ: ADJ n

2 If you **elect** to do something, you choose to do it; a formal use. *Those electing to smoke will be seated at the rear.* VERB V to-inf

3 **Elect** is added after words such as 'president' or 'governor' to indicate that a person has been elected to the post but has not officially started to carry out the duties involved; a formal use. *...the date when the president-elect takes office.* ADJ: n ADJ

election /ɪlekʃᵊn/ **elections** ◆◆◆◆◆

1 An **election** is a process in which people vote to choose a person or group of people to hold an official position. *...Poland's first fully free elections for more than fifty years... During his election campaign he promised to put the economy back on its feet... The final election results will be announced on Friday... Many residents say they have little or no idea who's standing for election.* N-VAR

2 The **election** of a particular person or group of people is their success in winning an election. *...the election of the Labour government in 1964. ...Vaclav Havel's election as president of Czechoslovakia... In Illinois, the Democrat candidate is the favorite to win election to the Senate.* N-UNCOUNT: usu with poss

electioneering /ɪlekʃənɪərɪŋ/. **Electioneering** is the activities that politicians and their supporters carry out in order to persuade people to vote for them or their political party in an election, for example making speeches and visiting voters. N-UNCOUNT =campaigning

elective /ɪlektɪv/ **electives**

1 An **elective** post or committee is one to which people are appointed as a result of winning an election; a formal use. *Buchanan has never held elective office.* ADJ: usu ADJ n

2 **Elective** surgery is surgery that you choose to have in advance rather than wait for it to become essential, for example a hip replacement or a hysterectomy; a formal use. *Hospitals have reduced resources for elective surgery.* ADJ: usu ADJ n

3 In American English, an **elective** is a subject which a student can choose to study as part of his or her course. *Electives are offered in Tai Chi and advanced dance exercise.* N-COUNT =option

elector /ɪlektəʳ/ **electors.** An **elector** is a person who has the right to vote in an election. *Greek electors go to the polls on Sunday.* ◆◇◇◇◇ N-COUNT: usu pl =voter

electoral /ɪle̲ktərəl/. **Electoral** is used to describe things that are connected with elections. *The Mongolian Democratic Party is campaigning for electoral reform. ...Italy's electoral system of proportional representation.* ♦ **electorally** *He believed that the policies were both wrong and electorally disastrous.* ◆◆◆◇◇ ADJ: ADJ n; ADV: ADV adj/-ed, ADV after v, ADV with cl

ele̲ctoral re̲gister, electoral registers. In Britain, an **electoral register** is an official list of all the people who have the right to vote in an election. *Many students are not on the electoral register.* N-COUNT: usu *the* N in sing =electoral roll

ele̲ctoral ro̲ll, electoral rolls. In Britain, an **electoral roll** is the same as an **electoral register**. N-COUNT

electorate /ɪle̲ktərət/ **electorates.** The **electorate** of a country or area is all the people in it who have the right to vote in an election. *He has the backing of almost a quarter of the electorate. ...the Maltese electorate.* ◆◆◇◇◇ N-COUNT-COLL

electric /ɪle̲ktrɪk/ ◆◆◆◇◇

1 An **electric** device or machine works by means of electricity, rather than using some other source of power. *...her electric guitar.* ADJ: usu ADJ n

2 An **electric** current, voltage, or charge is one that is produced by electricity. ADJ: ADJ n

3 **Electric** plugs, sockets, or power lines are designed to carry electricity. ADJ: ADJ n

4 The **electric** is the supply of electricity to a house or other place; an informal use. *An average electric bill might go up $2 or $3 per month... We don't have meters, not like the gas and the electric.* N-UNCOUNT: usu N n, *the* N =electricity

5 If you describe the atmosphere of a place or event as **electric**, you mean that people are in a state of great excitement. *The mood in the hall was electric.* ADJ-GRADED =charged

electrical /ɪle̲ktrɪkᵊl/ ◆◆◇◇◇

1 **Electrical** goods, equipment, or appliances work by means of electricity. *...shipments of electrical equipment. ...electrical appliances.* ♦ **electrically** /ɪle̲ktrɪkli/ *...electrically-powered vehicles.* ADJ: usu ADJ n; ADV: ADV -ed

2 **Electrical** systems or components supply or use electricity. ADJ: usu ADJ n

3 **Electrical** energy is energy in the form of electricity. ♦ **electrically** *...electrically charged particles... The researchers stimulated the muscle electrically.* ADJ: usu ADJ n; ADV: usu ADV adj

4 **Electrical** industries, engineers, or workers are involved in the production and supply of electricity or electrical goods. ADJ: ADJ n

ele̲ctrical engine̲er, electrical engineers. An **electrical engineer** is a person who uses scientific knowledge to design, construct, and maintain electrical devices. N-COUNT

ele̲ctrical enginee̲ring. Electrical engineering is the designing, constructing, and maintenance of electrical devices. N-UNCOUNT

ele̲ctric bla̲nket, electric blankets. An **electric blanket** is a blanket with wires inside it which carry an electric current that keeps the blanket warm. N-COUNT

ele̲ctric-blu̲e. Something that is **electric-blue** is very bright blue in colour. COLOUR

ele̲ctric cha̲ir, electric chairs. The **electric chair** is a method of execution, used especially in the United States, in which a person is strapped to a special chair and killed by a powerful electric current. N-COUNT: usu *the* N in sing

electrician /ɪlektrɪʃᵊn, i̲:lek-/ **electricians.** An **electrician** is a person whose job is to install and repair electrical equipment. ◆◇◇◇◇ N-COUNT

electricity /ɪlektrɪ̲sɪti, i̲:lek-/. **Electricity** is a form of energy that can be carried by wires and is used for heating and lighting, and to provide power for machines. *We moved into a cabin with electricity but no running water... The electricity had been cut off.* ◆◆◆◇◇ N-UNCOUNT

electrics /ɪle̲ktrɪks/. In British English, You can refer to a system of electrical wiring as the **electrics**. *Plumbing and electrics are installed to a high standard.* N-PLURAL

ele̲ctric sho̲ck, electric shocks. If you get an **electric shock**, you get a sudden painful feeling when you touch something which is connected to a supply of electricity. N-COUNT

electrification /ɪle̲ktrɪfɪke̲ɪʃᵊn/. The **electrification** of a house, town, or area is the connecting of that place with a supply of electricity. *...rural electrification.* ● See also **electrify.** N-UNCOUNT

electrified /ɪle̲ktrɪfaɪd/. An **electrified** fence or other barrier has been connected to a supply of electricity, so that a person or animal that touches it will get an electric shock. *The house was set amid dense trees and surrounded by an electrified fence.* ADJ: ADJ n

electrify /ɪle̲ktrɪfaɪ/ **electrifies, electrifying, electrified** ◆◇◇◇◇

1 If people **are electrified** by an event or experience, it makes them feel very excited and surprised. *The world was electrified by his courage and resistance.* ♦ **electrifying** *He gave an electrifying performance.* VB: usu passive =thrill; be V-ed; ADJ-GRADED

2 When a railway system or railway line **is electrified,** electric cables are put over the tracks, or electric rails are put beside them, so that the trains can be powered by electricity. *The west-coast line was electrified as long ago as 1974. ...the electrified section of the Lancashire and Yorkshire Railway.* ♦ **electrification** *...the electrification of the Oxted to Uckfield line.* VB: usu passive; be V-ed; V-ed; N-UNCOUNT

electro- /ɪle̲ktroʊ-/. **Electro-** is used to form words that refer to electricity or processes involving electricity. *...electro-chemical phenomena. ...electro-magnetic energy.* PREFIX

electrocardiogram /ɪle̲ktroʊka̲:ʳdioʊgræm/ **electrocardiograms.** If someone has an **electrocardiogram**, doctors use special equipment to measure the electric currents produced by that person's heart in order to see whether it is working normally. N-COUNT

electrocute /ɪle̲ktrəkju:t/ **electrocutes, electrocuting, electrocuted**

1 If someone **is electrocuted**, they are accidentally killed or badly injured when they touch something connected to a source of electricity. *Three people were electrocuted by falling power-lines... He accidentally electrocuted himself.* VERB; be V-ed; V pron-refl

2 If a criminal **is electrocuted**, he or she is executed by means of an electrical apparatus. *He was electrocuted for a murder committed when he was 17.* ♦ **electrocution** /ɪle̲ktrəkju̲:ʃᵊn/ **electrocutions** *The court pronounced him guilty and sentenced him to death by electrocution.* VB: usu passive; be V-ed; N-VAR

electrode /ɪle̲ktroud/ **electrodes.** An **electrode** is a small piece of metal or other substance that is used to take an electric current to or from a source of power, a piece of equipment, or a living body. *Two electrodes which measure changes in the body's surface moisture are attached to the palms of your hands.* ◆◇◇◇◇ N-COUNT

electrolysis /ɪlektrɒ̲lɪsɪs, i̲:-/. **Electrolysis** is the process of passing an electric current through a substance in order to produce chemical changes in the substance; a technical term in science. N-UNCOUNT

electrolyte /ɪle̲ktrəlaɪt/ **electrolytes.** An **electrolyte** is a substance, usually a liquid, which electricity can pass through; a technical use in science. N-COUNT

electromagnetic /ɪle̲ktroʊmægne̲tɪk/. **Electromagnetic** is used to describe the electrical and magnetic forces or effects produced by an electric current. *...electromagnetic fields.* ◆◇◇◇◇ ADJ: usu ADJ n

electron /ɪle̲ktrɒn/ **electrons.** An **electron** is a tiny particle of matter that is smaller than an atom and has a negative electrical charge; a technical term in physics. ◆◆◇◇◇ N-COUNT

electronic /ɪlektrɒ̲nɪk, i̲:-/ ◆◆◆◇◇

1 An **electronic** device is one that has transistors or silicon chips which control and change the electric current passing through the device. *...expensive electronic equipment.* ADJ: ADJ n

2 An **electronic** process or activity involves the use of electronic devices. *...electronic surveillance. ...electronic music.* ♦ **electronically** *Data is transmitted electronically. ...an electronically controlled dishwasher.* ADJ: usu ADJ n; ADV: ADV with v

electronic mail. **Electronic mail** is the same as **email**. N-SING

electronics /ɪlektrɒnɪks/ ◆◆◇◇◇

1 **Electronics** is the technology of using transistors and silicon chips, especially in devices such as radios, televisions, and computers. *...Europe's three main electronics companies. ...cheaper, better consumer electronics.* N-UNCOUNT

2 You can refer to electronic devices, or the part of a piece of equipment that consists of electronic devices, as the **electronics**. *All the electronics are housed in a waterproof box.* N-PLURAL: oft *the* N

electronic tagging. **Electronic tagging** is a system whereby a criminal or a person on bail has an electronic device attached to them which enables the police to know if they leave a particular area. N-UNCOUNT

electroplate /ɪlektroʊpleɪt/ **electroplates, electroplating, electroplated.** Something that **is electroplated** is covered with a layer of silver or another metal. This is done by dipping it in a special liquid through which an electric current is passed. *The whole knife shone as if it had been electroplated.* VB: usu passive; be V-ed

elegant /elɪgənt/ ◆◆◆◇◇

1 If you describe a person or thing as **elegant**, you mean that they are pleasing and graceful in appearance or style. *Patricia looked beautiful and elegant as always. ...an elegant restaurant.* ADJ-GRADED =stylish ♦ **elegance** *...Princess Grace's understated elegance... The furniture managed to combine practicality with elegance.* N-UNCOUNT ♦ **elegantly** *...a tall, elegantly dressed man with a mustache.* ADV-GRADED

2 If you describe a piece of writing, an idea, or a plan as **elegant**, you mean that it is simple, clear, and clever. *The document impressed me with its elegant simplicity.* ADJ-GRADED ♦ **elegantly** *...an elegantly simple idea.* ADV-GRADED

elegiac /elɪdʒaɪək/. Something that is **elegiac** expresses or shows sadness; a literary word. *The music has a dreamy, elegiac quality.* ADJ-GRADED

elegy /elɪdʒi/ **elegies.** An **elegy** is a sad poem, often about someone who has died. *...a touching elegy for a lost friend.* N-COUNT

element /elɪmənt/ **elements** ◆◆◆◆◇

1 The different **elements** of something are the different parts it contains. *The exchange of prisoners of war was one of the key elements of the UN's peace plan.* N-COUNT: usu pl, usu with supp =constituent ≠whole

2 A particular **element** of a situation, activity, or process is an important quality or feature that it has or needs. *Fitness has now become an important element in our lives.* N-COUNT: with supp =factor

3 When you talk about **elements** within a society or organization, you are referring to groups of people who have similar aims, beliefs, or habits. *The government must weed out criminal elements from within the security forces. ...the hooligan element.* N-COUNT: usu pl, supp N ≠individual

4 If something has an **element** of a particular quality or emotion, it has a certain amount of this quality or emotion. *These reports clearly contain elements of propaganda.* N-COUNT: usu sing, N *of* n

5 An **element** is a substance such as gold, oxygen, or carbon that consists of only one type of atom; a technical use in chemistry. N-COUNT ≠compound

6 The **element** in an electric fire or water heater is the metal part which changes the electric current into heat. *With its unique heating element it makes perfect coffee.* N-COUNT: usu sing

7 You can refer to the weather, especially wind and rain, as **the elements**. *The area where most refugees are waiting is exposed to the elements.* N-PLURAL: *the* N

8 If you say that someone is **in** their **element**, you mean that they are in a situation they enjoy, or are doing something that they enjoy and do well. If you say that someone is **out of** their **element**, you mean that they are in a situation that they do not enjoy. *My stepmother was in her element, organizing everything... Maybe it's because they're so out of their element that they feel the need to talk.* PHRASE: v-link PHR

elemental /elɪmentᵊl/. **Elemental** feelings and types of behaviour are simple, basic, and forceful; a literary word. *...the elemental life they would be living in this new colony.* ◆◇◇◇◇ ADJ-GRADED =basic

elementary /elɪmentri/. Something that is **elementary** is very simple, straightforward, and basic. *Literacy now includes elementary computer skills... His acting is about as elementary as you can get.* ◆◇◇◇◇ ADJ-GRADED: usu ADJ n =basic

elementary school, elementary schools. In the United States, an **elementary school** is a school where children are taught for the first six or eight years of their education. *The move from elementary school to middle school or junior high can be difficult.* ◆◇◇◇◇ N-VAR

elephant /elɪfənt/ **elephants.** An **elephant** is a very large animal with a long, flexible nose called a trunk, which it uses to pick up things. Elephants live in India and Africa. • See also **white elephant**. ◆◆◇◇◇ N-COUNT

elephantine /elɪfæntaɪn/. If you describe something as **elephantine**, you mean that you think it is large and clumsy; used showing disapproval. *...elephantine clumsiness... His legs were elephantine and his body obese.* ADJ-GRADED PRAGMATICS

elevate /elɪveɪt/ **elevates, elevating, elevated** ◆◆◇◇◇

1 When someone or something achieves a more important rank or status, you can say that they **are elevated** to it; a formal use. *He was elevated to the post of prime minister.* VB: usu passive =promote; be V-ed *to* n ♦ **elevation** /elɪveɪʃᵊn/ *The Prime Minister is known to favour the elevation of more women to the Cabinet... After his elevation to the papacy, he reigned for two years.* N-UNCOUNT: usu with poss, N *to* n

2 If you **elevate** something to a higher status, you consider it to be better or more important than it really is. *Don't elevate your superiors to superstar status.* VERB; V n *to* n

3 To elevate **something** means to increase it in amount or intensity; a formal use. *Emotional stress can elevate blood pressure. ...overweight individuals who have elevated cholesterol levels.* VERB =raise; V n; V-ed

4 If you **elevate** something, you raise it above a horizontal level; a formal use. *Jack elevated the gun at the sky.* VERB; V n

elevated /elɪveɪtɪd/

1 A person, job, or role that is **elevated** is very important or of very high rank. *His career has blossomed and that has given him a certain elevated status.* ADJ: usu ADJ n

2 If thoughts or ideas are **elevated**, they are on a high moral or intellectual level. *...the magazine's elevated British tone.* ADJ-GRADED: usu ADJ n

3 If land or buildings are **elevated**, they are raised up higher than the surrounding area. *An elevated platform on the stage collapsed during rehearsals.* ADJ: usu ADJ n =raised

elevation /elɪveɪʃᵊn/ **elevations**

1 An **elevation** is the front, back, or side of a building, or a drawing of one of these; a technical term in architecture. *...the addition of two-storey wings on the north and south elevations.* N-COUNT: with supp

2 The **elevation** of a place is its height above sea level. *We're probably at an elevation of about 13,000 feet above sea level.* N-COUNT: usu with supp =altitude

3 An **elevation** is a piece of ground that is higher than the area around it. N-COUNT

elevator /elɪveɪtəʳ/ **elevators.** In American English, an **elevator** is device that carries people up and down inside buildings. The usual British word is **lift**. ◆◇◇◇◇ N-COUNT

eleven /ɪlevᵊn/ **elevens.** **Eleven** is the number 11. *...the Princess and her eleven friends.* ◆◆◆◆◆ NUM

eleven-plus; also spelled **eleven plus**. The **eleven plus** is an exam which is taken by children in Britain at about the age of eleven. N-SING: oft *the* N

elevenses /ɪlevᵊnzɪz/. In British English, **elevenses** is a short break when you have a cup of tea or coffee, and sometimes biscuits, at around eleven o'clock in the morning; an informal word. N-UNCOUNT

eleventh /ɪlevᵊnθ/. The **eleventh** item in a series is the one that you count as number eleven. *We were working on the eleventh floor.* ◆◆◆◆◇ ORD

eleventh hour. If someone does something at **the eleventh hour**, they do it at the last possible N-SING: usu *at the* N, N n moment. *He postponed his trip at the eleventh hour. ...last night's eleventh hour agreement.*

elf /elf/ **elves.** In fairy stories, **elves** are small magical beings who play tricks on people.
N-COUNT: usu pl

elfin /elfɪn/. If you describe someone as **elfin**, you think that they are attractive because they are small and have delicate features. *...a little boy with an elfin face.*
ADJ-GRADED: usu ADJ n
PRAGMATICS

elicit /ɪlɪsɪt/ **elicits, eliciting, elicited** ◆◇◇◇◇

1 If you **elicit** a response or a reaction, you do or say something which makes other people respond or react. *Mr Delors elicited no response from Dr Kohl when he called for quick action to reduce interest rates... Yeltsin's firing of Yakovlev elicited a storm of protest in the Russian press.*
VERB
V n

2 If you **elicit** a piece of information, you get it by asking the right questions; a formal use. *They promised to make enquiries for us, but several phone calls elicited no further information.*
VERB
V n

elide /ɪlaɪd/ **elides, eliding, elided**

1 If you **elide** something, especially a distinction, you miss it out or ignore it; a formal use. *These habits of thinking elide the difference between what is common and what is normal.*
VERB
V n

2 In linguistics, if you **elide** a word, you do not pronounce or write it fully. *...the man who wrote to complain that you've started eliding the word 'not' or 'have'.*
VERB
=contract
V n

eligible /elɪdʒɪbᵊl/ ◆◆◇◇◇

1 Someone who is **eligible** to do something is qualified or able to do it, for example because they are old enough. *Almost half the population are eligible to vote in today's election... You could be eligible for a university scholarship.* ♦ **eligibility** /elɪdʒəbɪlɪti/ *The rules covering eligibility for benefits changed in the 1980s.*
ADJ-GRADED: usu v-link ADJ, usu ADJ for n, ADJ to-inf
N-UNCOUNT: oft N for n

2 An **eligible** man or woman is not yet married and is thought by many people to be a suitable partner. *He's the most eligible bachelor in Japan.*
ADJ-GRADED: usu ADJ n

eliminate /ɪlɪmɪneɪt/ **eliminates, eliminating, eliminated** ◆◆◆◇◇

1 To **eliminate** something, especially something you do not want or need, means to remove it completely; a formal use. *The Sex Discrimination Act has not eliminated discrimination in employment... Academic departments are being eliminated... If you think you may be allergic to a food or drink, eliminate it from your diet.* ♦ **elimination** /ɪlɪmɪneɪʃᵊn/ *...the prohibition and elimination of chemical weapons.*
VERB
V n
V n from n
N-UNCOUNT: usu N of n

2 When a person or team **is eliminated** from a competition, they are defeated and so take no further part in the competition. *I was eliminated from the 400 metres in the semi-finals... If you are eliminated in the show-jumping then you are out of the complete competition.*
V-PASSIVE
=knock out
be V-ed from n
be V-ed

3 If someone says that they **have eliminated** an enemy, they mean that they have killed them. By using the word eliminate, they are trying to make the action sound more positive than if they used the word 'kill'. *He declared war on the government and urged right-wingers to eliminate their opponents... The radio station claimed that 87,000 'reactionaries' had been eliminated.*
VERB
PRAGMATICS
V n

eliminator /ɪlɪmɪneɪtəʳ/ **eliminators.** In sport, an **eliminator** is a match or competition which decides which team or player is to go through to the next stage of a particular competition. *He meets tough Canadian Razor Ruddock in a world title eliminator at London's Earls Court on Saturday.*
N-COUNT: usu n N

elite /ɪliːt, eɪ-/ **elites** ◆◆◇◇◇

1 You can refer to the most powerful, rich, or talented people within a particular group, place, or society as the **elite**. *...a government comprised mainly of the elite. ...China's intellectual elite.*
N-COUNT

2 **Elite** people or organizations are considered to be the best of their kind. *...the elite troops of the President's bodyguard.*
ADJ-GRADED: ADJ n

elitism /ɪliːtɪzəm, eɪ-/

1 **Elitism** is the feeling of superiority someone has when they believe they are part of an elite. *Will severe selection standards create elitism and threaten the Olympic ethic of participation?... Many critics blame the arrogance and elitism of gallery owners.*
N-UNCOUNT

2 **Elitism** is the belief that a society or country should be ruled by a small group of people who are superior to everyone else. *Oxford was holding a conference against elitism yesterday.*
N-UNCOUNT

elitist /ɪliːtɪst, eɪ-/ **elitists** ◆◇◇◇◇

1 If you describe systems, practices, or ideas as **elitist**, you believe that they favour only the most powerful, rich, or talented people within a group, place, or society; used showing disapproval. *Labour has criticised government policy on Hong Kong as elitist and divisive.*
ADJ-GRADED
PRAGMATICS

2 If you describe an activity or profession as **elitist**, you mean that it is enjoyed or practised only by the most powerful, rich, or talented people within a group, place, or society; used showing disapproval. *Skiing is old-fashioned, elitist and boring... The legal profession is starting to be less elitist and more representative.*
ADJ-GRADED
PRAGMATICS

3 If you say that someone is an **elitist**, you mean that they believe that a society or country should be ruled by a small group of people who they consider to be the most powerful, rich, or talented; used showing disapproval. *A natural elitist, he has never understood the populist side of Mr Salinas's political personality.*
N-COUNT
PRAGMATICS

4 An **elitist** is someone who believes that they are part of an elite; used showing disapproval. *...intellectual elitists.*
N-COUNT
PRAGMATICS

elixir /ɪlɪksəʳ/ **elixirs.** An **elixir** is a liquid that is considered to have magical powers; a literary word. *...the elixir of life.*
N-COUNT: oft N of n

Elizabethan /ɪlɪzəbiːθᵊn/. **Elizabethan** means belonging to or connected with England in the second half of the sixteenth century, when Elizabeth the First was Queen. *...Elizabethan England. ...the Elizabethan theatre.*
◆◇◇◇◇
ADJ: usu ADJ n

elk /elk/ **elks; elk** can also be used as the plural form. The **elk** is the largest type of deer. Elks have big, flattened antlers and live in Northern Europe and Asia.
N-VAR

ellipse /ɪlɪps/ **ellipses.** An **ellipse** is an oval shape like a flattened circle; a formal word. *The Earth orbits in an ellipse.*
N-COUNT

ellipsis /ɪlɪpsɪs/. **Ellipsis** means leaving out words rather than repeating them unnecessarily; for example, saying 'I want to go but I can't' instead of 'I want to go but I can't go'. **Ellipsis** is a technical term in linguistics.
N-UNCOUNT

elliptical /ɪlɪptɪkᵊl/

1 Something that is **elliptical** is oval, like a flattened circle; a formal use. *...the moon's elliptical orbit... The stadium is elliptical in plan.*
ADJ-GRADED

2 **Elliptical** references to something are indirect, rather than clear and explicit; a formal use. *...Kirsty Gunn's austere, elliptical account of a childhood tragedy. ...elliptical references to problems best not aired in public.* ♦ **elliptically** /ɪlɪptɪkli/ *He spoke only briefly and elliptically about the mission.*
ADJ-GRADED
=oblique
≠direct
ADV-GRADED: ADV after v

elm /elm/ **elms.** An **elm** is a tree that has broad leaves which it loses in winter. ▶ **Elm** is the wood of this tree.
◆◇◇◇◇
N-VAR
N-UNCOUNT

elocution /eləkjuːʃᵊn/. **Elocution** lessons are lessons in which someone is taught to speak clearly and in an accent that is considered to be standard and acceptable. *When I was 11 my mother sent me to elocution lessons.*
N-UNCOUNT

elongate /iːlɒŋgeɪt, AM ɪlɔːŋ-/ **elongates, elongating, elongated.** If you **elongate** something or if it **elongates**, you stretch it so that it becomes longer; a formal word. *'Mom,' she intoned, elongating the word until it sounded like a foghorn... Corn is treated when the stalk starts to elongate.*
V-ERG
=lengthen
V n
V

elongated /iːlɒŋgeɪtɪd, AM ɪlɔːŋ-/. If something is **elongated**, it is very long and thin, often unnaturally so. *The light from my candle threw his elongated shadow on the walls.*
ADJ-GRADED

elope /ɪloʊp/ **elopes, eloping, eloped.** When two people **elope** they go away secretly together
V-RECIP

to get married. *My girlfriend Lynn and I eloped... In 1912 he eloped with Frieda von Richthofen.* pl-n V / V *with* n

eloquent /eləkwənt/ ◆◇◇◇◇

1 Speech or writing that is **eloquent** is well expressed and effective in persuading people. *I heard him make a very eloquent speech at that dinner.* ADJ-GRADED =expressive
♦ **eloquence** *...the eloquence of his prose.* N-UNCOUNT
♦ **eloquently** *Jan speaks eloquently about her art.* ADV-GRADED

2 A person who is **eloquent** is good at speaking and able to persuade people; used showing approval. *He was eloquent about his love of books. ...one particularly eloquent German critic.* ADJ-GRADED PRAGMATICS ♦ **eloquence** *I wish I'd had the eloquence of Helmut Schmidt.* N-UNCOUNT

else /els/ ◆◆◆◆◆

1 You use **else** after words such as 'anywhere', 'someone', and 'what', to refer in a vague way to another person, place, or thing. *If I can't make a living at painting, at least I can teach someone else to paint... We had nothing else to do on those long trips... What else have you had for your birthday?... There's not much else I can say.* ADJ: pron-indef/quest ADJ ► Also an adverb. *I never wanted to live anywhere else.* ADV: adv ADV

2 You use **else** after words such as 'everyone', 'everything', and 'everywhere' to refer in a vague way to all the other people, things, or places except the one you are talking about. *As I try to be truthful, I expect everyone else to be truthful... Cigarettes are in short supply, like everything else here.* ADJ: pron-indef ADJ ► Also an adverb. *London seems so much dirtier than everywhere else.* ADV: adv ADV

3 You use **or else** after stating a logical conclusion, to indicate that what you are about to say is evidence for that conclusion. *At least that Krayev's a decent bloke, or else he'd have slung us out for that kind of work... Evidently no lessons have been learnt or else the government would not have handled the problem so sloppily.* PHR-CONJ-COORD =otherwise

4 You use **or else** to introduce a statement that indicates the unpleasant results that will occur if someone does or does not do something. *This time we really need to succeed or else people will start giving us funny looks... Make sure you are strapped in very well, or else you will fall out.* PHR-CONJ-COORD =otherwise

5 You use **or else** to introduce the second of two possibilities when you do not know which one is true. *You are either a total genius or else you must be absolutely raving mad... It's likely someone gave her a lift, or else that she took a taxi.* PHR-CONJ-COORD

6 **Above all else** is used to emphasize that a particular thing is more important than other things. *Above all else I hate the cold.* PHRASES PHR with cl PRAGMATICS

7 You can say **'if nothing else'** to indicate that what you are mentioning is, in your opinion, the only good thing in a particular situation. *If nothing else, you'll really enjoy meeting them.* PHR with cl =at least

8 You say **'or else'** after a command to warn someone that if they do not obey, you will be angry and may harm or punish them. *Behave, or else!... He told us to put it right, or else.* cl PHR PRAGMATICS

elsewhere /elshweəʳ/. **Elsewhere** means in other places or to another place. *Almost 80 percent of the state's residents were born elsewhere... They were living rather well, in comparison with people elsewhere in the world... But if you are not satisfied then go elsewhere... Until the doctor arrived from elsewhere on the ward, Amy was in charge.* ◆◆◆◇◇ ADV: ADV after v, n ADV, ADV with cl, *be* ADV, *from* ADV, oft ADV prep/adv

ELT /iː el tiː/. **ELT** is the teaching of English to people whose first language is not English. **ELT** is an abbreviation for 'English Language Teaching'. N-UNCOUNT

elucidate /ɪluːsɪdeɪt/ **elucidates, elucidating, elucidated.** If you **elucidate** something, you make it clear and easy to understand; a formal word. *Haig went on to elucidate his personal principle of war... There was no need for him to elucidate.* VERB =clarify V n / V ♦ **elucidation** /ɪluːsɪdeɪʃᵊn/ *...Gerald's attempts at elucidation.* N-UNCOUNT

elude /ɪluːd/ **eludes, eluding, eluded** ◆◇◇◇◇

1 If something that you want **eludes** you, you fail to obtain it. *Sleep eluded her... At 62, Brian found the celebrity and status that had eluded him for so long.* VB: no passive =escape V n

2 If you **elude** someone or something, you avoid them or escape from them. *He eluded the police for 13 years.* VERB =escape V n

3 If a fact or idea **eludes** you, you do not succeed in understanding it, realizing it, or remembering it. *The appropriate word eluded him.* VB: no passive =escape V n

elusive /ɪluːsɪv/. Something or someone that is **elusive** is difficult to find, describe, remember, or achieve. *In London late-night taxis are elusive and far from cheap.* ◆◇◇◇◇ ADJ-GRADED ♦ **elusiveness** *...the elusiveness of her character.* N-UNCOUNT

elves /elvz/. **Elves** is the plural of **elf**.

em- /ɪm-/. Often pronounced /em-/, particularly in American English. **Em-** is a form of **en-** that is used before b-, m-, and p-. *The person who embodies democracy at the local level is the mayor... I want to empower the businessman.* PREFIX

emaciated /ɪmeɪsieɪtɪd, -meɪʃ-/. A person or animal that is **emaciated** is extremely thin and weak because of illness or lack of food. *...horrific television pictures of emaciated prisoners.* ADJ-GRADED

email /iːmeɪl/; also spelled **E-mail**. **Email** is a system of sending written messages electronically from one computer to another. **Email** is an abbreviation of 'electronic mail'. N-UNCOUNT

emanate /eməneɪt/ **emanates, emanating, emanated** ◆◇◇◇◇

1 If a quality or feeling **emanates** from you, or if you **emanate** a quality or feeling, you give people a strong sense that you have that quality or feeling; a formal use. *Intelligence and cunning emanated from him... He emanates sympathy.* V-ERG =radiate V *from* n / V n

2 If something **emanates** from somewhere, it comes from there; a formal use. *The heady aroma of wood fires emanated from the stove. ...reports emanating from America.* VERB V *from* n Also V

emanation /eməneɪʃᵊn/ **emanations.** An **emanation** is a form of energy or a mass of tiny particles that comes from something; a formal word. N-COUNT

emancipate /ɪmænsɪpeɪt/ **emancipates, emancipating, emancipated.** If people **are emancipated**, they are freed from unpleasant or degrading social, political, or legal restrictions; a formal word. *Catholics were emancipated in 1792... That war preserved the Union and emancipated the slaves... Newly emancipated states in Eastern Europe want to join the European Community.* ◆◇◇◇◇ VERB =liberate *be* V-ed / V n / V-ed ♦ **emancipation** /ɪmænsɪpeɪʃᵊn/ *...the emancipation of women.* N-UNCOUNT: oft N *of* n

emancipated /ɪmænsɪpeɪtɪd/. If you describe someone as **emancipated**, you mean that they behave in a less restricted way than is traditional in their society. *She is an emancipated woman.* ADJ-GRADED =liberated

emasculate /ɪmæskjʊleɪt/ **emasculates, emasculating, emasculated**

1 If you say that someone or something **is emasculated**, you disapprove of the fact that they have been made weak and ineffective. *Left-wing dissidents have been emasculated and marginalised... The company tried to emasculate the unions... Since Japan's defeat, the military has remained largely emasculated.* VERB PRAGMATICS =weaken *be* V-ed / V n / V-ed ♦ **emasculation** /ɪmæskjʊleɪʃᵊn/ *...the emasculation of fundamental freedoms.* N-UNCOUNT

2 If you say that a man **is emasculated**, you disapprove of the fact that he loses his male role, identity, or qualities, especially because a woman he has a close relationship with is powerful or assertive. *Tosh was known to be a man who feared no-one, yet he was clearly emasculated by his girlfriend.* VB: usu passive PRAGMATICS *be* V-ed

embalm /ɪmbɑːm/ **embalms, embalming, embalmed.** If a dead person **is embalmed**, their body is preserved using special substances. *His body was embalmed. ...the embalmed body of Lenin.* VB: usu passive *be* V-ed / V-ed ♦ **embalming** *People often look different after embalming.* N-UNCOUNT

embankment /ɪmbæŋkmənt/ **embankments.** An **embankment** is a thick wall or mound of earth that is built to carry a road or railway over an area of low ground, or to prevent water from a river or the sea from flooding the area. *They climbed a steep embankment. ...a railway embankment. ...Victoria Embankment.* ◆◇◇◇◇ N-COUNT: oft in names after n

embargo /ɪmbɑːʳgoʊ/ **embargoes, embargoing, embargoed** ◆◆◇◇◇

1 If one country or group of countries imposes an **embargo** against another, they prohibit trade with that country. *The United Nations imposed an arms embargo against the country... He has called on the government to lift its embargo on trade with Vietnam.* N-COUNT: usu with supp =ban

2 If goods of a particular kind **are embargoed**, people are not permitted to import them from a particular country or export them to a particular country. *The fruit was embargoed... They embargoed oil shipments to the U.S... A lot of embargoed goods were still crossing the border.* VERB =ban be V-ed V n V-ed

embark /ɪmbɑːʳk/ **embarks, embarking, embarked** ◆◆◇◇◇

1 If you **embark** on something new, difficult, or exciting, you start doing it. *He's embarking on a new career as a writer... The government embarked on a programme of radical economic reform.* VERB V *on/upon* n

2 When someone **embarks** on a ship, they go on board before the start of a voyage. *They travelled to Portsmouth, where they embarked on the battle cruiser HMS Renown... Bob ordered brigade HQ to embark.* ♦ **embarkation** /ɛmbɑːʳkeɪʃᵊn/ *Embarkation was scheduled for just after 4 pm.* VERB V *on* n V N-UNCOUNT

embarrass /ɪmbærəs/ **embarrasses, embarrassing, embarrassed** ◆◇◇◇◇

1 If something or someone **embarrasses** you, they make you feel shy or ashamed. *His clumsiness embarrassed him... It embarrassed him that he had no idea of what was going on.* VERB V n *it* V n that

2 If something **embarrasses** a politician or political party, it causes problems for them. *The Republicans are trying to embarrass the president by thwarting his economic program... The Government has been embarrassed by the affair.* VERB V n

embarrassed /ɪmbærəst/. A person who is **embarrassed** feels shy, ashamed, or guilty about something. *He looked a bit embarrassed. ...an embarrassed silence.* ◆◆◇◇◇ ADJ-GRADED: usu v-link ADJ

embarrassing /ɪmbærəsɪŋ/ ◆◆◇◇◇

1 Something that is **embarrassing** makes you feel shy or ashamed. *That was an embarrassing situation for me... Men find it embarrassing to be honest.* ADJ-GRADED =uncomfortable, awkward ♦ **embarrassingly** *The lyrics of the song are embarrassingly banal... Stephens had beaten him embarrassingly easily.* ADV-GRADED: usu ADV adj/adv

2 Something that is **embarrassing** to a politician or a political party causes problems for them. *He has put the Bonn government in an embarrassing position... The speech was deeply embarrassing to Cabinet ministers.* ADJ-GRADED: oft ADJ *to* n

embarrassment /ɪmbærəsmənt/ **embarrassments** ◆◆◇◇◇

1 Embarrassment is a feeling of shyness, shame, or guilt. *It is a source of embarrassment to Londoners that the standard of pubs is so low... I think I would have died of embarrassment... We apologise for any embarrassment this may have caused.* N-VAR: oft N prep

2 An **embarrassment** is an action, event, or situation which causes problems for a politician, political party, government, or other public group. *The poverty figures were undoubtedly an embarrassment to the president.* N-COUNT: usu with supp

3 If you refer to a person as **an embarrassment**, you mean that you disapprove of them but cannot avoid your connection with them. *You have been an embarrassment to us from the day Douglas married you.* N-SING: *a* N

4 If you say that someone has an **embarrassment of riches**, you mean that they have so many good things that these things are a problem. *The art gallery's problem is an embarrassment of riches, with nowhere to put most of them.* PHRASE

embassy /ɛmbəsi/ **embassies.** An **embassy** is a group of government officials, headed by an ambassador, who represent their government in a foreign country. The building in which they work is also called an **embassy**. *The American Embassy has already complained... Mr Cohen held discussions at the embassy with one of the rebel leaders.* ◆◆◆◇◇ N-COUNT: oft *the* adj N

embattled /ɪmbætᵊld/ ◆◇◇◇◇

1 If you describe a person, group, or organization as **embattled**, you mean that they are having a lot of problems or difficulties. *The embattled president also denied recent claims that he was being held hostage by his own soldiers.* ADJ-GRADED: usu ADJ n =beleaguered

2 An **embattled** area is one that is involved in the fighting in a war, especially one that is surrounded by enemy forces. *The commander of British forces in Bosnia was yesterday stranded close to the embattled town of Zepce.* ADJ: ADJ n

embed /ɪmbɛd/ **embeds, embedding, embedded** ◆◇◇◇◇

1 If an object **embeds** itself in a substance or thing, it becomes fixed there firmly and deeply. *One of the bullets passed through Andrea's chest before embedding itself in a wall.* ♦ **embedded** *The fossils at Dinosaur Cove are embedded in hard sandstones... There is glass embedded in the cut.* VERB V n *in* n Also V n prep ADJ-GRADED: oft ADJ *in* n

2 If something such as an attitude or feeling **is embedded** in a society or system, or in someone's personality, it becomes a permanent and noticeable feature of it. *This agreement will be embedded in a state treaty to be signed soon by Bonn and East Berlin.* ♦ **embedded** *I think that hatred of the other is deeply embedded in our society.* VB: usu passive be V-ed *in* n ADJ-GRADED: oft ADJ *in* n

embellish /ɪmbɛlɪʃ/ **embellishes, embellishing, embellished** ◆◇◇◇◇

1 If something **is embellished** with decorative features or patterns, it has those features or patterns on it and they make it look more attractive. *The stern was embellished with carvings in red and blue... Ivy leaves embellish the front of the dresser... Embellish basic covers and curtains with borders, ties and fringing.* VERB be V-ed *with* n V n

2 If you **embellish** a story, you make it more interesting by adding details which may be untrue. *I launched into the parable, embellishing the story with invented dialogue and extra details... Irving popularized the story in a dramatic and embellished account.* VERB V n V-ed

embellishment /ɪmbɛlɪʃmənt/ **embellishments.** An **embellishment** is a decoration added to something to make it seem more attractive or interesting. *...Renaissance embellishments... Florence is full of public buildings with little bits of decoration and embellishment.* N-VAR

ember /ɛmbəʳ/ **embers.** The **embers** of a fire are small pieces of wood or coal that remain and glow with heat after the fire has finished burning. N-COUNT: usu pl

embezzle /ɪmbɛzᵊl/ **embezzles, embezzling, embezzled.** If someone **embezzles** money that their organization or company has placed in their care, they take it and use it illegally for their own purposes. *One former director embezzled $34 million in company funds.* VERB V n Also V

embezzlement /ɪmbɛzᵊlmənt/. **Embezzlement** is the crime or activity of embezzling money. ◆◇◇◇◇ N-UNCOUNT

embittered /ɪmbɪtəʳd/. If you describe someone as **embittered**, you mean that they feel angry and resentful because of harsh, unpleasant, and unfair things that have happened to them. *He had turned into an embittered, hardened adult... Gerald turned sour and embittered when he felt people were not dealing honestly with him.* ADJ-GRADED

emblazoned /ɪmbleɪzᵊnd/. If something is **emblazoned** with a design, words, or letters, they are clearly drawn, printed, or sewn on it. *The republic's new flag was emblazoned with the ancient symbol of the Greek Macedonian dynasty... Jackie was sporting a T-shirt with 'Mustique' emblazoned on it.* ADJ: usu v-link ADJ, usu ADJ *with* n, ADJ *on/across* n

emblem /ɛmbləm/ **emblems** ◆◇◇◇◇

1 An **emblem** is a design representing a country or organization. *...the emblem of the Soviet Union. ...the Red Cross emblem.* N-COUNT: usu with supp

2 An **emblem** is something that represents a quality or idea. *The eagle was an emblem of strength and courage.* N-COUNT: usu N *of* n =symbol

emblematic /ɛmbləmætɪk/

1 If something, such as an object in a picture, is **emblematic** of a particular quality or an idea, it ADJ: usu v-link ADJ, usu ADJ *of* n symbolically represents the quality or idea. *Dogs are emblematic of faithfulness... In some works, flowers take on a powerful emblematic quality.* =symbolic

2 If you say that something is **emblematic** of a state of affairs, you mean that it is characteristic of it and represents its most typical features. *The killing in Pensacola is emblematic of a lot of the violence that is happening around the world.* ADJ: usu v-link ADJ of n =representative

embodiment /ɪmbɒdimənt/. If you say that someone or something is the **embodiment** of a quality or idea, you mean that that is their most noticeable characteristic or the basis of all they do; a formal word. *A baby is the embodiment of vulnerability.* ◆◇◇◇◇ N-SING: usu the N of n

embody /ɪmbɒdi/ **embodies, embodying, embodied** ◆◇◇◇◇

1 If someone or something **embodies** an idea or quality, they are a symbol or expression of that idea or quality. *Jack Kennedy embodied all the hopes of the 1960s... For twenty-nine years, Checkpoint Charlie embodied the Cold War... That stability was embodied in the Gandhi family.* VERB =represent V n be V-ed in/by n

2 If something **is embodied** in a particular thing, the second thing contains or consists of the first. *The proposal has been embodied in a draft resolution... Albanian Radio has given details of a new draft constitution which embodies reforms first called for by President Ramiz Alia... Mr Clinton is outspoken in his support for a multilateral trading system embodied by the GATT.* VERB be V-ed in/by n V n V-ed

embolden /ɪmboʊldᵊn/ **emboldens, emboldening, emboldened.** If you **are emboldened** by something, it makes you feel confident enough to behave in a particular way. *The Prime Minister was steadily emboldened by the discovery that he faced no opposition... Four days of non-stop demonstrations have emboldened the anti-government protesters.* VERB be V-ed V n

embossed /ɪmbɒst, AM -bɔːst/. If a surface such as paper or wood is **embossed** with a design, the design stands up slightly from the surface. *The paper on the walls was pale gold, embossed with swirling leaf designs.* ADJ: usu v-link ADJ, usu ADJ with n

embrace /ɪmbreɪs/ **embraces, embracing, embraced** ◆◆◇◇◇

1 If you **embrace** someone, you put your arms around them and hold them tightly, usually in order to show your love or affection for them. You can also say that two people **embrace** each other or that they **embrace**. *Penelope came forward and embraced her sister... At first people were sort of crying for joy and embracing each other... He threw his arms round her and they embraced passionately.* V-RECIP =hug V n (non-recip) pl-n V
▶ Also a noun. *...a young couple locked in an embrace.* N-COUNT

2 If you **embrace** a change, political system, or idea, you accept it and start supporting it or believing in it wholeheartedly; a formal use. *He embraces the new information age... The new rules have been embraced by government watchdog organizations.* VERB V n
▶ Also a noun. *The marriage signalled James's embrace of the Catholic faith.* N-SING: usu with supp

3 If something **embraces** a group of people, things, or ideas, it includes them in a larger group or category; a formal use. *...a theory that would embrace the whole field of human endeavour.* VERB V n

embroider /ɪmbrɔɪdəʳ/ **embroiders, embroidering, embroidered** ◆◇◇◇◇

1 If something such as clothing or cloth **is embroidered** with a design, the design is stitched into it. *The collar was embroidered with very small red strawberries... Matilda was embroidering an altar cloth covered with flowers and birds... I have a pillow with my name embroidered on it. ...hand embroidered tablecloths.* VERB be V-ed with/in n V n V-ed Also V

2 If you **embroider** a story or account of something, or if you **embroider** on it, you try to make it more interesting by adding details which may be untrue. *He told some lies and sometimes just embroidered the truth... She embroidered on this theme for about ten minutes.* VERB V n V on n

embroidery /ɪmbrɔɪdəri/ **embroideries** ◆◇◇◇◇

1 **Embroidery** consists of designs stitched into cloth. *The shorts had blue embroidery over the pockets... The panel contains an embroidery.* N-VAR

2 **Embroidery** is the activity of stitching designs onto cloth. *She learned sewing, knitting and embroidery.* N-UNCOUNT

embroil /ɪmbrɔɪl/ **embroils, embroiling, embroiled.** If someone **embroils** you in a fight or an argument, they get you deeply involved in it. *Any hostilities could result in retaliation and further embroil U.N. troops in fighting.* VERB V n in n Also V n

embroiled /ɪmbrɔɪld/ ◆◇◇◇◇

1 If you become **embroiled** in a fight or argument, you become deeply involved in it. *The Government insisted that troops would not become embroiled in battles in Bosnia.* ADJ-GRADED: v-link ADJ, usu ADJ in n

2 If you become **embroiled** with a person, you become involved in a relationship with them that causes you problems. *As Smith became embroiled with his new lover, the marriage was called off.* ADJ-GRADED: v-link ADJ, usu ADJ with n

embryo /embrioʊ/ **embryos** ◆◆◇◇◇

1 An **embryo** is an unborn animal or human being in the very early stages of development. *The embryo lives in the amniotic cavity. ...the remarkable resilience of very young embryos.* N-COUNT

2 An **embryo** idea, system, or organization is in the very early stages of development, but is expected to grow stronger. *They are an embryo party of government... It was an embryo idea rather than a fully worked proposal.* ADJ: ADJ n

3 Something that is **in embryo** is at a very early stage of its development. *These developments were foreseen in embryo more than a decade ago.* PHRASE: v-link PHR

embryonic /embriɒnɪk/. An **embryonic** process, idea, organization, or organism is one at a very early stage in its development; a formal word. *...Romania's embryonic democracy. ...the embryonic European central bank. ...embryonic plant cells.* ADJ-GRADED: usu ADJ n

emcee /emsiː/ **emcees.** In American English, an **emcee** is the same as a **master of ceremonies**. N-COUNT

emerald /emərəld/ **emeralds** ◆◇◇◇◇

1 An **emerald** is a precious stone which is clear and bright green. N-COUNT

2 Something that is **emerald** is bright green in colour. *...an emerald valley.* COLOUR

emerge /ɪmɜːʳdʒ/ **emerges, emerging, emerged** ◆◆◆◆◇

1 To **emerge** means to come out from an enclosed or dark space such as a room or a vehicle, or from a position where you could not be seen. *Richard was waiting outside the door as she emerged... The postman emerged from his van soaked to the skin. ...holes made by the emerging adult beetle.* VERB V V from n V-ing

2 If you **emerge from** a difficult or bad experience, you come to the end of it. *There is growing evidence that the economy is at last emerging from recession. ...their plans to emerge from bankruptcy by February of next year.* VERB V from n

3 If a fact or result **emerges** from a period of thought, discussion, or investigation, it becomes known as a result of it. *...the growing corruption that has emerged in the past few years... It soon emerged that neither the July nor August mortgage repayment had been collected... The emerging caution over numbers is perhaps only to be expected.* VERB V it V that V-ing

4 If someone or something **emerges** as a particular thing, they become recognised as that thing; used mainly in journalism. *Mr Shevardnadze has emerged as a major figure in the reform movement... Vietnam has emerged as the world's third-biggest rice exporter... New leaders have emerged.* VERB V as n V

5 When something such as an organization or an industry **emerges**, it comes into existence; used mainly in journalism. *...the new republic that emerged in October 1917. ...the emerging democracies of Eastern Europe.* VERB V V-ing

emergence /ɪmɜːʳdʒᵊns/. The **emergence** of something is the process or event of its coming into existence. *...the emergence of new democracies in East and Central Europe.* ◆◆◇◇◇ N-UNCOUNT: with supp, usu N of n

emergency /ɪmɜːʳdʒᵊnsi/ **emergencies** ◆◆◆◆◇
1 An **emergency** is an unexpected and difficult or dangerous situation, especially an accident, which arises suddenly and which requires quick action to deal with it. *He deals with emergencies promptly... The hospital will cater only for emergencies.* N-COUNT =crisis
2 An **emergency** action is one that is done or arranged quickly and not in the normal way, because an emergency has occurred. *The Prime Minister has called an emergency meeting of parliament... She made an emergency appointment.* ADJ: ADJ n
3 **Emergency** equipment or supplies are those intended for use in an emergency. *The plane is carrying emergency supplies for refugees... They escaped through an emergency exit and called the police.* ADJ: ADJ n

emergency services. The **emergency services** are the public organizations whose job is to take quick action to deal with emergencies when they occur, especially the fire brigade, the police, and the ambulance service. ◆◇◇◇◇ N-PLURAL: usu *the* N

emergent /ɪmɜːʳdʒᵊnt/. An **emergent** country, political movement, or social group is one that is becoming powerful or coming into existence; used mainly in written English. *...an emergent state. ...an emergent nationalist movement.* ADJ: ADJ n

emeritus /ɪmerɪtəs/. **Emeritus** is used with a professional title to indicate that the person bearing it has retired but keeps the title as an honour. *...emeritus professor of physics... He will continue as chairman emeritus.* ADJ: ADJ n, n ADJ

emetic /ɪmetɪk/ **emetics**
1 An **emetic** is something that is given to someone to swallow, in order to make them vomit. N-COUNT
2 Something that is **emetic** makes you vomit. *Caution: large doses of this remedy are emetic.* ADJ

emigrant /emɪgrənt/ **emigrants.** An **emigrant** is a person who has left their own country to live in another country. Compare **immigrant**. ◆◇◇◇◇ N-COUNT

emigrate /emɪgreɪt/ **emigrates, emigrating, emigrated.** If you **emigrate**, you leave your native country to live in another country. *He emigrated to Belgium... They planned to emigrate.* ◆◆◇◇◇ VERB V *to* n V
♦ **emigration** /emɪgreɪʃᵊn/ *...the huge emigration of workers to the West.* N-UNCOUNT: usu with supp

émigré /emɪgreɪ/ **émigrés;** also spelled **emigre**. An **émigré** is someone who has left their own country and lives in a different country for political reasons. *Several hundred Bosnian refugees and emigres demonstrated outside the main entrance. ...a Polish émigré family.* ◆◇◇◇◇ N-COUNT =immigrant

eminence /emɪnəns/ ◆◇◇◇◇
1 **Eminence** is the quality of being very well-known and highly respected. *Many of the pilots were to achieve eminence in the aeronautical world... Beveridge was a man of great eminence.* N-UNCOUNT
2 You use expressions such as **Your Eminence** or **His Eminence** when you are addressing or referring to a Roman Catholic cardinal. *'Your Eminence,' Pantieri broke in, 'I wonder if you would allow me a word.'... His Eminence Cardinal Hume will celebrate Mass.* N-VOC: poss N, also PRON: poss PRON

eminent /emɪnənt/. An **eminent** person is well-known and respected, especially because they are good at their profession. *...an eminent scientist.* ◆◇◇◇◇ ADJ-GRADED: usu ADJ n

eminently /emɪnəntli/. You use **eminently** in front of an adjective describing a positive quality in order to emphasize the quality expressed by that adjective. *His books on diplomatic history were eminently readable... His family was eminently respectable.* ◆◇◇◇◇ ADV-GRADED: ADV adj/-ed PRAGMATICS =highly, very

emir /emɪəʳ/ **emirs.** An **emir** is a Muslim ruler. *...the Emir of Kuwait.* ◆◇◇◇◇ N-COUNT

emirate /emərət, AM ɪmɪərət/ **emirates.** An **emirate** is a country that is ruled by an emir. ◆◇◇◇◇ N-COUNT

emissary /emɪsəri, AM -seri/ **emissaries.** An **emissary** is a messenger or representative sent by one government or leader to another; a formal word. *...the President's special emissary to Hanoi.* N-COUNT

emission /ɪmɪʃᵊn/ **emissions.** An **emission** of something such as gas or radiation is the release of it into the atmosphere; a formal word. *The emission of gases such as carbon dioxide should be stabilised at their present level... Sulfur emissions from steel mills become acid rain.* ◆◆◇◇◇ N-VAR

emit /ɪmɪt/ **emits, emitting, emitted** ◆◇◇◇◇
1 If something **emits** heat, light, gas, or a smell, it produces it and sends it out by means of a physical or chemical process; a formal use. *The new device emits a powerful circular column of light. ...the amount of carbon dioxide emitted.* VERB V n
2 To **emit** a sound or noise means to produce it; a formal use. *Polly blinked and emitted a long, low whistle.* VERB V n

emollient /ɪmɒliənt/ **emollients**
1 An **emollient** is a liquid or cream which you put on your skin to soften it; a formal use. N-MASS
2 An **emollient** cream or other substance softens and soothes skin; a formal use. ADJ: ADJ n
3 If you describe someone, especially a politician, as **emollient**, you mean that they try to be tactful to people and to reduce conflict; a formal use. *The central character is a deceptively emollient senior figure in a Conservative Government.* ADJ-GRADED

emolument /ɪmɒljʊmənt/ **emoluments.** **Emoluments** are money or other forms of payment which a person receives for doing work; a formal word. *He could earn up to £1m a year in salary and emoluments from many directorships.* N-COUNT: usu pl

emotion /ɪmoʊʃᵊn/ **emotions** ◆◆◆◇◇
1 An **emotion** is a feeling such as happiness, love, fear, anger, or hatred, which can be caused by the situation that you are in or the people you are with. *Happiness was an emotion that Reynolds was having to relearn... Her voice trembled with emotion.* N-VAR =feeling
2 **Emotion** is the part of a person's character that consists of their feelings, as opposed to their thoughts. *...the split between reason and emotion.* N-UNCOUNT

emotional /ɪmoʊʃənᵊl/ ◆◆◆◇◇
1 **Emotional** means concerned with emotions and feelings. *I needed this man's love, and the emotional support he was giving me... Victims are left with emotional problems that can last for life.* ADJ: usu ADJ n =psychological
♦ **emotionally** *Are you saying that you're becoming emotionally involved with me?* ADV: ADV adj/-ed
2 An **emotional** situation or issue is one that causes people to have strong feelings. *It's a very emotional issue. How can you advocate selling the ivory from elephants?* ♦ **emotionally** *In an emotionally charged speech, he said he was resigning.* ADJ-GRADED =emotive ADV-GRADED: ADV adj/-ed
3 If someone is or becomes **emotional** they show their feelings very openly, especially because they are upset. *He is a very emotional man... I don't get as emotional as I once did.* ADJ-GRADED

emotionless /ɪmoʊʃᵊnləs/. If you describe someone as **emotionless**, you mean that they do not show any feelings or emotions. *He stood emotionless as he heard the judge pass sentence.* ADJ-GRADED ≠emotional

emotive /ɪmoʊtɪv/. An **emotive** situation or issue is likely to make people feel strong emotions. *Embryo research is an emotive issue.* ◆◇◇◇◇ ADJ-GRADED: usu ADJ n =emotional

empathetic /empəθetɪk/. Someone who is **empathetic** has the ability to share another person's feelings or emotions as if they were their own; a formal word. *...Clinton's skills as an empathetic listener.* ADJ-GRADED

empathize /empəθaɪz/ **empathizes, empathizing, empathized;** also spelled **empathise** in British English. If you **empathize** with someone, you understand their situation, problems, and feelings, because you have been in a similar situation. *I clearly empathize with the people who live in those neighborhoods... Parents must make use of their natural ability to empathize.* VERB V *with* n V

empathy /empəθi/. **Empathy** is the ability to share another person's feelings and emotions as if they were your own. *Having begun my life in a children's home I have great empathy with the little ones.* ◆◇◇◇◇ N-UNCOUNT: oft N *with/for* n

emperor /empərəʳ/ **emperors.** An **emperor** is a man who rules an empire or is the head of state in an empire. ◆◆◇◇◇ N-COUNT; N-TITLE

emphasis /emfəsɪs/ **emphases** /emfəsiːz/ ◆◆◆◇◇
1 **Emphasis** is special or extra importance that is given to an activity or to a part or aspect of something. *Too much emphasis is placed on research... Grant puts a special emphasis on weather in his paintings.*
N-VAR: oft N *on* n =stress
2 **Emphasis** is extra force that you put on a syllable, word, or phrase when you are speaking in order to make it seem more important. *'Of course, Vassios,' Leonidas said with emphasis... The emphasis is on the first syllable of the last word.*
N-VAR

emphasize /emfəsaɪz/ **emphasizes, emphasizing, emphasized;** also spelled **emphasise** in British English. To **emphasize** something means to indicate that it is particularly important or true, or to draw special attention to it. *Mummery emphasized the difference between the interests of the individual and the interests of the community... Her tight black jeans emphasize her bird-like legs... Mr Menem emphasized that his government will stick to its program... Discuss pollution with your child, emphasizing how nice a clean street, lawn, or park looks.*
◆◆◆◇◇ VERB
V n
V that
V *how*

emphatic /ɪmfætɪk/ ◆◇◇◇◇
1 An **emphatic** response or statement is one made in a forceful way, because the speaker feels very strongly about what they are saying. *His response was immediate and emphatic... I answered both questions with an emphatic 'Yes'.*
ADJ-GRADED
2 If you are **emphatic** about something, you use forceful language which shows that you feel very strongly about what you are saying. *The rebels are emphatic that this is not a surrender... He is especially emphatic about the value of a precise routine.*
ADJ-GRADED: v-link ADJ, oft ADJ that, ADJ *about* n
3 An **emphatic** win or victory is one in which the winner has won by a large amount or distance. *Yesterday's emphatic victory was their fifth in succession.*
ADJ-GRADED: usu ADJ n

emphatically /ɪmfætɪkli/ ◆◇◇◇◇
1 If you say something **emphatically**, you say it in a forceful way which shows that you feel very strongly about what you are saying. *'No fast food', she said emphatically... Mr Craxi has emphatically denied the charges.*
ADV-GRADED: ADV with v
2 You use **emphatically** to emphasize the statement you are making. *Making people feel foolish is emphatically not my strategy... Politics is most emphatically back on the agenda.*
ADV-GRADED: ADV with cl/group, ADV before v
PRAGMATICS

empire /empaɪəʳ/ **empires** ◆◆◆◇◇
1 An **empire** is a number of individual nations that are all controlled by the government or ruler of one particular country. *...the Roman Empire.*
N-COUNT
2 You can refer to a group of companies controlled by one person as an **empire**. *...the big Mondadori publishing empire.*
N-COUNT: with supp

empirical /ɪmpɪrɪkəl/. **Empirical** evidence or study relies on practical experience rather than theories. *There is no empirical evidence to support his thesis.* ♦ **empirically** *...empirically based research... They approached this part of their task empirically.*
◆◇◇◇◇ ADJ: usu ADJ n
ADV: usu ADV adj/-ed, ADV after v

empiricism /ɪmpɪrɪsɪzəm/. **Empiricism** is the belief that people should rely on practical experience and experiments, rather than on theories, as a basis for knowledge; a formal word. ♦ **empiricist, empiricists** *He was an unswerving empiricist with little time for theory.*
N-UNCOUNT
N-COUNT

emplacement /ɪmpleɪsmənt/ **emplacements.** **Emplacements** are specially prepared positions from which a heavy gun can be fired; a technical term. *There are gun emplacements every five-hundred yards along the road.*
N-COUNT: usu pl, usu supp N

employ /ɪmplɔɪ/ **employs, employing, employed** ◆◆◆◇◇
1 If a person or company **employs** you, they pay you to work for them. *The company employs 18 staff... More than 3,000 local workers are employed in the tourism industry... The government counted 27,600,000 employed persons in West Germany.*
VERB
V n
be V-ed *in/as* n
V-ed
Also V n to-inf
2 If you **employ** certain methods, materials, or expressions, you use them. *The tactics the police are now to employ are definitely uncompromising. ...the vocabulary that she employs. ...the approaches and methods employed in the study.*
VERB =use
V n
V-ed
Also V n *as* n
3 If someone or someone's time **is employed** in doing something, they are using the time they have to do that thing. *Your time could be usefully employed in attending to professional matters... The journalists would be much better employed in trying to explain to us how the astronomical legal costs of the cases can be justified.*
VB: usu passive
be V-ed *in* -ing/n
4 If you are **in the employ of** someone or something, you work for them. *Others hinted that he was in the employ of the KGB... Those in his employ were careful never to enrage him.*
PHRASE

employable /ɪmplɔɪəbəl/. Someone who is **employable** has skills or abilities that are likely to make someone want to give them a job. *People need basic education if they are to become employable. ...employable adults.*
ADJ-GRADED

employee /ɪmplɔɪiː/ **employees.** An **employee** is a person who is paid to work for an organization or for another person. *He is an employee of Fuji Bank... Many of its employees are women. ...a government employee.*
◆◆◆◆◇ N-COUNT

employer /ɪmplɔɪəʳ/ **employers.** Your **employer** is the person or organization that you work for. *He had been sent to Rome by his employer... The telephone company is the country's largest employer.*
◆◆◆◇◇ N-COUNT

employment /ɪmplɔɪmənt/ ◆◆◆◇◇
1 **Employment** is the fact of having a paid job. *She was unable to find employment... He regularly drove from his home to his place of employment.*
N-UNCOUNT
2 **Employment** is the fact of employing someone. *...the employment of children under nine.*
N-UNCOUNT
3 **Employment** is the availability of work in a country or area. *...economic policies designed to secure full employment.*
N-UNCOUNT ≠unemployment

employment agency, employment agencies. An **employment agency** is a company whose business is to help people to find work and help employers to find the workers they need.
N-COUNT

emporium /empɔːriəm/ **emporiums** or **emporia** /empɔːriə/. An **emporium** is a shop; a formal word.
N-COUNT

empower /ɪmpaʊəʳ/ **empowers, empowering, empowered** ◆◇◇◇◇
1 If someone **is empowered** to do something, they have the authority or power to do it; a formal use. *The army is now empowered to operate on a shoot-to-kill basis... His position does not empower him to cite our views without consultation.*
VERB =authorize
be V-ed to-inf
V n to-inf
Also V n
2 If someone or something **empowers** you, they give you the means to achieve something, for example to become stronger or more successful. *Empowering the underprivileged lies in assuring them that education holds the real source of power... What I'm trying to do is to empower people, to give them ways to help them get well.*
VERB
V n

empowerment /ɪmpaʊəʳmənt/. The **empowerment** of a person or group of people is the process of giving them power and status in a particular situation. *This government believes very strongly in the empowerment of women.*
◆◇◇◇◇ N-UNCOUNT: oft *the* N *of* n

empress /emprɪs/ **empresses.** An **empress** is a woman who rules an empire or who is the wife of an emperor.
◆◇◇◇◇ N-COUNT; N-TITLE

emptiness /emptinəs/ ◆◇◇◇◇
1 A feeling of **emptiness** is an unhappy or frightening feeling that nothing is worthwhile, especially when you are very tired or have just experienced something upsetting. *The result later in life may be feelings of emptiness and depression.*
N-UNCOUNT
2 The **emptiness** of a place is the fact that there is nothing in it. *...the emptiness of the desert.*
N-UNCOUNT
3 An **emptiness** is a very large area of land, sea, or space that has nothing in it; a literary use. *I drove for a while across this fearsome emptiness.*
N-SING

empty /empti/ **emptier, emptiest; empties, emptying, emptied** ◆◆◆◇◇
1 An **empty** place, vehicle, or container is one that has no people or things in it. *The room was bare*
ADJ-GRADED: oft ADJ *of* n

and empty. *...empty cans of lager... The roads were nearly empty of traffic.*

2 An **empty** gesture, threat, or relationship has no real value or meaning. *His father had threatened disinheritance, but both men had known it was an empty threat. ...to ensure the event is not perceived as an empty gesture.* ADJ: usu ADJ n

3 If you describe a person's life or a period of time as **empty**, you mean that nothing interesting or valuable happens in it. *My life was very hectic but empty before I met him.* ADJ-GRADED: usu v-link ADJ

4 If you feel **empty**, you feel unhappy and have no energy, usually because you are very tired or have just experienced something upsetting. *I felt empty and hollow; defeated... I feel so empty, my life just doesn't seem worth living any more.* ADJ-GRADED: usu *feel* ADJ, also ADJ n

5 If you **empty** a container, or **empty** something out of it, you remove its contents, especially by tipping it up. *I emptied the ashtray... Empty the noodles and liquid into a serving bowl... He emptied the contents out into the palm of his hand.* VERB V n V n prep V n with *out*

6 If someone **empties** a room or place, or if it **empties**, everyone that is in it goes away. *The stadium emptied at the end of the first day of athletics. ...a woman who could empty a pub full of drunks just by lifting one fist.* V-ERG V V n

7 A river or canal that **empties into** a lake, river, or sea flows into it. *The Washougal empties into the Columbia River near Portland.* VERB V *into* n

8 **Empties** are bottles or containers which no longer have anything in them. N-COUNT: usu pl

empty-handed. If you come away from somewhere **empty-handed**, you have failed to get what you wanted. *Delegates from the warring sides held a new round of peace talks but went away empty-handed... Shirley returned home empty-handed from her shopping trip.* ◆◇◇◇◇ ADJ: ADJ after v

empty-headed. If you describe someone as **empty-headed**, you mean that they are not very intelligent and often do silly things. *...a pretty, empty-headed little thing, barely out of school.* ADJ-GRADED

emu /iːmjuː/ **emus;** the plural can be **emus** or **emu**. An **emu** is a large Australian bird which cannot fly. N-COUNT

emulate /emjʊleɪt/ **emulates, emulating, emulated.** If you **emulate** something or someone, you imitate them because you admire them a great deal; a formal word. *Sons are traditionally expected to emulate their fathers.* ♦ **emulation** /emjʊleɪʃən/ *...a role model worthy of emulation.* ◆◇◇◇◇ VERB V n N-UNCOUNT

emulsifier /ɪmʌlsɪfaɪəʳ/ **emulsifiers.** An **emulsifier** is a substance used in food manufacturing which helps to combine liquids of different thicknesses. N-MASS

emulsify /ɪmʌlsɪfaɪ/ **emulsifies, emulsifying, emulsified.** When two liquids of different thicknesses **emulsify** or when they **are emulsified**, they combine; a technical term, used especially in cookery. *It is the pressure which releases the coffee oils; these emulsify and give the coffee its rich, velvety texture... Whisk the cream into the mixture to emulsify it... Beeswax acts as an emulsifying agent. ...a creamy sludge of emulsified oil.* V-ERG V V n V-ing V-ed

emulsion /ɪmʌlʃən/ **emulsions** ◆◇◇◇◇

1 **Emulsion** or **emulsion paint** is a water-based paint, which is not shiny when it dries. It is used for painting walls and ceilings. *...an undercoat of white emulsion paint. ...a matt emulsion.* N-MASS

2 An **emulsion** is a liquid or cream which is a mixture of two or more liquids, such as oil and water, which do not naturally mix together. N-MASS

3 In photography, **emulsion** is a substance that is used to make photographic film sensitive to light. N-MASS

en- /ɪn-/. Also pronounced /en-/, particularly in American English. **En-** is added to words to form verbs that describe the process of putting someone into a particular state, condition, or place, or to form adjectives and nouns that describe that process or those states and conditions. *People with disabilities are now doing many things to enrich their lives. ...the current campaign to enthrone him as our national bard... It is the first enthronement since 1928. ...a more enlightened leadership.* PREFIX

enable /ɪneɪbəl/ **enables, enabling, enabled** ◆◆◆◇◇

1 If someone or something **enables** you to do a particular thing, they give you the opportunity to do it. *The new test should enable doctors to detect the disease early. ...a new charter for training to enable young people to make the most of their potential.* ♦ **enabling** *Researchers describe it as an enabling technology.* VERB V n to-inf ADJ

2 To **enable** something to happen means to make it possible for it to happen. *The hot sun enables the grapes to reach optimum ripeness... A series of holes in the side panels enables the position of the shelves to be adjusted... The working class is still too small to enable a successful socialist revolution.* VERB V n to-inf V n

3 To **enable** someone to do something means to give them permission or the right to do it. *...the republic's legislation which enables young people to do a form of alternative service.* ♦ **enabling** *Some protection for victims must be written into the enabling legislation.* VERB V n to-inf ADJ: ADJ n

enact /ɪnækt/ **enacts, enacting, enacted** ◆◆◇◇◇

1 When a government or authority **enacts** a proposal, they make it into a law; a technical use. *The authorities have failed so far to enact a law allowing unrestricted emigration... The bill would be submitted for public discussion before being enacted as law.* VERB V n

2 If people **enact** a story or play, they perform it by acting. *She often enacted the stories told to her by her father.* VERB =perform V n

3 If a particular event or situation **is enacted**, it happens, especially as a repetition of something that has happened before; used mainly in journalism. *It was a scene which was enacted month after month for eight years.* VB: usu passive *be* V-ed

enactment /ɪnæktmənt/ **enactments** ◆◇◇◇◇

1 The **enactment** of a law is the process in a parliament or legislative assembly by which it is agreed upon and made official; a technical use. *We support the call for the enactment of a Bill of Rights.* N-VAR: usu N *of* n

2 The **enactment** of a play or story is the performance of it by an actor or group of actors; a formal use. *The main building was also used for the enactment of mystery plays.* N-VAR: usu N *of* n =performance

enamel /ɪnæməl/ **enamels** ◆◇◇◇◇

1 **Enamel** is a substance like glass which can be heated and put onto metal, glass, or pottery in order to decorate or protect it. *...a white enamel saucepan on the oil stove. ...enamel baths.* N-MASS: oft N n

2 **Enamel** is a hard, shiny paint that is used especially for painting metal and wood. *...enamel polymer paints... He relied on translucent enamels to produce vivid, glowing pictures.* N-MASS: oft N n

3 **Enamel** is the hard white substance that forms the outer part of a tooth. N-UNCOUNT

enamelled /ɪnæməld/; spelled **enameled** in American English. An **enamelled** object is decorated or covered with enamel. *...enamelled plates.* ADJ: ADJ n

enamelling /ɪnæməlɪŋ/; spelled **enameling** in American English. **Enamelling** is the decoration of something such as jewellery with enamel. N-UNCOUNT

enamoured /ɪnæməʳd/; spelled **enamored** in American English.

1 If you say that you are **enamoured** of something, you mean that you are impressed by it and like or admire it a lot. If you say that you are not **enamoured** of something, you mean that you have a low opinion of it and dislike or disapprove of it. A formal use. *I became totally enamored of the wildflowers there... The religious conservatives are not enamoured of the West and its values... Foreign students tend to be less enamoured of jobs in big business consultancy than many of their American counterparts.* ADJ-GRADED: usu v-link ADJ, usu ADJ *of/with* n, oft with brd-neg PRAGMATICS

2 If you are **enamoured** of a person, you are in love with them; a literary use. *I remember being very young and being totally enamored of him.* ADJ-GRADED: usu v-link ADJ, usu ADJ *of/with* n

en bloc /ɒn blɒk/. If a group of people do something **en bloc**, they do it altogether and at the same time. If a group of people or things are ADV: ADV after v, n ADV =en masse considered **en bloc**, they are considered as a whole. *An enlarged Latin group would be in a stronger position to negotiate en bloc with the United States... The selectors should resign en bloc... Now the governors en bloc are demanding far more consultation and rights over contractual approval.*

encamped /ɪnkæmpt/. If people, especially soldiers, are **encamped** somewhere, they have set up camp there. *Railways could now bring food to encamped armies... He made his way back to the farmyard where his regiment was encamped.* ADJ

encampment /ɪnkæmpmənt/ **encampments.** An **encampment** is a group of tents or other shelters in a particular place, especially when they are used by soldiers, refugees, or gypsies. *...an encampment of 2,000 legionnaires... The men were able to enter the military encampment while the soldiers slept.* N-COUNT: usu with supp

encapsulate /ɪnkæpsjʊleɪt/ **encapsulates, encapsulating, encapsulated.** If something **encapsulates** particular facts or ideas, it represents all the most important aspects of those facts or ideas in a very small space or in a single object or event. *A Wall Street Journal editorial encapsulated the views of many conservatives... His ideas were later encapsulated in a book strangely called Democratic Ideals and Reality.* ◆◇◇◇◇ VERB; V n; be V-ed in n; Also V n in n
♦ **encapsulation** /ɪnkæpsjʊleɪʃən/ **encapsulations** *...a witty encapsulation of modern America.* N-COUNT: usu sing, usu N of n

encase /ɪnkeɪs/ **encases, encasing, encased.** If a person or an object **is encased** in something, they are completely covered or surrounded by it. *When nuclear fuel is manufactured it is encased in metal cans... These weapons also had a heavy brass guard which encased almost the whole hand... It will actually be cheaper to leave the machine encased in concrete to one side of the tunnel, than to take it apart and bring it back to Britain... The original plan was to encase a small amount of a radioactive substance in a protective steal container.* ◆◇◇◇◇ VERB; be V-ed in n; V n; V-ed; V n in/with n

-ence /-əns/ or **-ency** /-ənsi/. **-ence** and **-ency** are added to adjectives, usually in place of -ent, to form nouns. These nouns refer to states, qualities, attitudes, or behaviour. For example, 'affluence' is the state of being affluent, and 'complacency' is the attitude of someone who is complacent. Nouns like these are often not defined in this dictionary, but are treated with the related adjective. SUFFIX

enchant /ɪntʃɑːnt, -tʃænt/ **enchants, enchanting, enchanted** ◆◇◇◇◇

1 If you **are enchanted** by someone or something, they cause you to have feelings of great delight or pleasure. *Dena was enchanted by the house... She enchanted you as she has so many others.* VERB; be V-ed; V n
♦ **enchanted** *Don't expect young children to be as enchanted with the scenery as you are.* ADJ-GRADED

2 In fairy stories and legends, to **enchant** someone or something means to put a magic spell on them. *King Arthur hid his treasures here and Merlin enchanted the cave so that nobody should ever find them. ...Celtic stories of cauldrons and enchanted vessels.* VERB; V n; V-ed

enchanting /ɪntʃɑːntɪŋ, -tʃænt-/. If you describe someone or something as **enchanting**, you mean that they are attractive, delightful, or charming. *She's an absolutely enchanting child... The overall effect is enchanting.* ◆◇◇◇◇ ADJ-GRADED

enchantment /ɪntʃɑːntmənt, -tʃænt-/ **enchantments**

1 If you say that something has **enchantment**, you mean that it makes you feel great delight or pleasure. Your **enchantment** with something is the fact of your feeling great delight and pleasure because of it. *The wilderness campsite had its own peculiar enchantment... Percy's enchantment with orchids dates back to 1951.* N-UNCOUNT

2 In fairy stories and legends, an **enchantment** is a magic spell. N-COUNT =spell

enchantress /ɪntʃɑːntrɪs, -tʃænt-/ **enchantresses**

1 If you call a woman an **enchantress**, you mean that men find her extremely attractive and fascinating. *...a sexy, husky-voiced enchantress.* N-COUNT: usu sing

2 In fairy stories and legends, an **enchantress** is a woman who uses magic to put spells on people and things. N-COUNT

encircle /ɪnsɜːʳkəl/ **encircles, encircling, encircled.** To **encircle** something or someone means to surround or enclose them, or to go round them. *A forty-foot-high concrete wall encircles the jail... By 22nd November the Sixth Army was encircled.* ◆◇◇◇◇ VERB =surround; V n

enclave /eŋkleɪv/ **enclaves.** An **enclave** is an area within a country or a city that is inhabited by people of a different nationality or culture from the inhabitants of the surrounding country or city. *Nagorno-Karabakh is an Armenian enclave inside Azerbaijan.* ◆◇◇◇◇ N-COUNT: usu with supp

enclose /ɪnkloʊz/ **encloses, enclosing, enclosed** ◆◆◇◇◇

1 If a place or object **is enclosed** by something, the place or object is inside that thing or completely surrounded by it. *The rules state that samples must be enclosed in two watertight containers... Enclose the pot in a clear polythene bag... The surrounding land was enclosed by an eight foot wire fence. ...the enclosed waters of the Baltic.* VERB; be V-ed in n; V n in n; V-ed; V-ed; Also V n

2 If you **enclose** something with a letter, you put it in the same envelope as the letter. *I have enclosed a cheque for £10... He tore open the creamy envelope that had been enclosed in the letter... The enclosed leaflet shows how Service Care can ease all your worries.* VERB; V n; V-ed

enclosed /ɪnkloʊzd/. An **enclosed** community of monks or nuns does not have any contact with the outside world. *...monks and nuns from enclosed orders.* ADJ: usu ADJ n

enclosure /ɪnkloʊʒəʳ/ **enclosures.** An **enclosure** is an area of land that is surrounded by a wall or fence and that is used for a particular purpose. *This enclosure was so vast that the outermost wall could hardly be seen.* ◆◇◇◇◇ N-COUNT

encode /ɪnkoʊd/ **encodes, encoding, encoded.** If you **encode** a message or some information, you put it into a code or express it in a different form or system of language. *The two parties encode confidential data in a form that is not directly readable by the other party... We compared the human mind to a computer which actively seeks information to process, encodes it and stores it for future use.* ◆◇◇◇◇ VERB =encrypt ≠decode; V n

encompass /ɪnkʌmpəs/ **encompasses, encompassing, encompassed** ◆◇◇◇◇

1 If something **encompasses** particular things, it includes them. *...the extra services, which start next September and encompass a wide range of special interests... His repertoire encompassed everything from Bach to Schoenberg.* VERB =cover, include; V n

2 To **encompass** a place means to completely surround or cover it. *Encompassing over a million square miles, this remote and mountainous domain presides over the rest of Asia... The map shows the rest of the western region, encompassing nine states.* VERB; V n

encore /ɒŋkɔːʳ, -kɔːʳ/ **encores, encoring, encored** ◆◇◇◇◇

1 An **encore** is a short extra performance at the end of a longer one, which an entertainer gives because the audience asks for it. *Lang's final encore last night was 'Barefoot'.* N-COUNT

2 If an entertainer **encores**, they perform an encore; an informal use. *They encore with a superlative version of The Who's 'The Kids Are Alright'.* VERB; V

3 **'Encore'** is the word shouted by classical concert audiences when they want a performer to perform an encore. CONVENTION

encounter /ɪnkaʊntəʳ/ **encounters, encountering, encountered** ◆◆◆◇◇

1 If you **encounter** problems or difficulties, you experience them. *Every day of our lives we encounter* VERB; V n

major and minor stresses of one kind or another... Environmental problems they found in Poland were among the worst they encountered.

2 If you **encounter** someone, you meet them, usually unexpectedly; a formal use. *Did you encounter anyone in the building?... Renata wrote him that she had encountered her long-estranged father.* VERB =meet V n

3 An **encounter** with someone is a meeting with them, particularly one that is unexpected or significant. *The author tells of a remarkable encounter with a group of South Vietnamese soldiers.* N-COUNT: usu with supp

4 An **encounter** is a particular type of experience. *...a sexual encounter. ...his first serious encounter with alcohol.* N-COUNT: usu with supp

encourage /ɪnkʌrɪdʒ, AM -kɜːr-/ **encourages, encouraging, encouraged** ◆◆◆◆◇

1 If you **encourage** someone, you give them confidence, for example by letting them know that what they are doing is good and telling them that they should continue to do it. *When things aren't going well, he encourages me, telling me not to give up.* VERB V n

2 If someone **is encouraged by** something that happens, it gives them hope or confidence. *Investors were encouraged by the news... Mr Major said he had been encouraged by recent Irish statements about the issue..* ♦ **encouraged** *Mayor Elias Freij said he had a good meeting with Mr Baker which left him very encouraged and optimistic... I am encouraged that more physicians are asking questions in these meetings and coming to workshops.* VB: usu passive be V-ed by n; ADJ-GRADED: v-link ADJ, oft ADJ that

3 If you **encourage** someone to do something, you try to persuade them to do it, for example by telling them that it would be a pleasant thing to do, or by trying to make it easier for them to do it. You can also **encourage** an activity. *We want to encourage people to go fishing, not put them off... Herbie Hancock was encouraged by his family to learn music at a young age... Their task is to help encourage private investment in Russia... Participation is encouraged at all levels.* VERB V n to-inf V n

4 If something **encourages** a particular activity or state, it causes it to happen or increase. *...a natural substance that encourages cell growth... Such secrecy breeds and encourages fear and suspicion... Slow music encourages supermarket-shoppers to browse longer but spend more.* VERB V n V n to-inf

encouragement /ɪnkʌrɪdʒmənt, AM -kɜːr-/ **encouragements. Encouragement** is the activity of encouraging someone, or something that is said or done in order to encourage them. *I also had friends who gave me a great deal of encouragement... Thanks for your advice and encouragement. ...the notion that tax encouragements and the like would be sufficient to increase people's appetite for supporting charity.* ◆◆◇◇◇ N-VAR: oft N of n

encouraging /ɪnkʌrɪdʒɪŋ, AM -kɜːr-/. Something that is **encouraging** gives people hope or confidence. *There are encouraging signs of an artistic revival... The results have been encouraging... It was encouraging that he recognised the dangers facing the company.* ♦ **encouragingly** *The people at the next table watched me eat and smiled encouragingly... Against all expectations, the theatre reopened to encouragingly large audiences... But, most encouragingly, there'd been no sign of any recurrence of the hallucinations.* ◆◆◇◇◇ ADJ-GRADED: oft it v-link ADJ that; ADV-GRADED: ADV after v, ADV adj, ADV with cl

encroach /ɪnkroʊtʃ/ **encroaches, encroaching, encroached** ◆◇◇◇◇

1 If one thing **encroaches** on another, the first thing spreads or becomes stronger, and slowly begins to restrict the power, range, or effectiveness of the second thing; used in formal English showing disapproval. *Any attempt to encroach upon presidential prerogatives in this domain was quickly and firmly resisted... The new institutions do not encroach on political power... For some time the movie industry had loftily chosen to ignore the encroaching competition of television.* VERB PRAGMATICS V on/upon n V-ing Also V

2 If something **encroaches** on a place, it spreads and takes over more and more of that place; a formal use. *The rhododendrons encroached ever more on the twisting drive... I turned into the dirt road and followed it through encroaching trees and bushes.* VERB V on n V-ing Also V prep/adv, V

encroachment /ɪnkroʊtʃmənt/ **encroachments.** You can describe the action or process of encroaching on something as **encroachment**, especially when you disapprove of it. *It's a sign of the encroachment of commercialism in medicine... The problem was to safeguard sites from encroachment by property development.* N-VAR: usu with supp PRAGMATICS

encrustation /ɪŋkrʌsteɪʃən/ **encrustations.** An **encrustation** is a hard and thick layer on the surface of something that has built up over a long period of time. N-VAR

encrusted /ɪnkrʌstɪd/. If an object is **encrusted** with something, its surface is covered with a layer of that thing. *...a blue uniform coat that was thickly encrusted with gold loops.* ▸ Also a combining form. *...a jewel-encrusted ring. ...snow-encrusted mountain paths.* ADJ-GRADED: oft ADJ with n; COMB in ADJ: ADJ n

encumber /ɪnkʌmbəʳ/ **encumbers, encumbering, encumbered**

1 If you **are encumbered** by something, it prevents you from moving freely or doing what you want. *No soldiers ever marched with less to encumber them... It is still labouring under the debt burden that it was encumbered with in the 1980s.* ♦ **encumbered** *The rest of the world is less encumbered with legislation... I'm sure we all wish to be less encumbered by rules which we think unnecessary and restricting.* VERB =burden V n be V-ed with n; ADJ-GRADED: v-link ADJ, usu ADJ with/by n

2 If a place **is encumbered** with things, it contains so many of them that it is difficult to move freely there. *The narrow quay was encumbered by hundreds of carts.* VERB be V-ed prep

encumbrance /ɪnkʌmbrəns/ **encumbrances.** An **encumbrance** is something or someone that encumbers you. *Magdalena considered the past an irrelevant encumbrance. Only the future mattered, only the task ahead.* N-COUNT =burden

-ency. See **-ence.**

encyclical /ɪnsɪklɪkəl/ **encyclicals.** An **encyclical** is an official letter written by the Pope and sent to all Roman Catholic bishops, usually in order to make a statement about the official teachings of the Church. N-COUNT

encyclopedia /ɪnsaɪkləpiːdiə/ **encyclopedias;** also spelled **encyclopaedia** in British English. An **encyclopedia** is a book or set of books in which facts about many different subjects or about one particular subject are arranged for reference, usually in alphabetical order. ◆◇◇◇◇ N-COUNT: usu with supp

encyclopedic /ɪnsaɪkləpiːdɪk/; also spelled **encyclopaedic** in British English. If you describe something as **encyclopedic**, you mean that it is very full, complete, and thorough in the amount of knowledge or information that it has. *He had an encyclopaedic knowledge of drugs. ...an almost overwhelmingly encyclopaedic volume.* ADJ-GRADED: usu ADJ n =comprehensive

end /end/ **ends, ending, ended** ◆◆◆◆◆

1 **The end** of something such as a period of time, an event, a book, or a film is the last part of it or the final point in it. *The £5 banknote was first issued at the end of the 18th century... The report is expected by the end of the year... You will have the chance to ask questions at the end.* N-SING: the N, usu prep N, N of n

2 When a situation, process, or activity **ends**, or when something or someone **ends** it, it reaches its final point and stops. *The meeting quickly ended and Steve and I left the room... Talks have resumed to try to end the fighting... She began to weep. That ended our discussion.* ♦ **ending** *The ending of a marriage by death is different in many ways from an ending occasioned by divorce.* V-ERG V V n; N-SING: usu the N of n

3 An **end** to something or the **end** of it is the act or result of stopping it so that it does not continue any longer. *The French government today called for an end to the violence... I was worried she would walk out or bring the interview to an end... Francis fined him two weeks' wages and said: 'That's the end of the matter.'* N-COUNT: usu sing, oft N to/of n

4 If you say that someone or something **ends** a V-ERG

period of time in a particular way, you are indicating what the final part of it or the final situation was like. You can also say that a period of time **ends** in a particular way. *The markets ended the week on a quiet note... British Gas shares ended the day 1p up at 287p... The evening ended with a dramatic display of fireworks.* V n prep/adv V prep Also V n *by*-ing, V n -ing

5 If a period of time **ends**, it reaches its final point. *Its monthly reports on program trading usually come out about three weeks after each month ends... They hired eight college graduates to start work after the college year ends in March.* VERB V

6 If something such as a book, speech, or performance **ends** with a particular thing or the writer or performer **ends** it with that thing, its final part consists of the thing mentioned. *His statement ended with the words: 'Pray for me.'... The book ends on a lengthy description of Hawaii... Dawkins ends his discussion with a call for liberation... The memo ends: 'I am sorry if this seems a trifling point about which to be writing to you.'* V-ERG V *with/on* n V n *with/on* n V with quote

7 If a situation or event **ends** in a particular way, it has that particular result. *The incident could have ended in tragedy... The match ended in a draw... Our conversations ended with him saying he would try to be more understanding... My own view is that we can have a relationship without worrying where it will end... Shares ended 1.7 per cent firmer on the Frankfurt exchange.* VERB V *in* n V *with* n -ing V adv/adj

8 The two **ends** of something long and narrow are the two points or parts of it that are furthest away from each other. *The company is planning to place surveillance equipment at both ends of the tunnel... A typical fluorescent lamp is a tube with metal electrodes at each end.* N-COUNT: with supp

9 The **end** of a long, narrow object such as a finger or a pencil is the tip or smallest edge of it, usually the part that is furthest away from you. *He tapped the ends of his fingers together... She let the long cone of ash hang at the end of her cigarette.* N-COUNT: usu with supp, oft N *of* n =tip

10 If an object **ends with** or **in** a particular thing, it has that thing on its tip or point, or as its last part. *It has three pairs of legs, each ending in a large claw.* VERB V *with/in* n

11 A journey, road, or river that **ends** at a particular place stops there and goes no further. *The road ended at a T-junction... The journey ends in the ancient city of Marrakesh.* VERB V prep/adv Also V

12 **End** is used to refer to either of the two extreme points of a scale, or of something that you are considering as a scale. *At the other end of the social scale was the grocer, the village's only merchant... The agreement has been criticised by extremists groups on both ends of the political spectrum.* N-COUNT: with supp, oft N *of* n

13 The other **end** is one of two places that are connected because people are communicating with each other by telephone or writing, or are travelling from one place to the other. *When he answered it, Ferguson was at the other end... There was silence at the other end of the line... Make sure to meet them at the other end.* N-COUNT: supp N

14 If you refer to a particular **end** of a project or piece of work, you mean a part or aspect of it, for example a part of it that is done by a particular person or in a particular place; used in spoken English. *You take care of your end, kid, I'll take care of mine... Let's go up to the office and settle the business end of things.* N-COUNT: usu sing, usu supp N

15 An **end** is the purpose for which something is done or towards which you are working. *The police force is being manipulated for political ends... Now the government is trying another policy designed to achieve the same end.* N-COUNT: usu supp N

16 If you say that something **ends** at a particular point, you mean that it is applies or exists up to that point, and no further. *Helen is also 25 and from Birmingham, but the similarity ends there... Does responsibility end at the fitting of car seats?* VERB V adv/prep

17 You can refer to someone's death as their **end**, especially when you are talking about the way that they died or might die; a literary use. *Soon after we had spoken to this man he had met a violent end.* N-COUNT: usu sing, usu supp N

18 If you **end** by doing something or **end** in a particular state, you do that thing or get into that state even though you did not originally intend to. *They ended by making themselves miserable... They'll probably end back on the streets.* VERB V *by*-ing V adv/prep

19 If someone **ends it all**, they commit suicide. *He grew suicidal, thinking up ways to end it all.* PHRASES V inflects

20 If you describe something as, for example, the deal **to end all** deals or the film **to end all** films, you mean that it is a very important or successful deal or film and that compared to it all other deals or films would seem trivial or second-rate. *It was going to be a party to end all parties. ...the sale to end all sales at Harrods.* n PHR n

21 If something is **at an end**, it has finished and will not continue. *The court has passed sentence and the matter is now at an end... The recession is definitely at an end.* v-link PHR

22 If something **comes to an end**, it stops. *The cold war came to an end.* V inflects

23 You say **at the end of the day** when you are talking about what happens after a long series of events or what appears to be the case after you have considered the relevant facts; an informal expression. *At the end of the day it's up to the Germans to decide... At the end of the day, the board's not going to be too concerned with three or four more dollars.* PHR with cl PRAGMATICS

24 If you say that someone **has gone off the deep end**, you mean that their mind has stopped working in a normal way and their behaviour has become very strange as a result; an informal expression. *I'm not sure she believes me. She probably just thinks I've gone off the deep end.* V inflects

25 If you **are thrown in at the deep end**, you are put in a completely new situation or given something difficult to do without any help or preparation. If you **jump in at the deep end**, you go into a completely new situation or begin to do something difficult without any help or preparation; used mainly in British English. *It's a superb job. You get thrown in at the deep end and it's all down to you... The reason many people fail on diets is that they jump in at the deep end, making a complete change to their eating habits.* V inflects

26 If you do something to **the bitter end** or to **the very end**, you continue to do it for as long as you can, although it may be very unpleasant or dangerous. *We will fight to the bitter end to ensure our children get what is rightfully theirs.* *to/until* PHR

27 You say **in the end** when you are saying what is the final result of a series of events, or what is your final conclusion after considering all the relevant facts. *I toyed with the idea of calling the police, but in the end I didn't... Benny thought the president was sincere and sensitive, but, in the end, that's not what counts.* PHR with cl PRAGMATICS

28 If you consider something to be **an end in itself**, you do it because it seems desirable and not because it is likely to lead to something else. *While he had originally traveled in order to study, traveling had become an end in itself.* usu v-link PHR

29 If you have to **keep** your **end up**, or to **keep up** your **end** of something, you have to do something as well as other people, or as well as you are expected to do it; an informal use. *I had to keep my end up with other professors in the faculty... He had trouble keeping up his end of a technical discussion.* V inflects

30 If you find it difficult to **make ends meet**, you can only just manage financially because you hardly have enough money for the things you need. *With Betty's salary they barely made ends meet.* *make* inflects

31 **No end** means a lot; an informal expression. *The problem was causing the poor woman no end of misery... Teachers inform me that Tracey's behaviour has improved no end.* PHR after v, oft PHR *of* n

32 When something happens for hours, days, weeks, or years **on end**, it happens continuously and without stopping for the amount of time that is mentioned. *He is a wonderful companion and we can talk for hours on end... I spend days on end in this studio.* pl-n PHR

33 Something that is **on end** is upright, instead of in its normal or natural position, for example lying down, flat, or on its longest side. PHR after v

34 To **put an end to** something means to cause it to stop. *Only a political solution could put an end to the violence.* V inflects, PHR n

35 If a process or person has reached **the end of the road**, they are unable to progress any further. *Given the results of the vote, is this the end of the road for the hardliners in Congress?* PHR after v, v-link PHR *for* n

36 If you say that something will happen or be true **until the end of time** or **to the end of time**, you are emphasizing that it will always happen or always be true. *We can assume that the moon will continue to go around the earth until the end of time... I'll love her till the end of time.* PHR after v PRAGMATICS

37 If you say that something bad is **not the end of the world**, you are trying to stop yourself or someone else being so upset by it, by suggesting that it is not the worst thing that could happen. *Obviously I'd be disappointed if we don't make it, but it wouldn't be the end of the world.* V inflects, oft *it* v-link PHR if PRAGMATICS

38 • **the end of your tether**: see **tether**. • to **burn the candle at both ends**: see **candle**. • to **make** your **hair stand on end**: see **hair**. • **a means to an end**: see **mean**. • to **be on the receiving end**: see **receive**. • to **get the wrong end of the stick**: see **stick**. • to **come to a sticky end**: see **sticky**. • to **be at your wits' end**: see **wit**.

end up PHRASAL VERB

1 If someone or something **ends up** somewhere, they eventually arrive there, usually by accident. *The result was that the engine ended up at the bottom of the canal... She fled with her children, moving from neighbour to neighbour and ending up in a friend's cellar.* =finish up; V P prep/adv

2 If you **end up** doing something or **end up** in a particular state, you do that thing or get into that state even though you did not originally intend to. *If you don't know what you want, you might end up getting something you don't want... Every time they went dancing they ended up in a bad mood... She could have ended up a millionairess.* =finish up; V P -ing; V P prep/adv; V P n

endanger /ɪndeɪndʒəʳ/ **endangers, endangering, endangered.** To **endanger** something or someone means to put them in a situation where they might be harmed or destroyed completely. *The debate could endanger the proposed Mideast peace talks. ...endangered species such as lynx, wolf and several species of vulture.* ◆◆◇◇◇ VERB; V n; V-ed

endear /ɪndɪəʳ/ **endears, endearing, endeared.** If something **endears** you **to** someone or if you **endear** yourself **to** them, you become popular with them and well liked by them. *Their taste for gambling has endeared them to Las Vegas casino owners... He has endeared himself to the American public.* ◆◇◇◇◇ VERB; V n *to* n; V pron-refl *to* n

endearing /ɪndɪərɪŋ/. If you describe someone's behaviour as **endearing**, you mean that it causes you to feel very fond of them. *She has such an endearing personality... Henry's lisp is so endearing.* ♦ **endearingly** *He admits endearingly to doubts and hesitations... She is endearingly free of pretensions.* ◆◇◇◇◇ ADJ-GRADED: v-link ADJ; ADV-GRADED: ADV with v, ADV adj

endearment /ɪndɪəʳmənt/ **endearments.** An **endearment** is a loving or affectionate word or phrase that you say to someone you love. *No term of endearment crossed their lips. ...flattering endearments.* N-VAR

endeavour /ɪndevəʳ/ **endeavours, endeavouring, endeavoured;** spelled **endeavor** in American English. ◆◆◇◇◇

1 If you **endeavour** to do something, you try very hard to do it; a formal use. *I will endeavour to arrange it... They are endeavouring to protect trade union rights.* VERB =strive; V to-inf

2 An **endeavour** is an attempt to do something, especially something new or original; a formal use. *His first endeavours in the field were wedding films. ...the benefits of investment in scientific endeavour.* N-VAR: usu with supp, oft N to-inf

endemic /endemɪk/ ◆◇◇◇◇

1 If a disease or illness is **endemic** in a place, it is frequently found among the people who live there; a technical term in medicine. *Polio was then endemic among children my age.* ADJ ≠epidemic

2 If you say that a condition or problem is **endemic**, you mean that it is very common and strong, and cannot be dealt with easily; used mainly in written English. *Discrimination against Catholics is endemic in Northern Ireland's institutions. ...powerful radicals with an endemic hatred and fear of the West.* ADJ-GRADED

ending /endɪŋ/ **endings** ◆◆◇◇◇

1 You can refer to the last part of a book, story, play, or film as the **ending**, especially when you are considering the way that the story ends. *The film has a Hollywood happy ending.* N-COUNT: oft supp N

2 The **ending** of a word is the last part of it. *...common word endings, like 'ing' in walking.* N-COUNT: with supp

3 See also **nerve ending**.

endive /endɪv, AM -daɪv/ **endives**

1 Endive is a type of plant with crisp curly leaves that is eaten in salads. N-VAR

2 In American English, **endive** is type of a plant with crunchy sharp-tasting leaves that is eaten in salads. The British word is **chicory**. N-VAR

endless /endləs/. If you say that something is **endless**, you mean that it is very large or lasts for a very long time, and it seems as if it will never stop. *They turned into an endless street... The war was endless.* ♦ **endlessly** *They talk about it endlessly. ...endlessly long arcades of shops.* ◆◆◇◇◇ ADJ-GRADED; ADV-GRADED: ADV after v, ADV adj

endocrine /endəkraɪn/. The **endocrine** system is the system of glands that produce hormones which go directly into the bloodstream, such as the pituitary or thyroid glands; a technical term in medicine. ADJ: ADJ n

endorse /ɪndɔːʳs/ **endorses, endorsing, endorsed** ◆◆◇◇◇

1 If you **endorse** someone or something, you say publicly that you support or approve of them. *I can endorse their opinion wholeheartedly. ...policies agreed by the Labour Party and endorsed by the electorate.* VERB; V n

2 In Britain, if someone's driving licence **is endorsed**, an official record is made on it that they have been found guilty of a driving offence. *For failing to report the accident, his licence was endorsed... He also had his licence endorsed with eight penalty points.* V-PASSIVE; *be* V-ed; *have* n V-ed

3 When you **endorse** a cheque, you write your name on the back of it so that it can be paid into someone else's bank account. *The payee of the cheque must endorse the cheque.* VERB; V n

4 If you **endorse** a product or company, you appear in advertisements for it. *The twins endorsed a line of household cleaning products.* VERB; V n

endorsement /ɪndɔːʳsmənt/ **endorsements** ◆◇◇◇◇

1 An **endorsement** is a statement or action which shows that you support or approve of something or someone. *That adds up to an endorsement of the status quo... This is a powerful endorsement for his softer style of government.* N-COUNT: oft N *of/for* n

2 In Britain, an **endorsement** is a note on someone's driving licence saying that they have been found guilty of a driving offence. N-COUNT

3 An **endorsement** for a product or company involves appearing in advertisements for it or showing support for it. N-COUNT

endow /ɪndaʊ/ **endows, endowing, endowed** ◆◇◇◇◇

1 You say that someone **is endowed** with a particular desirable ability, characteristic, or possession when they have it by chance or by birth. *You are endowed with wealth, good health and a lively intellect.* VB: usu passive =be blessed; *be* V-ed *with* n

2 If you **endow** something **with** a particular feature or quality, you provide it with that feature or quality. *Herbs have been used for centuries to endow a whole range of foods with subtle flavours.* VERB =imbue; V n *with* n

3 If someone **endows** an institution, scholarship, or project, they provide a large amount of money which will produce the annual income needed to pay for it. *The ambassador has endowed a $1 million public-service fellowships program.* VERB; V n

endowment /ɪndaʊmənt/ **endowments** ◆◆◇◇◇
1 An **endowment** is a gift of money that is made to an institution or community in order to provide it with an annual income. *The company revived the finances of the Oxford Union with a generous £1m endowment.* [N-COUNT]
2 If someone has an **endowment** of a particular quality or ability, they possess it naturally; a formal use. [N-COUNT: usu with supp]
3 In finance, an **endowment** policy or mortgage is an insurance policy or mortgage which you pay towards each year and which then provides you with a large sum of money at the end of a fixed period; used in British English. [N-COUNT: usu N n]

end product, end products. The **end product** of something is the thing that is produced or achieved by means of it. *It is the end product of exhaustive research and development.* [N-COUNT: oft N of n]

end result, end results. The **end result** of an activity or a process is the final result or outcome that it produces. *The end result is very good and very successful... The end result of this will be unity.* ◆◇◇◇◇ [N-COUNT: usu the N]

endurance /ɪndjʊərəns, AM -dʊr-/. **Endurance** is the ability to continue with an unpleasant or difficult situation, experience, or activity over a long period of time. *The exercise obviously will improve strength and endurance. ...his powers of endurance.* ◆◇◇◇◇ [N-UNCOUNT]

endure /ɪndjʊəʳ, AM -dʊr/ **endures, enduring, endured** ◆◆◇◇◇
1 If you **endure** a painful or difficult situation, you experience it and do not avoid it or give up, usually because you cannot. *The company endured heavy financial losses. ...unbearable pain, which they had to endure in solitude because not even the doctors could get near them.* [VERB =undergo; V n]
2 If something **endures**, it continues to exist without any loss in quality or importance. *Somehow the language endures and continues to survive.* [VERB =last; V] ♦ **enduring** *This chance meeting was the start of an enduring friendship.* [ADJ-GRADED: usu ADJ n]

enema /enɪmə/ **enemas.** If someone has an **enema**, a liquid is put into their rectum in order to empty their bowels, for example before they have an operation. [N-COUNT]

enemy /enəmi/ **enemies** ◆◆◆◇◇
1 If someone is your **enemy**, they hate you or want to harm you. [N-COUNT]
2 If someone is your **enemy**, they are opposed to you and to what you think or do. *The Government's political enemies were quick to pick up on this series of disasters.* [N-COUNT]
3 The **enemy** is an army or other force that is opposed to you in a war, or a country with which your country is at war. *The enemy were pursued for two miles... He searched the skies for enemy bombers.* [N-SING-COLL: the N, N n]
4 If one thing is the **enemy of** another thing, the second thing cannot happen or succeed because of the first thing; a formal use. *Reform, as we know, is the enemy of revolution.* [N-COUNT: usu sing, N of n]

energetic /enəʳdʒetɪk/ ◆◆◇◇◇
1 If you are **energetic** in what you do, you have a lot of enthusiasm and determination. *Blackwell is 59, strong looking, enormously energetic and accomplished... The next government will play an energetic role in seeking multilateral nuclear disarmament.* [ADJ-GRADED] ♦ **energetically** /enəʳdʒetɪkli/ *He talked on energetically... He had worked energetically all day on his new book.* [ADV-GRADED: ADV with v]
2 An **energetic** person is very active and does not feel at all tired. An **energetic** activity involves a lot of physical movement and power. *Ten year-olds are incredibly energetic. ...an energetic exercise routine.* [ADJ-GRADED] ♦ **energetically** *Gretchen chewed energetically on the gristled steak.* [ADV-GRADED: ADV with v]

energize /enəʳdʒaɪz/ **energizes, energizing, energized;** also spelled **energise** in British English. To **energize** someone means to give them the enthusiasm and determination to do something. *He helped energize and mobilize millions of people around the nation... I am completely energized and feeling terrific.* ◆◇◇◇◇ [VERB; V n; be V-ed] ♦ **energizing** *Acupuncture has a harmonizing and energizing effect on mind and body.* [ADJ-GRADED]

energy /enəʳdʒi/ **energies** ◆◆◆◆◇
1 **Energy** is the ability and strength to do active physical things and the feeling that you are full of physical power and life. *He was saving his energy for next week's race in Belgium... We try to boost our energy by eating.* [N-UNCOUNT]
2 **Energy** is determination and enthusiasm about doing things; used showing approval. *At 54 years old her energy and looks are magnificent... You have drive and energy for those things you are interested in.* [N-UNCOUNT; PRAGMATICS]
3 Your **energies** are your efforts and attention, which you can direct towards a particular aim. *She had started to devote her energies to teaching rather than performing... We must concentrate our energies on treating addiction first.* [N-COUNT: usu pl, poss N]
4 **Energy** is the power from sources such as electricity and coal that makes machines work or provides heat. *...those who favour nuclear energy... Oil shortages have brought on an energy crisis... It doesn't take much to improve the energy efficiency of your home.* [N-UNCOUNT: oft N n]

enervated /enəʳveɪtɪd/. If you feel **enervated**, you feel tired and weak; a formal word. *Warm winds make many people feel enervated and depressed.* [ADJ-GRADED]

enervating /enəʳveɪtɪŋ/. Something that is **enervating** makes you feel tired and weak; a formal word. *Life was hard and enervating.* [ADJ-GRADED]

enfant terrible /ɒnfɒn teriːblə/ **enfants terribles.** If you describe someone as an **enfant terrible**, you mean that they are clever but unconventional, and often cause problems or embarrassment for their friends or families; a fairly formal expression. *He became known as the enfant terrible of British theater.* [N-COUNT: usu sing, usu the N of n]

enfeebled /ɪnfiːbᵊld/. If someone or something is **enfeebled**, they have become very weak; a formal word. *He finds himself politically enfeebled as never before... A strike at the already enfeebled newspaper would almost certainly prove fatal.* [ADJ-GRADED =weakened]

enfold /ɪnfoʊld/ **enfolds, enfolding, enfolded**
1 If something **enfolds** an object or person, they cover, surround, or are wrapped around that object or person; a literary use. *Aurora felt the opium haze enfold her... Wood was now comfortably enfolded in a woolly dressing-gown.* [VERB; V n; be V-ed in n; Also V n in n]
2 If you **enfold** someone or something, you hold them close in a very gentle, loving way; a literary use. *Thack came up behind him, enfolding him in his arms.* [VERB; V n in n; Also V n]

enforce /ɪnfɔːʳs/ **enforces, enforcing, enforced** ◆◆◇◇◇
1 If people in authority **enforce** a law or a rule, they make sure that it is obeyed, usually by punishing people who do not obey it. *Until now, the government has only enforced the ban with regard to American ships... The measures are being enforced by Interior Ministry troops.* [VERB; V n]
2 To **enforce** something means to force or cause it to be done or to happen. *They struggled to limit the cost by enforcing a low-tech specification... David is now living in Beirut again after an enforced absence.* [VERB; V n; V-ed]

enforceable /ɪnfɔːʳsəbᵊl/. If something such as a law or agreement is **enforceable**, it can be enforced. *...the creation of legally enforceable contracts... This Human Rights Act is enforceable in the ordinary courts.* [ADJ-GRADED]

enforcement /ɪnfɔːʳsmənt/. If someone carries out the **enforcement** of an act or rule, they enforce it. *The doctors want stricter enforcement of existing laws, such as those banning sales of cigarettes to children.* ◆◆◇◇◇ [N-UNCOUNT: oft N of n]

enfranchise /ɪnfræntʃaɪz/ **enfranchises, enfranchising, enfranchised.** To **enfranchise** someone means to give them the right to vote in elections; a formal word. *The company voted to enfranchise its 120 women members... If the city's* [VERB; V n] *foreign residents are enfranchised, they won't be able to vote until 1996.*

enfranchisement /ɪnfræntʃaɪzmənt/. **Enfranchisement** is the condition of someone being enfranchised; a formal word. *...the enfranchisement of the country's blacks.* N-UNCOUNT: oft N *of* n

engage /ɪngeɪdʒ/ **engages, engaging, engaged** ◆◆◆◇◇

1 If you **engage in** an activity, you do it or are actively involved with it; a formal use. *I have never engaged in the drug trade... You can engage in croquet on the south lawn.* VERB V *in* n

2 If something **engages** you or your attention or interest, it keeps you interested in it and thinking about it. *They never learned skills to engage the attention of the others.* VERB V n

3 If you **engage** someone **in** conversation, you have a conversation with them. *They tried to engage him in conversation... We want to engage recognized leaders in discussion.* VERB V n *in* n

4 If you **engage with** something or **with** a group of people, you get involved with that thing or group and feel that you are connected with it or have real contact with it. *She found it hard to engage with office life... She had vowed to go out of her way to engage with the Irish people at local community level.* VERB V *with* n
♦ **engagement** *And she, too, suffers from a lack of critical engagement with the literary texts.* N-UNCOUNT: usu N *with* n

5 If you **engage** someone to do a particular job, you appoint them to do it; a formal use. *We engaged the services of a recognised engineer... He had been able to engage some staff.* VERB V n

6 When a part of a machine or other mechanism **engages** or when you **engage** it, it moves into a position where it fits into something else. *Press the lever until you hear the catch engage. ...a lesson in how to engage the four-wheel drive.* V-ERG V, V n

7 When a military force **engages** the enemy, it attacks them and starts a battle. *It could engage the enemy beyond the range of hostile torpedoes.* VERB V n

8 See also **engaged, engaging**.

engaged /ɪngeɪdʒd/ ◆◆◇◇◇

1 Someone who is **engaged in** or **engaged on** a particular activity is doing that thing; a formal use. *The police said they found the three engaged in target practice. ...the various projects he was engaged on.* ADJ: v-link ADJ *in/on* n

2 When two people are **engaged**, they have agreed to marry each other. *We got engaged on my eighteenth birthday... He was engaged to Miss Julia Maria Boardman. ...the engaged couple.* ADJ: usu v-link ADJ, oft ADJ *to* n

3 In British English, if a telephone or a telephone line is **engaged**, it is already being used by someone else so that you are unable to speak to the person you are phoning. The usual American word is **busy**. *The line is engaged... We tried to call you back but you were engaged.* ADJ: v-link ADJ

4 If a public toilet is **engaged**, it is already being used by someone else; used mainly in British English. The American term is **occupied**. ADJ: v-link ADJ

engagement /ɪngeɪdʒmənt/ **engagements** ◆◆◇◇◇

1 An **engagement** is an arrangement that you have made to do something at a particular time; a formal use. *He had an engagement at a restaurant in Greek Street at eight. ...business-related social engagements.* N-COUNT

2 An **engagement** is an agreement that two people have made with each other to get married. *I've broken off my engagement to Arthur... Announcing our engagement was a relief.* N-COUNT: usu sing, usu poss N

3 You can refer to the period of time during which two people are engaged as their **engagement**. *I felt our engagement was quite an unhappy time.* N-COUNT: usu sing, usu poss N

4 A military **engagement** is an armed conflict between two enemies. *The constitution prohibits them from military engagement on foreign soil.* N-VAR

5 See also **engage**.

engagement ring, engagement rings. An **engagement ring** is a ring worn by a woman when she is engaged to be married. N-COUNT

engaging /ɪngeɪdʒɪŋ/. An **engaging** person or thing is pleasant, interesting, and entertaining. *...one of her most engaging and least known novels... He was engaging company.* ◆◇◇◇◇ ADJ-GRADED

engender /ɪndʒendəʳ/ **engenders, engendering, engendered.** If someone or something **engenders** a particular feeling, atmosphere, or situation, they cause it to occur; a formal word. *It helps engender a sense of common humanity... Mr Bowles could engender delight in students and musicians alike.* ◆◇◇◇◇ VERB V n

engine /endʒɪn/ **engines** ◆◆◆◆◇

1 The **engine** of a car or other vehicle is the part that produces the power which makes the vehicle move. *He got into the driving seat and started the engine. ...an engine failure that forced a jetliner to crash-land in a field.* N-COUNT

2 An **engine** is also the large vehicle that pulls a railway train. *In 1941, the train would have been pulled by a steam engine.* N-COUNT

-engined /-endʒɪnd/. **-engined** combines with other words to show the number or type of engines that something has. *...the world's biggest twin-engined airliner. ...a petrol-engined Ford Transit.* COMB in ADJ

engineer /endʒɪnɪəʳ/ **engineers, engineering, engineered** ◆◆◆◇◇

1 An **engineer** is a person who uses scientific knowledge to design, construct, and maintain engines and machines or structures such as roads, railways, and bridges. • See also **chemical engineer, civil engineer, electrical engineer, sound engineer**. N-COUNT

2 An **engineer** is a person who repairs mechanical or electrical devices. *They send a service engineer to fix the disk drive.* N-COUNT

3 An **engineer** is a person who is responsible for maintaining the engine of a ship while it is at sea. N-COUNT

4 When a vehicle, bridge, or building **is engineered**, it is planned and constructed using scientific methods. *Many of Kuwait's spacious freeways were engineered by W S Atkins... He needed to make his car look different from its better designed and engineered rivals.* VB: usu passive be V-ed, V-ed

5 If you **engineer** an event or situation, you arrange for it to happen, in a clever or indirect way. *He could stand no more and engineered an escape... Some people believe that his murder was engineered by Stalin.* VERB V n

engineering /endʒɪnɪərɪŋ/. **Engineering** is the work involved in designing and constructing engines and machinery, or structures such as roads and bridges. **Engineering** is also the subject studied by people who want to do this work. *...the design and engineering of aircraft and space vehicles. ...graduates with degrees in engineering.* • See also **chemical engineering, civil engineering, electrical engineering, genetic engineering.** ◆◆◆◇◇ N-UNCOUNT

English /ɪŋglɪʃ/ ◆◆◆◆◇

1 **English** means belonging or relating to England, or to its people or language. It is also often used to mean belonging or relating to Great Britain, although many people object to this. *...the English way of life... English students are forced to learn too much too soon.* ADJ
► **The English** are English people. *The English don't care for people like that.* N-PLURAL: the N

2 **English** is the language spoken by people who live in Great Britain and Ireland, the United States, Canada, Australia, and many other countries. *Their knowledge of written English is certainly better... He uses tapes of this program to teach English. ...the English-speaking world.* N-UNCOUNT

3 See also **Queen's English**.

English breakfast, English breakfasts. An **English breakfast** is a breakfast consisting of cooked food such as bacon, eggs, sausages, and tomatoes. It also includes toast and tea or coffee. N-COUNT

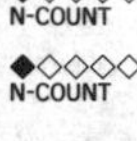

Englishman /ɪŋglɪʃmən/ **Englishmen.** An **Englishman** is a man who comes from England. ◆◇◇◇◇ N-COUNT

Englishwoman /ɪŋglɪʃwʊmən/ **Englishwomen.** An **Englishwoman** is a woman who comes from England. ◆◇◇◇◇ N-COUNT

engorged /ɪngɔːʳdʒd/. Something that is **engorged** is swollen, usually because it has been ADJ: oft ADJ *with* n filled with a particular fluid. *...the tissues become engorged with blood.*

engrave /ɪngreɪv/ **engraves, engraving, engraved.** ◆◇◇◇◇ VERB If you **engrave** something with a design or inscription, or if you **engrave** a design on it, you cut the design into its surface. *Your wedding ring can be engraved with a personal inscription at no extra cost... Harrods will also engrave your child's name on the side... I'm having 'John Law' engraved on the cap. ...a bottle engraved with her name. ...an engraved crystal goblet.* (be V-ed with n; V n on/in n; have n V-ed prep; V-ed; Also V n, V n with quote)

engraved /ɪngreɪvd/. ADJ: v-link ADJ *in/on/upon* n [PRAGMATICS] =etched If you say that something is **engraved** on your mind or memory or on your heart, you are emphasizing that you will never forget it, because it has made a very strong impression on you. *Her image is engraved upon my heart... The drowning at Chappaquiddick, now more than 20 years ago, is still engraved in the collective memory of America.*

engraver /ɪngreɪvəʳ/ **engravers.** N-COUNT An **engraver** is someone who cuts designs or inscriptions on metal, glass, or wood.

engraving /ɪngreɪvɪŋ/ **engravings**

1 N-COUNT An **engraving** is a picture or design that has been cut into a surface.

2 N-COUNT An **engraving** is a picture that has been printed from a plate on which designs have been cut. *...a color engraving of oranges and lemons.*

engrossed /ɪngroʊst/. ADJ-GRADED: usu v-link ADJ, usu ADJ *in* n If you are **engrossed** in something, it holds your attention completely. *Tony didn't notice because he was too engrossed in his work.*

engrossing /ɪngroʊsɪŋ/. ADJ-GRADED [PRAGMATICS] Something that is **engrossing** is very interesting and holds your attention completely. *He is an engrossing subject for a book.*

engulf /ɪngʌlf/ **engulfs, engulfing, engulfed** ◆◇◇◇◇

1 VERB (V n) If one thing **engulfs** another, it completely covers or hides it, often in a sudden and unexpected way. *A seven-year-old boy was found dead after a landslide engulfed a block of flats... The flat is engulfed in flames.*

2 VERB (V n) If a feeling or emotion **engulfs** you, you are strongly affected by it. *...the pain that engulfed him... He looked around his dark, cluttered office and was engulfed by a feeling of emptiness.*

enhance /ɪnhɑːns, -hæns/ **enhances, enhancing, enhanced.** ◆◆◆◇◇ VERB (V n) To **enhance** something means to improve its value, quality, or attractiveness. *They'll be keen to enhance their reputation abroad... The superb sets are enhanced by Bobby Crossman's marvellous costumes.*

enhancement /ɪnhɑːnsmənt, -hæns-/ **enhancements.** ◆◇◇◇◇ N-VAR: usu with supp, oft N *of* n The **enhancement** of something is the improvement of it in relation to its value, quality, or attractiveness; a formal word. *Music is merely an enhancement to the power of her words... He was concerned with the enhancement of the human condition.*

enhancer /ɪnhɑːnsəʳ, -hæns-/ **enhancers.** N-COUNT: usu n N An **enhancer** is a substance or a device which makes a particular thing look, taste, or feel better. *Cinnamon is an excellent flavour enhancer.*

enigma /ɪnɪgmə/ **enigmas.** ◆◇◇◇◇ N-COUNT: usu sing =mystery If you describe something or someone as an **enigma**, you mean they are mysterious or difficult to understand. *Iran remains an enigma for the outside world... ...a story which makes clear the modern enigma of spirituality.*

enigmatic /enɪgmætɪk/. ◆◇◇◇◇ ADJ-GRADED Someone or something that is **enigmatic** is mysterious and difficult to understand. *Haley studied her, an enigmatic smile on his face... She starred in one of Welles's most enigmatic films.* ♦ **enigmatically** ADV-GRADED: ADV after v, ADV -ed/adj *'Corbiere didn't deserve this,' she said enigmatically.*

enjoin /ɪndʒɔɪn/ **enjoins, enjoining, enjoined**

1 VERB (V n to-inf; V n; V-ed) If you **enjoin** someone to do something, you order them to do it. If you **enjoin** an action or attitude, you order people to do it or have it. This is a formal use. *She enjoined me strictly not to tell anyone else... It is true that Islam enjoins tolerance; there's no doubt about that... The positive neutrality enjoined on the force has now been overtaken by events.*

2 VERB (V n *from* -ing/n; V n) In American English, if a judge **enjoins** someone from doing something, they order them not to do it. If a judge **enjoins** an action, they order people not to do it. This is a formal use. *The judge enjoined Varityper from using the ad in any way. ...a preliminary injunction enjoining the practice.*

enjoy /ɪndʒɔɪ/ **enjoys, enjoying, enjoyed** ◆◆◆◆◇

1 VERB (V n/-ing) If you **enjoy** something, you find pleasure and satisfaction in doing it or experiencing it. *Ross had always enjoyed the company of women... He was a guy who enjoyed life to the full... I enjoyed playing cricket.*

2 VERB (V pron-refl) If you **enjoy** yourself, you do something that you like doing or you take pleasure in the situation that you are in. *I must say I am really enjoying myself at the moment.*

3 VERB (V n) If you **enjoy** something such as a right, benefit, or privilege, you have it; a formal word. *The average German will enjoy 40 days' paid holiday this year... He enjoys a reputation for honesty.*

enjoyable /ɪndʒɔɪəbəl/. ◆◆◇◇◇ ADJ-GRADED Something that is **enjoyable** gives you pleasure. *It was much more enjoyable than I had expected. ...the most enjoyable activity they did.* ♦ **enjoyably** ADV-GRADED: ADV adj, ADV with v *...an enjoyably nasty thriller. ...the place in which he has enjoyably spent his working life.*

enjoyment /ɪndʒɔɪmənt/. ◆◇◇◇◇ N-UNCOUNT: oft N *of* n **Enjoyment** is the feeling of pleasure and satisfaction that you have when you do or experience something that you like. *I apologise if your enjoyment of the movie was spoiled. ...her enjoyment of the beauty of the countryside.*

enlarge /ɪnlɑːʳdʒ/ **enlarges, enlarging, enlarged** ◆◆◇◇◇

1 V-ERG (V n; V) When you **enlarge** something or when it **enlarges**, it becomes bigger. *...the plan to enlarge Ewood Park into a 30,000 all-seater stadium... The glands in the neck may enlarge.* ♦ **enlarged** ADJ-GRADED *The UN secretary-general yesterday recommended an enlarged peacekeeping force.*

2 VERB (V n) To **enlarge** a photograph means to develop a bigger print of it. *...newly-weds wishing to enlarge snaps of their big day.*

3 VERB =expand (V *on/upon* n; Also V) If you **enlarge** on something that has been mentioned, you give more details about it; a formal use. *Mr Dienstbier was enlarging on proposals he made last night... I wish to enlarge upon a statement made by Gary Docking.*

enlargement /ɪnlɑːʳdʒmənt/ **enlargements** ◆◇◇◇◇

1 N-UNCOUNT: usu with supp, oft N *of* n The **enlargement** of something is the process or result of making it bigger. *There is insufficient space for enlargement of the buildings. ...the Community's enlargement.*

2 N-COUNT An **enlargement** is a photograph that has been made bigger.

enlighten /ɪnlaɪtən/ **enlightens, enlightening, enlightened.** ◆◇◇◇◇ VB: no cont (V n) To **enlighten** someone means to give them more knowledge and greater understanding about something; a formal use. *A few dedicated doctors have fought for years to enlighten the profession... I cannot remember how the trains turned round to return to London. Could you please enlighten me?* ♦ **enlightening** ADJ-GRADED: usu ADJ n *A representative from Shaldon Wildlife Trust gave an enlightening talk on the work done at the animal park... It can be an enormously enlightening and exciting experience.*

enlightened /ɪnlaɪtənd/.  ◆◇◇◇◇ ADJ-GRADED: usu ADJ n [PRAGMATICS] If you describe someone or their attitudes as **enlightened**, you mean that they have sensible, modern attitudes and ways of dealing with things; used showing approval. *A number of enlightened landowners have recently set an example by making land available at less than normal market value. ...an enlightened policy.*

enlightenment /ɪnlaɪtənmənt/ ◆◇◇◇◇

1 N-UNCOUNT **Enlightenment** means the act of enlightening or the state of being enlightened. *Stella had a moment of enlightenment.*

2 N-UNCOUNT In some religions, **enlightenment** is a state in

which you understand the true nature of the world. *Meditation may bring not only a sense of deep peace, but also spiritual enlightenment.*

enlist /ɪnlɪst/ **enlists, enlisting, enlisted** ◆◇◇◇◇

1 If someone **enlists** or **is enlisted**, they join the army, navy, or air force. *Michael Hughes of Lackawanna, Pennsylvania, enlisted in the 82nd Airborne 20 years ago... He enlisted as a private in the Mexican War... Three thousand men were enlisted... He decided to enlist.*
V-ERG; V in n; V as n; be V-ed; V

2 If you **enlist** the help of someone, you persuade them to help or support you in doing something. *I had to cut down a tree and enlist the help of seven neighbours to get it out of the garden!... I've read that you've enlisted some 12-year-olds to help out in your campaign... The prince has also enlisted his two daughters in the effort to avoid the press.*
VERB; V n; V n to-inf

enlisted /ɪnlɪstɪd/. An **enlisted** man or woman is a member of the American army or navy who is below the rank of an officer.
ADJ: usu ADJ n

enlistment /ɪnlɪstmənt/ **enlistments**

1 Enlistment is the act of joining the army, navy, or air force. *Canadians seek enlistment in the US Marines because they don't see as much opportunity in the Canadian armed forces.*
N-UNCOUNT: also N in pl

2 Enlistment is the period of time for which someone is a member of one of the armed forces. *On completion of my term of enlistment I decided to leave and return to civilian life.*
N-VAR =service

enliven /ɪnlaɪvᵊn/ **enlivens, enlivening, enlivened.** To **enliven** events, situations, or people means to make them more lively or cheerful. *I love the way a good flirtation can enliven the most mundane situation... Even the most boring meeting was enlivened by Dan's presence.*
◆◇◇◇◇ VERB; V n

en masse /ɒn mæs/. If a group of people do something **en masse**, they do it all together and at the same time. *The people marched en masse. ...the arrival en masse of the Latin American delegates.*
◆◇◇◇◇ ADV: ADV after v, n ADV

enmeshed /ɪnmeʃt/. If you are **enmeshed** in something or with something, usually something bad, you are involved in it and you cannot easily escape from it. *The way the European Community is becoming increasingly enmeshed in the Yugoslav crisis. ...as her life gets enmeshed with Andrew's.*
ADJ-GRADED: v-link ADJ, usu ADJ *in/with* n; PRAGMATICS

enmity /enmɪti/ **enmities. Enmity** is a long-lasting feeling of hatred towards someone. *I think there is an historic enmity between them... President Mitterrand arrived in Hanoi yesterday to bury old colonial and cold war enmities.*
N-VAR: usu with supp, oft N *between* pl-n

ennoble /ɪnnoʊbᵊl/ **ennobles, ennobling, ennobled**

1 Something that **ennobles** someone or something makes them more dignified and morally better; a literary use. *Instead, our focus should be on the enduring fundamental principles of life that ennoble mankind.* ♦ **ennobling** *...lofty rhetoric about the ennobling and civilizing power of education.*
VERB; V n; ADJ-GRADED

2 If someone **is ennobled**, they are made a member of the nobility; a formal use. *...the son of a financier who had been ennobled for arranging an important government loan in 1836. ...the newly ennobled Lord Archer.*
VB: usu passive; be V-ed; V-ed

ennui /ɒnwiː/. **Ennui** is a feeling of tiredness, boredom, and dissatisfaction; a literary word.
N-UNCOUNT

enormity /ɪnɔːʳmɪti/ **enormities**

1 If you refer to the **enormity** of something that you consider to be a problem or difficulty, you are referring to its very great size, extent, or seriousness. *I was numbed by the enormity of the responsibility... He was anxious about the enormity of the task ahead.*
N-UNCOUNT: usu *the* N *of* n; PRAGMATICS

2 If you refer to the **enormity** of an event, you are emphasizing that it is terrible and frightening. *It makes no sense to belittle the enormity of the disaster which has occurred.*
N-UNCOUNT: usu N *of* n; PRAGMATICS

3 An **enormity** is an action that is considered totally unacceptable; a formal use. *...the enormities they committed. ...the enormity of what slavery meant.*
N-COUNT: oft N *of* n

enormous /ɪnɔːʳməs/ ◆◆◆◇◇

1 Something that is **enormous** is extremely large in size or amount. *The main bedroom is enormous... There is, of course, an enormous amount to see.*
ADJ-GRADED

2 You can use **enormous** to emphasize the great degree or extent of something. *It was an enormous disappointment. ...his enormous capacity for brutality.* ♦ **enormously** *This book was enormously influential... The new database will help horse breeders enormously.*
ADJ: usu ADJ n; PRAGMATICS; ADV: ADV adj, ADV with v

enough /ɪnʌf/ ◆◆◆◆◆

1 Enough means as much as you need or as much as is necessary. *They had enough cash for a one-way ticket... There aren't enough tents to shelter them from the start of the rainy season.* ▶ Also an adverb. *I was old enough to work and earn money... Do you believe that sentences for criminals are tough enough at present?... She graduated with high enough marks to apply for university.* ▶ Also a pronoun. *Although the UK says efforts are being made, they are not doing enough.* ▶ Also a quantifier. *All parents worry about whether their child is getting enough of the right foods.* ▶ Also an adjective. *It was downright panic – the frozen expressions on the faces of the actors was proof enough of that.*
DET: DET n-uncount/pl-n; ADV: adj/adv ADV, ADV after v, oft ADV to-inf; PRON; QUANT: QUANT *of* def-n; ADJ: n ADJ

2 If you say that something is **enough**, you mean that you do not want it to continue any longer or get any worse. *I met him only the once, and that was enough... I think I have said enough... You've got enough to think about for the moment.* ▶ Also a quantifier. *Ann had heard enough of this... He had messed up enough of these occasions to give rise to some anxieties.* ▶ Also a determiner. *I've had enough problems with the police, I don't need this... Would you shut up, please! I'm having enough trouble with these children!* ▶ Also an adverb. *I'm serious, things are difficult enough as they are.*
PRON; QUANT: QUANT *of* def-n; DET: DET pl-n/n-uncount; ADV: adj ADV

3 You can also use **enough** to say that something is the case to a moderate or fairly large degree. *Winter is a common enough German surname... I got this phone call from a gentleman, who seemed sincere enough... The rest of the evening passed pleasantly enough.*
ADV: adj/adv ADV

4 You use **enough** in expressions such as **strangely enough** and **interestingly enough** to indicate that you think a fact is strange or interesting. *Strangely enough, the last thing he thought of was his beloved Tanya... Her latest conquest is an Italian who, interestingly enough, doesn't speak a word of his native language.*
ADV: adv ADV with cl

5 If you say **'enough is enough'**, you mean that you want something that is happening to stop. *Stop asking questions! You should know when enough is enough.*
PHRASES; V inflects

6 If you say that you **have had enough**, you mean that you are unhappy with a situation and you want it to stop. *I've had enough – there are limits even for the patience of a saint!... I had had enough of other people for one night.*
V inflects, oft PHR *of* n

7 If you say **'enough said'**, you mean that what you have just said is sufficient to make a point clear, and that there is no need to say any more. *It's about a girl from Liverpool. Enough said... My husband is a jazz musician. Enough said.*
CONVENTION; PRAGMATICS; =say no more

8 You say **'that's enough'** to tell someone, especially a child, to stop behaving in a silly, noisy, or unpleasant way.
CONVENTION; PRAGMATICS

9 • **fair enough**: see **fair.** • **sure enough**: see **sure.**

enquire /ɪnkwaɪəʳ/. See **inquire.**

enquirer /ɪnkwaɪərəʳ/. See **inquirer.**

enquiry /ɪnkwaɪəri/. See **inquiry.**

enrage /ɪnreɪdʒ/ **enrages, enraging, enraged.** If you **are enraged** by something, it makes you extremely angry. *Craig Tibbles, a tree surgeon, was enraged by news of plans to demolish the pub... He enraged the government by renouncing the agreement.* ♦ **enraged** *I began getting more and more enraged at my father... The enraged crowd stoned the car, then set it on fire.*
◆◇◇◇◇ VERB; be V-ed by n; V n; ADJ-GRADED

enrapture /ɪnræptʃəʳ/ **enraptures, enrapturing, enraptured.** If something or someone
VERB =enchant

enraptures you, you think they are wonderful or fascinating; a literary word. *The place at once enraptured me... The 20,000-strong audience listened, enraptured... He played to an enraptured audience at the Queen Elizabeth Hall.* Vn V-ed

enrich /ɪnrɪtʃ/ **enriches, enriching, enriched** ◆◇◇◇◇
1 To **enrich** something means to improve its quality, usually by adding something to it. *An extended family enriches life in many ways... It is important to enrich the soil prior to planting.* ♦ **-enriched** *...nutrient-enriched water.* VERB Vn COMB in ADJ
2 To **enrich** someone means to increase the amount of money that they have. *He will drain, rather than enrich, the country... Those who know how to use the system can enrich themselves at the expense of the very people who work for those companies.* VERB Vn
3 To **enrich** a nuclear fuel such as uranium means to increase the number of atoms of a particular kind in it, so that it can be used to produce more energy or a greater explosion; a technical term. *It was actually used for enriching uranium to weapons-grade levels.* VERB Vn

enrichment /ɪnrɪtʃmənt/. **Enrichment** is the act of enriching someone or something or the state of being enriched. *...with all the different groups contributing to the enrichment of society.* ◆◇◇◇◇ N-UNCOUNT: usu with supp

enrol /ɪnroʊl/ **enrols, enrolling, enrolled;** spelled **enroll** in American English. If you **enrol** or **are enrolled** on a course, you officially join it and pay a fee for it. *Cherny was enrolled at the University in 1945... She enrolled on a local Women Into Management course... At 33 he enrolled in a glass-making degree course at London's Royal College of Art... I thought I'd enrol you with an art group at the school.* ◆◇◇◇◇ V-ERG be V-ed prep V prep V n prep Also V

enrolment /ɪnroʊlmənt/ **enrolments;** spelled **enrollment** in American English.
1 **Enrolment** is the act of enrolling at an institution or on a course. *A fee is charged for each year of study and is payable at enrolment.* N-UNCOUNT
2 An **enrolment** is the number of people who are enrolled at an institution or on a course. *By 1922 the public schools had an enrolment of nearly 16,000 students.* N-COUNT: usu sing

en route /ɒn ruːt/. See **route**.

ensconced /ɪnskɒnst/. If you are **ensconced** somewhere, you are settled there firmly or comfortably and have no intention of moving or leaving. *Brian was ensconced behind the bar... She looked at Miss Melville, snugly ensconced among her new friends.* ADJ: v-link ADJ prep/adv

ensemble /ɒnsɒmbəl/ **ensembles** ◆◇◇◇◇
1 An **ensemble** is a group of musicians, actors, or dancers who regularly perform together. *...an ensemble of young musicians... He has also formed an exciting ensemble from his dancers.* N-COUNT: usu sing
2 In the arts, **ensemble** acting or playing is the fact or technique of playing or performing well together; a technical use. *Foote's most recent play, 'Dividing the Estate,' is an ensemble piece.* ADJ: ADJ n
3 An **ensemble** of things or people is a group of things or people considered as a whole rather than as separate individuals; a formal use. *The state is an ensemble of political and social structures.* N-COUNT: usu sing, oft N of n =collection
4 An **ensemble** is a set of clothes which have been chosen to look nice together; a formal use. *...elegant designs, including navy and white ensembles and extravagant feathered hats.* N-COUNT: usu sing =outfit

enshrine /ɪnʃraɪn/ **enshrines, enshrining, enshrined.** If something such as an idea or a right **is enshrined** in something such as a constitution or law, it is protected by it. *His new relationship with Germany is enshrined in a new non-aggression treaty... The apartheid system which enshrined racism in law still existed.* ◆◇◇◇◇ VERB be V-ed in n V n prep

enshroud /ɪnʃraʊd/ **enshrouds, enshrouding, enshrouded.** To **enshroud** something means to cover it completely so that it can no longer be seen; a literary word. *...dispiriting clouds that enshrouded us in twilight. ...the culture of secrecy which enshrouds our politics.* VERB V n in n V n

ensign /ensaɪn, ensən/ **ensigns** ◆◇◇◇◇
1 An **ensign** is a flag flown on a ship to show what country the ship belongs to. N-COUNT
2 An **ensign** is a junior officer in the United States Navy. *He had been a naval ensign stationed off Cuba. ...Ensign Smith.* N-COUNT; N-TITLE

enslave /ɪnsleɪv/ **enslaves, enslaving, enslaved**
1 To **enslave** someone means to make them into a slave. *They've been enslaved and had to do what they were told... I'd die myself before I'd let anyone enslave your folk ever again. ...George Gordon, born to an enslaved African mother and European landowner-farmer.* VERB be V-ed V n V-ed
2 To **enslave** a person or society means to trap them in a situation from which they cannot escape. *...the various cultures, cults and religions that have enslaved human beings for untold years... It would be a tragedy if, instead of that liberation, both sexes were enslaved, as men have always been, to the god of work.* VERB V n be V-ed to n Also V n to n

enslavement /ɪnsleɪvmənt/
1 **Enslavement** is the act of making someone into a slave or the state of being a slave. *The enslavement of African people must be the biggest crime in the whole of history... Her book about her experience of enslavement contributed to the abolition of the British Slave Trade.* N-UNCOUNT: oft N of n
2 **Enslavement** is the state of being caught or trapped in a situation from which it is difficult to escape. *...the analysis of women's enslavement to appearance. ...the enslavement to technology.* N-UNCOUNT: oft poss N, adj N, N to n

ensnare /ɪnsneəʳ/ **ensnares, ensnaring, ensnared**
1 If you **ensnare** someone, you gain power or control over them, especially by using dishonest or deceitful methods. *Feminism is simply another device to ensnare women... We find ourselves ensnared in employment acts which do not help resolve industrial disputes.* VERB V n V-ed
2 If an animal **is ensnared**, it is caught in a trap or snare. *The spider must wait for prey to be ensnared on its web... Fiona's foot ensnared itself in a trailing root.* VERB be V-ed on/in n V n on/in n

ensue /ɪnsjuː, AM suː/ **ensues, ensuing, ensued.** If something **ensues**, it happens immediately after another event, usually as a result of it. *If the Europeans did not reduce subsidies, a trade war would ensue... A brief but embarrassing silence ensued.* ◆◇◇◇◇ VB: no cont =follow V

ensuing /ɪnsjuːɪŋ, AM -suː-/ ◆◇◇◇◇
1 **Ensuing** events happen immediately after other events. *The ensuing argument had been bitter. ...any ensuing problems.* ADJ: ADJ n
2 **Ensuing** months or years follow the time you are talking about. *The two companies grew tenfold in the ensuing ten years.* ADJ: det ADJ

en suite /ɒn swiːt/. If a bedroom has an **en suite** bathroom, there is a bathroom next to the bedroom which can only be reached by a door in the bedroom, and which is intended only to be used by the people using that bedroom. An **en suite** bedroom has an en suite bathroom. *The master bedroom has its own en suite bathroom. ...a small hotel with 14 en suite bedrooms.* ADJ: ADJ n

ensure /ɪnʃʊəʳ/ **ensures, ensuring, ensured.** To **ensure** something, or to **ensure** that something happens, means to make certain that it happens; a formal word. *Britain's negotiators had ensured that the treaty which resulted was a significant change in direction... Ensure that it is written into your contract... South Africa's parliament has decided to abolish the President's Council, which ensures the supremacy of the National Party.* ◆◆◆◆◇ VERB V that V n

entail /ɪnteɪl/ **entails, entailing, entailed.** If one thing **entails** another, it involves it or causes it; a formal word. *Such a decision would entail a huge political risk in the midst of the presidential campaign... The changed outlook entails higher economic growth than was previously assumed... The job of a choreologist entails teaching dancers* ◆◇◇◇◇ VERB V n V -ing V n -ing *the technique and performance of dance movements... I'll never accept parole because that entails me accepting guilt.*

entangle /ɪntæŋgəl/ **entangles, entangling, entangled** ◆◇◇◇◇

1 If something **is entangled** in something such as a rope, wire, or net, it is caught in it very firmly. *Unfortunately, he managed to entangle his large feet with the small rudder bar.* ♦ **entangled** *Divers battled for hours to try to free a whale that became entangled in crab nets.* VERB; V n *with/in* n; Also V n; ADJ: oft ADJ *in/with* n

2 If something **entangles** you in problems or difficulties, it causes you to become involves in problems or difficulties from which it is hard to escape. *That kind of bill is sure to entangle the members in endless wrangling.* ♦ **entangled** *People in more primitive stages of development are less entangled in mental activities and problems which exist in more progressive societies.* VERB; V n *in/with* n; ADJ-GRADED: v-link ADJ, oft ADJ *in/with* n

entanglement /ɪntæŋgəlmənt/ **entanglements**

1 An **entanglement** is a complicated or adulterous sexual relationship; used showing disapproval. *Many women lurch from one entanglement to the next.* N-COUNT; PRAGMATICS

2 You can refer to a difficult or complicated situation as an **entanglement**; especially if you think it involves deception or illegal or immoral actions. *They see the inclusion of ground forces as a military and political entanglement the Government probably doesn't want... The legal entanglements of Noriega do not end in Miami.* N-VAR

3 If objects become entangled, you can refer to this as **entanglement**. *The main tow cable was clipped to the underside of the rear fuselage to avoid entanglement with the propeller. ...a barrier with barbed wire entanglements.* N-VAR

entente /ɒntɒnt/ **ententes.** An **entente** or an **entente cordiale** is a friendly agreement between two or more countries. *The French entente with Great Britain had already been significantly extended... Electoral pacts would not work, but an entente cordiale might.* N-VAR

enter /entər/ **enters, entering, entered** ◆◆◆◆◇

1 When you **enter** a place such as a room or building, you go into it or come into it; a formal use. *He entered the room briskly and stood near the door... Before entering the bathroom, he emptied his dirty laundry into the hamper... As soon as I entered, they stopped and turned my way.* VERB; V n; V

2 If you **enter** an organization or institution, you start to work there or become a member of it. *He entered the BBC as a general trainee... She entered a convent.* VERB; V n

3 If something new **enters** your mind, you suddenly think about it. *Whenever thoughts of his baby daughter enter his mind a magnetic smile appears on Jeremy's face... Dreadful doubts began to enter my mind.* VERB; =cross; V n

4 If you say it did not **enter** your head that something was the case, you mean that you did not think of that thing although you should have done. *It never enters his mind that anyone is better than him... Though it had always been within her power to detach herself, it had not seriously entered her head to do so.* VB: with neg; *it* V n that; *it* V n to-inf

5 If someone or something **enters** a particular situation or period of time, they start to be in it or part of it. *China enters a new five-year plan period next year. ...as the war enters its second month... A million young people enter the labour market each year... Tragedy entered the picture when their son Rudolph committed suicide at Mayerling... The phrase has already entered the language.* VERB; V n

6 If you **enter** a competition, race, or examination, you officially state that you will compete or take part in it. *I run so well I'm planning to enter some races... As a boy soprano he entered for many competitions, winning several gold medals... To enter, simply complete the coupon on page 150.* VERB; V n; V *for* n; V

7 If you **enter** someone for a race or competition, you officially state that they will compete or take part in it. *His wife Marie secretly entered him for the Championship. ...some of the 150 projects entered for the awards.* VERB; V n *for* n; V-ed; Also V n

8 If you **enter** something in a notebook, register, or financial account, you write it down. *Each week she meticulously entered in her notebooks all sums received... Prue entered the passage in her notebook, then read it aloud again.* VERB; V n with prep/adv; V n prep/adv; Also V n

9 To **enter** information into a computer or database means to record it there, for example by typing it on a keyboard. *When a baby is born, they enter that baby's name into the computer... Postcodes will be entered into the statisticians' computers... A lot less time is now spent entering the data.* VERB; V n *into* n; V n

enter into PHRASAL VERB

1 If you **enter into** something such as an agreement, discussion, or relationship with someone, you become involved in it. You can also say that two people **enter into** something. A formal expression. *I have not entered into any financial agreements with them... We entered into meaningful discussions with them weeks ago... There has been some talk recently that the United States and Canada may enter into an agreement that would allow easier access to jobs across the border. ...when a mutually beneficial contract is freely entered into by two adults... No correspondence will be entered into.* RECIP; V P n *with* n; pl-n V n; *be* V-ed P (non-recip)

2 If one thing **enters into** another, it is a factor in it; a formal expression. *There were also other factors that entered into the orchestration.* V P n

enterprise /entərpraɪz/ **enterprises** ◆◆◆◇◇

1 An **enterprise** is a company or business, often a small one. *There are plenty of small industrial enterprises. ...the integration of farming enterprises.* N-COUNT: usu with supp, oft adj N

2 An **enterprise** is something new, difficult, or important that you do or try to do. *...the first Director of such a novel enterprise... Horse breeding is indeed a risky enterprise.* N-COUNT: usu supp N; =venture

3 **Enterprise** is the activity of managing companies and businesses and starting new ones. *He is still involved in voluntary work promoting local enterprise. ...a national program of subsidies to private enterprise.* N-UNCOUNT: usu supp N

4 **Enterprise** is the ability to think of new and effective things to do, together with an eagerness to do them; used showing approval. *...the spirit of enterprise worthy of a free and industrious people. ...the group's lack of enterprise.* N-UNCOUNT

enterprising /entərpraɪzɪŋ/. An **enterprising** person is willing to try out new, unusual ways of doing or achieving something. *Debra is a very enterprising young black business-woman who is involved in a lot of activities... Some enterprising members found ways of reducing their expenses or raising their incomes.* ◆◇◇◇◇ ADJ-GRADED: usu ADJ n

entertain /entərteɪn/ **entertains, entertaining, entertained** ◆◆◆◇◇

1 If a performer, performance, or activity **entertains** you, it amuses you, interests you, or gives you pleasure. *...games and ideas to entertain children... They were entertained by top singers, dancers and celebrities... Children's television not only entertains but also teaches.* ♦ **entertaining** *To generate new money the sport needs to be more entertaining. ...this is a surprisingly entertaining film... Miro is the most inventive and entertaining of surrealist painters.* VERB; V n; V; ADJ-GRADED

2 If you **entertain** people, you give them food and hospitality, for example by inviting them to your house. *I don't like to entertain guests anymore... You weren't allowed to entertain men in your rooms even with a chaperone... The Monroes continued to entertain extravagantly.* ♦ **entertaining** *...a cosy area for entertaining and relaxing.* VERB; V n; V; N-UNCOUNT

3 If you **entertain** an idea or suggestion, you allow yourself to consider it as possible or as worth thinking about seriously; a formal use. *I feel how foolish I am to entertain doubts... I wouldn't entertain the idea of such an unsociable job.* VERB; V n

entertainer /entərteɪnər/ **entertainers.** An **entertainer** is a person whose job is to entertain audiences, for example by telling jokes, singing, ◆◇◇◇◇ N-COUNT or dancing. *Some have called him the greatest entertainer of the twentieth century.*

entertainment /entəʳteɪnmənt/ **entertainments.** **Entertainment** consists of performances of plays and films, and activities such as reading and watching television, that give people pleasure. *...the world of entertainment and international stardom... There were feasts and banquets, theatrical entertainments and sporting competitions between local groups.* ◆◆◆◇◇ N-VAR

enthral /ɪnθrɔːl/ **enthrals, enthralling, enthralled;** the spellings **enthrall** and **enthralls** are used in American English. If you **are enthralled** by something, you enjoy it and give it your complete attention and interest. *The passengers were enthralled by the scenery... He enthralled audiences in Prague, Vienna, and Paris... In real-life, the band have memorable songs and a stage vigour that enthrals... The fans sat enthralled in the darkened cinema.* ◆◇◇◇◇ VERB =engross; be V-ed; V n; V; V-ed
♦ **enthralling** *...an enthralling race.* ADJ-GRADED

enthrone /ɪnθroʊn/ **enthrones, enthroning, enthroned**

1 When kings, queens, emperors, or bishops **are enthroned**, they officially take on their role during a ceremony in which they are placed on a throne; a formal use. *Emperor Akihito of Japan has been enthroned in Tokyo... He is expected to be enthroned early next year as the spiritual leader of the Church of England.* VB: usu passive; be V-ed; be V-ed as n

2 To **enthrone** an idea means to give it a prominent place in your life or thoughts because you think it is very important; a formal use. *He was forcing the State to enthrone a particular brand of modernism. ...the religious fundamentalism now enthroned in American life.* VERB; V n; V-ed

enthronement /ɪnθroʊnmənt/ **enthronements.** The **enthronement** of a king, queen, emperor, or bishop is a ceremony in which they officially take on their role. *...the enthronement of their new emperor.* N-COUNT: usu sing, usu with poss

enthuse /ɪnθjuːz, AM -θuːz/ **enthuses, enthusing, enthused** ◆◇◇◇◇

1 If you **enthuse** about something, you talk about it in a way that shows how excited and thrilled you are about it. *Elizabeth David enthuses about the taste, fragrance and character of Provencal cuisine... 'I've found the most wonderful house to buy!' she enthused.* VERB; V about/over n; V with quote; Also V that

2 If you **are enthused** by something, it makes you feel excited and enthusiastic. *I was immediately enthused... Conference participants were clearly enthused by their presence, and the two women responded by listening intently... Find a hobby or interest which enthuses you.* VERB; be V-ed; V n; Also V

enthusiasm /ɪnθjuːziæzəm, AM -θuː-/ **enthusiasms** ◆◆◆◇◇

1 **Enthusiasm** is great eagerness to be involved in a particular activity which you like and enjoy or which you think is important. *The lack of enthusiasm for unification among most West Germans fills him with disappointment... Their skill, enthusiasm and running has got them in the team.* N-VAR: oft N for n/-ing

2 An **enthusiasm** is an activity or subject that interests you very much and that you spend a lot of time on. *Draw him out about his current enthusiasms and future plans.* N-COUNT: oft with poss =interest

enthusiast /ɪnθjuːziæst, AM -θuː-/ **enthusiasts.** An **enthusiast** is a person who is very interested in a particular activity or subject and who spends a lot of time on it. *He is a great sports enthusiast. ...keep-fit enthusiasts.* ◆◆◇◇◇ N-COUNT: usu with supp

enthusiastic /ɪnθjuːziæstɪk, AM -θuː-/. If you are **enthusiastic** about something, you show how much you like or enjoy it by the way that you behave and talk. *Tom was very enthusiastic about the place... Bob Dole seemed less than enthusiastic about the proposed move.* ◆◆◇◇◇ ADJ-GRADED: oft ADJ about n =excited
♦ **enthusiastically** /ɪnθjuːziæstɪkli, AM -θuː-/. *The announcement was greeted enthusiastically.* ADV-GRADED: usu ADV with v, also ADV adj

entice /ɪntaɪs/ **entices, enticing, enticed.** To **entice** someone to go somewhere or to do something means to try to persuade them to go to that place or to do that thing. *The high streets have been quiet this year as shops have battled to entice hard-pressed customers over the threshold... Child murderers in the past have very often carried photographs of young children to entice their victims away... They'll entice thousands of doctors to move from the cities to the rural areas by paying them better salaries.* ◆◇◇◇◇ VERB =lure; V n prep; V n with adv; V n to-inf; Also V n

enticement /ɪntaɪsmənt/ **enticements.** An **enticement** is something which persuades or tempts people to do a particular thing. *Among other enticements, they advertized that they would take guests to Ramsgate for the day.* N-VAR =inducement

enticing /ɪntaɪsɪŋ/. Something that is **enticing** is extremely attractive and tempts you to get it or to become involved with it. *A prospective premium of about 30 per cent on their initial investment is enticing. ...many enticing illustrations.* ◆◇◇◇◇ ADJ-GRADED
♦ **enticingly** *...laying out their stall enticingly.* ADV-GRADED

entire /ɪntaɪəʳ/. You use **entire** when you want to emphasize that you are referring to the whole of something, for example, the whole of a place, time, or population. *He had spent his entire life in China as a doctor... There are only 60 swimming pools in the entire country... The entire family was staring at him, waiting for him to speak... I cried the entire three weeks; I never stopped... The entire world must take notice of something like this.* ◆◆◆◆◇ ADJ: det ADJ PRAGMATICS =whole

entirely /ɪntaɪəʳli/ ◆◆◆◇◇

1 **Entirely** means completely and not just partly. *...an entirely new approach... Fraud is an entirely different matter... Their price depended almost entirely on their scarcity... I failed in my career as a writer of fiction entirely because of deficiencies in the education system.* ADV: ADV adj, ADV with v, ADV with cl/group =completely, totally

2 **Entirely** is also used to emphasize what you are saying. *I agree entirely... The official Chinese spokesman asserted that the coup was entirely a domestic affair of the Soviet people.* ADV: ADV with v, ADV group

3 People sometimes use the expression **not entirely** to reduce the force of a strong statement, especially a critical one. *They are not entirely happy with his criticism of the president... We shall see that this is not entirely true... She claimed the unemployment figures were not entirely unexpected... This government is not entirely free of suspicion.* ADV: not ADV, ADV group PRAGMATICS

entirety /ɪntaɪərɪti/. If something is used or affected **in its entirety**, the whole of it is used or affected. *The peace plan has not been accepted in its entirety by all parties. ...a number of cities were now to be bombed in their entirety.* ◆◇◇◇◇ PHRASE: PHR after v

entitle /ɪntaɪtəl/ **entitles, entitling, entitled** ◆◆◆◇◇

1 If you **are entitled** to something, you have the right to have it or do it. *If the warranty is limited, the terms may entitle you to a replacement or refund... They are entitled to first class travel... It entitles you to withdraw cash at two Post Offices of your choice.* VERB; V n to-inf

2 If the title of something such as a book, film, or painting is, for example, 'Sunrise', you can say that it **is entitled** 'Sunrise'. *Chomsky's review is entitled 'Psychology and Ideology'. ...a performance entitled 'United States'.* VB: usu passive; be V-ed quote; V-ed quote

entitlement /ɪntaɪtəlmənt/ **entitlements.** An **entitlement** to something is the right to have it or do it; a formal word. *They lose their entitlement to benefit when they start work.* ◆◇◇◇◇ N-VAR: oft N to n

entity /entɪti/ **entities.** An **entity** is something that exists separately from other things and has a clear identity of its own; a formal word. *...the earth as a living entity... North and South will remain separate entities within a commonwealth until the year 2000.* ◆◆◇◇◇ N-COUNT: usu supp N

entomb /ɪntuːm/ **entombs, entombing, entombed**

1 If something **is entombed**, it is buried or permanently trapped by something; a formal word. *The city was entombed in volcanic lava... The Tel, an artificial mountain, entombs Jericho's ancient past.* VERB; be V-ed in n; V n; Also V n in n

2 When a person's dead body **is entombed**, it is VB: usu passive

buried in a grave or put into a tomb; a formal use. *Neither of them had any idea how long the body had been entombed.* be V-ed

entomology /entəmɒlədʒi/. **Entomology** is the study of insects. ♦ **entomologist** /entəmɒlədʒɪst/ **entomologists** ...*a research entomologist.* N-UNCOUNT N-COUNT

entourage /ɒntʊrɑːʒ/ **entourages.** A famous or important person's **entourage** is the group of assistants, servants, or other people who travel with them. *Peter the Great shocked London by his wild behaviour and that of his entourage when he visited England in 1698... He was accompanied by an entourage of a dozen police officers.* ◆◇◇◇◇ N-COUNT: usu poss N, N *of* n

entrails /entreɪlz/. The **entrails** of people or animals are their inside parts, especially their intestines. *He cut out the steaming entrails.* N-PLURAL =innards

entrance 1 noun uses

entrance /entrəns/ **entrances** ◆◆◆◇◇

1 The **entrance** to a place is the way into it, for example a door or gate. *Beside the entrance to the church, turn right... He was driven out of a side entrance with his hand covering his face... A marble entrance hall leads to a sitting room.* N-COUNT: oft N *to/into/of* n =entry

2 You can refer to someone's arrival in a place as their **entrance**, especially when you think that they are trying to be noticed and admired. *If she had noticed her father's entrance, she gave no indication.* N-COUNT: usu sing, usu with poss =entry

3 When a performer makes his or her **entrance** on to the stage, he or she comes on to the stage. *He made his entrance into the parade ring.* N-COUNT: usu sing, usu with poss, oft N *on/into* n

4 If you gain **entrance** to a particular place, you manage to get in there; a fairly formal use. *Hewitt had gained entrance to the Hall by pretending to be a heating engineer.* N-UNCOUNT: oft N *to* n =entry

5 If you gain **entrance** to a particular profession, society, or institution, you are accepted as a member of it. *Entrance to universities and senior secondary schools was restricted. ...entrance exams for the French civil service.* N-UNCOUNT: oft N *to/into* n

6 If you make an **entrance** into a particular activity or system, you succeed in becoming involved in it. *The acquisition helped BCCI make its initial entrance into the US market. ...his entrance into politics in 1933.* N-SING: oft N *into* n =entry

entrance 2 verb use

entrance /ɪntrɑːns, -træns/ **entrances, entrancing, entranced.** If something or someone **entrances** you, they cause you to feel delight and wonder, often so that all your attention is taken up and you cannot think about anything else. *As soon as I met Dick, he entranced me because he has a lovely voice... Last Friday she entranced the audience with her classical Indian singing.* ◆◇◇◇◇ VERB =enchant V n

♦ **entranced** *I became entranced with the idea... For the next three hours we sat entranced as the train made its way up the mountains... He is entranced by the kindness of her smile.* ADJ-GRADED: v-link ADJ, ADJ after v, ADJ n

♦ **entrancing** *The light reflected off the stone, creating a golden glow he found entrancing.* ADJ-GRADED

entrance fee, entrance fees. An **entrance fee** is a sum of money which you pay before you go into somewhere such as a cinema or museum, or which you have to pay in order to join an organization or institution. *The entrance fee is £9.50.* N-COUNT

entrance hall, entrance halls. An **entrance hall** is the area behind the main door of a large house, hotel, or other large building. Rooms, staircases, and corridors are reached from the entrance hall. N-COUNT =foyer

entrant /entrənt/ **entrants** ◆◇◇◇◇

1 An **entrant** is a person who has recently become a member of an institution such as a university. ...*a young school entrant.* N-COUNT: with supp

2 An **entrant** is a person who is taking part in a competition. *All items entered for the competition must be the entrant's own work.* N-COUNT =contestant

entrap /ɪntræp/ **entraps, entrapping, entrapped.** If you **entrap** someone or something, you trick or deceive them and make them believe or do something wrong. *The police have been given extra powers to entrap drug traffickers... He overturned the conviction, saying the defendant was entrapped... He claimed the government had entrapped him into doing something that he would not have done otherwise.* VERB V n V n *into* n/-ing

entrapment /ɪntræpmənt/. **Entrapment** is the practice of arresting someone by using unfair or illegal methods; legal term. *It was an entrapment, a ruse plotted by rival Russian naval officers to sully his honor.* N-UNCOUNT

entreat /ɪntriːt/ **entreats, entreating, entreated.** If you **entreat** someone to do something, you ask them very humbly and seriously to do it; a formal word. *Trevor Steven entreated them to delay their departure... 'Call me Earl!' he entreated... I earnestly entreat that we don't get caught out again.* VERB =implore V n to-inf V with quote V that Also V n, V n with quote

entreaty /ɪntriːti/ **entreaties.** An **entreaty** is a humble, serious request; a formal word. *The FA has resisted all entreaties to pledge its support to the campaign.* N-VAR: oft N *to* n

entrée /ɒntreɪ/ **entrées;** also spelled **entree.**

1 If you have an **entrée** to a social group, you are accepted and made to feel welcome by them. *She had an entree into the city's cultivated society.* N-COUNT: oft N *into* n

2 At restaurants or formal banquets, the **entrée** is the main course, or sometimes a dish before the main course. *Dinner features a hot entrée of chicken, veal, or lamb.* N-COUNT

entrench /ɪntrentʃ/ **entrenches, entrenching, entrenched.** If something such as power, a custom, or an idea **is entrenched**, it is firmly established, so that it would be difficult to change it. ...*a series of measures designed to entrench democracy and the rule of law... The Hong Kong entrepreneurs are now using the last years of British colonialism to entrench themselves in Hong Kong's expanding service sector.* ◆◇◇◇◇ VERB V n V pron-refl

♦ **entrenched** *The recession remains deeply entrenched.* ADJ-GRADED

entrenchment /ɪntrentʃmənt/ **entrenchments**

1 **Entrenchments** are a series of trenches which are dug for defence by soldiers in war. N-COUNT: usu pl

2 **Entrenchment** means the firm establishment of a system or your own position in a situation. *In South Africa, the entrenchment of democratic norms will be that much harder.* N-UNCOUNT

entrepreneur /ɒntrəprənɜːʳ/ **entrepreneurs.** An **entrepreneur** is a person who sets up businesses and business deals. ◆◆◇◇◇ N-COUNT

entrepreneurial /ɒntrəprənɜːriəl/. **Entrepreneurial** means having the qualities that are needed for people to succeed as entrepreneurs. ...*her prodigious entrepreneurial flair.* ◆◇◇◇◇ ADJ-GRADED: usu ADJ n

entrepreneurship /ɒntrəprənɜːʳ/. **Entrepreneurship** is the state of being an entrepreneur, or the activities associated with being an entrepreneur. N-UNCOUNT

entropy /entrəpi/. **Entropy** is a state of disorder, confusion, and disorganization; a formal word. N-UNCOUNT

entrust /ɪntrʌst/ **entrusts, entrusting, entrusted.** If you **entrust** something important to someone or **entrust** them with it, you make them responsible for looking after it or dealing with it. *If parents wanted to entrust their prized child to the best surgeons, they traveled to Bologna's famous medical school... He was forced to entrust an assistant with the important task of testing and demonstrating aircraft to prospective customers... They can be entrusted to solve major national problems.* ◆◇◇◇◇ VERB V n *to* n V n *with* n be V-ed to-inf Also V *to* n n

entry /entri/ **entries** ◆◆◆◆◇

1 If you gain **entry** to a particular place, you are able to go in. *Bill was among the first to gain entry to Buckingham Palace when it opened to the public recently... Non-residents were refused entry into Lhasa without authority from their own district... The point of entry into Zambia would be the Chirundu border post... Entry to the museum is free. ...entry fees to places of scientific interest.* N-UNCOUNT: usu N *to/into* n =entrance

• The words **No Entry** are used on signs to indicate that you are not allowed to go into a particular area or go through a particular door or gate. PHRASE

2 You can refer to someone's arrival in a place as their **entry**, especially when you think that they are N-COUNT: usu sing, usu with poss

trying to be noticed and admired. *He made his triumphal entry into Mexico City.* [=entrance]

3 Someone's **entry** into a particular society or group is their joining of it. *He described Britain's entry into the European Exchange Rate Mechanism as an historic move. ...people who cannot gain entry to the owner-occupied housing sector.* [N-UNCOUNT: oft N *into/to* n =entrance]

4 An **entry** in a diary, account book, computer file, or reference book is a short piece of writing in it. *Violet's diary entry for 20 April 1917 records Brigit admitting to the affair... Many entries relate to the two world wars.* [N-COUNT]

5 A **entry** for a competition is a piece of work, for example a story or drawing, or the answers to a set of questions, which you complete in order to take part in the competition. *The closing date for entries is 31st December.* [N-COUNT]

6 Journalists sometimes use **entry** to refer to the total number of people taking part in an event or competition. For example, if a competition has an entry of twenty people, twenty people take part in it. *Prize-money of nearly £90,000 has attracted a record entry of 14 horses from Britain and Ireland... Our competition has attracted a huge entry.* [N-SING: with supp, oft N *of* n]

7 **Entry** in a competition is the act of taking part in it. *Entry to this competition is by invitation only. ...an entry form.* [N-UNCOUNT: oft n *in/to* n]

8 The **entry** to a place is the way into it, for example a door or gate. [N-COUNT: usu sing =entrance]

entwine /ɪntwaɪn/ **entwines, entwining, entwined**

1 If one thing **is entwined** with another thing, or if you **entwine** two things, the two things are twisted around each other. *His dazed eyes stare at the eels, which still writhe and entwine... Facing each other, the giraffes were managing to entwine their necks in the most astonishing manner... He entwined his fingers with hers. ...with silk ribbons and flowers entwined in their hair.* [V-RECIP-ERG; pl-n V; V pl-n; V n *with* n; V-ed; Also V *with* n, V n (non-recip)]

2 If two things **entwine** or **are entwined**, they closely resemble or are linked to each other, and they are difficult to separate or identify. *The book entwines the personal and the political to chart the history of four generations of the family... Once, years ago, he told me our lives should entwine.* [V-ERG =entangled; V pl-n; pl-n V] ♦ **entwined** *Fuji Heavy Industries, which makes Subaru cars, is becoming increasingly entwined with Nissan. ...the entwined lives of Dorothy Gale and Judy Garland.* [ADJ-GRADED: oft ADJ *with* n]

E number /iː nʌmbəʳ/ **E numbers.** In British English, **E numbers** are artificial substances which are added to some foods and drinks to improve their flavour or colour or to make them last longer. They are called 'E numbers' because they are represented in Europe by code names which begin with the letter 'E'. [N-COUNT]

enumerate /ɪnjuːməreɪt, AM -nuː-/ **enumerates, enumerating, enumerated.** When you **enumerate** a list of things, you name each one in turn. *I enumerate the work that will have to be done.* [VERB =itemize; V n]

enunciate /ɪnʌnsieɪt/ **enunciates, enunciating, enunciated**

1 When you **enunciate** a word or part of a word, you pronounce it clearly; a formal use. *His voice was harsh as he enunciated each word carefully... She enunciates very slowly and carefully.* [VERB; V n; V] ♦ **enunciation** /ɪnʌnsieɪʃᵊn/ *... his grammar always precise, his enunciation always perfect.* [N-UNCOUNT]

2 When you **enunciate** a thought, idea, or plan, you express it very clearly and precisely; a formal use. *He was ever ready to enunciate his views to all who would listen.* [VERB; V n] ♦ **enunciation** *...the enunciation of grand moral principles.* [N-UNCOUNT]

envelop /ɪnveləp/ **envelops, enveloping, enveloped.** If one thing **envelops** another, it covers or surrounds it completely. *That lovely, rich fragrant smell of the forest enveloped us... Perhaps, for an enveloping sense of well-being, we should live in round buildings.* [◆◇◇◇◇ VERB; V n; V-ing]

envelope /envəloʊp, ɒn-/ **envelopes.** An **envelope** is the rectangular paper cover in which you sent a letter to someone through the post. [◆◆◇◇◇ N-COUNT]

enviable /enviəbᵊl/. You describe something such as a quality as **enviable** when someone else has it and you wish that you had it too. *Japan, unlike other big economies, is in the enviable position of having a budget surplus... They have enviable reputations as athletes.* [◆◇◇◇◇ ADJ-GRADED: usu ADJ n]

envious /enviəs/. If you are **envious** of someone else, you envy them. *I don't think I'm envious of your success... Do I sound envious? I pity them, actually. ...envious thoughts.* [◆◇◇◇◇ ADJ-GRADED: oft ADJ *of* n] ♦ **enviously** *'You haven't changed,' I am often enviously told.* [ADV-GRADED: ADV with v]

environment /ɪnvaɪərənmənt/ **environments** [◆◆◆◆◇]

1 Someone's **environment** is all the circumstances, people, things, and events around them that influence their life. *Pupils in our schools are taught in a safe, secure environment... The moral characters of men are formed not by heredity but by environment... The twins were separated at birth and brought up in entirely different environments.* [N-VAR]

2 Your **environment** consists of the particular natural surroundings in which you live or exist, considered in relation to their physical characteristics or weather conditions. *If our environment cools, then messages from the skin alert the body's thermostat. ...the maintenance of a safe environment for marine mammals.* [N-COUNT: usu sing, with supp]

3 **The environment** is the natural world of land, sea, air, plants, and animals. *...Labour's spokesman on the environment. ...persuading people to respect the environment.* [N-SING: *the* N]

environmental /ɪnvaɪərənmentᵊl/ [◆◆◆◆◇]

1 **Environmental** means concerned with the protection of the natural world of land, sea, air, plants, and animals. *...economic and environmental legislation. ...the environmental claims being made for some products... Environmental groups plan to stage public protests during the conference.* [ADJ: ADJ n] ♦ **environmentally** *He veered away from the most environmentally sound option. ...the high price of environmentally friendly goods.* [ADV: ADV adj]

2 **Environmental** means relating to or caused by the surroundings in which someone lives or something exists. *It protects against environmental hazards such as wind and sun... The form the human family takes is a response to environmental pressures.* [ADJ: ADJ n]

environmentalism /ɪnvaɪərənmentᵊlɪzəm/. **Environmentalism** is used to describe actions and policies which show a concern with protecting and preserving the natural environment, for example, by preventing pollution. [N-UNCOUNT]

environmentalist /ɪnvaɪərənmentəlɪst/ **environmentalists.** An **environmentalist** is a person who is concerned with protecting and preserving the natural environment, for example by preventing pollution. [◆◆◇◇◇ N-COUNT]

environs /ɪnvaɪərənz/. The **environs** of a place consist of the area immediately surrounding it; a formal word. *...the environs of Paris... The town and its environs are inviting, with recreational attractions and art museums.* [N-PLURAL: with poss]

envisage /ɪnvɪzɪdʒ/ **envisages, envisaging, envisaged.** If you **envisage** something, you imagine that it is true, real, or likely to happen. *He envisages the possibility of establishing direct diplomatic relations in the future... He had never envisaged spending the whole of his working life in that particular job... Personally, I envisage them staying together.* [◆◆◇◇◇ VERB =imagine, envision; V n; V -ing; V n -ing; Also V that]

envision /ɪnvɪʒᵊn/ **envisions, envisioning, envisioned.** If you **envision** something, you envisage it; used mainly in American English. *In the future we envision a federation of companies... Most people do stop at this point, not envisioning that there is anything beyond.* [◆◇◇◇◇ VERB =imagine, envision; V n; V that; Also V wh]

envoy /envɔɪ/ **envoys** [◆◆◇◇◇]

1 An **envoy** is someone who is sent as a messenger, especially from one government or political group to another. [N-COUNT: with supp =emissary]

2 An **envoy** is a diplomat in an embassy who is immediately below the ambassador in rank. N-COUNT

envy /envi/ **envies, envying, envied** ◆◆◇◇◇

1 **Envy** is the feeling you have when you wish you could have the same thing or quality that someone else has. *Gradually he began to acknowledge his feelings of envy towards his mother... They gazed in a mixture of envy and admiration at the beauty of the statue.* N-UNCOUNT

2 If you **envy** someone, you wish that you had the same things or qualities that they have. *I don't envy the young ones who've become TV superstars and know no other world... I have a rich brother and a lot of people envy the fact... He envied Caroline her peace... 'You must've seen the world by now,' said Frannie, 'I envy you that.'* VERB Vn Vnn

3 If a thing or quality is **the envy of** someone, they wish very much that they could have or achieve it. *Britain is now the envy of the world's record companies. ...an economic expansion that was the envy of many other states.* N-SING: the N of n

4 • **green with envy**: see **green**.

enzyme /enzaɪm/ **enzymes.** An **enzyme** is a chemical substance that is found in living creatures which produces changes in other substances without being changed itself; a technical term in biology and medicine. ◆◆◇◇◇ N-COUNT

eon /iːɒn/. See **aeon**.

EP /iː piː/ **EPs.** An EP is a record which is designed to be played at either 33 rpm or 45 rpm and which lasts for about 8 minutes on each side. **EP** is an abbreviation for 'extended play'. ◆◇◇◇◇ N-COUNT

epaulette /epəlet/ **epaulettes;** spelled **epaulet** in American English. **Epaulettes** are decorations worn on the shoulders of certain uniforms, especially military ones. N-COUNT: usu pl

épée /eɪpeɪ/ **épées.** An **épée** is a thin, light sword that is used in the sport of fencing. N-COUNT

ephemera /ɪfemərə/

1 You can refer to things which last for only a short time as **ephemera**; a literary use. N-UNCOUNT

2 **Ephemera** is used to refer to things people collect such as old postcards, posters, and bus tickets which were only intended to last a short time when they were produced. *...one of Britains best known private collections of tickets and other printed ephemera. ...Victorian ephemera.* N-UNCOUNT: oft adj N

ephemeral /ɪfemərəl/. If you describe something as **ephemeral**, you mean that it lasts only for a very short time; a formal word. *He talked about the country's ephemeral unity being shattered by the defeat... These paintings are in some ways a reminder that earthly pleasures are ephemeral.* ADJ-GRADED =transient

epic /epɪk/ **epics** ◆◆◇◇◇

1 An **epic** is a long book, poem, or film, whose story extends over a long period of time or tells of great events. *...the Middle High German epic, 'Nibelungenlied', written about 1200... At three hours and 21 minutes, it is an over-long, standard Hollywood epic.* ▶ Also an adjective. *...epic narrative poems... Like 'Gone With The Wind' it's an unashamed epic romance.* N-COUNT: usu supp N; ADJ: usu ADJ n

2 If you describe something as **epic**, you mean that it is very impressive or ambitious, for example in its size or the length of time it lasts. *...Columbus's epic voyage of discovery.* ADJ: usu ADJ n

epicentre /episentəʳ/ **epicentres;** spelled **epicenter** in American English. The **epicentre** of an earthquake is the place on the earth's surface directly above the point where it starts, and is the place where it is felt most strongly. *The earthquake had its epicentre two-hundred kilometres north-east of the capital.* N-COUNT: usu with poss

epicure /epɪkjʊəʳ/ **epicures.** An **epicure** is someone who enjoys eating food that is of very good quality, especially unusual or rare food; a formal word. N-COUNT =gourmet

epicurean /epɪkjʊəriːən/. **Epicurean** food is of very good quality, especially unusual or rare food; a formal word. *Saddle of lamb is an epicurean dish for major celebrations.* ADJ: usu ADJ n

epidemic /epɪdemɪk/ **epidemics** ◆◆◇◇◇

1 If there is an **epidemic** of a particular disease somewhere, it affects a very large number of people there and spreads quickly to other people. *A flu epidemic is sweeping through Moscow. ...a killer epidemic of yellow fever.* N-COUNT: oft n N, N of n

2 If an activity that you disapprove of is increasing or spreading rapidly, you can refer to this as an **epidemic** of that activity. *...an epidemic of serial killings... Drug experts say it could spell the end of the crack epidemic.* N-COUNT: with supp, oft N of n PRAGMATICS

epidermis /epɪdɜːʳmɪs/. Your **epidermis** is the thin, protective, outer layer of your skin. N-SING

epidural /epidjʊərəl, AM -dʊr-/ **epidurals.** An **epidural** is a type of anaesthetic which is injected into a person's spine so that they cannot feel anything from the waist downwards. Epidurals are sometimes given to women when they are giving birth. N-COUNT

epigram /epɪgræm/ **epigrams.** An **epigram** is a short saying or poem which expresses an idea in a very clever and amusing way. N-COUNT

epilepsy /epɪlepsi/. **Epilepsy** is a brain condition which causes a person to suddenly lose consciousness and sometimes to have fits. ◆◇◇◇◇ N-UNCOUNT

epileptic /epɪleptɪk/ **epileptics**

1 Someone who is **epileptic** suffers from epilepsy. *He was epileptic and refused to take medication for his condition.* ▶ Also a noun. *His wife is an epileptic.* ADJ-GRADED; N-COUNT

2 An **epileptic** fit is caused by epilepsy. *He suffered an epileptic fit... Paula had never seen an epileptic seizure.* ADJ: ADJ n

epilogue /epɪlɒg, AM -lɔːg/ **epilogues.** An **epilogue** is a passage or speech which is added to the end of a book or play as a conclusion. N-COUNT: usu the N in sing

Epiphany /ɪpɪfəni/. **Epiphany** is a Christian festival which is celebrated on the 6th of January. It commemorates the arrival of the wise men who came to see Jesus Christ soon after he was born. N-UNCOUNT

episcopal /ɪpɪskəpᵊl/

1 **Episcopal** means relating to a branch of the Anglican Church in Scotland and the USA. *She was a staunch member of the Scottish Episcopal Church. ...the Episcopal bishop of New York.* ADJ: ADJ n

2 **Episcopal** means relating to bishops; a formal use. *Episcopal conferences exerted a strong influence during the Second Vatican Council. ...a set of red episcopal vestments.* ADJ: ADJ n

Episcopalian /ɪpɪskəpeɪliən/ **Episcopalians**

1 **Episcopalian** means belonging to the Episcopal Church. ADJ: ADJ n

2 An **Episcopalian** is a member of the Episcopal Church. N-COUNT

episode /epɪsoʊd/ **episodes** ◆◆◇◇◇

1 You can refer to an event or a short period of time as an **episode** if you want to suggest that it is important or unusual, or has some particular quality. *This episode is bound to be a deep embarrassment for Washington... Unfortunately it was a rather sordid episode of my life.* N-COUNT: usu with supp

2 An **episode** of something such as a television serial or a story in a magazine is one of the separate parts in which it is broadcast or published. *Actor James Doohan is to make a comeback in an episode of TV's 'Star Trek'. ...the famous twentieth century novel 'Ulysses', to be read in 18 episodes starting next week.* N-COUNT: oft N of n =instalment

3 An **episode** of an illness is short period in which a person who suffers from it is affected by it particularly badly; a medical use. *...people who'd suffered a third episode of depression in two years... the new drug lessens the severity of pneumonia episodes.* N-COUNT: usu with supp =attack

episodic /epɪsɒdɪk/

1 Something that is **episodic** occurs at irregular and infrequent intervals; a formal use. *...episodic attacks of fever.* ADJ-GRADED =periodic

2 An **episodic** piece of writing or film consists of a series of events, often events which seem random or unconnected. *...an episodic narrative of unrelated characters connected only by time and place.* ADJ-GRADED

epistle /ɪpɪsᵊl/ **epistles**
1 An **epistle** is a letter; a literary use. *...a brief but poignant epistle.* N-COUNT: supp N
2 In the Bible, the **Epistles** are a series of books in the New Testament which were originally written as letters from the Apostles to early Christians. N-COUNT: usu N *to* n

epistolary /ɪpɪstələri, AM -leri/. An **epistolary** novel or story is one that is written as a series of letters; a formal word. *It's written in epistolary form. ...Laclos's famous epistolary novel.* ADJ: ADJ n

epitaph /epɪtɑːf, -tæf/ **epitaphs.** An **epitaph** is a short description, thought, or message about someone who is dead, often carved on their gravestone. N-COUNT

epithet /epɪθet/ **epithets.** An **epithet** is an adjective or short, descriptive phrase which is used in criticism or praise of someone. *...the religious issue which led to the epithet 'bible-basher'.* N-COUNT: usu with supp

epitome /ɪpɪtəmi/. If you say that a person or thing is the **epitome** of something, you are emphasizing that they are the best possible example of a particular type of person or thing. *Maureen was the epitome of sophistication... The Dorchester Hotel is the epitome of luxury in the heart of London.* ◆◇◇◇◇ N-SING: usu *the* N *of* n PRAGMATICS

epitomize /ɪpɪtəmaɪz/ **epitomizes, epitomizing, epitomized;** also spelled **epitomise** in British English. If you say that something or someone **epitomizes** a particular thing, you mean that they are a perfect example of it. *Lyonnais cooking is epitomized by the so-called 'bouchons'. ...the sleek lift that epitomized the hotel's glossy decor.* ◆◇◇◇◇ VERB *be* V-ed *by* n V n

epoch /iːpɒk, AM epək/ **epochs** ◆◇◇◇◇
1 If you refer to a long period of time as an **epoch**, you mean that important events or great changes took place during it. *The birth of Christ was the beginning of a major epoch of world history.* N-COUNT: usu with supp
2 An **epoch** is a very long period of time in the earth's development, marked by particular physical or biological characteristics; a technical use in geography. *Two main glacial epochs affected both areas during the last 100 million years of Precambrian times.* N-COUNT: usu supp N

epoch-making. An **epoch-making** change or declaration is considered to be the extremely important because it is likely to have a significant effect on a particular period of time. *It was meant to sound like an epoch-making declaration. ...the epoch-making changes now taking place in Eastern Europe.* ADJ: usu ADJ n

eponymous /ɪpɒnɪməs/. An **eponymous** hero or heroine is the character in a play or book whose name is the title of that play or book; a formal word. *He fell in love with the eponymous heroine.* ◆◇◇◇◇ ADJ: ADJ n

Epsom salts /epsəm sɔːlts/. **Epsom salts** is a kind of white powder which you can mix with water and drink as a medicine to help you empty your bowels. N-UNCOUNT

equable /ekwəbᵊl/
1 If you describe someone as **equable**, you mean that they are calm, cheerful, and fair with other people, even in difficult circumstances. *He was a man of the most equable temper... He was a fine person to work with and he was very equable and a patient man.* ♦ **equably** *She wasn't prepared to respond equably to Richardson's mood, and she spoke curtly.* ADJ-GRADED; ADV-GRADED: ADV after v
2 An **equable** climate stays at an even temperature and has no sudden changes. *The climate has grown more equable and the crop yields have risen.* ADJ-GRADED

equal /iːkwəl/ **equals, equalling, equalled;** spelled **equaling, equaled** in American English. ◆◆◆◇◇
1 If two things are **equal** or if one thing is **equal** to another, they are the same in size, number, standard, or value. *Investors can borrow an amount equal to the property's purchase price. ...in a population having equal numbers of men and women... Research and teaching are of equal importance.* ADJ: oft ADJ *to* n
2 If different groups of people have **equal** rights or are given **equal** treatment, they have the same rights or are treated the same as each other, regardless of their differences. *We will be justly demanding equal rights at work. ...the commitment to equal opportunities. ...new legislation allowing building societies to compete on equal terms with their competitors.* ADJ-GRADED: usu ADJ n
3 If you say that people are **equal**, you mean that they have or should have the same rights and opportunities as each other. *We are equal in every way... At any gambling game, everyone is equal.* ADJ-GRADED: v-link ADJ
4 Someone who is your **equal** has the same ability, status, or rights as you have. *She was one of the boys, their equal... You should have married somebody more your equal.* N-COUNT: poss N
5 If someone is **equal to** a particular job or situation, they have the necessary ability, strength, or courage to deal successfully with it. *She was determined that she would be equal to any test the corporation put to them... The guards were equal to anything.* ADJ-GRADED: v-link ADJ *to* n
6 If something **equals** a particular number or amount, it is the same as that amount or the equivalent of that amount. *9 percent interest less 7 percent inflation equals 2 percent... The average pay rise equalled 1.41 times inflation.* V-LINK V amount
7 To **equal** something or someone means to be as good or as great as them. *The victory equalled Southend's best in history... No amount of money can equal memories like that.* VERB V n
8 If you say that someone or something **has no equal**, you think that there is nothing that is as good as them or that reaches the same standard. *As a pastor, it can be argued he has no equal... The film demands attention, and has no equal in cinema history.* PHRASES V inflects PRAGMATICS
9 If you say **'other things being equal'** or **'all things being equal'** when talking about a possible situation, you mean if nothing unexpected happens or if there are no other factors which affect the situation. *It appears reasonable to assume that, other things being equal, most hostel tenants would prefer single to shared rooms... All things being equal, should it matter who earns most money?* PHR with cl PRAGMATICS

equality /ɪkwɒlɪti/. **Equality** is the same status, rights, and responsibilities for all the members of a society, group, or family. *...equality of the sexes.* ◆◆◇◇◇ N-UNCOUNT

equalize /iːkwəlaɪz/ **equalizes, equalizing, equalized;** also spelled **equalise** in British English. ◆◇◇◇◇
1 To **equalize** a situation means to give everyone the same rights or opportunities, for example in education, wealth, or social status. *Women in Indonesia have secured modern divorce laws that equalize the rights of husbands and wives... Such measures are needed to equalize wage rates between countries.* ♦ **equalization** /iːkwəlaɪzeɪʃᵊn/ *...the equalization of parenting responsibilities between men and women.* VERB V n; N-UNCOUNT: also *a* N, oft N *of* n
2 In sports such as football, if a player **equalizes**, he or she scores a goal that makes the scores of the two teams equal. *Keegan equalized with only 16 minutes remaining... They showed little sign of equalising the Portsmouth striker's glorious 55th-minute shot.* VERB V V n

equalizer /iːkwəlaɪzəʳ/ **equalizers.** In sports such as football, an **equalizer** is a goal or a point that makes the scores of the two teams equal; used in British English. ◆◇◇◇◇ N-COUNT: usu sing

equally /iːkwəli/ ◆◆◆◇◇
1 **Equally** means in sections, amounts, or spaces that are the same size as each other. *A bank's local market share tends to be divided equally between the local branch and branches located elsewhere... Try to get into the habit of eating at least three small meals a day, at equally spaced intervals.* ADV: ADV after v, ADV -ed
2 **Equally** means to the same degree or extent. *All these techniques are equally effective... Success doesn't only depend on what you do. What you don't do is equally important.* ADV: ADV adj/adv, ADV before v =just as
3 **Equally** is used to introduce another comment on the same topic, which balances or contrasts with the previous comment. *Subscribers should be allowed call-blocking services, but equally, they* ADV: ADV with cl PRAGMATICS

should be able to choose whether to accept calls from blocked numbers.

equals sign, equals signs. An **equals sign** is the sign =, which is used in arithmetic to indicate that two numbers or sets of numbers are equal. N-COUNT

equanimity /ekwənɪmɪti, iːk-/. **Equanimity** is a calm state of mind and attitude to life, so that you never lose your temper or become upset; a formal word. *His sense of humour allowed him to face adversaries with equanimity... The defeat was taken with equanimity by the leadership.* N-UNCOUNT: oft *with* N

equate /ɪkweɪt/ **equates, equating, equated.** ◆◇◇◇◇ If you **equate** one thing with another, or if you say that one thing **equates** with another, you believe that they are strongly connected, for example because you think that they are the same thing or that one causes the other. *I'm always wary of men wearing suits, as I equate this with power and authority... The author doesn't equate liberalism and conservatism... The principle of hierarchy does not equate to totalitarian terror.* V-ERG; V n *with* n; V pl-n; V *to/with* n
♦ **equation** *The equation of gangsterism with business in general in Coppola's film was intended to be subversive.* N-UNCOUNT: oft N *of* n *with* n

equation /ɪkweɪʒən/ **equations** ◆◆◇◇◇
1 An **equation** is a mathematical statement saying that two amounts or values are the same, for example 6x4=12x2. N-COUNT
2 An **equation** is a situation or problem in which two or more parts have to be considered together so that the whole situation or problem can be understood or explained. *The equation is simple: research breeds new products... The party fears the equation between higher spending and higher taxes.* N-COUNT

equator /ɪkweɪtər/. **The equator** is an imaginary line around the middle of the earth at an equal distance from the North Pole and the South Pole. ◆◇◇◇◇ N-SING: *the* N

equatorial /ekwətɔːriəl, AM iː-/. Something that is **equatorial** is near or at the equator. *...the equatorial island with a hundred and twenty thousand people living there.* ADJ: usu ADJ n

equerry /ɪkweri, AM ekwəri/ **equerries.** An **equerry** is an officer of a royal household or court who acts as a personal assistant to a member of the royal family. N-COUNT: oft N *to* n

equestrian /ɪkwestriən/. **Equestrian** means connected with the activity of riding horses. *...his equestrian skills.* ◆◇◇◇◇ ADJ: usu ADJ n

equestrianism /ɪkwestriənɪzəm/. **Equestrianism** refers to sports such as show jumping and dressage which involve people demonstrating their skill at riding and controlling a horse. N-UNCOUNT

equidistant /iːkwɪdɪstənt/. A place that is **equidistant** from two other places is the same distance away from each of these places. *Horsey is equidistant from Great Yarmouth and Mundesley.* ADJ: usu v-link ADJ, usu ADJ *from/between* n

equilateral /iːkwɪlætərəl/. A shape or figure that is **equilateral** has sides that are all the same length; a mathematical term. *...its outline roughly forms an equilateral triangle.* ADJ: usu ADJ n

equilibrium /iːkwɪlɪbriəm/ **equilibria** ◆◇◇◇◇
1 **Equilibrium** is a balance between several different influences or aspects of a situation; a formal use. *Stocks seesawed ever lower until prices found some new level of equilibrium... For the economy to be in equilibrium, income must equal expenditure.* N-VAR
2 Someone's **equilibrium** is their normal calm state of mind. *I paused in the hall to take three deep breaths to restore my equilibrium... He had recovered his equilibrium and even his good humour, somehow.* N-UNCOUNT: oft poss N

equine /ekwaɪn, AM iːk-/. **Equine** means connected with or relating to horses. *The event has been cancelled this spring due to the outbreak of equine influenza in the stables.* ◆◇◇◇◇ ADJ: ADJ n

equinox /iːkwɪnɒks, ek-/ **equinoxes.** An **equinox** is one of the two days in the year when day and night are of equal length. *In the Chinese calendar, the Spring Equinox always occurs in the second month and the Autumn Equinox in the eighth month.* N-COUNT: oft supp N

equip /ɪkwɪp/ **equips, equipping, equipped** ◆◆◇◇◇
1 If you **equip** a person or thing with something, you give them the tools or equipment that are needed. *They become obsessed with trying to equip their vehicles with gadgets to deal with every possible contingency... Owners of restaurants would have to equip them to admit disabled people... The country did not possess the modern guns to equip the reserve army properly.* VERB; V n *with* n; V n to-inf; V n
♦ **equipped** *...well-equipped research buildings... The greenhouses come equipped with a ventilating system and aluminium screen door... Each caravan is equipped for four persons.* ADJ
2 If something **equips** you for a particular task or experience, it gives you the skills and attitudes you need for it, especially by educating you in a particular way. *Relative poverty, however, did not prevent Martin from equipping himself with an excellent education... A basic two-hour first aid course would equip you to deal with any of these incidents.* VERB; V n *with* n; V n to-inf; Also V n *for* n/-ing
♦ **equipped** *Some students unburden themselves of emotional problems that faculty members feel ill equipped to handle... When they leave school, they will be equipped for obtaining office jobs.* ADJ: v-link ADJ to-inf, v-link ADJ *for* n/-ing

equipment /ɪkwɪpmənt/. **Equipment** consists of the things which are used for a particular purpose, for example a hobby or job. *...computers, electronic equipment and machine tools. ...outdoor playing equipment.* ◆◆◆◆◇ N-UNCOUNT

equitable /ekwɪtəbəl/. Something that is **equitable** is fair and reasonable in a way that gives equal treatment to everyone. *He has urged them to come to an equitable compromise that gives Hughes his proper due... We believe you can redistribute this money in a way that's equitable to take care of the poor of the inner city.* ◆◇◇◇◇ ADJ-GRADED =even-handed
♦ **equitably** *...a real attempt to allocate scarce resources more equitably.* ADV-GRADED: ADV after v, ADV -ed

equity /ekwɪti/ ◆◆◆◇◇
1 Your **equity** is the sum of your assets, for example the value of your house, once your debts have been subtracted from it; a technical use in finance. *To capture his equity, Murphy must either sell or refinance. ...a Personal Equity Plan.* ● See also **negative equity**. N-UNCOUNT
2 **Equity** is the quality of being fair and reasonable in a way that gives equal treatment to everyone. *We base this call on grounds of social justice and equity.* N-UNCOUNT

equivalence /ɪkwɪvələns/. If there is **equivalence** between two things, they have the same use, function, size, or value. *...the equivalence of science and rationality.* N-UNCOUNT

equivalent /ɪkwɪvələnt/ **equivalents** ◆◆◆◇◇
1 If one amount or value is the **equivalent** of another, they are the same. *The equivalent of two tablespoons of polyunsaturated oils is ample each day... Even the cheapest car costs the equivalent of 70 years' salary for a government worker.* ▶ Also an adjective. *A unit is equivalent to a glass of wine or a single measure of spirits... They will react with hostility to the price rises and calls for equivalent wage increases are bound to be heard.* N-SING: oft N *of* n; ADJ-GRADED: oft ADJ *to* n =equal
2 The **equivalent** of someone or something is a person or thing that has the same function in a different place, time, or system. *...the civil administrator of the West Bank and his equivalent in Gaza. ...the Red Cross emblem, and its equivalent in Muslim countries, the Red Crescent.* ▶ Also an adjective. *...a decrease of 10% in property investment compared with the equivalent period in 1991.* N-COUNT: usu with poss =counterpart; ADJ
3 You can use **equivalent** to emphasize the great or severe effect of something. *His party has just suffered the equivalent of a near-fatal heart attack.* N-SING: *the* N *of* n PRAGMATICS

equivocal /ɪkwɪvəkəl/
1 If you are **equivocal**, you are deliberately vague or ambiguous in what you say, because you want to avoid speaking the truth or making a decision; a formal use. *Many were equivocal about the idea... His equivocal response has done nothing to dampen the speculation.* ADJ-GRADED

2 If something is **equivocal**, it is difficult to understand, interpret, or explain, often because it has aspects that seem to contradict each other; a formal use. *Research in this area is somewhat equivocal... He was tortured by an awareness of the equivocal nature of his position.* ADJ-GRADED

equivocate /ɪkwɪvəkeɪt/ **equivocates, equivocating, equivocated.** When someone **equivocates** they deliberately use vague and ambiguous language in order to deceive people or to avoid speaking the truth. *He is equivocating a lot about what is going to happen if and when there are elections... He had asked her once again about her finances. And again she had equivocated.* VERB V about/over n V
♦ **equivocation** /ɪkwɪvəkeɪʃᵊn/ *Why doesn't the President say so without equivocation?* N-UNCOUNT: usu without N

er /ɜːʳ/. **Er** is used to represent the sound that people make when they hesitate, especially while they decide what to say next. *I would challenge the, er, suggestion that we're in third place... People that are addicted to drugs get er help from the government one way or another.* ◆◆◆◆◆

-er /-əʳ/
1 You add **-er** to adjectives that have one or two syllables in order to form comparative adjectives. For example the comparative of 'hard' is 'harder'; the comparative of 'happy' is 'happier'. It is also added to some adverbs that do not end in -ly in order to form comparative adverbs. For example, the comparative of 'soon' is 'sooner'. SUFFIX
2 You add **-er** to verbs to form nouns which refer to a person, animal, or thing that does the action described by the verb; for example a 'reader' is someone who reads and a 'money-saver' is something that saves money. SUFFIX
3 You add **-er** to words to form nouns which refer to a person who is associated or involved with the thing described by the word; for example a 'pensioner' is someone who is entitled to a pension. SUFFIX
4 You add **-er** to nouns to form nouns or adjectives which refer to things with a particular characteristic or feature; for example a 'three-wheeler' is a vehicle with three wheels. SUFFIX
5 You add **-er** to words to form nouns which refer to a person with a particular job. For example, someone who works in a mine is a 'miner'. SUFFIX
6 You add **-er** to the names of some places to form nouns which refer to a person who comes from that place. For example, someone who comes from London is a 'Londoner'. SUFFIX

era /ɪərə/ **eras.** You can refer to a period of history or a long period of time as an **era** when you want to draw attention to a particular feature or quality that it has. *...the nuclear era. ...the Reagan-Bush era... It was an era of austerity.* ◆◆◆◇◇ N-COUNT: usu supp N, N of n =age

eradicate /ɪrædɪkeɪt/ **eradicates, eradicating, eradicated.** To **eradicate** something means to get rid of it completely; a formal word. *They are already battling to eradicate illnesses such as malaria and tetanus... If tedious tasks could be eradicated, the world would be much better place.* ◆◇◇◇◇ VERB =eliminate V n
♦ **eradication** /ɪrædɪkeɪʃᵊn/ *Many Czechs and Slovaks would like to see the eradication of their country's Communist past.* N-UNCOUNT: oft N of n

erase /ɪreɪz, AM ɪreɪs/ **erases, erasing, erased** ◆◇◇◇◇
1 If you **erase** a thought or feeling, you destroy it completely so that you can no longer remember something or no longer feel a particular emotion. *They are desperate to erase the memory of that last defeat in Cardiff... Love was a word he'd erased from his vocabulary since Susan's going.* VERB V n V n from n
2 If you **erase** sound which has been recorded on a tape or information which has been stored in a computer, you completely remove or destroy it. *He was found by the girls in the studio tearfully erasing all the tapes he'd slaved over... It appears the names were accidentally erased from computer disks.* VERB =wipe V n be V-ed from n Also V n from n
3 If you **erase** something such as writing or a mark, you remove it usually by rubbing it with a cloth. *It was unfortunate that she had erased the message.* VERB =rub out V n

eraser /ɪreɪzəʳ, AM -reɪs-/ **erasers.** In American English or formal British English, an **eraser** is an object, usually a piece of rubber, which is used for rubbing out writing. *...a large, flat, pink India-rubber eraser.* N-COUNT =rubber

erasure /ɪreɪʒəʳ, AM -reɪʃ-/. The **erasure** of something is the removal, loss, or destruction of it; a formal use. *It does not represent a further erasure of the UK's thin manufacturing base. ...the final and cataclysmic erasure of all the remaining dinosaurs 65 million years ago.* N-UNCOUNT: oft N of n

ere /eəʳ/. **Ere** means the same as 'before'; an old-fashioned, literary word. *It was not long ere a call came from the house and recalled me from my reflections... Take the water ere the clock strikes twelve.* CONJ-SUBORD

erect /ɪrekt/ **erects, erecting, erected** ◆◆◇◇◇
1 If people **erect** something such as a building, bridge, or barrier, they build it or create it; a formal use. *Opposition demonstrators have erected barricades in roads leading to the parliament building... The building was erected in 1900-1901 for the Glasgow Parish Council... We all unconsciously erect barriers against intimacy.* VERB =build V n
2 If you **erect** a system, a theory, or an institution, you create it. *Japanese proprietors are erecting a complex infrastructure of political influence throughout America... He erected a new doctrine of precedent. ...the whole edifice of free trade which has been erected since the Second World War.* VERB =put up V n
3 People or things that are **erect** are straight and upright. *Stand reasonably erect, your arms hanging naturally... Her head was erect and her back was straight. ...the short, stiff, erect stems of almost bead-like blue flowers.* ADJ-GRADED

erection /ɪrekʃᵊn/ **erections** ◆◇◇◇◇
1 If a man has an **erection** his penis is stiff, swollen, and sticking up because he is sexually aroused. N-COUNT
2 The **erection** of something is the act of building it or placing it in an upright position. *...the erection of temporary fencing to protect hedges under repair. ...the erection of the first temple.* N-UNCOUNT: oft N of n

ergo /ɜːʳgoʊ/. In formal English, some people use **ergo** instead of 'therefore' to introduce a clause in which they mention something that is the consequence or logical result of what they have just said. *Neither side would have an incentive to start a war. Ergo, peace would reign.* ADV: ADV with cl =therefore

ergonomics /ɜːʳgənɒmɪks/. **Ergonomics** is the study of how equipment and furniture can be arranged in order that people can do work or other activities more efficiently and comfortably. N-UNCOUNT

ermine /ɜːʳmɪn/. **Ermine** is expensive white fur that is obtained from stoats. N-UNCOUNT: oft N n

erode /ɪroʊd/ **erodes, eroding, eroded** ◆◆◇◇◇
1 If rock or soil **erodes** or **is eroded** by the weather, sea, or wind, it cracks and breaks so that it is gradually destroyed. *By 1980, Miami beach had all but totally eroded... Once exposed, soil is quickly eroded by wind and rain.* ♦ **eroded** *...the deeply eroded landscape.* V-ERG =wear away V be V-ed Also V n ADJ-GRADED
2 If someone's authority, right, or confidence **erodes** or **is eroded**, it is gradually destroyed or removed; a formal use. *His critics say his fumbling of the issue of reform has eroded his authority... America's belief in its own God-ordained uniqueness started to erode.* V-ERG V n V
3 If the value of something **erodes** or **is eroded** by something such as inflation or age, its value decreases. *Competition in the financial marketplace has eroded profits... The value of the dollar began to erode rapidly just around this time.* V-ERG V n V

erogenous /ɪrɒdʒɪnəs/. An **erogenous** part of your body is one where sexual pleasure can be felt or caused; a formal word. *Your body contains many erogenous zones, areas that lead to a feeling of sexual excitement when they are caressed.* ADJ-GRADED: usu ADJ n

erosion /ɪroʊʒᵊn/ ◆◇◇◇◇
1 **Erosion** is the gradual destruction and removal of rock or soil in a particular area by rivers, the sea, or the weather. *As their roots are strong and penetrating, they prevent erosion. ...erosion of the river valleys. ...soil erosion.* N-UNCOUNT
2 The **erosion** of a person's authority, rights, or N-UNCOUNT:

confidence is the gradual destruction or removal of them. *...the erosion of confidence in world financial markets. ...an erosion of presidential power.* usu N *of* n

3 The **erosion** of support, values, or money is a gradual decrease in its level or standard. *...the erosion of moral standards. ...a dramatic erosion of support for the program.* N-UNCOUNT: usu N *of* n

erotic /ɪrɒtɪk/ ◆◆◇◇◇

1 If you describe something as **erotic**, you mean that it involves sexual feelings or arouses sexual desire. *It might sound like some kind of wild fantasy, but it wasn't an erotic experience at all. ...photographs of nude women in erotic poses. ...the erotic thriller starring Madonna and Willem Dafoe.* ADJ-GRADED
♦ **erotically** /ɪrɒtɪkli/ *The film is shot seductively, erotically... He may get a woman erotically obsessed with him but he will never get her love.* ADV-GRADED: ADV with v, ADV adj

2 **Erotic** art shows situations that involve naked people or sexual acts, and is intended to produce feelings of sexual pleasure. *Erotic paintings also became a fine art.* ADJ: ADJ n

erotica /ɪrɒtɪkə/. **Erotica** means works of art that show or describe people engaged in sexual activity, and which are intended to arouse sexual feelings in the viewer or reader. N-UNCOUNT

eroticism /ɪrɒtɪsɪzəm/. **Eroticism** is sexual excitement, or the quality of being able to arouse sexual excitement; a formal word. *...the relationship between evil and eroticism... Almost all of Massenet's works are pervaded with an aura of eroticism.* N-UNCOUNT

err /ɜːʳ/ **errs, erring, erred** ◆◇◇◇◇

1 If you **err**, you make a mistake; an old-fashioned, formal use. *It criticises the main contractor for seriously erring in its original estimates... If you make a threat be sure to carry it out if he errs again.* VERB V *in* n V

2 If you say that **to err is human**, you mean that it is natural for human beings to make mistakes. *To err is human, and nobody likes a perfect person.* PHRASES

3 If you are uncertain what to do, and you **err on the side of** caution, for example, you decide to act in a cautious way, rather than do other things that are possible. *They may be wise to err on the side of caution... He probably erred on the conservative rather than the generous side.* V inflects

errand /erənd/ **errands** ◆◇◇◇◇

1 An **errand** is a short trip that you make in order to do a job for someone, for example when you go to a shop to buy something for them. *She went off on some errand... She had a more urgent errand.* N-COUNT

2 If you **run an errand** for someone, you do or get something for them, usually by making a short trip somewhere. *Run an errand for me, will you? Go find Roger for me... Frank drifted into running dodgy errands for a seedy local villain.* PHRASE: V inflects

errant /erənt/. **Errant** is used to describe someone whose actions are considered unacceptable or wrong by other people. For example, an **errant** husband is unfaithful to his wife; a formal word. *Usually his cases involved errant husbands and wandering wives... His errant son at Dartmouth ran up debts of £225.* ADJ: ADJ n

erratic /ɪrætɪk/. Something that is **erratic** does not follow a regular pattern, but happens at unexpected times or moves along in an irregular way. *Argentina's erratic inflation rate threatens to upset the plans. ...the family's erratic affairs.* ◆◇◇◇◇ ADJ-GRADED =unpredictable
♦ **erratically** /ɪrætɪkli/ *Police stopped him for driving erratically.* ADV-GRADED

erroneous /ɪroʊniəs/. Beliefs, opinions, or methods that are **erroneous** are incorrect or only partly correct. *Some people have the erroneous notion that one can contract AIDS by giving blood... They have arrived at some erroneous conclusions.* ◆◇◇◇◇ ADJ-GRADED
♦ **erroneously** *It had been widely and erroneously reported that Armstrong had refused to give evidence.* ADV: ADV with v

error /erəʳ/ **errors** ◆◆◆◇◇

1 An **error** is something you have done which is considered to be incorrect or wrong, or which should not have been done. *NASA discovered a mathematical error in its calculations... MPs attacked lax management and errors of judgment.* N-VAR: oft N prep

2 If you do something **in error** or if it happens **in error** you do it or it happens because you have made a mistake, especially in your judgement. *The plane was shot down in error by a NATO missile.* PHRASES usu PHR after v

3 If someone sees **the error of** their **ways**, they realize or admit that they have made a mistake or behaved badly. *I wanted an opportunity to talk some sense into him and try to make him see the error of his ways.* PHR after v

ersatz /eəʳzæts/

1 If you describe something as **ersatz**, you dislike it because it is not genuine and is a poor imitation of something better; used in written English. *...an ersatz Victorian shopping precinct... The ersatz spontaneity of 'Sunday Love' sounds especially hollow.* ADJ: usu ADJ n PRAGMATICS =fake

2 An **ersatz** product is a product of poor quality that is used as a substitute for something that is not available; an old-fashioned use. *There were few provisions available in exchange for food stamps: ersatz coffee, macaroni, small cubes of margarine.* ADJ: ADJ n =substitute

erstwhile /ɜːʳstʰwaɪl/. You use **erstwhile** to describe someone that used to be the type of person indicated, but no longer is; a formal word. *Erstwhile workers may have become managers... He fled to America with Phyllis Burton, an erstwhile friend of his wife's.* ◆◇◇◇◇ ADJ: ADJ n =one-time

erudite /erʊdaɪt, AM erjə-/. If you describe someone as **erudite**, you mean that they have or show great academic knowledge. You can also use **erudite** to describe something such as a book or a style of writing; a formal word. *He was never dull, always erudite and well informed. ...an original and highly erudite style.* ADJ-GRADED

erudition /erʊdɪʃən, AM erjə-/. **Erudition** is great academic knowledge; a formal word. *His erudition was apparently endless.* N-UNCOUNT

erupt /ɪrʌpt/ **erupts, erupting, erupted** ◆◆◇◇◇

1 When a volcano **erupts**, it throws out a lot of hot, molten lava, ash, and steam. *The volcano erupted in 1980, devastating a large area of Washington state... Scientists say Mount Pinatubo could erupt again soon.* VERB V
♦ **eruption** /ɪrʌpʃən/ **eruptions** *...the volcanic eruption of Tambora in 1815.* N-VAR: usu with supp

2 If violence or fighting **erupts**, it suddenly begins or intensifies in an unexpected, violent way; used mainly in journalism. *Heavy fighting erupted there today after a two-day cease-fire... Violence erupted as the boys were driven away in two police vans.* VERB =break out V
♦ **eruption** *...this sudden eruption of violence.* N-COUNT

3 When people in a place suddenly become angry or violent, you can say that they **erupt** or that the place **erupts**; used mainly in journalism. *In Los Angeles, the neighborhood known as Watts erupted into riots... This region which had been relatively calm erupted in violence again this spring.* VERB V *into/in* n Also V

4 You say that if someone **erupts** when they suddenly have a change in mood, usually becoming quite noisy. *Then, without warning, she erupts into laughter... Union leaders erupted in fury last night over the proposed pay restraints.* VERB V *into/in* n Also V
♦ **eruption** *...an eruption of despair.* N-COUNT

5 If your skin **erupts**, sores or spots suddenly appear there; a medical use. *At the end of the second week, my skin erupted in pimples.* VERB V *in/into* n Also V
♦ **eruption** *...eruptions of adolescent acne. ...an unpleasant skin eruption.* N-COUNT: with supp

escalate /eskəleɪt/ **escalates, escalating, escalated.** If a bad or unpleasant situation **escalates** or if someone or something **escalates** it, it becomes greater in size, seriousness, or intensity; used mainly in journalism. *Both unions and management fear the dispute could escalate... The protests escalated into five days of rioting... Defeat could cause one side or other to escalate the conflict.* ◆◆◇◇◇ V-ERG V V *into* n V n
♦ **escalation** /eskəleɪʃən/ **escalations** *The threat of nuclear escalation remains. ...a sudden escalation of violence.* N-VAR

escalator /eskəleɪtəʳ/ **escalators.** An **escalator** is a moving staircase on which people can go from one level of a building to another. N-COUNT

escalope /eskəlɒp, AM ɪskɑːləp/ **escalopes.** An **escalope** is a thin boneless slice of meat or fish; used mainly in British English. N-COUNT: usu with supp

escapade /eskəpeɪd/ **escapades.** An **escapade** is an exciting and rather dangerous adventure. *...the scene of Robin Hood's escapades.* N-COUNT

escape /ɪskeɪp/ **escapes, escaping, escaped** ◆◆◆◆◇

1 If you **escape** from a place, you succeed in getting away from it. *A prisoner has escaped from a jail in northern England... They are reported to have escaped to the other side of the border... He was fatally wounded as he tried to escape.* ♦ **escaped** *Officers mistook Stephen for an escaped prisoner.* VB: no passive; V from n; V to n; V; ADJ

2 Someone's **escape** is the act of escaping from a particular place or situation. *The man made his escape.* N-COUNT: usu poss N

3 You can say that you **escape** when you survive something such as an accident. *The two officers were extremely lucky to escape serious injury... The man's girlfriend managed to escape unhurt... He narrowly escaped with his life when suspected right-wing extremists fired shots into his office.* ► Also a noun. *I hear you had a very narrow escape on the bridge.* VERB; V n; V adj; V prep; N-COUNT

4 If something is an **escape**, it is a way of avoiding difficulties or responsibilities. *But for me television is an escape. ...an escape from the depressing realities of wartime.* N-COUNT: usu sing

5 You can use **escape** to describe things which allow you to avoid difficulties or problems. For example, an **escape route** is an activity or opportunity that lets you improve your situation. An **escape clause** is part of an agreement that allows you to avoid having to do something that you do not want to do. *We all need the occasional escape route from the boring, routine aspects of our lives... This has, in fact, turned out to be a wonderful escape clause for dishonest employers everywhere.* ADJ: ADJ n

6 If something **escapes** you or **escapes** your attention, you do not know about it, do not remember it, or do not notice it. *It was an actor whose name escapes me for the moment... Blonde and slender, she was too striking to escape their attention.* VERB; V n

7 When gas, liquid, or heat **escapes**, it leaks from a pipe, container, or place. *Leave a vent open to let some moist air escape.* VERB; V

8 See also **fire escape**.

escapee /ɪskeɪpiː/ **escapees.** An **escapee** is a person who has escaped from somewhere, especially from prison. N-COUNT

escapism /ɪskeɪpɪzəm/. If you describe an activity or type of entertainment as **escapism**, you mean that it makes people think about pleasant things instead of the uninteresting or unpleasant aspects of their life. *Horoscopes are merely harmless escapism from an ever-bleaker world.* N-UNCOUNT

escapist /ɪskeɪpɪst/. **Escapist** ideas, activities, or types of entertainment make people think about pleasant or unlikely things instead of the uninteresting or unpleasant aspects of their life. *...a little escapist fantasy.* ADJ-GRADED

escapologist /eskəpɒlədʒɪst/ **escapologists.** An **escapologist** is someone who entertains audiences by being tied up and placed in a dangerous situation, then escaping from it. N-COUNT

escarpment /ɪskɑːʳpmənt/ **escarpments.** An **escarpment** is a wide, steep slope on a ridge or mountain. N-COUNT

eschew /ɪstʃuː/ **eschews, eschewing, eschewed.** If you **eschew** something, you deliberately avoid doing it or becoming involved in it; a formal word. *Although he appeared to enjoy a jet-setting life, he eschewed publicity and avoided nightclubs.* ◆◇◇◇◇ VERB =avoid; V n

escort, escorts, escorting, escorted. The noun is pronounced /eskɔːʳt/. The verb is pronounced /ɪskɔːʳt/. ◆◆◇◇◇

1 An **escort** is a person who travels with someone in order to protect or guard them. *He arrived with a police escort shortly before half past nine.* ● If someone is taken somewhere **under escort**, they are accompanied by guards, either because they have been arrested or because they need to be protected. *A man was injured when gunmen attacked a group of Hindus being taken under police escort to the city outskirts.* N-COUNT; PHRASE: PHR after v

2 An **escort** is a person who accompanies another person of the opposite sex to a social event. Sometimes people are paid to be escorts. *My sister needed an escort for a company dinner.* N-COUNT

3 If you **escort** someone somewhere, you accompany them there, usually in order to make sure that they leave a place or get to their destination. *I escorted him to the door... The vessel was escorted to an undisclosed port.* VERB; V n prep/adv

Eskimo /eskɪmoʊ/ **Eskimos.** An **Eskimo** is a member of the group of peoples who live in Alaska, Northern Canada, eastern Siberia, and other parts of the Arctic. These peoples now usually call themselves Inuits or Aleuts, and the term Eskimo is sometimes considered offensive. ◆◇◇◇◇ N-COUNT =Inuit

ESL /iː es el/. **ESL** is an abbreviation for 'English as a second language'. ESL is taught to people whose native language is not English but who live in a society in which English is the main language or one of the main languages.

esophagus /ɪsɒfəgəs/. See **oesophagus**.

esoteric /iːsoʊterɪk, AM esə-/. If you describe something as **esoteric**, you mean it is known, understood, or appreciated by only a small number of people; a formal word. *...esoteric knowledge. ...a spoiled aristocrat with pretentious airs and esoteric tastes.* ◆◇◇◇◇ ADJ-GRADED

esp. **esp.** is a written abbreviation for **especially**.

ESP /iː es piː/ ◆◇◇◇◇

1 **ESP** is the teaching of English to students whose first language is not English but who need it for a particular job or profession or for some other purpose. **ESP** is an abbreviation for 'English for specific purposes' or 'English for special purposes'. N-UNCOUNT

2 **ESP** is an abbreviation for **extra-sensory perception**. N-UNCOUNT

especial /ɪspeʃᵊl/. **Especial** means exceptional or special in some way; a formal word. *The authorities took especial interest in him because of his trade union work.* ADJ: ADJ n =special

especially /ɪspeʃᵊli/ ◆◆◆◆◇

1 You use **especially** to emphasize that what you are saying applies more to one person, thing, or area than to any others. *Millions of wild flowers colour the valleys, especially in April and May... Re-apply sunscreen every two hours, especially if you have been swimming.* ADV: ADV with cl/group PRAGMATICS =particularly

2 You use **especially** to emphasize a characteristic or quality. *Babies lose heat much faster than adults, and are especially vulnerable to the cold in their first month.* ADV: ADV adj/adv PRAGMATICS

Esperanto /espəræntoʊ/. **Esperanto** is an invented language which consists of parts of several European languages, and which was designed to help people from different countries communicate with each other. N-UNCOUNT

espionage /espiənɑːʒ/. **Espionage** is the activity of finding out the political, military, or industrial secrets of your enemies or rivals by using spies; a formal word. *The authorities have arrested several people suspected of espionage. ...industrial espionage.* ● See also **counter-espionage**. ◆◇◇◇◇ N-UNCOUNT =spying

esplanade /esplәneɪd, AM -nɑːd/ **esplanades.** The **esplanade**, usually in a seaside town, is a wide, open road where people walk for pleasure. N-COUNT: usu *the* N in sing

espousal /ɪspaʊzᵊl/. A government's or person's **espousal** of a particular policy, cause, or belief is their strong support of it; a formal word. *...the Slovene leadership's espousal of the popular causes of reform and nationalism.* N-SING: usu poss N *of* n

espouse /ɪspaʊz/ **espouses, espousing, espoused.** If you **espouse** a particular policy, cause, or belief, you become very interested in it and give your support to it; a formal word. *She ran away with him to Mexico and espoused the revolutionary cause.* ◆◇◇◇◇ VERB =take up; V n

espresso /espresoʊ/ **espressos.** **Espresso** coffee is made by forcing steam or boiling water through ground coffee beans. *...Italian espresso coffee.* ► An **espresso** is a cup of espresso coffee.
N-UNCOUNT; N-COUNT

esprit de corps /espriː də kɔːʳ/. **Esprit de corps** is a feeling of loyalty and pride that is shared by the members of a group who consider themselves to be different from other people in some special way; a formal expression.
N-UNCOUNT

espy /ɪspaɪ/ **espies, espying, espied.** If you **espy** something, you see or notice it; an old-fashioned word. *Here, from a window, did Guinevere espy a knight standing in a woodman's cart.*
VERB; V n

Esq. **Esq.** is used after men's names as a written abbreviation for 'esquire'. *...Harold T. Cranford Esq.*

esquire /ɪskwaɪəʳ, AM eskwaɪr/. **Esquire** is a formal title that can be used after a man's name if he has no other title, especially on an envelope that is addressed to him.
N-TITLE

essay /eseɪ/ **essays, essaying, essayed.** The noun is pronounced /eseɪ/. The verb is pronounced /e seɪ/. ◆◆◇◇◇

1 An **essay** is a short piece of writing on one particular subject written by a student. *We asked Jason to write an essay about his hometown and about his place in it.*
N-COUNT

2 An **essay** is a short piece of writing on one particular subject that is written by a writer for publication. *...Thomas Malthus's essay on population.*
N-COUNT: oft N *on* n

3 If you **essay** something, you try to do it; a formal use. *Sinclair essayed a smile but it could hardly have been rated as a success.* ► Also a noun. *His first essay in running a company was a notoriously tough undertaking.*
VERB; V n; N-COUNT: usu N *in* n

essayist /eseɪɪst/ **essayists.** An **essayist** is a writer who writes essays for publication.
N-COUNT

essence /esᵊns/ **essences** ◆◆◇◇◇

1 The **essence** of something is its basic and most important characteristic which gives it its individual identity. *The essence of consultation is to listen to, and take account of, the views of those consulted. ...the essence of life... Others claim that Ireland's very essence is expressed through the language.* • You use **in essence** to emphasize that you are talking about the most important or central aspect of an idea, situation, or event; a formal expression. *Though off-puttingly complicated in detail, local taxes are in essence simple.* • If you say that something **is of the essence**, you mean that it is absolutely necessary in order for a particular action to be successful; a formal expression. *Time is of the essence... Speed was of the essence in a project of this type.*
N-UNCOUNT: usu N *of* n; PHRASE: PHR with cl/group PRAGMATICS; PHRASE: V inflects =crucial

2 **Essence** is a very concentrated liquid that is used for flavouring food or for its smell. *...a few drops of vanilla essence. ...exotic bath essences.*
N-MASS

essential /ɪsenʃᵊl/ **essentials** ◆◆◆◆◇

1 Something that is **essential** is extremely important or absolutely necessary to a particular subject, situation, or activity. *It was absolutely essential to separate crops from the areas that animals used as pasture... As they must also sprint over short distances, speed is essential... Jordan promised to trim the city budget without cutting essential services.*
ADJ-GRADED: oft *it* v-link ADJ to-inf =crucial

2 The **essentials** are the things that are absolutely necessary for the situation you are in or for the task you are doing. *The flat contained the basic essentials for bachelor life.*
N-COUNT: usu pl

3 The **essential** aspects of something are its most basic or important aspects. *Most authorities agree that play is an essential part of a child's development... In this trial two essential elements must be proven: motive and opportunity.*
ADJ-GRADED =fundamental

4 The **essentials** are the most important principles, ideas, or facts of a particular subject. *...the essentials of everyday life, such as eating and exercise... This has stripped the contest down to its essentials. ...the bare essentials.*
N-PLURAL

essentially /ɪsenʃəli/ ◆◆◆◇◇

1 You use **essentially** to emphasize a quality that someone or something has, and to say that it is their most important or basic quality; a formal use. *It's been believed for centuries that great writers, composers and scientists are essentially quite different from ordinary people... Essentially, vines and grapes need water, heat and light.*
ADV-GRADED: ADV with cl/group PRAGMATICS =fundamentally

2 You use **essentially** to indicate that what you are saying is basically true, although some parts of it are wrong or more complicated than has been stated; a formal use. *His analysis of urban use of agricultural land has been proved essentially correct... Essentially, the West has only two options... The company won the contract by essentially saying it would do the job for free.*
ADV: ADV with cl/group, ADV with v PRAGMATICS

-est /-ɪst/. You add **-est** to many short adjectives to form superlatives. For example, the superlative of 'hard' is 'hardest'; the superlative of 'happy' is 'happiest'. You also add it to some adverbs that do not end in -ly. For example, the superlative of 'soon' is 'soonest'.
SUFFIX

establish /ɪstæblɪʃ/ **establishes, establishing, established** ◆◆◆◆◇

1 If someone **establishes** something such as an organization, a type of activity, or a set of rules, they create it or introduce it in such a way that it is likely to last for a long time. *The UN has established detailed criteria for who should be allowed to vote... The School was established in 1989 by an Italian professor.*
VERB =set up, found; V n

2 If you **establish** contact or communication with someone, you start to have contact or communication with them. You can also say that two people, groups, or countries **establish** contact or communication; a formal use. *We had already established contact with the museum... China and Saudi Arabia have announced they are establishing formal diplomatic relations.*
V-RECIP; V n *with* n; pl-n V

3 If you **establish** that something is true, you discover facts that show that it is definitely true; a formal use. *Medical tests established that she was not their own child... It will be essential to establish how the money is being spent... An autopsy was being done to establish the cause of death... It was established that the missile had landed on a test range in Australia.* ♦ **established** *That link is an established medical fact.*
VERB =ascertain; V that; V wh; V n; *it be* V-ed that; ADJ-GRADED: usu ADJ n

4 If you **establish** yourself, your reputation, or a good quality that you have, you succeed in doing something, and achieve respect or a secure position as a result of this. *This is going to be the show where up-and-coming comedians will establish themselves... He has established himself as a pivotal figure in US politics... We shall fight to establish our innocence.*
VERB; V pron-refl; V pron-refl *as* n; V n; Also V n *as* n

established /ɪstæblɪʃt/. If you use **established** to describe something such as an organization, you mean that it is officially recognized or generally approved of because it has existed for a long time. *Their religious adherence is not to the established church. ...qualified lawyers with established and prestigious business addresses. ...the established names of Paris fashion.*
◆◆◇◇◇ ADJ-GRADED: usu ADJ n

establishment /ɪstæblɪʃmənt/ **establishments** ◆◆◆◇◇

1 The **establishment** of an organization or system is the act of creating it or beginning it; a formal use. *The establishment of the regional government in 1980 did not end terrorism. ...discussions to explore the establishment of diplomatic relations.*
N-SING: usu N *of* n =creation

2 An **establishment** is a shop, business, or organization occupying a particular building or place; a formal use. *...a scientific research establishment... Shops and other commercial establishments in Srinagar remain closed today.*
N-COUNT: usu with supp

3 You refer to the people who have power and influence in the running of a country or organization as the **establishment**. *Shopkeepers would once have been pillars of the Tory establishment... What do you expect? This is the Establishment we're taking on. ...a terrorist hit-list of prominent British establishment figures.*
N-COUNT: usu *the* N in sing

estate /ɪsteɪt/ **estates** ◆◆◆◆◇

1 An **estate** is a large area of land in the country which is owned by a person, family, or organization. *...a shooting party on Lord Wyville's estate in Yorkshire.* N-COUNT

2 In Britain, people sometimes use **estate** to refer to a housing estate or an industrial estate. *He used to live on the estate.* N-COUNT

3 Someone's **estate** is all the money and property that they leave behind them when they die; a legal use. *His estate was valued at $150,000.* N-COUNT: oft poss N

4 In British English, an **estate** is an estate car. The American term is **station wagon**. N-COUNT

5 See also **housing estate**, **industrial estate**, **real estate**.

estate agent, estate agents. In British English, an **estate agent** is someone who works for a company that sells houses and land for people. The American word is **realtor**. ◆◆◇◇◇ N-COUNT

estate car, estate cars. In British English, an **estate car** is a car with a long body, a door at the rear, and space behind the back seats. The American term is **station wagon**. N-COUNT

esteem /ɪstiːm/ **esteems, esteeming, esteemed** ◆◆◇◇◇

1 **Esteem** is the admiration and respect that you feel towards another person; a formal use. *He is held in high esteem by colleagues in the construction industry... Their public esteem has never been lower... He said he retained immense regard and esteem for the prime minister.* N-UNCOUNT

2 If you **esteem** someone or something, you respect or admire them; a formal use. *I greatly esteem your message in the midst of our hard struggle.* VERB V n

3 See also **self-esteem**.

esteemed /ɪstiːmd/. You use **esteemed** to describe someone who you greatly admire and respect; a formal word. *He was esteemed by his neighbours... It is indeed an honour to serve my country in such an esteemed position.* ADJ-GRADED

esthete /iːsθiːt, AM es-/. See **aesthete**.

esthetic /iːsθetɪk, AM esθ-/. See **aesthetic**.

estimable /estɪməbᵊl/. If you describe someone or something as **estimable**, you mean that they deserve admiration; a formal word. *You know I promised the estimable Miss Cartwright to look after you.* ADJ-GRADED: usu ADJ n =admirable

estimate, estimates, estimating, estimated. ◆◆◆◆◇ The verb is pronounced /estɪmeɪt/. The noun is pronounced /estɪmət/.

1 If you **estimate** a quantity or value, you make an approximate judgement or calculation of it. *Try to estimate how many steps it will take to get to a close object... I estimate that total cost for treatment will go from $9,000 to $12,500... He estimated the speed of the winds from the degree of damage... Some analysts estimate its current popularity at around ten per cent... His personal riches were estimated at £368 million.* VERB =guess V wh V that V n V n *at* amount Also V with quote ♦ **estimated** *There are an estimated 90,000 gangsters in the country.* ADJ: *an* ADJ amount

2 An **estimate** is an approximate calculation of a quantity or value. *...the official estimate of the election result... This figure is five times the original estimate... A recent estimate was that factories were undermanned by about 30 per cent.* N-COUNT: usu with supp, oft N *of/for* n

3 An **estimate** is a judgement about a person or situation which you make based on the available evidence. *I hadn't been far wrong in my estimate of his grandson's capabilities.* N-COUNT: oft with poss, N *of* n

4 An **estimate** from someone who you employ to do a job for you, such as a builder or a plumber, is a written statement of how much the job is likely to cost. *The shop also offers a curtain-making and fitting service. Quotes and estimates can be prepared by computer on the spot.* N-COUNT

estimation /estɪmeɪʃᵊn/ **estimations**

1 Your **estimation** of a person or situation is the opinion or impression that you have formed about them; a formal use. *He has gone down considerably in my estimation. ...Lee Dixon, the best player on the pitch in his manager's estimation.* N-SING: usu with poss =judgement

2 An **estimation** is an approximate calculation of a quantity or value. *In fact, the first group were absolutely correct in their estimation of this man's height. ...estimations of pre-tax profits of £12.25 million.* N-COUNT: oft N *of* n =estimate

estranged /ɪstreɪndʒd/ ◆◇◇◇◇

1 If you refer to someone as the **estranged** wife or husband of their partner, you mean that they are no longer living together, and usually they are not in communication with each other; a formal use. *...his estranged wife.* ADJ: usu ADJ n

2 If you are **estranged** from your family or friends, you have quarrelled with them and are not communicating with them; a formal use. *He was laid to rest yesterday without a final goodbye from his estranged son... Joanna, 30, spent most of her twenties virtually estranged from her father.* ADJ-GRADED: oft ADJ *from* n

3 If you describe someone as **estranged** from something such as society or their profession, you mean that they no longer seem involved in it; a formal use. *Arran became increasingly estranged from the mainstream of Hollywood.* ADJ-GRADED: v-link ADJ, usu ADJ *from* n

estrangement /ɪstreɪndʒmənt/ **estrangements.** **Estrangement** is the state of being estranged from someone or the length of time for which you are estranged; a formal word. *The trip will bring to an end years of estrangement between the two countries... That day marked the beginning of a 20-year estrangement.* N-VAR

estrogen /iːstrədʒᵊn, AM est-/. See **oestrogen**.

estuary /estʃʊri, AM estʃueri/ **estuaries.** An **estuary** is the wide part of a river where it joins the sea. *...naval maneouvres in the Clyde estuary.* ◆◇◇◇◇ N-COUNT: oft in names after n

et al. /et æl/. **et al.** is used after a name or a list of names to indicate that other people are also involved. It is used especially when referring to books or articles which were written by more than two people. *...Blough et al.* ◆◆◇◇◇

etc /et setrə/. **etc** is used at the end of a list to indicate that you have mentioned only some of the items involved and have not given a full list. **Etc** is a written abbreviation for 'et cetera'. *She knew all about my schoolwork, my hospital work etc. ...a packed programme of events – shows, dances, coach tours, sports, etc.* ◆◆◆◇◇

etcetera /etsetrə/; also spelled **et cetera**. See **etc**.

etch /etʃ/ **etches, etching, etched** ◆◇◇◇◇

1 If a line or pattern **is etched** into a surface, it is cut into the surface by means of acid or a sharp tool. You can also say that a surface **is etched** with a line or pattern. *Crosses were etched into the walls... The acid etched holes in the crystal surface... Windows are etched with the vehicle identification number... The stained-glass panels are etched and then handpainted using traditional methods.* VERB be V-ed *into/in/on* n V n *into/in/on* n be V-ed *with* n be V-ed

2 If you say that feelings **are etched** on someone's face, you mean that the person is very strongly affected by them, and you can see this in their appearance; a literary use. *His grief was etched into every line of his face... Every line etched on her face told a story of personal anguish.* VB: usu passive be V-ed *into/on* n V-ed

3 If something **is etched** on your memory, you remember it very clearly, usually because it has some special importance for you; a literary use. *The ugly scene in the study was still etched in her mind... This stark image will remain etched in the memory of a generation of Berliners.* V-PASSIVE =be engraved be V-ed *into/in/on* n

etching /etʃɪŋ/ **etchings.** An **etching** is a picture printed from a metal plate that has had a design cut into it with acid. N-COUNT

eternal /ɪtɜːʳnᵊl/ ◆◆◇◇◇

1 Something that is **eternal** lasts for ever. *Whoever believes in Him shall not perish but have eternal life. ...the quest for eternal youth.* ADJ =everlasting ♦ **eternally** *She is eternally grateful to her family for their support... The whole universe exists eternally in that one infinite being.* ADV: ADV adj, ADV with v

2 If you describe something as **eternal**, you mean that it seems to last for ever, often because you think it is boring or annoying. *In the background was that eternal hum.* ADJ =interminable, never-ending

3 **Eternal** truths, values, and questions never change and are believed to be always true and to be ADJ: ADJ n

relevant in all situations. *...the eternal truths of the Indian subcontinent. ...the eternal question.*

eternal triangle, eternal triangles. You use the expression **the eternal triangle** to refer to an emotional relationship involving love and jealousy between two men and a woman or two women and a man. N-COUNT: usu sing

eternity /ɪtɜːʳnɪti/ ◆◇◇◇◇

1 **Eternity** is time without an end or a state of existence outside time, especially the state which some people believe they will pass into after they have died. *I have always found the thought of eternity terrifying. ...laying him to rest for all eternity.* N-UNCOUNT

2 If you say that a situation lasted for **an eternity**, you mean that it seemed to last an extremely long time, usually because it was boring or unpleasant. *The war continued for an eternity... The ringing went on for what seemed an eternity, and then someone answered.* N-SING: a N =age

ether /iːθəʳ/

1 **Ether** is a colourless liquid that burns easily. It is used in industry as a solvent and in medicine as an anaesthetic. *...a sweetish smell of ether and iodine.* N-UNCOUNT

2 The air is sometimes referred to as **the ether**, usually when talking about sounds being communicated or broadcast through it; a literary use. *...vocals floating through the ether.* N-SING: the N

ethereal /ɪθɪəriəl/ ◆◇◇◇◇

1 If you describe someone or something as **ethereal**, you mean that they have a delicate beauty; a formal use. *She's the prettiest, most ethereal romantic heroine in the movies. ...gorgeous, hauntingly ethereal melodies.* ADJ-GRADED

2 **Ethereal** means unrelated to practical things and the real world; a formal use. *...the ethereal nature of romantic fiction. ...in the ethereal realm of the divine.* ADJ-GRADED

ethic /eθɪk/ **ethics** ◆◆◇◇◇

1 **Ethics** are moral beliefs and rules about right and wrong. *Its members are bound by a rigid code of ethics which includes confidentiality... Refugee workers said such action was a violation of medical ethics.* N-PLURAL

2 Someone's **ethics** are the moral principles about right and wrong behaviour which they believe in. *You sense his personal ethics to be very close to the surface... He told the police that he had thought honestly about the ethics of what he was doing.* N-PLURAL: with supp

3 **Ethics** is the study of questions about what is morally right and wrong. *...the teaching of ethics and moral philosophy.* N-UNCOUNT

4 An **ethic** of a particular kind is an idea or moral belief that influences the behaviour, attitudes, and philosophy of a group of people. *...the ethic of public service. ...an indomitable work ethic and determination to succeed.* N-SING: with supp

ethical /eθɪkəl/ ◆◆◇◇◇

1 **Ethical** means relating to beliefs about right and wrong. *...the moral and ethical standards in the school. ...the medical, nursing and ethical issues surrounding terminally-ill people.* ♦ **ethically** /eθɪkli/ *Attorneys are ethically and legally bound to absolute confidentiality.* ADJ: usu ADJ n; ADV: ADV adj/-ed, ADV after v

2 If you describe something as **ethical**, you mean that morally right or morally acceptable. *...ethical investment schemes... Does the party think it is ethical to link tax policy with party fund-raising?* ♦ **ethically** *Mayors want local companies to behave ethically.* ADJ-GRADED; ADV-GRADED: ADV after v

Ethiopian /iːθioʊpiən/ **Ethiopians. Ethiopian** means belonging or relating to Ethiopia, or to its people, language, or culture. ► An **Ethiopian** is an Ethiopian citizen, or a person of Ethiopian origin. ◆◆◆◆◇ ADJ; N-COUNT

ethnic /eθnɪk/ ◆◆◆◇◇

1 **Ethnic** means connected with or relating to different racial or cultural groups of people. *...a survey of Britain's ethnic minorities. ...ethnic tensions.* ♦ **ethnically** /eθnɪkli/ *...a predominantly young, ethnically mixed audience.* ADJ: usu ADJ n; ADV: usu ADV -ed/adj

2 You can use **ethnic** to describe people who belong to a particular racial or cultural group but who, usually, do not live in the country where most members of that group live. *There are still several million ethnic Germans in Russia.* ♦ **ethnically** *...a large ethnically Albanian population.* ADJ: ADJ n; ADV: ADV adj

3 **Ethnic** clothing, music, or food is characteristic of the traditions of a particular ethnic group, and different from what is usually found in modern Western culture. *...the original flavours of ethnic dishes. ...a magnificent range of ethnic fabrics.* ADJ-GRADED

ethnic cleansing. When journalists refer to **ethnic cleansing**, they are referring to the process of using violent methods to force certain groups of people out of a particular area or country. *In late May, government forces began the 'ethnic cleansing' of the area around the town. ...the obnoxious policy of ethnic cleansing.* ◆◇◇◇◇ N-UNCOUNT PRAGMATICS

ethnicity /eθnɪsɪti/ **ethnicities. Ethnicity** is the state or fact or belonging to a particular ethnic group. *He said his ethnicity had not been important to him.* N-VAR

ethnocentric /eθnoʊsentrɪk/. If you describe something as **ethnocentric**, you disagree with it because it is based on the belief that one particular race or nationality of people is superior to all others. *Her work is open to the criticism that it is ethnocentric.* ADJ-GRADED PRAGMATICS

ethnographic /eθnəgræfɪk/. **Ethnographic** refers to things that are connected with or relate to ethnography. ADJ

ethnography /eθnɒgrəfi/. **Ethnography** is the branch of anthropology in which different cultures are studied and described. N-UNCOUNT

ethos /iːθɒs/. An **ethos** is the set of ideas and attitudes that is associated with a particular group of people or a particular type of activity; a formal word. *The whole ethos of the hotel is effortless service. ...the traditional public service ethos.* ◆◇◇◇◇ N-SING: usu with supp

etiology /iːtiɒlədʒi/ **etiologies;** also spelled **aetiology**. The **etiology** of a disease or a problem is the study of its causes. *...the etiology of psychiatric disorder.* N-VAR: oft the N of n

etiquette /etɪket/. **Etiquette** is a set of customs and rules for polite behaviour, especially among a particular class of people or in a particular profession. *This was such a great breach of etiquette, he hardly knew what to do. ...the rules of diplomatic etiquette.* ◆◇◇◇◇ N-UNCOUNT =protocol

etymological /etɪməlɒdʒɪkəl/. **Etymological** means concerned with or relating to etymology; a formal word. *'Gratification' and 'gratitude' have the same etymological root.* ADJ: usu ADJ n

etymology /etɪmɒlədʒi/ **etymologies**

1 **Etymology** is the study of the origins and historical development of words. N-UNCOUNT

2 The **etymology** of a particular word is its history. N-COUNT

EU /iː juː/. The **EU** is an organization of European countries which have joint policies on matters such as trade, agriculture, and finance. EU is an abbreviation for 'European Union'. N-PROPER

eucalyptus /juːkəlɪptəs/; **eucalyptus** is both the singular and the plural form. A **eucalyptus** is an evergreen tree, originally from Australia, that is grown to provide timber, gum, and an oil that is used in medicines. ◆◇◇◇◇ N-VAR: oft N n

Eucharist /juːkərɪst/. The **Eucharist** is the Christian religious ceremony in which Christ's last meal with his disciples is celebrated by the consecration of bread and wine. N-SING: usu the N

eugenics /juːdʒenɪks/. **Eugenics** is the study of methods to improve the human race by carefully selecting parents who will produce the strongest children; a technical term. N-UNCOUNT

eulogize /juːlədʒaɪz/ **eulogizes, eulogizing, eulogized;** also spelled **eulogise** in British English. If you **eulogize** someone or something, you praise them very highly; a formal word. *Barry Davies eulogized Keegan's part in the operation... Taylor eulogised about Steven's versatility.* VERB =rhapsodize; V n; V prep

eulogy /juːlədʒi/ **eulogies**

1 A **eulogy** is a speech or piece of writing that N-COUNT

praises someone or something very much; a formal word. =tribute

2 In American English, a **eulogy** is a speech, usually at a funeral, in which a person who has just died is praised. N-COUNT

eunuch /juːnək/ **eunuchs.** A **eunuch** is a man who has been castrated. N-COUNT

euphemism /juːfəmɪzəm/ **euphemisms** ◆◇◇◇◇

1 A **euphemism** is a polite, pleasant, or neutral word or expression that is used to refer to something which people may find upsetting or embarrassing to talk about, for example sex, the human body, or death. *The term 'comfort women' is the euphemism they applied to women put in army brothels.* N-COUNT

2 If you describe a word or expression as a **euphemism** for something unpleasant, you are criticizing its use because it hides the unpleasantness, and deliberately give a wrong impression. *The term 'early retirement' is nearly always a euphemism for redundancy nowadays.* N-COUNT: oft N *for* n

euphemistic /juːfəmɪstɪk/. If you describe language as **euphemistic**, you mean that it uses polite, pleasant, or neutral words and expressions to refer to things which people find unpleasant, upsetting, or embarrassing. *...a formal and euphemistic way of saying that someone has been lying.* ♦ **euphemistically** /juːfəmɪstɪkli/. *...political prisons, called euphemistically 're-education camps'.* ADJ-GRADED: usu ADJ n; ADV-GRADED: ADV with v

euphoria /juːfɔːriə/. **Euphoria** is a feeling of intense happiness and excitement. *There was euphoria after the elections... After the euphoria of yesterday's celebrations, the country will come down to earth today.* ◆◇◇◇◇ N-UNCOUNT: oft N *of/over* n =elation

euphoric /juːfɒrɪk, AM -fɔːr-/. If you are **euphoric**, you feel intense happiness and excitement. *It had received euphoric support from the public.* ◆◇◇◇◇ ADJ-GRADED =elated

Eurasian /jʊəreɪʒən/ **Eurasians**

1 **Eurasian** means concerned with or relating to both Europe and Asia. *...the whole of the Eurasian continent.* ADJ

2 A **Eurasian** is a person who has one European and one Asian parent or who is of mixed European and Asian ancestry. ► Also an adjective. *She married into a leading Eurasian family in Hong Kong.* N-COUNT; ADJ

eureka /jʊriːkə/. Someone might say **'eureka'** when they suddenly find or realize something, or when they solve a problem; an old-fashioned word. *'Eureka! I've got it!'* EXCLAM

Euro- /jʊərou-/. **Euro** is used to form words that describe or refer to something which is connected with Europe or with the EU. *...German Euro-MPs.* PREFIX

Eurocentric /jʊəroʊsentrɪk/. If you describe something as **Eurocentric**, you disapprove of it because it focuses on Europe and the needs of European people, often with the result that people in other parts of the world suffer in some way. *...the insultingly Eurocentric bias in the education system.* ADJ-GRADED PRAGMATICS

Eurocrat /jʊəroʊkræt/ **Eurocrats.** Journalists use **Eurocrats** to refer to the civil servants and other people who work in the administration of the European Union. N-COUNT

Europe /jʊərəp/ ◆◆◆◆◇

1 **Europe** is the continent which is joined to Asia in the east, and which is to the north of Africa and the Mediterranean Sea and to the east of the Atlantic Ocean. You can also use **Europe** to refer to the people who live there. *...central Europe. ...one of Europe's finest players... Europe was afraid to leave high-technology industry entirely in American hands.* N-PROPER

2 In British English, **Europe** can refer to all of Europe except for the United Kingdom. *More than four out of ten cars produced in the UK are for the export market, mainly to Europe.* N-PROPER

3 People use **Europe** to refer to all the countries that are members of the European Union. *Britain should stay in Europe, helping to build the policies we wish to see.* N-PROPER

European /jʊərəpiːən/ **Europeans** ◆◆◆◆◇

1 **European** means belonging or relating to, or coming from Europe. *...in some other European countries.* ADJ: usu ADJ n

2 A **European** is a person who comes from Europe. N-COUNT

euthanasia /juːθəneɪziə, AM -ʒə/. **Euthanasia** is the practice of killing someone painlessly in order to stop their suffering when they are dying or have an incurable illness. Euthanasia is illegal in most countries. ◆◇◇◇◇ N-UNCOUNT

evacuate /ɪvækjueɪt/ **evacuates, evacuating, evacuated** ◆◆◇◇◇

1 To **evacuate** someone means to send them to a place of safety, away from a dangerous building, town, or area. *They were planning to evacuate the seventy American officials still in the country... Since 1951, 18,000 people have been evacuated from the area.* ♦ **evacuation** /ɪvækjueɪʃən/ **evacuations** *...the evacuation of the sick and wounded... An evacuation of the city's four-million inhabitants is planned for later this week.* VERB V n; N-VAR

2 If people **evacuate** a place, they move out of it for a period of time, especially because it is dangerous. *The fire is threatening about sixty homes, and residents have evacuated the area... Officials ordered the residents to evacuate.* ♦ **evacuation** /ɪvækjueɪʃən/ **evacuations** *...the mass evacuation of the Bosnian town of Srebrenica... Burning sulfur from the wreck has forced evacuations from the area.* VERB V n V; N-VAR

evacuee /ɪvækjuiː/ **evacuees.** An **evacuee** is someone who has been sent away from a dangerous place to somewhere safe, especially during a war. ◆◇◇◇◇ N-COUNT

evade /ɪveɪd/ **evades, evading, evaded** ◆◇◇◇◇

1 If you **evade** something, you find a way of not doing something that you really ought to do. *By his own admission, he evaded taxes as a Florida real-estate speculator... Delegates accused them of trying to evade responsibility for the failures of the past five years.* VERB V n

2 If you **evade** a question or a topic, you avoid talking about it or dealing with it. *Mr Portillo denied he was evading the question... Too many companies, she says, are evading the issue.* VERB V n

3 If you **evade** someone or something, you move so that you can avoid meeting them or avoid being touched or hit. *Under the pretence of lighting a candle, she evades him and disappears... She turned and gazed at the river, evading his eyes... He managed to evade capture because of the breakdown of a police computer.* VERB V n

4 If something such as success, glory, or love **evades** you, you do not manage to have it; a literary use. *Happiness, which had been so elusive in Henry's life, still evaded him... When she sat down at her desk she found that the words evaded her.* VERB V n

evaluate /ɪvæljueɪt/ **evaluates, evaluating, evaluated.** If you **evaluate** something or someone, you consider them in order to make a judgement about them, for example about how good or bad they are. *They will first send in trained nurses to evaluate the needs of the individual situation... The market situation is difficult to evaluate.* ♦ **evaluation** /ɪvæljueɪʃən/ **evaluations** *...the opinions and evaluations of college supervisors... Evaluation is standard practice for all training arranged through the school.* ◆◆◇◇◇ VERB =assess V n; N-VAR

evaluative /ɪvæljuətɪv/. Something that is **evaluative** is based on an assessment of the values, qualities, and significance of a particular person or thing; a formal word. *...ten years of evaluative research.* ADJ-GRADED

evanescent /evənesənt/. Something that is **evanescent** gradually disappears from sight or memory; a formal or literary word. *...the evanescent scents of summer herbs, flowers or exotic spices.* ADJ-GRADED =ephemeral

evangelical /iːvændʒelɪkəl/ ◆◇◇◇◇

1 **Evangelical** people and beliefs are Christian ADJ

and emphasize the importance of the Bible and the need for personal belief in Christ in order to obtain salvation. *...an evangelical Christian.*

2 If you describe someone's behaviour as **evangelical**, you mean that it is very enthusiastic. *Mr Yeutter spoke up often and fiercely, with an almost evangelical fervour, on the subject of Europe's export subsidies.* ADJ-GRADED: usu ADJ n

evangelism /ɪvændʒəlɪzəm/. **Evangelism** is the teaching of Christianity, especially to people who are not Christians. N-UNCOUNT

evangelist /ɪvændʒəlɪst/ **evangelists.** An **evangelist** is a person who travels from place to place in order to try to convert people to Christianity. ◆◇◇◇◇ N-COUNT

evangelize /ɪvændʒəlaɪz/ **evangelizes, evangelizing, evangelized;** also spelled **evangelise** in British English. If someone **evangelizes** a group or area, they try to convert people to their religion, especially Christianity. *Irish monks had settled there in the seventh century to establish the Celtic church and evangelize the North.* VERB =proselytize V n Also V

evaporate /ɪvæpəreɪt/ **evaporates, evaporating, evaporated** ◆◇◇◇◇

1 When a liquid **evaporates**, or **is evaporated**, it changes from a liquid state to a gas, because its temperature has increased. *Moisture is drawn to the surface of the fabric so that it evaporates... The water is evaporated by the sun.* ♦ **evaporation** /ɪvæpəreɪʃᵊn/ *High temperatures also result in high evaporation from the plants... The soothing, cooling effect is caused by the evaporation of the sweat on the skin.* V-ERG V be V-ed Also V n N-UNCOUNT

2 If a feeling, plan, or activity **evaporates**, it gradually becomes weaker and eventually disappears completely. *My anger evaporated and I wanted to cry... Your dreams always seem to evaporate, and nothing ever quite matches expectations... The project evaporated and Harry was left high and dry.* VERB V

evaporated milk. **Evaporated milk** is thick sweetened milk that is sold in tins. N-UNCOUNT

evasion /ɪveɪʒᵊn/ **evasions** ◆◇◇◇◇

1 If you accuse someone of **evasion**, you mean that they are deliberately not doing something that they are supposed to, especially when they are avoiding doing it through trickery. *Many Koreans were angered at what they saw as an evasion of responsibility... He was arrested for tax evasion.* N-VAR: usu with supp, oft N of n, n N

2 If you accuse someone of **evasion** when they have been asked a question, you mean that they are deliberately avoiding giving a clear direct answer. *We want straight answers. No evasions... Ted grinned in evasion and cleared his throat.* N-VAR

evasive /ɪveɪsɪv/ ◆◇◇◇◇

1 If you describe someone as **evasive**, you mean that they deliberately avoid giving clear direct answers to questions. *He was evasive about the circumstances of his first meeting with Stanley Dean... Direct questions would almost certainly result in evasive answers.* ♦ **evasively** *'Until I can speak to your husband I can't come to any conclusion about that,' Millson said evasively.* ♦ **evasiveness** *She looked at him closely to see if his evasiveness was intentional.* ADJ-GRADED ADV: ADV with v N-UNCOUNT: oft poss N

2 If you **take evasive action**, you deliberately move away from someone or something in order to avoid meeting them or being hit by them. *At least four high-flying warplanes had to take evasive action.* PHRASES V inflects

eve /iːv/ **eves.** The **eve** of a particular event or occasion is the day before it, or the period of time just before it; used mainly in journalism. *...on the eve of his 27th birthday.* ● See also **Christmas Eve, New Year's Eve.** ◆◆◇◇◇ N-COUNT: usu sing, usu *the* N *of* n

even 1 discourse uses

even /iːvᵊn/ ◆◆◆◆◆

1 You use the word **even** to suggest that what comes just after or just before it in the sentence is rather surprising. *He kept calling me for years, even after he got married... Even dark-skinned women should use sunscreens... I cannot come to a decision about it now or even give any indication of my own views... He didn't even hear what I said.* ADV: ADV with cl/group, ADV before v PRAGMATICS

2 You use **even** with comparative adjectives and adverbs to emphasize a quality that someone or something has. *It was on television that he made an even stronger impact as an interviewer... During his second day Edward looked even more pale and quiet than on his first... Stan was speaking even more slowly than usual.* ADV: ADV compar PRAGMATICS

3 You use **even if** or **even though** to indicate that a particular fact does not make the rest of your statement untrue. *Cynthia is not ashamed of what she does, even if she ends up doing something wrong... Even though I'm supposed to be working by myself, there are other people who I can interact with.* PHR-CONJ-SUBORD

4 If one thing happens **even as** something else happens, they both happen at exactly the same time; a literary use. *Even as she said this, she knew it was not quite true... He had been aware, even as he slept, of the noise of the engine.* PHR-CONJ-SUBORD

5 You use **even so** to introduce a surprising fact which relates to what you have just said; used mainly in spoken English. *The bus was only half full. Even so, a young man asked Nina if the seat next to her was taken... She has never given up her nationality. Even so, her opponents argue that she is not a true Burmese.* PHRASES PHR with cl PRAGMATICS =nevertheless

6 You use **even then** to say that something is the case in spite of what has just been stated or whatever the circumstances may be. *Peace could come only gradually, in carefully measured steps. Even then, it sounds almost impossible to achieve... She was at her prettiest in her late teens, but even then she always had somebody who was prettier.* PHR with cl PRAGMATICS

even 2 adjective uses

even /iːvᵊn/ ◆◆◇◇◇

1 An **even** measurement or rate stays at about the same level. *How important is it to have an even temperature when you're working?... Another use of the AGC type of circuit is to hold the brightness of TV pictures at an even level.* ♦ **evenly** *Stock is added evenly during the first 18 minutes while the mixture cooks... He looked at Ellen, breathing evenly in her sleep.* ADJ-GRADED: usu ADJ n =steady ADV: usu ADV after v

2 An **even** surface is smooth and flat. *The tables are fitted with a glass top to provide an even surface.* ADJ-GRADED =level

3 If there is an **even** distribution or division of something, each person, group, or area involved has an equal amount. *Divide the dough into 12 even pieces and shape each piece into a ball... Many are tired of being unpopular because of their wealth and would encourage more even distribution of it.* ♦ **evenly** *The meat is divided evenly and boiled in a stew... Within manufacturing, the loss of jobs has been far more evenly spread across the regions... The blood vessels in the skin are not evenly distributed around the face and neck.* ADJ-GRADED: usu ADJ n =equal ADV-GRADED: ADV after v, ADV -ed =equally

4 An **even** contest or competition is equally balanced between the two sides who are taking part. *It was an even game. ...an even match between eight nations.* ♦ **evenly** *They must choose between two evenly matched candidates for governor.* ADJ-GRADED: usu ADJ n ADV-GRADED: ADV -ed

5 If you are **even** with someone, you do not owe them anything, such as money or a favour; an informal use. *You don't owe me. I don't owe you. We're even.* ADJ: v-link ADJ

6 If your voice is **even**, you are speaking in a very controlled way which makes it difficult for people to tell what your feelings are; a literary use. *My voice surprised me; it was even and emotionless.* ♦ **evenly** *'Is Mary Ann O.K?'—'She's fine,' she said evenly.* ADJ-GRADED =steady, calm ADV-GRADED: ADV after v

7 An **even** number can be divided exactly by the number two. ADJ: usu ADJ n

8 If there is an **even** or **evens** chance that something will happen, it is equally likely that it will happen or will not happen; used in British English. *They have a more than even chance of winning the next election... You've then got an evens chance of doubling your money at a stroke.* ● See also **evens**. ADJ-GRADED: ADJ n =fifty-fifty

9 When a company or a person running a business **breaks even**, they make neither a profit nor a loss. *The airline hopes to break even next year and return to profit the following year... The theatre needs to fill* PHRASES V inflects

over ninety per cent of its seats every night just to break even.

10 If you say that you are going to **get even** with someone, you mean that you are going to cause them the same amount of harm or annoyance as they have caused you; an informal expression. *I'm going to get even with you for this... Don't get angry, get even.* V inflects, oft PHR *with* n

11 • to **be on an even keel**: see **keel**.

even 3 phrasal verb uses

even /iːvᵊn/ **evens, evening, evened** ◆◇◇◇◇

even out. If something **evens out**, or if you **even** it **out**, the differences between the different parts of it are reduced. *Relative rates of house price inflation have evened out across the country... Foundation make-up evens out your skin tone and texture.* PHRASAL VERB ERG =balance out V P V P n (not pron) Also V n P

even up. To **even up** a contest or game means to make it more equally balanced than it was. *The nation's electronics industry made important strides this year to even up its balance of trade... I would like to see the championship evened up a little bit more.* PHRASAL VERB =balance V P n (not pron) V-ed P Also V n P

even-handed; spelled **evenhanded** in American English. If someone is **even-handed**, they are completely fair, especially when they are judging other people or dealing with two groups of people. *...an even-handed approach to the war on drugs... The administration wants to ensure the meetings appear evenhanded.* ♦ **even-handedly** *He insists that the police are acting even-handedly.* ♦ **even-handedness** *...the carefully modulated even-handedness which is the hallmark of the Queen's public utterances.* ADJ-GRADED =unbiased; ADV-GRADED: ADV with v; N-UNCOUNT

evening /iːvnɪŋ/ **evenings.** The **evening** is the part of each day between the end of the afternoon and the time when you go to bed. *All he did that evening was sit around the flat... Supper is from 5.00 to 6.00 in the evening... Towards evening the carnival entered its final stage.* ◆◆◆◆◇ N-VAR

evening class, evening classes. An **evening class** is a course for adults that is taught in the evening rather than during the day. *Jackie has been learning flamenco dancing at an evening class for three years.* N-COUNT

evening dress, evening dresses

1 **Evening dress** consists of the formal clothes that people wear to formal occasions in the evening. N-UNCOUNT

2 An **evening dress** is a special dress, usually a long one, that a woman wears to a formal occasion in the evening. N-COUNT

evens /iːvᵊnz/

1 In a race or contest, if you bet on a horse or competitor that is quoted at **evens**, you will win a sum of money equal to your bet if that horse or competitor wins; used mainly in British English. *He won his first race by six lengths at evens and his second at 5-2 on... The Martell Cup Chase was won by the evens favourite Toby Tobias.* N-UNCOUNT

2 If there is an **evens** chance that something will happen, it is equally likely that it will happen or will not happen; used mainly in British English. *You've then got an evens chance of doubling your money at a stroke.* ADJ-GRADED: ADJ n =fifty-fifty

evensong /iːvᵊnsɒŋ, AM -sɔːŋ/. **Evensong** is the evening service in the Church of England. N-UNCOUNT

event /ɪvent/ **events** ◆◆◆◆◆

1 An **event** is something that happens, especially when it is unusual or important. You can use **events** to describe all the things that are happening in a particular situation. *...the events of Black Wednesday. ...in the wake of recent events in Europe... A new book by Grass is always an event.* N-COUNT

2 An **event** is a planned and organized occasion, for example a social gathering or a sports match. *The cross-country section of the three-day event was held here yesterday. ...major sporting events. ...our programme of lectures and social events.* N-COUNT: usu with supp

3 An **event** is one of the races or competitions that are part of an organized occasion such as a sports meeting. *A solo piper opens Aberdeen Highland Games at 10am and the main events start at 1pm.* N-COUNT

4 You use **in the event of, in the event that,** and **in that event** when you are talking about a possible future situation, especially when you are planning what to do if it occurs. *The bank has agreed to give an immediate refund in the unlikely event of an error being made... In the event that any part of the deal may be blocked, the rest would go ahead.* PHRASE

5 You say **in any event** after you have been discussing a situation, in order to indicate that what you are saying is true or possible, in spite of anything that has happened or may happen. *In any event, the bowling alley restaurant proved quite acceptable.* PHRASE: PHR with cl PRAGMATICS =anyway

6 In British English, you say **in the event** after you have been discussing what could have happened in a particular situation, in order to indicate that you are now describing what actually did happen. *'Don't underestimate us', Norman Willis warned last year. There was, in the event, little danger of that.* PHRASE: PHR with cl PRAGMATICS

even-tempered. If someone is **even-tempered**, they are usually calm and do not easily get angry. *He was normally a very even-tempered person... They seem less tense, more even-tempered.* ADJ-GRADED =equable

eventful /ɪventfʊl/. If you describe an event or a period of time as **eventful**, you mean that a lot of interesting, exciting, or important things have happened during it. *Her eventful life included holding senior positions in the Colonial Service... It was an eventful and controversial race... Our next journey was longer and much more eventful.* ADJ-GRADED

eventual /ɪventʃuəl/. You use **eventual** to indicate that something happens or is the case at the end of a process or period of time. *There are many who believe that civil war will be the eventual outcome of the racial tension in the country... The eventual aim is the reunification of Korea.* ◆◆◇◇◇ ADJ: ADJ n PRAGMATICS =ultimate

eventuality /ɪventʃuælɪti/ **eventualities.** An **eventuality** is a possible future event or result, especially one that is unpleasant or surprising; a formal word. *Every eventuality is covered, from running out of petrol to needing water.* ◆◇◇◇◇ N-COUNT: with supp =possibility

eventually /ɪventʃuəli/ ◆◆◆◆◇

1 **Eventually** means in the end, especially after a lot of delays, problems, or arguments. *Eventually, the army caught up with him in Latvia... The flight eventually got away six hours late.* ADV: ADV with cl, ADV before v PRAGMATICS =finally

2 **Eventually** means at the end of a situation or process or as the final result of it. *Eventually your child will leave home to lead her own life as a fully independent adult... She sees the bar as a starting point and eventually plans to run her own chain of country inns.* ADV: ADV with cl, ADV before v PRAGMATICS =ultimately

ever /evəʳ/ ◆◆◆◆◆

Ever is an adverb which you use to add emphasis in negative sentences, commands, questions, and conditional structures.

1 **Ever** means at any time. It is used in questions and negative statements. *I'm not sure I'll ever trust people again... Neither of us had ever skied... Have you ever experienced failure?... I don't know if you ever read any of his books... I forbid you ever to use that word!... You won't hear from Gaston ever again.* ADV: ADV before v, ADV adv ≠never

2 You use **ever** in expressions such as **'did you ever'** and **'have you ever'** to express surprise or shock at something you have just seen, heard, or experienced, especially when you expect people to agree with you. *Have you ever seen anything like it?... Did you ever hear anyone sound so peculiar?* ADV: in questions, ADV before v PRAGMATICS

3 You use **ever** after comparatives and superlatives to emphasize the degree to which something is true or when you are comparing a present situation with the past or the future. *She's got a great voice and is singing better than ever... Japan is wealthier and more powerful than ever before... He feels better than he has ever felt before... 'Fear Of Music' remains among the best albums ever for many music fans... This is the most awful evening I can ever remember.* ADV: ADV after compar *than*, ADV after adj-superl PRAGMATICS

4 You use **ever** to indicate that a person is showing a particular quality that is typical of them; used in ADV: ADV adj/n =always

written English. *He was ever careful to check his scripts... Mother, ever the peacemaker, pointed her finger at my little brother and said, 'See? Now stop!'*

5 You use **ever** to mean increasingly. *They grew ever further apart... I think the amount of work will increase and that it will become ever more complex.* ADV: ADV adj/adv

6 You can use **ever** for emphasis after 'never'; an informal use. *I can never, ever, forgive myself... Felix has never, ever confided in me.* ADV: ADV before v PRAGMATICS

7 You use **ever** in questions beginning with words such as 'why', 'when', and 'who' when you want to emphasize your surprise or shock. *Why ever didn't you tell me?... When ever am I going to see you again?... Who ever heard of a thing like that?* ADV: quest ADV PRAGMATICS

8 If something has been the case **ever since** a particular time, it has been the case all the time from then until now. *He's been there ever since you left!... Ever since we moved last year, I worry a lot about whether I can handle this new job... 'Have you been chatting for long?'—'Ever since you left.'* PHR-CONJ-SUBORD ► Also an adverb. *I simply gave in to him, and I've regretted it ever since... In 1985 her first collection received rave reviews from Women's Wear Daily. Ever since, applause has never ceased.* ADV: ADV after v, ADV with cl

9 In informal British English, you use **ever** in the expressions **ever such** and **ever so** to emphasize that someone or something has a particular quality, especially when you are expressing enthusiasm or gratitude. *When I met Derek he was very lively and ever such a good dancer... This is in ever such good condition... I like him ever so much... I'm ever so grateful... I saw him pause ever so slightly.* ADV: ADV *such/so* PRAGMATICS

10 See also **forever**.

11 You use the expression **all** someone **ever does** when you want to emphasize that they do the same thing all the time, and this annoys you. *All she ever does is whinge and complain... All he ever does is discuss the same boring list of medications.* PHRASES V inflects PRAGMATICS

12 You say **as ever** in order to indicate that something or someone's behaviour is not unusual because it is like that all the time or very often. *As ever, the meals are primarily fish-based... He was by himself, alone, as ever.* PHR with cl

13 You can write **'Yours ever'** or **'Ever yours'** at the end of a letter before you sign your name, as an affectionate way of ending the letter; used in old-fashioned British English. CONVENTION

14 ● **hardly ever**: see **hardly**.

ever- /evəʳ-/. You use **ever** in adjectives such as **ever-increasing** and **ever-present**, to show that something exists or continues all the time. *...the ever-increasing traffic on our roads. ...an ever-changing world of medical information... He is always eager for new experiences and ever-willing to experiment.* COMB in ADJ

evergreen /evəʳgriːn/ **evergreens.** An **evergreen** is a tree or bush which has green leaves all the year round. *Holly, like ivy and mistletoe, is an evergreen.* ◆◇◇◇◇ N-COUNT ► Also an adjective. *Plant evergreen shrubs around the end of the month.* ADJ: usu ADJ n

everlasting /evəʳlɑːstɪŋ, -læst-/

1 Something that is **everlasting** never comes to an end. *...a message of peace and everlasting life.* ADJ =eternal

2 If you describe something as **everlasting**, you mean that it seems never to change or end; a literary word. *I have loved you with an everlasting love!... Sometimes the work can feel unrewarding and everlasting.* ADJ =endless

ever more; also spelled **evermore. Ever more** means for all the time in the future. *They will bitterly regret what they have done for ever more... The editor's decision is final and shall evermore remain so.* ◆◇◇◇◇ ADV: ADV with v, oft *for* ADV =always

every /evri/ ◆◆◆◆◆

1 You use **every** to indicate that you are referring to all the members of a group or all the parts of something and not only some of them. *Every village has a green, a church, a pub and a manor house... Record every expenditure you make. ...mediterranean fish of every shape and hue... We need help, every kind of help. ...recipes for every occasion.* DET: DET sing-n ► Also an adjective. *His every utterance will be scrutinized... He will find his every step more harshly spotlighted than has been the case previously.* ADJ: poss ADJ n

2 You also use **every** in order to say how often something happens or to indicate that something happens at regular intervals. *We were made to attend meetings every day... A burglary occurs every three minutes in London... She will need to have the therapy repeated every few months... They meet here every Friday morning.* DET

3 You use **every** in front of a number when you are saying what proportion of people or things something happens to or applies to. *Two out of every three Britons already own a video recorder... About one in every 20 people have clinical depression... For every £1 we spend on food, on average we spend 22p on tobacco.* DET: *out of/in/for* DET amount

4 You can use **every** before some nouns, for example 'sign', 'effort', 'reason', and 'intention' in order to emphasize what you are saying. *The Congressional Budget Office says the federal deficit shows every sign of getting larger... I think that there is every chance that you will succeed... The Chinese Foreign Minister was making every effort to secure a peaceful settlement... Every care has been taken in compiling this list.* DET: DET sing-n PRAGMATICS ≠no

5 If you say that someone's **every** whim, wish, or desire will be satisfied, you are emphasizing that everything they want will happen or be provided. *Dozens of servants had catered to his every whim.* ADJ: poss ADJ n PRAGMATICS

6 You use **every** in the expressions **every now and then, every now and again, every once in a while,** and **every so often** in order to indicate that something happens occasionally. *Stir the batter every now and then to keep it from separating... Every so often the horse's heart and lungs are checked.* PHRASES PHR after v, PHR with cl

7 If something happens **every other day** or **every second day**, for example, it happens one day, then does not happen the next day, then happens the day after that, and so on. You can also say that something happens **every third week, every fourth year**, and so on. *I went home every other week... It has been snowing, roughly every third day, for as long as I've had the flu.* PHR after v, PHR with cl

8 ● **every bit as** good **as**: see **bit**.

everybody /evribɒdi/. **Everybody** means the same as **everyone**. ◆◆◆◆◇

everyday /evrideɪ/. You use **everyday** to describe something which happens or is used every day, or forms a regular and basic part of your life, so it is not especially interesting or unusual. *In the course of my everyday life, I had very little contact with teenagers. ...opportunities for improving fitness in your everyday routine. ...the everyday problems of living in the city... A paint finish can transform something everyday and mundane into something more elaborate.* ◆◆◇◇◇ ADJ: usu ADJ n

everyman /evrimæn/. **Everyman** is used to refer to people in general. If you say, for example, that a character in a film or book is an **everyman**, you mean that the character has experiences and emotions that are like those of any ordinary person. *Douglas plays a frustrated American everyman who suddenly loses control under the pressure of daily life.* N-SING

everyone /evriwʌn/. The form **everybody** is also used. ◆◆◆◆◇

1 You use **everyone** or **everybody** to refer to all the people in a particular group. *Everyone in the street was shocked when they heard the news... When everyone else goes home around 7 p.m. Lynn is still in high gear... Not everyone thinks that the government is being particularly generous.* PRON-INDEF: oft PRON *else* ≠no one, nobody

2 You use **everyone** or **everybody** to refer to all people. *Everyone wrestles with self-doubt and feels like a failure at times... Everyone needs some free time for rest and relaxation... You can't keep everybody happy.* PRON-INDEF ≠no one, nobody

everything /evriθɪŋ/ ◆◆◆◆◆

1 You use **everything** to refer to all the objects, activities, or facts in a particular situation. *He'd gone to Seattle long after everything else in his life had changed... Early in the morning, hikers* PRON-INDEF: oft PRON *else* ≠nothing

pack everything that they will need for the day's hike... Everything in the building had gone silent.

2 You use **everything** to refer to all possible or likely actions, activities, or situations. *'This should have been decided long before now.'—'We can't think of everything.'... Cathy thought that she had the answer to everything... Noel and I do everything together... Are you doing everything possible to reduce your budget?*
PRON-INDEF

3 You use **everything** to refer to a whole situation or to life in general. *She says everything is going smoothly... Is everything all right?... Everything's going to be just fine.*
PRON-INDEF =things

4 If you say that someone or something is **everything**, you mean you consider them to be the most important thing in your life, or the most important thing that there is. *I love him. He is everything to me... Crime cases were something that agents solved, and to him the case was everything... Money isn't everything.*
PRON-INDEF: oft PRON *to* n =all ≠nothing

5 If you say that someone or something has **everything**, you mean they have all the things or qualities that most people consider to be desirable. *This man had everything. He had the house, the sailboat and a full life with friends and family... It was a garden that had everything. It was rich and wild and beautiful, and exciting.*
PRON-INDEF

6 You say **'and everything'** after mentioning a particular thing or list of things to indicate that they are only examples and that other things are also involved; an informal use. *He had a bed and a fireplace and everything... We become friends and everything, and we call each other on the phone all the time.*
PHRASE: cl PHR

everywhere /e̱vriʰweəʳ/ ◆◆◆◇◇

1 You use **everywhere** to refer to a whole area or to all the places in a particular area. *Working people everywhere object to paying taxes... We went everywhere together... Dust is everywhere... Tap water is drinkable everywhere in the Algarve... People come here from everywhere to see these lights.*
ADV-INDEF: n ADV, ADV after v, *be* ADV, oft *from* ADV, ADV cl/group

2 You use **everywhere** to refer to all the places that someone goes to. *Bradley is still accustomed to travelling everywhere in style... Everywhere he went he was introduced as the current United States Open Champion.*
ADV-INDEF: ADV after v, oft ADV cl/prep

3 You use **everywhere** to emphasize that you are talking about a large number of places, or all possible places. *I saw her picture everywhere... I looked everywhere. I couldn't find him.*
ADV-INDEF: ADV after v, *be* ADV, ADV with cl PRAGMATICS

4 If you say that someone or something is **everywhere**, you mean that they are present in a place in very large numbers. *There were cartons of cigarettes everywhere... Clothes were everywhere; hanging out of drawers, strewn across the floor, even spilling from the wastepaper basket.*
ADV-INDEF: *be* ADV, ADV after v

evict /ɪvɪ̱kt/ **evicts, evicting, evicted.** If someone **is evicted** from the place where they are living, they are forced to leave it, usually because they have broken a law or contract. *They were evicted from their apartment after their mother became addicted to drugs... In the first week, the city police evicted ten families... If you don't keep up payments you could be evicted.*
◆◇◇◇◇ VERB
be V-ed *from* n
V n
Also V n *from* n

eviction /ɪvɪ̱kʃᵊn/ **evictions. Eviction** is the act or process of officially forcing someone to leave a house or piece of land. *He was facing eviction, along with his wife and family... He also criticised the evictions for being violent and ruthless. ...an eviction order.*
◆◇◇◇◇ N-VAR

evidence /e̱vɪdəns/ **evidences, evidencing, evidenced** ◆◆◆◆◇

1 Evidence is anything that you see, experience, read, or are told that causes you to believe that something is true or has really happened. *Ganley said he'd seen no evidence of widespread fraud... There is a lot of evidence that stress is partly responsible for disease... To date there is no evidence to support this theory.*
N-UNCOUNT: oft N *of/for* n, N that, N to-inf

2 Evidence is the information which is used in a court of law to try to prove something. **Evidence** is obtained from documents, objects, or witnesses; a technical term in law. *The evidence against him was purely circumstantial. ...enough evidence for a successful prosecution.*
N-UNCOUNT: oft N *against* n

3 If you **give evidence** in a court of law or an official enquiry, you officially say what you know about people or events, or describe an occasion at which you were present. *The forensic scientists who carried out the original tests will be called to give evidence... Cabin crew have been giving evidence at the M1 aircrash enquiry.*
PHRASE: V inflects =testify

4 If a particular feeling, ability, or attitude **is evidenced** by something or someone, it is seen or felt; a formal use. *He's wise in other ways too, as evidenced by his reason for switching from tennis to golf... She was not calculating and evidenced no specific interest in money.*
VERB
be V-ed *by* n
V n

5 If someone or something **is in evidence**, they are present and can be clearly seen. *Few soldiers were in evidence... Poverty and bad housing conditions are still very much in evidence.*
PHRASE: V inflects

evident /e̱vɪdənt/ ◆◆◇◇◇

1 If something is **evident**, you notice it easily and clearly. *His footprints were clearly evident in the heavy dust... The threat of inflation is already evident in bond prices. ...the best-publicised cases of evident injustice.*
ADJ-GRADED =noticeable, unmistakeable

2 You use **evident** to emphasize your certainty about a situation or fact and your interpretation of it. *It was evident that she had once been a beauty... The cities are bombarded day after day in an evident effort to force their surrender.*
ADJ-GRADED: oft *it* v-link ADJ that/wh PRAGMATICS =obvious

3 See also **self-evident**.

evidently /e̱vɪdəntli/ ◆◆◇◇◇

1 You use **evidently** to say that something is obviously true, for example because you have seen evidence of it yourself. *The man wore a bathrobe and had evidently just come from the bathroom... The two Russians evidently knew each other.*
ADV-GRADED: ADV with cl/group, ADV before v =clearly, obviously

2 You use **evidently** to show that you think something is true or have been told something is true, but that you are not sure, because you do not have enough information or proof. *From childhood, he was evidently at once rebellious and precocious... Ellis evidently wished to negotiate downwards after Atkinson had set the guidelines.*
ADV-GRADED: ADV with cl/group, ADV before v

3 You can use **evidently** to introduce a statement or opinion and to emphasize that you feel that it is true or correct; a formal use. *Quite evidently, it has nothing to do with social background.*
ADV-GRADED: ADV with cl PRAGMATICS

evil /i̱ːvᵊl/ **evils** ◆◆◆◇◇

1 Evil is a powerful force that some people believe to exist, and which causes wicked and bad things to happen. *We are still being attacked by the forces of evil... There's always a conflict between good and evil in his plays.*
N-UNCOUNT ≠good

2 Evil is used to refer to all the wicked and bad things that happen in the world. *He could not, after all, stop all the evil in the world. ...those who see television as the root of all evil.*
N-UNCOUNT

3 If you refer to an **evil**, you mean a very unpleasant or harmful situation or activity. *Apartheid is even a greater evil... Higher taxes may be a necessary evil. ...a lecture on the evils of alcohol.*
N-COUNT

4 If you describe someone as **evil**, you mean that they are very wicked by nature and take pleasure in doing things that harm other people. *...the country's most evil terrorists... She's an evil woman.*
ADJ-GRADED

5 If you describe something as **evil**, you mean that you think it causes a great deal of harm to people and is morally bad. *After 1760 few Americans refrained from condemning slavery as evil... They are setting an evil example for their children.*
ADJ-GRADED

6 If you describe something as **evil**, you mean that you think it is influenced by the devil. *I think this is an evil spirit at work... According to local folklore it is an evil place.*
ADJ-GRADED

7 If you describe a smell as **evil**, you think it is very unpleasant. *It left behind it a puff of smoke and a suffocatingly evil smell.*
ADJ-GRADED

8 If you say that someone is putting off or postponing **the evil day** or **the evil hour**, you mean that they will have to do something unpleasant and that
PHRASES usu v PHR

they are trying to avoid doing it for as long as possible. *You can simply go on putting off the evil day and eventually find yourself smoking as much as ever.*

9 If you have two choices, but think that they are both bad, you can describe the one which is less bad as **the lesser of two evils**, or the **lesser evil**. *People voted for him as the lesser of two evils... One suspects that hydro power is still the lesser evil.*

evildoer /iːvᵊlduːəʳ/ **evildoers;** also spelled **evil-doer**. If you describe someone as an **evildoer**, you mean that they are wicked, and that they deliberately cause harm or suffering to others; an old-fashioned or literary word. N-COUNT

evil eye

1 Some people believe that **the evil eye** is a magical power to cast a spell on someone or something by looking at them, so that bad things happen to them. N-SING: *the*N

2 If you say that someone is giving you the **evil eye**, you mean that they are looking at you in an unpleasant way, usually because they are jealous of you or because they dislike you. *When we go out, girls are always giving me the evil eye.* N-SING: usu *the*N

evince /ɪvɪns/ **evinces, evincing, evinced.** If someone or something **evinces** a particular feeling or quality, they show that feeling or quality, often indirectly; a formal word. *The entire production evinces authenticity and a real respect for the subject matter... The new president has so far evinced no such sense of direction.* VERB; V n

eviscerate /ɪvɪsəreɪt/ **eviscerates, eviscerating, eviscerated**

1 To **eviscerate** a person or animal means to remove their internal organs, such as their heart, lungs, and stomach; a formal use. *...strangling and eviscerating rabbits for the pot.* VERB; V n

2 If you say that something will **eviscerate** an organization or system, you are emphasizing that it will make the organization or system much weaker or much less powerful. *Democrats say the petition will eviscerate state government.* VERB PRAGMATICS; V n

evocation /iːvəkeɪʃᵊn, ev-/ **evocations.** An **evocation** of something involves creating an image or impression of it; a formal word. *...a perfect evocation of the period.* N-VAR: usu N *of*n

evocative /ɪvɒkətɪv/. If you describe something as **evocative**, you mean that it is good or interesting because it produces pleasant memories, ideas, emotions, and responses in people; a formal word. *Her story is sharply evocative of Italian provincial life. ...the evocative power of cinema.* ♦ **evocatively** *...the collection of islands evocatively known as the South Seas.* ◆◇◇◇◇ ADJ-GRADED: oft ADJ *of*n; ADV-GRADED: ADV with v

evoke /ɪvoʊk/ **evokes, evoking, evoked.** To **evoke** a particular memory, idea, emotion, or response means to cause it to occur; a formal word. *...the scene evoking memories of those old movies... A sense of period was evoked by complementing pictures with appropriate furniture.* ◆◆◇◇◇ VERB; V n

evolution /iːvəluːʃᵊn, ev-/ **evolutions** ◆◆◇◇◇

1 Evolution is a process of gradual change that takes place over many generations, during which species of animals, plants, or insects slowly change some of their physical characteristics. *...the evolution of plants and animals. ...the theory of evolution by natural selection. ...human evolution.* N-UNCOUNT

2 Evolution is a process of gradual and uninterrupted development in a particular situation or thing over a period of time; a formal use. *...a crucial period in the evolution of modern physics. ...an accurate account of his country's evolution... His long life comprised a series of evolutions.* N-VAR: usu with supp

evolutionary /iːvəluːʃənri, AM -neri/. **Evolutionary** means relating to a process of gradual change and development. *...an evolutionary process. ...a period of evolutionary change.* ◆◇◇◇◇ ADJ: usu ADJ n

evolve /ɪvɒlv/ **evolves, evolving, evolved** ◆◆◇◇◇

1 When animals or plants **evolve**, they gradually change and develop into different forms. *The bright plumage of many male birds was thought to have evolved to attract females... Maize evolved from a wild grass in Mexico. ...when amphibians evolved into reptiles.* VERB; V; V *from*n; V *into*n

2 If something **evolves** or you **evolve** it, it gradually develops over a period of time into something different and usually more advanced. *...a tiny airline which eventually evolved into Pakistan International Airlines... Popular music evolved from folk songs... As medical knowledge evolves, beliefs change... This was when he evolved the working method from which he has never departed.* V-ERG; V *into*n; V *from*n; V; V n

ewe /juː/ **ewes.** A **ewe** is a adult female sheep. N-COUNT

ewer /juːəʳ/ **ewers.** A **ewer** is a large jug with a wide opening; an old-fashioned word. N-COUNT

ex /eks/ **exes.** Someone's **ex** is the person they used to be married to or used to have a romantic or sexual relationship with; an informal word. *He's different from my ex. ...one of her exes.* N-COUNT: usu poss N

ex- /eks-/. **ex-** is added to nouns to show that someone or something is no longer the thing referred to by that noun. For example, someone's ex-husband is no longer their husband. *...my ex-wife. ...ex-President Reagan. ...an ex-soldier.* PREFIX

exacerbate /ɪgzæsəʳbeɪt/ **exacerbates, exacerbating, exacerbated.** If something **exacerbates** a problem or bad situation, it makes it worse; a formal word. *Mr Powell-Taylor says that depopulation exacerbates the problem... Longstanding poverty has been exacerbated by racial divisions.* ♦ **exacerbation** /ɪgzæsəʳbeɪʃᵊn/ *...the exacerbation of global problems.* ◆◇◇◇◇ VERB =aggravate; V n; N-UNCOUNT: usu *the*N *of*n

exact /ɪgzækt/ **exacts, exacting, exacted** ◆◆◆◆◇

1 Exact means correct in every detail. For example, an **exact** copy is the same in every detail as the thing it is copied from. *I don't remember the exact words... The exact number of protest calls has not been revealed... It's an exact copy of the one which was found in Ann Alice's room.* ♦ **exactly** *Try to locate exactly where the smells are entering the room... The system worked perfectly, exactly as his training and plans had led him to expect... What exactly goes wrong with those suffering from senile dementia?... Both drugs will be exactly the same... Barton couldn't remember exactly.* ADJ-GRADED: usu ADJ n =precise ≠approximate; ADV-GRADED: usu ADV with cl/group, also ADV after v =precisely ≠approximately

2 You use **exact** before a noun to emphasize that you are referring to that particular thing and no other, especially something that has a particular significance. *I hadn't really thought about it until this exact moment... Do you really think I could get the exact thing I want?... It may be that you will feel the exact opposite of what you expected.* ♦ **exactly** *These are exactly the people who do not vote... He knew exactly what he was doing.* ADJ: ADJ n PRAGMATICS; ADV: ADV n/wh =precisely, just

3 If you describe someone as **exact**, you mean that they are very careful and detailed in their work, thinking, or methods. *Formal, exact and obstinate, he was also cold, suspicious, touchy and tactless.* ADJ-GRADED =meticulous

4 When someone **exacts** something, they demand and obtain it from someone else, especially because they are in a superior or more powerful position; a formal use. *Already he has exacted a written apology from the chairman of the commission... They, too, would be likely to exact a high price for their cooperation.* VERB; V n *from/for*n

5 If someone **exacts** revenge on a person, they have their revenge on them. *She uses the media to help her exact a terrible revenge.* VERB; V n; Also V n *on*n

6 If something **exacts** a high price, it has a bad effect on a person or situation. *The sheer physical effort had exacted a heavy price... The strain of a violent ground campaign will exact a toll on troops.* VERB; V n; V n *on*n

7 See also **exactly**.

8 You say **to be exact** to indicate that you are now giving more detailed information or a slight correction that relates to what you have been saying. *A small number – five, to be exact – have been bad... I consider myself to be a liberal democrat, or to be more exact, a democratic liberal.* PHRASE: PHR with cl/group PRAGMATICS

exacting /ɪgzæktɪŋ/. You use **exacting** to describe something or someone that demands hard work and a great deal of care. *The Duke was not well enough to carry out such an exacting task...* ADJ-GRADED: usu ADJ n

Privately they seem to have the same exacting standards.

exactitude /ɪgzæktɪtjuːd, AM -tuːd/. **Exactitude** is the quality of being very accurate and careful; a formal word. *This was an extension of the exactitude he expected to find in all dimensions of daily life.* N-UNCOUNT

exactly /ɪgzæktli/ ◆◆◆◇◇

1 You use **exactly** before an amount, number, or position to emphasize that it is no more, no less, or no different from what you are stating. *Each corner had a guard tower, each of which was exactly ten meters in height... Agnew's car pulled into the driveway at exactly five o'clock... It seems logical to keep a moving subject exactly in the middle of the picture.* ADV: usu ADV num, also ADV prep/adv PRAGMATICS =just, precisely

2 If you say **'Exactly'**, you are agreeing with someone or emphasizing the truth of what they say. If you say **'Not exactly'**, you are telling them politely that they are wrong in part of what they are saying. *Eve nodded, almost approvingly. 'Exactly.'... 'We don't know the answer to that.'—'Exactly – so shut up and stop speculating.'... 'And you refused?'—'Well, not exactly. I couldn't say yes.'* ADV as reply PRAGMATICS =precisely

3 You use **not exactly** to indicate that a meaning or situation is slightly different from what people think or expect. *He's not exactly homeless, he just hangs out in this park.* ADV: *not* ADV, usu ADV group PRAGMATICS

4 You use **not exactly** to emphasize in a rather ironic or sarcastic way what is being said. *This is not exactly what the Church needed just at this moment... She was not exactly a beautiful woman.* ADV: *not* ADV, usu ADV group PRAGMATICS

5 You use **exactly** with a question to show that you disapprove of what the person you are talking to is doing or saying. *What exactly do you mean?... Exactly what are you looking for?* ADV: ADV with quest PRAGMATICS =precisely

6 See also **exact**.

exactness /ɪgzæktnəs/. **Exactness** is the quality of being very accurate and precise. *He recalls his native Bombay with cinematic exactness.* N-UNCOUNT: usu with supp

exact science. If you say that a particular activity is not an **exact science**, you mean that there are no set rules to follow or it does not produce entirely accurate results. *Forecasting floods is not an exact science.* N-SING: usu with brd-neg

exaggerate /ɪgzædʒəreɪt/ **exaggerates, exaggerating, exaggerated** ◆◆◇◇◇

1 If you **exaggerate**, you indicate that something is, for example, worse or more important than it really is. *He thinks I'm exaggerating... Don't exaggerate... Sheila admitted that she did sometimes exaggerate the demands of her job.* ♦ **exaggeration** /ɪgzædʒəreɪʃən/ **exaggerations** *Like many stories about him, it smacks of exaggeration... It would be an exaggeration to call the danger urgent.* VERB V V n N-VAR

2 If something **exaggerates** a situation, quality, or feature, it makes the situation, quality, or feature appear greater, more obvious, or more important than it really is. *These figures exaggerate the loss of competitiveness... The dress exaggerates her wasp waist and enlarges her bosom.* VERB V n

exaggerated /ɪgzædʒəreɪtɪd/. Something that is **exaggerated** is or seems larger, better, worse, or more important than it actually needs to be. *They should be sceptical of exaggerated claims for what such courses can achieve... Western fears, he insists, are greatly exaggerated.* ♦ **exaggeratedly** *...an exaggeratedly feminine appearance... She laughed exaggeratedly at their jokes.* ◆◆◇◇◇ ADJ-GRADED ADV-GRADED: ADV adj/-ed, ADV after v

exalt /ɪgzɔːlt/ **exalts, exalting, exalted.** To **exalt** someone or something means to praise them very highly; a formal use. *However difficult she might have been, this book exalts her as both mother and muse... His work exalts all those virtues that we, as Americans, are taught to hold dear.* ♦ **exaltation** *The poem, which appeared in 1890, is an exaltation of married love.* ◆◇◇◇◇ VERB V n N-UNCOUNT: also *a* N, usu N *of* n

exaltation /egzɔːlteɪʃən/. **Exaltation** is an intense feeling of great joy and happiness; a formal word. *The city was swept up in the mood of exaltation.* • See also **exalt**. N-UNCOUNT =exhilaration

exalted /ɪgzɔːltɪd/ ◆◇◇◇◇

1 Someone or something that is at an **exalted** level is at a very high level, especially with regard to rank or importance; a formal use. *...at the exalted level of Olympic competition... You must decide how to make the best use of your exalted position.* ADJ-GRADED: usu ADJ n =lofty

2 If you feel **exalted**, you feel full of great joy and happiness; a formal use. *You do get very excited and exalted by the power of their speeches.* ADJ-GRADED: usu v-link ADJ

exam /ɪgzæm/ **exams.** An **exam** is a formal test that you take to show your knowledge or ability in a particular subject, or to obtain a qualification. *This time he passed his A-level history exam... Kate's exam results were excellent.* ◆◆◇◇◇ N-COUNT =examination

examination /ɪgzæmɪneɪʃən/ **examinations.** An **examination** is the same as an **exam**; a formal use. • See also **examine**. ◆◆◆◇◇ N-COUNT

examine /ɪgzæmɪn/ **examines, examining, examined** ◆◆◆◆◇

1 If you **examine** something, you look at it carefully. *He examined her passport and stamped it... Forensic scientists are examining what police believe to have been the bombers' car.* ♦ **examination** /ɪgzæmɪneɪʃən/ **examinations** *The Navy is to carry out an examination of the wreck tomorrow... They have also searched offices in Sheffield and taken away documents for examination.* VERB V n N-VAR =inspection

2 If a doctor **examines** you, he or she looks at your body, feels it, or does simple tests in order to check how healthy you are. *Another doctor examined her and could still find nothing wrong... He was examined again and then prescribed a different herbal medicine.* ♦ **examination** *He was later discharged after an examination at Westminster Hospital... Further examination is needed to exclude the chance of disease.* VERB V n N-VAR

3 If an idea, proposal, or plan **is examined**, it is considered very carefully. *I have given the matter much thought, examining all the possible alternatives... The plans will be examined by EC environment ministers.* ♦ **examination** *The government said it was studying the implications, which 'required very careful examination and consideration'.* VERB V n N-VAR

4 If you **are examined**, you are given a formal test in order to show your knowledge of a subject. *...learning to cope with the pressures of being judged and examined by our teachers.* VB: usu passive *be* V-ed

examinee /ɪgzæmɪniː/ **examinees.** An **examinee** is someone who is taking an exam; a formal word. N-COUNT

examiner /ɪgzæmɪnər/ **examiners.** An **examiner** is a person who sets or marks an examination. • See also **medical examiner.** ◆◇◇◇◇ N-COUNT

example /ɪgzɑːmpəl, -zæmp-/ **examples** ◆◆◆◆◆

1 An **example** of something is a particular situation, object, or person that illustrates a point you are making, or that supports an argument, theory, or opinion. *The doctors gave numerous examples of patients being expelled from hospital... Listed below are just a few examples of some of the family benefits available.* N-COUNT: oft N *of* n PRAGMATICS

2 An **example** of a particular class of objects or styles is something that has many of the typical features of such a class or style, and that you consider clearly represents it. *Symphonies 103 and 104 stand as perfect examples of early symphonic construction... The plaque illustrated in Figure 1 is an example of his work at this time.* N-COUNT: oft N *of* n =illustration

3 You use **for example** to introduce and emphasize something that illustrates a point you are making, or that supports an argument, theory, or opinion. *...'educational toys' that are designed to promote the development of, for example, children's spatial ability... Take, for example, the simple sentence: 'The man climbed up the hill'... A few simple precautions can be taken, for example ensuring that desks are the right height.* PHRASE: PHR with cl/group PRAGMATICS =for instance

4 If you refer to a person or their behaviour as an **example** to other people, you mean that he or she behaves in a good or correct way that other people should copy. *He is a model professional and an example to the younger lads... Their example shows us what we are all capable of.* N-COUNT: oft N *to* n

5 In a dictionary entry, an **example** is a phrase or sentence which shows how a particular word is used. The examples usually come after the definition or translation of the word. *The examples are unique to this dictionary.* N-COUNT

6 If you **follow** someone's **example**, you behave in the same way as they did in the past, or in a similar way, especially because you admire them. *Following the example set by her father, she has fulfilled her role and done her duty... She should remember that she is a mother and a public figure and that others may follow her example.* PHRASES V inflects

7 To **make an example of** someone who has done something wrong means to punish them severely as a warning to other people not to do the same thing. *Let us at least see our courts make an example of these despicable criminals.* V inflects, PHR n

8 If you **set an example**, you encourage or inspire people by your behaviour to behave or act in a similar way. *An officer's job was to set an example... He is setting an example which other aristocrats and leading Britons should follow.* V inflects

exasperate /ɪgzɑːspəreɪt, -zæs-/ **exasperates, exasperating, exasperated.** If someone or something **exasperates** you, they annoy you and make you feel frustrated or upset. *The sheer futility of it all exasperates her.* ♦◇◇◇◇ VERB; V n ♦ **exasperation** /ɪgzɑːspəreɪʃən, -zæs-/ *Mahoney clenched his fist in exasperation... There was a trace of exasperation in his voice.* N-UNCOUNT

exasperated /ɪgzɑːspəreɪtɪd, -zæs-/. If you describe someone as **exasperated**, you mean that they are feeling frustrated or angry because of something that is happening or something that someone else is doing. *Bertha was exasperated at the delay... The president was clearly exasperated by the whole saga... Welland gave an exasperated sigh and turned back.* ♦◇◇◇◇ ADJ-GRADED: oft ADJ *by/with/at* n

exasperating /ɪgzɑːspəreɪtɪŋ, -zæs-/. If you describe someone or something as **exasperating**, you mean that you feel angry or frustrated by them or by what they do. *Hardie could be exasperating to his colleagues... She really is the most exasperating woman.* ADJ-GRADED: usu v-link ADJ

excavate /ekskəveɪt/ **excavates, excavating, excavated** ♦◇◇◇◇

1 When archaeologists or other people **excavate** a piece of land, they remove earth carefully from it and look for things such as pots, bones, or buildings which are buried there, in order to discover information about the past. *A new Danish expedition is again excavating the site in annual summer digs.* VERB; V n ♦ **excavation** /ekskəveɪʃən/ **excavations** *...the excavation of a bronze-age boat by the Canterbury Archaeological Trust... In time these new excavations will require conservation.* N-VAR

2 To **excavate** means to dig a hole in the ground, for example in order to build there. *A contractor was hired to drain the reservoir and to excavate soil from one area for replacement with clay.* VERB; V n ♦ **excavation** *Our new habitation was an excavation made in the earth. ...the excavation of canals.* N-VAR

excavator /ekskəveɪtəʳ/ **excavators.** An **excavator** is a very large machine that is used for digging, for example on a building site. N-COUNT

exceed /ɪksiːd/ **exceeds, exceeding, exceeded** ♦♦◇◇◇

1 If something **exceeds** a particular amount or number, it is greater or larger than that amount or number; a formal use. *Its research budget exceeds $700 million a year... The demand for places at some schools exceeds the supply... His performance exceeded all expectations.* VERB; V n

2 If you **exceed** a limit or rule, you go beyond it, even though you are not supposed to or it is against the law; a formal use. *Even Diana has been stopped by the police and warned that she was exceeding the speed limit... I would be exceeding my powers if I ordered the march to be halted.* VERB; V n

exceedingly /ɪksiːdɪŋli/. **Exceedingly** means very or very much; an old-fashioned word. *We had an exceedingly good lunch... This was an exceedingly difficult decision to take... I have a case that troubles me exceedingly.* ♦◇◇◇◇ ADV: usu ADV adj, also ADV after v; =extremely

excel /ɪksel/ **excels, excelling, excelled.** If someone **excels** in something or **excels** at it, they are very good at doing it. *Caine has always been an actor who excels in irony... Mary was a better rider than either of them and she excelled at outdoor sports... Academically he began to excel... I think Krishnan excelled himself in all departments of his game.* ♦◇◇◇◇ VERB; V in n; V at n; V; V pron-refl

excellence /eksələns/. If someone or something has the quality of **excellence**, they are extremely good at something. *...the top US award for excellence in journalism and the arts. ...a school once noted for its academic excellence.* ● See also **par excellence.** ♦♦◇◇◇ N-UNCOUNT

Excellency /eksələnsi/ **Excellencies.** You use expressions such as **Your Excellency** or **His Excellency** when you are addressing or referring to officials of very high rank, for example ambassadors or governors. *I am reluctant to trust anyone totally, your Excellency... His excellency the President will be waiting for you in the hall.* ♦◇◇◇◇ N-VOC: poss N; PRON: poss PRON; PRAGMATICS

excellent /eksələnt/ ♦♦♦♦◇

1 Something that is **excellent** is very good indeed. *The recording quality is excellent... Luckily, Sue is very efficient and does an excellent job as Fred's personal assistant.* ADJ ♦ **excellently** *They're both playing excellently... The tournament was excellently organised.* ADV-GRADED: ADV after v, ADV adj/-ed

2 Some people say **'Excellent!'** to show that they approve of something. EXCLAM

except /ɪksept/ ♦♦♦♦◇

1 You use **except** to introduce the only thing or person that a statement does not apply to, or a fact that prevents a statement from being completely true. *I wouldn't have accepted anything except a job in Europe... I don't take any drugs whatsoever, except aspirin for colds... Children who take exams early will be allowed to drop a subject except in the case of maths, English and science.* PREP ► Also a conjunction. *Freddie would tell me nothing about what he was writing, except that it was to be a Christmas play... The log cabin stayed empty, except when we came... Ida would not speak to him except to answer questions... Nothing more to do now except wait.* CONJ-SUBORD: oft CONJ that/when/where/if

2 You use **except for** to introduce the only thing or person that prevents a statement from being completely true. *He hadn't eaten a thing except for one forkful of salad... Everyone was late, except for Richard.* PHR-PREP =apart from

excepted /ɪkseptɪd/. You use **excepted** after you have mentioned a person or thing to show that you do not include them in the statement you are making; a formal word. *Jeremy excepted, the men seemed personable... You normally receive 4 treatments each day, Sundays excepted.* ADV: n ADV

excepting /ɪkseptɪŋ/. You use **excepting** to introduce the only thing that prevents a statement from being completely true; a formal word. *The source of meat for much of this region (excepting Japan) has traditionally been the pig.* PREP =except for

exception /ɪksepʃən/ **exceptions** ♦♦♦◇◇

1 An **exception** is a particular thing, person, or situation that is not included in a general statement, judgement, or rule. *Few guitarists can sing as well as they can play; Eddie, however, is an exception... There were no floral offerings at the ceremony, with the exception of a single red rose... The law makes no exceptions... With few exceptions, guests are booked for week-long visits.* N-COUNT: oft *with the* N *of* n, *with* N

2 If you make a general statement, and then say that something or someone is **no exception**, you are emphasizing that they are included in that statement. *Marketing is applied to everything these days, and books are no exception... Most people have no real idea how to change to healthy food, and Maureen was no exception.* PHRASES v-link PHR; PRAGMATICS

3 When you are referring to an example which contradicts a general argument or statement that you are making, you can say that it is **the exception** *exception* and V inflect, usu v-link PHR; PRAGMATICS

that proves the rule, in order to avoid difficulty or spoiling your argument. *On the surface, selling arms to a country that sponsors terrorism is clearly wrong, but it's the exception sometimes that proves the rule.*

4 If you **take exception to** something, you feel offended or annoyed by it, usually with the result that you complain about it. *He also took exception to having been spied on... And the problem is that they take exception to any kind of noise whatsoever.* V inflects =object

5 You use **with the exception of** to introduce a thing or person that is not included in a general statement that you are making. *Yesterday was a day off for everybody, with the exception of Lawrence... In virtually every sport, with the possible exception of women's gymnastics, the players are now bigger and stronger than before.* PREP

6 You use **without exception** to emphasize that the statement you are making is true in all cases. *The vehicles are without exception old, rusty and dented... Almost without exception those convicted were our friends and colleagues.* PHR with cl/group, PHR after v PRAGMATICS

exceptional /ɪksepʃənᵊl/ ◆◆◇◇◇

1 You use **exceptional** to describe someone or something that has particular quality, usually a good quality, to an unusually high degree. *...children with exceptional ability... His translation is exceptional in its poetic quality.* ♦ **exceptionally** *He's an exceptionally talented dancer and needs to practice several hours every day... The conditions under ground were exceptionally hot.* ADJ-GRADED PRAGMATICS =extraordinary; ADV: ADV adj/adv =extremely

2 Exceptional situations and incidents are unusual and only likely to happen very rarely; a formal use. *...if the courts hold that this case is exceptional... School governors have the discretion to allow parents to withdraw pupils in exceptional circumstances.* ♦ **exceptionally** *Exceptionally, in times of emergency, we may send a team of experts... At your request we may agree, exceptionally, to work outside usual working hours.* ADJ-GRADED =unusual; ADV: ADV with cl =unusually

excerpt, excerpts, excerpted. The noun is pronounced /eksɜːʳpt/. The verb is pronounced /eksɜːʳpt/. ◆◆◆◇◇

1 An **excerpt** is a short piece of writing or music which is taken from a larger piece. *...an excerpt from Tchaikovsky's Nutcracker.* N-COUNT: oft N *from* n =extract

2 If a long piece of writing or music **is excerpted**, short pieces from it are printed or played on their own. *The readings you heard earlier were excerpted from a new oral history of Pearl Harbor.* V-PASSIVE be V-ed *from* n

excess, excesses. The noun is pronounced /ɪkses/. The adjective is pronounced /ekses/. ◆◆◆◇◇

1 An **excess** of something is a larger amount than is needed, allowed, or usual. *An excess of houseplants in a small flat can be oppressive... Polyunsaturated oils are essential for health. Excess is harmful, however.* N-VAR: with supp, usu *a* N *of* n

2 Excess is used to describe amounts that are greater than what is needed, allowed, or usual. *After cooking the fish, pour off any excess fat... The major reason for excess weight is excess eating.* ADJ: ADJ n =surplus

3 Excess is behaviour that is unacceptable because it is considered too extreme or immoral. *She said she was sick of her life of excess. ...adolescent excess. ...the bloody excesses of warfare and empire-building.* N-UNCOUNT: also N in pl

4 Excess is used to refer to additional amounts of money that need to be paid for services and activities that were not originally planned or taken into account; a formal use. *...a letter demanding an excess fare of £20... Staff who have to travel farther can claim excess travel expenses.* ADJ: ADJ n

5 In British English, the **excess** on an insurance policy is a sum of money which the insured person has to pay towards the cost of a claim. The insurance company pays the rest; a technical term in finance. *The company wanted £1,413 for a policy with a £250 excess for under-21s.* N-COUNT: usu sing

6 In excess of means more than a particular amount; a formal expression. *Avoid deposits in excess of £20,000 in any one account... The energy value of dried fruits is considerably in excess of that of fresh items.* PHRASES PREP: PREP amount

7 If you do something **to excess** you do it too much; used showing disapproval. *I was reasonably fit, played a lot of tennis, and didn't smoke or drink to excess... Red meat, eaten to excess, is very high in fat and calories.* PHR after v

excessive /ɪksesɪv/. If you describe the amount or level of something as **excessive**, you disapprove of it because it is more or higher than is necessary or reasonable. *...the alleged use of excessive force by police... The government says that local authority spending is excessive.* ◆◆◇◇◇ ADJ-GRADED PRAGMATICS

♦ **excessively** *Managers are also accused of paying themselves excessively high salaries... Mum had started taking pills and drinking excessively.* ADV: ADV adj, ADV with v

exchange /ɪkstʃeɪndʒ/ **exchanges, exchanging, exchanged** ◆◆◆◆◇

1 If two or more people **exchange** things of a particular kind, they give them to each other at the same time. *We exchanged addresses and Christmas cards... The two men exchanged glances... He exchanged a quick smile with her then entered the lift.* V-RECIP =swap; pl-n V; V n *with* n

► Also a noun. *He ruled out any exchange of prisoners with the militants... There was also a brief exchange of views on the Gulf crisis.* N-COUNT: oft N *of* pl-n

2 If you **exchange** something or **exchange** it for something else, you replace it with something else, especially something that is better or more satisfactory. *...the chance to sell back or exchange goods... If the car you have leased is clearly unsatisfactory, you can always exchange it for another.* VERB =swap; V n; V n *for* n

3 An **exchange** is a brief conversation, usually an angry one; a formal use. *There've been some bitter exchanges between the two groups.* N-COUNT =conversation

4 An **exchange** of fire, for example, is an incident in which people use guns or missiles against each other; a military term. *There was an exchange of fire during which the gunman was wounded... This could intensify the risk of a nuclear exchange.* N-COUNT: oft N *of* n

5 An **exchange** is an arrangement in which people from two different countries visit each other's country, to strengthen links between them. *...a series of sporting and cultural exchanges with Seoul. ...educational exchanges for young people... I'm going to go on an exchange visit to Paris.* N-COUNT: usu adj N

6 Exchange is used in the names of some places where people used to trade and do business with each other. *...the Royal Exchange.* N-IN-NAMES: *the* supp N

7 The **exchange** is the same as the **telephone exchange**. N-COUNT: usu *the* N

8 See also **corn exchange**, **foreign exchange**, **stock exchange**.

9 If you do something for someone or give them something **in exchange**, you do it or give it because they did something for you or gave you something. *It is illegal for public officials to solicit gifts or money in exchange for favors... He paid her a huge salary. In exchange, he was assured of her vote.* PHRASE: usu PHR *for* n, PHR with cl =in return

exchange rate, exchange rates. The **exchange rate** of a country's unit of currency is the amount of another country's currency that you get in exchange for it. ◆◆◆◇◇ N-COUNT

Exchequer /ɪkstʃekəʳ/. **The Exchequer** is the department in the British government which is responsible for receiving, issuing, and accounting for money belonging to the state. ◆◇◇◇◇ N-PROPER: *the* N

excise, excises, excising, excised. The noun is pronounced /eksaɪz/. The verb is pronounced /ɪksaɪz/. ◆◇◇◇◇

1 Excise is a tax that the government of a country puts on particular goods, such as cigarettes and alcoholic drinks, which are produced for sale in its own country. *...this year's rise in excise duties... These products are excused VAT and excise in their country of origin.* N-VAR: usu N n

2 If someone **excises** something, they remove it deliberately and completely; a formal use. *...a personal crusade to excise racist and sexist references in newspapers. ...the question of permanently excising madness from the world.* ♦ **excision** /ɪksɪʒən/ VERB; V n; V n *from* n; N-VAR

excisions *The authors demanded excision of foreign words.*

excitable /ɪksaɪtəbᵊl/. If you describe someone as **excitable**, you mean that they behave in a rather nervous way and become excited very easily. *Mary sat beside Elaine, who today seemed excitable... The staff were somewhat alarmed by the man, who was in an excitable state.* ADJ-GRADED
♦ **excitability** /ɪksaɪtəbɪlɪti/ *She has always been more inclined to excitability and impatience.* N-UNCOUNT

excite /ɪksaɪt/ **excites, exciting, excited** ◆◆◇◇◇
1 If something **excites** you, it makes you feel very happy, eager, or enthusiastic. *I only take on work that excites me, even if it means turning down lots of money... We'd not been excited by anything for about three years... Where the show really excites is in the display of avant-garde photography.* VERB V n V
2 If something **excites** a particular feeling, emotion, or reaction in someone, it causes them to experience it. *By all accounts, the monarchy does not excite strong feelings among the majority of Romanians... Daniel's early exposure to motor racing did not excite his interest... Reports of the plot of this unusual film tend to excite revulsion.* VERB =arouse V n
3 If something or someone **excites** you, they cause you to feel sexual desire. *Don't try exciting your partner with dirty magazines.* ♦ **excited** *She makes you feel warm and comfortable, and maybe a little excited.* ♦ **exciting** *...a sexually exciting thought.* VERB V n *with* n Also V n ADJ-GRADED ADJ-GRADED
4 To **excite** a physical object such as an atomic particle or an organ in your body means to increase the amount of energy, movement, or activity in it; a technical use in science. *The amount of nicotine in these nicotine substitutes can be enough to excite the heart.* ♦ **excited** *...when an electron drops from an excited state to a less excited state.* VERB V n ADJ-GRADED

excited /ɪksaɪtɪd/ ◆◆◇◇◇
1 If you are **excited**, you are so happy that you cannot relax, especially because you are thinking about something pleasant that is going to happen to you. *I'm very excited about the possibility of playing for England's first team... I was so excited when I went to sign the paperwork I could hardly write. ...an excited teenager on a trek through the London shops.* ♦ **excitedly** *'You're coming?' he said excitedly. 'That's fantastic! That's incredible!'* ADJ-GRADED: usu v-link ADJ, oft ADJ *about* n ADV-GRADED: ADV with v
2 If you are **excited**, you are very worried or angry about something, and so you are very alert and cannot relax. *I don't think there's any reason to get excited about inflation... Excited voices were shouting that the road was blocked by soldiers.* ♦ **excitedly** *Larry rose excitedly to the edge of his seat, shook a fist at us and spat.* ADJ-GRADED =agitated ADV-GRADED: ADV with v

excitement /ɪksaɪtmənt/ **excitements.** You use **excitement** to refer to the state of being excited, or to something that excites you. *Everyone is in a state of great excitement. ...the excitement of a thunderstorm... This game had its challenges, excitements and rewards.* ◆◆◇◇◇ N-VAR

exciting /ɪksaɪtɪŋ/. If something is **exciting**, it makes you feel very happy or enthusiastic. *The race itself is very exciting... This voyage was the most exciting adventure of their lives... Jackie was an exciting player to watch.* ♦ **excitingly** *He is an excitingly original writer.* ◆◆◆◇◇ ADJ-GRADED =thrilling ADV-GRADED: usu ADV adj

exclaim /ɪkskleɪm/ **exclaims, exclaiming, exclaimed.** Writers sometimes use **exclaim** to show that someone is speaking suddenly, loudly, or emphatically, often because they are excited, shocked, or angry. *'He went back to the lab', Iris exclaimed impatiently... He exclaims that it must be a typing error.* ◆◇◇◇◇ VERB =cry V with quote V that

exclamation /ekskləmeɪʃᵊn/ **exclamations.** An **exclamation** is a sound, word, or sentence that is spoken suddenly, loudly, or emphatically and that expresses excitement, admiration, shock, or anger; a formal word. *Sue gave an exclamation as we got a clear sight of the house.* N-COUNT

exclamation mark, exclamation marks. An **exclamation mark** is the sign (!) which is used in writing to show that a word, phrase, or sentence is an exclamation; used mainly in British English. The usual American expression is **exclamation point**. N-COUNT

exclude /ɪkskluːd/ **excludes, excluding, excluded** ◆◆◇◇◇
1 If you **exclude** someone from a place or activity, you prevent them from entering it or taking part in it. *The Academy excluded women from its classes... The army should be excluded from political life... Many of the youngsters feel excluded.* VERB V n *from* n V-ed Also V n
2 If you **exclude** something that has some connection with what you are doing, you deliberately do not use it or consider it. *They eat only plant foods, and take care to exclude animal products from other areas of their lives... In some schools, Christmas carols are being modified to exclude any reference to Christ.* VERB V n *from* n V n
3 To **exclude** a possibility means to decide or prove that it is wrong and not worth considering. *I cannot entirely exclude the possibility that some form of pressure was applied to the neck. ...the pathological evidence, which does not exclude suicide.* VB: usu with brd-neg V n
4 To **exclude** something such as the sun's rays or harmful germs means to prevent them physically from reaching or entering a particular place. *This was intended to exclude the direct rays of the sun... They have spent $3 million building fences around the National Park to exclude such pests.* VERB =keep out V n

excluding /ɪkskluːdɪŋ/. You use **excluding** before mentioning a person or thing to show that you are not including them in your statement. *The families questioned, excluding those on income support, have a net income of £200.20 a week... Excluding water, half of the body's weight is protein.* ◆◇◇◇◇ PREP ≠including

exclusion /ɪkskluːʒᵊn/ **exclusions** ◆◆◇◇◇
1 The **exclusion** of something is the act of deliberately not using, allowing, or considering it. *It calls for the exclusion of all commercial lending institutions from the college loan program... Certain exclusions and limitations apply.* N-VAR: oft N *of* n
2 **Exclusion** is the act of preventing someone from entering a place or taking part in an activity. *...women's exclusion from political power... The Tory rebels were privately furious yesterday at their exclusion.* N-UNCOUNT: usu with poss, oft N *from* n
3 You can say that something happens **to the exclusion of** something else when you want to suggest that the first thing happens to such a great extent or in such a dominant way that it prevents the second thing from being considered or being present. *Diane had dedicated her life to caring for him to the exclusion of all else.* PHRASE: usu PHR after v, PHR n

exclusionary /ɪkskluːʒᵊnri/. Something that is **exclusionary** excludes a particular person or group of people; a formal word. *She highlighted exclusionary business practices.* ADJ-GRADED

exclusive /ɪkskluːsɪv/ **exclusives** ◆◆◇◇◇
1 If you describe something as **exclusive**, you mean that it is limited to people who have a lot of money or who belong to a high social class, and is therefore not available to everyone. *He is already a member of Britain's most exclusive club... The City was criticised for being too exclusive and uncompetitive.* ♦ **exclusiveness** *...a rising middle class, which objected to the exclusiveness of the traditional elite.* ♦ **exclusivity** /ekskluːsɪvɪti/ *While residents enjoy the exclusivity of their homes, they take more pride in their advanced degrees and ambitious jobs.* ADJ-GRADED N-UNCOUNT N-UNCOUNT: oft *the* N *of* n
2 Something that is **exclusive** is used or owned by only one person or group, and not shared with anyone else. *Our group will have exclusive use of a 60-foot boat... Many of their cheeses are exclusive to our stores in Britain.* ♦ **exclusivity** *Only 250 are to be sold in Europe, so exclusivity is guaranteed.* ADJ: oft ADJ *to* n N-UNCOUNT
3 If a newspaper, magazine, or broadcasting organization describes one of its articles or reports as **exclusive**, they mean that it is a special article or report which appears in no other publication or on no other channel. *He told the magazine in an exclusive interview: 'All my problems stem from* ADJ: usu ADJ n

drink'. ► An **exclusive** is an exclusive article or report. *Some papers thought they had an exclusive.* N-COUNT

4 If a company states that its prices, goods, or services are **exclusive** of something, that thing is not included in the stated price, although it usually still has to be paid for. *All charges for service are exclusive of value added tax... Skiing weekends cost £58 (exclusive of travel and accommodation).* ADJ: usu v-link ADJ *of* n ≠inclusive

5 If two things are **mutually exclusive**, they are separate and very different from each other, so that it is impossible for them to exist or happen together. *They both have learnt that ambition and successful fatherhood can be mutually exclusive.* PHRASE: v-link PHR

exclusively /ɪkskluːsɪvli/. **Exclusively** is used to refer to situations or activities that involve only the thing or things mentioned, and nothing else. *...an exclusively male domain... Instruction in these subjects in undergraduate classes is almost exclusively by lecture.* ◆◆◇◇◇ ADV: ADV with cl/group, ADV with v

excommunicate /ekskəmjuːnɪkeɪt/ **excommunicates, excommunicating, excommunicated.** If a Roman Catholic or member of the Orthodox Church is **excommunicated**, it is publicly and officially stated that the person is no longer allowed to be a member of the Church. This is a punishment for some very great wrong that they have done. *Eventually, he was excommunicated along with his mentor... In 1766 he excommunicated the village for its 'depraved diversion.'* VERB be V-ed V n ♦ **excommunication** /ekskəmjuːnɪkeɪʃən/ **excommunications** *...the threat of excommunication.* N-VAR

excoriate /ɪkskɔːrieɪt/ **excoriates, excoriating, excoriated.** To **excoriate** a person or organization means to criticize them severely or condemn their actions, usually in public; a formal word. *He proceeded to excoriate me in front of the nurses.* VERB =berate V n

excrement /ekskrɪmənt/. **Excrement** is the solid waste that is passed out of a person or animal's body through their bowels; a formal word. *The cage smelled of excrement.* N-UNCOUNT

excrescence /ɪkskresəns/ **excrescences.** If you describe something such as a building, addition, or development as an **excrescence**, you strongly disapprove of it because you think it is unnecessary, bad, or ugly; a literary word. *The main dining room is nothing more than a utilitarian addition to the original building, an architectural excrescence... The trade union block vote is an excrescence on democracy.* N-COUNT: usu with supp, oft N *on* n PRAGMATICS =blot

excreta /ɪkskriːtə/. **Excreta** is the waste matter, such as urine or faeces, which is passed out of a person or animal's body; a formal word. N-UNCOUNT

excrete /ɪkskriːt/ **excretes, excreting, excreted.** When a person or animal **excretes** waste matter from their body, they get rid of it, for example in faeces, urine, or sweat; a technical term in biology. *Your open pores excrete sweat and dirt... Calcium is excreted in the urine and stools.* ◆◇◇◇◇ VERB V n Also V ♦ **excretion** /ɪkskriːʃən/ **excretions** *...the excretion of this drug from the body.* N-UNCOUNT: also N in pl

excruciating /ɪkskruːʃieɪtɪŋ/ ◆◇◇◇◇

1 If you describe something as **excruciating**, you are emphasizing that it is extremely painful, either physically or emotionally. *I was in excruciating pain and one leg wouldn't move... Her search for love has often caused her excruciating misery and loneliness.* ADJ-GRADED PRAGMATICS =unbearable ♦ **excruciatingly** *He found the transition to boarding school excruciatingly painful... The ball hit him excruciatingly in the most sensitive part of his anatomy.* ADV-GRADED: usu ADV adj, also ADV after v

2 If you describe something as **excruciating**, you mean that it is very unpleasant to experience, for example because it is very boring or embarrassing. *Meanwhile, the boredom is excruciating... There was a moment of excruciating silence.* ADJ-GRADED ♦ **excruciatingly** *The dialogue is excruciatingly embarrassing. ...the one where the children's chorus goes on excruciatingly about 'Grocer Jack'.* ADV-GRADED: usu ADV adj, also ADV with v

excursion /ɪkskɜːʳʃən, AM -ʒən/ **excursions** ◆◇◇◇◇

1 You can refer to a short journey as an **excursion**, especially if it is made for pleasure or enjoyment. *In Bermuda, Sam's father took him on an excursion to a coral barrier.* N-COUNT =trip

2 An **excursion** is a tour or visit to an interesting place, especially one that is arranged or recommended by a holiday company or tourist organization. *We also recommend a full day optional excursion to the Upper Douro... Another pleasant excursion is Malaga, 18 miles away.* N-COUNT =outing

3 If you describe an activity as an **excursion** into something, you mean that it is an attempt by someone to develop or understand something new that they have not experienced before. *...Radio 3's latest excursion into ethnic music, dance and literature... The few excursions into stylistic experiment do not entirely come off.* N-COUNT: usu N *into* n, oft poss N

excusable /ɪkskjuːzəbəl/. If you say that someone's wrong words or actions are **excusable**, you mean that they can be understood and forgiven. *I then realised that he had made a simple but excusable historical mistake.* ADJ-GRADED =understandable

excuse, excuses, excusing, excused. The noun is pronounced /ɪkskjuːs/. The verb is pronounced /ɪkskjuːz/. ◆◆◆◇◇

1 An **excuse** is a reason which you give in order to explain why something has been done or has not been done, or in order to avoid doing something. *It is easy to find excuses for his indecisiveness... Once I had had a baby I had the perfect excuse to stay at home... If you stop making excuses and do it you'll wonder what took you so long.* N-COUNT: oft N *for* n/-ing, N to-inf =justification ● If you say that there is **no excuse** for something, you are emphasizing that it should not happen, or expressing disapproval that it has happened. *There's no excuse for behaviour like that... Solitude was no excuse for sloppiness.* PHRASE: v-link PHR, oft PHR *for* n/-ing PRAGMATICS

2 To **excuse** someone or **excuse** their behaviour means to provide reasons or a justification for their actions, especially when other people disapprove of these actions. *He excused himself by saying he was 'forced to rob to maintain my wife and cat'... That doesn't excuse my mother's behaviour.* VERB =justify V n *by*-ing V n

3 If you **excuse** someone for something wrong that they have done, you forgive them for it. *Many people might have excused them for shirking some of their responsibilities.* VERB =forgive V n *for* n/-ing Also V n, V n n

4 If someone **is excused** from a duty or responsibility, they are told that they do not have to carry it out. *She is usually excused from her duties during the school holidays... Some MPs will have been officially excused attendance.* VB: usu passive be V-ed *from* n/-ing be V-ed n

5 If you **excuse** yourself, you use a phrase such as 'Excuse me' as a polite way of saying that you are about to leave. *He excused himself and went up to his room.* VERB V pron-refl

6 You say **'Excuse me'** when you want to politely get someone's attention, especially when you are about to ask them a question. *Excuse me, but are you Mr Honig?* PHRASES CONVENTION PRAGMATICS =pardon me

7 You use **excuse me** to apologize to someone when you have disturbed or interrupted them. *Excuse me interrupting, but there's a thing I feel I've got to say.* CONVENTION PRAGMATICS

8 You use **excuse me** or a phrase such as **if you'll excuse me** as a polite way of indicating that you are about to leave, or to indicate that you are about to stop talking to someone because you need to deal with something else. *'Excuse me,' she said to Jarvis, and left the room... Now if you'll excuse me, I've got work to do.* CONVENTION PRAGMATICS

9 You use **excuse me, but** to indicate that you are about to disagree with someone or express a contradictory point of view. *Excuse me, but isn't this the man who deserted Labour, joined the SDP and is now supporting the Tories?* CONVENTION PRAGMATICS

10 You use **excuse me** to apologize when you have done something slightly embarrassing or impolite, such as burping, hiccupping, or sneezing. CONVENTION PRAGMATICS =pardon me

11 In American English, you say **'Excuse me?'** to show that you want someone to repeat what they have just said. The usual British expression is **pardon** or **I beg your pardon.** CONVENTION PRAGMATICS

ex-dir<u>e</u>ctory. In British English, if a person or his or her telephone number is **ex-directory**, the number is not listed in the telephone directory, and the telephone company will refuse to give it to people who ask for it. The usual American word is **unlisted**. ADJ

execrable /<u>e</u>ksɪkrəbᵊl/. If you describe something as **execrable**, you mean that it is very bad or unpleasant; a formal word. *Accusing us of being disloyal to cover his own sorry behavior is truly execrable. ...an execrable meal of boiled greens, mashed potato and supermarket meat pie.* ADJ-GRADED =deplorable

execute /<u>e</u>ksɪkjuːt/ **executes, executing, executed** ◆◆◆◇◇

1 To **execute** someone means to kill them as a punishment for a serious crime. *He said nobody had been executed as a direct result of the events... One group claimed to have executed the American hostage... This boy's father had been executed for conspiring against the throne.* VERB be V-ed, V n, be V-ed for n/-ing ♦ **execution** /eksɪkj<u>uː</u>ʃᵊn/ **executions** *Execution by lethal injection is scheduled for July 30th.* N-VAR

2 If you **execute** a plan, you carry it out; a formal use. *We are going to execute our campaign plan to the letter.* VERB V n ♦ **execution** *US forces are fully prepared for the execution of any action once the order is given by the president.* N-UNCOUNT

3 If you **execute** a difficult action or movement, you successfully perform it. *I executed the hairpin turn high on the sheer western face of the mountains... The landing was skilfully executed.* VERB V n

4 When someone **executes** a work of art, they make or produce it, using an idea as a basis. *Morris executed a suite of twelve drawings in 1978... A well-executed shot of a tall ship is a joy to behold.* VERB V n, V-ed ♦ **execution** *The earliest statues tend to be the most raw and immediate in execution and feeling.* N-UNCOUNT

executioner /<u>e</u>ksɪkj<u>uː</u>ʃənəʳ/ **executioners.** An **executioner** is a person who has the job of executing criminals. N-COUNT

executive /ɪgz<u>e</u>kjʊtɪv/ **executives** ◆◆◆◆◇

1 An **executive** is someone who is employed by a business at a senior level. Executives decide what the business should do, and ensure that it is done. *...an advertising executive. Her husband is a senior bank executive.* N-COUNT

2 The **executive** sections and tasks of an organization are concerned with the making of decisions and with ensuring that decisions are carried out. *A successful job search needs to be as well organised as any other executive task... I don't envisage I will take an executive role, but rather become a consultant on merchandise and marketing.* ADJ: ADJ n

3 **Executive** goods are expensive goods designed or intended for people who are executives or who are at a similar social or economic level; used mainly in British English. *...an executive briefcase. ...a chain of shops specialising in pricey executive toys. ...executive cars.* ADJ: ADJ n

4 **The executive** of an organization such as a political party is a committee within that organization which has the authority to make decisions and ensures that these decisions are carried out. *...the executive of the National Union of Students... Some executive members have called for his resignation.* N-SING: the N, N n

5 **The executive** is the part of the government of a country that is concerned with carrying out decisions or orders, as opposed to the part that makes laws or the part that deals with criminals. *The government, the executive and the judiciary are supposed to be separate... The matter should be resolved by the executive branch of government.* N-SING: the N, N n

executor /ɪgz<u>e</u>kjʊtəʳ/ **executors.** An **executor** is someone whose name you write in your will when you want them to be responsible for dealing with your affairs after your death; a legal term. ◆◇◇◇◇ N-COUNT

exegesis /<u>e</u>ksɪdʒ<u>iː</u>sɪs/ **exegeses** /<u>e</u>ksɪdʒ<u>iː</u>siːz/. An **exegesis** is an explanation and interpretation of a piece of writing, especially a religious piece of writing, after very careful study; a formal word. *...the kind of academic exegesis at which Isaacs excels. ...a substantial exegesis of his work.* N-VAR: usu with supp, oft N of n

exemplar /ɪgz<u>e</u>mplɑːʳ/ **exemplars**

1 An **exemplar** is someone or something that is considered to be so good that they should be copied or imitated; a formal use. *...since they viewed their new building as an exemplar of taste.* N-COUNT: oft N of n =example

2 An **exemplar** is a typical example of a group or class of things; a formal use. *One of the wittiest exemplars of the technique was M. C. Escher.* N-COUNT: oft N of n

exemplary /ɪgz<u>e</u>mpləri/ ◆◇◇◇◇

1 If you describe someone or something as **exemplary**, you mean that you consider them to be excellent or extremely good. *Underpinning this success has been an exemplary record of innovation.* ADJ-GRADED: usu ADJ n

2 An **exemplary** punishment is an unusually harsh one which is intended to discourage other people from committing similar crimes. *He demanded exemplary sentences for those behind the violence.* ADJ: usu ADJ n

exemplify /ɪgz<u>e</u>mplɪfaɪ/ **exemplifies, exemplifying, exemplified.** If something or someone **exemplifies** something such as a situation, quality, or class of things, they are a typical example of it; a formal word. *The room's style exemplifies Conran's ideal of 'beauty and practicality'. ...the emotional expressiveness of modern dance as exemplified by the work of Martha Graham.* ◆◇◇◇◇ VERB V n, V-ed

exempt /ɪgz<u>e</u>mpt/ **exempts, exempting, exempted** ◆◆◇◇◇

1 If someone or something is **exempt** from a particular rule, duty, or obligation, they are not affected or bound by it. *Men in college were exempt from military service... Children under two years are exempt.* ADJ: usu v-link ADJ, usu ADJ from n ► Also a combining form. *The fund was in danger of losing its tax-exempt status.* COMB in ADJ

2 To **exempt** a person or thing from a particular rule, duty, or obligation means to state officially that they are not bound or affected by it. *South Carolina claimed the power to exempt its citizens from the obligation to obey federal law... Companies with fifty-five or fewer employees would be exempted from the requirements.* VERB V n from n, Also V n ♦ **exemption** /ɪgz<u>e</u>mpʃᵊn/ **exemptions** *...the exemption of employer-provided health insurance from taxation. ...new exemptions for students and the low-paid.* N-VAR: oft N from n

exercise /<u>e</u>ksəʳsaɪz/ **exercises, exercising, exercised** ◆◆◆◆◇

1 If you **exercise** something such as your authority, your rights, or a good quality, you use it or put it into effect; a formal use. *They are merely exercising their right to free speech... 'The powers delegated to me,' the President said, 'will be exercised with due responsibility.'... Britain has warned travellers to exercise prudence and care.* VERB V n ► Also a noun. *Social structures are maintained through the exercise of political and economic power... Leadership does not rest on the exercise of force alone.* N-SING: N of n

2 When you **exercise**, you move your body energetically in order to get fit and to remain healthy. *She exercises two or three times a week... Never keep on exercising if you have even the slightest chest pain... To gradually reduce weight at the same time as exercising the body does a great deal to improve one's health.* VERB V, V n ► Also a noun. *Lack of exercise can lead to feelings of depression and exhaustion... Aerobic exercise moves our entire body and uses most major muscles.* N-UNCOUNT

3 If a movement or activity **exercises** a part of your body, it keeps it strong, healthy, or in good condition. *They call rowing the perfect sport. It exercises every major muscle group.* VERB V n

4 **Exercises** are a series of movements or actions which you do in order to get fit, remain healthy, or practise for a particular physical activity. *These stomach exercises will tighten abdominal muscles... I do special neck and shoulder exercises... That's when I try to meditate or do some deep-breathing exercises.* N-COUNT: usu pl

5 **Exercises** are military activities and operations which are not part of a real war, but which allow the armed forces to practise for a real war. *There* N-COUNT: usu pl, also on N =manoeuvres

have been reports that the South might scale down its joint military exercises with the United States... The military truck was taking 14 men on exercise in a remote area of Norway.

6 An **exercise** is a short activity or piece of work that you do, for example in school, which is designed to help you learn a particular skill. *Try working through the opening exercises in this chapter... He took up piano lessons, combining standard classical exercises with his own attempts at Gershwin.* N-COUNT

7 If you describe an activity as an **exercise** in a particular quality or result, you mean that it has that quality or result, especially when it was not intended to have it. *Her morning was an exercise in indecision. She tried on everything in her closet but couldn't remember what he'd liked... As an exercise in stating the obvious, this could scarcely be faulted... Think what a waste of taxpayers' money the whole exercise was.* N-COUNT: usu sing, usu N *in* n/-ing

8 If something **exercises** you or your mind, you think or talk about it a great deal, especially because you are worried or concerned about it. *This has been a major problem exercising the minds of scientists around the world... The proper role of appeal judges is an issue that has long exercised the finest legal minds.* VERB V n

exercise book, exercise books. An **exercise book** is a small book with blank pages that pupils and students use for writing in. N-COUNT

exert /ɪgzɜːʳt/ **exerts, exerting, exerted** ◆◆◇◇◇

1 If someone or something **exerts** influence, authority, or pressure, they use it in a strong or determined way, especially in order to produce an effect on someone or something; a formal use. *He exerted considerable influence on the thinking of the scientific community on these issues... The cyst was causing swelling and exerting pressure on her brain.* VERB V n

2 If you **exert** yourself, you make a great physical or mental effort, or work hard to do something. *Youngsters get so absorbed that they don't realise how much they're exerting themselves, visually and mentally... Do not exert yourself unnecessarily.* VERB V pron-refl

♦ **exertion, exertions** *He clearly found the physical exertion exhilarating... Thanks to the exertions of a few sensible and courageous men, the compromise was accepted.* N-UNCOUNT: also N in pl

ex gratia /eks greɪʃə/. In British English, an **ex gratia** payment is one that is given as a favour or gift and not because it is legally necessary; a formal expression. *Otherwise, they would not feel compelled to make ex gratia payments to customers they have wronged.* ADJ: usu ADJ n

exhale /ekshеɪl/ **exhales, exhaling, exhaled.** ◆◇◇◇◇ When you **exhale**, you breathe out the air that is in your lungs; a formal word. *Hold your breath for a moment and exhale... Wade exhaled a cloud of smoke and coughed.* VERB =breathe out ≠inhale V V n ♦ **exhalation** /ekshəleɪʃən/ **exhalations** *Milton let out his breath in a long exhalation. ...the quick exhalation of breath through expanded nostrils.* N-VAR

exhaust /ɪgzɔːst/ **exhausts, exhausting, exhausted** ◆◆◆◇◇

1 If something **exhausts** you, it makes you so tired, either physically or mentally, that you have no energy left. *Don't exhaust him... He took to walking long distances in an attempt to physically exhaust himself.* VERB V n ♦ **exhausted** *She was too exhausted and distressed to talk about the tragedy.* ADJ-GRADED =worn out ♦ **exhausting** *It was an exhausting schedule she had set herself.* ADJ-GRADED =gruelling

2 If you **exhaust** something such as money or food, you use or finish it all. *We have exhausted all our material resources... They said that food supplies were almost exhausted.* VERB V n V-ed

3 If you **have exhausted** a subject or topic, you have talked about it so much that there is nothing more to say about it. *She and Chantal must have exhausted the subject of babies and clothes.* VERB V n

4 The **exhaust** or the **exhaust pipe** is the pipe which carries the gas or steam out of the engine of a car, lorry, or motorbike. The more usual American word is **tailpipe**. N-COUNT

5 **Exhaust** is the gas or steam that is produced when the engine of a vehicle such as a car, lorry, or motorbike, is running. *...the exhaust from a car engine... The city's streets are filthy and choked with exhaust fumes. ...the concentration of car exhausts in the Los Angeles area.* N-UNCOUNT: also N in pl

exhaustion /ɪgzɔːstʃən/. **Exhaustion** is the state of being so tired that you have no energy left. *Staff say he is suffering from exhaustion. ...nervous exhaustion.* ◆◇◇◇◇ N-UNCOUNT

exhaustive /ɪgzɔːstɪv/. If you describe a study, search, or list as **exhaustive**, you mean that it is very thorough and complete. *This is by no means an exhaustive list but it gives an indication of the many projects taking place... The author's treatment of the subject is exhaustive.* ◆◇◇◇◇ ADJ-GRADED =comprehensive ♦ **exhaustively** *Hawley said these costs were scrutinised exhaustively by independent accountants. ...an exhaustively researched, sensitively written account.* ADV-GRADED: usu ADV with v, also ADV adj

exhibit /ɪgzɪbɪt/ **exhibits, exhibiting, exhibited** ◆◆◇◇◇

1 If someone or something shows a particular quality, feeling, or type of behaviour, you can say that they **exhibit** it; a formal use. *He has exhibited symptoms of anxiety and overwhelming worry... Two cats or more in one house will also exhibit territorial behaviour... The economy continued to exhibit signs of decline in September.* VERB =demonstrate, show V n

2 When a painting, sculpture, or object of interest **is exhibited**, it is put in a public place such as a museum or art gallery, so that people can come to look at it. You can also say that animals **are exhibited** in a zoo. *His work was exhibited in the best galleries in America, Europe and Asia. ...a massive elephant exhibited by London Zoo in the late 19th Century.* VB: usu passive *be* V-ed V-ed ♦ **exhibition** *Five large pieces of the wall are currently on exhibition in London.* N-UNCOUNT: usu *for/on* N

3 When artists **exhibit**, they show their work in public. *By 1936 she was exhibiting at the Royal Academy.* VERB V

4 An **exhibit** is a painting, sculpture, or object of interest that is displayed to the public in a museum or art gallery. *Shona showed me round the exhibits.* N-COUNT

5 In American English, an **exhibit** is a public display of paintings, sculpture, or objects of interest, for example in a museum or art gallery. The British word is **exhibition**. *Another friend sent me two tickets to an exhibit at the Metropolitan Museum of Art.* N-COUNT

6 An **exhibit** is an object that a lawyer shows in court as evidence in a legal case. N-COUNT

7 If you say that someone **exhibits** something, you mean that they are showing it openly or publicly in order to be admired, noticed, or believed. *Other women seemed content and even exhibited their bellies with pride... He seems to want to exhibit his shame.* VERB =show off V n

exhibition /eksɪbɪʃən/ **exhibitions** ◆◆◆◇◇

1 An **exhibition** is a public event at which pictures, sculptures, or other objects of interest are displayed, for example at a museum or art gallery. *...an exhibition of expressionist art. ...an exhibition on the natural history of the area.* N-COUNT

2 An **exhibition of** a particular skilful activity is a display or example of it that people notice or admire. *He responded in champion's style by treating the fans to an exhibition of power and speed.* N-SING: N *of* n =show of

3 See also **exhibit**.

exhibitionism /eksɪbɪʃənɪzəm/. If you describe someone's behaviour as **exhibitionism**, you disapprove of it because they try to get people's attention all the time, especially by boasting or by trying to make people notice their talents and abilities. *There is an element of exhibitionism in the parents' performance too.* N-UNCOUNT

exhibitionist /eksɪbɪʃənɪst/ **exhibitionists.** If you describe someone as an **exhibitionist**, you mean that they try to get people's attention all the time, especially by boasting or trying to make people notice their talents or abilities. N-COUNT

exhibitor /ɪgzɪbɪtəʳ/ **exhibitors.** An **exhibitor** is a person whose work is being shown in an exhibition. *Schedules will be sent out to all exhibitors.* ◆◇◇◇◇ N-COUNT

exhilarated /ɪgzɪləreɪtɪd/. If you are **exhilarated** by something, it makes you feel very happy and excited; a formal word. *He felt strangely exhilarated by the brisk, blue morning... By the week's end I was exhilarated and confused.* ADJ-GRADED: usu v-link ADJ =elated

exhilarating /ɪgzɪləreɪtɪŋ/. If you describe an experience or feeling as **exhilarating**, you mean that it makes you feel very happy and excited. *It was exhilarating to be on the road again and his spirits rose. ...in the exhilarating days of German unification.* ◆◇◇◇◇ ADJ-GRADED

exhilaration /ɪgzɪləreɪʃən/. **Exhilaration** is a strong feeling of excitement and happiness. N-UNCOUNT

exhort /ɪgzɔːrt/ **exhorts, exhorting, exhorted.** If you **exhort** someone to do something, you try hard to persuade or encourage them to do it; a formal word. *Kennedy exhorted his listeners to turn away from violence... He exhorted his companions, 'Try to accomplish your aim with diligence'.* ◆◇◇◇◇ VERB =urge V n to-inf V n with quote ♦ **exhortation** /egzɔːrteɪʃən/ **exhortations** *Foreign funds alone are clearly not enough, nor are exhortations to reform.* N-VAR

exhume /ekshjuːm, AM ɪgzuːm/ **exhumes, exhuming, exhumed.** If a dead person's body **is exhumed**, it is taken out of the ground where it is buried, especially so that it can be examined in order to find out how the person died; a formal word. *His remains have been exhumed from a cemetery in Queen's, New York City.* VB: usu passive =disinter be V-ed ♦ **exhumation** /egzjuːmeɪʃən/ **exhumations** *Detectives ordered the exhumation when his wife said she believed he had been killed.* N-VAR

exigency /eksɪdʒənsi/ **exigencies.** The **exigencies** of a situation or a job are the demands or difficulties that you have to deal with as part of it; a formal word. *The reduction was caused by the exigencies of a wartime economy.* N-COUNT: usu pl, usu N *of* n

exile /eksaɪl, egz-/ **exiles, exiling, exiled** ◆◆◆◇◇

1 If someone is living in **exile**, they are living in a foreign country because they cannot live in their own country, usually for political reasons. *He is now living in exile in Egypt... He returned from exile earlier this year. ...after nearly six years of exile... During his exile, he also began writing books.* N-UNCOUNT: usu prep N

2 If someone **is exiled**, they are living in a foreign country because they cannot live in their own country, usually for political reasons. *He was exiled from the Soviet Union 18 years ago... They threatened to exile her in southern Spain. ...Haiti's exiled president.* VERB be V-ed *from* n V n V-ed Also V n *from* n

3 An **exile** is someone who has been exiled. N-COUNT

4 If you say that someone **has been exiled** from a particular place or situation, you mean that they have been sent away from it or removed from it against their will. *He has been exiled from the first team and forced to play in third team matches... Michael was exiled to the kitchen for supper.* ► Also a noun. *Rovers lost 4-1 and began their long exile from the First Division.* VB: usu passive =banish be V-ed *from* n be V-ed prep/adv N-UNCOUNT: oft N *from* n

exist /ɪgzɪst/ **exists, existing, existed** ◆◆◆◆◇

1 If something **exists**, it is present in the world as a real thing. *He thought that if he couldn't see something, it didn't exist... Research opportunities exist in a wide range of pure and applied areas of entomology... When Alfred Adler first postulated in 1908 that there existed an inborn instinct of aggression Freud argued against it.* VB: no cont V *there* V n

2 To **exist** means to live, especially under difficult conditions or with very little food or money. *I exist from one visit to the next... I was barely existing. ...the problems of having to exist on unemployment benefit.* VERB V V *on* n

existence /ɪgzɪstəns/ **existences** ◆◆◆◇◇

1 The **existence** of something is the fact that it is present in the world as a real thing. *...the existence of other galaxies... The Congress of People's Deputies in effect voted itself out of existence... The recent education white paper seems to threaten the very existence of education authorities.* N-UNCOUNT: usu with supp

2 You can refer to someone's way of life as an **existence**, especially when they live under difficult conditions. *You may be stuck with a miserable existence for the rest of your life... Their day-to-day existence was routine.* N-COUNT: with supp

existent /ɪgzɪstənt/. You can describe something as **existent** when it exists; a formal word. *Their remedy lay within the range of existent technology.* • See also **non-existent.** ◆◇◇◇◇ ADJ =existing

existential /egzɪstenʃəl/

1 **Existential** means relating to human existence and experience; a formal use. *Existential questions requiring religious answers still persist.* ADJ: ADJ n

2 You use **existential** to describe fear, anxiety, and other feelings that are caused by thinking about human existence and death; a formal use. *'What if there's nothing left at all?' he cries, lost in some intense existential angst.* ADJ: ADJ n

existentialism /egzɪstenʃəlɪzəm/. **Existentialism** is a philosophical belief which stresses the importance of human experience, and says that everyone is responsible for the results of their own actions; a technical term. N-UNCOUNT

existentialist /egzɪstenʃəlɪst/ **existentialists**

1 An **existentialist** is a person who agrees with the philosophy of existentialism. N-COUNT

2 If you describe a person or their philosophy as **existentialist**, you mean that their beliefs are based on existentialism. *...drawing on her existentialist theories.* ADJ

existing /ɪgzɪstɪŋ/. **Existing** is used to describe something which is now present, available, or in operation, especially when you are contrasting it with something which is planned for the future. *...the need to improve existing products and develop new lines... Existing timbers are replaced or renewed... This facility is open to both new and existing borrowers.* ◆◆◆◇◇ ADJ: ADJ n

exit /egzɪt, eksɪt/ **exits, exiting, exited** ◆◆◇◇◇

1 The **exit** is the doorway through which you can leave a public building. *He picked up the case and walked towards the exit... There's a fire exit by the downstairs ladies room.* N-COUNT

2 An **exit** on a motorway is a place where traffic can leave it. *Take the A422 exit at Old Stratford.* N-COUNT: with supp

3 If you refer to someone's **exit**, you are referring to the way that they left a room or building, or the fact that they left it; a formal use. *I made a hasty exit and managed to open the gate.* N-COUNT: usu adj N =departure

4 If you refer to someone's **exit**, you are referring to the way that they left a situation or activity, or the fact that they left it; a formal use. *...after England's exit from the European Championship... They suggested that she make a dignified exit in the interest of the party.* N-COUNT: oft N *from* n =departure

5 If you **exit** from a room or building, you leave it; a formal use. *She exits into the tropical storm... As I exited the final display, I entered a hexagonal room... She walked into the front door of a store and exited from the rear.* VERB V V n V *from* n

exit visa, exit visas. An **exit visa** is an official stamp in someone's passport, or an official document, which allows them to leave the country that they are visiting or living in. ◆◇◇◇◇ N-COUNT

exodus /eksədəs/. If there is an **exodus** of people from a place, a lot of people leave that place at the same time. *Lieutenant Malcolm said she saw no sign that the exodus from Haiti was abating... The medical system is facing collapse because of an exodus of doctors.* ◆◇◇◇◇ N-SING: oft N *of* n

ex officio /eks ɒfɪʃiou/. **Ex officio** is used to describe something such as a rank or privilege that someone is entitled to because of the job or position they have; a formal word. *...ex officio members of the Advisory Council. They gave me an ex-officio degree.* ADJ: ADJ n

exonerate /ɪgzɒnəreɪt/ **exonerates, exonerating, exonerated.** If a court, report, or person in authority **exonerates** someone, they officially say or show that that person is not responsible for something wrong or unpleasant that has happened; a formal word. *The official report basically exonerated everyone... An investigation exonerated the school from any blame and recommended only a couple of minor changes.* VERB V n V n *from* n ♦ **exoneration** N-UNCOUNT

/ɪgzɒnəreɪʃᵊn/ *They expected complete exoneration for their clients.*

exorbitant /ɪgzɔːʳbɪtənt/. If you describe something such as a price or fee as **exorbitant**, you are emphasizing that it is much greater than it should be. *Exorbitant housing prices have created an acute shortage of affordable housing for the poor.* ♦ **exorbitantly** *...exorbitantly high salaries.*
ADJ-GRADED PRAGMATICS =excessive; ADV

exorcism /ekˌsɔːʳsɪzəm/ **exorcisms. Exorcism** is the removing of evil spirits from a person or place by the use of prayer. *The exorcism was broadcast on television.*
N-VAR

exorcist /ekˌsɔːʳsɪst/ **exorcists.** An **exorcist** is someone who performs exorcisms.
N-COUNT

exorcize /ekˌsɔːʳsaɪz/ **exorcizes, exorcizing, exorcized;** also spelled **exorcise** in British English.

1 If you **exorcize** a painful or unhappy memory, you succeed in removing it from your mind. *He confronted his childhood trauma and tried to exorcise the pain... The birth of my second daughter has finally exorcised these feelings of guilt.*
VERB; V n

2 To **exorcize** an evil spirit or to **exorcize** a place or person means to force the spirit to leave the place or person by means of prayers and religious ceremonies. *They came to our house and exorcised me... Last year, a 15-year-old girl, alleged to be possessed by the devil, was exorcised live on TV.*
VERB; V n

exotic /ɪgzɒtɪk/. Something that is **exotic** is unusual and interesting, usually because it comes from or is related to a distant country. *...brilliantly coloured, exotic flowers... She flits from one exotic location to another.* ♦ **exotically** *...exotically beautiful scenery.*
◆◆◇◇◇ ADJ-GRADED; ADV-GRADED

exotica /ɪgzɒtɪkə/. You use **exotica** to refer to objects which you think are unusual and interesting, usually because they come from or are related to a distant country.
N-PLURAL

exoticism /ɪgzɒtɪsɪzəm/. **Exoticism** is the quality of seeming unusual or interesting, usually because of associations with a distant country.
N-UNCOUNT

expand /ɪkspænd/ **expands, expanding, expanded**
◆◆◆◇◇

1 If something **expands**, or someone or something **expands** it, it becomes larger. *Engineers noticed that the pipes were not expanding as expected... The money supply expanded by 14.6 per cent in the year to September... We have to expand the size of the image. ...a rapidly expanding universe. ...strips of expanded polystyrene.*
V-ERG; V; V n; V-ing; V-ed

2 If something such as a business, organization, or service **expands**, or if you **expand** it, it becomes bigger and includes more people, goods, or activities. *The popular ceramics industry expanded towards the middle of the 19th century... The interest rate's coming down. I'll be able to expand or stay in business... I owned a bookshop and desired to expand the business... Health officials are proposing to expand their services by organising counselling.*
V-ERG; V; V n

expand on or **expand upon.** If you **expand on** or **expand upon** something, you give more information or details about it when you write or talk about it. *The president used today's speech to expand on remarks he made last month. ...a view that I will expand upon below.*
PHRASAL VERB =enlarge on; V P n

expanse /ɪkspæns/ **expanses.** An **expanse** of something, usually sea, sky, or land, is a very large amount of it. *...a vast expanse of grassland.*
◆◇◇◇◇ N-COUNT: usu N *of* n

expansion /ɪkspænʃᵊn/ **expansions. Expansion** is the process of becoming greater in size, number, or amount. *...the rapid expansion of private health insurance. ...a new period of economic expansion... The company has abandoned plans for further expansion.*
◆◆◆◇◇ N-VAR: oft N *of* n =growth

expansionary /ɪkspænʃənri/.

1 **Expansionary** economic policies are intended to expand the economy of a country. *They demanded a more expansionary economy to combat rising unemployment.*
ADJ-GRADED: usu ADJ n

2 **Expansionary** policies or actions are intended to increase the amount of land that a particular country rules; used showing disapproval. *In those days they shared America's concerns about Soviet expansionary objectives.*
ADJ-GRADED: usu ADJ n PRAGMATICS

expansionism /ɪkspænʃənɪzəm/. If you refer to a country's **expansionism**, you disapprove of its policy of increasing its land or power. *Soviet expansionism was considered a real threat.*
N-UNCOUNT PRAGMATICS

expansionist /ɪkspænʃənɪst/. If you describe a country or organization as **expansionist**, you disapprove of it because it has a policy of increasing its land or power. *...the intended victim of his expansionist foreign policy.*
ADJ-GRADED PRAGMATICS

expansive /ɪkspænsɪv/
◆◇◇◇◇

1 If something is **expansive**, it covers or includes a large area or many things; a formal use. *There also are several swing sets and an expansive grassy play area... They have played an expansive style of rugby.*
ADJ: ADJ n

2 If you are **expansive**, you talk a lot, or are friendly or generous, because you are feeling happy and relaxed. *He was becoming more expansive as he relaxed... The premier was in expansive mood.* ♦ **expansively** *'I'm here to make them feel good,' he says expansively.*
ADJ-GRADED; ADV-GRADED: usu ADV with v

3 If you describe something such as a period of time or an economy as **expansive**, you mean that it is associated with growth or expansion. *First of all, there must exist an active and expansive market economy, which is a necessary but not sufficient condition for progress.*
ADJ-GRADED: usu ADJ n

expat /ekspæt/ **expats.** An **expat** is the same as an **expatriate**; used in informal British English. *...exclusive country clubs for British expats.*
N-COUNT

expatriate /ekspætriət, -peɪt-/ **expatriates.** An **expatriate** is someone who is living in a country which is not their own. *...British expatriates in Spain.* ► Also an adjective. *The French military is preparing to evacuate women and children of expatriate families.*
◆◇◇◇◇ N-COUNT; ADJ: ADJ n

expect /ɪkspekt/ **expects, expecting, expected**
◆◆◆◆◆

1 If you **expect** something to happen, you believe that it will happen. *...a council workman who expects to lose his job in the next few weeks... They no longer expect corporate profits to improve... The talks are expected to continue until tomorrow... Few expected that he would declare his candidacy for the Democratic nomination for the presidency... It is expected that the new owner will change the yacht's name... They expect a gradual improvement in sales of new cars.*
VERB; V to-inf; V n to-inf; V that; *it be* V-ed that; V n

2 If you **are expecting** something or someone, you believe that they will be delivered to you or come to you soon, often because this has been arranged earlier. *I am expecting several important letters but nothing has arrived... I wasn't expecting a visitor... We were expecting him home again any day now.*
VB: usu cont; V n

3 If you **expect** something, or **expect** someone to do something, you believe that it is your right to have that thing, or that person's duty to do it for you. *He wasn't expecting our hospitality... I do expect to have some time to myself in the evenings... I wasn't expecting you to help... Is this a rational thing to expect of your partner, or not?... She realizes now she expected too much of Helen.*
VERB; V n; V to-inf; V n to-inf; V n *of* n; V amount *of* n

4 If you tell someone not to **expect** something, you mean that they are being too hopeful or optimistic, and that that thing is unlikely to happen as they have planned or imagined; used in spoken English. *Don't expect an instant cure... You cannot expect to like all the people you will work with... Don't expect me to come and visit you there.*
VB: with brd-neg PRAGMATICS; V n; V to-inf; V n to-inf

5 If you say that a woman **is expecting** a baby, or that she **is expecting**, you mean that she is pregnant. *She was expecting another baby... I hear Dawn's expecting again.*
VB: only cont; V n; V

6 You say **'I expect'** to suggest that a statement is probably correct, or a natural consequence of the present situation, although you have no definite knowledge; used in spoken English. *I expect you can guess what follows... I expect you're tired... 'Will Joe be here at Christmas?'—'I expect so.'... 'I don't think you have much of a case.'—'I expect not.'*
PHRASES; PHR that, PHR *so/not* PRAGMATICS

7 You can say **'What can you expect?'** or **'What do**
PRAGMATICS

you expect?' to emphasize that there is nothing surprising about a situation or a person's behaviour, especially if you find this disappointing. *It tastes artificial, but at that price what can you expect?... If a guy hunts and owns guns, what do you expect?*

expectancy /ɪkspektənsi/. **Expectancy** is the feeling or hope that something exciting, interesting, or good is about to happen. *The supporters had a tremendous air of expectancy.* • See also **life expectancy**. ◆◇◇◇◇ N-UNCOUNT =anticipation

expectant /ɪkspektənt/ ◆◇◇◇◇

1 If someone is **expectant**, they are excited because they think something interesting is about to happen. *An expectant crowd gathered... She turned to me with an expectant look on her face.* ADJ-GRADED

♦ **expectantly** *The others waited, looking at him expectantly.* ADV: ADV after v

2 An **expectant** mother or father is someone whose baby is going to be born soon. ADJ: ADJ n

expectation /ekspekteɪʃən/ **expectations** ◆◆◆◇◇

1 Your **expectations** are your strong hopes or beliefs that something will happen or that you will get something that you want. *Students' expectations were as varied as their expertise... The car has been General Motors' most visible success story, with sales far exceeding expectations... The Chancellor's statement lowers expectations of an early election... Contrary to general expectation, he announced that all four had given their approval.* N-UNCOUNT: also N in pl

2 A person's **expectations** are strong beliefs which they have about the proper way someone should behave or something should happen. *Stephen Chase had determined to live up to the expectations of the Company. ...the expectation that the grieving process should have a time limit on it.* N-COUNT: usu pl

expectorant /ɪkspektərənt/ **expectorants.** An **expectorant** is a cough medicine that helps to loosen phlegm in your chest; a formal or medical term. N-COUNT

expediency /ɪkspiːdiənsi/. **Expediency** means doing what is convenient rather than what is morally right; a formal word. *It seems political expediency, rather than absolute economic need, will determine who gains from the conflict... This was a matter less of morals than of expediency.* N-UNCOUNT =convenience

expedient /ɪkspiːdiənt/ **expedients** ◆◇◇◇◇

1 An **expedient** is an action that achieves a particular purpose, but may not be morally right. *Surgical waiting lists were reduced by the simple expedient of striking off all patients awaiting varicose vein operations... The story was a temporary expedient.* N-COUNT: usu sing, oft N *of*-ing

2 If it is **expedient** to do something, it is useful or convenient to do it, even though it may not be morally right. *Governments frequently ignore human rights abuses in other countries if it is politically expedient to do so.* ADJ-GRADED: oft *it* v-link ADJ to-inf

expedite /ekspɪdaɪt/ **expedites, expediting, expedited.** If you **expedite** something, you cause it to be done more quickly; a formal word. *The government has been extremely reluctant to expedite investigations that might result in his trial... We tried to help you expedite your plans.* VERB =speed up; V n

expedition /ekspɪdɪʃən/ **expeditions** ◆◆◇◇◇

1 An **expedition** is an organized journey that is made for a particular purpose such as exploration. *...Byrd's 1928 expedition to Antarctica.* N-COUNT: oft N *to* n

2 You can refer to a group of people who are going on an expedition as an **expedition**. *Forty-three members of the expedition were killed.* N-COUNT

3 An **expedition** is a short journey or outing that you make for pleasure. *Caroline joined them on the shopping expeditions. ...a fishing expedition.* N-COUNT =trip

expeditionary force /ekspɪdɪʃənri fɔːʳs, AM -neri/ **expeditionary forces.** An **expeditionary force** is a group of soldiers who are sent to fight in a foreign country; a military expression. N-COUNT

expeditious /ekspɪdɪʃəs/. **Expeditious** means quick and efficient; a formal word. *The judge said that arbitration was a fair and expeditious decision-making process.* ADJ-GRADED

♦ **expeditiously** *The matter has certainly been handled expeditiously by the authorities.* ADV-GRADED: ADV with v

expel /ɪkspel/ **expels, expelling, expelled** ◆◆◇◇◇

1 If someone **is expelled** from a school or organization, they are officially told to leave because they have behaved badly. *More than five-thousand secondary school students have been expelled for cheating. ...the mother of a 14-year-old boy expelled from school for refusing to take a shower.* VB: usu passive; be V-ed; V-ed

2 If people **are expelled** from a place, they are made to leave it, often by force. *An American academic was expelled from China yesterday... They were told at first that they should simply expel the refugees.* VERB; be V-ed; V n

3 To **expel** something means to force it out from a container or from your body. *Daily brushing of the skin helps the skin expel toxins... As the lungs exhale this waste, gas is expelled into the atmosphere.* VERB; V n

expend /ɪkspend/ **expends, expending, expended.** To **expend** something, especially energy, time, or money, means to use it or spend it; a formal word. *Children expend a lot of energy and may need more high-energy food than adults.* ◆◇◇◇◇ VERB; V n

expendable /ɪkspendəbəl/. If you regard someone or something as **expendable**, you think it is acceptable to get rid of them, abandon them, or allow them to be destroyed when they are no longer needed; a formal word. *Once our services cease to be useful to them, we're expendable... During the recession, training budgets were seen as an expendable luxury. ...an expendable rocket.* ADJ-GRADED

expenditure /ɪkspendɪtʃəʳ/ **expenditures** ◆◆◇◇◇

1 **Expenditure** is the spending of money on something, or the money that is spent on something; a formal use. *Policies of tax reduction must lead to reduced public expenditure... They should cut their expenditure on defence... An expenditure for clothing will qualify as a trade or business expense.* N-VAR

2 **Expenditure of** something such as time or energy is the using of that thing for a particular purpose; a formal use. *The financial rewards justified the expenditure of effort.* N-UNCOUNT: N *of* n

expense /ɪkspens/ **expenses** ◆◆◆◇◇

1 **Expense** is the money that something costs you or that you need to spend in order to do something. *He's bought a specially big TV at vast expense so that everyone can see properly... To avoid extra expense and mess later on, try to decide on fittings before the plastering's finished... It was not a fortune but would help to cover household expenses.* N-UNCOUNT: also N in pl

2 **Expenses** are amounts of money that you spend while doing something in the course of your work, which will be paid back to you afterwards. *As a member of the International Olympic Committee her fares and hotel expenses were paid by the IOC... Can you claim this back on expenses?* N-PLURAL: oft poss N

3 If you do something **at** someone's **expense**, they provide the money for it. *Should architects continue to be trained for five years at public expense?... Teachers who signed up did so out of personal choice and at their own expense.* PHRASES; PHR after v

4 If someone laughs or makes a joke **at** your **expense**, they do it to make you seem foolish. *I think he's having fun at our expense.* PHR after v

5 If you achieve something **at the expense of** someone, you do it in a way which might cause them some harm or disadvantage. *But skeptics worry that costs may be trimmed at the expense of the patient... According to this study, women have made notable gains at the expense of men.* PHR after v, PHR n

6 If you say that someone does something **at the expense of** another thing, you are expressing concern at the fact that they are not doing the second thing, because the first thing uses all their resources. *They are worth having but not at the expense of better services... The orchestra has more discipline now, but at the expense of spirit.* PHR after v, PHR n; PRAGMATICS

7 If you **go to** the **expense** of doing something, you do something which costs a lot of money. If you **go to** great **expense** to do something, you spend a lot of money in order to achieve it. *Why go to the expense of buying an electric saw when you can hire* V inflects, oft PHR *of*-ing, PHR to-inf; PRAGMATICS

one?... It was said that he went to great expense to install a lift in the building.
8 • to spare no expense: see **spare**.

expense account, expense accounts. An **expense account** is an arrangement between an employer and an employee which allows the employee to spend the company's money on things relating to their job, for example travelling or looking after clients. *He put Elizabeth's motel bill and airfare on his expense account. ...expense account lunches.* N-COUNT

expensive /ɪkspensɪv/. If something is **expensive**, it costs a lot of money. *Wine's so expensive in this country... I get very nervous because I'm using a lot of expensive equipment.* ♦♦♦♦◇ ADJ-GRADED =costly ≠cheap

♦ **expensively** *She was expensively dressed, with fine furs and jewels... They do a third-rate job very expensively.* ADV-GRADED: ADV -ed, ADV after v ≠cheaply

experience /ɪkspɪəriəns/ **experiences, experiencing, experienced** ♦♦♦♦♦

1 **Experience** is knowledge or skill in a particular job or activity, which you have gained because you have done that job or activity for a long time. *He has also had managerial experience on every level... He's counting on his mother to take care of the twins for him; she's had plenty of experience with them.* N-UNCOUNT: usu with supp

2 **Experience** is used to refer to the past events, knowledge, and feelings that make up someone's life or character. *I should not be in any danger here, but experience has taught me caution... She had learned from experience to take little rests in between her daily routine... 'If you act afraid, they won't let go,' he says, speaking from experience.* N-UNCOUNT

3 An **experience** is something that happens to you or something that you do, especially something important that affects you. *Moving had become a common experience for me... His only experience of gardening so far proved immensely satisfying... Many of his clients are unbelievably nervous, usually because of a bad experience in the past.* N-COUNT: usu with supp

4 If you **experience** a particular situation, you are in that situation or it happens to you. *We had never experienced this kind of holiday before and had no idea what to expect... British business is now experiencing a severe recession.* VERB V n

5 If you **experience** a feeling, you feel it or are affected by it. *Widows seem to experience more distress than do widowers.* ► Also a noun. *...the experience of pain.* VERB V n N-SING: the N of n

experienced /ɪkspɪəriənst/. If you describe someone as **experienced**, you mean that they have been doing a particular job or activity for a long time, and therefore know a lot about it or are very skilful at it. *...lawyers who are experienced in these matters... It's a team packed with experienced and mature professionals... Perhaps I'm a bit more experienced about life than my contemporaries.* ♦♦◇◇◇ ADJ-GRADED: oft ADJ in n/-ing

experiential /ɪkspɪəriənʃəl/. **Experiential** means relating to or resulting from experience; a formal word. *Learning has got to be active and experiential. ...the rediscovery of the experiential path of religious truth.* ADJ

experiment, experiments, experimenting, experimented. The noun is pronounced /ɪksperɪmənt/. The verb is pronounced /ɪksperɪment/. ♦♦♦◇◇

1 An **experiment** is a scientific test which is done in order to discover what happens to something in particular conditions. *The astronauts are conducting a series of experiments to learn more about how the body adapts to weightlessness. ...a proposed new law on animal experiments... This question can be answered only by experiment.* N-VAR

2 If you **experiment with** something or **experiment on** it, you do a scientific test on it in order to discover what happens to it in particular conditions. *In 1857 Mendel started experimenting with peas in his monastery garden... The scientists have experimented on the tiny neck arteries of rats... The scientists have already experimented at each other's test sites.* ♦ **experimentation** /ɪksperɪmenteɪʃən/ *...the ethical aspects of animal experimentation.* VERB V with/on n V N-UNCOUNT

♦ **experimenter, experimenters** *When the experimenters repeated the tests on themselves, they observed an exactly opposite effect.* N-COUNT

3 An **experiment** is the trying out of a new idea or method in order to see what it is like and what effects it has. *As an experiment, we bought Ted a watch. ...the country's five year experiment in democracy... She needs plenty of room for experiment in her life.* N-VAR

4 To **experiment** means to try out a new idea or method to see what it is like and what effects it has. *...if you like cooking and have the time to experiment... He believes that students should be encouraged to experiment with bold ideas.* VERB V V with n

♦ **experimentation** *Decentralization and experimentation must be encouraged... His stories about his sexual experimentation were more bravado than fact.* N-UNCOUNT

experimental /ɪksperɪmentəl/ ♦♦◇◇◇

1 Something that is **experimental** is new or uses new ideas or methods, and might be modified later if it is unsuccessful. *...an experimental air conditioning system... He tends to write bizarre and highly experimental pieces of music... The technique is experimental, but the list of its practitioners is growing.* ADJ-GRADED

2 **Experimental** means using, used in, or resulting from scientific experiments. *...the main techniques of experimental science. ...the use of experimental animals... We have experimental and observational evidence concerning things which happened before and after the origin of life.* ♦ **experimentally** *...an ecology laboratory, where communities of species can be studied experimentally under controlled conditions.* ADJ: ADJ n ADV: ADV with v

3 An **experimental** action is done in order to see what it is like, or what effects it has. *The British Sports Minister is reported to be ready to argue for an experimental lifting of the ban.* ADJ: usu ADJ n

♦ **experimentally** *This system is being tried out experimentally at many universities... Before opening the front door he lifted the cases experimentally.* ADV: ADV with v

expert /ekspɜːʳt/ **experts** ♦♦♦♦◇

1 An **expert** is a person who is very skilled at doing something or who knows a lot about a particular subject. *Our team of experts will be on hand to offer help and advice between 12 noon and 7pm daily. ...a yoga expert. ...an expert on trade in that area.* N-COUNT: oft n N, N on n =specialist

2 Someone who is **expert** at doing something is very skilled at it. *The Japanese are expert at lowering manufacturing costs... There is a great deal to learn from Hal's expert approach.* ♦ **expertly** *Shopkeepers expertly rolled spices up in bay leaves.* ADJ-GRADED: oft ADJ at -ing =skilled ADV-GRADED: ADV with v

3 If you say that someone has **expert** hands or an **expert** eye, you mean that they are very skilful or experienced in using their hands or eyes for a particular purpose. *When the horse suffered a back injury Harvey cured it with his own expert hands... The symptoms are very mild and it takes an expert eye to see them.* ADJ-GRADED: ADJ n

4 **Expert** advice or help is given by someone who has studied a subject thoroughly or who is very skilled at a particular job. *You'll also get expert advice on keeping your hair in good condition... We'll need an expert opinion... The good news is that expert help is now available.* ADJ: ADJ n

expertise /ekspɜːʳtiːz/. **Expertise** is special skill or knowledge that is acquired by training, study, or practice. *The problem is that most local authorities lack the expertise to deal sensibly in this market.* ♦♦◇◇◇ N-UNCOUNT

expiate /ekspieɪt/ **expiates, expiating, expiated.** If you **expiate** guilty feelings or bad behaviour, you do something to indicate that you are sorry for what you have done; a formal word. *It seemed that Alice was expiating her father's sins with her charity work.* ♦ **expiation** /ekspieɪʃən/ *They went through an often painful process of evaluation and expiation.* VERB V n Also V for n N-UNCOUNT

expiration /ekspɪreɪʃən/. The **expiration** of a fixed period of time is its ending; a formal word. N-UNCOUNT: oft the N of n

He met with officials a few hours before the expiration of the midnight deadline.

expire /ɪkspaɪəʳ/ **expires, expiring, expired** ◆◆◇◇◇

1 When something such as a contract, deadline, or visa **expires**, it comes to an end or is no longer valid. *He had lived illegally in the United States for five years after his visitor's visa expired.* — VERB =run out; V

2 When someone **expires**, they die; a literary use. *He endured excruciating agonies before he finally expired.* — VERB =die; V

expiry /ɪkspaɪəri/. The **expiry** of something such as a contract, deadline, or visa is the time that it comes to an end or stops being valid. *...the expiry of a fixed term contract... Make a note of credit card numbers and check expiry dates.* — N-UNCOUNT: oft N *of*n, N n

explain /ɪkspleɪn/ **explains, explaining, explained** ◆◆◆◆◇

1 If you **explain** something, you give details about it or describe it so that it can be understood. *Not every judge, however, has the ability to explain the law in simple terms... Don't sign anything until your solicitor has explained the contract to you... Professor Griffiths explained how the drug appears to work... 'He and Mrs Stein have a plan,' she explained... I explained that each person has different ideas of what freedom is.* — VERB; V n; V n *to*n; V wh; V with quote; V that; Also V, V *to*n that/wh

2 If you **explain** something that has happened, you give people reasons for it, especially in an attempt to justify it. *'Let me explain, sir.'—'Don't tell me about it. I don't want to know.'... Before she ran away, she left a note explaining her actions... Hospital discipline was broken. Amy would have to explain herself... Explain why you didn't telephone... The receptionist apologized for the delay, explaining that it had been a hectic day.* — VERB; V; V n; V pron-refl; V why; V that; Also V n *to*n, V with quote

explain away. If someone **explains away** a mistake or a bad situation they are responsible for, they try to indicate that it is unimportant or that it is not really their fault. *He evaded her questions about the war and tried to explain away the atrocities... I had noticed blood on my husband's clothing but he explained it away.* — PHRASAL VERB, PRAGMATICS; V P n (not pron); V n P

explanation /ekspləneɪʃᵊn/ **explanations** ◆◆◆◇◇

1 If you give an **explanation** of something that has happened, you give people reasons for it, especially in an attempt to justify it. *She told the court she would give a full explanation of the prosecution's decision on Monday... There was a hint of schoolboy shyness in his explanation... 'It's my ulcer,' he added by way of explanation.* — N-COUNT: also *of/in* N

2 If you say there is an **explanation** for something, you mean that there is a reason for it. *The deputy airport manager said there was no apparent explanation for the crash... Digging further into the medical literature, I found out there was a scientific explanation for all this... It's the only explanation I can think of.* — N-COUNT: oft N *for*n =reason

3 If you give an **explanation** of something, you give details about it or describe it so that it can be understood. *Haig was immediately impressed by Charteris's expertise and by his lucid explanation of the work.* — N-COUNT: oft N *of*n

explanatory /ɪksplænətəri, AM -tɔːri/. **Explanatory** statements or theories are intended to make people understand something by describing it or giving the reasons for it; a formal word. *These statements are accompanied by a series of explanatory notes... The concept was later seen to have explanatory power.* — ◆◇◇◇◇ ADJ-GRADED: usu ADJ n

expletive /ɪkspliːtɪv/ **expletives.** An **expletive** is a rude word or expression such as 'Damn!' which you say when you are annoyed, excited, or in pain; a formal word. — N-COUNT =swear word

explicable /ɪksplɪkəbᵊl, AM eksplɪk-/. If something is **explicable**, it can be explained and understood because it is logical or sensible; a formal word. *The older I grow, the stranger and less explicable the world appears to me.* — ADJ-GRADED

explicate /eksplɪkeɪt/ **explicates, explicating, explicated.** To **explicate** something means to explain it and make it clear; a formal word. *We shall have to explicate its basic assumptions before we can assess its implications.* ♦ **explication** /eksplɪkeɪʃᵊn/ **explications** *The jury listened to his impassioned explication of article 306... McKen criticises the lack of explication of what the term 'areas' means.* — VERB; V n; N-VAR

explicit /ɪksplɪsɪt/ ◆◆◇◇◇

1 Something that is **explicit** is expressed or shown clearly and openly, without any attempt to hide anything. *Sexually explicit scenes in films and books were taboo under the Communist system. ...explicit references to age in recruitment advertising.* ♦ **explicitly** *The play was the first commercially successful work dealing explicitly with homosexuality... Their intention is not to become involved in explicitly political activities.* ♦ **explicitness** *When the book was published, the energy and explicitness caught the popular imagination.* — ADJ-GRADED =overt; ADV-GRADED: ADV with v, ADV adj =overtly; N-UNCOUNT

2 If you are **explicit** about something, you speak about it very openly and clearly. *He was explicit about his intention to overhaul the party's internal voting system.* ♦ **explicitly** *She has been talking very explicitly about AIDS to these groups.* — ADJ-GRADED: v-link ADJ, oft ADJ *about*n; ADV-GRADED: ADV with v

explode /ɪksploʊd/ **explodes, exploding, exploded** ◆◆◆◇◇

1 If an object such as a bomb **explodes** or if someone or something **explodes** it, it bursts loudly and with great force, often causing damage or injury. *They were clearing up when the second bomb exploded... A school bus was hit by gunfire which exploded the fuel tank.* — V-ERG; V; V n

2 If someone **explodes**, they express strong feelings suddenly and violently. *Do you fear that you'll burst into tears or explode with anger in front of her?... 'What happened!' I exploded... George caught the look and decided that Bess had better leave before she exploded.* — VERB; V *with*n; V with quote; V

3 If something **explodes**, it increases suddenly and rapidly in number or intensity. *The population explodes to 40,000 during the tourist season... Investment by Japanese firms has exploded.* — VERB; V *to*n; V

4 If someone **explodes** a theory or myth, they prove that it is wrong or impossible. *Electricity privatisation has exploded the myth of cheap nuclear power... Such rumours have only recently been exploded.* — VERB; V n

5 If something **explodes**, it makes a sudden very loud noise; used in literary English. *She heard laughter explode, then die.* — VERB; V

exploit, exploits, exploiting, exploited. The verb is pronounced /ɪksplɔɪt/. The noun is pronounced /eksplɔɪt/. ◆◆◆◇◇

1 If you say that someone **is exploiting** you, you think that they are treating you unfairly by using your work or ideas and giving you very little in return. *Critics claim he exploited black musicians for personal gain. ...the plight of the exploited sugar cane workers.* ♦ **exploitation** /eksplɔɪteɪʃᵊn/ *Extra payments should be made to protect the interests of the staff and prevent exploitation.* — VERB; V n; V-ed; N-UNCOUNT

2 If you say that someone **is exploiting** a situation, you disapprove of them because they are using it to gain an advantage for themselves, rather than trying to help other people or do what is right. *The government and its opponents compete to exploit the troubles to their advantage.* ♦ **exploitation** *...the exploitation of the famine by local politicians.* — VERB, PRAGMATICS; V n; N-SING: N *of*n

3 If you **exploit** something, you use it well, and achieve something or gain an advantage from it. *You'll need a good aerial to exploit the radio's performance... Cary is hoping to exploit new opportunities in Europe... So you feel that your skills have never been fully appreciated or exploited?* — VERB; V n

4 To **exploit** resources or raw materials means to develop them and use them for industry or commercial activities. *I think we're being very short sighted in not exploiting our own coal.* ♦ **exploitation** *...the planned exploitation of its potential oil and natural gas reserves.* — VERB; V n; N-UNCOUNT: usu N *of*n

5 If you refer to someone's **exploits**, you mean the brave, interesting, or amusing things that they have done. *His wartime exploits were later made into a film and a television series.* — N-COUNT: usu pl, with poss

exploitable /ɪksplɔɪtəbᵊl/
1 If something is **exploitable**, it can be used or developed commercially to make a profit. *Exploitable raw materials were in short supply... Of 27 new wells drilled, 16 have proved exploitable.* ADJ-GRADED
2 An **exploitable** situation can be used by someone to their own advantage. *Your hope was I'd make some exploitable mistake. Admit it.* ADJ-GRADED

exploitative /ɪksplɔɪtətɪv/. If you describe something as **exploitative**, you disapprove of it because it treats people unfairly by using their work or ideas for its own advantage, and giving them very little in return; a formal word. *The expansion of Western capitalism incorporated the Third World into an exploitative world system.* ADJ-GRADED PRAGMATICS

exploiter /ɪksplɔɪtəʳ/ **exploiters.** If you refer to people as **exploiters**, you disapprove of them because they exploit other people in an unfair and uncaring way; a formal word. *They were accused of being exploiters and counter-revolutionaries.* N-COUNT PRAGMATICS

exploratory /ɪksplɒrətri, AM -plɔːrətɔːri/. ◆◇◇◇◇ **Exploratory** actions are done in order to discover something or to learn the truth about something. *Exploratory surgery revealed her liver cancer... The Prime Minister's talks with the leaders of the Democratic Party were largely exploratory.* ADJ

explore /ɪksplɔːʳ/ **explores, exploring, explored** ◆◆◆◇◇
1 If you **explore** a place, you travel around it to find out what it is like. *I just wanted to explore Paris, read Sartre, listen to Sidney Bechet... After exploring the old part of town there is a guided tour of the cathedral... We've come to this country, let's explore!* VERB V n V
♦ **exploration** /ekspləreɪʃᵊn/ **explorations** *We devote several days to the exploration of the magnificent Maya sites of Copan... We set out on this voyage of exploration with an open mind.* N-VAR
2 If you **explore** an idea or suggestion, you think about it or comment on it in detail, in order to assess it carefully. *The secretary is expected to explore ideas for post-war reconstruction of the area... The film is eloquent as it explores the relationship between artist and instrument.* ♦ **exploration** *I looked forward to the exploration of their theories.* VERB =investigate V n N-VAR
3 If people **explore** an area **for** a substance such as oil or minerals, they study the area and do tests on the land to see whether they can find it. *Central to the operation is a mile-deep well, dug originally to explore for oil... The government is allowing the areas of inshore coastal waters to be explored for oil and gas.* ♦ **exploration** *Oryx is a Dallas-based oil and gas exploration and production concern.* VERB V *for* n be V-ed *for* n Also V n *for* n N-UNCOUNT
4 If you **explore** something with your hands or fingers, you touch it to find out what it feels like. *He explored the wound with his finger, trying to establish its extent.* VERB V n

explorer /ɪksplɔːrəʳ/ **explorers.** ◆◇◇◇◇ An **explorer** is someone who travels to places about which very little is known, in order to discover what is there. N-COUNT

explosion /ɪkspləʊʒᵊn/ **explosions** ◆◆◆◇◇
1 An **explosion** is a sudden, violent burst of energy, for example one caused by a bomb. *After the second explosion, all of London's main train and subway stations were shut down... Three people have been killed and more than 40 injured in a bomb explosion in northwest Spain.* N-COUNT =blast
2 **Explosion** is the act of deliberately causing a bomb or similar device to explode. *Bomb disposal experts blew up the bag in a controlled explosion... France has carried out an underground nuclear explosion on Mururoa Atoll in the South Pacific.* N-VAR =detonation
3 An **explosion** is a large rapid increase in the number or amount of something. *The study also forecast an explosion in the diet soft-drink market... He explains that there was an explosion of courses through the 1960s... The spread of the suburbs has triggered a population explosion among America's deer.* N-COUNT: with supp
4 An **explosion** is a sudden violent expression of someone's feelings, especially anger; a literary use. *Every time they met, Myra anticipated an explosion... It was an explosion of anger against the practises of the occupying forces.* N-COUNT =outburst
5 An **explosion** is a sudden serious outbreak of political protest or violence. *They warned him that a referendum might cause an explosion in the country. ...the explosion of protest and violence sparked off by the killing of seven workers.* N-COUNT
6 An **explosion** is a sudden very loud noise; a literary use. *There was an explosion of music.* N-COUNT

explosive /ɪkspləʊsɪv/ **explosives** ◆◆◇◇◇
1 An **explosive** is a substance or device that can cause an explosion. *...one-hundred-and-fifty pounds of Semtex explosive... There were traces of explosives in the bedroom.* N-VAR
2 Something that is **explosive** is capable of causing an explosion. *The explosive device was timed to go off at the rush hour... Highly explosive gas is naturally found in coal mines.* ♦ **explosively** *Hydrogen is explosively flammable when mixed with oxygen.* ADJ-GRADED ADV: ADV adj, ADV after v
3 An **explosive** growth is a sudden, rapid increase in the size or quantity of something. *The explosive growth in casinos is one of the most conspicuous signs of Westernisation.* ♦ **explosively** *These transactions grew explosively in the early 1980s.* ADJ-GRADED ADV-GRADED: ADV after v, ADV adj
4 An **explosive** situation is likely to have difficult, serious, or dangerous effects. *He appeared to be treating the potentially explosive situation with some sensitivity... Nobody knows what explosive arguments the future of Europe will bring.* ♦ **explosively** *A referendum next year would coincide explosively with the election campaign.* ADJ-GRADED: usu ADJ n ADV-GRADED: ADV after v
5 If you describe someone as **explosive**, you mean that they tend to express sudden violent anger. *She was unpredictable, explosive, impulsive and easily distracted... He's inherited his father's explosive temper.* ♦ **explosively** *'Are you mad?' David asked explosively.* ADJ-GRADED =fiery ADV: ADV after v, ADV adj
6 A sudden loud noise can be described as **explosive**. *He made a loud, explosive noise of disgust. ...an explosive drumbeat.* ♦ **explosively** *The sound of her own chewing and swallowing were explosively loud.* ADJ-GRADED ADV: ADV adj, ADV after v

exponent /ɪkspəʊnənt/ **exponents** ◆◇◇◇◇
1 An **exponent** of an idea, theory, or plan is a person who supports and explains it, and who tries to persuade other people that it is a good idea; a formal use. *...a leading exponent of test-tube baby techniques.* N-COUNT: usu N *of* n =advocate
2 An **exponent** of a particular skill or activity is a person who is good at it. *...the great exponent of expressionist dance, Kurt Jooss. ...judo exponent Karen Briggs.* N-COUNT: with supp

exponential /ekspənenʃᵊl/. **Exponential** means growing or increasing very rapidly; a formal word. *The policy tried to check the exponential growth of public expenditure.* ♦ **exponentially** *The quantity of chemical pollutants has increased exponentially.* ADJ: usu ADJ n =explosive ADV: ADV after v

export, exports, exporting, exported. ◆◆◆◆◇ The verb is pronounced /ɪkspɔːʳt/. The noun is pronounced /ekspɔːʳt/.
1 To **export** products or raw materials means to sell them to another country. *The nation also exports beef... They expect the antibiotic products to be exported to Southeast Asia and Africa... To earn foreign exchange we must export.* ► Also a noun. *...the production and export of cheap casual wear... A lot of our land is used to grow crops for export. ...illegal arms exports.* VERB ≠import V n be V-ed *to* n V Also V n *to* n N-UNCOUNT: also N in pl
2 **Exports** are goods which are sold to another country and sent there. *He did this to promote American exports... Ghana's main export is cocoa.* N-COUNT ≠import
3 To **export** something means to introduce it into another country or make it happen there. *It has exported inflation at times. ...hecklers who said the deal would export jobs to Mexico.* VERB ≠import V n V n *to* n
4 In computing, if you **export** files or information from one type of software into another type, you change their format so that they can be used in the new software. *Files can be exported in ASCII or PCX formats.* VERB ≠import be V-ed Also V n

exportable /ɪkspɔːʳtəbəl/. **Exportable** products are suitable for being exported. *They are reliant on a very limited number of exportable products.* ADJ

exporter /ekspɔːʳtəʳ, ɪkspɔːʳtəʳ/ **exporters.** An **exporter** is a country, firm, or person that sells and sends goods to another country. *France is the world's second-biggest exporter of agricultural products.* ◆◇◇◇◇ N-COUNT: usu with supp ≠importer

expose /ɪkspoʊz/ **exposes, exposing, exposed** ◆◆◆◇◇

1 To **expose** something that is usually hidden means to uncover it so that it can be seen. *Lowered sea levels exposed the shallow continental shelf beneath the Bering Sea... For an instant his whole back was exposed. ...the exposed brickwork.* VERB V n V-ed

2 To **expose** a person or situation means to reveal that they are bad or immoral in some way. *The Budget does expose the lies ministers were telling a year ago... After the scandal was exposed, Dr Bailey committed suicide... He has simply been exposed as an adulterer and a fool.* VERB V n be V-ed as n/adj Also V n as n/adj

3 If someone **is exposed to** something dangerous or unpleasant, they are put in a situation in which it might affect them. *They had not been exposed to most diseases common to urban populations... A wise mother never exposes her children to the slightest possibility of danger. ...people exposed to high levels of radiation.* VERB be V-ed to n V n to n V-ed

4 If someone **is exposed to** an idea or feeling, usually a new one, they are given experience of it, or introduced to it. *...local people who've not been exposed to glimpses of Western life before... These units exposed children to many viewpoints of a given issue.* VERB be V-ed to n V n to n

5 A man who **exposes** himself shows people his genitals in a public place, usually because he is mentally or emotionally disturbed. *Smith admitted indecently exposing himself on Wimbledon Common.* VERB V pron-refl

exposé /ekspoʊzeɪ, AM ekspoʊzeɪ/ **exposés.** An **exposé** is a film or piece of writing which reveals the truth about a situation or person, especially something involving shocking facts. *The movie is an exposé of prison conditions in the South.* N-COUNT: oft N of n

exposed /ɪkspoʊzd/. If a place is **exposed**, it has no natural protection against bad weather or enemies, for example because it has no trees or is on very high ground. *...an exposed hillside in Connecticut... This part of the west coast of Scotland is very exposed to Atlantic winds.* ◆◇◇◇◇ ADJ-GRADED

exposition /ekspəzɪʃən/ **expositions** ◆◇◇◇◇

1 An **exposition** of an idea or theory is a detailed explanation or account of it; a formal use. *The fullest exposition of Coleridge's thought can be found in the Statesman's Manual.* N-COUNT: oft N of n

2 An **exposition** is an exhibition in which something such as goods or works of art are shown to the public. *...an art exposition.* N-COUNT =exhibition

expostulate /ɪkspɒstʃʊleɪt/ **expostulates, expostulating, expostulated.** If you **expostulate**, you express strong disagreement with someone; a formal word. *'For heaven's sake!' Dot expostulated. 'They're cheap and they're useful.'... For a moment I thought she was going to expostulate... His family expostulated with him.* VERB =protest V with quote V V with n

exposure /ɪkspoʊʒəʳ/ **exposures** ◆◆◆◇◇

1 **Exposure** to something dangerous means being in a situation where it might affect you. *Exposure to lead is known to damage the brains of young children. ...the potential exposure of people to nuclear waste.* N-UNCOUNT: usu N to n

2 **Exposure** is the harmful effect on your body caused by very cold weather. *He was suffering from exposure and shock but his condition was said to be stable... At least two people died of exposure in Chicago overnight.* N-UNCOUNT

3 The **exposure** of a well-known person is the revealing of the fact that they are bad or immoral in some way. *...the exposure of Anthony Blunt as a former Soviet spy... Their sporting reputation has suffered enormously from Johnson's exposure.* N-UNCOUNT: usu with poss =unmasking

4 **Exposure** is publicity that a person, company, or product receives. *All the candidates have been getting an enormous amount of exposure on television and in the press.* N-UNCOUNT =publicity

5 In photography, an **exposure** is a single photograph. *Larger drawings tend to require two or three exposures to cover them.* N-COUNT

6 In photography, the **exposure** is the amount of light that is allowed to enter a camera when taking a photograph. *A tripod also lets you shoot long exposures at night. ...an exposure of 1/18sec at f/11... Against a deep blue sky or dark storm-clouds, you may need to reduce the exposure.* N-VAR

expound /ɪkspaʊnd/ **expounds, expounding, expounded.** If you **expound** an idea or opinion, you give a clear and detailed explanation of it; a formal word. *Schmidt continued to expound his views on economics and politics.* ► **Expound on** means the same as **expound**. *Lawrence expounded on the military aspects of guerrilla warfare.* ◆◇◇◇◇ VERB =explain V n PHRASAL VERB V P n

express /ɪkspres/ **expresses, expressing, expressed** ◆◆◆◆◇

1 When you **express** an idea or feeling, or **express** yourself, you show what you think or feel by saying or doing something. *He expressed grave concern at American attitudes... Sumner would greet us with frowns and grimaces, doing his best to express wordless disapproval... He expresses himself easily in English... Children may find it easier to express themselves in a letter than in a formal essay.* VERB V n V pron-refl

2 If an idea or feeling **expresses** itself in some way, it can be clearly seen in someone's actions or in its effects on a situation. *The anxiety of the separation often expresses itself as anger towards the child for getting lost.* VERB =manifest V pron-refl prep

3 If you **express** a quantity or mathematical problem in a particular way, you write it using particular symbols, figures, or equations; a technical use in mathematics. *We can express that equation like that... It is expressed as a percentage.* VERB =show V n prep

4 An **express** command or order is one that is clearly and deliberately stated; a formal use. *The ship was sunk on express orders from the Prime Minister.* ♦ **expressly** *He has expressly forbidden her to go out on her own.* ADJ: ADJ n =explicit ADV: ADV before v

5 If you refer to an **express** intention or purpose, you are emphasizing that it is a deliberate and specific one that you have before you do something. *I had obtained my first camera for the express purpose of taking railway photographs.* ADJ: ADJ n PRAGMATICS =specific

♦ **expressly** *...projects expressly designed to support cattle farmers... Bleasdale had written the role expressly for Robert Lindsay.* ADV: ADV before v, ADV prep/to-inf

6 **Express** is used to describe special services which are provided by companies or organizations such as the Post Office, in which things are sent or done faster than usual for a higher price. *A special express service is available by fax... It was sent to us by express mail.* ► Also an adverb. *Send it express.* ADJ: ADJ n ADV

7 An **express** or an **express** train is a fast train which stops at very few stations. *Punctually at 7.45, the express to Kuala Lumpur left Singapore station... He had boarded an express for Rome.* N-COUNT: oft N to/for n

8 An **express** is a fast bus or coach which goes from one place to another directly or with very few stops. N-COUNT

expression /ɪkspreʃən/ **expressions** ◆◆◆◇◇

1 The **expression** of ideas or feelings is the showing of them through words, actions, or artistic activities. *Laughter is one of the most infectious expressions of emotion... From Cairo came expressions of regret at the attack. ...the rights of the individual to freedom of expression... Her concern has now found expression in the new environmental protection act.* N-VAR: usu N of n

2 Your **expression** is the way that your face looks at a particular moment. It shows what you are thinking or feeling. *The civil servant's expression, however, did not change, not so much as by a flicker... Levin sat there, an expression of sadness on his face... The face is entirely devoid of expression.* N-VAR: usu with supp, oft poss N

3 **Expression** is the showing of feeling when you are acting, singing, or playing a musical instru- N-UNCOUNT

ment. *I don't sing perfectly in tune, but I think I put more expression into my lyrics than a lot of other singers do.*
4 An **expression** is a word or phrase. *She spoke in a quiet voice but used remarkably coarse expressions.* N-COUNT
5 An **expression** is a symbol or equation which represents a quantity or problem; a technical use in mathematics. *This forms the basis for our mathematical expression for the electric field.* N-COUNT

expressionism /ɪkspreʃənɪzəm/. **Expressionism** is a style of art, literature, and music which uses symbolism and exaggeration in order to represent emotions rather than representing physical reality. N-UNCOUNT

expressionist /ɪkspreʃənɪst/ **expressionists**
1 An **expressionist** is an artist, writer, or composer who uses the style of expressionism. *He was a Belgian expressionist, of the same school as Chagall.* N-COUNT
2 Expressionist artists, writers, composers, or works use the style of expressionism. *...an extraordinary collection of expressionist paintings.* ADJ: usu ADJ n

expressionless /ɪkspreʃənləs/. If you describe someone's face as **expressionless**, you mean that they are not showing their feelings. ADJ-GRADED

expressive /ɪkspresɪv/ ◆◇◇◇◇
1 If you describe a person or their behaviour as **expressive**, you mean that their behaviour clearly indicates their feelings or intentions. *You can train people to be more expressive... She had almost the same look on her small, usually expressive face. ...the present fashion for intuitive, expressive painting.* ♦ **expressively** *He moved his hands expressively.* ♦ **expressiveness** *Crying is part of our natural expressiveness.* ADJ-GRADED PRAGMATICS; ADV-GRADED: ADV with v; N-UNCOUNT
2 If something is **expressive of** particular ideas or qualities, it has features which indicate or demonstrate them; a formal use, used in written English. *Perhaps all his poems were really love poems, expressive of love for someone... Its history is expressive of the character and development of the people who possess it.* ADJ-GRADED: v-link ADJ *of* n

expressway /ɪkspreswei/ **expressways.** An **expressway** is a wide road that is specially designed so that a lot of traffic can move along it very quickly. N-COUNT

expropriate /eksproupriet/ **expropriates, expropriating, expropriated.** If a government or other authority **expropriates** someone's property, they take it away from them for public use; a technical word in law. *The Bolsheviks expropriated the property of the landowners.* VERB; V n
♦ **expropriation** /eksprouprieɪʃən/ **expropriations** *...the expropriation of property... Ownership is not clear because of expropriations in the Nazi and communist eras.* N-VAR: oft N *of* n

expulsion /ɪkspʌlʃən/ **expulsions** ◆◆◇◇◇
1 Expulsion is the expelling of someone from a school, university, or organization. *Her hatred of authority led to her expulsion from high school. ...the high number of school expulsions... This led to his suspension and, finally, expulsion from the party in 1955.* N-VAR: usu with supp
2 Expulsion is the expelling of someone from a place; a formal use. *...the expulsion of Yemeni workers. ...a new wave of mass expulsions.* N-VAR: usu with supp
3 Expulsion is the expelling of something from a container or from your body; a formal use. *...the expulsion of waste products. ...their expulsion from the digestive tract.* N-UNCOUNT: usu with supp

expunge /ɪkspʌndʒ/ **expunges, expunging, expunged.** If you **expunge** something, you get rid of it completely, because it causes problems or bad feelings; a formal word. *The revolutionaries expunged domestic opposition and mobilized their resources for the war... The experience was something he had tried to expunge from his memory... His name was expunged from the record books.* VERB; V n; V n *from* n

expurgate /ekspəʳgeɪt/ **expurgates, expurgating, expurgated.** If someone **expurgates** a piece of writing, they remove parts of it before it is published because they think those parts will offend or shock people; a formal word. *He heavily expurgated the work in its second edition.* VERB =censor; V n
♦ **expurgated** *It was first published in 1914 in a highly expurgated version.* ADJ-GRADED

exquisite /ɪkskwɪzɪt, ekskwɪzɪt/ ◆◆◇◇◇
1 Something that is **exquisite** is extremely beautiful or pleasant, especially in a delicate or refined way. *The Indians brought in exquisite beadwork to sell... Mr Zhang's photography is exquisite. ...her exquisite manners.* ♦ **exquisitely** *...exquisitely crafted dolls' houses. ...an exquisitely beautiful young woman.* ADJ-GRADED; ADV-GRADED: usu ADV adj/-ed
2 Exquisite is used to emphasize that a feeling or quality is very great or intense; a literary use. *The words issuing from her lips gave exquisite pleasure as they flowed over him... She peeled it with exquisite care.* ADJ: ADJ n PRAGMATICS

ex-serviceman, ex-servicemen. In British English, an **ex-serviceman** is a man who used to be in a country's army, navy, or air force. The American word is **veteran.** N-COUNT

ext. Ext. is the written abbreviation for **extension** when it is used to refer to a particular telephone number. ◆◆◇◇◇ N-VAR: N num =extension

extant /ekstænt, ekstənt/. If something is **extant**, it is still in existence, in spite of being very old; a formal word. *Two fourteenth-century manuscripts of this text are still extant... The oldest extant document is dated 1492.* ADJ =surviving

extemporize /ɪkstempəraɪz/ **extemporizes, extemporizing, extemporized;** also spelled **extemporise** in British English. If you **extemporize**, you speak, act, or perform something immediately, without rehearsing or preparing it beforehand; a formal word. *He completely departed from the text and extemporized in a very energetic fashion.* VERB =improvise; V

extend /ɪkstend/ **extends, extending, extended** ◆◆◆◆◇
1 If you say that something, usually something large, **extends** for a particular distance or **extends** from one place to another, you are indicating its size or position. *The caves extend for some 18 kilometres... The main stem will extend to around 12ft, if left to develop naturally... Our personal space extends about 12 to 18 inches around us... The high-speed train service is planned to extend from Paris to Bordeaux... The new territory would extend over one-fifth of Canada's land mass.* VERB =stretch; V *for* amount; V *to* amount; V amount; V *from* n *to* n; V *over* n; Also V *to* n
2 If an object **extends from** a surface or place, it sticks out from it. *Billing's legs extended from the bushes and Anthony tripped over them as he retraced his steps.* VERB =protrude from; V *from* n
3 If an event or activity **extends** over a period of time, it continues for that time. *...a playing career in first-class cricket that extended from 1894 to 1920... The courses are based on a weekly two-hour class, extending over a period of 25 weeks.* VERB; V *from* n *to* n; V *over* n; Also V *to* n
4 If something **extends** to a group of people, things, or activities, it includes or affects them. *The service also extends to wrapping and delivering gifts... The talks will extend to the church, human rights groups and other social organizations... His influence extends beyond the TV viewing audience.* VERB; V *to* n/-ing; V *beyond* n
5 If you **extend** something, you make it longer or bigger. *This year they have introduced three new products to extend their range... The building was extended in 1500. ...an extended exhaust pipe.* VERB; V n; V-ed
6 If a piece of equipment or furniture **extends**, its length can be increased. *... a table which extends to accommodate extra guests... The table extends to 220cm.* VERB; V; V *to* amount
7 If you **extend** something, you make it last longer than before or end at a later date. *They have extended the deadline by twenty-four hours. ...an extended contract.* VERB; V n; V-ed
8 If you **extend** something **to** other people or things, you make it include or affect more people or things. *It might be possible to extend the technique to other crop plants.* VERB; V n *to* n
9 If someone **extends** their hand, they stretch out their arm and hand to shake hands with someone; VERB =stretch out

used in written English. *The man extended his hand: 'I'm Chuck'.* V n

extendable /ɪkstendəbᵊl/. Something that is **extendable** can be made longer. *These were hung in place with extendable rods.* ADJ: usu ADJ n

extended /ɪkstendɪd/. If something happens for an **extended** period of time, it happens for a long period of time. *Obviously, any child who receives dedicated teaching over an extended period is likely to improve.* • See also **extend**. ◆◇◇◇◇ ADJ: ADJ n =lengthy

extended family, extended families. An **extended family** is a family group which includes relatives such as uncles, aunts, and grandparents, as well as parents, children, and brothers and sisters. *The pregnant woman in such a community has the support of all the womenfolk in her extended family.* ◆◇◇◇◇ N-COUNT

extension /ɪkstenʃᵊn/ **extensions** ◆◆◇◇◇

1 An **extension** is a new room or building which is added to an existing building or group of buildings. N-COUNT

2 An **extension** is a new section of a road or rail line that is added to an existing road or line. *...the Jubilee Line extension.* N-COUNT: usu with supp

3 An **extension** is an extra period of time for which something lasts or is valid, usually as a result of official permission. *He first entered Britain on a six-month visa, and was given a further extension of six months... Ian Lentern has been granted a three-year extension.* N-COUNT

4 Something that is an **extension** of something else is a development of it that includes or affects more people, things, or activities. *Many Filipinos see the bases as an extension of American colonial rule... That's the logical extension of my approach.* N-COUNT: usu N *of* n

5 An **extension** is a telephone line that is connected to the switchboard of a company or institution, and that has its own number. The written abbreviation 'ext.' is also used. *She can get me on extension 308... For further information, please contact 414 3925, extension 2253.* N-COUNT: also N num

6 An **extension** is a part which is connected to a piece of equipment in order to make it reach something further away. *...a 30-foot extension cord... Some of the best extensions are made from sections of rod tube or drainpipe.* N-COUNT

extensive /ɪkstensɪv/ ◆◆◆◇◇

1 Something that is **extensive** covers or includes a large physical area. *...an extensive tour of Latin America... When built, the palace and its grounds were more extensive than the city itself.* ADJ-GRADED

♦ **extensively** *Mark, however, needs to travel extensively with his varied business interests.* ADV-GRADED: ADV after v

2 Something that is **extensive** covers a wide range of details, ideas, or items. *Developments in South Africa receive extensive coverage in The Sunday Telegraph. ...the extensive research into public attitudes to science... The facilities available are very extensive.* ♦ **extensively** *...the extensively reported trial... All these issues have been extensively researched in recent years.* ADJ-GRADED; ADV-GRADED: ADV after v, ADV adj/-ed

3 If something is **extensive**, it is very great. *The blast caused extensive damage, shattering the front hall and the ground-floor rooms... The security forces have extensive powers of search and arrest... Mr Marr makes extensive use of exclusively Scottish words.* ♦ **extensively** *Hydrogen is used extensively in industry for the production of ammonia.* ADJ-GRADED; ADV-GRADED: ADV after v

extent /ɪkstent/ ◆◆◆◇◇

1 If you are talking about how great, important, or serious a difficulty or situation is, you can refer to the **extent** of it. *The government itself has little information on the extent of industrial pollution... Growing up with him soon made me realise the extent of his determination... The full extent of the losses was disclosed yesterday.* N-SING: with supp, usu *the* N *of* n =magnitude

2 The **extent** of something is its length, area, or size. *Industry representatives made it clear that their commitment was only to maintain the extent of forests, not their biodiversity.* N-SING: with supp, usu *the* N *of* n

3 You use expressions such as **to a large extent, to some extent**, or **to a certain extent** in order to indicate that something is partly true, but not entirely true. *It was and, to a large extent, still is a good show... To some extent this was the truth... To a certain extent it's easier for men to get work... This also endangers American interests in other regions, although to a lesser extent... To an extent, that is the reason for the meeting.* PHRASES PHR with cl PRAGMATICS

4 You use expressions such as **to what extent, to that extent**, or **to the extent that** when you are discussing how true a statement is, or in what ways it is true. *It's still not clear to what extent this criticism is originating from within the ruling party... To that extent they helped bring about their own destruction... He could only be sorry to the extent that this affected his grandchildren... The extent to which it helped to promote Britain's broader strategic interests was sometimes questionable... We may not be able to do it to the extent that we would like.* PRAGMATICS

5 You use expressions such as **to the extent of, to the extent that**, or **to such an extent that** in order to emphasize that a situation has reached a difficult, dangerous, or surprising stage. *Ford kept his suspicions to himself, even to the extent of going to jail for a murder he obviously didn't commit... I became pregnant but this man was very violent towards me to the extent that I lost our baby... It has increased to such an extent that Ghana can now export maize.* PRAGMATICS

extenuating /ɪkstenjueɪtɪŋ/. If you say that there are **extenuating** circumstances for a bad situation or wrong action, you mean that there are reasons or factors which partly excuse it; a formal word. *The defendants decide to admit their guilt, but insist that there are extenuating circumstances.* ADJ: usu ADJ n =mitigating

exterior /ɪkstɪəriəʳ/ **exteriors** ◆◇◇◇◇

1 The **exterior** of something is its outside surface. *In one ad the viewer scarcely sees the car's exterior... The exterior of the building was a masterpiece of architecture, elegant and graceful.* N-COUNT: usu sing =outside

2 You can refer to someone's usual appearance or behaviour as their **exterior**, especially when it is very different from their real character. *According to Mandy, Pat's tough exterior hides a shy and sensitive soul.* N-COUNT: usu sing, usu with supp, oft poss N =facade

3 You use **exterior** to refer to the outside parts of something or things that are outside something. *The exterior walls were made of pre-formed concrete. ...the oven's exterior surfaces.* ADJ: ADJ n =outer, outside

exterminate /ɪkstɜːʳmɪneɪt/ **exterminates, exterminating, exterminated.** To **exterminate** a group of people or animals means to kill all of them. *A huge effort was made to exterminate the rats... They have a real fear that they'll be exterminated in the ongoing civil war... Man is exterminating too many species for zoos to be much help.* ◆◇◇◇◇ VERB =annihilate; V n

♦ **extermination** /ɪkstɜːʳmɪneɪʃᵊn/ *...the extermination of hundreds of thousands of their brethren.* N-UNCOUNT: oft N *of* n, N n

exterminator /ɪkstɜːʳmɪneɪtəʳ/ **exterminators.** An **exterminator** is a person whose job is to kill animals such as rats or mice, because they are a nuisance or a danger. *One hundred million rats are killed each year by pest exterminators.* N-COUNT

external /ɪkstɜːʳnᵊl/ ◆◆◇◇◇

1 **External** is used to indicate that something is on the outside of something or someone, or exists, happens, or comes from outside something. *...a much reduced heat loss through external walls. ...internal and external allergic reactions.* ADJ: usu ADJ n ≠internal

♦ **externally** *Vitamins can be applied externally to the skin. ...externally imposed conditions.* ADV: usu ADV with v

2 **External** means involving or intended for foreign countries. *...the commissioner for external affairs. ...Jamaica's external debt. ...the republic's external borders.* ♦ **externally** *...protecting the value of the mark both internally and externally.* ADJ: ADJ n; ADV: usu ADV after v

3 **External** means happening or existing in the world in general and affecting you in some way. *...a reaction to external events... Such events occur only when the external conditions are favorable.* ADJ: ADJ n

4 **External** examiners, accountants, or evaluators come into an organization from outside in order to do a job there that must be done fairly and ADJ: ADJ n =outside

impartially, or to check that a job was done properly; used mainly in British English. ♦ **externally** ADV: ADV -ed *There must be externally moderated tests.*

5 If medicine is **for external use**, it is intended to be used only on the outside of your body, and not to be eaten or drunk. PHRASE: v-link PHR, PHR after v

externalize /ɪkstɜːʳnəlaɪz/ **externalizes, externalizing, externalized;** also spelled **externalise** in British English. VERB ≠internalize If you **externalize** your ideas or feelings, you express them openly, in words or actions; a formal word. V n *For the Prime Minister, externalising the problem would divert attention from his domestic troubles... These are people who tend to externalize blame when anything goes wrong at work.*

externals /ɪkstɜːʳnəlz/. N-PLURAL When you talk about **externals**, you are referring to the features of a situation that are obvious but not important or central. *All that the tourists see are the externals of our faith.*

extinct /ɪkstɪŋkt/ ◆◇◇◇◇

1 A species of animal or plant that is **extinct** no longer has any living members, either in the world or in a particular place. ADJ *It is 250 years since the wolf became extinct in Britain. ...the bones of extinct animals.*

2 If a particular kind of worker, way of life, or type of activity is **extinct**, it no longer exists, because of changes in society. ADJ *If the current trend continues, black farmers in the United States may be extinct by the end of this decade... Herbalism had become an all but extinct skill in the Western world.*

3 An **extinct** volcano is one that does not erupt or is not expected to erupt any more. ADJ *Its tallest volcano, long extinct, is Olympus Mons.*

extinction /ɪkstɪŋkʃᵊn/ ◆◇◇◇◇

1 The **extinction** of a species of animal or plant is the death of all its remaining living members. N-UNCOUNT *An operation is beginning to try to save a species of crocodile from extinction... Many species have been shot to the verge of extinction.*

2 If someone refers to the **extinction** of a way of life or type of activity, they mean that the way of life or activity ceases to exist. N-UNCOUNT *The loggers say their jobs are faced with extinction because of declining timber sales.*

extinguish /ɪkstɪŋgwɪʃ/ **extinguishes, extinguishing, extinguished** ◆◇◇◇◇

1 If you **extinguish** a fire or a light, you stop it burning or shining; a formal use. VERB =put out V n *It took about 50 minutes to extinguish the fire... The lights are extinguished as soon as the news conference is over.*

2 If something **extinguishes** a feeling or idea, it destroys it. VERB V n *The message extinguished her hopes of Richard's return.*

extinguisher /ɪkstɪŋgwɪʃəʳ/ **extinguishers.** N-COUNT An **extinguisher** is the same as a **fire extinguisher**.

extn. N-VAR **Extn.** means the same as **ext**.

extol /ɪkstoʊl/ **extols, extolling, extolled.** ◆◇◇◇◇ VERB If you **extol** something or someone, you praise them enthusiastically. V n *Now experts are extolling the virtues of the humble potato... They kept extolling my managerial skills.*

extort /ɪkstɔːʳt/ **extorts, extorting, extorted**

1 If someone **extorts** money from you, they get it from you using force, threats, or other unfair or illegal means. VERB =extract V n from n V n *Corrupt government officials were extorting money from him... Her kidnapper extorted a £175,000 ransom for her release.*

2 If someone **extorts** something from you, they get it from you with difficulty or by using unfair means. VERB V n *Some magistrates have abused their powers of arrest to extort confessions.*

extortion /ɪkstɔːʳʃᵊn/. ◆◇◇◇◇ N-UNCOUNT **Extortion** is the crime of obtaining something from someone, especially money, by using force or threats. *He has been charged with extortion and abusing his powers.*

extortionate /ɪkstɔːʳʃᵊnət/. ADJ-GRADED PRAGMATICS =outrageous If you describe something such as a price as **extortionate**, you are emphasizing that it is much greater than it should be.

extortionist /ɪkstɔːʳʃᵊnɪst/ **extortionists.** N-COUNT An **extortionist** is someone who commits the crime of obtaining something from someone by using force or threats.

extra /ekstrə/ **extras** ◆◆◆◆◇

1 You use **extra** to describe an amount, person, or thing that is added to others of the same kind, or that can be added to others of the same kind. ADJ: ADJ n =additional *Police warned motorists to allow extra time to get to work... Extra staff have been taken on to cover busy periods... There's an extra blanket in the bottom drawer of the cupboard.*

2 If something is **extra**, you have to pay more money for it in addition to what you are already paying for something. ADJ: v-link ADJ *For foreign orders postage is extra... The price of your meal is extra.* ▶ Also a pronoun. PRON *Many of the additional features now cost extra... She won't pay any extra.* ▶ Also an adverb. ADV *You may be charged 10% extra for this service.*

3 **Extras** are additional amounts of money that are added to the price that you have to pay for something. N-COUNT: usu pl *She is disgusted by big hotels adding so many extras to the bill that it nearly doubles... There are no hidden extras.*

4 **Extras** are things which are not necessary in a situation, activity, or object, but which make it more comfortable, useful, or enjoyable. N-COUNT: usu pl *Optional extras include cooking tuition at a top restaurant... They are also spending much less on extras like meals in restaurants.*

5 The **extras** in a film are the people who play unimportant parts, for example as members of a crowd. N-COUNT

6 You can use **extra** in front of adjectives and adverbs to emphasize the quality that they are describing; an informal use. ADV: ADV adj/adv PRAGMATICS =especially *I'd have to be extra careful... What makes a magnificent garden extra special?... We were all told to try extra hard to be nice to him.*

7 ● to **go the extra mile**: see **mile**.

extra- /ekstrə-/. PREFIX **extra-** is used to form adjectives indicating that something is outside something or is not part of something; a formal word. *The move was extra-constitutional... They competed for power through a combination of parliamentary and extra-parliamentary methods... The report says torture was widespread, as were extra-judicial executions by government troops.*

extract, extracts, extracting, extracted. ◆◆◇◇◇ The verb is pronounced /ɪkstrækt/. The noun is pronounced /ekstrækt/.

1 To **extract** a substance means to obtain it from something else, for example by using industrial or chemical processes. VERB V n be V-ed from n V-ed Also V n from n *...the traditional method of pick and shovel to extract coal... Citric acid can be extracted from the juice of oranges, lemons, limes or grapefruit. ...looking at the differences in the extracted DNA.* ♦ **extraction** N-UNCOUNT: oft the N of n *Petroleum engineers plan and manage the extraction of oil.*

2 If you **extract** something from a place, you take it out or pull it out; a literary use. VERB V n from n V n *He extracted a small notebook from his hip pocket... Patterson went straight to the liquor cabinet and extracted a bottle of Scotch... She reached into the wardrobe and extracted another tracksuit.*

3 When a dentist **extracts** a tooth, he or she removes it from the patient's mouth. VERB V n have n V-ed *A dentist may decide to extract the tooth to prevent recurrent trouble... She is to go and have a tooth extracted at 3 o'clock today.* ♦ **extraction, extractions** N-VAR *In those days, dentistry was basic. Extractions were carried out without anaesthetic.*

4 If you say that someone **extracts** something, you disapprove of them because they take it for themselves to gain an advantage, often by taking it away from someone else. VERB PRAGMATICS V n from n *...the capitalist system, which extracts huge profits from arms production at the tax-payers' expense... He sought to extract the maximum political advantage from the cut in interest rates... His development policies have extracted cash from the city centre.*

5 If you **extract** information or a response VERB

from someone, you get it from them with difficulty, because they are unwilling to say or do what you want. *He made the mistake of trying to extract further information from our director... He used her cash card, and the PIN number he had extracted from her, to take £200 from cashpoints.*
=elicit from
V n *from* n

6 If you **extract** a particular piece of information, you obtain it from a larger amount or source of information. *I've simply extracted a few figures... Britain's trade figures can no longer be extracted from export-and-import documentation at ports. ...files of data extracted from the departmental archives.*
VERB
V n
be V-ed *from* n
V-ed
Also V n *from* n

7 If part of a book or text **is extracted** from it, that part is printed or published; used in journalism. *This material has been extracted from 'Collins Good Wood Handbook'.*
V-PASSIVE
be V-ed *from* n
Also *be* V-ed

8 An **extract** from a book or piece of writing is a small part of it that is printed or published separately. *Read this extract from an information booklet about the work of an airline cabin crew.*
N-COUNT: usu N *from* n

9 An **extract** is a substance that has been obtained from something else, for example by means of a chemical or industrial process. *Blend in the lemon extract, lemon peel and walnuts... Saponaria is a plant extract which acts as a natural tonic.*
N-MASS: oft n N

10 See also **yeast extract.**

extraction /ɪkstrækʃᵊn/. If you say, for example, that someone is of French **extraction**, you mean that they or their family originally came from France; a formal use. *Her real father was of Italian extraction... He married a young lady of Indian extraction.*
N-UNCOUNT: with supp
=origin, descent

extractor /ɪkstræktəʳ/ **extractors**

1 An **extractor** or **extractor fan** is a device that is fixed to a window or wall to draw smells, steam, or hot air out of a room or building; used mainly in British English.
N-COUNT

2 An **extractor** is a device that squeezes liquid out of something. *Push the leaves through a juice extractor until you have about four tablespoons of juice.*
N-COUNT: with supp

extracurricular /ekstrə kərɪkjʊləʳ/; also spelled **extra-curricular**, especially in American English.

1 **Extracurricular** activities are activities for students that are not part of their course; a formal use. *Each child had participated in extracurricular activities at school. ...extra-curricular sport.*
ADJ: ADJ n

2 **Extracurricular** activities are activities that someone does that are not part of their normal work; an informal use. *The money he made from these extra-curricular activities enabled him to pursue other ventures.*
ADJ: ADJ n

extradite /ekstrədaɪt/ **extradites, extraditing, extradited.** If someone **is extradited**, they are officially sent back to their own country to be tried for a crime that they have been accused of; a formal word. *He was extradited to Britain from the Irish Republic to face explosives charges... The authorities refused to extradite him.*
◆◆◇◇◇
VERB
be V-ed *to/from* n
V n

♦ **extradition** /ekstrədɪʃᵊn/ **extraditions** *A New York court turned down the British government's request for his extradition... There were no plans to reopen extradition proceedings against him.*
N-VAR

extra-marital; also spelled **extramarital**. An **extra-marital** affair is a sexual relationship between a married person and another person who is not their husband or wife. *Her husband has admitted having an extra-marital affair. ...an extra-marital relationship.*
ADJ: usu ADJ n

extra-mural. **Extra-mural** courses are courses at a college or university which are taken mainly by part-time students. *I took my first extra-mural course in 1948 in Coventry, even though I was working in Birmingham... Adult education is run in cooperation with the extra-mural departments of the universities.*
ADJ: usu ADJ n

extraneous /ɪkstreɪniəs/. **Extraneous** things are not relevant or essential to the situation you are involved in or the subject you are talking about; a formal word. *We ought not to bring in extraneous matters in trying to find a basis for a settlement... I can choose to ignore these extraneous thoughts or certainly choose not to act on them.*
ADJ: usu ADJ n

extraordinaire /ekstrɔːʳdɪneəʳ/. If you describe someone as being, for example, a **musician extraordinaire**, you are saying in a slightly humorous way that you think they are an extremely good musician. *...George Kuchar, film-maker extraordinaire.*
ADJ: n ADJ

extraordinary /ɪkstrɔːʳdənri, AM -neri/
◆◆◆◇◇

1 If you describe something or someone as **extraordinary**, you mean that they have some extremely good or special quality. *We've made extraordinary progress as a society in that regard... The task requires extraordinary patience and endurance... Rozhdestvensky is an extraordinary musician.* ♦ **extraordinarily** /ɪkstrɔːʳdənrɪli, AM -nerɪli/ *She's extraordinarily disciplined.*
ADJ-GRADED: usu ADJ n
PRAGMATICS
=exceptional, remarkable, amazing
ADV-GRADED: ADV adj
=exceptionally

2 If you describe something as **extraordinary**, you mean that it is very unusual or surprising. *What an extraordinary thing to happen!... His decision to hold talks is extraordinary because it could mean the real end of the war.* ♦ **extraordinarily** *Apart from the hair, he looked extraordinarily unchanged... Extraordinarily, the favourites for the title lie at the bottom of the table.*
ADJ-GRADED
PRAGMATICS
=remarkable, amazing
ADV-GRADED: ADV adj/adv, ADV with cl
=remarkably

3 An **extraordinary** meeting is arranged specially to deal with a particular situation or problem, rather than happening regularly; a formal use. *...at an extraordinary meeting of the sport's ruling body... Representatives of the colonies met in an extraordinary congress.*
ADJ: ADJ n

extrapolate /ɪkstræpᵊleɪt/ **extrapolates, extrapolating, extrapolated.** If you **extrapolate from** known facts, you use them as a basis for general statements about a situation or about what is likely to happen in the future; a formal word. *Extrapolating from his American findings, he reckons about 80% of these deaths might be attributed to smoking... It is unhelpful to extrapolate general trends from one case.*
VERB
V *from* n
V n *from* n

♦ **extrapolation** /ɪkstræpəleɪʃᵊn/ **extrapolations** *His estimate of half a million HIV positive cases was based on an extrapolation of the known incidence of the virus.*
N-VAR

extra-sensory perception. **Extra-sensory perception** means knowing things in a supernatural way, rather than as a result of using your ordinary senses such as sight and hearing. Some people believe this is possible. The abbreviation 'ESP' is also used.
N-UNCOUNT

extraterrestrial /ekstrətɪrestriəl/ **extraterrestrials;** also spelled **extra-terrestrial.**

1 **Extraterrestrial** means happening, existing, or coming from somewhere beyond the planet Earth; a formal use. *NASA has started a 10-year search for extraterrestrial intelligence. ...extraterrestrial rocks.*
ADJ: usu ADJ n

2 **Extraterrestrials** are living creatures that some people think exist or may exist in another part of the universe.
N-COUNT

extra time. In British English, if a sports match such as a game of football or hockey goes into **extra time**, the game continues for a set period after it would usually have ended because both teams have the same score. The American term is **overtime**. *Cambridge won 2-0 after extra time.*
◆◇◇◇◇
N-UNCOUNT

extravagance /ɪkstrævəgəns/ **extravagances**
◆◇◇◇◇

1 **Extravagance** is the spending of more money than is reasonable or than you can afford. *...gross mismanagement and financial extravagance... When the company went under, tales of his extravagance surged through the industry.*
N-UNCOUNT
=overspending

2 An **extravagance** is something that you spend money on but cannot really afford. *Her only extravagance was horses... Why waste money on such extravagances?*
N-COUNT

extravagant /ɪkstrævəgənt/
◆◇◇◇◇

1 Someone who is **extravagant** spends more money than they can afford or uses more of something than is reasonable. *We are not extravagant; restaurant meals are a luxury and designer clothes are out... I hope you don't think I'm extravagant but I've had the electric fire on for most of the day.*
ADJ-GRADED

♦ **extravagantly** *The day before they left Jeff had shopped extravagantly for presents for the whole family.* ADV-GRADED: ADV with v

2 Something that is **extravagant** costs more money than you can afford or uses more of something than is reasonable. *Her Aunt Sallie gave her an uncharacteristically extravagant gift... Baking a whole cheese in pastry may seem extravagant. ...her extravagant lifestyle.* ADJ-GRADED ♦ **extravagantly** *They claim Labour's plans would be extravagantly expensive and over-bureaucratic.* ADV-GRADED: ADV adj/-ed

3 **Extravagant** behaviour is extreme behaviour that is often done for a particular effect. *He was extravagant in his admiration of Hellas... They may make extravagant shows of generosity and concern for others.* ADJ-GRADED =unrestrained ♦ **extravagantly** *She had on occasions praised him extravagantly... The shop windows were filled with extravagantly bizarre clothes and outrageous displays.* ADV-GRADED: ADV with v, ADV adj

4 **Extravagant** claims or ideas are unrealistic or impractical; used showing disapproval. *They have to compete by adorning their products with ever more extravagant claims... Don't be afraid to consider apparently extravagant ideas.* ADJ-GRADED: usu ADJ n PRAGMATICS =absurd

5 **Extravagant** entertainments or designs are elaborate and impressive. *...the wildest and most extravagant London parties. ...painting extravagant and bold designs onto wooden frames.* ADJ-GRADED: usu ADJ n ♦ **extravagantly** *The day before announcing his farewell to business, Sir James talked to me in his extravagantly elegant Paris home.* ADV-GRADED: ADV adj/-ed

extravaganza /ɪkstrævəgænzə/ **extravaganzas.** An **extravaganza** is a very elaborate and expensive show or performance. *...a magnificent firework extravaganza. ...an all-night musical extravaganza.* ◆◇◇◇◇ N-COUNT: usu sing, with supp =spectacular

extreme /ɪkstriːm/ **extremes** ◆◆◆◇◇

1 **Extreme** means very great in degree or intensity. *The girls were afraid of snakes and picked their way along with extreme caution. ...people living in extreme poverty. ...the author's extreme reluctance to generalise.* ADJ-GRADED: usu ADJ n =great

2 You use **extreme** to describe situations and behaviour which are much more severe or unusual than you would expect, especially when you disapprove of them because of this. *The extreme case was Poland, where 29 parties won seats... It is hard to imagine Lineker capable of anything so extreme... The scheme has been condemned as extreme.* ADJ-GRADED PRAGMATICS

3 You use **extreme** to describe opinions, beliefs, or political movements which you disapprove of because they are very different from those that most people would accept as reasonable or normal. *This extreme view hasn't captured popular opinion. ...the racist politics of the extreme right.* ADJ-GRADED: usu ADJ n PRAGMATICS ≠moderate

4 You can use **extremes** to refer to situations or types of behaviour that have opposite qualities to each other, especially when each situation or type of behaviour has such a quality to the greatest degree possible. *...a 'middle way' between the extremes of success and failure, wealth and poverty... They can withstand extremes of temperature and weather without fading or cracking.* N-COUNT: usu pl, oft N *of* n

5 The **extreme** end or edge of something is its furthest end or edge. *...the room at the extreme end of the corridor. ...winds from the extreme north.* ADJ-GRADED: ADJ n =far

6 If someone **goes to extremes, takes** something **to extremes**, or **carries** something **to extremes**, they do or say something in a way that people consider to be unacceptable, unreasonable, or foolish. *The police went to the extremes of installing the most advanced safety devices in the man's house... The doctor told me not to mention dieting to her in case she took it to the extreme... There is a sense of shame, sometimes carried to extremes.* PHRASES V and N inflect

7 You use **in the extreme** after an adjective in order to emphasize what you are saying, especially when you want to indicate that it is something which is undesirable or very surprising; a formal expression. *It is proving controversial in the extreme... Our rows become unhealthy in the extreme.* adj PHR PRAGMATICS

extremely /ɪkstriːmli/. You use **extremely** in front of adjectives and adverbs to emphasize that the specified quality is present to a very great degree. *My mobile phone is extremely useful... These headaches are extremely common... Three of them are working extremely well.* ◆◆◆◆◇ ADV: ADV adj/adv PRAGMATICS =exceedingly, very

extremis /ɪkstriːmɪs/. See **in extremis.**

extremism /ɪkstriːmɪzəm/. **Extremism** is the behaviour or beliefs of extremists. *Greater demands were being placed on the police by growing violence and left and right-wing extremism.*  N-UNCOUNT

extremist /ɪkstriːmɪst/ **extremists** 

1 If you describe someone as an **extremist**, you disapprove of them because they try to bring about political change by using violent or extreme methods. *He said the country needed a strong intelligence service to counter espionage, terrorism and foreign extremists... A previously unknown extremist group has said it carried out Friday's bomb attack. ...a marked rise in extremist violence.* N-COUNT PRAGMATICS

2 If you say that someone has **extremist** views, you disapprove of them because they believe in bringing about change by using violent or extreme methods. ADJ: usu ADJ n PRAGMATICS

extremity /ɪkstremɪti/ **extremities**

1 The **extremity** of something is its furthest end or edge; a formal use. *...a small port on the north-western extremity of the Iberian peninsula. ...the extremities of the aeroplane.* N-COUNT: with supp

2 Your **extremities** are the ends or outermost parts of your body, especially your hands and feet. *He found that his extremities grew cold... Exercise is very important as it keeps the circulation moving and warms the extremities.* N-PLURAL: oft with poss

3 The **extremity** of a situation or of someone's behaviour is the degree to which it is severe, unusual, or unacceptable. *In spite of the extremity of her seclusion she was sane... In the past, the Tibetans had been protected by their forbidding geography and the extremities of their climate... Only in extremity, when his defences had been reduced by six weeks of bombing, was he ready to leave.* N-UNCOUNT: also N in pl, oft N *of* n

extricate /ekstrɪkeɪt/ **extricates, extricating, extricated**

1 If you **extricate** yourself or another person **from** a difficult or serious situation, you free yourself or the other person from it. *It represents a last ditch attempt by the country to extricate itself from its economic crisis... She tugged on Hart's arm to extricate him from the circle of men with whom he'd been talking.* VERB =free V pron-refl *from* n V n *from* n

2 If you **extricate** someone or something from a place where they are trapped or caught, you succeed in freeing them; a formal use. *...extricate the survivors... He endeavoured to extricate the car, digging with his hands in the blazing sunshine.* VERB =free V n

extrinsic /ɪkstrɪnzɪk, AM -sɪk/. **Extrinsic** reasons, forces, or factors exist outside the person or situation they affect; a formal word. *Nowadays there are fewer extrinsic pressures to get married.* ADJ: ADJ n =external ≠intrinsic

extrovert /ekstrəvɜːʳt/ **extroverts.** Someone who is **extrovert** is very active, lively, and sociable; used mainly in British English. The usual American word is **extroverted.** *His footballing skills and extrovert personality won the hearts of the public.* ◆◇◇◇◇ ADJ-GRADED =outgoing ≠introverted ► Also a noun. *He was a showman, an extrovert who revelled in controversy.* N-COUNT ≠introvert

extroverted /ekstrəvɜːʳtɪd/. Someone who is **extroverted** is very active, lively, and sociable; used mainly in American English. The usual British word is **extrovert.** *Some young people who were easy-going and extroverted as children become self-conscious in early adolescence.* ADJ-GRADED =outgoing ≠introverted

extrude /ɪkstruːd/ **extrudes, extruding, extruded.** If a substance **is extruded**, it is forced or squeezed out through a small opening; a formal word or a technical word in engineering and manufacturing. *These crystals are then embedded in a plastic, and the plastic is extruded as a wire... I work in the extruded tube business.* VB: usu passive *be* V-ed V-ed

extrusion /ɪkstruːʒᵊn/ **extrusions. Extrusion** is the act or process of extruding something; a for- N-VAR mal word or a technical word in engineering and manufacturing.

exuberance /ɪgzjuːbərəns, AM -zuːb-/ ◆◇◇◇◇

1 **Exuberance** is behaviour which is energetic, excited, and cheerful. *Her burst of exuberance and her brightness overwhelmed me.* N-UNCOUNT =ebullience, effervescence

2 If you talk about the **exuberance** of something, you like it because it is lively, exciting, and full of energy and life. *The sheer exuberance of the sculpture was exhilarating.* N-UNCOUNT: oft N *of*n =vitality

exuberant /ɪgzjuːbərənt, AM -zuːb-/ ◆◇◇◇◇

1 If you are **exuberant**, you are full of energy, excitement, and cheerfulness. *So the exuberant young girl with dark hair and blue eyes decided to become a screen actress.* ♦ **exuberantly** *They both laughed exuberantly.* ADJ-GRADED =effervescent, lively; ADV-GRADED

2 If you describe something as **exuberant**, you like it because it is lively, exciting, and full of energy and life. *This is bold and exuberant cooking.* ♦ **exuberantly** *...exuberantly decorated.* ADJ-GRADED PRAGMATICS; ADV-GRADED

exude /ɪgzjuːd, AM -zuːd/ **exudes, exuding, exuded** ◆◇◇◇◇

1 If someone **exudes** a quality or feeling, or if it **exudes**, they show that they have it to a great extent; a formal use. *The guerrillas exude confidence. Every town, they say, is under their control... She exudes an air of relaxed calm... A dogged air of confidence exuded.* V-ERG =radiate; V n; V

2 If something **exudes** a liquid or smell or if a liquid or smell **exudes** from it, the liquid or smell comes out of it slowly and steadily; a formal use. *Nearby was a factory which exuded a pungent smell... People have already died from licking the fluid that exudes from the cane toad's back.* V-ERG; V n; V

exult /ɪgzʌlt/ **exults, exulting, exulted.** If you **exult** in a triumph or success that you have had, you feel and show great happiness and pleasure because of it; used in written English. *He was exulting in a win at the show earlier that day... Some individual investors exulted at the record... I exulted and wept for joy... 'This is what I've longed for during my entire career,' Kendall exulted.* ♦ **exultation** /egzʌlteɪʃən/ *I felt a tremendous sense of relief and exultation.* VERB; V *in/at*n; V; V with quote; N-UNCOUNT

exultant /ɪgzʌltənt/. If you are **exultant**, you feel very happy and triumphant; a formal word. *An exultant party leader said: 'We had a first class candidate and ran a first-rate campaign. He will be an excellent MP.'* ♦ **exultantly** *'We cannot lose the war!' he shouted exultantly.* ADJ-GRADED =delighted; ADV: ADV with v

eye /aɪ/ **eyes, eyeing** or **eying, eyed** ◆◆◆◆◆

1 Your **eyes** are the parts of your body with which you see. *I opened my eyes and looked... Maria's eyes filled with tears. ...a tall, thin white-haired lady with piercing dark brown eyes... He is now blind in one eye.* N-COUNT: oft poss N in pl

2 If you **eye** someone or something in a particular way, you look at them carefully in that way. *Sally eyed Claire with interest... We eyed each other thoughtfully... Martin eyed the bottle at Marianne's elbow.* VERB; V n prep/adv; V n

3 You use **eye** when you are talking about a person's ability to judge things or about the way in which they are considering or dealing with things. *William was a man of discernment, with an eye for quality... Their chief negotiator turned his critical eye on the United States... It did not take his practised eye long to notice that he was not the only one who was hanging about... He first learnt to fish under the watchful eye of his grandmother.* N-COUNT: usu sing, with supp, oft *a* N *for*n

4 An electric **eye** or infra-red **eye** is a device which can recognize the presence of people or objects by detecting the light or heat coming from them. *An infra-red eye is said to detect the movement of any animal within an angle of 110 degrees at up to 10 metres.* N-COUNT: adj N

5 People sometimes talk about the **eye** of the camera when they are talking about something being filmed or photographed, or the way something appears in a photograph or film. *I was again using the cold, unflinching eye of the camera to probe a sick society.* N-SING: usu with poss

6 An **eye** on a potato is one of the dark spots from which new stems grow. N-COUNT

7 An **eye** is a small metal loop which a hook fits into, as a fastening on a piece of clothing. N-COUNT

8 The **eye** of a needle is the small hole at one end which the thread passes through. N-COUNT

9 **The eye of** a storm, tornado, or hurricane is the centre of it. *The eye of the hurricane hit Florida just south of Miami.* N-SING: *the* N *of*n =centre

10 See also **black eye, private eye, shut-eye.**

11 If you say that something happens **before** your **eyes, in front of** your **eyes**, or **under** your **eyes**, you are emphasizing or saying that it happens where you can see it clearly or while you are watching it, and often implying that it is surprising or unpleasant. *A lot of them died in front of our eyes... We are under the eyes of both sides all the time.* PHRASES; usu PHR after v, v-link PHR; PRAGMATICS

12 If you **cast** your **eye** or **run** your **eye** over something, you look at it or read it quickly. *I would be grateful if he could cast an expert eye over it and tell me what he thought of it... If you run your eye up and down these columns you will see that the value of some of them declined.* V inflects, PHR prep

13 If something **catches** your **eye**, you suddenly notice it. *As she turned back, a movement across the lawn caught her eye.* ● See also **eye-catching.** V inflects

14 If you **catch** someone's **eye**, you do something to attract their attention, so that you can speak to them or ask them something. *I tried to catch Chrissie's eye to find out what she was playing at.* V inflects

15 To **clap eyes on** someone or something, or **set** or **lay eyes on** them, means to see them; an informal expression. *That's probably the most bare, bleak, barren and inhospitable island I've ever had the misfortune to clap my eyes on... What was he doing when you last set eyes on him?* V inflects, oft after superl, oft with brd-neg =see

16 If you **make eye contact** with someone, you look at them at the same time as they look at you, so that you are both aware that you are looking at each other. If you **avoid eye contact** with someone, you deliberately do not look straight at them because you feel awkward or embarrassed. *She was looking at me across the room, and we made eye contact several times... I spent a fruitless ten minutes walking up and down the high street, desperately avoiding eye contact with passers-by.* PHR after v

17 If you **close** your **eyes to** something bad or if you **shut** your **eyes to** it, you ignore it. *Most governments must simply be shutting their eyes to the problem.* V inflects, PHR n =ignore

18 If you **cry** your **eyes out**, you cry very hard; an informal expression. V inflects

19 You say **'an eye for an eye'** or **'an eye for an eye and a tooth for a tooth'** to refer to the idea that people should be punished according to the way in which they offended, for example if they hurt someone, they should be hurt equally badly in return. *...a very simple punishment code based on an-eye-for-an-eye.*

20 If you say that there is a type of something, especially a type of scenery, **as far as the eye can see**, you are emphasizing that it extends to the horizon and there is a lot of it. *Here, massive dunes stretched in every direction as far as the eye could see... There are pine trees as far as the eye can see.* PRAGMATICS

21 If you say that someone **has an eye for** something, you mean that they are good at noticing it or making judgements about it. *Susan has a keen eye for detail, so each dress is beautifully finished off.* V inflects

22 You use expressions such as **in his eyes** or **to** her **eyes** to indicate that you are reporting someone's opinion and that other people might think differently. *The other serious problem in the eyes of the new government is communalism... Richard Dorrington was, in their eyes, a very sensible and reliable man... The practice of religion in America sometimes seems strange to European eyes.* PHR with cl-group PRAGMATICS

23 If you **keep** your **eyes open** or **keep an eye out** for someone or something, you watch for them carefully; an informal expression. *I ask the mounted patrol to keep their eyes open... You and your* V inflects, oft PHR *for*n

friends keep an eye out – if there's any trouble we'll make a break for it.
24 If you tell someone to **keep** their **eyes peeled** for something, you are telling them to watch very carefully for it; an informal expression. V inflects, oft PHR *for* n PRAGMATICS
25 If you **keep an eye on** something or someone, you watch them carefully, for example to make sure that they are satisfactory or safe, or not causing trouble. *I'm sure you will appreciate that we must keep a careful eye on all our running costs... I went for a run there, keeping an eye on the children the whole time... They're using villagers to keep an eye on each other, to spy on each other.* V inflects, PHR n
26 If you **make eyes at** someone, you look at them in a way which shows that you are romantically attracted to them and which is intended to get their attention; an informal, old-fashioned expression. V inflects, PHR n
27 You say **'there's more to** this **than meets the eye'** when you think a situation is not as simple as it seems to be. *I have to admit this whole business is very puzzling. Even your father says he thinks there is a lot more to it than meets the eye.*
28 If something, especially something surprising or impressive, **meets your eyes**, you see it. *The first sight that met my eyes on reaching the front door was the church enveloped in flames.* V inflects
29 If you say that **all eyes are on** something or that the **eyes of the world are on** something, you mean that everyone is paying careful attention to it and what will happen; used in journalism. *But come September, all eyes will be on the Maastricht referendum in France... The eyes of the world were now on the police.* V inflects, PHR n
30 If someone **has** their **eye on** you, they are watching you carefully to see what you do. *As the boat plodded into British waters and up the English Channel, Customs had their eye on her.* V inflects, PHR n
31 If you **have** your **eye on** something, you want to have it; an informal expression. *If you're saving up for a new outfit you've had your eye on, cheap dinners for a month might let you buy it.* V inflects, PHR n
32 If you say that you did something **with** your **eyes open**, you mean that you were fully aware of the problems and difficulties that you were likely to have. *We want all our members to undertake this trip responsibly, with their eyes open.* PHR after v
33 If something **opens** your **eyes**, it makes you aware that something is different from the way that you thought it was. *Watching your child explore the world about her can open your eyes to delights long forgotten.* V inflects, oft PHR *to* n
34 If you **see eye to eye** with someone, you agree with them and have the same opinions and views. *Yuriko saw eye to eye with Yul on almost every aspect of the production... We've never seen eye to eye.* RECIP: V inflects, PHR *with* n, pl-n PHR
35 If you say that someone or something is at **the eye of the storm**, you mean they are the main subject of a disagreement or controversy. *The bowlers at the eye of the storm were nowhere in evidence. ...the minister in the eye of the storm.* usu prep PHR
36 When you **take** your **eyes off** the thing you have been watching or looking at, you stop looking at it. *She took her eyes off the road to glance at me... Nina couldn't take her eyes off Philip.* V inflects, PHR n
37 If someone sees or considers something **through** your **eyes**, they consider it in the way that you do, from your point of view. *She tried to see things through his eyes... The story is told through the eyes of Inspector Simon Potter.* PHR after v
38 If you say that you are **up to** your **eyes** in something, you are emphasizing that you have a lot of it to deal with, and often that you are very busy; an informal expression. *I am up to my eyes in work... The women are just up to their eyes in debt.* v-link PHR, usu PHR *in* n PRAGMATICS
39 • **apple of** your **eye**: see **apple.** • to **turn a blind eye**: see **blind.** • to **feast** your **eyes**: see **feast.** • to **look** someone **in the eye**: see **look.** • **in your mind's eye**: see **mind.** • the **naked eye**: see **naked.** • to **pull the wool over** someone's **eyes**: see **wool.**

eye up. If someone **eyes** you **up**, they look at you in a way that shows they consider you attractive or sexy; used in informal British English. *...a slob called Drew who spends all day eyeing up the women and making lewd comments... The women sit in the corner and men eye them up.* PHRASAL VERB =ogle V P n (not pron) V n P

eyeball /aɪbɔːl/ **eyeballs, eyeballing, eyeballed** ◆◇◇◇◇
1 Your **eyeballs** are your whole eyes, rather than just the part which can be seen between your eyelids. N-COUNT
2 If you **eyeball** someone or something, you stare at them; an informal use. *The guard eyeballed him pretty hard despite his pass.* VERB V n
3 In informal English, if you are **eyeball to eyeball** with someone, you are in their presence and involved in a meeting, dispute, or contest with them. You can also talk about having an **eyeball to eyeball** meeting or confrontation. *...the young thug who stands eyeball-to-eyeball with his victim. ...proposals that the two armies end their eyeball to eyeball confrontation and withdraw.* PHRASES PHR after v, v-link PHR, PHR n, oft PHR *with* n =face to face
4 You use **up to** the **eyeballs** to emphasize that someone is in an undesirable state to a very great degree. *...driving around Los Angeles drugged up to the eyeballs... He is out of a job and up to his eyeballs in debt.* usu v-link PHR, adj/-ed PHR, PHR *in* n PRAGMATICS

eyebrow /aɪbraʊ/ **eyebrows** ◆◆◇◇◇
1 Your **eyebrows** are the lines of hair which grow above your eyes. N-COUNT: usu pl, oft poss N
2 If something causes you to **raise an eyebrow** or to **raise** your **eyebrows**, it causes you to feel surprised or disapproving. *An intriguing item on the news pages caused me to raise an eyebrow over my morning coffee... He raised his eyebrows over some of the suggestions... He was looking at her with his eyebrows raised questioningly.* PHRASE: V inflects

eye-catching. Something that is **eye-catching** is very noticeable. *...a series of eye-catching ads.* ◆◇◇◇◇ ADJ-GRADED =striking

-eyed /-aɪd/. **-eyed** combines with adjectives to form adjectives which indicate the colour, shape, or size of a person's eyes, or indicate the kind of expression that they have. *...a blonde-haired, blue-eyed little girl... She watched open-eyed as the plane took off. ...watched by large crowds, sad-eyed and silent.* COMB in ADJ

eyeful /aɪfʊl/ **eyefuls.** If you get an **eyeful** of something, especially of something that you would not normally see, you are able to get a good look at it; an informal word. *Then she bent over and gave him an eyeful of her tattoos.* N-COUNT: usu sing, oft N *of* n

eyelash /aɪlæʃ/ **eyelashes.** Your **eyelashes** are the hairs which grow on the edges of your eyelids. ◆◇◇◇◇ N-COUNT: usu pl

eyelet /aɪlɪt/ **eyelets.** An **eyelet** is a small hole with a metal or leather ring round it which is made in cloth, for example a sail or a tent flap. You can put cord, rope, or string through it. N-COUNT

eyelid /aɪlɪd/ **eyelids.** Your **eyelids** are the two flaps of skin which cover your eyes when they are closed. • **not bat an eyelid**: see **bat.** ◆◇◇◇◇ N-COUNT: usu pl

eyeliner /aɪlaɪnəʳ/ **eyeliners;** also spelled **eye-liner. Eyeliner** is a special kind of pencil which some women use on the edges of their eyelids next to their eyelashes in order to look more attractive. N-MASS

eye-opener, eye-openers. If you describe something as an **eye-opener**, you mean that it surprises you and that you learn something new from it; an informal word. *This summer's tour was an eye-opener for her. For the first time ever, the halls were not fully booked... Writing these scripts has been quite an eye-opener to me. It proves that one can do anything if the need is urgent.* N-COUNT: usu sing, usu *a* N =revelation

eye patch, eye patches. An **eye patch** is a piece of material which you wear over your eye when you have damaged or injured it. N-COUNT

eyepiece /aɪpiːs/ **eyepieces.** The **eyepiece** of a microscope or telescope is the piece of glass at one end, where you put your eye in order to look through the instrument. N-COUNT

eye shadow, eye shadows; also spelled **eyeshadow. Eye shadow** is a substance which you N-MASS can paint on your eyelids in order to make them a different colour.

eyesight /aɪsaɪt/. Your **eyesight** is your ability to see. *He suffered from poor eyesight and could no longer read properly.* ◆◇◇◇◇ N-UNCOUNT: usu supp N

eye socket, eye sockets. Your **eye sockets** are the two hollow bony parts on either side of your face, where your eyeballs are. N-COUNT

eyesore /aɪsɔːʳ/ **eyesores.** You describe a building or place as an **eyesore** when it is extremely ugly and you dislike it or disapprove of it. *Poverty leads to slums, which are an eyesore and a health hazard.* N-COUNT: usu sing

eye strain. If you suffer from **eye strain**, you feel pain around your eyes or at the back of your eyes, because you are very tired or should be wearing glasses. N-UNCOUNT

eye teeth. If you say that you would **give** your **eye teeth** for something, you mean that you want it very much and you would do anything to get it; an informal expression. *She has the job most of us would give our eye teeth for.* PHRASE: V inflects

eyewitness /aɪwɪtnəs/ **eyewitnesses.** An **eyewitness** is a person who was present at an event and can therefore describe it, for example in a law court. *Eyewitnesses say the police then opened fire on the crowd... Many of the papers have dramatic eye-witness accounts of the fighting.* ◆◇◇◇◇ N-COUNT

eyrie /ɪəri, AM eri/ **eyries;** spelled **aerie** in American English.

1 If you refer to a place such as a house or a castle as an **eyrie**, you mean is it built high up and is difficult to reach; a literary use. *I sit here marooned in my 48th floor eyrie in the sky, utterly alone.* N-COUNT: with supp

2 An **eyrie** is the nest of an eagle, falcon, or other similar bird, that is usually built high up in rough, mountainous country. N-COUNT

F f

F, f /ef/ **F's, f's**

1 **F** is the sixth letter of the English alphabet. N-VAR

2 In music, **F** is the fourth note in the scale of C major. N-VAR

3 **f.** is an abbreviation for 'following'. It is written after a page or line number in a cross-reference in order to indicate that you are referring to both the page or line mentioned and the next one. You use **ff.** when you are referring to the page or line mentioned and two or more following pages or lines.

4 **F** or **f** is an abbreviation for words beginning with f, such as 'female', 'feminine', 'franc', and 'false', and 'Fahrenheit'. *Heat the oven to 400 degrees F.*

fab /fæb/. If you say that something is **fab**, you are emphasizing that you think it is very good; an informal use. *The dancing is fab.* ◆◇◇◇◇ ADJ-GRADED PRAGMATICS =great

fable /feɪbəl/ **fables** ◆◇◇◇◇

1 A **fable** is a story which teaches a moral lesson. Fables sometimes have animals as the main characters. *...the fable of the tortoise and the hare... Each tale has the timeless quality of fable.* N-VAR =legend

2 You can describe a statement or explanation that is untrue but that many people believe as **fable**. *Is reincarnation fact or fable? ...little-known horticultural facts and fables.* N-VAR =myth

fabled /feɪbəld/. If you describe something or someone as **fabled**, especially something or someone remarkable, you mean that they are well known because they are often talked about or a lot of stories are told about them. *You cannot go home without visiting the fabled art collections of the Prado. ...the fabled city of Troy.* ADJ: ADJ n =legendary

fabric /fæbrɪk/ **fabrics** ◆◆◆◇◇

1 **Fabric** is cloth or other material produced by weaving together cotton, nylon, wool, silk, or other threads. Fabrics are used for making things such as clothes, curtains, and sheets. *...small squares of red cotton fabric... Whatever your colour scheme, there's a fabric to match.* N-MASS

2 The **fabric** of a society or system is its basic structure, with all the customs and beliefs that make it work successfully. *The fabric of society has been deeply damaged by the previous regime... Years of civil war have wrecked the country's infrastructure and destroyed its social fabric.* N-SING: with supp, usu *the* N *of* n

3 The **fabric** of a building is its walls, roof, and the materials with which it is built. *Condensation will eventually cause the fabric of the building to rot away.* N-SING: usu *the* N *of* n

fabricate /fæbrɪkeɪt/ **fabricates, fabricating, fabricated** ◆◇◇◇◇

1 If someone **fabricates** information, they invent it in order to deceive people. *All four claim that officers fabricated evidence against them... Eleven key Communist officials were hanged on fabricated charges.* ♦ **fabrication** /fæbrɪkeɪʃən/ **fabrications** *She described the interview with her in an Italian magazine as a 'complete fabrication'... China calls the report pure fabrication.* VERB V n V-ed N-VAR =invention

2 If something **is fabricated** from different materials or substances, it is made out of those materials or substances. *All the tools are fabricated from high quality steel. ...a plant which fabricates airplane components.* ♦ **fabrication** *More than 200 improvements, many of them major, were made in the design and fabrication of the shuttle.* VERB =manufacture be V-ed *from* n V n Also V n *from* n N-SING

fabulous /fæbjʊləs/ ◆◆◇◇◇

1 If you describe something as **fabulous**, you are emphasizing that you like it a lot or think that it is very good; an informal use. *This is a fabulous album. It's fresh, varied, fun... The scenery and weather were fabulous.* ADJ-GRADED PRAGMATICS =wonderful

2 If you talk about someone's **fabulous** beauty, for example, or their **fabulous** success, you are emphasizing that they are extremely beautiful or extremely successful. *Despite his fabulous wealth, he is very much a man of the people.* ♦ **fabulously** *...their fabulously rich parents.* ADJ-GRADED: usu ADJ n PRAGMATICS ADV-GRADED: ADV adj/adv

facade /fəsɑːd/ **facades;** also spelled **façade.** ◆◇◇◇◇

1 The **facade** of a building, especially a large one, is its front wall or the wall that faces the street. N-COUNT =frontage

2 A **facade** is an outward appearance which is deliberately false and gives you a wrong impression about someone or something. *They hid the troubles plaguing their marriage behind a facade of family togetherness.* N-SING: oft N *of* n =show, semblance

face 1 noun uses

face /feɪs/ **faces** ◆◆◆◆◆

1 Your **face** is the front part of your head from your chin to the top of your forehead, where your mouth, eyes, nose, and other features are. *He rolled down his window and stuck his face out... A strong wind was blowing right in my face... He was going red in the face and breathing with difficulty... She had a beautiful face.* N-COUNT: oft poss N

2 If your **face** is happy, sad, or serious, for example, the expression on your face shows that you are happy, sad, or serious. *He was walking around with a sad face... The priest frowned into the light, his face puzzled.* N-COUNT: poss N, adj N

3 The **face** of a cliff, mountain, or building is a vertical surface or side of it. *Harrer was one of the first to climb the north face of the Eiger... He scrambled 200 feet up the cliff face.* N-COUNT: with supp, oft N *of* n

4 The **face** of a clock or watch is the surface with the numbers or hands on it, which shows the time.
N-COUNT

5 If you say that **the face of** an area, institution, or field of activity is changing, you mean its appearance or nature is changing. *...the changing face of the British countryside... This would change the face of Malaysian politics.*
N-SING: *the* N *of* n

6 If you refer to something as **the** particular **face of** an activity, belief, or system, you mean that it is one particular aspect of it, in contrast to other aspects. *Brothels, she insists, are the acceptable face of prostitution... With the collapse of communism, the ugly face of capitalism to some extent is appearing again.*
N-SING: *the* adj N *of* n

7 If you lose **face**, you do something or experience something which makes you appear weak and makes people respect or admire you less. If you do something in order to save **face**, you do it in order to avoid appearing weak and losing people's respect or admiration. *England doesn't want a war but it doesn't want to lose face... To cancel the airport would mean a loss of face for the present governor... Children have an almost obsessive need to save face in front of their peers.*
N-UNCOUNT

8 See also **about-face, face value, poker face**.

9 If something that you have planned **blows up in** your **face**, it goes wrong unexpectedly, with the result that you suffer. *Can't you see this could blow up in your face?*
PHRASES V inflects =backfire

10 If you say that someone can do something **until** they are **blue in the face**, you are emphasizing that however much they do it, it will not make any difference. *You can criticise him until you're blue in the face, but you'll never change his personality.*
V inflects PRAGMATICS

11 If someone or something is **face down**, their face or front points downwards. If they are **face up**, their face or front points upwards. *All the time Stephen was lying face down and unconscious in the bath tub... Charles laid down his cards face up.*
PHR after v, v-link PHR

12 You can use the expression **'on the face of the earth'** to mean 'in the whole world', when you are emphasizing a statement that you are making or making a very exaggerated statement. *No human being on the face of the earth could do anything worse than what he did.*
n PHR, usu after adj-super/brd-neg PRAGMATICS

13 If you say that something will be wiped **off the face of the earth** or disappear **from the face of the earth**, you mean that it will stop existing. *If a nuclear war breaks out, every living thing will be wiped off the face of the Earth.*
PHR after v

14 If you come **face to face** with someone, you meet them and can talk to them or look at them directly. *We were strolling into the town when we came face to face with Jacques Dubois... It was the first face-to-face meeting between the two men.*
PHR after v, PHR n, oft PHR *with* n

15 If you come **face to face with** a difficulty or reality, you cannot avoid it and have to deal with it. *Eventually, he came face to face with discrimination again... I was gradually being brought face to face with the fact that I had very little success.*
PHR after v, PHR n

16 If an action or belief **flies in the face of** accepted ideas or rules, it seems to completely oppose or contradict them. *...scientific principles that seem to fly in the face of common sense... He said that the decision flew in the face of natural justice.*
V inflects, PHR n

17 If you take a particular action or attitude **in the face of** a problem or difficulty, you respond to that problem or difficulty in that way. *The Prime Minister has called for national unity in the face of the violent anti-government protests... Roosevelt was defiant in the face of the bad news.*
PREP

18 If someone **laughs in** your **face**, they are openly disrespectful towards you. *With juveniles under eighteen, there's little we can do. We can't keep them in custody. They just laugh in your face.*
V and N inflect

19 If you have **a long face**, you look very unhappy or serious. *He came to me with a very long face.*
N inflects

20 If you **make a face** or **pull a face**, you show a feeling such as dislike, disgust, or defiance by putting an exaggerated expression on your face, for example by sticking out your tongue. *Opening the door, she made a face at the musty smell... Kathryn pulled a face at Thomasina behind his back.*
V and N inflect, oft PHR *at* n

21 You say **on the face of it** when you are describing how something seems when it is first considered, in order to suggest that people's opinion may change when they know or think more about the subject. *On the face of it that seems to make sense. But the figures don't add up... It is, on the face of it, difficult to see how the West could radically change its position.*
PHR with cl

22 If you **put a brave face on** a bad situation or **put on a brave face**, you try not to show how disappointed or upset you are about the situation. In American English the expression **'put on a good face'** is also used. *Friends will see you are putting on a brave face and might assume you've got over your grief... Scientists are putting a good face on the troubles.*
V inflects, oft PHR n

23 You can say that someone **has set** their **face against** something to indicate that they are stubbornly opposed to it, especially when you want to suggest that they are wrong; used mainly in British English. *This Government has set its face against putting up income tax.*
V inflects, PHR n/-ing

24 If you **show** your **face** somewhere, you go there and see people, although you are not welcome, are rather unwilling to go, or have not been there for some time. *If she shows her face again back in Massachusetts she'll find a warrant for her arrest waiting... I felt I ought to show my face at her father's funeral.*
V inflects, PHR adv/prep

25 If you manage to keep **a straight face**, you manage to look serious, although you want to laugh. *What went through Tom's mind I can't imagine, but he did manage to keep a straight face... You have to wonder how anyone could say that seriously and with a straight face.*
PHR after v, *with* PHR

26 If you say something **to** someone's **face**, you say it openly in their presence. *Her opponent called her a liar to her face.*
PHR after v

27 If a feeling **is written all over** your **face** or **is written across** your **face**, it is very obvious to other people from your expression. *Relief and gratitude were written all over his face... I could just see the pain written across her face.*
V inflects

28 • to **shut the door in** someone's **face**: see **door**. • to **have egg on** your **face**: see **egg**. • to **cut off** your **nose to spite** your **face**: see **nose**. • **shut your face**: see **shut**. • **a slap in the face**: see **slap**.

face 2 verb and phrasal verb uses

face /feɪs/ **faces, facing, faced** ◆◆◆◆◆

1 If someone or something **faces** a particular thing, person, or direction, they are positioned opposite that thing or person or are looking in that direction. *They stood facing each other... The garden faces south.*
VERB V n V adv/prep

2 If you **face** someone or something, you turn so that you are looking at them. *She stood up from the table and faced him... Stand up. Face the wall.*
VERB V n

3 If you have to **face** a person or group, you have to stand or sit in front of them and talk to them, although it may be difficult and unpleasant. *Christie looked relaxed and calm as he faced the press... He was hauled in to face the judge.*
VERB V n

4 If you **face** or **are faced** with something difficult or unpleasant, or if it **faces** you, it is going to affect you and you have to deal with it. *Williams faces life in prison if convicted of attempted murder... The immense difficulties facing European businessmen in Russia were only too evident... We are faced with a serious problem.*
VERB V n be V-ed *with* n

5 If you **face** the truth, a fact, or a problem, you accept that it is true or really exists and respond to it in a suitable way, although you would prefer to ignore it. If you **face** someone with the truth, a fact, or a problem, you try to make them accept that it is true or really exists. *Although your heart is breaking, you must face the truth that a relationship has ended... He accused the Government of refusing to face facts about the economy... He called a family conference and faced them with the problems.*
VERB V n V n *with* n

► **Face up to** means the same as **face**. *I have grown*
PHRASAL VERB V P P n

up now and I have to face up to my responsibilities... They were having to face up to the fact that they had lost everything.

6 If you cannot **face** something, you do not feel able to do it because it seems so difficult or unpleasant. *I couldn't face the prospect of spending a Saturday night there, so I decided to press on... My children want me with them for Christmas Day, but I can't face it... I couldn't face seeing anyone.* VB: with neg V n/-ing

7 You use the expression **'let's face it'** when you are stating a fact or making a comment about something which you think your listener may find unpleasant or be unwilling to admit. *She was always attracted to younger men. But, let's face it, who is not?* PHRASE: PHR with cl PRAGMATICS

face down. In American English, if you **face** someone **down**, you oppose them or beat them by being confident and looking at them boldly. *He's confronted crowds before and faced them down.* PHRASAL VERB V n P Also V P n (not pron)

face up to. See **face** 5. PHRASAL VERB

facecloth /feɪsklɒθ, AM -klɔːθ/ **facecloths;** also spelled **face cloth**. A **facecloth** is the same as a **face flannel** or **washcloth**. N-COUNT

face cream, face creams. Face cream is a thick substance that you rub into your face in order to keep it soft. N-MASS

-faced /-feɪst/. **-faced** combines with adjectives to form other adjectives that describe someone's face or expression. *...a slim, thin-faced man... The committee walked out, grim-faced and shocked.* • See also **ashen-faced**, **bare-faced**, **po-faced**, **poker-faced**, **red-faced**, **shamefaced**, **straight-faced**, **two-faced**. COMB in ADJ-GRADED

face flannel, face flannels. In British English, a **face flannel** is a small cloth made of towelling which you use for washing yourself. The usual American word is **washcloth**. N-COUNT

faceless /feɪsləs/. If you describe someone or something as **faceless**, you dislike them because they have no character or individuality. *Ordinary people are at the mercy of faceless bureaucrats.* ◆◇◇◇◇ ADJ: usu ADJ n PRAGMATICS

facelift /feɪslɪft/ **facelifts;** also spelled **face lift**.

1 If you give a place or thing a **facelift**, you do something that will make it look better or more attractive. *Nothing gives a room a faster facelift than a coat of paint.* N-COUNT: usu sing

2 A **facelift** is an operation in which a surgeon tightens the skin on someone's face in order to make them look younger. N-COUNT

face pack, face packs. A **face pack** is a thick substance which you spread on your face, allow to dry for a short time, and then remove, in order to clean your skin thoroughly. N-COUNT

face powder, face powders. Face powder is a very fine soft powder that you can put on your face in order to make it look smoother. N-MASS =powder

face-saver, face-savers. A **face-saver** is an action or excuse which prevents damage to your reputation or the loss of people's respect for you; used in journalism. N-COUNT

face-saving. A **face-saving** action is one which prevents damage to your reputation or prevents the loss of people's respect for you. *The decision appears to be a face-saving compromise which will allow the government to remain in office.* ADJ: ADJ n

facet /fæsɪt, -set/ **facets** ◆◇◇◇◇

1 A **facet** of something is a single part or aspect of it. *The caste system shapes nearly every facet of Indian life.* N-COUNT: oft N *of* n

2 The **facets** of a diamond or other precious stone are the flat surfaces that have been cut on its outside. N-COUNT

facetious /fəsiːʃəs/. If you say that someone is being **facetious**, you are criticizing them because they are making humorous remarks or saying things that they do not mean in a situation where they ought to be serious. *The woman eyed him coldly. 'Don't be facetious,' she said.* ADJ-GRADED PRAGMATICS =flippant

♦ **facetiously** *Al facetiously described himself as the Last Angry Man.* ADV-GRADED: ADV with v

face to face. See **face**.

face value ◆◇◇◇◇

1 The **face value** of things such as coins, banknotes, investment bonds, or tickets is the amount of money that they are worth, and that is written on them. *Tickets were selling at twice their face value.* N-SING

2 If you take something **at face value**, you accept it and believe it without thinking about it very much, even though it might be misleading or untrue. *Public statements from the various groups involved should not necessarily be taken at face value.* PHRASE: PHR after v

facial /feɪʃəl/ **facials** ◆◆◇◇◇

1 Facial means appearing on or being part of your face. *Cross didn't answer; his facial expression didn't change... I ended up in hospital with facial injuries.* ADJ: ADJ n

2 A **facial** is a sort of beauty treatment in which someone's face is massaged, and creams and other substances are rubbed into it. N-COUNT

facie /feɪʃi/. See **prima facie**.

facile /fæsaɪl, AM -səl/. If you describe someone's arguments or suggestions as **facile**, you are criticizing them because their ideas are too simple and indicate a lack of careful, intelligent thinking. *I hated him suggesting facile solutions when I knew very well that the problem was extremely complex.* ADJ-GRADED PRAGMATICS =shallow

facilitate /fəsɪlɪteɪt/ **facilitates, facilitating, facilitated.** To **facilitate** an action or process, especially one that you would like to happen, means to make it easier or more likely to happen. *The new airport will facilitate the development of tourism... He argued that the economic recovery had been facilitated by his tough stance.* ◆◇◇◇◇ VERB =help, further V n

facilitator /fəsɪlɪteɪtəʳ/ **facilitators.** A **facilitator** is a person or organization that helps another person or organization to do or to achieve a particular thing; a formal word. N-COUNT

facility /fəsɪlɪti/ **facilities** ◆◆◆◆◇

1 Facilities are buildings, pieces of equipment, or services that are provided for a particular purpose. *What recreational facilities are now available?... The problem lies in getting patients to a medical facility as soon as possible.* N-COUNT: usu pl, usu with supp

2 A **facility** is something such as an additional service provided by an organization or an extra feature on a machine which is useful but not essential. *It is very useful to have an overdraft facility... One of the new models has the facility to reproduce speech as well as text.* N-COUNT: with supp, oft n N, N to-inf

3 If you have a **facility** for something, for example learning a language, you find it easy to do. *He and Marcia shared a facility for languages... Smell is a very basic sense but humans have lost much of the facility to use it properly.* N-COUNT: usu sing, usu N *for* n, N to-inf

facing /feɪsɪŋ/ **facings**

1 Facing is fabric which is stitched inside the cuffs, collars, or seams of a piece of clothing in order to make them look neat and strengthen them. N-UNCOUNT

2 The **facings** of a garment such as a jacket or coat are its collar and cuffs when they are made of a different fabric from the main part. N-PLURAL

3 A **facing** on a wall is a layer of stone, concrete, or other material that is spread over its surface in order to make it look attractive. N-VAR

facsimile /fæksɪmɪli/ **facsimiles**

1 A **facsimile** of something is an copy or imitation of it; a formal use. *...a facsimile of his writing desk. ...a facsimile edition of Beethoven's musical manuscripts.* N-COUNT: oft N *of* n, N n

2 A **facsimile** is the same as a **fax**; a formal use. N-COUNT

fact /fækt/ **facts** ◆◆◆◆◆

1 You use **the fact that** after some verbs or prepositions, especially in expressions such as **in view of the fact that**, **apart from the fact that**, and **despite the fact that**, to link the verb or preposition with a clause. *His chances do not seem good in view of the fact that the Chief Prosecutor has already voiced his public disapproval... Despite the fact that the disease is so prevalent, treatment is still far from satisfactory... No amount of encouragement can hide the fact that talking about very personal issues with a stranger is intimidating... In Rome, meeting him* PHRASE: prep PHR cl, v PHR cl PRAGMATICS *every morning, he soon became aware of the fact that Erter was ill.*

2 You use **the fact that** instead of a simple that-clause either for emphasis or because the clause is the subject of your sentence. *My family now accepts the fact that I don't eat sugar or bread... The fact that he had left her of his own accord proved to me that everything he'd said was true.*
PHRASE: PHR cl, oft v PHR cl, prep PHR cl PRAGMATICS

3 You use **in fact**, **in actual fact**, or **in point of fact** to indicate that you are giving more detailed information about what you have just said. *We've had a pretty bad time while you were away. In fact, we very nearly split up this time... He apologised as soon as he realised what he had done. In actual fact he wrote a nice little note to me... Mr Major didn't go to university. In fact he left school at 16.*
PHRASE: PHR with cl PRAGMATICS

4 You use **in fact**, **in actual fact**, or **in point of fact** to introduce or draw attention to a comment that modifies, contradicts, or contrasts with a previous statement. *That sounds rather simple, but in fact it's very difficult... They complained that they had been trapped inside the police station, but in fact most were seen escaping over the adjacent roofs to safety in nearby buildings... Why had she ever trusted her? In point of fact she never had, she reminded herself.*
PHRASE: PHR with cl PRAGMATICS =actually

5 When you refer to something as a **fact** or as **fact**, you mean that you think it is true or correct. *...a statement of verifiable historical fact... How much was fact and how much fancy no one knew.*
N-VAR

6 **Facts** are pieces of information that can be discovered. *There is so much information you can almost effortlessly find the facts for yourself... His opponent swamped him with facts and figures... The lorries always left for China in the dead of night when there were few witnesses around to record the fact.*
N-COUNT

7 You use **as a matter of fact** to introduce a statement that gives more details about what has just been said, or an explanation or modification of it. *The local people saw all the suffering to which these deportees were subjected. And, as a matter of fact, the local people helped the victims of these deportations... 'I guess you haven't eaten yet'. 'As a matter of fact, I have,' said Hunter.*
PHRASES PHR with cl PRAGMATICS =actually

8 If you say that you know something **for a fact**, you are emphasizing that you are completely certain that it is true. *I know for a fact that baby corn is very expensive in Europe... I know for a fact that Graham has kept in close touch with Alan.*
PHR after v PRAGMATICS

9 You use **the fact is** or **the fact of the matter is** to introduce and draw attention to a summary or statement of the most important point about what you have been saying. *The fact is blindness hadn't stopped the children doing many of the things that sighted children enjoy... I found that election rallies were being very poorly attended. But the fact of the matter is that they're not terribly interested in this election.*
V inflects, PHR cl PRAGMATICS

10 You say **the fact remains** that something is the case when you want to emphasize that the situation must be realized and accepted. *The fact remains that inflation, however you measure it, is unacceptably high... His admirers claim that he came to power perfectly legally, but the fact remains that he did so by exploiting an illegal situation.*
V inflects, PHR that PRAGMATICS

11 You say **and that's a fact** to emphasize the truth or correctness of a statement that you have just made; an informal expression. *We aren't playing well as a team, and that's a fact... He is a dull writer and that's a fact.*
cl PHR PRAGMATICS

12 You say **is that a fact?** as a response to a statement which you find surprising, interesting, or unlikely; an informal expression. *'I'm still staff colonel.'—'Is that a fact?'*
CONVENTION PRAGMATICS

fact-finding. A **fact-finding** mission or visit is one whose purpose is to get information about a particular situation, especially for an official group. *A UN fact-finding mission is on its way to the region.*
◆◇◇◇◇ ADJ: ADJ n

faction /fækʃən/ **factions**
◆◆◆◇◇

1 A **faction** is an organized group of people within a larger group, which opposes some of the ideas of the larger group and fights for its own ideas. *A peace agreement will be signed by the leaders of the country's warring factions.*
N-COUNT

2 **Faction** is also used to describe argument and disagreement within a group of people. *Faction and self-interest appear to be the norm.*
N-UNCOUNT

factional /fækʃənəl/. **Factional** arguments or disputes involve two or more small groups from within a larger group. *...factional disputes between the various groups that make up the leadership.*
◆◇◇◇◇ ADJ: usu ADJ n

factionalism /fækʃənəlɪzəm/. **Factionalism** refers to arguments or disputes between two or more small groups from within a larger group. *There has been a substantial amount of factionalism within the movement.*
N-UNCOUNT

fact of life, facts of life
◆◇◇◇◇

1 You say that something which is not pleasant is a **fact of life** when there is nothing you can do to change it so you must accept it. *Stress is a fact of life from time to time for all of us.*
N-COUNT

2 If you tell a child about **the facts of life**, you tell him or her about sexual intercourse and how babies are born. *There comes a time when children need to know more than the basic facts of life.*
N-PLURAL: the N

factor /fæktəʳ/ **factors, factoring, factored**
◆◆◆◆◇

1 A **factor** is one of the things that affects an event, decision, or situation. *Physical activity is an important factor in maintaining fitness.*
N-COUNT

2 If an amount increases by a **factor** of two, for example, or by a **factor** of eight, then it becomes two times bigger or eight times bigger. *The cost of butter quadrupled and bread prices increased by a factor of five.*
N-COUNT: usu sing, usu a N of num

3 You can use **factor** to refer to a particular level on a scale of measurement. *A suncream with a protection factor of 8 allows you to stay in the sun without burning.*
N-SING: usu a N of num

4 A **factor** of a whole number is a smaller whole number which can be multiplied with another whole number to produce the first whole number; a technical use in mathematics.
N-COUNT

factor in or **factor into.** If you **factor** a particular cost or element **into** a calculation you are making, or if you **factor it in**, you include it; used mainly in American English. *Using a computer model they factored in the costs of transplants for those women who die... You'd better consider this and factor this into your decision making.*
PHRASAL VERB V P n (not pron) V n P n Also V n P

factory /fæktri/ **factories.** A **factory** is a large building where machines are used to make large quantities of goods. *He owned furniture factories in New York State.*
◆◆◆◆◇ N-COUNT: oft n N

factory farming. In British English, people use **factory farming** to refer to a system of farming which involves keeping animals indoors with very little space, and giving them special foods so that they grow more quickly or produce more eggs or milk; used showing disapproval.
N-UNCOUNT PRAGMATICS

factory floor. The factory floor refers to the workers in a factory, as opposed to the managers. It can also refer to the area where they work. *He had worked on the factory floor for 16 years.*
N-SING: the N

factory ship, factory ships. A **factory ship** is a large fishing boat which has equipment for processing the fish that are caught, for example by cleaning or freezing them, before it returns to port.
N-COUNT

factotum /fæktoutəm/ **factotums.** A **factotum** is a servant who is employed to do a wide variety of jobs for someone; a formal use.
N-COUNT

fact sheet, fact sheets. A **fact sheet** is a short, printed document with information about a particular subject, especially a summary of information that has been given on a radio or television programme.
N-COUNT

factual /fæktʃuəl/. Something that is **factual** is concerned with facts or contains facts, rather than giving theories or personal interpretations. *The editorial contained several factual errors... Any comparison that is not strictly factual runs*
◆◇◇◇◇ ADJ-GRADED

the risk of being interpreted as subjective. ♦ **factually** *I learned that a number of statements in my talk were factually wrong. ...telling me coolly and factually the story of her life in prison.* [ADV-GRADED: ADV adj/-ed, ADV after v]

faculty /fækəlti/ **faculties** ◆◆◇◇◇

1 Your **faculties** are your physical and mental abilities. *He was drunk and not in control of his faculties... It is also a myth that the faculty of hearing is greatly increased in blind people.* [N-COUNT: usu pl, oft poss N, N *of* n]

2 In some universities or colleges, a **faculty** is a group of related departments. All the staff in these departments can also be referred to as **faculty** or the **faculty**. *...the Faculty of Social and Political Sciences... How can faculty improve their teaching so as to encourage creativity?* [N-VAR]

fad /fæd/ **fads.** You use **fad** to refer to an activity or topic of interest that is very popular for a short time, but which people become bored with very quickly. *Hamnett does not believe environmental concern is a passing fad.* ◆◇◇◇◇ [N-COUNT =craze]

faddish /fædɪʃ/. If you describe something as **faddish**, you mean that it has no real value and that it will not remain popular for very long. *It is hard to stand up to your children when they are screaming for faddish footwear.* [ADJ-GRADED]

faddy /fædi/. If you describe someone as **faddy**, you mean that they have very strong likes and dislikes, especially about what they eat, which you think are rather silly; used in British English. *My boys have always been faddy eaters.* [ADJ-GRADED PRAGMATICS =fussy]

fade /feɪd/ **fades, fading, faded** ◆◆◆◇◇

1 When a coloured object **fades** or when the light **fades** it, it gradually becomes paler. *All colour fades – especially under the impact of direct sunlight... No matter how soft the light is, it still plays havoc, fading carpets and curtains in every room. ...fading portraits of the Queen and Prince Philip.* ♦ **faded** *...a girl in a faded dress. ...faded painted signs on the sides of some of the buildings.* [V-ERG V V n V-ing ADJ-GRADED]

2 When light **fades**, it slowly becomes less bright. When a sound **fades**, it slowly becomes less loud. *Seaton lay on his bed and gazed at the ceiling as the light faded... The sound of the last bomber's engines faded into the distance.* [VERB V V *into* n]

3 When something that you are looking at **fades**, it slowly becomes less bright or clear until it disappears. *They observed the comet for 70 days before it faded from sight... They watched the familiar mountains fade into the darkness.* ► **Fade away** means the same as **fade**. *We watched the harbour and then the coastline fade away into the morning mist.* [VERB V *from/into* n PHRASAL VERB V P *into* n Also V P]

4 If someone or something **fades**, for example, into the background, they become hardly noticeable or very unimportant. *She had a way of fading into the background when things got rough... The most prominent poets of the Victorian period had all but faded from the scene.* ► **Fade away** means the same as **fade**. *Margaret Thatcher will not fade away into quiet retirement.* [VERB V *into/from* n PHRASAL VERB V P *into* n Also V P]

5 If memories, feelings, or possibilities **fade**, they slowly become less intense or less strong. *Sympathy for the rebels, the government claims, is beginning to fade... Prospects for peace had already started to fade. ...fading memories of better days.* [VERB V V-ing]

6 If someone's smile **fades**, they slowly stop smiling. *Jay nodded, his smile fading.* [VERB V]

fade away See **fade** 3 and 4. [PHRASAL VERB]

fade out [PHRASAL VERB]

1 When something **fades out**, it slowly becomes less noticeable or less important until it disappears completely. *He thought her campaign would probably fade out soon in any case.* [V P Also V P *of* n]

2 When light, an image or a sound **fades out**, it disappears after gradually becoming weaker. *You'll need to be able to project two images onto the screen as the new one fades in and the old image fades out.* [V P Also V P *of* n]

faecal /fiːkəl/; spelled **fecal** in American English. **Faecal** means referring or relating to faeces; a formal word. *One of the ways the parasite spreads is through fecal matter.* [ADJ]

faeces /fiːsiːz/; spelled **feces** in American English. **Faeces** is the solid waste substance that people and animals get rid of from their body by excreting it through the anus; a formal word. ◆◇◇◇◇ [N-UNCOUNT =excrement]

faff /fæf/ **faffs, faffing, faffed**

faff about or **faff around.** In informal British English, if you say that someone is **faffing about** or **faffing around**, you mean that they are doing things in a disorganized way and not achieving very much. *It was annoying to watch them faffing around when a more direct response was required.* [PHRASAL VERB V P]

fag /fæg/ **fags** ◆◇◇◇◇

1 In informal British English, a **fag** is a cigarette. [N-COUNT]

2 In informal American English, a **fag** is a homosexual; an offensive use. [N-COUNT]

fag end, fag ends; also spelled **fag-end.**

1 In informal British English, a **fag end** is the last part of a cigarette, which people throw away when they have smoked the rest. [N-COUNT =butt]

2 In informal British English, if you refer to the last part or only remaining part of something as the **fag end** of it, you dislike it, are tired of it, or think it is unimportant. *He never had much confidence in his judgement at the fag-end of the working day.* [N-COUNT: usu sing, N *of* n PRAGMATICS]

faggot /fægət/ **faggots.** In very informal American English, a **faggot** is a homosexual man; an offensive use. [N-COUNT]

Fahrenheit /færənhaɪt/. **Fahrenheit** is a scale for measuring temperature, in which water freezes at 32 degrees and boils at 212 degrees. It is represented by the symbol °F. *By mid-morning, the temperature was already above 100 degrees Fahrenheit.* ► Also a noun. *He was asked for the boiling point of water in Fahrenheit.* [ADJ: n/num ADJ N-UNCOUNT]

fail /feɪl/ **fails, failing, failed** ◆◆◆◆◆

1 If you **fail** to do something that you were trying to do, you are unable to do it or do not succeed in doing it. *The Workers' Party failed to win a single governorship... He failed in his attempt to take control of the company... Many of us have tried to lose weight and failed miserably... The truth is, I'm a failed comedy writer really.* [VERB ≠succeed V to-inf V *in* n V V-ed]

2 If an activity, attempt, or plan **fails**, it is not successful. *We tried to develop plans for them to get along, which all failed miserably... He was afraid the revolution they had started would fail... After a failed military offensive, all government troops and police were withdrawn from the island.* [VERB ≠succeed V V-ed]

3 If someone or something **fails** to do a particular thing that they should have done, they do not do it; a formal use. *Some schools fail to set any homework... He failed to file tax returns for 1982... The bomb failed to explode.* [VERB V to-inf]

4 If something **fails**, it stops working properly, or does not do what it is supposed to do. *The lights mysteriously failed, and we stumbled around in complete darkness... In fact many food crops failed because of the drought.* [VERB V]

5 If a business, organization, or system **fails**, it becomes unable to continue in operation or in existence. *So far this year, 104 banks have failed. ...a failed hotel business... Who wants to buy a computer from a failing company?* [VERB V V-ed V-ing]

6 If something such as your health or a physical quality **is failing**, it is becoming gradually weaker or less effective. *He was 58, and his health was failing rapidly... Here in the hills, the light failed more quickly... An apparently failing memory is damaging for a national leader.* [VERB V V-ing]

7 If someone **fails** you, they do not do what you had expected or trusted them to do. *We waited twenty-one years, don't fail us now. ...communities who feel that the political system has failed them.* [VERB V n]

8 If someone **fails in** their duty or **fails in** their responsibilities, they do not do everything that they have a duty or a responsibility to do. *Lawyers are accused of failing in their duties to advise clients of their rights... If we did not report what was happening in the country, we would be failing in our duty.* [VERB V *in* n]

9 If a quality or ability that you have **fails** you or if it **fails**, it is not great or good enough in a particular situation to enable you to do what you need or [VERB]

want to do. *For once, the artist's fertile imagination failed him... Their courage failed a few steps short and they came running back.*
V n
V

10 If someone **fails** a test or examination, they perform badly in it and do not reach the standard that is required. *I lived in fear of failing my end-of-term exams.* ▶ Also a noun. *It's the difference between a pass and a fail.*
VERB ≠pass
V n
N-COUNT

11 You say **if all else fails** to suggest what could be done in a certain situation if all the other things you have tried are unsuccessful. *If all else fails, I could always drive a truck.*
PHRASES
PHR with cl

12 You can use **I fail to see** or **I fail to understand** in order to introduce a statement which indicates that you do not agree with what someone has said or done; a formal expression. *That's how it was in my day and I fail to see why it should be different now.*
PHR wh
PRAGMATICS

13 You use **without fail** to emphasize that something always happens. *He attended every meeting without fail.*
PHR with cl
PRAGMATICS
=without exception

14 You use **without fail** to emphasize an order or a promise. *On the 30th you must without fail hand in some money for Alex... Tomorrow without fail he would be at the old riverside warehouse.*
PHR with cl
PRAGMATICS

failing /feɪlɪŋ/ **failings** ◆◇◇◇◇

1 The **failings** of someone or something are their faults or unsatisfactory features. *Like many in Russia, she blamed the country's failings on futile attempts to catch up with the West... He had invented an imaginary son, in order to make up for his real son's failings.*
N-COUNT: usu pl, oft with poss
=shortcoming

2 You say **failing that** to introduce an alternative, in case what you have just said is not possible. *Find someone who will let you talk things through, or failing that, write down your thoughts.*
PHRASE: PHR with cl/group

fail-safe; also spelled **failsafe**. Something that is **fail-safe** is designed or made in such a way that nothing dangerous can happen if a part of it goes wrong. *The camera has a built-in failsafe device which prevents it from working if the right signals aren't received.*
ADJ: usu ADJ n

failure /feɪljəʳ/ **failures** ◆◆◆◆◇

1 **Failure** is a lack of success in doing or achieving something, especially in relation to a particular activity. *This policy is doomed to failure... Three attempts on the British 200-metre record also ended in failure. ...feelings of failure.*
N-UNCOUNT ≠success

2 If something is a **failure**, it is not a success. *The marriage was a failure and they both wanted to be free of it... His six-year transition programme has by no means been a complete failure.*
N-COUNT ≠success

3 If you say that someone is a **failure**, you mean that they have not succeeded in a particular activity, or that they are unsuccessful at everything they do. *Elgar received many honors and much acclaim and yet he often considered himself a failure... I just felt I had been a failure in my personal life.*
N-COUNT ≠success

4 Your **failure** to do a particular thing is the fact that you do not do it, even though you were expected to do it. *She accused the Foreign Office of disgraceful failure to support British citizens arrested overseas... They see their failure to produce an heir as a curse from God.*
N-UNCOUNT: N to-inf, oft poss N

5 If there is a **failure** of something, for example a machine or part of the body, it goes wrong and stops working or developing properly. *There were also several accidents mainly caused by engine failures on take-off... He was being treated for kidney failure... Researchers found an almost total crop failure and a severe shortage of drinking water.*
N-VAR: with supp, oft n N

6 If there is a **failure** of a business or bank, it is no longer able to continue operating. *Business failures rose 16% last month.*
N-VAR: with supp
=collapse

7 If you say that someone has a **failure of** a particular quality or ability, you mean that they do not have enough of it. *There is, too, a simple failure of imagination... He remained on his knees for a long time afterwards, ashamed by his failure of nerve.*
N-VAR: N *of* n

faint /feɪnt/ **fainter, faintest; faints, fainting, fainted** ◆◆◇◇◇

1 A **faint** sound, colour, mark, feeling, or quality has very little strength or intensity. *He became aware of the soft, faint sounds of water dripping... The room held the faint, sweet odour of pipe tobacco... He could see faint lines in her face... There was still the faint hope deep within him that she might never need to know.* ♦ **faintly** *He was already asleep in the bed, which smelled faintly of mildew... She felt faintly ridiculous.*
ADJ-GRADED: usu ADJ n
ADV-GRADED: usu ADV after v, also ADV adj
=slightly

2 A **faint** attempt at something is one that is made without proper effort and with little enthusiasm. *Caroline made a faint attempt at a laugh... A faint smile crossed the Monsignor's face and faded quickly... Ten years ago today the US Center for Disease Control published the first faint warnings of a worldwide epidemic.* ♦ **faintly** *John smiled faintly and shook his head.*
ADJ-GRADED: ADJ n
ADV-GRADED: ADV after v

3 If you **faint**, you lose consciousness for a short time, especially because of hunger, pain, heat, or shock. *She suddenly fell forward on to the table and fainted... I thought he'd faint when I kissed him.* ▶ Also a noun. *She slumped to the ground in a faint.*
VERB =pass out
V
N-COUNT: oft *in a* N

4 Someone who is **faint** feels weak and unsteady as if they are about to lose consciousness. *Other signs of angina are nausea, sweating, feeling faint and shortness of breath.* ♦ **faintness** *One patient suffered headaches, nausea, and faintness.*
ADJ-GRADED: v-link ADJ
N-UNCOUNT

faintest /feɪntɪst/. You can use **faintest** for emphasis in negative statements. For example, if you say that someone hasn't the **faintest** idea what to do, you are emphasizing that they do not know what to do. *I haven't the faintest idea how to care for a snake... He said yesterday that there was not 'the faintest possibility' that the government would bring in such a measure.*
ADJ-SUPERL: ADJ n, with neg
PRAGMATICS
=slightest, remotest

faint-hearted; also spelled **fainthearted**.

1 If you describe someone or their behaviour as **faint-hearted**, you mean that they are not very confident and do not take strong action because they are afraid of failing. *This is no time to be faint-hearted... The voters may be ready to punish the politicians who devised a faint-hearted solidarity pact.*
ADJ-GRADED

2 If you say that something is **not for the faint-hearted**, you mean that it is an extreme or very unusual example of its kind, and is not suitable for people who like only safe and familiar things. *It's a film about a serial killer and not for the faint-hearted.*
PHRASE: usu v-link PHR

fair /feəʳ/ **fairer, fairest; fairs** ◆◆◆◆◇

1 Something or someone that is **fair** is reasonable, right, and just. *It didn't seem fair to leave out her father... Do you feel they're paying their fair share?... Independent observers say the campaign's been very much fairer than expected... I wanted them to get a fair deal... An appeals court had ruled that they could not get a fair trial in Los Angeles.* ♦ **fairly** *...demonstrating concern for employees and solving their problems quickly and fairly... In a society where water was precious, it had to be shared fairly between individuals.*
ADJ-GRADED: oft *it* v-link ADJ to-inf
ADV-GRADED: usu ADV after v, also ADV -ed

2 A **fair** amount, degree, size, or distance is quite a large amount, degree, size, or distance. *My neighbours across the street travel a fair amount... My mother's brother lives a fair distance away so we don't see him and his family very often.*
ADJ: ADJ n

3 A **fair** guess or idea about something is one that is likely to be correct. *It's a fair guess to say that the damage will be extensive... I have a fair idea of how difficult things can be.*
ADJ: ADJ n
=reasonable

4 If you describe someone or something as **fair**, you mean that they are average in standard or quality, neither very good nor very bad. *Reimar had a fair command of English.*
ADJ
=adequate

5 Someone who is **fair**, or who has **fair** hair, has light-coloured hair. *Both children were very like Robina, but were much fairer than she was.* ▶ Also a combining form. *...a tall, fair-haired Englishman.*
ADJ-GRADED
COMB in ADJ-GRADED

6 **Fair** skin is very pale and usually burns easily. *It's important to protect my fair skin from the sun.* ▶ Also a combining form. *Fair-skinned people who*
ADJ-GRADED
COMB in ADJ-GRADED

spend a great deal of time in the sun have the greatest risk of skin cancer.

7 When the weather is **fair**, it is quite sunny and not raining; a formal use. *Weather conditions were fair.*
ADJ-GRADED =fine

8 In British English, a **fair** is an event held in a park or field at which people pay to ride on various machines for amusement or try to win prizes in games. The usual American word is **carnival**. *...all the fun of the fair.*
N-COUNT =funfair

9 A **fair** is an event at which people display and sell goods, especially goods of a particular type. *He travels to agricultural shows and country fairs demonstrating his skills. ...an antiques fair.* • See also **craft fair**, **trade fair**.
N-COUNT: oft n N

10 You use **fair** in expressions such as **to be fair** and **let's be fair** when you want to add a favourable comment about someone or something that you have just mentioned and to correct an unfair, unreasonable, or false impression that you might have given. *To be fair, the team is young and not yet settled... And, let us be fair, some MPs do work hard.*
PHRASES PHR with cl PRAGMATICS =in all fairness

11 You use **fair enough** when you want to say that a statement, decision, or action seems reasonable to a certain extent, but that perhaps there is more to be said or done. *If you don't like it, fair enough, but that's hardly a justification to attack the whole thing... Fair enough, you didn't have a perfectly happy childhood: but your childhood is over now.*
PHR with cl PRAGMATICS

12 You say **fair enough** to acknowledge what someone has just said and to indicate that you understand it. *'I'm taking it to our local police station.'—'Oh right, fair enough.'... 'The message was addressed to me and I don't see why I should show it to you.'—'Fair enough.'*
CONVENTION PRAGMATICS =OK

13 If you say that someone **plays fair**, you mean that they behave or act in a reasonable and honest way. *The government is not playing fair, one union official told me.*
V inflects

14 You use **fair** in expressions such as **It would be fair to say** in order to introduce a statement which you believe to be true and reasonable. *It would be fair to say he had one or two unhappy moments out there... I think it's fair to say that it didn't sound quite right.*
PHR that PRAGMATICS

15 If you say that someone won a competition **fair and square**, you mean that they won honestly and without cheating. *There are no excuses. We were beaten fair and square.*
PHR after v

16 • **a fair crack of the whip**: see **crack**.

fair game. If you say that someone is **fair game**, you mean that it is acceptable to criticize or attack them, usually because of the way that they behave. *Politicians were always considered fair game by cartoonists.*
N-UNCOUNT

fairground /fɛəʳgraʊnd/ **fairgrounds.** A **fairground** is an area of land where a funfair is held.
◆◇◇◇◇ N-COUNT

fairly /fɛəʳli/
◆◆◆◇◇

1 **Fairly** means to quite a large degree. For example, if you say that something is **fairly** old, you mean that it is old but not very old. *Both ships are fairly new (five years old and one year old respectively)... We did fairly well but only fairly well.*
ADV: ADV adj/adv =quite

2 You use **fairly** instead of 'very' to add emphasis to an adjective or adverb without making it sound too forceful. *Were you always fairly bright at school?... You've got to be fairly single-minded about it... I'll have no income and no home and will need a job fairly badly.*
ADV: ADV adj/adv PRAGMATICS =pretty

3 **Fairly** is used to emphasize that something happens to a very great degree or extent. *He fairly flew across the room... For him, the place is fairly boiling with humanity... 'Get the hell out of my hospital!' Rosen fairly screamed.*
ADV: ADV before v PRAGMATICS =positively

4 You use **fairly** to suggest that a statement is probably or possibly true, and therefore deserves to be accepted or considered. *It can no doubt be fairly argued that Sir John, whose pay is linked to performance, is entitled to every penny... After I had read the book I could fairly claim to be an expert.*
ADV-GRADED: ADV before v =justifiably

5 See also **fair**.

fairness /fɛəʳnəs/
◆◇◇◇◇

1 **Fairness** is the quality of being reasonable, right, and just. *He says the new document will guarantee fairness for blacks in Georgia. ...concern about the fairness of the election campaign.*
N-UNCOUNT

2 You use **fairness** in expressions such as **in fairness to** and **in all fairness** when you want to add a favourable comment about someone or something that you have just mentioned and to correct an unfair, unreasonable, or false impression that you might have given. *In fairness to Bates, he always made it very clear that Webb was only on trial until the end of the season... There is much more to be said, in all fairness, on both sides of the issue.*
PHRASE: PHR with cl PRAGMATICS =to be fair

fair play. If you refer to someone's attitude or behaviour as **fair play**, you approve of it because it shows respect and tolerance towards everyone, even towards people who are thought to be wrong or deserving of punishment. *...a legal system that is unmatched anywhere in the world for its justice and sense of fair play.*
◆◇◇◇◇ N-UNCOUNT PRAGMATICS

fair sex; also spelled **fairer sex**. If a man talks about **the fair sex**, he is referring to women in general; an old-fashioned expression.
N-SING: *the* N

fairway /fɛəʳweɪ/ **fairways.** The **fairway** on a golf course is the long strip of short grass between each tee and green.
◆◇◇◇◇ N-COUNT: usu *the* N

fair-weather. You use **fair-weather** to refer to someone who offers help to someone, or who takes part in a particular activity, only when it is easy or pleasant for them to do so; used showing disapproval. *The Queen has told Canadians she's not just a fair-weather friend of Canada's.*
ADJ: ADJ n PRAGMATICS

fairy /fɛəri/ **fairies**
◆◆◇◇◇

1 A **fairy** is an imaginary creature with magical powers. Fairies are often portrayed as small people with wings.
N-COUNT

2 If someone describes a man as a **fairy**, they mean that he is a homosexual and they disapprove of this; an offensive use.
N-COUNT PRAGMATICS

fairy godmother. If you call a woman your **fairy godmother**, you are saying in a humorous way that she has been very helpful in your life, often at times when you thought you had problems that could not be solved. *The woman I regarded as my fairy godmother was Sybil. She was wonderful to me.*
N-SING: poss N

fairyland /fɛərilænd/ **fairylands**

1 **Fairyland** is the imaginary place where fairies live.
N-UNCOUNT

2 If you describe a place as a **fairyland**, you mean that it has a delicate beauty. *If you came with me to one of my toy shops, you'd think you were stepping into a fairyland.*
N-VAR

fairy lights. In British English, **fairy lights** are small, coloured electric lights that are hung up as decorations, for example on a Christmas tree.
N-PLURAL

fairy story, fairy stories. A **fairy story** is the same as a **fairy tale**.
N-COUNT

fairy tale, fairy tales; also spelled **fairytale**.
◆◇◇◇◇

1 A **fairy tale** is a story for children involving magical events and imaginary creatures. *She was like a princess in a fairy tale.*
N-COUNT =fairy story

2 A **fairy tale** place or situation is so wonderful that you can hardly believe that it is real. *...an excursion to the fairy-tale castle of Neuschwanstein... She loved him so much: it was a fairytale romance.*
ADJ: ADJ n

fait accompli /feɪt əkɒmpli, AM - ækɔːmpliː/ **faits accomplis.** If something is a **fait accompli**, it has already been decided or done and cannot be changed; a formal expression. *They became increasingly annoyed that they were being presented with a fait accompli.*
N-COUNT: usu sing

faith /feɪθ/ **faiths**
◆◆◆◇◇

1 If you have **faith** in someone or something, you feel confident about their ability or goodness. *She had placed a great deal of faith in Mr Penleigh... People have lost faith in the British Parliament.*
N-UNCOUNT: usu N *in* n =confidence

2 A **faith** is a particular religion, for example Christianity, Buddhism, or Islam. *England shifted officially from a Catholic to a Protestant faith in the 16th century.*
N-COUNT: also no det, usu adj N

3 **Faith** is strong religious belief in a particular God.
N-UNCOUNT

Umberto Eco's loss of his own religious faith is reflected in his novels.

4 If you **break faith with** someone you made a promise to or something you believed in, you stop acting in a way that supports them. *Mr Field accused the Labour leader of breaking faith with working people by failing to fight the tax.* PHRASES V inflects

5 If you do something **in good faith**, you seriously believe that what you are doing is right, honest, or legal, even though this may not be the case. *This report was published in good faith but we regret any confusion which may have been caused.* PHR after v

6 If you **keep faith with** someone you have made a promise to or something you believe in, you continue to support them even when it is difficult to do so. *President Francois Mitterrand will try to persuade his countrymen to keep faith with the European ideal.* V inflects, PHR n

7 • See also **article of faith, leap of faith.**

faithful /feɪθfʊl/ **faithfuls** ◆◆◇◇◇

1 Someone who is **faithful** to a person, organization, idea, or activity remains firm in their dedication to them or support for them. *She had been faithful to her promise to guard this secret... Older Americans are among this country's most faithful voters.* ADJ-GRADED: oft ADJ *to* n ▶ **The faithful** are people who are faithful to someone or something. *He spends his time making speeches at factories or gatherings of the Party faithful.* N-PLURAL: the N ♦ **faithfully** *He has since 1965 faithfully followed and supported every twist and turn of government policy.* ADV-GRADED: ADV with v

2 Someone who is **faithful** to their husband, wife, or lover does not have a sexual relationship with anyone else. *She insisted that she had remained faithful to her husband... I'm very faithful when I love someone.* ADJ-GRADED: oft ADJ *to* n ≠unfaithful

3 **The faithful** are the group of people who believe in a particular religion. *The faithful revered him then as a prophet.* N-PLURAL: the N

4 A **faithful** account, translation, adaptation, or copy of something represents or reproduces the original accurately. *Colin Welland's screenplay is faithful to the novel. ...faithful copies of household items used in the mid-1800s.* ADJ-GRADED: oft ADJ *to* n ♦ **faithfully** *When I adapt something I translate from one meaning to another as faithfully as I can.* ADV-GRADED: ADV with v

5 You can refer to something that has been used or has existed for a long time as an **old faithful**, especially when it is something you can rely on. *We tested a selection of vacuum cleaners, from old faithfuls to those with the latest features.* PHRASE: N inflects

faithfully /feɪθfʊli/. In British English, when you start a formal or business letter with 'Dear Sir' or 'Dear Madam', you write **Yours faithfully** before your signature at the end. The usual American expression is **Sincerely yours.** • See also **faithful.** ◆◆◇◇◇ CONVENTION

faith healing; also spelled **faith-healing. Faith healing** is the treatment of a sick person by someone who believes that they are able to heal people through prayer or a supernatural power. N-UNCOUNT

faithless /feɪθləs/. If you say that someone is **faithless**, you mean that they are disloyal or dishonest. *She decided to divorce her increasingly faithless and unreliable husband.* ADJ-GRADED

fake /feɪk/ **fakes, faking, faked** ◆◆◇◇◇

1 A **fake** fur or a **fake** painting, for example, is a fur or painting that has been made to look valuable or genuine, in order to deceive people. *The bank manager is said to have issued fake certificates.* ADJ: usu ADJ n ▶ A **fake** is something that is fake. *It is filled with famous works of art, and every one of them is a fake.* N-COUNT

2 If someone **fakes** something, they try to make it look valuable or genuine, although in fact it is not. *It's safer to fake a tan with make-up rather than subject your complexion to the harsh rays of the sun... He faked his own death last year to collect on a $1 million insurance policy. ...faked evidence.* VERB V n V-ed

3 Someone who is a **fake** is not what they claim to be, for example because they do not have the qualifications that they claim to have. N-COUNT =fraud

4 If you **fake** a feeling, emotion, or reaction, you pretend that you are experiencing it when you are not. *Jon faked nonchalance... Maturity and emotional sophistication can't be faked.* VERB V n

falcon /fɔːlkən, fælk-/ **falcons.** A **falcon** is a bird of prey that can be trained to hunt other birds and animals. N-COUNT

falconer /fɔːlkənəʳ, fælk-/ **falconers.** A **falconer** is someone who trains and uses falcons for hunting. N-COUNT

falconry /fɔːlkənri, fælk-/. **Falconry** is the skill of training falcons to hunt, and the sport of using them to hunt. N-UNCOUNT

fall /fɔːl/ **falls, falling, fell, fallen** ◆◆◆◆◆

1 If someone or something **falls**, they move quickly downwards onto or towards the ground, by accident or because of a natural force. *Her father fell into the sea after a massive heart attack... Prince Charles has again fallen from his horse... Bombs fell in the town... I ought to seal the boxes up. I don't want the books falling out... Twenty people were injured by falling masonry.* VERB V prep V V *out/off* V-ing ▶ Also a noun. *The helmets are designed to withstand impacts equivalent to a fall from a bicycle.* N-COUNT: oft N *from* n

2 If a person or structure that is standing somewhere **falls**, they move from their upright position, so that they are then lying on the ground. *The woman gripped the shoulders of her man to stop herself from falling... We watched buildings fall on top of people and pets... He lost his balance and fell backwards.* VERB V V prep/adv ▶ Also a noun. *Mrs Briscoe had a bad fall last week.* N-COUNT ▶ **Fall down** means the same as **fall.** *I hit him so hard he fell down... Children jumped from upper floors as the building fell down around them.* PHRASAL VERB V P ♦ **fallen** *A number of roads have been blocked by fallen trees.* ADJ: ADJ n

3 When rain or snow **falls**, it comes down from the sky. *Winds reached up to 100mph in some places with an inch of rain falling within 15 minutes.* VERB V ▶ Also a noun. *One night there was a heavy fall of snow.* N-COUNT: N *of* n • See also **rainfall, snowfall.**

4 If you **fall** somewhere, you allow yourself to drop there in a hurried or disorganized way, often because you are very tired. *Totally exhausted, he tore his clothes off and fell into bed... In the morning I got as far as the sofa and fell on to it.* VERB V prep

5 If something **falls**, it decreases in amount, value, or strength. *Output will fall by 6% in the EC... Her weight fell to under seven stones... Between July and August, oil product prices fell 0.2 per cent... The number of prosecutions has stayed static and the rate of convictions has fallen. ...a time of falling living standards and emerging mass unemployment.* VERB =drop ≠rise V *by* n V *to/from* n V amount V V-ing ▶ Also a noun. *There was a sharp fall in the value of the pound.* N-COUNT: usu sing

6 If a powerful or successful person **falls**, they suddenly lose their power or position. *Regimes fall, revolutions come and go, but places never really change... The moment Mrs Thatcher fell from power has left a lasting imprint on the world's memory.* VERB V V *from* n ▶ Also a noun. *Following the fall of the military dictator in March, the country has had a civilian government... Her rise has mirrored his fall.* N-SING: with poss ≠rise

7 If a place **falls** in a war or election, an enemy army or a different political party takes control of it. *Croatian army troops retreated from northern Bosnia and the area fell to the Serbs... With the announcement 'Paphos has fallen!' a cheer went up from the assembled soldiers.* VERB V *to* n V ▶ Also a noun. *...the fall of Rome.* N-SING: usu N *of* n

8 If someone **falls** in battle, they are killed; a literary use. *Another wave of troops followed the first, running past those who had fallen.* VERB V

9 You can use **fall** to show that someone or something passes into another state. For example, if someone **falls ill**, they become ill, and if something **falls into disrepair**, it is then in a state of disrepair. *It is almost impossible to visit Florida without falling in love with the state... 'Business to Business' was taken over by another company after it fell into debt... I took Moira to the cinema, where she fell asleep... Almost without exception these women fall victim to exploitation.* V-LINK V *in/into/out of* n V adj V n

10 If you say that something or someone **falls into** VERB

a particular group or category, you mean that they belong in that group or category. *The problems generally fall into two categories... Both women fall into the highest-risk group.* V into n

11 If the responsibility or blame for something **falls on** someone, they have to take the responsibility or the blame for it; used in written English. *That responsibility falls on the local office of the United Nations High Commissioner for Refugees... A vastly disproportionate burden falls on women for child care... A lot of suspicion fell on her.* VERB V on n

12 If silence or a feeling of sadness or tiredness **falls** on a group of people, they become silent, sad, or tired; used in written English. *The bus was stopped and silence fell on the passengers as the police checked identity cards.* VERB =descend V on/over n

13 If a celebration or other special event **falls on** a particular day or date, it happens to be on that day or date. *...the oddly named Quasimodo Sunday which falls on the first Sunday after Easter.* VERB V on n

14 When light or shadow **falls** on something, it covers it. *Nancy, out of the corner of her eye, saw the shadow that suddenly fell across the doorway.* VERB V across/over/on n

15 If someone's hair or a garment **falls** in a certain way, it hangs downwards in that way. *Her hair was dressed in soft waves, falling on her cheek in a manner fashionable in the early 1930s.* VERB V prep/adv

16 If you say that someone's eyes **fell** on something, you mean they suddenly noticed it; used in written English. *As he laid the flowers on the table, his eye fell upon a note in Grace's handwriting.* VERB V on/upon n

17 When night or darkness **falls**, night begins and it becomes dark. *As darkness fell outside, they sat down to eat at long tables.* VERB V

18 You can refer to a waterfall as the **falls**. *The falls have always been an insurmountable obstacle for salmon and sea trout. ...Niagara Falls.* N-PLURAL: oft in names after n

19 In American English, **fall** is the season between summer and winter when the weather becomes cooler. The British word is **autumn**. *He was elected judge in the fall of 1991... The Supreme Court will not hear the case until next fall.* N-VAR

20 In the Christian religion, **the Fall** was the occasion when Adam and Eve sinned and God made them leave the Garden of Eden. N-PROPER: the N

21 In some sports such as judo and wrestling, a **fall** is the act of throwing or forcing your opponent to the floor. N-COUNT

22 In cricket, when a wicket **falls**, the team who are fielding get one of the batsmen out. *The last seven wickets fell for ten runs.* VERB V

23 See also **fallen**.

24 If something **falls open**, it opens accidentally. *By chance the book beside him fell open to St. Paul's warning to the Romans... The basket that she was carrying fell open.* PHRASES V inflects, oft PHR at/to n

25 If you say that people **are falling over themselves** to do something, you mean that they are very keen to do it, and often you mean that you disapprove of this; an informal expression. *Within days of his death those same people were falling over themselves to denounce him.* V inflects, oft cont PRAGMATICS

26 To **fall to pieces**, or in British English to **fall to bits**, means the same as to **fall apart**. *At that point the radio handset fell to pieces.* V inflects

27 • to **fall on** your **feet**: see **foot**. • to **fall foul of** someone: see **foul**. • to **fall flat**: see **flat**. • to **fall from grace**: see **grace**. • to **fall into place**: see **place**. • to **fall short**: see **short**. • to **fall into step**: see **step**. • to **fall into** the **trap**: see **trap**. • to **fall by the wayside**: see **wayside**.

fall about. If you say that people **are falling about**, you mean that they are laughing a lot about something; an informal British expression. *Dan fell about and slapped his thighs... The men at the table fell about laughing.* PHRASAL VERB V P V P -ing Also V P with n

fall apart PHRASAL VERB

1 If something **falls apart**, it breaks into pieces because it is old or badly made. *The work was never finished and bit by bit the building fell apart.* V P

2 If an organization or system **falls apart**, it becomes disorganized or unable to work effectively, or breaks up into its different parts. *Europe's monetary system is falling apart... I've tried everything to stop our marriage falling apart.* =break down V P

3 If you say that someone **is falling apart**, you mean that they are becoming emotionally disturbed and are unable to think calmly or to deal with the difficult or unpleasant situation that they are in; an informal expression. *I was falling apart. I wasn't getting any sleep.* =crack up V P

fall away PHRASAL VERB

1 If something **falls away** from the thing it is attached to, it breaks off. *Officials say that one or two engines fell away from the plane shortly after take-off.* V P from n Also V P

2 If you say that land **falls away**, you mean it slopes downwards from a particular point. *On either side of the tracks the ground fell away sharply.* V P

3 If the degree, amount, or size of something **falls away**, it decreases. *His coalition may hold a clear majority but this could quickly fall away... Demand began to fall away.* =fall off V P

fall back PHRASAL VERB

1 If you **fall back**, you move backwards a short distance away from someone or something. *He fell back in embarrassment when he saw that Ross had no hair at all... The congregation fell back from them slightly as they entered.* V P V P from n

2 If an army **falls back** during a battle or war, it retreats. *The Prussian garrison at Charleroi was falling back.* V P

fall back on. If you **fall back on** something, you do it or use it after other things have failed. *Unable to defeat him by logical discussion, she fell back on her old habit of criticizing his speech... When necessary, instinct is the most reliable resource you can fall back on.* PHRASAL VERB =resort to V P P n

fall behind PHRASAL VERB

1 If you **fall behind**, you do not make progress or move forward as fast as other people. *Evans had rheumatic fever, missed school and fell behind... Boris is falling behind all the top players.* V P n

2 If you **fall behind** with something or let it **fall behind**, you do not do it or produce it when you should, according to an agreement or schedule. *He faces losing his home after falling behind with the payments... Thousands of people could die because the relief effort has fallen so far behind... Construction work fell behind schedule.* V P with n V P V P n

fall down PHRASAL VERB

1 See **fall** 2.

2 If an argument, organization, or person **falls down** on a particular point, they are weak or unsatisfactory on that point. *The UN, the US and the EC have all fallen down on their obligations towards the new world order... That is where his argument falls down.* =fail V P on n V P

fall for PHRASAL VERB

1 If you **fall for** someone, you are strongly attracted to them and start loving them. *He was fantastically handsome – I just fell for him right away.* V P n

2 If you **fall for** a lie or trick, you believe it or are deceived by it. *It was just a line to get you out here, and you fell for it!... I told him I would think about it and asked for his telephone number. He didn't fall for that one.* V P n

fall in PHRASAL VERB

1 If a roof or ceiling **falls in**, it collapses and falls to the ground. *Part of my bedroom ceiling has fallen in; I sleep downstairs.* V P

2 If you **fall in** behind or beside someone who is walking along, you start walking behind them or beside them. *Prentice saw Goss fall in behind the informer.* V P behind/beside n

fall into. If you **fall into** conversation or a discussion with someone, usually someone you have just met, you start having a conversation or discussion with them. *Over breakfast at my motel, I fell into conversation with the owner of a hardware shop.* PHRASAL VERB V P n

fall in with PHRASAL VERB

1 If you **fall in with** an idea, plan, or system, you accept it and do not try to change it. *Carmen's reluctance to fall in with Driver's plans led to trouble.* V P P n

2 If you **fall in with** someone, you become friends with them and start seeing them a lot. *At university, Taylor had fallen in with a small clique of literature students.* VPPn

fall off PHRASAL VERB
1 If something **falls off**, it separates from the thing to which it was attached and moves towards the ground. *When your exhaust falls off, you have to replace it.* =drop off VP
2 If the degree, amount, or size of something **falls off**, it decreases. *Unemployment is rising again and retail buying has fallen off.* ● See also **falling-off**. =fall away VP

fall on. If you **fall on** something when it arrives or appears, you eagerly seize it or welcome it. *They fell on the sandwiches with alacrity.* PHRASAL VERB VPn

fall out PHRASAL VERB
1 If something such as a person's hair or a tooth **falls out**, it separates from their body. *Her hair started falling out as a result of radiation treatment.* VP
2 If you **fall out** with someone, you have an argument and stop being friendly with them. You can also say that two people **fall out**. *She fell out with her husband... Mum and I used to fall out a lot.* RECIP VP with n pl-n VP
3 See also **fallout**.

fall over. If a person or object that is standing **falls over**, they accidentally move from their upright position so that they are then lying on the ground or on the surface supporting them. *If he drinks more than two glasses of wine he falls over.* PHRASAL VERB VP

fall through. If an arrangement, plan, or deal **falls through**, it fails to happen. *They wanted to turn the estate into a private golf course and offered £20 million, but the deal fell through.* PHRASAL VERB VP

fall to PHRASAL VERB
1 If a responsibility, duty, or opportunity **falls to** someone, it becomes their responsibility, duty, or opportunity. *He's been very unlucky that no chances have fallen to him... It fell to me to get rid of them.* VPn *it* VPn to-inf
2 If someone **falls to** doing something, they start doing it; used in written English. *When she had departed, they fell to fighting among themselves.* =begin VP-ing

fallacious /fəleɪʃəs/. If an idea, argument, or reason is **fallacious**, it is wrong because it is based on a fallacy; a formal word. *Their main argument is fallacious, and their conclusions untenable.* ADJ-GRADED =false

fallacy /fæləsi/ **fallacies.** A **fallacy** is an idea which many people believe to be true, but which is in fact false because it is based on incorrect information or faulty reasoning. *It's a fallacy that the affluent give relatively more to charity than the less prosperous... It exposes the fallacy of short-term industrial gain at long-term environmental expense.* ◆◇◇◇◇ N-VAR: oft N that, N of n/-ing

fallback /fɔːlbæk/. Someone's **fallback** position is what they will do if their plans do not succeed, or if something unexpected happens; used by journalists. *Yesterday's vote itself was a retreat from an earlier fallback position.* ADJ: ADJ n

fallen /fɔːlən/
1 **Fallen** is the past participle of **fall**.
2 **The fallen** are soldiers who have died in battle; a literary expression. *Work began on establishing the cemeteries as permanent memorials to the fallen.* N-PLURAL: *the* N =dead
3 In the Christian religion, **fallen** can be used to describe people or angels after the time when they sinned and were punished by God. *...Lucifer, the fallen angel.* ADJ: ADJ n
4 In the past, people described a woman who was considered to have lost her respectability and virtue because she had had sex with someone who she was not married to as a **fallen** woman; an old-fashioned use showing disapproval. ADJ: ADJ n PRAGMATICS =loose
5 See also **fall**.

fall guy, fall guys. If someone is the **fall guy**, they are blamed for something which they did not do or which is not their fault; an informal expression. *He claims he was made the fall guy for the affair.* N-COUNT =scapegoat

fallible /fælɪbᵊl/. If you say that someone or something is **fallible**, you mean that they are not perfect and are likely to make mistakes or to fail in what they are doing; a formal word. *They are only human and all too fallible... The system has proved fallible time after time... Human reason is a fallible guide.* ♦ **fallibility** /fælɪbɪlɪti/ *Errors may have been made due to human fallibility... The fallibility of science is one of the great betrayals of our times.* ADJ-GRADED ≠infallible N-UNCOUNT: usu with supp

falling-off. If there is a **falling-off** of an activity, there is a decrease in its amount or intensity. *There has been a falling off in box office income and other earnings.* ◆◇◇◇◇ N-SING: N of/in n =decline

fallopian tube /fəloupiən tjuːb, AM - tuːb/ **fallopian tubes.** A woman's **fallopian tubes** are the two tubes in her body along which eggs pass from her ovaries to her uterus. ◆◇◇◇◇ N-COUNT

fallout /fɔːlaut/ ◆◇◇◇◇
1 **Fallout** is the radiation that affects a particular place or area after a nuclear explosion has taken place. *They were exposed to radioactive fallout during nuclear weapons tests.* N-UNCOUNT
2 If you refer to the **fallout** from something that has happened, you mean the unpleasant consequences that follow it. *Grundy lost his job in the fallout from the incident.* N-UNCOUNT: oft N *from* n

fallow /fælou/
1 **Fallow** land has been dug or ploughed but nothing has been sown or planted in it, especially so that its quality or strength has a chance to improve. *...great red barns in empty fallow fields... The fields lay fallow.* ADJ
2 A **fallow** period is a time when very little is being achieved. *There followed something of a fallow period professionally, until a job came up in the summer.* ADJ: usu ADJ n

fallow deer; fallow deer is both the singular and the plural form. A **fallow deer** is a small deer that has a reddish coat which develops white spots in summer. N-COUNT

false /fɔːls/ ◆◆◆◇◇
1 If something is **false**, it is incorrect, untrue, or mistaken. *It was quite clear the President was being given false information by those around him... You do not know whether what you're told is true or false... His sister said he had deliberately given the hospital a false name and address.* ♦ **falsely** *It's about a man who is falsely accused of a crime and is trying to find the true criminal.* ♦ **falsity** /fɔːlsɪti/ *...with no clear knowledge of the truth or falsity of the issues involved.* ADJ ≠true, genuine ADV: ADV with v =wrongly N-UNCOUNT: oft *the* N of n
2 You use **false** to describe objects which are artificial but which are intended to look like the real thing or to be used instead of the real thing. *...the items she'd secreted in the false bottom of her suitcase. ...a set of false teeth... I was wearing false eyelashes and a sweater two sizes too small.* ADJ: usu ADJ n =artificial ≠real
3 If you describe a person or their behaviour as **false**, you are criticizing them for being insincere or for hiding their real feelings. *She bowed her head and smiled in false modesty... 'Thank you,' she said with false enthusiasm... Even to himself the geniality rang false and he came to a stop.* ♦ **falsely** *He was falsely jovial, with his booming, mirthless laugh... 'This food is divine,' they murmur, falsely.* ADJ-GRADED PRAGMATICS =genuine ADV-GRADED: ADV adj, ADV after v

false alarm, false alarms. When you think something dangerous is about to happen, but then discover that you were mistaken, you can say that it was a **false alarm**. *...a bomb threat that turned out to be a false alarm.* N-COUNT

false beginner, false beginners. In language teaching, a **false beginner** is someone who starts studying a language as a beginner even though they have studied it before. N-COUNT

falsehood /fɔːlshʊd/ **falsehoods**
1 **Falsehood** is the quality or fact of being untrue or of being a lie. *She called the verdict a victory of truth over falsehood.* N-UNCOUNT ≠truth
2 A **falsehood** is a lie; a formal use. *He accused them of knowingly spreading falsehoods about him.* N-COUNT

false move. You use **one false move** to introduce the very serious or disastrous consequences which will result if someone makes a mistake, PHRASE even a very small one. *One false move and I knew Sarah would be dead.*

false positive, false positives. A **false positive** is a mistaken result of a scientific test. For example, if the result of a pregnancy test is a false positive, it indicates that a woman is pregnant when she is not. *...a high rate of false positive results.* N-COUNT: oft N n

false start, false starts ◆◇◇◇◇
1 A **false start** is an attempt to start something, such as a speech, project, or plan, which fails because you were not properly prepared or ready to begin. *Any economic reform, he said, faced false starts and mistakes.* N-COUNT
2 If there is a **false start** at the beginning of a race, one of the competitors moves before the starter has given the signal. N-COUNT

falsetto /fɔːlsetoʊ/ **falsettos.** If a man sings or speaks in a **falsetto**, his voice is high-pitched, and higher than a man's normal voice. *He sang to himself in a soft falsetto... Even though it's high, it's not a falsetto voice.* N-COUNT: usu sing, oft *in* N, N n

falsify /fɔːlsɪfaɪ/ **falsifies, falsifying, falsified.** ◆◇◇◇◇ VERB
If someone **falsifies** something, they change it in a misleading way or add untrue details to it in order to deceive people. *The charges against him include fraud, bribery, and falsifying business records.* V n ♦ **falsification** /fɔːlsɪfɪkeɪʃᵊn/ **falsifications** *...recent concern about the falsification of evidence in court.* N-VAR: usu N *of* n

falter /fɔːltəʳ/ **falters, faltering, faltered** ◆◇◇◇◇
1 If something **falters**, it loses power or strength in an uneven way, or no longer makes much progress. *Normal life is at a standstill, and the economy is faltering... The car was out of sight around a bend in moments, but the engine did not falter or slow down... A faltering economy and a recent wave of labour unrest have affected the new party's popularity.* VERB V V-ing
2 If you **falter**, you lose your confidence or concentration and stop doing something or start making mistakes. *I have not faltered in my quest for a new future... As he neared the house his steps faltered.* VERB V
3 If your voice **falters** when you are speaking, you hesitate or pause, because you are unsure about what you are saying or are upset. *Her voice faltered and she had to stop a moment to control it.* VERB V

faltering /fɔːltərɪŋ/. A **faltering** attempt, effort, or movement is hesitant and uncertain because the person doing it is nervous or weak, or does not really know what to do. *'Now I feel I can do it,' he said in faltering English... Leaning on Jon, Michael took faltering steps to the bathroom.* ADJ =hesitant

fame /feɪm/. If you achieve **fame**, you become very well-known. *At the height of his fame, his every word was valued... The film earned him international fame. ...her rise to fame and fortune as a dramatist.* • **claim to fame**: see **claim**. ◆◆◇◇◇ N-UNCOUNT

famed /feɪmd/. If people, places, or things are **famed**, they are very well-known. *The city is famed for its outdoor restaurants. ...the famed Brazilian photographer Sebastiao Salgado.* ◆◇◇◇◇ ADJ-GRADED: oft ADJ *for* n =renowned

familial /fəmɪliəl/. **Familial** means relating to families in general, or typical of a family; a formal word. *There was a familial comfort to the place.* ADJ: usu ADJ n

familiar /fəmɪliəʳ/ ◆◆◆◇◇
1 If someone or something is **familiar** to you, you recognize them or know them well. *He talked of other cultures as if they were more familiar to him than his own... They are already familiar faces on our TV screens. ...the familiar names of long-established local firms.* ♦ **familiarity** /fəmɪliærɪti/ *Tony was unnerved by the uncanny familiarity of her face.* ADJ-GRADED: oft ADJ *to* n; N-UNCOUNT
2 If you are **familiar with** something, you know or understand it well. *Lesinko is quite familiar with Central Television. He worked there for 25 years... Most people are familiar with this figure from Wagner's opera.* ♦ **familiarity** *The enemy would always have the advantage of familiarity with the rugged terrain.* ADJ-GRADED: v-link ADJ *with* n; N-UNCOUNT: usu N *with* n
3 If someone you do not know well behaves in a **familiar** way towards you, they treat you very informally in a way that you might find offensive; used showing disapproval. *The driver of that taxi-cab seemed to me familiar to the point of impertinence... John's 'crime' was being too familiar with the manager and calling him Gouldy.* ♦ **familiarity** *She needed to control her surprise at the easy familiarity with which her host greeted the head waiter.* ♦ **familiarly** *'Gerald, isn't it?' I began familiarly.* ADJ-GRADED PRAGMATICS; N-UNCOUNT; ADV-GRADED

familiarity /fəmɪliærɪti/ **Familiarity** is used especially in the expression **familiarity breeds contempt** to say that if you know a person or situation very well, you can easily lose respect for that person or become careless in that situation. *Familiarity with evil breeds not contempt but acceptance.* • See also **familiar**. ◆◇◇◇◇ PHRASE: V inflects

familiarize /fəmɪliəraɪz/ **familiarizes, familiarizing, familiarized;** also spelled **familiarise** in British English. If you **familiarize** yourself **with** something, or if someone **familiarizes** you **with** it, you learn about it and start to understand it. *I was expected to familiarise myself with the keyboard... The goal of the experiment was to familiarize the people with the new laws.* VERB V pron-refl *with* n V n *with* n

familiarly /fəmɪljəʳli/. If you say that something or someone is **familiarly known** as a particular thing or **familiarly called** a particular thing, you are giving the name that people use informally to refer to it. *...Ann Hamilton's father, familiarly known as 'Dink'.* PHRASE

family /fæmɪli/ **families** ◆◆◆◆◆
1 A **family** is a group of people who are related to each other, especially parents and their children. *There's room in there for a family of five... His family are completely behind him, whatever he decides... To him the family is the core of society... Does he have any family?* N-COUNT-COLL
2 When people talk about a **family**, they sometimes mean children. *They decided to start a family. ...couples with large families.* N-COUNT-COLL
3 When people talk about their **family**, they sometimes mean their ancestors. *Her family came to Los Angeles at the turn of the century. ...homes where their families had lived for generations. ...the history of mental illness in the family.* N-COUNT-COLL
4 You can use **family** to describe things that belong to a particular family. *He returned to the family home... I was working in the family business.* ADJ: ADJ n
5 You can use **family** to describe things that are designed to be used or enjoyed by both parents and children. *It had been designed as a family house... A wedding is a family event.* ADJ: ADJ n
6 A **family** of animals or plants is a group of related species. *...foods in the cabbage family, such as Brussels sprouts.* N-COUNT: with supp

family doctor, family doctors. A **family doctor** is a doctor who does not specialize in any particular area of medicine, but who has a medical practice in which he or she treats all types of illness. *Only your family doctor can refer you to a surgeon.* ◆◇◇◇◇ N-COUNT: oft poss N =GP

family man, family men
1 A **family man** is a man who is very fond of his wife and children and likes to spend a lot of time with them. *I'm very much a family man and need to be close to those I love.* N-COUNT
2 A **family man** is a man who has a wife and children. *I am a family man with a mortgage.* N-COUNT

family name, family names. Your **family name** is your surname. N-COUNT

family planning. **Family planning** is the practice of using contraception to control the number of children you have. *...a family planning clinic.* ◆◇◇◇◇ N-UNCOUNT: oft N n

family tree, family trees. A **family tree** is a chart that shows all the people in a family over many generations and their relationship to one another. N-COUNT

famine /fæmɪn/ **famines.** **Famine** is a serious shortage of food in a country, which may cause many deaths. *Thousands of refugees are trapped* ◆◆◇◇◇ N-VAR *by war, drought and famine... The civil war is obstructing distribution of famine relief by aid agencies.*

famished /fæmɪʃt/. If you are **famished**, you are very hungry; an informal word. *Isn't dinner ready? I'm famished.* ADJ: usu v-link ADJ =starving

famous /feɪməs/. Someone or something that is **famous** is very well known. *New Orleans is famous for its cuisine. ...England's most famous landscape artist, John Constable.* ◆◆◆◆◇ ADJ-GRADED: oft ADJ *for* n

famously /feɪməsli/ ◆◇◇◇◇

1 You use **famously** to refer to a fact that is well known, usually because it is remarkable or extreme. *Authors are famously ignorant about the realities of publishing... As Wren's epitaph famously declares, the cathedral itself is his monument.* ADV: usu ADV adj, also ADV with v

2 If you get on, or get along, **famously** with someone, you are very friendly with each other and enjoy meeting and being together; an old-fashioned, informal use. *I got on famously with Leary from the first time we met.* ADV: ADV after v

fan /fæn/ **fans, fanning, fanned** ◆◆◆◆◇

1 If you are a **fan** of someone or something, especially a famous person or a sport, you like them very much and are very interested in them. *If you're a Billy Crystal fan, you'll love this movie... As a boy he was a Manchester United fan... I am a great fan of rave music.* N-COUNT: usu n N, N *of* n

2 A **fan** is a flat object that you hold in your hand and wave in order to move the air and make yourself feel cooler. N-COUNT

3 If you **fan** yourself or your face when you are hot, you wave a fan or other flat object in order to make yourself feel cooler. *She would have to wait in the truck, fanning herself with a piece of cardboard... Mo kept bringing me out refreshments and fanning me as it was that hot.* VERB V pron-refl V n

4 A **fan** is a piece of electrical or mechanical equipment with revolving blades which keeps a room or machine cool or which gets rid of unpleasant smells. *He cools himself in front of an electric fan. ...an extractor fan.* N-COUNT: oft supp N

5 You can describe anything that has the shape of a wide 'V' with a semicircle above it as a **fan**. *...its fan of tail feathers. ...a conservatory with an ornate fan-shaped roof.* N-COUNT

6 If you **fan** a fire, you wave something flat next to it in order to make it burn more strongly. If a wind or draught **fans** a fire, it blows on it and makes it burn more strongly. *Kneeling in front of the open hearth, old Maria was fanning the smoldering fire... During the afternoon burning period hot winds fan the flames.* VERB V n

7 If someone **fans** an emotion such as fear, hatred, or passion, they deliberately do things to make people feel the emotion more strongly. *He said students were fanning social unrest with their violent protests. ...economic problems which often fan hatred.* VERB =fuel V n

8 ● to **fan the flames**: see **flame**. ● **the shit hit the fan**: see **shit**.

fan out PHRASAL VERB

1 If a group of people or things **fan out**, they move forwards away from a particular point in different directions. *The main body of British, American, and French troops had fanned out to the west... We fanned out from the farmhouse in twos and threes.* =spread out VP

2 If something **fans out** or if you **fan** it **out**, it spreads out or opens out into a flat, semicircular shape. *She suddenly raised her arms and spun, so the dress's full skirt fanned out in a bright circle... Korontzis picked up his hand slowly and fanned out the cards one by one... She lay on her back, her black hair fanned out over the pillow.* ERG VP V P n (not pron) V-ed P Also V n P

fanatic /fənætɪk/ **fanatics** ◆◇◇◇◇

1 If you describe someone as a **fanatic**, you disapprove of them because you consider their behaviour or opinions to be very extreme, for example in the way they support particular religious or political ideas. *I am not a religious fanatic but I am a Christian.* N-COUNT PRAGMATICS =extremist

2 If you say that someone is a **fanatic**, you mean that they are very enthusiastic about a particular activity, sport, or way of life; used in informal English. *Both Rod and Phil are football fanatics.* N-COUNT: usu n N =enthusiast

3 **Fanatic** means the same as **fanatical**. ADJ-GRADED

fanatical /fənætɪkəl/. If you describe someone as **fanatical**, you disapprove of them because you consider their behaviour or opinions to be very extreme. *As a boy he was a fanatical patriot.* ◆◇◇◇◇ ADJ-GRADED PRAGMATICS

♦ **fanatically** *He's fanatically hostile to trade unions.* ADV-GRADED: ADV adj, ADV with v

fanaticism /fənætɪsɪzəm/. **Fanaticism** is fanatical behaviour or the quality of being fanatical; used showing disapproval. *...a protest against intolerance and religious fanaticism.* N-UNCOUNT PRAGMATICS =extremism

fan belt, fan belts. In a car engine, the **fan belt** is the belt that drives the fan which keeps the engine cool. N-COUNT

fancier /fænsiəʳ/ **fanciers.** An animal or plant **fancier** is a person who breeds animals or plants of a particular type or who is very interested in them. *...pigeon fanciers.* ● See also **fancy**. ◆◇◇◇◇ N-COUNT: supp N

fanciful /fænsɪfʊl/ ◆◇◇◇◇

1 If you describe an idea as **fanciful**, you disapprove of it because you think it comes from someone's imagination, and is therefore unrealistic or unlikely to be true. *...fanciful ideas about Martian life... Designing silicon chips to mimic human organs sounds fanciful.* ADJ-GRADED PRAGMATICS

2 If you describe the appearance of something as **fanciful**, you mean that it is unusual and elaborate rather than plain and simple. *The economic gloom of the early 1980s was relieved by fanciful architecture.* ADJ-GRADED

fan club, fan clubs ◆◇◇◇◇

1 A **fan club** is an organized group of people who all admire the same person or thing, for example a pop singer or pop group. Members of the fan club receive information and can take part in activities such as trips to concerts. N-COUNT

2 If you say that you are a member of someone's **fan club**, you mean that you like them a lot or approve of them strongly. *He has charmed most of them into membership of his fan club.* N-SING: usu poss N

fancy 1 wanting, liking, or thinking

fancy /fænsi/ **fancies, fancying, fancied** ◆◆◆◇◇

1 If you **fancy** something, you want to have it or to do it; used mainly in informal British English. *What do you fancy doing, anyway?... Do you fancy going to see a movie sometime?... I just fancied a drink.* VERB V -ing V n

2 A **fancy** is a liking or desire for someone or something, especially one that does not last long. *She did not suspect that his interest was just a passing fancy.* N-COUNT: usu with supp =whim

3 If you **fancy** someone, you feel attracted to them, especially in a sexual way; an informal use. *The boys would tease you to death if they didn't fancy you... I think he thinks I fancy him or something.* VERB V n

4 If you **fancy** yourself as a particular kind of person or doing a particular thing, you like the idea of being that kind of person or doing that thing. *So you fancy yourself as the boss someday?... I didn't fancy myself wearing a kilt.* VERB V pron-refl *as* n V pron-refl -ing

5 If you say that someone **fancies** themselves as a particular kind of person, you mean that they think, often wrongly, that they have the good qualities which that kind of person has. *She fancies herself a bohemian... She knew Felix fancied himself as a connoisseur. ...a flighty young woman who really fancies herself.* VERB V pron-refl n V pron-refl *as* n V pron-refl

6 If you say that you **fancy** a particular competitor or team in a competition, you think they will win; used in British English. *You have to fancy Bath because they are the most consistent team in England... I fancy England and Yugoslavia to win through.* VERB V n V n to-inf

7 If you **fancy** that something is the case, you think or suppose that it is so. *When Ferris looked up he fancied that he saw a shadow pass close to the window... She fancied he was trying to hide a smile.* VERB =imagine V that

8 A **fancy** is an idea that is unlikely, untrue, or imaginary; a literary use. *His last book is a bold, at times surrealistic mixture of fact and fancy. ...a* N-VAR =fantasy

childhood fancy. ...whims and fancies. • **flight of fancy**: see **flight**.

9 You say **'fancy'** or **'fancy that'** when you want to express surprise or disapproval. *Fancy coming to a funeral in brown boots!... 'Fancy that!' smiled Conti.*
EXCLAM PRAGMATICS

10 If you **take a fancy to** someone or something, you start liking them, usually for no understandable reason. *Sylvia took quite a fancy to him... The King took a fancy to ordering disguises and masks.*
PHRASES V inflects, PHR n/-ing

11 If something **takes** your **fancy** or **tickles** your **fancy**, you like it a lot when you see it or think of it. *She makes most of her own clothes, copying any fashion which takes her fancy.*
V inflects

fancy 2 elaborate or expensive

fancy /fænsi/ **fancier, fanciest** ◆◇◇◇◇

1 If you describe something as **fancy**, you mean that it is special, unusual, or elaborate, for example because it has a lot of decoration. *It was packaged in a fancy plastic case with attractive graphics. ...fancy jewellery.*
ADJ-GRADED: usu ADJ n

2 If you describe something as **fancy**, you mean that it is very expensive or of very high quality, and you often dislike it because of this; an informal use. *He owned a fancy house out on Lake Agaway... They sent me to a fancy private school.*
ADJ-GRADED: usu ADJ n PRAGMATICS

fancy dress. **Fancy dress** is clothing that you wear for a party at which everyone tries to look like a famous person or a person from a story, from history, or from a particular profession. *Guests were told to come in fancy dress... He turned up at the fancy dress party as a footballer.*
N-UNCOUNT: oft N n

fancy-free. • **footloose and fancy-free**: see **footloose**.

fandango /fændæŋgoʊ/ **fandangos.** A **fandango** is a Spanish dance in which two people dance very close together.
N-COUNT: oft *the* N

fanfare /fænfeəʳ/ **fanfares** ◆◇◇◇◇

1 A **fanfare** is a short, loud tune played on trumpets or other similar instruments to announce a special event. *The ceremony opened with a fanfare of trumpets.*
N-COUNT

2 If something happens with a **fanfare**, it happens or is announced with a lot of publicity. If something happens without a **fanfare**, it happens without a lot of fuss or publicity. Used mainly in journalism. *The company was privatised with a fanfare of publicity in 1986... The departure of the South Korean prime minister was marked with little fanfare.*
N-VAR: oft N *of* n

fang /fæŋ/ **fangs.** **Fangs** are the two long, sharp, upper teeth that some animals have. *The cobra sank its venomous fangs into his hand.*
◆◇◇◇◇ N-COUNT: usu pl

fanlight /fænlaɪt/ **fanlights.** A **fanlight** is a small window over a door or above another window.
N-COUNT

fanny /fæni/ **fannies**

1 In American English, someone's **fanny** is their bottom; an informal use which some people find offensive.
N-COUNT: usu poss N

2 In British English, a woman's **fanny** is her genitals; an informal use which some people find offensive.
N-COUNT: usu poss N

fantasia /fænteɪziə, AM -ʒə/ **fantasias.** A **fantasia** is a piece of music that is not written in a traditional or fixed form; a technical term in music.
N-COUNT: usu sing

fantasist /fæntəzɪst/ **fantasists.** A **fantasist** is someone who constantly tells lies about their life and achievements in order to make them sound more exciting than they really are. *Singleton was a fantasist who claimed to have a karate blackbelt.*
N-COUNT

fantasize /fæntəsaɪz/ **fantasizes, fantasizing, fantasized;** also spelled **fantasise** in British English. ◆◇◇◇◇

1 If you **fantasize** about an event or situation that you would like to happen, you give yourself pleasure by imagining that it is happening, although it is untrue or unlikely to happen. *I fantasised about writing music... Her husband died in 1967, although she fantasised that he was still alive.*
VERB V *about* n/-ing V that Also V -ing

2 If someone **fantasizes**, they try to excite themselves sexually by imagining a particular person or situation. *Research has shown that men are likely to fantasize far more frequently than women... I tried to fantasize about Christine: those wondering blue eyes, that coppery red hair of hers.*
VERB V V *about/over* n Also V n

fantastic /fæntæstɪk/. The form **fantastical** is also used for meaning 3. ◆◆◇◇◇

1 If you say that something is **fantastic**, you are emphasizing that you think it is very good or that you like it a lot; an informal use. *I have a fantastic social life... I thought she was fantastic.*
ADJ-GRADED PRAGMATICS =great

2 A **fantastic** amount or quantity is an extremely large one; an informal use. *...fantastic amounts of money.* ♦ **fantastically** /fæntæstɪkli/ *...a fantastically expensive restaurant.*
ADJ: ADJ n ADV: ADV adj/adv

3 You describe something as **fantastic** or **fantastical** when it seems strange and wonderful or unlikely. *Unlikely and fantastic legends grew up around a great many figures, both real and fictitious... The book has many fantastical aspects.*
ADJ-GRADED

fantasy /fæntəzi/ **fantasies;** also spelled **phantasy.** ◆◆◆◇◇

1 A **fantasy** is a pleasant situation or event that you think about and that you want to happen, especially one that is unlikely to happen. *...fantasies of romance and true love.*
N-COUNT =dream

2 You can refer to a story or situation that someone creates from their imagination and that is not based on reality as **fantasy**. *The film is more of an ironic fantasy than a horror story.*
N-VAR

3 **Fantasy** is the activity of imagining things. *...a world of imagination, passion, fantasy, reflection.*
N-UNCOUNT

fanzine /fænziːn/ **fanzines.** A **fanzine** is a magazine for people who are fans of, for example, a particular pop group or football team. Fanzines are written by people who are fans themselves, rather than by professional journalists.
◆◇◇◇◇ N-COUNT

far /fɑːʳ/ **farther** or **further, farthest** or **furthest.** ◆◆◆◆◆

Far has two comparatives, **farther** and **further**, and two superlatives, **farthest** and **furthest**. **Farther** and **farthest** are used mainly in sense 1, and are dealt with here. **Further** and **furthest** are dealt with in separate entries.

1 If one place, thing, or person is **far** away from another, there is a great distance between them. *I know a nice little Italian restaurant not far from here... They came from as far away as Florida... Both of my sisters moved even farther away from home... They lay in the cliff top grass with the sea stretching out far below... Is it far?*
ADV-GRADED: ADV after v, v-link ADV, usu ADV prep/adv ≠near

2 If you ask how **far** a place is, you are asking what distance it is from you or from another place. If you ask how **far** someone went, you are asking what distance they travelled, or what place they reached. *How far is Pawtucket from Providence?... How far is it to Malcy?... How far can you throw?... You can only judge how high something is when you know how far away it is... She followed the tracks as far as the road.*
ADV-GRADED: *how* ADV, *as/so* ADV *as*, ADV-compar *than*

3 When there are two things of the same kind in a place, the **far** one is the one that is a greater distance from you. *He had wandered to the far end of the room... A narrow steep path leads down into a valley and up the far side.*
ADJ: ADJ n ≠near

4 You can use **far** to refer to the part of an area or object that is the greatest distance from the centre in a particular direction. For example, the **far** north of a country is the part of it that is the greatest distance to the north. *I've spent a lot of time walking around Britain from the far north of Scotland down to Cornwall... I wrote the date at the far left of the blackboard.*
ADJ: ADJ n

5 A time or event that is **far** away in the future or the past is a long time from the present or from a particular point in time. *...hidden conflicts whose roots lie far back in time... I can't see any farther than the next six months... The first day of term, which seemed so far away at the start of the summer holidays, is looming.*
ADV-GRADED: ADV after v, v-link ADV, usu ADV adv/prep

6 You can use **far** to talk about the extent or degree to which something happens or is true. *How far did the film tell the truth about Barnes Wallis? The*
ADV-GRADED: ADV with v, usu *how* ADV =to what extent

answer is: not very far at all... It is not clear how far the rebels are acting under Mr Guseinov's orders.

7 You can talk about how **far** someone or something gets to describe the progress that they make. *Discussions never progressed very far... Think of how far we have come in a little time... I don't think Mr Cavanagh would get far with that trick.* ADV-GRADED: ADV with v, oft *how* ADV

8 You can talk about how **far** a person or action goes to describe the degree to which someone's behaviour or actions are extreme. *It's still not clear how far the Russian parliament will go to implement its own plans... Competition can be healthy, but if it is pushed too far it can result in bullying... This time he's gone too far.* ADV-GRADED: ADV with v

9 You can use **far** in expressions like **'I wouldn't go that far'** and **'I would go so far'** to indicate to what extent you agree with something. *'Does it sound like music?'—'I wouldn't go that far.'... I would go so far as to say it's positively neurotic.* ADV-GRADED: ADV after v PRAGMATICS

10 You can use **far** to mean 'very much' when you are comparing two things and emphasizing the difference between them. For example, you can say that something is **far better** or **far worse** than something else to indicate that it is very much better or worse. You can also say that something is, for example, **far too big** to indicate that it is very much too big. *Women who eat plenty of fresh vegetables are far less likely to suffer anxiety or depression... Clinton really does understand that far better than George Bush does... These trials are simply taking far too long... It now has debts reported to be far in excess of one thousand million pounds.* ADV: usu ADV compar, ADV *too* adj/adv, also ADV adv/prep PRAGMATICS

11 You can describe people with extreme left-wing or right-wing political views as the **far** left or the **far** right. *The far right is now a greater threat than the extreme left... Anti-racist campaigners are urging the Government to ban all far-Right groups.* ADJ: ADJ n =extreme

12 You can use **far** in expressions like **'as far as I know'** and **'so far as I remember'** to indicate that you are not absolutely sure of the statement you are about to make or have just made, and you may be wrong. *It only lasted a couple of years, as far as I know... So far as I am aware, no proper investigation has ever been carried out into the subject.* ADV-GRADED: *as/so* ADV *as* PRAGMATICS

13 You use the expression **far and away** when you are comparing something or someone with others of the same kind, in order to emphasize how great the difference is between them. For example, you can say that something is **far and away the best** to indicate that it is definitely the best. *Rangers are far and away the best team in Scotland.* PHRASES PHR *the* adj-superl PRAGMATICS =easily

14 You use the expression **by far** when you are comparing something or someone with others of the same kind, in order to emphasize how great the difference is between them. For example, you can say that something is **by far the best** or **the best by far** to indicate that it is definitely the best. *By far the most important issue for them is unemployment... It was better by far to be clear-headed.* PHR with compar/superl PRAGMATICS

15 If you say that something is **far from** a particular thing or **far from** being the case, you are emphasizing that it is not that particular thing or not at all the case, especially when people expect or assume that it is. *It was obvious that much of what they recorded was far from the truth... Far from being relaxed, we both felt so uncomfortable we hardly spoke... It is still far from clear exactly what the Thais intend to do.* PHR n/-ing/adj, oft v-link PHR PRAGMATICS

16 You can use the expression **'far from it'** to emphasize a negative statement that you have just made. *Being dyslexic does not mean that one is unintelligent. Far from it.* PRAGMATICS =on the contrary

17 You say **far be it from me** to disagree, or **far be it from me** to criticize, when you are disagreeing or criticizing and you want to appear less hostile. *Far be it from me to criticise, but shouldn't their mother take a share of the blame?* PHR to-inf PRAGMATICS

18 If you say that something is good **as far as it goes** or true **so far as it goes**, you mean that it is good or true only to a limited extent. *His plan for tax relief is fine as far as it goes but will not be sufficient to get the economy moving again.* PHR with cl

19 If you say that someone **will go far**, you mean that they will be very successful in their career. *I was very impressed with the talent of Michael Ball. He will go far.*

20 Someone or something that is **far gone** is in such a bad state or condition that not much can be done to help or improve them. *In his last few days the pain seemed to have stopped, but by then he was so far gone that it was no longer any comfort... Many of the properties are in a desperate state but none is too far gone to save.* v-link PHR

21 Someone or something that is **not far wrong**, **not far out**, or **not far off** is almost correct or almost accurate. *I hadn't been far wrong in my estimate... Robertson is not far off her target.* v-link PHR, oft PHR *in* n

22 You can use the expression **'as far as I can see'** when you are about to state your opinion of a situation, or have just stated it, to indicate that it is your personal opinion. *That's the problem as far as I can see... As far as I can see there are only two reasons for such an action.* PHR with cl PRAGMATICS

23 If you say that something only goes **so far** or can only go **so far**, you mean that its extent, effect, or influence is limited. *Their loyalty only went so far... The church can only go so far in secular matters.* PHR after v

24 If you tell or ask someone what has happened **so far**, you are telling or asking them what has happened up until the present point in a situation or story, and often implying that something different might happen later. *It's been quiet so far... So far, they have met with no success... Which one have you enjoyed most so far?* PHR with cl

25 You can say **so far so good** to express satisfaction with the way that a situation or activity is progressing, developing, or happening.

26 **Thus far** means up until the present point in a situation or story; a formal expression. *Thus far, the two prime ministers have achieved no concrete results.* PHR with cl

27 If people come from **far and wide**, they come from a large number of places, some of them far away. If things spread **far and wide**, they spread over a very large area or distance. Used mainly in written English. *Volunteers came from far and wide... His fame spread far and wide.* *from* PHR, PHR after v

28 If you say that someone **won't go far wrong** or **can't go far wrong** with a particular thing or course of action, you mean that it is likely to be successful or satisfactory. *If you remember these three golden rules you won't go far wrong.*

29 • **as far as** I am **concerned**: see **concern**. • **a far cry from**: see **cry**. • **in so far as**: see **insofar as**. • **near and far**: see **near**.

faraway /fɑːrəweɪ/; also spelled **far-away**. ◆◇◇◇◇

1 A **faraway** place is a long distance from you or from a particular place. *They have just returned from faraway places with wonderful stories to tell. ...photographs of a far away country.* ADJ-GRADED: ADJ n =distant

2 If you describe someone or their thoughts as **faraway**, you mean that they are thinking about something that is very different from the situation around them. *She smiled with a faraway look in her eyes.* ADJ-GRADED: ADJ n =dreamy

farce /fɑːʳs/ **farces** ◆◇◇◇◇

1 A **farce** is a humorous play in which the characters become involved in complicated and unlikely situations. N-COUNT

2 **Farce** is the style of acting and writing that is typical of farces. *The plot often borders on farce.* N-UNCOUNT

3 If you describe a situation or event as a **farce**, you mean that it is so disorganized or ridiculous that you cannot take it seriously. *The elections have been reduced to a farce.* N-SING: also no det PRAGMATICS =shambles

farcical /fɑːʳsɪkəl/. If you describe a situation or event as **farcical**, you mean that it is so silly or extreme that you are unable to take it seriously. *...a farcical nine months' jail sentence imposed yesterday on a killer.* ADJ-GRADED PRAGMATICS

fare /feəʳ/ **fares, faring, fared** 

1 A **fare** is the money that you pay for a journey that you make, for example, in a bus, train, or taxi. *He could barely afford the railway fare. ...taxi fares.* N-COUNT

2 The **fare** at a restaurant or cafe is the type of food that is served there; used mainly in written English. *The fare has much improved since Hugh has taken charge of the kitchen. ...traditional Portuguese fare in a traditional setting.* N-UNCOUNT

3 If you say that someone or something **fares** well or badly, you are referring to the degree of success they achieve in a particular situation or activity. *It is unlikely that the marine industry will fare any better in September... Some later expeditions fared better, though they were no better equipped.* VERB =do V adv

Far East. The **Far East** is used to refer to all the countries of Eastern Asia, including China, Japan, North and South Korea, and Indochina. ◆◇◇◇◇ N-PROPER: the N

farewell /feəʳwel/ **farewells. Farewell** means goodbye; an old-fashioned or literary word. ▶ Also a noun. *They said their farewells at the cafe.* ◆◆◇◇◇ CONVENTION N-COUNT

far-fetched. If you describe a story or idea as **far-fetched**, you are criticizing it because you think it is unlikely to be true or practical. *The storyline was too far-fetched and none of the actors was particularly good.* ADJ-GRADED PRAGMATICS =unrealistic

far-flung, farther-flung, farthest-flung

1 **Far-flung** places are a very long distance away from where you are or from important places. *Ferries are a lifeline to the far-flung corners of Scotland. ...one of the farthest-flung outposts of the old Roman Empire.* ADJ-GRADED: ADJ n =remote

2 If you describe something such as organization or system as **far-flung**, you mean that it extends over a very large area. *...a far-flung network of conspirators.* ADJ: ADJ n

farm /fɑːʳm/ **farms, farming, farmed** ◆◆◆◆◇

1 A **farm** is an area of land, together with the buildings on it, that is used for growing crops or raising animals, usually in order to sell them. *Farms in France are much smaller than those in the United States or even Britain.* N-COUNT

2 If you **farm** an area of land, you grow crops or keep animals on it. *They farmed some of the best land in Scotland... He has lived and farmed in the area for 46 years.* VERB V n V

3 A mink **farm** or a fish **farm**, for example, is a place where a particular kind of animal or fish is bred and kept in large quantities in order to be sold. *...trout fresh from a local trout farm.* N-COUNT: n N

farm out. If you say that someone **farms out** work, especially work that you would normally expect them to do themselves, you mean that they give it to other people to do. *The move is consistent with a trend for corporate legal staffs to do more work in-house, instead of farming it out to law firms... We can take advantage of new technology more quickly by farming out computer operations... They've tended to farm out work to consultants.* PHRASAL VERB V n P *to* n V P n (not pron) V P n (not pron) *to* n Also V n P

farmer /fɑːʳməʳ/ **farmers.** A **farmer** is a person who owns or manages a farm. ◆◆◆◆◇ N-COUNT

farmhand /fɑːʳmhænd/ **farmhands;** also spelled **farm hand**. A **farmhand** is a person who is employed to work on a farm. N-COUNT

farmhouse /fɑːʳmhaus/ **farmhouses;** also spelled **farm house**. A **farmhouse** is the main house on a farm, usually where the farmer lives. ◆◇◇◇◇ N-COUNT

farming /fɑːʳmɪŋ/. **Farming** is the activity of growing crops or keeping animals on a farm. ◆◆◇◇◇ N-UNCOUNT

farmland /fɑːʳmlænd/ **farmlands. Farmland** is land which is farmed, or which is suitable for farming. ◆◇◇◇◇ N-UNCOUNT: also N in pl

farmyard /fɑːʳmjɑːʳd/ **farmyards.** On a farm, the **farmyard** is an area of land near the farmhouse which is enclosed by walls or buildings. N-COUNT

far off, further off, furthest off ◆◇◇◇◇

1 If you describe a moment in time as **far off**, you mean that it is a long time from the present, either in the past or the future. *In those far off days it never entered anyone's mind that she could be Prime Minister... European political and monetary union is further off than ever.* ADJ-GRADED =distant

2 If you describe something as **far off**, you mean that it is a long distance from you or from a particular place. *...stars in far-off galaxies.* ▶ Also an adverb. *The band was playing far off in their blue and yellow uniforms.* ADJ-GRADED ADV-GRADED: ADV after v

far out; also spelled **far-out**. If you describe something as **far out**, you mean that it is very strange or extreme; an informal use. *Fantasies cannot harm you, no matter how bizarre or far out they are.* ◆◇◇◇◇ ADJ-GRADED: usu v-link ADJ

farrago /fərɑːgou/ **farragoes** or **farragos.** If you describe something as a **farrago**, you are critical of it because you think it is a confused mixture of different types of things. *Professor Brian Cox has described the report as 'a farrago of wild emotional outbursts, confused arguments and extravagant rhetoric'.* N-COUNT: oft N *of* n PRAGMATICS =hotchpotch

far-reaching. If you describe actions, events, or changes as **far-reaching**, you mean that they have a very great influence and affect a great number of things. *The economy is in danger of collapse unless far-reaching reforms are implemented.* ◆◇◇◇◇ ADJ-GRADED =sweeping

farrier /færiəʳ/ **farriers.** A **farrier** is a person who fits horseshoes onto horses. N-COUNT

far-sighted

1 If you describe someone as **far-sighted**, you admire them because they understand what is likely to happen in the future, and consequently make wise decisions and plans. *Haven't far-sighted economists been telling us for some time now that in the future we will work less, not more?... The White House has welcomed the Chinese decision and described it as a far-sighted, significant step.* ADJ-GRADED PRAGMATICS

2 In American English, **far-sighted** people cannot see things clearly that are close to them, and therefore need to wear glasses. The usual British expression is **long-sighted.** ADJ-GRADED ≠near-sighted

fart /fɑːʳt/ **farts, farting, farted** ◆◇◇◇◇

1 If someone **farts**, air is forced out of their body through their anus; an informal use which some people find offensive. *He'd been farting all night.* ▶ Also a noun. *...a loud fart.* VERB V N-COUNT

2 If someone describes another person as an old **fart**, they are showing that they think the person is boring and that they do not respect the person; an offensive use. N-COUNT: usu adj N PRAGMATICS

farther /fɑːʳðəʳ/. **Farther** is a comparative form of **far.**

farthest /fɑːʳðɪst/. **Farthest** is a superlative form of **far.**

farthing /fɑːʳðɪŋ/ **farthings.** In Britain until 1961, a **farthing** was a coin that was worth a quarter of an old penny. N-COUNT

fascia /feɪʃə/ **fascias**

1 In British English, in a car, the **fascia** is the part surrounding the instruments and dials; a formal use. N-COUNT: usu sing

2 In British English, the **fascia** on a shop front is the flat surface above the shop window, on which the name of the shop is written. N-COUNT: usu sing

fascinate /fæsɪneɪt/ **fascinates, fascinating, fascinated.** If something **fascinates** you, it interests and delights you so much that your thoughts tend to concentrate on it. *Politics fascinated Franklin's father... She fascinated him, both on and off stage.* ◆◇◇◇◇ VERB V n

fascinated /fæsɪneɪtɪd/. If you are **fascinated** by something, you find it very interesting and attractive, and your thoughts tend to concentrate on it. *I sat on the stairs and watched, fascinated... A new generation of scientists became fascinated by dinosaurs.* ◆◇◇◇◇ ADJ-GRADED: usu v-link ADJ, oft ADJ *by/with* n

fascinating /fæsɪneɪtɪŋ/. If you describe something as **fascinating**, you find it very interesting and attractive, and your thoughts tend to concentrate on it. *Madagascar is the most fascinating place I have ever been to... Her perceptions and intuitions about human nature were fascinating.* ◆◆◇◇◇ ADJ-GRADED

fascination /fæsɪneɪʃᵊn/ **fascinations** ◆◇◇◇◇

1 **Fascination** is the state of being greatly interested in or delighted by something. *I've had a lifelong fascination with the sea and with small boats.* N-UNCOUNT: oft N *with/of/for* n

2 A **fascination** is something that fascinates N-COUNT

people. *...a series focusing on the fascinations of the British Museum.*

fascism /fæʃɪzəm/. **Fascism** is a set of right-wing political beliefs that includes strong control of society and the economy by the state, a powerful role for the armed forces, and the prevention of political opposition. ◆◆◇◇◇ N-UNCOUNT

fascist /fæʃɪst/ **fascists** ◆◆◇◇◇

1 You use **fascist** to describe organizations, ideas, or systems which follow the principles of fascism. *...an upsurge of support for extreme rightist, nationalist and fascist organisations. ...the threatening nature of fascist ideology.* ADJ: usu ADJ n ► A **fascist** is someone who has fascist views. N-COUNT

2 If you refer to someone as a **fascist**, you are expressing disapproval of the fact that they have extreme views on something, and do not tolerate alternative views. *...the so-called health fascists who would meddle in their lives and regulate their calorie intake.* N-COUNT PRAGMATICS

fashion /fæʃᵊn/ **fashions, fashioning, fashioned** ◆◆◆◆◇

1 **Fashion** is the area of activity that involves styles of clothing and appearance. *There are 20 full-colour pages of fashion for men... The fashion world does not mind what the real world thinks.* N-UNCOUNT

2 A **fashion** is a style of clothing or a way of behaving that is popular at a particular time. *In the early seventies I wore false eyelashes, as was the fashion... Queen Mary started the fashion for blue and white china in England... He stayed at the top through all changes and fashions in pop music.* N-COUNT: oft *the* N

3 If you do something in a particular **fashion** or after a particular **fashion**, you do it in that way. *There is another drug called DHE that works in a similar fashion... It is happening in this fashion because of the obstinacy of one woman.* ● See also **parrot-fashion**. N-SING: with supp =manner

4 If you **fashion** an object or a work of art, you make it; a formal use. *Stone Age settlers fashioned necklaces from sheeps' teeth.* VERB V n

5 See also **old-fashioned**.

6 If you say that something was done **after a fashion**, you mean that it was done, but not very well. *She was educated – after a fashion – by a governess at home... He knew the way, after a fashion.* PHRASES

7 If something is **in fashion**, it is popular and approved of at a particular time. If it is **out of fashion**, it is not popular or approved of. *That sort of house is back in fashion... Marriage seems to be going out of fashion.*

fashionable /fæʃənəbᵊl/. Something or someone that is **fashionable** is popular or approved of at a particular time. *It became fashionable to eat certain kinds of fish... Chelsea Harbour is renowned for its fashionable restaurants.* ◆◆◇◇◇ ADJ-GRADED ♦ **fashionably** *...women who are perfectly made up and fashionably dressed.* ADV-GRADED: usu ADV adj/-ed

fast /fɑːst, fæst/ **faster, fastest; fasts, fasting, fasted** ◆◆◆◆◇

1 **Fast** means happening, moving, or doing something at great speed. You also use **fast** in questions or statements about speed. *...fast cars with flashing lights and sirens... Brindley was known as a very, very fast driver... The party aims to attract votes from the business and professional communities, which want a faster pace of political reform... The only question is how fast the process will be.* ADJ-GRADED =quick ≠slow ► Also an adverb. *They work terrifically fast... It would be nice to go faster and break the world record... He thinks they're not adapting fast enough... Barnes also knows that he is fast running out of time... How fast were you driving?... How fast would the disease develop?* ADV-GRADED: ADV with v =quickly ≠slowly

2 You use **fast** to say that something happens without any delay. *When you've got a crisis like this you need professional help – fast!... We'd appreciate your leaving as fast as possible.* ADV-GRADED: ADV after v =soon, swiftly ► Also an adjective. *That would be an astonishingly fast action on the part of the Congress.* ADJ-GRADED: ADJ n =swift

3 If a watch or clock is **fast**, it is showing a time that is later than the real time. *That clock's an hour fast.* ADJ-GRADED: v-link ADJ

4 The **fast** lane on a motorway or other road is intended for the vehicles which are travelling at the greatest speeds. *A man was killed as he walked down the fast lane of a motorway yesterday.* ADJ: ADJ n ≠slow

5 If you hold something **fast**, you hold it tightly and firmly. If something is stuck **fast**, it is stuck very firmly and cannot move. *She climbed the staircase cautiously, holding fast to the rail... The tanker is stuck fast on the rocks.* ADV-GRADED: ADV after v =firmly

6 If you hold **fast** to a principle or idea, or if you stand **fast**, you do not change your mind about it, even though people are trying to persuade you to. *We can only try to hold fast to the age-old values of honesty, decency and concern for others... He told supporters to stand fast over the next few vital days.* ADV-GRADED: ADV after v =firmly

7 If colours or dyes are **fast**, they do not come out of the fabrics they are used on when they get wet. *The fabric was ironed to make the colours fast.* ADJ-GRADED: usu v-link ADJ

8 A **fast** way of life is one which involves a lot of enjoyable and expensive or dangerous activities. *Life in Detroit no longer satisfied him; he wanted the fast life of California.* ADJ: ADJ n =exciting ≠dull

9 If you **fast**, you eat no food for a period of time, usually for either religious or medical reasons, or as a protest. *I fasted for a day and half and asked God to help me.* VERB ≠gorge V ► Also a noun. *The fast is broken at sunset, traditionally with dates and water.* N-COUNT ♦ **fasting** *...the Muslim holy month of fasting and prayer.* N-UNCOUNT ≠feasting

10 Someone who is **fast asleep** is completely asleep. *When he went upstairs five minutes later, she was fast asleep.* PHRASES v-link PHR, PHR after v

11 If you say that someone **is playing fast and loose**, you are expressing disapproval of them for behaving in a deceitful, immoral, or irresponsible way. *There have been people who have played fast and loose with the rules.* V inflects PRAGMATICS

12 If you say that someone **has pulled a fast one** on you, you mean that they have cheated or tricked you; an informal expression. *No doubt someone had pulled a fast one on her over a procedural matter.* V inflects

13 ● **make a fast buck**: see **buck**.

fast-breeder reactor, fast-breeder reactors. A **fast-breeder reactor** or a **fast-breeder** is a kind of nuclear reactor that produces more plutonium than it uses. N-COUNT

fasten /fɑːsᵊn, fæs-/ **fastens, fastening, fastened** ◆◇◇◇◇

1 When you **fasten** something, you do it up or close it by means of buttons or a strap, buckle, or other device. If something **fastens** with buttons, straps, or buckles, you do it up or close it by means of buttons, straps, or buckles. *She got quickly into her Mini and fastened the seat-belt... Her long fair hair was fastened at the nape of her neck by an elastic band. ...the dress, which fastens with a long back zip.* V-ERG =do up ≠unfasten V n *be* V-ed prep V prep Also V n prep

2 If you **fasten** one thing to another, you attach the first thing to the second, for example with a piece of string or tape. *There were no instructions on how to fasten the carrying strap to the box... Mamma fastened the picture on the wall.* VERB =attach V n prep/adv

3 If someone or something **fastens** your attention on a particular thing or your attention **fastens** on it, you start to concentrate on it, often to the exclusion of everything else. *More and more her memory and all her thoughts fastened on one event... The discovery has fastened public attention on the possibilities of DNA analysis for resolving mysteries.* V-ERG =focus V *on* n V n *on* n

4 If someone or something **fastens** on a particular thing, they start to concentrate on it. *The international press, which fastened on Ethiopian starvation in 1984 and 1985, said almost nothing about the Sudan... It's a gross over-simplification to fasten on to the red deer as a threat to the environment.* VERB V *on/onto* n

5 If someone **fastens** on you, they keep following, talking to, or staying with you, when you want them to go away. *He's fastening on that poor girl like a leech.* VERB =latch onto V *on/onto* n

6 See also **fastening**.

fastener /fɑːsənəʳ, fæs-/ **fasteners.** A **fastener** is a device such as a button, zip, or small hook that fastens something, especially clothing. N-COUNT

fastening /fɑːsənɪŋ, fæs-/ **fastenings.** A **fastening** is something such as a clasp, cord, or latch that you use to fasten something. *The sundress has a neat back zip fastening.* N-COUNT: oft n N

fast food. **Fast food** is hot food, such as hamburgers and chips, that you obtain from particular types of restaurant, and which is served quickly after you order it. *James works as assistant chef at a fast food restaurant... Most of the time we just ate snacks and fast food.* ◆◇◇◇◇ N-UNCOUNT: oft n N

fast forward, fast forwards, fast forwarding, fast forwarded; also spelled **fast-forward.**
1 If you put a video or cassette tape on **fast forward**, you make the tape go forwards. Compare **rewind.** *Before recording onto a new tape, wind it on fast forward, then rewind... I really tried with this film, but kept pushing the fast-forward button – I found it unwatchable.* N-UNCOUNT: oft *on* N
2 When you **fast forward** the tape in a video or tape recorder or when you **fast forward**, you make the tape go forwards. Compare **rewind.** *Just fast forward the video... He fast-forwarded the tape past the explosion... The urge to fast-forward is almost irresistible.* VERB V n V n prep/adv V Also V prep/adv

fastidious /fæstɪdiəs/ ◆◇◇◇◇
1 If you say that someone is **fastidious**, you mean that they pay great attention to detail because they like everything to be very neat, accurate, and orderly. *...her fastidious attention to historical detail... He was fastidious about his appearance.* ADJ-GRADED =meticulous
♦ **fastidiously** *He fastidiously copied every word of his notes on to clean paper.* ADV-GRADED
2 If you say that someone is **fastidious**, you mean that they are concerned about cleanliness to an extent that many people consider to be too fussy. *Be particularly fastidious about washing your hands before touching food.* ♦ **fastidiously** *Ernestine kept her daughters fastidiously clean.* ADJ-GRADED ADV-GRADED

fastness /fɑːstnəs, fæst-/ **fastnesses.** A **fastness** is a place, such as a fortress, which is considered safe because it is difficult to reach or easy to defend against attack; a literary word. *In his 80s, from the rural fastness of his farm, he preached the simple life.* N-COUNT: with supp

fast track; also spelled **fast-track.** The **fast track** to a particular goal, especially in politics or in your career, is the quickest route to achieving it. *Many Croats and Slovenes saw independence as the fast track to democracy... He was told that, at 28, he was too old for fast-track promotion.* ◆◇◇◇◇ N-SING: oft N *to* n, N n

fat /fæt/ **fatter, fattest; fats** ◆◆◆◆◇
1 If you say that a person or animal is **fat**, you mean that they have a lot of flesh on their body and that they weigh too much. You usually use the word **fat** when you think that this is a bad thing. *I could eat what I liked without getting fat... After five minutes, the fat woman in the seat in front of me was asleep.* ADJ-GRADED PRAGMATICS =overweight ≠thin
♦ **fatness** *No one knows whether a child's tendency towards fatness is inherited or due to the food he eats.* N-UNCOUNT
2 **Fat** is the extra flesh that animals and humans have under their skin, which is used to store energy and to help keep them warm. *Because you're not burning calories, everything you eat turns to fat.* N-UNCOUNT
3 **Fat** is a solid or liquid substance obtained from animals or vegetables, which is used in cooking. *When you use oil or fat for cooking, use as little as possible. ...vegetable fats, such as coconut oil and palm oil.* N-MASS
4 **Fat** is a substance contained in foods such as meat, cheese, and butter which forms an energy store in your body. *An easy way to cut the amount of fat in your diet is to avoid eating red meats... Most low-fat yogurts are about 40 calories per 100g.* N-MASS
5 A **fat** object, especially a book, is very thick or wide. *...'Europe in Figures', a fat book published on September 22nd... He took out his fat wallet and peeled off some notes.* ADJ-GRADED =thick ≠thin, slim
6 A **fat** profit or fee is a large one; an informal use. *They are set to make a big fat profit.* ADJ-GRADED: ADJ n
7 If you say that there is **fat chance** of something happening, you mean that you do not believe that it will happen; an informal expression used mainly in spoken English. *'Would your car be easy to steal?'—'Fat chance. I've got a device that shuts down the gas and ignition.'* PHRASES oft PHR *of* n
8 If you say that a person or organization **has grown fat** on something, you are criticising the fact that they have become very rich as a result of it. *Liverpool grew fat on the basis of the slave trade.* V inflects, oft PHR *on* n PRAGMATICS
9 If you say that something is **a fat lot of good** or **a fat lot of help**, you are saying rudely that it is no good or no help at all; an informal expression. *'I think we should go in and hammer them.'—'And a fat lot of good that would do us.'* PRAGMATICS

fatal /feɪtəl/ ◆◆◇◇◇
1 A **fatal** action has very undesirable effects. *It would clearly be fatal for Europe to quarrel seriously with America... He made the fatal mistake of compromising early.* ♦ **fatally** *Failure now could fatally damage his chances in the future.* ADJ-GRADED ADV-GRADED: ADV with v
2 A **fatal** accident or illness causes someone's death. *...the fatal stabbing of a police sergeant... A hospital spokesman said she had suffered a fatal heart attack.* ♦ **fatally** *The dead soldier is reported to have been fatally wounded in the chest.* ADJ ADV: usu ADV with v

fatalism /feɪtəlɪzəm/. **Fatalism** is a feeling that you cannot control events or prevent unpleasant things from happening, especially when this feeling stops you from acting decisively or making an effort. *There's a certain mood of fatalism now among the radicals.* N-UNCOUNT =resignation

fatalistic /feɪtəlɪstɪk/. If someone is **fatalistic** about something, especially an unpleasant event or situation, they feel that they cannot change or control it, and therefore that there is no purpose in trying. *People we spoke to today were really rather fatalistic about what's going to happen.* ADJ-GRADED: oft ADJ *about* n =resigned

fatality /fətælɪti/ **fatalities** ◆◇◇◇◇
1 A **fatality** is a death caused by an accident or by violence; a formal use. *Drunk driving fatalities in this country have declined more than 10 percent over the past 10 years.* N-COUNT
2 **Fatality** is the feeling or belief that human beings cannot influence or control events. *...with a feeling of fatality.* N-UNCOUNT

fat cat, fat cats. If you refer to a businessman or politician as a **fat cat**, you are indicating that you disapprove of the way they use their wealth and power. *...the fat cats who run the bank. ...fat-cat corporate types.* N-COUNT PRAGMATICS

fate /feɪt/ **fates** ◆◆◆◇◇
1 **Fate** is a power that some people believe controls and decides everything that happens, in a way that cannot be prevented or changed. You can also refer to **the fates.** *I see no use quarrelling with fate. ...the fickleness of fate... It was just one of those times when you wonder whether the fates conspire against you.* N-UNCOUNT: also N in pl
2 A person's or thing's **fate** is what happens to them. *The Russian Parliament will hold a special session later this month to decide his fate... He seems for a moment to be again holding the fate of the country in his hands... The Casino, where she had often danced, had suffered a similar fate. ...the terrible fate awaiting humanity.* N-COUNT: oft with poss =destiny
3 If something **seals** a person's or thing's **fate**, it makes it certain that they will fail or that something unpleasant will happen to them. *The call for a boycott could be enough to seal the fate of next week's general election... And yesterday the Zoo's fate was sealed, largely due to two months of ever-dwindling entrance figures.* • to **tempt fate**: see **tempt.** PHRASE: V inflects

fated /feɪtɪd/. If you say that someone is **fated** to do something, or that something is **fated**, especially something unpleasant, you mean that it seems to have been decided by fate before it happens, and nothing can be done to avoid or change it. *He was fated not to score. ...stories of* ◆◇◇◇◇ ADJ: oft ADJ to-inf =doomed *desperation, fated love, treachery and murder.* • See also **ill-fated**.

fateful /feɪtfʊl/. If an action, or a time when a particular event occurred, is described as **fateful**, it is considered to have an important, and often disastrous, effect on future events. *It was a fateful decision, one which was to break the Government.* ◆◇◇◇◇ ADJ-GRADED: usu ADJ n =momentous

father /fɑːðəʳ/ **fathers, fathering, fathered** ◆◆◆◆◆

1 Your **father** is the man who made your mother pregnant with you. You can also call someone your **father** if he brings you up as if he was this man. *His father was a painter... He would be a good father to my children. ...Mr Stoneman, a father of five.* N-FAMILY

2 When a man **fathers** a child, he makes a woman pregnant and their child is born. *She claims Mark fathered her child... He fathered at least three children by the wives of other men.* VERB V n, V n *by* n

3 The man who invented or started something is sometimes referred to as the **father of** that thing. *...Max Dupain, regarded as the father of modern photography. ...Mahatma Gandhi, the founding father of independent India.* N-COUNT: N *of* n

4 In some Christian churches, priests are addressed or referred to as **Father**. *I would like your advice on a matter of conscience, Father. ...Father William.* N-VOC; N-TITLE; N-COUNT

5 Christians often refer to God as **our Father** or address him as **Father**. *...Our Father in Heaven.* N-PROPER: *our* N; N-VOC

Father Christmas. **Father Christmas** is an imaginary old man with a long white beard and a red coat. Traditionally, young children in many countries are told that he brings their Christmas presents. N-PROPER =Santa Claus

father figure, father figures; also spelled **father-figure**. Someone who is a **father figure** is thought of as taking the place of a father and being the person you can turn to for advice, support, guidance, and help. *She believed her daughter needed a father-figure... He became a father figure to the whole company.* N-COUNT

fatherhood /fɑːðəʳhʊd/. **Fatherhood** is the state of being a father. *...the joys of fatherhood.* N-UNCOUNT

father-in-law, fathers-in-law. Someone's **father-in-law** is the father of their husband or wife. ◆◇◇◇◇ N-COUNT: usu poss N

fatherland /fɑːðəʳlænd/ **fatherlands.** If someone is very proud of the country where they or their ancestors were born, they sometimes refer to it as the **fatherland**. The word **fatherland** is particularly associated with Germany. *They were willing to serve the fatherland in its hour of need.* ◆◇◇◇◇ N-COUNT: usu sing

fatherless /fɑːðəʳləs/. You describe children as **fatherless** when their father has died or does not live with them. *...widows and fatherless children... They were left fatherless.* ADJ

fatherly /fɑːðəʳli/. **Fatherly** feelings or actions are like those of a kind father. *His voice filled with fatherly concern... He took my arm in a fatherly way.* ADJ-GRADED: usu ADJ n =paternal

Father's Day. **Father's Day** is the third Sunday in June, when children give cards and presents to their fathers to show that they love them. N-UNCOUNT

fathom /fæðəm/ **fathoms, fathomed** ◆◇◇◇◇

1 A **fathom** is a measurement of 1.8 metres or 6 feet, used when referring to the depth of water. *We sailed into the bay and dropped anchor in five fathoms of water.* N-COUNT: oft num N

2 If you cannot **fathom** something, you are unable to understand it, although you think carefully about it. *I really couldn't fathom what Steiner was talking about... Jeremy's passive attitude was hard to fathom.* ► **Fathom out** means the same as **fathom**. *We're trying to fathom out what's going on... I'm having difficulty using my video editing equipment and can't fathom out the various connections.* VB: no cont, oft with brd-neg; V wh; V n; PHRASAL VERB V P wh; V P n (not pron); Also V n P

fathomless /fæðəmləs/. Something that is **fathomless** cannot be measured or understood because it gives the impression of being very deep, obscure, or complicated. *...the fathomless space of the universe... The silence was fathomless and overwhelming.* ADJ

fatigue /fətiːg/ **fatigues** ◆◆◇◇◇

1 **Fatigue** is a feeling of extreme physical or mental tiredness. *She continued to have severe stomach cramps, aches, fatigue, and depression... Clarke says his team could have lasted another 15 days before fatigue would have begun to take a toll.* N-UNCOUNT =exhaustion

2 You can say that people are suffering from a particular kind of **fatigue** when they have been doing something for a long time and feel they can no longer continue to do it. *...compassion fatigue caused by endless TV and celebrity appeals. ...the result of four months of battle fatigue.* N-UNCOUNT: with supp, usu n N

3 **Fatigues** are clothes that soldiers wear when they are doing routine jobs or when they are on the battlefield. *He never expected to return home wearing US combat fatigues.* N-PLURAL

4 **Fatigue** in metal or wood is a weakness in it that is caused by repeated stress. Fatigue can cause the metal or wood to break. *The problem turned out to be metal fatigue in the fuselage.* N-UNCOUNT: usu n N

fatigued /fətiːgd/. If you are feeling **fatigued**, you are suffering from extreme physical or mental tiredness. *Winter weather can leave you feeling fatigued and tired.* ADJ-GRADED: usu v-link ADJ =exhausted

fatiguing /fətiːgɪŋ/. Something that is **fatiguing** makes you feel extremely physically or mentally tired. *Jet travel is undeniably fatiguing.* ADJ-GRADED: usu v-link ADJ =exhausting

fatten /fætᵊn/ **fattens, fattening, fattened**

1 If an animal **is fattened**, or if it **fattens**, it becomes fatter as a result of eating more. *The cattle are being fattened for slaughter... The creature continued to grow and fatten.* V-ERG *be* V-ed; V; Also V n

2 If you say that someone **is fattening** something such as a business or its profits, you mean that they are increasing the value of the business or its profits, in a way that you disapprove of. *They have kept the price of sugar artificially high and so fattened the company's profits.* ► **Fatten up** means the same as **fatten**. *The Government is making the taxpayer pay to fatten up a public sector business for private sale.* VERB PRAGMATICS; V n; PHRASAL VERB V P n (not pron); Also V n P

fatten up. To **fatten up** an animal or person means to make them fatter, by forcing or encouraging them to eat more food. *They fattened up ducks and geese... You're too skinny – we'll have to fatten you up.* • See also **fatten** 2. PHRASAL VERB V P n (not pron); V n P

fattening /fætənɪŋ/. Food that is **fattening** is considered to make people fat easily. *Some foods are more fattening than others.* ADJ-GRADED

fatty /fæti/ **fatties; fattier, fattiest** ◆◆◇◇◇

1 **Fatty** food contains a lot of fat. *Don't eat fatty food or chocolates... The report dispels the myth that Northerners have a fattier diet than people in the south.* ADJ-GRADED: usu ADJ n

2 **Fatty** acids or **fatty** tissues, for example, contain or consist of fat; a technical use in science. *...fatty acids... The woman lost about 1.8kg of fatty tissue during the week's fast.* ADJ: ADJ n

3 If you call someone a **fatty**, you are criticizing or insulting them for being fat; an informal use which some people find offensive. *Consuming this amount of food could turn these fit players into fatties... 'Get another one, Fatty,' said Jerry.* N-COUNT PRAGMATICS

fatuous /fætʃuəs/. If you describe a person, action, or remark as **fatuous**, you think that they are extremely silly, showing a lack of intelligence or thought; a formal word. *The Chief was left speechless by this fatuous remark.* ADJ-GRADED PRAGMATICS =idiotic

fatwa /fætwɑː/ **fatwas;** also spelled **fatwah**. A **fatwa** is a religious decree issued by a Muslim leader. N-COUNT

faucet /fɔːsɪt/ **faucets.** In American English, a **faucet** is a device that controls the flow of a liquid or gas from a pipe or container. Sinks and baths have faucets attached to them. The usual British word is **tap**. *She turned off the faucet and dried her hands.* N-COUNT

fault /fɔːlt/ **faults, faulting, faulted** ◆◆◆◇◇

1 If a bad or undesirable situation is your **fault**, you caused it or are responsible for it. *There was no escaping the fact: it was all his fault... A few borrowers* N-SING: with poss

will find themselves in trouble with their repayments through no fault of their own.

2 A **fault** is a mistake in what someone is doing or in what they have done. *It is a big fault to think that you can learn how to manage people in business school.*
N-COUNT: usu with supp =error, mistake

3 A **fault** in someone or something is a weakness or imperfection in them. *His manners had always made her blind to his faults. ...a short delay due to a minor technical fault... Pilots were trying to repair a fault in the plane when it crashed... For all its faults, the film presents a clear message.*
N-COUNT: usu with supp, oft poss N =failing

4 If you cannot **fault** someone, you cannot find any reason for criticizing them or the things that they are doing. *You can't fault them for lack of invention... It is hard to fault the way he runs his own operation.*
VB: with brd-neg
V n for n/-ing
V n

5 A **fault** is a large crack in the surface of the earth. *...the San Andreas Fault.*
N-COUNT

6 A **fault** in tennis is a service that is wrong according to the rules.
N-COUNT

7 If someone or something is **at fault**, they are to blame or are responsible for a particular situation that has gone wrong. *He could never accept that he had been at fault... There are no indications that standard security arrangements were at fault.*
PHRASES v-link PHR =to blame

8 If you **find fault** with something or someone, you look for mistakes and complain about them. *I was disappointed whenever the cook found fault with my work.*
V inflects, usu PHR *with* n =criticize

9 If you say that someone has a particular good quality **to a fault**, you are emphasizing that they have more of this quality than is usual or necessary. *Jefferson was generous to a fault... Others will tell you that she is modest to a fault, funny, clever and warm.*
usu adj PHR [PRAGMATICS]

faultless /fɔːltləs/. Something that is **faultless** is perfect and has no mistakes at all. *...Mary Thomson's faultless and impressive performance on the show... Hans's English was faultless.* ♦ **faultlessly** *Howard was faultlessly dressed in a dark blue suit.*
◆◇◇◇◇ ADJ =flawless
ADV: ADV with v, ADV adj

faulty /fɔːlti/
◆◇◇◇◇

1 A **faulty** piece of equipment has something wrong with it and is not working properly. *The money will be used to repair faulty equipment.*
ADJ-GRADED =imperfect

2 If you describe someone's argument or reasoning as **faulty**, you mean that it is wrong or contains errors, usually because they have not been thinking logically. *Their interpretation was faulty – they had misinterpreted things.*
ADJ =flawed

faun /fɔːn/ **fauns.** A **faun** is an imaginary creature which is like a man with goat's legs and horns.
N-COUNT

fauna /fɔːnə/ **faunas.** Animals, especially the animals in a particular area, can be referred to as **fauna**; a technical use in biology. *...the flora and fauna of the African jungle... Brackish waters generally support only a small range of faunas.*
◆◇◇◇◇ N-COUNT-COLL

faux pas /foʊ pɑː/ **faux pas.** A **faux pas** is a socially embarrassing action or mistake; a formal word. *It was not long before I realised the enormity of my faux pas.*
N-COUNT =gaffe, blunder

favour /feɪvəʳ/ **favours, favouring, favoured;** spelled **favor** in American English.
◆◆◆◆◇

1 If you regard something or someone with **favour**, you like or support them. *It remains to be seen if the show will still find favour with a 1990s audience... China will probably look with favour on continuing Burmese military rule... He has won favour with a wide range of interest groups.*
N-UNCOUNT

2 If you do someone a **favour**, you do something for them even though you do not have to. *I've come to ask you to do me a favour... These are gestures of genuine friendship with no favours expected in return.*
N-COUNT

3 If you say that one person gives or sells their **favours** to another, you mean that they have sex; a formal use. *In her extreme youth, Maria had sold her sexual favours for money.*
N-PLURAL: usu poss N

4 If you **favour** something, you prefer it to the other choices available. *The French say they favour a transition to democracy... He favours bringing the UN into touch with 'modern realities'.* ♦ **favoured** *The favoured candidate will probably emerge after private discussions.*
VERB
V n
V -ing
ADJ-GRADED =preferred

5 If you **favour** someone, you treat them better or more kindly than you treat other people. *Miss Bhutto has accused the President of favouring her rivals... Another possibility is that parents favour chicks that are strong.* ♦ **favoured** *Her younger brother was the favoured child, encouraged and admired by both parents.*
VERB
V n
ADJ-GRADED: usu ADJ n

6 If you are **in favour** of something, you support it and think that it is a good thing. *I wouldn't be in favour of income tax cuts... Yet this is a Government which proclaims that it is all in favour of openness... The vote passed with 111 in favour and 25 against.*
PHRASES oft v-link PHR, PHR *of* n

7 If someone makes a judgement **in** your **favour**, they say that you are right about something. *If the commission rules in Mr Welch's favour the case will go to the European Court of Human Rights.*
PHR after v

8 If something is **in** your **favour**, it helps you or gives you an advantage. *The protection that farmers have enjoyed amounts to a bias in favour of the countryside... Firms are trying to shift the balance of power in the labour market back in their favour.*
n PHR, PHR after v, v-link PHR

9 If one thing is rejected **in favour of** another, the second thing is done or chosen instead of the first. *He dropped socialism in favour of enterprise and the market economy.*
PHR n, usu PHR after v

10 If someone or something is **in favour**, people like or support them. If they are **out of favour**, people no longer like or support them.
v-link PHR

favourable /feɪvərəbᵊl/; spelled **favorable** in American English.
◆◆◇◇◇

1 If your opinion or your reaction is **favourable** to something, you agree with it and approve of it. *His recently completed chapel for Fitzwilliam is attracting favourable comment... In Switzerland, banks and big companies are favourable to EC membership.* ♦ **favourably** /feɪvərəbli/; *He listened intently, and responded favourably to both my suggestions... He was quite favourably impressed with the new French commander.*
ADJ-GRADED: ADJ n, v-link ADJ *to* n
ADV-GRADED: ADV with v

2 If something makes a **favourable** impression on you or is **favourable to** you, you like it and approve of it. *His ability to talk tough while eating fast made a favourable impression on his dining companions... These terms were favourable to India.*
ADJ-GRADED: oft ADJ *to* n =positive, good

3 **Favourable** conditions make something more likely to succeed or seem more attractive. *It's believed the conditions in which the elections are being held are too favourable to the government. ...favourable weather conditions.* ♦ **favourably** *Japan is thus favourably placed to maintain its lead as the most successful manufacturing nation.*
ADJ-GRADED: oft ADJ *to* n/-ing =good
ADV-GRADED: ADV -ed, ADV after v

4 If you make a **favourable** comparison between two things, you say that the first is better than or as good as the second. *The film bears favourable technical comparison with Hollywood productions costing 10 times as much.* ♦ **favourably** *Britain's overall road safety record compares favourably with that of other European countries.*
ADJ-GRADED: usu ADJ n
ADV-GRADED: usu ADV after v, also ADV -ed

favourite /feɪvərɪt/ **favourites;** spelled **favorite** in American English.
◆◆◆◆◇

1 Your **favourite** thing or person of a particular type is the one you like most. *He celebrated by opening a bottle of his favourite champagne... Her favourite writer is Hans Christian Andersen.* ► Also a noun. *The Liverpool Metropole is my favourite. I love those huge, anonymous hotels.* ● If you refer to something as an **old favourite**, you mean that it has been in existence for a long time and everybody knows it or likes it. *Everyone must be familiar with the old favourite among roses, Crystal Palace.*
ADJ: ADJ n
N-COUNT: usu with poss
PHRASE

2 If you describe one person as the **favourite** of another, you mean that the second person likes the first person a lot and treats them with special kindness. *...Robert Carr, Earl of Somerset, a favourite of King James I... The Prime Minister is no favourite of the tabloids.*
N-COUNT: usu with poss

3 The **favourite** in a race or contest is the runner or
N-COUNT:

competitor that is expected to win. In a team game, the team that is expected to win is referred to as the **favourites**. *The Belgian Cup has been won by the favourites F.C. Liege.* usu *the*N

favouritism /feɪvərɪtɪzəm/; spelled **favoritism** in American English. If you accuse someone of **favouritism**, you disapprove of them because they unfairly help or favour one person or group much more than another. *Maria loved both the children. There was never a hint of favouritism.* N-UNCOUNT PRAGMATICS =bias

fawn /fɔːn/ **fawns, fawning, fawned** ◆◇◇◇◇

1 Fawn is a pale yellowish-brown colour. *Tania was standing there in her light fawn coat.* COLOUR

2 A **fawn** is a very young deer. *The fawn ran to the top of the ridge.* N-COUNT

3 If you say that someone **fawns** over a powerful or rich person, you disapprove of them because they flatter that person and like to be with him or her. *People fawn over you when you're famous... Nauseatingly fawning journalism that's all it is.* VERB PRAGMATICS V *over/on/around*n V-ing

fax /fæks/ **faxes, faxing, faxed** ◆◆◇◇◇

1 A **fax** or a **fax machine** is a piece of equipment used to copy documents by sending information electronically along a telephone line, and to receive copies that are sent in this way. *...a modern reception desk with telephone and fax... These days, cartoonists send in their work by fax.* N-COUNT: also *by*N =facsimile

2 If you **fax** a document to someone, you send it from one fax machine to another. *I faxed a copy of the agreement to each of the investors... Did you fax him a reply?... Pop it in the post, or get your secretary to fax it... I faxed 10 hotels in the area to check room size.* VERB V n *to*n V n n V n

3 You can refer to a copy of a document that is transmitted by a fax machine as a **fax**. *I sent him a long fax, saying I didn't need a maid. ...a 2,000 word fax message.* N-COUNT =facsimile

faze /feɪz/ **fazes, fazed.** If something **fazes** you, it surprises, shocks, or frightens you, so that you do not know what to do; an informal word. *Big concert halls do not faze Melanie... He wasn't a bit fazed by the fact that I was gay.* VB: no cont, oft with brd-neg V n

FBI /ef biː aɪ/. **The FBI** is a government agency in the United States that investigates crimes in which a national law is broken or in which the country's security is threatened. **FBI** is an abbreviation for 'Federal Bureau of Investigation'. ◆◆◇◇◇ N-PROPER: *the*N

fealty /fiːəlti/. In former times, if someone swore **fealty** to their ruler, they promised to be loyal to him or her. N-UNCOUNT =allegiance

fear /fɪəʳ/ **fears, fearing, feared** ◆◆◆◆◆

1 Fear is the unpleasant feeling you have when you think that you are in danger. *I was sitting on the floor shivering with fear because a bullet had been fired through a window. ...boyhood memories of sickness and fear of the dark... London Zoo is running hypnosis programmes to help people overcome their fear of spiders.* N-VAR: oft N *of*n/-ing =terror, dread

2 If you **fear** someone or something, you are frightened because you think that they will harm you. *It seems to me that if people fear you they respect you.* VERB =be afraid of V n

3 A **fear** is a thought that something unpleasant might happen or might have happened. *These youngsters are motivated not by a desire to achieve, but by fear of failure... Then one day his worst fears were confirmed... His fears might be groundless. ...the fear that once a war began it would soon pass beyond the ability of either side to manage it.* N-VAR: with supp, oft N *of*n/-ing, N that

4 If you **fear** something unpleasant or undesirable, you are worried that it might happen or might have happened. *She had feared she was going down with pneumonia or bronchitis... More than two million refugees have fled the area, fearing attack by loyalist forces.* VERB V that V n

5 If you say that there is a **fear** that something unpleasant or undesirable will happen, you mean that you think it is possible or likely. *There was no fear that anything would be misunderstood... There is a fear that the freeze on bank accounts could prove a lasting deterrent to investors.* N-VAR: oft N that, N *of*n/-ing =risk, chance

6 If you **fear for** someone or something, you are very worried because you think that they might be in danger. *Carla fears for her son... He fled on Friday, saying he feared for his life.* VERB V *for*n

7 If you have **fears for** someone or something, you are very worried because you think that they might be in danger. *He also spoke of his fears for the future of his country's culture. ...fear for her own safety.* N-VAR: N *for*n

8 If you **fear** to do something, you are afraid to do it or you do not wish to do it. *She pursed her lips together, as though fearing to betray her news... Old people fear to leave their homes.* VERB =be afraid V to-inf

9 You say you **fear** that a situation is the case when the situation is unpleasant or undesirable, and when you want to express sympathy, sorrow, or regret about it; a formal use. *I fear that a land war now looks very probable... 'Is anything left at all?'—'I fear not.'* VERB PRAGMATICS =regret V that V *so/not*

10 If you are **in fear of** doing or experiencing something unpleasant or undesirable, you are very worried that you might have to do it or experience it. *The elderly live in fear of assault and murder.* PHRASES PHR n/-ing, usu v-link PHR, PHR after v

11 If you take a particular course of action **for fear of** something, you take the action in order to prevent that thing happening. *She was afraid to say anything to them for fear of hurting their feelings... No one dared shoot for fear of hitting Pete.* PHR n/-ing, PHR with cl

12 You say **'fear not'** or **'never fear'** to someone when you are telling them not to worry or be frightened; an old-fashioned expresssion. *Fear not, Darlene will protect me... You'll get the right training, never fear.* usu PHR with cl =don't worry

13 In informal British English, you use **'no fear'** to emphasize that you do not want to do something. *When I asked him if he wanted to change his mind, William said 'No fear.'* CONVENTION PRAGMATICS =not likely

14 If someone or something **puts the fear of God into** you, they frighten or worry you, often deliberately. *At some time or other Eve had obviously put the fear of God into her.* V inflects

fearful /fɪəʳfʊl/ ◆◆◇◇◇

1 If you are **fearful** of something, you are afraid of it; a formal use. *Bankers were fearful of a world banking crisis... I had often been very fearful, very angry, and very isolated.* ♦ **fearfully** *'What are you going to do to me?' Alex asked fearfully.* ADJ-GRADED: usu v-link ADJ, oft ADJ *of*n, ADJ that ADV: usu ADV after v, also ADV with cl

2 You use **fearful** to emphasize how serious or bad a situation is; a formal use. *The region is in a fearful recession. ...the fearful consequences which might flow from unilateral military moves.* ADJ-GRADED: ADJ n PRAGMATICS =terrible

3 Fearful is used to emphasize that something is very bad; an old-fashioned, informal use. *You gave me a fearful shock!... 'It sounds the most fearful hard work,' Sybil said later.* ♦ **fearfully** *This is fearfully expensive compared with the last one I bought.* ADJ-GRADED: ADJ n PRAGMATICS ADV: ADV adj

fearless /fɪəʳləs/. If you say that someone is **fearless**, you mean that they are not afraid at all, and you admire them for this. *...his fearless campaigning for racial justice.* ♦ **fearlessly** *...an honest and fearlessly outspoken politician.* ◆◇◇◇◇ ADJ-GRADED PRAGMATICS =intrepid ADV: ADV adj, ADV with v

fearsome /fɪəʳsəm/. **Fearsome** is used to describe things that are frightening, for example because of their large size or extreme nature. *He had developed a fearsome reputation for intimidating people. ...a fearsome array of weapons.* ◆◇◇◇◇ ADJ-GRADED =formidable

feasible /fiːzəbəl/. If something is **feasible**, it can be done, made, or achieved. *She questioned whether it was feasible to stimulate investment in these regions... That may be fine for the US, but it's not feasible for a mass European market.* ♦ **feasibility** /fiːzəbɪlɪti/ *The committee will study the feasibility of setting up a national computer network.* ◆◇◇◇◇ ADJ-GRADED: oft ADJ to-inf =practicable N-UNCOUNT: oft N *of*n

feast /fiːst/ **feasts, feasting, feasted** ◆◆◇◇◇

1 A **feast** is a large and special meal. *Lunch was a feast of meat and vegetables, cheese, yoghurt and fruit, with unlimited wine... The fruit was often served at wedding feasts... On the following day a feast was given in King John's honour.* N-COUNT =banquet

2 If you **feast** on a particular food, you eat a large amount of it with great enjoyment. *They feasted well into the afternoon on mutton and corn stew... Starving dogs feasted on the human corpses.* VERB V *on*n

3 If you **feast**, you take part in a feast. *Only a few* VERB *feet away, their captors feasted in the castle's banqueting hall.* ♦ **feasting** *The feasting, drinking, dancing and revelry continued for several days.* V N-UNCOUNT

4 You can refer to a large number of good, interesting, or enjoyable things as a **feast** of things. *This new series promises a feast of special effects and set designs... Chicago provides a feast for the ears of any music lover.* N-SING: with supp, usu N *of*n =cornucopia

5 A **feast** is a day or time of the year when a special religious celebration takes place. *The Jewish feast of Passover began last night... It's the first time since Communist rule was imposed on the republic that the feast day has been celebrated.* N-COUNT =festival

6 If you **feast** your **eyes on** something, you look at it for a long time with great attention because you find it very attractive. *She stood feasting her eyes on the view.* PHRASE: V inflects

feat /fiːt/ **feats.** If you refer to an action, or the result of an action, as a **feat**, you admire it because it is an impressive and difficult achievement. *A racing car is an extraordinary feat of engineering.* • **no mean feat** see **mean.** ◆◆◇◇◇ N-COUNT PRAGMATICS =accomplishment

feather /feðəʳ/ **feathers.** ◆◆◇◇◇

1 A bird's **feathers** are the soft covering on its body. Each **feather** consists of a lot of smooth hairs on each side of a thin stiff centre. *...a hat that she had made herself from black ostrich feathers. ...a feather bed.* • See also **feathered.** N-COUNT

2 If you describe two people as **birds of a feather**, you mean that they have very similar characteristics, interests, or beliefs. *She and my mother were birds of a feather.* PHRASES usu v-link PHR

3 If you describe something that someone has achieved as a **feather in** their **cap**, you mean that they can be proud of it or that it might bring them some advantage. *Harry's appointment to this important post was a feather in his cap.* usu v-link PHR

4 • to **feather one's nest**: see **nest.** • to **ruffle** someone's **feathers**: see **ruffle.**

feather-bedding. If you accuse an organization or company of **feather-bedding**, you disapprove of the fact that it allows work to be done slowly or inefficiently so that the jobs of all its employees are protected; an informal expression. *These industries are notorious for low productivity and feather-bedding.* N-UNCOUNT PRAGMATICS

feather boa. See **boa.**

feather duster, feather dusters. A **feather duster** is a stick with a bunch of real or artificial feathers attached to one end. It is used for dusting and cleaning things. N-COUNT

feathered /feðəʳd/ ◆◇◇◇◇

1 If you describe something as **feathered**, you mean that it has feathers on it. *Her mother was the proud lady in the feathered hat.* ADJ

2 Birds are sometimes referred to as our **feathered friends.** PHRASE

featherweight /feðəʳweɪt/ **featherweights.** A **featherweight** is a professional boxer who weighs between 53.5 and 57 kilograms, which is one of the lowest weight ranges. ◆◇◇◇◇ N-COUNT

feathery /feðəri/

1 If something is **feathery**, it has an edge divided into a lot of thin parts so that it looks soft. *The foliage was soft and feathery.* ADJ-GRADED

2 **Feathery** is used to describe things that are soft and light. *...flurries of small, feathery flakes of snow.* ADJ-GRADED

feature /fiːtʃəʳ/ **features, featuring, featured** ◆◆◆◆◇

1 A **feature** of something is an interesting or important part or characteristic of it. *Patriotic songs have long been a feature of Kuwaiti life... The spacious gardens are a special feature of this property... Perhaps the most unusual feature in the room is an extraordinary pair of candles.* N-COUNT: with supp, oft N *of*n

2 Your **features** are your eyes, nose, mouth, and other parts of your face. *His features seemed to change... Her features were strongly defined.* N-PLURAL: usu poss N

3 When something such as a film or exhibition **features** someone or something, they are an important part of it. *It's a great movie and it features a Spanish actor who is going to be a world star within a year... The hour-long programme will be updated each week and feature highlights from recent games... This spectacular event, now in its 5th year, features a stunning catwalk show.* VERB =include V n

4 If someone or something **features** in something such as a show, exhibition, or magazine, they are an important part of it. *Jon featured in one of the show's most thrilling episodes.* VERB V *in/on*n

5 A **feature** is a special article in a newspaper or magazine, or a special programme on radio or television. *We are delighted to see the Sunday Times running a long feature on breast cancer. ...a special feature on the fund-raising project.* N-COUNT: oft N *on*n

6 A geographical **feature** is something noticeable in a particular area of country, for example a hill, river, or valley. N-COUNT

feature film, feature films. A **feature film** is a full-length film about a fictional situation, as opposed to a short film or a documentary. ◆◇◇◇◇ N-COUNT =movie

featureless /fiːtʃəʳləs/. If you say that something is **featureless**, you mean that it has no interesting features or characteristics. *Malone looked out at the grey-green featureless landscape.* ADJ-GRADED =nondescript

Feb. **Feb.** is a written abbreviation for **February.** ◆◆◇◇◇

febrile /fiːbraɪl/. **Febrile** behaviour is intensely and nervously active; a literary word. *The news plunged the nation into a febrile, agitated state.* ADJ-GRADED =feverish

February /febjuəri, AM -jueri/ **Februaries. February** is the second month of the year in the Western calendar. *He joined the Army in February 1943... His exhibition opens on 5 February... Last February the tribunal agreed he had been the victim of racial discrimination.* ◆◆◆◆◇ N-VAR

fecal. /fiːkᵊl/; See **faecal.**

feces /fiːsiːz/. See **faeces.**

feckless /fekləs/. If you describe someone as **feckless**, you mean that they lack determination or strength, and are unable to do anything properly; a formal word. *He regarded the young man as feckless and irresponsible.* ADJ-GRADED =incompetent

fecund /fiːkənd, fek-/

1 When you are talking about living things or natural processes, **fecund** means the same as fertile; a formal use. *The pampas are still among the most fecund lands in the world... Large animals are less fecund than small ones.* ♦ **fecundity** /fɪkʌndɪti/ *...an island famous for the profusion and fecundity of its bird life.* ADJ-GRADED =fertile N-UNCOUNT

2 If you describe something as **fecund**, you approve of it because it produces a lot of good or useful things; a formal use. *It has now become clear how extraordinarily fecund a decade was the 1890s.* ♦ **fecundity** *...the extraordinary fecundity and vitality of the city.* ADJ-GRADED PRAGMATICS =productive N-UNCOUNT

fed /fed/ **feds**

1 **Fed** is the past tense and past participle of **feed.** See also **fed up.**

2 The **feds** are agents for the American security agency, the FBI; an informal word. N-COUNT: usu pl

federal /fedərəl/ **federals** ◆◆◆◆◇

1 A **federal** country or system of government is one in which the different states or provinces of the country have important powers to make their own laws and decisions. *Five of the six provinces are to become autonomous regions in a new federal system of government.* ADJ-GRADED: ADJ n

2 Some people use **federal** to describe a system of government which they disapprove of, in which the different states or provinces are controlled by a strong central government. *He does not believe in a federal Europe with centralising powers.* ADJ-GRADED: ADJ n PRAGMATICS

3 **Federal** also means belonging or relating to the national government of a federal country rather than to one of the states within it. *The federal government controls just 6% of the education budget. ...a federal judge.* ♦ **federally** *...residents of public housing and federally subsidized apartments.* ADJ: ADJ n ADV: ADV -ed

4 **Federals** are the same as **feds.** N-COUNT

federalism /fedərəlɪzəm/. **Federalism** is belief in or support for a federal system of government, or this system itself. *They argue that the amendment undermines Canadian federalism.* ◆◇◇◇◇ N-UNCOUNT

federalist /fedərəlɪst/ **federalists.** Someone or something that is **federalist** believes in, supports, or follows a federal system of government. *...the federalist idea of Europe.* ► Also a noun. *Many Quebeckers are federalists.* ◆◇◇◇◇ ADJ; N-COUNT

federated /fedəreɪtɪd/. **Federated** states or societies are ones that have joined together for a common purpose. *Whether to stay in the federated state or become independent is a decision that has to be made by the people.* ◆◇◇◇◇ ADJ: ADJ n, v-link ADJ *to* n

federation /fedəreɪʃᵊn/ **federations** ◆◆◆◇◇

1 A **federation** is a federal country. *...the Russian Federation.* N-COUNT

2 A **federation** is a group of societies or other organizations which have joined together, usually because they share a common interest. *...the British Athletic Federation... The organization emerged from a federation of six national agencies.* N-COUNT: usu with supp, oft in names

fedora /fɪdɔːrə/ **fedoras.** A **fedora** is a type of hat which has a brim and is made from a soft material such as velvet. N-COUNT

fed up. If you are **fed up**, you are unhappy, bored, or tired of something, especially something that you have been experiencing for a long time; an informal expression. *I am fed up with reading how women should dress to please men... He had become fed up with city life... I'm just fed up and I don't know what to do.* ◆◆◇◇◇ ADJ-GRADED: v-link ADJ, oft ADJ *with/of* n/-ing =cheesed off

fee /fiː/ **fees** ◆◆◆◆◇

1 A **fee** is a sum of money that you pay to be allowed to do something. *He hadn't paid his television licence fee.* N-COUNT

2 A **fee** is the amount of money that a person or organization is paid for a particular job or service that they provide. *Find out how much your surveyor's and solicitor's fees will be.* N-COUNT

feeble /fiːbᵊl/ **feebler, feeblest** ◆◇◇◇◇

1 If you describe someone or something as **feeble**, you mean that they are weak. *He told them he was old and feeble and was not able to walk so far... The feeble light of a tin lamp.* ♦ **feebly** *His left hand moved feebly at his side.* ADJ-GRADED; ADV-GRADED: ADV with v

2 If you describe someone as **feeble**, you are criticizing them because they are afraid of taking strong action or seem to make no effort. *He said that the Government had been feeble. ...some rather feeble traditionalists.* ADJ-GRADED PRAGMATICS =ineffectual

3 If you describe something that someone says as **feeble**, you mean that it is not very good or convincing. *This is a particularly feeble argument.* ♦ **feebly** *I said 'Sorry', very feebly, feeling rather embarrassed.* ADJ-GRADED =pathetic; ADV-GRADED: ADV with v =weakly

feed /fiːd/ **feeds, feeding, fed** ◆◆◆◆◇

1 If you **feed** a person or animal, you give them food to eat and sometimes actually put it in their mouths. *We brought along pieces of old bread and fed the birds... She fed him a cookie... He fed me on barbecue ribs, and talked to me non-stop... He spooned the ice cream into a cup and fed it to her.* ► Also a noun in British English. *She's had a good feed.* ♦ **feeding, feedings** *The feeding of dairy cows has undergone a revolution.* VERB V n, V n n, V n *on/with* n, V n *to* n, Also V pron-refl; N-COUNT; N-VAR

2 To **feed** a family or a community means to supply food for them. *Feeding a hungry family can be expensive . ...a food reserve large enough to feed the Sudanese population for many months.* VERB V n

3 When an animal **feeds**, it eats or drinks something. *After a few days the caterpillars stopped feeding... Slugs feed on decaying plant and animal material.* VERB V, V *on/off* n

4 When a baby **feeds** or when you **feed** it, it drinks breast milk. *When a baby is thirsty, it feeds more often... I knew absolutely nothing about handling or feeding a baby.* V-ERG V, V n

5 Animal **feed** is food given to animals, especially farm animals. *The grain just rotted and all they could use it for was animal feed. ...poultry feed.* N-MASS: usu n N

6 To **feed** something to a place, means to supply it to that place in a steady flow. *...blood vessels that feed blood to the brain. ...gas fed through pipelines.* VERB V n prep

7 If you **feed** something into a container or piece of equipment, you put it into it. *He took the compact disc from her, then fed it into the player... She was feeding documents into a paper shredder.* VERB V n prep

8 If someone **feeds** you false or secret information, they deliberately tell it to you. *He was surrounded by people who fed him ghastly lies... At least one British officer was feeding him with classified information.* VERB V n n, V n *with* n, Also V n *to* n

9 If you **feed** someone's dislike or desire for something, you make it stronger. *The divorce was painfully public, feeding her dislike of the press.* VERB V n

10 If you **feed** a plant, you add substances to it to make it grow well. *Feed plants to encourage steady growth.* VERB V n

11 If one thing **feeds** on another, it becomes stronger as a result of the other thing's existence. *The drinking and the guilt fed on each other.* VERB V *on* n

12 To **feed** information into a computer means to gradually put it into it. *An automatic weather station feeds information on wind direction to the computer.* VERB V n *into/to* n

13 • to **bite the hand that feeds** you: see **bite**. • **another mouth to feed**: see **mouth**.

feed up. If you **feed** someone **up**, you make them eat extra food so that they put on weight. *She is too thin. Feed her up a bit.* PHRASAL VERB V n P, Also V P n (not pron)

feedback /fiːdbæk/ ◆◆◇◇◇

1 If you get **feedback** on your work or progress, someone tells you how well or badly you are doing, and how you could improve. If you get good feedback you have worked or performed well. *Continue to ask for feedback on your work... I was getting great feedback from my boss.* N-UNCOUNT: oft N prep

2 **Feedback** is the unpleasant whistling sound you get in a piece of electrical equipment when part of its power goes back into it. N-UNCOUNT

feeder /fiːdəʳ/ **feeders** ◆◆◇◇◇

1 A **feeder** road, railway, or river is a smaller one that leads to a more important one. *...the feeder road leading to the airport.* ADJ: ADJ n

2 **Feeder** airline and railway services connect major routes and local destinations. *...a feeder to British Airways's transatlantic destinations.* N-COUNT: usu N n

3 A **feeder** school or team provides students or players for a larger or more important one. *...children coming up from two infant feeder schools.* N-COUNT: oft N n

4 A **feeder** is a container that you fill with food for birds or animals. N-COUNT: oft n N

feeding bottle, feeding bottles; also spelled **feeding-bottle.** A **feeding bottle** is a plastic bottle with a special rubber top through which a baby can suck milk or another liquid. N-COUNT

feeding ground, feeding grounds. The **feeding ground** of a group of animals or birds, is the place where they find food and eat. *The mud is a feeding ground for large numbers of birds.* N-COUNT: usu with supp

feel /fiːl/ **feels, feeling, felt** ◆◆◆◆◆

1 If you **feel** a particular emotion or physical sensation, you experience it. *I am feeling very depressed... I will always feel grateful to that little guy... I remember feeling sick. ...soldiers who once felt proud to wear their uniforms... Suddenly I felt a sharp pain in my shoulder... You won't feel a thing... I felt as if all my strength had gone... I felt like I was being kicked in the teeth every day.* V-LINK V adj, V n, V as if, V like

2 If you talk about how an experience or event **feels**, you talk about the emotions and sensations connected with it. *It feels good to have finished a piece of work... The speed at which everything moved felt strange... Within five minutes of arriving back from holiday, it feels as if I've never been away... It felt like I'd had two babies instead of one... Preparing for that first trial felt like learning the rules of a new game.* V-LINK: no cont *it* V adj to-inf/that, V adj, *it* V as if, *it* V like, V *like*-ing/n

3 If you talk about how an object **feels**, you talk about the physical quality that you notice when you touch or hold it. For example, if something **feels** soft, you notice that it is soft when you touch it. *The metal felt smooth and cold... The ten-foot oars felt heavy and awkward... When the clay feels like putty, it is ready to use.* ► Also a noun. *He remembered the feel of her skin... Linen raincoats have a crisp, papery feel.* V-LINK: no cont V adj, V *like* n; N-SING: usu with supp

4 If you talk about how the weather **feels**, you describe the weather, especially the temperature or whether or not you think it is going to rain or snow. *It felt wintry cold that day.*
V-LINK: no cont; *it* V adj; Also *it* V like/as if

5 If you **feel** an object, you touch it deliberately with your hand, so that you learn what it is like, for example what shape it is or whether it is rough or smooth. *The doctor felt his head... When dry, feel the surface and it will no longer be smooth... Feel how soft the skin is in the small of the back... Her eyes squeezed shut , she felt inside the tin, expecting it to be bare.*
VERB; V n; V wh; V prep/adv

6 If you can **feel** something, you are aware of it because it is touching you. *Through several layers of clothes I could feel his muscles... He felt her leg against his.*
VB: no cont; =sense; V n; V n prep/adv

7 If you **feel** something happening, you become aware of it because of the effect it has on your body. *She felt something being pressed into her hands... He felt something move beside him... She felt herself lifted from her feet... Tremors were felt 250 miles away.*
VERB; =sense; V n -ing; V n inf; V pron-refl -ed; *be* V-ed

8 If you **feel** yourself doing something or being in a particular state, you are aware that something is happening to you which you are unable to control. *I felt myself blush... If at any point you feel yourself becoming tense, make a conscious effort to relax... I actually felt my heart quicken.*
VERB; =sense; V pron-refl inf; V pron-refl -ing; V n inf; Also V n -ing

9 If you **feel** something such as the presence of someone or something, you become aware of it, even though you cannot see or hear it. *He felt her eyes on him... Suddenly, I felt a presence behind me... I could feel that a man was watching me very intensely... He almost felt her wincing at the other end of the telephone.*
VB: no cont; =sense; V n; V that; V n -ing

10 If you **feel** that something is the case, you have a strong idea in your mind that it is the case. *I feel that not enough is being done to protect the local animal life... I feel certain that it will all turn out well... She felt herself to be part of a large business empire... I never felt myself a real child of the sixties.*
VB: no cont; =think; V that; V adj that; V n to-inf; V pron-refl n

11 If you **feel** that you should do something, you think that you should do it. *I feel I should resign... He felt that he had to do it... You need not feel obliged to contribute... They felt under no obligation to maintain their employees.*
VB: no cont; V that; V -ed to-inf; V *under* n

12 If you talk about how you **feel** about something, you talk about your opinion, attitude, or reaction to it. *We'd like to know what you feel about abortion... How do you feel about going back to the neighborhood?... She feels guilty about spending less time lately with her two kids... He feels deep regret about his friend's death.*
VB: no cont; V *about* n; V adj/adv *about* n; V n *about* n

13 If you **feel** like doing something or having something, you want to do it or have it because you are in the right mood for it and think you would enjoy it. *Neither of them felt like going back to sleep... Could we take a walk? I feel like a little exercise.*
VERB; V *like* -ing/n

14 If you **feel** the effect or result of something, you experience it. *The charity is still feeling the effects of revelations about its one-time president... The real impact will be felt in the developing world.*
VERB; =notice; V n

15 The **feel** of something, for example a place, is the general impression that it gives you. *The room has a warm, cosy feel. ...a book that takes on the feel of an epic.* • If you **get the feel of** something, for example a place or a new activity, you become familiar with it. *He wanted to get the feel of the place.*
N-SING: with supp; PHRASE: V inflects, PHR n

16 See also **feeling**, **felt**. • to **feel** something **in your bones**: see **bone**. • **feel free**: see **free**.

feel for
PHRASAL VERB

1 If you **feel for** something, for example in the dark, you try to find it by moving your hand around until you touch it. *I felt for my wallet and papers in my inside pocket... I slumped down in my usual armchair and felt around for the newspaper.*
=grope for; V P n; V adv/prep P n

2 If you **feel for** someone, you have sympathy for them. *She cried on the phone and things like that and I really felt for her.*
=feel sorry for; V P n

feeler /fiːləʳ/ **feelers**

1 An insect's **feelers** are the two thin stalks on its head with which it touches and senses things around it.
N-COUNT: usu pl; =antenna

2 You can use **feelers** to refer to careful, discreet contacts with people in order to get information from them, or to find out what their reaction will be to a later suggestion. If you put out **feelers**, you make such contacts. *When vacancies occur, the office puts out feelers to the universities.*
N-PLURAL

feelgood /fiːlgʊd/

1 A **feelgood** film is a film which presents people and life in a way which makes the people who watch it feel happy and optimistic. *This could be the feelgood movie of the autumn. ...a bright and enjoyable feelgood romance.*
ADJ: ADJ n

2 When journalists refer to **the feelgood factor**, they mean that people are feeling hopeful and optimistic about the future. *There were obvious signs of the feelgood factor in the last survey taken in the wake of the election result.*
PHRASE

feeling /fiːlɪŋ/ **feelings** ◆◆◆◆◇

1 A **feeling** is an emotion, such as anger or happiness. *It gave me a feeling of satisfaction... Strong feelings of pride welled up in me... I think our main feeling would be of an immense gratitude... He was unable to contain his own destructive feelings.*
N-COUNT: usu with supp, oft N *of* n

2 Your **feelings** about something are the things that you think and feel about it, or your attitude towards it. *She has strong feelings about the alleged growth in violence against female officers... I have also begun to reassess my own feelings about being a woman... I think that sums up the feelings of most discerning and intelligent Indians... He made no real secret of his feelings to his friends.*
N-PLURAL: with supp, oft with poss, oft N *about* n/-ing; =opinions

3 When you refer to someone's **feelings**, you are talking about the things that might embarrass, offend, or upset them. For example, if you hurt someone's **feelings**, you upset them by something that you say or do. *He was afraid of hurting my feelings... He has no respect, no regard for anyone's feelings... What about my feelings?*
N-PLURAL: usu poss N

4 **Feeling** is a way of thinking and reacting to things which is emotional and spontaneous rather than logical and rational. *He was prompted to a rare outburst of feeling. ...a voice that trembles with feeling.*
N-UNCOUNT; =emotion

5 **Feeling** for someone is love, affection, sympathy, or concern for them. *Thomas never lost his feeling for Harriet... It's incredible that Peter can behave with such stupid lack of feeling.*
N-UNCOUNT: oft N *for* n

6 If you have a **feeling** of hunger, tiredness, or other physical sensation, you experience it. *I also had a strange feeling in my neck... Focus on the feeling of relaxation... He experienced feelings of claustrophobia from being in a small place.*
N-COUNT: usu with supp, oft N *of* n; =sensation

7 **Feeling** in part of your body is the ability to experience the sense of touch in this part of the body. *After the accident he had no feeling in his legs.*
N-UNCOUNT

8 If you have a **feeling** that something is the case or that something is going to happen, you think that is probably the case or that it is probably going to happen. *You have a feeling about people, and I just felt she was going to be good... I have a feeling that everything will come right for us one day.*
N-COUNT: usu with supp, oft N *about* n, N that

9 **Feeling** is used to refer to a general opinion that a group of people has about something. *There is still some feeling in the art world that the market for such works may be declining... It seemed that anti-Fascist feeling was being suppressed.*
N-UNCOUNT: with supp, oft N that

10 If you have a **feeling of** being in a particular situation, you feel that you are in that situation. *I had the terrible feeling of being left behind to bring up the baby while he had fun.*
N-SING: N *of*-ing; =sensation

11 If you have **a feeling for** something, you have an understanding of it or a natural ability to do it. *Try to get a feeling for the people who live here... You seem to have a feeling for drawing.*
N-SING: *a* N *for* n

12 If something such as a place or book creates a particular kind of **feeling**, it creates a particular kind of atmosphere. *That's what we tried to portray in the book, this feeling of opulence and grandeur.*
N-SING: with supp; =air

13 See also **feel**.

14 **Bad feeling** or **ill feeling** is resentment, bitterness, or anger which exists between people, for
PHRASES: oft PHR *between* n

example after they have had an argument. *There's been some bad feeling between the two families.*

15 Hard feelings are feelings of anger or bitterness towards someone who you have had an argument with or who has upset you. If you say **'no hard feelings'**, you are making an agreement with someone not to be angry or bitter about something. *I don't want any hard feelings between our companies... He held out his large hand. 'No hard feelings, right?'*

16 You say **'I know the feeling'** to show that you understand and sympathize with the problem or difficult experience that someone is telling you about. CONVENTION PRAGMATICS

17 If you **have mixed feelings** about something or someone, you feel uncertain about them because you can see both good and bad points about them. V inflects, usu PHR *about* n

feelingly /fiːlɪŋli/. If someone says something **feelingly**, they say it in a way which shows that they have very strong feelings about what they are saying. *'It's what I want,' she said feelingly... She spoke more feelingly of her horses than she did of her own children.* ADV-GRADED: ADV after v =emotionally

feet /fiːt/. **Feet** is the plural of **foot**.

feign /feɪn/ **feigns, feigning, feigned.** If someone **feigns** a particular feeling, attitude, or physical condition, they try to make other people think that they have it or are experiencing it, although this is not true; a formal word. *One morning, I didn't want to go to school, and decided to feign illness... 'Giles phoned this morning,' Mirella said with feigned indifference.* ◆◇◇◇◇ VERB =affect; V n; V-ed; Also V to-inf

feint /feɪnt/ **feints, feinting, feinted**

1 In sport or military conflict, if someone **feints**, they make a brief movement in a different direction from the one they intend to follow, as a way of confusing or deceiving their opponent. *I feinted to the left, then to the right... They feinted and concentrated forces against the most fortified line of the enemy side.* ► Also a noun. *He placed the ball and tried a couple of feints.* VERB; V prep/adv; V; N-COUNT

2 Feint is used to refer to paper that has pale lines across it for writing on. N-UNCOUNT

feisty /faɪsti/. If you describe someone as **feisty**, you mean that they are tough, independent, and spirited, often when you would not expect them to be, for example because they are old or ill. *The soldier looked incredulously at the feisty child... At 66, she was as feisty as ever.* ◆◇◇◇◇ ADJ-GRADED =spunky

felicitous /fɪlɪsɪtəs/. If you describe a remark or idea as **felicitous**, you approve of it because it seems particularly suitable or well-chosen in the circumstances; a formal word. *Her prose style is not always felicitous; she tends to repetition.* ADJ-GRADED =apposite

felicity /fɪlɪsɪti/

1 Felicity is great happiness and pleasure; a literary use. *...joy and felicity.* N-UNCOUNT =joy

2 Felicity is the quality of being good, pleasant, or desirable; a literary use. *...his conversational manner and easy verbal felicity.* N-UNCOUNT

feline /fiːlaɪn/ **felines**

1 Feline means belonging or relating to the cat family. ADJ: ADJ n

2 A **feline** is an animal that belongs to the cat family. *The 14lb feline is so fat she can hardly walk.* N-COUNT =cat

3 You can use **feline** to describe someone's appearance or movements if they are elegant or graceful in a way that makes you think of a cat; a literary use. *...a woman with large feline eyes and a sexy voice... She moves with feline grace.* ADJ-GRADED: usu ADJ n =catlike

fell /fel/ **fells, felling, felled** ◆◇◇◇◇

1 Fell is the past tense of **fall**.

2 If trees **are felled**, they are cut down. *Badly infected trees should be felled and burned.* VB: usu passive *be* V-ed

3 If you **fell** someone, you knock them down, for example in a fight. *...a blow on the forehead which felled him to the ground.* VERB V n

4 ● **in one fell swoop**: see **swoop**.

fella /felə/ **fellas;** also spelled **feller**. You can refer to a man as a **fella**; an informal word. *He's an intelligent man and a nice fella... 'You're a funny feller,' Fairbairn said grumpily.* ◆◇◇◇◇ N-COUNT: usu with supp =fellow

fellatio /fəleɪʃioʊ/. **Fellatio** is oral sex which involves someone using their mouth to stimulate their partner's penis. N-UNCOUNT

fellow /feloʊ/ **fellows** ◆◆◆◆◇

1 You use **fellow** to describe people who are in the same situation as you, or people you feel you have something in common with. *She discovered to her pleasure, a talent for making her fellow guests laugh... Even in jail, my fellow inmates treated me with kindness.* ADJ: ADJ n

2 A **fellow** is a man or boy; an old-fashioned, informal use. *By all accounts, Rodger would appear to be a fine fellow.* N-COUNT =chap

3 Your **fellows** are the people who you work with, do things with, or who are like you in some way; a formal use. *He stood out in terms of competence from all his fellows... People looked out for one another and were concerned about the welfare of their fellows.* N-PLURAL: poss N =comrades

4 A **fellow** of a society or academic institution is a member of it. It is an honour to be a **fellow** of such a society. *...the fellows of the Zoological Society of London.* N-COUNT: usu N *of* n

fellow feeling; also spelled **fellow-feeling. Fellow feeling** is sympathy and friendship that exists between people who have shared similar experiences or difficulties. N-UNCOUNT

fellowship /feloʊʃɪp/ **fellowships** ◆◇◇◇◇

1 A **fellowship** is a group of people that join together for a common purpose or interest. *...the National Schizophrenia Fellowship... At Merlin's instigation, Arthur founds the Fellowship of the Round Table.* N-COUNT: with supp

2 A **fellowship** at a university is a post which involves research work. *He was offered a research fellowship at Clare College.* N-COUNT

3 Fellowship is a feeling of friendship that people have when they are talking or doing something together and sharing their experiences. *...a sense of community and fellowship.* N-UNCOUNT =companionship

felon /felən/ **felons.** A **felon** is a person who is guilty of committing a felony; a legal term. *He's a convicted felon.* N-COUNT

felony /feləni/ **felonies.** In countries where the legal system distinguishes between very serious crimes and less serious ones, a **felony** is a very serious crime such as armed robbery; a legal term. *He pleaded guilty to six felonies.* ◆◇◇◇◇ N-COUNT

felt /felt/

1 Felt is the past tense and past participle of **feel**.

2 Felt is a thick cloth made from wool or other fibres packed tightly together. N-UNCOUNT

felt-tip, felt-tips. A **felt-tip** or a **felt-tip pen** is a pen which has a piece of fibre as a nib. N-COUNT

fem. fem. is a written abbreviation for **female** or **feminine**.

female /fiːmeɪl/ **females** ◆◆◆◆◇

1 Someone who is **female** is a woman or a girl. *...a sixteen-piece dance band with a female singer... Their aim is equal numbers of male and female MPs by the year 2000... Only 13 per cent of consultants are female.* ♦ **femaleness** *They are under pressure to negate their femaleness.* ADJ ≠male; N-UNCOUNT

2 Women and girls are sometimes referred to as **females** when they are being considered as a type. *But the average young female in this country now is stylish and remarkably confident... Hay fever affects males more than females.* N-COUNT ≠male

3 Female matters and things relate to, belong to, or affect women rather than men. *...female infertility. ...a purveyor of female undergarments... I realize there's no consensus on what are male or female values.* ADJ: ADJ n =women's ≠male

4 You can refer to any creature that can lay eggs or produce babies from its body as a **female**. *Each female will lay just one egg in April or May.* ► Also an adjective. *...the scent given off by the female aphid to attract the male.* N-COUNT ≠male; ADJ ≠male

5 A **female** flower or plant contains the part that will become the fruit when it is fertilized; a technical term in biology. *Figs have male and female flowers.* ADJ: usu ADJ n ≠male

feminine /fe̲mɪnɪn/ ◆◆◇◇◇
1 **Feminine** qualities and things relate to or are considered typical of women, in contrast to men. *...male leaders worrying about their women abandoning traditional feminine roles. ...a manufactured ideal of feminine beauty.*
ADJ: usu ADJ n =female
2 Someone or something that is **feminine** has qualities that are considered typical of women, especially prettiness or gentleness. *I've always been attracted to very feminine women who are not overpowering, the delicate English-rose type... The bedroom has a light, feminine look.*
ADJ-GRADED ≠masculine
3 In some languages, a **feminine** noun, pronoun, or adjective has a different form from a masculine or neuter one, or behaves in a different way.
ADJ

femininity /fe̲mɪnɪ̲nɪti/ ◆◇◇◇◇
1 A woman's **femininity** is the fact that she is a woman. *...the drudgery behind the ideology of motherhood and femininity.*
N-UNCOUNT ≠masculinity
2 **Femininity** means the qualities that are considered to be typical of women. *I wonder if there isn't a streak of femininity in him, a kind of sweetness.*
N-UNCOUNT ≠masculinity

feminism /fe̲mɪnɪzəm/. **Feminism** is the belief and aim that women should have the same rights, power, and opportunities as men. *Feminism may have liberated the feminists, but it has still to change the lives of the majority of women. ...Barbara Johnson, that champion of radical feminism.*
◆◇◇◇◇ N-UNCOUNT

feminist /fe̲mɪnɪst/ **feminists** ◆◆◇◇◇
1 A **feminist** is a person who believes in and supports feminism. *Only 16 per cent of young women in a 1990 survey considered themselves feminists. ...a daunting feminist academic.*
N-COUNT
2 **Feminist** groups, ideas, and activities are involved in feminism. *...the concerns addressed by the feminist movement. ...the reconstruction of history from a feminist perspective.*
ADJ: ADJ n

feminize /fe̲mɪnaɪz/ **feminizes, feminizing, feminized;** also spelled **feminise** in British English. To **feminize** something means to make it into something that involves mainly women or is thought suitable for or typical of women; a formal word. *...their governments' policies of feminizing low-paid factory work. ...a feminised pinstriped suit.*
VERB V n V-ed

femme fatale /fæm fətɑ̲ːl/ **femmes fatales.** If a woman has a reputation as a **femme fatale**, she is considered to be very attractive sexually, and likely to cause problems for any men who are attracted to her.
N-COUNT: usu sing

femur /fi̲ːməʳ/ **femurs.** Your **femur** is the large bone in the upper part of your leg.
N-COUNT

fen /fe̲n/ **fens. Fen** is used to refer to an area of low, flat, wet land, especially in the east of England. *...the flat fen lands near Cambridge.*
◆◇◇◇◇ N-VAR

fence /fe̲ns/ **fences, fencing, fenced** ◆◆◆◇◇
1 A **fence** is a barrier between two areas of land, made of wood or wire supported by posts. *Villagers say the fence would restrict public access to the hills.*
N-COUNT
2 If you **fence** an area of land, you surround it with a fence. *The first task was to fence the wood to exclude sheep... Thomas was playing in a little fenced area full of sand.*
VERB =close off V n V-ed
3 A **fence** in show jumping or horse racing is a frame or artificial hedge that horses have to jump over.
N-COUNT =hurdle
4 A **fence** is a person who receives stolen property and then sells it; an informal use. *He originally acted as a fence for another gang before turning to burglary himself.*
N-COUNT
5 If one country tries to **mend fences** with another, it tries to end a disagreement or quarrel with the other country. You can also say that two countries **mend fences**. *The Soviet Union, I think, is going to try and mend fences with Japan by some gesture over the northern islands... In 1979 China and Vietnam fought a border war, but now the two sides are mending fences.*
PHRASES RECIP: V inflects, PHR *with* n, pl-n PHR
6 If you **sit on the fence**, you avoid supporting a particular side in a discussion or argument. *They are sitting on the fence and refusing to commit themselves... He's not afraid of making decisions and a man who never sits on the fence.*
V inflects

fence in PHRASAL VERB
1 If you **fence** something **in**, you surround it completely with a fence. *He plans to fence in about 100 acres of his ranch five miles north of town.*
V P n
2 If you **are fenced in** by someone or something, they are so close to you that you are unable to move or leave. *She was basically fenced in by what the military wanted to do... He put his hand on the post behind her so that he had her fenced in and could look down on her.*
usu passive *be* V-ed P V-ed P

fence off. If you **fence off** an area of land, you build a fence round it. *When she and Luther got their house, they would fence off a lawn and raise roses from cuttings... They had to evict some gypsies today and I had to go and fence the area off.*
PHRASAL VERB =close off V P n V n P

fencing /fe̲nsɪŋ/ ◆◇◇◇◇
1 **Fencing** is a sport in which two competitors fight each other using very thin swords. The ends of the swords are covered and the competitors wear protective clothes, so that they do not hurt each other.
N-UNCOUNT
2 Materials such as wood or wire that are used to make fences are called **fencing**. *...old wooden fencing.*
N-UNCOUNT

fend /fe̲nd/ **fends, fending, fended.** If you have to **fend for** yourself, you have to look after yourself without relying on help from anyone else. *The woman and her young baby had been thrown out and left to fend for themselves.*
◆◇◇◇◇ VERB =take care of V *for* pron-refl

fend off PHRASAL VERB
1 If you **fend off** unwanted questions, problems, or people, you stop them from affecting you or defend yourself from them, but often only for a short time and without dealing with them completely. *He looked relaxed and determined as he fended off questions from the world's Press... He had struggled to pay off creditors but couldn't fend them off any longer.*
=deflect V P n (not pron) V n P
2 If you **fend off** someone who is attacking you, you use your arms or something such as a stick to defend yourself from their blows. *He raised his hand to fend off the blow.*
V P n (not pron) Also V n P

fender /fe̲ndəʳ/ **fenders** ◆◇◇◇◇
1 A **fender** is a low metal wall built around a fireplace, which stops any coals that fall out of the fire from rolling onto the carpet. *...a brass fender.*
N-COUNT =guard
2 A **fender** is the same as a **fireguard**.
N-COUNT
3 In American English, the **fenders** of a car are the parts of the body over the wheels. The British word is **wing**. *The only damage was to the front fender and headlight.*
N-COUNT
4 The **fenders** of a boat are objects which hang against the outside and protect it from damage when it comes next to a harbour wall or another boat.
N-COUNT

fennel /fe̲nəl/. **Fennel** is a plant with a crisp rounded base and feathery leaves. It can be eaten as a vegetable or used as a herb.
◆◇◇◇◇ N-UNCOUNT

feral /fe̲rəl, fɪ̲ər-/
1 **Feral** animals are wild animals that are not owned or controlled by anyone, especially ones that belong to species which are normally owned and kept by people; a formal use. *...feral cats.*
ADJ: usu ADJ n ≠domesticated
2 If you describe something or someone as **feral**, you mean that they seem wild, fierce, and uncontrolled; a literary use. *...the prowling, feral guitars underpinned by metronomic drum beats.*
ADJ: usu ADJ n =savage

ferment, ferments, fermenting, fermented. The noun is pronounced /fɜ̲ːʳment/. The verb is pronounced /fəʳme̲nt/.
◆◇◇◇◇
1 **Ferment** is excitement and trouble caused by change or uncertainty. *The whole country has been in a state of political ferment for some months.*
N-UNCOUNT =uproar
2 If a food, drink, or other natural substance **ferments**, or if it **is fermented**, a chemical change takes place in it so that alcohol is produced. This process forms part of the production of alcoholic drinks such as wine and beer. *The dried grapes are allowed to ferment until there is no sugar left and the wine is dry... To serve the needs of bakers, manufacturers ferment the yeast to produce a more*
V-ERG V V n V-ed

concentrated product. ...partially fermented wine. N-UNCOUNT
♦ **fermentation** /fɜːʳmenteɪʃᵊn/ *Yeast is essential for the fermentation that produces alcohol.*

fern /fɜːʳn/ **ferns.** A **fern** is a plant that has long stems with feathery leaves and no flowers. There are many types of fern. ◆◇◇◇◇ N-VAR

ferocious /fəroʊʃəs/ ◆◇◇◇◇
1 A **ferocious** animal, person, or action is very fierce and violent. *By its very nature a lion is ferocious... The police had had to deal with some of the most ferocious violence ever seen on the streets of London.* ADJ-GRADED =fierce ♦ **ferociously** *She kicked out ferociously.* ADV-GRADED
2 A **ferocious** war, argument, or other form of conflict involves a great deal of aggression, bitterness, and determination. *Fighting has been ferocious... A ferocious battle to select a new parliamentary candidate is in progress.* ADJ-GRADED ♦ **ferociously** *These days he is ferociously competitive.* ADV-GRADED: ADV adj, ADV with v
3 If you describe actions or feelings as **ferocious**, you mean that they are intense and determined. *Lindbergh was startled at the ferocious depth of anti-British feeling.* ADJ-GRADED ♦ **ferociously** *He set himself ferociously tough standards; and he was ardently devoted to ballet.* ADV-GRADED: ADV adj

ferocity /fərɒsɪti/. The **ferocity** of something is its fierce or violent nature. *The armed forces seem to have been taken by surprise by the ferocity of the attack.* ◆◇◇◇◇ N-UNCOUNT =violence

ferret /ferɪt/ **ferrets, ferreting, ferreted** ◆◇◇◇◇
1 A **ferret** is a small, fierce animal related to the weasel, which is used for hunting rabbits and rats. N-COUNT
2 If you **ferret** about for something, you look for it in a lot of different places or in a place where it is hidden; an informal British expression. *She nonetheless continued to ferret about for possible jobs... She ferreted among some papers.* VERB =search; V about/around; V prep

ferret out. If you **ferret out** some information, you discover it by searching for it very thoroughly; an informal expression. *The team is trying to ferret out missing details... I leave it to the reader to ferret these out.* PHRASAL VERB =search out; V P n (not pron); V n P

ferrous /ferəs/. **Ferrous** means containing or relating to iron. *...ferrous metals. ...ferrous chloride.* ADJ: ADJ n

ferrule /feruːl, AM -rᵊl/ **ferrules.** A **ferrule** is a metal or rubber cap that is fixed onto the end of a stick or post in order to prevent it from splitting or wearing down; a formal word. N-COUNT

ferry /feri/ **ferries, ferrying, ferried** ◆◆◇◇◇
1 A **ferry** is a boat that transports passengers and sometimes also vehicles, usually across rivers or short stretches of sea. *They had recrossed the River Gambia by ferry.* N-COUNT: also by N
2 If a vehicle **ferries** people or goods, it transports them, usually by means of regular journeys between the same two places. *Every day, a plane arrives to ferry guests to and from Bird Island Lodge... It was still dark when five coaches started to ferry the miners the 140 miles from the Silverhill colliery... A helicopter ferried in more soldiers to help in the search.* VERB =transport; V n prep/adv; V n amount; V n with adv; Also V n

ferryboat /feribout/ **ferryboats.** A **ferryboat** is a boat used as a ferry. N-COUNT

fertile /fɜːʳtaɪl, AM -tᵊl/ ◆◆◇◇◇
1 Land or soil that is **fertile** is able to support the growth of a large number of strong healthy plants. *...fertile soil. ...the rolling fertile countryside of East Cork.* ADJ-GRADED =rich ♦ **fertility** /fɜːʳtɪlɪti/ *He was able to bring large sterile acreages back to fertility.* N-UNCOUNT
2 A **fertile** mind or imagination is able to produce a lot of good, original ideas. *...a product of Flynn's fertile imagination... A chess player must have a fertile imagination and rich sense of fantasy.* ADJ-GRADED: usu ADJ n =prolific
3 A situation or environment that is **fertile** in relation to a particular activity or feeling encourages the activity or feeling. *...a fertile breeding ground for this kind of violent racism.* ADJ-GRADED: ADJ n
4 A person or animal that is **fertile** is able to reproduce and have babies or young. *The operation cannot be reversed to make her fertile again.* ADJ-GRADED ≠sterile ♦ **fertility** *Doctors will tell you that pregnancy is the only sure test for fertility.* N-UNCOUNT ≠sterility

fertilize /fɜːʳtɪlaɪz/ **fertilizes, fertilizing, fertilized;** spelled **fertilise** in British English. ◆◇◇◇◇
1 When a woman or female animal or her egg **is fertilized**, a sperm from the male joins with the egg, causing the process of reproduction to begin. A female plant **is fertilized** when its reproductive parts come into contact with pollen from the male plant. *Certain varieties cannot be fertilised with their own pollen. ...the normal sperm levels needed to fertilise the female egg... Pregnancy begins when the fertilized egg is implanted in the wall of the uterus.* VERB =inseminate; be V-ed with n; V n; V-ed; Also V n with n ♦ **fertilization** /fɜːʳtɪlaɪzeɪʃᵊn/ *The average length of time from fertilization until birth is about 266 days.* N-UNCOUNT
2 To **fertilize** land means to improve its quality in order to make plants grow well on it, by spreading manure or a chemical mixture on it. *The faeces contain nitrogen and it is that which fertilises the desert soil. ...chemically fertilized fields.* VERB =enrich; V n; V-ed

fertilizer /fɜːʳtɪlaɪzəʳ/ **fertilizers;** spelled **fertiliser** in British English. **Fertilizer** is a substance such as manure or a chemical mixture that you spread on the ground in order to make plants grow more successfully. *...farming without any purchased chemical, fertilizer or pesticide... Work in a balanced fertiliser before planting.* ◆◆◇◇◇ N-MASS

fervent /fɜːʳvᵊnt/. A **fervent** person has or shows strong feelings about something, and is very sincere and enthusiastic about it. *...a fervent admirer of Morisot's work. ...the fervent hope that matters will be settled promptly.* ◆◇◇◇◇ ADJ-GRADED: usu ADJ n =ardent ♦ **fervently** *Their claims will be fervently denied.* ADV-GRADED: usu ADV with v

fervour /fɜːʳvəʳ/; spelled **fervor** in American English. **Fervour** for something is a very strong feeling for or belief in it; a formal word. *They were concerned only with their own religious fervour.* ◆◇◇◇◇ N-UNCOUNT: usu with supp =enthusiasm

fester /festəʳ/ **festers, festering, festered** ◆◇◇◇◇
1 If you say that a situation, problem, or feeling **is festering**, you disapprove of the fact that it is being allowed to grow more unpleasant or full of anger, because it is not being properly recognized or dealt with. *Resentments are starting to fester. ...festering wounds of the legacy of British imperialism.* VERB PRAGMATICS; V; V-ing
2 If a wound **festers**, it becomes infected, making it worse. *The wound is festering, and gangrene has set in. ...with many of the children being afflicted by festering sores.* VERB; V; V-ing
3 In British English, if you say that food **is festering**, you mean that it is decaying in a very unpleasant way. *The chops will fester and go to waste. ...stale sauces festering in fridges.* VERB =rot; V

festival /festɪvᵊl/ **festivals** ◆◆◆◆◇
1 A **festival** is an organized series of events such as musical concerts or drama productions. *Numerous Umbrian towns hold their own summer festivals of music, theatre, and dance... There are over 350 films in the Edinburgh Film Festival this year.* N-COUNT
2 A **festival** is a day or time of the year when people have a holiday from work and celebrate some special event, often a religious event. *Shavuot is a two-day festival for Orthodox Jews and a one-day festival for Reform and Israeli Jews.* N-COUNT

festive /festɪv/ ◆◇◇◇◇
1 Something that is **festive** is special, colourful, or exciting, especially because of a holiday or celebration. *The town has a festive holiday atmosphere... The Captain's Party on Saturday evening is the cruise's most festive event.* ADJ-GRADED: usu ADJ n =joyous
2 **Festive** means relating to a holiday or celebration, especially Christmas. *With Christmas just around the corner, starting your festive cooking now will give cakes and puddings time to mature... The government's armed forces have halved their strength for the festive break.* ADJ: ADJ n

festive season. People sometimes refer to the Christmas period as the **festive season**. *For many of us, the festive season can be one of the most stressful times of the year.* N-SING: usu the N =Christmas

festivity /festɪvɪti/ **festivities** ◆◇◇◇◇
1 **Festivity** is the celebration of something in a N-UNCOUNT

happy way. *There was a general air of festivity and abandon.*
2 **Festivities** are events that are organized in order to celebrate something. *The festivities included a huge display of fireworks.* N-COUNT: usu pl =celebrations

festoon /festuːn/ **festoons, festooning, festooned.** ◆◇◇◇◇ If something **is festooned** with, for example, lights, balloons, or flowers, large numbers of these things are hung from it or wrapped around it, especially in order to decorate it. *The temples are festooned with lights. ...a lamppost festooned in political stickers.* ► Also a noun. *...a grand amphitheater, whose huge columns were wreathed with festoons of laurel and of magnolia.* VB: usu passive =bedeck; be V-ed with/in n; V-ed; N-COUNT: usu pl, usu N of n

fetal /fiːtəl/. See **foetal**.

fetch /fetʃ/ **fetches, fetching, fetched** ◆◆◇◇◇
1 If you **fetch** something or someone, you go and get them from the place where they are. *Sylvia fetched a towel from the bathroom... Fetch me a glass of water... The caddie ran over to fetch something for him.* VERB; V n; V n n; V n for n
2 If something **fetches** a particular sum of money, it is sold for that amount. *The painting is expected to fetch between two and three million pounds.* VERB =raise; V n
3 See also **far-fetched, fetching.**
4 If you **fetch and carry**, you perform simple, often boring tasks for someone, such as collecting and carrying things for them. *I helped out in the tents fetching and carrying.* PHRASES; Vs inflect

fetch up. If you **fetch up** somewhere, you arrive there, especially when you have not planned to go there; an informal expression. *He spent the first few months on a walking and sketching tour, before fetching up in Dublin.* PHRASAL VERB =end up; V P prep/adv

fetching /fetʃɪŋ/. If you describe someone or something as **fetching**, you think that they look very attractive. *Sue was sitting up in bed, looking very fetching in a flowered bedjacket... Agassi wore a fetching outfit in purple and green.* ADJ-GRADED

fete /feɪt/ **fetes, feting, feted;** spelled **fête** in American English. ◆◇◇◇◇
1 A **fete** is an event that is usually held outdoors and includes competitions, entertainments, and the selling of second-hand or homemade goods. N-COUNT
2 If someone **is feted**, they are celebrated, welcomed, or admired by the public. *Anouska Hempel, the British dress designer, was feted in New York this week at a spectacular dinner... The metamorphosis from anxious wife to feted author was rapid and dramatic.* VB: usu passive; be V-ed; V-ed

fetid /fetɪd, fiː-/; also spelled **foetid** in British English. **Fetid** water or air has a very strong unpleasant smell; a formal use. *The football pitch is flooded with fetid rainwater, stinking to heaven. ...the fetid stench of the slave ship.* ADJ-GRADED: usu ADJ n =stinking

fetish /fetɪʃ/ **fetishes** ◆◇◇◇◇
1 If someone has a **fetish**, they have an unusually strong liking or need for a particular object or activity, as a way of getting sexual pleasure. *...rubber and leather fetishes. ...fetish wear for sexual arousal.* N-COUNT: oft n N
2 If you say that someone has a **fetish** for doing something, you disapprove of the fact that they do it very often or enjoy it very much. *The Conservatives said Labour had a fetish for increasing taxes.* N-COUNT: usu with supp; PRAGMATICS; =fixation
3 In some cultures, a **fetish** is an object, especially a carved object, which is considered to have religious importance or magical powers. N-COUNT

fetishism /fetɪʃɪzəm/. **Fetishism** involves a person having a strong liking or need for a particular object or activity which gives them sexual pleasure and excitement. N-UNCOUNT

fetishist /fetɪʃɪst/ **fetishists.** A **fetishist** is a person who has a strong liking or need for a particular object or activity in order to experience sexual pleasure and excitement. *...a foot fetishist.* N-COUNT: usu n N

fetlock /fetlɒk/ **fetlocks.** A horse's **fetlock** is the back part of its leg, just above the hoof. N-COUNT

fetter /fetəʳ/ **fetters, fettering, fettered**
1 If you say that you **are fettered** by something, you dislike it because it prevents you from behaving or moving in a free and natural way; a literary use. *...a private trust which would not be fettered by bureaucracy... The black mud fettered her movements.* VERB; PRAGMATICS; =hamper; be V-ed; V n
2 You can use **fetters** to refer to things such as rules, traditions, or responsibilities that you dislike because they prevent you from behaving in the way you want; a literary use. *...the fetters of social convention.* N-PLURAL: usu with supp, oft N of n; PRAGMATICS; =constraints
3 Especially in former times, **fetters** were chains for a prisoner's feet. *He saw a boy in fetters in the dungeons.* N-COUNT: usu pl

fettle /fetəl/. If you say that someone or something is **in fine fettle**, you are emphasizing that they are in very good health or condition; an informal expression. *You seem in fine fettle.* PHRASE: v-link PHR, PHR after v; PRAGMATICS

fetus /fiːtəs/. See **foetus**.

feud /fjuːd/ **feuds, feuding, feuded** ◆◇◇◇◇
1 A **feud** is a quarrel in which two people or groups remain angry with each other for a long time, although they are not always fighting or arguing. *...a long and bitter feud between the state government and the villagers.* N-COUNT =vendetta
2 If one person or group **feuds** with another, they have a quarrel that lasts a long time. You can also say that two people or groups **feud**. *He feuded with his ex-wife... Their families had feuded since their teenage daughters quarrelled two years ago.* V-RECIP; V with n; pl-n V

feudal /fjuːdəl/. **Feudal** means relating to the system or the time of feudalism. *...the emperor and his feudal barons.* ◆◇◇◇◇ ADJ: ADJ n

feudalism /fjuːdəlɪzəm/. **Feudalism** was a system in which people were given land and protection by people of higher rank, and worked and fought for them in return. N-UNCOUNT

fever /fiːvəʳ/ **fevers** ◆◆◇◇◇
1 If you have a **fever** when you are ill, you have a body temperature that is higher than usual and a quick heartbeat. *My Uncle Jim had a high fever... Symptoms of the disease include fever and weight loss.* • See also **hay fever, rheumatic fever, scarlet fever.** N-VAR =temperature
2 A **fever** is also extreme excitement or agitation about something. *Angie waited in a fever of excitement.* N-COUNT: usu with supp =frenzy

fevered /fiːvəʳd/
1 **Fevered** is used to describe feelings of great excitement, and the activities that result from them; used in written English. *Meg was in a state of fevered anticipation. ...fevered speculation over the leadership.* ADJ-GRADED: usu ADJ n =feverish
2 If a person or their brow is **fevered**, they are suffering from a fever; a literary use. *He applied fragrant compresses to her fevered brow.* ADJ-GRADED: usu ADJ n

feverish /fiːvərɪʃ/ ◆◇◇◇◇
1 **Feverish** activity is done extremely quickly, often in a state of agitation because you want to finish it as soon as possible. *The breakthrough followed some feverish last minute negotiations with Mr Shamir's prospective partners.* ♦ **feverishly** *City workers and volunteers are working feverishly to remove the heavy snow from the roofs of homes.* ADJ-GRADED =frantic; ADV-GRADED: ADV with v
2 **Feverish** emotion is characterized by extreme agitation or excitement. *He will be attending next week's American Grammy Awards in feverish anticipation. ...a state of feverish excitement.* ADJ: ADJ n
3 If you are **feverish**, you are suffering from a fever. *A feverish child refuses to eat and asks only for cold drinks... She looked feverish, her eyes glistened.* ♦ **feverishly** *He slept feverishly all afternoon and into the night.* ADJ-GRADED; ADV-GRADED: ADV with v

fever pitch. If something is at **fever pitch**, it is in an extremely active or excited state. *Frances kept talking, her mind at fever pitch... Campaigning is reaching fever pitch for elections on November 6.* N-UNCOUNT: oft at N

few /fjuː/ **fewer, fewest** ◆◆◆◆◆
1 You use **a few** to indicate that you are talking about a small number of people or things. You can also say **a very few**. *I gave a dinner party for a few close friends... We had a few drinks afterwards... Here are a few more ideas to consider... She was silent for a few seconds.* ► Also a pronoun. *Doctors* DET: DET pl-n =a couple of; PRON

work an average of 90 hours a week, while a few are on call for up to 120 hours... A strict diet is appropriate for only a few. ▶ Also a quantifier. *There are many ways eggs can be prepared; here are a few of them. ...a little tea-party I'm giving for a few of the teachers.* QUANT: QUANT *of* def-pl-n =some

2 You use **few** after adjectives and determiners to indicate that you are talking about a small number of things or people. *The past few weeks of her life had been the most pleasant she could remember... The leaders are expected to fly to Mecca in the next few days to seal the agreement. ...in the last few chapters... A train would pass through there every few minutes at that time of day.* ADJ: adj/det ADJ n =couple of

3 You use **few** to emphasize that there are only a small number of people or things. You can use 'so', 'too' and 'very' in front of **few**. *She had few friends, and was generally not functioning up to her potential... Few members planned to vote for him... Very few firms collect the tax, even when they're required to do so by law.* DET: DET pl-n PRAGMATICS =many ▶ Also a pronoun. *The trouble is that few want to buy, despite the knockdown prices on offer. ...a true singing and songwriting talent that few suspected.* PRON ▶ Also a quantifier. *Few of the beach houses still had lights on... Few of the volunteers had military experience.* QUANT: QUANT *of* def-pl-n ▶ Also an adjective. *...spending her few waking hours in front of the TV... His memories of his father are few.* ADJ

4 **The few** means a small set of people considered as separate from the majority, especially because they share a particular opportunity or quality that the others do not have. *This should not be an experience for the few. ...a system built on academic excellence for the few.* N-SING: *the* N

5 You use **as few as** before a number to suggest that it is surprisingly small. *One study showed that even as few as ten cigarettes a day can damage fertility... The factory may make as few as 1,500 cars this year.* PHRASES PHR num

6 Things that are **few and far between** are very rare or uncommon. *Successful women politicians are few and far between... In this economic climate new ideas were few and far between.* v-link PHR =rare, uncommon

7 You use **a good few** and **not a few** when you are referring to quite a lot of things or people. *I think a good few of the others were like me, a bit confused... I've made this argument, and not a few people would disagree with me.* PHR n, PHR *of* n =many

8 If you say that someone **has had a few too many** or **has had a few**, you mean that they have drunk too many alcoholic drinks. *A breathalyzer tells you you've a had a few too many.* V inflects

9 You use **no fewer than** to emphasize that a number is surprisingly large. *No fewer than thirteen foreign ministers attended the session.* PHR num PRAGMATICS

fey /feɪ/. If you describe someone as **fey**, you mean that they behave in a shy, childish, or unpredictable way, and you are often suggesting that this is unnatural or insincere; a literary word. *They are no longer anything like as fey and reserved as they once were... Her fey charm and eccentric ways were legendary.* ADJ-GRADED =whimsical

fez /fez/ **fezzes.** A **fez** is a round, red hat with no brim, which has a flat top with a tassel hanging from it. N-COUNT

ff. ◆◇◇◇◇

1 In a book or journal, when **ff.** is written after a particular page or line number, it means 'and the following pages or lines'. *...p. 173 ff.*

2 In a piece of music **ff** is a written abbreviation for 'fortissimo'.

fiancé /fiɒnseɪ, AM fiːɑːnseɪ/ **fiancés.** A woman's **fiancé** is the man to whom she is engaged to be married. ◆◇◇◇◇ N-COUNT: usu poss N

fiancée /fiɒnseɪ, AM fiːɑːnseɪ/ **fiancées.** A man's **fiancée** is the woman to whom he is engaged to be married. ◆◇◇◇◇ N-COUNT: usu poss N

fiasco /fiæskoʊ/ **fiascos.** If you describe an event or attempt to do something as a **fiasco**, you are emphasizing that it fails completely. *The blame for the Charleston fiasco did not lie with him... It was a bit of a fiasco.* ◆◇◇◇◇ N-COUNT: usu with supp PRAGMATICS =debacle

fiat /fiːæt, faɪ-/ **fiats.** If something is done by **fiat**, it is done because of an official order given by someone in authority; a formal use. *He has tried to impose solutions to the country's problems by fiat.* N-COUNT: also *by* N

fib /fɪb/ **fibs, fibbing, fibbed**

1 A **fib** is a small, unimportant lie; an informal use. *She told innocent fibs like anyone else.* N-COUNT =untruth

2 If someone **is fibbing**, they are telling lies; an informal use. *He laughs loudly when I accuse him of fibbing.* VERB V

fibre /faɪbəʳ/ **fibres;** spelled **fiber** in American English. ◆◆◇◇◇

1 A **fibre** is a thin thread of a natural or artificial substance, especially one that is used to make cloth or rope. *If you look at the paper under a microscope you will see the fibres. ...a variety of coloured fibres.* N-COUNT =strand

2 A particular **fibre** is a type of cloth or other material that is made from or consists of threads. *The ball is made of rattan - a natural fibre.* N-VAR

3 **Fibre** consists of the parts of plants or seeds that your body cannot digest. Fibre is useful because it makes food pass quickly through your body. *Most vegetables contain fibre.* N-UNCOUNT

4 A **fibre** is a thin piece of flesh like a thread which connects nerve cells in your body or which muscles are made of. *...the nerve fibres.* N-COUNT

5 If you say that you feel something **with every fibre of** your **being**, you mean that you feel it very deeply; a literary use. *I wanted to be an actress with every fibre of my being.* ● See also **moral fibre.** PHRASE

fibreglass /faɪbəʳglɑːs, -glæs/; spelled **fiberglass** in American English.

1 **Fibreglass** is plastic strengthened with short, thin threads of glass. N-UNCOUNT

2 **Fibreglass** is a material made from short, thin threads of glass which can be used to stop heat escaping. N-UNCOUNT

fibre optics; spelled **fiber optics** in American English. The form **fibre optic** is used as a modifier.

1 **Fibre optics** is the use of long thin threads of glass to carry information in the form of light. N-UNCOUNT

2 **Fibre optic** means relating to or involved in fibre optics. *...fibre optic cables.* ADJ: ADJ n

fibroid /faɪbrɔɪd/ **fibroids.** **Fibroids** are lumps of fibrous tissue that form in a woman's uterus, often causing pain. N-COUNT: usu pl

fibrous /faɪbrəs/. A **fibrous** object or substance contains a lot of fibres or fibre, or looks as if it does. *Blood vessels are made up of layers of muscular, elastic and fibrous tissue.* ADJ-GRADED: usu ADJ n

fibula /fɪbjʊlə/ **fibulae.** Your **fibula** is the outer bone of the two bones in the lower part of your leg; a medical term. N-COUNT

fickle /fɪkəl/ ◆◇◇◇◇

1 If you describe someone as **fickle**, you disapprove of them because they keep changing their mind about what they like or want. *The group has been notoriously fickle in the past.* ADJ-GRADED PRAGMATICS =capricious ♦ **fickleness** *...the fickleness of businessmen and politicians.* N-UNCOUNT: usu N *of* n

2 If you say that something is **fickle**, you mean that it often changes and is unreliable. *Orta's weather can be fickle.* ADJ-GRADED ≠dependable

fiction /fɪkʃən/ **fictions** ◆◆◇◇◇

1 **Fiction** refers to books and stories about imaginary people and events, rather than books about real people or events. *Immigrant tales have always been popular themes in fiction... Diana is a writer of historical fiction.* ● See also **science fiction.** N-UNCOUNT: also N in pl ≠non-fiction

2 A statement or account that is **fiction** is not true. *The truth or fiction of this story has never been truly determined.* N-UNCOUNT ≠fact

3 If something is a **fiction**, it is not true, although people sometimes pretend that it is true. *Total recycling is a fiction.* N-COUNT ≠fact

fictional /fɪkʃənəl/. **Fictional** characters or events occur only in stories, plays, or films and never actually existed or happened. *It is drama featuring fictional characters... Ulverton is a fictional village on the Wessex Downs.* ◆◇◇◇◇ ADJ: usu ADJ n =imaginary

fictionalize /fɪkʃənəlaɪz/ **fictionalizes, fictionalizing, fictionalized;** also spelled **fictionalise** in British English. To **fictionalize** an account of something that really happened means to tell it as a story, with some details changed or added. *We had to fictionalize names. ...a fictionalised account of a true and horrific story.*
VERB · V n · V-ed

fictitious /fɪktɪʃəs/ ◆◇◇◇◇
1 Fictitious is used to describe something that is false or does not exist, although some people claim that it is true or exists. *We're interested in the source of these fictitious rumours.*
ADJ: usu ADJ n =non-existent
2 A **fictitious** character, thing, or event occurs in a story, play, or film but never really existed or happened. *The persons and events portrayed in this production are fictitious.*
ADJ =imaginary

fiddle /fɪdᵊl/ **fiddles, fiddling, fiddled** ◆◇◇◇◇
1 If you **fiddle with** an object, you keep moving it or touching it with your fingers. *Harriet fiddled with a pen on the desk.*
VERB · V *with* n
2 If you **fiddle with** something, you change it in minor ways. *She told Whistler that his portrait of her was finished and to stop fiddling with it.*
VERB · V *with* n
3 If you **fiddle with** a machine, you adjust it. *He turned on the radio and fiddled with the knob until he got a talk show.*
VERB · V *with* n
4 If someone **fiddles** financial documents, they alter them dishonestly so that they get money for themselves; an informal use. *He's been fiddling the books... Stop fiddling your expenses account.*
VERB · V n
5 A **fiddle** is a dishonest action or scheme in which someone gets money for themselves; used mainly in informal British English. *Police investigating a £1 million car insurance fiddle arrested 16 people yesterday. ...legitimate businesses that act as covers for tax fiddles.*
N-COUNT: oft supp N =swindle
6 If something is **a fiddle**, it is quite difficult to do because it involves small or complicated objects; used mainly in informal British English. *I found out how to fix the tray on – a bit of a fiddle.*
N-SING: *a* N
7 Some people call violins **fiddles**, especially when they are used to play folk music. *Hardy as a young man played the fiddle at local dances.*
N-VAR: oft *the* N =violin
8 Someone who is as **fit as a fiddle** is very healthy and full of energy. *I'm as fit as a fiddle – with energy to spare.*
PHRASES · v-link PHR
9 If someone is **on the fiddle**, they get money by doing illegal or dishonest things; used mainly in informal British English.
v-link PHR
10 If you say that someone **is fiddling while** Rome **burns**, you mean that they are not dealing with a difficult or dangerous situation but instead are doing useless things or pretending that nothing is wrong.
V inflects
11 If you **play second fiddle** to someone, your position is less important than theirs in something that you are doing together. *She hated the thought of playing second fiddle to Rose.*
V inflects, oft PHR *to* n

fiddle about or **fiddle around.** The form **fiddle about** is mainly used in British English.
PHRASAL VERB
1 If you **fiddle about** or **fiddle around** with a machine, you do things to it to try and make it work. *Two of them got out to fiddle around with the engine.*
=tinker · V P *with* n · Also V P
2 If someone **fiddles about** or **fiddles around**, they waste time doing unimportant things instead of dealing with important problems. *He wants lawmakers to basically stop fiddling around as the country moves closer to breaking up... He wastes time fiddling about with minor matters.*
V P · V P *with* n
3 If you say that someone is **fiddling about with** or **fiddling around with** something, you mean that they are changing it in a way that you disapprove of. *Right now in Congress, they're fiddling around with the budget and so on... One always wonders when a man starts fiddling about with his Will.*
V P P n

fiddler /fɪdləʳ/ **fiddlers** ◆◇◇◇◇
1 A **fiddler** is someone who plays the violin, especially one who plays folk music. *And the fiddler played another little tune.*
N-COUNT =violinist
2 A **fiddler** is someone who lies or dishonestly alters financial documents in order to get money for themselves; used mainly in informal British English. *Other benefits such as dole money could be frozen and there will be a huge push to weed out fiddlers.*
N-COUNT

fiddlesticks /fɪdᵊlstɪks/. Some people say **fiddlesticks** as an impolite way of showing that they disagree with what someone has just said; an old-fashioned expression. *'Fiddlesticks!' said Lucy, cutting him short.*
EXCLAM =nonsense

fiddling /fɪdəlɪŋ/
1 Fiddling is the practice of getting money dishonestly by altering financial documents; an informal use. *Salomon's fiddling is likely to bring big trouble for the firm.*
N-UNCOUNT
2 Violin playing, especially of folk music, is sometimes referred to as **fiddling**.
N-UNCOUNT
3 You can describe something as **fiddling** if it is small, unimportant, or difficult to do. *One reason it gives for the lack of progress is the daunting amount of fiddling technical detail.*
ADJ-GRADED: usu ADJ n

fiddly /fɪdəli/ **fiddlier, fiddliest.** Something is **fiddly** is difficult to do or use, because it involves small or complicated objects. *It was a time-consuming and fiddly job... Fish can be fiddly to cook.*
ADJ-GRADED: oft ADJ to-inf

fidelity /fɪdelɪti/ ◆◇◇◇◇
1 Fidelity is loyalty to a person, organization, or set of beliefs; a formal use. *I had to promise fidelity to the Queen.*
N-UNCOUNT: oft N *to* n =loyalty ≠disloyalty
2 Fidelity is being loyal to your husband, wife, or partner by not having a sexual relationship with anyone else. *Wanting fidelity implies you're thinking about a major relationship.*
N-UNCOUNT =faithfulness
3 The **fidelity** of something such as a report or translation is its degree of accuracy; a formal use. *...the fidelity of these early documents.*
N-UNCOUNT: with poss, oft N *to* n =accuracy

fidget /fɪdʒɪt/ **fidgets, fidgeting, fidgeted**
1 If you **fidget**, you keep moving your hands or feet slightly or changing your position slightly, for example because you are nervous, bored, or excited. *Brenda fidgeted in her seat.* ► **Fidget around** and **fidget about** mean the same as **fidget**. *There were two new arrivals, fidgeting around, waiting to ask questions.*
VERB · V · PHRASAL VERB · V P
2 If you **fidget with** something, you keep moving it or touching it with your fingers with small movements, for example because you are nervous or bored. *He fidgeted with his tie... The priest fidgeted nervously with his black rosary beads.*
VERB · V *with* n

fidgety /fɪdʒɪti/. Someone who is **fidgety** keeps fidgeting, for example because they are nervous or bored.
ADJ-GRADED

fief /fiːf/ **fiefs.** In former times, a **fief** was a piece of land given to someone by their lord, to whom they had a duty to provide particular services in return.
N-COUNT

field /fiːld/ **fields, fielding, fielded** ◆◆◆◆◇
1 A **field** is an area of grass, for example in a park or on a farm. A **field** is also an area of land on which a crop is grown. *...a field of wheat... They went for walks together in the fields.*
N-COUNT
2 A sports **field** is an area of grass where sports are played. *...a football field... Gavin Hastings was helped from the field with ankle injuries.*
N-COUNT
3 A **field** is an area of land or sea bed under which large amounts of a particular mineral have been found. *...an extensive natural gas field in Alaska.*
N-COUNT: usu supp N
4 A magnetic, gravitational, or electric **field** is the area in which that particular force is strong enough to have an effect. *Some people are worried that electromagnetic fields from electric power lines could increase the risk of cancer.*
N-COUNT: usu supp N
5 A particular **field** is a particular subject of study or type of activity. *Exciting artistic breakthroughs have recently occurred in the fields of painting, sculpture and architecture... Each of the authors of the tapes is an expert in his field.*
N-COUNT: usu with supp =discipline
6 You can refer to the area where fighting or other military action in a war takes place as the **field** or the **field** of battle. *We never defeated them on the field of battle. ...the need for politicians to leave day-to-day decisions to commanders in the field.*
N-COUNT: usu *the* N, oft N *of* n

7 Your **field** of vision or your visual **field** is the area that you can see without turning your head. *Our field of vision is surprisingly wide.* N-COUNT: with supp

8 The **field** is a way of referring to all the competitors taking part in a particular race or sports contest. *Going into the fourth lap, the two most broadly experienced riders led the field... The field were so close that they would have caught us if I hadn't begun the sprint. ...one of the strongest fields ever assembled for the Women's Bowling Association championship.* N-COUNT-COLL: usu sing, the N

9 You use **field** to describe work or study that is done in a real, natural environment rather than in a theoretical way or in controlled conditions. *I also conducted a field study among the boys about their attitude to relationships... Our teachers took us on field trips to observe plants and animals, firsthand... The man offering help is a field worker.* ADJ: ADJ n

10 In a game of cricket, baseball, or rounders, the team that **is fielding** is trying to catch the ball, while the other team is trying to hit it. *When we are fielding, the umpires keep looking at the ball.* VB: usu cont; V; Also V n ♦ **fielding** *Their bowling performance was very good, their fielding very sharp and their batting impressive.* N-UNCOUNT

11 If you say that someone **fields** a question or enquiry, you mean that they answer it or deal with it, usually successfully; used in journalism. *He was later shown on television, fielding questions.* VERB; V n

12 If a sports team **fields** a particular number or type of players, the players are chosen to play for the team on a particular occasion. *England intend fielding their strongest team in next month's World Youth Championship.* VERB; V n

13 If a candidate in an election is representing a political party, you can say that the party **is fielding** that candidate; used in journalism. *Mr Hata says he hopes to field 100 candidates in the general election next month.* VERB =put up; V n

14 See also **coalfield**, **minefield**, **playing field**, **snowfield**.

15 If someone **is having a field day**, they are very busy doing something that they enjoy, even though it may be hurtful for other people. *In our absence the office gossips are probably having a field day... I suspect that the lawyers are going to have a field day before it's all sorted out.* PHRASES; V inflects

16 Work or study that is done **in the field** is done in a real, natural environment rather than in a theoretical way or in controlled conditions. *Both Jersey and London zoos are doing major conservation work in captivity and in the field.* usu PHR after v

17 If you say that someone **leads the field** in a particular activity, you mean that they are better, more active, or more successful than everyone else who is involved in it. *When it comes to picking up awards they lead the field by miles.* V inflects

18 If someone **plays the field**, they have a number of different romantic or sexual relationships; an informal expression. *He gave up playing the field and married a year ago.* V inflects

fielder /fiːldəʳ/ **fielders.** A **fielder** is a player in cricket, baseball, or rounders who is fielding or one who has a particular skill at fielding. *The fielders crouch around the batsman's wicket.* ◆◇◇◇◇ N-COUNT

field event, field events. A **field event** is an athletics contest such as the high jump or throwing the discus or javelin, rather than a race. N-COUNT

field-glasses; also spelled **field glasses**. **Field-glasses** are binoculars; a formal expression. N-PLURAL: also *a pair of* N

field marshal, field marshals; also spelled **field-marshal.** A **field marshal** is an officer in the army who has the highest rank. ◆◇◇◇◇ N-COUNT; N-TITLE

field mouse, field mice; also spelled **field-mouse.** A **field mouse** is a mouse with a long tail that lives in fields and woods. N-COUNT

field sport, field sports. Hunting, shooting birds, and fishing with a rod are referred to as **field sports** when they are done mainly for pleasure. N-COUNT: usu pl

field-test, field-tests, field-testing, field-tested. If you **field-test** a new piece of equipment, you test it in a real, natural environment. *We've field-tested them ourselves and are happy that they work.* VERB; V n ► Also a noun. *Field tests are to be carried out at Blair Castle and Burghley.* N-COUNT

fieldwork /fiːldwɜːʳk/. **Fieldwork** is the gathering of information about something in a real, natural environment, rather than in a place of study such as a laboratory or classroom. *...anthropological fieldwork.* N-UNCOUNT

fiend /fiːnd/ **fiends**

1 If you describe someone as a **fiend**, you mean that they are extremely wicked or cruel; used in written English. *...such a saint to his patients and such a fiend to his children.* N-COUNT =monster

2 **Fiend** can be used after a noun to refer to a person who is very interested in the thing mentioned, and enjoys having a lot of it or doing it often. *...if you're a heavy coffee drinker or strong-tea fiend.* N-COUNT: n N

fiendish /fiːndɪʃ/

1 A **fiendish** plan, action, or device is very clever or imaginative; an informal use. *...a fiendish plot.* ADJ-GRADED: usu ADJ n =devilish ♦ **fiendishly** *This figure is reached by a fiendishly clever equation.* ADV: usu ADV adj

2 A **fiendish** problem or task is very difficult and challenging; an informal use. *A rather neat option allows you to design your own fiendish puzzle. ...the fiendish difficulty of the questions.* ADJ-GRADED: ADJ n =infernal ♦ **fiendishly** *America's trade laws are fiendishly complex.* ADV: ADV adj

3 A **fiendish** person enjoys being cruel. *This was a fiendish act of wickedness.* ADJ-GRADED: usu ADJ n

fierce /fɪəʳs/ **fiercer, fiercest** ◆◆◆◇◇

1 A **fierce** animal or person is very aggressive or angry. *They look like the teeth of some fierce animal.* ADJ-GRADED =ferocious ♦ **fiercely** *'I don't know,' she said fiercely.* ADV-GRADED

2 **Fierce** feelings or actions are very intense or enthusiastic, or involve great activity. *Competition has been fierce to win a stake in Skoda... A fierce battle has been raging all day in the Croatian town of Pakrac... He inspires fierce loyalty in his friends.* ADJ-GRADED ♦ **fiercely** *He has always been ambitious and fiercely competitive.* ADV-GRADED: ADV adj, ADV with v

3 **Fierce** conditions are very intense, great, or strong. *Polish climbers were trapped by a fierce storm which went on for five days.* ADJ-GRADED ♦ **fiercely** *As I arrived a lorry had just been set on fire and was burning fiercely.* ADV-GRADED: ADV with v, ADV adj

fiery /faɪəri/ **fieriest** ◆◇◇◇◇

1 If you describe something as **fiery**, you mean that it is burning strongly or contains fire; a literary use. *A helicopter crashed in a fiery explosion in Vallejo.* ADJ: usu ADJ n =flaming

2 You can use **fiery** for emphasis when you are referring to bright colours such as red or orange; a literary use. *A large terracotta pot planted with Busy Lizzie provides a fiery bright red display.* ADJ-GRADED: usu ADJ n PRAGMATICS

3 If you describe food or drink as **fiery**, you mean that it has a very strong hot or spicy taste; used in written English. *A fiery combination of chicken, chillies and rice.* ADJ-GRADED: usu ADJ n =spicy

4 If you describe someone as **fiery**, you mean that they express very strong emotions, especially anger, in their behaviour or speech; used in written English. *She was a fiery, brilliant and unyielding intellectual and politician... She had a fiery temper and liked to get her own way.* ADJ-GRADED: usu ADJ n

fiesta /fiestə/ **fiestas.** A **fiesta** is a time of public entertainment and parties, usually on a special religious holiday, especially in Spain or Latin America. N-COUNT

fife /faɪf/ **fifes.** A **fife** is a small pipe-shaped musical instrument. *...a fife and drum band.* N-COUNT

fifteen /fɪftiːn/ **fifteens** ◆◆◆◆◆

1 **Fifteen** is the number 15. NUM

2 A rugby-union team can be referred to as a **fifteen**. N-COUNT-COLL

fifteenth /fɪftiːnθ/. The **fifteenth** item in a series is the one that you count as number fifteen. ◆◆◆◆◇ ORD

fifth /fɪfθ/ **fifths** ◆◆◆◆◇

1 The **fifth** item in a series is the one that you count as number five. *Joe has recently returned from his fifth trip to Australia.* ORD

2 A **fifth** is one of five equal parts of something. *India spends over a fifth of its budget on defence.* FRACTION

fifth columnist, fifth columnists. A **fifth columnist** is someone who secretly supports and helps the enemies of the country or organization they are in.
N-COUNT =traitor

fiftieth /fɪftiəθ/. The **fiftieth** item in a series is the one that you count as number fifty.
◆◆◆◆◇ ORD

fifty /fɪfti/ **fifties.**
◆◆◆◆◆

1 Fifty is the number 50.
NUM

2 When you talk about the **fifties**, you are referring to numbers between 50 and 59. For example, if you are **in your fifties**, you are aged between 50 and 59. If the temperature is **in the fifties**, the temperature is between 50 and 59 degrees. *I probably look as if I'm in my fifties rather than my seventies.*
N-PLURAL

3 The fifties is the decade between 1950 and 1959. *He began performing in the early fifties, singing and playing guitar.*
N-PLURAL: the N

fifty-fifty

1 If something such money or property is divided or shared **fifty-fifty** between two people, each person gets half of it; an informal use. *The proceeds of the sale are split fifty-fifty.* ▶ Also an adjective. *The new firm was owned on a fifty-fifty basis by the two parent companies.*
ADV: ADV after v; ADJ

2 If there is a **fifty-fifty** chance of something happening, it is equally likely to happen as it is not to happen; an informal use. *You've got a fifty-fifty chance of being right.*
ADJ: usu ADJ n

fig /fɪg/ **figs**
◆◇◇◇◇

1 A **fig** is a soft sweet fruit that grows in hot countries. It is full of tiny seeds and is often eaten dried.
N-COUNT

2 A **fig** or a **fig tree** is a tree on which figs grow.
N-COUNT

3 If you say that someone doesn't **care a fig** or doesn't **give a fig** about something, you are emphasizing that they think it is unimportant or that they are not interested in it; an old-fashioned, informal expression. *I do not give a fig what society thinks.*
PHRASE: with brd-neg, V inflects, oft PHR about/for n PRAGMATICS

fig.

1 In books and magazines, **fig.** is used as an abbreviation for **figure** in order to tell the reader which illustration or diagram is being referred to. *Draw the basic outlines in black felt-tip pen (see fig 4).*

2 In some dictionaries and language books, **fig.** is used as an abbreviation for **figurative**.

fight /faɪt/ **fights, fighting, fought**
◆◆◆◆◆

1 If you **fight** something unpleasant, you try in a determined way to prevent it or stop it happening. *Mother Teresa is an elderly nun who has devoted her life to fighting poverty... More units to fight forest fires are planned... I've spent a lifetime fighting against racism and prejudice.* ▶ Also a noun. *...the fight against drug addiction.*
VERB V n V against n; N-COUNT: oft N against n

2 If you **fight** for something, you try in a determined way to get it or achieve it. *Our Government should be fighting for an end to food subsidies... Lee had to fight hard for his place on the expedition... I told him how we had fought to hold on to the company... The team has fought its way to the cup final.* ▶ Also a noun. *I too am committing myself to continue the fight for justice.*
VERB V for n V to-inf V way prep/adv; N-COUNT: usu N for n =battle

3 If an army or group **fights** a battle with another army or group, or **fights** another army or group, they oppose each other with weapons. You can also say that two armies or groups **fight** a battle. *The two men fought a battle over land and water rights... In the latest incident at the weekend police fought a gun battle with a gang which used hand grenades against them... The Sioux had always fought other tribes for territorial rights.*
V-RECIP pl-n V n over/for n V n with n V n for/over n Also pl-n V, V n

4 If a person or army **fights** in a battle or a war, they take part in it. *He fought in the war and was taken prisoner by the Americans... If I were a young man I would sooner go to prison than fight for this country... My father did leave his university to fight the Germans... Last month rebels fought their way into the capital.* ● See also **dogfight.** ♦ **fighting** *More than nine hundred people have died in the fighting.*
VERB V V for n V n V way prep/adv; N-UNCOUNT

5 If one person **fights** with another, or **fights** them, the two people hit or kick each other because they want to hurt each other. You can also say that two people **fight**. *As a child she fought with her younger sister... I did fight him, I punched him but it was like hitting a wall... He wrenched the crutch from Jacob, who didn't fight him for it... I refuse to act that way when my kids fight... You get a lot of unruly drunks fighting each other.* ▶ Also a noun. *He had had a fight with Smith and bloodied his nose.*
V-RECIP V with n V n V n for n pl-n V pl-n V pron-recip; N-COUNT: oft N with n

6 If one person **fights** with another, or **fights** them, they have an angry disagreement or quarrel. You can also say that two people **fight**; an informal use. *She was always arguing with him and fighting with him... Gwendolen started fighting her teachers... Mostly, they fight about paying bills.* ▶ Also a noun. *We think maybe he took off because he had a big fight with his dad the night before.*
V-RECIP =quarrel, argue V with n V n pl-n V about/over n Also pl-n V; N-COUNT

7 If you **fight** your way to a place, you move towards it with great difficulty, for example because there are a lot of people or obstacles in your way. *I fought my way into a carriage just before the doors closed... Peter fought his way through a blizzard to save one of the chickens.*
VERB =battle V way prep/adv

8 A **fight** is a boxing match. *This was Hyer's last fight, for no one else challenged him... The referee stopped the fight.*
N-COUNT =bout

9 To **fight** means to take part in a boxing match. *In a few hours' time one of the world's most famous boxers will be fighting in Britain for the first time... I'd like to fight him because he's undefeated and I want to be the first man to beat him... I'd like to fight him for the title.*
VERB V V n V n for n

10 If you **fight** an election, you are a candidate in the election and try to win it. *The former party treasurer helped raise almost £40 million to fight the election campaign.*
VERB V n

11 You can use **fight** to refer to a contest such as an election or a sports match; used in journalism. *In the fight for the US Presidency, round two was a disaster for George Bush.*
N-COUNT: usu sing =contest

12 If you **fight** a case or a court action, you persevere in suing someone, or put forward a defence when you are sued or charged with something. *Watkins sued the Army and fought his case in various courts for 10 years... The newspaper is fighting a damages action brought by the actress.*
VERB V n

13 Fight is the desire or ability to keep fighting. *I thought that we had a lot of fight in us.*
N-UNCOUNT

14 If you **fight** an emotion or desire, you try very hard not to feel it, show it, or act on it, but do not always succeed. *I desperately fought the urge to giggle... He fought with the urge to smoke one of the cigars he'd given up awhile ago... He fought to be patient with her.*
VERB =resist V n V with n V to-inf

15 If you **fight for breath**, you try to breathe but find it very difficult.
PHRASES V inflects

16 If you have a **fighting chance** of doing or achieving something, it is possible that you will do or achieve it, but only if you make a great effort or are very lucky. *When they didn't shoot at me right away, I figured I had a fighting chance.*
usu PHR after v

17 In British English, if you describe someone as **fighting fit**, you are emphasizing that they are very fit or healthy. *After a good night's sleep I feel fighting fit again.*
v-link PHR PRAGMATICS

18 Someone who **is fighting for** their **life** is making a great effort to stay alive, either when they are being physically attacked or when they are very ill. *He is still fighting for his life in hospital.*
V inflects

19 ● to **fight a losing battle**: see **battle.** ● **fight to the finish**: see **finish.** ● to **fight fire with fire**: see **fire.** ● to **fight shy**: see **shy.**

fight back
PHRASAL VERB

1 If you **fight back** against someone or something that is attacking or harming you, you resist them actively or attack them. *The teenage attackers fled when the two men fought back... We should take some comfort from the ability of the judicial system to fight back against corruption.*
V P V P against n

2 If you **fight back** an emotion or a desire, you try very hard not to feel it, show it, or act on it. *She fought back the tears.*
=hold back V P n (not pron) Also V n P

fight down. If you **fight down** an emotion or a desire, you try very hard not to feel it, show it, or act on it. *Meg fought down the desire to run... He looked*
PHRASAL VERB =hold back V P n (not pron)

at the telephone, fighting down first the despair and then the anger. Also V n P

fight off PHRASAL VERB

1 If you **fight off** something, for example an illness or an unpleasant feeling, you succeed in getting rid of it and in not letting it overcome you. *Unfortunately these drugs are quite toxic and hinder the body's ability to fight off infection... All day she had fought off the impulse to telephone Harry.* =overcome; V P n (not pron) Also V n P

2 If you **fight off** someone who has attacked you, you fight with them, and succeed in making them go away or stop attacking you. *The woman fought off the attacker.* V P n (not pron) Also V n P

fight out. If two people or groups **fight** something **out**, they fight or argue until one of them wins. *Instead of retaliating, he gets up and walks away leaving his team-mates to fight it out... Malcolm continued to fight it out with Julien from his self-imposed exile in Paris.* PHRASAL VERB RECIP; pl-n V *it*P; V *it*P *with* n; Also pl-n V P n (not pron), V P n *with* n

fightback /faɪtbæk/. A **fightback** is an effort made by a person or group of people to get back into a strong position when they seem likely to lose something such as an election or an important sports match; used in British journalism. *The West Indies have staged a dramatic fightback on the first day of the fifth test.* N-SING

fighter /faɪtəʳ/ **fighters** ◆◆◆◇◇

1 A **fighter** or a **fighter plane** is a fast military aircraft that is used for destroying other aircraft. N-COUNT

2 If you describe someone as a **fighter**, you approve of them because they continue trying to achieve things in spite of great difficulties or opposition. *From the start it was clear this tiny girl was a real fighter.* N-COUNT PRAGMATICS

3 A **fighter** is a person who physically fights another person. *...a tough little street fighter.* N-COUNT

4 See also **fire fighter**, **freedom fighter**, **prize fighter**.

fig leaf, fig leaves

1 A **fig leaf** is a large leaf which comes from the fig tree. A fig leaf is sometimes used in painting and sculpture to cover the genitals of a nude body. N-COUNT

2 In journalism, **fig leaf** is sometimes used to refer disapprovingly to something which is intended to conceal or prevent an embarrassing and shameful situation. *This deal is little more than a fig leaf for the continued destruction of the landscape.* N-COUNT: usu with supp PRAGMATICS

figment /fɪgmənt/ **figments.** If you say that something is a **figment of** someone's **imagination**, you mean that it does not really exist and that they are just imagining it. *The attack wasn't just a figment of my imagination.* PHRASE: Ns inflect, usu v-link PHR

figurative /fɪgərətɪv, AM -gjər-/ ◆◇◇◇◇

1 If you use a word or expression in a **figurative** sense, you use it with a more abstract or imaginative meaning than its ordinary literal one. *...an event that will change your route – in both the literal and figurative sense.* ♦ **figuratively** *Europe, with Germany literally and figuratively at its centre, is still at the start of a remarkable transformation.* ADJ: usu ADJ n ≠literal; ADV: ADV with cl/group, ADV with v

2 **Figurative** art is a style of art in which people and things are shown realistically, as they actually look. *His career spanned some 50 years and encompassed both abstract and figurative painting.* ADJ: usu ADJ n ≠abstract

figure /fɪgəʳ, AM -gjər/ **figures, figuring, figured** ◆◆◆◆◆

1 A **figure** is a particular amount expressed as a number, especially a statistic. *It would be very nice if we had a true figure of how many people in this country haven't got a job... It will not be long before the inflation figure starts to fall... New Government figures predict that one in two marriages will end in divorce.* N-COUNT

2 A **figure** is any of the ten written symbols from 0 to 9 that are used to represent a number. N-COUNT =digit

3 An amount or number that is in single **figures** is between nought and nine. An amount or number that is in double **figures** is between ten and ninety-nine. You can also say, for example, that an amount or number is in three **figures** when it is between one hundred and nine hundred and ninety-nine. *Inflation, which has usually been in single figures, is running at more than 12%... Crawley, with 14, was the only other player to reach double figures... The thermometer nudged three figures yesterday in Rome.* N-PLURAL: adj/num N

4 You refer to someone that you can see as a **figure** when you cannot see them clearly or when you are describing them. *Alistair saw the dim figure of Rose in the chair... She waited, standing on the bridge, until his figure vanished against the grey backdrop of the Palace... A figure in a blue dress appeared in the doorway.* N-COUNT: usu with supp, oft N *of* n =form

5 In art, a **figure** is a person in a drawing or a painting, or a statue of a person. *...a life-size bronze figure of a brooding, hooded woman.* N-COUNT

6 Your **figure** is the shape of your body. *Take pride in your health and your figure... Janet was a natural blonde with a good figure.* N-COUNT: with supp, oft poss/adj N

7 Someone who is referred to as a **figure** of a particular kind is a person who is well-known and important in some way. *The movement is supported by key figures in the three main political parties.* N-COUNT: with supp =personage

8 If you say that someone is, for example, a mother **figure** or a hero **figure**, you mean that other people regard them as the type of person stated or suggested. *Men often feel the need for a mother figure who is not in fact related to them... Mr Heseltine is a great hero figure to many Conservatives... Local police chiefs should re-emerge as figures of authority and reassurance in their areas.* N-COUNT: with supp, usu n N, N *of* n

9 In books and magazines, the diagrams which help to explain or illustrate information are referred to as **figures**. *If you look at a world map (see Figure 1) you can identify the major wine-producing regions... Figure 1.15 shows which provinces lost populations between 1910 and 1920.* N-COUNT: also N num =diagram

10 In geometry, a **figure** is a shape, especially a regular shape. *Draw a pentagon, a regular five-sided figure.* N-COUNT: usu supp N

11 If you **figure** that something is the case, you think or guess that it is the case; an informal use. *She figured that both she and Ned had learned a lot from the experience.* VERB; V that

12 If you say 'That **figures**' or 'It **figures**', you mean that the fact referred to is not surprising; an informal expression. *When I finished, he said, 'Yeah. That figures'... Work it out and you'll find it figures.* VERB; *that*/*it* V Also *it* V that

13 If someone or something **figures** in something, they appear or are included in it. *Human rights violations figured prominently in the report.* VB: no passive; V *in* n Also V *as* n

14 If you say that someone **cuts a** particular **figure**, you mean that they appear to other people in the way described. *Today she cuts a lonely figure.* PHRASES; V inflects

15 If you describe someone as a **figure of fun**, you mean that people think they are ridiculous. *The man has become an unlikely figure of fun.* *figure* inflects

16 If you **keep your figure**, you stay slim. If you **lose your figure**, you become rather fat. *You'll lose your girlish figure if you don't watch out.* V and N inflect

17 When you **put a figure on** an amount, you say exactly how much it is. *No one will put a figure on the final cost of this reconstruction.* V inflects, PHR n, usu with brd-neg

figure on. If you **figure on** something, you plan that it will happen or assume that it will happen when making your plans; an informal expression. *Jack worked as hard as he could to build his business, but he hadn't figured on a few obstacles.* PHRASAL VERB =bargain for; V P n/-ing

figure out. If you **figure out** a solution to a problem or the reason for something, you succeed in solving it or understanding it; an informal expression. *It took them about one month to figure out how to start the equipment... They're trying to figure out the politics of this whole situation... I don't have to be a detective to figure that out.* PHRASAL VERB =work out; V P wh/that; V P n (not pron); V n P

-figure. **-figure** combines with a number, usually 'five', 'six', or 'seven', to form adjectives which say how many figures are in a number. These adjectives usually describe a large amount of money. For example, a six-figure sum is between 100,000 and 999,999. *Columbia Pictures paid him a six-figure sum for the film rights. ...collectors' pieces which change hands for five-figure sums.* COMB in ADJ: ADJ n

figure eight, figure eights. In American English, a **figure eight** is something that has the shape of the number 8, for example a knot or a movement done by a skater. The usual British word is **figure of eight**. N-COUNT

figurehead /fɪgəʳhed, AM -gjəʳ-/ **figureheads** ◆◇◇◇◇
1 If someone is the **figurehead** of an organization or movement, they are recognized as being its leader, although they have little real power. *The President will be little more than a figurehead.* N-COUNT
2 A **figurehead** is a large wooden model of a person that was put just under the pointed front of a sailing ship in former times. N-COUNT

figure of eight, figures of eight. In British English, **figure of eight** is something that has the shape of the number 8, for example a knot or a movement done by a skater. The usual American word is **figure eight**. N-COUNT

figure of speech, figures of speech. A **figure of speech** is an expression or word that is used with a figurative rather than a literal meaning. *Of course I'm not. It was just a figure of speech.* N-COUNT

figure skating. **Figure skating** is skating in an attractive pattern, usually with spins and jumps included. N-UNCOUNT

figurine /fɪgərɪːn, AM -gjər-/ **figurines.** A **figurine** is a small ornamental model of a person. N-COUNT

filament /fɪləmənt/ **filaments.** A **filament** is a very thin piece or thread of something, for example the piece of wire inside a light bulb. N-COUNT

filch /fɪltʃ/ **filches, filching, filched.** If you say that someone **filches** something, you mean they steal it, especially when you do not consider this to be a very serious crime; an informal word. *I filched some notes from his wallet.* VERB =swipe V n

file /faɪl/ **files, filing, filed** ◆◆◆◆◇
1 A **file** is a box or folder in which letters or documents are kept. *He sat behind a table on which were half a dozen files. ...a file of insurance papers.* N-COUNT
2 A **file** is a collection of information about a particular person or thing. *There was stuff in that file that was private between me and Dr Denny... We already have files on people's tax details, mortgages and poll tax... You must record and keep a file of all expenses.* N-COUNT: oft N of/on n =dossier
3 If you **file** a document, you put it in the correct file. *A secretary can file papers as efficiently as a floppy disk can store them... They are all filed alphabetically under author.* VERB V n
4 In computing, a **file** is a set of related data that has its own name. N-COUNT
5 If you **file** a formal or legal accusation, complaint, or request, you make it officially. *A number of them have filed formal complaints against the police... I filed for divorce on the grounds of adultery a few months later.* VERB V n V for n
6 When someone **files** a report or a news story, they send or give it to their employer. *Catherine Bond filed that report for the BBC from Nairobi... He had to rush back to the office and file a housing story before the secretaries went home.* VERB =send V n
7 When a group of people **files** somewhere, they walk one behind the other in a line. *She paused as the group of children filed out of the house... Slowly, people filed into the room and sat down.* VERB V prep/adv
8 A **file** is a hand tool which is used for rubbing hard objects to make them smooth, shape them, or cut through them. N-COUNT
9 If you **file** an object, you smooth it, shape it, or cut it with a file. *Manicurists are skilled at shaping and filing nails.* VERB V n
10 See also **nail file, rank and file**.
11 Something that is **on file** or **on** someone's **files** is recorded or kept in a file or in a collection of information. *His fingerprints were on file in Washington... We'll keep your details on file... It is one of the most desperate cases on her files.* PHRASES v-link PHR, PHR after v
12 A group of people who are walking or standing **in single file** or **single file** are in a line, one behind the other. *We were walking in single file to the lake.* PHR after v

file away. If you **file away** a document, you put it in the correct file. *When at home, most evenings would be spent reading, cutting up and filing away his photographs... The details are filed away by his three secretaries for future reference.* PHRASAL VERB V P n (not pron) Also V n P

filial /fɪliəl/. You can use **filial** to describe the duties, feelings, or relationships which exist between a son or daughter and his or her parents; a formal word. *His father would accuse him of neglecting his filial duties... Right now I'm in need of a little filial affection.* ADJ: ADJ n

filibuster /fɪlɪbʌstəʳ/ **filibusters, filibustering, filibustered** ◆◇◇◇◇
1 A **filibuster** is a long slow speech made to use up time so that a vote cannot be taken and a law cannot be passed; used mainly in American English. *Senator Seymour has threatened a filibuster to block the bill.* N-COUNT
2 If a politician **filibusters**, he or she makes a long slow speech in order to use up time so that a vote cannot be taken and a law cannot be passed. *They simply threatened to filibuster until the Senate adjourns... A group of senators plans to filibuster a measure that would permit drilling in Alaska.* VERB V V n

filigree /fɪlɪgriː/. The word **filigree** is used to refer to delicate ornamental designs made with gold or silver wire. N-UNCOUNT: oft N n

filing cabinet, filing cabinets. A **filing cabinet** is a piece of office furniture, usually made of metal, which has drawers in which files are kept. N-COUNT

Filipino /fɪlɪpiːnoʊ/ **Filipinos** ◆◇◇◇◇
1 **Filipino** means belonging or relating to the Philippines, or to its people or culture. *...a group of Filipino girls.* ADJ
2 A **Filipino** is a person who comes from the Philippines. N-COUNT

fill /fɪl/ **fills, filling, filled** ◆◆◆◆◇
1 If you **fill** a container or area, or if it **fills**, an amount of something enters it that is enough to make it full. *Fill a saucepan with water and bring to a slow boil... She made sandwiches, filled a flask and put sugar in... The victims' lungs fill quickly with fluid... The boy's eyes filled with tears... While the bath was filling, he padded about in his underpants.* ▸ **Fill up** means the same as **fill**. *Pass me your cup, Amy, and I'll fill it up for you... Warehouses at the frontier between the two countries fill up with sacks of rice and flour.* V-ERG ≠empty V n with n V n V with n V PHRASAL VERB ERG V n P V P with n Also V P
2 If something **fills** a space, it is so big, or there are such large quantities of it, that there is very little room left. *He cast his eyes at the rows of cabinets that filled the enormous work area... The text fills 231 pages.* ▸ **Fill up** means the same as **fill**. *...the complicated machines that fill up today's laboratories.* ♦ **filled** *...four museum buildings filled with historical objects.* ♦ **-filled** *...the flower-filled courtyard of an old Spanish colonial house.* VERB V n PHRASAL VERB V P n (not pron) Also V n P ADJ-GRADED COMB in ADJ
3 If you **fill** a crack or hole, you put a substance into it in order to make the surface smooth again. *Fill small holes with wood filler in a matching colour... The gravedigger filled the grave.* ▸ **Fill in** means the same as **fill**. *If any cracks have appeared in the tart case, fill these in with raw pastry.* VERB V n with n V n PHRASAL VERB V n P Also V P n (not pron)
4 If a sound, smell, or light **fills** a space, or the air, it is very strong or noticeable. *In the parking lot of the school, the siren filled the air... All the light bars were turned on which filled the room with these rotating beams of light... The barn was filled with the sour-sweet smell of fresh dung.* ♦ **-filled** *...another sunshine-filled day. ...those whose work forces them to be in dusty or smoke-filled environments.* VERB V n V n with n V-ed COMB in ADJ
5 If something **fills** you with an emotion, or if an emotion **fills** you, you experience this emotion strongly. *I admired my father, and his work filled me with awe and curiosity... He looked at me without speaking, and for the first time I could see the pride that filled him... He stared at his favourite child, dismayed, filled with fear.* VERB V n with n V n V-ed
6 If you **fill** a period of time with a particular activity, you spend the time in this way. *If she wants a routine to fill her day, let her do community work.* ▸ **Fill up** means the same as **fill**. *On Thursday night she went to her yoga class, glad to have something to fill up the evening.* VERB V n Also V n with n PHRASAL VERB V P n (not pron) Also V n P

7 If something **fills** a need or a gap, it puts an end to this need or gap by existing or being active. *...properly organized and staffed day-care programs fill a need which allows family structures to remain intact... She brought him a sense of fun, of gaiety that filled a gap in his life.* VERB V n

8 If something **fills** a role, position, or function, they have that role or position, or perform that function, often successfully. *Dena was filling the role of diplomat's wife with the skill she had learned over the years.* VERB =fulfil V n

9 If a company or organization **fills** a job vacancy, they choose someone to do the job. If someone **fills** a job vacancy, they accept a job that they have been offered. *Mr Dinkins is finding it hard to recruit competent people to fill the vacancies... A vacancy has arisen which I intend to fill.* VERB V n

10 If you **fill** yourself with food, you eat so much that you do not feel hungry. *They joked and drank coffee and filled themselves with chocolate cake.* VERB =stuff V pron-refl *with* n

11 A play, film, or performer that **fills** a theatre, concert hall, or cinema attracts a very large audience. *Children are enthralled by his stories; he has been known to fill theatre halls in Australia.* VERB V n

12 When a dentist **fills** someone's tooth, he or she puts a filling in it. *It is almost impossible to find a dentist who will fill a tooth on the National Health.* VERB V n

13 If you **fill** an order or a prescription, you provide the things that are asked for; used mainly in American English. *A pharmacist can fill any prescription if, in his or her judgment, the prescription is valid.* VERB V n

14 If you **have had** your **fill of** something, you have had enough of it, and do not want to experience it any more or do it any more. *We feel that we have had our fill of disappointments and emotional upsets.* PHRASE: V inflects

15 • to **fill the bill**: see **bill**.

fill in PHRASAL VERB

1 If you **fill in** a form or other document requesting information, you write information in the spaces on it. *If you want your free copy of the Patients' Charter fill this form in... Fill in the coupon and send it first class to the address shown.* =fill out V n P V P n (not pron)

2 If you **fill in** a shape, you cover the area inside the lines with colour or shapes so that none of the background is showing. *When you have both filled in your patterns, you may want to share these with each other... With a lip pencil, outline lips and fill them in.* V P n (not pron) V n P

3 If you **fill** someone **in**, you give them more details about something that you know about; an informal expression. *I didn't give Reid all the details yet – I'll fill him in... He filled her in on Wilbur Kantor's visit.* V n P V n P *on* n

4 If you **fill in** for someone, you do the work or task that they normally do because they are unable to do it. *Vice-presidents' wives would fill in for first ladies.* =stand in V P *for* n

5 If you **are filling in** time, you are using time that is available by doing something that is not very important. *That's not a career. She's just filling in time as far as I can see, until she gets married.* usu passive V P n (not pron)

6 See also **fill** 3.

fill out PHRASAL VERB

1 To **fill out** a form means the same as to **fill in** a form. *Fill out the application carefully, and keep copies of it.* =fill in V P n (not pron) Also V n P

2 If a fairly thin person **fills out**, they become fatter. *A girl may fill out before she reaches her full height.* V P

fill up PHRASAL VERB

1 If you **fill up** or **fill** yourself **up** with food, you eat so much that you do not feel hungry. *Fill up on potatoes, bread and pasta, which are high in carbohydrate and low in fat... When you are happy about yourself you won't need to fill yourself up with food.* V P *on/with* n V pron-refl P *with* n

2 A type of food that **fills** you **up** makes you feel that you have eaten a lot, even though you have only eaten a small amount. *Potatoes fill us up without overloading us with calories.* V n P

3 See also **fill** 1, 2, 6.

filler /fɪlər/ **fillers** ◆◇◇◇◇

1 **Filler** is a substance used for filling cracks or holes, especially in walls, car bodies, or wood. N-MASS

2 You can describe something as a **filler** when it is being used or done because there is a need for something and nothing better is available; an informal use. N-COUNT =stopgap

3 If you say that something is, for example, a stadium **filler** or a floor **filler**, you mean that it is likely to attract crowds to a stadium or onto a dance floor; an informal use. N-COUNT: n N

4 See also **stocking filler**.

fillet /fɪlɪt, AM fɪleɪ/ **fillets, filleting, filleted** ◆◇◇◇◇

1 **Fillet** is a strip of tender meat, especially beef, that has no bones in it. *...fillet of beef with shallots. ...chicken breast fillets.* N-VAR: usu with supp

2 A **fillet** of fish is the side of a fish with the bones removed. *...anchovy fillets... I ordered a fine fillet of salmon.* N-COUNT: usu with supp

3 When you **fillet** fish or meat, you prepare it by taking the bones out. *Don't be afraid to ask your fishmonger to fillet flat fish.* VERB V n

filling /fɪlɪŋ/ **fillings** ◆◇◇◇◇

1 A **filling** is a small amount of metal or plastic that a dentist puts in a hole in a tooth to prevent further decay. *The longer your child can go without needing a filling, the better.* N-COUNT

2 The **filling** in something such as a cake, pie, or sandwich is a substance or mixture that is put inside it. *Spread some of the filling over each cold pancake and then either roll or fold.* N-MASS

3 The **filling** in a piece of soft furniture, a cushion, or a quilt is the soft substance inside it. *...second-hand sofas with old-style foam fillings.* N-MASS

4 Food that is **filling** makes you feel full when you have eaten it. *Although it is tasty, crab is very filling.* ADJ-GRADED

filling station, filling stations. A **filling station** is a place where you can buy petrol and oil for your car. The more usual American term is **gas station**. N-COUNT

fillip /fɪlɪp/ **fillips.** If someone or something gives a **fillip** to an activity or person, they suddenly stimulate or improve them; used in written English. *The news gave a fillip to the telecommunications sector... This will prove a much-needed fillip to racecourses and the racing industry in general.* N-COUNT: usu sing, oft N *to/for* n =boost

filly /fɪli/ **fillies.** A **filly** is a young female horse. N-COUNT

film /fɪlm/ **films, filming, filmed** ◆◆◆◆◆

1 A **film** consists of moving pictures that have been recorded so that they can be shown at the cinema or on television. A film tells a story, or shows a real situation. *Everything about the film was good. Good acting, good story, good fun. ...a government health film about the dangers of smoking.* N-COUNT =movie picture

2 If you **film** something, you use a camera to take moving pictures which can be shown on a screen or on television. *He had filmed her life story... Considering the restrictions under which she filmed, I think she did a commendable job.* VERB V n V

3 **Film** of something is moving pictures of a real event that are shown on television or on a screen. *They have seen news film of families queueing in Russia to buy a loaf of bread.* N-UNCOUNT =footage

4 A **film** is also the narrow roll of plastic that is used in a camera to take photographs. *The photographers had already shot a dozen rolls of film.* N-VAR

5 The making of cinema films, considered as a form of art or a business, can be referred to as **film** or **films**. *Film is a business with limited opportunities for actresses... She wanted to set up her own company to invest in films.* N-UNCOUNT, also N in pl

6 A **film** of powder, liquid, or grease is a very thin layer of it. *The sea is coated with a film of raw sewage.* N-COUNT: usu sing, usu with supp

7 Plastic **film** is a very thin sheet of plastic used to wrap and cover things. *Cover with plastic film and refrigerate for 24 hours.* N-UNCOUNT: usu adj N

8 See also **clingfilm**.

filmic /fɪlmɪk/. **Filmic** means related to films; a formal word. *...a new filmic style. ...the filmic potential of the landscape.* ADJ: ADJ n

filming /fɪlmɪŋ/. **Filming** is the activity of making a film including the acting, directing, and camera-work. *Filming was due to start next month.* ◆◇◇◇◇ N-UNCOUNT

film-maker, **film-makers;** also spelled **filmmaker**. A **film-maker** is someone involved in making films, in particular a director or producer. *...Italian film-makers like Sergio Leone.* ◆◇◇◇◇ N-COUNT

film star, **film stars.** A **film star** is a famous actor or actress who appears in films. ◆◇◇◇◇ N-COUNT

filmy /fɪlmi/ **filmier, filmiest.** A **filmy** fabric or substance is very thin and almost transparent. *...pictures of women wearing filmy nightgowns.* ADJ-GRADED: usu ADJ n =see-through

Filofax /faɪləfæks/ **Filofaxes.** A **Filofax** is a type of personal filing system in the form of a small book with pages that can easily be added or removed. **Filofax** is a trademark. N-COUNT

filter /fɪltəʳ/ **filters, filtering, filtered** ◆◆◇◇◇

1 To **filter** a substance means to pass it through a device which is designed to remove certain particles contained in it. *The best prevention for cholera is to boil or filter water, and eat only well-cooked food.* VERB V n

2 A **filter** is a device through which a substance is passed when it is being filtered. *...a paper coffee filter.* N-COUNT

3 A **filter** is a device through which sound or light is passed and which blocks or reduces particular sound or light frequencies. *You might use a yellow filter to improve the clarity of a hazy horizon.* N-COUNT

4 If light or sound **filters** into a place, it comes in faintly or slowly, either through a small or partly covered opening, or from a long distance away. *Light filtered into my kitchen through the soft, green shade of the honey locust tree.* VERB V *into/through* n

5 When news or information **filters** through to people, it gradually reaches them. *It took months before the findings began to filter through to the politicians... News of the attack quickly filtered through the college. ...as indications filter in from polling stations. ...the horror stories which were beginning to filter out of Germany.* VERB V *through to* n, V *through* n, V *in*, V *out of* n

6 In British English, a traffic **filter** is a traffic signal or lane which controls the movement of traffic wanting to turn left or right. N-COUNT

filter out. To **filter out** something from a substance or from light means to remove it by passing the substance or light through something acting as a filter. *Children should have glasses which filter out UV rays... Plants and trees filter carbon dioxide out of the air and produce oxygen.* PHRASAL VERB VP n (not pron), V n P *of/from* n, Also V n P

filter tip, filter tips. A **filter tip** is a small device at the end of a cigarette that reduces the amount of nicotine passing into the smoker's body. **Filter tips** are cigarettes that are manufactured with these devices. N-COUNT

filth /fɪlθ/ ◆◇◇◇◇

1 **Filth** is a disgusting amount of dirt. *The living-room floor was littered with filth and tin cans... Thousands of tons of filth and sewage pour into the Ganges every day.* N-UNCOUNT =muck

2 People refer to words or pictures, usually ones relating to sex, as **filth** when they think they are very disgusting and rude. *The dialogue was all filth and innuendo. ...pornographic filth.* N-UNCOUNT PRAGMATICS =smut

filthy /fɪlθi/ **filthier, filthiest** ◆◇◇◇◇

1 Something that is **filthy** is very dirty indeed. *He never washed, and always wore a filthy old jacket.* ADJ-GRADED =grimy

2 If you describe something as **filthy**, you mean that you think it is morally very unpleasant and disgusting, sometimes in a sexual way. *Apparently, well known actors were at these filthy parties... The play was full of filthy foul language.* ADJ-GRADED PRAGMATICS

3 **Filthy** weather is very cold, wet, and windy; an old-fashioned informal use. *...a filthy wet night.* ADJ-GRADED =foul

4 ● **filthy rich**: see **rich**.

filtration /fɪltreɪʃən/. **Filtration** is the process of filtering a substance. *This enzyme would make the filtration of beer easier. ...water filtration systems.* N-UNCOUNT

fin /fɪn/ **fins** ◆◆◇◇◇

1 A fish's **fins** are the flat objects which stick out of its body and help it to swim and keep its balance. N-COUNT

2 A **fin** on something such as an aeroplane, rocket, or bomb is a flat part which sticks out and which is intended to help control its movement. N-COUNT

final /faɪnəl/ **finals** ◆◆◆◆◆

1 In a series of events, things, or people, the **final** one is the last one. *Astronauts will make a final attempt today to rescue a communications satellite from its useless orbit... This is the fifth and probably final day of testimony before the Senate Judiciary Committee... On the last Saturday in September, I received a final letter from Clive.* ADJ: det ADJ =last

2 **Final** means happening at the end of an event or series of events. *You must have been on stage until the final curtain... The countdown to the Notting Hill Carnival is in its final hours.* ADJ: ADJ n

3 You can use **final** to emphasize that a situation has a particular quality to a very great or severe degree; used in written English. *Only a few go through the final humiliation of meeting the bailiff at the door.* ADJ: ADJ n PRAGMATICS =ultimate

4 If a decision or someone's authority is **final**, it cannot be changed or questioned. *The judges' decision is final... The White House has the final say... I'm not going, and that's final.* ADJ

5 The **final** is the last game or contest in a series, which decides the overall winner. *...the Scottish Cup Final... Pakistan's Jansher Khan has won the men's final at the Singapore Open.* ● See also **quarter-final, semi-final**. N-COUNT

6 The **finals** of a sporting tournament consist of a smaller tournament that includes only players or teams that have won earlier games. The finals decide the winner of the whole tournament. *Poland know they have a chance of qualifying for the World Cup Finals.* N-PLURAL

7 When a student takes his or her **finals**, he or she takes the last and most important examination in a university or college course. *Anna sat her finals in the summer.* N-PLURAL: oft poss N

finale /fɪnɑːli, -næli/ **finales** ◆◇◇◇◇

1 The **finale** of a show, piece of music, or series of shows is the last part of it or the last one of them, especially when this is exciting or impressive. *... the finale of Shostakovich's Fifth Symphony... Tonight's light show is the grand finale of a month-long series of events.* N-COUNT: usu with supp

2 If you say that an event provides a particular kind of **finale** to something, you mean that it provides it with a particular kind of ending. *...the dramatic finale to America's seven-year hostage crisis... It was a sad finale to an otherwise spectacular career.* N-COUNT: usu sing, oft N *to* n =conclusion

finalise /faɪnəlaɪz/. See **finalize**.

finalist /faɪnəlɪst/ **finalists.** A **finalist** is someone who reaches the last stages of a competition or tournament by doing well or winning in its earlier stages. *The twelve finalists will be listed in the Sunday Times.* ◆◇◇◇◇ N-COUNT

finality /faɪnælɪti/. **Finality** is the quality of being final and irreversible. If you say something with **finality**, you say it in a way that shows that you have made up your mind about something and do not want to discuss it further; a formal word. *Young Children have difficulty grasping the finality of death... 'Not this time, Faye,' he replied with finality.* N-UNCOUNT: oft N *of* n

finalize /faɪnəlaɪz/ **finalizes, finalizing, finalized;** also spelled **finalise** in British English. If you **finalize** something such as a plan or an agreement, you complete the arrangements for it, especially by discussing it with other people. *Negotiators from the three countries finalized the agreement in August... We are saying nothing until all the details have been finalised... They have not finalized the deal with the government.* ◆◇◇◇◇ VERB V n, V n *with* n

finally /faɪnəli/ ◆◆◆◆◇

1 You use **finally** to suggest that something happens after a long period of time, usually later than you wanted or expected it to happen. *The word was finally given for us to get on board... The food finally arrived at the end of last week and distribution began... Finally, after ten hours of negotiations, the gunman gave himself up.* ADV: ADV before v, ADV with cl =at last

2 You use **finally** to indicate that something is last in a series of actions or events. *The action slips from comedy to melodrama and finally to tragedy.* ADV: ADV with cl/group =lastly

3 You use **finally** in speech or writing to introduce a final point, question, or topic. *Finally, who needs the theatre?... And finally, a word about the winner and runner-up.*
ADV: ADV with cl PRAGMATICS =in conclusion

finance /faɪnæns, fɪnæns/ **finances, financing, financed** ◆◆◆◆◇

1 When someone **finances** something such as a project or an expensive purchase, they provide the money that is needed to pay for it. *The fund has been used largely to finance the construction of federal prisons... Government expenditure is financed by taxation and by borrowing.* ► Also a noun. *A United States delegation is in Japan seeking finance for a major scientific project.*
VERB V n N-UNCOUNT

2 **Finance** is the commercial or government activity of managing money, debt, credit, and investment. *...a major player in the world of high finance... The report recommends an overhaul of public finances. ...the Venezuelan Finance Minister, Mr Roberto Pocaterra.*
N-UNCOUNT: also N in pl

3 You can refer to the amount of money that you have and how well it is organized as your **finances**. *Be prepared for unexpected news concerning your finances... In general, women manage the day-to-day finances but leave most longer-term decisions to men... Finance is usually the biggest problem for students.*
N-UNCOUNT: also N in pl, oft with poss

financial /faɪnænʃəl, fɪn-/. **Financial** means relating to or involving money. *The company is in financial difficulties. ...the government's financial advisers.* ♦ **financially** *She would like to be more financially independent... She's been struggling financially for years... Financially, things are a bit tight.*
◆◆◆◆◆ ADJ: usu ADJ n =monetary ADV: ADV adj/-ed, ADV after v, ADV with cl

financial year, financial years. In British English, a **financial year** is a period of twelve months, used by government, business, and other organizations, according to which they plan and assess their budgets, profits, and losses. The usual American term is **fiscal year**. *...33,000 possible job losses in the coming financial year.*
◆◇◇◇◇ N-COUNT: usu sing, usu with supp =fiscal year

financier /faɪnænsiəʳ, fɪn-/ **financiers.** A **financier** is a person, company, or government that provides money for projects or enterprises.
◆◇◇◇◇ N-COUNT

finch /fɪntʃ/ **finches.** A **finch** is a small bird with a short strong beak.
◆◇◇◇◇ N-COUNT

find /faɪnd/ **finds, finding, found** ◆◆◆◆◆

1 If you **find** someone or something, you see them or learn where they are. *The police also found a pistol... They have spent ages looking at the map and can't find a trace of anywhere called Darrowby... I wonder if you could find me a deck of cards?*
VERB V n V n n Also V n *for* n

2 If you **find** something that you need or want, you succeed in achieving or obtaining it. *Many people here cannot find work... So far they have not found a way to fight the virus... He has to apply for a permit and we have to find him a job... Does this mean that they haven't found a place for him?*
VERB =get V n V n n V n *for* n Also V n *for* n to-inf

3 If something **is found** in a particular place or thing, it exists in that place. *Two thousand of France's 4,200 species of flowering plants are found in the park... Fibre is found in cereal foods, beans, fruit and vegetables.*
V-PASSIVE *be* V-ed

4 If you **find** someone or something in a particular situation or doing a particular thing, they are in that situation or doing that thing when you see them or come into contact with them. *They found her walking alone and depressed on the beach... She returned to her east London home to find her back door forced open... Thrushes are a protected species so you will not find them on any menu.*
VERB =discover V n -ing V n -ed V n prep/adv

5 If you **find** yourself doing something, you are doing it without deciding or intending to do it. *It's not the first time that you've found yourself in this situation... I found myself having more fun than I had had in years... It all seemed so far away from here that he found himself quite unable to take it in.*
VERB V pron-refl prep/adv V pron-refl -ing V pron-refl adj

6 If a time or event **finds** you in a particular situation or doing a particular thing, you are in that situation or doing that thing at the time mentioned or when the event occurs; used mainly in written English. *Daybreak found us on a cold, clammy ship... His lunch did not take long to arrive and found him poring over a notepad covered with scrawls.*
VB: no passive, no cont V n prep V n -ing

7 If you **find** that something is the case, you become aware of it or realize that it is the case. *The two biologists found, to their surprise, that both groups of birds survived equally well... At my age I would find it hard to get another job... We find her evidence to be based on a degree of oversensitivity... I've never found my diet a problem.*
VERB V that V *it* adj to-inf V n to-inf V n n

8 When a court or jury decides that a person on trial is guilty or innocent, you say that the person **has been found** guilty or not guilty. *She was found guilty of manslaughter and put on probation for two years... When they found us guilty, I just went blank.*
VERB *be* V-ed adj V n adj

9 You can use **find** to express your reaction to someone or something. *I find most of the young men of my own age so boring... We're sure you'll find it exciting!... I find it ludicrous that nothing has been done to protect passengers from fire... But you'd find him a good worker if you showed him what to do.*
VERB V n adj V *it* adj that V n n

10 If you **find** a feeling such as pleasure or comfort in a particular thing or activity, you experience the feeling mentioned as a result of this thing or activity. *How could anyone find pleasure in hunting and killing this beautiful creature?... I was too tired and frightened to find comfort in that familiar promise.*
VERB =feel V n *in* -ing V n *in* n

11 If you **find** the time or money to do something, you succeed in making or obtaining enough time or money to do it. *I was just finding more time to write music... My sister helped me find the money for a private operation.*
VERB V n

12 If you describe someone or something that has been discovered as a **find**, you mean that they are valuable, interesting, good, or useful. *Another of his lucky finds was a pair of candle-holders... His discovery was hailed as the botanical find of the century.*
N-COUNT: usu adj N

13 See also **finding, found.**

14 If you **find** your **way** somewhere, you successfully get there by choosing the right way to go. *He was an expert at finding his way, even in strange surroundings... After a while I pulled myself to my feet and found my way to the street.*
PHRASES V inflects, oft PHR prep/adv

15 If something **finds** its **way** somewhere, it comes to that place, especially by chance. *It is one of the very few Michelangelos that have found their way out of Italy... The most unlikely objects found their way into his design and look absolutely right where he placed them.*
V inflects, PHR adv/prep

16 • to **find fault with**: see **fault**. • to **find one's feet**: see **foot**.

find out
PHRASAL VERB

1 If you **find** something **out**, you learn something that you did not already know, especially by making a deliberate effort to do so. *It makes you want to watch the next episode to find out what's going to happen... I was relieved to find out that my problems were due to a genuine disorder... Yesterday, the men's families held a news conference in their campaign to find out the truth... As soon as we found this out, we closed the ward... He began by reading everything he could find out about heroin.*
=discover V P wh V P that V P n (not pron) V n P V P *about* n Also V P

2 If you **find** someone **out**, you discover that they have been doing something dishonest. *Her face was so grave, I wondered for a moment if she'd found me out.*
V n P

finder /faɪndəʳ/ **finders.** You can refer to someone who finds something as the **finder** of that thing. *The finder of a wallet who takes it home may be guilty of theft... Every stray dog has to be taken by its finder to the police.*
◆◇◇◇◇ N-COUNT

fin de siècle /fæn də siɛklə/; also spelled **fin-de-siècle. Fin de siècle** is used to describe something that is thought to be typical of the end of the nineteenth century, especially when it is considered stylish or exaggerated; used in written English. *He has never been averse to savouring a little fin de siècle decadence.*
ADJ: ADJ n

finding /faɪndɪŋ/ **findings** ◆◆◇◇◇
1 Someone's **findings** are the information they get or the conclusions they come to as the result of an investigation or some research. *One of the main findings of the survey was the confusion about the facilities already in place... We hope that manufacturers will take note of the findings and improve their products accordingly.* N-COUNT: usu pl, usu with supp
2 The **findings** of a court are the decision that it reaches after a trial or an inquiry into some matter. *The government hopes the court will announce its findings before the end of the month.* N-COUNT: usu pl, usu with poss =judgement

fine 1 adjective uses

fine /faɪn/ **finer, finest** ◆◆◆◆◇
1 You use **fine** to describe something that you admire and think is very good. *There is a fine view of the countryside... This is a fine book. ...London's finest art deco cinema.* ADJ-GRADED: usu ADJ n ♦ **finely** *They are finely engineered boats.* ADV-GRADED: ADV -ed
2 If you say that you are **fine**, you mean that you are in good health or reasonably happy. *Lina is fine and sends you her love and best wishes.* ADJ-GRADED: v-link ADJ
3 If you say that something is **fine**, you mean that it is satisfactory or acceptable. *The skiing is fine... Everything was going to be just fine... It's fine to ask questions as we go along, but it's better if you wait until we have finished.* ▸ Also an adverb. *All the instruments are working fine.* ADJ-GRADED: usu v-link ADJ, oft *it* v-link ADJ to-inf =great, OK ADV-GRADED
4 You say '**fine**' or '**that's fine**' to show that you do not object to an arrangement, action, or situation that has been suggested. *If competition is the best way to achieve it, then, fine... If you don't want to give it to me, that's fine, I don't mind... 'It'll take me a couple of days.' – 'That's fine with me.'* CONVENTION PRAGMATICS =OK
5 Something that is **fine** is very delicate, narrow, or small. *The heat scorched the fine hairs on her arms... The ship has come to rest on the fine sand.* ADJ-GRADED: usu ADJ n ≠coarse ♦ **finely** *Chop the ingredients finely and mix them together.* ADV-GRADED: ADV with v ≠coarsely ♦ **fineness** *That fineness of the tip is what controls the resolution of the image.* N-UNCOUNT
6 **Fine** objects or clothing are of good quality, delicate, and expensive. *We waited in our fine clothes... She'll wear fine jewellery wherever she goes.* ADJ-GRADED: usu ADJ n
7 A **fine** adjustment, detail, or distinction is very delicate, small, or exact. *The market likes the broad outline but is reserving judgment on the fine detail.* ADJ-GRADED: usu ADJ n =delicate ♦ **finely** *They had to take the finely balanced decision to let the visit proceed... This is a fast-moving but finely observed drama.* ADV-GRADED: usu ADV -ed, also ADV after v ♦ **fineness** *...a sense of quality and fineness of detail.* N-UNCOUNT: oft N *of* n
8 A **fine** person is someone you consider good, moral, and admirable. *I was with fine people doing a good job... He was an excellent journalist and a very fine man.* ADJ-GRADED: usu ADJ n
9 When the weather is **fine**, it is sunny and not raining. *He might be doing a spot of gardening if the weather is fine.* ADJ-GRADED =fair

fine 2 punishment

fine /faɪn/ **fines, fining, fined** ◆◆◆◇◇
1 A **fine** is a punishment in which a person is ordered to pay a sum of money because they have done something illegal or broken a rule. N-COUNT
2 If someone **is fined**, they are punished by being ordered to pay a sum of money because they have done something illegal or broken a rule. *She was fined £150 and banned from driving for one month... An east London school has set a precedent by fining pupils who break the rules.* VERB be V-ed V n

fine art, fine arts. ◆◇◇◇◇
1 Painting and sculpture, in which objects are produced that are beautiful rather than useful, can be referred to as **fine art** or as the **fine arts**. *He deals in antiques and fine art. ...the university of Cairo's faculty of fine arts.* N-UNCOUNT: also N in pl
2 If you **have got** something **down to a fine art**, you are able to do it in a very skilful or efficient way because you have had a lot of experience of doing it. PHRASE: V inflects

fine print. In a contract or agreement, the **fine print** is the same as the **small print**. N-UNCOUNT: usu *the* N

finery /faɪnəri/. If someone is dressed in their **finery**, they are wearing the elegant and impressive clothes and jewellery that they wear on special occasions; a literary word. *I used to watch the brides arriving in their white wedding dresses and the guests in all their finery.* N-UNCOUNT

finesse /fɪnes/. If you do something with **finesse**, you do it with great skill and flair. *...handling momentous diplomatic challenges with tact and finesse.* ◆◇◇◇◇ N-UNCOUNT

fine-tooth comb; also spelled **fine tooth comb.** If you say that you will **go over** something **with a fine-tooth comb** or **go through** something **with a fine-tooth comb**, you are emphasizing that you will search it thoroughly or examine it very carefully. *We went over that area with a fine-tooth comb.* PHRASE: V inflects PRAGMATICS

fine-tune, fine-tunes, fine-tuning, fine-tuned. If you **fine-tune** something, you make very small and precise adjustments to it in order to make it as successful or effective as it possibly can be. *We do not try to fine-tune the economy on the basis of short-term predictions... Computers allow the plans to be fine-tuned and to be altered quickly.* VERB V n ♦ **fine-tuning** *There's a lot of fine-tuning to be done yet.* N-UNCOUNT

finger /fɪŋgəʳ/ **fingers, fingering, fingered** ◆◆◆◆◇
1 Your **fingers** are the four long jointed parts at the end of each hand. *She suddenly held up a small, bony finger and pointed across the room... She ran her fingers through her hair... There was a ring on each of his fingers.* • See also **light-fingered**. N-COUNT
2 The **fingers** of a glove are the parts that a person's fingers fit into. N-COUNT: usu pl
3 A **finger of** something such as smoke or land is an amount of it that is shaped rather like a finger. *...a thin finger of land that separates Pakistan from the former Soviet Union... Cover the base with a single layer of sponge fingers.* • See also **fish finger**. N-COUNT: N *of* n, n N =strip
4 If you **finger** something, you touch or feel it with your fingers. *He fingered the few coins in his pocket... Self-consciously she fingered the emeralds at her throat.* VERB V n
5 If you **finger** a person or organization, you tell someone, usually the police, that the person or organization has done something illegal or wrong; an informal use. *Police and prosecutors manipulated the eyewitnesses so they would finger Aldo... People who have fingered crack houses and fingered drug dealers have been assassinated.* VERB V n
6 A **finger** of a strong alcoholic drink is an amount of it which, when it is in a glass, is the same size as the width of a person's finger. *I poured two final fingers of bourbon into my glass.* N-COUNT: usu N *of* n
7 If you **get your fingers burnt** or **burn your fingers**, you suffer because something you did or were involved in was a failure or a mistake. *He has had his fingers burnt by deals that turned out badly... Mr Walesa burned his fingers by promising he would give every Pole 100m zlotys to start a business.* PHRASES V inflects
8 If you **cross** your **fingers**, you put one finger on top of another and hope for good luck. If you say that someone **is keeping their fingers crossed**, you mean they are hoping for good luck. *He crossed his fingers, asking for luck for the first time in his life... I'm keeping my fingers crossed that they turn up soon.* V inflects
9 If you say that someone did not or must not **lay a finger on** a particular person or thing, you are emphasizing that they did not or must not touch or harm that person or thing at all. *I must make it clear I never laid a finger on her.* V inflects, usu with brd-neg, PHR n PRAGMATICS
10 If you say that someone does not **lift a finger** or **raise a finger** to do something, especially to help someone, you are critical of them because they do nothing. *She never lifted a finger around the house... They will not lift a finger to help their country.* V inflects, with brd-neg PRAGMATICS
11 If you say that someone has **a finger in every pie**, you mean they are involved in a lot of things. *He very much likes to have a finger in every pie... He's a man with fingers in a lot of pies.* Ns inflect
12 If you **point the finger at** someone or **point an accusing finger at** someone, you blame them or V inflects, PHR n

accuse them of something. *He said he wasn't pointing an accusing finger at anyone in the government or the army.*

13 To **point the finger of suspicion** or **blame at** someone means to make people suspect them of doing something or blame them for doing something. *Forensic evidence points the finger of suspicion firmly at him.* V inflects, PHR n

14 If you tell someone to **pull** their **finger out** or to **get** their **finger out**, you are telling them rudely that you want them to start doing some work or making an effort; an informal expression. *Isn't it about time that you pulled your finger out?* V inflects PRAGMATICS

15 If you **put** your **finger on** something, for example a reason or problem, you see and identify exactly what it is. *Midge couldn't quite put her finger on the reason... He could never quite put his finger on who or what was responsible for all this.* V inflects, PHR n/wh

16 If someone or something **slips through** your **fingers**, you just fail to catch them, get them, or keep them. *Money has slipped through his fingers all his life... You mustn't allow a golden opportunity to slip through your fingers or you will regret it later.* V inflects

17 • to **have green fingers**: see **green**. • **finger on the pulse**: see **pulse**.

fingering /fɪŋgərɪŋ/. **Fingering** is the method of using the most suitable finger to play each note when you are playing a musical instrument, especially the piano. N-UNCOUNT

fingermark /fɪŋgəʳmɑːʳk/ **fingermarks.** A **fingermark** is a mark which is made when someone puts a dirty or greasy finger onto a clean surface. N-COUNT

fingernail /fɪŋgəʳneɪl/ **fingernails;** also spelled **finger-nail.** Your **fingernails** are the thin hard areas at the end of each of your fingers. ◆◇◇◇◇ N-COUNT =nails

fingerprint /fɪŋgəʳprɪnt/ **fingerprints, fingerprinting, fingerprinted** ◆◇◇◇◇

1 **Fingerprints** are marks made by a person's fingers which show the lines on the skin. Everyone's fingerprints are different, so they can be used to identify criminals. *The detective discovered no fewer than 35 fingerprints. ...his fingerprint on the murder weapon.* N-COUNT: usu pl • If the police **take** someone's **fingerprints**, they make that person press their fingers onto a pad covered with ink, and then onto paper, so that they know what that person's fingerprints look like. *They were photographed and had their fingerprints taken.* PHRASE: V inflects

2 If someone **is fingerprinted**, the police take their fingerprints. *He took her to jail, where she was fingerprinted and booked.* VB: usu passive be V-ed

3 If the police **fingerprint** an object, they put a layer of special dust on it so that any greasy fingerprints that are on it can be seen. *Let's fingerprint the canoe, see if we come up with anything.* VERB V n

fingertip /fɪŋgəʳtɪp/ **fingertips;** also spelled **finger-tip.** ◆◇◇◇◇

1 Your **fingertips** are the ends of your fingers. *The fat and flour are rubbed together with the fingertips as for pastry.* N-COUNT: usu pl

2 If you say that something is **at** your **fingertips**, you approve of the fact that you can reach it easily or that it is easily available to you. *I had the information at my fingertips and hadn't used it.* PHRASE PRAGMATICS

finicky /fɪnɪki/. If you say that someone is **finicky**, you mean that they are fussy and difficult to please; used showing disapproval. *Even the most finicky eater will find something appetizing here.* ADJ-GRADED PRAGMATICS =picky

finish /fɪnɪʃ/ **finishes, finishing, finished** ◆◆◆◆◇

1 When you **finish** doing or dealing with something, you do or deal with the last part of it, so that there is no more for you to do or deal with. *As soon as he'd finished eating, he excused himself... Mr Gould was given a standing ovation and loud cheers when he finished his speech... I've practically finished the ironing.* VERB V n/-ing ► In American English, **finish up** means the same as **finish**. *We waited a few minutes outside his office while he finished up his meeting.* PHRASAL VERB V P n (not pron)

2 When you **finish** something that you are making or producing, you reach the end of making or producing it, so that it is complete. *The consultants had been working to finish a report this week.* VERB =complete V n ► **Finish off** and, in American English, **finish up** mean the same as **finish**. *Now she is busy finishing off a biography of Queen Caroline. ...the amount of stuff required to finish up a movie.* PHRASAL VERB V P n (not pron)

3 When something such as a course, film, or sale **finishes**, especially at a planned time, it ends. *The teaching day finishes at around 4pm... When a play finishes its run, many of the costumes are hired out to amateur dramatics companies and schools.* VERB =end V at/on/by n V n Also V

4 You say that someone or something **finishes** a period of time or an event in a particular way to indicate what the final part of it or the final situation was like. You can also say that a period of time or an event **finishes** in a particular way. *The two of them finished by kissing each other goodbye... The evening finished with the welcoming of three new members... A buggy ferries you down to the main restaurant to finish the evening with a dance on the beach... The American dollar finished the day up against foreign currencies... The last track finishes this compilation beautifully.* V-ERG V by -ing V with n V n with n V n adj/adv Also V n by -ing, V n prep, V prep

5 If someone **finishes** second, for example, in a race or competition, they are in second place at the end of the race or competition. *He finished second in the championship four years in a row.* VERB V ord/prep

6 To **finish** means to reach the end of saying something. *Her eyes flashed, but he held up a hand. 'Let me finish.'* VERB V

7 **The finish** of something is the end of it or the last part of it. *I intend to continue it and see the job through to the finish... From start to finish he believed in me, often more than I did myself.* N-SING: the N, with poss =end

8 The **finish** of a race is the end of it. *Win a trip to see the finish of the Tour de France!... The replays of the close finish showed Ottey finished ahead of the Olympic champion.* N-COUNT

9 If the surface of something that has been made has a particular kind of **finish**, it has the appearance or texture mentioned. *The finish and workmanship of the woodwork was excellent.* N-COUNT: usu with supp

10 See also **finished**.

11 A **fight to the finish** is one in which one of the people or groups fighting is killed or completely defeated. *The conflict in the North and East of the island was a fight to the finish.* PHRASES

12 If you add **the finishing touches** to something, you add or do the last things that are necessary to complete it. *Right up until the last minute, workers were still putting the finishing touches on the pavilions... The only finishing touch most of these puddings need is a custard sauce.* N inflects

finish off PHRASAL VERB

1 If you **finish off** something that you have been eating or drinking, you eat or drink the last part of it with the result that there is none left. *Kelly finished off his coffee... He took the bottle from her hands and finished it off in one long swallow.* =polish off V P n (not pron) V n P

2 If someone **finishes off** someone or something that is already badly injured or damaged, they kill or destroy them. *They meant to finish her off, swiftly and without mercy.* V n P

3 See **finish** 2.

finish up PHRASAL VERB

1 If you **finish up** in a particular place or situation, you are in that place or situation after doing or experiencing several things. *They had met by chance at university and finished up getting married... He's probably going to finish up in jail for business fraud.* =end up V P -ing V P prep

2 If you **finish up** something that you have been eating or drinking, you eat or drink the last part of it. *Finish up your drinks now, please.* V P n (not pron) Also V n P

3 See also **finish** 1, 2.

finish with. If you **finish with** someone or something, you stop dealing with them, being involved with them, or being interested in them. *My boyfriend was threatening to finish with me... 'Have you finished with me?' Luke asked, when he had listened to Armstrong's report of his evidence.* PHRASAL VERB V P n

finished /fɪnɪʃt/ ◆◆◇◇◇

1 Someone who is **finished with** something is no longer dealing with it or is no longer interested in it. *One suspects he will be finished with boxing.* ADJ: v-link ADJ *with* n

2 Something that is **finished** no longer exists or is no longer happening. *I go back on the dole when the shooting season's finished.* ADJ: v-link ADJ =over

3 Someone or something that is **finished** is no longer important, powerful, or effective. *Her power over me is finished... He confessed: 'I thought I was finished.'* ADJ: v-link ADJ

4 Something that is **finished** or **finished off** in a particular way has been given a particular appearance or decoration. *The dining room is finished in deep red... Each dress is beautifully finished off with piped seams and fitted underskirts.* ADJ: v-link ADJ prep, oft adv ADJ

finishing school, finishing schools. A **finishing school** is a private school where rich or upper-class young women are taught manners and other social skills that are considered to be suitable for them. *At 16 Jill was sent to a Swiss finishing school. ...where the Princess of Wales attended finishing school.* N-VAR

finite /faɪnaɪt/ ◆◇◇◇◇

1 Something that is **finite** has a definite fixed size or extent; a formal use. *...a finite set of elements... Only a finite number of situations can arise... The fossil fuels (coal and oil) are finite resources.* ADJ ≠infinite

2 A **finite** clause is a clause based on a verb group which indicates tense, such as 'went', 'is waiting', or 'will be found', rather than on an infinitive or a participle. Compare **non-finite.** ADJ: usu ADJ n

Finn /fɪn/ **Finns.** The **Finns** are the people of Finland. ◆◇◇◇◇ N-COUNT

Finnish /fɪnɪʃ/ ◆◆◆◆◇

1 Finnish means belonging or relating to Finland or to its people, language, or culture. *Mr Skubiszewski met the Finnish President.* ADJ

2 Finnish is the language spoken in Finland. N-UNCOUNT

fiord /fjɔːʳd, fiːɔːʳd/. See **fjord.**

fir /fɜːʳ/ **firs.** A **fir** or a **fir** tree is a tall evergreen tree that has thin needle-like leaves and produces cones. ◆◇◇◇◇ N-VAR

fire 1 burning, heat, or enthusiasm

fire /faɪəʳ/ **fires, firing, fired** ◆◆◆◆◇

1 Fire is the hot, bright flames produced by things that are burning. *They saw a big flash and a huge ball of fire reaching hundreds of feet into the sky... Many students were trapped by smoke and fire on an upper floor.* N-UNCOUNT

2 A **fire** or **fire** is an occurrence of uncontrolled burning which destroys buildings, forests, or other things. *87 people died in a fire at the Happy Land Social Club... A forest fire is sweeping across portions of north Maine this evening... Much of historic Rennes was destroyed by fire in 1720.* N-VAR =conflagration

3 A **fire** is a burning pile of wood, coal, or other fuel that you make, for example to use for heat, light, or cooking. *There was a fire in the grate... After the killing, he calmly lit a fire to destroy evidence.* N-COUNT

4 A **fire** is a device that uses electricity or gas to give out heat and warm a room; used mainly in British English. *The gas fire was still alight... She switched on one bar of the electric fire.* N-COUNT: oft n N

5 When a pot or clay object **is fired**, it is heated at a high temperature in a special oven, as part of the process of making it. *After the pot is dipped in this mixture, it is fired... I have watched the potters mold, fire and paint their bowls, plates and vases with sacred designs.* ♦ **firing, firings** *When soft woods are used for the firing, the clay turns dark from the smoke.* VERB *be* V-ed V n N-VAR

6 When the engine of a motor vehicle **fires**, an electrical spark is produced which causes the fuel to burn and the engine to work. *The engine fired and we moved off.* VERB V

7 If a machine **is fired with** a particular fuel, it operates by means of that fuel. *The engines were fired with coal and needed water to keep the steam up.* VB: usu passive *be* V-ed *with* n

8 If you **fire** someone with enthusiasm, you make them feel very enthusiastic. If you **fire** someone's imagination, you make them feel interested and excited. *...the potential to fire the imagination of an entire generation... It was Allen who fired this rivalry with real passion... Both his grandfathers were fired with an enthusiasm for public speaking... By Monday, Senor Menem had returned, apparently fired with new determination.* VERB V n V n *with* n *be* V-ed *with* n V-ed

9 You can use **fire** to refer in an approving way to someone's energy and enthusiasm. *I went to hear him speak and was very impressed. He seemed so full of fire... His punishing schedule seemed to dim his fire at times.* N-UNCOUNT PRAGMATICS =passion

10 If an object or substance **catches fire**, it starts burning. *My home catches fire and everything is destroyed... The aircraft caught fire soon after take-off.* PHRASES V inflects =ignite

11 If a situation or event **catches fire**, it begins to be exciting and successful. *The play only really catches fire once Aschenbach falls in love.* V inflects =ignite

12 If you **fight fire with fire**, you deal with people attacking or threatening you by using similar methods to the ones that they are using. *The only way they can deal with crime is to fight fire with fire.* V inflects

13 If you say that someone has **fire in** their **belly**, you are expressing approval of them because they are energetic, enthusiastic, and passionate. *In Stirling, Wilson had thundered out, a man with fire in his belly.* *belly* inflects, PHR after v, *with* PHR PRAGMATICS

14 If something is **on fire**, it is burning and being damaged or destroyed by an uncontrolled fire. *The captain radioed that the ship was on fire.* v-link PHR =burning

15 If you say that someone is **on fire**, you mean they are very enthusiastic, excited, or passionate about something. *He was on fire with this marvelous sight.* usu v-link PHR, PHR *with* n =burning

16 If you say that someone **is playing with fire**, you mean that they are doing something dangerous that may result in great harm for them and cause many problems. *Schulte warned government and industrial leaders that those who even venture to think about mass layoffs are playing with fire.* V inflects

17 If you **set fire to** something or if you **set** it **on fire**, you start it burning in order to damage or destroy it. *They set fire to vehicles outside that building... Lightning set several buildings on fire.* V inflects =ignite

18 ● **have irons on the fire**: see **iron.** ● **like a house on fire**: see **house.** ● **there's no smoke without fire**: see **smoke.**

fire 2 shooting or attacking

fire /faɪəʳ/ **fires, firing, fired** ◆◆◆◆◇

1 If someone **fires** a gun or a bullet, or if they **fire**, a bullet is sent from a gun that they are using. *Seven people were wounded when soldiers fired rubber bullets to disperse crowds... New guns firing high explosive shells were incorporated into the battlefield... The gun was fired and Beaton was wounded a second time... Seventeen people were killed when security forces fired on demonstrators... They were firing. I screamed at them to stop.* ♦ **firing** *They were under constant firing from the guns... The firing continued even while the protestors were fleeing.* VERB V n V *on* n V N-UNCOUNT =shooting

2 You can use **fire** to refer to the shots fired from a gun or guns. *His car was raked with fire from automatic weapons... The two were reportedly killed in an exchange of fire during a police raid.* N-UNCOUNT =shooting

3 If you **fire** an arrow, you send it from a bow. *He fired an arrow into a clearing in the forest.* VERB =shoot V n

4 If you **fire** questions at someone, you ask them a lot of questions very quickly, one after another. *They were bombarded by more than 100 representatives firing questions on pollution.* VERB V n

5 You can use **fire** to refer to someone's strong criticisms of something. *He concentrates his fire on the defects of the Maastricht treaty.* N-UNCOUNT: poss N =attack

6 If you **draw fire** from someone, you cause them to shoot at you, for example because they think that you are threatening them. *Crowds elsewhere drew fire from troops.* PHRASES V inflects

7 If you **draw fire** for something that you have done, you cause people to criticize you or attack you because of it. *The council recently drew fire for its intervention in the dispute... The campaign is drawing fire from anti-smoking advocates.* V inflects

8 If you **hang fire**, you delay making a decision about something. *All I can suggest is that you just hang fire and wait a minute or two and try again... Last week, banks and building societies were hanging fire on interest rates.* V inflects =wait

9 If someone **holds** their **fire** or **holds fire**, they stop shooting or they wait before they start shooting. *Devereux ordered his men to hold their fire until the ships got closer.* V inflects

10 If you **hold fire** in a situation, you delay before taking decisive action. *Observers reckon the Bank of England will hold fire until nearer the Budget.* V inflects =hold back

11 If you are in the **line of fire**, you are in a position where someone is aiming their gun at you. If you move into their **line of fire**, you move into a position between them and the thing they were aiming at. *He cheerfully blows away any bad guy stupid enough to get in his line of fire... The man and his son had been pushed into the line of fire by their captors.*

12 If you **open fire** on someone, you start shooting at them. *Then without warning, the troops opened fire on the crowd.* V inflects, oft PHR *on* n

13 If you **return fire** or you **return** someone's **fire**, you shoot back at someone who has shot at you. *The soldiers returned fire after being attacked.* V inflects

14 If you come **under fire** or are **under fire**, someone starts shooting at you. *The Belgians fell back as the infantry came under fire. ...sending aid to cities which have been under fire for weeks now.* usu v PHR, v-link PHR

15 If you come **under fire** from someone or are **under fire**, they criticize you strongly. *The president's plan first came under fire from critics who said he hadn't included enough spending cuts.* usu v PHR, v-link PHR

16 • **fire from the hip**: see **hip**.

fire away. If someone wants to say something or ask you something, you can say **'fire away'** as a way of showing that you are ready for them to speak; an informal expression. *'May I ask you something?'—'Sure. Fire away.'* PHRASAL VERB only imper PRAGMATICS =shoot, go on V P

fire off PHRASAL VERB

1 If you **fire off** a shot, you send a bullet or other missile from a gun. *A gunman fired off a volley of shots into the air... Cecil now began to panic and fired off two distress rockets. ...an illustration of a guy firing a huge cannon off into the distance.* V P n (not pron) V n P

2 If you **fire off** a letter, question, or remark, you send or say it very quickly, often as part of a series. *He immediately fired off an angry letter to his ministry colleagues... Ordinary officers fired off a string of angry demands to the government, to improve their pay, status, and conditions.* V P n (not pron)

fire 3 dismissal

fire /faɪəʳ/ **fires, firing, fired.** If an employer **fires** you, he or she dismisses you from your job. *If he hadn't been so good at the rest of his job, I probably would have fired him... She was sent a box of chocolates along with a letter saying she was fired.* ♦ **firing** *There was yet another round of firings.* ♦♦◇◇◇ VERB =sack V n; N-COUNT

fire alarm, fire alarms. A **fire alarm** is a device that makes a noise, for example with a bell, to warn people when there is a fire. N-COUNT

firearm /faɪərɑːʳm/ **firearms. Firearms** are guns; a formal word. *He was also charged with illegal possession of firearms... He was jailed for firearms offences.* ♦◇◇◇◇ N-COUNT: usu pl

fireball /faɪəʳbɔːl/ **fireballs.** A **fireball** is a ball of fire, for example one at the centre of a nuclear explosion. N-COUNT

firebomb /faɪəʳbɒm/ **firebombs;** also spelled **fire bomb**. A **firebomb** is a bomb that burns after it has exploded. N-COUNT

firebrand /faɪəʳbrænd/ **firebrands.** If you describe someone as a **firebrand**, especially someone who is very active in politics, you mean that they are always trying to make people take strong action. *...his reputation as a young firebrand.* N-COUNT

firebreak /faɪəʳbreɪk/ **firebreaks;** also spelled **fire break**. A **firebreak** is an area of open land in a wood or forest that has been created to stop a fire from spreading. N-COUNT

fire brigade, fire brigades. The **fire brigade** is an organization which has the job of putting out fires; used especially to refer to the people who actually fight the fires. *Get everyone out and call the fire brigade... Seven fire brigades were deployed to contain the blaze.* ♦◇◇◇◇ N-COUNT-COLL: usu *the* N

firecracker /faɪəʳkrækəʳ/ **firecrackers.** A **firecracker** is a firework that makes several loud bangs when it is lit. N-COUNT =banger

-fired /-faɪeʳd/. **-fired** combines with nouns which refer to fuels to form adjectives which describe power stations, machines, or devices that operate by means of that fuel. *Coal-fired power stations are among the worst offenders in the production of sulphur gases... Most of the food is cooked on a large wood-fired oven.* COMB in ADJ: usu ADJ n

fire department, fire departments. In American English, **the fire department** is an organization which has the job of putting out fires. The British term is **fire service**. N-COUNT-COLL: usu *the* N

fire drill, fire drills. When there is a **fire drill** in a particular building, the people who work or live there practise what to do if there is a fire. N-VAR

fire-eater, fire-eaters. Fire-eaters are performers who put flaming rods into their mouths in order to entertain people. N-COUNT

fire engine, fire engines. A **fire engine** is a large vehicle that carries firemen and equipment for putting out fires. N-COUNT

fire escape, fire escapes; also spelled **fire-escape**. A **fire escape** is a metal staircase or ladder on the outside of a building, which can be used to escape from the building if there is a fire. N-COUNT

fire extinguisher, fire extinguishers; also spelled **fire-extinguisher**. A **fire extinguisher** is a metal cylinder which contains water or chemicals at high pressure which can put out fires. N-COUNT

firefight /faɪəʳfaɪt/ **firefights.** A **firefight** is a battle in a war which involves the use of guns rather than bombs or any other sort of weapon; used mainly by journalists. *U.S. Marines a firefight with local gunmen this morning.* N-COUNT

fire fighter, fire fighters; also spelled **fire-fighter**. **Fire fighters** are people whose job is to put out fires. N-COUNT: usu pl =fireman

fire fighting. **Fire fighting** is the work of putting out fires. *There was no fire-fighting equipment.* N-UNCOUNT: oft N n

firefly /faɪəʳflaɪ/ **fireflies;** also spelled **fire fly**. A **firefly** is an insect that glows in the dark. N-COUNT

fireguard /faɪəʳgɑːʳd/ **fireguards;** also spelled **fire-guard**. A **fireguard** is a screen made of strong wire mesh that you put round a fire so that people cannot accidentally burn themselves. N-COUNT

fire hydrant, fire hydrants; also spelled **fire-hydrant**. A **fire hydrant** is a pipe in the street from which fire fighters can obtain water for putting out a fire. N-COUNT

firelight /faɪəʳlaɪt/. **Firelight** is the light that comes from a fire. *In the firelight his head gleamed with sweat.* N-UNCOUNT: also *the* N

fireman /faɪəʳmən/ **firemen.** A **fireman** is a person, usually a man, whose job is to put out fires. ♦◇◇◇◇ N-COUNT =firefighter

fireplace /faɪəʳpleɪs/ **fireplaces.** In a room, the **fireplace** is the place where a fire can be lit and the area on the wall and floor surrounding this place. ♦◇◇◇◇ N-COUNT

firepower /faɪəʳpaʊəʳ/. The **firepower** of an army, ship, tank, or aircraft is the amount of ammunition it can fire. *The US also had superior firepower... America has enough firepower in the area to mount sustained air strikes.* ♦◇◇◇◇ N-UNCOUNT

fireproof /faɪəʳpruːf/. Something that is **fireproof** cannot be damaged by fire. *...soldiers wearing fireproof clothing.* ADJ

fire-retardant. Fire-retardant substances make the thing that they are applied to burn more slowly. *The landing strip was coated with fire-retardant foam.* ADJ =flame-retardant.

fire sale, fire sales

1 A **fire sale** is an event in which goods are sold N-COUNT

cheaply because the shop or warehouse they were in has been damaged by fire.

2 If you describe a sale of goods or other assets as a **fire sale**, you mean that everything is being sold very cheaply. *They're likely to hold big fire sales to liquidate their inventory... Experts say it's just not worth selling out at current fire-sale prices.*
N-COUNT: oft N n

fire service, fire services. In British English, **the fire service** is an organization which has the job of putting out fires. The American term is **fire department**. *Crowds of youths prevented the fire service from dealing with the blaze.*
N-COUNT-COLL: usu *the* N

fireside /faɪəʳsaɪd/ **firesides.** If you sit by the **fireside** in a room, you sit near the fire. *...winter evenings by the fireside. ...cosy fireside chats.*
N-COUNT: usu sing

fire station, fire stations. A **fire station** is a building where fire engines are kept, and where fire fighters wait until they are called to put out a fire.
N-COUNT

firestorm /faɪəʳstɔːʳm/ **firestorms;** also spelled **fire storm.**

1 A **firestorm** is a fire that is burning uncontrollably, usually in a place that has been bombed.
N-COUNT

2 In American English, if you say that there is a **firestorm** of protest or criticism, you are emphasizing that there is a great deal of very fierce protest or criticism. *The speech has resulted in a firestorm of controversy.*
N-COUNT: usu with supp PRAGMATICS

fire truck, fire trucks. In American English, a **fire truck** is a large vehicle that carries firemen and equipment for putting out fires. The British term is **fire engine**.
N-COUNT

firewood /faɪəʳwʊd/. **Firewood** is wood that has been cut into pieces so that it can be burned on a fire.
◆◇◇◇◇ N-UNCOUNT

firework /faɪəʳwɜːʳk/ **fireworks** ◆◇◇◇◇

1 **Fireworks** are small objects that are lit to entertain people on special occasions. They contain chemicals and burn brightly or attractively, often with a loud noise, when you light them. *Berlin people drank champagne, set off fireworks and tooted their car horns. ...a firework display.*
N-COUNT: usu pl

2 You use **fireworks** to refer to an occasion on which fireworks are lit to entertain people. *On the night of the fireworks we had a really good spot.*
N-PLURAL

3 An exciting and impressive performance or piece of writing can be referred to as **fireworks**. *It is given a typically thoughtful production with just enough theatrical fireworks.*
N-PLURAL: usu with supp

firing line, firing lines; also spelled **firing-line.**

1 If you are in the **firing line** in a conflict, you are in a position where someone is aiming their gun at you. *Any hostages in the firing line would have been sacrificed... He was sure he would pin down the enemy between two firing lines.*
N-COUNT: usu *the* N in sing, usu prep N

2 If you say that someone is in **the firing line**, you mean that they are being criticized, blamed, or attacked for something. *Foreign banks are in the firing line too... Young players found themselves too much in the firing line.*
N-SING: *the* N, usu *in/out of* N

firing squad, firing squads. A **firing squad** is a group of soldiers who are ordered to shoot and kill a person who has been found guilty of committing a crime.
N-COUNT: also *by* N

firm /fɜːʳm/ **firms, firming, firmed; firmer, firmest** ◆◆◆◆◆

1 A **firm** is an organization which sells or produces something or which provides a service which people pay for. *The firm's employees were expecting large bonuses. ...a firm of heating engineers.*
N-COUNT =company

2 If something is **firm**, it does not change much in shape when it is pressed but is not completely hard. *Fruit should be firm and in excellent condition... Choose a soft, medium or firm mattress to suit their individual needs.* ♦ **firmness** *Vegetables should retain some firmness and should not be soggy and waterlogged.*
ADJ-GRADED =solid ≠soft, flabby; N-UNCOUNT ≠softness

3 If something is **firm**, it does not shake or move when you put weight or pressure on it, because it is strongly made or securely fastened. *If you have to climb up, use a firm platform or a sturdy ladder.* ♦ **firmly** *The front door is locked and all the windows are firmly shut.*
ADJ-GRADED =secure; ADV-GRADED: ADV -ed, ADV after v

4 If someone's grip is **firm** or if they perform a physical action in a **firm** way, they do it with quite a lot of force or pressure but also in a controlled way. *The quick handshake was firm and cool... He managed to grasp the metal, get a firm grip of it and heave his body upwards.* ♦ **firmly** *She held me firmly by the elbow and led me to my aisle seat.* ♦ **firmness** *Tim stretched out a hand in apology and was comforted by the firmness with which Marc gripped it.*
ADJ-GRADED =strong; ADV-GRADED: ADV after v; N-UNCOUNT

5 If you describe someone as **firm**, you mean they behave in a way that shows that they are not going to change their mind, or that they are the person who is in control. *She had to be firm with him. 'I don't want to see you again.'... Perhaps they need the guiding hand of a firm father figure.* ♦ **firmly** *'A good night's sleep is what you want,' he said firmly.* ♦ **firmness** *...a manner that combines friendliness with compassion and firmness.*
ADJ-GRADED: oft ADJ *with* n; ADV-GRADED: ADV with v; N-UNCOUNT

6 A **firm** decision or opinion is definite and unlikely to change. *He made a firm decision to leave Fort Multry by boat... It is my firm belief that an effective partnership approach between police and the public is absolutely necessary.* ♦ **firmly** *Political values and opinions are firmly held, and can be slow to change... He is firmly convinced that it is vital to do this.* ♦ **firmness** *What's impressed me has been his considerable firmness of purpose.*
ADJ-GRADED: usu ADJ n =definite; ADV-GRADED: ADV -ed, ADV after v =strongly; N-UNCOUNT

7 **Firm** evidence or information is based on facts and so is likely to be true. *This man may have killed others but unfortunately we have no firm evidence... There's unlikely to be firm news about the convoy's progress for some time.*
ADJ-GRADED: ADJ n =hard, definite

8 You use **firm** to describe control or a basis or position when it is strong and unlikely to be ended or removed. *Although the Yakutians are a minority, they have firm control of the territory... The company, a household name in the states, has a firm foothold in the British market.* ♦ **firmly** *This tradition is also firmly rooted in the past... It placed reggae music firmly in the mainstream of world culture.*
ADJ-GRADED: usu ADJ n =secure; ADV-GRADED: ADV -ed, ADV after v =securely

9 If people are **firm** friends, they have been close friends for a long time and their friendship is likely to continue. *The couple met about two years ago and soon became firm friends.*
ADJ-GRADED: ADJ n

10 If a price, value, or currency is **firm**, it is not decreasing in value or amount. *Cotton prices remain firm and demand is strong... The shares held firm at 280p... Firm prices and stability will allow both producers and consumers to plan confidently.* ♦ **firmness** *...the firmness of the franc against other currencies.*
ADJ-GRADED =solid, steady; N-UNCOUNT: usu N *of* n

11 If you **firm** soil around a plant, you press it so that it is fairly solid rather than loose. *Firm more soil over the roots and water thoroughly.*
VERB V n prep/adv

12 If someone **stands firm**, they refuse to surrender or change their mind about something. *The council is standing firm against the barrage of protest... The President has appealed to his European partners to stand firm on the issue.*
PHRASE: V inflects

firm up PHRASAL VERB

1 If you **firm up** something or if it **firms up**, it becomes firmer and more solid, and less flabby or floppy. *This treatment helps tone the body, firm up muscles and tighten the skin... I now go swimming five times a week, which helps firm me up... The mixture will seem too wet at this stage, but it will firm up when chilled.*
ERG V P n (not pron) V n P V P

2 If you **firm** something **up** or if it **firms up**, it becomes clearer, stronger, or more definite. *Looking to the future, the Conservatives will firm up their plans for a cleaner, greener, safer Britain... The ground rules have been firmed up... At least the bank situation had firmed up.*
ERG V P n (not pron) V P Also V n P

3 If a financial institution **firms up** the price or value of something, they take action to protect and maintain its price or value. *OPEC has agreed to freeze its global oil production slightly in order to firm up crude prices.*
V P n (not pron)

firmament /fɜːʳməmənt/

1 **The firmament** is the sky or heaven; a literary use. *There are no stars in the firmament.* [N-SING: the N]

2 If you talk about **the firmament** in a particular organization or field of activity, you mean the top of it. *He was rich, and a rising star in the political firmament.* [N-SING: the N, usu with supp]

first /fɜːʳst/ **firsts** ◆◆◆◆◆

1 The **first** thing, person, event, or period of time is the one that happens or comes before all the others of the same kind. *She lost 16 pounds in the first month of her diet. ...the first few flakes of snow... Two years ago Johnson came first in the one hundred metres at Seoul.* ▶ Also a pronoun. *The second paragraph startled me even more than the first... He put me through a series of exercises to improve my car control. The first was to drive on simulated ice.* [ORD ≠last] [PRON]

2 If you do something **first**, you do it before anyone else does, or before you do anything else. *I do not remember who spoke first, but we all expressed the same opinion... First, tell me what you think of my products... Routine questions first, if you don't mind.* [ADV: ADV with v, ADV with cl/group]

3 When something happens or is done for the **first** time, it has never happened or been done before. *This is the first time she has experienced disappointment... It was the first occasion when they had both found it possible to keep a rendezvous.* ▶ Also an adverb. *Anne and Steve got engaged two years after they had first started going out... I met him first at his house where we had a chat.* [ORD] [ADV: ADV with v]

4 An event that is described as **a first** has never happened before and is important or exciting. *It is a first for New York. An outdoor exhibition of Fernando Botero's sculpture on Park Avenue.* [N-SING: a N, oft N for n]

5 **The first** you hear of something or the **first** you know about it is the time when you first become aware of it. *We heard it on the TV last night – that was the first we heard of it... When Mark arrived home that afternoon, it was the first he knew for sure of the surprise party.* [PRON: the PRON that]

6 You use **first** when you are talking about what happens in the early part of an event or experience, in contrast to what happens later. *When he first came home he wouldn't say anything about what he'd been doing.* ▶ Also an ordinal. *She told him that her first reaction was disgust... My first feeling on getting into the cabin was one of dislike to everything I saw.* [ADV: ADV before v =initially] [ORD: usu poss ORD]

7 In order to emphasize your determination not to do a particular thing, you can say that rather than do it, you would do something else **first**. *Marry that fat son of a fat cattle dealer? She would die first!* [ADV: ADV after v PRAGMATICS]

8 You use **first** when you are about to give the first in a series of items. *Certain basic guidelines can be given. First, have a heating engineer check the safety of the heating system.* [ADV: ADV with cl/group PRAGMATICS =firstly]

9 The **first** thing, person, or place in a line is the one that is nearest to you or nearest to the front. *Before him, in the first row, sat the President... First in the queue were two Japanese students.* [ORD ≠last]

10 You use **first** to refer to the best or most important thing or person of a particular kind. *The first duty of any government must be to protect the interests of the taxpayers... Imagine winning the local lottery first prize of £5,000. ...first team football.* [ORD]

11 **First** is used in the title of a job or position whose holder has a higher rank than anyone else with the same basic job title. *...the First Lord of the Admiralty. ...the first mate of a British tanker.* [ORD]

12 In British universities, a **first** is an honours degree of the highest standard. *...an Oxford Blue who took a First in Constitutional History.* [N-COUNT: oft N in n]

13 You use **first of all** to introduce the first of a number of things that you want to say. *The cut in the interest rates has not had very much impact in California for two reasons. First of all, banks are still afraid to loan.* [PHRASES PHR with cl/group PRAGMATICS]

14 You use **at first** when you are talking about what happens in the early stages of an event or experience, or just after something else has happened, in contrast to what happens later. *At first, he seemed surprised by my questions... I had some difficulty at first recalling why we were there.* [PHR with cl =initially]

15 If you say that someone or something **comes first** for a particular person, you mean they treat or consider that person or thing as more important than anything else. *There's no time for boyfriends, my career comes first.* [V inflects]

16 You say **'first come first served'** to indicate that a group of people or things will be dealt with or given something in the order in which they arrive. *There will be five buses, first come first served.*

17 **From the first** means ever since something started. *You knew about me from the first, didn't you?... I thought from the first that she was a little unsure about that marriage.* [PHR with cl]

18 If you learn or experience something **at first hand**, you experience it yourself or learn it directly rather than being told about it by other people. *He arrived in Natal to see at first hand the effects of the recent heavy fighting.* [PHR after v =from the outset]

19 If you say that you **do not know the first thing about** something, you are emphasizing that you know absolutely nothing about it. *You don't know the first thing about farming.* [V inflects PRAGMATICS]

20 You use **first off** to introduce the first of a number of things that you want to say; an informal expression. *First off, huge apologies for last months' confusing report.* [PHR with cl PRAGMATICS]

21 If you **put** someone or something **first**, you treat or consider them as more important than anything else. *Somebody has to think for the child and put him first.* [V inflects =firstly]

22 You say **'first things first'** when you are talking about something that should be done or dealt with before anything else because it is the most important. *Let's see if we can't find something to set the mood. First things first; some music.*

23 ● **first and foremost**: see **foremost**.

-first /-fɜːʳst/. **-first** combines with nouns like 'head' and 'feet' to indicate that someone moves with the part that is mentioned pointing in the direction in which they are moving. *He fell head first into a wheelie-bin from the balcony of his fifth-floor flat.* [COMB in ADV: ADV after v]

first aid. **First aid** is simple medical treatment given as soon as possible to a person who is injured or who suddenly becomes ill. *There are many emergencies which need prompt first aid treatment. ...a first aid kit.* ◆◇◇◇◇ [N-UNCOUNT: oft N n]

first born; also spelled **first-born**. Someone's **first born** is their first child. *Isobel will always have a special place in my heart; she was my first-born... He was the first-born son.* [N-SING: oft N n]

first-class; also spelled **first class**. ◆◆◇◇◇

1 If you describe something or someone as **first-class**, you mean that they are excellent and of the highest quality. *The food was first-class... She has a first-class brain and is a damned good writer.* [ADJ =first-rate]

2 You use **first-class** to describe something that is in the group that is considered to be of the highest standard. *He officially announced his retirement from first-class cricket yesterday... Harriet graduated with a first class degree in literature... The Altea is a newly built first-class hotel.* [ADJ: ADJ n]

3 **First-class** accommodation on a train, aeroplane, or ship is the best and most expensive type of accommodation. *...first-class carriage... He won himself two first-class tickets to fly to Dublin. ...first-class passengers.* ▶ Also an adverb. *She had never flown first class before.* ▶ **First-class** is the first-class accommodation on a train, aeroplane, or ship. *He paid for and was assigned a cabin in first class.* [ADJ: ADJ n] [ADV: ADV after v] [N-UNCOUNT]

4 In Britain, **first-class** postage is the quicker and more expensive type of postage. In the United States, **first-class** postage is the type of postage that is used for sending letters and postcards. *Two first class stamps, please... The price of mailing a first-class letter will not be increasing this year.* ▶ Also an adverb. *It took six days to arrive despite being posted first class.* [ADJ: ADJ n] [ADV: ADV after v]

first cousin, first cousins. Someone's **first cousin** is the same as their **cousin**. Compare **second cousin.** N-COUNT: oft with poss

first degree, first degrees. People who have gained a higher qualification after completing a basic university degree such as a BA or a BSc refer to that basic degree as their **first degree.** *He was born in Zimbabwe where he completed his first degree in economics. He then acquired an MSc (Econ) from LSE and an MBA from Harvard.* N-COUNT

first-degree

1 In the United States, **first-degree** is used to describe crimes that are considered to be the most serious of their kind. For example, **first-degree** murder is when a murder is planned before it is carried out. *She was charged with first-degree murder... He pleaded guilty to a charge of first-degree robbery.* ADJ: ADJ n

2 A **first-degree** burn is one of the least severe kind, where only the surface layer of the skin has been burnt. ADJ: ADJ n

first ever; also spelled **first-ever.** Something that is the **first ever** one of its kind has never happened before. *It's the first-ever meeting between leaders of the two countries.* ◆◇◇◇◇ ADJ: usu ADJ n

first floor, first floors ◆◇◇◇◇

1 In British English, the **first floor** of a building is the floor immediately above the one at ground level. The American expression is **second floor.** N-COUNT: usu *the* N in sing

2 In American English, the **first floor** of a building is the one at ground level. The British expression is **ground floor.** N-COUNT: usu *the* N in sing

first fruits. The **first fruits** of a project or activity are the earliest results or profits. *The deal is one of the first fruits of a liberalization of foreign investment law.* N-PLURAL: usu N *of* n

first hand; also spelled **first-hand** or **firsthand.** ◆◇◇◇◇

1 **First hand** information or experience is gained or learned directly, rather than from other people or from books. *School trips give children firsthand experience not available in the classroom.* ► Also an adverb. *We've been through Germany and seen first-hand what's happening there.* ADJ: ADJ n; ADV: ADV after v

2 • **at first hand**: see **first.**

First Lady, First Ladies ◆◇◇◇◇

1 The **First Lady** in a country or state is the wife of the president or state governor, or a woman who performs the official duties normally performed by the wife. *America's First Lady stood on the sweeping staircase of the White House.* N-COUNT: usu *the* N in sing

2 If you refer to a woman as the **first lady of** something, you mean that you consider her to be better at the thing mentioned than any other person. *...the first lady of song, Ella Fitzgerald.* N-COUNT: usu sing, N *of* n

first language, first languages. Someone's **first language** is the language that they learnt first and speak best; used especially when someone speaks more than one language. N-COUNT

firstly /fɜːrstli/. You use **firstly** in speech or writing when you want to give a reason, make a point, or mention an item that will be followed by others connected with it. *The programme is now seven years behind schedule as a result, firstly of increased costs, then of technical problems... Vitamin C has many roles to play in weight control. Firstly, it is needed for hormone production.* ◆◇◇◇◇ ADV: ADV with cl/group PRAGMATICS =in the first place

first name, first names. Your **first name** is the first of the names that were given to you when you were born. You can also refer to all of your names except your surname as your **first names.** *Her first name was Mary. I don't know what her surname was.* • If two people are **on first name terms,** they know each other well enough to call each other by their first names, rather than having to use a more formal title. *The two were said to have been on first-name terms... Jim has been in the company for many years, and is on first-name terms with many of the board directors.* ◆◇◇◇◇ N-COUNT: usu poss N; PHRASE: usu v-link PHR, oft PHR *with* n

first night, first nights. The **first night** of a show, play, or performance is the first public performance of it. ◆◇◇◇◇ N-COUNT: oft N n

first offender, first offenders. A **first offender** is a person who has been found guilty of a crime for the first time. N-COUNT

first-past-the-post. A **first-past-the-post** electoral system is one in which the candidate who gets most votes wins. ADJ: ADJ n

first person. A statement in **the first person** is a statement about yourself, or about yourself and someone else. The subject of a statement like this is 'I' or 'we'. *He tells the story in the first person... His books are always first person narratives.* ◆◇◇◇◇ N-SING: *the* N

first-rate; also spelled **first rate.** If you say that something or someone is **first-rate,** you mean that they are excellent and of the highest quality. *People who used his service knew they were dealing with a first-rate professional.* ◆◇◇◇◇ ADJ =first-class

first school, first schools. In Britain, a **first school** is a school for children aged between five and eight or nine. N-COUNT

first-timer, first-timers. A **first-timer** is someone who does something for the first time. *Gabrielle entered this year's charts faster than any first-timer before her.* N-COUNT

First World War. **The First World War** or the **First War** is the major war that was fought between 1914 and 1918 in Europe. ◆◆◇◇◇ N-PROPER: *the* N

fiscal /fɪskəl/. **Fiscal** is used to describe something that relates to government money or public money, especially taxes. *...in 1987, when the government tightened fiscal policy.* ♦ **fiscally** *The scheme would be fiscally dangerous... Many members are determined to prove that they are fiscally responsible.* • See also **procurator fiscal.** ◆◆◆◇◇ ADJ: ADJ n =financial; ADV: usu ADV adj, also ADV after v

fiscal year, fiscal years. The **fiscal year** is the same as the **financial year.** *...the budget for the coming fiscal year.* ◆◇◇◇◇ N-COUNT: usu sing, usu with supp

fish /fɪʃ/ **fishes, fishing, fished.** The form **fish** is usually used for the plural, but **fishes** can also be used. ◆◆◆◆◇

1 A **fish** is a creature that lives in water and has a tail and fins. There are many different kinds of fish. *An expert angler was casting his line and catching a fish every time... The fish were counted and an average weight recorded.* N-COUNT

2 **Fish** is the flesh of a fish eaten as food. *Does dry white wine go best with fish?* N-UNCOUNT

3 If you **fish,** you try to catch fish, either for food or as a form of sport or recreation. *Brian remembers learning to fish in the River Cam.* VERB V

4 If you **fish** a particular area of water, you try to catch fish in it. *On Saturday we fished the River Arno.* VERB V n

5 If you say that someone is **fishing** for information or praise, you disapprove of the fact that they are trying to get it from someone in an indirect way. *He didn't want to create the impression that he was fishing for information... She may be fishing for a compliment and welcome your reassurance... 'Lucinda, you don't have to talk to him!' Mike shouted. 'He's just fishing.'* VERB PRAGMATICS V *for* n; V

6 See also **fishing.**

7 If you feel **like a fish out of water,** you do not feel comfortable or relaxed because you are in an unusual or unfamiliar situation; an informal expression. *I think he thought of himself as a country gentleman and was like a fish out of water in Birmingham.* PHRASE: v-link PHR

8 If you tell someone that **there are plenty more fish in the sea,** you are comforting them by saying that although their relationship with someone has failed, there are many other people they can have relationships with; an informal expression. PHRASE PRAGMATICS

fish out. If you **fish** something **out** from somewhere, you take or pull it out, often after searching for it for some time; an informal use. *Kelly fished out another beer from his cooler... She fished out a pair of David's socks for her cold feet.* PHRASAL VERB V P n (not pron) Also V n P

fish and chip shop, fish and chip shops. In Britain, a **fish and chip shop** is a shop which sells hot food such as fish and chips, fried chicken, sausages, and meat pies. The food is cooked N-COUNT =chippy in the shop and people take it away to eat at home or in the street.

fish cake, fish cakes; also spelled **fishcake**. A **fish cake** is a mixture of fish and mashed potato that is made into a round flat shape, covered in breadcrumbs, and fried. N-COUNT

fisherman /fɪʃəʳmən/ **fishermen.** A **fisherman** is a person who catches fish as a job or for sport. ◆◆◇◇◇ N-COUNT

fishery /fɪʃəri/ **fisheries** ◆◆◇◇◇

1 **Fisheries** are areas of the sea where fish are caught in large quantities for commercial purposes. *...the fisheries off Newfoundland.* N-COUNT: usu pl =fishing ground

2 A **fishery** is a place where fish are bred and reared. N-COUNT =fish farm

fish finger, fish fingers; also spelled **fish-finger**. **Fish fingers** are small oblong pieces of fish covered in breadcrumbs. They are usually sold in frozen form. N-COUNT: usu pl

fishing /fɪʃɪŋ/. **Fishing** is the sport, hobby, or business of catching fish. *Despite the poor weather the fishing has been pretty good. ...a fishing boat.* ◆◆◆◇◇ N-UNCOUNT

fishing rod, fishing rods; also spelled **fishing-rod**. A **fishing rod** is a long thin pole which has a line and hook attached to it and which is used for catching fish. N-COUNT

fishing tackle; also spelled **fishing-tackle**. **Fishing tackle** consists of all the equipment that is used in the sport of fishing, such as fishing rods, lines, hooks, and bait. N-UNCOUNT

fish knife, fish knives. A **fish knife** is a knife that you use when you eat fish. It has a wide flat blade and does not have a sharp edge. N-COUNT

fishmonger /fɪʃmʌŋgəʳ/ **fishmongers**

1 A **fishmonger** is a shopkeeper who sells fish; used mainly in British English. N-COUNT

2 The **fishmonger** or the **fishmonger's** is a shop where fish is sold; used mainly in British English. *Purchase your oysters from a reputable fishmonger.* N-COUNT: oft *the* N

fishnet /fɪʃnet/. **Fishnet** tights or stockings are made from a stretchy fabric which has wide holes between its strands, rather like the holes in a fishing net. N-UNCOUNT: usu N n

fish slice, fish slices; also spelled **fish-slice**. In British English, a **fish slice** is a kitchen tool which consists of a flat part with slits in it attached to a handle. It is used for turning or serving fish or other food that is cooked in a frying pan. The usual American word is **spatula**. N-COUNT

fishwife /fɪʃwaɪf/ **fishwives.** In British English, if you say that someone is behaving like a **fishwife**, you mean that they are shouting a great deal and behaving in a very unpleasant and bad-tempered way. N-COUNT

fishy /fɪʃi/

1 A **fishy** taste or smell reminds you of fish. ADJ-GRADED

2 If you describe a situation as **fishy**, you feel that someone is not telling the truth or behaving completely honestly; an informal use. *There seems to be something fishy going on.* ADJ-GRADED =suspicious, odd

fission /fɪʃᵊn/. Nuclear **fission** is the splitting of the nucleus of an atom to produce a large amount of energy or cause a large explosion. N-UNCOUNT

fissure /fɪʃəʳ/ **fissures.** A **fissure** is a deep crack in something, especially in rock or in the ground. N-COUNT

fist /fɪst/ **fists** ◆◆◇◇◇

1 Your hand is referred to as your **fist** when you have bent your fingers in towards the palm in order to hit someone, to make an angry gesture, or to hold something. *Angry protestors with clenched fists shouted their defiance... Gary clutched a penny in his fist.* N-COUNT

2 An **iron fist** policy or approach is one which deals with people and situations in a very strict and ruthless way. *The iron-fist policy towards the fundamentalists is unlikely to be interrupted.* ● **hand over fist**: see **hand**. PHRASE: usu PHR n

fistful /fɪstfʊl/ **fistfuls.** A **fistful** of things is the number of them that you can hold in your fist. *Mandy handed him a fistful of coins.* N-COUNT: usu N *of* n

fisticuffs /fɪstikʌfs/. **Fisticuffs** is fighting in which people try to hit each other with their fists; an old-fashioned word. N-UNCOUNT

fit 1 being right or going in the right place

fit /fɪt/ **fits, fitting, fitted** ◆◆◆◆◇

In American English the form **fit** is used in the present tense and sometimes also as the past tense and past participle of the verb.

1 If something **fits**, it is the right size and shape to go onto a person's body or onto a particular object. *The sash, kimono, and other garments were made to fit a child... She has to go to the men's department to find trousers that fit at the waist... Line a tin with lightly-greased greaseproof paper, making sure the corners fit well.* VERB V n V prep/adv

2 If something is a good **fit**, it fits well. *Eventually he was happy that the sills and doors were a reasonably good fit.* N-SING: adj N

3 If you **are fitted for** a particular piece of clothing, you try it on so that the person who is making it can see where it needs to be altered. *She was being fitted for her wedding dress.* VB: usu passive *be* V-ed *for* n

4 If something **fits** somewhere, it can be put there or is designed to be put there. *...a pocket computer which is small enough to fit into your pocket... He folded his long legs to fit under the table... The crowd was too large to fit inside the hall. ...filters are available that fit over the lens of suitable cameras.* VERB =go V prep/adv

5 If you **fit** something into a particular space or place, you put it there. *...she fitted her key in the lock... Who could cut the millions of stone blocks and fit them together?... When the crown has been made you go back and the dentist will fit it into place.* VERB V n prep/adv

6 If you **fit** something somewhere, you attach it there, or put it there carefully and securely. *Fit hinge bolts to give extra support to the door lock... Peter had built the overhead ladders and the next day he fitted them to the wall... Home spas or mini whirlpools massage and relax, and can be fitted into the bath.* VERB V n V n prep

7 If something **fits** something else or **fits** into it, it is compatible with that thing or able to be part of it. *Her daughter doesn't fit the current feminine ideal... Fostering is a full-time job and you should carefully consider how it will fit into your career... There's something about the way he talks of her that doesn't fit.* VERB V n V *in/into* n V

8 You can say that something **fits** a particular person or thing when it is appropriate or suitable for them or it. *The punishment must always fit the crime.* VERB =match V n

9 If something is **fit** for a particular purpose, it is suitable for that purpose. *Of the seven bicycles we had, only two were fit for the road. ...safety measures intended to reassure consumers that the meat is fit to eat... Follow our guide to making your home a fit place to work, rest and play.* ADJ: oft ADJ *for* n, ADJ to-inf, ADJ n to-inf, ADJ n *for* n

10 If someone is **fit** to do something, they have the appropriate qualities or skills that will allow them to do it. *You're not fit to be a mother!... In a word, this government isn't fit to rule... I'm over 60 now and only fit for gardening and sleeping in a chair... He was not a fit companion for their skipper that particular morning.* ♦ **fitness** *There is a debate about his fitness for the highest office... If you have suffered from a serious medical condition, then you should consult your doctor about your fitness to travel.* ADJ: oft ADJ to-inf, ADJ *for* n, ADJ n *for* n, ADJ n to-inf; N-UNCOUNT: N *for* n, N to-inf

11 If something **fits** someone for a particular task or role, it makes them good enough or suitable for it; a formal use. *...a man whose past experience fits him for the top job in education... It is not a person's gender that fits them to be a minister but what is in their hearts.* VERB V n *for* n V n to-inf

12 If you say that something or someone is **fit** to produce some extreme result, you are emphasizing the extreme nature of that thing or that person's activity; an informal use. *The stink was fit to knock you down. ...hour after hour, the same exercises until you're fit to drop!* ► Also an adverb. ADJ: v-link ADJ to-inf PRAGMATICS ADV:

Wally was laughing fit to burst... You're shivering fit to die, Gracie. ADV after v, ADV to-inf

13 If you say that someone **sees fit** to do something, you mean that they are entitled to do it, but that you disapprove of their decision to do it. *He's not a friend, you say, yet you saw fit to lend him money.* PHRASE: V inflects PRAGMATICS

14 See also **fitted, fitting.** • **fit the bill**: see **bill.** • **fit like a glove**: see **glove.** • **not in a fit state**: see **state.**

fit in PHRASAL VERB

1 If you manage to **fit** a person or task **in**, you manage to find time to deal with them. *We work long hours both outside and inside the home and we rush around trying to fit everything in... I find that I just can't fit in regular domestic work.* V n P, V P n (not pron)

2 If you **fit in** as part of a group, you seem to belong there because you are similar to the other people in it. *She was great with the children and fitted in beautifully.* V P

3 If you say that someone or something **fits in**, you understand how they form part of a particular situation or system. *He knew where I fitted in and what he had to do to get the best out of me... This fits in with what you've told me.* V P, V P *with* n

fit into PHRASAL VERB

1 If you **fit into** a particular group, you seem to belong there because you are similar to the other people in it. *It's hard to see how he would fit into the team.* V P n (not pron)

2 If something **fits into** a particular situation or system, that seems to be the right place for it. *Most film locations broadly fit into two categories; those on private property and those in a public place.* =slot into, V P n

fit out or **fit up.** The form **fit up** is mainly used in British English. If you **fit** someone or something **out**, or you **fit** them **up**, you provide them with equipment and other things that they need. *We helped to fit him out for a trip to the Baltic... I suggest we fit you up with an office suite... They spent 18 million pounds of Government funds fitting out the London headquarters.* PHRASAL VERB =equip, V n P *for* n, V n P *with* n, V P n (not pron), Also V n P

fit 2 healthy

fit /fɪt/ **fitter, fittest.** ◆◆◆◇◇

1 Someone who is **fit** is healthy and physically strong. *An averagely fit person can master easy ski runs within a few days.* ♦ **fitness** *...women who regularly engage in sports and fitness activities... Squash was once thought to offer all-round fitness.* ADJ-GRADED ≠unfit; N-UNCOUNT: oft N n

2 • **fit as a fiddle**: see **fiddle.** • **fighting fit**: see **fight.**

fit 3 uncontrollable movements or emotions

fit /fɪt/ **fits** ◆◆◇◇◇

1 If someone has a **fit** they suddenly lose consciousness and their body makes uncontrollable movements. *About two in every five epileptic fits occur during sleep... Once a fit has started there is nothing you can do to stop it.* N-COUNT =seizure

2 If you have a **fit of** coughing or laughter, you suddenly start coughing or laughing in an uncontrollable way. *Halfway down the cigarette she had a fit of coughing... It was so unreal that I broke into a fit of giggles.* N-COUNT: with supp, N *of* n =bout

3 If you do something in a **fit of** anger or panic, you are very angry or afraid when you do it. *Pattie shot Tom in a fit of jealous rage.* N-COUNT: N *of* n

4 If you say that someone will **have a fit** when they hear about something, you mean that they will be very angry or shocked; an informal expression. *Will Mrs Winterton have a fit if we add one more to the guest list at this late stage?... He'd have a fit if he knew what we were up to!* PHRASES V inflects =go mad

5 Someone who is **in fits** is laughing uncontrollably. *He was a much more entertaining person, who used to have us all in fits.* v-link PHR =stitches

6 Something that happens **in fits and starts** or **by fits and starts** keeps happening and then stopping again. *My slimming attempts tend to go in fits and starts... Military technology advances by fits and starts.* PHR after v =fitfully, spasmodically

fitful /fɪtfʊl/. Something that is **fitful** happens for irregular periods of time or occurs at irregular times, rather than being continuous. *Colin drifted off into a fitful sleep... The government is making slow and fitful progress in these negotiations.* ♦ **fitfully** *The sun shone fitfully and then light snow blew into our faces.* ADJ ≠continuous; ADV: ADV with v

fitted /fɪtɪd/ ◆◇◇◇◇

1 A **fitted** piece of clothing is designed so that it is the same size and shape as your body rather than being loose. *...baggy trousers with fitted jackets.* ADJ: usu ADJ n =tailored

2 A **fitted** piece of furniture, for example a cupboard, is designed to fill a particular space and is fixed in place. *I've re-carpeted our bedroom and added fitted wardrobes.* ADJ: usu ADJ n

3 A **fitted** carpet is cut to the same shape as a room so that it covers the floor completely. *...fitted carpets, central heating and double glazing.* ADJ: ADJ n

4 A **fitted** sheet has the corners sewn so that they fit over the corners of the mattress and do not have to be folded. ADJ: ADJ n

5 Someone who is **fitted** to do something or for something has the right qualities for it. *Helen was ill fitted to fulfil her daughter's ideal of a gentle mother-figure.* ADJ-GRADED: v-link ADJ to-inf =suited

6 If a room is **fitted** with objects, those objects are in the room and are normally fixed in place. *Bedrooms are fitted with alarm pull cords to alert the manager in an emergency.* ADJ: v-link ADJ *with* n, ADJ n

fitter /fɪtəʳ/ **fitters.** A **fitter** is a person whose job is to put together, adjust, or install machinery or equipment. *George was a fitter at the shipyard.* N-COUNT

fitting /fɪtɪŋ/ **fittings** ◆◆◇◇◇

1 A **fitting** is one of the smaller parts on the outside of a piece of equipment or furniture, for example a handle or a tap. *...brass light fittings. ...industrial fittings for kitchen and bathroom... He has made fittings for antique cars.* N-COUNT: usu with supp

2 **Fittings** are things, for example cookers or electric fires, that are fixed inside a building, but that can be removed if necessary. N-PLURAL

3 Something that is **fitting** is right or suitable. *A solitary man, it was perhaps fitting that he should have died alone... The President's address was a fitting end to a bitter campaign.* ♦ **fittingly** *...a fittingly eccentric figure. ...the four-storeyed, and fittingly named, High House... Fittingly, she will spend her year off training her voice to sing blues and jazz.* ADJ-GRADED =appropriate, proper; ADV-GRADED: ADV adj, ADV before v, ADV with cl =appropriately

4 If someone has a **fitting**, they try on a piece of clothing that is being made for them to see if it fits. *She lunched and shopped went for fittings for clothes she didn't need.* N-COUNT

-fitting /-fɪtɪŋ/. **-fitting** combines with adjectives or adverbs such as 'close', 'loose', or 'tightly' to show that something is the size indicated in relation to the thing it is on, in, or next to. *...loose-fitting night clothes. ...glass bottles with tight-fitting caps.* COMB in ADJ-GRADED

five /faɪv/ **fives** ◆◆◆◆◆

1 **Five** is the number 5. NUM

2 In Britain, **fives** is a ball game in which you hit the ball with your hands or a bat against three walls of a court. N-UNCOUNT

3 See also **high five.**

fiver /faɪvəʳ/ **fivers.** In British English, a **fiver** is a five pound note; an informal word. *...blank videos for a fiver each.* ◆◇◇◇◇ N-COUNT

fix /fɪks/ **fixes, fixing, fixed** ◆◆◆◇◇

1 If something **is fixed** somewhere, it is attached there firmly or securely. *It is fixed on the wall... Most blinds can be fixed directly to the top of the window-frame... He fixed a bayonet to the end of his rifle.* VERB =fasten, *be* V-ed prep/adv, V n prep/adv

2 If you **fix** something, for example a date, price, or policy, you decide and say exactly what it will be. *He's going to fix a time when I can see him... The date of the election was fixed... The prices of milk and cereals, are fixed annually.* VERB =set, settle, V n

3 If you **fix** something for someone, you arrange for it to happen or you organize it for them. *I've fixed it for you to see Bonnie Lachlan... It's fixed. He's going to meet us at the airport... They thought that their relatives would be able to fix the visas... He vanished after you fixed him with a job... We fixed for the* VERB =sort, V *it for* n to-inf, *be* V-ed, V n, V n *with* n, V *for* n to-inf, V that

team to visit our headquarters... They'd fixed yesterday that Mike'd be in late today.

4 If you **fix** something which is damaged or which does not work properly, you repair it. *He cannot fix the electricity... If something is broken, we get it fixed.*
VERB =mend V n *get/have* n V-ed

5 If you **fix** a problem or a bad situation, you deal with it and make it satisfactory. *It's not too late to fix the problem, although time is clearly getting short... Fixing a 40-year-old wrong does not mean, however, that history can be undone.*
VERB =mend V n V-ing

6 You can refer to a solution to a problem as a **fix**; an informal use, used mainly in American English. *Many of those changes could just be a temporary fix.* • See also **quick fix**.
N-COUNT: usu adj N

7 If you **fix** your eyes **on** someone or something or if your eyes **fix on** them, you look at them with complete attention. *She fixes her steel-blue eyes on an unsuspecting local official... Her soft brown eyes fixed on Kelly... The child kept her eyes fixed on the wall behind him.*
V-ERG V n *on* n V *on* n V-ed

8 If you **fix** someone with a particular kind of expression, you look at them in that way; used mainly in literary English. *He took her hand and fixed her with a look of deep concern... He fixed me with a lopsided grin.*
VB: no passive =fasten V n *with* n

9 If you **fix** your attention **on** someone or something, you think about them with complete attention. *Fix your attention on the practicalities of financing your schemes... Attention is fixed on the stock market... She kept her mind fixed on the practical problems which faced her.*
VERB =fasten V n *on* n V-ed

10 If someone or something **is fixed in** your mind, you remember them well, for example because they are very important, interesting, or unusual. *Leonard was now fixed in his mind... Amy watched the child's intent face eagerly, trying to fix it in her mind.*
VERB =be fastened *be* V-ed *in* n V n *in* n

11 If someone **fixes** a gun, camera, or radar **on** something, they point it at that thing. *The US crew fixed its radar on the Turkish ship... The bore of the gun remained fixed on me.*
VERB =aim, train V n *on* n

12 If you **fix** the position of something, you find out exactly where it is, usually by using radar or electronic equipment. *He had not been able to fix his position... The satellite fixes positions by making repeated observations of each star. ...accurate position fixing.* ► Also a noun. *The army hasn't been able to get a fix on the transmitter.*
VERB =pinpoint V n V-ing N-COUNT: usu N *on* n

13 If you get **a fix on** someone or something, you have a clear idea or understanding of them; an informal use. *It's been hard to get a steady fix on what's going on.*
N-SING: *a* N *on* n

14 If you **fix** some food or a drink for someone, you make it or prepare it for them. *Sarah fixed some food for us... Let me fix you a drink... Scotty stayed behind to fix lunch.*
VERB V n *for* n V n n V n

15 If you **fix** your hair, clothes, or make-up, you arrange or adjust them so you look neat and well-groomed; an informal use. *'I've got to fix my hair,' I said and retreated to my bedroom... She called a cab, fixed her face, and scrawled a hasty note to Brian.*
VB: no passive =tidy V n

16 If you have your teeth **fixed**, you have dental treatment to make your teeth even, straight, and white; an informal use. *The PR man suggested that I might benefit from getting my teeth fixed... I wonder if Tom ever had his teeth fixed anywhere else?*
VB: usu passive V-ed

17 If someone **fixes** a race, election, contest, or other event, they make unfair or illegal arrangements or use trickery to affect the result; used showing disapproval. *They offered opposing players bribes to fix a decisive league match against Valenciennes... We didn't 'fix' anything. It'll be seen as it happens... The debate seems, in retrospect, to have been fixed from the beginning. ...this week's report of match-fixing.* ► Also a noun. *It's all a fix, a deal they've made.*
VERB PRAGMATICS =rig V n V-ing N-COUNT

18 If you accuse someone of **fixing** prices, you accuse them of making unfair arrangements to charge a particular price for something, rather than allowing market forces to decide it. *...a suspected cartel that had fixed the price of steel for the construction market... The company is currently in dispute with the government over price fixing.*
VERB PRAGMATICS V n V-ing

19 An injection of an addictive drug such as heroin can be referred to as a **fix**; an informal use.
N-COUNT

20 In informal English, you can use **fix** to refer to an amount of something which a person gets or wants and which helps them physically or psychologically to survive. *It turned the country into an 'aid junkie', heavily dependent on its annual fix of dollars... The trouble with her is she needs her daily fix of publicity... I need my fix of sugar, sweets, and chocolate. ...a quick energy fix.*
N-COUNT: with supp, oft N *of* n, n N =dose

21 If you are in **a fix**, you are in a difficult situation, especially one that you have caused for yourself; an informal use. *He was in a fix... The government has really got itself into a fix... This will put us in a very difficult economic fix.*
N-SING: *a* N, usu *in/into* N =mess

22 To **fix** something such as a dye or photographic image means to treat or react with it chemically so that it does not fade or disappear. *Certain pigment colours were painted on to dry plaster using tempera (where egg yolk is used to fix the pigment)... The main aim of inbreeding is to standardise, to fix desirable inherited characteristics and to dispel undesirable ones.*
VERB =stabilize V n

23 If you say that you will **fix** someone, you mean that you will stop their activities permanently; an informal use. *That'll fix him.*
VERB =put paid to V n

24 In informal American English, if you say that you **are fixing** to do something, you mean that you are planning or intending to do it. *I'm fixing to go to graduate school... He would know when I was fixing to leave. He'd wait by the front door.*
VB: only cont V to-inf

25 See also **fixed, fixings.**

fix on. If you **fix on** a particular thing, you decide that it is the one you want and will have. *The Vietnamese government has fixed on May 19th to celebrate his anniversary.*
PHRASAL VERB V P n

fix up
PHRASAL VERB

1 If you **fix** something **up**, you arrange it. *I fixed up an appointment to see her... Accommodation is never fixed up in advance.*
V P n (not pron) Also V n P

2 If you **fix** something **up**, you do work that is necessary in order to make it more suitable or attractive. *I've fixed up Matthew's old room... The whole block is being fixed up.*
=do up V P n (not pron) Also V n P

3 If you **fix** someone **up with** something they need, you provide it for them. *We'll fix him up with a tie... He was fixed up with a job.*
V n P *with* n Also V n P

fixated /fɪkseɪtɪd, fɪkseɪtɪd/. If you accuse someone of being **fixated** on a particular thing, you mean that they think about it to an extreme and excessive degree. *The danger is we'll get so fixated on the technology that we will substitute hardware for people.* ► Also a combining form. *...a pop-fixated music journalist.*
ADJ-GRADED: v-link ADJ *on/with/by* n COMB in ADJ-GRADED

fixation /fɪkseɪʃᵊn/ **fixations.** If you accuse someone of having a **fixation** on something or someone, you mean they think about a particular subject or person to an extreme and excessive degree. *The country's fixation on the war may delay a serious examination of domestic needs.*
N-COUNT: usu sing, usu with supp

fixative /fɪksətɪv/ **fixatives. Fixative** is a liquid used to preserve the surface of things such as a drawings or photographs.
N-MASS

fixed /fɪkst/ ◆◆◆◇◇

1 You use **fixed** to describe something which stays the same and does not or cannot vary. *They issue a fixed number of shares that trade publicly. ...a world without fixed laws... Tickets will be printed with fixed entry times.*
ADJ: usu ADJ n =set ≠varying

2 If you say that someone has **fixed** ideas or opinions, you mean that they rarely change their ideas and opinions, although perhaps they should. *...people who have fixed ideas about things.*
ADJ-GRADED: usu ADJ n ≠flexible

3 If someone has a **fixed** smile on their face, they are smiling even though they do not feel happy or pleased. *I had to go through the rest of the evening with a fixed smile on my face.*
ADJ

4 Someone who is of **no fixed address**, or in British English **no fixed abode**, does not have a perma-
PHRASE: *of/with* PHR, v PHR

nent place to live; a formal use. *They are not able to get a job interview because they have no fixed address... He's of no fixed abode and we found him on the streets.*
5 See also **fix**.

fixedly /fɪksɪdli/. If you stare **fixedly** at someone or something, you look at them steadily and continuously for a period of time. *I stared fixedly at the statue... She was aware that he was watching her fixedly.*
ADV-GRADED: ADV after v =intently

fixer /fɪksəʳ/ **fixers.** If journalists refer to someone as a **fixer**, they mean that he or she is the sort of person who solves problems and gets things done. *John Wakeham seems certain to become the fixer the Prime Minister will need at election time.*
N-COUNT

fixings /fɪksɪŋz/
1 In American English, **fixings** are extra items that are used to decorate or complete something, especially a meal. *He bought a hot dog and had it covered with all the fixings.*
N-PLURAL
2 Fixings are items such as screws, nuts, and bolts which are used to fix things such as furniture together. *Have you got all the screws and fixings you need?*
N-PLURAL

fixity /fɪksɪti/. If you talk about the **fixity** of something, you talk about the fact that it does not change or weaken; used in written English. *I have been working on exploding the myth of fixity of meaning... She believed in the fixity of the class system.*
N-UNCOUNT: oft N *of* n

fixture /fɪkstʃəʳ/ **fixtures** ◆◆◇◇◇
1 Fixtures are pieces of furniture or equipment, for example baths and sinks, which are fixed inside a house or other building and which stay there if you move. *...a detailed list of what fixtures and fittings are included in the purchase price.*
N-COUNT: usu pl
2 A **fixture** is a sports event which takes place on a particular date; used in British English. *City won this fixture 3-0 last season.*
N-COUNT
3 If you describe someone or something as a **fixture** in a particular place or occasion, you mean that they always seem to be there. *She was a fixture in New York's nightclubs... The cordless kettle may now be a fixture in most kitchens.*
N-COUNT: usu N *in* n

fizz /fɪz/ **fizzes, fizzing, fizzed** ◆◇◇◇◇
1 If a drink **fizzes**, it produces lots of little bubbles of gas and makes a hissing sound. *After a while their mother was back, holding a tray of glasses that fizzed.* ► Also a noun. *I wonder if there's any fizz left in the lemonade.*
VERB
V
N-UNCOUNT
2 If something such as an engine **fizzes**, it makes a hissing sound. *When I started the engine it sparked, fizzed and went dead.*
VERB
V
3 If you say that someone puts **fizz** into something, you mean that they make it more interesting or exciting. *A Brazilian public relations firm has brought some fizz into his campaign.*
N-UNCOUNT =sparkle
4 Champagne or sparkling wine is sometimes called **fizz**; an informal use. *...a bottle of fizz.*
N-UNCOUNT

fizzle /fɪzᵊl/ **fizzles, fizzling, fizzled.** If something **fizzles**, it ends in a weak or disappointing way after starting off strongly. *Our relationship fizzled into nothing.* ► To **fizzle out** means the same as to **fizzle**. *The railway strike fizzled out on its second day as drivers returned to work.*
VERB
V *into/to* n
Also V
PHRASAL VERB =peter out
V P

fizzy /fɪzi/ **fizzier, fizziest. Fizzy** drinks are drinks that contain small bubbles of carbon dioxide. They make a hissing sound when you pour them; used mainly in British English. *...fizzy water. ...a can of fizzy drink.*
ADJ-GRADED: usu ADJ n

fjord /fjɔːʳd, fiːɔːʳd/ **fjords;** also spelled **fiord.** A **fjord** is a strip of sea that comes into the land between high cliffs, especially in Norway.
N-COUNT: oft in names after n

flab /flæb/. If you say that someone has **flab**, you mean they have loose flesh on their body because they are rather fat, especially when you are being critical of them. *Don had a hefty roll of flab overhanging his waistband.*
N-UNCOUNT PRAGMATICS

flabbergasted /flæbəʳgɑːstɪd, -gæst-/. If you say that you are **flabbergasted** by something, you are emphasising that you are extremely surprised by it. *Everybody was flabbergasted when I announced I was going to emigrate to Australia.*
ADJ-GRADED: usu v-link ADJ, oft ADJ *by* n, ADJ to-inf
PRAGMATICS

flabby /flæbi/ **flabbier, flabbiest**
1 Flabby people are rather fat, with loose flesh over their bodies. *He doesn't do anything physical. So he must be flabby and unfit... My bulging thighs and flabby stomach made me depressed.*
ADJ-GRADED
2 If you describe something as **flabby**, you are criticizing it for being inefficient or wasteful. *You hear talk about American business being flabby.*
ADJ-GRADED PRAGMATICS ≠lean

flaccid /flæsɪd, flæksɪd/. You use **flaccid** to describe a part of someone's body when it is unpleasantly soft and not hard or firm. *I picked up her wrist. It was limp and flaccid.*
ADJ-GRADED =limp

flag /flæg/ **flags, flagging, flagged** ◆◆◆◇◇
1 A **flag** is a piece of cloth which can be attached to a pole and which is used as a sign, signal, or symbol of something, especially of a particular country. *The Marines climbed to the roof of the embassy building to raise the American flag... They had raised the white flag in surrender.*
N-COUNT
2 A **flag** is a small piece of paper or cloth attached to a stick or pin which is sold on a flag day or used as a marker.
N-COUNT
3 Journalists sometimes refer to the **flag** of a particular country or organization as a way of referring to the country or organization itself and its values or power. *Joining John Whitaker will be his brother Michael also riding under the British flag... The airport was opened by Canadian troops operating under the flag of the United Nations.*
N-COUNT: with supp, usu adj N, N *of* n
4 If you **flag** or if your spirits **flag**, you begin to lose enthusiasm or energy. *His enthusiasm was in no way flagging... By 4,000m he was beginning to flag.*
VERB
V
5 A **flag** is the same as a **flagstone**.
N-COUNT
6 See also **flagged**.
7 If you **fly the flag**, you show that you are proud of your country, or that you support a particular cause, especially when you are in a foreign country or when few other people do. *Steve Crabb can fly the flag with distinction for Britain in Barcelona.*
PHRASE: V inflects

flag down. If you **flag down** a vehicle, especially a taxi, you wave at it as a signal for the driver to stop. *They flagged down a passing family who stopped to help them... They flagged a car down.*
PHRASAL VERB =hail
V P n (not pron)
V n P

flag day, flag days. In Britain, a **flag day** is a day on which people collect money for a charity from people in the street. People are given a small sticker to wear to show that they have given money.
N-COUNT

Flag Day. In the United States, **Flag Day** is the 14th of June, the anniversary of the day in 1777 when the Stars and Stripes became the official U.S. flag.
N-UNCOUNT

flagellation /flædʒəleɪʃᵊn/. **Flagellation** is the act of beating yourself or someone else, usually as a religious punishment; a formal word. *There is a ceremony of prayer and flagellation before the dancing begins.*
N-UNCOUNT

flagged /flægd/. A **flagged** path or area of ground is paved with flagstones. *She sat on a chair in the flagged yard.*
ADJ

flagon /flægən/ **flagons**
1 A **flagon** is a wide bottle in which cider or wine is sold.
N-COUNT
2 A **flagon** is a jug with a narrow neck in which wine or another drink is served.
N-COUNT

flagpole /flægpoul/ **flagpoles.** A **flagpole** is a tall pole on which a flag can be displayed. *The new Namibian flag was hoisted up the flagpole.*
N-COUNT

flagrant /fleɪgrənt/. You can use **flagrant** to describe an action, situation, or someone's behaviour that you find extremely bad or shocking in a very obvious way. *The judge called the decision 'a flagrant violation of international law'... His failure to turn his attention to flagrant wastes of public money is inexcusable.* ♦ **flagrantly** *It is a situation where basic human rights are being flagrantly abused.*
◆◇◇◇◇
ADJ-GRADED: ADJ n =blatant
ADV-GRADED: usu ADV with v, also ADV adj =blatantly

flagship /flægʃɪp/ **flagships** ◆◇◇◇◇
1 A **flagship** is the most important ship in a fleet of
N-COUNT

ships, especially the one on which the commander of the fleet is sailing.

2 The **flagship** of a group of things that are owned or produced by a particular organization is the most important one. *The hospital has been the government's flagship, leading the health service reforms... The company plans to open a flagship store in New York this month.* N-COUNT: oft with poss

flagstaff /flægstɑːf, -stæf/ **flagstaffs.** A **flagstaff** is the same as a **flagpole**. N-COUNT

flagstone /flægstoun/ **flagstones. Flagstones** are large, flat, square pieces of stone which are used for paving. N-COUNT: usu pl

flag-waving. You can use **flag-waving** to refer to the expression of patriotic feelings in a loud or exaggerated way, especially when you disapprove of this. *The real costs of the war have been ignored in the flag-waving of recent months.* N-UNCOUNT PRAGMATICS

flail /fleɪl/ **flails, flailing, flailed** ◆◇◇◇◇

1 If your arms or legs **flail** or if you **flail** them about, they wave about in an energetic but uncontrolled way. *His arms were flailing in all directions... He gave a choked cry, flailed his arms wildly for a moment, and then went over the edge.* ▶ **Flail around** means the same as **flail**. *He starting flailing around and hitting Vincent in the chest.* V-ERG V V n PHRASAL VERB VP

2 A **flail** is a tool which consists of a piece of wood or metal that can swing freely from a handle. Flails are used to thresh grain. N-COUNT

flail around. See **flail** 1. PHRASAL VERB

flair /fleəʳ/ ◆◇◇◇◇

1 If you have a **flair for** a particular thing, you have a natural ability to do it well. *...a friend who has a flair for languages.* N-SING: N *for* n =talent, gift

2 If you have **flair**, you do things in an original, interesting, and stylish way. *Their work has all the usual punch, panache and flair you'd expect.* N-UNCOUNT =style, panache

flak /flæk/. If you get a lot of **flak** from someone, they criticize you severely. If you take the **flak**, you get the blame for something; an informal word. *The President is getting a lot of flak for that... In recent years they have attracted more than their fair share of flak from the press.* ◆◇◇◇◇ N-UNCOUNT

flake /fleɪk/ **flakes, flaking, flaked** ◆◇◇◇◇

1 A **flake** is a small thin piece of something, especially one that has broken off a larger piece. *...flakes of paint... Large flakes of snow began swiftly to fall. ...oat flakes.* N-COUNT: usu with supp, oft N *of* n, n N

2 If something such as paint **flakes**, small thin pieces of it come off. *They can see how its colours have faded and where paint has flaked.* ▶ **Flake off** means the same as **flake**. *The surface corrosion was worst where the paint had flaked off.* VERB V PHRASAL VERB VP

3 If a food such as fish flakes, or if you **flake** it, it breaks into small thin pieces. *Fry until the fish flakes... Skin, bone and flake the fish. ...flaked almonds.* V-ERG V V n V-ed

flake off. See **flake** 2. PHRASAL VERB

flake out. If you **flake out**, you collapse, go to sleep, or totally relax because you are very tired; an informal expression. *If he flakes out before I get back, just cover him with a blanket... Ireland is not for you if you want to flake out on a beach.* PHRASAL VERB VP

flak jacket, flak jackets. A **flak jacket** is a thick sleeveless jacket that soldiers and policemen sometimes wear to protect themselves against bullets. N-COUNT

flaky /fleɪki/

1 Something that is **flaky** breaks easily into small thin pieces or tends to come off in small thin pieces. *...a small patch of red, flaky skin.* ADJ-GRADED

2 If you describe an idea, argument, or person as **flaky**, you mean that they are rather eccentric and unreliable; used showing disapproval. *He wondered if the idea wasn't just a little too flaky, a little too outlandish.* ADJ-GRADED PRAGMATICS

flambée /flɒmbeɪ, AM flɑːmbeɪ/ **flambées, flambéeing, flambéed.** Food that **is flambéed** has been cooked in flaming brandy, rum, or other alcoholic drink. *It would be natural to expect every dish to be flambed in Cognac, for this is the region of the finest brandies.* VERB be V-ed in n Also V n in n, V n

flamboyant /flæmbɔɪənt/. If you say that someone or something is **flamboyant**, you mean that they are very noticeable, stylish, and exciting. *Freddie Mercury was a flamboyant star of the British hard rock scene. ...his lightning speed and flamboyant, aggressive style of play... He wears flamboyant clothes more suited to a rock star than a literary figure.* ♦ **flamboyance** *Campese was his usual mixture of flamboyance and flair.* ♦ **flamboyantly** *She dressed flamboyantly so that everyone would remember her.* ◆◇◇◇◇ ADJ-GRADED N-UNCOUNT ADV-GRADED: ADV with v, ADV adj

flame /fleɪm/ **flames, flaming, flamed** ◆◆◇◇◇

1 A **flame** is a hot bright stream of burning gas that comes from something that is burning. *The heat from the flames was so intense that roads melted. ...a huge ball of flame.* N-VAR

2 If someone's face **flames**, it suddenly looks red, usually because they are angry; used in written English. *Her cheeks flamed an angry red... Christopher's listening face flamed at the contempt.* VERB V colour V

3 You can refer to a feeling of passion or anger as a **flame** of passion or a **flame** of anger. *...that burning flame of love.* N-COUNT: with supp

4 See also **flaming, old flame**.

5 If something **bursts into flames** or **bursts into flame**, it suddenly starts burning fiercely. *She managed to scramble out of the vehicle as it burst into flames.* PHRASES V inflects

6 If someone or something **fans the flames** of a situation or feeling, usually a bad one, they make it more intense or extreme in some way. *He accused the Tories of 'fanning the flames of extremism'.* V inflects

7 If something **goes up in flames**, it starts to burn fiercely and is destroyed. *Fires broke out everywhere, the entire city went up in flames.* V inflects

8 Something that is **in flames** is on fire. v-link PHR

flamenco /fləmeŋkou/ **flamencos. Flamenco** is a Spanish dance that is danced to a special type of guitar music. ◆◇◇◇◇ N-VAR

flameproof /fleɪmpruːf/; also spelled **flame-proof. Flameproof** cooking dishes can withstand direct heat, so they can be used, for example, on top of a cooker or under a grill. ADJ: usu ADJ n

flame-retardant. Flame-retardent is the same as **fire-retardant**. ADJ

flame-thrower, flame-throwers; also spelled **flame thrower**. A **flame-thrower** is a gun that can send out a stream of burning liquid and that is used as a weapon or for clearing plants from an area of ground. N-COUNT

flaming /fleɪmɪŋ/ ◆◇◇◇◇

1 **Flaming** is used to describe something that is burning and producing a lot of flames. *The plane, which was full of fuel, scattered flaming fragments over a large area.* ADJ: usu ADJ n =blazing

2 Something that is **flaming** red or orange is bright red or orange in colour. *He has flaming red hair.* ADJ: ADJ n

3 A **flaming** row or a **flaming** temper, for example, is a very angry row or a very bad temper. *She has had a flaming row with her lover.* ADJ: ADJ n

4 Some people use **flaming** as a mild swear word when they are annoyed. *Farmers don't need much prompting to tell you that 'flaming dog owners' are the scourge of their lives.* ▶ Also an adverb. *Oh God, you get so flaming worked up about everything.* ADJ: ADJ n ADV: ADV adj/adv

flamingo /fləmɪŋgou/ **flamingos** or **flamingoes.** A **flamingo** is a bird with pink feathers, long thin legs, a long neck, and a curved beak. Flamingos live near water in warm countries. N-COUNT

flammable /flæməbᵊl/. **Flammable** chemicals, gases, cloth, or other things catch fire and burn easily. *...flammable liquids such as petrol or paraffin.* ADJ-GRADED =inflammable ≠non-flammable

flan /flæn/ **flans.** A **flan** is a food that has a base and sides of pastry or sponge cake. The base is filled with fruit or savoury food. N-VAR

flange /flændʒ/ **flanges.** A **flange** is a projecting edge on an object. Its purpose is to strengthen the object or to connect it to another object. N-COUNT

flank /flæŋk/ **flanks, flanking, flanked** ◆◆◇◇◇

1 An animal's **flank** is its side, between the ribs and the hip. *He put his hand on the dog's flank.* N-COUNT

2 A **flank** of an army or naval force is one side of it when it is organized for battle. *The assault element, led by Captain Ramirez, opened up from their right flank.* N-COUNT

3 The side of anything large can be referred to as its **flank**. *They continued along the flank of the mountain.* N-COUNT: usu N *of* n

4 If something **is flanked** by things, it has them on both sides of it, or sometimes on one side of it. *The altar was flanked by two Christmas trees... Bookcases flank the bed... She crossed the room and sat in the armchair flanking the window seat... He walks briskly, flanked by heavily armed guards.* VERB *be* V-ed *by* n V n V-ed

flannel /flænᵊl/ **flannels** ◆◇◇◇◇

1 **Flannel** is a lightweight cloth used for making clothes. *He wore a faded red flannel shirt.* N-UNCOUNT: oft N n

2 **Flannels** are men's trousers made of flannel. *...respectable young chaps, dressed in flannels and blazers.* N-PLURAL: also *a pair of* N

3 In British English, a **flannel** is a small cloth that you use for washing yourself. The American word is **washcloth.** N-COUNT

4 If you describe what someone has said as **flannel**, you disapprove because they have said a lot but they avoided telling you what you wanted to know. *No amount of flannel could disguise that this was, at best, a minimalist solution.* N-UNCOUNT PRAGMATICS =waffle

flap /flæp/ **flaps, flapping, flapped** ◆◆◇◇◇

1 If something such as a piece of cloth or paper **flaps** or if you **flap** it, it moves quickly up and down or from side to side, often making a snapping sound. *Grey sheets flapped on the clothes line... They would flap bath towels from their balconies as they chatted.* V-ERG =flutter V V n

2 If a bird or insect **flaps** its wings or if its wings **flap**, the wings move quickly up and down. *The bird flapped its wings furiously... A pigeon emerges, wings flapping noisily, from the tower.* V-ERG V pl-n V

3 If you **flap** your arms, you move them quickly up and down as if they were the wings of a bird. *...a kid running and flapping her arms.* VERB V n

4 A **flap** of cloth or skin, for example, is a flat piece of it that can move freely up and down or from side to side because it is held or attached by only one edge. *He drew back the tent flap and strode out into the blizzard. ...a loose flap of skin.* N-COUNT: usu with supp

5 A **flap** on the wing of an aircraft is an area along the edge of the wing that can be raised or lowered to control the movement of the aircraft. *...the sudden slowing as the flaps were lowered.* N-COUNT

6 A **flap** is a sudden noise or movement made by a bird's wing or by a piece of paper or cloth when it flaps. *Nothing to be heard but the soft flap of a silk banner.* N-COUNT =flutter

7 Someone who is in **a flap** is in a state of great excitement, worry, or panic; an informal use. *Why did people get in a flap over nuclear energy?... Wherever he goes there's always a flap.* N-SING: *a* N, oft *in a* N

flapjack /flæpdʒæk/ **flapjacks**

1 In British English, **flapjacks** are thick chewy biscuits made from oats, butter, and syrup. N-VAR

2 In American English, **flapjacks** are thin, flat, circular pieces of cooked batter made of milk, flour, and eggs. Flapjacks are usually rolled up or folded and eaten hot with a sweet or savoury filling. N-COUNT

flare /fleəʳ/ **flares, flaring, flared** ◆◆◇◇◇

1 A **flare** is a small device that produces a bright flame. Flares are used as signals, for example on ships. *...a ship which had fired a distress flare.* N-COUNT

2 If a fire **flares**, the flames suddenly become larger. *Camp fires flared like beacons in the dark.* ► **Flare up** means the same as **flare.** *Don't spill too much fat on the barbecue as it could flare up.* VERB V PHRASAL VERB V P

3 If something such as trouble, violence, or conflict **flares**, it starts or becomes more violent. *Even as the President appealed for calm, trouble flared in several American cities.* ► **Flare up** means the same as **flare**. *Dozens of people were injured as fighting flared up.* VERB V PHRASAL VERB V P

4 If people's tempers **flare**, they get angry. *Tempers flared and harsh words were exchanged.* VERB V

5 If someone's nostrils **flare** or if they **flare** them, their nostrils become wider, often because the person is angry or upset. *I turned to Jacky, my nostrils flaring in disgust... He stuck out his tongue and flared his nostrils.* V-ERG V V n

6 If something such as a dress **flares**, it spreads outwards at one end to form a wide shape. *...a simple black dress, cut to flare from the hips.* VERB V

7 See also **flared, flares.**

flare up. If a disease or injury **flares up**, it suddenly returns or becomes painful again. *Students often find that their acne flares up before and during exams.* • See also **flare** 2, 3, **flare-up.** PHRASAL VERB V P

flared /fleəʳd/. **Flared** trousers or skirts are wider at the hem or at the bottom of the legs than at the top. *In the 1970s they all had flared trousers.* ADJ-GRADED: usu ADJ n

flare-up, flare-ups. If there is a **flare-up** of violence or of an illness, it suddenly starts or gets worse. *There's been a flare-up of violence in South Africa. ...a flare-up in her arthritis.* ◆◇◇◇◇ N-COUNT: usu *a* N *of/in* n

flash /flæʃ/ **flashes, flashing, flashed** ◆◆◆◇◇

1 A **flash** is a sudden burst of light or of something shiny or bright. *A sudden flash of lightning lit everything up for a second... The wire snapped at the wall plug with a blue flash and the light fused... A jay emerged from the juniper bush in a flash of blue feathers.* N-COUNT: usu with supp

2 If a light **flashes** or if you **flash** a light, it shines with a sudden bright light, especially as quick, regular flashes of light. *Lightning flashed among the distant dark clouds... He lost his temper after a driver flashed her headlights as he overtook... He flashed his light into the boat and saw the fishing-line... He saw the flashing lights of the highway patrol car in his driving mirror.* V-ERG V V n V-ing

3 You talk about a **flash of** something when you are saying that it happens very suddenly and unexpectedly. *'What did Moira tell you?' Liz demanded with a flash of anger... When pursued, he made his escape with a flash of speed... The essays could do with a flash of wit or humor.* N-COUNT: with supp, N *of* n =burst

4 If something **flashes** past or by, it moves past you so fast that you cannot see it properly. *It was a busy road, cars flashed by every few minutes. ...the ball flashed across the face of the goal.* VERB V prep/adv

5 If something **flashes through** or **into** your mind, you suddenly think about it. *A ludicrous thought flashed through Harry's mind... Those lines of Milton flashed into my mind.* VERB V *through/into* n

6 If you **flash** something such as an identity card, you show it to people quickly and then put it away again; an informal use. *Halim flashed his official card, and managed to get hold of a soldier to guard the Land Rover.* VERB V n

7 If a picture or message **flashes** up on a screen, or if you **flash** it onto a screen, it is displayed there briefly or suddenly, and often repeatedly. *The figures flash up on the scoreboard... The words 'Good Luck' were flashing on the screen... Researchers flash two groups of different letters on a computer screen... The screen flashes a message: Try again... A list of items is repeatedly flashed up on the screen.* V-ERG V *up* V prep V n prep V n *be* V-ed *up* Also V n *up*

8 If you **flash** news or information to a place, you send it there quickly by computer, satellite, or other telecommunication system. *They had told their offices to flash the news as soon as it broke... This is, of course, international news and soon it was being flashed around the world.* VERB V n *be* V-ed prep/adv Also V n prep/adv

9 If you **flash** a look or a smile at someone, you suddenly look at them or smile at them; used in written English. *I flashed a look at Sue... Meg flashed Cissie a grateful smile.* VERB V n *at* n V n n

10 If someone's eyes **flash**, they suddenly show a strong emotion, especially anger; used mainly in written or literary English. *Her dark eyes flashed and she spoke rapidly.* VERB =glitter V

11 **Flash** is the use of flashbulbs to give more light when taking a photograph. *He was one of the first people to use high speed flash in bird photography.* N-UNCOUNT: oft N n

12 A **flash** is the same as a **flashlight**; used in American English. *Stopping to rest, Pete shut off the flash.* N-COUNT

13 If you describe something as **flash**, you mean ADJ-GRADED

that it looks expensive, fashionable, and new; an informal use. *...a flash uptown restaurant... You can go for a 'rostrum' system, which sounds flash, but can be assembled quite cheaply if you buy used equipment.* =smart

14 If you describe an achievement or success as **a flash in the pan**, you mean that it is unlikely to be repeated and is not an indication of future achievements or successes; used showing disapproval. *People will be looking in to see how good we are now and whether our success has just been a flash in the pan.* PHRASES usu v-link PHR PRAGMATICS =one-off

15 If you say that something happens **in a flash**, you mean that it happens suddenly and lasts only a very short time. *The answer had come to him in a flash... It was done in a flash.* usu PHR after v

16 If you say that someone reacts to something **quick as a flash**, you mean that they react to it extremely quickly. *Quick as a flash, the man said, 'I have to, don't I?'*

flash back. If your mind **flashes back** to something in the past, you remember it or think of it briefly or suddenly. *His mind kept flashing back to the previous night... Thoughts inevitably flash back to 1914, when trouble in this part of the Balkans led all the way to world war.* ● See also **flashback**. PHRASAL VERB =return V P *to* n Also V P

flashback /flæʃbæk/ **flashbacks** ◆◇◇◇◇

1 In a film, novel, or play, a **flashback** to the past is a scene that returns to events in the past. *There is even a flashback to the murder itself.* N-COUNT: oft N *to* n

2 If you have a **flashback** to a past experience, you have a sudden and vivid memory of it. *He has recurring flashbacks to the night his friends died.* N-COUNT: oft N *to* n

flashbulb /flæʃbʌlb/ **flashbulbs;** also spelled **flash bulb**. A **flashbulb** is a small lightbulb that can be fixed to a camera. It makes a bright flash of light so that you can take photographs indoors. N-COUNT

flash card, flash cards; also spelled **flashcard**. **Flash cards** are cards which are sometimes used in the teaching of reading or a foreign language. Each card has words or a picture on it. N-COUNT

flasher /flæʃəʳ/ **flashers.** A **flasher** is a man who deliberately exposes his genitals to people in public places, especially in front of women; an informal use. N-COUNT

flash flood, flash floods. A **flash flood** is a sudden rush of water over dry land, usually caused by a great deal of rain. N-COUNT

flashgun /flæʃgʌn/ **flashguns.** A **flashgun** is a device that you can attach to, or that is part of, a camera and that causes a flashbulb to work automatically when the shutter opens. N-COUNT

flashlight /flæʃlaɪt/ **flashlights.** A **flashlight** is a small electric light which gets its power from batteries and which you can carry in your hand; used mainly in American English. The usual British word is **torch**. *Len studied it a moment in the beam of his flashlight... The troopers, by flashlight, were searching the immediate area.* ◆◇◇◇◇ N-COUNT: also *by* N =torch

flashpoint /flæʃpɔɪnt/ **flashpoints**

1 A **flashpoint** is the moment at which conflict, especially political conflict, reaches a climax and becomes violent. *The immediate flashpoint was Wednesday's big rally in the city centre... There are still plenty of potential flashpoints in relations between the two countries.* N-VAR =crisis

2 A **flashpoint** is a place which people think is dangerous because political trouble may start there and then spread to other towns or countries. *The more serious flashpoints are outside the capital... It could become the next Balkan flashpoint.* N-COUNT =danger spot

flashy /flæʃi/ **flashier, flashiest.** If you describe a person or thing as **flashy**, you mean they are smart and noticeable, but in a rather vulgar way; an informal word, used showing disapproval. *He was much less flashy than his brother. ...a flashy sports car.* ◆◇◇◇◇ ADJ-GRADED PRAGMATICS

flask /flɑːsk, flæsk/ **flasks** ◆◇◇◇◇

1 A **flask** is a bottle which you use for carrying drinks around with you. *He took out a metal flask from a canvas bag.* ► A **flask of** liquid is the flask and the liquid which it contains. *There's some sandwiches here and a flask of coffee.* N-COUNT N-COUNT: N *of* n

2 A **flask** is a bottle or other container which is used in science laboratories and industry for holding liquids. *Flasks for the transport of spent fuel are extremely strong containers made of steel or steel and lead.* N-COUNT

3 See also **hip flask, vacuum flask**.

flat /flæt/ **flats; flatter, flattest** ◆◆◆◆◇

1 In British English, a **flat** is a set of rooms for living in, usually on one floor and part of a larger building. A flat usually includes a kitchen and bathroom. The usual American word is **apartment**. *Sara lives with her husband and children in a flat in central London... It started a fire in a block of flats... Later on, Victor from flat 10 called.* N-COUNT: also N num =apartment

2 Something that is **flat** is level, smooth, or even, rather than sloping, curved, or bumpy. *Tiles can be fixed to any surface as long as it's flat, firm and dry... After a moment his right hand moved across the cloth, smoothing it flat. ...windows which a thief can reach from a drainpipe or flat roof... The sea was calm, perfectly flat.* ADJ-GRADED

3 **Flat** means horizontal and not upright. *Two men near him threw themselves flat... As heartburn is usually worse when you're lying down in bed, you should avoid lying flat.* ADJ: ADJ n, v-link ADJ, ADJ after v

4 A **flat** object is not very tall or deep in relation to its length and width. *Ellen is walking down the drive with a square flat box balanced on one hand. It's a health food pizza, she declares.* ADJ-GRADED: usu ADJ n =shallow ≠deep

5 **Flat** land is level, with no high hills or other raised parts. *To the north lie the flat and fertile farmlands of the Solway plain... The landscape became wider, flatter and very scenic... The highway stretched out flat and straight ahead.* ♦ **flatness** *Notice the flatness and the rich, red earth.* ADJ-GRADED: ADJ n, v-link ADJ, ADJ after v N-UNCOUNT

6 A low flat area of uncultivated land, especially a marsh, can be referred to as **flats** or a **flat**. *The salt marshes and mud flats attract large numbers of waterfowl.* N-COUNT: usu pl, usu n N

7 You can refer to one of the broad flat surfaces of an object as **the flat of** that object. *He slammed the counter with the flat of his hand. ...eight cloves, of garlic crushed with the flat of a knife.* N-COUNT: usu sing, *the* N *of* n

8 **Flat** shoes have no heels or very low heels. *People wear slacks, sweaters, flat shoes, and all manner of casual attire for travel.* ADJ-GRADED: usu ADJ n ≠high-heeled

9 A **flat** tyre, ball, or balloon does not have enough air in it. ADJ-GRADED

10 A **flat** is a tyre that does not have enough air in it. *Then, after I finally got back on the highway, I developed a flat.* N-COUNT

11 A drink that is **flat** is no longer fizzy. *Could this really stop the champagne from going flat?* ADJ-GRADED ≠effervescent

12 A **flat** battery has lost some or all of its electrical charge. *His car alarm had been going off for two days and, as a result, the battery was flat.* ADJ-GRADED ≠charged

13 If you have **flat** feet, the arches of your feet are too low. *The condition of flat feet runs in families.* ADJ-GRADED

14 A **flat** denial, refusal, or rejection is definite and firm, and is unlikely to be changed. *The Foreign Ministry has issued a flat denial of any involvement... She is likely to give you a flat refusal.* ♦ **flatly** *Michael flatly denied virtually every rumour... He flatly refused to discuss it... I could use some money, Sarah told him flatly.* ADJ: ADJ n ADV: usu ADV with v, also ADV adj

15 If you say that something happened, for example, in ten seconds **flat** or ten minutes **flat**, you are emphasizing that it happened surprisingly quickly and only took ten seconds or ten minutes. *'You're sitting behind an engine that'll move you from 0 to 60mph in six seconds flat... I had it all explained to me in two minutes flat.* ADJ: num n ADJ PRAGMATICS

16 A **flat** rate, price, or percentage is one that is fixed and which applies in every situation. *Fees are charged at a flat rate, rather than on a percentage basis... Sometimes there's a flat fee for carrying out a particular task... Medicare is preparing to cut all payments by a flat 2%.* ADJ: ADJ n =fixed ≠variable

17 If trade or business is **flat**, it is slow and inactive, rather than busy and improving or increasing. ADJ-GRADED =sluggish ≠active,

During the first eight months of this year, sales of big pickups were up 14 while car sales stayed flat... For the country overall, house prices have remained flat. busy

18 If you describe something as **flat**, you mean that it is dull and not exciting or interesting. *The past few days have seemed comparatively flat and empty... It is a long time since a party leader delivered such a dreadfully flat speech as he did yesterday.* ADJ-GRADED
♦ **flatness** *Kenworthy detected a certain flatness in the days that followed.* N-UNCOUNT

19 You use **flat** to describe someone's voice when they are saying something without expressing any emotion. *'Whatever you say,' he said in a deadly flat voice. 'I'll sit here and wait.'... Her voice was flat, with no question or hope in it.* ADJ-GRADED ♦ **flatly** *'I know you,' he said flatly, matter-of-fact, neutral in tone.* ADV-GRADED: ADV after v

20 Flat is used after a letter representing a musical note to show that the note should be played or sung half a tone lower than the note which otherwise corresponds to that letter. **Flat** is often represented by the symbol ♭ after the letter. *...Schubert's B flat Piano Trio (Opus 99).* ADJ: n ADJ ≠sharp

21 If someone sings **flat** or if a musical instrument is **flat**, their singing or the instrument is slightly lower in pitch than it should be. *Her vocal range was, to say the least of it, limited, and she had a distressing tendency to sing flat.* ADV-GRADED: ADV after v ≠sharp ► Also an adjective. *He had been fired because his singing was flat.* ADJ-GRADED

22 If you say that something is **as flat as a pancake**, you are emphasizing that it is completely flat. *My home state of Illinois is flat as a pancake... The economy is still as flat as a pancake.* PHRASES v-link PHR PRAGMATICS

23 If you **fall flat** on your face, you fall over. *A man walked in off the street and fell flat on his face, unconscious.* V inflects, oft PHR *on* n

24 If an event or attempt **falls flat** or **falls flat on** its **face**, it is unsuccessful. *Liz meant it as a joke but it fell flat... If it wasn't for the main actress, Ellen Barkin, the plot would have fallen flat on its face.* V inflects =fail

25 If you say that you are **flat broke**, you mean that you have no money at all; an informal expression. *Two years later he is flat broke and on the dole.* v-link PHR =penniless

26 If you do something **flat out**, you do it as fast or as hard as you can; used mainly in British English. *Everyone is working flat out to try to trap those responsible... They hurtled across the line in a flat-out sprint.* PHR after v, PHR n =all out

27 You use **flat out** to emphasize that something is completely the case; used mainly in informal American English. *That allegation is a flat-out lie... They say the industry is flat out lying about the effects of deregulation.* PHR n/adj, PHR with v PRAGMATICS =utter, complete

28 On the flat means on level ground. *He had angina and was unable to walk for more than 200 yards on the flat.*

29 • **in a flat spin**: see **spin**.

flat cap, flat caps. A **flat cap** is the same as a **cloth cap**. N-COUNT

flatfish /flætfɪʃ/; **flatfish** is both the singular and the plural form. **Flatfish** are sea fish with flat wide bodies, for example plaice or sole. N-VAR

flat-footed

1 If you are **flat-footed**, the arches of your feet are too low. *All babies look flat-footed and when they walk the whole sole touches the ground... He'll grow up flat-footed.* ADJ-GRADED: v-link ADJ, ADJ n, ADJ after v

2 If you describe a person or action as **flat-footed**, you think they are clumsy, awkward, or foolish. *In contrast to the often flat-footed writing, the movie's structure has a certain elegance to it... The government could be caught flat-footed.* ADJ-GRADED: ADJ n, v-link ADJ, ADJ after v ≠graceful

flatmate /flætmeɪt/ **flatmates;** also spelled **flatmate**. In British English, someone's **flatmate** is a person who shares a flat with them. N-COUNT: usu poss N

flat pack, flat packs; also spelled **flat-pack**. In British English, **flat pack** furniture is furniture such as wardrobes and cupboards which is sold in ready-cut pieces along with screws and instructions about how to put it together. *The flat-pack units are by Gower kitchens... It arrives as a flat pack and is bolted together on site.* N-COUNT: usu N n

flat racing. Flat racing is horse racing which does not involve jumping over fences. N-UNCOUNT

flatten /flætᵊn/ **flattens, flattening, flattened** ♦◇◇◇◇

1 If you **flatten** something or if it **flattens**, it becomes flat or flatter. *He carefully flattened the wrappers and put them between the leaves of his book... The dog's ears flattened slightly as Cook spoke his name. ...the pitiful shacks built of cardboard boxes, corrugated iron sheets and flattened oil drums.* V-ERG V n V V-ed ► **Flatten out** means the same as **flatten**. *The hills flattened out just south of the mountain... We now think prices will flatten out towards the end of this year... Peel off the blackened skin, flatten the pepper out and trim it into edible pieces.* PHRASAL VERB ERG V P V n P Also V P n (not pron)

2 To **flatten** something such as a building, town, or plant means to destroy it by knocking it down or crushing it. *...explosives capable of flattening a five-storey building. ...bombing raids flattened much of the area. ...areas of flattened corn.* VERB V n V-ed

3 If you **flatten** yourself against something, you press yourself flat against it, for example to avoid getting in the way or being seen. *He flattened himself against a brick wall as I passed.* VERB V pron-refl *against/on* n Also V pron-refl

4 If you **flatten** someone, you make them fall over by hitting them violently. *'I've never seen a woman flatten someone like that,' said a crew member. 'She knocked him out cold.'* VERB V n

5 If you **flatten** someone in a fight, contest, or argument, you defeat them completely. *In the squash court his chief aim is to flatten me... A large percentage of these forces had been flattened by the assault.* VERB =defeat V n

flatter /flætəʳ/ **flatters, flattering, flattered** ♦◇◇◇◇

1 If someone **flatters** you, they praise you in an exaggerated way that is not sincere, because they want to please you or to persuade you to do something; used showing disapproval. *I knew she was just flattering me. ...a story of how the president flattered and feted him into taking his side.* VERB PRAGMATICS =softsoap V n V n *into*-ing

2 If you **flatter** yourself that something good is the case, you believe that it is true, although others may disagree. If someone says to you **'you're flattering yourself'** or **'don't flatter yourself'**, they mean that they disagree with your good opinion of yourself. *I flatter myself that this campaign will put an end to the war... I flatter myself I've done it all rather well... You flatter yourself. Why would we go to such ludicrous lengths?* VERB V pron-refl that V pron-refl

3 If something **flatters** you, it makes you appear more attractive. *Orange and khaki flatter those with golden skin tones... My philosophy of fashion is that I like to make the kind of clothes that flatter.* VERB V n V

4 See also **flat, flattered, flattering**.

flattered /flætəʳd/ ♦◇◇◇◇

1 If you are **flattered** by something that has happened, you are pleased about it because it makes you feel important or special. *She was flattered by Roberto's long letter... I am flattered that they should be so supportive... She didn't know whether to feel flattered or indignant.* ADJ-GRADED: v-link ADJ, oft ADJ *by* n, ADJ that/to-inf

2 People sometimes use **flattered** when they are expressing thanks in formal situations. *We're flattered and honoured to receive this Doris Day Award.* ADJ-GRADED: v-link ADJ, oft ADJ that/to-inf PRAGMATICS

flattering /flætərɪŋ/ ♦◇◇◇◇

1 If something is **flattering**, it makes you appear more attractive. *Some styles are so flattering that they instantly become classics. ...a refreshing new look that's flattering to skins of all ages... It wasn't a very flattering photograph.* ADJ-GRADED ≠unflattering ♦ **flatteringly** *The bold necklace flatteringly lightens her skin tone.* ADV-GRADED

2 If someone's remarks are **flattering**, they praise you and say nice things about you. *There were pleasant and flattering obituaries about him... The press was flattering.* ADJ-GRADED ≠unflattering

3 If you describe something as **flattering**, you mean that it pleases you and makes you feel important or special. *It is all terribly flattering and she is trying to reply to every single letter personally... Colin chuckled at the flattering response... It was flattering to be told how indispensable his taste and talent were.* ADJ-GRADED: oft *it* v-link ADJ to-inf =pleasing

flattery /flætəri/. **Flattery** consists of flattering words or behaviour; used showing disapproval. *He is ambitious and susceptible to flattery.* N-UNCOUNT PRAGMATICS

flatulence /flætʃʊləns/. **Flatulence** is too much gas in a person's intestines, which causes an uncomfortable feeling. N-UNCOUNT =wind

flatware /flætweəʳ/. **Flatware** is the same as **cutlery**; used in American English. N-UNCOUNT

flaunt /flɔːnt/ **flaunts, flaunting, flaunted** ◆◇◇◇◇

1 If you say that someone **flaunts** their possessions, abilities, or qualities, you mean that they display them in a very obvious way in, especially in order to try to obtain other people's admiration; used showing disapproval. *They drove around in Rolls-Royces, openly flaunting their wealth... One secret he learned very early on was not to flaunt his success.* VERB PRAGMATICS =show off V n

2 If you say that someone **is flaunting** themselves, you disapprove of them because they are behaving in an excessively confident and flirtatious way. *'She's asking for trouble, flaunting herself like that. Did you see the way Major Winston was looking at her?' ...beach-boys flaunting themselves in designer swimwear.* VERB PRAGMATICS V pron-refl

flautist /flɔːtɪst/ **flautists.** In British English, a **flautist** is someone who plays the flute. The usual American word is **flutist**. N-COUNT

flavour /fleɪvəʳ/ **flavours, flavouring, flavoured;** spelled **flavor** in American English. ◆◆◆◇◇

1 The **flavour** of a food or drink is its taste. *This cheese has a crumbly texture with a strong flavour... I always add some paprika for extra flavour. ...drinks of rich colours and strong flavours.* N-VAR

2 If something is orange **flavour** or beef **flavour**, it is made to taste of orange or beef. *...salt and vinegar flavour crisps. ...now available in three new flavours.* N-COUNT: oft n N

3 If you **flavour** food or drink, you add something to it to give it a particular taste. *Flavour your favourite dishes with exotic herbs and spices... Lime preserved in salt is a north African speciality which is used to flavour chicken dishes.* VERB V n *with* n V n

4 You can refer to a special quality that something has as its **flavour**. For example, if something has an Italian flavour it reminds you of Italian things. *...a car with a flavour that is distinctly Italian. ...clothes with a nostalgic Forties flavour.* N-COUNT: usu with supp

5 If something gives you a **flavour** of a subject, situation, or event, it gives you a general idea of what it is like. *The book gives you a flavour of what alternative therapy is about.* N-SING: oft *a* N *of* n =taste

6 If you think that something or someone is very popular at a particular time, you can say that they are **flavour of the month**. *Hats were very much flavour of the month... Middlesex cricketers Gatting and Emburey are hardly flavour of the month.* PHRASE: usu v-link PHR =popular

flavoured /fleɪvəʳd/; spelled **flavored** in American English. If a food is **flavoured**, various ingredients have been added to it so that it has a distinctive flavour. *...meat flavoured with herbs... Many of these recipes are highly flavoured.* ◆◇◇◇◇ ADJ-GRADED: oft ADJ *with* n

-flavoured /-fleɪvəʳd/; spelled **-flavored** in American English. **-flavoured** is used after nouns such as strawberry and chocolate to indicate that a food or drink is flavoured with strawberry or chocolate. *...strawberry-flavoured sweets. ...fruit-flavored sparkling water.* COMB in ADJ: usu ADJ n

flavouring /fleɪvərɪŋ/ **flavourings;** spelled **flavoring** in American English. **Flavourings** are substances that are added to food or drink to give it a particular taste. *Our range of herbal teas contain no preservatives, colourings or artificial flavourings. ...lemon flavoring.* N-VAR

flavourless /fleɪvəʳləs/; also spelled **flavorless**. **Flavourless** food is uninteresting because it does not taste strongly of anything. ADJ

flaw /flɔː/ **flaws** ◆◇◇◇◇

1 A **flaw** in something such as a theory or argument is a mistake in it, which causes it to be less effective or valid. *There were, however, a number of crucial flaws in his monetary theory... Almost all of these studies have serious flaws.* N-COUNT: oft N *in* n

2 A **flaw** in someone's character is an undesirable quality that they have. *The only flaw in his character seems to be a short temper.* N-COUNT: oft N *in* n =defect

3 A **flaw** in something such as a pattern or material is a fault in it that should not be there. N-COUNT =imperfection

flawed /flɔːd/. Something that is **flawed** has a mark, fault, or mistake in it. *...the unique beauty of a flawed object... These tests were so seriously flawed as to render the results meaningless.* ◆◇◇◇◇ ADJ-GRADED

flawless /flɔːləs/. If you say that something or someone is **flawless**, you mean that they are extremely good and that there are no faults or problems with them. *She attributed her flawless complexion to the moisturiser she used... Discovery's takeoff this morning from Cape Canaveral was flawless.* ♦ **flawlessly** *Each stage of the battle was carried off flawlessly.* ◆◇◇◇◇ ADJ-GRADED =perfect ADV-GRADED: ADV with v, ADV adj

flax /flæks/. **Flax** is a plant with blue flowers. Its stem is used for making thread, rope, and cloth, and its seeds are used for making linseed oil. N-UNCOUNT

flaxen /flæksᵊn/. **Flaxen** hair is pale yellow in colour. ADJ: ADJ n

flay /fleɪ/ **flays, flaying, flayed**

1 When someone **flays** an animal or person, they remove their skin, usually when they are dead. *They had to flay the great, white, fleecy animals and cut them up for food... To remain together was like volunteering to be flayed alive.* VERB V n

2 If you **flay** someone, you criticize them severely for their beliefs, policies, or actions. *He flayed Mr Rao's government for not moving fast enough on economic reform.* VERB V n

flea /fliː/ **fleas.** A **flea** is a very small jumping insect that has no wings and feeds on the blood of humans or animals. ◆◇◇◇◇ N-COUNT

flea market, flea markets. A **flea market** is an outdoor market selling cheap second-hand goods and sometimes also antiques. N-COUNT

fleapit /fliːpɪt/ **fleapits;** also spelled **flea-pit**. In informal British English, if you refer to a cinema or theatre as a **fleapit**, you mean that it is old and does not look very clean or tidy. N-COUNT

fleck /flek/ **flecks. Flecks** are small marks on a surface, or objects that look like small marks. *He went to the men's room to wash flecks of blood from his shirt... His hair is dark grey with flecks of ginger.* ◆◇◇◇◇ N-COUNT: usu pl, oft N *of* n =speck

flecked /flekt/. Something that is **flecked** with something is marked or covered with small flecks of it. *His hair was increasingly flecked with grey.* ► Also a combining form. *He was attired in a plain, mud-flecked uniform.* ADJ: oft ADJ *with* n =streaked COMB in ADJ

fled /fled/. **Fled** is the past tense and past participle of **flee**.

fledgling /fledʒlɪŋ/ **fledglings** ◆◇◇◇◇

1 A **fledgling** is a young bird that has its feathers and is learning to fly. N-COUNT

2 You use **fledgling** to describe a person, organization, or system that is new or without experience. *...the sound practical advice he gave to fledgling writers. ...Russia's fledgling democracy.* ADJ: ADJ n

flee /fliː/ **flees, fleeing, fled.** If you **flee** from something or someone, or **flee** a person or thing, you escape from them; used in written English. *He slammed the bedroom door behind him and fled... In 1984 he fled to Costa Rica to avoid military service. ...refugees who have fled from wars, famine and persecution... The Home Secretary wants to protect the rights of refugees fleeing persecution or torture... Thousands have been compelled to flee the country in makeshift boats.* ◆◆◆◇◇ VB: no passive V V prep/adv V n

fleece /fliːs/ **fleeces, fleecing, fleeced** ◆◇◇◇◇

1 A sheep's **fleece** is the coat of wool that covers it. N-COUNT

2 A **fleece** is the wool, in a single piece, that is cut off one sheep during shearing. N-COUNT

3 If you **fleece** someone, you get a lot of money from them by tricking or overcharging them; an informal use. *She claims he fleeced her out of thousands of pounds.* VERB =swindle V n *out of* n Also V n

fleecy /fliːsi/

1 **Fleecy** clothes, blankets, or other objects are ADJ:

made of a soft slightly fluffy material. *...fleecy walking jackets.* usu ADJ n

2 Something that is **fleecy** is light, soft, and fluffy in appearance. *It was a lovely afternoon with a blue sky and a few fleecy white clouds.* ADJ-GRADED

fleet /fliːt/ **fleets** ◆◆◆◇◇

1 A **fleet** is a group of ships organized to do something together, for example to fight battles or to catch fish. *The damage inflicted upon the British fleet was devastating. ...restaurants supplied by local fishing fleets.* N-COUNT: usu supp N

2 A **fleet** of vehicles is a group of them, especially when they all belong to a particular organization or business, or when they are all going somewhere together. *With its own fleet of trucks, the company delivers most orders overnight... A fleet of ambulances took the injured to hospital.* N-COUNT: oft N of n

fleeting /fliːtɪŋ/. **Fleeting** is used to describe something which lasts only for a very short time. *The girls caught only a fleeting glimpse of the driver... She wondered for a fleeting moment if he would put his arm around her.* ◆◇◇◇◇ ADJ-GRADED: usu ADJ n =brief ♦ **fleetingly** *A smile passed fleetingly across his face... I think I saw her, fleetingly, at a football match.* ADV: usu ADV with v, also ADV adj

Fleet Street. **Fleet Street** is used to refer to British national newspapers and to the journalists who work for them. *He was the highest-paid sub-editor in Fleet Street. ...Fleet Street journalists.* ◆◇◇◇◇ N-PROPER

Flemish /flemɪʃ/ ◆◇◇◇◇

1 **Flemish** means belonging or relating to the region of Flanders in northern Europe, or to its people, language, or culture. *...a splendid collection of Dutch, French and Flemish art. ...this picturesque Flemish town.* ADJ

2 **Flemish** is a language spoken in Belgium. N-UNCOUNT

flesh /fleʃ/ **fleshes, fleshing, fleshed** ◆◆◇◇◇

1 **Flesh** is the soft part of a person's or animal's body between the bones and the skin. *Illness had wasted the flesh from her tall, willowy body. ...the pale pink flesh of trout and salmon.* N-UNCOUNT

2 You can use **flesh** to refer to human skin and the human body, especially when you are considering it in a sexual way. *...the warmth of her flesh. ...the sins of the flesh.* N-UNCOUNT

3 The **flesh** of a fruit or vegetable is the soft inner part of it. *Cut the flesh from the olives and discard the stones.* N-UNCOUNT

4 You use **flesh and blood** to emphasize that someone has human feelings or weaknesses, often when contrasting them with machines. *I'm only flesh and blood, like anyone else. ...skills of a precision unmatched by any flesh and blood worker.* PHRASES PRAGMATICS

5 If you say that someone is your **own flesh and blood**, you are emphasizing that they are a member of your family. *The kid, after all, was his own flesh and blood. He deserved a second chance.* usu v-link PHR PRAGMATICS

6 If something **makes** your **flesh creep** or **makes** your **flesh crawl**, it makes you feel horrified or revolted. *It makes my flesh creep to think of it... I was heading on a secret mission that made my flesh crawl.* *make* inflects

7 If you meet or see someone **in the flesh**, you actually meet or see them, rather than, for example, seeing them in a film or on television. *Charles' appeal is best observed in the flesh... The first thing viewers usually say when they see me in the flesh is 'You're smaller than you look on TV.'* usu PHR after v, v-link PHR =in person

8 If you **put flesh on** something, you add details and more information to it. *This is an attempt to put flesh on what has been a very bare skeleton plan up to now.* V inflects, PHR n

9 ● **pound of flesh**: see **pound**.

flesh out. If you **flesh out** something such as a story or plan, you add details and more information to it. *He talked with him for an hour and a half, fleshing out the details of his original five-minute account... He has since fleshed out his story.* PHRASAL VERB V P n (not pron) Also V n P

flesh-coloured; spelled **flesh colored** in American English. Something that is **flesh-coloured** is yellowish pink in colour. ADJ

flesh wound, flesh wounds. A **flesh wound** is a wound that breaks the skin but does not damage the bones or any of the body's important internal organs. N-COUNT

fleshy /fleʃi/

1 If you describe someone as **fleshy**, you mean that they are slightly too fat. *He was well-built, but too fleshy to be impressive.* ADJ-GRADED

2 **Fleshy** parts of the body or **fleshy** plants are thick and soft. *...the fleshy part of the thigh. ...fleshy fruits like apples, plums, pears, peaches.* ADJ-GRADED

flew /fluː/. **Flew** is the past tense of **fly**.

flex /fleks/ **flexes, flexing, flexed** ◆◇◇◇◇

1 A **flex** is an electric cable containing two or more wires that is connected to an electrical appliance; used mainly in British English. N-VAR

2 If you **flex** your muscles or parts of your body, you bend, move, or stretch them for a short time in order to exercise them. *He slowly flexed his muscles and tried to stand.* VERB V n

3 ● to **flex** your **muscles**: see **muscle**.

flexible /fleksɪbᵊl/ ◆◆◆◇◇

1 A **flexible** object or material can be bent easily without breaking. *...brushes with long, flexible bristles.* ADJ-GRADED =pliable ♦ **flexibility** /fleksɪbɪlɪti/ *The flexibility of the lens decreases with age; it is therefore common for our sight to worsen as we get older.* N-UNCOUNT =elasticity

2 Something or someone that is **flexible** is able to change easily and adapt to different conditions and circumstances as they occur; used showing approval. *Look for software that's flexible enough for a range of abilities. ...flexible working hours.* ADJ-GRADED PRAGMATICS =adaptable ♦ **flexibly** /fleksɪbli/ *It would seem more sensible to apply standards flexibly rather than rigidly.* ADV-GRADED: ADV with v ♦ **flexibility** *The flexibility of distance learning would be particularly suited to busy managers.* N-UNCOUNT =adaptability

flexitime /fleksitaɪm/; also spelled **flexi-time**. The word **flextime** is used instead in American English. **Flexitime** or **flextime** is a system that allows employees to vary the time that they start or finish work, provided that an agreed total number of hours are spent at work. N-UNCOUNT

flick /flɪk/ **flicks, flicking, flicked** ◆◆◇◇◇

1 If something **flicks** in a particular direction, or if someone **flicks** it, it moves with a short, sudden movement. *His tongue flicked across his lips... The man's gun flicked up from beside his thigh... His glance flicked round my face and came to rest on my eyes... He flicked his cigarette out of the window.* ► Also a noun. *...a flick of a paintbrush.* V-ERG V prep/adv V n prep/adv Also V, V n N-COUNT: oft a N of n

2 If you **flick** something away, or off something else, you remove it with a quick movement of your hand or finger. *Shirley flicked a speck of fluff from the sleeve of her black suit... Alan stretched out his hand and flicked the letter away.* VERB V n from/off n V n away

3 If you **flick** something such as a whip or a towel, or **flick** something with it, you hold one end of it and move your hand quickly up and then forward, so that the other end moves. *He helped her up before flicking the reins... She sighed and flicked a dishcloth at the counter... The jockey said he tended to flick horses with the whip.* ► Also a noun. *...a flick of the whip.* VERB V n V n prep V n with n N-COUNT

4 If you **flick** a switch, or **flick** an electrical appliance on or off, you press the switch sharply so that it moves into a different position and works the equipment. *He flicked a light-switch on the wall beside the door... Sam was flicking a flashlight on and off... Pearle flicked off the TV.* VERB V n V n with on/off

5 If you **flick through** a book or magazine, you turn its pages quickly, for example to get a general idea of its contents or to look for a particular item. If you **flick through** television channels, you continually change channels very quickly, for example using a remote control. *She was flicking through some magazines on a table... I'll just flick through the pages until I find the right section... He switched on the television, flicking through the channels in a search for something to hold his interest.* ► Also a noun. *I thought I'd have a quick flick through some recent issues.* VERB V through n N-SING: a N

flicker /flɪkəʳ/ **flickers, flickering, flickered** ◆◇◇◇◇

1 If a light or flame **flickers**, it shines unsteadily. *Fluorescent lights flickered, and then the room was* VERB V *brilliantly, blindingly bright... A television flickered in the corner.* ▶ Also a noun. *Looking through the cabin window I saw the flicker of flames.* N-COUNT

2 A **flicker** of emotion or feeling is one that is experienced or visible only faintly and for a very short time. *He felt a flicker of regret... He looked at me, a flicker of amusement in his cold eyes.* N-COUNT: usu sing, oft N *of* n =glimmer

3 If an expression **flickers** across your face, it appears very briefly; used in written English. *A smile flickered across Vincent's grey features. ...a shadow of disquiet flickering over his face.* VERB V *across/over* n

4 If someone's eyes **flicker** towards something, they look at it quickly; used in written English. *Dirk's eyes flickered towards the pistol... His dark eyes flickered over her face.* VERB V prep/adv

5 If something **flickers**, it makes very slight, quick movements. *In a moment her eyelids flickered, then opened... A few moments later Mrs Tenney's eyelids flickered open.* VERB V V adj

flick-knife, flick-knives; also spelled **flick knife**. In British English, a **flick-knife** is a knife with a blade in the handle that springs out when a button is pressed. The usual American word is **switchblade**. N-COUNT

flier /flaɪəʳ/. See **flyer**.

flight /flaɪt/ **flights** ◆◆◆◆◇

1 A **flight** is a journey made by flying, usually in an aeroplane. *The flight will take four hours.* N-COUNT

2 You can refer to an aeroplane carrying passengers on a particular journey as a particular **flight**. *I'll try to get on the flight down to Karachi tonight... BA flight 286 was two hours late.* N-COUNT: also N num

3 **Flight** is the action of flying, or the ability to fly. *These hawks are magnificent in flight, soaring and circling for long periods... Supersonic flight could become a routine form of travel in the 21st century.* N-UNCOUNT

4 A **flight of** birds is a group of them flying together. *A flight of green parrots shot out of the cedar forest.* N-COUNT: N *of* n

5 **Flight** is the act of running away from a dangerous or unpleasant situation or place. *Frank was in full flight when he reached them... The family was often in flight, hiding out in friends' houses. ...her hurried flight from the palace in a cart.* N-UNCOUNT: oft *in* N

6 A **flight** of steps or stairs is a set of steps or stairs that lead from one level to another without changing direction. *We walked in silence up a flight of stairs and down a long corridor.* N-COUNT: usu N *of* n

7 An idea or statement that is very imaginative but complicated, silly, or impractical can be referred to as a **flight of fancy**. *Cockburn engaged in a flight of fancy, never once allowing facts to get in the way.* PHRASES *flight* inflects

8 If someone **takes flight**, they run away from an unpleasant situation or place. *He was contacted by telephone and told of the raid and decided to take flight almost immediately.* V inflects =flee

flight attendant, flight attendants. On an aeroplane, the **flight attendants** are the people whose job is to look after the passengers and serve their meals. N-COUNT

flight deck, flight decks; also spelled **flight-deck**.

1 On an aircraft carrier, the **flight deck** is the flat open surface on the deck where aircraft take off and land. N-COUNT

2 On a large aeroplane, the **flight deck** is the area at the front where the pilot works and where all the controls are. N-COUNT

flightless /flaɪtləs/. A **flightless** bird or insect is unable to fly because it does not have the necessary type of wings. *...a flightless dinosaur.* ADJ: ADJ n

flight lieutenant, flight lieutenants; also spelled **flight-lieutenant**. In the British air force, a **flight lieutenant** is an officer of the rank below squadron leader. N-COUNT; N-TITLE

flight recorder, flight recorders. On an aeroplane, the **flight recorder** is the same as the **black box**. N-COUNT

flighty /flaɪti/ **flightier, flightiest.** If you say that someone is **flighty**, you disapprove of them because they are not very serious or reliable and keep changing from one activity, idea, or partner to another. *Isabelle was a frivolous little fool, vain and flighty.* ADJ-GRADED PRAGMATICS

flimsy /flɪmzi/ **flimsier, flimsiest** ◆◇◇◇◇

1 A **flimsy** object is weak because it is made of a weak material, or is badly made. *...a flimsy wooden door. ...a pair of inelegant and flimsy shoes.* ADJ-GRADED

2 **Flimsy** cloth or clothing is thin and does not give much protection. *...a very flimsy pink chiffon nightgown.* ADJ-GRADED

3 If you describe something such as evidence or an excuse as **flimsy**, you mean that it is not very good or convincing. *The charges were based on very flimsy evidence.* ADJ-GRADED =weak, unconvincing

flinch /flɪntʃ/ **flinches, flinching, flinched** ◆◇◇◇◇

1 If you **flinch**, you make a small sudden movement, especially when something surprises you or hurts you. *Murat had looked into the eyes of the firing squad without flinching... The sharp surface of the rock caught at her skin, making her flinch.* VERB V

2 If you **flinch** from something unpleasant, you are unwilling to do it or think about it, or you avoid doing it. *The world community should not flinch in the face of this challenge... He has never flinched from harsh financial decisions.* VERB =shy away V V *from* n

fling /flɪŋ/ **flings, flinging, flung** ◆◆◇◇◇

1 If you **fling** something somewhere, you throw it there using a lot of force. *The woman flung the cup at him... He once seized my knitting, flinging it across the room.* VERB V n prep/adv

2 If you **fling** yourself somewhere, you move or jump there suddenly and with a lot of force. *He flung himself to the floor.* VERB V pron-refl prep/adv

3 If you **fling** a part of your body in a particular direction, especially your arms or head, you move it there suddenly. *She flung her arms around my neck and kissed me.* VERB =throw V n prep/adv

4 If you **fling** someone to the ground, you push them very roughly so that they fall over. *The youth got him by the front of his shirt and flung him to the ground.* VERB V n prep/adv

5 If you **fling** something into a particular place or position, you put it there in a quick or angry way. *Peter flung his shoes into the corner... He flung it down on the desk.* VERB V n prep/adv

6 If you **fling** yourself into a particular activity, you do it with a lot of enthusiasm and energy. *She flung herself into her career... I flung myself into poetry.* VERB V pron-refl *into* n

7 If two people have a **fling**, they have a brief sexual relationship; an informal use. *She claims she had a brief fling with him 30 years ago.* N-COUNT: oft N *with* n =affair

8 A **fling** is a short period of enjoyment, especially the last one that you will get an opportunity to have. *...that last fling before you finally give up and take up a job.* N-SING

9 **Fling** can be used instead of 'throw' in many expressions that usually contain 'throw'.

flint /flɪnt/ **flints**

1 **Flint** is a very hard greyish-black stone that was used in prehistoric times for making tools. *...a flint arrowhead. ...eyes the colour of flint.* N-UNCOUNT

2 A **flint** is a small piece of flint which can be struck with a piece of steel to produce sparks. N-COUNT

flintlock /flɪntlɒk/ **flintlocks.** A **flintlock** gun is a type of gun that was used in former times. It is fired by pressing a trigger which causes a spark struck from a flint to light gunpowder. N-COUNT: oft N n

flinty /flɪnti/. If you describe a person or someone's character or expression as **flinty**, you mean they are harsh and show no emotion. *...her flinty stare. ...a man of flinty determination.* ADJ-GRADED =stony, hard

flip /flɪp/ **flips, flipping, flipped** ◆◆◇◇◇

1 If you **flip** a device or machine on or off, or if you **flip** a switch, you turn it on or off by pressing or turning the switch quickly. *He didn't flip on the headlights until he was two blocks away... Then he walked out, flipping the lights off... He flipped the timer switch.* VERB =flick V n with *on/off* V n

2 If you **flip** through the pages of a book, for example, you quickly turn over the pages in order to find a particular one or to get an idea of the contents. *He was flipping through a magazine in the living* VERB V *through* n V n

room... He flipped the pages of the diary and began reading the last entry.

3 If something **flips** over, or if you **flip** it over or into a different position, it moves or is moved into a different position. *The plane then flipped over and burst into flames... He flipped it neatly on to the plate.* V-ERG V adv/prep V n prep/adv

4 If you **flip** something, especially a coin, you use your thumb to make it turn over and over, as it goes through the air. *I pulled a coin from my pocket and flipped it... I flipped a butt out of the window and drove on.* ► Also a noun. *...having gambled all on the flip of a coin.* VERB =toss V n V n prep N-SING: N *of* n

5 If someone **flips**, they suddenly become extremely upset or angry because of something that has happened; an informal use. *He got so provoked that he flipped.* VERB =snap V

6 If you say that someone is being **flip**, you disapprove of them because you think that what they are saying shows they are not being serious enough about something. *...a flip answer... The tone of the book is sometimes too flip.* ADJ-GRADED PRAGMATICS =flippant, glib

flip-flop, flip-flops, flip-flopping, flip-flopped

1 **Flip-flops** are sandals which are held on your foot by a V-shaped strap that goes between your big toe and the toe next to it. They are often called **thongs** in American English. N-PLURAL

2 If you say that someone, especially a politician, **flip-flops** on a decision, you are critical of them because they change their decision, so that they do or think the opposite; used mainly in informal American English. *He has been criticized for flip-flopping on several key issues... He seemed so sure of his decision, how could he flip-flop so dramatically now?* ► Also a noun. *The President's flip-flops on taxes made him appear indecisive.* VERB PRAGMATICS V *on* n V N-COUNT

flippant /flɪpənt/. If you describe a person or what they say as **flippant**, you are criticizing them because you think they are not taking something as seriously as they should. *Don't be flippant, damn it! This is serious!... He now dismisses that as a flippant comment.* ♦ **flippancy** *She must have thought that there was some flippancy in his tone, for she said, 'Andrew, I wish you'd take this seriously'.* ♦ **flippantly** *He answered carelessly and flippantly.* ADJ-GRADED PRAGMATICS =flip, glib N-UNCOUNT ADV-GRADED: ADV with v

flipper /flɪpəʳ/ **flippers**

1 **Flippers** are flat pieces of rubber that you can wear on your feet to help you swim more quickly, especially underwater. N-COUNT: usu pl

2 The **flippers** of an animal that lives in water, for example a seal or a penguin, are the two or four flat limbs which it uses for swimming. N-COUNT: usu pl

flipping /flɪpɪŋ/. Some people use **flipping** to emphasize what they are saying, especially when they are annoyed; an informal word used in spoken British English. *This is such a flipping horrible picture.* ► Also an adjective. *I even washed the flipping bed sheets yesterday.* ADV: ADV adj PRAGMATICS =flaming ADJ: ADJ n

flip side; also spelled **flipside.**

1 **The flip side** of a record is the side that does not have the main song on it. *'What's on the flip side?'* N-SING: *the* N

2 The **flip side** of an argument or idea is the opposite argument or idea. *The trade deficit is the flip side of a rapidly expanding economy.* N-SING

flirt /flɜːʳt/ **flirts, flirting, flirted** ◆◇◇◇◇

1 If you **flirt** with someone, you behave as if you are sexually attracted to them, in a playful or not very serious way. *Dad's flirting with all the ladies, or they're all flirting with him, as usual... He flirts outrageously.* ♦ **flirtation** /flɜːʳteɪʃən/ **flirtations** *...a professor who has a flirtation with a student... She was aware of his attempts at flirtation.* V-RECIP V *with* n V (non-recip) N-VAR: oft N *with* n

2 Someone who is a **flirt** likes to flirt a lot. N-COUNT

3 If you **flirt** with the idea of something, you consider it but do not do anything about it. *My mother used to flirt with Socialism... They flirted with the idea of making records throughout the 1980s.* ♦ **flirtation** *...his brief flirtation with fame.* VERB V *with* n N-VAR

flirtatious /flɜːʳteɪʃəs/. Someone who is **flirtatious** behaves towards someone else, in a not very serious way, as if they are sexually attracted to them. *He was dashing, self-confident and flirtatious.* ADJ-GRADED

flirty /flɜːʳti/

1 If you describe someone as **flirty**, you mean that they behave towards people in a way which suggests they are sexually attracted to them, usually in a playful or not very serious way. *She is amazingly flirty and sensual... She had an appealing flirty smile.* ADJ-GRADED

2 **Flirty** clothes are feminine and sexy. *The skirts were knee-skimming and flirty.* ADJ-GRADED

flit /flɪt/ **flits, flitting, flitted** ◆◇◇◇◇

1 If you **flit** around or **flit** between one place and another, you go to lots of places without staying for very long in any of them. *Laura flits about New York hailing taxis at every opportunity. ...flitting between Florence, Rome and Bologna.* VERB =dash V prep/adv

2 If someone **flits** from one thing or situation to another, they move or turn their attention from one to the other very quickly. *She flits from one dance partner to another... He's prone to flit between subjects with amazing ease.* VERB V *from* n *to* n V prep

3 If something such as a bird or a bat **flits** about, it flies quickly from one place to another. *...the parrot that flits from tree to tree.* VERB V prep/adv

4 If an expression **flits** across your face or an idea **flits** through your mind, it is there for a short time and then goes again. *He was unable to prevent a look of interest from flitting across his features... Images and memories of the evening flitted through her mind.* VERB V *across* n V *through* n

float /floʊt/ **floats, floating, floated** ◆◆◆◇◇

1 If something or someone **is floating** in a liquid, they are in the liquid, on or just below the surface, and are being supported by it. You can also **float** something on a liquid. *They noticed fifty and twenty dollar bills floating in the water. ...barges floating quietly by the grassy river banks... They'll spend some time floating boats in the creek.* V-ERG V *in* n V prep/adv V n Also V n prep/adv

2 Something that **floats** lies on or just below the surface of a liquid when it is put in it and does not sink. *Empty things float.* VERB ≠sink V

3 A **float** is a light object that is used to help someone or something float. N-COUNT

4 A **float** is a small object attached to a fishing line which floats on the water and moves when a fish has been caught. N-COUNT

5 Something that **floats** in or through the air hangs in it or moves slowly and gently through it. *The white cloud of smoke floated away. ...the sun's rays lighting up the dust floating in the air.* VERB V prep/adv

6 If a sound or smell **floats** to a place quite far away, it can be heard or smelled faintly by people there; a literary use. *Sublime music floats on a scented summer breeze to the spot where you lie on the lush grass... The smells of delicious foods floated all around him.* VERB V prep/adv

7 If you **float** somewhere, you walk there very lightly and gracefully; a literary use. *Caroline floated up the aisle on her father's arm.* VERB V prep/adv

8 If you **float** a project, plan, or idea, you suggest it for others to think about. *The French had floated the idea of placing the diplomatic work in the hands of the UN.* VERB V n

9 If a company director **floats** his or her company, he or she starts to sell shares in it to the public. *He floated his firm on the stock market... The advisers are delaying the key decision on whether to float 60 per cent or 100 per cent of the shares.* VERB V n *on* n V n

10 If a government **floats** its country's currency or allows it to **float**, it allows the currency's value to change freely in relation to other currencies; a technical term in economics. *A decision by the Finns to float their currency sent a shudder through the foreign exchanges... 59 per cent of people believed the pound should be allowed to float freely.* V-ERG V n V

11 A **float** is a lorry on which displays and people in special costumes are carried in a festival procession. ● See also **milk float**. N-COUNT

12 A **float** is a small amount of coins and notes of low value that someone has before they start sell- N-SING

ing things so that they are able to give customers change if necessary.

float around. A rumour or idea that **is floating around** is often heard or talked about. *There are still some unfounded fears floating around out there about cancer being contagious.* PHRASAL VERB V P

floating voter, floating voters. In British English, a **floating voter** is a person who is not a firm supporter of any political party. N-COUNT

flock /flɒk/ **flocks, flocking, flocked** ◆◆◇◇◇

1 A **flock** of birds, sheep, or goats is a group of them. *They kept a small flock of sheep... They are gregarious birds and feed in flocks.* N-COUNT-COLL: usu N *of* n

2 You can refer to a group of people or things as a **flock of** them to emphasize that there are a lot of them. *These cases all attracted flocks of famous writers. ...his flock of advisers.* N-COUNT-COLL: N *of* n PRAGMATICS

3 If people **flock** to a particular place or event, a very large number of them go there, usually because it is pleasant or interesting. *The public have flocked to the show... The criticisms will not stop people flocking to see the film... His greatest wish must be that huge crowds flock into the beautiful park.* VERB V *to* n V to-inf V prep/adv

4 A clergyman's **flock** is the group of Christians who come to his church or live in the area that he has responsibility for; an old-fashioned use. N-COUNT: oft poss N =congregation

floe /fləʊ/. See **ice floe**.

flog /flɒg/ **flogs, flogging, flogged** ◆◇◇◇◇

1 If someone tries to **flog** something, they try to sell it; an informal word used in British English. *They are trying to flog their house.* VERB V n

2 If someone **is flogged**, they are hit very hard with a whip or stick as a punishment. *In these places people starved, were flogged, were clubbed to death... Flog them soundly.* ♦ **flogging, floggings** *He gets dragged off to court and sentenced to a flogging and life imprisonment... He urged the restoration of hanging and flogging.* VERB *be* V-ed V n N-VAR

3 If you say that someone **is flogging a dead horse**, you mean that they are trying to achieve something impossible; an informal expression. PHRASE: V inflects

flood /flʌd/ **floods, flooding, flooded** ◆◆◆◇◇

1 If there is a **flood**, a large amount of water covers an area which is usually dry, for example when a river overflows or a pipe bursts. *More than 70 people were killed in the floods, caused when a dam burst... This is the type of flood dreaded by cavers... Over 25 people drowned when a schoolbus tried to cross a river and flood waters swept through.* N-VAR

2 If something such as a river or a burst pipe **floods** an area that is usually dry or if the area **floods**, it becomes covered with water. *The Chicago River flooded the city's underground tunnel system... The kitchen flooded.* ♦ **flooded** *People have been mobilised to build defences and drain flooded land as heavy rains continue to fall.* V-ERG V n V ADJ

3 If a river **floods**, it overflows, especially after very heavy rain. *...the relentless rain that caused twenty rivers to flood... Many streams have flooded their banks, making some roads impassable.* VERB =overflow V V n

4 If you say that a **flood** of people or things arrive somewhere, you are emphasizing that a very large number of them arrive there. *The administration is trying to stem the flood of refugees out of Haiti and into Florida... He received a flood of letters from irate constituents.* N-COUNT: usu N *of* n PRAGMATICS =tide, torrent

5 If you say that people or things **flood** into a place, you are emphasizing that they arrive there in large numbers. *Large numbers of immigrants flooded into the area... Enquiries flooded in from all over the world. ...the refugees flooding out of Bosnia.* VERB PRAGMATICS =pour V prep/adv

6 If you **flood** a place with a particular type of thing, or if a particular type of thing **floods** a place, the place becomes full of so many of them that it cannot hold or deal with any more. *...a policy aimed at flooding Europe with exports... Brokers expect the markets to be flooded with the shares... German cameras at knock-down prices flooded the British market.* ♦ **flooded** *...the danger of Europe becoming flooded with low-cost agricultural imports.* VERB =saturate V n *with* n V n ADJ

7 If an emotion, feeling, or thought **floods** you, or you **are flooded** with it, you suddenly feel it very intensely. If feelings or memories **flood back**, you suddenly remember them very clearly. A literary use. *A wave of happiness flooded me... Mary Ann was flooded with relief... It was probably the shock which had brought all the memories flooding back.* VERB V n *be* V-ed *with* n V adv

8 If light **floods** a place or **floods** into it, it suddenly fills it. *The afternoon light flooded the little rooms... Morning sunshine flooded in through the open curtains.* VERB PRAGMATICS =stream V n V prep/adv

9 See also **flash flood**.

10 If a river is **in flood**, it is overflowing because it has more water in it than normal. PHRASES v-link PHR

11 If you say that someone was in **floods of tears**, you are emphasizing that they were crying with great intensity because they were very upset. *The pain was so bad that I would be in floods of tears... She attempted to articulate her grief from behind a flood of tears.* *flood* inflects, usu *in* PHR PRAGMATICS

flood out. If people, places, or things **are flooded out**, the water from a flood makes it impossible for people to stay in that place or to use that thing. *Train lines were flooded out... The river flooded them out every few years.* PHRASAL VERB *be* V-ed P V n P

floodgates /flʌdgeɪts/. If events **open the floodgates** to something, they make it possible for that thing to happen much more often or much more seriously than before. *A decision against the cigarette companies could open the floodgates to many more lawsuits... Would it not set a precedent? Would it not open the floodgates?* PHRASE: V inflects, usu PHR *to/for* n

flooding /flʌdɪŋ/. If **flooding** occurs, an area of land that is usually dry is covered with water after heavy rain or after a river or lake overflows. *The flooding, caused by three days of torrential rain, is the worst in sixty-five years.* ◆◇◇◇◇ N-UNCOUNT

floodlight /flʌdlaɪt/ **floodlights, floodlighting, floodlit** ◆◇◇◇◇

1 **Floodlights** are very powerful lamps that are used outside to light public buildings, sports grounds, and other places at night. N-COUNT: usu pl

2 If a building or place **is floodlit**, it is lit by floodlights. *In the evening the facade is floodlit... A police helicopter hovered above, floodlighting the area. ...a floodlit forecourt.* VERB *be* V-ed V n V-ed

floor /flɔː/ **floors, flooring, floored** ◆◆◆◆◇

1 The **floor** of a room is the part of it that you walk on. *Jack's sitting on the floor watching TV... We painted the wooden floor with a white stain.* N-COUNT: usu *the* N in sing

2 A **floor** of a building is all the rooms that are on a particular level. *It is on the fifth floor of the hospital... They occupied the first two floors of the tower.* N-COUNT: usu supp N =storey

3 The ocean **floor** is the ground at the bottom of an ocean. The valley **floor** is the ground at the bottom of a valley. *They spend hours feeding on the ocean floor. ...a two-hour climb from the valley floor.* N-COUNT: usu sing, with supp, oft n N

4 The place where official debates and discussions are held, especially between members of parliament or councillors, is referred to as the **floor**. *...the issues were debated on the floor of the House.* N-COUNT: usu *the* N in sing

5 In a debate or discussion, **the floor** is the people who are listening to the arguments being put forward but who are not among the main speakers. *The president is taking questions from the floor.* N-SING-COLL: *the* N

6 The **floor** of a stock exchange is the large open area where trading is done. *...the dealing floor at Standard Chartered Bank.* N-COUNT: usu sing, with supp

7 The **floor** in a place such as a club or disco is the area where people dance. N-COUNT

8 If you **are floored** by something, you are unable to respond to it because you are so surprised by it. *He was floored by the announcement... He seemed floored by a string of scandals.* VB: usu passive *be* V-ed V-ed

9 If someone **is floored**, especially in boxing, they are hit so hard that they fall over. *He was floored twice in the second round.* VB: usu passive *be* V-ed

10 See also **floored, flooring; dance floor, first floor, ground floor, shop floor**.

11 If you **take the floor**, you start speaking in a debate or discussion. If you **are given the floor**, you are allowed to do this. *Ministers took the floor to de-* PHRASES V inflects

nounce the decision to suspend constitutional rule... Only members would be given the floor.
12 If you **take to the floor**, you start dancing at a dance or disco. *The happy couple and their respective parents took to the floor.* V inflects
13 If you say that prices or sales have fallen **through the floor**, you mean that they have suddenly decreased. *Property prices have dropped through the floor... Last year, sales went through the floor.* PHR after v
14 If you **wipe the floor with** someone, you defeat them completely in a competition or discussion; an informal expression. *He could wipe the floor with the Prime Minister.* V inflects, PHR n
15 • **factory floor**: see **factory**.

floorboard /flɔːʳbɔːʳd/ **floorboards.** **Floorboards** are the long pieces of wood that a wooden floor is made up of. ◆◇◇◇◇ N-COUNT: usu pl

floored /flɔːʳd/. A room or part of a room that is **floored** with a particular material has a floor made of that material. *The aisle was floored with ancient bricks.* ► Also a combining form. *They had to cross the large marble-floored hall.* ADJ; COMB in ADJ

flooring /flɔːrɪŋ/ **floorings.** **Flooring** is a material that is used to make the floor of a room. *Quarry tiles are a popular kitchen flooring.* ◆◇◇◇◇ N-MASS

floor show, floor shows; also spelled **floorshow**. A **floor show** is a series of performances by dancers, singers, or comedians at a night club. N-COUNT

floozy /fluːzi/ **floozies.** If you refer to a woman as a **floozy**, you disapprove of the fact that she has sexual relations with a lot of different men and wears vulgar or gaudy clothes; a fairly old-fashioned word. N-COUNT PRAGMATICS

flop /flɒp/ **flops, flopping, flopped** ◆◆◇◇◇
1 If you **flop** into a chair, for example, you sit down suddenly and heavily because you are so tired. *Bunbury flopped down upon the bed and rested his tired feet... She flopped, exhausted, on to a sofa.* VERB =collapse V prep/adv
2 If something **flops** onto something else, it falls there heavily or untidily. *The briefcase flopped onto the desk... His hair flopped over his left eye.* VERB V prep/adv
3 If something is a **flop**, it is completely unsuccessful. *It is the public who decide whether a film is a hit or a flop.* N-COUNT: oft adj N =failure
4 If something **flops**, it is completely unsuccessful. *The film flopped badly at the box office.* VERB V

floppy /flɒpi/. Something that is **floppy** is loose rather than stiff, and tends to hang downwards. *...the girl with the floppy hat and glasses.* ◆◇◇◇◇ ADJ-GRADED

floppy disk, floppy disks; also spelled **floppy disc** in British English. A **floppy disk** is a small magnetic disk that is used for storing computer data and programs. Floppy disks are used especially with personal computers. N-COUNT

flora /flɔːrə/. You can refer to plants as **flora**, especially the plants growing in a particular area; a formal word. *...the variety of food crops and flora which now exists in Dominica.* ◆◇◇◇◇ N-UNCOUNT-COLL

floral /flɔːrəl/ ◆◇◇◇◇
1 A **floral** fabric or design has flowers on it. *...a bright yellow floral fabric.* ADJ: usu ADJ n
2 You can use **floral** to describe something that contains flowers or is made of flowers. *...eye-catching floral arrangements.* ADJ: ADJ n

florid /flɒrɪd, AM flɔːr-/
1 If you describe something as **florid**, you disapprove of the fact that it is complicated and extravagant rather than plain and simple. *...florid language.* ADJ-GRADED PRAGMATICS =ornate
2 Someone who is **florid** always has a red face. *Jacobs was a stout, florid man.* ADJ-GRADED

florin /flɒrɪn, AM flɔːr-/ **florins.** A **florin** was a British coin that was worth two shillings. N-COUNT

florist /flɒrɪst, AM flɔːr-/ **florists**
1 A **florist** is a shopkeeper who arranges and sells flowers and sells indoor plants. N-COUNT
2 A **florist** or a **florist's** is a shop where flowers and indoor plants are sold. N-COUNT: oft *the* N

floss /flɒs, AM flɔːs/. You can use **floss** to refer to fine soft threads of some kind. *Craft Resources also sells yarn and embroidery floss.* • See also **candyfloss**. N-UNCOUNT

flotation /floʊteɪʃən/ **flotations** ◆◇◇◇◇
1 The **flotation** of a company is the selling of shares in it to the public. N-VAR
2 A **flotation** compartment helps something to float because it is filled with air or gas. ADJ: ADJ n

flotilla /flətɪlə/ **flotillas.** A **flotilla** is a group of small ships, usually military ships. N-COUNT

flotsam /flɒtsəm/
1 **Flotsam** is rubbish or wreckage, for example bits of wood, that is floating on the sea or has been left by the sea on the shore. *The water was full of flotsam and refuse.* N-UNCOUNT
2 You can use **flotsam** to refer to people who do not have homes or jobs and perhaps have had to leave their own country; used especially in journalism. *He was another of the city's flotsam.* N-UNCOUNT
3 You can use **flotsam and jetsam** to refer to small or unimportant items that are found together, especially ones that have no connection with each other. *...cornflake packets, bottles, and all the flotsam and jetsam of the kitchen. ...flotsam and jetsam on the beach.* PHRASE

flounce /flaʊns/ **flounces, flouncing, flounced**
1 If you **flounce** somewhere, you walk there quickly with exaggerated movements, in a way that shows you are annoyed or upset. *She flounced out of my room in a huff... She will flounce and argue when asked to leave the room.* VERB V adv/prep V
2 A **flounce** is a deep frill around the edge of something, for example a skirt, dress, tablecloth, or curtain. *...a gown with a flounce round the hem.* N-COUNT =frill

flounder /flaʊndəʳ/ **flounders, floundering, floundered** ◆◆◇◇◇
1 If something **is floundering**, it has many problems and may soon fail completely. *What a pity that his career was left to flounder... The economy was floundering.* VERB =founder V
2 If you say that someone **is floundering**, you are criticizing them for not being decisive or for not knowing what to say or do. *Right now, you've got a president who's floundering, trying to find some way to get his campaign jump-started... I know that you're floundering around, trying to grasp at any straw.* VERB PRAGMATICS =dither V V *around*
3 If you **flounder** in water or mud, you move in an uncontrolled way, trying not to sink. *Three men were floundering about in the water.* VERB V adv/prep Also V
4 A **flounder** is a flat fish that you can eat. The plural can be either **flounder** or **flounders**. ► **Flounder** is this fish eaten as food. *Mr. Dambar had loaded his plate with stuffed flounder.* N-VAR N-UNCOUNT

flour /flaʊəʳ/ **flours, flouring, floured** ◆◆◇◇◇
1 **Flour** is a white or brown powder that is made by grinding grain. It is used to make bread, cakes, and pastry. N-MASS
2 If you **flour** a cooking utensil or food, you cover it with flour. *Lightly flour a rolling pin... Remove the dough from the bowl and put it on a floured surface.* VERB V n V-ed

flourish /flʌrɪʃ, AM flɜːr-/ **flourishes, flourishing, flourished** ◆◆◇◇◇
1 If something **flourishes**, it is successful, active, or widespread, and developing quickly and strongly. *Business flourished and within six months they were earning 18,000 roubles a day... Racism and crime still flourish in the ghetto.* ♦ **flourishing** *London quickly became a flourishing port.* VERB =thrive ≠decline V; ADJ-GRADED =thriving
2 If a plant or animal **flourishes**, it grows well or is healthy because the conditions are right for it. *The plant flourishes particularly well in slightly harsher climes.* ♦ **flourishing** *Britain has the largest and most flourishing fox population in Europe.* VERB =thrive V; ADJ-GRADED =thriving
3 If you **flourish** an object, you wave it about in a way that makes people notice it. *He flourished the glass to emphasize the point.* ► Also a noun. *He took his peaked cap from under his arm with a flourish and pulled it low over his eyes.* VERB V n; N-COUNT
4 If you do something with a **flourish**, you do in a showy way so that people notice it. *She tended to finish dancing with a flourish.* N-COUNT
5 A **flourish** is a curly line or piece of decoration. N-COUNT

He scrawled his name across the bill, underlining it with a showy flourish. =swirl, curlicue

floury /flaʊəri/

1 Something that is **floury** is covered with flour or tastes of flour. *She wiped her floury hands on her apron. ...floury scones.* ADJ-GRADED

2 **Floury** potatoes go fluffy and break up when they are cooked. ADJ-GRADED: usu ADJ n

flout /flaʊt/ **flouts, flouting, flouted.** If you **flout** something such as a law, an order, or an accepted way of behaving, you deliberately disobey it or do not follow it. *...illegal campers who persist in flouting the law... Building regulations have been habitually flouted.* ◆◇◇◇◇ VERB =defy ≠obey V n

flow /floʊ/ **flows, flowing, flowed** ◆◆◆◆◇

1 If a liquid, gas, or electrical current **flows** somewhere, it moves there steadily and continuously. *A stream flowed gently down into the valley... The current flows into electric motors that drive the wheels. ...compressor stations that keep the gas flowing.* ► Also a noun. *It works only in the veins, where the blood flow is slower.* VERB V adv/prep V N-VAR: with supp

2 If a number of people or things **flow** from one place to another, they move there steadily in large groups, usually without stopping. *Large numbers of refugees continue to flow from the troubled region into the no-man's land... Troops would patrol major roads to ensure that traffic flows freely throughout the country.* ► Also a noun. *She watched the frantic flow of cars and buses along the street... It would monitor traffic flows and provide feedback to motorists.* VERB =move V prep/adv N-VAR: with supp

3 If information or money **flows** somewhere, it moves freely between people or organizations. *A lot of this information flowed through other police departments... An interest rate reduction is needed to get more money flowing and create jobs.* ► Also a noun. *...the opportunity to control the flow of information.* • See also **cash flow**. VERB V prep/adv V N-VAR: with supp

4 If an emotion **flows** through someone, they feel it very intensely, often so that it is apparent to other people; a literary use. *In that moment a surge of hatred flowed through my blood... Waves of emotion flowed across his huge face.* VERB =surge V prep

5 If a quality or situation **flows** from something, it comes from it or results naturally from it. *Undesirable consequences flow from these misconceptions. ...the psychological effects that can flow from childhood experiences of sexual abuse.* VERB =result from V from n

6 If someone's words **flow**, they are spoken smoothly and continuously without hesitation. *His words flowed more readily.* VERB V

7 If someone's hair or clothing **flows** about them, it hangs freely and loosely; a literary use. *...a long white dress which flowed over her body. ...long black flowing hair.* VERB V prep V-ing

8 If you say that something **flows** or that a place **flows** with it, you are indicating that there is a great deal of that thing in the place. *The wine flowed and we danced the night away... The square was packed, and the cobbled streets flowed with coloured petals.* VERB V V with n

9 Someone who is **in full flow** is talking fluently and easily and seems likely to go on talking for some time. *He had been replying for some 40 minutes already and was still in full flow.* PHRASES v-link PHR

10 If you say that an activity, or the person who is performing the activity, is **in full flow**, you mean that the activity has started and is being carried out with a great deal of energy and enthusiasm. *Lunch at Harry's Bar was in full flow when Irene made a splendid entrance... The Everton keeper needed all his courage to thwart a charging Vinny Jones in full flow.* v-link PHR

11 If you **go with the flow**, you let things happen or let other people tell you what to do, rather than trying to control what happens yourself. *There's nothing I can do about the problem, so I might as well go with the flow.* V inflects

flow chart, flow charts. A **flow chart** or a **flow diagram** is a diagram which represents the sequence of actions in a particular process or activity. N-COUNT

flower /flaʊəʳ/ **flowers, flowering, flowered** ◆◆◆◆◇

1 A **flower** is the part of a plant which is often brightly coloured, grows at the end of a stem, and only survives for a short time. *Each individual flower is tiny. ...large, purplish-blue flowers.* N-COUNT

2 A **flower** is a stem of a plant with one or more flowers on it when it has been picked, usually with others, for example to give as a present or to put in a vase. *...a bunch of flowers sent by a new admirer.* N-COUNT: usu pl

3 **Flowers** are small plants that are grown for their flowers as opposed to trees, shrubs, and vegetables. *...a lawned area surrounded by screening plants and flowers... The flower garden will be ablaze with colour every day.* N-COUNT: usu pl

4 When a plant or tree **flowers**, its flowers appear and open. *Several of these rhododendrons will flower this year for the first time.* VERB V

5 When something **flowers**, for example a political movement or a relationship, it gets stronger and more successful. *Their relationship flowered.* VERB =blossom V

6 Someone or something that is described as **the flower** of something is the best part or example of it; a literary use. *Those killed have been described as the flower of Polish manhood.* N-SING: the N of n

7 When a plant is **in flower** or when it has come **into flower**, its flowers have appeared and opened. *Some of the daffodils are still in flower... As one plant fades, another comes into flower.* PHRASE: usu v-link PHR, PHR after v

8 See also **flowered**.

flower arranging. Flower arranging is the art or hobby of placing cut flowers in vases in a way which makes them look attractive. N-UNCOUNT

flowerbed /flaʊəʳbed/ **flowerbeds;** also spelled **flower bed**. A **flowerbed** is an area of ground in a garden or park which has been specially prepared so that flowers can be grown in it. N-COUNT

flowered /flaʊəʳd/. **Flowered** paper or cloth has a pattern of flowers on it. *She was wearing a pretty flowered cotton dress.* ADJ: ADJ n =floral

flowering /flaʊərɪŋ/ ◆◇◇◇◇

1 The **flowering** of something such as an idea or artistic style is the development of its popularity and success. *He may be happy with the flowering of new thinking, but he has yet to contribute much to it himself. ...the flowering of creative genius.* N-UNCOUNT: usu N of n =blossoming

2 **Flowering** shrubs, trees, or plants are those which produce noticeable flowers. ADJ: ADJ n

flowerpot /flaʊəʳpɒt/ **flowerpots;** also spelled **flower pot**. A **flowerpot** is a container that is used for growing plants. N-COUNT =plant pot

flower power. When journalists talk about **flower power**, they are referring to hippies and the culture associated with hippies in the late 1960s and early 1970s. *...the era of flower power. ...the flower power generation.* N-UNCOUNT

flowery /flaʊəri/

1 A **flowery** smell is strong and sweet. *Amy thought she caught the faintest drift of Isabel's flowery perfume.* ADJ-GRADED

2 **Flowery** cloth, paper, or china has a lot of flowers printed or painted on it. *The baby, dressed in a flowery jumpsuit, waved her rattle.* ADJ-GRADED: usu ADJ n =floral

3 **Flowery** speech or writing contains long or literary words and expressions. *They were using uncommonly flowery language.* ADJ-GRADED =fancy

flown /floʊn/. **Flown** is the past participle of **fly**.

fl. oz. **fl. oz** is a written abbreviation for **fluid ounce**. ◆◇◇◇◇ =fluid ounce

flu /fluː/. **Flu** is an illness which is similar to a bad cold but more serious. It often makes you feel very weak and your muscles ache. *I got flu... He had come down with the flu.* ◆◇◇◇◇ N-UNCOUNT: also the N =influenza

fluctuate /flʌktʃueɪt/ **fluctuates, fluctuating, fluctuated.** If something **fluctuates**, it changes a lot in an irregular way. *Body temperature can fluctuate if you are ill. ...the fluctuating price of oil.* ♦ **fluctuation** /flʌktʃueɪʃᵊn/ **fluctuations** *Don't worry about tiny fluctuations in your weight... The calculations do not take into account any fluctuation in the share price.* ◆◇◇◇◇ VERB V V-ing N-VAR: usu N in/of n

flue /fluː/ **flues.** A **flue** is a pipe or shaft that acts as a chimney, taking fumes and smoke away N-COUNT from a heating appliance such as a boiler or a stove.

fluent /flu:ənt/ ◆◇◇◇◇

1 Someone who is **fluent** in a particular language, can speak the language easily and correctly, with no hesitation or inaccuracy. You can also say that someone speaks **fluent** French, Chinese, or other language. *She studied eight foreign languages but is fluent in only six of them... He speaks fluent Russian.* ♦ **fluency** *To work as a translator, you need fluency in at least one foreign language.* ♦ **fluently** *He spoke three languages fluently.* ADJ-GRADED: oft ADJ *in* n / N-UNCOUNT / ADV-GRADED

2 If your speech, reading, or writing is **fluent**, you speak, read, or write easily, smoothly, and clearly with no hesitation or mistakes. *He had emerged from being a hesitant and unsure candidate into a fluent debater.* ♦ **fluency** *His son was praised for speeches of remarkable fluency.* ♦ **fluently** *Alex didn't read fluently till he was nearly seven.* ADJ-GRADED / N-UNCOUNT / ADV-GRADED: ADV with v

fluff /flʌf/ **fluffs, fluffing, fluffed** ◆◇◇◇◇

1 **Fluff** consists of soft threads or fibres in the form of small, light balls or lumps. For example, you can refer to the fur of a small animal as **fluff**. *...the nestbox which contained two chicks: just small grey balls of fluff... She noticed some bits of fluff on the sleeve of her sweater.* N-UNCOUNT: oft n *of* N

2 If you **fluff** something that you are trying to do, you are unsuccessful or you do it badly; an informal use. *She fluffed her interview at Oxford.* VERB / V n

3 If you **fluff** things such as cushions or feathers, you get a lot of air into them, for example by shaking or brushing them, in order to make them seem larger and lighter. *She stood up and fluffed her hair, wiggling her fingers through it and then throwing it back.* ► **Fluff up** means the same as **fluff**. *Take the pan off the heat and cover for 5 minutes to fluff up the rice.* VERB / V n / PHRASAL VERB V P n (not pron) Also V n P

fluffy /flʌfi/ **fluffier, fluffiest** ◆◇◇◇◇

1 If you describe something such as a towel or a toy animal as **fluffy**, you mean that it is very soft and woolly. *...fluffy white towels... It's a very fluffy kind of wool.* ADJ-GRADED =soft

2 A cake or other food that is **fluffy** is very light because it has a lot of air in it. *Cream together the margarine and sugar with a wooden spoon until light and fluffy.* ADJ-GRADED

fluid /flu:ɪd/ **fluids** ◆◆◇◇◇

1 A **fluid** is a liquid; a formal use. *The blood vessels may leak fluid, which distorts vision... Make sure that you drink plenty of fluids. ...fluid retention.* N-MASS

2 **Fluid** movements or lines or designs are smooth and graceful. *His painting became less illustrational and more fluid. ...long, fluid dresses.* ♦ **fluidity** /flu:ɪdɪti/ *She dances with an exquisite fluidity of movement.* ADJ-GRADED =flowing / N-UNCOUNT

3 A situation that is **fluid** is unstable and is likely to change often. *The situation is extremely fluid and it can be changing from day to day.* ♦ **fluidity** *...the complexity and fluidity of the crisis.* ADJ-GRADED: usu v-link ADJ =changeable / N-UNCOUNT

fluid ounce, fluid ounces. A **fluid ounce** is a measurement of liquid. There are twenty fluid ounces in a British pint, and sixteen in an American pint. N-COUNT: num N, oft N *of* n

fluke /flu:k/ **flukes.** If you say that something good is a **fluke**, you mean that it happened accidentally rather than by being planned or arranged; an informal word. *The discovery was something of a fluke... By sheer fluke, one of the shipowner's employees was in the city.* ◆◇◇◇◇ N-COUNT: usu sing, also *by* N

flummox /flʌməks/ **flummoxes, flummoxing, flummoxed.** If someone **is flummoxed** by something, they are confused by it and do not know what to do or say. *The two leaders were flummoxed by the suggestion.* ♦ **flummoxed** *No wonder Josef was feeling a bit flummoxed.* VB: usu passive / be V-ed / ADJ-GRADED

flung /flʌŋ/. **Flung** is the past tense and past participle of **fling**.

flunk /flʌŋk/ **flunks, flunking, flunked.** If you **flunk** an exam or a course, you fail to reach the required standard; an informal word used mainly in American English. *Your son is upset because he flunked a history exam.* VERB =fail / V n

flunkey /flʌŋki/ **flunkeys;** also spelled **flunky**.

1 Someone who refers to a servant as a **flunkey** is expressing their dislike for a job that involves doing things for an employer that ordinary people do for themselves. N-COUNT PRAGMATICS =lackey

2 If you refer to someone as a **flunkey**, you disapprove of the fact that they associate themselves with someone who is powerful and carry out small, unimportant jobs for them in the hope of being rewarded. N-COUNT PRAGMATICS =hanger-on

fluorescent /flʊəresᵊnt/ ◆◇◇◇◇

1 A **fluorescent** surface, substance, or colour has a very bright appearance when light is directed onto it, as if it is actually shining itself. *...a piece of fluorescent tape.* ♦ **fluorescence** *...the green fluorescence it gives off under ultraviolet radiation.* ADJ: usu ADJ n / N-UNCOUNT

2 A **fluorescent** light shines with a very hard, bright light and is usually in the form of a long strip. *Fluorescent lights flickered, and then the room was brilliantly, blindingly bright.* ADJ: usu ADJ n

fluoridation /flʊərɪdeɪʃᵊn/. **Fluoridation** is the action or process of adding fluoride to a water supply. *...fluoridation of the water supply in Strathclyde region.* N-UNCOUNT

fluoride /flʊəraɪd/. **Fluoride** is a mixture of chemicals that is sometimes added to drinking water and toothpaste because it is considered to be good for people's teeth. ◆◇◇◇◇ N-UNCOUNT

flurry /flʌri, AM flɜ:ri/ **flurries** ◆◇◇◇◇

1 A **flurry** of something such as activity or speculation is a short intense period of it. *...a flurry of diplomatic activity aimed at ending the war.* N-COUNT: usu N *of* n

2 A **flurry** of something such as snow is a small amount of it that suddenly appears for a short time and moves in a quick, swirling way. N-COUNT: oft N *of* n

flush /flʌʃ/ **flushes, flushing, flushed** ◆◆◇◇◇

1 If you **flush**, your face goes red because you are hot or ill, or because you are feeling a strong emotion such as embarrassment or anger. *Do you sweat a lot or flush a lot?... He turned away embarrassed, his face flushing red.* ► Also a noun. *There was a slight flush on his cheeks.* ♦ **flushed** *Her face was flushed with anger.* VERB / V / V colour / N-COUNT / ADJ-GRADED: oft ADJ *with* n

2 When someone **flushes** a toilet after using it, they fill the toilet bowl with water in order to clean it, usually by pressing a handle or pulling a chain. You can also say that a toilet **flushes**. *She flushed the toilet and went back in the bedroom. ...the sound of the toilet flushing.* ► Also a noun. *He heard the flush of a toilet.* V-ERG / V n / V / N-COUNT: usu sing

3 If you **flush** something down the toilet, you get rid of it by putting it into the toilet bowl and flushing the toilet. *He was found trying to flush banknotes down the toilet.* VERB / V n *down* n

4 If you **flush** a part of your body, you clean it or make it healthier by using a large amount of liquid to get rid of dirt or harmful substances. *Flush the eye with clean cold water for at least 15 minutes... Water is ideal to flush the kidneys and the urinary tract.* ► **Flush out** means the same as **flush**. *...an 'alternative' therapy that gently flushes out the colon to remove toxins.* VERB =cleanse / V n / PHRASAL VERB V P n (not pron) Also V n P

5 If you **flush** dirt or a harmful substance out of a place, you get rid of it by using a large amount of liquid. *That won't flush out all the sewage, but it should unclog some stinking drains.* VERB / V n with *out*

6 If you **flush** people or animals out of a place where they are hiding, you find or capture them by forcing them to come out of that place. *They flushed them out of their hiding places... The Guyana Defence Force is engaged in flushing out illegal Brazilian miners operating in the country.* VERB / V n *out of* n / V n with *out*

7 If one object or surface is **flush** with another, they are at the same height or distance from something else, so that they form a single smooth surface. *Make sure the tile is flush with the surrounding tiles.* ADJ: v-link ADJ, oft ADJ *with* n =level

8 If you are **flush** with money, you have a lot of it, usually only for a short time; an informal use. *At that time, many developing countries were flush with dollars earned from exports... If we're feeling flush we'll probably give them champagne.* ADJ-GRADED: v-link ADJ, usu ADJ *with* n

9 The **flush of** something is an intense feeling of excitement or pleasure that you have when you are experiencing it and for a short time afterwards. *...the first flush of young love. ...in the flush of victory in the spring of 1945.* N-SING: N *of* n

10 A **flush of** something is a large quantity of it that comes suddenly or quickly. *...the flush of recent victories. ...a flush of memories.* N-SING: N *of* n =spate

flush out. See **flush** 4. PHRASAL VERB

flushed /flʌʃt/. If you say that someone is **flushed with** success or triumph, you mean that they are very excited by their success or triumph. *Grace was flushed with the success of the venture... The publishers were flushed with triumph when they secured rights to her novel.* ADJ-GRADED: v-link ADJ *with* n =elated

fluster /flʌstəʳ/ **flusters, flustering, flustered.** VERB If you **fluster** someone, you make them feel nervous and confused by rushing them and preventing them from concentrating on what they are doing. *The General refused to be flustered... She was a very calm person. Nothing could fluster her.* ♦ **flustered** *She was so flustered that she forgot her reply.* be V-ed; V n; ADJ-GRADED: usu v-link ADJ

flute /fluːt/ **flutes.** A **flute** is a musical instrument of the woodwind family. You play it by blowing over a hole near one end while holding it sideways to your mouth. ◆◇◇◇◇ N-VAR: oft *the* N

fluted /fluːtɪd/. Something that is **fluted** has round, shallow grooves cut or shaped into it. *She leaned against the fluted wooden post of the porch.* ADJ: usu ADJ n =grooved

fluting /fluːtɪŋ/. If you describe someone's voice as **fluting**, you mean that it goes up and down a lot, and usually that it is high pitched. *Her voice, small and fluting, stopped abruptly. ...a fluting and melodic Scottish accent.* ADJ

flutist /fluːtɪst/ **flutists.** In American English, a **flutist** is someone who plays the flute. The usual British word is **flautist**. N-COUNT

flutter /flʌtəʳ/ **flutters, fluttering, fluttered** ◆◇◇◇◇

1 If something thin or light **flutters**, or if you **flutter** it, it moves up and down or from side to side with a lot of quick, light movements. *Her chiffon skirt was fluttering in the night breeze. ...a butterfly fluttering its wings. ...the fluttering white lace handkerchief.* ► Also a noun. *...a flutter of white cloth.* V-ERG; V; V n; V-ing; N-COUNT

2 If something light such as a small bird or a piece of paper **flutters** somewhere, it moves through the air with small quick movements. *The paper fluttered to the floor... The birds were active, whirring and fluttering among the trees.* VERB; V adv/prep; V

3 If you have a **flutter**, you have a small bet on something such as a horse race; an informal British use. *I had a flutter on five horses.* N-COUNT: oft N *on* n =bet

4 If you say that someone **flutters** somewhere, you mean that they walk there with quick, light movements, often in a silly way or in a way which suggests that they are nervous. *She'd been fluttering about in the kitchen.* VERB; V adv/prep

5 If your heart or stomach **flutters**, you experience a strong feeling of excitement or anxiety. *The look in his eyes made my heart flutter.* VERB; V

flux /flʌks/ **fluxes** ◆◇◇◇◇

1 If something is in a state of **flux**, it is constantly changing. *Education remains in a state of flux which will take some time to settle down. ...a period of economic flux.* N-UNCOUNT: oft *in* N =instability

2 You can refer to a flowing mass as a **flux**; a technical use in physics. *...the flux of cosmic rays.* N-VAR: oft N *of* n

fly /flaɪ/ **flies, flying, flew, flown** ◆◆◆◆◆

1 A **fly** is a small insect with two wings. There are many kinds of flies, and the most common are black in colour. N-COUNT

2 When something such as a bird, insect, or aircraft **flies**, it moves through the air. *The planes flew through the clouds... The bird flew away.* VERB; V prep/adv; Also V

3 If you **fly** somewhere, you travel there in an aircraft. *He flew to Los Angeles... He flew back to London... Mr Baker flew in from Moscow.* VERB; V prep/adv

4 When someone **flies** an aircraft, they control its movement in the air. *Parker had successfully flown both aircraft... He flew a small plane to Cuba... His inspiration to fly came even before he joined the Army.* ♦ **flying** *...a flying instructor.* VERB; V n; V n prep/adv; V; N-UNCOUNT

5 To **fly** someone or something somewhere means to take or send them there in an aircraft. *It may be possible to fly the women and children out on Thursday... The relief supplies are being flown from a warehouse in Pisa.* VERB; V n adv/prep

6 If something such as your hair **is flying** about, it is moving about freely and loosely in the air. *His long, uncovered hair flew back in the wind... She was running down the stairs, her hair flying.* VERB; V adv/prep; V

7 If you **fly** a flag or if it **is flying**, you display it at the top of a pole. *They flew the flag of the African National Congress... A Chinese flag was flying on the new military HQ.* V-ERG; V n; V

8 If you say that someone or something **flies** in a particular direction, you are emphasizing that they move there with a lot of speed or force. *She flew to their bedsides when they were ill... I flew downstairs... There are bullets flying around your head.* VERB; PRAGMATICS; V prep/adv

9 If you tell someone that you must **fly**, you are indicating that you have to leave in a great hurry. *I must fly or I'll miss my plane... I'll have to fly.* VERB; PRAGMATICS; V

10 If rumours or allegations **are flying** around a place, they are being discussed a great deal and by a lot of people within a short period of time. *Rumours had been flying around the workrooms all morning... Rumours were flying about possible deals.* VERB; V prep/adv; V

11 The front opening on a pair of trousers is referred to as the **fly**, or in British English the **flies**. It usually consists of a zip or row of buttons behind a band of cloth. N-COUNT

12 In fishing, a **fly** is a model of a small winged insect that is used as a bait. N-COUNT

13 See also **flying**; **tsetse fly**.

14 If you say that someone wouldn't **hurt a fly** or wouldn't **harm a fly**, you are emphasizing that they are very kind and gentle. *Ray wouldn't hurt a fly. ...a lovely girl, who would not have harmed a fly.* PHRASES; with brd-neg, V inflects; PRAGMATICS

15 If you **let fly**, you attack someone, either physically by hitting them, or with words by insulting them. *A simmering row ended with her letting fly with a stream of obscenities.* V inflects =fly at

16 If you do something **on the fly**, you do it automatically, without thinking about it; an informal expression. *It was all pretty much done on the fly.* PHR after v

17 If you **send** someone or something **flying** or if they **go flying**, they move through the air and fall down with a lot of force. *The blow sent the young man flying.* V inflects, PHR after v

18 If you say that you would like to be **a fly on the wall** in a situation that does not involve you, you mean that you would like to see or hear what happens in that situation. *What I'd give to be a fly on the wall when Davis finds out what's happened to his precious cargo.* • See also **fly-on-the-wall**. v-link PHR

19 • to **fly the coop**: see **coop**. • **as the crow flies**: see **crow**. • to **fly in the face of**: see **face**. • to **fly the flag**: see **flag**. • to **fly off the handle**: see **handle**. • **a fly in the ointment**: see **ointment**. • **pigs might fly**: see **pig**. • **sparks fly**: see **spark**. • **time flies**: see **time**.

fly at. If you **fly at** someone, you attack them, either physically by hitting them, or with words by insulting them. *She flew at him for making a very anti-British remark.* PHRASAL VERB =let fly; V P n

fly into. If you **fly into** a rage or a panic, you suddenly become very angry or anxious and show this in your behaviour. *Losing a game would cause him to fly into a rage.* PHRASAL VERB; V P n

flyaway /flaɪəweɪ/. **Flyaway** hair is very soft and fine. *...her flyaway blond hair.* ADJ-GRADED: usu ADJ n

flyby /flaɪbaɪ/ **flybys;** also spelled **fly-by**. A **flyby** is a flight made by an aircraft or a spacecraft over a particular place in order to record detailed observations about it. N-COUNT

fly-by-night. If you describe a business organization or a businessman as a **fly-by-night** operator, you are criticizing them because they want to make money very quickly, and they do not care about the quality or honesty of the service ADJ: ADJ n; PRAGMATICS =cowboy they offer; an informal word. *...fly-by-night operators who do shoddy work, overcharge or fail to complete jobs.*

flyer /flaɪəʳ/ **flyers;** also spelled **flier.** ◆◇◇◇◇

1 A **flyer** is a pilot of an aircraft. N-COUNT

2 You can refer to someone who travels by aeroplane as a **flyer.** *...regular business flyers. ...nervous fliers.* N-COUNT: usu supp N

3 A **flyer** is a small printed notice which is used to advertise a particular company, service, or event. N-COUNT =handbill

4 See also **high-flyer.**

fly-fishing; also spelled **fly fishing. Fly-fishing** is a method of fishing in which a silk or nylon model of a small winged insect is used as bait. N-UNCOUNT

flying /flaɪɪŋ/ ◆◇◇◇◇

1 A **flying** animal has wings and is able to fly. *...species of flying insects.* ADJ: ADJ n

2 If someone or something **gets off to a flying start**, or **makes a flying start**, they start something very well, for example a race or a new job. *Advertising revenue in the new financial year has got off to a flying start... Hendry made a flying start to the final.* PHRASE: V inflects

flying doctor, flying doctors. A **flying doctor** is a doctor, especially in Australia, who travels by aircraft to visit patients who live in distant or isolated areas. N-COUNT

flying fish, flying fishes. Flying fish can also be used as the plural form. **Flying fish** are a type of fish that live in warm seas. They have large fins that enable them to move forward in the air when they jump out of the water. N-VAR

flying saucer, flying saucers. A **flying saucer** is a round, flat object which some people say they have seen in the sky and which they believe to be a spacecraft from another planet. N-COUNT

Flying Squad. In Britain, **the Flying Squad** is a group of police officers who are always ready to travel quickly to the scene of a serious crime. *...weapons seized by the Flying Squad last year.* N-PROPER-COLL: the N

flying visit, flying visits. A **flying visit** is a visit that only lasts a very short time. N-COUNT

flyleaf /flaɪliːf/ **flyleaves.** The **flyleaf** of a book is a page at the front that has nothing printed on it, or just the title and the author's name. N-COUNT

fly-on-the-wall. A **fly-on-the-wall** documentary is made by filming people as they do the things they normally do, rather than by interviewing them or asking them to talk directly to the camera. *...a fly-on-the-wall documentary about the Queen's life.* • **a fly on the wall**: see **fly.** ADJ: ADJ n

flyover /flaɪoʊvəʳ/ **flyovers**

1 In British English, a **flyover** is a structure which carries one road over the top of another road. The usual American word is **overpass.** N-COUNT

2 In American English, a **flyover** is a flight by a group of aircraft in a special formation which takes place on a ceremonial occasion or as a display. The usual British word is **flypast.** N-COUNT

flypast /flaɪpɑːst, -pæst/ **flypasts;** also spelled **fly-past.** In British English, a **flypast** is a flight by a group of aircraft in a special formation which takes place on a ceremonial occasion or as a display. The usual American word is **flyover.** N-COUNT

flywheel /flaɪhwiːl/ **flywheels.** A **flywheel** is a heavy wheel that is part of some engines. It stores regulates the engine's rotation, making it operate at a steady speed. N-COUNT

FM /ef em/. **FM** is a method of transmitting radio waves that can be used to broadcast high quality stereo. FM is an abbreviation for 'frequency modulation'. ◆◆◇◇◇

foal /foʊl/ **foals, foaling, foaled** ◆◇◇◇◇

1 A **foal** is a very young horse. N-COUNT

2 When a female horse **foals**, it gives birth. *The mare is due to foal today.* VERB V

foam /foʊm/ **foams, foaming, foamed** ◆◇◇◇◇

1 **Foam** consists of a mass of small bubbles that are formed when air and a liquid are mixed together. *The water curved round the rocks in great bursts of foam.* N-UNCOUNT =froth

2 **Foam** is used to refer to various kinds of manufactured products which have a soft, light texture like a thick liquid. *...shaving foam.* N-MASS =cream

3 **Foam** or **foam rubber** is soft rubber full of small holes which is used, for example, to make mattresses and cushions. *...modern three-piece suites filled with foam rubber... We had given him a large foam mattress to sleep on.* N-MASS

4 If a liquid **foams**, it is full of small bubbles and keeps moving slightly. *I let the water run into it and we watched as it foamed and bubbled. ...ravines with foaming rivers rushing through them.* VERB =froth V V-ing

5 If you say that someone **is foaming at the mouth**, you mean that they are very angry. *Stewart was foaming at the mouth about an incident the previous afternoon.* PHRASE: V inflects

foamy /foʊmi/. A **foamy** liquid has a mass of small bubbles on its surface or consists of a mass of bubbles. *The ocean raged, slamming its foamy waves against the black, jagged rocks... Whisk the egg whites until they are foamy but not stiff.* ADJ-GRADED =frothy

fob /fɒb/ **fobs, fobbing, fobbed.** A **fob** is a chain which attaches a watch to a man's waistcoat. N-COUNT

fob off. If someone **fobs** you **off**, they tell you something just to stop you asking questions or asking for something, especially when this is not really what you wanted; used showing disapproval. *I've asked her about it but she fobs me off... Don't be fobbed off with excuses.* PHRASAL VERB PRAGMATICS V n P be V-ed P with n

focal /foʊkəl/ ◆◇◇◇◇

1 **Focal** is used to describe something that relates to the point where a number of rays or lines meet. *...the focal plane of the telescope.* ADJ: ADJ n

2 **Focal** is used to describe something that is very important. *Until 1940 Shanghai was the greatest modern city of China and the focal centre of the Far East.* ADJ: ADJ n

focal point, focal points. The **focal point** of something is the thing that people concentrate on or pay most attention to. *...the focal point for the town's many visitors – the Royal Shakespeare Theatre.* ◆◇◇◇◇ N-COUNT

focus /foʊkəs/ **foci** /foʊsaɪ/ **focuses, focusing, focused.** The spellings **focusses, focussing, focussed** are also used. The plural of the noun can be either **foci** or **focuses.** ◆◆◆◆◇

1 If you **focus** on a particular topic or if your attention **is focused** on it, you concentrate on it and think about it, discuss it, or deal with it, rather than dealing with other topics. *The research effort has focused on tracing the effects of growing levels of five compounds... He is currently focusing on assessment and development... Today he was able to focus his message exclusively on the economy... Many of the papers focus their attention on the controversy surrounding statements reportedly made by the Foreign Secretary.* V-ERG =concentrate V on n V n on n

2 The **focus** of something is the main topic or main thing that it is concerned with. *The UN's role in promoting peace is increasingly the focus of international attention... The new system is the focus of controversy... Her children are the main focus of her life.* N-COUNT: usu sing, usu with supp

3 Your **focus** on something is the special attention that you pay it. *He said his sudden focus on foreign policy was not motivated by presidential politics... The report's focus is on how technology affects human life rather than business... IBM has also shifted its focus from mainframes to personal computers.* N-COUNT: usu sing, usu with supp, oft N on n

4 If you say that something has a **focus**, you mean that you can see a purpose in it. *Somehow, though, their latest LP has a focus that the others have lacked... Suddenly all of the bizarre and seemingly isolated examples took on a meaningful focus.* N-UNCOUNT

5 If you **focus** your eyes or if your eyes **focus**, your eyes adjust so that you can clearly see the thing that you want to look at. If you **focus** a camera, telescope, or other instrument, you adjust it so that you can see clearly through it. *Kelly couldn't focus his eyes well enough to tell if the figure was male or female... His eyes slowly began to focus on what looked like a small dark ball... He found the binoculars and focused them on the boat... Had she kept* V-ERG V n V on n V n on n V-ed Also V

the camera focused on the river bank she might have captured a vital scene.

6 You use **focus** to refer to the fact of adjusting your eyes or a camera, telescope, or other instrument, and to the degree to which you can see clearly. *His focus switched to the little white ball... Together these factors determine the depth of focus... It has no manual focus facility.* N-UNCOUNT

7 If you **focus** rays of light on a particular point, you pass them through a lens or reflect them from a mirror so that they meet at that point. *Magnetic coils focus the electron beams into fine spots.* VERB V n prep

8 The **focus** of a number of rays or lines is the point at which they meet; a technical use. N-COUNT

9 If an image or a camera, telescope, or other instrument is **in focus**, the edges of what you see are clear and sharp. *Pictures should be in focus, with realistic colours and well composed groups.* PHRASES v-link PHR, PHR after v ≠out of focus

10 If something is **in focus**, it is being discussed or its purpose and nature are clear. *This aggression is the real issue the world should be concerned about. We want to keep that in focus... These issues have been brought into sharp focus by the Gulf crisis.* v-link PHR, PHR after v ≠out of focus

11 If an image or a camera, telescope, or other instrument is **out of focus**, the edges of what you see are unclear or blurred. *In some of the pictures the subjects are out of focus while the background is sharp. ...a lot of out-of-focus photographs.* v-link PHR, PHR after v ≠in focus

12 If something is **out of focus**, it is not being discussed or its purpose or nature is not clear. *The deficit in the US balance of payments put these considerations out of focus... The movement towards democracy in Latin America and the foreign debt problems that have plagued it have gone out of focus.* v-link PHR, PHR after v ≠in focus

focused /foʊkəst/; also spelled **focussed**. If you describe someone or something as **focused**, you approve of the fact that they have a clear and definite purpose. *I spent the next year just wandering. I wasn't focused... The band's third album seems more disciplined and focussed... The voting is now more focused.* ADJ-GRADED: usu v-link ADJ PRAGMATICS =purposeful

fodder /fɒdəʳ/ ◆◇◇◇◇

1 **Fodder** is food that is given to cows, horses, and other animals. *...fodder for horses... The alfalfa plant is widely used as animal fodder.* N-UNCOUNT =feed

2 If you say that something is **fodder** for a particular purpose, you mean that it is useful for that purpose and perhaps nothing else; used showing disapproval. *The press conference simply provided more fodder for another attack on his character... Old movies were the cheapest broadcast fodder.* N-UNCOUNT: usu with supp PRAGMATICS

foe /foʊ/ **foes.** Someone's **foe** is their enemy; used in written English. ◆◇◇◇◇ N-COUNT

foetal /fiːtəl/; also spelled **fetal**. **Foetal** is used to describe something that relates to or is like a foetus. *...an early stage of foetal development... His legs were curled beneath him in a foetal position.* ADJ: ADJ n

foetid /fiːtɪd/. See **fetid**.

foetus /fiːtəs/ **foetuses;** also spelled **fetus**. A **foetus** is an unborn animal or human being in its later stages of development. *Pregnant women who are heavy drinkers risk damaging the unborn foetus.* ◆◇◇◇◇ N-COUNT

fog /fɒg/ **fogs, fogging, fogged** ◆◆◇◇◇

1 When there is **fog**, there are tiny drops of water in the air which form a thick cloud and make it difficult to see things. *The crash happened in thick fog... These ocean fogs can last for days.* N-VAR

2 A **fog** is an unpleasant cloud of something such as smoke inside a building or room. *...a fog of stale cigarette smoke.* N-SING: usu N *of* n

3 You can use **fog** to refer to a situation which stops people from being able to notice things, understand things, or think clearly. *The most basic facts about him are lost in a fog of mythology and folklore... Synchronizing these attacks may also be difficult in the fog of war... His mind was in a fog when he finally got up.* N-SING: oft *in* N, N *of* n

4 If a window, mirror, or other glass surface **fogs**, or **is fogged**, it becomes covered with very small drops of water so that you cannot see things clearly through it or in it. *The windows fogged immediately... Water had fogged his diving mask and he couldn't remember how to clear it... The car windows were fogged with vapor.* ▶ **Fog up** means the same as **fog**. *The car windows fogged up... It'd fog up their telescopes... His hair was all wet and his glasses were fogged up.* V-ERG V V n V-ed PHRASAL VERB ERG V P V P n (not pron) V-ed P

fog bank, fog banks. A **fog bank** is an area of thick fog, especially at sea. N-COUNT

fogbound /fɒgbaʊnd/; also spelled **fog-bound**. If you are **fogbound** in a place or if the place is **fogbound**, thick fog makes it dangerous or impossible to go anywhere. *He was fog-bound at London airport. ...a fogbound motorway.* ADJ

fogey /foʊgi/ **fogies** or **fogeys** also spelled **fogy**. If you describe someone as a **fogey** or an **old fogey**, you mean that they are a boring, old-fashioned person; an informal word. *I don't want to sound like I'm some old fogy.* N-COUNT PRAGMATICS

foggy /fɒgi/ **foggier, foggiest** ◆◇◇◇◇

1 When it is **foggy**, there is fog. *It's quite foggy now... Conditions were damp and foggy after morning sleet.* ADJ-GRADED: oft *it* v-link ADJ

2 If you say that you **haven't the foggiest** or you **haven't the foggiest idea**, you are emphasizing that you do not know something; an informal expression. *I did not have the foggiest idea what he meant... 'How often does it need to be changed?'—'Haven't the foggiest.'* PHRASE: V inflects PRAGMATICS

foghorn /fɒghɔːʳn/ **foghorns;** also spelled **fog horn**. A **foghorn** is a loud siren that is used to warn ships about the position of land and other ships in fog. N-COUNT

fogy /foʊgi/. See **fogey**.

foible /fɔɪbəl/ **foibles.** A **foible** is a habit or characteristic that someone has which is considered rather strange, foolish, or bad but which is also considered unimportant and allowable. *...human foibles and weaknesses.* N-COUNT =quirk

foil /fɔɪl/ **foils, foiling, foiled** ◆◆◇◇◇

1 **Foil** consists of sheets of metal as thin as paper. It is used to wrap food in. *Pour cider around the meat and cover with foil. ...aluminium foil.* N-UNCOUNT

2 If you **foil** someone's plan or attempt to do something, for example to commit a crime, you succeed in stopping them from doing what they want; used in journalism. *A brave police chief foiled an armed robbery on a jewellers' by grabbing the raiders' shotgun... The idea of building a roof terrace was also foiled by the planning authorities.* VERB =thwart V n

3 If you refer to one thing or person as a **foil** for another, you approve of the fact that they contrast with each other and go well together, often in a way that makes the second thing or person seem better or less harmful. *He thought of her serenity as a foil for his intemperance... A cold beer is the perfect foil for a curry.* N-COUNT: usu sing, N *for* n PRAGMATICS =complement

4 A **foil** is a thin light sword used in fencing, which has a button on its tip to prevent injury. N-COUNT

foist /fɔɪst/ **foists, foisting, foisted**

foist on. If you say that someone **foists** something **on** you, or **foists** it **upon** you, you dislike the way that they force you to listen to it or experience it. *I don't see my role as foisting my beliefs on them... What this amounts to is foisting onto women the responsibility for reducing 'the opportunities for crime' by changing their behaviour.* PHRASAL VERB PRAGMATICS V n P n V P n n (not pron)

fold /foʊld/ **folds, folding, folded** ◆◆◆◇◇

1 If you **fold** something such as a piece of paper or cloth, you bend it so that one part covers another part, often pressing the edge so that it stays in place. *He folded the paper carefully... Fold the omelette in half... Fold the blanket back. ...a folded towel.* VERB V n V n prep/adv V-ed

2 A **fold** in a piece of paper or cloth is a bend that you make in it when you put one part of it over another part and press the edge. *Make another fold and turn the ends together.* N-COUNT =crease

3 The **folds** in a piece of cloth are the curved shapes which are formed when it is not hanging or lying flat. *The priest fumbled in the folds of his gown.* N-COUNT: usu pl

4 If a piece of furniture or equipment **folds** or if you V-ERG

can **fold** it, you can make it smaller or flatter by bending or closing parts of it. *The back of the bench folds forward to make a table... This portable seat folds flat for easy storage... Check if you can fold the buggy without having to remove the raincover. ...a folding beach chair.* V adv/prep V adj V n V-ing ► **Fold up** means the same as **fold**. *When not in use it folds up out of the way... Fold the ironing board up so that it is flat.* PHRASAL VERB ERG V P V n P

5 If you **fold** your arms or hands, you bring them together and cross or link them, for example over your chest or in your lap. *Meer folded his arms over his chest and turned his head away... Mrs Ringrose sat down and folded her hands in her lap.* VERB V n

6 If a business or organization **folds**, it is unsuccessful and has to close. *But as other shops fold, the march of the superstores continues... 2,500 small businesses were folding each week.* VERB V

7 When someone joins an organization or group, you can say that they have come into the **fold**. When they leave the organization or group, you can say that they leave the **fold**. *The EC brought Spain, Greece and Portugal into the fold... He might find it difficult to return to the family fold even when he realizes his mistake.* N-SING: *the*/poss N, usu *the* supp N

fold in or **fold into.** In cooking, if you **fold in** an ingredient or **fold** it **into** the other ingredients, you mix it very gently into the other ingredients. *Fold in the flour... Fold the cream into the egg yolk mixture.* PHRASAL VERB V P n (not pron) V n P n

fold up. If you **fold** something **up**, you make it into a smaller, neater shape by folding it, usually several times. *She folded it up, and tucked it into her purse... He folded up his paper and put it away.* PHRASAL VERB V n P V P n (not pron)
• See also **fold** 4, **fold-up**.

-fold /-foʊld/. **-fold** combines with numbers to form adverbs which say how much an amount has increased by. For example, if an amount increases **fourfold**, it is four times greater than it was originally. *By the late eighties their number had grown fourfold... Pretax profit surged almost twelvefold.* SUFFIX ► Also an adjective. *One survey revealed a threefold increase in breast cancer.* ADJ: ADJ n

folder /foʊldəʳ/ **folders.** A **folder** is a thin piece of cardboard in which you can keep loose papers. ◆◇◇◇◇ N-COUNT

fold-up. A **fold-up** piece of furniture or equipment is one that is specially designed so that it can be folded into a smaller shape for storage. *...a fold-up bed.* ADJ: ADJ n

foliage /foʊliɪdʒ/. The leaves of a plant are referred to as its **foliage**. *...shrubs with grey or silver foliage.* ◆◇◇◇◇ N-UNCOUNT

folio /foʊlioʊ/ **folios.** A **folio** is a book made with paper of a large size, used especially in the early centuries of European printing. *Richard told me of three 16th-century folio volumes on alchemy.* N-COUNT

folk /foʊk/ **folks; folk** can also be used as the plural form for meaning 1. ◆◆◆◇◇

1 You can refer to people as **folk** or **folks**. *Country folk can tell you that there are certain places which animals avoid... These are the folks from the local TV station. ...old folks.* N-PLURAL: usu with supp =people

2 You can refer to your close family, especially your mother and father, as your **folks**; an informal use. *I've been avoiding my folks lately.* N-PLURAL: usu poss N

3 You can use **folks** as a term of address when you are talking to several people; an informal use. *'It's a question of money, folks,' I announced... This is it, folks: the best record guide in the business.* N-VOC

4 **Folk** art and customs are traditional or typical of a particular community or nation. *...South American folk art. ...traditional Chinese folk medicine.* ADJ: ADJ n

5 **Folk** music is music which is traditional or typical of a particular community or nation. *...Irish folk music... He'd included a few folk songs from Barbados and Jamaica.* ADJ: ADJ n ► Also a noun. *...a variety of music including classical, jazz, and folk.* N-UNCOUNT

6 **Folk** can be used to describe something that relates to the beliefs and opinions of ordinary people. *Jack was a folk hero in the Greenwich Village bars... Folk psychology comes closer to the obvious truth than the most sophisticated theories.* ADJ-UNGRADED: ADJ n =popular

folklore /foʊklɔːʳ/. **Folklore** is the traditional stories, customs, and habits of a particular community or nation. *In Chinese folklore the bat is an emblem of good fortune.* ◆◇◇◇◇ N-UNCOUNT

folk song, folk songs; also spelled **folksong**. A **folk song** is a traditional song that is typical of a particular community or nation. N-COUNT

folksy /foʊksi/.

1 If you describe something as **folksy**, you mean that it is simple and has a style characteristic of folk craft and tradition. You sometimes use **folksy** to show disapproval of something because it seems so unsophisticated or primitive. *...folksy country furniture.* ADJ-GRADED: usu ADJ n

2 In American English, if you describe someone as **folksy**, you mean that they are friendly and informal in their behaviour. *...an elderly, folksy postman.* ADJ-GRADED: usu ADJ n =affable

follicle /fɒlɪkəl/ **follicles.** A **follicle** is one of the small hollows in the skin which hairs grow from. ◆◇◇◇◇ N-COUNT

follow /fɒloʊ/ **follows, following, followed** ◆◆◆◆◆

1 If you **follow** someone who is going somewhere, you move along behind them because you want to go to the same place. *We followed him up the steps into a large hall... Please follow me, madam... They took him into a small room and I followed.* VERB V n prep/adv V n V Also V *after* n

2 If you **follow** someone who is going somewhere, you move along behind them without their knowledge, in order to catch them or find out where they are going. *She realized that the Mercedes was following her... I think we're being followed.* VERB =trail V n

3 If you **follow** someone to a place where they have recently gone and where they are now, you go to join them there. *He followed Janice to New York, where she was preparing an exhibition.* VERB V n *to* n

4 An event, activity, or period of time that **follows** a particular thing happens or comes after that thing, at a later time. *...the rioting and looting that followed the verdict... I remember nothing else about the days following Daddy's death... He was arrested in the confusion which followed... Other problems may follow... Eyewitnesses spoke of a noise followed by a huge red light.* VERB =come after V n V V-ed

5 If you **follow** one thing with another, you do or say the second thing after you have done or said the first thing. *Her first major role was in Martin Scorsese's 'Goodfellas' and she followed this with a part in Spike Lee's 'Jungle Fever'.* VERB V n *with* n ► **Follow up** means the same as **follow**. *The book proved such a success that the authors followed it up with 'The Messianic Legacy'.* PHRASAL VERB V n P *with* n Also V P n (not pron) *with* n

6 If it **follows** that a particular thing is the case, that thing is a logical result of something else being true or being the case. *Just because a bird does not breed one year, it does not follow that it will fail the next... If the explanation is right, two things follow... It is easy to see the conclusions described in the text follow from this equation.* VERB *it* V that V V *from* n

7 If you refer to the words that **follow** or **followed**, you are referring to the words that come next or came next in a piece of writing or speech. *What follows is an eye-witness account... There followed a list of places where Hans intended to visit... General analysis is followed by five case studies.* VERB PRAGMATICS V *there* V n *be* V-ed *by* n

8 If you **follow** a path, route, or set of signs, you go somewhere using the path, route, or signs to direct you. *If they followed the road, they would be certain to reach a village... All we had to do was follow the map... I followed the signs to Metrocity.* VERB V n V n prep/adv

9 If something such as a path or river **follows** a particular route or line, it goes along that route or line. *Our route follows the Pacific coast through densely populated neighbourhoods... The Lot river follows a winding and tortuous course.* VERB V n

10 If you **follow** something with your eyes, or if your eyes **follow** it, you watch it as it moves or you look along its route or course. *Ann's eyes followed a police car as it drove slowly past.* VERB V n

11 Something that **follows** a particular course of development happens or develops in that way. *His release turned out to follow the pattern set by that of the other six hostages.* VERB V n

12 If you **follow** advice, an instruction, or a recipe, you act or do something in the way that it indicates. *Take care to follow the instructions carefully... No two chefs follow the same recipe.*
VERB
V n

13 If you **follow** what someone else has done, you do it too because you think it is a good thing or because you want to copy them. *His admiration for the athlete did not extend to the point where he would follow his example in taking drugs... Where eastern Germany goes the rest will surely follow.*
VERB
V n
V

14 If you **follow** someone in what you do, you do the same thing or job as they did previously. *He followed his father and became a surgeon... Anni-Frid's son has followed her into the music business.*
VERB
V n
V n *into* n

15 If you **follow** something such as an explanation or the plot of a film, you understand it as it continues and develops. *Do you follow the plot so far?... I'm afraid I don't follow.*
VERB
=understand
V n
V

16 If you **follow** something, you take an interest in it and keep informed about what happens. *Do you follow the football at all?... She was following Laura's progress closely.*
VERB
=keep up with
V n

17 A story, film, or TV programme that **follows** someone or something is about their experiences over a particular period of time. *The film follows the fortunes of two women.*
VERB
V n

18 If you **follow** a score or written copy of a play, you read it while you listen to it being performed. *...an annotated version of Mozart's opera that allows the listener to follow the score.*
VERB
V n

19 If you **follow** a particular religion or political belief, you have that religion or belief. *'Do you follow any particular religion?'—'Yes, we're all Hindus.'.*
VERB
V n

20 See also **following**.

21 You use **as follows** in writing or speech to introduce something such as a list, description, or explanation. *The winners are as follows: E. Walker; R. Foster; R. Gates; A. Mackintosh... This can be done if you proceed as follows.*
PHRASES
v-link PHR,
PHR after v
PRAGMATICS

22 You use **followed by** to say what comes after something else in a list or ordered set of things. *Potatoes are still the most popular food, followed by white bread.*
PHR n
PRAGMATICS

23 After mentioning one course of a meal, you can mention the next course by saying what you will have **to follow** or what there will be **to follow**. *He decided on roast chicken and vegetables, with apple pie to follow.*
n PHR
PRAGMATICS

24 • to **follow in** someone**'s footsteps**: see **footstep**. • to **follow** your **nose**: see **nose**. • to **follow suit**: see **suit**.

follow through. If you **follow through** an action, plan, or idea or **follow through** with it, you continue doing or thinking about it until it is completed, or until you have achieved everything possible. *The leadership has been unwilling to follow through the implications of these ideas... I was trained to be an actress but I didn't follow it through... He decided to follow through with his original plan.*
PHRASAL VERB
=pursue
V P n (not pron)
V n P
V P *with* n/-ing
Also V P,
V P *on* n

follow up. If you **follow up** something that has been said, suggested, or discovered, you try to find out more about it or take action about it. *State security police are following up several leads... An officer took a statement from me, but no one's bothered to follow it up.* • See also **follow** 5, **follow-up**.
PHRASAL VERB
=investigate
V P n (not pron)
V n P

follower /fɒləʊə^r/ **followers.** A **follower** of a particular person, group, or belief is someone who supports or admires this person, group, or belief. *...followers of the Zulu Inkatha movement. ...the Democratic Party's most loyal followers.* • See also **camp follower**.
◆◆◇◇◇
N-COUNT:
usu with poss
=supporter

following /fɒləʊɪŋ/ **followings**
◆◆◆◆◇

1 **Following** a particular event means after that event. *In the centuries following Christ's death, Christians genuinely believed the world was about to end... Following a day of medical research, the conference focused on educational practices.*
PREP

2 The **following** day, week, or year is the day, week, or year after the one you have just mentioned. *The following day the picture appeared on the front pages of every newspaper in the world... We went to dinner the following Monday evening... The following year she joined the Royal Opera House.*
ADJ:
det ADJ
≠previous

3 You use **following** to refer to something that you are about to mention. *Write down the following information: name of product, type, date purchased and price... The method of helping such patients is explained in the following chapters.* ► **The following** refers to the thing or things that you are about to mention. *The following is a paraphrase of what was said... Do you use any of the following? Pager, Answering machine, Mobile phone, Car phone.*
ADJ:
det ADJ
PRAGMATICS
PRON:
the PRON

4 A person or organization that has a **following** has a group of people who support or admire their beliefs or actions. *Australian rugby league enjoys a huge following in New Zealand.*
N-COUNT:
with supp,
usu adj N

5 If a boat or vehicle has a **following** wind, the wind is moving in the same direction as the boat or vehicle. *The following wind and eastward running tide had given us a very pleasant, lazy sail.*
ADJ:
ADJ n
=headwind

follow-on. A **follow-on** is something which is done as a continuation of something done previously, or in addition to it. *This course for bridge players with some experience is intended as a follow-on to the Beginners' course.*
◆◇◇◇◇
N-SING:
also no det,
usu N *to* n

follow-through, follow-throughs
◆◇◇◇◇

1 A **follow-through** is the completion of an action or planned series of actions. *...the task of finding a durable solution to the refugee problem as a follow-through to the very temporary measures.*
N-UNCOUNT:
also *a* N,
oft N prep

2 A **follow-through** is the completion of a movement such as hitting a ball. *Focus on making a short, firm follow-through.*
N-VAR

follow-up, follow-ups. A **follow-up** is something that is done as a continuation or second part of something done previously. *They are recording a follow-up to their successful 1989 album... One man was arrested during the raid and another during a follow-up operation.*
◆◆◇◇◇
N-VAR:
oft N n

folly /fɒli/ **follies**
◆◇◇◇◇

1 If you say that a particular action or way of behaving is **folly** or a **folly**, you mean that it is foolish. *It's sheer folly to build nuclear power stations in a country that has dozens of earthquakes every year. ...a reminder of the follies of war.*
N-VAR:
oft N *of* n/-ing,
it v-link N to-inf

2 A **folly** is an imitation castle, temple, or other unusual building that is built as a decoration in a large garden or park.
N-COUNT

foment /fəʊment/ **foments, fomenting, fomented.** If someone or something **foments** trouble, especially in the form of a riot or other disturbance, they cause it to develop; a formal word. *They accused strike leaders of fomenting violence.*
VERB
=incite
V n

fond /fɒnd/ **fonder, fondest**
◆◆◇◇◇

1 If you are **fond of** someone, you feel affection for them. *I am very fond of Michael... She was especially fond of a little girl named Betsy.* ♦ **fondness** *...a great fondness for children.*
ADJ-GRADED:
v-link ADJ *of* n
N-UNCOUNT

2 You use **fond** to describe people or their behaviour when they show affection. *...a fond father... He gave him a fond smile.* ♦ **fondly** *Liz saw their eyes meet fondly across the table.*
ADJ-GRADED:
ADJ n
ADV-GRADED:
ADV after v

3 If you are **fond of** something, you like it or you like doing it very much. *He was fond of marmalade... She is fond of collecting rare carpets.* ♦ **fondness** *I've always had a fondness for jewels. ...his fondness for cooking.*
ADJ-GRADED:
v-link ADJ *of* n/-ing
N-UNCOUNT:
usu N *for* n/-ing

4 If you have **fond** memories of someone or something, you remember them with pleasure. *I have very fond memories of living in our village.* ♦ **fondly** *My dad took us there when I was about four and I remembered it fondly.*
ADJ-GRADED:
ADJ n
=pleasant
ADV-GRADED:
ADV with v

5 You use **fond** to describe hopes, wishes, or beliefs which you think are foolish because they seem unlikely to be fulfilled. *My fond hope is that we will be ready by Christmastime.* ♦ **fondly** *I fondly imagined that surgery meant a few stitches and an overnight stay in hospital.*
ADJ:
ADJ n
ADV:
ADV with v

fondant /fɒndənt/. **Fondant** is a sweet paste made from sugar and water. *...a pack of eight fondant cakes.*
N-UNCOUNT:
oft N n

fondle /fɒndᵊl/ **fondles, fondling, fondled.** If you **fondle** someone or something, you touch them gently with a stroking movement, usually in a sexual way. *He tried to kiss her and fondle her.* VERB Vn

fondue /fɒndjuː, AM -duː/ **fondues.** A **fondue** is a sauce made from melted cheese into which you dip bread or a pot of hot oil into which you dip pieces of meat or vegetables. *They stopped at a little cafe and had a fondue.* N-VAR

font /fɒnt/ **fonts**
1 In printing, a **font** is a set of characters of the same style and size. N-COUNT
2 In a church, a **font** is a bowl which holds the water used for baptisms. N-COUNT

food /fuːd/ **foods** ◆◆◆◆◆
1 **Food** is what people and animals eat. *Enjoy your food. ...supplies of food and water. ...emergency food aid. ...frozen foods.* • See also **convenience food**, **fast food**, **health food**, **junk food**, **wholefood**. N-MASS
2 If you are **off** your **food**, you do not want to eat, usually because you are ill. *It's not like you to be off your food.* PHRASES v-link PHR
3 If you give someone **food for thought**, you make them think carefully about something. *Lord Fraser's speech offers much food for thought... Developments in your career may give you food for thought.* usu PHR after v

food chain, food chains. The **food chain** is a series of living things which are linked to each other because each thing feeds on the one next to it in the series. *The whole food chain is affected by the over use of chemicals in agriculture.* ◆◇◇◇◇ N-COUNT: usu sing

foodie /fuːdi/ **foodies;** also spelled **foody**. **Foodies** are people who enjoy cooking and eating different kinds of food; an informal word. *Other neighbourhoods in the city offer foodies a choice of Chinese, Portuguese or Greek food.* N-COUNT

food mixer, food mixers; also spelled **foodmixer**. A **food mixer** is a piece of electrical equipment that is used to mix food such as cake mixture. N-COUNT

food poisoning. If you get **food poisoning**, you become ill because you have eaten food that has gone bad. *He had suffered a serious case of food poisoning over the Christmas holidays.* ◆◇◇◇◇ N-UNCOUNT

food processor, food processors. A **food processor** is a piece of electrical equipment that is used to mix, chop, whisk, or liquidize food. ◆◇◇◇◇ N-COUNT

food stamp, food stamps. In the United States, **food stamps** are vouchers that are given to people with low incomes and that can be exchanged for food. ◆◇◇◇◇ N-COUNT: usu pl

foodstuff /fuːdstʌf/ **foodstuffs. Foodstuffs** are substances which people eat. *...basic foodstuffs such as sugar, cooking oil and cheese.* ◆◇◇◇◇ N-VAR: usu pl

food value, food values. The **food value** of a particular food is a measure of how good it is for you. Food value is usually measured in vitamins, minerals, or calories. N-VAR

fool /fuːl/ **fools, fooling, fooled** ◆◆◆◇◇
1 If you call someone a **fool**, you are indicating that you think they are not at all sensible and show a lack of good judgement. *'You fool!' she shouted... He'd been a fool to get involved with her!* N-COUNT =idiot
2 **Fool** is used, mainly in informal American English, to describe an action or person that is not at all sensible and shows a lack of good judgement. *What a damn fool thing to do!... What can that fool guard be thinking of?* ADJ: ADJ n
3 If someone **fools** you, they deceive or trick you. *Art dealers fool a lot of the people... Don't be fooled by his appearance... They tried to fool you into coming after us.* VERB =trick, con Vn Vn *into*-ing
4 If you say that someone **is fooling with** something or someone, you mean that the way they are behaving is likely to cause problems. *What are you doing fooling with such a staggering sum of money?... He kept telling her that here you did not fool with officials.* VERB V *with* n
5 In the courts of kings and queens in medieval Europe, the **fool** was the person whose job was to do silly things in order to make people laugh. N-COUNT: usu *the* N =jester
6 **Fool** is a British dessert made by mixing fruit puree with whipped cream or with custard. *...gooseberry fool.* N-VAR
7 If you **make a fool of** someone, you make them seem silly by telling people about something stupid that they have done, or by tricking them. *Your brother is making a fool of you... He'd been made a fool of.* PHRASES V and N inflect
8 If you **make a fool of** yourself, you behave in a way that makes other people think that you are silly or lacking in good judgement. *He was drinking and making a fool of himself.* V and N inflect
9 If you say to someone '**More fool** you' when they tell you what they have done or what they plan to do, you are indicating that you think that it is silly and shows a lack of good judgement. *Most managers couldn't care less about information technology. More fool them.* PRAGMATICS
10 If you **play the fool** or **act the fool**, you behave in a playful, childish, and foolish way, usually in order to make other people laugh. *They used to play the fool together, calling each other silly names and giggling.* V inflects =mess about
11 • to **suffer fools gladly**: see **suffer**.

fool about or **fool around.** The form **fool about** is mainly used in British English. If you **fool about** or **fool around**, you behave in a playful, childish, and silly way, often in order to make people laugh. *Stop fooling about, man... They fooled around for the camera.* PHRASAL VERB =mess about VP

fool around PHRASAL VERB
1 If you **fool around**, you behave in a silly, dangerous, or irresponsible way. *They were fooling around on an Army firing range... Have you been fooling around with something you shouldn't?* VP VP *with* n
2 If someone **fools around** with another person, especially when one of them is married, they have a casual sexual relationship. *Never fool around with the clients' wives... Her husband was fooling around.* VP *with* n VP

foolhardy /fuːlhɑːʳdi/. If you describe behaviour as **foolhardy**, you disapprove of it because it is extremely risky. *When he tested an early vaccine on himself, some described the act as foolhardy... It was foolhardy to have refused.* ♦ **foolhardiness** *What he once took as boldness he will now judge as foolhardiness.* ADJ-GRADED: oft *it* v-link ADJ to-inf PRAGMATICS N-UNCOUNT =recklessness

foolish /fuːlɪʃ/ ◆◆◇◇◇
1 If someone's behaviour or action is **foolish**, it is not sensible and shows a lack of good judgement. *It would be foolish to raise hopes unnecessarily... It is foolish to risk skin cancer.* ♦ **foolishly** *He admitted that he had acted foolishly.* ♦ **foolishness** *They don't accept any foolishness when it comes to spending money.* ADJ-GRADED: oft *it* v-link ADJ to-inf ADV: usu ADV with v N-UNCOUNT
2 If you look or feel **foolish**, you look or feel so silly or ridiculous that people are likely to laugh at you. *I just stood there feeling foolish and watching him... I didn't want him to look foolish and be laughed at.* ♦ **foolishly** *He saw me standing there, grinning foolishly at him.* ADJ-GRADED: usu v-link ADJ =ridiculous ADV-GRADED: ADV after v

foolproof /fuːlpruːf/. Something such as a plan or a machine that is **foolproof** is so well designed, easy to understand, or easy to use that it cannot go wrong or be used wrongly. *The system is not 100 per cent foolproof... I spent the day working out a foolproof plan to save him.* ADJ-GRADED

foolscap /fuːlzkæp/. In Britain, **foolscap** is paper which is about 34 centimetres by 43 centimetres in size. N-UNCOUNT

fool's gold
1 **Fool's gold** is a substance that is found in rock and that looks very like gold. N-UNCOUNT
2 If you say that a plan for getting money is **fool's gold**, you mean that it is foolish to carry it out because you are sure that it will fail or cause problems. *The British establishment seems to be off on another quest for fool's gold.* N-UNCOUNT PRAGMATICS

fool's paradise. If you say that someone is living in **a fool's paradise**, you are criticizing them N-SING: *a* N PRAGMATICS because they are not aware that their present happy situation is likely to change and get worse. *...living in a fool's paradise of false prosperity.*

foot /fʊt/ **feet** ◆◆◆◆◆

1 Your **feet** are the parts of your body that are at the ends of your legs, and that you stand on. *She stamped her foot again. ...a foot injury. ...his aching arms and sore feet.* ♦ **-footed** *She was bare-footed. ...pink-footed geese.* N-COUNT; COMB in ADJ

2 The **foot** of something is the part that is farthest from its top. *David called to the children from the foot of the stairs. ...the foot of Highgate Hill... A single word at the foot of a page caught her eye.* N-SING: usu *the* N *of* n =bottom ≠head, top

3 The **foot** of a bed is the end nearest to the feet of the person lying in it. *Friends stood at the foot of the bed, looking at her with serious faces.* N-SING: usu *the* N *of* n ≠head

4 A **foot** is a unit for measuring length, height, or depth, and is equal to 12 inches or 30.48 centimetres. When you are giving measurements, the form 'foot' is often used as the plural instead of the plural form 'feet'. *This beautiful and curiously shaped lake lies at around fifteen thousand feet. ...a shopping and leisure complex of one million square feet... He occupies a cell 10 foot long, 6 foot wide and 10 foot high... I have to give my height in feet and inches.* N-COUNT: usu num N, oft num N adj

5 A **foot** brake or **foot** pump is operated by your foot rather than by your hand. *I tried to reach the foot brakes but I couldn't.* ADJ: ADJ n

6 A **foot** patrol or **foot** soldiers move or operate by walking, rather than in vehicles or on horseback. *Paratroopers and foot-soldiers entered the building on the government's behalf.* ADJ: ADJ n =infantry

7 In poetry, a **foot** is one of the basic units of rhythm into which a line is divided. N-COUNT

8 See also **footing**.

9 If you get **cold feet** about something, you become nervous or frightened about it because you think it will fail. *The Government is getting cold feet about the reforms.* PHRASES V inflects, oft PHR *about* n

10 If you say that someone **is finding** their **feet** in a new situation, you mean that they are starting to feel confident and to deal with things successfully. *I don't know anyone in England but I am sure I will manage when I find my feet... Once he had found his feet he was able to deal with any problem.* V inflects =cope

11 If you say that someone has their **feet on the ground**, you approve of the fact that they have a sensible and practical attitude towards life, and do not have unrealistic ideas. *In that respect he needs to keep his feet on the ground and not get carried away... Kevin was always level-headed with both feet on the ground.* usu v PHR PRAGMATICS

12 If you go somewhere **on foot**, you walk, rather than using any form of transport. *We rowed ashore, then explored the island on foot for the rest of the day.* =walking

13 If you are **on** your **feet**, you are standing up. *Everyone was on their feet applauding wildly.* usu v-link PHR =upright

14 If you say that someone or something is **on** their **feet** again after an illness or difficult period, you mean that they have recovered and are back to normal. *You need someone to take the pressure off and help you get back on your feet... He said they all needed to work together to put the country on its feet again.* v-link PHR, PHR after v

15 If you say that someone always **falls** or **lands on** their **feet**, you mean that they are always successful or lucky, although they do not seem to achieve this by their own efforts. *He has good looks and charm, and always falls on his feet... While I struggle through life, she lands on her feet.* V inflects

16 If you say that **the boot is on the other foot** or **the shoe is on the other foot**, you mean that a situation has been reversed completely, so that the person who was in the better position before is now in the worse one. *You're not in a position to remove me. The boot is now on the other foot.* V inflects

17 If you **put** your **best foot forward**, you act in a cheerful, determined way; an old-fashioned expression. *Put your best foot forward and work on the assumption that there is an acceptable solution to every problem you are likely to face.* V inflects

18 If someone **puts** their **foot down**, they use their authority in order to stop something happening. *He had planned to go skiing on his own in March but his wife had decided to put her foot down.* V inflects

19 If someone **puts** their **foot down** when they are driving, they drive as fast as they can. *I asked the driver to put his foot down for Nagchukha.* V inflects

20 If someone **puts** their **foot in it**, they make a mistake which embarrasses or offends people; an informal expression. *Our chairman has really put his foot in it, poor man, though he doesn't know it.* V inflects

21 If you **put** your **feet up**, you relax or have a rest, especially by sitting or lying with your feet supported off the ground. *After supper he'd put his feet up and read. It was a pleasant prospect.* V inflects =rest

22 If you never **put a foot wrong**, you never make any mistakes. *When he's around, we never put a foot wrong... He hardly put a foot wrong in defence and was fine in attack.* V inflects, with brd-neg

23 If you say that someone **sets foot** in a place, you mean that they enter it or reach it, and you are emphasizing the significance of their action. If you say that someone never **sets foot** in a place, you are emphasizing that they never go there. *...the day the first man set foot on the moon... A little later I left that place and never set foot in Texas again.* V inflects, oft with brd-neg PRAGMATICS

24 If someone has to **stand on** their **own two feet**, they have to be independent and manage their lives without help from other people. *My father didn't mind whom I married, so long as I could stand on my own two feet and wasn't dependent on my husband.* V inflects

25 If you get or rise **to** your **feet**, you stand up. *Malone got to his feet and followed his superior out of the suite... The delegates cheered and rose to their feet... He sprang to his feet and ran outside.* v PHR

26 If you say that someone is **under** your **feet**, you are annoyed because they are with you or near you, and being a nuisance to you. *The children were running about under everybody's feet.* usu PHR after v

27 If someone **gets off on the wrong foot** in a new situation, they make a bad start by doing something in completely the wrong way. *Even though they called the election and had been preparing for it for some time, they got off on the wrong foot.* V inflects

28 • **drag** your **feet**: see **drag**. • **feet of clay**: see **clay**. • **foot the bill**: see **bill**. • **foot in the door**: see **door**. • **shoot** yourself **in the foot**: see **shoot**. • **sweep** someone **off their feet**: see **sweep**. • **vote with** your **feet**: see **vote**. • **hand and foot**: see **hand**.

footage /fʊtɪdʒ/. **Footage** of a particular event is a film of it or the part of a film which shows this event. *They are planning to show exclusive footage from this summer's festivals.* ◆◆◇◇◇ N-UNCOUNT

foot-and-mouth disease. Foot-and-mouth disease or **foot-and-mouth** is a serious and highly infectious disease that affects cattle, sheep, pigs, and goats. N-UNCOUNT

football /fʊtbɔːl/ **footballs** ◆◆◆◆◇

1 In British English, **football** is a game played by two teams of eleven players using a round ball. Players kick the ball to each other and try to score goals by kicking the ball into a large net. The American word is **soccer**. *Several boys were still playing football on the waste ground. ...Arsenal Football Club. ...Italian football fans.* N-UNCOUNT =soccer

2 In American English, **football** is a game played by two teams of eleven players using an oval ball. Players carry the ball in their hands or throw it to each other as they try to score goals that are called touchdowns. The British term is **American football**. *Two blocks beyond our school was a field where boys played football... This year's national college football championship was won by Princeton.* N-UNCOUNT

3 A **football** is a ball that is used for playing football. N-COUNT

footballer /fʊtbɔːləʳ/ **footballers.** In British English, a **footballer** is a person who plays foot- ◆◆◇◇◇ N-COUNT ball, especially as a profession. The American term is 'soccer player'.

footballing /fʊtbɔːlɪŋ/. In British English, **footballing** means relating to the playing of the game that British people call football. *My two years at Farnham were the best of my footballing life.* ◆◇◇◇◇ ADJ: ADJ n

football pools. In British English, if you do **the football pools**, you take part in a gambling competition in which people try to win money by guessing the results of football matches. N-PLURAL: *the* N =pools

footbridge /fʊtbrɪdʒ/ **footbridges.** A **footbridge** is a narrow bridge for people travelling on foot. N-COUNT

foot-dragging. When journalists talk about a particular person's or organization's **foot-dragging**, they are suggesting that the person or organization is deliberately slowing down a plan or process; used showing disapproval. *Their bargaining position with America has been weakened by their foot-dragging over the Gulf... He accused the company of 'shameful foot-dragging'.* N-UNCOUNT PRAGMATICS

-footed /-fʊtɪd/. **-footed** combines with words such as 'heavy', 'light', or 'leaden' to form adjectives which indicate how someone moves. *A slim, light-footed little man... He was a nimble-footed boy of ten.* • See also **foot**, **flat-footed**, **sure-footed**. COMB in ADJ

footfall /fʊtfɔːl/ **footfalls.** A **footfall** is the sound that is made by someone walking each time they take a step; a literary word. *She heard the priest's familiar, flat footfall on the staircase.* N-COUNT

foothills /fʊthɪlz/. The **foothills** of a mountain or a range of mountains are the lower hills or mountains around its base. *Pasadena lies in the foothills of the San Gabriel mountains.* ◆◇◇◇◇ N-PLURAL: oft N *of* n

foothold /fʊthoʊld/ **footholds** ◆◇◇◇◇

1 A **foothold** is a strong or favourable position from which further advances or progress may be made. *If British business is to have a successful future, companies must establish a firm foothold in Europe.* N-COUNT: oft adj N, N *in* n

2 A **foothold** is a place such as a ledge, crevice, or hollow where you can safely put your foot when climbing. *He lowered his legs until he felt he had a solid foothold on the rockface beneath him.* N-COUNT: oft adj N, N *on* n

footing /fʊtɪŋ/ ◆◇◇◇◇

1 If something is put on a particular **footing**, it is defined, established, or changed in a particular way, often so that it is able to develop or exist successfully. *The new law will put official corruption on the same legal footing as treason. ...research that is aimed at placing training on a more scientific footing.* N-UNCOUNT: with supp, usu *on* N =basis

2 If you are on a particular kind of **footing** with someone, you have that kind of relationship with them. *They decided to put their relationship on a more formal footing... They are now trying to compete on an equal footing.* N-UNCOUNT: with supp, usu *on* N =basis

3 If a country or armed force is **on a war footing**, it is ready to fight a war. *The president placed the republic on a war footing.* PHRASE: v-link PHR, PHR after v

4 You refer to your **footing** when you are referring to your position and how securely your feet are placed on the ground. For example, if you lose your **footing**, your feet slip and you fall. *He was cautious of his footing, wary of the edge... He lost his footing and slid into the water.* N-UNCOUNT: poss N

footlights /fʊtlaɪts/. In a theatre, the **footlights** are the row of lights along the front of the stage. N-PLURAL

footloose /fʊtluːs/

1 If you describe someone as **footloose**, you mean that they have no responsibilities or commitments, and are therefore free to do what they want and go where they want. *People that are single tend to be more footloose.* ADJ-GRADED ≠tied down

2 If you describe someone as **footloose and fancy-free**, you mean that they are not married or in a similar relationship, and you therefore consider them to have very few responsibilities or commitments. *In the eyes of the public, a divorced man is footloose and fancy-free.* PHRASE: usu v-link PHR

footman /fʊtmən/ **footmen.** A **footman** is a male servant who typically does jobs such as opening doors or serving food, and who often wears a special uniform. N-COUNT

footnote /fʊtnoʊt/ **footnotes** ◆◇◇◇◇

1 A **footnote** is a note at the bottom of a page in a book which provides more detailed information about something that is mentioned on that page. N-COUNT

2 If you refer to what you are saying as a **footnote** to what has just been said, you mean that you are adding a comment which gives some extra information about it. *As a footnote, I should add that there was one point on which his bravado was more than justified.* N-COUNT PRAGMATICS

3 If you describe an event as a **footnote**, you mean that it is relatively unimportant although it will probably be remembered. *I'm afraid that Marx will now become a footnote in history.* N-COUNT

footpath /fʊtpɑːθ, -pæθ/ **footpaths.** A **footpath** is a path for people to walk on, especially in the countryside. ◆◇◇◇◇ N-COUNT

footplate /fʊtpleɪt/ **footplates.** On a steam train, the **footplate** is the platform on the engine where the driver and fireman stand; used mainly in British English. N-COUNT: usu *the* N in sing

footprint /fʊtprɪnt/ **footprints.** A **footprint** is a mark in the shape of a foot that a person or animal makes in or on a surface. ◆◇◇◇◇ N-COUNT

footsie /fʊtsi/. If someone **plays footsie** with you, they touch your feet with their own feet, for example under a table, often as a playful way of expressing their romantic or sexual feelings towards you; an informal expression. PHRASE: V inflects, usu PHR *with* n

foot soldier, foot soldiers. The **foot soldiers** of a particular organization are people who seem unimportant and who do not have a high position but who do a large amount of very important and often very boring work. N-COUNT

footsore /fʊtsɔːʳ/. If you are **footsore**, you have sore or tired feet after walking a long way. *It was hot and I was footsore.* ADJ-GRADED

footstep /fʊtstep/ **footsteps** ◆◇◇◇◇

1 A **footstep** is the sound or mark that is made by someone walking each time their foot touches the ground. *I heard footsteps outside.* N-COUNT: usu pl

2 If you **follow in** someone's **footsteps**, you do the same things as they did earlier. *My father is extremely proud that I followed in his footsteps and became a doctor.* PHRASE: V inflects

footstool /fʊtstuːl/ **footstools.** A **footstool** is a low stool that you can rest your feet on when you are sitting in a chair. N-COUNT

footwear /fʊtweəʳ/. **Footwear** refers to things that people wear on their feet, for example shoes, boots, and sandals. *Today the sports footwear industry is worth £1.7 billion in the UK alone.* ◆◇◇◇◇ N-UNCOUNT

footwork /fʊtwɜːʳk/

1 **Footwork** is the way in which you move your feet, especially in sports such as boxing, football, or tennis, or in dancing. *This exercise improves your coordination, balance, timing and footwork.* N-UNCOUNT: usu supp N

2 If you refer to someone's **footwork** in a difficult situation, you mean the clever way they deal with it. *In the end, his brilliant legal footwork paid off.* N-UNCOUNT: supp N

foppish /fɒpɪʃ/. If you describe a man as **foppish**, you disapprove of the fact that he is vain and dresses in fancy, extravagant clothes; an old-fashioned word. ADJ-GRADED PRAGMATICS

for /fəʳ, STRONG fɔːʳ/ ◆◆◆◆◆

In addition to the uses shown below, **for** is used after some verbs, nouns, and adjectives in order to introduce extra information, and in phrasal verbs such as 'account for' and 'make up for'. It is also used with some verbs that have two objects in order to introduce the second object.

1 If something is **for** someone, they are intended to have it or benefit from it. *Isn't that enough for you?... I have some free advice for you. ...that intense need to care for your baby. ...a table for two... Your mother is only trying to make things easier for you... What have you got for me this morning, Patrick?...* PREP

He wanted all the running of the business for himself.

2 If you work or do a job **for** someone, you are employed by them. *I knew he worked for a security firm... Have you had any experience writing for radio? ...a buyer for one of the largest chain stores in the south.*
PREP

3 If you speak or act **for** a particular group or organization, you represent them. *She appears nightly on the television news, speaking for the State Department. ...the spokesman for the Democrats.*
PREP =on behalf of

4 If someone does something **for** you, they do it so that you do not have to do it. *If your pharmacy doesn't stock the product you want, have them order it for you... I hold a shop door open for an old person... He picked the bracelet up for me.*
PREP

5 If you feel a particular emotion **for** someone, you feel it on their behalf. *This is the best thing you've ever done – I am so happy for you!... He felt a great sadness for this little girl.*
PREP: adj/n PREP

6 If you feel a particular emotion **for** someone or something, they are the object of that emotion, and you feel it when you think about them. *John, I'm sorry for Steve, but I think you've made the right decisions... Mack felt a pitiless contempt for her.*
PREP: adj/n PREP

7 You use **for** after words such as 'time', 'space', 'money', or 'energy' when you say how much there is or whether there is enough of it in order to be able to do or use a particular thing. *Many new trains have space for wheelchair users... It would take three to six hours for a round trip. ...a huge room with plenty of room for books. ...the high level of concentration required for sixth form study... Chris couldn't even raise the energy for a smile.*
PREP

8 If something is **for** sale, hire, or use, it is available to be sold, hired, or used. *...fishmongers displaying freshwater fish for sale... Skis are available for hire on a daily basis. ...a room for rent. ...a comfortable chair, suitable for use in the living room.*
PREP

9 You use **for** when you state or explain the purpose of an object, action, or activity. *...drug users who use unsterile equipment for injections of drugs... The knife for cutting sausage was sitting in the sink. ...economic aid for the future reconstruction of the country.*
PREP: PREP n/-ing

10 You use **for** after nouns expressing reason or cause. *He's soon to make a speech in parliament explaining his reasons for going... The county hospital could find no physical cause for Sumner's problems... He has now been formally given the grounds for his arrest.*
PREP: n PREP n/-ing

11 You can use **for** to introduce a clause which gives the reason why you made the statement in the main clause; a literary use. *He had a great desire to have a home of his own for he had always lived with my grandmother.*
CONJ-SUBORD =as, since

12 You can use **for** to introduce the cause of the fact that you have just mentioned; a literary use. *...doing jobs that others turn down for lack of skill... They cannot sleep for hunger.*
PREP =because of

13 **For** is used in conditional sentences, in expressions such as **'if not for'** and **'were it not for'**, to introduce the only thing which prevents the main part of the sentence from being true. *If not for John, Brian wouldn't have learned the truth... The earth would be a frozen ball if it were not for the radiant heat of the sun... She might have forgotten her completely had it not been for recurrent nightmares.*
PREP

14 You use **for** to say how long something lasts or continues. *The toaster remained on for more than an hour... For a few minutes she sat on her bed watching the clock... He smoked one and a half packs of cigarettes a day for about 25 years... They talked for a bit.*
PREP: PREP amount

15 You use **for** to say how far something extends. *We drove on for a few miles... Great clouds of black smoke were rising for several hundred feet or so.*
PREP: PREP amount

16 If something is bought, sold, or done **for** a particular price or amount, that price or amount is the cost of buying, selling, or doing it. *We got the bus back to Tange for 30 cents... The Martins sold their house for about 1.4 million pounds... The doctor was prepared to do the operation for a large sum.*
PREP: PREP amount

17 If something is planned **for** a particular time, it is planned to happen then. *...the Welsh Boat Show, planned for July 30-August 1... Marks & Spencer will be unveiling its latest fashions for autumn and winter... The party was scheduled for 7:00.*
PREP

18 If you do something **for** a particular occasion, you do it on that occasion or to celebrate that occasion. *He asked his daughter what she would like for her birthday... I'll be home for Christmas.*
PREP

19 If you leave **for** a particular place or if you take a bus, train, plane, or boat **for** a place, you are going there. *They would be leaving for Rio early the next morning.*
PREP

20 You use **for** when you make a statement about something in order to say how it affects or relates to someone, or what their attitude to it is. *What matters for most scientists is money and facilities... For her, books were as necessary to life as bread... It would be excellent experience for him to travel a little.*
PREP

21 After some adjective, noun, and verb phrases, you use **for** to introduce the subject of the action indicated by the following infinitive verb. *It might be possible for a single woman to be accepted as a foster parent... I had made arrangements for my affairs to be dealt with by one of my children... He held out his glass for an old waiter to refill.*
PREP: PREP n to-inf

22 You use **for** when you say that an aspect of something or someone is surprising in relation to other aspects of them. *He was tall for an eight-year-old... He had too much money for a young man.*
PREP

23 If you say that you are **for** a particular activity, you mean that this is what you want or intend to do. *Right, who's for a toasted sandwich then?... 'What'll it be?' Paul said.—'I'm for halibut.'*
PREP: v-link PREP n/-ing

24 If you say that something is not **for** you, you mean that you do not enjoy it or that it is not suitable for you; an informal use. *Wendy decided the sport was not for her... Not for me the settled life... I'm afraid German beer isn't for me.*
PREP: with neg

25 If it is **for** you to do something, it is your responsibility or right to do it. *I wish you would come back to Washington with us, but that's for you to decide... It is not for me to arrange such matters.*
PREP: PREP n to-inf

26 If you are **for** something, you agree with it or support it. *Are you for or against public transport?... I'm for a government that the people respect and that respects the people... No, I'm not for abolishing prizes and denying novelists their money.*
PREP: v-link PREP n/-ing ≠against

27 You use **for** after words such as 'argue', 'case', 'evidence', or 'vote' in order to introduce the thing that is being supported or proved. *Another union has voted for industrial action in support of a pay claim... The case for nuclear power is impressive... We have no real, objective, scientific evidence for our belief. ...committees arguing for increased support of technical education.* ▶ Also an adverb. *833 delegates voted for, and only 432 against.*
PREP: n/v PREP n ≠against
ADV: ADV after v

28 **For** is the preposition that is used after some nouns, adjectives, or verbs in order to introduce more information or to indicate what a quality, thing, or action relates to. *Reduced-calorie cheese is a great substitute for cream cheese... Car park owners should be legally responsible for protecting vehicles... Be prepared for both warm and cool weather... Make sure you have ample time to prepare for the new day ahead... Special bus and rail services are being laid on to cater for the crowds... He was destined for a career in the Bank of England.*
PREP: n/adj/v PREP n/-ing

29 You use **for** with 'every' when you are stating a ratio, to introduce the less important thing in the ratio. *For every farm job that is lost, two or three other jobs in the area are put at risk... Where there had been one divorce for every 100 marriages before the war, now there were five.*
PREP PRAGMATICS

30 You can use **for** in expressions such as **pound for pound** or **mile for mile** when you are making comparisons between the values or qualities of different things. *...the Antarctic, mile for mile one of*
PREP: n PREP n

the planet's most lifeless areas... He insists any tax cut be matched dollar-for-dollar with cuts in spending.

31 If one word or expression has the same meaning as a second word or expression, you can say that the first one is another word or expression **for** the second one. *The technical term for sunburn is erythema... Cancer is derived from the Greek word for crab, karkinos.* PREP

32 You use **for** in cross-references when you mention information which will be found somewhere else. *For further information on the life of William James Sidis, see Amy Wallace, 'The Prodigy'.* PREP PRAGMATICS

33 If you say that you are **all for** doing something, you agree or strongly believe that it should be done, but you are also often suggesting that other people disagree with you or that there are practical difficulties. *I am all for cutting carbon dioxide emissions, but that would be much more easily achieved by giving subsidies to windpower, than with nuclear power... He is all for players earning what they can while they are in the game... I was all for it, but Wolfe said no.* PHRASES v-link PHR, PHR -ing/n =in favour of

34 If you **are for it** or if you **are in for it** you are going to be in trouble because of something you have done; an informal expression. V inflects

35 You use expressions such as **for the first time** and **for the last time** when you are talking about how often something has happened. *Mr Lukman is visiting the United States for the second time this year... For the first time in my career, I was failing.* PHR with cl

36 • **as for**: see **as**. • **but for**: see **but**. • **for all**: see **all**.

forage /fɒrɪdʒ, AM fɔːr-/ **forages, foraging, foraged** ◆◇◇◇◇

1 If someone **forages for** something, they search busily for it. *They were forced to forage for clothing and fuel.* VERB V for n

2 When animals **forage**, they search for food. *We disturbed a wild boar that had been foraging by the roadside... The cat forages for food.* VERB V V for n

3 **Forage** is crops that are grown as food for cattle and horses. *...the amount of forage needed to feed one cow and its calf.* N-UNCOUNT

foray /fɒreɪ, AM fɔːreɪ/ **forays** ◆◇◇◇◇

1 If you make a **foray** into a new or unfamiliar type of activity, you start to become involved in it. *Emporio Armani, the Italian fashion house, has made a discreet foray into furnishings. ...her first forays into politics.* N-COUNT: oft poss N, usu N into n

2 You can refer to a short journey that you make as a **foray** if it seems to involve excitement or risk, for example because it is to an unfamiliar place or because you are looking for a particular thing. *Most guests make at least one foray into the town... A foray to your supermarket will supply all the ready-made foods for an excellent picnic.* N-COUNT: usu N into/to n

3 If a group of soldiers make a **foray** into enemy territory, they make a quick attack there, and then return to their own territory. *These base camps were used by the PKK guerrillas to make forays into Turkey.* N-COUNT: oft N into n =raid

forbade /fəʳbæd, -beɪd/. **Forbade** is the past tense of **forbid**.

forbear /fɔːʳbeəʳ/ **forbears, forbearing, forbore, forborne.** If you **forbear** to do something, you do not do it although you have the opportunity or the right to do it; a formal word. *I forbore to comment on this... Protesters largely forbore from stone-throwing and vandalism.* VERB V to-inf V from -ing/n

forbearance /fɔːʳbeərəns/. If you say that someone has shown **forbearance**, you admire them for showing self-control and patience when something happens that would give them the right to be very upset or angry; a formal word. *She remembered the example of fortitude and forbearance given by her father when her mother had died.* N-UNCOUNT PRAGMATICS

forbearing /fɔːʳbeərɪŋ/. Someone who is **forbearing** shows self-control and patience at a time when they would have a right to be very upset or angry; a formal word, used showing approval. ADJ-GRADED PRAGMATICS =long-suffering

forbid /fəʳbɪd/ **forbids, forbidding, forbade, forbidden** ◆◆◇◇◇

1 If you **forbid** someone to do something, or if you **forbid** an activity, you order that it must not be done. *They'll forbid you to marry... She was shut away and forbidden to read... Brazil's constitution forbids the military use of nuclear energy.* VERB =prohibit V n to-inf V n

2 If something **forbids** a particular course of action or state of affairs, it makes it impossible for the course of action or state of affairs to happen. *His own pride forbids him to ask Arthur's help... Custom forbids any modernisation.* VERB V n to-inf V n

3 • **God forbid**: see **God**. • **heaven forbid**: see **heaven.**

forbidden /fəʳbɪdᵊn/ ◆◆◇◇◇

1 If something is **forbidden**, you are not allowed to do it or have it. *Smoking was forbidden everywhere... It is forbidden to drive faster than 20mph.* ADJ: usu v-link ADJ, oft it v-link ADJ to-inf

2 A **forbidden** place is one that you are not allowed to visit or enter. *This was a forbidden area for foreigners.* ADJ: usu ADJ n =out of bounds

3 **Forbidden** is used to describe things that people strongly disapprove of or feel guilty about, so that they are very rarely mentioned or talked about. *The war was a forbidden subject... Men fantasise as a substitute for acting out forbidden desires... Divorce? It was such a forbidden word.* ADJ-GRADED: usu ADJ n =taboo

forbidden fruit, forbidden fruits. Forbidden fruit is a source of pleasure that involves breaking a rule or doing something that you are not supposed to do. *...the forbidden fruit of an illicit romance.* N-VAR

forbidding /fəʳbɪdɪŋ/. If you describe a person, place, or thing as **forbidding**, you mean they have a severe, unfriendly, or threatening appearance. *There was something a little severe and forbidding about her face. ...a huge, forbidding building.* ADJ-GRADED

force /fɔːʳs/ **forces, forcing, forced** ◆◆◆◆◆

1 If someone **forces** you to do something, they make you do it even though you do not want to, for example by threatening you. *He was charged with abducting a taxi driver and forcing him to drive a bomb to Downing Street... He was forced to resign by Russia's conservative parliament at the beginning of December... I cannot force you in this. You must decide... They were grabbed by three men who appeared to force them into a car.* VERB V n to-inf V n V n prep/adv

2 If a situation or event **forces** you to do something, it makes it necessary for you to do something that you would not otherwise have done. *A back injury forced her to withdraw from Wimbledon... He turned right, down a dirt road that forced him into four-wheel drive... She finally was forced to the conclusion that she wouldn't get another paid job in her field.* VERB V n to-inf V n into/to/out of n

3 If someone **forces** something **on** or **upon** you, they make you accept or use it when you would prefer not to. *To force this agreement on the nation is wrong.* VERB =impose V n on/upon n

4 If you **force** something into a particular position, you use a lot of strength to make it move there. *They were forcing her head under the icy waters, drowning her.* VERB V n prep/adv

5 If someone **forces** a lock, a door, or a window, they break it violently in order get into a building without using a key. *That evening police forced the door of the flat and arrested Mr Roberts... He tried to force the window open but it was jammed shut.* VERB V n V n adj

6 If someone uses **force** to do something, or if it is done by **force**, strong and violent physical action is taken in order to achieve it. *The government decided against using force to break-up the demonstrations. ...the guerrillas' efforts to seize power by force.* N-UNCOUNT

7 **Force** is the power or strength which something has. *The force of the explosion shattered the windows of several buildings... It looked as though the storm had an awful lot of force.* N-UNCOUNT =power

8 If you refer to someone or something as a **force** in a particular type of activity, you mean that they N-COUNT: with supp, oft N in/behind

have a strong influence on it. *Today's march has made it clear that the FLN is still a big political force in the country... The band are still as innovative a force in British music as they were when they started... One of the driving forces behind this recent expansion is the growth of services.*

9 The **force** of something is the powerful effect or quality that it has. *He changed our world through the force of his ideas... Perhaps your force of argument might have made some difference.* — N-UNCOUNT: oft N *of* n

10 You can use **forces** to refer to processes and events that do not appear to be caused by human beings, and are therefore difficult to understand or control. *...the protection of mankind against the forces of nature: epidemics, predators, floods, hurricanes... The principle of market forces was applied to some of the countries most revered institutions... Is it really the Holy Spirit moving me, or is it some evil force?* — N-COUNT: usu pl, usu with supp

11 In physics, a **force** is the pulling, attracting, or pushing effect that something has on something else. *...the earth's gravitational force. ...protons and electrons trapped by magnetic forces in the Van Allen belts.* — N-VAR

12 The word **force** is used before a number to indicate a wind of a particular speed or strength, especially a very strong wind. *The airlift was conducted in force ten winds... Northerly winds will increase to force six by midday.* — N-UNCOUNT: N num

13 If you **force** a smile or a laugh, you manage to smile or laugh, but with an effort because you are unhappy. *Joe forced a smile, but underneath he was a little disturbed... 'Why don't you offer me a drink?' he asked, with a forced smile.* — VERB; V n; V-ed

14 Forces are groups of soldiers or military vehicles that are organized for a particular purpose. *...the deployment of American forces in the region.* — N-COUNT: usu pl

15 The **forces** means the army, the navy, or the air force, or all three. *The more senior you become in the forces, the more likely you are to end up in a desk job.* — N-PLURAL

16 The **force** is sometimes used to mean the police force. *It was hard for a police officer to make friends outside the force.* — N-SING: det N

17 See also **air force**, **armed forces**, **labour force**, **peacekeeping**, **task force**, **tour de force**, **workforce**.

18 If something happens **by force of** a particular quality, action, or set of circumstances, it happens because of the nature or intensity of that quality, action, or set of circumstances. *...converting the sceptics by force of argument. ...its promise to free Kuwait by force of arms.* — PHRASES; PHR n

19 If you do something from **force of habit**, you do it because you have always done it in the past, rather than because you have thought carefully about it. *He looked around from force of habit, but nobody paid any attention to him... Unconsciously, by force of habit, she plugged the coffee pot in.* — usu *from/by* PHR

20 A law, rule, or system that is **in force** exists or is being used. *Martial law is in force in the Tibetan capital Lhasa... Although the new tax is already in force, you have until November to lodge an appeal.* — v-link PHR; =in strength

21 When people do something **in force**, they do it in large numbers. *Voters turned out in force for their first taste of multi-party elections.* — PHR after v

22 If you **join forces** with someone, you work together in order to achieve a common aim or purpose. *Both groups joined forces to persuade voters to approve a tax break for the industry... William joined forces with businessman Nicholas Court to launch the new vehicle.* — RECIP: V inflects, pl-n PHR, PHR *with* n

23 If you **force** your **way** through or into somewhere, you have to push or break things that are in your way in order to get there. *The miners were armed with clubs as they forced their way through a police cordon... He forced his way into a house shouting for help.* — V inflects, oft PHR *through/into* n

24 • to **force someone's hand**: see **hand**.

force back. If you **force back** an emotion or desire, you manage, with an effort, not to experience it. *Nancy forced back tears. She wasn't going to cry in front of all those people.* — PHRASAL VERB; V P n (not pron); Also V n P

forced /fɔːʳst/ ◆◇◇◇◇

1 A **forced** action is something that you do because someone else makes you do it. *A system of forced labour was used on the cocoa plantations.* — ADJ: ADJ n

2 A **forced** action is something that you do because circumstances make it necessary. *He made a forced landing on a highway.* — ADJ: ADJ n

3 If you describe something as **forced**, you mean it does not happen naturally and easily. *...a forced smile... She called him darling. It sounded so forced.* — ADJ-GRADED; ≠natural

force-feed, force-feeds, force-feeding, force-fed. If you **force-feed** a person or animal, you make them eat or drink by pushing food or drink down their throat. *Production of the foie gras pate involves force-feeding geese and ducks so that their livers swell.* — VERB; V n

forceful /fɔːʳsfʊl/ ◆◇◇◇◇

1 If you describe someone as **forceful**, you approve of them because they express their opinions and wishes in a strong, emphatic, and confident way. *He was a man of forceful character, with considerable insight and diplomatic skills.* ♦ **forcefully** *Mrs. Dambar was talking very rapidly and somewhat forcefully.* ♦ **forcefulness** *She had inherited her father's forcefulness.* — ADJ-GRADED; PRAGMATICS; ADV-GRADED: ADV with v; N-UNCOUNT

2 Something that is **forceful** has a very powerful effect and causes you to think or feel something very strongly. *Clinton promised last year that he would take forceful action to stop the suffering... For most people a heart attack is a forceful reminder that they are mortal.* ♦ **forcefully** *Daytime television tended to remind her too forcefully of her own situation.* — ADJ-GRADED; =strong; ADV-GRADED: ADV with v

3 A **forceful** point or argument in a discussion is one that is good, valid, and convincing. — ADJ-GRADED; =powerful

forceps /fɔːʳseps/. **Forceps** are an instrument consisting of two long narrow arms. Forceps are used by a doctor to hold things. — N-PLURAL: also *a pair of* N

forcible /fɔːʳsɪbəl/. **Forcible** action involves physical force or violence. *Reports are coming in of the forcible resettlement of villagers from the countryside into towns.* ♦ **forcibly** *Two student leaders were forcibly removed from the university president's office.* — ◆◇◇◇◇; ADJ: usu ADJ n; ADV: ADV with v

ford /fɔːʳd/ **fords, fording, forded** ◆◇◇◇◇

1 A **ford** is a shallow place in a river or stream where it is possible to cross safely without using a boat. — N-COUNT

2 If you **ford** a river or stream, you cross it without using a boat, usually at a shallow point. *They were guarding the bridge, so we forded the river.* — VERB; V n

fore /fɔːʳ/ ◆◇◇◇◇

1 If someone or something comes **to the fore** in a particular situation or group, they become important or popular. *A number of low-budget independent films brought new directors and actors to the fore.* — PHRASE: PHR after v

2 Fore is used to refer to parts at the front of an animal, ship, or aircraft. *There had been no direct damage in the fore part of the ship. ...a swelling appeared below his near fore knee.* — ADJ: ADJ n; =front

3 If something is **fore** in a boat or plane, it is at the front of it. *Our yacht was well equipped with two double cabins fore and aft... He loosened his very strong hold on the ship's rail and glanced fore and aft.* — ADV: n ADV, ADV after v; ≠aft

forearm /fɔːrɑːʳm/ **forearms.** Your **forearm** is the part of your arm between your elbow and your wrist. — ◆◇◇◇◇; N-COUNT: oft poss N

forearmed /fɔːʳwɔːʳnd/. If you say '**Forewarned is forearmed**', you are saying that if you know about a problem or situation in advance, you will be able to deal with it when you need to. — PHRASE

forebear /fɔːʳbeəʳ/ **forebears.** Your **forebears** are your ancestors; a literary word. *I'll come back to the land of my forebears.* — N-COUNT: usu with poss; =forefather

foreboding /fɔːʳbəʊdɪŋ/ **forebodings**

1 Foreboding is a strong feeling that something — N-VAR

terrible is going to happen. *His triumph was overshadowed by an uneasy sense of foreboding.*
2 If you describe something as **foreboding**, you mean that it makes you feel that something terrible is going to happen. *Prisons like Strangeways, built more than 100 years ago, were intended to look grim and foreboding places.* ADJ-GRADED

forecast /fɔːʳkɑːst, -kæst/ **forecasts, forecasting, forecasted.** The forms **forecast** and **forecasted** can both be used for the past tense and past participle. ◆◆◆◇◇
1 A **forecast** is a prediction or statement of what is expected to happen in the future, especially in relation to a particular event or situation. *...a forecast of a 2.25 per cent growth in the economy... He delivered his election forecast... In mid-Atlantic, even if you should happen to have a forecast of heavy weather to come, there is nowhere to hide.* N-COUNT: usu with supp
2 If you **forecast** future events, you say what you think is going to happen in the future. *They forecast a humiliating defeat for the Prime Minister... He forecasts that average salary increases will remain around 4 per cent.* VERB V n V that
3 See also **weather forecast**.

forecaster /fɔːʳkɑːstəʳ, -kæst-/ **forecasters.** A **forecaster** is someone who uses detailed knowledge about a particular activity in order to work out what they think will happen in that activity in the future. *Some of the nation's top economic forecasters say the economic recovery is picking up speed.* ● See also **weather forecaster.** ◆◇◇◇◇ N-COUNT

foreclose /fɔːʳklouz/ **forecloses, foreclosing, foreclosed.** If the person or organization that lent someone money **forecloses**, they take possession of a property that was bought with the borrowed money, for example because regular repayments have not been made; a technical term. *The bank foreclosed on the mortgage for his previous home.* ♦ **foreclosure, foreclosures** *If they can't keep up the payments, they face foreclosure... If interest rates go up, won't foreclosures rise?* VERB V on n Also V N-VAR

forecourt /fɔːʳkɔːʳt/ **forecourts.** The **forecourt** of a large building or petrol station is the open area at the front of it; used mainly in British English. *I locked the bike in the forecourt of the Kirey Hotel. ... gas station forecourts.* N-COUNT: oft N of n, n N

forefather /fɔːʳfɑːðəʳ/ **forefathers.** Your **forefathers** are your ancestors, especially your male ancestors; a literary word. *They were determined to go back to the land of their forefathers.* N-COUNT: usu pl, usu poss N =forebear

forefinger /fɔːʳfɪŋgəʳ/ **forefingers.** Your **forefinger** is the finger that is next to your thumb. *He took the pen between his thumb and forefinger.* ◆◇◇◇◇ N-COUNT: oft poss N =index finger

forefoot /fɔːʳfʊt/ **forefeet.** A four-legged animal's **forefeet** are its two front feet. *Moles have powerful forefeet for digging.* N-COUNT: usu pl

forefront /fɔːʳfrʌnt/ ◆◇◇◇◇
1 If you are at **the forefront** of a campaign or other activity, you have a leading and influential position in it. *They have been at the forefront of the campaign for political change.* N-SING: the N, usu at/in/to N, N of/in n/-ing
2 If something is at **the forefront** of people's minds or attention, they think about it a lot because it is particularly important to them. *The pension issue was not at the forefront of his mind in the spring of 1985.* N-SING: the N, usu at/in/to N of n

forego /fɔːʳgou/ **foregoes, foregoing, forewent, foregone;** also spelled **forgo.** If you **forego** something, you decide to do without it, although you would like it; a formal word. *Keen skiers are happy to forego a summer holiday to go skiing.* VERB =do without V n

foregoing /fɔːʳgouɪŋ, fɔːʳgou-/. You can refer to what has just been stated or mentioned as **the foregoing**; a formal word. *You might think from the foregoing that the French want to phase accents out. Not at all.* ► Also an adjective. *The foregoing paragraphs were written in 1985.* PRON: the PRON ADJ: ADJ n =preceding

foregone /fɔːʳgɒn/
1 **Foregone** is the past participle of **forego**.
2 If you say that a particular result is **a foregone conclusion**, you mean you are certain that it will happen. *Most voters believe the result is a foregone conclusion... It's almost a foregone conclusion that you'll get what you want.* PHRASE: usu v-link PHR, oft it v-link PHR that

foreground /fɔːʳgraund/ **foregrounds, foregrounding, foregrounded** ◆◇◇◇◇
1 The **foreground** of a picture or scene you are looking at is the part or area of it that appears nearest to you. *He is the bowler-hatted figure in the foreground of Orpen's famous painting.* N-VAR: oft in the N =focus on ≠background
2 If something or someone is in the **foreground**, or comes to the **foreground**, they receive a lot of attention. *This is another worry that has come to the foreground in recent years.* N-SING: usu the N, oft in/to N
3 To **foreground** certain features of a situation means to make them the most important part of a description or account; a formal use. *His book foregrounds three events in which police relations with the media were central.* VERB =highlight V n

forehand /fɔːʳhænd/ **forehands.** A **forehand** is a shot in tennis or squash in which the palm of your hand faces the direction in which you are hitting the ball. *Agassi saw his chance and, with another lightning forehand, reached match point.* N-COUNT

forehead /fɒrɪd, fɔːʳhed/ **foreheads.** Your **forehead** is the area at the front of your head between your eyebrows and your hair. ◆◆◇◇◇ N-COUNT: oft poss N =brow

foreign /fɒrɪn, AM fɔːr-/ ◆◆◆◆◆
1 Something or someone that is **foreign** comes from or relates to a country that is not your own. *...in Frankfurt, where a quarter of the population is foreign... She was on her first foreign holiday without her parents. ...a foreign language... It is the largest ever private foreign investment in the Bolivian mining sector.* ADJ
2 In politics and journalism, **foreign** is used to describe people, jobs, and activities relating to countries that are not the country of the person or government concerned. *...the German foreign minister... I am the foreign correspondent in Washington of La Tribuna newspaper of Honduras. ...the effects of US foreign policy in the 'free world'.* ADJ: ADJ n
3 A **foreign** object is something that has got into something else, usually by accident, and should not be there; a formal use. *The patient's immune system would reject the transplanted organ as a foreign object.* ADJ: usu ADJ n
4 Something that is **foreign** to a particular person or thing is not typical of them or is unknown to them. *The very notion of price competition is foreign to many schools... The whole thing is foreign to us.* ADJ-GRADED: usu v-link ADJ to n

foreign body, foreign bodies. A **foreign body** is an object that has come into something else, usually by accident, and should not be in it; a formal expression. *...a foreign body in the eye.* N-COUNT

foreigner /fɒrɪnəʳ, AM fɔːr-/ **foreigners.** A **foreigner** is someone who belongs to a country that is not your own. Some people believe this word is slightly offensive. *They are discouraged from becoming close friends with foreigners.* ◆◆◆◇◇ N-COUNT

foreign exchange, foreign exchanges ◆◆◇◇◇
1 **Foreign exchanges** are the institutions or systems involved with changing one currency into another. *On the foreign exchanges, the US dollar is up point forty-five.* N-PLURAL
2 **Foreign exchange** is used to refer to foreign currency that is obtained through the foreign exchange system. *...an important source of foreign exchange. ...foreign-exchange traders.* N-UNCOUNT: oft N n

Foreign Office, Foreign Offices. The **Foreign Office** is the government department, especially in Britain, which has responsibility for the government's dealings and relations with foreign governments. *...a Foreign Office spokesman.* ◆◆◇◇◇ N-COUNT: the N, oft N n

foreknowledge /fɔːʳnɒlɪdʒ/. If you have **foreknowledge** of an event or situation, you have some knowledge of it before it actually happens. *She has maintained that the General had foreknowledge of the plot.* N-UNCOUNT: oft N of n

foreleg /fɔːʳleg/ **forelegs.** A four-legged animal's **forelegs** are its two front legs. N-COUNT: usu pl

forelock /fɔːʳlɒk/ **forelocks**
1 A **forelock** is a piece of hair that falls over your forehead. People often used to pull their forelocks to show respect for other people of a higher class than they were. *He touched his forelock in mock deference.* N-COUNT
2 If you say that a person **tugs their forelock** to another person, you are criticizing them for showing too much respect to the second person or being unnecessarily worried about their opinions; used mainly in British English. PHRASE: V and N inflect, oft PHR *to* n PRAGMATICS

foreman /fɔːʳmən/ **foremen** ◆◇◇◇◇
1 A **foreman** is a person, especially a man, in charge of a group of workers. *He still visited the dairy daily, but left most of the business details to his manager and foreman.* N-COUNT
2 The **foreman** of a jury is the person who is chosen as their leader. *There was applause from the public gallery as the foreman of the jury announced the verdict.* N-COUNT

foremost /fɔːʳmoust/ ◆◇◇◇◇
1 The **foremost** thing or person in a group is the most important or best. *He was one of the world's foremost scholars of ancient Indian culture... The military government is waging a war of words against its supposed enemies. Foremost among these are the foreign media.* ADJ
2 You use **first and foremost** to emphasize the most important quality of something or someone. *It is first and foremost a trade agreement... I see myself, first and foremost, as a working artist.* PHRASE: PHR n/prep, PHR with cl, PHR after v PRAGMATICS

forename /fɔːʳneɪm/ **forenames.** In formal English, your **forename** is your first name, as opposed to your surname. You can also refer to all of your names other than your surname as your **forenames.** N-COUNT: oft poss N =first name

forenoon /fɔːʳnuːn/. The **forenoon** is the morning; an old-fashioned word. N-SING

forensic /fərensɪk/ ◆◇◇◇◇
1 **Forensic** is used to describe the scientific data and procedures that pathologists, laboratory technicians, and other scientists work with when they help the police to solve crimes. *They were convicted on forensic evidence alone... Forensic experts searched the area for clues. ...the use of genetic data for forensic science.* ADJ: ADJ n
2 **Forensic** means relating to the legal profession. *He won admiration for his forensic skills in cross-examining ministers. ...a forensic psychiatrist.* ADJ: ADJ n

foreplay /fɔːʳpleɪ/. **Foreplay** is activity such as kissing and stroking when it takes place before sexual intercourse. N-UNCOUNT

forerunner /fɔːʳrʌnəʳ/ **forerunners.** If you describe something or someone as the **forerunner** of something or someone similar, you mean they existed before them and either influenced their development or were a sign of what was going to happen. *...a machine which, in some respects, was the forerunner of the modern helicopter... Some respiratory symptoms can be the forerunners of asthma.* ◆◇◇◇◇ N-COUNT: oft N *of* n =precursor

foresee /fɔːʳsiː/ **foresees, foreseeing, foresaw, foreseen.** If you **foresee** something, you expect and believe that it will happen. *He did not foresee any problems. ...a dangerous situation which could have been foreseen... He could never have foreseen that one day his books would sell in millions.* ◆◆◇◇◇ VERB =predict V n V that Also V wh

foreseeable /fɔːʳsiːəbᵊl/ ◆◇◇◇◇
1 If a future event is **foreseeable,** you know that it will happen or that it can happen, because it is a natural or obvious consequence of something else that you know. *It seems to me that this crime was foreseeable and this death preventable... One of the principles of our legal system is that people are accountable for the foreseeable consequences of their actions.* ADJ-GRADED
2 If you say that something will happen **for the foreseeable future,** you think that it will continue to happen for a long time. *Profit and dividend growth looks like being above average for the foreseeable future.* PHRASES usu PHR after v, PHR with cl
3 If you say that something will happen **in the foreseeable future** you mean that you think it will happen fairly soon. *So, might they finally have free elections in the foreseeable future?* usu PHR after v, PHR with cl

foreshadow /fɔːʳʃædou/ **foreshadows, foreshadowing, foreshadowed.** If something **foreshadows** an event or situation, it suggests that it will happen. *The disappointing sales figures foreshadow more redundancies... The change proposed last month was foreshadowed in the March Budget.* VERB V n

foreshore /fɔːʳʃɔːʳ/ **foreshores.** Beside the sea, a lake, or a wide river, the **foreshore** is the part of the shore which is between the highest and lowest points reached by the water. N-COUNT: usu sing

foreshorten /fɔːʳʃɔːʳtᵊn/ **foreshortens, foreshortening, foreshortened**
1 To **foreshorten** someone or something is to draw them, photograph them, or see them in a distorted way or from a strange angle so that parts of them seem closer together than they really are. This technique is sometimes used in art to give the illusion of perspective. *She could see herself in the reflecting lenses, which had grotesquely foreshortened her. ...a steeply foreshortened view.* VERB V n V-ed
2 If something or someone **foreshortens** something, they make it shorter than it would otherwise be; a literary use. *She felt that her husband's unexpected promotion foreshortened his life. ...a foreshortened version of the opera.* VERB =shorten V n V-ed

foresight /fɔːʳsaɪt/. Someone's **foresight** is their ability to see what is likely to happen in the future and to take appropriate action; used showing approval. *He was later criticised for his lack of foresight... They had the foresight to invest in new technology.*  N-UNCOUNT PRAGMATICS

foreskin /fɔːʳskɪn/ **foreskins.** A man's **foreskin** is the skin that covers the end of his penis. N-VAR

forest /fɒrɪst, AM fɔːr-/ **forests** ◆◆◆◇◇
1 A **forest** is a large area where trees grow close together. *Parts of the forest are still dense and inaccessible. ...25 million hectares of forest.* N-VAR
2 A **forest** of tall or narrow objects is a group of them standing or sticking upright; a literary use. *They descended from the planes into a forest of microphones and cameras.* N-COUNT: with supp, usu N *of* n

forestall /fɔːʳstɔːl/ **forestalls, forestalling, forestalled.** If you **forestall** someone, you realize what they are likely to do and prevent them from doing it. *O'Leary made to open the door, but Bunbury forestalled him by laying a hand on his arm... Large numbers of police were in the square to forestall any demonstrations.* ◆◇◇◇◇ VERB =stop V n

forested /fɒrɪstɪd, AM fɔːr-/. A **forested** area is an area covered in trees growing closely together. *The road snaked through forested mountains, past the village of San Antonio. ...a thickly forested valley... Only 8 per cent of Britain is forested.* ADJ-GRADED

forester /fɒrɪstəʳ, AM fɔːr-/ **foresters.** A **forester** is a person whose job is to look after the trees in a forest and to plant new ones. N-COUNT

forestry /fɒrɪstri, AM fɔːr-/. **Forestry** is the science or skill of growing and taking care of trees in forests, especially in order to obtain wood. ◆◇◇◇◇ N-UNCOUNT

foretaste /fɔːʳteɪst/ **foretastes.** If you describe an event as a **foretaste** of a future situation, you mean that it suggests to you what that future situation will be like. *It was a foretaste of things to come... This is but a foretaste of what the emerging technologies will enable us to do.* N-COUNT: usu *a* N *of* n =indication

foretell /fɔːʳtel/ **foretells, foretelling, foretold.** If you **foretell** a future event, you predict that it will happen. *...prophets who have foretold the end of the world.* VERB V n Also V that/wh, V *of* n

forethought /fɔːʳθɔːt/. If you act with **forethought,** you think carefully before you act about what will be needed, or about what the consequences will be. *With a little forethought many accidents could be avoided.* N-UNCOUNT

foretold /fɔːʳtould/. **Foretold** is the past participle of **foretell.**

forever /fərevəʳ/; also spelled **for ever** for meanings 1, 2, and 3. ◆◆◇◇◇
1 If you say that something will happen or continue **forever**, you mean that it will always happen or continue. *I think that we will live together forever... It was great fun but we knew it wouldn't go on for ever... I will forever be grateful for his considerable input.* ADV: ADV with v
2 If something has gone or changed **forever**, it has gone or changed completely and permanently. *The old social order was gone forever... Their lives changed forever.* ADV: ADV after v =for good
3 If you say that something takes **forever** or lasts **forever**, you are emphasizing that it takes or lasts a very long time, or that it seems to; an informal use. *The drive seemed to take forever... They didn't cost anything and they lasted forever.* ADV: ADV after v PRAGMATICS =ages
4 If you say that someone is **forever** doing a particular thing, especially something which annoys or amuses you, you are emphasizing that they do it very often; an informal use. *He was forever attempting to arrange deals... I was forever dragging him away from the fireplace.* ADV: ADV before v-cont PRAGMATICS =always, constantly
5 You use **forever** to emphasize that someone always has or shows the quality mentioned. *Katherine was forever secretive... To this end the young child is forever watchful.* ADV: ADV adj PRAGMATICS =ever, eternally

forewarn /fɔːʳwɔːʳn/ **forewarns, forewarning, forewarned.** If you **forewarn** someone about something, you warn them in advance that it is going to happen. *The Macmillan Guide had forewarned me of what to expect.* • **forewarned is forearmed**: see **forearmed.** VERB =alert; V n of/about n; Also V n that, V n

forewent /fɔːʳwent/. **Forewent** is the past tense of **forego**.

foreword /fɔːʳwɜːʳd/ **forewords.** The **foreword** to a book is an introduction by the author or by someone else. N-COUNT: oft N to n

forfeit /fɔːʳfɪt/ **forfeits, forfeiting, forfeited** ◆◇◇◇◇
1 If you **forfeit** something, you lose it or are forced to give it up because you have broken a rule or done something wrong. *He was ordered to forfeit more than £1.5m in profits... He argues that murderers forfeit their own right to life.* VERB; V n
2 If you **forfeit** something, you give it up voluntarily, especially so that you can achieve something else. *He has forfeited a lucrative fee but feels his well-being is more important... Do you think that they would forfeit profit in the name of safety?* VERB; V n
3 A **forfeit** is something that you have to give up because you have done something wrong. *That is the forfeit he must pay.* N-COUNT =penalty

forfeiture /fɔːʳfɪtʃəʳ/ **forfeitures. Forfeiture** is the action of forfeiting something; a legal word. *...the forfeiture of illegally obtained profits... Both face maximum forfeitures of about $1.2 million.* N-VAR: oft N of n

forgave /fəʳgeɪv/. **Forgave** is the past tense of **forgive**.

forge /fɔːʳdʒ/ **forges, forging, forged** ◆◆◇◇◇
1 If one person or institution **forges** an alliance or relationship with another, or if two people or institutions **forge** an alliance or relationship, they create it with a lot of hard work, hoping that it will be strong or lasting. You can also say that one person or institution **forges** a relationship between two other people or institutions. *The Prime Minister is determined to forge a good relationship with America's new leader... They agreed to forge closer economic ties... The programme aims to forge links between higher education and small businesses... The Community was trying to forge a common foreign and security policy.* V-RECIP =form; V n with n; pl-n V n; NON-RECIP: V n between pl-n; V n
2 If you say that someone **has forged** something that you approve of, you mean that you admire them for having done something difficult. *The project will help inmates forge new careers... Tito forged a unique model of communism after breaking with Stalin in 1948.* VERB; V n
3 If someone **forges** something such as a banknote, a document, or a painting, they copy it or make it so that it looks genuine, in order to deceive people. *He admitted seven charges including forging passports... She alleged that Taylor had forged her signature on the form... They used forged documents to leave the country.* ♦ **forger, forgers** *...the most prolific art forger in the country.* VERB; V n; V-ed; N-COUNT
4 A **forge** is a place where someone makes metal goods and equipment by heating pieces of metal and then shaping them. *...the blacksmith's forge. ...Woodbury Blacksmith & Forge Co.* N-COUNT: oft in names
5 If someone **forges** an object out of metal, they heat the metal and then hammer and bend it into the required shape. *To forge a blade takes great skill.* VERB; V n

forge ahead. If you **forge ahead** with something, you continue with it and make a lot of progress with it. *He again pledged to forge ahead with his plans for reform... The two companies forged ahead, innovating and expanding.* PHRASAL VERB; V P with n; V P

forgery /fɔːʳdʒəri/ **forgeries** ◆◇◇◇◇
1 Forgery is the crime of forging money, documents, or paintings. *He was found guilty of forgery.* N-UNCOUNT
2 You can refer to a forged document, banknote, or painting as a **forgery**. *The letter was a forgery.* N-COUNT

forget /fəʳget/ **forgets, forgetting, forgot, forgotten** ◆◆◆◆◇
1 If you **forget** something or **forget** how to do something, you cannot think of it or think how to do it, although you knew it or knew how to do it in the past. *Sometimes I improvise and change the words because I forget them... She forgot where she left the car and it took us two days to find it.* VERB ≠remember; V n; V wh
2 If you **forget** something or **forget** to do it, you fail to think about it or fail to remember to do it, for example because you are thinking about other things. *She never forgets her daddy's birthday... She forgot to lock her door one day and two men got in... Don't forget that all dogs need a supply of fresh water to drink... She forgot about everything but the sun and the wind and the salt spray.* VERB ≠remember; V n; V to-inf; V that; V about n
3 If you **forget** something that you had intended to bring with you, you do not bring it because you did not think about it at the right time. *Once when we were going to Paris, I forgot my passport.* VERB; V n; Also V about n
4 If you **forget** something or someone, you deliberately put them out of your mind and do not think about them any more. *I hope you will forget the bad experience you had today... I can't forget what happened... I found it very easy to forget about Sumner... She tried to forget that sometimes she heard them quarrelling.* VERB; V n; V about n; V that
5 If you **forget** yourself, you behave in an unrestrained or unacceptable way, which is not the way in which you usually behave. *He was so fascinated by her beauty that he forgot himself and leaned across to touch her.* VERB; V pron-refl
6 You say **'Forget it'** in reply to someone as a way of telling them not to worry or bother about something, or as an emphatic way of saying no to a suggestion. *'Sorry, Liz. I think I was a bit rude to you.'—'Forget it, but don't do it again!'... 'You want more?' roared Claire. 'Forget it, honey.'* PHRASES CONVENTION PRAGMATICS
7 You say **not forgetting** a particular thing or person when you want to include them in something that you have already talked about. *The first thing is to support as many shows as one can, not forgetting the small local ones.* PHR n PRAGMATICS

forgetful /fəʳgetfʊl/. Someone who is **forgetful** often forgets things. *My mother has become very forgetful and confused recently.* ♦ **forgetfulness** *Her forgetfulness is due to advancing age.* ADJ-GRADED =absent-minded; N-UNCOUNT

forget-me-not, forget-me-nots. A **forget-me-not** is a small plant with tiny blue flowers. N-COUNT

forgettable /fəʳgetəbəl/. If you describe something or someone as **forgettable**, you are emphasizing that they do not have any qualities that make them special, unusual, or interesting. *He has acted in three forgettable action films... He was average height, average build, with mousy hair and a forgettable face.* ADJ-GRADED PRAGMATICS ≠unforgettable

forgivable /fəʳgɪvəbəl/. If you say that something bad is **forgivable**, you mean that you can understand it and can forgive it in the circumstances. *His sense of humour makes all else* ADJ-GRADED ≠unforgivable

forgivable... This was a blunder by Mr Baker, but it was a forgivable one.

forgive /fəʳgɪv/ **forgives, forgiving, forgave, forgiven** ◆◆◇◇◇

1 If you **forgive** someone who has done something wrong, or **forgive** a bad deed that someone has done, you stop being angry with them and no longer want to punish them. *Hopefully she'll understand and forgive you, if she really loves you... She'd find a way to forgive him for the theft of the money... Still, for those flashes of genius, you can forgive him anything.* VERB V n V n for n/-ing V n n Also V

2 If you say that someone could **be forgiven for** doing something, you mean that they were wrong or mistaken, but not seriously, because many people would have done the same thing in those circumstances. *Looking at the figures, you could be forgiven for thinking the recession is already over... If the research which enticed them to Britain is removed, they can be forgiven for feeling betrayed.* V-PASSIVE =be excused for be V-ed for -ing/n

3 **Forgive** is used in polite expressions and apologies like '**forgive me**' and '**forgive my ignorance**' when you are saying or doing something that might seem rude, silly, or complicated. *Forgive me, I don't mean to insult you... I do hope you'll forgive me but I've got to leave... 'Forgive my manners,' she said calmly. 'I neglected to introduce myself.'* VERB PRAGMATICS V n

4 If an organization such as a bank **forgives** someone's debt, they agree not to ask for that money to be repaid. *The American Congress has agreed to forgive Egypt's military debt.* VERB V n

forgiveness /fəʳgɪvnəs/. If you ask for **forgiveness**, you ask to be forgiven for something wrong that you have done. *I offered up a short prayer for forgiveness. ...a spirit of forgiveness and national reconciliation.* ◆◇◇◇◇ N-UNCOUNT

forgiving /fəʳgɪvɪŋ/. Someone who is **forgiving** is willing to forgive. *Voters can be remarkably forgiving of presidents who fail to keep their campaign promises... I don't think people are in a very forgiving mood.* ADJ-GRADED

forgo /fɔːʳgoʊ/. See **forego**.

forgot /fəʳgɒt/. **Forgot** is the past tense of **forget**.

forgotten /fəʳgɒtᵊn/. **Forgotten** is the past participle of **forget**.

fork /fɔːʳk/ **forks, forking, forked** ◆◆◇◇◇

1 A **fork** is an implement that you eat food with. It consists of three or four long thin prongs on the end of a handle. *...knives and forks.* N-COUNT

2 If you **fork** food **into** your mouth or **onto** a plate, you put it there using a fork. *Ann forked some fish into her mouth... He forked an egg onto a piece of bread and folded it into a sandwich.* VERB V n into/onto n

3 A garden **fork** is a large tool that you use to break up soil when you are gardening. It consists of three or four long prongs attached to a long handle. N-COUNT

4 If you **fork** something such as manure or hay, you move it from one place to another using a garden fork. *They started me off in the gardens as a handyman. Digging, forking manure, that kind of thing... Farmers cut the hay, fork it on to a cart and then store it in barns.* VERB V n V n prep

5 A **fork** in a road, path, or river is a point at which it divides into two parts and forms a 'Y' shape. *We arrived at a fork in the road... The road divides; you should take the right fork. ...the fork of the Delaware and Lehigh rivers.* N-COUNT: usu with supp

6 If a road, path, or river **forks**, it forms a fork. *Beyond the village the road forked... The path dipped down to a sort of cove, and then it forked in two directions.* VB: no cont V V prep/adv

7 If you **fork** in a particular direction when you are travelling along a road or path, you choose one of the forks in it and travel down it. *Just before the town boundary fork left onto a minor road.* VERB V prep/adv

8 See also **tuning fork**.

fork out. If you **fork out** for something, you spend a lot of money on it; an informal expression. *He will have to fork out for private school fees for Nina... You don't ask people to fork out every time they drive up the motorways... Britons fork out more than a billion pounds a year on toys.* PHRASAL VERB V P for/on n V P V P n for/on n

forked /fɔːʳkt/. Something that divides into two parts and forms a 'Y' shape can be described as **forked**. *Jaegers are swift black birds with long forked tails.* ADJ: usu ADJ n

forked lightning. **Forked lightning** is lightning that is in the form of jagged lines of bright light that divide into two or more parts near the ground. N-UNCOUNT

forkful /fɔːʳkfʊl/ **forkfuls.** You can refer to an amount of food on a fork as a **forkful** of food. *I put a forkful of fillet steak in my mouth... He lingered over the chocolate cake, letting each forkful slowly dissolve in his mouth.* N-COUNT: usu N of n

fork-lift truck, fork-lift trucks. A **fork-lift truck** or a **fork-lift** is a small vehicle with two movable parts on the front that are used to lift heavy loads. N-COUNT

forlorn /fɔːʳlɔːʳn/ ◆◇◇◇◇

1 If someone is **forlorn**, they are lonely and unhappy. *One of the demonstrators, a young woman, sat forlorn on the pavement... He looked a forlorn figure as he limped off after 26 minutes.* ♦ **forlornly** *A Dutch newspaper photographed the president waiting forlornly in the rain.* ADJ-GRADED: ADJ n, v-link ADJ, ADJ after v ADV-GRADED: ADV with v

2 If a place is **forlorn**, it is deserted or uncared for, or has little in it. *They headed inland on a forlorn road that was rutted and pocked... The once glorious palaces stood empty and forlorn.* ♦ **forlornly** *It is stranded somewhat forlornly in the middle of the plain.* ADJ-GRADED =desolate ADV-GRADED: ADV with v

3 If you describe a hope or attempt as a **forlorn** hope or attempt, you think that it has no chance of success or is the result of desperation. *Peasants have left the land in the forlorn hope of finding a better life in cities. ...a forlorn effort to keep from losing my mind.* ♦ **forlornly** *His father forlornly hoped someone might have seen them.* ADJ-GRADED: usu ADJ n ADV-GRADED: ADV with v

form /fɔːʳm/ **forms, forming, formed** ◆◆◆◆◆

1 A **form** of something is a type or kind of it. *He contracted a rare form of cancer... Doctors are willing to take some form of industrial action... I am against hunting in any form.* N-COUNT: with supp, oft N of n

2 When something can exist or happen in several possible ways, you can use **form** to refer to one particular way in which it exists or happens. *Valleys often take the form of deep canyons... They received a benefit in the form of a tax reduction... In its present form, the law could lead to new injustices.* N-COUNT: with supp, oft N of n

3 When a particular shape **forms** or **is formed**, people or things move or are arranged so that this shape is made. *A queue forms outside Peter's study... They formed a circle and sang 'Auld Lang Syne'... The General gave orders for the cadets to form into lines.* V-ERG V V n V into n Also V n into n

4 The **form** of something is its shape. *...the form of the body.* N-COUNT: with supp

5 You can refer to something that you can see as a **form** if you cannot see it clearly, or if its outline is the clearest or most striking aspect of it. *She thought she'd never been so glad to see his bulky form.* N-COUNT: usu with supp

6 If something is arranged or changed so that it becomes similar to a thing with a particular structure or function, you can say that it **forms** that thing. *These panels folded up to form a screen some five feet tall... All the buildings have names and form a half circle.* VERB V n

7 If something consists of particular things, people, or features, you can say that they **form** that thing. *...the articles that formed the basis of Randolph's book... Cereals form the staple diet of an enormous number of people around the world.* VERB V n

8 If you **form** an organization, group, or company, you start it. *They tried to form a study group on human rights... They formed themselves into teams.* VERB V n V pron-refl into n

9 When something natural **forms** or **is formed**, it begins to exist and develop. *The stars must have formed 10 to 15 billion years ago... Huge ice sheets were formed.* V-ERG V be V-ed

10 If you **form** something such as a relationship with someone, or if you **form** a habit or an idea, V-ERG

you begin to have it and develop it. If a relationship, a habit, or an idea **forms**, it begins to exist and develop. *This should help him form a relationship with me... She had formed the habit of giving herself freely to men. ...an idea formed in his mind.* V n / V

11 If you say that something **forms** a person's character or personality, you mean that it has a strong influence on them and causes them to develop in a particular way. *Anger at injustice formed his character.* VERB =mould / V n

12 In sport, **form** refers to the ability or success of a person or animal over a period of time. *His form this season has been brilliant... Leconte showed good form.* N-UNCOUNT: usu supp N

13 A **form** is a paper with questions on it and spaces marked where you should write the answers. Forms usually ask you to give details about yourself, for example when you are applying for a job or joining an organization. *You will be asked to fill in a form with details of your birth and occupation. ...application forms.* N-COUNT

14 See also **sixth form**.

15 If you say that it is **bad form** to behave in a particular way, you mean that it is rude and impolite; used in British English. *It was thought bad form to discuss business on social occasions.* PHRASES usu PHR after v, v-link PHR

16 If you say that someone is **in good form**, you mean that they seem healthy and cheerful; used in British English. v-link PHR

17 If you say that someone is **off form**, you think they are not performing as well as they usually do; used in British English. v-link PHR =below par

18 If you say that someone is **on form**, you think that they are performing their usual activity very well; used in British English. *Robert Redford is back on form in his new movie 'Sneakers'.* v-link PHR

19 When something **takes form**, it develops or begins to be visible. *As plans took form in her mind, she realized the need for an accomplice... The face of Mrs Lisbon took form in the dimness.* V inflects

20 If someone or something behaves **true to form**, they do what is expected and is typical of them. *Before the train had left the outskirts of London he behaved true to form and began a conversation... My luck was running true to form... True to form, she kept her guests waiting for more than 90 minutes.* v PHR, PHR with cl

formal /fɔːʳməl/ ◆◆◆◆◇

1 **Formal** speech or behaviour is very correct and serious rather than relaxed and friendly, and is used especially in official situations. *He wrote a very formal letter of apology to Douglas... Business relationships are necessarily a bit more formal.* ADJ-GRADED ≠informal ♦ **formally** *He took her back to Vincent Square in a taxi, saying goodnight formally on the doorstep.* ADV-GRADED: ADV with v ♦ **formality** *Lillith's formality and seriousness amused him.* N-UNCOUNT

2 A **formal** action, statement, or request is an official one. *The European Community began formal talks on enlargement... No formal announcement had been made. ...a formal application.* ADJ: ADJ n ≠informal ♦ **formally** *Diplomats haven't formally agreed to Anderson's plan... They are now formally separated and they will continue to lead their own lives.* ADV: ADV with v

3 **Formal** occasions are ones at which people wear smart clothes and behave correctly in accordance with particular conventions. *One evening the film company arranged a formal dinner after the play.* ADJ-GRADED: usu ADJ n ≠informal

4 **Formal** clothes are very smart clothes that are suitable for formal occasions. *They wore ordinary ties instead of the more formal high collar and cravat.* ADJ-GRADED: ADJ n ≠informal, casual ♦ **formally** *It was really too warm for her to dress so formally.* ADV-GRADED: ADV after v, ADV -ed

5 Something that is done, written, or studied in a **formal** way has a very ordered, organized method or style. *This does not encourage the child to analyse the environment in a formal way... Classic Greek drama was written in verse, usually in an elevated and formal style. ...a formal methodology.* ADJ-GRADED

6 **Formal** education or training is given officially, usually in a school, college, or university. *Although his formal education stopped after primary school, he was an avid reader... Leroy didn't have any formal dance training.* ADJ: ADJ n ♦ **formally** *Mr Dawe was the ancient, formally trained head gardener.* ADV: ADV -ed

7 A **formal** garden or room is arranged in a very regular and controlled way, especially according to certain conventions of design. *...a formal herb garden... The Coronata wallpaper lends a formal air to the dining room.* ADJ ≠informal

8 See also **formality**.

formaldehyde /fɔːʳmældihaɪd/. **Formaldehyde** is a strong-smelling gas, used especially to preserve specimens in biology. N-UNCOUNT

formalise /fɔːʳməlaɪz/. See **formalize**.

formalism /fɔːʳməlɪzəm/. **Formalism** is a style, especially in art, in which great attention is paid to the outward form or appearance rather than to the inner reality or significance of things. *...the rigid formalism of classical ballet.* N-UNCOUNT ♦ **formalist** *...art based on formalist principles.* ADJ: ADJ n

formality /fɔːʳmælɪti/ **formalities** ◆◇◇◇◇

1 If you say that an action or procedure is just a **formality**, you mean that it is done only because it is normally done, and that it will not have any real effect on the situation. *Ingrid considered her marriage to Roberto not a mere formality but a sanctification of their relationship.* N-COUNT

2 **Formalities** are formal actions or procedures that are conventionally carried out as part of an activity or event. *They are whisked through the immigration and customs formalities in a matter of minutes.* N-COUNT: usu pl

3 See also **formal**.

formalize /fɔːʳməlaɪz/ **formalizes, formalizing, formalized;** also spelled **formalise** in British English. If you **formalize** a plan, idea, arrangement, or system, you make it formal and official. *A recent treaty signed by Russia, Canada and Japan formalized an agreement to work together to stop the pirates... She feels the time has come to formalise her relationship with Tempelsman.* ◆◇◇◇◇ VERB / V n ♦ **formalization** /fɔːʳməlaɪzeɪʃən/ **formalizations** *The formalization of co-operation between the republics would produce progress.* N-VAR: oft N of n

format /fɔːʳmæt/ **formats, formatting, formatted** ◆◆◇◇◇

1 The **format** of something is the way or order in which it is arranged and presented. *I had met with him to explain the format of the programme and what we had in mind. ...a large-format book.* N-COUNT

2 The **format** of a piece of computer software or a musical recording is the type of equipment on which it is designed to be used or played. For example, the formats in which a musical recording is normally available are vinyl, CD, and cassette. *His latest album is available on all formats.* N-COUNT

3 To **format** a computer disk means to run a program so that the disk can be written on. VERB: V n

formation /fɔːʳmeɪʃən/ **formations** ◆◆◇◇◇

1 The **formation** of something is the starting or creation of it. *It's expected that Mr Mugabe will announce the formation of a new government.* N-UNCOUNT: with supp, usu the N of n =creation

2 The **formation** of an idea, habit, relationship, or character is the process of developing and establishing it. *My profession had an important influence in the formation of my character and temperament.* N-UNCOUNT: with supp =development

3 If people or things are in **formation**, they are arranged in a particular pattern as they move. *He was flying in formation with seven other jets... They saw a squadron of fifteen motorcycle policemen driving in V-formation... The dancers step into a formation which represents the human being.* N-COUNT: also a N, usu in N

4 A rock or cloud **formation** is rock or cloud of a particular shape or structure. *...a vast rock formation shaped like a pillar... Enormous cloud formations formed a purple mass.* N-COUNT: n N

formative /fɔːʳmətɪv/. A **formative** period of time or experience is one that has an important and lasting influence on a person's character and attitudes. *She was born in Barbados but spent her formative years growing up in east London.* ◆◇◇◇◇ ADJ-GRADED: usu ADJ n

former /fɔːʳməʳ/ 

1 **Former** is used to describe someone who used to ADJ:

have a particular job, position, or role, but no longer has it. *The unemployed executives include former sales managers, directors and accountants. ...former President Richard Nixon.* ADJ n =ex-

2 Former is used to refer to countries which no longer exist or whose boundaries have changed. *...the former Soviet Union. ...the former Yugoslavia.* ADJ: ADJ n

3 Former is used to describe something which used to belong to someone or which used to be a particular thing. *...the former home of Sir Christopher Wren. ...a former monastery.* ADJ: ADJ n

4 Former is used to describe a situation or period of time which came before the present one; a formal use. *He would want you to remember him as he was in former years.* ADJ: ADJ n

5 When two people, things, or groups have just been mentioned, you can refer to the first of them as **the former**. *Given the choice between a pure white T-shirt and a more expensive, dirty cream one, most people can be forgiven for choosing the former... If the family home and joint pension rights are of equal value, the wife may choose the former and the husband the latter.* PRON: *the* PRON ≠latter

formerly /fɔːʳməʳli/. If something happened or was true **formerly**, it happened or was true in the past. *He had formerly been in the Navy. ...east Germany's formerly state-controlled companies.* ◆◆◇◇◇ ADV: ADV with cl/group, ADV before v

Formica /fɔːʳmaɪkə/. **Formica** is a hard plastic that is used for covering surfaces such as kitchen tables or worktops. **Formica** is a trademark. N-UNCOUNT

formidable /fɔːʳmɪdəbᵊl, fəʳmɪd-/. If you describe something or someone as **formidable**, you mean that you feel slightly frightened by them because they are very impressive or considerable. *We have a formidable task ahead of us... Marsalis has a formidable reputation in both jazz and classical music... She looked every bit as formidable as her mother.* ♦ **formidably** *Sofia was attractive and formidably intelligent.* ◆◆◇◇◇ ADJ-GRADED =daunting; ADV: ADV adj

formless /fɔːʳmləs/. Something that is **formless** does not have a clear or definite structure or shape. *A series of largely formless images rushed across the screen.* ADJ =amorphous

formula /fɔːʳmjʊlə/ **formulae** or **formulas** ◆◆◆◇◇

1 A **formula** is a plan that is devised as a way of dealing with a particular problem. *It is difficult to imagine how the North and South could ever agree on a formula to unify the divided peninsula. ...a peace formula.* N-COUNT: usu with supp

2 A **formula for** a particular situation, usually a good one, is a course of action or a combination of actions that is certain or likely to result in that situation. *After he was officially pronounced the world's oldest man, he offered this simple formula for a long and happy life... Clever exploitation of the latest technology would be a sure formula for success... Socialism does not after all offer a magic formula for prosperity and human dignity.* N-SING: N *for* n =recipe

3 A **formula** is a group of letters, numbers, or other symbols which represents a scientific or mathematical rule. *He developed a mathematical formula describing the distances of the planets from the Sun.* N-COUNT

4 In science, the **formula** for a substance is a list of the amounts of various substances which make up that substance, or an indication of the atoms that it is composed of. N-COUNT

5 Formula is used followed by a number to indicate a particular type of racing car or something relating to that type of car. *...Formula 1 racing cars. ...Formula 3000 racing.* N-UNCOUNT: N num

6 Formula is a powder which you mix with water to make artificial milk for babies. *...bottles of formula.* N-UNCOUNT

formulaic /fɔːʳmjʊleɪɪk/. If you describe a way of saying or doing something as **formulaic**, you are criticizing it because it is not original and has been used many times before in similar situations. *His paintings are contrived and formulaic.* ADJ-GRADED PRAGMATICS ≠original

formulate /fɔːʳmjʊleɪt/ **formulates, formulating, formulated** ◆◆◇◇◇

1 If you **formulate** something such as a plan or proposal, you invent it, thinking about the details carefully. *Little by little, he formulated his plan for escape.* VERB =devise V n

2 If you **formulate** a thought, opinion, or idea, you express it or describe it using particular words. *I was impressed by the way he could formulate his ideas.* VERB =express V n

formulation /fɔːʳmjʊleɪʃᵊn/ **formulations** ◆◇◇◇◇

1 The **formulation** of something such as a medicine or a beauty product is the way in which different ingredients are combined to make it. You can also say that the finished product is a **formulation**. *There have been problems with the formulation of the vaccine... You can buy a formulation containing royal jelly, pollen and vitamin C.* N-VAR =formula

2 The **formulation** of something such as policy or plans is the way that they have been devised and thought out. *...the process of policy formulation and implementation.* N-UNCOUNT

3 Formulation or a **formulation** is the way in which you express your thoughts and ideas. *Freedom, said the Soviet President, in a formulation that could have come from any American leader, was the pivotal element of his reforms.* N-VAR =form of words

fornicate /fɔːʳnɪkeɪt/ **fornicates, fornicating, fornicated.** To **fornicate** means to have sex with someone who you are not married to; a formal or Biblical word used showing disapproval. V-RECIP: pl-n V, V *with* n, V (non-recip) PRAGMATICS ♦ **fornication** /fɔːʳnɪkeɪʃᵊn/ *Fornication is a crime in some American states.* N-UNCOUNT

forsake /fəʳseɪk/ **forsakes, forsaking, forsook** /fəʳsʊk/ **forsaken** ◆◇◇◇◇

1 If you **forsake** someone, you leave them when you should have stayed, or stop helping them or looking after them; a literary use, used showing disapproval. *I still love him and I would never forsake him. ...children who've been forsaken by individual teachers... I don't want him to feel forsaken and unhappy.* VERB PRAGMATICS V n V-ed

2 If you **forsake** something, you stop doing it, using it, or having it; a literary use. *He doubted their claim to have forsaken military solutions to the civil war... But that didn't make her forsake her ideals... She forsook her notebook for new technology.* VERB V n V n *for* n

3 If you **forsake** a place or a thing, you leave it or go away from it; a literary use. *At 53 he has no plans to forsake the hills.* VERB V n

4 See also **God-forsaken**.

forsaken /fəʳseɪkᵊn/. A **forsaken** place is not lived in, used, or looked after; a literary word. *The delta region of the Rio Grande river was a forsaken land of thickets and swamps. ...a forsaken church and a derelict hotel.* ADJ: ADJ n

forswear /fɔːʳsweəʳ/ **forswears, forswearing, forswore, forsworn.** If you **forswear** something, you promise that you will stop doing it, having it, or using it; a formal or literary word. *The party was offered a share of government if it forswore violence.* VERB =renounce V n

forsythia /fɔːʳsaɪθiə, AM -sɪθ-/ **forsythias. Forsythia** is a bush that has spiky yellow flowers on it. The flowers appear in the spring before the leaves have grown. N-VAR

fort /fɔːʳt/ **forts** ◆◆◇◇◇

1 A **fort** is a strong building or a place with a wall or fence around it where soldiers can stay and be safe from the enemy. N-COUNT: oft in names

2 If you **hold the fort** for someone, you look after things for them while they are somewhere else or busy doing something else. *His business partner is holding the fort while he is away.* PHRASE: V inflects, oft PHR *for* n

forte /fɔːʳteɪ/ **fortes.** Pronounced /fɔʳt/ for meaning 1 in American English.

1 You can say that a particular activity is your **forte** if you are very good at it. *Originality was never his forte.* N-COUNT: usu sing, poss N =strong point

2 A piece of music that is played **forte** is played loudly; a technical term in music. ADV: ADV after v

forth /fɔːʳθ/ ◆◆◆◇◇

In addition to the uses shown below, **forth** is also used in the phrasal verbs 'put forth' and 'set forth'.

1 When someone goes **forth** from a place, they ADV:

leave it; a literary use. *Go forth into the desert... I came forth to take the air.* — ADV after v =out

2 If one thing brings **forth** another, the first thing produces the second; a literary use. *Nature herself brings forth new forms of life... My reflections brought forth no conclusion.* — ADV: ADV after v

3 When someone or something is brought **forth**, they are brought to a place or moved into a position where people can see them; a literary use. *Pilate ordered Jesus to be brought forth... He brought forth a small gold amulet from beneath his robe.* — ADV: ADV after v =out

4 • **back and forth**: see **back**. • to **hold forth**: see **hold**.

forthcoming /fɔːʳθkʌmɪŋ/ ◆◆◇◇◇

1 A **forthcoming** event is planned to happen soon. *He will stand again in the forthcoming election.* — ADJ: ADJ n

2 If something that you want, need, or expect is **forthcoming**, it is given to you or it happens; a formal use. *They promised that the money would be forthcoming... We must first see some real evidence. So far it is not been forthcoming... One source predicts no major shift in policy will be forthcoming at the committee hearings.* — ADJ: v-link ADJ

3 If you say that someone is **forthcoming**, you mean that they willingly give information when you ask them. — ADJ-GRADED: usu v-link ADJ

forthright /fɔːʳθraɪt/. If you describe someone as **forthright**, you admire them because they show clearly and strongly what they think and feel. — ◆◇◇◇◇ ADJ-GRADED PRAGMATICS =direct

forthwith /fɔːʳθwɪθ/. **Forthwith** means immediately; a formal word. *I could have you arrested forthwith!* — ADV: ADV with v =immediately

fortieth /fɔːʳtiəθ/. The **fortieth** item in a series is the one that you count as number forty. — ◆◆◆◆◇ ORD

fortification /fɔːʳtɪfɪkeɪʃən/ **fortifications.** **Fortifications** are buildings, walls, or ditches that are built to protect a place against attack. *The government has started building fortifications along its eastern border.* • See also **fortify**. — N-COUNT: usu pl =defence

fortified wine, fortified wines. **Fortified wine** is an alcoholic drink such as sherry or port that is made by mixing wine with a small amount of brandy or strong alcohol. — N-MASS

fortify /fɔːʳtɪfaɪ/ **fortifies, fortifying, fortified** ◆◇◇◇◇

1 To **fortify** a place means to make it stronger and less easy to attack, often by building a wall or ditch round it. *...British soldiers working to fortify an airbase in Bahrain.* — VERB, V n ♦ **fortified** *He remains barricaded inside his heavily-fortified mansion. ...fortified castles and villages.* — ADJ-GRADED

2 If food or drink **is fortified**, another substance is added to it to make it healthier or stronger. *It has also been fortified with vitamin C... All sherry is made from wine fortified with brandy. ...fortified cereal products.* — VB: usu passive, be V-ed with n, V-ed ♦ **fortification** *In some countries, iron fortification of foods is carried out to reduce iron deficiency.* — N-UNCOUNT

3 If you **are fortified** by something such as food, drink, or an idea, it makes you feel more cheerful, determined, or energetic. *The volunteers were fortified by their patriotic belief... They will be laying on liquid refreshment to revitalise flagging energies and fortify brides-to-be for the shopping extravaganza ahead... Would you care for some tea, or even a light meal, to fortify yourself before your adventure?... They drove on fortified with still more Scotch.* — VERB =sustain, be V-ed, V n, V pron-refl, V-ed

4 To **fortify** something means to make it more powerful and more likely to succeed; a formal use. *His declared agenda is to raise standards in schools, fortify parent power and decentralise control.* — VERB =strengthen, V n

fortissimo /fɔːʳtɪsɪmoʊ/. A piece of music that is played **fortissimo** is played very loudly; a technical term in music. — ADV: ADV after v

fortitude /fɔːʳtɪtjuːd, AM -tuːd/. If you say that someone has shown **fortitude**, you admire them for being brave, calm, and uncomplaining when they have experienced something unpleasant or painful; a formal word. *He suffered a long series of illnesses with tremendous dignity and fortitude.* — N-UNCOUNT PRAGMATICS =courage, grit

fortnight /fɔːʳtnaɪt/ **fortnights.** A **fortnight** is a period of two weeks; used mainly in British English. *I hope to be back in a fortnight.* — ◆◆◇◇◇ N-COUNT

fortnightly /fɔːʳtnaɪtli/. In British English, a **fortnightly** event or publication happens or appears once a fortnight. The American word is **biweekly**. *They are now holding their fortnightly meetings at The New Invention Victory Club. ...an exciting new fortnightly magazine.* — ADJ: ADJ n ► Also an adverb. *They recently put my rent up and I pay it fortnightly. ...Overseas Jobs Express, published fortnightly.* — ADV: ADV after v

fortress /fɔːʳtrɪs/ **fortresses.** A **fortress** is a castle or other large strong building, or a well-protected place, which is intended to be difficult for enemies to enter. *...a 13th-century fortress.* — ◆◇◇◇◇ N-COUNT =stronghold

fortuitous /fɔːʳtjuːɪtəs, AM -tuː-/. You can describe something as **fortuitous** if it happens, by chance, to be very successful or pleasant. *Their success is the result of a fortuitous combination of circumstances.* — ADJ-GRADED =lucky

fortunate /fɔːʳtʃʊnɪt/. If you say that someone or something is **fortunate**, you mean that they are lucky. *He was extremely fortunate to survive... Central London is fortunate in having so many large parks and open spaces... It was fortunate that the water was shallow... She is in the fortunate position of having plenty of choice.* — ◆◆◇◇◇ ADJ-GRADED: oft ADJ to-inf, ADJ in -ing, it v-link ADJ that

fortunately /fɔːʳtʃʊnɪtli/. **Fortunately** is used to introduce or indicate a statement about an event or situation that is good. *Fortunately, the weather that winter was reasonably mild... Fortunately for me, my friend saw that something was seriously wrong... Bombs had hit the building a number of times but fortunately no one was hurt.* — ◆◆◇◇◇ ADV-GRADED: ADV with cl, oft ADV for n =luckily

fortune /fɔːʳtʃuːn/ **fortunes** ◆◆◆◇◇

1 You can refer to a large sum of money as a **fortune** or a small **fortune** to emphasize how large it is. *We had to eat out all the time. It ended up costing a fortune... He made a small fortune in the London property boom.* — N-COUNT PRAGMATICS

2 Someone who has a **fortune** has a very large amount of money. *He made his fortune in car sales... Having spent his rich wife's fortune, the Major ended up in a debtors' prison.* — N-COUNT: oft poss N

3 **Fortune** or good **fortune** is good luck. Ill **fortune** is bad luck. *Government ministers are starting to wonder how long their good fortune can last.* — N-UNCOUNT

4 If you talk about someone's **fortunes** or the **fortunes** of something, you are talking about the extent to which they are doing well or being successful. *The electoral fortunes of the Liberal Democratic party may decline... She kept up with the fortunes of the Reeves family... The company had to do something to reverse its sliding fortunes.* — N-PLURAL: with poss

5 If you talk about the way someone or something is treated by **fortune**, you are referring to the good or bad luck that they have. *He is certainly being smiled on by fortune.* — N-UNCOUNT

6 When someone **tells** your **fortune**, they tell you what they think will happen to you in the future, which they say is shown, for example, by the lines on your hand. — PHRASE: V inflects

fortune cookie, fortune cookies. A **fortune cookie** is a biscuit which contains a piece of paper which is supposed to say what will happen to you in the future. Fortune cookies are often served in Chinese restaurants. — N-COUNT

fortune-teller, fortune-tellers. A **fortune-teller** is a person who tells you what they think will happen to you in the future, after looking at something such as the lines on your hand. — N-COUNT

forty /fɔːʳti/ **forties.** 

1 **Forty** is the number 40. • **forty winks**: see **wink**. — NUM

2 When you talk about the **forties**, you are referring to numbers between 40 and 49. For example, if you are **in your forties**, you are aged between 40 and 49. If the temperature is **in the forties**, the temperature is between 40 and 49 degrees. *He was a big man in his forties, smartly dressed in a suit and tie.* — N-PLURAL

3 **The forties** is the decade between 1940 and 1949. — N-PLURAL:

Steel cans were introduced sometime during the forties.
the N

forum /fɔːrəm/ **forums** ◆◆◇◇◇

1 A **forum** is a place, situation, or group in which people exchange ideas and discuss issues, especially important public issues. *Members of the council agreed that it still had an important role as a forum for discussion... The organisation would provide a forum where problems could be discussed.*
N-COUNT: with supp, oft N for n/-ing

2 In ancient Roman towns, the **forum** was a square where people met to discuss business and political matters.
N-COUNT

forward /fɔːʳwəʳd/ **forwards, forwarding, forwarded** ◆◆◆◆◇

In addition to the uses shown below, **forward** is also used in phrasal verbs such as 'bring forward' and 'look forward to'. In British English, **forwards** is often used as an adverb instead of **forward** , in senses 1, 4, and 7.

1 If you move or look **forward**, you move or look in a direction that is in front of you. In British English, you can also move or look **forwards.** *He came forward with his hand out. 'Mr and Mrs Selby?' he enquired... She fell forwards on to her face... He continued to walk, didn't look at the car, kept his face forward.*
ADV: ADV after v ≠backwards

2 **Forward** means in a position near the front of something such as a building or a vehicle. *The best seats are in the aisle and as far forward as possible... The other car had a 3-inch lower driving seat and had its engine mounted further forward.* ▶ Also an adjective. *Reinforcements were needed to allow more troops to move to forward positions.*
ADV-GRADED: be ADV, ADV after v
ADJ-GRADED: ADJ n

3 If one thing is **forward of** another, especially on a ship or aircraft, the first thing is in front of the second thing or further ahead. *Forward of the main cabin are the guest cabins... Sixty-one small parachute symbols were painted on the left side just forward of the wing.*
PHR-PREP ≠behind

4 If you say that someone looks **forward**, you approve of them because they think about what will happen in the future and plan for it. In British English, you can also say that someone looks **forwards**. *Now the leadership wants to look forward, and to outline a strategy for the rest of the century... People should forget and look forwards... Manchester United has always been a forward-looking club.* ▶ Also an adjective. *The university system requires more forward planning.*
ADV: usu ADV after v, also ADV adj PRAGMATICS
ADJ: ADJ n

5 If you put a clock or watch **forward**, you change the time shown on it so that it shows a later time, for example when the time changes to summer time. *When we put the clocks forward in March we go into British Summer Time.*
ADV: ADV after v

6 When you are referring to a particular time, if you say that something was true **from** that time **forward**, you mean that it became true at that time, and continued to be true afterwards. *Velazquez's work from that time forward was confined largely to portraits of the royal family.*
ADV: from n ADV =on

7 You use **forward** to indicate that something progresses or improves. In British English, you can also use **forwards**. *The European Community aimed at moving forward on economic and monetary union... They just couldn't see any way forward... Space scientists and astronomers have taken another step forwards.*
ADV: ADV after v, n ADV

8 If you **forward** something, you cause it to progress or improve; used in written English. *The music is used to forward the plot, not simply to keep the toes tapping. ...the scientist who has done the most to forward the cause of public understanding over the year.*
VERB =further
V n

9 If something or someone is put **forward**, or comes **forward**, they are suggested or offered as suitable for a particular purpose. *Over the years several similar theories have been put forward... Next month the Commission is to bring forward its first proposals for action... He was putting himself forward as a Democrat... Investigations have ground to a standstill because no witnesses have come forward.*
ADV: ADV after v

10 If a letter or message **is forwarded** to someone, it is sent to the place where they are, after having been sent to a different place earlier. *When he's out on the road, office calls are forwarded to the cellular phone in his truck... A hospital appointment letter for Jane was forwarded from the clinic.*
VERB =send on
be V-ed from/to n
Also V n, V n from/to n

11 If you describe someone as **forward**, you mean that they speak very confidently and frankly, but that they do not always show enough respect for the feelings or the position of the person they are talking to. *He's very forward and confident and chats happily to other people.* ♦ **forwardness** *Rather taken aback by such forwardness, I slammed down the phone.*
ADJ-GRADED: usu v-link ADJ
N-UNCOUNT

12 In football, rugby, or hockey, a **forward** is a player whose usual position is in the opponents' half of the field, and whose usual job is to attack or score goals. ● See also **centre-forward.**
N-COUNT

13 ● **backwards and forwards**: see **backwards.** ● to **look forward to** something: see **look.**

forwarding address, forwarding addresses. A **forwarding address** is an address that you give to someone when you go and live somewhere else so that they can send your mail on to you. *The former owner had not left any forwarding address.*
N-COUNT

forward-looking. If you describe a person or organization as **forward-looking**, you approve of the fact that they think about the future or have modern ideas. *...the need for the party to be forward-looking, to identify with changing attitudes among voters.*
ADJ-GRADED PRAGMATICS

forwards /fɔːʳwəʳdz/. See **forward.**

forwent /fɔːʳwent/. **Forwent** is the past tense of **forego.**

fossil /fɒsəl/ **fossils.** A **fossil** is the hardened remains of a prehistoric animal or plant that are found inside a rock.
◆◆◇◇◇ N-COUNT

fossil fuel, fossil fuels; also spelled **fossil-fuel. Fossil fuel** is fuel such as coal, oil, or peat that is formed from the decayed remains of plants or animals.
◆◇◇◇◇ N-MASS

fossilize /fɒsɪlaɪz/ **fossilizes, fossilizing, fossilized;** also spelled **fossilise** in British English.

1 If the remains of an animal or plant **fossilize** or **are fossilized**, they become hard and form fossils, instead of decaying completely. *The most important parts, the flowers, rarely fossilise... The survival of the proteins depends on the way in which bones are fossilised. ...fossilized dinosaur bones.*
V-ERG
V
be V-ed
V-ed

2 If you say that ideas, attitudes, or ways of behaving **have fossilized** or **have been fossilized**, you are criticizing the fact that they are fixed and unlikely to change, in spite of changing situations or circumstances. *What they seem to want to do in fact is fossilize the particular environment in which people live and work... Needs change while policies fossilize.* ♦ **fossilized** *Efforts have been made to breathe some new life into these fossilized organisations.*
V-ERG PRAGMATICS
V n
V
ADJ-GRADED

foster /fɒstəʳ, AM fɔːst-/ **fosters, fostering, fostered** ◆◆◇◇◇

1 **Foster** parents are people who officially take a child into their family for a period of time, without becoming the child's legal parents. The child is referred to as their **foster** child. *Little Jack was placed with foster parents... The foster mother was a wonderful, warm person.*
ADJ: ADJ n

2 If you **foster** a child, you take it into your family for a period of time, without becoming its legal parent. *She has since gone on to find happiness by fostering more than 100 children.*
VERB
V n

3 To **foster** something such as an activity or idea means to help it to develop. *He said that developed countries had a responsibility to foster global economic growth to help new democracies... Its cash crisis has been fostered by declining property values.*
VERB
V n

fought /fɔːt/. **Fought** is the past tense and past participle of **fight.**

foul /faʊl/ **fouler, foulest; fouls, fouling, fouled** ◆◆◇◇◇

1 If you describe something as **foul**, you mean it is dirty and smells or tastes unpleasant. *...foul polluted water... The pot-pourri of smells in the air was quite foul.* ADJ-GRADED =disgusting

2 **Foul** language is offensive and contains swear words or rude words. *He was sent off for using foul language in a match last Sunday... He had a foul mouth.* ADJ-GRADED: usu ADJ n =filthy

3 If someone has a **foul** temper or is in a **foul** mood, they become angry or violent very suddenly and easily. *Collins was in a foul mood even before the interviews began.* ADJ-GRADED: usu ADJ n =bad

4 **Foul** weather is unpleasant, windy, and stormy. ADJ-GRADED

5 If a place **is fouled** by someone or something, they make it dirty. *A village's entire beach and harbor can be fouled by a single rotting whale... Two oil-related accidents near Los Angeles have fouled the ocean and the skies there.* VERB be V-ed V n

6 If an animal **fouls** a place, it drops faeces onto the ground. *It is an offence to let your dog foul a footpath.* VERB V n

7 If a machine or vehicle **fouls** part of its mechanism or if something such as a rope **fouls** the mechanism, the mechanism can no longer work properly because something has become twisted or knotted around it. *The freighter fouled its propeller in fishing nets.* VERB V n

8 In a game or sport, if a player **fouls** another player, they touch them or obstruct them in a way which is not allowed according to the rules. *Middlesbrough's Jimmy Phillips was sent off for fouling Steve Tilson.* VERB V n

9 A **foul** is an act in a game or sport that is not allowed according to the rules. *He picked up his first booking for a 45th-minute foul on Bull.* ► Also an adjective. *...a foul tackle.* N-COUNT: oft N on n ADJ: ADJ n

10 If you **cry foul**, you claim that someone, especially an opponent or rival, has acted illegally or unfairly. *Deprived of the crushing victory it was confidently expecting, the party cried foul.* PHRASES V inflects

11 If someone tries to achieve something **by fair means or foul**, they use every means possible in order to achieve it, and they do not care if their behaviour is dishonest or unfair. *They will only be satisfied if they regain control – by fair means or foul.* PHR after v

12 If you **fall foul of** someone or **run foul of** someone, you do something which gets you into trouble with them; used mainly in British English. *He had fallen foul of the FBI. ...teenagers who run foul of the law.* V inflects, PHR n =run afoul of

foul up. If you **foul up** something such as a plan, you spoil it by doing something wrong or stupid. *There are serious risks that laboratories may foul up these tests.* PHRASAL VERB =mess up V P n (not pron) Also V n P

foul-mouthed. If you describe someone as **foul-mouthed**, you disapprove of them because their language is offensive and contains unacceptable words such as swear words and rude words. *He's a coarse, foul-mouthed bully.* ADJ-GRADED PRAGMATICS

foul play

1 **Foul play** is criminal violence or activity that results in a person's death. *The report says it suspects foul play was involved in the deaths of two journalists.* N-UNCOUNT

2 **Foul play** is unfair or dishonest behaviour, especially during a sports match. *Players were warned twice for foul play.* N-UNCOUNT

foul-up, foul-ups. You can call something that has gone badly wrong as a result of someone's mistakes or carelessness a **foul-up**; used in informal English. *A series of technical foul-ups delayed the launch of the new product.* N-COUNT =bungle

found /faʊnd/ **founds, founding, founded** ◆◆◆◇◇

1 **Found** is the past tense and past participle of **find**.

2 When an institution, company, or organization **is founded** by someone or by a group of people, they get it started, often by providing the necessary money. *The Independent Labour Party was founded in Bradford on January 13, 1893... He founded the Centre for Journalism Studies at University College Cardiff... The business, founded by Dawn and Nigel, suffered financial setbacks.* ♦ **founding** *I have been a member of The Sunday Times Wine Club since its founding in 1973.* ♦ **foundation** /faʊndeɪʃᵊn/ *...the 150th anniversary of the foundation of Kew Gardens.* VERB =set up, establish be V-ed V n V-ed N-SING: with poss N-SING: with poss

3 When a town, important building, or other place **is founded** by someone or by a group of people, they cause it to be built. *The town was founded in 1610.* VB: usu passive be V-ed

4 See also **founded, founding.**

foundation /faʊndeɪʃᵊn/ **foundations** ◆◆◆◇◇

1 The **foundation** of something such as a belief or way of life is the things on which it is based. *Best friends are the foundation of my life... The issue strikes at the very foundation of our community... This laid the foundations for later modern economic growth.* ● If an event **shakes the foundations** of a society or a system of beliefs, it causes great uncertainty and makes people question their most deeply held beliefs. *The destruction of war and the death of millions of young people shook the foundations of Western idealism... Emotional conflict may shake the foundations of even the strongest relationship.* N-COUNT: usu the N of/for n PHRASE: V inflects

2 The **foundations** of a building or other structure are the layer of bricks or concrete below the ground that it is built on. N-PLURAL

3 A **foundation** is an organization which provides money for a special purpose such as research or charity. *...the National Foundation for Educational Research.* N-COUNT

4 If a story, idea, or argument has no **foundation**, there are no facts to prove that it is true. *The allegations were without foundation... Each complaint is analysed very closely, and if it has no foundation it is rejected.* N-UNCOUNT: with brd-neg

5 **Foundation** is a skin-coloured cream that is put on the face before the rest of the make-up is put on. N-MASS

6 See also **found.**

foundation course, foundation courses. In Britain, a **foundation course** is a course that you do at some colleges and universities in order to prepare yourself for a longer or more advanced course. N-COUNT

foundation stone, foundation stones

1 A **foundation stone** is a large smooth block of stone built into a large public building near the bottom. The foundation stone is usually unveiled at a ceremony when the building is complete, and it usually has words cut into it which record the occasion. *The Princess of Wales laid the foundation stone for the extension to the Cathedral.* N-COUNT: oft with poss

2 The **foundation stone** for something is the basic, fundamental part which its existence or success depends on. *...these foundation stones of the future; education, training, research, development.* N-COUNT: usu N of n

founded /faʊndɪd/. If something is **founded on** a particular thing, it is based on it. *The criticisms are founded on facts as well as on convictions... His game is founded on power and determination.* ◆◇◇◇◇ ADJ: v-link ADJ on n

founder /faʊndəʳ/ **founders, foundering, foundered** ◆◆◆◇◇

1 The **founder** of an institution, organization, or building is the person who got it started or caused it to be built, often by providing the necessary money. *He was one of the founders of the university's medical faculty.* N-COUNT: usu with poss

2 If something such as a plan or project **founders**, it fails because of a particular point, difficulty, or problem. *The talks have foundered, largely because of the reluctance of some members of the government to do a deal with criminals.* VERB =fail V

3 If a ship **founders**, it fills with water and sinks. *Three ships foundered in heavy seas.* VERB V

founder member, founder members. A **founder member** of a club, group, or organization is one of the first members, often one who was involved in setting it up. ◆◇◇◇◇ N-COUNT: usu N of n

founding /faʊndɪŋ/. **Founding** means relating to the starting of a particular institution or organization. *The committee held its founding congress in the capital, Riga... He is founding director of The Conservation Foundation.* • See also **found**. ◆◇◇◇◇ ADJ: ADJ n

founding father, founding fathers ◆◇◇◇◇
1 The **founding father** of an institution, organization, or idea is the person who sets it up or who first develops it; a literary expression. N-COUNT: oft N of n =founder
2 The **Founding Fathers** of the United States were the members of the American Constitutional Convention of 1787. N-PROPER-PLURAL

foundling /faʊndlɪŋ/ **foundlings.** A **foundling** is a baby that has been abandoned by its parents, often in a public place, and that has then been found by someone; an old-fashioned word. N-COUNT

foundry /faʊndri/ **foundries.** A **foundry** is a place where metal or glass is melted and formed into particular shapes. N-COUNT

fount /faʊnt/ **founts.** If you describe a person or thing as the **fount of** something, you are saying that they are an important source or supply of it; a literary word. *To the young boy his father was the fount of all knowledge.* N-COUNT: usu sing, N of n =source

fountain /faʊntɪn/ **fountains** ◆◆◇◇◇
1 A **fountain** is an ornamental feature in a pool or lake which consists of a jet of water that is forced up into the air by a pump. N-COUNT
2 A **fountain** of a liquid is an amount of it which is sent up into the air and falls back; a literary use. *The volcano spewed a fountain of molten rock 650 feet in the air.* N-COUNT: usu N of n =jet
3 If you describe a person or thing as a **fountain of** something, you mean they are an important source of it and supply a lot of it; a literary use. *You are a fountain of ideas.* N-COUNT: N of n
4 If a plant produces a **fountain of** flowers, leaves, or branches, it has a lot of stems, leaves, or branches which curve in an arch; a literary use. N-COUNT: N of n

fountain pen, fountain pens. A **fountain pen** is a pen with a nib that is supplied with ink from a container inside the pen. N-COUNT

four /fɔːʳ/ **fours** ◆◆◆◆◆
1 **Four** is the number 4. *Judith is married with four children.* NUM
2 In cricket, if a player hits a **four**, they score four runs by hitting the ball along the ground so that it crosses the boundary at the edge of the playing area. *Taylor hit 13 fours and batted for 140 minutes.* N-COUNT
3 A **four** is a narrow racing boat that is rowed by a team of four people. N-COUNT
4 If you are **on all fours**, your knees, feet, and hands are on the ground. *She crawled on all fours over to the window.* PHRASE: PHR after v, v-link PHR

four-letter word, four-letter words. A **four-letter word** is a short word that people consider to be rude or offensive, usually because it refers to sex or other bodily functions. N-COUNT =swear word

four-poster bed, four-poster beds. A **four-poster bed** or a **four-poster** is a large old-fashioned bed that has a tall post at each corner and curtains that can be drawn around it. N-COUNT

foursome /fɔːʳsəm/ **foursomes.** A **foursome** is a group of four people or things. *The London-based foursome are set to release their fourth single this month.* ◆◇◇◇◇ N-COUNT-COLL

four-square; also spelled **foursquare**.
1 If you say that someone stands **four-square** behind something or something, you mean that they are firm in their support of that person or thing. *They stood four-square behind their chief, and they would not accept pressure on him to resign... He was still certain that Franklin was four-square for reform.* ADJ: v-link ADJ prep
2 A **four-square** building or structure is square in shape and looks solid and well-built. ADJ: usu ADJ n

fourteen /fɔːʳtiːn/. **Fourteen** is the number 14. *I'm fourteen years old.* ◆◆◆◆◆ NUM

fourteenth /fɔːʳtiːnθ/. The **fourteenth** item in a series is the one that you count as number fourteen. ◆◆◆◆◇ ORD

fourth /fɔːʳθ/ **fourths** ◆◆◆◆◇
1 The **fourth** item in a series is the one that you count as number four. *Last year's winner Greg Lemond of the United States is in fourth place.* ORD
2 In American English, a **fourth** is one of four equal parts of something. The British word is **quarter**. *Three-fourths of the public say they favor a national referendum on the issue.* FRACTION

fourth dimension. In physics, **the fourth dimension** is time. The other three dimensions are length, breadth, and height. N-SING: the N

fourthly /fɔːʳθli/. You say **fourthly** when you want to make a fourth point or give a fourth reason for something. *Fourthly, the natural enthusiasm of the student teachers should be maintained.* ADV: ADV with cl PRAGMATICS

Fourth of July. In the United States, the **Fourth of July** is a public holiday when people celebrate the Declaration of Independence in 1776. *On the Fourth of July, my husband and our friends drove into the city to see the fireworks. ...a Fourth of July picnic.* N-SING: usu the N

fowl /faʊl/ **fowls; fowl** can also be used as the plural form. A **fowl** is a bird, especially one that can be eaten as food, such as a duck or a chicken. *Carve the fowl into 8 pieces. ...ducks and many other animals and fowl.* ◆◇◇◇◇ N-COUNT

fox /fɒks/ **foxes, foxing, foxed** ◆◆◇◇◇
1 A **fox** is a wild animal which looks like a dog and has reddish-brown fur, a pointed face and ears, and a thick tail. Foxes eat smaller animals. N-COUNT
2 If you **are foxed** by something, you cannot understand it or solve it; used in informal British English. *I admit I was foxed for some time... Only once did we hit on a question which foxed one of these formidable experts... They're a bit foxed by the colours of the riders' jerseys and hats.* VERB be V-ed V n V-ed
3 If you describe someone as a **fox**, you mean they are very clever, cunning, and deceitful. *Enrico was too good, an old fox, cunning.* N-SING

foxglove /fɒksglʌv/ **foxgloves.** A **foxglove** is a tall plant that has pink or white flowers shaped like bells growing up the stem. N-VAR

foxhole /fɒkshoʊl/ **foxholes.** A **foxhole** is a small pit which soldiers dig as a shelter from the enemy and from which they can shoot. N-COUNT

foxhound /fɒkshaʊnd/ **foxhounds.** A **foxhound** is a type of dog that is trained to hunt foxes. N-COUNT

fox-hunting; also spelled **foxhunting**. **Fox-hunting** is a sport in which people riding horses chase a fox across the countryside. Dogs called hounds are used to find the fox. N-UNCOUNT

foxy /fɒksi/ **foxier, foxiest**
1 If you describe someone as **foxy**, you mean that they are deceitful in a clever, secretive way. *He had wary, foxy eyes.* ADJ-GRADED =crafty
2 If a man calls a woman **foxy**, he means that she is physically attractive; used in informal, mainly American, English. *...a foxy blonde in a turtleneck sweater.* ADJ-GRADED

foyer /fɔɪəʳ, fwaɪeɪ/ **foyers.** A **foyer** is the large area where people meet or wait just inside the main doors of a building such as a theatre, cinema, or hotel. *I went and waited in the foyer.* ◆◇◇◇◇ N-COUNT =lobby

Fr ◆◇◇◇◇
1 **Fr** is a written abbreviation for **French** or **franc**.
2 **Fr** is a written abbreviation for **Father** when it is used in titles before the name of a Catholic priest.

fracas /frækɑː, AM freɪkəs/. A **fracas** is a rough, noisy quarrel or fight. N-SING =brawl

fractal /fræktəl/ **fractals.** In geometry, a **fractal** is an irregular shape which is made up of a large number of smaller shapes which are all identical to each other. N-COUNT: oft N n

fraction /frækʃən/ **fractions** ◆◆◇◇◇
1 A **fraction** is a tiny amount or proportion of something. *She hesitated for a fraction of a second before responding... Here's how to eat like the stars, at a fraction of the cost... I opened my eyes just a fraction.* N-COUNT: oft N of n
2 A **fraction** is a number that can be expressed as a ratio of two whole numbers. For example, $\frac{1}{2}$ and $\frac{1}{3}$ N-COUNT

are both fractions. *The students had a grasp of decimals, percentages and fractions.*

fractional /frækʃənᵊl/. If something is **fractional**, it is very small in size or degree. *...a fractional hesitation.* ♦ **fractionally** /frækʃənli/ *Murphy, Sinclair's young team-mate, was fractionally behind him.* ◇◇◇◇◇ ADJ-GRADED: usu ADJ n; ADV: ADV group

fractious /frækʃəs/. If you describe someone as **fractious**, you disapprove of them because they become upset or angry very quickly about small unimportant things. *...fractious national movements. ...in a fractious mood... The children were predictably fractious.* ADJ-GRADED PRAGMATICS

fracture /fræktʃəʳ/ **fractures, fracturing, fractured** ◆◆◇◇◇

1 A **fracture** is a slight crack or break in something, especially a bone. *At least one-third of all women over ninety have sustained a hip fracture.* N-COUNT

2 If something such as a bone **is fractured** or **fractures**, it gets a slight crack or break in it. *You've fractured a rib, maybe more than one... One strut had fractured and been crudely repaired in several places... He suffered a fractured skull.* V-ERG V n V V-ed

3 If something such as an organization or society **is fractured** or **fractures**, it splits so that it is then in several parts or ceases to exist; a formal use. *His policy risks fracturing the coalition... It might be a society that could fracture along class lines.* ♦ **fractured** *...in a world of fractured cultures and global interdependence.* V-ERG V n V ADJ-GRADED

fragile /frædʒaɪl, AM -dʒᵊl/ ◆◆◇◇◇

1 If you describe a situation as **fragile**, you mean that it is weak or uncertain, and unlikely to be able to resist strong pressure or attack; used in journalism. *The fragile economies of several southern African nations could be irreparably damaged... The Prime Minister's fragile government was on the brink of collapse... His overall condition remained fragile.* ♦ **fragility** /frədʒɪlɪti/ *By mid-1988 there were clear indications of the extreme fragility of the Right-wing coalition.* ADJ-GRADED =unstable N-UNCOUNT: oft N of n

2 Something that is **fragile** is easily broken or damaged. *He leaned back in his fragile chair.* ♦ **fragility** *Older drivers are more likely to be seriously injured because of the fragility of their bones.* ADJ-GRADED ≠sturdy N-UNCOUNT: oft N of n

3 Something that is **fragile** is very delicate or fine in appearance. *The haircut emphasised her fragile beauty.* ADJ-GRADED =delicate

4 If someone feels **fragile**, they feel weak, for example because they are ill or have drunk too much alcohol. *He felt irritated and strangely fragile, as if he were recovering from a severe bout of flu.* ADJ-GRADED: usu v-link ADJ

fragment, fragments, fragmenting, fragmented. The noun is pronounced /frægmənt/. The verb is pronounced /frægment/. ◆◆◇◇◇

1 A **fragment** of something is a small piece or part of it. *The only reminder of the shooting is a few fragments of metal in my shoulder... She read everything, digesting every fragment of news. ...glass fragments.* N-COUNT: oft N of n =piece

2 If something **fragments** or **is fragmented**, it breaks or separates into small pieces or parts. *The clouds fragmented and out came the sun... Fierce rivalries have traditionally fragmented the region... By the first century BC, Buddhism was in danger of fragmenting into small sects.* ♦ **fragmentation** /frægmenteɪʃᵊn/ *...the extraordinary fragmentation of styles on the music scene.* ♦ **fragmented** *Europe had become infinitely more unstable and fragmented.* V-ERG V V n V *into* n N-UNCOUNT: oft N of n ADJ-GRADED =divided

fragmentary /frægməntəri, AM -teri/. Something that is **fragmentary** is made up of small or unconnected pieces. *Any action on the basis of such fragmentary evidence would be foolish.* ADJ-GRADED

fragrance /freɪgrəns/ **fragrances** ◆◆◇◇◇

1 A **fragrance** is a pleasant or sweet smell. *A shrubby plant with a strong characteristic fragrance. ...the fragrance of his cologne.* N-VAR: usu with supp

2 **Fragrance** is a pleasant-smelling liquid which people put on their bodies to make themselves smell nice. *The advertisement is for a male fragrance.* N-MASS =perfume

fragrant /freɪgrənt/. Something that is **fragrant** has a pleasant, sweet smell. *...fragrant oils and perfumes... The air was fragrant with the smell of orange blossoms.* ◆◇◇◇◇ ADJ-GRADED: oft ADJ *with* n

frail /freɪl/ **frailer, frailest** ◆◇◇◇◇

1 Someone who is **frail** is not very strong or healthy. *She lay in bed looking particularly frail.* ADJ-GRADED =weak

2 Something that is **frail** is easily broken or damaged. *The frail craft rocked as he clambered in.* ADJ-GRADED =fragile

frailty /freɪlti/ **frailties**

1 If you refer to the **frailties** or **frailty** of people, you are referring to their weaknesses. *...the frailties of human nature. ...a triumph of will over human frailty.* N-VAR

2 **Frailty** is the condition of being weak in health. *She died after a long period of increasing frailty.* N-UNCOUNT

frame /freɪm/ **frames, framing, framed** ◆◆◆◇◇

1 The **frame** of a picture or mirror consists of the wood, metal, plastic, or glass part that is fitted around or over it, especially when it is displayed or hung on a wall. *Estelle kept a photograph of her mother in a silver frame on the kitchen mantelpiece. ...a pair of picture frames.* N-COUNT

2 The **frame** of an object such as a building, chair, or window is the arrangement of wooden, metal, or plastic bars between which other material is fitted, and which give the object its strength and shape. *He supplied housebuilders with modern timber frames... With difficulty he released the mattress from the metal frame, and groped beneath it... We painted our table to match the window frame in the bedroom.* N-COUNT

3 The **frames** of a pair of glasses are all the metal or plastic parts of it, but not the lenses. *He was wearing new spectacles with gold wire frames.* N-COUNT: usu pl

4 You can refer to someone's body as their **frame**, especially when you are describing the general shape of their body. *Their belts are pulled tight against their bony frames.* N-COUNT: oft poss N

5 A **frame** of cinema film is one of the many separate photographs that it consists of. *Standard 8mm projects at 16 frames per second.* N-COUNT

6 In the United States and some other countries, a **frame** building is one in which wooden beams and boards form an important part of the structure. *He lives in a white-painted frame house behind a picket fence up in Connecticut.* ADJ: ADJ n

7 When a picture or photograph **is framed**, it is put in a frame. *The picture is now ready to be mounted and framed... On the wall is a large framed photograph.* VB: usu passive *be* V-ed V-ed

8 If an object **is framed** by a particular thing, it is surrounded by that thing in a way that makes the object more striking or attractive to look at. *The swimming pool is framed by tropical gardens... An elegant occasional table is framed in the window.* VB: usu passive *be* V-ed prep

9 If someone **frames** something such as a set of rules, a plan, or a system, they create and develop it; used in written English. *After the war, a convention was set up to frame a constitution.* VERB =put together V n

10 If someone **frames** something in a particular style or kind of language, they express it in that way. *The story is framed in a format that is part thriller, part love story... He framed this question three different ways in search of an answer.* VERB *be* V-ed prep/adv V n n

11 If someone **frames** an innocent person, they make other people think that that person is guilty of a crime, by lying or inventing evidence. *I need to find out who tried to frame me... He claimed that he had been framed by the police.* VERB V n

12 See also **cold frame**.

frame of mind, frames of mind. Your **frame of mind** is the mood that you are in, which causes you to have a particular attitude to something. *Lewis was not in the right frame of mind to continue.* ◆◇◇◇◇ N-COUNT: usu sing, with supp

frame of reference, frames of reference. A **frame of reference** is a particular set of beliefs, ideas, or observations on which you base your judgement of things. *We know we're dealing with someone with a different frame of reference.* N-COUNT: usu with supp

frame-up, frame-ups. A **frame-up** is a situation where someone pretends that an innocent person has committed a crime by deliberately lying or inventing evidence; an informal word. *He was innocent and the victim of a frame-up.* N-COUNT

framework /fre͟ɪmwɜːʳk/ **frameworks** ◆◆◇◇◇
1 A **framework** is a particular set of rules, ideas, or beliefs which you use in order to deal with problems or to decide what to do. *...within the framework of federal regulations.* N-COUNT: usu adj N, N of n
2 A **framework** is a structure that forms a support or frame for something. *...wooden shelves on a steel framework.* N-COUNT: usu supp N

franc /fræ͟ŋk/ **francs.** The **franc** is the unit of currency that is used in France, Switzerland, Belgium, and some other countries where French is spoken. *The price of grapes has shot up to 32 francs a kilo.* ► **The franc** is also used to refer to the currency systems of France, Switzerland, Belgium, and some other countries where French is spoken. *In Paris the French franc is suffering from uncertainty surrounding the new government.* ◆◆◇◇◇ N-COUNT: num N; N-SING: the N

franchise /fræ͟ntʃaɪz/ **franchises franchising franchised** ◆◆◇◇◇
1 A **franchise** is an authority that is given by an organization to someone, allowing them to sell its goods or services or to participate in an activity which the organization controls. *...the television franchise. ...the franchise to build and operate the tunnel... Talk to other franchise holders and ask them what they think of the parent company.* N-COUNT: oft n N, N to n, N n
2 If a company **franchises** its business, it sells franchises to other companies, allowing them to sell its goods or services. *She has recently franchised her business... Though the service is available only in California, its founder Michael Cane says he plans to franchise it in other states... It takes hundreds of thousands of dollars to get into the franchised pizza business.* ♦ **franchising** *One of the most important aspects of franchising is the reduced risk of business failure it offers to franchisees.* VERB: V n, V-ed; N-UNCOUNT
3 **Franchise** is the right to vote in an election, especially one in which people elect a parliament. *...the introduction of universal franchise... The 1867 Reform Act extended the franchise to much of the male working class.* N-UNCOUNT: also the N

franchisee /fræntʃaɪzi͟ː/ **franchisees.** A **franchisee** is a person or group of people who buy a particular franchise. ◆◇◇◇◇ N-COUNT

franchiser /fræ͟ntʃaɪzəʳ/ **franchisers.** A **franchiser** is an organization which sells franchises. N-COUNT

frank /fræ͟ŋk/ **franker, frankest; franks, franking, franked** ◆◆◇◇◇
1 If someone is **frank**, they state or express things in an open, honest, and straightforward way. *'It is clear that my client has been less than frank with me,' said his lawyer... They had a frank discussion about the issue.* ♦ **frankly** *You can talk frankly to me... He now frankly admits that much of his former playboy lifestyle was superficial.* ♦ **frankness** *The reaction to his frankness was hostile.* ADJ-GRADED: oft ADJ about/with n =candid; ADV-GRADED: ADV with v; N-UNCOUNT: oft with poss
2 When a letter or parcel **is franked**, it is marked with a symbol that shows that the proper charge has been paid or that no stamp is needed. *The letter was franked in London on August 6. ...a self-addressed, franked envelope.* VB: usu passive; be V-ed; V-ed
3 You can say **'to be frank'** or **'to be frank with you'** to introduce a statement which is your honest opinion, especially when the person you are talking to might not like it. *To be frank, he could also be a bit of a bore... To be frank with you, Harvey, I may have made a mistake.* PHRASE: PHR with cl PRAGMATICS

frankfurter /fræ͟ŋkfɜːʳtəʳ/ **frankfurters.** A **frankfurter** is a type of smoked sausage. N-COUNT

frankincense /fræ͟ŋkɪnsens/. **Frankincense** is a substance which is obtained from a tree and which is burned as incense. N-UNCOUNT

frankly /fræ͟ŋkli/. You use **frankly** when you are expressing an opinion or feeling to emphasize that you mean what you are saying, especially when the person you are speaking to may not like it. *'You don't give a damn about my feelings, do you.'—'Quite frankly, I don't.'... Frankly, Thomas, this question of your loan is beginning to worry me... I was frankly astonished at the degree to which different singers can affect the interpretation of a song.* ● See also **frank**. ◆◆◇◇◇ ADV-GRADED: ADV with cl, ADV adj/-ed PRAGMATICS

frantic /fræ͟ntɪk/ ◆◆◇◇◇
1 If you are **frantic**, you are behaving in a wild and desperate way because you are frightened or worried. *A bird had been locked in and was by now quite frantic.* ♦ **frantically** /fræ͟ntɪkli/ *She clutched frantically at Emily's arm.* ADJ-GRADED =frenzied; ADV-GRADED: ADV with v
2 If an activity is **frantic**, things are done hurriedly and in an energetic but disorganized way. *A busy night in the restaurant can be frantic in the kitchen.* ♦ **frantically** *We have been frantically trying to save her life.* ADJ-GRADED; ADV-GRADED: ADV with v

fraternal /frətɜ͟ːʳnəl/
1 **Fraternal** actions show strong links of friendship between two people or groups of people; a formal use. *...the fraternal assistance of our colleagues and comrades... He said he hoped the issue could be solved in a fraternal way.* ADJ-GRADED: usu ADJ n
2 **Fraternal** twins are twins born from two eggs, so they are not identical. They may be different sexes and may look different from each other. ADJ: usu ADJ n

fraternity /frətɜ͟ːʳnɪti/ **fraternities** ◆◇◇◇◇
1 **Fraternity** refers to friendship and mutual support between people who feel they are closely linked to each other; a formal use. *Bob needs the fraternity of others who share his mission.* N-UNCOUNT =comradeship
2 You can refer to people who have the same profession or the same interests as a particular **fraternity**. *...the spread of stolen guns among the criminal fraternity. ...the sailing fraternity.* N-COUNT: usu supp N =set
3 In the United States, a **fraternity** is a society of male university or college students. N-COUNT

fraternize /fræ͟təʳnaɪz/ **fraternizes, fraternizing, fraternized;** also spelled **fraternise** in British English. If you **fraternize** with someone, you associate with them in a friendly way. *At these conventions, executives fraternized with the key personnel of other banks... Mrs Zuckerman does not fraternize widely... The recession has created an atmosphere where disparate groups fraternise in an atmosphere of mutual support.* V-RECIP =socialize; V with n; V (non-recip); pl-n V

fratricidal /frætrɪsa͟ɪdəl/. A **fratricidal** war or conflict is one in which people kill members of their own society or social group. ADJ: ADJ n

fratricide /fræ͟trɪsaɪd/. If someone commits **fratricide**, they kill their brother; a formal word. N-UNCOUNT

fraud /frɔ͟ːd/ **frauds** ◆◆◆◇◇
1 **Fraud** is the crime of gaining money or financial benefits by deceit or trickery. *He was jailed for two years for fraud and deception... Tax frauds are dealt with by the Inland Revenue.* N-VAR
2 A **fraud** is something or someone that deceives people in a way that is illegal or dishonest. *Unfortunately the portraits were frauds... He believes many 'psychics' are frauds who rely on perception and subtle deception.* N-COUNT
3 If you call someone or something a **fraud**, you are criticizing them because you think that they are not genuine, or are less good than they claim or appear to be. *You're a fraud and a spy, Simons. ...all those fashion frauds who think they are being original by raiding the tired old styles of the '60s and '70s... UNITA is denouncing the vote as a fraud.* N-COUNT PRAGMATICS

fraudster /frɔ͟ːdstəʳ/ **fraudsters.** A **fraudster** is someone who commits the crime of fraud; mainly used in British journalism. N-COUNT

fraudulent /frɔ͟ːdʒʊlənt/. A **fraudulent** activity is deliberately deceitful, dishonest, or untrue. *...fraudulent claims about being a nurse.* ♦ **fraudulently** *All 5,000 of the homes were fraudulently obtained... The report concludes that I acted neither fraudulently nor improperly.* ◆◇◇◇◇ ADJ: usu ADJ n; ADV: ADV with v

fraught /frɔ͟ːt/ ◆◇◇◇◇
1 If a situation or action is **fraught with** problems or risks, it is filled with them. *The earliest opera-* ADJ: v-link ADJ with n

tions employing this technique were fraught with dangers.

2 If you say that a situation or action is **fraught**, you mean that it is worrying or stressful. *It has been a somewhat fraught day.* ADJ-GRADED

fray /freɪ/ **frays, fraying, frayed** ◆◇◇◇◇

1 If something such as cloth or rope **frays**, or if something **frays** it, its threads or fibres start to come apart from each other and spoil its appearance. *The fabric is very fine or frays easily... The stitching had begun to fray at the edges... Her washing machine tends to fray edges on intricate designs. ...fraying edges in the stair carpet... He wore frayed jeans and cowboy shirts.* V-ERG V V at n V n V-ing V-ed

2 If your nerves or your temper **fray**, or if something **frays** them, you feel irritable and nervous because of mental strain and anxiety. *Tempers began to fray as the two teams failed to score... This kind of living was beginning to fray her nerves.* ♦ **frayed** *Nerves became severely frayed when air traffic problems delayed the flight.* V-ERG V V n ADJ-GRADED

3 **The fray** is an exciting or challenging activity, situation, or argument that you are involved in. *There will have to be a second round of voting when new candidates can enter the fray... He would be inspiring young people to get into the political fray.* N-SING: the N

4 If you say that something **is fraying at the edges** or **is fraying around the edges**, you mean that it has an uncertain, unstable, or untidy quality, for example because it is gradually being spoiled or destroyed. *There are signs that the alliance is now fraying at the edges... Their marriage is getting a little frayed around the edges... The champion, too, looked frayed at the edges.* PHRASE: V inflects

freak /friːk/ **freaks, freaking, freaked** ◆◆◇◇◇

1 A **freak** event or action is one that is a very unusual or extreme example of its type. *Weir broke his leg in a freak accident playing golf... The ferry was hit by a freak wave off the North Wales coast.* ADJ: ADJ n =bizarre, chance

2 If you describe someone as a particular kind of **freak**, you are emphasizing that they are very enthusiastic about that particular thing or activity, often to the point where they are obsessed with it; an informal use. *Oat bran became the darling of health freaks last year. ...computer freaks.* • See also **control freak**. N-COUNT: n N =fanatic

3 People are sometimes referred to as **freaks** when their behaviour or attitude is very different from that of the majority of other people; used showing disapproval. *However, outside of these institutions the black thinking woman is looked upon as a freak... Not so long ago, transsexuals were regarded as freaks.* N-COUNT PRAGMATICS

4 If you refer to someone as a **freak**, you mean that they are physically abnormal in some way; an offensive use. N-COUNT

5 If someone **freaks**, or if something **freaks** them, they suddenly feel extremely surprised, upset, angry, or confused; an informal use. *I saw five cop cars pull into the driveway. And I literally freaked... I think they got freaked by women laughing at them.* ► **Freak out** means the same as **freak**. *I remember the first time I went onstage. I freaked out completely... I think our music freaks people out sometimes... It sort of frightens me. I guess I am kind of freaked out by it.* V-ERG V get V-ed Also V n PHRASAL VERB V P V n P be V-ed P Also V P n (not pron)

freak out. See **freak** 5. PHRASAL VERB

freakish /friːkɪʃ/. Something that is **freakish** is remarkable because it is not normal or natural. *...his freakish voice varying from bass to soprano.* ADJ-GRADED: usu ADJ n

freaky /friːki/ **freakier, freakiest.** If someone or something is **freaky**, they are very unusual in some way; an informal word. *This guy bore a really freaky resemblance to Jones.* ADJ-GRADED =weird, strange

freckle /frekᵊl/ **freckles. Freckles** are small light brown spots on someone's skin, especially on their face. *He had short ginger-coloured hair and freckles.* N-COUNT: usu pl

freckled /frekᵊld/. If a part of your body is **freckled**, it has freckles on it. *...a slight man with auburn hair and a freckled face.* ADJ-GRADED

free /friː/ **freer, freest; frees, freeing, freed** ◆◆◆◆◆

1 If something is **free**, you can have it or use it without paying for it. *The seminars are free, with lunch provided. ...a free brochure with details of gift vouchers.* • **free of charge**: see **charge**. ADJ

2 Someone or something that is **free** is not restricted, controlled, or limited, for example by rules, customs, or other people. *The government will be free to pursue its economic policies... The elections were free and fair... Economists argued that freer markets would quickly revive the region's economy... He fears that until state subsidies are removed, Russia will never have a truly free press... Dogs were allowed to roam free and 48 sheep were killed.* ♦ **freely** *They cast their votes freely and without coercion on election day... Merchandise can now circulate freely among the 12 EC countries.* ADJ-GRADED: oft ADJ to-inf ADV-GRADED: ADV with v

3 If you **free** someone of something that is unpleasant or restricting, you remove it from them. *It will free us of a whole lot of debt... The 30-year-old star is trying to free himself from his recording contract.* VERB V n of/from n

4 Someone who is **free** is no longer a prisoner or a slave. *He walked from the court house a free man... More than ninety prisoners have been set free so far under a government amnesty.* ADJ: ADJ n, v-link ADJ, ADJ after v

5 To **free** a prisoner or a slave means to let them go or release them from prison. *Israel is set to free more Lebanese prisoners... The act had a specific intent, to protect freed slaves from white mobs.* VERB V n V-ed

6 If someone or something is **free of** or **free from** an unpleasant or unwanted thing, they do not have it or they are not affected by it. *...a future far more free of fear... She retains her slim figure and is free of wrinkles... The filtration system provides the crew with clean air free from fumes.* ADJ: v-link ADJ of/from n =without

7 A sum of money or type of goods that is **free of** tax or duty is one that you do not have to pay tax on. • See also **duty-free**, **interest-free**, **tax-free**. ADJ: v-link ADJ of n

8 If something **frees** someone or something, it makes them available for a task or function that they were previously unavailable for. *Toolbelts free both hands and lessen the risk of dropping hammers... His deal with Disney will run out shortly, freeing him to pursue his own project... There were more civilians working for the police, freeing officers from desk jobs.* ► **Free up** means the same as **free**. *It can handle even the most complex graphic jobs, freeing up your computer for other tasks.* VERB V n V n to-inf V n from/of/for n PHRASAL VERB V P n (not pron) Also V n P

9 If you have a **free** period of time or are **free** at a particular time, you are not working or occupied then. *She spent her free time shopping... I used to write during my free periods at school... I am always free at lunchtime.* ADJ

10 If something such as a table or seat is **free**, it is not being used or occupied by someone, or is not reserved for someone to use. *There was only one seat free on the train... They took the only free table which was just inside the door.* ADJ

11 If you get something **free** or if it gets **free**, it is no longer trapped by something or attached to something. *The severe conditions hampered attempts to pull the vessel free of the rig... He pulled his arm free, and strode for the door... The shark was writhing around wildly, trying to get free.* ADJ: v n ADJ, v-link ADJ, oft ADJ of n

12 If you **free** someone or something, you remove or loosen them from the place in which they have been trapped or become fixed. *It took firemen two hours to cut through the drive belt to free him... He managed to free one hand to ward off a punch.* VERB V n

13 When someone is using one hand or arm to hold or move something, their other hand or arm is referred to as their **free** one. *He snatched up the receiver and his free hand groped for the switch on the bedside lamp... She checked her fall with her free arm.* ADJ: ADJ n

14 If you say that someone is **free with** something such as advice or money, you mean they give a lot of it, sometimes when it is not wanted; used showing disapproval. *They weren't always so free with their advice... They would often be free with criticism, some of it unjustified.* ADJ-GRADED: v-link ADJ with n PRAGMATICS

15 You say **'feel free'** to someone who has asked you if they can do something as an informal way of giving your permission. You say **'feel free to** do something' as an informal way of telling someone that you do not mind them doing it. *Go right ahead. Feel free... If you have any questions at all, please feel free to ask me.* PHRASES oft PHR to-inf PRAGMATICS

16 If you do something or get something **for free**, you do it without being paid or get it without having to pay for it; an informal expression. *I wasn't expecting you to do it for free... Why waste £250 when you could get it for free?* PHR after v

17 You say you will express a critical opinion about something **for free** to emphasize how strongly you feel about it. *I'll tell you one thing for free: I can't stand him.* v n PHR PRAGMATICS

18 • to **give someone a free hand**: see **hand**.

free up PHRASAL VERB

1 See **free** 8.

2 To **free up** a market, economy, or system means to make it operate with fewer restrictions and controls. *...policies for freeing up markets and extending competition.* V P n (not pron) Also V n P

-free /-friː/. **-free** combines with nouns to form adjectives that indicate that something does not have the thing mentioned, or has only a little of it. For example, sugar-free drinks do not contain any sugar, and lead-free petrol is made using only a small amount of lead. *...a salt-free diet.* COMB in ADJ

free agent, free agents

1 If you say that someone is a **free agent**, you are emphasizing that they can do whatever they want to do, because they are not responsible to anyone or for anyone. *We are not free agents; we abide by the decisions of our president.* N-COUNT PRAGMATICS

2 If a sports player is a **free agent**, he or she is free to sign a contract with any team. N-COUNT

free and easy; also spelled **free-and-easy**. Someone or something that is **free and easy** is casual, informal, and tolerant. *...the free and easy atmosphere of these cafés.* ADJ-GRADED =easy-going, laid-back

freebie /friːbi/ **freebies.** A **freebie** is something that you are given, usually by a company, without having to pay for it; an informal word. ◆◇◇◇◇ N-COUNT

freedom /friːdəm/ **freedoms** ◆◆◆◆◇

1 **Freedom** is the state of being allowed to do what you want to do. **Freedoms** are instances of this. *...freedom of speech... They want greater political freedom... Today we have the freedom to decide our own futures... The United Nations Secretary-General has spoken of the need for individual freedoms and human rights.* N-UNCOUNT: also N in pl

2 When prisoners or slaves are set free or escape, they gain their **freedom**. *...the agreement worked out by the UN, under which all hostages and detainees would gain their freedom.* N-UNCOUNT: oft poss N =liberty

3 **Freedom from** something you do not want means not being affected by it. *...all the freedom from pain that medicine could provide. ...freedom from government control.* N-UNCOUNT: N *from* n

4 If someone is given **the freedom of** a city, they are officially given the right to do anything they want in it, as an honour. *He was given the Freedom of the City of Dublin by the Lord Mayor.* N-SING: *the* N *of* n

freedom fighter, freedom fighters. If you refer to someone as a **freedom fighter**, you mean that they belong to a group that is trying to overthrow the government of their country using violent methods, and you agree with or approve of this. ◆◇◇◇◇ N-COUNT PRAGMATICS

free enterprise. Free enterprise is an economic system in which businesses compete for profit without much government control. ◆◇◇◇◇ N-UNCOUNT

free fall, free falls; also spelled **free-fall**.

1 In economics, if the value or price of something goes into **free fall**, it starts to fall uncontrollably. *Sterling went into free fall... The price did a free fall.* N-VAR: oft *into/in* N

2 In parachuting, **free fall** is the part of the jump before the parachute opens. N-UNCOUNT

free-floating. Free-floating things or people are able to move freely and are not controlled or directed by anything. *...a system of free-floating exchange rates.* ADJ: ADJ n ≠restricted

freefone /friːfoʊn/; also spelled **freephone**. In British English, a **freefone** telephone number is one which you can dial without having to pay for the call. The American word is **toll-free. Freefone** is a trademark. *...London's Freefone emergency housing helpline.* N-UNCOUNT: usu N num, N n

free-for-all, free-for-alls

1 A **free-for-all** is a situation in which several people or groups are trying to get something for themselves and there are no controls on how they do it. N-SING

2 A **free-for-all** is a disorganized fight or argument which lots of people join. N-COUNT

free form; also spelled **free-form**. A **free form** work of art or piece of music has not been created according to a standard style or convention. *...free-form jazz.* ADJ: ADJ n

freehand /friːhænd/. A **freehand** drawing is drawn without using instruments such as a ruler or a pair of compasses. *...freehand sketches.* ADJ: ADJ n ► Also an adverb. *Use a template or stencil or simply do it freehand.* ADV: ADV after v

freehold /friːhoʊld/ **freeholds**

1 If you have the **freehold** of a building or piece of land, it is yours for life and there are no conditions regarding your ownership. *People owning leasehold homes will be given a new right to buy the freehold of their property.* N-VAR

2 If a building or piece of land is **freehold**, you can own it for life. *The property register will also say whether the property is freehold or leasehold.* ADJ

freeholder /friːhoʊldəʳ/ **freeholders.** A **freeholder** is someone who owns the freehold to a particular piece of land. N-COUNT

free house, free houses. In Britain, a **free house** is a pub which is not owned by a particular brewery and which can sell whatever beers it chooses to sell. N-COUNT

free kick, free kicks. In a game of football, when there is a **free kick**, the ball is given to a member of one side to kick without opposition because a member of the other side has broken a rule. ◆◇◇◇◇ N-COUNT

freelance /friːlɑːns, -læns/ **freelances, freelancing, freelanced** ◆◇◇◇◇

1 Someone who does **freelance** work or who is, for example, a **freelance** journalist or photographer is not employed by one organization, but is paid for each piece of work they do by the organization they do it for. *Michael Cross is a freelance journalist... Jill was starting to get some freelance writing jobs from trade magazines... She had a baby and decided to go freelance.* ADJ: usu ADJ n ► Also an adverb. *He is now working freelance from his home in Hampshire.* ADV: ADV after v

2 A **freelance** is the same as a **freelancer**. N-COUNT

3 If you **freelance**, you do freelance work. *She has freelanced as a writer and researcher and has worked as a TV critic for 'Today' newspaper.* VERB V *as* n Also V

freelancer /friːlɑːnsəʳ, -læns-/ **freelancers.** A **freelancer** is someone who does freelance work. N-COUNT

freeloader /friːloʊdəʳ/ **freeloaders.** If you refer to someone as a **freeloader**, you disapprove of them because they take advantage of other people's generosity, for example by accepting food or accommodation from them, without giving anything in return; an informal word. N-COUNT PRAGMATICS

free love. A belief in **free love** is the belief that it is acceptable and good to have sexual relationships without marrying, often several relationships at the same time; an old-fashioned expression. N-UNCOUNT

freely /friːli/ ◆◆◇◇◇

1 You use **freely** to indicate that something happens or is done many times or in large quantities, often without restraint. *We have referred freely to his ideas... George was spending very freely. ...the United States, where consumer goods are freely available.* ADV-GRADED: ADV after v, ADV adj

2 If you can talk **freely**, you can talk without needing to be careful about what you say. *She wondered* ADV-GRADED: ADV after v =unreservedly

whether he had someone to whom he could talk freely.

3 If someone gives or does something **freely**, they give or do it willingly, without being ordered or forced to do it. *Danny shared his knowledge freely with anyone interested... Williams freely admits he lives for racing.* ADV-GRADED: ADV with v =willingly, voluntarily

4 If something or someone moves **freely**, they move easily and smoothly, without any obstacles or resistance. *The clay court was slippery and he was unable to move freely... You must allow the clubhead to swing freely.* ADV-GRADED: ADV after v

5 See also **free**.

freeman /friːmən/ **freemen.** Someone who is a **freeman** of a particular city has been given a special honour by that city, known as the freedom of the city. *Peter was made a Freeman of the City of London.* N-COUNT: usu N *of* n

free-marketeer, free-marketeers. A **free-marketeer** is someone, especially a politician, who is in favour of letting market forces regulate the economy. N-COUNT

Freemason /friːmeɪsᵊn/ **Freemasons.** A **Freemason** is a man who is a member of a large secret society. Freemasons promise to help each other, and use a system of secret signs in order to recognize each other. N-COUNT

freemasonry /friːmeɪsᵊnri/

1 **Freemasonry** is the organization of the Freemasons and their beliefs and practices. *He was very active in Freemasonry.* N-UNCOUNT

2 **Freemasonry** is the friendly feeling that exists between people who are of the same kind or who have the same interests. *...the freemasonry of sailors.* N-UNCOUNT: also *a* N, usu with supp

free pass, free passes. A **free pass** is an official document that allows a person to travel or to enter a particular building without having to pay. N-COUNT

freephone. See **freefone.**

free port, free ports. A **free port** is a port or airport where goods can be brought in from foreign countries without payment of duty if they are going to be exported again. N-COUNT

Freepost /friːpoust/. **Freepost** is a system in Britain which allows you to send mail to certain organizations without paying for the postage. 'Freepost' is written on the envelope as part of the address. N-UNCOUNT

freer /friːəʳ/. **Freer** is the comparative of **free.**

free-range. Free-range means relating to a system of keeping animals in which they can move and feed freely on an area of open ground. *...free-range eggs.* ADJ: usu ADJ n

freesia /friːʒə/ **freesias. Freesias** are small plants with yellow, pink, white, or purple tubular flowers. N-VAR

free spirit, free spirits. If you describe someone as a **free spirit**, you admire them because they are independent and live as they want to live rather than in a conventional way. N-COUNT PRAGMATICS

freest /friːɪst/. **Freest** is the superlative of **free.**

free-standing. A **free-standing** piece of furniture or other object is not fixed to anything, or stands on its own away from other things. *...a free-standing cooker.* ADJ

freestyle /friːstaɪl/. **Freestyle** is used to describe sports competitions, especially in swimming, wrestling, and skiing, in which competitors can use any style or method that they like when they take part. *...the 100m freestyle swimming event. ...the reigning European Freestyle Champion. ...freestyle skiing.* ► Also a noun. *She won the 800 metres freestyle.* ◆◇◇◇◇ ADJ: ADJ n; N-SING

free-thinker, free-thinkers. If you refer to someone as a **free-thinker**, you admire them because they work out their own ideas rather than accepting generally accepted views. N-COUNT PRAGMATICS

freeway /friːweɪ/ **freeways.** In American English, a **freeway** is a major road that has been specially built for fast travel over long distances. Freeways have several lanes and special places where traffic gets on and leaves. The usual British word is **motorway.** *The speed limit on the freeway is 55mph. ...Boston's freeway system.* ◆◇◇◇◇ N-COUNT

freewheel /friːʰwiːl/ **freewheels, freewheeling, freewheeled;** also spelled **free-wheel.** If you **freewheel**, you travel, usually downhill, on a bicycle without using the pedals, or in a vehicle without using the engine. *He freewheeled back down the course.* VERB V adv/prep Also V

freewheeling /friːʰwiːlɪŋ/; also spelled **free-wheeling.** If you refer to someone's **freewheeling** lifestyle or attitudes, you mean that they behave in a casual, relaxed way without feeling restricted by rules or accepted ways of doing things. *He has given up his freewheeling lifestyle to settle down with his baby daughter. ...an update on corporate affairs delivered in Johnson's unique, freewheeling style.* ADJ: usu ADJ n

free will ◆◇◇◇◇

1 If you believe in **free will**, you believe that people have a choice in what they do and that their actions have not been decided in advance by God or Fate. *...the free will of the individual.* N-UNCOUNT

2 If you do something **of** your **own free will**, you do it by choice and not because you are forced to do it. *Would Bethany return of her own free will, as she had promised, or would she have to be fetched?* PHRASE: PHR after v

freeze /friːz/ **freezes, freezing, froze, frozen** ◆◆◆◇◇

1 If a liquid or a substance containing a liquid **freezes**, or if something **freezes** it, it becomes solid because of low temperatures. *If the temperature drops below 0°C, water freezes... The ground froze solid. ...the discovery of how to freeze water at higher temperatures. ...frozen puddles.* V-ERG V V adj V n V-ed

2 If you **freeze** something such as food, you preserve it by storing it at a temperature below freezing point. You can also talk about how well food **freezes.** *You can freeze the soup at this stage... Most fresh herbs will freeze successfully.* V-ERG V n V adv

3 If something such as a pipe or machine **freezes**, it becomes blocked or stiff with ice or frozen liquid. *The water pipes will freeze.* VERB V

4 When **it freezes** outside, the temperature falls below freezing point. *What if it rained and then froze all through those months?* ► Also a noun. *The trees were damaged by a freeze in December.* VERB *it* V N-COUNT

5 If you **freeze**, you feel extremely cold. *The windows didn't fit at the bottom so for a while we froze even in the middle of summer... Your hands will freeze doing this.* VERB V

6 If someone who is moving **freezes**, they suddenly stop and become completely still and quiet; used mainly in written English. *She froze when the beam of the flashlight struck her.* VERB V

7 If the government or a company **freeze** things such as prices or wages, they state officially that they will not allow them to increase for a fixed period of time. *They want the government to freeze prices... Wages have been frozen and workers laid off.* ► Also a noun. *A wage freeze was imposed on all staff earlier this month. ...a freeze on the prices of consumer goods.* VERB V n N-COUNT: with supp

8 If a government **freezes** a plan or process, they state officially that they will not allow it to continue for a period of time. *Britain has already frozen its aid programme... Diplomatic relations were frozen until August this year.* ► Also a noun. *...a freeze in nuclear weapons programs.* VERB V n N-COUNT: with supp

9 If someone in authority **freezes** something such as a bank account, fund, or property, they obtain a legal order which states that it cannot be used or sold for a particular period of time. *The governor's action freezes 300,000 accounts... Under these laws, he said, Mr. Rice's assets could have been frozen.* ► Also a noun. *...a freeze on private savings.* VERB V n N-COUNT: with supp

10 See also **freezing, frozen.**

freeze out. If you **freeze** someone **out** of an activity or situation, you prevent them from being involved in it by creating difficulties or by being unfriendly. *He has sworn that he will freeze Cuba out of the world economy.* PHRASAL VERB V n P *of* n Also V n P

freeze over. If something **freezes over**, it becomes covered with a layer of ice or other frozen PHRASAL VERB substance. *The air temperature was well below freezing, and lakes and rivers froze over... The lakes are still frozen over.* V P V-ed P

freeze up. If something **freezes up** or if something **freezes** it **up**, it becomes completely covered or blocked with ice. *...lavatories that often freeze up in winter... Ice could freeze up their torpedo release mechanisms.* PHRASAL VERB ERG V P V P n (not pron) Also V n P

freeze-dried. **Freeze-dried** food has been preserved by a process of rapid freezing and drying. *...freeze-dried instant mashed potato. ...freeze-dried coffee granules.* ADJ

freeze-frame, freeze-frames

1 A **freeze-frame** from a film is an individual picture from it, produced by stopping the film or video tape at that point. *6-millimetre film was used because it offered clearer freeze frames than video tape.* N-COUNT

2 If you watch a film in **freeze-frame**, you watch it using a facility that allows you to stop the film to look at an individual picture. *The jury watched the tape dozens of times in slow motion and in freeze frame. ...the freeze-frame button on the remote control.* N-UNCOUNT: oft *in* N, N n

freezer /friːzəʳ/ **freezers.** A **freezer** is a large container like a fridge in which the temperature is kept below freezing point so that you can store food inside it for long periods. ◆◇◇◇◇ N-COUNT =deep freeze

freezing /friːzɪŋ/ ◆◇◇◇◇

1 If you say that something is **freezing** or **freezing cold**, you are emphasizing that it is very cold. *The cinema was freezing. ...a freezing January afternoon.* ADJ PRAGMATICS

2 If you say that you are **freezing** or **freezing cold**, you emphasizing that you feel very cold. *'You must be freezing,' she said.* ADJ: v-link ADJ PRAGMATICS

3 **Freezing** means the same as **freezing point**. *It's 15 degrees below freezing.* N-UNCOUNT

4 See also **freeze**.

freezing point, freezing points; also spelled **freezing-point**.

1 **Freezing point** is 0° Celsius, the temperature at which water freezes; often used when talking about the weather. *The temperature remained below freezing point throughout the day.* N-UNCOUNT: usu *above/below/to* N

2 The **freezing point** of a particular substance is the temperature at which it freezes. N-COUNT: usu with poss

freight /freɪt/ **freights, freighting, freighted** ◆◆◇◇◇

1 **Freight** is the movement of goods by lorries, trains, ships, or aeroplanes. *France derives 16% of revenue from air freight.* N-UNCOUNT

2 **Freight** is goods that are transported by lorries, trains, ships, or aeroplanes. *...26 tons of freight... 90% of managers wanted to see more freight carried by rail.* N-UNCC'INT

3 When goods **are freighted**, they are transported in large quantities over a long distance. *From these ports the grain is freighted down to Addis Ababa.* VB: usu passive *be* V-ed adv/prep

freight car, freight cars. On a train, a **freight car** is a wagon in which goods are transported. N-COUNT

freighter /freɪtəʳ/ **freighters.** A **freighter** is a large ship or aeroplane that is designed for carrying freight. ◆◇◇◇◇ N-COUNT

freight train, freight trains. A **freight train** is a train on which goods are transported. N-COUNT

French /frentʃ/ ◆◆◆◆◇

1 **French** means belonging or relating to France, or its people, language, or culture. *The French parliament has adopted laws banning advertisements for tobacco... All the staff are French.* ADJ

2 The **French** are the people who come from France. *Two-thirds of the French are in favour of limiting foreign imports into Europe.* N-PLURAL

3 **French** is the language spoken by people who live in France and in parts of some other countries, including Belgium, Canada, and Switzerland. *The villagers spoke French.* N-UNCOUNT

French bean, French beans. In British English, **French beans** are long very narrow beans that are green in colour and are eaten as a vegetable. They grow on a tall climbing plant and are the cases that contain the seeds of the plant. The American expression is **string beans.** N-COUNT: usu pl

French bread. **French bread** is white bread which is baked in long, thin, crusty loaves. N-UNCOUNT

French Canadian, French Canadians; also spelled **French-Canadian.**

1 **French Canadian** means belonging or relating to people who come from the part of Canada where French is spoken. *French-Canadian nationalism was fuelled in the 1960s. ...a young French-Canadian artist.* ADJ

2 **French Canadians** are Canadians whose native language is French. *Up to seventy per cent of French Canadians favour Quebec independence.* N-COUNT

French door, French doors. **French doors** are the same as **French windows.** N-COUNT: usu pl

French dressing. **French dressing** is a thin sauce made of oil, vinegar, salt, and spices which you put on salad. N-UNCOUNT

French fries. **French fries** are long, thin pieces of potato fried in oil or fat. N-PLURAL

French horn, French horns. A **French horn** is a musical instrument of the brass family. It is shaped like a long metal tube wound round in a circle with a wide funnel at one end. You play the French horn by blowing into the mouthpiece and moving valves in order to obtain different notes. N-VAR: oft *the* N =horn

French loaf, French loaves. In British English, a **French loaf** is a long, thin, crusty loaf of white bread. N-COUNT =baguette

Frenchman /frentʃmən/ **Frenchmen.** A **Frenchman** is a man who comes from France. ◆◆◇◇◇ N-COUNT

French polish. **French polish** is a type of varnish which is painted onto wood so that the wood has a hard shiny surface. N-UNCOUNT

French window, French windows. **French windows** are a pair of glass doors which you go through into a garden or onto a balcony. N-COUNT: usu pl =French door

Frenchwoman /frentʃwʊmən/ **Frenchwomen.** A **Frenchwoman** is a woman who comes from France. ◆◆◇◇◇ N-COUNT

frenetic /frɪnetɪk/. If you describe an activity as **frenetic**, you mean that it is fast and energetic, but rather uncontrolled. *...the frenetic pace of life in New York... This frenetic activity is the sign of a worried man.* ◆◇◇◇◇ ADJ-GRADED =frantic ♦ **frenetically** /frɪnetɪkli/ *Steve and I worked frenetically to ensure that everything would go smoothly.* ADV: usu ADV with v

frenzied /frenzid/. **Frenzied** activities or actions are wild, excited, and uncontrolled. *...the frenzied activity of the general election... The man was stabbed to death in a frenzied attack.* ◆◇◇◇◇ ADJ-GRADED: usu ADJ n =frantic

frenzy /frenzi/ **frenzies.** **Frenzy** or a **frenzy** is great excitement or wild behaviour that often results from losing control of your feelings. *'Get out!' she ordered in a frenzy... The country was gripped by a frenzy of nationalism.* ◆◇◇◇◇ N-VAR: oft N *of* n

frequency /friːkwənsi/ **frequencies** ◆◆◇◇◇

1 The **frequency** of an event is the number of times it happens during a particular period. *The frequency of Kara's phone calls increased rapidly... The tanks broke down with increasing frequency.* N-UNCOUNT

2 The **frequency** of a sound wave or a radio wave is the number of times it vibrates within a specified period of time; a technical use in physics. *You can't hear waves of such a high frequency. ...a frequency of 24 kilohertz. ...low frequency waves.* N-VAR

frequent, frequents, frequenting, frequented. The adjective is pronounced /friːkwənt/. The verb is pronounced /frɪkwent/. ◆◆◆◆◇

1 If something is **frequent**, it happens often. *Bordeaux is on the main Paris-Madrid line so there are frequent trains... He is a frequent visitor to the house.* ADJ-GRADED ♦ **frequently** *Iron and folic acid supplements are frequently given to pregnant women.* ADV-GRADED: usu ADV with v

2 If someone **frequents** a particular place, they regularly go there; a formal use. *I hear he frequents Kenny's, the Cajun restaurant in Hampstead.* VERB V n

fresco /freskoʊ/ **frescoes** or **frescos.** A **fresco** is a picture that is painted on a plastered wall when the plaster is still wet. ● See also **alfresco**. ◆◇◇◇◇ N-COUNT

fresh /freʃ/ **fresher, freshest** ◆◆◆◆◇

1 A **fresh** thing or amount replaces or is added to a previous thing or amount. *He asked Strathclyde police, which carried out the original investigation, to make fresh inquiries... I need a new challenge and a fresh start somewhere else.* — ADJ: ADJ n =new

2 Something that is **fresh** has been done, made, or experienced recently. *There were no fresh car tracks or footprints in the snow... A puppy stepped in the fresh cement... With the memory of the bombing fresh in her mind, Eleanor became increasingly agitated.* — ADJ-GRADED

3 **Fresh** food has been picked or produced recently, and has not been preserved, for example by being tinned or frozen. *...locally caught fresh fish. ...fresh fruit.* — ADJ-GRADED ♦ **freshness** *With oysters, as with all seafood, freshness equals quality.* — N-UNCOUNT

4 If you describe something as **fresh**, you like it because it is new and exciting. *These designers are full of fresh ideas. ...a fresh image.* — ADJ-GRADED =original ♦ **freshness** *There was a freshness and enthusiasm about the new students.* — N-UNCOUNT

5 If you describe something as **fresh**, you mean that it is pleasant, bright, and clean in appearance. *Gingham fabrics always look fresh and pretty.* — ADJ-GRADED ♦ **freshness** *...the crisp freshness of laundered clothes.* — N-UNCOUNT

6 If something smells, tastes, or feels **fresh**, it is clean, cool, or refreshing. *The air was fresh and for a moment she felt revived.* — ADJ-GRADED: usu ADJ n ♦ **freshness** *...the freshness of early morning.* — N-UNCOUNT

7 **Fresh** water is water that is not salty, for example the water from rivers, lakes, or reservoirs. *Fresh water and other commodities are in short supply.* — ADJ

8 If you say that the weather is **fresh**, you mean that it is fairly cold and windy. *It was a fine, fresh summer morning, with a bit of a wind... Outside the breeze was fresh and from the north.* — ADJ-GRADED

9 **Fresh** colours are clear, bright, and fairly light. *...a semi-circular mosaic, its startling colours still fresh.* — ADJ-GRADED

10 If someone has a **fresh** face or complexion, their skin looks healthy. *His fresh complexion made him look younger than he was.* — ADJ-GRADED =glowing

11 If you feel **fresh**, you feel full of energy and enthusiasm. *It's vital we are as fresh as possible for those matches... I nearly always wake up fresh and rested.* — ADJ-GRADED: usu v-link ADJ

12 If you **are fresh from** a particular place or experience, you have just come from that place or you have just had that experience. You can also say that someone **is fresh out of** a place. *I returned to the office, fresh from Heathrow... Fresh from their semi-final win over Germany, Britain took a promising early lead... From what I've heard he started wheeling and dealing fresh out of college.* — ADJ: v-link ADJ *from/out of* n =straight

13 If you are **fresh out of** something, you have recently used the last of it and have none left; an informal expression. *When I needed a tape to record an interview on I found I was fresh out of cassettes.* — PHRASE: PHR n

fresh- /freʃ-/. **Fresh-** is added to past participles in order to form adjectives which describe something as having been recently made or done. *...a vase of fresh-cut flowers. ...a meadow of fresh-mown hay.* — COMB in ADJ: ADJ n

fresh air. You can describe the air outside as **fresh air**, especially when you mean that it is good for you because it is not polluted. *'Let's take the baby outside,' I suggested. 'We all need some fresh air.'* — ◆◇◇◇◇ N-UNCOUNT: also *the* N

freshen /freʃən/ **freshens, freshening, freshened.** If the wind **freshens**, it becomes stronger and colder. *The wind had freshened.* — VERB V

freshen up — PHRASAL VERB

1 If you **freshen** something **up**, you make it clean and pleasant in appearance or smell. *A thorough brushing helps to freshen up your mouth... My room needed a lick of paint to freshen it up.* — V P n (not pron), V n P

2 If you **freshen up**, you wash your hands and face and make yourself look neat and tidy. *After Martine had freshened up, they went for a long walk.* — V P

fresher /freʃəʳ/ **freshers**

1 **Fresher** is the comparative form of **fresh**.

2 In informal British English, **freshers** are students who have just started their first year at university or college. The usual American term is **freshmen**. — N-COUNT: usu pl

freshly /freʃli/. If something is **freshly** made or done, it has been recently made or done. *...freshly baked bread. ...freshly cut grass.* — ◆◆◇◇◇ ADV: ADV -ed =recently

freshman /freʃmən/ **freshmen.** In America, a **freshman** is a student who is in his or her first year at university or college. — ◆◇◇◇◇ N-COUNT

freshwater /freʃwɔːtəʳ/. A **freshwater** lake contains water that is not salty, usually in contrast to the sea. **Freshwater** creatures live in lakes, ponds, and rivers which are not salty. *...Lake Balaton, the largest freshwater lake in Europe... The perch is a freshwater fish.* — ◆◇◇◇◇ ADJ: ADJ n

fret /fret/ **frets, fretting, fretted** ◆◇◇◇◇

1 If you **fret** about something, you worry about it. *I was working all hours and constantly fretting about everyone else's problems... But congressional staffers fret that the project will eventually cost billions more... Don't fret, Mary. This is all some crazy mistake, and Max will fix it.* — VERB =worry, V *about/over* n, V that, V

2 The **frets** on a stringed instrument such as a guitar are the metal ridges across its neck. — N-COUNT

fretful /fretfʊl/. If someone is **fretful**, they behave in a way that shows that they worried or unhappy about something. *Don't assume your baby automatically needs feeding if she's fretful.* — ADJ-GRADED

fretwork /fretwɜːʳk/. **Fretwork** is wood or metal that has been decorated by cutting bits of it out to make a pattern. — N-UNCOUNT: oft N n

Freudian /frɔɪdiən/. **Freudian** means relating to the ideas and methods of the psychiatrist Freud, especially to his ideas about people's subconscious sexual feelings. *...the Freudian theory about daughters falling in love with their father.* — ADJ: usu ADJ n

Freudian slip, Freudian slips. If someone accidentally says something that reveals their subconscious feelings, especially their sexual feelings, this is referred to as a **Freudian slip**. — N-COUNT

Fri. **Fri.** is a written abbreviation for **Friday**. — ◆◆◇◇◇

friar /fraɪəʳ/ **friars.** A **friar** is a member of one of several Catholic religious orders. — ◆◇◇◇◇ N-COUNT

friction /frɪkʃən/ **frictions** ◆◇◇◇◇

1 If there is **friction** between people, there is disagreement and argument between them. *Sara sensed that there had been friction between her children... The plan is likely only to aggravate ethnic frictions.* — N-UNCOUNT: also N in pl =conflict

2 **Friction** is the force that makes it difficult for things to move freely when they are touching each other. *The pistons are graphite-coated to reduce friction.* — N-UNCOUNT =resistance

3 **Friction** is the rubbing of one object against another. *...the friction of his leg against hers.* — N-UNCOUNT

Friday /fraɪdeɪ, -di/ **Fridays.** **Friday** is the day after Thursday and before Saturday. *Mr Heath is intending to go to the Middle East on Friday. ...Friday 6 November... I get home at half seven on a Friday.* — ◆◆◆◆◇ N-VAR

fridge /frɪdʒ/ **fridges.** A **fridge** is a large metal container which is kept cool, usually by electricity, so that food that is put in it stays fresh. The more usual American word is **refrigerator**. — ◆◆◇◇◇ N-COUNT =refrigerator

friend /frend/ **friends** ◆◆◆◆◆

1 A **friend** is someone who you know well and like, but who is not related to you. *I had a long talk about this with my best friend... She never was a close friend of mine. ...Sara's old friend, Ogden.* — N-COUNT

2 If you are **friends** with someone, you are their friend and they are yours. *I still wanted to be friends with Alison... We remained good friends... Sally and I became friends.* — N-PLURAL: oft N *with* n

3 The **friends** of a country, cause, organization, or a famous politician are the people and organizations who help and support them. *...the friends of Bosnia. ...The Friends of Birmingham Royal Ballet.* — N-PLURAL: oft in names

4 If one country refers to another as a **friend**, they mean that the other country is not an enemy of — N-COUNT =ally

theirs. *The president said that Japan is now a friend and international partner.*
5 If you **make friends** with someone, you begin a friendship with them. You can also say that two people **make friends**. *He has made friends with the kids on the street... Dennis made friends easily... He had made a friend of both girls.* PHR-RECIP: V inflects, usu PHR *with* n

friendless /frendləs/. Someone who is **friendless** has no friends. *The boy was unhappy because he thought he was friendless.* ADJ

friendly /frendli/ **friendlier, friendliest; friendlies** ◆◆◆◇◇
1 If someone is **friendly**, they behave in a pleasant, kind way, and like to be with other people. *Godfrey had been friendly to me. ...a man with a pleasant, friendly face... Robert has a friendly relationship with his customers. ...a friendly atmosphere... Your cat isn't very friendly.* ♦ **friendliness** *She also loves the friendliness of the people.* ADJ-GRADED =affable, amiable; N-UNCOUNT
2 If you are **friendly** with someone, you like each other and enjoy spending time together. *I'm friendly with his mother... Asmus became friendly with a number of writers and appeared in print as a literary critic.* ADJ-GRADED: v-link ADJ, usu ADJ *with* n
3 You can describe another country or their government as **friendly** when they have good relations with your own country rather than being an enemy. *...a worsening in relations between the two previously friendly countries.* ADJ-GRADED
4 In sport, a **friendly** is a match which is not part of a competition, and is played for entertainment or practice, often without any serious effort to win. *Athletic Bilbao agreed to play a friendly at Real Sociedad.* ► Also a noun. *Austria beat Hungary 3-nil in a friendly match at Salzburg on Wednesday.* N-COUNT; N-COUNT

-friendly /-frendli/
1 **-friendly** combines with nouns to form adjectives which describe things that are not harmful to the specified part of the natural world. *Palm oil is environment-friendly. ...ozone-friendly fridges.* COMB in ADJ
2 **-friendly** combines with nouns to form adjectives which describe things which are intended for or suitable for the specified person, especially things that are easy for them to understand, appreciate, or use. *...customer-friendly banking facilities.* COMB in ADJ
• See also **user-friendly**.

friendly society, friendly societies. In Britain, a **friendly society** is an organization to which people regularly pay small amounts of money and which then gives them money when they retire or when they are ill. N-COUNT

friendship /frendʃɪp/ **friendships** ◆◆◆◇◇
1 A **friendship** is a relationship between two or more friends. *Giving advice when it's not called for is the quickest way to end a good friendship... She struck up a close friendship with Desiree during the week of rehearsals... After seven years of friendship, she still couldn't tell when he was kidding.* N-VAR
2 You use **friendship** to refer in a general way to the state of being friends, or the feelings that friends have for each other. *...a hobby which led to a whole new world of friendship and adventure.* N-UNCOUNT
3 If you have someone's **friendship**, they are your friend. *He had the friendship of Terry Jones and the respect of John Cleese... Steve really values your friendship more than anything else.* N-SING: with poss
4 **Friendship** is a relationship between two countries in which they help and support each other. *The President set the targets for the future to promote friendship with East Europe... They were reaching out the hand of friendship to their former adversaries of the Cold War... Restoring ties with Israel would not affect Bulgaria's traditional friendships with other countries.* N-VAR =goodwill

frieze /friːz/ **friezes.** A **frieze** is a decoration high up on the walls of a room or just under the roof of a building. It consists of a long panel of carving or a long strip of paper with a picture or pattern on it. N-COUNT

frigate /frɪgət/ **frigates.** A **frigate** is a fairly small naval ship that can move at fast speeds. Frigates are often used to protect other ships. ◆◇◇◇◇ N-COUNT

frigging /frɪgɪŋ/. Some people use **frigging** to emphasize that they are angry or annoyed about something; an informal word which some people find offensive. ADJ: ADJ n PRAGMATICS

fright /fraɪt/ **frights** ◆◇◇◇◇
1 **Fright** is a sudden feeling of fear, especially the fear that you feel when something unpleasant surprises you. *The steam pipes rattled suddenly, and Franklin uttered a shriek and jumped with fright... The birds smashed into the top of their cages in fright... To hide my fright I asked a question.* N-UNCOUNT
2 A **fright** is an experience which makes you suddenly afraid. *The snake picked up its head and stuck out its tongue which gave everyone a fright... The last time you had a real fright, you nearly crashed the car.* N-COUNT: usu sing =scare
3 If a person or animal **takes fright** at something, they are suddenly frightened by it, and want to run away or to stop doing what they are doing. *An untrained horse had taken fright at the sound of gunfire... When costs soared, the studio took fright and recalled the company from Rome.* • **the fright of your life**: see **life**. PHRASE: V inflects

frighten /fraɪtᵊn/ **frightens, frightening, frightened** ◆◆◇◇◇
1 If something or someone **frightens** you, they cause you to suddenly feel afraid, anxious, or nervous. *He knew that Soli was trying to frighten him, so he smiled to hide his fear... Most children are frightened by the sight of blood.* VERB =scare; V n
2 If something **frightens the life out of** you, **frightens the wits out of** you, or **frightens** you **out of your wits**, it causes you to feel suddenly afraid or gives you a very unpleasant shock. *Fairground rides are intended to frighten the life out of you.* PHRASE: V inflects

frighten away or **frighten off** PHRASAL VERB
1 If you **frighten away** a person or animal or **frighten** them **off**, you make them afraid so that they run away or stay some distance away from you. *The fishermen said the company's seismic survey was frightening away fish... He fired into the air, hoping that the noise would frighten them off.* V P n (not pron); V n P
2 To **frighten** someone **away** or **frighten** them **off** means to make them nervous so that they decide not to become involved with a particular person or activity. *Building society repossessions have frightened buyers off... The government is convinced that the bombers want to frighten away foreign investors.* =put off; V n P; V P n (not pron)

frighten into. If you **frighten** someone **into** doing something they would not normally do, you make them do it by making them afraid not to do it. *He was a bully. He tried to frighten people into doing what he wanted.* PHRASAL VERB; V n P -ing/n

frighten off. See **frighten away**. PHRASAL VERB

frightened /fraɪtᵊnd/. If you are **frightened**, you are anxious or afraid, often because of something that has just happened or that you think may happen. *She was frightened of flying... Miriam was too frightened to tell her family what had happened.* ◆◆◇◇◇ ADJ-GRADED: oft v-link ADJ *of* n/-ing, ADJ to-inf

frightening /fraɪtənɪŋ/. If something is **frightening**, it makes you feel afraid, anxious, or nervous. *It was a very frightening experience and they were very courageous... The number of youngsters involved in crime is frightening.* ♦ **frighteningly** *The country is frighteningly close to possessing nuclear weapons.* ◆◆◇◇◇ ADJ-GRADED =alarming; ADV-GRADED: usu ADV adj

frightful /fraɪtful/ ◆◇◇◇◇
1 **Frightful** means very bad or unpleasant; an old-fashioned use. *My father was unable to talk about the war, it was so frightful.* ADJ-GRADED =terrible
2 **Frightful** is used to emphasize the extent or degree of something, usually something bad; an old-fashioned, informal use. *He got himself into a frightful muddle... What frightful gossips people are, even one's best friends.* ♦ **frightfully** *I'm most frightfully sorry about this... You're frightfully good at this sort of thing.* ADJ: ADJ n PRAGMATICS =dreadful; ADV: ADV adj/adv =terribly

frigid /frɪdʒɪd/
1 **Frigid** means extremely cold. *A snowstorm hit the West today, bringing with it frigid temperatures...* ADJ-GRADED =freezing

The water was too frigid to allow him to remain submerged for long.
2 If a woman is **frigid**, she finds it difficult to become sexually aroused or responsive. *My husband says I am frigid.* ♦ **frigidity** /frɪdʒɪdɪti/ *After years of frigidity Angie had her first passionate affair.* ADJ-GRADED: usu v-link ADJ N-UNCOUNT
3 If you describe the atmosphere in a place or someone's behaviour as **frigid**, you mean that it is very formal and unfriendly. *He presided at all councils of ministers, where the atmosphere could be frigid on occasions... 'Well, dear,' her hostess would reply with a frigid smile.* ADJ-GRADED PRAGMATICS =chilly

frill /frɪl/ **frills** ◆◇◇◇◇
1 A **frill** is a long narrow strip of cloth or paper with many folds in it, which is attached to something as a decoration. *...net curtains with frills.* N-COUNT
2 If you describe something as having no **frills**, you mean that it has no extra features, but is acceptable or good if you want something simple; used showing approval. *This booklet restricts itself to facts without frills. ...plain, simple cooking in no-frills surroundings.* N-COUNT: usu with brd-neg, usu pl PRAGMATICS

frilled /frɪld/. A **frilled** item of clothing is decorated with a frill or frills. *...a frilled shirt and floppy cravat.* ADJ: ADJ n

frilly /frɪli/. **Frilly** items of clothing or fabric have a lot of frills on them. *...maids in frilly aprons.* ADJ-GRADED: usu ADJ n

fringe /frɪndʒ/ **fringes** ◆◆◇◇◇
1 In British English, a **fringe** is hair which is cut so that it hangs over your forehead. The usual American word is **bangs**. N-COUNT
2 A **fringe** is a decoration attached to clothes, or other objects such as lampshades, consisting of a row of hanging strips or threads. *The jacket had leather fringes.* N-COUNT
3 To be on the **fringe** or the **fringes** of a place means to be on the outside edge of it, or to be in one of the parts that are farthest from its centre. *...black townships located on the fringes of the city... They lived together in a mixed household on the fringe of a campus.* N-COUNT: usu *on the* N *of* n
4 The **fringe** or the **fringes** of an activity or organization are its less important, least typical, or most extreme parts, rather than its main and central part. *The Communist Party has always been on the fringe of British politics.* N-COUNT: usu pl, *the* N *of* n
5 **Fringe** groups or events are less important or established than other related groups or events, or are unofficial. *The monarchists are a small fringe group who quarrel fiercely among themselves. ...the numerous fringe meetings held during the party conference.* ADJ: ADJ n

fringe benefit, fringe benefits
1 **Fringe benefits** are extra things that some people get from their job in addition to their salary, for example a car. N-COUNT: usu pl
2 The **fringe benefits** of doing something are the extra advantages which you get from it, although you may not have expected them and they were not the main reason for doing it. *His support was one of the nicest fringe benefits of pursuing this research.* N-COUNT: oft N *of*-ing/n =bonus

fringed /frɪndʒd/ ◆◇◇◇◇
1 **Fringed** clothes, curtains, or lampshades are decorated with fringes. *Emma wore a fringed scarf round her neck.* ADJ: ADJ n
2 If a place or object **is fringed with** something, that thing forms a border around it or is situated along its edges. *Her eyes were large and brown and fringed with incredibly long lashes. ...tiny islands fringed with golden sand.* ADJ: v-link ADJ *with* n =edged

frippery /frɪpəri/ **fripperies.** If you refer to something as **frippery**, you disapprove of it because it is trivial, extravagant, and only done or worn to impress people; used mainly in British English. *...all the fripperies with which the Edwardian woman indulged herself. ...a sombre display, with no frills or frippery.* N-UNCOUNT: also N in pl PRAGMATICS

Frisbee /frɪzbi/ **Frisbees.** A **frisbee** is a light plastic disc that one person throws to another as a game. **Frisbee** is a trademark. N-COUNT

frisk /frɪsk/ **frisks, frisking, frisked.** If someone **frisks** you, they search you, usually with their hands in order to see if you are hiding a weapon or something else such as drugs in your clothes. *Drago pushed him up against the wall and frisked him.* VERB =body-search V n

frisky /frɪski/ **friskier, friskiest.** A **frisky** animal or person is energetic and playful, and may be difficult to control. *His horse was feeling frisky, and he had to hold the reins tightly.* ADJ-GRADED =spirited

frisson /friːsɒn, AM friːsoʊn/ **frissons.** A **frisson** is a short, sudden feeling of excitement or fear. *A frisson of apprehension rippled round the theatre.* N-COUNT: usu with supp, oft N *of* n

fritter /frɪtəʳ/ **fritters, frittering, frittered. Fritters** are round pieces of fruit, vegetables, or meat that are dipped in batter and fried. *...apple fritters.* N-COUNT: usu n N

fritter away. If someone **fritters away** time or money, they waste it on unimportant and unnecessary things. *The firm soon started frittering away the cash it was generating... I seem to fritter my time away at coffee mornings.* PHRASAL VERB =squander V P n (not pron) V n P

frivolity /frɪvɒlɪti/ **frivolities.** If you refer to an activity as a **frivolity**, you think that it is amusing and rather silly, rather than serious and sensible. *There is a serious message at the core of all this frivolity... He was one of my most able pupils, but far too easily distracted by frivolities.* N-VAR

frivolous /frɪvələs/ ◆◇◇◇◇
1 If you describe someone as **frivolous**, you mean they behave in a silly or light-hearted way, rather than being serious and sensible. *I just decided I was a bit too frivolous to be a doctor... Isabelle was a frivolous little fool, vain and flighty.* ADJ-GRADED
2 If you describe an activity as **frivolous**, you disapprove of it because it is not useful and wastes time or money. *The group says it wants politicians to stop wasting public money on what it believes are frivolous projects.* ADJ-GRADED PRAGMATICS =futile

frizz /frɪz/. **Frizz** is frizzy hair. *Manic brushing will only cause frizz.* N-UNCOUNT

frizzy /frɪzi/ **frizzier, frizziest. Frizzy** hair is very thickly and stiffly curled. *Carol's hair had a slightly frizzy perm.* ADJ-GRADED

fro /froʊ/. ● **to and fro**: see **to**.

frock /frɒk/ **frocks.** A **frock** is a woman's or girl's dress; an old-fashioned word. ◆◇◇◇◇ N-COUNT

frock coat, frock coats; also spelled **frock-coat.** A **frock coat** was a long coat that was worn by men in the 19th century. N-COUNT

frog /frɒg, AM frɔːg/ **frogs** ◆◇◇◇◇
1 A **frog** is a small creature with smooth skin, big eyes, and long back legs which it uses for jumping. Frogs usually live near water. N-COUNT
2 Some people refer to French people as **Frogs**; an informal use which some people find offensive. N-COUNT

frogman /frɒgmən, AM frɔːg-/ **frogmen.** A **frogman** is someone whose job involves diving and working underwater, especially in order to mend or search for something. Frogmen wear special rubber suits and shoes, and carry equipment to help them to breathe underwater. N-COUNT =diver

frog-march, frog-marches, frog-marching, frog-marched; also spelled **frogmarch**. If you **are frog-marched** somewhere, someone takes you there by force, holding you by the arms or another part of your body so that you have to walk along with them. *He was frog-marched through the kitchen and out into the yard. ...arresting the men and frog-marching them to the local police station.* VERB *be* V-ed prep/adv V n prep/adv

frogspawn /frɒgspɔːn, AM frɔːg-/; also spelled **frog spawn. Frogspawn** is a soft jelly-like substance which contains the eggs of a frog. N-UNCOUNT

fro-ing. See **to-ing and fro-ing**.

frolic /frɒlɪk/ **frolics, frolicking, frolicked.** When people or animals **frolic** they play or move in a lively, happy, and carefree way. *Tourists sunbathe and frolic in the ocean. ...lambs frolicking in the fields.* ► Also a noun. *There relationship is never short on fun and frolic.* ◆◇◇◇◇ VERB V N-VAR

from /frəm, STRONG frɒm, AM frʌm/ ◆◆◆◆◆
In addition to the uses shown below, **from** is used in phrasal verbs such as 'date from' and 'grow away from'.
1 If something comes **from** a particular person or thing, or if you get something **from** them, they give or provide it to you, or they are the source of it. *He appealed for information from anyone who saw the attackers. ...an anniversary present from his wife... The results were taken from six surveys... The dirt from the fields drifted like snow.* PREP
2 Someone who comes **from** a particular place lives in that place or originally lived there. Something that comes **from** a particular place was made in that place. *...an art dealer from Zurich... Katy Jones is nineteen and comes from Birmingham. ...wines from Coteaux d'Aix-en-Provence.* PREP
3 A person **from** a particular organization works for that organization. *...a representative from the Israeli embassy. ...Colonel Milan Gvero, who is from the federal Defense Ministry in Belgrade.* PREP
4 If someone or something moves or is moved **from** a place, they leave it or are removed, so that they are no longer there. *Soviet troops withdrew from Afghanistan last year... The guests watched as she fled from the room.* PREP
5 If you take one thing or person **from** another, you move that thing or person so that they are no longer with the other or attached to the other. *In many bone transplants, bone can be taken from other parts of the patient's body... Remove the bowl from the ice and stir in the cream.* PREP
6 If you take something **from** an amount, you reduce the amount by that much. *The £103 is deducted from Mrs Adams' salary every month... Three from six leaves three.* PREP
7 **From** is used in expressions such as **away from** or **absent from** to say that someone or something is not present in a place where they are usually found. *Her husband worked away from home a lot... Jo was absent from the house all the next day.* PREP
8 If you return **from** a place or an activity, you return after being in that place or doing that activity. *My son Colin has just returned from Amsterdam. ...a group of men travelling home from a darts match.* PREP
9 If you are back **from** a place or activity, you have left it and have returned to your former place. *Our economics correspondent, James Morgan, is just back from Germany... One afternoon when I was home from school, he asked me to come to see a movie with him.* PREP
10 If you see or hear something **from** a particular place, you are in that place when you see it or hear it. *Visitors see the painting from behind a plate glass window... Viewed from above, the valleys form the shape of a man.* PREP: PREP n, PREP prep, PREP adv
11 If something hangs or sticks out **from** an object, it is attached to it or held by it. *Hanging from his right wrist is a heavy gold bracelet. ...large fans hanging from ceilings... He saw the corner of a magazine sticking out from under the blanket.* PREP: v PREP n
12 You can use **from** when giving distances. For example, if a place is fifty miles **from** another place, the distance between the two places is fifty miles. *The centre of the town is 4 kilometres from the station. ...a small park only a few hundred yards from Zurich's main shopping centre... How far is it from here?* PREP: amount PREP n
13 If a road or railway line goes **from** one place to another, you can travel along it between the two places. *...the road from St Petersburg to Tallinn.* PREP
14 **From** is used, especially in the expression **made from**, to say what substance has been used to make something. *...bread made from white flour. ...a luxurious resort built from the island's native coral stone.* PREP: v PREP n =out of
15 You can use **from** when you are talking about the beginning of a period of time. *She studied painting from 1926 and also worked as a commercial artist... Breakfast is available to fishermen from 6 a.m... From 1922 till 1925 she lived in Prague.* PREP
16 You say **from** one thing **to** another when you are stating the range of things that are possible, or when saying that the range of things includes everything in a certain category. *There are 94 countries represented in Barcelona, from Algeria to Zimbabwe... Over 150 companies will be there, covering everything from finance to fixtures and fittings.* PREP: PREP n/-ing
17 If something changes **from** one thing to another, it stops being the first thing and becomes the second thing. *The expression on his face changed from sympathy to surprise... Unemployment has fallen from 7.5 to 7.2%... I made a switch from butter to olive oil for much of my cooking.* PREP
18 You use **from** after some verbs and nouns when mentioning the cause of something. *The problem simply resulted from a difference of opinion... He is suffering from eye ulcers, brought on by the intense light in Australia... They really do get pleasure from spending money on other people... Most of the wreckage from the 1985 quake has been cleared.* PREP: PREP n/-ing
19 You use **from** when you are giving the reason for an opinion. *She knew from experience that Dave was about to tell her the truth... He sensed from the expression on her face that she had something to say... I guessed from his name that Jose must have been Spanish.* PREP
20 **From** is used after verbs with meanings such as 'protect', 'free', 'keep', and 'prevent' to introduce the action that does not happen, or that someone does not want to happen. *Such laws could protect the consumer from harmful or dangerous remedies... 300 tons of Peruvian mangoes were kept from entering France.* PREP

frond /frɒnd/ **fronds.** A **frond** is a long leaf or piece of seaweed which has an edge divided into lots of thin parts. *...palm fronds.* N-COUNT: usu with supp

front /frʌnt/ **fronts, fronting, fronted** ◆◆◆◆◆
1 The **front** of something is the part of it that faces you, or that faces forward, or that you normally see or use. *One man sat in an armchair, and the other sat on the front of the desk... Stand at the front of the line... Her cotton dress had ripped down the front.* N-COUNT: usu sing, oft *the* N *of* n ≠back
2 The **front** of a building is the side or part of it that faces the street. *Attached to the front of the house, there was a large veranda.* N-COUNT: usu sing, oft *the* N *of* n
3 A person's or animal's **front** is the part of their body between their head and their legs that is on the opposite side to their back. *If you lie your baby on his front, he'll lift his head and chest up.* N-SING: poss N ≠back
4 **Front** is used to refer to the side or part of something that is towards the front or nearest to the front. *I went out there on the front porch... She was only six and still missing her front teeth... Children may be tempted to climb into the front seat while the car is in motion.* ADJ: ADJ n ≠back
5 The **front** page of a newspaper is the outside of the first page, where the main news stories are printed. *The Guardian's front page carries a photograph of the two foreign ministers... The violence in the Gaza Strip makes the front page of most of the newspapers.* • See also **front-page**. ADJ: ADJ n
6 In British English, **the front** is a road next to the sea in a seaside town. *...a stroll on the front... Amy went out for a last walk along the sea front.* N-SING: *the* N
7 In a war, the **front** is a line where two opposing armies are facing each other. *Sonja's husband is fighting at the front.* • See also **front line**. N-COUNT: usu *the* N in sing
8 If you say that something is happening on a particular **front**, you mean that it is happening with regard to a particular situation or field of activity. *...research across a wide academic front... We're moving forward on a variety of fronts.* N-COUNT
9 If someone puts on a particular kind of **front**, they pretend to have a particular quality. *Michael kept up a brave front both to the world and in his home... His laugh-a-minute image is just a front to hide his deep unhappiness.* N-COUNT: usu adj N
10 An organization or activity that is a **front** for one that is illegal or secret is used to hide it. *...a firm later identified by the police as a front for crime syndicates... He said the present civilian government is just a front for the old military regime.* N-COUNT: usu N *for* n =cover

11 In weather forecasting, a **front** is the line where a mass of cold air meets a mass of warm air. *The snow signaled the arrival of a front, and a high-pressure area seemed to be settling in... A very active cold front brought dramatic weather changes to Kansas on Wednesday.* N-COUNT

12 The word **Front** is often used in the titles of political organizations with a particular aim. *...the People's Liberation Front.* N-IN-NAMES: *the* supp N

13 A building or area of land that **fronts** a particular place or **fronts** onto it is next to it and faces it. *...real estate, which includes undeveloped land fronting the city convention center... There are some delightful Victorian houses fronting on to the pavement. ...quaint cottages fronted by lawns and flowerbeds.* VERB =face V n V *onto* n V-ed

14 In British English, the person who **fronts** an organization is the most senior person in it. *He fronted a formidable band of guerilla fighters against the Pakistan army... The commission, fronted by Sir Isaac Hayatali, was set up in June 1992.* VERB V n V-ed

15 The person who **fronts** a pop group or rock band is the main singer. *He also fronted a group called Haircuts That Kill. ...the debut single from the new five-piece fronted by singer Melissa Heathcoate.* VERB V n V-ed

16 If a person or thing is **in front**, they are ahead of others in a moving group, or further forward than someone or something else. *Officers will crack down on lunatic motorists who speed or drive too close to the car in front... 'What's with this guy?' demanded an American voice in the row in front.* PHRASES

17 Someone who is **in front** in a competition or contest at a particular point is winning at that point. *Richard Dunwoody is in front in the jockeys' title race... Some preliminary polls show him out in front in the race.* PHR after v, v-link PHR =leading

18 If someone or something is **in front of** a particular thing, they are facing it, ahead of it, or close to the front part of it. *She sat down in front of her dressing-table mirror to look at herself... Something darted out in front of my car, and my car hit it... A police car was parked in front of the house.* PREP

19 If you do or say something **in front of** someone else, you do or say it when they are present. *They never argued in front of their children... He has been brought up not to swear in front of women.* PREP

20 On the home front or **on the domestic front** means with regard to your own country rather than foreign countries; used in journalism. *Its present economic ills on the home front are largely the result of overspending... On the domestic front, the president got his way with his budget proposals.* PHR with cl

frontage /frʌntɪdʒ/ **frontages.** A **frontage** of a building is a wall which faces a public place such as a street or a river. *The restaurant has a river frontage.* N-COUNT: also no det

frontal /frʌntəl/ ◆◇◇◇◇

1 Frontal means relating to or involving the front of something, for example the front of an army, a vehicle, or the brain; a formal use. *Military leaders are not expecting a frontal assault by the rebels... He pioneered the surgical technique called frontal lobotomy.* ADJ: usu ADJ n

2 A **frontal** attack or challenge criticizes or threatens something in a very strong, direct way. *He launches a frontal attack on working-class organizations.* ADJ: usu ADJ n =head on

3 See also **full-frontal**.

front bench, front benches. In Britain, the **front bench** or people who sit on the **front bench** are members of Parliament who are ministers in the Government or who hold official positions in an opposition party. *Some of the Government front bench still believe our relationship with the US is paramount. ...Labour's front bench spokesperson on the inner cities.* N-COUNT-COLL

frontbencher /frʌntbentʃəʳ/ **frontbenchers.** In Britain, a **frontbencher** is a member of Parliament who is a minister in the Government or who holds an official position in an opposition party. N-COUNT: usu supp N

front burner. If an issue is on the **front burner**, it receives a lot of attention because it is considered to be more urgent or important than other issues. *Bosnia continues to be on the front burner... We have an urgent front-burner public health problem.* N-SING: usu *on the* N ≠back burner

front door, front doors. The **front door** of a house or other building is the main door, which is usually in the wall that faces a street. ◆◆◇◇◇ N-COUNT

frontier /frʌntɪəʳ, -tɪəʳ/ **frontiers** ◆◆◇◇◇

1 In British English, a **frontier** is a border between two countries. The usual American word is **border**. *It wasn't difficult then to cross the frontier.* N-COUNT

2 You use **frontier** to refer to the border of an area of unclaimed land, or to a region beyond its border. *...a far-flung outpost on the frontier.* N-COUNT

3 The **frontiers** of something, especially knowledge, are the limits to which it extends. *...pushing back the frontiers of science. ...technological frontiers.* N-COUNT: usu pl, usu N *of* n, adj N

frontispiece /frʌntɪspiːs/ **frontispieces.** The **frontispiece** of a book is a picture at the beginning, opposite the page with the title on. N-COUNT: usu sing

front line, front lines; also spelled **front-line.** ◆◆◇◇◇

1 The **front line** is the place where two opposing armies are facing each other and where fighting is going on. *...a massive concentration of soldiers on the front line.* N-COUNT: usu *the* N

2 A **front line** state shares a border with a country that it is at war with or is in conflict with. *...the front-line states bordering South Africa.* ADJ: ADJ n

3 Someone who is **in the front line** has to play a very important part in defending or achieving something. *Information officers are in the front line of putting across government policies.* PHRASE: v-link PHR, PHR after v

front man, front men. If you say that someone is a **front man** for a group or organization, you mean that their role is to represent and give a good impression of it to the public, especially when it is not very respectable or popular; used showing disapproval. *Mr Walesa accused his rival of being a front man for former members of the Communist secret police.* N-COUNT: oft N *for* n PRAGMATICS

front-page. A **front-page** article or picture appears on the front page of a newspaper because it is very important or interesting. *...a front-page article in last week's paper.* ◆◆◇◇◇ ADJ: ADJ n

front-runner, front-runners. In a competition or contest, the **front-runner** is the person who seems most likely to win it. *Neither of the front-runners in the presidential election is a mainstream politician.* ◆◇◇◇◇ N-COUNT =favourite

frost /frɒst, AM frɔːst/ **frosts** ◆◇◇◇◇

1 When there is **frost** or a **frost**, the temperature outside falls below freezing point and the ground becomes covered in ice crystals. *There is frost in the ground and snow is forecast... The wind had veered to north, bringing clear skies and a keen frost.* N-VAR

2 When someone says that there are a particular number of **degrees of frost** they mean that the temperature is that number of degrees below freezing point. *We had 11 degrees of frost last night.* PHRASE

frostbite /frɒstbaɪt, AM frɔːst-/. **Frostbite** is a condition in which parts of your body, such as your fingers or toes, become seriously damaged as a result of being very cold. *The survivors suffered from frostbite.* N-UNCOUNT

frostbitten /frɒstbɪtən, AM frɔːst-/. If a person or a part of their body is **frostbitten**, they are suffering from frostbite. ADJ

frosted /frɒstɪd, AM frɔːst-/

1 Frosted glass has had its surface roughened so that you cannot see through it clearly. *The top half of the door to his office was of frosted glass.* ADJ

2 Frosted means covered with frost. *...the frosted trees.* ADJ

3 Frosted means covered with something that looks like frost. *...frosted blue eye shadow.* ADJ

4 In American English, **frosted** means covered with icing. The usual British word is **iced**. *...a plate of frosted cupcakes.* ADJ

frosting /frɒstɪŋ, AM frɔːst-/. In American English, **frosting** is a sweet substance made from powdered sugar that is used to cover and decorate cakes. The usual British word is **icing**. *...a huge pastry with green frosting on it.* N-UNCOUNT

frosty /frɒsti, AM frɔːsti/ **frostier, frostiest** ◆◇◇◇◇
1 If the weather is **frosty**, the temperature is below freezing. *...sharp, frosty nights.* ADJ-GRADED =icy
2 You describe the ground or an object as **frosty** when it is covered with frost. *The street was deserted except for a cat lifting its paws off the frosty stones.* ADJ-GRADED =icy
3 If you describe someone's behaviour as **frosty**, you think it is unfriendly. *The president may get a frosty reception in New Hampshire... The relationship has obviously become frosty.* ADJ-GRADED =unfriendly ♦ **frostily** /frɒstɪli, AM frɔːst-/ *The Prime Minister smiled again, this time a trifle frostily.* ADV-GRADED: ADV with v ♦ **frostiness** *There was a certain frostiness in his smile.* N-UNCOUNT

froth /frɒθ, AM frɔːθ/ **froths, frothing, frothed** ◆◇◇◇◇
1 **Froth** is a mass of small bubbles on the surface of a liquid. *...the froth of bubbles on the top of a glass of beer... The froth is blown away.* N-UNCOUNT =foam
2 If a liquid **froths**, small bubbles appear on its surface. *The sea froths over my feet... Add a little of the warmed milk and allow to froth a little.* VERB V prep V
3 If you say that someone **is frothing**, or that they **are frothing** at the mouth, you are emphasizing that they are very angry or excited about something; used in written English. *'No! No! Never!' he froths... This story has many ingredients which make any news editor froth at the mouth with excitement.* VERB PRAGMATICS =foam V with quote V prep Also V
4 If you refer to an activity or object as **froth**, you disapprove of it because it appears exciting or attractive, but has very little real value or importance. *Loads of verve, but no substance at all, just froth... Falling in love the first time is all froth and fantasy.* N-UNCOUNT PRAGMATICS

frothy /frɒθi, AM frɔːθi/ **frothier, frothiest.** A **frothy** liquid has lots of bubbles on its surface. *...frothy milk shakes.* ADJ-GRADED: usu ADJ n

frown /fraʊn/ **frowns, frowning, frowned.** When someone **frowns**, their eyebrows become drawn together, because they are annoyed, worried, or puzzled, or because they are concentrating. *Nancy shook her head, frowning... He frowned at her anxiously. ...a frowning man.* ◆◆◇◇◇ VERB V V at n V-ing ► Also a noun. *There was a deep frown on the boy's face.* N-COUNT

frown upon or **frown on.** If something **is frowned upon** or **is frowned on** people disapprove of it. *This practice is frowned upon as being wasteful... Many teachers frown on such practices.* PHRASAL VERB be V-ed P V P n (not pron)

froze /froʊz/. **Froze** is the past tense of **freeze**.

frozen /froʊzᵊn/ ◆◆◇◇◇
1 **Frozen** is the past participle of **freeze**.
2 If the ground is **frozen** it has become very hard because the weather is very cold. *It was bitterly cold now and the ground was frozen hard. ...the frozen bleakness of the Far North.* ADJ
3 **Frozen** food has been preserved by being kept at a very low temperature. *Frozen fish is a very healthy convenience food. ...frozen desserts like ice cream.* ADJ: usu ADJ n
4 If you say that you are **frozen**, or a part of your body is **frozen**, you are emphasizing that you feel very cold. *He put one hand up to his frozen face... I'm frozen to the bone out here.* ADJ PRAGMATICS ● **Frozen stiff** means the same as **frozen**. *It was cold and damp; he pulled up his collar and was aware of being frozen stiff.* PHRASE: v-link PHR
5 If you describe someone as **frozen**, you mean that their body is fixed in a particular position, for example because they are very worried or afraid. *One boy, aged about 11, looks frozen with fright... Katherine was frozen in horror.* ADJ: oft ADJ in/with n

frugal /fruːgᵊl/ ◆◇◇◇◇
1 People who are **frugal** or who live **frugal** lives do not eat much or spend much money on themselves. *She lives a frugal life.* ADJ-GRADED =thrifty ♦ **frugality** *We must practise the strictest frugality and economy.* N-UNCOUNT ♦ **frugally** *We lived fairly frugally... He frugally saved various bits of the machine in carefully marked boxes.* ADV-GRADED: ADV with v
2 A **frugal** meal is small and inexpensive. *The diet was frugal: cheese and water, rice and beans.* ADJ-GRADED

fruit /fruːt/ **fruits, fruiting, fruited.** The plural of the noun can be either **fruit** or **fruits**, but is usually **fruit**. ◆◆◆◆◇
1 **Fruit** or a **fruit** is something which grows on a tree or bush and which contains seeds or a stone covered by a substance that you can eat. The plural is either fruit or fruits. *Fresh fruit and vegetables provide fibre and vitamins. ...bananas and other tropical fruits... Try to eat at least one piece of fruit a day.* N-VAR
2 If a plant **fruits**, it produces fruit; a technical use in horticulture. *The scientists will study the variety of trees and observe which are fruiting.* VERB V
3 The **fruits** or the **fruit** of someone's work or activity are the good things that result from it. *The team have really worked hard and Mansell is enjoying the fruits of that labour... The findings are the fruit of more than three years research.* N-COUNT: usu the N of n
4 See also **dried fruit**, **forbidden fruit**, **kiwi fruit**, **passion fruit**.
5 If the effort that you put into something or a particular way of doing something **bears fruit**, it is successful and produces good results. *Eleanor's work among the women will, I trust, bear fruit... He was naturally disappointed when the talks failed to bear fruit.* PHRASES V inflects
6 **The first fruits** or **the first fruit** of a project or activity are its earliest results or profits. *This project is one of the first fruits of commercial co-operation between the two countries.* oft PHR of n

fruit bowl, fruit bowls. A **fruit bowl** is a large bowl in which fruit is kept and displayed. N-COUNT

fruitcake /fruːtkeɪk/ **fruitcakes;** also spelled **fruit cake**. A **fruitcake** is a cake that contains raisins, currants, and other dried fruit. N-VAR

fruit cocktail, fruit cocktails. Fruit cocktail is a mixture of pieces of different kinds of fruit eaten as part of a meal. N-VAR

fruitful /fruːtfʊl/ ◆◇◇◇◇
1 Something that is **fruitful** produces good and useful results. *We had a long, happy, fruitful relationship... The talks had been fruitful, but much remained to be done.* ADJ-GRADED =successful ♦ **fruitfully** *...taking their skills where they can be applied most fruitfully.* ADV-GRADED: ADV with v
2 **Fruitful** land or trees produce a lot of crops. *...a landscape that was fruitful and lush.* ADJ-GRADED =fertile

fruition /fruɪʃᵊn/. If something comes to **fruition**, it starts to succeed and produce the results that were intended or hoped for; a formal word. *These plans take time to come to fruition... His hopes for a new political party have little chance of reaching fruition.* ◆◇◇◇◇ N-UNCOUNT: usu to N

fruitless /fruːtləs/. **Fruitless** actions, events, or efforts do not achieve anything at all. *It was a fruitless search... Talks have so far have been fruitless.* ◆◇◇◇◇ ADJ-GRADED =unproductive ♦ **fruitlessly** *Four years of negotiation ended fruitlessly last December.* ADV: ADV with v

fruit machine, fruit machines. In British English, a **fruit machine** is a machine used for gambling. You put money into it and if a particular combination of symbols, especially fruit, appears, you win money. N-COUNT

fruit salad, fruit salads. Fruit salad is a mixture of pieces of different kinds of fruit. It is usually eaten as a dessert. N-VAR

fruity /fruːti/ **fruitier, fruitiest** ◆◇◇◇◇
1 Something that is **fruity** smells or tastes of fruit. *This shampoo smells fruity and leaves the hair beautifully silky. ...a lovely rich fruity wine.* ADJ-GRADED
2 A **fruity** voice or laugh is pleasantly rich and deep. *Jerrold laughed again, a solid, fruity laugh.* ADJ-GRADED: usu ADJ n

frumpy /frʌmpi/. If you describe a woman or her clothes as **frumpy**, you mean that her clothes are dull and unfashionable. *I looked so frumpy next to these women. ...bulky, frumpy clothes.* ADJ-GRADED =dowdy

frustrate /frʌstreɪt, AM frʌstreɪt/ **frustrates, frustrating, frustrated** ◆◆◆◇◇
1 If something **frustrates** you, it upsets or angers VERB

you because you are unable to do anything about the problems it creates. *These questions frustrated me... Doesn't it frustrate you that audiences in the theatre are so restricted?* ♦ **frustrated** *Roberta felt frustrated and angry. ...voters who are frustrated with the council.* ♦ **frustrating** *It was frustrating to be out of government for the next four years.* ♦ **frustration** /frʌstreɪʃᵊn/ **frustrations** *The results show the level of frustration among hospital doctors. ...a man fed up with the frustrations of everyday life.*
V n / ADJ-GRADED: usu v-link ADJ / ADJ-GRADED: usu v-link ADJ / N-VAR

2 If someone or something **frustrates** a plan or attempt to do something, they prevent it from succeeding. *The government has deliberately frustrated his efforts to gain work permits for his foreign staff. ...her frustrated attempt to become governor.*
VERB / V n / V-ed

fry /fraɪ/ **fries, frying, fried** ◆◆◆◇◇
1 When you **fry** food, you cook it in a pan that contains hot fat or oil. *Fry the breadcrumbs until golden brown. ...fried rice.*
VERB / V n / V-ed
2 **Fry** are very small, young fish.
N-PLURAL
3 **Fries** are the same as **French fries**.
N-PLURAL
4 See also **small fry**.

fry up. If you **fry up** food, you fry it, especially in order to make a quick, casual meal; an informal expression. *I fried up the beef... She cuts and fries the mixture up into a potato doughnut called Quin-Kuria.* ● See also **fry-up**.
PHRASAL VERB / V P n(not pron) / V n P

frying pan, frying pans. A **frying pan** is a flat metal pan with a long handle, in which you fry food.
◆◇◇◇◇ N-COUNT

fry-up, fry-ups. In British English, a **fry-up** is a meal consisting of a mixture of foods such as sausages, bacon, and eggs that have been fried; an informal expression.
N-COUNT

ft. ft. is a written abbreviation for **feet** or **foot**. *Flying at 1,000 ft, he heard a peculiar noise from the rotors. ...an area of 2,750 sq ft.*
◆◆◇◇◇ N-COUNT: num N

fuchsia /fjuːʃə/ **fuchsias.** A **fuchsia** is a plant or a small bush which has pink, purple, or white flowers. The flowers hang downwards, with their outer petals curved backwards.
◆◇◇◇◇ N-VAR

fuck /fʌk/ **fucks, fucking, fucked** ◆◆◇◇◇
Fuck is a rude and offensive word which you should avoid using.
1 **Fuck** is used to express anger or annoyance.
EXCLAM
2 If someone uses an expression such as '**Fuck it**', '**Fuck you**', or '**Fuck that**', they are expressing anger or the fact that they do not care about someone or something.
EXCLAM
3 To **fuck** someone means to have sex with them.
V-RECIP
► Also a noun.
N-COUNT
4 **Fuck all** is used to mean 'nothing at all'.
PHRASE

fuck about or **fuck around.** The form **fuck about** is mainly used in British English. To **fuck about** or **fuck around** means to behave in a way that is silly, stupid, or unnecessary.
PHRASAL VERB / V P

fuck off. Telling someone to **fuck off** is an insulting way of telling them to go away.
PHRASAL VERB / usu imper, V P

fuck up. If you **fuck** something **up**, you make a mess of it.
PHRASAL VERB / V n P, V P n (not pron)

fucker /fʌkəʳ/ **fuckers.** If someone calls a person a **fucker**, they are insulting them; a rude and offensive word which you should avoid using.
N-COUNT / PRAGMATICS

fucking /fʌkɪŋ/. **Fucking** is used to emphasize a word or phrase, especially when feeling angry or annoyed; a rude and offensive word which you should avoid using.
◆◆◇◇◇ ADJ: ADJ n; ADV: ADV adj

fuddy-duddy /fʌdi dʌdi/ **fuddy-duddies.** If you describe someone as a **fuddy-duddy**, you are criticizing or making fun of them because they are old-fashioned in their appearance or attitudes. *He didn't want all those old fuddy-duddies around.* ► Also an adjective. *Perhaps we did acquire a somewhat fuddy-duddy image in the later years.*
N-COUNT / PRAGMATICS / ADJ-GRADED: ADJ n

fudge /fʌdʒ/ **fudges, fudging, fudged** ◆◇◇◇◇
1 **Fudge** is a soft brown sweet that is made from butter, cream, and sugar.
N-UNCOUNT
2 If you **fudge** something, you avoid making a clear and definite decision, distinction, or statement about it. *Both have fudged their calculations and avoided specifics. ...certain issues that can no longer be fudged.*
VERB / V n

fuel /fjuːəl/ **fuels, fuelling, fuelled;** spelled **fueling**, **fueled** in American English. ◆◆◆◆◇
1 **Fuel** is a substance such as coal, oil, or petrol that is burned to provide heat or power. *They ran out of fuel... Delays were caused by the discovery of dangerous fuel leaks.*
N-MASS
2 If something **fuels** something such as speculation, controversy, or inflation, it makes it increase or become more intense. *The result will inevitably fuel speculation about the Prime Minister's future... The economic boom was fueled by easy credit.*
VERB =feed / V n / be V-ed
3 If something **adds fuel to** a conflict or debate, or **adds fuel to the fire**, it makes the conflict or debate more intense. *His comments are bound to add fuel to the debate... The decision to raise tariffs on imports will only add fuel to the fire.*
PHRASE: V inflects

fuelled /fjuːəld/; spelled **fueled** in American English. A machine or vehicle that **is fuelled by** a particular substance works by burning that substance. *It is less polluting than power stations fuelled by oil, coal and gas.*
ADJ: v-link ADJ by n

fug /fʌg/. In British English, people refer to the atmosphere somewhere as a **fug** when it is airless, and usually smoky and rather smelly. *...the fug of cigarette smoke.*
N-SING: oft N of n

fugitive /fjuːdʒɪtɪv/ **fugitives.** A **fugitive** is someone who is running away or hiding, usually in order to avoid being caught by the police. *The rebel leader was a fugitive from justice. ...the fugitive train robber.*
◆◇◇◇◇ N-COUNT

fugue /fjuːg/ **fugues.** A **fugue** is a piece of music that begins with a simple tune which is then repeated by other voices or instrumental parts with small variations; a technical term in music.
N-COUNT

-ful /-fʊl/ **-fuls.** You use **-ful** to form nouns that refer to the quantity of a substance that an object contains or can contain. For example, a handful of sand is the amount of sand that you can hold in your hand. *...a spoonful of brown sugar.*
SUFFIX

fulcrum /fʊlkrəm/. If you say that someone or something is the **fulcrum** of an activity or situation, you are emphasizing that they have a very important effect on what happens; a formal use. *He will shortly become the fulcrum of the England team... The decision is the strategic fulcrum of the Budget.*
N-SING: oft N of n / PRAGMATICS / =pivot

fulfil /fʊlfɪl/ **fulfils, fulfilling, fulfilled;** also spelled **fulfill** and **fulfills**, especially in American English. ◆◆◆◇◇
1 If you **fulfil** something such as a promise, dream, or ambition, you do what you said or hoped you would do. *President Kaunda fulfilled his promise of announcing a date for the referendum.*
VERB =carry out / V n
2 To **fulfil** a task, role, or requirement means to do or be what is required, necessary, or expected. *Without them you will not be able to fulfil the tasks you have before you... All the necessary conditions were fulfilled.*
VERB / V n
3 If something **fulfils** you, or if you **fulfil** yourself, you feel happy and satisfied with what you are doing or with what you have achieved. *The war was the biggest thing in her life and nothing after that quite fulfilled her... They don't like the idea that women can fulfil themselves without the assistance of a man.* ♦ **fulfilled** *She has courageously continued to lead a fulfilled life... I feel more fulfilled doing this than I've ever done.* ♦ **fulfilling** *...a fulfilling career... I found it all very fulfilling.*
VERB =satisfy / V n / V pron-refl / ADJ-GRADED / ADJ-GRADED

fulfilment /fʊlfɪlmənt/; also spelled **fulfillment**, especially in American English. ◆◇◇◇◇
1 **Fulfilment** is a feeling of satisfaction that you get from doing or achieving something, especially something useful. *...professional fulfilment.*
N-UNCOUNT =satisfaction
2 The **fulfilment** of a promise, threat, request, hope, or duty is the event or act of it happening or being made to happen. *Visiting Angkor was the fulfilment of a childhood dream.*
N-UNCOUNT: usu N of n =realization

full /fʊl/ **fuller, fullest** ◆◆◆◆◆
1 If something is **full**, it contains as much of a substance or as many objects as it can. *Once the con-*
ADJ-GRADED ≠empty

tainer is full, it stays shut until you turn it clockwise. ...a full tank of petrol.

2 If a place or thing **is full of** things or people, it contains a large number of them. *The case was full of clothes... The streets are still full of debris from two nights of rioting. ...a useful recipe leaflet full of ideas for using the new cream.* ADJ-GRADED: v-link ADJ *of* n =filled

3 If someone or something **is full of** a particular feeling or quality, they have a lot of it. *I feel full of confidence and so open to possibilities... Mom's face was full of pain. ...an exquisite mousse, incredibly rich and full of flavour.* ADJ-GRADED: v-link ADJ *of* n

4 You say that a place or vehicle is **full** when there is no space left in it for any more people or things. *The main car park was full when I left about 10.45... They stay here a few hours before being sent to refugee camps, which are now almost full... The bus was completely full, and lots of people were standing.* ADJ-GRADED: usu v-link ADJ =packed

5 If your hands or arms are **full**, you are carrying or holding as much as you can carry. *Sylvia entered, her arms full of packages... People would go into the store and come out with their arms full.* ADJ-GRADED: v-link ADJ =loaded

6 If you feel **full**, you have eaten or drunk so much that you do not want anything else. *It's healthy to eat when I'm hungry and to stop when I'm full.* ADJ-GRADED: v-link ADJ
♦ **fullness** *High fibre diets give the feeling of fullness.* N-UNCOUNT

7 You use **full** before a noun to indicate that you are referring to all the details, things, or people that it can possibly include. *Full details will be sent to you once your application has been accepted... May I have your full name?... Is full employment any longer achievable?* ADJ: ADJ n =maximum

8 **Full** is used to describe a sound, light, or physical force which is being produced with the greatest possible power or intensity. *From his study came the sound of Mahler, playing at full volume... Officials say the operation will be carried out in full daylight... Then abruptly he revved the engine to full power.* ADJ: ADJ n ► Also an adverb. *...a two-seater Lotus, parked with its headlamps full on.* ADV: ADV adv

9 You use **full** to emphasize the completeness, intensity, or extent of something. *We should conserve oil and gas by making full use of other energy sources... Television cameras are carrying the full horror of this war into homes around the world... The lane leading to the farm was in full view of the house windows... By the time the tests took place, the athletes had had a full 17 hours notice.* ADJ: ADJ n PRAGMATICS

10 A **full** statement or report contains a lot of information and detail. *Mr Primakov gave a full account of his meeting with the President. ...the enormous detail in this very full document.* ADJ-GRADED: usu ADJ n

11 If you say that someone has or leads a **full** life, you approve of the fact that they are always busy and do a lot of different things. *You will be successful in whatever you do and you will have a very full and interesting life.* ADJ-GRADED: usu ADJ n PRAGMATICS

12 You use **full** to emphasize the force or directness with which someone or something is hit or looked at. *The burning liquid hit him full in the right eye... She kissed him full on the mouth... She looked him full in the face as she spoke.* ADV: ADV prep PRAGMATICS

13 You use **full** to refer to something which gives you all the rights, status, or importance for a particular position or activity, rather than just some of them. *How did the meeting go, did you get your full membership?... She sent her provisional licence with the test certificate to have it upgraded to a full licence.* ADJ: ADJ n

14 A **full** flavour is strong and rich. *Italian plum tomatoes have a full flavour, and are best for cooking.* ADJ: ADJ n

15 If you describe a part of someone's body as **full**, you mean that it is rounded and rather large. *The Juno Collection specialises in large sizes for ladies with a fuller figure. ...his strong chin, his full lips, his appealing mustache.* ADJ-GRADED: usu ADJ n

16 A **full** skirt or sleeve is wide and has been made from a lot of fabric. *My wedding dress has a very full skirt so I need to wear a good quality net petticoat.* ADJ-GRADED: usu ADJ n
♦ **fullness** *The coat has raglan sleeves, and is cut to give fullness at the back.* N-UNCOUNT

17 When there is a **full** moon, the moon appears as a bright, complete circle. ADJ: usu ADJ n

18 You say that something has been done or described **in full** when everything that was necessary has been done or described. *The medical experts have yet to report in full... We guarantee to reply in full within 10 working days.* PHRASES PHR after v =fully

19 If you say that someone **knows full well** that something is true, especially something unpleasant, you are emphasizing that they are definitely aware of it, although they may behave as if they are not. *He knew full well he'd be ashamed of himself later.* V inflects PRAGMATICS

20 Something that is done or experienced **to the full** is done to as great an extent as is possible. *She probably has a good mind, which should be used to the full... There's only one thing we should do with love; experience it to the full for as long as it lasts.* PHR after v

21 If you say to someone, 'you're **full of** yourself', you disapprove of them because they appear very pleased with themselves, thinking that they are very clever, special, or important. *He's full of himself, sharp and aggressive and sometimes he comes over badly.* V inflects PRAGMATICS

22 • to **be full of beans**: see **bean**. • **full blast**: see **blast**. • to **come full circle**: see **circle**. • to **have** your **hands full**: see **hand**. • **in full swing**: see **swing**.

full-back, full-backs; also spelled **fullback**. In rugby or football, a **full-back** is a defending player whose position is towards the goal which their team is defending. ◆◇◇◇◇ N-COUNT

full-blooded. Full-blooded behaviour and actions are carried out with great commitment and enthusiasm. *Experts are agreed that full-blooded market reform is the only way to save the economy.* ADJ: ADJ n ≠half-hearted ♦ **full-bloodedly** *Maxim Gorky was lucky in the sense that he had no artistic, moral or political dilemmas to resolve. He was of the revolution, and he put his art full-bloodedly at its service.* ADV-GRADED

full-blown. Full-blown means having all the characteristics of a particular type of thing or person. *Before becoming a full-blown director, he worked as the film editor on Citizen Kane.* ◆◇◇◇◇ ADJ: ADJ n

full board; also spelled **full-board**. If the price at a hotel includes **full board**, it includes all your meals; used mainly in British English. N-UNCOUNT

full dress. Someone who is in **full dress** is wearing all the clothes needed for a ceremony or formal occasion. *...full dress uniform.* N-UNCOUNT

full-flavoured; spelled **full-flavored** in American English. **Full-flavoured** food or wine has a pleasant fairly strong taste. *This full-flavoured white wine ages well.* ADJ-GRADED

full-fledged. Full-fledged means the same as **fully-fledged.** ADJ

full-frontal; also spelled **full frontal**.

1 If there is **full-frontal** nudity in a photograph or film, you can see the whole of the front part of someone's naked body, including the genitals. *Why is full-frontal male nudity still so scarce in films?* ADJ: usu ADJ n

2 If you use **full-frontal** to describe someone's criticism or way of dealing with something, you are emphasizing that it is very strong and direct. *The Tories believe a full-frontal attack on the opposition leader is their best hope... They are eager to confront their guests with full frontal interrogations about their marriages.* ADJ: usu ADJ n PRAGMATICS

full-grown. An animal or plant that is **full-grown** has reached its full adult size and stopped growing. *...a full-grown male orang-utan.* ADJ

full house, full houses. If a theatre has a **full house** for a particular performance, it has as large an audience as it can hold. *...playing to a full house.* N-COUNT

full-length ◆◇◇◇◇

1 A **full-length** book, record, or film is the normal length, rather than being shorter than normal. *...his first full-length recording in well over a decade.* ADJ: ADJ n

2 A **full-length** coat or skirt is long enough to reach ADJ:

the lower part of a person's leg, almost to the ankles. A full-length sleeve reaches a person's wrist. ADJ n

3 **Full-length** curtains or other furnishings reach to the floor. ADJ: ADJ n

4 A **full-length** mirror or portrait shows the whole of a person. ADJ: ADJ n

5 Someone who is lying **full-length**, is lying down flat and stretched out. *She stretched herself out full-length.* ADV: ADV after v

full marks

1 In British English, if you get **full marks** in a test or exam, you get everything right and gain the maximum number of marks. *Most people in fact got full marks in one question and zero in the other.* N-PLURAL

2 In British English, if you say that someone gets **full marks** for something, you are praising them for being very clever or for showing some other good quality. *Full marks for honesty, perhaps, but a fail for diplomacy.* N-PLURAL: usu N for n

fullness /fʊlnɒs/

1 See **full**.

2 If you say that something will happen **in the fullness of time**, you mean that it will eventually happen after a long time or after a long series of events. *How he finally reached the South Pole is a mystery that will be revealed in the fullness of time.* PHRASE: PHR with cl, PHR after v

full-page. A **full-page** advertisement, picture, or article in a newspaper or magazine uses a whole page. ◆◇◇◇◇ ADJ: ADJ n

full-scale ◆◇◇◇◇

1 **Full-scale** means as complete, intense, or great in extent as possible. *...the possibility of a full-scale nuclear war.* ADJ: ADJ n ≠partial

2 A **full-scale** drawing or model is the same size as the thing that it represents. *...working, full-scale prototypes.* ADJ: ADJ n

full-size or **full-sized.** A **full-size** or **full-sized** model or picture is the same size as the thing or person that it represents. *I made a full-size cardboard model.* ◆◇◇◇◇ ADJ: ADJ n

full stop, full stops. In British English, a **full stop** is the punctuation mark (.) which you use at the end of a sentence when it is not a question or exclamation; the American expression is **period**. N-COUNT

full-strength. See **strength**.

full-throated. A **full-throated** sound coming from someone's mouth, such as a shout or a laugh, is very loud. *...full-throated singing.* ADJ: ADJ n

full-time; also spelled **full time**. ◆◆◇◇◇

1 **Full-time** work or study involves working or studying for the whole of each normal working week rather than for part of it. *...a full-time job. ...full-time staff.* ► Also an adverb. *Deirdre works full-time.* ADJ: usu ADJ n; ADV: ADV after v

2 If you describe a regular activity or task as **a full-time job**, you mean that it takes up so much of your time it is like doing a paid job. *The way she did it, mothering was a full-time job.* PHRASE: usu v-link PHR

3 In games such as football, **full time** is the end of a match; used in British English. *The score at full-time was Arsenal 1, Sampdoria 1.* N-UNCOUNT

full-timer, full-timers. A **full-timer** is someone who works full-time. *The company employs six full-timers and one part-time worker.* N-COUNT

full up; also spelled **full-up**.

1 Something that is **full up** has no space left for any more people or things. *The prisons are all full up.* ADJ: v-link ADJ

2 If you are **full up** you have eaten or drunk so much that you do not want to eat or drink anything else; an informal use. ADJ-GRADED: v-link ADJ

fully /fʊli/ ◆◆◆◆◇

1 **Fully** means to the greatest degree or extent possible. *She was fully aware of my thoughts... I don't fully agree with that.* ADV: ADV adj, ADV with v =completely

2 You use **fully** to say that a process is completely finished. *He had still not fully recovered.* ADV: ADV with v

3 If you describe, answer, or deal with something **fully**, you leave out nothing that should be mentioned or dealt with. *Fiers promised to testify fully and truthfully... Major elements of these debates are discussed more fully later in this book.* ADV-GRADED: ADV with v

4 **Fully** is used to emphasize how great an amount is; used in written English. *Fully 30% of the poor could not even afford access to illegal shanties.* ADV: ADV amount PRAGMATICS

fully-fledged. **Fully-fledged** means complete or fully developed. *Hungary is to have a fully-fledged Stock Exchange from today.* ◆◇◇◇◇ ADJ: ADJ n

fulminate /fʊlmɪneɪt, fʌl-/ **fulminates, fulminating, fulminated.** If you **fulminate** against someone or something, you criticize them angrily; a formal word. *They all fulminated against the new curriculum.* ♦ **fulmination** /fʊlmɪneɪʃ°n, fʌl-/ **fulminations** *...fulminations against the government.* VERB; V against/about n; N-VAR

fulsome /fʊlsəm/. If you describe expressions of praise, apology, or gratitude as **fulsome**, you disapprove of them because they are exaggerated and elaborate, so that they sound insincere. *Newspapers have been fulsome in their praise of the former president.* ♦ **fulsomely** *She chatted to them about the show and praised them fulsomely.* ADJ-GRADED PRAGMATICS =extravagant; ADV-GRADED: ADV with v

fumble /fʌmb°l/ **fumbles, fumbling, fumbled** ◆◇◇◇◇

1 If you **fumble** for something or **fumble** with something, you try and reach for it or hold it in a clumsy way. *She crept from the bed and fumbled for her dressing gown... He fumbled with the buttons at the neck... He fumbled his one-handed attempt to light his cigarette.* VERB; V for/with/in n; V n

2 When you are trying to say something, if you **fumble** for the right words, you speak in a clumsy and unclear way. *I fumbled for something to say... He fumbled his lines, not knowing what he was going to say.* VERB; V for n; V n; Also V

fume /fjuːm/ **fumes, fuming, fumed** ◆◇◇◇◇

1 **Fumes** are the unpleasant and often unhealthy smoke and gases that are produced by fires or by things such as chemicals, fuel, or cooking. *...car exhaust fumes... They have been protesting about fumes from a chlorine factory.* N-PLURAL

2 If you **fume** over something, you express impatience and anger about it. *He was still fuming over the remark... 'It's monstrous!' Jackie fumed... The old man fumed and threatened.* VERB; V over/at/about n; V with quote; V

fumigate /fjuːmɪgeɪt/ **fumigates, fumigating, fumigated.** If you **fumigate** something, you disinfect it using special chemicals, usually in order to get rid of germs or insects. *I shall fumigate the greenhouse before planting the biannuals.* ♦ **fumigation** /fjuːmɪgeɪʃ°n/ *Methods of control involved poisoning and fumigation.* VERB; V n; N-UNCOUNT

fun /fʌn/ ◆◆◆◆◇

1 You refer to an activity or situation as **fun** if you think it is pleasant and enjoyable and it causes you to feel happy. *This year promises to be terrifically good fun... It was such a success and we had so much fun doing it... It could be fun to watch them... You still have time to join in the fun.* N-UNCOUNT

2 If you say that someone is **fun**, you mean you enjoy being with them because they say and do interesting or amusing things. *Liz was wonderful fun to be with.* N-UNCOUNT

3 If you describe something as a **fun** thing, you mean that you think it is enjoyable. If you describe someone as a **fun** person, you mean that you enjoy being with them; an informal use. *It was a fun evening... What a fun person he is!* ADJ-GRADED: ADJ n =entertaining

4 Someone who is a **figure of fun** is considered ridiculous, so that people laugh at them or make jokes about them. PHRASES figure inflects, v-link PHR

5 If you do something **for fun** or **for the fun of it**, you do it in order to enjoy yourself rather than because it is important or necessary. *I took my M. A. just for fun really... He had just come for the fun of it.* PHR after v

6 You can refer to playful behaviour as **fun and games**, especially if you disapprove of it because you think it is irresponsible; an informal expression. *Police suspected that the boys, whose fun and games hurt a lot of people, were on drugs.* PRAGMATICS

7 If you do something **in fun**, you do it as a joke or for amusement, without intending to cause any harm. *Don't say such things, even in fun.* PHR after v, v-link PHR

8 If you **make fun of** someone or something or **poke fun at** them, you laugh at them, tease them, V inflects, PHR n =laugh at,

or make jokes about them in a way that causes them to seem ridiculous. *Don't make fun of me... She poked fun at people's shortcomings.* [ridicule]

function /fʌŋkʃᵊn/ **functions, functioning, functioned** ◆◆◆◆◇

1 The **function** of something or someone is the useful thing that they do or are intended to do. *The main function of the merchant banks is to raise capital for industry.* [N-COUNT: with supp =purpose, role]

2 If a machine or system **is functioning**, it is working or operating. *The authorities say the prison is now functioning normally... Conservation programs cannot function without local support.* [VERB V]

3 If someone or something **functions** as a particular thing, they do the work or fulfil the purpose of that thing. *On weekdays, one third of the room functions as workspace.* [VERB V as n]

4 A **function** is a series of operations that a computer performs, for example when a single key is pressed; a technical word in computing. [N-COUNT]

5 If you say that one thing is a **function** of another, you mean that its amount or nature depends on the other thing; a formal use. *Investment is a function of the interest rate.* [N-COUNT: usu sing, N of n]

6 A **function** is a large formal dinner or party. [N-COUNT]

functional /fʌŋkʃənᵊl/ ◆◇◇◇◇

1 **Functional** things are useful rather than decorative. *...modern, functional furniture... The decor is functional.* [ADJ-GRADED]

2 **Functional** means relating to the way in which something works or operates, or relating to how useful it is. *...rules defining the territorial boundaries and functional limits of the local state.* [ADJ: ADJ n] ♦ **functionally** *The Indian cavalry under Haig became a functionally efficient unit... It satisfies the user's requirements both functionally and emotionally.* [ADV: ADV adj, ADV with v]

3 **Functional** equipment works or operates in the way that it is supposed to. *We have fully functional smoke alarms on all staircases.* [ADJ =operational]

functionalism /fʌŋkʃənəlɪzəm/. **Functionalism** is the idea that the most important aspect of something, especially the design of a building or piece of furniture, is how it is going to be used or its usefulness; a technical word. [N-UNCOUNT] ♦ **functionalist, functionalists.** [N-COUNT]

functionary /fʌŋkʃənəri, AM -neri/ **functionaries.** A **functionary** is a person whose job is to do administrative work, especially for a government or a political party; a formal word. [N-COUNT]

fund /fʌnd/ **funds, funding, funded** ◆◆◆◆◆

1 **Funds** are amounts of money that are available to be spent, especially money that is given to an organization or person for a particular purpose. *The concert will raise funds for research into Aids. ...government funds.* • See also **fund-raising.** [N-PLURAL]

2 A **fund** is an amount of money that is collected or saved for a particular purpose. *...a pension fund. ...a scholarship fund for undergraduate engineering students.* • See also **trust fund.** [N-COUNT: oft n N]

3 When a person or organization **funds** something, they provide money for it. *The Bush Foundation has funded a variety of faculty development programs... The airport is being privately funded by a construction group. ...a new privately funded scheme.* [VERB V n, V-ed] ♦ **-funded** *...government-funded institutions.* [COMB in ADJ]

4 If you have a **fund of** something, you have a lot of it. *He is possessed of the most brilliant talents and an extraordinary fund of energy.* [N-COUNT: N of n =reserve]

fundamental /fʌndəmentᵊl/ ◆◆◆◇◇

1 You use **fundamental** to describe things, activities, and principles that are very important or essential. They affect the basic nature of other things or are the most important element upon which other things depend. *Our constitution embodies all the fundamental principles of democracy... A fundamental human right is being withheld from these people... Technical skill is a fundamental basis for most, if not all, great art.* [ADJ-GRADED: usu ADJ n =basic]

2 You use **fundamental** to describe something which exists at a deep and basic level, and is therefore likely to continue. *But on this question, the two leaders have very fundamental differences... Amnesty says there are fundamental flaws in their military justice system.* [ADJ-GRADED: usu ADJ n =profound]

3 If one thing **is fundamental to** another, it is absolutely necessary to it, and the second thing cannot exist, succeed, or be imagined without it. *He believes better relations with China are fundamental to the well-being of the area... The method they pioneered remains fundamental to research into the behaviour of nerve cells.* [ADJ: v-link ADJ to n =vital]

4 You can use **fundamental** to show that you are referring to what you consider to be the most important aspect of a situation, and that you are not concerned with less important details. *The fundamental problem lies in their inability to distinguish between reality and invention... It was not simply a practical matter, but a fundamental question of principle.* [ADJ: ADJ n =basic]

5 **Fundamental** research into a subject is concerned with gaining knowledge about the subject itself, rather than with its practical applications. *Industry leaders want scientists to engage in fundamental research, not applied research.* [ADJ: ADJ n]

fundamentalism /fʌndəmentəlɪzəm/. **Fundamentalism** is the belief in the original form of a religion or theory, without accepting any later ideas. *Religious fundamentalism was spreading in the region.* ◆◆◇◇◇ [N-UNCOUNT] ♦ **fundamentalist, fundamentalists** *He will try to satisfy both wings of the party, the fundamentalists and the realists. ...fundamentalist Christians.* [N-COUNT: oft N n]

fundamentally /fʌndəmentəli/ ◆◇◇◇◇

1 You use **fundamentally** for emphasis when you are stating an opinion, or when you are making an important or general statement about something. *Fundamentally, women like him for his sensitivity and charming vulnerability... He can be very charming, but he is fundamentally a bully... Fundamentally, it was a conventional bomber, but it had a number of interesting innovations.* [ADV-GRADED: ADV with cl/group PRAGMATICS =basically]

2 You use **fundamentally** to indicate that something affects or relates to the deep, basic nature of something. *He disagreed fundamentally with the President's judgement... I don't think it has fundamentally altered the sport... Environmentalists say the treaty is fundamentally flawed.* [ADV-GRADED: ADV with v =profoundly]

fundamentals /fʌndəmentəlz/. The **fundamentals** of something are its simplest, most important elements, ideas, or principles, in contrast to more complicated or detailed ones. *...teaching small children the fundamentals of road safety... They agree on fundamentals, like the need for further political reform.* ◆◇◇◇◇ [N-PLURAL: usu the N, oft N of n =basics]

funding /fʌndɪŋ/. **Funding** is money which a government or organization provides for a particular purpose. *They hope for government funding for the scheme... Many colleges have seen their funding cut.* ◆◆◆◇◇ [N-UNCOUNT]

fundraiser /fʌndreɪzəʳ/ **fundraisers**

1 A **fundraiser** is an event which is intended to raise money for a particular purpose, for example, for a charity. *Organize a fundraiser for your church.* [N-COUNT]

2 A **fundraiser** is someone who works to raise money for a particular purpose, for example, for a charity. *Sir Anthony was a keen fundraiser for the Liberal Democrats.* [N-COUNT]

fund-raising. **Fund-raising** is the activity of collecting money to support a charity or political campaign or organization. *Encourage her to get involved in fund-raising for charity.* ◆◇◇◇◇ [N-UNCOUNT]

funeral /fjuːnərəl/ **funerals** ◆◆◇◇◇

1 A **funeral** is the ceremony that is held when the body of someone who has died is buried or cremated. *His funeral will be on Thursday at Blackburn Cathedral... He was given a state funeral.* [N-COUNT]

2 If someone says to you **'It's your funeral'**, they think your decision or your actions will have bad consequences for you, but they are unwilling to interfere; an informal expression. *None of my business, I guess. It's your funeral.* [PHRASE]

funeral director, funeral directors. A **funeral director** is a person whose job is to arrange funerals. N-COUNT

funeral home, funeral homes. In American English, a **funeral home** is a place where a funeral director works and where dead people are prepared for burial or cremation. The British expression is **funeral parlour.** N-COUNT

funeral parlour, funeral parlours. In British English, a **funeral parlour** is a place where a funeral director works and where dead people are prepared for burial or cremation. The American expression is **funeral home.** N-COUNT

funerary /fjuːnərəri, AM -reri/. **Funerary** means relating to funerals, burials, or cremations. *...funerary monuments.* ADJ: ADJ n

funereal /fjuːnɪəriəl/. A **funereal** tone, atmosphere, or colour is very sad and serious and would be suitable for a funeral. *He addressed the group in funereal tones.* ADJ-GRADED: usu ADJ n =solemn

funfair /fʌnfeəʳ/ **funfairs.** In British English, a **funfair** is an event held in a park or field at which people pay to ride on various machines for amusement or try to win prizes in games. The usual American word is **carnival.** *We all love to frighten ourselves by going on hair-raising rides at funfairs.* N-COUNT =fair

fungal /fʌŋgᵊl/. **Fungal** means caused by, consisting of, or relating to fungus. *Athlete's foot is a fungal infection.* ◆◇◇◇◇ ADJ: usu ADJ n

fungi /fʌŋgiː, fʌndʒaɪ/. **Fungi** is the plural of **fungus.**

fungicide /fʌŋgɪsaɪd, fʌndʒ-/ **fungicides.** A **fungicide** is a chemical that can be used to kill fungus or to prevent it from growing. N-MASS

fungus /fʌŋgəs/ **fungi.** A **fungus** is a plant that has no flowers, leaves, or green colouring, such as a mushroom or a toadstool. Other types of fungus such as mould are extremely small and look like a fine powder. ◆◇◇◇◇ N-MASS

funicular /fjuːnɪkjʊləʳ/. A **funicular** or a **funicular railway** is a type of railway which goes up a very steep hill or mountain. A machine at the top of the slope pulls the carriage up the rails by a steel rope. N-SING

funk /fʌŋk/ **funks, funking, funked** ◆◇◇◇◇

1 **Funk** is a style of dance music based on jazz and blues, with a strong, repeated bass part. *...a mixture of experimental jazz, soul and funk.* N-UNCOUNT

2 If someone is in a **funk**, they are frightened, especially because they are in a situation they cannot control. *He was in a blue funk! Worse than me!... My face went crimson (which it does out of sheer funk).* N-VAR =panic

3 If you **funk** something, you avoid doing it because you are afraid; used mainly in British English. *If he funks it, he will confirm the impression of cowardice given by his recent letter.* VERB V n

funky /fʌŋki/ **funkier, funkiest** ◆◇◇◇◇

1 **Funky** jazz, blues, or pop music has a very strong, repeated bass part. *It's a funky sort of rhythm.* ADJ-GRADED

2 If you describe something or someone as **funky**, you like them because they are unconventional or unusual; an informal use, used mainly in American English. *It had a certain funky charm, I guess, but it wasn't much of a place to raise a kid.* ADJ-GRADED

funnel /fʌnᵊl/ **funnels, funnelling, funnelled;** spelled **funneling, funneled** in American English. ◆◇◇◇◇

1 A **funnel** is an object with a wide, circular top that tapers to a short tube at the bottom. Funnels are used to pour liquids into containers which have a small opening, for example bottles. N-COUNT

2 A **funnel** is a metal chimney on a ship or railway engine powered by steam. *...a merchantman with three masts and two funnels.* N-COUNT

3 You can describe as a **funnel** something that is narrow, or narrow at one end, through which a substance flows and is directed. *These fires create convection funnels, and throw a lot of particles into the upper atmosphere.* N-COUNT

4 If something **funnels** somewhere or **is funnelled** there, it is directed through a narrow space. *The winds came from the north, across the plains, funnelling down the valley... High tides in the North Sea were funnelled down into the English Channel by a storm.* V-ERG V adv/prep be V-ed adv/prep Also V n adv/prep

5 If you **funnel** money, goods, or information from one place or group to another, you cause it to be sent there as it becomes available. *Its Global Programme on AIDS funnelled money from donors to governments... He secretly funnelled credit-card information to counterfeiters.* VERB =channel V n prep/adv

funnily /fʌnɪli/. You use **funnily enough** to indicate that, although something is surprising, it is true or really happened. *Funnily enough I can remember what I had for lunch on July 5th, 1906, but I've forgotten what I had for breakfast today.* PHRASE: PHR with cl PRAGMATICS =surprisingly

funny /fʌni/ **funnier, funniest; funnies** ◆◆◆◇◇

1 Someone or something that is **funny** is amusing and likely to make you smile or laugh. *Wade was smart and not bad-looking, and he could be funny when he wanted to... I'll tell you a funny story.* ADJ-GRADED =amusing, comic

2 If you describe something as **funny**, you mean that you think it is strange, surprising, or puzzling. *Children get some very funny ideas sometimes!... There's something funny about him... It's funny how love can come and go.* ADJ-GRADED: oft it v-link ADJ how/that =odd, curious

3 If you feel **funny**, you feel slightly ill; an informal use. *My head had begun to ache and my stomach felt funny.* ADJ-GRADED: usu feel ADJ

4 In American English, **the funnies** are newspaper comic strips; an informal use. N-PLURAL: the N

5 **Funny business** is dishonest or unacceptable behaviour; an informal expression. *...an inquiry into funny business in Ireland's biggest export industry.* PHRASE =tricks

funny bone, funny bones. Your **funny bone** is the part of your elbow which gives you a tingling feeling if it is hit; an informal expression. N-COUNT: usu sing

fur /fɜːʳ/ **furs, furring, furred** ◆◆◇◇◇

1 **Fur** is the thick and usually soft hair that grows on the bodies of many mammals. *This creature's fur is short, dense and silky.* N-MASS

2 **Fur** is the fur-covered skin of an animal that is used to make clothing or rugs. *She had on a black coat with a fur collar... Women are also wearing fur again. ...the trading of furs from Canada.* N-VAR: oft N n

3 A **fur** is a coat made from real or synthetic fur, or a piece of fur worn like a shawl or scarf. *There were women in furs and men in comfortable overcoats.* N-COUNT

4 **Fur** is a synthetic fabric that looks like fur and is used, for example, to make clothing, soft toys, and seat covers. N-MASS

5 If an event sets the **fur flying**, it causes a great argument. *Last week's meeting of the 1922 Committee set the fur flying again on the Tory backbenches... The fur will really fly over this.* PHRASE: V inflects

fur up. In British English, if your veins or arteries **fur up** or **are furred up**, they become blocked, so that your blood cannot flow properly. *Three of my veins had furred up and I needed a triple bypass... Oxidized cholesterol may be responsible for furring up the arteries.* PHRASAL VERB ERG V P V P n (not pron)

furious /fjʊəriəs/ ◆◆◇◇◇

1 Someone who is **furious** is extremely angry. *He is furious at the way his wife has been treated... I am furious that it has taken so long to uncover what really happened.* ♦ **furiously** *He stormed out of the apartment, slamming the door furiously behind him.* ADJ-GRADED: usu v-link ADJ, oft ADJ at/with n, ADJ that ADV-GRADED: usu ADV with v

2 **Furious** is also used to describe something that is done with great energy, effort, speed, or violence. *A furious gunbattle ensued.* ♦ **furiously** *Officials worked furiously to repair the centre court.* ADJ: usu ADJ n ADV: usu ADV with v

furl /fɜːʳl/ **furls, furling, furled.** When you **furl** something made of fabric such as an umbrella, sail, or flag, you roll or fold it up because it is not going to be used. *An attempt was made to furl the headsail. ...a furled umbrella.* VERB V n V-ed

furlong /fɜːʳlɒŋ, AM -lɔːŋ/ **furlongs.** A **furlong** is an imperial unit of length that is equal to 220 yards or 201.2 metres. ◆◇◇◇◇ N-COUNT: usu num N

furlough /fɜːʳloʊ/ **furloughs, furloughing, furloughed**

1 In American English, if workers are given **furlough**, they are told to stay away from work for a N-VAR

certain period because there is not enough for them to do. *This could mean a massive furlough of government workers.*
2 In American English, if people who work for a particular organization **are furloughed**, they are given a furlough. *We regret to inform you that you are being furloughed indefinitely... The factories have begun furloughing hundreds of workers.* VERB =lay off be V-ed V n
3 In American English, when soldiers are given **furlough**, they are given official permission to leave the area where they are fighting for a certain period. *I was at home on furlough.* N-VAR

furnace /fɜːʳnɪs/ **furnaces** ◆◇◇◇◇
1 A **furnace** is a container or enclosed space in which a very hot fire is made, for example to melt metal, burn rubbish, or produce steam. N-COUNT
2 If you say that a place is a **furnace**, you mean that it is very hot there: an informal use. *How can we walk? It's a furnace out there.* N-SING

furnish /fɜːʳnɪʃ/ **furnishes, furnishing, furnished** ◆◇◇◇◇
1 If you **furnish** a room or building, you put furniture and furnishings into it. *Many proprietors try to furnish their hotels with antiques.* VERB V n *with* n Also V n
2 If you **furnish** someone with something, you provide or supply it; a formal use. *They'll be able to furnish you with the rest of the details.* VERB V n *with* n

furnished /fɜːʳnɪʃt/ ◆◇◇◇◇
1 A **furnished** room or house is available to be rented together with the furniture in it. *Eleanor moved into a small furnished apartment.* ADJ
2 When you say that a room or house is **furnished** in a particular way, you are describing the kind or amount of furniture that it has in it. *We took tea by lamplight in his sparsely furnished house... All 300 elegantly furnished rooms have private bath.* ADJ: adv ADJ

furnishings /fɜːʳnɪʃɪŋz/. The **furnishings** of a room or house are the furniture, curtains, carpets, and decorations such as pictures. ◆◇◇◇◇ N-PLURAL

furniture /fɜːʳnɪtʃəʳ/ ◆◆◆◇◇
1 **Furniture** consists of large movable objects such as tables, chairs, or beds that are used in a room for sitting on or for putting things on or in. *Each piece of furniture in their home suited the style of the house.* N-UNCOUNT
2 If you describe someone or something as **part of the furniture**, you are suggesting humorously that they have been somewhere such as their workplace for such a long time that it is hard to imagine the place without them; an informal expression. PHRASE: v-link PHR

furore /fjʊrɔːri, fjʊərɔːʳ/; spelled **furor** in American English. A **furore** is a very angry or excited reaction by people to something. *The disclosure has already caused a furore among MPs. ...an international furore over the plan.* ◆◇◇◇◇ N-SING: usu with supp, oft adj N, N *over* n =uproar

furrier /fʌriəʳ, AM fɜːr-/ **furriers.** A **furrier** is a person who makes or sells clothes made from fur. N-COUNT

furrow /fʌroʊ, AM fɜːr-/ **furrows, furrowing, furrowed** ◆◇◇◇◇
1 A **furrow** is a long, thin line in the earth which a farmer makes in order to plant seeds or to allow water to flow along. N-COUNT
2 A **furrow** is a deep, fairly wide line in the surface of something. *Dirt bike trails crisscrossed the grassy furrows.* N-COUNT
3 A **furrow** is a deep fold or line in the skin of someone's face. *He was his old self again, except for the deep furrows that marked the corners of his mouth.* N-COUNT =wrinkle
4 If someone **furrows** their brow or forehead or if it **furrows**, deep folds appear in it because they are frowning; used in written English. *My bank manager furrowed his brow, fingered his calculator and finally pronounced 'Aha!'... Midge's forehead furrowed as she saw that several were drinking... Fatigue and stress quickly result in a dull complexion and a furrowed brow.* V-ERG =crease V n V V-ed
5 In British English, if you say that someone **ploughs** a particular **furrow** or **ploughs** their **own furrow**, you mean that their activities or interests are different or isolated from those of other people. *Cale has ploughed a more esoteric furrow as a recording artist... The Syrian government is more than adept at ploughing its own diplomatic furrow.* PHRASE: V inflects

furry /fɜːri/ ◆◇◇◇◇
1 A **furry** animal is covered with thick, soft hair. *I learnt how to stalk along the kangaroo pads till I could almost touch their thick furry tails.* ADJ: usu ADJ n
2 If you describe something as **furry**, you mean that it has a soft rough texture like fur. *...his herringbone tweed coat with its furry lining.* ADJ: usu ADJ n
3 If you have a **furry** tongue, your tongue it is covered with a layer of a soft greyish-white substance, usually because you are unwell. ADJ: usu ADJ n

further /fɜːʳðəʳ/ **furthers, furthering, furthered** ◆◆◆◆◆
Further is a comparative form of **far**. It is also a verb.
1 **Further** means to a greater extent or degree. *Inflation is below 5% and set to fall further... The rebellion is expected to further damage the country's image... The government's economic policies have further depressed living standards.* ADV-COMPAR: ADV with v
2 If you go or get **further** with something, or take something **further**, you make some progress. *They lacked the scientific personnel to develop the technical apparatus much further.* ADV-COMPAR: ADV with v
3 If someone goes **further** in a discussion, they make a more extreme statement or deal with a point more thoroughly. *On February 7th the Post went further, claiming that Mr Wood had grabbed and kissed another 13 women... To have a better comparison, we need to go further and address such issues as repairs and insurance.* ADV-COMPAR: ADV after v
4 A **further** thing, number of things, or amount of something is an additional thing, number of things, or amount. *His speech provides further evidence of his increasingly authoritarian approach... They believed there were likely to be further attacks... There was nothing further to be done for this man.* ADJ: ADJ n, pron-indef ADJ =more
5 **Further** means a greater distance than before or than something else. *Now we live further away from the city centre... He came to a halt at crossroads fifty yards further on... An old man shuffled out of a doorway further along the corridor... Further to the south are some of the island's loveliest unspoilt coves.* ADV-COMPAR: ADV adv/prep
6 **Further** is used in expressions such as **'further back'** and **'further ahead'** to refer to a point in time that is earlier or later than the time you are talking about. *Looking still further ahead, by the end of the next century world population is expected to be about ten billion.* ADV-COMPAR: ADV adv/prep
7 If you **further** something, you help it to progress, to be successful, or to be achieved. *Demaci was jailed in the early 1960s on charges of furthering the cause of Albanian nationalism... Education needn't only be about furthering your career.* VERB V n
8 You use **further** to introduce a statement that relates to the same general topic and that gives additional information or makes an additional point; a formal use. *Dodd made no appeal of his death sentence and, further, instructed his attorney to sue anyone who succeeds in delaying his execution.* ADV: ADV with cl PRAGMATICS =moreover
9 **Further to** is used in letters in expressions such as **'further to your letter'** or **'further to our conversation'**, in order to indicate what you are referring to in the letter; a formal British use. *Further to your letter, I agree that there are some presentational problems, politically speaking.* PHR-PREP PRAGMATICS =with reference to

furtherance /fɜːʳðərəns/. The **furtherance** of something is the activity of helping it to be successful or be achieved; a formal word. *The thing that matters is the furtherance of research in this country.* N-UNCOUNT: N *of* n =advancement

further education. **Further education** is the education of people who have left school but who are not at a university or a college of education; used mainly in British English. The usual American term is **continuing education**. *She is now in further education with new career pos-* ◆◇◇◇◇ N-UNCOUNT sibilities ahead of her... Most further-education colleges offer A-level courses.*

furthermore /fɜːʳðəʳmɔːʳ/. **Furthermore** is used to introduce a piece of information or opinion that adds to or supports the previous one; a formal word. *Furthermore, they claim that any such interference is completely ineffective.* ◆◆◇◇◇ ADV: ADV with cl PRAGMATICS =moreover

furthermost /fɜːʳðəʳmoʊst/. The **furthermost** one of a number of similar things is the one that is the greatest distance away from a place. *We walked to the furthermost point and then sat on the sand dunes.* ADJ: ADJ n

furthest /fɜːʳðɪst/ ◆◇◇◇◇
Furthest is a superlative form of **far**.

1 **Furthest** means to a greater or more extreme extent or degree than ever before or than anything or anyone else. *The south of England, where prices have fallen furthest, will remain the weakest market... These institutional reforms have gone furthest in Poland.* ADV-SUPERL: ADV with v

2 **Furthest** means at a greater distance from a particular point than anyone or anything else, or for a greater distance than anyone or anything else. *The risk of thunder is greatest in those areas furthest from the coast... Amongst those who have travelled furthest to take part in the Festival are a group from Northern Ireland.* ADV-SUPERL: n ADV, ADV after v, be ADV, ADV prep/adv ► Also an adjective. *...the furthest point from earth that any controlled spacecraft has ever been.* ADJ-SUPERL: ADJ n

furtive /fɜːʳtɪv/. If you describe someone's behaviour as **furtive**, you disapprove of them behaving as if they want to keep something secret or hidden. *With a furtive glance over her shoulder, she unlocked the door and entered the house.* ◆◇◇◇◇ ADJ-GRADED PRAGMATICS
♦ **furtively** *He walked towards the summerhouse, at first furtively, then with more confidence.* ADV-GRADED: usu ADV with v, also ADV adj

fury /fjʊəri/ ◆◆◇◇◇

1 **Fury** is violent or very strong anger. *She screamed, her face distorted with fury and pain.* N-UNCOUNT =wrath

2 If you are **in a fury**, you are very angry. *I had reacted in a fury of grief... He rose to his feet in a fury to leave no doubt about where he stood on the issue.* PHRASE: PHR after v, PHR with cl

fuse /fjuːz/ **fuses, fusing, fused** ◆◇◇◇◇

1 A **fuse** is a safety device in an electric plug or circuit. It contains a piece of wire which melts when there is a fault so that the flow of electricity stops. *The fuse blew as he pressed the button to start the motor... Remove the circuit fuse before beginning electrical work.* N-COUNT

2 When an electric device **fuses** or when you **fuse** it, it stops working because of a fault. *The wire snapped at the wall plug and the light fused... We pursued my grandmother round the house hoping she wasn't going to fuse anything.* V-ERG V Vn

3 A **fuse** is a device on a bomb or firework which delays the explosion so that people can move a safe distance away. *A bomb was deactivated at the last moment, after the fuse had been lit.* N-COUNT

4 When things **fuse** or **are fused**, they join together physically or chemically, usually to become one thing. You can also say that one thing **fuses** with another. *The skull bones fuse between the ages of fifteen and twenty-five... Conception occurs when a single sperm fuses with an egg... Manufactured glass is made by fusing various types of sand... Their solution was to isolate specific clones of B cells and fuse them with cancer cells... The flakes seem to fuse together and produce ice crystals.* V-RECIP-ERG pl-n V, V with n, V pl-n, V n with n, pl-n V together, Also V pl-n together

5 If something **fuses** two different qualities, ideas, or things, it causes them to join together, especially in order to form a pleasing or satisfactory combination. *His music of that period fused the rhythms of jazz with classical forms... What they have done is fuse two different types of entertainment, the circus and the rock concert... Past and present fuse.* V-RECIP-ERG =combine V n with n, V pl-n, pl-n V, Also V with n

6 If you **blow a fuse**, you suddenly become very angry and are unable to stay calm. *For all my experience, I blew a fuse in the quarter-final and could have been sent off.* PHRASES V inflects

7 If someone or something **lights the fuse** of a particular situation or activity, they do something which suddenly gets it started. *Hopes for an early cut in German interest rates lit the market's fuse early on.* V inflects

8 If you say that someone **has a short fuse** or is **on a short fuse** you mean that they are quick to react angrily when something goes wrong. *I have a very short fuse and a violent temper.* V inflects

fuse box, fuse boxes. The **fuse box** is the box that contains the fuses for all the electric circuits in a building. It is usually fixed to a wall. N-COUNT: oft *the* N in sing

fused /fjuːzd/. If an electric plug or circuit is **fused**, it has a fuse in it. ADJ

fuselage /fjuːzɪlɑːʒ/ **fuselages.** The **fuselage** is the main body of an aeroplane, missile, or rocket. It is usually cylindrical in shape. ◆◇◇◇◇ N-COUNT

fusillade /fjuːzɪleɪd, AM -lɑːd/. A **fusillade** of shots or objects is a large number of them fired or thrown at the same time. *Both were killed in a fusillade of bullets fired at close range.* N-SING: usu N *of* n

fusion /fjuːʒən/ **fusions** ◆◇◇◇◇

1 A **fusion** is something new that is created by joining together different qualities, ideas, or things. *His previous fusions of jazz, pop and African melodies have proved highly successful.* N-COUNT: oft N *of* pl-n

2 The **fusion** of two or more things involves joining them together to form one thing. *His final reform was the fusion of regular and reserve forces.* N-VAR: oft N *of* pl-n =merging

3 **Fusion** is the process in which atomic particles combine and produce a large amount of nuclear energy; a technical use in science. *...research into nuclear fusion.* N-UNCOUNT

fuss /fʌs/ **fusses, fussing, fussed** ◆◆◇◇◇

1 **Fuss** is anxious or excited behaviour which serves no useful purpose. *I don't know what all the fuss is about... He just gets down to work without any fuss.* N-SING: also no det =bother

2 If you **fuss**, you worry or behave in a nervous, anxious way about unimportant matters or rush around doing unnecessary things. *Carol fussed about getting me a drink... My wife was fussing over the food and clothing we were going to take... She fussed with a wisp of hair over her ear... A team of waiters began fussing around the table... 'Stop fussing,' he snapped.* VERB =flap V *about*, V *over* n, V prep, V, Also V n

3 If you **fuss over** someone, you pay them a lot of attention and do things to make them happy or comfortable. *Auntie Hilda and Uncle Jack couldn't fuss over them enough.* VERB V *over* n

4 If you **make a fuss** or **kick up a fuss** about something, you become angry or excited about it and complain; an informal expression. *I don't know why everybody makes such a fuss about a few mosquitoes... I kick up a fuss if my wife wants to spend time alone.* PHRASES V inflects

5 In British English, if you **make a fuss of** someone, you pay them a lot of attention and do things to make them happy or comfortable. *When I arrived my nephews made a big fuss of me.* V inflects, PHR n

fussed /fʌst/. In British English, if you say you **are not fussed** about something, you mean you do not mind about it or do not mind what happens; an informal word. *I'm not fussed as long as we get where we want to go.* ADJ-GRADED: with brd-neg, v-link ADJ =bothered

fussy /fʌsi/ **fussier, fussiest** ◆◇◇◇◇

1 Someone who is **fussy** is very concerned with unimportant details and is difficult to please. *She is not fussy about her food... Her aunt was small, with a rather fussy manner.* ADJ-GRADED: oft ADJ *about* n ♦ **fussily** *She adjusted her coloured head scarf fussily... He was once described as a fussily accurate test pilot.* ADV-GRADED: ADV with v, ADV adj ♦ **fussiness** *There's a lack of fussiness about the way he works.* N-UNCOUNT

2 If you describe things such as clothes and furniture as **fussy**, you are criticizing them because they are too elaborate or detailed. *We are not very keen on floral patterns and fussy designs.* ADJ-GRADED PRAGMATICS ♦ **fussily** *...the fussily ornate Jubilee Room at the House of Commons.* ADV-GRADED: ADV adj/-ed

fusty /fʌsti/ **fustier, fustiest**

1 If you describe something or someone as **fusty**, you disapprove of them because they are old-fashioned in attitudes or ideas. *The fusty old establishment refused to recognise the demand for popular music.* ADJ-GRADED PRAGMATICS

2 A **fusty** place or thing has a stale smell. *...fusty old carpets.* ADJ-GRADED: usu ADJ n

futile /fjuːtaɪl, AM -təl/. If you say that something is **futile**, you mean there is no point in doing it, usually because it has no chance of succeeding. *He brought his arm up in a futile attempt to ward off the blow... It would be futile to sustain his life when there is no chance of any improvement.* ◆◇◇◇◇ ADJ-GRADED: oft it v-link ADJ to-inf =pointless

futility /fjuːtɪlɪti/. **Futility** is a total lack of purpose or usefulness. *...the injustice and futility of terrorism.* N-UNCOUNT: oft N of n/-ing

futon /fuːtɒn/ **futons.** A **futon** is a piece of furniture which consists of a thin mattress on a low wooden frame which can be used as a bed or folded up to make a chair. N-COUNT

future /fjuːtʃər/ **futures** ◆◆◆◆◆

1 **The future** is the period of time that will come after the present, or the things that will happen then. *The spokesman said no decision on the proposal was likely in the immediate future... He was making plans for the future... I had little time to think about what the future held for me.* N-SING: the N ≠past

2 **Future** things will happen or exist after the present time. *She said if the world did not act conclusively now, it would only bequeath the problem to future generations... Meanwhile, the domestic debate on Denmark's future role in Europe rages on. ...the future King and Queen.* • **for future reference**: see **reference**. ADJ: ADJ n

3 Someone's **future**, or the **future** of something, is what will happen to them or what they will do after the present time. *His future as prime minister depends on the outcome of the elections... Graeme remains a supremely talented cricketer and must still have a splendid future in the game. ...a proposed national conference on the country's political future... Young people are an investment for our future.* N-COUNT: usu sing, usu with supp

4 If you say that someone or something has a **future**, you mean that they are likely to be successful or to survive. *These abandoned children have now got a future... There's no future in this relationship.* N-COUNT: usu a N in sing

5 When people trade in **futures**, they buy stocks and shares, commodities such as coffee or oil, or foreign currency at a price that is agreed at the time of purchase for items which are delivered some time in the future. *This report could spur some buying in corn futures when the market opens today... Futures prices recovered from sharp early declines to end with moderate losses.* N-PLURAL: usu with supp

6 The **future** tense of a verb is the one used to talk about things that are going to happen. In English, verb groups consisting of 'will' or 'shall' and the base form of a verb are sometimes called the future tense. The **future perfect** tense of a verb is used to talk about things that will have happened at some time in the future. ADJ: ADJ n

7 You use **in future** when saying what will happen from now on, which will be different from what has previously happened. *In future the President will be chosen by the people instead of by the National Assembly... I asked her to be more careful in future.* PHRASES

8 If you wonder what the future **holds**, you wonder what will happen in the future. *We wondered what the future would hold for our baby son.* V inflects

9 If you say that someone's **future lies** in a particular place or activity, you think they will be most successful or happy in that place or doing that activity. *Armstrong is uncertain where his long-term future lies... He came back because he believed his future lay with her.* V inflects

futurism /fjuːtʃərɪzəm/. **Futurism** was a modern artistic and literary movement in the early twentieth century. N-UNCOUNT

futurist /fjuːtʃərɪst/ **futurists**

1 **Futurists** were artists and writers who were followers of futurism. N-COUNT

2 A **futurist** is someone who makes predictions about what is going to happen, on the basis of facts about what is happening now; used mainly in American English. *Futurists agree that these trends will grow as telecommunications networks become cheaper and more efficient.* N-COUNT =futurologist

futuristic /fjuːtʃərɪstɪk/ ◆◇◇◇◇

1 Something that is **futuristic** looks or seems very modern and unusual, like something from the future. *The theatre is a futuristic steel and glass structure. ...futuristic cars.* ADJ-GRADED

2 A **futuristic** film or book tells a story that is set in the future, when things are different. *...the futuristic hit film, 'Terminator 2'.* ADJ: ADJ n

futurology /fjuːtʃərɒlədʒi/. **Futurology** is the activity of trying to predict what is going to happen, on the basis of facts about what is happening now. *The way a good investor does really well is by engaging in successful futurology.* N-UNCOUNT =forecasting

♦ **futurologist** /fjuːtʃərɒlədʒɪst/ **futurologists** *In his March 1984 report Wanger analyzed some predictions made by futurologists in 1972.* N-COUNT =forecaster

fuzz /fʌz/

1 **Fuzz** is a mass of short, curly hairs. *He had a baby fuzz round his jaw.* N-UNCOUNT

2 The **fuzz** are the police; an old-fashioned, informal use. N-PLURAL: usu the N

fuzzy /fʌzi/ **fuzzier, fuzziest** ◆◇◇◇◇

1 **Fuzzy** hair sticks up in a soft, curly mass. *He had fuzzy black hair and bright black eyes.* ADJ-GRADED =frizzy

2 If something is **fuzzy**, it has a covering that feels soft and like fur. *...fuzzy material.* ADJ-GRADED

3 A **fuzzy** picture, image, or sound is unclear and hard to see or hear. *A couple of fuzzy pictures have been published. ...fuzzy bass lines.* ADJ-GRADED =indistinct

4 If you or your thoughts are **fuzzy**, you are confused and cannot think clearly. *He had little patience for fuzzy ideas.* ADJ-GRADED ≠clear

5 You describe something as **fuzzy** when it is vague and not clearly defined. *The border between science fact and science fiction gets a bit fuzzy.* ADJ-GRADED =unclear

6 **Fuzzy** logic is a type of computer logic that is supposed to imitate the way that humans think, for example by adapting to changing circumstances rather than always following the same procedure. *...domestic appliances that also use fuzzy logic to mimic the way a person would do the job manually. ...research on fuzzy systems.* ADJ-UNGRADED: ADJ n

Gg

G, g /dʒiː/ **G's, g's**

1 **G** is the seventh letter of the English alphabet. N-VAR

2 In music, **G** is the fifth note in the scale of C major. N-VAR

3 A **G** is a measurement of the rate of acceleration in something such as a space rocket. One G is equivalent to the earth's gravitational pull. N-COUNT

4 A **G** is a thousand pounds or dollars; a very informal use, mainly in American English. N-COUNT: usu a/num N =grand

5 **G** or **g** is used as an abbreviation for words beginning with g, such as 'gram', 'gallon', and 'German'. *Oranges contain only 35 calories per 100g.*

gab /gæb/. If you say that someone has **the gift of the gab**, or in American English **the gift of gab**, you mean that they have the ability to speak PHRASE easily, confidently, and in a persuasive way; an informal expression. *They are naturally good salesmen with the gift of the gab.*

gabardine /gæbəʳdiːn, AM -diːn/ **gabardines;** also spelled **gaberdine.**
1 Gabardine is a fairly thick cloth which is used for making coats, suits, and other clothes. *...a demure white blouse and long, straight gabardine skirt.* [N-UNCOUNT: also N in pl, oft N n]
2 A **gabardine** is a coat made from gabardine. [N-COUNT]

gabble /gæbəl/ **gabbles, gabbling, gabbled.** If you **gabble**, you say things so quickly that it is difficult for people to understand you; an informal word. *Marcello sat on his knee and gabbled excitedly... She gabbles on about drug dealers and journalists... One of the soldiers gabbled something and pointed at the front door.* [VERB =babble; V; V adv; V n; Also V with quote]

gable /geɪbəl/ **gables.** A **gable** is the triangular part at the top of the end wall of a building, between the two sloping sides of the roof. [N-COUNT]

gabled /geɪbəld/. A **gabled** building or roof has a gable. *...the entrance of an attractive gabled house. ...steeply gabled roofs.* [ADJ: usu ADJ n]

gad /gæd/ **gads, gadding, gadded.** If you **gad** about, you go to a lot of different places looking for amusement and entertainment; an informal word, used mainly in British English. *Don't think you'll keep me here while you gad about... Elizabeth was off gadding in Italy.* [VERB =gallivant; V *about/out*; V]

gadfly /gædflaɪ/ **gadflies.** If you refer to someone as a **gadfly**, you believe that they deliberately annoy or challenge other people, especially people in authority. *It still remains to be seen whether Buchanan will be just a gadfly or a real threat to the president.* [N-COUNT]

gadget /gædʒɪt/ **gadgets.** A **gadget** is a small machine or device which does something useful. You sometimes refer to something as a **gadget** when you are suggesting that it is complicated and unnecessary. *...sales of kitchen gadgets including toasters, kettles and percolators. ...the latest gadget for the technology obsessed: pocket-sized computers that you write on with a pen.* [◆◇◇◇◇ N-COUNT: usu with supp =appliance]

gadgetry /gædʒɪtri/. If you refer to a particular kind of **gadgetry**, you mean small machines or devices of that kind which do something useful. You sometimes use **gadgetry** when you are suggesting that the machines and devices are complicated and unnecessary. *In the days before domestic gadgetry and time-saving appliances, food preparation took up most of the day. ...a passion for the latest electronic gadgetry.* [N-UNCOUNT: oft adj N]

Gaelic /geɪlɪk, gælɪk/ ◆◇◇◇◇
1 Gaelic is a language spoken by people in parts of Scotland and Ireland. *We weren't allowed to speak Gaelic at school.* ► Also an adjective. *...the Gaelic language.* [N-UNCOUNT; ADJ: usu ADJ n]
2 Gaelic means coming from or relating to the parts of Scotland and Ireland where Gaelic is spoken. *...an evening of Gaelic music and drama.* [ADJ: usu ADJ n]

gaff /gæf/ **gaffs**
1 On a boat, a **gaff** is a pole which is attached to a mast in order to support a particular kind of sail. [N-COUNT: oft N n]
2 A **gaff** is a pole with a spike or hook at one end, which is used for catching large fish. [N-COUNT =spear, harpoon]
3 See also **gaffe.**

gaffe /gæf/ **gaffes;** also spelled **gaff.**
1 A **gaffe** is a stupid or careless mistake, for example when you say or do something that offends or upsets people. *He made an embarrassing gaffe at the convention last weekend. ...social gaffes committed by high-ranking individuals.* [N-COUNT =blunder]
2 If you **blow the gaffe** or **blow the gaff**, you tell someone something that other people wanted you to keep secret; used in informal British English. [PHRASE: V inflects =let slip]

gaffer /gæfəʳ/ **gaffers.** In informal British English, people use **gaffer** to refer to the foreman, supervisor, or other person in charge of the workers at a factory, building-site, or other place of work. *The gaffer said he'd been fined for not doing the contract on time.* [N-COUNT: usu *the* N in sing; N-VOC =boss]

gag /gæg/ **gags, gagging, gagged** ◆◇◇◇◇
1 A **gag** is something such as a piece of cloth that is tied around or put inside someone's mouth in order to stop them from speaking. *His captors had put a gag of thick leather in his mouth.* [N-COUNT]
2 If someone **gags** you, they tie a piece of cloth around your mouth in order to stop you from speaking or shouting. *I gagged him with a towel.* [VERB; V n]
3 If a person **is gagged** by someone in authority, they are prevented from expressing their opinion or from publishing certain information; used showing disapproval. *Judges must not be gagged.* [VERB; *be* V-ed; Also V n]
4 If you **gag**, you choke and nearly vomit; an informal use. *I knelt by the toilet and gagged.* [VERB; V]
5 A **gag** is a joke, especially one told by a professional comedian; an informal use. *...a gag about policemen giving evidence in court.* [N-COUNT: usu with supp]

gaga /gɑːgɑː/. If you say that someone is **gaga** or has gone **gaga**, you mean that they are senile; used in very informal British English. *I do it because if you don't keep your brain working you go gaga.* [ADJ-GRADED: v-link ADJ =dotty]

gaggle /gægəl/ **gaggles.** You can use **gaggle** to refer to a group of people, usually when you want to express disapproval or contempt for them. *A gaggle of journalists sit in a hotel foyer waiting impatiently.* [N-COUNT-COLL: usu N *of* n; PRAGMATICS]

gaiety /geɪɪti/. **Gaiety** is a feeling, attitude, or atmosphere of liveliness and fun; an old-fashioned word. *Music rang out adding to the gaiety and life of the market.* [N-UNCOUNT =joy]

gaily /geɪli/
1 If you do something **gaily**, you do it in a lively, happy way. *Magda laughed gaily.* [ADV-GRADED: ADV with v]
2 Something that is **gaily** coloured or **gaily** decorated is coloured or decorated in a bright, pretty way. *He put on a gaily coloured shirt. ...gaily painted front doors.* [ADV-GRADED: ADV -ed =brightly]

gain /geɪn/ **gains, gaining, gained** ◆◆◆◆◇
1 If a person or place **gains** something such as an ability or quality, they gradually get more of it. *Students can gain valuable experience by working on the campus radio or magazine... While it has lost its tranquility, the area has gained in liveliness.* [VERB; V n; V *in* n]
2 If you **gain** from something such as an event or situation, you get some advantage or benefit from it. *The company didn't disclose how much it expects to gain from the two deals... There is absolutely nothing to be gained by feeling bitter... It is sad that a major company should try to gain from other people's suffering.* [VERB =profit; V n *from/by* n/-ing; V *from* n]
3 To **gain** something such as weight or speed means to have an increase in that particular thing. *Some people do gain weight after they stop smoking... The BMW started coming forward, passing the other cars and gaining speed as it approached... She gained some 25lb in weight during her pregnancy.* ► Also a noun. *News on new home sales is brighter, showing a gain of nearly 8% in June... Excessive weight gain doesn't do you any good.* [VERB ≠lose; V n; V amount; Also V; N-VAR: usu with supp =increase]
4 If you **gain** something, you obtain it, especially after a lot of hard work or effort. *They realise that passing exams is no longer enough to gain a place at university... Their efforts helped the hostages gain their freedom.* [VERB =acquire; V n; V n]
5 If you do something **for gain**, you do it in order to get some advantage or profit for yourself; a formal phrase, used showing disapproval. *...buying art solely for financial gain.* [PHRASES; PHR after v]
6 If something such as an idea or an ideal **gains ground**, it gradually becomes more widely known or more popular. *There are strong signs that his views are gaining ground... The Christian right has been steadily gaining ground in state politics.* [V inflects]
7 If you do something in order to **gain time**, you do it in order to give yourself enough time to think of an excuse or a way out of a difficult situation. *He believes Croatia agreed to the truce in order to gain time to buy desperately needed weapons.* [V inflects, oft PHR to-inf]

gain on. If you **gain on** someone or something that is moving in front of you, you gradually get closer to them. *In some places he was quicker and at others I'd gain on him... The Mercedes began to gain on the van.* [PHRASAL VERB; V P n]

gainer /geɪnəʳ/ **gainers.** A **gainer** is a person or organization who gains something from a particular situation. *Overall, there were more losers than gainers... Tuesday's notable gainer was Sony, which reached a high of 9,070 yen.* N-COUNT: oft adj N ≠loser

gainful /geɪnfʊl/. If you are in **gainful** employment, you have a job for which you are paid and which is not against the law; a formal word. *The lack of money comes from lack of opportunities for gainful employment.* ♦ **gainfully** *Both parents were gainfully employed.* ADJ: ADJ n; ADV: ADV -ed

gainsay /geɪnseɪ/ **gainsays, gainsaying, gainsaid.** If you say that nobody can **gainsay** something, you mean that it is true or obvious and that everyone would agree with it, although there may be other things connected with it that are more doubtful; a formal word. *However much people have criticised her style and some of her policies no one will gainsay her courage... There is no gainsaying the fact that they have been responsible for a truly great building.* VB: with brd-neg PRAGMATICS =deny; V n

gait /geɪt/ **gaits.** A particular kind of **gait** is a particular way of walking; used in written English. *...a tubby little man in his fifties, with sparse hair and a rolling gait... His movements were decidedly clumsy, and his gait peculiarly awkward.* ◆◇◇◇◇ N-COUNT: usu sing, usu with supp

gaiter /geɪtəʳ/ **gaiters. Gaiters** are tight coverings, made of cloth, worn on the legs below the knees. Gaiters were commonly worn in former times, but are now mainly worn by clergymen or as part of a ceremonial uniform. N-COUNT: usu pl

gal /gæl/ **gals. Gal** is used in written English to represent the word 'girl' as it is pronounced in a particular accent. *...a Southern gal who wants to make it in the movies.* ◆◇◇◇◇ N-COUNT; N-VOC

gal; also spelled **gal. gal** is a written abbreviation for 'gallon' or 'gallons'. *Diesel cost 60p/gal in some places.*

gala /gɑːlə, AM geɪlə/ **galas.** A **gala** is a special public celebration, entertainment, performance, or festival. *...a gala evening at the Royal Opera House.* ◆◇◇◇◇ N-COUNT: oft N n

galactic /gəlæktɪk/. **Galactic** means relating to galaxies. ADJ: ADJ n

galaxy /gæləksi/ **galaxies;** also spelled **Galaxy.** ◆◆◇◇◇

1 A **galaxy** is a huge group of stars and planets that extends over many millions of miles. *Astronomers have discovered a distant galaxy.* N-COUNT

2 The Galaxy is the huge group of stars and planets to which the Earth and the Solar System belong. *The Galaxy consists of 100 billion stars.* N-PROPER: *the* N

3 If you talk about **a galaxy of** people from a particular profession, you mean a group of them who are all famous or important. *He is one of a small galaxy of Dutch stars on German television.* N-SING: N *of* n =array

gale /geɪl/ **gales** ◆◇◇◇◇

1 A **gale** is a very strong wind. *...forecasts of fierce gales over the next few days.* N-COUNT

2 You can refer to the loud noise made by a lot of people all laughing at the same time as a **gale of** laughter or **gales** of laughter. *This was greeted with gales of laughter from the audience.* N-COUNT: N *of* n =outburst

gale-force. A **gale-force** wind is a very strong wind. *...bad weather with heavy rain and gale-force winds of up to seventy miles per hour.* ADJ: ADJ n

gall /gɔːl/ **galls, galling, galled** ◆◇◇◇◇

1 You can use **gall** to refer to someone's behaviour when you disapprove of it because it is bold or risky, or does not show enough respect for someone or something. *I daresay he thought he was above the law. I can't get over the gall of the fellow... She had the gall to suggest that I might supply her with information about what Steve was doing.* N-UNCOUNT: oft *the* N *of* n, *the* N to-inf PRAGMATICS =nerve

2 If someone's action **galls** you, it makes you feel very angry or annoyed, often because it is unfair to you and you cannot do anything about it. *It must have galled him that Bardo thwarted each of these measures... It was their serenity, their insouciance which galled her most.* ♦ **galling** *It was especially galling to be criticised by this scoundrel.* VERB =irk; *it* V n that; V n; Also *it* V n to inf; ADJ-GRADED: usu v-link ADJ

3 A **gall** is an abnormal growth on the surface of a plant that is caused by an insect, disease, fungus, or injury. N-COUNT

gallant /gælənt/. Also pronounced /gəlænt/ for meaning 3. ◆◇◇◇◇

1 If someone is **gallant**, they behave bravely and honourably in a dangerous or difficult situation; an old-fashioned use. *The gallant soldiers lost their lives so that peace might reign again.* ♦ **gallantly** *The town responded gallantly to the War.* ADJ-GRADED =brave; ADV-GRADED: ADV with v =bravely

2 In written English, a **gallant** effort or fight is one in which someone tried very hard to do something difficult, although in the end they failed; used showing approval. *He died at the age of 82, after a gallant fight against illness... Ireland's gallant attempt to win the series was thwarted by Scotland.* ♦ **gallantly** *The Spaniard gallantly fought off 11 set points before Seles won 8-6.* ADJ-GRADED: ADJ n PRAGMATICS =valiant, brave; ADV-GRADED: ADV with v =valiantly

3 If someone is **gallant**, they are kind, polite, and considerate towards other people; used mainly in old-fashioned English about men and their behaviour towards women. *Douglas was a complex man, thoughtful, gallant, and generous.* ♦ **gallantly** *He gallantly kissed Marie's hand as we prepared to leave.* ADJ-GRADED =courteous; ADV-GRADED: ADV with v =courteously

gallantry /gæləntri/

1 Gallantry is bravery shown by someone who is in danger, for example when they are fighting in a war; an old-fashioned or formal word. *For his gallantry he was awarded a Victoria Cross.* N-UNCOUNT =bravery

2 Gallantry is kind, polite, and considerate behaviour towards other people, especially women; an old-fashioned use. *It's that time of year again, when thoughts turn to romance and gallantry.* N-UNCOUNT =courtesy

gall bladder, gall bladders. Your **gall bladder** is the organ in your body which contains bile and is next to your liver. N-COUNT

galleon /gæliən/ **galleons.** A **galleon** is a sailing ship with three masts. Galleons were used mainly in the fifteenth to seventeenth centuries. N-COUNT

gallery /gæləri/ **galleries** ◆◆◆◇◇

1 A **gallery** is a place that has permanent exhibitions of works of art in it. *...an art gallery. ...the National Gallery.* N-COUNT: oft in names after n

2 A **gallery** is a building or room where works of art are exhibited and sometimes sold. *The painting is in the gallery upstairs.* N-COUNT

3 A **gallery** is a raised area at the back or at the sides of a large room or hall. People often stand or sit in the gallery to get a good view of what is happening. *A crowd already filled the gallery.* N-COUNT

4 The gallery in a theatre or concert hall is a raised area like a large balcony that usually contains the cheapest seats. *They had been forced to find cheap tickets in the gallery.* • If you **play to the gallery**, you do something in public in a way which you hope will impress people. *Walesa has a tendency generally to play to the gallery.* N-COUNT: usu *the* N in sing; PHRASE: V inflects

5 A **gallery** is an underground passage in a mine or cave. *Four miners were killed when a gallery collapsed.* N-COUNT

galley /gæli/ **galleys** ◆◇◇◇◇

1 On a ship or aircraft, the **galley** is the kitchen. N-COUNT

2 In former times, a **galley** was a ship with sails and a lot of oars, which was often rowed by slaves or prisoners. N-COUNT

Gallic /gælɪk/. **Gallic** means the same as **French.** You sometimes use **Gallic** to describe ideas, feelings, or actions that you think are very typical of France and French people. *The proposal has provoked howls of Gallic indignation... Mme Arlette gave a Gallic shrug.* ◆◇◇◇◇ ADJ-GRADED: usu ADJ n =French

gallivant /gælɪvænt/ **gallivants, gallivanting, gallivanted.** If you **are gallivanting** around, you go to a lot of different places looking for amusement and entertainment; a rather old-fashioned word. *...the past couple of months while Mick has been gallivanting round the world.* VERB =gad; V prep/adv; Also V

gallon /gælən/ **gallons.** A **gallon** is a unit of measurement for liquids that is equal to eight pints. In Britain, it is equal to 4.564 litres. In America, it is equal to 3.785 litres. *...80 million* ◆◆◇◇◇ N-COUNT: oft N *of* n *gallons of water a day. ...a gasoline tax of 4.3 cents a gallon.*

gallop /gæləp/ **gallops, galloping, galloped** ◆◇◇◇◇
1 When a horse **gallops**, it runs very fast so that all four legs are off the ground at the same time in each stride. If you **gallop** a horse, you make it gallop. *The horses galloped away... Staff officers galloped fine horses down the road.* V-ERG V adv/prep V n prep/adv
2 If you **gallop**, you ride a horse that is galloping. *Major Winston galloped into the distance.* VERB V prep/adv
3 A **gallop** is a ride on a horse that is galloping. *I was forced to attempt a gallop.* N-SING
4 If something such as a process **gallops**, it develops very quickly and is often difficult to control. *China's economy galloped ahead. ...galloping inflation.* VERB V adv V-ing
5 If you **gallop**, you run somewhere very quickly; an informal use. *They are galloping around the garden playing football.* VERB V prep Also V n
6 If you do something **at a gallop**, you do it very quickly. *I read the book at a gallop.* PHRASE: PHR after v

gallows /gælouz/; **gallows** is both the singular and the plural form. A **gallows** is a wooden frame used to execute criminals by hanging. N-COUNT

gallstone /gɔːlstoun/ **gallstones.** A **gallstone** is a small, painful lump which can develop in your gall bladder. N-COUNT

galore /gəlɔːʳ/. You use **galore** to emphasize that something you like exists in very large quantities; an informal word used in written English. *You'll be able to win prizes galore. ...a popular resort with beaches galore and a large marina.* ◆◇◇◇◇ ADJ: n ADJ PRAGMATICS

galoshes /gəlɒʃɪz/. **Galoshes** are waterproof shoes, usually made of rubber, which you wear over your ordinary shoes to prevent them getting wet. N-PLURAL

galvanize /gælvənaɪz/ **galvanizes, galvanizing, galvanized;** also spelled **galvanise** in British English. To **galvanize** someone means to cause them to take action, for example by making them feel very excited, afraid, or angry. *The aid appeal has galvanised the German business community... They have been galvanised into collective action — militarily, politically and economically.* ◆◇◇◇◇ VERB =stir V n be V-ed into n/-ing Also V n into n/-ing

galvanized /gælvənaɪzd/; also spelled **galvanised**. You use **galvanized** to describe metal, especially iron and steel, which has been covered with zinc in order to protect it from rust and other damage. *...corrosion-resistant galvanized steel. ...75mm galvanised nails.* ADJ: usu ADJ n

gambit /gæmbɪt/ **gambits**
1 A **gambit** is an action or set of actions, which you carry out in order to try to gain an advantage in a situation or game. *He sees the proposal as more of a diplomatic gambit than a serious defense proposal... Campaign strategists are calling the plan a clever politic gambit.* N-COUNT: usu with supp =ploy, tactic
2 A **gambit** is a remark which you make to someone in order to start or continue a conversation with them. *His favourite opening gambit is: 'You are so beautiful, will you be my next wife?'... Bernard sat like a zombie, making no response to Tom's conversational gambits.* N-COUNT: usu with supp =remark, ploy

gamble /gæmbəl/ **gambles, gambling, gambled** ◆◆◇◇◇
1 A **gamble** is a risky action or decision that you take in the hope of gaining money, success, or an advantage over other people. *Yesterday, he named his cabinet and took a big gamble in the process. ...the French president's risky gamble in calling a referendum.* N-COUNT =risk
2 If you **gamble** on something, you take a risky action or decision in the hope of gaining money, success, or an advantage over other people. *Few firms will be willing to gamble on new products... They are not prepared to gamble their careers on this matter... Who wants to gamble with the life of a friend?.* VERB V on n/-ing V n on n V with n Also V, V n, V that
3 If you **gamble** an amount of money, you bet it in a game such as cards or on the result of a race or competition. People who **gamble** usually do it frequently. *Most people visit Las Vegas to gamble their hard-earned money... John gambled heavily on the horses... Britain is the only country in Europe that allows minors to gamble... He gambled away his family estates on a single throw of the dice.* VERB =bet V n V on n V V n with away

gambler /gæmbləʳ/ **gamblers** ◆◇◇◇◇
1 A **gambler** is someone who gambles regularly, for example in card games or horse racing. N-COUNT
2 If you describe someone as a **gambler**, you mean that they are ready to take risks in order to gain advantages or success. *He had never been afraid of failure: he was a gambler, ready to go off somewhere else and start all over again.* N-COUNT =risk-taker

gambling /gæmblɪŋ/. **Gambling** is the act or activity of betting money, for example in card games or on horse racing. *Gambling is a form of entertainment. ...gambling casinos.* ◆◆◇◇◇ N-UNCOUNT

gambol /gæmbəl/ **gambols, gambolling, gambolled;** spelled **gamboling, gamboled** in American English. If animals or people **gambol**, they run or jump about in a playful way. *They gamboled down the passageway. ...the sight of newborn lambs gambolling in the fields.* VERB =frisk, frolic V prep/adv

game /geɪm/ **games** ◆◆◆◆◆
1 A **game** is an activity or sport usually involving skill, knowledge, or chance, in which you follow fixed rules and try to win against an opponent or to solve a puzzle. *...the wonderful game of football. ...a playful game of hide-and-seek. ...a video game.* N-COUNT
2 A **game** is one particular occasion on which a game is played. *England's first game of the new season is a friendly against Spain... He regularly watched our games from the stands... We won three games against Australia.* N-COUNT =match
3 A **game** is a part of a match, for example in tennis or bridge, consisting of a fixed number of points. *She won six games to love in the second set. ...the last three points of the second game.* N-COUNT
4 **Games** are an organized event in which competitions in several sports take place. *...the 1996 Olympic Games at Atlanta.* N-PLURAL
5 In British English, **games** are organized sports activities that children do at school. *At his grammar school he is remembered for being bad at games but good in debates.* N-PLURAL =sport
6 Someone's **game** is the degree of skill or the style that they use when playing a particular game. *Once I was through the first set my game picked up... He was having a splendid game in central midfield.* N-SING: usu poss N
7 You can describe a situation that you do not treat seriously as a **game**. *Many people regard life as a game: you win some, you lose some... It's a cat-and-mouse game to him, and I'm the mouse.* N-COUNT
8 You can use **game** to describe a way of behaving in which a person uses a particular plan, usually in order to gain an advantage for himself or herself. *When the uncertainties become greater than the certainties, we end up in a game of bluff... Until now, the Americans have been playing a very delicate political game.* N-COUNT: usu with supp
9 Wild animals or birds that are hunted for sport and sometimes cooked and eaten are referred to as **game**. *As men who shot game for food, they were natural marksmen.* N-UNCOUNT
10 If you say that someone is **game** or **game for** something, you mean that they are willing to do something new, unusual, or risky. *After all this time he still had new ideas and was game to try them... He said he's game for a similar challenge next year.* ADJ-GRADED: v-link ADJ, oft ADJ to-inf, ADJ for n
11 See also **gamely**.
12 If someone or something **gives the game away**, they reveal a secret or reveal their feelings, and this puts them at a disadvantage. *She'd never been to a posh mansion, and was afraid she might give the game away... The faces of the two conspirators gave the game away!* PHRASES V inflects
13 If you are **new to** a particular **game**, you have not done a particular activity or been in a particular situation before. *Don't forget that she's new to this game and will take a while to complete the task.* v-link PHR
14 If a man or woman is **on the game**, he or she is v-link PHR

working as a prostitute; an informal British expression.

15 If you beat someone **at** their **own game**, you use the same methods that they have used, but more successfully, so that you gain an advantage over them. *He must anticipate the maneuvers of the other lawyers and beat them at their own game... The police knew that to trap the killer they had to play him at his own game.* PHR after v

16 If you say that something is **all part of the game**, you are telling someone not to be surprised or upset by something, because it is a normal part of the situation that they are in. *For investors, risks are part of the game.* v-link PHR

17 If you say that someone is **playing games** or **playing silly games**, you are emphasizing your disapproval of the fact that they are not treating a situation seriously and that you are annoyed with them. *This seemed to annoy Professor Steiner. 'Don't play games with me' he thundered... From what I know of him he doesn't play silly games.* V inflects PRAGMATICS

18 If you say **the game is up**, you mean that someone's secret plans or activities have been revealed and therefore must stop because they cannot succeed. *Some thought they would hold out until Sunday. The realists knew that the game was already up.* V inflects

game bird, game birds. Game birds are birds which are shot for food or for sport. *The sauce is good with other roasted game birds, too, not just pheasant.* N-COUNT: usu pl

Gameboy /geɪmbɔɪ/ **Gameboys.** A **Gameboy** is a small portable computer that is specially designed for people to play games on. **Gameboy** is a trademark. N-VAR

gamekeeper /geɪmkiːpəʳ/ **gamekeepers.** A **gamekeeper** is a person who takes care of the wild animals or birds that are kept on someone's land for hunting. N-COUNT

gamely /geɪmli/. If you do something **gamely**, you do it bravely or with a lot of effort. *Mary Ann smiled at her gamely... He gamely defended his organisation's decision.* ADV-GRADED: ADV with v =resolutely

game plan, game plans; also spelled **gameplan.**

1 In sport, a team's **game plan** is the strategy they intend to use during a match in order to win it. *Leeds kept quiet, stuck to their game plan and quietly racked up the points.* N-COUNT: usu poss N

2 Someone's **game plan** is the actions they intend to do and the policies they intend to adopt in order to achieve a particular thing; use mainly in journalism. *If he has a game plan for winning the deal, only he understands it... He is unlikely to alter his game plan.* N-COUNT: oft poss N

gamesmanship /geɪmzmənʃɪp/. **Gamesmanship** is the art or practice of winning a game by clever methods and tactics which are not against the rules but are very close to cheating. *...a remarkably successful piece of diplomatic gamesmanship.* N-UNCOUNT

gamine /gæmiːn/. If you describe a girl or a woman as **gamine**, you mean that she is attractive in a boyish way. *She had a gamine charm which men found irresistibly attractive.* ▶ Also a noun. *Critics remarked upon her childlike beauty, describing her as a snub-nosed gamine.* ADJ-GRADED: usu ADJ n =boyish; N-SING

gaming /geɪmɪŋ/. **Gaming** means the same as **gambling**, especially at cards, roulette, and other games of chance. *...offences connected with vice, gaming and drugs. ...the most fashionable gaming club in London.* ◆◇◇◇◇ N-UNCOUNT: oft N n

gamma /gæmə/ **gammas.** **Gamma** is the third letter of the Greek alphabet. ◆◇◇◇◇ N-VAR

gamma rays. **Gamma rays** are a type of electromagnetic radiation that has a shorter wavelength and higher energy than X-rays. N-PLURAL

gammon /gæmən/. In British English, **gammon** is smoked or salted meat, similar to bacon, from the back leg or the side of a pig. N-UNCOUNT

gamut /gæmət/

1 The gamut of something is the complete range of things of that kind, or a wide variety of things of that kind. *Varied though the anthology may claim to be, it does not cover the whole gamut of Scottish poetry... As the story unfolded throughout the past week, I experienced the gamut of emotions: shock, anger, sadness, disgust, confusion.* N-SING: usu *the* N *of* n =range, variety

2 To **run the gamut** of something means to include, express, or experience all the different things of that kind, or a wide variety of them. *The show runs the gamut of 20th century design... The reviews for 'On a Clear Day' ran the gamut from contempt to qualified rapture.* PHRASE: V inflects

gander /gændəʳ/ **ganders.** A **gander** is a male goose. N-COUNT

gang /gæŋ/ **gangs, ganging, ganged** ◆◆◆◇◇

1 A **gang** is a group of people, especially young people, who go around together and often deliberately cause trouble. *During the fight with a rival gang he lashed out with his flick knife... Gang members were behind a lot of the violence... He was attacked by a gang of youths.* N-COUNT

2 A **gang** is a group of criminals who work together to commit crimes. *Police were hunting for a gang who had allegedly stolen fifty-five cars. ...an underworld gang. ...a gang of masked robbers.* N-COUNT

3 The **gang** is a group of friends who frequently meet; an informal use. *Come on over, we've got lots of the old gang here.* N-SING: usu *the* N

4 A **gang** is a group of manual workers who work together. *...a gang of labourers.* N-COUNT: oft N *of* n

gang up. If people **gang up** on someone, they unite against them for a particular reason, for example in a fight or argument; used in informal English. *Harrison complained that his colleagues ganged up on him... All the other parties ganged up to keep them out of power... All the girls in my class seemed to gang up against me.* PHRASAL VERB: V P *on* n, V P to-inf, V P *against* n

gangland /gæŋlænd/. **Gangland** is used to describe activities or people that are involved in organized crime. *It's been suggested they were gangland killings... Her younger brother, Raffaele, is one of Italy's top gangland bosses.* ADJ: ADJ n =underworld

gangling /gæŋglɪŋ/. **Gangling** is used to describe a young person, especially a man, who is tall, thin, and clumsy in their movements. *His gangling, awkward gait has earned him the name Spiderman. ...his gangling, bony frame.* ADJ: ADJ n

gangly /gæŋgli/. If you describe someone as **gangly**, you mean that they are tall and thin and have a slightly awkward or clumsy manner. *...a gangly youth dressed in jeans and trainers.* ADJ-GRADED: usu ADJ n =gangling

gangplank /gæŋplæŋk/ **gangplanks.** The **gangplank** is a short bridge or platform that can be placed between the side of a ship or boat and the shore, so that people can get on or off. N-COUNT: usu *the* N in sing =gangway

gangrene /gæŋgriːn/. **Gangrene** is the decay that can occur in a part of a person's body if the blood stops flowing to it, for example as a result of illness or injury. *Once gangrene has developed the tissue is dead and the only hope is to contain the damage.* N-UNCOUNT

gangrenous /gæŋgrɪnəs/. **Gangrenous** is used to describe a part of a person's body that has been affected by gangrene. *...patients with gangrenous limbs.* ADJ

gangster /gæŋstəʳ/ **gangsters.** A **gangster** is a member of an organized group of violent criminals. ◆◇◇◇◇ N-COUNT

gangway /gæŋweɪ/ **gangways**

1 The **gangway** is the gangplank leading onto a ship. *He led me to the gangway and then to his cabin.* N-COUNT: usu *the* N in sing

2 The **gangway** is a passage left between rows of seats, for example in a theatre or aircraft, for people to walk along; used mainly in British English. *A man in the gangway suddenly stood up to reach for something in the overhead locker.* N-COUNT: usu *the* N in sing =aisle

gantry /gæntri/ **gantries.** A **gantry** is a high metal structure that supports a crane, a set of road signs, railway signals, or other equipment. *On top of the gantry the American flag flew. ...the lighting gantries.* N-COUNT

gaol /dʒeɪl/ **gaols, gaoling, gaoled;** also spelled **jail.** See **jail.**
gaoler /dʒeɪləʳ/ **gaolers;** See **jailer.**
gap /gæp/ **gaps** ◆◆◆◇◇
1 A **gap** is a space between two things or a hole in the middle of something solid. *He pulled the thick curtains together, leaving just a narrow gap. ...the wind tearing through gaps in the window frames.* N-COUNT
2 A **gap** is a period of time when you are not busy or when you stop doing something that you normally do. *There followed a gap of four years, during which William joined the Army.* N-COUNT: oft N *of* n =hiatus
3 If there is something missing from a situation that prevents it being complete or satisfactory, you can say that there is a **gap**. *China can't fill the economic gap left by the cut in Soviet support... Like a good businessman, Stewart identified a gap in the market.* N-COUNT: usu with supp
4 A **gap** between two groups of people, things, or sets of ideas is a big difference between them. *...the gap between rich and poor... America's trade gap widened... Britain needs to bridge the technology gap between academia and industry.* N-COUNT: with supp, oft N *between* pl-n =gulf
gape /geɪp/ **gapes, gaping, gaped** ◆◇◇◇◇
1 If you **gape**, you look at someone or something in surprise, usually with an open mouth. *His secretary stopped taking notes to gape at me... He was not the type to wander round gaping at everything like a tourist. ...a grotesque face with its gaping mouth.* VERB =gawk V *at* n V-ing Also V
2 If you say that something such as a hole or a wound **gapes**, you are emphasizing that it is big or wide. *The front door was missing. A hole gaped in the roof.* ♦ **gaping** *The aircraft took off with a gaping hole in its fuselage... The doctors took shrapnel out of a gaping wound in her back.* VERB PRAGMATICS V ADJ: usu ADJ n
gap-fill, gap-fills. In language teaching, a **gap-fill** test is an exercise in which words are removed from a text and replaced with spaces. The learner has to fill each space with the missing word or a suitable word. N-COUNT: usu N n =cloze
gap-toothed. If you describe a person or their smile as **gap-toothed**, you mean that some of that person's teeth are missing; used in written English. *The old man's face broke into a broad, gap-toothed grin.* ADJ: usu ADJ n
garage /gærɑːʒ, -rɪdʒ, AM gərɑːʒ/ **garages** ◆◆◇◇◇
1 A **garage** is a building in which you keep a car. A garage is often built next to or as part of a house. N-COUNT
2 A **garage** is a place where you can get your car repaired, buy a car, or buy petrol. *Nancy took her car to a local garage for a check-up... Nelson Garage has the used car you're after.* N-COUNT: oft in names after n
garb /gɑːʳb/. You can refer to the clothes someone is wearing as their **garb** when you want to draw attention to these clothes, for example because they are unusual; used in written English. *At 9.30 p.m. a familiar figure in civilian garb came out of the main entrance... He wore the garb of a scout, not a general.* N-UNCOUNT: oft *in* adj N, oft with poss =attire
garbage /gɑːʳbɪdʒ/ ◆◇◇◇◇
1 **Garbage** is rubbish, especially waste from a kitchen; used in American English. *I don't remember what day the garbage is collected. ...rotting piles of garbage.* N-UNCOUNT =rubbish
2 If someone says that an idea or opinion is **garbage**, they are emphasizing that they believe it is untrue or unimportant; an informal use. *I personally think this is complete garbage... Furious government officials branded her story 'garbage'.* N-UNCOUNT PRAGMATICS =rubbish
garbage can, garbage cans. In American English, a **garbage can** is a container that you put rubbish into. The usual British word is **dustbin.** *A bomb planted in a garbage can exploded early today.* N-COUNT
garbed /gɑːʳbd/. If someone is **garbed** in particular clothes, they are wearing those clothes; a literary word. *He was garbed in sweater, tweed jacket, and flying boots.* ► Also a combining form. *...the small blue-garbed woman with a brown wrinkled face.* ADJ: v-link ADJ *in* n, adv ADJ COMB in ADJ: usu ADJ n
garbled /gɑːʳbəld/. A **garbled** message or report contains confused or wrong details, often because it is spoken by someone who is nervous or in a hurry. *The Coastguard needs to decipher garbled messages in a few minutes. ...his own garbled version of the El Greco story.* ADJ-GRADED =jumbled
garden /gɑːʳdᵊn/ **gardens, gardening, gardened** ◆◆◆◆◇
1 A **garden** is a piece of land next to someone's house where they grow flowers, vegetables, or other plants. A **garden** often includes a lawn. In American English, the word **yard** is often used instead of **garden**. *...the full glare of sunshine in a beautiful garden.* N-COUNT
2 If you **garden**, you do work in your garden such as weeding or planting. *Jim gardened at the homes of friends on weekends.* ♦ **gardening** *I have taken up gardening again.* VERB V N-UNCOUNT
3 **Gardens** are places like a park that have areas of plants, trees, and grass, and that people can visit and walk around. *The Gardens are open from 10.30am until 5pm. ...Kensington Gardens.* N-PLURAL
4 **Gardens** is sometimes used as part of the name of a street. *He lives at 9, Acacia Gardens.* N-IN-NAMES
garden centre, garden centres. A **garden centre** is a large shop, usually with an outdoor area, where you can buy things for your garden such as plants and gardening tools. ◆◇◇◇◇ N-COUNT
gardener /gɑːʳdənəʳ/ **gardeners** ◆◆◇◇◇
1 A **gardener** is a person who is paid to work in someone else's garden. N-COUNT
2 A **gardener** is someone who enjoys working in their own garden growing flowers or vegetables. *The majority of sweet peas are still bred by enthusiastic amateur gardeners.* N-COUNT
gardenia /gɑːʳdiːniə/ **gardenias.** A **gardenia** is a type of large, white, or yellow flower with a very pleasant smell. A **gardenia** is also the bush on which these flowers grow. N-COUNT
garden party, garden parties. A **garden party** is a formal party that is held out of doors, especially in a large private garden, during the afternoon. *A garden party at Buckingham Palace was beyond my wildest expectations.* N-COUNT: usu sing
gargantuan /gɑːʳgæntʃuən/. If you say that something is **gargantuan**, you are emphasizing that it is very large; used mainly in written English. *...a marketing event of gargantuan proportions. ...a gargantuan corruption scandal.* ADJ-GRADED: usu ADJ n PRAGMATICS =huge, colossal
gargle /gɑːʳgᵊl/ **gargles, gargling, gargled**
1 If you **gargle**, you wash your mouth and throat by filling your mouth with a liquid, making a bubbling noise in your throat, then spitting out the liquid. *Try gargling with salt water as soon as a cough begins... At the sink, Neil noisily gargled something medicinal.* VERB V V n
2 A **gargle** is a liquid, such as a medicine or a mouthwash, which is used for gargling. *The mixture can be used as a gargle several times a day.* N-COUNT: usu sing
gargoyle /gɑːʳgɔɪl/ **gargoyles.** A **gargoyle** is a decorative stone carving on old buildings. It is usually shaped like the head of a strange and ugly creature, and water drains through it from the roof of the building. N-COUNT
garish /geərɪʃ/. You describe something as **garish** when you dislike it because it is very bright in an unattractive, showy way. *They climbed the garish purple-carpeted stairs... Residents have boycotted the restaurant because of its garish, illuminated signs.* ♦ **garishly** *...a garishly patterned three-piece suite.* ◆◇◇◇◇ ADJ-GRADED PRAGMATICS =gaudy ADV-GRADED: ADV adj/-ed
garland /gɑːʳlənd/ **garlands, garlanding, garlanded** ◆◇◇◇◇
1 A **garland** is a circular decoration made from flowers and leaves. People sometimes wear garlands of flowers on their heads or around their necks. *They wore blue silk dresses with cream sashes and garlands of summer flowers in their hair.* N-COUNT: usu pl, oft N *of* n
2 If people, places, or objects **are garlanded**, people hang garlands or similar decorations around them. *Players and officials were garlanded with flowers... The wagons were decorated with flowers and pulled by garlanded horses.* VB: usu passive =festoon, deck *be* V-ed *with* n V-ed

garlic /gɑːʳlɪk/. **Garlic** is the small, white, round bulb of a plant that is related to the onion plant. Garlic has a very strong smell and taste and is used in cooking. *...a clove of garlic.* ◆◆◇◇◇ N-UNCOUNT

garlicky /gɑːʳlɪki/. Something that is **garlicky** tastes or smells of garlic. *...a garlicky salad. ...garlicky breath.* ADJ-GRADED: usu ADJ n

garment /gɑːʳmənt/ **garments.** A **garment** is a piece of clothing; used especially in contexts where you are talking about the manufacture or sale of clothes. *Many of the garments have the customers' name tags sewn into the linings... New autumn ranges are going well here, with garment sales up 31%.* ◆◆◇◇◇ N-COUNT

garner /gɑːʳnəʳ/ **garners, garnering, garnered.** If someone has collected or gained something useful or valuable, you can say that they **have garnered** it; a formal word. *Durham had garnered three times as many votes as Carey... He has garnered extensive support for his proposals... His priceless collection of Chinese art and artefacts was garnered over three decades.* ◆◇◇◇◇ VERB =gather, acquire V n

garnet /gɑːʳnɪt/ **garnets.** A **garnet** is a hard, shiny stone that is used in making jewellery. Garnets can be red, yellow, or green in colour. N-COUNT

garnish /gɑːʳnɪʃ/ **garnishes, garnishing, garnished** ◆◇◇◇◇

1 A **garnish** is a small amount of salad, herbs, or other food that is used to decorate cooked or prepared food. *...a garnish of chopped raw onion, tomato and fresh coriander... Reserve some watercress for garnish.* N-VAR

2 If you **garnish** cooked or prepared food, you decorate it with a garnish. *She had finished the vegetables and was garnishing the roast.* VERB V n

garret /gærɪt/ **garrets.** A **garret** is a small room at the top of a house, especially one that is rented to a writer, artist, or other lodger. N-COUNT =attic

garrison /gærɪsᵊn/ **garrisons, garrisoning, garrisoned** ◆◇◇◇◇

1 A **garrison** is a group of soldiers whose task is to guard the town or building where they live. *...a five-hundred man French army garrison.* N-COUNT-COLL

2 A **garrison** is the buildings which the soldiers live in. *The approaches to the garrison have been heavily mined.* N-COUNT

3 To **garrison** a place means to put soldiers there in order to protect it. You can also say that soldiers **are garrisoned** in a place. *British troops still garrisoned the country... No other soldiers were garrisoned there. ...the large, heavily garrisoned towns.* VERB V n be V-ed V-ed

garrotte /gərɒt/ **garrottes, garrotting, garrotted**

1 If someone **is garrotted**, they are killed by being strangled or having their neck broken, using a device such as a piece of wire or a metal collar. *The two guards had been garrotted.* VERB be V-ed Also V n

2 A **garrotte** is a piece of wire or a metal collar used to garrotte someone. N-COUNT

garrulous /gærələs/. If you describe someone as **garrulous**, you mean that they talk a great deal, especially about unimportant things. *I found her in conversation with Mrs Williams, a garrulous old woman who lived next door.* ADJ-GRADED =talkative ≠taciturn

garter /gɑːʳtəʳ/ **garters.** A **garter** is a piece of elastic worn round the top of a stocking or sock in order to prevent it slipping down. N-COUNT

gas /gæs/ **gases, gasses, gassing, gassed.** The form **gases** is the plural of the noun. The form **gasses** is the third person singular of the verb. ◆◆◆◆◇

1 **Gas** is a substance like air that is neither liquid nor solid and burns easily. It is used as a fuel for fires, cookers, and central heating. *Coal is actually cheaper than gas... Shell signed a contract to develop oil and gas reserves near Archangel.* N-UNCOUNT

2 A **gas** is any substance that is neither liquid nor solid, for example oxygen or hydrogen. *Helium is a very light gas. ...a huge cloud of gas and dust from the volcanic eruption.* N-VAR

3 **Gas** is a poisonous gas that can be used as a weapon. *...mustard gas... The problem was that the exhaust gases contain many toxins.* N-MASS

4 **Gas** is a gas used for medical purposes, for example to make patients feel less pain or go to sleep during an operation; an informal use. *...an anaesthetic gas used by many dentists.* N-MASS

5 In American English, **gas** is the fuel which is used to drive motor vehicles. The British word is **petrol**. *...a tank of gas. ...gas stations.* N-UNCOUNT

6 To **gas** a person or animal means to kill them by making them breathe poisonous gas. *Her husband ran a pipe from her car exhaust to the bedroom in an attempt to gas her.* VERB V n

7 Some speakers of American English say that a situation or an event is **a gas** when it is very lively, amusing, and enjoyable; an informal use. *It was really a gas to find someone I could talk with.* N-SING: a N

8 See also **greenhouse gas, laughing gas, natural gas, tear gas, gas chamber, gas mask.**

9 If you **step on the gas** when you are driving a vehicle, you go faster; an informal expression, used mainly in American English. PHRASE: V inflects

gas chamber, gas chambers. A **gas chamber** is a room that has been specially built so that it can be filled with poisonous gas in order to kill people or animals. N-COUNT

gaseous /gæsiəs, geɪʃəs/. You use **gaseous** to describe something which is in the form of a gas, rather than a solid or liquid. *Freon exists both in liquid and gaseous states.* ADJ: usu ADJ n

gas fire, gas fires. A **gas fire** is a fire that produces heat by burning gas. N-COUNT

gas guzzler, gas guzzlers; also spelled **gas-guzzler**. If you say that a car is a **gas guzzler** you mean that it is not economical to run because it uses so much petrol. *They say gas guzzlers are contributing to air pollution.* N-COUNT

gash /gæʃ/ **gashes, gashing, gashed** ◆◇◇◇◇

1 A **gash** is a long, deep cut in your skin or in the surface of something. *There was an inch-long gash just above his right eye.* N-COUNT

2 If you **gash** something, you accidentally make a long and deep cut in it. *He gashed his leg while felling trees.* VERB V n

gasket /gæskɪt/ **gaskets.** A **gasket** is a flat piece of soft material that you put between two joined surfaces in a pipe or engine in order to make sure that gas and oil cannot escape. N-COUNT

gaslight /gæshouldəʳ/ **gaslights;** also spelled **gas light**. A **gaslight** is a lamp that produces light by burning gas. *The gaslights in the passage would be on, turned low.* ▶ **Gaslight** is also the light that the lamp produces. *He would show his collection by gaslight.* N-COUNT N-UNCOUNT

gasman /gæsmæn/ **gasmen.** The **gasman** is a man whose job is to install and repair gas appliances and read gas meters; an informal word. N-COUNT: usu *the* N in sing

gas mask, gas masks. A **gas mask** is a device that you wear over your face in order to protect yourself from poisonous gases. ◆◇◇◇◇ N-COUNT

gasoline /gæsəliːn/. **Gasoline** is the same as **petrol**; used mainly in American English. ◆◆◇◇◇ N-UNCOUNT

gasometer /gæsɒmɪtəʳ/ **gasometers.** A **gasometer** is a very large metal container that is usually part of a gasworks. It stores gas until it is needed, then supplies it through pipes to buildings for purposes such as heating and cooking. N-COUNT

gasp /gɑːsp, gæsp/ **gasps, gasping, gasped** ◆◆◇◇◇

1 A **gasp** is a short quick breath of air that you take in through your mouth, especially when you are surprised, shocked, or in pain. *An audible gasp went round the court as the jury announced the verdict... She gave a small gasp of pain.* N-COUNT: usu with supp

2 When you **gasp**, you take a short quick breath through your mouth, especially when you are surprised, shocked, or in pain. *She gasped for air and drew in a lungful of water... I heard myself gasp and cry out.* VERB V for n V Also V with quote

3 If you describe something as **the last gasp**, you are emphasizing that it is the final action of something or that it happens in the final possible moment. *With the collapse of that strike we saw the* PHRASE: usu PHR of n, PHR n PRAGMATICS

last gasp of trades unionism... He snatched a last gasp winner.

gas ring, gas rings. A **gas ring** is a circular gas pipe on a cooker, which has several holes in it and directs the flames under pans. N-COUNT =burner

gas station, gas stations. In American English, a **gas station** is a place where gasoline is sold. ◆◇◇◇◇ N-COUNT =filling station

gassy /gæsi/ **gassier, gassiest.** Something that is **gassy** contains a lot of bubbles or gas. *The champagne was sweet and too gassy.* ADJ-GRADED =fizzy

gastric /gæstrɪk/. You use **gastric** to describe processes, pain, or illnesses that occur in someone's stomach; a medical term. *He suffered from diabetes and gastric ulcers.* ◆◇◇◇◇ ADJ: ADJ n

gastroenteritis /gæstroʊentəraɪtɪs/; also spelled **gastro-enteritis. Gastroenteritis** is an illness in which the lining of your stomach and intestines becomes swollen and painful; a medical term. N-UNCOUNT

gastronome /gæstrənoʊm/ **gastronomes.** A **gastronome** is someone who enjoys preparing and eating good food, especially unusual or expensive food; a literary word. N-COUNT =gourmet

gastronomic /gæstrənɒmɪk/. **Gastronomic** is used to describe things that are concerned with good food; a formal word. *Paris is the gastronomic capital of the world... She is sampling gastronomic delights along the Riviera.* ADJ: ADJ n

gastronomy /gæstrɒnəmi/. **Gastronomy** is the activity and knowledge involved in preparing and appreciating good food; a formal word. *Burgundy has always been considered a major centre of gastronomy.* N-UNCOUNT

gasworks /gæswɜːʳks/ **gasworks;** also spelled **gas works.** A **gasworks** is a factory where gas is made, usually from coal, so that it can be used as a fuel. N-COUNT

gate /geɪt/ **gates** ◆◆◆◇◇

1 A **gate** is a structure like a door which is used at the entrance to a field, a garden, or the grounds of a building. *He opened the gate and started walking up to the house.* N-COUNT

2 In an airport, a **gate** is an exit through which passengers reach their aeroplane. *Passengers with hand luggage can go straight to the departure gate to check in there.* N-COUNT

3 **Gate** is used in the names of streets that stand on the site of an old gate into a city. *...9 Palace Gate.* N-IN-NAMES

4 The **gate** at a sporting event such as a football match is the total number of people who attend it. *Their average gate is less than 23,000.* N-COUNT =attendance

gateau /gætoʊ/ **gateaux.** A **gateau** is a very rich, elaborate cake, especially one with cream in it; used mainly in British English. *...a large slice of gateau. ...a huge selection of gateaux, cakes and pastries.* N-VAR

gatecrash /geɪtkræʃ/ **gatecrashes, gatecrashing, gatecrashed.** If someone **gatecrashes** a party or other social event, they go to it, even though they have not been invited; an informal word. *Scores of people tried desperately to gatecrash the party... He had gatecrashed but he was with other people we knew and there was no problem.* ♦ **gatecrasher, gatecrashers** *Panic set in as gatecrashers tried to force their way through the narrow doors and corridor.* VERB V n V N-COUNT

gatehouse /geɪthaʊs/ **gatehouses.** A **gatehouse** is a small house next to a gate in the boundary of a park or country estate. N-COUNT

gatekeeper /geɪtkiːpəʳ/ **gatekeepers.** A **gatekeeper** is a person who is in charge of a gate and who allows people through it; an old-fashioned word. N-COUNT

gate money. **Gate money** is the total amount of money that is paid by the spectators who attend a sports match or other event. *We gave the gate money to the St John Ambulance brigade.* N-UNCOUNT =gate

gatepost /geɪtpoʊst/ **gateposts.** A **gatepost** is a post in the ground which a gate is hung from, or which it is fastened to when it is closed. N-COUNT

gateway /geɪtweɪ/ **gateways** ◆◇◇◇◇

1 A **gateway** is an entrance where there is a gate. *He walked across the park and through a gateway.* N-COUNT

2 A **gateway to** somewhere is a place which you go through because it leads you to a much larger place. *Lyons is the gateway to the Alps for motorists driving out from Britain.* N-COUNT: usu N *to* n

3 If something is a **gateway to** a job, career, or other activity, it gives you the opportunity to make progress or get further success in that activity. *The prestigious title offered a gateway to success in the highly competitive world of modelling.* N-COUNT: with supp, usu N *to* n =passport

gather /gæðəʳ/ **gathers, gathering, gathered** ◆◆◆◆◇

1 If people **gather** somewhere or if someone or something **gathers** them there, they come together in a group. *In the evenings, we gathered around the fireplace and talked... The man signalled for me to gather the children together.* V-ERG =congregate V prep/adv V n with *together* Also V

2 If you **gather** things, you collect them together so that you can use them. *I suggest we gather enough firewood to last the night... She stood up and started gathering her things together.* ► **Gather up** means the same as **gather**. *When Sutcliffe had gathered up his papers, he went out... He gathered the leaves up off the ground.* VERB =collect V n V n *together* PHRASAL VERB V P n (not pron) V n P

3 If you **gather** information or evidence, you collect it, especially over a period of time and after a lot of hard work. *...a private detective using a hidden tape recorder to gather information... This would help the prosecutor gather evidence against him which could be used in court.* VERB =collect, amass V n

4 If something **gathers** speed, momentum, or force, it gradually becomes faster or more powerful. *Demands for his dismissal have gathered momentum in recent weeks... The raft gathered speed as the current dragged it toward the falls.* VERB =gain V n

5 When you **gather** something such as your strength, courage, or thoughts, you make an effort to prepare yourself to do something. *You must gather your strength for the journey.* ► **Gather up** means the same as **gather**. *She was gathering up her courage to approach him when he called to her.* VERB =muster V n PHRASAL VERB V P n (not pron) Also V n P

6 You use **gather** in expressions such as **'I gather'**, **'from what I can gather'** and **'as far as I can gather'** when you are introducing information that you have found out, especially when you have found it out in an indirect way. *I gather his report is highly critical of the trial judge... 'He speaks English,' she said to Graham. 'I gathered that.'... From what I could gather, he was trying to raise money by organising festivals.* VERB PRAGMATICS V that V n

7 If you **gather** fabric or cloth, you make a row of very small pleats in it by sewing a thread through it and then pulling the thread tight. *Gather the skirt at the waist.* ► Also a noun. *Try soft gathers at the waist on trousers.* VERB V n N-PLURAL

8 ● to **gather dust**: see **dust**.

gather up. See **gather** 2, 5. PHRASAL VERB

gatherer /gæðərəʳ/ **gatherers.** A **gatherer** is someone who collects or gathers a particular thing. *The brazil nut gatherers were paid only 2 to 3 percent of the New York wholesale price. ...professional intelligence gatherers.* N-COUNT: usu n N

gathering /gæðərɪŋ/ **gatherings** ◆◆◇◇◇

1 A **gathering** is a group of people meeting together for a particular purpose. *...the twenty-second annual gathering of the South Pacific Forum.* N-COUNT

2 If you refer to the **gathering** dusk, darkness, or gloom, you mean that the light is gradually decreasing, usually because it is nearly night. *The lighthouse beam was quite distinct in the gathering dusk.* ● See also **gather**. ADJ: ADJ n

gator /geɪtəʳ/ **gators;** also spelled **'gator.** A **gator** is the same as an **alligator**; used in informal American English. N-COUNT =alligator

gauche /goʊʃ/. If you describe someone as **gauche**, you mean that they are awkward and uncomfortable in the company of other people. *We're all a bit gauche when we're young.... She was a rather gauche, provincial creature.* ADJ-GRADED =shy, awkward

gaudy /gɔːdi/ **gaudier, gaudiest.** If something is **gaudy**, it is very bright-coloured and showy; ◆◇◇◇◇ ADJ-GRADED =garish often used to express disapproval and to suggest that it is vulgar. *...her gaudy orange-and-purple floral hat. ...gaudy tropical butterflies.*

gauge /geɪdʒ/ **gauges, gauging, gauged** ◆◆◇◇◇

1 If you **gauge** the speed or strength of something, or if you gauge an amount, you measure or calculate it, often by using a device of some kind. *He gauged the wind at over thirty knots... Distance is gauged by journey time rather than miles.* VERB V n

2 A **gauge** is a device that measures the amount or quantity of something and shows the amount measured. *...temperature gauges. ...pressure gauges.* N-COUNT: oft n N

3 If you **gauge** people's actions, feelings, or intentions in a particular situation, you carefully consider and judge them. *Our correspondent was in the Kremlin to hear Mr. Gorbachev's speech and gauged the reaction to it... His mood can be gauged by his reaction to the most trivial of incidents.* VERB =assess V n

4 A **gauge** of someone's feelings or a situation is a fact or event that can be used to judge them. *The index is the government's chief gauge of future economic activity.* N-SING: usu N *of*n =measure

5 A **gauge** is the distance between the two rails on a railway line. *...a narrow gauge railway.* N-COUNT: usu n N

6 A **gauge** is the thickness of something, especially metal or wire. N-COUNT

gaunt /gɔːnt/ ◆◇◇◇◇

1 If someone looks **gaunt**, they look very thin, usually because they have been very ill or worried. *Looking gaunt and tired, he denied there was anything to worry about.* ADJ-GRADED =drawn, pinched

2 If you describe a building as **gaunt**, you mean it is bare and unattractive; a literary use. *Above on the hillside was a large, gaunt, grey house.* ADJ-GRADED: ADJ n

gauntlet /gɔːntlɪt/ **gauntlets** ◆◇◇◇◇

1 **Gauntlets** are long, thick, protective gloves. *...a pair of pale yellow leather driving gauntlets.* N-COUNT: usu pl

2 If you **pick up the gauntlet** or **take up the gauntlet**, you accept the challenge that someone has made. *She picked up the gauntlet in her incisive Keynote Address to the Conference... Whoever decides to take up the gauntlet and challenge the Prime Minister will have a tough battle.* PHRASES V inflects

3 If you **run the gauntlet**, you go through an unpleasant experience in which a lot of people criticize or attack you. *The trucks tried to drive to the British base, running the gauntlet of marauding bands of gunmen.* V inflects, oft PHR *of*n

4 If you **throw down the gauntlet** to someone, you say or do something that challenges them to argue or compete with you. *Luxury car firm Jaguar has thrown down the gauntlet to competitors by giving the best guarantee on the market.* V inflects, oft PHR *to*n

gauze /gɔːz/. **Gauze** is a type of light, soft cloth with tiny holes in it. *Extract the juice by straining it through a piece of gauze or a sieve.* N-UNCOUNT

gauzy /gɔːzi/. **Gauzy** material is light, soft, and thin, so that you can see through it. *...thin, gauzy curtains stirred by a breeze.* ADJ: ADJ n =filmy

gave /geɪv/. **Gave** is the past tense of **give**.

gavel /gævəl/ **gavels.** A **gavel** is a small wooden hammer that someone such as a judge, auctioneer, or chairman of a meeting bangs on a table to get people's attention. *'Let's take a ten-minute recess', the judge said, pounding his gavel.* N-COUNT: usu sing, oft poss N

gawd /gɔːd/. **Gawd** is used in written English to represent the word 'god' pronounced in a particular accent or tone of voice, especially in phrases expressing boredom, irritation, or shock; an informal word. *I thought, oh my gawd!* EXCLAM

gawk /gɔːk/ **gawks, gawking, gawked.** If someone **gawks** at someone or something, they stare at them in a rude, stupid, or unthinking way; an informal word. *The youth continued to gawk at her and did not answer... Tens of thousands came to gawk.* VERB =gape V *at*n V

gawky /gɔːki/. If you describe someone, especially a teenager, as **gawky**, you mean they are awkward and clumsy. *...a gawky lad with spots.* ADJ-GRADED =ungainly

gawp /gɔːp/ **gawps, gawping, gawped.** In British English, to **gawp** means the same as to **gawk**; an informal word. *At weekends the roads are jammed with holidaymakers coming to gawp at the parade... Thorpe could only stand and gawp.* VERB V *at*n V

gay /geɪ/ **gays; gayer, gayest** ◆◆◆◆◇

1 A **gay** person is homosexual. *The quality of life for gay men has improved over the last two decades. ...the gay community.* ► **Gays** are homosexual people, especially homosexual men. *Irish lesbians and gays are celebrating a reform of the Republic's laws.* ♦ **gayness** *...Mike's admission of his gayness.* ADJ: usu ADJ n ≠straight N-PLURAL N-UNCOUNT

2 A **gay** person is fun to be with because they are lively and cheerful; an old-fashioned use. *I am happy and free, in good health, gay and cheerful.* ADJ-GRADED

3 A **gay** object is brightly coloured and pretty to look at; an old-fashioned use. *I like gay, relaxing paintings.* ADJ-GRADED =cheerful

gay liberation. **Gay liberation** is a political movement, started in the 1970s, to fight prejudice and discrimination against gay people. N-UNCOUNT

gaze /geɪz/ **gazes, gazing, gazed** ◆◆◇◇◇

1 If you **gaze** at someone or something, you look steadily at them for a long time, for example because you find them attractive or interesting, or because you are thinking about something else. *...gazing at herself in the mirror... Sitting in his wicker chair, he gazed reflectively at the fire... The girls stood still, gazing around the building, trying to picture life there fifty years before.* VERB =stare V *at*n V prep/adv

2 You can talk about someone's **gaze** as a way of describing how they are looking at something, especially when they are looking steadily at it. *The Monsignor turned his gaze from the flames to meet the Colonel's... She felt increasingly uncomfortable under the woman's steady gaze... The interior was shielded from the curious gaze of passersby.* N-COUNT: usu sing, usu with poss

3 If someone or something is **in the public gaze**, they are receiving a lot of attention from the general public. *You won't find a couple more in the public gaze than Michael and Lizzie.* PHRASE

gazebo /gəziːboʊ, AM -zeɪ-/ **gazebos.** A **gazebo** is a small building with open sides. Gazebos are often put up in gardens so that people can sit in them to enjoy the view. N-COUNT

gazelle /gəzel/ **gazelles.** A **gazelle** is a type of small African or Asian antelope. Gazelles move very quickly and gracefully. N-COUNT

gazette /gəzet/ **gazettes** ◆◇◇◇◇

1 **Gazette** is often used in the names of newspapers or journals. *...the Arkansas Gazette.* N-IN-NAMES: n N

2 A **gazette** is an official publication in which information such as honours, public appointments, and important decisions are announced. N-COUNT: oft adj N

gazetteer /gæzɪtɪəʳ/ **gazetteers.** A **gazetteer** is a book or a part of a book which lists and describes places. N-COUNT

gazump /gəzʌmp/ **gazumps, gazumping, gazumped.** In British English, if you **are gazumped** by someone, they agree to sell their house to you, but then sell it to someone else who offers to pay a higher price; an informal word, used showing disapproval. *In France you cannot be gazumped... During the 1980s property boom, gazumping was common.* VB: usu passive PRAGMATICS *be* V-ed V-ing

GB /dʒiː biː/. **GB** is an abbreviation for **Great Britain.** ◆◆◇◇◇ =Great Britain

GBH /dʒiː biː eɪtʃ/. In British English, **GBH** is an abbreviation for **grievous bodily harm.** N-UNCOUNT

GCE /dʒiː siː iː/ **GCEs**

1 **GCE** O levels are British educational qualifications which schoolchildren used to take at the age of fifteen or sixteen. In 1988, GCE O levels, together with CSEs, were replaced by GCSEs. **GCE** is an abbreviation for 'General Certificate of Education.' *Pupils were encouraged to obtain some GCE qualifications and stay on for sixth-form work.* ADJ: ADJ n

2 **GCE** A levels are British educational qualifications which schoolchildren take when they are seventeen or eighteen years old. People usually need GCE A levels if they want to go to university in Britain. GCE is an abbreviation for 'General Certificate of Education.' *GCE 'A' Level results will be published on Thursday.* ADJ: ADJ n

3 GCEs are GCE O levels. *He's got eight GCEs... The group had been studying the book for GCE.* N-VAR

GCSE /dʒiː siː es iː/ **GCSEs. GCSEs** are British educational qualifications which schoolchildren take when they are fifteen or sixteen years old. The GCSE examination was introduced in 1988 to replace the GCE O level and CSE examinations. **GCSE** is an abbreviation for 'General Certificate of Secondary Education'. *She quit school as soon as she had taken her GCSEs. ...GCSE candidates... I have a GCSE in Religious Studies.* ◆◇◇◇◇ N-VAR

gdn, gdns. gdn is a written abbreviation for **garden**, for example in addresses, or in advertisements for houses that are for sale. *The Piazza, Covent Gdn, WC2. ...flat, private gdn, close to station.* =garden

GDP /dʒiː diː piː/. **GDP** is an abbreviation for 'gross domestic product', which is the total value of goods and services produced within a country in a year; a technical term in economics. ◆◆◇◇◇ N-UNCOUNT

gear /gɪəʳ/ **gears, gearing, geared** ◆◆◆◇◇

1 In a machine or vehicle, a **gear** is a device or system which controls the rate at which the energy being used is converted into motion. Gears usually consist of moving wheels and levers which fit together. *He accelerated smoothly through the gears. ...a truck changing gears far out on the highway.* N-COUNT

2 A **gear** is the range of speed or power which a vehicle has when a particular gear is used. *On hills, he must use low gears... The car was in fourth gear... He put the truck in gear and drove on.* N-COUNT: also *in* N

3 The **gear** involved in a particular activity is the equipment or special clothing that you use. *About 100 officers in riot gear were needed to break up the fight. ...fishing gear... They helped us put our gear back into the van.* N-UNCOUNT

4 **Gear** means clothing; an informal use. *I used to wear trendy gear but it just looked ridiculous.* N-UNCOUNT =clothes

5 Some people refer to illegal drugs, especially heroin, as **gear**; an informal use. *Are these people using gear and amphetamines at the same time?* N-UNCOUNT

6 If someone or something is **geared to** or **towards** a particular purpose, they are organized or designed in order to achieve that purpose. *Colleges are not always geared to the needs of mature students... My training was geared towards winning gold in Munich.* ADJ-GRADED: v-link ADJ, usu ADJ *to/towards* n/-ing

gear up. If someone **is gearing up for** a particular activity, or **is geared up to** it, they are preparing to do it. *All the parties will be gearing up for a general election... The factory was geared up to make 1,100 cars a day.* PHRASAL VERB usu passive V P *for/to* n *be* V-ed to-inf

gearbox /gɪəʳbɒks/ **gearboxes.** A **gearbox** is the system of gears in an engine or vehicle. ◆◇◇◇◇ N-COUNT =transmission

gear lever, gear levers. In British English, a **gear lever** or a **gear stick** is the lever that you use to change gear in a car or other vehicle. The usual American term is **gearshift.** N-COUNT

gearshift /gɪəʳʃɪft/ **gearshifts;** also spelled **gear shift**. In a vehicle, the **gearshift** is the same as the **gear lever**; used mainly in American English. N-COUNT

gear stick. See **gear lever.**

gee /dʒiː/. In informal American English, people sometimes say **gee** in order to express a strong reaction to something or to introduce a remark or response. *Gee, it's hot... Gee thanks, Stan.* ◆◇◇◇◇ EXCLAM PRAGMATICS

geek /giːk/ **geeks.** If you call someone, usually a man or a boy, a **geek**, you are saying in a rather unkind way that you think they are rather stupid and weak; an informal word used especially by young people. N-COUNT PRAGMATICS =drip

geese /giːs/. **Geese** is the plural of **goose.**

gee whiz /dʒiː ʰwɪz/; also spelled **gee whizz.**

1 In informal American English, people sometimes say **gee whiz** in order to express a strong reaction to something or to introduce a remark or response. *Gee whiz, they carried on and on, they loved the evening.* EXCLAM PRAGMATICS

2 You use **gee whiz** to describe something that is new, exciting, and impressive, but that is perhaps more complicated or showy than it needs to be; used mainly in informal American English. *The trend now is towards 'lifestyle' electronics — black, shiny gee-whiz things that people like to own.* ADJ: ADJ n PRAGMATICS

geezer /giːzəʳ/ **geezers.** Some people use **geezer** to refer to a man; an informal and old-fashioned word, used mainly in British English. *...an old bald geezer in a posh raincoat.* ◆◇◇◇◇ N-COUNT =bloke

Geiger counter /gaɪgəʳ kaʊntəʳ/ **Geiger counters.** A **Geiger counter** is a device which detects and measures radioactivity. N-COUNT

geisha /geɪʃə/ **geishas.** A **geisha** is a Japanese woman who is specially trained in music, dancing, and the art of conversation. Her job is to entertain men. N-COUNT

gel /dʒel/ **gels, gelling, gelled;** also spelled **jell.** ◆◆◇◇◇

1 If people **gel** with each other, they work well together because their skills and personalities are compatible. *They have gelled very well with the rest of the side... Taylor has long felt Shearer and Hirst are the most likely to gel... Their partnership gelled and scriptwriting for television followed.* V-RECIP V with n pl-n V V (non-recip)

2 If a vague shape, thought, or creation **gels**, it becomes clearer or more definite. *Even if her interpretation has not yet gelled into a satisfying whole, she displays real musicianship... It was not until 1974 that his ability to write gelled again.* VERB V *into* n V

3 **Gel** is a thick jelly-like substance, especially one used to keep your hair in a particular style. N-MASS

gelatine /dʒelɪtiːn, AM -tᵊn/ **gelatines;** also spelled **gelatin. Gelatine** is a clear tasteless powder that is used to make liquids become firm, for example when you are making jelly. N-MASS

gelatinous /dʒɪlætɪnəs/. **Gelatinous** substances or mixtures are wet and sticky. *Pour a cup of the gelatinous mixture into the blender.* ADJ

gelding /geldɪŋ/ **geldings.** A **gelding** is a male horse which has been castrated in order to make it less aggressive or to make it jump better in races or competitions. ◆◇◇◇◇ N-COUNT

gelignite /dʒelɪgnaɪt/. **Gelignite** is an explosive substance that is similar to dynamite; used mainly in British English. N-UNCOUNT

gem /dʒem/ **gems** ◆◇◇◇◇

1 A **gem** is a jewel or stone that is used in jewellery. *The mask is formed of a gold-platinum alloy inset with emeralds and other gems.* N-COUNT

2 If you describe something or someone as a **gem**, you mean that they are especially pleasing, good, or helpful. *...a gem of a hotel, Castel Clara... Miss Famous, as she was called, was a gem.* N-COUNT: oft N *of* n

Gemini /dʒemɪnaɪ, AM -niː/ **Geminis** ◆◆◇◇◇

1 **Gemini** is one of the twelve signs of the zodiac. Its symbol is a pair of twins. People who are born approximately between 21st May and 20th June come under this sign. N-UNCOUNT

2 A **Gemini** is a person whose sign of the zodiac is Gemini. N-COUNT

gemstone /dʒemstoʊn/ **gemstones.** A **gemstone** is a jewel or stone used in jewellery. N-COUNT =gem

gen /dʒen/ **gens, genning, genned.** If you have some **gen** on something, you have some information about it; used in old-fashioned, informal British English. *You don't have any inside gen on the hijack, do you?* N-UNCOUNT: oft N *on/about* n =info

gen up on. If you **gen up on** something, you find out as much as possible about it; used in old-fashioned, informal British English. *He genned up on the flora and fauna of Malaya.* PHRASAL VERB V P P n

Gen. **Gen**. is a written abbreviation for **General.** *...the late dictator, Gen. Franco.*

gendarme /ʒɒndɑːʳm/ **gendarmes.** A **gendarme** is a member of the French police force. N-COUNT

gender /dʒendəʳ/ **genders** ◆◆◇◇◇

1 A person's **gender** is the fact that they are male or female. *Women are sometimes denied opportunities solely because of their gender. ...groups that are traditionally discriminated against on grounds of gender, colour, race, or age.* N-VAR =sex

2 You can refer to all male people or all female people as a particular **gender**. *While her observations may be true about some men, they could hardly apply to the entire gender. ...the different abilities and skills of the two genders.* N-COUNT =sex

3 In grammar, the **gender** of a noun, pronoun, or adjective is whether it is masculine, feminine, or neuter. A word's gender can affect its form and behaviour. In English, only personal pronouns such as 'she', reflexive pronouns such as 'itself', and possessive determiners such as 'his' have gender. *In both Welsh and Irish the word for 'moon' is of feminine gender.* N-VAR

gene /dʒiːn/ **genes.** A **gene** is the part of a cell in a living thing which controls its physical characteristics, growth, and development. Genes can change and reproduce themselves and they are passed on from one generation to another, for example from parents to their children. ◆◆◆◇◇ N-COUNT

genealogy /dʒiːniælədʒi/ **genealogies**

1 **Genealogy** is the study of the history of families, especially through studying historical documents to discover the relationships between particular people and their families. ♦ **genealogical** /dʒiːniəlɒdʒɪkəl/ *He had engaged in genealogical research on his family shortly before the War.* N-UNCOUNT; ADJ: ADJ n

2 A **genealogy** is the history of a family over several generations, for example describing who each person married and who their children were. *He had sat and repeated his family's genealogy to her, twenty minutes of nonstop names.* N-COUNT: usu with poss =family history

genera /dʒenərə/. **Genera** is the plural of **genus.**

general /dʒenrəl/ **generals** ◆◆◆◆◆

1 A **general** is a high-ranking officer in the armed forces, usually in the army. *The General's visit to Sarajevo is part of preparations for the deployment of extra troops.* N-COUNT; N-TITLE; N-VOC

2 If you talk about the **general** situation somewhere or talk about something in **general** terms, you are describing the situation as a whole rather than considering its details or exceptions. *The figures represent a general decline in employment. ...the general deterioration of English society... She recounted in very general terms some of the events of recent months... As a general rule, burglars are wary about gaining entry from the front or side of a building.* ADJ-GRADED: ADJ n

3 You use **general** to describe several items or activities when there are too many of them or when they are not important enough to mention separately. *£2,500 for software is soon swallowed up in general costs... His firm took over the planting and general maintenance of the park last March.* ADJ: ADJ n =overall

4 You use **general** to describe something that involves or affects most people, or most people in a particular group. *The project should raise general awareness about bullying.* ADJ-GRADED: ADJ n ≠specific

5 If you describe something as **general**, you mean that it is not restricted to any one thing or area. *...a general ache radiating from the back of the neck. ...a general sense of well-being. ...raising the level of general physical fitness.* ADJ: ADJ n

6 A **general** business offers a variety of services or goods rather than just one particular kind. *They ran the general store and the farm dairy.* ADJ: ADJ n

7 **General** is used to describe a person's job, usually as part of their title, to indicate that they have complete responsibility for the administration of an organization or business. *He joined Sanders Roe, moving on later to become General Manager.* ADJ: ADJ n

8 **General** workers do a variety of jobs which require no special skill or training. *The farm employed a tractor driver and two general labourers.* ADJ: ADJ n =unskilled

9 **General** is used to describe a person who has an average amount of knowledge or interest in a particular subject. *This book is intended for the general reader rather than the student.* ADJ-GRADED: ADJ n =lay

10 See also **generally.**

11 You use **in general** to indicate that you are talking about something as a whole, rather than about part of it. *I think we need to improve our educational system in general... She had a confused idea of life in general.* PHRASES n PHR =generally

12 You say **in general** to indicate that you are referring to most people or things in a particular group. *People in general will support us... She enjoys a sterling reputation in law enforcement circles and among the community in general.* n PHR

13 You say **in general** to indicate that a statement is true in most cases. *In general, it was the better-educated voters who voted Yes in the referendum.* PHR with cl =on the whole

general election, general elections. A **general election** is an election at which all the citizens of a country vote for people to represent them in the national parliament. ◆◆◆◇◇ N-COUNT

generalise /dʒenrəlaɪz/. See **generalize.**

generalissimo /dʒenrəlɪsɪmoʊ/ **generalissimos.** In some countries, a **generalissimo** is the supreme commander of combined military, naval, and air forces, especially one who has political as well as military power. N-COUNT; N-TITLE

generality /dʒenəræləti/ **generalities**

1 A **generality** is a general statement that covers a range of things, rather than being concerned with specific instances; a formal use. *I'll start with some generalities and then examine a few specific examples... He avoided this tricky question and talked in generalities.* N-COUNT

2 The **generality** of a statement or description is the fact that it is a general one, rather than a specific, detailed one. *That there are problems with this kind of definition is hardly surprising, given its level of generality.* N-UNCOUNT

3 If someone refers to **the generality of** a group of people, they mean the majority of that group; a formal use. *When the generality of the electorate is doing badly, the mood will grow pessimistic.* QUANT: QUANT of n =majority

generalization /dʒenrəlaɪzeɪʃən/ **generalizations;** also spelled **generalisation.** A **generalization** is a statement that seems to be true in most situations or for most people, but that may not be completely true in all cases. *He is making sweeping generalisations to get his point across... The evaluation of conduct involves some amount of generalization.* ◆◇◇◇◇ N-VAR

generalize /dʒenrəlaɪz/ **generalizes, generalizing, generalized;** also spelled **generalise** in British English. ◆◇◇◇◇

1 If you **generalize**, you say something that seems to be true in most situations or for most people, but that may not be completely true in all cases. *Critics love to generalise, to formulate trends into which all new work must be fitted, however contradictory... It's hard to generalize about Cole Porter because he wrote so many great songs that were so varied.* VERB V V prep

2 If you **generalize** something such as an idea or concept, you apply it more widely than its original context, as if it was true in many other situations. *A child first labels the household pet cat as a 'cat' and then generalises this label to other animals that look like it.* VERB V n across/to n Also V n

generalized /dʒenrəlaɪzd/; also spelled **generalised.** ◆◇◇◇◇

1 **Generalized** means involving many different things, rather than one or two specific things. *...a generalised discussion about admirable singers. ...generalised feelings of inadequacy.* ADJ-GRADED: usu ADJ n =general ≠specific

2 You use **generalized** to describe medical conditions or problems which affect the whole of someone's body, or the whole of a part of their body; a technical term in medicine. *She experienced an increase in generalized aches and pains. ...generalised muscle disorders.* ADJ: usu ADJ n ≠local

general knowledge. General knowledge is knowledge about many different things, as opposed to detailed knowledge about one particular subject. N-UNCOUNT

generally /dʒenrəli/ ◆◆◆◆◇

1 You use **generally** to summarize a situation, activity, or idea without referring to the particular details of it. *University teachers generally have admitted a lack of enthusiasm about their subjects... Both President Bush and Bill Clinton have spoken generally about the need to limit spending.* ADV-GRADED: ADV with cl/group, ADV with v

2 You use **generally** to say that something happens or is used on most occasions but not on every occasion. *As women we generally say and feel too* ADV: ADV with cl/group, ADV with v

much about these things... In the diet, it is generally true that the darker the fruit the higher its iron content... The warmer a place is, generally speaking, the more types of plants and animals it will usually support. =usually

general practice, general practices

1 **General practice** is the work of a doctor who usually treats sick people at a surgery or in their homes, rather than in a hospital, and who does not specialize in a particular type of medicine; used mainly in British English. *In recent years, doctors have been trained specifically for general practice.* N-UNCOUNT

2 A **general practice** is a place or organization where the doctors who are involved in general practice work; used mainly in British English. *The sample was selected from the medical records of two general practices.* N-COUNT

general practitioner, general practitioners. A **general practitioner** is the same as a **GP**; a formal expression. N-COUNT

general public. You can refer to the people in a society as **the general public**, especially when you are contrasting people in general with a small group. *These charities depend on the compassionate feelings and generosity of the general public... Unemployment is 10 percent among the general public and about 40 percent among North African immigrants.* ◆◇◇◇◇ N-SING-COLL: the N

general strike, general strikes. A **general strike** is a situation where most or all of the workers in a country are on strike and are refusing to work. ◆◇◇◇◇ N-COUNT

generate /dʒenəreɪt/ **generates, generating, generated** ◆◆◆◇◇

1 To **generate** something means to cause it to begin and develop. *The Employment Minister said the reforms would generate new jobs. ...the excitement generated by the changes in Eastern Europe.* VERB =create V n V-ed

2 To **generate** a form of energy or power means to produce it. *...schemes to generate power from landfill gas.* VERB V n

generation /dʒenəreɪʃᵊn/ **generations** ◆◆◆◆◇

1 A **generation** is all the people in a group or country who are of a similar age, especially when they are considered as having the same experiences or attitudes. *...the younger generation of Party members... David Mamet has long been considered the leading American playwright of his generation.* N-COUNT: with supp

2 A **generation** is the period of time, usually considered to be about thirty years, that it takes for children to grow up and become adults and have children of their own. *Within a generation flight has become the method used by many travellers.* N-COUNT

3 You can use **generation** to refer to a stage of development in the design and manufacture of machines or equipment. *...a new generation of IBM/Apple computers.* N-COUNT: N of n

4 **Generation** is used to indicate how long members of your family have had a particular nationality. For example, second generation means that you were born in the country you live in, but your parents were not. *...second generation Asians in Britain... She is a first generation American.* ADJ: ord ADJ n

5 **Generation** is also the production of a form of energy or power from fuel or another source of power such as water. *Japan has announced plans for a sharp rise in its nuclear power generation.* N-UNCOUNT: with supp

generational /dʒenəreɪʃənəl/. **Generational** means relating to a particular generation, or to the relationship between particular generations. *People's lifestyles are usually fixed by generational habits and fashions. ...a generational conflict within the Asian community.* ADJ: usu ADJ n

generation gap, generation gaps. If you refer to the **generation gap**, you are referring to a difference in attitude and behaviour between older people and younger people, which may cause them to argue or may prevent them from understanding each other fully. N-COUNT =divide

generative /dʒenərətɪv/

1 If something is **generative**, it is capable of producing something or causing it to develop; a formal use. *...the generative power of the sun.* ADJ =reproductive

2 In linguistics, **generative** is used to describe linguistic theories or models which are based on the idea that a single set of rules can explain how all the possible sentences of a language are formed; a technical use. *...a new approach to linguistics called Generative Grammar.* ADJ: ADJ n

generator /dʒenəreɪtəʳ/ **generators** ◆◆◇◇◇

1 A **generator** is a machine which produces electricity. N-COUNT

2 A **generator** of something is a person, organization, product, or situation which produces it or causes it to happen. *The US economy is still an impressive generator of new jobs... The company has been a very good cash generator.* N-COUNT: with supp, oft N of n

generic /dʒɪnerɪk/ **generics** ◆◇◇◇◇

1 You use **generic** to describe something that refers or relates to a whole class of similar things; a fairly formal use. *Parmesan is a generic term used to describe a family of hard Italian cheeses.* ADJ: usu ADJ n ≠specific ♦ **generically** *...a drift away from news towards what are known generically as 'features' – the pages devoted to commentaries, opinions and the arts. ...something generically called 'rock 'n' roll'.* ADV: usu ADV after v, ADV -ed/adj, also ADV with cl

2 A **generic** drug or other product is one that does not have a trademark and that is known by a general name, rather than the manufacturer's name; a technical use. *They encourage doctors to prescribe cheaper generic drugs instead of more expensive brand names.* ADJ: usu ADJ n =unbranded ≠branded ► Also a noun. *The program saved $11 million in 1988 by substituting generics for brand-name drugs.* N-COUNT

3 People sometimes use **generic** to refer to something that is exactly typical of the kind of thing mentioned, and that has no special or unusual characteristics; a fairly informal use. *...generic California apartments, the kind that have white walls and white drapes and were built five years ago.* ADJ: ADJ n =archetypal

generosity /dʒenərɒsɪti/. If you refer to someone's **generosity**, you mean that they are generous, especially in doing or giving more than is usual or expected. *There are stories about his generosity, the massive amounts of money he gave to charities. ...a man of unwavering integrity and great generosity of spirit.* ◆◇◇◇◇ N-UNCOUNT ≠meanness

generous /dʒenərəs/ ◆◆◆◇◇

1 A **generous** person gives more of something, especially money, than is usual or expected. *German banks are more generous in their lending... The gift is generous by any standards.* ADJ-GRADED ≠mean ♦ **generously** *We would like to thank all the judges who gave so generously of their time.* ADV-GRADED: ADV with v

2 A **generous** person is friendly, helpful, and willing to see the good qualities in someone or something. *He was always generous in sharing his enormous knowledge... It would have been agreeable if Mr Ross could have been generous enough to congratulate his successor on his decision.* ADJ-GRADED ♦ **generously** *The students generously gave them instruction in social responsibility.* ADV-GRADED: ADV with v

3 A **generous** amount of something is much larger than is usual or necessary. *...a generous six weeks of annual holiday... He should be able to keep his room tidy with the generous amount of storage space.* ADJ-GRADED =lavish ♦ **generously** *Season the steaks generously with salt and pepper.* ADV-GRADED: ADV -ed, ADV after v

genesis /dʒenɪsɪs/. The **genesis** of something is its beginning, birth, or creation; a formal word. *The project had its genesis two years earlier... His speech was an exposition of the genesis of the conflict.* N-SING: usu with poss =origin

gene therapy. **Gene therapy** is the use of genetic material to treat disease. ◆◇◇◇◇ N-UNCOUNT

genetic engineering. **Genetic** engineering is the science or activity of changing the genetic structure of an animal, plant, or other organism in order to make it stronger or more suitable for a particular purpose. *Scientists have used genetic engineering to protect tomatoes against the effects of freezing.* ◆◇◇◇◇ N-UNCOUNT

genetic fingerprinting. **Genetic fingerprinting** is a method of identifying people using a substance called DNA. DNA is present in every part of our bodies, and everybody's DNA is different.
N-SING

geneticist /dʒɪnetɪsɪst/ **geneticists.** A **geneticist** is a person who studies or specializes in genetics.
N-COUNT

genetics /dʒɪnetɪks/. The form **genetic** is used as a modifier. ◆◆◇◇◇

1 Genetics is the study of heredity and how qualities and characteristics are passed on from one generation to another by means of genes.
N-UNCOUNT

2 You use **genetic** to describe something that is concerned with genetics or with genes. *Cystic fibrosis is the most common fatal genetic disease in the United States.* ♦ **genetically** /dʒɪnetɪkli/ *Some people are genetically predisposed to diabetes. ...fetuses that are genetically abnormal.*
ADJ
ADV: usu ADV adj

genial /dʒiːniəl/. Someone who is **genial** is kind and friendly. *Bob was always genial and welcoming... He was a warm-hearted friend and genial host.* ♦ **genially** *'If you don't mind,' Mrs. Dambar said genially.* ♦ **geniality** /dʒiːniælɪti/ *He soon recovered his habitual geniality.*
◆◇◇◇◇ ADJ-GRADED =amiable
ADV-GRADED
N-UNCOUNT

genie /dʒiːni/ **genies**

1 In stories from Arabia and Persia, a **genie** is a spirit which appears and disappears by magic and obeys the person who controls it.
N-COUNT

2 If you say that **the genie is out of the bottle** or that someone **has let the genie out of the bottle**, you mean that something that people wanted has caused a situation to change and that now it cannot go back to what it was before. *As for unconventional weapons, the genie is unfortunately already out of the bottle.*
PHRASE: V inflects

genital /dʒenɪtəl/ **genitals** ◆◇◇◇◇

1 Someone's **genitals** are their external sexual organs.
N-PLURAL

2 Genital means relating to a person's external sexual organs. *Wear loose clothing in the genital area.*
ADJ: ADJ n

genitalia /dʒenɪteɪliə/. A person's or animal's **genitalia** are their external sexual organs; a technical term in biology.
N-PLURAL

genitive /dʒenɪtɪv/. In the grammar of some languages, **the genitive**, or **the genitive case**, is a noun case which is used primarily to show possession. In English grammar, a noun or name with 's added to it, for example 'dog's' or 'Anne's', is sometimes called **the genitive form**.
N-SING: *the* N

genius /dʒiːniəs/ **geniuses** ◆◆◇◇◇

1 Genius is very great ability or skill in a particular subject or activity. *This is the mark of her real genius as a designer... The man had genius and had made his mark in the aviation world... Its very title is a stroke of genius.*
N-UNCOUNT

2 A **genius** is a highly talented, creative, or intelligent person. *Chaplin was not just a genius, he was among the most influential figures in film history.*
N-COUNT

genocidal /dʒenəsaɪdəl/. **Genocidal** means relating to genocide or carrying out genocide; a fairly formal word. *They have been accused of genocidal crimes.*
ADJ: usu ADJ n

genocide /dʒenəsaɪd/. **Genocide** is the deliberate murder of a whole community or race; a formal word. *They have alleged that acts of genocide and torture were carried out.*
◆◇◇◇◇ N-UNCOUNT

genome /dʒenoʊm/ **genomes.** A **genome** is the particular number and combination of certain chromosomes necessary to form the single nucleus of a living cell; a technical term in biology and genetics.
◆◇◇◇◇ N-COUNT

genre /ʒɒnrə/ **genres.** A **genre** is a particular type of literature, painting, music, film, or other art form which people consider as a class because it has special characteristics; a fairly formal word. *...his love of films and novels in the horror genre.*
◆◆◇◇◇ N-COUNT

gent /dʒent/ **gents** ◆◇◇◇◇

1 Gent is an informal and old-fashioned word for **gentleman**. *Mr Blake was a gent. He knew how to behave.*
N-COUNT

2 In informal British English, people sometimes refer to a public toilet for men as **the gents**.
N-SING-COLL: usu *the* N

3 Gents is used when addressing men in an informal, humorous way, especially in the expression 'ladies and gents'. *Don't be left standing, ladies and gents, while a bargain slips past your eyes.*
N-VOC

genteel /dʒentiːl/ ◆◇◇◇◇

1 If you describe someone as **genteel**, you mean they are respectable, well-bred, and refined; an old-fashioned use. *It was a place to which genteel families came in search of health and quiet. ...two maiden ladies with genteel manners and voices.*
ADJ-GRADED ≠vulgar

2 If you describe a place or area as **genteel**, you mean it is quiet, refined, and traditional, but you may be suggesting that it is old-fashioned, dull, or pretentious. *...the town of Eastbourne – a genteel resort on the south coast.*
ADJ-GRADED: usu ADJ n ≠vulgar

gentian /dʒenʃən/ **gentians.** A **gentian** is a small plant with a blue or purple flower shaped like a trumpet which grows in mountain regions.
N-COUNT

Gentile /dʒentaɪl, AM -təl/ **Gentiles;** also spelled **gentile.** A **Gentile** is a person who is not Jewish; used when you are talking about non-Jewish people in contrast to Jewish people. *Blacks, whites, Hispanics, Jews, Gentiles, Protestants and Catholics have joined hands to form a new democratic coalition.* ▶ Also an adjective. *...a flood of Jewish and Gentile German refugees.*
N-COUNT =goy, non-Jew
ADJ: usu ADJ n

gentility /dʒentɪlɪti/

1 Gentility is used to refer to people of high social status, and their typical way of life; an old-fashioned use. *All the gentility of London was there... He surrounds himself with all the trappings of gentility – dogs, horses, and fine paintings.*
N-UNCOUNT =nobility

2 Gentility is polite, well-mannered, and refined behaviour; an old-fashioned use. *He treated her with scrupulous gentility during the brief periods he spent at home.*
N-UNCOUNT =courtesy

3 If you talk about the **gentility** of a place, you mean that it is quiet, refined, and traditional, but you may be suggesting that it is also old-fashioned or dull; used mainly in written English. *The hotel has an air of faded gentility. ...Thruxton, set in the gentility of English pastureland.*
N-UNCOUNT: with supp ≠vulgarity

gentle /dʒentəl/ **gentler, gentlest** ◆◆◆◇◇

1 Someone who is **gentle** is kind, mild, and calm. *My son was a quiet and gentle man who liked sports and enjoyed life... Michael's voice was gentle and consoling.* ♦ **gently** *She smiled gently at him... 'I'm sorry to disturb you,' Webb said gently.* ♦ **gentleness** *...the gentleness with which she treated her pregnant mother.*
ADJ-GRADED
ADV-GRADED: ADV with v
N-UNCOUNT

2 Gentle actions or movements are performed in a calm and controlled manner, with little force. *...a gentle game of tennis... His movements were gentle and deliberate.* ♦ **gently** *Patrick took her gently by the arm and led her to a chair.*
ADJ-GRADED
ADV-GRADED

3 If you describe the weather, especially the wind, as **gentle**, you mean it is pleasant and calm and not harsh or violent. *The blustery winds of spring had dropped to a gentle breeze.* ♦ **gently** *Light airs blew gently out of the south-east.*
ADJ-GRADED
ADV-GRADED: ADV with v

4 A **gentle** slope or curve is not steep or severe. *...gentle, rolling meadows... There were two passes over 13,000 feet but the slopes were gentle.* ♦ **gently** *With its gently rolling hills it looks like Tuscany... Green meadows sloped gently up from the road.*
ADJ-GRADED
ADV-GRADED: ADV after v, ADV adj

5 A **gentle** heat is a fairly low heat. *Cook for 30 minutes over a gentle heat.* ♦ **gently** *Add the onion and cook gently for about 5 minutes.*
ADJ-GRADED
ADV-GRADED: ADV with v

gentleman /dʒentəlmən/ **gentlemen** ◆◆◆◇◇

1 A **gentleman** is a man who comes from a family of high social standing. *...this wonderful portrait of English gentleman Joseph Greenway.*
N-COUNT

2 If you say that a man is a **gentleman**, you mean he is well-behaved, educated, and refined in his manners. *He was always such a gentleman.*
N-COUNT

3 You can address men as **gentlemen**, or refer politely to them as **gentlemen**. *This way, please, ladies and gentlemen... It seems this gentleman was waiting for the doctor.*
N-COUNT; N-VOC PRAGMATICS

4 A gentleman's agreement or **a gentlemen's**
PHRASE

agreement is an informal agreement in which people trust one another to do what they have promised. The agreement is not written down and does not have any legal force. *We had no contract; it was done by a gentleman's agreement... She made a gentleman's agreement with her buyer.*

gentlemanly /dʒentəlmənli/. If you describe a man's behaviour as **gentlemanly**, you approve of him because he has perfect manners and is very well-behaved. *He was respected by all who knew him for his kind and gentlemanly consideration.*
ADJ-GRADED: usu ADJ n PRAGMATICS =courteous

gentlewoman /dʒentəlwʊmən/ **gentlewomen.** A **gentlewoman** is a woman of high social standing, or a woman who is cultured, educated, and refined; an old-fashioned word. *She decided to set up a training scheme for 'gentlewomen who aspired to be teachers'.*
N-COUNT =lady

gentry /dʒentri/. The **gentry** are people of high social status or high birth; an old-fashioned word, used mainly in British English. *Most of the country estates were built by the landed gentry during the late 19th century.*
◆◇◇◇◇ N-PLURAL

genuflect /dʒenjʊflekt/ **genuflects, genuflecting, genuflected**

1 If you **genuflect**, you bend one or both knees and bow, especially in church, as a sign of respect; a formal use. *He genuflected in front of the altar.*
VERB
V

2 You can say that someone **is genuflecting** to something when they are giving it a great deal of attention and respect, especially if you think it does not deserve this; used mainly in journalism showing disapproval. *They refrained from genuflecting to the laws of political economy.*
VERB PRAGMATICS =bow
V to n Also V prep

genuine /dʒenjuɪn/
◆◆◆◇◇

1 **Genuine** is used to describe people and things that are exactly what they appear to be, and are not fake or an imitation. *There was a risk of genuine refugees being returned to Vietnam. ...genuine leather... They're convinced the picture is genuine.*
ADJ: usu ADJ n =real ≠fake

2 **Genuine** refers to things such as emotions that are real and not pretended. *There was genuine joy in this room... If this offer is genuine I will gladly accept it.* ♦ **genuinely** *He was genuinely surprised.* ♦ **genuineness** *He needed at least three days to assess the genuineness of their intentions.*
ADJ-GRADED =sincere
ADV-GRADED
N-UNCOUNT: usu with supp

3 If you describe a person as **genuine**, you approve of them because they are honest, truthful, and sincere in the way they live and in their relationships with other people. *She is very caring and very genuine.* ♦ **genuineness** *I have no doubt about their genuineness.*
ADJ-GRADED PRAGMATICS
N-UNCOUNT

genus /dʒenəs, AM dʒiː-/ **genera.** A **genus** is a class of similar things, especially a group of animals or plants that includes several closely related species; a technical term in biology.
N-COUNT

geographer /dʒiɒgrəfəʳ/ **geographers.** A **geographer** is a person who studies geography or is an expert in it.
N-COUNT

geographical /dʒiːəgræfɪkəl/. The form **geographic** /dʒiːəgræfɪk/ is also used. **Geographical** or **geographic** means concerned with or relating to geography. *Its geographical location stimulated overseas mercantile enterprise. ...a vast geographical area.* ♦ **geographically** /dʒiːəgræfɪkli/ *It is geographically more diverse than any other continent.*
◆◆◇◇◇ ADJ: usu ADJ n
ADV

geography /dʒiɒgrəfi/
◆◆◇◇◇

1 **Geography** is the study of the countries of the world and of such things as land formations, seas, climate, towns, and population.
N-UNCOUNT

2 The **geography** of a place is the way that features such as rivers, mountains, towns, or streets are arranged within it. *...policemen who knew the local geography. ...a pictorial journey through the history, geography and culture of the Caribbean.*
N-UNCOUNT: usu with poss

geological /dʒiːəlɒdʒɪkəl/. **Geological** means relating to geology. *With geological maps, books and atlases you can find out all the proven sites of precious minerals. ...a lengthy geological survey.* ♦ **geologically** /dʒiːəlɒdʒɪkli/. *At least 10,000 of these hectares are geologically unsuitable for housing.*
◆◇◇◇◇ ADJ: usu ADJ n
ADV

geology /dʒiɒlədʒi/
◆◇◇◇◇

1 **Geology** is the study of the Earth's structure, surface, and origins. *He was visiting professor of geology at the University of Jordan.* ♦ **geologist, geologists** *Geologists have studied the way that heat flows from the earth.*
N-UNCOUNT
N-COUNT

2 The **geology** of an area is the structure of its land, together with the types of rocks and minerals that exist within it. *...an expert on the geology of south-east Asia.*
N-UNCOUNT: usu with poss

geometric /dʒiːəmetrɪk/. The form **geometrical** /dʒiːəmetrɪkəl/ is also used.
◆◇◇◇◇

1 **Geometric** or **geometrical** patterns or shapes consist of regular shapes or lines. *Geometric designs were popular wall decorations in the 14th century.* ♦ **geometrically** /dʒiːəmetrɪkli/ *...a few geometrically planted trees.*
ADJ: usu ADJ n
ADV

2 **Geometric** or **geometrical** means relating to or involving the principles of geometry. *Euclid was trying to convey his idea of a geometrical point.*
ADJ: usu ADJ n

geometry /dʒiɒmɪtri/
◆◇◇◇◇

1 **Geometry** is the branch of mathematics concerned with the properties and relationships of lines, angles, curves, and shapes. *...the very ordered way in which mathematics and geometry describe nature.*
N-UNCOUNT

2 The **geometry** of an object is its shape or the relationship of its parts to each other; a formal use. *They have tinkered with the geometry of the car's nose.*
N-UNCOUNT: usu with poss

geophysical /dʒiːoʊfɪzɪkəl/. **Geophysical** means relating to geophysics.
ADJ: usu ADJ n

geophysicist /dʒiːoʊfɪzɪsɪst/ **geophysicists.** A **geophysicist** is someone who studies or specializes in geophysics.
N-COUNT

geophysics /dʒiːoʊfɪzɪks/. **Geophysics** is the branch of geology that uses physics to examine the earth's structure, climate, and oceans.
N-UNCOUNT

geopolitical /dʒiːoʊpəlɪtɪkəl/. **Geopolitical** means relating to or concerned with geopolitics. *Hungary and Poland have suffered before because of their unfortunate geopolitical position on the European map.*
ADJ: usu ADJ n

geopolitics /dʒiːoʊpɒlɪtɪks/. **Geopolitics** is the activity or study of politics on a worldwide scale, especially as it affects relations between countries. *The shape of geopolitics has been decisively altered by the democracies' victories in the Gulf War and the Cold War.*
N-UNCOUNT

Georgian /dʒɔːʳdʒən/. **Georgian** means belonging to or connected with Britain in the eighteenth century, when there were three kings called George. *...the restoration of his Georgian house.*
◆◆◇◇◇ ADJ

geranium /dʒɪreɪniəm/ **geraniums.** A **geranium** is a plant with clusters of small red, pink, or white flowers. It is usually grown in gardens, or in pots inside people's houses.
◆◇◇◇◇ N-COUNT

gerbil /dʒɜːʳbɪl/ **gerbils.** A **gerbil** is a small, furry rodent that is often kept as a pet.
N-COUNT

geriatric /dʒeriætrɪk/ **geriatrics**
◆◇◇◇◇

1 **Geriatric** is used to describe things relating to the illnesses and medical care of old people; a medical use. *There is a question mark over the future of geriatric care... The geriatric and mental patients will be moved out within three months.*
ADJ: ADJ n

2 **Geriatrics** is the study of the illnesses that affect old people and the medical care of old people.
N-UNCOUNT

3 If you describe someone as a **geriatric**, you are being disrespectful, and implying that they are old and that their mental or physical condition is poor; an informal use. *He will complain about having to spend time with such a boring bunch of geriatrics. ...how can it be acceptable to have a load of geriatric judges deciding what should happen?*
N-COUNT: oft N n PRAGMATICS

germ /dʒɜːʳm/ **germs**
◆◇◇◇◇

1 A **germ** is a very small organism that causes disease. *Chlorine is widely used to kill germs. ...a germ that destroyed hundreds of millions of lives.*
N-COUNT

2 The **germ of** something such as an idea is something which developed or might develop into that
N-SING: N of n

thing. *The germ of an idea took root in Rosemary's mind... This was the germ of a book.*
3 See also **wheatgerm**.

German /dʒɜːʳmən/ **Germans** ◆◆◆◆◇
1 **German** means belonging or relating to Germany. *...a cut in German interest rates. ...the German government.* ADJ
▶ A **German** is a person who comes from Germany. *Horst, a German from Hamburg, was a true original.* N-COUNT
2 **German** is the language used in Germany, Austria, and parts of Switzerland. *I heard a very angry man talking in German.* N-UNCOUNT

germane /dʒɜːʳmeɪn/. Something that is **germane** to a situation or idea is connected with it in an important way; a formal word. *...the suppression of a number of documents which were very germane to the case... Fenton was a good listener, and his questions were germane.* ADJ-GRADED: oft ADJ *to* n =relevant

Germanic /dʒɜːʳmænɪk/
1 If you describe someone or something as **Germanic**, you think that their appearance or behaviour is typical of German people or things. *He asked in his Germanic English if I was enjoying France.* ADJ-GRADED
2 **Germanic** is used to describe the ancient culture and language of the peoples of northern Europe. *...the Germanic tribes of pre-Christian Europe.* ADJ

German measles. **German measles** is a disease which causes you to have a cough, a sore throat, and red spots on your skin. N-UNCOUNT =rubella

germinate /dʒɜːʳmɪneɪt/ **germinates, germinating, germinated** ◆◇◇◇◇
1 If a seed **germinates** or if it **is germinated**, it starts to grow; a technical use in biology. *Some seed varieties germinate fast, so check every day or so... First, the researchers germinated the seeds.* V-ERG =develop V V n
♦ **germination** /dʒɜːʳmɪneɪʃᵊn/ *The poor germination of your seed could be because the soil was too cold.* N-UNCOUNT: usu with supp
2 If an idea, plan, or feeling **germinates**, it comes into existence and begins to develop; a formal use. *He wrote to Eliot about a 'big book' that was germinating in his mind.* VERB V Also V *into* n

germ warfare. **Germ warfare** is the use of germs in a war in order to cause disease in enemy troops, or to destroy crops that they might use as food. *...an international treaty banning germ warfare.* N-UNCOUNT

gerontology /dʒerəntɒlədʒi/. **Gerontology** is the study of the process by which we get old, how our bodies change, and the problems that old people have. N-UNCOUNT

gerrymandering /dʒerimændərɪŋ/. **Gerrymandering** is the act of altering political boundaries in order to give an unfair advantage to one political party or group of people; used showing disapproval. *With the help of skilful gerrymandering, the Party has never lost an election since.* N-UNCOUNT PRAGMATICS

gerund /dʒerʌnd/ **gerunds.** A **gerund** is a noun formed from a verb which refers to an action, process, or state. In English, gerunds end in '-ing', for example 'running' and 'thinking'. N-COUNT

gestalt /gəʃtælt/. A **gestalt** is something that you see or think of that has particular qualities when you consider it as a whole which are not apparent when you consider only the separate parts of it; a formal word which is used especially as a technical term in psychology. *...the visual strength of the gestalt.* N-SING

gestation /dʒesteɪʃᵊn/
1 **Gestation** is the process in which babies grow inside their mother's body before they are born; a technical term in biology. *...the seventeenth week of gestation... The gestation period can be anything between 95 and 150 days.* N-UNCOUNT
2 **Gestation** is the process in which an idea or plan develops; a formal use. *...the prolonged period of gestation of this design.* N-UNCOUNT =development

gesticulate /dʒestɪkjʊleɪt/ **gesticulates, gesticulating, gesticulated.** If you **gesticulate**, you make movements with your arms or hands, often while you are describing something that is difficult to express in words; used mainly in written English. *A man with a paper hat upon his head was gesticulating wildly... The architect was gesticulating at a hole in the ground.* VERB =gesture V V prep
♦ **gesticulation** /dʒestɪkjʊleɪʃᵊn/ **gesticulations** *We communicated mainly by signs, gesticulation and mime.* N-UNCOUNT: also N in pl

gestural /dʒestʃərəl/. **Gestural** means consisting of or relating to gestures and movement; a formal word. *There is a frank gestural quality to much of this early work.* ADJ: usu ADJ n

gesture /dʒestʃəʳ/ **gestures, gesturing, gestured** ◆◆◆◇◇
1 A **gesture** is a movement that you make with a part of your body, especially your hands, to express emotion or information. *Sarah made a menacing gesture with her fist... He throws his hands open in a gesture which clearly indicates his relief.* N-COUNT
2 A **gesture** is something that you say or do in order to express your attitude or intentions, often something that you know will not have much effect. *He questioned the government's commitment to peace and called on it to make a gesture of good will... There's no greater gesture of love than having someone's name tattooed on your body... As a gesture to security, cars were fitted with special locks.* N-COUNT: oft N *of* n
3 If you **gesture**, you use movements of your hands or head in order to tell someone something or draw their attention to something. *I gestured towards the boathouse, and he looked inside... He gestures, gesticulates, and moves with the grace of a dancer.* VERB V prep V

get 1 changing, causing, moving, or reaching

get /get/ **gets, getting, got** or **gotten** ◆◆◆◆◆
In most of its uses **get** is a fairly informal word. **Gotten** is an American form of the past tense and past participle.
1 You use **get** with adjectives to mean 'become'. For example, if someone **gets cold**, they become cold, and if they **get angry**, they become angry. *The boys were getting bored... There's no point in getting upset... From here on, it can only get better.* V-LINK V adj
2 If you **get** into a particular state or situation, you cause or allow yourself to be in that state or situation. If you **get** out of a state or situation, you are then no longer in it. *Half the pleasure of an evening out is getting ready... They tried to get in touch with her... Perhaps I shouldn't say that – I might get into trouble... How did we get into this recession, and what can we do to get out of it?* V-LINK V adj V prep/adv
3 To **get** someone or something into a particular state or situation means to cause them to be in that state or situation. *I don't know if I can get it clean... What got me interested was looking at an old New York Times... Brian will get them out of trouble.* VERB V n adj V n prep
4 If you **get** someone to do something, you cause them to do it by asking, persuading, or telling them to do it. *...a long campaign to get US politicians to take the Aids epidemic more seriously... How did you get him to pose for this picture?* VERB =persuade V n to-inf
5 If you **get** something done, you cause it to be done. *I might benefit from getting my teeth fixed... It was best to get things done quickly.* VERB V n -ed
6 To **get** somewhere means to move there. *I got off the bed and opened the door... How can I get past her without her seeing me?... I heard David yelling and telling them to get back.* VERB V prep/adv
7 When you **get** to a place, you arrive there. *Generally I get to work at 9.30am... It was dark by the time she got home.* VERB =reach V *to* n V adv
8 To **get** something or someone into a place or position means to cause them to move there, although this may be difficult. *Mack got his wallet out... Go and get your coat on... The UN was supposed to be getting aid to where it was most needed.* VERB V n with adv V n prep
9 **Get** is often used in place of 'be' as an auxiliary verb to form passives. *Does she ever get asked for her autograph?... A pane of glass got broken.* AUX AUX -ed
10 If you **get** to do something, you eventually or gradually reach a stage at which you do it. *Miller and Ferlinghetti got to be friends... No one could figure out how he got to be so wealthy.* VERB V to-inf

11 If you **get** to do something, you manage to do it or have the opportunity to do it. *They say you can get to be prime minister without O levels, these days... Do you get to see him often?... They get to stay in nice hotels.* VERB V to-inf

12 You can use **get** in expressions like **get moving**, **get going**, and **get working** when you want to tell people to begin moving, going, or working quickly. *I aim to be off the lake before dawn, so let's get moving... We need to get thinking, talking and acting on this before it is too late.* VERB =start V-ing

13 If you **get** to a particular stage in your life or in something you are doing, you reach that stage. *We haven't got to the stage of a full-scale military conflict... If she gets that far, Jane may get legal aid to take her case to court... It got to the point where I was so ill I was waiting to die.* VERB V to n V adv it V to n

14 You can use **get** to talk about the progress that you are making. For example, you can say that you are **getting somewhere** to mean that you are making progress, and you can say that something **won't get you anywhere** to mean it will not help you to progress at all. *Radical factions say the talks are getting nowhere and they want to withdraw... My perseverance was getting me somewhere.* VERB V adv V n adv

15 When it **gets** to a particular time, it is that time. If it **is getting** towards a particular time, it is approaching that time. *It got to after 1am and I was exhausted... It was getting towards evening when we got back... It's getting late.* V-LINK it V to n it V towards n it V adj

16 If something that has continued for some time **gets to** you, it starts causing you to suffer. *That's the first time I lost my cool in 20 years in this job. This whole thing's getting to me.* VERB V to n

17 If something **gets** you, it annoys you; an informal use. *What gets me is the attitude of so many of the people.* VB: no passive V n

get 2 obtaining, receiving, or catching

get /get/ **gets, getting, got** or **gotten** ◆◆◆◆◆

1 If you **get** something that you want or need, you obtain it. *I got a job at the sawmill... The problem was how to get enough food to sustain life... It is impossible to get help, so she is doing everything herself... He had been having trouble getting a hotel room... I asked him to get me some information.* VERB V n V n n Also V n for n

2 If you **get** something, you receive it or are given it. *I'm getting a bike for my birthday... He gets a lot of letters from women... They get a salary of $11,000 a year.* VERB V n

3 If you **get** someone or something, you go and bring them to a particular place. *I came down this morning to get the newspaper... Go and get me a large brandy... Go and get your daddy for me.* VERB =fetch V n V n n V n for n

4 If you **get** a meal, you prepare it. *She was getting breakfast as usual.* VERB V n

5 If you **get** a particular result, you obtain it from some action that you take, or from a calculation or experiment. *You could run that race again and get a different result each time... What do you get if you multiply six by nine?* VERB V n

6 If you **get** a particular price for something that you sell, you obtain that amount of money by selling it. *He can't get a good price for his crops.* VERB V n for n

7 If you **get** the time or opportunity to do something, you have the time or opportunity to do it. *You get time to think in prison. ...whenever I get the chance I go to Maxim's for dinner.* VERB V n

8 If you **get** an idea, impression, or feeling, you begin to have that idea, impression, or feeling as you learn or understand more about something. *I get the feeling that you're an honest man... The study is an attempt to get a better idea of why people live where they do... Doctors can get the wrong impression from even an accurate description.* VERB V n

9 If you **get** something such as a feeling or benefit from an activity or experience, the activity or experience causes you to have that feeling or benefit. *Charles got a shock when he saw him... She gets enormous pleasure out of working freelance... I would like to take pictures professionally because I get so much out of it.* VERB V n V n out of/from n/-ing

10 If you **get** a look, view, or glimpse of something, you manage to see it. *Young men climbed on buses and fences to get a better view... Crowds shouted and pushed to get a glimpse of their hero.* VERB =obtain V n

11 If a place **gets** a particular type of weather, it has that type of weather. *Riyadh, the Saudi capital, got 25 mm of rain in just 12 hours... Northern Kentucky is likely to get snow mixed with sleet.* VERB V n

12 If you **get** a joke or **get** the point of something that is said, you understand it. *Did you get that joke, Ann? I'll explain later... You don't seem to get the point.* VERB V n

13 If you **get** an illness or disease, you become ill with it. *When I was five I got measles.* VERB V n

14 When you **get** a train, bus, plane, or boat, you leave a place on a particular train, bus, plane, or boat. *It'll be two pounds to get the bus... What time are you getting your train?* VERB =catch V n

15 If you **get** a person or animal, you succeed in catching, killing, or hitting them. *Take it easy. We've got him. He's not going to kill anyone else.* VERB V n

16 If you **get** a newspaper or magazine, you regularly buy it. *We don't get a paper... We already get The Times.* VERB =take V n

17 If you can **get** a particular radio or television channel, you are able to receive broadcasts from it on your radio or television. *I only get Channel 7.* VERB V n

18 See also **getting, got**.

get 3 phrases and phrasal verbs

get /get/ **gets, getting, got, gotten** ◆◆◆◆◆

1 You can say that something is, for example, **as good as you can get** to mean that it is as good as it is possible for that thing to be. You can say that you want something **as small as you can get it** to mean that you want it to be as small as it is possible to make it. *Consort has a population of 714 and is about as rural and isolated as you can get. ...the diet that is as near to perfect as you can get it.* PHRASES v-link PHR, PHR after v

2 If you say **you can't get away from** something or **there is no getting away from** something, you are emphasizing that it is true, even though people might prefer it not to be true; an informal expression. *There is no getting away from the fact that he is on the left of the party.* PHR n PRAGMATICS

3 If you **get away from it all**, you have a holiday in a place that is very different from the place where you normally live and work. *...the ravishing island of Ischia, where rich Italians get away from it all.* V inflects

4 **Get** is used in expressions like **get stuffed** and **get lost** which are offensive ways of expressing contempt for someone, disagreement with someone, or refusal to do something. CONVENTION PRAGMATICS

5 You can say, for example, **'How lucky can you get?'** or **'How stupid can you get?'** to express your surprise that anyone could be as lucky or stupid as the person that you are talking about; an informal expression. *I mean, how crazy can you get?* PRAGMATICS

6 If you **tell** someone **where to get off**, you tell them in a rather rude way that you are not going to do or agree to what they want; an informal expression. *If somebody tried to do that to you, you'd just go right up to them and tell them where to get off.* *tell* inflects

7 In spoken English, you can use **you get** instead of 'there is' or 'there are' to say that something exists, happens, or can be experienced. *You get a lot of youngsters hanging around the Common... That's where you get some differences of opinion.* PHR n

get about PHRASAL VERB

1 If you **get about**, you go to different places and visit different people. *So you're getting about a bit again? Not shutting yourself away?* V P

2 The way that someone **gets about** is the way that they walk or go from one place to another. *When he went out of town on business, his wife, a friend, or an associate helped him to get about.* V P

3 If news **gets about**, it becomes well known as a result of being told to lots of people; used mainly in British English. *How did the rumours get about?... The story had soon got about that he had been suspended.* =get around V P

get across. When an idea **gets across** or when you **get** it **across**, you succeed in making other people understand it. *Officers felt their point of* PHRASAL VERB ERG =get over V P to n

view was not getting across to ministers... I had created a way to get my message across while using as few words as possible. V n P Also V P

get ahead. PHRASAL VERB If you want to **get ahead**, you want to be successful in your career. *He wanted safety, security, a home, and a chance to get ahead.* =get on V P

get along PHRASAL VERB

1 If you **get along with** someone, you have a friendly relationship with them. You can also say that two people **get along**. *It's impossible to get along with him... Although at one point their voices were raised they seemed to be getting along fine.* RECIP =get on V P *with* n pl-n V P

2 Get along means the same as **get by**. *You can't get along without water... Many older people cannot get along on just their Social Security checks.* =manage, survive V P prep

get around or **get round** PHRASAL VERB

1 To **get around** a problem or difficulty, or **get round** it, means to overcome it. *None of these countries has found a way yet to get around the problem of the polarization of wealth.* =get over V P n

2 If you **get around** a rule or law, or **get round** it, you find a way of doing something that the rule or law is intended to prevent, without actually breaking it. *Although tobacco ads are prohibited, companies get around the ban by sponsoring music shows.* =circumvent V P n

3 If news **gets around** or **gets round**, it becomes well known as a result of being told to lots of people. *They threw him out because word got around that he was taking drugs... I'll see that it gets round that you've arrived.* =get about V P *it* V P that

4 See also **get round.**

get around. PHRASAL VERB If you **get around**, you visit a lot of different places as part of your way of life. *He claimed to be a journalist, and he got around.* V P

get around to or **get round to.** PHRASAL VERB When you **get around to** doing something that you have delayed doing or have been too busy to do, you finally do it. *I said I would write to you, but as usual I never got around to it... I've got bags of photographs and one day I'll get round to putting them in an album.* V P P n/-ing

get at PHRASAL VERB

1 To **get at** something means to succeed in reaching it. *A goat was standing up against a tree on its hind legs, trying to get at the leaves.* V P n

2 If you **get at** the truth about something, you succeed in discovering it. *We want to get at the truth. Who killed him? And why?* =find out V P n

3 If you **get at** someone, you keep criticizing or teasing them in an unkind way; an informal British expression. *They don't like my moustache and my long hair, they get at me whenever they can.* =pick on V P n

4 If you ask someone what they **are getting at**, you are asking them to explain what they mean, usually because you think that they are being unpleasant or are suggesting something that is untrue. *'What are you getting at now?' demanded Rick.* usu cont =insinuate V P

get away PHRASAL VERB

1 If you **get away**, you succeed in leaving a place or a person's company. *She'd gladly have gone anywhere to get away from the cottage... I wanted a divorce. I wanted to get away.* =escape V P *from* n V P

2 If you **get away**, you go away for a period of time in order to have a holiday. *He is too busy to get away.* V P

3 When someone or something **gets away**, or when you **get** them **away**, they escape. *Dr Dunn was apparently trying to get away when he was shot... I wanted to get her away to somewhere safe.* ERG V P V n P

4 If you **get away** from an old-fashioned or restrictive way of doing or thinking about something, you manage to do or think about it in a new way. *We want to get away from the politics of outdated dogmatism and class confrontation.* V P *from* n Also V P

get away with. PHRASAL VERB If you **get away with** doing something wrong or risky, you do not suffer any punishment or other bad consequences because of it. *The criminals know how to play the system and get away with it... This is one of the few jobs you can do and get away with being completely drunk.* V P P n/-ing

get back PHRASAL VERB

1 If someone or something **gets back** to a state they were in before, they are then in that state again. *Then life started to get back to normal... I couldn't get back to sleep.* =return V P *to* n Also V P *into* n

2 If you **get back** to a subject that you were talking about before, you start talking about it again. *It wasn't until we had sat down to eat that we got back to the subject of Tom Halliday.* =return V P *to/onto* n

3 If you **get** something **back** after you have lost it or after it has been taken from you, you then have it again. *You have 14 days in which you can cancel the contract and get your money back.* V n P Also V P n (not pron)

4 If you **get back at** someone or **get** them **back**, you do something unpleasant to them in order to have revenge for something unpleasant that they did to you; an informal expression. *My wife has left me and I wanted to get back at the first woman I saw... I'm going to get you back so badly you're never going to be able to show your face again.* V P *at* n V n P

get back to. PHRASAL VERB If you **get back to** an activity, you start doing it again after you have stopped doing it. *I think I ought to get back to work.* V P P n

get by. PHRASAL VERB If you can **get by** with the few resources you have, you can manage to live or do things satisfactorily. *I'm a survivor. I'll get by... Melville managed to get by on a small amount of money.* =survive V P V P *on* n

get down PHRASAL VERB

1 If something **gets** you **down**, it makes you unhappy. *At times when my work gets me down, I like to fantasize about being a farmer.* V n P

2 If you **get down**, you lower your body until you are sitting, kneeling, or lying on the ground. *She got down on her hands and knees on the floor... 'Get down!' she yelled. 'Somebody's shooting!'* V P *on* n V P

3 If you **get** something **down**, especially something that has just been said or something that you have been thinking about, you write it down. *The idea has been going around in my head for quite a while and now I am getting it down on paper.* V n P Also V P n (not pron)

4 If you **get** food or medicine **down**, you swallow it, especially with difficulty; an informal expression. *I bit into a hefty slab of bread and cheese. When I had got it down I started talking.* V n P Also V P n (not pron)

get down to. PHRASAL VERB If you **get down to** something, especially something that requires a lot of attention, you begin doing it. *With the election out of the way, the government can get down to business.* V P P n

get in PHRASAL VERB

1 If a political party or a politician **gets in**, they are elected. *If the Conservatives get in they might decide to change it.* V P

2 If you **get** something **in**, you manage to do it at a time when you are very busy doing other things. *I plan to get a few lessons in.* V n P

3 To **get** crops or the harvest **in** means to gather them from the land and take them to a particular place. *We didn't get the harvest in until Christmas, there was so much snow.* V n P

4 When a train, bus, or plane **gets in**, it arrives. *We would have come straight here, except our flight got in too late.* V P

5 If you **get** something **in**, you eventually manage to succeed in saying it, usually when a lot of people are talking at the same time or one person is talking non-stop. *It was hard to get a word in.* V n P

get in on. PHRASAL VERB If you **get in on** something that other people are already involved in, you take part in it; an informal expression. *Now baseball is trying to get in on the European market.* V P P n

get into PHRASAL VERB

1 If you **get into** a particular kind of work or activity, you manage to become involved in it. *He was eager to get into politics.* V P n

2 If you **get into** a school, college, or university, you are accepted there as a pupil or student. *I was working hard to get into Cambridge.* V P n

3 If you ask what has **got into** someone, you mean that they are behaving in an unexpected way; an informal expression. *He didn't know what could have got into him, to steal a watch all of a sudden.* V P n

get in with. PHRASAL VERB PRAGMATICS If someone tries to **get in with** you, they try to become friendly with you because they think that they will get some advantage out of you, for example because you are powerful; used showing disapproval. *She did everything she could to get in with the people she thought would make her look important.* VPPn

get off PHRASAL VERB

1 If someone who has broken a law or rule **gets off**, they are not punished, or are given only a very small punishment. *He is likely to get off with a small fine.* VP with n

2 If you **get off**, you leave a place because it is time to leave. *At eight I said 'I'm getting off now.'* VP

3 If you tell someone to **get off** a piece of land or **get off** the premises, you are telling them to leave, because they have no right to be there and you do not want them there. *I told you. Get off the farm.* VPn

4 You can tell someone to **get off** when they are touching something and you do not want them to. *I kept telling him to get off... 'Get off me!' I screamed.* VP VPn

5 If you **get off**, or **get off to sleep**, you succeed in falling asleep. VP

get off on. If you **get off on** something, you are very excited by it; an informal expression. *I'm an exhibitionist, and I get off on the entertainment we give people.* PHRASAL VERB VPPn

get off with. If you **get off with** someone, you have a romantic or sexual encounter with them; used in informal British English. *I got off with a cute boy from Nottingham.* PHRASAL VERB VPPn

get on PHRASAL VERB

1 If you **get on** with someone, you like them and have a friendly relationship with them. *The host fears the guests won't get on... What are your neighbours like? Do you get on with them?* RECIP =get along pl-n VP VP with n

2 If you **get on** with something, you continue with something that you have started doing or you start something that you were about to do. *Jane got on with her work... Let's get on.* VP with n VP

3 If you say how someone **is getting on**, you are saying how much success they are having with what they are trying to do. *Livy's getting on very well in Russian. She learns very quickly... When he came back to see me I asked how he had got on.* VP adv

4 If you try to **get on**, you try to be successful in your career; used mainly in British English. *Politics is seen as a man's world. It is very difficult for women to get on.* =get ahead VP

5 If someone **is getting on**, they are getting old; an informal expression. *I'm nearly 31 and that's getting on a bit for a footballer.* usu cont VP

get on to PHRASAL VERB

1 If you **get on to** a topic when you are speaking, you start talking about it. *We got on to the subject of relationships.* VPPn

2 If you **get on to** someone, you contact them in order to ask them to do something or to give them some information; used mainly in British English. *I got on to him and explained some of the things I had been thinking of.* VPPn

get out PHRASAL VERB

1 If you **get out**, you leave a place because you want to escape from it, or because you are made to leave it. *They probably wanted to get out of the country... I told him to leave and get out.* VP of n VP

2 If you **get out**, you go to places and meet people, usually in order to have a more enjoyable life. *Get out and enjoy yourself, make new friends.* =go out VP

3 If you **get out** of an organization or a commitment, you withdraw from it. *I wanted to get out of the group, but they wouldn't let me... Getting out of the contract would be no problem.* =pull out VP of n Also VP

4 If news or information **gets out**, it becomes known. *If word got out now, a scandal could be disastrous... Once the news gets out that Armenia is in a very critical situation, I think the world will respond.* VP VP that

get out of. If you **get out of** doing something that you do not want to do, you succeed in avoiding doing it. *It's amazing what people will do to get out of paying taxes.* PHRASAL VERB =avoid VPP-ing/n

get over PHRASAL VERB

1 If you **get over** an unpleasant or unhappy experience or an illness, you recover from it. *It took me a very long time to get over the shock of her death.* VPn

2 If you **get over** a problem or difficulty, you overcome it. *How would they get over that problem, he wondered?* =get round VPn

3 If you **get** your message **over** to people, they hear and understand it. *We have got to get the message over to the young that smoking isn't cool.* =get across VnP to n

get over with. If you want to **get** something unpleasant **over with**, you want to do it or finish experiencing it quickly, since you cannot avoid it. *The sooner we start, the sooner we'll get it over with.* PHRASAL VERB VnPP

get round PHRASAL VERB

1 See **get around**.

2 If you **get round** someone, you persuade them to allow you to do or have something by pleasing them or flattering them. *Max could always get round her.* VPn

get round to. See **get around to.** PHRASAL VERB

get through PHRASAL VERB

1 If you **get through** a task or an amount of work, especially when it is difficult, you complete it. *I think you can get through the first two chapters.* VPn

2 If you **get through** a difficult or unpleasant period of time, you manage to live through it. *It is hard to see how people will get through the winter... We couldn't get through a day without arguing.* =last VPn

3 If you **get through** a large amount of something, you use it up; used mainly in British English. *We've got through a lot of tyres... You'll get through at least ten nappies a day.* VPn

4 If you **get through** to someone, you succeed in making them understand something that you are trying to tell them. *An old friend might well be able to get through to her and help her... The message was finally getting through to him.* VP to n Also VP

5 If you **get through** to someone, you succeed in contacting them on the telephone. *Look, I can't get through to this number... I've been trying to ring up all day and I couldn't get through.* VP to n VP

6 If you **get through** an examination or **get through**, you pass it. *Did you have to get through an entrance examination?* VPn Also VP

7 If a law or proposal **gets through**, it is officially approved by something such as a parliament or committee. *He would be very disappointed if his referendum law failed to get through... Such a radical proposal would never get through parliament.* VP VPn

get together PHRASAL VERB

1 When people **get together**, they meet in order to discuss something or to spend time together. *This is the only forum where East and West can get together.* • See also **get-together**. VP

2 If you **get** something **together**, you organize it. *Paul and I were getting a band together, and we needed a new record deal.* VnP

3 If you **get** an amount of money **together**, you succeed in getting all the money that you need in order to pay for something. *Now you've finally got enough money together to put down a deposit on your dream home.* =scrape together VnP Also VPn (not pron)

get up PHRASAL VERB

1 When someone who is sitting or lying down **gets up**, they rise to a standing position. *I got up and walked over to where he was.* =stand up VP

2 When you **get up**, you get out of bed. *They have to get up early in the morning.* VP

3 If you **get** yourself **up** in a particular kind of clothing, you dress in that clothing. *They knew how to get themselves up in those days. ...an old tramp got up in a velvet smoking-jacket.* V pron-refl P V-ed P

4 See also **get-up**.

get up to. If you say that someone **gets up to** something, you mean that they do it and you do not approve of it; mainly used in spoken British English. *They get up to all sorts behind your back.* PHRASAL VERB PRAGMATICS VPPn

getaway /getəweɪ/ **getaways;** also spelled **get-away.** ◆◇◇◇◇

1 If someone makes a **getaway**, they leave a place in a hurry, especially after committing a crime. *They made their getaway along a pavement on a stolen motorcycle. ...the burglar's getaway car.* N-COUNT: usu sing, oft N n =escape

2 A **getaway** is a short holiday somewhere, or a place where you can go for a short holiday; an in- N-COUNT =break formal use in journalism. *Weekend tours are ideal for families who want a short getaway.*

getting /ɡetɪŋ/
1 **Getting** is the present participle of **get**.
2 **Getting on for** means the same as **nearly**; mainly used in spoken British English. *I've been trying to give up smoking for getting on for two years now... It was getting on for two o'clock.* PHR-PREP

get-together, get-togethers. A **get-together** is an informal meeting or party, usually arranged for a particular purpose. *...a get-together I had at my home.* N-COUNT

get-up, get-ups. If you refer to a set of clothes as a **get-up**, you think that they are unusual or ridiculous; an informal word. *Naturally he couldn't work in this get-up.* ◆◇◇◇◇ N-COUNT PRAGMATICS

geyser /ɡiːzəʳ/ **geysers.** A **geyser** is a hole in the Earth's surface from which hot water and steam are forced out, usually at irregular intervals of time. N-COUNT

Ghanaian /ɡɑːneɪən/ **Ghanaians.** Something that is **Ghanaian** belongs or relates to Ghana or to its people. *...the Ghanaian capital, Accra. ...Ghanaian children.* ▶ **Ghanaians** are people who are Ghanaian. *Among the people in this area are Ghanaians and Nigerians.* ◆◆◆◆◇ ADJ; N-COUNT

ghastly /ɡɑːstli, ɡæstli/ ◆◇◇◇◇
1 If you describe someone or something as **ghastly**, you mean that you dislike them a great deal; an informal use. *...a mother accompanied by her ghastly unruly child. ...a ghastly pair of white shoes... This wallpaper is absolutely ghastly; we'll have to replace it.* ADJ-GRADED =awful
2 A **ghastly** experience or situation is one that you find very unpleasant, usually because it makes you unhappy or embarrassed; an informal use. *...those of us who see shopping as a ghastly ordeal... It was the worst week of my life. It was ghastly.* ADJ-GRADED =hideous
3 **Ghastly** events, situations, or news involve suffering or death. *We are appealing to them to stop this ghastly war. ...a particularly ghastly murder.* ADJ-GRADED =horrendous
4 Something that is **ghastly** is extremely severe in its effects. *By 8.40 the pain started and by 9.15 it was ghastly... Perhaps I was making yet another ghastly mistake.* ADJ-GRADED =awful
5 If someone looks **ghastly**, they look very ill or unhappy. *She looked ghastly, frail, thin and colourless.* ADJ-GRADED: v-link ADJ =dreadful

gherkin /ɡɜːʳkɪn/ **gherkins. Gherkins** are small green cucumbers that have been pickled in vinegar; used mainly in British English. N-COUNT

ghetto /ɡetoʊ/ **ghettos** or **ghettoes.** A **ghetto** is a part of a town or city in which many poor people or many people of a particular race, religion, or nationality live in isolation from the majority group in the town or city. *...the black ghettos of New York and Los Angeles. ...the gang kids who will never escape the ghetto.* ◆◆◇◇◇ N-COUNT

ghost /ɡoʊst/ **ghosts, ghosting, ghosted** ◆◆◇◇◇
1 A **ghost** is the spirit of a dead person that someone believes they can see or feel. *...the ghost of Marie Antoinette... The village is haunted by the ghosts of the dead children.* N-COUNT: oft N of n
2 The **ghost of** something, especially of something bad that has happened, is the memory of it. *The President is using the two visits to lay the ghosts of the Munich Agreement. ...the ghost of anti-Americanism.* N-COUNT: N of n
3 A **ghost of** something is a faint trace of it. *He gave the ghost of a smile... Here and there a ghost of a track led off to a cottage buried in the trees.* N-SING: N of n
4 If a book or other piece of writing **is ghosted**, it is written by a writer for another person, for example a politician or sportsman, who then publishes it as his or her own work. *I published his autobiography, which was very competently ghosted by a woman journalist from the Daily Mail... I ghosted a series of five articles for Neil Kinnock.* VERB =ghost-write; be V-ed; V n
5 If someone **does not stand** or **does not have a ghost of a chance** of doing something, they have very little chance of succeeding in it; an informal expression. *He doesn't stand a ghost of a chance of selling the house.* PHRASES v PHR, with neg
6 If someone **gives up the ghost**, they stop trying to do something because they no longer believe they can do it successfully; an informal expression. *Economics required George Bush to give up the ghost on what was a campaign pledge.* V inflects =give up

ghostly /ɡoʊstli/ ◆◇◇◇◇
1 Something that is **ghostly** seems unreal or unnatural and may be frightening because of this. *The moon shone, shedding a ghostly light on the fields. ...Sonia's ghostly laughter.* ADJ: usu ADJ n
2 A **ghostly** presence is the ghost or spirit of a dead person. *...the ghostly presences which haunt these islands... Charles is haunted by ghostly children.* ADJ: ADJ n

ghost story, ghost stories. A **ghost story** is a story about ghosts. N-COUNT

ghost town, ghost towns. A **ghost town** is a town which used to be busy and prosperous but is now poor and deserted. *Mogadishu is said to be a virtual ghost town, deserted by two-thirds of its residents.* N-COUNT

ghost-write, ghost-writes, ghost-writing, ghost-wrote, ghost-written; also spelled **ghost write**. If a book or other piece of writing **is ghost-written**, it is written by a writer for another person, for example a politician or sportsman, who then publishes it as his or her own work. *Articles were ghost-written by company employees.* VB: usu passive =ghost; be V-ed

ghost-writer, ghost-writers. A **ghost-writer** is someone who writes a book or other published work instead of the person who is named as the author. *I suspect she'll be writing it herself; she doesn't need a ghost-writer.* N-COUNT

ghoul /ɡuːl/ **ghouls**
1 A **ghoul** is an imaginary evil spirit. **Ghouls** are said to steal bodies from graves and eat them. N-COUNT
2 If you describe someone as a **ghoul**, you disapprove of them because they show an unnatural interest in things such as torture, death, or dead bodies. N-COUNT PRAGMATICS

ghoulish /ɡuːlɪʃ/
1 If you describe someone as **ghoulish**, you disapprove of them because they show an unnatural interest in death or human suffering. If you describe something as **ghoulish**, you disapprove of it because it is produced by someone's unnatural interest in death and human suffering. *They are there only to satisfy their ghoulish curiosity. ...the ghoulish modern passion for torture.* ADJ-GRADED: usu ADJ n PRAGMATICS
2 Something that is **ghoulish** looks or behaves like a ghoul. *...the ghoulish apparitions at the window.* ADJ-GRADED: usu ADJ n

GHQ /dʒiː eɪtʃ kjuː/. In British English, **GHQ** is used to refer the place where the people who organize military forces or a military operation work. **GHQ** is an abbreviation for 'General Headquarters' and is a military term. *...the dispatches he was carrying from GHQ to the Eighth Army.* N-UNCOUNT

GI /dʒiː aɪ/ **GIs.** A **GI** is a soldier in the United States army. ◆◇◇◇◇ N-COUNT

giant /dʒaɪənt/ **giants** ◆◆◆◇◇
1 Something that is described as **giant** is much larger or more important than most others of its kind. *...Italy's giant car maker, Fiat. ...a giant oak table. ...a giant step towards unification with the introduction of monetary union.* ADJ: ADJ n =huge
2 The word **giant** is often used to refer to any large, successful business organization or country; used in journalism. *...Japanese electronics giant Sony. ...one of Germany's industrial giants, Daimler-Benz.* N-COUNT: usu n N
3 A **giant** is an imaginary person who is very big and strong, especially one mentioned in myths and children's stories. *...a Nordic saga of giants.* N-COUNT
4 You can refer to someone, especially a man, as a **giant**, if you are impressed by them, either because they seem important or powerful or because they are physically large. *He has enormous charisma. He is a giant of a man... The biggest man in the patrol, a giant of a man, lifted Mattie on to his shoulders.* N-COUNT: usu a N of n PRAGMATICS
5 You can refer to someone, for example a famous musician or writer, as a **giant**, if they are generally N-COUNT: usu N of n

regarded as being one of the most important or successful people in their field. *...the giant of opera, Luciano Pavarotti... He was without question one of the giants of Japanese literature.*

giantess /dʒaɪəntes/ **giantesses.** In myths and children's stories, a **giantess** is an imaginary woman who is very big and strong. N-COUNT

giant-killer, giant-killers; also spelled **giant killer.** Journalists sometimes call a sportsperson or team a **giant-killer** when they have achieved an unexpected victory over a much stronger opponent. *Giant-killers Yeovil became the most successful non-league club in history with their 5-2 win at Torquay.* N-COUNT

giant-killing, giant-killings. In sport, when a weaker team or competitor beats a much stronger, well-known team or competitor, journalists sometimes refer to their success as a **giant-killing**. *Scarborough are aiming to pull off a repeat of their giant-killing act against Chelsea three years ago.* N-COUNT: usu N n

giant-sized. An object that is **giant-sized** is much bigger than objects of its kind usually are. *...a giant-sized TV.* ADJ: usu ADJ n

gibber /dʒɪbəʳ/ **gibbers, gibbering, gibbered.** If you say that someone **is gibbering**, you mean that they are talking very fast and in a confused manner; an informal word. *Everyone is gibbering insanely, nerves frayed as showtime approaches... I was a gibbering wreck by this stage.* VERB =babble V V-ing

gibberish /dʒɪbərɪʃ/. If you describe someone's words or ideas as **gibberish**, you mean that they do not make any sense. *When he was talking to a girl he could hardly speak, and when he did speak he talked gibberish.* N-UNCOUNT =nonsense

gibbet /dʒɪbɪt/ **gibbets.** A **gibbet** is a gallows; an old-fashioned word. N-COUNT =gallows

gibbon /gɪbən/ **gibbons.** A **gibbon** is an ape with very long arms and no tail that lives in southern Asia. N-COUNT

gibe /dʒaɪb/. See **jibe**.

giblets /dʒɪblɪts/. **Giblets** are the parts such as the heart and liver that you remove from inside a chicken or other bird before you cook and eat it. Some people cook the giblets separately to make soup or a sauce. N-PLURAL

giddy /gɪdi/ **giddier, giddiest** ◆◇◇◇◇

1 If you feel **giddy**, you feel unsteady and think that you are about to fall over, usually because you are not well. *He felt giddy and light-headed.* ♦ **giddiness** *A wave of giddiness swept over her.* ADJ-GRADED =dizzy N-UNCOUNT

2 If you feel **giddy** with delight or excitement, you feel so happy or excited that you find it hard to think or act normally. *Anthony was giddy with self-satisfaction... Being there gave me a giddy pleasure.* ♦ **giddiness** *There's almost a giddiness surrounding the talks in Houston.* ADJ-GRADED N-UNCOUNT

gift /gɪft/ **gifts** ◆◆◆◇◇

1 A **gift** is something that you give someone as a present. *...a gift of £50.00... They believed the unborn child was a gift from God. ...gift shops.* N-COUNT

2 If someone has a **gift** for doing something, they have a natural ability for doing it. *As a youth he discovered a gift for teaching... I had the gift of shattering glass with my singing.* N-COUNT: oft N *for/of* -ing/n

3 ● **God's gift**: see **God**.

gifted /gɪftɪd/ ◆◇◇◇◇

1 Someone who is **gifted** has a natural ability to do something well. *He's the most gifted player at Highbury... He was witty, amusing and gifted with a sharp business brain.* ADJ-GRADED =talented

2 A **gifted child** is more intelligent than average. *...a state program for gifted children.* ADJ-GRADED

gift-wrapped. A **gift-wrapped** present is wrapped in pretty paper. ADJ: usu ADJ n

gig /gɪg/ **gigs, gigging, gigged** ◆◆◇◇◇

1 A **gig** is a live performance by a pop or jazz musician, comedian, or disk jockey; an informal use. *The two bands join forces for a gig at the Sheffield Arena on November 28... He supplemented his income with occasional comedy gigs.* N-COUNT =show

2 When musicians or other performers **gig**, they perform live in public; an informal use. *By the time he was 15, Scott had gigged with a handful of well-known small bands. ...ten years of gigging in bars and clubs all over Kentucky.* VERB =perform V V-ing

gigantic /dʒaɪgæntɪk/. If you describe something as **gigantic**, you are emphasizing that it is extremely large in size, amount, or degree; an informal word. *Her love for the tenor is of gigantic proportions... He looked gigantic in the solid glare from my torch.* ◆◇◇◇◇ ADJ-GRADED PRAGMATICS =colossal

giggle /gɪgᵊl/ **giggles, giggling, giggled** ◆◆◇◇◇

1 If someone **giggles**, they laugh in a childlike, helpless way, because they are amused, nervous, or embarrassed. *Both girls began to giggle... 'I beg your pardon?' she giggled. ...a giggling little girl.* ► Also a noun. *She gave a little giggle.* VERB =titter V V with quote V-ing N-COUNT

2 If you say that someone has **the giggles**, you mean they cannot stop giggling; an informal use. *I was so nervous I got the giggles... She had a fit of the giggles.* N-PLURAL: *the* N

3 If you say that something is **a giggle**, you mean it is fun or is amusing; used mainly in informal British English. *I might buy one for a friend's birthday as a giggle.* N-SING: *a* N

giggly /gɪgəli/. Someone who is **giggly** keeps laughing in a childlike, helpless way, because they are amused, nervous, or drunk. *Ray was very giggly and joking all the time. ...giggly girls.* ADJ-GRADED

gigolo /dʒɪgəloʊ/ **gigolos.** A **gigolo** is a man who is paid to be the lover and companion of a rich and usually older woman; used showing disapproval. N-COUNT: usu sing PRAGMATICS

gild /gɪld/ **gilds, gilding, gilded** ◆◇◇◇◇

1 If you **gild** a surface, you cover it in a thin layer of gold or gold paint. *Carve the names and gild them. ...gilded statues.* VERB V n V-ed

2 If you say that someone is **gilding the lily**, you mean that they are spoiling something that is already beautiful or perfect by trying to improve it or by praising it too highly. *Gilding the lily of what is basically a romantic comedy, the director falls a little short of his best mark.* PHRASE: V inflects

gilding /gɪldɪŋ/. **Gilding** is a layer of gold or gold paint that is put on something. *The gilding is extremely lavish.* N-UNCOUNT

gill /gɪl/ **gills.** **Gills** are the organs on the sides of fish and other water creatures through which they breathe. N-COUNT: usu pl

gilt /gɪlt/ **gilts** ◆◆◇◇◇

1 A **gilt** object is covered with a thin layer of gold or gold paint. *...marble columns and gilt spires.* ADJ: usu ADJ n

2 In British English, **gilts** are gilt-edged stocks or securities. N-COUNT

gilt-edged. In British English, **gilt-edged** stocks or securities are issued by the government for people to invest in for a fixed period of time at a fixed rate of interest. ADJ: ADJ n =gilts

gimlet /gɪmlɪt/. If you say that someone has **gimlet** eyes, you mean that they look at people or things very carefully, and seem to notice every detail; used in written English. *...his gimlet eyes and sardonic, deadpan style.* ADJ: ADJ n-

gimmick /gɪmɪk/ **gimmicks.** A **gimmick** is an unusual and unnecessary feature or action whose purpose is to attract attention or publicity; used showing disapproval. *It is just a public relations gimmick... The exhibition is informative, up to date, and mercifully free of gimmicks.* ◆◇◇◇◇ N-COUNT PRAGMATICS

gimmickry /gɪmɪkri/. If you describe features or actions as **gimmickry**, you disapprove of them because they are not necessary or useful, and their only purpose is to attract attention or publicity. *Privatisation and gimmickry are not the answer to improving Britain's rail service.* N-UNCOUNT PRAGMATICS

gimmicky /gɪmɪki/. If you describe something as **gimmicky**, you disapprove of it because it has features which are not necessary or useful, and whose only purpose is to attract attention or publicity; an informal word. *The campaign was gimmicky, but it had a serious side to it.* ADJ-GRADED PRAGMATICS

gin /dʒɪn/ **gins.** **Gin** is a strong colourless alcoholic drink made from grain and juniper berries. ◆◇◇◇◇ N-MASS N-COUNT
▶ A **gin** is a glass of gin. *...another gin and tonic.*

ginger /dʒɪndʒəʳ/ ◆◇◇◇◇
1 **Ginger** is the root of a plant that is used to flavour food. It has a sweet spicy flavour and is often sold in powdered form. N-UNCOUNT
2 **Ginger** is used to describe things that are orangey-brown in colour. *She was a mature lady with dyed ginger hair.* COLOUR

ginger ale, ginger ales. **Ginger ale** is a fizzy non-alcoholic drink flavoured with ginger, which is often mixed with an alcoholic drink. *I live mostly on coffee and ginger ale.* ▶ A glass of ginger-ale can be referred to as a **ginger ale**. N-MASS N-COUNT

ginger beer, ginger beers. **Ginger beer** is a drink that is made from syrup and ginger and is sometimes slightly alcoholic. N-MASS

gingerbread /dʒɪndʒəʳbred/. **Gingerbread** is a sweet cake or biscuit that is flavoured with ginger. The biscuits are often made in the shape of a man or an animal. N-UNCOUNT

ginger group, ginger groups. In British English, a **ginger group** is a group of people who have similar ideas and who work together, especially within a larger organization, to try to persuade others to accept or approve of their ideas. *...the Democratic Platform, the radical ginger group in the party... I set up a ginger group on the environment.* N-COUNT: usu sing

gingerly /dʒɪndʒəʳli/. If you do something **gingerly**, you do it in a careful, hesitant manner, usually because you expect it to be dangerous, unpleasant, or painful; used in written English. *She was touching the dressing gingerly with both hands... I drove gingerly past the security check points.* ◆◇◇◇◇ ADV-GRADED: ADV with v =cautiously

gingery /dʒɪndʒəri/. Something, especially hair, that is **gingery** is slightly ginger in colour. ADJ-GRADED

gingham /gɪŋəm/. **Gingham** is cotton cloth which has a woven pattern of small squares, usually in white and one other colour. *...a gingham apron. ...gingham check shorts.* N-UNCOUNT

ginseng /dʒɪnseŋ/. **Ginseng** is the root of a plant found in China, Korea, and America which some people believe is good for your health. N-UNCOUNT

gipsy /dʒɪpsi/. See **gypsy**.

giraffe /dʒɪrɑːf, -ræf/ **giraffes.** A **giraffe** is a large African animal with a very long neck, long legs, and dark patches on its body. N-COUNT

gird /gɜːʳd/ **girds, girding, girded.** If you **gird** yourself **for** a battle or contest, you prepare yourself for it; a literary word. *Washington has girded itself for terrorist retaliation.* • If you **gird** your **loins**, you prepare to do something difficult or dangerous; a literary expression. *Conservation organisations are girding their loins to take on the government.* VERB V pron-refl for n PHRASE: V inflects

girder /gɜːʳdəʳ/ **girders.** A **girder** is a long, thick piece of steel or iron that is used in the framework of buildings and bridges. N-COUNT

girdle /gɜːʳdəl/ **girdles, girdling, girdled**
1 A **girdle** is a piece of women's underwear that fits tightly around the stomach and hips. N-COUNT
2 Something that **girdles** something else surrounds it; a literary use. *Weather satellites have observed a ring of volcanic ash girdling the earth... The old town centre is girdled by a boulevard lined with trees.* VERB V n be V-ed by/with n

girl /gɜːʳl/ **girls** ◆◆◆◆◆
1 A **girl** is a female child. *...an eleven year old girl... I must have been a horrid little girl.* N-COUNT
2 You can refer to someone's daughter as a **girl**. *We had a little girl.* N-COUNT
3 Young women are often referred to as **girls**. Some people find this use offensive. *...a pretty twenty-year old girl.* N-COUNT
4 Some people refer to a man's girlfriend as his **girl**; an informal use. *I've been with my girl for nine years.* N-COUNT

girlfriend /gɜːʳlfrend/ **girlfriends** ◆◆◇◇◇
1 Someone's **girlfriend** is a girl or woman with whom they are having a romantic or sexual relationship. *He had been going out with his girlfriend for seven months... Has he got a girlfriend?* N-COUNT: oft poss N
2 A **girlfriend** is a female friend. *I met a girlfriend for lunch.* N-COUNT

Girl Guide, Girl Guides; also spelled **girl guide.**
1 In Britain, the Guides used to be called **the Girl Guides.** N-PROPER-COLL: the N
2 A **Girl Guide** was a girl who was a member of the Girl Guides. N-COUNT =Guide

girlhood /gɜːʳlhʊd/. **Girlhood** is the period of a female person's life during which she is a girl. *Even in her girlhood her friends had nicknamed her 'the immodest Violet'... Her girlhood dream had been to study painting.* N-UNCOUNT: oft poss N

girlie /gɜːʳli/. **Girlie** magazines or calendars show photographs of naked or almost naked women which are intended to please men; an informal word. ADJ: ADJ n

girlish /gɜːʳlɪʃ/. If you describe a woman as **girlish**, you mean she behaves, looks, or sounds like a young girl, for example because she is shy, excited, or lively. *She gave a little girlish giggle.* ADJ-GRADED: usu ADJ n

Girl Scout, Girl Scouts
1 In the United States, **the Girl Scouts** is an organization similar to **the Guides.** N-PROPER-COLL: the N
2 **A Girl Scout** is a girl who is a member of the Girl Scouts. N-COUNT

giro /dʒaɪərəʊ/ **giros;** also spelled **Giro.**
1 In Britain, a **giro** or a **giro cheque** is a cheque that is given by the government to a person who is unemployed or ill. *He lived on an invalidity pension which came as a weekly giro.* N-COUNT
2 In Britain, **giro** is a system in which banks and post offices will directly transfer money from one person's account into another person's account when they receive instructions to do so. *There will be no further costs as long as the receiving bank is part of the giro network.* N-UNCOUNT

girth /gɜːʳθ/ **girths**
1 The **girth** of an object, for example a person's or an animal's body, is its width or thickness, considered as the measurement around its circumference; a formal use. *A girl he knew had upset him by commenting on his increasing girth.* N-VAR: with supp, oft poss N
2 A **girth** is a leather strap which is fastened firmly around the middle of a horse to keep the saddle or load in the right place. N-COUNT

gist /dʒɪst/. **The gist of** a speech, conversation, or piece of writing is its general meaning. *He related the gist of his conversation to Naseby.* N-SING: the N of n

git /gɪt/ **gits.** In British English, if someone refers to another person as a **git**, they are expressing their dislike and lack of respect for that person; an offensive word. N-COUNT: usu adj N PRAGMATICS

give 1 used with nouns describing actions

give /gɪv/ **gives, giving, gave, given** ◆◆◆◆◆
1 You can use **give** with nouns that refer to physical actions. The whole expression refers to the performing of the action. For example, **She gave a smile** means almost the same as 'She smiled'. *She stretched her arms out and gave a great yawn... Giving a sigh, she fell to her knees at my feet... He gave her a fond smile... He reached for her hand and gave it a reassuring squeeze.* VB: no cont V n V n n
2 You use **give** to say that a person provides a service or performs an action for someone else. For example, if you **give** someone a lift, you take them somewhere in your car. *I gave her a lift back out to her house... He was given mouth-to-mouth resuscitation... Sophie asked her if she would like to come and give art lessons.* VERB V n n V n
3 You use **give** with nouns that refer to information, opinions, or greetings to indicate that something is communicated. For example, if you **give** someone some news, you tell it to them. *He gave no details... Would you like to give me your name?... He asked me to give his regards to all of you... He gave the cause of death as haemorrhaging following a stab wound.* VERB V n V n n V n to n V n as n
4 If you **give** someone or something a length of time, an amount, or a value, you estimate that they VERB

will last that time or have that amount or value. *A BBC poll gave the Labour Party a 2 per cent lead.* V n n

5 People use **give** in expressions such as **I don't give a damn** to emphasize that they do not care about something; an informal use. *I don't give a toss if the music press don't like us.* VB: no cont, no passive, with brd-neg V n

6 If someone or something **gives** you a particular idea or impression, it causes you to have that idea or impression. *They gave me the impression that they were doing exactly what they wanted in life... The examiner's final report does not give an accurate picture.* VERB V n n V n

7 If someone or something **gives** you a particular physical or emotional feeling, it makes you experience it. *He gave me a shock... It will give great pleasure to the many thousands of children who visit the hospital each year.* VERB V n n V n *to* n Also V n

8 If you **give** a performance or speech, you perform or speak in public. *Kotto gives a stupendous performance... I am sure you remember Mrs Butler who gave us such an interesting talk last year.* VERB V n V n n

9 If you **give** something thought or attention, you think about it, concentrate on it, or deal with it. *I've been giving it some thought... Priority will be given to those who apply early.* VERB V n n V n *to* n/-ing

10 If you **give** a party or other social event, you organize it. *That evening, I gave a dinner party for a few close friends.* VERB =have V n

give 2 transferring

give /gɪv/ **gives, giving, gave, given** ◆◆◆◆◆

1 If you **give** someone something that you own or have bought, you provide them with it, so that they have it or can use it. *They gave us T-shirts and stickers... Many leading industrialists gave money to the Conservative Party either personally or through their companies... This recipe was given to me years ago by a farmer's wife.* VERB V n n V n *to* n

2 If you **give** someone something that you are holding or that is near you, you pass it to them, so that they are then holding it. *Give me that pencil... He pulled a handkerchief from his pocket and gave it to him.* VERB V n n V n *to* n

3 To **give** someone or something a particular power or right means to allow them to have it. *...a citizen's charter giving rights to gays... Critics have said Mr Yeltsin is giving too much power to the republics... The draft would give the president the power to appoint the central bank's chairman.* VERB =grant V n *to* n V n n

give 3 other uses, phrases, and phrasal verbs

give /gɪv/ **gives, giving, gave, given** ◆◆◆◆◆

1 If something **gives**, it collapses or breaks under pressure. *My knees gave under me... That damn wagon axle gave and fell on me.* VERB V

2 You say that you **are given** to understand or believe that something is the case when you do not want to say how you found out about it, or who told you; a formal use. *We were given to understand that he was ill... He has been given to believe that there may be a future for him and Maria together.* V-PASSIVE *be* V-ed to-inf

3 See also **given**.

4 If someone **gives as good as** they **get**, they fight or argue as well as the person they are fighting or arguing with. *As Blair stepped up the pressure, Major gave as good as he got.* PHRASES Vs inflect

5 You use **give** in phrases such as **I'd give anything, I'd give my right arm**, and **what wouldn't I give** to emphasize that you are very keen to do or have something. *I'd give anything to be like you.* usu PHR to-inf PRAGMATICS

6 You use **give me** to say that you would rather have one thing than another, especially when you have just mentioned the thing that you do not want. *I've never had anything barbecued and I don't want it. Give me a good roast dinner any day.* PHR n

7 If you say that something requires **give and take**, you mean that people must compromise for it to be successful. *...a happy relationship where there's a lot of give and take.*

8 **Give or take** is used to indicate that an amount is approximate. For example, if you say that something is fifty years old, **give or take** a few years, you mean that it is approximately fifty years old. *They grow to a height of 12 ins – give or take a couple of inches.* PHR amount

9 You say **I'll give you that** to indicate that you admit that someone has a particular characteristic or ability. *You're a bright enough kid, I'll give you that.* cl PHR PRAGMATICS

10 ● to **give the game away**: see **game**. ● to **give up the ghost**: see **ghost**. ● to **give** someone **hell**: see **hell**. ● to **give** something **up as a bad job**: see **job**. ● to **give** your **life**: see **life**. ● to **give notice**: see **notice**. ● to **give rise to**: see **rise**. ● to **give way**: see **way**.

give away PHRASAL VERB

1 If you **give away** something that you own, you give it to someone, rather than selling it, often because you no longer want it. *He was giving his collection away for nothing... We have six copies of the book to give away.* ≠keep V n P V P n (not pron)

2 If someone **gives away** an advantage, they accidentally cause their opponent or enemy to have that advantage. *We gave away a silly goal... Military advantages should not be given away.* =concede V P n (not pron) Also V n P

3 If you **give away** information that should be kept secret, you reveal it to other people. *She would give nothing away... They felt like they were giving away company secrets.* =divulge V n P V P n (not pron)

4 To **give** someone or something **away** means to show their true nature or identity, which is not obvious. *Although they are pretending hard to be young, grey hair and cellulite give them away... I was never tempted for a moment to give her away.* =betray V n P Also V P n (not pron)

5 In a Christian wedding ceremony, if someone **gives** the bride **away**, they officially present her to her husband. This is traditionally done by the bride's father. V n P

give back. If you **give** something **back**, you return it to the person who gave it to you. *I gave the textbook back to him... You gave me back the projector... I gave it back politely.* PHRASAL VERB V n P *to* n V n P n (not pron) V n P

give in PHRASAL VERB

1 If you **give in**, you admit that you are defeated or that you cannot do something. *All right. I give in. What did you do with the ship?* V P

2 If you **give in**, you agree to do something that you do not want to do. *I pressed my parents until they finally gave in and registered me for skating classes... Officials say they won't give in to the workers' demands.* V P V P *to* n

give off or **give out.** If something **gives off** or **gives out** a gas, heat, or a smell, it produces it and sends it out into the air. *...natural gas, which gives off less carbon dioxide than coal... Substances such as ammonia give out heat when they dissolve.* PHRASAL VERB =emit V P n (not pron) Also V n P

give out PHRASAL VERB

1 If you **give out** a number of things, you distribute them among a group of people. *They were giving out leaflets at the Prime Minister's former school.* V P n (not pron) Also V n P

2 If you **give out** information, you make it known to people. *He wouldn't give out any information... How often do you give your phone number out?* V P n (not pron) V n P

3 If a piece of equipment or part of the body **gives out**, it stops working. *All machines give out eventually... One of his lungs gave out entirely.* V P

4 If you **give out** something such as a scream or a sigh, you sigh, scream, or make some other sound; used in written English. *He gave out a scream of pain.* =let out V P n (not pron)

5 See **give off**.

give over. If you tell someone to **give over**, you are telling them to stop doing something, usually because they are annoying you; an informal expression. *Tell him to give over... She gave over teasing and grinned at him.* PHRASAL VERB V P V P -ing/n

give over to or **give up to.** If something **is given over** or **given up to** a particular use, it is used entirely for that purpose. *Much of the garden was given over to vegetables... One third of their entire site is given up to a water-purification plant.* PHRASAL VERB usu passive *be* V-ed P P n

give up PHRASAL VERB

1 If you **give up** something, you stop doing it or having it. *Coastguards had given up all hope of finding the two divers alive. ...smokers who give up before 30.* V P n/-ing V P Also V n P

2 If you **give up**, you decide that you cannot do something and stop trying to do it. *After a fruitless morning sitting at his desk he had given up.* VP

3 If you **give up** your job, you resign from it. *She gave up her job to join her husband's campaign... He is thinking of giving up teaching.* V P n/-ing (not pron) Also V n P, VP

4 If you **give up** something that you have or that you are entitled to, you allow someone else to have it. *Georgia refuses to give up any territory... One of the men with him gave up his place on the bench.* V P n (not pron) Also V n P

5 If you **give** yourself **up**, you let the police or other people know where you are, after you have been hiding from them. *A 28-year-old man later gave himself up and will appear in court today.* V pron-refl P Also V n P

give up on. If you **give up on** something, you decide that you will never succeed in doing it, understanding it, or changing it, and you stop trying to. *He urged them not to give up on peace efforts.* PHRASAL VERB V P P n

give up to. See **give over to.** PHRASAL VERB

give-and-take. See **give.**

giveaway /gɪvəweɪ/ **giveaways;** also spelled **give-away.** ◆◇◇◇◇

1 A **giveaway** is something that makes you realize the truth about a particular person or situation. *The only giveaway was the look of amusement in her eyes.* N-SING

2 A **giveaway** is something that a company or organization gives to someone, usually in order to encourage people to buy a particular product. *Next week TODAY is celebrating with a great giveaway of FREE garden seeds.* N-COUNT

3 When you talk about **giveaway** prices, you are emphasizing that the prices are very low. *Wine and food of superlative quality are available everywhere at giveaway prices.* ADJ: ADJ n PRAGMATICS

given /gɪvən/ ◆◆◆◇◇

1 **Given** is the past participle of **give.**

2 If you talk about, for example, any **given** position or a **given** time, you mean the particular position or time that you are discussing. *In chess there are typically about 36 legal moves from any given board position... The bank discovered that in a given period, only a proportion of its borrowers would ask for their money in the form of cash.* ADJ: det ADJ =particular

3 **Given** is used when indicating a possible situation in which someone has the opportunity or ability to do something. For example, **given the chance** means 'if I had the chance'. *Write down the sort of thing you would like to do, given the opportunity... Given patience, successful breeding of this species can be achieved.* PREP

4 If you say **given that** something is the case, you mean taking that fact into account. *This may seem an odd view to take, given that I am strongly in favour of the Maastricht treaty.* PHR-CONJ-SUBORD =considering

5 If you say **given** something, you mean taking that thing into account. *Given the uncertainty over Leigh's future I was left with little other choice.* PREP

6 If you are **given to** doing something, you often do it; a formal use. *I am not very given to emotional displays.* ADJ-GRADED: v-link ADJ *to* -ing/n

given name, given names. A **given name** is a person's first name, which they are given at birth in addition to their surname; a formal expression. N-COUNT: oft with poss =first name

giver /gɪvər/ **givers.** You can refer to a person or organization that gives or supplies a particular thing as a **giver** of that thing. *Germany is the largest giver of aid among the wealthy countries of the West. ...a complex social ritual that says a lot about both the giver and the receiver.* ▶ Also a combining form. *If the money-givers do not have specific projects in view, they can sponsor a writing prize, perhaps, or a new recording studio.* ◆◇◇◇◇ N-COUNT COMB in N-COUNT

gizmo /gɪzmoʊ/ **gizmos.** A **gizmo** is a device or machine which performs a particular task, usually in a new and efficient way. People often use **gizmo** to refer to a device or machine when they do not know what it is really called. *...a plastic gizmo for holding a coffee cup on the dashboard.* N-COUNT: usu with supp

glacé /glæseɪ, AM -seɪ/. **Glacé** fruits are fruits that have been preserved in a thick sugary syrup and then dried. *Use pieces of glacé cherry and chopped nuts to decorate.* ADJ: ADJ n =candied

glacial /gleɪʃəl/ ◆◇◇◇◇

1 **Glacial** means relating to or produced by glaciers or ice; a technical use in geography. *...a true glacial landscape with U-shaped valleys. ...rising sea levels at the end of the last glacial period.* ADJ: usu ADJ n

2 If you say that a person, action, or atmosphere is **glacial**, you are emphasizing that they are very unfriendly or hostile. *The Duchess's glare was glacial... Inside the jeep the atmosphere was glacial.* ADJ-GRADED PRAGMATICS =cold, icy

3 If you say that something moves or changes at a **glacial** pace, you are emphasizing that it moves or changes very slowly; used mainly in written English. *One has to join another queue moving at glacial speed.* ADJ-GRADED: usu ADJ n PRAGMATICS

4 If you describe someone, usually a woman, as **glacial**, you mean they are very beautiful and elegant, but do not show their feelings. *Her glacial beauty is magnetic.* ADJ: usu ADJ n

glacier /glæsiər, AM gleɪʃər/ **glaciers.** A **glacier** is a huge mass of ice which moves very slowly, often down a mountain valley. ◆◇◇◇◇ N-COUNT

glad /glæd/ ◆◆◆◇◇

1 If you are **glad** about something, you are happy and pleased about it. *I'm glad I relented in the end... The people seem genuinely glad to see you... I ought to be glad about what happened... I'd be glad if the boys slept a little longer so I could do some ironing.* ♦ **gladly** *Mallarme gladly accepted the invitation.* ♦ **gladness** *...a night of joy and gladness, of sorrow and recollection.* ADJ-GRADED: v-link ADJ, oft ADJ that, ADJ to-inf, ADJ *of/about* n ADV-GRADED: ADV with v N-UNCOUNT

2 If you say that you will be **glad** to do something, usually for someone else, you mean that you are willing and eager to do it. *I'll be glad to show you everything... We should be glad to answer any questions.* ♦ **gladly** *The counselors will gladly baby-sit during their free time.* ADJ-GRADED: v-link ADJ to-inf PRAGMATICS =happy ADV: ADV with v

3 **Glad tidings** means good news; a literary expression. *...the bringer of glad tidings.* PHRASE

gladden /glædən/ **gladdens, gladdening, gladdened**

1 If you say that something **gladdens** someone's **heart**, you mean that it makes them feel pleased and hopeful; used in written English. *...a conclusion that should gladden the hearts of all animal-rights activists.* PHRASE: V and N inflect

2 If something **gladdens** you, it makes you feel happy and pleased; a literary use. *Charles's visit surprised him and gladdened him.* VERB ≠sadden V n

glade /gleɪd/ **glades.** A **glade** is a grassy space without trees in a wood or forest; a literary word. *...a woodland glade.* N-COUNT =clearing

gladiator /glædieɪtər/ **gladiators**

1 In the time of the Roman Empire, a **gladiator** was a man who had to fight against other men or wild animals in order to entertain an audience. N-COUNT

2 You can refer to a sports player or a performer as a **gladiator** in order to emphasize how brave or dangerous their actions are; used in journalism. *As the gladiators rolled away from the starting gates, a gasp went up when the Scottish cyclist's left foot clicked out of the pedal.* N-COUNT PRAGMATICS

glad-rags. You can refer to clothes that you wear to parties and other special occasions as your **glad-rags**; an informal word. N-PLURAL

glamor /glæmər/. See **glamour.**

glamorize /glæməraɪz/ **glamorizes, glamorizing, glamorized;** also spelled **glamorise** in British English. If someone **glamorizes** something, they make it look or seem more attractive than it really is, especially in a film, book, or programme; used showing disapproval. *Filmmakers have often been accused of glamorizing organized crime. ...a glamorised view of the past.* VERB PRAGMATICS V n V-ed

glamorous /glæmərəs/. If you describe someone or something as **glamorous**, you mean that they are more attractive, exciting, or interesting than ordinary people or things. *...some of the world's most beautiful and glamorous women...* ◆◆◇◇◇ ADJ-GRADED

The south coast is less glamorous but full of clean and attractive hotels.

glamour /glæməʳ/; spelled **glamor** in American English. **Glamour** is the quality of being more attractive, exciting, or interesting than ordinary people or things. *...the glamour of show biz.* ◆◆◇◇◇ N-UNCOUNT =glitter

glance /glɑːns, glæns/ **glances, glancing, glanced** ◆◆◆◇◇

1 If you **glance** at something or someone, you look at them very quickly and then look away again immediately. *He glanced at his watch... I glanced back.* VERB V prep/adv

2 If you **glance through** or **at** a newspaper, report, or book, you spend a short time looking at it without reading it very carefully. *I picked up the phone book and glanced through it... I never even glanced at the political page of a daily paper.* VERB V through/at n

3 A **glance** is a quick look at someone or something. *Trevor and I exchanged a glance. ...stealing a quick glance at her watch.* N-COUNT

4 If you see something **at a glance**, you see or recognize it immediately, and without having to think or look carefully. *One could tell at a glance that she was a compassionate person.* PHRASES

5 If you say that something is true or seems to be true **at first glance**, you mean that it seems to be true when you first see it or think about it, but that your first impression may be wrong. *At first glance, organic farming looks much more expensive for the farmer.* PHR with cl

6 If you **steal a glance** at someone or something, you look at them quickly so that nobody sees you looking. *He stole a glance at the clock behind her.* V and N inflect, oft PHR at n

glance off. If an object **glances off** something, it hits it at an angle and bounces away in another direction. *My fist glanced off his jaw.* PHRASAL VERB V P n

glancing /glɑːnsɪŋ, glæns-/. A **glancing** blow is one that hits something at an angle rather than from directly in front. *The car struck him a glancing blow on the forehead.* ADJ: ADJ n

gland /glænd/ **glands.** A **gland** is an organ in the body which produces chemical substances for the body to use or get rid of. *...the hormones secreted by our endocrine glands. ...sweat glands.* ◆◆◇◇◇ N-COUNT: usu supp N

glandular /glændʒʊləʳ/. **Glandular** means relating to or affecting your glands; a technical term in biology. *...the amount of fat and glandular tissue in the breasts.* ADJ: usu ADJ n

glandular fever. **Glandular fever** is a disease which causes swollen glands, fever, and a sore throat. N-UNCOUNT

glare /gleəʳ/ **glares, glaring, glared** ◆◆◇◇◇

1 If you **glare** at someone, you look at them with an angry expression on your face. *The old woman glared at him... Jacob glared and muttered something. ...glaring eyes.* VERB V at n V V-ing

2 A **glare** is an angry, hard, and unfriendly look. *His glasses magnified his irritable glare.* N-COUNT

3 If the sun or a light **glares**, it shines with a very bright light which is difficult to look at. *The sunlight glared. ...glaring searchlight beams.* VERB V V-ing

4 **Glare** is very bright light that is difficult to look at. *...the glare of a car's headlights... Special-purpose glasses reduce glare.* N-UNCOUNT: usu with supp

5 If someone is in **the glare of** publicity or public attention, they are constantly being watched and talked about by a lot of people. *Norma is said to dislike the glare of publicity... She attacked police in the full glare of TV cameras.* N-SING: the N of n

glaring /gleərɪŋ/. If you describe something bad as **glaring**, you are emphasizing that it is very obvious and easily seen or noticed. *I never saw such a glaring example of misrepresentation.* ◆◇◇◇◇ ADJ-GRADED: usu ADJ n PRAGMATICS =blatant

♦ **glaringly** *It was glaringly obvious... He told a glaringly different story.* • See also **glare**. ADV-GRADED

glasnost /glæznɒst/. **Glasnost** is a policy of making a government more open and accountable to its people and other nations. The word **Glasnost** was originally used to describe the policies of President Gorbachev in the former Soviet Union in the 1980s. ◆◇◇◇◇ N-UNCOUNT

glass /glɑːs, glæs/ **glasses** ◆◆◆◆◇

1 **Glass** is a hard transparent substance that is used to make things such as windows and bottles. *...a pane of glass. ...a sliding glass door.* N-UNCOUNT

2 A **glass** is a container made from glass, which you can drink from and which does not have a handle. *Grossman raised the glass to his lips.* ► The contents of a glass can be referred to as a **glass** of something. *...a glass of milk.* N-COUNT N-COUNT: usu N of n

3 **Glass** is used to mean objects made of glass, for example drinking containers and bowls. *There's a glittering array of glass to choose from at markets.* N-UNCOUNT =glassware

4 **Glasses** are two lenses in a frame that some people wear in front of their eyes in order to help them see better. *He took off his glasses.* N-PLURAL =spectacles

5 See also **dark glasses, magnifying glass.**

glass ceiling, glass ceilings. When people refer to a **glass ceiling**, they are talking about the attitudes and traditions in a society that prevent women from rising to the top jobs. *In her current role she broke through the glass ceiling as the first woman to reach senior management level in the company... They're now seeing their daughters hitting the glass ceiling and they are horrified at the effects.* N-COUNT: usu sing

glassed-in. A **glassed-in** room or building has windows instead of walls. *...an attractive, glassed-in restaurant with a view of Water Street.* ADJ: usu ADJ n

glass fibre; spelled **glass fiber** in American English. **Glass fibre** is a cloth made from short thin threads of glass. It is used to keep heat in or to strengthen plastic. N-UNCOUNT

glasshouse /glɑːshaʊs, glæs-/ **glasshouses.** A **glasshouse** is a greenhouse, especially a large one which is used for the commercial production of fruit, flowers, or vegetables; used mainly in British English. N-COUNT

glassware /glɑːsweəʳ, glæs-/. **Glassware** consists of objects made of glass, such as bowls, drinking containers, and ornaments. N-UNCOUNT

glassy /glɑːsi, glæsi/

1 If you describe something as **glassy**, you mean that it is very smooth and shiny, like glass; used in written English. *The water was glassy. ...glassy green pebbles.* ADJ-GRADED

2 If you describe someone's eyes or expression as **glassy**, you mean that they are showing no feeling, emotion, or awareness; used mainly in written English. *He was very still, his eyes glassy... Henry gave Paul a glassy-eyed stare.* ADJ-GRADED =vacant

glaucoma /glɔːkoʊmə, AM glaʊ-/. **Glaucoma** is an eye disease which can cause people to go gradually blind. N-UNCOUNT

glaze /gleɪz/ **glazes, glazing, glazed** ◆◇◇◇◇

1 A **glaze** is a thin layer of liquid which is put on a piece of pottery and becomes hard and shiny when the pottery is heated in a very hot oven. *...hand-painted French tiles with decorative glazes.* N-COUNT

2 A **glaze** is a thin layer of beaten egg, milk, or other liquid that you spread onto food in order to make the surface shine and look attractive. *Brush the glaze over the top and sides of the hot cake.* N-COUNT

3 When you **glaze** food such as bread or pastry, you spread a layer of beaten egg, milk, or other liquid onto it before you cook it in order to make its surface shine and look attractive. *Glaze the pie with beaten egg.* VERB V n

glaze over. If your eyes **glaze over**, they become dull and lose all expression, usually because you are bored or are thinking about something else. *...movie actors whose eyes glaze over as soon as the subject wavers from themselves.* PHRASAL VERB V P

glazed /gleɪzd/ ◆◇◇◇◇

1 If you describe someone's eyes as **glazed**, you mean that their expression is dull or dreamy, usually because they are tired or are having difficulty concentrating on something. *Doctors with glazed eyes sat chain-smoking in front of a television set... There was a glazed look in her eyes.* ADJ-GRADED: usu ADJ n =glassy

2 **Glazed** pottery is covered with a thin layer of a hard shiny substance. ADJ: usu ADJ n

3 A **glazed** window or door has glass in it. ADJ

glazier /gleɪziəʳ, AM -ʒər/ **glaziers.** A **glazier** is someone whose job is fitting glass into windows and doors. N-COUNT

gleam /gliːm/ **gleams, gleaming, gleamed** ◆◆◇◇◇
1 If an object or a surface **gleams**, it reflects light because it is shiny and clean. *His black hair gleamed in the sun. ...a gleaming red sports car.* VERB V V-ing
2 You can refer to the light reflected from something as a **gleam**; used in written English. *...the gleam of the dark river... In the light that fell on her from the hall her fair hair had a golden gleam.* N-SING
3 If a light or the sun or moon **gleams**, it shines faintly; used in written English. *Neon lights gleamed in the deepening mists.* VERB V
4 A **gleam of** light is a pale, clear light; used in written English. *...the gleam of the headlights.* N-COUNT: N of n
5 If your eyes **gleam**, they look bright and show that you are excited or happy; used in written English. *His eyes gleamed almost wickedly.* VERB =glisten, shine V
6 If someone has a **gleam** in their eye, their eyes show a particular feeling; used in written English. *There was a gleam in her eye when she looked at me.* N-SING
7 A **gleam of** something is a faint sign of it. *There was a gleam of hope for a peaceful settlement. ...gleams of wit.* N-COUNT: N of n =glimmer
8 If you say that something is only **a gleam in** someone's **eye** at present, you mean that it is only being planned or considered, and has not yet been properly begun. *The product is still only a gleam in an engineer's eye.* PHRASE: usu v-link PHR

glean /gliːn/ **gleans, gleaning, gleaned.** If you **glean** something such as information or knowledge, you learn or collect it slowly and patiently, and perhaps indirectly. *At present we're gleaning information from all sources... 10,000 pages of evidence were gleaned from hundreds and hundreds of interviews.* ◆◇◇◇◇ VERB =gather V n from n V n

glee /gliː/. **Glee** is a feeling of happiness and excitement, often caused by someone else's misfortune; used mainly in written English. *His victory was greeted with glee by his fellow American golfers... There was much glee among journalists over the leaked letter.* ◆◇◇◇◇ N-UNCOUNT: oft with N =delight

gleeful /gliːfʊl/. Someone who is **gleeful** is happy and excited, often because of someone else's misfortune; used in written English. *He took an almost gleeful delight in showing how wrong they can be.* ♦ **gleefully** *I spent the rest of their visit gleefully boring them with tedious details.* ◆◇◇◇◇ ADJ-GRADED ADV-GRADED: ADV with v

glen /glen/ **glens.** A **glen** is a deep, narrow valley, especially in the mountains of Scotland or Ireland. N-COUNT: oft in names

glib /glɪb/. If you describe what someone says as **glib**, you disapprove of it because it implies that something is simple or easy, or that there are no problems involved, when this is not the case. *...the glib talk of 'past misery'... Mr. Lewis takes an insufferably glib attitude toward it all.* ♦ **glibly** *We talk glibly of equality of opportunity.* ADJ-GRADED PRAGMATICS ADV-GRADED: ADV with v

glide /glaɪd/ **glides, gliding, glided** ◆◇◇◇◇
1 If you **glide** somewhere, you move silently and in a smooth and effortless way. *Waiters glide between tightly packed tables bearing trays of pasta.* VERB V prep/adv
2 When birds or aeroplanes **glide**, they float on air currents. *Our only companion is the wandering albatross, which glides effortlessly and gracefully behind the yacht.* VERB V prep/adv Also V

glider /glaɪdəʳ/ **gliders.** A **glider** is an aircraft without an engine, which flies by floating on air currents. ◆◇◇◇◇ N-COUNT

gliding /glaɪdɪŋ/. **Gliding** is the sport or activity of flying in a glider. N-UNCOUNT

glimmer /glɪməʳ/ **glimmers, glimmering, glimmered** ◆◇◇◇◇
1 If something **glimmers**, it produces or reflects a faint, gentle, often unsteady light. *The lights of Truro glimmer outside my window. ...the glimmering ocean.* VERB V V-ing
2 A **glimmer** is a faint, gentle, often unsteady light. *In the east there is the slightest glimmer of light.* N-COUNT =flicker
3 A **glimmer of** something is a faint sign of it. *Despite an occasional glimmer of hope, this campaign has not produced any results... He is celebrating his first glimmer of success.* N-COUNT: N of n =gleam

glimmering /glɪmərɪŋ/ **glimmerings.** A **glimmering of** something is a faint sign of it. *...a glimmering of understanding. ...the first glimmerings of civilization.* N-COUNT: N of n

glimpse /glɪmps/ **glimpses, glimpsing, glimpsed** ◆◆◇◇◇
1 If you get a **glimpse** of someone or something, you see them very briefly and not very well. *Some of the fans had waited 24 hours outside the Hyde Park Hotel to catch a glimpse of their heroine.* N-COUNT: usu N of n
2 If you **glimpse** someone or something, you see them very briefly and not very well. *She glimpsed a group of people standing on the bank of a river.* VERB V n
3 A **glimpse** of something is a brief experience of it or an idea about it that helps you understand or appreciate it better. *As university campuses become increasingly multi-ethnic, they offer a glimpse of the conflicts society will face tomorrow. ...a glimpse into the future.* N-COUNT: usu N of n

glint /glɪnt/ **glints, glinting, glinted** ◆◇◇◇◇
1 If something **glints**, it produces or reflects a quick flash of light; used in written English. *The sea glinted in the sun... Sunlight glinted on his spectacles. ...the glinting ripples of water.* VERB =glisten V V on/off n V-ing
2 A **glint** is a quick flash of light; used in written English. *...a glint of silver. ...glints of sunlight.* N-COUNT: usu N of n
3 If someone's eyes **glint**, they shine and express a particular emotion; used in written English. *Her eyes glinted wildly... A mischievous spark glinted in his eyes.* VERB =gleam V
4 A **glint** in someone's eyes is a brightness that expresses a particular emotion. *He came up to me with the glint of triumph in his eye.* N-SING =gleam

glisten /glɪsᵊn/ **glistens, glistening, glistened** ◆◇◇◇◇
1 If something **glistens**, it shines or sparkles, usually because it is wet or oily. *The calm sea glistened in the sunlight... Darcy's face was white and glistening with sweat. ...tubs of glistening olives.* VERB =gleam V V with n V-ing
2 If you say that someone's eyes **glisten**, you mean their eyes shine, for example because they are about to cry, or because they are happy or excited; used in written English. *'I shall go, leave him.' Laura Stebbing stopped, her eyes glistening... His sunken eyes glistened with delight.* VERB V V with n

glitch /glɪtʃ/ **glitches.** A **glitch** is a problem which stops something from working properly or being successful; an informal word. *Manufacturing glitches have limited the factory's output, and costs are still far too high.* N-COUNT =hitch, problem

glitter /glɪtəʳ/ **glitters, glittering, glittered** ◆◆◇◇◇
1 If something **glitters**, light comes from or is reflected off different parts of it every moment. *The bay glittered in the sunshine... The Palace glittered with lights.* VERB =sparkle V V prep
2 If someone's eyes **glitter**, they are bright and express a particular emotion, for example excitement or greed; used in written English. *His eyes glittered with a tense amusement.* VERB =gleam V
3 **Glitter** consists of tiny shining pieces of metal. It is glued to things for decoration. *Decorate the tunic with sequins or glitter.* N-UNCOUNT
4 You can use **glitter** to refer to superficial attractiveness or to the glamour and excitement connected with something. *She was blinded by the glitter and the glamour of her own life.* N-UNCOUNT

glitterati /glɪtərɑːti/. Journalists use **glitterati** to refer to rich and famous people such as actors and rock stars. *The glitterati of Hollywood are flocking to Janet Vaughan's nail salon.* N-PLURAL

glittering /glɪtərɪŋ/. You use **glittering** to indicate that something is very impressive or successful. *...a brilliant school pupil destined for a glittering academic career. ...a champagne breakfast for a glittering array of celebrities.* ◆◇◇◇◇ ADJ-GRADED: ADJ n =dazzling

glittery /glɪtəri/. Something that is **glittery** shines with a lot of very small points of light. *...a gold suit and a glittery bow tie.* ADJ-GRADED

glitz /glɪts/. You use **glitz** to refer to something that you think is exciting and attractive in a N-UNCOUNT showy and rather superficial way. *...the glitz of Beverly Hills. ...the glitz with which France celebrated the bicentenary of its revolution.*

glitzy /glɪtsi/ **glitzier, glitziest.** ◆◇◇◇◇ If you describe something as **glitzy**, you mean that it is exciting and attractive in a showy and rather superficial way. *...Aspen, Colorado, one of the glitziest ski resorts in the world.* ADJ-GRADED

gloat /gloʊt/ **gloats, gloating, gloated.** ◆◇◇◇◇ If you say that someone **is gloating**, you are being critical of the arrogant and uncaring way in which they show pleasure at their own success or at other people's failure. *Anti-abortionists are gloating over the court's decision... This is nothing to gloat about.* VERB PRAGMATICS =crow V over/about n Also V

glob /glɒb/ **globs.** A **glob** of something soft or liquid is a small round amount of it; an informal word. *...oily globs of soup.* N-COUNT: usu N of n =blob

global /gloʊbᵊl/ ◆◆◆◇◇

1 You can use the word **global** to describe something that happens in all parts of the world or affects all parts of the world. *...a global ban on nuclear testing... On a global scale, AIDS may well become the leading cause of infant death.* ♦ **globally** *...a globally familiar trade name.* ADJ: usu ADJ n =worldwide ADV

2 A **global** view or vision of a situation is one in which all the different aspects of it are considered. *...the global view, the ability to make wider decisions based on a knowledge of all the facts, not just some of them. ...a global vision of contemporary societies.* ADJ-GRADED: usu ADJ n

globalize /gloʊbəlaɪz/ **globalizes, globalizing, globalized;** also spelled **globalise** in British English. When industry **globalizes** or **is globalized**, companies from one country link with companies from another country in order to do business with them. *One way to lower costs will be to forge alliances with foreign companies or to expand internationally through appropriate takeovers - in short, to 'globalise'.* ♦ **globalization** /gloʊbəlaɪzeɪʃᵊn/ *Trends toward the globalization of industry have dramatically affected food production in California.* V-ERG V Also V n N-UNCOUNT

global warming. ◆◆◇◇◇ The problem of the gradual rise in the earth's temperature is referred to as **global warming**. It happens because the heat that is absorbed from the sun cannot leave the atmosphere because the level of carbon dioxide and other gases is too high. *The threat of global warming will eventually force the US to slow down its energy consumption.* N-UNCOUNT

globe /gloʊb/ **globes** ◆◆◇◇◇

1 You can refer to the world as the **globe** when you are emphasizing how big it is or that something happens in many different parts of it. *...bottles of beer from every corner of the globe... 70% of our globe's surface is water.* N-SING: usu the N =planet

2 A **globe** is a ball-shaped object with a map of the world on it. It is usually fixed on a stand. *...a globe of the world... Three large globes stand on the floor.* N-COUNT

3 Any ball-shaped object can be referred to as a **globe**. *The overhead light was covered now with a white globe.* N-COUNT: usu with supp

globe artichoke, globe artichokes. Globe artichokes are round green vegetables that have fleshy leaves arranged like the petals of a flower. Each leaf can be removed and the fleshy bottom part of it eaten. N-VAR =artichoke

globe-trot, globe-trots, globe-trotting, globe-trotted; also spelled **globetrot**. If someone spends their time **globe-trotting**, they spend a lot of time travelling to different parts of the world; an informal word. *The son of a diplomat, he has spent much of his life globe-trotting.* ♦ **globe-trotting** *...globe-trotting academic superstars.* ♦ **globe-trotter, globe-trotters** *TV globe-trotter Alan Whicker was nearly burned alive by an angry mob in Egypt.* VB: usu cont V ADJ N-COUNT

globular /glɒbjʊləʳ/. A **globular** object is shaped like a ball; a formal word. *The globular seed capsule contains numerous small seeds.* ADJ: usu ADJ n

globule /glɒbjuːl/ **globules. Globules** of a liquid or of a soft substance are tiny round particles of it. *...globules of saliva... Our bone marrow contains fat in the form of small globules.* N-COUNT: usu pl, oft N of n =droplet

glockenspiel /glɒkənʃpiːl/ **glockenspiels.** A **glockenspiel** is a musical instrument which consists of metal bars of different lengths arranged like the keyboard of a piano. You play the glockenspiel by hitting the bars with wooden hammers. N-COUNT: oft the N

gloom /gluːm/ ◆◆◇◇◇

1 **The gloom** is a state of partial darkness somewhere. *...the gloom of a foggy November morning... I was peering about me in the gloom.* N-SING: the N, oft in/into N

2 **Gloom** is a feeling of unhappiness or despair. *...the deepening gloom over the economy... A gloom descended on the group.* N-UNCOUNT: also a N

gloomy /gluːmi/ **gloomier, gloomiest** ◆◆◇◇◇

1 If a place is **gloomy**, it is almost dark so that you cannot see very well. *Inside it's gloomy after all that sunshine... All the electric lamps in this huge gloomy church were extinguished.* ADJ-GRADED

2 If people are **gloomy**, they are unhappy and have no hope. *Miller is gloomy about the fate of the serious playwright in America.* ♦ **gloomily** *He tells me gloomily that he has been called up for army service.* ADJ-GRADED =despondent ADV-GRADED: ADV with v

3 If a situation is **gloomy**, it does not give you much hope of success or happiness. *...a gloomy picture of an economy sliding into recession... Officials say the outlook for next year is gloomy.* ADJ-GRADED =grim

glorified /glɔːrɪfaɪd/. You use **glorified** to indicate that something is less important or impressive than its name suggests. For example, if you describe a lake as a **glorified** pond, you mean that it is really no bigger than a pond. *Sometimes they tell me I'm just a glorified waitress... Some observers see Parliament as nothing but a glorified talk-shop.* ADJ: ADJ n =jumped up

glorify /glɔːrɪfaɪ/ **glorifies, glorifying, glorified** ◆◇◇◇◇

1 If you say that someone **glorifies** something, you mean that they praise it or make it seem good or special, usually when it is not. *...the outrageous video which glorifies the antics of soccer's hard men. ...the banning of songs glorifying war and racism.* ♦ **glorification** /glɔːrɪfɪkeɪʃᵊn/ *...the glorification of violence. ...a glorification of the past.* VERB =glamorize V n N-UNCOUNT

2 If you **glorify** God, you express His greatness by speech or action, for example by singing hymns of praise. *We are all committed to serving the Lord and glorifying His name in the best way we know.* VERB =praise V n

glorious /glɔːriəs/ ◆◆◇◇◇

1 If you describe something as **glorious**, you are emphasizing that it looks very beautiful and impressive, usually because it is very colourful or very large; a literary use. *...a glorious rainbow in the air... She had missed the glorious blooms of the Mediterranean spring. ...a glorious Edwardian opera house.* ♦ **gloriously** *A tree, gloriously lit by autumn, pressed against the windowpane.* ADJ-GRADED PRAGMATICS =magnificent ADV-GRADED: usu ADV adj

2 If you describe something as **glorious**, you are emphasizing that it is wonderful and it makes you feel very happy. *The win revived glorious memories of his championship-winning days... We opened the windows and let in the glorious evening air.* ♦ **gloriously** *...her gloriously happy love life.* ADJ-GRADED =heavenly ADV-GRADED

3 A **glorious** career, victory, or occasion involves great fame or success. *Harrison had a glorious career spanning more than six decades... Her future could be more glorious even than her past.* ♦ **gloriously** *But the mission was successful, gloriously successful.* ADJ-GRADED =illustrious ADV-GRADED: usu ADV adj

4 When you describe the weather as **glorious**, you mean it is hot and sunny. *I got dressed and emerged into glorious sunshine... The sun was out again, and it was a glorious day.* ♦ **gloriously** *For a change, it was a gloriously sunny day.* ADJ-GRADED ADV-GRADED: ADV adj

glory /glɔːri/ **glories, glorying, gloried** ◆◆◇◇◇

1 **Glory** is the fame and admiration that you gain by doing something impressive. *Walsham had his moment of glory when he won a 20km race... Bobby Moore led England to World Cup glory in 1966.* N-UNCOUNT

2 A person's **glories** are the occasions when they have done something people greatly admire which makes them famous. *The album sees them re-living past glories but not really breaking any new ground. ...the military glories of Frederick the Great.* N-PLURAL: with supp

3 The **glory** of something is its great beauty or impressiveness. *The glory of the idea blossomed in his mind... The Church saw that music could fill men's souls with wonderment for the glory of God.* N-UNCOUNT: with poss, usu *the* N *of* n

4 The **glories** of a culture or place are the things that people admire most about it. *...a tour of Florence, to enjoy the artistic glories of the Italian Renaissance... One of the glories of the island has always been its bird population.* N-COUNT: usu pl, with supp, usu *the* N *of* n

5 If you **glory in** a situation or activity, you enjoy it very much. *The workers were glorying in their new-found freedom... He does not glory in his past successes and looks forward to achieving more.* VERB =revel V *in* n

6 If you go out in **a blaze of glory**, you do something very dramatic at the end of your career or your life which makes you famous. *I am never going back to prison. I am going to make national news headlines and go out in a blaze of glory.* PHRASE: oft *in* PHR

gloss /glɒs, AM glɔːs/ **glosses, glossing, glossed** ◆◇◇◇◇

1 A **gloss** is a bright shine on the surface of something. *Sheets of rain were falling and produced a black gloss on the asphalt.* N-SING =sheen

2 Gloss is an appearance of attractiveness or good quality which sometimes hides less attractive features or poor quality. *Television commercials might seem more professional but beware of mistaking the gloss for the content.* N-UNCOUNT

3 If you put **a gloss** on a bad situation, you try to make it seem more attractive or acceptable by giving people a false explanation or interpretation of it. *He used his diary to put a fine gloss on the horrors the regime perpetrated... The whole idea was to give history a happy gloss.* N-SING: *a* N, usu N *on* n

4 Gloss is the same as **gloss paint**. N-MASS

5 Gloss is a type of shiny makeup. *She brushed gloss on to her eyelids. ...lip glosses.* N-MASS

6 If you **gloss** a difficult word or idea, you provide an explanation of it. *Older editors glossed 'drynke' as 'love-potion'.* VERB V n *as* n Also V n

gloss over. If you **gloss over** a problem, a mistake, or an embarrassing moment, you try and make it seem unimportant by ignoring it or by dealing with it very quickly. *Some foreign governments appear happy to gloss over continued human rights abuses.* PHRASAL VERB V P n (not pron) Also V n P

glossary /glɒsəri, AM glɔːs-/ **glossaries.** A **glossary** of special, unusual, or technical words or expressions is an alphabetical list of them giving their meanings, for example at the end of a book on a particular subject. N-COUNT

glossies /glɒsiz, AM glɔːs-/. The **glossies** are expensive magazines for women which are printed on thick, glossy paper; an informal British word. N-PLURAL

gloss paint. **Gloss paint** is paint that forms a shiny surface when it dries. N-UNCOUNT

glossy /glɒsi, AM glɔːsi/ ◆◇◇◇◇

1 Glossy means smooth and shiny. *...glossy black hair... The leaves were dark and glossy.* ADJ-GRADED

2 You can describe something as **glossy** if you think that it has been designed to look attractive but is of little practical value or may have hidden defects. *...a glossy new office... British TV commercials are glossy and sophisticated.* ADJ-GRADED

3 Glossy magazines, brochures, books, and photographs are produced on expensive, shiny paper. *...a glossy magazine called 'Women Today'.* ADJ: ADJ n

glove /glʌv/ **gloves** ◆◆◇◇◇

1 Gloves are pieces of clothing which cover your hands and wrists and have individual sections for each finger. You wear gloves to keep your hands warm or dry or to protect them. *He stuck his gloves in his pocket. ...a pair of white cotton gloves.* N-COUNT

2 If you say that something **fits like a glove**, you are emphasizing that it fits exactly. PHRASE: V inflects PRAGMATICS

3 See also **kid gloves.** • **hand in glove**: see **hand**.

glove compartment, glove compartments. The **glove compartment** in a car is a small cupboard or shelf below the front windscreen. N-COUNT

gloved /glʌvd/. A **gloved** hand has a glove on it; used mainly in written English. *His gloved hand held up a computer disk.* ADJ: usu ADJ n

glow /gloʊ/ **glows, glowing, glowed** ◆◆◇◇◇

1 A **glow** is a dull, steady light, for example the light produced by a fire when there are no flames. *The cigarette's red glow danced about in the darkness... The rising sun casts a golden glow over the fields.* N-COUNT: usu sing

2 A **glow** is a pink colour on a person's face, usually because they are healthy or have been exercising. *The moisturiser gave my face a healthy glow that lasted all day.* N-SING: usu *a* N

3 If you feel a **glow** of satisfaction or achievement, you have a strong feeling of pleasure because of something that you have done or that has happened. *Exercise will give you a glow of satisfaction at having achieved something... He basked in the glow of adulation as US troops returned victorious from the Gulf War.* N-SING: oft N *of* n

4 If something **glows**, it produces a dull, steady light. *The night lantern glowed softly in the darkness... Even the mantel above the fire glowed white.* VERB V V adj

5 If a place **glows** with a colour or a quality, it is bright, attractive, and colourful. *Used together these colours will make your interiors glow with warmth and vitality. ...carved wood bathed in glowing colors and gold leaf.* VERB V *with* n V-ing Also V

6 If something **glows**, it looks bright because it is reflecting light. *The instruments glowed in the bright orange light... The fall foliage glowed red and yellow in the morning sunlight.* VERB V V adj

7 If someone's skin **glows**, it looks pink because they are healthy or excited, or have been doing physical exercise. *Her freckled skin glowed with health again. ...a glowing complexion.* VERB V *with* n V-ing Also V

8 If someone **glows** with an emotion such as pride or pleasure, the expression in their face shows how they feel. *The expectant mothers that Amy had encountered positively glowed with pride.* VERB V *with* n Also V

9 See also **glowing**.

glower /glaʊəʳ/ **glowers, glowering, glowered.** If you **glower** at someone or something, you look at them angrily. *He glowered at me but said nothing... He glowered and glared, but she steadfastly refused to look his way.* VERB =glare V *at* n V Also V adv/prep

glowering /glaʊərɪŋ/

1 If you describe a person as **glowering**, you mean they look angry and bad tempered; used in written English. *...his glowering good looks.* ADJ-GRADED: usu ADJ n

2 If you describe a place as **glowering**, you mean that it looks dark and threatening; used in written English. *...glowering castle walls.* ADJ-GRADED: usu ADJ n

glowing /gloʊɪŋ/. A **glowing** description or opinion about someone or something praises them highly or supports them strongly. *The media has been speaking in glowing terms of the relationship between the two countries... The premieres of his plays brought in glowing reviews.* ◆◇◇◇◇ ADJ-GRADED: usu ADJ n

glow-worm, glow-worms. In British English, a **glow-worm** is a type of beetle. The females and young glow-worms have special organs on their bodies which produce a greenish light. N-COUNT

glucose /gluːkoʊz, -oʊs/. **Glucose** is a type of sugar that gives you energy. ◆◇◇◇◇ N-UNCOUNT

glue /gluː/ **glues, glueing** or **gluing, glued** ◆◆◇◇◇

1 Glue is a sticky substance used for joining things together, often for repairing broken things. *...a tube of glue. ...high quality glues.* N-MASS

2 If you **glue** one object to another, you stick them together using glue. *Glue the fabric around the window... The material is cut and glued in place... They are glued together.* VERB V n prep/adv *be* V-ed *together*

3 If you say that someone **is glued to** something, you mean that they are giving it all their attention. *They are all glued to the Olympic Games.* • If you say that someone **keeps** their **eyes glued to** something, you mean that they are watching it with all their attention. *He kept his eyes glued to the clock.* V-PASSIVE *be* V-ed *to* n PHRASE: V inflects

glue sniffing. **Glue sniffing** is the dangerous practice of inhaling the vapour from glue in order to become intoxicated. N-UNCOUNT

glum /glʌm/ **glummer, glummest.** Someone who is **glum** is sad and quiet because they are disappointed or unhappy about something. *She was very glum and was obviously missing her children.* ♦ **glumly** *When Eleanor returned, I was still sitting glumly on the settee.* ◆◇◇◇◇ ADJ-GRADED: usu v-link ADJ =forlorn; ADV-GRADED: ADV with v

glut /glʌt/ **gluts, glutting, glutted** ◆◇◇◇◇
1 If there is a **glut** of something, there is so much of it that it cannot all be sold or used. *There's a glut of agricultural products in Western Europe. ...a world oil glut.* N-COUNT: usu sing, usu with supp =surplus
2 If a market **is glutted** with something, there is a glut of that thing. *The region is glutted with hospitals... 1948 was not a good year to be seeking employment. Soldiers returning from the war had glutted the job market.* VERB be V-ed with n, V n

glutamate /gluːtəmeɪt/. See **monosodium glutamate.**

gluten /gluːtᵊn/. **Gluten** is a substance found in cereal grains such as wheat. N-UNCOUNT

glutinous /gluːtɪnəs/. Something that is **glutinous** is very sticky. *The sauce was glutinous and tasted artificial. ...soft and glutinous mud.* ADJ-GRADED

glutton /glʌtᵊn/ **gluttons**
1 If you think that someone eats too much and is greedy, you can say they are a **glutton**. *I can't control my eating. It's hard when people don't understand and call you a glutton.* N-COUNT
2 If you say that someone is a **glutton for** something, you mean that they enjoy or need it very much. *He was a glutton for hard work... Ivy must be a glutton for punishment.* N-COUNT: N for n

gluttonous /glʌtənəs/. If you think that someone eats too much and is greedy, you can say they are **gluttonous**. *...a selfish, gluttonous and lazy person.* ADJ-GRADED

gluttony /glʌtəni/. **Gluttony** is the act or habit of eating too much and being greedy. *I was brought up to believe chocolate stimulated the sin of gluttony.* N-UNCOUNT

glycerine /glɪsərɪn/; spelled **glycerin** in American English. **Glycerine** is a thick, sweet, colourless liquid that is used especially in making medicine, explosives, and antifreeze for cars. N-UNCOUNT

gm, gms. The plural can be **gm** or **gms**. **gm** is a written abbreviation for **gram**. *...450 gm (1 lb) mixed soft summer fruits.* ◆◆◇◇◇

GMT /dʒiː em tiː/. **GMT** is an abbreviation for 'Greenwich Mean Time', the standard time in Great Britain which is used to calculate the time in the rest of the world. *New Mexico is seven hours behind GMT.* ◆◆◇◇◇

gnarled /nɑːʳld/
1 A **gnarled** tree is twisted and oddly shaped because it is old. *...a large and beautiful garden full of ancient gnarled trees.* ADJ-GRADED
2 If you describe someone as **gnarled**, you mean they look very old because their skin is wrinkled or rough, or their body is bent or twisted. If someone has **gnarled** hands, their hands are twisted as a result of old age or illness. *...gnarled old men... His hands were gnarled with arthritis.* ADJ-GRADED

gnash /næʃ/ **gnashes, gnashing, gnashed.** If you say that someone **is gnashing** their **teeth**, you mean they are angry or frustrated about something. *If Blythe heard that piece, I bet he was gnashing his teeth... If you couldn't attend either of the concerts and are currently gnashing your teeth at having missed out, don't despair... There will be wailing and gnashing of teeth whatever criteria the Arts Council employ for this exercise.* PHRASE: V inflects

gnat /næt/ **gnats.** A **gnat** is a very small flying insect that bites people and usually lives near water. N-COUNT

gnaw /nɔː/ **gnaws, gnawing, gnawed** ◆◇◇◇◇
1 If people or animals **gnaw** something or **gnaw** at it, they bite it repeatedly. *Woodlice attack living plants and gnaw at the stems... Melanie gnawed a long, painted fingernail.* VERB V at/on n, V n
2 If a feeling or thought **gnaws at** you, it causes you to keep worrying; a literary use. *Doubts were already gnawing away at the back of his mind... Mary Ann's exhilaration gave way to gnawing fear.* VERB =nag, V at n, V-ing

gnome /noʊm/ **gnomes.** In children's stories, a **gnome** is an imaginary creature that is like a tiny old man with a beard and pointed hat. In Britain people sometimes have small statues of gnomes in their gardens. ◆◇◇◇◇ N-COUNT

gnomic /noʊmɪk/. A **gnomic** remark is brief and seems wise but is difficult to understand; used in written English. *In the gnomic words of Wittgenstein, 'The human body is the best picture of the human soul'.* ADJ-GRADED: usu ADJ n

GNP /dʒiː en piː/ **GNPs.** In economics, a country's **GNP** is the total value of all the goods produced and services provided by that country in one year. **GNP** is an abbreviation for 'Gross National Product'. *By 1973 the government deficit equalled thirty per cent of GNP.* ◆◆◇◇◇ N-VAR

gnu /nuː/ **gnus.** A **gnu** is a large African antelope. N-COUNT

go 1 moving or leaving

go /goʊ/ **goes, going, went, gone** ◆◆◆◆◆
In most cases the past participle of **go** is **gone**, but occasionally you use 'been': see **been**.
1 When you **go** somewhere, you move or travel there. *We went to Rome... Gladys had just gone into the kitchen... I went home at the weekend... Four of them had gone off to find help... It took us an hour to go three miles.* VERB V prep/adv, V amount
2 When you **go**, you leave the place where you are. *Let's go... She's going tomorrow.* VERB V
3 You use **go** to say that someone leaves the place where they are and does an activity, often a leisure activity. *We went swimming very early... Maybe they've just gone shopping... He went for a walk.* VERB V -ing, V for n
4 When someone **goes** to do something, they move somewhere in order to do it, and they do it. In British English, someone can also **go and** do something. In American English, someone can also **go** do something, but you say that someone **went and** did something. *His second son, Paddy, had gone to live in Canada... I must go and see this film... Go ask whoever you want.* VERB V to-inf, V and v, V inf
5 If you **go to** school, work, or church, you attend it regularly as part of your normal life. *She will have to go to school... His son went to a top university in America.* VERB V to n
6 When you say where a road or path **goes**, you are saying where it begins or ends, or what places it is in. *There's a mountain road that goes from Blairstown to Millbrook Village.* VERB =lead, V prep/adv
7 You can use **go** in expressions such as **'don't go telling everybody'**, in order to express disapproval of the kind of behaviour you mention, or to tell someone not to behave in that way. *You don't have to go running upstairs every time she rings... Don't you go thinking it was your fault.* VB: with brd-neg, PRAGMATICS, V -ing
8 You can use **go** to indicate how extreme an action, idea, or result is, or what level it reaches or passes. For example, you can say that an action **goes further than** something else or **goes beyond** it to indicate that it is more extreme or reaches a higher level. *He went even further in his speech to the conference... Some physicists have gone so far as to suggest that the entire Universe is a sort of gigantic computer.* VERB V adv/prep
9 If you say that a period of time **goes** quickly or slowly, you mean that it seems to pass quickly or slowly. *The weeks go so quickly!* VERB =pass, V adv
10 If you say where money **goes**, you are saying what it is spent on. *Most of my money goes on bills... The money goes to projects chosen by the wider community.* VERB V prep/adv
11 If you say that something **goes to** someone, you mean that it is given to them. *A lot of credit must go to the chairman and his father... The job went to Yuri Skokov, a capable administrator.* VERB V to n
12 If someone **goes on** television or radio, they take part in a television or radio programme. *The Turkish president has gone on television to defend strin-* VERB V on n

gent new security measures... We went on the air, live, at 7.30.*

13 If something **goes**, someone gets rid of it. *The Institute of Export now fears that 100,000 jobs will go... If people stand firm against the tax, it is only a matter of time before it has to go.* VERB V

14 If someone **goes**, they leave their job, usually because they are forced to. *He had made a humiliating tactical error and he had to go.* VERB V

15 If something **goes into** something else, it is put in it as one of the parts or elements that form it. *...the really interesting ingredients that go into the dishes that we all love to eat.* VERB V *into/in* n

16 If something **goes** in a particular place, it fits in that place or should be put there because it is the right size or shape. *He was trying to push it through the hole and it wouldn't go. ...This knob goes here.* VERB V; V prep/adv

17 If something **goes** in a particular place, it belongs there or should be put there, because that is where you normally keep it. *The shoes go on the shoe shelf... 'Where does everything go?'* VERB V prep/adv

18 If you say that one number **goes into** another number a particular number of times, you are dividing the second number by the first. *Six goes into thirty five times.* VERB V *into* num; Also V num

19 If one of a person's faculties, such as their sight or hearing, **is going**, it is getting weak and they may soon lose it completely. *His eyes are going; he says he has glaucoma... Lately he'd been making mistakes; his nerve was beginning to go.* VERB =fail; V

20 If something such as a light bulb or a part of an engine **is going**, it is no longer working properly and will soon need to be replaced. *I thought it looked as though the battery was going.* VERB V

21 If you say that someone **is going** or **has gone** you are saying in a gentle, indirect way that they are dying or are dead. *'Any hope?'—'No, he's gone.'* VERB V

go 2 link verb uses

go /gəʊ/ **goes, going, went, gone** ◆◆◆◆◆

1 You can use **go** to say that someone or something changes to another state or condition. For example, if someone **goes crazy**, they become crazy, and if something **goes green**, it changes colour and becomes green. *I'm going bald... You'd better serve it to them before it goes cold... 50,000 companies have gone out of business.* V-LINK V adj; V prep

2 You can use **go** when indicating whether or not someone wears or has something. For example, if someone **goes barefoot**, they do not wear any shoes. *The baby went naked on the beach... But if you arm the police won't more criminals go armed?* V-LINK V adj

3 You can use **go** to say that something does not have a particular thing done to it. For example, if something **goes unheard**, nobody hears it, and if it **goes unseen**, nobody sees it. *As President, he affirmed that no tyranny went unnoticed.* V-LINK V -ed

go 3 other verb uses, noun uses, and phrases

go /gəʊ/ **goes, going, went, gone** ◆◆◆◆◆

1 You use **go** to talk about how successful an event or situation is. For example, if you say that an event or situation **went well**, you mean that it was successful, and if you ask how something **is going**, you are asking how much success people are having with it. *She says everything is going smoothly... How did it go at the hairdresser's?* VERB V adv

2 If a machine or device **is going**, it is working. *What about my copier? Can you get it going again?... You do not want to get stuck on the motorway with a car that won't go.* VERB V

3 If a bell **goes**, it makes a noise, usually as a signal for you to do something. *The bell went for the break.* VERB V

4 If something **goes with** something else, or if two things **go together**, they look or taste nice together. *I was searching for a pair of grey gloves to go with my new gown... I can see that some colours go together and some don't... Wear something else. This won't go.* V-RECIP V *with* n; pl-n V *together*; V (non-recip); Also V

5 You use **go** to introduce something you are quoting. For example, you say **the story goes** or **the argument goes** just before you quote all or part of it. *The story goes that she went home with him that night... The story goes like this... As the saying goes, 'There's no smoke without fire.'.* VERB V that; V prep; V with quote

6 You use **go** when indicating that something makes or produces a sound. For example, if you say that something **goes 'bang'**, you mean it produces the sound 'bang'. *She stopped in front of a painting of a dog and she started going 'woof woof'... His back tyre just went 'pop' on a motorway.* VERB V with sound

7 You can use **go** instead of 'say' when you are quoting what someone has said or what you think they will say; an informal use. *They say 'Tom, shut up' and I go 'No, you shut up'... He goes to me: 'Oh, what do you want?'* VERB V with quote; V *to* n with quote

8 A **go** is an attempt at doing something. *I always wanted to have a go at football... She won on her first go... Her hair was bright orange. It took us two goes to get the colour right.* N-COUNT: oft N *at* n/-ing =try

9 If it is your **go** in a game, it is your turn to do something, for example to play a card or move a piece. *I'm two behind you but it's your go... Now whose go is it?* N-COUNT: poss N =turn

10 See also **going, gone**.

11 If you **go all out** to do something or **go all out** for something, you make the greatest possible effort to do it or get it; an informal expression. *They will go all out to get exactly what they want... They're ready to go all out for the Premier League title next season.* PHRASES V inflects, PHR to-inf, PHR *for* n

12 If people say **'anything goes'**, they mean that anything people say or do is considered acceptable, and usually they mean that they do not approve of this. *In the 90s, almost anything goes.*

13 You use expressions like **as things go** or **as bosses go** when you are describing one person or thing and comparing them with other things of the same kind; an informal expression. *This is a straightforward case, as these things go... He's good company, as small boys go.* PHR with cl

14 If you do something **as** you **go along**, you do it gradually, without preparing it beforehand. *Learning how to become a parent takes time. It's a skill you learn as you go along.* PHR after v

15 If you say that someone **has gone and done** something, you are expressing your annoyance at the foolish thing they have done. *Well, he's gone and done it again, hasn't he?... Somebody goes and does something mindless like that and just destroys everything for you.* V s inflect PRAGMATICS

16 If you say **'Go for it'** to someone, you are encouraging them to increase their efforts to achieve or win something; an informal expression. CONVENTION PRAGMATICS

17 If someone **has a go at** you, they criticize you, often in a way that you feel is unfair; used mainly in informal British English. *Some people had a go at us for it, which made us more angry.* V inflects, PHR n

18 If someone asks **'Where do we go from here?'** they are asking what should be done next, usually because a problem has not been solved very satisfactorily. CONVENTION

19 If you say that someone is **making a go of** something such as a business or relationship, you mean that they are having some success with it. *I knew we could make a go of it and be happy.* V inflects, PHR n

20 If you say that someone is always **on the go**, you mean that they are always busy and active; used mainly in informal British English. *I got a new job this year where I am on the go all the time.* usu v-link PHR, PHR after v

21 If you **have** something **on the go**, you have started it and are busy doing it. *Do you like to have many projects on the go at any one time?* V inflects, usu PHR after v

22 You can say **'My heart goes out to him'** or **'My sympathy goes out to her'** to express the strong sympathy you have for someone in a difficult or unpleasant situation. *My heart goes out to Mrs Adams and her fatherless children.* V inflects

23 If you say that there are a particular number of things **to go**, you mean that they still remain to be dealt with. *I still had another five operations to go.* amount PHR

24 If you say that there is a certain amount of time **to go**, you mean that there is that amount of time left before something happens or ends. *There is a week to go until the first German elections.* amount PHR, oft PHR prep

25 If you are in a cafe or restaurant and ask for an n PHR item of food **to go**, you mean that you want to take it away with you and not eat it there. *Large fries to go.*

go 4 phrasal verbs

go /gou/ **goes, going, went, gone** ◆◆◆◆◆

go about PHRASAL VERB

1 The way you **go about** a task or problem is the way you approach it and deal with it. *I want him back, but I just don't know how to go about it.* =approach V P n/-ing

2 When you **are going about** your normal activities, you are doing them. *We were simply going about our business when we were pounced upon by these police officers.* V P n

3 If you **go about** in a particular way, you behave or dress in that way, often as part of your normal life. *He used to go about in a black cape... He went about looking ill and unhappy.* =go around V P prep V P -ing

go after. If you **go after** something, you try to get it, catch it, or hit it. *We're not going after civilian targets.* PHRASAL VERB V P n

go against PHRASAL VERB

1 If a person or their behaviour **goes against** your wishes, beliefs, or expectations, their behaviour is the opposite of what you want, believe in, or expect. *Changes are being made here which go against my principles and I cannot agree with them.* V P n

2 If a decision, vote, or result **goes against** you, you do not get the decision, vote, or result that you wanted. *The prime minister will resign if the vote goes against him... Everything began to go against us.* V P n

go ahead PHRASAL VERB

1 If someone **goes ahead** with something, they begin to do it or make it, especially after planning, promising, or asking permission to do it. *The district board will vote today on whether to go ahead with the plan.* =proceed V P *with* n Also V P

2 If a process or an organized event **goes ahead**, it takes place or is carried out. *The event will go ahead as planned in Sheffield next summer.* V P

go along PHRASAL VERB

1 If you **go along** to a meeting, event, or place, you attend or visit it. *I went along to the meeting... You should go along and have a look.* V P *to* n V P *and* inf

2 If you describe how something **is going along**, you describe how it is progressing. *Things were going along fairly well.* usu cont V P adv

go along with PHRASAL VERB

1 If you **go along with** a rule, decision, or policy, you accept it and obey it. *The main political parties in Cambodia are likely to go along with the plan.* V P P n

2 If you **go along with** a person or an idea, you agree with them. *'I don't think a government has properly done it for about the past twenty-five years.'—'I'd go along with that.'* V P P n

go around or **go round** PHRASAL VERB

1 If you **go around** or **go round** to someone's house, you go to visit them at their house; used mainly in British English. *I asked them to go around to the house to see if they were there... Mike went round to see them.* V P *to* n V P to-inf

2 If you **go around** or **go round** in a particular way, you behave or dress in that way, often as part of your normal life. *I had got in the habit of going around with bare feet... If they went around complaining publicly, they might not find it so easy to get another job.* V P prep V P -ing Also V P adj

3 If a piece of news or a joke **is going around** or **going round**, it is being told by many people in the same period of time. *There's a nasty sort of rumour going around about it.* =circulate V P

4 If there is enough of something to **go around** or **go round**, there is enough of it to be shared among a group of people, or to do all the things for which it is needed. *Meat cannot be rationed, because there would still not be enough to go around.* V P

go around with or **go round with.** If you **go around with** or **go round with** a person or group of people, you regularly meet them and go to different places with them; used mainly in British English. *I went around with them, but never felt like one of them.* PHRASAL VERB =hang around V P P n

go at. If you **go at** a task or activity, you start doing it in an energetic, enthusiastic way. *He sank the spade into the ground, and went at it.* PHRASAL VERB V P n

go away PHRASAL VERB

1 If you **go away**, you leave a place or a person's company. *I think we need to go away and think about this.* V P

2 If you **go away**, you leave a place and spend a period of time somewhere else, especially as a holiday. *When you go away on holiday, you need to take extra security precautions... Why don't you and I go away this weekend?* V P

go back PHRASAL VERB

1 If something **goes back** to a particular time in the past, it was made or started at that time. *The feud with the Catholics goes back to the 11th century... Our association with him goes back four years.* V P *to* n V P n

2 If someone **goes back** to a time in the past, they begin to discuss or consider events that happened at that time. *If you go back to 1960, you'll find that very few jobs were being created.* V P *to* n Also V P n

go back on. If you **go back on** a promise or agreement, you do not do what you promised or agreed to do. *The budget crisis has forced the President to go back on his word.* PHRASAL VERB V P P n

go back to PHRASAL VERB

1 If you **go back to** a task or activity, you start doing it again after you have stopped doing it for a period of time. *I now look forward to going back to work as soon as possible... Amy went back to studying.* V P P n/-ing

2 If you **go back to** a particular point in a lecture, discussion, or book, you start to discuss it. *Let me just go back to the point I was making.* V P P n

go before PHRASAL VERB

1 Something that has **gone before** has happened or been discussed at an earlier time. *This is a rejection of most of what has gone before.* V P

2 When people, problems, or cases **go before** a judge, tribunal, or court of law, they are brought or discussed there as part of an official or legal process. *The case went before Mr Justice Henry on December 23 and was adjourned.* V P n

go by PHRASAL VERB

1 If you say that time **goes by**, you mean that it passes. *My grandmother was becoming more and more sad and frail as the years went by.* =go on V P

2 If you **go by** something, you use it as a basis for a judgement or action. *If they prove that I was wrong, then I'll go by what they say.* V P n

go down PHRASAL VERB

1 If a price, level, or amount **goes down**, it becomes lower or less than it was. *Income from sales tax went down... Crime has gone down 70 percent... Average life expectancy went down from about 70 to 67.7.* =fall V P V P amount V P *from/to/by* n

2 If you **go down** on your knees or on all fours, you lower your body until it is supported by your knees, or by your hands and knees. *I went down on my knees and prayed for guidance.* =get down V P *on* n

3 In sport, if a person or team **goes down**, they are defeated in a match or contest. *They went down 2-1 to Australia.* =lose V P num Also V P

4 In sport, if a team **goes down**, they move to a lower division in a league; used in British English. *Only two go down at the end of this season.* ≠go up V P

5 If you say that a remark, idea, or type of behaviour **goes down** in a particular way, you mean that it gets a particular kind of reaction from a person or group of people. *Solicitors advised their clients that a tidy look went down well with the magistrates.* V P adv

6 When the sun **goes down**, it goes below the horizon. *...the glow left in the sky after the sun has gone down.* =set V P

7 If a ship **goes down**, it sinks. If a plane **goes down**, it crashes out of the sky. *Their aircraft went down during a training exercise.* V P

8 If a computer **goes down**, it stops functioning temporarily. *The main computers went down for 30 minutes.* V P

go down as. If you say that an event or action PHRASAL VERB will **go down as** a particular thing, you mean that it will be regarded, remembered, or recorded as that thing. *It will go down as one of the highlights of my* VPPn *career... The riots of the early '80s must go down as a significant event in British history.*

go down with. If you **go down with** an illness or PHRASAL VERB a disease, you catch it; an informal expression. =catch VPPn *Three members of the band went down with flu.*

go for PHRASAL VERB

1 If you **go for** a particular thing or way of doing =select something, you choose it. *People tried to persuade* VPn *him to go for a more gradual reform programme.*

2 If you **go for** someone or something, you like them very much; an informal use. *I tend to go for* VPn *large dark men.*

3 If you **go for** someone, you attack them. *Pantieri* VPn *went for him, gripping him by the throat.*

4 If you say that a statement you have made about one person or thing also **goes for** another person or thing, you mean that the statement is also true of this other person or thing. *It is illegal to dishon-* VPn *our bookings; that goes for restaurants as well as customers.*

go in. If the sun **goes in**, a cloud comes in front of PHRASAL VERB it and it can no longer be seen. *The sun went in,* VP *and the breeze became cold.*

go in for. If you **go in for** a particular activity, you PHRASAL VERB decide to do it as a hobby or interest. *They go in for* VPPn *tennis and bowls.*

go into PHRASAL VERB

1 If you **go into** something, you describe or examine it fully or in detail. *It was a private conversation* VPn *and I don't want to go into details about what was said.*

2 If you **go into** something, you decide to do it as your job or career. *Mr Pok has now gone into the* VPn *tourism business.*

3 If an amount of time, effort, or money **goes into** something, it is spent or used to do it, get it, or make it. *Is there a lot of effort and money going into* VPn *this sort of research?*

go off PHRASAL VERB

1 If you **go off** someone or something, you stop liking them; used mainly in informal British English. VPn *'Why have they gone off him now?'—'It could be something he said.'... I started to go off the idea.*

2 If an explosive device or a gun **goes off**, it explodes or fires. *A few minutes later the bomb went* VP *off, destroying the vehicle.*

3 If an alarm bell **goes off**, it makes a sudden loud noise. *Then the fire alarm went off. I just grabbed* VP *my clothes and ran out.*

4 If an electrical device **goes off**, it stops operating. VP *As the water came in the windows, all the lights went off.*

5 If you say how an organized event **went off**, you are saying whether everything happened in the way that was planned or hoped. *The meeting went* VP adv/prep *off all right... The voting went off without any undue irregularities.*

6 Food or drink that has **gone off** has become stale, sour, or rotten; used mainly in British English. VP *Don't eat that! It's mouldy. It's gone off!*

go off with PHRASAL VERB

1 If someone **goes off with** another person, they leave their husband, wife, or lover and have a relationship with that person. *I suppose Carolyn went* VPPn *off with some man she'd fallen in love with.*

2 If someone **goes off with** something that belongs to someone else, they leave a place and take it with them. *He's gone off with my passport.* VPPn

go on PHRASAL VERB

1 If you **go on** doing something, or **go on with** an =continue activity, you continue to do it. *Unemployment is* VP-ing *likely to go on rising this year... I'm all right here. Go* VP *with*n VP *on with your work... I don't want to leave, but I can't go on.*

2 If something **is going on**, it is happening. *While* =take place VP *this conversation was going on, I was listening with earnest attention... I don't know what's going on.*

3 If a process or institution **goes on**, it continues to =continue happen or exist. *The population failed to under-* VP *stand the necessity for the war to go on.*

4 If you say that a period of time **goes on**, you mean =go by that it passes. *Renewable energy will become pro-* VP *gressively more important as time goes on.*

5 If you **go on** to do something, you do it after you have done something else. *Alliss retired from golf* VP to-inf *in 1969 and went on to become a successful broadcaster... She went on to say that she had discussed it with the Canadian foreign minister.*

6 If you **go on** to a place, you go to it from the place that you have reached. *He goes on to Holland to-* VP prep/adv *morrow.*

7 If you **go on**, you continue saying something or talking about something. *Meer cleared his throat* VP *several times before he went on... 'Go on,' Chee said.* VP with quote *'I'm interested.'*

8 If you **go on about** something, or in British English **go on at** someone, you continue talking about the same thing, often in an annoying way; an informal use. *Expectations have been raised with the* VP *about*n *Government going on about choice and market* VP *at*n to-inf Also VP *at*n *forces... She's always going on at me to have a baby.*

9 In informal English, you say **'Go on'** to someone only imper to persuade or encourage them to do something. PRAGMATICS VP *Go on, it's fun.*

10 If you talk about the information you have to **go on**, you mean the information you have available to base an opinion or judgement on. *But you have* VPn *to go on the facts... There's not much to go on.*

11 If an electrical device **goes on**, it begins operat- =come on ing. *A light went on at seven every evening.* VP

go out PHRASAL VERB

1 If you **go out**, you leave your home in order to do ≠stay in something enjoyable, for example to go to a party, a bar, or the cinema. *I'm going out tonight.* VP

2 If you **go out** with someone, the two of you spend RECIP time together socially, and have a romantic or sexual relationship. *I once went out with a French* VP *with*n *man... They've only been going out for six weeks.* pl-n VP

3 If you **go out** to do something, you make a deliberate effort to do it. *You do not go out to injure op-* VP to-inf *ponents... It will be a marvellous occasion and they* VP *and*inf *should go out and enjoy it.*

4 If a light **goes out**, it stops shining. *The bedroom* VP *light went out after a moment.*

5 If something that is burning **goes out**, it stops burning. *The fire seemed to be going out.* VP

6 If a message **goes out**, it is announced, published, or sent out to people. *Word went out that a* VP *column of tanks was on its way.*

7 When a television or radio programme **goes out**, it is broadcast; used mainly in British English. *The* VP *series goes out at 10.30pm, Fridays, on Channel 4.*

8 If a type of thing **goes out**, it ceases to exist or be used, usually because it is replaced by something else. *Miners are not unskilled: wielding picks went* VP *out years ago... The weapons had gone out of use.* VP *of*n

9 When the tide **goes out**, the water in the sea ≠come in gradually moves back to a lower level. *The tide was* VP *going out.*

go out of. If a quality or feeling **goes out of** some- PHRASAL VERB one or something, they no longer have it. *The fun* VPPn *had gone out of it.*

go over. If you **go over** a document, incident, or PHRASAL VERB problem, you examine, discuss, or think about it very carefully and systematically. *I won't know* VPn *how successful it is until an accountant has gone over the books.*

go over to PHRASAL VERB

1 If someone or something **goes over to** a different way of doing things, they change to it. *The Armed* VPPn *Forces could do away with conscription and go over to a volunteer system.*

2 If you **go over to** a group or political party, you =defect to join them after previously belonging to an opposing group or party. *Only a small number of tanks* VPPn *and paratroops have gone over to his side.*

go round. **Go round** means the same as **go** PHRASAL VERB **around**.

go through PHRASAL VERB

1 If you **go through** an experience or a period of

time, especially an unpleasant or difficult one, you experience it. *He was going through a very difficult time... South Africa was going through a period of irreversible change.* VPn

2 If you **go through** a lot of things such as papers or clothes, you look at them, usually in order to sort them into groups or to search for a particular item. *It was evident that someone had gone through my possessions.* VPn

3 If you **go through** a list, story, or plan, you read or check it from beginning to end. *Going through his list of customers is a massive job.* VPn

4 When someone **goes through** a routine, procedure, or series of actions, they perform it in the way they usually do. *Every night, they go through the same routine: he throws open the bedroom window, she closes it.* VPn

5 If a law, agreement, or official decision **goes through**, it is approved by a parliament or committee. *The bill might have gone through if the economy was growing.* =get through VP

go through with. If you **go through with** an action you have decided on, you do it, even though it may be very unpleasant or difficult for you. *Richard pleaded for Belinda to reconsider and not to go through with the divorce.* PHRASAL VERB VPPn

go towards. If an amount of money **goes towards** something, it is used to pay part of the cost of that thing. *One per cent of total public spending should eventually go towards the arts... Half of the money will go towards paying for the United States' presence in the Gulf.* PHRASAL VERB VPn/-ing

go under PHRASAL VERB

1 If a business or project **goes under**, it becomes unable to continue in operation or in existence. *If one firm goes under it could provoke a cascade of bankruptcies.* =fail VP

2 If a boat, ship, or person in a sea or river **goes under**, they sink below the surface of the water. *The ship went under, taking with her all her crew.* =sink VP

go up PHRASAL VERB

1 If a price, amount, or level **goes up**, it becomes higher or greater than it was. *Interest rates went up... The cost has gone up to $1.95 a minute... Prices have gone up 61 percent since deregulation.* =rise VP VP *to/from/by* n VP amount

2 When a building, wall, or other structure **goes up**, it is built or fixed in place. *He noticed a new building going up near Whitaker Park.* VP

3 If something **goes up**, it explodes or starts to burn, usually suddenly and with great intensity. *I was going to get out of the building in case it went up... The hotel went up in flames.* VP VP *in*n

4 If a shout or cheer **goes up**, it is made by a lot of people together. *A cheer went up from the other passengers.* =rise VP

5 In sport, if a team **goes up**, they move to a higher division in a league; used in British English. *I fancy Leicester to go up.* ≠go down VP

go with PHRASAL VERB

1 If one thing **goes with** another thing, the two things officially belong together, so that if you get one, you also get the other. *...the lucrative £150,000 salary that goes with the job.* =accompany VPn

2 If one thing **goes with** another thing, it is usually found or experienced together with the other thing. *It takes away some of the stigma that goes with being on the dole.* VPn

3 If someone **goes with** another person, they have sex with that person; an informal use. VPn

go without. If you **go without** something that you need or usually have or do, you do not get it or do it. *I have known what it is like to go without food for days... The embargo won't hurt us because we're used to going without.* PHRASAL VERB VPn/-ing VP

goad /goʊd/ **goads, goading, goaded** ◆◇◇◇◇

1 If you **goad** someone, you deliberately make them feel angry or irritated, often causing them to react by doing something. *He wondered if the psychiatrist was trying to goad him into some unguarded response... Charles was always goading me.* ► Also a noun. *Her presence was just one more goad to Joanna's unravelling nerves.* VERB Vn *into*n/-ing Vn N-COUNT

2 If you describe something as a **goad**, you mean it makes someone do something or react in some way. *This activity happens on account of the goad of a cold climate.* N-SING =spur

3 A **goad** is a sharp, pointed stick that is used for driving cattle. N-COUNT

go-ahead ◆◆◇◇◇

1 If you give someone **the go-ahead**, or give **the go-ahead** to a plan or project, you give permission or approval to someone to start doing something. *The Greek government today gave the go-ahead for five major road schemes.* N-SING: *the*N

2 A **go-ahead** person or organization is ambitious and tries hard to succeed, often by using new methods; used mainly in British English. *Fairview Estate is one of the oldest and the most go-ahead wine producers in South Africa.* ADJ-GRADED: ADJ n

goal /goʊl/ **goals** ◆◆◆◆◇

1 In games such as football or hockey, the **goal** is the space into which the players try to get the ball in order to score a point for their team. *The Spaniards put all their strokes past Mason in the England goal to emerge 5-4 winners.* N-COUNT

2 In games such as football or hockey, a **goal** is an instance in which a player gets the ball into the goal, or the point that is scored by doing this. *They scored five goals in the first half of the match... The scorer of the winning goal.* N-COUNT

3 Something that is your **goal** is something that you hope to achieve, especially when much time and effort will be needed. *It's a matter of setting your own goals and following them... The goal is to raise as much money as possible.* N-COUNT =target

goalie /goʊli/ **goalies.** A **goalie** is a goalkeeper; an informal word. N-COUNT =goalkeeper

goalkeeper /goʊlkiːpəʳ/ **goalkeepers.** A **goalkeeper** is the player in a sports team whose job is to guard the goal. ◆◆◇◇◇ N-COUNT =goalie

goalkeeping /goʊlkiːpɪŋ/. In games such as football and hockey, **goalkeeping** refers to the activity of playing in goal. *They were thankful for the excellent goalkeeping of John Lukic.* N-UNCOUNT

goalless /goʊlləs/. In soccer, a **goalless** draw is a match which ends with neither team having scored a goal. *The fixture ended in a goalless draw... The semi-final finished goalless after extra time.* ADJ

goal line, goal lines; also spelled **goal-line.** In games such as football and hockey, a **goal line** is one of the lines at each end of the pitch on which the goalposts stand. N-COUNT

goalmouth /goʊlmaʊθ/ **goalmouths.** In soccer, the **goalmouth** is the area just in front of the goal. N-COUNT

goalpost /goʊlpoʊst/ **goalposts;** also spelled **goal post.**

1 A **goalpost** is one of the two upright wooden posts that are connected by a crossbar and form the goal in games such as football and hockey. N-COUNT

2 If you accuse someone of **moving the goalposts**, you mean that they have changed the rules in a situation or an activity, especially to benefit themselves and to make the situation or activity harder for everyone else involved; used showing disapproval. *They seem to move the goal posts every time I meet the conditions which are required.* PHRASE: V inflects PRAGMATICS

goat /goʊt/ **goats.** A **goat** is a farm animal or a wild animal that is about the size of a sheep. Goats have horns, and hairs on their chin which resemble a beard. ◆◆◇◇◇ N-COUNT

goat cheese, goat cheeses; also spelled **goat's cheese. Goat cheese** is cheese made from goat's milk. N-MASS

goatee /goʊtiː/ **goatees.** A **goatee** is a very short pointed beard that a man wears on his chin but not on his cheeks. N-COUNT

gob /gɒb/ **gobs, gobbing, gobbed**

1 In British English, a person's **gob** is their mouth; a informal use which some people find offensive. *Shut your gob.* N-COUNT

2 A **gob** of a thick, unpleasant liquid is a small amount of it; an informal use. *...a gob of spit.* N-COUNT: N *of*n

3 If someone **gobs**, they spit; used in informal British English. *At a concert in Leeds, some punks gobbed at them and threw beer cans.*
[VERB; V prep; Also V]

gobbet /gɒbɪt/ **gobbets**
1 A **gobbet** of something soft, especially food, is a small lump or piece of it. *...gobbets of meat.*
[N-COUNT]
2 A **gobbet** of information is a small piece of it.
[N-COUNT]

gobble /gɒbᵊl/ **gobbles, gobbling, gobbled.** If you **gobble** food, you eat it quickly and greedily. *Pete gobbled all the beef stew.* ► **Gobble down** and **gobble up** mean the same as **gobble**. *There were dangerous beasts in the river that might gobble you up.*
[◆◇◇◇◇; VERB; V n; PHRASAL VERB; V n P; Also V P n (not pron)]

gobble down. See **gobble**.
[PHRASAL VERB]

gobble up
[PHRASAL VERB]
1 If a group or organization **gobbles up** a smaller group or organization, it takes control of it or destroys it. *Banc One of Ohio has built an empire in the mid-west by gobbling up smaller banks.*
[V P n (not pron); Also V n P]
2 If someone or something **gobbles up** something such as money, they use or waste a lot of it. *The firm's expenses gobbled up 44% of revenues.*
[V P n (not pron); Also V n P]
3 See also **gobble**.

gobbledygook /gɒbᵊldiguːk/; also spelled **gobbledegook**. If you describe a speech or piece of writing as **gobbledygook**, you mean that it seems like nonsense to you because it uses official, technical, or complicated language, an informal word; used showing disapproval. *When he asked questions, the answers came back in Wall Street gobbledygook.*
[N-UNCOUNT; PRAGMATICS]

go-between, go-betweens. A **go-between** is a person who takes messages between people who are unable or unwilling to meet each other. *He will act as a go-between to try and work out an agenda.*
[◆◇◇◇◇; N-COUNT; =intermediary]

goblet /gɒblɪt/ **goblets.** A **goblet** is a type of cup without handles and usually with a long stem.
[N-COUNT]

goblin /gɒblɪn/ **goblins.** In fairy stories, a **goblin** is a small, ugly creature which usually enjoys causing trouble.
[N-COUNT]

gobsmacked /gɒbsmækt/. If you say that you were **gobsmacked** by something, you are emphasizing how amazed and surprised you were by it; an informal word, used in British English. *I was really gobsmacked when I saw your picture of a model wearing a hat with a toy airplane on it.*
[ADJ-GRADED; PRAGMATICS; =stunned]

god /gɒd/ **gods**
[◆◆◆◆◇]
1 The name **God** is given to the spirit or being who is worshipped as the creator and ruler of the world, especially by Jews, Christians, and Muslims. *He believes in God... God bless you.*
[N-PROPER]
2 People sometimes use **God** in exclamations to emphasize something that they are saying, or to express surprise, fear, or excitement. Some people find this offensive. *God, how I hated him!... Oh my God he's shot somebody... Good God, it's Mr Harper!... God Almighty, Hart, you scared me silly.*
[CONVENTION]
3 In many religions, a **god** is one of the spirits or beings that are believed to have power over a particular part of the world or nature. *...Pan, the God of nature. ...Zeus, king of the gods.*
[N-COUNT]
4 Someone who is admired very much by a person or group of people, and who influences them a lot, can be referred to as a **god**. *To his followers he was a god.*
[N-COUNT]
5 see also **act of God**.
6 If you say **God forbid**, you are expressing your hope that something will not happen. *If, God forbid, something goes wrong, I don't know what I would do.*
[PHRASES; PHR with cl; PRAGMATICS; =heaven forbid]
7 If you say that a person or thing is **God's gift to** someone or something, you approve of them because you think they are good for them; an informal use. You can say that a person thinks they are **God's gift to** someone else, if you disapprove of that person because they are arrogant and conceited; an informal use. *Technology is God's gift to all nations alike... Are men god's gift to women? Some of them think they are.*
[v-link PHR; PRAGMATICS]
8 If you want to say that something unpleasant will happen to someone if they do a particular thing, you can say **God help them**. If you want to warn someone not to do a particular thing because something unpleasant will happen to them if they do it, you can say **God help you**; an informal expression. *God help him if he gets in my way... The boss says you must wear a tie. And God help you if you don't.*
[PHR n; PRAGMATICS; =heaven help]
9 If you feel sorry for someone because they are in a difficult or unpleasant situation, especially if you think that nobody can help them, you can say **God help them**; an informal expression. *'God help them,' he said. 'They're beyond help.'*
[PHR n; =heaven help]
10 If you say **God help us**, you mean that you have negative feelings about the person or situation you are talking about; an informal expression. *Where is the rising star with the talent to replace the Beatles or Dylan or even, God help us, Madonna?*
[PHR with cl; PRAGMATICS; =heaven help]
11 You can say **God knows**, **God only knows**, or **God alone knows** when you do not know something, in order to emphasize that you feel annoyed, angry, worried, surprised, or disappointed by it. *Gunga spoke God knows how many languages... God alone knows what she thinks.*
[PHR wh; PRAGMATICS]
12 If someone says **God knows** in reply to a question that they do not know the answer to, they are emphasising how angry, annoyed, or disappointed they feel. *'Where is he now?' 'God knows.'*
[PRAGMATICS]
13 The term **a man of God** is sometimes used to refer to Christian priests or ministers. *I am a man of God.*
14 If someone uses such expressions as **what in God's name**, **why in God's name**, or **how in God's name**, they are emphasizing how angry, annoyed, or surprised they are; an informal expression. *What in God's name do you expect me to do?... Why in God's name did you have to tell her?.*
[PRAGMATICS]
15 If you say that someone **plays God**, you mean that you disapprove of them because they act as if they have unlimited power and can do anything they want. *You have no right to play God in my life!*
[V inflects; PRAGMATICS]
16 You say **please God** to emphasize a strong hope, wish, or desire that you have. *Please God, let him telephone me now.*
[usu PHR with cl; PRAGMATICS]
17 You can use **God** in expressions such as **I hope to God**, or **I wish to God**, or **I swear to God**, in order to emphasize what you are saying. *I hope to God they are paying you well... I wish to God I hadn't met you.*
[usu v PHR that; PRAGMATICS]
18 If you say **God willing**, you are saying that something will happen if all goes well. *God willing, there will be a breakthrough.*
19 • **put the fear of God into** someone: see **fear**. • **honest to God**: see **honest**. • **in the lap of the gods**: see **lap**. • **for God's sake**: see **sake**. • **thank God**: see **thank**.

god-awful; also spelled **godawful**. If someone says that something is **god-awful**, they mean that they think it is very unpleasant; an informal word which some people find offensive.
[ADJ-GRADED: usu ADJ n; PRAGMATICS]

godchild /gɒdtʃaɪld/ **godchildren.** In the Christian religion, if a younger person is your **godchild**, you agreed to take responsibility for their religious upbringing when they were baptized.
[N-COUNT: usu with poss]

goddammit /gɒddæmɪt/; also spelled **goddamnit** or **goddamn it**. Some people say **goddammit** in order to express anger, annoyance, or irritation; an informal word which some people find offensive.
[EXCLAM; PRAGMATICS]

goddamn /gɒdæm/; also spelled **goddam**. The form **goddamned** is also used. Some people use **goddamn** in order to emphasize how angry, irritated, surprised, or excited they are; an informal word which some people find offensive. ► Also an adverb.
[◆◇◇◇◇; ADJ: ADJ n; PRAGMATICS; ADV: ADV adj]

goddamned /gɒdæmd/. **Goddamned** means the same as **goddamn**; an offensive word.
[◆◇◇◇◇; ADJ: usu ADJ n]

goddaughter /gɒddɔːtəʳ/ **goddaughters;** also spelled **god-daughter**. A **goddaughter** is a female godchild.
[N-COUNT: usu with poss]

goddess /gɒdes/ **goddesses.** In many religions, a **goddess** is a female spirit or being that is
[◆◆◇◇◇; N-COUNT]

believed to have power over a particular part of the world or nature. *...Diana, the goddess of war.*

godfather /gɒdfɑːðəʳ/ **godfathers** ◆◇◇◇◇
1 A **godfather** is a male godparent. N-COUNT
2 A powerful man who is at the head of a criminal organization is sometimes referred to as a **godfather**. *...the feared godfather of the Mafia.* N-COUNT
3 A man who began or developed a type or music or an activity is sometimes referred to as the **godfather of** that music or activity; used in journalism. *...the godfather of soul, James Brown.* N-COUNT: N *of* n

God-fearing. Someone who is **God-fearing** is religious and behaves according to the moral rules of their religion. *They brought up their children to be God-fearing Christians.* ADJ: usu ADJ n

God-forsaken. If you say that somewhere is a **God-forsaken** place, you mean that you dislike it a lot because you find it very boring and depressing. *I don't want to stay here, in this job and in this God-forsaken country.* ADJ: ADJ n PRAGMATICS

Godhead /gɒdhed/. The **Godhead** is the divine nature of God. *The matter of this universe is taken up into the Godhead.* N-SING: usu *the* N

godless /gɒdləs/. If you say that a person or group of people is **godless**, you mean that you disapprove of them and think that they are amoral because they do not believe in God. *...a godless and alienated society.* ♦ **godlessness** *For them, Moscow was not just the seat of communist godlessness, it was an enemy.* ADJ-GRADED: usu ADJ n PRAGMATICS; N-UNCOUNT

godlike /gɒdlaɪk/. A **godlike** person or a person with **godlike** qualities is admired or respected very much as if he or she were perfect. *His energy and talent elevate him to godlike status. ...a godlike being with curly hair... They were godlike in their wisdom and compassion.* ADJ: usu ADJ n

godliness /gɒdlinəs/
1 **Godliness** is the quality of being godly. N-UNCOUNT
2 If someone says that **cleanliness is next to godliness**, they are referring to the idea that people have a moral duty to keep themselves and their homes clean. PHRASE

godly /gɒdli/. A **godly** person is someone who is deeply religious and shows obedience to the rules of their religion. *...a learned and godly preacher. ...the godly life.* ADJ-GRADED: usu ADJ n

godmother /gɒdmʌðəʳ/ **godmothers.** A **godmother** is a female godparent. N-COUNT: usu with poss

godparent /gɒdpeərənt/ **godparents.** In the Christian religion, if you are the **godparent** of a younger person, you agreed to take responsibility for their religious upbringing when they were baptized. N-COUNT: usu with poss

godsend /gɒdsend/. If you describe something as **a godsend**, you are emphasizing that it helps you very much. *Pharmacists are a godsend when you don't feel sick enough to call the doctor.* N-SING: *a* N PRAGMATICS

godson /gɒdsʌn/ **godsons.** A **godson** is a male godchild. N-COUNT: usu with poss

Godspeed /gɒdspiːd/; also spelled **godspeed**. The term **Godspeed** is sometimes used in order to wish someone success and safety, especially if they are about to go on a long and dangerous journey; a formal word. *I know you will join me in wishing them Godspeed.* CONVENTION

-goer /-goʊəʳ/ **-goers. -goer** is added to words such as 'theatre', 'church', and 'film' to form nouns which describe people who regularly go to that type of place or event. *They are regular church-goers... Excited party-goers often don't have very big appetites.* COMB in N-COUNT

gofer /goʊfəʳ/ **gofers.** A **gofer** is a person whose job is to do simple but rather boring tasks for someone. *He'd been in the entertainment business since starting as a gofer to TV producer Aaron Spelling in the early 1960s.* N-COUNT =dogsbody

go-getter, go-getters. If you say that someone is a **go-getter**, you approve of them because they are very ambitious and energetic. N-COUNT PRAGMATICS

goggle /gɒgəl/ **goggles, goggling, goggled** ◆◇◇◇◇
1 If you **goggle** at something, you stare at it with your eyes wide open, usually because you are surprised by it; an informal use. *She goggled at me... He goggled in bewilderment.* VERB =stare; V *at* n; V
2 **Goggles** are large glasses that fit closely to your face around your eyes to protect them from such things as water, wind, dust, or sparks. N-PLURAL: also *a pair of* N

goggle-eyed
1 If you say that someone is **goggle-eyed**, you mean that they are very surprised or interested by something. *Johnson stared goggle-eyed at Kravis's sumptuous quarters.* ADJ: ADJ n, ADJ after v, v-link ADJ =wide-eyed
2 If you say that someone is **goggle-eyed**, you disapprove of the fact that they watch television a lot; an informal British use. ADJ PRAGMATICS

go-go ◆◇◇◇◇
1 A **go-go** dancer is a young woman whose job involves dancing to pop music in nightclubs wearing very few clothes. ADJ: ADJ n
2 In American English, a **go-go** period of time is a time when people make a lot of money and businesses are growing; an informal use. *Current economic activity is markedly slower than during the go-go years of the mid to late 1980s.* ADJ: ADJ n

going /goʊɪŋ/ ◆◆◆◆◆
1 If you say that something **is going to** happen, you mean that it will happen in the future, usually quite soon. *I think it's going to be successful... You're going to enjoy this... I'm going to have to tell him the truth... Are they going to be alright?* PHR-MODAL
2 You say that you **are going to** do something to express your intention or determination to do it. *I'm going to go to bed... He announced that he's going to resign... I was not going to compromise.* PHR-MODAL
3 If you talk about the **going**, you are talking about how easy or difficult someone is finding it to do something. You can also say that something is, for example, **hard going** or **tough going**. *He has her support to fall back on when the going gets tough... Though the talks had been hard going at the start, they had become more friendly.* N-UNCOUNT: *the* N, adj N
4 In horse-racing and horse-riding, when you talk about **the going**, you are talking about the condition of the surface the horses are running on. *The going was soft; some horses found it hard work.* N-UNCOUNT: oft *the* N
5 The **going** rate or the **going** salary is the usual amount of money that you expect to pay or receive for something. *She says that's the going rate for a house this big... That's about half the going price on world oil markets.* ADJ: ADJ n
6 See also **go**.
7 If someone or something **has** a lot **going for** them, they have a lot of advantages. *This area has a lot going for it... I wish I could show you the things you've got going for you.* PHRASES V inflects, PHR n
8 When you **get going**, you start doing something or start a journey, especially after a delay. *Now what about that shopping list? I've got to get going.* V inflects
9 If you say that someone should do something **while the going is good**, you are advising them to do it while things are going well and they still have the opportunity, because you think it will become much more difficult to do. *Those with capital should rent now while the going is good.* V inflects
10 If you **keep going**, you continue doing things or doing a particular thing. *I like to keep going. I hate to sit still.* V inflects
11 If you can **keep going** with the money you have, you can manage to live on it. *Things were difficult, and we needed her wages to keep going.* V inflects
12 If you say that something that has been achieved is **good going** or **not bad going**, you mean that it is better than usual or than expected; used mainly in informal British English. *4,000 copies of Wuthering Heights went in two days. That's not bad going for a book that has been on the market for 145 years.* usu v-link PHR, oft PHR *for* n
13 If you say that something is enough **to be going on with**, you mean that it is enough for your needs at the moment, although you will need something better at some time in the future; used mainly in British English. *It was a good enough description for Mattie to be going on with.* usu PHR after v
14 You can use **going on** before a number to say PHR num

that something has almost reached that number. For example, you can say that someone is **going on 40** to indicate that they are nearly 40. *We've been married for going on two years... This is 1980 going on 1981.*
15 • **comings and goings**: see **coming**. • **going concern**: see **concern**.

-going /-gəʊɪŋ/
1 -going is added to nouns such as 'theatre', 'church', and 'film' to form nouns which describe the activity of going to that type of place or event. *It is the cinema-going public who decide whether a film is a blockbuster or not. ...his party-going days as a student.* COMB in N-UNCOUNT: oft N n
2 -going is added to nouns such as 'ocean', 'sea', and 'road' to form adjectives which describe vehicles that are designed for that type of place. *...one of the largest ocean-going liners in the world. ...a new range of road-going bicycles.* COMB: COMB in ADJ: usu ADJ n
3 -going is added to nouns that refer to directions to form adjectives which describe things that are moving in that direction. *There is a strong west-going tide, even one mile offshore... The material can absorb outward-going radiation from the Earth.* COMB: COMB in ADJ: usu ADJ n
4 See also **easy-going**, **ongoing**, **outgoing**, **thoroughgoing**.

going-over
1 If you give someone or something a **going-over**, you examine them in order to make sure that they are all right; an informal use. *Michael was given a complete going-over and then treated for glandular fever.* N-SING
2 A **going-over** is a violent attack on or criticism of someone; an informal use. *He gets a terrible going-over in these pages.* N-SING =pasting

goings-on. If you describe events or activities as **goings-on**, you mean that they are strange, interesting, amusing, or rather dishonest; an informal word. *The Swiss girl had found out about the goings-on in the factory. ...strange goings-on between Cantrell and his men.* N-PLURAL

goitre /gɔɪtəʳ/. **Goitre** is a disease of the thyroid gland that makes a person's neck very swollen. N-VAR

go-kart, go-karts; also spelled **go-cart**. A **go-kart** is a very small motor vehicle with four wheels, used for racing. N-COUNT

go-karting. Go-karting is the sport of racing or riding on go-karts. N-UNCOUNT

gold /gəʊld/ **golds** ◆◆◆◆◇
1 Gold is a valuable, yellow-coloured metal that is used for making jewellery and ornaments, and as an international currency. *...a sapphire set in gold... The price of gold was going up. ...gold coins.* N-UNCOUNT
2 Gold is jewellery and other things that are made of gold. *We handed over all our gold and money.* N-UNCOUNT
3 Something that is **gold** is a bright yellow colour, and is often shiny. *I'd been wearing Michel's black and gold shirt.* COLOUR
4 A **gold** is the same as a **gold medal**; an informal use. *My aim is to represent Britain at the Olympics and win the gold... This Saturday the British star is going for gold in the Winter Olympics.* N-VAR
5 If you say that a child is being **as good as gold**, you are emphasizing that they are behaving very well and are not causing you any problems. *The boys were as good as gold on our walk.* PHRASES v-link PHR, PHR after v PRAGMATICS
6 If you say that someone has **a heart of gold**, you are emphasizing that they are very good, kind, and considerate. *They are all good boys with hearts of gold. They would never steal.* *heart* inflects, v PHR, *with* PHR
7 People sometimes refer to money that someone hopes they will get in the future as **a pot of gold** or **a crock of gold**. *I would rather be honest with people than tell them that there is going to be some pot of gold at the end of the rainbow.*
8 • See also **fool's gold**. • to **strike gold**: see **strike**. • **worth** one's **weight in gold**: see **weight**.

gold dust
1 Gold dust is gold in the form of a fine powder. N-UNCOUNT
2 If you say that a type of thing is **like gold dust** or is **gold dust**, you mean that it is very difficult to obtain, usually because everyone wants it; used mainly in British English. *Tickets were like gold dust.* N-UNCOUNT

golden /gəʊldᵊn/ ◆◆◆◇◇
1 Something that is **golden** is bright yellow in colour; a literary use. *She combed and arranged her golden hair. ...an endless golden beach.* ADJ
2 Golden things are made of gold; a literary use. *...a golden chain with a golden locket.* ADJ: usu ADJ n
3 If you describe something as **golden**, you mean it is wonderful because it is likely to be successful and rewarding, or because it is the best of its kind. *He says there's a golden opportunity for peace which must be seized... She shines as an athlete. She is truly a golden girl.* ADJ: ADJ n

golden age, golden ages. A **golden age** is a period of time during which a very high level of achievement is reached in a particular field of activity, especially in art or literature. *You grew up in the golden age of American children's books.* ◆◇◇◇◇ N-COUNT: oft N *of* n

golden handshake, golden handshakes. A **golden handshake** is a large sum of money that a company gives to an employee when he or she leaves, as a reward for long service or good work; used mainly in British English. N-COUNT

golden jubilee, golden jubilees. A **golden jubilee** is the 50th anniversary of an important or special event. *The company is celebrating its golden jubilee.* N-COUNT

golden oldie, golden oldies. People sometimes refer to something that is still successful or popular even though it is quite old as a **golden oldie**; an informal word. N-COUNT

golden rule, golden rules. A **golden rule** is an important thing to remember to do in order to be successful at something. *Hanson's golden rule is to add value to whatever business he buys.* N-COUNT

golden syrup. In Britain, **golden syrup** is a type of sweet food in the form of a thick, sticky, yellow liquid. Golden syrup can be spread on bread, or used to make cakes and puddings. N-UNCOUNT

golden wedding, golden weddings. A **golden wedding** or a **golden wedding anniversary** is the fiftieth anniversary of a wedding. N-COUNT

goldfish /gəʊldfɪʃ/; **goldfish** is both the singular and the plural form. A **goldfish** is a small gold or orange-coloured fish which is often kept as a pet in a bowl or a garden pond. ◆◇◇◇◇ N-COUNT

gold medal, gold medals. A **gold medal** is a medal made of gold which is awarded as first prize in a contest or competition. ◆◆◇◇◇ N-COUNT

goldmine /gəʊldmaɪn/. If you describe something such as a business or idea as a **goldmine**, you mean that it produces large profits. *The book is a goldmine... A-level students have become a goldmine for schools.* N-SING

gold-plated. Something that is **gold-plated** is covered with a very thin layer of gold. *...marble bathrooms with gold-plated taps.* ADJ

gold-rimmed. Gold-rimmed spectacles have a frame of gold or gold-coloured metal. ADJ: usu ADJ n

goldsmith /gəʊldsmɪθ/ **goldsmiths.** A **goldsmith** is a person whose job is making jewellery and other objects using gold. N-COUNT

golf /gɒlf/. **Golf** is a game in which you use long sticks called clubs to hit a small, hard ball into holes that are spread out over a large area of grassy land. ◆◆◆◇◇ N-UNCOUNT

golf ball, golf balls. A **golf ball** is a small, hard white ball which people use when they are playing golf. ◆◇◇◇◇ N-COUNT

golf club, golf clubs ◆◇◇◇◇
1 A **golf club** is a long, thin, metal stick with a piece of wood or metal at one end that you use to hit the ball in golf. N-COUNT
2 A **golf club** is a social organization which provides a golf course and a clubhouse for its members. N-COUNT

golf course, golf courses; also spelled **golf-course**. A **golf course** is a large area of grass which is specially designed for people to play golf on. ◆◇◇◇◇ N-COUNT

golfer /gɒlfəʳ/ **golfers.** A **golfer** is a person who plays golf for pleasure or as a profession. ◆◆◇◇◇ N-COUNT

golfing /gɒlfɪŋ/ ◆◇◇◇◇
1 **Golfing** is used to describe things that involve the playing of golf or that are used while playing golf. *He was wearing a cream silk shirt and a tartan golfing cap. ...a golfing holiday in Spain.* ADJ: ADJ n
2 **Golfing** is the activity of playing golf. *You can play tennis or go golfing.* N-UNCOUNT

golly /gɒli/
1 Some people say **golly** to indicate that they are very surprised by something; an informal and old-fashioned use. *'Golly,' he says, 'Isn't it exciting!'* EXCLAM PRAGMATICS
2 Some people say **by golly** to emphasize that something did happen or should happen; an informal and old-fashioned use. *By golly we can do something about it this time.* EXCLAM PRAGMATICS

gondola /gɒndələ/ **gondolas.** A **gondola** is a long narrow boat that is used especially in Venice. It has a flat bottom and curves upwards at both ends. A person stands at one end of the boat and uses a long pole to move and steer it. N-COUNT

gone /gɒn, AM gɔːn/ ◆◆◆◆◇
1 **Gone** is the past participle of **go**.
2 When someone is **gone**, they have left the place where you are and are no longer there. When something is **gone**, it is no longer present or no longer exists. *While he was gone she had tea with the Colonel... He's already been gone four hours!... By morning the smoke will be all gone.* ADJ: v-link ADJ
3 If you say it is **gone** a particular time, you mean it is later than that time; used in informal British English. *It was just gone 7 o'clock this evening when I finished.* PREP =after, past

goner /gɒnəʳ, AM gɔːn-/ **goners.** If you say that someone is a **goner**, you mean that they are about to die, or are in such danger that nobody can save them; an informal word. *She fell so heavily I thought she was a goner.* N-COUNT

gong /gɒŋ, AM gɔːŋ/ **gongs** ◆◇◇◇◇
1 A **gong** is a large, flat, circular piece of metal that you hit with a hammer to make a sound like a loud bell. Gongs are sometimes used as musical instruments, or to give a signal that it is time to do something. *On the stroke of seven, a gong summons guests into the dining-room.* N-COUNT
2 In British English, people sometimes refer to a medal or an award as a **gong**; an informal use, mainly in journalism. *Spike Milligan has finally got the gong he had been promised. ...peerages, knighthoods and other assorted gongs.* N-COUNT

gonna /gɒnə, AM gɔːnə/. **Gonna** is used in written English to represent the words **going to** when they are pronounced informally. *Then what am I gonna do?*

gonorrhoea /gɒnəriːə/; spelled **gonorrhea** in American English. **Gonorrhoea** is a sexually transmitted disease. N-UNCOUNT

goo /guː/. You can use **goo** to refer to any thick, sticky substance, for example mud or paste; an informal word. *...a sticky goo of pineapple and coconut.* N-UNCOUNT

good /gʊd/ **better, best** ◆◆◆◆◆
1 **Good** means pleasant or enjoyable. *We had a really good time together... I know they would have a better life here... There's nothing better than a good cup of hot coffee... It's so good to hear your voice after all this time.* ADJ-GRADED ≠bad
2 **Good** means of a high quality, standard, or level. *Exercise is just as important to health as good food... His parents wanted Raymond to have the best possible education... The train's average speed was no better than that of our bicycles. ...good quality furniture.* ADJ-GRADED ≠poor
3 If you are **good at** something, you are skilful and successful at doing it. *He was very good at his work... I'm not very good at singing... He is one of the best players in the world... I always played football with my older brother because I was good for my age.* ADJ-GRADED: oft ADJ at n/-ing ≠bad, poor
4 If you describe a piece of news, an action, or an effect as **good**, you mean that it is likely to result in benefit or success. *President Bush called the report very good news for the US economy... I had the good fortune to be selected... This is not a good example to set other children... I think the response was good.* ADJ-GRADED: usu ADJ n ≠bad
5 A **good** idea, reason, method, or decision is a sensible or valid one. *They thought it was a good idea to make some offenders do community service... There is good reason to doubt this... Could you give me some advice on the best way to do this?* ADJ-GRADED: usu ADJ n =sound, valid ≠bad, poor
6 If you say that **it is good** that something should happen or **good** to do something, you mean it is desirable, acceptable, or right. *I think it's good that some people are going... It is always best to choose organically grown foods if possible.* ADJ-GRADED: usu v-link ADJ, oft *it* v-link ADJ that/to-inf ≠bad
7 A **good** estimate or indication of something is an accurate one. *We have a fairly good idea of what's going on... This is a much better indication of what a school is really like... Laboratory tests are not always a good guide to what happens in the world.* ADJ-GRADED: usu ADJ n ≠poor
8 If you get a **good** deal or a **good** price when you buy or sell something, you receive a lot in exchange for what you give. *Whether such properties are a good deal will depend on individual situations... The merchandise is reasonably priced and offers exceptionally good value.* ADJ-GRADED: usu ADJ n
9 If something is **good for** a person or organization, it benefits them. *Rain water was once considered to be good for the complexion... Nancy chose the product because it is better for the environment.* ADJ-GRADED: v-link ADJ *for* n =beneficial ≠bad
10 If something is done for the **good** of a person or organization, it is done in order to benefit them. *Furlaud urged him to resign for the good of the country... Victims want to see justice done not just for themselves, but for the greater good of society... I'm only telling you this for your own good!* N-SING: with poss =benefit
11 If someone or something is **no good** or is **not any good**, they are not satisfactory or are of a low standard. *If the weather's no good then I won't take any pictures... I was never any good at maths.* N-UNCOUNT: with brd-neg
12 If you say that doing something is **no good** or does **not** do **any good**, you mean that doing it is not of any use or will not bring any success. *It's no good worrying about it now... We gave them water and kept them warm, but it didn't do any good... There is no way to measure these effects; the chances are it did some good.* N-UNCOUNT: usu with brd-neg
13 **Good** is what is considered to be right according to moral standards or religious beliefs. *Good and evil may co-exist within one family.* N-UNCOUNT ≠evil
14 Someone who is **good** is morally correct in their attitudes and behaviour. *The Dalai Lama is a good man... For me to think I'm any better than a homeless person on the street is ridiculous.* ADJ-GRADED ≠bad, evil
15 Someone, especially a child, who is **good** obeys rules and instructions and behaves in a socially correct way. *The children were very good... I'm going to be a good boy now... Both boys had good manners, politely shaking hands.* ADJ-GRADED ≠bad
16 Someone who is **good** is kind and thoughtful. *You are good to me... Her good intentions were thwarted almost immediately... Just ask the Admiral if he will be good enough to drop me a note.* ADJ-GRADED
17 Someone who is in a **good** mood is cheerful and pleasant to be with. *People were in a pretty good mood... He exudes natural charm and good humour... A relaxation session may put you in a better frame of mind.* ADJ-GRADED: usu ADJ n ≠bad
18 If people are **good** friends, they get on well together and are very close. *She and Gavin are good friends... She's my best friend, and I really love her.* ADJ-GRADED: ADJ n
19 A person's **good** eye, arm, or leg is the one that is healthy and strong, if the other one is injured or weak. *He turned his good eye on me and laughed.* ADJ: ADJ n ≠bad
20 You use **good** to emphasize the great extent or degree of something. *We waited a good fifteen minutes... This whole thing's got a good bit more dangerous.* ADJ: a ADJ n
21 You say **'Good'** or **'Very good'** to express pleasure, satisfaction, or agreement with something that has been said or done, especially when you are in a position of authority. *'Are you all right?'—'I'm* CONVENTION PRAGMATICS

fine.'—'Good. So am I.'... Oh good, Tom's just come in... 'Strike Force Three are here, sir.'—'Good.'
22 See also **best, better, goods.**
23 **'As good as'** can be used to mean 'almost.' *His career is as good as over... The vote as good as kills the chance of real reform.* PHRASES v-link PHR adj/-ed/v =practically
24 If you do something for **the common good**, you do it for the benefit or advantage of everyone. *...communities working together for the common good... Many of them placed self-interest before the common good.* oft *for* PHR
25 If you say that something will **do** someone **good**, you mean that it will benefit them or improve them. *The outing will do me good... It's probably done you good to get away for a few hours... You don't do anybody any good by getting yourself arrested.* V inflects, oft *it* PHR if/to-inf
26 If something changes or disappears **for good**, it never changes back or reappears as it was before. *The days of big-time racing at Herne Hill had gone for good... A few shots of this drug cleared up the disease for good.* PHR after v
27 People say **'Good for you'** to express approval of your actions. *'He has a girl now, who he lives with.'—'Good for him.'* CONVENTION
28 If someone **is good for** something, you can rely on them to provide that thing. *Joe was always good for a colorful quote... She heard her father shouting that her mother was stupid, useless, and good for nothing but her money.* V inflects, PHR n
29 If you say **it's a good thing**, or in British English **it's a good job**, that something is the case, you mean that it is fortunate. *It's a good thing you aren't married... It's a good job it happened here rather than on the open road.* V inflects
30 If you **make good** some damage, a loss, or a debt, you try to repair the damage, replace what has been lost, or repay the debt. *It may cost several billion roubles to make good the damage.* V inflects, PHR n =put right
31 If someone **makes good** a threat or promise or **makes good on** it, they do what they have threatened or promised to do; used mainly in American English. *Certain that he was going to make good his threat to kill her now, Darlene brandished the gun... He was confident the allies would make good on their pledges.* V inflects, PHR n, PHR *on* n
32 If someone **makes good**, they become successful, famous, or rich. *Both men are poor boys made good.* V inflects
33 If you say that something or someone is **as good as new**, you mean that they are in a very good condition or state, especially after they have been damaged or ill. *I only ever use that on special occasions so it's as good as new... In a day or so he will be as good as new.* usu v-link PHR
34 You use **good old** before the name of a person, place, or thing when you are referring to them in an affectionate way. *Good old Harry. Reliable to the end... There is nothing wrong with good old cauliflower cheese.* PHR n PRAGMATICS
35 • to **be in someone's good books**: see **book**. • **good deal**: see **deal**. • **in good faith**: see **faith**. • **so far so good**: see **far**. • **a good few**: see **few**. • **good as gold**: see **gold**. • **good gracious**: see **gracious**. • **good grief**: see **grief**. • **good heavens**: see **heaven**. • **for good or ill**: see **ill**. • **good job**: see **job**. • **good lord**: see **lord**. • **for good measure**: see **measure**. • **the good old days**: see **old**. • **good question**: see **question**. • **in good shape**: see **shape**. • to **stand someone in good stead**: see **stead**. • **in good time**: see **time**. • **too good to be true**: see **true**. • to **be as good as one's word**: see **word**.

good afternoon. You say **'Good afternoon'** when you are greeting someone in the afternoon; a formal expression. CONVENTION PRAGMATICS

goodbye /gʊdbaɪ/ **goodbyes;** also spelled **good-bye.** ◆◆◇◇◇
1 You say **'Goodbye'** to someone when you or they are leaving, or at the end of a telephone conversation. CONVENTION PRAGMATICS
2 When you say your **goodbyes**, you say something such as 'goodbye' when you leave. *He said his goodbyes knowing that a long time would pass before he would see his child again... I said a hurried goodbye and walked home in the cold... Perry and I exchanged goodbyes.* N-COUNT: usu supp N
3 When you **say goodbye** to someone, you say something such as 'Goodbye', 'Bye', or 'See you', when you or they are leaving. You can also **wave goodbye** to someone. *He left without saying goodbye... He wanted to say goodbye to you... They came to the front door to wave goodbye.* PHRASES V inflects, oft PHR *to* n
4 If you **say goodbye to** something that you want or usually have, or **wave goodbye to** it, you accept that you are not going to get it or have it any more, or do something that means you will not have it. *He has probably said goodbye to his last chance of Olympic gold... We can wave goodbye to the sort of protection that people at work need and deserve.* V inflects, PHR n
5 • to **kiss** something **goodbye**: see **kiss**.

good day. People sometimes say **'Good day'** instead of 'Hello' or 'Goodbye'. *Well, I'd better be off. Good day to you.* ◆◇◇◇◇ CONVENTION PRAGMATICS

good evening. You say **'Good evening'** when you are greeting someone in the evening; a formal expression. ◆◆◇◇◇ CONVENTION PRAGMATICS

good-for-nothing, good-for-nothings. If you describe someone as **good-for-nothing**, you think that they are lazy or irresponsible. *...a good-for-nothing fourteen-year-old son who barely knows how to read and count.* ► Also a noun. *...lazy good-for-nothings.* ADJ: ADJ n =lazy N-COUNT

Good Friday. Good Friday is the day on which Christians remember the crucifixion of Jesus Christ. It is the Friday before Easter Sunday. N-UNCOUNT

good-humoured. A **good-humoured** person or atmosphere is pleasant and cheerful. *Charles was brave and remarkably good-humoured... It was a good humoured conference.* ADJ-GRADED

goodie /gʊdi/. See **goody**.

good-looking, better-looking, best-looking. Someone who is **good-looking** has an attractive face. *Cassandra noticed him because he was good-looking. ...a good-looking woman.* ◆◆◇◇◇ ADJ-GRADED

goodly /gʊdli/. A **goodly** amount or part of something is a fairly large amount or part of it, often more than was expected; a formal word. *The Central Intelligence Agency employed a goodly number of expert professionals in this particular field... Laski spent a goodly part of his lecturing life in American universities.* ADJ: ADJ n =substantial

good morning. You say **'Good morning'** when you are greeting someone in the morning; a formal expression. ◆◆◆◇◇ CONVENTION PRAGMATICS

good-natured. A **good-natured** person or animal is naturally friendly and does not get angry easily. *Bates looks like a good-natured lad... He was good natured about it, he didn't fuss.* ◆◇◇◇◇ ADJ-GRADED

goodness /gʊdnəs/ ◆◆◇◇◇
1 People sometimes say **'goodness'** or **'my goodness'** to express surprise. *Goodness, I wonder if he knows... My goodness, he's earned millions in his career.* • **for goodness sake**: see **sake**. • **thank goodness**: see **thank**. EXCLAM PRAGMATICS
2 **Goodness** is the quality of being kind, helpful, and honest. *He retains a faith in human goodness.* N-UNCOUNT

goodnight /gʊdnaɪt/; also spelled **good night**. ◆◇◇◇◇
1 You say **'Goodnight'** to someone late in the evening before one of you goes home or goes to sleep. CONVENTION PRAGMATICS
2 If you **say goodnight** to someone or **kiss** them **goodnight**, you say something such as 'Goodnight' to them or kiss them before one of you goes home or goes to sleep. *Eleanor went upstairs to say goodnight to the children... Both men rose to their feet and kissed her goodnight. ...a goodnight kiss.* N-UNCOUNT

goods /gʊdz/ ◆◆◆◆◇
1 **Goods** are things that are made to be sold. *Money can be exchanged for goods or services. ...a wide range of consumer goods.* N-PLURAL
2 If you **deliver the goods** or **come up with the goods**, you do what is expected or required of you; an informal expression. PHRASE: V inflects

goods train, goods trains. In British English, a **goods train** is a train that transports goods and not people. The American term is **freight train.** N-COUNT

good-tempered. A **good-tempered** person or animal is naturally friendly and pleasant and does not easily get angry or upset. *He was a happy, good-tempered child. ...a horse which is quiet and good tempered.* ADJ-GRADED =good-natured

goodwill /gʊdwɪl/. **Goodwill** is a friendly or helpful attitude towards other people, countries, or organizations. *I invited them to dinner, a gesture of goodwill... They depend on the goodwill of visitors to pick up rubbish.* ◆◆◇◇◇ N-UNCOUNT

goody /gʊdi/ **goodies;** also spelled **goodie.** ◆◇◇◇◇

1 You can refer to pleasant, exciting, or attractive things as **goodies**; an informal use. *...a little bag of goodies... Birmingham, the 'UK City of Music', will be parading its finest artistic goodies.* N-COUNT: usu pl

2 You can refer to the heroes or the morally good characters in a film or story as the **goodies**. You can also refer to the **goodies** in a situation in real life; an informal use. *...the thriller, a genre which depends on goodies and baddies... There are few goodies and baddies in this industrial dispute.* N-COUNT: usu pl ≠baddy

3 People, especially children, say **goody** in order to express their pleasure or approval of something; an informal use. *Oh, goody, I like games.* EXCLAM PRAGMATICS

goody bag, goody bags. A **goody bag** is a bag of gifts or free samples, often given away by manufacturers in order to encourage people to try their products; an informal word. N-COUNT

goody-goody, goody-goodies. If you call someone a **goody-goody**, you dislike them because they behave extremely well in order to please people in authority; an informal word. N-COUNT PRAGMATICS

gooey /guːi/ **gooier, gooiest**

1 If you describe a food or other substance as **gooey**, you mean that it is very soft and sticky; an informal use. *These cakes are fudgy, gooey, and delicious. ...a lovely, gooey, sticky mess.* ADJ-GRADED

2 **Gooey** is sometimes used to describe very foolish, exaggerated ways of expressing love or affection; an informal use. *I'm gonna write you a long, gooey letter... Women went gooey over him.* ADJ-GRADED

goof /guːf/ **goofs, goofing, goofed**

1 If someone **goofs**, they make a foolish mistake and often fail to achieve what they wanted; an informal use. *We had goofed by fitting the antenna to the stern of the boat.* ► Also a noun. *But was it, in fact, a hideous goof?* VERB V N-COUNT

2 If you call someone a **goof**, you think they are foolish or are easily deceived; an informal use. *I could write for TV as well as any of those goofs.* N-COUNT PRAGMATICS =fool, idiot

goof around. If someone **goofs around**, they spend their time doing foolish things; an informal expression. *They just goof around, roll around on the floor and fight.* PHRASAL VERB =mess around V P

goof off. If someone **goofs off**, they spend their time doing nothing, often when they should be working; an informal expression. *My work duty is this afternoon, so I'm gonna goof off for a while.* PHRASAL VERB =skive off V P

goofy /guːfi/ **goofier, goofiest.** If you describe someone or something as **goofy**, you think they are rather silly or ridiculous; an informal word used mainly in American English. *...a goofy smile.* ADJ-GRADED

googly /guːgli/ **googlies.** When a cricketer bowls a **googly**, he or she spins the ball and makes it bounce in a different direction from the direction that the batsman is expecting. N-COUNT

goon /guːn/ **goons**

1 In informal American English, a **goon** is a person who is paid to hurt or threaten people. *He and the other goon began to beat me up.* N-COUNT =thug

2 If you call someone a **goon**, you think they behave in a silly way; an old-fashioned use. N-COUNT PRAGMATICS

goose /guːs/ **geese** ◆◆◇◇◇

1 A **goose** is a large bird that has a long neck and webbed feet. Geese are often kept on farms for their meat. N-COUNT

2 **Goose** is the meat from a goose that has been cooked. *...roast goose.* N-UNCOUNT

3 See also **wild goose chase**.

4 If you **cook** someone**'s goose**, you prevent their plans from succeeding. *He said that what they were up to would cook Krasky's goose.* PHRASES V inflects

5 If someone **kills the goose that lays the golden egg**, they harm or destroy the person or thing that gives them their money, power, or advantage. *Unregulated tourism can kill the goose that laid their golden egg.* Vs inflect

6 If you say **what's sauce for the goose is sauce for the gander**, you mean what is acceptable for one person in a particular situation should be acceptable for another person in a similar situation.

gooseberry /gʊzbəri, AM guːsberi/ **gooseberries.** A **gooseberry** is a small green fruit that has a sharp taste and is covered with tiny hairs. N-COUNT

goose bumps. If you get **goose bumps**, the hairs on your skin stand up so that it is covered with tiny bumps. You get goose bumps when you are cold, frightened, or excited. *She still got goose bumps whenever he walked into the room.* N-PLURAL =goose pimples

goose pimples. **Goose pimples** are the same as **goose bumps**. N-PLURAL

goose-step, goose-steps, goose-stepping, goose-stepped. When soldiers **goose-step**, they lift their legs high and do not bend their knees as they march. *...photos of soldiers goose-stepping beside fearsome missiles.* VERB V

gopher /goʊfəʳ/ **gophers.**

1 A **gopher** is a small animal which looks a bit like a rat and lives in holes in the ground. Gophers are found in Canada and the USA. N-COUNT

2 In computing, **Gopher** is a program that collects information for you from many databases across the Internet network. N-PROPER; also N-COUNT

gore /gɔːʳ/ **gores, goring, gored** ◆◆◇◇◇

1 If someone **is gored** by an animal, they are badly wounded by its horns or tusks. *Carruthers had been gored by a rhinoceros... He was gored to death in front of his family.* VB: usu passive be V-ed be V-ed to n

2 **Gore** is unpleasant-looking blood from a person or animal, for example after they have been involved in an accident; a literary use. *There were pools of blood and gore on the pavement.* N-UNCOUNT

gorge /gɔːʳdʒ/ **gorges, gorging, gorged** ◆◇◇◇◇

1 A **gorge** is a deep, narrow valley with very steep sides, usually where a river passes through mountains or an area of hard rock. N-COUNT =ravine

2 If you **gorge on** something or **gorge** yourself on it, you eat lots of it in a very greedy way. *I could spend each day gorging on chocolate... Three men are gorging themselves on grouse and water melon.* VERB V on n V pron-refl on n Also V

gorgeous /gɔːʳdʒəs/ ◆◆◇◇◇

1 If you say that something is **gorgeous**, you mean that it gives you a lot of pleasure or is very attractive; an informal use. *...gorgeous mountain scenery... It's a gorgeous day... Some of the Renaissance buildings are gorgeous.* ♦ **gorgeously** *She has a gorgeously warm speaking voice.* ADJ-GRADED =lovely ADV: ADV adj/-ed

2 If you describe someone as **gorgeous**, you are emphasizing that you find them very sexually attractive; an informal use. *The cosmetics industry uses gorgeous women to sell its skincare products... All the girls in my house are mad about Ryan, they think he's gorgeous.* ADJ-GRADED =beautiful

3 If you describe things such as clothes and colours as **gorgeous**, you mean they are bright, rich, and impressive. *...a red-haired man in the gorgeous uniform of a Marshal of the Empire.* ♦ **gorgeously** *...gorgeously embroidered clothing.* ADJ-GRADED: usu ADJ n ADV-GRADED: ADV adj/-ed

gorilla /gərɪlə/ **gorillas.** A **gorilla** is a very large ape. It has long arms, black fur, and a black face. ◆◇◇◇◇ N-COUNT

gormless /gɔːʳmləs/. In British English, if you say that someone is **gormless**, you think that they are stupid because they do not understand things very well; an informal use. ADJ-GRADED PRAGMATICS

gorse /gɔːʳs/. **Gorse** is a dark green European bush that has small yellow flowers and sharp prickles. N-UNCOUNT

gory /gɔːri/. **Gory** situations involve people being injured or dying in a horrible way. *...the gory details of Mayan human sacrifices. ...the gory death scenes.* ADJ-GRADED: usu ADJ n

gosh /gɒʃ/. Some people say '**Gosh**' when they are surprised; an old-fashioned word. *Gosh, there's a lot of noise.* ◆◇◇◇◇ EXCLAM

gosling /gɒzlɪŋ/ **goslings.** A **gosling** is a baby goose. N-COUNT

go-slow, go-slows. A **go-slow** is a protest by workers in which they deliberately work slowly in order to cause problems for their employers; used in British English. N-COUNT

gospel /gɒspəl/ **gospels** ◆◆◇◇◇

1 In the New Testament of the Bible, the **Gospels** are the four books which describe the life and teachings of Jesus Christ. *...the parable in St Matthew's Gospel. ...an illustrated and illuminated manuscript of the four gospels.* N-COUNT: oft in names

2 In the Christian religion, **the gospel** refers to the message and teachings of Jesus Christ, as explained in the New Testament. *I didn't shirk my duties. I visited the sick and I preached the gospel.* N-SING: the N

3 You can use **gospel** to refer to a particular way of thinking that a person or group believes in very strongly and that they urge others to accept. *It taught only materialism, the gospel of mammon. ...the gospel according to my mom.* N-COUNT: usu N of n, N according to n-proper =doctrine

4 **Gospel** or **gospel music** is a style of religious music that uses strong rhythms and vocal harmony. It is especially popular among black Christians in the southern United States of America. *I had to go to church, so I grew up singing gospel... The group perform variations on soul and gospel music.* N-UNCOUNT

5 If you take something as **gospel**, or as **gospel truth**, you believe that it is completely true. *The results were not to be taken as gospel... He wouldn't say this if it weren't the gospel truth.* N-UNCOUNT: usu as N

gossamer /gɒsəməʳ/. You use **gossamer** to indicate that something is very light, thin, delicate, or fragile; a literary word. *...the daring gossamer dresses of sheer black lace.* ADJ: ADJ n

gossip /gɒsɪp/ **gossips, gossiping, gossiped** ◆◆◇◇◇

1 **Gossip** is informal conversation, often about other people's private affairs. *He spent the first hour talking gossip... There has been much gossip about the possible reasons for his absence... Don't you like a good gossip?* N-UNCOUNT: also a N

2 If you **gossip with** someone, you talk informally, especially about other people or local events. You can also say that two people **gossip.** *We spoke, debated, gossiped into the night... Eva gossiped with Sarah... Mrs Lilywhite never gossiped.* V-RECIP pl-n V, V with n, V (non-recip)

3 If you describe someone as a **gossip**, you disapprove of them because they enjoy talking informally to people about the private affairs of others. *He was a vicious gossip.* N-COUNT PRAGMATICS

gossip column, gossip columns. A **gossip column** is a part of a newspaper or magazine where the activities and private lives of famous people are discussed. *The jet-setting couple made frequent appearances in the gossip columns.* N-COUNT

gossipy /gɒsɪpi/

1 If you describe a book or account as **gossipy**, you mean it is informal and full of interesting but often unimportant news or information about people. *...a chatty, gossipy account of Forster's life.* ADJ-GRADED: usu ADJ n

2 If you describe someone as **gossipy**, you are critical of them because they talk about other people's private lives a great deal. *...gossipy old women.* ADJ-GRADED: usu ADJ n PRAGMATICS

got /gɒt/ ◆◆◆◆◆

1 **Got** is the past tense and past participle of **get**.

2 In spoken English, you use **have got** when you are saying that someone owns, possesses, or is holding a particular thing, or when you are mentioning a quality or characteristic that someone or something has. In informal American English, the 'have' is sometimes omitted. *I've got a coat just like this... She hasn't got a work permit... Have you got any ideas?... Every city's got its good and bad points... After a pause he asked, 'You got any identification?'* PHRASES have inflects, PHR n =have

3 In spoken English, you use **have got to** when you are saying that something is necessary or must happen in the way stated. In informal American English, the 'have' is sometimes omitted. *I'm not happy with the situation, but I've just got to accept it... There has got to be a degree of flexibility... See, you got to work very hard.* MODAL =must

4 In spoken English, people sometimes use **have got to** in order to emphasize that they are certain that something is true, because of the facts or circumstances involved. In informal American English, the 'have' is sometimes omitted. *Bill Clinton's got to be happy with these results.* MODAL PRAGMATICS =must

Gothic /gɒθɪk/ ◆◇◇◇◇

1 **Gothic** is used to describe a style of architecture or church art, dating from the Middle Ages, that is distinguished by tall pillars, high curved ceilings, and pointed arches. *a vast, lofty Gothic cathedral. ...Gothic stained glass windows... The images were gothic or Byzantine rather than classical.* ADJ: usu ADJ n

2 **Gothic** is used to describe stories in which strange, mysterious adventures happen in dark and lonely places such as the ruins of a castle. *This novel is not science fiction, nor is it Gothic horror.* ADJ: usu ADJ n

3 **Gothic** is used to describe a style of printing or writing in which the letters are very ornate. German books and signs often used to be written in Gothic script. ADJ: usu ADJ n

gotta /gɒtə/. **Gotta** is used in written English to represent the words 'got to' when they are pronounced informally, with the meaning 'have to' or 'must'. *Prices are high and our kids gotta eat.*

gotten /gɒtən/. **Gotten** is the past participle of **get** in American English. • See also **ill-gotten gains.**

gouge /gaʊdʒ/ **gouges, gouging, gouged** ◆◇◇◇◇

1 If you **gouge** something, you make a hole or a long cut in it, usually with a pointed object. *He gouged her cheek with a screwdriver. ...quarries which have gouged great holes in the hills.* ► Also a noun. *...a muddy gouge in the ground.* VERB V n prep N-COUNT

2 A **gouge** is a tool which is used for cutting and shaping wood. N-COUNT

3 If you say that a business **gouges** its customers, you disapprove of it because it forces them to pay an unfairly high price for its goods or services; an informal use, used mainly in American English. *Banks and credit-card companies have been accused of gouging their customers.* ♦ **gouging** *The airline industry has charged the oil companies with price gouging.* VERB PRAGMATICS V n N-UNCOUNT

gouge out. To **gouge out** a piece or part of something means to cut, dig, or force it from the surrounding surface. You can also **gouge out** a hole or trench. *He has accused her of threatening to gouge his eyes out. ...stripping off the soil and gouging out bauxite, gold or iron ore.* PHRASAL VERB V n P, V P n (not pron)

gourd /gʊəʳd, gɔːʳd/ **gourds**

1 A **gourd** is a large fruit that is similar to a marrow. You can also use the word **gourd** to refer to the plant on which this fruit grows. N-COUNT

2 A **gourd** is a container made from the hard dry skin of a gourd fruit. Gourds are often used to carry water or for decoration. *The shop imports goods such as painted gourd containers.* N-COUNT

gourmand /gʊəʳmɒnd/ **gourmands.** A **gourmand** is a person who enjoys eating and drinking in large amounts; a formal word, used showing disapproval. *The food here satisfies gourmands rather than gourmets.* N-COUNT PRAGMATICS

gourmet /gʊəʳmeɪ/ **gourmets** ◆◇◇◇◇

1 **Gourmet** food is nicer or more unusual or sophisticated than ordinary food, and is often more expensive. *Flavored coffee is sold at gourmet food stores and coffee shops... The couple share a love of gourmet cooking. ...a gourmet dinner.* ADJ: ADJ n =gastronome

2 A **gourmet** is someone who enjoys good food, and who knows a lot about food and wine. N-COUNT

gout /gaʊt/. **Gout** is a disease which causes people's joints to swell painfully, especially in their toes. N-UNCOUNT

Gov., Govs. Gov. is a written abbreviation for **Governor.** *...Gov. Thomas Kean of New Jersey.* N-TITLE

govern /gʌvəʳn/ **governs, governing, governed** ◆◆◆◇◇

1 To **govern** a place such as a country, or its people, VERB

means to be officially in charge of the place, and to have responsibility for making laws, managing the economy, and controlling public services. *They go to the polls on Friday to choose the people they want to govern their country... Their citizens are very thankful they are not governed by a dictator.*
=rule
V n

2 If a situation or activity **is governed** by a particular factor, rule, or force, it is controlled by or depends on that factor, rule, or force. *Marine insurance is governed by a strict series of rules and regulations... The government has altered the rules governing eligibility for unemployment benefit.*
VERB
be V-ed by n
V n

governance /gʌvəʳnəns/ ◆◇◇◇◇

1 The **governance** of a country is the way in which it is governed; a formal use. *They believe that a fundamental change in the governance of Britain is the key to all other necessary changes.*
N-UNCOUNT

2 The **governance** of a company or organization is the way in which it is managed or administered; a formal use. *...a dramatic move away from the traditional view of governance in American education.*
N-UNCOUNT

governess /gʌvəʳnes/ **governesses.** A **governess** is a woman who is employed by a family to live with them and educate their children.
◆◇◇◇◇
N-COUNT

governing /gʌvəʳnɪŋ/. A **governing** body or organization is one which controls or regulates a particular activity. *The league became the governing body for amateur fencing in the U.S.*
◆◇◇◇◇
ADJ: ADJ n
=ruling

government /gʌvəʳnmənt/ **governments** ◆◆◆◆◆

1 The **government** of a country is the group of people who are responsible for governing it. *...The Government are to carry out a review of the Shops Act in the autumn. ...democratic governments in countries like Britain and the US. ...fighting between government forces and left-wing rebels.*
N-COUNT-COLL

2 **Government** consists of the activities, methods, and principles involved in governing a country or other political unit. *The first four years of Socialist government were completely disastrous. ...our system of government.*
N-UNCOUNT

governmental /gʌvəʳnmentᵊl/. **Governmental** means relating to a particular government, or to the practice of governing a country. *...a governmental agency for providing financial aid to developing countries.*
◆◆◇◇◇
ADJ: ADJ n

governor /gʌvəʳnəʳ/ **governors** ◆◆◆◆◇

1 In some systems of government, a **governor** is a person who is in charge of the political administration of a region or state. *He was governor of the province in the late 1970s... Governor William Livingston addressed the New Jersey Assembly.*
N-COUNT; N-TITLE

2 A **governor** is a member of a committee which controls an organization such as a school or a hospital. *Governors are using the increased powers given to them to act against incompetent headteachers. ...the chairman of the BBC board of governors.*
N-COUNT

3 In some institutions, the **governor** is the most senior official, who is in charge of the institution. *The incident was reported to the prison governor.*
N-COUNT

Governor-General, Governors-General. A **Governor-General** is a person who is sent to a former colony as the chief representative of the country which used to control that colony. *...the former Governor-General of New Zealand.*
N-COUNT: oft the N of n

governorship /gʌvnəʳʃɪp/ **governorships.** The **governorship** of a particular country or state is the position of being its governor. **Governorship** is also used to refer to the period of time a particular person spends being the governor of a country or state. *The governorship went to a Democrat, Mrs Anne Richards... He had worked closely with the President during his governorship.*
N-COUNT

govt. govt is a written abbreviation for **government**.
=government

gown /gaʊn/ **gowns** ◆◆◇◇◇

1 A **gown** is a dress, usually a long dress, which women wear on formal occasions. *The new ball gown was a great success. ...wedding gowns.*
N-COUNT

2 A **gown** is a loose black cloak worn on formal occasions by people such as lawyers and academics. *...an old headmaster in a flowing black gown.*
N-COUNT

GP /dʒiː piː/ **GPs.** A **GP** is a doctor who does not specialize in any particular area of medicine, but who has a medical practice in which he or she treats all types of illness. **GP** is an abbreviation for 'general practitioner'. *Her husband called their local GP.*
◆◆◇◇◇
N-COUNT: oft poss N

grab /græb/ **grabs, grabbing, grabbed** ◆◆◆◇◇

1 If you **grab** something, you take it or pick it up suddenly and roughly. *I managed to grab her hand... I grabbed him by the neck.*
VERB
V n
V n by/round n

2 If you **grab at** something, you try to grab it. *He was clumsily trying to grab at Alfred's arms.* ► Also a noun. *I made a grab for the knife... Mr Penrose made a grab at his collar.*
VERB
V at n
N-COUNT: usu sing, N for/at n

3 If you **grab** someone who is walking past, you succeed in getting their attention; an informal use. *Grab that waiter, Mary Ann.*
VERB
V n

4 If you **grab** someone's attention, you do something in order to make them notice you. *I jumped on the wall to grab the attention of the crowd.*
VERB
V n

5 If you **grab** something such as food, drink, or sleep, you manage to get some quickly; an informal use. *Grab a beer.*
VERB
V n

6 If you **grab** something such as a chance or opportunity, or **grab at** it, you take advantage of it eagerly. *She grabbed the chance of a job interview... He grabbed at the opportunity to buy his castle.*
VERB
=seize
V n
V at n

7 A **grab for** something such as power or fame is an attempt to gain it. *...a grab for personal power.*
N-COUNT: usu sing, N for n

8 ● **grab hold**: see **hold**. See also **smash-and-grab**.

9 If something is **up for grabs**, it is available to anyone who is interested; an informal expression. *The famous Ritz hotel is up for grabs for £100m.*
PHRASE: usu v-link PHR

grace /greɪs/ **graces, gracing, graced** ◆◆◇◇◇

1 If someone moves with **grace**, they move in a smooth, controlled, and attractive way. *He moved with the grace of a trained boxer... Ballet classes are important for poise and grace.*
N-UNCOUNT: usu with supp

2 If someone behaves with **grace**, they behave in a pleasant, polite, and dignified way, even when they are upset or being treated unfairly. *The new King seemed to be carrying out his duties with grace and due decorum... The young woman had grace beyond her years.*
N-UNCOUNT

3 The **graces** are the ways of behaving and doing things which are considered polite and well-mannered; used mainly in old-fashioned or British English. *Despite the hardships of prairie life she remembered the graces she'd learned in her girlhood... Her reading and her social graces had made her a very pleasant companion.*
N-PLURAL: oft the N, adj N

4 You use **grace** in expressions such as **a day's grace** and **a month's grace** to show that you have been given that amount of time before something happens or before you are expected to do something such as finish a job or pay a bill. *She wanted a couple of days' grace to get the maisonette cleaned before she moved in... We have only a few hours' grace before the soldiers come.*
N-UNCOUNT: usu supp N

5 If you say that something **graces** a place, you mean that it makes the place more pleasant or attractive; a formal use. *He went to the beautiful old Welsh dresser that graced this homely room... Her shoulders were graced with mink and her fingers sparkled with diamonds.*
VERB
V n
be V-ed with/by n

6 If you say that someone important **will grace** an event or an organization, you mean that they have kindly agreed to be present at the event or to be part of the organization; a formal use. *He had been invited to grace a function at the evening college.*
VERB
V n

7 In Christianity and some other religions, **grace** is the kindness that God shows to people because he loves them. *It was only by the grace of God that no one died.*
N-UNCOUNT

8 When someone says **grace** before or after a meal, they say a prayer in which they thank God for the food and ask him to bless it. *Leo, will you say grace? ...a Latin grace.*
N-VAR

9 You use expressions such as **Your Grace** and **His Grace** when you are addressing or referring to a
N-VOC; N-PROPER: det-poss N

duke, duchess, or archbishop. *Your Grace, I have a great favour to ask of you.*

10 See also **coup de grace, saving grace.**

11 If you refer to someone's **fall from grace**, you are talking about the fact they are suddenly no longer approved of or popular, often because they have done something wrong or unacceptable. You can also say that someone **has fallen from grace**. *The reasons for his apparent fall from grace are not clear... All went well at first, and I was in high favour; but presently I fell from grace.* PHRASES

12 If you refer to someone's **fall from grace**, you are talking about the immoral act, often the act of adultery, that they have committed. If someone **falls from grace**, they do something immoral. *She'd taken her husband's fall from grace with courage and forgiveness... The next time you fall from grace will be the last time.*

13 If you say that someone **had the grace** or **had the good grace** to do something, you mean that they showed by their behaviour that they were ashamed of something bad that they had done earlier; used showing approval. *He did not even have the grace to apologise.* V inflects, PHR to-inf

14 If you are talking about someone who is in an unfortunate situation and you say **'There but for the grace of God go I'**, you mean that it is only by luck or God's goodness that you are not in the same situation as them and you sympathize with them.

15 If you do something unpleasant **with good grace** or **with a good grace**, you do it cheerfully and without complaining. If you do something **with bad grace** or **with a bad grace**, you do it unwillingly and unenthusiastically. *He accepted the decision with good grace, and wished me the very best of luck... With appallingly bad grace I packed up and we drove north.* PHR after v

16 If you are in someone's **good graces**, they are pleased with you. *You're so eager to stay in the good graces of the King that nothing else matters to you.* PHR with poss

17 • **airs and graces**: see **air.**

graceful /greɪsfʊl/ ◆◇◇◇◇

1 Someone or something that is **graceful** moves in a smooth and controlled way which is attractive to watch. *His movements were so graceful they seemed effortless. ...graceful ballerinas.* ♦ **gracefully** *She stepped gracefully onto the stage.* ADJ-GRADED ≠graceless; ADV-GRADED: ADV with v

2 Something that is **graceful** is attractive because it has a pleasing shape or style. *A graceful medieval cathedral... His handwriting, from earliest young manhood, was flowing and graceful.* ♦ **gracefully** *She loved the gracefully high ceiling, with its white-painted cornice.* ADJ-GRADED ≠graceless; ADV: ADV adj/-ed

3 If a person's behaviour is **graceful**, it is polite, kind, and pleasant, especially in a difficult situation. *Aubrey could think of no graceful way to escape Corbet's company... He was charming, cheerful, and graceful under pressure.* ♦ **gracefully** *We managed to decline gracefully.* ADJ-GRADED; ADV-GRADED: ADV with v

graceless /greɪsləs/

1 Something that is **graceless** is unattractive and not at all interesting or charming. *It was a massive, graceless house.* ADJ-GRADED ≠graceful

2 A **graceless** movement is clumsy and uncontrolled. *...a graceless pirouette.* ♦ **gracelessly** *He dropped gracelessly into a chair opposite her.* ADJ-GRADED; ADV-GRADED: ADV with v

3 If you describe someone as **graceless**, you mean that their behaviour is impolite and unrefined. *She couldn't stand his blunt, graceless manner.* ♦ **gracelessly** *The task fell to Mr Harris to deliver this bad news. It was gracelessly done.* ADJ-GRADED; ADV-GRADED: ADV with v

gracious /greɪʃəs/ ◆◇◇◇◇

1 If you describe someone, especially someone you think is superior to you, as **gracious**, you mean that they are very well-mannered and pleasant; a formal use. *She is a lovely and gracious woman.* ADJ-GRADED =courteous

2 If you describe the behaviour of someone in a position of authority as **gracious**, you mean that they behave in a polite and considerate way. *She closed with a gracious speech of thanks.* ♦ **graciously** *Hospitality at the Presidential guest house was graciously declined.* ADJ-GRADED; ADV-GRADED: ADV with v

3 You use **gracious** to describe the comfortable way of life of wealthy people. *He drove through the gracious suburbs with the swimming pools and tennis courts.* ADJ-GRADED: usu ADJ n

4 Some people say **good gracious** or **goodness gracious** in order to express surprise or annoyance. *Good gracious, look at that specimen will you?* EXCLAM PRAGMATICS

gradation /grədeɪʃən, AM greɪ-/ **gradations.** **Gradations** are small differences or changes in things; a formal word. *But TV images require subtle gradations of light and shade.* N-COUNT: usu pl, with supp

grade /greɪd/ **grades, grading, graded** ◆◆◆◇◇

1 If something **is graded**, its quality is judged or classified. It is often given a number or a name that indicates how good or bad it is. *Dust masks are graded according to the protection they offer... South Point College does not grade the students' work. ...a three-tier grading system.* VERB be V-ed; V n; V-ing

2 The **grade** of a product is its quality, especially when this has been officially judged or classified. *...a good grade of plywood. ...a grade II listed building.* ► Also a combining form. *...weapons-grade plutonium. ...aviation fuel and high-grade oil.* N-COUNT: with supp, oft adj N, N num; COMB in ADJ

3 Your **grade** in an examination or piece of written work is the mark you get, usually in the form of a letter or number, that indicates your level of achievement. *...GCSE O level, grade B... What grade are you hoping to get?... There was a lot of pressure on you to obtain good grades.* N-COUNT: with supp, oft adj N, N num

4 Your **grade** in a company or organization is your level of importance or your rank. *Staff turnover is particularly high among junior grades.* N-COUNT: with supp

5 In the United States, a **grade** is a group of classes in which all the children are of a similar age. When you are five years old you go into the first grade and you leave school after the twelfth grade. *Mr White teaches first grade in south Georgia.* N-COUNT: usu with supp, oft ord N

6 In American English, a **grade** is a slope. The usual British word is **gradient**. *Trekking is rated as moderate involving some steep grades.* N-COUNT

7 If someone **makes the grade**, they succeed, especially by reaching a particular standard; an informal expression. *She had a strong desire to be a dancer but failed to make the grade.* PHRASE: V inflects =succeed

grade crossing, grade crossings. In American English, a **grade crossing** is a place where a railroad track crosses a road at the same level. The usual British word is **level crossing**. N-COUNT

graded /greɪdɪd/. In this dictionary, a **graded** adjective or adverb is one which is sometimes used with an adverb or phrase indicating degree. 'Clever' is an example of a graded adjective. ADJ: usu ADJ n

graded reader, graded readers. A **graded reader** is a story which has been adapted for people learning to read or learning a foreign language. Graded readers avoid using difficult grammar and vocabulary. N-COUNT

-grader /-greɪdər/ **-graders. -grader** combines with words such as 'first' and 'second' to form nouns which refer to a child or young person who is in a particular grade in the American education system. *Randy Stillwell is a sixth-grader at the Latta School just outside of Ada.* COMB in N-COUNT

grade school, grade schools. In the United States, a **grade school** is the same as an **elementary school.** *I was just in grade school at the time, but I remember it perfectly.* N-VAR: oft *in* N

gradient /greɪdiənt/ **gradients** ◆◇◇◇◇

1 A **gradient** is a slope, or the degree to which the ground slopes. The more usual American word is **grade**. *...a gradient of 1 in 3... The courses are long and punishing, with steep gradients.* N-COUNT

2 The **gradient** of a graph or series of measurements is the rate at which one set of amounts changes in relation to another. N-COUNT: with supp

gradual /grædʒuəl/. A **gradual** change or process occurs in small stages over a long period of time, rather than suddenly. *Losing weight is a slow, gradual process... You can expect her progress at school to be gradual rather than brilliant.* ◆◆◇◇◇ ADJ-GRADED

gradually. If something changes or is done **gradually**, it changes or is done in small stages over a long period of time, rather than suddenly. *Electricity lines to 30,000 homes were gradually being restored yesterday... Gradually we learned to cope.* ◆◆◆◇◇ ADV-GRADED: ADV with v

graduate, graduates, graduating, graduated. The noun is pronounced /grædʒuət/. The verb is pronounced /grædʒueɪt/. ◆◆◆◇◇

1 In Britain, a **graduate** is a person who has successfully completed a degree at a university or college and has received a certificate that shows this. *In 1973, the first Open University graduates received their degrees. ...graduates in engineering.* N-COUNT: usu with supp, oft N *in/from/* of n

2 In the United States, a **graduate** is a student who has successfully completed high school and has received a certificate or diploma. *The top one-third of all high school graduates are entitled to an education at the California State University.* N-COUNT: usu supp N

3 In Britain, when a student **graduates** from university, they have successfully completed a degree course and receive a certificate that shows this, usually at a special ceremony. *She graduated in English and Drama from Manchester University.* VERB V prep Also V

4 In the United States, when a student **graduates** or when their university, college, or school **graduates** them, they have successfully completed their studies and receive a certificate or diploma that shows this, usually at a special ceremony. *When the boys graduated from high school, Ann moved to a small town in Vermont... In 1986, American universities graduated a record number of students with degrees in computer science.* V-ERG V prep V n Also V

5 If you **graduate** from one thing to another, you go from a less important job or position to a more important one. *Bruce graduated to chef at the Bear Hotel... From commercials she quickly graduated to television shows.* VERB =progress V *to/from* n

graduated /grædʒueɪtɪd/

1 **Graduated** means increasing by regular amounts or grades. *The US military wants to avoid the graduated escalation that marked the Vietnam War.* ADJ: ADJ n

2 **Graduated** jars are marked with lines and numbers which show particular measurements. *...a graduated tube marked in millimetres.* ADJ: ADJ n

graduate school, graduate schools. In the United States, a **graduate school** is a department in a university or college where postgraduate students are taught. *She was in graduate school, studying for a master's degree in social work.* N-VAR

graduation /grædʒueɪʃᵊn/ **graduations** ◆◇◇◇◇

1 **Graduation** is the successful completion of a course of study at a university, college, or school, for which you receive a degree or diploma. *They asked what his plans were after graduation... Upon graduation he joined a small law firm.* N-UNCOUNT

2 A **graduation** is a special ceremony at university, college, or school, at which degrees and diplomas are given to students who have successfully completed their studies. *...the graduation ceremony at Yale... At my brother's high school graduation the students recited a poem.* N-COUNT: usu sing, oft N n

3 A **graduation** is a line or number on a container or measuring instrument which marks a particular measurement. *...medicine bottles with graduations on them.* N-COUNT

graffiti /grəfiːti/. **Graffiti** are words or pictures that are written or drawn in public places, for example on walls or posters. Graffiti are usually rude, funny, or political. *Buildings old and new are thickly covered with graffiti... There's no vandalism, no graffiti, no rubbish left lying about.* ◆◇◇◇◇ N-UNCOUNT-COLL

graft /grɑːft, græft/ **grafts, grafting, grafted** ◆◇◇◇◇

1 A **graft** is a piece of healthy skin or bone, or a healthy organ, which is attached to a damaged part of your body by a medical operation in order to replace it. *I am having a skin graft on my arm soon.* N-COUNT: oft supp N

2 If a piece of healthy skin or bone or a healthy organ **is grafted** onto a damaged part of your body, it is attached to that part of your body by a medical operation. *The top layer of skin has to be grafted onto the burns.* VB: usu passive be V-ed *onto/on* n

3 If a part of one plant or tree **is grafted** onto another plant or tree, they are joined together so that they will become one plant or tree, often in order to produce a new variety. *Pear trees are grafted on quince rootstocks.* VERB be V-ed *on/onto* n

4 If you **graft** one idea or system on to another, you try to join one to the other. *The Japanese tried to graft their own methods on to this different structure.* VERB V n *onto* n

5 In informal British English, **graft** means hard work. *His career has been one of hard graft.* N-UNCOUNT

6 In politics, **graft** is used to refer to the activity of using power or authority to obtain money dishonestly; used mainly in American English. *...another politician accused of graft.* N-UNCOUNT

Grail /greɪl/ ◆◇◇◇◇

1 The **Grail** or the **Holy Grail** is the cup that was used by Jesus Christ at the Last Supper. In medieval times, many people tried to find the Grail without success. N-PROPER

2 If you describe something as a **grail** or a **holy grail**, you mean it is something that someone is trying very hard to obtain or achieve. *The discovery is being hailed as The Holy Grail of astronomy, with scientists claiming it has solved one of space's most troubling enigmas.* N-SING: oft *the* N *of* n

grain /greɪn/ **grains** ◆◆◆◇◇

1 A **grain** of wheat, rice, or other cereal crop is a seed from it. *...a grain of wheat. ...rice grains.* N-COUNT: usu with supp

2 **Grain** is a cereal crop, especially wheat or corn, that has been harvested and is used for food or in trade. *...a bag of grain. ...the best grains.* N-MASS

3 A **grain of** something such as sand or salt is a tiny hard piece of it. *...a grain of sand.* ♦ **-grained** *...coarse-grained salt.* N-COUNT COMB in ADJ-GRADED

4 A **grain of** a quality is a very small amount of it. *There's more than a grain of truth in that.* N-SING: N *of* n

5 **The grain** of a piece of wood is the direction of its fibres. You can also refer to the pattern of lines on the surface of the wood as **the grain**. *Brush the paint generously over the wood in the direction of the grain.* ♦ **-grained** *...a hard, heavy, straight-grained wood.* N-SING: *the* N COMB in ADJ-GRADED

6 If you say that an idea or action **goes against the grain**, you mean that it is very difficult for you to accept it or do it, because it conflicts with your previous ideas, beliefs, or principles. *Privatisation goes against the grain of their principle of opposition to private ownership of industry.* PHRASE: V inflects

grainy /greɪni/

1 A **grainy** photograph looks as if it is made up of lots of spots, which make the lines or shapes in it difficult to see. *...grainy black and white photos.* ADJ-GRADED

2 **Grainy** means having a rough surface or texture, or containing small bits of something. *...the grainy tree trunk... Do not use a grainy mustard.* ADJ: usu ADJ n ≠smooth

gram /græm/ **grams;** also spelled **gramme.** A **gram** is a unit of weight. One thousand grams are equal to one kilogram. *...a camcorder which weighs just 760 grams.* ◆◆◇◇◇ N-COUNT

-gram /-græm/ **-grams. -gram** combines with nouns to form other nouns which refer to someone who dresses up as the specified type of person in order to a bring a message to someone else, as a practical joke. *Halfway through the evening, a Gorillagram burst into the office. ...a striptease nun-a-gram.* COMB in N-COUNT

grammar /græməʳ/ **grammars** ◆◆◇◇◇

1 **Grammar** is the ways that words can be put together in order to make sentences. *He doesn't have mastery of the basic rules of grammar. ...the difference between Sanskrit and Tibetan grammar.* N-UNCOUNT

2 Someone's **grammar** is the way in which they obey or do not obey the rules of grammar when they write or speak. *His vocabulary was sound and his grammar excellent. ...a deterioration in spelling and grammar among teenagers.* N-UNCOUNT: oft supp N

3 A **grammar** is a book that describes the rules of a language. *...an advanced English grammar.* N-COUNT

4 A particular **grammar** is a particular theory that N-VAR:

is intended to explain the rules of a language. *Transformational grammars are more restrictive.* with supp

grammarian /grəmeəriən/ **grammarians.** A **grammarian** is someone who studies the grammar of a language and writes books about it or teaches it. N-COUNT

grammar school, grammar schools. A **grammar school** is a school in Britain for children aged between eleven and eighteen who have a high academic ability. *He is in the third year at Leeds Grammar School.* ◆◇◇◇◇ N-VAR: oft in names after n

grammatical /grəmætɪkəl/

1 **Grammatical** is used to indicate that something relates to grammar. *Should the teacher present grammatical rules to students? ...grammatical errors.* ♦ **grammatically** *...grammatically correct language.* ADJ: ADJ n; ADV: ADV adj/-ed

2 If someone's language is **grammatical**, it is considered correct because it obeys the rules of grammar. *...a new test to determine whether students can write grammatical English.* ♦ **grammatically** *...studies showing that up to one in five undergraduates cannot write grammatically.* ADJ; ADV: ADV after v

gramme /græm/. See **gram**.

gramophone /græməfoun/ **gramophones.** A **gramophone** is an old-fashioned type of record player; used mainly in British English. *...a wind-up gramophone with a big horn. ...gramophone records.* N-COUNT

gran /græn/ **grans.** In informal British English, some people refer to or address their grandmother as **gran**. *My gran's given us some apple jam.* ◆◇◇◇◇ N-FAMILY

granary /grænəri/ **granaries**

1 A **granary** is a building which is used for storing grain. *The granaries containing last year's harvest are nearly empty.* N-COUNT

2 You can refer to the part of a country or region where a large amount of corn is grown as the **granary of** that country or region. *The wheat lands that made North Africa the granary of the Roman Empire are now largely desert.* N-SING: N of n

3 In Britain, **Granary** bread contains whole grains of wheat. **Granary** is a trademark. ADJ: ADJ n

grand /grænd/ **grander, grandest; grands.** The form **grand** is used as the plural for meaning 8. ◆◆◆◆◇

1 If you describe a building or a landscape as **grand**, you mean that it looks splendid because its size or appearance is very impressive. *This grand building in the center of town used to be the hub of the capital's social life... The scenery of South Island is on a grand scale.* ADJ-GRADED =majestic

2 **Grand** plans or actions are ambitious and intended to achieve important results. *Mr Rocard hoped to take the first step in his grand scheme for a realignment of the party... The grand design of Europe's monetary union is already agreed.* ADJ-GRADED

3 If you describe people or things such as their jobs or appearances as **grand**, you disapprove of them because they think they are important or socially superior. *He is grander and even richer than the Prince of Wales... The Duke of Clarence will be there, and many of your grander friends.* ADJ-GRADED PRAGMATICS

4 If you describe an activity or experience as **grand**, you mean that it is very pleasant and enjoyable. *Few museums could rival the Old Royal Observatory at Greenwich for a grand day out... The dinner was a grand success... He was having a grand time meeting new sorts of people.* ADJ =great

5 If you describe someone or something as **grand**, you mean that you admire or approve of them very much; used in informal spoken English. *He was a grand bloke. We used to have some good times on the river.* ADJ-GRADED PRAGMATICS =great, wonderful

6 A **grand** total is one that is the final amount or the final result of a calculation. *It came to a grand total of £220,329.* ADJ: ADJ n

7 **Grand** is often used in the names of buildings such as hotels, especially when they are very large. *They stayed at The Grand Hotel, Budapest.* ADJ: ADJ n

8 A **grand** is a thousand dollars or a thousand pounds; an informal use. *They're paying you ten grand now for those adaptations of old plays.* N-COUNT: usu a/num N

9 A **grand** is the same as a **grand piano**. N-COUNT: usu sing

10 See also **grandly**.

grandad /grændæd/ **grandads;** also spelled **granddad**. Your **grandad** is your grandfather; an informal word. *My grandad is 85.* N-FAMILY

grandaddy /grændædi/ **grandaddies;** also spelled **granddaddy**. Some people refer to or address their grandfather as **grandaddy**; an informal word used in American English. N-FAMILY =grandad

grandchild /græntʃaɪld/ **grandchildren.** Someone's **grandchild** is the child of their son or daughter. *Mary loves her grandchildren.* ◆◆◇◇◇ N-COUNT: oft poss N

granddad /grændæd/. See **grandad**.

granddaughter /grændɔːtəʳ/ **granddaughters.** Someone's **granddaughter** is the daughter of their son or daughter. *...a drawing of my granddaughter Amelia.* ◆◇◇◇◇ N-COUNT: usu with poss

grandee /grændiː/ **grandees.** A **grandee** is a Spanish prince of the highest rank; an old-fashioned word. N-COUNT

grandeur /grændʒəʳ/ ◆◇◇◇◇

1 **Grandeur** is the quality in something, for example in a building or in scenery, which makes it seem impressive and often elegant. *Mrs Thatcher was in her element amid the grandeur of the country mansion... ...a car that almost matched the Bentley in its grandeur.* N-UNCOUNT: oft the N of n

2 Someone's **grandeur** is the great importance and social status that they have, or think they have. *He is wholly concerned with his own grandeur... He condemned the Prime Minister's ridiculous 'delusions of grandeur'.* N-UNCOUNT: oft poss N

grandfather /grændfɑːðəʳ/ **grandfathers.** Your **grandfather** is the father of your father or mother. *His grandfather was a professor.* ◆◆◇◇◇ N-FAMILY

grandfather clock, grandfather clocks. A **grandfather clock** is an old-fashioned type of clock in a tall wooden case which stands upright on the floor. N-COUNT

grandiloquent /grændɪləkwənt/. If you describe language or behaviour as **grandiloquent**, you are critical of it because it is very formal, literary, or exaggerated, and is used by people when they want to seem impressive; a formal word. *She attacked her colleagues for indulging in 'grandiose and grandiloquent language'. ...grandiloquent claims from Tory ministers.* ADJ-GRADED PRAGMATICS

grandiose /grændious/. If you describe something as **grandiose**, you mean it is bigger or more elaborate than necessary; used showing disapproval. *The sad truth is that not one of Kim's grandiose plans has even begun.* ◆◇◇◇◇ ADJ-GRADED PRAGMATICS

grand jury, grand juries. A **grand jury** is a jury, usually in the United States, which considers a criminal case in order to decide if someone should be tried in a court of law. *They have already given evidence before a grand jury in Washington.* ◆◇◇◇◇ N-COUNT

grandly /grændli/

1 You use **grandly** to say that the name of a place or thing makes it sound much more impressive than it really is. *The grandly named European Cricketer Cup is based at Worksop College... Lucille's home was very grandly called a chateau, though in truth it was nothing more than a large moated farm.* ADV-GRADED: ADV adj, ADV before v

2 You say that someone speaks or behaves **grandly** when you disapprove of them because they are trying to impress other people. *This, the EEA grandly declared, would require a diplomatic conference.* ADV-GRADED: usu ADV with v, also ADV adj PRAGMATICS

grandma /grænmɑː/ **grandmas.** Your **grandma** is your grandmother; an informal word. *Grandma was from Scotland.* ◆◇◇◇◇ N-FAMILY

Grandmaster /grændmɑːstəʳ, -mæst-/ **Grandmasters.** In chess, a **Grandmaster** is a player who has achieved a very high standard in tournaments. N-COUNT; N-TITLE

grandmother /grænmʌðəʳ/ **grandmothers.** Your **grandmother** is the mother of your father or mother. *My grandmothers are both widows.* ◆◆◇◇◇ N-FAMILY

grandpa /grænpɑː/ **grandpas.** Your **grandpa** is your grandfather; an informal word. *Grandpa was not yet back from the war.*
N-FAMILY =grandad

grandparent /grænpeərənt/ **grandparents.** Your **grandparents** are the parents of your father or mother. *Tammy was raised by her grandparents.*
◆◇◇◇◇ N-COUNT: usu pl, oft poss N

grand piano, grand pianos. A **grand piano** is a large piano whose strings are set horizontally to the ground. Grand pianos are used especially for giving concerts and making recordings.
N-COUNT

Grand Prix /grɒn priː, AM grænd -/ **Grands Prix** or **Grand Prix.** A **Grand Prix** is one of a series of races for very powerful racing cars; also used sometimes in the names of competitions in other sports. *He never won the British Grand Prix.*
◆◆◇◇◇ N-COUNT: usu with supp

Grand Slam, Grand Slams
◆◇◇◇◇
1 In sport, a **Grand Slam** tournament is a major one. *...her 39 Grand Slam titles.* ► Also a noun. *It's my first Grand Slam and I was hoping to make a good impression.*
ADJ: ADJ n; N-COUNT
2 If someone wins a **Grand Slam**, they win all the major tournaments in a season in a particular sport, for example in rugby or tennis. *They won the Grand Slam in 1990.*
N-COUNT

grandson /grænsʌn/ **grandsons.** Someone's **grandson** is the son of their son or daughter. *My grandson's birthday was on Tuesday.*
◆◇◇◇◇ N-COUNT: oft with poss

grandstand /grændstænd/ **grandstands.** A **grandstand** is a covered stand with rows of seats for spectators at sporting events.
◆◇◇◇◇ N-COUNT

Grand Tour, Grand Tours; also spelled **grand tour.** The **Grand Tour** was a journey round the main cities of Europe that young men from rich families used to make as part of their education. *Every traveller on the Grand Tour had to visit Florence.*
N-COUNT

granite /grænɪt/ **granites. Granite** is a very hard rock used in building.
◆◇◇◇◇ N-MASS

granny /græni/ **grannies;** also spelled **grannie.** Some people refer to their grandmother as **granny**; an informal word. *...my old granny.*
◆◇◇◇◇ N-FAMILY

grant /grɑːnt, grænt/ **grants, granting, granted**
◆◆◆◆◇
1 A **grant** is an amount of money that a government or other institution gives to an individual or to an organization for a particular purpose such as education or home improvements. *They'd got a special grant to encourage research... Unfortunately, my application for a grant was rejected.*
N-COUNT
2 If someone in authority **grants** you something, or if something **is granted** to you, you are allowed to have it. *France has agreed to grant him political asylum... The local council in Brent in northwest London has granted the Freedom of the Borough to Mr Nelson Mandela... Permission was granted a few weeks ago.*
VERB =give; V n n; V n to n; be V-ed
3 If you **grant** that something is true, especially someone else's opinion or an unpleasant fact, you accept that it is true; a formal use. *The magistrates granted that the RSPCA was justified in bringing the action.*
VERB; V that
4 If you say that someone **takes** you **for granted,** you are complaining that they benefit from your help, efforts, or presence without showing that they are grateful. *What right has the family to take me for granted, Martin?... The officials felt taken for granted and grumbled loudly.*
PHRASES; *take* inflects
5 If you **take** something **for granted**, you believe that it is true or accept it as normal without thinking about it. *I was amazed that virtually all the things I took for granted up north just didn't happen in London.*
take inflects
6 If you **take it for granted** that something is the case, you believe that it is true or you accept it as normal without thinking about it. *He seemed to take it for granted that he should speak as a representative.*
take inflects, PHR that

granted /grɑːntɪd, græntɪd/. You use **granted** or **granted that** at the beginning of a clause to say that something is true, before you make a comment on it. *Granted that the firm has not broken the law, is the law what it should be?* ► Also an adverb. *Granted, he doesn't look too bad for his age, though there's nothing about his character that would appeal to me.*
CONJ-SUBORD; PRAGMATICS; ADV: ADV with cl =true

grant-maintained. In Britain, a **grant-maintained school** is one which receives money directly from the national government rather than from a local authority.
◆◇◇◇◇ ADJ: usu ADJ n

granular /grænjʊləʳ/. **Granular** substances are composed of a lot of granules, or feel or look as if they are composed of a lot of granules; a formal word. *...a granular fertiliser.*
ADJ: usu ADJ n

granulated sugar /grænjʊleɪtɪd ʃʊgəʳ/. **Granulated sugar** is sugar that is in the form of crystal-like grains. You add it to drinks such as tea and coffee or use it in cooking.
N-UNCOUNT

granule /grænjuːl/ **granules. Granules** are small round pieces of something. *She was spooning coffee granules into cups.*
N-COUNT: usu pl, oft supp N

grape /greɪp/ **grapes**
◆◆◇◇◇
1 **Grapes** are small green or dark purple fruit which grow in bunches. Grapes can be eaten raw, used for making wine, or dried.
N-COUNT
2 If you describe someone's attitude as **sour grapes**, you mean that they say something is worthless or undesirable because they want it themselves but cannot have it. *These accusations have been going on for some time now, but it is just sour grapes.*
PHRASE: usu v-link PHR, PHR after v

grapefruit /greɪpfruːt/ **grapefruits.** The plural can be either **grapefruit** or **grapefruits**. A **grapefruit** is a large, round, yellow fruit, similar to an orange, that has a sharp, slightly bitter taste.
◆◇◇◇◇ N-VAR

grapevine /greɪpvaɪn/ **grapevines**
◆◇◇◇◇
1 If you hear or learn something on **the grapevine**, you hear it or learn it in casual conversation with other people. *He'd doubtless heard rumours on the grapevine... I had heard through the grapevine that he was quite critical of what we were doing.*
N-SING: usu *on/through the* N
2 A **grapevine** is a climbing plant on which grapes grow.
N-COUNT

graph /grɑːf, græf/ **graphs.** A **graph** is a mathematical diagram which shows the relationship between two or more sets of numbers or measurements.
◆◇◇◇◇ N-COUNT

graphic /græfɪk/ **graphics**
◆◆◇◇◇
1 If you say that a description or account of something unpleasant is **graphic**, you are emphasizing that it is clear and detailed. *The descriptions of sexual abuse are graphic. ...graphic scenes of drug taking.* ♦ **graphically** /græfɪkli/ *Here, graphically displayed, was confirmation of the entire story.*
ADJ-GRADED =explicit; ADV-GRADED; ADV with v
2 **Graphic** means concerned with drawing or pictures, especially in publishing, industry, or computing. *...the graphic design department. ...fine and graphic arts.*
ADJ: ADJ n
3 **Graphics** is the activity of drawing or making pictures, especially in publishing, industry, or computing. *...a computer manufacturer which specialises in graphics.*
N-UNCOUNT
4 **Graphics** are drawings and pictures that are composed using simple lines and sometimes strong colours. *The articles are noticeably shorter with strong headlines and graphics... The Agriculture Department today released a new graphic to replace the old symbol.*
N-COUNT: usu pl

graphical /græfɪkᵊl/. A **graphical** representation of something uses graphs or similar visual devices to represent statistics or figures. *A graphical representation of results is shown in figure 1. ...a graphical map of Britain showing the party gains in each area.*
ADJ: ADJ n

graphic design. **Graphic design** is the art of designing advertisements, magazines, and books by combining pictures and words.
N-UNCOUNT

graphic designer, graphic designers. A **graphic designer** is a person who designs advertisements, magazines, and books by combining pictures and words. *She asked her son, a graphic designer, to create letterheads and stationery.*
N-COUNT

graphite /græfaɪt/. **Graphite** is a hard black substance that is a form of carbon. It has many
◆◇◇◇◇ N-UNCOUNT

uses, for example in pencils, in lightweight sports equipment, and in nuclear reactors.

graphology /græfɒlədʒi/. **Graphology** is the science of examining people's handwriting in order to discover what sort of personality they have. N-UNCOUNT

graph paper. **Graph paper** is paper that has small squares printed on it so that you can use it for drawing graphs. N-UNCOUNT

grapple /græpᵊl/ **grapples, grappling, grappled** ◆◇◇◇◇

1 If you **grapple** with a problem or difficulty, you try hard to solve it. *The economy is just one of several critical problems the country is grappling with... Both cricketers grappled to establish a lively tempo.* VERB V *with* n V to-inf

2 If you **grapple** with someone, you take hold of them and struggle with them, as part of a fight. You can also say that two people **grapple**. *He was grappling with an alligator in a lagoon... They grappled desperately for control of the weapon.* V-RECIP =wrestle V *with* n pl-n V

grasp /grɑːsp, græsp/ **grasps, grasping, grasped** ◆◆◇◇◇

1 If you **grasp** something, you take it in your hand and hold it very firmly. *He grasped both my hands... She was trying to grasp at something.* ● See also **grasping**. VERB V n V *at* n

2 A **grasp** is a very firm hold or grip. *His hand was taken in a warm, firm grasp.* N-SING: with supp

3 If you say that something is in someone's **grasp**, you disapprove of the fact that they possess or control it. If something slips from your **grasp**, you lose it or lose control of it. *The people in your grasp are not guests, they are hostages... She allowed victory to slip from her grasp. ...the task of liberating a number of states from the grasp of tyrants.* N-SING: with poss, oft *in/from* N PRAGMATICS

4 If you **grasp** something that is complicated or difficult to understand, you understand it. *The Government has not yet grasped the seriousness of the crisis... He instantly grasped that Stephen was talking about his wife.* VERB V n V that

5 A **grasp** of something is an understanding of it. *They have a good grasp of foreign languages.* N-SING: with supp, usu N *of* N

6 If you say that something is **within** someone's **grasp**, you mean that it is very likely that they will achieve it. *Peace is now within our grasp.* PHRASE: v-link PHR

grasping /grɑːspɪŋ, græsp-/. If you describe someone as **grasping**, you disapprove of them because they want to get and keep as much money as possible and are unwilling to spend it. *...a greedy grasping drug-ridden individual... They were grasping and manipulative.* ADJ-GRADED PRAGMATICS

grass /grɑːs, græs/ **grasses, grassing, grassed** ◆◆◆◇◇

1 **Grass** is a very common plant consisting of large numbers of thin, spiky, green leaves covering the surface of the ground. *Small things stirred in the grass around the tent... The lawn contained a mixture of grasses.* N-MASS

2 If you talk about **the grass**, you are referring to an area of ground that is covered with grass, for example in your garden. *In the old days, there were strict fines for walking on the grass or missing a study period... I'm going to cut the grass.* N-SING: usu *the* N

3 **Grass** is the same as **marijuana**; an informal use. *I started smoking grass when I was about sixteen.* N-UNCOUNT =dope

4 In informal British English, if you say that one person **grasses on** another, you disapprove of the fact that the first person tells the police or other authorities about something criminal or wrong which the second person has done. *His wife wants him to grass on the members of his own gang... He was repeatedly attacked by other inmates, who accused him of grassing.* ► **Grass up** means the same as **grass**. *How many of them are going to grass up their own kids to the police?* VERB PRAGMATICS =inform V *on* n V PHRASAL VERB V P n (not pron) Also V n P

5 In informal British English, if you call someone a **grass**, you disapprove of them because they tell the police or other authorities about criminal activities that they know about. N-COUNT PRAGMATICS =informer

6 If you say to someone that **the grass is greener** somewhere else, you are reminding them that other people's situations always seem better or more attractive than your own, but may not really be so. *He was very happy with us but wanted to see if the grass was greener elsewhere.* PHRASES V inflects

7 If you say that someone is being **put out to grass**, you mean they are no longer being employed because they are considered to be too old or no longer useful; an informal expression. *Mr Galpin, brought in when the old guard were put out to grass, yesterday unveiled an 11% jump in profits.* V inflects

grass over. If an area of ground **is grassed over**, grass is planted all over it. *The asphalt playgrounds have been grassed over or sown with flowers.* PHRASAL VERB usu passive *be* V-ed P

grass up. See **grass** 4. PHRASAL VERB

grasshopper /grɑːshɒpəʳ, græs-/ **grasshoppers.** A **grasshopper** is an insect with long back legs that jumps high into the air and makes a high, vibrating sound. N-COUNT

grassland /grɑːslænd, græs-/ **grasslands.** **Grassland** is land covered with wild grass. *...areas of open grassland.* ◆◇◇◇◇ N-UNCOUNT: also N in pl, usu supp N

grass roots; also spelled **grass-roots** or **grassroots**. The **grass roots** of an organization or movement are the ordinary people who form the main part of it, rather than its leaders. *You have to join the party at grass-roots level from what I understand.* ◆◇◇◇◇ N-PLURAL: oft N n

grassy /grɑːsi, græs-/ **grassier, grassiest.** A **grassy** area of land is covered in grass. *Its buildings are half-hidden behind grassy banks.* ◆◇◇◇◇ ADJ-GRADED: usu ADJ n

grata /grɑːtə/. See **persona non grata**.

grate /greɪt/ **grates, grating, grated** ◆◆◇◇◇

1 A **grate** is a framework of metal bars in a fireplace, which holds the coal or wood. *A wood fire burned in the grate.* N-COUNT

2 If you **grate** food such as cheese or carrots, you rub it over a metal tool called a grater so that the food is shredded into very small pieces. *Grate the cheese into a mixing bowl. ...grated carrot.* VERB V n V-ed

3 When something **grates**, it rubs against something else making a harsh, unpleasant sound. *His chair grated as he got to his feet... The gun barrel grated against the floor.* VERB V V *against/on* n

4 If something such as someone's behaviour **grates on** you or **grates**, it makes you feel annoyed. *His manner always grated on me... What truly grates is the painful banter.* VERB V *on* n V

5 See also **grating**.

grateful /greɪtfʊl/. If you are **grateful** for something that someone has given you or done for you, you have warm, friendly feelings towards them and wish to thank them. *She was grateful to him for being so good to her... I should like to extend my grateful thanks to all the volunteers.* ◆◆◇◇◇ ADJ-GRADED: usu v-link ADJ, usu ADJ *to* n, ADJ *for* n/-ing

♦ **gratefully** *'That's kind of you, Sally,' Claire said gratefully.* ADV-GRADED: ADV with v

grater /greɪtəʳ/ **graters.** A **grater** is a kitchen tool which has a rough surface that you use for shredding food into very small pieces. N-COUNT

gratify /grætɪfaɪ/ **gratifies, gratifying, gratified** ◆◇◇◇◇

1 If you **are gratified** by something, it gives you pleasure or satisfaction; a formal use. *Mr. Dambar was gratified by his response... The figures are likely to gratify ministers anxious to portray the council tax as acceptable.* VERB *be* V-ed V n

♦ **gratified** *He was gratified to hear that his idea had been confirmed... They were gratified that America kept its promise.* ADJ-GRADED: oft ADJ to-inf, ADJ that

♦ **gratifying** *We took a chance and we've won. It's very gratifying. ...a gratifying development.* ADJ-GRADED

♦ **gratification** /grætɪfɪkeɪʃᵊn/ *He is waiting for them to recognise him and eventually they do, much to his gratification.* N-UNCOUNT

2 If you **gratify** your own or another person's desire, you do what is necessary to please yourself or them; a formal use. *We gratified our friend's curiosity... Every whim will be gratified.* ♦ **gratification** *...sexual gratification.* VERB =satisfy V n N-UNCOUNT

grating /greɪtɪŋ/ **gratings**

1 A **grating** is a flat metal frame with rows of bars across it, which is fastened over a window or over a hole in a wall or the ground. *...an open grating in the sidewalk.* N-COUNT

2 A **grating** sound is harsh and unpleasant. *She recognized the grating voice of Dr. Sarnoff.*
ADJ-GRADED: usu ADJ n

gratis /grætɪs, grɑːt-/. If something is done or provided **gratis**, it does not have to be paid for. *David gives the first consultation gratis.* ► Also an adjective. *What I did for you was free, gratis, you understand?*
ADV: ADV after v =free
ADJ =free

gratitude /grætɪtjuːd, AM -tuːd/. **Gratitude** is the state of feeling grateful. *...a sense of gratitude... I wish to express my gratitude to Kathy Davis for her immense practical help.*
◆◇◇◇◇ N-UNCOUNT: oft N *for/to* n

gratuitous /grətjuːɪtəs, AM -tuː-/. If you describe something as **gratuitous**, you mean that it is unnecessary, and often harmful or upsetting. *There's too much crime and gratuitous violence on TV. ...his insistence on offering gratuitous advice.* ♦ **gratuitously** *They wanted me to change the title to something less gratuitously offensive.*
◆◇◇◇◇ ADJ-GRADED =needless
ADV: ADV adj, ADV with v

gratuity /grətjuːɪti, AM -tuː-/ **gratuities**

1 A **gratuity** is a gift of money to someone who has done something for you; a formal use. *The porter expects a gratuity.*
N-COUNT =tip

2 In British English, a **gratuity** is large gift of money given to someone when they leave their employment, especially when they leave the armed forces; a formal use. *He is taking a gratuity from the Navy.*
N-COUNT

grave, graves; graver, gravest. Pronounced /greɪv/, except for meaning 5, when it is pronounced /grɑːv/.
◆◆◆◇◇

1 A **grave** is a place where a dead person is buried. *They used to visit her grave twice a year.*
N-COUNT

2 You can refer to someone's death as their **grave** or to death as the **grave**. *...drinking yourself to an early grave... Most men would rather go to the grave than own up to feelings of dependency.*
N-COUNT: oft *to* N, oft poss/adj N

3 A **grave** event or situation is very serious, important, and worrying. *He said that the situation in his country is very grave... I have grave doubts that the documents tell the whole story.* ♦ **gravely** *They had gravely impaired the credibility of the government.*
ADJ-GRADED
ADV: ADV adj, ADV with v

4 A **grave** person is quiet and serious in their appearance or behaviour. *William was up on the roof for some time and when he came down he looked grave... Anxiously, she examined his unusually grave face.* ♦ **gravely** *'I think I've covered that business more than adequately,' he said gravely.*
ADJ-GRADED
ADV-GRADED: ADV with v, ADV adj

5 In some languages such as French, a **grave** accent is a symbol that is placed over a vowel in a word to show how the vowel is pronounced. For example, the word 'mère' has a grave accent over the first 'e'.
ADJ: ADJ n

6 If you say that someone **is digging** their **own grave**, you are warning them that they are doing something foolish or dangerous that will cause their own failure. *The magazine isn't trying to ruin his career, the man's digging his own grave by refusing an interview.*
PHRASES V and N inflect

7 If you say that someone who is dead would **turn in** their **grave** at something that is happening now, you mean that they would be very shocked or upset by it, if they were alive. *Darwin must be turning in his grave at the thought of what is being perpetrated in his name.*
V and N inflect

8 • **from the cradle to the grave**: see **cradle**.

gravedigger /greɪvdɪgəʳ/ **gravediggers.** A **gravedigger** is a person whose job is to dig the graves in which dead people can be buried.
N-COUNT

gravel /grævᵊl/. **Gravel** consists of very small stones. It is often used to make paths. *...a gravel path leading to the front door.*
◆◇◇◇◇ N-UNCOUNT: oft N n

gravelled /grævᵊld/; spelled **graveled** in American English. A **gravelled** path, road, or area has a surface made of gravel.
ADJ: ADJ n

gravelly /grævəli/

1 A **gravelly** voice is low and rather rough and harsh. *There's a triumphant note in his gravelly voice.*
ADJ-GRADED: usu ADJ n

2 An **gravelly** area of land is covered in or full of small stones. *Water runs through the gravelly soil very quickly.*
ADJ-GRADED

graveside /greɪvsaɪd/ **gravesides.** You can refer to the area around a grave as the **graveside**, usually when you are talking about the time when someone is buried. *Both women wept at his graveside.*
N-COUNT: usu sing, oft *at* N

gravestone /greɪvstoʊn/ **gravestones.** A **gravestone** is a large stone with words carved into it, which is placed on a grave.
N-COUNT =tombstone

graveyard /greɪvjɑːʳd/ **graveyards**
◆◇◇◇◇

1 A **graveyard** is an area of land, sometimes near a church, where dead people are buried. *They made their way to a graveyard to pay their traditional respects to the dead.*
N-COUNT =cemetery

2 If you call a place a **graveyard** of particular things, you are expressing disapproval or disappointment that there are many broken or unwanted things of that kind there, or that many of those things have been destroyed there. *This had once been the greatest port in the world, now it was a graveyard of rusting cranes.*
N-COUNT: usu sing, oft N *of* n PRAGMATICS

3 If you call an event or place the **graveyard** for particular people or their hopes, you mean that those people have often failed in such events or in that place; used in written English. *Europe has been the graveyard for American golfers recently.*
N-COUNT: usu N *for/of* n

gravitas /grævɪtæs/. If you say that someone has **gravitas**, you mean that you respect them because they seem serious and intelligent; a formal word. *...Douglas Hurd, the Foreign Secretary, whose gravitas during the Gulf crisis won much admiration.*
N-UNCOUNT

gravitate /grævɪteɪt/ **gravitates, gravitating, gravitated.** If you **gravitate** towards a particular place, thing, or activity, you are attracted by it and go to it or get involved in it. *Traditionally young Asians in Britain have gravitated towards medicine, law and engineering.*
VERB
V *towards/to* n
Also V prep/adv

gravitation /grævɪteɪʃᵊn/. **Gravitation** is the force which causes objects to be attracted towards each other because they have mass; a technical term in physics.
N-UNCOUNT

gravitational /grævɪteɪʃənᵊl/. **Gravitational** means relating to or resulting from the force of gravity. *If a spacecraft travels faster than 11 km a second, it escapes the earth's gravitational pull.*
◆◇◇◇◇ ADJ: ADJ n

gravity /grævɪti/
◆◆◇◇◇

1 **Gravity** is the force which causes things to drop to the ground. *Arrows would continue to fly forward forever in a straight line were it not for gravity, which brings them down to earth.*
N-UNCOUNT

2 **Gravity** is the same as gravitation. *By changing the position of your body so that the pull of gravity is reversed, you feel more energetic.* • See also **centre of gravity**.
N-UNCOUNT

3 The **gravity** of a situation or event is its extreme importance or seriousness. *The president said those who grab power through violence deserve punishment which matches the gravity of their crime... Not all acts of vengeance are of equal gravity.*
N-UNCOUNT: oft N *of* n

4 The **gravity** of someone's behaviour or speech is the extremely serious way in which they behave or speak. *There was an appealing gravity to everything she said.*
N-UNCOUNT

gravy /greɪvi/ **gravies. Gravy** is a sauce made from the juices that come from meat when it cooks.
◆◇◇◇◇ N-MASS

gravy boat, gravy boats. A **gravy boat** is a long narrow jug that is used to serve gravy.
N-COUNT

gravy train, gravy trains. If journalists think an organization or person earns too much money for the work that it does, they sometimes say that it is on the **gravy train**. *We were disgusted when bosses awarded themselves a massive pay rise. How can they get on the gravy train, but ask us to take a wage freeze?*
N-COUNT: oft *on the* N

gray /greɪ/. See **grey**.

graze /greɪz/ **grazes, grazing, grazed**
◆◆◇◇◇

1 When animals **graze** or **are grazed**, they eat the grass or other plants that are growing in a particular place. You can also say that a field **is grazed** by animals. *Five cows graze serenely around a massive oak... The hills have been grazed by sheep because they were too steep to be ploughed... Several horses*
V-ERG
V
be V-ed
V n
V -ing

grazed the meadowland. ...a large herd of grazing animals.

2 If you **graze** a part of your body, you injure your skin by scraping against something. *I had grazed my knees a little.* ♦ **grazed** *...grazed arms and legs.* VERB V n ADJ

3 A **graze** is a small wound caused by scraping against something. *He put a piece of sticking plaster on a graze behind Ken's ear.* N-COUNT

4 If something **grazes** another thing, it touches that thing lightly as it passes by. *A bullet had grazed his arm... Wright managed a shot but it grazed the near post and rolled harmlessly across the goal.* VERB =brush V n

grazing /greɪzɪŋ/. **Grazing** or **grazing land** is land on which animals graze. *He had nearly a thousand acres of grazing and arable land.* N-UNCOUNT

GRE /dʒiː ɑːr iː/. The **GRE** is the examination which you have to pass to be able to join a graduate degree programme in the United States; an abbreviation for 'Graduate Record Examination'. N-PROPER

grease /griːs/ **greases, greasing, greased** ◆◇◇◇◇

1 **Grease** is a thick, oily substance which is put on the moving parts of cars and other machines in order to make them work smoothly. *...grease-stained hands.* N-UNCOUNT =oil

2 If you **grease** a part of a car, machine, or device, you put grease on it in order to make it work smoothly. *I greased front and rear hubs and adjusted the brakes.* VERB =oil V n

3 **Grease** is an oily substance that is produced by your skin. *His hair is thick with grease.* N-UNCOUNT

4 **Grease** is animal fat that is produced by cooking meat. You can use **grease** for cooking. *He could smell the bacon grease.* N-UNCOUNT

5 If you **grease** a baking tray, you smear it with animal fat or vegetable oil in order to prevent food sticking to it. *Grease two sturdy baking sheets and heat the oven to 400 degrees... Place the frozen rolls on a greased baking tray.* VERB =oil V n V-ed

6 See also **elbow grease**.

greasepaint /griːspeɪnt/. **Greasepaint** is an oily substance used by actors as make-up. N-UNCOUNT

greaseproof paper /griːspruːf peɪpəʳ/. In British English, **greaseproof paper** is a special kind of paper which does not allow grease or oil to pass through it. It is mainly used in cooking or to wrap food. N-UNCOUNT

greasy /griːsi, -zi/ **greasier, greasiest.** Something that is **greasy** has grease on it or in it. *...the problem of greasy hair... He propped his elbows upon a greasy counter.* ◆◇◇◇◇ ADJ-GRADED

greasy spoon, greasy spoons. If you think a café is small, cheap, and unattractively decorated, you can call it a **greasy spoon**; an informal expression. *...a run-down greasy spoon called the Step Inn Cafe.* N-COUNT

great /greɪt/ **greater, greatest; greats** ◆◆◆◆◆

1 You use **great** to describe something that is very large. **Great** is more formal than **big**. *The room had a great bay window. ...a great hall as long and high as a church.* ADJ-GRADED: ADJ n

2 **Great** means large in amount or degree. *I'll take great care of it... Benjamin Britten did not live to a great age.* ADJ-GRADED

3 You use **great** to describe something that is important, famous, or exciting. *...the great cultural achievements of the past... America can be great again.* ♦ **greatness** *A nation must take certain risks to achieve greatness.* ADJ-GRADED N-UNCOUNT

4 You can describe someone who is successful and famous for their actions, knowledge, or skill as **great**. *Wes Hall was once one of the West Indies' great cricketers. ...the great George Padmore.* ♦ **greatness** *Abraham Lincoln achieved greatness.* ADJ-GRADED: usu ADJ n N-UNCOUNT

5 The **greats** in a particular subject or field of activity are the people who have been most successful or famous in it; used in journalism. *...all the greats of Hollywood. ...cycling's all-time greats.* N-PLURAL: with supp

6 If you refer to the **greats** of popular modern music, you are referring to records that have been successful and that continue to be popular; used in journalism. *...a medley of rock'n'roll greats.* N-PLURAL

7 If you describe someone or something as **great**, you approve of them or admire them; an informal use. *Arturo has this great place in Cazadero... They're a great bunch of guys... I think she's great.* ADJ PRAGMATICS

8 If you **feel great**, you feel very healthy, energetic, and enthusiastic. *I feel just great.* ADJ: feel ADJ

9 You use **great** in order to emphasize the size or degree of a characteristic or quality. *...a great big Italian wedding. ...her sense of colour and great eye for detail.* ADJ-GRADED PRAGMATICS

10 You say **great** in order to emphasize that you are pleased or enthusiastic about something. *Oh great! That'll be good for Fergus.* EXCLAM PRAGMATICS

11 You say **great** in order to emphasize that you are angry or annoyed about something. *'Oh great,' I thought. 'Just what I need.'* EXCLAM PRAGMATICS

12 **Great** is used as part of the name of a species of plant or animal when there is another species of the same plant or animal which is smaller and has different characteristics. *...the great bustard.* ● See also **greater**. N-IN-NAMES

great- /greɪt-/. **Great-** is used before some nouns that refer to relatives. Nouns formed in this way refer to a relative who is a further generation away from you. For example, your great-aunt is the aunt of one of your parents. *...Davis's great-grandmother.* PREFIX

Great Britain /greɪt brɪtᵊn/. **Great Britain** is the island consisting of England, Scotland, and Wales, which together with Northern Ireland makes up the United Kingdom. ◆◆◇◇◇ N-PROPER =GB

greatcoat /greɪtkoʊt/ **greatcoats;** also spelled **great coat.** A **greatcoat** is a long thick overcoat that is worn especially as part of a uniform. *...an army greatcoat.* N-COUNT

greater /greɪtəʳ/ ◆◆◇◇◇

1 **Greater** is the comparative of **great**.

2 **Greater** is used with the name of a large city to refer to the city together with the surrounding urban and suburban area. *...Greater London.* ADJ: ADJ n

3 **Greater** is used with the name of a country to refer to a larger area which includes that country and other land which used to belong to it, or which some people believe should belong to it. *President Gligorov and President Milosevic both want to prevent the creation of a greater Albania.* ADJ: ADJ n

greatly /greɪtli/. You use **greatly** to emphasize the degree or extent of something; a formal word. *People would benefit greatly from a pollution-free vehicle... We were greatly honoured that Sheik Hasina took the trouble to visit us.* ◆◆◇◇◇ ADV-GRADED: ADV with v, ADV adj PRAGMATICS

Grecian /griːʃᵊn/. **Grecian** is used to describe something which is in the style of things from ancient Greece. *...elegant Grecian columns. ...a vaguely Grecian gown of flowing blue.* ADJ: usu ADJ n =Greek

greed /griːd/. **Greed** is the desire to have more of something, such as food or money, than is necessary or fair. *...an insatiable greed for personal power... I get fed up with other people's greed.* ◆◇◇◇◇ N-UNCOUNT =avarice

greedy /griːdi/ **greedier, greediest.** If you describe someone as **greedy**, you mean that they want to have more of something such as food or money than is necessary or fair. *He attacked greedy bosses for awarding themselves big rises... She is greedy and selfish.* ♦ **greedily** *Livy ate the pasties greedily and with huge enjoyment.* ◆◇◇◇◇ ADJ-GRADED ADV-GRADED: ADV with v

Greek /griːk/ **Greeks** ◆◆◆◆◇

1 **Greek** means belonging or relating to Greece. *In the Greek general election, the New Democracy party has claimed victory. ...the Greek army.* ADJ

2 A **Greek** is a person who comes from Greece. *He had looked through the house for the two Greeks.* N-COUNT

3 **Greek** is the language used in Greece. *I had to learn Greek.* N-UNCOUNT

4 **Greek** or **Ancient Greek** was the language used in Greece in ancient times. *Teachers warn today that Latin, Greek and other classics will be squeezed out of school timetables.* N-UNCOUNT

green /griːn/ **greens; greener, greenest** ◆◆◆◆◆

1 **Green** is the colour of grass or leaves. *...shiny red and green apples... Yellow and green together make a pale green.* COLOUR

2 A place that is **green** is covered with grass, plants, and trees and not with houses or factories. *Cairo has only thirteen square centimetres of green space for each inhabitant.* ♦ **greenness** *...the lush greenness of the river valleys.* ADJ-GRADED / N-UNCOUNT

3 Green issues and political movements relate to or are concerned with the protection of the environment. *The power of the Green movement in Germany has made that country a leader in the drive to recycle more waste materials.* ADJ: ADJ n

4 If you say that someone or something is **green**, you mean they harm the environment as little as possible. *...trying to persuade governments to adopt greener policies... Our children are being educated to be green in everything they do.* ♦ **greenness** *A Swiss company offers to help environmental investors by sending teams round factories to ascertain their greenness.* ADJ-GRADED / N-UNCOUNT

5 Greens are members of green political movements. *The Greens see themselves as a radical alternative to the two major British political parties.* N-COUNT: usu pl

6 A **green** is a smooth, flat area of grass around a hole on a golf course. *...the 18th green.* N-COUNT

7 A **green** is an area of land covered with grass, especially in a town or in the middle of a village. *...the village green.* N-COUNT

8 Green is used in the names of places that contain or used to contain an area of grass. *...Bethnal Green.* N-IN-NAMES: n N

9 You can refer to the cooked green leaves of vegetables such as spinach or cabbage as **greens**; used mainly in informal British English. *Eat your greens.* N-PLURAL

10 You can describe fruit and vegetables as **green** when they are unripe and not ready to be eaten. *Pick and ripen any green fruits in a warm dark place.* ADJ-GRADED

11 If you say that someone is **green**, you mean that they have had very little experience of life or a particular job. *He was a young lad, very green, very immature.* ADJ-GRADED

12 If you say that someone is **green with envy**, you mean that they are very envious indeed. PHRASES v-link PHR

13 In British English, if you say that someone has **green fingers**, you mean that they are very good at gardening and their plants grow well. The American expression is **a green thumb**. *You don't need green fingers to fill your home with lush leaves.*

14 If someone in authority gives a **green light** to something, they give permission for it to happen or be done. *Senators gave the green light to her nomination... They see the lifting of martial law as a green light for further protests.* oft PHR *to/for* n, PHR to-inf

greenback /griːnbæk/ **greenbacks.** In American English, a **greenback** is a banknote such as a dollar bill; an informal word. N-COUNT

green bean, green beans. Green beans are long narrow beans that are green in colour and are eaten as a vegetable. They grow on a tall climbing plant and are the cases that contain the seeds of the plant. N-COUNT: usu pl

green belt, green belts. A **green belt** is an area of land with fields or parks around a town or city, where people are not allowed to build houses or factories by law; used mainly in British English. N-COUNT

Green Beret, Green Berets. A **Green Beret** is a British or American commando; an informal use. N-COUNT

green card, green cards. A **green card** is a document showing that someone who is not a citizen of the United States has permission to live and work there. *Nicollette married Harry so she could get a green card.* N-COUNT

greenery /griːnəri/. Plants that make a place look attractive are referred to as **greenery**. *They have ordered a bit of greenery to brighten up the new wing at Guy's Hospital.* ◆◇◇◇◇ N-UNCOUNT

greenfly /griːnflaɪ/ **greenflies.** The plural can be either **greenfly** or **greenflies**. **Greenfly** are small green winged insects that damage plants. N-COUNT

greengage /griːngeɪdʒ/ **greengages.** A **greengage** is a greenish-yellow coloured plum with a sweet taste; used mainly in British English. N-COUNT

greengrocer /griːngrəʊsəʳ/ **greengrocers**

1 A **greengrocer** is a shopkeeper who sells fruit and vegetables; used mainly in British English. *...a greengrocer's daughter from Birmingham.* N-COUNT

2 In British English, a **greengrocer** or a **greengrocer's** is a shop where fruit and vegetables are sold. *...the outside display of the local greengrocer.* N-COUNT: oft *the* N

greenhouse /griːnhaʊs/ **greenhouses** ◆◆◇◇◇

1 A **greenhouse** is a glass building in which you grow plants that need to be protected from bad weather. N-COUNT

2 Greenhouse means relating to or causing the greenhouse effect. *...the consequences of the buildup of greenhouse gases.* ADJ: ADJ n

greenhouse effect. The **greenhouse effect** is the problem caused by a build-up of gases such as carbon dioxide in the air around the earth. These gases trap the heat from the sun, and cause a gradual rise in the temperature of the Earth's atmosphere. ◆◇◇◇◇ N-SING: *the* N

greenhouse gas, greenhouse gases. Greenhouse gases are the gases which are responsible for causing the greenhouse effect. The main greenhouse gas is carbon dioxide. ◆◇◇◇◇ N-VAR

greening /griːnɪŋ/. Journalists talk about the **greening** of a particular person or organization when they want to say that that person or organization is becoming more aware of environmental issues. *1990 was supposed to be the year for the greening of China.* N-SING: also no det, oft N *of* n

greenish /griːnɪʃ/. **Greenish** means slightly green in colour. *...his cold greenish eyes.* ► Also a combining form. *...greenish-yellow flowers.* ADJ / COMB in COLOUR

Green Paper, Green Papers. In Britain, a **Green Paper** is a document containing ideas about a particular subject that is published by the Government so that people can discuss them before any decisions are made. N-COUNT

Green Party. The **Green Party** is a political party that is particularly concerned about protecting the environment. ◆◇◇◇◇ N-PROPER: *the* N

green pepper, green peppers. A **green pepper** is an unripe pepper that is used in cooking or eaten raw in salads. N-COUNT

green revolution; also spelled **Green Revolution**. The **green revolution** is the increase in agricultural production in developing countries that has been made possible by the use of new types of crops and new farming methods. N-SING: usu *the* N

greenroom /griːnruːm/ **greenrooms;** also spelled **green room**. A **greenroom** is a room in a theatre or television studio where performers can rest. N-COUNT

green salad, green salads. A **green salad** is a salad made mainly with lettuce and other green vegetables. N-VAR

Greenwich Mean Time /grenɪtʃ miːn taɪm/. See **GMT**.

greeny /griːni/. **Greeny** means slightly green in colour. *...greeny sea water.* ► Also a combining form. *...a lightweight, greeny grey wool suit.* ADJ / COMB in COLOUR

greet /griːt/ **greets, greeting, greeted** ◆◆◇◇◇

1 When you **greet** someone, you express friendliness or pleasure when you meet them, or when they arrive, for example by saying 'Hello' or shaking hands with them. *She liked to be home to greet Steve when he came in from school.* VERB / V n

2 If something **is greeted** in a particular way, people react to it in that way. *The European Court's decision has been greeted with dismay by fishermen... It is unlikely that this suggestion will be greeted enthusiastically in the Baltic States.* VB: usu passive / be V-ed *with/by* n / be V-ed adv

3 If you **are greeted** by something, it is the first thing you notice in a particular place; a literary use. *I was greeted by a shocking sight... The savoury smell greeted them as they went through the door.* VERB / be V-ed *by* n / V n

greeting /griːtɪŋ/ **greetings** ◆◇◇◇◇

1 A **greeting** is something friendly that you say or do when you meet someone. *His greeting was familiar and friendly... They exchanged greetings... He raised a hand in greeting.* N-VAR

2 'Greetings' is an old-fashioned greeting. CONVENTION

greetings card, greetings cards; also spelled **greeting card.** A **greetings card** is a folded card with a picture on the front and greetings inside that you give or send to someone, for example on their birthday. N-COUNT

gregarious /grɪgeəriəs/
1 Someone who is **gregarious** enjoys being with other people. *She is such a gregarious and outgoing person.* ADJ-GRADED ≠shy
2 **Gregarious** animals or birds normally live in large groups. *Snow geese are very gregarious birds.* ADJ-GRADED

gremlin /gremlɪn/ **gremlins.** A **gremlin** is a tiny imaginary evil spirit that people say is the cause of a problem, especially in a machine, which they cannot explain properly or locate. *The microphones went dead as if the technical gremlins had struck again.* N-COUNT

grenade /grɪneɪd/ **grenades.** A **grenade** or a **hand grenade** is a small bomb that can be thrown by hand. *A hand grenade was thrown at an army patrol.* ◆◇◇◇◇ N-COUNT

grew /gruː/. **Grew** is the past tense of **grow.**

grey /greɪ/ **greyer, greyest;** spelled **gray** in American English. ◆◆◆◆◆
1 **Grey** is the colour of ashes or of clouds on a rainy day. *...a grey suit..* COLOUR
2 You use **grey** to describe the colour of people's hair when it changes from its original colour, usually as they get old, and before it becomes white. *...my grey hair... Eddie was going grey.* ADJ-GRADED
3 If the weather is **grey**, there are many clouds in the sky and the light is dull. *It was a grey, wet April Sunday.* ♦ **greyness** *...winter's greyness.* ADJ-GRADED N-UNCOUNT
4 If you describe a situation as **grey**, you mean that it is dull, unpleasant, or difficult. *Brazilians look gloomily forward to a New Year that even the president admits will be grey and cheerless.* ♦ **greyness** *In this new world of greyness there is an attempt to remove all risks.* ADJ-GRADED =bleak N-UNCOUNT
5 If you describe someone or something as **grey**, you think that they are boring and unattractive, and very similar to other things or other people. *...little grey men in suits.* ♦ **greyness** *Journalists are frustrated by his apparent greyness.* ADJ-GRADED PRAGMATICS N-UNCOUNT: with supp

grey area, grey areas; spelled **gray area** in American English. If you refer to something as a **grey area**, you mean that it is unclear, for example because nobody is sure how to deal with it or who is responsible for it, or it falls between two separate categories of things. *At the moment, the law on compensation is very much a grey area. ...jobs in that gray area between blue-collar laborers and white-collar professionals, jobs such as teachers and computer programmers.* N-COUNT

greyhound /greɪhaʊnd/ **greyhounds.** A **greyhound** is a dog with a thin body and long thin legs, which can run very fast. Greyhounds sometimes run in races and people bet on them. ◆◇◇◇◇ N-COUNT

greyish /greɪɪʃ/; spelled **grayish** in American English. **Greyish** means slightly grey in colour. *The building was of greyish plaster and looked old.* ► Also a combining form. *...greyish green leaves.* ADJ COMB in COLOUR

grid /grɪd/ **grids** ◆◇◇◇◇
1 A **grid** is something which is in a pattern of straight lines that cross over each other, forming squares. On maps the grid is used to help you find a particular thing or place. *...a grid of ironwork. ...a grid of narrow streets... Many canals were built along map grid lines.* ● See also **cattle grid.** N-COUNT
2 A **grid** is a network of wires and cables by which sources of power, such as electricity, are distributed throughout a country or area. *...breakdowns in communications and electric power grids.* N-COUNT
3 The **grid** or the **starting grid** is the starting line on a car-racing track. *The Ferrari of Alain Prost will be second on the grid.* N-COUNT

griddle /grɪdᵊl/ **griddles.** A **griddle** is a round, flat, heavy piece of metal which is placed on a stove or fire and used for cooking. N-COUNT

gridiron /grɪdaɪəᵊn/. American football is sometimes referred to as **gridiron.** *...the greatest quarterback in gridiron history.* N-UNCOUNT

gridlock /grɪdlɒk/ ◆◇◇◇◇
1 **Gridlock** is the situation that exists when all the roads in a particular place are so full of vehicles that none of them can move. *Thousands of troops and civilians have been reported leaving the Iraqi city of Basra, causing gridlock there.* N-UNCOUNT
2 You can use **gridlock** to refer to a situation in an argument or dispute when neither side is prepared to give in, so no agreement can be reached. *He agreed that these policies will lead to gridlock in the future.* N-UNCOUNT =deadlock

grief /griːf/ **griefs** ◆◆◇◇◇
1 **Grief** is a feeling of extreme sadness. *...a huge outpouring of national grief for the victims of the shootings... Their grief soon gave way to anger.* N-VAR
2 If something **comes to grief**, it is unsuccessful. *So many marriages have come to grief over lack of money.* PHRASES V inflects
3 If someone **comes to grief**, they harm themselves, sometimes fatally. *Thomas and his balloon partner almost came to grief when foolishly they took off in an easterly gale.* V inflects
4 Some people say **'Good grief'** to express surprise or disbelief. *'He's been arrested for theft and burglary.'—'Good grief!'* EXCLAM PRAGMATICS

grief-stricken. If someone is **grief-stricken,** they are extremely sad about something that has happened; a formal word. *...the grief-stricken family... The Queen was grief-stricken over his death.* ADJ-GRADED

grievance /griːvᵊns/ **grievances.** If you have a **grievance** about something that has happened or been done, you believe that it was unfair. *They had a legitimate grievance... The main grievance of the drivers is the imposition of higher fees for driving licences and certificates of proficiency. ...a deep sense of grievance.* ◆◇◇◇◇ N-VAR: usu with supp

grieve /griːv/ **grieves, grieving, grieved** ◆◇◇◇◇
1 If you **grieve** over something, especially someone's death, you feel very sad about it. *He's grieving over his dead wife and son... I didn't have any time to grieve... Margery's grieving family battled to come to terms with their loss.* VERB V prep V V-ing
2 If you **are grieved** by something, it makes you unhappy or upset. *He was deeply grieved by the sufferings of the common people... I was grieved to hear of the suicide of James... It grieved me to see the poor man in such distress.* VERB be V-ed by/at n be V-ed to-inf it V n to-inf Also V n

grievous /griːvəs/ ◆◇◇◇◇
1 If you describe something such as a loss as **grievous**, you mean that it is extremely serious or worrying in its effects. *Their loss would be a grievous blow to our engineering industries... Mr Morris said the victims had suffered from a very grievous mistake.* ♦ **grievously** *Birds, sea-life and the coastline all suffered grievously.* ADJ-GRADED: usu ADJ n ADV-GRADED: ADV with v
2 A **grievous** injury to your body is one that causes you great pain and suffering. *He survived in spite of suffering grievous injuries.* ♦ **grievously** *Nelson Piquet, three times world champion, was grievously injured.* ADJ-GRADED: usu ADJ n ADV-GRADED: ADV with v, ADV adj

grievous bodily harm. If someone is accused of **grievous bodily harm**, they are accused of causing very serious physical injury to someone; a legal term. *They were both found guilty of causing grievous bodily harm.* N-UNCOUNT

griffin /grɪfɪn/ **griffins;** also spelled **griffon.** In mythology, a **griffin** is a winged monster with the body of a lion and the head of an eagle. N-COUNT

grill /grɪl/ **grills, grilling, grilled** ◆◆◇◇◇
1 A **grill** is a part of a cooker which produces strong heat that cooks food placed underneath it. *Place the omelette under a gentle grill until the top is set.* N-COUNT
2 A **grill** is a flat frame of metal bars on which food can be cooked over a fire. ● See also **grille.** N-COUNT
3 A **grill** is a dish which consists of food that has been grilled, especially meat. *...a mixed grill.* N-COUNT
4 When you **grill** food or when food **grills**, it is cooked using very strong heat directly above or be- V-ERG

low it. *Grill the meat for 20 minutes each side... Apart from peppers and aubergines, many other vegetables grill well. ...grilled chicken.* ♦ **grilling** *The breast can be cut into portions for grilling.*
V n
V adv
V-ed
N-UNCOUNT

5 If you **grill** someone about something, you ask them a lot of questions for a long period of time; an informal use. *Grill your travel agent about the facilities for families with children... The police grilled him for hours.* ♦ **grilling, grillings** *They gave him a grilling about the implications of a united Europe.*
VERB
=interrogate
V n *about/on* n
V n
N-COUNT

grille /grɪl/ **grilles;** also spelled **grill**. A **grille** is a framework of metal bars or wire which is placed in front of a window or a piece of machinery, in order to protect it or to protect people.
N-COUNT

grim /grɪm/ **grimmer, grimmest** ◆◆◇◇◇

1 A situation or piece of information that is **grim** is unpleasant, depressing, and difficult to accept. *They painted a grim picture of growing crime... There was further grim economic news yesterday... The mood could not have been grimmer.* ♦ **grimness** *...an unrelenting grimness of tone.*
ADJ-GRADED
N-UNCOUNT

2 A place that is **grim** is unattractive and depressing in appearance. *The city might be grim at first, but there is a vibrancy and excitement. ...the tower blocks on the city's grim edges.*
ADJ-GRADED

3 If a person or their behaviour is **grim**, they are very serious or stern, usually because they are worried about something; a literary use. *She was a stout, grim woman with a turned-down mouth... Her expression was grim and unpleasant.* ♦ **grimly** *'It's too late now to stop him,' Harris said grimly.*
ADJ-GRADED
ADV-GRADED

4 If you say that something is **grim**, you think that it is awful, ugly, or depressing; an informal use. *Everton and Wimbledon battled out a grim, goalless draw last night.*
ADJ-GRADED

grimace /grɪmeɪs, grɪməs/ **grimaces, grimacing, grimaced.** If you **grimace**, you twist your face in an ugly way because you are displeased, disgusted, or in pain. *She started to sit up, grimaced, and sank back weakly against the pillow... She grimaced at Cerezzi, then turned to Brenda.* ► Also a noun. *He took another drink of his coffee. 'Awful,' he said with a grimace.*
◆◇◇◇◇
VERB
=pull a face
V
V *at* n
N-COUNT

grime /graɪm/. **Grime** is dirt which has collected on the surface of something. *Kelly got the grime off his hands before rejoining her in the kitchen.*
N-UNCOUNT

Grim Reaper. **The Grim Reaper** is an imaginary character who looks like a skeleton wearing a long, black cloak with a hood and who carries a scythe. The Grim Reaper represents death.
N-SING:
the N

grimy /graɪmi/ **grimier, grimiest.** Something that is **grimy** is very dirty. *...a grimy industrial city.*
ADJ-GRADED

grin /grɪn/ **grins, grinning, grinned** ◆◆◇◇◇

1 When you **grin**, you smile broadly. *He grins, delighted at the memory... Sarah tried several times to catch Philip's eye, but he just grinned at her. ...a statue of a grinning old man cutting the throat of a deer.*
VERB
V
V *at* n
V-ing

2 A **grin** is a broad smile. *...a big grin on her face... Bobby looked at her with a sheepish grin.* ● to **wipe the grin off someone's face**: see **wipe**.
N-COUNT:
oft adj N

3 If you **grin and bear it**, you accept a difficult or unpleasant situation without complaining because you know there is nothing you can do to make things better. *If your flatmate has an unfortunate liking for everything kitsch, you may have to grin and bear it... A writer has to grin and bear bad reviews.*
PHRASE:
Vs inflect

grind /graɪnd/ **grinds, grinding, ground** ◆◆◇◇◇

1 If you **grind** a substance such as corn, you crush it between two hard surfaces or with a machine until it becomes a fine powder. *Store the peppercorns in an airtight container and grind the pepper as you need it. ...the odor of fresh ground coffee.* ► **Grind up** means the same as **grind**. *He makes his own paint, grinding up the pigment with a little oil.*
VERB
V n
V-ed
PHRASAL VERB
V P n (not pron)
Also V n P

2 If you **grind** something into a surface, you press and rub it hard into the surface using small circular or sideways movements. *'Well,' I said, grinding my cigarette nervously into the granite step.* ● If you **grind** your **teeth**, you rub your upper and lower teeth together as though you are chewing something. *If you know you're grinding your teeth, particularly at night, see your dentist.*
VERB
V n prep
PHRASE:
V inflects
V n

3 If you **grind** something, you make it smooth or sharp by rubbing it against a hard surface. *It was beyond my ability to grind a blade this broad... The tip can be ground to a much sharper edge to cut smoother and faster.*
VERB
V n
be V-ed *to* n
Also V n *to* n

4 If a vehicle **grinds** somewhere, it moves there very slowly and noisily. *Tanks had crossed the border at five fifteen and were grinding south.*
VERB
V adv/prep

5 The **grind** of a machine is the harsh, scraping noise that it is making, usually because it is old or is being overworked. *The grind of heavy machines could get on their nerves.*
N-SING:
oft N *of* n

6 If you refer to routine tasks or activities that you have to do as the **grind**, you are emphasizing that they are boring and take up a lot of time and effort; an informal use. *The daily grind of government is done by Her Majesty's Civil Service... Life continues to be a terrible grind for the ordinary person.*
N-SING:
oft adj N

7 See also **grinding**.

8 If a country's economy or something such as a process **grinds to a halt**, it gradually becomes slower or less active until it stops. *The peace process has ground to a halt while Israel struggles to form a new government.*
PHRASES
V inflects

9 If a vehicle **grinds to a halt**, it stops slowly and noisily. *The tanks ground to a halt after a hundred yards because the fuel had been siphoned out.*
V inflects

10 ● to have **an axe to grind**: see **axe**. ● to **come to a grinding halt**: see **grinding**.

grind down. If you say that someone **grinds** you **down**, you mean that they treat you very harshly and cruelly, reducing your confidence or your will to resist them. *'You see,' said Hughes, 'there's people who want to humiliate you and grind you down.'*
PHRASAL VERB
PRAGMATICS
V n P

grind on. If you say that something **grinds on**, you disapprove of the fact that it continues to happen in the same way for a long time. *Civil war in the Sudan has been grinding on for nine years.*
PHRASAL VERB
PRAGMATICS
V P

grind out. To **grind** something **out** means to produce it in a boring or routine manner; an informal expression. *Were it not for this misfortune, he might never have been forced into the business of grinding out novels to support his family.*
PHRASAL VERB
V P n (not pron)
Also V n P

grind up. See **grind** 1.
PHRASAL VERB

grinder /graɪndəʳ/ **grinders** ◆◇◇◇◇

1 In a kitchen, a **grinder** is a device for crushing food such as coffee or meat into small pieces or into a powder. *...an electric coffee grinder.*
N-COUNT:
oft n N

2 A **grinder** is a machine or tool for sharpening, smoothing, or polishing the surface of something.
N-COUNT:
oft supp N

grinding /graɪndɪŋ/

1 If you describe a bad situation as **grinding**, you mean it never gets better, changes, or ends. *Their grandfather had left his village in order to escape the grinding poverty. ...the grinding difficulty of getting to the stadium.* ♦ **grindingly** *Nursing was ill-paid and grindingly hard work.*
ADJ:
ADJ n
ADV:
ADV adj

2 If you say that something comes **to a grinding halt**, you are emphasizing that it stops very suddenly, especially before it was meant to. *A car will come to a grinding halt if you put water in the petrol tank.*
PHRASE:
PHR after v
PRAGMATICS

3 See also **grind**.

grindstone /graɪndstoʊn/ **grindstones.** A **grindstone** is a large round stone that turns like a wheel and is used for sharpening knives and tools.
N-COUNT

gringo /grɪŋgoʊ/ **gringos. Gringo** is sometimes used by people from Latin America to refer to foreigners, especially people from the United States and Britain; an offensive word.
N-COUNT

grip /grɪp/ **grips, gripping, gripped** ◆◆◆◇◇

1 If you **grip** something, you take hold of it with your hand and continue to hold it firmly. *She gripped the rope.*
VERB
V n

2 A **grip** is a firm, strong hold on something. *His strong hand eased the bag from her grip.*
N-COUNT:
oft poss N

3 Someone's **grip** on someone or something is the power and control they have over them. *The*
N-SING:
with supp,
oft N *on* n

president maintains an iron grip on his country. ...a series of measures aimed at tightening his grip on the Soviet economy.

4 If something **grips** you, it affects you very strongly. *Pain gripped him... The entire community has been gripped by fear.* VERB V n

5 If you **are gripped** by something such as a story or a series of events, your attention is concentrated on it and held by it. *The nation is gripped by the dramatic story.* ♦ **gripping** *The film turned out to be a gripping thriller.* VB: usu passive be V-ed ADJ-GRADED =riveting

6 If things such as shoes or car tyres have **grip**, they do not slip. *...a new way of reinforcing rubber which gives car tyres better grip.* N-UNCOUNT

7 A **grip** is a bag that is smaller than a suitcase, and that you use when you are travelling. N-COUNT

8 If you **get to grips with** a problem or if you **come to grips with** it, you consider it seriously, and start taking action to deal with it. *The government's first task is to get to grips with the economy.* PHRASES V inflects, PHR n

9 If you **get a grip** on yourself, you make an effort to control or improve your behaviour or work. V inflects

10 If a person, group, or place is **in the grip of** something, they are being severely affected by it. *Britain is still in the grip of recession. ...a region in the grip of severe drought.* v-link PHR, PHR n

11 If you **lose** your **grip**, you become less efficient and less confident, and less able to deal with things. V inflects

12 If you say that someone has **a grip on reality**, you mean they recognize the true situation and do not have mistaken ideas about it. *Shakur loses his fragile grip on reality and starts blasting away at friends and foe alike.* usu PHR after v

gripe /graɪp/ **gripes, griping, griped** ◆◇◇◇◇

1 If you say that someone **is griping**, you mean they are annoying you because they keep on complaining about something; an informal use. *Why are football players griping when the average salary is half a million dollars? ...griping about high prices.* ♦ **griping** *Still, the griping went on.* VERB PRAGMATICS =complain V V about n N-UNCOUNT

2 A **gripe** is a complaint about something; an informal use. *My only gripe is that one main course and one dessert were unavailable.* N-COUNT =complaint

griping /graɪpɪŋ/. A **griping** pain is a sudden, stabbing pain in your stomach or bowels. ADJ: ADJ n

grisly /grɪzli/ **grislier, grisliest;** also spelled **grizzly**. If you describe something as **grisly**, you mean that it is extremely nasty and horrible; used especially of things involving death and violence. *He was insane when he carried out the grisly murders. ...a grizzly crime.* ◆◇◇◇◇ ADJ-GRADED: usu ADJ n =gruesome

grist /grɪst/. If you say that something is **grist to the mill**, you mean that it is useful for a particular purpose or helps support someone's point of view. PHRASE: v-link PHR, oft PHR of/for n

gristle /grɪsᵊl/. **Gristle** is a tough, rubbery substance found in meat, especially in meat of poor quality, which is unpleasant to eat. N-UNCOUNT

grit /grɪt/ **grits, gritting, gritted** ◆◇◇◇◇

1 **Grit** is very small pieces of stone. It is often put on roads in winter to make them less slippery. *He felt tiny bits of grit and sand peppering his knees.* N-UNCOUNT

2 If someone has **grit**, they have the determination and courage to continue doing something even though it is very difficult. *If they gave gold medals for grit, Karen would be right up there on the winners' podium.* N-UNCOUNT

3 **Grits** are coarsely ground grains of corn which are eaten for breakfast or as part of a meal in the southern United States. N-PLURAL

4 If you **grit** your teeth, you press your upper and lower teeth tightly together, usually because you are angry about something. *Gritting my teeth, I did my best to stifle one or two remarks... 'It is clear that my client has been less than frank with me,' said his lawyer, through gritted teeth.* VERB V n V-ed

5 If you **grit your teeth**, you make up your mind to carry on even if the situation is very difficult. *There is going to be hardship, but we have to grit our teeth and get on with it.* PHRASE: V inflects

gritty /grɪti/ **grittier, grittiest** ◆◇◇◇◇

1 Something that is **gritty** contains grit, is covered with grit, or has a texture like that of grit. *The sheets fell on the gritty floor, and she just let them lie.* ADJ-GRADED

2 Someone who is **gritty** is determined and courageous. *We have to prove how gritty we are. ...a gritty determination to avoid humiliation.* ADJ-GRADED

3 A **gritty** description or portrayal of a tough or unpleasant situation shows it in a very realistic way. *...gritty social comment... His most celebrated work is the film classic, 'Woman in the Dunes,' a gritty look at survival in an extreme environment.* ADJ-GRADED: usu ADJ n

grizzled /grɪzᵊld/. A **grizzled** person or a person with **grizzled** hair has hair that is grey or streaked with grey. *...a grizzled old age pensioner... He was an old man with grey, grizzled hair.* ADJ: usu ADJ n

grizzly /grɪzli/ **grizzlies**

1 A **grizzly** or a **grizzly bear** is a large, fierce, greyish-brown bear. *...two grizzly bear cubs.* N-COUNT

2 If children are **grizzly**, they whine or cry a lot, often because they are unwell or tired; an informal use. *All babies need quiet times on their own and get grizzly if they've had too much stimulation.* ADJ-GRADED: usu v-link ADJ

3 See also **grisly**.

groan /groʊn/ **groans, groaning, groaned** ◆◆◇◇◇

1 If you **groan**, you make a long, low sound because you are experiencing a strong physical feeling, especially pain, or because you want to indicate your disapproval or unhappiness about something. *Slowly, he opened his eyes. As he did so, he began to groan with pain... They glanced at the man on the floor, who began to groan... She was making small groaning noises.* ► Also a noun. *She heard him let out a pitiful, muffled groan... As his ball flew wide, there was a collective groan from the stands.* VERB =moan V with n V V-ing N-COUNT =moan

2 If you **groan** something, you say it in a low, unhappy voice. *'My leg – I think it's broken,' Eric groaned.* VERB V with quote

3 If you **groan** about something, you complain about it; an informal use. *His parents were beginning to groan about the price of college tuition.* ► Also a noun. *Listen sympathetically to your child's moans and groans about what she can't do.* VERB V about n Also V, V that N-COUNT

4 If wood **groans**, it makes a loud creaking sound, because it is being pushed, pressed, or moved. *The timbers groan and creak and the floorboards shift.* VERB V

5 If you say that something such as a table **groans** under the weight of food, you are emphasizing that there is a lot of food on it. *The bar counter groans under the weight of huge plates of the freshest fish. ...tables groaning with ethnic foodstuffs.* VERB PRAGMATICS V under/with n V-ing

6 If you say that someone or something **is groaning under** the weight of something, you disapprove of the fact that there is too much of that thing. *Consumers were groaning under the weight of high interest rates... Bookshelves groan under the burden of books on threats to the environment.* VB: usu cont PRAGMATICS V under n

grocer /groʊsəʳ/ **grocers** ◆◇◇◇◇

1 A **grocer** is a shopkeeper who sells foods such as flour, sugar, and tinned foods. *She was a Brazilian grocer's daughter.* N-COUNT

2 A **grocer** or a **grocer's** is a shop where foods such as flour, sugar, and tinned foods are sold. *I go to our local grocer and buy butter and cornflakes.* N-COUNT: oft the N

grocery /groʊsəri/ **groceries** ◆◇◇◇◇

1 In American English, a **grocery** or a **grocery store** is a grocer's shop. *They went to the grocery store to buy bananas.* N-COUNT

2 **Groceries** are foods you buy at a grocer's or at a supermarket such as flour, sugar, and tinned foods. *Mama came in the back door carrying two bags of groceries.* N-PLURAL

grog /grɒg/. **Grog** is a drink made by diluting a strong spirit, such as rum or whisky, with water. N-UNCOUNT

groggy /grɒgi/ **groggier, groggiest.** If you feel **groggy**, you feel weak and rather ill; an informal use. *She was feeling a bit groggy when I saw her.* ADJ-GRADED: usu v-link ADJ

groin /grɔɪn/ **groins.** Your **groin** is the part of your body where your legs meet your abdomen. ◆◇◇◇◇ N-COUNT

groom /gruːm/ **grooms, grooming, groomed** ◆◇◇◇◇

1 A **groom** is the same as a **bridegroom**. *...the bride and groom.* N-COUNT

2 A **groom** is someone whose job is to look after the horses in a stable and to keep them clean. N-COUNT

3 If you **groom** an animal, you clean its fur, usually by brushing it. *The horses were exercised and groomed with special care.* VERB V n

4 If you **are groomed** for a special job, someone prepares you for it by teaching you the skills you will need. *George was already being groomed for the top job... Marshall was groomed to run the family companies.* VB: usu passive be V-ed for n be V-ed to-inf

groomed /gruːmd/. You use **groomed** in expressions such as **well groomed** and **badly groomed** to say how neat, clean, and smart a person is. *...a very well groomed man... She always appeared perfectly groomed.* ADJ: usu adv ADJ

grooming /gruːmɪŋ/. **Grooming** refers to the things that people do to keep themselves clean and make their face, hair, and skin look nice. *...a growing concern for personal grooming. ...five new men's grooming products.* ◆◇◇◇◇ N-UNCOUNT: oft N n

groove /gruːv/ **grooves** ◆◆◇◇◇

1 A **groove** is a deep line cut into a surface. *Prior to assembly, grooves were made in the shelf, base and sides to accommodate the back panel.* N-COUNT

2 In popular music, a **groove** is a rhythm; an informal use. *...Latin and African grooves.* N-COUNT: usu supp N

grooved /gruːvd/. Something that is **grooved** has grooves on its surface. *The inscriptions are as fresh and deep-grooved as if they had been cut only last week.* ADJ

groovy /gruːvi/ **groovier, grooviest.** If you describe something as **groovy**, you mean that it is attractive, fashionable, or exciting; an old-fashioned, informal word. *...the grooviest club in London.* ◆◇◇◇◇ ADJ-GRADED

grope /grəʊp/ **gropes, groping, groped** ◆◇◇◇◇

1 If you **grope** for something that you cannot see, you try to find it by moving your hands around in order to feel it. *With his left hand he groped for the knob, turned it, and pulled the door open... Bunbury groped in his breast pocket for his wallet.* VERB =fumble V for n V adv/prep

2 If you **grope** your way to a place, you move there, holding your hands in front of you and feeling the way because you cannot see anything. *I didn't turn on the light, but groped my way across the room.* VERB =feel V way prep/adv

3 If you **grope** for something, for example the solution to a problem, you try to think of it, when you have no real idea what it could be. *He groped for solutions to the problems facing the country... She groped for a simple word to express a simple idea.* VERB V for n Also V towards n

♦ **groping, gropings** *They continue their groping towards a constitutional settlement.* N-VAR

4 If one person **gropes** another, they touch or grab their body in a rough, sexual way; used in informal English showing disapproval. *He would try to grope her breasts and put his hand up her skirt.* ► Also a noun. *It took a good few gropes for me to realise that he was doing this on purpose.* VERB PRAGMATICS V n N-COUNT

gross /grəʊs/ **grosser, grossest; grosses, grossing, grossed.** The plural of the number is **gross**. ◆◆◆◇◇

1 You use **gross** to describe something unacceptable or unpleasant to a very great amount, degree, or intensity. *The company were guilty of gross negligence. ...an act of gross injustice.* ♦ **grossly** *Funding of education had been grossly inadequate for years... Lexicographers are still grossly underpaid.* ADJ: ADJ n ADV-GRADED: ADV -ed/adj

2 If you say that someone's speech or behaviour is **gross**, you think it is very rude or unacceptable. *He abused the Admiral in the grossest terms... I feel disgusted and wonder how I could ever have been so gross.* ADJ-GRADED PRAGMATICS

3 If you describe something as **gross**, you think that it is very ugly and lacks good taste. *He wears really gross holiday outfits.* ADJ-GRADED PRAGMATICS

4 If you describe someone as **gross**, you are emphasizing that they are extremely fat and unattractive. *The figures (or lack of them) that many men cut on any beach can be so gross... I only resist things like chocolate if I feel really gross.* ADJ-GRADED: v-link ADJ PRAGMATICS

5 **Gross** means the total amount of something, especially money, before any necessary deductions are made. *...a fixed rate account guaranteeing 10.4% gross interest or 7.8% net until October.* ► Also an adverb. *Interest is paid gross, rather than having tax deducted. ...a father earning £20,000 gross a year.* ADJ: ADJ n ADV: ADV after v

6 **Gross** means the total amount of something, after all the relevant amounts have been added together. *National Savings gross sales in June totalled £709 million.* ADJ: ADJ n

7 **Gross** means the total weight of something, including its container or wrapping. *The aeroplane is said to have a gross weight of only 20,900 lbs.* ADJ: ADJ n

8 If a person or a business **grosses** a particular amount of money, they earn that amount of money before tax has been deducted. *I'm a factory worker who grossed £8,900 last year... So far the films have grossed more than £590 million.* VERB V n

9 A **gross** is a group of 144 things. *In all honesty he could not have justified ordering more than twelve gross of the disks.* NUM: usu a/num NUM

gross domestic product, gross domestic products. A country's **gross domestic product** is the total value of all the goods it has produced and the services it has provided in a particular year. ◆◇◇◇◇ N-VAR

grotesque /grəʊtesk/ **grotesques** ◆◇◇◇◇

1 You say that something is **grotesque** when it is so unnatural, unpleasant, and exaggerated that it upsets or shocks you. *...the grotesque disparities between the wealthy few and nearly everyone else. ...a country where grotesque abuses are taking place.* ADJ-GRADED PRAGMATICS =gross

♦ **grotesquely** *He called it the most grotesquely tragic experience that he's ever had.* ADV-GRADED

2 If someone or something is **grotesque**, they are very ugly. *They tried to avoid looking at his grotesque face and his crippled body.* ♦ **grotesquely** *...grotesquely deformed beggars.* ADJ-GRADED =hideous ADV-GRADED: ADV adj/-ed

3 A **grotesque** is a very ugly or deformed person, especially one in a novel or painting. *Grass's novels are peopled with outlandish characters: grotesques, clowns, scarecrows, dwarfs.* N-COUNT

grotto /grɒtəʊ/ **grottoes** or **grottos.** A **grotto** is a small cave with interesting or attractively shaped rocks. *Water trickles through an underground grotto.* N-COUNT

grotty /grɒti/ **grottier, grottiest.** In informal British English, if you describe something as **grotty**, you mean that it is unpleasant or of poor quality and you dislike it strongly. *...a grotty little flat in Camden.* ADJ-GRADED PRAGMATICS

grouch /graʊtʃ/ **grouches**

1 A **grouch** is someone who is always complaining in a bad-tempered way; an informal use. *He's an old grouch but she puts up with him.* N-COUNT

2 A **grouch** is a bad-tempered complaint; an informal use. *One of the biggest grouches is the new system of payment.* N-COUNT =whinge, grumble

grouchy /graʊtʃi/. If someone is **grouchy**, they are very bad-tempered and complain a lot; an informal word. *Your grandmother has nothing to stop her from being bored, grouchy and lonely.* ADJ-GRADED

ground /graʊnd/ **grounds, grounding, grounded** ◆◆◆◆◆

1 **The ground** is the surface of the earth or the floor of a room. *Forty or fifty women were sitting cross-legged on the ground... We slid down the roof and dropped to the ground.* ● Something that is **below ground** is under the earth's surface or under a building. Something that is **above ground** is on top of the earth's surface. *People were making for the air-raid shelters below ground.* N-SING: the N PHRASE

2 If you say that something takes place on the **ground**, you mean it takes place on the surface of the earth and not in the air. *Coordinating airline traffic on the ground is as complicated as managing the traffic in the air... All ground forces have not arrived in the Persian Gulf.* N-SING: oft N n

3 The **ground** is the soil and rock on the earth's surface. *The ground had eroded. ...the marshy ground of the river delta.* N-SING: usu the N

4 You can refer to land as **ground**, especially when it has very few buildings or when it is considered to N-UNCOUNT: usu with supp

be special in some way. *...a stretch of waste ground... This memorial stands on sacred ground.*

5 You can use **ground** to refer to an area of land, sea, or air which is used for a particular activity. *...Indian hunting grounds... The best fishing grounds are around the islands.* N-COUNT: supp N

6 A **ground** is an area of land which is specially designed and made for playing sport or for some other activity. *...the city's football ground. ...a parade ground.* N-COUNT: supp N

7 The **grounds** of a large or important building are the garden or area of land which surrounds it. *...the palace grounds. ...the grounds of the University.* N-PLURAL: usu with supp, oft N *of* n, n N

8 You can use **ground** to refer to a place or situation in which particular methods or ideas can develop and be successful. *The company has maintained its reputation as the developing ground for new techniques... Colonialism is especially fertile ground for nationalist ideas.* N-VAR: with supp, oft N *for* n

9 You can use **ground** in expressions such as **on shaky ground** and **the same ground** to refer to a particular subject, area of experience, or basis for an argument. *Sensing she was on shaky ground, Marie changed the subject... The French are on solid ground when they argue that competitiveness is no reason for devaluation... It's often necessary to go over the same ground more than once.* N-UNCOUNT: supp N, oft *on* adj N

10 **Ground** is used in expressions such as **gain ground**, **lose ground**, and **give ground** in order to indicate that someone obtains or loses an advantage which they have in a particular situation, activity, or argument; used in journalism. *There are signs that the party is gaining ground in the latest polls... The US dollar lost more ground.* N-UNCOUNT

11 If you say that something is **a ground for** or **grounds for** a particular feeling or course of action, you mean that it is a reason or justification for it. If you say that you are doing something **on the grounds** of a particular thing, you are giving the reason for your action. *In the interview he gave some grounds for optimism... The court overturned that decision on the grounds that the Prosecution had withheld crucial evidence... Owen was against it, on the grounds of expense.* N-VAR: N *for* n, *on* N with supp

12 If an argument, belief, or opinion **is grounded** in something, that thing is used as a justification for it. *Her argument was grounded in fact... They believe the soul is immortal, grounding this belief on the Divine nature of the human spirit.* VERB =base; be V-ed *in/on* n; V n *in/on* n

13 If an aircraft or its passengers **are grounded**, they are made to stay on the ground and are not allowed to take off. *The civil aviation minister ordered all the planes to be grounded... A hydrogen leak forced NASA to ground the space shuttle.* VERB be V-ed; V n

14 When parents **ground** a child, they forbid them to go out and enjoy themselves for a period of time, as a punishment. *Thompson grounded him for a month, and banned television.* VERB V n

15 If a ship or boat **is grounded** or if it **grounds**, it touches the bottom of the sea, lake, or river it is on, and is unable to move off. *Residents have been told to stay away from the region where the ship was grounded... The boat finally grounded on a soft, underwater bank. ...a grounded oil tanker.* V-ERG be V-ed; V; V-ed

16 In American English, the **ground** in an electric plug or piece of electrical equipment is the wire through which electricity passes into the ground and which makes the equipment safe. The British word is **earth**. N-COUNT: usu sing

17 **Ground** is the past tense and past participle of **grind**.

18 See also **grounding**; **home ground**.

19 If you **break new ground**, you do something completely different or you do something in a completely different way; used showing approval. *Gellhorn may have broken new ground when she filed her first report on the Spanish Civil War.* PHRASES V inflects PRAGMATICS

20 If you say that a town or building **is burnt to the ground** or **is razed to the ground**, you are emphasizing that it has been completely destroyed by fire. *The town was razed to the ground after the French Revolution.* V inflects PRAGMATICS

21 If two people or groups find **common ground**, they agree about something, especially when they do not agree about other things.

22 If you **go to ground**, you hide somewhere where you cannot easily be found. *Citizens of East Beirut went to ground in basements and shelters.* V inflects

23 The **middle ground** between two groups, ideas, or plans involves things which do not belong to either of these groups, ideas, or plans but have elements of each, often in a less extreme form. *Clinton seemed to be searching for the middle ground between suburban voters and traditional Democratic supporters from minority groups.* oft PHR *between* n

24 If something such as a project gets **off the ground**, it begins or starts functioning. *We help small companies to get off the ground.* PHR after v, v-link PHR

25 If you are **on** your **own ground**, you are in a place or situation in which you feel confident because you are very familiar with it. *On her own ground she knows exactly what she's doing.* PHR with cl, v-link PHR

26 If you **prepare the ground** for a future event, course of action, or development, you make it easier for it to happen. *...a political initiative which would prepare the ground for war.* V inflects

27 If you **shift** your **ground** or **change** your **ground**, you change the basis on which you are arguing. V inflects

28 If you **stand** your **ground** or **hold** your **ground**, you continue to support a particular argument or to have a particular opinion when other people are opposing you or trying to make you change your mind. *The spectacle of Sakharov standing his ground and speaking his mind gave me hope.* V inflects

29 If you **stand** your **ground** or **hold** your **ground**, you do not run away from a situation, but face it bravely. *She had to force herself to stand her ground when she heard someone approaching.* V inflects

30 If you say that something such as a person, job, or piece of clothing **suits** someone **down to the ground**, you are emphasizing that it is completely suitable or appropriate for them; an informal expression. V inflects PRAGMATICS

31 If people or things of a particular kind are **thin on the ground**, there are very few of them; used mainly in British English. *Good managers are often thin on the ground.* v-link PHR

32 • to **have one's ear to the ground**: see **ear**.

groundbreaking /graʊndbreɪkɪŋ/; also spelled **ground-breaking**. You use **groundbreaking** to describe things which you think are significant because they provide new and positive ideas, and influence the way people think about things. *...his groundbreaking novel on homosexuality. ...groundbreaking research.* ADJ: usu ADJ n

groundcloth /graʊndklɒθ/ **groundcloths.** In American English, a **groundcloth** is a piece of waterproof material which you put on the ground to sleep on when you are camping. The usual British word is **groundsheet**. N-COUNT =groundsheet

ground crew, ground crews. At an airport, the people who look after the planes when they are on the ground are called the **ground crew**. *The airport ground crew tried to dissuade the pilot from taking off.* N-COUNT-COLL =ground staff

ground floor, ground floors. In British English, the **ground floor** of a building is the floor that is level or almost level with the ground outside. *She showed him around the ground floor of the empty house... Jenny now lives in a terraced ground floor flat.* ◆◇◇◇◇ N-COUNT: usu *the* N in sing

groundhog /graʊndhɒg, AM -hɔːg/ **groundhogs.** A **groundhog** is a type of small animal with reddish-brown fur and a bushy tail. Groundhogs hibernate in winter. They are found in North America. N-COUNT

grounding /graʊndɪŋ/. If you have a **grounding** in a subject, you know the basic facts or principles of that subject, especially as a result of a particular course of training or instruction. *The degree provides a thorough grounding in both mathematics and statistics.* ◆◇◇◇◇ N-SING: oft N *in* n

groundless /graʊndləs/. If you say that a fear, accusation, or story is **groundless**, you mean that it is not based on evidence and is unlikely to be true or valid. *Fears that the world was about to run out of fuel proved groundless... A ministry official described the report as groundless.* ADJ: usu v-link ADJ ≠well-founded

ground level. If something is at **ground level**, it is at the same level as the ground, as opposed to being higher up or below the surface. *The hotel is set on three floors. There's a bar and cafe at ground level... The remaining block of woodland is cut down to ground level.* ◆◇◇◇◇ N-UNCOUNT: oft prep N

groundnut /graʊndnʌt/ **groundnuts.** A **groundnut** is a peanut; used mainly in British English. N-COUNT

ground plan, ground plans
1 A **ground plan** is a plan of the ground floor of a building. N-COUNT
2 A **ground plan** is a basic plan for future action. N-COUNT

ground rent, ground rents. Ground rent is rent that is paid by the owner of a flat or house to the owner of the land on which it is built; used mainly in British English. *How much is the annual ground rent?... Ground rents are likely to escalate over time.* N-VAR

ground rule, ground rules. The **ground rules** for something are the basic principles on which future action will be based. *The panel says the ground rules for the current talks should be maintained.* ◆◇◇◇◇ N-COUNT: usu pl, oft N *for/of* n

groundsheet /graʊndʃiːt/ **groundsheets.** In British English, a **groundsheet** is a piece of waterproof material which you put on the ground to sleep on when you are camping. The usual American word is **groundcloth**. N-COUNT =groundcloth

groundsman /graʊndzmən/ **groundsmen.** A **groundsman** is a person whose job is to look after a park or sports ground; used mainly in British English. N-COUNT

ground staff
1 The people who are paid to maintain a sports ground are called the **ground staff**. *The ground staff do all they can to prepare the pitch.* N-COUNT-COLL
2 At an airport, the **ground staff** are the airline employees who do not fly with the planes, but who work in the airport building helping passengers and providing information. *There had been a strike amongst British Airways ground staff.* N-COUNT-COLL =ground crew

groundswell /graʊndswel/. In newspapers, a sudden growth of public feeling or support for something is often called a **groundswell**. *There is undoubtedly a groundswell of support for the idea of a strong central authority... The groundswell of opinion is in favour of a referendum.* N-SING: with supp, usu N *of* n

groundwater /graʊndwɔːtəʳ/. **Groundwater** is water that is found under the ground. Groundwater has usually passed down through the soil and become trapped by rocks. *The groundwater is only feet beneath the city streets.* N-UNCOUNT

groundwork /graʊndwɜːʳk/. The **groundwork** for something is the early work on it which forms the basis for further work. *Yesterday's meeting was to lay the groundwork for the task ahead... These courses provide the groundwork of statistical theory.* ◆◇◇◇◇ N-SING: *the* N, oft *the* N *for* n

group /gruːp/ **groups, grouping, grouped** ◆◆◆◆◆
1 A **group** of people or things is a number of people or things which are together in one place at one time. *The trouble involved a small group of football supporters... The students work in groups on complex problems.* N-COUNT-COLL: oft N *of* n
2 A **group** is a set of people who have the same interests or objectives, and who organize themselves to work or act together. *...the Minority Rights Group... Members of an environmental group are staging a protest inside a chemical plant.* N-COUNT: usu supp N
3 A **group** is a set of people, organizations, or things which are considered together because they have something in common. *She is among the most promising players in her age group... As a group, today's old people are still relatively deprived.* N-COUNT: usu supp N
4 A **group** is a number of separate commercial or industrial firms which all have the same owner. *The group made a pre-tax profit of £1.05 million. ...a French-based insurance group.* N-COUNT: usu supp N
5 A **group** is a number of musicians who perform together, especially ones who play popular music. *At school he played bass in a pop group called The Urge. ...Billy Bragg's backing group.* N-COUNT =band
6 If a number of things or people **are grouped together** or **group together**, they are together in one place or within one organization or system. *The fact sheets are grouped into seven sections... That's a proposal being canvassed by the WEU, which groups together the nine leading European NATO members... We want to encourage them to group together to act as a big purchaser.* V-ERG *be* V-ed prep V pl-n with *together* V *together* Also V n prep
7 See also **grouping; blood group, ginger group, pressure group.**

groupie /gruːpi/ **groupies.** A **groupie** is someone, especially a young woman, who is very keen on a particular pop group, singer, or other famous person, and keeps following them around. N-COUNT

grouping /gruːpɪŋ/ **groupings.** A **grouping** is a set of people or things that have something in common. *There were two main political groupings pressing for independence.* ◆◇◇◇◇ N-COUNT: usu with supp

group therapy. **Group therapy** is a form of psychiatric treatment in which a group of people discuss their problems with each other. ◆◇◇◇◇ N-UNCOUNT

grouse /graʊs/ **grouses, grousing, groused.** ◆◇◇◇◇ The form **grouse** is used as the plural for meaning 1.
1 A **grouse** is a small fat bird. Grouse are often shot for sport and can be eaten. *The party had been to the grouse moors that morning... There was grouse-shooting in the autumn and pheasant-shooting in the winter.* ► **Grouse** is the flesh of this bird eaten as food. *The menu included roast grouse and smoked salmon with oysters.* N-COUNT: oft N n / N-UNCOUNT
2 If you **grouse**, you complain. *'How come we never know what's going on?' he groused... When they groused about the parking regulations, they did it with good humor.* VERB V with quote V *about* n Also V that, V
3 A **grouse** is a complaint. *There have been grouses about the economy, interest rates and house prices.* N-COUNT

grove /groʊv/ **groves** ◆◆◇◇◇
1 A **grove** is a group of trees that are close together. *...open fields and groves of trees. ...an olive grove.* N-COUNT: usu with supp
2 **Grove** is often used as part of the name of a street. *...47 Canada Grove, Bognor Regis.* N-IN-NAMES

grovel /grɒvᵊl/ **grovels, grovelling, grovelled;** spelled **groveling, groveled** in American English.
1 If you say that someone **grovels**, you mean they behave very humbly towards another person, for example because they are frightened or because they want something; used showing disapproval. *I don't grovel to anybody... Speakers have been shouted down, classes disrupted, teachers made to grovel. ...a letter of grovelling apology.* VERB PRAGMATICS V *to/before* n V V-ing
2 If you **grovel**, you crawl on the ground, for example in order to find something. *We grovelled around the club on our knees.* VERB V prep/adv Also V

grow /groʊ/ **grows, growing, grew, grown** ◆◆◆◆◆
1 When people, animals, and plants **grow**, they increase in size and change physically over a period of time. *We stop growing at maturity.* VERB V
2 If a plant or tree **grows** in a particular place, it is alive there. *The station had roses growing at each end of the platform.* VERB V
3 If you **grow** a particular type of plant, you put seeds or young plants in the ground and look after them as they develop. *I always grow a few red onions... Lettuce was grown by the Ancient Romans.* VERB V n
4 When someone's hair **grows**, it gradually becomes longer. Your nails also **grow**. *Then the hair began to grow again and I felt terrific.* VERB V
5 If someone **grows** their hair, or **grows** a beard or moustache, they stop cutting their hair or shaving so that their hair becomes longer. You can also **grow** your nails. *I'd better start growing my hair.* VERB V n
6 If someone **grows** mentally, they change and develop in character or attitude. *They began to grow as persons.* VERB V
7 You use **grow** to say that someone or something V-LINK

gradually changes until they have a new quality, feeling, or attitude. *I grew a little afraid of the guy next door... He's growing old... He grew to love his work.* V adj V to-inf

8 If an amount, feeling, or problem **grows**, it becomes greater or more intense. *The number of unemployed people in Poland has grown by more than a quarter in the last month... Opposition grew and the government agreed to negotiate. ...a growing number of immigrants.* VERB V V-ing

9 If one thing **grows into** another, it develops or changes until it becomes that thing. *The boys grew into men... This political row threatens to grow into a full blown crisis.* VERB V *into* n

10 If something such as an idea or a plan **grows out of** something else, it develops from it. *The idea for this book grew out of conversations with Philippa Brewster.* VERB V *out of* n

11 If the economy or a business **grows**, it increases in wealth, size, or importance. *The economy continues to grow. ...a fast growing business.* VERB V V-ing

12 If a crystal **grows**, or if a scientist **grows** it, it forms from a solution. *...crystals of natralite that grow in cavities in the rock... We tried to grow some copper sulphate crystals with our children.* V-ERG V V n

13 See also **grown**.

grow apart. If people who have a close relationship **grow apart**, they gradually start to have different interests and opinions from each other, and their relationship starts to fail. *He and his wife grew apart... It sounds as if you have grown apart from Tom.* PHRASAL VERB RECIP pl-n V P V P *from* n

grow away from. If you **grow away from** someone, you gradually have fewer interests and opinions in common with them. *He's never grown away from the people amongst whom he was brought up.* PHRASAL VERB V P P n

grow into. When a child **grows into** an item of clothing, they become taller or bigger so that it fits them properly. *It's a bit big, but she'll soon grow into it.* PHRASAL VERB V P n

grow on. If someone or something **grows on** you, you start to like them more and more. *Slowly and strangely, the place began to grow on me.* PHRASAL VERB V P n

grow out. If you **grow out** a hairstyle or let it **grow out**, you let your hair grow so that the style changes or so that you can cut off the part that you do not want. *I also let my hair go darker and grew out my fringe... The red rinse had grown out completely.* PHRASAL VERB ERG V P n (not pron) V P

grow out of PHRASAL VERB

1 If you **grow out of** a type of behaviour or an interest, you stop behaving in that way or having that interest, as you develop or change. *Most children who stammer grow out of it.* V P P n

2 When a child **grows out of** an item of clothing, they become so tall or big that it no longer fits them properly. *You've grown out of your shoes again.* V P P n

grow up PHRASAL VERB

1 When someone **grows up**, they gradually change from being a child into being an adult. *She grew up in Tokyo.* • See also **grown-up**. V P

2 If you tell someone to **grow up**, you are telling them to stop behaving in a silly or childish way; an informal use. *It's time you grew up.* usu imper PRAGMATICS V P

3 If something **grows up**, it starts to exist and becomes larger or more important. *A variety of heavy industries grew up alongside the port.* V P

grower /grəʊəʳ/ **growers.** A **grower** is a person who grows large quantities of a particular plant or crop in order to sell them. *England's apple growers are fighting an uphill battle against foreign competition.* ◆◆◇◇◇ N-COUNT: usu supp N

growing pains

1 If a person or organization suffers from **growing pains**, they experience temporary difficulties and problems at the beginning of a particular stage of development. *There's some sympathy for this new country's growing pains, but that sympathy is fast wearing out. ...the growing pains of teenagers experiencing their first taste of adulthood.* N-PLURAL: usu with poss

2 If children suffer from **growing pains**, they have pain in their muscles or joints that is caused by unusually fast growth. N-PLURAL

growing season, growing seasons. The **growing season** in a particular country or area is the period in each year when the weather and temperature is right for plants and crops to grow. *Any farmer or gardener knows that a milder winter means a longer growing season.* N-COUNT: usu sing

growl /graʊl/ **growls, growling, growled** ◆◇◇◇◇

1 When a dog or other animal **growls**, it makes a low rumbling noise, usually because it is angry. *The dog was biting, growling and wagging its tail.* ▶ Also a noun. *Their noise modulated to a concerted menacing growl punctuated by sharp yaps.* VERB V N-COUNT

2 If someone **growls** something, they say something in a low, rough, and angry voice; used in written English. *His fury was so great he could hardly speak. He growled some unintelligible words at Pete... 'I should have killed him,' Sharpe growled.* ▶ Also a noun. *...with an angry growl of contempt for her own weakness.* VERB V n V with quote N-COUNT

3 If you say that something **growls**, you mean that it makes a deep rumbling noise. *My stomach growled... The car growls along rutted streets.* ▶ Also a noun. *Acceleration is accompanied by a resonating growl from the gearbox.* VERB V V prep N-COUNT

grown /grəʊn/. A **grown** man or woman is one who is fully developed and mature, both physically and mentally. *Few women can understand a grown man's love of sport... Dad, I'm a grown woman. I know what I'm doing.* • See also **full-grown**. ◆◇◇◇◇ ADJ: ADJ n

grown-up, grown-ups; also spelled **grownup**. The syllable **up** is not stressed when it is a noun. ◆◇◇◇◇

1 A **grown-up** is an adult; used by or to children. *Jan was almost a grown-up... Tell children to tell a grown-up if they're being bullied.* N-COUNT

2 Someone who is **grown-up** is physically and mentally mature and no longer dependent on their parents or another adult. *I seem to have everything anyone could want – a good husband, a lovely home, grown-up children who're doing well.* ADJ

3 If you say that someone is **grown-up**, you mean that they behave in an adult way, often when they are in fact still a child. *She's very grown up.* ADJ-GRADED: usu v-link ADJ

4 **Grown-up** things seem suitable for or typical of adults; an informal use. *Her songs tackle grown-up subjects... She talked in a grown-up manner.* ADJ-GRADED

growth /grəʊθ/ **growths** ◆◆◆◆◇

1 The **growth** of something such as an industry, organization, or idea is its development in size, wealth, or importance. *...the growth of nationalism. ...Japan's enormous economic growth. ...high growth rates.* N-UNCOUNT: oft N *of* n

2 The **growth** in something is the increase in it. *A steady growth in the popularity of two smaller parties may upset the polls... The area has seen a rapid population growth... The market has shown annual growth of 20 per cent for several years.* N-UNCOUNT: also a N, oft supp N, N *in* n, N *of* amount

3 A **growth** industry, area, or market is one which is increasing in size or activity. *Computers and electronics are growth industries and need skilled technicians.* ADJ: ADJ n

4 Someone's **growth** is the development and progress of their character. *...the child's emotional and intellectual growth... Different teachers make different contributions to a student's growth.* N-UNCOUNT: usu supp N

5 **Growth** in a person, animal, or plant is the process of increasing in physical size and development. *...hormones which control fertility and body growth... Cells divide and renew as part of the human growth process.* N-UNCOUNT: usu with supp

6 You can use **growth** to refer to plants which have recently developed or which developed at the same time. *This helps to ripen new growth and makes it flower profusely... Pinch out the tips of the young growths to make for compact, bushy plants.* N-VAR

7 A **growth** is a lump that grows inside or on a person, animal, or plant, and that is caused by a disease or other abnormality. *This type of surgery could even be used to extract cancerous growths.* N-COUNT

growth industry, growth industries. A **growth industry** is an area of business or trade which is growing in size and is making a lot of N-COUNT money. *Japanese government officials are predicting that foreign travel will be one of that country's major growth industries in the coming decade.*

grub /grʌb/ **grubs, grubbing, grubbed** ◆◇◇◇◇

1 A **grub** is a young insect which has just come out of an egg and looks like a short fat worm. N-COUNT

2 Grub is food; an informal use. *Get yourself some grub and come and sit down.* N-UNCOUNT =nosh

3 If you **grub** around, you search for something; an informal use. *I simply cannot face grubbing through all this paper.* VERB V adv/prep

grub up or **grub out.** If you **grub up** trees or plants, or **grub** them **out**, you dig them out of the ground, usually because they are no longer wanted. *Farmers are grubbing up ancient varieties of crops... One by one, orchards were grubbed up.* PHRASAL VERB V P n Also V n P

grubby /grʌbi/ **grubbier, grubbiest** ◆◇◇◇◇

1 A **grubby** person or object is rather dirty. *His white coat was grubby and stained. ...kids with grubby faces.* ADJ-GRADED =grimy

2 If you call an activity or someone's behaviour **grubby**, you mean that it is not completely honest or respectable and you disapprove of it. *...the grubby business of politics.* ADJ-GRADED PRAGMATICS

grudge /grʌdʒ/ **grudges.** If you have or bear a **grudge** against someone, you have unfriendly feelings towards them because of something they did in the past. *He appears to have a grudge against certain players... There is no doubt it was an accident and I bear no grudges.* ◆◇◇◇◇ N-COUNT: oft N *against* n

grudge match, grudge matches. You can call a contest between two people or groups a **grudge match** when they dislike each other. *This is something of a grudge match against a long-term enemy.* N-COUNT

grudging /grʌdʒɪŋ/. A **grudging** feeling or action is one that is positive, but is felt or done very unwillingly. *He even earned his opponents' grudging respect... There seems to be a grudging acceptance of the situation.* ♦ **grudgingly** *The film studio grudgingly agreed to allow him to continue working.* ◆◇◇◇◇ ADJ-GRADED: usu ADJ n =reluctant; ADV-GRADED: ADV with v =reluctantly

gruel /gruːəl/. **Gruel** is a simple, cheap food made by boiling oats with water or milk. N-UNCOUNT

gruelling /gruːəlɪŋ/; spelled **grueling** in American English. A **gruelling** activity is extremely difficult and tiring to do. *He had complained of exhaustion after his gruelling schedule over the past week... This flight was more gruelling than I had expected!* ◆◇◇◇◇ ADJ-GRADED =exhausting

gruesome /gruːsəm/. Something that is **gruesome** is extremely unpleasant and shocking. *There has been a series of gruesome murders in the capital.* ♦ **gruesomely** *He has spent periods in prison, where he was gruesomely tortured. ...a gruesomely compelling series of interviews.* ◆◇◇◇◇ ADJ-GRADED: usu ADJ n =grisly; ADV-GRADED: ADV adj, ADV with v

gruff /grʌf/

1 A **gruff** voice sounds low and rough. *He picked up the phone expecting to hear the chairman's gruff voice.* ♦ **gruffly** *'Well, never mind now,' he said gruffly and turned to Robbie.* ADJ-GRADED; ADV-GRADED

2 If you describe someone as **gruff**, you mean that they seem rather unfriendly or bad-tempered. *His gruff exterior concealed one of the kindest hearts.* ADJ-GRADED

grumble /grʌmbᵊl/ **grumbles, grumbling, grumbled** ◆◇◇◇◇

1 If someone **grumbles**, they complain about something in a bad-tempered and discontented way. *I shouldn't grumble about Mum – she's lovely really... Taft grumbled that the law so favored the criminal that trials seemed like a game of chance... 'This is inconvenient,' he grumbled... It's simply not in her nature to grumble.* ► Also a noun. *My grumble is with the structure and organisation of the material.* ♦ **grumbling, grumblings** *There have been grumblings about the party leader.* VERB =moan, whinge V *about/at* n V that V with quote V; N-COUNT; N-VAR

2 If something **grumbles**, it makes a low continuous sound; a literary use. *It was quiet now, the thunder had grumbled away to the west... The dogs made a noise, a rough, grumbling sound.* ► Also a noun. *One could often hear, far to the east, the grumble of guns.* VERB =rumble V adv/prep V-ing Also V; N-SING: usu N *of* n

grumpy /grʌmpi/ **grumpier, grumpiest.** If you say that someone is **grumpy**, you mean that they are bad-tempered and miserable. *Some folk think I'm a grumpy old man.* ♦ **grumpily** *'I know, I know,' said Ken, grumpily, without looking up.* ◆◇◇◇◇ ADJ-GRADED; ADV-GRADED: ADV with v

grunge /grʌndʒ/. **Grunge** is the name of a fashion and of a type of music. People who wear **grunge** wear clothes which look scruffy and old, and they deliberately try to look as if they do not care about money or fashion. **Grunge** music is guitar-based and is very loud. ◆◆◇◇◇ N-UNCOUNT: oft N n

grunt /grʌnt/ **grunts, grunting, grunted** ◆◇◇◇◇

1 If you **grunt**, you make a low rough noise, especially because you are annoyed or uninterested. *The driver grunted, convinced that Michael was crazy... 'Rubbish,' I grunted... He grunted his thanks.* ► Also a noun. *Their replies were no more than grunts of acknowledgement.* VERB V V with quote V n; N-COUNT: oft N *of* n

2 When an animal **grunts**, it makes a low rough noise. *...the sound of a pig grunting.* VERB V

G-string /dʒiː strɪŋ/ **G-strings.** A **G-string** is a narrow band of cloth that is worn between a person's legs to cover his or her sexual organs, and that is held up by a narrow string round the waist. N-COUNT

guano /gwɑːnoʊ/. **Guano** is the excrement of sea birds and bats. It is used as a fertilizer. N-UNCOUNT

guarantee /gærəntiː/ **guarantees, guaranteeing, guaranteed** ◆◆◆◆◇

1 If one thing **guarantees** another, the first is certain to cause the second thing to happen. *Surplus resources alone do not guarantee growth. ...a man whose fame guarantees that his calls will nearly always be returned.* VERB V n V that Also V n n

2 Something that is a **guarantee** of something else makes it certain that it will happen or that it is true. *A famous old name on a firm is not necessarily a guarantee of quality... There is still no guarantee that a formula could be found.* N-COUNT: oft N *of* n, N that

3 If you **guarantee** something, you promise that it will definitely happen, or that you will do or provide it for someone. *Most states guarantee the right to free and adequate education... All students are guaranteed campus accommodation for their first year... We guarantee that you will find a community with which to socialise... We guarantee to refund your money if you are not delighted with your purchase. ...a guaranteed income of £3.6 million.* ► Also a noun. *The Editor can give no guarantee that they will fulfil their obligations... California's state Constitution includes a guarantee of privacy.* VERB V n *be* V-ed n V that V to-inf V-ed Also V n n, V n that; N-COUNT: oft N that, N *of* n

4 A **guarantee** is a written promise by a company that if a product that they sell or work that they do has any faults within a particular time, it will be repaired, replaced, or redone free of charge. *Whatever a guarantee says, when something goes wrong, you can still claim your rights from the shop... It was still under guarantee.* N-COUNT: also *under* N

5 If a company **guarantees** its product or work, they provide a guarantee for it. *Some builders guarantee their work... All Dreamland's electric blankets are guaranteed for three years. ... parts of guaranteed quality.* VERB V n V-ed

6 A **guarantee** is money or something valuable which you give to someone to show that you will do what you have promised. *Males between 18 and 20 had to leave a deposit as a guarantee of returning to do their military service.* N-COUNT: usu N *of* n/-ing

guaranteed /gærəntiːd/. If you say that something is **guaranteed** to happen, you mean that you are certain that it will happen. *Reports of this kind are guaranteed to cause anxiety... It's guaranteed that my colleagues think I'm deranged... Success is not guaranteed.* ● See also **guarantee**. ◆◆◇◇◇ ADJ: v-link ADJ, usu ADJ to-inf, *it* v-link ADJ that

guarantor /gærəntɔːʳ/ **guarantors.** A **guarantor** is a person who gives a guarantee or who is bound by one; a legal term. N-COUNT

guard /gɑːʳd/ **guards, guarding, guarded** ◆◆◆◆◇

1 If you **guard** a place, person, or object, you stand near them in order to watch and protect them. *Gunmen guarded homes near the cemetery with* VERB V n V-ed *shotguns... The two warlords met at the heavily guarded American Embassy.*

2 If you **guard** someone, you watch them and keep them in a particular place to stop them from escaping. *Marines with rifles guarded them... He is being guarded by a platoon of police.* VERB V n

3 A **guard** is someone such as a soldier, police officer, or prison officer who is guarding a particular place or person. *The prisoners overpowered their guards and locked them in a cell.* N-COUNT

4 A **guard** is a specially organized group of people, such as soldiers or policemen, who protect or watch someone or something. *We have a security guard around the whole area... A heavily armed guard of police have sealed off the city centre.* N-SING-COLL

5 A **guard** is a person whose job is to travel on a train in order to assist passengers, check tickets, and ensure that the train travels safely and punctually; used mainly in British English. N-COUNT

6 If you **guard** some information or advantage that you have, you try to protect it or keep it for yourself. *He closely guarded her identity. ...a threat to China's jealously guarded unity.* VERB V n V-ed

7 A **guard** is a protective device which covers a part of someone's body or a dangerous part of a piece of equipment. *...the chin guard of my helmet... A blade guard is fitted to protect the operator.* N-COUNT: usu with supp

8 Some regiments in the British Army, or the soldiers in them, are referred to as **Guards**. *...the Grenadier Guards.* N-IN-NAMES

9 You use **guard** to refer to someone's attitude of caution or distrust towards someone or something. For example, if you lower your **guard**, you relax when you should be careful and alert, often with unpleasant consequences. *The ANC could not afford to lower its guard until everything had been carried out... You can't let your guard down... I don't think we have to worry too much as long as we keep our guard up and use common sense.* N-SING: poss N

10 See also **guarded**; **bodyguard**, **coastguard**, **lifeguard**, **old guard**.

11 If someone **catches** you **off guard**, they surprise you by doing something when you are not expecting it. If something **catches** you **off guard**, it surprises you by happening when you are not expecting it. *Charm the audience and catch them off guard... The invitation had caught me off guard.* PHRASES V inflects

12 If you **mount guard** or if you **mount a guard**, you organize people to watch or protect a person or place. *They've even mounted guard outside the main hotel in the capital... Police mounted round-the-clock guards on properties last night.* V and N inflect

13 If you are **on** your **guard** or if you are **on guard**, you are being very careful because you think a situation might become difficult or dangerous. *The police have questioned him thoroughly, and he'll be on his guard... He is constantly on guard against any threat of humiliation.* usu v-link PHR

14 If someone is **on guard**, they are on duty and responsible for guarding a particular place or person. *Police were on guard at Barnet town hall.* usu v-link PHR

15 If you **stand guard**, you stand near a particular person or place because you are responsible for watching or protecting them. *One young policeman stood guard outside the locked embassy gates.* V inflects

16 If someone is **under guard**, they are being guarded. *Three men were arrested and one was under guard in hospital.* v-link PHR, PHR after v

guard against. If you **guard against** something, you are careful to prevent it from happening, or to avoid being affected by it. *The armed forces were on high alert to guard against any retaliation.* PHRASAL VERB V P n

guard dog, guard dogs. A **guard dog** is a fierce dog that has been specially trained to protect a particular place. N-COUNT

guarded /gɑːrdɪd/. If you describe someone as **guarded**, you mean that they are careful not to show their feelings or give away information. *The boy gave him a guarded look... In the office, Dr. Lahey seemed less guarded, more relaxed.* ADJ-GRADED =cagey, cautious

♦ **guardedly** *'I am happy, so far,' he says guardedly... They are guardedly optimistic that the market is on the road to recovery.* ADV-GRADED: usu ADV with v, ADV adj, also ADV with cl

guardian /gɑːrdiən/ **guardians** ◆◆◇◇◇

1 A **guardian** is someone who has been legally appointed to look after the affairs of another person, for example a child or someone who is mentally ill. N-COUNT: usu with poss

2 If you consider someone a defender or protector of something, you can call them its **guardian**. *They perceive the church as the guardian of the mysteries of faith... Some guardians of the public's morals are too touchy about what we should laugh at.* N-COUNT: usu N *of* n

guardian angel, guardian angels. A **guardian angel** is a spirit who is believed to protect and guide a particular person. N-COUNT

guardianship /gɑːrdiənʃɪp/. **Guardianship** is the position of being a guardian. *...depriving mothers of the guardianship of their children.* N-UNCOUNT: usu with poss

guard of honour, guards of honour; spelled **guard of honor** in American English. A **guard of honour** is an official parade of troops, usually to celebrate or honour a special occasion, such as the visit of a head of state. N-COUNT

guardrail /gæːrdreɪl/ **guardrails;** also spelled **guard rail**. A **guardrail** is a railing that is placed along the edge of something such as a staircase, path, or boat, so that people can hold onto it or so that they do not fall over the edge. N-COUNT

guardsman /gɑːrdzmən/ **guardsmen;** also spelled **Guardsman**. ◆◇◇◇◇

1 In Britain, a **guardsman** is a soldier who is a member of one of the regiments of Guards. N-COUNT

2 In the United States, a **guardsman** is a soldier who is a member of the National Guard. N-COUNT

guard's van, guard's vans. In British English, the **guard's van** of a train is a small carriage or part of a carriage in which the guard travels. N-COUNT =brake van

guava /gwɑːvə/ **guavas.** A **guava** is a round yellow tropical fruit with pink or white flesh and hard seeds. N-VAR

gubernatorial /guːbərnətɔːriəl/. **Gubernatorial** means relating to or connected with the post of governor. *...a well- known Dallas lawyer and former Texas gubernatorial candidate.* ADJ: ADJ n

guerrilla /gərɪlə/ **guerrillas;** also spelled **guerilla**. A **guerrilla** is someone who fights as part of an unofficial army, usually against an official army or police force. *The guerrillas threatened to kill their hostages. ...a guerrilla war.* ◆◆◆◇◇ N-COUNT: oft N n

guess /ges/ **guesses, guessing, guessed** ◆◆◆◆◇

1 If you **guess** something, you give an answer or provide an opinion which may not be true because you do not have definite knowledge about the matter concerned. *The suit was faultless: Wood guessed that he was a very successful publisher or a banker... You can only guess at what mental suffering they endure... Paula reached for her camera, guessed distance and exposure, and shot two frames... Guess what I did for the whole of the first week... If she guessed wrong, it meant twice as many meetings the following week.* VERB V that V *at* n/wh V n V wh V adv Also V with quote

2 If you **guess** that something is the case, you correctly form the opinion that it is the case, although you do not have definite knowledge about it. *By now you will have guessed that I'm back in Ireland... As you've probably guessed, the problem was electrical... He should have guessed what would happen... Someone might have guessed our secret and passed it on.* VERB V that V wh V n

3 A **guess** is an attempt to give an answer or provide an opinion which may not be true because you do not have definite knowledge about the matter concerned. *My guess is that Mandela probably will emerge as the next president... He'd taken her pulse and made a guess at her blood pressure... Well, we can hazard a guess at the answer.* N-COUNT: oft N that, N *at* n, N *as to* n/wh

4 If you say that something is **anyone's guess** or **anybody's guess**, you mean that no-one can be certain about what is really true; an informal expression. *Just when this will happen is anyone's guess... It's anybody's guess what happened.* PHRASES v-link PHR

5 You say **at a guess** to indicate that what you are saying is only an estimate or what you believe to be PHR with cl true, rather than being a definite fact. *At a guess he's been dead for two days.*

6 You say **I guess** to indicate slight uncertainty or reluctance about what you are saying; an informal expression, used mainly in American English. *I guess she thought that was pretty smart... I guess he's right... 'I think you're being paranoid.'—'Yeah. I guess so.'* PHR with cl, PHR *so/not* PRAGMATICS

7 If someone **keeps** you **guessing**, they do not tell you what you want to know. *The author's intention is to keep everyone guessing until the bitter end... She was keeping everyone guessing about the latest love in her life.* V inflects

8 You say **guess what** to draw attention to something exciting, surprising, or interesting that you are about to say; an informal expression. *Guess what, I just got my first part in a movie.* CONVENTION PRAGMATICS

guesstimate /gestɪmət/ **guesstimates.** A **guesstimate** is an approximate calculation which is based mainly or entirely on guesswork; an informal word. N-COUNT

guesswork /geswɜːʳk/. **Guesswork** is the process of trying to guess or estimate something without knowing all the facts or information. *The question of who planted the bomb remains a matter of guesswork.* N-UNCOUNT

guest /gest/ **guests, guesting, guested** ◆◆◆◆◇

1 A **guest** is someone who is visiting you or is at an event because you have invited them. *She was a guest at the wedding... Their guests sipped drinks on the veranda.* N-COUNT

2 A **guest** is someone who visits a place or organization or appears on a radio or television show because they have been invited to do so. *...a frequent chat show guest... Dr Gerald Jeffers is the guest speaker... They met when she made a guest appearance in the hit TV show Minder.* N-COUNT

3 A **guest** is someone who is staying in a hotel. *I was the only hotel guest... Hotels operate a collection service for their guests from the airports.* N-COUNT

4 If someone **guests for** someone or **guests on** something, they perform or take part in a game or programme on a particular occasion because they have been invited to do so. *He guested for one or two League sides... The band have recently guested on records by Ringo Starr and Tears For Fears.* VERB V prep

5 If you say **be my guest** to someone, you are giving them permission to do something. *If anybody wants to work on this, be my guest.* CONVENTION PRAGMATICS

guest book, guest books. A **guest book** is a book in which guests write their names and addresses when they have been staying in someone's house or in a hotel. N-COUNT

guest house, guest houses; also spelled **guesthouse.** ◆◇◇◇◇

1 In Britain, a **guest house** is a small hotel. N-COUNT

2 In American English, a **guest house** is a small house in the grounds of a large house, where visitors can stay. N-COUNT

guest of honour, guests of honour; spelled **guest of honor** in American English. If you say that someone is the **guest of honour** at a dinner or other social occasion, you mean that they are the most important guest. N-COUNT: usu sing

guest room, guest rooms. A **guest room** is a bedroom in a house or hotel for visitors or guests to sleep in. N-COUNT

guff /gʌf/. If you say that what someone has said or written is **guff**, you think that it is nonsense; an informal word. N-UNCOUNT PRAGMATICS

guffaw /gʌfɔː/ **guffaws, guffawing, guffawed**

1 A **guffaw** is a very loud, hearty laugh. *He bursts into a loud guffaw.* N-COUNT

2 To **guffaw** means to laugh loudly and heartily. *As they guffawed loudly, the ticket collector arrived... 'Ha, ha,' everyone guffawed. 'It's one of Viv's shock tactics.'* VERB V V with quote Also V *at* n

guidance /gaɪdᵊns/. **Guidance** is help and advice. *...an opportunity for young people to improve their performance under the guidance of professional coaches... The nation looks to them for guidance.* ◆◆◇◇◇ N-UNCOUNT: oft *the* N *of* n, supp N

guidance system, guidance systems. The **guidance system** of a missile or rocket is the device which controls its course. *The guidance systems didn't work and the missile couldn't hit its target.* N-UNCOUNT: oft N n

guide /gaɪd/ **guides, guiding, guided** ◆◆◆◆◇

1 A **guide** is a book that gives you information or instructions to help you do or understand something. *Our 10-page guide will help you to change your life for the better. ...the Pocket Guide to Butterflies of Britain and Europe.* N-COUNT: oft in names

2 A **guide** is a book that gives tourists information about a town, area, or country. *The Rough Guide to Paris lists accommodation for as little as £20 a night.* N-COUNT: oft in names =guidebook

3 A **guide** is someone who shows tourists around places such as museums or cities. *We've arranged a walking tour of the city with your guide.* N-COUNT

4 If you **guide** someone around a city, museum, or building, you show it to them and explain points of interest. *...a young Egyptologist who guided us through tombs and temples with enthusiasm... After breakfast, we set off on a guided tour of Paris.* VERB V n adv/prep V-ed

5 A **guide** is someone who shows people the way to a place in a difficult or dangerous region. *The mountain people say that, with guides, the journey can be done in fourteen days.* N-COUNT

6 A **guide** is something that can be used to help you plan your actions or to form an opinion about something. *As a rough guide, a horse needs 2.5 per cent of his body weight in food every day... When selecting fresh fish, let your taste buds be your guide.* N-COUNT: usu sing

7 If you **guide** someone or something somewhere, you go there with them in order to show them the way. *He took the bewildered Elliott by the arm and guided him out... Khandoo guided me through the dark alleys until the smell told me we had arrived.* VERB =lead V n adv/prep

8 If you **guide** a vehicle somewhere, you control it carefully to make sure that it goes in the right direction. *Captain Shelton guided his plane down the runway and took off.* VERB V n adv/prep

9 If something **guides** you somewhere, it gives you the information you need in order to go in the right direction. *They sailed across the Baltic and North Seas with only a compass to guide them.* VERB V n

10 If something or someone **guides** you, they influence your actions or decisions. *He should have let his instinct guide him... Development has been guided by a concern for the ecology of the area... My mother, whose guiding principle in life was doing right, had a far greater influence on me.* VERB V n V-ing

11 If you **guide** someone through something that is difficult to understand or to achieve, you help them to understand it or to achieve success in it. *A free helpline to guide businessmen through the maze of government and EC grants has been set up in Glasgow... The 42-year-old Scot has guided the team to victory in three of their last five games.* VERB V n adv/prep

Guide, Guides

1 In Britain, **the Guides** is an organization for girls which teaches them to become disciplined, practical, and self-sufficient. In the United States, there is a similar organization called the **Girl Scouts**. N-PROPER-COLL: *the* N

2 In Britain, a **Guide** is a girl who is a member of the Guides. N-COUNT

guidebook /gaɪdbʊk/ **guidebooks;** also spelled **guide book.**

1 A **guidebook** is a book that gives tourists information about a town, area, or country. N-COUNT =guide

2 A **guidebook** is a book that gives you information or instructions to help you do or understand something. *In 1987 Congressional Quarterly published a series of guidebooks to American politics.* N-COUNT =guide

guided missile, guided missiles. A **guided missile** is a missile whose direction can be controlled while it is in the air. N-COUNT

guide dog, guide dogs. A **guide dog** is a dog that has been trained to lead a blind person. N-COUNT

guided writing. In language teaching, when students do **guided writing** activities, they are given an outline in words or pictures to help them write. *...some guided writing tasks.* N-UNCOUNT: oft N n

guideline /gaɪdlaɪn/ **guidelines** ◆◆◇◇◇

1 If an organization issues **guidelines** on something, it issues official advice about how to do it. *The government should issue clear guidelines on the content of religious education... The accord also lays down guidelines for the conduct of American drug enforcement agents.* — N-COUNT: usu pl

2 A **guideline** is something that can be used to help you plan your actions or to form an opinion about something. *The effects of the sun can be significantly reduced if we follow certain guidelines... A written IQ test is merely a guideline.* — N-COUNT

guild /gɪld/ **guilds.** A **guild** is an organization of people who do the same job or who have the same occupation. *...the Writers' Guild of America.* — ◆◆◇◇◇ N-COUNT: oft in names, N *of* n

guilder /gɪldəʳ/ **guilders.** A **guilder** is a unit of money that is used in the Netherlands. ▶ **The guilder** is also used to refer to the Dutch currency system. *During last year's turmoil in the foreign-exchange markets, when even the franc was shaken, the guilder remained unperturbed.* — N-COUNT: num N; N-SING: *the* N

guildhall /gɪldhɔːl/ **guildhalls.** A **guildhall** is a building near the centre of a town where members of a guild used to meet in former times. — ◆◇◇◇◇ N-COUNT

guile /gaɪl/. **Guile** is the quality of being very cunning and good at deceiving people. *His cunning and guile were not attributes I would ever underestimate... I love children's innocence and lack of guile.* — N-UNCOUNT

guileless /gaɪlləs/. If you describe someone as **guileless**, you approve of them because they behave openly and truthfully and do not try to deceive people; a literary word. *Daphne was so guileless, that Claire had no option but to believe her.* — ADJ-GRADED, PRAGMATICS, =straight

guillotine /gɪlətiːn/ **guillotines, guillotining, guillotined**

1 A **guillotine** is a device used to execute people, especially in France in the past. A sharp blade was raised up on a frame and dropped onto the person's neck. *One after the other Danton, Robespierre and the rest went to the guillotine.* — N-COUNT: also *by* N

2 If someone **is guillotined**, they are killed with a guillotine. *After Marie Antoinette was guillotined, her lips moved in an attempt to speak.* — VB: usu passive, *be* V-ed

3 A **guillotine** is a device used for cutting and trimming paper. — N-COUNT

guilt /gɪlt/ ◆◆◇◇◇

1 **Guilt** is an unhappy feeling that you have because you have done something wrong or think that you have done something wrong. *Her emotions had ranged from anger to guilt in the space of a few seconds... Some cancer patients experience strong feelings of guilt.* — N-UNCOUNT

2 **Guilt** is the fact that you have done something wrong or illegal. *The trial is concerned only with the determination of guilt according to criminal law... You weren't convinced of Mr Matthews' guilt.* — N-UNCOUNT

guilt complex, guilt complexes. If you say that someone has a **guilt complex** about something, you mean that they feel very guilty about it, in a way that you consider is exaggerated, unreasonable, or unnecessary. — N-COUNT, PRAGMATICS

guilty /gɪlti/ **guiltier, guiltiest** ◆◆◆◇◇

1 If you feel **guilty**, you feel unhappy because you think that you have done something wrong or have failed to do something which you should have done. *I feel so guilty, leaving all this to you... When she saw me she looked guilty.* — ADJ-GRADED: usu v-link ADJ, oft ADJ *about* n ♦ **guiltily** *He glanced guiltily over his shoulder.* — ADV-GRADED: ADV with v

2 **Guilty** is used of an action or fact that you feel guilty about. *Many may be keeping it a guilty secret... I leave with a guilty sense of relief.* ● **guilty conscience**: see **conscience**. — ADJ: ADJ n

3 If someone is **guilty** of a crime or offence, they have committed that crime or offence. *They were found guilty of murder... He pleaded guilty to causing actual bodily harm.* — ADJ: oft ADJ *of* n/-ing

4 If someone is **guilty** of doing something wrong, they have done something wrong. *He claimed Mr Brooke had been guilty of a 'gross error of judgment'... They will consider whether or not he has been guilty of serious professional misconduct.* — ADJ: oft ADJ *of* n/-ing

guinea /gɪni/ **guineas.** A **guinea** is an old British unit of money that was worth £1.05. Guineas are still sometimes used, for example in auctions. — ◆◇◇◇◇ N-COUNT

guinea fowl; guinea fowl is both the singular and the plural. A **guinea fowl** is a large grey African bird. — N-COUNT

guinea pig, guinea pigs; also spelled **guinea-pig.** ◆◇◇◇◇

1 If someone is used as a **guinea pig** in an experiment, something is tested on them that has not been tested on people before. *Dr Roger Altounyan used himself as a human guinea pig to perfect a treatment which has since saved the lives of countless people... Nearly 500,000 pupils are to be guinea pigs in a trial run of the new 14-plus exams.* — N-COUNT

2 A **guinea pig** is a small furry animal without a tail. Guinea pigs are often kept as pets. — N-COUNT

guise /gaɪz/ **guises.** You use **guise** to refer to the outward appearance or form of someone or something, which is often temporary or different from their real nature. *He turned up at a fancy dress Easter dance in the guise of a white rabbit... I see myself at different moments of history, in various guises and occupations.* — ◆◇◇◇◇ N-COUNT: with supp, oft *in/under the* N *of* n

guitar /gɪtɑːʳ/ **guitars.** A **guitar** is a musical instrument with six strings and a long neck. An **acoustic guitar** has a hollow wooden body. An **electric guitar** has a solid wooden body and is played using electricity. You play the guitar by plucking or strumming the strings. — ◆◆◆◇◇ N-VAR: oft *the* N

guitarist /gɪtɑːrɪst/ **guitarists.** A **guitarist** is someone who plays the guitar. — ◆◆◇◇◇ N-COUNT

gulch /gʌltʃ/ **gulches.** A **gulch** is a long narrow valley with steep sides which has been made by a stream flowing through it; used mainly in American English. *...California Gulch.* — N-COUNT: oft in names

gulf /gʌlf/ **gulfs**

1 A **gulf** is an important or significant difference between two people, things, or groups. *Within society, there is a growing gulf between rich and poor. ...the gulf between rural and urban life.* — N-COUNT: oft N *between* pl-n

2 A **gulf** is a large area of sea which extends a long way into the surrounding land. *Hurricane Andrew was last night heading into the Gulf of Mexico.* — N-COUNT

Gulf. **The Gulf** is used to refer to the Persian Gulf and the countries around it. *...the Gulf crisis... Despite the Gulf war, oil has continued to flow. ...the oil wells of the Gulf.* — ◆◆◆◆◇ N-PROPER: *the* N, oft N n

gull /gʌl/ **gulls.** A **gull** is a common sea bird. — N-COUNT

gullet /gʌlɪt/ **gullets.** Your **gullet** is the tube which goes from your mouth to your stomach. — N-COUNT

gulley /gʌli/. See **gully.**

gullible /gʌlɪbᵊl/. If you describe someone as **gullible**, you mean they are easily tricked because they are too trusting. *What point is there in admitting that the stories fed to the gullible public were false?... I'm so gullible I would have believed him.* — ◆◇◇◇◇ ADJ-GRADED, PRAGMATICS ♦ **gullibility** /gʌləbɪlɪti/ *Was she taking part of the blame for her own gullibility?* — N-UNCOUNT: oft with poss

gully /gʌli/ **gullies;** also spelled **gulley.** A **gully** is a long narrow valley with steep sides. *The bodies of the three climbers were located at the bottom of a steep gully.* — ◆◇◇◇◇ N-COUNT

gulp /gʌlp/ **gulps, gulping, gulped** ◆◇◇◇◇

1 If you **gulp** something, you eat or drink it very quickly by swallowing large quantities of it at once. *She quickly gulped her tea.* — VERB: V n

2 If you **gulp**, you swallow air, often making a noise in your throat as you do so, because you are nervous or excited; used in written English. *I gulped, and then proceeded to tell her the whole story... 'I'm sorry,' he gulped.* — VERB: V, V with quote

3 If you **gulp** air, you breathe in a large amount of air quickly through your mouth. *She gulped air into her lungs... He slumped back, gulping for air.* — VERB: V n *into* n, V *for* n

4 A **gulp** of air, food, or drink, is a large amount of it that you swallow at once. *I took in a large gulp of air... When his whisky came he drank half of it in one gulp.* — N-COUNT: oft N *of* n

gulp down. If you **gulp down** food or drink, you — PHRASAL VERB quickly eat or drink it all by swallowing large quantities of it at once. *She gulped down a mouthful of coffee... He'd gulped it down in one bite.* V P n V n P

gum /gʌm/ **gums, gumming, gummed** ◆◆◇◇◇

1 **Gum, chewing gum** or **bubble gum** is a substance, often mint-flavoured, which you chew for a long time but do not swallow. *She chewed gum and liked parties. ...two large boxes of chewing gum.* N-MASS

2 Your **gums** are the areas of firm, pink flesh inside your mouth, which your teeth grow out of. *The toothbrush gently removes plaque without damaging the gums or causing bleeding. ...gum disease.* N-COUNT: usu pl

3 **Gum** is a type of glue that is used to stick two pieces of paper together; used mainly in British English. *He was holding up a pound note that had been torn in half and stuck together with gum.* N-MASS
♦ **gummed** *Our local stationer was selling gummed labels for $9.95 per box of 700.* ADJ: usu ADJ n

4 If you **gum** one thing to another, you stick the two things together; used in British English. *He selected a blond moustache, carefully gummed it into place and trimmed it a little... It is a mild infection in which a baby's eyelashes can become gummed together.* VERB V n prep/adv V-ed

5 A **gum** is a chewy sweet which feels like firm rubber and usually tastes of fruit. *...a quarter pound of wine gums.* N-COUNT

6 **Gum** is a sticky substance which comes from the eucalyptus tree or from various other trees and shrubs. N-MASS

7 people sometimes say **'By gum'** to emphasize a point that they are making; used in old-fashioned British English. *By gum, my phone bills have shot up.* EXCLAM PRAGMATICS

gum up. If you **gum up** something, you prevent it from operating properly or efficiently; an informal expression. *Regulators may gum up an efficient system... The house price chain is gummed up.* PHRASAL VERB V P n (not pron) Also V n P

gumboot /gʌmbuːt/ **gumboots. Gumboots** are long rubber boots which you wear to keep your feet dry; an old-fashioned word used in British English. N-COUNT: usu pl =wellington

gummy /gʌmi/. Something that is **gummy** is sticky. *My eyes are gummy; my mouth is sticky and sour; my fingers seem glued together.* ADJ-GRADED =sticky

gumption /gʌmpʃᵊn/

1 If someone has **gumption**, they are able to think what it would be sensible to do in a particular situation, and they do it; an informal word. *We now find that common sense, or what used to be called gumption, is a thing of the past.* N-UNCOUNT

2 If someone has the **gumption** to do something, they have the courage or the audacity to do it. *He suspected that deep down, she admired him for having the gumption to disagree with her.* N-UNCOUNT: oft *the* N to-inf

gun /gʌn/ **guns, gunning, gunned** ◆◆◆◆◇

1 A **gun** is a weapon from which bullets or other things are fired. *He produced a gun and he came into the house... The inner-city has guns and crime and drugs and deprivation. ...gun control laws.* N-COUNT

2 A starting **gun** is an object like a gun that is used to make a noise to signal the start of a race. *The starting gun blasted and they were off.* N-COUNT

3 In American English, if you **gun** an engine or a vehicle, you make it start or go faster by pressing on the accelerator pedal. *They gunned the 32-valve, V-8 engine to 157 miles per hour.* VERB V n

4 See also **airgun, machine-gun, shotgun, submachine gun.**

5 If you come out **with guns blazing** or **with all guns blazing**, you put all your effort and energy into trying to achieve something. *The company came out with guns blazing... Starting out with all guns blazing, Ipswich were a goal ahead after only 10 minutes.* PHRASES PHR after v

6 If you **jump the gun**, you do something before everyone else or before the proper or right time; an informal use. *It wasn't due to be released until September 10, but some booksellers have jumped the gun and decided to sell it early.* V inflects

7 If you **stick to your guns**, you continue to have your own opinion about something even though other people are trying to tell you that you are wrong; an informal use. *He should have stuck to his guns and refused to meet her.* V inflects

gun down. If someone **is gunned down**, they are shot and severely injured or killed. *He had been gunned down and killed at point-blank range.* PHRASAL VERB usu passive *be* V-ed P

gun for. If someone **is gunning for** you, they are trying to find a way to harm you or cause you trouble; an informal expression. *You knew that they were gunning for you, but did you ever imagine that it would be as bad as this?* PHRASAL VERB only cont V P n

gunboat /gʌnbout/ **gunboats.** A **gunboat** is a small ship which has several large guns fixed on it. N-COUNT

gun dog, gun dogs; also spelled **gundog.** A **gun dog** is a dog that has been trained to work with a hunter or gamekeeper, especially to find and carry back birds or animals that have been shot. N-COUNT

gunfire /gʌnfaɪəʳ/. **Gunfire** is the repeated shooting of guns. *The sound of gunfire and explosions grew closer.* ◆◇◇◇◇ N-UNCOUNT

gunge /gʌndʒ/. You use **gunge** to refer to a soft, sticky substance, especially if it is unpleasant; used in informal British English. *He had painted the floors with some kind of black gunge.* N-UNCOUNT

gunman /gʌnmən/ **gunmen.** A **gunman** is a man who uses a gun to commit a crime such as murder or robbery. *Two policemen were killed when gunmen opened fire on their patrol vehicle.* ◆◆◇◇◇ N-COUNT

gunner /gʌnəʳ/ **gunners.** A **gunner** is a member of the armed forces who is trained to use guns. ◆◇◇◇◇ N-COUNT

gunnery /gʌnəri/. **Gunnery** is the activity of firing large guns; a technical military term. *During the Second World War the area was used for gunnery practice.* N-UNCOUNT: usu N n

gunpoint /gʌnpɔɪnt/. If you are held **at gunpoint**, someone is threatening to shoot and kill you if you do not obey them. *She and her two daughters were held at gunpoint by a gang who burst into their home.* ◆◇◇◇◇ PHRASE: PHR after v

gunpowder /gʌnpaʊdəʳ/. **Gunpowder** is an explosive substance which is used to make fireworks or cause explosions. N-UNCOUNT

gun-runner, gun-runners; spelled **gunrunner** in American English. A **gun-runner** is someone who takes or sends guns into a country secretly and illegally. N-COUNT

gun-running. Gun-running is the activity of taking or sending guns into a country secretly and illegally. N-UNCOUNT

gunship /gʌnʃɪp/ **gunships.** See **helicopter gunship.**

gunshot /gʌnʃɒt/ **gunshots** ◆◇◇◇◇

1 **Gunshot** is used to refer to bullets that are fired from a gun. *They had died of gunshot wounds. ...avoiding the volleys of gunshot.* N-UNCOUNT: usu N n

2 A **gunshot** is the firing of a gun or the sound of a gun being fired. *They heard thousands of gunshots... A balloon popped, sounding like a gunshot.* N-COUNT

gunsmith /gʌnsmɪθ/ **gunsmiths.** A **gunsmith** is someone who makes and repairs guns. N-COUNT

guppy /gʌpi/ **guppies.** A **guppy** is a small, brightly-coloured tropical fish. N-COUNT

gurgle /gɜːʳgᵊl/ **gurgles, gurgling, gurgled** ◆◇◇◇◇

1 If water **is gurgling**, it is making the sound that it makes when it flows quickly and unevenly through a narrow space. *...a narrow stone-edged channel along which water gurgles unseen.* ► Also a noun. *We could hear the swish and gurgle of water against the hull.* VERB V adv/prep N-COUNT

2 If someone, especially a baby, **is gurgling**, they are making a sound in their throat similar to the gurgling of water. *Henry gurgles happily in his baby chair.* ► Also a noun. *There was a gurgle of laughter on the other end of the line.* VERB V N-COUNT

guru /guːruː/ **gurus** ◆◇◇◇◇

1 If you refer to someone as a **guru**, you mean that some people regard them as an expert or leader. *Fashion gurus dictate crazy ideas such as squeezing oversized bodies into tight trousers.* N-COUNT: oft n N

2 A **guru** is a religious and spiritual leader and teacher, especially in Hinduism. N-COUNT; N-TITLE

gush /gʌʃ/ **gushes, gushing, gushed** ◆◇◇◇◇
1 When liquid **gushes** out of something, or when something **gushes** a liquid, the liquid flows out very quickly and in large quantities. *Piping-hot water gushed out... A supertanker continues to gush oil off the coast of Spain.* V-ERG V adv/prep V n
2 A **gush** of liquid is a sudden, rapid flow of liquid, or a quantity of it that suddenly flows out. *I heard a gush of water.* N-SING: usu N of n
3 If someone **gushes**, they express their admiration or pleasure in an exaggerated way. *'Oh, it was brilliant,' he gushes... He gushed about his love for his wife.* ♦ **gushing** *He delivered a gushing speech.* VERB V with quote V prep ADJ-GRADED
4 You can use **gush** in expressions such as **a gush of enthusiasm** to refer to a sudden intense feeling or an expression of a feeling. *She felt a gush of pure affection for her mother... Their initial gush of sympathy gradually dried up.* N-SING: N of n

gusset /gʌsɪt/ **gussets.** A **gusset** is a small strip or triangle of cloth sewn into a garment to make it wider, stronger, or more comfortable. N-COUNT

gust /gʌst/ **gusts, gusting, gusted** ◆◇◇◇◇
1 A **gust** is a short, strong, sudden rush of wind. *A gust of wind drove down the valley... A hurricane-force gust blew off part of a church tower.* N-COUNT: oft N of n
2 When the wind **gusts**, it blows with short, strong, sudden rushes. *The wind gusted again... The wind gusted up to 164 miles an hour.* VERB V V prep/adv
3 If you feel a **gust of** emotion, you feel the emotion suddenly and intensely. *...a small gust of pleasure.* N-COUNT: N of n

gusto /gʌstoʊ/. If you do something with **gusto**, you do it with energetic and enthusiastic enjoyment. *Hers was a minor part, but she played it with gusto.* N-UNCOUNT: usu *with* N

gusty /gʌsti/. **Gusty** is used to describe weather in which there are very strong, irregular winds. *Weather forecasts predict more hot weather, gusty winds and lightning strikes.* ADJ-GRADED: usu ADJ n

gut /gʌt/ **guts, gutting, gutted** ◆◆◇◇◇
1 A person's or animal's **guts** are all the organs inside them. *One of the crew started shovelling a foul-smelling gruel of ground-up fish guts overboard.* N-PLURAL
2 When someone **guts** a dead animal or fish, they prepare it for cooking by removing all the organs from inside it. *It is not always necessary to gut the fish prior to freezing.* VERB V n
3 **The gut** is the tube inside the abdomen of a person or animal through which food passes while it is being digested. N-SING: *the*/poss N
4 **Guts** is the will and courage to do something which is difficult or unpleasant, or which might have unpleasant results; an informal use. *The new Chancellor has the guts to push through unpopular tax increases... It takes more guts than I've usually got to go and see him.* N-UNCOUNT
5 A **gut** feeling is based on instinct or emotion rather than reason. *Let's have your gut reaction to the facts as we know them.* N-SING: usu N n
6 You can refer to someone's stomach as their **gut**, especially when it is very large and sticks out; an informal use. *His gut sagged out over his belt.* • See also **beer gut**. N-COUNT: usu sing
7 The **guts** of something, for example a subject or a machine, are the key elements of it, which make it work; an informal use. *She has a reputation for getting at the guts of a subject and never pulling her punches... The guts of the reactor have to be hauled out of the pressure vessel.* N-PLURAL: N of n
8 To **gut** a building means to destroy the inside of it so that only its outside walls remain. *Over the weekend, a firebomb gutted a building where 60 people lived... A factory stands gutted and deserted.* VERB V n V-ed
9 **Gut** is string made from part of the stomach of an animal. Traditionally, it is used to make the strings of sports rackets or musical instruments such as violins. N-UNCOUNT
10 See also **gutted**.
11 To **bust a gut** means to work very hard trying to achieve something; an informal expression. *You can bust a gut sixteen hours a day, seven days a week, but if your product is lousy, you've wasted your time.* PHRASES V inflects
12 If you **hate** someone's **guts**, you dislike them very much indeed; an informal expression. *We hate each other's guts.* V inflects PRAGMATICS
13 If someone **spills** their **guts**, they tell you everything about something secret or private; an informal expression. *People call in and just spill their guts about whatever's bothering them on the job or in a relationship.* V inflects
14 If you say that you **are working your guts out** or **slogging your guts out**, you are emphasizing that you are working as hard as you can, usually in an attempt to achieve something in as short a time as possible; an informal expression. *Most have worked their guts out and made sacrifices.* V inflects PRAGMATICS

gutless /gʌtləs/. If you describe someone as **gutless**, you think they have a weak character and lack courage or determination. *By attacking me, by attacking my wife, he has proved himself to be a gutless coward.* ADJ-GRADED PRAGMATICS

gutsy /gʌtsi/ **gutsier, gutsiest**
1 If you describe someone as **gutsy**, you mean they show courage or determination; an informal word; used showing approval. *I've always been drawn to tough, gutsy women... They admired his gutsy and emotional speech.* ADJ-GRADED PRAGMATICS
2 If you describe something as **gutsy**, you mean that it is powerful, substantial, and vivid; an informal use. *...the rich, gutsy flavours of mature autumn vegetables... 'The Commitments' is the gutsy story of a Dublin rock band.* ADJ-GRADED

gutted /gʌtɪd/. If you are **gutted**, you feel extremely disappointed or depressed about something that has happened; used in informal British English. *Birmingham City supporters will be absolutely gutted if he leaves the club.* ADJ-GRADED: v-link ADJ

gutter /gʌtəʳ/ **gutters, guttering, guttered** ◆◇◇◇◇
1 The **gutter** is the edge of a road next to the pavement, where rain water collects and flows away. *It is supposed to be washed down the gutter and into the city's vast sewerage system.* N-COUNT: usu *the* N
2 A **gutter** is a plastic or metal channel fixed to the lower edge of the roof of a building, which rain water drains into. *Did you fix the gutter?* N-COUNT
3 You can use **the gutter** to refer to a condition of life in which you are poor and have no self-respect. *Instead of ending up in jail or in the gutter he was remarkably successful.* N-SING: *the* N
4 If a flame **gutters**, it burns unsteadily and weakly; a literary use. *The flames guttered. ...a guttering candle.* VERB V V-ing
5 See also **gutter press**.

guttering /gʌtərɪŋ/. **Guttering** consists of the plastic or metal channels fixed to the lower edge of the roof of a building, which rain water drains into. N-UNCOUNT

gutter press. If you refer to particular newspapers and magazines as **the gutter press**, you disapprove of them because they contain more stories about sex, crime, and people's private affairs than about international, political, or economic affairs. *'The Tory gutter press prints only distortions and lies,' she said.* N-SING: *the* N PRAGMATICS

guttural /gʌtərᵊl/. **Guttural** sounds are harsh sounds that are produced at the back of a person's throat. *Joe had a low, guttural voice with a mid-Western accent.* ADJ-GRADED

guv /gʌv/. **Guv** is sometimes used in informal British English to address a man, especially a customer or someone you are doing a service for. *Hey, thanks, guv.* N-VOC

guvnor /gʌvnəʳ/ **guvnors;** also spelled **guv'nor. Guvnor** is sometimes used in informal British English to refer to or address a man who is in a position of authority over you, for example your employer or father. *People seem to forget that the guvnor's horses have not been well.* N-COUNT; N-VOC

guy /gaɪ/ **guys** ◆◆◆◆◇
1 A **guy** is a man; an informal use. *I was working with a guy from Manchester.* • See also **wise guy**. N-COUNT
2 Americans sometimes address a group of people, N-VOC;

whether they are male or female, as **guys** or **you guys**; an informal use. *Hi, guys. How are you doing?... Mom wants to know if you guys still have that two-person tent.* N-PLURAL: you N

3 A **guy** is the same as a **guy rope**. N-COUNT

4 In Britain, a **guy** is a model of a man that is made from old clothes stuffed with straw or rags. Guys are burned on bonfires as part of the celebrations for Guy Fawkes Night. N-COUNT

Guy Fawkes Night /gaɪ fɔːks naɪt/. In Britain, **Guy Fawkes Night** is the evening of 5th November, when many people have bonfire parties and let off fireworks. It was originally a time when people remembered Guy Fawkes' attempt to blow up the Houses of Parliament in 1605. Guy Fawkes Night is often referred to as 'Bonfire Night'. N-UNCOUNT =Bonfire Night

guy rope, guy ropes. A **guy rope** is a rope or wire that has one end fastened to a tent or pole and the other end fixed to the ground, so that it keeps the tent or pole in position. N-COUNT =guy

guzzle /gʌzᵊl/ **guzzles, guzzling, guzzled**

1 If you **guzzle** something, you drink it or eat it quickly and greedily; an informal use. *Melissa had chain-smoked all evening and guzzled gin and tonics like they were lemonade.* VERB V n Also V

2 If you say that a vehicle **guzzles** fuel, you mean that it uses a lot of it in a way that is wasteful and unnecessary. *The plane was deafeningly noisy, guzzled fuel, and left a trail of smoke.* VERB V n ♦ **-guzzling** *The boom of the 1980s led to a taste for petrol-guzzling cars. ...big energy-guzzling houses.* COMB in ADJ: ADJ n

gym /dʒɪm/ **gyms** ◆◆◇◇◇

1 A **gym** is a club, building, or large room, usually containing special equipment, where people go to do physical exercise or get fit. *While the lads are golfing, I work out in the gym. ...the school gym.* N-COUNT

2 Gym is the activity of doing physical exercises in a gym, especially at school; an informal use. *...gym classes.* N-UNCOUNT: oft N n

gymkhana /dʒɪmkɑːnə/ **gymkhanas.** A **gymkhana** is an event in which people ride horses in competition. N-COUNT

gymnasium /dʒɪmneɪziəm/ **gymnasiums** or **gymnasia.** A **gymnasium** is the same as a **gym**; a formal word. ◆◇◇◇◇ N-COUNT =gym

gymnast /dʒɪmnæst/ **gymnasts.** A **gymnast** is someone who is trained in gymnastics. N-COUNT

gymnastics /dʒɪmnæstɪks/. The form **gymnastic** is used as a modifier. ◆◇◇◇◇

1 Gymnastics consists of physical exercises that develop your strength, co-ordination, and agility. *...the British Amateur Gymnastics Association.* N-UNCOUNT

2 Gymnastic is used to describe things relating to gymnastics. *...gymnastic exercises.* ADJ: ADJ n

3 You can use **gymnastics** to refer to an activity where someone shows great agility and flexibility. *Hers is the kind of voice that excels at vocal gymnastics... They are the only ones whose brains are supple enough for the mental gymnastics required.* N-UNCOUNT: adj N

gynaecology /gaɪnɪkɒlədʒi/; spelled **gynecology** in American English. **Gynaecology** is the branch of medical science which deals with women's diseases and medical conditions. ◆◇◇◇◇ N-UNCOUNT ♦ **gynaecologist, gynaecologists** *Gynaecologists at Aberdeen Maternity Hospital have successfully used the drug on 60 women.* N-COUNT ♦ **gynaecological** /gaɪnɪkəlɒdʒɪkᵊl/ *Breast examination is a part of a routine gynaecological examination.* ADJ: ADJ n

gypsum /dʒɪpsəm/. **Gypsum** is a soft white substance which looks like chalk and which is used to make plaster of Paris. N-UNCOUNT

gypsy /dʒɪpsi/ **gypsies;** also spelled **gipsy**. A **gypsy** is a member of a race of people who travel from place to place, usually in caravans, rather than living in one place. ◆◆◇◇◇ N-COUNT =Romany ► Also an adjective. *...the largest gypsy community of any country.* ADJ: usu ADJ n

gyrate /dʒaɪreɪt, AM dʒaɪreɪt/ **gyrates, gyrating, gyrated**

1 If you say that a person or their body **is gyrating**, you mean that they are dancing or moving their body in a sexually suggestive way. *The woman began to gyrate to the music. ...a room stuffed full of gasping, gyrating bodies.* VERB V V-ing ♦ **gyration** /dʒaɪreɪʃᵊn/ **gyrations** *Prince continued his enthusiastic gyrations on stage.* N-COUNT: usu pl

2 To **gyrate** means to turn round and round in a circle, usually very fast. *The aeroplane was gyrating about the sky in a most unpleasant fashion.* VERB V prep Also V

3 If things such as prices or currencies **gyrate**, they move up and down in a rapid and uncontrolled way; used in journalism. *Interest rates began to gyrate up towards 20 per cent in 1980 and then down and up again.* VERB V adv/prep Also V ♦ **gyration** *The gyrations of the currency markets show why tougher controls are now needed.* N-COUNT: usu pl, with supp

gyroscope /dʒaɪrəskoʊp/ **gyroscopes.** A **gyroscope** is a device that contains a disc rotating on an axis that can turn freely in any direction, so that the disc maintains the same position whatever the position or movement of the surrounding structure. N-COUNT

H h

H, h /eɪtʃ/ **H's, h's** /eɪtʃɪz/

1 H is the eighth letter of the English alphabet. N-VAR

2 H or **h** is an abbreviation for words beginning with h, such as 'hour', 'height', 'hospital', and 'hard'.

ha /hɑː/; also spelled **hah**. **Ha** is used in writing to represent a noise that people make to show they are surprised, annoyed, or pleased about something. *Ha! said Wren. Think I'd trust you?... Hah! Just as I suspected.* ● See also **ha ha**. ◆◇◇◇◇ EXCLAM

ha. ha. is a written abbreviation for **hectare**.

habeas corpus /heɪbiəs kɔːʳpəs/. **Habeas corpus** is a law that exists in many countries. It states that a person cannot be kept in prison unless he or she has been brought before a judge or a magistrate, who must decide whether it is lawful for that person to be kept in prison. N-UNCOUNT

haberdasher /hæbəʳdæʃəʳ/ **haberdashers**

1 In British English, a **haberdasher** or a **haberdasher's** is a shop where small articles for sewing and dressmaking are sold. N-COUNT

2 In American English, a **haberdasher** is a shopkeeper who makes and sells men's clothes. The British word is **tailor**. N-COUNT

3 In American English, a **haberdasher** or a **haberdasher's** is a shop where men's clothes are sold. The British word is **tailor** or **tailor's**. N-COUNT

haberdashery /hæbəʳdæʃəri/

1 In British English, **haberdashery** is small articles for sewing and dressmaking such as buttons, zips, thread, and ribbons which are sold in a haberdasher's shop. N-UNCOUNT

2 In American English, **haberdashery** is men's clothing sold in a shop, or a shop selling men's clothing. N-UNCOUNT

habit /hæbɪt/ **habits** ◆◆◆◇◇

1 A **habit** is something that you do often or regularly. *He has an endearing habit of licking his lips* N-VAR: oft N of -ing *when he's nervous... Many people add salt to their food out of habit, without even tasting it first. ...a survey on eating habits in the UK.*

2 A **habit** is an action which is considered bad that someone does repeatedly and finds it difficult to stop doing. *A good way to break the habit of eating too quickly is to put your knife and fork down after each mouthful... After twenty years as a chain smoker Mr Nathe has given up the habit.* N-COUNT: oft N *of*-ing

3 A drug **habit** is an addiction to a drug such as heroin or cocaine. *She became a prostitute in order to pay for her cocaine habit.* N-COUNT: supp N

4 A **habit** is a piece of clothing shaped like a long loose dress, which a nun or monk wears. N-COUNT

5 If you say that someone is **a creature of habit**, you mean that they usually do the same thing at the same time each day, rather than doing new and different things. PHRASES *creature* inflects, usu v-link PHR

6 If you are **in the habit of** doing something, you do it regularly or often. If you get **into the habit of** doing something, you begin to do it regularly or often. *They were in the habit of giving two or three dinner parties a month... I got into the habit of calling in on Gloria on my way home from work.* v-link PHR -ing

7 If you **make a habit of** doing something, you do it regularly or often. *You can phone me at work as long as you don't make a habit of it.* V inflects, PHR -ing/n

8 If someone has a particular **habit of mind**, they usually think in that particular way. *In accent, mannerism and habit of mind he appeared to be completely Eastern European.* *habit* inflects

habitable /hæbɪtəbᵊl/. If a place is **habitable**, it is good enough for people to live in. *Making the house habitable was a major undertaking.* ADJ-GRADED

habitat /hæbɪtæt/ **habitats.** The **habitat** of an animal or plant is the natural environment in which it normally lives or grows. *In its natural habitat, the hibiscus will grow up to 25ft... Few countries have as rich a diversity of habitat as South Africa.* ◆◆◇◇◇ N-VAR: usu supp N =home

habitation /hæbɪteɪʃᵊn/ **habitations**

1 **Habitation** is the activity of living somewhere; a formal use. *The recent survey found that 20 per cent of private-rented dwellings are unfit for human habitation... Signs of habitation appeared and the fields gave way to houses.* N-UNCOUNT

2 A **habitation** is a place where people live; a formal use. *Behind the habitations, the sandstone cliffs rose abruptly to the north and west.* N-COUNT

habitual /həbɪtʃuəl/ ◆◇◇◇◇

1 A **habitual** action, state, or way of behaving is one that someone usually does or has, especially one that is considered to be typical or characteristic of them. *He soon recovered his habitual geniality... If bad posture becomes habitual, you risk long-term effects.* ♦ **habitually** *His mother had a patient who habitually flew into rages. ...her habitually prim expression.* ADJ; ADV: ADV with v, ADV adj

2 You use **habitual** to describe someone who usually or often does a particular thing. *She was a habitual daydreamer... Three out of four of them would become habitual criminals if actually sent to jail.* ADJ: ADJ n

habituated /həbɪtʃueɪtɪd/. If you are **habituated** to something, you have got used to it; a formal word. *Hong-Kongers are habituated to the idea of learning from the person above how to do the work... More people are habituated to cigarettes than to drugs or alcohol in this country.* ADJ-GRADED: usu v-link ADJ, usu ADJ *to* n

habitué /həbɪtʃueɪ/ **habitués.** Someone who is a **habitué** of a particular place often visits that place; a formal word. *Kiki and Man Ray, who lived just down the street, were habitués of this bar.* N-COUNT: usu with supp, oft N *of* n =regular

hack /hæk/ **hacks, hacking, hacked** ◆◆◇◇◇

1 If you **hack** something or **hack** at it, you cut it with strong, rough strokes using a sharp tool such as an axe or knife. *An armed gang barged onto the train and began hacking and shooting anyone in sight... Some were hacked to death with machetes... Matthew desperately hacked through the leather.* VERB; V n; *be* V-ed prep/adv; V prep

► **Hack away** means the same as **hack**. *He started to hack away at the tree bark.* PHRASAL VERB V P *at* n

2 If you **hack** your way through something such as a jungle or wood or **hack** a path through it, you clear a path through it by cutting and chopping trees, bushes, or anything else that is in your way. *We undertook the task of hacking our way through the jungle.* VERB V n prep/adv

3 If you **hack** at or **hack** something which is too large, too long, or too expensive, you reduce its size, length, or cost by cutting out or getting rid of large parts of it. *He hacked away at the story, throwing out much of the flashback material and eliminating one character entirely.* VERB V adv/prep Also V n

4 If you refer to a professional writer, such as a journalist, as a **hack**, you disapprove of them because they write for money without worrying very much about the quality of their writing. *...tabloid hacks, always eager to find victims in order to sell newspapers. ...a hack writer of cheap romances.* N-COUNT PRAGMATICS

5 If you refer to a politician as a **hack**, you disapprove of them because they have gained power by being loyal and obedient to their party and not because they are particularly talented or popular. *Far too many party hacks from the old days still hold influential jobs.* N-COUNT: oft supp N PRAGMATICS

6 When someone **hacks into** a computer system, they break into the system, especially in order to get secret or confidential information that is stored there. *The saboteurs had demanded money in return for revealing how they hacked into the systems.* ♦ **hacking** *...the common and often illegal art of computer hacking.* VERB V *into* n; N-UNCOUNT

7 If you **hack** or **go hacking**, you go for a ride on horseback; used mainly in British English. *The children could be seen hacking across the hillside on their ponies.* ♦ **hacking** *Hacking is a major activity in the horse world.* VB: oft cont V prep/adv; N-UNCOUNT

8 A **hack** is a ride on horseback; used mainly in British English. N-COUNT

9 A **hack** is a horse which people can hire from a stable to go out riding. N-COUNT

10 If you say that someone **can't hack it** or **couldn't hack it**, you mean that they do not or did not have the qualities needed to do a task or cope with a situation; an informal expression. *You have to be strong and confident and never give the slightest impression that you can't hack it... Smith tries to convince them that he can hack it as a police chief.* PHRASE =not be up to it

11 See also **hacking**.

hack away. See **hack** 1. PHRASAL VERB

hack off. If you **hack** something **off**, you cut it off with strong, rough strokes using a sharp tool such as an axe or knife. *Kim even hacked off her long hair... Surgeons saved a man's arm after it was hacked off at the elbow.* PHRASAL VERB V P n (not pron)

hacker /hækəʳ/ **hackers** ◆◇◇◇◇

1 A computer **hacker** is someone who tries to break into computer systems, especially in order to get secret or confidential information that is stored there. N-COUNT

2 A computer **hacker** is someone who uses a computer a lot, especially so much that they have no time to do anything else. N-COUNT

hacking /hækɪŋ/. A **hacking** cough is a dry, painful cough with a harsh, unpleasant sound. *The quiet was broken by Astley's hacking cough.* ADJ: ADJ n
• See also **hack**.

hacking jacket, hacking jackets. A **hacking jacket** is a jacket made of tweed. Hacking jackets are often worn by people who go horse riding; used mainly in British English. N-COUNT

hackles /hækᵊlz/. If something **raises** your **hackles** or makes your **hackles rise**, it makes you feel angry and hostile. *Oh boy, this record's going to raise a few hackles... You could see her hackles rising as she heard him outline his plan.* PHRASE: V inflects

hackneyed /hæknid/. If you describe something as **hackneyed**, you disapprove of it because it has been used, seen, or heard many times before. *The style was dull, the only metaphor was hackneyed... They take refuge in hackneyed, well-* ADJ-GRADED PRAGMATICS *tried moves which fail to impress. ...hackneyed postcard snaps of lochs and glens.*

hacksaw /hæksɔː/ **hacksaws.** A **hacksaw** is a small saw used for cutting metal. N-COUNT

had. The auxiliary verb is pronounced /həd, STRONG hæd/. For the main verb, and for the meanings 2 to 5, the pronunciation is /hæd/.
1 Had is the past tense and past participle of **have.**
2 Had is sometimes used instead of 'if' to begin a clause which refers to a situation that might have happened but did not. For example, the clause 'had he been elected' means the same as 'if he had been elected'. *Had he succeeded, he would have acquired a monopoly... Had I known what the problem was, we could have addressed it.* AUX; AUX n -ed
3 If you **have been had**, someone has tricked you, for example by selling you something at too high a price; an informal expression. *If your customer thinks he's been had, you have to make him happy.* PHRASES; *be* inflects
4 If you say that someone **has had it**, you mean they are in very serious trouble or have no hope of succeeding; an informal expression. *Unless she loses some weight, she's had it... He wants actors who can speak Welsh. Obviously I've had it.* AUX inflects
5 If you say that you **have had it**, you mean that you are very tired of something or very annoyed about it, and do not want to continue doing it or it to continue happening; an informal expression. *I've had it. Let's call it a day... I've had it with that kind of treatment of Americans.* AUX inflects

haddock /hædək/; **haddock** is both the singular and the plural form. **Haddock** are a type of edible sea fish that are found in the North Atlantic. *...fishing boats which normally catch a mix of cod, haddock and whiting.* ► **Haddock** is this fish eaten as food. *Use Scottish smoked haddock if you can.* ◆◇◇◇◇ N-VAR; N-UNCOUNT

Hades /heɪdiːz/. In Greek mythology, **Hades** was a place under the earth where people's souls went after they had died. N-PROPER =the underworld

hadn't /hædᵊnt/. In informal English, **had not** is usually said or written as **hadn't**.

haemoglobin /hiːməgloʊbɪn/; spelled **hemoglobin** in American English. **Haemoglobin** is the red substance in blood, which combines with oxygen and carries it around the body; a technical term in biology. ◆◇◇◇◇ N-UNCOUNT

haemophilia /hiːməfɪliə/; spelled **hemophilia** in American English. **Haemophilia** is a medical condition in which a person's blood does not clot properly, so that they continue to bleed for a long time if they are injured. N-UNCOUNT

haemophiliac /hiːməfɪliæk/ **haemophiliacs;** spelled **hemophiliac** in American English. A **haemophiliac** is a person who suffers from haemophilia. ◆◇◇◇◇ N-COUNT

haemorrhage /hemərɪdʒ/ **haemorrhages, haemorrhaging, haemorrhaged;** spelled **hemorrhage** in American English. ◆◇◇◇◇
1 A **haemorrhage** is serious bleeding from broken blood vessels inside a person's body. *Shortly after his admission into hospital he had a massive brain haemorrhage and died... These drugs will not be used if hemorrhage is the cause of the stroke.* N-VAR
2 If someone **is haemorrhaging**, they are bleeding heavily because of broken blood vessels inside their body. *I haemorrhaged badly after the birth of all three of my sons... If this is left untreated, one can actually haemorrhage to death.* ♦ **haemorrhaging** *A post mortem showed he died from shock and haemorrhaging.* VERB; V; V to n; N-UNCOUNT
3 A **haemorrhage of** people or resources is a rapid loss of them from a group or place, seriously weakening its position. *He said the move would definitely stem the haemorrhage of talent and enterprise from the colony.* N-SING: N of n
4 If a group or place **is haemorrhaging** people or resources, or if people or resources **are haemorrhaging** from a group or place, the group or place is rapidly losing people or resources and is becoming weak. *Venice is haemorrhaging the very resource which could save it: its own people... The figures showed that cash was haemorrhaging from the conglomerate.* V-ERG; V n; V from n

haemorrhoid /hemərɔɪdz/ **haemorrhoids;** spelled **hemorrhoids** in American English. **Haemorrhoids** are painful swellings that can appear in the veins inside the anus; a medical term. N-COUNT: usu pl =piles

hag /hæg/ **hags.** If someone refers to a woman as a **hag**, they mean that she is ugly, old, and unpleasant; an offensive word. *I hope the old hag has gone out to do her grocery shopping and hasn't come back yet.* N-COUNT =bag

haggard /hægəʳd/. Someone who looks **haggard** has a tired expression and shadows under their eyes, especially because they are ill or have not had enough sleep. *He was pale and a bit haggard... Nick glanced around at the haggard faces watching him.* ADJ-GRADED

haggis /hægɪs/ **haggises.** A **haggis** is a large Scottish sausage, usually shaped like a ball, which is made from minced sheep's meat contained inside the skin from a sheep's stomach. N-VAR

haggle /hægᵊl/ **haggles, haggling, haggled.** If you **haggle**, you argue about something before reaching an agreement, especially about the cost of something that you are buying. *Ella showed her the best places to go for a good buy, and taught her how to haggle with used furniture dealers... Meanwhile, as the politicians haggle, the violence worsens... Of course he'll still haggle over the price.* ► Also a noun. *She laughed again, enjoying the haggle.* ♦ **haggling** *After months of haggling, they recovered only three-quarters of what they had lent.* ◆◇◇◇◇ V-RECIP; V with n; pl-n V; V (non-recip); N-COUNT; N-UNCOUNT

hah /hɑː/. See **ha.**

ha ha; also spelled **ha ha ha.** ◆◇◇◇◇
1 Ha ha or **ha ha ha** is used in writing to represent the sound that people make when they laugh. *I dropped my bag at the officer's feet. The bank notes fell out. 'Ha ha ha!' he laughed. 'Black market, uh?'* EXCLAM
2 People sometimes say **'ha ha'** sarcastically, when they are not amused by what you have said, or do not believe it. *John Lennon: 'Well, I would say, "I'm baking bread," you know.'—'And they say, "Ha, ha, what are you really doing?"'.* EXCLAM

hail /heɪl/ **hails, hailing, hailed** ◆◆◇◇◇
1 If a person, event, or achievement **is hailed** as important or successful, they are praised publicly. *Faulkner has been hailed as the greatest American novelist of his generation... US magazines hailed her as the greatest rock'n'roll singer in the world... The deal was hailed by the Defence Secretary.* VERB; be V-ed as n; V n as n; be V-ed; Also be V-ed n
2 Hail consists of small balls of ice that fall like rain from the sky. *A sharp short-lived storm with heavy hail affected Hastings.* N-UNCOUNT
3 When **it hails**, hail falls like rain from the sky. *It started to hail, huge great stones.* VERB; it V
4 A **hail of** things, usually small objects, is a large number of them that hit you at the same time and with great force. *The victim was hit by a hail of bullets... The riot police were met with a hail of stones and petrol bombs.* N-SING: N of n
5 Someone who **hails from** a particular place was born there or lives there; a formal use. *I hail from Brighton... The band hail from Glasgow.* VERB; V from n
6 If someone or something **hails from** a particular background, they come from it; a formal use. *This is a film which seems to hail from the hippie era.* VERB; V from n
7 If you **hail** someone, you call to them; a literary use. *Jill saw him and hailed him... Suddenly, a voice hailed us and there was Miss Quigley.* VERB; V n
8 If you **hail** a taxi or a cab, you wave at it in order to stop it and ask the driver to take you somewhere. *I hurried away to hail a taxi.* VERB; V n
9 Hail is used as a word of greeting; used in old-fashioned English. *Hail to the new champion Bengali D'Albret.* CONVENTION

Hail Mary, Hail Marys. A **Hail Mary** is a prayer to the Virgin Mary that is said by worshipping Roman Catholics. N-COUNT =Ave Maria

hailstone /heɪlstoʊn/ **hailstones. Hailstones** are the small balls of ice that fall from the sky N-COUNT: usu pl when it hails. *He was woken by a shower of hailstones sometime in the night.*

hailstorm /heɪlstɔːʳm/ **hailstorms;** also spelled **hail storm**. A **hailstorm** is a storm during which it hails. N-COUNT

hair /heəʳ/ **hairs** ◆◆◆◆◇

1 Your **hair** is all the fine thread-like material that grows in a mass on your head. *I wash my hair every night... He has black hair. ...a girl with long blonde hair... I get some grey hairs but I pull them out.* N-VAR: usu supp N

2 **Hair** is all the short, fine, thread-like material that grows on different parts of your body. *The majority of men have hair on their chest... It tickled the hairs on the back of my neck.* N-VAR

3 **Hair** is the rough, thread-like material that covers the body of an animal such as a dog, or makes up a horse's mane and tail. *I am allergic to cat hair. ...dog hairs on the carpet.* N-VAR

4 **Hairs** are very fine thread-like pieces of material that grow on some insects and plants. *The stinging nettle has a square stem and little hairs.* N-COUNT: usu pl

5 If you **let** your **hair down**, you relax completely and enjoy yourself. *...the world-famous Oktoberfest, a time when everyone in Munich really lets their hair down.* PHRASES V inflects

6 Something that **makes** your **hair stand on end** shocks or horrifies you. *This was the kind of smile that made your hair stand on end.* V inflects

7 If you say that someone has **not a hair out of place**, you are emphasizing that they are extremely smart and neatly dressed. *She had a lot of make-up on and not a hair out of place.* PRAGMATICS

8 If you say that someone faced with a shock or a problem **does not turn a hair**, you mean that they do not show any surprise or fear, and remain completely calm. *No one seems to turn a hair at the thought of the divorced Princess marrying.* V inflects =bat an eyelid

9 If you say that someone **is splitting hairs**, you mean that they are making unnecessary distinctions between things when the differences between them are so small they are not important. *Don't split hairs. You know what I'm getting at.* V inflects =quibble

hairbrush /heəʳbrʌʃ/ **hairbrushes.** A **hairbrush** is a brush that you use to brush your hair. N-COUNT

hair care; also spelled **haircare**. **Hair care** is all the things people do to keep their hair clean, healthy-looking, and attractive. *He will share his professional knowledge of haircare. ...an American maker of hair-care products.* N-UNCOUNT

haircut /heəʳkʌt/ **haircuts** ◆◇◇◇◇

1 If you have a **haircut**, someone cuts your hair for you. *Your hair is all right; it's just that you need a haircut.* N-COUNT

2 A **haircut** is the style in which your hair has been cut. *Who's that guy with the funny haircut?* N-COUNT

hairdo /heəʳduː/ **hairdos.** A **hairdo** is the style in which your hair has been cut and arranged; an informal word. *How do you like my new hairdo? ...a teenager with a punk hairdo.* N-COUNT =hairstyle

hairdresser /heəʳdresəʳ/ **hairdressers** ◆◇◇◇◇

1 A **hairdresser** is a person who cuts, colours, and arranges people's hair. N-COUNT

2 A **hairdresser** or a **hairdresser's** is a shop where a hairdresser works. *I work in this new hairdresser's.* N-COUNT

hairdressing /heəʳdresɪŋ/. **Hairdressing** is the job or activity of cutting, colouring, and arranging people's hair. *...personal services such as hairdressing and dry cleaning... Gloria runs a hairdressing salon.* N-UNCOUNT

hairdryer /heəʳdraɪəʳ/ **hairdryers;** also spelled **hairdrier**. A **hairdryer** is a machine that you use to dry your hair. N-COUNT

-haired /-heəʳd/. **-haired** combines with adjectives to describe the length, colour, or type of hair that someone has. *He was a small, dark-haired man.* COMB in ADJ-GRADED

hairgrip /heəgrɪp/ **hairgrips;** also spelled **hair-grip**. A **hairgrip** is a small piece of metal or plastic bent back on itself, which someone uses to hold their hair in position; used mainly in British English. N-COUNT =hairpin

hairless /heəʳləs/. A part of your body that is **hairless** has no hair on it. *...a smooth and hairless body.* ADJ ≠hairy

hairline /heəʳlaɪn/ **hairlines**

1 Your **hairline** is the edge of the area where your hair grows on your head. *Joanne had a small dark birthmark near her hairline... His hairline had receded slightly over the years.* N-COUNT: usu sing, oft poss N

2 A **hairline** crack or gap is very narrow or fine. *There's a hairline crack in the rim of that jar... He suffered a hairline fracture of the right index finger.* ADJ: ADJ n

hairnet /heəʳnet/ **hairnets.** A **hairnet** is a small net that some women wear over their hair in order to keep it tidy. N-COUNT

hairpiece /heəʳpiːs/ **hairpieces.** A **hairpiece** is a piece of false hair that some people wear on their head if they are bald or if they want to make their own hair seem longer or thicker. N-COUNT

hairpin /heəʳpɪn/ **hairpins**

1 A **hairpin** is a small piece of metal or plastic bent back on itself which someone uses to hold their hair in position. N-COUNT =hairgrip

2 A **hairpin** is the same as a **hairpin bend**. N-COUNT

hairpin bend, hairpin bends. A **hairpin bend** or a **hairpin** is a very sharp bend in a road, where the road turns back and heads in the opposite direction. N-COUNT

hair-raising. A **hair-raising** experience, event, or story is very frightening but can also be exciting. *...hair-raising rides at funfairs... Her truck is a very large pickup which she drives at hair-raising speeds.* ADJ-GRADED

hair's breadth. A **hair's breadth** is a very small degree or amount. *The dollar fell to within a hair's breadth of its all-time low... He did not swerve a hair's breadth from the decision he had made.* N-SING: aN

hair shirt, hair shirts

1 A **hair shirt** is a shirt made of rough uncomfortable cloth which some religious people used to wear to punish themselves. *He was sent barefoot wearing only a hair shirt into the wilderness as a penance.* N-COUNT

2 If you say that someone is wearing a **hair shirt**, you mean that they are trying to punish themselves to show they are sorry for something they have done. *No one is asking you to put on a hair shirt and give up all your luxuries.* N-COUNT

hairspray /heəʳspreɪ/ **hairsprays. Hairspray** is a sticky substance that you spray out of a can onto your hair in order to hold it in place. N-MASS =lacquer

hairstyle /heəʳstaɪl/ **hairstyles.** Your **hairstyle** is the style in which your hair has been cut or arranged. *I think her new short hairstyle looks simply great.* ◆◇◇◇◇ N-COUNT =hairdo

hairstylist /heəʳstaɪlɪst/ **hairstylists;** also spelled **hair stylist**. A **hairstylist** is someone who cuts and arranges people's hair, especially in order to get them ready for a photograph or film. *...her personal hair stylist.* N-COUNT

hair-trigger. If you describe something as **hair-trigger**, you mean that it is likely to change very violently and suddenly. *His boozing, arrogance, and hair-trigger temper have often led him into ugly nightclub brawls... A hair-trigger situation has been created which could lead to an outbreak of war at any time.* ADJ: ADJ n

hairy /heəri/ **hairier, hairiest** ◆◇◇◇◇

1 Someone or something that is **hairy** is covered with hairs. *He was wearing shorts which showed his long, muscular, hairy legs... The plant has serrated and hairy leaves.* ADJ-GRADED ≠hairless

2 If you describe a situation as **hairy**, you mean that it is exciting, worrying, and rather frightening; an informal use. *His driving was a bit hairy.* ADJ-GRADED =hair-raising

hake /heɪk/; **hake** is both the singular and the plural form. A **hake** is a big fish similar to a cod. N-VAR

► Hake is this fish eaten as food. N-UNCOUNT

halcyon /hælsiən/. A **halcyon** time is a time in the past that was peaceful or happy; a literary word. *It was all a far cry from those halcyon days* ◆◇◇◇◇ ADJ: ADJ n *in 1990, when he won three tournaments on the European tour.*

hale /heɪl/. If you describe people, especially people who are old, as **hale**, you mean that they are healthy; an old-fashioned word. *But even should he reappear tomorrow looking hale and hearty, his long absence will have cast a shadow over his position.* ◆◇◇◇◇ ADJ-GRADED: usu v-link ADJ

half /hɑːf, AM hæf/ **halves** /hɑːvz, AM hævz/ ◆◆◆◆◆

1 Half of an amount or object is one of two equal parts that together make up the whole number, amount, or object. *They need an extra two and a half thousand pounds to complete the project... More than half of all households report incomes above £35,000... Cut the tomatoes in half vertically... The bridge was re-built in two halves... The tough market would lead to 400 jobs being cut in the first half of this year.* FRACTION ▶ Also a predeterminer. *We just sat and talked for half an hour or so... They had only received half the money promised... She's half his age.* PREDET ▶ Also an adjective. *...£4.75 for a half chicken tandoori. ...a half measure of fresh lemon juice... Steve barely said a handful of words during the first half hour.* ADJ: ADJ n

2 You use **half** to say that something is only partly the case or happens to only a limited extent. *His eyes were half closed... His refrigerator frequently looked half empty... She'd half expected him to withdraw from the course.* ADV: ADV adj, ADV before v

3 In games such as football and rugby, matches are divided into two equal periods of time which are called **halves**. *The only goal was scored by Jakobsen early in the second half.* N-COUNT: usu ord N

4 A **half** is half a pint of a drink such as beer or cider; used mainly in British English. *...a half of lager and a sandwich.* N-COUNT

5 A **half** is a half-price ticket for a child on a bus or train; used mainly in British English. N-COUNT

6 You use **half** to say that someone has parents of different nationalities. For example, if you are **half** German, one of your parents is German. *She was half Italian and half English.* ADV: ADV adj

7 You use **half past** to refer to a time that is thirty minutes after a particular hour. *'What time were you planning lunch?'—'Half past twelve, if that's convenient.'... I think I got there about four and left about half past.* PHR-PREP: usu PREP num

8 Half means the same as **half past**; an informal use. *They are supposed to be here at about half four.* PREP: PREP num

9 You can use the word **half** before an adjective describing an extreme quality, as a way of emphasizing and exaggerating something; an informal use. *He felt half dead with tiredness... All this time I've been half sick about you and why you wouldn't write.* ADV: ADV adj PRAGMATICS ▶ **Half** can also be used in this way with a noun referring to a long period of time or a large quantity. *I thought about you half the night... He wouldn't know what he was saying half the time... One phone call and half the city's police force will be around to arrest you.* PREDET

10 In informal British English, **half** is sometimes used in negative statements, with an affirmative meaning, to emphasize a particular fact or quality. For example, if you say **'he isn't half lucky'**, you mean that he is very lucky. *You don't half sound confident... I didn't half get into trouble... She eventually decided the acting profession wasn't half bad... My kick wasn't half a bad effort for an old man... 'There'd been a tremendous amount of poverty around and presumably this made some impact then.'—'Oh not half.'* ADV: with neg, usu ADV before v, ADV adj/adv, ADV n, also ADV as reply PRAGMATICS

11 You use **not half** to emphasize a negative quality that someone has. *You're not half the man you think you are... Poor old Henry, and not half as clever as he'd thought.* ADV: with neg, ADV n, ADV *as/so* adj PRAGMATICS

12 When you use an expression such as **a problem and a half** or **a meal and a half**, you are emphasizing that your reaction to it is either very favourable or very unfavourable. *'It's a full-time job, isn't it'—'Job and a half.'* PHRASES usu v-link PHR PRAGMATICS

13 If you talk about your **better half** or your **other half** you mean your husband, your wife, or the person of the opposite sex that you live with; an informal expression. *My career, my children and my other half might become too much to cope with.* poss PHR

14 If you increase something **by half**, half of the original amount is added to it. If you decrease it **by half**, half of the original amount is taken away from it. *The number of 7 year olds who read poorly has increased by half over the past 5 years... Cutting food intake by half is an incredibly difficult thing for anyone to do.* PHR after v

15 If you say that someone never **does things by halves**, you mean that they always do things very thoroughly. *In Italy they rarely do things by halves. When designers latch on to a theme, they work it through thoroughly, producing the world's most wearable clothes in the most beautiful fabrics.* with brd-neg, V inflects

16 If two people **go halves** they divide the cost of something equally between them. *He's constantly on the phone to his girlfriend. We have to go halves on the phone bill which drives me mad.* V inflects, oft PHR *on* n

17 • **half the battle**: see **battle**. • **half an ear**: see **ear**. • **too clever by half**: see **clever**.

half-baked. If you describe an idea, opinion, or plan as **half-baked**, you mean that it has not been properly thought out, and so is stupid or impractical. *This is another half-baked scheme that isn't going to work... I didn't want to make things worse by coming up with half-baked notions.* ADJ-GRADED: usu ADJ n

half board; also spelled **half-board**. If you stay at a hotel and have **half board**, you have your breakfast and evening meal at the hotel, but not your lunch; used mainly in British English. N-UNCOUNT

half-brother, half-brothers. Someone's **half-brother** is a boy or man who has either the same mother or the same father as they have. ◆◇◇◇◇ N-COUNT

half-caste, half-castes. Someone who is **half-caste** has parents who come from different races. Some people find this word offensive and use the term 'mixed race' instead. *He has two half-caste children.* ADJ ▶ A **half-caste** is someone who is half-caste. N-COUNT

half-day half-days; also spelled **half day**. A **half-day** is a day when you work only in the morning or in the afternoon, but not all day. ◆◇◇◇◇ N-COUNT

half-hearted. If someone does something in a **half-hearted** way, they do it without any real effort, interest, or enthusiasm. *Joanna had made one or two half-hearted attempts to befriend Graham's young wife. ...a half-hearted apology... In truth, her application was a bit half-hearted.* ◆◇◇◇◇ ADJ-GRADED ♦ **half-heartedly** *I can't do anything half-heartedly. I have to do everything 100 per cent.* ADV-GRADED: ADV with v

half-life half-lives; also spelled **half life**. The **half-life** of a radioactive substance is the amount of time that it takes to lose half its radioactivity. N-COUNT

half-mast. If a flag is flying **at half-mast**, it is flying from the middle of the pole, not the top, as a sign of mourning for someone who has died. *Flags have been flying at half-mast, and schools, offices and businesses have been closed.* PHRASE: usu PHR after v

half measure half measures; also spelled **half-measure**. If someone refers to policies or actions as **half measures**, they are critical of them because they think that they are not forceful enough and are therefore of little value. *They have already declared their intention to fight on rather than settle for half-measures.* N-COUNT: usu pl PRAGMATICS

halfpenny /heɪpni/ **halfpennies** or **halfpence** /heɪpəns/. A **halfpenny** was a small British coin which was worth one half of a penny. N-COUNT

half-price ◆◇◇◇◇

1 If something is **half-price**, it costs only half what it usually costs. *Main courses are half price from 12.30pm to 2pm... Mind you, a half-price suit still cost $400... We can get in half-price.* ADJ: v-link ADJ, ADJ n, ADJ after v

2 If something is sold at **half-price**, it is sold for only half of what it usually costs. *By yesterday she was selling off stock at half price... They normally charge three hundred pounds but we got it for half price.* N-UNCOUNT: usu *at/for* N

half-sister, half-sisters. Someone's **half-sister** is a girl or woman who has either the same mother or the same father as they have. N-COUNT: oft poss N

half-term half-terms; also spelled **half term.** In Britain, **half-term** is a short holiday in the middle of a school term. *There was no play school at half term, so I took them both to the cinema. ...the half-term holidays.* N-VAR: oft at N

half-timbered. **Half-timbered** is used to describe old buildings that have wooden beams showing in the brick and plaster walls, both on the inside and the outside of the building. ADJ

half-time; also spelled **half time. Half-time** is the short period of time between the two parts of a sporting event such as a football match, when the players have a short rest. ◆◆◇◇◇ N-UNCOUNT

half-truth, half-truths; also spelled **half truth.** If you describe statements as **half-truths**, you mean that they are only partly based on fact and are intended or likely to deceive people. *The article had been full of errors and half truths that he felt slandered him.* N-COUNT

halfway /hɑːfweɪ, AM hæf-/; also spelled **half-way.** ◆◆◇◇◇

1 **Halfway** means in the middle of a place or between two points, at an equal distance from each of them. *Half-way across the car-park, he noticed she was walking with her eyes closed... He was halfway up the ladder... She was halfway down when she heard the noise.* ADV: usu ADV prep/adv, also ADV after v

2 **Halfway** means in the middle of a period of time or of an event. *By then, it was October and we were more than halfway through our tour.* ► Also an adjective. *Welsh international Matthew Postle was third fastest at the halfway point.* ADV: ADV prep/adv; ADJ: ADJ n

3 If you **meet** someone **halfway**, you accept some of the points they are making so that you can come to an agreement with them. *The Democrats are willing to meet the president halfway.* PHRASE: V inflects =compromise

4 **Halfway** means fairly or reasonably; an informal use. *You need hard currency to get anything halfway decent... All I had to do was be halfway cool.* ADV: ADV adj

halfway house, halfway houses

1 A **halfway house** is a compromise between two things. *A halfway house between the theatre and cinema is possible. Olivier built one in his imaginative 'Henry V' in 1945.* N-SING =compromise

2 A **halfway house** is a home for people such as former prisoners, mental patients, or drug addicts who can stay there for a limited period of time to get used to life outside prison or hospital. N-COUNT

half-wit, half-wits

1 If you describe someone as a **half-wit**, you think they have behaved in a stupid, silly, or irresponsible way; an informal use. N-COUNT PRAGMATICS =fool

2 A **half-wit** is a person who has little intelligence; an old-fashioned use. N-COUNT

half-witted. If you describe someone as **half-witted**, you think they are very stupid, silly, or irresponsible; an informal word. ADJ-GRADED PRAGMATICS

half-yearly

1 **Half-yearly** means happening in the middle of a calendar year or a financial year; used mainly in British English. *This is the half-yearly meeting of the interim committee. ...the Central Bank's half-yearly report on the state of the economy.* ADJ: ADJ n

2 A company's **half-yearly** profits are the profits that it makes in six months. *The company announced a half-yearly profit of just £2 million.* ADJ: ADJ n

3 **Half-yearly** means happening twice a year, with six months between each event. *...half-yearly payments.* ADJ: usu ADJ n

halibut /hælɪbət/ **halibut** is both the singular and the plural form. A **halibut** is a large flat fish. ► **Halibut** is this fish eaten as food. N-VAR; N-UNCOUNT

halitosis /hælɪtoʊsɪs/. If someone has **halitosis**, their breath smells unpleasant; a formal word. N-UNCOUNT =bad breath

hall /hɔːl/ **halls** ◆◆◆◇◇

1 In a house or flat, the **hall** is the area just inside the front door, into which some of the other rooms open. *The lights were on in the hall and in the bedroom.* ● See also **entrance hall.** N-COUNT =entrance hall, hallway

2 A **hall** is a large room or building which is used for public events such as concerts, exhibitions, and meetings. *Its 300 inhabitants will be celebrating with a dance in the village hall... We picked up our conference materials and filed into the lecture hall... It was brilliant to hear George Harrison in concert at the Royal Albert Hall last week.* ● See also **city hall, town hall.** N-COUNT: oft n N

3 Students who live in **hall** live in university or college accommodation. *I lived in hall during my first and second years.* N-COUNT: also prep N

4 **Hall** is sometimes used as part of the name of a large house on a country estate. *He died at Holly Hall, his wife's family home... Matthew was up at the Hall this morning.* N-IN-NAMES: also the N

5 See also **music hall.**

hallelujah /hælɪluːjə/; also spelled **alleluia.**

1 **Hallelujah** is used in hymns and some other types of religious worship as an exclamation of praise and thanks to God. EXCLAM

2 You can use **hallelujah** as an exclamation of joy when something you have been waiting a long time for finally happens. *Hallelujah! College days are over!* EXCLAM

hallmark /hɔːlmɑːrk/ **hallmarks** ◆◇◇◇◇

1 The **hallmark** of something or someone is their most typical quality or feature. *It's a technique that has become the hallmark of Amber Films... The killing had the hallmarks of a professional assassination... His designs show a love of simplicity which is very much his hallmark.* N-COUNT: usu with poss

2 A **hallmark** is an official mark put on things made of gold, silver, or platinum that indicates the quality of the metal, where the object was made, and who made it. N-COUNT

hallo /hæloʊ/. See **hello.**

hall of residence, halls of residence. Halls of residence are blocks of rooms or flats, usually built by universities or colleges, in which students live during the termtime; used mainly in British English. The usual American term is **dormitory.** N-COUNT

hallowed /hæloʊd/

1 **Hallowed** is used to describe something that is respected and admired, usually because it is old, important, or has a good reputation. *The hallowed turf of Twickenham is the venue for the Middlesex Rugby Sevens Finals... They protested that there was no place for a school of commerce in their hallowed halls of learning.* ADJ-GRADED: ADJ n

2 **Hallowed** is used to describe something that is considered to be holy. *...hallowed ground.* ADJ-GRADED: ADJ n

Halloween /hæloʊwiːn/; also spelled **Hallowe'en. Halloween** is the night of the 31st of October and is traditionally said to be the time when ghosts and witches can be seen. On Halloween, children often dress up as ghosts and witches. *He had insisted that she come up to Lawford for the Halloween party.* ◆◇◇◇◇ N-UNCOUNT

hallucinate /həluːsɪneɪt/ **hallucinates, hallucinating, hallucinated.** If you **hallucinate**, you see things that are not really there, either because you are ill or because you have taken a drug. *Hunger made him hallucinate... If you stared long enough and hard, you could even begin to hallucinate the appearance of small islands.* VERB: V; V n; Also V that

hallucination /həluːsɪneɪʃən/ **hallucinations** ◆◇◇◇◇

1 A **hallucination** is the experience of seeing something that is not really there because you are ill or have taken a drug. *The drug induces hallucinations at high doses... Hallucination is common in patients who have suffered damage to the brain.* N-VAR

2 A **hallucination** is something that is not real that someone sees because they are ill or have taken a drug. *Perhaps the footprint was a hallucination.* N-COUNT

hallucinatory /həluːsɪnətri, AM -tɔːri/. **Hallucinatory** is used to describe something that is like a hallucination or is the cause of a hallucination. *It was an unsettling show. There was a hallucinatory feel from the start... He had confessed to supplying Charley with hallucinatory drugs.* ADJ: usu ADJ n

hallucinogen /həluːsɪnədʒen/ **hallucinogens.** A **hallucinogen** is a substance such as a drug which makes you hallucinate. N-COUNT

hallucinogenic /həluːsɪnədʒenɪk/. A **hallucinogenic** drug is one that causes you to hallucinate. ADJ: usu ADJ n

hallway /hɔːlweɪ/ **hallways.** A **hallway** is the entrance hall of a house or other building. ◆◇◇◇◇ N-COUNT =hall

halo /heɪloʊ/ **haloes** or **halos** ◆◇◇◇◇

1 A **halo** is a circle of light that is shown in pictures round the head of a holy figure such as a saint or angel. N-COUNT

2 A **halo** is a circle of light round a person or thing, or something that looks like a circle of light. *The sun had a faint halo round it... She angrily slung a scarf around her head, flattening her halo of hair.* N-COUNT: oft N *of* n

halt /hɔːlt/ **halts, halting, halted** ◆◆◆◇◇

1 When a person or a vehicle **halts** or when something **halts** them, they stop moving in the direction they were going and stand still. *They halted at a short distance from the house... The engine note changed as the aircraft landed, taxied and halted... She held her hand out flat, to halt him.* V-ERG V V n

2 When something such as growth, development, or activity **halts** or when you **halt** it, it stops completely. *Striking workers halted production at the auto plant yesterday... He criticised the government for failing to halt economic decline... The flow of assistance to Vietnam's fragile economy from its ideological allies has virtually halted.* V-ERG V n V

3 **'Halt!'** is a military order to stop walking or marching and stand still. *The colonel ordered 'Halt!'* VB: only imper PRAGMATICS V

4 A **halt** is a very small station on a country railway line, which often consists only of a short platform and no building; used mainly in British English. N-COUNT

5 If someone **calls a halt** to something such as an activity, they decide not to continue with it or to end it immediately. *The Russian government had called a halt to the construction of a new project in the Rostov region.* PHRASES V inflects, oft PHR *to* n

6 If someone or something comes **to a halt**, they stop moving. *Sofia and Alex came to a halt and both tried to regain their breath... The elevator creaked to a halt at the ground floor.* PHR after v

7 If something such as growth, development, or activity comes or grinds **to a halt** or is brought **to a halt**, it stops completely. *Her political career came to a halt in December 1988... Air traffic in Poland has been brought to a halt by an air traffic controllers' strike.* PHR after v

halter /hɔːltəʳ/ **halters.** A **halter** is a piece of leather or rope that is fastened round the head of a horse so that it can be led easily. N-COUNT

halting /hɔːltɪŋ/. If you speak or do something in a **halting** way, you speak or do it slowly and with a lot of hesitation, usually because you are uncertain about what to say or do next. *In a halting voice she said that she wished to make a statement... The officer replied in halting German... Russia's efforts to attract investment have been halting and confused.* ♦ **haltingly** *She spoke haltingly of her deep upset and hurt... Kenya is moving haltingly towards democracy.* ADJ-GRADED =hesitant; ADV-GRADED: ADV with v

halve /hɑːv, AM hæv/ **halves, halving, halved** ◆◆◇◇◇

1 When you **halve** something or when it **halves**, it is reduced to half its previous size or amount. *Dr Lee believes that men who exercise can halve their risk of cancer of the colon... The work force has been halved in two years... Meanwhile, sales of vinyl records halved in 1992 to just 6.7m.* V-ERG V n V

2 If you **halve** something, you divide it into two equal parts. *Halve the pineapple and scoop out the inside.* VERB V n

3 **Halves** is the plural of **half.**

ham /hæm/ **hams, hamming, hammed** ◆◆◇◇◇

1 **Ham** is meat from the top of the back leg of a pig, specially treated so that it can be kept for a long period of time. *...a huge baked ham. ...ham sandwiches. ...a dozen slices of ham.* N-VAR

2 A **ham** is a person whose hobby consists of using special radio equipment to talk to other people with the same hobby, often people who are in other countries. *I became a ham radio operator at the age of eleven.* N-COUNT

3 A **ham** actor is someone who acts badly, exaggerating every emotion and gesture. N-COUNT: oft N n

4 If actors or actresses **ham it up**, they exaggerate every emotion and gesture when they are acting, often deliberately because they think that the audience will be more amused. *Thrusting themselves into the spirit of the farce, they ham it up like mad.* PHRASE: V inflects

hamburger /hæmbɜːʳgəʳ/ **hamburgers.** A **hamburger** is minced meat which has been shaped into a flat disc. Hamburgers are fried or grilled and then eaten, often in a bread roll. ◆◇◇◇◇ N-COUNT

ham-fisted. If you describe someone as **ham-fisted**, you mean that they are clumsy, especially in the way that they use their hands. *They can all be made in minutes by even the most ham-fisted of cooks.* ADJ-GRADED

hamlet /hæmlɪt/ **hamlets.** A **hamlet** is a very small village. ◆◇◇◇◇ N-COUNT

hammer /hæməʳ/ **hammers, hammering, hammered** ◆◆◇◇◇

1 A **hammer** is a tool that consists of a heavy piece of metal at the end of a handle. It is used, for example, to hit nails into a piece of wood or a wall, or to break things into pieces. *He used a hammer and chisel to chip away at the wall.* N-COUNT

2 If you **hammer** an object such as a nail, you hit it with a hammer. *To avoid damaging the tree, hammer a wooden peg into the hole... Another bloke would be hammering outside.* ▶ **Hammer in** means the same as **hammer.** *The workers kneel on the ground and hammer the small stones in.* ♦ **hammering** *The noise of hammering was dulled by the secondary glazing.* VERB V n prep/adv V Also V n; PHRASAL VERB V n P Also V P n (not pron); N-UNCOUNT

3 If you **hammer** on a surface, you hit it several times in order to make a noise, or to emphasize something you are saying when you are angry. *We had to hammer and shout before they would open up... A crowd of reporters was hammering on the door... He hammered his two clenched fists on the table.* ♦ **hammering** *As he said it, there was a hammering outside.* VERB =pound V V *on* n V n *on* n; N-SING

4 If you **hammer** something such as an idea into people or you **hammer** at it, you keep repeating it forcefully so that it will have an effect on people. *He hammered it into me that I had not suddenly become a rotten goalkeeper... Recent advertising campaigns from the industry have hammered at these themes.* VERB V n *into* n V *at* n

5 If you say that someone **hammers** another person, you mean that they attack, criticize, or punish the other person severely; used mainly in British English. *The report hammers the private motorist... If we turned up late we would be hammered by everybody.* ♦ **hammering** *Parents have taken a terrible hammering.* VERB V n; N-SING

6 If you say that businesses **are being hammered**, you mean that they are being unfairly harmed, for example by a change in taxes or by bad economic conditions; used mainly in British English. *Look at the numbers of small businesses that are being hammered unmercifully... The company has been hammered by the downturn in the construction and motor industries.* V-PASSIVE *be* V-ed

7 In sports, if you say that you **hammered** someone, you mean that you defeated them completely and easily; used in British journalism. *He hammered the young left-hander in four straight sets.* ♦ **hammering** *Our cricketers are suffering their ritual hammering at the hands of the Aussies.* VERB =thrash V n; N-SING =thrashing

8 If someone's heart **is hammering**, it is beating very fast, usually because they are frightened; a literary use. *My heart was hammering. The footsteps had stopped outside my door.* VERB =pound V

9 In machines and instruments, a **hammer** is a part that hits another part. For example, in a gun the hammer causes the explosion which makes the bullet shoot out of it, and in a piano the hammers hit the strings and cause the sounds; a technical use. N-COUNT

10 In athletics, a **hammer** is a heavy weight on a N-COUNT

piece of wire, which the athlete throws as far as possible. ▶ The **hammer** also refers to the sport of throwing the hammer. *Events like the hammer and the discus are not traditional crowd-pullers in the West.*
N-SING: theN

11 If you say that someone was going at something **hammer and tongs**, you mean that they were doing it with great energy and enthusiasm. *He loved gardening. He went at it hammer and tongs as soon as he got back from work.*
PHRASES
PHR after v

12 If you say that two people are going at it **hammer and tongs**, you mean they are arguing violently or making love passionately. *They yell, shout and argue. For six hours a night they go at it, hammer and tongs.*
PHR after v

13 If you say that something goes, comes, or is **under the hammer**, you mean that it is going to be sold at an auction; used mainly in British English. *Ian Fleming's original unpublished notes are to go under the hammer at London auctioneers Sotheby's.*
PHR after v

hammer away. If you **hammer away** at a task or activity, you work at it constantly and with great energy. *Palmer kept hammering away at his report.*
PHRASAL VERB
V P *at*n

hammer in. See **hammer** 2.
PHRASAL VERB

hammer out. If people **hammer out** an agreement or treaty, they succeed in producing it after a long or difficult discussion. *I think we can hammer out a solution... The details of the latest deal were hammered out by the American secretary of state and his Soviet counterpart.*
PHRASAL VERB
V P n (not pron)
Also V n P

hammock /hæmək/ **hammocks.** A **hammock** is a piece of strong cloth or netting which is hung between two supports and used as a bed.
N-COUNT

hamper /hæmpəʳ/ **hampers, hampering, hampered** ◆◆◇◇◇

1 If someone or something **hampers** you, they make it difficult for you to do what you are trying to do. *The bad weather hampered rescue operations... I was hampered by a lack of information.*
VERB
V n

2 A **hamper** is a basket containing a selection of nice food that is given to people as a present. *...a luxury food hamper.*
N-COUNT

3 A **hamper** is a large basket with a lid, used especially for carrying food in. *...a picnic hamper.*
N-COUNT

hamster /hæmstəʳ/ **hamsters.** A **hamster** is a small rodent similar to a mouse, which is often kept as a pet.
N-COUNT

hamstring /hæmstrɪŋ/ **hamstrings, hamstringing, hamstrung** ◆◇◇◇◇

1 A **hamstring** is a tendon behind your knee which joins the muscles of your thigh to the bones of your lower leg. *Webster has not played since suffering a hamstring injury in the opening game.*
N-COUNT

2 If you **hamstring** someone, you make it very difficult for them to take any action. *If he becomes the major opposition leader, he could hamstring a conservative-led coalition.*
VERB
V n

hand 1 noun uses and phrases

hand /hænd/ **hands** ◆◆◆◆◆

1 Your **hands** are the parts of your body at the end of your arms. Each hand has four fingers and a thumb. *I put my hand into my pocket and pulled out the letter... Sylvia, camera in hand, asked, 'Where do we go first?'*
N-COUNT

2 The **hand** of someone or something is their influence in an event or situation. *The hand of the military authorities can be seen in the entire electoral process... The study will strengthen the hand of congressmen who want stricter enforcement of the 14-year-old Act.*
N-SING: with poss

3 If you say that something is in a particular person's **hands**, you mean that they are looking after it, own it, or are responsible for it. *I feel that possibly the majority of these dogs are in the wrong hands... He is leaving his north London business in the hands of a colleague... We're in safe hands... The franchises are unlikely to pass into private hands much before 1995.*
N-PLURAL: usu *in/into*N

4 If you ask someone for **a hand** with something, you are asking them to help you in what you are doing. *I could see you'd want a hand with the children... Come and give me a hand in the garden... We gave him a hand bringing it back.*
N-SING: aN, oft N *with*n

5 A **hand** is someone, usually a man, who does hard physical work, for example in a factory or on a farm, as part of a group of people who all do similar work. *He now works as a farm hand... He met mill hands, miners and farm labourers.*
N-COUNT: usu with supp

6 If someone asks an audience to give someone **a hand**, they are asking the audience to clap loudly, usually before or after that person performs. *Let's give 'em a big hand.*
N-SING: aN

7 If a man asks for a woman's **hand** in marriage, he asks her or her parents for permission to marry her; an old-fashioned use. *He came to ask Usha's father for her hand in marriage.*
N-COUNT: usu sing, poss N, oft N *in*n

8 In a game of cards, your **hand** is the set of cards that you are holding in your hand at a particular time or the cards that are dealt to you at the beginning of the game. *He carefully inspected his hand.*
N-COUNT

9 A **hand** is a measurement of four inches, which is used for measuring the height of a horse from its front hooves to its shoulders. *I had a very good 14.2 hands pony, called Brandy.*
N-COUNT: usu num N

10 The **hands** of a clock or watch are the thin pieces of metal or plastic that indicate what time it is.
N-COUNT

11 Your **hand** is the style in which you write with a pen or pencil; a literary word. *The manuscripts were written in the composer's own hand.*
N-SING: usu poss N =handwriting

12 If something is **at hand**, **near at hand**, or **close at hand**, it is very near in place or time. *Having the right equipment at hand will be enormously helpful... Realizing that his retirement was near at hand, he looked for some additional income.*
PHRASES
PHR after v, v-link PHR =to hand

13 If someone experiences a particular kind of treatment, especially unpleasant treatment, **at the hands of** a person or organization, they receive it from them. *Too many East Germans suffered at the hands of the Stasi.*
PREP: PREP n

14 If you do something **by hand**, you do it using your hands rather than a machine. *Each pleat was stitched in place by hand.*
PHR after v =manually

15 When something **changes hands**, its ownership changes, usually because it is sold to someone else. *The firm has changed hands many times over the years.*
V inflects

16 If you have someone **eating out of** your **hand**, they are completely under your control. *Parker could have customers eating out of his hand.*
V and N inflect

17 If someone is bound **hand and foot**, both their hands and both their feet are tied together.
usu -ed PHR

18 If you **force** someone's **hand**, you force them to act sooner than they want to, or to act in public when they would prefer to keep their actions secret. *He blamed the press for forcing his hand.*
V and N inflect

19 If you **have** your **hands full** with something, you are very busy because of it. *She had her hands full with new arrivals.*
V inflects, oft PHR *with*n

20 If someone gives you **a free hand**, they give you the freedom to use your own judgement and to do exactly as you wish. *He gave Stephanie a free hand in the decoration.*
PHR after v

21 If you say that someone is making or losing money **hand over fist**, you mean that they are getting or losing a lot of money very quickly.
PHR after v

22 If you **get** your **hands on** something or **lay** your **hands on** something, you manage to find it or obtain it, usually after some difficulty; an informal expression. *Patty began reading everything she could get her hands on.*
V inflects, PHR n =get hold of

23 If you work **hand in glove** with someone, you work very closely with them. *The UN inspectors work hand in glove with the western intelligence agencies.*
usu PHR *with*n

24 If two people are **hand in hand**, they are holding each other's nearest hand, usually while they are walking or sitting together. People often do this to show their affection for each other. *I saw them making their way, hand in hand, down the path.*
usu PHR after v, PHR with cl

25 If two things go **hand in hand**, they are closely connected and cannot be considered separately from each other. *For us, research and teaching go*
usu PHR after v, v-link PHR, oft PHR *with*n

hand in hand... Hand in hand with the police inquiries the government has also announced a full investigation.

26 If you **have a hand in** something such as an event or activity, you are involved in it. *He thanked all who had a hand in his release.*
V inflects, PHR n

27 If someone such as the ruler of a country treats people with a **heavy hand**, they are very strict and severe with them. *Henry and Richard both ruled with a heavy hand.*
usu *with* PHR

28 If two people are **holding hands**, they are holding each other's nearest hand, usually while they are walking or sitting together. People often do this to show their affection for each other. *She approached a young couple holding hands on a bench.*
RECIP: V inflects, pl-n PHR, PHR *with* n

29 If you ask someone to **hold** your **hand** at an event that you are worried about, you ask them to support you by being there with you; an informal expression. *I don't need anyone to hold my hand.*
V and N inflect

30 In a competition, if someone has games or matches **in hand**, they have more games or matches left to play than their opponent and therefore have the possibility of scoring more points; used mainly in British English. *Wales are three points behind Romania in the group but have a game in hand.*
n PHR

31 If you have time **in hand**, you have more time than you need; used mainly in British English. *Hughes finished with 15 seconds in hand.*
usu *with* amount PHR

32 The job or problem **in hand** is the job or problem that you are dealing with at the moment. *The business in hand was approaching some kind of climax.*
n PHR, v-link PHR

33 If a situation is **in hand**, it is under control. *The Olympic organisers say that matters are well in hand.*
v-link PHR, PHR after v

34 If you do something to **keep** your **hand in**, you practise a skill or hobby occasionally in order to remain fairly good at it; an informal expression. *He still plays keyboards for a local band to keep his hand in.*
V and N inflect

35 If you are **on** your **hands and knees**, you are kneeling down and bending forward so that your knees, feet, and the palms of your hands are all on the ground. *Chris crawled on his hands and knees out onto the highway.*
v-link PHR, PHR after v =on all fours

36 If you **lend** someone **a hand**, you help them. *I'd be glad to lend a hand.*
V inflects

37 If someone **lives hand to mouth** or **lives from hand to mouth**, they have hardly enough food or money to live on. • See also **hand-to-mouth.**
V inflects

38 If you tell someone to **keep their hands off** something or someone or to **take their hands off** it, you are telling them in a rather aggressive way not to touch it or interfere with it. *Keep your hands off my milk.*
V inflects, PHR n PRAGMATICS

39 If you do not know something **off hand**, you do not know it without having to ask anyone else or look it up in a book; used in spoken English. *I can't think of any off hand.*
usu with brd-neg, PHR after v

40 If you have a problem or responsibility **on your hands**, you have to deal with it. If it is **off your hands**, you no longer have to deal with it. *They now have yet another drug problem on their hands... She would like the worry of dealing with her affairs taken off her hands.*
PHR after v

41 If someone or something is **on hand**, they are near and able to be used if they are needed. *The Bridal Department will have experts on hand to give you all the help and advice you need... There was simply no cash on hand to meet the cost of food.*
PHR after v, v-link PHR =available

42 You use **on the one hand** to introduce the first of two contrasting points, facts, or ways of looking at something. It is always followed later by 'on the other hand' or 'on the other'. *On the one hand, if the body doesn't have enough cholesterol, we would not be able to survive. On the other hand, if the body has too much cholesterol, the excess begins to line the arteries.*
PHR with cl PRAGMATICS

43 You use **on the other hand** to introduce the second of two contrasting points, facts, or ways of looking at something. *Well, all right, hospitals lose money. But, on the other hand, if people are healthy, don't think of it as losing money; think of it as saving lives.*
PRAGMATICS

44 If a person or a situation gets **out of hand**, you are no longer able to control them. *His drinking had got out of hand.*
v-link PHR

45 If you dismiss or reject something **out of hand**, you do it quickly and suddenly without any thought of changing your mind. *I initially dismissed the idea out of hand.*
PHR after v =out of control

46 If you **play into** someone's **hands**, you do something which they want you to do and which places you in their power; used mainly in journalism. *He is playing into the hands of racists.*
V inflects

47 If you **show** your **hand**, you show how much power you have and the way you intend to act. *Events in Russia are now forcing Mr Clinton to show his hand.*
V and N inflect

48 If you **take** something or someone **in hand**, you take control or responsibility over them, especially in order to improve them. *I hope that Parliament will soon take it in hand... He had thought her worth taking in hand.*
V inflects

49 If someone **throws up** their **hands**, they express their anger, frustration, or disgust when a situation becomes so bad that they can no longer accept it. *She threw up her hands in despair... Or are they just going to throw up their hands and say you're asking too much?*
V inflects

50 If you say that your **hands are tied**, you mean that something is preventing you from acting in the way that you want to. *Politicians are always saying that they want to help us but their hands are tied... Her hands were tied by the way that the US constitution is structured.*
V inflects

51 If you have something **to hand** or **near to hand**, you have it with you or near you, ready to use when needed. *You may want to keep this brochure safe, so you have it to hand whenever you may need it.*
PHR after v, v-link PHR =at hand

52 If you **try** your **hand** at an activity, you attempt to do it, usually for the first time. *After he left school, he tried his hand at a variety of jobs – bricklayer, cinema usher, coal man.*
V and N inflect, usu PHR *at* n/-ing =have a go

53 If you **turn** your **hand to** something such as a practical activity, you learn about it and do it for the first time. *...a person who can turn his hand to anything.*
V and N inflect, PHR n

54 If you **wash** your **hands of** someone or something, you refuse to be involved with them any more or to take responsibility for them. *He seems to have washed his hands of the job.*
V inflects, PHR n

55 If you **win hands down**, you win very easily.
V inflects

56 • **with one's bare hands**: see **bare.** • **to overplay one's hand**: see **overplay.** • **to shake** someone's **hand**: see **shake.** • **to shake hands**: see **shake.**

hand 2 verb uses

hand /hæ̲nd/ **hands, handing, handed** ◆◆◆◆◇

1 If you **hand** something to someone, you pass it to them. *He handed me a little rectangle of white paper... He took a thick envelope from an inside pocket and handed it to me.*
VERB
V n n
V n *to* n

2 You say things such as **You have to hand it to her** or **You've got to hand it to them** when you admire someone for their skills or achievements and you think they deserve a lot of praise; an informal expression. *You've got to hand it to Melissa, she certainly gets around.*
PHRASE

hand around. See **hand round.**
PHRASAL VERB

hand back. If you **hand back** something that you have borrowed or taken from someone, you return it to them. *The management handed back his few possessions... He took a saxophone from the Salvation Army but was caught and had to hand it back... He handed the book back to her... He unlocked her door and handed her back the key.*
PHRASAL VERB =give back
V P n (not pron)
V n P
V n P *to* n
V n P n (not pron)
Also V P n *to* n

hand down
PHRASAL VERB

1 If you **hand down** something such as knowledge, a possession, or a skill, you give or leave it to people who belong to a younger generation. *The idea of handing down his knowledge from generation to*
=pass on
V P n (not pron)
V-ed P
Also V n P

generation is important to Mclean. ...a Ukrainian folk heritage handed down from their parents.

2 When a particular decision **is handed down** by someone in authority, it is given by them; used mainly in journalism. *Tougher sentences are being handed down these days... She is expected soon to hand down a ruling.* be V-ed P; V P n (not pron); Also V n P

hand in PHRASAL VERB

1 If you **hand in** something such as homework or something that you have found, you give it to a teacher, police officer, or some other person in authority. *I'm supposed to have handed in a first draft of my dissertation... My advice to anyone who finds anything on a bus is to hand it in to the police.* V P n (not pron); V n P

2 If you **hand in** your notice or resignation, you tell your employer, in speech or in writing, that you no longer wish to work for them. *I handed my notice in on Saturday... All eighty opposition members of parliament have handed in their resignation.* V n P; V P n (not pron)

hand on. If you **hand** something **on**, you give it or leave it to someone else, often someone who replaces you. *The government is criticised for not handing on information about missing funds... His chauffeur-driven car and company mobile phone will be handed on to his successor.* PHRASAL VERB =pass on; V P n (not pron); be V-ed P to n; Also V P n to n

hand out PHRASAL VERB

1 If you **hand** something **out** to people, you give each person in a group one of a set of similar or identical things. *One of my jobs was to hand out the prizes... Food is still being handed out.* =give out; V P n (not pron); Also V n P

2 When people in authority **hand out** something such as advice or permission to do something, they give it. *I listened to a lot of people handing out a lot of advice... Planning permission is handed out sparingly.* V P n (not pron); Also V n P

3 See also **handout**.

hand over PHRASAL VERB

1 If you **hand** something **over** to someone, you pass it to them. *He also handed over a letter of apology from the Prime Minister... 'I've got his card.' Judith said, handing it over.* V P n (not pron); V n P

2 When you **hand over** someone such as a prisoner to someone else, you give the control of and responsibility for them to that other person. *They would just catch the robbers and hand them over to the police... This morning Mrs Parish was formally handed over to the British High Commissioner.* V n P to n; Also V n P, V P n (not pron)

3 If you **hand over** to someone or **hand** something **over** to them, you give them the responsibility for dealing with a particular situation or problem. *The present leaders have to decide whether to stand down and hand over to a younger generation... I wouldn't dare hand this project over to anyone else... They would like to hand over their financial affairs to another body.* V P to n; V n P to n; V P n to n; Also V n P, V P n

hand round or **hand around.** If you **hand round** or **hand around** something such as food, you pass it from one person to another in a group. *John handed round the plate of sandwiches. ...the free Jamaican cigars that were always handed around at official functions... Dean produced another bottle and handed it round.* PHRASAL VERB =distribute; V P n (not pron); V n P

hand- /hænd-/. **Hand-** combines with past participles to indicate that something has been made by someone using their hands or using tools rather than by machines. *...handcrafted jewelry. ...handbuilt cars.* COMB in ADJ: COMB -ed

handbag /hændbæg/ **handbags.** A **handbag** is a small bag which a woman uses to carry things such as her money and keys in when she goes out. ◆◇◇◇◇ N-COUNT

handball /hændbɔːl/; also spelled **hand-ball.**

1 In Britain, **handball** is a team sport in which the players try to score goals by throwing or hitting a large ball with their hand. N-UNCOUNT

2 In the United States and some other countries, **handball** is a sport in which players try to score points by hitting a small ball against a wall with their hand. N-UNCOUNT

3 In British English, **handball** is the foul of touching the ball with your hand during a football game. *He got sent off for deliberate handball in the 32nd minute.* N-UNCOUNT: also a N

handbill /hændbɪl/ **handbills.** A **handbill** is a small printed notice which is used to advertise a particular company, service, or event. *He was distributing handbills announcing his lecture when Nora caught her first glimpse of him.* N-COUNT

handbook /hændbʊk/ **handbooks.** A **handbook** is a book that gives you advice and instructions about a particular subject, tool, or machine. *If you have not kept a pet parrot before, it would be wise to purchase a handbook on the subject. ...the AA Members' Handbook.* ◆◇◇◇◇ N-COUNT: usu with supp =manual

handbrake /hændbreɪk/ **handbrakes.** A **handbrake** is a brake which is operated by a long lever moved by the hand of the person driving a vehicle. N-COUNT

handcart /hændkɑːʳt/ **handcarts;** also spelled **hand-cart.** A **handcart** is a small two-wheeled cart which is pushed or pulled along and is used for transporting goods. N-COUNT =barrow

handcuff /hændkʌf/ **handcuffs, handcuffing, handcuffed** ◆◇◇◇◇

1 **Handcuffs** are two metal rings which are joined together and can be locked round someone's wrists, usually by the police during an arrest. *He was led away to jail in handcuffs.* N-PLURAL: also a pair of N

2 If you **handcuff** someone, you put handcuffs around their wrists. *They tried to handcuff him but, despite his injuries, he fought his way free.* VERB V n

-hander /-hændəʳ/ **-handers. -hander** combines with words like 'two' or 'three' to form nouns which indicate how many people are involved in a particular activity, especially a play or a film; used mainly in British English. *...a two-hander play... Williams's play is a tense contemporary three-hander about two murderers and a bank-robber.* • See also **left-hander, right-hander.** COMB in N-COUNT: oft N n

handful /hændfʊl/ **handfuls** ◆◆◇◇◇

1 A **handful** of people or things is a small number of them. *He surveyed the handful of customers at the bar... One spring morning a handful of potential investors assembled in Quincy.* N-SING: usu N of n

2 A **handful** of something is the amount of it that you can hold in your hand. *She scooped up a handful of sand and let it trickle through her fingers.* N-COUNT: usu N of n

3 If you say that someone, especially a child, is a **handful**, you mean that they are difficult to control; an informal use. *Zara can be a handful sometimes.* N-SING

hand grenade, hand grenades. A **hand grenade** is the same as a **grenade.** ◆◇◇◇◇ N-COUNT

handgun /hændgʌn/ **handguns;** also spelled **hand gun.** A **handgun** is a gun that you can hold, carry, and fire with one hand. ◆◇◇◇◇ N-COUNT

hand-held; also spelled **handheld.** A **hand-held** camera or a **hand-held** computer is small and light enough to be used while you are holding it. *Saivonsac shot the entire film with a hand-held camera. ...a hand-held electric mixer.* ◆◇◇◇◇ ADJ: usu ADJ n

handhold /hændhoʊld/ **handholds.** A **handhold** is a small hole or hollow in something such as rock or a wall that you can put your hand in if you are trying to climb it. *I found handholds and hoisted myself along.* N-COUNT

handicap /hændikæp/ **handicaps, handicapping, handicapped** ◆◆◇◇◇

1 A **handicap** is a physical or mental disability. *He lost his leg when he was ten, but learnt to overcome his handicap.* N-COUNT

2 A **handicap** is an event or situation that places you at a disadvantage and makes it harder for you to do something. *She was away from school for 15 weeks, a handicap she could have done without... Being a foreigner was not a handicap.* N-COUNT

3 If an event or a situation **handicaps** someone or something, it places them at a disadvantage and makes it harder for them to do something. *Greater levels of stress may seriously handicap some students... The industrial injuries scheme takes into account the actual disability and whether it handicaps a person in working.* VERB V n

4 In golf, a **handicap** is an advantage given to someone who is not a good player, in order to make the players more equal. As you improve, your handicap gets lower. *I see your handicap is down from 16 to 12.* N-COUNT

5 In horse racing, a **handicap** is a race in which some competitors are given a disadvantage of extra weight in an attempt to give everyone an equal chance of winning. N-COUNT

handicapped /hændikæpt/. Someone who is **handicapped** has a physical or mental disability that prevents them living a totally normal life. *I'm going to work two days a week teaching handicapped kids to fish... Alex was mentally handicapped.* ► You can refer to people who are handicapped as **the handicapped**. *...measures to prevent discrimination against the handicapped.* ◆◆◇◇◇ ADJ-GRADED N-PLURAL: the N

handicraft /hændikrɑːft, -kræft/ **handicrafts**

1 **Handicrafts** are activities such as embroidery and pottery which involve making things with your hands in a skilful way. N-COUNT: usu pl

2 **Handicrafts** are the objects that are produced by people doing handicrafts. *She sells handicrafts to the ever dwindling number of tourists.* N-COUNT: usu pl

handiwork /hændiwɜːʳk/. You can refer to something that you have done or made yourself as your **handiwork**. *The architect stepped back to admire his handiwork... While the government said the fire was accidental, residents of the town alleged it was the handiwork of the security forces.* N-UNCOUNT: usu with poss

handkerchief /hæŋkəʳtʃɪf/ **handkerchiefs.** A **handkerchief** is a small square piece of fabric which you use for blowing your nose. ◆◇◇◇◇ N-COUNT

handle /hændᵊl/ **handles, handling, handled** ◆◆◆◆◇

1 A **handle** is a small round object or a lever that is attached to a door and is used for opening and closing it. *I turned the handle and found the door was open.* N-COUNT

2 A **handle** is the part of an object such as a tool, bag, or cup that you hold in order to be able to pick up and use the object. *The handle of a cricket bat protruded from under his arm. ...a broom handle.* N-COUNT

3 If you say that someone can **handle** a problem or situation, you mean that they have the ability to deal with it successfully. *To tell the truth, I don't know if I can handle the job... She cannot handle pressure... You must learn how to handle your feelings.* VERB =cope with V n

4 If you talk about the way that someone **handles** a problem or situation, you mention whether or not they are successful in achieving the result they want. *I think I would handle a meeting with Mr. Siegel very badly... She admitted to herself she didn't know how to handle the problem.* ♦ **handling** *The family has criticized the military's handling of Robert's death.* VERB V n adv N-UNCOUNT: usu N of n

5 If you **handle** a particular area of work, you have responsibility for it. *She handled travel arrangements for the press corps during the presidential campaign... The investigation is being handled by Scotland Yard's anti terrorist branch.* VERB V n

6 When you **handle** something such as a weapon, vehicle, or animal, you use it or control it, especially by using your hands. *I had never handled an automatic.* VERB V n

7 If something such as a vehicle **handles** well, it is easy to use or control. *His ship had handled like a dream!* VERB V adv/prep

8 When you **handle** something, you hold it or move it with your hands. *Wear rubber gloves when handling cat litter.* VERB V n

9 If you have a **handle** on a subject or problem, you have a way of approaching it that helps you to understand it or deal with it; an informal use. *When you have got a handle on your anxiety you can begin to control it.* N-SING: a N on n

10 If you **fly off the handle**, you suddenly and completely lose your temper; an informal expression. *He flew off the handle at the slightest thing.* PHRASE: V inflects

handlebar /hændᵊlbɑːʳ/ **handlebars.** The **handlebar** or **handlebars** of a bicycle consist of a curved metal bar with handles at each end which are used for steering. N-COUNT

handlebar moustache **handlebar moustaches;** also spelled **handlebar mustache**. A **handlebar moustache** is a long bushy moustache with curled ends. N-COUNT

handler /hændləʳ/ **handlers** ◆◇◇◇◇

1 A **handler** is someone whose job is to be in charge of and control an animal. *Fifty officers, including frogmen and dog handlers, are searching for her.* N-COUNT: usu supp N

2 A **handler** is someone whose job is to deal with a particular type of object. *...baggage handlers at Gatwick airport.* N-COUNT: usu n N

hand luggage. When you travel by air, your **hand luggage** is the luggage you have with you in the plane, rather than the luggage that is carried in the hold. N-UNCOUNT

handmade /hændmeɪd/; also spelled **handmade.** ◆◇◇◇◇

1 **Handmade** objects have been made by someone using their hands or using tools rather than by machines. *As they're handmade, each one varies slightly. ...handmade chocolates.* ADJ

2 If something **is handmade**, it is made by someone using their hands or using tools rather than by machines. *The beads they use are handmade in the Jura mountains in central France... These exquisitely ornate boxes and cabinets have been handmade and hand-painted by Indian craftspeople.* V-PASSIVE be V-ed

handmaiden /hændmeɪdᵊn/ **handmaidens**

1 A **handmaiden** is a female servant; an old-fashioned or literary use. N-COUNT

2 If one thing is the **handmaiden** of another, the first thing plays a lesser but important supportive role to the second. *He disliked the idea that science should be a handmaiden to commerce.* N-COUNT: N of/to n

hand-me-down, hand-me-downs

1 **Hand-me-downs** are things, especially clothes, which have been used by someone else before you and which have been given to you for your use. *Edward wore Andrew's hand-me-downs.* N-COUNT: usu pl

2 **Hand-me-down** is used to describe things, especially clothes, which have been used by someone else before you and which have been given to you for your use. *Most of the boys wore hand-me-down military shirts from their fathers. ...hand-me-down tennis rackets.* ADJ: ADJ n

handout /hændaʊt/ **handouts** ◆◇◇◇◇

1 A **handout** is a gift of money, clothing, or food, which is given free to poor people. *Soldiers oversee the food handouts... Each family is being give a cash handout of six thousand rupees.* N-COUNT

2 If you call money that is given to someone a **handout**, you disapprove of it because you believe that the person who receives it has done nothing to earn or deserve it. *Many saw Labour as proposing government handouts for the undeserving... The president called foreign aid a handout that fosters dependence on wealthy nations.* N-COUNT PRAGMATICS

3 A **handout** is a document which gives information about a particular organization, event, or person and is used to publicize that organization, event, or person. *Official handouts describe the Emperor as 'particularly noted as a scholar'.* N-COUNT

4 A **handout** is a paper containing a summary of information or topics which will be dealt with in a lecture or talk. N-COUNT

handover /hændoʊvəʳ/ **handovers.** The **handover** of something is when possession or control of it is given by one person or group of people to another. *He said they would attach conditions to the handover of the base... The handover is expected to be completed in the next ten years.* ◆◇◇◇◇ N-COUNT: usu sing, oft N of n

hand-pick **hand-picks, hand-picking, hand-picked;** also spelled **handpick**. If someone **is hand-picked**, they are very carefully chosen by someone in authority for a particular purpose or a particular job. *He was hand-picked for this job by the Admiral... Diana hand-picked Patrick Demarchelier to photograph her for the front cover of Vogue. ...his hand-picked successor.* VERB be V-ed V n V-ed

handrail /hændreɪl/ **handrails.** A **handrail** is a long piece of metal or wood which is fixed near stairs or places where people could slip and fall, and which people can hold on to for support. **N-COUNT**

handset /hændset/ **handsets**
1 The **handset** of a telephone is the part that you hold next to your face in order to speak and listen. **N-COUNT**
2 You can refer to a device such as the remote controls of a television or stereo as a **handset**. **N-COUNT**

handshake /hændʃeɪk/ **handshakes.** If you give someone a **handshake**, you take their right hand with your own right hand and hold it firmly or move it up and down, as a sign of greeting or to show that you have agreed about something such as a business deal. *John smiled and gave him a hearty handshake... He has a strong handshake.* • See also **golden handshake**. **◆◇◇◇◇ N-COUNT**

handsome /hænsəm/ **◆◆◇◇◇**
1 A **handsome** man has an attractive face with regular features. *...a tall, dark, handsome sheep farmer.* **ADJ-GRADED =good-looking**
2 A **handsome** woman has an attractive appearance with features that are large and regular rather than small and delicate and that are considered to show strength of character. *...an extremely handsome woman with a beautiful voice.* **ADJ-GRADED**
3 A **handsome** sum of money is a large or generous amount; a formal word. *They will make a handsome profit on the property.* **ADJ-GRADED: ADJ n** ♦ **handsomely** *He was rewarded handsomely for his efforts.* **ADV-GRADED: ADV with v**
4 A place such as a building or garden that is **handsome** is large and well made with an attractive appearance. *...the ports of Dubrovnik and Zadar, with their handsome Renaissance buildings.* **ADJ-GRADED**
♦ **handsomely** *The drawing-room is handsomely proportioned.* **ADV-GRADED: ADV -ed**
5 If someone has a **handsome** win or a **handsome** victory, they achieve it by a large margin. *The opposition won a handsome victory in the election.* **ADJ: ADJ n**
♦ **handsomely** *The car ran perfectly to the finish, and we won handsomely.* **ADV: ADV after v**

hands-on. Hands-on experience or work involves actually doing a particular thing, rather than just talking about it or getting someone else to do it. *Ninety-nine per cent of primary pupils now have hands-on experience of computers... This hands-on management approach often stretches his workday from 6 a.m. to 11 p.m.* **◆◇◇◇◇ ADJ-GRADED: usu ADJ n**

handstand /hændstænd/ **handstands.** If you do a **handstand**, you balance yourself upside down on your hands with your body and legs straight up in the air. **N-COUNT**

hand-to-hand; also spelled **hand to hand. Hand-to-hand** fighting is fighting where the people are very close together, using either their hands or weapons such as knives. *There was, reportedly, hand-to-hand combat in the streets... He suffered two broken ribs in a fierce hand-to-hand battle.* **ADJ: ADJ n**

hand-to-mouth; also spelled **hand to mouth.** A **hand-to-mouth** existence is a way of life in which you have hardly enough food or money to live on. *Unloved and uncared-for, they live a meaningless hand to mouth existence.* **ADJ-GRADED** ► Also an adverb. *I just can't live hand-to-mouth, it's too frightening.* **ADV: ADV after v**

hand tool, hand tools. Hand tools are fairly simple tools which you use with your hands, and which are usually not powered. **N-COUNT**

handwriting /hændraɪtɪŋ/. Your **handwriting** is your style of writing with a pen or pencil. *The address was in Anna's handwriting... I have to admit that I have bad handwriting.* **◆◇◇◇◇ N-UNCOUNT: oft poss N**

handwritten /hændrɪtᵊn/. A piece of writing that is **handwritten** is one that someone has written using a pen or pencil rather than by typing it. **◆◇◇◇◇ ADJ**

handy /hændi/ **handier, handiest** **◆◆◇◇◇**
1 Something that is **handy** is useful. *The book gives handy hints on looking after indoor plants... Credit cards can be handy – they mean you do not have to carry large sums of cash.* **ADJ-GRADED** • If something **comes in handy**, it is useful in a particular situation. *That key will come in handy if you lock yourself out... The $20 check came in very handy.* **PHRASE: V inflects**
2 A thing or place that is **handy** is nearby and convenient. *It would be good to have a pencil and paper handy... Keep handy a lightweight sweater or cardigan... This lively town is handy for Londoners.* **ADJ-GRADED: usu v-link ADJ**
3 Someone who is **handy with** a particular tool is skilful at using it; an informal use. *If you're handy with a needle you could brighten up your sweater with giant daisies.* **ADJ-GRADED: v-link ADJ with n**

handyman /hændimæn/ **handymen.** A **handyman** is a man who earns money by doing small jobs for people such as making and repairing things in their houses. You can also describe a man who is good at making things or repairing things in his home as a **handyman**. **N-COUNT**

hang /hæŋ/ **hangs, hanging, hung, hanged.** **◆◆◆◆◇** The form **hung** is used as the past tense and participle. The form **hanged** is used as the past tense for meaning 5.
1 If something **hangs** in a high place or position, or if you **hang** it there, it is attached there so it does not touch the ground. *Notices painted on sheets hang at every entrance... A light-bulb hanging from the ceiling filled the room with a cold yellow light... The curtains will be hanging there for years... I was left hanging by my finger-tips over a drop of hundreds of feet. ...small hanging lanterns... They saw a young woman come out of the house to hang clothes on a line.* **V-ERG V prep/adv V-ing V n prep/adv Also V n, V** ► **Hang up** means the same as **hang**. *I found his jacket, which was hanging up in the hallway... Some prisoners climbed onto the roof and hung up a banner.* **PHRASAL VERB ERG V P V P n (not pron) Also V n P**
2 If a piece of clothing or fabric **hangs** in a particular way or position, that is how it is worn or arranged. *...a ragged fur coat that hung down to her calves... Look for a suit made from good, sturdy cloth to ensure it hangs well... She stood with her hands on her hips, the shawl hanging loose from her shoulders.* **VERB V adv/prep V adj**
3 If something **hangs** loose or **hangs** open, it is partly fixed in position, but is not firmly held, supported, or controlled, often in such a way that it moves freely. *...her long golden hair which hung loose about her shoulders... The window sashes were missing, the doors hung open, or were gone altogether... She froze, her mouth hanging open.* **VERB V adj**
4 If something such as a wall **is hung with** pictures or other objects, they are attached to it. *The walls were hung with huge modern paintings. ...a line of wall hooks hung with old anoraks and mud-stained overalls.* **VB: usu passive be V-ed with n V-ed**
5 If someone **is hanged** or if they **hang**, they are killed, usually as a punishment, by having a rope tied around their neck and the support taken away from under their feet. *The five were expected to be hanged at 7 am on Tuesday... It is right that their murderers should hang... He hanged himself two hours after arriving at a mental hospital.* **V-ERG be V-ed V V pron-refl Also V n**
♦ **hanging, hangings** *Four steamboat loads of spectators came to view a hanging in New Orleans.* **N-VAR**
6 If something such as someone's breath or smoke **hangs** in the air, it remains there without appearing to move or change position. *His breath was hanging in the air before him... A haze of expensive perfume hangs around her.* **VERB =linger V prep/adv**
7 If a possibility **hangs over** you, it worries you and makes your life unpleasant or difficult because you think it might happen. *A constant threat of unemployment hangs over thousands of university researchers... A question mark hangs over many of their futures.* **VERB V over n**
8 **Hang** is used in expressions such as **hang it** and **hang the money** to indicate that you are not concerned about something or the consequences of doing something; an informal use. *Oh hang it, Geoff, you have been so nice and gone to all that bother, let's make it two bottles... Once the Americans decide to do a thing, they do it well, and hang the cost.* **VB: only imper V it V n**
9 See also **hanging, hung**.

10 If you **get the hang of** something such as a skill or activity, you begin to understand or realize how to do it; an informal expression. *It's a bit tricky at first till you get the hang of it.* PHRASES V inflects: PHR n

11 If you tell someone to **hang in there** or to **hang on in there**, you are encouraging them to keep trying to do something and not to give up even though it might be difficult; an informal expression. *Hang in there and you never know what is achievable.* V inflects PRAGMATICS

12 If you **let it all hang out**, you relax completely and enjoy yourself without worrying about hiding your emotions or behaving politely; an informal expression. *let* inflects

13 • to **hang by a thread**: see **thread.** • to **hang on** someone's **every word**: see **word.**

hang around or **hang round;** the form **hang about** is also used in British English. PHRASAL VERB

1 If you **hang around, hang about**, or **hang round**, you stay in the same place doing nothing, usually because you are waiting for something or someone; an informal expression. *He got sick of hanging around waiting for me... On Saturdays we hang about in the park. ...those people hanging round the streets at 6 am with nowhere to go.* V P -ing V P V P n

2 If you **hang around, hang about**, or **hang round** with someone or in a particular place, you spend a lot of time with that person or in that place; an informal expression. *They usually hung around together most of the time... Helen used to hang round with the boys. ...the usual young crowd who hung around the cafe day in and day out.* V P *together* V P *with* n V P n

hang back PHRASAL VERB

1 If you **hang back**, you move or stay slightly behind a person or group, usually because you are nervous about something. *I saw him step forward momentarily but then hang back, nervously massaging his hands.* V P

2 If a person or organization **hangs back**, they do not do something immediately. *They will then hang back on closing the deal... Even his closest advisers believe he should hang back no longer.* V P *on* n V P

hang on PHRASAL VERB

1 If you ask someone to **hang on**, you ask them to wait or stop what they are doing or saying for a moment; an informal expression. *Can you hang on for a minute?... Hang on a sec. I'll come with you.* PRAGMATICS =hold on V P V P n

2 If you **hang on**, you manage to survive, achieve success, or avoid failure in spite of great difficulties or opposition. *Without the support of my parents I would have probably cracked up completely. But I managed to hang on... Manchester United hung on to take the Cup.* V P

3 If you **hang on** to or **hang onto** something that gives you an advantage, you succeed in keeping it for yourself, and prevent it from being taken away or given to someone else. *The British driver was unable to hang on to his lead... The President has been trying hard to hang onto power... The company has been struggling to hang onto its sales force.* V P *to* n V P n

4 If you **hang on** to or **hang onto** something, you hold it very tightly, for example to stop it falling or to support yourself. *She was conscious of a second man hanging on to the rail. ...a flight stewardess who helped save the life of a pilot by hanging onto his legs... He hangs on tightly, his arms around my neck.* =cling on to V P *to* n V P n V P

5 If you **hang on** to or **hang onto** something, you keep it for a longer time than you would normally expect; an informal expression. *You could, alternatively, hang onto it in the hope that it will be worth millions in 10 years time... In the present climate, owners are hanging on to old ships.* V P n V P *to* n

6 If one thing **hangs on** another, it depends on it in order to be successful. *Much hangs on the success of the collaboration between the Group of Seven governments and Brazil.* =depend V P n

hang out PHRASAL VERB

1 If you **hang out** clothes that you have washed, you hang them on a clothes line to dry. *I was worried I wouldn't be able to hang my washing out.* V n P Also V P n (not pron)

2 If you **hang out** in a particular place or area, you go and stay there for no particular reason, or spend a lot of time there; an informal expression used mainly in American English. *I often used to hang out in supermarkets... We can just hang out and have a good time.* • See also **hangout.** V P adv/prep V P

hang round. See **hang around.** PHRASAL VERB

hang together PHRASAL VERB

1 If two people or groups **hang together**, they stay with each other and support each other even though they may disagree on some things. *He urged his supporters to hang together.* =stick together V P

2 If things such as ideas or the parts of something **hang together**, they are properly organized and fit together reasonably. *Her ideas don't always hang together very well as a plot.* V P

hang up PHRASAL VERB

1 See **hang** 1.

2 If you **hang up** or you **hang up** the phone, you end a phone call and put back the receiver. If you **hang up** on someone you are speaking to on the phone, you end the phone call suddenly and unexpectedly by putting back the receiver. *Mum hung up the phone... Don't hang up!... He said he'd call again, and hung up on me.* V P n (not pron) V P V P *on* n

3 You can use **hang up** to indicate that someone stops doing a particular sport or activity that they have regularly done over a long period. For example, when a footballer **hangs up** his boots, he stops playing football. *Keegan announced he was hanging up his boots for good... Looking back, she feels she should never have hung up her backpack.* V P n (not pron) Also V n P

4 See also **hang-up, hung up.**

hangar /hæŋəʳ/ **hangars.** A **hangar** is a large building in which aircraft are kept. ◆◇◇◇◇ N-COUNT

hangdog /hæŋdɒg, AM -dɔːg/; also spelled **hang-dog.** If you say that someone has a **hangdog** expression on their face, you mean that they look sad, and often guilty or ashamed. *'Everybody missed her,' Stan said with a hangdog look.* ADJ-GRADED: usu ADJ n

hanger /hæŋəʳ/ **hangers.** A **hanger** is the same as a **coat hanger.** ◆◇◇◇◇ N-COUNT

hanger-on, hangers-on. If you describe someone as a **hanger-on**, you are critical of them because they are trying to be friendly with a richer or more important person, especially in order to gain an advantage for themselves. *Five thousand delegates, with 30,000 assorted hangers-on, will descend on the city.* N-COUNT PRAGMATICS

hang-glider hang-gliders; also spelled **hang glider.**

1 A **hang-glider** is a glider for one person, with which they can fly in the air. It consists of a large piece of cloth over a frame which you hang from in a harness. N-COUNT

2 A **hang glider** is a person who flies using a hang-glider. N-COUNT

hang-gliding. Hang-gliding is the activity of flying in a hang-glider. N-UNCOUNT

hanging /hæŋɪŋ/ **hangings.** A **hanging** is a large piece of cloth that you put as a decoration on a wall. *...a giant antique embroidered hanging.* N-COUNT: usu with supp

hanging basket, hanging baskets. A **hanging basket** is a basket with small ropes or chains attached so that it be hung from a hook. Hanging baskets are usually used for displaying plants or storing fruit and vegetables. N-COUNT

hangman /hæŋmæn/ **hangmen.** A **hangman** is a man whose job is to execute people by hanging them. N-COUNT

hangout /hæŋaʊt/ **hangouts.** If a place is a **hangout** for a particular group of people, they spend a lot of time there because they can relax and meet other people there; an informal word. *By the time he was sixteen, Malcolm already knew most of London's teenage hangouts.* N-COUNT: with supp =haunt

hangover /hæŋoʊvəʳ/ **hangovers** ◆◇◇◇◇

1 If someone wakes up with a **hangover**, they feel sick and have a headache because they have drunk a lot of alcohol the night before. N-COUNT

2 Something that is a **hangover** from the past is an idea or way of behaving which people used to have in the past but which people no longer generally N-COUNT: with supp, usu N *from* n have. *As a hangover from rationing, they mixed butter and margarine.*

hang-up, hang-ups. If you have a **hang-up** about something, you have a feeling of fear, anxiety, or embarrassment about it; an informal word. *I don't have any hang-ups about my body.* ◆◇◇◇◇ N-COUNT =inhibition

hank /hæŋk/ **hanks.** A **hank** of wool, rope, or string is a loosely-wound length of it. N-COUNT: oft N *of* n

hanker /hæŋkəʳ/ **hankers, hankering, hankered.** If you **hanker** after something, you want it very much. *In 1969 I hankered after a floor-length brown suede coat.* VERB V *after/for* n Also V to-inf

hankering /hæŋkərɪŋ/ **hankerings.** A **hankering** for something is a desire or longing for it. *From time to time we all get a hankering for something a little different... Have you always had a hankering to be an actress?* N-COUNT: usu N *for/after* n, N to-inf

hanky /hæŋki/ **hankies;** also spelled **hankie.** A **hanky** is the same as a handkerchief; an informal word. N-COUNT

hanky-panky /hæŋki pæŋki/

1 In British English, **hanky-panky** is used to refer to improper but not very serious sexual activity between two people; an informal word. *Does this mean no hanky-panky after lights out?* N-UNCOUNT

2 In American English, if you describe behaviour as **hanky-panky**, you disapprove of it because it involves mischief, trickery, or dishonesty, and often because it is done in secret. The British word is **jiggery-pokery**. *The government has been offering tax credits, accelerated depreciation, and other economic hanky-panky.* N-UNCOUNT PRAGMATICS

hansom /hænsəm/ **hansoms.** In former times, a **hansom** or a **hansom cab** was a horse-drawn carriage with two wheels and a fixed hood. N-COUNT

Hanukkah /hɑːnʊkə/; also spelled **Hanukah.** **Hanukkah** is a Jewish festival that commemorates the re-dedication of the Temple in Jerusalem in 165 B.C. It begins in November or December and lasts for eight days. N-UNCOUNT =Chanukah

haphazard /hæphæzəʳd/. if you describe something as **haphazard**, you are critical of it because it is not at all organized or is not arranged according to a plan. *The investigation does seem haphazard... He had never seen such a haphazard approach to filmmaking as Roberto's.* ◆◇◇◇◇ ADJ-GRADED PRAGMATICS =casual

♦ **haphazardly** *She looked at the books jammed haphazardly in the shelves.* ADV-GRADED: usu ADV with v

hapless /hæpləs/. A **hapless** person is unlucky; a formal word. *...his hapless victim.* ◆◇◇◇◇ ADJ: ADJ n

happen /hæpən/ **happens, happening, happened** ◆◆◆◆◆

1 Something that **happens** occurs or is done without being planned. *We cannot say for sure what will happen... The accident happened close to Martha's Vineyard.* VERB V

2 If something **happens**, it occurs as a result of a situation or course of action. *She wondered what would happen if her parents found her... He trotted to the truck and switched on the ignition. Nothing happened.* VERB V

3 When something, especially something unpleasant, **happens to** you, it takes place and affects you. *If we had been spotted at that point, I don't know what would have happened to us... It's the best thing that ever happened to me.* VERB V *to* n

4 If you **happen** to do something, you do it by chance. If it **happens** that something is the case, it occurs by chance. *We happened to discover we had a friend in common... I looked in the nearest paper, which happened to be the Daily Mail... If it happens that I'm wanted badly somewhere, my mother will take the call and phone through to me here.* VERB V to-inf *it* V that

5 You use **as it happens** in order to introduce a statement, especially one that is rather surprising. *She called Amy to see if she had any idea of her son's whereabouts. As it happened, Amy had.* PHRASE: V inflects, PHR with cl PRAGMATICS

happening /hæpənɪŋ/ **happenings** ◆◇◇◇◇

1 **Happenings** are things that happen, often in a way that is unexpected or hard to explain. *The Budapest office plans to hire freelance reporters to cover the latest happenings.* N-COUNT: usu pl, usu with supp =incident

2 If you describe something or someone as **happening**, you mean that they are exciting or lively, and involved in the newest fashions or trends; an informal use. *...a definitive area-by-area guide to the hip and happening bands. ...the most happening place at the moment, the Que Club.* ADJ-GRADED

happenstance /hæpənstæns/. If you say that something happened by **happenstance**, you mean that it happened because of certain circumstances, although it was not planned by anyone; a literary word. *I came to live at the farm by happenstance.* N-UNCOUNT: also *a* N, oft *by* N =chance

happily /hæpɪli/. You can add **happily** to a statement to indicate that you are glad that something happened. *Happily, his neck injuries were not serious... Happily, Lisa Martineau takes an opposite approach.* • See also **happy**. ◆◇◇◇◇ ADV-GRADED: ADV with cl =fortunately

happy /hæpi/ **happier, happiest** ◆◆◆◆◇

1 Someone who is **happy** has feelings of pleasure, usually because something nice has happened or because they feel satisfied with their life. *Marina was a confident, happy child... I'm just happy to be back running... Her face relaxed into a happy smile.* ADJ-GRADED

♦ **happily** *Albert leaned back happily and lit a cigarette.* ADV-GRADED: usu ADV with v ♦ **happiness** *I think mostly she was looking for happiness.* N-UNCOUNT

2 A **happy** time, place, or relationship is full of happy feelings and pleasant experiences, or has an atmosphere in which people feel happy. *Except for her illnesses, she had had a particularly happy childhood... It had always been a happy place... We have a very happy marriage.* ADJ-GRADED: usu ADJ n

3 If you are **happy** about a situation or arrangement, you are satisfied with it, for example because you think that something is being done in the right way. *If you are not happy about a repair, go back and complain... He's happy that I deal with it myself... When he got old he was really quite happy to let the department run itself.* ADJ-GRADED: v-link ADJ, ADJ *about/with* n/-ing, ADJ that, ADJ to-inf

4 If you say you are **happy** to do something, you mean that you are very willing to do it. *I'll be happy to answer any questions if there are any... That's a risk I'm happy to take.* ADJ-GRADED: v-link ADJ, usu ADJ to-inf ♦ **happily** *If I've caused any offence over something I have written, I will happily apologise.* ADV-GRADED: ADV with v =gladly

5 **Happy** is used in greetings and other conventional expressions to say that you hope someone will enjoy a special occasion. *Happy Birthday!... Happy Christmas!* • **many happy returns**: see **return**. ADJ-GRADED: ADJ n

6 A **happy** coincidence is one that results in something pleasant happening. *By happy coincidence, Robert met Richard and Julia and discovered they were experiencing similar problems.* ADJ-GRADED: ADJ n

happy-go-lucky. Someone who is **happy-go-lucky** enjoys life and does not worry about the future. ADJ-GRADED =easy going

happy hour, happy hours. In a pub, **happy hour** is a period when drinks are sold more cheaply than usual to encourage people to come to the pub. N-VAR

hara-kiri /hærə kɪri/. In former times, **hara-kiri** was a Japanese method of suicide in which a man cut his own stomach open in order to avoid dishonour. N-UNCOUNT

harangue /həræŋ/ **harangues, haranguing, harangued**

1 If someone **harangues** you, they try to persuade you to accept their opinions or ideas in a forceful way. *An argument ensued, with various band members joining in and haranguing Simpson and his girlfriend for over two hours.* VERB V n Also V

2 A **harangue** is a long, forceful speech that someone makes to try and persuade other people to accept their opinions. N-COUNT: usu with supp

harass /hærəs, həræs/ **harasses, harassing, harassed.** If someone **harasses** you, they trouble or annoy you, for example by attacking you repeatedly or by causing you as many problems as they can. *A woman reporter complained one of them sexually harassed her in the locker room... We are almost routinely harassed by the police.* ◆◇◇◇◇ VERB V n

harassed /hærəst, həræst/. If you are **harassed**, you are anxious and tense because you have too much to do or too many problems to cope with. *This morning, looking harassed and drawn, Lewis tendered his resignation.* ◆◇◇◇◇ ADJ-GRADED

harassment /hærəsmənt, həræs-/. **Harassment** is behaviour which is intended to trouble or annoy someone, for example repeated attacks on them or attempts to cause them problems. *Another survey found that 51 per cent of women had experienced some form of sexual harassment in their working lives. ...racial harassment... The MMD has accused the police of harassment.* ◆◆◇◇◇ N-UNCOUNT: oft adj N

harbinger /hɑːʳbɪndʒəʳ/ **harbingers.** Something that is a **harbinger** of something else is a sign that it is going to happen; a literary word. *The November air stung my cheeks, a harbinger of winter.* N-COUNT: usu N *of* n =herald

harbour /hɑːʳbəʳ/ **harbours, harbouring, harboured;** spelled **harbor** in American English. ◆◆◆◇◇

1 A **harbour** is an area of the sea at the coast which is partly enclosed by land or strong walls, so that boats can be left there safely. *She led us to a room with a balcony overlooking the harbour... The ship was permitted to tie up in Boston harbour.* N-COUNT: oft in names after n

2 If you **harbour** an emotion, thought, or secret, you have it in your mind over a long period of time. *He might have been murdered by a former client or someone harbouring a grudge... Townsend harbours no regrets.* VERB V n

3 If a person or country **harbours** someone who is wanted by the police, they let them stay in their house or country and offer them protection. *Accusations of harbouring terrorist suspects were raised against the former Hungarian leadership.* VERB V n

harbourmaster /hɑːʳbəʳmɑːstəʳ, -mæs-/ **harbourmasters;** spelled **harbormaster** in American English. A **harbourmaster** is the official in charge of a harbour. N-COUNT

hard /hɑːʳd/ **harder, hardest** ◆◆◆◆◆

1 Something that is **hard** is very firm and stiff to touch and is not easily bent, cut, or broken. *He shuffled his feet on the hard wooden floor... Something cold and hard pressed into the back of his neck.* ♦ **hardness** *He felt the hardness of the iron railing press against his spine.* ADJ-GRADED ≠soft; N-UNCOUNT: oft with poss

2 Something that is **hard** is very difficult to do or deal with. *It's hard to tell what effect this latest move will have... She found it hard to accept some of the criticisms directed towards her and her work... Our traveller's behaviour on the journey is hard to explain... That's a very hard question.* ADJ-GRADED: oft *it* v-link ADJ to-inf, ADJ to-inf =difficult ≠easy

3 If you work **hard** doing something, you are very active or work intensely, with a lot of effort. *I'll work hard. I don't want to let him down... Am I trying too hard?.* ► Also an adjective. *I admired him as a true scientist and hard worker.* ADV-GRADED: ADV after v; ADJ-GRADED: ADJ n

4 Hard work involves a lot of activity and effort. *Coping with three babies is very hard work. ...a hard day's work... Their work is hard and unglamorous, and most people would find it boring.* ADJ-GRADED

5 If you look, listen, or think **hard**, you do it carefully and with a great deal of attention. *He looked at me hard... You had to listen hard to hear the old man breathe... People are having to think hard about their holiday plans.* ► Also an adjective. *It might be worth taking a long hard look at you frustrations and resentments.* ADV-GRADED: ADV after v; ADJ-GRADED: usu ADJ n

6 If you strike or take hold of something **hard**, you strike or take hold of it with a lot of force. *I kicked a dustbin very hard and broke my toe.* ► Also an adjective. *He gave her a hard push which toppled her backwards into an armchair.* ADV-GRADED: ADV after v; ADJ-GRADED: ADJ n

7 You can use **hard** to indicate that someone does something or something happens intensely and for quite a long time. *I've never seen Terry laugh so hard... It was snowing hard by then.* ADV-GRADED: ADV after v

8 If a person or their expression is **hard**, they show no kindness or sympathy. *His father was a hard man... Kate realized that the previous hard look on her face had been a mask.* ADJ-GRADED: usu ADJ n ≠gentle

9 If you are **hard on** someone, you treat them severely or unkindly. *Don't be so hard on him.* ► Also an adverb. *He said the security forces would continue to crack down hard on the protestors.* ADJ-GRADED: v-link ADJ *on* n ≠soft; ADV-GRADED: ADV after v

10 If you say that something is **hard on** a person or thing, you mean it affects them in a way that is likely to cause them damage or suffering. *The grey light was hard on the eyes... These last four years have been hard on them.* ADJ-GRADED: v-link ADJ *on* n

11 If you have a **hard** life or a **hard** period of time, your life or that period is difficult and unpleasant for you. *It had been a hard life for her... Those were hard times.* ♦ **hardness** *In America, people don't normally admit to the hardness of life.* ADJ-GRADED =tough; N-UNCOUNT: N *of* n

12 A **hard** winter or a **hard** frost is very cold and severe. *Insulate plants from hard frost by lining the greenhouse with polythene... I am expecting a long, hard winter.* ADJ-GRADED: usu ADJ n ≠mild

13 Hard colours or sounds are harsh or bright and unpleasant to see or hear. *The sea was a hard blue.* ADJ-GRADED: usu ADJ n

14 Hard evidence or facts are definitely true and do not need to be questioned. *He wanted more hard evidence... Yeltsin has no hard information that any American POWs are still alive.* ADJ: ADJ n

15 Hard water contains a lot of lime so that it leaves a whitish coating on kettles. ADJ-GRADED

16 Hard drugs are very strong illegal drugs such as heroin or cocaine. ADJ: ADJ n

17 In phonetics, a **hard** sound is one such as 'c' or 'g' as pronounced in the words 'cat' or 'give', and not as in the words 'cinema' or 'gin'. ADJ ≠soft

18 If one thing is **hard by** another, it is very close to it; an old-fashioned expression. *Paradise Street was a short, crowded street near the railway station and hard by the factory.* PHRASES PREP

19 If you feel **hard done by**, you feel that you have not been treated fairly; used mainly in British English. *The hall porter was feeling hard done by at having to extend his shift.* v-link PHR

20 If you say that something is **hard going**, you mean it is difficult and requires a lot of effort. *The talks had been hard going at the start.* usu v-link PHR

21 To be **hard hit** by something means to be affected very severely by it. *California's been particularly hard hit by the recession.* usu v-link PHR

22 If someone **plays hard to get**, they pretend not to be interested in another person or in what someone is trying to persuade them to do. *I wanted her and she was playing hard to get.* V inflects

23 If someone is **hard put** or **hard pushed** to do something, they have great difficulty doing it. *Mr Morton is undoubtedly cleverer than Mr Kirkby, but he will be hard put to match his popularity.* usu v-link PHR to-inf

24 If you **take** something **hard**, you are very upset or depressed by it. *Maybe I just took it too hard.* V inflects

25 If you **learn** something **the hard way**, you have to make mistakes or face difficulties before you can improve the way that you do things or improve your behaviour. *Wales' young stars are learning the hard way that mistakes at international level are ruthlessly punished.* V inflects

26 ● to **drive a hard bargain**: see **bargain.** ● to **follow hard on the heels of**: see **heel.** ● **as hard as nails**: see **nail.** ● **a hard nut to crack**: see **nut.**

hard and fast. If you say that there are no **hard and fast** rules, or that there is no **hard and fast** information about something, you are indicating that there are no fixed or definite rules or facts. *There are no hard and fast rules, but rather traditional guidelines as to who pays for what... At the moment there's no hard and fast timetable.* ADJ: usu with brd-neg, usu ADJ n =definite

hardback /hɑːʳdbæk/ **hardbacks.** A **hardback** is a book which has a stiff hard cover. Compare **paperback** and **softback**. *'The Secret History' was published in hardback last October.* ◆◇◇◇◇ N-COUNT: also *in* N

hard-bitten. If you describe someone as **hard-bitten**, you are critical of them because they do not show much emotion or have much sympathy for other people, usually because they have experienced many unpleasant things. *...a cynical hard-bitten journalist.* ADJ-GRADED: usu ADJ n PRAGMATICS =tough

hardboard /hɑːʳdbɔːʳd/. **Hardboard** is a material which is made by pressing very small N-UNCOUNT pieces of wood very closely together to form a thin, slightly flexible sheet.

hard-boiled; also spelled **hard boiled**. ◆◇◇◇◇

1 A **hard-boiled** egg has been boiled in its shell until the yolk and the white are hard. ADJ ≠soft-boiled

2 You use **hard-boiled** to describe someone who is tough and does not show much emotion. *She's hard-boiled, tough and funny.* ADJ-GRADED =cynical, tough

hard cash. **Hard cash** is money in the form of notes and coins as opposed to a cheque or a credit card. N-UNCOUNT

hard copy, hard copies. A **hard copy** of a document is a printed version of it, rather than a version that is stored on a computer. *...eight pages of hard copy.* N-VAR

hard core; also spelled **hardcore**. ◆◇◇◇◇

1 You can refer to the members of a group who are the most committed to its activities or who are the most involved in them as a **hard core** of members or as the **hard-core** members. *We've got a hard core of customers that have stood by us... A hard-core group of right-wing senators had hoped to sway their colleagues.* N-SING: oft N *of*n, N n

2 **Hard-core** pornography is pornography that shows sex in a very explicit, violent, or unpleasant way. Compare **soft-core**. ADJ: ADJ n

3 **Hard core** consists of pieces of broken stone that are used as a base on which to build roads; used mainly in British English. N-UNCOUNT

hard currency, hard currencies. A **hard currency** is one which is unlikely to lose its value and so is considered to be a good one to have or to invest in. *The government is running short of hard currency to pay for imports.* ◆◇◇◇◇ N-VAR

hard disk, hard disks; also spelled **hard disc**. A computer's **hard disk** is a stiff magnetic disk on which data and programs can be stored. A computer with a hard disk can store more data and run more complicated programs than one which uses floppy disks. N-COUNT

hard-drinking. If you describe someone as a **hard-drinking** person, you mean that they frequently drink large quantities of alcohol. *She had transformed him from being a hard-drinking womaniser into a devoted husband and father.* ADJ-GRADED: ADJ n

hard-edged. If you describe something such as a style, play, or article as **hard-edged**, you mean you admire it because it is powerful, critical, or unsentimental. *...his fiery, hard-edged acoustic jazz style... His hard-edged stories are torn right from the violent heart of America.* ADJ-GRADED PRAGMATICS =uncompromising

harden /hɑːʳdᵊn/ **hardens, hardening, hardened** ◆◆◇◇◇

1 When something **hardens** or when you **harden** it, it becomes stiff or firm. *Mould the mixture into shape while hot, before it hardens... Give the cardboard two or three coats of varnish to harden it.* V-ERG V, V n

2 When you **harden** your ideas or attitudes or when they **harden**, they become fixed and you become more determined than ever that you will not change them. *Their action can only serve to harden the attitude of landowners... The bitter split which has developed within Solidarity is likely to harden further into separation.* ♦ **hardening** *...a hardening of the government's attitude towards rebellious parts of the army.* V-ERG V n, V; N-SING: usu N *of*n

3 When prices and economies **harden**, they become much more stable than they were. *Property prices are just beginning to harden again.* VERB V

4 When events **harden** people or when people **harden**, they become less easily affected emotionally and less sympathetic and gentle than they were before. *Her years of drunken bickering hardened my heart... She was hardened by the rigours of the Siberian steppes... All of a sudden my heart hardened against her.* V-ERG V n, V *against*n

5 If you say that someone's face or eyes **harden**, you mean that their face or eyes become sterner and more serious, usually because they have become angry about something. *His smile died and the look in his face hardened.* VERB V

hardened /hɑːʳdᵊnd/. If you describe someone as **hardened**, you mean that they have had so much experience of something bad or unpleasant that they are no longer affected by it in the way that other people would be. *...hardened criminals. ...hardened politicians.* ADJ-GRADED: usu ADJ n

hard hat, hard hats. A **hard hat** is a hat made from a hard material, which people wear to protect their heads on building-sites or in factories, or when riding a horse. N-COUNT

hard-headed. You use **hard-headed** to describe someone who is practical and determined to get what they want or need, and who does not allow emotions to affect their actions. *...a hard-headed and shrewd businesswoman... They are taking a hard-headed commercial decision.* ADJ-GRADED =tough

hard-hearted. You describe someone as **hard-hearted** when you disapprove of the fact that they have no sympathy for other people and do not care if people are hurt or made unhappy. *You would have to be pretty hard-hearted not to feel something for him.* ADJ-GRADED PRAGMATICS =unfeeling

hard-hitting. If journalists describe a report or speech as **hard-hitting**, they approve of it because it talks about difficult or controversial matters in a bold and direct way. *In a hard-hitting speech to the IMF, he urged third world countries to undertake sweeping reforms. ...a hard-hitting account of violence in the home.* ◆◇◇◇◇ ADJ-GRADED: usu ADJ n

hard labour; spelled **hard labor** in American English. **Hard labour** is hard physical work which people have to do as punishment for a crime. *The sentence of the court was twelve years' hard labour, to be served in a British prison.* N-UNCOUNT

hard left; also spelled **hard-left**. You use **hard left** to describe those members of a left wing political group or party who have the most extreme political beliefs and ideals; used mainly in British English. *...the hard-left view that foreign forces should not have been sent.* N-SING: *the*N, oft N n

hardline /hɑːʳdlaɪn/; also spelled **hard-line**. If you describe someone's policy or attitude as **hardline**, you mean that it is strict or extreme, and they refuse to change it. *The United States has taken a lot of criticism for its hard-line stance. ...a hardline Communist state.* ◆◆◇◇◇ ADJ-GRADED

hardliner /hɑːʳdlaɪnəʳ/ **hardliners.** The **hardliners** in a group such as a political party are the people who support a strict, fixed set of ideas that are often extreme, and who refuse to accept any change in them. *Communist hardliners accused him of being too liberal.* ◆◆◇◇◇ N-COUNT: usu pl

hard luck

1 If you say that someone had some **hard luck**, or that a situation was **hard luck** on them, you mean that something bad happened to them and you are implying that it was not their fault; an informal use. *We had a bit of hard luck this season... It was jolly hard luck on him, wasn't it?* N-UNCOUNT =bad luck

2 If someone says that a bad situation affecting you is just your **hard luck**, they do not care about it or think you should be helped, often because they think it is your fault; an informal use. *The shop assistants didn't really want to discuss the matter, saying it was just my hard luck.* N-UNCOUNT: poss N =tough luck

3 You can say **'hard luck'** to someone to show that you are sorry they have not got or done something that they had wanted to get or do; an informal expression. *Hard luck, chaps, but don't despair too much.* CONVENTION PRAGMATICS =tough luck

hardly /hɑːʳdli/ ◆◆◆◆◇

1 You use **hardly** to modify a statement when you want to emphasize that it is only a small amount or detail which makes it true, and that therefore it is best to consider the opposite statement as being true. *I hardly know you... Nick, on the sofa, hardly slept... He was given hardly 24 hours to pack his bags... Their two faces were hardly more than eighteen inches apart.* ADV-BRD-NEG: ADV before v, ADV group, oft ADV amount =scarcely, barely

2 You use **hardly** in expressions such as **hardly ever, hardly any**, and **hardly anyone** to mean almost never, almost none, or almost no-one. *We ate* ADV-BRD-NEG: ADV *ever/any* =scarcely

chips every night, but hardly ever had fish... Most of the others were so young they had hardly any experience... Hardly anyone slept that night.

3 You use **hardly** before a noun group and a verb, followed by a negative statement in order to emphasize that something is usually the case. For example, if you say 'hardly a day goes by when I don't eat fruit', you mean that you eat fruit almost every day. *Hardly a day goes by without a visit from someone.* ADV-BRD-NEG: ADV n PRAGMATICS =scarcely

4 When you say you can **hardly** do something, you are emphasizing that it is very difficult for you to do it. *I can hardly believe it's been over eight years since you used to go camping at Cedar Creek... My garden was covered with so many butterflies that I could hardly see the flowers.* ADV-BRD-NEG: *can/could* ADV inf PRAGMATICS =scarcely

5 If you say **hardly** had one thing happened when something else happened, you mean that the first event was followed immediately by the second. *He had hardly collected the papers on his desk when the door burst open... Hardly had he returned to London than an anonymous well-wisher called to say he was about to be raided by Customs & Excise.* ADV-BRD-NEG: ADV before v PRAGMATICS =no sooner

6 You use **hardly** to mean 'not' when you want to suggest that you are expecting your listener or reader to agree with your comment. *We have not seen the letter, so we can hardly comment on it... It's hardly surprising his ideas didn't catch on... The growth rate for 1980-89 was 2.2%. Hardly the stuff of economic miracles.* ADV-BRD-NEG: ADV before v, ADV group PRAGMATICS

7 You use **'hardly'** to mean 'no', especially when you want to express surprise or annoyance at a statement that you disagree with. *'They all thought you were marvellous!'—'Well, hardly.'... 'We could almost have seen it,'—'Hardly, darling – in the dark and from a distance of a good hundred feet?'* CONVENTION PRAGMATICS

hard-nosed. You use **hard-nosed** to describe someone who is tough and realistic, and who takes decisions on practical grounds rather than emotional ones; an informal word. *This requires a hard-nosed government, willing to do unpopular things to turn principle into practice.* ADJ-GRADED: usu ADJ n =unsentimental

hard of hearing. Someone who is **hard of hearing** is not able to hear properly. ADJ-GRADED: usu v-link ADJ

hard porn. **Hard porn** is pornography that shows sex in a very explicit, violent, or unpleasant way. N-UNCOUNT

hard-pressed; also spelled **hard pressed.** ◆◇◇◇◇

1 If someone is **hard-pressed**, they are under a great deal of strain and worry, usually because they have not got enough money; used in journalism. *The region's hard-pressed consumers are spending less on luxuries.* ADJ-GRADED

2 If you will be **hard-pressed** to do something, you will have great difficulty doing it. *This year the airline will be hard-pressed to make a profit.* ADJ-GRADED: v-link ADJ to-inf =hard put

hard right; also spelled **hard-right**. You use **hard right** to describe those members of a right wing political group or party who have the most extreme beliefs and ideals; used mainly in British English. *...the appearance of hard-right political groupings.* N-SING: *the* N, oft N n

hard sell. A **hard sell** is a method of selling in which the salesperson puts a lot of pressure on someone to make them buy something. *...a double-glazing firm whose hard-sell techniques were exposed by a consumer programme.* N-SING: oft N n

hardship /hɑːʳdʃɪp/ **hardships. Hardship** is a situation in which your life is difficult or unpleasant, often because you do not have enough money. *Many people are suffering economic hardship... One of the worst hardships is having so little time to spend with one's family.* ◆◆◇◇◇ N-VAR =privation

hard shoulder, hard shoulders. The **hard shoulder** is the area at the side of a motorway where you are allowed to stop if your car breaks down; used mainly in British English. N-COUNT: usu *the* N in sing

hard up; also spelled **hard-up**. If you are **hard up**, you have very little money; an informal word. *Her parents were very hard up.* ADJ-GRADED ≠well-off

hardware /hɑːʳdweəʳ/ ◆◆◇◇◇

1 In computer systems, **hardware** refers to the machines themselves as opposed to the programs which tell the machines what to do: compare **software**. N-UNCOUNT

2 Military **hardware** is the machinery and equipment that is used by the armed forces, such as tanks, aircraft, and missiles. N-UNCOUNT: usu adj N

3 **Hardware** refers to tools and equipment that are used in the home and garden, for example saucepans, screwdrivers, and lawnmowers. N-UNCOUNT

hardware store, hardware stores. In American English, a **hardware store** is a shop where articles for the house and garden such as tools, nails, and pans are sold. The British word is **ironmonger**. N-COUNT

hard-wearing; also spelled **hard wearing**. Something that is **hard-wearing** is strong and well made so that it lasts for a long time and stays in good condition even though it is used a lot; used mainly in British English. *...hard-wearing cotton shirts.* ADJ =strong, durable

hardwood /hɑːʳdwʊd/ **hardwoods. Hardwood** is wood such as oak, teak, and mahogany, which is very strong and hard and is used especially for floors. *...imports of tropical hardwood. ...hardwood floors.* ◆◇◇◇◇ N-MASS: oft N n ≠softwood

hardworking /hɑʳdwɜːʳkɪŋ/. If you describe someone as **hardworking**, you mean that they work very hard. *He was hardworking and energetic.* ADJ-GRADED

hardy /hɑːʳdi/ **hardier, hardiest** ◆◆◇◇◇

1 Plants that are **hardy** are able to survive frost and cold weather. *The silver-leaved varieties of cyclamen are not quite as hardy.* ♦ **hardiness** *...the hardiness of other species that have blue flowers.* ADJ-GRADED N-UNCOUNT

2 People and animals that are **hardy** are strong and able to endure difficult conditions. *They grew up to be farmers, round-faced and hardy... Hardy antelope wander in from the desert.* ♦ **hardiness** *...the hardiness, endurance, and courage of my companions... These Pacific oysters are known for their hardiness.* ADJ-GRADED N-UNCOUNT

3 If you describe a group of people as **hardy**, you mean that they have been very patient or loyal, or have been trying hard to do something in difficult conditions. *...the ten hardy supporters who had made the trek to Dublin from Riga.* ADJ-GRADED: usu ADJ n =trusty

hardy perennial, hardy perennials

1 A **hardy perennial** is a plant that lives for several years, because it is strong enough to survive a cold winter. N-COUNT

2 You can describe something such as a book or a song as a **hardy perennial** when people keep reading or listening to it over a number of years; used mainly in British English. *...hardy perennials which continue to sell, year in, year out.* N-COUNT

hare /heəʳ/ **hares, haring, hared** ◆◇◇◇◇

1 A **hare** is an animal like a rabbit but larger with long ears, long legs, and a small tail. ► **Hare** is the flesh of this animal eaten as food. N-VAR N-UNCOUNT

2 If you **hare** off somewhere, you go there very quickly; an informal use. *...an over-protective mother who keeps haring off to ring the babysitter.* VERB V adv/prep

hare-brained; also spelled **harebrained**. You use **hare-brained** to describe a scheme or theory which you consider to be very foolish and which you think is unlikely to be successful or true. *This isn't the first hare-brained scheme he's had.* ADJ-GRADED: usu ADJ n PRAGMATICS =crackpot ≠sensible

harem /hɑːriːm, AM herəm/ **harems**

1 A **harem** is a group of wives or mistresses belonging to a wealthy man, especially in some Muslim societies. N-COUNT

2 A **harem** is a part of a building where a harem lives. N-COUNT

haricot bean /hærɪkoʊ biːn/ **haricot beans. Haricot beans** are small white beans that are eaten as a vegetable. They are often sold dried rather than fresh. N-COUNT: usu pl

hark /hɑːʳk/ **harks, harking, harked. 'Hark!'** means 'Listen!'; an old-fashioned word. *Hark. I hear the returning footsteps of my love.* ◆◇◇◇◇ EXCLAM

hark back to PHRASAL VERB

1 If you say that one thing **harks back to** another

thing in the past, you mean it is similar to it or takes it as a model. *...pitched roofs, which hark back to the Victorian era.* VPPn

2 When people **hark back to** something in the past, they remember it or remind someone of it. *The result devastated me at the time. Even now I hark back to it.* VPPn

harlequin /hɑːʳlɪkwɪn/. You use **harlequin** to describe something that has a lot of different colours, often in a diamond pattern; used in written English. *...the striking harlequin floor.* ADJ: ADJ n

harlot /hɑːʳlət/ **harlots.** If someone describes a woman as a **harlot**, they disapprove of her because she is a prostitute, or because she looks or behaves like a prostitute; an old-fashioned word. N-COUNT PRAGMATICS

harm /hɑːʳm/ **harms, harming, harmed** ◆◆◆◇◇

1 To **harm** a person or animal means to cause them physical injury, usually on purpose. *The hijackers seemed anxious not to harm anyone.* VERB =injure, hurt Vn

2 **Harm** is physical injury to a person or an animal which is usually caused on purpose. *All dogs are capable of doing harm to human beings.* N-UNCOUNT: oft N to n =injury

3 To **harm** a thing, or sometimes a person, means to damage them or make them less effective or successful than they were. *...a warning that the product may harm the environment... Low-priced imports will harm the industry.* VERB =damage, ruin Vn

4 **Harm** is the damage to something which is caused by a particular course of action. *The abuse of your powers does harm to all other officers who do their job properly... To cut taxes would probably do the economy more harm than good.* N-UNCOUNT

5 If you say that someone or something **will come to no harm** or that **no harm will come** to them, you mean that they will not be hurt or damaged in any way. *There is always a lifeguard to ensure that no one comes to any harm... 'Go back and make sure that no harm comes to him,' he said quietly.* PHRASES V inflects

6 If you say **it does no harm** to do something or **there is no harm** in doing something, you mean that it might be worth doing, and you will not be blamed for doing it. *They are not always willing to take on untrained workers, but there's no harm in asking.* V inflects

7 If you say that something would **do no harm**, or **do** someone **no harm**, you are recommending a course of action which you think is worthwhile, helpful, or useful. *It would do her no harm to try them until we found the one which suited her best.* V inflects PRAGMATICS

8 If you say that there is **no harm done**, you are telling someone not to worry about something that has happened because it has not caused any serious injury or damage. *There, now, you're all right. No harm done.* usu v-link PHR PRAGMATICS

9 If someone is put **in harm's way**, they are caused to be in a dangerous situation; used mainly in American English. *These men were never told how they'd been put in harm's way... They could be in harm's way if military action becomes necessary.* PHR after v, v-link PHR =endanger

10 If someone or something is **out of harm's way**, they are in a safe place away from danger or from the possibility of being damaged. *For parents, it is an easy way of keeping their children entertained, or simply out of harm's way... Workers scrambled to carry priceless objects out of harm's way.* v-link PHR, PHR after v

harmful /hɑːʳmfʊl/. Something that is **harmful** has a bad effect on something else, especially on a person's health. *...the harmful effects of smoking... It believed the affair was potentially harmful to British aviation.* ◆◆◇◇◇ ADJ-GRADED: oft ADJ to n =damaging ≠harmless

harmless /hɑːʳmləs/ ◆◆◇◇◇

1 Something that is **harmless** does not have any bad effects, especially on people's health. *Industry has been working at developing harmless substitutes for these gases... This experiment was harmless to the animals.* ♦ **harmlessly** *Another missile exploded harmlessly outside the town.* ADJ-GRADED =safe ≠harmful ADV: ADV with v

2 If you describe someone or something as **harmless**, you mean that they are not important and therefore unlikely to annoy other people or cause trouble. *He seemed harmless enough... I would not want to deny them a harmless pleasure.* ♦ **harmlessly** *It started harmlessly enough, with a statement from the Secretary of State for Social Security.* ADJ-GRADED =inoffensive ADV: ADV after v

harmonic /hɑːʳmɒnɪk/ **harmonics** ◆◇◇◇◇

1 **Harmonic** means composed, played, or sung using two or more notes which sound right and pleasing together. *I had been looking for ways to combine harmonic and rhythmic structures.* ADJ: usu ADJ n

2 **Harmonics** are musical notes which can be produced on certain instruments. Harmonics are higher and quieter than the main note being played. N-COUNT: usu pl =overtone

harmonica /hɑːʳmɒnɪkə/ **harmonicas.** A **harmonica** is a small musical instrument. You play the harmonica by moving it across your lips and blowing and sucking air through it. N-COUNT: oft the N =mouth organ

harmonious /hɑːʳmoʊniəs/ ◆◇◇◇◇

1 A **harmonious** relationship, agreement, or discussion is friendly and peaceful. *Their harmonious relationship resulted in part from their similar goals. ...the most harmonious European Community summit for some time.* ♦ **harmoniously** *To live together harmoniously as men and women is an achievement.* ADJ-GRADED =amicable, cordial ADV-GRADED: ADV after v

2 Something that is **harmonious** has parts which go well together and which are in proportion to each other. *The architecture is harmonious and no building is over five or six floors high. ...a harmonious balance of mind, body, and spirit.* ♦ **harmoniously** *...a pure, harmoniously proportioned face. ...stone paths that blend harmoniously with the scenery.* ADJ-GRADED =balanced ADV-GRADED: ADV adj, ADV after v

3 Musical notes that are **harmonious** produce a pleasant sound when played together. *...the mysterious skill involved in producing harmonious sounds.* ADJ-GRADED

harmonize /hɑːʳmənaɪz/ **harmonizes, harmonizing, harmonized;** also spelled **harmonise** in British English. ◆◇◇◇◇

1 If two or more things **harmonize** with each other, they fit in well with each other. *...slabs of pink and beige stone that harmonize with the carpet... Barbara White and her mother like to listen to music together, though their tastes don't harmonize.* V-RECIP V with n pl-n V

2 When governments or organizations **harmonize** laws, systems, or regulations, they agree in a friendly way to make them the same or similar. *How far will members have progressed towards harmonising their economies?* ♦ **harmonization** /hɑːʳmənaɪzeɪʃən/ *Air France pilots called a strike over the European harmonisation of their working hours. ...fiscal harmonization.* VERB Vn N-UNCOUNT: usu with supp

3 When people **harmonize**, they sing or play notes which are different from the main tune but which sound nice with it. *Bremer and Garland harmonize on the title song, 'Meet Me in St. Louis'.* VERB V

harmony /hɑːʳməni/ **harmonies** ◆◆◇◇◇

1 If people are living in **harmony** with each other, they are in a state of peaceful agreement and co-operation. *...the notion that man should dominate nature rather than live in harmony with it... He projected himself as the protector of national unity and harmony.* N-UNCOUNT =accord, unity

2 **Harmony** is the pleasant combination of different notes of music played at the same time. *...complex vocal harmonies. ...singing in harmony.* N-VAR

3 The **harmony** of something is the way in which its parts are combined into a pleasant arrangement. *...the ordered harmony of the universe... He looked more relaxed, as if some of the harmony from his surroundings had flowed into him.* N-UNCOUNT

harness /hɑːʳnɪs/ **harnesses, harnessing, harnessed** ◆◇◇◇◇

1 If you **harness** something such as an emotion or natural source of energy, you bring it under your control and use it. *...the movement's ability to harness the anger of all Ukrainians... Turkey plans to harness the waters of the Tigris and Euphrates rivers for big hydro-electric power.* VERB Vn

2 A **harness** is a set of straps which fit under a person's arms and fasten round their body in order to N-COUNT

keep a piece of equipment in place or to prevent the person moving from a place.

3 A **harness** is a set of leather straps and metal links fastened round a horse's head or body so that the horse can have a carriage fastened to it. N-COUNT

4 If a horse or other animal **is harnessed**, a harness is put on it, especially so that it can pull a carriage, cart, or plough. *On Sunday the horses were harnessed to a heavy wagon for a day-long ride over the Border.* VB: usu passive be V-ed to n Also be V-ed

5 People or things who work or who are **in harness** work together and co-operate in order to achieve their aim; used mainly in British English. *At Opera North he will be in harness with Paul Daniel, the conductor appointed music director last year.* PHRASE: v-link PHR, PHR after v

6 If you say that someone is **in harness**, you mean that they are working, often after a break or absence. *You can rest for three or four months and then the longing for work will return and you will be right back in harness.* PHRASE: PHR after v, v-link PHR

harp /hɑːʳp/ **harps, harping, harped.** A **harp** is a large musical instrument consisting of a row of strings stretched from the top to the bottom of a frame. You play the harp by plucking the strings with your fingers. ◆◇◇◇◇ N-VAR: oft the N

harp on. If you say that someone **harps on** a subject, or **harps on** about it, you mean that they keep on talking about it in a way that other people find annoying. *Jones harps on this theme more than on any other... She concentrated on the good parts of her trip instead of harping on about the bad.* PHRASAL VERB V P n V P about n Also V P

harpist /hɑːʳpɪst/ **harpists.** A **harpist** is someone who plays the harp. N-COUNT

harpoon /hɑːʳpuːn/ **harpoons, harpooning, harpooned**

1 A **harpoon** is a weapon like a spear with a long rope attached to it, which is fired or thrown by people hunting whales or large sea fish. N-COUNT

2 To **harpoon** a whale or large fish means to hit or pierce it with a harpoon. *Norwegian whalers said yesterday they had harpooned a female minke whale.* VERB V n

harpsichord /hɑːʳpsɪkɔːʳd/ **harpsichords.** A **harpsichord** is a musical instrument rather like a small piano. When you press the keys, the strings are plucked mechanically rather than hit by hammers as in a piano. N-VAR: oft the N

harpy /hɑːʳpi/ **harpies**

1 In classical mythology, the **harpies** were creatures with the bodies of birds and the faces of women. They flew quickly and were cruel and greedy. N-COUNT: usu pl, oft the N

2 If you refer to a woman as a **harpy**, you mean that she is very cruel or violent. *Murderous women are not presented by Trollope as harpies or monsters but as ordinary people provoked to excessive acts.* N-COUNT PRAGMATICS

harridan /hærɪdən/ **harridans.** If you call a woman a **harridan**, you are saying in a rather cruel way that you think she is bossy and unpleasant; a formal word. *She was a mean old harridan.* N-COUNT PRAGMATICS

harrow /hæroʊ/ **harrows.** A **harrow** is a piece of farm equipment consisting of a row of spikes fixed to a heavy frame. When it is pulled over ploughed land, the spikes break up large lumps of soil. N-COUNT

harrowing /hæroʊɪŋ/. A **harrowing** experience is extremely upsetting or disturbing. *You've had a harrowing time this past month. ...harrowing pictures of the children who had been murdered.* ◆◇◇◇◇ ADJ-GRADED: usu ADJ n =disturbing

harry /hæri/ **harries, harrying, harried.** If someone **harries** you, they keep asking you to do something, attacking you, or trying to get something from you. *He is increasingly active in harrying the government in late-night debates.* ◆◇◇◇◇ VERB =hassle V n
♦ **harried** *...harried businessmen scurrying from one crowded office to another.* ADJ-GRADED =worried

harsh /hɑːʳʃ/ **harsher, harshest** ◆◆◇◇◇

1 **Harsh** climates or conditions are very difficult for people, animals, and plants to live in. *The weather grew harsh, chilly and unpredictable. ...the harsh desert environment. ...after the harsh experience of the war.* ♦ **harshness** *...the harshness of their living conditions.* ADJ-GRADED =severe ≠mild N-UNCOUNT =severity

2 **Harsh** actions or speech are unkind and show no understanding or sympathy. *...the cold, harsh cruelty of her husband... He said many harsh and unkind things about his opponents.* ♦ **harshly** *She's been told that her husband is being harshly treated in prison... 'Why didn't you tell me before?' asked Hunter harshly.* ♦ **harshness** *...treating him with great harshness.* ADJ-GRADED =cruel, severe ADV-GRADED: ADV with v N-UNCOUNT =severity

3 Something that is **harsh** is so hard, bright, or rough that it seems unpleasant or harmful. *Tropical colours may look rather harsh in our dull northern light. ...harsher detergents that can leave hair brittle.* ♦ **harshness** *...as the wine ages, losing its bitter harshness.* ADJ-GRADED N-UNCOUNT

4 **Harsh** voices and sounds are ones that are rough and unpleasant to listen to. *It's a pity she has such a loud harsh voice.* ♦ **harshly** *Chris laughed harshly.* ♦ **harshness** *Then in a tone of abrupt harshness, he added, 'Open these trunks!'.* ADJ-GRADED ≠soft, gentle ADV-GRADED: ADV with v N-UNCOUNT

5 If you talk about **harsh** realities or facts, or the **harsh** truth, you are emphasizing that they are true or real, although they are unpleasant and many other people try to avoid thinking about them. *The harsh truth is that luck plays a big part in who will live or die.* ADJ-GRADED PRAGMATICS =grim, bitter

harvest /hɑːʳvɪst/ **harvests, harvesting, harvested** ◆◆◇◇◇

1 **The harvest** is the gathering of a crop. *There was about 300 million tons of grain in the fields at the start of the harvest.* N-SING: the N

2 A **harvest** is the crop that is gathered in. *...a bumper potato harvest... Millions of people are threatened with starvation as a result of drought and poor harvests.* N-COUNT

3 When you **harvest** a crop, you gather it in. *Many farmers are refusing to harvest the cane. ...freshly harvested beetroot.* ♦ **harvesting** *The Soviet Union had a record grain crop but tremendous losses occurred during harvesting.* VERB V n V-ed N-UNCOUNT

4 If you **harvest** a large number of things, you collect them, often by making great efforts; a literary use. *In his new career as a restaurateur he has blossomed and harvested many awards.* VERB =collect V n

5 If you **reap** the **harvest**, you benefit or suffer from the results of your past actions or of someone else's past actions. *Russia is reaping the vicious harvest of 74 years of Soviet rule.* PHRASE: V inflects

harvester /hɑːʳvɪstəʳ/ **harvesters**

1 A **harvester** is a machine which cuts and often collects ripe crops such as wheat, maize, or vegetables. • See also **combine harvester**. N-COUNT

2 You can refer to a person who cuts, picks, or gathers crops as a **harvester**. N-COUNT

harvest festival, harvest festivals. A **harvest festival** is a special Christian church service held every year to thank God for the harvest. N-VAR

has. The auxiliary verb is pronounced /həz STRONG hæz/. The main verb is usually pronounced /hæz/. **Has** is the third person singular of the present tense of **have**.

has-been, has-beens. If you describe someone as a **has-been**, you are indicating in an unkind way that they were important or respected in the past, but they are not now. *...the so-called experts and various has-beens who foist opinions on us.* N-COUNT PRAGMATICS

hash /hæʃ/ ◆◇◇◇◇

1 If you **make a hash of** a job or task, you do it very badly; an informal expression. *The Government made a total hash of things and squandered a small fortune... Watson had made a thorough hash of it.* PHRASE: V inflects, PHR n/-ing =bungle

2 **Hash** is a dish made from meat cut into small lumps and fried with other ingredients such as onions or potato. *...corned beef hash.* N-UNCOUNT: oft n N

3 **Hash** is hashish; an informal use. N-UNCOUNT

hash browns also spelled **hashed browns**. **Hash browns** or **hashed browns** are potatoes that have been chopped into small pieces and cooked on a grill or in a frying pan. N-PLURAL

hashish /hæʃiːʃ/. **Hashish** is a drug made from the hemp plant which people usually smoke like a cigarette to make them feel relaxed. N-UNCOUNT

hasn't /hæzᵊnt/. In informal English, **has not** is usually said or written as **hasn't.**

hasp /hɑːsp hæsp/ **hasps.** A **hasp** is a flat piece of metal with a slot in it, fastened to the edge of a door or lid. To close the door or lid, you push the slot over a metal loop fastened to the other section and put a padlock through the loop. N-COUNT

hassle /hæsᵊl/ **hassles, hassling, hassled** ◆◇◇◇◇

1 A **hassle** is a situation that is difficult and involves problems, effort, or arguments with people; an informal use. *I don't think it's worth the money or the hassle... Weddings are so much hassle that you need a good break afterwards. ...a day spent travelling, with all the usual hassles at airport check-in.* N-VAR =aggro

2 If someone **hassles** you, they cause problems for you, often by repeatedly telling you or asking you to do something, in an annoying way; an informal use. *Then my husband started hassling me... If you are tired of being hassled by unreasonable parents, leave home and pay your own way.* VERB V n

hassock /hæsək/ **hassocks.** A **hassock** is a cushion for kneeling on in a church; used mainly in British English. N-COUNT

hast /hæst/. **Hast** is an old-fashioned way of saying or writing the present tense of 'have'. **Hast** was used only with the word **thou.**

haste /heɪst/ ◆◇◇◇◇

1 **Haste** is the quality of doing something quickly, sometimes too quickly so that you are careless and make mistakes. *In their haste to escape the rising water, they dropped some expensive equipment... The translations bear the signs of inaccuracy and haste.* N-UNCOUNT =rush

2 If you do something **in haste**, you do it quickly and hurriedly, and sometimes carelessly. *Don't act in haste or be hot-headed, but do try to sort things out before the 23rd.* PHRASES PHR after v

3 If someone is told to **make haste**, they are told to do something quickly and not waste time; an old-fashioned expression. *As Simon was under orders to make haste, some days they covered thirty miles.* V inflects =hurry

hasten /heɪsᵊn/ **hastens, hastening, hastened** ◆◇◇◇◇

1 If you **hasten** an event or process, often an unpleasant one, you make it happen faster or sooner. *But if he does this, he may hasten the collapse of his own country.* VERB =precipitate V n

2 If you **hasten** to do something, you are quick to do it. *She more than anyone had hastened to sign the contract.* VERB V to-inf

3 If you **hasten** to say something, you quickly add something to what you have just said in order to prevent it being misunderstood. *Naturally, it'll go back. But without Murray's little note, I hasten to add... 'There's no threat in this, Freddie,' Arnold hastened to say... He hastened to assure me that there was nothing traumatic to report.* VERB =be quick V to-inf

4 If you **hasten** somewhere, you hurry there; a literary use. *One of them, the first to alight, hastened with quicksilver steps towards me.* VERB =hurry V prep/adv

hasty /heɪsti/ ◆◆◇◇◇

1 A **hasty** movement, action, or statement is sudden, and often done in reaction to something that has just happened. *One company is giving its employees airplane tickets in the event they need to make a hasty escape.* ♦ **hastily** /heɪstɪli/ *'It may be satisfying, but it's not fun.' 'No, I'm sure it's not,' said Virginia hastily. 'I didn't mean that.'* ADJ-GRADED: usu ADJ n =swift, quick ADV-GRADED: ADV with v =swiftly

2 A **hasty** event or action is one that is completed more quickly than normal. *After the hasty meal, the men had moved forward to take up their positions.* ♦ **hastily** *He said good night hastily, promising that he would phone Hans in the morning... The survivors were recovering in hastily erected tents.* ADJ-GRADED: usu ADJ n =quick, hurried ADV-GRADED: ADV with v =hurriedly

3 If you describe a person or their behaviour as **hasty**, you mean that they are acting too quickly, without thinking carefully, for example because they are angry; used showing disapproval. *So let's not be hasty. After all, he can't run away... A number of the United States' allies had urged him not to take a hasty decision.* ♦ **hastily** *I decided that nothing should be done hastily, that things had to be sorted out carefully.* ADJ-GRADED PRAGMATICS =rash ADV-GRADED: ADV with v

hat /hæt/ **hats** ◆◆◆◇◇

1 A **hat** is a head covering, often with a brim round it, which is usually worn out of doors to give protection from the weather. N-COUNT

2 If you say that someone is wearing a particular **hat**, you mean that they are performing a particular role at that time. If you say that they wear several **hats**, you mean that they have several roles or jobs. *...putting on my nationalistic hat... Now, he is a headmaster, serves on the MCC committee, and is an active linguist. 'I can wear three different hats this week,' he says happily. ...various problems, including too many people wearing too many hats.* N-COUNT: with supp

3 If you say that you are ready to do something **at the drop of a hat**, you mean that you are willing to do it immediately, without hesitating. *India is one part of the world I would go to at the drop of a hat.* PHRASES PHR after v

4 If you tell someone to **keep** a piece of information **under** their **hat**, you are asking them not to tell anyone else about it. *Look, if I tell you something, will you promise to keep it under your hat?... He kept it all very much under his hat.* V inflects

5 If you say that something or someone is **old hat**, you mean that they have existed or been known for a long time, and they have become uninteresting and boring. *The younger generation tell me that religion is 'old hat' and science has proved this.* v-link PHR

6 In British English, if you **pass the hat around**, you collect money from a group of people, for example in order to give someone a present. In American English, you just say **pass the hat**. *Professors are passing the hat to help staff in their department.* V inflects

7 If you say that you **take** your **hat off to** someone, you mean that you admire them for something that they have done. *I take my hat off to Mr Clarke for taking this action... I was impressed by that, you have to take your hat off to the guy.* V inflects, PHR n PRAGMATICS

8 If you say **'Hats off to** someone', you are expressing admiration for them. *Hats off to them for supporting the homeless.* CONVENTION PRAGMATICS

9 If you say that someone **pulled** something **out of** the **hat**, you mean that they did something very unexpected and surprising which helped them to succeed, often when they appeared to be failing. *Southampton had somehow managed to pull another Cup victory out of the hat.* V inflects

10 In competitions, if you say that the winners will be drawn or picked **out of the hat**, you mean that they will be chosen at random, so that they all have an equal chance of winning. *The first 10 correct entries drawn out of the hat will win a pair of tickets, worth £20 each.* PHR after v

11 • to **knock** something **into a cocked hat**: see **cocked hat**.

hatband /hætbænd/ **hatbands.** A **hatband** is a strip of cloth that is put round a hat above the brim as a decoration. N-COUNT

hatbox /hætbɒks/ **hatboxes.** A **hatbox** is a cylindrical box in which a hat can be carried and stored. N-COUNT

hatch /hætʃ/ **hatches, hatching, hatched** ◆◆◇◇◇

1 When a baby bird, insect, or other animal **hatches**, or when it **is hatched**, it comes out of its egg by breaking the shell. *As soon as the two chicks hatch, they leave the nest burrow... The young disappeared soon after they were hatched.* V-ERG V be V-ed Also V n

2 When an egg **hatches** or when a bird, insect, or other animal **hatches** an egg, the egg breaks open and a baby comes out. *The eggs hatch after a week or ten days... During these periods the birds will lie on the cage floor as if trying to lay or hatch eggs.* ► **Hatch out** means the same as **hatch**. *Seeing the eggs hatch out for the first time is a moment that I will never forget.* V-ERG V V n PHRASAL VERB V P Also V n P, V P n (not pron)

3 If you **hatch** a plot or a scheme, you think of it and work it out. *He has accused opposition parties of hatching a plot to assassinate the Pope.* VERB V n

4 A **hatch** is an opening in the deck of a ship, which N-COUNT

is used by people for coming on deck or going below deck, or during loading and unloading cargo. You can also refer to the door or covering of this opening as a **hatch**. *He stuck his head up through the hatch... All deck fittings, windows, hatches and doors had been fastened.*

5 A **hatch** is an opening in a wall, especially between a kitchen and a dining room, which you can pass something such as food through; used mainly in British English. N-COUNT

6 If someone **battens down the hatches**, they prepare themselves so that they will be able to withstand a coming difficulty or crisis. *Many firms are battening down the hatches and preparing to ride out the storm.* PHRASE: V inflects

hatch out. See **hatch** 2. PHRASAL VERB

hatchback /hætʃbæk/ **hatchbacks.** A **hatchback** is a car with an extra door at the back which opens upwards. N-COUNT

hatchery /hætʃəri/ **hatcheries.** A **hatchery** is a place where people control the hatching of eggs, especially fish eggs. N-COUNT

hatchet /hætʃɪt/ **hatchets** ◆◇◇◇◇

1 A **hatchet** is a small axe that you can hold in one hand. N-COUNT

2 Someone with a **hatchet** face has a long, narrow face with sharp features. *...an old naval sergeant, with a hatchet face and drooping moustaches.* ADJ: ADJ n

3 If two people **bury the hatchet**, they become friendly again after a quarrel or disagreement. PHR-RECIP: V inflects

hatchet job, hatchet jobs. To do a **hatchet job** on someone or something means to say or write something mentioning many bad things about them, which harms their reputation; an informal expression. *Unfortunately, his idea of bold journalism was a hatchet job, portraying the staff in a negative light.* N-COUNT: usu sing, oft N *on* n =attack

hatchet man, hatchet men. If you use **hatchet man** to describe a man employed by a person, company, or organization, you disapprove of him because his job is to destroy things or do unpleasant tasks. *They reckoned he was a hatchet man, out to shred the workforce and crush the union.* N-COUNT PRAGMATICS

hatchway /hætʃweɪ/ **hatchways.** A **hatchway** is the same as a hatch. N-COUNT

hate /heɪt/ **hates, hating, hated** ◆◆◆◇◇

1 If you **hate** someone or something, you have an extremely strong feeling of dislike for them. *Most people hate him, but they don't dare to say so, because he still rules the country... I hated myself for writing that letter.* ▶ Also a noun. *I was 17 and filled with a lot of hate... It is difficult to bear the agony of our loved ones' anger and hate. ...eyes that held a look of chronic hate.* ♦ **hated** *He's probably the most hated man in this county.* VERB =detest, loathe ≠love V n; N-UNCOUNT =hatred; ADJ-GRADED: ADJ n =detested

2 If you say that you **hate** something such as a particular activity, you mean that you find it very unpleasant. *Ted hated parties, even gatherings of people he liked individually... She hated hospitals and didn't like the idea of having an operation... He hates to be interrupted during training... He hated coming home to the empty house... I hate it when people accuse us of that... I would hate him to think I'm trying to trap him... She hates me having any fun and is quite jealous and spoiled.* VB: no cont =dislike ≠like V n, V to-inf, V -ing, V *it* wh, V n to-inf, V n -ing

3 You can use **hate** in expressions like **I hate to trouble you** or **I hate to bother you** when you are apologizing to someone for interrupting them or asking them to do something. *I hate to rush you but I have another appointment later on.* VB: no cont PRAGMATICS V to-inf

4 You can use **hate** in expressions such as **I hate to say it** or **I hate to tell you** when you want to express regret about what you are about to say, because you think it is unpleasant or should not be the case. *I hate to tell you this, but tomorrow's your last day... I hate to admit it, but you were right.* VB: no cont PRAGMATICS V to-inf

5 ● to **hate** someone's **guts**: see **gut**.

6 You can use **hate** in expressions like **I hate to see** or **I hate to think** when are emphasizing that you find a situation or an idea unpleasant. *I just hate to see you doing this to yourself.* VB: no cont PRAGMATICS V to-inf

7 You can use **hate** in expressions like **I'd hate to think** when you hope that something is not true or that something will not happen. *I'd hate to think my job would not be secure if I left it temporarily.* VB: no cont V to-inf

hate campaign, hate campaigns. A **hate campaign** is a series of actions which are intended to harm or upset someone, or to make other people have a low opinion of them. *The media has waged a virulent hate campaign against her.* N-COUNT: usu sing

hateful /heɪtfʊl/

1 Someone or something that is **hateful** is extremely unpleasant; an old-fashioned use. *I'm sorry I didn't mean that. It was a hateful thing to say.* ADJ-GRADED =horrid

2 Someone who is **hateful** hates someone else. *These are not necessarily hateful, malicious people. ...a lying, hateful and racist campaign.* ADJ-GRADED

hate mail; also spelled **hate-mail**. If someone receives **hate mail**, they receive unpleasant or threatening letters. N-UNCOUNT

hater /heɪtəʳ/ **haters.** If you call someone a **hater of** something, you mean that they strongly dislike that thing. *Braccio was a hater of idleness.* ▶ Also a combining form. *He was reputed to be a woman-hater... A mustache-hater, he is said once to have made an employee shave before he got a raise.* N-COUNT: N *of* n; COMB in N-COUNT

hath /hæθ/. **Hath** is an old-fashioned way of saying or writing 'has'.

hatpin /hætpɪn/ **hatpins.** A **hatpin** is a metal pin which can be pushed through a woman's hat and through her hair to keep the hat in position. N-COUNT

hatred /heɪtrɪd/. **hatreds. Hatred** is an extremely strong feeling of dislike for someone or something. *Her hatred of them would never lead her to murder... My hatred for her is so intense it seems to be destroying me... He been accused of inciting racial hatred.* ◆◆◇◇◇ N-UNCOUNT: also N in pl, oft N *of/for* n ≠love

hatstand /hætstænd/ **hatstands.** A **hatstand** is an upright pole with hooks at the top on which hats can be hung. N-COUNT

hat-trick hat-tricks; also spelled **hat trick**. A **hat-trick** is a series of three achievements, especially in a sports match, for example three goals scored by the same person in a football match. *I scored a hat-trick against Arsenal.* ◆◇◇◇◇ N-COUNT

haughty /hɔːti/. You use **haughty** to describe someone's behaviour or appearance when you disapprove of the fact that they seem to be very proud and to think that they are better than other people. *He spoke in a haughty tone.* ♦ **haughtily** /hɔːtɪli/ *Toni looked at him rather haughtily.* ADJ-GRADED: usu ADJ n PRAGMATICS =disdainful ≠humble; ADV-GRADED: usu ADV with v

haul /hɔːl/ **hauls, hauling, hauled** ◆◆◇◇◇

1 If you **haul** something which is heavy or difficult to move, you move it using a lot of effort. *A crane had to be used to haul the car out of the stream... He hauled himself to his feet... She hauled up her bedroom window and leaned out.* VERB V n prep/adv, V adv n, Also V n

2 If someone **is hauled** before a court, a tribunal, or someone in authority, they are made to appear before them because they are accused of having done something wrong. *She was hauled before magistrates for refusing to reveal her age to a policeman... He was hauled before the managing director and fired.* ▶ **Haul up** means the same as **haul**. *He was hauled up before the Board of Trustees... She was late for her wedding after being hauled up for speeding.* VB: usu passive *be* V-ed *before* n; PHRASAL VERB: usu passive

3 A **haul** of something illegal such as drugs or explosives is an amount of them found and seized by police or customs, or seized by thieves in a robbery. *The size of the drugs haul shows that the international trade in heroin is still flourishing. ...the biggest haul of cannabis ever seized.* N-COUNT: with supp

4 If you say that a task or a journey is a **long haul**, you mean that it takes a long time and a lot of effort. *Revitalising the Romanian economy will be a long haul.* PHRASE

haulage /hɔːlɪdʒ/. **Haulage** is the business of transporting goods by road; used mainly in British English. *The haulage company was a carrier of machine parts to Turkey.* N-UNCOUNT: usu with supp

hauler /hɔːləʳ/ **haulers.** In American English, a **hauler** is a company or a person that transports goods by road. The British word is **haulier.** N-COUNT

haulier /hɔːliəʳ/ **hauliers.** In British English, a **haulier** is a company or a person that transports goods by road. The American word is **hauler.** *A road haulier's tool of trade is the truck.* N-COUNT

haunch /hɔːntʃ/ **haunches**

1 If you squat **on** your **haunches**, you lower yourself towards the ground so that your legs are bent under you and you are balancing on your feet. *Edgar squatted on his haunches... Ferris was crouched down on his haunches.* PHRASE: V PHR

2 The **haunches** of an animal or person consist of the area of the body which includes the hips, the buttocks, and the tops of the legs. N-COUNT: usu pl

haunt /hɔːnt/ **haunts, haunting, haunted** ◆◆◇◇◇

1 If something unpleasant **haunts** you, you keep thinking or worrying about it over a long period of time. *The decision to leave her children now haunts her... He would always be haunted by that scene in Well Park.* VERB V n

2 Something that **haunts** a person or organization regularly causes them problems over a long period of time. *The stigma of being a bankrupt is likely to haunt him for the rest of his life.* VERB =plague V n

3 A place that is the **haunt** of a particular person is one which they often visit because they enjoy going there. *The Channel Islands are a favourite summer haunt for UK and French yachtsmen alike.* N-COUNT: with supp

4 A ghost or spirit that **haunts** a place or a person regularly appears in the place, or is seen by the person and frightens them. *His ghost is said to haunt some of the rooms, banging a toy drum.* VERB V n

haunted /hɔːntɪd/ ◆◇◇◇◇

1 A **haunted** building or other place is one where a ghost regularly appears. *Tracy said the cabin was haunted. ...a haunted house.* ADJ

2 Someone who has a **haunted** expression looks very worried or troubled. *She looked so haunted, I almost didn't recognize her.* ADJ-GRADED =troubled ≠calm

haunting /hɔːntɪŋ/. **Haunting** sounds, images, or words remain in your thoughts because they are very beautiful or sad. *...the haunting calls of wild birds in the mahogany trees. ...haunting prose.* ♦ **hauntingly** *Each one of these ancient towns is hauntingly beautiful.* ◆◇◇◇◇ ADJ-GRADED: usu ADJ n =poignant; ADV-GRADED: usu ADV adj

haute couture /oʊt kuːtjʊəʳ/. **Haute couture** refers to the designing and making of high-quality fashion clothes, or to the clothes themselves; a formal expression. N-UNCOUNT

hauteur /oʊtɜːʳ, AM hoʊtʊr/. **Hauteur** is proud and arrogant behaviour; a formal word, used showing disapproval. *Once, she had been put off by his hauteur. Now, she was struck by his energy.* N-UNCOUNT PRAGMATICS =haughtiness

have 1 auxiliary verb uses

have /həv, STRONG hæv/ **has, having, had** ◆◆◆◆◆

In spoken English forms of **have** are often contracted, for example **I have** is contracted to **I've** and **has not** is contracted to **hasn't**. For explanations of the use of inflected forms and contractions, see the individual entries.

1 You use the forms **have** and **has** with a past participle to form the present perfect tense of verbs. *Alex has already gone... I've just seen a play that I can highly recommend... My term hasn't finished yet... What have you found so far?... This is something which you might have forgotten... Frankie hasn't been feeling well for a long time.* AUX; AUX -ed; AUX *been* -ing

2 You use the form **had** with a past participle to form the past perfect tense of verbs. *When I met her, she had just returned from a job interview... By Friday at 5:30 p.m., I still hadn't heard from Lund... Miss Windham said she had spoken to them over the weekend.* AUX; AUX -ed

3 **Have** is used in question tags. *You haven't sent her away, have you?... It's happened, hasn't it?... They hadn't invented sequencers back in those days, had they?* AUX; cl AUX n

4 You use **have** when you are confirming or contradicting a statement containing 'have', 'has', or 'had', or giving a negative or positive answer to a question. *'You'd never seen the Marilyn Monroe film?'—'No I hadn't.'... 'Have you been to York before?'—'Yes we have.'* AUX

5 The form **having** with a past participle can be used to introduce a clause in which you mention an action which had already happened before another action began. *He arrived in San Francisco, having left New Jersey on January 19th... Having been told by his doctor that he was overweight, he's eating all the fibre and fruit he can.* AUX; AUX -ed

have 2 used with nouns describing actions

have /hæv/ **has, having, had** ◆◆◆◆◆

Have is used in combination with a wide range of nouns, where the meaning of the combination is mostly given by the noun.

1 You can use **have** followed by a noun to talk about an action or event, when it would also be possible to use a verb. For example, you can say **'I had a look at the photos'** instead of 'I looked at the photos.' *I went out and had a walk around... She rested for a while, then had a wash and changed her clothes... I'll have a think about that... Sit down and have a good cry... They were having a long wait for someone to serve them.* VB: no passive; V n

2 In normal spoken or written English, people use **have** with a wide range of nouns when it is clear from the context what it means, often instead of a more specific verb. For example people are more likely to say **'we had ice-cream'** or **'he's had a shock'** than 'we ate ice-cream', or 'he's suffered a shock'. *Come and have a meal with us tonight... We will be having a meeting to decide what to do... She had an operation on her knee at the clinic... His visit had a great effect on them.* VB: no passive; V n

have 3 other verb uses and phrases

have /hæv/ **has, having, had** ◆◆◆◆◆

For meanings 1-4, people often use **have got** instead of **have**, especially in spoken English. In this case, **have** is pronounced as an auxiliary verb. For more information and examples of the use of 'have got', see **got**.

1 You use **have** when you are saying that someone or something owns, possesses, or holds a particular thing, or when you are mentioning one of their qualities or characteristics. *Oscar had a new bicycle... I want to have my own business... She had no job and no money... You have beautiful eyes... Her house had a balcony... Do you have any brothers and sisters?... I have a good friend who's a teacher... I have no doubt at all in my own mind about this... I just had a feeling that it was Santero on the telephone... Have you any valuables anywhere else in the house?... I have my microphone with me.* VB: no passive =have got; V n; V n adv/prep

2 If you **have** something to do, you are responsible for doing it or must do it. *He had plenty of work to do... I have some important calls to make.* VB: no passive =have got; V n to-inf

3 You can use **have** to say that something exists or happens, where it would also be possible to use an impersonal structure with 'there is'. For example, you can say **'you have no alternative'** instead of 'there is no alternative', or **'he had a good view from his window'** instead of 'there was a good view from his window.' *He had two tenants living with him... We haven't any shops on the island... First we had clock-radios, now there's the clock-radio-telephone... You have a lot of people that are very upset with what happened.* VB: no passive =have got; V n

4 If you **have** something such a part of your body in a particular position or state, it is in that position or state. *Mary had her eyes closed... They had the curtains open... He had his shirt buttoned... As I was working, I had the radio on... He had his hand on Maria's shoulder.* VB: no passive =have got; V n adj/adv/prep

5 If you **have** something done, someone does it for you or you arrange for it to be done. *I had your rooms cleaned and aired... They killed him, or had him killed... You've had your hair cut, it looks great... I don't think most nine-year-olds have their teeth brushed.* VB: no passive; V n -ed

6 If someone or something **has** something happen to them, usually something unpleasant, it happens VB: no passive

to them. *We had our money stolen... The dance hall once even had its roof blown off in World War II.* Vn-ed

7 If you **have** someone do something or doing something, you persuade, cause, or order them to do it. *If you happen to talk to him, have him call me... The bridge is not as impressive as some guides would have you believe... Mr Gower had had us all working so hard.* VB: no passive Vn inf Vn-ing

8 If someone **has** you by a part of your body, they are holding you there and they are trying to hurt you or force you to go somewhere. *When the police came, Larry had him by the ear and was beating his head against the pavement.* VB: no passive =have got Vn by n

9 If you **have** something from someone, they give it to you. *You can have my ticket... Can I have your name please?... We have had some help from the Government... I had comments from people in all age groups.* VB: no passive Vn

10 If you **have** an illness or disability, you suffer from it. *I had a headache... He might be having a heart attack... She has epilepsy.* VB: no passive Vn

11 If a woman **has** a baby, she gives birth to it. If she **is having** a baby, she is pregnant. *My wife has just had a baby boy... She's having another baby.* VB: no passive Vn

12 You can use **have** in expressions like **I won't have it** or **I'm not having that**, to mean that you will not allow or put up with something. *She wanted to be alone. They wouldn't have it... I'm not having any of that nonsense... I will not have the likes of you dragging down my reputation.* VB: with neg PRAGMATICS Vn Vn-ing

13 You can use **has it** in expressions like **'rumour has it that'** or **'as legend has it'** when you are quoting something that you have heard, but you do not necessarily think it is true. *Rumour has it that tickets were being sold for £300... He could not possibly have been poisoned as popular legend has it.* PHRASES V inflects, oft PHR that

14 If someone **has it in for** you, they do not like you and they want to make life difficult for you. *He's always had it in for the Dawkins family.* V inflects, PHR n

15 If you **have it in** you, you have abilities and skills which you do not usually use and which only show themselves in a difficult situation. *'You were brilliant!' he said. 'I didn't know you had it in you.'... He has it in him to succeed.* V inflects, PHR pron, oft PHR pron to-inf

16 In British English, to **have it off** with someone or **have it away** with someone means to have sex with them; an informal expression which some people find offensive. *She's having it off with the gardener.* RECIP: V inflects, PHR with n, pl-n V

17 If you **are having** someone **on**, you are pretending that something is true when it is not true, for example as a joke or in order to tease them; used in informal British English. *Malone's eyes widened. 'You're having me on, Liam.'* be inflects =pull someone's leg

18 If you **have it out** or **have things out** with someone, you discuss a problem or disagreement very openly with them, even if it means having an argument, because you think this is the best way to solve the problem. *Why not have it out with your critic, discuss the whole thing face to face?* V inflects, oft PHR with n

19 • to **be had**: see **had**. • to **have had it**: see **had**. • to **melt** someone's **heart**: see **melt**.

have 4 modal phrases

have /hæv, hæf/ **has, having, had** ◆◆◆◆◆

1 You use **have to** when you are saying that something is necessary, obligatory, or must happen. If you do not **have to** do something, it is not necessary or obligatory for you to do it. *He had to go to Germany... We'll have to find a taxi... You have to be careful what you say on telly... They didn't have to pay tax.* PHR-MODAL =must

2 You can use **have to** in order to say that you feel certain that something is true or will happen. *There has to be some kind of way out... That has to be the biggest lie ever told.* PHR-MODAL =must

haven /heɪvᵊn/ **havens.** A **haven** is a place where people or animals feel safe, secure, and happy. *It's a real haven at the end of a busy working day. ...Lake Baringo, a freshwater haven for a mixed variety of birds.* • See also **safe haven**. ◆◆◇◇◇ N-COUNT: oft N for/of n =refuge

have-nots. If you refer to two groups of people as **haves and have-nots**, you mean that the first group are very wealthy and the second group are very poor. You can also refer generally to poor people as **have-nots**. *The stark contrast between the haves and have-nots has always existed but in a recession the injustices become more painful... The position of the have-nots in our society could deteriorate even further.* PHRASE

haven't /hævᵊnt/. In informal English, **have not** is usually spoken or written as **haven't**.

haversack /hævərsæk/ **haversacks.** A **haversack** is a canvas bag that is usually worn over one shoulder; used mainly in British English. N-COUNT

haves /hævz/. • **haves and have-nots**: see **have-nots**.

havoc /hævək/ ◆◇◇◇◇

1 **Havoc** is chaos, disorder, and confusion. *Rioters caused havoc in the centre of the town.* N-UNCOUNT =chaos

2 If one thing **plays havoc with** another or **wreaks havoc on** it, it prevents it from continuing or functioning as normal, or damages it. *Drug addiction soon played havoc with his career... The weather played havoc with airline schedules... Stress can wreak havoc on the immune system.* PHRASE: V inflects, PHR n

haw /hɔː/ **haws, hawing, hawed**

1 **Haws** are the red berries produced by hawthorn trees in autumn. N-COUNT

2 Writers sometimes use **'haw haw'** to show that one of their characters is laughing, especially in a rather unpleasant or superior way. *Look at the plebs! Getting all muddy! Haw haw haw!* EXCLAM

3 If you **hum and haw** or **hem and haw**, you take a long time to say something because you cannot think of the right words, or because you are not sure what to say. *Tim hemmed and hawed, but finally told his boss the truth.* PHRASE: Vs inflect

hawk /hɔːk/ **hawks, hawking, hawked** ◆◆◇◇◇

1 A **hawk** is a large bird with a short, hooked bill, sharp claws, and very good eyesight. Hawks catch and eat small birds and animals. N-COUNT

2 If you refer to someone as a **hawk**, you mean that they believe in using force and violence to achieve something, rather than using more peaceful or diplomatic methods; used mainly in American English. *Both hawks and doves have expanded their conditions for ending the war.* N-COUNT ≠dove

3 If someone **hawks** goods, they sell them by walking through the streets or knocking at people's houses, and asking people to buy them; used in American English and old-fashioned British English. *...vendors hawking trinkets.* VERB =peddle Vn

4 If you say that someone **is hawking** something, you disapprove of the fact that they are asking people in a rather forceful manner to buy it, rather than waiting for people to contact them. *Developers will be hawking cut-price flats and houses.* VERB PRAGMATICS Vn

► **Hawk around** means the same as **hawk**; used mainly in British English. *He is hawking around a 15-minute, £5,000 promotional video... Most of the women were hawking food around the various prisons.* PHRASAL VERB VPn (not pron) VnP

5 If someone **hawks**, they clear phlegm from their throat before spitting it out; an old-fashioned use. *He hawked and spat.* VERB V

6 If you **watch** someone **like a hawk**, you observe them very carefully, usually to make sure that they do not make a mistake or do something you do not want them to do. PHRASE: V inflects

hawk around. See **hawk** 5. PHRASAL VERB

hawker /hɔːkər/ **hawkers.** You can use **hawker** to refer to a person who tries to sell things by calling at people's homes or standing in the street; used showing disapproval. *...as soon as she saw that it was a visitor and not a hawker or tramp at her door.* ◆◇◇◇◇ N-COUNT PRAGMATICS =peddler

hawkish /hɔːkɪʃ/. Journalists use **hawkish** to describe politicians or governments who are in favour of using force to achieve something, rather than using peaceful and diplomatic methods. *He is one of the most hawkish members of the new cabinet.* ADJ-GRADED ≠dovish

hawser /hɔːzər/ **hawsers.** A **hawser** is a large heavy rope, especially one used on a ship. N-COUNT

hawthorn /hɔːθɔːʳn/ **hawthorns.** A **hawthorn** is a small tree which has sharp thorns and produces white or pink flowers. *Much of the track had become overgrown with hawthorn.* ◆◇◇◇◇ N-VAR

hay /heɪ/ ◆◇◇◇◇
1 **Hay** is grass which has been cut and dried so that it can be used to feed animals. *...bales of hay. ...traditional hay making methods.* N-UNCOUNT
2 If you say that someone **is making hay** or **is making hay while the sun shines**, you mean that they are taking advantage of a situation that is favourable to them while they have the chance to. *We shared a prescience of the coming war, and were determined to make hay while we could.* PHRASE: V inflects

hay fever. If someone suffers from **hay fever**, their nose, throat, and eyes become inflamed, usually because they are allergic to the pollen of some grasses or flowers. ◆◇◇◇◇ N-UNCOUNT

haystack /heɪstæk/ **haystacks**
1 A **haystack** is a large, firmly-built pile of hay, often covered with a straw roof to protect it, which is left in the field until it is needed. N-COUNT
2 If you are trying to find something and say that it is like looking for **a needle in a haystack**, you mean that you are very unlikely indeed to find it. PHRASE

haywire /heɪwaɪəʳ/. If something goes **haywire**, it becomes completely disordered or out of control; an informal word. *Many Americans think their legal system has gone haywire.* ADJ-GRADED: v-link ADJ

hazard /hæzəʳd/ **hazards, hazarding, hazarded** ◆◆◇◇◇
1 A **hazard** is something which could be dangerous to you, your health or safety, or your plans or reputation. *A new report suggests that chewing-gum may be a health hazard... Oil leaking from a barge in the Mississippi River poses a hazard to the drinking water of New Orleans.* N-COUNT: oft N *to/for*n, N *of*n
2 If you **hazard** someone or something, you put them into a situation which might be dangerous for them, because of something you are trying to achieve or a plan you are trying to follow; used in formal British English. *He could not believe that, had the Englishman known how much he was at risk, he would have hazarded his grandson.* VERB =endanger V n
3 If you **hazard** or if you **hazard** a guess, you make a suggestion about something which is only a guess and which you know might be wrong. *I would hazard a guess that they'll do fairly well in the next election... 'Fifteen or sixteen?' Mrs Dearden hazarded.* VERB V n V with quote Also V that

hazardous /hæzəʳdəs/. Something that is **hazardous** is dangerous, especially to people's health or safety. *They have no way to dispose of the hazardous waste they produce... Passive smoking can be hazardous to health.* ◆◇◇◇◇ ADJ-GRADED =dangerous ≠safe

haze /heɪz/ **hazes** ◆◇◇◇◇
1 **Haze** is light mist, caused by particles of water or dust in the air, which prevents you from seeing distant objects clearly. Haze often forms in hot weather. *They vanished into the haze near the horizon... The sun smouldered through a thin summer haze. ...the shimmering heat haze.* N-VAR
2 If there is a **haze** of something such as smoke or steam, you cannot see clearly through it; a literary use. *Dan smiled at him through a haze of smoke and steaming coffee... A thick haze of acrid smoke hung in the air.* N-SING: usu N *of*n
3 If someone is in a **haze**, they are not thinking clearly or not really noticing what is happening around them. *His mind was a haze of fear and confusion. ...asking people to recollect a vanished past through a nostalgic haze.* N-SING: with supp, oft adj N, N *of*n =blur

hazel /heɪzəl/ **hazels** ◆◇◇◇◇
1 A **hazel** is a small tree which produces nuts that you can eat. N-VAR
2 **Hazel** eyes are greenish-brown in colour. COLOUR

hazelnut /heɪzəlnʌt/ **hazelnuts. Hazelnuts** are nuts from a hazel tree, which can be eaten. N-COUNT

hazy /heɪzi/ **hazier, haziest** ◆◇◇◇◇
1 **Hazy** weather conditions are those in which things are difficult to see, because of light mist, hot air, or dust. *The air was thin and crisp, filled with hazy sunshine and frost... The floodlights were hazy behind the slanting rain.* ADJ-GRADED ≠clear
2 If you are **hazy** about ideas or details, or if they are **hazy**, you are uncertain or confused about them. *I'm a bit hazy about that... I have only a hazy memory of what he was really like... She had only a hazy idea of Britain's prison problems... Many details remain hazy.* ADJ-GRADED ≠clear
3 If things seem **hazy**, or if you feel **hazy**, you cannot see things clearly or distinctly, for example because you are feeling ill. *My vision has grown so hazy... She sipped the wine. Everything was hazy now, except for Nick's face... It's as if I'm living in a hazy dream world.* ADJ-GRADED

H-bomb, H-bombs. An **H-bomb** is a bomb in which energy is released from hydrogen atoms. N-COUNT

he /hi, STRONG hiː/ ◆◆◆◆◆
He is a third person singular pronoun. **He** is used as the subject of a verb.
1 You use **he** to refer to a man, boy, or male animal. *He could never quite remember all our names... He lives in Rapid City, South Dakota... Rex did all sorts of tricks. I cried when he died.* PRON-SING
2 In written English, writers sometimes use **he** to refer to a person without saying whether that person is a man or a woman. Some people dislike this use and prefer to use 'he or she' or 'they'. *The teacher should encourage the child to proceed as far as he can, and when he is stuck, ask for help.* PRON-SING
3 In some religions, **He** is used to refer to God. PRON-SING

H.E. H.E. is a written abbreviation for 'His Excellency' or 'Her Excellency' and is used as part of the title of an important official such as an ambassador. *I went to a really splendid reception at the Italian Embassy given by H.E. the Italian Ambassador.* N-TITLE

head /hed/ **heads, heading, headed** ◆◆◆◆◆
1 Your **head** is the top part of your body, which has your eyes, mouth, and brain in it. *She turned her head away from him... He took a puff on his pipe and shook his head.* ▶ You can also use **head** as a measure of distance, equal to the length of a person's or animal's head. *The third gorilla was taller by a head.* N-COUNT N-SING: aN
2 You can use **head** to refer to your mind and your mental abilities. *I can't get that song out of my head. ...an exceptional analyst who could do complex maths in his head.* N-COUNT
3 The **head** of a line of people or vehicles is the front of it, or the first person or vehicle in the line. *...the head of the queue... We took our place at the head of the convoy.* N-SING: with supp
4 If someone or something **heads** a line or procession, they are at the front of it. *The parson, heading the procession, had just turned right towards the churchyard.* VERB V n
5 If something **heads** a list or group, it is at the top of it. *Running a business heads the list of ambitions among the 1,000 people interviewed by Good Housekeeping magazine.* VERB V n
6 The **head** of something is the highest or top part of it. *...the head of the stairs... Every day a different name was placed at the head of the chart.* N-SING: usu N *of*n =top
7 The **head** of something long and thin is the end which is wider than or a different shape from the rest, and which is often considered to be the most important part. *There should be no exposed screw heads... Keep the head of the club the same height throughout the swing. ...a flower head.* N-COUNT: usu with supp
8 The **head** of a school is the teacher who is in charge of a school; used mainly in British English. *She is full of admiration for the head and teachers.* N-COUNT =head teacher
9 The **head** of a company or organization is the person in charge of it and in charge of the people in it. *Heads of government from more than 100 countries gather in Geneva tomorrow. ...the head waiter.* N-COUNT: with supp
10 If you **head** a department, company, or organization, you are the person in charge of it. *...Michael Williams, who heads the department's Office of Civil Rights. ...the ruling Socialist Party, headed by Dr Franz Vranitzky.* VERB V n V-ed
11 The **head** of a spot or boil is the part of it which N-COUNT

goes yellow and has pus in it when it is about to burst.

12 The **head** on a glass of beer is the layer of small bubbles that form on the top of the beer.
N-COUNT: usu sing

13 You can use **head** to describe how many animals of a particular type a farmer has. For example, if they have fifty **head of** cattle, they have fifty cows.
N-PLURAL: num N of n

14 If you have a bad **head**, you have a headache; used in informal British English. *I had a terrible head and was extraordinarily drunk.*
N-COUNT: usu sing, with supp

15 When you are tossing a coin and it comes down **heads**, you can see the side of the coin which has a head on it, for example the head of the king or president. *'We might toss up for it,' suggested Ted. 'If it's heads, then we'll talk.'... Heads or tails?*
ADV: be ADV, ADV after v ≠tails

16 If you **are heading** for a particular place or in a particular direction, you are going towards that place or in that direction. In American English, you can also say that you **are headed** for a particular place or in a particular direction. *He headed for the bus stop. ...an Iraqi vessel heading for the port of Basra... It is not clear how many of them will be heading back to Saudi Arabia tomorrow... She and her child boarded a plane headed to where her family lived... He could just as well have hitched a ride on a train or a truck headed west.*
VERB
V for n
V adv/prep
V-ed

17 If something or someone **is heading for** a particular result, the situation they are in is developing in a way that makes that result very likely. In American English, you can also say that something or someone **is headed** for a particular result. *The latest talks aimed at ending the civil war appear to be heading for deadlock... He said anyone giving orders without respecting the wishes of his people is heading for disaster... The centuries-old ritual seems headed for extinction.*
VERB
V for/towards n
V-ed

18 If a piece of writing **is headed** a particular title, it has that title written at the beginning of it. *One chapter is headed, 'Beating the Test'.*
VB: usu passive
be V-ed quote

19 If you **head** a ball, you hit it with your head in order to make it go in a particular direction. *He headed the ball across the face of the goal.*
VERB
V n prep/adv
Also V n

20 See also **heading**.

21 You use **a head** or **per head** after stating a cost or amount in order to indicate that that cost or amount is for each person in a particular group. *This simple chicken dish costs less than £1 a head... Ethiopia, for instance uses the equivalent of just twenty kilos of oil per head a year.*
PHRASES
amount PHR =per person

22 **From head to foot** means all over your body. *Colin had been put into a bath and been scrubbed from head to foot.*
oft be V-ed PHR

23 If you a have a **head for** something, you can deal with it easily in your mind. For example, if you have a **head for figures**, you can understand and do arithmetic easily, and if you have a **head for heights**, you can climb to a great height without feeling afraid. *I don't have a head for business. ...an extraordinarily effective organiser with a remarkable head for figures.*
have/with PHR, PHR n

24 If you **get** a fact or idea **into** your **head**, you suddenly realize or think that it is true and you usually do not change your opinion about it. *Once they get an idea into their heads, they never give up.*
V and N inflect

25 If you say that someone has **got** something **into** their **head**, you mean that they have finally understood or accepted it, and you are usually criticizing them because it has taken them a long time to do this. *Managers have at last got it into their heads that they can no longer rest content with inefficient operations.*
V and N inflect
PRAGMATICS

26 If you **give** someone their **head**, you allow them to do what they want to do, without trying to advise or stop them. *He recognised ability and gave people their heads.*
V and N inflect

27 If alcoholic drink **goes to** your **head**, it makes you feel drunk. *That wine was strong, it went to your head.*
V and N inflect

28 If you say that something such as praise or success **goes to** someone**'s head**, you mean that they become arrogant or conceited as a result of it. *Foord is definitely not a man to let a little success go to his head.*
V and N inflect

29 If you are **head over heels** or **head over heels in love**, you are very much in love. *I was very attracted to men and fell head over heels many times.*
v PHR, v-link PHR

30 If you **keep** your **head**, you remain calm in a difficult situation. If you **lose** your **head**, you panic or do not remain calm in a difficult situation. *She was able to keep her head and not panic... She lost her head and started screaming at me.*
V and N inflect =keep your cool

31 If you **knock** something **on the head**, you stop doing something or stop something happening; used mainly in British English. *When we stop enjoying ourselves we'll knock it on the head.*
V inflects

32 Phrases such as **laugh** your **head off**, **scream** your **head off**, and **shout** your **head off** can be used to emphasize that you are laughing, screaming, or shouting very much. *He carried on telling a joke, laughing his head off.*
N inflects
PRAGMATICS

33 If you say that someone is **off** their **head**, you mean that they have taken so many drugs that they do not know what they are doing; used mainly in informal British English.
N inflects, usu v-link PHR =out of your tree

34 If you say that someone is **off** their **head**, you think that their ideas or behaviour are very strange, foolish, or dangerous; used mainly in informal British English. *He's gone completely off his head.*
N inflects, usu v-link PHR
PRAGMATICS

35 If you **stand** an idea or argument **on its head** or **turn** it **on its head**, you think about it or treat it in a completely new and different way. *Theirs was a nonconformist relationship which turned the standard notion of marriage on its head.*
V inflects

36 If something such as an idea, joke, or comment goes **over** someone's **head**, it is too difficult for them to understand. *I admit that a lot of the ideas went way over my head.*
v-link PHR, PHR after v

37 If someone does something **over** your **head**, they do it without consulting you. *He was reprimanded for trying to go over the heads of senior officers.*
v-link PHR, PHR after v

38 If you say that something unpleasant or embarrassing rears its **ugly head**, you mean that it has appeared or is present, often after having been absent for some time. *There was a problem which reared its ugly head about a week after she moved back in... The scourge of racial tyranny should never again be allowed to raise its ugly head.*
V inflects

39 If you **stand on** your **head**, you turn your body upside down and rest all your weight on the top part of your head and your hands with your feet directly above you.
V and N inflect

40 If you say you cannot **make head or tail of** something, you are emphasizing that you cannot understand it at all; an informal expression. *I couldn't make head nor tail of the damn film.*
usu with brd-neg, V inflects, PHR n
PRAGMATICS

41 If you **take it into** your **head** to do something, you suddenly decide to do it. *He suddenly took it into his head to go out to Australia to stay with his son.*
V and N inflect, usu PHR to-inf

42 If a problem or disagreement **comes to a head** or if you **bring** it **to a head**, it reaches a state where you have to do something urgently about it. *These problems came to a head in September when five of the station's journalists were sacked.*
V inflects

43 If you **bang** peoples' **heads together** or **knock** their **heads together**, you tell them off for doing something wrong or for not doing something they were asked to do; used mainly in British English. *It is now high time he banged his colleagues' heads together.*
V inflects

44 If two or more people **put** their **heads together**, they talk about a problem they have and try to solve it. *So everyone put their heads together and eventually an amicable arrangement was reached.*
V inflects

45 If you **keep** your **head above water**, you avoid getting into difficulties, especially in business. *We are keeping our head above water, but our cash flow position is not too good.*
V inflects

46 If you say that **heads will roll** as a result of something bad that has happened, you mean that people will be punished for it, especially by losing
V inflects

their jobs. *The group's problems have led to speculation that heads will roll.*

47 Head is used in a large number of expressions which are explained under other words in the dictionary. For example, the expression 'off the top of your head' is explained at 'top'.

head off PHRASAL VERB

1 If you **head off** a person, animal, or vehicle, you move to a place in front of them and make them change the direction they are moving in. *He changed direction swiftly, turned into the hallway and headed her off.* =intercept; V n P; Also V P n (not pron)

2 If you **head** something **off**, especially something unpleasant, you take action before it is expected to happen in order to prevent it from happening. *He would ask Congress to intervene and head off a strike... You have to be good at spotting trouble on the way and heading it off.* V P n (not pron); V n P

headache /hedeɪk/ **headaches** ◆◆◇◇◇

1 If you have a **headache**, you have a pain in your head. *I have had a terrible headache for the last two days.* N-COUNT

2 If you say that something is a **headache**, you mean that it causes you difficulty or worry. *The airline's biggest headache is the increase in the price of aviation fuel... This is a real headache for us.* N-COUNT =problem

headband /hedbænd/ **headbands;** also spelled **head band**. A **headband** is a narrow strip of material which you can wear around your head across your forehead, for example to keep hair or sweat out of your eyes. N-COUNT

headboard /hedbɔːʳd/ **headboards.** A **headboard** is an upright board at the end of a bed where you lay your head. N-COUNT

head boy, head boys. The **head boy** of a school is the boy who is the leader of the prefects and who often represents the school on public occasions; used mainly in British English. N-COUNT

head-butt, head-butts, head-butting, head-butted; also spelled **headbutt**. If someone **head-butts** you, they hit you with the top of their head. *He was said to have head-butted one policeman and stamped on another's hand.* ► Also a noun. *The cuts on Colin's head could only have been made by head-butts.* VERB; V n; N-COUNT

head count, head counts. If you do a **head count**, you count the number of people present. You can also use **head count** to talk about the number of people that are present at an event, or that an organization employs. N-COUNT

headdress /heddres/ **headdresses;** also spelled **head-dress**. A **headdress** is something that is worn on a person's head for decoration. N-COUNT

headed notepaper. **Headed notepaper** is notepaper which has the name and address of the person or organization sending the letter printed at the top; used mainly in British English. N-UNCOUNT

header /hedəʳ/ **headers.** In football, a **header** is the act of hitting the ball in a particular direction with your head. ◆◇◇◇◇ N-COUNT

head-first; also spelled **headfirst**. If you move **head-first** in a particular direction, your head is the part of your body that is furthest forward as you are moving. *He had apparently fallen head-first down the stairwell... My mate dived headfirst through a window and I ran down the hallway.* ADV: ADV after v

headgear /hedgɪəʳ/; also spelled **head gear**. You use **headgear** to refer to hats or other things worn on the head. N-UNCOUNT

head girl, head girls. The **head girl** of a school is the girl who is the leader of the prefects and who often represents the school on public occasions; used mainly in British English. N-COUNT

headhunt /hedhʌnt/ **headhunts, headhunting, headhunted.** If someone who works for a particular company **is headhunted**, they leave that company because another company has approached them and offered them another job with better pay and higher status. *He was headhunted by Barkers last October to build an advertising team... They may headhunt her for the vacant position of Executive Producer.* VERB; be V-ed; V n

headhunter /hedhʌntəʳ/ **headhunters;** also spelled **head-hunter**. A **headhunter** is a person who tries to persuade someone to leave their job and take another job which has better pay and more status. N-COUNT

heading /hedɪŋ/ **headings.** A **heading** is the title of a piece of writing, which is written or printed at the top of the page. *...helpful chapter headings.* • See also **head**. ◆◇◇◇◇ N-COUNT

headlamp /hedlæmp/ **headlamps.** A **headlamp** is a headlight; used mainly in British English. N-COUNT

headland /hedlənd/ **headlands.** A **headland** is a narrow piece of land which sticks out from the coast into the sea. N-COUNT

headless /hedləs/. If the body of a person or animal is **headless**, the head has been cut off. ADJ

headlight /hedlaɪt/ **headlights.** A vehicle's **headlights** are the large powerful lights at the front. ◆◇◇◇◇ N-COUNT

headline /hedlaɪn/ **headlines** ◆◆◆◇◇

1 A **headline** is the title of a newspaper story, printed in large letters at the top of the story, especially on the front page. *The Sydney Morning Herald carried the headline: 'Sorry Ma'am, Most Australians Want a Republic'... I'm sick of reading headlines involving the Kennedys in sex scandals.* N-COUNT

2 The **headlines** are the main points of the news which are read on radio or television. *I'm Claudia Polley with the news headlines.* N-PLURAL

3 Someone or something that **hits the headlines** or **grabs the headlines** gets a lot of publicity from the media. *El Salvador first hit the world headlines at the beginning of the 1980s... In sport, it's usually men who grab the headlines.* PHRASE: V inflects

headlined /hedlaɪnd/. If a newspaper or magazine article is **headlined** a particular thing, that is the headline that introduces it. *The Sunday Times ran an article headlined 'The X Brothers'.* ◆◇◇◇◇ ADJ: v-link ADJ quote

headlong /hedlɒŋ, AM -lɔːŋ/ ◆◇◇◇◇

1 If you move **headlong** in a particular direction, you move there very quickly. *He ran headlong for the open door.* ► Also an adjective. *The army was in headlong flight.* ADV: ADV after v; ADJ: ADJ n

2 If you fall or move **headlong**, you fall or move with your head furthest forward. *She missed her footing and fell headlong down the stairs.* ADV: ADV after v =head first

3 If you rush **headlong** into something, you do it quickly without thinking carefully about it. *Do not leap headlong into decisions... The country, they say, will inevitably now plunge headlong into decadence.* ► Also an adjective. *...the headlong rush to independence.* ADV: ADV after v; ADJ: ADJ n

headman /hedmən/ **headmen.** A **headman** is the chief or leader of a tribe in a village. N-COUNT

headmaster /hedmɑːstəʳ, -mæst-/ **headmasters.** A **headmaster** is a man who is the head teacher of a school; used mainly in British English. ◆◇◇◇◇ N-COUNT

headmistress /hedmɪstrɪs/ **headmistresses.** A **headmistress** is a woman who is the head teacher of a school; used mainly in British English. ◆◇◇◇◇ N-COUNT

head of state, heads of state. A **head of state** is the leader of a country, for example a president, king, or queen. ◆◆◇◇◇ N-COUNT

head-on ◆◆◇◇◇

1 If two vehicles hit each other **head-on**, they hit each other with their fronts pointing towards each other. *Pulling out to overtake, the car collided head-on with a van.* ► Also an adjective. *Their car was in a head-on smash with an articulated lorry.* ADV: ADV after v; ADJ: ADJ n

2 A **head-on** conflict or disagreement is firm and direct, without any compromises. *The only victors in a head-on clash between the president and the assembly would be the hardliners on both sides.* ► Also an adverb. *Once again, I chose to confront the issue head-on.* ADJ: ADJ n; ADV: ADV after v

headphones /hedfoʊnz/. **Headphones** are a pair of padded speakers which you wear over your ears in order to listen to a radio, record player, or tape recorder without other people hearing it. ◆◇◇◇◇ N-PLURAL: also *a pair of* N

headquartered /hedkwɔːʳtəʳd/. If an organization **is headquartered in** a particular place, that is where its main offices are. *The company is headquartered in Chicago.* V-PASSIVE be V-ed in/at n

headquarters /hedkwɔːʳtəʳz/. The **headquarters** of an organization are its main offices. *...fraud squad officers from London's police headquarters... The building is the headquarters of the family firm.* ◆◆◆◇◇ N-SING-COLL =HQ

headrest /hedrest/ **headrests.** A **headrest** is the part of the back of a seat on which you can lean your head, especially one on the front seat of a car. N-COUNT

headroom /hedruːm/. **Headroom** is the amount of space below a roof or bridge. *The forecabin, with 6ft headroom, also has plenty of room to stand and get dressed.* N-UNCOUNT

headscarf /hedskɑːʳf/ **headscarves.** A **headscarf** is a scarf which is worn on the head, especially by women. N-COUNT

headset /hedset/ **headsets.** A **headset** is a piece of equipment, attached to a radio or a telephone, that has two earpieces and which you can wear on your head so that your hands are free while you are listening. N-COUNT

headship /hedʃɪp/ **headships.** A **headship** is the position of being the head of a school, college, or department. *I feel sure you'll be offered the headship.* N-COUNT

head start, head starts; also spelled **headstart.** If you have a **head start** on other people, you have an advantage over them in something such as a competition or race. *Hungarian businessmen have had a head start over most of their Eastern European neighbors... A good education gives your child a head start in life.* ◆◇◇◇◇ N-COUNT: usu sing, oft N on/over n

headstone /hedstoun/ **headstones.** A **headstone** is a large stone which stands at one end of a grave, usually with the name of the dead person carved on it. N-COUNT =grave stone

headstrong /hedstrɒŋ, AM -strɔːŋ/. If you refer to someone as **headstrong**, you are slightly critical of the fact that they are determined to do what they want. *He's young, very headstrong, but he's a good man underneath.* ADJ-GRADED PRAGMATICS =stubborn, wilful

head teacher, head teachers; also spelled **headteacher.** A **head teacher** is a teacher who is in charge of a school; used mainly in British English. ◆◇◇◇◇ N-COUNT =head

headway /hedweɪ/. If you **make headway**, you progress towards achieving something. *He is not disappointed at the failure to make headway towards resolving their differences... There was concern in the city that police were making little headway in the investigation.* ◆◇◇◇◇ PHRASE: oft with brd-neg, V inflects =progress

headwind /hedwɪnd/ **headwinds;** also spelled **head-wind.** A **headwind** is a wind which blows in the opposite direction to the one in which you are moving. N-COUNT

headword /hedwɜːʳd/ **headwords.** A **headword** is a word which is followed by a phrase or paragraph which explains the word's meaning, especially in a dictionary. N-COUNT

heady /hedi/ **headier, headiest.** A **heady** drink, atmosphere, or experience strongly affects your senses, for example by making you feel drunk or excited. *...in the heady days just after their marriage... I felt heady and euphoric.* ◆◇◇◇◇ ADJ-GRADED: usu ADJ n

heal /hiːl/ **heals, healing, healed** ◆◆◆◇◇

1 When a broken bone or other injury **heals** or when someone or something **heals** it, it becomes healthy and normal again. When someone **is healed** of an illness, or when they **heal**, they recover. *Within six weeks the bruising had gone, but it was six months before it all healed... If they'd operated and pinned her arm at once, she might have healed by now... No doctor has ever healed a broken bone: he or she sets them... Therapies like acupuncture do work and many people have been healed by them.* V-ERG V V n

2 When someone **is healed** from their emotional pain or wounds, or when they **heal**, they feel normal and happy again. *A year later, she had healed to the point of at least being able to consider a romantic relationship with another man... Only by fully experiencing the depth of our pain can we be healed from it and be done with it.* V-ERG V be V-ed from n Also V n

3 If you **heal** something such as a rift or a wound, or it **heals**, the situation is restored to its former state after it has been damaged. *Today Sophie and her sister have healed the family rift and visit their family every weekend... The psychological effects on the United States were immense and in Washington the wounds have still not fully healed.* V-ERG V n V

heal up. When an injury **heals up**, it becomes completely healthy again. *Before too long my lung abscess healed up.* PHRASAL VERB V P

healer /hiːləʳ/ **healers.** A **healer** is a person who heals people. ◆◇◇◇◇ N-COUNT

health /helθ/ ◆◆◆◆◆

1 A person's **health** is the condition of their body and the extent to which it is free from illness or is able to resist illness. *Tea contains caffeine. It's bad for your health.* N-UNCOUNT: oft with poss

2 Health is a state in which a person is not suffering from any illness and is feeling well. *In hospital they nursed me back to health.* N-UNCOUNT

3 When you **drink to** someone's **health** or **drink** their **health**, you have a drink as a sign of wishing them health and happiness. *In the village pub, regulars drank the health of John and his father.* PHRASE: V inflects

4 The **health** of something such as an organization or a system is its success and the fact that it is working well. *There's no way to predict the future health of the banking industry.* N-UNCOUNT =prosperity

health centre health centres; spelled **health center** in American English. A **health centre** is a building in which the doctors of a particular district have offices where their patients can visit them. N-COUNT =surgery

health farm, health farms. A **health farm** is a sort of hotel where people can go if they want to get fitter. Health farms have facilities such as swimming pools and gyms, and they serve special food; used mainly in British English. N-COUNT

health food, health foods. Health foods are natural foods without artificial ingredients which people buy because they consider them to be good for them. ◆◇◇◇◇ N-MASS: oft N n =whole food

healthful /helθfʊl/. Something that is **healthful** is good for your health. *Does the college cafeteria provide a healthful diet?... Chinese cooking is both low in calories and healthful.* ADJ-GRADED =healthy

health visitor, health visitors. In Britain, a **health visitor** is a nurse whose job is to visit people in their homes and offer advice on matters such as how to look after very young babies or people with physical disabilities. N-COUNT

healthy /helθi/ **healthier, healthiest** ◆◆◆◇◇

1 Someone who is **healthy** is well and is not suffering from any illness. *Most of us need to lead more balanced lives to be healthy and happy... She had a normal pregnancy and delivered a healthy child.* ADJ-GRADED
♦ **healthily** /helθɪli/ *What I really want is to live healthily for as long as possible.* ADV-GRADED: usu ADV after v

2 If a feature or quality that you have is **healthy**, it makes you look well or shows that you are well. *...the glow of healthy skin. ...young adults with healthy appetites.* ADJ-GRADED: usu ADJ n

3 Something that is **healthy** is good for your health. *...a great healthy outdoor pursuit. ...a healthy diet.* ADJ-GRADED: usu ADJ n

4 A **healthy** organization or system is successful. *...an economically healthy socialist state.* ADJ-GRADED: usu ADJ n

5 A **healthy** amount of something is a large amount that shows success. *He predicts a continuation of healthy profits in the current financial year. ...a healthy bank account.* ADJ-GRADED: usu ADJ n =substantial

6 If you have a **healthy** attitude about something, you show good sense. *She has a refreshingly healthy attitude to work... It's very healthy to be afraid when there's something to be afraid of.* ADJ-GRADED: oft it v-link ADJ to-inf
♦ **healthily** *I had never seen bombing on such a scale, and I was healthily apprehensive.* ADV: ADV adj

heap /hiːp/ **heaps, heaping, heaped** ◆◆◇◇◇

1 A **heap** of things is a pile of them, especially a pile arranged in a rather untidy way. *...a heap of bricks. ...a compost heap... He has dug up the tiles that cover the floor and left them in a heap.* N-COUNT: oft N *of* n =mound

2 If you **heap** things in a pile, you arrange them in a large pile. *Mrs. Madrigal heaped more carrots onto Michael's plate.* VERB V n prep/adv ▶ **Heap up** means the same as **heap**. *Off to one side, the militia was heaping up wood for a bonfire.* PHRASAL VERB V P n (not pron) Also V n P

3 If you **heap** praise or criticism **on** someone or something, you give them a lot of praise or criticism. *The head of the navy heaped scorn on both the methods and motives of the conspirators.* VERB =shower V n *on/upon* n

4 Heaps of something or a **heap of** something is a large quantity of it; an informal use. *You have heaps of time. ...a job that might suit someone with heaps of experience... Mansell managed to get himself in a whole heap of trouble.* QUANT: QUANT *of* n-uncount/pl-n =loads

5 Someone who is **at the bottom of the heap** or **at the top of the heap** is low down or high up in the structure of society or of an organization, considered in terms of their status, their quality of life, and how successful they have been. *...those at the top of the social heap... Ordinary workers in state industry, once favoured, suddenly found themselves at the bottom of the heap.* PHRASES usu v-link PHR, PHR after v

6 If someone collapses **in a heap**, they fall heavily and untidily and do not move. *Twelve weeks ago, the young striker collapsed in a heap after a heavy tackle.* v PHR, v-link PHR

heaped /hiːpt/ ◆◇◇◇◇

1 A **heaped** spoonful has the contents of the spoon piled up above the edge. *Add one heaped tablespoon of salt.* ADJ: ADJ n

2 A container or a surface that is **heaped with** things has a lot of them in it or on it in a pile, often so many that it cannot hold any more. *The large desk was heaped with papers. ...ashtrays heaped with cigarette butts.* ADJ: v-link ADJ *with* n

hear /hɪəʳ/ **hears, hearing, heard** /hɜːʳd/ ◆◆◆◆◆

1 When you **hear** a sound, you become aware of it through your ears. *She heard no further sounds... The trumpet can be heard all over their house... They heard the protesters shout: 'No more fascism!'... And then we heard the bells ringing out... I'm not hearing properly.* VERB V n V n inf V n -ing V

2 If you **hear** something such as a lecture or a piece of music, you listen to it. *You can hear commentary on the match in about half an hour's time... I don't think you've ever heard Doris talking about her emotional life before. ...if she can hear it played by a professional orchestra.* VERB =listen to V n V n -ing V n -ed Also V n inf

3 If you say that you can **hear** something that you heard in the past or might hear in the future, especially someone saying something, you mean that you are able to imagine hearing it in your mind. *Can't you just hear John Motson now?... 'I was hot', I could still hear Charlotte say with her delicious French accent.* VB: no cont V n V n inf

4 When a judge or a court of law **hears** a case, or evidence in a case, they listen to it officially in order to make a decision about it; a formal use. *The jury have heard evidence from defence witnesses... He had to wait months before his case was heard.* VERB V n

5 If you **hear** from someone, you receive a letter or telephone call from them. *Drop us a line, it's always great to hear from you... The police are anxious to hear from anyone who may know her.* VERB V *from* n

6 In a debate or discussion, if you **hear from** someone, you listen to them giving their opinion or information. *What are you hearing from people there?* VERB V *from* n

7 If you **hear** some news or information about something or someone, you find out about it by someone telling you, or from the radio or television. *My mother heard of this school through Leslie. ...the rumours I've been hearing about for years... He had heard that the trophy had been sold... I had waited to hear the result... Have you heard anything of the other Englishman?* VERB V *of/about* n V that V n V n *of/about* n

8 If you **have heard** of something or someone, you know about them, but not in great detail. *Many people haven't heard of reflexology. ...people who, maybe, had hardly heard the word till a year or two ago.* VB: no cont V *of* n V n

9 If you say that you **have heard** something **before**, you mean that you are not interested in it, or do not believe it, or are not surprised about it, because you already know about it or have experienced it. *Furness shrugs wearily. He has heard it all before... 'How many times have I heard that before?' Merchant complained angrily.* PHRASES V inflects

10 If you say **'Do you hear?'** or **'Did you hear me?'** to someone, you are telling them in an angry or forceful way to pay attention to what you are saying. *If you don't get out I'll call the police. Do you hear?... Leave her alone! Do you hear me?* CONVENTION PRAGMATICS

11 During political debates and public meetings, people sometimes say **'Hear hear!'** to express their agreement with what the speaker is saying; a formal use in British English. CONVENTION PRAGMATICS

12 If you say that you **can't hear** yourself **think**, you are complaining and emphasizing that there is a lot of noise, and that it is disturbing you or preventing you from doing something; an informal expression. *For God's sake shut up. I can't hear myself think!... If you're sitting in the front yard, you can't hear yourself think because the traffic is getting very, very bad.* usu with brd-neg PRAGMATICS

13 If you say that you **won't hear of** someone doing something, you mean that you refuse to let them do it. *I've always wanted to be an actor but Dad wouldn't hear of it... He even thought about moving from the village. But his friends wouldn't hear of it.* PHR n PRAGMATICS

14 ● **you could have heard a pin drop**: see **pin**.

hear out. If you **hear** someone **out**, you listen to them without interrupting them until they have finished saying everything that they want to say. *MPs heard him out in silence... Perhaps, when you've heard me out, you'll appreciate the reason for secrecy... He shows keen interest in his friends, hearing out their problems and offering counsel.* PHRASAL VERB V n P V P n (not pron)

hearer /hɪərəʳ/ **hearers.** Your **hearers** are the people who are listening to you speak; a formal word. *He knew that his hearers wanted to hear this story... Communication of whatever sort involves not just a speaker but a hearer too.* N-COUNT =listener ≠speaker

hearing /hɪərɪŋ/ **hearings** ◆◆◆◇◇

1 A person's or animal's **hearing** is the sense which makes it possible for them to be aware of sounds. *His mind still seemed clear and his hearing was excellent.* N-UNCOUNT: oft poss N

2 A **hearing** is an official meeting which is held in order to collect facts about an incident or problem. *After more than two hours of pandemonium, the judge adjourned the hearing until next Tuesday.* N-COUNT

3 See also **hard of hearing**.

4 If someone gives you **a fair hearing** or **a hearing**, they listen to you when you give your opinion about something. *Weber gave a fair hearing to anyone who held a different opinion.* PHRASES usu PHR after v

5 If someone says something **in** your **hearing** or **within** your **hearing**, you can hear what they say because they are with you or near you. *No one spoke disparagingly of her father in her hearing.* usu PHR after v

hearing aid, hearing aids. A **hearing aid** is a device which people with hearing difficulties wear in their ear to enable them to hear better. N-COUNT =deaf aid

hearsay /hɪəʳseɪ/. **Hearsay** is information which you have been told indirectly, but which you do not personally know to be true. *Much of what was reported to them was hearsay... Rumour, myth and hearsay obscure the truth after months of bloodshed.* N-UNCOUNT =rumour ≠fact

hearse /hɜːʳs/ **hearses.** A **hearse** is a large car that carries the coffin at a funeral. N-COUNT

heart /hɑːʳt/ **hearts** ◆◆◆◆◇

1 Your **heart** is the organ in your chest that pumps the blood around your body. People also use **heart** to refer to the area of their chest that is closest to their heart. *The bullet had passed less than an inch from Andrea's heart... The only sound inside was* N-COUNT *the beating of his heart... He gave a sudden cry of pain and put his hand to his heart.*

2 You can refer to someone's **heart** when you are talking about their deep feelings and beliefs; a literary use. *Alik's words filled her heart with pride... I just couldn't bring myself to admit what I knew in my heart to be true.*
N-COUNT: usu with poss

3 You use the word **heart** when you are talking about someone's character and attitude towards other people, especially when they are kind and generous. *She loved his brilliance and his generous heart... She's got a good heart but she's calculating.*
N-VAR: usu adj N in sing PRAGMATICS

4 If you refer to things of **the heart**, you mean love and relationships. *This is an excellent time for affairs of the heart.*
N-SING: *the* N

5 The **heart of** something is the most central and important part of it. *The heart of the problem is supply and demand... Money lies at the heart of the debate over airline safety.*
N-SING: N *of* n =crux

6 The **heart** of a place is its centre. *...a busy dentists' practice in the heart of London's West End.*
N-SING: usu N *of* n

7 The **heart** of a lettuce, cabbage, or other vegetable is its centre leaves.
N-COUNT: with supp

8 A **heart** is a shape that is used as a symbol of love: ♥. *...heart-shaped chocolates.*
N-COUNT

9 **Hearts** is one of the four suits in a pack of playing cards. Each card in the suit is marked with one or more symbols in the shape of a heart.
N-UNCOUNT-COLL

10 A **heart** is one of the thirteen playing cards in the suit of hearts.
N-COUNT

11 If you feel or believe something **with all** your **heart**, you feel or believe it very strongly. *My own family I loved with all my heart.*
PHRASES PHR after v, PHR with cl PRAGMATICS

12 If you say that someone is a particular kind of person **at heart**, you mean that that is what they are really like, even though they may seem very different. *He was a very gentle boy at heart.*
PHR with cl

13 If you say that someone has your interests or your welfare **at heart**, you mean that they are concerned about you and that is why they are doing something. *She told him she only had his interests at heart.*
usu *have* n PHR

14 If someone **breaks** your **heart**, they make you very sad and unhappy, usually because they end a love affair or close relationship with you; a literary expression.
V and N inflect PRAGMATICS

15 If something **breaks** your **heart**, it makes you feel very sad and depressed, especially because people are suffering but you can do nothing to help them; a literary expression. *It really breaks my heart to see them this way.*
V and N inflect, oft PHR to-inf PRAGMATICS

16 If you say that someone has a **broken heart**, you mean that they are deeply upset and sad, for example because a love affair has ended unhappily; a literary expression. *She never recovered from her broken heart.*
N inflects

17 If you know something such as a poem **by heart**, you have learnt it so well that you can remember it without having to read it. *Mack knew this passage by heart.*
PHR after v

18 If someone has a **change of heart**, their attitude towards something changes. *A Bosnian family divided by immigration regulations is to be reunited in Britain after a change of heart by the Home Office... Why the change of heart?*
change inflects

19 If something such as a subject or project is **close to** your **heart** or **near to** your **heart**, it is very important to you and you are very interested in it and concerned about it. *This is a subject very close to my heart.*
N inflects, oft v-link PHR

20 If you can do something **to** your **heart's content**, you can do it as much as you want. *I was delighted to be able to eat my favorite dishes to my heart's content.*
PHR after v

21 You can say **'cross my heart'** when you want someone to believe that you are telling the truth. You can also ask **'cross your heart?'**, when you are asking someone if they are really telling the truth; used in spoken English. *And I won't tell any of the other girls anything you tell me about it. I promise, cross my heart.*
CONVENTION

22 If you say something **from the heart** or **from the bottom of** your **heart**, you sincerely mean what you say. *He spoke with confidence, from the heart... I don't want to go away without thanking you from the bottom of my heart.*
PHR after v =sincerely

23 If something **gives** you **heart**, it makes you feel more confident or happy about something. *It gave me heart to see one thug get what he deserves.*
V inflects

24 If you want to do something but do **not have the heart** to do it, you do not do it because you know it will make someone unhappy or disappointed. *We knew all along but didn't have the heart to tell her.*
V inflects, usu PHR to-inf

25 If you believe or know something **in your heart of hearts**, that is what you really believe or think, even though it may sometimes seem that you do not. *I know in my heart of hearts that I am the right man for that mission.*
PHR after v, PHR with cl

26 If your **heart isn't in** the thing you are doing, you have very little enthusiasm for it, usually because you are depressed or are thinking about something else. *I tried to learn some lines but my heart wasn't really in it.*
V and N inflect, PHR n/-ing

27 If you **lose heart**, you become sad and depressed and are no longer interested in something, especially because it is not progressing as you would like. *He appealed to his countrymen not to lose heart.*
V inflects PRAGMATICS

28 If you **lose** your **heart** to someone, you fall in love with them; a literary expression.
V and N inflect, oft PHR *to* n

29 If your **heart is in** your **mouth**, you feel very excited, worried, or frightened. *My heart was in my mouth when I walked into her office.*
V and Ns inflect

30 If you **open** your **heart** or **pour out** your **heart** to someone, you tell them your most private thoughts and feelings. *She opened her heart to millions yesterday and told how she came close to suicide.*
V and N inflect, usu PHR *to* n

31 If you say that someone's **heart is in the right place** you mean that they are kind, considerate, and generous, although you may disapprove of other aspects of their character. *He is a bit of a wide boy but his heart is in the right place.*
heart and V inflect

32 If you have **set** your **heart on** something, you want it very much or want to do it very much. *He had always set his heart on a career in the fine arts.*
V and N inflect, PHR n/-ing

33 If you **wear** your **heart on** your **sleeve**, you openly show your feelings or emotions rather than keeping them hidden.
V and N inflect

34 If you put your **heart and soul** into something, you do it with a great deal of enthusiasm, dedication, and pleasure. *He will always be successful when he puts his mind to something, because he puts his heart and soul into it.*
PRAGMATICS

35 If you **take heart** from something, you are made to feel encouraged and optimistic by it.
V inflects, oft PHR *from* n

36 If you **take** something **to heart**, for example someone's behaviour, you are deeply affected and upset by it. *If someone says something critical I take it to heart.*
V inflects

heartache /hɑːʳteɪk/ **heartaches;** also spelled **heart-ache**. **Heartache** is very great sadness and emotional suffering; used mainly in journalism. *...after suffering the heartache of her divorce from her first husband. ...all the joys and heartaches of parenthood.*
◆◇◇◇◇ N-VAR

heart attack, heart attacks ◆◆◇◇◇

1 If someone has a **heart attack**, their heart begins to beat very irregularly or stops completely. *He died of a heart attack brought on by overwork.*
N-COUNT

2 If you say that someone will have **a heart attack** about something, you are emphasizing that they will be very shocked or angry; an informal use. *She'll have a heart attack if I tell her.*
N-SING: *a* N PRAGMATICS

heartbeat /hɑːʳtbiːt/ **heartbeats** ◆◇◇◇◇

1 Your **heartbeat** is the regular movement of your heart as it pumps blood around your body. *Your baby's heartbeat will be monitored continuously.*
N-SING: oft poss N

2 A **heartbeat** is one of the movements of your heart. *Smoking could lead to irregular heartbeats.*
N-COUNT

heartbreak /hɑːʳtbreɪk/ **heartbreaks. Heartbreak** is very great sadness and emotional suffering, especially after the end of a love affair or close relationship. *...suffering and heartbreak for*
◆◇◇◇◇ N-VAR

those close to the victims... Recent events had obviously been a heartbreak for him.

heartbreaking /hɑːʳtbreɪkɪŋ/. Something that is **heartbreaking** makes you feel extremely sad and upset. *This year we won't even be able to buy presents for our grandchildren. It's heartbreaking.* ADJ-GRADED

heartbroken /hɑːʳtbroukən/. Someone who is **heartbroken** is very sad and emotionally upset. *Was your daddy heartbroken when they got a divorce?* ADJ-GRADED =broken-hearted

heartburn /hɑːʳtbɜːʳn/. **Heartburn** is a painful burning sensation in your chest, caused by indigestion. N-UNCOUNT

-hearted /-hɑːʳtɪd/. **-hearted** combines with adjectives such as 'kind' or 'cold' to form adjectives which indicate that someone has a particular character or personality or is in a particular mood. *They are now realising just how much they owe to kind-hearted strangers... That Harriet is a cold-hearted bitch... I tried to be light-hearted.* COMB in ADJ-GRADED

hearten /hɑːʳtᵊn/ **heartens, heartening, heartened.** ◆◇◇◇◇ If someone **is heartened** by something, it encourages them and makes them cheerful. *He will have been heartened by the telephone opinion poll published yesterday... The news heartened everybody.* VERB =cheer *be* V-ed V n
♦ **heartened** *I feel heartened by her progress... The British government is heartened that Germany shares its enthusiasm.* ADJ-GRADED: v-link ADJ, oft ADJ *by* n, ADJ that
♦ **heartening** *It has been very heartening to see new writing emerging... This is heartening news.* ADJ-GRADED: oft *it* v-link ADJ to-inf

heart failure. ◆◇◇◇◇ **Heart failure** is a serious medical condition in which someone's heart does not work as well as it should, sometimes stopping completely so that they die. *He remained in a critical condition after suffering heart failure.* N-UNCOUNT

heartfelt /hɑːʳtfelt/. ◆◇◇◇◇ **Heartfelt** is used to describe a deep or sincere feeling or wish, or the expression of this feeling or wish. *My heartfelt sympathy goes out to all the relatives.* ADJ-GRADED: usu ADJ n =deep

hearth /hɑːʳθ/ **hearths** ◆◇◇◇◇
1 The **hearth** is the floor of a fireplace, which sometimes extends into the room. *It was winter and there was a huge fire roaring in the hearth.* N-COUNT
2 A person's home and family life can be referred to as their **hearth and home**; a literary expression. *...a man who leaves his hearth and home to labour as a miner in the inhospitable north.* PHRASE

hearth rug, hearth rugs; also spelled **hearthrug**. A **hearth rug** is a rug which is put in front of a fireplace. N-COUNT

heartland /hɑːʳtlænd/ **heartlands** ◆◇◇◇◇
1 Journalists use **heartland** or **heartlands** to refer to the area or region where a particular set of activities or beliefs is most significant. *...his six-day bus tour around the industrial heartland of America... Worst-hit areas were Tory heartlands in London and the South-East. ...the heartlands of the service industries.* N-COUNT: with supp, oft adj N, N *of* n =stronghold
2 In written English, the most central area of a country or continent can be referred to as its **heartland** or **heartlands**. *We then headed west towards the heartland of Tibet... For many, the essence of French living is to be found in the rural heartlands.* N-COUNT: with supp

heartless /hɑːʳtləs/. If you describe someone as **heartless**, you mean that they are cruel and unkind, and have no sympathy for anyone or anything. *I couldn't believe they were so heartless... It was a heartless thing to do.* ADJ-GRADED =cruel ≠kind

heart-rending; also spelled **heartrending**. You use **heart-rending** to describe something that causes you to feel great sadness and pity. *...heart-rending pictures of refugees... I heard the most heartrending screams and moans.* ADJ-GRADED: usu ADJ n =heartbreaking

heartstrings /hɑːʳtstrɪŋz/. If you say that someone or something tugs at your **heartstrings**, you mean that they cause you to feel strong emotions, usually sadness or pity. *She knows exactly how to tug at readers' heartstrings.* N-PLURAL: oft with poss

heart-throb, heart-throbs. If you describe a man as a **heart-throb**, you mean that he is physically very attractive, so that a lot of women fall in love with him. N-COUNT

heart-to-heart, heart-to-hearts. A **heart-to-heart** is an intimate conversation between two people, especially close friends, in which feelings and personal problems are talked about. *I've had a heart-to-heart with him... Before the wedding, I had a heart-to-heart talk with my mother.* N-COUNT: oft N n

heart-warming. Something that is **heart-warming** causes you to feel happy, usually because something nice has happened to people. *...the heart-warming story of enemies who discover a shared humanity.* ADJ-GRADED =cheering

hearty /hɑːʳti/ **heartier, heartiest** ◆◇◇◇◇
1 **Hearty** people or actions are loud, cheerful, and energetic. *Wade was a hearty, bluff, athletic sort of guy... He gave a hearty laugh.* ADJ-GRADED =jovial
♦ **heartily** *He laughed heartily.* ADV-GRADED: ADV after v
2 **Hearty** feelings or opinions are strongly felt or strongly held. *With the last sentiment, Arnold was in hearty agreement.* ADJ-GRADED: usu ADJ n
♦ **heartily** *I heartily agree with her favourable comments on Germany and France. ...most Afghans are heartily sick of war.* ADV: ADV with v, ADV adj
3 A **hearty** meal is large and very satisfying. *The men ate a hearty breakfast. ...a hearty soup delicately flavoured with nutmeg.* ADJ-GRADED: usu ADJ n
♦ **heartily** *He ate heartily but would drink only beer.* ADV-GRADED: ADV after v

heat /hiːt/ **heats, heating, heated** ◆◆◆◆◇
1 When you **heat** something, you raise its temperature, for example by using a flame or a special piece of equipment. *Meanwhile, heat the tomatoes and oil in a pan. ...a gas that absorbs the sun's energy and heats the air above it. ...heated swimming pools.* VERB V n V-ed
2 **Heat** is warmth or the quality of being hot. *The seas store heat and release it gradually during cold periods... Its leaves drooped a little in the fierce heat of the sun.* N-UNCOUNT
3 The **heat** is very hot weather. *As an asthmatic, he cannot cope with the heat and humidity... This heat is killing me.* N-UNCOUNT: also *the* N
• **The heat of the day** is the hottest part of the day, especially when this is very hot. *The town square's empty in the heat of the day.* PHRASE
4 The **heat** of something is the temperature of something that is warm or that is being heated. *Warm the milk to blood heat... Adjust the heat of the barbecue by opening and closing the air vents.* N-UNCOUNT: with supp
5 You use **heat** to refer to a source of heat, for example a cooking ring or the heating system of a house. *Immediately remove the pan from the heat... Some apartment buildings don't have their heat turned on till the end of this week.* N-SING
6 You use **heat** to refer to a state of strong emotion, especially of anger or excitement. *It was all done in the heat of the moment and I have certainly learned by my mistake... 'Look here,' I said, without heat, 'all I did was to walk down a street and sit down.'* N-UNCOUNT: oft N *of* n
7 **The heat of** a particular activity is the point when there is the greatest activity or excitement. *Last week, in the heat of the election campaign, the Prime Minister left for America.* N-SING: *the* N *of* n
8 A **heat** is one of a series of races or competitions. The winners of a heat take part in another race or competition, against the winners of other heats. *...the heats of the men's 100m breaststroke.* • See also **dead heat**. N-COUNT
9 In British English, when a female animal is **on heat**, she is in a state where she is ready for mating. The American term is **in heat**. PHRASE: v-link PHR

heat up PHRASAL VERB
1 When you **heat** something **up**, especially food which has already been cooked and allowed to go cold, you make it hot. *Freda heated up a pie for me but I couldn't face it.* =warm up V P n (not pron) Also V n P
2 When a situation **heats up**, things start to happen much more quickly and with increased interest and excitement among the people involved. *Then in the last couple years, the movement for democracy began to heat up.* =hot up ≠cool off V P
3 When something **heats up**, it gradually becomes hotter. *In the summer when her mobile home heats up like an oven, the car is Annemarie's refuge.* =cool down V P

heated /hiːtɪd/ ◆◆◇◇◇

1 A **heated** discussion or quarrel is one where the people involved are angry and excited. *It was a very heated argument and they were shouting at each other... Our discussions were rather heated.* ADJ-GRADED ≠calm

2 If someone gets **heated about** something, they get angry and excited about it. *You will understand that people get a bit heated about issues such as these... The baron became increasingly heated over the hypocrisy of it all.* ♦ **heatedly** *The crowd continued to argue heatedly about the best way to tackle the problem.* ADJ-GRADED: v-link ADJ about/over n =worked up; ADV-GRADED: ADV with v

heater /hiːtəʳ/ **heaters.** A **heater** is a piece of equipment or a machine which is used to raise the temperature of something, especially of the air inside a room or a car. *There's an electric heater in the bedroom.* ◆◇◇◇◇ N-COUNT

heath /hiːθ/ **heaths.** A **heath** is an area of open land covered with rough grass or heather and with very few trees or bushes; used mainly in British English. ◆◇◇◇◇ N-COUNT =moor

heathen /hiːðən/ **heathens**

1 Some people refer to people who have no religion, or who have a religion that is not Christianity, Judaism, or Islam, as **heathens**; an old-fashioned use which often shows disapproval. *She called us all heathens and hypocrites.* N-COUNT PRAGMATICS =pagan

2 Some people use **heathen** to describe people who they consider to be heathens and things belonging or relating to these people and their way of life; an old-fashioned use which often shows disapproval. *He preached the Gospel to the heathen locals from this spot. ...a heathen temple.* ► **The heathen** are heathen people. *They first set out to convert the heathen.* ADJ: usu ADJ n PRAGMATICS =pagan; N-PLURAL: the N

heather /heðəʳ/. **Heather** is a low, spreading plant with small purple, pink, or white flowers that grows wild on hills or moorland. ◆◇◇◇◇ N-UNCOUNT

heating /hiːtɪŋ/ ◆◆◇◇◇

1 **Heating** is the process of heating a building or room, considered especially from the point of view of how much this costs. *You can still find cottages for £150 a week, including heating. ...heating bills.* N-UNCOUNT

2 **Heating** is the system and equipment that is used to heat a building. *There is no heating in the shed, so the dogs would be bitterly cold at night... I wish I knew how to turn on the heating.* • See also **central heating.** N-UNCOUNT

heat stroke; also spelled **heatstroke**. **Heat stroke** is the same as **sunstroke**. N-UNCOUNT

heatwave /hiːtweɪv/ **heatwaves;** also spelled **heat wave** in American English. A **heatwave** is a period of time during which the weather is much hotter than usual. N-COUNT

heave /hiːv/. The forms **heaves, heaving, heaved** are used for meanings 1 to 4, and for the phrasal verb. The forms **heaves, heaving, hove** are used for meaning 5. ◆◇◇◇◇

1 If you **heave** something heavy or difficult to move somewhere, you push, pull, or lift it using a lot of effort. *It took five strong men to heave it up a ramp and lower it into place... He heaved Barney to his feet... He heaved himself up off his stool.* ► Also a noun. *It took only one heave to hurl him into the river.* VERB; V n prep/adv; N-COUNT

2 If something **heaves**, it moves up and down with large regular movements. *His chest heaved, and he took a deep breath. ...the grey, heaving seas.* VERB; V; V-ing

3 If you **heave**, or if your stomach **heaves**, you vomit or feel sick. *He gasped and heaved and vomited again... My stomach heaved and I felt sick.* VERB; V

4 If you **heave** a sigh, you give a big sigh. *Mr Collier heaved a sigh and got to his feet.* VERB; V n

5 When something **heaves into view** or **heaves into sight**, it appears; used in written English. *The train that now hove into view was clearly of a much older vintage.* PHRASE: V inflects

6 • to **heave a sigh of relief**: see **sigh**.

heave to. When a boat or ship **heaves to**, it stops moving; a technical term in sailing. *Captain Cornish repeated his order to heave to.* PHRASAL VERB; V P

heaven /hevən/ **heavens** ◆◆◆◇◇

1 In some religions, **heaven** is said to be the place where God lives, where good people go when they die, and where everyone is always happy. It is usually imagined as being high up in the sky. *I believed that when I died I would go to heaven and see God.* N-PROPER =paradise

2 You can use **heaven** to refer to a place or situation that you like very much; an informal use. *We went touring in Wales and Ireland. It was heaven... I was in cinematic heaven.* N-UNCOUNT =paradise

3 **The heavens** are the sky; an old-fashioned use. *He walked out into the middle of the road, looking up at the heavens. ...a detailed map of the heavens.* N-PLURAL: the N =sky, skies

4 See also **seventh heaven**.

5 You say **'Heaven forbid!'** to emphasize that you very much hope that something will not happen; used mainly in spoken British English. *Heaven forbid that he should leave because of me!* PHRASES; PHR that PRAGMATICS

6 You say **'Good heavens!'** to express surprise or to emphasize that you agree or disagree with someone; an informal use. In British English, you can also just say **'Heavens!'**. *Good Heavens! That explains a lot!... 'I thought you were bringing it.'—'Heavens, no.'* EXCLAM PRAGMATICS =good grief

7 You say **'Heaven help** someone' when you fear that something bad is going to happen to them, often because you disapprove of what they are doing or the way they are behaving; used in informal spoken British English. *If this makes sense to our leaders, then heaven help us all... Heaven help the man she marries.* PHR n PRAGMATICS

8 You can say **'Heaven knows'** to emphasize that you do not know something, or that you find something very surprising; used mainly in informal British English. *Heaven knows what they put in it.* PHR wh PRAGMATICS

9 You can say **'Heaven knows'** to emphasize something that you feel or believe very strongly; used mainly in informal British English. *Heaven knows they have enough money... This gained me some thinking time, and heaven knows I needed it.* PHR with cl PRAGMATICS

10 If you **move heaven and earth** to do something, you try as hard as you can to do it. *They would move heaven and earth to stop me if they could.* V inflects, usu PHR to-inf

11 You can use **in heaven's name** in questions beginning with 'what', 'when', 'who', 'why', 'when', and 'how' to add emphasis in a way that shows that you are very angry or surprised; used mainly in informal spoken British English. *Where in heaven's name was she?* quest PHR PRAGMATICS =on earth

12 If **the heavens open**, it suddenly starts raining very heavily; a literary use. *The match had just begun when the heavens opened and play was suspended.* V inflects

13 • **for heaven's sake**: see **sake**. • **thank heaven**: see **thank**.

heavenly /hevənli/ ◆◇◇◇◇

1 **Heavenly** things are things that are connected with the religious idea of heaven. *...heavenly beings whose function it is to serve God.* ADJ: usu ADJ n

2 Something that is **heavenly** is very pleasant and enjoyable; an informal use. *The idea of spending two weeks with him may seem heavenly.* ADJ-GRADED =blissful

heavenly body, heavenly bodies. A **heavenly body** is a planet, star, moon, or other natural object in space. N-COUNT

heaven-sent; also spelled **heaven sent**. You use **heaven-sent** to describe something such as an opportunity which is unexpected, but which is very welcome because it occurs at just the right time. *It will be a heaven-sent opportunity to prove himself.* ADJ: usu ADJ n

heavenward /hevənwəʳd/. The form **heavenwards** is also used. **Heavenward** means towards the sky or to heaven; used in written English. *He rolled his eyes heavenward in disgust.* ADV: ADV after v =upward

heavily /hevɪli/. If someone says something **heavily**, they say it in a slow way which shows a feeling such as sadness, tiredness, or annoyance. *'I didn't even think about her,' he said heavily.* • See also **heavy**. ADV: ADV after v ≠lightly

heavy /hevi/ **heavier, heaviest; heavies** ◆◆◆◆◇

1 Something that is **heavy** weighs a lot. *These scissors are awfully heavy... Gosh, that was a heavy bag!... The mud stuck to her boots, making her feet heavy and her legs tired.* ♦ **heaviness** *...a sensation of warmth and heaviness in the muscles.* ADJ-GRADED ≠light N-UNCOUNT

2 You use **heavy** to ask or talk about how much someone or something weighs. *How heavy are you?... Protons are nearly 2000 times as heavy as electrons.* ADJ-GRADED: how ADJ, as ADJ as, ADJ-compar than

3 **Heavy** means great in amount, degree, or intensity. *Heavy fighting has been going on... The State fails to recognize the heavy responsibility that parents take on... He worried about her heavy drinking. ...lengthy jail sentences and heavy fines... The traffic along Fitzjohn's Avenue was heavy.* ♦ **heavily** *It has been raining heavily all day. ...groups of riot police and heavily armed members of a special anti-robbery squad.* ♦ **heaviness** *...the heaviness of the blood loss.* ADJ-GRADED: usu ADJ n ADV-GRADED: ADV after v, ADV -ed/adj N-UNCOUNT

4 Someone or something that is **heavy** is solid or thick in appearance or structure, or is made of a thick material. *We talk in her Belgrade flat, full of heavy old brown furniture... He was short and heavy... Put the sugar and water in a heavy pan and heat slowly. ...a heavy cream silk blouse.* ♦ **heavily** *He was a big man of about forty, wide-shouldered and heavily built.* ADJ-GRADED ≠light ADV-GRADED: ADV -ed

5 A **heavy** substance is thick in texture. *It is advisable to mix coarse grit into heavy soil to improve drainage. ...11 million gallons of heavy crude oil.* ADJ-GRADED: usu ADJ n ≠light

6 A **heavy** meal is large in amount and often difficult to digest. *He had been feeling drowsy, the effect of an unusually heavy meal.* ADJ-GRADED =filling ≠light

7 Something that is **heavy with** things is full of them or loaded with them; a literary use. *The air is heavy with moisture... She brought in a tray heavy with elegant sandwiches, scones and cakes.* ADJ-GRADED: v-link ADJ with n =laden

8 If a person's breathing is **heavy**, it is very loud and deep. *Her breathing became slow and heavy.* ♦ **heavily** *She sank back on the pillow and closed her eyes, breathing heavily as if asleep.* ADJ-GRADED ≠light, shallow ADV-GRADED: ADV after v

9 A **heavy** movement or action is done with a lot of force or pressure. *...a heavy blow on the back of the skull... The plane made a heavy landing.* ♦ **heavily** *I sat down heavily on the ground beside the road... A man stumbled heavily against the side of the car.* ADJ-GRADED: ADJ n ≠gentle ADV-GRADED: ADV after v ≠gently

10 A **heavy** machine or piece of military equipment is very large and very powerful. *...government militia backed by tanks and heavy artillery. ...armoured personnel carriers and other heavy vehicles.* ADJ: ADJ n

11 If you describe a period of time or a schedule as **heavy**, you mean it involves a lot of work. *It's been a heavy day and I'm tired... Hopefully, Max would be able to spend a few days with them, depending on his heavy schedule.* ADJ-GRADED: usu ADJ n =busy

12 **Heavy** work requires a lot of strength or energy. *These days, the business is thriving and Philippa employs two full-timers for the heavy work.* ADJ-GRADED: usu ADJ n

13 If someone or something is **heavy on** something, they use a lot of it, which is sometimes a bad thing. *Tanks are heavy on fuel, destructive to roads and difficult to park. ...Linda, a platinum blonde, heavy on the lipstick. ...salads heavy on carrots.* ADJ-GRADED: v-link ADJ on n PRAGMATICS

14 Air or weather that is **heavy** is unpleasantly still, hot, and damp. *The outside air was heavy and moist and sultry.* ADJ-GRADED =oppressive ≠cool, fresh

15 If you describe a person's face as **heavy**, you mean that it looks sad, tired, or unfriendly; a literary use. *Many of them were policemen, with their heavy faces and cropped hair.* ADJ-GRADED

16 If your heart is **heavy**, you are sad about something; a literary use. *Mr Maddison handed over his resignation letter with a heavy heart.* ADJ-GRADED ≠light

17 A situation that is **heavy** is serious and difficult to cope with; an informal use. *I don't want any more of that heavy stuff.* ADJ-GRADED =serious

18 A **heavy** is a large strong man who is employed to protect a person or place, often by using violence; an informal use. *They had employed heavies to evict shop squatters from neighbouring sites.* N-COUNT

19 ● to make **heavy weather of** something: see **weather.** ● **a heavy hand**: see **hand.**

heavy-duty. A **heavy-duty** piece of equipment is very strong and can be used a lot. *...a heavy duty polythene bag... Cut the lobster shells into small pieces with heavy-duty scissors.* ◆◇◇◇◇ ADJ: usu ADJ n

heavy-handed ◆◇◇◇◇

1 If you say that someone's behaviour is **heavy-handed**, you mean that they are unnecessarily forceful, rough, and thoughtless. *...heavy-handed police tactics... The demonstration had been dealt with in a violent and heavy handed way... You can't be heavy handed. You have to make people aware that you understand their concerns.* ADJ-GRADED ≠gentle

2 If someone is **heavy handed** with something, they use too much of it or use it in a clumsy way. *It all depends on how heavy-handed you are with the paprika... In fact she tends to be a little heavy-handed when she wears make-up.* ADJ-GRADED: oft ADJ with n

heavy industry, heavy industries. Heavy industry is industry in which large machines are used to produce raw materials or to make large objects. *...the policy of redirecting investment to heavy industries like steel and energy.* ◆◇◇◇◇ N-VAR ≠light industry

heavy metal heavy metals ◆◇◇◇◇

1 **Heavy metal** is a type of very loud rock music with a fast beat. People who play and listen to heavy metal music usually have long hair and wear black leather or denim clothes. *...a German heavy metal band named The Scorpions.* N-UNCOUNT: oft N n

2 A **heavy metal** is a metallic element with a high density. Many heavy metals are poisonous; a technical use in science. *...the toxic heavy metal, cadmium.* N-COUNT

heavy-set. Someone who is **heavy-set** has a large solid body. ADJ =thick-set

heavyweight /heviweɪt/ **heavyweights** ◆◆◇◇◇

1 A **heavyweight** is a boxer weighing more than 175 pounds and therefore in the heaviest class. *Lewis is now among the top three or four heavyweights in the world.* N-COUNT

2 If you refer to a person or organization as a **heavyweight**, you mean that they have a lot of influence, experience, and importance in a particular field, subject, or activity. *He was a political heavyweight. ...jazz heavyweights.* N-COUNT: oft supp N

Hebrew /hiːbruː/ **Hebrews** ◆◇◇◇◇

1 **Hebrew** is a language that was spoken by Jews in former times. A modern form of Hebrew is spoken now in Israel. *He is a fluent speaker of Hebrew.* N-UNCOUNT

2 A **Hebrew** was a person in former times who was Jewish and lived in Israel. *...the exodus of the Hebrews from Egypt.* N-COUNT

3 **Hebrew** means belonging to or relating to the Hebrew language or people. *...the respected Hebrew newspaper Haarez... He sits puzzling over ancient Hebrew texts.* ADJ

heck /hek/ ◆◇◇◇◇

1 You say **'heck!'** to express slight irritation or surprise; an informal use. *Heck, if you don't like it, don't vote for him... Oh, heck. What can I write about?* EXCLAM PRAGMATICS

2 People use **a heck of** to emphasize how big something is or how much of it there is; an informal expression. *They're spending a heck of a lot of money... The truth is, I'm in one heck of a mess.* PHRASES PHR n PRAGMATICS

3 You use **the heck** in expressions such as **'what the heck'** and **'how the heck'** in order to emphasize a question, especially when you are puzzled or annoyed. Used in informal English. *What the heck's that?... The question was, where the heck was he?* quest PHR PRAGMATICS

4 You say **'what the heck'** to indicate your acceptance of a situation that is unsatisfactory in some way but cannot be avoided or changed; an informal expression. *What the heck, I thought, I'll give it a whirl.* PHR with cl PRAGMATICS

heckle /hekəl/ **heckles, heckling, heckled.** If people in an audience **heckle** public speakers or performers, they interrupt them, for example by making rude remarks. *They heckled him and interrupted his address with angry questions... He* ◆◇◇◇◇ VERB =barrack V n V

was insulted and heckled mercilessly... A small group of youths stayed behind to heckle and shout abuse. ► Also a noun. *The offending comment was in fact a heckle from an audience member.* N-COUNT
♦ **heckling** *The ceremony was disrupted by unprecedented heckling and slogan-chanting.* N-UNCOUNT =barracking
♦ **heckler** /heklə^r/ **hecklers** *As he began his speech, a heckler called out asking for his opinion on gun control.* N-COUNT

hectare /hekteə^r/ **hectares.** A **hectare** is a measurement of an area of land which is equal to 10,000 square metres, or 2.471 acres. ◆◇◇◇◇ N-COUNT: usu num N

hectic /hektɪk/. A **hectic** situation is one that is very busy and involves a lot of rushed activity. *Despite his hectic work schedule, Benny has rarely suffered poor health... The two days we spent there were enjoyable but hectic.* ◆◇◇◇◇ ADJ-GRADED =busy

hector /hektə^r/ **hectors, hectoring, hectored.** If someone **hectors** you, they try to make you do something by bothering you and talking to you aggressively; used showing disapproval. *I suppose you'll hector me until I phone him.* VERB PRAGMATICS =bully V n
♦ **hectoring** *In a loud, hectoring tone, Alan told us that he wasn't going to waste time discussing nonsense.* ADJ-GRADED: usu ADJ n =bullying

he'd /hɪd, hiːd/
1 **He'd** is the usual spoken form of 'he had', especially when 'had' is an auxiliary verb. *Steve had told her that he'd been in an accident on Wednesday night... He'd never learnt to read.*
2 **He'd** is a spoken form of 'he would'. *He'd come into the clubhouse every day, sit down, and read the paper for a while.*

hedge /hedʒ/ **hedges, hedging, hedged** ◆◆◇◇◇
1 A **hedge** is a row of bushes or small trees, usually along the edge of a garden, field, or road. N-COUNT
2 If you **hedge** against something unpleasant or unwanted that might affect you, especially losing money, you do something which will protect you from it. *You can hedge against redundancy or illness with insurance... Today's clever financial instruments make it possible for firms to hedge their risks.* VERB V against n V n
3 Something that is a **hedge against** something unpleasant will protect you from its effects. *Gold is traditionally a hedge against inflation.* N-COUNT: N against n
4 If you **hedge**, you avoid answering a question or committing yourself to a particular action or decision. *They hedged in answering various questions about the operation... 'I can't give you an answer now,' he hedged.* VERB V V with quote
5 If you **hedge** your **bets**, you reduce the risk of losing a lot by supporting more than one person or thing in a situation where they are opposed to each other. *Hawker Siddeley tried to hedge its bets by diversifying into other fields... Forecasters are hedging their bets about the outcome of this Saturday's Louisiana governor's race.* PHRASE: V inflects

hedge about or **hedge around.** If you say that something such as an offer **is hedged about** or **is hedged around with** rules or conditions, you mean that there are so many rules or conditions that it seems as if the person making the offer is deliberately trying to make it difficult for other people to accept. *The offer was hedged around with conditions... Many reduced fares are hedged around with restrictions.* PHRASAL VERB PASSIVE be V-ed P with n

hedgehog /hedʒhɒg, AM -hɔːg/ **hedgehogs.** A **hedgehog** is a small brown animal with sharp spikes covering its back. ◆◇◇◇◇ N-COUNT

hedgerow /hedʒroʊ/ **hedgerows.** A **hedgerow** is a row of bushes, trees, and plants, usually growing along a bank bordering a country lane or between fields. *He crouched behind a low hedgerow... More than a hundred thousand miles of hedgerow have been lost since 1945.* ◆◇◇◇◇ N-VAR

hedonism /hiːd^{ə}nɪzəm/. **Hedonism** is the belief that gaining pleasure is the most important thing in life; a formal word. N-UNCOUNT

hedonist /hiːdənɪst/ **hedonists.** A **hedonist** is someone who believes that having pleasure is the most important thing in life; a formal word. N-COUNT

hedonistic /hiːdənɪstɪk/. **Hedonistic** means relating to hedonism; a formal word. *...the hedonistic pleasures of the South... The cookery course was serious and hedonistic at the same time.* ADJ-GRADED

heed /hiːd/ **heeds, heeding, heeded** ◆◇◇◇◇
1 If you **heed** someone's advice or warning, you pay attention to it and do what they suggest; a formal use. *But few at the conference in London last week heeded his warning... Chris would have been well advised to heed the old saying 'Never bite the hand that feeds you.'* VERB =take note of V n
2 If you **take heed of** what someone says or if you **pay heed to** them, you pay attention to them and consider carefully what they say; used in formal English. *He pays too much heed these days to my nephew Tom, and Tom is no great thinker... But what if the government takes no heed?* PHRASE: V inflects, oft PHR *to/of* n =pay attention to

heedless /hiːdləs/. If you are **heedless** of someone or something, you do not take any notice of them; a formal word. *Heedless of time or any other consideration, they began to search the underwater cave... She was rummaging through the letters, scattering them about the table in her heedless haste.* ADJ: oft ADJ of n

heel /hiːl/ **heels, heeling, heeled** ◆◆◇◇◇
1 Your **heel** is the back part of your foot, just below your ankle. N-COUNT
2 The **heel** of a shoe is the raised part on the bottom at the back. *He kicked it shut with the heel of his boot. ...the shoes with the high heels.* N-COUNT
3 **Heels** are women's shoes that are raised very high at the back. *...two well-dressed ladies in high heels... Today, the old adage that you shouldn't wear heels with trousers doesn't apply.* N-PLURAL
4 The **heel** of a sock or stocking is the part that covers your heel. N-COUNT
5 The **heel of** your hand is the rounded pad at the bottom of your palm. *He shoved the heel of his hand against the side of my face.* N-COUNT: N of n
6 See also **Achilles heel.**
7 If a person or an animal is **at** your **heels**, they are following close behind you. *She strode off down the restaurant with Cavendish following close at her heels.* PHRASES
8 If you **bring** someone **to heel**, you force them to obey you. *It's still not clear how the president will use his power to bring the republics to heel.* V inflects
9 If you **click** your **heels**, you make a sharp sound with the heels of your shoes, especially by knocking them together, often as part of a military salute. *Nonetheless, he remained a courtly European who still clicked his heels when he met a lady.* V inflects
10 If you are **cooling** your **heels**, someone is deliberately keeping you waiting, so that you get bored or impatient; an informal expression. *Cohen didn't mention that he had Ted Forstmann cooling his heels in a back room.* V inflects
11 If you **dig** your **heels in** or **dig in** your **heels**, you refuse to do something such as change your opinions or plans, especially when someone is trying very hard to make you do so. *It was really the British who, by digging their heels in, prevented any last-minute deal.* V inflects
12 If you say that one event follows **hard on the heels of** another or **hot on the heels of** another, you mean that one happens very quickly or immediately after another. *Unfortunately, bad news has come hard on the heels of good... The visit follows hot on the heels of their season at the Edinburgh International Festival.* PHR after v, PHR n
13 If you say that someone is **hot on** your **heels**, you are emphasizing that they are chasing you and are not very far behind you. *They sped through the American southwest with the law hot on their heels.* usu v-link PHR
14 If you are **kicking** your **heels**, you are having to wait around with nothing to do, so that you get bored or impatient; used in informal British English. *The authorities wouldn't grant us permission to fly all the way down to San Francisco, so I had to kick my heels at Tunis Airport.* V inflects
15 If you **turn on** your **heel** or **spin on** your **heel**, you suddenly turn round, especially because you V inflects

are angry or surprised. *He simply turned on his heel and walked away.*

16 If you **take to** your **heels**, you run away; a literary expression. *He stood, for a moment, staring defiantly back at her, then took to his heels.* V inflects =flee

17 • **head over heels**: see **head**. • to **drag** your **heels**: see **drag**.

heel over. When something **heels over**, it leans over very far as if it is about to fall over. *The little sailing-boat moved briskly along, heeling over under a nice breeze.* PHRASAL VERB V P

hefty /hefti/ **heftier, heftiest** ◆◇◇◇◇

1 **Hefty** means large in size, weight, or amount; an informal use. *Though quite a hefty woman, she would come to meetings wearing a tight shirt, shorts and high socks... If he is found guilty he faces a hefty fine.* ADJ-GRADED: usu ADJ n

2 A **hefty** movement is forceful and vigorous; an informal use. *Lambert leapt out, pulled the wheel straight and gave Luckwell a hefty shove to send him on his way.* ADJ-GRADED: usu ADJ n

hegemony /hɪgeməni, AM -dʒem-/. **Hegemony** is the domination or control by one country, organization, or social group over a group of others, especially if it is a member of that group; a formal word. ◆◇◇◇◇ N-UNCOUNT

heifer /hefəʳ/ **heifers.** A **heifer** is a young cow that has not yet had a calf. N-COUNT

height /haɪt/ **heights** ◆◆◆◇◇

1 The **height** of a person or thing is their size or length from the bottom to the top. *Her weight is about normal for her height... I am 5'6" in height... The wave here has a length of 250 feet and a height of 10 feet... He was a man of medium height. ...a garden containing all sorts of trees and shrubs of varying heights and shades.* N-VAR: oft with poss, amount *in* N, N *of* amount

2 **Height** is the quality of being tall. *She admits that her height is intimidating for some men.* N-UNCOUNT

3 A particular **height** is the distance that something is above the ground or above something else mentioned. *At the speed and height at which he was moving, he was never more than half a second from disaster. ...a test in which a 6.3 kilogram weight was dropped on it from a height of 1 metre... The corridors there were painted chocolate-brown to shoulder height... The chains were at different heights on the wall.* N-VAR

4 A **height** is a high position or place above the ground. *From a height, it looks like a desert... I'm not afraid of heights. ...the Golan Heights.* N-COUNT

5 When an activity, situation, or organization is **at** its **height**, it is at its most successful, powerful, or intense. *During the early sixth century emigration from Britain to Brittany was at its height... At its height Bletchley Park employed 12,000 people... He was struck down at the height of his career... At the height of the summer season there can be up to 42,000 people in Benidorm.* N-SING: *at* N with poss =peak

6 If you say that something is **the height of** a particular quality, you are emphasizing that it has that quality to the greatest degree possible. *The hip-hugging black and white polka-dot dress was the height of fashion... I think it's the height of bad manners to be dressed badly... This is the height of hooliganism.* N-SING: *the* N *of* n PRAGMATICS

7 If something reaches great **heights**, it becomes very extreme or intense. *...the mid-1980s, when prices rose to absurd heights... Recently the speculation has reached new heights... One wondered what heights of ecstasy the winner reached.* N-PLURAL: with supp, oft adj N, N *of* n

heighten /haɪtᵊn/ **heightens, heightening, heightened.** If something **heightens** a feeling or if the feeling **heightens**, the feeling increases in degree or intensity. *The move has heightened tension in the state... These latest murders have heightened fears of further attacks... Cross's interest heightened. ...a heightened awareness of the dangers that they now face.* ◆◆◇◇◇ V-ERG =intensify V n V V-ed

heinous /heɪnəs/. If you describe something such as a crime as **heinous**, you mean that it is extremely evil or horrible; a formal word. *Her life has been permanently blighted by his heinous crime... They are capable of the most heinous acts.* ADJ-GRADED: usu ADJ n =evil, monstrous

heir /eəʳ/ **heirs.** An **heir** is someone who has the right to inherit a person's money, property, or title when that person dies. *His heir, Lord Doune, cuts a bit of a dash in the city. ...the heir to the throne.* ◆◆◇◇◇ N-COUNT: oft with poss, oft N *to* n =successor

heir apparent, heirs apparent. When journalists refer to someone as the **heir apparent** to a particular job or position, they mean that that person is expected to take over the job or position when the person who currently holds it resigns. *...Mr Ozawa, the heir apparent to the leadership... He was seen as Mr Olsen's heir apparent.* N-COUNT: usu sing, oft *the* N *to* n, poss N

heiress /eərɪs/ **heiresses.** An **heiress** is a woman or girl who has the right to inherit property or a title, or who has inherited it, especially when this involves great wealth. *...the heiress to a jewellery empire. ...an American heiress.* N-COUNT: oft N *to* n

heirloom /eəʳluːm/ **heirlooms.** An **heirloom** is an ornament or other object that has belonged to a family for a very long time and that has been handed down from one generation to another. N-COUNT

heist /haɪst/ **heists.** A **heist** is a burglary or robbery, especially a very daring one. N-COUNT: oft n N

held /held/. **Held** is the past tense and past participle of **hold**.

helicopter /helɪkɒptəʳ/ **helicopters.** A **helicopter** is an aircraft that is capable of hovering or moving vertically and horizontally, by means of large overhead blades which rotate. ◆◆◆◇◇ N-COUNT =chopper

helicopter gunship, helicopter gunships. A **helicopter gunship** is a helicopter with large guns attached to it. N-COUNT

helipad /helipæd/ **helipads.** A **helipad** is a place where helicopters can land and take off. N-COUNT

heliport /helipɔːʳt/ **heliports.** A **heliport** is an airport for helicopters. N-COUNT

helium /hiːliəm/. **Helium** is a very light gas that is colourless and has no smell. ◆◇◇◇◇ N-UNCOUNT

helix /hiːlɪks/ **helixes.** A **helix** is a spiral shape or form; a technical term. *Coil the fibre into a helix.* N-COUNT

hell /hel/ **hells** ◆◆◆◇◇

1 In some religions, **hell** is the place where the Devil lives, and where wicked people are sent to be punished when they die. Hell is usually imagined as being under the ground and full of flames. N-PROPER; N-COUNT

2 If you say that a particular situation or place is **hell**, you are emphasizing that it is extremely unpleasant; an informal use. *...the hell of the Siberian labor camps... Bullies can make your life hell. ...the hells of grief and shame and lost love.* N-VAR PRAGMATICS =torture

3 **Hell** is a swear word used by some people when they are angry or excited, or when they want to emphasize what they are saying; an informal use which some people find offensive. *'Hell, no!' the doctor snapped.* EXCLAM PRAGMATICS

4 You can use **as hell** after an adjective or adverb to emphasize the adjective or adverb; an informal expression. *The men might be armed, but they sure as hell weren't trained... I am angry as hell.* PHRASES adj PHR

5 If you say that a place or a situation is **hell on earth** or a **hell on earth**, you are emphasizing that it is extremely unpleasant or that it causes great suffering. *Very longstanding couples have relationships that are worth celebrating, even if their years together have been hell on earth.* oft v-link PHR =living hell

6 If someone does something **for the hell of it**, or **just for the hell of it**, they do it for fun or for no particular reason; used in informal English. *I started shouting in German, just for the hell of it... It was stupid, just vandalism for the hell of it.* usu PHR with cl, PHR after v, n PHR =for fun, for kicks

7 If you say that you will do something **until hell freezes over**, you are emphasizing that you will do it for a very long time or for ever. *He says he'll sit there until hell freezes over before he'll pay them one cent.* PHR after v PRAGMATICS

8 You can use **from hell** after a noun when you are emphasizing that something or someone is extremely unpleasant or evil; an informal expression. *He's a child from hell... She is the bitch from hell. ...the holiday from hell.* n PHR

9 If you say that someone **gives** you **hell**, you are emphasizing that they shout at you very angrily because of something you have done wrong; an informal expression. *My father saw this in the newspaper and he gave me absolute hell.* V inflects

10 If you say that something **is giving** you **hell**, you are emphasizing that it is causing you a lot of trouble. If you say that a part of your body **is giving** you **hell**, you are emphasizing that it is very painful. Used in informal English. *My back's giving me hell, let me tell you!... The children give her hell, particularly the older boys.* V inflects PRAGMATICS

11 If you tell someone to **go to hell**, you are angrily telling them to go away and leave you alone; an informal expression which some people find offensive. *'Well, you can go to hell!' He swept out of the room.* PRAGMATICS =get lost

12 If you say that someone can **go to hell**, you are emphasizing angrily that you do not care about them and that they will not stop you doing what you want; an informal expression which some people find offensive. *Peter can go to hell. It's my money and I'll leave it to who I want... I'm going to do as I please and let 'em all go to hell.* PRAGMATICS =get lost

13 If you say that someone is going **hell for leather**, you are emphasizing that they are doing something or moving very quickly, and often recklessly; an informal expression. *The first horse often goes hell for leather, hits a few fences but gets away with it... They've been going hell for leather, trying to record as much as they can.* usu v PHR PRAGMATICS

14 Some people say **like hell** to emphasize that they strongly disagree with you or are strongly opposed to what you say; an informal expression. *'I'll go myself.'—'Like hell you will!'* usu PHR cl PRAGMATICS

15 Some people use **like hell** to emphasize how strong an action or quality is; an informal expression. *It hurts like hell... I missed her like hell.* PHR after v PRAGMATICS

16 If you describe a place or situation as a **living hell**, you are emphasizing that it is extremely unpleasant. *School is a living hell for some children.* v-link PHR PRAGMATICS

17 If you say that **all hell breaks loose**, you are emphasizing that a lot of arguing or fighting suddenly starts; an informal expression. *He had an affair, I found out and then all hell broke loose.* V inflects PRAGMATICS

18 If you talk about **a hell of a lot of** something, or **one hell of a lot of** something, you mean that there is a large amount of it: an informal use which some people find offensive. *The manager took a hell of a hell of a lot of money out of the club.* usu PHR *of* n/-ing

19 Some people use **a hell of** or **one hell of** to emphasize that something is very good, very bad, or very big. Used in informal English. *Whatever the outcome, it's going to be one hell of a fight.* PHR n PRAGMATICS =a helluva

20 If you tell someone to **get the hell out** of a place, you are telling them angrily or urgently to leave that place immediately; an informal expression which some people find offensive. *Get the hell out of my way... I got the hell out of Glasgow and I can honestly say I will never go back.* V inflects, oft PHR *of* n PRAGMATICS

21 Some people use **the hell out of** for emphasis after verbs such as 'scare', 'irritate', and 'beat'; an informal expression. *I patted the top of her head in the condescending way I knew irritated the hell out of her... Those cops beat the hell out of me.* v PHR n PRAGMATICS

22 If you say **there'll be hell to pay**, you are emphasizing that there will be serious trouble; an informal expression. *There would be hell to pay when Ferguson and Tony found out about it.* V inflects PRAGMATICS

23 If you say that one thing **plays hell** with another, you are emphasizing that the first thing has a bad effect on the second or causes great confusion; an informal expression. In British English, you can also say that one thing **plays merry hell** with another. *Lord Beaverbrook, to put it bluntly, played hell with the war policy of the R.A.F... Slugs play merry hell with emerging shoots.* V inflects, usu PHR *with* n PRAGMATICS

24 If you say that someone **raises hell**, you are emphasizing that they protest strongly and angrily about a situation in order to persuade other people to correct it or improve it; an informal expression. *She came in and raised hell. Her son's sports bag was missing... The only way to preserve democracy is to raise hell about its shortcomings.* V inflects PRAGMATICS

25 People sometimes use **the hell** for emphasis in questions, after words such as 'what', 'where', and 'why', often in order to express anger; an informal expression which some people find offensive. *Where the hell have you been?... Why the hell should I know about Dadinha?... What the hell's going on?* quest PHR PRAGMATICS =on earth

26 If you **go through hell**, or if someone **puts** you **through hell**, you have a very difficult or unpleasant time; used in informal English. *All of you seem to have gone through hell making this record... I put Brian through hell.* V inflects

27 If you say you **hope to hell** or **wish to hell** that something is true, you are emphasizing that you strongly hope or wish it is true; used in informal English. *I hope to hell you're right.* V inflects, PHR that PRAGMATICS

28 If you say that you will do something **come hell or high water**, you are emphasizing that you are determined to do it, in spite of the difficulties involved. *I've always managed to get into work come hell or high water and I will continue to do so.* usu PHR after v PRAGMATICS

29 You can say **'what the hell'** when you decide to do something in spite of the doubts that you have about it; an informal expression. *What the hell, I thought, at least it will give the lazy old man some exercise.* PRAGMATICS

30 If you say **'to hell with'** something, you are emphasizing that you do not care about something and that it will not stop you from doing what you want to do; an informal expression. *To hell with this, I'm getting out of here... To hell with grades and qualifications.* PHR n PRAGMATICS

he'll /hɪl, hiːl/. **He'll** is the usual spoken form of 'he will'. *By the time he's twenty he'll know everyone worth knowing in Washington.*

hell-bent; also spelled **hellbent.** If you are **hell-bent** on doing something, you are determined to do it, whatever the consequences might be. *He accused Ford of being hell-bent on achieving its cuts by whatever means. ...a side hell-bent on a place in the Premier League.* ADJ: usu v-link ADJ, usu ADJ *on* -ing/n

Hellenic /helenɪk, -liː-/. **Hellenic** is used to describe the people, language, and culture of Ancient Greece. ADJ: usu ADJ n

hellhole /helhoul/ **hellholes.** If you call a place a **hellhole**, you mean that it is extremely unpleasant, usually because it is dirty and uncomfortable. *...stuck in this hellhole of a jail.* N-COUNT

hellish /helɪʃ/

1 You describe something as **hellish** to emphasize that it is extremely unpleasant; an informal use. *The atmosphere in Washington is hellish... I'm sure you will remember from the hellish years of your boyhood.* ADJ-GRADED PRAGMATICS

2 You use **hellish** to emphasize an unpleasant quality or its great extent; an old-fashioned, informal use. *It's hellish cold up here in winter.* ADV: ADV adj

hello /heloʊ/ **hellos;** also spelled **hallo** or **hullo.** ◆◆◆◇◇

1 You say **'Hello'** to someone when you are greeting them or when you are meeting them for the first time in the course of a day. *Hello, Trish. I won't shake hands, because I'm filthy... Do you want to pop your head in and say hallo to my girlfriend?* CONVENTION PRAGMATICS
► Also a noun. *The salesperson greeted me with a warm hello.* N-COUNT

2 You say **'Hello'** to someone at the beginning of a telephone conversation, either when you answer the phone or before you give your name or say why you are phoning. *A moment later, Cohen picked up the phone. 'Hello?'... Hallo, may I speak to Frank, please.* CONVENTION PRAGMATICS

3 Radio or television presenters often say **'Hello'** at the beginning of a programme, as part of the introduction. CONVENTION PRAGMATICS

4 You can call **'hello'** to attract someone's attention. *She could see the open door of a departmental office. 'Hello! Excuse me. This is the department of French, isn't it?'... Very softly, she called out: 'Hallo? Who's there?'* CONVENTION

helluva /heləvə/. Some people say **a helluva** or **one helluva** to emphasize that something is very ADJ: *a/one* ADJ n PRAGMATICS

good, very bad, or very big; used in informal English. *It taught me a helluva lot about myself... The man did one helluva job getting it all together.*
=a hell of a

helm /he̲lm/ **helms**
◆◇◇◇◇

1 The **helm** of a boat or ship is its wheel or tiller and the position from which the boat is controlled. *I got into our dinghy while Willis took the helm and positioned the boat for the photograph.*
N-COUNT: usu sing

2 You can say that someone is at **the helm** when they are in a position of leadership or control. *He has been at the helm of Lonrho for 31 years. ...Yutaka Kume, who took the helm as Nissan's president in June 1985.*
N-SING: *the*N

helmet /he̲lmɪt/ **helmets.** A **helmet** is a close-fitting hat made of a strong material which you wear to protect your head. • See also **crash helmet.**
◆◆◇◇◇ N-COUNT

helmsman /he̲lmzmən/ **helmsmen.** The **helmsman** of a boat is the person who is steering it.
N-COUNT

help /he̲lp/ **helps, helping, helped**
◆◆◆◆◆

1 If you **help** someone, you make it easier for them to do something, for example by doing part of the work for them or by giving them advice or money. *He has helped to raise a lot of money... My mum used to help cook the meals for the children... America's priority is to help nations defend themselves... You can of course help by giving them a donation directly... I was only trying to help... If you're not willing to help me, I'll find somebody who will.*
VERB
V to-inf/inf
V n inf/to-inf
V
V n

► Also a noun. *Thanks very much for your help... Always ask the pharmacist for help... Some of them have qualified for help with monthly payments.*
N-UNCOUNT =assistance

2 If you say that something **helps**, you mean that it makes something easier to do or get, or that it improves a situation to some extent. *The right style of swimsuit can help to hide, minimise or emphasise what you want it to... Building more motorways and by-passes will help the environment by reducing pollution and traffic jams in towns and cities... Understanding these rare molecules will help chemists to find out what is achievable... I could cook your supper, though, if that would help.*
VERB
V to-inf/inf
V n
V n to-inf/inf
V

3 If you **help** someone go somewhere or move in some way, you give them support so that they can move more easily. *Martin helped Tanya over the rail... I allowed her to help me to my feet... Come and help me up!... She helped her sit up in bed so she could hold her baby.*
VERB
V n prep/adv
V n inf/to-inf

4 If you **help** yourself, you try to get yourself out of a difficult situation rather than accept it and think you can do nothing to change it. *He tries to help people with problems, but firmly believes they should do more to help themselves.*
VERB
V pron-refl

5 If you say that someone or something has been **a help** or has been some **help**, you mean that they have helped you to do something that you were having difficulty with. *Thank you. You've been a great help already. ...a quality which will be a help rather than a hindrance to them... She's been a lot of help... The books were not much help.*
N-SING: *a*N, also no det

6 **Help** is the assistance that someone gives when they go to rescue a person who is in danger. You shout **'help!'** when you are in danger in order to attract someone's attention so that they can come and rescue you. *He was screaming for help... 'Help!' I screamed, turning to run.*
N-UNCOUNT

7 If you **help** yourself to something, you serve yourself or you take it for yourself. If someone tells you to **help** yourself, they are telling you politely to serve yourself anything you want or to take anything you want. *There's bread on the table. Help yourself... Just help yourself to leaflets.*
VERB
PRAGMATICS
V pron-refl
V pron-refl *to* n

8 If someone **helps** themself **to** something, they steal it; an informal use. *Has somebody helped himself to some film star's diamonds?*
VERB
V pron-refl *to* n

9 See also **helping.**

10 If you **can't help** the way you feel or behave, you cannot control it or stop it happening. You can also say that you **can't help** yourself. *I can't help feeling sorry for the poor man... 'Please don't cry.'—'I can't help it.'... Jerry and Lise know their romance inflicts hurt on others, but they can't help themselves... He can't help a suppressed giggle.*
PHRASES
V inflects, PHR -ing, PHR *it*, PHR pron-refl, PHR n

11 If you say you **can't help** thinking something, you are expressing your opinion in an indirect way, often because you think it seems rude. *I can't help feeling that this may just be another of her schemes... I could not help but think this is a very queer life.*
V inflects, PHR -ing, PHR *but* inf
PRAGMATICS

12 If someone or something **is of help**, they make something easier or make a situation better to some extent. *Can I be of help to you?*
V inflects

help off with. If you **help** someone **off with** an item of clothing, you help them take it off; used mainly in British English. *He helped her off with her robe.*
PHRASAL VERB
V n P P n

help on with. If you **help** someone **on with** an item of clothing, you help them put it on; used mainly in British English. *'I'll get you a cab,' I said as I helped her on with her coat.*
PHRASAL VERB
V n P P n

help out. If you **help** someone **out**, you help them by doing some work for them or by lending them some money. *I help out with the secretarial work... All these presents came to more money than I had, and my mother had to help me out... He thought you'd been brought in from Toronto to help out the local police.*
PHRASAL VERB
V P *with* n
V n P
V P n (not pron)
Also V P

helper /he̲lpəʳ/ **helpers.** A **helper** is a person who helps another person or group with a job they are doing.
◆◇◇◇◇ N-COUNT =assistant

helpful /he̲lpfʊl/
◆◆◇◇◇

1 If you describe someone as **helpful**, you mean that they help you in some way, such as doing part of your job for you or by giving you advice or information. *The staff in the London office are helpful but only have limited information... James is a very helpful and cooperative lad... Thank you, you've been most helpful.* ♦ **helpfully** *They had helpfully provided us with instructions on how to find the house... 'Perhaps you could check the book?' Moira said helpfully.* ♦ **helpfulness** *The level of expertise and helpfulness is far higher in smaller shops.*
ADJ-GRADED
ADV-GRADED: ADV with v
N-UNCOUNT

2 If you describe information or advice as **helpful**, you mean that it is useful for you. *The catalog includes helpful information on the different bike models available... The following information may be helpful to readers.*
ADJ-GRADED ≠unhelpful

3 Something that is **helpful** makes a situation more pleasant or more easy to tolerate. *A predominantly liquid diet for a day or two may be helpful... It is often helpful to have your spouse in the room when major news is expected... Group discussion is also immensely helpful in convincing patients that they can choose a course that feels right to them.*
ADJ-GRADED: oft *it* v-link ADJ to-inf, ADJ *for* n/-ing, ADJ *in*-ing/n

helping /he̲lpɪŋ/ **helpings**

1 A **helping** of food is the amount of it that you get in a single serving. *She gave them extra helpings of ice-cream.*
N-COUNT: usu with supp, oft N *of* n, adj N

2 You can refer to an amount of something, especially a quality, as a **helping of** that thing; an informal use. *It took a generous helping of entrepreneurial confidence to persevere during this incident.*
N-COUNT: N *of* n, usu adj N *of* n =amount

helpless /he̲lpləs/. If you are **helpless**, you do not have the strength or power to do anything useful or to control or protect yourself. *Parents often feel helpless, knowing that all the cuddles in the world won't stop the tears... The officials who supervised the camps were generally sympathetic to the refugees' plight, but were helpless to do very much about it... Once aboard we were soon helpless with laughter at the absurdity of it... They are not merely helpless victims... Many people felt helpless against the violence... He smiled wanly, his hands making a helpless gesture.* ♦ **helplessly** *Their son watched helplessly as they vanished beneath the waves... Police and National Guardsmen stood by helplessly as looters stripped businesses bare.* ♦ **helplessness** *I remember my feelings of helplessness... He was wary of letting strangers observe his helplessness.*
◆◆◇◇◇ ADJ-GRADED: oft ADJ to-inf, ADJ *against/with* n
ADV-GRADED: usu ADV with v, also ADV adj
N-UNCOUNT

helpline /he̲lplaɪn/ **helplines.** A **helpline** is a special telephone service that people can call to
◆◇◇◇◇ N-COUNT

get advice about a particular subject; used mainly in British English.

helpmate /helpmeɪt/ **helpmates.** If you say that one person is another person's **helpmate,** you mean that they help the other person in their life or work, especially by doing boring but necessary jobs for them such as cooking and cleaning; an old-fashioned word. N-COUNT

helter-skelter /heltəʳ skeltəʳ/. You use **helter-skelter** to describe something that is hurried and disorganized, especially when things happen very quickly, one after the other. *He now faces another crisis in his helter-skelter existence.* ADJ: ADJ n
▶ Also an adverb. *...a panic-stricken crowd running helter-skelter to get away from the tear gas.* ADV: ADV after v =pell-mell

hem /hem/ **hems, hemming, hemmed** ◆◇◇◇◇
1 A **hem** on something such as a sheet, cloth, or piece of clothing is an edge that is folded over and stitched down to make it neat and to prevent it fraying. The **hem** of a skirt or dress is the hem along its lower edge. N-COUNT
2 If you **hem** something, you form a hem along its edge. *Hem the lower edges and hand stitch the facing along the hem edge... Each dress is hemmed and scrupulously checked for imperfections.* VERB V n
3 ● **hem and haw**: see **haw.**

hem in PHRASAL VERB
1 If a place **is hemmed in** by mountains, barriers, or other places, it is surrounded by them; used especially when this seems undesirable or claustrophobic. *Manchester is hemmed in by greenbelt countryside and by housing and industrial areas... The brick path to the door was hemmed in on either side by tall, unkempt boxwood hedges.* usu passive; be V-ed P *by* n
2 If someone **is hemmed in** or if someone **hems** them **in,** they are prevented from moving or changing, for example because they are surrounded by people or obstacles. *BG's competitors complain that they are hemmed in by rigid, legal contracts... Derek told him to get round to the front of the parade to hem her in.* be V-ed P *by* n; V n P

he-man, he-men. A **he-man** is a strong and virile man, especially one who likes to show everyone how strong and virile he is; an informal word. N-COUNT

hemisphere /hemɪsfɪəʳ/ **hemispheres** ◆◇◇◇◇
1 A **hemisphere** is one half of the earth. *...the depletion of the ozone layer in the northern hemisphere.* N-COUNT: usu supp N
2 A **hemisphere** is one half of the brain. *In most people, the left hemisphere is bigger than the right.* N-COUNT: usu supp N

hemline /hemlaɪn/ **hemlines.** The **hemline** of a dress or skirt is its lower edge; sometimes used to refer to how long the dress or skirt is. *Mickey favoured tight skirts with a hemline at the knee.* N-COUNT

hemlock /hemlɒk/. **Hemlock** is a poisonous plant. N-UNCOUNT

hemoglobin /hiːməgloʊbɪn/. See **haemoglobin.**
hemophilia /hiːməfɪliæk/. See **haemophilia.**
hemophilic /hiːməfɪliə/. See **haemophilic.**
hemorrhage /hemərɪdʒ/. See **haemorrhage.**
hemorrhoid /hemərɔɪd/. See **haemorrhoid.**

hemp /hemp/. **Hemp** is a plant grown in Asia. It is used for making rope or the drug cannabis. ◆◇◇◇◇ N-UNCOUNT

hen /hen/ **hens** ◆◆◇◇◇
1 A **hen** is a female chicken. People often keep hens in order to eat or sell their eggs. N-COUNT
2 The female of any bird can be referred to as a **hen.** *...ostrich hens.* N-COUNT

hence /hens/ ◆◆◇◇◇
1 You use **hence** to indicate that the statement you are about to make is a consequence of what you have just said; a formal use. *The trade imbalance is likely to rise again in 1990. Hence a new set of policy actions will be required soon... Whatever is hidden is harmful (hence revelation equals security)... European music happens to use a scale of eight notes, hence the use of the term octave... The Socialist Party was profoundly divided and hence very weak.* ADV: ADV cl/group =therefore, thus
2 You use **hence** in expressions such as **'several years hence'** or **'six months hence'** to refer to a time in the future, especially a long time in the future; a formal use. *The gases that may be warming the planet will have their main effect many years hence. ...the much larger peacekeeping force that is meant to be fully deployed five months hence.* ADV: amount ADV PRAGMATICS

henceforth /hensfɔːʳθ/. **Henceforth** means from this time onwards; a formal word. *Henceforth, parties which fail to get 5% of the vote will not be represented in parliament... We were finally released with a formal warning that we were henceforth barred from the base.* ◆◇◇◇◇ ADV: ADV with cl =henceforward, from now on

henceforward /hensfɔːʳwəʳd/. **Henceforward** means from this time on; a formal word. *Henceforward France and Britain had a common interest... He announced that it would henceforward be the custom to give him five rands each time a cow was slaughtered.* ADV: ADV with cl =henceforth, from now on

henchman /hentʃmən/ **henchmen.** If you refer to someone as another person's **henchman,** you mean that they work for or support the other person, especially by doing unpleasant, violent, or dishonest things on their behalf. N-COUNT: usu poss N PRAGMATICS =heavy

henhouse /henhaʊs/ **henhouses.** A **henhouse** is a special building where hens are kept. N-COUNT

henna /henə/. **Henna** is a reddish-brown dye that is made from the leaves of a shrub. It is used especially for colouring hair or skin. N-UNCOUNT

hen night, hen nights. In Britain, a **hen night** is a party for a woman who is getting married very soon, to which only women are invited. N-COUNT

hen party, hen parties. A **hen party** is a party to which only women are invited; used mainly in British English. N-COUNT

hen-pecked; also spelled **henpecked.** You use **hen-pecked** to describe a man when you disapprove of the fact that his wife, or another woman, is always telling him what to do or telling him that he has done something wrong; an informal word. ADJ-GRADED: usu ADJ n PRAGMATICS

hepatitis /hepətaɪtɪs/. **Hepatitis** is a serious disease which affects the liver. ◆◇◇◇◇ N-UNCOUNT

heptathlon /heptæθlɒn/ **heptathlons.** The **heptathlon** is an athletics competition for women in which each athlete competes in seven different events. N-COUNT

her /həʳ, STRONG hɜːʳ/ ◆◆◆◆◆
Her is a third person singular pronoun. **Her** is used as the object of a verb or a preposition. **Her** is also a possessive determiner.
1 You use **her** to refer to a woman, girl, or female animal. *I went in the room and told her I had something to say to her... Catherine could not give her the advice she most needed... I really thought I'd lost her. Everybody kept asking me, 'Have you found your cat?'* PRON-SING: v PRON, prep PRON ▶ Also a possessive determiner. *Liz travelled round the world for a year with her boyfriend James... We admire her courage, compassion and dedication. ...a black dog, her hair erect along the centre of her back.* DET-POSS
2 In written English, writers sometimes use **her** to refer to a person without saying whether that person is a man or a woman. Some people dislike this use and prefer to use 'him or her' or 'them'. *Talk to your baby, play games, and show her how much you enjoy her company.* PRON-SING: v PRON, prep PRON ▶ Also a possessive determiner. *The non-drinking, non smoking model should do nothing to risk her reputation.* DET-POSS
3 In formal or written English, **her** is sometimes used to refer to a country or nation. ▶ Also a possessive determiner. *Our reporter looks at reactions to Britain's apparently deep-rooted distrust of her EC partner.* PRON-SING: v PRON, prep PRON DET-POSS
4 In informal English, people sometimes use **her** to refer to a car or a machine. People also sometimes use **her** to refer to a ship. *Kemp got out of his car. 'Just fill her up, thanks.'* PRON-SING: v PRON, prep PRON ▶ Also a possessive determiner. *This dramatic photograph was taken from Carpathia's deck by one of her passengers.* DET-POSS

herald /herəld/ **heralds, heralding, heralded** ◆◆◇◇◇
1 Something that **heralds** a future event or situation is a sign that it is going to happen or appear; a formal use. *...the sultry evening that heralded the* VERB V n

end of the baking hot summer... Their discovery could herald a cure for some forms of impotence.

2 Something that is a **herald** of a future event or situation is a sign that it is going to happen or appear; a formal use. *I welcome the report as a herald of more freedom, not less... For her, it was the herald of summer.* N-COUNT: N *of* n

3 If an important event or action **is heralded** by people, announcements are made about it so that it is publicly known and expected; a formal use. *Janet Jackson's new album has been heralded by a massive media campaign... Tonight's clash between Real Madrid and Arsenal is being heralded as the match of the season.* • See also **much-heralded**. VB: usu passive *be* V-ed *by* n *be* V-ed *as* n

4 In former times, a **herald** was a person who delivered and announced important messages. N-COUNT =messenger

heraldic /hərælдɪk/. **Heraldic** means relating to heraldry. *...religious and heraldic symbols.* ADJ: ADJ n

heraldry /herəldri/. **Heraldry** is the study of coats of arms and of the history of the families who are entitled to have them. N-UNCOUNT

herb /hɜːʳb, AM ɜːʳb/ **herbs.** A **herb** is a plant whose leaves are used in cookery to add flavour to food, or as a medicine. ◆◆◇◇◇ N-COUNT

herbaceous /hɜːʳbeɪʃəs, AM ɜːʳb-/. **Herbaceous** plants are soft and fleshy rather than hard and woody. ◆◇◇◇◇ ADJ: ADJ n

herbaceous border, herbaceous borders. A **herbaceous border** is a flower bed containing a mixture of plants that flower every year. N-COUNT

herbal /hɜːʳbəl, AM ɜːʳb-/ **herbals** ◆◇◇◇◇

1 **Herbal** means made from or using herbs. *...herbal teas. ...herbal remedies for colds.* ADJ: ADJ n

2 A **herbal** is a book which describes herbs or other plants, and their uses as medicines or in cooking. N-COUNT

herbalism /hɜːʳbəlɪzəm, AM ɜːʳb-/. **Herbalism** is the practice of using herbs to treat illnesses. N-UNCOUNT

herbalist /hɜːʳbəlɪst, AM ɜːʳb-/ **herbalists.** A **herbalist** is a person who grows or sells herbs that are used in medicine. N-COUNT

herbicide /hɜːʳbɪsaɪd, AM ɜːʳb-/ **herbicides.** A **herbicide** is a chemical that is used to destroy plants, especially weeds. ◆◇◇◇◇ N-MASS

herbivore /hɜːʳbɪvɔːʳ, AM ɜːʳb-/ **herbivores.** A **herbivore** is an animal that only eats plants. N-COUNT

herculean /hɜːʳkjʊliːən/; also spelled **Herculean**. A **herculean** task or ability is one that requires extremely great strength or effort; a literary word. *Finding a lawyer may seem like a Herculean task if you live in a big city because there are so many of them.* ADJ-GRADED: usu ADJ n =formidable

herd /hɜːʳd/ **herds, herding, herded** ◆◆◇◇◇

1 A **herd** is a large group of animals of one kind that live together. *Chobe is also renowned for its large herds of elephant and buffalo. ...dairy herds.* N-COUNT: oft n N, N *of* n

2 If you say that someone has joined **the herd** or follows **the herd**, you are criticizing them because you think that they behave just like everyone else and do not think for themselves. *They are individuals; they will not follow the herd.* N-SING: *the* N PRAGMATICS =pack

3 If you **herd** people somewhere, you make them move there in a group. *He began to herd the prisoners out... The group was herded into a bus.* VERB =shepherd V n prep/adv

4 If you **herd** animals, you make them move along as a group. *Stefano used a motor cycle to herd the sheep... A boy herded half a dozen camels down towards the water trough.* VERB V n V n prep/adv

herdsman /hɜːʳdzmən/ **herdsmen.** A **herdsman** is a man who looks after a herd of animals such as cattle or goats. N-COUNT

here /hɪəʳ/ ◆◆◆◆◆

1 You use **here** when you are referring to the place where you are. *I'm here all by myself and I know I'm going to get lost... Well, I can't stand here chatting all day. ...the growing number of skiers that come here... Sheila was in here a minute ago... My name is Roseanne and I'm in here for heroin addiction... I'm not going to stay here. I'm out of here, back down to San Diego... When Mommy comes, just tell her I'm up here.* ADV: *be* ADV, ADV after v, prep ADV ≠there

2 You use **here** when you are pointing towards a place that is near you, in order to draw someone else's attention to it. *...if you will just sign here... Come and sit here, Lauren... 'From there, pulling a line to here,' he said, making invisible drawings in the air... 'It's on the right-hand side of the shopping centre.'—'Okay. Fine.'—'Oh it's here.'* ADV: ADV after v, prep ADV, *be* ADV

3 You use **here** in order to indicate that the person or thing that you are talking about is near you or is being held by you. *My friend here writes for radio... I have here at my side Mr. Glenn Williams... I have a little book here by a lady called Mystic Meg.* ADV: n ADV, ADV after v

4 You use **here** to refer to people in general and their life on Earth. *...where we have come from, where we are going to, or what our purpose here is, if any... Who are we? What are we doing here?* ADV: n ADV, ADV after v

5 If you say that you are **here** to do something, that is your role or function. *I'm here to help you... I'm not here to listen to your complaints.* ADV: *be* ADV to-inf

6 You use **here** in order to draw attention to something or someone who has just arrived in the place where you are, or to draw attention to the place you have just arrived at. *'Here's the taxi,' she said politely... 'Mr Cummings is here,' she said, holding the door open... Here comes your husband... 'Okay, here we are,' she said, and inserted her key in the lock... Here's my apartment.* ADV: ADV with *be*, ADV before v

7 You use **here** to refer to a particular point or stage of a situation or subject that you have come to or that you are dealing with. *Both sides will have to sell the agreement to their people. It's here that the real test will come... It's here that we come up against the difference of approach... The book goes into recent work in greater detail than I have attempted here... Here I think it is appropriate to draw your attention to one very specific feature of socialism.* ADV: *it* v-link ADV that, ADV with v, ADV with cl

8 You use **here** to refer to a period of time, a situation, or an event that is present or happening now. *Here comes the summer... Economic recovery is here... Here is your opportunity to acquire a luxurious one bedroom starter home.* ADV: ADV before v, ADV with *be*

9 You use **here** at the beginning of a sentence in order to draw attention to something or to introduce something. *From Nairobi here's our East Africa correspondent, Colin Blane... Here is a summer soup that is almost a meal in itself... Now here's what I want you to do... So here's what I think.* ADV: ADV *be* n/wh

10 You use **here** when you are offering or giving something to someone. *You know you can phone me – here's my mother's number... Here's your coffee, just the way you like it... Here's my card. You know where to find me... Here's some letters I want you to sign... Here's your cash.* ADV: ADV *be* n PRAGMATICS

11 You say **'here we are'** or **'here you are'** when the statement that you are making about someone's character or situation is unexpected. *Here you are, saying these terrible things... Here we are, pretending we're winning.* PHRASES V inflects, PHR with cl PRAGMATICS

12 You say **'here we are'** when you have just found something that you have been looking for. *I rummaged through the drawers and came up with Amanda's folder. 'Here we are.'* CONVENTION

13 You say **'here goes'** when you are about to do or say something difficult or unpleasant. *Dr Culver nervously muttered 'Here goes,' and gave the little girl an injection.* CONVENTION PRAGMATICS

14 You use expressions such as **'here we go'**, **'here we go again'**, or **'here I go again'** in order to indicate that something is happening again in the way that you expected, especially something unpleasant; used in informal English. *'Police! Open up!'—'Oh well,' I thought, 'here we go.'... At first, he was told he was too young and I thought, 'Oh, boy, here we go again.'... Here I go again, confusing the issue.* PRAGMATICS

15 You use **here and now** to emphasize that something is happening at the present time, rather than in the future or past, or that you would like it to happen at the present time. *I'm a practicing physician trying to help people here and now... Instead of staying in the here and now, you bring up similar instances from the past.* PRAGMATICS

16 If something happens **here and there**, it happens in several different places. *I do a bit of teach-* PHR with cl, PHR after v

ing here and there... He could only understand a word here and there.

17 You use expressions such as **'here's to us'** and **'here's to your new job'** as a toast in order to wish success to a venture or happiness to a person. *He raised his glass. 'Here's to neighbors.'... Tony smiled and lifted his glass. 'Here's to you, Amy.'* CONVENTION PRAGMATICS

hereabouts /hɪərəbaʊts/. You use **hereabouts** to indicate that you are talking about something near you or in the same area as you. *It's a bit chilly and empty hereabouts... The mountains hereabouts reach heights of over 2000 metres.* ADV: ADV after v, n ADV =here

hereafter /hɪərɑːftəʳ, -æft-/

1 **Hereafter** means from this time onwards; used in formal written English. *My new plan seems admirable—hereafter for three years my name will not appear at all.* ADV: ADV with cl =henceforth, from now on

2 In legal documents and in written English, **hereafter** is used to introduce information about an abbreviation that will be used in the rest of the text to refer to the person or thing just mentioned. *Michel Foucault (1972), The Archaeology of Knowledge; hereafter this text will be abbreviated as AK.* ADV: ADV with cl PRAGMATICS

3 The **hereafter** is sometimes used to refer to the time after you have died, or to the life which some people believe you have after you have died. ▸ Also an adverb. *He had a sense of mission in both the temporal world and in the life hereafter... Its message is that what a man does in this life has a bearing on what happens to him hereafter.* N-SING: usu *the* N ADV: n ADV, ADV with cl

hereby /hɪəʳbaɪ/

1 You use **hereby** in formal statements and documents to indicate that what you are saying has official status and will take effect immediately. *I hereby sentence you for life after all the charges against you have been proven true... You are hereby appointed Sub-Lieutenant RNVR of HMS Tartar... I hereby agree that I will never divulge such information to anyone who is not authorized to receive it.* ADV: ADV before v PRAGMATICS

2 In formal English, you use **hereby** to draw attention to what you are saying or suggesting, and to emphasize your sincerity. *I would hereby like to point out that editorial alterations to my story were made in order to make it suit a different reader from the one I originally had in mind... I hereby predict this fetish will be the death of economics.* ADV: ADV before v PRAGMATICS

hereditary /hɪredɪtri/ ◆◇◇◇◇

1 A **hereditary** characteristic or illness is passed on to a child from its parents before it is born. *Cystic fibrosis is the commonest fatal hereditary disease... In men, hair loss is hereditary.* ADJ

2 A title or position in society that is **hereditary** is one that is passed on as a right from parent to child. *...the position of the head of state is hereditary... British Prime Ministers are traditionally offered hereditary peerages.* ADJ

heredity /hɪredɪti/. **Heredity** is the process by which features and characteristics are passed on from parents to their children before the children are born. *Heredity is not a factor in causing the cancer.* N-UNCOUNT

herein /hɪərɪn/

1 **Herein** means in this document, text, or book; used in formal written English. *The statements and views expressed herein are those of the author and are not necessarily those of the Wilson Centre... The argument contained herein takes exactly the opposite point of view... Most of the experiences herein concern cancer.* ADV: ADV after v, n ADV PRAGMATICS

2 In formal written English, you can use **herein** to introduce a clause where you state an opinion or analysis that relates to your main topic, usually when you go on to explain it in more detail. *The point is that people grew unaccustomed to thinking and acting in a responsible and independent way. Herein lies another big problem.* ADV: ADV cl PRAGMATICS =here

heresy /herɪsi/ **heresies** ◆◇◇◇◇

1 **Heresy** is a belief or action that most people think is wrong, because it disagrees with beliefs that are generally accepted. *It might be considered heresy to suggest such a notion.* N-VAR

2 **Heresy** is a belief or action which seriously disagrees with the principles of a particular religion. *He said it was a heresy to suggest that women should not conduct services.* N-VAR

heretic /herɪtɪk/ **heretics**

1 A **heretic** is someone whose beliefs or actions are considered wrong by most people, because they disagree with beliefs that are generally accepted. *He was considered a heretic and was ridiculed and ostracized for his ideas.* N-COUNT

2 A **heretic** is a person who belongs to a particular religion, but whose beliefs or actions seriously disagree with the principles of that religion. *Thousands of heretics were burned at the stake.* N-COUNT

heretical /hɪretɪkəl/

1 A belief or action that is **heretical** is one that most people think is wrong because it disagrees with beliefs that are generally accepted. *I made the then heretical suggestion that it might be cheaper to design new machines.* ADJ

2 A belief or action that is **heretical** is one that seriously disagrees with the principles of a particular religion. *The Church regards spirit mediums and people claiming to speak to the dead as heretical.* ADJ

heretofore /hɪəʳtuːfɔːʳ/. **Heretofore** means before this time; used in formal English, especially American English. *They reported that clouds are an important and heretofore uninvestigated contributor to the climate.* ADV: usu ADV with v, also ADV adj, ADV with cl =hitherto, previously

herewith /hɪəʳwɪð/. In formal written English, **herewith** means with this document, text, or book. You can use **herewith** in a letter to say that you are enclosing something with it. *We demand that by 9 a.m. the regime free the 236 revolutionary prisoners whose names are listed herewith... I return herewith your papers.* ADV: usu ADV with v, also n ADV, ADV n, ADV with cl PRAGMATICS

heritage /herɪtɪdʒ/ **heritages.** A country's **heritage** is all the qualities, traditions, or features of life that have been continued over many years and passed on from one generation to another, especially ones that are of historical importance or that have had a strong influence on society. *The historic building is as much part of our heritage as the paintings. ...the rich heritage of Russian folk music.* ◆◆◇◇◇ N-VAR: usu with supp, oft poss N

hermaphrodite /hɜːʳmæfrədaɪt/ **hermaphrodites.** A **hermaphrodite** is a person, animal, or flower that has both male and female reproductive organs; a technical term in biology. N-COUNT

hermetic /hɜːʳmetɪk/ ◆◇◇◇◇

1 If a container has a **hermetic** seal, the seal is very tight so that no air can get in or out. *This would permit air to enter, breaking the hermetic seal of the jar.* ♦ **hermetically** /hɜːʳmetɪkli/ *The batteries are designed to be leak-proof and hermetically sealed.* ADJ: ADJ n =airtight ADV: ADV -ed, ADV after v

2 You use **hermetic** to describe something which you disapprove of because it seems to be socially, physically, or intellectually separate from other people and things in society; used in written English. *Its film industry operates in its own curiously hermetic way... Their work is more cosily hermetic than ever.* ADJ-GRADED PRAGMATICS

hermit /hɜːʳmɪt/ **hermits.** A **hermit** is a person who lives alone, away from people and society. ◆◇◇◇◇ N-COUNT

hernia /hɜːʳniə/ **hernias.** A **hernia** is a medical condition which is often caused by strain or injury. It results in one of your inner organs sticking through a weak point in the surrounding tissue. ◆◇◇◇◇ N-VAR

hero /hɪərou/ **heroes** ◆◆◆◇◇

1 The **hero** of a book, play, film, or story is the main male character, who usually has good qualities. *The hero of Doctor Zhivago dies in 1929. ...the author's decision to make his hero a photographer.* N-COUNT =protagonist ≠villain

2 A **hero** is someone, especially a man, who has done something brave, new, or good, and who is therefore greatly admired by a lot of people. *He called Mr Mandela a hero who had inspired millions. ...the goalscoring hero of the British hockey team... They think you're some sort of hero.* N-COUNT

3 If you describe someone as your **hero** you mean that you admire them a greal deal, usually because of a particular quality or skill that they have. *My* N-COUNT: usu sing, with poss =idol

boyhood hero was Bobby Charlton... No matter, he remained the hero of the crowds.

heroic /hɪrouɪk/ **heroics** ◆◆◇◇◇

1 If you describe a person or their actions as **heroic**, you admire them because they show extreme bravery. *The heroic sergeant risked his life to rescue 29 fisherman from their blazing trawler... His heroic deeds were celebrated in every corner of India.* ADJ-GRADED: usu ADJ n =courageous

♦ **heroically** /hɪrouɪkli/ *He had acted heroically during the liner's evacuation.* ADV-GRADED: ADV with v

2 If you describe an action or event as **heroic**, you admire it because it involves great effort or determination to succeed. *The company has made heroic efforts at cost reduction... He finally faltered in the last game of a heroic match... Their dogged single-mindedness is almost heroic.* ♦ **heroically** *Single parents cope heroically in doing the job of two people.* ADJ-GRADED PRAGMATICS; ADV: usu ADV with v, also ADV adj

3 A **heroic** event or character is one that occurs in a story and involves a hero or his actions. *...a story fraught with perils, deaths, and heroic deeds.* ADJ: usu ADJ n

4 **Heroics** are actions involving bravery, courage, or determination. *...the man whose aerial heroics helped save the helicopter pilot... England need heroics from the captain now.* N-PLURAL

5 If you describe someone's actions or plans as **heroics**, you mean that they are foolish or dangerous because they are too difficult or brave for the situation in which they occur; used in spoken English, showing disapproval. *He said his advice was: 'No heroics, stay within the law'... Cut it out, Perry. You've performed your heroics. It's all over now.* N-PLURAL: usu with brd-neg PRAGMATICS

heroin /herouɪn/. **Heroin** is a powerful drug which some people take for pleasure, but which they can become addicted to. ◆◆◇◇◇ N-UNCOUNT

heroine /herouɪn/ **heroines** ◆◆◇◇◇

1 The **heroine** of a book, play, film, or story is the main female character, who usually has admirable qualities. *The heroine is a senior TV executive.* N-COUNT =protagonist ≠villain

2 A **heroine** is a woman who has done something brave, new, or good, and who is therefore greatly admired by a lot of people. *The national heroine of the day was Xing Fen, winner of the first Gold medal of the Games.* N-COUNT

3 If you describe a woman as your **heroine**, you mean that you admire her greatly, usually because of a particular quality or skill that she has. *My heroine was Elizabeth Taylor.* N-COUNT: usu sing, with poss PRAGMATICS =idol

heroism /herouɪzəm/. **Heroism** is great courage and bravery. *...individual acts of heroism.* ◆◇◇◇◇ N-UNCOUNT

heron /herən/ **herons.** A **heron** is a large bird which has long legs and a long beak, and which eats fish. N-COUNT

hero-worship, hero-worships, hero-worshipping, hero-worshipped; the noun is also spelled **hero worship**.

1 **Hero-worship** is a very great admiration of someone and a belief that they are special or perfect. *Singer Brett Anderson inspires old-fashioned hero-worship.* N-UNCOUNT

2 If you **hero-worship** someone, you admire them a great deal and think they are special or perfect. *He was amused by the way younger actors started to hero-worship and copy him.* VERB V n

herpes /hɜːʳpiːz/. **Herpes** is a disease which causes painful red spots to appear on the skin. ◆◇◇◇◇ N-UNCOUNT

herring /herɪŋ/ **herrings.** The plural can be either **herring** or **herrings**. A **herring** is a long silver-coloured fish. Herring live in large groups in the sea. ► **Herring** is a piece of this fish eaten as food. • See also **red herring**. ◆◇◇◇◇ N-VAR; N-UNCOUNT

herringbone /herɪŋboun/. **Herringbone** is a pattern used in fabrics or brickwork, which appears as parallel rows of zigzag lines. N-UNCOUNT: oft N n

hers /hɜːʳz/ ◆◆◇◇◇

Hers is a third person possessive pronoun.

1 You use **hers** to indicate that something belongs or relates to a woman, girl, or female animal. *His hand as it shook hers was warm and firm... He'd never seen eyes as green as hers... Professor Camm was a great friend of hers... Hers was the suggestion I acted upon.* PRON-POSS

2 In written English, writers sometimes use **hers** to refer to a person without saying whether that person is a man or a woman. Some people dislike this use and prefer to use 'his or hers' or 'theirs'. *The author can report other people's results which more or less agree with hers.* PRON-POSS

3 In formal or written English, **hers** is sometimes used to refer to a country or nation. PRON-POSS

4 In informal English, people sometimes use **hers** to refer to a car or a machine. People also sometimes use **hers** to refer to a ship. PRON-POSS

herself /həʳself/. ◆◆◆◆◆

Herself is a third person singular reflexive pronoun. **Herself** is used when the object of a verb or preposition refers to the same person as the subject of the verb, except in meaning 5.

1 You use **herself** to refer to a woman, girl, or female animal. *She let herself out of the room... Jennifer believes she will move out on her own when she is financially able to support herself... Robin didn't feel good about herself.* PRON-REFL: v PRON, prep PRON

2 In written English, writers sometimes use **herself** to refer to a person without saying whether that person is a man or a woman. Some people dislike this use and prefer to use 'himself or herself' or 'themselves'. *How can anyone believe stories for which she feels herself to be in no way responsible?* PRON-REFL

3 In formal or written English, **herself** is sometimes used to refer to a country or nation. *Britain's dream of herself began to fade.* PRON-REFL

4 In informal English, people sometimes use **herself** to refer to a car or a machine. People also use **herself** to refer to a ship. *The ship adjusted herself to the roll and rhythm of the sea.* PRON-REFL

5 You use **herself** to emphasize the person or thing that you are referring to. **Herself** is sometimes used instead of 'her' as the object of a verb or preposition. *She's so beautiful herself... Has anyone thought of consulting Bethan herself?... She herself was not a keen gardener.* PRON-REFL-EMPH PRAGMATICS

he's /hɪz, hiːz/. **He's** is the usual spoken form of 'he is' or 'he has', especially when 'has' is an auxiliary verb. *He's working maybe twenty-five hours a week... From day one he's been a great asset to the company.*

hesitant /hezɪtᵊnt/. If you are **hesitant** about doing something, you do not do it quickly or immediately, usually because you are uncertain, embarrassed, or worried. *She was hesitant about coming forward with her story... His advisers are rightfully hesitant to let the United States be sucked into the conflict. ...a quiet hesitant voice.* ◆◇◇◇◇ ADJ-GRADED: oft ADJ *about* n, ADJ to-inf

♦ **hesitancy** /hezɪtənsi/ *A trace of hesitancy showed in Dr. Stockton's eyes.* ♦ **hesitantly** *'Would you do me a favour?' she asked hesitantly.* N-UNCOUNT =reluctance; ADV-GRADED: ADV with v

hesitate /hezɪteɪt/ **hesitates, hesitating, hesitated** ◆◆◇◇◇

1 If you **hesitate**, you pause slightly while you are doing or saying something, or just before you do or say it, usually because you are uncertain, embarrassed, or worried about it. *The telephone rang. Catherine hesitated, debating whether to answer it... She hesitated a long time and then she said 'Yes'.* VERB V

♦ **hesitation** /hezɪteɪʃᵊn/ **hesitations** *Asked if he would go back, Mr Searle said after some hesitation, 'I'll have to think about that'... Mirella approached him and, after a brief hesitation, shook his hand.* N-VAR

2 If you **hesitate** to do something, you are unwilling to do it, usually because you are worried or not quite certain whether it is correct or right. If you do not **hesitate** to do something, you do it very willingly or with great certainty. *Some parents hesitate to take these steps because they suspect that their child is exaggerating... I hesitated to apply the word 'vulnerable' to him but it came into my mind... I will not hesitate to take unpopular decisions.* VERB V to-inf

3 You can use **hesitate** in expressions such as **'don't hesitate to call me'**, or **'don't hesitate to contact us'**, when you are telling someone that they should do something, and that they should not worry about disturbing other people if they do. *In the event of difficulties, please do not hesitate to* VB: only imper, with neg PRAGMATICS V to-inf

contact our Customer Service Department... Please don't hesitate to tell either Mr Schrader or myself should you feel ill again... Do not hesitate to laugh at anything you find amusing.

hesitation /hezɪteɪʃᵊn/ **hesitations.** ◆◇◇◇◇

1 Hesitation is an unwillingness to do something, or a delay in doing it, because you are uncertain, worried, or embarrassed about it. *He promised there would be no more hesitations in pursuing reforms. ...the prime minister's hesitation to accept a ceasefire.* • See also **hesitate**. [N-VAR: oft N *in*-ing]

2 If you say that you **have no hesitation** in doing something, you are emphasizing that you will do it immediately or willingly because you are certain that it is the right thing to do. *The board said it had no hesitation in unanimously rejecting the offer... Some of us had careers, but we had no hesitation in giving them up to work alongside our husbands.* [PHRASES: V inflects, usu PHR *in*-ing; PRAGMATICS]

3 If you say that someone does something **without hesitation**, you are emphasizing that they do it immediately and willingly. *The great majority of players would, of course, sign the contract without hesitation... The boy followed without hesitation.* [usu PHR after v, PHR with cl; PRAGMATICS]

hessian /hesiən, AM heʃən/. **Hessian** is a thick rough fabric that is used for making sacks; used mainly in British English. [N-UNCOUNT]

heterodox /hetərədɒks/. **Heterodox** beliefs, opinions, or ideas are different from the accepted or official ones; a formal word. [ADJ =unorthodox]

heterogeneous /hetərədʒiːniəs/. A **heterogeneous** group consists of many different types of things or people; a formal word. *...a rather heterogeneous collection of studies from diverse origins. ...the heterogeneous society of today.* [ADJ-GRADED: usu ADJ n =diverse ≠homogeneous]

heterosexual /hetərouseksʃuəl/ **heterosexuals** ◆◆◇◇◇

1 A **heterosexual** relationship is a sexual relationship between a man and a woman. [ADJ: usu ADJ n]

2 Someone who is **heterosexual** is sexually attracted to people of the opposite sex. ► Also a noun. *In Denmark the age of consent is fifteen for both heterosexuals and homosexuals.* [ADJ; N-COUNT]

♦ **heterosexuality** /hetərouseksʃuælɪti/ *...a challenge to the assumption that heterosexuality was 'normal'.* [N-UNCOUNT]

het up /het ʌp/. If you get **het up** about something, you get very excited or anxious about it; an informal word. *I used to get very het up about things.* [ADJ-GRADED: v-link ADJ, oft ADJ *about* n =worked up]

heuristic /hjuərɪstɪk/. A **heuristic** method of learning involves discovery and problem-solving techniques, using reasoning and past experience. [ADJ]

hew /hjuː/ **hews, hewing, hewed, hewn.** The past participle can be either **hewed** or **hewn**.

1 If you **hew** stone or wood, you cut it, for example with an axe; an old-fashioned use. *He felled, peeled and hewed his own timber.* [VERB =chop; V n]

2 If something **is hewn** from stone or wood, it is cut or formed from stone or wood; an old-fashioned or literary use. *...the rock from which the lower chambers and subterranean passageways have been hewn. ...medieval monasteries hewn out of the rockface.* [VB: usu passive =cut; be V-ed *from/out of* n; V-ed]

3 See also **rough-hewn**.

hexagon /heksəgən, AM -gɔːn/ **hexagons.** A **hexagon** is a geometric shape that has six straight sides. [N-COUNT]

hexagonal /heksægənᵊl/. A **hexagonal** object or shape has six straight sides. [ADJ]

hey /heɪ/. In informal situations, you say or shout **'hey'** to attract someone's attention, or to show surprise, interest, or annoyance. *'Hey! Look out!' shouted Patty... Hey, can I ask you a question?* ◆◆◇◇◇ [CONVENTION; PRAGMATICS]

heyday /heɪdeɪ/. Someone's **heyday** is the time when they are most powerful, successful, or popular. *In its heyday, the studio's boast was that it had more stars than there are in heaven.* ◆◇◇◇◇ [N-SING: with poss]

hi /haɪ/. In informal situations, you say **'hi'** to greet someone. *'Hi, Liz' she said shyly.* ◆◆◆◇◇ [CONVENTION; PRAGMATICS]

hiatus /haɪeɪtəs/. A **hiatus** is a pause in which nothing happens, or a gap where something is missing; a formal word. *Diplomatic efforts to reach a settlement resume today after a two-week hiatus... There was an hiatus in his acting life.* [N-SING: usu with supp, oft N *in/of* n]

hibernate /haɪbəʳneɪt/ **hibernates, hibernating, hibernated.** Animals that **hibernate** spend the winter in a state like a deep sleep. *Dormice are nocturnal creatures and hibernate from October to May... Hibernating insects begin to move.* [VERB; V; V-ing]

hibiscus /hɪbɪskəs, AM haɪ-/; **hibiscus** is both the singular and the plural. A **hibiscus** is a tropical bush that has large, brightly-coloured bell-shaped flowers. [N-VAR]

hiccup /hɪkʌp/ **hiccups, hiccuping** or **hiccupping, hiccuped** or **hiccupped;** also spelled **hiccough.** ◆◇◇◇◇

1 You can refer to a small problem or difficulty as a **hiccup**, especially if it does not last very long or is easily put right. *A recent sales hiccup is nothing to panic about... Despite the occasional hiccup, the US and Laos have had quite cordial relations.* [N-COUNT: usu with supp, oft n N, N *in* n]

2 When you have **hiccups**, you make repeated sharp sounds in your throat, often because you have been eating or drinking too quickly. *A young baby may frequently get a bout of hiccups during or soon after a feed.* [N-UNCOUNT: also *the* N]

3 A **hiccup** is a sound of the kind that you make when you have hiccups. [N-COUNT]

4 When you **hiccup**, you make repeated sharp sounds in your throat. *She was still hiccuping from the egg she had swallowed whole.* [VERB; V]

hick /hɪk/ **hicks.** If you refer to someone as a **hick**, you think they are uneducated and stupid because they come from the countryside. *He is an obnoxious hick. ...a crummy little hick hotel.* [N-COUNT: oft N n; PRAGMATICS]

hid /hɪd/. **Hid** is the past tense of **hide**.

hidden /hɪdᵊn/ ◆◆◇◇◇

1 Hidden is the past participle of **hide**.

2 Hidden facts, feelings, activities, or problems are not easy to notice or discover. *Under all the innocent fun, there are hidden dangers, especially for children... The precise details of the origins of life remain hidden.* [ADJ]

3 A **hidden** place is difficult to find. *As you descend, suddenly you see at last the hidden waterfall.* [ADJ =concealed]

hidden agenda, hidden agendas. If you say that someone has a **hidden agenda**, you are criticizing them because you think they are secretly trying to achieve or cause a particular thing, while they appear to be doing something else. *Labour's hidden agenda was that it wanted political campaigning to be funded by the taxpayer... Is there a hidden agenda?* [N-COUNT; PRAGMATICS]

hide /haɪd/ **hides, hiding, hid, hidden** ◆◆◆◇◇

1 If you **hide** something or someone, you put them in a place where they cannot easily be seen or found. *He hid the bicycle in the hawthorn hedge... They could see that I was terrified, and hid me until the coast was clear.* [VERB =conceal; V n]

2 If you **hide** or if you **hide** yourself, you go somewhere where you cannot easily be seen or found. *At their approach the little boy scurried and hid... They hid themselves behind a tree.* [VERB; V; V pron-refl]

3 If you **hide** your face, you press your face against something or cover your face with something, so that people cannot see it. *She hid her face under the collar of his jacket and she started to cry... He hid his face in his hands. again, lost in his own thoughts.* [VERB; V n]

4 If you **hide** what you feel or know, you keep it a secret, so that no one knows about it. *Lee tried to hide his excitement... I have absolutely nothing to hide, I have done nothing wrong... Alison was not the sort of person to hide anything from her dad.* [VERB; V n]

5 If something **hides** an object, it covers it and prevents it from being seen. *The man's heavy moustache hid his upper lip completely... The compound was hidden by trees and shrubs.* [VERB; V n]

6 A **hide** is a place which is built to look like its surroundings. Hides are used by people who want to watch or photograph animals and birds without being seen by them; used mainly in British English. [N-COUNT]

7 A **hide** is the skin of a large animal such as a cow, horse, or elephant, which can be used for making leather. *...the process of tanning animal hides. ...kangaroo hide.* N-VAR =skin

8 See also **hidden, hiding.**

hide-and-seek. Hide-and-seek is a children's game in which one player covers his or her eyes until the other players have hidden themselves, and then he or she tries to find them. N-UNCOUNT

hideaway /haɪdəweɪ/ **hideaways.** A **hideaway** is a place where you go to hide or to get away from other people. *The bandits fled to a remote mountain hideaway. ...the £3 million hideaway holiday home on the exclusive island of Mustique.* N-COUNT

hidebound /haɪdbaʊnd/. If you describe someone or something as **hidebound**, you are criticizing them for keeping to outdated traditions, rather than changing or accepting new ideas. *The men are hidebound and reactionary... The economy was hidebound by public spending and private monopolies.* ADJ-GRADED: oft ADJ *by* n PRAGMATICS

hideous /hɪdiəs/ ◆◇◇◇◇

1 If you say that someone or something is **hideous**, you mean that they are very ugly or unattractive. *She saw a hideous face at the window and screamed. ...hideous new Europe architecture, and horrible metal sculptures.* ADJ-GRADED =monstrous, horrible

2 You can describe an event, experience, or action as **hideous** when you mean that it is very unpleasant, painful, or difficult to bear. *His family was subjected to a hideous attack by the gang... It's been a perfectly hideous day.* ADJ-GRADED =horrendous

hideously /hɪdiəsli/

1 You use **hideously** to emphasize that something is very ugly or unattractive. *Everything is hideously ugly... He has been left hideously disfigured by plastic surgery.* ADV: usu ADV adj/-ed, also ADV after v PRAGMATICS

2 You can use **hideously** to emphasize that something is very unpleasant or unacceptable. *...a hideously complex program. ...a simple but undoubtedly hideously expensive black suit.* ADV-GRADED: ADV adj/-ed PRAGMATICS =horrendously

hideout /haɪdaʊt/ **hideouts.** A **hideout** is a place where someone goes secretly because they do not want anyone to find them, for example if they are running away from the police. N-COUNT

hiding /haɪdɪŋ/ **hidings** ◆◆◇◇◇

1 If someone is in **hiding**, they have secretly gone somewhere where they cannot be seen or found. *Gray is thought to be in hiding near the France/Italy border... Hundreds of people are said to have gone into hiding to avoid arrest... The duchess is expected to come out of hiding to attend the ceremony.* N-UNCOUNT: prep N

2 If you give someone a **hiding**, you punish them by hitting them many times; an informal use. N-COUNT =beating

3 In informal British English, if you say that someone who is trying to achieve something is **on a hiding to nothing**, you are emphasizing that they have absolutely no chance of being successful. *As regards commercial survival, a car manufacturer capable of making only 50,000 cars a year is on a hiding to nothing.* PHRASE: v-link PHR PRAGMATICS

hiding place, hiding places. A **hiding place** is a place where someone or something can be hidden, or where they are hiding. ◆◇◇◇◇ N-COUNT

hierarchical /haɪərɑːʳkɪkəl/. A **hierarchical** system or organization is one in which people have different ranks or positions, depending on how important they are. *...the traditional hierarchical system of military organization.* ◆◇◇◇◇ ADJ-GRADED: usu ADJ n

hierarchy /haɪərɑːʳki/ **hierarchies** ◆◆◇◇◇

1 A **hierarchy** is a system of organizing people into different ranks or levels of importance, for example in society or in a company. *Like most other American companies with a rigid hierarchy, workers and managers had strictly defined duties... She rose up the Tory hierarchy by the local government route... Even in the desert there was a kind of social hierarchy.* N-VAR: usu with supp

2 The **hierarchy** of an organization such as the Church is the group of people who manage and control it. N-COUNT-COLL: with supp

3 A **hierarchy** of ideas and beliefs involves organizing them into a system or structure; a formal use. *...the notion of 'cultural imperialism', implies a hierarchy of cultures, some of which are stronger than others.* N-COUNT: usu N *of* n

hieroglyph /haɪərəglɪf/ **hieroglyphs. Hieroglyphs** are symbols in the form of pictures, which are used in some writing systems, especially those of ancient Egypt. N-COUNT =hieroglyphics

hieroglyphics /haɪərəglɪfɪks/

1 **Hieroglyphics** are symbols in the form of pictures which are used in some writing systems, for example those of ancient Egypt. N-PLURAL =hieroglyphs

2 You can use **hieroglyphics** to refer to something that has been written, but that you cannot understand; an informal use. *I've never come across hieroglyphics like the handwriting of Peter Smallwood.* N-PLURAL

hi-fi /haɪ faɪ/ **hi-fis.** A **hi-fi** is a set of equipment on which you play records and tapes, and which produces stereo sound of very good quality. ◆◇◇◇◇ N-VAR

higgledy-piggledy /hɪgəldi pɪgəldi/. If you say that things are **higgledy-piggledy**, you mean that they are very muddled, untidy, or disorganized; an informal word. *Books are often stacked in higgledy-piggledy piles on the floor.* ADJ-GRADED =jumbled, untidy ► Also an adverb. *A whole valley of boulders tossed higgledy-piggledy as though by some giant.* ADV-GRADED: ADV after v

high /haɪ/ **higher, highest; highs** ◆◆◆◆◆

1 Something that is **high** extends a long way from the bottom to the top when it is upright. You do not use the word **high** to describe people, animals, or plants. *...a house, with a high wall all around it... Mount Marcy is the highest mountain in the Adirondacks. ...distraught people who have threatened to jump from high buildings. ...high-heeled shoes... The gate was too high for a man of his age to climb.* ADJ-GRADED ≠low ► Also an adverb. *...wagons packed high with bureaus, bedding, and cooking pots.* ADV-GRADED: ADV after v

2 You use **high** to talk or ask about how much something upright measures from the bottom to the top. *...an elegant bronze horse only nine inches high... The grass in the yard was waist high... Measure your garage: how high is the door?* ADJ: amount ADJ, n ADJ, *how* ADJ, *as* ADJ *as*, ADJ-compar *than*

3 If something is **high**, it is a long way above the ground, above sea level, or above a person or thing. *I looked down from the high window... The bridge was high, jacked up on wooden piers... The sun was high in the sky, blazing down on us... In Castel Molo, high above Taormina, you can sample the famous almond wine made there.* ADJ-GRADED: oft ADJ prep ≠low ► Also an adverb. *...being able to run faster or jump higher than other people.* ADV-GRADED: ADV after v ● If something is **high up**, it is a long way above the ground, above sea level, or above a person or thing. *His farm was high up in the hills. ...grapes grown high up on the cliff... We saw three birds circling very high up.* PHRASE: oft PHR prep ≠low down

4 You can use **high** to indicate that something is great in amount, degree, or intensity. *The European country with the highest birth rate is Ireland... Official reports said casualties were high... The higher the risk of lending money, the higher is the interest rate demanded by the lenders... High winds have knocked down trees and power lines... Commercialisation has given many sports a higher profile.* ADJ-GRADED ≠low ► Also an adverb. *He expects the unemployment figures to rise even higher in coming months.* ADV-GRADED: ADV after v ● You can use phrases such as **'in the high 80s'** to indicate that a number or level is, for example, more than 85 but not as much as ninety. PHRASE ≠low

5 If a food or other substance is **high in** a particular ingredient, it contains a large amount of that ingredient. *Don't indulge in rich sauces, fried food and thick pastry as these are high in fat. ...a superb compost, high in calcium.* ADJ-GRADED: v-link ADJ *in* n ≠low

6 If something reaches a **high** of a particular amount or degree, that is the greatest it has ever been. *Traffic from Jordan to Iraq is down to a dozen loaded lorries a day, compared with a high of 200 a day... Sales of Russian vodka have reached an all-time high.* N-COUNT: oft N *of* amount ≠low

7 If you say that something is a **high** priority or is **high** on your list, you mean that you consider it to ADJ-GRADED: oft ADJ *on* n ≠low

be one of the most important things you have to do or deal with. *The Labour Party has not made the issue a high priority... Economic reform is high on the agenda.*

8 Someone who is **high** in a particular profession or society, or has a **high** position, has a very important position and has great authority and influence. *Was there anyone particularly high in the administration who was an advocate of a different policy?... Every single one of the arms companies is controlled by the families of high officials. ...corruption in high places. ...high social class.* ● Someone who is **high up** in a profession or society has a very important position. *His cousin is somebody quite high up in the navy... You've offended somebody very high up.*
ADJ-GRADED: v-link ADJ *in* n, ADJ n
PHRASE: oft PHR *in* n

9 You can use **high** to describe something that is advanced or complex. *Neither Anna nor I are interested in high finance. ...the rise of Japan's high technology industries.*
ADJ: ADJ n

10 If you aim **high**, you try to obtain or to achieve the best that you can. *You should not be afraid to aim high in the quest for an improvement in your income... We just do not set our sights high enough.*
ADV-GRADED: ADV after v

11 If someone has a **high** reputation, or people have a **high** opinion of them, people think they are very good in some way, for example at their work. *She has always had a high reputation for her excellent short stories... People have such high expectations of you.*
ADJ-GRADED ≠low

12 If the quality or standard of something is **high**, it is very good indeed. *This is high quality stuff... His team were of the highest calibre... Schools award scholarships for high academic achievement.*
ADJ-GRADED

13 If someone has **high** principles, they are morally good. *He was a man of the highest principles.*
ADJ-GRADED: usu ADJ n

14 A **high** sound or voice is close to the top of a particular range of notes. *Her high voice really irritated Maria.*
ADJ-GRADED ≠low

15 When a river is **high**, it contains much more water than usual. *The waters of the Yangtze River are dangerously high for the time of year.*
ADJ-GRADED ≠low

16 If your spirits are **high**, you feel happy and excited. *Her spirits were high with the hope of seeing Nick in minutes rather than hours.*
ADJ-GRADED ≠low

17 If someone is **high** on drink or drugs, they are affected by the alcoholic drink or drugs they have taken; an informal use. *He was too high on drugs and alcohol to remember them.*
ADJ: v-link ADJ, usu ADJ *on* n

18 A **high** is a feeling or mood of great excitement, stimulation, and happiness; an informal use.
N-COUNT

19 If you say that something came from **on high**, you mean that it came from a person or place of great authority. *Orders had come from on high that extra care was to be taken during this week.*
PHRASES usu *from* PHR

20 If you say that you were left **high and dry**, you are emphasizing that you were left in a difficult situation and were unable to do anything about it; an informal expression. *Schools with better reputations will be flooded with applications while poorer schools will be left high and dry.*
PHR after v, v-link PHR PRAGMATICS

21 If you refer to the **highs and lows** of someone's life or career, you are referring to the successful or happy times, and the unsuccessful or bad times.
oft PHR *of* n =ups and downs

22 If you say that you looked **high and low** for something, you are emphasizing that you looked for it in every place that you could think of.
PHR after v PRAGMATICS

23 ● **in high dudgeon**: see **dudgeon**. ● **come hell or high water**: see **hell**. ● **to be high time**: see **time**.

-high /-haɪ/. **-high** combines with words such as 'knee' or 'shoulder' to indicate that someone or something reaches as high as the point that is mentioned. *The grass was knee-high.* ► Also a combining form. *The Tibetans lifted the man with the flag shoulder-high.*
COMB in ADJ
COMB in ADV: ADV after v

high and mighty. If you describe someone as **high and mighty**, you disapprove of them because they consider themselves to be very important and are confident that they are always right. *I think you're a bit too high and mighty yourself.* ► **The high and mighty** are people who are high and mighty. *The press mogul befriended the high and mighty in Britain.*
ADJ-GRADED PRAGMATICS =arrogant
N-PLURAL: *the* N

highborn /haɪbɔːʳn/; also spelled **high-born**. If someone is **highborn**, their parents are members of the nobility; an old-fashioned word.
ADJ-GRADED

highbrow /haɪbraʊ/ **highbrows**

1 If you say that a book or discussion is **highbrow**, you mean that it is intellectual, academic, and is often difficult to understand. *...highbrow classical music... He presents his own highbrow literary programme.*
ADJ-GRADED ≠lowbrow

2 If you describe someone as **highbrow**, you mean that they are interested in serious subjects of a very intellectual nature; often used showing disapproval. *Highbrow critics sniff that the programme was 'too sophisticated' to appeal to most viewers.* ► Also a noun. *...the sniggers of the highbrows.*
ADJ-GRADED: usu ADJ n PRAGMATICS ≠lowbrow
N-COUNT

high chair, high chairs. A **high chair** is a chair with long legs for a small child to sit in while they are eating.
N-COUNT

high-class; spelled **high class** in American English. If you describe something as **high-class**, you mean that it is of very good quality or of superior social status. *...a high-class jeweller's.*
◆◇◇◇◇ ADJ-GRADED: usu ADJ n

high command, high commands. The **high command** is the group that consists of the most senior officers in a nation's armed forces.
◆◇◇◇◇ N-COUNT-COLL: oft supp N

High Commission, High Commissions. A **High Commission** is an office which houses a High Commissioner and his or her staff, or group of officials who work there.
◆◇◇◇◇ N-COUNT: oft *the* adj N

High Commissioner, High Commissioners
◆◇◇◇◇

1 A **High Commissioner** is a senior representative who is sent by one Commonwealth country to live in another in order to work as an ambassador.
N-COUNT: oft *the* adj N

2 A **High Commissioner** is the head of an international commission. *...the United Nations High Commissioner for Refugees.*
N-COUNT: usu N *for* n, supp N

High Court, High Courts. In England and Wales, the **High Court** is a court of law which deals with very serious or important cases.
◆◆◇◇◇ N-COUNT: usu sing

higher /haɪəʳ/. A **higher** degree or diploma is a qualification of an advanced standard or level. *...a higher diploma in hotel management.* ● See also **high**.
ADJ: ADJ n

higher education. **Higher education** is education at universities and colleges.
◆◆◇◇◇ N-UNCOUNT

high explosive, high explosives. High explosive is an extremely powerful explosive substance.
N-VAR

highfalutin /haɪfəluːtɪn/. People sometimes use **highfalutin** to describe behaviour that they dislike because it seems pompous, pretentious, false, or foolish; an old-fashioned, informal word. *This isn't highfalutin art-about-art. It's marvellous and adventurous stuff.*
ADJ-GRADED =pretentious

high five, high fives; also spelled **high-five**. If you give someone a **high five**, you jump into the air and slap their outstretched hand, especially after a victory or as a greeting.
N-COUNT

high-flier. See **high-flyer**.

high-flown. High-flown language is very grand, formal, or literary; used showing disapproval. *It is highly probable that many of the Service's personnel were put off by such high-flown rhetoric.*
ADJ-GRADED: usu ADJ n PRAGMATICS

high-flyer, high-flyers; spelled **high-flier** in American English. A **high-flyer** is someone who is very ambitious and who is likely to be very successful in their career.
N-COUNT

high-flying. A **high-flying** person is very ambitious and is likely to be successful in their career. *...her high-flying newspaper-editor husband.*
◆◇◇◇◇ ADJ-GRADED: usu ADJ n

high ground
◆◇◇◇◇

1 When journalists say that a person or organization has **the high ground** in an argument or dispute, they mean that that person or organization has an advantage. *The President must seek to regain the high ground in the political debate... How do we recapture the intellectual high ground?*
N-SING: *the* N, oft *the* adj N

2 If you say that someone has taken the **moral high ground**, you mean that they consider that their policies and actions are morally superior to the
PHRASE: PHR after v

policies and actions of their rivals. *The Republicans took the moral high ground with the message that they were best equipped to manage the authority... Now we stand on the moral high ground. We can defend ethically and morally everything we stand for.*

high-handed. If you say that someone is **high-handed**, you disapprove of them because they use their authority in an unnecessarily forceful way without considering other people's feelings. *He wants to be seen as less bossy and high-handed. ...his allegedly high-handed organisation of government business in parliament.* ♦ **high-handedness** *They have been accused of secrecy and high-handedness in their dealings.* ADJ-GRADED PRAGMATICS =overbearing; N-UNCOUNT

high-heeled. **High-heeled** shoes have high heels. ADJ: ADJ n ≠flat

high heels. **High heels** are high-heeled shoes. *...a tall girl in high heels.* ◆◇◇◇◇ N-PLURAL

high jinks. **High jinks** is lively, excited behaviour in which people do things for fun; an old-fashioned, informal expression. N-UNCOUNT-COLL =horseplay

high jump. The **high jump** is an athletics event which involves jumping over a raised bar. N-SING: usu *the* N

highlands /haɪləndz/. **Highlands** are mountainous areas of land. ◆◇◇◇◇ N-PLURAL

high life. You use the **high life** to refer to an exciting and luxurious way of living that involves a great deal of entertainment, going to parties, and eating good food. *Ironically, the Hollywood high life that he had thought he wanted and needed had proved hollow... Most large cities are good for business and high life, but not for families on holiday.* N-SING: also no det

highlight /haɪlaɪt/ **highlights, highlighting, highlighted** ◆◆◆◇◇

1 If someone or something **highlights** a point or problem, they emphasize it or make you think about it. *Last year Collins wrote a moving ballad which highlighted the plight of the homeless... Once again, the 'Free Press' prefers not to highlight these facts... Two events have highlighted the tensions in recent days.* VERB =emphasize; V n

2 The **highlights** of an event, activity, or period of time are the most interesting or exciting parts of it. *...a match that is likely to prove one of the highlights of the tournament... The highlight of my day used to be cooking Meg a meal when she came in from work... I don't want to watch the game now. I'll just wait till the highlights come on later tonight.* N-COUNT: oft N *of* n

3 **Highlights** in a person's hair are thin streaks of lighter colour that have usually been made by dyeing parts of the hair. N-PLURAL

highlighter /haɪlaɪtəʳ/ **highlighters**

1 **Highlighter** is a pale-coloured cosmetic that someone puts above their eyes or on their cheeks to emphasize the shape of their face. N-MASS

2 A **highlighter** is a felt-tip pen with brightly coloured ink that is used to mark parts of a document. N-COUNT

highly /haɪli/ ◆◆◆◆◇

1 **Highly** is used before some adjectives to mean 'very'. *Mr Singh was a highly successful salesman... It seems highly unlikely that she ever existed. ...the highly controversial nuclear energy programme.* ADV: ADV adj PRAGMATICS =very

2 You use **highly** to indicate that someone has an important position in an organization or set of people. *...a highly placed government advisor. ...highly ranked soccer teams.* ADV-GRADED: ADV -ed

3 If someone is **highly** paid, they receive a large salary. *He was the most highly paid member of staff.* ADV-GRADED: ADV -ed

4 If you think **highly** of something or someone, you think they are very good indeed. *Daphne and Michael thought highly of the school. ...one of the most highly regarded chefs in the French capital.* ADV-GRADED: ADV after v, ADV -ed

highly-strung. If someone is **highly-strung**, they are very nervous and easily upset. *He was sensitive and highly-strung, and she had always tried to shield him from his father's sarcasm and violence.* ADJ-GRADED =sensitive

high mass. **High mass** is a church service held in a Catholic church in which there is more ceremony than in an ordinary mass. N-UNCOUNT

high-minded. If you say that someone is **high-minded**, you think they have strong moral principles. *The President's hopes for the country were high-minded, but too vague... She belonged to a high-minded group of ladies who met and discussed Works of Literature.* ADJ-GRADED

Highness /haɪnɪs/ **Highnesses.** Expressions such 'Your **Highness**' or 'His **Highness** are used to address or refer to a member of the royal family other than a king or queen. *That would be best, Your Highness... Her Royal Highness the Duchess of Kent opened an art exhibition recently.* ◆◇◇◇◇ N-VOC: poss N; PRON: poss PRON PRAGMATICS

high noon

1 **High noon** means the same as noon; a literary use. N-UNCOUNT

2 Journalists sometimes use **high noon** to refer to a crisis or event which is likely to decide finally what is going to happen in a conflict or situation. *It looks like high noon for the nation's movie theaters. The film business used to be considered recession proof, but that was before the age of the home video.* N-UNCOUNT: usu with supp, oft N *for/of* n

high-performance. A **high-performance** car or other product goes very fast or does a lot. *...the thrill of taking an expensive high-performance car to its limits. ...high-performance computers.* ADJ-GRADED: ADJ n

high-pitched; also spelled **high pitched.** A **high-pitched** sound is high and shrill. *A woman squealed in a high-pitched voice.* ◆◇◇◇◇ ADJ-GRADED =piercing

high point, high points. The **high point** of an event or period of time is the most exciting or enjoyable part of it. *The high point of this trip was a day at the races in Balgriffin.* ◆◇◇◇◇ N-COUNT: usu with supp, oft N *of/in* n =highlight

high-powered ◆◇◇◇◇

1 A **high-powered** machine or piece of equipment is very powerful and efficient. *...high powered lasers. ...high-powered binoculars.* ADJ-GRADED: usu ADJ n

2 If you describe a job or activity as **high-powered**, you mean that it carries a lot of responsibility or status, and needs a high degree of expertise. *I had a very high-powered senior job in publishing.* ADJ-GRADED: usu ADJ n

3 If you describe someone as **high-powered**, you mean that they have a high-powered job or are involved in a high-powered activity. *Her father is a very high-powered solicitor in London... A high-powered American team of officials is visiting India and Pakistan next week.* ADJ-GRADED: usu ADJ n

high priest, high priests. If you call a man the **high priest** of a particular thing, you are saying in a slightly mocking way that he is considered by people to be expert in that thing. *...the high priest of cheap periodical fiction.* N-COUNT: usu N *of* n PRAGMATICS

high priestess, high priestesses. If you call a woman the **high priestess** of a particular thing, you are saying in a slightly mocking way that she is considered by people to be expert in that thing. *...the American high priestess of wit.* N-COUNT: usu N *of* n PRAGMATICS

high-profile. A **high-profile** person or a **high-profile** event attracts a lot of attention or publicity. *...high-profile singers like Prince and Madonna. ...the high-profile reception being given to Mr Arafat.* ◆◇◇◇◇ ADJ-GRADED: usu ADJ n

high-ranking. A **high-ranking** person has an important position in a particular organization. *...a high-ranking officer in the medical corps.* ◆◇◇◇◇ ADJ: ADJ n

high-rise, high-rises. **High-rise** buildings are modern buildings which are very tall and have many storeys. *...high-rise apartment blocks. ...high-rise office buildings.* ► A **high-rise** is a high-rise building. *That big high-rise above us is where Brian lives.* ◆◇◇◇◇ ADJ: ADJ n; N-COUNT

high road, high roads

1 In British English, a **high road** is a main road. The usual American word is **highway**. *The gutters either side of the paved high road were gurgling and even flooding.* N-COUNT: usu sing

2 You say that something is the **high road** to a particular situation when it seems likely to lead to that situation. *This is the high road to disaster.* N-SING: usu *the* N *to* n

3 If you say that someone is taking the **high road** in a situation, you mean that they are taking the most positive and careful course of action; used mainly N-SING: usu *the* N

in American English. *US diplomats say the president is likely to take the high road in his statements about trade.*

high-roller high-rollers; also spelled **high roller.** When journalists refer to **high rollers**, they are referring to people who are very rich and who spend money in an extravagant or risky way, especially by gambling. N-COUNT

high school, high schools ◆◆◇◇◇

1 In Britain, a **high school** is a school for children aged between eleven and eighteen. *...Sunderland High School.* N-VAR: oft in names after n

2 In the United States, a **high school** is a school for children aged between fourteen and eighteen. *...an 18-year-old inner-city kid who dropped out of high school. ...the high school football team.* N-VAR: oft in names after n

high season. The **high season** is the time of year when a holiday resort, hotel, or tourist attraction receives most visitors; used mainly in British English. *A typical high-season week in a chalet costs about £470.* N-SING: also no det ≠low season

high-sounding. **High-sounding** language and ideas seem very grand and important, although often they are not at all important; used showing disapproval. *... high-sounding decrees designed to impress foreigners and attract foreign capital.* ADJ-GRADED: usu ADJ n PRAGMATICS

high-spirited

1 Someone who is **high-spirited** is very lively and easily excited. ADJ-GRADED ≠placid

2 A **high-spirited** horse is difficult to control because it is very lively, active, or nervous. ADJ-GRADED

high spot, high spots. The **high spot** of an event or activity is the most exciting or enjoyable part of it. *Rough weather would have denied us a landing on the island, for me the high spot of the entire cruise.* N-COUNT: oft N of n =highlight, high point

high street, high streets ◆◆◇◇◇

1 The **high street** of a town is the main street where most of the shops and banks are; used mainly in British English. *Vegetarian restaurants and health food shops are springing up in every high street. ...West Bromwich high street.* N-COUNT: oft in names after n

2 **High street** banks and retailers are companies which have branches in the main shopping areas of most towns; used mainly in British English. *The scanners are available from high street stores.* ADJ: ADJ n

high summer. **High summer** is the middle of summer. N-UNCOUNT

high tea, high teas. In Britain, some people have **high tea** in the late afternoon instead of having dinner or supper later in the evening. N-VAR

high tech; also spelled **hi tech.** **High tech** activities or equipment involve or result from the use of high technology. *...such high-tech industries as computers or telecommunications. ...the latest high-tech medical gadgetry.* ◆◆◇◇◇ ADJ-GRADED: usu ADJ n

high technology. **High technology** is the practical use of advanced scientific research and knowledge, especially in relation to electronics and computers, and the development of new advanced machines and equipment. ◆◇◇◇◇ N-UNCOUNT

high-tension. A **high-tension** electricity cable is one which is able to carry a very powerful current. ADJ: ADJ n

high tide. At the coast, **high tide** is the time when the sea is at its highest level because the tide is in. N-UNCOUNT ≠low tide

high treason. **High treason** is a very serious crime which involves putting your country or its head of state in danger. N-UNCOUNT

high-up, high-ups ◆◇◇◇◇

1 In informal English, a **high-up** is an important person who has a lot of authority and influence. N-COUNT

2 • **high up**: see **high**.

high water. **High water** is the time at which the water in a river or sea is at its highest level as a result of the tide. *Fishing is possible for a couple of hours either side of high water.* • **come hell or high water**: see **hell**. ◆◇◇◇◇ N-UNCOUNT =high tide

high-water mark; also spelled **high water mark.**

1 **The high-water mark** is the level reached in a particular place by the sea at high tide or by a river in flood. N-SING: the N

2 The **high-water mark** of a process is its highest or most successful stage of achievement. *This was almost certainly the high-water mark of her career... This period represented a high water mark for liberal denominations.* N-SING: with supp, oft N of/for n

highway /haɪweɪ/ **highways.** A **highway** is a main road, especially one that connects towns or cities; used mainly in American English. *I crossed the highway, dodging the traffic.* ◆◆◇◇◇ N-COUNT

Highway Code. In Britain, **the Highway Code** is an official booklet published by the Department of Transport, which contains the rules which tell people how to use public roads safely. N-SING: the N

highwayman /haɪweɪmən/ **highwaymen.** In former times, **highwaymen** were robbers on horseback who used to threaten to shoot travellers if they did not hand over their money and valuable possessions. N-COUNT

high wire, high wires; also spelled **high-wire.**

1 A **high wire** is a length of rope or wire stretched tight high above the ground and used for balancing acts. N-COUNT =tightrope

2 Journalists talk about a person being on a **high wire** or performing a **high-wire** act when he or she is involved in a delicate, tricky situation, and is dealing with it cleverly. *What could have been a mere intellectual high wire act becomes a wholly unexpected delight.* N-SING: oft N n

hijack /haɪdʒæk/ **hijacks, hijacking, hijacked** ◆◇◇◇◇

1 If someone **hijacks** a plane or other vehicle, they illegally take control of it by force while it is travelling from one place to another. *Two men tried to hijack a plane on a flight from Riga to Murmansk... Almost 250 trucks were hijacked before they reached central Bosnia... The hijacked plane exploded in a ball of fire.* ► Also a noun. *Every minute during the hijack seemed like a week.* ♦ **hijacking, hijackings** *There have been at least ten attempted hijackings in the Soviet Union.* VERB V n V-ed N-COUNT N-COUNT

2 If you say that someone **has hijacked** something, you disapprove of the way in which they have taken control of it when they had no right to do so. *A peaceful demonstration had been hijacked by anarchists intent on causing trouble.* VERB PRAGMATICS V n

hijacker /haɪdʒækəʳ/ **hijackers.** A **hijacker** is a person who hijacks a plane or other vehicle. ◆◇◇◇◇ N-COUNT

hike /haɪk/ **hikes, hiking, hiked** ◆◆◇◇◇

1 A **hike** is a long walk in the country, especially one that you go on for pleasure. N-COUNT =walk

2 If you **hike**, you go for a long walk in the country. *You could hike through the Fish River Canyon – it's entirely up to you... We plan to hike the Samaria Gorge.* ♦ **hiking** *...some harder, more strenuous hiking on cliff pathways. ...heavy hiking boots.* VERB =walk V prep/adv V n Also V N-UNCOUNT: oft N n

3 A **hike** is a sudden or large increase in prices, rates, taxes, or quantities; an informal use. *...a sudden 1.75 per cent hike in Italian interest rates... His economic plan, with its tax hikes and spending cuts, will slow the economy.* N-COUNT: usu supp N =rise

4 To **hike** prices, rates, taxes, or quantities means to increase them suddenly or by a large amount; an informal use. *It has now been forced to hike its rates by 5.25 per cent... TSB's monthly credit card rate is now hiked from 1.95% to 2.05%... The federal government hiked the tax on hard liquor.* ► **Hike up** means the same as **hike**. *The insurers have started hiking up premiums by huge amounts... Big banks were hiking their rates by up to 15 per cent.* VERB =raise V n PHRASAL VERB V P n (not pron) V n P

hike up. If you **hike up** your clothing, you pull or lift it up quickly or roughly, especially so you can move more easily. *He hiked up his trouser legs... I hiked my nightgown right up and I ran.* • See also **hike** 4. PHRASAL VERB =hitch up V P n (not pron) V n P

hiker /haɪkəʳ/ **hikers.** A **hiker** is a person who is going for a long walk in the countryside for pleasure. N-COUNT

hilarious /hɪleəriəs/. If something is **hilarious**, it is extremely funny and makes you laugh a lot. *We thought it was hilarious when we first heard about it... He had a fund of hilarious tales on the* ◆◇◇◇◇ ADJ-GRADED *subject.* ♦ **hilariously** *She found it hilariously funny... Safire writes hilariously of being banished from presidential favor.* ADV-GRADED: usu ADV adj, ADV with v, also ADV with cl

hilarity /hɪlærɪti/. **Hilarity** is great amusement and laughter. N-UNCOUNT

hill /hɪl/ **hills** ◆◆◆◇◇

1 A **hill** is an area of land that is higher than the land that surrounds it. *...the shady street that led up the hill to the office building. ...the Black Hills of Dakota.* N-COUNT: oft in names

2 If you say that someone is **over the hill**, you are saying rudely that they are old and no longer fit, attractive, or capable of doing useful work; an informal expression. *He doesn't take kindly to suggestions that he is over the hill.* PHRASE: usu v-link PHR PRAGMATICS =past it

hillbilly /hɪlbɪli/ **hillbillies.** If you refer to someone as a **hillbilly**, you think they are uneducated and stupid because they come from the countryside; used in American English. N-COUNT PRAGMATICS

hillock /hɪlək/ **hillocks.** A **hillock** is a small hill. N-COUNT

hillside /hɪlsaɪd/ **hillsides.** A **hillside** is the sloping side of a hill. ◆◇◇◇◇ N-COUNT

hilltop /hɪltɒp/ **hilltops.** A **hilltop** is the top of a hill. *The Morrison's home stood on a wooded hilltop. ...a medieval hilltop village.* ◆◇◇◇◇ N-COUNT: oft N n

hilly /hɪli/ **hillier, hilliest.** A **hilly** area has many hills. *The areas where the fighting is taking place are hilly and densely wooded.* ◆◇◇◇◇ ADJ-GRADED

hilt /hɪlt/ **hilts**

1 The **hilt** of a sword, dagger, or knife is its handle. *...the hilt of the small, sharp knife.* N-COUNT

2 **'To the hilt'** and **'up to the hilt'** mean to the maximum extent possible or as fully as possible; used in informal English to emphasize an action or situation. *The men who wield the power are certainly backing him to the hilt... James was overdrawn and mortgaged to the hilt... She was in this right up to the hilt.* PHRASE: usu PHR after v PRAGMATICS

him /hɪm/ ◆◆◆◆◆

Him is a third person singular pronoun. **Him** is used as the object of a verb or a preposition.

1 You use **him** to refer to a man, boy, or male animal. *John's aunt died suddenly and left him a surprisingly large sum... Is Sam there? Let me talk to him... On his arrival, Elaine met him at the bus station... My brother had a lovely dog. I looked after him for about a week.* PRON-SING: v PRON, prep PRON

2 In written English, writers sometimes use **him** to refer to a person without saying whether that person is a man or a woman. Some people dislike this use and prefer to use 'him or her' or 'them'. *If the child encounters 'hear', we should show him that this is the base word in 'hearing' and 'hears'.* PRON-SING: v PRON, prep PRON

3 In some religions, **Him** is used to refer to God. *God will help you if you turn to Him in humility and trust.* PRON-SING: v PRON, prep PRON

himself /hɪmself/ ◆◆◆◆◆

Himself is a third person singular reflexive pronoun. **Himself** is used when the object of a verb or preposition refers to the same person as the subject of the verb, except in meaning 4.

1 You use **himself** to refer to a man, boy, or male animal. *He poured himself a whisky and sat down in the chair... A driver blew up his car and himself after being stopped at a police checkpoint... William went away muttering to himself.* PRON-REFL: v PRON, prep PRON

2 In written English, writers sometimes use **himself** to refer to a person without saying whether that person is a man or a woman. Some people dislike this use and prefer to use 'himself or herself' or 'themselves'. *The child's natural way of expressing himself is play... The student is invited to test each item for himself by means of specific techniques.* PRON-REFL: v PRON, prep PRON

3 In some religions, **Himself** is used to refer to God. *He thanked God for concealing Himself from the wise and revealing Himself to the simple.* PRON-REFL: v PRON, prep PRON

4 You use **himself** to emphasize the person or thing that you are referring to. **Himself** is sometimes used instead of 'him' as the object of a verb or preposition. *The Prime Minister himself is on a visit to Peking... He himself had joined the others straight from the office... There's no work and no future for students like himself.* PRON-REFL-EMPH PRAGMATICS

hind /haɪnd/ **hinds** ◆◇◇◇◇

1 An animal's **hind** legs are at the back of its body. *Suddenly the cow kicked up its hind legs.* ADJ: ADJ n =rear

2 A **hind** is a female deer, especially one of the red deer family. N-COUNT =doe

hinder /hɪndəʳ/ **hinders, hindering, hindered** ◆◇◇◇◇

1 If something **hinders** you, it makes it more difficult for you to do something or make progress. *Does the fact that your players are part-timers help or hinder you?... Further investigation was hindered by the loss of all documentation on the case.* VERB V n

2 If something **hinders** your movement, it makes it difficult for you to move forward or move around. *A thigh injury increasingly hindered her mobility... Landslides and bad weather are continuing to hinder the arrival of relief supplies to the area.* VERB V n

Hindi /hɪndi/. **Hindi** is a language that is spoken by people in northern India. It is also one of the official languages of India. N-UNCOUNT

hindquarters /haɪndkwɔːʳtəz/; also spelled **hind quarters**. The **hindquarters** of a four-legged animal are its back part, including its two back legs. N-PLURAL: oft with poss

hindrance /hɪndrəns/ **hindrances**

1 A **hindrance** is a person or thing that makes it more difficult for you to do something. *The higher rates have been a hindrance to economic recovery... You would be more of a hindrance than a help.* N-COUNT: oft N to n ≠help

2 **Hindrance** is the act of hindering someone or something. *They boarded their flight to Paris without hindrance.* N-UNCOUNT

hindsight /haɪndsaɪt/. **Hindsight** is the ability to understand and realize something about an event after it has happened, although you did not understand or realize it at the time. *With hindsight, we'd all do things differently... Even with the benefit of hindsight, I doubt I would change anything if I had my time again.* ◆◇◇◇◇ N-UNCOUNT: oft with/in N =in retrospect

Hindu /hɪnduː, hɪnduː/ **Hindus** ◆◆◇◇◇

1 A **Hindu** is a person who believes in Hinduism and follows its teachings. N-COUNT

2 **Hindu** is used to describe things that belong or relate to Hinduism. *...a Hindu temple.* ADJ: usu ADJ n

Hinduism /hɪnduːɪzəm/. **Hinduism** is an Indian religion. It has many gods and teaches that people have another life on earth after they die. N-UNCOUNT

hinge /hɪndʒ/ **hinges, hinging, hinged.** A **hinge** is a piece of metal, wood, or plastic that is used to join a door to its frame or to join two things together so that one of them can swing freely. *The top swung open on well-oiled hinges.* ◆◇◇◇◇ N-COUNT

hinge on. Something that **hinges on** one thing or event depends entirely on it. *The plan hinges on a deal being struck with a new company... A lot hinges on how we are viewed by overseas investors.* PHRASAL VERB V P n/-ing/wh

hinged /hɪndʒd/. Something that is **hinged** is joined to another thing, or joined together, by means of a hinge. *The mirror was hinged to a surrounding frame... The hinged seat lifts up to reveal a useful storage space.* ADJ

hint /hɪnt/ **hints, hinting, hinted** ◆◆◆◇◇

1 A **hint** is a suggestion about something that is made in an indirect way. *The Minister gave a strong hint that the government were thinking of introducing tax concessions for mothers... I'd dropped a hint about having an exhibition of his work up here... The statement gave no hint as to what the measures would be.* ● If you **take a hint**, you understand something that is suggested to you indirectly. *'I think I hear the telephone ringing.'—'Okay, I can take a hint.'* N-COUNT: oft N that; PHRASE: V inflects

2 If you **hint** at something, you suggest it in an indirect way. *She suggested a trip to the shops and hinted at the possibility of a treat of some sort... Criticism is hinted at, but never made explicit... Was he hinting that there could be some connection between drugs and Ian's disappearance?... The President hinted he might make some changes in the government.* VERB V at n V that

3 A **hint** is a helpful piece of advice, usually about how to do something. *Here are some helpful hints* N-COUNT: usu supp N =tip

to make your journey easier... I'm hoping to get some fashion hints.

4 A **hint** of something is a very small amount of it. *She added only a hint of vermouth to the gin... I glanced at her and saw no hint of irony on her face.* N-SING: N of n =trace

hinterland /hɪntəʳlænd/ **hinterlands.** The **hinterland** of a piece of coastline or a large river is the area of land behind it or around it. *...the French Mediterranean coast and its hinterland.* ◆◇◇◇◇ N-COUNT: usu sing, usu with supp

hip /hɪp/ **hips** ◆◆◆◇◇

1 Your **hips** are the two areas at the sides of your body between the tops of your legs and your waist. *Tracey put her hands on her hips and sighed.* N-COUNT: oft poss N
♦ **-hipped** *He is broad-chested and narrow-hipped.* COMB in ADJ

2 You refer to the bones between the tops of your legs and your waist as your **hips.** N-COUNT: oft poss N

3 If you say that someone is **hip**, you mean that they are very modern and follow all the latest fashions, for example in clothes and ideas; an informal use. *...a hip young character with tight-cropped blond hair and stylish glasses.* ADJ-GRADED =trendy

4 A **hip** is a rosehip. N-COUNT

5 If a large group of people want to show their appreciation or approval of someone, one of them says **Hip hip** and they all shout **hooray.** PHRASES EXCLAM

6 If you say that someone **shoots from the hip** or **fires from the hip**, you mean that they react to situations or give their opinion very quickly, without stopping to think. *Judges don't have to shoot from the hip. They have the leisure to think, to decide.* V inflects

hip flask, hip flasks. A **hip flask** is a small metal container in which brandy, whisky, or other spirits can be carried. N-COUNT

hip-hop. **Hip-hop** is a form of popular culture which started among young black people in the United States in the 1980s. It includes rap music and graffiti art. ◆◇◇◇◇ N-UNCOUNT: oft N n

hippie /hɪpi/ **hippies;** also spelled **hippy**. **Hippies** were young people in the 1960s and 1970s who rejected conventional ways of living, dressing, and behaving, and tried to live a life based on peace and love. Hippies usually had long hair and many took drugs. ◆◇◇◇◇ N-COUNT

hippo /hɪpoʊ/ **hippos.** A **hippo** is a hippopotamus; an informal word. N-COUNT

Hippocratic oath /hɪpəkrætɪk oʊθ/ **Hippocratic oaths.** The **Hippocratic oath** is a solemn promise made by newly qualified doctors, saying that they will follow the standards set by their profession and try to preserve life. N-COUNT

hippopotamus /hɪpəpɒtəməs/ **hippopotamuses.** A **hippopotamus** is a very large African animal with short legs and thick, hairless skin. Hippopotamuses live near rivers. N-COUNT

hippy /hɪpi/. See **hippie.**

hipster /hɪpstəʳ/ **hipsters**

1 If you refer to someone as a **hipster**, you mean that they are very fashionable, often in a way that you think is rather silly. *...a swaggering hipster with a fondness for Teddy Boy clothes.* N-COUNT

2 **Hipsters** are trousers which are designed so that the highest part of them is around your hips, rather than around your waist; used mainly in British English. N-PLURAL: oft N n

hire /haɪəʳ/ **hires, hiring, hired** ◆◆◆◇◇

1 If you **hire** someone, you employ them or pay them to do a particular job for you. *Sixteen of the contestants have hired lawyers and are suing the organisers... The rest of the staff have been hired on short-term contracts... He will be in charge of all hiring and firing at PHA. ...the mystery assassin (who turned out to be a hired killer).* VERB V n V-ing V-ed

2 If you **hire** something, you pay money to the owner so that you can use it for a period of time; used mainly in British English. *To hire a car you must produce a passport and a current driving licence... Her hired car was found abandoned at Beachy Head.* VERB =rent V n V-ed

3 You use **hire** to refer to the activity or business of hiring something; used mainly in British English. *They booked our hotel, and organised car hire... Hire of skis, boots and clothing, are all available. ...a day's outing by hire car to the southern coast of Crete.* N-UNCOUNT: usu n N, N of n, N n =rental
● If something is **for hire**, it is available for you to hire; used mainly in British English. *Fishing tackle is available for hire and tuition can be arranged.* PHRASE: usu v-link PHR =to rent

hire out. If you **hire out** something such as a car or a person's services, you allow them to be used in return for payment. *Companies hiring out narrow boats report full order books... His agency hires out security guards and bodyguards.* PHRASAL VERB V P n (not pron) Also V n P

hireling /haɪəʳlɪŋ/ **hirelings.** If you refer to someone a **hireling**, you disapprove of them because they do not care who they work for and they are willing to do illegal or immoral things as long as they are paid. N-COUNT PRAGMATICS

hire purchase. In British English, **hire purchase** is a way of buying goods gradually. You make regular payments to the seller until, after some time, you have paid the full price and the goods belong to you. The usual American term is **installment plan**. *...the serious problem of hire purchase and credit card debts. ...buying a car on hire purchase.* N-UNCOUNT: oft N n

hirsute /hɜːʳsjuːt, AM -suːt/. If a man is **hirsute**, he is hairy; a formal word. ADJ-GRADED

his. The determiner is pronounced /hɪz/. The pronoun is pronounced /hɪz/. **His** is a third person singular possessive determiner. **His** is also a possessive pronoun. ◆◆◆◆◆

1 You use **his** to indicate that something belongs or relates to a man, boy, or male animal. *Brian splashed water on his face, then brushed his teeth... He spent a large part of his career in Hollywood... The past 10 years have been the happiest and most fulfilling of his life... The dog let his head thump on the floor again.* DET-POSS
► Also a possessive pronoun. *He had taken advice, but the decision was his... Anna reached out her hand to him and clasped his.* PRON-POSS

2 In written English, writers sometimes use **his** to refer to a person without saying whether that person is a man or a woman. Some people dislike this use and prefer to use 'his or her' or 'their'. *Formerly, the relations between a teacher and his pupils were dominated by fear on the part of the pupils... Everyone should receive a fair price for the product of his labour.* DET-POSS
► Also a possessive pronoun. *The student going to art or drama school will be even more enthusiastic about further education than the university student. His is not a narrow mind, but one eager to grasp every facet of anything he studies.* PRON-POSS

3 In some religions, **His** is used to refer to God. *...humble faith in God, and trust in His Church.* DET-POSS
► Also a possessive pronoun. *In what way do you feel called to serve God as a clergyman? Is it your way, or His?* PRON-POSS

Hispanic /hɪspænɪk/ **Hispanics.** A **Hispanic** person is a citizen of the United States of America who originally came from Latin America, or whose family originally came from Latin America. *...a group of Hispanic doctors in Washington... The former mayor of San Antonio is Hispanic.* ◆◆◇◇◇ ADJ
► A **Hispanic** is someone who is Hispanic. N-COUNT

hiss /hɪs/ **hisses, hissing, hissed** ◆◇◇◇◇

1 To **hiss** means to make a sound like a long 's'. *The tires of Lenny's bike hissed over the wet pavement as he slowed down... My cat hisses when I step on its tail... Caporelli made a small hissing sound of irritation.* VERB V prep V V-ing
► Also a noun. *...the hiss of water running into the burnt pan... The CD banished for ever all the hisses and crackles that had plagued disc recordings until then.* N-COUNT
♦ **hissing** *...a silence broken only by a steady hissing from above my head.* N-UNCOUNT

2 If you **hiss** something, you say it in a strong, angry whisper. *'Now, quiet,' my mother hissed... 'Stay here,' I hissed at her.* VERB V with quote V *at/to* n with quote

3 If people **hiss** at someone such as a performer or a person making a speech, they express their disapproval or dislike of that person by making long loud 's' sounds. *One had to listen hard to catch the words of the President's speech as the delegates booed and hissed... Some local residents whistled* VERB V V *at* n Also V n

and hissed at them as they entered. ► Also a noun. *After a moment the barracking began. First came hisses, then shouts.* N-COUNT: usu pl =hissing

historian /hɪstɔːriən/ **historians.** A **historian** is a person who specializes in the study of history, and who writes books and articles about it. ◆◆◇◇◇ N-COUNT

historic /hɪstɒrɪk, AM -tɔːr-/. Something that is **historic** is important in history, or likely to be considered important at some time in the future. *...the historic changes in the Soviet Union. ...a fourth historic election victory.* ◆◆◆◇◇ ADJ: usu ADJ n

historical /hɪstɒrɪkəl, AM -tɔːr-/ ◆◆◆◇◇

1 **Historical** people, situations, or things existed in the past and are considered to be a part of history. *...an important historical figure. ...the historical impact of Western capitalism on the world... In Buda, several historical monuments can be seen.* ♦ **historically** *Historically, royal marriages have been cold, calculating affairs.* ADJ: ADJ n; ADV

2 **Historical** books, films, or pictures describe or represent people, situations, or things that existed in the past. *He is writing a historical novel about nineteenth-century France. ...another great Eisenstein historical film.* ADJ: ADJ n

3 **Historical** information, research, and discussion is related to the study of history. *...historical records. ...modern historical research.* ADJ: ADJ n

4 If you look at an event within a **historical** context, you look at what was happening at that time and what had happened previously, in order to assess what the event means and how important it is. *It was this kind of historical context that Morris brought to his work... The Telegraph puts the union in a historical perspective.* ADJ: ADJ n

history /hɪstəri/ **histories** ◆◆◆◆◆

1 You can refer to the events of the past as **history**. You can also refer to the past events which concern a particular topic or place as its history. *The Catholic Church has played a prominent role throughout Polish history. ...the most evil mass killer in history. ...the history of Birmingham. ...religious history.* N-UNCOUNT: usu with supp

• Someone who **makes history** does something that is considered to be important and significant in the development of the world or of a particular society. *Willy Brandt made history by visiting East Germany in 1970.* PHRASE: V inflects • If someone or something **goes down in history**, people in the future remember them because of particular actions that they have done or because of particular events that have happened. *Bradley will go down in history as Los Angeles' longest serving mayor. ...a day that will go down in history.* PHRASE: V inflects

2 **History** is a subject studied in schools, colleges, and universities that deals with events that have happened in the past. N-UNCOUNT

3 A **history** is an account of events that have happened in the past. *...his magnificent history of broadcasting in Canada. ...oral histories taken from elderly people in Rochester.* N-COUNT: with supp, oft N *of* n

4 If a person or a place has a **history** of something, it has been very common or has happened frequently in their past. *He had a history of drink problems... The boy's mother had a history of abusing her children.* N-COUNT: usu sing, usu *a* N *of* n/-ing =record

5 Someone's **history** is the set of facts that are known about their past. *He couldn't get a new job because of his medical history. ...an exhibition documenting the personal history of Anne Frank.* N-COUNT: with poss

6 If you say that an event, thing, or person is **history**, you mean that they are no longer important. *The Charlottetown agreement is history.* N-UNCOUNT

7 If you are telling someone about an event and say **the rest is history**, you mean that you do not need to tell them what happened next because everyone knows about it already. *We met at college, the rest is history.* PHRASE

8 See also **natural history**.

histrionic /hɪstriɒnɪk/. If you refer to someone's behaviour as **histrionic**, you are critical of it because it is very dramatic, exaggerated, and insincere. *Dorothea let out a histrionic groan.* ADJ-GRADED: usu ADJ n PRAGMATICS

histrionics /hɪstriɒnɪks/. If you disapprove of someone's dramatic and exaggerated behaviour, you can describe it as **histrionics**. *When I explained everything to my mum and dad, there were no histrionics.* N-PLURAL PRAGMATICS

hit /hɪt/ **hits, hitting.** The form **hit** is used in the present tense and is the past and present participle. ◆◆◆◆◆

1 If you **hit** someone or something, you deliberately touch them with a lot of force, with your hand or an object held in your hand. *Find the exact grip that allows you to hit the ball hard... She hit him hard across his left arm... Police at the scene said Dr Mahgoub had been hit several times in the head.* VERB =strike V n

2 When one thing **hits** another, it touches it with a lot of force. *The car had apparently hit a traffic sign before skidding out of control... She hit the last barrier and sprawled across the track.* VERB =strike V n

3 If a bomb or missile **hits** its target, it reaches it. *...multiple-warhead missiles that could hit many targets at a time... The hospital had been hit with heavy artillery fire.* ► Also a noun. *First a house took a direct hit and then the rocket exploded.* VERB V n; N-COUNT

4 If something **hits** a person, place, or thing, it affects them very badly; used in journalism. *The plan to charge motorists £75 a year to use the motorway is going to hit me hard... About two-hundred people died in the earthquake which hit northern Peru... Special schools were hardest hit.* VERB V n

5 When a feeling or an idea **hits** you, it suddenly affects you or comes into your mind. *It hit me that I had a choice... Then the answer hit me. It had been staring me in the face.* VERB *it* V n that; V n

6 If you **hit** a particular high or low point on a scale of something such as success or health, you reach it; used in journalism. *The number of 16-year-old school-leavers hit its lowest point for over 30 years... Oil prices hit record levels yesterday.* VERB V n

7 If a record, film, or play is a **hit**, it is very popular and successful. *The song became a massive hit in 1945. ...the surprise hit video of the year.* N-COUNT: oft N n ≠flop

8 If two people **hit it off**, they like each other and become friendly as soon as they meet. *They hit it off straight away, Daddy and Walter... How well did you hit it off with one another?* PHRASES RECIP: V inflects, pl-n PHR, PHR *with* n

9 If you **make a hit** with someone, they like you or are impressed by you when they meet you. *He made a hit with Lady Sopwith... She sends her best wishes – you've obviously made a hit there.* V inflects, oft PHR *with* n

10 • to **hit the bottle**: see **bottle**. • to **hit the headlines**: see **headline**. • to **hit home**: see **home**. • to **hit the nail on the head**: see **nail**. • to **hit the road**: see **road**. • to **hit the roof**: see **roof**. • to **hit** someone **for six**: see **six**.

hit back PHRASAL VERB

1 If you **hit back** when someone hits you, or **hit** them **back**, you hit them in return. *Some violent men beat up their sons, until the boys are strong enough to hit back... If somebody hit me, I'd hit him back.* VP; V n P

2 If you **hit back** at someone who has criticized or harmed you, you criticize or harm them in return; used in journalism. *The President has hit back at those who have criticised his economic reforms... British Rail immediately hit back with their own cheap fares scheme.* =retaliate V P *at* n; V P

hit on or **hit upon.** If you **hit on** an idea or a solution to a problem, or **hit upon** it, you think of it. *After running through the numbers in every possible combination, we finally hit on a solution.* PHRASAL VERB =stumble on V P n

hit out PHRASAL VERB

1 If you **hit out** at someone, you try to hit them, although you may miss them; used mainly in British English. *I used to hit out at my husband and throw things at him... I had never punched anybody in my life but I hit out and gave him a black eye.* =lash out V P *at* n; V P

2 If you **hit out** at someone or something, you criticize them strongly because you do not agree with them; used in journalism. *The President took the opportunity to hit out at what he sees as foreign interference... Brazilian soccer boss Carlos Parreira* V P *at/against* n; V P

hit out angrily last night after his side were barred from training at Wembley.

hit upon. See **hit on.** PHRASAL VERB

hit and miss; also spelled **hit-and-miss.** Something that is **hit and miss** or **hit or miss** happens in an unplanned way, so that you cannot predict what the result will be. *Our tester found its efficiency a bit hit-and-miss at first... Farming can thus be very much a hit-and-miss affair.* ADJ-GRADED

hit-and-run

1 A **hit-and-run** accident is an accident in which the driver of a vehicle hits someone and then drives away without stopping. *...the victim of a hit-and-run accident. ...a hit-and-run driver in a stolen car.* ADJ: ADJ n

2 A **hit-and-run** attack on an enemy position relies on surprise and speed for its success. *The rebels appear to be making hit-and-run guerrilla style attacks on military targets.* ADJ: ADJ n

hitch /hɪtʃ/ **hitches, hitching, hitched** ◆◇◇◇◇

1 A **hitch** is a slight problem or difficulty which causes a short delay. *After some technical hitches the show finally got under way... The five-hour operation went without a hitch.* N-COUNT =snag

2 If you **hitch, hitch** a lift, or **hitch** a ride, you hitch-hike; an informal use. *There was no garage in sight, so I hitched a lift into town... Jean-Phillippe had hitched all over Europe in the 1960s.* VERB V n V

3 If you **hitch** something onto something else, you hook it or fasten it there. *Last night we hitched the horse to the cart and moved here.* VERB V n *onto/to* n

4 If you **get hitched**, you get married; an informal expression. *The report shows that fewer couples are getting hitched.* PHRASE: V inflects

hitch up. If you **hitch up** a piece of clothing such as a skirt or pair of trousers, you pull it up into a higher position. *She leapt from the car, hitched up her dress and sprinted down the road after him... He hitched his trousers up over his potbelly.* PHRASAL VERB V P n (not pron) V n P

hitchhike /hɪtʃhaɪk/ **hitchhikes, hitchhiking, hitchhiked;** also spelled **hitch-hike.** If you **hitchhike**, you travel by getting lifts from passing vehicles without paying. *Neff hitchhiked to New York during his Christmas vacation... They had an eighty-mile journey and decided to hitchhike... She decided hitchhiking was her best method of escape.* ♦ **hitchhiker, hitchhikers** *On my way to Vancouver one Friday night I picked up a hitchhiker.* VERB V prep/adv V V-ing N-COUNT

hi tech. See **high tech.**

hither /hɪðəʳ/

1 Hither means to the place where you are; an old-fashioned word. *He has sent hither swarms of officers to harass our people.* ADV: ADV after v =here

2 In British English, **hither and thither** means in many different directions or places, and in a disorganized way. The usual American expression is **hither and yon.** *Refugees run hither and thither in search of safety. ...the awful amount of time I spend moving things hither and yon every year!* PHRASE: PHR after v

hitherto /hɪðəʳtuː/. You use **hitherto** to indicate that something was true up until the time you are talking about, although it may no longer be the case; a fairly formal word. *The polytechnics have hitherto been at an unfair disadvantage in competing for pupils and money... Hitherto, the main emphasis has been on the need to resist aggression... The helicopter is the first in the world to be designed to serve three hitherto very distinct markets.* ◆◇◇◇◇ ADV: ADV after v, ADV with cl, ADV adj/-ed PRAGMATICS

hit list, hit lists ◆◇◇◇◇

1 If someone has a **hit list** of people or things, they are intending to take action concerning those people or things. *Some banks also have a hit list of people whom they threaten to sue for damages. ...America's hit list of countries targeted for unfair trade practices.* N-COUNT: oft poss N, N *of* n

2 A **hit list** is a list that terrorists or gangsters make, containing the names of people they intend to have killed. N-COUNT

hitman /hɪtmæn/ **hitmen;** also spelled **hit man.** A **hitman** is a man who is hired by someone in order to kill people. N-COUNT

hit or miss. See **hit and miss.**

hit parade. The **hit parade** is the list of pop records which have sold most copies over the previous week or month; an old-fashioned expression. *Suede are once again riding high in the hit parade with their new single.* N-SING: *the* N =charts

hitter /hɪtəʳ/ **hitters** ◆◇◇◇◇

1 In sport, a **hitter** is someone who is good at hitting the ball. *The Georgian, aged 19, is not one of the game's big hitters.* N-COUNT

2 If you refer to someone such as a politician or a businessman as a heavy **hitter** or a big **hitter**, you mean that they are powerful and influential. *...friendships with heavy hitters like European industrialist Carlo De Benedetti.* N-COUNT: adj N

HIV /eɪtʃ aɪ viː/ ◆◆◆◇◇

1 HIV is a virus which reduces people's resistance to illness and can cause AIDS. **HIV** is an abbreviation of 'human immunodeficiency virus'. N-UNCOUNT: oft N n

2 If someone is **HIV positive**, they are infected with the HIV virus, and may develop AIDS. If someone is **HIV negative**, they have been tested for the virus and are not infected with it. PHRASE: v-link PHR

hive /haɪv/ **hives, hiving, hived** ◆◇◇◇◇

1 A **hive** is the same as a **beehive.** *This year I got 100 pounds of honey from two hives.* N-COUNT

2 If you describe a place as a **hive** of activity, you approve of the fact that there is a lot of activity there or that people are busy working there. *In the morning the house was a hive of activity... Stuart Tannahill's shed is a veritable hive of photographic creativity.* N-COUNT: N *of* n PRAGMATICS

3 Hives is a condition in which patches of your skin become red and very uncomfortable and itchy. N-UNCOUNT

hive off. If someone **hives off** part of a business, they transfer it to new ownership, usually by selling it; used mainly in British English. *Klockner plans to hive off its loss-making steel businesses... Lufthansa had originally planned to hive off its domestic operations into a subsidiary, Lufthansa Express.* PHRASAL VERB V P n (not pron) V P n (not pron) *into/to* n Also V n P, V n P *into/to* n

hiya /haɪjə/. You can say **'hiya'** when you are greeting someone; an informal word. *Hiya. How are you?* CONVENTION PRAGMATICS =hi

HM /eɪtʃ em/. **HM** is the written abbreviation for 'Her Majesty's' or 'His Majesty's'; it is used as part of the name of some British government organizations, or as part of a person's title. *...his enlistment in HM Armed Forces. ...HM Chief Inspector of Fire Services.* ◆◇◇◇◇

h'm; also spelled **hm. H'm** is used in writing to represent a noise that people make when they are hesitating, for example because they are thinking about something. PRAGMATICS

HMS /eɪtʃ em es/. **HMS** is used before the names of ships in the British Royal Navy; it is an abbreviation for 'Her Majesty's Ship' or 'His Majesty's Ship'. *...launching HMS Warrior.* ◆◇◇◇◇ N-IN-NAMES: N n

HNC /eɪtʃ en siː/ **HNCs.** An **HNC** is a group of examinations in technical subjects which you can take at a British college; it is an abbreviation for 'Higher National Certificate'. *...passing his HNC in computer studies.* N-VAR

hoard /hɔːʳd/ **hoards, hoarding, hoarded** ◆◇◇◇◇

1 If you **hoard** things such as food or money, you save or store them, often in secret, because they are valuable or important to you. *They've begun to hoard food and gasoline and save their money... Consumers did not spend and create jobs; they hoarded... The tea was sweetened with a hoarded tin of condensed milk.* ♦ **hoarder, hoarders** *Most hoarders have favorite hiding places.* VERB V n V V-ed N-COUNT

2 A **hoard** is a store of things that you have saved and that are valuable or important to you or you do not want other people to have. *The case involves a hoard of silver and jewels valued at up to $40m.* N-COUNT: oft N *of* n =cache

hoarding /hɔːʳdɪŋ/ **hoardings.** A **hoarding** is a very large board at the side of a road or on the side of a building, which is used for displaying N-COUNT =billboard advertisements and posters; used mainly in British English. The usual American word is **billboard**. *An advertising hoarding on the platform caught her attention.*

hoarse /hɔːʳs/ **hoarser, hoarsest.** If your voice is **hoarse** or if you are **hoarse**, your voice sounds rough and unclear, for example because your throat is sore. *'So what do you think?' she said in a hoarse whisper... Nick's voice was hoarse with screaming... The small British crowd roared themselves hoarse, waving their Union Jacks.* ◆◇◇◇◇ ADJ-GRADED
♦ **hoarsely** *'Thank you,' Maria said hoarsely.* ADV-GRADED
♦ **hoarseness** *Hoarseness is very common in the winter season.* N-UNCOUNT

hoary /hɔːri/. If you describe a problem or subject as **hoary**, you mean that it is old and familiar. *...the hoary old myth that women are unpredictable.* ADJ-GRADED: usu ADJ n

hoax /hoʊks/ **hoaxes.** A **hoax** is a trick in which someone tells people something that is not true, for example that there is a bomb somewhere, or that a forged work of art is genuine. *A series of bomb hoaxes has disrupted Christmas shopping in the city centre... He denied making the hoax call but was convicted after a short trial.* ◆◇◇◇◇ N-COUNT: usu with supp, oft N n

hoaxer /hoʊksəʳ/ **hoaxers.** A **hoaxer** is someone who carries out a hoax; used mainly in British English. N-COUNT

hob /hɒb/ **hobs.** A **hob** is a surface on top of a cooker or set into a work surface, which can be heated in order to cook things on it in pots and pans; used mainly in British English. ◆◇◇◇◇ N-COUNT

hobble /hɒbᵊl/ **hobbles, hobbling, hobbled** ◆◇◇◇◇
1 If you **hobble**, you walk in an awkward way with small steps, for example because your foot is injured. *He got up slowly and hobbled over to the coffee table... The swelling had begun to go down, and he was able, with pain, to hobble.* VERB V adv/prep V
2 To **hobble** something or someone means to make it more difficult for them to be successful or to achieve what they want. *The poverty of 10 million citizens not only demeans our society but its cost also hobbles our economy.* VERB =hinder V n

hobby /hɒbi/ **hobbies.** A **hobby** is an activity that you enjoy doing in your spare time. *My hobbies are letter writing, football, music, photography, and tennis.* ◆◆◇◇◇ N-COUNT =pastime

hobby-horse, hobby-horses; also spelled **hobbyhorse**. You describe a subject or idea as your **hobby-horse** if you have strong feelings on it and like talking about it whenever you have the opportunity. *Honesty is a favourite hobby-horse for Courau.* N-COUNT

hobbyist /hɒbiɪst/ **hobbyists.** You can refer to person who is very interested in a particular hobby and spends a lot of time on it as a **hobbyist**. N-COUNT

hobnob /hɒbnɒb/ **hobnobs, hobnobbing, hobnobbed.** In informal English, if you disapprove of the way in which someone is spending a lot of time with a group of people, especially rich and powerful people, you can say that he or she **is hobnobbing** with them. *This gave Bill an opportunity to hobnob with the company's president, board chairman, and leading executives.* VERB PRAGMATICS V with n Also V

hobo /hoʊboʊ/ **hobos** or **hoboes**
1 In American English, a **hobo** is a person who has no home, especially one who travels from place to place and gets money by begging. The usual British word is **tramp**. N-COUNT
2 In American English, a **hobo** is a worker, especially a farm worker, who goes from place to place in order to find work. N-COUNT

hock /hɒk/ **hocks**
1 **Hock** is a type of dry white wine from Germany; used mainly in British English. *...a glass of hock.* N-MASS
2 The **hock** of an animal, especially a horse, is the joint in its back leg that points backwards. N-COUNT
3 A **hock** is a piece of meat from above the foot of an animal, especially a pig. *...ham hocks with garlic and mustard sauce.* N-COUNT: usu n N
4 If someone is **in hock**, they are in debt. *Even company directors on £100,000 a year can be deeply in hock to the banks.* PHRASES v-link PHR, oft PHR to n
5 If you are **in hock to** someone, you are obliged to do things for them because they have given you money or support. *It is almost impossible for the prime minister to stand magisterially above the factions. He always seems in hock to one or another.* v-link PHR n

hockey /hɒki/. **Hockey** is an outdoor game played between two teams of 11 players who use long curved sticks to hit a small ball and try to score goals. *She played hockey for the national side. ...the British hockey team.* • See also **ice hockey**. ◆◆◇◇◇ N-UNCOUNT: oft N n

hocus-pocus /hoʊkəs poʊkəs/. If you describe something as **hocus-pocus**, you disapprove of it because you think it is false and intended to trick or deceive people. *It is unlikely he would have mistaken hocus-pocus for genuine knowledge.* N-UNCOUNT PRAGMATICS =trickery

hod /hɒd/ **hods.** A **hod** is a container that is used by someone on a building site for carrying bricks. N-COUNT

hodgepodge /hɒdʒpɒdʒ/; also spelled **hodge-podge**. In informal English, especially American English, a **hodgepodge** is a confused or disorderly mixture of different types of things. The usual British word is **hotch-potch**. *...a hodgepodge of maps, small tools, and notebooks.* N-SING: usu with supp, oft N of n =jumble

hoe /hoʊ/ **hoes, hoeing, hoed** ◆◇◇◇◇
1 A **hoe** is a gardening tool with a long handle and a small square blade, which you use to remove small weeds and break up the surface of the soil. N-COUNT
2 If you **hoe** a field or crop, you use a hoe on the weeds or soil there. *I have to feed the chickens and hoe the potatoes... Today he was hoeing in the vineyard.* VERB V n V
3 If you say that someone has **a hard row to hoe** or **a tough row to hoe**, you mean that they are in a difficult situation and have many problems to deal with. PHRASE: N inflects

hog /hɒg, AM hɔːg/ **hogs, hogging, hogged** ◆◇◇◇◇
1 A **hog** is a pig. In British English, **hog** usually refers to a large male pig that has been castrated, but in American English it can refer to any kind of pig. *We picked the corn by hand and we fed it to the hogs and the cows... Johnny Warrick has a hog farm in Alabama.* N-COUNT
2 If you **hog** something, you take all of it in a greedy or impolite way; an informal use. *Have you done hogging the bathroom?... Now, Bert, quit hogging the limelight.* VERB V n
3 See also **road hog**.
4 If you **go the whole hog**, you do something bold or extravagant in the most complete way possible; an informal expression. *Well, I thought, I've already lost half my job, I might as well go the whole hog and lose it completely.* PHRASE: V inflects

Hogmanay /hɒgmənei/. **Hogmanay** is New Year's Eve in Scotland and the celebrations that take place at that time. N-UNCOUNT

hogwash /hɒgwɒʃ, AM hɔːg-/. If you describe what someone says as **hogwash**, you think it is nonsense; an informal word. *Sugar said it was a 'load of hogwash' that he was not interested in football.* N-UNCOUNT =rubbish

ho ho; also spelled **ho ho ho**. **Ho ho** or **ho ho ho** is used in writing to represent the sound that people make when they laugh. *'Ha, ha, ho, ho,' he chortled.* EXCLAM

ho hum /hoʊ hʌm/
1 You can use **ho hum** when you want to show that you think something is not interesting, remarkable, or surprising in any way. *My general reaction to this news might be summed up as 'ho-hum'... The music is generally terrific but the scripting and acting are a bit ho-hum.* PHRASES PRAGMATICS
2 You can say **ho hum** to show that you accept or are resigned to an unpleasant situation. *Ho hum, another nice job down the drain.* EXCLAM PRAGMATICS =oh well

hoi polloi /hɔɪ pəlɔɪ/. If someone refers to the **hoi polloi**, they are referring scornfully to ordinary people, in contrast to rich, well-educated, or upper-class people; often used ironically or hu- N-PLURAL PRAGMATICS =riff-raff morously. *Monstrously inflated costs are designed to keep the hoi polloi at bay.*

hoist /hɔɪst/ **hoists, hoisting, hoisted** ◆◇◇◇◇

1 If you **hoist** something heavy somewhere, you lift it or pull it up there. *Hoisting my suitcase on to my shoulder, I turned and headed toward my hotel... Grabbing the side of the bunk, he hoisted himself to a sitting position.*
VERB V n prep/adv V pron-refl prep/adv Also V n

2 If something heavy **is hoisted** somewhere, it is lifted there using a machine such as a crane. *A twenty-foot steel pyramid is to be hoisted into position on top of the tower... Then a crane hoisted him on to the platform.*
VERB be V-ed prep/adv V n prep/adv

3 A **hoist** is a machine for lifting heavy things.
N-COUNT

4 If you **hoist** a flag or a sail, you pull it up to its correct position by using ropes. *One protester climbed on the roof to hoist the Soviet flag.*
VERB V n

5 • **hoist with** your **own petard**: see **petard**.

hokum /hoʊkəm/. If you describe something as **hokum**, you think it is nonsense; an informal word. *The book is enjoyable hokum.*
N-UNCOUNT =nonsense

hold 1 physically touching, supporting, or containing

hold /hoʊld/ **holds, holding, held** ◆◆◆◆◇

1 When you **hold** something, you carry or support it, using your hands or your arms. *Hold the knife at an angle... She is holding her journal and a pen... He held the pistol in his right hand... Hold the baby while I load the car.* ► Also a noun. *He released his hold on the camera.*
VERB V n prep/adv V n
N-COUNT: usu sing

2 **Hold** is used in expressions such as **grab hold of**, **catch hold of**, and **get hold of**, to indicate that you close your hand tightly around something, for example to stop something moving or falling. *I was woken up by someone grabbing hold of my sleeping bag... A doctor and a nurse caught hold of his arms... Mother took hold of the barking dogs by their collars.*
N-UNCOUNT: N of n

3 When you **hold** someone, you put your arms round them, usually because you want to show them how much you like them or because you want to comfort them. *If only he would hold her close to him.*
VERB V n adv Also V n

4 If you **hold** someone in a particular position, you use force to keep them in that position and stop them from moving. *He then held the man in an armlock until police arrived... I'd got two nurses holding me down.*
VERB V n prep V n with adv Also V n

5 A **hold** is a particular way of keeping someone in a position using your own hands, arms, or legs. *...use of an unauthorized hold on a handcuffed suspect.*
N-COUNT

6 When you **hold** a part of your body, you put your hand on or against it, often because it hurts. *Soon she was crying bitterly about the pain and was holding her throat.*
VERB V n

7 When you **hold** a part of your body in a particular position, you put it into that position and keep it there. *Hold your hands in front of your face... He walked at a rapid pace with his back straight and his head held erect.*
VERB V n prep/adv V-ed Also V n adj

8 If one thing **holds** another in a particular position, it keeps it in that position. *...the wooden wedge which held the heavy door open... They used steel pins to hold everything in place.*
VERB V n with adv V n prep

9 If one thing is used to **hold** another, it is used to store it. *Two knife racks hold her favourite knives. ...the large cardboard and wooden cases used to hold my new appliances.*
VERB =store V n

10 In a ship or aeroplane, a **hold** is a place where cargo or luggage is stored. *A fire had been reported in the cargo hold.*
N-COUNT: oft n N

11 If a place **holds** something, it keeps it available for reference or for future use. *The Small Firms Service holds an enormous amount of information on any business problem... We have reviewed the data that we hold for the area.*
VERB V n

12 If something **holds** a particular amount of something, it can contain that amount. *The small bottles don't seem to hold much... One CD-ROM disk can hold over 100,000 pages of text.*
VB: no cont V n

13 If you can **hold** your drink, you are able to drink large quantities of alcohol without becoming ill or getting drunk. *...but you had to be able to hold your liquor.*
VERB V n

14 If a vehicle **holds** the road well, it remains in close contact with the road and can be controlled safely and easily. *For an early Ford I thought the car handled and held the road really well.*
VERB V n adv Also V n

15 See also **holding**.

hold 2 having or doing

hold /hoʊld/ **holds, holding, held** ◆◆◆◆◆

Hold is often used to indicate that someone or something has the particular thing, characteristic, or attitude that is mentioned. Therefore it takes most of its meaning from the word that follows it.

1 **Hold** is used with words and expressions indicating an opinion or belief, to show that someone has a particular opinion or believes that something is true. *He held firm opinions which usually conflicted with my own... He holds certain expectations about the teacher's role... Current thinking holds that obesity is more a medical than a psychological problem... The public, meanwhile, hold architects in low esteem. ...a widely held opinion.*
VB: no cont V n V that V n in n V-ed

2 **Hold** is used with words such as 'fear' or 'mystery' to indicate someone's feelings towards something, as if those feelings were a characteristic of the thing itself. *Death doesn't hold any fear for me... It held more mystery than even the darkest jungle... This approach, more than any other, holds promise for true reform.*
VB: no passive V n for n V n

3 **Hold** is used with nouns such as 'office', 'power', and 'responsibility' to indicate that someone has a particular position of power or authority. *She has never held ministerial office... I'd seen it before in people who held immense power.*
VERB =have V n

4 **Hold** is used with nouns such as 'permit', 'degree', or 'ticket' to indicate that someone has a particular document that allows them to do something. *Applicants should normally hold a good Honours degree... He did not hold a firearm certificate... Passengers holding tickets will receive refunds.*
VERB V n

5 **Hold** is used with nouns such as 'party', 'meeting', 'talks', 'election', and 'trial' to indicate that people are organizing a particular activity. *The country will hold democratic elections within a year... The German sports federation said it would hold an investigation. ...the club, which was licensed to hold parties.* ♦ **holding** *They also called for the holding of multi-party general elections.*
VERB V n
N-UNCOUNT: N of n

6 **Hold** is used with nouns such as 'conversation', 'interview', and 'consultation' to indicate that two or more people meet and discuss something. *The Prime Minister, is holding consultations with his colleagues to finalise the deal... The engineer and his son held frequent consultations concerning technical problems... They can't believe you can even hold a conversation.*
V-RECIP V n with n pl-n V V n (non-recip)

7 **Hold** is used with nouns such as 'shares' and 'stock' to indicate that someone owns a particular proportion of a business. *The group said it continues to hold 1,774,687 Vons shares... The Fisher family holds 40% of the stock.*
VERB V n

8 **Hold** is used with words such as 'lead' or 'advantage' to indicate that someone is winning or doing well in a contest. *He continued to hold a lead in Angola's presidential race... Mestel holds a slight advantage.*
VERB V n

9 **Hold** is used with nouns such as 'attention' or 'interest' to indicate that what you do or say keeps someone interested or listening to you. *If you want to hold someone's attention, look them directly in the eye but don't stare... Couldn't I hold Philippe's interest?*
VERB =keep V n

10 If you **hold** someone responsible, liable, or accountable for something, you will blame them if anything goes wrong. *It's impossible to hold any individual responsible. ...shareholders who want to hold corporate directors more accountable for their actions.*
VERB V n adj

11 See also **holding**.

hold 3 controlling or remaining

hold /hould/ **holds, holding, held** ◆◆◆◆◇

VERB
1 If someone **holds** you in a place, they keep you there as a prisoner or hostage and do not allow you to leave. *The inside of a van was as good a place as any to hold a kidnap victim... Somebody is holding your wife hostage... Japan had originally demanded the return of two seamen held on spying charges.*
V n / V n n / V-ed

VERB
2 If people such as an army or a violent crowd **hold** a place, they control it by using force. *Demonstrators have been holding the square since Sunday.*
V n
COMB in ADJ
► Also a combining form. *...enemy-held territory.*

N-SING: usu N over/on n
3 If you have a **hold** over someone, you have power or control over them, for example because you know something about them you can use to threaten them or because you are in a position of authority. *It's always useful to have a hold over a fellow like Carl May... He had ordered his officers to keep an exceptionally firm hold over their men... Because he once loved her, she still has a hold on him.*

VB: no passive =hold on
4 If you ask someone to **hold**, or to **hold** the line, when you are answering a telephone call, you are asking them to wait for a short time, for example so that you can find the person they want to speak to. *Could you hold the line and I'll just get my pen... A telephone operator asked him to hold.*
V n / V

VERB
5 If you **hold** telephone calls for someone, you do not allow the caller to speak to that person, and you take a message instead. *He tells his secretary to hold his calls.*
V n

V-ERG
6 If something **holds** at a particular value or level, or **is held** there, it stays or is kept at that value or level. *OPEC production is holding at around 21.5 million barrels a day... They were expecting the jobless rate to hold steady... The Prime Minister yesterday ruled out Government action to hold down petrol prices... The company forecasts that its 1992 dividend will be held at 3p a share. ...provided the pound holds its value against the deutschmark.*
V prep/adv/adj / V n with adv / V n prep/adj / V n / Also V

VERB
7 If you **hold** a sound or musical note, you continue making it. *...a voice which hit and held every note with perfect ease and clarity.*
V n

VERB
8 If you **hold** something such as the departure of a train, you delay it. *A London Underground spokesman defended the decision to hold the train until police arrived.*
V n

VERB
9 If an offer or invitation still **holds**, it is still available for you to accept. *Does your offer still hold?*
V

VERB
10 If a good situation **holds**, it continues and does not get worse or fail. *Our luck couldn't hold for ever... Would the weather hold?... Will the ceasefire hold?*
V

VERB
11 If an argument or theory **holds**, it is true or valid, even after close examination. *Today, most people think that argument no longer holds... The theory could still hold.*
V
PHRASAL VERB
► To **hold up** means the same as to **hold**. *Democrats say arguments against the bill won't hold up.*
V P

VERB
12 If part of a structure **holds**, it does not fall or break although there is a lot of force or pressure on it. *How long would the roof hold?*
V

VERB
13 If laws and rules **hold**, they exist and remain in force. *These laws also hold for universities.*
V

VERB
14 If you say that you **hold to** a particular opinion or belief, you are stating firmly that you continue to have that opinion or belief; a formal use. *I hold to my belief that people should be allowed to have private lives... Would you still hold to that view?*
V to n

VERB =keep
15 If you **hold to** a promise or to high standards of behaviour, you keep that promise or continue to behave according to those standards; a formal use. *Will the President be able to hold to this commitment?... Not all men are as honorable or hold to the same standards as Sam. ...whether youngsters in a multicultural society can really be expected to hold to uniformity in their speech.*
V to n

VERB
16 If someone or something **holds** you **to** a promise or to high standards of behaviour, they make you keep that promise or those standards. *I would say it's almost time to hold him to that promise... Don't hold me to that... It does hold you to certain standards of fairness.*
V n to n

17 See also **holding**.

hold 4 phrases

hold /hould/ **holds, holding, held** ◆◆◆◆◇

PHRASES
V inflects, oft PHR on n
1 If you **hold forth** on a subject, you speak confidently and for a long time about it, especially to a group of people. *Barry was holding forth on something.*

V inflects, PHR n
2 If you **get hold of** an object or information, you obtain it, usually after some difficulty. *It is hard to get hold of guns in this country.*

V inflects, PHR n
3 If you **get hold of** a fact or a subject, you learn about it and understand it well; used in informal British English. *He first had to get hold of some basic facts.*

V inflects, PHR n
4 If you **get hold of** someone, you manage to contact them. *The only electrician we could get hold of was miles away.*

CONVENTION =stop
5 If you say **'Hold it'**, you are telling someone to stop what they are doing and to wait. *Hold it! Don't move!*

PHR after v, v-link PHR
6 If you put something **on hold**, you decide not to do it, deal with it, or change it now, but to leave it till later. *He put his retirement on hold to work 16 hours a day, seven days a week to find a solution... He described their foreign policy as on hold.*

V inflects
7 If you **hold** your **own**, you are able to resist someone who is attacking or opposing you. *Croatia could not hold its own against either the federal airforce or the federal artillery.*

V inflects, oft PHR *against* n
8 If you can do something well enough to **hold** your **own**, you do not appear foolish when you are compared with someone who is generally thought to be very good at it. *She can hold her own against almost any player.*

V inflects =keep still
9 If you **hold still**, you do not move. *Can't you hold still for a second?*

V inflects, oft PHR of n
10 If something **takes hold**, it finally gains complete control or influence over something or someone. *She felt a strange excitement taking hold of her... She was determined not to let the illness take hold again.*

V inflects, oft PHR prep =hang on
11 If you **hold tight** you put your hand round or against something in order to prevent yourself from falling over. A bus driver might say **'Hold tight!'** to you if you are standing on a bus when it is about to move. *He held tight to the rope... Climb on to my back and hold tight.*

V inflects
12 If you **hold tight**, you do not immediately start a course of action that you have been planning or thinking about. *The unions have circulated their branches, urging members to hold tight until a national deal is struck.*

13 • to **hold** something **at bay**: see **bay**. • to **hold** your **breath**: see **breath**. • **can't hold a candle to**: see **candle**. • to **hold** something **in check**: see **check**. • to **hold court**: see **court**. • to **hold fast**: see **fast**. • to **hold the fort**: see **fort**. • **what the future holds**: see **future**. • to **hold** your **ground**: see **ground**. • to **hold** your **peace**: see **peace**. • to **hold** someone **to ransom**: see **ransom**. • to **hold sway**: see **sway**. • to **hold** your **tongue**: see **tongue**.

hold 5 phrasal verbs

hold /hould/ **holds, holding, held** ◆◆◆◆◇

PHRASAL VERB
hold against. If you **hold** something **against** someone, you let something which they did in the past influence your present attitude towards them and cause you to deal more severely with them than you would otherwise have done. *Bernstein lost the case, but never held it against Grundy.*
V n P n

PHRASAL VERB
hold back

ERG
1 If you **hold back** or something **holds** you **back**, you hesitate before you do something because you are not sure whether it is the right thing to do. *The administration had several reasons for holding back... Melancholy and mistrust of men hold her back.*
V P / V n P / Also V P n (not pron)

=inhibit
2 To **hold** someone or something **back** means to prevent someone from doing something or to prevent something from happening. *Stagnation in home sales is holding back economic recovery... Jake wanted to wake up, but sleep held him back.*
V P n (not pron) / V n P

3 If you **hold** something **back**, you keep it in reserve to use later. *Farmers apparently hold back produce in the hope that prices will rise.* VPn (not pron) Also VnP

4 If you **hold** something **back**, you do not tell someone the full details about something. *You seem to be holding something back.* VnP Also VPn (not pron)

5 If you **hold back** something such as tears or laughter, or if you **hold back**, you make an effort to stop yourself from showing how you feel. *She kept trying to hold back her tears... He could no longer hold back convulsive laughter... I was close to tears with frustration, but I held back.* VPn (not pron) VP Also VnP

hold down PHRASAL VERB

1 If you **hold down** a job or a place in a team, you manage to keep it. *He never could hold down a job... Constant injury problems had made it tough for him to hold down a regular first team place.* oft with brd-neg VPn (not pron) Also VnP

2 If you **hold** someone **down**, you keep them under control and do not allow them to have much freedom or power or many rights. *Everyone thinks there is some vast conspiracy wanting to hold down the younger generation.* VPn (not pron) Also VnP

hold in. If you **hold in** an emotion or feeling, you do not allow yourself to express it, often making it more difficult to deal with. *Depression can be traced to holding in anger... Go ahead and cry. Don't hold it in.* PHRASAL VERB PRAGMATICS VPn (not pron) VnP

hold off PHRASAL VERB

1 If you **hold off** doing something, you delay doing it or delay making a decision about it. *The hospital staff held off taking Rosenbaum in for an X-ray... They have threatened military action but held off until now.* VP -ing VP

2 If you **hold off** a challenge in a race or competition, you do not allow someone to overtake you. *Alesi drove his Tyrrell magnificently, holding off a tremendous challenge from Gerhard Berger.* VPn (not pron) Also VnP

hold on or **hold onto** PHRASAL VERB

1 If you **hold on**, or **hold onto** something, you keep your hand on it or around it, for example to prevent the thing from falling or to support yourself. *His right arm was extended up beside his head, still holding on to a coffee cup... He was struggling to hold onto a rock on the face of the cliff... Despite her aching shoulders, Nancy held on.* VP to n VPn VP

2 If you **hold on**, you manage to achieve success or avoid failure in spite of great difficulties or opposition. *Juanito scored for the Spaniards with only two minutes left, but the Romanians held on... This Government deserved to lose power a year ago. It held on... You helped me to hold on at times when I didn't think I could even go on trying.* VP

3 If you ask someone to **hold on**, you are asking them to wait for a short time; used in spoken English. *The manager asked him to hold on while he investigated... Hold on a minute.* VP

hold on to or **hold onto** PHRASAL VERB

1 If you **hold on to** something that gives you an advantage, you succeed in keeping it for yourself, and prevent it from being taken away or given to someone else. *Jane is determined to hold on to her fortune... Firms are now keen to hold on to the people they recruit. ...a politician who knew how to hold onto power.* VPPn VPn

2 If you **hold on to** something, you keep it for a longer time than would normally be expected; used in spoken English. *Do you think you could hold on to that report for the next day or two?... People hold onto letters for years and years.* VPPn VPn

3 If you **hold on to** your beliefs, ideas, or principles, you continue to believe in them and do not change or abandon them if others try to influence you or if circumstances cause you to doubt them. *He was imprisoned for 19 years yet held on to his belief in his people.* VPPn

hold out PHRASAL VERB

1 If you **hold out** your hand or something you have in your hand, you move your hand away from your body, for example to shake hands with someone or because someone is giving you something. *'I'm Nancy Drew,' she said, holding out her hand... Max held out his cup for a refill.* VPn (not pron) Also VnP

2 If you **hold out** for something, you refuse to accept something which you do not think is adequate, and you continue to demand more. *I should have held out for a better deal... He can only hold out a few more weeks.* VP for n VP

3 If you say that someone **is holding out** on you, you think that they are refusing to give you information that you want; an informal expression. *He had always believed that kids could sense it when you held out on them.* VP on n Also VP

4 If you **hold out**, you manage to resist an enemy or opponent in difficult circumstances and refuse to surrender. *The guerrillas were holding out in the Paghman valley... One prisoner was still holding out on the roof of the jail.* VP

5 If you **hold out** hope of something happening, you hope that in the future something will happen as you want it to. *He still holds out hope that they could be a family again.* VPn (not pron)

hold over PHRASAL VERB

1 If you **hold** something **over** someone, you use it in order to threaten them or make them do what you want. *Did Laurie know something, and hold it over Felicity?* VnPn

2 If something is **held over**, it does not happen or it is not dealt with until a future date. *Further voting might be held over until tomorrow... We would have held the story over until the next day.* be V-ed P VnP Also VPn (not pron)

hold together. When you **hold** people **together** or when they **hold together**, people who have different aims, attitudes, or interests manage to live or work together without arguing or disagreeing. *Her 13-year-old daughter is holding the family together... Mr Major sought to hold together the warring factions in his party... The coalition will never hold together for six months.* PHRASAL VERB ERG PRAGMATICS VnP VPn (not pron) VP

hold up PHRASAL VERB

1 If you **hold up** your hand or something you have in your hand, you move it upwards into a particular position and keep it there. *She held up her hand stiffly... Hold it up so that we can see it.* VPn (not pron) VnP

2 If one thing **holds up** another, it is placed under the other thing in order to support it and prevent it from falling. *Mills have iron pillars all over the place holding up the roof... Her legs wouldn't hold her up.* VPn (not pron) VnP

3 To **hold up** a person or process means to make them late or delay them. *Why were you holding everyone up?... Continuing violence could hold up progress towards reform.* =delay VnP VPn (not pron)

4 If someone **holds up** a place such as a bank or a shop, they point a weapon at someone there to make them give them money or valuable goods. *A thief ran off with hundreds of pounds yesterday after holding up a petrol station.* =rob VPn (not pron) Also VnP

5 If you **hold up** something such as someone's behaviour, you make it known to other people, so that they can criticize or praise it. *She said the picture that had appeared in a Sunday newspaper had held her up to ridicule... He had always been held up as an example to the younger ones.* VnP to n be V-ed P as n Also VnP as n

6 If something such as a type of business **holds up** in difficult conditions, it stays in a reasonably good state. *Children's wear is one area that is holding up well in the recession.* VP

7 If an argument or theory **holds up**, it is true or valid, even after close examination. *I'm not sure if the argument holds up, but it's stimulating.*

8 See also **hold-up**.

hold with. If you do not **hold with** an activity or action, you do not approve of it. *I don't hold with the way they do things nowadays.* PHRASAL VERB with brd-neg VPn

holdall /hoʊldɔːl/ **holdalls;** also spelled **hold-all**. N-COUNT
A **holdall** is a large bag made of nylon, canvas, or leather, which you use to carry your clothes and other belongings, for example when you are travelling; used mainly in British English.

holder /hoʊldəʳ/ **holders** ◆◆◆◇◇

1 A **holder** is someone who owns or has something. *This season the club has had 73,500 season-ticket holders. ...Peter Koech, the record holder in the 3, 000 metres steeplechase. ...the holders of the European Football Championship.* N-COUNT: n N, N of n

2 A **holder** is a container in which you put an object, usually in order to protect it or to keep it in place. *...a toothbrush holder. ...a cigarette holder.* N-COUNT: usu n N

holding /hoʊldɪŋ/ **holdings** ◆◆◇◇◇

1 If you have a **holding** in a company, you own shares in it. *That would increase Olympia & York's holding to 35%... Sid's amazing wealth comes from holdings in oil, gas, land and property.* N-COUNT: with supp =investment

2 A **holding** is an area of farm land which is owned or rented by the person who cultivates it. N-COUNT

3 The **holdings** of a place such as a museum, library, or art gallery is the collection of items such as books or paintings which are kept there. *Because of the nature of the museum's holdings the focus is on Europe.* N-PLURAL

4 A **holding** operation or action is a temporary one that is intended to keep a situation under control and to prevent it from becoming worse. *A garden is, at best, a holding operation against nature.* ADJ: ADJ n

holdout /hoʊldaʊt/ **holdouts.** In American English, a **holdout** is someone who refuses to agree or act with other people in a particular situation and by doing so stops the situation from progressing or being resolved. *France has been the holdout in trying to negotiate an end to the dispute.* N-COUNT

hold-up, hold-ups ◆◇◇◇◇

1 A **hold-up** is a situation in which someone is threatened with a weapon in order to make them hand over money or valuables. N-COUNT =raid

2 A **hold-up** is something which causes a delay. N-COUNT

3 A **hold-up** is the stopping or very slow movement of traffic, sometimes caused by an accident which happened earlier. *They arrived late due to a motorway hold-up.* N-COUNT

hole /hoʊl/ **holes, holing, holed** ◆◆◆◆◇

1 A **hole** is a hollow space in something solid, with an opening on one side. *He took a shovel, dug a hole, and buried his once-prized possessions... The builders had cut holes into the soft stone to support the ends of the beams. ...a 60ft hole.* N-COUNT

2 A **hole** is an opening in something that goes right through it. *These tiresome creatures eat holes in the leaves... Armed robbers broke into the jeweller's through a hole in the wall. ...kids with holes in the knees of their jeans.* N-COUNT: oft N *in* n

3 A **hole** is the home or hiding place of a mouse, rabbit, or other small animal. *...a rabbit hole.* N-COUNT

4 A **hole** in a law, theory, or argument is a fault or weakness that it has. *There were some holes in that theory, some unanswered questions.* N-COUNT: oft N *in* n =flaw

5 If you refer to a place as a **hole**, you are emphasizing that you think it is very unpleasant; an informal use. *Why don't you leave this awful hole and come to live with me?* N-COUNT: usu adj N PRAGMATICS =dump

6 A **hole** is also one of the nine or eighteen sections of a golf course. *I played nine holes with Gary Player today.* N-COUNT

7 A **hole** is one of the places on a golf course that the ball must drop into, usually marked by a flag. N-COUNT

8 If you **hole** in a game of golf, you hit the ball so that it goes into the hole. *He holed from nine feet at the 18th... Frost holed a bunker shot from 50 feet to snatch the title by one stroke.* VERB V V n

9 If something such as a building or ship **is holed**, holes are made in it by guns or other weapons; used mainly in British English. *Blocks of flats have been holed and some shells have fallen within the historic ramparts.* VB: usu passive *be* V-ed

10 If you say that you **need** something or someone **like a hole in the head**, you are emphasizing that you do not want them and that they would only add to the problems that you already have; an informal expression. *We need more folk heroes like we need a hole in the head.* PHRASES V inflects PRAGMATICS

11 If you say that you are **in a hole**, you mean that you are in a difficult or embarrassing situation; an informal expression. *He admitted that the government was in 'a dreadful hole'.* v-link PHR

12 If you get **a hole in one** in golf, you get the golf ball into the hole with a single stroke. *All they ever dream about is getting a hole in one.* usu v PHR

13 If you **pick holes in** an argument or theory, you find weak points in it so that it is no longer valid; an informal expression. *He then goes on to pick holes in the article before reaching his conclusion.* V inflects

hole up. If you **hole up** somewhere, you hide or shut yourself there, usually so that people cannot find you or disturb you; an informal expression. *His creative process involves holing up in his Paris flat with the phone off the hook.* PHRASAL VERB V P

holed up. If you are **holed up** somewhere, you are hiding or staying there, usually so that other people cannot find or disturb you; an informal expression. *If he had another well-stocked hideaway like this, he could stay holed up for months... I wanted to spend Sundays holed up together in our flat.* ADJ: v-link ADJ

hole-in-the-wall. In British English, a **hole-in-the-wall** machine is a machine built into the wall of a bank or other building, which allows people to take out money from their bank account by using a special card; an informal expression. *Since hole-in-the-wall cash machines were introduced in the 1970s, banks have claimed unauthorised withdrawals could never happen.* N-SING: usu N n =cash dispenser

holiday /hɒlɪdeɪ/ **holidays, holidaying, holidayed** ◆◆◆◆◇

1 In British English, a **holiday** is a period of time during which you relax and enjoy yourself away from home. People sometimes refer to their holiday as their holidays. The American word is **vacation**. *I've just come back from a holiday in the United States... We rang Duncan to ask where he was going on holiday, but he had already gone away... Ischia is a popular seaside holiday resort... We're going to Scotland for our holidays.* N-COUNT: also *on/from* N

2 A **holiday** is a day when people do not go to work or school because of a religious or national festival. *New Year's Day is a public holiday throughout Britain... Bad weather has caused dozens of flight cancellations over the holiday weekend.* • See also **bank holiday**. N-COUNT: usu with supp

3 In British English, the **holidays** are the time when children do not have to go to school. The American word is **vacation**. *...the first day of the school holidays.* N-PLURAL: usu *the* N, oft n N

4 In British English, if you have a particular number of days' or weeks' **holiday**, you do not have to go to work for that number of days or weeks. The American word is **vacation**. *Every worker will be entitled to four weeks' paid holiday a year.* N-UNCOUNT

5 In British English, if you **are holidaying** in a place away from home, you are on holiday there. The American word is **vacation**. *Sampling the local cuisine is one of the delights of holidaying abroad... Vacant rooms on the campus were being used by holidaying families.* VB: oft cont V prep/adv V-ing

holiday camp, holiday camps. In Britain, a **holiday camp** is a place which provides holiday accommodation and entertainment for large numbers of people. N-COUNT

holidaymaker /hɒlɪdeɪmeɪkəʳ/ **holidaymakers;** also spelled **holiday-maker**. In British English, a **holidaymaker** is a person who is away from their home on holiday. The American word is **vacationer**. ◆◇◇◇◇ N-COUNT

holier-than-thou. If you describe someone as **holier-than-thou**, you disapprove of them because they seem to believe that they are more religious or have better moral qualities than anyone else. *He has always sounded holier-than-thou. ...those with holier-than-thou attitudes.* ADJ-GRADED PRAGMATICS =self-righteous

holiness /hoʊlinəs/

1 **Holiness** is the state or quality of being holy. *The holiness of God reveals one's own sin... We were immediately struck by this city's holiness.* N-UNCOUNT: usu with supp

2 You say **Your Holiness** or **His Holiness** when you address or refer respectfully to the Pope or to leaders of some other religions. *The President received His Holiness at the White House.* N-VOC: poss N; PRON: poss PRON PRAGMATICS

holism /hoʊlɪzəm/. **Holism** is the belief that everything in nature is connected in some way; a formal word. N-UNCOUNT

holistic /hoʊlɪstɪk/. **Holistic** means based on the principles of holism; a formal word. *...practitioners of holistic medicine.* ◆◇◇◇◇ ADJ: usu ADJ n

holler /hɒlə^r/ **hollers, hollering, hollered.** If you **holler**, you shout loudly; an informal word, used mainly in American English. *The audience whooped and hollered... 'Watch out!' he hollered... In a minute he'll be hollering at me for coming in late... Cal hollered for help... Nick hollered for her to pick up her orders.* ▶ Also a noun. *On the ship's deck, after the whoops and hollers, the butchering begins.* ▶ **Holler out** means the same as **holler**. *I holler out the names, someone shouts a number... I heard him holler out, 'Somebody bombed the Church.'* ◆◇◇◇◇ VERB =shout, yell; V; V with quote; V at/for n; V for n to-inf; Also V n; N-COUNT; PHRASAL VERB V P n; V P with quote; Also V P

hollow /hɒloʊ/ **hollows, hollowing, hollowed** ◆◆◇◇◇

1 Something that is **hollow** has a space inside it, as opposed to being solid all the way through. *...a hollow tree. ...a hollow cylinder.* ADJ

2 A surface that is **hollow** curves inwards. *He looked young, dark and sharp-featured, with hollow cheeks.* ADJ-GRADED

3 A **hollow** is a hole inside a tree. *I made my home there, in the hollow of a dying elm.* N-COUNT

4 A **hollow** is an area that is lower than the surrounding surface. *Below him the town lay warm in the hollow of the hill. ...where water gathers in a hollow and forms a pond.* N-COUNT: oft N of/in/between n

5 If you describe a statement, situation, or person as **hollow**, you mean they have no real value, worth, or effectiveness. *Any threat to bring in the police is a hollow one. ...a hollow man who's coasted on charm for far too long.* ♦ **hollowness** *One month before the deadline we see the hollowness of these promises.* ADJ: usu ADJ n =empty; N-UNCOUNT: oft N of/behind n

6 If someone gives a **hollow** laugh, they laugh in a way that shows that they do not really find something amusing. *Murray Pick's hollow laugh had no mirth in it.* ADJ: ADJ n

7 A **hollow** sound is dull and echoing. *...the hollow sound of a gunshot.* ADJ: ADJ n

8 If something **is hollowed**, its surface is made to curve inwards or downwards. *The mule's back was hollowed by the weight of its burden. ...her high, elegantly hollowed cheekbones.* VB: usu passive be V-ed; V-ed

hollow out. If you **hollow** something **out**, you remove the inside part of it. *Someone had hollowed out a large block of stone... Bake some big red peppers and hollow them out.* PHRASAL VERB V P n (not pron); V n P

holly /hɒli/ **hollies. Hollies** are a group of evergreen trees and shrubs which have hard, shiny, prickly leaves, and also have bright red berries in winter. ◆◇◇◇◇ N-VAR

Hollywood /hɒliwʊd/. You use **Hollywood** to refer to the American film industry that is based in Hollywood, California, and also to the lifestyles of the rich and famous people living there. *...a major Hollywood studio. ...Hollywood film stars. ...a satire on Hollywood life.* 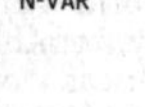 N-PROPER: oft N n

holocaust /hɒləkɔːst/ **holocausts** ◆◇◇◇◇

1 A **holocaust** is an event in which there is large-scale destruction and loss of life, especially in war. *A nuclear holocaust seemed a very real possibility in the '50s.* N-VAR

2 **The holocaust** is used to refer to the killing by the Nazis of millions of Jews during the Second World War. *...an Israeli-based fund for survivors of the holocaust and their families.* N-SING: the N

hologram /hɒləgræm/ **holograms.** A **hologram** is a three-dimensional photographic image created by laser beams. N-COUNT

hols /hɒlz/. In informal British English, some people refer to their holidays as their **hols**. *Where did you go for your hols? ...during the summer hols.* N-PLURAL: usu supp N =holidays

holster /hoʊlstə^r/ **holsters.** A **holster** is a holder for a pistol or revolver, which is worn either on a belt around someone's waist or on a strap around their shoulder. N-COUNT

holy /hoʊli/ **holier, holiest** ◆◆◆◇◇

1 If you describe something as **holy**, you mean that it is considered to be special because it is connected with God or a particular religion. *To them, as to all Tibetans, this is a holy place. ...Yom Kippur, the holiest day in the Jewish calendar.* ADJ-GRADED: usu ADJ n

2 If you describe someone as **holy**, you mean that they lead a pure and good life which is dedicated to God or to a particular religion. *The Indians think of him as a holy man, a combination of doctor and priest.* ADJ-GRADED

3 **Holy** is used in exclamations such as 'Holy cow!' and 'Holy smoke!' to express an emotion such as surprise or panic. ADJ: ADJ n PRAGMATICS

4 See also **holier-than-thou.**

Holy Communion. **Holy Communion** is the most important religious service in the Christian church, in which people share bread and wine as a symbol of the Last Supper and the crucifixion of Christ. N-UNCOUNT

Holy Father. In the Catholic Church, **the Holy Father** is the Pope. N-PROPER: the N

Holy Ghost. **The Holy Ghost** is the same as the **Holy Spirit.** N-PROPER: the N

holy of holies /hoʊli əv hoʊliz/. A **holy of holies** is a place that is so sacred that only particular people are allowed to enter; often used in informal English to refer ironically to a place where only a few special people can go. *...the holy of holies in the Temple. ...the Aldeburgh Festival, the holy of holies in the contemporary British music scene.* N-SING =sanctum

holy orders; also spelled **Holy Orders**. Someone who is in **holy orders** is a member of the Christian clergy. *He took holy orders in 1935.* N-PLURAL

Holy Spirit. In the Christian religion, **the Holy Spirit** is one of the three aspects of God, together with God the Father and God the Son. N-PROPER: the N =Holy Ghost

Holy Week. In the Christian religion, **Holy Week** is the week before Easter, when Christians remember the events leading up to the crucifixion of Christ. N-UNCOUNT

homage /hɒmɪdʒ/. **Homage** is respect shown towards someone or something you admire, or to someone who is in authority. *Palace has released two marvellous films that pay homage to our literary heritage... At his coronation he received the homage of kings from Wales, Northumbria and Scotland.* ◆◇◇◇◇ N-UNCOUNT: usu N to n

home 1 noun, adjective, and adverb uses

home /hoʊm/ **homes** ◆◆◆◆◆

1 Someone's **home** is the house or flat where they live. *Last night they stayed at home and watched TV... The General divided his time between his shabby offices in Carlton Gardens and his home in Hampstead. ...the allocation of land for new homes.* N-COUNT: oft poss N, also at N

2 You can use **home** to refer in a general way to the house, town, or country where someone lives now or where they were born, often to emphasize that they feel they belong in that place. *She gives frequent performances of her work, both at home and abroad... His father worked away from home for much of Jim's first five years... At seventeen, Daniele was told to leave home by her father... Ms Highsmith has made Switzerland her home... Warwick is home to some 550 international students... Brian decided to leave the UK and set up home in Southern Spain... He has moved back to his home town of Miami.* N-UNCOUNT

3 **Home** means to or at the place where you live. *His wife wasn't feeling too well and she wanted to go home... I'll telephone you as soon as I get home... Hi, Mom, I'm home!... Company officials say striking union members should stay home today.* ADV: ADV after v, be ADV

4 **Home** means made or done in the place where you live. *...cheap but healthy home cooking... All you have to do is make a home video.* ADJ: ADJ n

5 **Home** means relating to your own country as opposed to foreign countries. *Europe's software companies still have a growing home market. ...the Guardian's home news pages.* ADJ: ADJ n =domestic

6 A **home** is a large house or institution where a number of people live and are looked after, instead of living in their own houses or flats. They usually live there because they are too old or ill to look after N-COUNT

themselves. *It's going to be a home for handicapped children. ...an old people's home.*

7 You can refer to a family unit as a **home**. *She had, at any rate, provided a peaceful and loving home for Harriet... Single-parent homes are commonplace.* [N-COUNT]

8 If you refer to the **home** of something, you mean the place where it began or where it is most typically found. *This south-west region of France is the home of claret.* [N-SING: with supp, usu N *of* n]

9 If you find a **home** for something, you find a place where it can be kept. *The equipment itself is getting smaller, neater and easier to find a home for.* [N-COUNT: oft N *for* n]

10 If you press, drive, or hammer something **home**, you explain it to your listeners as firmly as possible. *It is now up to all of us to debate this issue and press home the argument.* [ADV: ADV after v]

11 When a team plays at **home**, they play a game on their own ground, rather than on the opposing team's ground. *I scored in both games against Barcelona; we drew at home and beat them away.* [N-UNCOUNT: usu *at* N] ▶ Also an adjective. *All three are Chelsea fans, and attend all home games together.* [ADJ: ADJ n ≠away]

12 If you feel **at home**, you feel comfortable and at ease in the place or situation that you are in. *He spoke very good English and appeared pleased to see us, and we soon felt quite at home... I am not completely at home in any Protestant Church.* [PHRASES v-link PHR]

13 To **bring** something **home** to someone means to make them understand how important or serious it is. *Their sobering conversation brought home to everyone present the serious and worthwhile work the Red Cross does.* [V inflects, usu PHR *to* n]

14 If you say that someone is **home and dry** in a contest or other activity, you mean that they have achieved victory or success, or you are certain that they will achieve it; used mainly in British English. *The prime minister and the moderates are not yet home and dry.* [v-link PHR]

15 If a situation or what someone says **hits home** or **strikes home**, people accept that it is real or true, even though it may be painful for them to realize. *Did the reality of war finally hit home, or were you able to keep it at bay?... Israeli officials say that message struck home.* [V inflects]

16 In British English, you can use **a home from home** to refer to a place in which you feel happy and at ease, just as if you were in your own home. In American English, you say **a home away from home**. *Many cottages are a home from home, offering microwaves, dishwashers, tvs and videos.* [usu v-link PHR] [PRAGMATICS]

17 If you say to a guest **'Make yourself at home'**, you are making them feel welcome and inviting them to behave in an informal, relaxed way. [CONVENTION] [PRAGMATICS]

18 If you say that something is **nothing to write home about**, you mean that it is not very interesting or exciting; an informal expression. *So a dreary Monday afternoon in Walthamstow is nothing to write home about, right?* [v-link PHR]

19 If something that is thrown or fired **strikes home**, it reaches its target; used in written English. *Only two torpedoes struck home.* [V inflects]

home 2 phrasal verb uses

home /hoʊm/ **homes, homing, homed** ◆◇◇◇◇

home in [PHRASAL VERB]

1 If you **home in** on one particular aspect of something, you give all your attention to it. *The critics immediately homed in on the group's essential members.* [V P *on* n, Also V P]

2 If something such as a weapon **homes in** on something else, the weapon is aimed at that thing and moves towards it with great accuracy. *Two rockets homed in on it from behind without a sound... A bank of telephoto lenses homed in on his nose.* ● See also **homing**. [V P *on* n, Also V P]

home birth, home births. If a woman has a **home birth**, she gives birth to her baby at home rather than in a hospital. [N-VAR]

home-brew. Home-brew is beer that is made in someone's home, rather than in a brewery. [N-UNCOUNT]

homecoming /hoʊmkʌmɪŋ/ **homecomings.** ◆◇◇◇◇ Your **homecoming** is your return to your home or your country, usually after a fairly long absence. *Her homecoming was tinged with sadness.* [N-VAR: oft poss N]

Home Counties; also spelled **home counties.** ◆◇◇◇◇ **The Home Counties** are the counties which surround London. *...a shy, self-employed computer salesman from the Home Counties. ...Home Counties villages.* [N-PROPER-PLURAL: *the* N]

home economics. Home economics is a school subject dealing with how to run a house well and efficiently. [N-UNCOUNT]

home ground, home grounds

1 A sports team's **home ground** is their own playing field, as opposed to that of other teams. *They are banned from playing on their home ground because of crowd trouble... Austria, playing on home ground in Vienna, took a 3-0 lead over Italy.* [N-VAR]

2 If you say that someone is **on** their **home ground**, you mean that they are in or near where they work or live, and feel confident and secure because of this. *Although he was on home ground, his campaign had been rocked by adultery allegations.* [PHRASE: v-link PHR, PHR after v]

home-grown. Home-grown fruit and vegetables have been grown in your garden, rather than a farm, or in your country rather than abroad. ◆◇◇◇◇ [ADJ: usu ADJ n]

home help, home helps. A **home help** is a person who is employed to help sick or old people with their housework; used mainly in British English. [N-COUNT]

homeland /hoʊmlænd/ **homelands** ◆◆◇◇◇

1 Your **homeland** is your native country; mainly used in written English. *Many are planning to return to their homeland.* [N-COUNT: usu poss N]

2 The **homelands** were regions within South Africa in which black South Africans had limited self-government. They are now part of the Republic of South Africa. [N-COUNT]

homeless /hoʊmləs/. **Homeless** people have nowhere to live. *...the growing number of homeless families... Hundreds were made homeless.* ◆◆◆◇◇ [ADJ] ▶ The **homeless** are people who are homeless. *...shelters for the homeless.* [N-PLURAL: *the* N] ♦ **homelessness** *The only way to solve homelessness is to provide more homes.* [N-UNCOUNT]

homely /hoʊmli/ ◆◇◇◇◇

1 If you describe a room or house as **homely**, you like it because it makes you feel comfortable and at ease, and is as you imagine a home should be. *I wanted a homely room but I wanted it to look smart, too... We try and provide a very homely atmosphere.* [ADJ-GRADED =cosy]

2 Homely food is simple and ordinary. *Scottish baking is homely, comforting and truly good.* [ADJ-GRADED =plain]

3 In British English, if you describe a woman as **homely**, you mean that she has a warm, comforting manner and looks like someone who would enjoy being at home and running a family. *Mrs Jones was a pleasant, homely person with a ready smile.* [ADJ-GRADED]

4 In American English, if you say that someone is **homely**, you mean that they are not very attractive to look at. *The man was homely, overweight, and probably only two or three years younger than Lou.* [ADJ-GRADED =plain]

home-made; also spelled **homemade**. Something that is **home-made** has been made in someone's home, rather than in a shop or factory. *The bread, pastry and mayonnaise are home-made... A home-made bomb exploded during the disturbances.* ◆◇◇◇◇ [ADJ]

homemaker /hoʊmmeɪkəʳ/ **homemakers.** A **homemaker** is a woman who spends a lot of time looking after her home and family. If you describe a woman as a **homemaker**, you usually mean that she does not have another job. [N-COUNT]

Home Office. The **Home Office** is the department of the British Government which is responsible for domestic affairs, including the police, immigration, and broadcasting. ◆◆◇◇◇ [N-PROPER: usu *the* N]

homeopath /hoʊmiəʊpæθ/ **homeopaths.** In British English, the spelling **homoeopath** is also used. A **homeopath** is someone who treats illness by homeopathy. [N-COUNT]

homeopathic /hoʊmioʊpæθɪk/. In British English, the spelling **homoeopathic** is also used. [ADJ: usu ADJ n]

Homeopathic means relating to or used in homeopathy. *...homeopathic remedies. ...a homeopathic doctor.*

homeopathy /hoʊmiɒpəθi/. In British English, the spelling **homoeopathy** is also used. **Homeopathy** is a way of treating an illness in which the patient is given very small amounts of a drug that produces signs of the illness in healthy people. N-UNCOUNT

home owner **home owners;** also spelled **homeowner.** A **home owner** is a person who owns the house or flat that they live in. ◆◇◇◇◇ N-COUNT

home rule. If a country or region has **home rule**, it has its own independent government and laws. *Home rule for Scotland would be accompanied by a similar measure for Wales.* N-UNCOUNT

Home Secretary, Home Secretaries. The **Home Secretary** is the member of the British government who is in charge of the Home Office. ◆◆◇◇◇ N-COUNT: usu *the* N in sing

home shopping; also spelled **home-shopping. Home shopping** is buying things by ordering them by post or telephone, rather than going to a shop to buy them. *...the most successful name in home shopping in the UK. ...the proliferation of home-shopping TV programmes.* N-UNCOUNT: oft N n

homesick /hoʊmsɪk/. If you are **homesick**, you feel unhappy because you are away from home and are missing your family, friends, and home very much. *She's feeling a little homesick.* ◆◇◇◇◇ ADJ-GRADED: usu v-link ADJ

♦ **homesickness** *There were inevitable bouts of homesickness.* N-UNCOUNT

homespun /hoʊmspʌn/

1 You use **homespun** to describe opinions or ideas that are simple and uncomplicated, especially ones that do not seem to have been thought out well. *The book is simple homespun philosophy.* ADJ: usu ADJ n

2 **Homespun** clothes are made from cloth that has been made at home, rather than in a factory. *Most of them still wore the homespun clothes in which they had left their farms.* N-UNCOUNT: usu N n

homestead /hoʊmsted/ **homesteads.** A **homestead** is a farmhouse, together with the land around it. ◆◇◇◇◇ N-COUNT

home straight or **home stretch**

1 **The home straight** or **the home stretch** is the last part of a race. *Wales take on Czechoslovakia in the home straight of the qualifying competition.* N-SING: *the* N

2 You can also refer to the last part of any activity that lasts for a long time as **the home straight** or **the home stretch**, especially if the activity is difficult or boring. *...as his two hours of banter, quips and anecdotes goes into the home straight.* N-SING: *the* N

hometown /hoʊmtaʊn/ **hometowns;** also spelled **home town.** Someone's **hometown** is the town where they live or the town that they come from. *I went to work as a painter in my hometown, Natrona Heights, Pennsylvania.* ◆◇◇◇◇ N-COUNT: with poss

home truth, home truths. Home truths are unpleasant facts that you learn about yourself, usually from someone else. *We held a team meeting after losing at Newcastle and a few home truths were spelled out.* N-COUNT: usu pl

homeward /hoʊmwəʳd/; also spelled **homewards.**

1 If you are on a **homeward** journey, you are on a journey towards your home. *She is ready for her homeward journey.* ADJ: ADJ n

2 If you are travelling **homeward** or **homewards**, you are travelling towards your home. 'Homewards' is not often used in American English. *John drove homeward through the lanes... They travelled happily homewards.* ADV: ADV after v

homeward bound. People or things that are **homeward bound** are on their way home. *I'd be homeward bound even before Grant arrived... The platforms groan with homeward-bound commuters.* ADJ

homework /hoʊmwɜːʳk/ ◆◇◇◇◇

1 **Homework** is school work that teachers give to pupils to do at home in the evening or at the weekend. *Have you done your homework, Gemma?* N-UNCOUNT

2 If you do your **homework**, you find out what you need to know in preparation for something. *Before you go near a stockbroker, do your homework.* N-UNCOUNT

homey /hoʊmi/. If you describe a place as **homey**, you mean that you feel comfortable and relaxed there; used mainly in informal American English. *...a large, homey dining room.* ADJ-GRADED =cosy, homely

homicidal /hɒmɪsaɪdᵊl/. **Homicidal** is used to describe someone who is dangerous because they are likely to kill someone. *That man is a homicidal maniac. ...an explosion of homicidal rage.* ADJ: usu ADJ n

homicide /hɒmɪsaɪd/ **homicides. Homicide** is the deliberate and unlawful killing of a person; used mainly in American English. *The police arrived at the scene of the homicide.* ◆◇◇◇◇ N-VAR =murder

homily /hɒmɪli/ **homilies.** A **homily** is a speech or piece of writing in which someone complains about the state of something or tells people how they ought to behave; a formal word. *...a receptive audience for his homily on moral values.* N-COUNT =sermon

homing /hoʊmɪŋ/

1 A weapon or piece of equipment that has a **homing** system is able to guide itself to a target or to give out a signal that guides people to it. *...infra-red homing missiles... All the royal cars are fitted with electronic homing devices.* ADJ: ADJ n

2 An animal that has a **homing** instinct has the ability to remember and return to a place where it has been in the past. *Then the pigeons ran into thick fog, and the famous homing instinct went to pot.* ADJ: ADJ n

homing pigeon, homing pigeons. A **homing pigeon** is trained to return to a particular place, especially in races with other pigeons. N-COUNT

homoeopath /hoʊmioʊpæθ/. See **homeopath.**

homogeneity /hɒmədʒəniːɪti, hoʊ-/. **Homogeneity** is the quality of being homogeneous. *The government panicked into imposing a kind of cultural homogeneity.* N-UNCOUNT =uniformity

homogeneous /hɒmədʒiːniəs, hoʊ-/ also spelled **homogenous. Homogeneous** is used to describe a group or thing which has members or parts that are all the same; a formal word. *The unemployed are not a homogeneous group... Russia is ethnically relatively homogeneous.* ◆◇◇◇◇ ADJ-GRADED =uniform ≠heterogeneous

homogenize /həmɒdʒənaɪz/ **homogenizes, homogenizing, homogenized;** also spelled **homogenise** in British English. If something **is homogenized**, it has been made homogeneous, so that all its parts seem the same; usually used in contexts where you are suggesting that this is undesirable, and variety is preferable. *Even Brussels bureaucrats can't homogenize national cultures and tastes.* VERB PRAGMATICS V n

♦ **homogenized** *...an increasingly homogenised and bland America.* ADJ-GRADED

♦ **homogenization** /həmɒdʒənaɪzeɪʃᵊn/ *They no longer worry about the homogenization of culture.* N-UNCOUNT

homogenized /həmɒdʒənaɪzd/; also spelled **homogenised** in British English. **Homogenized** milk is milk where the fat has been broken up so that is evenly distributed. ADJ

homogenous /həmɒdʒənəs/. **Homogenous** means the same as **homogeneous.** ADJ-GRADED

homophobia /hɒməfoʊbiə/. **Homophobia** is a strong and unreasonable dislike of homosexual people, especially homosexual men. ◆◇◇◇◇ N-UNCOUNT

homophobic /hɒməfoʊbɪk/. **Homophobic** means involving or related to a strong and unreasonable dislike of homosexual people, especially homosexual men. ◆◇◇◇◇ ADJ-GRADED

homophone /hɒməfoʊn/ **homophones. Homophones** are words with different meanings which are pronounced in the same way but are spelled differently. For example, 'write' and 'right' are homophones; a technical term in linguistics. N-COUNT

homo sapiens /hoʊmoʊ sæpienz/. **Homo sapiens** is used to refer to human beings, considered as a type of animal, in contrast to other species of ape or animal, or earlier evolutionary forms of humans. *What distinguishes homo sapiens from every other living creature is the mind.* N-UNCOUNT =mankind

homosexual /hɒmoʊsekʃuəl, AM hoʊ-/ **homosexuals** ◆◆◆◇◇

1 A **homosexual** relationship is a sexual relationship between people of the same sex. ADJ: usu ADJ n

2 Someone who is **homosexual** is sexually attracted to people of the same sex. *A fraud trial involving two homosexual lawyers was abandoned.* ▸ Also a noun. *The judge said that discrimination against homosexuals is deplorable.* ♦ **homosexuality** /hɒmoʊsekʃuælɪti, AM hoʊm-/ *...a place where gays could openly discuss homosexuality.* ADJ; N-COUNT; N-UNCOUNT

Hon. /ɒn/. **Hon.** is an abbreviation for 'honourable' and 'honorary' when they are used as part of a person's title. ◆◇◇◇◇ N-TITLE

hone /hoʊn/ **hones, honing, honed** ◆◇◇◇◇

1 If you **hone** something, for example a skill, technique, idea, or product, you carefully develop it over a long period of time so that it is exactly right for your purpose. *Leading companies spend time and money on honing the skills of senior managers... His body is honed and kept in trim with constant exercise.* VERB; V n

2 If you **hone** a blade, weapon, or tool, you sharpen it on a stone or with a special device; a technical word. *...four grinding wheels for honing fine edged tools and implements. ...a thin, honed blade.* VERB =sharpen, whet; V n; V-ed

honest /ɒnɪst/ ◆◆◆◇◇

1 If you describe someone as **honest**, you mean that they always tell the truth, and do not try to deceive people or break the law. *My dad was the most honest man I ever met... I know she's honest and reliable.* ♦ **honestly** *She fought honestly for a just cause and for freedom.* ADJ-GRADED; ADV-GRADED: ADV after v

2 If you are **honest** in a particular situation, you tell the complete truth or give your sincere opinion, even if this is not very pleasant. *I was honest about what I was doing... He had been honest with her and she had tricked him!... What do you think of the school, in your honest opinion?* ♦ **honestly** *It came as a shock to hear an old friend speak so honestly about Ted.* ADJ-GRADED =frank; ADV-GRADED: ADV with v

3 You say **'honest'** before or after a statement to emphasize that you are telling the truth and that you want people to believe you; an informal use. *I'm not sure, honest.* ADV: ADV with cl PRAGMATICS

4 Some people say **'honest to God'** to emphasize their feelings or to emphasize that something is really true; an informal expression. *I wish we weren't doing this, Lillian, honest to God, I really do... You wanna know the honest-to-God truth?* PHRASES PHR with cl, PHR n PRAGMATICS

5 You can say **'to be honest'** before or after a statement to emphasize that you are telling the truth about your own opinions or feelings, especially if you think these will disappoint the person you are talking to. *To be honest the house is not quite our style... I'd rather get it out the way, to be honest.* PHR with cl PRAGMATICS

honest broker, honest brokers. If a person or country acts as an **honest broker**, they try to help people resolve a dispute or arrange a deal by talking to all sides and finding out what they want, without favouring any one side. *The Scottish TUC has been acting as an honest broker in an attempt at unity between the three opposition parties.* N-COUNT: usu sing

honestly /ɒnɪstli/ ◆◆◇◇◇

1 You use **honestly** to emphasize that you are referring to your, or someone else's, true beliefs or feelings. *I honestly feel I cannot do any more to prove myself... I honestly don't know... But did you honestly think we wouldn't notice?* ADV: ADV before v PRAGMATICS

2 You use **honestly** to emphasize that you are telling the truth and that you want people to believe you; used in spoken English. *Honestly, I don't know anything about it... We didn't play with him, honestly we didn't.* ADV: ADV with cl

3 You use **honestly** to indicate that you are annoyed or impatient; used in spoken English. *Honestly, Nev! Must you be quite so crude!... Oh, honestly, I don't know what they will think of next.* ADV: ADV with cl =really

honesty /ɒnɪsti/ ◆◆◇◇◇

1 **Honesty** is the quality of being honest. *They said the greatest virtues in a politician were integrity, correctness and honesty.* N-UNCOUNT

2 **Honesty** is a plant with round flat silvery seed-pods. N-UNCOUNT

3 You say **in all honesty** when you are stating an opinion or fact that might be disappointing or upsetting, and when you want to soften its effect by emphasizing your sincerity. *In all honesty, aren't there already far too many pages of scientific research published every week?... But in all honesty, I wish it had never happened.* PHRASE: PHR with cl PRAGMATICS

honey /hʌni/ **honeys** ◆◆◇◇◇

1 **Honey** is a sweet, sticky, yellowish substance that is made by bees. N-VAR

2 You call someone **honey** as a sign of affection; used mainly in American English. *Honey, I don't really think that's a good idea.* N-VOC

honeybee /hʌnibiː/ **honeybees.** A **honeybee** is a bee that makes honey. N-COUNT

honeycomb /hʌnikoʊm/ **honeycombs.** A **honeycomb** is a wax structure consisting of rows of six-sided cells where bees store the honey. N-VAR

honeyed /hʌnid/

1 You can describe someone's voice or words as **honeyed** when they are saying something that is soothing and pleasant to listen to, especially if you want to suggest that they are insincere. *His gentle manner and honeyed tones reassured Andrew... They could not understand how anyone could believe her honeyed words.* ADJ: usu ADJ n

2 In written English, you can describe something as **honeyed** when it tastes or smells of honey, or is the pale yellowish colour of honey. *I could smell the honeyed ripeness of melons and peaches... Wait for the warm glow of sunset as it washes the stone to a honeyed hue.* ADJ-GRADED: usu ADJ n

honeymoon /hʌnimuːn/ **honeymoons, honeymooning, honeymooned** ◆◇◇◇◇

1 A **honeymoon** is a holiday taken by a man and a woman who have just got married. N-COUNT

2 When a newly married couple **honeymoon** somewhere, they go there on their honeymoon. *They honeymooned in Venice. ...honeymooning Japanese tourists.* VERB; V; V-ing

3 You can use **honeymoon** to refer to a period of time after the start of a new job or new government when everyone is pleased with the person or people concerned and is nice to them. *It's clear the post-Communist honeymoon in Poland is over... Brett is enjoying a honeymoon period with both press and public.* N-COUNT: usu with supp

honeypot /hʌnipɒt/ **honeypots.** When journalists refer to a place as a **honeypot**, they mean that a lot of people are attracted to it for a particular reason; used mainly in British English. *Like every other tourist honeypot, Bath is plagued by traffic problems.* N-COUNT: usu supp N

honeysuckle /hʌnisʌkᵊl/ **honeysuckles.** **Honeysuckle** is a climbing plant with sweet-smelling yellow, pink, or white flowers. N-VAR

honk /hɒŋk/ **honks, honking, honked.**

1 If you **honk** the horn of a vehicle or if the horn **honks**, you make the horn produce a short loud sound. *Drivers honked their horns in solidarity with the peace marchers... Horns honk. An angry motorist shouts. ...people yelling and honking at you to get out of the cab.* ▸ Also a noun. *She pulled to the right with a honk.* V-ERG =hoot; V n; V; N-COUNT

2 If a bird, person, or musical instrument **honks**, they make a short, loud, harsh noise. *If you're going to sneeze and honk all night, we'll never get any sleep... A lone mother Canada goose honked a warning to stay away from her nest. ...a honking saxophone playing gospel music.* ▸ Also a noun. *The honk of geese can be heard.* VERB; V; V n; V-ing; N-COUNT

honky-tonk /hɒŋki tɒŋk/ **honky-tonks**

1 In the United States, a **honky-tonk** is a cheap, shabby bar or nightclub. *For several years, Bill Wirtz has been performing in small clubs and honky-tonks from Maryland to the Carolinas. ...little honky-tonk bars in Texas.* N-COUNT: oft N n

2 Honky-tonk is the kind of piano music played in honky-tonks. *...the beat of honky-tonk pianos.* N-UNCOUNT: oft N n

honor /ɒnər/. See **honour**.

honorable /ɒnrəbəl/. See **honourable**.

honorarium /ɒnəreəriəm/ **honoraria** /ɒnəreəriə/ or **honorariums.** An **honorarium** is a fee that someone receives for doing something which is not a normal part of their job, for example giving a talk. *All sorts of people I found were getting honoraria for various extra duties that they had assigned to them.* N-COUNT

honorary /ɒnərəri, AM -reri/ ◆◇◇◇◇

1 An **honorary** title or membership of a group is given to someone without their needing to have the necessary qualifications, usually because of their public achievements. *He will be awarded the honorary degree in a ceremony at Newcastle University. ...an honorary member of the Golf Club.* ADJ: ADJ n

2 Honorary is used to describe an official job that is done without payment. *...the honorary secretary of the Cheshire Beekeepers' Association.* ADJ: ADJ n

honorific /ɒnərɪfɪk/. An **honorific** title or way of talking is used to show respect or honour to someone; a formal use. *He was given the honorific title of national chairman... All employees will refer to each other by the honorific suffix 'san'.* ADJ: ADJ n

honour /ɒnər/ **honours, honouring, honoured;** spelled **honor** in American English. ◆◆◆◇◇

1 Honour means doing what you believe to be right and being confident that you have done what is right. *The officers died faithful to Poland and to the honour of a soldier... I do not believe I can any longer serve with honour as a member of your government.* N-UNCOUNT

2 An **honour** is a special award that is given to someone, usually because they have done something good or because they are greatly respected. *Most of the high honours usually go to long-serving MPs loyal to the government... He was showered with honours – among them an Oscar in 1950.* N-COUNT

3 If someone **is honoured**, they are given public praise or an award for something they have done. *Two American surgeons were last week honoured with the 1990 Nobel Prize for Medicine and Physiology... Mr Reddy has been honoured by the Pope by being made a knight of St Gregory.* VB: usu passive *be* V-ed

4 If you describe doing or experiencing something as an **honour**, you mean you think it is something special and desirable. People often describe something as an **honour** to indicate in a polite and formal way how pleased they are to be doing it or experiencing it. *Five other cities including Manchester had been competing for the honour of staging the Games... Tchaikovsky was given a state funeral – the first commoner to be granted this honour... Michael said: 'It's an honour to finally work with her.'... Perhaps as it is so close to noon, you would do me the honour of having lunch with me.* N-SING: oft N *of*-ing, *it* v-link N to-inf PRAGMATICS

5 If you say that you would **be honoured** to do something, you are saying very politely and formally that you would be pleased to do it. If you say that you **are honoured** by something, you are saying that you are grateful for it and pleased about it. *Peter Alliss says he would be honoured to be asked... It's a very flattering offer, and I'm honoured by your confidence in me.* V-PASSIVE PRAGMATICS *be* V-ed to-inf *be* V-ed

6 To **honour** someone means to treat them or regard them with special attention and respect. *Her Majesty later honoured the Headmaster with her presence at lunch... Those right-wing people who most honour their monarch see no reason for any apology.* ♦ **honoured** *Mrs Patrick Campbell was an honoured guest.* VERB V n *with* n V n; ADJ-GRADED: ADJ n

7 If you **honour** an arrangement or promise, you do what you said you would do. *The two sides agreed to honour a new ceasefire... Walesa's opponents say he is making election promises he will be unable to honour.* VERB V n

8 Honours is a type of university degree which is of a higher standard than a pass or ordinary degree. *...an honours degree in business studies.* N-UNCOUNT: usu N n

9 Judges are sometimes called **your honour** or referred to as **his honour** or **her honour**. *I bring this up, your honor, because I think it is important to understand the background of the defendant. ...His Honour Judge Brodrick.* N-VOC: poss N; PRON: poss PRON

10 See also **guest of honour, lap of honour, maid of honour.**

11 If someone **does the honours** at a social occasion or public event, they act as host or perform some official function. *The two teams were introduced to the dignitaries with Lord Haslam of British Coal doing the honours.* PHRASES V inflects

12 If something is arranged **in honour of** a particular event, it is arranged in order to celebrate that event. *The Foundation is holding a dinner at the Museum of American Art in honour of the opening of their new show.* PREP

13 If something is arranged or happens **in** someone's **honour**, it is done specially to show appreciation of them. *Mr Mandela will attend an outdoor concert in his honour in the centre of Paris... The United Nations has issued a stamp in honour of Captain Alfred Dreyfus.* n PHR, PHR after v, PHR with cl

honourable /ɒnrəbəl/; spelled **honorable** in American English. ◆◇◇◇◇

1 If you describe people or actions as **honourable**, you mean that they are worthy of being respected or admired. *I believe he was an honourable man, dedicated to the people and his union... He argued that the only honorable course of action was death... However, their intentions are honourable.* ♦ **honourably** /ɒnrəbli/ *He also felt she had not behaved honorably in the leadership election.* ADJ-GRADED; ADV-GRADED: usu ADV with v

2 Honourable is used as a title before the names of some members of the nobility, judges, and some other officials. *...the Honourable Mr Justice Swinton Thomas.* ADJ: *the* ADJ n-proper

3 In debates in the British parliament, one member of parliament refers to another as the **honourable** member, the **honourable** gentleman, the **honourable** lady or their **honourable** friend. *...the Honourable Member for Billericay.* ADJ: ADJ n

honourable mention, honourable mentions; spelled **honorable mention** in American English. If something that you do in a competition is given an **honourable mention**, it receives special praise from the judges although it does not actually win a prize. N-COUNT

honours list honours lists. In Britain, the **honours list** is the list of people who have been selected to receive titles or decorations from the Queen in recognition of their achievements. *He has been made an MBE in the New Year Honours list.* N-COUNT: usu *the* N in sing, oft supp N

Hons /ɒnz/. In Britain, **Hons** is an abbreviation for 'Honours', used after the names of some university degrees, mainly first degrees. *...Kevin P Kearns, BA (Hons), University of Liverpool.*

hooch /huːtʃ/. **Hooch** is strong alcoholic drink; an informal word. N-UNCOUNT

hood /hʊd/ **hoods** ◆◇◇◇◇

1 A **hood** is a part of a coat which you can pull up to cover your head. It is in the shape of a triangular bag attached to the neck of the coat at the back. N-COUNT

2 A **hood** is a bag made of cloth, which is put over someone's head and face so that they cannot be recognized or so that they cannot see. N-COUNT

3 In American English, the **hood** of a car is the metal cover over the engine at the front. The British word is **bonnet**. N-COUNT

4 A **hood** is a covering on a vehicle or a piece of equipment, which is usually curved and can be moved; used mainly in British English. *Why aren't all lenses supplied with a lens hood?* N-COUNT: usu n N

hooded /hʊdɪd/ ◆◇◇◇◇

1 A **hooded** piece of clothing or furniture has a hood. *It was lit by hooded fluorescent lamps. ...a blue, hooded anorak.* ADJ: usu ADJ n

2 If someone has **hooded** eyes, their eyelids always look as though they are partly closed. *...sparkling, hooded blue eyes, and an impish grin.* ADJ: ADJ n

3 A **hooded** person is wearing a hood or a piece of ADJ:

clothing pulled down over their face, so they are difficult to recognize. *The class was held hostage by a hooded gunman.* ADJ n

hoodlum /huːdləm/ **hoodlums.** A **hoodlum** is a violent criminal, especially one who is part of a gang; an informal word. N-COUNT

hoodwink /hʊdwɪŋk/ **hoodwinks, hoodwinking, hoodwinked.** If someone **hoodwinks** you, they trick or deceive you. *People expect others to be honest, which is why conmen find it so easy to hoodwink people... Many people are hoodwinked by the so-called beauty industry.* VERB =con, take in V n

hoof /huːf/ **hoofs** or **hooves.** The **hooves** of an animal such as a horse are the hard, bony parts of its feet. *The horses' hooves often could not get a proper grip.* ◆◇◇◇◇ N-COUNT: usu pl

hoofer /huːfəʳ/ **hoofers.** A **hoofer** is a dancer, especially one who dances in musicals; an informal word. N-COUNT

hook /hʊk/ **hooks, hooking, hooked** ◆◆◆◇◇

1 A **hook** is a bent piece of metal or plastic that is used for catching or holding things, or for hanging things up. *One of his jackets hung from a hook. ...curtain hooks... He felt a fish pull at his hook.* N-COUNT

2 If you **hook** one thing to another, you attach it there using a hook. If something **hooks** somewhere, it can be hooked there. *Paul hooked his tractor to the car and pulled it to safety. ...one of those can openers that hooked onto the wall.* V-ERG V n *to/onto* V *onto* n Also V n prep, V prep

3 If you **hook** your arm, leg, or foot round an object, you place it like a hook round the object in order to move it or hold it. *She latched on to his arm, hooking her other arm around a tree... I hooked my left arm over the side of the dinghy.* VERB V n prep

4 If you **hook** a fish, you catch it with a hook on the end of a line. *At the first cast I hooked a huge fish, probably a tench.* VERB V n

5 A **hook** is a short sharp blow with your fist that you make with your elbow bent, usually in a boxing match. *Ribalta was demolished by the best punch Bruno has ever thrown, a fearsome right hook.* N-COUNT: usu adj N

6 If you **are hooked into** something, or **hook into** something, you get involved with it; used mainly in American English. *I'm guessing again now because I'm not hooked into the political circles... Eager to hook into a career but can't find one right for you?* V-ERG be/get V-ed *into* n V *into* n

7 If someone gets **off the hook** or if someone or something lets them **off the hook**, they manage to get out of the awkward or unpleasant situation that they are in. *Government officials accused of bribery and corruption get off the hook with monotonous regularity... His opponents have no intention of letting him off the hook until he agrees to leave office immediately.* PHRASES V inflects

8 If you take a phone **off the hook**, you take the receiver off the part that it normally rests on, so that the phone will not ring. PHR after v

9 In American English, if your phone **is ringing off the hook**, so many people are trying to telephone you that it is ringing constantly. *Since war broke out in the Middle East, the phones at donation centers have been ringing off the hook.* V inflects

10 • **by hook or by crook**: see **crook.** • **hook, line, and sinker**: see **sinker.**

hook up PHRASAL VERB

1 When someone **hooks up** a computer or other electronic machine, they connect it to other similar machines or to a central power supply. *...technicians who hook up computer systems and networks... He brought it down, hooked it up, and we got the generator going. ...if the machine is hooked up to an apartment's central wiring system.* V P n (not pron) V n P be V-ed P *to* n Also V n P *to* n

2 If one person, especially a musician, **hooks up** with another, the two people start working with each other. You can also say that two people **hook up**. *Anthrax have hooked up with Public Enemy for a metal/rap version of 'Bring On The Noise'... Seeing as how we got on so well together, it just seemed natural that we should hook up.* RECIP V P *with* n pl-n V P

hooked /hʊkt/ ◆◇◇◇◇

1 If you describe something as **hooked**, you mean that it is shaped like a hook. *He was thin and tall, with a hooked nose. ...hooked claws.* ADJ-GRADED: usu ADJ n

2 If you are **hooked** on something, you enjoy it so much that it takes up a lot of your interest and attention; an informal use. *Many of the leaders have become hooked on power and money... Open this book and read a few pages and you will be hooked.* ADJ: v-link ADJ, oft ADJ *on* n

3 If you are **hooked** on a drug, you are addicted to it; an informal use. *He spent a number of years hooked on cocaine, heroin and alcohol.* ADJ: v-link ADJ, oft ADJ *on* n

hooker /hʊkəʳ/ **hookers.** A **hooker** is a prostitute; used mainly in informal American English. ◆◇◇◇◇ N-COUNT

hook-up, hook-ups. A **hook-up** is a connection between two locations, systems, or pieces of equipment. *Water and electric hook-ups are available and facilities are good.* N-COUNT: usu supp N

hooky /hʊki/; also spelled **hookey**. If a child **plays hooky**, they stay away from school without permission; used mainly in informal American English. *...the misadventures of a happy-go-lucky boy who plays hooky from school.* PHRASE: V inflects =play truant

hooligan /huːlɪgən/ **hooligans.** If you describe young people as **hooligans**, you are critical of them because they behave in a noisy and violent way in a public place. *...riots involving football hooligans.* ◆◇◇◇◇ N-COUNT PRAGMATICS

hooliganism /huːlɪgənɪzəm/. **Hooliganism** is the behaviour and actions of hooligans. *...police investigating football hooliganism.* ◆◇◇◇◇ N-UNCOUNT PRAGMATICS

hoop /huːp/ **hoops** ◆◇◇◇◇

1 A **hoop** is a large ring made of wood, metal, or plastic. N-COUNT

2 In croquet, the **hoops** are the small metal arches which players hit the ball through. N-COUNT

3 A basketball **hoop** is the ring that players try to throw the ball into in order to get a point for their team. N-COUNT

4 If someone makes you **jump through hoops**, they make you do lots of difficult or boring things in order to please them or achieve something. *He had the duty receptionist almost jumping through hoops for him. But to no avail.* PHRASE: V inflects

hooped /huːpt/. If something is **hooped**, it is decorated with hoops or horizontal stripes, or it contains hoops as part of its structure; used mainly in British English. *A hooped arbour of iron rods was constructed from one wall to the other. ...emerald green and red hooped sleeves.* ADJ: ADJ n

hooray /hʊreɪ/. People sometimes shout **'Hooray!'** when they are very happy and excited about something. • **hip hip hooray**: see **hip.** EXCLAM

hoot /huːt/ **hoots, hooting, hooted** ◆◇◇◇◇

1 If you **hoot** the horn on a vehicle or if it **hoots**, it makes a loud noise on one note; used mainly in British English. *I never hoot my horn when I pick a girl up for a date... Somewhere in the distance a siren hooted... I can be very rude to motorists who hoot at me... It felt good to drive down the middle of the road, hooting at every junction.* ► Also a noun. *Mortlake strode on, ignoring the car, in spite of a further warning hoot.* V-ERG V n V V *at* n V N-COUNT

2 If you **hoot**, you make a loud high-pitched noise when you are laughing or showing disapproval. *The protesters chanted, blew whistles and hooted at the name of Governor Pete Wilson... Bev hooted with laughter.* ► Also a noun. *His confession was greeted with derisive hoots... This time she burst into hoots of laughter.* VERB V V *with* n N-COUNT: usu with supp

3 When an owl **hoots**, it makes a sound like a long 'oo'. *Out in the garden an owl hooted suddenly.* VERB V

4 If you say that someone or something is a **hoot**, you think they are very amusing; an informal use. *Michael Fish is my favourite. He's a hoot, a real character.* N-SING: a N

5 If you say that you **don't give a hoot** or **don't care two hoots** about something, you are emphasizing that you don't care at all about it; an informal expression. *Alan doesn't care two hoots about Irish politics... They just don't give a hoot.* PHRASE: V inflects, oft PHR *about/for* n, PHR wh PRAGMATICS

hooter /huːtəʳ/ **hooters**

1 A **hooter** is a device such as a horn or a siren that N-COUNT

makes a hooting noise; used mainly in old-fashioned British English.

2 In informal British English, you can refer to someone's nose as their **hooter**, especially if it is large. N-COUNT: usu with poss

hoover /huːvəʳ/ **hoovers, hoovering, hoovered** ◆◇◇◇◇

1 In British English, a **Hoover** is a **vacuum cleaner**. **Hoover** is a trademark. N-COUNT

2 If you **hoover** a carpet, you clean it using a vacuum cleaner; used mainly in British English. *She hoovered the study and the sitting-room.* VERB V n Also V

♦ **hoovering** *I finished off the hoovering upstairs.* N-UNCOUNT: also *the* N

hooves /huːvz/. **Hooves** is a plural of **hoof**.

hop /hɒp/ **hops, hopping, hopped** ◆◆◇◇◇

1 When you **hop**, you move along by jumping on one foot. *I hopped down three steps... Malcolm hopped rather than walked.* ► Also a noun. *'This really is a catching rhythm, huh?' he added, with a few little hops.* VERB V prep/adv V N-COUNT

2 When birds and some small animals **hop**, they move along by jumping on both feet. *A small brown fawn hopped across the trail in front of them.* ► Also a noun. *The rabbit got up, took four hops and turned round.* VERB V prep/adv N-COUNT

3 If you **hop** somewhere, you move there quickly or suddenly; an informal use. *My wife and I were the first to arrive and hopped on board... I hopped out of bed quickly.* VERB =jump V prep/adv

4 A **hop** is a short, quick journey, usually by plane; an informal use. *It is a three-hour drive from Geneva but can be reached by a 20-minute hop in a private helicopter.* N-COUNT

5 In informal English, a **hop** is a social event at which people mix together and dance in an informal way. *They were afraid of being turned down when they asked girls to dance at high school hops.* N-COUNT

6 **Hops** are flowers that are dried and used for making beer. N-COUNT: usu pl

7 If you tell someone to **hop it**, you are telling them in a rude way to go away; an informal British expression. *'Hop it', I snapped at the bloke. 'She's with me.'* PHRASES V inflects PRAGMATICS =clear off

8 Someone who is **hopping mad** is very angry; an informal expression. *The family's hopping mad that she left them nothing.* usu v-link PHR

9 If you are caught **on the hop**, you are surprised by someone doing something when you were not expecting them to and so you are not prepared for it; used in informal British English. *His plans almost caught security chiefs and hotel staff on the hop.* usu PHR after v

hope /hoʊp/ **hopes, hoping, hoped** ◆◆◆◆◆

1 If you **hope** that something is true, or you **hope** for something, you want it to be true or to happen, and you usually believe that it is possible or likely. *She had decided she must go on as usual, follow her normal routine, and hope and pray... He hesitates before leaving, almost as though he had been hoping for conversation... I hope to get a job within the next two weeks... The researchers hope that such a vaccine could be available in about ten years' time... 'We'll speak again.'—'I hope so.'... 'Will it happen again?'—'I hope not, but you never know.'* VERB V V *for* n V to-inf V that V *so/not*

2 If you say that you cannot **hope** for something, or if you talk about the only thing that you can **hope** to get, you mean that you are in a bad situation, and there is very little chance of improving it. *Things aren't ideal, but that's the best you can hope for... I always knew it was too much to hope for. ...these mountains, which no one can hope to penetrate.* ► Also a noun. *The only hope for underdeveloped countries is to become, as far as possible, self-reliant... The car was smashed beyond any hope of repair.* VB: with brd-neg V *for* n V to-inf N-VAR

3 **Hope** is a feeling of desire and expectation that things will go well in the future. *Now that he has become President, many people once again have hope for genuine changes in the system... But Kevin hasn't given up hope of being fit... Consumer groups still hold out hope that the president will change his mind... Thousands of childless couples are to be given new hope by the government.* N-UNCOUNT

4 If someone wants something to happen, and considers it likely or possible, you can refer to their **hopes** of that thing, or to their **hope** that it will happen. *They have hopes of increasing trade between the two regions... The delay in the programme has dashed Japan's hopes of commercial success in space... My hope is that, in the future, I will go over there and marry her.* N-COUNT: with supp, oft N *of* n/-ing, N that

5 If you think that the help or success of a particular person or thing will cause you to be successful or to get what you want, you can refer to them as your **hope**. *...England's last hope in the English Open Table Tennis Championships... Roemer represented the best hope for a businesslike climate in Louisiana.* N-COUNT: with supp

6 If you are in a difficult situation and do something and **hope for the best**, you hope that everything will happen in the way you want, although you know that it may not. *I took the risk and hoped for the best... Some companies are cutting costs and hoping for the best.* PHRASES V inflects

7 If you tell someone not to **get** their **hopes up**, or not to **build** their **hopes up**, you are warning them that they should not become too confident of progress or success. *There is no reason for people to get their hopes up over this mission... I don't want you to build your hopes up, but I'll have a word with Fred tomorrow.* V inflects PRAGMATICS

8 If you say that someone has **not** got **a hope in hell** of doing something, you are emphasizing that they will not be able to do it; an informal expression. *Everybody knows they haven't got a hope in hell of forming a government anyway.* PHR after v, v-link PHR, oft PHR *of*-ing

9 If you have **high hopes** or **great hopes** that something will happen, you are confident that it will happen. If you have **high hopes** or **great hopes** for someone or something, you are confident that they will be successful. *I had high hopes that Derek Randall might play an important part... Britain's three-day event team has high hopes of winning the Olympic gold medal... He had no great hopes for the success of his undertaking.* PHR after v, v-link PHR, usu PHR that, PHR *of* n/-ing, PHR *for* n

10 If you **hope against hope** that something will happen, you hope that it will happen, although it seems impossible. *She glanced about the hall, hoping against hope that Richard would be waiting for her.* V inflects, usu PHR that

11 You use **'I hope'** in expressions such as **'I hope you don't mind'** and **'I hope I'm not disturbing you'**, when you are being polite and want to make sure that you have not offended someone or disturbed them. *I hope you don't mind me coming to see you... I hope I haven't said anything to upset you.* PHR with cl PRAGMATICS

12 You say **'I hope'** when you want to warn someone not to do something foolish, something dangerous, or something that you disapprove of. *You're not trying to see him, I hope?... I hope you won't be too harsh with the girl... Are we starting that again? I most sincerely hope not.* PHR with cl, PHR *not* PRAGMATICS

13 You add **'I hope'** to what you are saying to make it sound more polite and less rude, abrupt, or definite. *You wouldn't hesitate, I hope... I'm the best man for the job, I hope... Fraulein Wendel is well, I hope?* PHR with cl PRAGMATICS

14 If you do one thing **in the hope** of another thing happening, you do it because you think it might cause or help the other thing to happen, which is what you want. *He was studying in the hope of being admitted to an engineering college... We will be analysing all the things she has told us in the hope that we can locate the person responsible.* PHR after v, PHR *of*-ing, PHR that

15 If you **live in hope** that something will happen, you continue to hope that it will happen, although it seems unlikely, and you realize that you are being foolish. *I just live in hope that one day she'll talk to me... My mother bought lots of tickets and lived in hope of winning the prize.* V inflects, oft PHR that, PHR *of*-ing

16 If you say **'Some hope'**, or **'Not a hope'**, you think there is no possibility that something will happen, although you may want it to happen; an informal expression. *The industry reckons it will* CONVENTION PRAGMATICS *see orders swell by 10% this financial year. Some hope.*

hoped-for. ◆◇◇◇◇ **Hoped-for** is used to describe something that people would like to happen, and which they usually think is likely or possible; used in journalism. *The hoped-for economic recovery in Britain did not arrive... The hoped-for result is to raise $106 million next year.* ADJ: ADJ n

hopeful /hoʊpfʊl/ **hopefuls** ◆◆◇◇◇

1 If you are **hopeful**, you are fairly confident that something that you want to happen will happen. *I am hopeful this misunderstanding will be rectified very quickly... Surgeons were hopeful of saving the sight in Sara's left eye.* ADJ-GRADED: usu v-link ADJ, oft ADJ that, ADJ of n/-ing ♦ **hopefully** *'Am I welcome?' He smiled hopefully, leaning on the door.* ADV-GRADED: ADV with v

2 If something such as a sign or event is **hopeful**, it makes you feel that what you want to happen will happen. *The leadership election has not been a hopeful sign for Labour's future. ...hopeful forecasts that the economy will improve.* ADJ-GRADED

3 A **hopeful** action is one that you do in the hope that you will get what you want to get. *We've chartered the aircraft in the hopeful anticipation that the government will allow them to leave.* ADJ: ADJ n

4 If you refer to someone as a **hopeful**, you mean that they have a particular ambition and it is possible that they will achieve it. *His soccer skills continue to be put to good use in his job as football coach to young hopefuls.* N-COUNT

hopefully /hoʊpfʊli/. ◆◆◇◇◇ You say **hopefully** when mentioning something that you hope will happen. Some careful speakers of English think that this use of **hopefully** is not correct, but it is very frequently used. *Both of them have been through an awful lot and hopefully now I can help them rebuild their lives... Hopefully, you won't have any problems after reading this.* ADV: ADV with cl/group

hopeless /hoʊpləs/ ◆◆◇◇◇

1 If you feel **hopeless**, you feel desperate because there seems to be no possibility of comfort or success. *He had not heard her cry before in this uncontrolled, hopeless way... The economic crisis makes jobs almost impossible to find and even able pupils feel hopeless about job prospects.* ADJ-GRADED ♦ **hopelessly** *I looked around hopelessly. ...a young woman hopelessly in love with a handsome hero.* ADV-GRADED: ADV after v, ADV prep ♦ **hopelessness** *She had a feeling of hopelessness about the future.* N-UNCOUNT

2 Someone or something thing that is **hopeless** is certain to fail or be unsuccessful. *I don't believe your situation is as hopeless as you think. If you love each other, you'll work it out... A doctor is there to treat and to cure, not to dismiss anyone as a hopeless case.* ADJ-GRADED

3 If someone is **hopeless** at something, they are very bad at it; an informal use. *I'd be hopeless at working for somebody else... I was fine at sports, but pretty hopeless academically.* ADJ-GRADED: oft ADJ at n

4 You use **hopeless** to emphasize how bad or inadequate something or someone is. *I don't drive and the buses are quite hopeless... Argentina's economic policies were a hopeless mess.* ADJ-GRADED ♦ **hopelessly** *The story is hopelessly confusing... They were on the other side of Berlin and Harry was hopelessly lost... By October 1990, when arrested, he was hopelessly in debt.* ADV-GRADED: usu ADV adj/-ed/prep, also ADV after v

hopper /hɒpəʳ/ **hoppers.** ◆◇◇◇◇ A **hopper** is a device shaped like a large funnel, into which substances such as grain, coal, or animal food can be put and from which they can be released when required. N-COUNT

hopscotch /hɒpskɒtʃ/. **Hopscotch** is a children's game which involves jumping between squares which are drawn on the ground. N-UNCOUNT

horde /hɔːʳd/ **hordes.** ◆◇◇◇◇ If you describe a crowd of people as a **horde**, you mean that the crowd is very large and excited and, often, rather frightening or unpleasant. *This attracts hordes of tourists to Las Vegas. ...a horde of people was screaming for tickets.* N-COUNT: usu N of n

horizon /həraɪzᵊn/ **horizons** ◆◆◇◇◇

1 The **horizon** is the line in the far distance where the sky seems to meet the land or the sea. *A grey smudge appeared on the horizon. That must be Calais, thought Fay... The sun had already sunk below the horizon.* N-SING: usu the N

2 Your **horizons** are the limits of what you want to do or of what you are interested or involved in. *As your horizons expand, these new ideas can give a whole new meaning to life... By embracing other cultures and genres, we actually broaden our horizons, rather than narrow any existing ones.* N-COUNT: usu pl

3 If something is **on the horizon**, it is almost certainly going to happen or be done quite soon. *With breast cancer, as with many common diseases, there is no obvious breakthrough on the horizon... Suddenly, with war on the horizon, the army seemed in danger of disintegration... There are glimmers of hope on the horizon.* PHRASES

horizontal /hɒrɪzɒntᵊl, AM hɔːr-/ **horizontals** ◆◇◇◇◇

1 Something that is **horizontal** is flat and level with the ground, rather than at an angle to it. *The board consists of vertical and horizontal lines... Swing the club back until it is horizontal.* ADJ ► Also a noun. *Do not raise your left arm above the horizontal.* N-SING: the N ♦ **horizontally** *The wind was cold and drove the snow at him almost horizontally. ...a horizontally striped tie.* ADV: ADV with v, ADV -ed

2 A **horizontal** is a line or structure that is horizontal. *The undulating planes and organic forms of the countryside provide relief from the hard horizontals and verticals of the urban scene.* N-COUNT

hormonal /hɔːʳmoʊnᵊl/. ◆◇◇◇◇ **Hormonal** means relating to or involving hormones. *...our individual hormonal balance.* ADJ: usu ADJ n

hormone /hɔːʳmoʊn/ **hormones.** ◆◆◇◇◇ A **hormone** is a chemical, usually occurring naturally in your body, that stimulates certain organs of your body. N-COUNT

hormone replacement. If a woman has **hormone replacement** therapy, she takes doses of the hormone oestrogen, usually in order to control the symptoms of the menopause. *She has been on Hormone Replacement Therapy for four years and looks fantastic.* N-UNCOUNT: usu N n

horn /hɔːʳn/ **horns** ◆◆◇◇◇

1 On a vehicle such as a car, the **horn** is the device that makes a loud noise as a signal or warning. *He sounded the car horn.* N-COUNT: oft supp N

2 The **horns** of an animal such as a cow or deer are the hard pointed things that grow from its head. *A mature cow has horns.* N-COUNT: usu pl

3 **Horn** is the hard substance that the horns of animals are made of. Horn is sometimes used to make objects such as spoons, buttons, or ornaments. ● See also **horn-rimmed**. N-UNCOUNT

4 A **horn** is a musical instrument of the brass family. It is shaped like a long metal tube wound round in a circle with a wide funnel at one end. You play the horn by blowing into the mouthpiece and moving valves in order to obtain different notes. N-COUNT: oft the N =French horn

5 A **horn** is a simple musical instrument consisting of a metal tube that is wide at one end and narrow at the other. You play it by blowing into it. *...a hunting horn.* N-COUNT

6 A **horn** is a hollow curved object that is narrow at one end and wide at the other. *...a wind-up gramophone with a big horn.* N-COUNT

7 See also **shoehorn**.

8 If two people **lock horns**, they argue about something. *During his six years in office, Seidman has often locked horns with lawmakers.* PHRASES RECIP: V inflects, pl-n PHR

9 If you are **on the horns of a dilemma**, you have to choose between two things which are both unpleasant or difficult. *The bird is caught on the horns of a dilemma. Should it attack the predator, even though it then risks its own life? Or should it get out while the going is good?* PHR after v =in a quandry

10 If someone **pulls in** their **horns** or **draws in** their **horns**, they start behaving more cautiously than they did before, especially by spending less money. *Customers are drawing in their horns at a time of high interest rates.* V inflects

11 ● **take the bull by the horns**: see **bull**.

horned /hɔːʳnd/. **Horned** animals have horns, or parts of their bodies that look like horns. *...horned cattle. ...the call of a horned lark.* ADJ: usu ADJ n

hornet /hɔːʳnɪt/ **hornets**

1 A **hornet** is a large wasp. Hornets live in nests and have a powerful sting. N-COUNT

2 If you say that someone has stirred up **a hornet's nest**, you mean that they have done something which has caused a lot of controversy or produced a situation which is extremely difficult to deal with; an informal expression. PHRASE: usu PHR after v PRAGMATICS

hornpipe /hɔːʳnpaɪp/ **hornpipes.** A **hornpipe** is a lively dance which was traditionally danced by sailors. N-COUNT

horn-rimmed. **Horn-rimmed** spectacles have plastic frames that look as though they are made of horn. *He wore heavy horn-rimmed glasses.* ADJ: ADJ n

horny /hɔːʳni/ **hornier, horniest** ◆◇◇◇◇

1 If you describe someone as **horny**, you mean that they are sexually aroused or easily aroused; an informal use. *But don't you get frustrated sometimes? I mean, don't you get a bit, you know, horny? ...horny adolescent boys.* ADJ-GRADED =randy

2 In informal British English, if you describe someone as **horny**, you mean that they are sexually attractive. *Let's face it, Keanu Reeves is horny.* ADJ-GRADED =sexy

3 Something that is **horny** is hard, strong, and made of horn or of a hard substance like horn. *His fingernails had grown long, and horny... This cuttlefish has a horny internal shell like a pen.* ADJ

horoscope /hɒrəskoup, AM hɔːr-/ **horoscopes.** Your **horoscope** is a forecast of events which some people believe will happen to you in the future. Horoscopes are based on the position of the stars when you were born. ◆◇◇◇◇ N-COUNT

horrendous /hərendəs, AM hɔːr-/ ◆◇◇◇◇

1 Something that is **horrendous** is very unpleasant or shocking. *He described it as the most horrendous experience of his life... The violence used was horrendous.* ADJ-GRADED =horrific

2 Some people use **horrendous** to describe something that is so big or great that they find it extremely unpleasant; an informal use. *Nor do their debts looks so horrendous when related to the value of their fixed assets. ...the usually horrendous traffic jams.* ♦ **horrendously** *Many outings can now be horrendously expensive for parents with a young family.* ADJ-GRADED =dreadful; ADV-GRADED: usu ADV adj/-ed, also ADV after v

horrible /hɒrɪbᵊl, AM hɔːr-/ ◆◆◇◇◇

1 If you describe something or someone as **horrible**, you do not like them at all; an informal use. *The record sounds horrible. ...a horrible small boy.* ♦ **horribly** /hɒrɪbli, AM hɔːr-/ *When trouble comes they behave selfishly and horribly.* ADJ-GRADED =horrid ≠lovely; ADV-GRADED: ADV with v

2 You can call something **horrible** when it causes you to feel great shock, fear, and disgust; an informal use. *Still the horrible shrieking came out of his mouth.* ♦ **horribly** *A two-year-old boy was horribly murdered.* ADJ-GRADED =frightful; ADV-GRADED: ADV with v

3 **Horrible** is used to emphasize how awful or unpleasant something is; an informal use. *That seems like a horrible mess that will drag on for years... Unless you respect other people's religions, horrible mistakes and conflict will occur.* ♦ **horribly** *Our plans have gone horribly wrong... You got horribly drunk.* ADJ-GRADED: ADJ n PRAGMATICS =awful; ADV-GRADED: ADV with v, ADV adj

horrid /hɒrɪd, AM hɔːr-/ ◆◇◇◇◇

1 If you describe something as **horrid**, you mean that it is very unpleasant indeed; a rather informal use. *What a horrid smell!... The winter was horrid.* ADJ-GRADED =horrible

2 If you describe someone as **horrid**, you mean that they behave in a very unpleasant, nasty way towards other people. *I must have been a horrid little girl... I love both my parents, but they're horrid to each other.* ADJ-GRADED: oft ADJ *to* n =horrible

horrific /hərɪfɪk, AM hɔːr-/ ◆◇◇◇◇

1 If you describe a physical attack, accident, or injury as **horrific**, you mean that it is very bad, so that people are shocked when they see it or think about it. *I have never seen such horrific injuries... The slaughter was horrific.* ♦ **horrifically** *He had been horrifically assaulted before he died.* ADJ-GRADED =horrendous; ADV-GRADED: ADV with v

2 If you describe something as **horrific**, you mean that it is so big that it is extremely unpleasant. *...piling up horrific extra amounts of money on top of your original debt.* ♦ **horrifically** *Opera productions are horrifically expensive.* ADJ-GRADED =horrendous; ADV-GRADED: ADV adj

horrify /hɒrɪfaɪ, AM hɔːr-/ **horrifies, horrifying, horrified.** If someone **is horrified**, they feel shocked, disappointed, or disgusted, usually because of something that they have seen or heard. *His family were horrified by the change. ...a crime trend that will horrify all parents.* ♦ **horrified** *When I saw these figures I was horrified... We are so horrified by the enormity of the crime that we want somebody brought to justice quickly.* ◆◆◇◇◇ VERB =appal; *be* V-ed; V n; ADV-GRADED

horrifying /hɒrɪfaɪɪŋ/. If you describe something as **horrifying**, you mean that it is shocking, alarming, or disgusting. *These were horrifying experiences... The scale of the problem is horrifying.* ♦ **horrifyingly** *...horrifyingly high levels of infant mortality... The two cars cartwheeled horrifyingly into the sand trap at the first corner.* ◆◇◇◇◇ ADJ-GRADED =appalling; ADV-GRADED: ADV adj, ADV with v

horror /hɒrəʳ, AM hɔːr-/ **horrors** ◆◆◆◇◇

1 **Horror** is a feeling of great alarm and dismay caused by something extremely unpleasant. *I felt numb with horror... As I watched in horror the boat began to power away from me.* N-UNCOUNT =terror

2 If you have a **horror of** something, you are afraid of it or dislike it very much. *...his horror of death.* N-SING: N *of* n

3 The **horror** of something, especially something that hurts people, is its very great unpleasantness, which is often frightening and shocking. *...the horror of this most bloody of civil wars.* N-SING: oft N *of* n

4 You can refer to extremely unpleasant or frightening experiences as **horrors**. *Can I possibly picture to you all the horrors we have undergone since I last wrote you?* N-COUNT: usu pl

5 If you refer to someone or something as a **horror**, you mean that you think they are very unpleasant or ugly; an informal use. *Our host was arrogant and offensive. How his sweet wife could tolerate such a horror was baffling.* N-COUNT PRAGMATICS

6 A **horror** film or story is intended to be very frightening. *...a psychological horror film.* ADJ: ADJ n

7 You can refer to an account of a very unpleasant experience or event as a **horror** story. *Almost everyone has a horror story to tell about 'cowboy' builders.* ADJ: ADJ n

8 **Horror of horrors** is used in a humorous way to refer to something that you consider to be the worst part of a situation; an informal expression. *The company has already boosted its share of the UK tea market with its round tea bags. Now it is successfully converting the nation to (horror of horrors) instant tea.* PHRASE: PHR with cl PRAGMATICS

horror-stricken /hɒrəʳstrɪkən/. **Horror-stricken** means the same as **horror-struck**. ADJ

horror-struck. If you describe someone as **horror-struck** or **horror-stricken**, you mean that they feel very great horror or dismay at something that has happened. *Nightingale had announced her nursing ambitions to her rich parents, they were horror-struck.* ADJ =appalled

hors d'oeuvre /ɔːʳdɜːʳv/ **hors d'oeuvres.** **Hors d'oeuvres** are dishes of cold foods that have been specially prepared and which are served in small portions before the main course of a meal. N-VAR =appetizers

horse /hɔːʳs/ **horses, horsing, horsed** ◆◆◆◆◇

1 A **horse** is a large animal which people can ride. Some horses are used for pulling ploughs and carts. *A small man on a grey horse had appeared.* N-COUNT

2 When you talk about **the horses**, you mean horse races in which people bet money on the horse which they think will win. *I will definitely be having a flutter on the horses that Gaye trains.* N-PLURAL: *the* N, usu *on the* N

3 A vaulting **horse** is a piece of sports equipment which gymnasts jump over. It is made of wood and the top is covered in a soft material such as leather. N-COUNT

4 **Horse** is heroin; an old-fashioned, informal use. N-UNCOUNT

5 If you hear something **from the horse's mouth**, you hear it from someone who knows that it is definitely true. *He has got to hear it from the horse's* PHRASE: v PHR

mouth. Then he can make a judgment as to whether his policy is correct or not.
6 See also **clothes horse**, **dark horse**, **rocking horse**, **seahorse**. • to **put the cart before the horse**: see **cart**.

horse around. If you **horse around**, you play roughly and rather carelessly, so that you could hurt someone or damage something; an informal expression. *Later that day I was horsing around with Katie when she accidentally stuck her finger in my eye.* PHRASAL VERB VP

horseback /hɔːʳsbæk/ ◆◇◇◇◇
1 If you do something on **horseback**, you do it while riding a horse. *In remote mountain areas, voters arrived on horseback.* N-UNCOUNT: usu *on/by* N
2 **Horseback** riding is the activity of riding a horse. *...a horseback ride into the mountains.* ▶ Also an adverb. *Many people in this area ride horseback.* ADJ: ADJ n =horse riding ADV

horse box horse boxes; also spelled **horse-box**. A **horse box** is a vehicle which is used to take horses from one place to another; used mainly in British English. N-COUNT

horse chestnut horse chestnuts; also spelled **horse-chestnut**.
1 A **horse chestnut** is a large tree which has leaves with several pointed parts and shiny reddish-brown nuts covered with a spiky case. N-COUNT
2 **Horse chestnuts** are the nuts of a horse chestnut tree. They are more commonly called **conkers**. N-COUNT

horse-drawn; also spelled **horsedrawn**. A **horse-drawn** carriage, cart, or other vehicle is one that is pulled by one or more horses. *The Queen arrives for the ceremony in a horse-drawn open-topped carriage.* ADJ: ADJ n

horsehair /hɔːʳsheəʳ/. **Horsehair** is hair which is taken from the tails or manes of horses, and was formerly used to stuff mattresses and furniture such as armchairs. N-UNCOUNT: oft N n

horseman /hɔːʳsmən/ **horsemen.** A **horseman** is a man who is riding a horse, or who rides horses well. *Gerald was a fine horseman.* ◆◇◇◇◇ N-COUNT: usu with supp

horsemanship /hɔːʳsmənʃɪp/. **Horsemanship** is the ability to ride horses well. N-UNCOUNT

horseplay /hɔːʳspleɪ/. **Horseplay** is rough play in which people push and hit each other, or behave in a silly way. *...the childish splashing and horseplay Mark indulged in.* N-UNCOUNT

horsepower /hɔːʳspaʊəʳ/. **Horsepower** is a unit of power used for measuring how powerful an engine is. *The engine has more than 4,000 horsepower. ...a 300-horsepower engine.* N-UNCOUNT: usu num N

horse racing; also spelled **horse-racing** or **horseracing**. **Horse racing** is a sport in which horses ridden by jockeys run in races, sometimes jumping over fences. ◆◇◇◇◇ N-UNCOUNT

horseradish /hɔːʳsrædɪʃ/
1 **Horseradish** is a small white vegetable that is the root of a crop. It has a very strong sharp taste and is often made into a sauce. *...1 tablespoon freshly grated horseradish.* N-UNCOUNT
2 **Horseradish** or **horseradish sauce** is a sauce made from horseradish. It is often eaten with roast beef. N-UNCOUNT

horse riding; also spelled **horse-riding**. **Horse riding** is the activity of riding a horse, especially for enjoyment or as a form of physical exercise; used mainly in British English. N-UNCOUNT

horseshoe /hɔːʳsʃuː/ **horseshoes** ◆◇◇◇◇
1 A **horseshoe** is a piece of metal shaped like a U, which is fixed with nails to a horse's hoof in order to protect it. N-COUNT
2 A **horseshoe** is an object which has the shape of a horseshoe. Cardboard or plastic horseshoes are sometimes given to people for their birthday or wedding because they are thought to bring good luck. *...a golden horseshoe suspended in midair.* N-COUNT

horse show, horse shows. A **horse show** is a sporting event in which people riding horses compete in order to demonstrate their skill and control. N-COUNT =gymkhana

horse-trading; also spelled **horsetrading**. If you describe discussions or negotiations as **horse-trading**, you disapprove of the way in which people are using secret, unofficial, and perhaps dishonest methods in order to get what they want; used especially in journalism. *...the anger and distaste many people feel at the political horse-trading involved in forming a government.* N-UNCOUNT PRAGMATICS

horsewhip /hɔːʳshwɪp/ **horsewhips, horsewhipping, horsewhipped;** also spelled **horse-whip**.
1 A **horsewhip** is a long, thin piece of leather on the end of a short, stiff handle. It is used to train and control horses. N-COUNT
2 If someone **horsewhips** an animal or a person, they hit them several times with a horsewhip in order to hurt or punish them. *He tied them up and then horsewhipped them, to 'tame' his catches before sending them off to zoos... These young louts deserve to be horse-whipped.* VERB V n

horsewoman /hɔːʳswʊmən/ **horsewomen.** A **horsewoman** is a woman who is riding a horse, or who rides horses well. *She developed into an excellent horsewoman.* N-COUNT

horsey /hɔːʳsi/; also spelled **horsy**.
1 Someone who is **horsey** is very keen on horses or spends a lot of time with horses because he or she is fond of them; an informal use. *Harry has been riding since he was a child and he comes from a very horsey family.* ADJ-GRADED
2 If you describe a woman as **horsey**, you are saying in a rather rude way that her face reminds you of a horse, for example because it is long and thin. *...his tall rather horsey wife.* ADJ-GRADED PRAGMATICS

horticultural /hɔːʳtɪkʌltʃərəl/. **Horticultural** means concerned with horticulture. *The horticultural show will take place in the old covered Victorian Market.* ◆◇◇◇◇ ADJ: usu ADJ n

horticulturalist /hɔːʳtɪkʌltʃərəlɪst/ **horticulturalists.** A **horticulturalist** is a person who grows flowers, fruit, and vegetables, especially as their job. N-COUNT

horticulture /hɔːʳtɪkʌltʃəʳ/. **Horticulture** is the study and practice of growing plants. N-UNCOUNT

hose /hoʊz/ **hoses, hosing, hosed** ◆◇◇◇◇
1 A **hose** is a long, flexible pipe made of rubber or plastic. Water is directed through a hose in order to do things such as put out fires, clean cars, or water gardens. *You've left the garden hose on... The firemen unwrapped their hoses and began dousing the scorched grain silos.* N-COUNT =hosepipe
2 A **hose** is a pipe made of rubber or plastic, along which a liquid or gas flows, for example from one part of an engine to another. *Water in the engine compartment is sucked away by a hose.* N-COUNT
3 If you **hose** something, you wash or water it using a hose. *We wash our cars and hose our gardens without even thinking of the water that uses.* VERB V n Also V
4 **Hose** is used to refer to tights, socks, and stockings; an old-fashioned or technical use. *If you have varicose veins, consider wearing elastic support hose.* • See also **panty hose**. N-UNCOUNT =hosiery
5 **Hose** is an old-fashioned men's garment that looks like a pair of very tight trousers. N-UNCOUNT

hose down. When you **hose** something or someone **down**, you clean them using a hose. *In one driveway a chauffeur wearing rubber boots was hosing down a limousine... When the children come in covered in sand you can just hose them down.* PHRASAL VERB V P n (not pron) V n P

hosepipe /hoʊzpaɪp/ **hosepipes.** A **hosepipe** is a hose that people use to water their gardens or for washing their cars; used mainly in British English. N-COUNT =hose

hosiery /hoʊziəri, AM -ʒəri/. You use **hosiery** to refer to tights, stockings, and socks, especially when they are on sale in shops; a formal term. N-UNCOUNT

hospice /hɒspɪs/ **hospices.** A **hospice** is a special hospital for people who are dying, where their practical and emotional needs are dealt with as well as their medical needs. *...a hospice for cancer patients... He died in March at St Julia's Hospice.* ◆◇◇◇◇ N-COUNT: oft in names after n

hospitable /hɒspɪtəbəl, hɒspɪt-/ ◆◇◇◇◇
1 A **hospitable** person is friendly, generous, and ADJ-GRADED

welcoming to guests or strangers. *The locals are hospitable and welcoming... He was very hospitable to me when I came to New York.* ≠unfriendly

2 A **hospitable** place, climate, or environment is one that allows or encourages the existence or development of particular people, things, or processes. *Even in summer this place did not look exactly hospitable: in winter, conditions must have been exceedingly harsh. ...hospitable political environments.* ADJ-GRADED ≠hostile

hospital /hɒspɪtᵊl/ **hospitals.** A **hospital** is a place where people who are ill are looked after by nurses and doctors. *Queen Elizabeth Hospital is a children's hospital with 120 beds... A couple of weeks later my mother went into hospital... He may be able to leave hospital early next week.* ◆◆◆◆◆ N-VAR

hospitality /hɒspɪtælɪti/ ◆◇◇◇◇

1 Hospitality is friendly, welcoming behaviour towards guests or towards strangers. *Every visitor to Georgia is overwhelmed by the kindness, charm and hospitality of the people.* N-UNCOUNT

2 Hospitality is the food, drink, and other privileges which some companies provide for their visitors or clients at major sporting or other public events. *A few of us in the press were there, goggle-eyed at the lavish hospitality. ...corporate hospitality tents.* N-UNCOUNT

hospitalize /hɒspɪtəlaɪz/ **hospitalizes, hospitalizing, hospitalized;** also spelled **hospitalise** in British English. If someone **is hospitalized**, they are sent or admitted to hospital. *Most people do not have to be hospitalized for asthma or pneumonia.* ◆◇◇◇◇ VB: usu passive, be V-ed ♦ **hospitalization** /hɒspɪtəlaɪzeɪʃᵊn/ *Occasionally hospitalization is required to combat dehydration.* N-UNCOUNT

host /hoʊst/ **hosts, hosting, hosted** ◆◆◆◆◆

1 The **host** at a party is the person who has invited the guests and provides the food, drink, or entertainment. *Apart from my host, I didn't know a single person there... Tommy Sopwith was always the perfect host.* N-COUNT

2 If someone **hosts** a party, dinner, or other function, they have invited the guests and provide the food, drink, or entertainment. *Tonight she hosts a ball for 300 guests. ...a banquet hosted by the president of Kazakhstan.* VERB, V n

3 A country, city, or organization that is the **host** of an event provides the facilities for that event to take place. *Barcelona was chosen to be host of the 1992 Olympic games. ...a preliminary qualifying tournament in Andorra involving the host country.* N-COUNT: oft N n

4 If a country, city, or organization **hosts** an event, they provide the facilities for the event to take place. *Cannes hosts the annual film festival.* VERB, V n

5 If a person or country **plays host to** an event or an important visitor, they host the event or the visit. *In 1987 Canada played host to the Commonwealth Conference... The Prime Minister played host to French Premier Jacques Chirac.* PHRASE: V inflects

6 The **host** of a radio or television show is the person who introduces it and talks to the people who appear in it. *I am host of a live radio programme.* N-COUNT: usu with supp =presenter

7 The person who **hosts** a radio or television show introduces it and talks to the people who appear in it. *Mr Beadle hosts a daily news quiz on GMTV.* VERB, V n

8 A **host** of things is a lot of them. *A host of problems may delay the opening of the Channel Tunnel... Today we have radios, TVs, and a whole host of gadgets powered by electricity.* QUANT =multitude

9 If an area is **host** to living things, those creatures live and feed in that area. *Uganda's beautiful highlands are host to a wide range of wildlife.* N-COUNT: usu N *to* n

10 The **host** of a parasite is the plant or animal it feeds off: a technical use. *When the eggs hatch the larvae eat the living flesh of the host animal.* N-COUNT: oft N n

11 The **Host** is the bread which is used to represent the body of Christ in Christian church services such as Holy Communion; a technical use. N-COUNT: usu sing, *the* N

hostage /hɒstɪdʒ/ **hostages** ◆◆◆◆◇

1 A **hostage** is someone who has been captured by a person or organization and who may be killed or injured if people do not do what that person or organization demands. *It is hopeful that two hostages will be freed in the next few days.* N-COUNT

2 If someone **is taken hostage** or **is held hostage**, they are captured and kept as a hostage. *He was taken hostage while on his first foreign assignment as a television journalist.* PHRASE: V inflects

3 If you say you are **hostage to** something, you mean that your freedom to take action is restricted by things that you cannot control. *With the reduction in foreign investments, the government will be even more a hostage to the whims of the international oil price... Wine growers say they've been held hostage to the interests of the cereal and soybean farmers.* N-VAR: N *to* n

hostel /hɒstᵊl/ **hostels.** A **hostel** is a large house where people can stay cheaply for a short period of time. Hostels are usually owned by local government authorities or charities; used mainly in British English. ● See also **youth hostel.** ◆◆◇◇◇ N-COUNT

hostelry /hɒstᵊlri/ **hostelries.** In British English, a **hostelry** is a pub or a hotel; a formal word. N-COUNT

hostess /hoʊstɪs/ **hostesses** ◆◇◇◇◇

1 The **hostess** at a party is the woman who has invited the guests and provides the food, drink, or entertainment. *The hostess introduced them... She was a superb hostess to us all.* N-COUNT

2 A **hostess** at a night club or dance hall is a woman who is paid by a man to be his companion for the evening. N-COUNT

hostile /hɒstaɪl, AM -tᵊl/ ◆◆◇◇◇

1 If you are **hostile** to another person or an idea, you disagree with them or disapprove of them, often showing this in your behaviour. *Many people felt they would be hostile to the idea of foreign intervention... The West has gradually relaxed its hostile attitude to this influential state... The Governor faced hostile crowds when he visited the town yesterday.* ADJ-GRADED: oft ADJ *to/towards* n =antagonistic ≠receptive

2 Someone who is **hostile** is unfriendly and aggressive. *Drinking may make a person feel relaxed and happy, or it may make her hostile, violent, or depressed... The prisoner eyed him in hostile silence.* ADJ-GRADED =aggressive ≠cordial

3 Hostile situations and conditions make it difficult for you to achieve something. *...some of the most hostile climatic conditions in the world... If this round of talks fails, the world's trading environment is likely to become increasingly hostile.* ADJ-GRADED

4 In a war, you use the word **hostile** to describe your enemy's forces, organizations, weapons, land, and activities. *The city is encircled by a hostile army... They were in hostile territory. ...hostile aircraft.* ADJ: ADJ n =enemy

hostilities /hɒstɪlɪtiz/. You can refer to fighting between two countries or groups who are at war as **hostilities**; a formal use. *The authorities have urged people to stock up on fuel in case hostilities break out.* ◆◇◇◇◇ N-PLURAL

hostility /hɒstɪlɪti/ ◆◆◇◇◇

1 Hostility is unfriendly or aggressive behaviour towards people or ideas. *The last decade has witnessed a serious rise in the levels of racism and hostility to Black and ethnic groups... Christabel looked at Ron with open hostility.* N-UNCOUNT: oft N *to/towards* n

2 Your **hostility** to something you do not approve of is your opposition to it. *There is hostility among traditionalists to this method of teaching history.* N-UNCOUNT: usu N *to/towards* n

hot /hɒt/ **hotter, hottest; hots, hotting, hotted** ◆◆◆◆◇

1 Something that is **hot** has a high temperature. *When the oil is hot, add the sliced onion... What he needed was a hot bath and a good sleep... Metal-handled pans can get really hot and burn you.* ADJ-GRADED ≠cold, cool

2 Hot is used to describe the weather or the air in a room or building when the temperature is high. *It was too hot even for a gentle stroll... It was a hot, humid summer day... My small greenhouse gets very hot when the sun is shining.* ADJ-GRADED ≠chilly, cold

3 If you are **hot**, you feel as if your body is at an unpleasantly high temperature. *I was too hot and tired to eat more than a few mouthfuls... My head was reeling. I felt hot all over.* ADJ-GRADED: usu v-link ADJ ≠cold

4 You use **hot** to talk or ask about how high the temperature of something is. *They are called in-* ADJ-GRADED: *how* ADJ, *as* ADJ *as*, *candescent lights, and their colour depends on how hot they are... Remember that the top of the oven will be hotter than the bottom.* ADJ-compar than

5 Hot food is intended to be eaten as soon as it is cooked, as opposed to food that you eat when it has cooled or that you do not cook at all. *If you live alone, you might not want to cook a hot meal every day.* ADJ: ADJ n ≠cold

6 You can say that food is **hot** when it has a strong, burning taste caused by spices such as chili or cayenne pepper. *...hot curries. ...a dish that's spicy but not too hot.* ADJ-GRADED =spicy ≠mild

7 A **hot** issue or topic is one that is very important at the present time and is receiving a lot of publicity; used in journalism. *The role of women in war has been a hot topic of debate in America since the Gulf conflict.* ADJ-GRADED: usu ADJ n

8 Hot news is new, recent, and fresh; an informal use. *Well, if you hear any hot news from Yugoslavia, you'll let us know, won't you.* ADJ-GRADED: usu ADJ n

9 You can use **hot** to describe something that is very exciting and that many people want to see, use, obtain, or become involved with; an informal use. *When I was in Chicago in 1990 a friend got me a ticket for the hottest show in town: the Monet Exhibition at the Art Institute... When I was last there, the hot place was the Royal Bachelors' Club.* ADJ-GRADED: usu ADJ n

10 You can use **hot** to describe something that no one wants to deal with, often because it has been illegally obtained and is very valuable or famous; an informal use. *If too much publicity is given to the theft of important works, the works will become too hot to handle and be destroyed.* ADJ-GRADED: usu v-link ADJ

11 You can describe a situation that is created by a person's behaviour or attitude as **hot** when it is unpleasant and difficult to deal with; an informal use. *When the streets get too hot for them, they head south in one stolen car after another.* ADJ-GRADED: usu v-link ADJ

12 A **hot** contest is one that is intense and involves a great deal of activity and determination; an informal use. *It took hot competition from abroad, however, to show us just how good Scottish cashmere really is.* ADJ-GRADED: usu ADJ n =fierce

13 If a person or team is the **hot** favourite, people think that they are most the likely to win a race or competition. *Labour is now hot favourite to win the election.* ADJ-GRADED: ADJ n

14 Someone who has a **hot** temper gets angry very quickly and easily. *His hot temper was making it increasingly difficult for others to work with him.* ADJ-GRADED: usu ADJ n
• See also **hot-tempered**.

15 If someone **blows hot and cold**, they keep changing their attitude towards something or someone, sometimes being very enthusiastic and at other times expressing no interest at all. *The media, meanwhile, has blown hot and cold on the affair.* PHRASES V inflects, oft PHR *on/over/about* n

16 If you are **hot and bothered**, you are so worried and anxious that you cannot think clearly or behave sensibly. *Ray was getting very hot and bothered about the idea.* v-link PHR, oft PHR *about* n =in a flap

17 If you say that one person **has the hots for** another, you mean that they feel a strong sexual attraction towards that person; an informal use. *I've had the hots for him ever since he came to college.* V inflects

hot up. When something **hots up**, a lot of activity and excitement starts to happen; used mainly in British English. *The bars rarely hot up before 1am or the night-clubs before 2am... Campaigning is expected to start hotting up today.* PHRASAL VERB V P

hot air. If you say that someone's claims or promises are just **hot air**, you are criticizing them because they are made mainly to impress people and have no real value or meaning; an informal expression. *His justification for the merger was just hot air... I'd come to the conclusion by then that he was all hot air.* ◆◇◇◇◇ N-UNCOUNT PRAGMATICS =empty talk

hot-air balloon, hot-air balloons. A **hot-air balloon** is a large balloon with a basket underneath in which people can travel. The balloon is filled with hot air in order to make it float in the air. N-COUNT

hotbed /hɒtbed/ **hotbeds.** If you say that somewhere is a **hotbed** of an undesirable activity, you are emphasizing that a lot of the activity is going on there or being started there. *...a state now known worldwide as a hotbed of racial intolerance.* N-COUNT: with supp, usu N *of* n PRAGMATICS

hot-blooded. If you describe someone as **hot-blooded**, you mean that they are very quick to express their emotions, especially anger and love. *His neighbors remembered him as a hot-blooded teenager, a self-styled ladies' man.* ADJ-GRADED: usu ADJ n ≠cold-blooded

hotch-potch /hɒtʃ pɒtʃ/; also **hotchpotch**. In informal British English, a **hotch-potch** is a confused or disorderly mixture of different types of things. The usual American word is **hodgepodge**. *The palace is a complete hotch-potch of architectural styles.* N-SING: usu with supp, oft N *of* n =jumble

hot dog, hot dogs. A **hot dog** is a long bread roll with a hot sausage inside it. ◆◇◇◇◇ N-COUNT

hotel /hoʊtel/ **hotels.** A **hotel** is a building where people stay, for example on holiday, paying for their rooms and meals. ◆◆◆◆◇ N-COUNT

hotelier /hoʊteliəʳ, AM oʊteljeɪ/ **hoteliers.** A **hotelier** is a person who owns or manages a hotel. ◆◇◇◇◇ N-COUNT

hot flash, hot flashes. A **hot flash** is the same as a **hot flush**; used in American English. N-COUNT

hot flush hot flushes. A **hot flush** is a sudden hot feeling in the skin which women often experience at the time of their menopause. N-COUNT

hot-foot, hot-foots, hot-footing, hot-footed; also spelled **hotfoot**. If you **hot-foot** it somewhere, you go there in a hurry; an informal word. *Richard was hot-footing it back to London, to process everything.* VERB =speed V *it* adv/prep

hothead /hɒthed/ **hotheads.** If you refer to someone as a **hothead**, you are criticizing them for doing things hastily, without thinking of the consequences; an informal word, used showing disapproval. *He is a hothead and a bully just like his dad.* N-COUNT PRAGMATICS

hot-headed. If you describe someone as **hot-headed**, you are criticizing them for acting hastily and without thinking of the consequences. ADJ-GRADED PRAGMATICS

hothouse /hɒthaʊs/ **hothouses**

1 A **hothouse** is a heated building, usually made of glass, in which plants and flowers can be grown. N-COUNT

2 You can refer to a situation or place as a **hothouse** when there is intense activity, especially intellectual or emotional activity. *The vast crowds make Rome a frantic hothouse at times. ...the reputation of the College as a hothouse of novel ideas.* N-COUNT: oft N n, N *of* n

hotline /hɒtlaɪn/ **hotlines;** also spelled **hot line.** ◆◇◇◇◇

1 A **hotline** is a telephone line that the public can use to contact an organization about a particular subject. Hotlines allow people to obtain information from an organization or to give the organization information. *...a telephone hotline for gardeners seeking advice... Anyone with information should contact the Anti-Terrorist Squad on the confidential freephone hotline.* N-COUNT

2 A **hotline** is a special, direct telephone line between the heads of government in different countries. *He used the Washington-Moscow hot line to put the suggestion to Mr Gorbachev.* N-COUNT

hotly /hɒtli/ ◆◇◇◇◇

1 If people discuss, argue, or say something **hotly**, they speak in a lively or angry way, because they feel strongly. *'You're a fool, then,' she said hotly... The bank hotly denies any wrongdoing.* ADV-GRADED: ADV with v =vehemently

2 If you are being **hotly** pursued, there is someone who is close behind you, moving very quickly, and determined to catch you. *He'd snuck out of America hotly pursued by the CIA.* ADV-GRADED: ADV with v =closely

hotplate /hɒtpleɪt/ **hotplates.** A **hotplate** is a flat surface, usually on a cooker. You heat it in order to cook food in pans or keep food warm. N-COUNT

hotpot /hɒtpɒt/ **hotpots;** also spelled **hot-pot**. In Britain, a **hotpot** is a dish made from a mixture of meat, vegetables, and gravy cooked slowly in the oven. *...lamb hotpot.* N-VAR =stew, casserole

hot potato, hot potatoes. If you describe a problem or issue as a **hot potato**, you mean that N-COUNT it is a very difficult and nobody wants to deal with it. *Birth-control was a political hot potato.*

hot seat. If you are in **the hot seat**, you are responsible for making important and difficult decisions; an informal expression. *He is to remain in the hot seat as chief executive.* PHRASE: usu *in/into* PHR

hotshot /hɒtʃɒt/ **hotshots.** If you refer to someone as a **hotshot**, you mean they are very good at a particular job and are going to be very successful, usually because they are very ambitious. *...a bunch of corporate hotshots... She's a hotshot broker on Wall Street.* N-COUNT: oft N n

hot spot **hot spots;** also spelled **hotspot.** ◆◇◇◇◇

1 You can refer to an exciting place where there is a lot of activity or entertainment as a **hot spot**; an informal use. *...a fancy Manhattan hot spot. ...a popular and lively package tour hotspot.* N-COUNT

2 You can refer to an area where there is some form of trouble such as fighting or political unrest as a **hot spot**; used in journalism. *There were many hot spots in the region, where fighting had been going on.* N-COUNT

hot stuff. If you think that someone or something is **hot stuff**, you find them exciting or sexually attractive; an informal word. *His love letters were hot stuff, apparently.* N-UNCOUNT

hot-tempered. If you describe someone as **hot-tempered**, you think they get angry very quickly and easily. *He is so hot tempered and excitable, like a bottle of soda water exploding.* ADJ-GRADED

hot tub, hot tubs. A **hot tub** is a very large, round bath in which several people can bathe together. N-COUNT

hot-water bottle, hot-water bottles; also spelled **hot water bottle.** A **hot-water bottle** is a rubber container that you fill with hot water and put in a bed to make it warm. N-COUNT

hot wire, hot wires, hot wiring, hot wired. To **hot wire** a car means to start its engine using a piece of wire rather than the key. Car thieves often hot wire cars in order to steal them. *A youth was inside the car, attempting to hot wire it.* VERB V n

houmous /huːməs/; also spelled **humous** or **hummus. Houmous** is a smooth food made from chick peas. It is often eaten with bread at the beginning of a meal. N-UNCOUNT

hound /haʊnd/ **hounds, hounding, hounded** ◆◆◇◇◇

1 A **hound** is a type of dog that is often used for hunting or racing. *Rainey's chief interest in life is hunting with hounds.* N-COUNT

2 If someone **hounds** you, they constantly disturb or pester you. *Newcomers are constantly hounding them for advice... From the start of the season, the Arsenal striker has been hounded by the press.* VERB V n

3 If someone **is hounded** out of a job or place, they are forced to leave it, often because other people are constantly criticizing them. *There is a general view around that he has been hounded out of office by the press.* VB: usu passive be V-ed out of/from n

hour /aʊəʳ/ **hours** ◆◆◆◆◆

1 An **hour** is a period of sixty minutes. *They waited for about two hours... I only slept about half an hour that night. ...a twenty-four hour strike... London was an hour away and by the time I arrived the operation had already been performed.* N-COUNT

2 People say that something takes or lasts **hours** to emphasize that it takes or lasts a very long time, or what seems like a very long time. *Getting there would take hours.* N-PLURAL PRAGMATICS =ages

3 A clock that strikes **the hour** strikes when it is exactly one o'clock, two o'clock, and so on. N-SING: the N

4 You can refer to a particular time or moment as a particular **hour**; a literary use. *...the hour of his execution... The gathering storm had made the day even darker than was usual at this hour.* N-SING: with supp =time

5 If you refer, for example, to someone's **hour** of need or **hour** of happiness, you are referring to the time in their life when they are or were experiencing that condition or feeling; a literary use. *He recalled her devotion to her husband during his hour of need. ...the darkest hour of my professional life.* N-COUNT: with supp

6 You can refer to the period of time during which something happens or operates each day as the **hours** during which it happens or operates. *...the hours of darkness... Phone us on this number during office hours. ...outside prison visiting hours.* N-PLURAL: with supp

7 If you refer to the **hours** involved in a job, you are talking about how long you spend each week doing it and when you do it. *I worked quite irregular hours... The job was easy; the hours were good.* N-PLURAL

8 See **eleventh hour, lunch hour, rush hour.**

9 If you do something **after hours**, you do it outside normal business hours or the time when you are usually at work. *...a local restaurant where steel workers unwind after hours... Daly kept this school open after hours so it doubled as a community center.* ● See also **after-hours.** PHRASES PHR after v, PHR n

10 If you say that something is done or happens **at all hours** of the day or night, you disapprove of it being done or happening at the time that it does or as often as it does. *She didn't want her fourteen-year-old daughter coming home at all hours of the morning. ...a neighbour's car alarm going off at all hours of the day and night.* PHR after v PRAGMATICS

11 If something happens **in the early hours** or **in the small hours**, it happens in the early morning after midnight. *Gibbs was arrested in the early hours of yesterday morning.*

12 If you say that someone does something **hour after hour**, you are emphasizing that they do it continually for a long time. *He and my mom were arguing every night, hour after hour.* PRAGMATICS

13 If something happens **on the hour**, it happens every hour at, for example, nine o'clock, ten o'clock, and so on, and not at any number of minutes past an hour. PHR after v

14 In American English, if you want to state the time exactly, you can give a number of minutes followed by **before the hour** or **past the hour.** v-link num PHR

15 Something that happens **out of hours** happens at a time that is not during the usual hours of business or work; used mainly in British English. *Teachers refused to run out of hours sports matches because they weren't being paid.* PHR after v, PHR n

hourglass /aʊəʳglɑːs/ **hourglasses;** also spelled **hour glass.** An **hourglass** is a device that was used to measure the passing of an hour. It has two round glass sections linked by a narrow channel, and contains sand which takes an hour to flow from the top section into the lower one. N-COUNT

hourly /aʊəʳli/ ◆◇◇◇◇

1 An **hourly** event happens once every hour. *He flipped on the radio to get the hourly news broadcast.* ▶ Also an adverb. *The hospital issued press releases hourly.* ADJ: ADJ n ADV: ADV after v

2 Your **hourly** earnings are the earnings that you make in one hour. *They have little prospect of finding new jobs with the same hourly pay.* ADJ: ADJ n

house, houses, housing, housed. The noun is pronounced /haʊs/. The verb is pronounced /haʊz/. The form **houses** is pronounced /haʊzɪz/. ◆◆◆◆◆

1 A **house** is a building in which people live, usually the people belonging to one family. *She has moved to a small house and is living off her meagre savings. ...her parents' house in Warwickshire.* N-COUNT

2 You can refer to all the people who live together in a house as the **house**. *If he set his alarm clock for midnight, it would wake the whole house... So I grew up with that feeling that the man is the head of the house.* N-SING: usu the N =household

3 **House** is used in the names of types of places where people go to eat and drink. *...a steak house. ...an old Salzburg coffee house.* N-COUNT: n N

4 **House** is used in the names of types of companies, especially ones which publish books, lend money, or design clothes. *Many of the clothes come from the world's top fashion houses... Eventually she was fired from her job at a publishing house.* N-COUNT: n N

5 **House** is sometimes used in the names of office buildings and large private homes. *I was to go to the very top floor of Bush House in Aldwych. ...Harewood House near Leeds.* N-IN-NAMES: n N

6 You can refer to the two main bodies of Britain's and the United States of America's parliament as N-COUNT

the **House** or a **House**. *Some members of the House and Senate worked all day yesterday... The Republicans have majorities in both Houses.*

7 In formal British English, you can refer to all the people at a debate as the **house**. *The club is planning a public debate on 'This house believes that journalism has not gained from the introduction of new technology'.* N-SING: *the/this* N

8 In a British school, a **house** is a group of children of different ages who compete against other groups in sports and other activities. Each house usually has a name. *He was a prefect and house captain.* N-COUNT

9 A **house** is a family which has been or will be important for many generations, especially the family of a king or queen. *...the Saudi Royal House. ...the House of Windsor.* N-COUNT: with supp

10 The **house** is the part of a theatre, cinema, or other place of entertainment where the audience sits. You can also refer to the audience at a particular performance as the **house**. *They played in front of a packed house.* N-COUNT

11 A restaurant's **house** wine is the cheapest wine it sells, which is not listed by name on the wine list. *Tweed ordered a carafe of the house wine. ...a bottle of house red or white.* ADJ: ADJ n

12 To **house** someone means to provide a house or flat for them to live in. *Part III of the Housing Act 1985 imposes duties on local authorities to house homeless people... Regrettably we have to house families in these inadequate flats.* VERB V n V n adv/prep

13 A building or container that **houses** something is the place where it is located or from where it operates. *The château itself is open to the public and houses a museum of motorcycles and cars. ...the office complex that used to house the Central Committee of the Communist Party.* VB: no cont V n

14 If you say that a building **houses** a number of people, you mean that is the place where they live or where they are staying. *The building will house twelve boys and eight girls... Their villas housed army officers now.* VB: no cont =accommodate V n

15 See also **boarding house**, **chapter house**, **clearing house**, **council house**, **doll's house**, **full house**, **opera house**, **public house**, **wendy house**, **White House**.

16 If a person or their performance in a play or concert **brings the house down**, the audience claps and cheers loudly for a long time because they are very pleased with the performance; an informal expression. *It's really an amazing dance. It just always brings the house down.* PHRASES V inflects

17 If two people **get on like a house on fire**, they quickly become close friends, for example because they have many interests in common; an informal expression. V inflects =hit it off

18 If you **keep house**, you do the cleaning and cooking for your household, and do not go out to work. *He lives with an aunt who keeps house for him.* V inflects, oft PHR *for* n

19 If you are given something in a restaurant or pub **on the house**, you do not have to pay for it. *The owner knew about the engagement and brought them glasses of champagne on the house.* v-link PHR, PHR after v

20 If you say you keep **open house**, you mean that visitors are always welcome at your house, whether they have been invited or not. *He used to keep open house on Sundays... This is a time for open house, and friends drop by to bring good wishes and share sweets, roasted nuts, and New Year Cake.* usu PHR after v

21 If someone **gets** their **house in order**, **puts** their **house in order**, or **sets** their **house in order**, they arrange their affairs and solve their problems. *He's got his house in order and made some tremendous decisions... The challenge for American leadership is this: Can we put our economic house in order?... Before you lecture me, Mr Abbey, I suggest you set your house in order.* V inflects

house arrest. ◆◇◇◇◇ If someone is under **house arrest**, they are officially ordered not to leave their home, because they are suspected of being involved in an illegal activity. *The main opposition leaders had been arrested or placed under house arrest... He was released from house arrest in China two years ago.* N-UNCOUNT: usu *under* N

houseboat /haʊsbout/ **houseboats.** A **houseboat** is a small boat on a river or canal which people live in. N-COUNT

housebound /haʊsbaʊnd/. Someone who is **housebound** is unable to go out of their house, usually because they are ill or cannot walk far. *If you are housebound, you can arrange for a home visit from a specialist adviser.* ADJ: usu v-link ADJ

houseboy /haʊsbɔɪ/ **houseboys.** A **houseboy** is a man or boy who cleans and does other jobs in someone else's house; an old-fashioned word. N-COUNT

housebreaker /haʊsbreɪkəʳ/ **housebreakers.** A **housebreaker** is someone who enters another person's house by force, for example by breaking the locks or windows, in order to steal their possessions. N-COUNT =burglar

housebreaking /haʊsbreɪkɪŋ/. **Housebreaking** is the crime of entering another person's house by force, for example by breaking the locks or windows, in order to steal their possessions. *...a huge increase in housebreaking and car theft.* N-UNCOUNT =burglary

housecoat /haʊskout/ **housecoats.** A **housecoat** is a long loose piece of clothing that some women wear over their underwear or nightclothes when they are at home during the day. N-COUNT =dressing gown

house guest, house guests. A **house guest** is a person who is staying at someone's house for a period of time. N-COUNT

household /haʊshould/ **households** ◆◆◆◇◇

1 A **household** is all the people in a family or group who live together in a house. *...growing up in a male-only household... Many poor households are experiencing real hardship.* N-COUNT

2 The **household** is your home and everything that is connected with looking after it. *My husband gave me cash to manage the household, but none of it was ever my own. ...household chores.* N-SING: oft N n

3 Someone or something that is a **household** name or word is very well known. *Today, fashion designers are household names... My agent told me, 'This'll make your name a household word.'* ADJ: ADJ n

4 In British English, the word **Household** is used in the names of groups of soldiers who have the job of protecting a king or queen and their family. *...the Household Cavalry Mounted Regiment.* ADJ: ADJ n

householder /haʊshouldəʳ/ **householders.** ◆◇◇◇◇ A **householder** is the legal owner or tenant of a house. *Millions of householders are eligible to claim the new council tax benefit.* N-COUNT

househusband /haʊshʌzbənd/ **househusbands;** also spelled **house husband**. A **househusband** is a married man who does not have a paid job, but instead looks after his home and children. N-COUNT

housekeeper /haʊskiːpəʳ/ **housekeepers.** ◆◇◇◇◇ A **housekeeper** is a person whose job is to cook, clean, and look after a house for its owner. N-COUNT

housekeeping /haʊskiːpɪŋ/ ◆◇◇◇◇

1 Housekeeping is the work and organization involved in running a home, including the shopping and cleaning. *I thought that cooking and housekeeping were unimportant, easy tasks.* N-UNCOUNT

2 The **housekeeping** is the money that you use to buy food, cleaning materials, and other things that you need in your home; used mainly in British English. *...the housekeeping money Jim gave her each week.* N-UNCOUNT: oft N n

house lights. In a theatre or cinema, when the **house lights** dim or go down, the lights where the audience sits are switched off. When the **house lights** come up, the lights are switched on. *The house lights dimmed, flickered and went out.* N-PLURAL: *the* N

housemaid /haʊsmeɪd/ **housemaids.** A **housemaid** is a female servant who does cleaning and other work in someone's house. N-COUNT

houseman /haʊsmən/ **housemen**

1 In British English, a **houseman** is a doctor who has a junior post in a hospital and who usually N-COUNT sleeps at the hospital. The American word is **intern.**

2 In American English, a **houseman** is a man who is a servant in a house. The British word is **manservant.** N-COUNT

housemaster /haʊsmɑːstəʳ, -mæs-/ **housemasters.** A **housemaster** is a male teacher who is in charge of one of the houses in a school; used mainly in British English. N-COUNT

housemate /haʊsmeɪt/ **housemates.** Your **housemate** is someone who shares a house with you. You do not use 'housemate' to refer to members of your family or your boyfriend or girlfriend. N-COUNT: usu poss N

House of Commons. **The House of Commons** is the more powerful of the two parts of parliament in Britain or Canada. Its members are elected by the adult population of the country. The building where the members meet is also called **the House of Commons**. *The House of Commons has overwhelmingly rejected demands to bring back the death penalty for murder... In 1950, the House of Commons was re-opened after it was bombed in 1941.* ◆◆◇◇◇ N-PROPER: the N

house of God, houses of God. A Christian church or chapel is sometimes referred to as a **house of God.** N-COUNT

House of Lords. **The House of Lords** is the less powerful of the two parts of parliament in Britain. Its members have the right of office because they belong to the nobility, they are bishops, or they hold very high positions in the legal system. The building where they meet is also called the **House of Lords**. *The legislation has majority support in the House of Commons but has twice been rejected by the House of Lords... I visited the House of Lords to hear my husband speak.* ◆◇◇◇◇ N-PROPER: the N

House of Representatives. **The House of Representatives** is the less powerful of the two parts of Congress in the United States, or the equivalent part of the system of government in some other countries. *The House of Representatives approved a new budget plan.* ◆◇◇◇◇ N-PROPER: the N

house owner, house owners; also spelled **house-owner**. A **house owner** is a person who owns a house. N-COUNT

house party, house parties. A **house party** is a party held at a big house in the country, usually at a weekend, where the guests stay for a few days. N-COUNT

house plant, house plants; also spelled **houseplant**. A **house plant** is a plant which is grown in a pot indoors. N-COUNT =pot plant

houseproud /haʊspraʊd/; also spelled **house-proud**. Someone who is **houseproud** spends a lot of time cleaning and decorating their house, because they want other people to admire it; used mainly in British English. ADJ-GRADED

houseroom /haʊsruːm/; also **house room**. If you say that you wouldn't **give** something **houseroom**, you are emphasizing that you do not want it or do not like it at all; used mainly in British English. PHRASE: V inflects, with brd-neg PRAGMATICS

Houses of Parliament. In Britain, **the Houses of Parliament** are the British parliament, which consists of two parts, the House of Commons and the House of Lords. The buildings where the British parliament does its work are also called **the Houses of Parliament**. *...issues aired in the Houses of Parliament... They marched past the Houses of Parliament on their way to a rally.* ◆◇◇◇◇ N-PROPER-COLL: the N

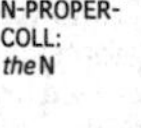

house-to-house; also spelled **house to house**. A **house-to-house** activity involves going to all the houses in an area one after another. *Security officers have carried out a number of house-to-house searches.* ► Also an adverb. *They're going house to house, rounding up the residents.* ◆◇◇◇◇ ADJ: ADJ n =door-to-door; ADV: ADV after v

housewares /haʊsweəʳz/. Some shops and manufacturers refer to objects on sale for use in your house as **housewares**, especially objects related to cooking and cleaning. N-PLURAL

housewarming /haʊswɔːʳmɪŋ/ **housewarmings.** A **housewarming** is a party that you give for friends when you have just moved to a new house. *I'm so sorry I missed the housewarming... I'd been to a housewarming party the night before.* N-COUNT: oft N n

housewife /haʊswaɪf/ **housewives.** A **housewife** is a married woman who does not have a paid job, but instead looks after her home and children. *Married at nineteen, she was a traditional housewife and mother of four children.* ◆◇◇◇◇ N-COUNT

housework /haʊswɜːʳk/. **Housework** is the work such as cleaning, washing, and ironing that you do in your home. ◆◇◇◇◇ N-UNCOUNT

housing /haʊzɪŋ/ **housings** ◆◆◆◆◇

1 You refer to the buildings in which people live as **housing** when you are talking about their standard, price, or availability. *...a shortage of affordable housing... Poor housing and family stress can affect both physical and mental health.* N-UNCOUNT =accommodation

2 **Housing** is the job of providing houses for people to live in. *...graduate courses in housing and public administration... If you are a council tenant call the housing department about it.* N-UNCOUNT

3 A **housing** is a case or covering which protects parts of a machine. *Both housings are waterproof to a depth of two metres.* N-COUNT

housing association, housing associations. In Britain, a **housing association** is an organization which owns houses and helps its members to rent or buy them more cheaply than on the open market. ◆◇◇◇◇ N-COUNT

housing development, housing developments. A **housing development** is the same as a **housing estate.** N-COUNT

housing estate, housing estates. In British English, a **housing estate** is a large number of houses or flats built close together at the same time. ◆◇◇◇◇ N-COUNT

housing project, housing projects. In American English, a **housing project** is a publicly funded and controlled housing estate for low-income families. ◆◇◇◇◇ N-COUNT

hove /hoʊv/. **Hove** is the past tense and past participle of **heave** in one of its meanings.

hovel /hɒvəl, AM hʌv-/ **hovels**

1 A **hovel** is a small hut, especially one which is dirty or needs a lot of repair. *They lived in a squalid hovel for the next five years.* N-COUNT =shack

2 You describe a house, room, or flat as a **hovel** to express your disapproval or dislike of it because it is dirty, untidy, and in poor condition. *I went for a living-in job, but the room I was given was a hovel.* N-COUNT PRAGMATICS =dump

hover /hɒvəʳ, AM hʌv-/ **hovers, hovering, hovered** ◆◆◇◇◇

1 To **hover** means to stay in the same position in the air without moving forwards or backwards. Many birds and insects can hover by moving their wings very quickly. *Beautiful butterflies hovered above the wild flowers... A police helicopter hovered overhead... Mist hovered in all the valleys.* VERB V

2 If you **hover**, you stay in one place and move slightly in a nervous way, for example because you cannot decide what to do. *Judith was hovering in the doorway... A waiter came and hovered... With no idea of what to do for my next move, my hand hovered over the board.* VERB V V prep/adv

3 If you **hover**, you are in an uncertain or unsettled situation or state of mind. *She hovered on the brink of death for three months as doctors battled to save her... Just as at the turn of the century, we hover between great hopes and great fears.* VERB V prep/adv Also V

4 If a something such as a price, value, or score **hovers** around a particular level, it stays at more or less that level and does not change much. *In September 1989 the exchange rate hovered around 140 yen to the dollar... His golf handicap hovered between 10 and 12.* VERB V prep/adv

hovercraft /hɒvəʳkrɑːft, AM hʌvəʳkræft/; **hovercraft** is both the singular and the plural. A **hover-** N-COUNT: also by N

craft is a vehicle that can travel across land and water. It floats above the land or water on a cushion of air. *Travelling at speeds of up to thirty five knots, these hovercraft can easily outpace most boats... The expedition made the journey to its source by hovercraft.*

how /haʊ/. The conjunction is pronounced /haʊ/. ◆◆◆◆◆

1 You use **how** to ask about the way in which something happens or is done. *How do I make payments into my account?... How do you manage to keep the place so tidy?... The law, your contracts, your public protect you, do they? How?... How are you going to plan for the future?* ► Also a conjunction. *I don't want to know how he died... Did you ever wonder how the top supermodels manage to look stunning?... I didn't know how to tell you.* QUEST; CONJ-SUBORD

2 You use **how** after certain adjectives and verbs to introduce a statement or fact, often something that you remember or expect other people to know about. *It's amazing how people collect so much stuff over the years... It's funny how I never seem to get a thing done on my day off... I remember how Grandma loved to cook, loved to fix special treats... It's important to become acutely aware of how your eating ties in with your stress level.* CONJ-SUBORD

3 You use **how** to ask questions about the quantity or degree of something. *How much money are we talking about?... How many full-time staff have we got?... How long will you be staying?... How old is your son now?... How fast were you driving?... How difficult is it to do business with the company?... 'How well do you know Mrs. O'Toole?' Ryan asked... No-one knows how many people have been killed since the war began... He was asked how serious the situation had become.* QUEST: QUEST *much/many*, QUEST adj/adv

4 You use **how** when you are asking someone whether something was successful or enjoyable. *How was your trip down to Orlando?... How did your date go?... Tell me about your clinical trials. How did they go?... Tell me how everything went off tonight... I wonder how Sam got on with him.* QUEST

5 You use **how** to ask about someone's health or to find out someone's news. *Hi! How are you doing?... How's Rosie?... How's the job?... She asked how he had been feeling... Susan introduced herself to him and asked him how he was.* QUEST

6 **'How do you do'** is a polite way of greeting someone when you meet them for the first time. *'How do you do, Mrs Bellingham,' Sam said.* CONVENTION PRAGMATICS

7 You use **how** when you want to say that it does not matter which way something is done; an informal use. *Two historical questions – you can answer them how you like... It's your life, so live it how you want!* CONJ-SUBORD =however

8 You use **how** to emphasize the degree to which something is true. *I didn't realize how heavy that shopping was going to be... Franklin told them all how happy he was to be in Britain again.* ADV: ADV adj/adv PRAGMATICS

9 You use **how** in exclamations to emphasize an adjective, adverb, or statement. *How strange that something so simple as a walk on the beach could suddenly mean so much... How anxiously she awaited my answer... How she must have talked last night!* ADV: ADV adj/adv/cl PRAGMATICS

10 You use **how** in expressions such as **'How can you...'** and **'How could you...'** to indicate that you disapprove of what someone has done or that you find it hard to believe. *How can you drink so much beer, Luke?... How could such a writer be taken seriously?... How could he be so indiscreet?* QUEST: QUEST *can/could* PRAGMATICS

11 You use **how** in expressions such as **'how about...'** or **'how would you like...'** when you are making an offer or a suggestion. *How about a cup of coffee?... You want Jeannie to make the appointment for you? How about the end of next week?... How would you like to have dinner one night?* QUEST PRAGMATICS =what about

12 If you ask someone **'How about you?'** you are asking them what they think or want. *Well, I enjoyed that. How about you two?... 'Something to drink?'—'No, thanks,' said Michael. He glanced at Wilfred. 'How about you?'* CONVENTION PRAGMATICS =what about you

13 If you say **'How about that?'** you are drawing attention to something that has been said or done that you think is surprising. *The twins made their appearance at three o'clock. How about that? Spot on time.* CONVENTION PRAGMATICS

14 You use **how about** to introduce a new subject which you think is relevant to the conversation you have been having. *Are your products and services competitive? How about marketing?* PHRASES PHR n PRAGMATICS =what about

15 You ask **'How come?'** or **'How so?'** when you are surprised by something and are asking why it happened or was said; an informal expression. *'They don't say a single word to each other.'—'How come?'... How come he hasn't been able to be as good this year?... 'She was weird.'—'How so?'* oft PHR cl PRAGMATICS

16 If you say **'How do you mean?'** to someone, you are asking them to explain or give more details of what they have just said; used in informal British English. *'The fuel gauge is broken.'—'Broken? How do you mean?'* PRAGMATICS =what do you mean

17 If you say **'How's that?'** to someone, you are asking whether something is acceptable or satisfactory. *Suppose we meet somewhere for a drink? I'll pay. How's that?* PRAGMATICS

howdy /haʊdi/. In American English, **'Howdy'** is an informal way of saying 'Hello'. CONVENTION

however /haʊevəʳ/ ◆◆◆◆◆

1 You use **however** when you are adding a comment which is surprising or which contrasts with what has just been said. *This was not an easy decision. It is, however, a decision that we feel is dictated by our duty... Some of the food crops failed. However, the cotton did quite well... Higher sales have not helped profits, however.* ADV: ADV with cl PRAGMATICS =nevertheless

2 You use **however** before an adjective or adverb to emphasize that the degree or extent of something cannot change a situation. *You should always strive to achieve more, however well you have done before... However hard she tried, nothing seemed to work... There is no sunset however beautiful, no joke however funny, no movie, no meal that I can enjoy only by myself... However much it hurt, he could do it.* ADV: ADV adj/adv, ADV *many/much* PRAGMATICS =no matter how

3 You use **however** when you want to say that it makes no difference how something is done. *However we adopt healthcare reform, it isn't going to save major amounts of money... Wear your hair however you want.* CONJ-SUBORD

4 You use **however** in expressions such as **or however long it takes** and **or however many there were** to indicate that the figure you have just mentioned may not be accurate but that the exact figure is not important. *The 20,000 or however many who come to watch would love to be out on the pitch... Wait 30 to 60 minutes or however long it takes.* ADV: ADV *many/much*, ADV adv

5 You can also use **however** to ask in an emphatic way how something has happened which you are very surprised about. Some speakers of English think that this form is incorrect and prefer to use 'how ever'. *However did you find this place in such weather?* QUEST PRAGMATICS =how

howitzer /haʊɪtsəʳ/ **howitzers.** A **howitzer** is a large gun with a short barrel, which fires shells high up into the air so that they will drop down onto the target. N-COUNT

howl /haʊl/ **howls, howling, howled** ◆◆◇◇◇

1 If an animal such as a wolf or a dog **howls**, it utters a long, loud, crying sound. *Somewhere in the streets beyond a dog suddenly howled, baying at the moon.* ► Also a noun. *The dog let out a savage howl and, wheeling round, flew at him.* VERB V; N-COUNT

2 If a person **howls**, they make a long, loud cry expressing pain, anger, or unhappiness. *He howled like a wounded animal as blood spurted from the gash... The baby was howling for her 3am feed.* ► Also a noun. *With a frantic howl she threw herself at the mesh.* VERB V, V *for* n; N-COUNT

3 When the wind **howls**, it blows hard and makes a loud noise. *The wind howled all night, but I slept a little... It sank in a howling gale.* VERB V, V-ing

4 If you **howl** something, you say it in a very loud VERB voice; an informal use. *'Get away, get away, get away' he howled... The crowd howled its approval.* V with quote V n

5 If you **howl** with laughter, you laugh very loudly. *Joe, Pink, and Booker howled with delight... The crowd howled, delirious.* ▶ Also a noun. *His stories caused howls of laughter.* VERB V with n V N-COUNT

howl down. If you **are howled down**, people prevent you from speaking or giving your opinion, often by shouting angrily; used mainly in British English. *The president was howled down by hundreds of opponents.* PHRASAL VERB usu passive =shout down be V-ed P

howler /haʊləʳ/ **howlers.** In British English, a **howler** is a stupid mistake; an informal word. *I felt as if I had made an outrageous howler.* N-COUNT =blunder

hp. **hp** is an abbreviation for 'horsepower'.

HP /eɪtʃ piː/. In British English, **HP** is an abbreviation for 'hire purchase'. *I have never bought anything on HP.* N-UNCOUNT: oft *on* N

HQ /eɪtʃ kjuː/ **HQs. HQ** is an abbreviation for 'headquarters'. *The regimental HQ is a tiny office manned by two retired officers.* ◆◇◇◇◇ N-VAR

hr, hrs. hr is a written abbreviations for 'hour'. *Let this cook on low for another 1 hr 15 mins.* ◆◇◇◇◇

HRH /eɪtʃ ɑːʳ eɪtʃ/. **HRH** is an abbreviation for 'His Royal Highness' or 'Her Royal Highness'; used as part of the title of a prince or princess. N-TITLE

HRT /eɪtʃ ɑːʳ tiː/. **HRT** is an abbreviation for 'hormone replacement therapy'. The treatment is given to women and involves taking doses of the hormone oestrogen, usually in order to control the symptoms of menopause. ◆◇◇◇◇ N-UNCOUNT

hub /hʌb/ **hubs** ◆◇◇◇◇

1 You can describe a place as a **hub** of an activity when it is a very important centre for that activity. *The island's social hub is the Cafe Sport... As a hub of finance and communications, Paris is now almost equal to London.* N-COUNT: usu with supp, oft N *of* n =centre

2 The **hub** of a wheel is the part at the centre. N-COUNT: oft N *of* n

hubbub /hʌbʌb/ **hubbubs**

1 A **hubbub** is a noise made by a lot of people all talking or shouting at the same time. *There was a hubbub of excited conversation from over a thousand people.* N-VAR: oft N *of* n

2 You can describe a situation where there is great confusion or excitement as a **hubbub**. *In all the hubbub over the election, one might be excused for missing yesterday's announcement.* N-SING: also no det

hubby /hʌbi/ **hubbies.** You can refer to a woman's husband as her **hubby**; an old-fashioned word. *Women in the North complain that their hubbies find it difficult to say 'I love you.'* N-COUNT: usu poss N

hubcap /hʌbkæp/ **hubcaps;** also **hub cap**. A **hubcap** is a metal or plastic disc that covers and protects the hub of a wheel on cars and lorries and other vehicles. N-COUNT

hubris /hjuːbrɪs/. If you accuse someone of **hubris**, you are accusing them of arrogant pride; a formal word. *...a tale of how an honourable man pursuing honourable goals was afflicted with hubris and led his nation towards catastrophe.* N-UNCOUNT =arrogance

huckster /hʌkstəʳ/ **hucksters.** In American English, if you refer to someone as a **huckster**, you are criticizing them for trying to sell useless or worthless things in a dishonest or aggressive way. *A huckster offered to sell Carnegie the formula for guaranteed success for $20,000.* N-COUNT PRAGMATICS

huddle /hʌdᵊl/ **huddles, huddling, huddled** ◆◇◇◇◇

1 If you **huddle** somewhere, you sit, stand, or lie there holding your arms and legs close to your body, usually because you are cold or frightened. *She huddled inside the porch as she rang the bell, but it was small and offered little protection... Myrtle sat huddled on the side of the bed, weeping.* VERB =hunch up V prep/adv V-ed

2 If people **huddle** together or **huddle** round something, they stand, sit, or lie close to each other, usually because they all feel cold or frightened. *Tired and lost, we huddled together. ...strangers huddling together for warmth... Hundreds of people huddled around a single transistor radio listening to the announcement... The survivors spent the night huddled around bonfires.* VERB =cluster V adv/prep V-ed

3 If people **huddle** in a group, they gather together to discuss something quietly or secretly. *Off to one side, Sticht, Macomber, Jordan, and Kreps huddled to discuss something... The president has been huddling with his most senior aides... Mr Perot was huddled with advisers at his house in Dallas.* V-RECIP pl-n V V *with* n V-ed

4 A **huddle** is a small group of people or things that are standing very close together or lying on top of each other, usually in a disorganized way. *We lay there: a huddle of bodies, gasping for air... Les kept seeing Eric and Tam in a huddle and he knew they were talking about him. ...the huddle of dark houses on the other side of the reservoir.* N-COUNT: oft N *of* n

hue /hjuː/ **hues** ◆◇◇◇◇

1 A **hue** is a colour; a literary use. *The same hue will look different in different light. ...a selection of tops in natural hues and fibres.* N-COUNT =shade

2 If people raise a **hue and cry** about something, they protest angrily about it. *Just as the show ended, he heard a huge hue and cry outside.* PHRASE

huff /hʌf/ **huffs, huffing, huffed** ◆◇◇◇◇

1 If you **huff**, you indicate that you are annoyed or offended about something, usually by the way that you say something. *'This', huffed Mr Buthelezi, 'was discrimination.'* VERB =puff V with quote

2 If someone is **in a huff**, they are behaving in a bad-tempered way because they are annoyed and offended; an informal expression. *After the row in a pub he drove off in a huff.* PHRASE: PHR after v, v-link PHR

3 If someone **huffs and puffs**, they express their annoyance or dissatisfaction with a decision or situation loudly but do not do anything to change it. *The British government huffed and puffed at the commission's decision.* PHRASE: Vs inflect

huffy /hʌfi/. Someone who is **huffy** is obviously annoyed or offended about something; an informal word. *I, in my turn, became embarrassed and huffy and told her to take the money back.* ♦ **huffily** /hʌfɪli/ *'I appreciate your concern for my feelings,' Bess said huffily, 'but I'm a big girl now'.* ADJ-GRADED ADV-GRADED: ADV with v

hug /hʌg/ **hugs, hugging, hugged** ◆◆◇◇◇

1 When you **hug** someone, you put your arms around them and hold them tightly, for example because you like them or are pleased to see them. You can also say that two people **hug** each other or that they **hug**. *She had hugged him exuberantly and invited him to dinner the next day... They hugged each other like a couple of lost children... We hugged and kissed.* ▶ Also a noun. *Syvil leapt out of the back seat, and gave him a hug.* V-RECIP =embrace V n (non-recip) pl-n V N-COUNT

2 If you **hug** something, you hold it close to your body with your arms tightly round it. *Shaerl trudged toward them, hugging a large box... She hugged her legs tight to her chest... She stood hugging her quilted jacket round her.* VERB V n V n adv/prep

3 Something that **hugs** the ground or a stretch of land or water stays very close to it; used mainly in written English. *The road hugs the coast for hundreds of miles... Our pilot reduced height until we hugged the ground.* VERB V n

4 See also **bear hug**.

huge /hjuːdʒ/ **huger, hugest** ◆◆◆◆◇

1 Something or someone that is **huge** is extremely large in size. *...a tiny little woman with huge black glasses... Several painters were working on a huge piece of canvas which would serve as the scenery... Our driver strolled up, huge and swarthy.* ADJ-GRADED =gigantic ≠minute

2 Something that is **huge** is extremely large in amount or degree. *I have a huge number of ties because I never throw them away... He is furious they are making huge profits out of the misery of young addicts.* ♦ **hugely** *In summer this hotel is a hugely popular venue for wedding receptions. ...a hugely successful businessman... She seemed to be enjoying herself hugely... I think she was hugely embarrassed by the whole scene.* ADJ-GRADED =enormous ADV-GRADED: ADV adj, ADV with v =enormously

3 Something that is **huge** exists or happens on a very large scale, and involves a lot of different people or things. *Another team is looking at the huge problem of debts between companies... The result was human suffering on a huge scale.* ADJ-GRADED =vast ≠minute

-hugging /-hʌgɪŋ/. **-hugging** combines with nouns to form adjectives which describe an item COMB in ADJ: usu ADJ n of clothing that fits very tightly and clearly reveals the shape of your body. *...a figure-hugging dress. ...hip-hugging flares.*

huh /hʌ, hɜː/. **Huh** is used in writing to represent a noise that people make at the end of a question if they want someone to agree with them, or if they want to indicate that they did not hear what someone has said and want them to repeat it. **Huh** is also used to show that someone is either surprised or unimpressed by something. *Can we just get on with it, huh?... Clever, huh?... Huh? What's going on? You want to tell me what I did?... Huh. What are you so excited about.* ◆◆◇◇◇

hulk /hʌlk/ **hulks** ◆◇◇◇◇
1 The **hulk** of something is the large, ruined remains of it. *...the ruined hulk of the old church tower... I could make out the gutted hulk of the tanker.* N-COUNT: oft N *of* n =wreck
2 You use **hulk** to describe anything which is large and seems threatening to you. *I followed his big hulk into the vestry.* N-COUNT: usu with supp

hulking /hʌlkɪŋ/. You use **hulking** to describe a person or object that is extremely large, heavy, or slow-moving, especially when they seem unnatural or threatening in some way. *When I woke up there was a hulking figure staring down at me... He came upon the hulking redbrick hospital.* ADJ: ADJ n

hull /hʌl/ **hulls, hulling, hulled** ◆◆◇◇◇
1 The **hull** of a boat or tank is the main body of it. *The hull had suffered extensive damage to the starboard side.* ♦ **-hulled** *...a steel-hulled narrowboat.* N-COUNT; COMB in ADJ
2 The **hull** of a soft fruit such as a strawberry is the stalk and ring of leaves at the base. N-COUNT
3 If you **hull** soft fruit such as strawberries, you remove the hulls from them. *Wash and hull the strawberries.* VERB; V n

hullabaloo /hʌləbəluː/. A **hullabaloo** is a lot of noise or fuss made by people who are angry or excited about something; an informal word. *I was scared by the hullabaloo over my arrival.* N-SING =rumpus

hullo /hʌlou/. See **hello**.

hum /hʌm/ **hums, humming, hummed** ◆◆◇◇◇
1 If something **hums**, it makes a low continuous noise. *The birds sang, the bees hummed... Within five hours, the equipment will be humming away again... There was a low humming sound in the sky.* ► Also a noun. *...the hum of traffic... There was a general hum of conversation around them.* VERB; V; V-ing; N-SING: oft *the* N *of* n
2 When you **hum** a tune, you sing it with your lips closed. *She was humming a merry little tune... He hummed to himself as he opened the trunk.* ♦ **humming** *The guard stopped his humming and turned his head sharply.* VERB; V n; V; N-UNCOUNT
3 If you say that a place **hums**, you mean that it is full of activity. *The place is really beginning to hum... On Saturday morning, the town hums with activity and life.* VERB; V; V *with* n
4 **Hum** is sometimes used to represent the sound people make when they are not sure what to say. *Hum, I am sorry but I thought you were French.* CONVENTION
5 • **ho hum**: see **ho**. • **hum and haw**: see **haw**.

human /hjuːmən/ **humans** ◆◆◆◆◆
1 **Human** means relating to or concerning people. *...the human body. ...human history.* ADJ: ADJ n
2 You can refer to people as **humans**, especially when you are comparing them with animals or machines. *Its rate of growth was fast - much more like that of an ape than that of a human.* N-COUNT
3 If you call feelings, errors, or people **human**, you mean that they are, or have, weaknesses which are typical of people rather than machines. *...an ever growing risk of human error... Damon, I'm only human. I can't know all.* ADJ-GRADED

human being, human beings. A **human being** is a man, woman, or child. ◆◆◇◇◇ N-COUNT

humane /hjuːmeɪn/ ◆◇◇◇◇
1 **Humane** people act in a kind, sympathetic, and compassionate way towards other people and animals, and try to do them as little harm as possible. *He was a thoughtful and humane man... It is the responsibility of a humane society to treat animals as well as it can... Amnesty calls on all parties to abide by international law on the humane treatment of prisoners.* ♦ **humanely** *Our horse had to be humanely destroyed after breaking his right foreleg.* ADJ-GRADED; ADV-GRADED: ADV with v
2 A **humane** activity is one that is thought to have a civilizing and improving effect on people. *We're helping with rescue, rehabilitation and humane education programmes to encourage local people to protect the seals. ...the humane values of socialism.* ADJ

humanise /hjuːmənaɪz/. See **humanize**.

humanism /hjuːmənɪzəm/. **Humanism** is the belief that people can achieve happiness and fulfilment without the need for religion. *The main theme of our discussion was humanism and politics.* ♦ **humanist, humanists** *He is a practical humanist, who believes in the dignity of mankind.* ◆◇◇◇◇ N-UNCOUNT; N-COUNT

humanistic /hjuːmənɪstɪk/. A **humanistic** idea, condition, or practice relates to humanism. *Religious values can often differ greatly from humanistic morals.* ADJ: usu ADJ n

humanitarian /hjuːmænɪteəriən/ **humanitarians.** If a person or society has **humanitarian** ideas or attitudes, or behaves in a **humanitarian** way, they try to avoid making people suffer or they help people who are suffering. *Air bombardment raised criticism on the humanitarian grounds that innocent civilians might suffer. ...humanitarian aid.* ► A **humanitarian** is someone who is humanitarian. *I like to think of myself as a humanitarian.* ◆◆◇◇◇ ADJ: usu ADJ n; N-COUNT

humanitarianism /hjuːmænɪteəriənɪzəm/. **Humanitarianism** is the concern that humanitarians have for the welfare of the human race. N-UNCOUNT

humanity /hjuːmænɪti/ **humanities** ◆◆◇◇◇
1 All the people in the world can be referred to as **humanity**. *They face charges of committing crimes against humanity. ...a young lawyer full of illusions and love of humanity.* N-UNCOUNT
2 A person's **humanity** is their state of being a human being, rather than an animal or an object; a formal use. *He was under discussion and it made him feel deprived of his humanity.* N-UNCOUNT: with poss
3 **Humanity** is the quality of being kind, thoughtful, and sympathetic towards others. *Her speech showed great maturity and humanity.* N-UNCOUNT
4 The **humanities** are the subjects such as history, philosophy, and literature which are concerned with human ideas and behaviour. *The number of students majoring in the humanities has declined by about half.* N-PLURAL: oft *the* N =arts

humanize /hjuːmənaɪz/ **humanizes, humanizing, humanized;** also spelled **humanise** in British English. If you **humanize** a situation or condition, you improve it by changing it in a way which makes it more suitable and pleasant for people. *Jo Robinson began by humanizing the waiting time at the health centre with tea-making and toys for children.* VERB; V n

humankind /hjuːmənkaɪnd/. **Humankind** is the same as **mankind**. N-UNCOUNT

humanly /hjuːmənli/
1 **Humanly** means relating to human beings. *A mother is not allowed to be humanly flawed; she has to be perfect.* ADV-GRADED: ADV adj/-ed, ADV after v
2 If something is **humanly possible**, it is possible for people to do it. *She has gained a reputation for creating books as perfect as is humanly possible... They had done everything humanly possible for their son.* PHRASE: v-link PHR, pron-indef PHR, *as* PHR

human nature. **Human nature** is the natural qualities and ways of behaviour that most people have. *It seems to be human nature to worry.* ◆◇◇◇◇ N-UNCOUNT

human race. **The human race** is the same as **mankind**. *Can the human race carry on expanding and growing the same way that it is now?* ◆◇◇◇◇ N-SING: *the* N

human resources. The department of **human resources** is the department within a company that is responsible for dealing with the recruiting, training, and welfare of the staff of that company or organization. ◆◇◇◇◇ N-UNCOUNT =personnel

human rights. **Human rights** are basic rights which many societies believe that all people ◆◆◆◇◇ N-PLURAL should have. *In the treaty both sides pledge to respect human rights.*

humble /hʌmbəl/ **humbler, humblest; humbles, humbling, humbled** ◆◆◇◇◇

1 A **humble** person is not proud and does not believe that they are better than other people. *He gave a great performance, but he was very humble... Andy was a humble, courteous and gentle man. ...a humble apology.* ADJ-GRADED =unassuming ≠proud ♦ **humbly** *'I'm a lucky man, undeservedly lucky,' he said humbly.* ADV-GRADED: ADV with v

2 People with low social status are sometimes described as **humble**. *Spyros Latsis started his career as a humble fisherman in the Aegean... He came from a fairly humble, poor background.* ADJ-GRADED: usu ADJ n =lowly

3 A **humble** place or thing is ordinary and not special in any way. *There are restaurants, both humble and expensive, that specialize in them... Varndell made his own reflector for these shots from a strip of humble kitchen foil.* ADJ-GRADED

4 People use the word **humble** in a phrase such as **in my humble opinion** as a polite way of emphasizing what they think, even though they do not feel humble about it. *It is, in my humble opinion, perhaps the best steak restaurant in Great Britain.* ADJ-GRADED PRAGMATICS =modest ♦ **humbly** *So may I humbly suggest we all do something next time.* ADV-GRADED: ADV before v

5 If you **eat humble pie**, you speak or behave in a way which tells people that you admit you were wrong about something. *Anson was forced to eat humble pie and publicly apologise to her.* PHRASE: V inflects

6 If you **humble** someone who is more important or powerful than you, you defeat them easily and humiliate them by doing so. *Honda won fame in the 1980s as the little car company that humbled the industry giants... Third-placed Barnet were humbled 3-0 at Crewe.* VERB V n

7 If something or someone **humbles** you, they make you realize that you are not as important, capable, or valuable as you thought you were. *Ted's words humbled me... I am sure millions of viewers were humbled by this story.* VERB V n ♦ **humbled** *I came away very humbled and recognizing that I, for one, am not well-informed.* ADJ-GRADED ♦ **humbling** *Giving up an addiction is a humbling experience.* ADJ-GRADED

humbug /hʌmbʌg/ **humbugs**

1 If you describe someone's language or behaviour as **humbug**, you mean that it is dishonest and intended to deceive people. *There was all the usual humbug and obligatory compliments from ministers... Britain's laws on homosexuality are hypocritical humbug.* N-UNCOUNT

2 You can also refer to a person as a **humbug** when you think they are being dishonest or insincere. *What a revolting humbug the man was!* N-COUNT

3 A **humbug** is a hard, striped sweet that tastes of peppermint. N-COUNT

humdinger /hʌmdɪŋər/ **humdingers.** If you describe someone or something as a **humdinger**, you mean that they are marvellous, impressive, or especially enjoyable; an informal word. *It should be a humdinger of a match... His latest novel is a humdinger.* N-COUNT: usu sing, oft a N of n PRAGMATICS

humdrum /hʌmdrʌm/. If you describe someone or something as **humdrum**, you mean that they are ordinary, dull, or boring. *...her lawyer husband, trapped in a humdrum but well-paid job... The new government seemed rather humdrum.* ADJ-GRADED PRAGMATICS =tedious

humid /hjuːmɪd/. You use **humid** to describe an atmosphere or climate that is very damp, and usually very hot. *Visitors can expect hot and humid conditions... The day is overcast and humid.* ◆◇◇◇◇ ADJ-GRADED =sticky, heavy ≠dry

humidifier /hjuːmɪdɪfaɪər/ **humidifiers.** A **humidifier** is a machine for increasing the amount of moisture in the air. *Use a humidifier in heated rooms to prevent dry air irritating your throat.* N-COUNT

humidity /hjuːmɪdɪti/ ◆◇◇◇◇

1 You say there is **humidity** when the air feels very heavy and damp. *The heat and humidity were insufferable.* N-UNCOUNT

2 **Humidity** is the amount of water in the air. *The humidity is relatively low.* N-UNCOUNT

humiliate /hjuːmɪlieɪt/ **humiliates, humiliating, humiliated.** To **humiliate** someone means to say or do something which makes them feel ashamed or stupid. *She had been beaten and humiliated by her husband... His teacher continually humiliates him in maths lessons.* ◆◇◇◇◇ VERB be V-ed V n ♦ **humiliated** *I have never felt so humiliated in my life.* ADJ-GRADED

humiliating /hjuːmɪlieɪtɪŋ/. If something is **humiliating**, it embarrasses you and makes you feel ashamed and stupid. *The Conservatives have suffered a humiliating defeat... It was so humiliating, a terrible blow to my self-esteem.* ◆◇◇◇◇ ADJ-GRADED =crushing ♦ **humiliatingly** *Thousands of men struggled humiliatingly for jobs... He was caught cheating during the Seoul Olympics and humiliatingly stripped of his title.* ADV: usu ADV after v, ADV adj/-ed, also ADV with cl

humiliation /hjuːmɪlieɪʃən/ **humiliations** ◆◆◇◇◇

1 **Humiliation** is the embarrassment and shame you feel when someone makes you appear stupid, or when you make a mistake in public. *She faced the humiliation of discussing her husband's affair.* N-UNCOUNT

2 A **humiliation** is an occasion or a situation in which you feel embarrassed and humiliated. *The result is a humiliation for the prime minister.* N-COUNT

humility /hjuːmɪlɪti/. Someone who has **humility** is not proud and does not believe they are better than other people. *...a deep sense of humility... For a long time he still thought like a millionaire but he has humility now.* ◆◇◇◇◇ N-UNCOUNT =modesty ≠pride

hummingbird /hʌmɪŋbɜːrd/ **hummingbirds.** A **hummingbird** is a small brightly coloured bird that is found in America, especially Central and South America. It has a long thin beak and powerful narrow wings that often make a humming sound as they vibrate. N-COUNT

hummock /hʌmək/ **hummocks.** A **hummock** is mound of earth, like a very small hill; a literary word. N-COUNT =hillock

hummus /hʊməs/. See **houmous.**

humor /hjuːmər/. See **humour.**

humorist /hjuːmərɪst/ **humorists.** A **humorist** is a writer who specializes in writing amusing things. *...a political humorist.* N-COUNT

humorous /hjuːmərəs/. If someone or something is **humorous**, they are amusing, especially in a clever or witty way. *He was quite humorous, and I liked that about him. ...a humorous magazine.* ◆◇◇◇◇ ADJ-GRADED ♦ **humorously** *He looked at me humorously as he wrestled with the door... Occasionally he made a humorously sardonic remark.* ADV-GRADED: ADV with v, ADV adj

humour /hjuːmər/ **humours, humouring, humoured;** spelled **humor** in American English. ◆◆◆◇◇

1 You can refer to the amusing things that people say as their **humour**. *Her humour and determination were a source of inspiration to others.* ● See also **sense of humour.** N-UNCOUNT: supp N

2 **Humour** is a quality in something that makes you laugh, for example in a situation, in someone's words or actions, or in a book or film. *She felt sorry for the man but couldn't ignore the humour of the situation.* N-UNCOUNT

3 If you are in a good **humour**, you feel cheerful and happy, and are pleasant to people. If you are in a bad **humour**, you feel bad-tempered and unhappy, and are unpleasant to people. *Christina was still not clear why he had been in such ill humour... Next day, Louis XIV was in the best of humours... Did the old boy drink? Could that have been the source of his good humour?* N-VAR: supp N =temper

4 If you do something with good **humour**, you do it cheerfully and pleasantly. *Hugo bore his illness with great courage and good humour.* N-UNCOUNT: adj N

5 If you **humour** someone who is behaving strangely, you try to please them or pretend to agree with them, so that they will not become upset. *She disliked Dido but was prepared to tolerate her for a weekend in order to humour her husband.* VERB V n

humourless /hjuːmərləs/; spelled **humorless** in American English. If you accuse someone of being **humourless**, you mean that they are very serious about everything and do not find things ADJ-GRADED PRAGMATICS =solemn amusing. *He was a straight-faced, humourless character.*

hump /hʌmp/ **humps, humping, humped** ◆◇◇◇◇

1 A **hump** is a small hill or raised area. *The path goes over a large hump by a tree before running near a road.* N-COUNT =mound

2 A camel's **hump** is the large lump on its back. *Camels rebuild fat stores in their hump.* N-COUNT

3 A **hump** is a large lump on a person's back, usually caused by illness or old age. N-COUNT: oft poss N

4 If you **hump** something heavy, you carry it from one place to another with great difficulty; used mainly in informal British English. *Charlie humped his rucksack up the stairs to his flat.* VERB =lug V n prep/adv Also V n

5 If someone **humps** someone else, they have sex with them; a rude and offensive use which you should avoid using. VERB: V n

6 If someone **gets the hump**, they get very annoyed about something; used mainly in informal British English. *Fans just get the hump when they lose.* PHRASE: V inflects

7 If you say that you are **over the hump**, you mean that you no longer have a problem or difficulty that was stopping you being successful or happy. *We're basically over the hump. We've got an economy that's likely to grow next year even more than it did in 1992.* PHRASE: usu v-link PHR, PHR after v

humpback /hʌmpbæk/ **humpbacks.** A **humpback** or a **humpback whale** is a large whale with a hump-shaped back and long flippers. N-COUNT

humped /hʌmpt/

1 If someone is **humped**, their back is bent so that their shoulders are further forward than usual and their head hangs down. *I was humped like an old lady.* ADJ

2 A **humped** bridge rises and falls very sharply so that it has a shape similar to a semi-circle; used mainly in British English. *...the humped iron bridge spanning the railway.* ADJ: ADJ n =humpback

humungous /hjuːmʌŋgəs/; also spelled **humungus**. If you describe something or someone as **humungous**, you are emphasizing that they are very large or important. *...a choppy guitar riff coming from humungous speakers... Barbra Streisand is such a humungous star.* ADJ PRAGMATICS

humus /huːməs/. **Humus** is the part of soil which consists of plant and animal remains that have begun to decompose. N-UNCOUNT

hunch /hʌntʃ/ **hunches, hunching, hunched** ◆◇◇◇◇

1 If you have a **hunch** about something, you are sure that it is correct or true, even though you do not have any proof; an informal use. *I had a hunch that Susan and I would work well together... Then Mr. Kamenar, acting on a hunch, ran a computer check at the Federal Election Commission.* N-COUNT

2 If you **hunch** forward, you raise your shoulders, put your head down, and lean forwards, often because you are cold, ill, or unhappy. *He got out his map of Yorkshire and hunched over it to read the small print.* VERB V adv/prep

3 If you **hunch** your shoulders, you raise them and lean forwards slightly. *Wes hunched his shoulders and leaned forward on the edge of the counter.* VERB V n

hunchback /hʌntʃbæk/ **hunchbacks.** A **hunchback** is an offensive word for a person who has a large lump on their back because their spine is deformed. N-COUNT

hunched /hʌntʃt/. If you are **hunched**, or **hunched up**, you are leaning forwards with your shoulders raised and your head down, often because you are cold, ill, or unhappy. *A solitary hunched figure emerged from Number Ten... He got a stiff neck and a sore back from sitting hunched up for so long.* ◆◇◇◇◇ ADJ

hundred /hʌndrəd/ **hundreds.** The plural form is **hundred** after a number, or after a word or expression referring to a number, such as 'several' or 'a few'. ◆◆◆◆◆

1 A **hundred** or one **hundred** is the number 100. *According to one official more than a hundred people have been arrested.* NUM: usu a/num NUM

2 If you refer to **hundreds of** things or people, you are emphasizing that there are very many of them. *Hundreds of tree species face extinction... Today you can buy hundreds of flavours of ice-cream.* ► Also a pronoun. *Hundreds have been killed in the fighting and thousands made homeless.* QUANT: QUANT of pl-n PRAGMATICS PRON

3 You can use **a hundred per cent** or **one hundred per cent** to emphasize that you agree completely with something or that it is completely right or wrong; an informal expression. *Are you a hundred per cent sure it's your neighbour?... I agree with you one hundred per cent.* PHRASE: PHR adj, PHR after v PRAGMATICS =absolutely

hundredth /hʌndrədθ/ **hundredths** ◆◇◇◇◇

1 The **hundredth** item in a series is the one that you count as number one hundred. *The bank celebrates its hundredth anniversary in December.* ORD

2 A **hundredth** of something is one of a hundred equal parts of it. *Mitchell beat Lewis by three-hundredths of a second.* FRACTION

hundredweight /hʌndrədweɪt/ **hundredweights.** When it has a number in front of it, the plural form is **hundredweight**. A **hundredweight** is a unit of weight that is equal to 112 pounds in Britain and to 100 pounds in the United States. *...a hundredweight of coal.* N-COUNT: oft N of n

hung /hʌŋ/

1 **Hung** is the past tense and past participle of most of the senses of **hang**.

2 A **hung** parliament, council, or jury consists of different groups of people who have different opinions, but none forms a majority, and so often no clear decisions can be made. *In the event of a hung Parliament he would still fight for everything in the manifesto... George's first trial ended in a hung jury.* ADJ: usu ADJ n

Hungarian /hʌŋgeəriən/ **Hungarians** ◆◆◆◆◇

1 **Hungarian** means belonging or relating Hungary, or to its people, language, or culture. *...the Hungarian government. ...a Hungarian bank clerk.* ADJ: usu ADJ n

2 A **Hungarian** is a Hungarian citizen, or a person of Hungarian origin. N-COUNT: usu pl

3 **Hungarian** is the language spoken by people who live in Hungary. N-UNCOUNT

hunger /hʌŋgəʳ/ **hungers, hungering, hungered** ◆◆◇◇◇

1 **Hunger** is the feeling of weakness or discomfort that you get when you need something to eat. *Hunger is the body's signal that levels of blood sugar are too low... Seized by morning hunger pangs, Robert made a beeline for the chocolate vending machine.* N-UNCOUNT

2 **Hunger** is a severe lack of food which causes suffering or death. *Three hundred people in this town are dying of hunger every day. ...a desire to alleviate hunger and suffering in the Third World.* N-UNCOUNT =starvation

3 If you have a **hunger** for something, you want or need it very much; a rather formal or literary use. *Geffen has a hunger for success that seems bottomless. ...his hunger to equal Vardon's record of six wins.* N-SING: also no det, with supp, oft N for n =craving

4 If you say that someone **hungers** for something or **hungers** after it, you are emphasizing that they want it very much; a formal use. *But Jules was not eager for classroom learning, he hungered for adventure.* VERB PRAGMATICS =hanker V for/after n Also V to-inf

hunger strike, hunger strikes. If someone goes on **hunger strike** or goes on a **hunger strike**, they refuse to eat as a way of protesting about something. *The protesters have been on hunger strike for 17 days... He has begun a hunger strike in protest over political violence in Karachi.* ◆◇◇◇◇ N-VAR

hungover /hʌŋoʊvəʳ/; also spelled **hung-over**. Someone who is **hungover** is unwell because they drank too much alcohol on the previous day. *He was still hungover on the 25-minute bus drive to work the following morning.* ADJ-GRADED: usu v-link ADJ

hungry /hʌŋgri/ **hungrier, hungriest** ◆◆◇◇◇

1 When you are **hungry**, you want some food because you have not eaten for some time and have an uncomfortable or painful feeling in your stomach. *My friend was hungry, so we drove to a shopping mall to get some food... She is reduced to stealing to feed her hungry family.* ADJ-GRADED ≠full ♦ **hungrily** /hʌŋgrɪli/ *James ate hungrily.* ADV-GRADED: ADV with v

2 If people **go hungry**, they suffer from hunger, either for a long period because they are poor or for a short period because they miss a meal. *Leonidas' family had been poor, he went hungry for years.* PHRASE: V inflects

3 If you say that someone is **hungry** for something, you are emphasizing that they want it very much; a literary use. *Susan was certainly hungry for a life different from the one she had made for herself... I left Oxford in 1961 hungry to be a critic.* ► Also a combining form. *...power-hungry politicians. ...land-hungry peasants.* ♦ **hungrily** *He looked at her hungrily. What eyes! What skin!* ADJ-GRADED: usu v-link ADJ *for* n, v-link ADJ to-inf =eager COMB in ADJ ADV-GRADED: ADV with v

hung up. If you say that someone is **hung up** about a particular person or thing, you are criticizing them for thinking or worrying too much about that person or thing; an informal word. *It was a time when people weren't so hung-up about health... Are you really that hung up on her?* ◆◇◇◇◇ ADJ-GRADED: v-link ADJ, usu ADJ *about/on* n PRAGMATICS

hunk /hʌŋk/ **hunks** ◆◇◇◇◇

1 A **hunk** of something is a large piece of it. *...a thick hunk of bread. ...hunks of wood.* N-COUNT: usu N *of* n

2 If you refer to a man as a **hunk**, you mean that he is big, strong, and sexually attractive; an informal use. *...a blond, blue-eyed hunk.* N-COUNT

hunker /hʌŋkəʳ/ **hunkers, hunkering, hunkered**

hunker down PHRASAL VERB

1 In American English, if you **hunker down**, you bend your knees so that you are in a squatting position. *Betty hunkered down on the floor... He ended up hunkering down beside her.* V P *on* n V P *beside* n

2 In American English, if you say that someone **hunkers down**, you mean that they are trying to avoid doing things that will make them noticed. *Their strategy for the moment is to hunker down and let the furor die.* =lie low VP

hunt /hʌnt/ **hunts, hunting, hunted** ◆◆◆◇◇

1 If you **hunt** for something or someone, you try to find them by searching carefully or thoroughly. *A forensic team was hunting for clues... Some new arrivals lose hope even before they start hunting for a job... Chryssa hunted for Patra, and found her busy at a corner of the site.* ► Also a noun. *The couple had helped in the hunt for the toddlers.* VERB =search V *for* n Also V N-COUNT =search

2 If you **hunt** a criminal or an enemy, you search for them in order to catch or harm them. *Detectives have been hunting him for seven months... Her irate husband was hunting him with a gun.* ► Also a noun. *Despite a nationwide hunt for the kidnap gang, not a trace of them was found.* VERB V n Also V *for* n N-COUNT: usu sing, oft N *for* n

3 When people or animals **hunt**, they chase and kill wild animals for food or as a sport. *As a child I learned to hunt and fish... A leopard hunts alone, and an injured leopard cannot hunt... He got up at four and set out on foot to hunt black grouse.* ► Also a noun. *He set off for a nineteen-day moose hunt in Nova Scotia.* VERB V V n Also V *for* n N-COUNT: oft n N

4 In Britain, when people **hunt**, they chase a fox on horseback and try to kill it as a sport. Dogs called hounds are used to find the fox. *She liked to hunt as often as she could.* ► Also a noun. *The hunt was held on land owned by the Duke of Marlborough.* VERB V Also V n N-COUNT

5 In Britain, a **hunt** is a group of people who meet regularly to hunt foxes. N-COUNT

6 See also **hunting, witch-hunt**.

hunt down. If you **hunt down** a criminal or an enemy, you find them after searching for them. *Last December they hunted down and killed one of the gangsters... Mr Major vowed that the terrorists would be hunted down... It took her four months to hunt him down.* PHRASAL VERB V P n (not pron) V n P

hunt out. If you **hunt out** something that is hidden or difficult to find, you search for it and eventually find it. *I'll try and hunt out the information you need... American consumers are accustomed to hunting out bargains and buying on price.* PHRASAL VERB V P n (not pron) Also V n P

hunter /hʌntəʳ/ **hunters** ◆◆◇◇◇

1 A **hunter** is a person who hunts wild animals for food or as a sport. *The hunters stalked their prey. ...a deer hunter.* N-COUNT

2 People who are searching for things of a particular kind are often referred to as **hunters**. *...job-hunters. ...treasure hunters.* ● See also **bargain hunter, headhunter**. N-COUNT: n N =seeker

3 A **hunter** is a type of fast strong horse that is used in Britain by people who hunt foxes. N-COUNT

hunting /hʌntɪŋ/ ◆◆◇◇◇

1 **Hunting** is the chasing and killing of wild animals by people or other animals, for food or as a sport. *Hunting is one of Italy's most popular sports... Deer hunting was banned in Scotland in 1959. ...a hunting accident.* N-UNCOUNT

2 **Hunting** is the activity of searching for a particular thing. *Job hunting should be approached as a job in itself.* ► Also a combining form. *Lee has divided his time between flat-hunting and travelling.* N-UNCOUNT: n N COMB in N-UNCOUNT

hunting ground, hunting grounds

1 If you say that a place is a good **hunting ground** for something, you mean that people who have a particular interest are likely to find something that they want there. *Other people's weddings are the perfect hunting ground for ideas... Auctions are good hunting grounds, but set yourself a price limit.* N-COUNT: oft N *for* n

2 A **hunting ground** is an area where people or animals chase and kill wild animals for food or as a sport. *Good hunting grounds are becoming harder to find.* N-COUNT

huntsman /hʌntsmən/ **huntsmen.** A **huntsman** is a person who hunts wild animals, especially one who hunts foxes on horseback using dogs. ◆◇◇◇◇ N-COUNT

hurdle /hɜːʳdᵊl/ **hurdles, hurdling, hurdled** ◆◆◇◇◇

1 A **hurdle** is a problem or difficulty that you must overcome in order to achieve something. *The first hurdle for many women returning to work is finding nursery places... The weather will be the biggest hurdle so I have to be ready.* N-COUNT: usu supp N =obstacle

2 **Hurdles** is a race in which people run and jump over a number of hurdles. You can use **hurdles** to refer to one or more races. *Davis won the 400m. hurdles in a new Olympic time of 49.3 sec.* N-COUNT-COLL

3 If you **hurdle**, you jump over something while you are running. *He crossed the lawn and hurdled the short fence... She learnt to hurdle by leaping over bales of hay on her family's farm.* VERB V n V Also V prep

4 If you say that someone or something has fallen **at the first hurdle**, you mean they have failed at the first difficulty that had to be overcome in order to be successful. *A deal between the White House and Congressional leaders has fallen at the first hurdle to a grassroots revolt in Congress.* PHRASE: PHR after v

hurdler /hɜːʳdləʳ/ **hurdlers.** A **hurdler** is an athlete whose special event is the hurdles. ◆◇◇◇◇ N-COUNT

hurl /hɜːʳl/ **hurls, hurling, hurled** ◆◆◇◇◇

1 If you **hurl** something, you throw it violently and with a lot of force. *Groups of angry youths hurled stones at police... One prisoner set fire to rags and hurled them into the courtyard... Simon caught the grenade and hurled it back... Gangs rioted last night, breaking storefront windows and hurling rocks and bottles.* VERB V n prep V n with adv V n

2 If you **hurl** abuse or insults at someone, you shout insults at them aggressively. *How would you handle being locked in the back of a cab while the driver hurled abuse at you?* VERB V n *at* n Also V n

hurly-burly /hɜːʳli bɜːʳli/. If you talk about the **hurly-burly** of a situation, you are emphasizing how noisy or busy it is. *No one expects him to get involved in the hurly-burly of campaigning.* N-SING: usu *the* N, oft N *of* n PRAGMATICS

hurray /hʊreɪ/; also spelled **hurrah**. See **hooray**.

hurricane /hʌrɪkən, AM hɜːrɪkeɪn/ **hurricanes.** A **hurricane** is an extremely violent wind or storm. ◆◆◇◇◇ N-COUNT

hurried /hʌrid, AM hɜːr-/ ◆◇◇◇◇

1 A **hurried** action is done quickly, because you do not have much time to do it in. *...a hurried breakfast.* ♦ **hurriedly** *...students hurriedly taking notes.* ADJ-GRADED: usu ADJ n ADV-GRADED: ADV with v

2 A **hurried** action is done suddenly, in reaction to something that has just happened. *Downing Street denied there had been a hurried overnight redrafting of the text.* ♦ **hurriedly** *The moment she saw it, she blushed and hurriedly left the room.* ADJ-GRADED: usu ADJ n ADV-GRADED: ADV with v

3 Someone who is **hurried** does things more quickly than they should because they do not have ADJ-GRADED: usu v-link ADJ =rushed much time to do them. *Parisians on the street often looked worried, hurried and unfriendly.*

hurry /hʌri, AM hɜːri/ **hurries, hurrying, hurried** ◆◆◇◇◇

1 If you **hurry** somewhere, you go there as quickly as you can. *Claire hurried along the road... When she finished work she had to hurry home and look after her son... Bob hurried to join him, and they rode home together.* VERB V prep/adv V

2 If you **hurry** to do something, you start doing it as soon as you can, or try to do it quickly. *Mrs Hardie hurried to make up for her tactlessness by asking her guest about his holiday.... There was no longer any reason to hurry.* VERB V to-inf V

3 If you are in a **hurry** to do something, you need or want to do something quickly. If you do something in a **hurry**, you do it quickly or suddenly. *Kate was in a hurry to grow up, eager for knowledge and experience... Eric left the barge in a hurry.* N-SING: usu *in a* N, oft N to-inf

4 To **hurry** something means the same as to **hurry up** something. *...Mr de Klerk's attempt to hurry the process of independence.* VERB V n

5 If you **hurry** someone to a place or into a situation, you try to make them go to that place or get into that situation quickly. *Rachel hurried him to his bed... They say they are not going to be hurried into any decision... I don't want to hurry you.* VERB =rush V n prep/adv V n

6 If you say to someone **'There's no hurry'** or **'I'm in no hurry'** you are telling them that there is no need for them to do something immediately. *I'll need to talk with you, but there's no hurry... 'I am in no particular hurry,' he insisted.* PHRASES PRAGMATICS

7 If you are **in no hurry** to do something, you are very unwilling to do it. *I love it at St Mirren so I'm in no hurry to go anywhere... 'It's a thrill I'm in no hurry for,' he smiles.* PHR after v, PHR to-inf, PHR *for* n PRAGMATICS

hurry up. If you tell someone to **hurry up**, you are telling them do something more quickly than they were doing. *Franklin told Howe to hurry up and take his bath; otherwise, they'd miss their train... Hurry up with that coffee, will you.* PHRASAL VERB V P V P *with* n Also V *it* P

hurry up or **hurry along.** If you **hurry** something **up** or **hurry** it **along**, you make it happen faster or sooner than it would otherwise have done. *...if you're not a traditionalist and you want to hurry up the process... Petter saw no reason to hurry the divorce along.* PHRASAL VERB =hasten V P n (not pron) V n P

hurt /hɜːrt/ **hurts, hurting, hurt** ◆◆◆◆◇

1 If you **hurt** yourself or **hurt** a part of your body, you feel pain because you have injured yourself. *Yasin had seriously hurt himself while trying to escape from the police... He had hurt his back in an accident.* VERB V pron-refl V n

2 If a part of your body **hurts**, you feel pain there. *His collar bone only hurt when he lifted his arm.* VERB V

3 If you are **hurt**, you have been injured. *His comrades asked him if he was hurt... They were dazed but did not seem to be badly hurt.* ADJ-GRADED: usu v-link ADJ

4 If you **hurt** someone, you cause them to feel pain. *I didn't mean to hurt her, only to keep her still... You're hurting my arm... Ouch. That hurt.* VERB V n V

5 If someone **hurts** you, they upset you by saying or doing something rude or inconsiderate. *He is afraid of hurting Bessy's feelings... She's afraid she's going to be hurt and that she'll never fall in love again... What hurts most is the betrayal, the waste.* VERB =upset V n V

6 If you are **hurt**, you are emotionally upset because of something that someone has said or done. *Yes, I was hurt, jealous... He gave me a slightly hurt look.* ADJ-GRADED =upset

7 If you say that you **are hurting**, you mean that you are experiencing emotional pain. *I am lonely and I am hurting.* VB: only cont V

8 You can say that something **hurts** someone or something when it has a bad effect on them or prevents them from succeeding. *The combination of hot weather and decreased water supplies is hurting many industries... They may fear hurting their husbands' careers.* VERB =damage V n

9 A feeling of **hurt** is a feeling that you have when you think that you have been treated badly or judged unfairly. *...feelings of hurt and anger, fear and despair... I was full of jealousy and hurt... There would be a hurt in her heart for a while, but in the end she would get over it.* N-VAR =pain

10 If you say something such as **'It won't hurt** to do something' or **'It never hurts** to do something', you are recommending something which you think is worth doing or is helpful or useful; an informal expression. *It never hurts to ask... It wouldn't hurt you to be a bit more serious.* PHRASE: V inflects, usu PHR to-inf PRAGMATICS

hurtful /hɜːrtfʊl/. If you say that someone's comments or actions are **hurtful**, you mean that they are unkind and upsetting. *Her comments can only be very hurtful to Mrs Green's family.* ADJ-GRADED PRAGMATICS =upsetting

hurtle /hɜːrtᵊl/ **hurtles, hurtling, hurtled.** If someone or something **hurtles** somewhere, they move there very quickly, often in a rough or violent way. *A pretty young girl came hurtling down the stairs.* ◆◇◇◇◇ VERB =plunge V prep

husband /hʌzbənd/ **husbands, husbanding, husbanded** ◆◆◆◆◇

1 A woman's **husband** is the man she is married to. *Eva married her husband Jack in 1957... Are they husband and wife?* N-COUNT: oft poss N

2 If you **husband** something valuable, you use it carefully and do not waste it; a literary word. *Husbanding precious resources was part of rural life.* VERB V n

husbandry /hʌzbəndri/. **Husbandry** is farming, especially when it is done carefully and well. *...soil-conserving methods of good husbandry.* N-UNCOUNT

hush /hʌʃ/ **hushes, hushing, hushed** ◆◇◇◇◇

1 You say **'Hush!'** to someone when you are asking or telling them to be quiet. *Hush, my love, it's all right.* CONVENTION PRAGMATICS

2 If you **hush** someone or they **hush**, they stop speaking or making a noise. *She tried to hush her noisy father... I had to box Max's ears to get him to hush.* V-ERG V n V

3 You say there is a **hush** in a place when everything is quiet and peaceful, or suddenly becomes quiet. *A hush fell over the crowd and I knew something terrible had happened.* N-SING: also no det =silence

hush up PHRASAL VERB

1 If someone **hushes** something **up**, they prevent other people from knowing about it. *The scandal has been discussed by the politburo, although the authorities have tried to hush it up... The Ministry desperately tried to hush up the whole affair.* V n P V P n (not pron)

2 If people in authority **hush** someone **up**, they try to stop that person revealing information which they want to keep secret. *The Conservative Government was only too quick to hush him up.* V n P

hushed /hʌʃt/ ◆◇◇◇◇

1 A **hushed** place is peaceful and much quieter and calmer than usual. *The house seemed muted, hushed as if it had been deserted... He liked a hushed and dignified atmosphere.* ADJ-GRADED =quiet ≠noisy

2 A **hushed** voice or **hushed** conversation is very quiet. *At first we spoke in hushed voices and crept about in order not to alarm them... We switched off the engine and discussed the situation in hushed whispers.* ADJ-GRADED: usu ADJ n =quiet

hush-hush. Something that is **hush-hush** is secret and not to be discussed with other people; an informal expression. *Apparently there's a very hush-hush project under way up north... They were desperate to keep the marriage hush-hush.* ADJ-GRADED =secret

hush money. If a person is paid **hush money**, someone gives them money not to reveal information they have which could be damaging or embarrassing; an informal expression. N-UNCOUNT

husk /hʌsk/ **husks.** A **husk** is the outer covering of a grain or a seed. N-COUNT

husky /hʌski/ **huskies** ◆◇◇◇◇

1 If someone's voice is **husky**, it sounds rough or hoarse, often in an attractive way. *His voice was husky with grief... Dietrich's deep, husky voice and smouldering eyes were her trademark.* ♦ **huskily** *'Ready?' I asked huskily.* ADJ-GRADED ADV-GRADED: ADV after v

2 If you describe a man as **husky**, you think that he is tall, strong, and attractive; an informal use. *...a very husky young man, built like a football player.* ADJ-GRADED: usu ADJ n

3 A **husky** is a strong, furry dog, which is used to pull sledges across snow. N-COUNT

hussy /hʌsi, AM hʌzi/ **hussies.** If someone refers to a girl or woman as a **hussy**, they are criticizing her for behaving in a shocking, immoral, or immodest way; an old-fashioned word, which is now often used humorously. N-COUNT PRAGMATICS

hustings /hʌstɪŋz/. In British English, the political campaigns and speeches before an election are sometimes referred to as the **hustings**. *With only days to go before elections in Pakistan, candidates are battling it out at the hustings.* N-PLURAL: usu *the* N

hustle /hʌsᵊl/ **hustles, hustling, hustled** ◆◇◇◇◇

1 If you **hustle** someone, you try to hurry them into doing something, for example by pulling or pushing them along. *The guards hustled Harry out of the car... There was no opportunity to ask anything more as the guards hustled us away.* VERB V n prep/adv

2 If you **hustle**, you go somewhere or do something hurriedly. *You'll have to hustle if you're to get home for supper... He hustled straight up the aircraft steps without looking round or waving goodbye... They had finished the exam and the teacher was hustling to get the papers gathered up.* VERB V V prep V to-inf

3 If someone **hustles**, they try to earn money or gain an advantage from a situation, often by using dishonest or illegal means; used mainly in American English. *We're expected to hustle and fight for what we want... I hustled some tickets from a magazine and off we went.* VERB V V n *from* n

4 **Hustle** is busy, noisy activity. *Shell Cottage, provides the perfect retreat from the hustle and bustle of London... She waited until they were beyond the hustle of the Washington Saturday night traffic.* N-UNCOUNT =bustle

hustler /hʌsləʳ/ **hustlers**

1 If you refer to someone as a **hustler**, you mean that they try to earn money or gain an advantage from situations they are in by using dishonest or illegal methods; an informal word. *...an insurance hustler.* N-COUNT

2 A **hustler** is a male prostitute. N-COUNT

hut /hʌt/ **huts** ◆◆◇◇◇

1 A **hut** is a small house with only one or two rooms, especially one which is made of wood, mud, grass, or stones. N-COUNT

2 A **hut** is a small shed or shelter in someone's garden, or a temporary building used by builders or repair workers. N-COUNT =shed

hutch /hʌtʃ/ **hutches.** A **hutch** is a cage, often made of wood, that rabbits or other small pet animals are kept in. N-COUNT

hyacinth /haɪəsɪnθ/ **hyacinths.** A **hyacinth** is a plant with a lot of small, sweet-smelling flowers growing closely around a single stem. It grows from a bulb and the flowers are usually blue, pink, or white. N-COUNT

hybrid /haɪbrɪd/ **hybrids** ◆◆◇◇◇

1 A **hybrid** is an animal or plant that has been bred from two different species of animal or plant; a technical use. *All these brightly coloured hybrids are so lovely in the garden. ...a hybrid between watermint and spearmint.* ► Also an adjective. *...the hybrid maize seed.* N-COUNT ADJ: ADJ n

2 You can use **hybrid** to refer to anything that is a mixture of other things, especially two other things. *...a hybrid of solid and liquid fuel.* ► Also an adjective. *...a hybrid system.* N-COUNT ADJ: ADJ n

hybridize /haɪbrɪdaɪz/ **hybridizes, hybridizing, hybridized;** also spelled **hybridise** in British English. If one species of plant or animal **hybridizes** or **is hybridized** with another, the species reproduce together to make a hybrid. You can also say that a species of plant or animal **hybridize** or **are hybridized**. *All sorts of colours will result as these flowers hybridise freely... Wild boar readily hybridises with the domestic pig... Hybridising the two species will reduce the red to orange... Some people will take the seeds and hybridize the resulting plants with others of their own.* V-RECIP-ERG pl-n V V *with* n V pl-n V n *with* n

hydrant /haɪdrənt/ **hydrants.** See **fire hydrant**.

hydrate /haɪdreɪt/ **hydrates, hydrating, hydrated**

1 A **hydrate** is a chemical compound that contains water. *...aluminium hydrate.* N-MASS: usu n/adj N

2 If a substance **hydrates** your skin, it makes it softer and moister, and prevents it from drying out. *After sun products will cool and hydrate your skin.* VERB =moisten V n

hydraulic /haɪdrɒlɪk, AM -drɔːl-/. Something that is **hydraulic** involves or is operated by a fluid that is under pressure, such as water or oil. ♦ **hydraulically** *...hydraulically operated pistons for raising and lowering the blade.* ◆◇◇◇◇ ADJ: ADJ n ADV: ADV with v

hydraulics /haɪdrɒlɪks, AM -drɔːl-/. **Hydraulics** is the study and use of systems that work using hydraulic pressure. N-UNCOUNT

hydrocarbon /haɪdroʊkɑːʳbᵊn/ **hydrocarbons.** A **hydrocarbon** is a chemical compound that is a mixture of hydrogen and carbon. ◆◇◇◇◇ N-COUNT

hydrochloric acid /haɪdrəklɔrɪk æsɪd/. **Hydrochloric acid** is a colourless, strong acid containing hydrogen and chlorine. N-UNCOUNT

hydroelectric /haɪdroʊɪlektrɪk/; also spelled **hydro-electric**. **Hydroelectric** means relating to or involving electricity made from the energy of running water. ADJ: ADJ n

hydro-electricity /haɪdroʊ ɪlektrɪsɪti/. **Hydro-electricity** is electricity made from the energy of running water. N-UNCOUNT

hydrofoil /haɪdrəfɔɪl/ **hydrofoils.** A **hydrofoil** is a boat which can travel above the surface of the water on a pair of winglike fins. You can also to refer to the fins themselves as **hydrofoils**. N-COUNT

hydrogen /haɪdrədʒᵊn/. **Hydrogen** is a colourless gas that is the lightest and commonest element in the universe. ◆◆◇◇◇ N-UNCOUNT

hydrogen bomb, hydrogen bombs. A **hydrogen bomb** is a nuclear bomb in which energy is released from hydrogen atoms. N-COUNT

hydrogen peroxide. **Hydrogen peroxide** is a chemical that is often used as a bleach for hair and as an antiseptic. N-UNCOUNT

hydroplane /haɪdrəpleɪn/ **hydroplanes.** A **hydroplane** is a speedboat which rises out of the water on winglike fins when it is travelling fast. N-COUNT

hydrotherapy /haɪdroʊθerəpi/. **Hydrotherapy** is a method of treating people with some diseases or injuries by making them swim or do exercises in water. N-UNCOUNT

hyena /haɪiːnə/ **hyenas.** A **hyena** is an animal that looks rather like a dog and makes a sound which is similar to a human laugh. Hyenas live in Africa and Asia. N-COUNT

hygiene /haɪdʒiːn/. **Hygiene** is the practice of keeping yourself and your surroundings clean, especially in order to prevent illness or the spread of diseases. *Be extra careful about personal hygiene.* ◆◇◇◇◇ N-UNCOUNT =cleanliness

hygienic /haɪdʒiːnɪk, AM haɪdʒienɪk/. Something that is **hygienic** is clean and unlikely to cause illness. *...a white, clinical-looking kitchen that was easy to keep clean and hygienic.* ADJ-GRADED

hygienist /haɪdʒiːnɪst/ **hygienists.** A **hygienist** or a **dental hygienist** is a person who is trained to clean people's teeth and to give them advice on how to look after their teeth and gums. N-COUNT

hymen /haɪmen/ **hymens.** A **hymen** is a piece of skin that often covers part of a girl's or woman's vagina and breaks, usually when she has sex for the first time; a technical term in medicine. N-COUNT

hymn /hɪm/ **hymns** ◆◇◇◇◇

1 A **hymn** is a religious song that Christians sing in church. *I like singing hymns. ...a hymn book.* N-COUNT

2 If you describe a film, book, or speech as a **hymn to** something, you mean that it praises or celebrates that thing. *...a hymn to freedom and rebellion... Edward Kennedy won the most emotional applause for his hymn to the lost ideal of equality.* N-COUNT: N *to* n

hymnal /hɪmnᵊl/ **hymnals.** A **hymnal** is a book of hymns; a formal word. N-COUNT

hype /haɪp/ **hypes, hyping, hyped** ◆◆◇◇◇

1 **Hype** is the intensive use of publicity and adver- N-UNCOUNT:

tising in order to make people aware of something such as a product or a politician's ideas; used showing disapproval. *We are certainly seeing a lot of hype by some companies... My products aren't based on advertising hype, they sell by word of mouth.* — usu supp N; PRAGMATICS

2 To **hype** a product means to advertise it using intensive methods of publicity; used showing disapproval. *We had to hype the film to attract the financiers... These gurus are being promoted by publishers and hyped in the business press.* ▶ **Hype up** means the same as **hype**. *The media seems obsessed with hyping up individuals or groups... He felt the film was hyped up too much.* — VERB; PRAGMATICS; V n; PHRASAL VERB; V P n (not pron); Also V n P

hype up. To **hype** someone **up** means to deliberately make them very excited about something. *Everyone at school used to hype each other up about men all the time.* ● See also **hype** 2. — PHRASAL VERB; V n P; Also V P n (not pron)

hyped up; also spelled **hyped-up**. If someone is **hyped up** about something, they are very excited or anxious about it; an informal expression. *We were both so hyped up about buying the house, we could not wait to get in there.* — ADJ-GRADED

hyper /haɪpəʳ/. If someone is **hyper**, they are very excited and energetic; an informal word. *I was incredibly hyper. I couldn't sleep.* — ◆◇◇◇◇ ADJ-GRADED: usu v-link ADJ =hyperactive

hyper- /haɪpəʳ-/. **Hyper-** is used to form adjectives that describe someone as having a lot or too much of a particular quality. *I hated my father. He was hyper-critical and mean... He is one of those lean, hyper-fit people.* — PREFIX

hyperactive /haɪpəræktɪv/. Someone who is **hyperactive** is unable to relax, and is always in a state of great agitation or activity. *His research was used in planning treatments for hyperactive children.* ♦ **hyperactivity** /haɪpəræktɪvɪti/ *...an extreme case of hyperactivity.* — ◆◇◇◇◇ ADJ; N-UNCOUNT

hyperbole /haɪpɜːʳbəli/. **Hyperbole** is a style of speech and writing where people exaggerate what they are saying in order to make something sound more impressive than it really is: a formal word. *...the hyperbole that portrays him as one of the greatest visionaries in the world.* — N-UNCOUNT =exaggeration

hyperbolic /haɪpəʳbɒlɪk/. If you describe language as **hyperbolic**, you mean that it is full of exaggeration in order to make something sound more impressive than it really is: a formal word. — ADJ: usu ADJ n =exaggerated

hyperinflation /haɪpərɪnfleɪʃən/; also spelled **hyper inflation**. **Hyperinflation** is very severe inflation. — N-UNCOUNT

hypermarket /haɪpəʳmɑːʳkɪt/ **hypermarkets.** A **hypermarket** is a very large supermarket; used mainly in British English. — N-COUNT

hypersensitive /haɪpəʳsensɪtɪv/

1 If you say that someone is **hypersensitive**, you mean that they get annoyed or offended very easily. *Student teachers were hypersensitive to any criticism of their performance.* — ADJ: oft ADJ *to/about* n =touchy

2 Someone who is **hypersensitive** is extremely sensitive to certain drugs or chemicals; a medical use. — ADJ: oft ADJ *to* n

hypertension /haɪpəʳtenʃən/. **Hypertension** is a medical condition in which a person has very high blood pressure. *He suffered from hypertension and accompanying heart problems.* — ◆◇◇◇◇ N-UNCOUNT

hypertext /haɪpəʳtekst/. In computing, **hypertext** is a way of structuring information in a database, so that users can find particular information without having to read from beginning or read to end. — N-UNCOUNT

hyperventilate /haɪpəʳventɪleɪt/ **hyperventilates, hyperventilating, hyperventilated.** If someone **hyperventilates**, they begin to breathe very fast in an uncontrollable way, usually because they are very frightened, tired, or excited. *I hyperventilate when they come near me with the needle.* ♦ **hyperventilation** /haɪpəʳventɪleɪʃən/ *Several notable researchers are studying the effects of hyperventilation.* — VERB; V; N-UNCOUNT

hyphen /haɪfən/ **hyphens.** A **hyphen** is the punctuation sign (-) used to join words together to make a compound. For example, the word 'left-handed' has a hyphen in it. People also use hyphens to show that a word has been broken in order to fit it onto a line. — N-COUNT

hyphenated /haɪfəneɪtɪd/. A word that is **hyphenated** is written with a hyphen between two or more of its parts. *...hyphenated names such as Wong-Shong or Li-Wong.* — ADJ

hypnosis /hɪpnoʊsɪs/ — ◆◇◇◇◇

1 **Hypnosis** is a state of unconsciousness in which a person seems to be asleep but can still see, hear, or respond to things said to them. *Bevin is now an adult and has re-lived her birth experience under hypnosis.* — N-UNCOUNT

2 **Hypnosis** is the art or practice of putting people into this state of unconsciousness. — N-UNCOUNT =hypnotism

hypnotherapist /hɪpnoʊθerəpɪst/ **hypnotherapists.** A **hypnotherapist** is a person who treats people by using hypnotherapy. — N-COUNT

hypnotherapy /hɪpnoʊθerəpi/. **Hypnotherapy** is the practice of hypnotizing people in order to help them solve problems, helping them for example to give up smoking or learn how to cope with irrational fears. — N-UNCOUNT

hypnotic /hɪpnɒtɪk/ — ◆◇◇◇◇

1 If someone is in a **hypnotic** state, they have been hypnotized. *The hypnotic state actually lies somewhere between being awake and being asleep.* — ADJ: usu ADJ n

2 Something that is **hypnotic** makes you feel as if you have been hypnotized. *His songs are often both hypnotic and reassuringly pleasant... Everyone is familiar with the TV screen's hypnotic power.* — ADJ-GRADED

hypnotise /hɪpnətaɪz/. See **hypnotize**.

hypnotism /hɪpnətɪzəm/. **Hypnotism** is the practice of hypnotizing people. *Dulcy also saw a psychiatrist who used hypnotism to help her deal with her fear.* ♦ **hypnotist, hypnotists** — N-UNCOUNT =hypnosis; N-COUNT

hypnotize /hɪpnətaɪz/ **hypnotizes, hypnotizing, hypnotized;** also spelled **hypnotise** in British English.

1 If someone **hypnotizes** you, they put you into a state of unconsciousness in which you seem to be asleep but can see or hear certain things or respond to things said to you. *A hypnotherapist will hypnotize you and will stop you from smoking... Surprisingly, the ability to hypnotize yourself can be learnt in a single session.* — VERB; V n; V pron-refl

2 If you **are hypnotized** by someone or something, you are so fascinated by them that you cannot think of anything else. *He's hypnotized by that black hair and that white face... Davey sat as if hypnotized by the sound of Nick's voice.* — VB: usu passive =mesmerized; *be* V-ed; V-ed

hypochondria /haɪpəkɒndriə/. If someone suffers from **hypochondria**, they continually worry about their health and imagine that they are ill, although there is really nothing wrong with them. — N-UNCOUNT

hypochondriac /haɪpəkɒndriæk/ **hypochondriacs.** A **hypochondriac** is a person who continually worries about their health, although there is nothing physically wrong with them. — N-COUNT

hypocrisy /hɪpɒkrɪsi/ **hypocrisies.** If you accuse someone of **hypocrisy**, you mean that they pretend to have qualities, beliefs, or feelings that they do not really have; used showing disapproval. *He accused newspapers of hypocrisy in their treatment of the story... You'll have little patience with the hypocrisy and double standards you encounter. ...the hypocrisies of middle-class provincial life.* — ◆◇◇◇◇ N-VAR; PRAGMATICS; ≠sincerity

hypocrite /hɪpəkrɪt/ **hypocrites.** If you accuse someone of being a **hypocrite**, you mean that they pretend to have qualities, beliefs, or feelings that they do not really have; used showing disapproval. *The magazine wrongly suggested he was a liar and a hypocrite.* — N-COUNT; PRAGMATICS

hypocritical /hɪpəkrɪtɪkəl/. If you accuse someone of being **hypocritical**, you mean that they pretend to have qualities, beliefs, or feelings that they do not really have; used showing disapproval. *It would be hypocritical to say I travel at 70mph simply because that is the law... If some-* —  ◆◇◇◇◇ ADJ-GRADED; PRAGMATICS; ≠sincere

one is being hypocritical then it is fair to expose that.

hypodermic /haɪpədɜːʳmɪk/ **hypodermics.** A **hypodermic** needle or syringe is a medical instrument with a hollow needle, which is used to give injections. ► Also a noun. *He lifted the hypodermic, depressed the plunger and inserted the needle in the vial.* ADJ: ADJ n; N-COUNT

hypotenuse /haɪpɒtənjuːz, AM -nuːs/ **hypotenuses.** The **hypotenuse** of a right-angled triangle is the side opposite its right angle; a technical term in geometry. N-COUNT: usu *the* N

hypothermia /haɪpoʊθɜːʳmiə/. If someone has **hypothermia**, their body temperature has become dangerously low as a result of being in severe cold for a long time; a medical term. N-UNCOUNT =exposure

hypothesis /haɪpɒθɪsɪs/ **hypotheses.** A **hypothesis** is an idea which is suggested as a possible explanation for a particular situation or condition, but which has not yet been proved to be correct; a formal word. *Work will now begin to test the hypothesis in rats... Different hypotheses have been put forward to explain why these foods are more likely to cause problems.* ◆◇◇◇◇ N-VAR =theory

hypothesize /haɪpɒθɪsaɪz/ **hypothesizes, hypothesizing, hypothesized;** also spelled **hypothesise** in British English. If you **hypothesize** that something will happen, you say that you think that thing will happen because of various facts you have considered; a formal word. *To explain this, they hypothesise that galaxies must contain a great deal of missing matter which cannot be detected... I have long hypothesized a connection between these factors.* VERB; V that; V n; Also V

hypothetical /haɪpəθetɪkəl/ **hypotheticals.** If something is **hypothetical**, it is based on possible ideas or situations rather than actual ones. *Let's look at a hypothetical situation in which Carol, a recovering cocaine addict, gets invited to a party. ...a purely hypothetical question.* ► A **hypothetical** is something that is hypothetical. *Well, at present we won't speculate on hypotheticals.* ♦ **hypothetically** /haɪpəθetɪkli/ *He was invariably willing to discuss the possibilities hypothetically... It bases its figures on what it might, hypothetically, be earning on past investment.* ◆◇◇◇◇ ADJ =theoretical; N-COUNT; ADV: usu ADV with v, ADV with cl, also ADV adj =theoretically

hysterectomy /hɪstərektəmi/ **hysterectomies.** A **hysterectomy** is a surgical operation to remove a woman's womb. ◆◇◇◇◇ N-COUNT

hysteria /hɪstɪəriə, AM -ster-/ ◆◇◇◇◇

1 **Hysteria** among a group of people is a state of uncontrolled excitement, anger, or panic. *No one could help getting carried away by the hysteria... Several were hurt in the panic. 'It was mass hysteria,' said Rev John Borders.* N-UNCOUNT

2 A person who is suffering from **hysteria** is in a state of violent and disturbed emotion as a result of shock; a medical use. *By now, she was screaming, completely overcome with hysteria.* N-UNCOUNT =hysterics

hysterical /hɪsterɪkəl/ ◆◇◇◇◇

1 Someone who is **hysterical** is in a state of uncontrolled excitement, anger, or panic. *Police and bodyguards had to form a human shield around him as the almost hysterical crowds struggled to approach him... He made headlines and received hysterical hate mail.* ♦ **hysterically** /hɪsterɪkli/ *I don't think we can go round screaming hysterically: 'Ban these dogs. Muzzle all dogs.'* ADJ-GRADED; ADV-GRADED: ADV with v, ADV adj/adv

2 Someone who is **hysterical** is in a state of violent and disturbed emotion that is usually a result of shock. *I suffered bouts of really hysterical depression accompanied by a strong desire to run away.* ♦ **hysterically** *I was curled up on the floor in a corner sobbing hysterically.* ADJ-GRADED; ADV-GRADED

3 **Hysterical** laughter is loud and uncontrolled; an informal use. *I had to rush to the loo to avoid an attack of hysterical giggles.* ♦ **hysterically** *She says she hasn't laughed as hysterically since she was 13.* ADJ: usu ADJ n; ADV: ADV with v

4 If you describe something or someone as **hysterical**, you think that they are very funny and they make you laugh a lot; an informal use. *Paul Mazursky was Master of Ceremonies, and he was pretty hysterical.* ♦ **hysterically** *It wasn't supposed to be a comedy but I found it hysterically funny.* ADJ-GRADED; ADV-GRADED: ADV adj

hysterics /hɪsterɪks/

1 If someone is in **hysterics** or is having **hysterics**, they are in a state of uncontrolled excitement, anger, or panic; an informal use. *I'm sick of your having hysterics, okay?... It is quite easy to get engulfed in the hysterics and you have to be careful.* N-PLURAL: oft *in* N

2 If someone is in **hysterics** or is having **hysterics**, they are in a state of violent and disturbed emotion that is usually a result of shock. *It was such a shock I had hysterics... I went into hysterics.* N-PLURAL: oft *in* N =hysteria

3 You can say that someone is in **hysterics** or is having **hysterics** when they are laughing loudly in an uncontrolled way; an informal use. *He'd often have us all in absolute hysterics.* N-PLURAL: oft *in* N

Ii

I, i /aɪ/ **I's, i's.** I is the ninth letter of the English alphabet. N-VAR

I /aɪ/. A speaker or writer uses **I** to refer to himself or herself. **I** is a first person singular pronoun. **I** is used as the subject of a verb. *Jim and I are getting married... She liked me, I think.* ◆◆◆◆◆ PRON-SING: PRON v

-ian. See **-an**.

ibid. **Ibid** is used in books and journals to indicate that a quotation is taken from the same source as the one previously mentioned. ◆◆◇◇◇ CONVENTION

-ibility, /-ɪbɪlɪti/ **-ibilities.** **-ibility** replaces '-ible' at the end of adjectives to form nouns referring to the state or quality described by the adjective. *...its commitment to increase the accessibility of the arts... Check your eligibility for State benefits... But the possibilities that emerged were not used to the full.* SUFFIX

ice /aɪs/ **ices, icing, iced** ◆◆◆◆◇

1 **Ice** is frozen water. *Glaciers are moving rivers of ice... The ice is melting.* N-UNCOUNT

2 **Ice** is pieces of ice that you use to keep food or drink cool. *...a bitter lemon with ice.* N-UNCOUNT

3 You use **ice** to refer to the frozen surface of a lake, river, or rink that people skate on. *Hans ground his skate blade against the ice.* N-UNCOUNT: usu *the* N

4 If you **ice** cakes or buns, you cover them with icing. *I've made the cake. I've iced and decorated it.* VERB =frost; V n

5 An **ice** is a portion of ice cream; used mainly in British English. *He's eaten a lot of choc ices.* N-COUNT =ice cream

6 See also **iced, icing.**

7 If you **break the ice** at a party or meeting, or in a new situation, you say or do something to make people feel relaxed and comfortable. *That sort of approach should go a long way toward breaking the ice... The major purpose of his trip was to break the ice, and his itinerary so far has been packed full.* • See also **ice-breaker.** PHRASES; V inflects

8 If you say that something **cuts no ice** with you, you mean that you are not impressed or influenced by it. *That sort of romantic attitude cuts no ice with money-men.* V inflects, oft PHR *with* n

9 If someone puts a plan or project **on ice**, they delay doing it. *There would be a three-month delay while the deal would be put on ice... The $40 million-a-month aid payments will remain on ice.* PHR after v, v-link PHR =shelve

10 If you say that someone is **on thin ice** or **is skating on thin ice**, you mean that they are doing something risky which may have serious or unpleasant consequences. *I had skated on thin ice on many assignments and somehow had, so far, got away with it.*

Ice Age. **The Ice Age** was a period of time lasting many thousands of years, during which a lot of the earth's surface was covered with ice. ◆◇◇◇◇ N-PROPER: *the*N

iceberg /aɪsbɜːʳg/ **icebergs.** An **iceberg** is a large tall mass of ice floating in the sea. • **the tip of the iceberg**: see **tip**. ◆◇◇◇◇ N-COUNT

ice-blue. **Ice-blue** is a very pale blue colour; a literary word. *...ash-blonde girls with ice-blue eyes.* COLOUR

icebox /aɪsbɒks/ **iceboxes;** also spelled **ice-box.** In American English, an **icebox** is the same as a **refrigerator**; a fairly old-fashioned word. N-COUNT

ice-breaker, ice-breakers; also spelled **icebreaker.**

1 An **ice-breaker** is a large ship which sails through frozen waters, breaking the ice as it goes, in order to create a passage for other ships. N-COUNT

2 An **ice-breaker** is something that someone says or does in order to make it easier for people have never met before to talk to each other. *This exercise can be quite a useful ice-breaker for new groups.* N-COUNT

ice bucket, ice buckets. An **ice bucket** is a container which holds ice cubes or cold water and ice. You can use it to provide ice cubes to put in drinks, or to put bottles of wine in and keep the wine cool. N-COUNT

ice cap, ice caps; also spelled **ice-cap.** An **ice-cap** is a thick layer of ice and snow that permanently covers an area of land, usually the area around the North or South Pole. *This could cause the ice caps to melt. ...the polar ice caps.* N-COUNT: usu *the*N

ice-cold

1 If you describe something as **ice-cold**, you are emphasizing that it is very cold. *...delicious ice-cold beer... The water was ice cold and my hands were completely blue.* ADJ

2 If you describe someone as **ice-cold**, you are emphasizing that they do not allow their emotions to affect them or that they lack feeling and friendliness. *...his ice-cold calculation... The gunman was young, with brown hair and 'an ice-cold stare'.* ADJ

ice cream, ice creams; also spelled **ice-cream.** ◆◆◇◇◇

1 **Ice cream** is a very cold sweet-tasting food made from frozen cream or from an artificial substitute for cream. It can also contain vanilla, chocolate, strawberry, or other flavourings. *I'll get you some ice cream. ...vanilla ice cream.* N-MASS

2 An **ice cream** is a portion of ice cream. Ice-creams are usually sold in a container, or in a cone made of thin biscuit. *Do you want an ice cream?... They stuffed themselves with ice creams, chocolate and lollies.* N-COUNT =ice

ice-cream soda, ice-cream sodas. An **ice-cream soda** is a dessert made from ice cream, fruit-flavoured syrup, and soda water. It is usually served in a tall glass. N-VAR

ice cube, ice cubes. An **ice cube** is a small square block of ice that you put into a drink in order to make it cold. ◆◇◇◇◇ N-COUNT

iced /aɪst/ ◆◇◇◇◇

1 An **iced** drink has been made very cold, often by putting ice in it. *...iced tea.* ADJ: ADJ n

2 An **iced** cake is covered with a layer of icing. *We were all given little iced cakes.* ADJ: usu ADJ n =frosted

ice floe, ice floes. An **ice floe** is a large area of ice floating in the sea. N-COUNT

ice hockey; also spelled **ice-hockey. Ice hockey** is a game like hockey played on ice. ◆◇◇◇◇ N-UNCOUNT

Icelander /aɪslændəʳ/ **Icelanders.** An **Icelander** is a person who comes from Iceland. N-COUNT

Icelandic /aɪslændɪk/ ◆◆◆◆◇

1 Something that is **Icelandic** belongs or relates to Iceland, to its people, or to its language. ADJ

2 **Icelandic** is the official language of Iceland. N-UNCOUNT

ice lolly, ice lollies; also spelled **ice-lolly.** In British English, an **ice lolly** is a piece of flavoured ice or ice cream on a stick. N-COUNT

ice pick, ice picks; also spelled **icepick.** An **ice pick** is a small pointed tool that you use for breaking ice. N-COUNT

ice rink, ice rinks. An **ice rink** is a level area of ice, usually inside a building, that has been made artificially and kept frozen so that people can skate on it. N-COUNT

ice-skate, ice-skates; also spelled **ice skate. Ice-skates** are boots with a thin metal bar underneath that people wear to move quickly on ice. N-COUNT

ice-skating; also spelled **ice skating.** If you go **ice-skating**, you move about on ice wearing ice-skates. This activity is also a sport. *They took me ice-skating on a frozen lake.* ► Also a noun. *I love watching ice-skating on television. ...British ice-skating champion Joanne Conway.* VB: only cont V N-UNCOUNT =skating

icicle /aɪsɪkᵊl/ **icicles.** An **icicle** is a long pointed piece of ice hanging down from a surface. It forms when water drips slowly off the surface, freezing as it falls. N-COUNT

icing /aɪsɪŋ/. ◆◇◇◇◇

1 **Icing** is a sweet substance made from powdered sugar that is used to cover and decorate cakes. *Paul made five-year-old Michelle a birthday cake with yellow icing.* N-UNCOUNT =frosting

2 If you describe something as **the icing on the cake**, you mean that it makes a good thing even better, but it is not essential. *Paul's two goals were the icing on the cake for what was a very good team display.* PHRASE: v-link PHR

icing sugar. In British English, **icing sugar** is very fine white sugar that is used for making icing and sweets. The usual American term is **confectioners' sugar.** ◆◇◇◇◇ N-UNCOUNT

-icity /-ɪsɪti/ **-icities. -icity** replaces '-ic' at the end of adjectives to form nouns referring to the state, quality, or behaviour described by the adjective. *...if someone disputes the authenticity of the document... He soon exhibited signs of eccentricity.* SUFFIX

icon /aɪkɒn/ **icons** ◆◇◇◇◇

1 If you describe something or someone as an **icon**, you mean that they are important as a symbol of something. *...Britain's favourite fashion icon, the Princess of Wales. ...Picasso and the other icons of modernism. ...the greatest icon of this century.* N-COUNT: usu with supp

2 An **icon** is a picture of Christ, the Virgin Mary, or a saint painted on a wooden panel. Icons are regarded as holy by some Christians. N-COUNT

3 An **icon** is a picture on a computer screen representing a particular computer function. If you want to use it, you move the cursor onto the icon using a mouse. N-COUNT

iconic /aɪkɒnɪk/. An **iconic** image or thing is important or impressive because it seems to symbolize something; a formal word. *Murphy's powerfully spoken Oedipus is an autocrat of iconic grandeur... The ads helped Nike to achieve iconic status.* ADJ

iconoclast /aɪkɒnəklæst/ **iconoclasts.** If you describe someone as an **iconoclast**, you mean that they often criticize beliefs and things that are generally accepted by society; a formal word. *Cage was an iconoclast. He refused to be bound by western musical traditions of harmony and structure.* N-COUNT

iconoclastic /aɪkɒnəklæstɪk/. If you describe someone or their words or ideas as **iconoclastic**, you mean that they contradict established beliefs; a formal word. *Is it utopian to hope that such iconoclastic ideas will gain ground?... His iconoclastic tendencies can get him into trouble.* ADJ-GRADED

iconography /aɪkənɒgrəfi/. The **Iconography** of a group of people consists of the symbols, pictures, and objects which represent their ideas N-UNCOUNT and way of life. *The pictures of the original moon landings are as much a part of the iconography of the Sixties as Beatles album covers. ...religious iconography.*

icy /aɪsi/ **icier, iciest** ◆◇◇◇◇
1 If you describe something as **icy** or **icy cold**, you mean that it is extremely cold. *An icy wind blew hard across the open spaces... His shoes and clothing were wet through and icy cold.* ADJ-GRADED
2 An **icy** road has ice on it. ADJ-GRADED
3 If you describe a person or their behaviour as **icy**, you mean that they are not affectionate or friendly, and they show their dislike or anger in a quiet, controlled way. *His response was icy.* ♦ **icily** *'You have nothing to say in the matter,' he said icily... The prison official is icily polite and bureaucratic.* ADJ-GRADED =cold, frosty ≠warm; ADV-GRADED: ADV after v, ADV adj

ID /aɪ diː/ **IDs.** If you have **ID** or an **ID**, you are carrying a document such as an identity card or driver's licence which proves that you are a particular person. *I had no ID on me so the police couldn't establish I was the owner of the car... Peter took out his wallet and showed his ID to the man... Registrars checked the ID cards of prospective voters.* ◆◇◇◇◇ N-VAR =identification

I'd /aɪd/
1 **I'd** is the usual spoken form of 'I had', especially when 'had' is an auxiliary verb. *I felt absolutely certain that I'd seen her before.*
2 **I'd** is the usual spoken form of 'I would'. *There are some questions I'd like to ask... He knows I'd love him whatever he did.*

idea /aɪdiːə/ **ideas** ◆◆◆◆◆
1 An **idea** is a plan, suggestion, or possible course of action. *It's a good idea to keep a stock of slimmers' meals for when you're too busy or tired to cook... I really like the idea of helping people... She told me she'd had a brilliant idea.* N-COUNT: oft adj N, N to-inf, N of n/-ing
2 An **idea** is an opinion or belief about what something is like or should be like. *Some of his ideas about democracy are entirely his own... There may be some truth in the idea that reading too many books ruins your eyes... My idea of physical perfection is to be very slender.* N-COUNT: usu N *about/on/of* n, N that =notion
3 If someone gives you an **idea of** something, they give you information about it without being very exact or giving a lot of detail. *This table will give you some idea of how levels of ability in a foreign language can be measured... Could you give us an idea of the range of complaints you've been receiving?... If you cannot remember the exact date give a rough idea of when it was.* N-SING: N *of* n/wh =impression
4 If you have an **idea** of something, you know about it to some extent. *By the end of the week you will have a clear idea of what your eating habits are... No one has any real idea how much the company will make next year.* N-SING: with supp
5 If you have an **idea** that something is the case, you think that it may be the case, although you are not certain. *I had an idea that he joined the army later, after university, but I may be wrong.* N-SING: N that =suspicion
6 **The idea** of an action or activity is its aim or purpose. *The idea is to lend money to homeowners who are unable to move because their houses are worth less than their mortgages.* N-SING: *the* N =objective
7 If you have the **idea of** doing something, you intend to do it. *He sent for a number of books he admired with the idea of re-reading them... I had to postpone ideas of a career and stay at home.* N-COUNT: N *of*-ing/n =intention
8 You can use **idea** in expressions such as **I've no idea** or **I haven't the faintest idea** to emphasize that you don't know something. *'Is she coming by coach?'—'Well I've no idea.'... We haven't the faintest idea where he is.* N-SING: with brd-neg PRAGMATICS =notion
9 If someone **gets the idea**, they understand how to do something or they understand what you are telling them; an informal expression. *It isn't too difficult once you get the idea... You're beginning to get the idea.* PHRASES V inflects
10 You can say **you have no idea** to emphasize how good or bad something is; an informal expression. *We are both so happy, you have no idea... You have no idea how depressed it made me.* V inflects, oft PHR wh PRAGMATICS

ideal /aɪdiːəl/ **ideals** ◆◆◆◇◇
1 An **ideal** is a principle, idea, or standard that seems very good and worth trying to achieve. *The party has drifted too far from its socialist ideals... I tried to live up to my ideal of myself.* N-COUNT: oft N *of* n
2 Your **ideal** of something is the person or thing that seems to you to be the best possible example of it. *Her features were almost the opposite of the Japanese ideal of beauty in those days... Throughout his career she remained his feminine ideal.* N-SING: oft poss N
3 The **ideal** person or thing for a particular task or purpose is the best possible person or thing for it. *She decided that I was the ideal person to take over the job... I really love the area and see it as an ideal place to start my managerial career... The conditions were ideal for racing.* ADJ-GRADED =perfect
4 An **ideal** society or world is the best possible one that you can imagine. *We do not live in an ideal world... In an ideal world, there would be no such thing as rubbish... Their ideal society collapsed around them into the Terror and then into the Counterrevolution.* ADJ: ADJ n

idealise /aɪdiːəlaɪz/. See **idealize.**

idealism /aɪdiːəlɪzəm/. **Idealism** is the beliefs and behaviour of someone who has ideals and who tries to base their behaviour on these ideals. *She never lost her respect for the idealism of the 1960s... This experience has tempered their idealism.* ♦ **idealist, idealists** *He is not such an idealist that he cannot see the problems.* ◆◇◇◇◇ N-UNCOUNT; N-COUNT

idealistic /aɪdiəlɪstɪk/. If you describe someone as **idealistic**, you mean that they have ideals, and base their behaviour on these ideals, even though this may be impractical and naive. *Idealistic young people died for a future that was stolen from them as soon as it became possible... Older mothers tend to be too idealistic about the pleasures of motherhood.* ◆◇◇◇◇ ADJ-GRADED

idealize /aɪdiːəlaɪz/ **idealizes, idealizing, idealized;** also spelled **idealise** in British English. If you **idealize** something or someone, you think of them, or represent them to other people, as being perfect or much better than they really are. *People idealize the past... I'm not trying to glorify or idealise women.* ♦ **idealized** *...an idealised image of how a parent should be... Men want to look like the idealized men depicted in advertisements.* ♦ **idealization** /aɪdiːəlaɪzeɪʃən/ **idealizations** *...Marie's idealisation of her dead husband.* ◆◇◇◇◇ VERB =romanticize; V n; ADJ-GRADED: usu ADJ n; N-VAR

ideally /aɪdiːəli/ ◆◆◇◇◇
1 If you say that **ideally** a particular thing should happen or be done, you mean that this is what you would like to happen or be done, but you know that this is may not be possible or practical. *People should, ideally, be persuaded to eat a diet with much less fat or oil.* ADV: ADV with cl/group =preferably
2 If you say that someone or something is **ideally** suited, **ideally** located, or **ideally** qualified, you mean that they are as well suited, located, or qualified as they could possibly be. *They were an extremely happy couple, ideally suited... The hotel is ideally situated for country walks... The General is ideally qualified for the job.* ADV: usu ADV -ed, also ADV after v =perfectly

identical /aɪdentɪkəl/. Things that are **identical** are exactly the same. *Nearly all the houses were identical... The two parties fought the last election on almost identical manifestos.* ♦ **identically** /aɪdentɪkli/ *...nine identically dressed female dancers.* ◆◆◇◇◇ ADJ: oft ADJ *to/with* n; ADV: usu ADV -ed/adj, also ADV after v

identical twin, identical twins. Identical twins are twins of the same sex who look exactly the same. N-COUNT: usu pl

identifiable /aɪdentɪfaɪəbəl/. Something or someone that is **identifiable** can be recognized. *In the corridor were four dirty, ragged bundles, just identifiable as human beings... Stan Dean, easily identifiable by his oddly-shaped hat, sat in a doorway... Where the risk is clearly identifiable, the tour operators should give advice to holidaymakers on their arrival.* ◆◇◇◇◇ ADJ-GRADED: oft ADJ *as/by/from* n =recognizable ≠unidentifiable

identification /aɪdentɪfɪkeɪʃᵊn/ **identifications** ◆◆◇◇◇

1 The **identification** of something is the recognition that it exists, is important, or is true. *Early identification of a disease can prevent death and illness... Their work includes the identification of genes which govern the growth rate and fertility... There should be some identification of goals, and how far these have been achieved.* N-VAR: oft N of n

2 Your **identification** of a particular person or thing is your ability to name them because you know them or recognize them. *Officials are awaiting positive identification before charging the men with war crimes... He's made a formal identification of the body. ...the Hamlyn identification guide to wild flowers of Britain.* N-VAR

3 If someone asks you for some **identification**, they want to see something such as a driving licence, which proves who you are. *The woman who was on passport control asked me if I had any further identification.* N-UNCOUNT =ID

4 The **identification** of one person or thing with another is the close association of one with the other. *Throughout the Balkans, there is a close identification of nationhood with language. ...the identification of Spain with Catholicism.* N-VAR: usu N of n with n =association

5 Identification with someone or something is the feeling of sympathy and support for them. *I need your full, emotional identification with the problem and with me... Marilyn had an intense identification with animals.* N-UNCOUNT: N with n =empathy

identify /aɪdentɪfaɪ/ **identifies, identifying, identified** ◆◆◆◆◇

1 If you can **identify** someone or something, you are able to recognize them or distinguish them from others. *There are a number of distinguishing characteristics by which you can identify a Hollywood epic... I tried to identify her perfume... A uniformed chauffeur identified me among the crowd.* VERB =recognize V n

2 If you **identify** someone or something, you name them or say who or what they are or what their purpose is. *Police have already identified around 10 murder suspects... The reporters identified one of the six Americans as an Army Specialist... They identified six plants as having potential for development into pharmaceutical drugs.* VERB =name V n V n as n/-ing

3 If you **identify** something, you discover or notice its existence. *Scientists claim to have identified chemicals produced by certain plants which have powerful cancer-combating properties... Having identified the problem, the question arises of how to overcome it.* VERB =discover V n

4 If a particular thing **identifies** someone or something, it makes them easy to recognize, by making them different in some way. *She wore a little nurse's hat on her head to identify her... His boots and purple beret identify him as commanding the Scottish Paratroops.* VERB =distinguish V n V n as -ing/n

5 If you **identify with** someone or something, you feel that you understand them or their feelings and ideas. *She would only play a role if she could identify with the character... I could speak their language and identify with their problems because I had been there myself.* VERB =empathize V with n

6 If you **identify** one person or thing **with** another, you think that they are closely associated or involved in some way. *Moore really hates to play the sweet, passive women that audiences have identified her with... The mood in Japan is changing, and candidates want to identify themselves with reform.* VERB =associate, equate V n with n V pron-refl with n

identikit /aɪdentɪkɪt/ **identikits.** In British English, an **identikit** or an **identikit picture** is a drawing, made up from a special set of smaller drawings, of the face of someone the police want to question. It is made from descriptions given to them by witnesses to a crime. Compare **photofit**. N-COUNT

identity /aɪdentɪti/ **identities** ◆◆◆◇◇

1 Your **identity** is who you are. *Abu is not his real name, but it's one he uses to disguise his identity... The police soon established his true identity and he was quickly found.* N-COUNT: with poss

2 The **identity** of a person or place is the characteristics they have that distinguish them from others. *I wanted a sense of my own identity. ...the distinct cultural, religious and national identity of many Tibetans.* N-VAR: usu with supp, oft with poss, adj N

identity card, identity cards. An **identity card** is a card with a person's name, photograph, date of birth, and other information on it. In some countries, people are required to carry identity cards in order to prove who they are. ◆◇◇◇◇ N-COUNT

identity parade, identity parades. In British English, an **identity parade** is a line of people who have been assembled in a police station. One of the people is a suspected criminal, and victims or witnesses of a crime try to identify that person. The usual American word is **line-up**. N-COUNT

ideogram /ɪdioʊgræm/ **ideograms**

1 An **ideogram** is a sign or symbol that represents a particular idea or thing rather than a word. The writing systems of Japan and China, for example, use ideograms. N-COUNT

2 In languages such as English which are written using letters and words, an **ideogram** is a sign or symbol that can be used to represent a particular word. %, @, and & are examples of ideograms. N-COUNT

ideological /aɪdiəlɒdʒɪkᵊl/. **Ideological** means relating to principles or beliefs. *Others left the Communist Party for ideological reasons... The ideological divisions between the parties aren't always obvious.* ♦ **ideologically** /aɪdiəlɒdʒɪkli/ *...an ideologically sound organisation... The army was ideologically opposed to the kind of economic solution proposed... Ideologically, there was nothing in common between them.* ◆◆◇◇◇ ADJ: usu ADJ n ADV: ADV adj/-ed, ADV with cl, ADV after v

ideologist /aɪdiɒlədʒɪst/ **ideologists.** An **ideologist** is someone who develops or supports a particular ideology. N-COUNT

ideologue /aɪdiəlɒg, AM -lɔːg/ **ideologues.** An **ideologue** is the same as an **ideologist**; a formal word. N-COUNT

ideology /aɪdiɒlədʒi/ **ideologies.** An **ideology** is a set of beliefs, especially the political beliefs on which people, parties, or countries base their actions. *...capitalist ideology.* ◆◆◇◇◇ N-VAR =philosophy

idiocy /ɪdiəsi/ **idiocies.** If you refer to the **idiocy** of something, you mean that you think it is very stupid. *...a powerful chapter on the idiocy of continuing government subsidies for environmentally damaging activities. ...his gentle, ironic analysis of the idiocies of Communist rule.* N-VAR: oft N of n/-ing PRAGMATICS =lunacy

idiom /ɪdiəm/ **idioms** ◆◇◇◇◇

1 A particular **idiom** is a particular style of something such as music, dance, or architecture; a formal use. *McCartney was also keen to write in a classical idiom, rather than a pop one... It was an old building in the local idiom.* N-COUNT: usu sing, with supp =style

2 An **idiom** is a group of words which have a different meaning when used together from the one they would have if you took the meaning of each word individually. *Proverbs and idioms may become worn with over-use... She is, in fact, a perfect illustration of the French idiom 'to be comfortable in one's own skin.'* N-COUNT =phrase

3 Idiom of a particular kind is the kind of language and grammatical structures that people use at a particular time or in a particular place; a formal use. *And nothing was so irritating as the confident way he used archaic idiom. ...her command of the Chinese idiom.* N-UNCOUNT =language

idiomatic /ɪdioʊmætɪk/. **Idiomatic** language uses words in a way that sounds natural to native speakers of the language. *Philippa was soon to acquire a remarkable command of idiomatic English.* ADJ-GRADED: usu ADJ n

idiosyncrasy /ɪdioʊsɪŋkrəsi/ **idiosyncrasies.** If you talk about the **idiosyncrasies** of someone or something, you are referring to their rather unusual habits or characteristics. *One of his idiosyncrasies was to wear thick orange gloves of the kitchen-sink variety... The bike has style, it has looks, it has its little idiosyncrasies... The book is a gem of Victorian idiosyncrasy.* N-VAR: usu with poss =eccentricity, peculiarity

idiosyncratic /ɪdiəʊsɪŋkrætɪk/. If you describe someone's actions or characteristics as **idiosyncratic**, you mean that they are rather unusual. *...a highly idiosyncratic personality. ...his erratic typing and idiosyncratic spelling.* ◆◇◇◇◇ ADJ-GRADED =eccentric, peculiar

idiot /ɪdiət/ **idiots** ◆◇◇◇◇

1 If you call someone an **idiot**, you are showing that you think they are very stupid or have done something very stupid; an offensive use. *I knew I'd been an idiot to stay there... You're an idiot!* N-COUNT PRAGMATICS =fool, moron

2 **Idiot** means stupid. *...a bunch of idiot journalists waiting to ask me stupid questions.* ADJ: ADJ n

3 An **idiot** is a person who is mentally ill or mentally handicapped; an old-fashioned, offensive use. *...the village idiot.* N-COUNT

idiotic /ɪdiɒtɪk/. If you call someone or something **idiotic**, you mean that they are very stupid or silly. *What an idiotic thing to say!* ♦ **idiotically** /ɪdiɒtɪkli/ *...his idiotically romantic views.* ADJ-GRADED PRAGMATICS =ridiculous ADV

idle /aɪdᵊl/ **idles, idling, idled** ◆◆◇◇◇

1 If people who were working are **idle**, they have no jobs or work. *Employees have been idle almost a month because of shortages.* ADJ: v-link ADJ ≠busy

2 If machines or factories are **idle**, they are not working or being used. *Now the machine is lying idle. ...factories that had been idle for years.* ADJ: v-link ADJ

3 If you say that someone is **idle**, you disapprove of them because they are not doing anything and you think they should be. *...idle bureaucrats who spent the day reading newspapers... I never met such an idle bunch of workers in all my life!* ♦ **idleness** *Idleness is a very bad thing for human nature.* ♦ **idly** *We were not idly sitting around.* ADJ PRAGMATICS =lazy N-UNCOUNT ADV: ADV with v

4 **Idle** is used to describe something that you do for no particular reason, often because you have nothing better to do. *Brian kept up the idle chatter for another five minutes. ...idle curiosity.* ♦ **idly** *We talked idly about magazines and baseball... 'Has there been an accident?' Gary asked, idly curious.* ADJ: ADJ n ADV: ADV with v, ADV adj

5 If you say that **it is idle** to do something, you mean that it is not worth doing it, because it will not achieve anything. *It would be idle to pretend the system is perfect.* ADJ: it v-link ADJ to-inf =futile

6 You refer to an **idle** threat or boast when you are referring to a threat or boast that do not think has been made seriously. *It was more of an idle threat than anything... His statement isn't merely an idle boast.* ADJ: ADJ n =empty

7 If you **idle**, you spend time in a lazy way, doing nothing in particular. *When they reached his house, Scobie idled a bit, finishing his cigarette... We spent many hours idling in one of the cafes that line three sides of the tiny piazza... He idled around afterwards, window shopping until about 5pm.* VERB =laze V V adv/prep

8 In American English, to **idle** a factory or other place of work means to close it down because there is no work to do or because the workers are on strike. To **idle** workers means to stop them working. *The strike has idled about 55,000 machinists... Officials say some of the idled assembly plants will resume production after the Labor Day holiday.* VERB V n V-ed

9 If an engine or vehicle **is idling**, the engine is running slowly and quietly because it is not in gear, and the vehicle is not moving. *Beyond a stand of trees a small plane idled... Her Daimler limo waits with its engine idling.* VERB =tick over V

idle away. If you **idle away** a period of time, you spend it doing very little. *Residents were mowing their lawns, washing their cars and otherwise idling away a pleasant, sunny day... He idled the time away in dreamy thought.* PHRASAL VERB V P n (not pron) V n P

idler /aɪdləʳ/ **idlers.** If you describe someone as an **idler**, you are criticizing them because you think they are lazy and should be working. *The Duke resents being seen as a moneyed idler.* N-COUNT PRAGMATICS =loafer

idol /aɪdᵊl/ **idols** ◆◇◇◇◇

1 If you refer to someone such as a film, pop, or sports star as an **idol**, you mean that they are greatly admired or loved by their fans. *A great cheer went up from the crowd as they caught sight of their idol... He looks more like a stockbroker than a teen idol.* N-COUNT: usu with supp =hero

2 An **idol** is a statue or other object that is worshipped by people who believe that it is a god. N-COUNT

3 If you refer to someone as a **fallen idol**, you mean that they have lost people's respect and admiration because of something bad that they have done. *He was once worshipped like a god but now Lenin is a fallen idol.* PHRASE: N inflects

idolatry /aɪdɒlətri/

1 Someone who practises **idolatry** worships idols; a formal use. N-UNCOUNT

2 If you refer to someone's admiration for a particular person as **idolatry**, you are being critical of it because you regard it as too great and unquestioning; a formal use. *His real view of Roosevelt stood well short of idolatry.* N-UNCOUNT PRAGMATICS

idolize /aɪdəlaɪz/ **idolizes, idolizing, idolized;** also spelled **idolise** in British English. If you **idolize** someone, you admire them very much. *Naomi idolised her father as she was growing up... A tall, soft-spoken woman, she is idolized by her young patients.* VERB =worship V n

idyll /ɪdɪl, AM aɪdᵊl/ **idylls.** If you describe a situation as an **idyll**, you mean that it is idyllic. *She finds that the sleepy town she moves to isn't the rural idyll she imagined... Though they still talked a lot, Harry felt that their idyll was drawing to an end.* N-COUNT

idyllic /ɪdɪlɪk, AM aɪd-/. If you describe something as **idyllic**, you mean that it is extremely pleasant, simple, and peaceful without any difficulties or dangers. *...an idyllic setting for a summer romance... Married life was not as idyllic as he had imagined.* ◆◇◇◇◇ ADJ-GRADED

i.e. /aɪ iː/. **i.e.** is used to introduce a word or sentence which makes clearer or makes explicit the meaning of what you have just said. *...strategic points – i.e. airports or military bases.* ◆◆◇◇◇ PRAGMATICS

-ied. See **-ed.**

-ier. See **-er.**

-iest. See **-est.**

if /ɪf/. Often pronounced /ɪf/ at the beginning of the sentence. ◆◆◆◆◆

1 You use **if** in conditional sentences to introduce the circumstances in which an event or situation might happen, might be happening, or might have happened. *She gets very upset if I exclude her from anything... You'll feel a lot better about yourself if you work on solutions to your upsetting situations... You can go if you want... If you would like to send a donation to Cobuild, please enclose a cheque with your coupon... If you went into town, you'd notice all the pubs have loud jukeboxes... What I did was right and if I had done anything less it would have been wrong... Fry remaining peppers, adding a little more dressing if necessary... Are you a student with a knack for coming up with great ideas? If so, we would love to hear from you.* CONJ-SUBORD

2 You use **if** in indirect questions where the answer is either 'yes' or 'no'. *He asked if I had left with you, and I said no... I wonder if I might have a word with Mr Abbot?* CONJ-SUBORD =whether

3 You use **if** to suggest that something might be slightly different from what you are stating in the main part of the sentence, for example that there might be slightly more or less of a particular quality. *Sometimes, that standard is quite difficult, if not impossible, to achieve... I'm working on my fitness and I will be ready in a couple of weeks, if not sooner... Many, if not most, scientific papers are presented orally at scientific meetings... What one quality, if any, do you like the most about your partner?... Meat was available once a week if at all.* CONJ-SUBORD: with neg

4 You use **if**, usually with 'can', 'could', 'may', or 'might', at a point in a conversation when you are politely trying to make a point, change the subject, or interrupt another speaker. *If I could just make another small point about the weightlifters in the Olympics... So, if we may return strictly to athletics again for a few minutes... But if I can interrupt, Joe, I don't think anybody here is personally blaming the Germans... Well, it's the old argument Max, which is a bit ridiculous if you don't mind me saying so...* CONJ-SUBORD PRAGMATICS

Well if you want my opinion, unless you do it soon you're gonna lose the opportunity and you'll be really sorry.

5 You use **if** at or near the beginning of a clause when politely asking someone to do something. *I wonder if you'd be kind enough to give us some information, please?... If you will just sign here, we will arrange for your bank to deduct your payments automatically.* CONJ-SUBORD PRAGMATICS

6 You use **if not** in front of a word or phrase to indicate that your statement does not apply to that word or phrase, but to something closely related to it that you also mention. *A number of recent advances hold out if not the hope of a cure, then at least the possibility of some drug which could stop the spread of the virus... She understood his meaning, if not his words, and took his advice.* PHR-CONJ-SUBORD PRAGMATICS =although not

7 You use **if** to introduce a subordinate clause in which you admit a fact which you regard as less important than the statement in the main clause. *If there was any disappointment it was probably temporary... Even if I'm overstating the case for nutrition, at least it will result in the woman being in charge of her own symptoms... So what if sometimes they stayed rather late, it doesn't mean anything.* CONJ-SUBORD

8 You use **if ever** with past tenses when you are introducing a description of a person or thing, to emphasize how appropriate it is. *I became a distraught, worried mother, a useless role if ever there was one... If ever there was the right person in the right job it was she... If ever a man needed your love, I need it.* PHR-CONJ-SUBORD PRAGMATICS

9 You use **if only** with past tenses to introduce what you think is a fairly good reason for doing something, although you realize it may not be a very good one. *She always writes me once a month, if only to scold me because I haven't answered her last letter yet... A one-to-one meeting with the US President was necessary, if only for a deeper exchange of views.* PHR-CONJ-SUBORD

10 You use **if only** to express a wish or desire, especially one that cannot be fulfilled. *If only you had told me that some time ago... If only it were that simple!... 'Hey, listen to me, all that 1980 nonsense is over.'—'If only, Timothy, if only.'* PHR-CONJ-SUBORD PRAGMATICS

11 You use **as if** when you are making a judgement about something that you see or notice. Your belief or impression might be correct, or it might be wrong. *The whole room looks as if it has been lovingly put together over the years... His heart was pounding, as if he were frightened.* PHR-CONJ-SUBORD =as though

12 You use **as if** to describe something or someone by comparing them with another thing or person. *He points two fingers at his head, as if he were holding a gun... The two cousins looked as if they'd been carved from blocks of ice.* PHR-CONJ-SUBORD =as though

13 You use **as if** to emphasize that something is not true; used in spoken English. *My husband, for some unknown reason, suggested that I loved my birds more than him: as if I would... Getting my work done! My God! As if it mattered.* PHR-CONJ-SUBORD PRAGMATICS =as though

14 You use **'if anything'** to introduce something which strengthens or changes the meaning of the statement you have just made, but only in a small or unimportant way. *Katie and I also lived with a friend and we got on OK. If anything it strengthened our relationship... Asthma drugs are not addictive and you don't need to keep increasing the dose. If anything, the reverse is true.* PHRASES PHR with cl PRAGMATICS

15 You use **'It's not as if'** to introduce a statement which, if it were true, might explain something puzzling, although in fact it is not true. *I am surprised by the degree of fuss she's making. It's not as if my personality has changed or vanished.* V inflects PRAGMATICS

16 You say **'if I were you'** to someone when you are giving them advice. *If I were you, Mrs Gretchen, I just wouldn't worry about it... What I'd do if I were you is be nice to him... I should lie down for a bit, if I were you.* PHR with cl PRAGMATICS

iffy /ɪfi/

1 If you say that something is **iffy**, you mean that it is not very good in some way; an informal use. *If your next record's a bit iffy, you're forgotten... He was from an iffy neighborhood.* ADJ-GRADED =dodgy

2 If something is **iffy**, it is uncertain; an informal use. *His political future has looked iffy for most of this year.* ADJ-GRADED =doubtful

-ify /-ɪfaɪ/ **-ifies, -ifying, -ified.** **-ify** is used at the end of verbs that refer to making something or someone different in some way. *More needs to be done to simplify the process of registering to vote... Water can be purified by boiling for five minutes.* SUFFIX

igloo /ɪgluː/ **igloos.** **Igloos** are dome-shaped houses built from blocks of snow by the Inuit people. N-COUNT

igneous /ɪgniəs/. **Igneous** rocks are formed by volcanic action; a technical term in geology. ADJ: ADJ n

ignite /ɪgnaɪt/ **ignites, igniting, ignited** ◆◇◇◇◇

1 When you **ignite** something or when it **ignites** it starts burning or explodes. *The bombs ignited a fire which destroyed some 60 houses... The blasts were caused by pockets of methane gas that ignited.* V-ERG V n V

2 If something or someone **ignites** your passions, they cause you to feel passionate about something; a literary use. *There was one teacher who really ignited my interest in words... The recent fighting in the area could ignite regional passions far beyond the borders.* VERB V n

ignition /ɪgnɪʃən/ **ignitions** ◆◇◇◇◇

1 In a car engine, the **ignition** is the part where the fuel is ignited. *The device automatically disconnects the ignition.* N-VAR

2 Inside a car, **the ignition** is the part where you turn the key so that the engine starts. N-SING: the N

3 **Ignition** is the process of something starting to burn. *The ignition of methane gas killed eight men.* N-UNCOUNT

ignoble /ɪgnoubəl/. If you describe someone's behaviour or circumstances as **ignoble**, you mean that you consider them dishonourable, shameful, or morally unacceptable; a formal word. *...ignoble thoughts. ...an ignoble episode from their country's past.* ADJ-GRADED PRAGMATICS

ignominious /ɪgnəmɪniəs/. If you describe someone's behaviour or circumstances as **ignominious**, you mean that they are shameful or very embarrassing; a formal word. *The recollection of their ignominious defeat was still fresh in his mind... Many thought that he was doomed to ignominious failure.* ADJ-GRADED =humiliating ♦ **ignominiously** *Their soldiers had to retreat ignominiously after losing hundreds of lives.* ADV-GRADED: ADV with v

ignominy /ɪgnəmɪni/. **Ignominy** is shame or public disgrace; a formal word. *...the ignominy of being made redundant... If they were caught, she would be thrown out in disgrace, dismissed with ignominy.* N-UNCOUNT: oft N of n/-ing =humiliation

ignoramus /ɪgnəreɪməs/ **ignoramuses.** If you describe someone as an **ignoramus**, you are being critical of them because they do not have the knowledge you think they ought to have. N-COUNT PRAGMATICS =dunce

ignorance /ɪgnərəns/. **Ignorance** of something is lack of knowledge about it. *I am beginning to feel embarrassed by my complete ignorance of non-European history... There is so much ignorance about mental illness... In my ignorance I had never heard country & western music.* ◆◆◇◇◇ N-UNCOUNT: oft N *of/about* n

ignorant /ɪgnərənt/ ◆◇◇◇◇

1 If you describe someone as **ignorant**, you mean that they are not very knowledgeable or well educated. If someone is **ignorant** of a fact, they do not know it. *People don't like to ask questions for fear of appearing ignorant... Many people are worryingly ignorant of the facts about global warming. ...ignorant peasants.* ADJ-GRADED: oft ADJ *of/about* n =uninformed

2 People are sometimes described as **ignorant** when they behave in an impolite or inconsiderate way. Some people think that it is not correct to use **ignorant** with this meaning. *I met some very ignorant people who called me all kinds of names.* ADJ-GRADED

ignore /ɪgnɔː/ **ignores, ignoring, ignored** ◆◆◆◆◇

1 If you **ignore** someone or something, you pay no attention to them. *She said her husband ignored her... The government had ignored his views on the subject... She ignored legal advice to drop the case...* VERB =disregard V n

For two decades her theatrical talents were ignored by the film industry.
2 If you say that an argument or theory **ignores** an important aspect of a situation, you are criticizing it because it fails to consider that aspect or to take it into account. *Such arguments ignore the question of where ultimate responsibility lay.* VERB =overlook V n

iguana /ɪgjuɑːnə, AM ɪgwɑːnə/ **iguanas.** An **iguana** is a type of large lizard found in America. N-COUNT

ikon /aɪkɒn/. See **icon**.

il-. Usually pronounced /ɪl/ before an unstressed syllable, and /ɪl/ before a stressed syllable. **Il-** is added to words that begin with the letter 'l' to form words with the opposite meaning. *...an awful illegible signature... He could face a charge of illegally importing weapons.* PREFIX

ilk /ɪlk/. If you talk about people or things of the same **ilk**, you mean people or things of the same type as a person or thing that has been mentioned. *He currently terrorises politicians and their ilk on 'Newsnight'... Where others of his ilk have battled against drugs or drink, Gabriel's problems seem to have centred on his marriage.* N-SING: supp N =kind

ill /ɪl/ **ills** ◆◆◆◆◇
1 Someone who is **ill** is suffering from a disease or a health problem. *In November 1941 Payne was seriously ill with pneumonia... I was feeling ill... If damp, musty buildings make you ill, mould is probably the cause... Two years ago my husband was declared to be terminally ill.* ► People who are ill in some way can be referred to as, for example, **the** mentally **ill**. *I used to work with the mentally ill... She became a nun and cared for the terminally ill for the rest of her life.* ADJ-GRADED: usu v-link ADJ =sick N-PLURAL: *the* adv N
2 Difficulties and problems are sometimes referred to as **ills**; a formal use. *His critics maintain that he's responsible for many of Algeria's ills. ...various potions that would cure all ills.* N-COUNT: usu pl, usu with supp =trouble
3 **Ill** is evil or harm; a literary use. *They say they mean you no ill.* N-UNCOUNT
4 **Ill** means the same as 'badly'; a formal use. *The company's conservative instincts sit ill with competition.* ADV-GRADED: ADV with v
5 You can use **ill** in front of some nouns to indicate that you are referring to something harmful or unpleasant; a formal use. *She had brought ill luck into her family... He says that he bears no ill feelings towards Johnson.* ADJ: ADJ n =bad
6 If you say that someone **can ill afford** to do something, or **can ill afford** something, you mean that they must not do it or must prevent it from happening because it would be harmful or embarrassing to them; a formal expression. *It's possible he won't play but I can ill afford to lose him... We can ill afford another scandal... It's an ignorance we can ill afford.* PHRASES PHR to-inf, PHR n
7 If something **bodes ill** or **augurs ill**, it gives you a reason to fear that something harmful might happen soon; a formal expression. *It's an ominous development that may bode ill for the Russian parliament.* V inflects, usu PHR *for* n
8 If you **fall ill** or **are taken ill**, you suddenly become ill. *Shortly before Christmas, he was mysteriously taken ill... She fell ill with measles.* V inflects
9 If you say that something is happening or will happen **for good or ill**, you mean that it is out of anyone's control whether it happens and what its effects will be; a formal expression. *Recent events should make everyone modest about saying what cannot happen there, for good or ill.* oft PHR with cl
10 ● to **speak ill of** someone: see **speak**.

ill- /ɪl-/. **Ill-** is added to words, especially adjectives and past participles, to add the meaning 'badly' or 'inadequately'. For example, 'ill-written' means badly written. *'It was an amazingly ill-disciplined attack,' he said.* COMB in ADJ-GRADED

I'll /aɪl/. **I'll** is the usual spoken form of 'I will' or 'I shall'. *I'll be leaving town in a few weeks... I'll explain tomorrow morning.*

ill-advised. If you describe something that someone does as **ill-advised**, you mean that it is not sensible or wise. *They would be ill-advised to do this... She said Mr Baker's remarks had been ill-advised... We deplore this lamentably ill-advised decision.* ADJ-GRADED: oft ADJ to-inf

ill-assorted. If you describe a group of people or things as an **ill-assorted** group, you mean that the people or things in the group do not suit one another or go well together. *His parents were an ill-assorted couple.* ADJ-GRADED

ill at ease; also spelled **ill-at-ease**. See **ease**.

ill-bred. If you say that someone is **ill-bred**, you mean that they have bad manners. *They seemed to her rather vulgar and ill-bred.* ADJ-GRADED =uncouth

ill effects; also spelled **ill-effects**. If something has **ill effects**, it causes problems or damage. *Some people are still suffering ill effects from the contamination of their water.* N-PLURAL

illegal /ɪliːgᵊl/ **illegals** ◆◆◆◇◇
1 If something is **illegal**, the law says that it is not allowed. *It is illegal to intercept radio messages... Birth control was illegal there until 1978... He has been charged with membership of an illegal organisation. ...illegal drugs. ...an illegal action.* ♦ **illegally** *They were yesterday convicted of illegally using a handgun... The previous government had acted illegally.* ♦ **illegality** /ɪlɪgælɪti/ **illegalities** *There is no evidence of illegality.* ADJ: oft *it* v-link ADJ to-inf =unlawful ADV: ADV with v N-VAR
2 **Illegal** immigrants or workers have travelled into a country or are working without official permission. ► Illegal immigrants or workers are sometimes referred to as **illegals**. *...a clothing factory where many other illegals also worked.* ADJ: ADJ n N-COUNT

illegible /ɪledʒɪbᵊl/. Writing that is **illegible** is so unclear that you cannot read it. ADJ-GRADED

illegitimacy /ɪlɪdʒɪtɪməsi/. **Illegitimacy** is the state of being born of parents who were not married to each other. *Divorce and illegitimacy mean an estimated 51 per cent of children will grow up without a father.* N-UNCOUNT

illegitimate /ɪlɪdʒɪtɪmət/ ◆◇◇◇◇
1 A person who is **illegitimate** was born of parents who were not married to each other. ADJ
2 **Illegitimate** is used to describe activities and institutions that are not in accordance with the law or with accepted standards of what is right. *He realized that, otherwise, the election would have been dismissed as illegitimate by the international community... They represented a ruthless and illegitimate regime that could not remain forever.* ADJ =illegal

ill-equipped. Someone who is **ill-equipped** to do something does not have the ability, the qualities, or the equipment necessary to do it. *Universities were ill-equipped to meet the massive intake of students... They often leave prison ill-equipped for life and work on the outside.* ADJ-GRADED: oft ADJ to-inf, ADJ *for* n

ill-fated. If you describe something as **ill-fated**, you mean that it ended or will end in an unsuccessful or unfortunate way. *England's footballers are back home after their ill-fated trip to Algeria.* ◆◇◇◇◇ ADJ: usu ADJ n =doomed

ill-fitting. An **ill-fitting** piece of clothing does not fit the person who is wearing it properly. *He wore an ill-fitting green corduroy suit.* ADJ: ADJ n

ill-founded. Something that is **ill-founded** is not based on any proper proof or evidence. *Suspicion and jealousy, however ill-founded, can poison a marriage.* ADJ-GRADED

ill-gotten gains. **Ill-gotten gains** are things that you have obtained by means of dishonesty or deceit. *But many leaders have invested their ill-gotten gains in several different countries.* N-PLURAL

ill health. Someone who suffers from **ill health** has an illness or keeps being ill. *He was forced to retire because of ill health... As a child she had suffered regular bouts of ill health.* ◆◇◇◇◇ N-UNCOUNT

illiberal /ɪlɪbərᵊl/. If you describe someone or something as **illiberal**, you are critical of them because they do not allow or approve of much freedom or choice of action. *...the sort of illiberal legislation which could only be justified by a serious emergency... His views are markedly illiberal.* ADJ-GRADED PRAGMATICS

illicit /ɪlɪsɪt/. An **illicit** activity or substance is not allowed by law or the social customs of a ◆◇◇◇◇ ADJ: usu ADJ n country. *Dante clearly condemns illicit love. ...information about the use of illicit drugs.*

illiteracy /ɪlɪtərəsi/. **Illiteracy** is the state of not knowing how to read or write. N-UNCOUNT

illiterate /ɪlɪtərət/ **illiterates** ◆◇◇◇◇

1 Someone who is **illiterate** does not know how to read or write. *A large percentage of the population is illiterate.* ► An **illiterate** is someone who is illiterate. *...an educational centre for illiterates.* ADJ; N-COUNT

2 If you describe someone as musically, technologically, or economically **illiterate**, you mean that they do not know much about music, technology, or economics. *Many senior managers are technologically illiterate.* ADJ: usu adv ADJ

ill-mannered. If you describe someone as **ill-mannered**, you are critical of them because they are impolite or rude; a formal word. *...this rude, ill-mannered individual who assumes he has the force of the law behind him... Chantal would have considered it ill-mannered to show surprise.* ADJ-GRADED PRAGMATICS ≠well-mannered

illness /ɪlnəs/ **illnesses** ◆◆◆◇◇

1 **Illness** is the fact or experience of being ill. *If your child shows any signs of illness, take her to the doctor... Mental illness is still a taboo subject.* N-UNCOUNT

2 An **illness** is a particular disease such as measles or pneumonia. *She returned to her family home to recover from an illness.* N-COUNT

illogical /ɪlɒdʒɪkəl/. If you describe an action, feeling, or belief as **illogical**, you are critical of it because you think that it is not rational and does not result from a logical and ordered way of thinking. *It is illogical to oppose the repatriation of economic migrants... She may think your reaction is crazy or illogical, but she cannot deny what you are feeling. ...his completely illogical arguments.* ♦ **illogically** /ɪlɒdʒɪkli/ *Illogically, I felt guilty.* ◆◇◇◇◇ ADJ-GRADED: oft *it* v-link ADJ to-inf PRAGMATICS =irrational, unreasonable; ADV-GRADED

ill-prepared. If you are **ill-prepared** for something, you have not made the correct preparations for it, for example because you are not expecting it to happen. *The government was ill-prepared for the problems it now faces... It was ill-prepared to meet this challenge.* ADJ-GRADED: usu v-link ADJ, oft ADJ *for* n, ADJ to-inf

ill-starred. If you describe something or someone as **ill-starred**, you mean that they were unlucky or unsuccessful; a literary word. *...an ill-starred attempt to create jobs in Northern Ireland.* ADJ: usu ADJ n

ill-tempered. If you describe someone as **ill-tempered**, you mean they are angry or hostile, and you may be implying that this is unreasonable. *He sounded like an ill-tempered child... It was a day of tense and often ill-tempered debate.* ADJ-GRADED

ill-timed. If you describe something as **ill-timed**, you mean that it happens or is done at the wrong time, so that it is damaging or rude. *Congressman Rostenkowski argued that the tax cut was ill-timed.* ADJ-GRADED =inopportune

ill-treat, ill-treats, ill-treating, ill-treated. If someone **ill-treats** you, they treat you badly or cruelly. *They thought Mr Smith had been ill-treating his wife... They said they had not been ill-treated but that their time in captivity had been miserable.* VERB =mistreat, abuse V n

ill-treatment. **Ill-treatment** is harsh or cruel treatment. *In spite of our worldwide campaign, ill-treatment of animals remains commonplace... The victims had either died as a result of their ill-treatment or had been left crippled.* N-UNCOUNT =abuse

illuminate /ɪluːmɪneɪt/ **illuminates, illuminating, illuminated** ◆◇◇◇◇

1 To **illuminate** something means to shine light on it and to make it brighter and more visible; a formal use. *No streetlights illuminated the street... The black sky was illuminated by forked lightning.* VERB =illumine V n

2 If you **illuminate** something that is unclear or difficult to understand, you make it clearer by explaining it carefully or giving information about it; a formal use. *Instead of formulas and charts, the two instructors use games and drawings to illuminate their subject.* ♦ **illuminating** *It is illuminating to compare how different sections of the national press have treated the story.* VERB =clarify V n; ADJ-GRADED: oft *it* v-link ADJ to-inf

illuminated /ɪluːmɪneɪtɪd/ ◆◇◇◇◇

1 Something that is **illuminated** is lit up, usually by electric lighting. *...an illuminated sign... Much of the ancient city is illuminated at night.* ADJ

2 **Illuminated** manuscripts, books, and official documents have brightly coloured drawings and designs round the writing. *...illuminated manuscripts from the 12th to 16th century.* ADJ: ADJ n =illustrated

illumination /ɪluːmɪneɪʃən/ **illuminations** ◆◇◇◇◇

1 **Illumination** is the lighting that a place has; a formal use. *The only illumination came from a small window high in the opposite wall.* N-UNCOUNT

2 In British English, **illuminations** are coloured lights which are put up in towns, especially at Christmas, in order to make them look more attractive at night. *...the famous Blackpool illuminations.* N-PLURAL

3 You can use **illumination** to describe an increased understanding of something, especially something of a religious or spiritual nature; a formal use. *...a sense of illumination... No further illumination can be had from Marxist theory.* N-UNCOUNT =enlightenment

illumine /ɪluːmɪn/ **illumines, illumining, illumined.** To **illumine** something means the same as to **illuminate** it; a literary word. *The interchange of ideas illumines the debate... By night, the perimeter wire was illumined by lights.* VERB V n

illusion /ɪluːʒən/ **illusions** ◆◆◇◇◇

1 An **illusion** is a false idea or belief. *Do not have any illusions that an industrial tribunal will right all employment wrongs... No one really has any illusions about winning the war.* N-VAR: oft N that, N *of* n/-ing =delusion

2 An **illusion** is something that appears to exist or be a particular thing but does not actually exist or is in reality something else. *Floor-to-ceiling windows can look stunning, giving the illusion of extra height... This eerie calm is an illusion.* N-COUNT: oft N *of* n/-ing

illusionist /ɪluːʒənɪst/ **illusionists.** An **illusionist** is a performer who performs tricks which create the illusion that something strange or impossible is happening, for example that a person has disappeared or been cut in half. N-COUNT

illusory /ɪluːzəri, -səri/. If you describe something as **illusory**, you mean that although it seems true or possible, it is in fact false or impossible. *Universalists argue that freedom is illusory. ...the illusory nature of nationhood.* ADJ-GRADED

illustrate /ɪləstreɪt/ **illustrates, illustrating, illustrated** ◆◆◆◇◇

1 If you say that something **illustrates** a situation that you are drawing attention to, you mean that it shows that the situation exists. *The example of the United States illustrates this point... This change is neatly illustrated by what has happened to the Arab League... The incident graphically illustrates how parlous their position is... The case also illustrates that some women are now trying to fight back.* VERB =demonstrate, exemplify V n V wh V that

2 If you use an example, story, or diagram to **illustrate** a point, you use it show that what you are saying is true or to make your meaning clearer. *Let me give another example to illustrate this difficult point... Throughout, she illustrates her analysis with excerpts from discussions.* ♦ **illustration** /ɪləstreɪʃən/ *Here, by way of illustration, are some extracts from our new catalogue.* VERB V n V n *with* n; N-UNCOUNT: usu prep N

3 If you **illustrate** a book, you put pictures, photographs or diagrams into it. *She went on to art school and is now illustrating a book... He has illustrated the book with black-and-white photographs.* ♦ **illustrated** *The book is beautifully illustrated throughout.* ♦ **illustration** *...the world of children's book illustration.* VERB V n V n *with* n; ADJ-GRADED; N-UNCOUNT

illustration /ɪləstreɪʃən/ **illustrations** ◆◆◆◇◇

1 An **illustration** is an example or a story which is used to make a point clear. *An illustration of China's dynamism is that a new company is formed in Shanghai every 11 seconds.* N-COUNT: oft N *of* n

2 An **illustration** in a book is a picture, design, or diagram. *She looked like a princess in a nineteenth-century illustration.* N-COUNT

3 See also **illustrate**.

illustrative /ɪləstrətɪv/. If you use something as an **illustrative** example, or for **illustrative** purposes, you use it to show that what you are saying is true or to make your meaning clearer; a formal word. *A second illustrative example was taken from The Observer newspaper... The following excerpt is illustrative of her interaction with students.* ADJ-GRADED: oft ADJ *of* n =explanatory

illustrator /ɪləstreɪtəʳ/ **illustrators.** An **illustrator** is an artist who draws pictures and diagrams for books and magazines. N-COUNT

illustrious /ɪlʌstriəs/. If you describe someone as an **illustrious** person, you mean that they are extremely well known because they have a high position in society or they have done something impressive. *...the most illustrious scientists of the century. ...his long and illustrious career.* ◆◇◇◇◇ ADJ-GRADED: usu ADJ n =distinguished

ill will; also spelled **ill-will. Ill will** is a feeling of hostility or spite that you have towards someone. *He didn't bear anyone any ill will... All this has created considerable ill-will towards the armed forces.* N-UNCOUNT =animosity

ill wind. You can describe an unfortunate event as an **ill wind** if someone benefits from it. The expression occurs in the proverb 'It's an ill wind that blows nobody any good', meaning that however bad something is, it usually has one or two good aspects. *Still, it's an ill wind, Mr Vicars; it sounds as if you have an unexpected holiday.* N-SING: usu *a* N

im-. Usually pronounced /ɪm-/ before an unstressed syllable, and /ɪm-/ before a stressed syllable. **Im-** is added to words that begin with 'm', 'p', or 'b' to form words with the opposite meaning. *He implied that we were emotionally immature... Don't stare at me – it's impolite!... The illness is triggered by a chemical imbalance in the brain.* PREFIX

I'm /aɪm/. **I'm** is the usual spoken form of 'I am'. *I'm sorry... I'm already late for my next appointment... I'm going out with an old friend.*

image /ɪmɪdʒ/ **images** ◆◆◆◆◇

1 If you have an **image** of something or someone, you have a picture or idea of them in your mind. *The image of art theft as a gentleman's crime is outdated... The words 'Cote d'Azur' conjure up images of sunny days in Mediterranean cafes.* N-COUNT: usu with supp

2 The **image** of a person, group, or organization is the way that they appear to other people. *The Prime Minister knows that his personal image is his greatest political asset... He has cultivated the image of an elder statesman... The tobacco industry has been trying to improve its image.* N-COUNT: oft with poss

3 An **image** is a picture or reflection of someone or something; a formal use. *...the way men respond to glamorous images of women on record sleeves... A computer in the machine creates an image on the screen.* N-COUNT

4 An **image** is a description of something in a poem or piece of creative writing; a formal use. *The natural images in the poem are meant to be suggestive of realities beyond themselves.* N-COUNT

5 If you **are the image of** someone else, you look very much like them. *Marianne's son was the image of his father.* PHRASE: V inflects

6 See also **mirror image.** • **spitting image**: see **spit.**

imagery /ɪmɪdʒri/ ◆◇◇◇◇

1 You can refer to the descriptions in something such as a poem or song, and the pictures they create in your mind, as its **imagery**; a formal use. *...the nature imagery of the ballad.* N-UNCOUNT

2 You can refer to pictures and representations of things as **imagery**, especially when they have symbolic significance; a formal use. *...artists whose imagery is in the surrealist mode.* N-UNCOUNT

imaginable /ɪmædʒɪnəbᵊl/ ◆◇◇◇◇

1 You use **imaginable** after a superlative such as 'best' or 'worst' to emphasize that something is extreme in some way. *...their imprisonment under some of the most horrible circumstances imaginable... He could not disguise that he had had the worst imaginable day for any minister.* ADJ: adj-superl n ADJ, adj-superl ADJ n PRAGMATICS =conceivable

2 You use **imaginable** after a word like 'every' or 'all' to emphasize that you are talking about all the possible examples of something. You use **imaginable** after 'no' to emphasize that something does not have the quality mentioned. *...all of the other imaginable ramifications of this technology... Parents encourage every activity imaginable. ...a place of no imaginable strategic value.* ADJ: ADJ n, n ADJ PRAGMATICS =possible

imaginary /ɪmædʒɪnəri, AM -neri/. An **imaginary** person, place, or thing exists only in your mind or in a story, and not in real life. *Lots of children have imaginary friends. ...creating an imaginary world.* ◆◇◇◇◇ ADJ: usu ADJ n

imagination /ɪmædʒɪneɪʃᵊn/ **imaginations** ◆◆◆◇◇

1 Your **imagination** is the ability that you have to form pictures or ideas in your mind of things that are new and exciting, or things that you have not experienced. *Antonia is a woman with a vivid imagination... Alistair had a logical mind, and little imagination... The Government approach displays a lack of imagination.* N-VAR

2 Your **imagination** is the part of your mind which allows you to form pictures or ideas of things that do not necessarily exist in real life. *Long before I ever went there, Africa was alive in my imagination.* N-COUNT: usu with supp =mind's eye

3 If you say that someone or something **captured** your **imagination**, you mean that you thought they were interesting or exciting when you saw them or heard them for the first time. *Italian football captured the imagination of the nation last season.* PHRASES V inflects =fascinate

4 If you say that something **stretches** your **imagination**, you mean that it is good because it makes you think about things that you hadn't thought about before. *Their films are exciting and really stretch the imagination.* V inflects

5 • **by no stretch of the imagination**: see **stretch.**

imaginative /ɪmædʒɪnətɪv/. If you describe someone or their ideas as **imaginative**, you are praising them because they are easily able to think of or create new or exciting things. *...an imaginative writer. ...hundreds of cooking ideas and imaginative recipes... They should adopt a more imaginative approach and investigate alternative uses for their property.* ♦ **imaginatively** *The hotel is decorated imaginatively and attractively.* ◆◆◇◇◇ ADJ-GRADED PRAGMATICS =inventive ≠unimaginative; ADV-GRADED: ADV with v

imagine /ɪmædʒɪn/ **imagines, imagining, imagined** ◆◆◆◆◇

1 If you **imagine** something, you think about it and your mind forms a picture or idea of it. *He could not imagine a more peaceful scene... She couldn't imagine living in a place like that... Can you imagine how she must have felt when Mary Brent turned up with me in tow?... Imagine you're lying on a beach, listening to the steady rhythm of waves lapping the shore... I can't imagine you being unfair to anyone, Leigh.* VERB =picture V n/-ing V wh V that V n -ing/prep

2 If you **imagine** that something is the case, you think that it is the case. *I imagine you're referring to Jean-Paul Sartre... We tend to imagine that the Victorians were very prim and proper... 'Was he meeting someone?'—'I imagine so.'* VERB =suppose V that V *so/not*

3 If you **imagine** something, you think that you have seen, heard, or experienced something, although actually you haven't. *Looking back on it now, I realised that I must have imagined the whole thing.* VERB =dream V n Also V that

imaging /ɪmɪdʒɪŋ/. **Imaging** is the process of forming or obtaining images by electronically tracing something such as sound waves, temperature, or chemicals, rather than by using light rays or ordinary photography. *Police and firemen were last night using thermal imaging cameras in a hunt for two missing children.* ◆◇◇◇◇ N-UNCOUNT

imaginings /ɪmædʒɪnɪŋz/. **Imaginings** are things that you think you have seen or heard, although actually you have not; a literary word. N-PLURAL

imam /ɪmɑːm/ **imams.** In Islam, an **imam** is a religious leader, especially the leader of a Muslim community or the person who lead the prayers in a mosque. ◆◇◇◇◇ N-COUNT

imbalance /ɪmbælǝns/ **imbalances.** If there is an **imbalance** in a situation, the things involved are not the same size, or are not the right size in proportion to each other. *...the imbalance between the two sides in this war. ...an international strategy to reduce trade imbalances.* ◆◇◇◇◇ N-VAR: oft N *in/between* pl-n =inequity

imbalanced /ɪmbælǝnst/. If you describe a situation as **imbalanced**, you mean that the elements within it are not evenly or fairly arranged. *...a markedly imbalanced geographical distribution of immigrants. ...the present imbalanced structure of world trade.* ADJ-GRADED =uneven

imbecile /ɪmbɪsiːl, AM -sǝl/ **imbeciles**

1 If you call someone an **imbecile**, you are showing that you think they are stupid or have done something stupid; an offensive use. *I don't want to deal with these imbeciles any longer.* N-COUNT PRAGMATICS =idiot

2 **Imbecile** means stupid. *It was an imbecile thing to do.* ADJ: ADJ n

3 An **imbecile** is a person who is mentally handicapped; an old-fashioned use which is now offensive. N-COUNT

imbibe /ɪmbaɪb/ **imbibes, imbibing, imbibed**

1 To **imbibe** alcohol means to drink it; a formal, often humorous use. *They were used to imbibing enormous quantities of alcohol... No one believes that current nondrinkers should be encouraged to start imbibing.* VERB V n V

2 If you **imbibe** ideas or arguments, you listen to them, accept them, and believe that they are right or true; a formal use. *As a clergyman's son he'd imbibed a set of mystical beliefs from the cradle.* VERB =absorb V n

imbroglio /ɪmbroʊlioʊ/ **imbroglios.** An **imbroglio** is a very confusing or complicated situation; a literary word. N-COUNT: usu with supp

imbue /ɪmbjuː/ **imbues, imbuing, imbued.** If someone or something **is imbued** with an idea, feeling, or quality, they become filled with it; a formal word. *As you listen, you notice how every single word is imbued with a breathless sense of wonder. ...men who can imbue their hearers with enthusiasm.* ♦ **imbued** *...a Guards officer imbued with a military sense of duty and loyalty.* ◆◇◇◇◇ VERB =infuse be V-ed *with* n V n *with* n ADJ: v-link ADJ *with* n

IMF /aɪ em ef/. **The IMF** is an international agency which is part of the United Nations. It tries to promote trade and improve economic conditions in the countries which belong to it, sometimes by lending them money. **IMF** is an abbreviation for 'International Monetary Fund'. ◆◆◇◇◇ N-PROPER: *the* N

imitate /ɪmɪteɪt/ **imitates, imitating, imitated** ◆◇◇◇◇

1 If you **imitate** someone, you copy what they do or produce. *...a genuine German musical which does not try to imitate the American model. ...a precedent which may be imitated by other activists in the future.* VERB V n

2 If you **imitate** a person or animal, you copy the way they speak or behave, usually because you are trying to be funny. *Clarence screws up his face and imitates the Colonel again.* VERB =mimic V n

imitation /ɪmɪteɪʃǝn/ **imitations** ◆◇◇◇◇

1 An **imitation** of something is a copy of it. *...the most accurate imitation of Chinese architecture in Europe.* N-COUNT: oft N *of* n

2 **Imitation** means copying someone else's actions. *They discussed important issues in imitation of their elders... Molly learned her golf by imitation.* N-UNCOUNT: oft *in* N *of* n

3 **Imitation** things are not genuine but are made to look as if they are. *...a complete set of Dickens bound in imitation leather.* ADJ: ADJ n

4 If someone does an **imitation** of another person, they copy the way they speak or behave, sometimes in order to be funny. *He gave his imitation of Queen Elizabeth's royal wave... I could do a pretty good imitation of him.* N-COUNT: usu N *of* n =impression

imitative /ɪmɪtǝtɪv, AM -teɪt-/. People and animals who are **imitative** copy others' behaviour. *Babies of eight to twelve months are generally highly imitative.* ADJ-GRADED

imitator /ɪmɪteɪtǝʳ/ **imitators.** An **imitator** is someone who copies what someone else does, or copies the way they speak or behave. *He doesn't take chances; that's why he's survived and most of his imitators haven't. ...a group of Elvis imitators.* N-COUNT

immaculate /ɪmækjʊlǝt/ ◆◇◇◇◇

1 If you describe something as **immaculate**, you are praising it because it is extremely clean, tidy, or neat. *Her front room was kept immaculate. ...the waiter, dressed in immaculate bow tie and suit.* ♦ **immaculately** *As always he was immaculately dressed.* ADJ-GRADED =spotless ADV-GRADED

2 If you say that something is **immaculate**, you are emphasizing that it is perfect, without any mistakes or flaws at all. *...goalkeeper Peter Schmeichel, who was immaculate under first-half pressure... The 1979 Chevrolet is in immaculate condition.* ♦ **immaculately** *The orchestra plays immaculately... It is difficult to praise this immaculately researched work too highly.* ADJ-GRADED PRAGMATICS =flawless ADV-GRADED: ADV with v

immanent /ɪmǝnǝnt/. If you say that a quality is **immanent** in a particular thing, you mean that the thing has that quality, and cannot exist or be imagined without it; a formal word. *...a radical analysis of hierarchy as the immanent principle of Western society... God is immanent in the world.* ADJ

immaterial /ɪmǝtɪǝriǝl/. If you say that something is **immaterial**, you mean that it is not important or not relevant. *Whether we like him or not is immaterial.* ◆◇◇◇◇ ADJ: v-link ADJ =irrelevant

immature /ɪmǝtjʊǝʳ, AM -tʊr/ ◆◇◇◇◇

1 Something or someone that is **immature** is not yet completely grown or fully developed. *The birds were in immature plumage... She is emotionally immature.* ♦ **immaturity** /ɪmǝtjʊǝrɪti, AM -tʊr-/ *In spite of some immaturity in the figure drawing and painting, it showed real imagination.* ADJ N-UNCOUNT

2 If you describe someone as **immature**, you are being critical of them because they do not behave in a sensible or responsible way. *...grossly immature drivers who flout the rules of the road... She's just being childish and immature.* ♦ **immaturity** *...his immaturity and lack of social skills.* ADJ-GRADED PRAGMATICS N-UNCOUNT

immeasurable /ɪmeʒǝrǝbǝl/. If you describe something as **immeasurable**, you are emphasizing how great it is; a formal word. *I felt an immeasurable love for him... His contribution is immeasurable, almost impossible to put into words.* ADJ PRAGMATICS

immeasurably /ɪmeʒǝrǝbli/. You use **immeasurably** to emphasize the degree or extent of a process or quality; a formal word. *They have improved immeasurably since the arrival of their Australian coach last November... The situation in 1989 was immeasurably more acute than it had been 25 years previously.* ADV: ADV with v, ADV adj PRAGMATICS =infinitely

immediacy /ɪmiːdiǝsi/. The **immediacy** of an event or situation is the quality that it has which makes it seem important or exciting because it is happening at the present time. *Do they understand the severity and the immediacy of the crisis that's facing timber workers?... The books that result have intensity and a fascinating immediacy, far beyond that of ordinary narrative.* N-UNCOUNT: oft N *of* n

immediate /ɪmiːdiǝt/ ◆◆◆◇◇

1 An **immediate** result, action, or reaction happens or is done without any delay. *These tragic incidents have had an immediate effect... My immediate reaction was just disgust.* ADJ: usu ADJ n =instant

2 **Immediate** needs and concerns exist at the present time and must be dealt with quickly. *Relief agencies say the immediate problem is not a lack of food, but transportation.* ADJ-GRADED: usu ADJ n =pressing

3 You use **immediate** to describe something or something that comes just before or just after something or someone else in a sequence. *In the immediate aftermath of the riots, a mood of hope and reconciliation sprang up... His immediate superior, General Geichenko, had singled him out for special mention.* ADJ: ADJ n

4 You use **immediate** to describe an area or position that is next to or very near a particular place or person. *Only a handful had returned to work in the immediate vicinity... I was seated at Sauter's immediate left.* ADJ: ADJ n

5 Your **immediate** family are the members of your family who are most closely related to you, for example your parents, children, brothers, and sisters. *The presence of his immediate family is obviously having a calming effect on him.* ADJ: ADJ n =close

immediately /ɪmiːdiətli/ ◆◆◆◆◇

1 If something happens **immediately**, it happens without any delay. *He immediately flung himself to the floor... Ingrid answered Peter's letter immediately.* ADV: ADV with v =at once

2 If something is **immediately** apparent, it can be seen or understood without any delay. *The cause of the accident was not immediately apparent.* ADV: ADV adj =instantly

3 Immediately is used to indicate that someone or something is closely and directly involved in a situation. *The man immediately responsible for this misery is the province's governor... We had the people immediately concerned in the plot.* ADV: ADV adj/-ed

4 Immediately is used to emphasize that something comes next, or is next to something else. *They wish to begin immediately after dinner... She always sits immediately behind the driver... Immediately to our right the old German summer resort was awakening.* ADV: ADV prep/adj =directly

5 If one thing happens **immediately** something else happens, it happens after that event, without any delay. *Immediately I've done it I feel completely disgusted with myself.* CONJ-SUBORD =as soon as

immemorial /ɪmɪmɔːriəl/

1 If you say that something has been happening **since time immemorial** or **from time immemorial**, you are emphasizing that it has been happening for many centuries; a literary expression. *It has remained virtually unchanged since time immemorial... From time immemorial there has been the belief that there are good and bad places to be.* PHRASE PRAGMATICS

2 You use **immemorial** to indicate that something has existed for many centuries; a literary use. *...a modern version of an immemorial myth.* ADJ: usu ADJ n =ancient

immense /ɪmens/. If you describe something as **immense**, you mean that it is extremely large or great. *...an immense cloud of smoke... With immense relief I stopped running.* ♦ **immensity** /ɪmensɪti/ *The immensity of the universe is difficult to grasp.* ◆◆◇◇◇ ADJ-GRADED: usu ADJ n =enormous; N-UNCOUNT: usu N *of* n

immensely /ɪmensli/. You use **immensely** to emphasize the degree or extent of a quality, feeling, or process. *Wind surfing can be strenuous but immensely exciting... I enjoyed this movie immensely.* ◆◇◇◇◇ ADV: usu ADV adj, also ADV after v PRAGMATICS =enormously

immerse /ɪmɜːʳs/ **immerses, immersing, immersed** ◆◇◇◇◇

1 If you **immerse** yourself in something that you are doing, you become completely involved in it. *Their commitments do not permit them to immerse themselves in current affairs as fully as they might wish.* ♦ **immersed** *He's really becoming immersed in his work.* VERB =engross V pron-refl *in* n; ADJ-GRADED: v-link ADJ *in* n

2 If something **is immersed** in a liquid, someone puts it into the liquid so that it is completely covered. *The electrodes are immersed in liquid.* VB: usu passive =submerged *be* V-ed *in* n

immersion /ɪmɜːʳʃᵊn/

1 Someone's **immersion in** a subject is their complete involvement in it. *...long-term assignments that allowed them total immersion in their subjects.* N-UNCOUNT: N *in* n

2 Immersion of something in a liquid means putting it into the liquid so that it is completely covered. *The wood had become swollen from prolonged immersion.* N-UNCOUNT: oft N *in* n

immigrant /ɪmɪgrənt/ **immigrants.** An **immigrant** is a person who has come to live in a country from some other country. *...illegal immigrants. ...immigrant visas.* ◆◆◆◇◇ N-COUNT =settler

immigrate /ɪmɪgreɪt/ **immigrates, immigrating, immigrated.** If someone **immigrates** to a particular country, they leave their native country to live in that country. *...a Russian-born professor who had immigrated to the United States... He immigrated from Ulster in 1848... 10,000 people are expected to immigrate in the next two years.* VB: no passive V *to* n V *from* n V

immigration /ɪmɪgreɪʃᵊn/ ◆◆◆◇◇

1 Immigration is the coming of people into a country in order to live and work there. *The government has decided to tighten its immigration policy. ...immigration into Europe.* N-UNCOUNT

2 Immigration or **immigration control** is the place at a port, airport, or international border where officials check the passports of people who wish to come into the country. N-UNCOUNT

imminent /ɪmɪnənt/. If you say that something is **imminent**, especially something unpleasant, you mean it is almost certain to happen very soon. *There appeared no imminent danger... They warned that an attack is imminent.* ♦ **imminence** *The imminence of war was on everyone's mind.* ◆◆◇◇◇ ADJ; N-UNCOUNT: usu N *of* n

immobile /ɪmoʊbaɪl, AM -bᵊl/ ◆◇◇◇◇

1 Someone or something that is **immobile** is completely still. *Joe remained as immobile as if he had been carved out of rock.* ♦ **immobility** /ɪmoʊbɪlɪti/ *Hyde maintained the rigid immobility of his shoulders.* ADJ-GRADED: usu v-link ADJ =motionless; N-UNCOUNT

2 Someone or something that is **immobile** is unable to move or unable to be moved. *A riding accident left him immobile. ...a very heavy or immobile object.* ♦ **immobility** *Again, the pain locked me into immobility.* ADJ: usu v-link ADJ; N-UNCOUNT

immobilize /ɪmoʊbɪlaɪz/ **immobilizes, immobilizing, immobilized;** also spelled **immobilise** in British English. To **immobilize** something or someone means to stop them from moving or operating. *A car alarm system that not only sounds off, but also immobilises the engine... The knee and ankle joints must be immobilized – this usually means up to six weeks in plaster.* VERB V n

immoderate /ɪmɒdərət/. If you describe something as **immoderate**, you disapprove of it because it is too extreme; a formal word. *He launched an immoderate tirade on Turner.* ADJ-GRADED: usu ADJ n PRAGMATICS =excessive

immodest /ɪmɒdɪst/

1 If you describe someone's behaviour as **immodest**, you mean that it shocks or embarrasses you because you think that it is rude. ADJ-GRADED: usu ADJ n

2 If you say that someone is **immodest**, you disapprove of the way in which they often boast about how good, important, or clever they are. *He could become ungraciously immodest about his own capacities.* ADJ-GRADED: usu v-link ADJ PRAGMATICS =boastful ≠modest

immoral /ɪmɒrᵊl, AM -mɔːr-/. If you describe someone or their behaviour as **immoral**, you believe that their behaviour is morally wrong. *...those who think that birth control and abortion are immoral.* ♦ **immorality** /ɪmərælɪti/ *...a reflection of our society's immorality.* ◆◇◇◇◇ ADJ-GRADED PRAGMATICS; N-UNCOUNT

immortal /ɪmɔːʳtᵊl/ **immortals** ◆◇◇◇◇

1 Someone or something that is **immortal** is famous and likely to be remembered for a long time. *...the immortal Reverend Dr Spooner. ...Wuthering Heights, Emily Bronte's immortal love story... Maybe my work is not immortal, but it will live for a while.* ▶ An **immortal** is someone who is immortal. *He called Moore 'one of the immortals of soccer'.* ♦ **immortality** /ɪmɔːʳtælɪti/ *Some people want to achieve immortality through their works.* ADJ; N-COUNT: usu pl; N-UNCOUNT

2 Someone or something that is **immortal** will live or last for ever and never die or be destroyed. *The pharaohs, after all, were considered gods and therefore immortal.* ▶ An **immortal** is an immortal being. *...porcelain figurines of the Chinese immortals.* ♦ **immortality** *The Greeks accepted belief in the immortality of the soul.* ADJ ≠mortal; N-COUNT: usu pl; N-UNCOUNT

3 If you refer to someone's **immortal** words, you mean they what they said is well-known or memorable, and you are usually about to quote it. *Everyone knows Teddy Roosevelt's immortal words, 'Speak softly and carry a big stick.'... Mr Mellor quoted the immortal line of Max Miller: Always quit when they are asking for more.* ADJ: ADJ n

immortalize /ɪmɔːʳtəlaɪz/ **immortalizes, immortalizing, immortalized;** also spelled **immortalise** in British English. If someone or something **is immortalized** in a story, film, or work of VERB art, they appear in that story, film, or work of art, and so will be remembered or are well-known; used in written English. *The town of Whitby was immortalised in Bram Stoker's famous Dracula story... D H Lawrence immortalised her in his novel 'Women in Love'. ...Colditz, the grim fortress immortalised by films and TV.* be V-ed / V n / V-ed

immovable /ɪmuːvəbᵊl/
1 An **immovable** object is fixed and cannot be moved. ADJ: usu ADJ n
2 If someone is **immovable** in their attitude to something, they will not change their mind. *On one issue, however, she was immovable.* ADJ: usu v-link ADJ =resolute

immune /ɪmjuːn/ ◆◆◆◇◇
1 If you are **immune** to a particular disease, you cannot be affected by it. *This blood test will show whether or not you're immune to the disease... Most adults are immune to Rubella.* ♦ **immunity** /ɪmjuːnɪti/ *Birds in outside cages develop immunity to airborne bacteria.* ADJ: v-link ADJ, usu ADJ *to* n; N-UNCOUNT: oft N *to* n
2 An **immune** response or reaction is a reaction by the body's immune system to something harmful that is affecting it; a technical use in biology. *It is hoped the procedure will trigger an immune response that will wipe out HIV-infected cells while leaving non-infected cells unharmed.* ADJ: ADJ n
3 If someone or something is **immune** to something that happens or is done, they are not affected by it. *Whilst Marc did gradually harden himself to the poverty, he did not become immune to the sight of death... Football is not immune to economic recession.* ADJ: v-link ADJ, usu ADJ *to* n
4 Someone or something that is **immune** from a particular process or situation is able to escape it. *Members of the Bundestag are immune from prosecution for corruption... No one is immune from scandal.* ♦ **immunity** *The police are offering immunity to witnesses who help identify the murderers.* • See also **diplomatic immunity**. ADJ: v-link ADJ, usu ADJ *from* n =exempt; N-UNCOUNT =exemption

immune system, immune systems. Your **immune system** consists of all the organs and processes in your body which protect you from illness and infection. ◆◆◇◇◇ N-COUNT: usu sing

immunize /ɪmjʊnaɪz/ **immunizes, immunizing, immunized;** also spelled **immunise** in British English. If people or animals **are immunized**, they are made immune to a particular disease, often by being given an injection. *We should require that every student is immunized against hepatitis B... The monkeys used in those experiments had previously been immunized with a vaccine made from killed infected cells... If parents decide not to have their child immunized, they are responsible for keeping their child as healthy as possible.* ♦ **immunization** /ɪmjʊnaɪzeɪʃᵊn/ **immunizations** *...universal immunization against childhood diseases... Only half of America's children get the full range of immunisations.* ◆◇◇◇◇ VB: usu passive =innoculate, vaccinate; be V-ed *against* n; be V-ed; have n V-ed; N-VAR =innoculation, vaccination

immutable /ɪmjuːtəbᵊl/. Something that is **immutable** will never change or cannot be changed; a formal word. *...the eternal and immutable principles of right and wrong.* ADJ

imp /ɪmp/ **imps.** In fairy stories, an **imp** is a small, magical creature that often causes trouble in a playful way. N-COUNT =sprite

impact, impacts, impacting, impacted. The noun is pronounced /ɪmpækt/. The verb is pronounced /ɪmpækt/. ◆◆◆◆◇
1 The **impact** that something has on a situation, process, or person is a sudden and powerful effect that it has on them. *They say they expect the meeting to have a marked impact on the future of the country... The major impact of this epidemic worldwide is yet to come... When an executive comes into a new job, he wants to quickly make an impact.* N-COUNT: usu sing, oft N *on* n
2 An **impact** is the action of one object hitting another, or the force with which one object hits another. *The plane is destroyed, a complete wreck: the pilot must have died on impact... A running track should be capable of absorbing the impact of a runner's foot landing on it.* N-VAR
3 To **impact** on a situation, process, or person means to affect them; used mainly in American English and journalism. *Such schemes mean little unless they impact on people... The Gulf crisis also impacted on the period to 28 September. ...the potential for women to impact the political process.* ♦ **impacted** *Somebody who is a foreign investor and more sensitive about the public profile will be more impacted by that pressure.* VERB =affect; V *on/upon* n; V n; ADJ-GRADED: usu v-link ADJ =affected
4 If one object **impacts** on another, it hits it with great force; a formal use. *...the sharp tinkle of metal impacting on stone... According to the air force, the missile merely impacted with the ground prematurely... When a large object impacts the Earth, it makes a crater similar to the craters which we see on the Moon.* VERB; V *on/upon/with* n; V n; Also V

impair /ɪmpeəʳ/ **impairs, impairing, impaired.** If something **impairs** something such as an ability or the functioning of something, it damages it or makes it worse; a formal word. *Consumption of alcohol impairs your ability to drive a car or operate machinery... His movements were painfully impaired by arthritis.* ♦ **impaired** *The blast left him with permanently impaired hearing.* ◆◇◇◇◇ VERB; V n; ADJ-GRADED

-impaired /-ɪmpeəʳd/. Someone who is **hearing-impaired**, for example, has a disability affecting their hearing. *More than 1 in 20 of the population is hearing-impaired to some extent.* ▶ **The hearing-impaired**, for example, are people who have a disability affecting their hearing. *...giving a voice to the speech-impaired.* COMB in ADJ; COMB in N-PLURAL: *the* N

impairment /ɪmpeəʳmənt/ **impairments.** If someone has an **impairment**, they have a condition which prevents their eyes, ears, or brain from working properly. *He has a visual impairment in the right eye.* N-VAR: usu with supp

impale /ɪmpeɪl/ **impales, impaling, impaled.** To **impale** something on a pointed object means to cause it to be pierced by that object. *Researchers observed one bird impale a rodent on a cactus... Lenny swayed for a moment, then dropped to the ground, impaling himself on his switchblade... The boy died after being impaled on railings when he slipped while playing.* VERB =skewer; V n *on* n; Also V n, V n *with* n

impart /ɪmpɑːʳt/ **imparts, imparting, imparted** ◆◇◇◇◇
1 If you **impart** information to people, you tell it to them; a formal use. *The ability to impart knowledge and command respect is the essential qualification for teachers... Think carefully before reading on. I am about to impart knowledge to you that you will never be able to forget.* VERB =convey; V n; V n *to* n
2 If someone or something **imparts** a particular quality to something, they give it that quality; a formal use. *She managed to impart great elegance to the unpretentious dress she was wearing... His production of Harold Pinter's play fails to impart a sense of excitement or danger.* VERB; V n *to* n; V n

impartial /ɪmpɑːʳʃᵊl/. Someone who is **impartial** is not directly involved in a particular situation, and is therefore able to give a fair opinion or decision about it. *As an impartial observer my analysis is supposed to be objective... Careers officers offer impartial advice, guidance and information to all pupils.* ♦ **impartiality** /ɪmpɑːʳʃiælɪti/ *...a justice system lacking impartiality by democratic standards.* ♦ **impartially** *He has vowed to oversee the elections impartially.* ◆◇◇◇◇ ADJ-GRADED =neutral ≠biased; N-UNCOUNT; ADV: ADV with v

impassable /ɪmpɑːsəbᵊl, -pæs-/. If a road, path, or route is **impassable**, it is impossible to travel over because it is blocked or in bad condition. ADJ

impasse /æmpæs, ɪm-/. If people are in a difficult position in which it is impossible to make any progress, you can refer to the situation as an **impasse**. *The company says it has reached an impasse in negotiations with the union.* ◆◇◇◇◇ N-SING =deadlock

impassioned /ɪmpæʃᵊnd/. If someone makes an **impassioned** speech or plea, they express their strong feelings about an issue in a forceful way; used in journalism and written English. *He made an impassioned appeal for peace.* ◆◇◇◇◇ ADJ-GRADED: usu ADJ n =fervent

impassive /ɪmpæsɪv/. If someone is **impassive** or their face is **impassive**, they are not showing ◆◇◇◇◇ ADJ-GRADED =emotionless any emotion; used in written English. *He searched Hill's impassive face for some indication that he understood... As the foreman of the jury announced the verdict, Miss Allan remained impassive.* ♦ **impassively** *The lawyer looked impassively at him and said nothing.* ADV: ADV with v

impatient /ɪmpeɪʃənt/ ◆◆◇◇◇

1 If you are **impatient**, you are annoyed because you have to wait too long for something. *He is impatient as the first hour passes and then another... The big clubs are becoming increasingly impatient at the rate of progress.* ADJ-GRADED: v-link ADJ ♦ **impatiently** *People have been waiting impatiently for a chance to improve the situation.* ADV-GRADED: ADV with v ♦ **impatience** /ɪmpeɪʃəns/ *There is considerable impatience with the slow pace of political change... Impatience is growing after three days in which nothing has been achieved.* N-UNCOUNT

2 If you are **impatient**, you are easily irritated by things. *Beware of being too impatient with others... He threw it aside with an impatient gesture and another oath and walked off.* ADJ-GRADED ♦ **impatiently** *'Come on, David,' Harry said impatiently.* ADV-GRADED: ADV with v ♦ **impatience** *There was a hint of impatience in his tone.* N-UNCOUNT

3 If you are **impatient** to do something or **impatient for** something to happen, you are eager to do it or for it to happen and do not want to wait. *He didn't want to tell Mr Morrisson why he was impatient to get home... They are impatient for jobs and security.* ADJ: v-link ADJ, ADJ to-inf, ADJ *for* n ♦ **impatience** *She showed impatience to continue the climb.* N-UNCOUNT

impeach /ɪmpiːtʃ/ **impeaches, impeaching, impeached.** ◆◇◇◇◇ VERB If a court or a group in authority **impeaches** a president or other senior official, it charges them with committing a crime which makes them unfit for office. *...an opposition move to impeach the President.* V n

impeachment /ɪmpiːtʃmənt/ **impeachments.** ◆◇◇◇◇ N-VAR The **impeachment** of a senior official is their trial for a crime which makes them unfit for office. *If his action proves to be unconstitutional, that would be grounds for impeachment.*

impeccable /ɪmpekəbəl/. ◆◇◇◇◇ ADJ-GRADED PRAGMATICS =faultless If you describe something such as someone's behaviour or appearance as **impeccable**, you are emphasizing that it is excellent and has no faults. *She had impeccable taste in clothes... Her academic credentials are impeccable.* ♦ **impeccably** /ɪmpekəbli/ *He was charming, considerate and impeccably mannered.* ADV-GRADED =faultlessly

impecunious /ɪmpɪkjuːniəs/. ADJ-GRADED =poor Someone who is **impecunious** has very little money; a formal word.

impede /ɪmpiːd/ **impedes, impeding, impeded.** ◆◇◇◇◇ VERB =hinder, hamper If you **impede** someone or something, you make their movement, development, or progress difficult; a formal word. *Debris and fallen rock are impeding the progress of the rescue workers.* V n

impediment /ɪmpedɪmənt/ **impediments** ◆◇◇◇◇

1 Something that is an **impediment** to a person or thing makes their movement, development, or progress difficult; a formal use. *He was satisfied there was no legal impediment to the marriage.* N-COUNT: oft N *to* n, also *without* N =obstruction

2 Someone who has a speech **impediment** has a disability which makes speaking difficult. *John's slight speech impediment made it difficult for his mother to understand him.* N-COUNT

impel /ɪmpel/ **impels, impelling, impelled.** VERB =force, compel When something such as an emotion **impels** you to do something, it affects you so strongly that you feel forced to do it. *...the courage and competitiveness which impels him to take risks...* V n to-inf *I felt impelled to go on speaking.* V-ed

impending /ɪmpendɪŋ/. ◆◇◇◇◇ ADJ: ADJ n An **impending** event is one that is going to happen very soon; a formal word. *On the morning of the expedition I awoke with a feeling of impending disaster... He'd spoken to Simon that morning of his impending marriage.*

impenetrable /ɪmpenɪtrəbəl/ ◆◇◇◇◇

1 If you describe something such as a barrier or a forest as **impenetrable**, you mean that it is impossible or very difficult to get through. *...the Caucasus range, an almost impenetrable barrier between Europe and Asia.* ADJ-GRADED: usu ADJ n =impassable

2 If you describe something such as a book or a theory as **impenetrable**, you are emphasizing that it is impossible or very difficult to understand. *His philosophical work is notoriously impenetrable. ...these impenetrable poems.* ADJ-GRADED PRAGMATICS =incomprehensible ♦ **impenetrably** *Every day computers churned out seven impenetrably detailed reports on product sales.* ADV-GRADED: ADV adj =incomprehensibly

imperative /ɪmperətɪv/ **imperatives** ◆◇◇◇◇

1 If it is **imperative** that something is done, that thing is extremely important and must be done; a formal use. *It was imperative that he act as naturally as possible... That's why it is imperative to know what your rights are at such a time... The events of the past few days make it imperative for her to act.* ADJ-GRADED: usu v-link ADJ =vital

2 An **imperative** is something that is extremely important and must be done; a formal use. *The most important political imperative is to limit the number of US casualties. ...the needs of those unable to respond to the imperatives of an enterprise culture.* N-COUNT: usu with supp

3 In grammar, a clause that is in **the imperative**, or in **the imperative** mood, contains the base form of a verb and usually has no subject. Examples are 'Go away' and 'Please be careful'. Clauses of this kind are typically used to tell someone to do something. N-SING: *the* N

4 An **imperative** is a verb in the base form that is used, usually without a subject, in an imperative clause. N-COUNT

imperceptible /ɪmpərseptɪbəl/. ADJ =indiscernible Something that is **imperceptible** is so small or slight that it is not noticed or cannot be seen. *Brian's hesitation was almost imperceptible.* ♦ **imperceptibly** /ɪmpərseptɪbli/ *The disease develops gradually and imperceptibly until it is too late to do anything about it.* ADV: usu ADV with v, also ADV adj =indiscernibly

imperfect /ɪmpɜːrfɪkt/ ◆◇◇◇◇

1 Something that is **imperfect** has faults and is not exactly as you would like it to be; a formal use. *We live in an imperfect world... They have a huge selection of perfect, slightly imperfect and discontinued cookers, fridges and so on. ...a child's imperfect understanding of what is going on between their parents.* ADJ-GRADED =faulty, flawed ≠perfect ♦ **imperfectly** *This effect was imperfectly understood by designers at that time. ...in a country whose language she spoke imperfectly.* ADV-GRADED: usu ADV -ed/adj

2 In grammar, **the imperfect** or **the imperfect** tense of a verb is used in describing continuous situations or repeated actions in the past. In English, the past continuous (as in 'I was reading') is sometimes called the **imperfect.** N-SING: *the* N

imperfection /ɪmpərfekʃən/ **imperfections** ◆◇◇◇◇

1 An **imperfection** in someone or something is a fault, weakness, or undesirable feature that they have. *He concedes that there are imperfections in the socialist system... I was obsessed by my physical imperfections.* N-VAR =flaw, failing

2 An **imperfection** in something is a small mark or damaged area which may spoil its appearance. *Optical scanners ensure that imperfections in the cloth are located and removed.* N-COUNT =flaw, blemish

imperial /ɪmpɪəriəl/ ◆◆◇◇◇

1 **Imperial** is used to refer to things or people that are or were connected with an empire. *...the Imperial Palace in Tokyo... They executed Russia's imperial family in 1918.* ADJ: ADJ n

2 The **imperial** system of measurement uses inches, feet, and yards to measure length, ounces, and pounds to measure weight, and pints and gallons to measure volume. ADJ: ADJ n

imperialism /ɪmpɪəriəlɪzəm/. ◆◇◇◇◇ N-UNCOUNT **Imperialism** is a system in which a rich and powerful country controls other countries, or a desire for control over other countries; often used showing disapproval.

imperialist /ɪmpɪəriəlɪst/ **imperialists.** ◆◇◇◇◇ ADJ: usu ADJ n **Imperialist** means relating to or based on imperialism; often used showing disapproval. *The developed nations have all benefited from their imperialist exploitation.* ► An **imperialist** is someone who has imperialist views. *He claims that imperialists* N-COUNT *are trying to re-establish colonial rule in the country.*

imperialistic /ɪmpɪəriəlɪstɪk/. If you describe a country as **imperialistic**, you disapprove of it because it wants control over other countries. *They were warlike and imperialistic.* ADJ PRAGMATICS

imperil /ɪmperɪl/ **imperils, imperilling, imperilled;** spelled **imperiling, imperiled** in American English. Something that **imperils** you puts you in danger; a formal word. *'You imperilled the lives of other road users by your driving,' the judge said.* VERB =endanger; V n

imperious /ɪmpɪəriəs/. If you describe someone as **imperious**, you mean that they have a proud manner and expect to be obeyed; used in written English. *Her attitude may be imperious at times but that is more than compensated by her bravery... From across the desk she gave him a witheringly imperious look.* ♦ **imperiously** *Imperiously she beckoned me out of the room.* ADJ-GRADED =haughty; ADV-GRADED: ADV with v

imperishable /ɪmperɪʃəbəl/. Something that is **imperishable** cannot disappear or be destroyed; a literary word. *My memories are within me, imperishable.* ADJ =enduring

impermanent /ɪmpɜːʳmənənt/. Something that is **impermanent** does not last for ever; a formal word. *To see him standing there, against the vacant sky, is to be reminded just how small and how impermanent we are.* ♦ **impermanence** /ɪmpɜːʳmənəns/ *He was convinced of the impermanence of his work.* ADJ-GRADED =transient ≠permanent; N-UNCOUNT

impermeable /ɪmpɜːʳmiəbəl/. Something that is **impermeable** will not allow fluid to pass through it; a formal word. *The canoe is made from an impermeable wood.* ADJ =impervious

impersonal /ɪmpɜːʳsənəl/ ◆◇◇◇◇

1 If you describe a place, organization, or activity as **impersonal**, you mean that it is not very friendly and makes you feel unimportant because it involves or is used by a large number of people. *Before then many children were cared for in large impersonal orphanages... The health service has been criticized for being too impersonal.* ADJ-GRADED

2 If you describe someone's behaviour as **impersonal**, you mean that they act towards other people in a detached way, not caring particularly who they are. *We must be as impersonal as a surgeon with his knife... I gave Coe an impersonal stare.* ♦ **impersonally** *The doctor treated Ted gently but impersonally.* ADJ-GRADED =objective, dispassionate; ADV-GRADED

3 An **impersonal** room, statistic, or label does not give any information about the character of the person to which it belongs or relates. *The rest of the room was neat and impersonal... History reduces the carnage to impersonal numbers.* ADJ-GRADED

impersonate /ɪmpɜːʳsəneɪt/ **impersonates, impersonating, impersonated.** If someone **impersonates** a person, they pretend to be that person, either to deceive people or to make people laugh. *He was returned to prison in 1977 for impersonating a police officer... Tom was a brilliant mimic who could impersonate most of the college staff.* ♦ **impersonation** /ɪmpɜːʳsəneɪʃən/ **impersonations** *She excelled at impersonations of his teachers, which provided great amusement for him.* ◆◇◇◇◇ VERB; V n; N-COUNT: oft N of n

impersonator /ɪmpɜːʳsəneɪtəʳ/ **impersonators.** An **impersonator** is a stage performer who impersonates famous people. N-COUNT =impressionist

impertinence /ɪmpɜːʳtɪnəns/ **impertinences.** If someone talks or behaves in a rather impolite and disrespectful way, you can call this behaviour **impertinence** or an **impertinence**; a formal word. *The sheer impertinence of this man is phenomenal!.* N-VAR =impudence, cheek

impertinent /ɪmpɜːʳtɪnənt/. If someone talks or behaves in a rather impolite and disrespectful way, you can say that they are being **impertinent**; a formal word. *Would it be impertinent to ask where exactly you were?... I don't like strangers who ask impertinent questions.* ADJ-GRADED: oft it v-link ADJ to-inf =impudent, cheeky

imperturbable /ɪmpəʳtɜːʳbəbəl/. If you describe someone as **imperturbable**, you mean that they remain calm and untroubled, even in a situation that is disturbing; used in written English. *Thomas, of course, was cool and aloof and imperturbable.* ADJ-GRADED

impervious /ɪmpɜːʳviəs/

1 Someone or something that is **impervious** to someone's actions is not affected or influenced by them. *She seems almost impervious to the criticism from all sides... The political system there has been impervious to all suggestions of change.* ADJ-GRADED: usu v-link ADJ, usu ADJ to n

2 Something that is **impervious** to water, heat, or a particular object is able to resist it or stop it passing through it. *The floorcovering you select will need to be impervious to water. ...a layer of impervious rock.* ADJ: oft ADJ to n =impermeable

impetuosity /ɪmpetʃuɒsɪti/. **Impetuosity** is the quality of being impetuous. *With characteristic impetuosity, he announced he was leaving school.* N-UNCOUNT

impetuous /ɪmpetʃuəs/. If you describe someone as **impetuous**, you mean that they are likely to act quickly and suddenly without thinking or being careful. *He was young and impetuous... He tended to react in a heated and impetuous way.* ADJ-GRADED PRAGMATICS =rash, impulsive

impetus /ɪmpɪtəs/. Something that gives a process **impetus** or an **impetus** makes it happen or progress more quickly. *This decision will give renewed impetus to the economic regeneration of east London... She was restless and needed a new impetus for her talent.* ◆◇◇◇◇ N-UNCOUNT: also a N, oft N for n =stimulus

impinge /ɪmpɪndʒ/ **impinges, impinging, impinged.** Something that **impinges** on you affects you to some extent; a formal word. *...the cuts in defence spending that have impinged on two of the region's largest employers.* VERB =encroach; V on/upon n

impious /ɪmpiəs/. If you describe someone as **impious**, you mean that they show a lack of respect or religious reverence; a formal word. ADJ-GRADED =irreverent

impish /ɪmpɪʃ/. If you describe someone or their behaviour as **impish**, you mean that they are rather cheeky or naughty in a playful way. *Gillespie is well known for his impish sense of humour.* ♦ **impishly** *He smiled at me impishly.* ADJ-GRADED; ADV-GRADED

implacable /ɪmplækəbəl/. If you say that someone is **implacable**, you mean that they have very strong feelings, usually feelings of hostility or disapproval, which you are unable to change. *...the threat of invasion by a ruthless and implacable enemy... The move has won the implacable opposition of many economists.* ♦ **implacably** *His union was implacably opposed to the privatization of the company.* ◆◇◇◇◇ ADJ-GRADED; ADV-GRADED: usu ADV -ed/adj, also ADV after v

implant, implants, implanting, implanted. The verb is pronounced /ɪmplɑːnt, -plænt/. The noun is pronounced /ɪmplɑːnt, -plænt/. ◆◇◇◇◇

1 To **implant** something into a person's body means to put it there, usually by means of a medical operation. *Doctors in Arizona say they have implanted an artificial heart into a 46-year-old woman... Two days later, they implanted the fertilized eggs back inside me. ...a surgically implanted birth-control device.* ♦ **implantation** /ɪmplɑːnteɪʃən, -plæn-/ *The embryos were tested to determine their sex prior to implantation.* VERB; V n in/into n; V n adv/prep; V-ed; N-UNCOUNT

2 An **implant** is something that is implanted into a person's body. *They felt a woman had a right to choose to have a breast implant.* N-COUNT

3 When an egg or embryo **implants** in the womb, it becomes established there and can then develop. *Non-identical twins are the result of two fertilised eggs implanting in the uterus at the same time.* ♦ **implantation** *...the 11 days required to allow for normal implantation of a fertilized egg.* VERB; V in n; Also V; N-UNCOUNT

4 If you **implant** an idea or attitude in people, you make it become accepted or believed. *The diagram implanted a dangerous prejudice firmly in the minds of countless economics students... Gregory's father had implanted in him an ambition to obtain an education... This would implant the idea that the communists are the legitimate rulers of the country.* VERB =sow; V n in/into n; V n

implausible /ɪmplɔːzɪbəl/. If you describe something as **implausible**, you believe that it is ADJ-GRADED unlikely to be true. *I had to admit it sounded like a convenient and implausible excuse... It seems implausible that the projects would have gone ahead without her backing.* ♦ **implausibly** *They are, rather implausibly, close friends.* ADV-GRADED

implement, implements, implementing, implemented. ◆◆◆◇◇
The verb is pronounced /ɪmplɪment/. The noun is pronounced /ɪmplɪmənt/.

1 If you **implement** something such as a plan, you ensure that what has been planned is done. *The government promised to implement a new system to control financial loan institutions... The report sets out strict inspection procedures to ensure that the recommendations are properly implemented.* VERB =carry out V n
♦ **implementation** /ɪmplɪmənteɪʃən/ *Very little has been achieved in the implementation of the peace agreement signed last January.* N-UNCOUNT: oft N *of* n

2 An **implement** is a tool or other piece of equipment; a formal use. *...knives and other useful implements. ...writing implements.* N-COUNT =tool

implicate /ɪmplɪkeɪt/ **implicates, implicating, implicated.** ◆◇◇◇◇ VERB
To **implicate** someone or something means to show or claim that they were involved in a crime or responsible for something bad. *Allegations had appeared in the press implicating the army and police in some of the killings... He was obliged to resign when one of his own aides was implicated in a financial scandal... He didn't find anything in the notebooks to implicate Stu.* • See also **implicated.** V n *in* n, V n
♦ **implication** *Implication in a murder finally brought him to the gallows.* N-UNCOUNT =ramification

implicated /ɪmplɪkeɪtɪd/. ◆◇◇◇◇ ADJ: v-link ADJ, usu ADJ *in* n
If someone or something is **implicated** in a crime or a bad situation, they are involved in it or responsible for it. *He has been defending charges that he was implicated in the failed coup against President Gorbachev... It is thought that this virus is implicated in the development of a number of illnesses.* • See also **implicate.**

implication /ɪmplɪkeɪʃən/ **implications** ◆◆◆◇◇

1 The **implications** of something are the things that are likely to happen as a result. *The Attorney General was aware of the political implications of his decision to prosecute... The low level of current investment has serious implications for future economic growth.* N-COUNT: usu pl, oft N *of/for* n

2 The **implication** of a statement, event, or situation is what it implies or suggests is the case. *The implication was obvious: vote for us or it will be very embarrassing for you... The implication that marital infidelity enhances a leader's credibility is preposterous.* N-COUNT =inference
• If you say that something is the case **by implication**, you mean that a statement, event, or situation implies that it is the case. *Now his authority and, by implication, that of the whole management team are under threat as never before.* PHRASE: PHR with cl/group

3 See also **implicate.**

implicit /ɪmplɪsɪt/ ◆◆◇◇◇

1 Something that is **implicit** is expressed in an indirect way. *It is taken as an implicit warning to the Moroccans not to continue or repeat the military actions they began a week ago... Branagh says that it was his intention to make explicit in the film what was only implicit in the play.* ADJ-GRADED =tacit ≠explicit
♦ **implicitly** *Mr Patten implicitly accepted that there would not be nationwide tests for 14-year-olds this summer.* ADV: ADV with v =tacitly ≠explicitly

2 If a quality or element is **implicit in** something, it is involved in it or is shown by it; a formal use. *Implicit in snobbery is timidity – being afraid to take a risk for fear of what your posh friends may think... Try and learn from the lessons implicit in the failure of your marriage.* ADJ: v-link ADJ *in* n =inherent

3 If you say that someone has an **implicit** belief or faith in something, you mean that they have complete faith in it and no doubts at all. *He had implicit faith in the noble intentions of the Emperor.* ADJ-GRADED: usu ADJ n =absolute
♦ **implicitly** *I trust him implicitly.* ADV-GRADED: ADV after v

implode /ɪmpləʊd/ **implodes, imploding, imploded**

1 If something **implodes**, it collapses into itself in a sudden and violent way. *The engine imploded... He has nightmares about the tanks imploding.* VERB V

2 If something such as an organization or a system **implodes**, it suddenly fails or ceases to exist. *...the possibility that the party will implode under its first experience of opposition.* VERB =collapse V

implore /ɪmplɔːr/ **implores, imploring, implored.** If you **implore** someone to do something, you desperately beg them to do it. *Opposition leaders this week implored the president to break the deadlock in parliament... 'Tell me what to do!' she implored him.* VERB =beg, plead V n to-inf, V n with quote, Also V with quote, V n

imploring /ɪmplɔːrɪŋ/. An **imploring** look, cry, or letter is one by which someone shows that they desperately want you to do something. *Frank looked at Jim with imploring eyes.* ADJ: ADJ n =pleading
♦ **imploringly** *Michael looked at him imploringly, eyes brimming with tears.* ADV: ADV after v

imply /ɪmplaɪ/ **implies, implying, implied** ◆◆◆◇◇

1 If you **imply** that something is the case, you say something which indicates that it is the case in an indirect way. *'Are you implying that I have something to do with those attacks?' she asked coldly... She felt undermined by the implied criticism.* VERB =suggest, hint V that, V-ed, Also V n

2 If an event or situation **implies** that something is the case, it makes you think it likely that it is the case. *Exports in June rose 1.5%, implying that the economy was stronger than many investors had realized... He stressed that the meeting in no way implies a resumption of contacts with the terrorists.* VERB =suggest V that, V n

impolite /ɪmpəlaɪt/. If you say that someone is **impolite**, you mean that they are rather rude and do not have good manners. *The Count acknowledged the two newcomers as briefly as was possible without being impolite... It would be most ungracious and impolite to refuse a simple invitation to supper with him.* ADJ-GRADED: oft *it* v-link ADJ to-inf =rude, uncivil ≠polite

imponderable /ɪmpɒndərəbəl/ **imponderables.** An **imponderable** is something unknown which it is difficult or impossible to estimate or make correct guesses about. *The big imponderable, of course, is what's going to happen to interest rates.* N-COUNT

import, imports, importing, imported. ◆◆◆◆◇ The verb is pronounced /ɪmpɔːrt/. The noun is pronounced /ɪmpɔːrt/.

1 To **import** products or raw materials means to buy them from another country for use in your own country. *Britain last year spent nearly £5000 million more on importing food than selling abroad... To import from Russia, a Ukrainian firm needs Russian roubles. ...imported goods from Mexico, China, and India.* VERB ≠export V n, V *from* n, V-ed
▶ Also a noun. *Germany, however, insists on restrictions on the import of Polish coal... On July 3rd the government slashed import duties on cars.* N-UNCOUNT: also N in pl ≠export
♦ **importation** /ɪmpɔːrteɪʃən/ *...restrictions concerning the importation of birds.* N-UNCOUNT: usu N *of* n

2 **Imports** are products or raw materials bought from another country for use in your own country. *...French farmers protesting about what they say are cheap imports from other European countries.* N-COUNT: usu pl ≠exports

3 The **import** of something is its importance; a formal use. *Who leads Canada is also of some import to the rest of the world... Such arguments are of little import.* N-UNCOUNT =consequence

4 The **import** of something is its meaning, especially when the meaning is not clearly expressed; a formal use. *I have already spoken about the import of his speech.* N-SING: with poss =content

importance /ɪmpɔːrtəns/ ◆◆◆◇◇

1 The **importance** of something is its quality of being significant, valued, or necessary in a particular situation. *China has been stressing the importance of its ties with third world countries... Safety is of paramount importance.* N-UNCOUNT: oft N *of* n

2 **Importance** means having influence, power, or status. N-UNCOUNT

important /ɪmpɔːrtənt/ ◆◆◆◆◆

1 Something that is **important** is very significant, is highly valued, or is necessary. *Her sons are the most important thing in her life... The planned general strike represents an important economic challenge to the government... This gold is every bit as* ADJ-GRADED: oft ADJ *to* n, *it* v-link ADJ to-inf/that

important to me as it is to you... It's important to answer her questions as honestly as you can... It was important that he rest. ♦ **importantly** *I was hungry, and, more importantly, my children were hungry.* ADV-GRADED

2 Someone who is **important** has influence or power within a society or a particular group. *He was the most important person on the island. ...an important figure in the media world.* ADJ-GRADED

importer /ɪmpɔːʳtəʳ/ **importers.** An **importer** is a country, firm, or person that buys goods from another country for use in their own country. *He made his money first as an importer of exotic food in west London.* ◆◇◇◇◇ N-COUNT: oft N *of* n

importunate /ɪmpɔːʳtʃʊnət/. If you describe someone as **importunate**, you think they are annoying because they keep trying to get something from you; a formal word. *His secretary shielded him from importunate visitors.* ADJ PRAGMATICS =troublesome

importune /ɪmpɔːʳtjuːn, AM -tuːn/ **importunes, importuning, importuned.** If someone **importunes** someone else, they ask that person for something or urge them to do something, in an annoying way; a formal word. *One can no longer walk the streets without seeing beggars importuning passers by.* VERB =pester V n Also V n to-inf, V n *for* n

impose /ɪmpoʊz/ **imposes, imposing, imposed** ◆◆◆◆◇

1 If you **impose** something on people, you use your authority to force them to accept it. *Britain was the first country to impose fines on airlines which bring passengers without proper immigration papers... A third of companies reviewing pay since last August have imposed a pay freeze of up to a year... The conditions imposed on volunteers were carefully designed to put off all but the keenest.* ♦ **imposition** /ɪmpəzɪʃᵊn/ *Cambridge cyclists are attempting to fight the imposition of a day-time ban on cycling in the city centre.* VERB V n *on* n V n V-ed N-UNCOUNT: oft N *of* n

2 If you **impose** your opinions or beliefs on other people, you try and make people accept them as a rule or as a model to copy. *Parents of either sex should beware of imposing their own tastes on their children.* VERB V n *on* n

3 If something **imposes** strain, pressure, or hardship on someone or something, it causes them to experience it. *The filming imposed an additional strain on her as she had little or no experience of using such a camera. ...the pressures imposed upon teachers by ceaseless curriculum reforms.* VERB =inflict V n *on* n V-ed

4 If someone **imposes** on you, they unreasonably expect you to do something for them which you do not want to do. *I was afraid you'd simply feel we were imposing on you... 'Mum thinks I should stop imposing on your hospitality, Leo,' said Grace.* ♦ **imposition, impositions** *I know this is an imposition. But please hear me out.* VERB V *on/upon* n N-COUNT

5 If someone **imposes** themselves on you, they force you to accept their company although you may not want to. *I didn't want to impose myself on my married friends.* VERB =foist V pron-refl *on* n

imposing /ɪmpoʊzɪŋ/. If you describe someone or something as **imposing**, you mean that they have an impressive appearance or manner. *He was an imposing man. ...the imposing wrought-iron gates at the entrance to the estate.* ◆◆◇◇◇ ADJ-GRADED

impossible /ɪmpɒsɪbᵊl/ ◆◆◆◆◇

1 Something that is **impossible** cannot be done or cannot happen. *It was impossible for anyone to get in because no one knew the password... He thinks the tax is impossible to administer... You shouldn't promise what's impossible... The new leader of the Russian Communist Party is facing an almost impossible task.* ► **The impossible** is something which is impossible. *They were expected to do the impossible... No one can achieve the impossible.* ♦ **impossibly** *Mathematical physics is an almost impossibly difficult subject.* ♦ **impossibility** /ɪmpɒsɪbɪlɪti/ **impossibilities** *...the impossibility of knowing absolute truth.* ADJ-GRADED: oft *it* v-link ADJ to-inf/that, ADJ to-inf =impracticable ≠possible N-SING: *the* N ADV: ADV adj N-VAR: oft *the* N *of* n

2 An **impossible** situation or an **impossible** position is one that is very difficult to deal with. *The Government was now in an almost impossible position.* ADJ: ADJ n =hopeless

3 If you describe someone as **impossible**, you are annoyed that their bad behaviour or strong views make them difficult to deal with. *The woman is impossible, thought Frannie.* ADJ-GRADED PRAGMATICS =intolerable

impostor /ɪmpɒstəʳ/ **impostors;** also spelled **imposter**. Someone who is an **impostor** is dishonestly pretending to be someone else in order to get something they want. *He was an imposter, who masqueraded as a doctor when he was totally unqualified.* N-COUNT

impotence /ɪmpətᵊns/ ◆◇◇◇◇

1 **Impotence** is a lack of power to influence people or events. *...a sense of impotence in the face of deplorable events.* N-UNCOUNT =powerlessness

2 **Impotence** is a man's sexual problem in which his penis fails to get hard or stay hard. *Impotence affects 10 million men in the US alone.* N-UNCOUNT

impotent /ɪmpətᵊnt/ ◆◇◇◇◇

1 If someone feels **impotent**, they feel that they have no power to influence people or events. *The aggression of a bully leaves people feeling hurt, angry and impotent... In impotent rage he got up and stalked up and down the flat.* ADJ-GRADED =powerless

2 If a man is **impotent**, he is unable to have sex normally, because his penis fails to get hard or stay hard. ADJ: usu v-link ADJ

impound /ɪmpaʊnd/ **impounds, impounding, impounded.** If something **is impounded** by policemen, customs officers or other officials, they officially take possession of it because a law or rule has been broken. *The ship was impounded under the terms of the UN trade embargo... The police moved in, arrested him and impounded the cocaine.* ◆◇◇◇◇ VERB =confiscate *be* V-ed V n

impoverish /ɪmpɒvərɪʃ/ **impoverishes, impoverishing, impoverished** ◆◇◇◇◇

1 Something that **impoverishes** a person or a country makes them poor. *We need to reduce the burden of taxes that impoverish the economy. ...a society impoverished by wartime inflation.* ♦ **impoverished** *The goal is to lure businesses into impoverished areas by offering them tax breaks.* VERB V n V-ed ADJ-GRADED

2 A person or thing that **impoverishes** something makes it worse in quality. *A top dressing of fertiliser should be added to improve growth as mint impoverishes the soil quickly.* VERB V n

impoverishment /ɪmpɒvərɪʃmənt/. **Impoverishment** is the state or process of being impoverished. *...a meeting of experts on how the impoverishment of Africa can be reversed... National isolation can only cause economic and cultural impoverishment.* N-UNCOUNT

impracticable /ɪmpræktɪkəbᵊl/. If something such as a course of action is **impracticable**, it is impossible to do. *Experts have told them that such measures would be highly impracticable and almost impossible to apply. ...naive and impracticable schemes for the resolution of international conflict.* ADJ-GRADED: usu v-link ADJ =impossible

impractical /ɪmpræktɪkᵊl/ ◆◇◇◇◇

1 If you describe an object, idea, or course of action as **impractical**, you mean that it is not sensible or realistic, and does not work well in practice. *When stalking subjects, a tripod is impractical... Once there were regularly scheduled airlines, it became impractical to make a business trip by ocean liner.* ADJ-GRADED: usu v-link ADJ, oft *it* v-link ADJ to-inf ≠practical

2 If you describe someone as **impractical**, you mean that they do not have the abilities or skills to do practical work such as making, repairing, or organizing things. *Geniuses are supposed to be difficult, eccentric and hopelessly impractical.* ADJ-GRADED: usu v-link ADJ

imprecation /ɪmprɪkeɪʃᵊn/ **imprecations.** An **imprecation** is a curse or insult; a formal word. N-VAR

imprecise /ɪmprɪsaɪs/. Something that is **imprecise** is not clear, accurate, or precise. *The charges were vague and imprecise, and defendants were rarely accused of carrying out any specific act... Utilitarianism is a very broad, imprecise concept that covers a multitude of underlying theoretical positions.* ADJ-GRADED =inexact

imprecision /ɪmprɪsɪʒᵊn/. **Imprecision** is the quality of being imprecise. *This served to hide the confusion and imprecision in their thinking.* N-UNCOUNT

impregnable /ɪmpregnəbᵊl/

1 If you describe a building or other place as **impregnable**, you mean it is so strong or inaccessible that it cannot be broken into or captured. *The old Dutch fort with its thick high walls looks virtually impregnable... In those impregnable mountains, the guerrillas could hold out for years.* ADJ =impenetrable

2 If you say that a person or group is **impregnable**, or their position is **impregnable**, you think they cannot be defeated by anyone, for example in political or financial competition or in a sporting contest. *The Bundesbank's seemingly impregnable position has begun to weaken.* ADJ =unassailable

impregnate /ɪmpregneɪt, AM ɪmpreg-/ **impregnates, impregnating, impregnated**

1 If someone or something **impregnates** a thing with a substance, they make the substance spread through it and stay in it. *Undercover officers found drug-making equipment used to impregnate paper with LSD. ...a block of plastic impregnated with a light-absorbing dye.* ♦ **-impregnated** *...nicotine-impregnated chewing gum.* VERB V n with n V-ed Also V n COMB in ADJ

2 When a man or a male animal **impregnates** a female, he makes her pregnant; a formal use. *For centuries, war entailed killing men and raping and impregnating the surviving women.* VERB V n

impresario /ɪmprɪsɑːrioʊ/ **impresarios.** An **impresario** is a person who arranges for plays, concerts, and other entertainments to be performed. N-COUNT

impress /ɪmpres/ **impresses, impressing, impressed** ◆◆◆◇◇

1 If something **impresses** you, you feel great admiration for it. *What impressed him most was their speed. ...a group of students who were trying to impress their girlfriends... Cannon's film impresses on many levels.* ♦ **impressed** *I was very impressed by one young man at my lectures... I'm very impressed with the new airport... He went away suitably impressed.* VERB V n V ADJ-GRADED: v-link ADJ, oft ADJ by/with n

2 If you **impress** something on someone, you make them understand its importance or degree. *I had always impressed upon the children that if they worked hard they would succeed in life... He said he'd be telephoning other Western leaders to impress on them the need to support Soviet reforms... I impressed on him what a huge honour he was being offered.* VERB V on/upon n that V on/upon n n V on/upon n wh

3 If something **impresses** itself on your mind, you notice and remember it. *But this change has not yet impressed itself on the minds of the British public.* VERB V pron-refl on n

4 If someone or something **impresses** you as a particular thing, usually a good one, they gives you the impression of being that thing. *Billy Sullivan had impressed me as a fine man.* VERB V n as n/-ing

impression /ɪmpreʃᵊn/ **impressions** ◆◆◆◇◇

1 Your **impression** of a person or thing is what you think they are like, usually after having seen or heard them. Your **impression** of a situation is what you think is going on. *What were your first impressions of college?... My impression is that they are totally out of control... There was a general impression that tomorrow meant a fresh start.* N-COUNT: oft poss N, N of n, N that =feeling

2 If someone or something gives a particular **impression**, they cause you to believe that something is the case, often when it is not actually the case. *I don't want to give the impression that I'm running away from the charges... He cleverly inserted mirrors above the window to create an impression of space.* N-SING: usu with supp, oft N that, N of n

3 An **impression** by someone is an amusing imitation of someone's behaviour or way of talking, usually someone well-known. *...doing impressions of Sean Connery and James Mason.* N-COUNT: oft N of n =impersonation

4 An **impression** of an object is a mark or outline that it has left after being pressed hard onto a surface. *...the world's oldest fossil impressions of plant life.* N-COUNT

5 If someone or something **makes an impression**, they have a strong effect on people or a situation. *He has told me his plans and he's made a good impression on me... The type of aid coming in makes no immediate impression on the horrific death rates.* PHRASES V inflects

6 If you are **under the impression** that something is the case, you believe that it is the case, usually when it is not actually the case. *He had apparently been under the impression that a military coup was in progress.* v-link PHR, usu PHR that

impressionable /ɪmpreʃənəbᵊl/. Someone who is **impressionable**, usually a young person, is not very critical and is therefore easy to influence. *The law is intended to safeguard young and impressionable viewers from exploitation. ...seven years old, which is apparently the age at which you are most impressionable.* ADJ-GRADED =suggestible

Impressionism /ɪmpreʃənɪzəm/. **Impressionism** is a style of painting developed in France between 1870 and 1900 which concentrated on showing the effects of light on things rather than on clear and exact detail. N-UNCOUNT

impressionist /ɪmpreʃənɪst/ **impressionists.** An **impressionist** is an entertainer who does amusing imitations of well-known people. ◆◇◇◇◇ N-COUNT

Impressionist, Impressionists

1 An **Impressionist** is an artist who painted in the style of Impressionism. *...the French Impressionists.* N-COUNT

2 An **Impressionist** painting is by an Impressionist or is in the style of Impressionism. ADJ: ADJ n

impressionistic /ɪmpreʃənɪstɪk/. An **impressionistic** work of art or piece of writing shows the artist's or writer's impressions of something rather than giving clear details. *His paintings had become more impressionistic as his eyesight dimmed.* ADJ-GRADED

impressive /ɪmpresɪv/. Something that is **impressive** impresses you, for example because it is great in size or degree, or is done with a great deal of skill. *It is an impressive achievement... The film's special effects are particularly impressive.* ♦ **impressively** *...an impressively bright and energetic American woman called Cathie Gould... The socialists performed impressively in the legislative elections.* ◆◆◆◇◇ ADJ-GRADED ≠unimpressive ADV-GRADED: ADV adj, ADV with v

imprint, imprints, imprinting, imprinted. The noun is pronounced /ɪmprɪnt/. The verb is pronounced /ɪmprɪnt/. ◆◇◇◇◇

1 If something leaves an **imprint** on a place or on your mind, it has a strong and lasting effect on it. *Few cities in America bear the imprint of Japanese money more than Los Angeles... Both King and Gandhi were tremendously brave men whose unique form of courage left a lasting imprint on their nations' histories.* N-COUNT: usu sing, usu N of/on n =stamp

2 When something **is imprinted** on your memory, it is firmly fixed in your memory so that you will not forget it. *As I arrived, the shimmering skyline of domes and minarets was imprinted on my memory... He repeated the names, as if to imprint them in his mind... He could not dislodge the images imprinted on his brain.* VERB be V-ed on/in n V n on/in n V-ed

3 An **imprint** is a mark or outline made by the pressure of one object on another. *It was the imprint of his little finger on a box of poisoned chocolates that finally sealed his fate.* N-COUNT

4 If a surface **is imprinted** with a mark or design, that mark or design is printed on the surface or pressed into it. *The firm carries a variety of binders that can be imprinted with your message or logo... They also left a card, imprinted with the name Sean Lynch. ...a racket with the club's badge imprinted on the strings.* VB: usu passive be V-ed with/on n V-ed

imprison /ɪmprɪzᵊn/ **imprisons, imprisoning, imprisoned.** If someone **is imprisoned**, they are locked up or kept somewhere, usually in prison as a punishment for a crime or for political opposition. *The local priest was imprisoned for 18 months on charges of anti-state agitation... Dutch colonial authorities imprisoned him for his part in the independence movement.* ◆◆◇◇◇ VERB be V-ed V n

imprisonment /ɪmprɪzᵊnmənt/. **Imprisonment** is the state of being imprisoned. *She was sentenced to seven years' imprisonment. ...the prospect of imprisonment.*
◆◆◇◇◇ N-UNCOUNT

improbable /ɪmprɒbəbᵊl/ ◆◇◇◇◇

1 Something that is **improbable** is unlikely to be true or to happen. *Ordered arrangements of large groups of atoms and molecules are highly improbable... It seems improbable that this year's figure will fall much below last year's 75,000.*
ADJ-GRADED: oft *it* v-link ADJ that =unlikely ≠probable, likely

♦ **improbability** /ɪmprɒbəbɪlɪti/ **improbabilities** *...the improbability of such an outcome.*
N-VAR

2 If you describe something as **improbable**, you mean it is strange, unusual, or ridiculous. *On the face of it, their marriage seems an improbable alliance. ...her improbable accent.*
ADJ-GRADED =unlikely

♦ **improbably** *The sea is an improbably pale turquoise... His financial situation forced him to go and teach in, improbably enough, Tulsa, Oklahoma.*
ADV-GRADED: ADV adj, ADV with v, ADV with cl =bizarrely

impromptu /ɪmprɒmptjuː, AM -tuː/. An **impromptu** action is one that you do without planning or organizing it in advance. *This afternoon the Palestinians held an impromptu press conference... The children put on an impromptu concert for the visitors.*
◆◇◇◇◇ ADJ: usu ADJ n =spontaneous

improper /ɪmprɒpəʳ/ ◆◇◇◇◇

1 **Improper** activities are illegal or dishonest; a formal use. *25 officers were investigated following allegations of improper conduct during the murder inquiry... Mr Matthews maintained that he had done nothing improper.*
ADJ =unlawful

♦ **improperly** *I acted neither fraudulently nor improperly.*
ADV-GRADED: ADV with v

2 **Improper** conditions or methods of treatment are not suitable or adequate for a particular purpose; a formal use. *The improper use of medicine could lead to severe adverse reactions.*
ADJ: ADJ n =inappropriate, inadequate

♦ **improperly** *The study confirmed many reports that doctors were improperly trained... He had become infected with Aids from an improperly sterilised needle.*
ADV: ADV with v

3 If you describe someone's behaviour as **improper**, you mean that it is rude or shocking; an old-fashioned use. *He would never be improper, he is always the perfect gentleman.*
ADJ-GRADED =indecent

♦ **improperly** *Fundamentalist groups have attacked women they regarded as improperly dressed.*
ADV-GRADED: ADV after v, ADV -ed

impropriety /ɪmprəpraɪɪti/ **improprieties. Impropriety** is improper behaviour; a formal word. *He resigned amid allegations of financial impropriety.*
N-VAR

improve /ɪmpruːv/ **improves, improving, improved** ◆◆◆◆◇

1 If something **improves** or if you **improve** it, it gets better. *Within a month, both the texture and condition of your hair should improve... The weather is beginning to improve... Time won't improve the situation... He improved their house.*
V-ERG; V; V n

2 If a skill you have **improves** or you **improve** a skill, you get better at it. *Their French has improved enormously... He said he was going to improve his football.*
V-ERG; V; V n

3 If you **improve** after an illness or an injury, your health gets better or you get stronger. *He had improved so much the doctor had cut his dosage.*
VERB =recover; V

4 If you **improve** on a previous achievement of your own or of someone else, you achieve a better standard or result. *We need to improve on our performance against France.*
VERB; V *on* n

improvement /ɪmpruːvmənt/ **improvements** ◆◆◆◇◇

1 If there is an **improvement** in something, it becomes better. If you make **improvements** to something, you make it better. *...the dramatic improvements in organ transplantation in recent years... There is considerable room for improvement in state facilities for treating the mentally handicapped.*
N-VAR

2 If you say that something is an **improvement** on a previous thing or situation, you mean that it is better than that thing. *The new Prime Minister is an improvement on his predecessor... The system we introduced in 1980 has been a great improvement.*
N-COUNT: usu sing, oft N *on* n

improvident /ɪmprɒvɪdənt/. If you describe someone as **improvident**, you are critical of them because they wasteful and does not think about the future; a formal word.
ADJ-GRADED PRAGMATICS

improvise /ɪmprəvaɪz/ **improvises, improvising, improvised** ◆◇◇◇◇

1 If you **improvise**, you make or do something using whatever you have or without having planned it in advance. *You need a wok with a steaming rack for this; if you don't have one, improvise... The vet had improvised a harness... The men huddled in holes in the sand or behind an improvised stone windbreak. ...tents improvised from sheets of heavy plastic draped over wooden poles.*
VERB; V; V n; V-ed

♦ **improvisation** /ɪmprəvaɪzeɪʃᵊn, AM -vɪz-/ **improvisations.** *Funds were not abundant and clever improvisation was necessary.*
N-VAR

2 When performers **improvise**, they invent the music or words as they play, sing, or speak. When they **improvise** on a tune or story, they invent variations of it. *I asked her what the piece was and she said, 'Oh, I'm just improvising'... Uncle Richard intoned a chapter from the Bible and improvised a prayer... I think that the art of a storyteller is to take the story and improvise on it. ...improvised comedy.*
VERB; V; V n; V *on* n; V-ed

♦ **improvisation** /ɪmprəvaɪzeɪʃᵊn, AM -vɪz-/ **improvisations** *...an improvisation on 'Jingle Bells'.*
N-VAR: oft N *on* n

imprudent /ɪmpruːdᵊnt/. If you describe someone's behavior as **imprudent**, you think it is not sensible or carefully thought out; a formal word. *...an imprudent investment he made many years ago... The Government of Jamaica consider it imprudent to abolish the death penalty.*
ADJ-GRADED =unwise

impudent /ɪmpjʊdənt/. If you describe someone as **impudent**, you mean they behave or speak rudely or disrespectfully, or do something they have no right to do; a formal word. *Some of them spoke pleasantly and were well behaved, while others were impudent and insulting.*
ADJ-GRADED =cheeky

♦ **impudence** *...when one sister had the impudence to wear the other's clothes.*
N-UNCOUNT =cheek

impugn /ɪmpjuːn/ **impugns, impugning, impugned.** If you **impugn** something such as someone's motives or integrity, you imply that they are not entirely honest or honorable; a formal word. *The Secretary's letter questions my veracity, impugns my motives, and tends to publicly discredit me... I request the judges to punish the accused severely, since they have impugned the honour of the Soviet Army.*
VERB =question; V n

impulse /ɪmpʌls/ **impulses** ◆◆◇◇◇

1 An **impulse** is a sudden desire to do something. *Unable to resist the impulse, he glanced at the sea again... He still couldn't understand the impulse that had made him confide in Cassandra... Wade resisted an impulse to smile.*
N-VAR: oft N to-inf

2 An **impulse** is a short electrical signal that is sent along a wire or nerve or through the air, usually as one of a series.
N-COUNT

3 An **impulse** buy or **impulse** purchase is something that you decide to buy when you see it, although you had not planned to buy it. *The curtains were an impulse buy.*
ADJ: ADJ n

4 If you do something **on impulse**, you suddenly decide to do it, without planning it. *Sean's a fast thinker, and he acts on impulse... After lunch she decided on impulse to take a bath.*
PHRASE: PHR after v

impulsive /ɪmpʌlsɪv/. If you describe someone as **impulsive**, you mean that they do things suddenly without thinking about them carefully first. *He is too impulsive to be a responsible prime minister... Avoid making an impulsive decision.*
◆◇◇◇◇ ADJ-GRADED

♦ **impulsively** *He studied her face for a moment, then said impulsively: 'Let's get married'... Impulsively she patted him on the arm.*
ADV-GRADED: ADV with v

♦ **impulsiveness** *...Walesa's flamboyant impulsiveness.*
N-UNCOUNT

impunity /ɪmpjuːnɪti/. If you say that someone does something **with impunity**, you disapprove of the fact that they are not punished for doing something bad. *Mr Kinnock said future aggressors would be able to act with impunity if the*
◆◇◇◇◇ PHRASE: PHR after v PRAGMATICS

objectives of the UN weren't met... These gangs operate with apparent impunity.

impure /ɪmpjʊəʳ/

1 A substance that is **impure** is not of good quality because it has other substances mixed with it. ADJ-GRADED

2 If you describe thoughts and actions as **impure**, you mean they are concerned with sex and you regard them as sinful; an old-fashioned use. ADJ-GRADED

impurity /ɪmpjʊərɪti/ **impurities**

1 Impurities are substances that are present in small quantities in another substance and make it dirty or of an unacceptable quality. *The air in the factory is filtered to remove impurities.* N-COUNT: usu pl

2 Impurity is the state of being no longer pure, especially sexually pure. N-UNCOUNT

impute /ɪmpjuːt/ **imputes, imputing, imputed.** VERB
If you **impute** something such as blame, a crime, or a change to a person or thing, you say that this person or thing is responsible for it or the cause of it; a formal word. *It is grossly unfair to impute blame to the United Nations.* V n to n

in 1 position or movement

in. The preposition is pronounced /ɪn/. The adverb is pronounced /ɪn/. ◆◆◆◆◆
In addition to the uses shown below, **in** is used after some verbs, nouns, and adjectives in order to introduce extra information. **In** is also used with verbs of movement such as 'walk' and 'push', and in phrasal verbs such as 'give in' and 'dig in'.

1 Someone or something that is **in** something else is enclosed by it or surrounded by it. If you put something **in** a container, you move it so that it is enclosed by the container. *He was in his car. ...clothes hanging in the wardrobe... Put the knives in the kitchen drawer... Mix the sugar and the water in a cup.* PREP

2 If something happens **in** a place, it happens there. *...spending a few days in a hotel... He had intended to take a holiday in America... Those rockets landed in the desert.* PREP

3 If you **are in**, you are present at your home or place of work. *My flatmate was in at the time... He has had to be in every day.* ADV: be ADV ≠out

4 When someone comes **in**, they enter a room or building. *She looked up anxiously as he came in... They shook hands and went in.* ADV: ADV after v

5 If a train, boat, or plane has come **in** or is **in**, it has arrived at a station, port, or airport. *We'd be watching every plane coming in from Melbourne... Look. The train's in. We'll have to run for it now.* ADV: ADV after v, be ADV

6 When the sea or tide comes **in**, the sea moves towards the shore rather than away from it. *She thought of the tide rushing in, covering the wet sand... If the tide was in they went swimming.* ADV: ADV after v, be ADV ≠out

7 Something that is **in** a window, especially a shop window, is just behind the window so that you can see it from outside. *The light in the window went out... There was a camera for sale in the window.* PREP

8 When you see something **in** a mirror, you see its reflection. *I couldn't bear to see my reflection in the mirror... He caught sight of his hair in a mirror.* PREP

9 If you are dressed **in** a piece of clothing, you are wearing it. *He was a big man, smartly dressed in a suit and tie. ...three women in black.* PREP: oft -ed PREP n

10 Something that is covered or wrapped **in** something else has that thing over or round its surface. *His legs were covered in mud. ...carrots wrapped in newspaper.* PREP: oft -ed PREP n

11 If there is something such as a crack or hole **in** something, there is a crack or hole somewhere on its surface. *There was a deep crack in the ceiling above him. ...an unsightly hole in the garden.* PREP

in 2 inclusion or involvement

in /ɪn/ ◆◆◆◆◆

1 If something is **in** a book, film, play, or picture, you can read it or see it there. *Don't stick too precisely to what it says in the book. ...one of the funniest scenes in the film.* PREP

2 If you are **in** something such as a play or a race, you are one of the people taking part. *Alf offered her a part in the play he was directing... The Princess had been invited to ride in a charity race... More than fifteen thousand people took part in the memorial service.* PREP

3 Something that is **in** a group or collection is a member of it or part of it. *The New England team are the worst in the league. ...the most spectacular painting in the collection.* PREP

4 You use **in** to specify a general subject or field of activity. *...those working in the defence industry. ...future developments in medicine and surgery.* PREP

in 3 time and numbers

in /ɪn/ ◆◆◆◆◆

1 If something happens **in** a particular year, month, or other period of time, it happens during that time. *...that early spring day in April 1949... Export orders improved in the last month... In the evening, the people assemble in the mosques... He believes food prices will go up in the future.* PREP

2 If something happens **in** a particular situation, it happens while that situation is going on. *His father had been badly wounded in the last war. ...issues you struggle with in your daily life.* PREP

3 If you do something **in** a particular period of time, that is how long it takes you to do it. *He walked two hundred and sixty miles in eight days.* PREP: PREP amount

4 If something will happen **in** a particular length of time, it will happen after that length of time. *I'll have some breakfast ready in a few minutes... They'll be back in a few months.* PREP: PREP amount

5 You use **in** to indicate roughly how old someone is. For example, if someone is **in** their fifties, they are between 50 and 59 years old. *...young people in their twenties. ...Molly, a tall woman in her early sixties.* PREP: PREP poss pl-num

6 You use **in** to indicate roughly how many people or things do something. *...men who came there in droves... The children were assembled in hundreds... The jugs were produced in their millions.* PREP: oft PREP num

7 You use **in** to express a ratio, proportion, or probability. *Last year, one in five boys left school without a qualification... He was told that he had a one in 500 chance of survival.* PREP: num PREP num

in 4 states and qualities

in /ɪn/ ◆◆◆◆◆

1 If something or someone is **in** a particular state or situation, that is their present state or situation. *The economy was in trouble... Dave was in a hurry to get back to work... Their equipment was in poor condition... One of their men was in danger.* PREP: v-link PREP n

2 You use **in** to indicate the feeling or desire which someone has when they do something, or which causes them to do it. *Simpson looked at them in surprise... Chris wept, crying freely in anger and grief... Carl pushed ahead in his eagerness to reach the wall.* PREP

3 If a particular quality or ability is **in** you, you naturally have it. *Violence is not in his nature... I couldn't find it in me to embrace him.* PREP: oft PREP pron to-inf

4 You use **in** when saying that someone or something has a particular quality. *He had all the qualities I was looking for in a partner... 'I don't agree,' she said, surprised at the strength in her own voice... There is artistry in what he does.* PREP

5 You use **in** to indicate how someone is expressing something. *Information is given to the patient verbally and in writing. ...lessons in languages other than Spanish. ...trying to speak in a casual voice. ...written in a simple but very expressive style.* PREP

6 You use **in** in expressions such as **in a row** or **in a ball** to describe the arrangement or shape of something. *The cards need to be laid out in two rows... Her ear, shoulder and hip are in a straight line... He was curled up in a ball.* PREP

7 If something is **in** a particular colour, it has that colour. *...white flowers edged in pink... He saw something written in black on the gravestones.* PREP: oft -ed PREP colour

8 You use **in** to specify which feature or aspect of something you are talking about. *The movie is nearly two hours in length... The oil is green in colour... There is a big difference in the amounts that banks charge. ...a real increase in the standard of living... The officers were rather slovenly in their methods.* PREP

in 5 other uses and phrases

in, ins. Pronounced /ɪn/ for meanings 1 and 3 to 7, and /ɪn/ for meaning 2. ◆◆◆◆◆

1 If you say that something is **in**, or is the **in** thing, you mean it is fashionable or popular; an informal use. *A few years ago jogging was the in thing... It is the 'in' place to go for a quick drink after work.* ADJ

2 You use **in** with a present participle to indicate that when you do something, something else happens as a result. *He shifted uncomfortably on his feet. In doing so he knocked over Steven's briefcase.* PREP: PREP -ing

3 If you say that someone **is in for** a shock or a surprise, you mean that they are going to experience it. *You might be in for a shock at the sheer hard work involved... When you venture outside, you are in for a surprise.* PHRASES V inflects, PHR n

4 If someone **has it in for** you, they dislike you and try to cause problems for you; an informal use. *The other kids had it in for me.* V inflects, PHR n

5 If you are **in on** something, you are involved in it or know about it. *I don't know. I wasn't in on that particular argument... I'm going to let you in on a little secret.* PREP: v-link PREP n, v n PREP n

6 You use **in that** to introduce an explanation of a statement you have just made. *I'm lucky in that I've got four sisters.* CONJ-SUBORD

7 The **ins and outs** of a situation are all the detailed points and facts about it. *...the ins and outs of high finance... Dietary experts can advise on the ins and outs of dieting.* usu *the* PHR *of* n/-ing

in. **in.** is a written abbreviation for **inch**. The plural can be 'in.' or 'ins'. *...30.4 x 25.4 cm (12 x 10 in)... It is 24 ins wide and 16 ins high.* ◆◆◇◇◇

in-. Usually pronounced /ɪn-/ before an unstressed syllable, and /ɪn-/ before a stressed syllable. **in-** is added to some adjectives, adverbs, and nouns to form other adjectives, adverbs, and nouns that have the opposite meaning. For example, something that is incorrect is not correct. *...incomplete answers. ...women who are insecure about themselves.* PREFIX

inability /ɪnəbɪlɪti/. If you refer to someone's **inability** to do something, you are referring to the fact that they are unable to do it. *Her inability to concentrate could cause an accident. ...the government's inability to provide basic services.* ◆◆◇◇◇ N-UNCOUNT: usu N to-inf, usu with poss ≠ability

inaccessible /ɪnəksesɪbᵊl/ ◆◇◇◇◇

1 An **inaccessible** place is very difficult or impossible to reach. *...people living in remote and inaccessible parts of China... The route took us through scenery quite inaccessible to the motorist.* ♦ **inaccessibility** /ɪnəksesɪbɪlɪti/ *Poor roads and inaccessibility make food distribution very difficult.* ADJ-GRADED: oft ADJ *to* n; N-UNCOUNT

2 If something is **inaccessible**, you are unable to see, use, or buy it. *Ninety-five per cent of its magnificent collection will remain inaccessible to the public... We gained a rich supply of data which would normally be inaccessible.* ♦ **inaccessibility** *The problem of inaccessibility of essential goods, especially of food, is reaching a crisis point.* ADJ-GRADED: usu v-link ADJ, oft ADJ *to* n =unavailable; N-UNCOUNT: oft N *of* n

3 Someone or something that is **inaccessible** is difficult or impossible to understand or appreciate. *A lot of contemporary music is virtually inaccessible. ...using language that is inaccessible to working people.* ♦ **inaccessibility** *White was fascinated by bizarre characters, which added to the inaccessibility of his literature.* ADJ-GRADED: usu v-link ADJ, oft ADJ *to* n; N-UNCOUNT

inaccuracy /ɪnækjʊrəsi/ **inaccuracies.** The **inaccuracy** of a statement or measurement is the fact that it is not accurate or correct. *He was disturbed by the inaccuracy of the answers... A reporter tries to guard against inaccuracies by checking with a variety of sources.* N-VAR ≠accuracy

inaccurate /ɪnækjʊrət/. If a statement or measurement is **inaccurate**, it is not accurate or correct. *The book is both inaccurate and exaggerated... The reports were based on inaccurate information.* ♦ **inaccurately** *He claimed his remarks had been reported inaccurately.* ◆◇◇◇◇ ADJ-GRADED ≠accurate; ADV-GRADED: ADV with v

inaction /ɪnækʃᵊn/. If you refer to someone's **inaction**, you disapprove of the fact that they are doing nothing. *He is bitter about the inaction of the other political parties.* ◆◇◇◇◇ N-UNCOUNT: oft with poss PRAGMATICS

inactive /ɪnæktɪv/. Someone or something that is **inactive** is not doing anything or is not working. *He certainly was not politically inactive... The satellite had been inactive since its launch two years ago.* ♦ **inactivity** /ɪnæktɪvɪti/ *The players have comparatively long periods of inactivity.* ◆◇◇◇◇ ADJ-GRADED ≠active; N-UNCOUNT ≠activity

inadequacy /ɪnædɪkwəsi/ **inadequacies** ◆◇◇◇◇

1 The **inadequacy** of something is the fact that there is not enough of it, or that it is not good enough. *...the inadequacy of the water supply... The inadequacies of the current system have already been recognised... This man drank rather heavily in an effort to come to terms with his own inadequacies.* N-VAR: oft *the* N *of* n =insufficiency ≠adequacy

2 If someone has feelings of **inadequacy**, they feel that they do not have the qualities and abilities necessary to do something or to cope with life in general. *The feeling of inadequacy was overpowering. ...his deep-seated sense of inadequacy.* N-UNCOUNT

inadequate /ɪnædɪkwət/ ◆◆◇◇◇

1 If something is **inadequate**, there is not enough of it or it is not good enough. *Supplies of food and medicines are inadequate... The problem goes far beyond inadequate staffing.* ♦ **inadequately** *The projects were inadequately funded.* ADJ-GRADED =insufficient ≠adequate; ADV-GRADED: ADV with v

2 If someone feels **inadequate**, they feel that they do not have the qualities and abilities necessary to do something or to cope with life in general. *I still feel inadequate, useless and mixed up... Mary Ann felt painfully inadequate in the crisis.* ADJ-GRADED: usu v-link ADJ =incapable

inadmissible /ɪnədmɪsɪbᵊl/

1 **Inadmissible** evidence cannot be used in a court of law. *The judge ruled that identification evidence presented by the prosecution was inadmissible.* ADJ ≠admissible

2 If you say that something that someone says or does is **inadmissible**, you think that it is totally unacceptable. *He said the use of force would be inadmissible.* ADJ-GRADED: usu v-link ADJ PRAGMATICS

inadvertent /ɪnədvɜːtənt/. An **inadvertent** action is one that you do without realizing what you are doing. *The government has said it was an inadvertent error.* ♦ **inadvertently** *You may have inadvertently pressed the wrong button.* ◆◇◇◇◇ ADJ =unintentional ≠deliberate; ADV: ADV with v

inadvisable /ɪnədvaɪzəbᵊl/. A course of action that is **inadvisable** should not be carried out because it is not wise or sensible. *For three days, it was inadvisable to leave the harbour.* ADJ-GRADED: oft *it* v-link ADJ to-inf =unwise ≠advisable

inalienable /ɪneɪljənəbᵊl/. If you say that someone has an **inalienable** right to something, you are emphasizing that they have a right to it which cannot be changed or taken away; a formal word. *He said the republic now had an inalienable right to self-determination.* ADJ: usu ADJ n

inane /ɪneɪn/. If you describe someone's behaviour or actions as **inane**, you think they are very silly or stupid. *He always had this inane grin... She started asking me inane questions.* ♦ **inanely** *He lurched through the bar, grinning inanely.* ♦ **inanity** /ɪnænɪti/ *...the inanity of the conversation.* ADJ-GRADED PRAGMATICS =idiotic; ADV-GRADED: ADV after v; N-UNCOUNT

inanimate /ɪnænɪmət/. An **inanimate** object is one that has no life. *He thinks that inanimate objects have a life of their own.* ADJ ≠animate

inapplicable /ɪnəplɪkəbᵊl, AM ɪnæplɪk-/. Something that is **inapplicable** to what you are talking about is not relevant or appropriate to it. *His theory was inapplicable to many underdeveloped economies.* ADJ-GRADED: usu v-link ADJ, oft ADJ *to* n =irrelevant ≠applicable

inappropriate /ɪnəproʊpriət/ ◆◆◇◇◇

1 Something that is **inappropriate** is not useful or suitable for a particular situation or purpose. *The industry is inappropriate to the region's present and future needs... There is no suggestion that clients have been sold inappropriate policies.* ♦ **inappropriately** *He was dressed inappropriately for the heat in a dark suit.* ADJ-GRADED =unsuitable ≠appropriate; ADV-GRADED: ADV with v

2 If you say that someone's speech or behaviour in a particular situation is **inappropriate**, you are criticising it because you think it is not suitable for that situation. *I feel the remark was inappropriate* ADJ-GRADED: oft ADJ *for* n, *it* v-link ADJ to-inf PRAGMATICS

for such a serious issue... It is inappropriate for a judge to belong to a discriminatory club.
♦ **inappropriately** *You have the law on your side if the bank is acting inappropriately. ...behavior that may appear inappropriately childish.* ADV-GRADED: ADV with v, ADV adj

inarticulate /ɪnɑːʳtɪkjʊlət/. If someone is **inarticulate**, they are unable to express themselves easily or well in speech. *Inarticulate and rather shy, he had always dreaded speaking in public... Kempton made an inarticulate noise at the back of his throat as if he were about to choke.* ADJ-GRADED ≠articulate

inasmuch as /ɪnəzmʌtʃ æz/; also spelled **in as much as**. You use **inasmuch as** to introduce a statement which explains something you have just said, and adds to it; a formal word. *We were doubly lucky inasmuch as my friend was living on the island and spoke Greek fluently.* PHR-CONJ-SUBORD PRAGMATICS =insofar as

inattention /ɪnətenʃᵊn/. A person's **inattention** is their lack of attention; used showing disapproval. *Vital evidence had been destroyed as a result of a moment's inattention.* N-UNCOUNT PRAGMATICS ≠attention

inattentive /ɪnətentɪv/. Someone who is **inattentive** is not paying complete attention to a person or thing, which often causes an accident or problems. ADJ-GRADED ≠attentive

inaudible /ɪnɔːdɪbᵊl/. If a sound is **inaudible**, you are unable to hear it. *His voice was almost inaudible... Animals are able to hear high-pitched sounds that are inaudible to humans.* ADJ ≠audible

inaugural /ɪnɔːgjʊrəl/. An **inaugural** meeting or speech is the first meeting of a new organization or the first speech by the new leader of an organization. *In his inaugural address, the President appealed for national unity.* ◆◇◇◇◇ ADJ: ADJ n

inaugurate /ɪnɔːgjʊreɪt/ **inaugurates, inaugurating, inaugurated** ◆◇◇◇◇

1 When a new leader **is inaugurated**, they are formally given their new position at an official ceremony. *The new President will be inaugurated on January 20.* ♦ **inauguration** /ɪnɔːgjʊreɪʃᵊn/ **inaugurations** *...the inauguration of the new Governor. ...his long inauguration speech.* VB: usu passive be V-ed N-VAR: oft N of n, N n

2 When a new building or institution **is inaugurated**, it is declared open in a formal ceremony. *A new centre for research on toxic waste was inaugurated today at Imperial College.* ♦ **inauguration** *They later attended the inauguration of the University.* VB: usu passive =open be V-ed N-COUNT: usu N of n

3 If you **inaugurate** a new system or service, you start it; a formal use. *Pan Am inaugurated the first scheduled international flight.* VERB V n

inauspicious /ɪnɔːspɪʃəs/. An **inauspicious** event is one that gives signs that success is unlikely; a formal word. *The meeting got off to an inauspicious start with one of the main participants failing to turn up.* ADJ-GRADED: usu ADJ n ≠auspicious

inboard /ɪnbɔːʳd/. An **inboard** motor or engine is inside a boat rather than attached to the outside; a technical use. ADJ: ADJ n ≠outboard

inborn /ɪnbɔːʳn/. **Inborn** qualities are natural ones which you are born with. *He had an inborn talent for languages... It is clear that the ability to smile is inborn.* ADJ: usu ADJ n =innate, inbred

inbound /ɪnbaʊnd/. An **inbound** flight is one that is arriving from another place. *...a special inbound flight from Honduras.* ADJ: usu ADJ n ≠outbound

inbred /ɪnbred/

1 **Inbred** means the same as **inborn**. *She had that inbred politeness, it was a part of her. ...behaviour patterns that are inbred.* ADJ =innate, inborn

2 People who are **inbred** have ancestors who are all closely related to each other. *The whole population is so inbred that no genetic differences remain... He came from an old inbred family.* ADJ: usu v-link ADJ

inbreeding /ɪnbriːdɪŋ/. **Inbreeding** is the repeated breeding of closely related animals or people. *In the 19th century, inbreeding nearly led to the extinction of the royal family.* N-UNCOUNT

inbuilt /ɪnbɪlt/; also spelled **in-built**. An **inbuilt** quality is one that someone or something has from the time they were born or produced; used mainly in British English. *The children had this inbuilt awareness that not everyone was as lucky as they were. ...the only answering machine with inbuilt fax and printer.* ADJ: usu ADJ n

inc. In written advertisements, **inc.** is an abbreviation for 'including'. *The hotel offers a two-night break for £210 per person, inc. breakfast and dinner.* =incl.

Inc. In the United States, **Inc.** is an abbreviation for 'Incorporated' when it is used after a company's name. *...BP America Inc.* ◆◆◆◇◇

incalculable /ɪnkælkjʊləbᵊl/. Something that is **incalculable** cannot be calculated or estimated because it is so great. *He warned that the effects of any war would be incalculable... This has done incalculable damage to his reputation.* ADJ =inestimable

incandescent /ɪnkændesᵊnt/

1 **Incandescent** substances or devices give out a lot of light when heated; a technical use in science. *...incandescent gases. ...incandescent light bulbs.* ADJ

2 If you describe someone or something as **incandescent**, you mean that they are very lively and impressive; a literary use. *Gill had an extraordinary, incandescent personality. ...an incandescent performance from Audrey Hepburn.* ♦ **incandescence** *She burned with an incandescence that had nothing to do with her looks.* ADJ: usu ADJ n N-UNCOUNT

3 If you say that someone is **incandescent** with rage, you mean that they are extremely angry; a literary use. *It makes me incandescent with fury.* ADJ: oft ADJ *with* n

incantation /ɪnkænteɪʃᵊn/ **incantations.** An **incantation** is a series of words that a person says or sings as a magic spell. *...huddled shapes whispering strange prayers and incantations.* N-COUNT =chant

incapable /ɪnkeɪpəbᵊl/ ◆◇◇◇◇

1 Someone who is **incapable of** doing something is unable to do it. *She seemed incapable of taking decisions... He was a man incapable of violence.* ADJ: v-link ADJ *of* -ing/n ≠capable

2 An **incapable** person is weak or stupid. *He lost his job for allegedly being incapable.* ADJ ≠capable

incapacitate /ɪnkəpæsɪteɪt/ **incapacitates, incapacitating, incapacitated.** If something **incapacitates** you, it weakens you in some way, so that you cannot do certain things; a formal word. *A serious fall incapacitated the 68-year-old congressman.* ♦ **incapacitated** *He is incapacitated and can't work.* VERB V n ADJ-GRADED: usu v-link ADJ

incapacity /ɪnkəpæsɪti/. The **incapacity** of a person, society, or system to do something is their inability to do it; a formal word. *...Europe's incapacity to take collective action... Patients with no mental incapacity can refuse treatment.* N-UNCOUNT: oft with poss, oft N to-inf =inability

incarcerate /ɪnkɑːʳsəreɪt/ **incarcerates, incarcerating, incarcerated.** If people **are incarcerated**, they are imprisoned; a formal word. *They were incarcerated for the duration of the war... It can cost $40,000 to $50,000 to incarcerate a prisoner for a year.* ♦ **incarceration** *...her mother's incarceration in a psychiatric hospital.* ◆◇◇◇◇ VERB =imprison be V-ed V n N-UNCOUNT =imprisonment

incarnate, incarnates, incarnating, incarnated. The adjective is pronounced /ɪnkɑːʳnɪt/. The verb is pronounced /ɪnkɑːʳneɪt/.

1 If you say that someone is a quality **incarnate**, you mean that they represent that quality or are typical of it in an extreme form. *She is evil incarnate... He is cynicism incarnate.* ADJ: n ADJ =personified

2 You use **incarnate** to say that something, especially a god or spirit, is represented in human form. *Why should God become incarnate as a male?... The pharaoh is Osiris, the moon bull incarnate.* ADJ: v-link ADJ, n ADJ, ADJ n

3 If you say that a quality **is incarnated** in a person, you mean that they represent that quality or are typical of it in an extreme form. *The iniquities of the regime are incarnated in one man. ...a writer who incarnates the changing consciousness of the Americas.* VERB =embody be V-ed in n V n

4 If you say that someone or something **is incarnated** in a particular form, you mean that they appear on earth in that form. *He was the god Vishnu incarnated on earth as a righteous king.* VB: usu passive be V-ed prep

incarnation /ɪnkɑːʳneɪʃᵊn/ **incarnations** ◆◇◇◇◇

1 If you say that someone is the **incarnation of** a particular quality, you mean that they represent that quality or are typical of it in an extreme form. N-COUNT: N of n =embodiment

The regime was the very incarnation of evil... She is a perfect incarnation of glamour.

2 An **incarnation** is an instance of being alive on earth in a particular form. Some religions believe that people have several incarnations in different forms. *She began recalling a series of previous incarnations... His industry and persistence suggest that he was an ant in a previous incarnation.*
N-COUNT

incautious /ɪnkɔːʃəs/. If you say that someone is **incautious**, you are criticizing them because they do or say something without thinking or planning; a formal word. *In case you think I was incautious, take a look at the map.*
ADJ-GRADED: usu ADJ n PRAGMATICS =rash, foolish ≠cautious

♦ **incautiously** *Incautiously, Crook had asked where she was.*
ADV-GRADED: ADV with v

incendiary /ɪnsendiəri, AM -eri/ **incendiaries** ◆◇◇◇◇

1 **Incendiary** weapons or attacks are ones that cause large fires. *Five incendiary devices were found in her house. ...incendiary attacks on shops.*
ADJ: ADJ n

2 An **incendiary** is an incendiary bomb. *A shower of incendiaries struck the Opera House.*
N-COUNT

incense, incenses, incensing, incensed. The noun is pronounced /ɪnsens/. The verb is pronounced /ɪnsens/. ◆◇◇◇◇

1 **Incense** is a substance that is burned for its sweet smell, often as part of a religious ceremony.
N-UNCOUNT

2 If you say that something **incenses** you, you mean that it makes you extremely angry. *This proposal will incense conservation campaigners.*
VERB =enrage V n

♦ **incensed** *Mum was incensed at his lack of compassion... He followed her, incensed that she'd dared to leave him alone.*
ADJ-GRADED: usu v-link ADJ, oft ADJ *at/by* n, ADJ that

incentive /ɪnsentɪv/ **incentives.** If something is an **incentive** to do something, it encourages you to do it. *There is little or no incentive to adopt such measures... Clinton's proposal would provide tax incentives for businesses to hire people from these areas.*
◆◆◇◇◇ N-VAR: oft N to-inf =inducement

inception /ɪnsepʃən/. The **inception** of an institution or activity is the start of it; a formal word. *Since its inception the company has produced 53 different aircraft designs.*
◆◇◇◇◇ N-UNCOUNT: with poss

incessant /ɪnsesənt/. An **incessant** process or activity is one that continues without stopping. *Incessant rain made conditions almost intolerable. ...his incessant demands for affection.*
◆◇◇◇◇ ADJ-GRADED: usu ADJ n =constant ≠intermittent

♦ **incessantly** *Dee talked incessantly about herself.*
ADV-GRADED: usu ADV with v

incest /ɪnsest/. **Incest** is the crime of two members of the same family having sexual intercourse, for example a father and daughter, or a brother and sister.
◆◇◇◇◇ N-UNCOUNT

incestuous /ɪnsestʃuəs/

1 An **incestuous** relationship is one involving sexual intercourse between two members of the same family, for example a father and daughter, or a brother and sister. *They accused her of an incestuous relationship with her father.*
ADJ

2 If you describe a group of people as **incestuous**, you disapprove of the fact that they are not interested in ideas or people from outside the group. *Its inhabitants are a close and incestuous lot... Hospitals are very incestuous places.*
ADJ-GRADED PRAGMATICS

inch /ɪntʃ/ **inches, inching, inched** ◆◆◆◇◇

1 An **inch** is an imperial unit of length, approximately equal to 2.54 centimetres. There are twelve inches in a foot. *...a candy tin 6 inches high and 8 inches in diameter. ...18 inches below the surface.*
N-COUNT: num N, oft N *of* n

2 To **inch** somewhere means to move there very slowly, carefully, or with difficulty. To **inch** something somewhere means to move it there very slowly, carefully, or with difficulty. *...a climber inching up a vertical wall of rock... He inched the van forward... An ambulance inched its way through the crowd.*
V-ERG V prep/adv V n prep/adv V *way* prep/adv

3 If you talk about **every inch** of an area, you are emphasizing that you mean the whole of it. *Every inch of shelf space was crammed with books... We are prepared to fight for every inch of territory.*
PHRASES usu PHR *of* n PRAGMATICS

4 If you say that someone looks **every inch** a certain type of person, you are emphasizing that they look exactly like that kind of person. *He looks every inch the City businessman, with his grey suit, dark blue shirt and blue tie... There stood Gertrude, looking every inch a star.*
v-link PHR n PRAGMATICS

5 If someone or something moves or does something **inch by inch**, they move or do it very slowly and carefully. *The car moved forward inch by inch... The police were searching the area inch by inch.*
PHR after v

inchoate /ɪnkoʊɪt/. If something is **inchoate**, it is recent or new, and vague or not yet properly developed; a formal word. *His dreams were senseless and inchoate. ...the inchoate mood of dissatisfaction with all politicians.*
ADJ =incoherent

incidence /ɪnsɪdəns/ **incidences.** The **incidence** of something bad, such as a disease, is the frequency with which it occurs, or the occasions when it occurs. *The incidence of breast cancer increases with age. ...the high incidence of child mortality. ...a couple of isolated incidences.*
◆◇◇◇◇ N-VAR

incident /ɪnsɪdənt/ **incidents.** An **incident** is something that happens, often something that is unpleasant; a formal word. *These incidents were the latest in a series of disputes between the two nations... 26 people have been killed in a dramatic shooting incident... The voting went ahead without incident.*
◆◆◆◆◇ N-COUNT: also *without* N

incidental /ɪnsɪdentəl/. If one thing is **incidental** to another, it is less important than the other thing or is not a major part of it. *The playing of music proved to be incidental to the main business of the evening... At the bottom of the bill, you will notice various incidental expenses such as faxes.*
◆◇◇◇◇ ADJ: oft ADJ *to* n

incidentally /ɪnsɪdentli/ ◆◆◇◇◇

1 You use **incidentally** to introduce a point which is not directly relevant to what you are saying, often a question or extra information that you have just thought of. *'I didn't ask you to come. Incidentally, why have you come?'... The tower, incidentally, dates from the twelfth century.*
ADV: ADV with cl PRAGMATICS =by the way

2 If something occurs only **incidentally**, it is less important than another thing or is not a major part of it. *The letter mentioned my great-aunt and uncle only incidentally.*
ADV: ADV with v

incidental music. In a film, play, or television programme, **incidental music** is music that is played to create a particular atmosphere.
N-UNCOUNT

incident room, incident rooms. In Britain, an **incident room** is a room used by the police while they are dealing with a major crime or accident. *Police have set up an incident room as they begin to investigate this morning's fire.*
N-COUNT: usu sing

incinerate /ɪnsɪnəreɪt/ **incinerates, incinerating, incinerated** ◆◇◇◇◇

1 When authorities **incinerate** rubbish or waste material, they burn it in a furnace. *The government is trying to stop hospitals incinerating their own waste.*
VERB V n

♦ **incineration** /ɪnsɪnəreɪʃən/ *...banning the incineration of lead batteries. ...an incineration plant.*
N-UNCOUNT

2 If people **are incinerated**, for example in a bomb attack or a fire, they are burnt to death. *The cars caught fire on impact and some of the victims were incinerated.*
VB: usu passive *be* V-ed

incinerator /ɪnsɪnəreɪtəʳ/ **incinerators.** An **incinerator** is a large furnace for burning rubbish.
◆◇◇◇◇ N-COUNT

incipient /ɪnsɪpiənt/. An **incipient** situation or quality is one that is starting to happen or develop; a formal word. *...an incipient economic recovery... There were signs of incipient panic.*
ADJ: ADJ n =impending

incise /ɪnsaɪz/ **incises, incising, incised.** If an object **is incised** with a design, the design is carefully cut into the surface of the object with a sharp instrument; a formal word. *After the surface is polished, a design is incised or painted. ...a set of chairs incised with Grecian scrolls.*
VB: usu passive *be* V-ed V-ed

incision /ɪnsɪʒən/ **incisions.** An **incision** is a sharp cut made in something, for example by a surgeon who is operating on a patient. *The technique involves making a tiny incision in the skin.*
N-COUNT =opening, cut

incisive /ɪnsaɪsɪv/. You use **incisive** to describe a person, their thoughts, or their speech when
◆◇◇◇◇ ADJ-GRADED PRAGMATICS

you approve of their ability to think and express their ideas clearly, briefly, and forcefully. *He is a very shrewd operator with an incisive mind... She's incredibly incisive, incredibly intelligent.*

incisor /ɪnsaɪzəʳ/ **incisors.** Your **incisors** are the teeth at the front of your mouth which you use for biting into food. N-COUNT

incite /ɪnsaɪt/ **incites, inciting, incited.** If someone **incites** people to behave in a violent or unlawful way, they encourage people to behave in that way, usually by making them excited or angry. *He incited his fellow citizens to take their revenge... The party agreed not to incite its supporters to violence... They pleaded guilty to possessing material likely to incite racial hatred.* ◆◇◇◇◇ VERB; V n to-inf; V n to n; V n

incitement /ɪnsaɪtmənt/ **incitements.** If someone is accused of **incitement** to violent or unlawful behaviour, they are accused of encouraging people to behave in that way, usually by making them excited or angry. *British law forbids incitement to murder... He still faces charges of incitement. ...an incitement to religious hatred.* N-VAR: oft N to n

incl.
1 In written advertisements, **incl.** is an abbreviation for 'including'. *...only £19.95 (incl. VAT and delivery). ...seven nights £403, incl flights.* =inc.
2 In written advertisements, **incl.** is an abbreviation for 'inclusive'. *Double room: £50 per week incl... Open 19th July-6th September, Sun to Thurs incl.*

inclement /ɪnklemənt/. **Inclement** weather is unpleasantly cold or stormy; a formal word. ADJ-GRADED ≠clement

inclination /ɪnklɪneɪʃən/ **inclinations.** An **inclination** is a feeling that makes you want to act in a particular way. *He had neither the time nor the inclination to think of other things... She showed no inclination to go... He set out to follow his artistic inclinations.* ◆◇◇◇◇ N-VAR: usu with supp, oft N to-inf, oft with brd-neg

incline, inclines, inclining, inclined. The verb is pronounced /ɪnklaɪn/. The noun is pronounced /ɪnklaɪn/.
1 If you **incline** to think or act in a particular way, or if something **inclines** you to it, you are likely to think or act in that way; a formal use. *I incline to the view that he is right. ...the factors which incline us towards particular beliefs... Many end up as team leaders, which inclines them to co-operate with the bosses... Those who fail incline to blame the world for their failure.* V-ERG; V to/towards n; V n to/towards n; V n to-inf; V to-inf
2 If you **incline** your head, you bend your neck so that your head is leaning forward; used in written English. *Jack inclined his head very slightly.* VERB; V n
3 An **incline** is land that slopes at an angle; a formal use. *He came to a halt at the edge of a steep incline.* N-COUNT =slope

inclined /ɪnklaɪnd/ ◆◆◇◇◇
1 If you are **inclined** to behave in a particular way, you often behave in that way, or you want to do so. *Nobody felt inclined to argue with Smith... He was inclined to self-pity... If you are so inclined, you can watch TV.* ADJ-GRADED: v-link ADJ, ADJ to-inf, ADJ to n, so ADJ
2 If you say that you are **inclined** to have a particular opinion, you mean that you hold this opinion but you are not expressing it strongly. *I am inclined to think that the ancient Greeks understood this better than we do... I am inclined to agree with Alan.* ADJ-GRADED: v-link ADJ to-inf; PRAGMATICS; =tend
3 Someone who is mathematically **inclined** or artistically **inclined**, for example, has a natural talent for mathematics or art. *Bratby's grandfather had been artistically inclined. ...the needs of academically inclined pupils.* ADJ: adv ADJ
4 See also **incline**.

include /ɪnkluːd/ **includes, including, included** ◆◆◆◆◆
1 If one thing **includes** another thing, it has the other thing as one of its parts. *A good British breakfast always includes sausages... The trip has been extended to include a few other events... The list includes many British internationals.* VERB; V n
2 If someone or something **is included** in a large group, system, or area, they become a part of it or are considered a part of it. *I had worked hard to be included in a project like this... The President is expected to include this idea in his education plan.* VERB; be V-ed in n; V n in n

included /ɪnkluːdɪd/. You use **included** to emphasize that a person or thing is part of the group of people or things that you are talking about. *All of us, myself included, had been totally committed to the Party... No city, Tel Aviv or Jerusalem included, is home to more Jews than New York... Food is included in the price.* ◆◆◆◆◇ ADJ: n ADJ, v-link ADJ

including /ɪnkluːdɪŋ/. You use **including** to introduce examples of people or things that are part of the group of people or things that you are talking about. *A number of international stars, including Joan Collins, are expected to attend. ...many conditions, including allergies, hyperactivity and tooth decay... Preparation time (not including chilling): 5 minutes.* ◆◆◆◆◆ PREP: PREP n/-ing; PRAGMATICS; ≠excluding

inclusion /ɪnkluːʒən/ **inclusions.** The **inclusion** of a person or thing in a group or collection of people or things is the act of making the person or thing a part of the group or collection. *...a confident performance which justified his inclusion in the team. ...the inclusion of the term 'couplehood' in a Dictionary of New Words.* ◆◇◇◇◇ N-VAR: usu with poss

inclusive /ɪnkluːsɪv/ ◆◇◇◇◇
1 If a price is stated to be **inclusive**, it includes all the charges connected with the goods or services offered. If a price is **inclusive** of postage and packing, it includes the charge for this. *All prices are inclusive of VAT. ...an inclusive price of £32.90.* ► Also an adverb. *...a special introductory offer of £5,995 fully inclusive.* ● See also **all-inclusive**. ADJ: oft ADJ of n; ADV: amount ADV
2 After stating the first and last item in a set of things, you can add **inclusive** to make it clear that the items stated are included in the set. *Training will commence on 5 October, running from Tuesday to Saturday inclusive. ...£5 for senior citizens and children (5 to 16 inclusive).* ADJ: n ADJ
3 If you describe a group or organization as **inclusive**, you mean that it allows all sorts of people to belong to it or use its facilities, rather than being restricted to a few rich, upper-class, or privileged people. *The academy is far more inclusive now than it used to be.* ADJ-GRADED ≠exclusive

incognito /ɪnkɒgniːtoʊ/. Someone who is **incognito** is using a false name or wearing a disguise, in order not to be recognized or identified. *Hotel inspectors have to travel incognito... He preferred to remain incognito.* ADJ: v-link ADJ, ADJ after v

incoherent /ɪnkoʊhɪərənt/ ◆◇◇◇◇
1 If someone is **incoherent**, they are talking in a confused and unclear way. *As the evening progressed, he became increasingly incoherent... The man was almost incoherent with fear... She dissolved into incoherent sobs.* ♦ **incoherence** *Beth's incoherence was enough to tell Amy that something was terribly wrong.* ♦ **incoherently** *He collapsed on the floor, mumbling incoherently.* ADJ-GRADED ≠coherent; N-UNCOUNT; ADV: ADV with v
2 If you say that something such as a policy is **incoherent**, you are criticizing the fact that it is unclear and illogical. *...an incoherent set of objectives.* ♦ **incoherence** *...the general incoherence of government policy.* ADJ-GRADED ≠coherent; N-UNCOUNT: oft N of n

income /ɪnkʌm/ **incomes.** A person's or organization's **income** is the money that they earn or receive, as opposed to the money that they have to spend or pay out. *Many families on low incomes will be unable to afford to buy their own home... To cover its costs, the company will need an annual income of £15 million... Over a third of their income comes from comedy videos.* ◆◆◆◆◇ N-VAR

incomer /ɪnkʌməʳ/ **incomers.** An **incomer** is someone who has recently come to live in a particular place or area; used in British English. N-COUNT

income support. In Britain, **income support** is money that the government gives regularly to people with no income or very low incomes. The old name for this money was **supplementary benefit**. *People on income support do not have to pay council tax.* ◆◇◇◇◇ N-UNCOUNT

income tax, income taxes. Income tax is a certain percentage of your income that you have to pay regularly to the government. ◆◆◇◇◇ N-VAR

incoming /ɪnkʌmɪŋ/ ◆◇◇◇◇

1 An **incoming** message or phone call is one that you receive. *We keep a tape of incoming calls.* ADJ: ADJ n ≠outgoing

2 An **incoming** plane or passenger is one that is arriving at a place. *The airport was closed for incoming flights.* ADJ: ADJ n ≠outgoing

3 An **incoming** official or government is one that has just been appointed or elected. *...the problems confronting the incoming government.* ADJ: ADJ n ≠outgoing

4 An **incoming** tide or wave is coming towards the shore. ADJ: ADJ n

incommunicado /ɪnkəmjuːnɪkɑːdoʊ/

1 If someone is being kept **incommunicado**, they are not allowed to talk to anyone outside the place where they are. *He was held incommunicado in prison for ten days before being released without charge.* ADJ: usu v n ADJ

2 If someone is **incommunicado**, they do not want to be disturbed, or are in a place where they cannot be contacted. *Yesterday she was incommunicado, putting the finishing touches to her autobiography... He is incommunicado in a secluded cottage in Wales.* ADJ: v-link ADJ

incomparable /ɪnkɒmprəbᵊl/

1 If you describe someone or something as **incomparable**, you mean that they are extremely good or impressive. *...a play starring the incomparable Edith Evans... The views from the house are incomparable.* ADJ

2 You use **incomparable** to emphasize that someone or something has a good quality to a great degree; a formal use. *It was a performance of incomparable brilliance. ...an area of incomparable beauty.* ♦ **incomparably** *...incomparably good brakes.* ADJ: ADJ n PRAGMATICS =superlative; ADV

incomparably /ɪnkɒmprəbli/. You can use **incomparably** to mean 'very much' when you are comparing two things and emphasizing the difference between them; a formal word. *South Africa seems incomparably richer than the rest of Africa... British industry is in incomparably better shape than at the beginning of the 1980s.* ADV: ADV compar PRAGMATICS =infinitely

incompatible /ɪnkəmpætɪbᵊl/ ◆◇◇◇◇

1 If one thing or person is **incompatible** with another, they are very different in important ways, and do not suit each other or agree with each other. *They feel strongly that their religion is incompatible with the Communist system... His behavior has been incompatible with his role as head of state... Their interests were mutually incompatible... We were totally incompatible.* ♦ **incompatibility** /ɪnkəmpætɪbɪlɪti/ *Incompatibility between the mother's and the baby's blood groups may cause jaundice.* ADJ: usu v-link ADJ, oft ADJ *with* n ≠compatible; N-UNCOUNT: usu N *between/of/with* n

2 If one type of computer or computer system is **incompatible** with another, they cannot use the same programs or be linked up together. *This made its mini-computers incompatible with its mainframes... Many institutions exchange information by hand because of incompatible computer systems.* ADJ: oft ADJ *with* n ≠compatible

incompetence /ɪnkɒmpɪtəns/. If you refer to someone's **incompetence**, you are criticizing them because they are unable to do their job or a task properly. *The incompetence of government officials is appalling. ...his incompetence in failing to conduct full inquiries.* ◆◇◇◇◇ N-UNCOUNT ≠competence

incompetent /ɪnkɒmpɪtənt/ **incompetents.** If you describe someone as **incompetent**, you are criticizing them because they are unable to do their job or a task properly. *The court declared him incompetent to manage his financial affairs... I was incompetent at playing the piano... He wants the power to sack incompetent teachers.* ▸ An **incompetent** is someone who is incompetent. *The Prince turned furiously on his staff. 'I'm surrounded by incompetents!'* ◆◇◇◇◇ ADJ-GRADED ≠competent; N-COUNT

incomplete /ɪnkəmpliːt/. Something that is **incomplete** is not yet finished, or does not have all the parts or details that it needs. *The clearing of rubbish and drains is still incomplete... European political union would be incomplete without a defence element... Some offices had incomplete information on spending.* ◆◇◇◇◇ ADJ-GRADED ≠complete

incomprehensible /ɪnkɒmprɪhensɪbᵊl/. Something that is **incomprehensible** is impossible to understand. *Her speech was almost incomprehensible. ...incomprehensible mathematics puzzles.* ◆◇◇◇◇ ADJ-GRADED ≠unintelligible

incomprehension /ɪnkɒmprɪhenʃᵊn/. **Incomprehension** is the state of being unable to understand something or someone. *Rosie had a look of incomprehension on her face. ...his incomprehension of what happened to his father... The incomprehension between the two men was mutual.* N-UNCOUNT

inconceivable /ɪnkənsiːvəbᵊl/. If you describe something as **inconceivable**, you think it is very unlikely to happen or be true. *It was inconceivable to me that Toby could have been my attacker... Until now, a devaluation of the dollar seemed inconceivable.* ◆◇◇◇◇ ADJ-GRADED: usu v-link ADJ, oft *it* v-link ADJ that =unthinkable

inconclusive /ɪnkənkluːsɪv/ ◆◇◇◇◇

1 If research or evidence is **inconclusive**, it has not proved anything. *Research has so far proved inconclusive... I find the evidence inconclusive.* ADJ-GRADED ≠conclusive

2 If a contest or conflict is **inconclusive**, it is not clear who has won or who is winning. *The past two elections were inconclusive. ...eight years of bloody and inconclusive war.* ADJ-GRADED

incongruity /ɪnkɒŋgruːɪti/ **incongruities.** The **incongruity** of something is its strangeness when considered together with other aspects of a situation; a formal word. *She smiled at the incongruity of the question. ...the almost absurd incongruity between her wealth and her lifestyle. ...the incongruities of life in war-time London.* N-VAR: oft N *of* n

incongruous /ɪnkɒŋgruəs/. Someone or something that is **incongruous** seems strange when considered together with other aspects of a situation; a formal word. *She was small and fragile and looked incongruous in an army uniform... The Indian temple is an incongruous sight in the Welsh border country.* ♦ **incongruously** *...a town of Western-style buildings perched incongruously in a high green valley.* ◆◇◇◇◇ ADJ-GRADED; ADV-GRADED: ADV after v, ADV adj/-ed

inconsequential /ɪnkɒnsɪkwenʃᵊl/. Something that is **inconsequential** is not important. *...a constant reminder of just how insignificant and inconsequential their lives were... Seemingly inconsequential details can sometimes contain significant clues.* ADJ-GRADED =unimportant

inconsiderable /ɪnkənsɪdərəbᵊl/. If you describe an amount or quality as **not inconsiderable**, you are emphasizing that it is, in fact, large or present to a large degree. *The production costs are a not inconsiderable £8 million... He was a man of great charm and not inconsiderable wit.* ADJ: with neg, usu ADJ n PRAGMATICS

inconsiderate /ɪnkənsɪdərət/. If you accuse someone of being **inconsiderate**, you mean that they do not take enough care over how their words or actions will affect other people. *Motorists were criticised for being inconsiderate to pedestrians. ...his inconsiderate behaviour.* ADJ-GRADED PRAGMATICS =thoughtless ≠considerate

inconsistency /ɪnkənsɪstənsi/ **inconsistencies** ◆◇◇◇◇

1 If you refer to someone's **inconsistency**, you are criticizing them for not behaving in the same way every time a similar situation occurs. *His worst fault was his inconsistency... The report accuses the judicial system of inconsistency and partiality.* N-UNCOUNT ≠consistency

2 If there are **inconsistencies** in two statements, one cannot be true if the other is true. *We were asked to investigate the alleged inconsistencies in his evidence. ...the complete inconsistency of his argument.* N-VAR =contradiction

inconsistent /ɪnkənsɪstənt/ ◆◇◇◇◇

1 If you describe someone as **inconsistent**, you are criticizing them for not behaving in the same way every time a similar situation occurs. *You are inconsistent and unpredictable. ...the leadership's hesitant and inconsistent behaviour.* ADJ-GRADED ≠consistent

2 Someone or something that is **inconsistent** does ADJ-GRADED

not stay the same, being sometimes good and sometimes bad. *We had a terrific start to the season, but recently we've been inconsistent... Moon, as great as he is, has had some inconsistent days.* ≠consistent

3 If two statements are **inconsistent**, one cannot possibly be true if the other is true. *The evidence given in court was inconsistent with what he had previously told them.* ADJ: oft ADJ *with* n ≠consistent

4 If something is **inconsistent with** a set of ideas or values, it does not fit in well with them or match them. *This legislation is inconsistent with what they call Free Trade... The outburst was inconsistent with the image he has cultivated.* ADJ-GRADED: v-link ADJ *with* n ≠consistent

inconsolable /ɪnkənsoʊləbəl/. If you say that someone is **inconsolable**, you mean that they are very sad and cannot be comforted. *When my mother died I was inconsolable.* ADJ

inconspicuous /ɪnkənspɪkjuəs/

1 Someone who is **inconspicuous** does not attract attention to themselves. *I'll try to be as inconspicuous as possible... He had ridden out of Cambridge, inconspicuous among the hundreds of young cyclists.* ♦ **inconspicuously** *I sat inconspicuously in a corner.* ADJ-GRADED =unobtrusive ≠conspicuous; ADV-GRADED: ADV after v

2 Something that is **inconspicuous** is not easily seen or does not attract attention because it is small, ordinary, or hidden away. *The studio is an inconspicuous grey building.* ADJ-GRADED =unobtrusive ≠conspicuous

incontinence /ɪnkɒntɪnəns/. **Incontinence** is the inability to control your bladder and bowels. *Incontinence is not just a condition of old age.* N-UNCOUNT

incontinent /ɪnkɒntɪnənt/. Someone who is **incontinent** is unable to control their bladder and bowels. *His diseased bladder left him incontinent.* ADJ

incontrovertible /ɪnkɒntrəvɜːʳtɪbəl/. **Incontrovertible** evidence or facts are absolutely certain and cannot be denied or disproved. *There is now incontrovertible evidence that the government is violating the agreement.* ♦ **incontrovertibly** *No solution is incontrovertibly right.* ADJ =indisputable; ADV

inconvenience /ɪnkənviːniəns/ **inconveniences, inconveniencing, inconvenienced** ◆◇◇◇◇

1 If someone or something causes **inconvenience**, they cause problems or difficulties for someone. *We apologize for any inconvenience caused during the repairs... The practical inconveniences of long hair are negligible.* N-VAR

2 If someone **inconveniences** you, they cause problems or difficulties for you. *He promised to be quick so as not to inconvenience them any further.* VERB V n

inconvenient /ɪnkənviːniənt/. Something that is **inconvenient** causes problems or difficulties for someone. *Can you come at 10.30? I know it's inconvenient for you, but I must see you... It's very inconvenient to have to wait so long... She arrived at an extremely inconvenient moment.* ♦ **inconveniently** *The Oriental is a comfortable hotel, but rather inconveniently situated.* ◆◇◇◇◇ ADJ-GRADED: oft ADJ *for* n =awkward ≠convenient; ADV-GRADED ≠conveniently

incorporate /ɪnkɔːʳpəreɪt/ **incorporates, incorporating, incorporated** ◆◆◇◇◇

1 If one thing **incorporates** another thing, it includes the other thing; a formal use. *The new cars will incorporate a number of major improvements.* VERB =include V n

2 If someone or something **is incorporated** into a large group, system, or area, they become a part of it; a formal use. *The agreement would allow the rebels to be incorporated into a new national police force... The party vowed to incorporate environmental considerations into all its policies.* ♦ **incorporation** /ɪnkɔːʳpəreɪʃən/ *...the incorporation of Piedmont Airlines and PSA into US Air.* VERB =include be V-ed *into* n, V n *into* n; N-UNCOUNT: usu N *of* n *into* n

incorrect /ɪnkərekt/ ◆◇◇◇◇

1 Something that is **incorrect** is wrong and untrue. *He denied that his evidence about the telephone call was incorrect... People often have incorrect information about food.* ♦ **incorrectly** *The magazine suggested, incorrectly, that he was planning to announce his retirement.* ADJ: oft *it* v-link ADJ to-inf; ADV: ADV with v

2 Something that is **incorrect** is not the thing that is required or is most suitable in a particular situation. *...injuries caused by incorrect posture. ...incorrect diet.* ♦ **incorrectly** *He was told that the doors had been fitted incorrectly.* ADJ-GRADED: usu ADJ n; ADV: ADV with v

incorrigible /ɪnkɒrɪdʒəbəl, AM -kɔːr-/. If you tell someone they are **incorrigible**, you are saying, often in a humorous way, that they have faults which will never change. *'Sue, you are incorrigible!' he said... Gamblers are incorrigible optimists.* ADJ

incorruptible /ɪnkərʌptɪbəl/. If you describe someone as **incorruptible**, you approve of the fact that they cannot be bribed or persuaded to do things that they should not do. *He was a sound businessman, totally reliable and incorruptible.* ADJ PRAGMATICS

increase, increases, increasing, increased. ◆◆◆◆◆ The verb is pronounced /ɪnkriːs/. The noun is pronounced /ɪnkriːs/.

1 If something **increases** or you **increase** it, it becomes greater in number, level, or amount. *The population continues to increase... Japan's industrial output increased by 2%... The company has increased the price of its cars... The increased investment will help stabilise the economy... We are experiencing an increasing number of problems.* V-ERG ≠decrease V; V *by/from/to* amount; V n; V-ed; V-ing

2 If there is an **increase** in the number, level, or amount of something, it becomes greater. *...a sharp increase in productivity... He called for an increase of 1p on income tax. ...an increase of violence along the border.* N-COUNT: oft N *in* n, N *of* amount =rise ≠decrease

3 If something is **on the increase**, it is becoming more frequent or greater in number or intensity. *Crime is on the increase.* PHRASE: v-link PHR

increasingly /ɪnkriːsɪŋli/. You can use **increasingly** to indicate that a situation or quality is becoming greater in intensity or more common. *He was finding it increasingly difficult to make decisions... There is an increasingly popular alternative... The U.S. has increasingly relied on Japanese capital... Increasingly, their goals have become more radical.* ◆◆◆◆◇ ADV: ADV adj, ADV with v, ADV with cl

incredible /ɪnkredɪbəl/ ◆◆◆◇◇

1 If you describe something or someone as **incredible**, you like them very much or are impressed by them, because they are extremely or unusually good. *The wildflowers will be incredible after this rain... Thanks for taking me, I had an incredible time... You're always an incredible help on these cases.* ♦ **incredibly** /ɪncredɪbli/ *Their father was incredibly good-looking.* ADJ-GRADED PRAGMATICS =fantastic; ADV-GRADED: ADV adj/adv

2 If you say that something is **incredible**, you mean that it is very unusual or surprising, and you cannot believe it is really true, although it may be. *It seemed incredible that people would still want to play football during a war... We should not dismiss as lies the incredible stories that children may tell us.* ♦ **incredibly** *Incredibly, some people don't like the name.* ADJ-GRADED: oft *it* v-link ADJ that =unbelievable ≠credible; ADV: usu ADV with cl

3 You use **incredible** to emphasize the degree, amount, or intensity of something. *We import an incredible amount of cheese from the Continent... There was an incredible din... It's incredible how much Francesca wants her father's approval... His panic was incredible.* ♦ **incredibly** *It was incredibly hard work.* ADJ-GRADED: usu ADJ n, also *it* v-link ADJ wh, v-link ADJ PRAGMATICS =amazing; ADV: ADV adj/adv

incredulity /ɪnkrɪdjuːlɪti, AM -duːl-/. If someone reacts with **incredulity** to something, they are unable to believe it because it is very surprising or shocking. *The announcement has been met with incredulity... The Vicar looked at him with open-mouthed incredulity.* N-UNCOUNT =disbelief

incredulous /ɪnkredʒʊləs/. If someone is **incredulous**, they are unable to believe something because it is very surprising or shocking. *'He made you do it?' Her voice was incredulous... There was a brief, incredulous silence.* ♦ **incredulously** *'You told Pete?' Rachel said incredulously. 'I can't believe it!'* ◆◇◇◇◇ ADJ-GRADED; ADV-GRADED: ADV with v

increment /ɪnkrɪmənt/ **increments**

1 An **increment** in something or in the value of something is an amount by which it increases; a formal use. *The average yearly increment in labour* N-COUNT: oft N *in/of* n

productivity in industry was 4.5 per cent... Each increment of knowledge tells us more of our world.
2 An **increment** is an amount by which your salary automatically increases after a fixed period of time; a formal use. *Many teachers qualify for an annual increment.* N-COUNT

incremental /ɪnkrɪmentᵊl/. **Incremental** is used to describe something that increases in value or worth, often by a regular amount; a formal use. *...our ability to add production capacity at relatively low incremental cost... We are seeking continuous, incremental improvements, not great breakthroughs.* ADJ: usu ADJ n

incriminate /ɪnkrɪmɪneɪt/ **incriminates, incriminating, incriminated.** If something **incriminates** you, it suggests that you are responsible for something bad, especially a crime. *He claimed that the drugs had been planted to incriminate him... They are afraid of incriminating themselves and say no more than is necessary.* ◆◇◇◇◇ VERB V n V pron-refl
♦ **incriminating** *Police had reportedly searched his flat and found incriminating evidence.* ADJ-GRADED: usu ADJ n

incubate /ɪnkjʊbeɪt/ **incubates, incubating, incubated** ◆◇◇◇◇
1 When birds **incubate** their eggs, they keep the eggs warm until the baby birds hatch. *The birds returned to their nests and continued to incubate the eggs.* ♦ **incubation** /ɪnkjʊbeɪʃᵊn/ *Male albatrosses share in the incubation of eggs.* VERB V n Also V N-UNCOUNT
2 When a germ in your body **incubates** or **is incubated**, it develops for a period of time before it starts making you feel ill. *The virus can incubate for up to ten days after the initial infection.* ♦ **incubation** *The illness has an incubation period of up to 11 days.* V-ERG V Also V n N-UNCOUNT: usu N n
3 If you say that plans or ideas **incubate**, you mean that they develop slowly after a lot of thought or discussion. *...the fateful decision which had doubtless been incubating in his mind for years.* VERB V

incubator /ɪnkjʊbeɪtəʳ/ **incubators**
1 An **incubator** is a piece of hospital equipment which helps weak or premature babies to survive. It consists of a transparent container and devices that control the oxygen, temperature, and humidity levels. N-COUNT
2 An **incubator** is a piece of equipment used to keep eggs or bacteria at the correct temperature for them to hatch or develop. N-COUNT

inculcate /ɪnkʌlkeɪt, AM ɪnkʌl-/ **inculcates, inculcating, inculcated.** If you **inculcate** an idea or opinion in someone's mind, you teach it to them by repeating it until it is fixed in their mind; a formal word. *You might try to inculcate a few ideas in him, to show him how wrong he's been... The aim is to inculcate business people with an appreciation of different cultures... Great care was taken to inculcate the values of nationhood and family.* VERB V n in n V n with n V n

incumbent /ɪnkʌmbənt/ **incumbents** ◆◆◇◇◇
1 An **incumbent** is someone who holds an official post at a particular time; a formal use. *In general, incumbents have a 94 per cent chance of being reelected.* ► Also an adjective. *...the only candidate who defeated an incumbent senator.* N-COUNT ADJ: ADJ n
2 If it is **incumbent** upon you to do something, it is your duty or responsibility to do it; a formal use. *It is incumbent upon all of us as loyal citizens to make an extra effort.* ADJ: it v-link ADJ upon/on n to-inf

incur /ɪnkɜːʳ/ **incurs, incurring, incurred.** If you **incur** something unpleasant, it happens to you because of something you have done; used in written English. *The government had also incurred huge debts... She falls in love and incurs the wrath of her father. ...the terrible damage incurred during the past decade.* ◆◆◇◇◇ VERB =sustain V n V-ed

incurable /ɪnkjʊərəbᵊl/ ◆◇◇◇◇
1 If someone has an **incurable** disease, they cannot be cured of it. *He is suffering from an incurable skin disease.* ♦ **incurably** /ɪnkjʊərəbli/ *...youngsters who are disabled, or incurably ill.* ADJ ADV: ADV adj
2 You can use **incurable** to indicate that someone has a particular quality or attitude and will not change. *Poor old William is an incurable romantic... You are either very young or an incurable optimist.* ♦ **incurably** *I know you think I'm incurably nosey, but the truth is I'm concerned about you.* ADJ: ADJ n =incorrigible ADV: ADV adj

incursion /ɪnkɜːʳʃᵊn, -ʒᵊn/ **incursions** ◆◇◇◇◇
1 An **incursion** into a country is a small, sudden military invasion of it; a formal use. *...armed incursions into border areas by rebel forces.* N-COUNT: oft N into n
2 If someone or something enters an area where you would not expect them to be, or where they have not been found before, you can call this an **incursion**, especially when you disapprove of their presence; a formal use. *Traditional crafts remain remarkably unchanged by the slow incursion of modern ways. ...his incursion into the sale of automated equipment to factories.* N-COUNT: oft N of n

indebted /ɪndetɪd/ ◆◇◇◇◇
1 If you say that you are **indebted to** someone for something, you mean that you are very grateful to them for something. *I am deeply indebted to him for his help.* ♦ **indebtedness** *...his indebtedness to Sir Geoffrey.* ADJ-GRADED: v-link ADJ to n N-UNCOUNT: usu N to n
2 **Indebted** countries, organizations, or people are ones that owe money to other countries, organizations, or people. *America's treasury secretary identified the most heavily indebted countries.* ♦ **indebtedness** *The company has reduced its indebtedness to just $15 million.* ADJ-GRADED: usu ADJ n N-UNCOUNT: usu with supp

indecency /ɪndiːsᵊnsi/.
1 If you talk about the **indecency** of something or someone, you are indicating that you find them morally or sexually offensive. *...the indecency of their language.* N-UNCOUNT
2 In law, an act of **indecency** is a sexual act for which you can be prosecuted. *They were found guilty of acts of gross indecency.* N-UNCOUNT

indecent /ɪndiːsᵊnt/ ◆◇◇◇◇
1 If you describe something as **indecent**, you mean that it is shocking and offensive, usually because it relates to sex or nakedness. *He accused Mrs Moore of making an indecent suggestion.* ♦ **indecently** *He behaved indecently. ...an indecently short skirt.* ADJ-GRADED =obscene ADV: ADV with v, ADV adj
2 If you describe the speed or amount of something as **indecent**, you are indicating, often in a humorous way, that it is much quicker or larger than is usual or desirable. *The opposition says the legislation was drafted with indecent haste.* ♦ **indecently** *...an indecently large office.* ADJ ADV

indecent assault. **Indecent assault** is the crime of attacking someone in a way which involves touching or threatening them sexually, but not forcing them to have sexual intercourse. N-UNCOUNT

indecent exposure. **Indecent exposure** is a criminal offence that is committed when someone exposes their genitals in public. N-UNCOUNT

indecipherable /ɪndɪsaɪfərəbᵊl/. If writing or speech is **indecipherable**, you cannot understand what the words are. *Maggie's writing was virtually indecipherable... He uttered little indecipherable sounds.* ADJ-GRADED

indecision /ɪndɪsɪʒᵊn/. If you say that someone suffers from **indecision**, you mean that they find it very difficult to make decisions. *After months of indecision, the government gave the plan the go-ahead on Monday... The team has been plagued by indecision and internal divisions.* ◆◇◇◇◇ N-UNCOUNT PRAGMATICS

indecisive /ɪndɪsaɪsɪv/ ◆◇◇◇◇
1 If you say that someone is **indecisive**, you mean that they find it very difficult to make decisions. *Michael was indecisive about how to decorate the room... He was criticised as a weak and indecisive leader.* ♦ **indecisiveness** *The mayor was criticized by radical reformers for his indecisiveness.* ADJ-GRADED PRAGMATICS ≠decisive N-UNCOUNT: oft with poss
2 An **indecisive** result in a contest or election is one which is not clear or definite. *An indecisive result would force a second round of voting... The outcome of the battle was indecisive.* ADJ =inconclusive

indeed /ɪndiːd/ ◆◆◆◆◇
1 You use **indeed** to confirm or agree with something that has just been said. *Later, he admitted that the payments had indeed been made... He did indeed keep important documents inside his hat...* ADV: ADV with v, ADV with cl/group PRAGMATICS

'Did you know him?'—'I did indeed.'... 'Know what I mean?'—'Indeed I do.'... 'Isn't it a gorgeous day, Father?'—'Yes, indeed!'... 'That's a topic which has come to the fore very much recently.'—'Indeed.'

2 You use **indeed** to introduce a further comment or statement which strengthens the point you have already made. *We have nothing against diversity; indeed, we want more of it... When we asked to see more we were refused. Indeed we were escorted away by men with guns.* ADV: ADV with cl PRAGMATICS =in fact

3 You use **indeed** at the end of a clause to give extra force to the word 'very', or to emphasize a particular word. *The engine began to sound very loud indeed... The wine was very good indeed... It's rare indeed for an Irish Prime Minister to visit Belfast.* ADV: adj ADV PRAGMATICS

4 You can use **indeed** as a way of repeating a question in order to emphasize it, especially when you do not know the answer; used in spoken English. *'Now where are the real villains?'—'Where indeed?'... 'And what do we do here?'—'What, indeed?'* ADV: quest ADV PRAGMATICS

indefatigable /ɪndɪfætɪgəbᵊl/. You use **indefatigable** to describe someone who never gets tired of doing something; a formal word. *His indefatigable spirit helped him to cope with his illness... He was indefatigable in his efforts to secure funding for new projects.* ♦ **indefatigably** /ɪndɪfætɪgəbli/ *She worked indefatigably and enthusiastically to interest the young in music.* ADJ =untiring, tireless; ADV: ADV with v, ADV adj

indefensible /ɪndɪfensɪbᵊl/

1 If you say that a statement, action, or idea is **indefensible**, you mean that it cannot be justified or supported because it is completely wrong or unacceptable. *His action was indefensible... She described the new policy as 'morally indefensible'.* ADJ-GRADED ≠defensible
▶ **The indefensible** is something which is indefensible. *To argue otherwise is trying to defend the indefensible.* N-SING

2 Places or buildings that are **indefensible** cannot be defended if they are attacked. *The checkpoint was abandoned as militarily indefensible.* ADJ

indefinable /ɪndɪfaɪnəbᵊl/. An **indefinable** quality or feeling cannot easily be described; used in written English. *There was something indefinable in her eyes... His head felt lighter in some indefinable way.* ADJ

indefinite /ɪndefɪnɪt/ ◆◇◇◇◇

1 If you describe a situation or period as **indefinite**, you mean that people have not decided when it will end. *The trial was adjourned for an indefinite period. ...an indefinite strike by government workers.* ADJ: usu ADJ n

2 Something that is **indefinite** is not exact or clear. *...at some indefinite time in the future. ...a handsome woman of indefinite age.* ADJ =indeterminate, uncertain

indefinite article, indefinite articles. The words 'a' and 'an' are sometimes called the **indefinite article**. N-COUNT

indefinitely /ɪndefɪnɪtli/. If a situation will continue **indefinitely**, it will continue for ever or until someone decides to change it or end it. *The visit has now been postponed indefinitely... I couldn't stay there indefinitely.* ◆◇◇◇◇ ADV: ADV with v

indefinite pronoun, indefinite pronouns. An **indefinite pronoun** is a pronoun such as 'someone', 'anything', or 'nobody', which you use to refer in a general way to a person or thing without saying who or what they are, or what kind of person or thing you mean. N-COUNT

indelible /ɪndelɪbᵊl/

1 If you say that something leaves an **indelible** impression, you mean that it is very unlikely to be forgotten. *My visit to India in 1986 left an indelible impression on me... The war has made an indelible mark on the world.* ♦ **indelibly** *The horrors he experienced are imprinted, perhaps indelibly, in his brain.* ADJ-GRADED: usu ADJ n; ADV: ADV with v

2 **Indelible** ink or an **indelible** stain cannot be removed, erased, or washed out. *It leaves indelible stains on clothes. ...written in indelible ink.* ADJ: usu ADJ n

indelicate /ɪndelɪkət/. If something or someone is **indelicate**, they are rude or embarrassing; a formal word. *She really could not touch upon such an indelicate subject.* ADJ-GRADED

indemnify /ɪndemnɪfaɪ/ **indemnifies, indemnifying, indemnified.** To **indemnify** someone against something bad happening means to promise to protect them, especially financially, if it happens; a formal word. *They agreed to indemnify the taxpayers against any loss... The printers were indemnified against legal action... It doesn't have the money to indemnify everybody.* VERB V n *against* n; V n

indemnity /ɪndemnɪti/ **indemnities** ◆◇◇◇◇

1 If something provides **indemnity**, it provides insurance or protection against damage or loss, especially in the form of financial compensation; a formal use. *They were charged with failing to have professional indemnity cover... Political exiles had not been given indemnity from prosecution.* N-UNCOUNT

2 An **indemnity** is an amount of money or goods that are received by someone as compensation for some damage or loss they have suffered; a formal use. *The government paid the family an indemnity for the missing pictures.* N-VAR

indent /ɪndent/ **indents, indenting, indented.** When you **indent** a line, you write or print it further away from the margin than the other lines. *...if you don't indent the second line.* VERB V n

indentation /ɪndenteɪʃᵊn/ **indentations**

1 An **indentation** is a space at the beginning of a line of writing, between the margin and the beginning of the writing. N-COUNT

2 An **indentation** is a dent in a surface or a notch on the edge of something. *Using a knife, make slight indentations around the edges of the pastry.* N-COUNT

indented /ɪndentɪd/. If something is **indented**, its edge or surface is uneven because parts of it have been worn away or cut away. *...a voyage down Chile's indented coastline.* ADJ-GRADED

indentured /ɪndentʃᵊrd/. In the past, an **indentured** worker was one who was forced to work for someone for a period of time, because of an agreement made by people in authority. *Daniel arrived in Maryland as an indentured servant.* ADJ: usu ADJ n

independence /ɪndɪpendəns/ ◆◆◆◆◇

1 If a country has or gains **independence**, it has its own government and is not ruled by any other country. *In 1816, Argentina declared its independence from Spain. ...the country's first elections since independence in 1962.* N-UNCOUNT

2 Someone's **independence** is the fact that they do not rely on other people. *He was afraid of losing his independence. ...a woman's independence, capability, and power.* N-UNCOUNT: oft poss N

Independence Day. A country's **Independence Day** is the day on which its people celebrate their independence from another country that ruled them in the past. *He died on Independence Day, 1831.* N-UNCOUNT

independent /ɪndɪpendənt/ **independents** ◆◆◆◆◆

1 If one thing or person is **independent** of another, they are separate and not connected, so the first one is not affected or influenced by the second. *Your questions should be independent of each other... We're going independent from the university and setting up our own group... Two independent studies have been carried out.* ♦ **independently** *...several people working independently in different areas of the world. ...biological processes which continue to function independently of any effort that we can make.* ADJ: oft ADJ *of/from* n =separate; ADV: usu ADV with v, also ADV adj, oft ADV *of/from* n =separately

2 If someone is **independent**, they are free to live as they want, because they do not need help and have no obligations to anyone. *Phil was now much more independent of his parents... She would like to be financially independent... There were benefits to being a single independent woman.* ♦ **independently** *...helping disabled students to live and study as independently as possible. ...the independently-minded females of the Nineties... He is independently wealthy.* ADJ-GRADED: oft ADJ *of/from* n ≠dependent; ADV: ADV after v, ADV adj/-ed

3 An **independent** school or other organization does not receive money from the government. *He* ADJ: usu ADJ n ≠state

taught chemistry at a leading independent school. ...an independent television station.

4 **Independent** countries and states are not ruled by other countries but have their own government. *...a fully independent state... Papua New Guinea became independent from Australia in 1975.* ADJ-GRADED: oft ADJ *from/of* n

5 An **independent** inquiry or opinion is one that involves people who are not connected with a situation, and should therefore be fair and unbiased. *The government ordered an independent inquiry into the affair... An independent opinion poll published today shows growing discontent with the government.* ADJ: ADJ n

6 An **independent** politician is one who does not represent any political party. *There's been a late surge of support for an independent candidate. ...the most powerful independent politician in France.* ADJ: usu ADJ n ▶ An **independent** is an independent politician. *Mr Fujimori, an independent, was almost unknown a month ago.* N-COUNT

indescribable /ɪndɪskraɪbəbᵊl/. You use **indescribable** to emphasize that a quality or condition is very intense or extreme, and therefore cannot be properly described. *...her indescribable joy when it was confirmed her son was alive... The stench from the sewer is indescribable.* ADJ PRAGMATICS =inexpressible ♦ **indescribably** /ɪndɪskraɪbəbli/. *...the treacherous and indescribably filthy conditions.* ADV: ADV adj

indestructible /ɪndɪstrʌktɪbᵊl/. If something is **indestructible**, it is very strong and cannot be destroyed. *This type of plastic is almost indestructible.* ADJ

indeterminacy /ɪndɪtɜːʳmɪnəsi/. The **indeterminacy** of something is its quality of being uncertain or vague; a formal word. *...the indeterminacy of language.* N-UNCOUNT

indeterminate /ɪndɪtɜːʳmɪnət/. If something is **indeterminate**, you cannot say exactly what it is. *Dr Amid was a man of indeterminate age... I hope to carry on for an indeterminate period.* ADJ-GRADED: usu ADJ n =indefinite

index /ɪndeks/ **indices, indexes, indexing, indexed.** **Indexes** is the usual plural, but the form **indices** can be used for meanings 1, 5, and 6. ◆◆◆◇◇

1 An **index** is a system by which changes in the value of something and the rate at which it changes can be recorded, measured, or interpreted. *The UK retail price index for October is expected to show an increase of 0.8 per cent. ...economic indices.* N-COUNT: with supp

2 An **index** is an alphabetical list that is printed at the back of a book and tells you on which pages important topics are referred to. *Curiously, the word 'gay' does not occur in the index... There's even a special subject index.* N-COUNT

3 If you **index** a book or a collection of information, you make an alphabetical list of the items in it. *A quarter of this vast archive has been indexed and made accessible to researchers... Painters and sculptors are indexed separately... She's indexed the book many different ways—by author, by age, and by illustrator.* VERB *be* V-ed V-ed V n

4 If a quantity or value **is indexed** to another, a system is arranged so that it increases or decreases whenever the other one increases or decreases. *Minimum pensions and wages are to be indexed to inflation.* VB: usu passive *be* V-ed *to* n

5 If one thing is an **index** of another, it indicates what the other thing will be like; a formal use. *Weeds are an index to the character of the soil.* N-COUNT: usu N *of/to* n

6 In mathematics, **indices** are the little numbers that show how many times you must multiply a number by itself. In the equation $3^2 = 9$, the number 2 is an index; a technical use. N-COUNT

7 See also **card index**.

index card, index cards. An **index card** is a small card on which you can write information. You can keep index cards together in a file, and arrange them in any order that you find useful. N-COUNT

index finger, index fingers. Your **index finger** is the finger that is next to your thumb. N-COUNT =forefinger

index-linked. **Index-linked** pensions, payments, or welfare benefits are calculated using the index which measures inflation or the cost of living, and therefore change as inflation or the cost of living changes; used mainly in British English. ADJ

Indian /ɪndiən/ **Indians** ◆◆◆◆◇

1 **Indian** means belonging or relating to India, or to its people or culture. *...the Indian government.* ADJ: usu ADJ n

2 An **Indian** is an Indian citizen, or a person of Indian origin. *...a study of Indians and Pakistanis living in Southall.* N-COUNT

3 **Indians** are the people who lived in North, South, or Central America before Europeans arrived, or their descendants; an old-fashioned use. *The South American Indians have been cooking and eating potatoes for well over two thousand years.* N-COUNT

4 See also **Anglo-Indian**.

Indian corn. **Indian corn** is the same as **maize**. N-UNCOUNT

Indian summer, Indian summers. You can refer to a period of unusually warm and sunny weather during the autumn as an **Indian summer**. N-COUNT

indicate /ɪndɪkeɪt/ **indicates, indicating, indicated** ◆◆◆◆◇

1 If one thing **indicates** another, the first thing shows that the second is true or exists. *A survey of retired people has indicated that most are independent and enjoying life... Our vote today indicates a change in United States policy... This indicates whether remedies are suitable for children.* VERB =show V that V n V wh

2 If you **indicate** an opinion, an intention, or a fact, you mention it in an indirect way. *Mr Rivers has indicated that he may resign. ...waiting for U.S. authorities to indicate their monetary policy plans.* VERB V that V n

3 If you **indicate** something to someone, you show them where it is, especially by pointing to it; a formal use. *He indicated a chair. 'Sit down.'... Pelham moved across to indicate a wall chart.* VERB V n

4 If one thing **indicates** something else, it is a sign of that thing. *Dreams can help indicate your true feelings... His language indicates a poor education.* VERB V n

5 If a technical instrument **indicates** something, it shows a measurement or reading. *The needles that indicate your height are at the top right-hand corner... The temperature gauge indicated that it was boiling.* VERB =show V n V that

6 When drivers **indicate**, they make lights flash on one side of their vehicle to show that they are going to turn in that direction; used mainly in British English. The usual American word is **signal**. *He told us when to indicate and when to change gear.* VERB =signal V n Also V

indication /ɪndɪkeɪʃᵊn/ **indications.** An **indication** is a sign which suggests, for example, what people are thinking or feeling. *All the indications are that we are going to receive reasonable support from abroad... He gave no indication that he was ready to compromise.* ◆◆◆◇◇ N-VAR =sign

indicative /ɪndɪkətɪv/ ◆◇◇◇◇

1 If one thing is **indicative** of another, it suggests what the other thing is likely to be; a formal use. *His action is indicative of growing concern about the shortage of skilled labour... Often physical appearance is indicative of how a person feels.* ADJ-GRADED: usu v-link ADJ, usu ADJ *of* n/wh =symptomatic

2 In grammar, a clause that is in **the indicative**, or in **the indicative mood**, has a subject followed by a verb group. Examples are 'I'm hungry' and 'She was followed'. Clauses of this kind are typically used to make statements. N-SING: *the* N =declarative

indicator /ɪndɪkeɪtəʳ/ **indicators** ◆◆◇◇◇

1 An **indicator** is a measurement or value which gives you an idea of what something is like. *...vital economic indicators, such as inflation, growth and the trade gap... The number of wells is a fair indicator of the demand for water.* N-COUNT: usu with supp

2 A car's **indicators** are the flashing lights that tell you that it is going to turn left or right; used mainly in British English. N-COUNT

indices /ɪndɪsiːz/. **Indices** is a plural form of **index**.

indict /ɪndaɪt/ **indicts, indicting, indicted.** If someone **is indicted** for a crime, they are officially charged with it; a legal term used mainly in American English. *He was later indicted on corruption charges... She has been indicted for* ◆◇◇◇◇ VB: usu passive =charge *be* V-ed *on* n *be* V-ed *for* -ing/n *possessing cocaine... The police said he'd been formally indicted on Saturday... Attorneys for the indicted officers tried to delay the trial.* (be V-ed; V-ed)

indictment /ɪndaɪtmənt/ **indictments** ◆◆◇◇◇

1 If you say that one thing is an **indictment** of another thing, you mean that it shows how bad the other thing is. *It's a sad indictment of society that policeman are regarded as easy targets by thugs.* N-COUNT: oft N *of* n

2 An **indictment** is a formal accusation that someone has committed a crime; a legal term used mainly in American English. *Prosecutors may soon seek an indictment on racketeering and fraud charges... The government's indictment against the three men alleged unlawful trading.* N-VAR: oft N *against* n =charge

indie /ɪndi/ **indies.** In informal British English, **indie** music refers to rock or pop music produced by new bands working with small, independent record companies, and is often considered to be more interesting and creative than music produced by well-known bands and large international companies. *...a multi-racial indie band.* ◆◆◇◇◇ ADJ: ADJ n ≠mainstream ► An **indie** is an indie band or record company. N-COUNT =major

indifference /ɪndɪfərəns/. If you accuse someone of **indifference** to something, you mean that they have a complete lack of interest in it. *...his callous indifference to the plight of his son. ...the prejudice and indifference which surround the Aids epidemic.* ◆◇◇◇◇ N-UNCOUNT: oft N *to* n ≠concern

indifferent /ɪndɪfərənt/ ◆◇◇◇◇

1 If you accuse someone of being **indifferent** to something, you mean that they have a complete lack of interest in it. *People have become indifferent to the suffering of others. ...the row over the police's indifferent attitude to the killings.* ADJ-GRADED: oft ADJ *to* n ≠concerned ♦ **indifferently** *'Not that it matters,' said Tench indifferently.* ADV-GRADED: ADV after v

2 If you describe something or someone as **indifferent**, you mean that their standard or quality is not very good, and often quite bad. *She had starred in several very indifferent movies... Much of the food we eat is of very poor or indifferent quality.* ADJ-GRADED =mediocre ♦ **indifferently** *...an eight-year-old girl who reads tolerably and writes indifferently.* ADV-GRADED: ADV with v

indigenous /ɪndɪdʒɪnəs/. **Indigenous** people or things belong to the country in which they are found, rather than coming there or being brought there from another country; a formal word. *...the country's indigenous population. ...animals that are indigenous to Asia.* ◆◇◇◇◇ ADJ =native

indigent /ɪndɪdʒənt/. Someone who is **indigent** is very poor; a formal word. ADJ-GRADED

indigestible /ɪndɪdʒestɪbᵊl/

1 Food that is **indigestible** cannot be digested easily. *Fried food is very indigestible.* ADJ-GRADED ≠digestible

2 If you describe facts or ideas as **indigestible**, you mean that they are difficult to understand, complicated, and dull. *...an extremely dense, indigestible and wordy book.* ADJ-GRADED

indigestion /ɪndɪdʒestʃᵊn/. If you have **indigestion**, you have pains in your stomach and chest that are caused by difficulties in digesting food. ◆◇◇◇◇ N-UNCOUNT

indignant /ɪndɪgnənt/. If you are **indignant**, you are shocked and angry, because you think that something is unjust or unfair. *He is indignant at suggestions that they were secret agents... MPs were indignant that the government had not consulted them... Sheena gave her an indignant look.* ◆◇◇◇◇ ADJ-GRADED: oft ADJ *at/about* n/-ing, ADJ that ♦ **indignantly** *'That is not true,' Erica said indignantly.* ADV-GRADED: ADV with v

indignation /ɪndɪgneɪʃᵊn/. **Indignation** is the feeling of shock and anger which you have when you think that something is unjust or unfair. *She was filled with indignation at the conditions under which miners were forced to work... No wonder he could hardly contain his indignation.* ◆◇◇◇◇ N-UNCOUNT

indignity /ɪndɪgnɪti/ **indignities.** If you talk about the **indignity** of doing something, you mean that doing it is humiliating or embarrassing; a formal word. *Later, he suffered the indignity of having to flee angry protesters... What sort of indignities would he be forced to endure?* ◆◇◇◇◇ N-VAR: oft *the* N *of* -ing/n =humiliation

indigo /ɪndɪgoʊ/. Something that is **indigo** is dark purplish blue in colour. *...the stars in the indigo sky... Indigo tattoos adorn her forehead.* ◆◇◇◇◇ COLOUR

indirect /ɪndaɪrekt, -dɪr-/ ◆◆◇◇◇

1 An **indirect** result or effect is not caused immediately and obviously by a thing or person, but happens because of something else that they have done. *Businesses are feeling the indirect effects from the recession that's going on elsewhere... Millions could die of hunger as an indirect result of the war... His influence has been profound, but it has been indirect.* ADJ: usu ADJ n ≠direct ♦ **indirectly** *Drugs are indirectly responsible for the violence... The president is indirectly elected by parliament... Indirectly, I did cause her death. I shouldn't have left her there.* ADV: usu ADV adj, ADV with v, also ADV with cl

2 An **indirect** route or journey does not use the shortest or easiest way between two places. *The goods went by a rather indirect route.* ADJ-GRADED ≠direct

3 Indirect remarks and information suggest something or refer to it, without actually mentioning it or stating it clearly. *His remarks amounted to an indirect appeal for economic aid... There were indirect references to his opponent... So far the evidence is only indirect.* ADJ-GRADED ♦ **indirectly** *He referred indirectly to the territorial dispute.* ADV: ADV with v

indirect object, indirect objects. An **indirect object** is an object which is used with a transitive verb to indicate who benefits from an action or gets something as a result. For example, in 'She gave him her address', 'him' is the indirect object. Compare **direct object**. N-COUNT

indirect question, indirect questions. An **indirect question** is the same as a **reported question**. N-COUNT

indirect speech. Indirect speech is the same as **reported speech**. N-UNCOUNT

indirect tax, indirect taxes. An **indirect tax** is a tax on goods and services which is added to their price. VAT and import duty are indirect taxes. Compare **direct tax**. N-COUNT

indirect taxation. Indirect taxation is a system in which a government raises money by means of indirect taxes. N-UNCOUNT

indiscipline /ɪndɪsɪplɪn/. If you refer to **indiscipline** in a group or team, you disapprove of their lack of discipline. *There is growing evidence of indiscipline among the troops. ...the team's indiscipline on the pitch.* N-UNCOUNT PRAGMATICS ≠discipline

indiscreet /ɪndɪskriːt/. If you describe someone as **indiscreet**, you mean that they do or say things in public which they should only do or say secretly or in private. *He is notoriously indiscreet about his private life... Had he been indiscreet in what he had said? ...the duchess's indiscreet behaviour.* ADJ-GRADED ≠discreet

indiscretion /ɪndɪskreʃᵊn/ **indiscretions.** If you talk about someone's **indiscretion**, you mean that they have done or said something that is risky, careless, or likely to upset people. *Occasionally they paid for their indiscretion with their lives. ...punishing me for an indiscretion committed a decade ago. ...rumours of his mother's youthful indiscretions.* N-VAR

indiscriminate /ɪndɪskrɪmɪnət/. If you describe an action as **indiscriminate**, you are critical of it because it does not involve any careful thought or choice. *The indiscriminate use of fertilisers is damaging to the environment. ...the indiscriminate killing of refugees.* ◆◇◇◇◇ ADJ-GRADED PRAGMATICS ≠selective ♦ **indiscriminately** *The men opened fire indiscriminately... I'm afraid this disease strikes indiscriminately.* ADV-GRADED: usu ADV with v, also ADV adj

indispensable /ɪndɪspensəbᵊl/. If you say that someone or something is **indispensable**, you mean that they are absolutely essential and other people or things cannot function without them. *She was becoming indispensable to him. ...the indispensable guide for any traveller in France.* ◆◇◇◇◇ ADJ-GRADED: oft ADJ *to* n =essential ≠dispensable

indisposed /ɪndɪspoʊzd/. If you say that someone is **indisposed**, you mean that they are not available because they are ill, or for a reason that you don't want to reveal; a formal use. *The speaker was regrettably indisposed.* ADJ: usu v-link ADJ =unwell

indisputable /ɪndɪspjuːtəbəl/. If you say that something is **indisputable**, you are emphasizing that it cannot be denied or proved wrong. *It is indisputable that birds in the UK are harbouring this illness... The indisputable fact is that computers carry out logical operations.* ♦ **indisputably** /ɪndɪspjuːtəbli/ *She has an indisputably lovely voice.*
◆◇◇◇◇ ADJ: oft *it* v-link ADJ that PRAGMATICS =undeniable, indubitable; ADV

indissoluble /ɪndɪsɒljʊbəl/. If you describe a relationship as **indissoluble**, you mean that it is permanent and cannot be ended; a formal word. *...an indissoluble link between church and state.*
ADJ

indistinct /ɪndɪstɪŋkt/. Something that is **indistinct** is unclear and difficult to see, hear, or recognize. *The lettering is fuzzy and indistinct. ...the indistinct murmur of voices.* ♦ **indistinctly** *He speaks so rapidly and indistinctly that many listeners haven't a clue what he is saying.*
ADJ-GRADED =unclear ≠distinct; ADV-GRADED: ADV after v

indistinguishable /ɪndɪstɪŋgwɪʃəbəl/. If one thing is **indistinguishable** from another, the two things are so similar that it is difficult to know which is which. *Replica weapons are indistinguishable from the real thing.*
◆◇◇◇◇ ADJ: usu v-link ADJ, oft ADJ *from* n ≠distinguishable

individual /ɪndɪvɪdʒuəl/ **individuals** ◆◆◆◆◇

1 **Individual** means relating to one person or thing, rather than to a large group. *...waiting for the group to decide rather than making individual decisions... Aid to individual countries would be linked to progress towards democracy... Divide the vegetables among four individual dishes.* ♦ **individually** *...cheeses which come in individually wrapped segments... There are 96 pieces and they are worth, individually and collectively, a lot of money.*
ADJ: ADJ n; ADV: usu ADV with v, ADV adj, also ADV with cl

2 An **individual** is a person. *...anonymous individuals who are doing good things within our community. ...the rights and responsibilities of the individual... A child's awareness of being an individual grows in stages during the pre-school years.*
N-COUNT

3 If you describe someone or something as **individual**, you mean that you admire them because they are very unusual and do not try to imitate other people or things. *It was really all part of her very individual personality... The language is highly individual.*
ADJ-GRADED PRAGMATICS

individualism /ɪndɪvɪdzʊlɪzəm/ ◆◇◇◇◇

1 You use **individualism** to refer to the behaviour of someone who likes to think and do things in their own way, rather than imitating other people. *He is struck by what he calls the individualism of American officers.*
N-UNCOUNT

2 **Individualism** is the belief that economics and politics should not be controlled by the state. *She sought a middle road between communism and individualism.*
N-UNCOUNT

individualist /ɪndɪvɪdʒʊlɪst/ **individualists**

1 If you describe someone as an **individualist**, you mean that they like to think and do things in their own way, rather than imitating other people. *Individualists say that you should be able to wear what you want.*
N-COUNT

2 **Individualist** means relating to the belief that economics and politics should not be controlled by the state. *...a party fundamentally committed to individualist and consumerist values.* ► An **individualist** is a person with individualist views. *They share with earlier individualists a fear of creeping socialism.*
ADJ: usu ADJ n; N-COUNT

individualistic /ɪndɪvɪdʒʊlɪstɪk/. If you say that someone is **individualistic**, you mean that they like to think and do things in their own way, rather than imitating other people. If you say that a society is **individualistic**, you mean that the people there are individualistic. *Most artists are very individualistic... Spain remains a very individualistic country.*
ADJ-GRADED

individuality /ɪndɪvɪdʒuælɪti/. The **individuality** of a person or thing consists of the qualities that make them different from other people or things. *People should be free to express their individuality... This will give your promotional material individuality and style.*
◆◇◇◇◇ N-UNCOUNT

individualize /ɪndɪvɪdʒʊlaɪz/ **individualizes, individualizing, individualized;** also spelled **individualise** in British English. To **individualize** a thing or person means to make them different from other things or people and to give them a recognizable identity; a formal word. *Unless a document is highly formal, individualize it by adding comments in the margins.* ♦ **individualized** *Doctors feel that a more individualized approach to patients should now be adopted.*
VERB =personalize; V n; ADJ-GRADED

indivisible /ɪndɪvɪzɪbəl/. If you say that something is **indivisible**, you mean that it cannot be divided into different parts. *Far from being separate, the mind and body form an indivisible whole, like the two sides of a coin.*
ADJ ≠divisible

Indo- /ɪndoʊ-/. **Indo-** combines with nationality adjectives to form adjectives which describe something as connected with both India and another country. *...Indo-Pakistani talks.*
PREFIX

indoctrinate /ɪndɒktrɪneɪt/ **indoctrinates, indoctrinating, indoctrinated.** If people **are indoctrinated**, they are taught a particular belief with the aim that they will reject other beliefs; used showing disapproval. *They have been completely indoctrinated... I wouldn't say that she was trying to indoctrinate us.* ♦ **indoctrination** /ɪndɒktrɪneɪʃən/ *...political indoctrination classes.*
VERB PRAGMATICS =brainwash; *be* V-ed; V n; N-UNCOUNT

indolence /ɪndələns/. **Indolence** means laziness; a formal word. *He was noted for his indolence.*
N-UNCOUNT

indolent /ɪndələnt/. Someone who is **indolent** is lazy; a formal word. *...indolent teenagers who won't lift a finger to help.*
ADJ-GRADED

indomitable /ɪndɒmɪtəbəl/. If you say that someone has an **indomitable** spirit, you admire them because they never give up or admit that they have been defeated; a formal word. *...the indomitable spirit of the Polish people. ...a woman of indomitable will... He was utterly indomitable.*
ADJ-GRADED PRAGMATICS

Indonesian /ɪndəniːʒən/ **Indonesians** ◆◆◆◆◇

1 **Indonesian** means belonging or relating to Indonesia, or to its people or culture.
ADJ

2 An **Indonesian** is an Indonesian citizen, or a person of Indonesian origin.
N-COUNT

3 People sometimes refer to the language spoken by people who live in Indonesia as **Indonesian**; an informal use.
N-UNCOUNT

indoor /ɪndɔːr/. **Indoor** activities or things are ones that happen or are used inside a building and not outside. *No smoking in any indoor facilities. ...an indoor market. ...indoor plants.*
◆◆◇◇◇ ADJ: ADJ n ≠outdoor

indoors /ɪndɔːrz/. If something happens **indoors**, it happens inside a building. *Since she was indoors, she had not been wearing a coat... I think perhaps we should go indoors... Spend an evening indoors watching TV.*
◆◇◇◇◇ ADV: *be* ADV, ADV after v ≠outdoors

indubitable /ɪndjuːbɪtəbəl, AM -duːb-/. You use **indubitable** to describe something when you want to emphasize that it is definite and cannot be doubted; a formal word. *His brilliance as a director and actor renders this film an indubitable classic.* ♦ **indubitably** *His behaviour was indubitably ill-judged.*
ADJ PRAGMATICS =indisputable; ADV

induce /ɪndjuːs, AM -duːs-/ **induces, inducing, induced** ◆◆◇◇◇

1 To **induce** a state or condition means to cause it. *Doctors said surgery could induce a heart attack. ...an economic crisis induced by high oil prices.*
VERB V n V-ed

2 If you **induce** someone to do something, you persuade or influence them to do it. *I would do anything to induce them to stay... More than 4,000 teachers were induced to take early retirement.*
VERB =persuade V n to-inf

3 If a doctor or midwife **induces** labour or birth, they cause a pregnant woman to start giving birth by using drugs or other medical means. *He might decide that it is best to induce labour.* ♦ **induction** *...if there are obvious medical reasons for induction.*
VERB V n; N-SING

-induced /-ɪndjuːst, AM -duːs-/. **-induced** combines with nouns to form adjectives which indicate that a state, condition, or illness is caused
COMB in ADJ

by a particular thing. *...stress-induced disorders. ...a drug-induced hallucination.*

inducement /ɪndjuːsmənt, AM -duːs-/ **inducements.** If someone is offered an **inducement** to do something, they are given or promised something such as gifts or special benefits, in order to persuade them to do it. *They offer every inducement to foreign businesses to invest in their states... Various inducements are offered to encourage employees to wear safety clothing.* ◆◇◇◇◇ N-COUNT: oft N to-inf =incentive

induct /ɪndʌkt/ **inducts, inducting, inducted**

1 If someone **is inducted** into a particular job, rank, or position, they are given the job, rank, or position in a formal ceremony; a formal word. *Six new members have been inducted into the Provincial Cabinet. ...as the Countess inducts Nina into the cult.* VERB be V-ed into n, V n into n, Also V n

2 In American English, if someone **is inducted** into the army, they are officially made to join the army. *In December he was inducted into the army.* VB: usu passive =conscript be V-ed into n

induction /ɪndʌkʃᵊn/ **inductions** ◆◇◇◇◇

1 Induction is a procedure or ceremony for introducing someone to a new job or way of life. *...the induction of the girls into the sport. ...Elvis' induction into the army. ...an induction course for new members.* N-VAR: oft with poss, N to/into n

2 Induction is a method of reasoning in which you use individual ideas or facts to give you a general rule or conclusion; a formal use. N-UNCOUNT

3 Induction is the process by which electricity or magnetism is passed between two objects or circuits without them touching each other; a technical use. N-UNCOUNT

4 See also **induce**.

inductive /ɪndʌktɪv/. **Inductive** reasoning is based on the process of induction. ADJ

indulge /ɪndʌldʒ/ **indulges, indulging, indulged** ◆◆◇◇◇

1 If you **indulge** in something or if you **indulge** yourself, you allow yourself to have or do something that you know you will enjoy. *Only rarely will she indulge in a glass of wine... He returned to Britain so that he could indulge his passion for football... You can indulge yourself without spending a fortune.* VERB V in n, V n, V pron-refl, Also V

2 If you **indulge** someone, you let them have or do what they want, even if this is not good for them. *He did not agree with indulging children.* VERB =spoil V n

indulgence /ɪndʌldʒᵊns/ **indulgences. Indulgence** means treating someone with special kindness, often when it is not a good thing. *The king's indulgence towards his sons angered the business community... For a moment he allowed himself the indulgence of examining his feelings for her... The car is one of my few indulgences.* ◆◇◇◇◇ N-VAR

indulgent /ɪndʌldʒᵊnt/. If you are **indulgent**, you treat a person with special kindness, often in a way that is not good for them. *His indulgent mother was willing to let him do anything he wanted.* ♦ **indulgently** *Ned smiled at him indulgently and said, 'Come on over when you feel like it.'* ◆◇◇◇◇ ADJ-GRADED; ADV-GRADED: usu ADV with v, also ADV adj

industrial /ɪndʌstriəl/ ◆◆◆◆◇

1 You use **industrial** to describe things which relate to or are used in industry. *...industrial machinery and equipment. ...a link between industrial chemicals and cancer.* ADJ: usu ADJ n

2 An **industrial** city or country is one in which industry is important or highly developed. *...ministers from leading western industrial countries.* ADJ: usu ADJ n

industrial action. If workers take **industrial action**, they join together and do something to show that they are unhappy with their pay or working conditions, for example refusing to work; used mainly in British English. *Prison officers will decide next week whether to take industrial action over staffing levels.* ◆◇◇◇◇ N-UNCOUNT

industrial estate, industrial estates. An **industrial estate** is an area which has been specially planned for a lot of factories; used mainly in British English. ◆◇◇◇◇ N-COUNT

industrialise /ɪndʌstriəlaɪz/. See **industrialize**.

industrialism /ɪndʌstriəlɪzəm/. **Industrialism** is the state of having an economy based on industry. N-UNCOUNT

industrialist /ɪndʌstriəlɪst/ **industrialists.** An **industrialist** is a powerful businessman who owns or controls large industrial companies or factories. *...prominent Japanese industrialists.* ◆◇◇◇◇ N-COUNT

industrialize /ɪndʌstriəlaɪz/ **industrializes, industrializing, industrialized;** also spelled **industrialise** in British English. When a country **industrializes** or **is industrialized**, it develops a lot of industries. *Energy consumption rises as countries industrialise... Stalin's methods had industrialized the Russian economy... Britain was the first nation to be industrialised.* ♦ **industrialization** /ɪndʌstriəlaɪzeɪʃᵊn/ *Industrialization began early in Spain.* ◆◆◇◇◇ V-ERG; V; V n; N-UNCOUNT

industrialized /ɪndʌstriəlaɪzd/; also spelled **industrialised**. An **industrialized** area or place is one which has a lot of industries. *Industrialized countries could reduce carbon dioxide emissions by 20 per cent. ...the industrialized world.* ◆◆◇◇◇ ADJ-GRADED: ADJ n

industrial relations. Industrial relations refers to the relationship between employers and employees in industry, and the political decisions and laws that affect it. *The offer is seen as an attempt to improve industrial relations... The new industrial relations legislation curbed the power of the unions.* ◆◇◇◇◇ N-PLURAL

industrious /ɪndʌstriəs/. If you describe someone as **industrious**, you mean they work very hard. *She was an industrious and willing worker.* ♦ **industriously** *Maggie paints industriously all through the summer.* ADJ-GRADED =hard-working; ADV-GRADED: ADV with v

industry /ɪndəstri/ **industries** ◆◆◆◆◆

1 Industry is the work and processes involved in collecting raw materials, and making them into products in factories. *British industry suffers through insufficient investment in research. ...in countries where industry is developing rapidly.* N-UNCOUNT

2 A particular **industry** consists of all the people and activities involved in making a particular product or providing a particular service. *...the motor vehicle and textile industries. ...the Scottish tourist industry.* N-COUNT: oft n N

3 If you refer to a social or political activity as an **industry**, you are criticizing it because you think it involves a lot of people in unnecessary or useless work. *Some Afro-Caribbeans are rejecting the whole race relations industry... The multibillion-dollar fitness industry rakes in fat profits from our hunger to look good.* N-COUNT: usu sing, the supp N PRAGMATICS

4 Industry is the fact of working very hard; a formal use. *No one doubted his ability, his industry or his integrity.* N-UNCOUNT

5 See also **captain of industry**, **cottage industry**, **service industry**.

inebriated /ɪniːbrieɪtɪd/. Someone who is **inebriated** has drunk too much alcohol; a formal word. *Scott was obviously inebriated by the time the dessert was served.* ADJ-GRADED

inedible /ɪnedɪbᵊl/. If you say that something is **inedible**, you mean you cannot eat it, for example because it tastes bad or is poisonous. *Detainees complained of being given food which is inedible. ...the unnecessary killing of large numbers of inedible fish.* ADJ-GRADED ≠edible

ineffable /ɪnefəbᵊl/. You use **ineffable** to say that something is so great or extreme that it cannot be described in words; a formal word. *...the ineffable sadness of many of the portraits.* ♦ **ineffably** /ɪnefəbli/ *Walters is ineffably entertaining. ...his ineffably powerful brain.* ADJ: usu ADJ n =indescribable; ADV: usu ADV adj

ineffective /ɪnɪfektɪv/. If you say that something is **ineffective**, you mean that it has no effect on a process or situation. *Economic reform will continue to be painful and ineffective... This is an ineffective method of controlling your dog.* ♦ **ineffectiveness** *...the ineffectiveness of some of the police's anti-crime strategies.* ◆◇◇◇◇ ADJ-GRADED ≠effective; N-UNCOUNT

ineffectual /ɪnɪfektʃuəl/. If someone or something is **ineffectual**, they fail to do what they are expected to do or are trying to do. *The mayor had become ineffectual in the struggle to clamp down on drugs. ...the well-meaning but ineffectual jobs programs of the past.* ♦ **ineffectually** *Her voice trailed off ineffectually.* ◆◇◇◇◇ ADJ-GRADED; ADV-GRADED

inefficient /ɪnɪfɪʃənt/. **Inefficient** people, organizations, systems, or machines do not use time, energy, or other resources in the best way. *Their communication systems are inefficient in the extreme. ...the closure of outdated and inefficient factories.* ♦ **inefficiency, inefficiencies** *The inefficiency of the distribution system has led to the loss of millions of tons of food.* ♦ **inefficiently** *Energy prices have been kept low, so energy is used inefficiently.* ◆◆◇◇◇ ADJ-GRADED PRAGMATICS ≠efficient; N-VAR; ADV-GRADED: ADV with v

inelegant /ɪnelɪgənt/. If you say that something is **inelegant**, you mean that it is not attractive or graceful. *The grand piano has been replaced with a small, inelegant electric model.* ADJ-GRADED ≠elegant

ineligible /ɪnelɪdʒəbəl/. If you are **ineligible** for something, you are not qualified for it or entitled to it; a formal word. *Defence contractors are ineligible for the EC subsidies... They were ineligible to remain in the USA because of their criminal records.* ADJ: usu v-link ADJ, oft ADJ *for* n, ADJ to-inf ≠eligible

ineluctable /ɪnɪlʌktəbəl/. You use **ineluctable** to describe something that you think cannot be denied or ignored; a formal word. *...Malthus's theories about the ineluctable tendency of populations to exceed resources.* ADJ: usu ADJ n =inescapable

inept /ɪnept/. If you say that someone is **inept**, you are criticizing them because they do something with a complete lack of skill. *He was inept and lacked the intelligence to govern... You are completely inept at writing. ...his inept handling of the army.* ◆◇◇◇◇ ADJ-GRADED PRAGMATICS ≠skilful

ineptitude /ɪneptɪtjuːd, AM -tuːd/. If you refer to someone's **ineptitude**, you are criticizing them because they do something with a complete lack of skill. *...the tactical ineptitude of the allied commander.* N-UNCOUNT PRAGMATICS ≠skill

inequality /ɪnɪkwɒlɪti/ **inequalities. Inequality** is the difference in social status, wealth, or opportunity between people or groups. *People are concerned about corruption and social inequality... Blacks have been hurt by racial inequalities in housing and education.* ◆◇◇◇◇ N-VAR ≠equality

inequitable /ɪnekwɪtəbəl/. If you say that something is **inequitable**, you are criticizing it because it is unfair or unjust; a formal word. *The welfare system is grossly inequitable and inefficient.* ADJ-GRADED PRAGMATICS ≠equitable

inequity /ɪnekwɪti/ **inequities.** If you refer to the **inequity** of something, you are criticizing it because it is unfair or unjust; a formal word. *Social imbalance worries him more than inequity of income. ...the inequities in our health care system.* N-VAR PRAGMATICS =inequality

ineradicable /ɪnɪrædɪkəbəl/. You use **ineradicable** to emphasize that a quality, fact, or situation is permanent and cannot be changed; a formal word. *The emotional wounds of early childhood leave ineradicable scars... Divorce is a permanent, ineradicable fact of modern life.* ADJ: usu ADJ n PRAGMATICS

inert /ɪnɜːʳt/ ◆◇◇◇◇

1 Something that is **inert** does not move at all and appears to be lifeless. *He covered the inert body with a blanket.* ADJ

2 If you describe something as **inert**, you are criticizing it because it is not very lively or interesting. *The novel itself remains oddly inert. ...her inert personality.* ADJ-GRADED PRAGMATICS

3 An **inert** substance is one which does not react with other substances; a technical use in chemistry. *...inert gases like neon and argon.* ADJ

inertia /ɪnɜːʳʃə/ ◆◇◇◇◇

1 If you have a feeling of **inertia**, you feel very lazy and unwilling to move or be active. *He resented her inertia, her lack of energy and self-direction... This might help you overcome inertia.* N-UNCOUNT =apathy

2 **Inertia** is the tendency of a physical object to remain still or to continue moving, unless a force is applied to it; a technical use in physics. N-UNCOUNT

inescapable /ɪnɪskeɪpəbəl/. If you describe a fact, situation, or activity as **inescapable**, you mean that it is difficult not to notice it or be affected by it. *The inescapable conclusion is that he was trying to avenge the death of his friend... A sense of imminent doom was inescapable.* ♦ **inescapably** /ɪnɪskeɪpəbli/ *It is inescapably clear that they won't turn round.* ◆◇◇◇◇ ADJ =unavoidable; ADV

inessential /ɪnɪsenʃəl/. If something is **inessential**, you do not need it. *We have omitted footnotes which we judged inessential to the text.* ADJ =unnecessary ≠essential

inestimable /ɪnestɪməbəl/. If you describe the value, benefit, or importance of something as **inestimable**, you mean that it is extremely great and cannot be calculated; a formal word. *Human life is of inestimable value... This gives the professional an inestimable advantage.* ADJ: usu ADJ n =incalculable

inevitability /ɪnevɪtəbɪlɪti/ **inevitabilities.** The **inevitability** of something is the fact that it is certain to happen and cannot be prevented or avoided. *We are all bound by the inevitability of death... Success is an inevitability for us.* ◆◇◇◇◇ N-VAR: oft N *of* n

inevitable /ɪnevɪtəbəl/. If something is **inevitable**, it is certain to happen and cannot be prevented or avoided. *If the case succeeds, it is inevitable that other trials will follow... The defeat had inevitable consequences for British policy.* ► **The inevitable** is something which is inevitable. *'It's just delaying the inevitable,' he said.* ◆◆◆◇◇ ADJ: oft *it* v-link ADJ that =unavoidable; N-SING: *the* N

inevitably /ɪnevɪtəbli/. If something will **inevitably** happen, it is certain to happen and cannot be prevented or avoided. *Technological changes will inevitably lead to unemployment... Inevitably, the proposal is running into difficulties.* ◆◆◇◇◇ ADV: usu ADV with v, also ADV with cl, ADV adj =unavoidably

inexact /ɪnɪgzækt/. Something that is **inexact** is not precise or accurate. *Both explanations were inexact... Forecasting was an inexact science.* ADJ-GRADED ≠exact

inexcusable /ɪnɪkskjuːzəbəl/. If you say that something is **inexcusable**, you are emphasizing that it cannot be justified or tolerated because it is extremely bad. *He said the killing of innocent people was inexcusable... The Home Office has been accused of inexcusable incompetence.* ♦ **inexcusably** /ɪnɪkskjuːzəbli/ *She had been inexcusably careless.* ADJ-GRADED PRAGMATICS =unpardonable, unforgivable; ADV-GRADED

inexhaustible /ɪnɪgzɔːstəbəl/. If there is an **inexhaustible** supply of something, there is so much of it that it cannot all be used up. *They seem to have an inexhaustible supply of ammunition... His energy was unbounded and his patience inexhaustible.* ADJ =endless

inexorable /ɪneksərəbəl/. You use **inexorable** to describe a process which cannot be prevented from continuing or progressing; a formal word. *...the seemingly inexorable rise in unemployment. ...his steady, inexorable decline.* ♦ **inexorably** /ɪneksərəbli/ *Spending on health is growing inexorably... The crisis is moving inexorably towards war.* ◆◇◇◇◇ ADJ-GRADED: usu ADJ n =relentless; ADV-GRADED: ADV with v

inexpensive /ɪnɪkspensɪv/. Something that is **inexpensive** does not cost very much. *There is a large variety of good inexpensive restaurants.* ◆◇◇◇◇ ADJ-GRADED =cheap ≠expensive

inexperience /ɪnɪkspɪəriəns/. If you refer to someone's **inexperience**, you mean that they have little knowledge or experience of a particular situation or activity. *Critics attacked the youth and inexperience of his staff.* N-UNCOUNT ≠experience

inexperienced /ɪnɪkspɪəriənst/. If you are **inexperienced**, you have little knowledge or experience of a particular situation or activity. *They are inexperienced when it comes to decorating... Routine tasks are often delegated to inexperienced young doctors.* ◆◇◇◇◇ ADJ-GRADED ≠experienced

inexpert /ɪnekspɜːʳt/. If you describe someone or something as **inexpert**, you mean that they show a lack of skill. *He was too inexperienced and too inexpert to succeed. ...inexpert needlework.* ADJ-GRADED ≠expert

inexplicable /ɪnɪksplɪkəbəl/. If something is **inexplicable**, you cannot explain why it happens or why it is true. *His behaviour was extraordinary* ◆◇◇◇◇ ADJ-GRADED =incomprehensible *and inexplicable... For some inexplicable reason, the investors decided to pull out.* ♦ **inexplicably** /ɪnɪksplɪkəbli/ *She suddenly and inexplicably announced her retirement... His wartime experiences were inexplicably absent from the diaries.* ADV-GRADED: usu ADV with v, also ADV adj, ADV with cl

inexpressible /ɪnɪkspresɪbᵊl/. An **inexpressible** feeling cannot be expressed in words because it is so strong. *He felt a sudden inexpressible loneliness.* ♦ **inexpressibly** /ɪnɪkspresɪbli/ *For some reason I feel inexpressibly sad.* ADJ =indescribable; ADV: ADV adj

in extremis /ɪn ɪkstriːmɪs/. If someone or something is **in extremis**, they are in a very difficult situation and have to use extreme methods; a formal expression used mainly in British English. *Yet now he was here, in extremis, to seek an alliance... The use of antibiotics is permitted only in extremis.* PHRASE: PHR with v

inextricable /ɪnɪkstrɪkəbᵊl, ɪnekstrɪk-/. If there is an **inextricable** link between things, they cannot be considered separately; a formal word. *There's an inextricable link between markets and cost... Thoreau viewed man as an inextricable part of nature... Art and life are inextricable.* ADJ-GRADED =inseparable

inextricably /ɪnekstrɪkəbᵊli/. If two or more things are **inextricably** linked, they cannot be considered separately; a formal word. *Our survival is inextricably linked to the survival of the rainforest.* ◆◇◇◇◇ ADV-GRADED: ADV with v

infallible /ɪnfælɪbᵊl/. If a person or thing is **infallible**, they are never wrong. *Although he was experienced, he was not infallible... She had an infallible eye for style.* ♦ **infallibility** /ɪnfælɪbɪlɪti/ *...exaggerated views of the infallibility of science.* ◆◇◇◇◇ ADJ ≠fallible; N-UNCOUNT

infamous /ɪnfəməs/. **Infamous** people or things are well-known because of something bad; a formal word. *...the infamous massacre of Indians at Wounded Knee... He was infamous for his anti-feminist attitudes.* ◆◇◇◇◇ ADJ: usu ADJ n, also v-link ADJ *for* n, v-link ADJ =notorious

infamy /ɪnfəmi/. **Infamy** is the state of being infamous; a formal word. *...one of the greatest acts of infamy in history... He enjoyed exaggerating his infamy.* N-UNCOUNT =notoriety

infancy /ɪnfənsi/ ◆◇◇◇◇

1 **Infancy** is the period of your life when you are a very young child. *...minute details of Deborah's infancy. ...the development of the mind from infancy onwards.* N-UNCOUNT: usu poss N, prep N

2 If something is in its **infancy**, it is new and has not developed very much. *Computing science was still in its infancy.* N-UNCOUNT: usu *in* poss N

infant /ɪnfənt/ **infants** ◆◆◇◇◇

1 An **infant** is a baby or very young child; a formal use. *...young mums with infants in prams... The family were forced to flee with their infant son. ...the infant mortality rate in Britain.* N-COUNT: oft N n

2 In British English, **infants** are children between the ages of five and seven, who go to an infant school. ► You use **the infants** to refer to a school or class for such children. *You've been my best friend ever since we started in the infants.* N-COUNT: usu pl; N-UNCOUNT: *the* N

3 **Infant** means designed especially for very young children. *...an infant carrier in the back of a car.* ADJ: ADJ n

4 An **infant** organization or system is new and has not developed very much. *The infant company was based in Germany. ...the infant health service.* ADJ: ADJ n

infanticide /ɪnfæntɪsaɪd/. **Infanticide** is the crime of killing a young child. N-UNCOUNT

infantile /ɪnfəntaɪl/

1 **Infantile** behaviour or illnesses are typical of very young children; a formal use. *...infantile aggression. ...children with infantile eczema.* ADJ: ADJ n

2 If you accuse someone or something of being **infantile**, you think that they are foolish and childish. *This kind of humour is infantile and boring.* ADJ-GRADED PRAGMATICS =childish

infantry /ɪnfəntri/. The **infantry** are soldiers who fight on foot rather than in tanks or on horses. *The infantry were advancing to attack the ridge... The enemy infantry was hiding. ...an infantry division. ...regiments of infantry.* ◆◆◇◇◇ N-UNCOUNT-COLL

infantryman /ɪnfəntrimən/ **infantrymen.** An **infantryman** is a soldier in an infantry regiment. N-COUNT

infant school, infant schools. In Britain, an **infant school** is a school for children between the ages of five and seven. N-VAR

infatuated /ɪnfætʃueɪtɪd/. If you are **infatuated** with a person or thing, you have strong feelings of love or passion for them which make you unable to think clearly or sensibly about them. *He was utterly infatuated with her... I became infatuated with the case.* ADJ-GRADED: oft ADJ *with* n PRAGMATICS =obsessed

infatuation /ɪnfætʃueɪʃᵊn/ **infatuations.** If you have an **infatuation** for a person or thing, you have strong feelings of love or passion for them which make you unable to think clearly or sensibly about them. *...his infatuation with bull-fighting. ...Daisy's infatuation for the doctor... Teenagers have their own infatuations.* N-VAR PRAGMATICS =obsession

infect /ɪnfekt/ **infects, infecting, infected** ◆◆◆◇◇

1 To **infect** people, animals, or plants means to cause them to have a disease or illness. *A single mosquito can infect a large number of people. ...objects used by an infected person. ...people infected with HIV.* ♦ **infection** /ɪnfekʃᵊn/ *...plants that are resistant to infection.* VERB V n V-ed Also V n *with* n; N-UNCOUNT

2 To **infect** a substance or area means to cause it to contain harmful germs or bacteria. *The birds infect the milk. ...a virus which is spread mainly by infected blood.* VERB =contaminate V n V-ed

3 When people, places, or things **are infected** by a feeling or influence, it spreads to them. *For an instant I was infected by her fear... He thought they might infect others with their bourgeois ideas... His urge for revenge would never infect her.* VERB *be* V-ed *by* n V n *with* n V n

infected /ɪnfektɪd/. An **infected** place is one where germs or bacteria are causing a disease to spread among people or animals. *In heavily infected areas, half the population become blind.* ADJ-GRADED: ADJ n

infection /ɪnfekʃᵊn/ **infections.** An **infection** is a disease caused by germs or bacteria. *Ear infections are common in pre-school children... Exactly which bacteria cause the infection is still unknown.* • See also **infect**. ◆◆◆◇◇ N-COUNT

infectious /ɪnfekʃəs/ ◆◇◇◇◇

1 A disease that is **infectious** can be caught by being near a person who is infected with it. Compare **contagious**. *...infectious diseases such as measles... These viruses affect children and are highly infectious.* ADJ-GRADED

2 If a feeling is **infectious**, it spreads to other people. *She radiates an infectious enthusiasm for everything she does... There was a peal of laughter down the phone, which Harry found infectious.* ADJ-GRADED

infective /ɪnfektɪv/. **Infective** means related to infection or likely to cause infection; a formal word. *...a mild and very common infective disease of children.* ADJ-GRADED: usu ADJ n

infer /ɪnfɜːʳ/ **infers, inferring, inferred** ◆◇◇◇◇

1 If you **infer** that something is the case, you decide that it is true on the basis of information that you already have. *I inferred from what she said that you have not been well... By measuring the motion of the galaxies in a cluster, astronomers can infer the cluster's mass.* VERB =deduce V that V n

2 Some people use **infer** to mean 'imply', but many people consider this use to be incorrect. *The police inferred, though they didn't exactly say it, that they found her behaviour rather suspicious.* VERB V that

inference /ɪnfərəns/ **inferences** ◆◇◇◇◇

1 An **inference** is a conclusion that you draw about something by using information that you already have about it. *There were two inferences to be drawn from her letter.* N-COUNT =conclusion

2 **Inference** is the act of drawing conclusions about something on the basis of information that you already have. *It had an extremely tiny head and, by inference, a tiny brain.* N-UNCOUNT

inferior /ɪnfɪəriəʳ/ **inferiors** ◆◆◇◇◇

1 Something that is **inferior** is not as good as something else. *The cassettes were of inferior quality... This resulted in overpriced and often inferior products... Comprehensive schools were perceived as inferior to grammar schools.* ADJ-GRADED: oft ADJ *to* n ≠superior

2 If one person is regarded as **inferior** to another, ADJ-GRADED:

they are regarded as less important because they have less status or ability. *He preferred the company of those who were intellectually inferior to himself. ...the inferior status of women in pre-revolutionary Russia... Most career women make me feel inferior.* ► Also a noun. *It was a gentleman's duty always to be civil, even to his inferiors.* ♦ **inferiority** /ɪnfɪəriɒrɪti, AM -ɔːr-/ *I found it difficult to shake off a sense of social inferiority.* — oft ADJ *to* n; ≠superior; N-COUNT; N-UNCOUNT

inferiority complex, inferiority complexes. Someone who has an **inferiority complex** feels that they are of less worth or importance than other people. — N-COUNT

infernal /ɪnfɜːʳnəl/

1 **Infernal** is used to emphasize that something is very annoying or unpleasant; an old-fashioned use. *The post office is shut, which is an infernal bore... They can't work in these infernal conditions.* — ADJ: ADJ n; PRAGMATICS

2 **Infernal** is used to describe things that relate to hell. *...the goddess of the infernal regions.* — ADJ: ADJ n

inferno /ɪnfɜːʳnoʊ/ **infernos.** If you refer to a fire as an **inferno**, you mean that it is burning fiercely and causing great destruction; used mainly in journalism. *Rescue workers fought to get to victims inside the inferno.* — ◆◇◇◇◇ N-COUNT: usu sing

infertile /ɪnfɜːʳtaɪl, AM -təl/ — ◆◇◇◇◇

1 A person or animal that is **infertile** is unable to produce babies. *According to one survey, one woman in eight is infertile.* ♦ **infertility** /ɪnfɜːʳtɪlɪti/ *Male infertility is becoming commonplace. ...couples receiving infertility treatment.* — ADJ; N-UNCOUNT

2 **Infertile** soil is of poor quality so that plants cannot grow in it. *The polluted waste is often dumped, making the surrounding land infertile.* — ADJ-GRADED; ≠fertile

infest /ɪnfest/ **infests, infesting, infested** — ◆◇◇◇◇

1 When pests such as insects or rats **infest** plants or a place, they spread in large numbers and cause damage. *...pests like aphids which infest cereal crops.* ♦ **infested** *The prison is infested with rats... In less than seven days the infested plants had recovered.* ♦ **-infested** *...the rat-infested slums where the plague flourished.* ♦ **infestation** /ɪnfesteɪʃən/ **infestations.** *The premises were treated for cockroach infestation... Parts of California are suffering from an infestation of oriental fruit flies.* — VERB; V n; ADJ: oft ADJ *with* n; COMB in ADJ; N-VAR: oft n N, N *of* n

2 If you say that people or things you disapprove of or regard as dangerous **are infesting** a place, you mean that there are large numbers of them in that place. *Crime and drugs are infesting the inner cities.* ♦ **infested** *The road further south was infested with bandits.* ♦ **-infested** *...the shark-infested waters of the Great Barrier Reef.* — VERB; PRAGMATICS; =overrun; V n; ADJ; COMB in ADJ

infidel /ɪnfɪdəl/ **infidels.** If one person refers to another as an **infidel**, the first person is hostile towards the second person because that person has a different religion or has no religion; a literary word. *...a holy war, to drive the infidels and the non-believers out of this holy land.* ► Also an adjective. *He promised to continue the fight against infidel forces.* — N-COUNT; PRAGMATICS; ADJ: ADJ n

infidelity /ɪnfɪdelɪti/ **infidelities. Infidelity** occurs when a person who is married or in a steady relationship has sex with another person. *George turned a blind eye to his partner's infidelities... I divorced him for infidelity.* — ◆◇◇◇◇ N-VAR

in-fighting. In-fighting is rivalry or quarrelling between members of the same group or organization. *...after a year of in-fighting between right-wingers and moderates in the party.* — N-UNCOUNT

infill /ɪnfɪl/ **infills, infilling, infilled**

1 To **infill** a hollow place or gap means to fill it; used mainly in British English. *The cave was too polluted to enter and the entrance was infilled by the landowner... It is wise to start infilling with a layer of gravel for drainage.* — VERB; be V-ed; V; Also V n

2 **Infill** is something which fills a hollow place or gap. *There is room for infill between the new outer suburbs. ...an infill panel between the top of the wardrobes and the ceiling.* — N-UNCOUNT: oft N n

infiltrate /ɪnfɪltreɪt/ **infiltrates, infiltrating, infiltrated** — ◆◇◇◇◇

1 If people **infiltrate** a place or organization, or **infiltrate** into it, they enter it secretly in order to spy on it or influence it. *Activists had infiltrated the student movement... The street protests had been infiltrated by people bent on violence... A reporter tried to infiltrate into the prison.* ♦ **infiltration** /ɪnfɪltreɪʃən/ **infiltrations** *...an inquiry into alleged infiltration by the far left group... The security zone was set up to prevent guerrilla infiltrations.* — VERB; V n; V *into/from* n; N-VAR

2 To **infiltrate** people **into** a place or organization means to get them into it secretly in order to spy on it or influence it. *He claimed that some countries have been trying to infiltrate their agents into the Republic.* — VERB; V n *into* n

infiltrator /ɪnfɪltreɪtəʳ/ **infiltrators.** An **infiltrator** is a person who has infiltrated a place or organization. — N-COUNT

infin. Infin. is an abbreviation for **infinitive.**

infinite /ɪnfɪnɪt/ — ◆◆◇◇◇

1 If you describe something as **infinite**, you are emphasizing that it is extremely great in amount or degree. *...an infinite variety of landscapes... With infinite care, John shifted position... The choice is infinite.* ♦ **infinitely** *His design was infinitely better than anything I could have done.* — ADJ; PRAGMATICS; =immense; ADV: ADV adj/adv

2 Something that is **infinite** has no limit, end, or edge. *...an infinite number of atoms... Obviously, no company has infinite resources. ...God's infinite mercy.* ► **The infinite** is something which is infinite. *...pondering on the infinite.* ♦ **infinitely** *A centimeter can be infinitely divided into smaller units.* — ADJ; =boundless; N-SING: *the* N; ADV: ADV with v

infinitesimal /ɪnfɪnɪtesɪməl/. Something that is **infinitesimal** is extremely small; a formal word. *...mineral substances present in infinitesimal amounts in the soil... There was an infinitesimal pause.* ♦ **infinitesimally** *...an infinitesimally small amount of the offending substance.* — ADJ; =minute; ADV: ADV adj/adv

infinitive /ɪnfɪnɪtɪv/ **infinitives.** The **infinitive** of a verb is the basic form, for example 'do', 'be', 'take', and 'eat'. The infinitive is often used with 'to' in front of it. — N-COUNT

infinitum /ɪnfɪnaɪtəm/. See **ad infinitum.**

infinity /ɪnfɪnɪti/ — ◆◇◇◇◇

1 **Infinity** is a number that is larger than any other number and can never be given an exact value. *These permutations multiply towards infinity... There is always an infinity of numbers between any two numbers.* — N-UNCOUNT: also *a* N *of* n

2 **Infinity** is a point that is further away than any other point and can never be reached. *...the darkness of a starless night stretching to infinity.* — N-UNCOUNT

infirm /ɪnfɜːʳm/. A person who is **infirm** is weak or ill, and usually old. *She moved with her aging, infirm husband into a retirement center.* ► **The infirm** are people who are infirm. *We are here to protect and assist the weak and infirm.* ♦ **infirmity** /ɪnfɜːʳmɪti/ **infirmities** *In spite of his age and infirmity, the old man is still producing plays and novels... Older people often try to ignore their infirmities.* — ADJ-GRADED; N-PLURAL: *the* N; N-VAR

infirmary /ɪnfɜːʳməri/ **infirmaries.** Some hospitals are called **infirmaries.** *Mrs Hardie had been taken to the infirmary in an ambulance. ...the Radcliffe Infirmary in Oxford.* — ◆◇◇◇◇ N-COUNT: oft in names after n

inflame /ɪnfleɪm/ **inflames, inflaming, inflamed.** If something **inflames** a situation or **inflames** people's feelings, it makes people angry or passionate about something; used mainly in journalism. *The General holds the rebels responsible for inflaming the situation... The shooting has only inflamed passions further.* — ◆◇◇◇◇ VERB; V n

inflamed /ɪnfleɪmd/. If part of your body is **inflamed**, it is red or swollen, usually as a result of an infection, injury, or illness; a formal word. *Symptoms include red, itchy and inflamed skin... Her eyes were sore and inflamed.* — ADJ-GRADED

inflammable /ɪnflæməbəl/. An **inflammable** material or chemical catches fire and burns easily. *A highly inflammable liquid escaped into the drilling equipment.* — ADJ-GRADED; =flammable

inflammation /ɪnfləmeɪʃən/ **inflammations.** An **inflammation** is a painful redness or swelling of a part of your body that results from an — ◆◇◇◇◇ N-VAR infection, injury, or illness; a formal word. *The drug can cause inflammation of the liver. ...throat inflammations.*

inflammatory /ɪnflæmətəri, AM -tɔːri/ ◆◇◇◇◇

1 If you accuse someone of saying or doing **inflammatory** things, you mean that what they say or do is likely to make people react very angrily. *...nationalist policies that are too drastic and inflammatory... She described his remarks as irresponsible, inflammatory and outrageous.* ADJ-GRADED PRAGMATICS

2 An **inflammatory** condition or disease is one in which the patient suffers from inflammation; a formal use. *...the inflammatory reactions that occur in asthma.* ADJ: ADJ n

inflatable /ɪnfleɪtəbᵊl/ **inflatables** ◆◇◇◇◇

1 An **inflatable** object is one that you fill with air when you want to use it. *...an inflatable dinghy... The children were playing on the inflatable castle.* ADJ: usu ADJ n

2 An **inflatable** is an inflatable object, especially a small boat. N-COUNT

inflate /ɪnfleɪt/ **inflates, inflating, inflated** ◆◇◇◇◇

1 If you **inflate** something such as a balloon or tyre, or if it **inflates**, it becomes bigger as it is filled with air or a gas. *Stuart jumped into the sea and inflated the liferaft... Don's lifejacket had failed to inflate.* V-ERG V n V

2 If you say that someone **inflates** the price of something, or that the price **inflates**, you mean that the price increases. *The promotion of a big release can inflate a film's final cost... Clothing prices have not inflated as much as automobiles.* V-ERG =increase V n V
♦ **inflated** *They had to buy everything at inflated prices at the ranch store.* ADJ-GRADED

3 If someone **inflates** the amount or effect of something, they say it is bigger, better, or more important than it really is, usually so that they can profit from it. *They inflated their clients' medical injuries and treatment to defraud insurance companies... Even his war record was fraudulently inflated.* VERB V n

inflation /ɪnfleɪʃᵊn/. **Inflation** is a general increase in the prices of goods and services in a country. *...rising unemployment and high inflation. ...an inflation rate of only 2.2%.* ◆◆◆◆◇ N-UNCOUNT

inflationary /ɪnfleɪʃənri, AM -neri/. **Inflationary** means connected with inflation or causing inflation. *The bank is worried about mounting inflationary pressures.* ◆◇◇◇◇ ADJ-GRADED: usu ADJ n

inflect /ɪnflekt/ **inflects, inflecting, inflected.** If a word **inflects**, its ending or form changes in order to show its grammatical function. If a language **inflects**, it has words in it that inflect. VERB: V
♦ **inflected** *Kings, ministers, and Brahmans spoke Sanskrit, the most esteemed and highly inflected language... In all dictionaries to date we give the headword and all the inflected forms.* ADJ-GRADED

-inflected /-ɪnflektɪd/

1 **-inflected** is used to form adjectives describing someone's voice or accent; a literary use. *'Sergeant, I should like a word with you,' said the newcomer, in a pleasantly-inflected baritone.* COMB in ADJ

2 **-inflected** is used to form adjectives describing the style of a piece of music or a performance; used in journalism. *...his attacking, gospel-inflected vocal style.* COMB in ADJ

inflection /ɪnflekʃᵊn/ **inflections;** also spelled **inflexion** in British English.

1 An **inflection** in someone's voice is a change in their tone or intonation as they are speaking; used in written English. *The man's voice was devoid of inflection... 'Seb?' he said, with a rising inflection.* N-VAR

2 In grammar, an **inflection** is a change in the form of a word that shows its grammatical function, for example a change that makes a noun plural or makes a verb into the past tense. N-VAR

inflexible /ɪnfleksɪbᵊl/ ◆◇◇◇◇

1 Something that is **inflexible** cannot be altered in any way, even if the situation changes. *Workers insisted the new system was too inflexible... Charles was a man of settled habits and inflexible routine.* ADJ-GRADED =rigid ≠flexible
♦ **inflexibility** /ɪnfleksɪbɪlɪti/ *The snag about an endowment mortgage is its inflexibility.* N-UNCOUNT

2 If you say that someone is **inflexible**, you are criticizing them because they refuse to change their mind or alter their way of doing things. *His opponents viewed him as stubborn, dogmatic, and inflexible.* ADJ-GRADED PRAGMATICS ≠flexible
♦ **inflexibility** *Joyce was irritated by the inflexibility of her colleagues.* N-UNCOUNT: oft with poss

inflexion /ɪnflekʃᵊn/. See **inflection**.

inflict /ɪnflɪkt/ **inflicts, inflicting, inflicted.** To **inflict** harm or damage on someone or something means to make them suffer it. *Rebels say they have inflicted heavy casualties on government forces. ...the damage being inflicted on Britain's industries by the recession... The dog then attacked her, inflicting serious injuries.* ◆◆◇◇◇ VERB V n on n V n
♦ **infliction** /ɪnflɪkʃᵊn/ *...without the unnecessary or cruel infliction of pain.* N-UNCOUNT: usu N of n

in-flight; also spelled **inflight**. **In-flight** services are ones that are provided on board an aeroplane. *...in-flight entertainment on long-haul aircraft... The in-flight movie was Casablanca. ...an inflight magazine.* ADJ: ADJ n

inflow /ɪnfloʊ/ **inflows.** If there is an **inflow** of money or people into a place, a large amount of money or people move into a place. *The Swiss wanted to discourage an inflow of foreign money. ...the inflow of immigrants from East Germany.* ◆◇◇◇◇ N-COUNT: usu N of n ≠outflow

influence /ɪnfluəns/ **influences, influencing, influenced** ◆◆◆◆◇

1 **Influence** is the power to make other people agree with your opinions or do what you want. *As Hugh grew older, she had less influence and couldn't control him... I have rather a large influence over a good many people... He denies exerting any political influence over them... The government should continue to use its influence for the release of all hostages.* N-UNCOUNT: oft N over n

2 If you **influence** someone, you use your power to make them agree with you or do what you want. *He is trying to improperly influence a witness... The angry crowds could influence the government... My dad influenced me to do electronics.* VERB =manipulate, persuade V n V n to-inf

3 If someone or something has an **influence** on people or situations, they affect the way people think or act, or what happens. *Van Gogh had a major influence on the development of modern painting... The Shropshire landscape was an influence on Owen too... Many other medications have an influence on cholesterol levels.* N-COUNT: usu with supp

4 If someone or something **influences** a person or situation, they have an effect on that person's behaviour or that situation. *We became the best of friends and he influenced me deeply... What you eat may influence your risk of getting cancer... They still influence what's played on the radio.* VERB V n V wh

5 Someone or something that is a good or bad **influence** on people has a good or bad effect on them. *I thought Sue would be a good influence on you... TV is a bad influence on people.* N-COUNT: usu sing, usu adj N, oft N on n

6 If you are **under the influence of** someone or something, you are being affected or controlled by them. *I fell under the influence of a history master... The very earliest sculptures were made under the influence of Greek art... He was arrested on suspicion of driving under the influence of alcohol.* PHRASES PHR n, usu v-link PHR, PHR after v

7 If someone is **under the influence**, their mind is affected by alcohol or drugs; an informal expression. *Police charged the man with driving under the influence... We find members of the opposite sex more attractive when under the influence.* v-link PHR

influential /ɪnfluenʃᵊl/. Someone or something that is **influential** has a lot of influence over people or events. *It helps to have influential friends. ...the influential position of president of the chamber... He had been influential in shaping economic policy. ...one of the most influential books ever written.* ◆◆◇◇◇ ADJ-GRADED: oft ADJ in-ing

influenza /ɪnfluenzə/. **Influenza** is the same as **flu**; a formal word. N-UNCOUNT

influx /ɪnflʌks/ **influxes.** An **influx** of people or things into a place is their arrival there in large numbers. *...problems caused by the influx of refugees. ...the influx of American popcorn into the British market.* ◆◇◇◇◇ N-COUNT: usu sing, oft N of n

info /ɪnfoʊ/. **Info** is information; an informal word. *For more info phone 414-3935.* ◆◇◇◇◇ N-UNCOUNT

infobahn /ɪnfoʊbɑːn/. **The infobahn** means the same as the information **superhighway**. N-SING: *the* N

infomercial /ɪnfoʊmɜːʳʃəl/ **infomercials.** An **infomercial** is a television programme in which a famous person gives information about a company's products or services, or a politician gives his or her opinions. The word is formed from 'information' and 'commercial'. *New $750,000 infomercials, featuring artists like Cher, have recently hit the screens... Perot hoped to run another series of campaign infomercials.* N-COUNT

inform /ɪnfɔːʳm/ **informs, informing, informed** ◆◆◆◇◇

1 If you **inform** someone of something, you tell them about it. *They would inform him of any progress they had made... My daughter informed me that she was pregnant... 'I just added a little soy sauce,' he informs us.* VERB V n *of* n, V n that, V n with quote, Also V n

2 If someone **informs on** a person, they give information about the person to the police or another authority, which causes the person to be suspected or proved guilty of doing something bad. *Somebody must have informed on us... Thousands of American citizens have informed on these organized crime syndicates.* VERB V *on* n

3 If a situation or activity **is informed** by an idea or a quality, that idea or quality is very noticeable in it; a formal use. *All great songs are informed by a certain sadness and tension... The concept of the Rose continued to inform the poet's work.* VERB *be* V-ed *by* n, V n

informal /ɪnfɔːʳməl/ ◆◆◇◇◇

1 **Informal** speech or behaviour is relaxed and friendly rather than serious, very correct, or official. *She is refreshingly informal... His friend was less good-looking, but a lot more informal and relaxed.* ♦ **informally** *She was always there at half past eight, chatting informally to the children.* ♦ **informality** /ɪnfɔːʳmælɪti/ *He was overwhelmed by their cheerfulness and friendly informality.* ADJ-GRADED: usu v-link ADJ ≠formal; ADV-GRADED: ADV after v; N-UNCOUNT

2 An **informal** situation is one which is relaxed and friendly and not very serious or official. *I would like it to be an informal occasion... The house has an informal atmosphere.* ♦ **informality** *Eleanor enjoyed the relative informality of island life.* ADJ-GRADED ≠formal; N-UNCOUNT

3 **Informal** clothes are casual and suitable for wearing when you are relaxing, but not on formal occasions. *Most of the time Jenny needs informal clothes... For lunch, dress is informal.* ♦ **informally** *Everyone dressed informally in shorts or faded jeans, and baggy sweatshirts.* ADJ-GRADED =casual ≠formal; ADV-GRADED

4 You use **informal** to describe something that is done unofficially or casually without planning. *The two leaders will retire to Camp David for informal discussions. ...an informal meeting of EC ministers... We had an informal party at a hotel, and people just flooded in.* ♦ **informally** *He began informally to handle Ted's tax affairs for him.* ADJ: usu ADJ n; ADV

informant /ɪnfɔːʳmənt/ **informants** ◆◇◇◇◇

1 An **informant** is someone who gives another person a piece of information; a formal use. N-COUNT

2 An **informant** is the same as an **informer**. N-COUNT

information /ɪnfəʳmeɪʃən/. **Information** about someone or something consists of facts about them. *Pat refused to give her any information about Sarah... Each centre would provide information on technology and training... For further information contact the number below. ...an important piece of information... The information was passed on to another government department.* ◆◆◆◆◆ N-UNCOUNT: oft N *about/on* n

informational /ɪnfəʳmeɪʃənəl/. **Informational** means relating to information; used in journalism. *...the informational needs of school-age children. ...informational television.* ADJ: ADJ n

information technology. **Information technology** is the theory and practice of using computers to store and analyse information. *...the information technology industry.* ◆◇◇◇◇ N-UNCOUNT

informative /ɪnfɔːʳmətɪv/. Something that is **informative** gives you useful information. *The adverts are not very informative... 'Holidays That Don't Cost the Earth' is a lively, informative read.* ◆◇◇◇◇ ADJ-GRADED

informed /ɪnfɔːʳmd/ ◆◇◇◇◇

1 Someone who is **informed** knows about a subject or what is happening in the world. *Informed people know the company is shaky. ...the importance of keeping the public properly informed.* • See also **well-informed.** ADJ-GRADED

2 When journalists talk about **informed** sources, they mean people who are likely to give correct information because of their private or special knowledge. *According to informed sources, those taken into custody include at least one major-general.* ADJ: ADJ n

3 An **informed** guess or decision is one that likely to be good, because it is based on definite knowledge or information. *An informed guess at his personal wealth was $1.25 billion... Science is now enabling us to make more informed choices about how we use common drugs.* ADJ-GRADED: ADJ n

4 See also **inform.**

informer /ɪnfɔːʳməʳ/ **informers.** An **informer** is someone who tells the police that another person has done something illegal or is about to do something illegal. *...two men suspected of being police informers.* ◆◇◇◇◇ N-COUNT

infotainment /ɪnfoʊteɪnmənt/. **Infotainment** is used to refer to radio or television programmes that are intended to be entertaining while providing useful information at the same time. The word is formed from 'information' and 'entertainment'; used mainly in British English. N-UNCOUNT

infra-red /ɪnfrə red/ ◆◇◇◇◇

1 **Infra-red** radiation is similar to light but has a longer wavelength, so we cannot see it without special equipment. ADJ: ADJ n

2 **Infra-red** equipment detects infra-red radiation. *...searching with infra-red scanners for weapons and artillery.* ADJ: ADJ n

infrastructure /ɪnfrəstrʌktʃəʳ/ **infrastructures.** The **infrastructure** of a country, society, or organization consists of the basic facilities such as transport, communications, power supplies, and buildings, which enable it to function. *...improvements in the country's infrastructure... The infrastructure, from hotels to transport, is old and decrepit.* ◆◆◇◇◇ N-VAR

infrequent /ɪnfriːkwənt/. If something is **infrequent**, it does not happen often. *John Marvell was paying one of his infrequent visits to London.* ♦ **infrequently** *The bridge is used infrequently. ...schools which, not infrequently, were made up of 80 per cent or more of ethnic minorities.* ◆◇◇◇◇ ADJ-GRADED =rare ≠frequent; ADV-GRADED: usu ADV with v, also ADV with cl/group

infringe /ɪnfrɪndʒ/ **infringes, infringing, infringed** ◆◇◇◇◇

1 If someone **infringes** a law or a rule, they break it or do something which disobeys it. *The film exploited his image and infringed his copyright... The jury ruled that he had infringed no rules.* VERB V n

2 If something **infringes** people's rights, it interferes with these rights and does not allow people the freedom they are entitled to. *They rob us, they infringe our rights, they kill us... It's starting to infringe on our personal liberties.* VERB V n, V *on* n

infringement /ɪnfrɪndʒmənt/ **infringements** ◆◇◇◇◇

1 An **infringement** is an action or situation that interferes with your rights and the freedom you are entitled to. *...infringement of privacy... They see it as an infringement on their own freedom of action.* N-VAR: usu N *of/on* n

2 An **infringement** of a law or rule is the act of breaking it or disobeying it. *There might have been an infringement of the rules... Infringement of the regulation is punishable by a fine.* N-VAR: usu N *of* n

infuriate /ɪnfjʊərieɪt/ **infuriates, infuriating, infuriated.** If something or someone **infuriates** you, they make you extremely angry. *Jimmy's presence had infuriated Hugh... The champion was infuriated by the decision... It infuriates us to have to deal with this particular mayor.* ♦ **infuriated** *He knew me well enough to realize how infuriated such a conversation would make me.* ◆◇◇◇◇ VERB =enrage V n, *it* V n to-inf, Also *it* V n that; ADJ-GRADED: usu v-link ADJ

infuriating /ɪnfjʊərieɪtɪŋ/. Something that is **infuriating** annoys you very much. *I was in the middle of typing when Robert rang. It was infuriating!... Steve accelerated with infuriating slowness.* ♦ **infuriatingly** *This book is infuriatingly repetitious... 'It seems obvious to me,' she said infuriatingly.*
◆◇◇◇◇ ADJ-GRADED =maddening
ADV-GRADED: usu ADV adj, also ADV with v

infuse /ɪnfjuːz/ **infuses, infusing, infused** ◆◇◇◇◇

1 To **infuse** a quality into someone or something, or to **infuse** them with a quality, means to fill them with it; a formal use. *Many of the girls seemed to be infused with excitement on seeing the snow... He argued that a union would infuse unnecessary conflict into the company's employee relations.*
VERB
be V-ed with n
V n into n
Also V n with n

2 If a quality **infuses** something, every part of that thing has that quality; a literary use. *A strange spirit infused the place.*
VERB
V n

3 If you **infuse** things such as tea leaves or herbs, or allow them to **infuse**, you put them in hot water for some time so that the water absorbs their flavour. You can also infuse things in other liquids. *...teas made by infusing the roots of herbs... Herbalists infuse the flowers in oil... Leave the tea to infuse.*
V-ERG
V n
V n in n
V

infusion /ɪnfjuːʒᵊn/ **infusions** ◆◇◇◇◇

1 If there is an **infusion** of one thing into another, the first thing is added to the other thing and makes it stronger or better; a formal use. *He brought a tremendous infusion of hope to the people. ...a series of capital infusions.*
N-VAR: usu N of n

2 An **infusion** is a liquid made by leaving herbs in hot water until the flavour is strong. *...a herbal infusion... This remedy contains infusions of five flowers.*
N-COUNT: usu with supp, also by N

-ing. /-ɪŋ/

1 **-ing** is added to verbs to form present participles. Present participles are used with auxiliary verbs to make continuous tenses. They are also used like adjectives, describing a person or thing as doing something. *He was walking along the street... Children sit round small tables, talking to each other... It was worth it to see all those smiling faces.*
SUFFIX

2 **-ing** is added to verbs to form uncount nouns referring to activities. *Gardening is very popular in Britain... This campaign is one of the most successful in the history of advertising.*
SUFFIX

ingenious /ɪndʒiːniəs/. Something that is **ingenious** is very clever and involves new ideas, methods, or equipment. *...a truly ingenious invention... Gautier's solution to the puzzle is ingenious.* ♦ **ingeniously** *The roof has been ingeniously designed to provide solar heating.*
◆◇◇◇◇ ADJ-GRADED
ADV-GRADED: usu ADV with v, also ADV adj

ingenue /ænʒeɪnjuː/ **ingenues.** An **ingenue** is a young, innocent girl in a play or film, or an actress who plays the part of young, innocent girls. *She's not really interested in any more ingenue roles.*
N-COUNT: usu sing

ingenuity /ɪndʒənjuːɪti, AM -nuː-/. **Ingenuity** is skill at working out how to achieve things or skill at inventing new things. *Inspecting the nest can be difficult and may require some ingenuity.*
◆◇◇◇◇ N-UNCOUNT

ingenuous /ɪndʒenjuəs/. If you describe someone as **ingenuous**, you mean that they are innocent, trusting, and incapable of deceiving anyone; a formal word. *He seemed too ingenuous for a reporter... With ingenuous sincerity, he captivated his audience.* ♦ **ingenuously** *Somewhat ingenuously, he explains how the crime may be accomplished... He smiled, eyes ingenuously wide.*
ADJ-GRADED ≠disingenuous
ADV-GRADED: ADV with v, ADV adj

ingest /ɪndʒest/ **ingests, ingesting, ingested.** When animals or plants **ingest** a substance, they take it into themselves, for example by eating or absorbing it; a technical term. *When we ingest a mineral it must be combined with an amino acid to be absorbed... The spores can also be ingested through open wounds.* ♦ **ingestion** /ɪndʒestʃən/ *Every ingestion of food can affect our mood or thinking processes.*
◆◇◇◇◇ VERB
V n
N-UNCOUNT

inglorious /ɪnglɔːriəs/. If you describe something as **inglorious**, you mean that it is rather shameful. *He wouldn't have accepted such an inglorious outcome.* ♦ **ingloriously** *If fighting worsens, the troops might be reinforced, or ingloriously withdrawn.*
ADJ-GRADED: usu ADJ n
ADV-GRADED: ADV with v

ingot /ɪŋgət/ **ingots.** An **ingot** is a lump of metal, usually shaped like a brick. *...gold ingots.*
N-COUNT: oft n N

ingrained /ɪngreɪnd/. **Ingrained** habits and beliefs are difficult to change or remove. *Morals tend to be deeply ingrained... From ingrained habit he paused to straighten up the bed.*
◆◇◇◇◇ ADJ-GRADED

ingratiate /ɪngreɪʃieɪt/ **ingratiates, ingratiating, ingratiated.** If someone tries to **ingratiate** themselves with you, they do things to try and make you like them; used showing disapproval. *Many politicians are trying to ingratiate themselves with her.*
VERB PRAGMATICS
V pron-refl with n
Also V pron-refl

ingratiating /ɪngreɪʃieɪtɪŋ/. If you describe someone or their behaviour as **ingratiating**, you mean that they try to make people like them; used showing disapproval. *He said this with an ingratiating smile at John... His fellow students had found him too ingratiating.*
ADJ-GRADED PRAGMATICS

ingratitude /ɪngrætɪtjuːd, AM -tuːd/. **Ingratitude** is lack of gratitude for something that has been done for you. *The Government could expect only ingratitude from the electorate.*
N-UNCOUNT ≠gratitude

ingredient /ɪngriːdiənt/ **ingredients** ◆◆◆◇◇

1 **Ingredients** are the things that are used to make something, especially all the different foods you use when you are cooking a particular dish. *Mix in the remaining ingredients.*
N-COUNT

2 An **ingredient** of a situation is one of the essential parts of it. *The meeting had all the ingredients of high political drama... I think that is one of the major ingredients in his success.*
N-COUNT: oft N of/in n

ingrown /ɪngroun/ or **ingrowing** /ɪngrouɪŋ/. An **ingrown** toenail, or in British English an **ingrowing** toenail, is one which is growing into your toe, often causing you pain.
ADJ

inhabit /ɪnhæbɪt/ **inhabits, inhabiting, inhabited.** If a place or region **is inhabited** by a group of people or a species of animal, those people or animals live there. *The valley is inhabited by the Dani tribe. ...the people who inhabit these islands. ...the beautifully coloured fish that inhabit the Egyptian reefs. ...a land primarily inhabited by nomads.*
◆◆◇◇◇ VERB
be V-ed
V n
V-ed

inhabitant /ɪnhæbɪtənt/ **inhabitants.** The **inhabitants** of a place are the people who live there. *...the inhabitants of Glasgow.*
◆◆◇◇◇ N-COUNT: usu pl

inhalation /ɪnhəleɪʃᵊn/ **inhalations.**

1 **Inhalation** is the process or act of breathing in, taking air and sometimes other substances into your lungs; a formal word. *...a complete cycle of inhalation and exhalation... Passengers suffering from smoke inhalation have been taken to hospital... Accidental inhalation of the powder can be harmful... Take several deep inhalations.*
N-VAR ≠exhalation

2 An **inhalation** is a treatment for colds and other illnesses in which you dissolve substances in hot water and breathe in the vapour. *Inhalations can soothe and control the cough... Inhalations of menthol may do the trick.*
N-COUNT

inhale /ɪnheɪl/ **inhales, inhaling, inhaled.** When you **inhale**, you breathe in. When you **inhale** something such as smoke, you take it into your lungs when you breathe in. *He took a long slow breath, inhaling deeply... He was treated for the effects of inhaling smoke.*
◆◇◇◇◇ VERB ≠exhale
V
V n

inhaler /ɪnheɪləʳ/ **inhalers.** An **inhaler** is a small device that helps you to breathe more easily if you have asthma or a bad cold. You put it in your mouth and breathe in deeply, and it sends a small amount of a drug into your lungs.
N-COUNT

inherent /ɪnherənt, -hɪər-/. The **inherent** qualities of something are the necessary and natural parts of it. *Stress is an inherent part of dieting. ...the dangers inherent in an outbreak of war.* ♦ **inherently** *Aeroplanes are not inherently dangerous... War is inherently a dirty business.*
◆◆◇◇◇ ADJ: usu ADJ n =intrinsic
ADV: usu ADV adj =intrinsically

inherit /ɪnherɪt/ **inherits, inheriting, inherited** ◆◆◇◇◇

1 If you **inherit** money or property, you receive it from someone who has died. *He has no son to*
VERB
V n

inherit his land. ...paintings that he inherited from his father. ...people with inherited wealth. V n *from* n V-ed

2 If you **inherit** something such as a task, problem, or attitude, you get it from the people who used to have it, for example because you have taken over their job or been influenced by them. *A future Labour government would inherit a difficult economic situation... Our legal system inherited laws from the English system. ...the inherited wisdoms contained in its social hierarchy.* VERB V n V n *from* n V-ed

3 If you **inherit** a characteristic or quality, you are born with it, because your parents or ancestors also had it. *We inherit from our parents many of our physical characteristics... Her children have inherited her love of sport... Stammering is probably an inherited defect.* VERB V n *from* n V n V-ed

inheritance /ɪnh̲erɪtᵊns/ **inheritances** ◆◇◇◇◇

1 An **inheritance** is money or property which you receive from someone who has died. *She feared losing her inheritance to her stepmother... Avoiding inheritance tax is straightforward.* N-VAR

2 If you get something such as job, problem, or attitude from someone who used to have it, you can refer to this as an **inheritance**. *...starvation and disease over much of Europe and Asia, which was Truman's inheritance as President.* N-COUNT: usu sing, with supp, oft with poss =heritage

3 Your **inheritance** is the particular characteristics or qualities which your family or ancestors had and which you are born with. *Eye colour shows more than your genetic inheritance, however.* N-SING: also no det, with supp

inheritor /ɪnh̲erɪtəʳ/ **inheritors**

1 The **inheritors** of something such as a tradition are the people who live or arrive after it has been established and are able to benefit from it. *...the proud inheritors of the Prussian military tradition.* N-COUNT: usu pl, usu N *of* n =heir

2 An **inheritor** is someone who inherits money or property from someone who has died; a legal use. *Two-thirds of inheritors promptly sold the houses they were left.* N-COUNT =heir

inhibit /ɪnh̲ɪbɪt/ **inhibits, inhibiting, inhibited** ◆◇◇◇◇

1 If something **inhibits** an event or process, it prevents it or slows it down. *Wine or sugary drinks inhibit digestion... The high cost of borrowing is inhibiting investment by industry in new equipment.* VERB V n

2 To **inhibit** someone from doing something means to prevent them from doing it, although they want to do it or should be able to do it. *It could end up inhibiting the poor from getting the medical care they need... Officers will be inhibited from doing their duty.* VERB V n *from* -ing/n

inhibited /ɪnh̲ɪbɪtɪd/. If you say that someone is **inhibited**, you mean they find it difficult to behave naturally and show their feelings, and that you think this is a bad thing. *Men are more inhibited about touching each other than women.* ◆◇◇◇◇ ADJ-GRADED: oft ADJ *about* n/-ing PRAGMATICS

inhibition /ɪnɪbɪ̲ʃᵊn/ **inhibitions. Inhibitions** are feelings of fear or embarrassment that make it difficult for you to behave naturally. *The whole point about dancing is to stop thinking and lose all your inhibitions... They behave with a total lack of inhibition.* ◆◇◇◇◇ N-VAR

inhospitable /ɪnhɒspɪ̲təbᵊl/

1 An **inhospitable** place is unpleasant to live in. *...the earth's most inhospitable regions. ...the island's inhospitable climate.* ADJ-GRADED: usu ADJ n ≠hospitable

2 If someone is **inhospitable**, they do not make people welcome when they visit. ADJ-GRADED ≠hospitable

inhuman /ɪnhju̲ːmən/ ◆◇◇◇◇

1 If you describe something as **inhuman**, you mean that it is extremely cruel or brutal. *The detainees are often held in cruel and inhuman conditions... The barbaric slaughter of whales is unnecessary and inhuman.* ADJ-GRADED: usu ADJ n

2 If you describe someone or something as **inhuman**, you mean that they are strange or bad because they do not seem human in some way. *...those inhuman shrieks that rent the air and chilled my heart.* ADJ-GRADED

inhumane /ɪ̲nhjʊme̲ɪn/. If you describe something as **inhumane**, you mean that it is extremely cruel. *He was kept under inhumane conditions... He got his first insight into how inhumane employers can be.* ADJ-GRADED ≠humane

inhumanity /ɪ̲nhjʊmænɪti/ **inhumanities. Inhumanity** is extreme cruelty. *...the inhumanity of war. ...man's inhumanity to man.* N-UNCOUNT: also N in pl, oft N *of* n

inimical /ɪnɪ̲mɪkᵊl/. Conditions that are **inimical** to something make it difficult for that thing to exist or do well; a formal word. *...a false morality that is inimical to human happiness. ...goals inimical to Western interests.* ADJ-GRADED: usu v-link ADJ, usu ADJ *to* n

inimitable /ɪnɪ̲mɪtəbᵊl/. You use **inimitable** to describe someone, especially a performer, when you like or admire them because of their special qualities; a formal word. *The major box office attraction was, of course, the inimitable Peter Hunningale... He makes his own point in his own inimitable way.* ADJ: usu ADJ n PRAGMATICS =unique

iniquitous /ɪnɪ̲kwɪtəs/. If you describe something as **iniquitous**, you mean that it is very unfair or morally bad; a formal word. *...an iniquitous fine.* ADJ-GRADED: usu ADJ n =wicked

iniquity /ɪnɪ̲kwɪti/ **iniquities. Iniquity** is wickedness or injustice; a formal word. *He rails against the iniquities of capitalism... A disco isn't exactly a den of iniquity.* N-VAR

initial /ɪnɪ̲ʃᵊl/ **initials, initialling, initialled;** spelled **initialing, initialed** in American English. ◆◆◆◇◇

1 You use **initial** to describe something that happens at the beginning of a process. *The initial reaction has been excellent... The aim of this initial meeting is to clarify the issues.* ADJ: ADJ n

2 **Initials** are the capital letters which begin each word of a name. For example, if your full name is Michael Dennis Stocks, your initials will be M.D.S. *...a silver Porsche car with her initials JB on the side.* N-COUNT: usu pl, oft poss N

3 If someone **initials** an official document, they write their initials on it, for example to show that they have seen it, agree with it, or authorize it. *Would you mind initialing this voucher?... The agreement was initialled in June.* VERB V n

initially /ɪnɪ̲ʃəli/. **Initially** means soon after the beginning of a process or situation, rather than in the middle or at the end of it. *Forecasters say the gales may not be as bad as they initially predicted... Initially, they were wary of Simon.* ◆◆◆◇◇ ADV: ADV with v, ADV with cl/group =originally

initiate, initiates, initiating, initiated. The verb is pronounced /ɪnɪ̲ʃieɪt/. The noun is pronounced /ɪnɪ̲ʃiət/. ◆◆◇◇◇

1 If you **initiate** something, you start it or cause it to happen. *They wanted to initiate a discussion on economics... The trip was initiated by the manager of the community centre.* VERB V n

2 If you **initiate** someone into something, you introduce them to a particular skill or type of knowledge and teach them about it. *He initiated her into the study of other cultures.* VERB V n *into* n Also V n

3 If someone **is initiated** into something such as a religion, secret society, or social group, they become a member of it by taking part in ceremonies at which they learn its special knowledge or customs. *In many societies, young people are formally initiated into their adult roles. ...the lengthy ceremony that initiated Golden Dawn members into the Second Order.* VERB be V-ed *into* n V n *into* n Also V n

4 An **initiate** is a person who has been accepted as a member by a particular group or club and been taught its secrets and skills. *Chen was an initiate of a Chinese spiritual discipline.* N-COUNT: oft N *of* n

initiation /ɪnɪ̲ʃie̲ɪʃᵊn/ **initiations** ◆◇◇◇◇

1 The **initiation** of something is the starting of it. *They announced the initiation of a rural development programme... There was a year between initiation and completion.* N-UNCOUNT: usu *the* N *of* n

2 Someone's **initiation** into a particular group is the act or process by which they officially become a member, often involving special ceremonies. *After initiation, the youths started to interact with the older members... This was my initiation into the peace movement. ...initiation ceremonies.* N-VAR: oft N *into* n, N n

initiative /ɪnɪ̲ʃətɪv/ **initiatives** 

1 An **initiative** is an important act or statement that is intended to solve a problem. *Government* N-COUNT: usu with supp, oft N to-inf

initiatives to help young people have been inadequate... There's talk of a new peace initiative.

2 In a fight or contest, if you have **the initiative**, you are in a better position than your opponents to decide what to do next. *We have the initiative; we intend to keep it... He paused enough to consider the options but never so long as to lose the initiative.* N-SING: *the*N

3 If you have **initiative**, you have the ability to decide what to do next and to do it, without needing other people to tell you what to do. *She was disappointed by his lack of initiative. ...workers who are able to sort out problems on their own initiative.* N-UNCOUNT

4 If you **take the initiative** in a situation, you are the first person to act, and are therefore able to control the situation. *We are the only power willing to take the initiative in the long struggle to end the war... She knew she had to take the initiative and maintain an aggressive game throughout.* PHRASE: V inflects

initiator /ɪnɪʃieɪtəʳ/ **initiators.** The **initiator** of a plan or process is the person who was responsible for thinking of it or starting it. *...one of the major initiators of the tumultuous changes in Eastern Europe... Live Aid initiator Bob Geldof has a new project.* N-COUNT: oft N *of*n

inject /ɪndʒekt/ **injects, injecting, injected** ◆◆◇◇◇

1 To **inject** someone with a substance such as a medicine, or to **inject** it into them, means to use a needle and a syringe to put it into their body. *His son was injected with strong drugs... The technique consists of injecting healthy cells into the weakened muscles... He needs to inject himself once a month.* VERB; *be* V-ed *with*n; V n *into*n; V pron-refl; Also V n, V n *with*n

2 If you **inject** a new, exciting, or interesting quality into a situation, you add it. *She kept trying to inject a little fun into their relationship... The result might inject more sense into future bargaining.* VERB; V n *into*n

3 If you **inject** money or resources into a business or organization, you provide more money or resources for it. *He has injected £5.6 billion into the health service.* VERB; V n *into*n

injection /ɪndʒekʃᵊn/ **injections** ◆◆◇◇◇

1 If you have an **injection**, a doctor or nurse puts a medicine into your body using a needle and a syringe. *They gave me an injection to help me sleep... It has to be given by injection, usually twice daily.* N-COUNT: also *by*N

2 An **injection** of money or resources into a business or organization is the act of providing more money or resources for it, to help it become more efficient or profitable. *An injection of cash is needed to fund some of these projects... The company is hoping to obtain a £250 million cash injection from the government.* N-COUNT: with supp, oft N *of*n

injudicious /ɪndʒʊdɪʃəs/. If you describe a person or something that they have done as **injudicious**, you are critical of them because they have shown very poor judgement; a formal word. *He blamed injudicious comments by bankers for last week's devaluation.* ADJ-GRADED =ill-advised

injunction /ɪndʒʌŋkʃᵊn/ **injunctions** ◆◇◇◇◇

1 An **injunction** is a court order, usually one telling someone not to do something; a legal use. *He took out a court injunction against the newspaper demanding the return of the document.* N-COUNT: usu with supp

2 An **injunction** to do something is an order or strong request to do it; a formal use. *We hear endless injunctions to managers to build commitment and a sense of community among their staff.* N-COUNT: with supp, oft N *to*n to-inf

injure /ɪndʒəʳ/ **injures, injuring, injured.** If you **injure** a person or animal, you damage some part of their body. *A number of bombs have exploded, seriously injuring at least five people... Several policemen were injured in the clashes. ...stiff penalties for motorists who kill, maim, and injure.* ◆◇◇◇◇ VERB; V n; V

injured /ɪndʒəʳd/ ◆◆◆◇◇

1 An **injured** person or animal has physical damage to part of their body, usually as a result of an accident or fighting. *The other injured man had a superficial stomach wound... Many of them will have died because they were so badly injured.* ADJ-GRADED =wounded
► **The injured** are people who are injured. *Army helicopters tried to evacuate the injured.* N-PLURAL: *the*N

2 If you feel **injured** or if your feelings are **injured**, you feel upset because you believe something unjust or unfair has been done to you. *...a look of injured pride. ...compensation for injured feelings.* ADJ-GRADED =hurt

injured party, injured parties. The **injured party** in a court case or in a dispute over unfair treatment is the person who is or claims to be the victim of the unfair treatment; a legal expression. *The injured party got some compensation.* N-COUNT: usu *the*N =victim

injurious /ɪndʒʊəriəs/. Something that is **injurious** to someone or their health, well-being, or reputation is harmful or damaging to them; a formal word. *His continuance in the office of prime minister was 'injurious to the health of the nation'... Stress in itself is not necessarily injurious.* ADJ-GRADED: oft ADJ *to*n =damaging, detrimental

injury /ɪndʒəri/ **injuries** ◆◆◆◆◇

1 An **injury** is damage done to a person's or an animal's body. *Four police officers sustained serious injuries in the explosion... The two other passengers escaped serious injury.* N-VAR

2 If someone suffers **injury** to their feelings, they are distressed by something; a legal use. *She was awarded £1,500 for injury to her feelings.* N-VAR: oft N *to*n

3 ● to **add insult to injury**: see **insult**.

injury time. **Injury time** is the period of time added to the end of a football match because play was interrupted during the match when players were injured; used mainly in British English. N-UNCOUNT

injustice /ɪndʒʌstɪs/ **injustices** ◆◆◇◇◇

1 **Injustice** is a lack of fairness in a situation. *They'll continue to fight injustice... They resented the injustices of the system.* N-VAR

2 If you say that someone has **done** you **an injustice**, you mean that they have been unfair in the way that they have judged you or treated you. *Calling them a bunch of capricious kids with half-formed ideas does them an injustice.* PHRASE: V inflects

ink /ɪŋk/ **inks, inking, inked** ◆◆◇◇◇

1 **Ink** is the coloured liquid used for writing or printing. *The letter was handwritten in black ink.* N-MASS

2 If you **ink** something, you put ink on it. *Ritter took his left hand and inked the fingertips.* VERB; V n

inkling /ɪŋklɪŋ/ **inklings.** If you have an **inkling** of something, you have a vague idea about it. *I had no inkling of his real purpose until much later... We had an inkling that something might be happening.* N-COUNT: usu sing, usu N *of*n/wh, N that/wh =suspicion

inkwell /ɪŋkwel/ **inkwells.** An **inkwell** is a container for ink on a desk. N-COUNT

inky /ɪŋki/

1 **Inky** means black or very dark blue; a literary use. *The moon was rising in the inky sky. ...the inky black of night.* ► Also a combining form. *...looking out over an inky blue ocean.* ADJ: usu ADJ n; COMB in COLOUR

2 If something is **inky**, it is covered in ink. *We learned to write really well, in spite of inky fingers and occasional blots.* ADJ

inlaid /ɪnleɪd/. An object that is **inlaid** has a design on it which is made by putting materials such as wood, gold, or silver into the surface of the object. *...a box delicately inlaid with little triangles.* ADJ: oft ADJ *with*n

inland. The adverb is pronounced /ɪnlænd/. The adjective is pronounced /ɪnlænd/. ◆◆◇◇◇

1 If something is situated **inland**, it is away from the coast, towards or near the middle of a country. If you go **inland**, you go away from the coast, towards the middle of a country. *The vast majority live further inland... It's about 15 minutes' drive inland from Cannes... The car turned away from the coast and headed inland.* ADV: *be* ADV, ADV after v, oft amount ADV

2 **Inland** areas, lakes, and places are not on the coast, but in or near the middle of a country. *...a rather quiet inland town.* ADJ: ADJ n

Inland Revenue. In Britain, the **Inland Revenue** is the government authority which collects income tax and some other taxes. ◆◇◇◇◇ N-PROPER

in-laws. Your **in-laws** are the parents and close relatives of your husband or wife. ◆◇◇◇◇ N-PLURAL: usu poss N

inlay /ɪnleɪ/ **inlays**

1 An **inlay** is a design or pattern on an object which N-VAR

is made by putting materials such as wood, gold, or silver into the surface of the object. *...an inlay of medieval glass. ...woodwork with mother-of-pearl and silver inlay.*

2 **Inlay** is the technique of putting designs or patterns onto the surfaces of objects. *...traditional craft skills such as weaving, wood inlay, embroidery and metalwork.* N-UNCOUNT

inlet /ɪnlet/ **inlets** ◆◇◇◇◇

1 An **inlet** is a narrow strip of water which goes from a sea or lake into the land. *...a sheltered inlet.* N-COUNT

2 An **inlet** is a part of a machine through which a flow of liquid enters. *...a blocked water inlet.* N-COUNT: usu n N

inmate /ɪnmeɪt/ **inmates.** The **inmates** of a prison or a psychiatric hospital are the prisoners or patients who are living there. ◆◆◇◇◇ N-COUNT

inmost /ɪnmoust/. **Inmost** means the same as **innermost**. *He knew in his inmost heart that he was behaving badly.* ADJ: ADJ n

inn /ɪn/ **inns.** An **inn** is a small hotel or pub, usually an old one; an old-fashioned word. *...the Waterside Inn.* ◆◆◇◇◇ N-COUNT: oft in names after n

innards /ɪnəʳdz/

1 The **innards** of a person or animal are the organs inside their body; an informal use. N-PLURAL: usu with poss

2 A machine's **innards** are the parts inside it; an informal use. N-PLURAL

innate /ɪneɪt/. An **innate** quality or ability is one which a person is born with. *Americans have an innate sense of fairness. ...a society in which individuals could develop their innate abilities and capacities.* ♦ **innately** *I believe everyone is innately psychic.* ◆◇◇◇◇ ADJ: usu ADJ n =inherent, natural; ADV: ADV adj

inner /ɪnəʳ/ ◆◆◆◇◇

1 The **inner** parts of something are the parts which are contained or are enclosed inside the other parts, and which are closest to the centre. *She got up and went into an inner office... Wade stepped inside and closed the inner door behind him.* ADJ: ADJ n ≠outer

2 Your **inner** feelings are feelings which you have but do not show to other people. *Loving relationships that a child makes will give him an inner sense of security... Michael needed to express his inner tensions.* ADJ: ADJ n

inner circle, inner circles. An **inner circle** is a group of people who have a lot of power or control in a group or organization, and who work together in secretive ways. *He was one of the inner circle of scientists who produced the atomic bomb.* ◆◇◇◇◇ N-COUNT: usu sing, oft N *of* n

inner city, inner cities; also spelled **inner-city**. You use **inner city** to refer to the areas in or near the centre of a large city where people live and where there are often social and economic problems. *...helping kids deal with the fear of living in the inner city... Schools in 20 inner-city areas produced the worst results in last year's tests.* ◆◆◇◇◇ N-COUNT

innermost /ɪnəʳmoust/

1 Your **innermost** thoughts and feelings are your most personal and secret ones. *...expressing your innermost feelings. ...revealing a company's innermost secrets.* ADJ: ADJ n =inmost

2 The **innermost** thing is the one that is nearest to the centre. *The innermost part of the eye is a large cavity filled with a jelly-like fluid... She put the receipt into the innermost pocket of her bag.* ADJ: ADJ n ≠outermost

inner tube, inner tubes. An **inner tube** is a rubber tube containing air which is inside a car tyre or a bicycle tyre. *I had to change the inner tube, in the mud and the snow.* N-COUNT

inning /ɪnɪŋ/ **innings.** An **inning** is a period in a game of baseball when one of the teams is at bat. ◆◆◇◇◇ N-COUNT

innings /ɪnɪŋz/; **innings** is both the singular and the plural form. An **innings** is a period in a game of cricket during which a particular team or player is batting. *The home side were all out for 50 in their second innings.* ◆◆◇◇◇ N-COUNT

innkeeper /ɪnkiːpəʳ/ **innkeepers.** An **innkeeper** is someone who owns or manages an inn; an old-fashioned word. N-COUNT

innocence /ɪnəsəns/ ◆◆◇◇◇

1 **Innocence** is the quality of having no experience or knowledge of the more complex or unpleasant aspects of life. *...the sweet innocence of youth... Youngsters are losing their childhood innocence too quickly.* N-UNCOUNT

2 If someone proves their **innocence**, they prove that they are not guilty of a crime. *He claims he has evidence which could prove his innocence.* N-UNCOUNT: oft poss N ≠guilt

innocent /ɪnəsənt/ **innocents** ◆◆◆◇◇

1 If someone is **innocent**, they did not commit a crime which they have been accused of. *He was sure that the man was innocent of any crime... The police knew from day one that I was innocent.* ADJ: oft ADJ *of* n ≠guilty

2 If someone is **innocent**, they have no experience or knowledge of the more complex or unpleasant aspects of life. *They seemed so young and innocent... He's curiously innocent about what this means to other people.* ▶ An **innocent** is someone who is innocent. *She had always regarded Ian as a hopeless innocent where women were concerned.* ♦ **innocently** *The baby gurgled innocently on the bed.* ADJ-GRADED =naive; N-COUNT; ADV-GRADED: usu ADV with v

3 **Innocent** people are those who are not involved in a crime, conflict, or other situation, but who nevertheless get injured or killed. *All those wounded were innocent victims... The war was killing innocent women and children.* ADJ: usu ADJ n

4 An **innocent** question, remark, or comment is not intended to offend or upset people, even if it does so. *It was probably an innocent question, but Michael got flustered, anyway.* ADJ-GRADED =harmless

innocently /ɪnəsəntli/. If you say that someone does or says something **innocently**, you mean that they are pretending to be naive or know nothing about a situation, although they are really being quite clever and know more than they say. *I tried to catch Chrissie's eye to find out what she was playing at, but she only smiled back at me innocently... 'Any chance you'd be heading out that way again, soon?' I asked innocently.* ● See also **innocent**. ◆◇◇◇◇ ADV-GRADED: ADV with v

innocuous /ɪnɒkjuəs/. Something that is **innocuous** is not at all harmful or controversial; a formal word. *Both mushrooms look innocuous but are in fact deadly... Even seemingly innocuous words are offensive in certain contexts.* ◆◇◇◇◇ ADJ-GRADED =inoffensive

innovate /ɪnəveɪt/ **innovates, innovating, innovated.** To **innovate** means to introduce changes and new ideas in the way something is done or made. *What sets Rice apart from most engineers is his constant desire to innovate and experiment.* VERB; V; Also V n

innovation /ɪnəveɪʃən/ **innovations** ◆◆◇◇◇

1 An **innovation** is a new thing or a new method of doing something. *They produced the first vegetarian beanburger – an innovation which was rapidly exported to Britain. ...the transformation wrought by the technological innovations of the industrial age.* N-COUNT

2 **Innovation** is the introduction of new ideas, methods, or things. *We must promote originality, inspire creativity and encourage innovation.* N-UNCOUNT

innovative /ɪnəveɪtɪv/ ◆◆◇◇◇

1 Something that is **innovative** is new and original. *...products which are cheaper, more innovative and more reliable than those of their competitors.* ADJ-GRADED

2 An **innovative** person introduces changes and new ideas. *He was one of the most creative and innovative engineers of his generation.* ADJ-GRADED

innovator /ɪnəveɪtəʳ/ **innovators.** An **innovator** is someone who introduces changes and new ideas. *He is an innovator in this field.* ◆◇◇◇◇ N-COUNT

innovatory /ɪnəveɪtəri, AM -tɔːri/. **Innovatory** means the same as **innovative**; used mainly in British English. *Only the opening sequence could claim to be genuinely innovatory.* ADJ-GRADED

innuendo /ɪnjuendou/ **innuendoes** or **innuendos.** **Innuendo** is indirect reference to something rude or unpleasant. *The report was based on rumours, speculation, and innuendo. ...magazines which are full of sexual innuendo.* ◆◇◇◇◇ N-VAR =insinuation

innumerable /ɪnjuːmərəbəl, AM -nuː-/. **Innumerable** means very many, or too many to be ◆◇◇◇◇ ADJ: usu ADJ n counted. *He has invented innumerable excuses, told endless lies.* =countless

inoculate /ɪnɒkjʊleɪt/ **inoculates, inoculating, inoculated.** To **inoculate** a person or animal means to inject a weak form of a disease into their body as a way of protecting them against the disease. *...a program to inoculate every child in the state... His dogs were inoculated against rabies.* ♦ **inoculation** /ɪnɒkjʊleɪʃᵊn/ **inoculations** *This may eventually lead to routine inoculation of children... An inoculation against cholera is recommended.* VERB =vaccinate V n be V-ed against n N-VAR: oft N against n

inoffensive /ɪnəfensɪv/. If you describe someone or something as **inoffensive**, you mean that they are not unpleasant or unacceptable in any way, but are perhaps rather dull. *He's a mild inoffensive man... It's a very nice song. Catchy, and inoffensive.* ADJ-GRADED =innocuous ≠offensive

inoperable /ɪnɒpərəbᵊl/. An **inoperable** tumour, for example, is one that cannot be removed or cured by a surgical operation; a formal word. ADJ

inoperative /ɪnɒpərətɪv/. An **inoperative** rule, principle, or tax is one that does not work any more or that cannot be made to work; a formal word. ADJ

inopportune /ɪnɒpəʳtjuːn, AM -tuːn/. If you describe something as **inopportune** or if you say that it happens at an **inopportune** time, you mean that it happens at an unfortunate or unsuitable time, and causes trouble or embarrassment because of this. *The dismissals came at an inopportune time, diverting attention from the match.* ADJ-GRADED

inordinate /ɪnɔːʳdɪnɪt/. If you describe something as **inordinate**, you are emphasizing that it is unusually or excessively great in amount or degree; a formal word. *They spend an inordinate amount of time talking. ...their inordinate number of pets.* ♦ **inordinately** *He is inordinately proud of his wife's achievements.* ◆◇◇◇◇ ADJ: usu ADJ n PRAGMATICS =excessive ADV: usu ADV adj/-ed

inorganic /ɪnɔːʳgænɪk/. **Inorganic** substances are substances such as stone and metal that do not come from living things. *...roofing made from organic and inorganic fibres.* ADJ: usu ADJ n ≠organic

in-patient, in-patients. An **in-patient** is someone who stays in hospital while they receive their treatment. N-COUNT ≠out-patient

input /ɪnpʊt/ **inputs, inputting,** The form **input** is used in the present tense and is the past tense and past participle. ◆◆◇◇◇

1 Input consists of information or resources that a group or project receives. *It's up to the teacher to provide a variety of types of input in the classroom... They may need some additional inputs and advice on how to improve the management of their farms.* N-VAR

2 Input is information that is put into a computer. *When the input has been converted to zeros and ones, the computer's CPU takes over.* N-UNCOUNT ≠output

3 If you **input** information into a computer, you feed it in, for example by typing it on a keyboard. *The computer acts as a word processor where the text of a speech can be input at any time.* VERB be V-ed

inquest /ɪnkwest/ **inquests** ◆◇◇◇◇

1 An **inquest** is an official inquiry into the cause of someone's death. *The inquest into their deaths opened yesterday in Enniskillen.* N-COUNT: oft N into n

2 You can refer to an investigation by the people involved into the causes of a defeat or failure as an **inquest**. *His plea came last night as party chiefs held an inquest into the election disaster.* N-COUNT: usu sing, usu N into n =inquiry

inquire /ɪnkwaɪəʳ/ **inquires, inquiring, inquired;** also spelled **enquire.** ◆◆◇◇◇

1 If you **inquire** about something, you ask for information about it; a formal use. *'Is something wrong?' he enquired... 'Who are you?' he enquired of the first man... I rang up to inquire about train times... He asked for his key and inquired whether there had been any messages for him... He was so impressed that he inquired the young shepherd's name.* VERB V with quote V of n with quote V about n V wh V n Also V for n, V of n wh, V

2 If you **inquire into** something, you investigate it carefully. *Inspectors were appointed to inquire into the affairs of the company.* VERB V into n/wh

inquire after. If you **inquire after** someone, you ask how they are or what they are doing; a formal expression. *Elsie called to inquire after my health.* PHRASAL VERB V P n (not pron)

inquirer /ɪnkwaɪərəʳ/ **inquirers;** also spelled **enquirer.**

1 An **inquirer** is a person who asks for information about something or someone; a formal use. *I send each inquirer a packet of information.* N-COUNT

2 Inquirer is used in the names of some newspapers and magazines. *...the National Enquirer.* N-IN-NAMES: the supp N

inquiring /ɪnkwaɪərɪŋ/; also spelled **enquiring.**

1 If you have an **inquiring** mind, you have a great interest in learning new things. *I have always had an enquiring mind where food is concerned... All this helps children to develop an inquiring attitude to learning.* ADJ-GRADED: ADJ n =inquisitive

2 If someone has an **inquiring** expression on their face, they are showing that they want to know something; used in written English. *'That's right, dear,' she said in reply to his enquiring glance.* ♦ **inquiringly** *She looked at me inquiringly. 'Well?'* ADJ: ADJ n =questioning ADV

inquiry /ɪnkwaɪəri/ **inquiries;** also spelled **enquiry.** Sometimes pronounced /ɪŋkwɪri/ in American English. ◆◆◆◇◇

1 An **inquiry** is a question which you ask in order to get some information. *He made some inquiries and discovered she had gone to the Continent... After a brief inquiry about the Christmas holiday, he returned to the subject of music.* N-COUNT

2 An **inquiry** is an official investigation. *This is the most difficult and shocking murder inquiry I have had to open in the last 25 years... The Democratic Party has called for an independent inquiry into the incident.* N-COUNT

3 Inquiry is the process of asking about or investigating something in order to find out more about it. *The investigation has suddenly switched to a new line of inquiry.* N-UNCOUNT

4 If someone **is helping the police with their inquiries**, the police are questioning them about a crime, but have not yet charged them with it. *Two men were helping police with their inquiries at Salisbury last night.* PHRASE: V inflects

5 See also **court of inquiry**.

inquisition /ɪnkwɪzɪʃᵊn/ **inquisitions.** An **inquisition** is an official investigation, especially one which is very thorough and uses harsh methods of questioning. N-COUNT

inquisitive /ɪnkwɪzɪtɪv/. An **inquisitive** person likes finding out about things, especially secret things. *Barrow had an inquisitive nature... Bears are very inquisitive and must be kept mentally stimulated.* ♦ **inquisitively** *Molly looked at Ann inquisitively. 'Where do you want to go?'* ♦ **inquisitiveness** *I liked children, loved their innocence and their inquisitiveness.* ◆◇◇◇◇ ADJ-GRADED ADV-GRADED: ADV after v N-UNCOUNT

inquisitor /ɪnkwɪzɪtəʳ/ **inquisitors.** An **inquisitor** is someone who is asking someone else a series of questions, especially in a rather hostile way or as part of an inquisition. N-COUNT

inquisitorial /ɪnkwɪzɪtɔːriᵊl/. If you describe something or someone as **inquisitorial**, you mean they resemble things or people in an inquisition. *The next hearings will be structured differently in order to minimize the inquisitorial atmosphere.* ADJ

inroads /ɪnroʊdz/. If one thing **makes inroads** into another, the first thing starts affecting or destroying the second. *In Italy, as elsewhere, television has made deep inroads into cinema.* ◆◇◇◇◇ PHRASE: V inflects, usu PHR into n

insane /ɪnseɪn/ ◆◇◇◇◇

1 Someone who is **insane** has a mind that does not work in a normal way, with the result that their behaviour is very strange. *Some people simply can't take it and they just go insane... Agnes was a battered woman who had killed, in self-defense, while temporarily insane.* ► **The insane** are people who are insane. *...the state hospital for the criminally insane.* ADJ: usu v-link ADJ =mad N-PLURAL: the N

2 If you describe a decision or action as **insane**, you ADJ-GRADED think it is very foolish or excessive. *He asked me what I thought and I said, 'Listen, this is completely insane.' ...insane jealousy.* ♦ **insanely** *I would be insanely jealous if Bill left me for another woman.* PRAGMATICS ADV-GRADED: usu ADV adj, also ADV with v

insanitary /ɪnsænɪtri, AM -teri/. If something such as a place is **insanitary**, it is so dirty that it is likely to have a bad effect on people's health; a formal word. *...the insanitary conditions of slums... British prisons remain disgracefully crowded and insanitary.* ADJ-GRADED =unhygienic, unsanitary

insanity /ɪnsænɪti/ ◆◇◇◇◇

1 **Insanity** is the state of being insane. *The film is a powerful study of a woman's descent into insanity... The defence pleaded insanity, but the defendant was found guilty and sentenced.* N-UNCOUNT =madness

2 If you describe a decision or action as **insanity**, you think it is very foolish. *It was a period of collective insanity, of legalized murder and mayhem. ...the final financial insanity of the 1980s.* N-UNCOUNT: usu with supp, oft N of n PRAGMATICS =lunacy

insatiable /ɪnseɪʃəbᵊl/. If someone has an **insatiable** desire for something, they want as much of it as they can possibly get. *A section of the reading public has an insatiable appetite for dirty stories about the famous... They were insatiable collectors.* ◆◇◇◇◇ ADJ =voracious

inscribe /ɪnskraɪb/ **inscribes, inscribing, inscribed** ◆◇◇◇◇

1 If you **inscribe** words on an object, you write or carve the words on the object. *Some galleries commemorate donors by inscribing their names on the walls... She and Mark read the words inscribed on the inner walls of the monument. ...stone slabs inscribed with Buddhist texts. ...a silver cigarette-case, inscribed 'To Laura, with all my love, Leonard'.* VERB V n on n V-ed on/with n V-ed quote

2 If you **inscribe** something in the front of a book or on a photograph, you write it there, often before giving it to someone. *On the back I had inscribed the words: 'Here's to Great Ideas! John'... The book is inscribed: To John Arlott from Laurie Lee.* VERB V n V-ed quote

inscription /ɪnskrɪpʃᵊn/ **inscriptions** ◆◇◇◇◇

1 An **inscription** is writing carved into something made of stone or metal, for example a gravestone, monument, or medal. *Above its doors was a Latin inscription: Non omnia possumus omnes... The silver medal bears the sovereign's head and the inscription 'For distinguished service'.* N-COUNT

2 An **inscription** is something written by hand in the front of a book or on a photograph. *The inscription reads: 'To Emma, with love from Harry'.* N-COUNT

inscrutable /ɪnskruːtəbᵊl/. If a person or their expression is **inscrutable**, it is very hard to know what they are really thinking or what they mean. *In some circumstances, it is important to keep a straight face and to remain inscrutable.* ADJ-GRADED

insect /ɪnsekt/ **insects.** An **insect** is a small animal that has six legs. Most insects have wings. Ants, flies, butterflies, and beetles are all insects. ◆◆◇◇◇ N-COUNT

insecticide /ɪnsektɪsaɪd/ **insecticides. Insecticide** is a chemical substance that is used to kill insects that are a nuisance, for example because they eat crops. *Spray the plants with insecticide.* ◆◇◇◇◇ N-MASS

insecure /ɪnsɪkjʊəʳ/ ◆◆◇◇◇

1 If you are **insecure**, you feel unsure of yourself because you think that you are not good enough or are not loved. *In effect she is punishing her parents for making her feel threatened and insecure... Most mothers are insecure about their performance as mothers.* ♦ **insecurity** /ɪnsɪkjʊərɪti/ **insecurities** *She is always assailed by self-doubt and emotional insecurity... His behaviour is an attempt to cover up his insecurities.* ADJ-GRADED: usu v-link ADJ ≠secure N-VAR

2 Something that is **insecure** is not safe or protected. *...low-paid, insecure jobs... Cellular phones are inherently insecure, as anyone can listen to and record conversations.* ♦ **insecurity** *...the increase in crime, which has created feelings of insecurity in the population. ...the harshness and insecurity of agricultural life.* ADJ-GRADED ≠secure N-UNCOUNT

inseminate /ɪnsemɪneɪt/ **inseminates, inseminating, inseminated**

1 To **inseminate** a woman or female animal means to put a male's sperm into her in order to make her pregnant. *The gadget is used to artificially inseminate cows.* ♦ **insemination** /ɪnsemɪneɪʃᵊn/ *The sperm sample is checked under the microscope before insemination is carried out.* VERB V n N-UNCOUNT

2 See also **artificial insemination.**

insensitive /ɪnsensɪtɪv/ ◆◇◇◇◇

1 If you describe someone as **insensitive**, you are criticizing them for being unaware of or unsympathetic to other people's feelings. *I feel my husband is very insensitive about my problem... My mother was a thinking woman, not an insensitive one.* ♦ **insensitivity** /ɪnsensɪtɪvɪti/ *I was ashamed and appalled at my clumsiness and insensitivity towards her.* ADJ-GRADED PRAGMATICS ≠sensitive N-UNCOUNT

2 Someone who is **insensitive** to a situation or requirement is unaware of its importance and does not react to it. *Women's and Latino organizations that say he is insensitive to civil rights.* ♦ **insensitivity** *...insensitivity to the environmental consequences.* ADJ-GRADED: usu ADJ to n N-UNCOUNT

3 Someone who is **insensitive** to a physical sensation is unable to feel it. *He had become insensitive to cold.* ADJ: usu v-link ADJ to n

inseparable /ɪnseprəbᵊl/ ◆◇◇◇◇

1 If one thing is **inseparable** from another, the things are so closely connected that they cannot be considered separately. *He firmly believes liberty is inseparable from social justice... For the ancient Mexicans, life and death were inseparable, two halves of the same whole.* ♦ **inseparably** *The doctrine of karma is inseparably linked with reincarnation... In his mind, religion and politics were inseparably intertwined.* ADJ: oft ADJ from n ADV: usu ADV -ed, also ADV after v

2 If you say that two people are **inseparable**, you are emphasizing that they are very good friends and spend a great deal of time together. *She and Kristin were inseparable.* ADJ-GRADED

insert, inserts, inserting, inserted. The verb is pronounced /ɪnsɜːʳt/. The noun is pronounced /ɪnsɜːʳt/. ◆◆◇◇◇

1 If you **insert** an object into something, you put the object inside it. *He took a small key from his pocket and slowly inserted it into the lock... Wait for a couple of minutes with your mouth closed before inserting the thermometer.* ♦ **insertion** /ɪnsɜːʳʃᵊn/ **insertions** *...the first experiment involving the insertion of a new gene into a human being.* VERB V n into n V n N-VAR

2 If you **insert** a comment into a piece of writing or a speech, you include it. *They joined with the monarchists to insert a clause calling for a popular vote on the issue.* ♦ **insertion** *He saw no point whatsoever in recording an item for insertion in the programme.* VERB V n Also V n into/in n N-VAR

3 An **insert** is something that is inserted somewhere, especially an advertisement on a piece of paper that is placed between the pages of a book or magazine. N-COUNT

in-service. If people working in a particular profession are given **in-service** training, they attend special courses to improve their skills or to learn about new developments in their field. *...the undoubted need for in-service training. ...in-service courses for people such as doctors, teachers, and civil servants.* ADJ: ADJ n

inset /ɪnset/ **insets**

1 Something that is **inset** with a decoration or piece of material has the decoration or material set inside it. *...a small gold pendant, shaped as a heart and inset with a diamond. ...the glass bricks inset high along the corridor's opposite wall.* ADJ: usu v-link ADJ, oft ADJ with n

2 An **inset** is a small picture, diagram, or map that is inside a larger one. *I frequently paint between 10 and 20 insets for my murals.* N-COUNT

inshore. The adverb is pronounced /ɪnʃɔːʳ/. The adjective is pronounced /ɪnʃɔːʳ/. If something is **inshore**, it is in the sea but quite close to the land. If something moves **inshore**, it moves from the sea towards the land. *A barge was close inshore about a hundred yards away... There was still a strong wind blowing inshore.* ► Also an adjective. *...inshore reefs and islands.* ◆◇◇◇◇ ADV: be ADV, ADV after v ≠offshore ADJ: ADJ n ≠offshore

inside /ɪnsaɪd/ **insides.** The preposition is usually pronounced /ɪnsaɪd/. ◆◆◆◆◇

The form **inside of** can also be used as a preposition. This form is more usual in American English.

1 Something or someone that is **inside** a place, container, or object is in it or is surrounded by it. *Inside the passport was a folded slip of paper... There is a telephone inside the entrance hall.* ▶ Also an adverb. *The couple chatted briefly on the doorstep before going inside... He ripped open the envelope and read what was inside... I could hear music coming from inside... At a table inside, a man and woman were awaiting her... Inside, clouds of cigarette smoke swirled from the booths along the walk.* ▶ Also an adjective. *...four-berth inside cabins with en suite bathroom and shower.*
PREP ≠outside; ADV: ADV after v, *be* ADV, *from* ADV, n ADV, ADV with cl ≠outside; ADJ: ADJ n

2 The **inside** of something is the part or area that its sides surround or contain. *The doors were locked from the inside... I painted the inside of the house the colours of an English garden... Kiwi fruit can be eaten by cutting off the tops and scooping out the insides with a teaspoon.* ▶ Also an adjective. *The popular papers all have photo features on their inside pages.* ▶ Also an adverb. *The potato cakes can be shallow or deep-fried until crisp outside and meltingly soft inside.*
N-COUNT: usu *the* N in sing ≠outside; ADJ: ADJ n; ADV: adj ADV

3 You can say that someone is **inside** when they are in prison; an informal use. *They've both done prison time – he's been inside three times.*
ADV: *be* ADV, ADV after v

4 On a wide road, the **inside** lanes are the ones which are closest to the edge of the road. *I was driving up at seventy miles an hour on the inside lane on the motorway.* ▶ Also a noun. *I overtook Charlie on the inside, and I accelerated all the way to the finish.*
ADJ: ADJ n =nearside ≠outside; N-SING: *the* N, oft *on the* N ≠outside

5 **Inside** information is obtained from someone who is involved in a situation and therefore knows a lot about it. *Sloane used inside diplomatic information to make himself rich... Keith Vass, editor, denies he had inside knowledge... It's fascinating to get the inside story so many years after this incident.*
ADJ: ADJ n

6 If you are **inside** an organization, you belong to it. *75 percent of chief executives come from inside the company... He hasn't looked very carefully into what was happening inside the Communist Party.* ▶ Also an adjective. *...a recent book about the inside world of pro football.* ▶ Also a noun. *McAvoy was convinced he could control things from the inside but he lost control.*
PREP; ADJ: ADJ n; N-SING: *the* N

7 Your **insides** are your internal organs, especially your stomach; an informal use.
N-PLURAL: usu poss N =innards

8 If you say that someone has a feeling **inside**, you mean that they have it but have not expressed it. *There is nothing left inside – no words, no anger, no tears... Do you get a feeling inside when you write something you like?* ▶ Also a preposition. *He felt a great weight of sorrow inside him... There was a little anger inside me.* ▶ Also a noun. *What is needed is a change from the inside, a real change in outlook and attitude.*
ADV: ADV after v, n ADV; PREP: usu n PREP pron; N-SING: *the* N

9 If you do something **inside** a particular time, you do it before the end of that time. *They should have everything working inside an hour... New Zealand were ahead inside five minutes.*
PREP: PREP amount =within

10 If something such as a piece of clothing is **inside out**, the part that is normally inside now faces outwards. *Her umbrella blew inside out.*
PHRASES PHR after v

11 If you say that you know something or someone **inside out**, you are emphasizing that you know them extremely well. *He knew the game inside out... We know each other inside out.*
v n PHR PRAGMATICS

12 If you say that something **has been turned inside out**, you mean that it is the opposite of what you expect or think it should be. *Edinburgh is an American city turned inside out: the rich in the middle, the poor around the outside... War turns morality inside out: killing and cruelty are virtues.*
V inflects

insider /ɪnsaɪdəʳ/ **insiders.** An **insider** is someone who is involved in a situation and who knows more about it than other people. *An insider said, 'Katharine has told friends it is time to end her career.'... German banks have more insider knowledge than most.*
◆◆◇◇◇ N-COUNT

insider dealing. **Insider dealing** is the practice of illegally buying or selling shares on the stock market for profit when someone knows more about a particular company than most people, often because they are involved with it in some way. *...illegal income gained through insider dealing.*
N-UNCOUNT

insidious /ɪnsɪdiəs/. Something that is **insidious** is unpleasant or dangerous and develops gradually without being noticed. *The changes are insidious, and will not produce a noticeable effect for 15 to 20 years... They focus on overt discrimination rather than insidious aspects of racism.* ♦ **insidiously** *Delusions are sometimes insidiously destructive.*
◆◇◇◇◇ ADJ-GRADED; ADV-GRADED: usu ADV adj

insight /ɪnsaɪt/ **insights**
◆◆◇◇◇

1 If you gain **insight** or an **insight** into a complex situation or problem, you gain an accurate and deep understanding of it. *The project would give scientists new insights into what is happening to the earth's atmosphere... I hope that this talk has given you some insight into the kind of work that we've been doing.*
N-VAR: usu N *into* n

2 If someone has **insight**, they are able to understand complex situations. *He was a man of forceful character, with considerable insight and diplomatic skills.*
N-UNCOUNT =understanding

insightful /ɪnsaɪtfʊl/. If you describe a person or their remarks as **insightful**, you mean that they show a very good understanding of people and situations. *She offered some really interesting, insightful observations.*
ADJ-GRADED PRAGMATICS =astute, perceptive

insignia /ɪnsɪgniə/; **insignia** is both the singular and the plural form. An **insignia** is a badge or sign which shows that a person or object belongs to a particular organization, often a military one. *...a scarlet tunic bearing the insignia of a captain in the Irish Guards.*
N-COUNT =emblem

insignificance /ɪnsɪgnɪfɪkəns/. **Insignificance** is the quality of being insignificant. *These prices pale into insignificance when compared with what was paid for two major works by the late Alfred Stieglitz... The event was regarded as of such insignificance that not one major newspaper carried a report.*
N-UNCOUNT ≠significance

insignificant /ɪnsɪgnɪfɪkənt/. Something that is **insignificant** is unimportant, especially because it is very small. *In 1949 Bonn was a small, insignificant city.*
◆◇◇◇◇ ADJ-GRADED ≠significant

insincere /ɪnsɪnsɪəʳ/. If you say that someone is **insincere**, you are being critical of them because they say things they do not really mean, usually pleasant, admiring, or encouraging things. *Some people are so terribly insincere you can never tell if they are telling the truth... John found himself surrounded by insincere flattery.* ♦ **insincerity** /ɪnsɪnserɪti/ *You need to sound enthusiastic without gushing. Too many superlatives lend a note of insincerity.*
ADJ-GRADED PRAGMATICS ≠sincere, genuine; N-UNCOUNT ≠sincerity

insinuate /ɪnsɪnjueɪt/ **insinuates, insinuating, insinuated**

1 If you say that someone **insinuates** that something is the case, you mean that they suggest in a very unpleasant way that it is the case; used showing disapproval. *The libel claim followed an article which insinuated that the President was lying... Are you insinuating that I smell?* ♦ **insinuation** /ɪnsɪnjueɪʃən/ **insinuations** *He speaks with rage of insinuations that there's a 'gay mafia' in Hollywood... I just don't think it's right to bring a good man down by rumour and insinuation.*
VERB PRAGMATICS =imply; V that; Also V n; N-VAR

2 If you say that someone **insinuates** themselves into a particular situation, you mean that they manage very cleverly to get into that situation; used showing disapproval. *...a thriller about a young man who insinuates himself into a millionaire's empire by assuming different identities.*
VERB PRAGMATICS =worm; V pron-refl *into* n; Also V n prep

insinuating /ɪnsɪnjueɪtɪŋ/. If you describe someone or what they say as **insinuating**, you mean that they hint that something is the case in
ADJ PRAGMATICS

a very unpleasant way; used showing disapproval. *Marcus kept making insinuating remarks... 'Yes.' My tone was insinuating. 'I heard she was a real friendly girl.'*

insipid /ɪnsɪpɪd/
1 If you describe food or drink as **insipid**, you dislike it because it has very little taste. *It tasted indescribably bland and insipid, like warmed cardboard.* ADJ-GRADED =bland, tasteless
2 If you describe someone or something as **insipid**, you mean they are dull and boring. *On the surface she seemed meek, rather insipid... They gave an insipid opening performance in a nil-nil draw with Peru.* ADJ-GRADED

insist /ɪnsɪst/ **insists, insisting, insisted** ◆◆◆◆◇
1 If you **insist** that something should be done, you say so very firmly and refuse to give in about it. If you **insist** on something, you say firmly that it must be done or provided. *My family insisted that I should not give in, but stay and fight... She insisted on being present at all the interviews... She insists on all her employees coming to the Christmas lunch she gives every year... I didn't want to join in, but Kenneth insisted.* VERB V that V *on*-ing/n V *on* n -ing V
2 If you **insist** that something is the case, you say so very firmly and refuse to say otherwise, even though other people do not believe you. *The president insisted that he was acting out of compassion, not political opportunism... 'It's not that difficult,' she insists... Crippen insisted on his innocence.* VERB V that V with quote V *on* n

insistence /ɪnsɪstəns/. Someone's **insistence** on something is the fact that they insist that it should be done or insist that it is the case. *...Raeder's insistence that naval uniform be worn... He admired your insistence on understanding things and making your point, even when he preferred his own... She had attended an interview, at her boyfriend's insistence.* ◆◆◇◇◇ N-UNCOUNT: oft N *on*-ing/n, N that

insistent /ɪnsɪstənt/ ◆◇◇◇◇
1 Someone who is **insistent** keeps insisting that a particular thing should be done or is the case. *Stalin was insistent that the war would be won and lost in the machine shops... He is most insistent on this point... 'When can I see him?' Her tone was insistent now.* ♦ **insistently** *'What is it?' his wife asked again, gently but insistently.* ADJ-GRADED: oft ADJ that, ADJ *on* n/-ing; ADV-GRADED: ADV with v
2 An **insistent** noise or rhythm keeps going on for a long time and holds your attention. *...the insistent rhythms of the Caribbean and Latin America.* ADJ-GRADED =unrelenting

in situ /ɪn sɪtjuː, AM - sɪtuː/. If something remains **in situ**, especially while something is done to it, it remains where it is; a formal expression. *Major works of painting, sculpture, mosaic and architecture were examined in situ in Venice.* ▶ Also an adjective. *...technical data derived from laboratory and in-situ experimentation.* ADV: ADV after v; ADJ: ADJ n

insofar as /ɪnsəfɑːr æz/; also spelled **in so far as**. You use **insofar as** to introduce a statement which explains and adds to something you have just said; a formal expression. *We are entering a period of less danger insofar as the danger of nuclear war between the superpowers is less.* ◆◇◇◇◇ PHR-CONJ-SUBORD =inasmuch as

insole /ɪnsoʊl/ **insoles.** The **insoles** of a pair of shoes are the soft layer of material inside each one, which the soles of your feet rest on. N-COUNT: usu pl

insolent /ɪnsələnt/. If you say that someone is being **insolent**, you mean they are being rude to someone they ought to be respectful to. *...her insolent stare... The officer stamped his boot. 'Don't be insolent with me, mademoiselle.'* ♦ **insolence** *The most frequent reasons for excluding a pupil were breaking school rules, insolence, and bad language.* ADJ-GRADED =impudent; N-UNCOUNT =impudence

insoluble /ɪnsɒljʊbəl/
1 An **insoluble** problem is so difficult that it is impossible to solve. *I pushed the problem aside; at present it was insoluble... It was an insoluble dilemma and one which I could do nothing about.* ADJ
2 If a substance is **insoluble**, it does not dissolve in a liquid. *Carotenes are insoluble in water and soluble in oils and fats.* ADJ ≠soluble

insolvency /ɪnsɒlvənsi/ **insolvencies. Insolvency** is the state of not having enough money to pay your debts; a formal word. *...eight mortgage companies, seven of which are on the brink of insolvency... The economy has entered a sharp downturn, and unemployment and insolvencies can be expected to increase.* ◆◇◇◇◇ N-VAR

insolvent /ɪnsɒlvənt/. A person or organization that is **insolvent** does not have enough money to pay their debts; a formal word. *Two years later, the bank was declared insolvent.* ◆◇◇◇◇ ADJ: usu v-link ADJ

insomnia /ɪnsɒmniə/. Someone who suffers from **insomnia** finds it difficult to sleep. ◆◇◇◇◇ N-UNCOUNT

insomniac /ɪnsɒmniæk/ **insomniacs.** An **insomniac** is a person who finds it difficult to sleep. N-COUNT

insouciance /ɪnsuːsiəns/. **Insouciance** is lack of concern shown by someone about something which they might be expected to take more seriously; a formal word. *He replied with characteristic insouciance: 'So what?'* N-UNCOUNT =nonchalance

insouciant /ɪnsuːsiənt/. An **insouciant** action or quality shows someone's lack of concern about something which they might be expected to take more seriously; a formal word. *...Andy Warhol, who worked with an insouciant disregard for the distinctions between painting, photography and film.* ADJ-GRADED =nonchalant

Insp. **Insp.** is the written abbreviation for 'Inspector' when it is used as a title. *...Insp John Downs.* N-TITLE

inspect /ɪnspekt/ **inspects, inspecting, inspected** ◆◆◆◇◇
1 If you **inspect** something, you look at every part of it carefully in order to find out about it or check that it is all right. *Elaine went outside to inspect the playing field... Cut the fruit in half and inspect the pips: if they are turning slightly brown it is ready for harvesting.* ♦ **inspection** /ɪnspekʃən/ **inspections** *'Excellent work,' he said when he had completed his inspection of the painted doors... From a distance, the birds appear mainly green in colour. However, closer inspection reveals that their chests are banded with yellow.* VERB =examine V n; N-VAR
2 When an official **inspects** a place or a group of people, they visit it and check it carefully, for example in order to find out whether regulations are being obeyed. *The Public Utilities Commission inspects us once a year... Each hotel is inspected and, if it fulfils certain criteria, is recommended.* ♦ **inspection** *Officers making a routine inspection of the vessel found fifty kilograms of the drug.* VERB V n; N-VAR

inspector /ɪnspektəʳ/ **inspectors** ◆◆◆◇◇
1 An **inspector** is a person, usually employed by a government agency, whose job is to find out whether people are obeying official regulations. *The mill was finally shut down by state safety inspectors.* N-COUNT
2 In Britain, an **inspector** is an officer in the police who is higher in rank than a sergeant and lower in rank than a superintendent. *Last week gunmen attacked Mogadishu airport killing a police inspector... I got on the phone to Inspector Joplin at Scotland Yard.* N-COUNT; N-TITLE; N-VOC

inspectorate /ɪnspektərət/ **inspectorates.** An **inspectorate** is a group of inspectors who are employed to work on the same issue or area; used mainly in British English. *...the Nuclear Installations Inspectorate.*  N-COUNT: usu with supp

inspiration /ɪnspɪreɪʃən/ **inspirations** 
1 **Inspiration** is a feeling of enthusiasm and encouragement you get from someone or something, which gives you new ideas or the desire to create something. *My inspiration comes from poets like Baudelaire and Jacques Prévert... What better way of finding inspiration for your own garden than by visiting others.* N-UNCOUNT
2 If you describe someone or something as an **inspiration**, you admire them because they fill people with enthusiasm or encouragement. *Powell's unusual journey to high office is an inspiration to millions... She was a great inspiration. She was the* N-SING: *a* N, oft N *to* n PRAGMATICS

person who impressed us with the importance of research.

3 If something or someone is the **inspiration** for a particular work of art or other creation, they are the source of the ideas in it or act as a model for it. *India's myths and songs are the inspiration for her books... The inspiration behind the reforms was a paper written in 1985.* N-SING: oft N *for/behind* n

4 If you suddenly have an **inspiration**, you suddenly think of an idea of what to do or say. *Alison had an inspiration. 'Wouldn't it be good if we made a tunnel out of hardboard'.* N-COUNT

inspirational /ɪnspɪreɪʃənəl/. Something that is **inspirational** provides you with inspiration. *Tolstoy was an inspirational figure in forming Gandhi's ideas about nonviolence... Cumbria was inspirational for Wordsworth.* ◆◇◇◇◇ ADJ-GRADED

inspire /ɪnspaɪəʳ/ **inspires, inspiring, inspired** ◆◆◇◇◇

1 If someone or something **inspires** you to do something, usually something new or unusual, they make you want to do it. *These herbs will inspire you to try out all sorts of exotic-flavoured dishes!... Our challenge is to motivate those voters and inspire them to join our cause... And what inspired you to change your name?* VERB =encourage V n to-inf

2 If someone or something **inspires** you, they give you new ideas and a strong feeling of enthusiasm. *In the 1960s, the electric guitar virtuosity of Jimi Hendrix inspired a generation.* VERB V n

3 If a work of art or an action **is inspired** by something, that thing is the source of the idea or the motivation for it. *The book was inspired by a real person, namely Tamara de Treaux. ...a political murder inspired by the same nationalist conflicts now wrecking the country.* ♦ **-inspired** *...Mediterranean-inspired ceramics in bright yellow and blue... Jamaica's socialist government is adopting US-inspired free market practices.* VB: usu passive *be* V-ed *by* n V-ed COMB in ADJ

4 Someone or something that **inspires** a particular emotion or reaction in people makes them feel this emotion or reaction. *The car's performance is effortless and its handling is precise and quickly inspires confidence.* VERB V n

inspiring /ɪnspaɪərɪŋ/. Something or someone that is **inspiring** is exciting and makes you feel strongly interested and enthusiastic. *...Edward Kennedy and Mario Cuomo, the party's most inspiring orators... England produced an effective, if not inspiring, performance against the CIS in Moscow.* ◆◇◇◇◇ ADJ-GRADED =stirring

Inst. **Inst.** is a written abbreviation for 'Institute'. *...the Liverpool Inst. of Higher Ed.* N-IN-NAMES

instability /ɪnstəbɪlɪti/ **instabilities. Instability** is a lack of stability in a person, place, or situation. *...unpopular policies, which resulted in social discontent and political instability. ...Caligula's inherent mental instability... The length of the fuselage was increased due to a degree of directional instability.* ◆◆◇◇◇ N-UNCOUNT: also N in pl ≠stability

install /ɪnstɔːl/ **installs, installing, installed** ◆◆◆◇◇

1 If you **install** a piece of equipment, you fit it or put it somewhere so that it is ready to be used. *They had installed a new phone line in the apartment.* ♦ **installation** *Hundreds of lives could be saved if the installation of alarms was more widespread.* VERB V n N-UNCOUNT: oft N *of* n

2 If someone is **installed** in a new job or important position, they are officially given the job or position, often in a special ceremony. *A new Catholic bishop was installed in Galway yesterday... Professor Sawyer was formally installed as President last Thursday... The army has promised to install a new government within a week.* ♦ **installation** *He sent a letter inviting Naomi to attend his installation as chief of his tribe.* VERB *be* V-ed *be* V-ed *as* n V n Also V n *as* n N-UNCOUNT: oft with poss, N *as* n

3 If you **install** yourself in a particular place, you settle there and make yourself comfortable; a formal use. *Before her husband's death she had installed herself in a modern villa.* VERB V pron-refl prep/adv

installation /ɪnstəleɪʃən/ **installations.** An **installation** is a place that contains equipment and machinery which are being used for a particular purpose. *The building was turned into a secret military installation. ...a nuclear installation.* ● See also **install**. ◆◆◇◇◇ N-COUNT: usu supp N

instalment /ɪnstɔːlmənt/ **instalments;** spelled **installment** in American English. ◆◇◇◇◇

1 If you pay for something in **instalments**, you pay small sums of money at regular intervals over a period of time, rather than paying the whole amount at once. *The first instalment of £1 per share is payable on application. ...the first month's interest instalment on the loan.* N-COUNT

2 An **instalment** of a story or plan is one of its parts that are published or carried out separately one after the other. *The next instalment of this four-part series deals with the impact of the war on the continent of Africa.* N-COUNT =part

instance /ɪnstəns/ **instances** ◆◆◆◆◇

1 You use **for instance** to introduce a particular event, situation, or person that is an example of what you are talking about. *In sub-Saharan Africa today, for instance, gross investment accounts for roughly 15% of national income... Let your child make some of the small decisions concerning his daily routine. For instance, allow him to choose what clothes he wears at the weekend.* PHRASE: PHR with cl/group PRAGMATICS =for example

2 An **instance** is a particular example or occurrence of something. *She cited an instance where their training had been a marvelous help in dealing with problems. ...an investigation into a serious instance of corruption.* N-COUNT

3 You say **in the first instance** to mention something that is the first step in a series of actions. *In the first instance your child will be seen by an ear, nose and throat specialist... The post was for one year in the first instance with possible renewal to a further year.* PHRASES PHR with cl PRAGMATICS

4 If you **do** something **at someone's instance**, you do it because they have ordered or requested you to do it; used in formal British English. *The rally was organised at the instance of two senior cabinet ministers.* usu PHR after v =at someone's request

instant /ɪnstənt/ **instants** ◆◆◆◇◇

1 An **instant** is an extremely short period of time. *For an instant, Catherine was tempted to flee... The pain disappeared in an instant.* N-COUNT: usu sing =moment

2 If you say that something happens at a particular **instant**, you mean that it happens at exactly the time you have been referring to, and you are usually suggesting that it happens quickly or immediately. *At that instant the museum was plunged into total darkness... In the same instant he flung open the car door.* N-SING: with supp, usu *at/in* N =moment

3 If you say that someone does something **the instant** something else happens, you are emphasizing that they do the first thing immediately after the second thing happens. *I had bolted the door the instant I had seen the bat.* PHR-CONJ-SUBORD PRAGMATICS =the minute

4 You use **instant** to describe something that happens immediately. *Mr Porter's book was an instant hit... He had taken an instant dislike to Mortlake.* ♦ **instantly** *The man was killed instantly... The songs are instantly recognisable.* ADJ: usu ADJ n =immediate ADV: ADV with v, ADV adj

5 **Instant** food is food that you can prepare very quickly, for example by just adding water. *He was stirring instant coffee into two mugs of hot water.* ADJ: ADJ n

instantaneous /ɪnstənteɪniəs/. Something that is **instantaneous** happens immediately and very quickly. *Death was not instantaneous because none of the bullets hit the heart.* ♦ **instantaneously** *Airbags inflate instantaneously on impact to form a cushion between the driver and the steering column.* ◆◇◇◇◇ ADJ-GRADED =immediate ADV: ADV with v

instead /ɪnsted/ ◆◆◆◆◇

1 If you do one thing **instead of** another, you do the first thing and not the second thing, as the result of a choice or a change of behaviour. *She had to spend nearly four months away from him that summer, instead of the usual two... Check-out workers in London will receive £7.17 an hour instead of £7.54... They raised prices and cut production, instead of cutting costs... Instead of going to work thinking that it will be totally boring, try to be positive.* PHR-PREP: PREP n/-ing =as opposed to

2 If you do not do something, but do something ADV:

else **instead**, you do the second thing and not the first thing, as the result of a choice or a change of behaviour. *He reached for the wine but did not drink, pushed it, instead, across the table towards Joanna... The kitchen might have been workable had Nicola kept it tidy; instead it was littered with pots and pans... My husband asked why I couldn't just forget about dieting all the time and eat normally instead.* ADV with cl

instep /ɪnstep/ **insteps.** Your **instep** is the middle part of your foot, where it arches upwards. N-COUNT

instigate /ɪnstɪgeɪt/ **instigates, instigating, instigated.** Someone who **instigates** an event causes it to happen. *Jenkinson instigated a refurbishment of the old gallery... The violence over the last forty-eight hours was instigated by ex-members of the secret police.* ◆◇◇◇◇ VERB =bring about V n
♦ **instigation** /ɪnstɪgeɪʃᵊn/ *The talks are taking place at the instigation of Germany... At Kukhar's instigation he joined the restaurant as an apprentice chef.* N-UNCOUNT: usu *at/on* N with poss

instigator /ɪnstɪgeɪtəʳ/ **instigators.** The **instigator** of an event is the person who instigates it. *He was accused of being the main instigator of the coup. ...the key instigators of reform.* N-COUNT: oft N *of* n

instil /ɪnstɪl/ **instils, instilling, instilled;** spelled **instill** in American English. If you **instil** an idea or feeling into someone, especially over a period of time, you make them think it or feel it. *They hope that their work will instil a sense of responsibility in children... They are the kind of young men who could instil fear on football terraces.* ◆◇◇◇◇ VERB =implant V n *in/into* n V n

instinct /ɪnstɪŋkt/ **instincts** ◆◆◇◇◇

1 Instinct is the natural tendency that a person or animal has to behave or react in a particular way. *I didn't have as strong a maternal instinct as some other mothers... The basis for training relies on the dog's natural instinct to hunt and retrieve... He always knew what time it was, as if by instinct.* N-VAR

2 If you have an **instinct** for something, you are naturally good at it or able to do it. *Farmers are increasingly losing touch with their instinct for managing the land... Irene is so incredibly musical and has a natural instinct to perform.* N-COUNT: oft N *for* n/-ing, N to-inf =aptitude

3 If it is your **instinct** to do something, you feel that it is right to do it. *I should've gone with my first instinct, which was not to do the interview... She hadn't followed her instinct and because of this Frank was dead.* N-VAR: usu with poss, oft N to-inf =gut feeling

4 Instinct is a feeling that you have that something is the case, rather than an opinion or idea based on facts. *There is scientific evidence to support our instinct that being surrounded by plants is good for health... He seems so honest and genuine and my every instinct says he's not.* N-VAR: oft N that =intuition

instinctive /ɪnstɪŋktɪv/. An **instinctive** feeling, idea, or action is one that you have or do without thinking or reasoning. *It's an absolutely instinctive reaction – if a child falls you pick it up... Ms Senatorova showed an instinctive feel for market economics.* ◆◆◇◇◇ ADJ =automatic, natural
♦ **instinctively** *Jane instinctively knew all was not well with her 10-month old son.* ADV: ADV with v

instinctual /ɪnstɪŋktʃuəl/. An **instinctual** feeling, action, or idea is one based on instinct. *The relationship between a parent and a child is instinctual and stems from basic human nature.* ADJ

institute /ɪnstɪtjuːt, AM -tuːt/ **institutes, instituting, instituted** ◆◆◆◆◇

1 An **institute** is an organization set up to do a particular type of work, especially research or teaching. You can also use **institute** to refer to the building the organization occupies. *...the National Cancer Institute. ...an elite research institute devoted to computer software... Directly in front of the institute is Kelly Ingram Park.* N-COUNT: oft in names

2 If you **institute** a system, rule, or course of action, you start it; a formal use. *We will institute a number of measures to better safeguard the public... Hormone replacement therapy is very important and should be instituted early.* VERB V n

institution /ɪnstɪtjuːʃᵊn, AM -tuː-/ **institutions** ◆◆◆◆◇

1 An **institution** is a large important organization such as a university, church, or bank. *Class size varies from one type of institution to another... The Hong Kong Bank is Hong Kong's largest financial institution.* N-COUNT: oft in names

2 An **institution** is a building where certain people are looked after, for example people who are mentally ill or children who have no parents. *He was transferred to Shoal Creek Mental Institution for an indefinite period... Larry has been in an institution since he was four... He visited various penal institutions in the United Kingdom in the late 1930s.* N-COUNT: oft in names

3 An **institution** is a custom or system that is considered an important or typical feature of a particular society or group, usually because it has existed for a long time. *I believe in the institution of marriage. ...the institution of the family.* N-COUNT: usu N *of* n

4 The **institution** of a new system is the act of starting it or bringing it in. *There was never an official institution of censorship in Albania. ...the institution of the forty-hour week.* N-UNCOUNT: usu N *of* n

institutional /ɪnstɪtjuːʃənᵊl, AM -tuː-/ ◆◆◇◇◇

1 Institutional means relating to a large organization, for example a university, bank, or church. *NATO remains the United States' chief institutional anchor in Europe... The share price will be determined by bidding from institutional investors.* ADJ: ADJ n

2 Institutional means relating to a building where people are looked after or held. *Outside the protected environment of institutional care he could not survive.* ADJ: ADJ n

3 An **institutional** value or quality is considered an important and typical feature of a particular society or group, usually because it has existed for a long time. *...social and institutional values.* ADJ: ADJ n

institutionalize /ɪnstɪtjuːʃənəlaɪz, AM -tuː-/ **institutionalizes, institutionalizing, institutionalized;** also spelled **institutionalise** in British English. ◆◇◇◇◇

1 If someone such as a sick or old person **is institutionalized**, they are sent to stay in a special hospital or home, usually for a long period. *She became seriously ill and had to be institutionalized for a lengthy period... She saw herself as a failure and had been institutionalized once for depression. ...institutionalized kids with medical problems.* VB: usu passive *be* V-ed V-ed
♦ **institutionalization** /ɪnstɪtjuːʃənəlaɪzeɪʃᵊn, AM -tuː-/ *For Arnie, institutionalization was necessary when his wife became both blind and violent.* N-UNCOUNT

2 To **institutionalize** something means to establish it as part of a culture, social system, or organization. *The goal is to institutionalize family planning into community life... In the first century there was no such thing as institutionalized religion.* VERB V n V-ed
♦ **institutionalization** *The political and economic situation demanded the institutionalization of social change.* N-UNCOUNT

instruct /ɪnstrʌkt/ **instructs, instructing, instructed** ◆◆◇◇◇

1 If you **instruct** someone to do something, you formally tell them to do it; a formal use. *The family has instructed solicitors to sue Thomson for compensation... 'Go and have a word with her, Ken,' Webb instructed... I want you to instruct them that they've got three months to get the details sorted out.* VERB V n to-inf V with quote V n that Also V n with quote

2 Someone who **instructs** people in a subject or skill teaches it to them. *He instructed family members in nursing techniques.* VERB V n *in/on* n Also V

instruction /ɪnstrʌkʃᵊn/ **instructions** ◆◆◆◇◇

1 An **instruction** is something that someone tells you to do. *Many Labour MPs defied a party instruction to vote against the Bill.* N-COUNT

2 If someone gives you **instruction** in a subject or skill, they teach it to you; a formal use. *Each candidate is given instruction in safety... All schoolchildren must now receive some religious instruction.* N-UNCOUNT: usu with supp

3 Instructions are clear and detailed information on how to do something. *This book gives instructions for making a wide range of skin and hand creams.* N-PLURAL =directions

instructional /ɪnstrʌkʃənᵊl/. **Instructional** books or films are meant to teach people something or to offer them help with a particular ADJ: usu ADJ n problem. *...instructional material designed to help you with your lifestyle... You may wish to take advantage of our instructional session.*

instructive /ɪnstrʌktɪv/. Something that is **instructive** gives useful information. *It's instructive to compare his technique with Alan Bennett's. ...an entertaining and instructive documentary.* ◆◇◇◇◇ ADJ-GRADED: oft *it* v-link ADJ to-inf

instructor /ɪnstrʌktəʳ/ **instructors.** An **instructor** is someone who teaches a skill such as driving or skiing. In American English, **instructor** can also be used to refer to a schoolteacher or to a low-ranking university teacher. *I recommend that you drive under tuition from an approved driving instructor.* ◆◆◇◇◇ N-COUNT: oft n N

instrument /ɪnstrəmənt/ **instruments** ◆◆◆◇◇

1 An **instrument** is a tool or device that is used to do a particular task, especially a scientific task. *...a thin tube-like optical instrument. ...instruments for cleaning and polishing teeth... The environment itself will at the same time be measured by about 60 scientific instruments.* N-COUNT: usu with supp

2 A musical **instrument** is an object such as a piano, guitar, or flute, which you play in order to produce music. *Learning a musical instrument introduces a child to an understanding of music.* N-COUNT: oft supp N

3 An **instrument** is a device that is used for making measurements of something such as speed, height, or sound, for example on a ship or plane or in a car. *The design of crucial instruments on the control panel will have to be improved. ...navigation instruments.* N-COUNT: oft supp N

4 Something that is an **instrument** for achieving a particular aim is used by people to achieve that aim. *The veto has been a traditional instrument of diplomacy for centuries.* N-COUNT: oft N *of* n

5 See also **stringed instrument, wind instrument.**

instrumental /ɪnstrəmentᵊl/ **instrumentals** ◆◇◇◇◇

1 Someone or something that is **instrumental** in a process or event helps to make it happen. *In his first years as chairman he was instrumental in raising the company's wider profile... Jesse Jackson was instrumental in the release of some of the hostages.* ADJ-GRADED: usu v-link ADJ, oft ADJ *in* -ing/n

2 **Instrumental** music is performed by instruments and not by voices. *...a cassette recording of vocal and instrumental music.* ▸ **Instrumentals** are pieces of instrumental music. *After a couple of brief instrumentals, he puts his guitar down.* ADJ: ADJ n; N-COUNT: usu pl

instrumentalist /ɪnstrəmentəlɪst/ **instrumentalists.** An **instrumentalist** is someone who plays a musical instrument. N-COUNT =musician

instrumentation /ɪnstrəmenteɪʃᵊn/ ◆◇◇◇◇

1 **Instrumentation** is a group or collection of instruments, usually ones that are part of the same machine. *Basic flight instrumentation was similar on both planes... Now with this particular piece of instrumentation, you can actually spot individual carbon atoms.* N-UNCOUNT

2 The **instrumentation** of a piece of music is the way in which it is written for different instruments. *Some of the instrumentation is exquisite, particularly for harp and flute.* N-UNCOUNT

instrument panel, instrument panels. The **instrument panel** of a plane, car, or machine is the panel where the dials and switches are located. *They had failed to recognise signs on their instrument panel indicating a serious problem in the left engine.* N-COUNT

insubordinate /ɪnsəbɔːʳdɪnət/. If you say that someone is **insubordinate**, you mean that they are disobedient; a formal word. *In industry, a worker who is grossly insubordinate is threatened with discharge.* ADJ-GRADED

insubordination /ɪnsəbɔːʳdɪneɪʃᵊn/. **Insubordination** is disobedience; a formal word. *Hansen and his partner were fired for insubordination.* N-UNCOUNT

insubstantial /ɪnsəbstænʃᵊl/. Something that is **insubstantial** is not large, solid, or strong. *Mars has an insubstantial atmosphere, consisting almost entirely of carbon dioxide... Her limbs were insubstantial, almost transparent.* ADJ-GRADED

insufferable /ɪnsʌfrəbᵊl/. If you say that someone or something is **insufferable**, you are emphasizing that they are very unpleasant or annoying; a formal word. *Everyone agreed that he was a most insufferable bore.* ♦ **insufferably** /ɪnsʌfrəbli/. *His letters are insufferably dull... He found most of them insufferably arrogant.* ADJ PRAGMATICS =unbearable; ADV: ADV adj

insufficient /ɪnsəfɪʃᵊnt/. Something that is **insufficient** is not large enough in amount or degree for a particular purpose; a formal word. *He decided there was insufficient evidence to justify criminal proceedings... These efforts were insufficient to contain the burgeoning crisis.* ♦ **insufficiency** /ɪnsəfɪʃᵊnsi/ *Late miscarriages are usually not due to hormonal insufficiency.* ♦ **insufficiently** *Food that is insufficiently cooked can lead to food poisoning.* ◆◆◇◇◇ ADJ: oft ADJ to-inf, ADJ *for* n =inadequate; N-UNCOUNT; ADV: ADV adj/-ed

insular /ɪnsjʊləʳ, AM -sə-/. If you say that someone is **insular**, you are being critical of them because they are unwilling to meet new people or to consider new ideas. *The old image of the insular, xenophobic Brit has altered dramatically with this new Euro-conscious generation.* ♦ **insularity** /ɪnsjʊlærɪti, AM -sə-/ *But at least they have started to break out of their old insularity.* ◆◇◇◇◇ ADJ-GRADED PRAGMATICS =blinkered; N-UNCOUNT

insulate /ɪnsjʊleɪt, AM -sə-/ **insulates, insulating, insulated** ◆◇◇◇◇

1 If a person or group **is insulated** from the rest of society or from outside influences, they are protected from them. *They wonder if their community is no longer insulated from big city problems... Their wealthy families had further insulated them from reality with the privilege that money could buy.* ♦ **insulation** *They lived in happy insulation from brutal facts.* VERB =shield; be V-ed *from/against* n; V n *from/against* n; N-UNCOUNT

2 To **insulate** something such as a building means to protect it from cold or noise by covering it or surrounding it in a thick layer. *It will take almost 25 years to insulate the homes of the six million households that require this assistance... Is there any way we can insulate our home from the noise?... Are your hot and cold water pipes well insulated? ...a garment lined with a light insulating material.* VERB; V n; V n *from/against* n; V-ed; V-ing

3 If a piece of equipment **is insulated**, it is covered with rubber or plastic to prevent electricity passing through it and giving the person using it an electric shock. *In order to make it safe, the element is electrically insulated. ...electrical insulating tape.* VERB; be V-ed; V-ing

insulation /ɪnsjʊleɪʃᵊn, AM -sə-/. **Insulation** is a thick layer of a substance that keeps something warm, especially a building. *High electricity bills point to a poor heating system or bad insulation... A wet suit provides excellent insulation.* • See also **insulate.** ◆◇◇◇◇ N-UNCOUNT

insulator /ɪnsjʊleɪtəʳ, AM -sə-/ **insulators.** An **insulator** is a material that insulates something. *Fat is an excellent insulator against the cold.* N-COUNT: usu sing

insulin /ɪnsjʊlɪn, AM -sə-/. **Insulin** is a substance that most people produce naturally in their body and which controls the level of sugar in their blood. *Sufferers from the more severe form of diabetes have faulty insulin-producing cells.* ◆◇◇◇◇ N-UNCOUNT

insult, insults, insulting, insulted. The verb is pronounced /ɪnsʌlt/. The noun is pronounced /ɪnsʌlt/. ◆◆◇◇◇

1 If someone **insults** you, they say something rude to you or offend you by doing or saying something which shows they have a low opinion of you. *I did not mean to insult you... Buchanan said he was insulted by the judge's remarks.* ♦ **insulted** *I mean, I was a bit insulted that they thought I needed bribing to shut up.* VERB; V n; ADJ-GRADED: usu v-link ADJ

2 An **insult** is a rude remark, or something a person says or does which insults you. *Their behaviour was an insult to the people they represent... The prison Governor criticised some of his officers who shouted insults at prisoners on the roof.* N-COUNT: oft N *to* n

3 You say **to add insult to injury** when mentioning an action or fact that makes an unfair or unacceptable situation even worse. *The driver of the car that killed Smith got a £250 fine and five penalty points on his licence. To add insult to injury, he drove away from court in his own car.* PHRASE: V inflects, PHR with cl

insulting /ɪnsʌltɪŋ/. Something that is **insulting** offends someone because it is rude or shows that someone has a low opinion of them. *The article was politically insensitive and possibly insulting to the families of British citizens... One of the apprentices made an insulting remark to a passing officer.* ♦ **insultingly** *UEFA said that their supporters had behaved insultingly... I have rarely read anything so insultingly sexist as this article.*
◆◇◇◇◇ ADJ-GRADED: oft ADJ *to* n =offensive; ADV-GRADED: ADV with v, ADV adj

insuperable /ɪnsuːpərəbᵊl/. A problem that is **insuperable** cannot be dealt with successfully; a formal word. *They are also to discuss ways to overcome ethnic antagonism before it becomes an insuperable obstacle to co-operation.*
ADJ =insurmountable

insupportable /ɪnsəpɔːʳtəbᵊl/. If you say that something is **insupportable**, you mean it is unbearable or unacceptable; a formal word. *Too much spending on rearmament would place an insupportable burden on the nation's productive capacity... Life without Anna had no savour, was tedious, insupportable.*
ADJ =intolerable

insurance /ɪnʃʊərəns/ **insurances** ◆◆◆◆◇
1 Insurance is an arrangement in which you pay money to a company, and they pay money to you if something unpleasant happens to you, for example if your property is stolen or damaged, or if you get a serious illness. *The insurance company paid out for the stolen jewellery and silver... The individual may take out insurance on the lenses, covering replacement if they are lost or damaged.* N-VAR: oft N n
2 If you do something as **insurance** against something unpleasant happening, you do it to protect yourself in case the unpleasant thing happens. *The country would continue to need a robust defence capability as insurance against the unexpected.* N-VAR: usu N *against* n

insure /ɪnʃʊəʳ/ **insures, insuring, insured** ◆◆◇◇◇
1 If you **insure** yourself or your property, you pay money to an insurance company so that, if you become ill or if your property is damaged or stolen, the company will pay you a sum of money. *For protection against unforeseen emergencies, you insure your house, your furnishings and your car... While many people insure against death, far fewer take precautions against long-term loss of income because of sickness... We automatically insure your furniture, belongings and decorations against theft, fire, vandalism or burst pipes.* VERB; V n; V *against/for* n; V n *against/for* n
2 If you **insure** yourself against something unpleasant that might happen in the future, you do something to protect yourself in case it happens, or to prevent it happening. *...if he can further insure himself against ambitious party rivals by achieving a strong election result in his home state next April... Mr Mandela said the demotion of the ministers concerned would not insure against any recurrence of such practices.* VERB; V pron-refl *against* n; V *against* n
3 See also **ensure**.

insured /ɪnʃʊəʳd/; **insured** is both the singular and the plural form. **The insured** is the person who is insured by a particular policy; a legal term. *Once the insured has sold his policy, he naturally loses all rights to it.*
N-COUNT: usu sing, *the* N

insurer /ɪnʃʊərəʳ/ **insurers.** An **insurer** is a company that sells insurance.
◆◆◇◇◇ N-COUNT

insurgency /ɪnsɜːʳdʒᵊnsi/ **insurgencies.** An **insurgency** is a violent attempt to oppose a country's government carried out by citizens of that country. *Insurgencies still cause trouble in Ethiopia.*
◆◇◇◇◇ N-VAR =uprising, insurrection

insurgent /ɪnsɜːʳdʒᵊnt/ **insurgents. Insurgents** are people who are fighting against the government or army of their own country; a formal word. *By early yesterday, the insurgents had taken control of the country's main military air base.*
◆◇◇◇◇ N-COUNT: usu pl =rebel

insurmountable /ɪnsəʳmaʊntəbᵊl/. A problem that is **insurmountable** is so great that it cannot be dealt with successfully. *Philadelphia's fiscal crisis doesn't seem like an insurmountable problem.*
ADJ =insuperable

insurrection /ɪnsərekʃᵊn/ **insurrections.** An **insurrection** is violent action that is taken by a large group of people against the rulers of their country, usually in order to remove them from office; a formal word. *They were plotting to stage an armed insurrection if negotiations with the government should fail... Those found guilty of rebellion and insurrection will be sentenced to life imprisonment.*
◆◇◇◇◇ N-VAR =uprising, insurgency

int. Int. is an abbreviation for **internal** or for **international**.
◆◇◇◇◇

intact /ɪntækt/. Something that is **intact** is complete and has not been damaged or changed. *Customs men put dynamite in the water to destroy the cargo, but most of it was left intact... If the family unit is still intact, the patient frequently does very well.*
◆◆◇◇◇ ADJ: usu v-link ADJ =in one piece

intake /ɪnteɪk/ **intakes** ◆◆◇◇◇
1 Your **intake** of a particular kind of food, drink, or air is the amount that you eat, drink, or breathe in. *Your intake of alcohol should not exceed two units per day... Reduce your salt intake.* N-SING: with supp, oft N *of* n
2 The people who are accepted into an organization or place at a particular time are referred to as a particular **intake**. *...one of this year's intake of students... There was a proposal in the United States to quadruple its annual intake of immigrants.* N-COUNT: usu sing, with supp, oft N *of* n
3 When there is **an intake of breath**, someone breathes in quickly and audibly, usually because they are shocked at something. *I heard, even over the babble of the crowd, a sharp, shocked intake of breath.* PHRASE

intangible /ɪntændʒɪbᵊl/ **intangibles.** Something that is **intangible** is abstract or is hard to define or measure. *...the intangible and non-material dimensions of our human and social existence.* ► You can refer to intangible things as **intangibles**. *That approach fails to take into consideration intangibles such as pride of workmanship, loyalty and good work habits.*
◆◇◇◇◇ ADJ-GRADED; N-PLURAL

integer /ɪntɪdʒəʳ/ **integers.** An **integer** is an exact whole number such as 1, 7, or 24 as opposed to a number with fractions or decimals; a technical term in mathematics.
N-COUNT

integral /ɪntɪgrəl/. Something that is an **integral** part of something is an essential part of that thing. *Rituals and festivals form an integral part of every human society... Anxiety is integral to the human condition.*
◆◇◇◇◇ ADJ: oft ADJ *to* n =basic, fundamental

integrate /ɪntɪgreɪt/ **integrates, integrating, integrated** ◆◆◆◇◇
1 If someone **integrates** into a social group, or **is integrated** into it, they behave in such a way that they become part of the group or are accepted into it. *He didn't integrate successfully into the Italian way of life... Integrating the kids with the community, finding them a role, is essential... The way Swedes integrate immigrants is, she feels, 100% more advanced... If they want to integrate, that's fine with me.* ♦ **integrated** *He thinks we are living in a fully integrated, supportive society.* ♦ **integration** /ɪntɪgreɪʃᵊn/ *Americans overwhelmingly support the integration of disabled people into mainstream society.*
V-ERG; V *into/with* n; V n *into/with* n; V n; V; ADJ-GRADED; N-UNCOUNT: usu with supp, oft N *of* n
2 If you **integrate** one thing with another, or one thing **integrates** with another, the first thing is combined with the second so that they become closely linked or form part of a whole idea or system. You can also say that two things **integrate**. *It believes that by integrating the rail lines with its buses it can make them pay... Ann wanted the conservatory to integrate with the kitchen... Little attempt was made to integrate the parts into a coherent whole... Talks will now begin about integrating the activities of both companies.* ♦ **integrated** *There is, he said, a lack of an integrated national transport policy. ...a more integrated approach to land uses in a rural environment.* ♦ **integration** *With Germany, France has been the prime mover behind closer European integration.*
V-RECIP-ERG; V n *with* n; V *with* n; V pl-n *into* n; V pl-n; Also pl-n V; ADJ-GRADED; N-UNCOUNT: usu with supp, oft adj N

integrated /ɪntɪgreɪtɪd/. An **integrated** institution is intended for use by all races or religious groups. *We believe that pupils of integrated schools will have more tolerant attitudes.* ● See also **integrate**.
ADJ: usu ADJ n ≠segregated

integrity /ɪntegrɪti/ ◆◆◇◇◇
1 If you have **integrity**, you are honest and firm in your moral principles. *I have always regarded him as a man of integrity... He was praised for his fairness and high integrity.* N-UNCOUNT
2 The **integrity** of something such as a group of people or a text is its state of being a united whole; a formal use. *Separatist movements are a threat to the integrity of the nation.* N-UNCOUNT: with poss

intellect /ɪntɪlekt/ **intellects** ◆◇◇◇◇
1 **Intellect** is the ability to understand or deal with ideas and information. *Do the emotions develop in parallel with the intellect?... The intellect is not the most important thing in life.* N-VAR
2 **Intellect** is the quality of being very intelligent or clever. *Her intellect is famed far and wide... The members of the committee described Gates as a man of keen intellect.* N-VAR: oft poss N
3 If you describe someone as an **intellect**, you mean that they are very intelligent. *My boss isn't a great intellect.* N-COUNT

intellectual /ɪntɪlektʃuəl/ **intellectuals** ◆◆◆◇◇
1 **Intellectual** means involving a person's ability to think and to understand ideas and information. *High levels of lead could damage the intellectual development of children... He has written seven thrillers, and clearly enjoys intellectual pursuits.* ADJ: ADJ n =mental
♦ **intellectually** *...intellectually satisfying work... Intellectually, I was completely prepared for that type of work.* ADV: usu ADV adj/-ed, ADV after v
2 An **intellectual** is someone who spends a lot of time studying and thinking about complicated ideas. *Teachers, artists and other intellectuals urged political parties to launch a united movement against the government.* ► Also an adjective. *They were very intellectual and witty. ...an intellectual elite.* N-COUNT; ADJ-GRADED

intelligence /ɪntelɪdʒəns/ ◆◆◆◇◇
1 **Intelligence** is the quality of being intelligent or clever. *She's a woman of exceptional intelligence.* N-UNCOUNT
2 **Intelligence** is the ability to think, reason, and understand instead of doing things automatically or by instinct. *Nerve cells, after all, do not have intelligence of their own.* N-UNCOUNT
3 **Intelligence** is information that is gathered by the government or the army about their country's enemies and their activities. *She first moved into the intelligence services 22 years ago... The purpose of intelligence is to provide information on how the enemy can be beaten... Why was military intelligence so lacking?* N-UNCOUNT: oft N n

intelligent /ɪntelɪdʒənt/ ◆◆◆◇◇
1 A person or animal that is **intelligent** has the ability to think, understand, and learn things quickly and well. *Susan's a very bright and intelligent woman who knows her own mind. ...lively and intelligent conversation... He ventured the opinion that 'whales are as intelligent as human beings'.* ADJ-GRADED =clever
♦ **intelligently** *They are incapable of thinking intelligently about politics.* ADV-GRADED: ADV with v, ADV adj
2 Something that is **intelligent** has the ability to think and understand instead of doing things automatically or by instinct. *Within a few years an intelligent computer will certainly be an indispensable diagnostic tool for every doctor in the country. ...the biggest-ever search for intelligent life elsewhere in the universe.* ADJ

intelligentsia /ɪntelɪdʒentsiə/. The **intelligentsia** in a country or community are the most educated people there, especially those interested in the arts, philosophy, and politics. *I was not high up enough in the intelligentsia to be invited to such exalted meetings.* ◆◇◇◇◇ N-SING-COLL: usu *the* N

intelligible /ɪntelɪdʒɪbəl/. Something that is **intelligible** can be understood. *The language of Darwin was intelligible to experts and non-experts alike... The woman moaned faintly but made no intelligible response.* ADJ-GRADED: oft ADJ *to* n ≠unintelligible

intemperate /ɪntempərət/. If you describe someone's behaviour or opinions as **intemperate**, you are critical of them because they are unreasonably strong and uncontrolled; a formal word. *The tone of the article is intemperate. ...the unwisely intemperate language of the party chairman.* ADJ-GRADED PRAGMATICS =extreme

intend /ɪntend/ **intends, intending, intended** ◆◆◆◆◇
1 If you **intend** to do something, you have decided or planned to do it. *She intends to do A levels and go to university... I didn't intend coming to Germany to work... We had always intended that the new series would be live.* VERB =plan V to-inf V -ing V that
2 If something **is intended** for a particular purpose, it has been planned to fulfil that purpose. If something **is intended** for a particular person, it has been planned to be used by that person or to affect them in some way. *This money is intended for the development of the tourist industry... Columns are usually intended in architecture to add grandeur and status... Originally, Hatfield had been intended as a leisure complex.* VB: usu passive =plan *be* V-ed *for* n *be* V-ed to-inf *be* V-ed *as* n
3 If you **intend** a particular idea or feeling in something that you say or do, you want to express it or want it to be understood. *He didn't intend any sarcasm... Burke's response seemed a little patronizing, though he undoubtedly hadn't intended it that way... This sounds like a barrage of accusation – I don't intend it to be... I think he intended it as a put-down comment.* VERB =mean V n V n n V n to-inf V n prep

intended /ɪntendɪd/. You use **intended** to describe the thing you are trying to achieve or person you are trying to affect. *The intended target had been a military building... Keith hoped the obvious sarcasm would have its intended effect... It's never occurred to me that the intended victim of the fire was Margaret.* ◆◇◇◇◇ ADJ: ADJ n

intense /ɪntens/ ◆◆◆◇◇
1 **Intense** is used to describe something that is very great or extreme in strength or degree. *He was sweating from the intense heat... Suddenly the room filled with intense light... Stevens's murder was the result of a deep-seated and intense hatred... His threats become more intense, agitated, and frequent.* ♦ **intensely** *The fast-food business is intensely competitive.* ♦ **intensity** /ɪntensɪti/ **intensities** *The attack was anticipated but its intensity came as a shock.* ADJ-GRADED =extreme; ADV-GRADED; N-VAR: usu with poss
2 If you describe an activity as **intense**, you mean that it is very serious and concentrated, and often involves doing a great deal in a short time. *The battle for third place was intense... The military on both sides are involved in intense activity.* ADJ-GRADED
3 If you describe the way someone looks at you as **intense**, you mean that they look at you very directly and seem to know what you are thinking or feeling. *I felt so self-conscious under Luke's mother's intense gaze... He gazed at me with those intense blue eyes.* ♦ **intensely** *He sipped his drink, staring intensely at me.* ADJ-GRADED =forceful; ADV-GRADED: ADV with v
4 If you describe a person as **intense**, you mean that they appear to concentrate very hard on everything that they do, and they feel and show their emotions in a very extreme way. *I know he's an intense player, but he does enjoy what he's doing... She is taller than I imagined, more adult, more intense.* ♦ **intensely** *Sometimes she expressed it intensely in moments of eloquent passion.* ♦ **intensity** *His intensity and the ferocity of his feelings alarmed me.* ADJ-GRADED =impassioned; ADV-GRADED: ADV with v; N-UNCOUNT

intensifier /ɪntensɪfaɪər/ **intensifiers.** An **intensifier** is a word such as 'very' or 'extremely' which you can put in front of an adjective or adverb in order to make its meaning stronger; a grammatical term. N-COUNT

intensify /ɪntensɪfaɪ/ **intensifies, intensifying, intensified.** If you **intensify** something or if it **intensifies**, it becomes greater in strength, amount, or degree. *Britain is intensifying its efforts to secure the release of three British hostages... The conflict is almost bound to intensify... Groups of refugees are on the move following intensified fighting in the region.* ♦ **intensification** /ɪntensɪfɪkeɪʃən/ *The country was on the verge of collapse because of the intensification of violent rebel attacks.* ◆◆◇◇◇ V-ERG =heighten V n V V-ed; N-UNCOUNT

intensive /ɪntensɪv/ ◆◆◇◇◇
1 An **intensive** activity involves the concentration of energy or people on one particular task in order to try to achieve a great deal in a short time. *...after several days and nights of intensive negotiations... Each counsellor undergoes an intensive training programme before beginning work.* ♦ **intensively** *Ruth's parents opted to educate her intensively at home.* ADJ-GRADED: usu ADJ n; ADV-GRADED: ADV with v
2 **Intensive** farming involves producing as many crops or animals as possible from your land, usually with the aid of chemicals. *Elsewhere large areas have been drained and levelled for industry or intensive farming. ...intensive methods of rearing poultry.* ♦ **intensively** *Will they farm the rest of their land less intensively?* ADJ-GRADED: usu ADJ n; ADV-GRADED: ADV with v

-intensive /-ɪntensɪv/. **-intensive** combines with nouns to form adjectives which indicate that an industry or activity involves the use of a lot of a particular thing. *...the development of capital-intensive farming. ...energy-intensive industries.* COMB in ADJ-GRADED

intensive care. If someone is in **intensive care**, they are being given extremely thorough care in a hospital because they are very ill or very badly injured. *She spent the night in intensive care after the operation.* ◆◇◇◇◇ N-UNCOUNT: usu *in* N

intent /ɪntent/ **intents** ◆◆◇◇◇
1 If you are **intent** on doing something, you are eager and determined to do it. *The rebels are obviously intent on keeping up the pressure... The play starred a well-known retired actress who was intent on a come-back.* ADJ-GRADED: v-link ADJ *on/upon* -ing/n
2 If someone does something in an **intent** way, they pay great attention to what they are doing; used in written English. *She looked from one intent face to another... Rodney had been intent on every word.* ♦ **intently** *He listened intently, then slammed down the phone.* ADJ-GRADED: oft ADJ *on/upon* n; ADV-GRADED: ADV after v
3 A person's **intent** is their intention to do something; a formal word. *The timing of this strong statement of intent on arms control is crucial... Two men will appear before Birmingham magistrates' court today charged with possession of arms with intent to endanger life.* N-VAR =intention
4 You say **to all intents and purposes** to suggest that a situation is not exactly as you describe it but the effect is the same as if it were. *To all intents and purposes he was my father.* PHRASE: usu PHR with cl

intention /ɪntenʃᵊn/ **intentions** ◆◆◆◇◇
1 An **intention** that you have is an idea or plan of what you are going to do. *Beveridge announced his intention of standing for parliament... It is my intention to remain in my position until a successor is elected... Unfortunately, his good intentions never seemed to last long.* N-VAR: oft N *of*-ing, N to-inf
2 If you say that you **have no intention of** doing something, you are emphasizing that you are not going to do it. If you say that you **have every intention of** doing something, you are emphasizing that you intend to do it. *We have no intention of buying American jets... Those close to him are convinced that he has every intention of staying on until the end of his seven-year term.* PHRASE: V inflects, PHR -ing PRAGMATICS

intentional /ɪntenʃənᵊl/. Something that is **intentional** is deliberate. *Women who are the victims of intentional discrimination will be able to get compensation... How can I blame him? It wasn't intentional.* ♦ **intentionally** *I've never intentionally hurt anyone... The figures are intentionally misleading.* ◆◇◇◇◇ ADJ =deliberate; ADV: ADV with v, ADV adj

inter /ɪntɜːʳ/ **inters, interring, interred.** When a dead person **is interred**, they are buried; a formal word. *...the spot where his bones were originally interred.* ◆◆◇◇◇ VERB; *be* V-ed Also V n

inter- /ɪntəʳ-/. **Inter-** combines with adjectives and nouns to form adjectives indicating that something moves, exists, or happens between two or more places, things, or groups of people. For example, inter-governmental relations are relations between governments. *He hopes to be able to announce a date for inter-party talks. ...a policy of encouraging inter-racial marriage.* PREFIX

interact /ɪntəræ̱kt/ **interacts, interacting, interacted** ◆◆◇◇◇
1 When people **interact** with each other or **interact**, they communicate as they work or spend time together. *While the other children interacted and played together, Ted ignored them. ...rhymes and songs to help parents interact with their babies.* ♦ **interaction** /ɪntəræ̱kʃᵊn/ **interactions** *This can sometimes lead to somewhat superficial interactions with other people. ...our experience of informal social interaction among adults.* V-RECIP; pl-n V, V *with* n; N-VAR: oft N prep
2 When people **interact** with computers, or when computers **interact** with other machines, information or instructions are exchanged. *Millions of people want new, simplified ways of interacting with a computer... There will be a true global village in which telephones, computers and televisions interact.* ♦ **interaction, interactions** *...experts on human-computer interaction.* VERB; V *with* n, pl-n V; N-VAR: usu with supp
3 When one thing **interacts** with another or two things **interact**, the two things affect each other's behaviour or condition. *You have to understand how cells interact... Atoms within the fluid interact with the minerals that form the grains.* ♦ **interaction** *...the interaction between physical and emotional illness.* V-RECIP; pl-n V, V *with* n; N-VAR: oft N prep

interactive /ɪntəræ̱ktɪv/ ◆◇◇◇◇
1 An **interactive** computer program or television system is one which allows direct communication between the user and the machine. *This will make videogames more interactive than ever.* ADJ-GRADED
2 If you describe a group of people or their activities as **interactive**, you mean that the people communicate with each other. *There is little evidence that this encouraged flexible, interactive teaching in the classroom.* ADJ-GRADED

inter alia /ɪntər e̱ɪliə/. You use **inter alia**, meaning 'among other things', when you want to say that there are other things involved apart from the one you are mentioning; a formal expression. *...a collector who had, inter alia, 900 engraved gems, 59 marble busts, and over 2,500 coins and medals.* PHRASE: PHR with cl PRAGMATICS

intercede /ɪntəʳsi̱ːd/ **intercedes, interceding, interceded.** If you **intercede** with someone, you talk to them in order to try to end a disagreement that they have with another person; a formal word. *They asked my father to intercede with the king on their behalf... He had occasionally tried to intercede for me... The Supreme Court will not intercede to overturn an election.* VERB; V *with* n, V *for* n, V

intercept /ɪntəʳse̱pt/ **intercepts, intercepting, intercepted.** If you **intercept** someone or something that is travelling from one place to another, you stop them before they get to their destination. *Gunmen intercepted him on his way to the airport... Dodd intercepted a ball intended for Smith... His letter was intercepted by the Secret Service.* ♦ **interception** /ɪntəʳse̱pʃᵊn/ **interceptions** *...the interception of a ship off the west coast of Scotland.* ◆◇◇◇◇ VERB =stop; V n; N-VAR

interceptor /ɪntəʳse̱ptəʳ/ **interceptors.** An **interceptor** is a fighter aircraft or ground based missile system designed to intercept and attack enemy planes. N-COUNT

intercession /ɪntəʳse̱ʃᵊn/ **intercessions. Intercession** is an act of interceding to try to end a disagreement or to try to persuade someone powerful to be merciful to a weaker person; a formal word. *There was always the possibility that his intercession could be of help to the tribe... Many claimed to have been cured as a result of the Madonna's intercessions.* N-VAR =intervention

interchange, interchanges, interchanging, interchanged. The noun is pronounced /ɪ̱ntəʳtʃeɪndʒ/. The verb is pronounced /ɪntəʳtʃe̱ɪndʒ/. ◆◇◇◇◇
1 If there is an **interchange** of ideas or information among a group of people, each person talks about his or her ideas or gives information to the others. *What made the meeting exciting was the interchange of ideas from different disciplines...* N-VAR: with supp, usu N *of* n =exchange

Ministers want to see more interchange between the private sector and the civil service.

2 If you **interchange** one thing with another, or you **interchange** two things, each thing takes the place of the other or is exchanged for the other. You can also say that two things **interchange**. *She likes to interchange her furnishings at home with the stock in her shop... Your task is to interchange words so that the sentence makes sense. ...the point where the illusions of the stage and reality begin to interchange.* ▸ Also a noun. *...the interchange of matter and energy at atomic or sub-atomic levels.*
V-RECIP-ERG; V n *with* n; V pl-n; pl-n V; Also V *with* n; N-VAR: oft N *of* n

3 An **interchange** on a motorway is a junction where it meets a main road or another motorway. N-COUNT: usu n N

interchangeable /ɪntəʳtʃeɪndʒəbəl/. Things that are **interchangeable** can be exchanged with each other without it making any difference. *His greatest innovation was the use of interchangeable parts... Many of his campaign proposals are interchangeable with the DLC's core beliefs.* ♦ **interchangeably** *These expressions are often used interchangeably, but they do have different meanings.*
◆◇◇◇◇ ADJ: oft ADJ *with* n; ADV: ADV after v

intercollegiate /ɪntəʳkəliːdʒət/. **Intercollegiate** means involving or related to more than one university; used in American English. *...the first intercollegiate gymnastics team championship.* ADJ: ADJ n

intercom /ɪntəʳkɒm/ **intercoms.** An **intercom** is a device like a small box with a microphone which is connected to a loudspeaker in another room. You use it to talk to the people in the other room. N-COUNT

interconnect /ɪntəʳkənekt/ **interconnects, interconnecting, interconnected.** Things that **interconnect** or **are interconnected** are connected to or with each other. You can also say that one thing **interconnects** with another. *The causes are many and may interconnect... Their lives interconnect with those of celebrated figures of the late eighteenth-century... The regions are interconnected by an excellent highway system. ...a huge mesh of interconnecting wires.*
V-RECIP-ERG; pl-n V; V *with* n; *be* V-ed; V-ing; Also V n *with* n

interconnection /ɪntəʳkənekʃən/ **interconnections.** If you say that there is an **interconnection** between two or more things, you mean that they are very closely connected; a formal word. *...the thematic interconnection between the stories. ...the alarming interconnection of drug abuse and AIDS infection.* N-VAR: oft N *between* pl-n

intercontinental /ɪntəʳkɒntɪnentəl/. **Intercontinental** is used to describe something that exists or happens between continents. *...intercontinental flights.* ADJ: ADJ n

intercourse /ɪntəʳkɔːʳs/ ◆◆◇◇◇

1 **Intercourse** is the act of having sex; a formal use. *...sexual intercourse... We didn't have intercourse.* N-UNCOUNT

2 Social **intercourse** is communication between people as they spend time together; an old-fashioned use. *There was social intercourse between the old and the young.* N-UNCOUNT: usu adj N =contact

intercut /ɪntəʳkʌt/ **intercuts, intercutting.** The form **intercut** is used in the present tense and is the past tense and past participle. If a film **is intercut with** particular images, those images appear regularly throughout the film; a technical word. *The film is set in a night club and intercut with images of gangland London... He intercuts scenes of Rex getting more and more desperate with scenes of the abductor with his family.*
VERB; *be* V-ed *with* n; V n *with* n

interdependence /ɪntəʳdɪpendəns/. **Interdependence** is the condition of a group of people or things that all depend on each other. *...the interdependence of nations. ...economic interdependence.* N-UNCOUNT

interdependent /ɪntəʳdɪpendənt/. People or things that are **interdependent** all depend on each other. *We live in an increasingly interdependent world.* ADJ-GRADED

interdict, interdicts, interdicting, interdicted. The verb is pronounced /ɪntəʳdɪkt/. The noun is pronounced /ɪntəʳdɪkt/.

1 If an armed force **interdicts** something or someone, they stop them and prevent them from moving. If they **interdict** a route, they block it or cut it off; a formal use, used mainly in American English. *Troops could be ferried in to interdict drug shipments. ...efforts to isolate the theater of operations by interdicting the bridges.*
VERB =intercept; V n

2 An **interdict** is an official order to ban, prevent, or restrict something; a formal use. *The National Trust has placed an interdict on jet-skis in Dorset, Devon and Cornwall.* N-COUNT =ban

interdiction /ɪntəʳdɪkʃən/. The **interdiction** of something is the official banning of it; a formal word. *...immigration control and the interdiction of drug traffic.* N-UNCOUNT: oft N *of* n =prohibition

interdisciplinary /ɪntəʳdɪsɪplɪnəri, AM -plɪneri/. **Interdisciplinary** means involving more than one academic subject. *...interdisciplinary courses combining psychology, philosophy and linguistics.* ADJ: usu ADJ n

interest /ɪntrəst, -tərest/ **interests, interesting, interested** ◆◆◆◆◆

1 If you have an **interest** in something, you want to learn or hear more about it. *There has been a lively interest in the elections in the last two weeks... His parents tried to discourage his interest in music, but he persisted... She'd liked him at first, but soon lost interest... Food was of no interest to her at all.* N-UNCOUNT: also *a* N

2 Your **interests** are the things that you enjoy doing. *Encourage your child in her interests and hobbies even if they're things that you know little about... He developed a wide range of sporting interests as a pupil at Millfield.* N-COUNT

3 If something **interests** you, it attracts your attention so that you want to learn or hear more about it or continue doing it. *That passage interested me because it seems to parallel very closely what you're doing in the novel... It may interest you to know that Miss Woods, the housekeeper, witnessed the attack.*
VERB; V n; *it* V n to-inf

4 If you are trying to persuade someone to buy something from you or do something for you, you can say that you are trying to **interest** them **in** it. *In the meantime I can't interest you in a new car, I suppose?... The group wasn't able to interest them in reproducing literature specifically for women.*
VERB; V n *in* n/-ing

5 If something is in the **interests** of a particular person or group, it will benefit them in some way. *Did those directors act in the best interests of their club?... The social worker would try to get her to see she was acting against the boy's interests.* N-COUNT: usu pl, usu *in* N with poss

6 You can use **interests** to refer to groups of people who you think use their power or money to benefit themselves. *The government accused unnamed 'foreign interests' of inciting the trouble... He resigned as finance minister only weeks before the election and stood against big-business interests.* N-COUNT: usu pl, supp N

7 A person or organization that has **interests** in a company or in a particular type of business owns shares in this company or this type of business. *Her other business interests include a theme park in Scandinavia and hotels in the West Country. ...the Hatch family, who controlled large dairy interests... Disney will retain a 51 percent controlling interest in the venture.* N-COUNT: usu with supp =concern

8 If a person, country, or organization has an **interest** in a possible event or situation, they want that event or situation to happen because they are likely to benefit from it. *The West has an interest in promoting democratic forces in Eastern Europe... Domestic consumers of petroleum products have an interest in a secure source of petroleum products.* N-COUNT: usu N *in* n/-ing

9 **Interest** is extra money that you receive if you have invested a sum of money, or extra money that you pay if you have borrowed money. *Does your current account pay interest?... This is an important step toward lower interest rates.* N-UNCOUNT: oft N n

10 See also **interested, interesting; compound interest, self-interest, vested interest.**

11 If you do something **in the interests of** a particular result or situation, you do it in order to achieve that result or maintain that situation. *...a call for all businessmen to work together in the interests of national stability.* ● to **have someone's interests at heart**: see **heart**. PHRASE: N inflects, PHR n

interested /ɪntrestɪd/ ◆◆◆◆◇
1 If you are **interested** in something, you think it is important and you are keen to learn more about it or spend time doing it. *I thought she might be interested in Paula's proposal... I think the young man is getting interested in gardening... I'd be interested to meet her.*
ADJ-GRADED: usu v-link ADJ, oft ADJ *in* n/-ing, ADJ to-inf
2 An **interested** party or group of people is affected by or involved in a particular event or situation. *The success was only possible because all the interested parties eventually agreed to the idea.*
ADJ: ADJ n
3 See also **self-interested**.

interest-free. An **interest-free** loan has no interest charged on it. *He was offered a £10,000 interest-free loan... Many stores are offering interest-free credit.* ► Also an adverb. *Customers allowed the banks to use their money interest-free.*
ADJ: usu ADJ n
ADV: ADV after v

interesting /ɪntrestɪŋ/. If you find something **interesting**, it attracts your attention, for example because you think it is exciting or unusual. *It was interesting to be in a different environment... The two halves of the town face each other, and both have interesting churches... His third album is by far his most interesting.*
◆◆◆◇◇ ADJ-GRADED: oft *it* v-link ADJ to-inf/that

interestingly /ɪntrestɪŋli/. You use **interestingly** to introduce a piece of information that you think is interesting or unexpected. *Interestingly enough, a few weeks later, Benjamin remarried... Interestingly, it is not clear which solution the prime minister favors.*
◆◇◇◇◇ ADV-GRADED: ADV with cl PRAGMATICS

interface /ɪntəʳfeɪs/ **interfaces, interfacing, interfaced** ◆◇◇◇◇
1 The **interface** between two subjects or systems is the area in which they affect each other or have links with each other; a formal use. *...a witty exploration of that interface between bureaucracy and the working world.*
N-COUNT
2 If you refer to the user **interface** of a particular piece of computing software, you are talking about its presentation on screen and how easy it is to operate; a technical use in computing. *...the development of better user interfaces.*
N-COUNT: usu n N
3 An **interface** is an electrical circuit which links one machine, especially a computer, with another; a technical use in computing and electronics.
N-COUNT
4 If one thing **interfaces** with another or if two things **interface**, they have connections with each other or interact. If you **interface** one thing with another, you connect the two things. This is a formal or technical use. *...the way we interface with the environment... Unless divisions consult with one another, the components they produce are not likely to interface smoothly... He had interfaced all this machinery with a master computer.*
V-RECIP-ERG
V *with* n, pl-n V, V n *with* n, Also V pl-n

interfere /ɪntəʳfɪəʳ/ **interferes, interfering, interfered** ◆◆◇◇◇
1 If you say that someone **interferes** in a situation, you mean they get involved in it although it does not concern them and their involvement is not wanted. *I wish everyone would stop interfering and just leave me alone... The UN cannot interfere in the internal affairs of any country.*
VERB PRAGMATICS =meddle
V, V *in/with* n
2 Something that **interferes with** a situation, activity, or process has a damaging effect on it. *Drug problems frequently interfered with his work... Alexander wasn't going to let a lack of space interfere with his plans... Smoking and drinking interfere with your body's ability to process oxygen.*
VERB
V *with* n

interference /ɪntəʳfɪərəns/ ◆◆◇◇◇
1 **Interference** by a person or group is their unwanted or unnecessary involvement in something. *The parliament described the decree as interference in the republic's internal affairs... Airlines will be able to set cheap fares without interference from the government.*
N-UNCOUNT: oft N *in/with* n, N *from* n PRAGMATICS =meddling
2 When there is **interference**, a radio signal is affected by other radio waves or electrical activity so that it cannot be received properly. *...electrical interference... They have been accused of deliberately causing interference to transmissions.*
N-UNCOUNT

interfering /ɪntəʳfɪərɪŋ/. If you describe someone as **interfering**, you are being critical of them because they try to get involved in other people's affairs or to give them advice, especially when the advice is not wanted. *When she was a child she had regarded her mother as an interfering busybody. ...interfering neighbours.*
ADJ: ADJ n  PRAGMATICS
=meddling

interim /ɪntərɪm/ ◆◆◆◇◇
1 **Interim** is used to describe something that is intended to be used until something permanent is done or established. *She was sworn in as head of an interim government in March. ...an interim report.*
ADJ: ADJ n
2 **In the interim** means until a particular thing happens or until a particular thing happened; a formal expression. *But, in the interim, we obviously have a duty to maintain law and order... He was to remain in jail in the interim.*
PHRASE: PHR with cl =in the meantime

interior /ɪntɪəriəʳ/ **interiors** ◆◆◆◇◇
1 The **interior** of something is the inside part of it. *The interior of the house was furnished with heavy, old-fashioned pieces... The boat's interior badly needed painting.*
N-COUNT: oft with poss
2 You use **interior** to describe something that is inside a building or vehicle. *The interior walls were painted green... There is more interior space than in some rival cars... He pulled the car over, turned on the interior light, examined the map.*
ADJ: ADJ n
3 The **interior** of a country or continent is the central area of it. *...a 5-day hike into the interior. ...the unknown interior of South America... The Yangzi river would give access to much of China's interior.*
N-SING: oft *the* N, oft with poss
4 A country's **interior** minister, ministry, or department deals with affairs within that country, such as law and order. *The French Interior Minister has intervened in a scandal over the role of a secret police force.*
ADJ: ADJ n
5 A country's minister or ministry of **the interior** deals with affairs within that country, such as law and order. *An official from the Ministry of the Interior said six people had died.*
N-SING
6 **Interior** thoughts or processes go on inside someone's head and are not expressed aloud. *She depicted the interior life of human beings, and particularly their moral stresses and strains. ...the mind's interior space.*
ADJ: ADJ n =inner

interior decoration. **Interior decoration** is the decoration of the inside of a house, using paints, wallpapers, carpets, and furnishings. *...plenty of advice on interior decoration and selecting carpets for your home.*
N-UNCOUNT

interior decorator **interior decorators.** An **interior decorator** is employed by someone to design and decorate the inside of their house by choosing paints, wallpapers, carpets, and furnishings.
N-COUNT

interior design. **Interior design** is the art or profession of designing how the inside of a house is going to be decorated by choosing paints, wallpapers, carpets, and furnishings.
◆◇◇◇◇ N-UNCOUNT

interior designer, **interior designers.** An **interior designer** is a person who designs how the inside of a house is going to be decorated by choosing paints, wallpapers, carpets, and furnishings.
◆◇◇◇◇ N-COUNT

interject /ɪntəʳdʒekt/ **interjects, interjecting, interjected.** If you **interject** something, you say it and interrupt someone else who is speaking; a formal word. *'Surely there's something we can do?' interjected Palin... He listened thoughtfully, interjecting only the odd word.*
VERB =interpose
V with quote, V n, Also V

interjection /ɪntəʳdʒekʃᵊn/ **interjections**
1 An **interjection** is something you say which interrupts someone else who is speaking. *...the moronic and insensitive interjections of the disc jockey.*
N-COUNT
2 In grammar, an **interjection** is a word or expression which you use to express a strong feeling such as surprise, pain, or horror.
N-COUNT

interlaced /ɪntəʳleɪst/. If things are **interlaced**, parts of one thing go over, under, or between parts of another; used in written English. *During my whole report, he sat with his eyes closed and his fingers interlaced. ...languid women, their flowing locks interlaced with flowers and vines.*
ADJ: oft ADJ *with* n =entwined

interlink /ɪntəʳlɪŋk/ **interlinks, interlinking, interlinked.** Things that **are interlinked** or **interlink** are linked with each other in some way. *Those two processes are very closely interlinked... The question to be addressed is interlinked with the question of human rights. ...a more integrated transport network, with bus, rail, and ferry services all interlinking... The play takes three Scottish tales and interlinks them.* V-RECIP-ERG =interconnect be V-ed be V-ed with n pl-n V V pl-n

interlock /ɪntəʳlɒk/ **interlocks, interlocking, interlocked** ◆◇◇◇◇

1 Things that **interlock** or **are interlocked** go between or through each other so that they are linked. *The parts interlock... Interlock your fingers behind your back... Joyce sits with her fingers interlocked under her chin. ...a series of interlocking rings.* V-RECIP-ERG pl-n V V pl-n V-ed V-ing Also V with n

2 If systems, situations, or plans **are interlocked** or **interlock**, they are very closely connected. *The problems of Israel, Lebanon, and the Gulf are tightly interlocked... The tragedies begin to interlock... Your girlfriend's fear of being abandoned seems to interlock with your fear of being found undesirable.* V-RECIP-ERG be V-ed pl-n V V with n Also V pl-n

interlocutor /ɪntəʳlɒkjʊtəʳ/ **interlocutors**

1 Your **interlocutor** is the person with whom you are having a conversation; a formal use. *Owen had the habit of staring motionlessly at his interlocutor.* N-COUNT: oft poss N

2 If a person or organization has a role as an **interlocutor** in talks or negotiations, they have a role as a representative, intermediary, or participant in them; a formal use. *...one of the Palestine Liberation Organization's principle interlocutors with Egypt. ...key interlocutors in the Middle East conference.* N-COUNT

interloper /ɪntəʳloʊpəʳ/ **interlopers.** If you describe someone as an **interloper**, you mean that they have come into a situation or a place where they are not wanted or do not belong. *She had no wish to share her father with any outsider and regarded us as interlopers.* N-COUNT =intruder

interlude /ɪntəʳluːd/ **interludes.** An **interlude** is a short period of time when an activity or situation stops and something else happens. *It was a happy interlude in the Kents' life. ...a chat-show with musical interludes.* ◆◇◇◇◇ N-COUNT =interval

intermarriage /ɪntəʳmærɪdʒ/ **intermarriages.** **Intermarriage** is marriage between people from different social, racial, or religious groups. *There was a great deal of intermarriage between members of the old and new ruling classes... Intermarriages were not uncommon.* N-UNCOUNT: also N in pl, oft N between pl-n

intermarry /ɪntəʳmæri/ **intermarries, intermarrying, intermarried.** When people from different social, racial, or religious groups **intermarry**, they marry each other. You can also say that one group **intermarries** with another group. *They were allowed to intermarry... Some of the traders settled and intermarried with local women.* V-RECIP pl-n V V with n

intermediary /ɪntəʳmiːdiəri/ **intermediaries.** An **intermediary** is a person who passes messages or proposals between two people or groups. *She wanted him to act as an intermediary in the dispute with Moscow.* ◆◇◇◇◇ N-COUNT =go-between

intermediate /ɪntəʳmiːdiət/ **intermediates** ◆◆◇◇◇

1 An **intermediate** stage, level, or position is one that occurs between two other stages, levels, or positions. *You should consider breaking the journey with intermediate stopovers at airport hotels. ...hourly trains to Perugia, Assisi, and intermediate stations.* ADJ: usu ADJ n

2 **Intermediate** is used to describe learners of something, who are no longer beginners, but are not yet advanced. *The Badminton Club holds coaching sessions for beginners and intermediate players on Friday evenings.* ► An **intermediate** is an intermediate learner. *The ski school coaches beginners, intermediates, and advanced skiers.* ADJ N-COUNT

interment /ɪntɜːʳmənt/ **interments.** The **interment** of a dead person is their burial; a formal word. N-VAR =burial

interminable /ɪntɜːʳmɪnəbəl/. If you describe something as **interminable**, you are emphasizing that it continues for a very long time and indicating that you wish it was shorter or would stop. *...an interminable meeting.* ♦ **interminably** *He talked to me interminably about his first wife.* ◆◇◇◇◇ ADJ PRAGMATICS =endless ADV: usu ADV after v

intermingle /ɪntəʳmɪŋgəl/ **intermingles, intermingling, intermingled.** When people or things **intermingle**, they mix with each other; a formal word. *This allows the two cultures to intermingle without losing their separate identities. ...an opportunity for them to intermingle with the citizens of other countries.* ♦ **intermingled** *The ethnic populations are so intermingled that there's bound to be conflict.* V-RECIP pl-n V V with n ADJ-GRADED: usu v-link ADJ

intermission /ɪntəʳmɪʃən/ **intermissions.** An **intermission** is a short interval between two parts of a film, play, or show. In American English, you can also say that something happens at, after, or during **intermission**. *I slipped out for a beer during the intermission... Fraser did not perform until after intermission.* N-COUNT: also prep N

intermittent /ɪntəʳmɪtənt/. Something that is **intermittent** happens occasionally rather than continuously. *After three hours of intermittent rain, the game was abandoned.* ♦ **intermittently** *The talks went on intermittently for three years.* ◆◇◇◇◇ ADJ-GRADED =sporadic ADV-GRADED: usu ADV with v

intern, interns, interning, interned. The verb is pronounced /ɪntɜːʳn/. The noun is pronounced /ɪntɜːʳn/. ◆◇◇◇◇

1 If someone **is interned**, they are put in prison or in a prison camp for political reasons. *He was interned as an enemy alien at the outbreak of the Second World War.* VB: usu passive be V-ed

2 In American English, an **intern** is an advanced student or a recent graduate, especially in medicine, who is being given practical training under supervision. N-COUNT

internal /ɪntɜːʳnəl/ ◆◆◆◇◇

1 **Internal** is used to describe things that exist or happen inside a country or organization. *The country stepped up internal security... We now have a Europe without internal borders... Mr Kelly posted his resignation letter to Mr Jones in the internal mail box.* ♦ **internally** *The state is not a unified and internally coherent entity.* ADJ: ADJ n ADV

2 **Internal** is used to describe things that exist or happen inside a particular person, object, or place. *The doctor said the internal bleeding had been massive... Some of the internal walls of my house are made of plasterboard.* ♦ **internally** *Evening primrose oil is used on the skin as well as taken internally... Internally, however, the two computers are so different that programs cannot be switched from one to the other.* ADJ: ADJ n ADV: usu ADV with v, also ADV with cl, ADV adj

internal combustion engine, internal combustion engines. An **internal combustion engine** is an engine that creates its energy by burning fuel inside itself. Most cars have internal combustion engines. N-COUNT

internalize /ɪntɜːʳnəlaɪz/ **internalizes, internalizing, internalized;** also spelled **internalise** in British English. If you **internalize** something such as a belief or a set of values, you make it become part of your attitude or way of thinking; a formal word. *Over time she internalized her parents' attitudes. ...a social order which depends on internalized feelings of what is right and wrong.* ♦ **internalization** /ɪntɜːʳnəlaɪzeɪʃən/ *...my internalisation of hatred, disgust and fear.* VERB V n V-ed N-UNCOUNT: usu with poss

international /ɪntəʳnæʃənəl/ **internationals** ◆◆◆◆◆

1 **International** means between or involving different countries. *...an international agreement against exporting arms to that country. ...Kuwait International Airport... The Cuban Government has asked for emergency aid from the international community.* ♦ **internationally** *There are only two internationally recognised certificates in Teaching English as a Foreign Language... I am one of the few young women who has made it as a writer financially and internationally.* ADJ: usu ADJ n ADV: usu ADV adj/-ed, also ADV with cl, ADV after v

2 In sport, an **international** is a match that is played between teams representing two different N-COUNT

countries; used mainly in British English. *...the midweek international against England.*

3 An **international** is a sportsman or sportswoman who plays in a match played between teams representing two different countries; used mainly in British English. *The two players, both former England internationals, had been at the club for 16 years.* N-COUNT: usu n N

internationalism /ɪntəʳnæʃənəlɪzəm/. **Internationalism** is the belief that countries should co-operate with one another and try to understand one another. N-UNCOUNT

internationalist /ɪntəʳnæʃənəlɪst/ **internationalists.** If someone has **internationalist** beliefs or opinions, they believe that countries should co-operate with one another and try to understand one another. *...a more genuinely internationalist view of US participation in peace-keeping.* ADJ ▶ An **internationalist** is someone who has internationalist views. N-COUNT

internationalize /ɪntəʳnæʃənəlaɪz/ **internationalizes, internationalizing, internationalized;** also spelled **internationalise** in British English. If an issue or a crisis is **internationalized**, it becomes the concern of many nations throughout the world; used by journalists. *A very real danger exists of the conflict becoming internationalised... They have been trying to internationalise the Kashmir problem.* VERB be V-ed V n ♦ **internationalization** /ɪntəʳnæʃənəlaɪzeɪʃən/ *...the internationalization of the crisis in Croatia.* N-UNCOUNT

international relations. The political relationships between different countries are referred to as **international relations**. *...peaceful and friendly international relations.* ◆◇◇◇◇ N-PLURAL

internecine /ɪntəʳniːsaɪn, AM -siːn/. An **internecine** conflict, war, or quarrel is one which takes place between opposing groups within a country or organization; a formal word. *The whole episode has drawn attention again to internecine strife in the ruling party.* ADJ: ADJ n

internee /ɪntɜːʳniː/ **internees.** An **internee** is a person who has been imprisoned for political reasons. N-COUNT

Internet /ɪntəʳnet/. **The Internet** is the world-wide network of computer links which allows computer users to connect with computers all over the world, and which carries electronic mail. N-PROPER: the N

internment /ɪntɜːʳnmənt/. **Internment** is imprisonment for political reasons. *They called for the return of internment without trial for terrorists. ...internment camps for dissidents.* N-UNCOUNT

interpersonal /ɪntəʳpɜːʳsənəl/. **Interpersonal** means relating to relationships between people. *...problems in interpersonal relationships... Training in interpersonal skills is essential.* ◆◇◇◇◇ ADJ: ADJ n

interplay /ɪntəʳpleɪ/. The **interplay** between two or more things or people is the way that they have an effect on each another or react to each other. *...the personal interplay between great entertainers and a live public. ...the interplay of political, economic, social and cultural factors.* N-UNCOUNT: usu N between/of pl-n =interaction

interpolate /ɪntɜːʳpəleɪt/ **interpolates, interpolating, interpolated.** If you **interpolate** a comment into a conversation or some words into a piece of writing, you put it in as an addition; a formal word. *Williams interpolated much spurious matter... These odd assertions were interpolated into the manuscript some time after 1400.* VERB =insert V n be V-ed into n

interpolation /ɪntɜːʳpəleɪʃən/ **interpolations.** An **interpolation** is an addition to a piece of writing; a formal word. *The interpolation appears to have been inserted very soon after the original text was finished.* N-COUNT =addition

interpose /ɪntəʳpoʊz/ **interposes, interposing, interposed**

1 If you **interpose** something between two people or things, you place it between them; a formal use. *Strong police forces had to interpose themselves between the two rival groups in the village... The work interposes a glass plate between two large circular mirrors.* VERB V pron-refl between pl-n V n between pl-n

2 If you **interpose**, you interrupt with a comment or question; a formal use. *'He rang me just now,' she interposed... Jacob was silent so long that Livvy interposed.* VERB V with quote V Also V n

interpret /ɪntɜːʳprɪt/ **interprets, interpreting, interpreted** ◆◆◇◇◇

1 If you **interpret** something in a particular way, you decide that this is its meaning or significance. *Even so, the move was interpreted as a defeat for Mr Gorbachev and a victory for Mr Yeltsin... The judge quite rightly says that he has to interpret the law as it's been passed... Both approaches agree on what is depicted in the poem, but not on how it should be interpreted.* VERB V n as n V n V n adv/prep

2 If you **interpret** what someone is saying, you translate it immediately into another language. *The chambermaid spoke little English, so her husband came with her to interpret... Three interpreters looked it over for about three or four hours and found that they could not interpret half of it.* VERB V V n

interpretation /ɪntɜːʳprɪteɪʃən/ **interpretations** ◆◆◇◇◇

1 An **interpretation** of something is an opinion about what it means. *The opposition Labour Party put a different interpretation on the figures... Analysis and interpretation is a very personal thing.* N-VAR

2 A performer's **interpretation** of something such as a piece of music or a role in a play is the particular way in which they choose to perform it. *...her full-bodied interpretation of the role of Micaela.* N-COUNT: with supp =portrayal, rendition

interpretative /ɪntɜːʳprɪtətɪv/. See **interpretive.**

interpreter /ɪntɜːʳprɪtəʳ/ **interpreters** ◆◆◇◇◇

1 An **interpreter** is a person whose job is to translate what someone is saying into another language. *Speaking through an interpreter, Aristide said that Haitians had hoped coups were behind them.* N-COUNT

2 The **interpreter** of something such as a piece of music is the person who performs it. *Over the years Freni has been one of the supreme interpreters of Puccini's heroines.* N-COUNT: oft N of n

interpretive /ɪntɜːʳprɪtɪv/. The form **interpretative** is also used. You use **interpretive** to describe something that provides an interpretation; a formal word. *History is an interpretive process.* ADJ: ADJ n

interregnum /ɪntəʳregnəm/. An **interregnum** is a period between the end of one person's time as ruler or leader and the coming to power of the next ruler or leader. N-SING

interrelate /ɪntəʳrɪleɪt/ **interrelates, interrelating, interrelated.** If two or more things **interrelate**, there is a connection between them and they have an effect on each other. *The body and the mind interrelate... Each of these cells have their specific jobs to do, but they also interrelate with each other. ...the way in which we communicate and interrelate with others... All things are interrelated.* V-RECIP =interconnect pl-n V pl-n V with pron-recip V with n V-ed

interrelationship /ɪntəʳrɪleɪʃənʃɪp/ **interrelationships.** An **interrelationship** is a close relationship between two or more things or people. *...to reach a deeper understanding of the interrelationships between unemployment, crime, and imprisonment. ...the interrelationship of biography and history. ...a family's interrelationships.* N-COUNT: oft N between/of pl-n

interrogate /ɪnterəgeɪt/ **interrogates, interrogating, interrogated.** If someone, especially a police officer, **interrogates** someone, they question them thoroughly for a long time in order to get some information from them. *I interrogated everyone even slightly involved.* ◆◇◇◇◇ VERB =question V n ♦ **interrogator, interrogators** *I was well aware of what my interrogators wanted to hear.* N-COUNT: oft poss N

interrogation /ɪnterəgeɪʃən/ **interrogations.** An **interrogation** is the act of interrogating someone. *...the right to silence in police interrogations. ...ill-treatment of suspects during interrogation.* ◆◇◇◇◇ N-VAR =questioning

interrogative /ɪntərɒgətɪv/ **interrogatives**

1 An **interrogative** gesture or tone of voice shows that you want to know the answer to a question; used in written English. *Donovan cocked an* ADJ-GRADED: usu ADJ n =questioning

interrogative eye at his companion, who nodded in reply.
2 In grammar, a clause that is in **the interrogative**, or in the **interrogative** mood, has its subject following 'do', 'be', 'have', or a modal verb. Examples are 'When did he get back?' and 'Are you all right?'. Clauses of this kind are typically used to ask questions. N-SING: *the*N
3 In grammar, an **interrogative** is a word such as 'who', 'how', or 'why', which can be used to ask a question. N-COUNT

interrupt /ɪntərʌpt/ **interrupts, interrupting, interrupted** ◆◆◇◇◇
1 If you **interrupt** someone who is speaking, you say or do something that causes them to stop. *Turkin tapped him on the shoulder. 'Sorry to interrupt, Colonel.'... He tried to speak, but she interrupted him.* VERB V V n ♦ **interruption** /ɪntərʌpʃən/ **interruptions** *The sudden interruption stopped Beryl in mid-flow.* N-VAR
2 If someone or something **interrupts** a process or activity, they stop it for a period of time. *He has rightly interrupted his holiday in Spain to return to London... The match took nearly three hours and was interrupted at times by rain.* VERB =disrupt V n ♦ **interruption** *...interruptions in the supply of food and fuel... Motherhood did not constitute much of an interruption to her career... I was able to get on with my work without interruption.* N-VAR: oft N *in/to* n =disruption
3 If something **interrupts** a line, surface, or view, it stops it from being continuous or makes it look irregular. *Taller plants interrupt the views from the house.* VERB V n

intersect /ɪntərsekt/ **intersects, intersecting, intersected**
1 If two or more lines or roads **intersect**, they meet or cross each other. You can also say that one line or road **intersects** another. *The orbit of this comet intersects the orbit of the Earth... The circles will intersect in two places... The centre of the city is full of tiny intersecting alley-ways.* V-RECIP V n pl-n V V-ing Also V *with* n
2 If one thing **intersects** with another or if two things **intersect**, the two things have a connection at a particular point. *...the ways in which historical events intersect with individual lives... Their histories intersect.* V-RECIP =overlap V *with* n pl-n V
3 If a place, area, or surface **is intersected** by things such as roads or lines, they cross it. *The centre of the city is intersected by three main waterways and several rail links.* VB: usu passive =cross *be* V-ed

intersection /ɪntərsekʃən/ **intersections.** An **intersection** is a place where roads or other lines meet or cross. *...at the intersection of two main canals. ...a busy highway intersection.* ◆◇◇◇◇ N-COUNT: oft N *of/with* n =junction

intersperse /ɪntərspɜːrs/ **intersperses, interspersing, interspersed.** If you **intersperse** one group of things **with** another or **among** another, you put or include the second things between or among the first things. *Originally the intention was to intersperse the historical scenes with modern ones. ...skillfully interspersing jokes and gossipy anecdotes among his instructions.* VERB V n *with* n V n *among* n

interspersed /ɪntərspɜːrst/. If one group of things are **interspersed with** another or **interspersed among** another, the second things occur between or among the first things. *...a series of bursts of gunfire, interspersed with single shots. ...a landscape of mixed forest interspersed with bamboo groves. ...reports of gruesome murder scenes interspersed among descriptions of comic farces.* ◆◇◇◇◇ ADJ: v-link ADJ prep, usu ADJ *with* n, ADJ *among* n

interstate /ɪntərsteɪt/ **interstates** ◆◇◇◇◇
1 Interstate means between states, especially the states of the United States. *...interstate highways. ...federal barriers to interstate banking.* ADJ: ADJ n
2 In the United States, an **interstate** is a major road linking states. *...a series of attacks on motorists along the interstate. ...the southbound lane of Interstate 75.* N-COUNT: also N num

interstellar /ɪntərstelər/. **Interstellar** means between the stars; a formal word. *...interstellar space.* ADJ: ADJ n

intertwine /ɪntərtwaɪn/ **intertwines, intertwining, intertwined** ◆◇◇◇◇
1 If two or more things **are intertwined** or **intertwine**, they are closely connected with each other in many ways. *Their destinies are intertwined... Three major narratives intertwine within Foucault's text, 'Madness and Civilisation'... He intertwines his personal reminiscences with the story of British television... Her fate intertwined with his.* V-RECIP-ERG =interweave *be* V-ed pl-n V V n *with* n V *with* n Also V pl-n
2 If two things **intertwine**, they are twisted together or go over and under each other. *Trees, undergrowth and creepers intertwined, blocking our way... Even the towels were embroidered with their three intertwined initials.* V-RECIP =entwine pl-n V V-ed Also V *with* n

interval /ɪntərvəl/ **intervals** ◆◆◇◇◇
1 An **interval** between two events or dates is the period of time between them. *The ferry service between Burnham and Wallasea Island has restarted after an interval of 12 years... There was a long interval of silence.* N-COUNT: oft N *of* n =gap
2 An **interval** during a play, concert, or game is a short break between two of the parts. *During the interval, wine was served... England were two goals behind at the interval.* N-COUNT
3 An **interval** is the difference in pitch between two musical notes; a technical term in music. N-COUNT
4 If something happens **at intervals**, it happens several times with gaps or pauses in between. *She woke him for his medicines at intervals throughout the night.* PHRASES PHR with v
5 If things are placed **at** particular **intervals**, there are spaces of a particular size between them. *Several red and white barriers marked the road at intervals of about a mile... The trees which gave the road its name stood at regular intervals along the kerb... At intervals there were red warning lights.* PHR with v

intervene /ɪntərviːn/ **intervenes, intervening, intervened** ◆◆◇◇◇
1 If you **intervene** in a situation, you become involved in it and try to change it. *The situation calmed down when police intervened... The Government is doing nothing to intervene in the crisis.* VERB V V *in* n
2 If you **intervene**, you interrupt a conversation in order to add something to it. *Hattie intervened and told me to stop it... 'I've told you he's not here,' Irena intervened.* VERB =interject V V with quote
3 If an event **intervenes**, it happens suddenly in a way that stops, delays, or prevents something from happening. *The South African mailboat arrived on Friday mornings unless bad weather intervened... I pray that death may not intervene to prevent our meeting with my darling children.* VERB V V to-inf

intervening /ɪntərviːnɪŋ/ ◆◇◇◇◇
1 An **intervening** period of time is one that separates two events or points in time. *During those intervening years Bridget had married her husband Robert... I had spent the intervening time in London, with Gretchen.* ADJ: ADJ n
2 An **intervening** object or area comes between two other objects or areas. *They had scoured the intervening miles of moorland.* ADJ: ADJ n

intervention /ɪntərvenʃən/ **interventions. Intervention** is the act of intervening, especially in order to influence a situation in some way. *...the role of the United States and its intervention in the internal affairs of many countries. ...military interventions.* ◆◆◆◇◇ N-VAR: oft N *in* n

interventionist /ɪntərvenʃənɪst/ **interventionists.** When journalist talk about **interventionist** policies, they are referring to policies which show an organization's desire to become involved in a problem or a crisis which does not concern it directly. *...the interventionist industrial policy of the Wilson government... The UN needs to become more interventionist to prevent human rights abuses and suffering.* ► An **interventionist** is someone who supports interventionist policies. ◆◇◇◇◇ ADJ-GRADED ≠laissez-faire N-COUNT

interview /ɪntərvjuː/ **interviews, interviewing, interviewed** ◆◆◆◆◇
1 An **interview** is a formal meeting at which someone is asked questions in order to find out if they N-VAR: oft N *for* n

are suitable for a job or a course of study. *When I went for my first interview for this job I arrived extremely early... The interview went well... Not everyone who writes in can be invited for interview.*

2 If you **are interviewed** for a particular job or course of study, someone asks you questions about yourself to find out if you suitable for it. *When Wardell was interviewed, he was impressive, and on that basis, he was hired... He was among the three candidates interviewed for the job.* VB: usu passive; be V-ed; V-ed; Also be V-ed for n

3 An **interview** is a conversation in which a journalist puts questions to someone such as a famous person or politician. *The trouble began when Allan gave an interview to the Chicago Tribune newspaper last month... There'll be an interview with Mr Hurd after the news.* N-COUNT

4 When a journalist **interviews** someone such as a famous person, they ask them a series of questions. *I seized the chance to interview Chris Hani about this issue.* VERB; V n

5 When the police **interview** someone, they ask them questions about a crime that has been committed. *The police interviewed the driver, but had no evidence to go on.* VERB =question; V n

interviewee /ɪntəʳvjuiː/ **interviewees.** An **interviewee** is a person who is being interviewed. ◆◇◇◇◇ N-COUNT

interviewer /ɪntəʳvjuəʳ/ **interviewers.** An **interviewer** is a person who is asking someone questions at an interview. ◆◇◇◇◇ N-COUNT

interweave /ɪntəʳwiːv/ **interweaves, interweaving, interwove, interwoven.** If two or more things **are interwoven** or **interweave**, they are very closely connected or are combined with each other. *For these people, land is inextricably interwoven with life itself... Complex family relationships interweave with a murder plot in this ambitious new novel... The programme successfully interweaves words and pictures... Social structures are not discrete objects; they overlap and interweave.* ◆◇◇◇◇ V-RECIP-ERG =intertwine; be V-ed with n; V with n; V pl-n; pl-n V; Also V n with n

intestinal /ɪntestɪnəl/. **Intestinal** means relating to the intestines; a formal word. ◆◇◇◇◇ ADJ: ADJ n

intestine /ɪntestɪn/ **intestines.** Your **intestines** are the tubes in your body through which food passes when it has left your stomach. *This area is always tender to the touch if the intestines are not functioning properly... This vitamin is absorbed through the walls of the small intestine.* ◆◇◇◇◇ N-COUNT

intimacy /ɪntɪməsi/ **intimacies** ◆◇◇◇◇

1 **Intimacy** between two people is a very close personal relationship between them. *...a means of achieving intimacy with another person.* N-UNCOUNT: oft N with/between n

2 **Intimacies** are things that you say or do to someone you have a very close personal relationship with. *...the intimacies of a love scene.* N-COUNT: usu pl

intimate, intimates, intimating, intimated. ◆◆◇◇◇ The adjective and noun are pronounced /ɪntɪmət/. The verb is pronounced /ɪntɪmeɪt/.

1 If you have an **intimate** friendship with someone, you know them very well and like them a lot. *I discussed with my intimate friends whether I would immediately have a baby.* ADJ-GRADED: usu ADJ n ► An **intimate** is an intimate friend. *They are to have an autumn wedding, an intimate of the couple confides.* N-COUNT: usu with poss ♦ **intimately** *He did not feel he had got to know them intimately.* ADV-GRADED: ADV after v, ADV -ed

2 If two people are in an **intimate** relationship, they are involved with each other in a loving or sexual way. *I just won't discuss my intimate relationships. ...their intimate moments with their boyfriends.* ADJ-GRADED: usu ADJ n ♦ **intimately** *You have to be willing to get to know yourself and your partner intimately.* ADV-GRADED: ADV after v

3 An **intimate** conversation or detail, for example, is very personal and private. *He wrote about the intimate details of his family life... I hate to interrupt your intimate conversation but we do have an assignment to discuss.* ADJ-GRADED: usu ADJ n =private ♦ **intimately** *It was the first time they had attempted to talk intimately.* ADV-GRADED: ADV after v

4 If you use **intimate** to describe an occasion or the atmosphere of a place, you like it because it is quiet and pleasant, and seems suitable for close conversations between friends. *...an intimate candlelit dinner for two.* ADJ-GRADED: usu ADJ n PRAGMATICS

5 An **intimate** connection between ideas or organizations, for example, is a very strong link between them. *...an intimate connection between madness and wisdom... France has kept the most intimate links with its former African territories.* ADJ-GRADED: usu ADJ n ♦ **intimately** *Property and equities are intimately connected in Hong Kong.* ADV-GRADED: ADV after v

6 An **intimate** knowledge of something is a deep and detailed knowledge of it. *He surprised me with his intimate knowledge of Kierkegaard and Schopenhauer.* ADJ-GRADED: usu ADJ n =thorough ♦ **intimately** *...a golden age of musicians whose work she knew intimately.* ADV-GRADED: usu ADV after v

7 If you **intimate** something, you say it in an indirect way; a formal use. *He went on to intimate that he was indeed contemplating a shake-up of the company... He had intimated to the French and Russians his readiness to come to a settlement.* VERB =hint; V that; V to n n; Also V n

intimation /ɪntɪmeɪʃən/ **intimations.** An **intimation** is an indirect suggestion or sign that something is likely to happen or be true; a formal word. *...intimations of mortality... I did not have any intimation that he was going to resign.* N-COUNT: usu N of n, N that

intimidate /ɪntɪmɪdeɪt/ **intimidates, intimidating, intimidated.** If you **intimidate** someone, you deliberately make them frightened enough to do what you want them to do. *Jones had set out to intimidate and dominate Paul... Attempts to intimidate people into voting for the governing party did not work.* ◆◆◇◇◇ VERB =browbeat; V n; V n into -ing ♦ **intimidation** /ɪntɪmɪdeɪʃən/ *...an inquiry into allegations of intimidation during last week's vote.* N-UNCOUNT

intimidated /ɪntɪmɪdeɪtɪd/. Someone who feels **intimidated** feels frightened and lacks confidence because of the people they are with or the situation they are in. *Women can come in here and not feel intimidated.* ◆◇◇◇◇ ADJ-GRADED: usu v-link ADJ

intimidating /ɪntɪmɪdeɪtɪŋ/. If you describe someone or something as **intimidating**, you mean that they are frightening and make people lose confidence. *He was a huge, intimidating figure.* ◆◇◇◇◇ ADJ-GRADED: usu ADJ n

into /ɪntuː/. Also pronounced /ɪntuː/, particularly before pronouns and for meaning 14. ◆◆◆◆◆

In addition to the uses shown below, **into** is used after some verbs and nouns in order to introduce extra information. **Into** is also used with verbs of movement, such as 'walk' and 'push', and in phrasal verbs such as 'enter into' and 'talk into'.

1 If you put one thing **into** another, you put the first thing inside the second. *Combine the remaining ingredients and put them into a dish... Until the 1980s almost all olives were packed into jars by hand.* PREP =in

2 If you go **into** a place or vehicle, you move from being outside it to being inside it. *I have no idea how he got into Iraq... She got up and went into an inner office... He got into bed and started to read.* PREP

3 If one thing goes **into** another, the first thing moves from the outside to the inside of the second thing, by breaking or damaging the surface of it. *Flavell had accidentally discharged a pistol, firing it into the ceiling... The rider came off and the handlebar went into his neck.* PREP

4 If one thing gets **into** another, the first thing enters the second and becomes part of it. *Poisonous smoke had got into the water supply... The money went into a common fund.* PREP

5 If you are walking or driving a vehicle and you bump **into** something or crash **into** something, you hit it accidentally. *A train from Kent plowed into the barrier at the end of the platform... Joanna heard him bump into the table and curse again.* PREP

6 When you get **into** a piece of clothing, you put it on. *She could change into a different outfit in two minutes... He put on his underwear and got into his suit.* PREP

7 If someone or something gets **into** a particular state, they start being in that state. *He had too much time on his hands and that caused him to get into trouble... I slid into a depression. ...the group's plunge into financial crisis earlier in the year.* PREP: v PREP n, n PREP n

8 If you talk someone **into** doing something, you PREP:

persuade them to do it. *Gerome tried to talk her into taking an apartment in Paris.* V n PREP n/-ing

9 If something changes **into** something else, it then has a new form, shape, or nature. *...to turn a nasty episode into a little bit of a joke. ...learning what she needs to know to grow into a competent adult. ...Irish fairytales that had been translated into English.* PREP

10 If something is cut or split **into** a number of pieces or sections, it is divided so that it becomes several smaller pieces or sections. *Sixteen teams are taking part, divided into four groups... Roll out the pastry and cut into narrow strips... Mr Botnar's business empire is split into two companies.* PREP

11 An investigation **into** a subject or event is concerned with that subject or event. *The concert will raise funds for research into Aids... We are beginning to have some insight into drug therapy.* PREP: n PREP n =about

12 If you move or go **into** a particular career or business, you start working in it. *In the early 1980s, it was easy to get into the rental business... He closed down the business and went into politics.* PREP

13 If something continues **into** a period of time, it continues until after that period of time has begun. *He had three children, and lived on into his sixties... The Open Golf Championship will be getting into its second day in a few hours.* PREP

14 If you are very interested in something and like it very much, you can say that you are **into** it; an informal use. *I'm into electronics myself.* PREP: v-link PREP n

intolerable /ɪntɒlərəbᵊl/. If you describe something as **intolerable**, you mean that it is so bad or extreme that no one can bear it or tolerate it. *They felt this would put intolerable pressure on them... Human rights abuses by any party are intolerable.* ♦ **intolerably** /ɪntɒlərəbli/ *...intolerably cramped conditions... Her leg ached intolerably.* ◆◇◇◇◇ ADJ-GRADED ≠tolerable; ADV-GRADED

intolerance /ɪntɒlərəns/. **Intolerance** is unwillingness to let other people act in a different way or hold different opinions from you; used showing disapproval. *...his intolerance of any opinion other than his own. ...religious intolerance.* ◆◇◇◇◇ N-UNCOUNT: usu with supp PRAGMATICS ≠tolerance

intolerant /ɪntɒlərənt/. If you describe someone as **intolerant**, you mean that they do not accept behaviour and opinions that are different from their own; used showing disapproval. *He was intolerant of both suggestions and criticisms. ...intolerant attitudes toward non-Catholics.* ADJ-GRADED: oft v-link ADJ *of* n PRAGMATICS ≠tolerant

intonation /ɪntəneɪʃᵊn/ **intonations.** Your **intonation** is the way that your voice rises and falls as you speak. *His voice had a very slight German intonation.* N-VAR

intone /ɪntoʊn/ **intones, intoning, intoned.** If you **intone** something, you say or recite it in a slow and serious way, with most of the words at one pitch; used in written English. *He quietly intoned several prayers... 'But Jesus is here!' the priest intoned.* ◆◇◇◇◇ VERB =chant V n V with quote

intoxicated /ɪntɒksɪkeɪtɪd/

1 Someone who is **intoxicated** is drunk; a formal use. *He appeared intoxicated, police said.* ADJ-GRADED =inebriated

2 If you are **intoxicated by** or **with** something such as a feeling or an event, you are so excited by it that you find it hard to think clearly and sensibly; a literary use. *They seem to have become intoxicated by their success... These leaders can become intoxicated with a sense of their own omnipotence.* ADJ-GRADED: v-link ADJ *by/with* n =carried away

intoxicating /ɪntɒksɪkeɪtɪŋ/

1 Intoxicating drink contains alcohol and can make you drunk. *...intoxicating liquor.* ADJ-GRADED: usu ADJ n

2 If you describe something as **intoxicating**, you mean that it makes you feel a strong sense of excitement or happiness; a literary use. *...the intoxicating fragrance of lilies... The music is pulsating and the atmosphere is intoxicating.* ADJ-GRADED

intoxication /ɪntɒksɪkeɪʃᵊn/

1 Intoxication is the state of being drunk; a formal use. *Intoxication interferes with memory and thinking, speech and coordination.* N-UNCOUNT

2 You use **intoxication** to refer to a quality that something has that makes you feel very excited; a literary use. *...the sheer intoxication of cinema.* N-UNCOUNT: oft N *of* n

intractable /ɪntræktəbᵊl/ ◆◇◇◇◇

1 Intractable people are very difficult to control or influence; a formal use. *What may be done to reduce the influence of intractable opponents?* ADJ-GRADED: usu ADJ n

2 Intractable problems or situations are very difficult to deal with; a formal use. *The economy still faces intractable problems.* ADJ-GRADED: usu ADJ n

intransigence /ɪntrænsɪdʒᵊns/. If you talk about someone's **intransigence**, you mean that they refuse to behave differently or to change their attitude to something; a formal word, used showing disapproval. *He often appeared angry and frustrated by the intransigence of both sides.* ◆◇◇◇◇ N-UNCOUNT: usu with poss PRAGMATICS ≠flexibility

intransigent /ɪntrænsɪdʒᵊnt/. If you describe someone as **intransigent**, you mean that they refuse to behave differently or to change their attitude to something; a formal word, used showing disapproval. *They put pressure on the Government to change its intransigent stance... The worry is that the radicals will grow more intransigent.* ADJ-GRADED PRAGMATICS ≠flexible

intransitive /ɪntrænsɪtɪv/. An **intransitive** verb does not have an object. ADJ ≠transitive

intravenous /ɪntrəviːnəs/. **Intravenous** foods or drugs are given to sick people through their veins, rather than their mouths; a technical term. *...an intravenous drip. ...intravenous drug users.* ♦ **intravenously** *Premature babies have to be fed intravenously.* ◆◇◇◇◇ ADJ: ADJ n; ADV: ADV after v

in tray, in trays; also spelled **in-tray**. An **in tray** is a shallow basket used in offices to put letters and documents in when they arrive or when they are waiting to be dealt with. N-COUNT ≠out tray

intrepid /ɪntrepɪd/. An **intrepid** person acts in a brave way; an old-fashioned word, often used humorously. *...an intrepid space traveller.* ◆◇◇◇◇ ADJ-GRADED: usu ADJ n =fearless

intricacies /ɪntrɪkəsiz/. The **intricacies** of something are its complicated details. *Rose explained the intricacies of the job.* N-PLURAL: usu N *of* n

intricacy /ɪntrɪkəsi/. **Intricacy** is the state of being made up of many small parts or details. *Garments are priced from $100 to several thousand dollars, depending on the intricacy of the work.* N-UNCOUNT: usu N *of* n =complexity

intricate /ɪntrɪkət/. You use **intricate** to describe something that has many small parts or details. *...intricate patterns and motifs.* ♦ **intricately** *...intricately carved sculptures.* ◆◇◇◇◇ ADJ-GRADED: usu ADJ n ≠simple; ADV-GRADED

intrigue, intrigues, intriguing, intrigued. The noun is pronounced /ɪntriːg/. The verb is pronounced /ɪntriːg/. ◆◇◇◇◇

1 Intrigue is the making of secret plans to harm or deceive people. *...political intrigue. ...a powerful story of intrigue, passion and betrayal. ...the plots and intrigues in the novel.* N-VAR: usu with supp

2 If something **intrigues** you, it interests you and you are curious about it. *The novelty of the situation intrigued him.* VERB =fascinate V n

intrigued /ɪntriːgd/. If you are **intrigued** by something, it interests you and you are curious about it. *They are intrigued by her story... I would be intrigued to hear others' views.* ◆◇◇◇◇ ADJ-GRADED: usu v-link ADJ, oft ADJ *by* n, ADJ to-inf

intriguing /ɪntriːgɪŋ/. If you describe someone or something as **intriguing**, you mean that they interest you and you are curious about them. *This intriguing book is both thoughtful and informative.* ♦ **intriguingly** *...the intriguingly-named newspaper Le Canard Enchainé (The Chained Duck).* ◆◆◇◇◇ ADJ-GRADED: usu ADJ n =fascinating; ADV-GRADED: ADV adj, ADV with v

intrinsic /ɪntrɪnsɪk/. If something has **intrinsic** value or **intrinsic** interest, it is valuable or interesting because of its basic nature or character, and not because of its connection with other things; a formal word. *Diamonds have little intrinsic value and their price depends almost entirely on their scarcity... The rate is determined by intrinsic qualities such as the land's slope.* ♦ **intrinsically** /ɪntrɪnsɪkli/ *Sometimes I wonder if people are intrinsically evil... It was intrinsically a very powerful ship.* ◆◇◇◇◇ ADJ: ADJ n; ADV: ADV adj, ADV with cl

introduce /ɪntrədjuːs, AM -duːs/ **introduces, introducing, introduced** ◆◆◆◆◇

1 To **introduce** something means to cause it to enter a place or exist in a system for the first time. *The* VERB V n

Government has introduced a number of other money-saving moves... I kept the birds indoors all winter and introduced them into an aviary the following June... The word 'Pagoda' was introduced to Europe by the 17th century Portuguese. V n into/to n
♦ **introduction** *What he is better remembered for is the introduction of the moving assembly-line in Detroit in 1913. ...the introduction of a privacy bill to prevent press intrusions into private lives.* N-UNCOUNT: usu N of n

2 If you **introduce** someone **to** something, you cause them to learn about it or experience it for the first time. *He introduced us to the delights of natural food.* ♦ **introduction** *His introduction to League football would have been gentler if he had started at a smaller club... It was Sergeant Miller's introduction to a crime which has occupied him for nearly nine years.* VERB; V n to n; N-SING: usu N to n

3 If you **introduce** one person to another, or you **introduce** two people, you tell them each other's names, so that they can get to know each other. If you **introduce** yourself to someone, you tell them your name. *Tim, may I introduce you to my uncle's secretary, Mary Waller?... Someone introduced us and I sat next to him... We haven't been introduced. My name is Nero Wolfe... Let me introduce myself.* VERB; V n to n; V pl-n; V pron-refl
♦ **introduction, introductions** *With considerable shyness, Elaine performed the introductions.* N-VAR

4 The person who **introduces** a television or radio programme speaks at the beginning of it, and often between the different items in it, in order to explain what the programme or the items are about. *'Health Matters' is introduced by Dick Oliver on BBC World Service.* VERB =present; be V-ed by n; Also V n

introduction /ɪntrədʌkʃᵊn/ **introductions** ◆◆◇◇◇

1 The **introduction** to a book or talk is the part that comes at the beginning and tells you what the rest of the book or talk is about. *Ellen Malos, in her introduction to 'The Politics of Housework', provides a summary of the debates.* N-COUNT: oft N to n =foreword

2 If you refer to a book as an **introduction** to a particular subject, you mean that it explains the basic facts about that subject. *On balance, the book is a friendly, down-to-earth introduction to physics. ...'Psychology and Language: An Introduction to Psycholinguistics'.* N-COUNT: usu N to n, oft in names

3 You can refer to a new product as an **introduction** when it becomes available in a place for the first time. *There are two among their recent introductions that have greatly impressed me.* N-COUNT

4 See also **introduce**.

5 If you say that someone or something **needs no introduction**, you mean that they are so well known that everyone knows who or what they are. *Michael Jackson, of course, needs no introduction.* PHRASE: V inflects

introductory /ɪntrədʌktəri/ ◆◇◇◇◇

1 An **introductory** remark, talk, or chapter in a book gives a small amount of general information about a particular subject, often before a more detailed explanation. *...an introductory course in religion and theology.* ADJ: ADJ n

2 An **introductory** offer or price on a new product is something such as a free gift or a low price that is meant to attract new customers. *...just out on the shelves at an introductory price of £2.99.* ADJ: ADJ n

introspection /ɪntrəspekʃᵊn/. **Introspection** is the examining of your own thoughts, ideas, and feelings. *He had always had his moments of quiet introspection.* N-UNCOUNT

introspective /ɪntrəspektɪv/. **Introspective** people spend a lot of time examining their own thoughts, ideas, and feelings. ADJ-GRADED

introvert /ɪntrəvɜːʳt/ **introverts**

1 An **introvert** is a quiet, shy person who finds it difficult to talk to people. N-COUNT ≠extrovert

2 **Introvert** means the same as **introverted**. *The music students here are a very introvert lot.* ADJ-GRADED

introverted /ɪntrəvɜːʳtɪd/. **Introverted** people are quiet and shy and find it difficult to talk to other people. *Machen was a lonely, introverted child.* ADJ-GRADED ≠extroverted

intrude /ɪntruːd/ **intrudes, intruding, intruded** ◆◇◇◇◇

1 If you say that someone **is intruding** into a particular place or situation, you mean that they are not wanted or welcome there. *The press has been blamed for intruding into people's personal lives in an unacceptable way... I don't want to intrude on your meeting... I hope I'm not intruding.* VERB; V into/on/upon n; V

2 If something **intrudes** on your mood or your life, it disturbs it or has an unwanted effect on it. *Do you feel anxious when unforeseen incidents intrude on your day?... There are times when personal feelings cannot be allowed to intrude.* VERB; V on/into/upon n; V

3 If someone **intrudes** into a place, they go there even though they are not allowed to be there. *An American officer on the scene said no one had intruded into the space he was defending... We believe they intruded on to the field of play... The voyage home began, but not before an intruding aeroplane had repeatedly circled the ship.* VERB; V into/onto n; V-ing

intruder /ɪntruːdəʳ/ **intruders.** An **intruder** is a person who goes into a place where they are not supposed to be. ◆◇◇◇◇ N-COUNT

intrusion /ɪntruːʒᵊn/ **intrusions** ◆◇◇◇◇

1 If someone disturbs you when you are in a private place or having a private conversation, you can call this event an **intrusion**. *I hope you don't mind this intrusion, Jon.* N-VAR

2 An **intrusion** is something that disturbs your mood or your life in an unwelcome way. *...intrusion into private grief... I felt it was a grotesque intrusion into our lives.* N-VAR: oft N into n

intrusive /ɪntruːsɪv/. Something that is **intrusive** disturbs your mood or your life in an unwelcome way. *The cameras were not an intrusive presence... Staff are courteous but never intrusive.* ◆◇◇◇◇ ADJ-GRADED

intuit /ɪntjuːɪt, AM -tuː-/ **intuits, intuiting, intuited.** If you **intuit** something, you guess what it is on the basis of your intuition or feelings, rather than on the basis of knowledge; a formal word. *They would confidently intuit your very thoughts... He was probably right to intuit that it was universal.* VERB; V n; V that

intuition /ɪntjuɪʃᵊn, AM -tu-/ **intuitions.** Your **intuition** or your **intuitions** are unexplained feelings you have that something is true even when you have no evidence or proof of it. *Her intuition was telling her that something was wrong... You can't make a case on your intuitions, Phil.* ◆◇◇◇◇ N-VAR =instinct

intuitive /ɪntjuːətɪv, AM -tuː-/. If you have an **intuitive** idea or feeling about something, you feel that it is true although you have no evidence or proof of it. *A positive pregnancy test soon confirmed her intuitive feelings.* ◆◇◇◇◇ ADJ-GRADED: usu ADJ n =instinctive
♦ **intuitively** *He seemed to know intuitively that I must be missing my mother... Some of the ideas are very intriguing and sound intuitively plausible.* ADV-GRADED: ADV with v, ADV adj

Inuit /ɪnjuɪt/ **Inuits;** the form **Inuit** can also be used for the plural. The **Inuit** are a race of people descended from the original inhabitants of Eastern Canada and Greenland. N-COUNT

inundate /ɪnʌndeɪt/ **inundates, inundating, inundated** ◆◇◇◇◇

1 If you say that you **are inundated** with things such as letters, demands, or requests, you are emphasizing that you receive so many of them that you cannot deal with them all. *Her office was inundated with requests for tickets... They have inundated me with fan letters.* VERB PRAGMATICS =swamp; be V-ed with n; V n with n; Also V n

2 If an area of land **is inundated**, it becomes covered with water. *Their neighborhood is being inundated by the rising waters of the Colorado River.* VB: usu passive =flood; be V-ed

inure /ɪnjʊəʳ/ **inures, inuring, inured.** If an experience **inures** you to something unpleasant, it makes you accustomed to it so that it no longer affects you; a formal word. *Pictures and accounts of the bombed cities had not inured the world to such sights.* VERB =accustom; V n to n
♦ **inured** *I'm already inured to the sound of the alarm.* ADJ-GRADED: v-link ADJ to n

invade /ɪnveɪd/ **invades, invading, invaded** ◆◆◇◇◇

1 To **invade** a country means to enter it by force with an army. *In autumn 1944 the allies invaded the Italian mainland at Anzio and Salerno... When the Romans and later the Normans came to Britain they did so as invading armies.* VERB; V n; V-ing; Also V

2 If you say that people or animals **invade** a place, you mean that they enter it in large numbers, often in a way that is unpleasant or difficult to deal with. *People invaded the streets in victory processions almost throughout the day... Every so often the kitchen would be invaded by ants.* VERB V n

3 ● to **invade** someone's **privacy**: see **privacy**.

invader /ɪnveɪdəʳ/ **invaders** ◆◇◇◇◇

1 **Invaders** are soldiers who are invading a country. *The invaders were only finally crushed when troops overcame them at Glenshiel in June 1719.* N-COUNT: usu pl

2 You can refer to a country or army that has invaded or is about to invade another country as an **invader**. *...action against a foreign invader.* N-COUNT: usu sing

invalid, invalids. The noun is pronounced /ɪnvəlɪd/. The adjective is pronounced /ɪnvælɪd/. ◆◇◇◇◇

1 An **invalid** is someone who needs to be cared for because they have an illness or disability. *I hate being treated as an invalid.* N-COUNT

2 If an action, procedure, or document is **invalid**, it cannot be accepted, because it breaks the law or some official rule. *The trial was stopped and the results declared invalid... We cannot accept liability if you are refused entry because of invalid documents.* ADJ ♦ **invalidity** /ɪnvəlɪdɪti/ *...the invalidity of the marriage ceremony.* N-UNCOUNT

3 An **invalid** argument or conclusion is wrong because it is based on a mistake. *We think that those arguments are rendered invalid by the hard facts on the ground.* ADJ

invalidate /ɪnvælɪdeɪt/ **invalidates, invalidating, invalidated**

1 To **invalidate** something such as an argument, conclusion, or result means to prove that it is wrong or cause it to be wrong. *Any form of physical activity will invalidate the results... Some of the other criticisms were invalidated years ago.* VERB V n

2 If something **invalidates** something such as a law, contract, or election, it causes it to be considered illegal. *An official decree invalidated the vote in the capital... A contract signed now might be invalidated at some future date.* VERB V n

invalidity /ɪnvəlɪdɪti/. **Invalidity** is the state of being an invalid. *The contributions employees pay give cover against sickness, including chronic invalidity... I live on an invalidity pension.* N-UNCOUNT

invaluable /ɪnvæljəbəl/. If you describe something as **invaluable**, you mean that it is extremely useful. *I was able to gain invaluable experience over that year... The research should prove invaluable in the study of linguistics... Their advice was invaluable to me at that stage of my work.* ◆◇◇◇◇ ADJ: oft ADJ in n/-ing, ADJ to n

invariable /ɪnveəriəbəl/. You use **invariable** to describe something that never changes. *It was his invariable custom to have one whisky before his supper.* ADJ: usu ADJ n =habitual

invariably /ɪnveəriəbli/. If something **invariably** happens or is **invariably** true, it always happens or is always true. *They almost invariably get it wrong... Their teamwork was invariably good... Invariably, he keeps the refrigerator well stocked... The Arc is invariably a fast-run race.* ◆◆◇◇◇ ADV: ADV with v, ADV with cl/group

invasion /ɪnveɪʒən/ **invasions** ◆◆◆◇◇

1 If there is an **invasion** of a country, a foreign army enters it by force. *...seven years after the Roman invasion of Britain... He was commander in chief during the invasion of Panama.* N-VAR: usu with supp, oft adj N, N of n

2 If you refer to the arrival of a large number of people or things as an **invasion**, you are emphasizing that they are unpleasant or difficult to deal with. *...this year's annual invasion of flies, wasps and ants... Seaside resorts such as Blackpool and Brighton are preparing for a tourist invasion.* N-VAR: oft N of n

3 If you describe an action as an **invasion**, you disapprove of it because it affects someone or something in a way that is not wanted. *Is reading a child's diary always a gross invasion of privacy? ...the first skirmish in the invasion of the British Parliament by Brussels.* N-VAR: usu N of n PRAGMATICS

invasive /ɪnveɪsɪv/ ◆◇◇◇◇

1 You use **invasive** to describe something undesirable which spreads very quickly and which is very difficult to stop from spreading. *They found invasive cancer during a routine examination.* ADJ-GRADED: usu ADJ n

2 **Invasive** medical procedures are procedures such as surgery or internal examinations which involve handling a patient's body in a way which might be stressful or upsetting. *Many people find the idea of any kind of invasive surgery unbearable.* ADJ-GRADED: usu ADJ n

invective /ɪnvektɪv/. **Invective** is rude and unpleasant things that people shout at people they hate or are angry with; a formal word. *A woman had hurled racist invective at the family... Crowley maintained a stream of invective and abuse against Waite.* N-UNCOUNT: usu with supp =abuse

inveigh /ɪnveɪ/ **inveighs, inveighing, inveighed.** If you **inveigh against** something, you criticize it strongly; a formal word. *A lot of his writings inveigh against luxury and riches.* VERB V against n

inveigle /ɪnveɪgəl/ **inveigles, inveigling, inveigled.** If you **inveigle** someone **into** doing something, you cleverly persuade them to do it when they do not really want to; a formal word. *She inveigles Paco into a plot to swindle Tania out of her savings.* VERB =cajole V n into n/-ing

invent /ɪnvent/ **invents, inventing, invented** ◆◆◇◇◇

1 If you **invent** something such as a machine or process, you are the first person to think of it or make it. *He invented the first electric clock... Writing had not been invented as yet.* VERB V n

2 If you **invent** a story or excuse, you try to make other people believe that it is true when in fact it is not. *I stood still, trying to invent a plausible excuse.* VERB V n

invention /ɪnvenʃən/ **inventions** ◆◆◇◇◇

1 An **invention** is a machine, device, or system that has been invented by someone. *It's been a tricky business marketing his new invention... The spinning wheel was a Chinese invention.* N-COUNT

2 **Invention** is the act of inventing something that has never been made or used before. *More than eight million books were printed within fifty years after the invention of the printing press. ...the invention of the telephone.* N-UNCOUNT: oft N of n

3 If you refer to someone's account of something as an **invention**, you think that it is untrue and that they have made it up. *In these and several other respects, there are many inventions and exaggerations... The story was certainly a favourite one, but it was undoubtedly pure invention.* N-VAR =fabrication

4 **Invention** is the ability to invent things or to have clever and original ideas. *Perhaps, with such powers of invention and mathematical ability, he will be offered a job in computers.* N-UNCOUNT =creativity

inventive /ɪnventɪv/. An **inventive** person is good at inventing things or has clever and original ideas. *...Stroman's ceaselessly inventive choreography... It inspired me to be more inventive with my own cooking.* ◆◇◇◇◇ ADJ-GRADED =creative ♦ **inventiveness** *He has surprised us before with his inventiveness.* N-UNCOUNT

inventor /ɪnventəʳ/ **inventors.** An **inventor** is a person who has invented something, or whose job is to invent things. *...Alexander Graham Bell, the inventor of the telephone.* ◆◇◇◇◇ N-COUNT

inventory /ɪnvəntri, AM -tɔːri/ **inventories** ◆◆◇◇◇

1 An **inventory** is a written list of all the objects in a particular place. *Before starting, he made an inventory of everything that was to stay.* N-COUNT

2 In American English, an **inventory** is a supply or stock of something. *...one inventory of twelve sails for each yacht.* N-VAR

inverse /ɪnvɜːʳs/

1 If there is an **inverse** relationship between two things, one of them becomes larger as the other becomes smaller; a technical use. *The tension grew in inverse proportion to the distance from their final destination.* ADJ: usu ADJ n ≠direct ♦ **inversely** *The size of the nebula at this stage is inversely proportional to its mass.* ADV: ADV adj/-ed, ADV after v

2 **The inverse** of something is its exact opposite; a formal use. *There is no sign that you bothered to consider the inverse of your logic.* N-SING: the N, usu N of n ► Also an adjective. *The hologram can be flipped to show the inverse image.* ADJ: ADJ n

inversion /ɪnvɜːʳʃən, -ʒən/ **inversions.** When there is an **inversion** of something, it is changed N-VAR: usu N of n into its opposite; a formal word. *It was the most scandalous inversion of the truth I have ever encountered. ...a strange inversion of priorities.*

invert /ɪnvɜːʳt/ **inverts, inverting, inverted** ◆◇◇◇◇

1 If you **invert** something, you turn it upside down or back to front; a formal use. *Invert the cake onto a cooling rack. ...a black inverted triangle.* VERB V n V-ed

2 If you **invert** something, you change it to its opposite; a formal use. *They may be hoping to invert the presumption that a defendant is innocent until proved guilty. ...a telling illustration of inverted moral values.* VERB V n V-ed

invertebrate /ɪnvɜːʳtɪbrət/ **invertebrates.** An **invertebrate** is a creature that does not have a spine, for example an insect, a worm, or an octopus; a technical term in biology. ► Also an adjective. *...invertebrate creatures.* N-COUNT ADJ

inverted commas

1 In British English, **inverted commas** are punctuation marks that are used in writing to show where speech or a quotation begins and ends. They are usually written or printed as (' ') or (" "). Inverted commas are also sometimes used round the titles of books, plays, or songs, or round a word or phrase that is being discussed. N-PLURAL =quotation marks

2 If you say **in inverted commas** after a word or phrase, you are indicating that you think the word or phrase is inaccurate or unacceptable in some way, or that you are quoting someone else; used in British English. *They're asked to make objective, in inverted commas, evaluations of these statements.* PHRASE PRAGMATICS

invest /ɪnvest/ **invests, investing, invested** ◆◆◆◇◇

1 If you **invest** in something, or if you **invest** a sum of money, you use your money in a way that you hope will increase its value, for example by paying it into a bank, or buying shares or property. *They intend to invest directly in shares... He invested all our profits in gold shares... When people buy houses they're investing a lot of money.* VERB V in n V n in n V n

2 When a government or organization **invests** in something, it gives or lends money for a purpose that it considers useful or profitable. *...the British government's failure to invest in an integrated transport system. ...the European Investment Bank, which has invested £100 million in Canary Wharf... Why does Japan invest, on average, twice as much capital per worker per year than the United States?* VERB V in n V n in n V n Also V

3 If you **invest in** something useful, you buy it, because it will help you to do something more efficiently or more cheaply. *The company has invested a six-figure sum in an electronic order-control system which is used to keep shops stocked... The easiest way to make ice cream yourself is to invest in an ice cream machine.* VERB V n in n V in n

4 If you **invest** time or energy in something, you spend a lot of time or energy on something that you consider to be useful or likely to be successful. *I would rather invest time in Rebecca than in the kitchen.* VERB V n in n

5 If you say that someone or something **is invested with** a particular quality, you mean that they seem to have that quality; a formal use. *The buildings are invested with a nation's history... A tsar was a living icon, invested with deep historical and religious significance.* VB: usu passive be V-ed with n V-ed

6 To **invest** someone **with** rights or responsibilities means to give them those rights or responsibilities legally or officially; a formal use. *The constitution had invested him with certain powers and he was determined to deploy them.* VERB V n with n

investigate /ɪnvestɪgeɪt/ **investigates, investigating, investigated.** If someone, especially an official, **investigates** an event, situation, or allegation, they try to find out what happened or what is the truth. *Gas officials are investigating the cause of an explosion which badly damaged a house in Hampshire... The two officers were being investigated by the director of public prosecutions... Police are still investigating how the accident happened.* ♦ **investigation** /ɪnvestɪgeɪʃən/ **investigations** *He ordered an investigation into the affair... He has been notified by magistrates that he is under investigation for corruption.* ◆◆◆◆◇ VERB =look into V n V wh Also V N-VAR: oft N into n

investigative /ɪnvestɪgətɪv, AM -geɪt-/. **Investigative** work, especially journalism, involves investigating things. *The paper has earned respect for its investigative journalism. ...an investigative reporter.* ◆◇◇◇◇ ADJ: usu ADJ n

investigator /ɪnvestɪgeɪtəʳ/ **investigators.** An **investigator** is someone who carries out investigations, especially as part of their job. ◆◆◇◇◇ N-COUNT

investigatory /ɪnvestɪgətri, AM -tɔːri/. **Investigatory** means the same as **investigative**. *At no time did I make an attempt to impede any investigatory effort.* ADJ: ADJ n

investiture /ɪnvestɪtʃəʳ/ **investitures.** An **investiture** is a ceremony in which someone is given an official title. *...Edward VIII's investiture as Prince of Wales in 1911.* N-COUNT

investment /ɪnvesmənt/ **investments** ◆◆◆◆◇

1 **Investment** is the activity of investing money. *He said the government must introduce tax incentives to encourage investment... One of the most important changes concerns the investment of pension contributions. ...investment bankers.* N-UNCOUNT: usu with supp, oft N in n

2 An **investment** is an amount of money that you invest, or the thing that you invest it in. *...an investment of twenty-eight million pounds... You'll be able to earn an average rate of return of 8% on your investments. ...people's desire to buy a house as an investment... Total foreign investment in America still constitutes only about 5% of U.S. assets.* N-VAR: usu with supp

3 If you describe something you buy as an **investment**, you mean that it will be useful, especially because it will help you to do a task more cheaply or efficiently. *When selecting boots, fine, quality leather will be a wise investment... A small-screen portable TV can be a good investment.* N-COUNT: usu sing, usu adj N

4 **Investment** of time or effort is the spending of time or effort on something in order to make it a success. *I worry about this big investment of time and money and effort not working.* N-UNCOUNT: usu N of n

investor /ɪnvestəʳ/ **investors.** An **investor** is a person or organization that buys shares or pays money into a bank in order to receive a profit. *The main investor in the project is the French bank Credit National.* ◆◆◆◆◇ N-COUNT

inveterate /ɪnvetərət/. If you describe someone as, for example, an **inveterate** liar or smoker, you mean that they have lied or smoked for a long time and are not likely to stop doing it. *Anderson has a reputation as an inveterate gambler. ...the inveterate laziness of these boys.* ADJ: ADJ n

invidious /ɪnvɪdiəs/

1 If you describe a task or job as **invidious**, you mean that it is unpleasant because it is likely to make you unpopular. *How did you manage to get yourself into this invidious position of having to reprimand others for your own faults?* ADJ-GRADED

2 An **invidious** comparison or choice between two things is an unfair one because the two things are not comparable or because there is only one thing that you can choose. *Police officers fear invidious comparisons... It is invidious to make a selection.* ADJ: oft it v-link ADJ to-inf =impossible

invigilate /ɪnvɪdʒɪleɪt/ **invigilates, invigilating, invigilated.** The person who **invigilates** an examination supervises the people who are taking it in order to ensure that it starts and finishes at the correct time, and that there is no cheating; used mainly in British English. *I've taught sixth formers and invigilated exams.* ♦ **invigilator, invigilators** *...an exam invigilator.* VERB V n N-COUNT

invigorate /ɪnvɪgəreɪt/ **invigorates, invigorating, invigorated**

1 If something **invigorates** you, it makes you feel refreshed and wide-awake. *Take a deep breath in to invigorate you... The shampoo contains lavender oil to invigorate the scalp.* ♦ **invigorated** *She seemed invigorated, full of life and energy.* VERB V n ADJ-GRADED: usu v-link ADJ

2 To **invigorate** a situation or a process means to make it more efficient or more effective. *...the promise that they would invigorate the economy...* VERB =stimulate V n

The tactic could well help invigorate a struggling campaign.

invigorating /ɪnvɪgəreɪtɪŋ/. If you describe something as **invigorating**, you mean that it makes you feel more energetic. *...the bright Finnish sun and invigorating northern air.* ◆◇◇◇◇ ADJ-GRADED

invincible /ɪnvɪnsɪbəl/ ◆◇◇◇◇

1 If you describe an army or sports team as **invincible**, you believe that they cannot be defeated. *When Sotomayor is on form he is virtually invincible.* ♦ **invincibility** /ɪnvɪnsɪbɪlɪti/ *...symbols of the invincibility of the Roman army.* ADJ-GRADED =unbeatable; N-UNCOUNT

2 If someone has an **invincible** belief or attitude, it cannot be changed. *He also had an invincible faith in the medicinal virtues of garlic.* ADJ: usu ADJ n =unshakable

inviolable /ɪnvaɪələbəl/

1 If a law or principle is **inviolable**, you must not break it; a formal use. *The game had a single inviolable rule: obstacles were to be overcome, not circumvented.* ADJ-GRADED

2 If a country say its borders are **inviolable**, it means they must not be changed or crossed without permission; a formal use. *Yesterday's resolution says the present Polish border is 'inviolable'.* ♦ **inviolability** /ɪnvaɪələbɪlɪti/ *Parliament has passed a motion recognising the inviolability of the country's current border with Poland.* ADJ; N-UNCOUNT

inviolate /ɪnvaɪələt/. If something is **inviolate**, it has not been or cannot be harmed or affected by anything; a formal word. *We believed our love was inviolate. ...their retreat into an inviolate private domain.* ADJ

invisible /ɪnvɪzɪbəl/ **invisibles** ◆◆◇◇◇

1 If you describe something as **invisible**, you mean that it cannot be seen, for example because it is transparent, hidden, or very small. *The lines were so finely etched as to be invisible from a distance... The belt is invisible even under the thinnest garments.* ♦ **invisibly** /ɪnvɪzɪbli/ *A thin coil of smoke rose almost invisibly into the sharp, bright sky.* ADJ-GRADED: usu v-link ADJ ≠visible; ADV: ADV with v

2 You can use **invisible** when you are talking about something that cannot be seen but has a definite effect. In this sense, **invisible** is often used before a noun which refers to something that can usually be seen. *All the time you are in doubt about the cause of your illness, you are fighting against an invisible enemy... Her father's face had suddenly tightened as though he was being strangled by invisible hands.* ♦ **invisibly** *...the tradition that invisibly shapes things in the present.* ADJ: ADJ n; ADV: ADV with v

3 If you say that you feel **invisible**, you are complaining that you are being ignored by other people. If you say that a particular problem or situation is **invisible**, you are complaining that it is not being considered or dealt with. *It was strange, how invisible a clerk could feel... The problems of the poor are largely invisible.* ♦ **invisibility** /ɪnvɪzɪbɪlɪti/ *She takes up the issue of the invisibility of women and women's concerns in society.* ADJ-GRADED; N-UNCOUNT

4 In stories, **invisible** people or things have a magic quality which makes people unable to see them. *...The Invisible Man.* ADJ

5 **Invisible** earnings are the money that a country makes as a result of services such as banking and tourism, rather than by producing goods; a technical use in economics. *The revenue from tourism is the biggest single item in the country's invisible earnings... The invisible trade surplus was £900 million lower than reported.* ADJ: ADJ n ≠visible

6 **Invisibles** are services such as banking and tourism, which provide a country's invisible earnings; used mainly in British English. N-PLURAL

invitation /ɪnvɪteɪʃən/ **invitations** ◆◆◆◇◇

1 An **invitation** is a written or spoken request to come to an event such as a party, a meal, or a meeting. *...an invitation to lunch... The Syrians have not yet accepted an invitation to attend... He's understood to be there at the personal invitation of President Daniel Arap Moi.* N-COUNT: oft N to-inf, N *to* n

2 An **invitation** is the card or paper on which an invitation is written or printed. *Hundreds of invitations are being sent out this week. ...gold embossed invitation cards.* N-COUNT =invite

3 If you believe that someone's action is likely to have a particular result, especially a bad one, you can refer to the action as an **invitation to** that result. *...a war that most liberal Democrats regarded as an invitation to disaster... Don't leave your shopping on the back seat of your car – it's an open invitation to a thief.* N-SING: N *to* n

invite, invites, inviting, invited. The verb is pronounced /ɪnvaɪt/. The noun is pronounced /ɪnvaɪt/. ◆◆◆◆◇

1 If you **invite** someone to something such as a party or a meal, you ask them to come to it. *She invited him to her 26th birthday party in New Jersey... I invited her in for a coffee... Neighbours have invited us out, given us clothes, and taken us on excursions... Barron invited her to accompany him to the races... Sometimes it seems right to invite an entire class of children so no one will feel left out... I haven't been invited. ...an invited audience of children from inner-city schools.* VERB V n prep/adv; V n to-inf; V n; V-ed

2 If you **are invited** to do something, you are formally asked or given permission to do it. *At a future date, managers will be invited to apply for a management buy-out... The person concerned would be shown the evidence in private and invited to stand down... If a new leader emerged, it would then be for the Queen to invite him to form a government... The Department is inviting applications from groups within the Borough.* VERB *be* V-ed to-inf; V n to-inf; V n

3 If something you say or do **invites** trouble or criticism, it makes trouble or criticism more likely. *I realise that an Englishman who generalises about Ireland invites trouble... Their refusal to compromise will inevitably invite more criticism from the UN.* VERB V n

4 An **invite** is an invitation to something such as a party or a meal; an informal use. *They haven't got an invite to the wedding.* N-COUNT

inviting /ɪnvaɪtɪŋ/. If you say that something is **inviting**, you mean that it has good qualities that attract you or make you want to experience it. *The February air was soft, cool, and inviting... There is an inviting restaurant with an outdoor terrace. ...an inviting smile.* ♦ **invitingly** *The waters of the tropics are invitingly clear.* • See also **invite**. ◆◇◇◇◇ ADJ-GRADED; ADV-GRADED: ADV adj, ADV with v

in vitro /ɪn viːtroʊ/. **In vitro** fertilization is a method of helping a woman to conceive by removing an egg from one of her ovaries and fertilizing it outside her body, then replacing the fertilized egg in her uterus. ADJ: ADJ n

invocation /ɪnvəkeɪʃən/ **invocations.** An **invocation** is an appeal to a god for help or forgiveness; a formal word. *...an invocation to the rising sun. ...an invocation for divine guidance.* N-VAR: oft N prep

invoice /ɪnvɔɪs/ **invoices, invoicing, invoiced** ◆◇◇◇◇

1 An **invoice** is a document that lists goods that have been supplied or services that have been done, and says how much money you owe for them. *We will then send you an invoice for the total course fees... His £700 invoice was settled immediately in cash.* N-COUNT: oft N *for* n =bill

2 If you **invoice** someone, you send them a bill for goods or services you have provided them with. *The agency invoices the client who then pays the full amount to the agency.* VERB =bill V n

invoke /ɪnvoʊk/ **invokes, invoking, invoked** ◆◇◇◇◇

1 If you **invoke** a law, you state that you are taking a particular action because that law allows or obliges you to. *The judge invoked an international law that protects refugees.* VERB V n

2 If you **invoke** something such as a principle, a saying, or a famous person, you refer to them in order to support your argument. *He invoked memories of Britain's near-disastrous disarmament in the 1930s to argue that the project could not be postponed... In political matters George Washington went out of his way to avoid invoking the authority of Christ.* VERB V n

3 If something such as a piece of music **invokes** a feeling or an image, it causes someone to have the VERB =evoke

feeling or to see the image. Many people consider this use to be incorrect. *'Appalachian Spring' by Aaron Copland invoked the atmosphere of the wide open spaces of the prairies.* V n

4 If someone **invokes** a god, they appeal to the god for help or forgiveness; a literary use. *The great magicians of old always invoked their gods with sacrifice.* VERB =call upon V n

involuntary /ɪnvɒləntri, AM -teri/ ◆◇◇◇◇

1 If you make an **involuntary** movement or exclamation, you make it suddenly and without intending to because you are unable to control yourself. *Another surge of pain in my ankle caused me to give an involuntary shudder.* ♦ **involuntarily** /ɪnvɒləntrəli, AM -teərɪli/ *His left eyelid twitched involuntarily.* ADJ; ADV: ADV with v

2 You use **involuntary** to describe an action or situation which is forced on someone. *...insurance policies that cover death, accident, sickness and involuntary unemployment... Involuntary repatriation of Haitians began this week.* ADJ =forced

involve /ɪnvɒlv/ **involves, involving, involved** ◆◆◆◆◇

1 If a situation or activity **involves** something, that thing is a necessary part or consequence of it. *Running a kitchen involves a great deal of discipline and speed... Nicky's job as a public relations director involves spending quite a lot of time with other people.* VERB =entail V n/-ing

2 If a situation or activity **involves** someone, they are taking part in it. *If there was a cover-up, it involved people at the very highest levels of government. ...a riot involving a hundred inmates... Detectives launched an operation involving Interpol and Nigerian police.* VERB V n

3 If you say that someone **involves** themselves **in** something, you mean that they take part in it, often in a way that is unnecessary or unwanted. *I seem to have involved myself in something I don't understand.* VERB V pron-refl *in* n

4 If you **involve** someone else **in** something, you get them to take part in it. *Noel and I do everything together, he involves me in everything... Before too long he started involving me in the more confidential aspects of the job.* VERB V n *in* n/-ing

5 If one thing **involves** you **in** another thing, especially something unpleasant or inconvenient, the first thing causes you to do or deal with the second. *A late booking may involve you in extra cost... This involved me in a round trip of over 400 miles.* VERB V n *in* n

involved /ɪnvɒlvd/ ◆◆◆◆◇

1 If you are **involved** in a situation or activity, you are taking part in it or have a strong connection with it. *If she were involved in business, she would make a strong chief executive... She became involved with political causes after the Chernobyl nuclear disaster... The Farmers' Club is an organisation for people involved in agriculture.* ADJ-GRADED: v-link ADJ, usu ADJ *in/with* n

2 If you are **involved** in something, you give a lot of time, effort, or attention to it. *The family were deeply involved in Jewish culture. ...women who are so involved in their careers that they have no time for friendship.* ADJ-GRADED: v-link ADJ, usu ADJ *in* n

3 The things **involved** in something such as a job or system are the necessary parts or consequences of it. *We believe the time and hard work involved in completing such an assignment are worthwhile... He cannot reveal how much money is involved in the scheme... Let's take a look at some of the figures involved.* ADJ: v-link ADJ, oft ADJ *in* n

4 If a situation or activity is **involved**, it has a lot of different parts or aspects, often making it difficult to understand, explain, or do. *The operations can be quite involved, requiring many procedures in order to restructure the anatomy.* ADJ-GRADED =complicated, complex

5 If one person is **involved** with another, especially someone they are not married to, they are having a sexual, loving, or intimate relationship. *During a visit to Kenya in 1928 he became romantically involved with a married woman.* ADJ-GRADED: oft v-link ADJ *with* n

involvement /ɪnvɒlvmənt/ **involvements** ◆◆◆◇◇

1 Your **involvement** in something is the fact that you are taking part in it. *You have no proof of my involvement in anything... She disliked his involvement with the group and disliked his friends.* N-UNCOUNT: oft N *in/with* n =participation

2 **Involvement** is the enthusiasm that you feel when you care deeply about something. *Ben has always felt a deep involvement with animals.* N-UNCOUNT =attachment

3 An **involvement** is a close relationship between two people, especially if they are not married to each other. *They were very good friends but there was no romantic involvement... Mahler was also known for his passionate involvements outside marriage.* N-VAR =attachment

invulnerable /ɪnvʌlnərəbᵊl/. If someone or something is **invulnerable**, they cannot be harmed or damaged. *Many daughters mistakenly assume that their mothers are invulnerable and all-powerful. ...a system that would make the U.S. invulnerable to nuclear attack.* ♦ **invulnerability** /ɪnvʌlnərəbɪlɪti/ *They have a sense of invulnerability to disease.* ADJ-GRADED: oft ADJ *to* n ≠vulnerable; N-UNCOUNT

inward /ɪnwəʳd/ ◆◇◇◇◇

1 Your **inward** thoughts or feelings are the ones that you do not express or show to other people. *I sighed with inward relief. ...a glow of inward satisfaction.* ♦ **inwardly** *Chantal smiled inwardly... Sara, while remaining outwardly amiable toward all concerned, was inwardly furious.* ADJ: ADJ n =inner; ADV: ADV with v, ADV adj

2 An **inward** movement is one towards the inside or centre of something. *...a sharp, inward breath like a gasp... The athlete takes off from one leg from an inward twist.* ADJ: ADJ n

3 See also **inwards**.

inward-looking. If you describe a people or society as **inward-looking**, you mean that they are more interested in themselves than in other people or societies; used showing disapproval. *...an insular and inward-looking community that doesn't like to be told what to think by outsiders.* ADJ-GRADED PRAGMATICS

inwards /ɪnwəʳdz/; the form **inward** is also used. In American English, **inward** is more usual. If something moves or faces **inwards**, it moves or faces towards the inside or centre of something. *She pressed back against the door until it swung inwards... Keeping your heels on the ground, turn your feet inwards.* ◆◇◇◇◇ ADV: ADV after v ≠outwards

in-your-face; also spelled **in-yer-face**. If you say that someone has an **in-your-face** attitude, you mean that they seem determined to behave in a way that is unconventional or slightly shocking, and that they do not care what people think of them; used in very informal English. *...the in-your-face defiance of groups such as ACTP and Queer Nation... More precisely, it's in-your-face feminism, and it's meant to shock.* ADJ-GRADED: usu ADJ n

iodine /aɪədiːn, AM -daɪn/. **Iodine** is a dark-coloured substance that is used in medicine and photography. ◆◇◇◇◇ N-UNCOUNT

ion /aɪən/ **ions.** **Ions** are electrically charged atoms; a technical term in science. ◆◇◇◇◇ N-COUNT: usu pl

-ion. See **-ation**.

ionizer /aɪənaɪzəʳ/ **ionizers;** also spelled **ioniser** in British English. An **ionizer** is a device which is meant to make the air in a room more healthy by removing positive ions. N-COUNT

iota /aɪoʊtə/.

1 If you say that there is not **an iota** or not **one iota** of something, you are emphasizing that there is not even a very small amount of it. *He's never before shown an iota of interest in any kind of social work that I know of.* QUANT: with brd-neg, QUANT *of* n-uncount PRAGMATICS =jot

2 You can use **an iota** or **one iota** to emphasize a negative statement. **Not an iota** or **not one iota** means not even to a small extent or degree. *Our credit standards haven't changed one iota.* PHRASE: with brd-neg, PHR after v PRAGMATICS =a jot

IOU /aɪ oʊ juː/ **IOUs.** An **IOU** is a written promise that you will pay back some money that you have borrowed. **IOU** is an abbreviation for 'I owe you'. N-COUNT

IQ /aɪ kjuː/ **IQs.** Your **IQ** is your level of intelligence, as indicated by a special test that you do. **IQ** is an abbreviation for 'intelligence quotient'. *He possesses an IQ of only 77... His IQ is above average. ...IQ tests.* ◆◇◇◇◇ N-VAR: usu with supp

ir-. Usually pronounced /ɪr-/ before an unstressed syllable, and /ɪr-/ before a stressed syllable. **Ir-** is added to words that begin with the letter 'r' to form words with the opposite meaning. *His behaviour was becoming increasingly irrational. ...its mixture of satirical wit, irreverence and spontaneity.* PREFIX

Iranian /ɪreɪniən/ **Iranians** ◆◆◆◆◇
1 **Iranian** means belonging or relating to Iran, or to its people or culture. *...an Iranian writer in her mid-forties.* ADJ
2 An **Iranian** is an Iranian citizen, or a person of Iranian origin. N-COUNT

Iraqi /ɪrɑːkiː, ɪrækiː/ **Iraqis** ◆◆◆◆◇
1 **Iraqi** means belonging or relating to Iraq, or to its people or culture. *...the Iraqi ambassador to the US.* ADJ
2 An **Iraqi** is an Iraqi citizen, or a person of Iraqi origin. N-COUNT

irascible /ɪræsɪbᵊl/. If you describe someone as **irascible**, you mean that they become angry very easily; used in written English. *He had an irascible temper.* ADJ-GRADED =quick-tempered

irate /aɪreɪt/. If someone is **irate**, they are very angry about something. *The owner was so irate he almost threw me out of the place... She then wrote an extremely irate letter to the New Statesman about me.* ADJ-GRADED =incensed, furious

ire /aɪəʳ/. **Ire** is anger; a formal word. *Their ire was directed mainly at Warrington and Wigan.* N-UNCOUNT =wrath

iridescent /ɪrɪdesᵊnt/. Something that is **iridescent** has many bright colours that seem to keep changing; a literary word. *...iridescent bubbles.* ADJ

iris /aɪərɪs/ **irises** ◆◇◇◇◇
1 The **iris** is the round coloured part of a person's eye. N-COUNT
2 An **iris** is a tall plant with long leaves and large purple, yellow, or white flowers. N-COUNT

Irish /aɪərɪʃ/ ◆◆◆◆◇
1 **Irish** means belonging or relating to Ireland, or to its people, language, or culture. **Irish** sometimes refers to the whole of Ireland, and sometimes only to the Republic of Ireland. *...the Prime Minister of the Irish Republic. ...traditional Irish music.* ADJ
2 The **Irish** are the people of Ireland, or of the Republic of Ireland. *The Irish educate proportionately more young people to university level than the British.* N-PLURAL: usu *the* N
3 **Irish** is a Celtic language spoken by people who live in Ireland, especially in the Republic of Ireland. N-UNCOUNT

Irishman /aɪərɪʃmən/ **Irishmen.** An **Irishman** is a man who is an Irish citizen or is of Irish origin. ◆◇◇◇◇ N-COUNT

Irishwoman /aɪərɪʃwʊmən/ **Irishwomen.** An **Irishwoman** is a woman who is an Irish citizen or is of Irish origin. ◆◇◇◇◇ N-COUNT

irk /ɜːʳk/ **irks, irking, irked.** If something **irks** you, it irritates or annoys you; a formal word. *The rehearsal process also irked him increasingly... She was irked by their behavior... I must admit it irks me to see this guy get all this free publicity... It irks them that some people have more of a chance than others for their voices to be heard.* VERB =infuriate V n *it* V n to-inf *it* V n that
♦ **irked** *Claire had seemed a little irked when he left.* ADJ-GRADED: v-link ADJ

irksome /ɜːʳksəm/. If something is **irksome**, it irritates or annoys you; a formal word. *...the irksome regulations.* ADJ-GRADED =infuriating

iron /aɪəʳn/ **irons, ironing, ironed** ◆◆◆◇◇
1 **Iron** is an element which usually takes the form of a hard, dark-grey metal. It is used to make steel, and also forms part of many tools, buildings, and vehicles. Very small amounts of iron occur in your blood and in food. *The huge, iron gate was locked. ...the highest grade iron ore deposits in the world... Some would call these odd pieces of iron and wood 'antiques'... Snails, like most things, need a small quantity of iron... He was a tall, lanky man with iron-grey hair.* ● See also **cast-iron, pig iron**. N-UNCOUNT: oft N n
2 An **iron** is an electrical device with a flat metal base. You heat it until the base is hot, then rub it over clothes to remove creases. N-COUNT
3 If you **iron** clothes, you remove the creases from them using an iron. *She used to iron his shirts... Don't you think there's something nice about a freshly ironed shirt?* ♦ **ironing** *I managed to get all the ironing done this morning.* VERB =press V n V-ed N-UNCOUNT
4 You can use **iron** to describe the character or behaviour of someone who is very firm in their decisions and actions, or who can control their feelings well. *...a man of icy nerve and iron will... She delighted in the nickname, the 'iron lady'.* ADJ: ADJ n
5 **Iron** is used in expressions such as **an iron hand** and **iron discipline** to describe strong, harsh, or unfair methods of control which do not allow people much freedom. *He died in 1985 after ruling Albania with an iron fist for 40 years. ...a people living permanently in the iron grip of poverty.* ADJ: ADJ n
6 If someone has a lot of **irons in the fire**, they are involved in several different activities or have several different plans. *Too many irons in the fire can sap your energy and prevent you from seeing which path to take.* PHRASES
7 If someone **pumps iron**, they exercise by lifting weights using special machines; an informal expression. V inflects

iron out. If you **iron out** difficulties, you resolve them and bring them to an end. *'It was in the beginning, when we were still ironing out problems,' a company spokesman said... The various groups had now managed to iron out their differences.* PHRASAL VERB =smooth out V P n (not pron) Also V n P

Iron Age. The **Iron Age** was a period of time which began when people started making things from iron about three thousand years ago. *...the remains of an Iron Age fort.* N-PROPER: *the* N

ironclad /aɪəʳnklæd/; also spelled **iron-clad**. If you describe a guarantee or plan as **ironclad**, you are emphasizing that it has been carefully put together, and that you think it is absolutely certain to work or be successful. *...ironclad guarantees of safe passage... The case for testing now is ironclad.* ADJ-GRADED =copper-bottomed

Iron Curtain ◆◇◇◇◇
1 People referred to the border that separated the Soviet Union and its East European allies from the Western European countries as **the Iron Curtain**. *The collapse of the Iron Curtain had immediate impact on the lives of everyone in Germany. ...when he travelled behind the Iron Curtain in the 1970s.* N-PROPER: *the* N
2 People used to refer to the Soviet Union and its East European allies as the **Iron Curtain** countries. ADJ: ADJ n

ironic /aɪrɒnɪk/ or **ironical** /aɪrɒnɪkᵊl/ ◆◆◇◇◇
1 When you make an **ironic** remark, you say something that you do not mean, as a joke. *At the most solemn moments he will flash a mocking smile or make an ironic remark... People used to call me Mr Popularity at high school, but they were being ironic.* ADJ-GRADED
2 If you say that it is **ironic** that something should happen, you mean that it is odd or amusing because it involves a contrast. *Does he not find it ironic that the sort of people his movie celebrates hardly ever watch this kind of movie?* ADJ-GRADED: oft *it* v-link ADJ that

ironically /aɪrɒnɪkli/ ◆◆◇◇◇
1 You use **ironically** to draw attention to a situation which is odd or amusing because it involves a contrast. *Ironically, for a man who hated war, he would have made a superb war cameraman.* ADV-GRADED: ADV with cl
2 If you say something **ironically**, you do not mean it and are saying it as a joke. *Classmates at West Point had ironically dubbed him Beauty.* ADV-GRADED: ADV with v

ironing board, ironing boards. An **ironing board** is a long narrow board covered with cloth on which you iron clothes. N-COUNT

ironist /aɪrənɪst/ **ironists.** An **ironist** is a person who uses a lot of irony. *Altman, probably the master ironist of modern American film, was evidently open to persuasion.* N-COUNT

ironmonger /aɪəʳnmʌŋgəʳ/ **ironmongers**
1 In British English, an **ironmonger** is a shopkeeper who sells articles for the house and garden such as tools, nails, and pans. N-COUNT
2 In British English, an **ironmonger** or an **ironmonger's** is a shop where articles for the house N-COUNT: oft *the* N

and garden such as tools, nails, and pans are sold. The usual American term is **hardware store**.

ironmongery /aɪəˈnmʌŋgəri/. In British English, **ironmongery** is articles for the house and garden such as tools, nails, and pans which are sold in an ironmonger's shop. — N-UNCOUNT =hardware

ironwork /aɪəˈnwɜːʳk/. Iron objects or structures are referred to as **ironwork**. *...the ironwork on the doors. ...an ironwork spiral staircase.* — N-UNCOUNT

irony /aɪrəni/ **ironies** ◆◆◇◇◇

1 **Irony** is a subtle form of humour which involves saying things that you do not mean. *They find only irony in the narrator's concern... Sinclair examined the closed, clever face for any hint of irony, but found none.* — N-UNCOUNT

2 If you talk about the **irony** of a situation, you mean that it is odd or amusing because it involves a contrast. *The irony is that many officials in Washington agree in private that their policy is inconsistent... Opposition parties lost no time in stressing the irony of his return to power after being rejected by voters in November.* — N-VAR: oft N *of/in* n

irradiate /ɪreɪdieɪt/ **irradiates, irradiating, irradiated.** ◆◇◇◇◇

1 If someone or something **is irradiated**, they are exposed to a large amount of radioactivity; a technical term. *He observed that leukaemia in children was more common if the fathers had been heavily irradiated. ...the Chernobyl disaster, which irradiated large parts of Europe.* ♦ **irradiation** /ɪreɪdieɪʃᵊn/ *...the harmful effects of irradiation and pollution.* — VERB; *be* V-ed; V n; N-UNCOUNT

2 If food **is irradiated**, it is treated with radiation to kill pests and make it last longer. *It's safe to eat foods that have been irradiated to prolong their shelf life. ...the risks and benefits of irradiated food.* ♦ **irradiation** *...doubts about the safety of food irradiation.* — VB: usu passive; *be* V-ed; V-ed; N-UNCOUNT: oft n N

irrational /ɪræʃənᵊl/. If you describe someone's feelings and behaviour as **irrational**, you mean they are not based on logical reasons or clear thinking. *...an irrational fear of science.* ♦ **irrationally** *People often behave irrationally, especially when in large masses... My husband is irrationally jealous over my past loves.* ♦ **irrationality** /ɪræʃənælɪti/ *...the irrationality of his behaviour.* — ◆◇◇◇◇ ADJ-GRADED =unreasonable ≠rational; ADV-GRADED: ADV with v, ADV adj, ADV with cl; N-UNCOUNT

irreconcilable /ɪrekənsaɪləbᵊl/

1 If two things such as opinions or proposals are **irreconcilable**, they are so different from each other that it is not possible to believe or have both of them; a formal use. *...incompatibility between two irreconcilable positions... These old concepts are irreconcilable with modern life.* — ADJ: oft ADJ *with* n =incompatible

2 An **irreconcilable** disagreement or conflict is so serious that it cannot be settled; a formal use. *...an irreconcilable clash of personalities.* — ADJ

irredeemable /ɪrɪdiːməbᵊl/. If someone or something has an **irredeemable** fault, it cannot be corrected; a formal word. *He is still, in the eyes of some, an irredeemable misogynist.* ♦ **irredeemably** /ɪrɪdiːməbli/ *The applicant was irredeemably incompetent.* — ADJ =incurable; ADV: ADV adj/-ed

irreducible /ɪrɪdjuːsɪbᵊl/. **Irreducible** things cannot be made simpler or smaller; a formal word. *...the irreducible complexity of human life.* — ADJ: usu ADJ n ≠reducible

irrefutable /ɪrɪfjuːtəbᵊl/. **Irrefutable** evidence, statements, or arguments cannot be denied or shown to be incorrect; a formal word. *The pictures provide irrefutable evidence of the incident... Her logic was irrefutable.* — ADJ =indisputable

irregular /ɪregjʊləʳ/ **irregulars** ◆◆◇◇◇

1 If events or actions occur at **irregular** intervals, the periods of time between them are of different lengths. *Cars passed at irregular intervals... She was taken to hospital suffering from an irregular heartbeat... He worked irregular hours.* ♦ **irregularly** *He was eating irregularly, steadily losing weight.* ♦ **irregularity** /ɪregjʊlærɪti/ **irregularities** *...a dangerous irregularity in her heartbeat.* — ADJ-GRADED ≠regular; ADV-GRADED: ADV with v; N-VAR

2 Something that is **irregular** is not smooth or straight, or does not form a regular pattern. *The paint was drying in irregular patches... He had bad teeth, irregular and discolored.* ♦ **irregularly** *Located off-center in the irregularly shaped lake was a fountain.* ♦ **irregularity** *...treatment of abnormalities or irregularities of the teeth.* — ADJ-GRADED =uneven ≠regular; ADV-GRADED: usu ADV -ed; N-VAR

3 **Irregular** behaviour is dishonest or not in accordance with the normal rules. *...the minister accused of irregular business practices... 'Will you do this for me, Leo? It's the only way.'—'It's highly irregular, Ralph.'* ♦ **irregularity** *...charges arising from alleged financial irregularities.* — ADJ-GRADED; N-VAR

4 An **irregular** verb, noun, or adjective does not inflect in the same way as most other verbs, nouns, or adjectives in the language. For example, 'break' is an irregular verb because its past form is 'broke', not 'breaked'. — ADJ ≠regular

5 **Irregular** troops do not belong to an official national army. *At least 17 different irregular units are engaged in the war.* ► **Irregulars** are irregular troops. — ADJ: ADJ n ≠regular; N-COUNT: usu pl

irrelevance /ɪrelɪvᵊns/ **irrelevances**

1 If you talk about the **irrelevance** of something, you mean that it is irrelevant. *...the utter irrelevance of the debate.* — N-UNCOUNT: oft N *of* n ≠relevance

2 If you describe something as an **irrelevance**, you have a low opinion of it because it is not important in a situation. *The Patriotic Front has been a political irrelevance since it was abandoned by its foreign backers.* — N-COUNT =irrelevancy

irrelevancy /ɪrelɪvᵊnsi/ **irrelevancies.** If you describe something as an **irrelevancy**, you have a low opinion of it because it is not important in a situation. *Why was he wasting her time with these irrelevancies?* — N-COUNT =irrelevance

irrelevant /ɪrelɪvᵊnt/ ◆◆◇◇◇

1 If you describe something such as a fact or remark as **irrelevant**, you mean that it is not connected with what you are discussing or dealing with. *...irrelevant details... The government decided that their testimony would be irrelevant to the case.* ♦ **irrelevantly** *She would have hated the suit, I thought irrelevantly.* — ADJ-GRADED: oft ADJ *to* n ≠relevant; ADV-GRADED: ADV with v, ADV with cl

2 If you say that something is **irrelevant**, you mean that it is not important in a situation. *Their old hard-won skills were irrelevant... The choice of subject matter is irrelevant... He said politics has become increasingly irrelevant to most Americans.* — ADJ-GRADED: oft ADJ *to* n

irreligious /ɪrɪlɪdʒəs/. An **irreligious** person does not accept the beliefs of any religion or opposes all religions. *...irreligious communists.* — ADJ-GRADED =atheistic

irremediable /ɪrɪmiːdiəbᵊl/. If a bad situation or change is **irremediable**, the situation cannot be improved; a formal word. *His memory suffered irremediable damage.* — ADJ =irreparable

irreparable /ɪreprəbᵊl/. **Irreparable** damage or harm is so bad that it cannot be repaired or put right; a formal word. *The move would cause irreparable harm to the organization.* ♦ **irreparably** /ɪreprəbli/ *She was given a new heart after her own was irreparably damaged by a virus.* — ◆◇◇◇◇ ADJ =irreversible; ADV: ADV with v, ADV -ed

irreplaceable /ɪrɪpleɪsəbᵊl/. **Irreplaceable** things are so special that they cannot be replaced if they are lost or destroyed. *...a rare and irreplaceable jewel... There's one man who's considered irreplaceable.* — ADJ ≠replaceable

irrepressible /ɪrɪpresɪbᵊl/. An **irrepressible** person is lively and energetic and never seems to be depressed. *...the irrepressible Viv Allen... Jon's exuberance was irrepressible.* ♦ **irrepressibly** /ɪrɪpresɪbli/ *Gavin was irrepressibly rebellious.* — ADJ-GRADED; ADV-GRADED: usu ADV adj/-ed

irreproachable /ɪrɪproʊtʃəbᵊl/. If you say that someone's character or behaviour is **irreproachable**, you mean that they behave so well that they cannot be criticized. — ADJ =impeccable

irresistible /ɪrɪzɪstɪbᵊl/ ◆◆◇◇◇

1 If you describe something such as a desire or force as **irresistible**, you mean that it is so powerful that it makes you act in a certain way, and there is nothing you can do to prevent this. *It proved an irresistible temptation to Hall to go back. ...irresistible pressure from the financial markets... They feel* — ADJ-GRADED =overwhelming

the case for change is irresistible. ♦ **irresistibly** /ɪrɪzɪstɪbli/ *I found myself irresistibly drawn to Steve's world.* ADV-GRADED: ADV with v

2 If you describe something or someone as **irresistible**, you mean that they are so good or attractive that you cannot stop yourself from liking them or wanting them; an informal use. *The music is irresistible. ...irresistible granary bread.* ADJ-GRADED
♦ **irresistibly** *She had a gamine charm which men found irresistibly attractive.* ADV-GRADED: ADV adj

irresolute /ɪrezəluːt/. Someone who is **irresolute** cannot decide what to do; a formal word. *The worst reason to launch an attack would be a fear of seeming irresolute... I stood irresolute beside my car.* ADJ-GRADED =indecisive

irrespective /ɪrɪspektɪv/. If you say that something happens or should happen **irrespective of** a particular thing, you mean that it is not affected or should not be affected by that thing; a formal expression. *...their commitment to a society based on equality for all citizens irrespective of ethnic origin... This service should be available to everybody, irrespective of whether they can afford it.* ◆◇◇◇◇ PHR-PREP =regardless of

irresponsible /ɪrɪspɒnsɪbᵊl/. If you describe someone as **irresponsible**, you are criticizing them because they do things without properly considering their possible consequences. *I felt that it was irresponsible to advocate the legalisation of drugs... It would be irresponsible of me not to advise my company to abandon this project... Many people have an irresponsible attitude towards marriage and relationships.* ◆◇◇◇◇ ADJ-GRADED: oft *it* v-link ADJ to-inf PRAGMATICS ≠responsible
♦ **irresponsibly** /ɪrɪspɒnsɪbli/ *They resent the implication that they have behaved irresponsibly.* ADV-GRADED: usu ADV with v
♦ **irresponsibility** /ɪrɪspɒnsɪbɪlɪti/ *I can only wonder at the irresponsibility of people who advocate such destruction to our environment.* N-UNCOUNT

irretrievable /ɪrɪtriːvəbᵊl/. If you talk about **irretrievable** damage or an **irretrievable** situation, you mean that the damage or situation is so bad that there is no possibility of putting it right; a formal word. *What a tragedy if the sport suffers irretrievable damage because this issue is ducked. ...a country in irretrievable decline.* ADJ ≠irreparable
♦ **irretrievably** /ɪrɪtriːvəbli/ *Eventually her marriage broke down irretrievably.* ADV: usu ADV with v

irreverent /ɪrevərənt/. If you describe someone as **irreverent**, you mean that they do not show respect for people or things that are generally respected; usually used showing approval. *She's irreverent, fun and hugely popular... Taylor combined great knowledge with an irreverent attitude to history.* ◆◇◇◇◇ ADJ-GRADED PRAGMATICS ≠deferential
♦ **irreverence** *His irreverence for authority marks him out as a troublemaker.* N-UNCOUNT
♦ **irreverently** *'Jobs for the boys,' said Crosby irreverently..* ADV-GRADED: ADV with v, ADV adj

irreversible /ɪrɪvɜːrsɪbᵊl/. If a change is **irreversible**, things cannot be changed back to the way they were before. *She could suffer irreversible brain damage if she is not treated within seven days... The reforms are irreversible.* ◆◇◇◇◇ ADJ ≠reversible
♦ **irreversibly** *Television has irreversibly changed our perception of the Royal Family.* ADV: ADV with v

irrevocable /ɪrevəkəbᵊl/. If a decision, action, or change is **irrevocable**, it cannot be changed or reversed; a formal word. *It may well be worth waiting for better times before making any irrevocable commitment... He said the decision was irrevocable.* ◆◇◇◇◇ ADJ
♦ **irrevocably** /ɪrevəkəbli/ *My relationships with friends have been irrevocably altered by their reactions to my illness.* ADV: usu ADV with v, also ADV adj

irrigate /ɪrɪgeɪt/ **irrigates, irrigating, irrigated.** To **irrigate** land means to supply it with water in order to help crops grow. *None of the water from Lake Powell is used to irrigate the area. ...strips of cultivated land irrigated by a maze of interconnected canals.* ◆◇◇◇◇ VERB V n V-ed
♦ **irrigation** /ɪrɪgeɪʃᵊn/ *The agricultural land is hilly and the irrigation poor. ...a sophisticated irrigation system.* N-UNCOUNT: oft N n

irritable /ɪrɪtəbᵊl/. If you are **irritable**, you are easily annoyed. *He had been waiting for over an hour and was beginning to feel irritable.* ◆◇◇◇◇ ADJ-GRADED =crotchety
♦ **irritably** /ɪrɪtəbli/ *'Why are you whispering?' he asked irritably... The judge shook his head irritably and Juicks hushed.* ADV-GRADED: ADV with v
♦ **irritability** /ɪrɪtəbɪlɪti/ *Patients usually suffer from memory loss, personality changes, and increased irritability.* N-UNCOUNT

irritant /ɪrɪtənt/ **irritants** ◆◇◇◇◇

1 If you describe something as an **irritant**, you mean that it keeps annoying you; a formal use. *He said the issue was not a major irritant.* N-COUNT =annoyance

2 An **irritant** is a substance which causes a part of your body to become tender, sore, or itchy; a formal use. *Many pesticides are irritants.* N-COUNT

irritate /ɪrɪteɪt/ **irritates, irritating, irritated** ◆◆◇◇◇

1 If something **irritates** you, it keeps annoying you. *Their attitude irritates me... Perhaps they were irritated by the sound of crying.* VERB =annoy V n
♦ **irritated** *Not surprisingly, her teacher is getting irritated with her.* ADJ-GRADED

2 If something **irritates** a part of your body, it causes it to itch or become sore. *Wear rubber gloves while chopping chillies as they can irritate the skin.* VERB V n

irritating /ɪrɪteɪtɪŋ/ ◆◇◇◇◇

1 Something that is **irritating** keeps annoying you. *They also have the irritating habit of interrupting.* ADJ-GRADED =annoying
♦ **irritatingly** *They can be irritatingly indecisive at times.* ADV-GRADED: usu ADV adj, also ADV with cl

2 An **irritating** substance can cause your body to itch or become sore. *In heavy concentrations, ozone is irritating to the eyes, nose and throat.* ADJ-GRADED: oft ADJ *to* n

irritation /ɪrɪteɪʃᵊn/ **irritations** ◆◆◇◇◇

1 **Irritation** is a feeling of annoyance, especially when something is happening that you cannot easily stop or control. *For the first time Leonard felt irritation at her methods... He tried not to let his irritation show as he blinked in the glare of the television lights.* N-UNCOUNT =annoyance

2 An **irritation** is something that keeps annoying you. *Don't allow a minor irritation in the workplace to mar your ambitions... He describes the tourists as an irritation.* N-COUNT =annoyance

3 **Irritation** in a part of your body is a feeling of slight pain and discomfort there. *These oils may cause irritation to sensitive skins... This is an irritation and inflammation of the edge of the eyelid.* N-VAR

is /ɪz/. **Is** is the third person singular of the present tense of **be**. **Is** is often abbreviated to **'s**.

-ise /-aɪz/. See **-ize**.

-ish /-ɪʃ/

1 **-ish** is added to adjectives to form adjectives which indicate that someone or something has a quality to a small extent. For example, if you say that something is largish, you mean it is fairly large. *She is tallish, brown-haired, and clear-skinned... With her was a youngish man in a dinner jacket. ...a tank of greenish water.* SUFFIX

2 **-ish** is added to nouns and names to form adjectives which indicate that someone or something is like a particular kind of person or thing. For example, 'childish' means like a child, or typical of a child. *She had entirely lost her girlish chubbiness. ...a man of monkish appearance. ...his affecting, Tom Petty-ish voice.* SUFFIX

3 **-ish** is added to words referring to times, dates, or ages to form words which indicate that the time or age mentioned is approximate. *I'll call you guys tomorrow. Noon-ish... The nurse was fiftyish.* SUFFIX

Islam /ɪzlɑːm, AM ɪslɑːm/ ◆◆◆◇◇

1 **Islam** is the religion of the Muslims, which teaches that there is only one God and that Mohammed is His prophet. N-UNCOUNT

2 Some people use **Islam** to refer to all the countries where Islam is the main religion. *...relations between Islam and the West.* N-UNCOUNT

Islamic /ɪzlæmɪk/. **Islamic** means belonging or relating to Islam. *...Islamic law. ...Islamic fundamentalists.* ◆◆◆◇◇ ADJ: ADJ n

island /aɪlənd/ **islands.** An **island** is a piece of land that is completely surrounded by water. *...a wonderful day trip to the picturesque island of Gozo... We spent a day on Caldey Island. ...the Canary Islands.* ◆◆◆◆◇ N-COUNT: oft in names

islander /aɪləndəʳ/ **islanders. Islanders** are people who live on an island. *The islanders endured centuries of exploitation. ...the Easter Islanders.* ◆◇◇◇◇ N-COUNT: usu pl

isle /aɪl/ **isles.** An **isle** is an island; a literary word, often used as part of an island's name. *...the paradise isle of Bali. ...the Isle of Man.* ◆◆◇◇◇ N-COUNT: oft in names

islet /aɪlət/ **islets.** An **islet** is a small island; a literary word. N-COUNT

-ism /-ɪzəm/ **-isms**

1 **-ism** is used to form uncount nouns that refer to political or religious movements and beliefs. *Buddhism has declined in both India and China. ...a time of growing Slovak nationalism.* SUFFIX

2 **-ism** is used to form uncount nouns that refer to attitudes and behaviour. *...an act of heroism... He didn't hide his pacifism.* SUFFIX

3 **-ism** is used to form nouns that refer to unfair or illegal discrimination against particular groups of people. *...discrimination based on racism, sexism and disability... Many women feel ageism is obstructing their career ambitions.* SUFFIX

isn't /ɪzᵊnt/. In informal English, **is not** is usually said or written as **isn't**.

isolate /aɪsəleɪt/ **isolates, isolating, isolated** ◆◇◇◇◇

1 To **isolate** a person or organization means to cause them to lose their friends or supporters. *This policy could isolate China from the other permanent members of the United Nations Security Council... Political influence is being used to shape public opinion and isolate critics.* ♦ **isolated** *They are finding themselves increasingly isolated within the teaching profession.* ♦ **isolation** /aɪsəleɪʃᵊn/ *Diplomatic isolation could lead to economic disaster. ...the public isolation of the Prime Minister.* VERB =cut off V n *from* n V n; ADJ-GRADED: usu v-link ADJ; N-UNCOUNT: usu with supp

2 If you **isolate** yourself, or if something **isolates** you, you become physically or socially separated from other people. *When he was thinking out a problem Tweed's habit was never to isolate himself in his room... His radicalism and refusal to compromise isolated him... Police officers had a siege mentality that isolated them from the people they served... But of course no one lives totally alone, isolated from the society around them.* VERB =cut off V pron-refl V n V n *from* n V-ed

3 If you **isolate** something such as an idea or a problem, you separate it from others that it is connected with, so that you can concentrate on it or consider it on its own. *Our anxieties can also be controlled by isolating thoughts, feelings and memories. ...attempts to isolate a single factor as the cause of the decline of Britain... Gandhi said that those who isolate religion from politics don't understand the nature of either.* VERB V n V n *from* n

4 To **isolate** a substance means to obtain it by separating it from other substances using scientific processes. *We can use genetic engineering techniques to isolate the gene that is responsible... Researchers have isolated a new protein from the seeds of poppies. ...the chemical isolated from brain tissue.* VERB V n V n *from* n V-ed

5 To **isolate** a sick person or animal means to keep them apart from other people or animals, so that their illness does not spread. *Patients will be isolated from other people for between three days and one month after treatment... You don't have to isolate them from the community.* VERB =quarantine *be* V-ed *from* n V n *from* n Also V n

isolated /aɪsəleɪtɪd/ ◆◆◇◇◇

1 An **isolated** place is a long way away from large towns and is difficult to reach. *Many of the refugee villages are in isolated areas... Aubrey's family's farm is very isolated.* ADJ-GRADED =cut off, remote

2 If you feel **isolated**, you feel lonely and without friends or help. *Men can feel isolated at work... Some patients may become very isolated and depressed.* ADJ-GRADED: usu v-link ADJ =cut off

3 An **isolated** example is an example of something that is not very common. *They said the allegations related to an isolated case of cheating.* ADJ: ADJ n =untypical

isolation /aɪsəleɪʃᵊn/ ◆◆◇◇◇

1 **Isolation** is the state of feeling alone and without friends or help. *Many deaf people have feelings of isolation and loneliness... He also talked briefly about the isolation he endured while in captivity.* ● See also **isolate**. N-UNCOUNT

2 If something is considered **in isolation** from other things that it is connected with, it is considered separately, and those other things are not considered. *Punishment cannot, therefore, be discussed in isolation from social and political theory.* PHRASES oft with brd-neg, PHR after v, oft PHR *from* n =separately

3 If someone does something **in isolation**, they do it without other people being present or without their help. *Malcolm, for instance, works in isolation but I have no doubts about his abilities.* PHR after v =alone

isolationism /aɪsəleɪʃənɪzəm/. If you refer to **isolationism**, you are referring to a country's policy of avoiding close relationships with other countries and of not taking sides in disputes between other countries. *...the perils of isolationism.* ♦ **isolationist, isolationists** *Not surprisingly, isolationists found thousands of willing recruits to their cause... The government had to overcome isolationist opposition to the plan.* N-UNCOUNT; N-COUNT: oft N n

isometrics /aɪsəmetrɪks/; the form **isometric** is used as a modifier. **Isometrics** or **isometric** exercises are exercises in which you make your muscles work against each other or against something else, for example by pressing your hands together. N-PLURAL

isotope /aɪsətoʊp/ **isotopes. Isotopes** are atoms which have the same atomic number but which have different physical properties because they do not have the same number of neutrons; a technical term in science. *...tritium, a radioactive isotope of hydrogen.* ◆◇◇◇◇ N-COUNT

Israeli /ɪzreɪli/ **Israelis** ◆◆◆◆◇

1 **Israeli** means belonging or relating to Israel, or to its people or culture. *...the Israeli government.* ADJ

2 An **Israeli** is an Israeli citizen, or a person of Israeli origin. N-COUNT

issue /ɪsjuː, ɪʃuː/ **issues, issuing, issued** ◆◆◆◆◆

1 An **issue** is an important subject that people are arguing about or discussing. *Agents will raise the issue of prize-money for next year's world championships... A key issue for higher education in the 1990's is the need for greater diversity of courses... Is it right for the Church to express a view on political issues?* ● See also **side issue**. N-COUNT: usu with supp =subject, matter

2 If something is **the issue**, it is the thing you consider to be the most important part of a situation or discussion. *I was earning a lot of money, but that was not the issue... She avoided the issue by ordering a turkey sandwich... Do not draw it on the chart, however, as this will confuse the issue... The real issue was never addressed.* N-SING: *the* N =the point

3 An **issue** of something such as a magazine or newspaper is the version of it that is published, for example, in a particular month or on a particular day. *The growing problem is underlined in the latest issue of the Lancet... I read Germaine Greer's article in the March issue with particular interest.* N-COUNT =edition

4 If you **issue** a statement or a warning, you make it known formally or publicly. *Last night he issued a statement denying the allegations... The government issued a warning that the strikers should end their action or face dismissal... Yesterday his kidnappers issued a second threat to kill him.* VERB =put out V n

5 If you **are issued with** something, it is officially given to you. *On your appointment you will be issued with a written statement of particulars of employment... Staff will be issued with new grey-and-yellow designer uniforms.* ► Also a noun. *...a standard army issue rifle.* VB: usu passive *be* V-ed *with* n; N-UNCOUNT: oft N n

6 When something such as a liquid, sound, or smell **issues from** something, it comes out of that thing; a formal use. *A tinny voice issued from a speaker.* VERB V *from* n

7 The question or point **at issue** is the question or point that is being argued about or discussed. *The problems of immigration were not the question at issue... One of the main points at issue is that the Community wants the representatives to be based in East Jerusalem.* PHRASES usu v-link PHR

8 If you **make an issue of** something, you try to make other people think about it or discuss it, because you are concerned or annoyed about it. *It* V inflects =make a big thing of

seemed the Colonel had no desire to make an issue of the affair.

9 If you **take issue with** someone or something they said, you disagree with them, and start arguing about it. *Sister Morrison might take issue with me on that matter... I will not take issue with the fact that we have a recession.* V inflects, PHR n =argue

-ist /-ɪst/ **-ists**

1 -ist is added to nouns instead of -ism in order to form count nouns and adjectives. The nouns refer to people who have particular beliefs. The adjectives describe something related to or based on particular beliefs. *Later he was to become famous as a pacifist. ...fascist organisations.* SUFFIX

2 -ist is used to form count nouns referring to people who do a particular kind of work. *Susi Arnott is a biologist.* SUFFIX

3 -ist is added to nouns referring to musical instruments, in order to form nouns that refer to people who play these instruments. *...Hungarian pianist Christina Kiss.* SUFFIX

isthmus /ɪsməs/ **isthmuses.** An **isthmus** is a narrow piece of land connecting two very large areas of land. *...the Isthmus of Panama.* N-COUNT: oft in names

it /ɪt/ ◆◆◆◆◆

It is a third person singular pronoun. **It** is used as the subject or object of a verb, or as the object of a preposition.

1 You use **it** to refer to an object, animal, or other thing that has already been mentioned. *He saw the grey Land-Rover down the by-pass. It was more than a hundred yards from him... It's a wonderful city, really. I'll show it to you if you want... My wife has become crippled by arthritis. She is embarrassed to ask the doctor about it... I took a lot of convincing that parenthood was a good idea and I didn't think I'd be much use at it.* PRON-SING

2 You use **it** to refer to a child or baby whose sex you do not know or whose sex is not relevant to what you are saying. *She could, if she wanted, compel him, through a court of law, to support the child after it was born... He threw the baby high in the air and it stopped crying.* PRON-SING

3 You use **it** to refer in a general way to a situation that you have just described. *He was through with sports, not because he had to be but because he wanted it that way... Antonia will not be jealous, or if she is, she will not show it.* PRON-SING

4 You use **it** before certain nouns, adjectives, and verbs to introduce your feelings or point of view about a situation. *It was nice to see Steve again... It's a pity you never got married, Sarah... It's funny how you remember things... It's good of him to spare the time to visit at all... Is it possible he'll phone you?... He found it hard to work with a microphone pointing at him... I know it's a good idea to use dental floss... It's up to us to change things we don't like... It seems that you are letting things get you down.* PRON-SING

5 You use **it** in passive clauses which report a situation or event. *It has been said that stress causes cancer... Yesterday it was reported that a number of people had been arrested in the capital... It was noted that within a year the incidence of illness had increased quite significantly.* PRON-SING

6 You use **it** with some verbs that need a subject or object, although there is no noun that it refers to. *Of course, as it turned out, three-fourths of the people in the group were psychiatrists... I like it here... We live in a world in which only the strongest can make it to the top.* PRON-SING

7 You use **it** as the subject of 'be', to say what the time, day, or date is. *It's three o'clock in the morning... It was a Monday, so she was at home... It's December 1989, in Las Vegas.* PRON-SING

8 You use **it** as the subject of a link verb to describe the weather, the light, or the temperature. *It was very wet and windy the day I drove over the hill to Milland... It's getting dark. Let's go inside... It was warm in the kitchen.* PRON-SING

9 You use **it** when you are telling someone who you are, or asking them who they are, especially at the beginning of a phone call. You also use **it** in statements and questions about the identity of other people. *'Who is it?' he called.—'It's your neighbor.'... Hello Freddy, it's only me, Maxine.* PRON-SING PRAGMATICS

10 When you are emphasizing or drawing attention to something, you can put that thing immediately after **it** and a form of the verb 'be'. *It's really the poor countries that don't have an economic base that have the worst environmental records... It's the country's Communist rulers who devised this system... It was I who found him there... It's my father they're accusing.* PRON PRAGMATICS

11 You use **it** in expressions such as **it's not that** or **it's not simply that** when you are giving a reason for something and are suggesting that there are several other reasons. *It's not that I didn't want to be with my family... It's not just that a gulf exists in living standards – there's a psychological ravine.* PHRASE PRAGMATICS

12 ● **if it wasn't for**: see **be**.

Italian /ɪtæliən/ **Italians** ◆◆◆◆◇

1 Italian means belonging or relating to Italy, or to its people, language, or culture. *I watch Italian football a lot.* ADJ

2 An **Italian** is an Italian citizen, or a person of Italian origin. N-COUNT

3 Italian is the language spoken in Italy, and in parts of Switzerland. N-UNCOUNT

italic /ɪtælɪk/ **italics**

1 Italics are letters which slope to the right. Italics are often used to emphasize a particular word or sentence. The examples in this dictionary are printed in italics. N-PLURAL

2 Italic letters slope to the right. *She addressed them by hand in her beautiful italic script.* ADJ: ADJ n

itch /ɪtʃ/ **itches, itching, itched** ◆◇◇◇◇

1 When you **itch** or when a part of your body **itches**, you have an unpleasant feeling on your skin that makes you want to scratch. *When someone has hayfever, the eyes and nose will stream and itch... My skin was hard and scaly and I itched. ...dry, itching skin.* ► Also a noun. *Scratch my back – I've got an itch.* ♦ **itching** *It may be that the itching is caused by contact with irritant material.* VERB V V-ing N-COUNT N-UNCOUNT

2 If you **are itching** to do something, you are very eager or impatient to do it; an informal use. *I was itching to get involved and to bring my own theories into practice... The general was itching for a fight.* ► Also a noun. *...cable TV viewers with an insatiable itch to switch from channel to channel.* VB: usu cont =be dying V to-inf V for n N-SING: usu N to-inf

itchy /ɪtʃi/

1 If a part of your body or something you are wearing is **itchy**, you have an unpleasant feeling on your skin that makes you want to scratch; an informal use. *...itchy, sore eyes... Wigs are itchy and uncomfortable.* ADJ-GRADED

2 If you have **itchy feet**, you have a strong desire to leave a place and to travel; an informal expression. *The thought gave me really itchy feet so within a couple of months I decided to leave.* PHRASE: usu PHR after v

it'd /ɪtəd/

1 It'd is a spoken form of 'it would'. *It'd be better for a place like this to remain closed.*

2 It'd is a spoken form of 'it had', especially when 'had' is an auxiliary verb. *I got home and Marcie was watching the news. It'd just started.*

item /aɪtəm/ **items** ◆◆◆◆◇

1 An **item** is one of a collection or list of objects. *The most valuable item on show will be a Picasso drawing... The menu includes the occasional offbeat item.* ● See also **collector's item**. N-COUNT

2 An **item** is one of a list of things for someone to do, deal with, or talk about. *The other item on the agenda is the tour.* N-COUNT =matter

3 An **item** is a report or article in a newspaper or magazine, or on television or radio. *There was an item in the paper about him.* N-COUNT

4 If you say that two people are an **item**, you mean that they are having a long-term romantic or sexual relationship; an informal use. *She and Gino were an item.* N-SING: a N =couple

itemize /aɪtəmaɪz/ **itemizes, itemizing, itemized;** also spelled **itemise** in British English. If you **itemize** a number of things, you make a list VERB of them. *Itemise your gear and mark major items with your name and post code. ...a fully itemised bill.* V n / V-ed

itinerant /aɪtɪnərənt/ **itinerants**

1 An **itinerant** worker or preacher travels around a region, working for short periods in different places; a formal use. *...an off-beat account of the author's experiences as an itinerant musician.* ADJ: ADJ n =travelling

2 An **itinerant** is someone whose way of life involves travelling around, usually someone who is poor and homeless; a formal use. N-COUNT

itinerary /aɪtɪnərəri, AM -eri/ **itineraries.** An **itinerary** is a plan of a journey, including the route and the places that you will visit. *The next place on our itinerary was Silistra.* ◆◇◇◇◇ N-COUNT

it'll /ɪtᵊl/. **It'll** is a spoken form of 'it will'. *It's ages since I've seen her so it'll be nice to meet her in town on Thursday.*

its /ɪts/ ◆◆◆◆◆

Its is a third person singular possessive determiner. You use **its** to indicate that something belongs or relates to a thing, place, or animal that has just been mentioned or whose identity is known. You can use **its** to indicate that something belongs or relates to a child or baby. *The British Labor Party concludes its annual conference today in Brighton. ...Japan, with its extreme housing shortage... The dog lifted its head, listening... I met one woman whose tiny baby had just died and whose other child was fighting for its life.* DET-POSS

it's /ɪts/

1 **It's** is the usual spoken form of 'it is'. *It's the best news I've heard in a long time.*

2 **It's** is the usual spoken form of 'it has', especially when 'has' is an auxiliary verb. *It's been such a long time since I played.*

itself /ɪtself/. ◆◆◆◆◆

1 **Itself** is used as the object of a verb or preposition when it refers to something that is the same thing as the subject of the verb. *Scientists have discovered remarkable new evidence showing how the body rebuilds itself while we sleep... Unemployment does not correct itself. ...the threat of Europe building trade business around itself... Their conversation tumbled over itself as they joked and drank coffee.* PRON-REFL: v PRON, prep PRON

2 You use **itself** to emphasize the thing you are referring to. *I think life itself is a learning process... The involvement of the foreign ministers was itself a sign of progress... He cheered up on Christmas Day itself.* PRON-REFL-EMPH PRAGMATICS

3 If you say that someone is, for example, politeness **itself** or kindness **itself**, you are emphasizing they are extremely polite or extremely kind. *I am never really happy staying in a hotel, although the management here have been kindness itself... Many men are charm itself... He is rarely satisfied with anything less than perfection itself.* PRON-REFL-EMPH: n PRON PRAGMATICS

4 • **by itself**: see **by** • **an end in itself**: see **end**.

ITV /aɪ tiː viː/ ◆◆◇◇◇

1 **ITV** refers to the group of British commercial television companies that broadcasts programmes on one channel. **ITV** is an abbreviation for 'Independent Television'. *ITV has set its sights on winning a younger and more upmarket audience. ...the managing directors of all 15 ITV companies.* N-PROPER-COLL

2 **ITV** is the television channel that is run by ITV. *The first episode will be shown tomorrow at 10.40pm on ITV. ...ITV viewers.* N-PROPER

-ity /-ɪti/ **-ities.** **-ity** is added to adjectives, sometimes in place of '-ious', to form nouns referring to the state, quality, or behaviour described by the adjective. *I, for one, admire his audacity... He enjoyed the tranquillity of village life. ...life with all its contradictions and complexities.* SUFFIX

IUD /aɪ juː diː/ **IUDs.** An **IUD** is a piece of plastic or metal which is put inside a woman's womb in order to prevent her from becoming pregnant. **IUD** is an abbreviation for 'intra-uterine device'. N-COUNT =coil

I've /aɪv/. **I've** is the usual spoken form of 'I have', especially when 'have' is an auxiliary verb. *I've been invited to meet with the American Ambassador... I've no other appointments.*

ivory /aɪvəri/ **ivories** ◆◆◇◇◇

1 **Ivory** is a type of bone, which forms most of the tusks of an elephant. It is valuable, and is often used for making carved ornaments. *...the international ban on the sale of ivory. ...intricate ivory carvings.* N-UNCOUNT

2 **Ivory** is a creamy-white colour. COLOUR

ivory tower, ivory towers. If you describe someone as living in an **ivory tower**, you mean that they have no knowledge or experience of the practical problems of everyday life; used showing disapproval. *They don't really, in their ivory towers, understand how pernicious drug crime is. ...ivory-tower intellectuals.* N-COUNT: usu prep N, N n PRAGMATICS

ivy /aɪvi/ **ivies.** **Ivy** is an evergreen plant that grows up walls or along the ground. ◆◇◇◇◇ N-VAR

Ivy League. **The Ivy League** is a group of eight important universities in the eastern part of the United States. *...an Ivy League college.* N-PROPER: *the* N

-ize /-aɪz/ **-izes, -izing, -ized;** also spelled **-ise** in British English. Verbs that can end in either '-ize' or '-ise' are dealt with in this dictionary at the '-ize' spelling. Many verbs ending in **-ize** describe processes by which things or people are brought into a new state. *The dispute could jeopardize the negotiations. ...a way of trying to regularize and standardize practice.* SUFFIX

J j

J, j /dʒeɪ/ **J's, j's**

1 **J** is the tenth letter of the English alphabet. N-VAR

2 **J** or **j** is an abbreviation for words beginning with j, such as 'joule' or 'Jack'.

jab /dʒæb/ **jabs, jabbing, jabbed** ◆◇◇◇◇

1 If you **jab** something into something, you push it there with a quick, sudden movement and with a lot of force. *He saw her jab her thumb on a red button—a panic button... A needle was jabbed into the baby's arm... Stern jabbed at me with his glasses... Nick jabbed his finger at the clothes on the bed.* VERB =stab; V n prep; be V-ed *into* n; V *at* n; V n *at* n

2 A **jab** is a sudden, sharp punch. *He was simply too powerful for his opponent, rocking him with a steady supply of left jabs.* N-COUNT

3 In informal British English, a **jab** is an injection of something into your blood to prevent illness. *...painful anti malaria jabs.* N-COUNT

4 In informal English, you can refer to a sudden and unpleasant critical remark as a **jab**. *They have been sniping at each other, with the Democrats taking jabs at the president's handling of foreign policy.* N-COUNT =swipe

jabber /dʒæbəʳ/ **jabbers, jabbering, jabbered.** If you say that someone **is jabbering**, you mean that they are talking very quickly and excitedly, and you cannot understand them; used showing disapproval. *The girl jabbered incomprehensibly, her voice rising to a screech like a parrot... After a minute or two I left them there jabbering away. ...a roomful of jabbering tourists.* VERB PRAGMATICS; V; V *away*; V-ing

jack /dʒæk/ **jacks, jacking, jacked** ◆◆◇◇◇
1 A **jack** is a device for lifting a heavy object off the ground, for example a car. N-COUNT
2 A **jack** is a playing card whose value is between a ten and a queen. A jack is usually represented by a picture of a young man. N-COUNT: oft N *of* n =knave
3 See also **jack-of-all-trades, Union Jack**.

jack in. In British English, if you **jack in** something such as an activity or a job, you stop doing it; an informal expression. *Four of the cast jacked it in about Christmas... After she jacked in the teaching, Jane got herself a job with a shipping line.* PHRASAL VERB V n P, V P n

jack up PHRASAL VERB
1 If you **jack up** a heavy object such as a car, you raise it off the ground using a jack. *They jacked up the car... All I had to do was get everyone out of the car, jack it up, and put on the spare.* V P n, V n P
2 If you say that someone or something **jacks up** the price or amount of something, you mean that the price or amount increases to an unreasonable or unacceptable level; an informal expression. *The plan would cost so much that the company would have to jack up its prices... Inflation has jacked up the rate of unemployment.* PRAGMATICS =hike, hike up V P n

jackal /dʒækɔːl/ **jackals.** A **jackal** is a wild animal that looks like a dog, has long legs and pointed ears, and lives in Africa and Southern Asia. N-COUNT

jackboot /dʒækbuːt/ **jackboots**
1 **Jackboots** are heavy boots that come up to the knee, such as the ones worn by some soldiers. N-COUNT: usu pl
2 If you say that a country or group of people is **under the jackboot**, you mean that they are suffering because of a dictator or an authoritarian government. PHRASE PRAGMATICS

jackdaw /dʒækdɔː/ **jackdaws.** A **jackdaw** is a large black and grey bird that is similar to a crow, and lives in Europe and Asia. N-COUNT

jacket /dʒækɪt/ **jackets** ◆◆◆◇◇
1 A **jacket** is a short coat with long sleeves. *...a black leather jacket.* N-COUNT
2 Potatoes baked in their **jackets** are baked without being peeled. N-COUNT: usu pl
3 The **jacket** of a book is the paper cover that protects the book. N-COUNT =dust jacket
4 In American English, a record **jacket** is the cover in which a record is kept. The British word is **sleeve**. N-COUNT
5 See also **bomber jacket, dinner jacket, hacking jacket, flak jacket, life jacket, sports jacket, strait-jacket**.

jacket potato, jacket potatoes. In British English, a **jacket potato** is a large potato that has been baked without being peeled. N-COUNT =baked potato

jack-in-the-box, jack-in-the-boxes. A **jack-in-the-box** is a child's toy that consists of a box with a doll inside it that springs out when the lid is opened. N-COUNT

jack-knife, jack-knifes, jack-knifing, jack-knifed. If an articulated truck **jack-knifes**, the trailer swings around at a sharp angle to the cab in an uncontrolled way as the truck is moving. *His vehicle jack-knifed, and crashed across all three lanes of the opposite carriageway.* VERB V

jack-of-all-trades, jacks-of-all-trades. If you refer to someone as a **jack-of-all-trades**, you mean that they are able to do a variety of different jobs. You are also often suggesting that they are not very good at any of these jobs. N-COUNT

jackpot /dʒækpɒt/ **jackpots** ◆◇◇◇◇
1 A **jackpot** is the most valuable prize in a game or lottery, especially when the game involves increasing the value of the prize until someone wins it. *A nurse who gambled £6 in a slot machine walked away with the biggest ever jackpot of more than £5 million.* N-COUNT: usu sing
2 If you **hit the jackpot**, you have a great success, for example by winning a lot of money or having a piece of good luck; an informal expression. PHRASE: V inflects =score

Jacobean /dʒækəbiːən/. A **Jacobean** building, piece of furniture, or work of art was built or produced in the style of the period between 1603 and 1625. *...a Jacobean manor house.* ADJ: usu ADJ n

Jacuzzi /dʒəkuːzi/ **Jacuzzis.** A **Jacuzzi** is a large circular bath which is fitted with a device that makes the water swirl around. **Jacuzzi** is a trademark. ◆◇◇◇◇ N-COUNT

jade /dʒeɪd/ ◆◇◇◇◇
1 **Jade** is a hard stone, usually green in colour, that is used for making jewellery and ornaments. N-UNCOUNT
2 Something that is **jade** or **jade green** is bright green in colour. COLOUR

jaded /dʒeɪdɪd/. If you are **jaded**, you feel bored, tired, and unenthusiastic, for example because you have had too much of the same thing. *We had both become jaded, disinterested, and disillusioned. ...his air of jaded cynicism.* ◆◇◇◇◇ ADJ-GRADED =bored

jagged /dʒægɪd/. Something that is **jagged** has a rough, uneven shape or edge with lots of sharp points. *...jagged black cliffs... A jagged scar runs through his lower lip.* ◆◇◇◇◇ ADJ-GRADED

jaguar /dʒægjuəʳ, AM -gwɑːr/ **jaguars.** A **jaguar** is a large animal of the cat family with dark spots on its back. N-COUNT

jail /dʒeɪl/ **jails, jailing, jailed;** the form **gaol** is also used in British English. ◆◆◆◇◇
1 A **jail** is a place where criminals are kept in order to punish them, or where people awaiting trial are kept. *Three prisoners escaped from a jail.* N-VAR =prison
2 If someone **is jailed**, they are put into jail. *He was jailed for twenty years.* VB: usu passive *be* V-ed

jailbird /dʒeɪlbɜːʳd/ **jailbirds.** If you refer to someone as a **jailbird**, you mean that they are in prison, or have been in prison; an old-fashioned, informal word. N-COUNT =convict

jailbreak /dʒeɪlbreɪk/ **jailbreaks.** A **jailbreak** is an escape from jail. N-COUNT

jailer /dʒeɪləʳ/ **jailers;** the form **gaoler** is also used in British English. A **jailer** is a person who is in charge of a jail and the prisoners in it; an old-fashioned word. N-COUNT =warder

jailhouse /dʒeɪlhaʊs/ **jailhouses.** In American English, a **jailhouse** is the same as a **prison**; an informal word. N-COUNT

jam /dʒæm/ **jams, jamming, jammed** ◆◆◇◇◇
1 In British English, **jam** is a food that is made by cooking fruit with a large amount of sugar. Usually you spread jam on bread. The usual American word is **jelly**. *...home-made jam.* N-MASS
2 If you **jam** something somewhere, you push or put it there roughly. *He picked his cap up off the ground and jammed it on his head... Pete jammed his hands into his pockets.* VERB V n prep
3 If something such as a part of a machine **jams**, or if something **jams** it, the part becomes fixed in position and is unable to move freely or work properly. *The second time he fired his gun jammed... A rope jammed the boat's propeller... Cracks appeared in the wall and a door jammed shut... The intake valve was jammed open... Every few minutes the motor cut-out as the machinery became jammed.* V-ERG V, V n, V adj, *be* V-ed adj, V-ed, Also V n adj
4 If vehicles **jam** a road, there are so many of them that they cannot move. *Hundreds of departing motorists jammed roads that had been closed during the height of the storm.* ► Also a noun. *400 trucks may sit in a jam for ten hours waiting to cross the limited number of bridges.* ♦ **jammed** *Nearby roads and the dirt track to the beach were jammed with cars.* VERB V n; N-COUNT; ADJ-GRADED: oft ADJ *with* n
5 If a lot of people **jam** a place, or **jam** into a place, they are pressed tightly together so that they can hardly move. *Hundreds of people jammed the boardwalk to watch... They jammed into buses provided by the Red Cross and headed for safety.* ♦ **jammed** *The stadium was jammed and they had to turn away hundreds of disappointed fans.* VERB =cram V n, V *into* n; ADJ-GRADED =packed
6 To **jam** a radio or electronic signal means to interfere with it and prevent it from being received or heard clearly. *They will try to jam the transmissions electronically.* ♦ **jamming** *The plane is used for electronic jamming and radar detection.* VERB V n; N-UNCOUNT: usu with supp
7 If you say that callers **are jamming** telephone VERB

lines, you are emphasizing that there are so many callers that the people answering the telephones find them difficult to deal with. *Hundreds of callers jammed the BBC switchboard for more than an hour... The telephone exchange has been jammed all day with people wanting to buy season tickets.* V n V-ed
8 If someone is **in a jam**, they are in a very difficult situation; an informal use. *They were in a real jam, Bob thought glumly.* N-SING: in N
9 When jazz or rock musicians **are jamming**, they are informally playing music that has not been written down or planned in advance; an informal use. *He was jamming with his saxophone.* ► Also a noun. *...a free-form jazz jam. ...a jam session.* VERB V N-COUNT
10 See also **traffic jam**.

Jamaican /dʒəmeɪkən/ **Jamaicans** ◆◆◇◇◇
1 **Jamaican** means belonging or relating to Jamaica or to its people or culture. *...the Jamaican community in Britain.* ADJ
2 A **Jamaican** is a person who comes from Jamaica. N-COUNT

jamb /dʒæm/ **jambs.** A **jamb** is a post that forms the side part or upright of a door frame or window frame. N-COUNT: usu n N

jamboree /dʒæmbəriː/ **jamborees.** A **jamboree** is a party, celebration, or other gathering where there is a large number of people and a lot of excitement, fun, and enjoyment. N-COUNT: usu sing

jam-jar, jam-jars; also spelled **jam jar.** A **jam-jar** is a glass jar which is used for keeping jam in; used mainly in British English. N-COUNT

jammy /dʒæmi/ **jammier, jammiest.** If you describe someone as **jammy**, you mean that they are very lucky because something good has happened to them, without their making much effort or deserving such luck; used in informal British English. *You'd think that at least he'd have the good grace to admit his blinding, jammy luck.* ADJ-GRADED: usu ADJ n

jam-packed. If somewhere is **jam-packed**, it is so full of people or things that there is no room for any more; an informal word. *His room was jam-packed with fruit, flowers, gifts etc.* ADJ-GRADED: oft ADJ *with* n =packed

Jan. **Jan.** is a written abbreviation for **January**. ◆◆◇◇◇

jangle /dʒæŋgəl/ **jangles, jangling, jangled** ◆◇◇◇◇
1 When objects strike against each other and make an unpleasant ringing noise, you can say that they **jangle** or **are jangled**. *Her bead necklaces and bracelets jangled as she walked... Jane took out her keys and jangled them. ...her jangling bracelets.* ► Also a noun. *...a jangle of bells.* V-ERG V V n V-ing N-SING
2 If you say that someone's nerves **are jangling**, or someone or something **jangles** them, you mean that they are very anxious. *Behind that quietness his nerves are jangling, he's in a terrible state... The caffeine in coffee can jangle the nerves and perhaps contribute to health problems.* V-ERG V V n

janitor /dʒænɪtəʳ/ **janitors.** A **janitor** is a person whose job is to look after a building; used mainly in American English. N-COUNT =caretaker

January /dʒænjəri, AM -jueri/ **Januaries. January** is the first month of the year in the Western calendar. *We always have snow in January... She was born on January 6, 1946... I haven't seen my own daughter since last January.* ◆◆◆◆◇ N-VAR

Japanese /dʒæpəniːz/. **Japanese** is both the singular and the plural form. ◆◆◆◆◇
1 **Japanese** means belonging or relating to Japan, or to its people, language, or culture. *Japanese firms are looking for a new breed of manager. ...a planned visit by the Japanese Prime Minister.* ADJ
2 The **Japanese** are the people of Japan. N-PLURAL
3 **Japanese** is the language spoken in Japan. N-UNCOUNT

jape /dʒeɪp/ **japes.** A **jape** is a silly trick that you play on someone which is quite funny and which does not really involve upsetting them; an old-fashioned word. N-COUNT =prank

jar /dʒɑːʳ/ **jars, jarring, jarred** ◆◆◇◇◇
1 A **jar** is a glass container with a lid that is used for storing food. *...yellow cucumbers in great glass jars.* ● See also **jam-jar**. N-COUNT
2 You can use **jar** to refer to a jar and its contents, or to the contents only. *She opened up a glass jar of plums. ...two jars of filter coffee.* N-COUNT: oft N *of* n
3 In informal British English, if you have a **jar**, you have a drink with friends in a pub. *They had a few jars together.* N-COUNT
4 If something **jars** on you, you find it unpleasant, disturbing, or shocking. *Sometimes a light remark jarred on her father. ...televised congressional hearings that jarred the nation's faith in the presidency... You shouldn't have too many colours in a small space as the effect can jar.* ♦ **jarring** *In the context of this chapter, Dore's comments strike a jarring note.* VERB V on n V n V ADJ-GRADED =grating
5 If an object **jars**, or if something **jars** it, the object moves with a fairly hard shaking movement. *The ship jarred a little... The impact jarred his arm.* V-ERG V V n

jargon /dʒɑːʳgən/. You use **jargon** to refer to words and expressions that are used in special or technical ways by particular groups of people, often making the language difficult to understand. *The manual is full of the jargon and slang of self-improvement courses. ...the reading habits of 600,000 C2 males (marketing jargon for skilled manual workers).* ◆◇◇◇◇ N-UNCOUNT

jasmine /dʒæzmɪn/ **jasmines. Jasmine** is a climbing plant which has small white or yellow flowers with a pleasant smell. ◆◇◇◇◇ N-VAR

jaundice /dʒɔːndɪs/. **Jaundice** is an illness that makes your skin and eyes become yellow. N-UNCOUNT

jaundiced /dʒɔːndɪst/. If you describe someone's attitudes or views as **jaundiced**, you mean that they are unenthusiastic, pessimistic, or cynical. *He has a somewhat jaundiced attitude... His view of the groups was less jaundiced than that of the prime minister.* ADJ-GRADED: usu ADJ n

jaunt /dʒɔːnt/ **jaunts.** A **jaunt** is a short journey which you go on for pleasure or excitement. N-COUNT =trip

jaunty /dʒɔːnti/ **jauntier, jauntiest.** If you describe someone or something as **jaunty**, you mean that they are full of confidence and energy. *...a jaunty little man... Tremain's novel is altogether jauntier, more various and energetic than these quotations imply.* ♦ **jauntily** /dʒɔːntɪli/ *He walked jauntily into the cafe... The Arsenal striker remains jauntily confident.* ◆◇◇◇◇ ADJ-GRADED: usu ADJ n ADV-GRADED: ADV with v, ADV adj

javelin /dʒævlɪn/ **javelins** ◆◇◇◇◇
1 A **javelin** is a long spear that is used in sports competitions. Competitors try to throw the javelin as far as possible. N-COUNT
2 You can refer to the competition in which the javelin is thrown as **the javelin**. *...Steve Backley who won the javelin.* N-SING: the N

jaw /dʒɔː/ **jaws** ◆◆◇◇◇
1 Your **jaw** is the lower part of your face below your mouth. The movement of your jaw is sometimes considered to express a particular emotion. For example, if your **jaw drops**, you are very surprised. *He thought for a moment, stroking his well-defined jaw... Meg's jaw dropped in amazement... His jaw was set, but his voice sounded thin and unsure.* N-COUNT: usu sing, poss N
2 A person's or animal's **jaws** are the two bones in their head which their teeth are attached to. *...a forest rodent with powerful jaws.* N-COUNT
3 If you talk about the **jaws of** something unpleasant such as death or hell, you are referring to a dangerous or unpleasant situation. *A family dog rescued a newborn boy from the jaws of death. ...caught in the jaws of world recession.* N-PLURAL: N *of* n =clutches
4 ● to **snatch defeat from the jaws of victory**: see **snatch.** ● to **snatch victory from the jaws of defeat**: see **snatch.**

jawbone /dʒɔːboun/ **jawbones;** also spelled **jaw bone.** A **jawbone** is the bone in the lower jaw of a person or animal. N-COUNT

jawline /dʒɔːlaɪn/ **jawlines;** also spelled **jaw line.** Your **jawline** is the part of your lower jaw which forms the outline of the bottom of your face. *...high cheekbones and strong jawline.* N-COUNT: usu sing

jay /dʒeɪ/ **jays.** A **jay** is a brownish-pink bird with blue and black wings that lives in Europe and Asia. ◆◇◇◇◇ N-COUNT

jaywalking /dʒeɪwɔːkɪŋ/. **Jaywalking** is the act of crossing a road or walking in a road in a care- N-UNCOUNT less and dangerous way. *The policemen threatened to arrest them for jaywalking.*

jazz /dʒæz/ **jazzes, jazzing, jazzed.** **Jazz** is a style of music that was invented by black American musicians in the early part of the twentieth century. Jazz music has very strong rhythms and often involves improvisation. *The pub has live jazz on Sundays. ...the great American jazz pianist George Shearing.* ◆◆◆◇◇ N-UNCOUNT: oft N n

jazz up PHRASAL VERB
1 If you **jazz** something **up**, you make it look more interesting, colourful, or exciting; an informal use. *Mary Ann had made an effort at jazzing up the chilly modern interiors... I don't think they're just jazzing it up for the media.* V P n (not pron) V n P
2 If someone **jazzes up** a piece of music, they change it in order to make it sound more like popular music or jazz. *Instead of playing it in the traditional style, she jazzed it up... Stephen and I are going to jazz up the love songs... The tune is basically the same as the old one, but considerably jazzed up.* V n P V P n (not pron) V-ed P

jazzy /dʒæzi/ **jazzier, jazziest** ◆◇◇◇◇
1 If you describe something as **jazzy**, you mean that it is colourful and modern. *...a check sports jacket, worn with a plain waistcoat and shirt and jazzy tie.* ADJ-GRADED: usu ADJ n
2 **Jazzy** music is music in the style of jazz. *'Pop-Pop' is her jazziest album ever.* ADJ-GRADED: usu ADJ n

jealous /dʒeləs/ ◆◆◇◇◇
1 If someone is **jealous**, they feel angry or bitter because they think that another person is trying to take a lover or friend, or a possession, away from them. *She got insanely jealous and there was a terrible fight.* ♦ **jealously** *The formula is jealously guarded.* ADJ-GRADED; ADV-GRADED: ADV with v
2 If you are **jealous** of another person's possessions or qualities, you feel angry or bitter because you do not have them. *She was jealous of his wealth... You're jealous because the record company rejected your idea.* ♦ **jealously** *Gloria eyed them jealously.* ADJ-GRADED: oft ADJ *of* n; ADV-GRADED: ADV after v

jealousy /dʒeləsi/ **jealousies** ◆◆◇◇◇
1 **Jealousy** is the feeling of anger or bitterness which someone has when they think that another person is trying to take a lover or friend, or a possession, away from them. *At first his jealousy only showed in small ways – he didn't mind me talking to other guys.* N-UNCOUNT: also N in pl
2 **Jealousy** is the feeling of anger or bitterness which someone has when they wish that they could have the qualities or possessions that another person has. *Her beauty causes envy and jealousy.* N-UNCOUNT: also N in pl

jeans /dʒiːnz/. **Jeans** are casual trousers that are usually made of strong blue denim. *She wore a very clean pair of blue jeans.* ◆◆◇◇◇ N-PLURAL: also *a pair of* N

Jeep /dʒiːp/ **Jeeps.** A **Jeep** is a small four-wheeled vehicle that can travel over rough ground and is often used by the American army. **Jeep** is a trademark. ◆◇◇◇◇ N-COUNT

jeer /dʒɪəʳ/ **jeers, jeering, jeered** ◆◇◇◇◇
1 If people **jeer** at someone, they show that they think that person is stupid and not worthy of respect by saying or shouting rude and insulting things to them. *The Soviet people who once cheered him on now jeer at him... His motorcade was jeered by angry residents... Demonstrators have jeered the mayor as he arrived for a week long visit... I didn't come here today to jeer: I want to give advice. ...mobs of jeering bystanders.* ♦ **jeering** *There was constant jeering and interruption from the floor.* VERB: V at n, *be* V-ed, V n, V, V-ing, Also V with quote; N-UNCOUNT
2 **Jeers** are rude and insulting things that people shout in order to show that they think someone is stupid and not worthy of respect. *He stared sullenly into space, pretending not to hear the jeers. ...the heckling and jeers of his audience.* N-COUNT: usu pl

Jehovah /dʒɪhoʊvə/. **Jehovah** is the name given to God in the Old Testament. N-PROPER

Jehovah's Witness, Jehovah's Witnesses. A **Jehovah's Witness** is a member of a religious organization which accepts some Christian ideas and believes that the world is going to end very soon. N-COUNT

jejune /dʒɪdʒuːn/
1 If you describe something or someone as **jejune**, you consider them to be very simple and unsophisticated; a formal use. *They were of great service in correcting my jejune generalizations.* ADJ-GRADED
2 If you describe something or someone as **jejune**, you mean they are dull and boring; an old-fashioned use. *We knew we were in for a pretty long, jejune evening.* ADJ-GRADED

jell /dʒel/. See **gel.**

jellied /dʒelid/. **Jellied** food is prepared and eaten in a jelly. *...jellied eels.* ADJ: ADJ n

Jell-O. In America, **Jell-O** is a clear food made from gelatine, fruit juice and sugar, which is eaten as a dessert. The usual British word is **jelly.** **Jell-O** is a trademark. N-UNCOUNT

jelly /dʒeli/ **jellies** ◆◇◇◇◇
1 In British English, **jelly** is a transparent, usually coloured food that is eaten as a dessert. It is made from gelatine, fruit juice, and sugar. The usual American word is **Jell-O.** *In the middle of the table stood a large bowl of jelly.* ► A container of jelly can be referred to as a **jelly.** *Dip the base of the bowls in hot water for a few seconds to loosen the jellies.* N-MASS; N-COUNT
2 In American English, **jelly** is jam. *I had two peanut butter and jelly sandwiches.* N-MASS
3 In British English, **jelly** is a kind of thin, clear jam. *Crabapple jelly is a fantastic complement to both hot and cold meats.* N-MASS
4 If you refer to a substance as a **jelly**, you mean that it is a thick, usually clear liquid. *...meat in jelly.* N-VAR
5 If your legs or arms feel like **jelly**, they feel very weak, usually because you are nervous or afraid. *My legs were like jelly when I realised I had won.* N-UNCOUNT
6 See also **royal jelly.**

jelly bean, jelly beans. **Jelly beans** are small coloured sweets with hard shells and jelly inside. They are popular in the United States. N-COUNT: usu pl

jellyfish /dʒelifɪʃ/; **jellyfish** is both the singular and the plural form. A **jellyfish** is a sea creature with a clear soft body and tentacles that can sting you. N-COUNT

jeopardize /dʒepəʳdaɪz/ **jeopardizes, jeopardizing, jeopardized;** also spelled **jeopardise** in British English. If someone or something **jeopardizes** a situation or activity, they do something that may destroy it or cause it to fail. *He has jeopardised the future of his government... The talks may still be jeopardized by disputes.* ◆◇◇◇◇ VERB =threaten, endanger; V n

jeopardy /dʒepəʳdi/. If someone or something is **in jeopardy**, they are in a dangerous situation where they might fail, be lost, or be destroyed. *A series of setbacks have put the whole project in jeopardy.* ◆◇◇◇◇ PHRASE: PHR after v, v-link PHR =at risk

jerk /dʒɜːʳk/ **jerks, jerking, jerked** ◆◆◇◇◇
1 If you **jerk** something or someone in a particular direction, or they **jerk** in a particular direction, they move a short distance very suddenly and quickly. *Mr Griffin jerked forward in his chair... The car jerked to a halt... 'This is Brady Coyne,' said Sam, jerking his head in my direction... Mike kept snatching him up by the collar and jerking him up... Eleanor jerked her wrist free... Foley raised his chin and jerked his neck as if his collar were too tight.* ► Also a noun. *He indicated the bedroom with a jerk of his head.* V-ERG: V adv/prep, V n adv/prep, V n adj, V n; N-COUNT
2 If you call someone a **jerk**, you are insulting them because you think they are stupid or you do not like them; an informal use. N-COUNT PRAGMATICS
3 See also **knee-jerk.**

jerk around. If you say that someone is **jerking** you **around**, you mean that they are not being honest with you about something; an informal expression. *Don't jerk me around, Mr Crook... We're being jerked around, and I don't like it.* PHRASAL VERB: V n P

jerk off. To **jerk off** means to masturbate; a rude and offensive expression. PHRASAL VERB: V P, V n P

jerkin /dʒɜːʳkɪn/ **jerkins.** A **jerkin** is a sleeveless jacket worn by men or women; an old-fashioned word. N-COUNT

jerky /dʒɜːʳki/ **jerkier, jerkiest.** **Jerky** movements are very sudden and abrupt and do not flow smoothly. *Mr Griffin made a jerky gesture.* [◆◇◇◇◇ ADJ-GRADED: usu ADJ n ≠smooth] ♦ **jerkily** /dʒɜːʳkɪli/ *Using his stick heavily, he moved jerkily towards the car.* [ADV: ADV with v] ♦ **jerkiness** *Avoid jerkiness by breathing easily throughout the whole exercise.* [N-UNCOUNT]

jerry-built /dʒeri bɪlt/. If you describe houses or blocks of flats as **jerry-built**, you are critical of the fact that they have been built very quickly and cheaply, without much care for safety or quality. *Workers at the plant speak of jerry-built equipment and grave technical short-comings... 'The place is a bit jerry-built. Last night the rain leaked through the roof and set off all the smoke detectors.'* [ADJ-GRADED PRAGMATICS]

jersey /dʒɜːʳzi/ **jerseys** [◆◆◆◇◇]
1 A **jersey** is a knitted piece of clothing that covers the upper part of your body and your arms and does not open at the front. Jerseys are usually worn over a shirt or blouse; an old-fashioned use. *His grey jersey and trousers were sodden with the rain.* [N-COUNT =jumper, sweater, pullover]
2 **Jersey** is a knitted, slightly stretchy fabric used especially to make women's clothing. *Sheila had come to dinner in a black jersey top.* [N-VAR: oft N n]

Jersey, Jerseys. A **Jersey cow** or a **Jersey** is a light brown cow that produces very creamy milk. [◆◇◇◇◇ N-COUNT: oft N n]

jest /dʒest/ **jests, jesting, jested** [◆◇◇◇◇]
1 A **jest** is something that you say that is intended to be amusing; a formal use. *It was a jest rather than a reproach... The men talk as cheerfully as ever; jests are bandied about freely.* [N-COUNT =joke] ● If you say something **in jest**, you do not mean it seriously, but want to be amusing. *Don't say that, even in jest... It was said in jest.* [PHRASE: PHR after v ≠seriously]
2 If you **jest**, you tell jokes or say amusing things; a formal use. *He enjoyed drinking and jesting with his cronies... A newspaper half jested: Had alcohol not already killed him, this would surely drive him to drink.* [VERB =joke V; V with quote]

jester /dʒestəʳ/ **jesters.** In the courts of kings and queens in medieval Europe, the **jester** was the person whose job was to do silly things in order to make people laugh. [N-COUNT =fool]

Jesuit /dʒezjuɪt, AM dʒeʒuɪt/ **Jesuits.** A **Jesuit** is a Catholic priest who belongs to the Society of Jesus, which does a lot of missionary work and is especially loyal to the Pope. [◆◇◇◇◇ N-COUNT]

Jesus /dʒiːzəs/ [◆◆◆◇◇]
1 **Jesus** or **Jesus Christ** is the name of the man who Christians believe was the son of God, and whose teachings are the basis of Christianity. [N-PROPER]
2 Some people use **Jesus** as a swear word used to express surprise, shock, or annoyance; an informal use which some people find offensive. [EXCLAM]

jet /dʒet/ **jets, jetting, jetted** [◆◆◆◇◇]
1 A **jet** is an aeroplane that is powered by jet engines. *Her private jet landed in the republic on the way to Japan... He had arrived from Jersey by jet. ...America's first jet aircraft.* ● See also **jump jet**. [N-COUNT: also by N]
2 If you **jet** somewhere, you travel there in a fast aeroplane. *He and his wife, Val, will be jetting off on a two-week holiday in America... They spend a great deal of time jetting around the world.* [VERB V adv/prep]
3 A **jet** of liquid or gas is a strong, fast, thin stream of it. *A jet of water poured through the windows.* [N-COUNT: oft N of n]
4 **Jet** is a hard black stone that is used in jewellery. [N-UNCOUNT]

jet aircraft; **jet aircraft** is both the singular and the plural form. A **jet aircraft** is an aircraft that is powered by one or more jet engines. [N-COUNT]

jet black; also spelled **jet-black**. Something that is **jet black** is a very intense black. *Their long jet-black hair was braided or swept up.* [ADJ]

jet engine, jet engines. A **jet engine** is an engine in which hot air and gases are pushed out at the back. Jet engines are used for most modern aeroplanes. [N-COUNT]

jet lag; also spelled **jetlag**. If you are suffering from **jet lag**, you feel tired and slightly confused after a long journey by aeroplane, especially after travelling between places that have a time difference of several hours. [◆◇◇◇◇ N-UNCOUNT]

jet-lagged. Someone who is **jet-lagged** is suffering from jet-lag. *I'm still a little jet-lagged.* [ADJ-GRADED: usu v-link ADJ]

jetliner /dʒetlaɪnəʳ/ **jetliners.** In American English, a **jetliner** is a large aeroplane, especially one which carries passengers. [N-COUNT]

jetsam /dʒetsəm/. See **flotsam.**

jet set; also spelled **jet-set**. You can refer to rich and successful people who live in a luxurious way as the **jet set**. *The winter sports bring the jet set from England.* [N-SING: usu the N]

jet-setting. You use **jet-setting** to describe people who are rich and successful and who have a luxurious lifestyle. *...the international jet-setting elite. ...his jet-setting lifestyle.* [ADJ: ADJ n]

jet stream, jet streams. The **jet stream** is a very strong wind that blows high in the earth's atmosphere and has an important influence on the weather; a technical term. [N-COUNT]

jettison /dʒetɪsən/ **jettisons, jettisoning, jettisoned** [◆◇◇◇◇]
1 If you **jettison** something, for example an idea or a plan, you deliberately reject it or decide not to use it. *He is already doing a lot to jettison Marxist-Leninist ideology... The Government seems to have jettisoned the plan.* [VERB =abandon V n]
2 If someone **jettisons** something that is not needed, they throw it away or get rid of it. *I had to jettison the first list and make a second list... The crew jettisoned their excess fuel and made an emergency landing.* [VERB =discard V n]

jetty /dʒeti/ **jetties.** A **jetty** is a wide stone wall or wooden platform where boats stop to let people get on or off, or to load or unload goods. [◆◇◇◇◇ N-COUNT: usu the N in sing]

Jew /dʒuː/ **Jews.** A **Jew** is a person who believes in and practises the religion of Judaism. Jews are considered to be the descendants of the ancient Hebrew people. [◆◆◆◇◇ N-COUNT]

jewel /dʒuːəl/ **jewels** [◆◆◇◇◇]
1 A **jewel** is a precious stone used to decorate valuable things that you wear, such as rings or necklaces. *...a golden box containing precious jewels.* ● See also **crown jewels.** [N-COUNT]
2 If you describe something or someone as a **jewel**, you mean that they are better, more beautiful, or more special than other similar things or than other people. *Walk down Castle Street and admire our little jewel of a cathedral... Alan, you're a jewel.* [N-COUNT: oft N of n =treasure]
3 If you refer to an achievement or thing as the **jewel in** someone's **crown**, you mean that it is considered to be their greatest achievement or the thing they can be most proud of. *His achievement is astonishing and this new book is the jewel in his crown.* [PHRASE: usu v-link PHR]

jewel case, jewel cases
1 A **jewel case** is a box for keeping jewels in. [N-COUNT]
2 A **jewel case** is the rigid plastic box in which a compact disc is kept. [N-COUNT]

jewelled /dʒuːəld/; spelled **jeweled** in American English. **Jewelled** items and ornaments are decorated with precious stones. [ADJ]

jeweller /dʒuːələʳ/ **jewellers;** spelled **jeweler** in American English. [◆◇◇◇◇]
1 A **jeweller** is a person who makes, sells, and repairs jewellery and watches. [N-COUNT]
2 A **jeweller** or a **jeweller's** is a shop where jewellery and watches are made, sold, and repaired. [N-COUNT]

jewellery /dʒuːəlri/; spelled **jewelry** in American English. **Jewellery** is ornaments that people wear, for example rings, bracelets, and necklaces. It is often made of a valuable metal such as gold, and sometimes decorated with precious stones. [◆◆◇◇◇ N-UNCOUNT]

Jewish /dʒuːɪʃ/. **Jewish** means belonging or relating to the religion of Judaism or to Jews. *...the Jewish festival of the Passover.* [◆◆◆◇◇ ADJ]

Jewishness /dʒuːɪʃnəs/. Someone's **Jewishness** is the fact that they are a Jew. [N-UNCOUNT: oft with poss]

Jewry /dʒʊəri, AM dʒuːri/. **Jewry** is all the people, or all the people in a particular place, who believe in and practise the religion of Judaism; a formal word. *There could be no better way to strengthen the unity of world Jewry.* [N-UNCOUNT: usu adj N]

jib /dʒɪb/ **jibs, jibbing, jibbed**
1 The **jib** is the small triangular sail that is sometimes used at the front of a sailing boat. N-COUNT: usu *the*N
2 If you **jib** at something, you are unwilling to do it or to accept it; an old-fashioned use. *...those who jib at the idea of selling their land.* VERB V at n/-ing Also V

jibe /dʒaɪb/ **jibes, jibing, jibed;** also spelled **gibe** for meanings 1 and 2. ◆◇◇◇◇
1 A **jibe** is a rude or insulting remark about someone that is intended to make them look foolish. *...a cheap jibe about his loss of hair... There is no longer any truth in the cruel jibe that early music is the last resort of the incompetent.* N-COUNT: oft N that
2 If someone **jibes**, they say something, often something rude or insulting, which is intended to make another person look foolish; used in written English. *'No doubt he'll give me the chance to fight him again,' he jibed, tongue in cheek.* VERB V with quote
3 In informal American English, if numbers, statements, or events **jibe**, they are exactly the same as each other or they are consistent with each other. *The numbers don't jibe... How did your expectations jibe with the reality?* V-RECIP =tally pl-n V V *with* n

jiffy /dʒɪfi/. If you say that you will do something **in a jiffy**, you mean that you will do it very quickly or very soon; an informal use. PHRASE: PHR after v

jig /dʒɪg/ **jigs, jigging, jigged** ◆◇◇◇◇
1 A **jig** is a lively folk dance. *She danced an Irish jig.* N-COUNT
2 To **jig** means to dance or move energetically, especially bouncing up and down. *You didn't just jig about by yourself, I mean you danced properly.* VERB V adv/prep Also V
3 A **jig** is a device that holds something in position when it is being machined by a tool such as a drill. N-COUNT

jiggery-pokery /dʒɪgəri poʊkəri/. In informal British English, if you describe behaviour as **jiggery-pokery**, you mean that it involves mischief, trickery, or dishonesty. The usual American word is **hanky panky**. *It seems astonishing that Bond got away with so much jiggery-pokery for as long as he did.* N-UNCOUNT

jiggle /dʒɪgᵊl/ **jiggles, jiggling, jiggled**
1 If you **jiggle** something, you move it quickly up and down or from side to side; an informal use. *He jiggled the doorknob noisily.* VERB V n
2 If someone or something **jiggles** around, they move quickly up and down or from side to side; an informal use. *He tapped his feet, hummed tunes and jiggled about... A roll of fat jiggled on the underside of her arm.* VERB V adv V

jigsaw /dʒɪgsɔː/ **jigsaws** ◆◇◇◇◇
1 A **jigsaw** or **jigsaw puzzle** is a picture on cardboard or wood that has been cut up into odd shapes. You have to make the picture again by putting the pieces together correctly. N-COUNT =puzzle
2 You can describe a complicated situation as a **jigsaw**. *...the jigsaw of high-level diplomacy.* N-COUNT

jihad /dʒihæd, AM -hɑːd/. A **jihad** is a holy war which Islam allows Muslims to fight against those who reject its teachings. ◆◇◇◇◇ N-SING

jilt /dʒɪlt/ **jilts, jilting, jilted.** If someone **is jilted** by the person who they are having a romantic relationship with, that person ends the relationship suddenly in a way which is surprising and upsetting; an informal use. *She was jilted by her first fiancé... Driven to distraction, he murdered the woman who jilted him... Police want to interview her jilted lover.* VERB =dump be V-ed V n V-ed Also V n

jingle /dʒɪŋgᵊl/ **jingles, jingling, jingled** ◆◆◇◇◇
1 When something **jingles** or when you **jingle** it, it makes a gentle ringing noise, like small bells. *Brian put his hands in his pockets and jingled some change... Her bracelets jingled like bells. ...jingling bottles.* ► Also a noun. *...the jingle of money in a man's pocket.* V-ERG V n V V-ing N-SING: oft N of n
2 A **jingle** is a short, simple tune, often with words, which is used to advertise a product or programme on radio or television. *...advertising jingles.* N-COUNT

jingoism /dʒɪŋgoʊɪzəm/. If you refer to people's behaviour as **jingoism**, you disapprove of it because it shows a strong and unreasonable belief in the superiority of their country, especially in support of a war against another country. N-UNCOUNT PRAGMATICS

jingoistic /dʒɪŋgoʊɪstɪk/. If you describe people's behaviour as **jingoistic**, you disapprove of it because it shows a strong and unreasonable belief in the superiority of their country, especially in support of a war against another country. *The press continued its jingoistic display.* ADJ: usu ADJ n PRAGMATICS

jink /dʒɪŋk/ **jinks, jinking, jinked.** If someone or something **jinks** somewhere, they move there quickly in an irregular way, rather than by moving in a straight line; used in informal British English. *As they reached the start-finish line Prost jinked right and drew abreast.* • See also **high jinks**. VERB V adv/prep Also V

jinx /dʒɪŋks/ **jinxes.** You can call something or someone that is considered to be unlucky or to bring bad luck a **jinx**. *He was beginning to think he was a jinx.* N-COUNT: usu sing

jinxed /dʒɪŋkst/. If something is **jinxed**, it is considered to be unlucky or to bring bad luck. ADJ-GRADED

jitters /dʒɪtəʳz/. If you have the **jitters**, you feel extremely nervous, for example because you have to do something important or because you are expecting important news; an informal word. *I had a case of the jitters during my first two speeches... Officials feared that any public announcements would only increase market jitters.* ◆◇◇◇◇ N-PLURAL: oft *the*N

jittery /dʒɪtəri/. If you say that someone is **jittery**, you mean that they feel nervous or are showing feelings of nervousness; an informal word. *International investors have become jittery about the country's economy.* ◆◇◇◇◇ ADJ-GRADED =jumpy, edgy, on edge

jive /dʒaɪv/ **jives, jiving, jived.** If you **jive**, you dance energetically, especially to jazz music or to rock and roll; an informal word. *I learnt to jive there when they got the jukebox.* VERB V

Jnr. **Jnr** is a written abbreviation for 'Junior', used in British English after a man's name to distinguish him from an older member of his family with the same name. In American English, the abbreviation **Jr.** is used. ◆◇◇◇◇ =Jr

job /dʒɒb/ **jobs** ◆◆◆◆◆
1 A **job** is the work that someone does to earn money. *Once I'm in America I can get a job... Thousands have lost their jobs... I felt the pressure of being the first woman in the job. ...overseas job vacancies.* N-COUNT
2 A **job** is a particular task. *He said he hoped that the job of putting together a coalition wouldn't take too much time... Save major painting jobs for the spring or summer.* N-COUNT: usu with supp, oft N *of*n, n N
3 The **job** of a particular person or thing is their duty or function. *Their main job is to preserve health rather than treat illness... His next job is get us to the World Cup finals... Drinking a lot helps the kidneys do their job.* N-COUNT: usu with poss
4 If you say that someone is doing a good **job**, or is making a good **job** of something, you mean that they are doing it well. *We could do a far better job of managing it than they have... You've done a fine job with Billy and Joey.* N-SING: usu adj N, oft N *of*-ing/n
5 If you say that you have a **job** doing something, you are emphasizing how difficult it is. *He may have a hard job selling that argument to investors... With all these different pensions, you're going to have a job to keep track.* N-SING: usu N -ing, N to-inf PRAGMATICS
6 See also **jobbing**; **day job**, **hatchet job**, **on-the-job**.
7 In British English, if you refer to work as **jobs for the boys**, you mean that the work is unfairly given to someone's friends, supporters, or relations, even though they may not be the best qualified people to do it. *The Party has been accused of creating a 'jobs for the boys' system of government.* PHRASES PRAGMATICS =cronyism
8 If you say that something is **just the job**, you mean that it is exactly what you wanted or needed; used in informal British English. *Not only is it just the job for travelling, but it's handy for groceries too.* usu v-link PHR
9 If someone is **on the job**, they are actually doing a particular job or task. *The top pay scale after five years on the job would reach $5.00 an hour... There was no formal training; they learned on the job.*
10 • **it's a good job**: see **good**. • **the job in hand**: see **hand**.

jobbing /dʒɒbɪŋ/. In British English, a **jobbing** worker does not work for someone on a regular basis, but does particular jobs when they are asked to. *...a jobbing builder.* ADJ: ADJ n

job centre, job centres; also spelled **jobcentre.** In Britain, a **job centre** is a place where people who are looking for work can go to get advice on finding a job, and to look at adverts placed by people who are looking for new employees. N-COUNT

jobless /dʒɒbləs/. Someone who is **jobless** does not have a job, although they would like one. *One in four people are now jobless in inner areas like Tottenham and Peckham. ...the number of jobless people.* ◆◆◇◇◇ ADJ =unemployed ► **The jobless** are people who are jobless. *They joined the ranks of the jobless.* N-PLURAL: the N ♦ **joblessness** *Concern over the rising level of joblessness was a feature of yesterday's debate.* N-UNCOUNT =unemployment

job lot, job lots. A **job lot** is a number of cheap things of low quality which are sold together, for example in auctions or second-hand shops. *I was lucky to get it as part of a job lot at a sale.* N-COUNT

job seeker, job seekers. The term **job seeker** is sometimes used by the government and journalists to refer to an unemployed person who is trying to get a job. N-COUNT

job sharing. Job sharing is the arrangement by which two people share the same job by working part-time, for example one person working in the mornings and the other in the afternoons. N-UNCOUNT

jobsworth /dʒɒbzwɜːʳθ/ **jobsworths.** In British English, if you call someone a **jobsworth**, you are critical of them because they are so concerned about the rules and regulations connected to their job that they are not prepared to break them in order to do something kind or sensible. *A surly jobsworth alerted security.* N-COUNT PRAGMATICS

jock /dʒɒk/ **jocks**

1 A **jock** is a young man who is very enthusiastic about a particular sport or other activity, and spends a lot of time doing it or involved with it; an informal use. *...an all-American football jock.* N-COUNT

2 A **jock** is the same as a **disc jockey**; an informal use. *...top Radio 1 jock Simon Bates.* N-COUNT

jockey /dʒɒki/ **jockeys, jockeying, jockeyed** ◆◆◇◇◇

1 A **jockey** is someone who rides a horse in a race. N-COUNT

2 If you say that someone **is jockeying** for something, you mean that they are using whatever methods they can in order to get it or do it before their competitors can get it or do it. *The rival political parties are already jockeying for power... Already, both sides are jockeying to belittle the other side.* VERB V for n V to-inf ● If someone **is jockeying for position**, they are using whatever methods they can in order to get into a better position than their rivals. PHRASE: V inflects

jockey shorts. Jockey shorts are men's underpants that are shaped like the shorts worn for playing sports, and cover the top of the thighs. Jockey Shorts is a trademark. N-PLURAL: also a pair of N =boxer shorts

jockstrap /dʒɒkstræp/ **jockstraps.** A **jockstrap** is a piece of clothing worn by sportsmen under their shorts or trousers to support their genitals. N-COUNT

jocular /dʒɒkjʊləʳ/. If you say that someone has a **jocular** manner, you mean that they are cheerful and often make jokes or try to make people laugh; a formal word. *He was in a less jocular mood than usual... The song was written in a light-hearted jocular way.* ADJ-GRADED =humorous

jodhpurs /dʒɒdpəʳz/; the form **jodhpur** is used as a modifier. **Jodhpurs** are trousers that people wear when they ride a horse. Jodhpurs are usually loose from the thigh to the knee and tight below the knee. *...a boy in jodhpurs.* N-PLURAL: also a pair of N

jog /dʒɒg/ **jogs, jogging, jogged** ◆◇◇◇◇

1 If you **jog**, you run slowly, often as a form of exercise. *I got up early the next morning to jog... He could scarcely jog around the block that first day.* VERB V ► Also a noun. *He went for another early morning jog.* N-COUNT ♦ **jogging** *It isn't the walking and jogging that got his weight down.* N-UNCOUNT

2 If you **jog** something, you push or bump it slightly so that it moves. *Avoid jogging the camera.* VERB V n

3 If something or someone **jogs** your **memory**, they cause you to suddenly remember something that you had forgotten. *Police have planned a reconstruction of the crime tomorrow in the hope this will jog the memory of passers-by.* PHRASE: V inflects

jogger /dʒɒgəʳ/ **joggers.** A **jogger** is a person who runs at a jogging pace as a form of exercise. N-COUNT

joie de vivre /ʒwɑː də viːvrə/. **Joie de vivre** is a feeling of happiness and enjoyment of life; a literary expression. *He has plenty of joie de vivre.* N-UNCOUNT

join /dʒɔɪn/ **joins, joining, joined** ◆◆◆◆◆

1 If one person or vehicle **joins** another, they move or go to the same place, for example so that both of them can do something together. *His wife and children moved to join him in their new home... The two policemen were joined by another policeman also carrying a pistol.* VERB V n

2 If you **join** an organization, you become a member of it or start work as an employee of it. *He joined the Army five years ago... She joined a dance company which took her around the world.* VERB V n

3 If you **join** an activity that other people are doing, you take part in it or become involved with it. *Telephone operators joined the strike and four million engineering workers are also planning action... The pastor requested the women present to join him in prayer... Last night the group which represents private contractors joined in condemning the Government's confused stance.* VERB V n V n in n/-ing V in -ing

4 If you **join** a queue, you stand at the end of it so that you are part of it. *Make sure you join the queue inside the bank.* VERB V n

5 To **join** two things means to fix or fasten them together. *The opened link is used to join the two ends of the chain. ...the conjunctiva, the skin which joins the eye to the lid. ...two springs that are joined together by a string.* VERB V pl-n V n prep/adv

6 If something such as a line or path **joins** two things, it connects them. *It has a dormer roof joining both gable ends... The car parks are joined by a footpath. ...a global highway of cables joining all the continents together.* VERB V pl-n V-ing

7 If two roads or rivers **join**, or if one road or river **joins** another, the two meet or come together at a particular point. *Do you know the highway to Tulsa? The airport road joins it. ...Allahabad, where the Ganges and the Yamuna rivers join.* V-RECIP V n pl-n V

8 A **join** is a place where two things are fastened or fixed together. N-COUNT

9 ● **join forces**: see **force**. ● **join the ranks**: see **rank**.

join in. If you **join in** an activity, you take part in it or become involved in it. *I hope that everyone will be able to join in the fun... The songs the woman will sing will be known by everyone present and all will join in as she sings.* PHRASAL VERB V P n V P

join up PHRASAL VERB

1 In British English, if someone **joins up**, they become a member of the army, the navy, or the air force. *When hostilities broke out he returned to England and joined up.* =enlist V P

2 If a person or thing **joins up** with another, they move or go to the same place. *Hawkins joined up with Mick in Malaga, and the two went touring around the countryside... Councils are joining up with their European counterparts in a number of special interest groups... They began to join up in communities and to contribute to the livelihood of other communities.* RECIP V P with n pl-n V P

joiner /dʒɔɪnəʳ/ **joiners.** A **joiner** is a person who makes wooden window frames, door frames, doors, and cabinets; used mainly in British English. Compare **carpenter.** N-COUNT

joinery /dʒɔɪnəri/. **Joinery** is the skill and work of a joiner; used mainly in British English. N-UNCOUNT

joint /dʒɔɪnt/ **joints** ◆◆◆◆◇

1 **Joint** means shared by or belonging to two or more people. *She and Frank had never gotten around to opening a joint account... Jackie and Ben came to a joint decision as to where they would live.* ADJ: ADJ n ♦ **jointly** *The Port Authority is an agency jointly run by New York and New Jersey.* ADV: ADV with v

2 A **joint** is a part of your body such as your elbow N-COUNT

or knee where two bones meet and are able to move together. *Her joints ache if she exercises.*

3 A **joint** is the place where two things are fastened or fixed together. ● See also **dovetail joint**. N-COUNT

4 In British English, a **joint** is a fairly large piece of meat which is suitable for roasting. The usual American word is **roast**. *He carved the joint of beef.* N-COUNT

5 You can refer to a place where people go for some form of entertainment as a **joint**; an informal use. *They had come to the world's most famous pick-up joint... She had always wanted to eat in a hamburger joint in Hollywood.* N-COUNT: usu supp N

6 A **joint** is a cigarette which contains cannabis; an informal use. N-COUNT =spliff, reefer

PHRASES

7 If something puts someone's **nose out of joint**, it upsets or offends them because it makes them feel less important or less valued; an informal use. *Barry had his nose put out of joint by Lucy's aloof sophistication... Her sister-in-law's nose is a little out of joint.* PHR after v, v-link PHR

8 If something is **out of joint**, it is not quite right or appropriate, or does not work quite as it should. *There was something out of joint in the situation. Something was strange... The electoral timetable seems to be out of joint with the need for change.* usu v-link PHR

jointed /dʒɔɪntɪd/

1 Something that is **jointed** has joints that move. *The glass cover for this is cleverly jointed in the middle.* ADJ

2 A **jointed** chicken or other bird has been cut into pieces so that it is ready to cook. ADJ

joint-stock company, joint-stock companies. A **joint-stock company** is a business company that is owned by the people who have bought shares in that company; a technical term in business. N-COUNT

joist /dʒɔɪst/ **joists. Joists** are long thick pieces of metal, wood, or concrete that form part of the structure of a building, usually to support a floor or ceiling. N-COUNT =beam

jojoba /hoʊhoʊbə/. **Jojoba** or **jojoba oil** is oil which is made from the seeds of the jojoba plant, which is a small tree that grows in the South West part of North America. Jojoba oil is used in many cosmetics such as shampoos. N-UNCOUNT

joke /dʒoʊk/ **jokes, joking, joked** ◆◆◆◇◇

1 A **joke** is something that is said or done to make you laugh, for example a funny story. *He debated whether to make a joke about shooting rabbits, but decided against it... No one told worse jokes than Claus.* N-COUNT: oft N *about* n

2 If you **joke**, you tell funny stories or say amusing things. *She would joke about her appearance... Lorna was laughing and joking with Trevor... The project was taking so long that Stephen joked that it would never be finished... 'Well, a beautiful spring Thursday would probably be a nice day to be buried on,' Nancy joked.* VERB V *about* n, V *with* n, V that, V with quote

3 A **joke** is something untrue that you tell another person in order to amuse yourself. *It was probably just a joke to them, but it wasn't funny to me.* N-COUNT

4 If you **joke**, you tell someone something that is not true in order to amuse yourself. *Don't get defensive, Charlie. I was only joking... 'I wish you made as much fuss of me,' Vera joked, going into the scullery to make some fresh tea.* VERB =kid, V, V with quote

5 If you say that something or someone is **a joke**, you think they are ridiculous and not worthy of respect; an informal use. *It's ridiculous, it's pathetic, it's a joke... The police investigation was a joke. A total cover-up.* N-SING: a N PRAGMATICS

PHRASES

6 If you say that an annoying or worrying situation is **beyond a joke**, you are emphasizing that it is worse than you think is fair or reasonable; used mainly in British English. *Giving an arsonist a lighter is beyond a joke... I'm not afraid of a fair fight but this is beginning to get beyond a joke.* v-link PHR, PHR after v PRAGMATICS

7 If you **make a joke of** something, you laugh at it even though it is in fact rather serious or sad. *I wish I had your courage, Michael, to make a joke of it like that.* V inflects, PHR n

8 If you describe a situation as **no joke**, you are emphasizing that it is very difficult or unpleasant; an informal expression. *Two hours on a bus is no joke, is it.* v-link PHR PRAGMATICS

9 If you say that **the joke is on** a particular person, you mean that they have been made to look very foolish by something. *'For once,' he said, 'the joke's on me. And it's not very funny.'* V inflects, PHR n

10 If you say that someone **cannot take a joke**, you are criticizing them for getting upset or angry at something you think is funny. *'What's the matter with you, Simon?' Curly said. 'Can't you take a joke?'* V inflects PRAGMATICS

11 You say **you're joking** or **you must be joking** to someone when they have just told you something that is so surprising or unreasonable that you find it difficult to believe; used in spoken English. *You're joking. Are you serious?... One hundred and forty quid for a pair of headphones, you've got to be joking!* CONVENTION PRAGMATICS =you're kidding

joker /dʒoʊkəʳ/ **jokers** ◆◇◇◇◇

1 Someone who is a **joker** likes making jokes or doing amusing things. *He is, by nature, a joker, a witty man with a sense of fun.* N-COUNT

2 The **joker** in a pack of playing cards is the card which does not belong to any of the four suits. N-COUNT

3 If you describe someone or something as **the joker in the pack**, you mean that they are different from the other people or things in their group, and can be unpredictable. PHRASE

jokey /dʒoʊki/. If something is done in a **jokey** way, it is intended to be amusing, rather than to have a serious meaning or intention; an informal word, used mainly in British English. *Bruno has not got his younger brother's jokey manner... He was still his old jokey self.* ADJ-GRADED: usu ADJ n ≠serious

jokingly /dʒoʊkɪŋli/. If you say or do something **jokingly**, you do it with the intention of amusing someone, rather than with any serious meaning or intention. *Sarah jokingly called her 'my monster'... She frowned at him, only half-jokingly.* ADV: ADV with v

jollity /dʒɒlɪti/. **Jollity** is cheerful behaviour; an old-fashioned word. *...the singing and jollity of the celebration.* N-UNCOUNT

jolly /dʒɒli/ **jollier, jolliest** ◆◆◇◇◇

1 Someone who is **jolly** is happy and cheerful in their appearance or behaviour. *She was a jolly, kindhearted woman.* ADJ-GRADED

2 A **jolly** event is lively and enjoyable. *I was looking forward to a jolly party... She had a very jolly time in Korea.* ADJ-GRADED: usu ADJ n

3 In British English, you can use **jolly** to give emphasis to an adjective or adverb; an informal, old-fashioned use. *She was jolly good at jigsaws... It was jolly hard work, but I loved it.* ADV: ADV adj/adv PRAGMATICS =very, extremely

4 In British English, you use **jolly well** to emphasize what you are saying, especially when you are annoyed or angry; an informal, old-fashioned expression. *We can hardly just tell him what we jolly well think of him can we?... She was jolly well not going to let them get away with it.* PHRASE: PHR before v, PHR adj PRAGMATICS

jolt /dʒoʊlt/ **jolts, jolting, jolted** ◆◇◇◇◇

1 If something **jolts** or if something **jolts** it, it moves suddenly and quite violently. *The wagon jolted again... The train jolted into motion... They were working frantically in the fear that an after-shock would jolt the house again.* ► Also a noun. *We were worried that one tiny jolt could worsen her injuries.* V-ERG V, V prep, V n; N-COUNT

2 If something **jolts** someone, it gives them an unpleasant surprise or shock. *A stinging slap across the face jolted her... Henderson was momentarily jolted by the news... It is tragic that it needs deaths to jolt authorities into action... She had drifted into a light sleep when an uproar from the hallway jolted her awake.* ► Also a noun. *The campaign came at a time when America needed such a jolt.* VERB V n, V n prep, V n adj; N-COUNT

Jordanian /dʒɔːʳdeɪniən/ **Jordanians** ◆◆◆◆◇

1 **Jordanian** means belonging or relating to the country of Jordan, or to its people or culture. ADJ

2 A **Jordanian** is a Jordanian citizen, or a person of Jordanian origin. N-COUNT

joss stick /dʒɒs stɪk/ **joss sticks.** A **joss stick** is a thin stick covered with a substance that burns very slowly and fills the air with a perfumed smell; used mainly in British English. N-COUNT

jostle /dʒɒsᵊl/ **jostles, jostling, jostled** ◆◇◇◇◇

1 If people **jostle** you, they bump against you or push you in a way that annoys you, usually because you are in a crowd and they are trying to get past you. *You get 2,000 people jostling each other and bumping into furniture... We spent an hour jostling with the crowds as we did our shopping... She was cheered and clapped by tourists who jostled to see her... Crowds of near hysterical men jostled their way through to try to find news of their wives and families.* VERB; V n; V prep/adv; V to-inf; V *way* adv/prep; Also V n prep/adv

2 If people or things **are jostling for** something such as attention or a reward, they are competing with other people or things in order to get it. *...the contenders who have been jostling for the top job... There is a wide spread of stories jostling for coverage on today's front pages.* VERB =compete; V *for* n

jot /dʒɒt/ **jots, jotting, jotted** ◆◇◇◇◇

1 If you **jot** something short such as an address somewhere, you write it down so that you will remember it. *Could you just jot his name on there.* VERB =note; V n prep/adv

► **Jot down** means the same as **jot**. *Keep a pad handy to jot down queries as they occur... Listen carefully to the instructions and jot them down.* PHRASAL VERB =note down; V P n (not pron); V n P

2 If you say that there is not **a jot** or not **one jot** of something, you are emphasizing that there is not even a very small amount of it; an old-fashioned use. *There is not a jot of evidence to say it does them any good... It makes not one jot of difference.* QUANT: with brd-neg, QUANT *of* n-uncount; PRAGMATICS; =a bit

3 You can use **a jot** or **one jot** to emphasize a negative statement. **Not a jot** or **not one jot** means not even to a small extent or degree. An old-fashioned use. *It doesn't affect my judgement one jot... It matters not a jot.* PHRASE: with brd-neg, PHR after v; PRAGMATICS

jotting /dʒɒtɪŋ/ **jottings. Jottings** are brief, informal notes that you write down. N-COUNT: usu pl =note

joule /dʒuːl/ **joules.** A **joule** is a unit of energy or work; a technical term in physics. N-COUNT

journal /dʒɜːʳnᵊl/ **journals** ◆◆◆◆◇

1 A **journal** is a magazine, especially one that deals with a specialized subject. *All our results are published in scientific journals.* N-COUNT

2 A **journal** is a daily or weekly newspaper. The word journal is often used in the name of the paper. *He was a newspaperman for The New York Times and some other journals. ...The Wall Street Journal.* N-COUNT

3 A **journal** is an account which you write of your daily activities. *Sara confided to her journal... On the plane he wrote in his journal.* N-COUNT =diary

journalism /dʒɜːʳnəlɪzəm/. **Journalism** is the job of collecting news or other information, and writing about it in newspapers or magazines or talking about it on television or radio. *He began a career in journalism, working for the North London Press Group... It was an accomplished piece of investigative journalism.* • See also **chequebook journalism**. ◆◆◇◇◇ N-UNCOUNT

journalist /dʒɜːʳnəlɪst/ **journalists.** A **journalist** is a person whose job is to collect news or other information, and write about it in newspapers or magazines or talk about it on television or radio. ◆◆◆◆◇ N-COUNT =reporter

journalistic /dʒɜːʳnəlɪstɪk/. **Journalistic** means relating to journalism, or produced by or typical of a journalist. *He began his journalistic career in the early eighties in Australia. ...journalistic descriptions of countries she visited.* ◆◇◇◇◇ ADJ: ADJ n

journey /dʒɜːʳni/ **journeys, journeying, journeyed** ◆◆◆◇◇

1 When you make a **journey**, you travel from one place to another. *There is an express service from Paris which completes the journey to Bordeaux in under 4 hours.* N-COUNT: oft supp N, N prep

2 You can refer to a person's experience of changing or developing from one state of mind to another as a **journey**. *How do we go about embarking on this 'inner journey' to understand ourselves?... My films try to describe a journey of discovery, both for myself and the watcher.* N-COUNT: with supp

3 If you **journey** somewhere, you travel there; a formal use. *In February 1935, Naomi journeyed to the United States for the first time... She has journeyed on horseback through Africa and Turkey.* VERB =travel; V *to* n; V prep/adv

4 If you **break** your **journey** somewhere, you stop there for a short time so that you can have a rest; used mainly in British English. *Because of the heat we broke our journey at a small country hotel.* PHRASE: V inflects, usu PHR prep/adv

journeyman /dʒɜːʳnimən/ **journeymen**

1 In former times, a **journeyman** was a worker who has finished learning a trade and who was employed by someone else rather than working on his or her own. N-COUNT

2 If you refer to someone, especially a sportsman or woman or an entertainer, as a **journeyman**, you mean that they have the basic skill which their job requires, but that they do not have much talent or originality; used mainly in journalism. *Douglas was a 29-year-old journeyman fighter, erratic in his previous fights.* N-COUNT: oft N n

joust /dʒaʊst/ **jousts, jousting, jousted**

1 When two or more people or organizations **joust**, they compete with each other for superiority; a literary use. *Sleep is the only escape for jurors as lawyers joust in the courtroom... The image of the white knight jousting with the oppressive tyranny of bureaucrats, oligarchs and politicians is tempting.* V-RECIP =spar; pl-n V; V *with* n

► Also a noun. *There were notable jousts with the Secretary of Commerce.* N-COUNT

2 In medieval times, when two knights on horseback **jousted**, they fought against each other using lances. *Knights joust and frolic.* ♦ **jousting** *...medieval jousting tournaments.* V-RECIP; pl-n V; Also V *with* n; N-UNCOUNT

jovial /dʒoʊviəl/. If you describe a person as **jovial**, you mean that they are happy and behave in a cheerful way; used in written English. *Father Whittaker appeared to be in a jovial mood... Grandma was plump and jovial.* ♦ **joviality** /dʒoʊviælɪti/ *...his old expansive joviality.* ♦ **jovially** *'No problem,' he said jovially.* ADJ-GRADED; N-UNCOUNT; ADV-GRADED: ADV with v

jowl /dʒaʊl/ **jowls**

1 You can refer to someone's lower cheeks as their **jowls**, especially when they hang down and cover their jawbones; a literary use. N-COUNT: usu pl

2 If you say that people or things are **cheek by jowl** with each other, you are indicating that they are very close to each other. *She and her family have to live cheek by jowl with these people.* PHRASE: usu v PHR, v-link PHR, PHR n, oft PHR *with* n

jowly /dʒaʊli/. Someone who is **jowly** has fat cheeks which hang downwards towards their jaw. *The man was jowly, unshaven, balding.* ADJ-GRADED

joy /dʒɔɪ/ **joys** ◆◆◆◇◇

1 **Joy** is a feeling of great happiness. *Salter shouted with joy. ...tears of joy.* N-UNCOUNT

2 A **joy** is something or someone that makes you feel happy or gives you great pleasure. *One can never learn all there is to know about cooking, and that is one of the joys of being a chef... It was a joy to see her looking so well.* N-COUNT: with supp =delight

3 In informal British English, if you get no **joy**, you do not have success or luck in achieving what you are trying to do. *They expect no joy from the vote itself... If you don't get any joy, get in touch with your local councillor.* N-UNCOUNT: with brd-neg

4 If you say that someone **is jumping for joy**, you mean that they are very pleased or happy about something. *He jumped for joy on being told the news.* • one's **pride and joy**: see **pride**. PHRASE: V inflects

joyful /dʒɔɪfʊl/ ◆◇◇◇◇

1 Something that is **joyful** causes happiness and pleasure; a formal use. *Giving birth to a child is both painful and joyful... A wedding is a joyful celebration of love.* ADJ-GRADED

2 Someone who is **joyful** is extremely happy; a formal use. *We're a very joyful people; we're very musical people and we love music.* ♦ **joyfully** *They greeted him joyfully.* ADJ-GRADED; ADV-GRADED

joyless /dʒɔɪləs/. Something that is **joyless** produces no happiness or pleasure; a formal word. *His work load, meanwhile, had become so enor-* ADJ-GRADED =miserable ≠joyous *mous that life seemed joyless... Eating in East Berlin used to be a hazardous and joyless experience.*

joyous /dʒɔɪəs/. **Joyous** means extremely happy; a literary word. *She had made their childhood so joyous and carefree. ...a joyous celebration of life.* ♦ **joyously** *Sarah accepted joyously.* ◆◇◇◇◇ ADJ-GRADED =joyful ≠joyless ADV-GRADED

joyride /dʒɔɪraɪd/ **joyrides.** If someone goes on a **joyride**, they steal a car and drive around in it at high speed. N-COUNT

joyrider /dʒɔɪraɪdəʳ/ **joyriders.** A **joyrider** is someone who steals cars in order to drive around in them at high speed. ◆◇◇◇◇ N-COUNT

joyriding /dʒɔɪraɪdɪŋ/. **Joyriding** is the crime of stealing a car and driving around in it at high speed. N-UNCOUNT

joystick /dʒɔɪstɪk/ **joysticks**
1 In some computer games, the **joystick** is the lever which the player uses in order to control the direction of the things on the screen. N-COUNT: usu sing
2 In an aeroplane, the **joystick** is the lever which the pilot uses in order to control the direction and height of the aeroplane; an informal use. N-COUNT: usu sing

JP /dʒeɪ piː/ **JPs.** In Britain, a **JP** is a **Justice of the Peace.** N-COUNT =magistrate

Jr; this abbreviation is usually followed by a full stop in American English. **Jr** is a written abbreviation for **Junior**. It is used after a man's name to distinguish him from an older member of his family with the same name. *...Harry Connick Jr.* ◆◆◇◇◇ =Jnr

jubilant /dʒuːbɪlənt/. If you are **jubilant**, you feel extremely happy because of a success. *Ferdinand was jubilant after making an impressive comeback from a month on the injured list. ...the jubilant crowds of Paris.* ◆◇◇◇◇ ADJ-GRADED =ecstatic

jubilation /dʒuːbɪleɪʃᵊn/. **Jubilation** is a feeling of great happiness and triumph, because of a success; a formal word. *His resignation was greeted by jubilation on the streets of Sofia. ...cheers of jubilation.* N-UNCOUNT

jubilee /dʒuːbɪliː/ **jubilees.** A **jubilee** is a special anniversary of an event, especially the 25th or 50th anniversary. *...Queen Victoria's jubilee.* • See also **golden jubilee, silver jubilee.** ◆◇◇◇◇ N-COUNT

Judaic /dʒuːdeɪɪk/. **Judaic** means belonging or relating to Judaism; a formal word. ADJ: ADJ n

Judaism /dʒuːdeɪɪzəm/. **Judaism** is the religion of the Jewish people. It is based on the Old Testament of the Bible and the Talmud. ◆◇◇◇◇ N-UNCOUNT

Judas /dʒuːdəs/ **Judases.** If you accuse someone of being a **Judas**, you are accusing them of being deceitful and betraying their friends or country. *The Soviet press called him a Judas in the service of the West.* N-COUNT PRAGMATICS =traitor

judder /dʒʌdəʳ/ **judders, juddering, juddered.** If something **judders**, it shakes and vibrates violently. *The lift started off, juddered, and went out of action... The car was juddering and vibrating as if it would explode.* VERB V

judge /dʒʌdʒ/ **judges, judging, judged** ◆◆◆◆◇
1 A **judge** is the person in a court of law who decides how the law should be applied, for example how criminals should be punished. *The judge adjourned the hearing until next Tuesday... Judge Mr Justice Schiemann jailed him for life.* N-COUNT; N-TITLE
2 A **judge** is a person who decides who will be the winner of a competition. *A panel of judges is now selecting the finalists.* N-COUNT
3 If you **judge** something such as a competition, you decide who or what is the winner. *Colin Mitchell will judge the entries each week... Entrants will be judged in two age categories: 5-10 years and 11-14 years... A grade B judge could only be allowed to judge alongside a qualified grade A judge.* ♦ **judging** *The judging was difficult as always.* VERB V n V N-UNCOUNT
4 If you **judge** something or someone, you form an opinion about them after you have examined the evidence or thought carefully about them. *It will take a few more years to judge the impact of these ideas... I am ready to judge any book on its merits... It's for other people to judge how much I have improved... The UN withdrew its relief personnel because it judged the situation too dangerous... I judged it to be one of the worst programmes ever screened.* VERB =evaluate, assess V n V n *on* n V wh V n adj V n to-inf
5 If you **judge** something, you guess its amount, size, or value or you guess what it is. *It is important to judge the weight of your washing load correctly... I judged him to be about forty... The shoreline could be dimly seen it was impossible to judge how far away it was.* VERB =estimate V n V n to-inf V wh
6 If someone is a good **judge** of something, they understand it and can make sensible decisions about it. If someone is a bad **judge** of something, they cannot do this. *I'm a pretty good judge of character... It would appear that my sister is a poor judge of masculine charm.* N-COUNT: usu sing, usu N *of* n
7 You use **judging by**, **judging from** or **to judge from** to introduce the reasons why you believe or think something. *Judging by the opinion polls, he seems to be succeeding... Judging from the way he laughed as he told it, it was meant to be humorous... To judge from his productivity, Mozart clearly enjoyed robust good health throughout his twenties.* PHRASES PREP PRAGMATICS
8 If you say that something is true **as far as** you **can judge** or **so far as** you **can judge**, you mean that you are assuming or guessing that it is true, although you do not know all the details and facts about it. *They were typed records of his bets, going back a couple of years as far as I could judge... The book, so far as I can judge, is remarkably accurate.* PHR with cl

judgment /dʒʌdʒmənt/ **judgments;** also spelled **judgement** in British English. ◆◆◆◇◇
1 A **judgment** is an opinion that you have or express after thinking carefully about something. *In your judgment, what has changed over the past few years?... How can he form any judgement of the matter without the figures?... I don't really want to make any judgments on the decisions they made.* N-VAR
2 **Judgment** is the ability to make sensible guesses about a situation or sensible decisions about what to do. *I respect his judgement and I'll follow any advice he gives me... He said that publication of the information was a serious error in judgment.* N-UNCOUNT: oft with poss
3 A **judgment** is a decision made by a judge or by a court of law. *The industry was awaiting a judgment from the European Court... The Court is expected to give its judgement within the next ten days.* N-VAR =verdict, ruling
4 If something is **against** your **better judgment**, you believe that it would be more sensible or better not to do it. *Against my better judgement I agreed... She had become so fond of him, almost against her better judgement.* PHRASES PHR with cl, PHR after v, v-link PHR
5 If you **pass judgment** on someone or something, you give your opinion about it, especially if you are making a criticism. *It's not for me to pass judgement, it's a personal matter between the two of you... It's very hard to pass judgement on yourself.* V inflects
6 If you **reserve judgment** on something, you refuse to give an opinion about it until you know more about it. *Doctors are reserving judgement on his ability to travel until later in the week.* V inflects, usu PHR *on* n
7 To **sit in judgment** means to decide whether or not someone is guilty of doing something wrong. *He argues very strongly that none of us has the right to sit in judgment.* V inflects

judgmental /dʒʌdʒmentᵊl/; also spelled **judgemental** in British English. If you say that someone is **judgmental**, you are critical of them because they form opinions on people and situations very quickly, when it would be better for them to wait until they know more about the person or situation. *We tried not to seem critical or judgmental while giving advice that would protect him from ridicule... You should not be judgemental about people and their differing sexualities.* ADJ-GRADED PRAGMATICS

judgment call, judgment calls; also spelled **judgement call**. If you refer to a decision as a **judgment call**, you mean that there are no firm rules or principles that can help you make it, so you simply have to rely on your own judgement and instinct; used mainly in American English. *Well, physicians make judgment calls every day.* N-COUNT

judicial /dʒuːdɪʃᵊl/. **Judicial** means relating to the legal system and to judgements made in a court of law. ...*an independent judicial inquiry... The last judicial hanging in Britain was in 1964. ...judicial decisions.* ♦ **judicially** *Even if the amendment is passed it can be defeated judicially.*
◆◆◇◇◇ ADJ: ADJ n
ADV: ADV with v

judiciary /dʒuːdɪʃəri, AM -ʃieri/. **The judiciary** is the branch of authority in a country which is concerned with justice and the legal system; a formal word. *The judiciary must think very hard before jailing non-violent offenders.*
◆◆◇◇◇ N-SING: *the* N

judicious /dʒuːdɪʃəs/. If you describe an action or decision as **judicious**, you approve of it because you think that it shows good judgement and sense; a formal word. *The President authorizes the judicious use of military force to protect our citizens.* ♦ **judiciously** *Modern fertilisers should be used judiciously.*
◆◇◇◇◇ ADJ-GRADED PRAGMATICS =wise
ADV-GRADED: ADV with v

judo /dʒuːdoʊ/. **Judo** is a Japanese sport or martial art in which two people fight and try to throw each other to the ground.
◆◇◇◇◇ N-UNCOUNT

jug /dʒʌg/ **jugs.** A **jug** is a cylindrical container with a handle and a lip or spout, used for holding and pouring liquids. ...*a handpainted ceramic jug.* ► A jug of liquid is the amount that the jug contains. ...*a jug of water.*
◆◇◇◇◇ N-COUNT =pitcher
N-COUNT =jugful

juggernaut /dʒʌgəʳnɔːt/ **juggernauts**

1 A **juggernaut** is a very large lorry; used mainly in British English.
N-COUNT

2 If you describe an organization or group as a **juggernaut**, you are critical of them because they are large and extremely powerful, and you think they are not being controlled properly. *The group became a sales juggernaut in the commodity options business.*
N-COUNT PRAGMATICS

juggle /dʒʌgᵊl/ **juggles, juggling, juggled**
◆◇◇◇◇

1 If you say that you **juggle** lots of different things, for example your work and your family, you are indicating that it is difficult to fit them all in so that you have enough time for all of them, or to arrange them so that they fit the pattern you want them to. *The management team meets several times a week to juggle budgets and resources... Mike juggled the demands of a family of 11 with a career as a TV reporter... Scientists are juggling with theories about how the giant lizards vanished from the earth.*
VERB
V n
V n *with* n
V *with* n

2 If you **juggle**, you entertain people by throwing things into the air, catching each one and throwing it up again so that there are several of them in the air at the same time. *Soon she was juggling five eggs... I can't juggle.* ♦ **juggling** *He can perform an astonishing variety of acts, including mime and juggling.*
VERB
V n
V
N-UNCOUNT

juggler /dʒʌgləʳ/ **jugglers.** A **juggler** is someone who juggles in order to entertain people.
N-COUNT

juggling act, juggling acts. If you say that a situation is a **juggling act**, you mean that someone is trying to do two or more things at once, and that they are finding it difficult to do those things properly. *Beth was doing precisely the tricky juggling act that a lot of women do. She was trying to be wife, mother, and employee, and feeling desperately tired and inadequate.*
N-COUNT

jugular /dʒʌgjʊləʳ/ **jugulars**

1 A **jugular** or **jugular** vein is one of the three important veins in your neck that carry blood from your head back to your heart.
N-COUNT

2 If you say that someone **went for the jugular**, you mean that they ruthlessly attacked another person's weakest points; an informal expression. *A look of disbelief crossed her face when Mr Black went for the jugular, asking intimate sexual questions.*
PHRASE: V inflects

juice /dʒuːs/ **juices**
◆◆◆◇◇

1 **Juice** is the liquid that can be obtained from a fruit. ...*fresh orange juice... Soak the couscous overnight in the juice of about six lemons.*
N-MASS: usu with supp

2 The **juices** of a joint of meat are the liquid that comes out of it when you cook it. *When cooked, drain off the juices and put the meat in a processor or mincer.*
N-PLURAL

3 The **juices** in your stomach are the fluids that help you to digest food.
N-PLURAL: with supp

juicy /dʒuːsi/ **juicier, juiciest**
◆◇◇◇◇

1 If food is **juicy**, it has a lot of juice in it and is very enjoyable to eat. ...*a thick, juicy steak.*
ADJ-GRADED

2 You can describe information as **juicy**, if it is exciting or scandalous; an informal use. *It provided some juicy gossip for a few days. ...the juicy details.*
ADJ-GRADED: usu ADJ n

jukebox /dʒuːkbɒks/ **jukeboxes;** also spelled **juke-box.** A **jukebox** is a record player in a place such as a pubs or a bar. You put a coin in and choose the record you want to hear. *My favorite song is on the jukebox.*
N-COUNT

Jul. **Jul.** is a written abbreviation for **July**. *'Eat before Jul 14' was stamped on the label.*
◆◆◇◇◇

July /dʒʊlaɪ/ **Julys. July** is the seventh month of the year in the Western calendar. *In late July 1914, he and Violet spent a few days with friends near Berwick-upon-Tweed... I expect you to report for work on July the twenty-eighth.*
◆◆◆◆◇ N-VAR

jumble /dʒʌmbᵊl/ **jumbles, jumbling, jumbled**
◆◇◇◇◇

1 A **jumble** of things is a lot of different things that are all mixed together in a disorganized or confused way. *The shoreline was made up of a jumble of huge boulders. ...a meaningless jumble of words.*
N-COUNT: usu sing, usu N *of* n =muddle

2 If you **jumble** things, or if they **jumble**, they become mixed together so that they are untidy or not in the correct order. *They jumble together shampoos, toys, chocolate, clothes, electronic goods and hair slides. ...a number of animals whose remains were jumbled together by scavengers and floods... Jumble spots and stripes to build a whole spectrum of blues... His thoughts jumbled and raced like children fighting.* ► To **jumble up** means the same as to **jumble**. *They had jumbled it all up into a heap... The bank scrambles all that money together, jumbles it all up and lends it out to hundreds and thousands of borrowers... The watch parts fell apart and jumbled up... There were six wires jumbled up, tied together, all painted black.*
V-ERG =mix
V n with *together*
V n
V
Also V n prep
PHRASAL VERB ERG
V n P prep/adv
V n P
V P
V-ed P
Also V P n (not pron)

3 In British English, **jumble** is old or unwanted things that people give away to charity. The American word is **rummage**. *She expects me to drive round collecting jumble for the church.*
N-UNCOUNT

jumbled /dʒʌmbᵊld/. If you describe things or ideas as **jumbled**, you mean that they are mixed up and not in order. *These jumbled priorities should be no cause for surprise... The Judaeo-Christian tradition is diverse, jumbled, contradictory, at every point inviting inquiry and debate.*
ADJ-GRADED =muddled

jumble sale, jumble sales. In British English, a **jumble sale** is a sale of cheap second-hand goods, usually held to raise money for charity. The usual American expression is **rummage sale**. *We are having a jumble sale at our school.*
N-COUNT

jumbo /dʒʌmboʊ/ **jumbos**
◆◇◇◇◇

1 **Jumbo** means very large; used mainly in advertising and in the names of products. ...*a jumbo box of tissues. ...grilled jumbo prawns.*
ADJ: ADJ n =giant

2 A **jumbo** or a **jumbo jet** is a very large jet aeroplane that can carry several hundred passengers. ...*a British Airways jumbo.*
N-COUNT

jump /dʒʌmp/ **jumps, jumping, jumped**
◆◆◆◆◇

1 If you **jump**, you bend your knees, push against the ground with your feet, and move quickly upwards into the air. *I jumped over the fence... They came into the front hall, stamping their boots and jumping up and down to knock the snow off... I'd jumped seventeen feet six in the long jump, which was a school record... Whoever heard of a basketball player who doesn't need to jump?* ► Also a noun. *The longest jumps by a man and a woman were witnessed in Sestriere, Italy, yesterday.*
VERB
V prep/adv
V n
V
N-COUNT

2 If you **jump** from something above the ground, you deliberately push yourself into the air so that you drop towards the ground. *He jumped out of a third-floor window... She has jumped from an aeroplane four times (with a parachute)... I jumped the last six feet down to the deck.*
VERB =leap
V prep/adv
V n
Also V

3 If you **jump** something such as a fence, you move quickly up and through the air over or across it. *He jumped the first fence beautifully.*
VERB
V n

4 If you **jump** somewhere, you move there quickly and suddenly. *Adam jumped from his seat at the girl's cry... She jumped to her feet and ran downstairs... 'I'll do it, Eleanor,' Angus said, jumping up.* VERB V prep/adv

5 If something makes you **jump**, it makes you make a sudden movement because you are frightened or surprised. *The phone shrilled, making her jump.* VERB V

6 If an amount or level **jumps**, it suddenly increases or rises by a large amount in a short time. *Sales jumped from $94 million to over $101 million... The number of crimes jumped by ten per cent last year... Shares in Euro Disney jumped 17p.* VERB V *to/from* amount V *by* amount V amount ► Also a noun. *A big jump in energy conservation could be achieved without much disruption of anyone's standard of living.* N-COUNT: with supp, usu N *in* n

7 If someone **jumps** a queue, they move to the front of it and are served or dealt with before it is their turn; used in British English. *The prince refused to jump the queue for treatment at the local hospital.* VERB V n

8 If someone **jumps** on you or **jumps** you, they attack you suddenly; an informal use. *A week later, the same guys jumped on me on our own front lawn... Two guys jumped me with clubs in the carpark.* VERB V on n V n

9 If you **jump at** an offer or opportunity, you accept it quickly and eagerly. *Members of the public would jump at the chance to become part owners of the corporation.* VB: no cont V at n

10 If someone **jumps on** you, they quickly criticize you if you do something that they do not approve of. *A lot of people jumped on me about that, you know.* VERB V on n

11 See also **bungee jumping**, **high jump**, **long jump**, **queue-jumping**, **show jumping**, **triple jump**.

12 In American English, if you **get a jump on** something or someone or **get the jump on** them, you gain an advantage over them, especially by doing something before they do it; used mainly in journalism. *Helicopters helped fire crews get a jump on the blazes... The idea is to get the jump on him.* PHRASES V inflects, PHR n

13 If you say that someone is **jumping up and down**, you mean they are very excited, happy, or angry about something. *I don't think a lot of people will jump up and down and say 'thank heavens'... Everybody still jumps up and down about being rid of tyrants.* V inflects

14 • to **jump on the bandwagon**: see **bandwagon**. • to **jump bail**: see **bail**. • to **jump to a conclusion**: see **conclusion**. • to **jump the gun**: see **gun**. • to **jump for joy**: see **joy**. • to **jump out of one's skin**: see **skin**.

jump in. If you **jump in**, you act quickly and decisively, often without thinking much about what you are doing. *The Government had to jump in and purchase millions of dollars worth of supplies.* PHRASAL VERB V P

jump out. If you say that something **jumps out** at you, you mean that it is easy to notice it because it is different from other things of its type. *Every so often one letter will jump out at you as being a bit different.* PHRASAL VERB V P at n Also V P

jumped-up. In informal British English, if you describe someone as **jumped-up**, you disapprove of them because they consider themselves to be more important than they really are. *He's nothing better than a jumped-up bank clerk!* ◆◇◇◇◇ ADJ: usu ADJ n PRAGMATICS

jumper /dʒʌmpəʳ/ **jumpers** ◆◆◇◇◇

1 In British English, a **jumper** is a warm knitted piece of clothing which covers the upper part of your body and your arms. *With her simple jumper and skirt, Isabel looked like a young girl again.* N-COUNT =sweater, pullover

2 In American English, a **jumper** is a sleeveless dress that is worn over a blouse or sweater. The usual British word is **pinafore**. *She wore a checkered jumper and had ribbons in her hair.* N-COUNT

3 If you refer to a person or a horse as a particular kind of **jumper**, you are describing how good they are at jumping or the way that they jump. *He is a terrific athlete and a brilliant jumper... Horses are not natural jumpers.* N-COUNT: usu adj N

4 A particular kind of **jumper** is an athlete who takes part in a particular jumping event. *Packer began her career as a long jumper.* N-COUNT: supp N

jumping-off point. A **jumping-off point** or a **jumping-off place** is a place, situation, or occasion which you use as the starting point for something. *Lectoure is a bustling market town and the best jumping-off point for a first visit to Le Gers.* N-SING =springboard

jump jet, jump jets. In British English, a **jump jet** is a jet aircraft that can take off and land vertically. N-COUNT

jump leads /dʒʌmp liːdz/. In British English, **jump leads** are two thick wires that can be used to start a car whose battery does not have enough power. The jump leads are used to connect the battery to the battery of another car that is working properly. N-PLURAL

jumpsuit /dʒʌmpsuːt/ **jumpsuits.** A **jump suit** is a piece of clothing in the form of a top and trousers in one continuous piece. *I was wearing a purple jumpsuit, high heeled shoes, and lots of makeup.* N-COUNT

jumpy /dʒʌmpi/. If you are **jumpy**, you are nervous or worried about something; an informal word. *I told myself not to be so jumpy... When he spoke his voice was jumpy.* ADJ-GRADED: usu v-link ADJ =jittery, edgy, on edge

Jun. **Jun.** is a written abbreviation for **June**. *...Wed 21 Jun.* ◆◆◇◇◇

junction /dʒʌŋkʃᵊn/ **junctions.** A **junction** is a place where roads or railway lines join. In American English, the more usual word is **intersection**, especially when referring to roads. *Follow the road to a junction and turn left... Leave the M1 at junction 25... There's a good British Rail link at Clapham Junction.* ◆◆◇◇◇ N-COUNT: oft in names

juncture /dʒʌŋktʃəʳ/ **junctures.** At a particular **juncture** means at a particular point in time, especially when it is a very important time in a process or series of events. *What's important at this juncture is the ability of the three republics to work together... We're at a critical juncture in terms of his domestic program.* N-COUNT: usu with supp, usu *at* N

June /dʒuːn/ **Junes.** **June** is the sixth month of the year in the Western calendar. *He spent two and a half weeks with us in June 1986... I am moving out on June 5... Last June I decided to take a trip to Marbella.* ◆◆◆◆◇ N-VAR

jungle /dʒʌŋgᵊl/ **jungles** ◆◆◇◇◇

1 A **jungle** is a forest in a tropical country where there large numbers of tall trees and plants grow very close together. *...the mountains and jungles of Papua New Guinea... The seventy square miles of the mountain area were covered entirely in dense jungle. ...a remote jungle area.* N-VAR

2 If you describe a place as a **jungle**, you are emphasizing that it is full of lots of things and very untidy. *...a jungle of stuffed sofas, stuffed birds, knick-knacks, potted plants.* N-SING: with supp PRAGMATICS

3 If you describe a situation as a **jungle**, you dislike it because it is complicated and difficult to get what you want from it. *Social security law and procedure remain a jungle of complex rules. ...the examination jungle.* N-SING: with supp PRAGMATICS

4 If you refer to **the law of the jungle**, you are referring to a situation in which there are no laws or rules to govern the way that people behave and people use force to get what they want. *If you make aggression pay, this becomes the law of the jungle... The law of the jungle demands: kill or be killed.* PHRASE

junior /dʒuːniəʳ/ **juniors** ◆◆◆◇◇

1 A **junior** official or employee holds a lower-ranking position in an organization or profession. *Junior and middle-ranking civil servants have pledged to join the indefinite strike. ...a junior minister attached to the prime minister's office.* ADJ-GRADED: usu ADJ n =senior ► Also a noun. *The Lord Chancellor has said legal aid work is for juniors when they start out in the law.* N-COUNT

2 If you are someone's **junior**, you are younger than they are. *She now lives with actor Denis Lawson, 10 years her junior.* N-SING: poss N

3 In American English, when there are two people N-IN-NAMES

in one family who have the same name, especially a father and son, **Junior** is sometimes used after the younger person's name to prevent confusion. The abbreviations **Jnr** and **Jr** are also used. *His son, Arthur Ochs Junior, is expected to succeed him as publisher.*

4 In the United States, a student in the third year of a high school or university course is called a **junior**. *Their youngest daughter Amy's a junior at the University of Evansville in Indiana... It was the summer before his junior year in high school.* N-COUNT

junior school, junior schools. In England and Wales, a **junior school** is a school for children between the ages of about seven and eleven. *...Middleton Road Junior School.* N-VAR: oft in names after n

juniper /dʒuːnɪpəʳ/ **junipers.** A **juniper** is an evergreen bush with purple berries which can be used in cooking and medicine. ◆◇◇◇◇ N-VAR

junk /dʒʌŋk/ **junks, junking, junked** ◆◆◇◇◇

1 If you describe a group of objects as **junk**, you think that they are old and useless; an informal use. *What are you going to do with all that junk, Larry?... The dining room's still full of junk.* N-UNCOUNT PRAGMATICS =rubbish

2 You can use **junk** to refer to old and second-hand goods that people buy and collect. *For unusual pictures, look out for old illustrated books in junk shops. ...the vast array of junk we had collected for display on our stall.* N-UNCOUNT: usu N n

3 If you **junk** something, you get rid of it or stop using it; an informal use. *Consumers will not have to junk their old cassettes to use the new format... The Socialists junked dogma when they came to office in 1982.* VERB =ditch, jettison V n

4 A **junk** is a Chinese sailing boat that has a flat bottom and square sails. N-COUNT

junk bond, junk bonds. If a company issues **junk bonds**, it borrows money from investors, usually at a high rate of interest, in order to finance a particular deal, for example the setting up or the taking over of a company. ◆◆◇◇◇ N-COUNT: usu pl

junket /dʒʌŋkɪt/ **junkets.** If you describe a trip or visit by an official or businessman as a **junket**, you disapprove of it because it is expensive, unnecessary, and often has been paid for with public money; an informal word. *He took frequent junkets with friends to exotic locales.* N-COUNT PRAGMATICS

junk food, junk foods. If you refer to food as **junk food**, you mean that it is quick and easy to prepare but is not good for your health. N-MASS

junkie /dʒʌŋki/ **junkies** ◆◇◇◇◇

1 A **junkie** is a drug addict; an informal use. N-COUNT

2 You can use **junkie** to refer to someone who is very interested in a particular activity, especially when they spend a lot of time on it; an informal use. *...a computer junkie.* N-COUNT: n N

junk mail. **Junk mail** is advertisements and publicity materials that you receive through the post which you have not asked for and which you do not want. *My junk mail always goes straight into the bin.* N-UNCOUNT

junkyard /dʒʌŋkjɑːʳd/ **junkyards.** A **junkyard** is the same as a **scrapyard**. N-COUNT

junta /dʒʌntə, hʊntə/ **juntas.** If you refer to a **junta**, you mean a military government that has taken power by force, and not through elections; used showing disapproval. ◆◇◇◇◇ N-COUNT-COLL PRAGMATICS

jurisdiction /dʒʊərɪsdɪkʃən/ **jurisdictions** ◆◇◇◇◇

1 **Jurisdiction** is the power that a court of law or an official has to carry out legal judgements or to enforce laws; a formal word. *The British police have no jurisdiction over foreign bank accounts.* N-UNCOUNT =authority

2 A **jurisdiction** is a state or other area in which a particular court and system of laws has authority; used in formal or American English. N-COUNT

jurisprudence /dʒʊərɪspruːdəns/. **Jurisprudence** is the study of law and the principles on which laws are based; a formal word. N-UNCOUNT

jurist /dʒʊərɪst/ **jurists.** A **jurist** is a person who is an expert on law; a formal word. *Patrick Devlin was an outstanding judge and brilliant jurist.* N-COUNT

juror /dʒʊərəʳ/ **jurors.** A **juror** is a member of a jury. ◆◇◇◇◇ N-COUNT

jury /dʒʊəri/ **juries** ◆◆◆◇◇

1 In a court of law, the **jury** is the group of people who have been chosen from the general public to listen to the facts about a crime and to decide whether the person accused is guilty or not. *The jury convicted Mr Hampson of all offences. ...the tradition of trial by jury.* N-COUNT-COLL: also *by* N

2 A **jury** is a group of people who choose the winner of a competition. *I am not surprised that the Booker Prize jury included it on their shortlist.* N-COUNT-COLL =panel

3 If you say that **the jury is out** or that **the jury is still out** on a particular subject, you mean that people in general have still not made a decision or formed an opinion about that subject. *The jury is out on whether or not this is true... The jury is still out on what kind of solutions we might undertake.* PHRASE: oft PHR *on* wh/n

just 1 adverb uses

just /dʒʌst/ ◆◆◆◆◆

1 You use **just** to say that something happened a very short time ago, or is starting to happen at the present time. For example, if you say that someone **has just arrived**, you mean that they arrived a very short time ago. *I've just bought a new house... The two had only just met and were barely friends... I just had the most awful dream... I'm only just beginning to take it in that he's still missing.* ADV: ADV before v

2 If you say that you are **just** doing something, you mean that you are doing it now and will finish it very soon. If you say that you are **just about to** do something, or **just going to** do something, you mean that you will do it very soon. *I'm just making the sauce for the cauliflower... I'm just going to walk down the lane now and post some letters... The Vietnam War was just about to end.* ADV: ADV before v, ADV *about/going* to-inf

3 You can also use **just** to emphasize that something is happening at exactly the moment of speaking or at exactly the moment that you are talking about. *Randall would just now be getting the Sunday paper... Just then the phone rang... I remember now. He arrived just at the moment it happened... Just as she prepared to set off to the next village, two friends arrived in a taxi.* ADV: ADV adv/prep, ADV *as/when* cl PRAGMATICS

4 You use **just** to indicate that something is no more important, interesting, or difficult, for example, than you say it is, especially when you want to correct a wrong idea that someone may get or has already got. *It's just a suggestion... It's not just a financial matter... I am sure you can tell just by looking at me that I am all right... The reason women are drinking is just because they like it.* ADV: ADV group/cl PRAGMATICS =only, simply

5 You use **just** to emphasize that you are talking about a small part or sample, not the whole of an amount. *That's just one example of the kind of experiments you can do... These are just a few of the many options available.* ADV: ADV n PRAGMATICS =only, merely

6 You use **just** to draw attention to how small an amount is or how short a length of time is. *Stephanie and David redecorated a room in just three days... Remember he's just fourteen years old.* ADV: ADV amount PRAGMATICS =only

7 You can use **just** in front of a verb to indicate that the result of something is unfortunate or undesirable and is likely to make the situation worse rather than better. *Leaving like I did just made it worse... They just hurt the people in their community, they didn't really solve any problem.* ADV: ADV before v PRAGMATICS =only

8 You use **just** to indicate that what you are saying is the case, but only by a very small degree or amount. *Her hand was just visible by the light from the sitting room... It was Colin's voice, only just audible... I arrived just in time for my flight to London... Jack took out his notes and talked for just under an hour... He could just reach the man's head with his right hand.* ADV: ADV adj/adv/prep, ADV before v =barely

9 You use **just** with 'might,' 'may,' and 'could', when you mean that there is a small chance of something happening, despite the fact that it is not very likely. *It's an old trick but it just might work... It may just be possible.* ADV: ADV with modal

10 You use **just** to emphasize the following word or phrase, in order to express feelings such as annoyance, admiration, or certainty. *She just won't relax... I knew you'd be here. I just knew... Isn't it fan-* ADV: ADV before v, ADV adj/n PRAGMATICS =simply *tastic? Just look at that!... Just think, we should be home this time tomorrow... I don't see the point in it really. It's just stupid... Isn't he just the most beautiful thing you ever saw?*

11 You use **just** with instructions, polite requests or statements of intention, to make your request or statement seem less difficult and problematical than someone might think. *Could you just give us a description of your cat?... Can you just lift the table for a second?... I'm just going to ask you a bit more about your father's business... Just add water, milk and butter... I'd just like to mention that, personally, I don't think it's wise... Just wait for me in the lounge.* ADV: ADV before v PRAGMATICS

12 You use **just** in expressions such as **just a minute**, **just a moment**, and **just a second** when you are asking someone to wait for a short time; used in spoken English. *'Let me in, Di.'—'Okay. Just a minute.'* ADV: ADV n PRAGMATICS =hold on

13 You can use **just** in expressions such as **just a minute**, **just a moment**, and **just a second** when you want to interrupt or stop someone, for example in order to disagree with them, explain something, or calm them down; used in spoken English. *Well, now just a second, I don't altogether agree with the premise.* ADV: ADV n PRAGMATICS

14 In spoken British English, you can use **just** with negative question tags, for example **'isn't he just?'** and **'don't they just!'**, to say that you agree completely with what has been said. *'That's crazy,' I said. 'Isn't it just?' he said... 'The manager's going to have some tough decisions to make.'—'Won't he just.'* ADV: with neg, cl ADV PRAGMATICS

15 If you say that you can **just** see or hear something, you mean that it is easy for you to imagine seeing or hearing it. *I can just see the nasty suspicious looks I'd be getting from you if we started whispering together... I can just hear her telling her friends, 'Well, I blame his mother!'* ADV: ADV before v =almost

16 You use **just** to mean exactly, when you are specifying something precisely or asking for precise information. *It is really not clear just why he became a Socialist... There are no statistics about just how many people won't vote... My arm hurts too, just here... That's Warwick Road, just opposite Earls Court tube station.* ADV: ADV cl/prep/adv =exactly

17 You use **just** to emphasize that a particular thing is exactly what is needed or fits a particular description exactly. *Kiwi fruit are just the thing for a healthy snack... 'Let's get a coffee somewhere.'—'I know just the place.' ...the bottle of whiskey that we had stashed behind the bookcase for just this eventuality.* ADV: ADV n PRAGMATICS =exactly

18 You use **just** in expressions such as **just like**, **just as...as**, and **just the same** when you are emphasizing the similarity between two things or two people. *Behind the facade they are just like the rest of us... He worked just as hard as anyone... At 62 years old, her voice sounded just the same as it did when she was 21.* ADV: ADV *like* n, ADV *as* adj/adv, ADV n PRAGMATICS

19 You use **just about** to indicate that what you are talking about is so close to being the case that it can be regarded as being the case. *There are those who believe that Nick Price is just about the best golfer in the world... What does she read? Just about everything... 'His memory must be completely back, then?'—'Just about.'* PHRASES PHR n/adj/adv =practically

20 You use **just about** to indicate that what you are talking about is in fact the case, but only by a very small degree or amount. *I can just about tolerate it at the moment... We've got just about enough time to get there.* PHR before v, PHR n/adj =only just

21 **Just on** is used to specify an exact number or amount; used mainly in British English. *Eve, squinting at the clock, saw it was just on 7 a.m... Many were retired people, and just on a fifth were in their fifties.* PHR amount

22 **Just so** is used to agree with or confirm a statement that has been made; a formal expression used in spoken British English. *'She has a large flat in Mayfair.'—'Just so.'* CONVENTION PRAGMATICS =quite, exactly

23 If things are **just so**, they are done or arranged exactly as they should be or exactly as someone wants them. *I do her hair, and it has to be just so.* usu v-link PHR

24 You use the expression **it's just that** when you are making a complaint, suggestion, or excuse, so that the person you are talking to will not get annoyed with you. *I'm sorry I struck you. I didn't mean to. It's just that I was so mad... Your hair is all right; it's just that you need a haircut.* PHR cl PRAGMATICS

25 • **just my luck**: see **luck**. • **just now**: see **now**. • **only just**: see **only**. • it **just goes to show**: see **show**. • **not just**: see **not**.

just 2 adjective use

just /dʒʌst/. If you describe a situation, action, or idea as **just**, you mean that it is right or acceptable according to particular moral principles, such as respect for all human beings; a formal use. *In a just society there must be a system whereby people can seek redress through the courts... She fought honestly for a just cause and for freedom... Was Pollard's life sentence just or was it too severe?* ♦ **justly** *They were not treated justly in the past... No government can justly claim authority unless it is based on the will of the people.* • to **get your just deserts**: see **desert**. ◆◇◇◇◇ ADJ-GRADED =fair ≠unjust; ADV-GRADED: ADV with v =fairly ≠unjustly

justice /dʒʌstɪs/ **justices** ◆◆◆◆◇

1 **Justice** is fairness in the way that people are treated. *He has a good overall sense of justice and fairness... He only wants freedom, justice and equality... There is no justice in this world!* N-UNCOUNT

2 The **justice** of a cause, claim, or argument is its quality of being reasonable, justifiable, or right. *We are a minority and must win people round to the justice of our cause.* N-UNCOUNT =legitimacy

3 **Justice** is the legal system that a country uses in order to deal with people who break the law. *Many in Toronto's black community feel that the justice system does not treat them fairly... A lawyer is part of the machinery of justice.* N-UNCOUNT: oft N n

4 In American English, a **justice** is a judge. *Thomas will be sworn in today as a justice on the Supreme Court.* N-COUNT

5 **Justice** is used before the names of judges. *A preliminary hearing was due to start today before Mr Justice Hutchison, but was adjourned.* N-TITLE

6 See also **miscarriage of justice**.

7 If a criminal is **brought to justice**, he or she is punished for a crime by being arrested and tried in a court of law. *They demanded that those responsible be brought to justice... She'd need proof to bring Jason to justice.* PHRASES V inflects

8 If someone or something **does justice** to a person or thing, they describe or reproduce them in a way that shows truly how good or valuable they are. *The photograph I had seen didn't do her justice... Most TV sets don't have the sound quality to do justice to the music.* V inflects

9 If you **do justice** to someone or something, you deal with them properly and completely. *No one article can ever do justice to the topic of fraud... It is impossible here to do justice to the complex history of the Legion.* V inflects, usu PHR *to* n

10 If you **do** yourself **justice**, you do something as well as you are capable of doing it. *I don't think he could do himself justice playing for England... I don't think I can win, but I want to do myself justice.* V inflects

11 If you describe someone's treatment or punishment as **rough justice**, you mean that it is not given according to the law; used mainly in British English. *Trial by television makes for very rough justice indeed.*

12 If you say that something is **rough justice** for someone, you mean that they have not been treated fairly; used mainly in British English. *It would have been rough justice had he been deprived of this important third European win.* v-link PHR

Justice of the Peace, Justices of the Peace. In Britain, a **Justice of the Peace** is a person who is not a lawyer but who is authorized to act as a judge in a local criminal law court. The abbreviation **JP** is also used. N-COUNT =magistrate

justifiable /dʒʌstɪfaɪəbəl/. An action, situation, emotion, or idea that is **justifiable** is acceptable or correct because there is a good reason for it. *The violence of the revolutionary years was justifiable on the grounds of political necessity. ...the strong and justifiable desire of the Baltic States for independence.* ♦ **justifiably** /dʒʌstɪfaɪəbli/ *He was justifiably proud of his achievements.* ◆◇◇◇◇ ADJ-GRADED: oft *it* v-link ADJ to-inf =legitimate ADV-GRADED

justification /dʒʌstɪfɪkeɪʃən/ **justifications.** A **justification** for something is an acceptable reason or explanation for it. *To me the only justification for a zoo is educational... I knew from the beginning that there was no justification for what I was doing.* ◆◆◇◇◇ N-VAR =defence, excuse

justified /dʒʌstɪfaɪd/ ◆◆◇◇◇

1 If you describe a decision, action, or idea as **justified**, you think it is reasonable and acceptable. *In my opinion, the decision was wholly justified.* ADJ-GRADED PRAGMATICS

2 If you think that someone is **justified in** doing something, you think that their reasons for doing it are good and valid. *He's absolutely justified in resigning. He was treated shamefully.* ADJ: v-link ADJ *in* -ing PRAGMATICS

justify /dʒʌstɪfaɪ/ **justifies, justifying, justified.** If someone or something **justifies** a particular decision, action, or idea, they show or prove that it is reasonable or necessary. *No argument can justify a war... Ministers agreed that this decision was fully justified by economic conditions.* ◆◆◆◇◇ VERB V n

justly /dʒʌstli/. You use **justly** to show that you approve of someone's attitude towards something, because it seems to be based on truth or reality. *Australians are justly proud of their native wildlife.* ● See also **just**. ADV: usu ADV adj, also ADV with v PRAGMATICS =justifiably

jut /dʒʌt/ **juts, jutting, jutted** ◆◇◇◇◇

1 If something **juts** out, it sticks out above or beyond a surface. *The northern end of the island juts out like a long, thin finger into the sea... Tombstones jutted out of the ground in broken clusters... He had clear blue eyes and a jutting chin.* VERB =stick out V adv/prep V-ing

2 If you **jut** a part of your body, especially your chin, or if it **juts**, you push it forward in an aggressive or determined way. *His jaw jutted stubbornly forward; he would not be denied... Gwen jutted her chin forward, her nose in the air, and did not bother to answer the teacher... Derek's jaw jutted with determination.* V-ERG V adv/prep V n adv/prep V Also V n

jute /dʒuːt/. **Jute** is a substance that is used to make cloth and rope. It comes from a plant which grows mainly in South-East Asia. N-UNCOUNT

juvenile /dʒuːvənaɪl/ **juveniles** ◆◆◇◇◇

1 A **juvenile** is a child or young person who is not yet old enough to be regarded as an adult; a formal use. *The number of juveniles in the general population has fallen by a fifth in the past 10 years.* N-COUNT

2 **Juvenile** activity or behaviour involves young people who are not yet adults. *Juvenile crime is increasing at a terrifying rate. ...a scheme to lock up persistent juvenile offenders.* ADJ: ADJ n =childish

3 If you describe someone's behaviour as **juvenile**, you are critical of it because you think that it is silly or immature. *It is juvenile to call your opponents the Democrat Party when you know they are the Democratic Party.* ADJ-GRADED PRAGMATICS

4 A **juvenile** is a young animal. N-COUNT

juvenile court, juvenile courts. A **juvenile court** is a court which deals with crimes committed by young people who are not yet old enough to be considered as adults. N-VAR

juvenile delinquency. **Juvenile delinquency** is vandalism and other criminal behaviour that is committed by young people who are not old enough to be legally considered as adults. N-UNCOUNT

juvenile delinquent, juvenile delinquents. A **juvenile delinquent** is a young person who is guilty of committing crimes, especially vandalism or violence. N-COUNT

juxtapose /dʒʌkstəpoʊz/ **juxtaposes, juxtaposing, juxtaposed.** If you **juxtapose** two contrasting objects, images, or ideas, you place them together or describe them together, so that the differences between them are strongly emphasized; a formal word. *The technique Mr Wilson uses most often is to juxtapose things for dramatic effect... Contemporary photographs are juxtaposed with a sixteenth century, copper Portuguese mirror. ...art's oldest theme: the celebration of life juxtaposed with the terror of mortality.* VERB V pl-n *be* V-ed *with* n V-ed Also V n *with* n

juxtaposition /dʒʌkstəpəzɪʃən/ **juxtapositions.** The **juxtaposition** of two contrasting objects, images, or ideas is the fact that they are placed together or described together, so that the differences between them are strongly emphasized; a formal word. *This juxtaposition of brutal reality and lyrical beauty runs through Park's stories.* ◆◇◇◇◇ N-VAR: usu N *of* n

Kk

K, k /keɪ/ **K's, k's**

1 **K** is the eleventh letter of the English alphabet. N-VAR

2 **K** or **k** is used as an abbreviation for words beginning with k, such as 'kilometre', 'kilobyte', or 'king'.

3 **K** or **k** is sometimes used to represent the number 1000, especially when referring to sums of money; an informal use. *I used to make over 40k.* NUM: usu num NUM

kaftan /kæftæn/ **kaftans.** See **caftan**.

kale /keɪl/. **Kale** is a vegetable that is similar to a cabbage. N-UNCOUNT

kaleidoscope /kəlaɪdəskoʊp/ **kaleidoscopes**

1 A **kaleidoscope** is a toy in the shape of a tube with a small hole at one end. If you look through the hole and turn the other end of the tube, you can see a pattern of colours which changes as you turn the tube round. N-COUNT

2 You can describe something that is made up of a lot of different and frequently changing colours or elements as a **kaleidoscope**. *...the vivid kaleidoscope of colours displayed in the plumage of the peacock. ...a kaleidoscope of different alliances, groupings and interests.* N-SING: usu with supp, oft N *of* n

kaleidoscopic /kəlaɪdəskɒpɪk/. If you describe something as **kaleidoscopic**, you mean that it consists of a lot of very different parts, such as different colours, patterns, or shapes. *...a kaleidoscopic range of fabrics by American design house, Robert Allen. ...a kaleidoscopic study of the shifting ideas and symbols of French nationhood.* ADJ: ADJ n

kamikaze /kæmɪkɑːzi/

1 If someone such as a soldier or terrorist performs a **kamikaze** act, they attack the enemy knowing that they will be killed doing it. *...kamikaze pilots who say they are ready to strike and bomb nuclear installation targets.* ADJ: ADJ n

2 You can use **kamikaze** to describe an action or attitude which involves doing something which is very dangerous and likely to harm the person who does it. *These are kamikaze jobs, the ones almost guaranteed to end your career... Tone down your kamikaze tendencies and take more prudent risks.* ADJ: ADJ n

kangaroo /kæŋgəruː/ **kangaroos.** A **kangaroo** is a large Australian animal which moves by jumping on its back legs. Female kangaroos carry their babies in a pouch on their stomachs. ◆◇◇◇◇ N-COUNT

kangaroo court, kangaroo courts. If you refer to a court or a meeting as a **kangaroo court**, you disapprove of it because it is unofficial or unfair, and is intended to find someone guilty. N-COUNT PRAGMATICS

kaput /kəpʊt/. If you say that something is **kaput**, you mean that it is completely broken, useless, or finished; an informal word. *'What's happened to your car?' – 'It's kaput.'... He finally admitted that his film career was kaput.* ADJ: usu v-link ADJ

karaoke /kærioʊki/. **Karaoke** is a form of entertainment in which a machine plays tapes of the tunes of pop songs, and people take it in turns to use a microphone to sing the words. ◆◇◇◇◇ N-UNCOUNT

karate /kərɑːti/. **Karate** is a Japanese martial art or sport in which people fight without weapons, using only their hands, elbows, feet, and legs. ◆◇◇◇◇ N-UNCOUNT

karma /kɑːʳmə/. In religions such as Hinduism and Buddhism that accept the idea of reincarnation, **karma** is the belief that your actions in this life affect all your future lives. ◆◇◇◇◇ N-UNCOUNT

kart /kɑːʳt/ **karts.** A **kart** is the same as a **go-kart**. N-COUNT

kayak /kaɪæk/ **kayaks.** A **kayak** is a boat like a canoe, used by the Inuit people and in the sport of canoeing. N-COUNT

kazoo /kəzuː/ **kazoos.** A **kazoo** is a small musical instrument that consists of a pipe with a hole in the side. You play the kazoo by blowing into it while humming. N-COUNT

kebab /kəbæb, AM -bɑːb/ **kebabs.** A **kebab** is a dish of Turkish or Greek origin, consisting of small pieces of grilled meat, and sometimes vegetables, either inside a pitta bread or on a long thin metal rod. N-VAR

kedgeree /kedʒəriː/. **Kedgeree** is a cooked dish consisting of rice, fish, and eggs. N-UNCOUNT

keel /kiːl/ **keels, keeling, keeled** ◆◇◇◇◇

1 The **keel** of a boat is the long, specially shaped piece of wood or steel along the bottom of it. N-COUNT

2 If you say that someone or something is **on an even keel**, you mean that they are working or progressing smoothly and steadily, without any sudden changes. *Jason had helped him out with a series of loans, until he could get back on an even keel.* PHRASE: PHR after v, v-link PHR

keel over. If someone **keels over**, they collapse because they are tired or ill; an informal use. *He then keeled over and fell flat on his back.* PHRASAL VERB VP

keen /kiːn/ **keener, keenest; keens, keening, keened** ◆◆◆◇◇

1 If you are **keen** on doing something, you very much want to do it. If you are **keen** that something should happen, you very much want it to happen. *You're not keen on going, are you?... Both companies were keen on a merger... I'm very keen that the European Community should be as open as possible to trade from Russia... She's still keen to keep in touch... I am not keen for her to have a bicycle.* ADJ-GRADED: v-link ADJ, ADJ *on* -ing/n, ADJ that, ADJ to-inf ♦ **keenness** *...Doyle's keenness to please. ...the country's keenness for better economic ties with China.* N-UNCOUNT: oft N to-inf =enthusiasm

2 If you are **keen on** something, you like it a lot and are very enthusiastic about it. *I got quite keen on the idea... I wasn't too keen on physics and chemistry.* ADJ-GRADED: v-link ADJ *on* n ♦ **keenness** *...his keenness for the arts.* N-UNCOUNT

3 You use **keen** to indicate that someone has a lot of enthusiasm for a particular activity and spends a lot of time doing it. *She was a keen amateur photographer... Many of you are keen on DIY.* ADJ-GRADED: ADJ n, v-link ADJ *on* n/-ing

4 If you describe someone as **keen**, you mean that they have an enthusiastic nature and are interested in everything that they do. *He's a very keen student and works very hard... You're all very keen.* ADJ-GRADED =enthusiastic ♦ **keenness** *...the keenness of the students.* N-UNCOUNT

5 A **keen** interest or emotion is one that it very intense. *He had retained a keen interest in the progress of the work. ...his keen sense of loyalty.* ADJ-GRADED: usu ADJ n ♦ **keenly** *She remained keenly interested in international affairs... This is a keenly awaited project.* ADV-GRADED: ADV adj, ADV with v

6 If you are a **keen** supporter of a cause, movement, or idea, you support it enthusiastically. *He's been a keen supporter of the Labour Party all his life... He is a keen advocate of park-and-ride schemes.* ADJ-GRADED: ADJ n

7 If you say that someone has a **keen** intellect, you mean that they are very clever and aware of what is happening around them. *They described him as a man of keen intellect... Mr Walsh has a keen appreciation of the priorities of the electorate... I can see you have a keen sense of humour.* ADJ-GRADED: ADJ n ♦ **keenly** *They're keenly aware that whatever they decide will set a precedent.* ADV-GRADED: ADV adj, ADV with v

8 If you have a **keen** eye or ear, you are able to notice things that are difficult to detect. *...an amateur artist with a keen eye for detail... Brand's keen ear caught the trace of an accent.* ADJ-GRADED: usu ADJ n =sharp ♦ **keenly** *Charles listened keenly. ...his keenly observed portrait.* ADV-GRADED: ADV with v

9 If you are **keen on** someone, you find them sexually attractive and want to get to know them better; an informal use. *Mick has always been very keen on Carla.* ADJ-GRADED: v-link ADJ *on* n

10 A **keen** fight or competition is one in which the competitors are all trying very hard to win, and it is not easy to predict who will win. *There is expected to be a keen fight in the local elections.* ADJ-GRADED ♦ **keenly** *The 1994 contest should be very keenly fought.* ADV-GRADED

11 **Keen** prices are low and competitive; used mainly in British English. *The company negotiates very keen prices with their suppliers.* ADJ-GRADED ♦ **keenly** *The shops also offer a keenly priced curtain-making service.* ADV-GRADED: ADV -ed

12 If someone **keens**, they make a wailing sound, usually as a sign of grief because someone has died; a literary use. *He tossed back his head and keened... Someone was making a low, keening noise.* VERB =wail V V-ing

13 If you say that someone is **mad keen** on something, you are emphasizing that they are very enthusiastic about it; an informal British expression. *So you're not mad keen on science then?... She was mad keen to go. ...a mad keen golfer.* PHRASE: v-link PHR, PHR n PRAGMATICS

keep /kiːp/ **keeps, keeping, kept** ◆◆◆◆◆

1 If someone **keeps** or **is kept** in a particular state, they remain in it. *The noise kept him awake... Reggie was being kept busy behind the bar... To keep warm they burnt wood in a rusty oil barrel... For several years I kept in touch with her.* V-LINK-ERG V n adj/prep V adj/prep

2 If you **keep** or you **are kept** in a particular position, or place, you remain in it. *Keep away from the doors while the train is moving... He kept his head down, hiding his features... It was against all orders to smoke, but a cigarette kept away mosquitoes... Doctors will keep her in hospital for at least another week.* V-ERG =stay V adv/prep V n with adv V n prep

3 If you **keep** or **are kept** off something or **keep** or **are kept** away from it, you avoid it. If you **keep** or **are kept** out of something, you avoid getting involved in it. *I managed to stick to the diet and keep off sweet foods... He's going to be a fantastic player if he keeps away from booze and women... The best way to keep babies off sugar is to go back to the natural diet and eat lots of fresh fruit.* V-ERG =stay V prep/adv V n prep/adv

4 If someone or something **keeps** you from doing something, they prevent you from doing it. *Embarrassment has kept me from doing all sorts of things... He kept her from being lonely... What can you do to keep it from happening again?* VERB =stop V n *from* -ing

5 If you try to **keep** from doing something, you try to stop yourself from doing it. *She bit her lip to keep from crying... He had to lean on Dan to keep from falling.* VERB V *from* -ing

6 If you **keep** something from someone, you do not tell them about it. *She knew that Gabriel was keeping something from her.* VERB V n *from* n

7 If you **keep** doing something, you do it repeatedly or continue to do it. If someone or something **keeps** you doing something, they cause you to do it repeatedly or to continue to do it. *I keep forgetting it's December... I turned back after a while, but he kept walking... I will let you have my answer tomorrow. I won't keep you waiting.* VERB V -ing V n -ing ▶ **Keep on** means the same as **keep**. *Did he give up or keep on trying?... My wife keeps on saying that I work too hard.* PHRASAL VERB VP -ing

8 **Keep** is used with some nouns to indicate that someone does something for a period of time or continues to do it. For example, if you **keep a grip** VERB

on something, you continue to hold or control it. *Until last year, the regime kept a tight grip on the country... One of them would keep a look-out on the road behind to warn us of approaching vehicles... His parents kept a vigil by his bedside as he was given brain and body scans.* V n

9 If you **keep** something, you continue to have it in your possession and do not throw it away, give it away, or sell it. *'I like this dress,' she said. 'Keep it. You can have it,' said Daphne... Lathan had to choose between marrying her and keeping his job.* VERB V n

10 If you **keep** something in a particular place, you always have it or store it in that place so that you can use it whenever you need it. *She kept her money under the mattress... She remembered where she kept the gun... To make it easier to contact us, keep this card handy.* VERB V n prep/adv V n adj

11 When you **keep** something such as a promise or an appointment, you do what you said you would do. *I'm hoping you'll keep your promise to come for a long visit... He had again failed to keep his word.* VERB V n

12 If you **keep** a record of a series of events, you write down details of it so that they can be referred to later. *Eleanor began to keep a diary... The volunteers kept a record of everything they ate for a week.* VERB V n

13 If you **keep** yourself or **keep** someone else, you support yourself or the other person by earning enough money to provide food, clothing, money, and other necessary things. *She could just about afford to keep her five kids... I just cannot afford to keep myself... He married an Armenian with a good dowry, who kept him in silk cravats.* VERB V n V pron-refl V n *in* n

14 Someone's **keep** is the cost of food and other things that they need in their daily life. *Ray will earn his keep on local farms while studying... I need to give my parents money for my keep.* N-SING: poss N

15 If you **keep** animals, you own them and take care of them. *I've brought you some eggs. We keep chickens... This mad writer kept a lobster as a pet.* VERB V n V n *as* n

16 If you **keep** a business such as a small shop or hotel, you own it and manage it. *His father kept a village shop.* VERB V n

17 If someone or something **keeps** you, they delay you and make you arrive somewhere later than expected. *Sorry to keep you, Jack... 'What kept you?'—'I went in the wrong direction.'* VERB V n

18 If food **keeps** for a certain length of time, it stays fresh and suitable to eat for that time. *Whatever is left over may be put into the refrigerator, where it will keep for 2-3 weeks.* VERB V

19 You can say or ask how someone **is keeping** as a way of saying or asking whether they are well. *She hasn't been keeping too well lately... How are you keeping these days?* VB: only cont V adv

20 A **keep** is the main tower of a medieval castle, in which people lived. N-COUNT

21 If you **keep at it**, you continue doing something that you have started, even if you are tired and would prefer to stop. *It may take a number of attempts, but it is worth keeping at it... 'Keep at it!' Thade encouraged me.* PHRASES V inflects =persevere

22 Something that is **for keeps** is permanent and will not change; an informal expression. *Ensure that whatever you gain now will be for keeps... He advised them to leave town for keeps.* v-link PHR, PHR after v =for good

23 If you **keep going**, you continue moving along or doing something that you have started, even if you are tired and would prefer to stop. *She forced herself to keep going... I was shouting: 'Keep going, keep going!'* *keep* inflects

24 If you say that something is **in keeping** with something else, you mean that it is appropriate or suitable in relation to that thing. If you say that something is **out of keeping** with something else, you mean that it is not suitable or appropriate in relation to that thing. *His office was in keeping with his station and experience... In keeping with tradition, the Emperor and Empress did not attend the ceremony... His own response to it seemed to be out of keeping with his earlier expressed opinions.* v-link PHR, PHR with cl, oft PHR *with* n

25 If you **keep it up**, you continue working or trying as hard as you have been in the past. *There are fears that he will not be able to keep it up when he gets to the particularly demanding third year... You're doing a great job! Keep it up!* V inflects

26 If you say that someone **is keeping up with the Joneses**, you are criticizing them or making fun of them for trying to have all the same possessions as their friends and neighbours, because they do not want to seem inferior to them. V inflects PRAGMATICS

27 If you **keep** something **to** yourself, you do not tell anyone else about it. *I have to tell someone. I can't keep it to myself... There's one thing you can do for me. But keep it to yourself.* V inflects

28 If you **keep** yourself **to** yourself or **keep to** yourself, you stay on your own most of the time and do not mix socially with other people. *He was a quiet man who kept himself to himself... Since she knows little Italian, she keeps to herself.* V inflects ≠socialize

29 • to **keep** someone **company**: see **company**. • to **keep your end up**: see **end**. • to **keep a straight face**: see **face**. • to **keep your hand in**: see **hand**. • to **keep your head**: see **head**. • to **keep house**: see **house**. • to **keep pace**: see **pace**. • to **keep the peace**: see **peace**. • to **keep a secret**: see **secret**. • to **keep time**: see **time**. • to **keep track**: see **track**.

keep back PHRASAL VERB

1 If you **keep back** part of something, you do not use or give away all of it, so that you still have some to use at a later time. *Roughly chop the vegetables, and keep back a little to chop finely and serve as a garnish.* =reserve V P n (not pron) Also V n P

2 If you **keep** some information **back**, you do not tell all that you know about something. *Neither of them is telling the whole truth. Invariably, they keep something back.* V n P Also V P n (not pron)

keep down PHRASAL VERB

1 If you **keep** the number, size, or amount of something **down**, you do not let it get bigger or go higher. *The prime aim is to keep inflation down... Administration costs were kept down to just £460.* V n P V P n (not pron)

2 If someone **keeps** a group of people **down**, they keep them in a state of powerlessness, and prevent them from being completely free. *No matter what a woman tries to do to improve her situation, there is some barrier or attitude to keep her down.* =oppress V n P Also V P n (not pron)

3 If you **keep** food or drink **down**, you manage to swallow it properly and not vomit, even though you feel sick. *I tried to give her something to drink but she couldn't keep it down.* V n P

keep in with. If you **keep in with** someone, you stay friendly with them, often in order to gain some advantage for yourself because they have power or influence; used mainly in British English. *I had to keep in with the people who mattered.* PHRASAL VERB V P P n

keep on PHRASAL VERB

1 See **keep** 7.

2 If you **keep** someone **on**, you continue to employ them, for example after they are old enough to retire or after other employees have lost their jobs. *Sometimes they keep you on a bit longer if there's no one quite ready to step into your shoes... A skeleton staff of 20 is being kept on.* V n P Also V P n (not pron)

keep on about. In informal British English, if you say that someone **keeps on about** something, you mean they continue to talk about it in a boring or repetitive way. *He kept on about me being 'defensive'.* PHRASAL VERB =go on about V P P n

keep on at. In informal British English, if you **keep on at** someone, you repeatedly ask them something or tell them something in a way that annoys them. *You've constantly got to keep on at people about that... She kept on at him to get some qualifications.* PHRASAL VERB =nag V P P n V P P n to-inf

keep to PHRASAL VERB

1 If you **keep to** a rule, plan, or agreement, you do exactly what you are expected or supposed to do. *You've got to keep to the speed limit... He had been unable to keep to his schedule.* =stick to V P n

2 If you **keep to** something such as a path or river, you do not move away from it as you go somewhere. *Please keep to the paths.* =stick to V P n

3 If you **keep to** a particular subject, you talk only =stick to about that subject, and do not talk about anything else. *Let's keep to the subject, or you'll get me too confused.* VPn

4 If you **keep** something **to** a particular number or quantity, you limit it to that number or quantity. *Keep costs to a minimum.* VnPn

keep up PHRASAL VERB

1 If you **keep up** with someone or something that is moving near you, you move at the same speed. *She shook her head and started to walk on. He kept up with her.* VP *with*n Also VP

2 If someone or something **keeps up** with something that is changing or increasing, they are able to cope with the change or increase, usually by changing or increasing at the same rate. *The union called the strike to press for wage increases which keep up with inflation... Things are changing so fast, it's hard to keep up.* VP *with*n VP

3 If you **keep up** with your work or with other people, you manage to do or understand all your work, or to do or understand it as well as other people. *Penny tended to work through her lunch hour in an effort to keep up with her work... Life here is tough for a parent whose kids aren't keeping up in school.* VP *with*n VP

4 If you **keep up** with what is happening, you make sure that you know about it. *She did not bother to keep up with the news.* VP *with*n Also VP

5 If you **keep** something **up**, you continue to do it or provide it. *I was so hungry all the time that I could not keep the diet up for longer than a month... They risk losing their homes because they can no longer keep up the repayments.* VnP VPn (not pron)

6 If you **keep** something **up**, you prevent it from growing less in amount, level, or degree. *There will be a major incentive among TV channels to keep standards up... Opposition forces are keeping up the pressure against the government.* =maintain VnP VPn (not pron)

keeper /kiːpəʳ/ **keepers** ◆◆◇◇◇

1 In football, the **keeper** is the same as the **goalkeeper**; used in informal British English. N-COUNT

2 A **keeper** at a zoo is a person who takes care of the animals. N-COUNT

3 The **keeper** of a museum or art gallery, or of one part of it, is the person who is responsible for the exhibits; used mainly in British English. N-COUNT =curator

4 If you say that you **are not** someone**'s keeper**, you mean that you are not responsible for what they do or for what happens to them. *'I don't know where he is,' Hughes replied. 'I'm not his keeper.'* PHRASE: V inflects

5 See also **keep**.

keep-fit; also spelled **keep fit**. **Keep-fit** is the activity of keeping your body in good condition by doing special exercises; used mainly in British English. ◆◇◇◇◇ N-UNCOUNT: oft N n

keepsake /kiːpseɪk/ **keepsakes.** A **keepsake** is a small present that someone gives you so that you will not forget them. N-COUNT =memento

keg /keg/ **kegs**

1 A **keg** is a small barrel used for storing something such as beer or other alcoholic drinks. N-COUNT: oft n N

2 In British English, **keg** is a kind of beer which is kept under pressure in a metal barrel. N-UNCOUNT

kelp /kelp/. **Kelp** is a type of seaweed. N-UNCOUNT

ken /ken/. If something is **beyond** your **ken**, you do not have enough knowledge to be able to understand it. *The subject matter was so technical as to be beyond the ken of the average layman.* PHRASE: usu v-link PHR

kennel /kenəl/ **kennels** ◆◇◇◇◇

1 A **kennel** is a small building made especially for a dog to sleep in. N-COUNT

2 **Kennels** or **a kennels** or **a kennel** is a place where dogs are bred and trained, or looked after when their owners are away. *The guard dog was now in kennels as it was not aggressive... Pauline runs a kennels... Once you have chosen a kennel, don't forget to make a booking for your pet.* N-COUNT: oft *in* N in pl

Kenyan /kenjən/ **Kenyans** ◆◆◆◆◇

1 **Kenyan** means belonging or relating to Kenya, or to its people or culture. ADJ

2 A **Kenyan** is a Kenyan citizen, or a person of Kenyan origin. N-COUNT

kept /kept/. **Kept** is the past tense and past participle of **keep**.

kerb /kɜːʳb/ **kerbs;** spelled **curb** in American English. The **kerb** is the raised edge of a pavement which separates it from the road. *Stewart stepped off the kerb.* ◆◇◇◇◇ N-COUNT: usu *the* N

kerb-crawling. Kerb-crawling is the activity of driving slowly along the side of a road in order to find and hire a prostitute; used in British English. N-UNCOUNT

kerchief /kɜːʳtʃɪf/ **kerchiefs.** A **kerchief** is a piece of cloth that you can wear on your head or round your neck; an old-fashioned word. N-COUNT

kerfuffle /kəʳfʌfəl/. A **kerfuffle** is noisy and disorderly behaviour often resulting from an argument; used in informal British English. *There was a bit of a kerfuffle during the race when a dog impeded the leading runners.* N-SING =commotion

kernel /kɜːʳnəl/ **kernels** ◆◇◇◇◇

1 The **kernel** of a nut is the part that is inside the shell. N-COUNT

2 The **kernel** of something is the central and most important part of it. *The kernel of that message was that peace must not be a source of advantage or disadvantage for anyone.* N-COUNT: usu sing, usu N *of*n =core, crux

3 A **kernel** of something is a small element of it. *For all I know, there may be a kernel of truth in what he says.* N-COUNT: usu sing, usu N *of*n =grain

kerosene /kerəsiːn/. **Kerosene** is a clear, strong-smelling liquid which is used as a fuel, for example in heaters and lamps; used especially in American English. ◆◇◇◇◇ N-UNCOUNT =paraffin

kestrel /kestrəl/ **kestrels.** A **kestrel** is a type of small falcon. N-COUNT

ketch /ketʃ/ **ketches.** A **ketch** is a type of sailing ship that has two masts. N-COUNT

ketchup /ketʃʌp/. **Ketchup** is a thick, cold sauce, usually made from tomatoes, that is sold in bottles. N-UNCOUNT

kettle /ketəl/ **kettles** ◆◇◇◇◇

1 A **kettle** is a covered container that you use for boiling water. It has a handle and a spout. *I'll put the kettle on and make us some tea.* N-COUNT ► A **kettle** of water is the amount of water contained in a kettle. *Pour a kettle of boiling water over the onions.* N-COUNT: usu N *of*n

2 If you say that something is **a different kettle of fish**, you mean that it is very different from another related thing that you are talking about; an informal expression. *Playing for the reserve team is a totally different kettle of fish.* PHRASE: v-link PHR

kettledrum /ketəldrʌm/ **kettledrums.** A **kettledrum** is a large drum which can be tuned to play a particular note. N-COUNT =timpani

key /kiː/ **keys, keying, keyed** ◆◆◆◆◇

1 A **key** is a specially shaped piece of metal that you place in a lock and turn in order to open or lock something such as a door or a suitcase, or to start or stop the engine of a vehicle. *They put the key in the door and entered... She reached for her coat and car keys.* N-COUNT

2 The **keys** on a computer keyboard or typewriter are the buttons that you press in order to operate it. N-COUNT: usu pl

3 The **keys** of a piano or organ are the long narrow pieces of wood or plastic that you press in order to play it. N-COUNT: usu pl

4 In music, a **key** is a scale of musical notes that starts on one specific note. *...the key of A minor.* N-VAR

5 The **key** on a map or diagram or in a technical book is a list of the symbols or abbreviations used and their meanings. *You will find a key at the front of the book.* N-COUNT

6 The **key** person or thing in a group is the most important one. *He is expected to be the key witness at the trial... Education is likely to be a key issue in the next election.* ADJ: ADJ n

7 The **key** to a desirable situation or result is the way in which it can be achieved. *The key to success is to be ready from the start... Diet and relaxation are two important keys to good health.* N-COUNT: usu N *to*n

8 • **under lock and key**: see **lock**. See also **master key**.

key in. If you **key** something **in**, you put informa- PHRASAL VERB tion into a computer or you give the computer a particular instruction by typing the information or instruction on the keyboard. *Brian keyed in his personal code.* =enter V P n (not pron) Also V n P

keyboard /kiːbɔːʳd/ **keyboards** ◆◆◇◇◇
1 The **keyboard** of a typewriter or computer is the set of keys that you press in order to operate it. N-COUNT
2 The **keyboard** of a piano or organ is the set of black and white keys that you press in order to play it. *Tanya's hands rippled over the keyboard.* N-COUNT
3 People sometimes refer to musical instruments that have a keyboard as **keyboards**. *...Sean O'Hagan on keyboards. ...the keyboard player.* N-COUNT: usu pl

keyboarder /kiːbɔːʳdəʳ/ **keyboarders.** A **keyboarder** is a person whose job is typing information into a computer or word processor. N-COUNT

keyboarding /kiːbɔːʳdɪŋ/. **Keyboarding** is the activity of typing information into a computer or word processor. N-UNCOUNT

keyboardist /kiːbɔːʳdɪst/ **keyboardists.** A **keyboardist** is someone who plays keyboard instruments, especially in popular music. N-COUNT

keyed up. If you are **keyed up**, you are very excited or nervous before an important or dangerous event. *I wasn't able to sleep that night, I was so keyed up.* ADJ-GRADED: v-link ADJ =tense

keyhole /kiːhoʊl/ **keyholes.** A **keyhole** is the hole in a lock that you put a key in. *I looked through the keyhole.* N-COUNT

keyhole surgery. **Keyhole surgery** is a surgical technique in which the surgeon inserts the instruments through small cuts in the patient's body, using as a guide an image provided by equipment inserted into the patient's body. N-UNCOUNT

keynote /kiːnoʊt/ **keynotes.** The **keynote** of a policy, speech, or idea is the main theme of it or the part of it that is emphasized the most. *He would be setting out his plans for the party in a keynote speech... Responsibility and moderation were to be the keynotes of their foreign policy.* ◆◇◇◇◇ N-COUNT: usu sing, oft N n, N of n

key ring, key rings; also spelled **keyring**. A **key ring** is a metal ring which you use to keep your keys together. You pass the ring through the holes in your keys. N-COUNT

keystone /kiːstoʊn/ **keystones**
1 A **keystone** is a stone at the top of an arch, which keeps the other stones in place by its weight and position; a technical term in architecture. N-COUNT
2 A **keystone** of a policy, system, or process is an important part of it, which is the basis for later developments. *The government's determination to beat inflation has so far been the keystone of its economic policy.* N-COUNT: usu sing, oft N *of/in* n

key word, key words. In language teaching, **key words** are the words in a course book which the writer suggests are the most important for the student to learn. N-COUNT: usu pl

kg. **Kg** is an abbreviation for **kilogram** or **kilograms**. ◆◇◇◇◇

khaki /kɑːki, AM kæki/ ◆◇◇◇◇
1 **Khaki** is a strong material of a greenish brown colour, used especially to make uniforms for soldiers. *On each side of me was a figure in khaki.* N-UNCOUNT
2 Something that is **khaki** is greenish brown in colour. *He was dressed in khaki trousers.* COLOUR

kHz. **kHz** is a written abbreviation for **kilohertz**. It is often written on radios beside a range of numbers to help you find a particular radio station. =kilohertz

kibbutz /kɪbʊts/ **kibbutzim** /kɪbʊtsiːm/. A **kibbutz** is a place of work in Israel, for example a farm or factory, where the workers live together and share all the duties and income. N-COUNT

kick /kɪk/ **kicks, kicking, kicked** ◆◆◆◆◇
1 If you **kick** someone or something, you hit them forcefully with your foot. *He kicked the door hard... He threw me to the ground and started to kick... He escaped by kicking open the window... The fiery actress kicked him in the shins... An ostrich can kick a man to death.* ► Also a noun. *He suffered a kick to the knee.* VERB V n V V n with adj V n *in* n V n *to* n N-COUNT
2 When you **kick** a ball or other object, you hit it with your foot so that it moves through the air. *I went to kick the ball and I completely missed it... He kicked the ball away... A furious player kicked his racket into the grandstand.* ► Also a noun. *Schmeichel swooped to save the first kick from Borisov.* VERB V n V n with adv V n prep N-COUNT
3 If you **kick** or **kick** your legs, you move your legs with very quick, small, and forceful movements, once or repeatedly. *They were dragged away struggling and kicking... First he kicked the left leg, then he kicked the right... He kicked his feet away from the window.* ► **Kick out** means the same as **kick**. *As its rider tried to free it, the horse kicked out and rolled over, crushing her.* VERB V V n V n adv/prep Also V prep PHRASAL VERB V P
4 If you **kick** your legs, you lift your legs up very high one after the other, for example when you are dancing. *...kicking his legs like a Can Can dancer... She begins dancing, kicking her legs high in the air.* VERB V n V n adj
5 If you **kick** a habit, you stop doing something that is bad for you and that you regularly do and find difficult to stop doing; an informal use. *She's kicked her drug habit and learned that her life has value... I've kicked cigarettes, heroin, and booze.* VERB V n
6 If something gives you **a kick**, it makes you feel very excited or very happy for a short period of time; an informal use. *I got a kick out of seeing my name in print.* N-SING: a N
7 If you say that someone **kicks** you **when** you **are down**, you think they are behaving unfairly because they are attacking you when you are in a weak position. *In the end I just couldn't kick Jimmy when he was down.* PHRASES V inflects
8 If you say that someone does something **for kicks**, you mean that they do it because they think it will be exciting; an informal expression. *They made a few small bets for kicks.* PHR after v =for fun
9 If you say that someone is dragged **kicking and screaming** into a particular course of action, you are emphasizing that they are very reluctant do something that other people think is necessary. *He had to be dragged kicking and screaming into action.* PHR after v, oft PHR *into* n/-ing PRAGMATICS
10 If you describe a situation as **a kick in the teeth,** you are emphasizing that it is a severe setback or disappointment; an informal expression. *We've been struggling for years and it's a real kick in the teeth to see a new band make it ahead of us.* usu v-link PHR, PHR after v PRAGMATICS =setback
11 You use **kick** yourself in expressions such as **I could have kicked myself** and **you're going to kick yourself** to indicate that you were annoyed or are going to be annoyed that you got something wrong. *I was still kicking myself for not paying attention... I immediately regretted having said this – I could have kicked myself.* V inflects
12 ● **alive and kicking**: see **alive**. ● **kick someone's ass**: see **ass**. ● **kick the bucket**: see **bucket**. ● **kick up a fuss**: see **fuss**.

kick against. If you **kick against** a situation you dislike but cannot control, you react against it in a violent, sudden, or extreme way; used mainly in British English. *North Sea operators kicked against legislation making them responsible for removing oil platforms at the end of their useful life.* PHRASAL VERB V P n

kick around PHRASAL VERB
1 If you **kick around** ideas or suggestions, you discuss them informally; an informal expression. *We kicked a few ideas around... They started to kick around the idea of an electric scraper.* =play with V n P V P n (not pron)
2 If you say that someone **kicks** you **around**, you do not like the way that they treat you because it is unfair; an informal expression. *I don't feel that anyone can kick me around anymore.* PRAGMATICS V n P

kick down or **kick in.** If someone **kicks** something **down** or if they **kick** it **in**, they hit it violently with their foot so that it falls over or breaks to pieces. *She was forced to kick down the front door... My neighbour's door had been kicked in.* PHRASAL VERB V P n (not pron) Also V n P

kick in. If something **kicks in**, it begins to take effect. *An energy saving mode automatically kicks in after a designated time to dim the screen and reduce power consumption... When you're confronted with the problem, emotions kick in, fear kicks in, and* PHRASAL VERB V P *you don't always do the rational and thought-out approach.* • See also **kick down**.

kick off PHRASAL VERB

1 In football, when the players **kick off**, they start a match by kicking the ball from the centre of the pitch. *Liverpool kicked off an hour ago.* VP

2 If an event, game, series, or discussion **kicks off**, or **is kicked off**, it begins. *The shows kick off on October 24th... The Mayor kicked off the party... We kicked off with a slap-up dinner.* ERG VP VP n (not pron) VP *with* n Also V n P

3 If you **kick off** your shoes, you shake your feet so that your shoes come off. *She stretched out on the sofa and kicked off her shoes.* VP n (not pron) Also V n P

4 To **kick** someone **off** an area of land means to force them to leave it; an informal expression. *We can't kick them off the island.* V n P n Also V n P

kick out. To **kick** someone **out** of a place means to force them to leave it; an informal expression. *The country's leaders kicked five foreign journalists out of the country... Her family kicked her out.* • See also **kick** 3. PHRASAL VERB V n P *of* n V n P Also V P n (not pron)

kick up PHRASAL VERB

1 If you **kick up** a fuss about something, you make it very obvious that you are annoyed or dissatisfied with it. *Those customers who have kicked up a fuss have received refunds... They kick up a rumpus and throw things at each other.* VP n (not pron)

2 If you **kick up** dust or dirt, you create a cloud of dust or dirt as you move along a dusty road. *He was kicking up dust every time he came out of the coppice.* VP n (not pron)

kickback /kɪkbæk/ **kickbacks.** A **kickback** is a sum of money that is paid to someone illegally, for example money which a company pays someone to arrange for the company to be chosen to do an important job. *Magistrates are investigating a nationwide web of alleged kickbacks and illegal party financing.* ◆◇◇◇◇ N-COUNT

kick-off, kick-offs ◆◇◇◇◇

1 In football, **kick-off** is the time at which a particular match starts. *The kick-off is at 1.30.* N-VAR

2 The **kick-off** of an event or activity is its beginning; an informal use. *The street is jammed with people awaiting the kick-off of the parade.* N-SING

kick-start, kick-starts, kick-starting, kick-started; also spelled **kickstart.** ◆◇◇◇◇

1 To **kick-start** a process that has stopped working or progressing is to take a course of action that will quickly start it going again. *The President has chosen to kick-start the economy by slashing interest rates.* ► Also a noun. *The housing market needs a kick-start.* VERB V n N-COUNT

2 If you **kick-start** a motorcycle, you press the lever that starts it with your foot. *He lifted the bike off its stand and kick-started it.* VERB V n

kid /kɪd/ **kids, kidding, kidded** ◆◆◆◆◇

1 You can refer to a child as a **kid**; an informal use. *They've got three kids... All the kids in my class could read.* N-COUNT

2 Young people who are no longer children are sometimes referred to as **kids**; an informal use. *There were gangs of kids on motorbikes roaming around... That's a lot for a kid of 22 to cope with.* N-COUNT; N-VOC

3 You can refer to your younger brother as your **kid** brother and your younger sister as your **kid** sister; an informal use. *My kid sister woke up and started crying.* ADJ: ADJ n

4 If you **are kidding**, you are saying something that is not really true, as a joke. *I'm not kidding, Frank. There's a cow out there, just standing around... I'm just kidding... Are you sure you're not kidding me?* VB: usu cont V V n

5 If you **kid** someone, you tease them. *He liked to kid Ingrid a lot... He used to kid me about being chubby.* VERB V n V n *about*-ing/n

6 If people **kid** themselves, they allow themselves to believe something that is not true because they wish that it was true. *We're kidding ourselves, Bill. We're not winning, we're not even doing well... I could kid myself that you did this for me, but it would be a lie.* VERB =fool V pron-refl V pron-refl that

7 A **kid** is a young goat. N-COUNT

8 You can say **'No kidding'** to emphasize that what you are saying is true, or that you mean it; an informal expression. *I'm scared. No kidding, really.* PHRASES CONVENTION PRAGMATICS

9 You can say **'No kidding?'** to show you are interested or surprised when someone tells you something; an informal expression. *'We won.'—'No kidding?'* CONVENTION PRAGMATICS

10 You can say **'you've got to be kidding'** or **'you must be kidding'** to someone if they have said something you think is ridiculous or completely untrue; an informal expression. *You've got to be kidding! I can't live here!... 'He's a mild inoffensive man isn't he?'—'Oh you've gotta be kidding.'* V inflects PRAGMATICS =you've got to be joking

11 You can say **'who is she kidding?'** or **'who is he trying to kid?'** if you think it is obvious that someone is not being sincere and does not mean what they say; an informal expression. *She played the role of a meek, innocent, shy girl. I don't know who she was trying to kid... 'Maybe tomorrow will be better,' I said, hanging up. 'Who am I kidding?' I told Wolfe. 'Tomorrow will be more of the same.'* V inflects

kiddie /kɪdi/ **kiddies;** also spelled **kiddy.** A **kiddie** is a very young child; an informal word. N-COUNT

kid gloves; the form **kid glove** is used as a modifier. If you treat someone or something with **kid gloves** or give them the **kid glove** treatment, you are very careful in the way you deal with them, for example because they are very delicate or easily upset, or because they could be dangerous. *In presidential campaigns, foreign policy is treated with kid gloves... Some artists have to be handled with kid gloves... We must take off the kid gloves and smash these evil monsters once and for all.* N-PLURAL: oft *with* N

kidnap /kɪdnæp/ **kidnaps, kidnapping, kidnapped** ◆◆◇◇◇

1 To **kidnap** someone is to take them away illegally and by force, and usually to hold them prisoner in order to demand something from their family, employer, or government. *Police in Brazil uncovered a plot to kidnap him... The aim of the terrorists is to kidnap rather than kill... The kidnapped man was said to have been seized by five people.* ♦ **kidnapper, kidnappers** *His kidnappers have threatened that they will kill him unless three militants are released from prison.* ♦ **kidnapping, kidnappings** *Two youngsters have been arrested and charged with kidnapping.* VERB =abduct V n V V-ed N-COUNT =abductor N-VAR

2 **Kidnap** or a **kidnap** is the crime of taking someone away by force. *Stewart denies attempted murder and kidnap... He was charged with the kidnap of a 25 year-old woman.* N-VAR =abduction

kidney /kɪdni/ **kidneys** ◆◆◇◇◇

1 Your **kidneys** are the organs in your body that filter waste matter from your blood and send it out of your body in your urine. N-COUNT

2 **Kidneys** are the kidneys of an animal, for example a lamb, calf, or pig, that are eaten as meat. *...lambs' kidneys. ...steak and kidney pie.* N-VAR

kidney bean, kidney beans. Kidney beans are small reddish brown beans that are eaten as a vegetable. They are the seeds of a bean plant. N-COUNT: usu pl

kill /kɪl/ **kills, killing, killed** ◆◆◆◆◆

1 If a person, animal, or other living thing **is killed**, something or someone causes them to die. *More than 1,000 people have been killed by the armed forces... Cattle should be killed cleanly and humanely... The earthquake killed 62 people... Heroin can kill.* ♦ **killing** *There is tension in the region following the killing of seven civilians.* VERB *be* V-ed V n V N-UNCOUNT: usu N *of* n

2 The act of killing an animal after hunting it is referred to as the **kill**. *After the kill the men and old women collect in an open space and eat a meal of whale meat.* N-COUNT: usu sing

3 If someone or something **kills** a project, activity, or idea, they completely destroy or end it. *His objective was to kill the space station project altogether... Public opinion may yet kill the proposal.* ► To **kill off** means the same as to **kill**. *He would soon launch a second offensive, killing off the peace process... The Government's financial squeeze had killed the scheme off.* VERB V n PHRASAL VERB V P n (not pron) V n P

4 If something **kills** pain, it weakens it so that it is VERB

no longer as strong as it was. *He was forced to take opium to kill the pain.* V n

5 If you say that something **is killing** you, you mean that it is causing you physical or emotional pain; an informal use. *My feet are killing me.* VB: only cont V pron

6 If you say that you **kill** yourself to do something, you are emphasizing that you make a great effort to do it, even though it causes you a lot of trouble or suffering; an informal use. *You shouldn't always have to kill yourself to do well.* VERB PRAGMATICS V pron-refl

7 If you say that you will **kill** someone for something they have done, you are emphasizing that you are extremely angry with them. *Tell Richard I'm going to kill him when I get hold of him.* VERB PRAGMATICS V n

8 If you say that something will not **kill** you, you mean that it is not really as difficult or unpleasant as it might seem; an informal use. *Three or four more weeks won't kill me!* VERB V pron

9 If you **are killing** time, you are doing something because you have some time available, not because you really want to do it. *I'm just killing time until I can talk to the other witnesses... To kill the hours while she waited, Ann worked in the garden.* VERB V n Also V n -ing

10 If you say that you will do something **if it kills** you, you are emphasizing that you are determined to do it even though it is extremely difficult or painful. *I'll make this marriage work if it kills me.* PHRASES V inflects, PHR with cl PRAGMATICS

11 If you say that you **killed** yourself **laughing**, you are emphasizing that you laughed a lot because you thought something was extremely funny; an informal expression. V inflects PRAGMATICS

12 If you **move in for the kill** or if you **close in for the kill**, you take advantage of a changed situation in order to do something that you have been preparing to do. *Seeing his chance, Dennis moved in for the kill.* V inflects

13 • to **kill two birds with one stone**: see **bird**. • **dressed to kill**: see **dressed**. • to **kill the goose that lays the golden egg**: see **goose**. • **to be killed outright**: see **outright**.

kill off PHRASAL VERB

1 See **kill** 3.

2 If you say that a group or an amount of something has **been killed off**, you mean that all of them or all of it have been killed or destroyed. *Their natural predators have been killed off... It is an effective treatment for the bacteria and does kill it off... All blood products are now heat treated to kill off any infection.* be V-ed P V n P V P n (not pron)

killer /kɪ̲lə^r/ **killers** ◆◆◆◇◇

1 A **killer** is a person who has killed someone, or who intends to kill someone. *The police are searching for his killers... He's a psychopath, a killer.* N-COUNT =murderer

2 You can refer to something that causes death or is likely to cause death as a **killer**. *Heart disease is the biggest killer of men in most developed countries.* N-COUNT

ki̲ller i̲nstinct, killer instincts. If you say that a sports player or politician has the **killer instinct**, you admire them for their toughness and determination to succeed. *He quit the sport when he realised he didn't have the killer instinct.* N-VAR PRAGMATICS

ki̲ller wha̲le, killer whales. A **killer whale** is a type of black and white whale. N-COUNT

killing /kɪ̲lɪŋ/ **killings** ◆◆◆◇◇

1 A **killing** is an act of deliberately killing a person. *This is a brutal killing.* N-COUNT =murder

2 If you **make a killing**, you make a large profit very quickly and easily; an informal expression. *They have made a killing on the deal.* PHRASE: V and N inflect

killjoy /kɪ̲ldʒɔɪ/ **killjoys.** If you call someone a **killjoy**, you are critical of them because they stop other people from enjoying themselves, often by reminding them of something unpleasant. *Don't be such a killjoy!... This is a classic example of the killjoy attitudes of officialdom.* N-COUNT PRAGMATICS =spoilsport

kiln /kɪ̲ln/ **kilns.** A **kiln** is an oven that is used to bake pottery, bricks, and timber in order to make them become hard. ◆◇◇◇◇ N-COUNT

kilo /ki̲ːloʊ/ **kilos.** A **kilo** is the same as a **kilogram**. *He'd lost ten kilos in weight. ...a kilo of rice.* ◆◇◇◇◇ N-COUNT: num N

kilo- /kɪ̲loʊ-/. **Kilo-** is added to some nouns that refer to units of measurement in order to form other nouns referring to units a thousand times bigger. *...100 kilojoules of energy. ...an explosion of around 20 kilotons.* PREFIX

kilobyte /kɪ̲ləbaɪt/ **kilobytes.** In computing, a **kilobyte** is one thousand bytes of data. N-COUNT

kilogram /kɪ̲ləgræm/ **kilograms;** also spelled **kilogramme.** A **kilogram** is a metric unit of weight. One kilogram is a thousand grams, or a thousandth of a metric ton, and is equal to 2.2 pounds. A **kilogram** of something is a quantity of it that weighs one kilogram. *...a parcel weighing around 4.5 kilograms. ...a kilogram of butter.* ◆◇◇◇◇ N-COUNT: num N, oft N of n =kilo

kilohertz /kɪ̲ləhɜː^rts/; **kilohertz** is both the singular and the plural form. A **kilohertz** is a unit of measurement of radio waves. One kilohertz is one thousand hertz. *Their instruments detected very faint radiowaves at a frequency of 3 kilohertz.* N-COUNT: num N

kilometre /kɪ̲ləmiːtə^r, kɪlɒ̲mɪtə^r/ **kilometres;** spelled **kilometer** in American English. A **kilometre** is a metric unit of distance or length. One kilometre is a thousand metres and is equal to 0.62 miles. *...about twenty kilometres from the border... The fire destroyed some 40,000 square kilometres of forest.* ◆◆◆◇◇ N-COUNT: num N

kilowatt /kɪ̲ləwɒt/ **kilowatts.** A **kilowatt** is a unit of power. One kilowatt is a thousand watts. *...a prototype system which produces 25 kilowatts of power.* N-COUNT: num N, oft N of n

ki̲lowatt-hour, kilowatt-hours. A **kilowatt-hour** is a unit of energy that is equal to the energy provided by a thousand watts in one hour. N-COUNT

kilt /kɪ̲lt/ **kilts.** A **kilt** is a short pleated skirt that men sometimes wear as part of their country's traditional costume, especially in Scotland. Kilts can also be worn by women and girls. N-COUNT

kimono /kɪmo̲ʊnoʊ, AM -nə/ **kimonos.** A **kimono** is an item of Japanese clothing. It is long, shaped like a coat, and has wide sleeves. N-COUNT

kin /kɪ̲n/. Your **kin** are your relatives; an old-fashioned word. *She has gone to live with her husband's kin.* • See also **kith and kin**, **next of kin.** ◆◇◇◇◇ N-PLURAL =relatives

kind 1 noun uses and phrases

kind /ka̲ɪnd/ **kinds** ◆◆◆◆◆

1 If you talk about a particular **kind** of thing, you are talking about one of the types or sorts of that thing. *The party needs a different kind of leadership... Had Jamie ever been in any kind of trouble?... I'm not the kind of person to get married... This book prize is the biggest of its kind in the world... Ear pain of any kind must never be ignored.* N-COUNT: usu N of n =sort

2 If you refer to someone's **kind,** you are referring to all the other people that are like them or that belong to the same class or set, especially when you disapprove of them. *I hate Lewis and his kind just as much as you do... I can take care of your kind.* N-COUNT: poss N PRAGMATICS =sort

3 You can use **all kinds of** to emphasize that there are a great number and variety of particular things or people. *Adoption can fail for all kinds of reasons... Donations came from all kinds of people... All kinds of remarkable things began to happen.* PHRASES PHR n PRAGMATICS =all sorts of

4 You use **kind of** when you want to say that something or someone can be roughly described in a particular way; used in spoken English. *It was kind of sad, really... She wasn't beautiful. But she was kind of cute... It kind of gives us an idea of what's happening.* PHR adj/adv/n, PHR before v =sort of

5 You can use **of a kind** to indicate that something is not as good as it might be expected to be, but that it seems to be the best that is possible in the circumstances. *There is good news of a kind for the Prime Minister... She finds solace of a kind in alcohol.* n PHR PRAGMATICS =of a sort

6 If you refer to someone or something as **one of a kind**, you mean that there is nobody or nothing else like them. *She's a very unusual woman, one of a kind. If she seems a little odd at times it's because her mind is on more important things.*

7 If you refer, for example, to **two, three,** or **four of a kind**, you mean two, three, or four similar people or things that seem to go well or belong together.

They were two of a kind, from the same sort of background.

8 If you respond or retaliate **in kind**, you react to something that someone has done to you, by doing the same thing to them. *They hurled defiant taunts at the riot police, who responded in kind.* PHR after v

9 If you pay a debt **in kind**, you pay it in the form of goods or services and not money. *Inflation and the shortage of banknotes has forced factories to pay their workers in kind. ...benefits in kind.* PHR after v, n PHR

kind 2 adjective uses

kind /kaɪnd/ **kinder, kindest** ◆◆◇◇◇

1 Someone who is **kind** behaves in a gentle, caring, and helpful way towards other people. *She is warmhearted and kind to everyone and everything... I must thank you for being so kind to me... It was very kind of you to come.* ♦ **kindly** *'You seem tired this morning, Jenny,' she said kindly.* ♦ **kindness** *He says he was treated with kindness by numerous officials.* ADJ-GRADED: oft ADJ *to* n, it v-link ADJ *of* n to-inf; ADV-GRADED: ADV after v; N-UNCOUNT

2 You can use **kind** in expressions such as **please be so kind as to** and **would you be kind enough to** in order to ask someone to do something in a firm but polite way. *Please be so kind as to see to it that all the alterations are made at once!... I wonder if you'd be kind enough to call him.* ADJ-GRADED: v-link ADJ PRAGMATICS

3 Something that is **kind** emphasizes the good qualities in something or someone, and perhaps makes them appear better than they really are. *Summer clothes are invariable less kind to fuller figures.* ADJ-GRADED =flattering

4 See also **kindly, kindness.**

kindergarten /kɪndəʳgɑːʳtᵊn/ **kindergartens.** A **kindergarten** is an informal kind of school for very young children, where they learn things by playing. *She's in kindergarten now.* ◆◇◇◇◇ N-COUNT: also *in/to/at* N =nursery

kind-hearted. If you describe someone as **kind-hearted**, you mean that they are kind, caring, and generous. *He was a warm, generous and kind-hearted man.* ADJ-GRADED =kind

kindle /kɪndᵊl/ **kindles, kindling, kindled**

1 If something **kindles** a particular emotion in someone, it makes them start to feel it. *The second world war kindled his enthusiasm for politics... These poems have helped kindle the imagination of generations of children.* VERB V n

2 If you **kindle** a fire, you light paper or wood in order to start it. *I came in and kindled a fire in the stove.* VERB V n

kindling /kɪndlɪŋ/. **Kindling** is small pieces of dry wood and other materials that you use to start a fire. N-UNCOUNT

kindly /kaɪndli/ ◆◆◇◇◇

1 A **kindly** person is kind, caring, and sympathetic. *He was a stern critic but an extremely kindly man.* ♦ **kindliness** *His kindliness and warmth made him particularly effective with staff welfare.* ADJ-GRADED: usu ADJ n; N-UNCOUNT

2 If someone **kindly** does something for you, they show thoughtfulness and care for you. *He kindly carried our picnic in a rucksack... He had very kindly asked me to the cocktail party that evening.* ADV-GRADED: ADV before v

3 If someone asks you to **kindly** do something, they are asking you in a way which shows that they have authority over you, or that they are angry with you; formal use. *Will you kindly obey the instructions I am about to give?* ADV: ADV before v PRAGMATICS

4 See also **kind.**

5 If you **look kindly on** or **look kindly upon** someone or something, you support them or approve of what they are doing. *Recent historical work looks kindly on the regime.* PHRASES V inflects, PHR n

6 If someone **does not take kindly to** something or someone, they do not like them. *She did not take kindly to being offered advice on her social life... It is hard to imagine her taking kindly to too much interference.* V inflects, PHR n/-ing

kindness /kaɪndnəs/ **kindnesses** ◆◇◇◇◇

1 Kindness is the quality of being gentle, caring, and helpful. *We have been treated with such kindness by everybody.* N-UNCOUNT

2 A **kindness** is a helpful or considerate act. N-COUNT

3 See also **kind.**

kindred /kɪndrɪd/

1 Your **kindred** are your family, and all the people who are related to you; an old-fashioned use. *The offender made proper restitution to the victim's kindred.* N-UNCOUNT: with poss =relatives

2 Kindred things are similar to each other; a formal use. *I recall many discussions with her on these and kindred topics.* ADJ: usu ADJ n =similar

kindred spirit, kindred spirits. A **kindred spirit** is a person who has the same view of life or the same interests as you. N-COUNT

kinetic /kɪnetɪk/. **Kinetic** is used to describe something that is concerned with movement; a technical term in physics. ADJ: usu ADJ n

kinetic energy. Kinetic energy is the energy that is produced when something moves; a technical term in physics. N-UNCOUNT

king /kɪŋ/ **kings** ◆◆◆◆◇

1 A **king** is a man who is the most important member of the royal family of his country, and who is considered to be the Head of State of that country. *The king and queen of Spain... In 1154, Henry II became King of England. ...King Albert.* N-TITLE; N-COUNT: oft *the* N *of* n

2 If you describe a man as **the king of** something, you mean that he is the most important person doing that thing or he is the best at doing it. *He's the king of unlicensed boxing... He was the king of the big love song.* N-COUNT: *the* N *of* n

3 A **king** is a playing card with a picture of a king on it. *...the king of diamonds.* N-COUNT: oft N *of* n

4 In chess, the **king** is the most important piece. When you are in a position to capture your opponent's king, you win the game. N-COUNT

5 If you say that someone **lives like a king**, you mean that they are able to live in a very comfortable or luxurious way. *Executives lived like kings. The top thirty-one executives were paid a total of $14.2 million.* ● **a king's ransom**: see **ransom.** PHRASE: V and N inflect

kingdom /kɪŋdəm/ **kingdoms** ◆◆◇◇◇

1 A **kingdom** is a country or region that is ruled by a king or queen. *The kingdom's power declined. ...the United Kingdom. ...the Kingdom of Denmark.* N-COUNT: usu sing, oft in names

2 A **kingdom** is a place or area that is thought to be under the control of a person or organization. *It was infamous as a kingdom of brigands, scoundrels, and slave-traders.* N-COUNT: usu N *of* n

3 All the animals, birds, and insects in the world can be referred to together as the animal **kingdom.** All the plants can be referred to as the plant **kingdom.** N-SING: usu n N

kingfisher /kɪŋfɪʃəʳ/ **kingfishers.** A **kingfisher** is a brightly-coloured bird which lives near rivers and lakes and catches fish. ◆◇◇◇◇ N-COUNT

kingly /kɪŋli/. **Kingly** means like a king, or related to the duties of a king; a literary word. *Waving his arms in a kingly manner, he led his company back to the royal dwellings... They thought that he should resume his kingly duties.* ADJ-GRADED: usu ADJ n

kingpin /kɪŋpɪn/ **kingpins.** If someone, especially a journalist, describes someone as the **kingpin** of an organization, they mean that they are the most important person involved in it. *...one of the alleged kingpins of Colombia's largest drugs ring. ...the Chicago crime kingpin.* N-COUNT: oft N *of* n, n N =linchpin

kingship /kɪŋʃɪp/. **Kingship** is the fact or position of being a king. *He was unfitted by temperament and education for the duties of kingship.* N-UNCOUNT

king-size; also spelled **king-sized.** A **king-size** or **king-sized** version of something is a larger size than the standard version, and may be the largest size available. *...a large bedroom with a king-size bed. ...king-size cigarettes.* ADJ: usu ADJ n

kink /kɪŋk/ **kinks, kinking, kinked**

1 A **kink** is a curve or twist in something which is otherwise or normally straight. *...a tiny black kitten with tufted ears and a kink in her tail.* N-COUNT: oft N *in* n

2 If something **kinks** or **is kinked**, it has, or it develops a curve or twist in it. *...her wet hair kinking in the breeze... Care when loading the roll is needed to prevent twisting or kinking the film... The kinked line in chart 1 represents this pattern.* V-ERG V V n V-ed

3 A **kink** is a particular quality or feature of a per- N-COUNT son's mind or character, especially one which is thought to be unusual or abnormal; an informal use. *What kink did he have in his character?*

4 If someone **works out the kinks** in a situation, they resolve the problems associated with it. *...working out the kinks of a potential trade agreement. ...joint sessions with her, to work out the kinks in the marriage.* PHRASE: V inflects

kinky /kɪŋki/ **kinkier, kinkiest**

1 If you describe something, usually a sexual practice or preference, as **kinky**, you mean that it is unusual and would be considered strange by most people; an informal use. *He had been engaging in some kind of kinky sexual activity. ...kinky underwear.* ADJ-GRADED

2 Something that is **kinky** has a lot of curves or twists. *He had red kinky hair.* ADJ-GRADED

kinship /kɪnʃɪp/

1 **Kinship** is the relationship between members of the same family; a literary use. *The ties of kinship may have helped the young man find his way in life. ...her kinship to the English King.* N-UNCOUNT

2 If you feel **kinship** with someone, you feel close to them, because you have a similar background or similar feelings or ideas; a literary use. *She evidently felt a sense of kinship with the woman. ...the warmth and kinship one farmer feels for another.* N-UNCOUNT =bond

kinsman /kɪnzmən/ **kinsmen.** Someone's **kinsman** is their male relative; a literary word. N-COUNT: oft with poss

kinswoman /kɪnzwʊmən/ **kinswomen.** Someone's **kinswoman** is their female relative; a literary word. N-COUNT: oft poss N

kiosk /kiːɒsk/ **kiosks** ◆◇◇◇◇

1 A **kiosk** is a small shop on the pavement, on the corner of a street, or in public place like a station. A kiosk sells things such as sandwiches or newspapers which you buy through an open window. *I was getting cigarettes at the kiosk.* N-COUNT

2 A **kiosk** or a **telephone kiosk** is a public telephone box; used mainly in British English. *He phoned me from a kiosk.* N-COUNT =telephone box

kip /kɪp/ **kips, kipping, kipped**

1 In informal British English, **kip** is sleep. *Mason went home for a couple of hours' kip.* N-SING: also no det =sleep

2 In informal British English, if you **kip** somewhere, usually somewhere that is not your own home or bed, you sleep there. *He moved from one friend's flat to another, first kipping on the floor of Theodore's studio.* VERB =sleep V prep/adv Also V

kipper /kɪpəʳ/ **kippers.** In British English, a **kipper** is a herring which has been preserved by being hung in smoke. N-COUNT

kirk /kɜːʳk/ **kirks.** In Scottish English, a **kirk** is a church. *...the eighteenth-century kirk across the road.* N-COUNT

Kirk. In Scotland, **the Kirk** is the Church of Scotland, the main church in Scotland. *...ministers of the Kirk.* N-PROPER: the N

kirsch /kɪəʳʃ/. **Kirsch** is a strong, colourless, alcoholic drink made from cherries which is drunk in small quantities, usually after a meal. N-UNCOUNT

kiss /kɪs/ **kisses, kissing, kissed** ◆◆◆◇◇

1 If you **kiss** someone, you touch them lightly with your lips to show affection or sexual desire, or to greet them or say goodbye. *She leaned up and kissed him on the cheek... She kissed me hard on the mouth... Her parents kissed her goodbye as she set off from their home... They kissed for almost half-a-minute... We kissed goodbye.* ► Also a noun. *I put my arms around her and gave her a kiss... We gave each other hugs and kisses every morning.* V-RECIP NON-RECIP: V n, V n n RECIP: pl-n V, pl-n V n; N-COUNT

2 If you **kiss** something, you touch it lightly with your lips, usually as a sign of reverence. *The men stepped forward to kiss the hand of their mentor... She bowed her head and kissed the Archbishop's ring.* VERB V n

3 If you say that something **kisses** another thing, you mean that it touches that thing very gently. *The wheels of the aircraft kissed the runway.* VERB V n

4 If you **blow** someone **a kiss** or **blow a kiss**, you touch the palm of your hand lightly with your lips, and then blow on your hand towards the person. You do this to show affection to the person when you can see them but not touch them, often when saying goodbye. *Maria blew him a kiss... Amy blew a kiss from the door.* PHRASES V inflects

5 If say that you **kiss something goodbye** or **kiss goodbye to** something, you accept the fact that you are going to lose it, although you do not want to; an informal expression. *I felt sure I'd have to kiss my dancing career goodbye.* V inflects

kiss and tell. If someone who has had a love affair with a famous person tells the story of that affair in public, for example in a newspaper or book, you can refer to this as a **kiss and tell** story. *...intimate photographs and kiss-and-tell revelations.* ADJ: ADJ n

kiss of death. If you say that a particular event is the **kiss of death** for something, you mean that it is certain to make them fail or be a disaster. *The government fears these accusations will be the kiss of death for foreign sales of other such goods.* N-SING: usu the N, oft N for/to n

kiss of life. If you give someone who has stopped breathing **the kiss of life**, you put your mouth onto their mouth and breathe into their lungs to make them start breathing again; used mainly in British English. *Julia was given the kiss of life but she could not be revived.* N-SING: the N

kit /kɪt/ **kits, kitting, kitted** ◆◆◇◇◇

1 A **kit** is a group of items that are kept together, often in the same container, because they are all used for similar purposes. *Make sure you keep a well-stocked first aid kit ready to deal with any emergency... The kit consisted of about twenty cosmetic items and a lady's shaver.* N-COUNT: oft n N

2 **Kit** is special clothing and equipment that you use when you take part in a particular activity, especially a sport; used mainly in British English. *I forgot my gym kit.* N-UNCOUNT: usu supp N

3 A **kit** is a set of parts that can be put together in order to make something. *Her popular potholder is also available in do-it-yourself kits.* N-COUNT

kit out. If someone or something **is kitted out**, they have everything they need at a particular time, such as clothing, equipment, or furniture; an informal British expression. *She was kitted out with winter coat, skirts, jumpers, nylon stockings... The place is kitted out in upmarket Italian cafe style.* PHRASAL VERB usu passive =fit out be V-ed P with n, be V-ed P in n

kitbag /kɪtbæg/ **kitbags.** A **kitbag** is a long narrow bag, usually made of canvas, in which soldiers or sailors keep clothing and personal belongings; used mainly in British English. N-COUNT

kitchen /kɪtʃɪn/ **kitchens.** A **kitchen** is a room that is used for cooking and for household jobs such as washing dishes. • See also **soup kitchen.** ◆◆◆◆◇ N-COUNT

kitchenette /kɪtʃɪnet/ **kitchenettes.** A **kitchenette** is a small kitchen, or a part of a larger room that is used for cooking. N-COUNT

kitchen garden, kitchen gardens. A **kitchen garden** is a part of the garden of a large country house in which vegetables, herbs, and fruit are grown. N-COUNT

kite /kaɪt/ **kites** ◆◇◇◇◇

1 A **kite** is an object, usually used as a toy, which is flown in the air. It consists of a light frame covered with paper or cloth and has a long string attached which you hold while the kite is flying. N-COUNT

2 A **kite** is a bird of prey which hunts and kills small animals for food. N-COUNT

3 If you say that someone is **flying a kite**, you are critical of them for putting forward new ideas just to see how people react, rather than with the intention of seeing those ideas put into practice; used mainly in British English. *The Government flies these kites of disinformation, then people feel grateful when the changes don't happen.* PHRASES V and N inflect PRAGMATICS

4 If you say that someone is **as high as a kite**, you mean that they feel very excited or that they are strongly affected by the alcohol or drugs that they have taken. *Jeremy is as high as a kite. Who knows how far he could go. He is playing well beyond his* v-link PHR *rankings... I felt so strange on the steroid injections. I was as high as a kite some of the time.*

Kitemark /kaɪtmɑːʳk/. In Britain, the **Kitemark** is a symbol like a small kite which is displayed on products that have been approved as meeting certain standards of safety and quality. N-SING

kith and kin /kɪθ ən kɪn/. Someone's **kith and kin** are their relatives. N-PLURAL

kitsch /kɪtʃ/. You can refer to a work of art or an object as **kitsch** if it is showy and in bad taste, for example because it has been made to appeal to people's sentimentality. *...a hideous ballgown verging on the kitsch... Collectors of Fifties kitsch should pop over to Brussels for the flea market.* ◆◇◇◇◇ N-UNCOUNT
► Also an adjective. *Blue and green eyeshadow has long been considered rather kitsch. ...kitsch pop culture.* ADJ-GRADED

kitten /kɪtᵊn/ **kittens.** A **kitten** is a very young cat. ◆◇◇◇◇ N-COUNT

kitty /kɪti/ **kitties**
1 A **kitty** is an amount of money consisting of contributions from several people, which is meant to be spent on things that these people will share or use together. *You haven't put any money in the kitty for three weeks.* N-COUNT: usu sing
2 A **kitty** is the total amount of money which is bet in a lottery or card game, and which is taken by the winner or winners. *Each month the total prize kitty is £13.5 million.* N-COUNT: usu sing
3 **Kitty** is sometimes used as an affectionate way of referring to a cat or kitten; an informal use. N-COUNT

kiwi /kiːwiː/ **kiwis** ◆◇◇◇◇
1 A **kiwi** is a type of bird that lives in New Zealand. Kiwis cannot fly. N-COUNT
2 In British and Australian English, people who come from New Zealand are sometimes referred to as **Kiwis**; an informal use which some people find offensive. N-COUNT

kiwi fruit, kiwi fruits; kiwi fruit can also be used as the plural form. A **Kiwi fruit** is a fruit with a brown hairy skin and green flesh. N-VAR

Kleenex /kliːneks/. **Kleenex** is both the singular and the plural form. A **Kleenex** is a piece of soft tissue paper that is used as a handkerchief. **Kleenex** is a trademark. *She reached for a Kleenex and blew her nose. ...a box of Kleenex.* N-COUNT =tissue

kleptomaniac /kleptəmeɪniæk/ **kleptomaniacs.** A **kleptomaniac** is a person who cannot control their desire to steal things, usually because of a medical condition. N-COUNT

km, kms; km can also be used as the plural form. **Km** is a written abbreviation for **kilometre**. ◆◆◇◇◇

knack /næk/ **knacks.** A **knack** is a particularly clever or skilful way of doing something successfully, especially something which most people find difficult. *He's got the knack of getting people to listen.* ◆◇◇◇◇ N-COUNT: usu sing, oft N *of/for* n/-ing

knacker /nækəʳ/ **knackers.** In informal British English, a **knacker** is someone who buys up old horses and then kills them for their meat, bones, or leather. *Her horse was a show jumper whom the family rescued from the knacker's yard.* N-COUNT

knackered /nækəʳd/
1 In informal British English, if you say that you are **knackered**, you are emphasizing that you are extremely tired. *I was absolutely knackered at the end of the match.* ADJ-GRADED: usu v-link ADJ PRAGMATICS
2 In informal British English, if you say that something is **knackered**, you mean that it is completely broken or worn out. *My tape player's knackered. ...faded pictures on a knackered TV set.* ADJ

knapsack /næpsæk/ **knapsacks.** A **knapsack** is a canvas or leather bag that you carry on your back or over your shoulder, for example when you are walking in the countryside. N-COUNT

knave /neɪv/ **knaves**
1 If someone calls a man a **knave**, they mean that he is dishonest and should not be trusted; an old-fashioned use. N-COUNT PRAGMATICS =rogue, scoundrel
2 In card games, **knave** is another word for **jack**; used mainly in British English. N-COUNT

knead /niːd/ **kneads, kneading, kneaded** ◆◇◇◇◇
1 When you **knead** dough or other food, you press and squeeze it with your hands so that it becomes smooth and ready to cook. *Lightly knead the mixture on a floured surface.* ♦ **kneading** *Just how much kneading is required depends on the sort of flour.* VERB V n N-UNCOUNT
2 If you **knead** a part of someone's body, you press or squeeze it with your fingers. *She felt him knead the aching muscles.* VERB V n

knee /niː/ **knees, kneeing, kneed** ◆◆◆◇◇
1 Your **knee** is the place where your leg bends. *He will receive physiotherapy on his damaged left knee. ...a knee injury.* N-COUNT: oft poss N
2 If something or someone is on your **knee** or on your **knees**, they are resting or sitting on the upper part of your legs when you are sitting down. *He sat with the package on his knees... I sat in the back of the taxi with my son on my knee.* N-COUNT: poss N, oft *on* N =lap
3 The **knee** on a piece of clothing is the part that covers your knee. *...jeans with holes at both knees.* N-COUNT
4 If you are on your **knees** you are in a kneeling position, with the lower part of your legs bent under you and your knees touching the ground, supporting the rest of your body. *She fell to the ground on her knees and prayed... She was on her knees in the kitchen.* N-PLURAL: poss N, usu *on/to* N
5 If you **knee** someone, you hit them using your knee. *Ian kneed him in the groin.* VERB V n
6 If a country or organization **is brought to its knees**, it is almost completely destroyed by someone or something. *The country was being brought to its knees by the loss of 2.4 million manufacturing jobs... Our aim is to bring this government to its knees, to force it to the negotiating table.* PHRASE: V inflects

kneecap /niːkæp/ **kneecaps;** also spelled **knee-cap**. Your **kneecaps** are the bones at the front of your knees. N-COUNT

knee-capping, knee-cappings; also spelled **kneecapping**. **Knee-capping** is the act of shooting someone in the knee, which is carried out by some terrorist organizations for revenge or as a form of punishment. N-VAR

knee-deep
1 Something that is **knee-deep** is as high as your knees. *The water was only knee-deep. ...knee-deep snow.* ADJ
2 If a person or a place is **knee-deep** in something such as water, the level of the water comes up to a person's knees. *They spent much of their time knee-deep in mud... They sometimes sank knee-deep into the marsh.* ADJ: v-link ADJ *in* n, ADJ after v

knee-high. Something that is **knee-high** is as tall or high as an adult's knees. *...a field of knee-high sunflowers.* ADJ

knee-jerk. If you call someone's response to a question or situation a **knee-jerk** reaction, you mean that they react to it in a very predictable way, without thinking about it; used showing disapproval. *The knee-jerk reaction to this is to call for proper security in all hospitals.* ADJ PRAGMATICS

kneel /niːl/ **kneels, kneeling, kneeled, knelt.** The forms **kneeled** and **knelt** can both be used for the past tense and past participle. When you **kneel**, you sit down with your weight on your knees and your legs bent underneath you. *She knelt by the bed and prayed... Other people were kneeling, but she just sat. ...a kneeling position.* ◆◇◇◇◇ VERB V prep/adv V V-ing
► **Kneel down** means the same as **kneel**. *She kneeled down beside him.* PHRASAL VERB V P

knees-up, knees-ups. In informal British English, a **knees-up** is a party or celebration. N-COUNT =shindig

knelt /nelt/. **Knelt** is a past tense and past participle of **kneel**.

knew /njuː, AM nuː/. **Knew** is the past tense of **know**.

knickers /nɪkəʳz/; the form **knicker** is used as a modifier. ◆◇◇◇◇
1 **Knickers** are a piece of underwear worn by women and girls which have holes for the legs and elastic around the waist to hold them up; used mainly N-PLURAL: also *a pair of* N

in British English. *She bought Ann two bras and six pairs of knickers.*
2 If you say that someone **is getting** their **knickers in a twist** about something, you are saying, in a humorous way, that they are getting annoyed or upset about it without good reason; an informal expression. *The company, which makes its money on 3,000 grocery lines has its knickers in a twist about Sunday trading.* PHRASE: V inflects

knick-knacks /nɪk næks/. **Knick-knacks** are small objects which people keep as ornaments or toys, rather than for a particular use. *Her flat is spilling over with knick-knacks.* N-PLURAL

knife /naɪf/ **knives, knifes, knifing, knifed;** **knives** is the plural form of the noun and **knifes** is the third person singular of the present tense of the verb. ◆◆◆◇◇
1 A **knife** is an implement used for cutting food. It consists of a flat sharp-edged piece of metal on the end of a handle. *...a knife and fork.* N-COUNT
2 A **knife** is a weapon that consists of a very sharp-edged piece of metal on the end of a handle. *Two robbers broke into her home, held a knife to her throat and stole her savings.* N-COUNT
3 To **knife** someone means to attack and injure them with a knife. *Dawson takes revenge on the man by knifing him to death... She was knifed in the back six times.* VERB V n prep Also V n
4 A surgeon's **knife** is an piece of equipment used to cut flesh and organs during operations. It is made of metal and has a very thin sharp edge. N-COUNT =scalpel ● If you go **under the knife**, you have an operation in a hospital. *Kelly was about to go under the knife when her surgeon stopped everything.* PHRASE: PHR after v
5 See also **carving knife, fish knife, flick knife, palette knife, paper knife, pocket knife, Stanley knife.**
6 If someone does something **like a knife through butter** or **like a hot knife through butter**, they do it very easily. *Spending by Japanese companies has left them more competitive than companies in other nations. They will be cutting through the competition like a hot knife through butter.* PHRASES *knife* inflects, PHR after v
7 If you have been in a place where there was a very tense atmosphere, you can say that you **could have cut** the atmosphere **with a knife**. *Officials hung the flag upside down. You could have cut the atmosphere with a knife.*
8 If a lot of people want something unpleasant to happen to someone, for example if they want them to lose their job, you can say that **the knives are out** for that person; used mainly in British English. *The Party knives are out for the leader.* V inflects, usu PHR *for* n
9 If you **twist the knife** or if you **turn the knife in** someone's **wound**, you do or say something to make an unpleasant situation they are in even more unpleasant. *Even as Mrs Thatcher is fighting to survive fellow EC leaders have been turning the knife in her wounds... It is the turn of Latvia to twist the knife.* V inflects

knife-edge; also spelled **knife edge.**
1 To be **on a knife-edge** means to be in a situation in which nobody knows what is going to happen next and in which one thing is just as likely to happen as another. *His future remains on a knife edge... The game is poised on a knife-edge. One mistake or one piece of good luck could decide it.* PHRASE: oft v-link PHR
2 You can use the word **knife-edge** to refer to something that is very exciting or tense because you do not know what is going to happen next. *Tonight's knife-edge vote could be uncomfortably close.* ADJ-GRADED: ADJ n

knifeman /naɪfmən/ **knifemen.** A **knifeman** is someone who has attacked or killed someone with a knife; mainly used in British journalism. *A crazed knifeman attacked three policewomen.* N-COUNT: usu sing

knifepoint /naɪfpɔɪnt/; also spelled **knife-point.** If you are attacked or robbed **at knifepoint**, someone threatens you with a knife while they attack or rob you; used in journalism. *A 15-year-old girl was attacked at knifepoint in a subway... He held her at knifepoint and threatened to kill her.* PHRASE: PHR after v

knifing /naɪfɪŋ/ **knifings.** A **knifing** is an incident in which someone is attacked and injured with a knife. ● See also **knife.** N-COUNT =stabbing

knight /naɪt/ **knights, knighting, knighted** ◆◆◇◇◇
1 In medieval times, a **knight** was a man of noble birth, who served his king or lord in battle. N-COUNT
2 If someone **is knighted**, they are given a knighthood. *He was knighted in the Queen's birthday honours list in June 1988.* VB: usu passive *be* V-ed
3 In chess, a **knight** is a piece which is shaped like a horse's head. N-COUNT
4 If you refer to a **knight in shining armour**, you mean someone who is kind and brave, and likely to rescue you from a difficult situation. *The love songs tricked us all into believing in happy endings and knights in shining armor.* PHRASE: *knight* inflects

knighthood /naɪthʊd/ **knighthoods.** A **knighthood** is a title that is given to a man by a British king or queen for his outstanding achievements or his service to his country. A man who has been given a knighthood can put 'Sir' in front of his name. ◆◇◇◇◇ N-COUNT

knightly /naɪtli/. **Knightly** describes something that is characteristic of a knight, especially something that shows chivalry, bravery, and fairness. *...the knightly arts of battle and courtliness.* ADJ: ADJ n

knit /nɪt/ **knits, knitting, knitted.** The past tense can be either **knit** or **knitted** for meaning 4. ◆◆◇◇◇
1 If you **knit** something, especially an article of clothing, you make it from wool or a similar thread by using two knitting needles or a machine. *I had endless hours to knit and sew... I have already started knitting baby clothes... She knitted him 10 pairs of socks to take with him... During the war, Joan helped her mother knit scarves for soldiers... She pushed up the sleeves of her grey knitted cardigan and got to work.* VERB V V n V n n V n *for* n V-ed Also V n *into* n ► Also a combining form. *Ferris wore a heavy knit sweater. ...a cotton-knit sweater. ...hand-knit garments.* COMB in ADJ: ADJ n ♦ **knitter, knitters** *Pattern charts with small print are often difficult for older knitters to use.* N-COUNT
2 If someone or something **knits** things or people together, they make them fit or work together closely and successfully. *The best thing about sport is that it knits the whole family close together... Ordinary people have some reservations about their president's drive to knit them so closely to their neighbors.* VERB V n with *together* V n *to/into* n Also V n ► Also a combining form. *...a closer-knit European Community. ...a tightly knit society.* COMB in ADJ-GRADED: usu ADJ n
3 When broken bones **knit**, the broken pieces grow together again. *The bone hasn't knitted together properly. ...broken bones that have failed to knit.* VERB V *together* V
4 If you **knit** your **brows** or **knit** your **eyebrows**, you frown because you are angry or worried; a literary expression. *They knitted their brows and started to grumble... Billy's eyebrows knitted together in a little frown.* PHRASE: V inflects

knitting /nɪtɪŋ/ ◆◇◇◇◇
1 **Knitting** is something, such as an article of clothing, that is being knitted. *She had been sitting with her knitting at her fourth-floor window.* N-UNCOUNT: usu poss N
2 **Knitting** is the action or process of knitting. *Take up a relaxing hobby, such as knitting. ...knitting patterns.* N-UNCOUNT: oft N n

knitting needle, knitting needles. Knitting needles are thin plastic or metal rods which you use when you are knitting. N-COUNT

knitwear /nɪtweəʳ/. **Knitwear** is clothing that has been knitted. *...expensive Italian knitwear.* N-UNCOUNT

knives /naɪvz/. **Knives** is the plural of **knife.**

knob /nɒb/ **knobs** ◆◇◇◇◇
1 A **knob** is a round handle on a door or drawer which you use in order to open or close it. *He turned the knob and pushed against the door.* N-COUNT
2 A **knob** is a rounded lump or ball on top of a post or stick. *A loose brass knob on the bedstead rattled.* N-COUNT
3 A **knob** is a round switch on a piece of machinery or equipment. *...the volume knob.* N-COUNT
4 A **knob of** butter is a small amount of it about the N-COUNT:

size of a walnut; used mainly in British English. *Top the steaming hot potatoes with a knob of butter.* N *of* n

knobbly /nɒbli/; the form **knobby** /nɒbi/ is also used. Something that is **knobbly** or **knobby** has lumps on it which stick out and make the surface uneven. *...knobbly knees. ...potatoes that are very knobbly and difficult to peel.* ADJ-GRADED

knock /nɒk/ **knocks, knocking, knocked** ◆◆◆◇◇

1 If you **knock** on something such as a door or window, you hit it, usually several times, to attract someone's attention. *She went directly to Simon's apartment and knocked on the door... Knock at my window at eight o'clock and I'll be ready... He knocked before going in.* ► Also a noun. *They heard a knock at the front door.* ♦ **knocking** *They were wakened by a loud knocking at the door.* VERB; V *on/at* n; V; N-COUNT; N-SING: also no det

2 If you **knock** something, you touch or hit it roughly, especially so that it falls or moves from its original position. *She accidentally knocked the tea tin off the shelf... The baby was knocked from his father's arms... Isabel rose so abruptly that she knocked down her chair... Buckets of roses had been knocked over.* ► Also a noun. *The bags have tough exterior materials to protect against knocks, rain and dust.* VERB; V n prep; V n with adv; Also V n; N-COUNT

3 If someone **knocks** two rooms or buildings into one, or **knocks** them together, they make them form one room or building by removing a wall. *They decided to knock the two rooms into one... The spacious kitchen was achieved by knocking together three small rooms.* VERB; V pl-n *into* n; V pl-n with *together*

4 To **knock** someone into a particular position or condition means to hit them very hard so that they fall over or become unconscious. *The third wave was so strong it knocked me backwards... They were knocked to the ground and robbed of their wallets... Someone had knocked him unconscious.* VERB; V n prep/adv; V n adj

5 To **knock** a particular quality or characteristic out of someone means to make them lose it. *The stories of his links with the actress had knocked the fun out of him... When they first joined for training many were starry eyed about just sailing around the world. We soon knocked that out of them... Those people hurt me and knocked my confidence.* VB: no cont; V n *out of* n; V n

6 If something **knocks**, it makes a repeated sharp banging noise. *The walls squeaked and the pipes knocked... His old truck, knocking and smoking, pulled down the road and out of sight.* VERB; V

7 If you **knock** something or someone, you criticize them and say unpleasant things about them; an informal use. *I'm not knocking them: if they want to do it, it's up to them... Never knock charter flights; they are opening up the world for budget-conscious travellers.* ♦ **knocker, knockers** *This season he's more determined that ever to prove the knockers wrong.* VERB; V n; N-COUNT

8 If someone or something receives a **knock**, they have an unpleasant experience which prevents them from achieving something or which causes them to change their attitudes or plans. *I can remember it feeling a real knock to my self-confidence that they said I wasn't academically up to being a teacher... The art market has suffered some severe knocks during the past two years.* N-COUNT =blow

9 To **knock** them **dead** means to impress people a great deal, especially with your appearance; an informal expression. *Glamorous make-up is best reserved for days when you want to go all out to knock 'em dead.* PHRASES; V inflects

10 If you tell someone to **knock it off**, you are telling them to stop doing something that is annoying you; an informal expression. *Will you just knock it off!* =cut it out

11 • to **knock** peoples' **heads together**: see **head**. • to **knock** something **on the head**: see **head**. • to **knock** someone or something **into shape**: see **shape**. • to **be knocked sideways**: see **sideways**.

knock about. See **knock around.** PHRASAL VERB

knock around; the form **knock about** is also used in British English. PHRASAL VERB

1 If someone **knocks** you **around** or **knocks** you **about**, they hit or kick you several times; mainly used in informal British English. *He lied to me constantly and started knocking me around.* V n P

2 If someone **knocks around** or **knocks about** somewhere, they spend time there, experiencing different situations or just passing time. *...reporters who knock around in troubled parts of the world... They knock around on weekends in grubby sweaters and pants... I know nothing about him except that he knocked about South Africa for a while.* V P prep/adv; V P; V P n

3 If someone or something is **knocking around** or **knocking about**, they are present in a particular place. *There were a couple of decent kits knocking around, but this wasn't one of them!... His paintings look as if they have been knocking around for centuries.* only cont; V P

4 If you **knock around** or **knock about** with someone, you spend your spare time with them, either because you are one of their friends or because you are their boyfriend or girlfriend. *I used to knock about with all the lads from round where Mum lives... They were knocking around together for about a year before they started living together.* RECIP; V P *with* n; pl-n V P *together*

knock back PHRASAL VERB

1 If you **knock back** a drink, especially an alcoholic one, you drink it quickly, and often in large amounts; an informal expression. *He was knocking back his 10th gin and tonic of the day... She poured some vodka into a glass and knocked it back in two swallows.* V P n (not pron); V n P

2 If an event, situation, or person **knocks** you **back**, they prevent you from progressing or achieving something; used mainly in British English. *It seemed as though every time we got rolling something came along to knock us back... That really knocked back any hope for further peace negotiations for a while.* V n P; V P n (not pron)

knock down or **knock over** PHRASAL VERB

1 If someone **is knocked down** or **is knocked over** by a vehicle or its driver, they are hit by a car and fall to the ground, and are often injured or killed. *He died in hospital after being knocked down by a car... A drunk driver knocked down and killed two girls... A car knocked him over.* =run over; *be* V-ed P; V P n (not pron); V n P

2 To **knock down** a building or part of a building means to demolish it. *Why doesn't he just knock the wall down?... They have since knocked down the shack and built a modern villa on the site.* =demolish; V n P; V P n (not pron)

knock off PHRASAL VERB

1 To **knock off** an amount from a price, time, or level means to reduce it by that amount. *Udinese have knocked 10% off admission prices... He has knocked 10 seconds off the world record... When pressed they knock off 10 per cent.* V amount P n; V P amount

2 If you **knock** something **off** a list or document, you remove it. *Tighter rules for benefit entitlement have knocked many people off the unemployment register.* V n P n; Also V n P

3 If someone **knocks** something **off**, they steal it; an informal British expression. *Cars can be stolen almost as easily as knocking off a bike.* V P n (not pron); Also V n P

4 When you **knock off**, you finish work at the end of the day or before a break; an informal expression. *If I get this report finished I'll knock off early... What time do you knock off?* V P

5 If someone **knocks** someone else **off**, they kill them; an informal expression. *He had many motives for wanting to knock off Yvonne... People don't just knock one another off like this unless there's big money at stake.* V P n (not pron); V n P

knock out PHRASAL VERB

1 To **knock** someone **out** means to cause them to become unconscious or to go to sleep. *He was arguing with his girlfriend and she hit him with a frying pan! Nearly knocked him out... The three drinks knocked him out... He had never been knocked out in a professional fight.* V n P; Also V P n (not pron)

2 If a person or team **is knocked out** of a competition, they are defeated in a game, so that they take no more part in the competition. *Henri Leconte has been knocked out in the quarter-finals of the Geneva Open... The Irish came so close to knocking* *be* V-ed P; V n P *of* n; Also V P n

know a lot more than other people. The American word is **know-it-all**.

know-how; also spelled **knowhow**. **Know-how** is knowledge of the methods or techniques of doing something, especially something technical or practical; an informal word. *He hasn't got the know-how to run a farm. ...technical know-how.* ◆◆◆◇◇ N-UNCOUNT: usu with supp =expertise

knowing /nouɪŋ/. A **knowing** gesture or remark is one that shows that you understand something, for example the way that someone is feeling or what they really mean, even though it has not been mentioned directly. *Ron gave her a knowing smile... Dan exchanged a knowing look with Harry.* ♦ **knowingly** *He smiled knowingly.* ADJ-GRADED: usu ADJ n; ADV-GRADED

knowingly /nouɪŋli/. If you **knowingly** do something wrong, you know that it is wrong but you do it anyway. *He repeated that he had never knowingly taken illegal drugs.* ◆◇◇◇◇ ADV-GRADED: ADV before v

know-it-all, know-it-alls. In informal American English, if you say that someone is a **know-it-all**, you are critical of them because they think they know a lot more than other people. The British word is **know-all**. N-COUNT PRAGMATICS

knowledge /nɒlɪdʒ/ ◆◆◆◆◇

1 **Knowledge** is information and understanding about a subject which a person has, or which all people have. *She disclaims any knowledge of her husband's business concerns. ...the quest for scientific knowledge.* N-UNCOUNT: usu with supp

2 If you say that something is true **to your knowledge** or **to the best of** your **knowledge**, you mean that you believe it to be true but it is possible that you do not know all the facts. *Alec never carried a gun to my knowledge... To the best of my knowledge, Gloria did not make these comments.* PHRASES PHR with cl/group

3 If you do something **safe in the knowledge** that something else is the case, you do the first thing confidently because you are sure of the second thing; used in written English. *On warm summer nights you can ventilate your room, safe in the knowledge that your window is secure.* PHR after v, usu PHR that

knowledgeable /nɒlɪdʒəbᵊl/. Someone who is **knowledgeable** has or shows a clear understanding of many different facts about the world or about a particular subject. *Do you think you are more knowledgeable about life than your parents were at your age?... If you don't know much about cars, take a knowledgeable friend along.* ♦ **knowledgeably** *Kaspar had spoken knowledgeably about the state of agriculture in Europe.* ◆◇◇◇◇ ADJ-GRADED =well-informed; ADV-GRADED: ADV after v

known /noun/

1 **Known** is the past participle of **know**.

2 You use **known** to describe someone or something that is clearly recognized by or familiar to all people or to a particular group of people. *...He was a known drug dealer... He became one of the best known actors of his day... Lead was one of the metals known to the ancient world... This plant has long been known for its medicinal qualities... The sport is still little known.* ADJ: ADJ n, v-link ADJ prep, v-link adv ADJ

3 If someone or something is **known for** a particular achievement or feature, they are familiar to many people because of that achievement or feature. *He is better known for his film and TV work.* ADJ: v-link ADJ *for* n/-ing

4 If you **let it be known** that something is the case, or you **let** something **be known**, you make sure that people know it or can find out about it. *The Prime Minister has let it be known that he is against it... He let his preference be known to the press.* PHRASE

knuckle /nʌkᵊl/ **knuckles, knuckling, knuckled.** Your **knuckles** are the rounded pieces of bone that form lumps on your hands where your fingers join your hands, and where your fingers bend. *Brenda's knuckles were white as she gripped the arms of the chair.* ● a **rap on the knuckles**: see **rap**. ◆◇◇◇◇ N-COUNT: usu pl, oft poss N

knuckle down. If someone **knuckles down**, they begin to work or study very hard, especially after a period when they have done very little work; an informal expression. *The only thing to do was knuckle down and get on with some serious hard work... He managed to knuckle down to his lessons long enough to pass his examination.* PHRASAL VERB VP VP *to*n/-ing

knuckle under. If you **knuckle under**, you do what someone else tells you to do or what a situation forces you to do, because you realize that you have no choice; an informal expression. *It is arguable whether the rebels will knuckle under... The United States, he said, did not knuckle under to demands.* PHRASAL VERB =give in VP VP *to*n

knuckle-duster, knuckle-dusters; also spelled **knuckleduster**. A **knuckle-duster** is a piece of metal that is designed to be worn on a person's hand as a weapon, so that if they hit someone they will hurt them badly; used mainly in British English. N-COUNT

KO /keɪ ou/ **KO's, KO'd**

1 **KO** is an abbreviation for **knockout**. *34 of his wins were KO's.* N-COUNT

2 To **KO** someone means to hit them so hard that they become unconscious; an informal expression. *He KO'd Nathan Mann in the third round.* VERB Vn

koala /kouɑːlə/ **koalas.** A **koala** or a **koala bear** is an Australian animal which looks like a small bear with grey fur and small tufted ears. N-COUNT

kohl /koul/. **Kohl** is a cosmetic used to darken the edge of a person's eyelids. N-UNCOUNT

kohlrabi /koulrɑːbi/; **kohlrabi** is both the singular and the plural form. **Kohlrabi** is a green vegetable that has a round ball of leaves like a cabbage. It has a thick stem that you boil in water before eating. N-VAR

kooky /kuːki/. Someone who is **kooky** is slightly strange or eccentric, but often in a way which makes you like them. *It's slightly kooky, but I love it... She's been mocked for her kooky ways.* ADJ-GRADED

Koran /kɔːrɑːn/. **The Koran** is the sacred book on which the religion of Islam is based. ◆◇◇◇◇ N-PROPER: *the*N

Koranic /kɔːrænɪk/. **Koranic** is used to describe something which belongs or relates to the Koran. *...Koranic schools.* ADJ: ADJ n

Korean /kəˈriːən/ **Koreans** ◆◆◆◆◇

1 **Korean** means belonging or relating to North or South Korea, or to their people, language, or culture. ADJ

2 A **Korean** is a North or South Korean citizen, or a person of North or South Korean origin. N-COUNT

3 **Korean** is the language spoken by people who live in North and South Korea. N-UNCOUNT

kosher /kouʃəʳ/

1 Something, especially food, that is **kosher** is approved of or permitted by the laws of Judaism. *...a kosher butcher.* ADJ

2 Something that is **kosher** is generally approved of or considered to be correct; an informal use. *I guessed something wasn't quite kosher... Acting was not considered a kosher trade for a girl from a well-to-do Victorian family.* ADJ-GRADED

kowtow /kautau/ **kowtows, kowtowing, kowtowed;** also spelled **kow-tow**. If you say that someone **kowtows** to someone else, you are critical of them for behaving very humbly towards that other person, because they are afraid of them or hope to get something from them; an informal word. *See how stupidly they kow-tow to persons higher in the hierarchy.* VERB PRAGMATICS V *to*n Also V

kph /keɪ piː eɪtʃ/. **kph** is an abbreviation for 'kilometres per hour'; it is used to indicate the speed of something such as a vehicle.

Kremlin /kremlɪn/. **The Kremlin** is the building in Moscow where Russian government business takes place. *...a two hour meeting in the Kremlin.* ◆◆◇◇◇ N-PROPER: *the*N

▶ **The Kremlin** is also used to refer to the central government of Russia and of the former Soviet Union. *The Kremlin is still insisting on a diplomatic solution to the crisis.* N-PROPER: *the*N

kudos /kjuːdɒs, AM kuːdouz/. **Kudos** is fame, glory, or admiration that someone gets as a result of a particular action or achievement. *It was always a fight as to which of them was going to get a case, because it meant kudos for whoever won it.* ◆◇◇◇◇ N-UNCOUNT

kung fu /kʌŋ fuː/. **Kung fu** is a Chinese martial art or sport in which people fight using only their bare hands and feet. *He decides to study kung fu. ...kung fu films.* N-UNCOUNT

Kuwaiti /kʊweɪti/ **Kuwaitis** ◆◆◆◆◇
1 ADJ **Kuwaiti** means belonging or relating to Kuwait, or to the people or culture of Kuwait.
2 N-COUNT A **Kuwaiti** is a Kuwaiti citizen, or a person of Kuwaiti origin. *...the wonderful hospitality that was offered to us by the Kuwaitis.*

KW; also spelled **kW. KW** is a written abbreviation for **kilowatt**.

Ll

L, l /el/ **L's, l's**
1 N-VAR **L** is the twelfth letter of the English alphabet.
2 N-VAR **L** is the symbol for 'learner driver'. In Britain, a large red 'L' on a white background is attached to cars in which people are learning to drive.
3 **L** or **l** is used as an abbreviation for words beginning with l, such as 'litre' and 'lire'.

La. **La** is a written abbreviation for **lane**, and is used especially in addresses and on maps or signs. *Andy's Records, 14-16 Lower Goat La., Norwich.*

lab /læb/ **labs** ◆◆◇◇◇
1 N-COUNT A **lab** is the same as a **laboratory**.
2 In Britain, **Lab** is the written abbreviation for **Labour**. *...Ron Brown MP for Edinburgh Leith (Lab).*

label /leɪbᵊl/ **labels, labelling, labelled;** spelled **labeling, labeled** in American English. ◆◆◆◇◇
1 N-COUNT A **label** is a piece of paper or plastic that is attached to an object in order to give information about it. *He peered at the label on the bottle.*
2 VB: usu passive; be V-ed; V-ed quote; V-ed *with* n — If something **is labelled**, a label is attached to it giving information about it. *The stuff has never been properly logged and labelled... The produce was labelled 'Made in China'... All the products are labelled with comprehensive instructions.*
3 VB: usu passive; PRAGMATICS; =brand; be V-ed *as* n; be V-ed *as* adj; be V-ed n; be V-ed adj — If you say that someone or something **is labelled** as a particular thing, you mean that people generally describe them that way and you think that this is unfair. *Too often the press are labelled as bad boys... Certain estates are labelled as undesirable... They are afraid to contact the social services in case they are labelled a problem family... If you venture from 'feminine' standards, you are labelled aggressive, hostile, mannish, and worse.*
4 N-COUNT: usu with supp — If you say that someone gets a particular **label**, you mean that people show disapproval of them by describing them with a critical word or phrase. *Her treatment of her husband earned her the label of the most hated woman in America.*
5 N-COUNT: usu supp N — You can refer to a company that produces and sells records as a particular **label**. *She landed a contract with record label EMI... It was on the Virgin label.*

labor /leɪbəʳ/. See **labour**.

laboratory /ləbɒrətri, AM læbrətɔːri/ **laboratories.** ◆◆◆◇◇
1 N-COUNT A **laboratory** is a building or a room where scientific experiments, analyses, and research are carried out.
2 N-COUNT A **laboratory** in a school, college, or university is a room containing scientific equipment where students are taught science subjects such as chemistry.
3 See also **language laboratory**.

Labor Day. N-UNCOUNT In the United States, **Labor Day** is a public holiday in honour of working people. It is the first Monday in September.

laborer /leɪbərəʳ/. See **labourer**.

laborious /ləbɔːriəs/. ◆◇◇◇◇ ADJ-GRADED If you describe a task or job as **laborious**, you mean that it takes a lot of time and effort. *Keeping the garden tidy all year round can be a laborious task.* ♦ **laboriously** ADV-GRADED: ADV with v *He sat behind a desk laboriously writing with an Army issue pen. ...the embroidery she'd worked on so laboriously during the long winter nights.*

labor union, labor unions. N-COUNT In American English, a **labor union** is an organization that has been formed by workers in order to represent their rights and interests to their employers, for example in order to improve working conditions or wages. The British term is **trade union**.

labour, /leɪbəʳ/ **labours, labouring, laboured;** spelled **labor** in American English. ◆◆◆◆◆
1 N-UNCOUNT: also N in pl, oft supp N — **Labour** is very hard work, usually physical work. *...the labour of seeding, planting and harvesting... The chef at the barbecue looked up from his labours; he was sweating.* • See also **hard labour**. • PHRASE If you do something as a **labour of love**, you do it because you really want to and not because of any reward you might get for it, even though it involves hard work. *Writing this book has been a great pleasure, a true labour of love.*
2 VERB; V — Someone who **labours** works hard using their hands. *...peasants labouring in the fields... Her husband laboured at the plant for 17 years.*
3 VERB; =struggle; V to-inf; V *under* n — If you **labour** to do something, you do it with difficulty. *For twenty-five years now he has laboured to build a religious community. ...a young man who's labouring under all kinds of other difficulties.*
4 N-UNCOUNT: oft supp N — **Labour** is used to refer to the workers of a country or industry, considered as a group. *Latin America lacked skilled labour. ...the struggle between capital and labour... They were cheap labour.*
5 N-UNCOUNT: oft poss N — The work done by a group of workers or by a particular worker is referred to as their **labour**. *Every man should receive a fair price for the product of his labour... The unemployed cannot withdraw their labour – they have no power.*
6 N-PROPER-COLL In Britain, people use **Labour** to refer to the **Labour Party**. *Labour will now have to try and reassess its position... They all vote Labour.*
7 ADJ A **Labour** politician or voter is a member of a Labour Party or votes for a Labour Party. *...a Labour MP... Millions of Labour voters will go unrepresented.*
8 VERB; V *under* n — If you **labour under** a delusion or misapprehension, you continue to believe something which is not true. *She laboured under the illusion that I knew what I was doing... You seem to be labouring under considerable misapprehensions.*
9 VERB; V n — If you **labour** a point or an argument, you keep making the same point or saying the same thing, although it is unnecessary. *I don't want to labour the point but there it is.*
10 N-UNCOUNT **Labour** is the last stage of pregnancy, in which the baby is gradually pushed out of the womb by the mother. *By the time people knew she was in labour, it was too late... Some women prefer to move about during labour.*

labour camp, labour camps; spelled **labor camp** in American English. N-COUNT A **labour camp** is a kind of prison, where the prisoners are forced to do hard, physical work, usually outdoors.

laboured /leɪbəʳd/
1 ADJ-GRADED If someone's breathing is **laboured**, it is slow and seems to take a lot of effort. *From his slow walk and laboured breathing, Ginny realized he was far from well.*
2 ADJ-GRADED If something such as someone's writing or speech is **laboured**, they have put too much effort

into it so it seems awkward and unnatural. *The prose of his official communications was so laboured, pompous and verbose... Daniel's few encounters with Gold had been characterized by a laboured politeness.*

labourer /leɪbərəʳ/ **labourers;** spelled **laborer** in American English. A **labourer** is a person who does a job which involves a lot of hard physical work; used mainly in British English. *He has worked as a labourer in factories and on building sites... Her husband had been a farm labourer.* ◆◇◇◇◇ N-COUNT: oft supp N

labour force, labour forces. The **labour force** consists of all the people who are able to work in a country or area, or all the people who work for a particular company. *Unemployment in Britain rose to 8.1% of the labour force.* ◆◇◇◇◇ N-COUNT: usu sing

labour-intensive. **Labour-intensive** industries or methods of making things involve a lot of workers. *Construction remains a relatively labour-intensive industry.* ADJ-GRADED

labour market, labour markets. When you talk about the **labour market**, you are referring to all the people who are able to work and want jobs in a country or area, in relation to the number of jobs there are available in that country or area. *The longer people have been unemployed, the harder it is for them to compete in the labour market.* ◆◇◇◇◇ N-COUNT: usu sing

Labour Party; spelled **Labor Party** in American English. In Britain, **the Labour Party** is the main left-of-centre party. It has always had an association with the trade unions. It believes in a fair distribution of wealth and power, and in public services such as free health care and education for everyone. *The Labour Party and the teaching unions have condemned the idea.* ◆◆◆◇◇ N-PROPER: the N

labour-saving. A **labour-saving** device or idea makes it possible for you to do something with less effort than usual. *...labour-saving devices such as washing machines.* ADJ: usu ADJ n

labrador /læbrədɔːʳ/ **labradors.** A **labrador** is a type of large dog with black or gold short dense hair. N-COUNT

laburnum /ləbɜːʳnəm/ **laburnums.** A **laburnum** or a **laburnum tree** is a small tree which has long stems of yellow flowers. N-VAR

labyrinth /læbɪrɪnθ/ **labyrinths** ◆◇◇◇◇

1 If you describe a place as a **labyrinth**, you mean that it is made up of a complicated series of paths or passages, through which it is difficult to find your way; a literary use. *...the labyrinth of corridors.* N-COUNT: oft N of n =maze

2 If you describe a situation, process, or area of knowledge as a **labyrinth**, you mean that it is very complicated; a formal use. *...a labyrinth of conflicting political and sociological interpretations.* N-COUNT: usu N of n =maze

labyrinthine /læbɪrɪnθaɪn/

1 If you describe a place as **labyrinthine**, you mean that it is like a labyrinth; a formal use. *The streets of the Old City are narrow and labyrinthine.* ADJ-GRADED: usu ADJ n

2 If you describe a situation, process, or field of knowledge as **labyrinthine**, you mean that it is very complicated and difficult to understand; a formal use. *...his failure to understand the labyrinthine complexities of the situation.* ADJ-GRADED: usu ADJ n

lace /leɪs/ **laces, lacing, laced** ◆◆◇◇◇

1 **Lace** is a very delicate cloth which is made with a lot of holes in it. It is made by twisting together very fine threads of cotton to form patterns. *She finally found the perfect gown, a beautiful creation trimmed with lace. ...a plain white lace bedspread.* N-UNCOUNT

2 **Laces** are thin pieces of material that are put through special holes in some types of clothing, especially shoes. The laces are tied together in order to tighten the clothing. *Barry was sitting on the bed, tying the laces of an old pair of running shoes.* N-COUNT: usu pl

3 If you **lace** something such as a pair of shoes, you tighten the shoes by pulling the laces through the holes, and usually tying them together. *I have a good pair of skates, but no matter how tightly I lace them, my ankles wobble.* ▸ **Lace up** means the same as **lace**. *He sat on the steps, and laced up his boots... Nancy was lacing her shoe up when the doorbell rang.* VERB =tie; V n; PHRASAL VERB V P n (not pron), V n P

4 To **lace** food or drink with a substance such as alcohol or a drug means to put a small amount of the substance into the food or drink. *She laced his food with sleeping pills.* VERB V n with n

5 If you **lace** your speech or writing with a particular quality or with words of a particular kind, you include a lot of that quality or those words in what you say or write. *Fred liked to lace his conversation with military terms. ...a speech laced with wry humour.* VERB V n with n, V-ed

6 If you **lace** your fingers together, you put the palms of your hands together and fold your fingers over, fitting the fingers of one hand between the fingers of the other. *He took to lacing his fingers together in an attempt to keep his hands still.* VERB V pl-n together, Also V pl-n

lace up. See **lace** 3. PHRASAL VERB

lacerate /læsəreɪt/ **lacerates, lacerating, lacerated.** If something **lacerates** your skin, it cuts it badly and deeply. *Its claws lacerated his thighs.* ♦ **lacerated** *She was suffering from a badly lacerated hand.* VERB V n, Also V; ADJ-GRADED

laceration /læsəreɪʃᵊn/ **lacerations.** **Lacerations** are deep cuts on your skin. *He had lacerations on his back and thighs.* N-COUNT: usu pl, oft N prep

lace-ups; the form **lace-up** is used as a modifier. **Lace-ups** are shoes which are fastened with laces; used mainly in British English. *Slip-on shoes are easier to put on than lace-ups... He was wearing black lace-up shoes.* N-PLURAL

lachrymose /lækrɪmous, -mouz/. Someone who is **lachrymose** cries very easily and very often; a literary word. *...the tears of lachrymose mourners.* ADJ-GRADED

lack /læk/ **lacks, lacking, lacked** ◆◆◆◆◇

1 If there is a **lack** of something, there is not enough of it or it does not exist at all. *Despite his lack of experience, he got the job... The charges were dropped for lack of evidence... He tricked his way into a job as a hospital doctor and killed a patient through lack of care... There is a lack of people wanting to start up new businesses.* N-UNCOUNT: also a N, usu N of n

2 If you say that someone or something **lacks** something, or that that thing **is lacking** in them, you mean they do not have any or enough of that thing. *It lacked the power of the Italian cars... He lacked the judgment and political acumen for the post of chairman... Certain vital information is lacking in the report.* V-ERG V n, V

3 See also **lacking**.

4 If you say there is **no lack of** something, you are emphasizing there is a great deal of it. *He said there was no lack of things for them to talk about... President Clinton displayed no lack of vigor when he began to speak.* PHRASE: PHR n, usu v-link PHR, v PHR; PRAGMATICS

lackadaisical /lækədeɪzɪkᵊl/. If you say that someone is **lackadaisical**, you mean that they are rather lazy and do not show much interest or enthusiasm in what they do. *Dr. Jonsen seemed a little lackadaisical at times. ...the lackadaisical attitude of a number of the principal players.* ADJ-GRADED

lackey /læki/ **lackeys.** If you describe someone as a **lackey**, you are critical of them because they follow someone's orders completely, without ever questioning them. *I'm not staying as a paid lackey to act as your yes-man.* N-COUNT; PRAGMATICS

lacking /lækɪŋ/. If something or someone **is lacking in** a particular quality, they do not have any of it or enough of it. *...if your hair is lacking in lustre and feeling dry... She felt nervous, increasingly lacking in confidence about herself... Why was military intelligence so lacking?* • See also **lack**. ◆◇◇◇◇ ADJ-GRADED: v-link ADJ, usu ADJ in n

lacklustre /læklʌstəʳ/; spelled **lackluster** in American English. If you describe something or someone as **lacklustre**, you mean that they have no brightness or liveliness. *He has already been blamed for his party's lackluster performance during the election campaign.* ◆◇◇◇◇ ADJ-GRADED

laconic /ləkɒnɪk/. If you describe someone as **laconic**, you mean that they use very few words to say something, so that they seem casual or un- ADJ-GRADED friendly. *Usually so laconic in the office, Dr. Lahey seemed less guarded, more relaxed... 'At least we weren't kidnapped.'—'I'm glad of that,' was the laconic response.* ♦ **laconically** /ləkɒnɪkli/ *A week or so later he laconically announced that Digby had been transferred to another post.* [ADV-GRADED: ADV with v]

lacquer /lækəʳ/ **lacquers** ◆◇◇◇◇

1 Lacquer is a special liquid which is painted on wood or metal in order to protect it and to make it shiny. *We put on the second coating of lacquer... Only the finest lacquers are used for finishes.* [N-MASS]

2 Lacquer is a clear sticky liquid which some women spray on their hair to hold their hairstyle in place; used mainly in British English. [N-MASS]

lacquered /lækəʳd/. **Lacquered** is used to describe things that have been coated or sprayed with lacquer. *...17th-century lacquered cabinets. ...perfectly lacquered hair and face powder.* [ADJ: ADJ n]

lacrosse /ləkrɒs, AM -krɔːs/. **Lacrosse** is an outdoor game in which players use long sticks with nets at the end to catch and throw a small ball, in order to try and score goals. [N-UNCOUNT]

lactation /lækteɪʃᵊn/. **Lactation** is the production of milk by women and female mammals during the period after they give birth; a formal word. [N-UNCOUNT]

lactic acid /læktɪk æsɪd/. **Lactic acid** is a type of acid which is found in sour milk and is also produced by your muscles when you have been exercising a lot. [N-UNCOUNT]

lactose /læktoʊs/. **Lactose** is a type of sugar which is found in milk and which is sometimes added to food. [N-UNCOUNT]

lacuna /ləkjuːnə/ **lacunae.** If you say that there is a **lacuna** in something such as a document or a person's argument, you mean that it does not deal with an important issue and is therefore not effective or convincing; a formal word. *There are still major lacunae in the material available.* [N-COUNT]

lacy /leɪsi/ **lacier, laciest** ◆◇◇◇◇

1 Lacy things are made from lace or have pieces of lace attached to them. *...lacy nightgowns.* [ADJ-GRADED: usu ADJ n]

2 Lacy is used to describe something that looks like lace, especially because it is very delicate. *...lacy ferns.* [ADJ-GRADED: usu ADJ n]

lad /læd/ **lads** ◆◆◆◇◇

1 A **lad** is a young man or boy; an informal use. *When I was a lad his age I would laugh at the strangest things... Come along, lad. Time for you to get home.* [N-COUNT; N-VOC]

2 In informal British English, some men refer to their group of friends or colleagues as **the lads.** *...having a drink with the lads... The lads don't join the union because they're frightened of being victimized.* [N-PLURAL: the N]

ladder /lædəʳ/ **ladders** ◆◆◇◇◇

1 A **ladder** is a piece of equipment used for climbing up something or down from something. It consists of two long pieces of wood, metal, or rope with steps fixed between them. [N-COUNT]

2 You can use **ladder** to refer to something such as a society, organization, or system which has different levels that people can progress up or drop down. *If they want to climb the ladder of success they should be given that opportunity... She admired her mother's sister for moving up the social ladder.* [N-SING: the N, usu with supp]

3 A **ladder** is a torn part in a woman's stocking or tights, where some of the vertical threads have broken, leaving only the horizontal threads. *Her hair was a mess and there was a ladder in her tights.* [N-COUNT]

laddie /lædi/ **laddies.** A **laddie** is a young man or boy; used especially in informal Scottish English. *...this little laddie, aged about four... Now then, laddie, what's the trouble?* [N-COUNT; N-VOC]

laden /leɪdᵊn/ ◆◇◇◇◇

1 If someone or something is **laden** with a lot of heavy things, they are holding or carrying them; a literary use. *I came home laden with cardboard boxes... The following summer the peach tree was laden with fruit... Heavily laden lorries were passing at a rate of one every three minutes.* [ADJ: oft ADJ with n]

2 If you describe a person or thing as **laden with** something, particularly something bad, you mean that they have a lot of it. *We're so laden with guilt... Many of their heavy industries are laden with debt.* [ADJ-GRADED: v-link ADJ with n]

-laden /-leɪdᵊn/. **-laden** combines with nouns to form adjectives which indicate that something has a lot of a particular thing or quality. *...a fat-laden meal. ...smoke-laden air. ...a technology-laden military.* [COMB in ADJ-GRADED: usu ADJ n]

la-di-da /lɑː di dɑː/; also spelled **lah-di-dah.** If you describe someone as **la-di-da**, you mean that they have an upper-class way of behaving, which you think seems unnatural and is only done to impress other people; an old-fashioned word used showing disapproval. *I wouldn't trust them in spite of all their la-di-da manners.* [ADJ-GRADED] [PRAGMATICS]

ladies' man. If you say that a man is a **ladies' man**, you mean that he enjoys flirting with women and that women find him attractive and enjoy his company; an old-fashioned expression. *He had quite a reputation as a ladies' man.* [N-SING: usu a N]

ladies' room. Some people refer to a public toilet for women as **the ladies' room.** *Where's the ladies' room?* [N-SING: usu the N =ladies]

ladle /leɪdᵊl/ **ladles, ladling, ladled**

1 A **ladle** is a large, round, deep spoon with a long handle, used for serving soup, stew, or sauce. [N-COUNT]

2 If you **ladle** food such as soup or stew, you serve it, especially with a ladle. *Barry held the bowls while Liz ladled soup into them... Mrs King went to the big black stove and ladled out steaming soup.* [VERB: V n prep, V n with adv, Also V n]

ladle out. If you **ladle out** something such as money, information, or advice, you give it freely and in large quantities. *She was constantly on the phone, ladling out inside details to reporters.* [PHRASAL VERB: V P n (not pron), Also V n P]

lady /leɪdi/ **ladies** ◆◆◆◆◇

1 You can use the word **lady** when you are referring to a woman, especially when you are showing politeness or respect. *She's a very sweet old lady... Shall we rejoin the ladies? ...a lady doctor. ...a cream-coloured lady's shoe.* • See also **old lady.** [N-COUNT =woman]

2 You can say **'ladies'** when you are addressing a group of women in a formal and respectful way. *Your table is ready, ladies, if you'd care to come through... Good afternoon, ladies and gentlemen.* [N-VOC] [PRAGMATICS]

3 A **lady** is a woman from the upper classes, especially in former times. *...the Empress and ladies of the Imperial Palace... Our governess was told to make sure we knew how to talk like English ladies.* [N-COUNT]

4 In Britain, **Lady** is a title used in front of the names of some female member of the nobility, or the wives of knights or peers. *Cockburn's arrival coincided with that of Sir Iain and Lady Noble... My dear Lady Mary, how very good to see you.* [N-TITLE]

5 If you say that a woman is a **lady**, you mean that she behaves in a polite, dignified, and graceful way. *His wife was great as well, beautiful-looking and a real lady... A lady always sits quietly with her hands in her lap.* [N-COUNT]

6 In informal British English, people sometimes refer to a public toilet for women as **the ladies.** *At Temple station, Charlotte rushed into the Ladies.* [N-SING: usu the N =ladies' room]

7 'Lady' is sometimes used by men as a form of address when they are talking to a woman that they do not know, especially in shops and in the street; used mainly in informal American English. *What seems to be the trouble, lady?... As she left the litter-strewn lot, an angry voice called out to her. 'Hey, lady!'* [N-VOC] [PRAGMATICS]

8 See also **First Lady, Our Lady.**

ladybird /leɪdibɜːʳd/ **ladybirds.** In British English, a **ladybird** is a small round beetle that is red with black spots. The American word is **ladybug.** [N-COUNT]

ladybug /leɪdibʌg/ **ladybugs.** See **ladybird.**

lady friend, lady friends. A man's **lady friend** is the woman with whom he is having a romantic or sexual relationship; an old-fashioned expression, used mainly in British English. [N-COUNT: usu poss N]

lady-in-waiting, ladies-in-waiting. A **lady-in-waiting** is a woman from the aristocracy or upper classes, who acts as a companion to a queen or princess. [N-COUNT]

lady-killer, lady-killers. If you refer to a man as a **lady-killer**, you mean that you think he is very successful at attracting women but quickly leaves them; an old-fashioned word. N-COUNT

ladylike /le͟ɪdilaɪk/. If you say that a woman or girl is **ladylike**, you mean that she behaves in a polite, dignified, and graceful way. *I hate to be blunt, Frankie, but she just didn't strike me as being very ladylike... She crossed the room with quick, ladylike steps.* ADJ-GRADED =genteel

Ladyship /le͟ɪdiʃɪp/ **Ladyships.** In British English, you use the expressions **Your Ladyship**, **Her Ladyship**, or **Their Ladyships** when you are addressing or referring to a female member of the nobility or the wife of a knight or peer. *Her Ladyship's expecting you, sir.* N-VOC; N-PROPER: det-poss N PRAGMATICS

lag /læ͟g/ **lags, lagging, lagged** ◆◆◇◇◇
1 If one thing or person **lags** behind another thing or person, their progress is slower than that of the other thing or person. *Britain still lags behind most of Europe in its provisions for women who want time off to have babies... The restructuring of the pattern of consumption in Britain also lagged behind... He now lags 10 points behind the champion... A poll for the Observer showed Labour on 39 per cent with the Tories lagging a point behind... Bush was lagging badly in the polls.* VERB V behind n V behind V amount behind n V amount behind V
2 A time **lag** or a **lag** of a particular length of time is a period of time between one event and another related event. *There's a time lag between infection with HIV and developing AIDS... Price rises have matched rises in the money supply with a lag of two or three months.* N-COUNT: with supp
3 If you **lag** the inside of a roof, a pipe, or a water tank, you cover it with a special material in order to prevent heat escaping from it or to prevent it from freezing; used mainly in British English. *If you have to take the floorboards up, take the opportunity to lag any pipes at the same time... Water tanks should be well lagged and the roof well insulated.* ● See also **lagging.** VERB V n

lager /lɑ͟ːgəʳ/ **lagers. Lager** is a type of light beer; used mainly in British English. *...a pint of lager... He claims to sell the widest range of beers and lagers in the world.* ► A glass of lager can be referred to as a **lager**. *Liz and Darren shared a lager and danced a little.* ◆◇◇◇◇ N-MASS N-COUNT

laggard /læ͟gəʳd/ **laggards.** If you describe a country, company, or product as a **laggard**, you mean that it is not performing as well as its competitors. *The company has developed a reputation as a technological laggard in the personal-computer arena.* N-COUNT

lagging /læ͟gɪŋ/. **Lagging** is special material which is used to cover pipes, water tanks, or the inside of a roof so that heat does not escape from them or so they do not freeze; used mainly in British English. N-UNCOUNT

lagoon /ləgu͟ːn/ **lagoons.** A **lagoon** is an area of calm sea water that is separated from the ocean by reefs or sandbanks. ◆◇◇◇◇ N-COUNT

lah-di-dah. See **la-di-da**

laid /le͟ɪd/. **Laid** is the past tense and past participle of **lay**.

laid-back. If you describe someone as **laid-back**, you mean that they behave in a calm relaxed way as if nothing will ever worry them; an informal word. *Nothing worried him, he was really laid back... Everyone here has a really laid-back attitude.* ◆◇◇◇◇ ADJ-GRADED

lain /le͟ɪn/. **Lain** is the past participle of **lie**.

lair /le͟əʳ/ **lairs**
1 A **lair** is a place where a wild animal lives, usually a place which is underground or well-hidden. *...a fox's lair.* N-COUNT: usu with poss
2 Someone's **lair** is the particular room or hiding place that they go to, especially when they want to get away from other people; an informal use. *Green recounts how he once went to see Bremner in his lair... The village was once a pirates' lair.* N-COUNT: usu with poss

laird /le͟əʳd/ **lairds.** A **laird** is a landowner in Scotland who owns a large area of land. ◆◇◇◇◇ N-COUNT

laissez-faire /le͟ɪseɪ fe͟əʳ, le͟s-/. **Laissez-faire** is the policy which is based on the idea that governments and the law should not interfere with business, finance, or the conditions of people's working lives. *...a policy of laissez faire. ...the doctrine of laissez-faire and unbridled individualism.* ► Also an adjective. *...the Government's laissez-faire attitude toward the use of motor vehicles. ...a laissez-faire policy.* ◆◇◇◇◇ N-UNCOUNT ADJ-GRADED: usu ADJ n

laity /le͟ɪɪti/. The **laity** are all the people involved in the work of a church who are not clergymen, monks, or nuns. *The Church and the laity were increasingly active in charity work... Clergy and laity alike are divided in their views.* ◆◇◇◇◇ N-SING-COLL: also no det

lake /le͟ɪk/ **lakes.** A **lake** is a large area of fresh water, surrounded by land. *They can go fishing in the lake... The Nile flows from Lake Victoria in East Africa north to the Mediterranean Sea.* ◆◆◆◇◇ N-COUNT: oft in names

lakeside /le͟ɪksaɪd/. The **lakeside** is the area of land around the edge of a lake. *They were out by the lakeside a lot. ...the picturesque Italian lakeside town of Lugano.* N-SING

lam /læ͟m/. If someone is **on the lam** or if they go **on the lam**, they are trying to escape or hide from someone such as the police or an enemy; an informal expression used mainly in American English. *He was on the lam for seven years.* PHRASE: v-link PHR, PHR after v

lama /lɑ͟ːmə/ **lamas.** A **lama** is a Buddhist priest or monk in Tibet and Mongolia. *It takes twenty to twenty-five years of study and meditation to qualify as a lama.* ◆◆◇◇◇ N-COUNT; N-TITLE

lamb /læ͟m/ **lambs** ◆◆◇◇◇
1 A **lamb** is a young sheep. ► **Lamb** is the flesh of a lamb eaten as food. *Laura was basting the leg of lamb.* N-COUNT N-UNCOUNT
2 People sometimes use **lamb** when they are addressing or referring to someone who they are fond of and who is gentle and lovable, for example a young child. *She came and put her arms around me. 'You poor lamb. What's wrong?'* N-COUNT PRAGMATICS
3 If you say that people do something or go somewhere **like lambs** or **like lambs to the slaughter**, you mean that they do something or go somewhere quietly and obediently, without causing any trouble, rather than trying to resist. *The pair surrendered to him like lambs... So long as the British behaved like lambs, the colonists would play the part of lions... We follow their every word like lambs to the slaughter.* PHRASES *lamb* inflects, PHR after v
4 ● **mutton dressed as lamb**: see **mutton.**

lambast /læmbæ͟st/ **lambasts, lambasting, lambasted;** also spelled **lambaste** /læmbe͟ɪst/. If you **lambast** someone, you criticize them severely, usually in public; a formal word. *Grey took every opportunity to lambast Thompson and his organization.* VERB V n

lambing /læ͟mɪŋ/. **Lambing** is the time in the spring when female sheep give birth to lambs. *Lambing is the climax of the sheep farmer's year. ...the lambing season.* N-UNCOUNT: oft N n

lame /le͟ɪm/ **lamer, lamest** ◆◇◇◇◇
1 If someone is **lame**, they are unable to walk properly and they limp because an injury or illness has damaged one or both of their legs. *He was aware that she was lame in one leg... David had to pull out of the Championships when his horse went lame.* ► **The lame** are people who are lame. *... the wounded and the lame of the last war.* ♦ **lameness** *Persistent damage or inadequate healing may lead to chronic lameness.* ADJ-GRADED N-PLURAL: the N N-UNCOUNT
2 If you describe an excuse, argument, or remark as **lame**, you mean that it is poor or weak. *He mumbled some lame excuse about having gone to sleep... All our theories sound pretty lame.* ♦ **lamely** *'Lovely house,' I said lamely.* ADJ-GRADED ADV-GRADED: ADV with v

lamé /lɑ͟ːmeɪ, AM læme͟ɪ/. **Lamé** is cloth that has threads of gold or silver woven into it, which make it sparkle. *...a silver lamé dress.* N-UNCOUNT: usu supp N

lame duck, lame ducks
1 If you describe someone or something as a **lame duck**, you are critical of them because they are not successful and need to be helped a lot. *Look, I'm* N-COUNT: oft N n PRAGMATICS

not one of your lame ducks... It is not proper to use British taxpayers' money to support lame-duck industries.

2 If you refer to a politician or a government as a **lame duck**, you mean that they have little real power, for example because their period of office is coming to an end. *He must recognise by now that he will be a one-term, increasingly lame duck president. ...a lame duck government.* N-COUNT: usu N n

lament /ləment/ **laments, lamenting, lamented** ◆◇◇◇◇

1 If you **lament** something, you express your sadness, regret, or disappointment about it. *Ken began to lament the death of his only son... He laments that people in Villa El Salvador are suspicious of the police... 'Prices are down 40 per cent since Christmas,' he lamented.* VERB V n V that V with quote Also V

2 Someone's **lament** is something that they say that expresses their sadness, regret, or disappointment about something. *She spoke of the professional woman's lament that a woman's judgment is questioned more than a man's.* N-COUNT: oft with poss

3 A **lament** is a poem, song, or piece of music which expresses sorrow that someone has died. *A singer on the country music station was singing a lament for the late, great Buddy Holly.* N-COUNT

lamentable /læməntəbᵊl, ləment-/. If you describe something as **lamentable**, you mean that it is very unfortunate or disappointing; a literary word. *This lamentable state of affairs lasted until 1947... His command of English was lamentable.* ADJ-GRADED PRAGMATICS

♦ **lamentably** /læməntəbli/ *There are still lamentably few women surgeons... They have failed lamentably... There are, lamentably, no set rules.* ADV: usu ADV adj, also ADV with v, ADV with cl

lamentation /læmenteɪʃᵊn/ **lamentations.** A **lamentation** is an expression of grief or great sorrow; a formal word. *It was a time for mourning and lamentation. ...special prayers and lamentations.* N-VAR

laminate /læmɪneɪt/ **laminates.** A **laminate** is a tough material that is made by bonding together two or more layers of a particular substance. *A new insulating laminate has just been designed by Attwater and Sons... Thick sections of the laminate can be produced without the risk of cracking.* N-MASS

laminated /læmɪneɪtɪd/

1 Material such as wood or plastic that is **laminated** consists of several thin sheets or layers that are stuck together. *Modern windscreens are made from laminated glass.* ADJ: usu ADJ n

2 A product that is **laminated** is covered with a thin sheet of something, especially clear or coloured plastic, in order to protect it. *The photographs were mounted on laminated cards. ...laminated work surfaces.* ADJ: usu ADJ n

lamp /læmp/ **lamps** ◆◆◇◇◇

1 A **lamp** is a light that works by using electricity or by burning oil or gas. *She switched on the bedside lamp... In the evenings we eat by the light of an oil lamp.* N-COUNT

2 A **lamp** is an electrical device which produces a special type of light or heat, used especially in medical or beauty treatment. *...a sun lamp. ...the use of infra-red lamps.* N-COUNT: usu supp N

lamplight /læmplaɪt/. **Lamplight** is the light produced by a lamp. *Her cheeks glowed red in the lamplight.* N-UNCOUNT

lampoon /læmpuːn/ **lampoons, lampooning, lampooned**

1 If you **lampoon** someone or something, you criticize them very strongly, using humorous means. *He entertained his readers by lampooning the pretensions of the rich... He was lampooned for his short stature and political views.* VERB V n

2 A **lampoon** is a piece of writing or speech which criticizes someone or something very strongly, using humorous means. *...his scathing lampoons of consumer culture. ...an attempt to cloak their idiotic ramblings in satire and lampoon.* N-VAR

lamp-post, lamp-posts. A **lamp-post** is a tall metal or concrete pole that is fixed beside a road and has a light at the top; used mainly in British English. The more usual American word is **street lamp** or **street light.** N-COUNT

lampshade /læmpʃeɪd/ **lampshades.** A **lampshade** is a covering that is fitted round or over an electric light bulb in order to protect it or decorate it, or to make the light less harsh. N-COUNT =shade

lance /lɑːns, læns/ **lances, lancing, lanced** ◆◇◇◇◇

1 If a boil on someone's body **is lanced**, it is pierced with a sharp instrument in order to let the pus drain out; a medical use. *It is a painful experience having the boil lanced.* VB: usu passive have n V-ed Also be V-ed

2 A **lance** is a long spear used in former times, especially by soldiers on horseback. *...the clang of lances striking armour.* N-COUNT

land /lænd/ **lands, landing, landed** ◆◆◆◆◆

1 **Land** is an area of ground, especially one that is used for a particular purpose such as farming or building. *Good agricultural land is in short supply. ...160 acres of land. ...a small piece of grazing land.* N-UNCOUNT

2 You can refer to an area of land which someone owns as their **land** or their **lands.** *Their home is on his father's land... His lands were poorly farmed.* N-COUNT: poss N

3 If you talk about **the land**, you mean farming and the way of life in farming areas, as opposed to in the cities. *Living off the land was hard enough at the best of times.* N-SING: the N

4 **Land** is the part of the world that is ground, rather than sea or air. *It isn't clear whether the plane went down over land or sea. ...a stretch of sandy beach that was almost inaccessible from the land.* N-UNCOUNT: also the N

5 You can use **land** to refer to a country or region, when you do not mean any particular country, when you are talking about an imaginary or ideal place, or when you are talking about your own country in an emotional or patriotic way; a literary use. *Her husband's body lies buried 2,000 miles away in a strange land. ...blessed lands of sun and sea and olive trees. ...America, land of opportunity. ...this land of free speech.* N-COUNT: with supp

6 When someone or something **lands**, they come down to the ground after moving through the air or falling. *He was sent flying into the air and landed 20ft away... Three mortar shells had landed close to a crowd of people.* VERB V

7 When someone **lands** a plane, ship, or spacecraft, or when it **lands**, it arrives somewhere after a journey. *The jet landed after a flight of just under three hours... He landed his troops on the western shore... The crew finally landed the plane on its belly on the soft part of the runway.* V-ERG V V n

8 To **land** goods somewhere means to successfully unload them there at the end of a journey, especially by ship; used mainly in British English. *The vessels will have to land their catch at designated ports. ...a five-man gang which landed the huge shipment on the Cornwall coast.* VERB V n

9 If you **land** in an unpleasant situation or place or if something **lands** you in it, something causes you to be in it; an informal use. *He landed in a psychiatric ward... This is not the first time his exploits have landed him in trouble.* V-ERG V in n V n in n

10 If someone or something **lands** you with a difficult situation, they cause you to have to deal with the difficulties involved; used mainly in informal British English. *The other options simply complicate the situation and could land him with more expense.* VERB =saddle V n with n

11 If something **lands** somewhere, it arrives there unexpectedly, often causing problems; an informal use. *Two days later the book had already landed on his desk... This was the weekend that the war finally landed on their doorstep.* VERB =arrive V prep/adv

12 If you **land** a fish, you succeed in catching it and getting it out of the water. *One angler landed fish of 10 lb and 9 lb on the same day.* VERB =catch V n

13 If you **land** something that is difficult to get and that many people want, you are successful in getting it; an informal use. *He landed a place on the graduate training scheme... His flair with hair soon landed him a part-time job at his local barbers.* VERB =get V n V n n

14 If someone **lands** a blow or punch or if their blow or punch **lands**, they hit someone. *De Leon* V-ERG V n prep *landed a punch on the Italian's mouth after the end of the eleventh round... I could hear the blows landing as he appealed for help.* V Also V n

15 ● to **land on** your **feet**: see **foot**.

land up. If you say that you **land up** in a place or situation, you mean that you arrive in it after a long journey or at the end of a long series of events; used mainly in informal British English. *Half of those who went east seem to have landed up in southern India... We landed up at the Las Vegas at about 6.30.* PHRASAL VERB =end up, wind up V P prep/adv

landed /lændɪd/. **Landed** means owning or including a large amount of land, especially land that has belonged to the same family for several generations. *Most of them were the nobility and the landed gentry. ...the erosion of the aristocracy's landed wealth.* ADJ: ADJ n

landfall /lændfɔːl/ **landfalls. Landfall** is the first piece of land which you see or arrive at after a voyage at sea; a literary word. *By the time we had made landfall the boat looked ten years older!* N-VAR

landfill /lændfɪl/ **landfills** ◆◇◇◇◇

1 **Landfill** is a method of disposing of very large amounts of rubbish by digging a large deep hole and burying it. *...the environmental costs of landfill.* N-UNCOUNT

2 A **landfill** is a large deep hole in which very large quantities of rubbish are disposed of. *The rubbish in modern landfills does not rot. ...the cost of disposing of refuse in landfill sites.* N-COUNT: oft N n

landing /lændɪŋ/ **landings** ◆◆◇◇◇

1 In a house or other building, the **landing** is the area at the top of the staircase which has rooms leading off it. *I ran out onto the landing.* N-COUNT: usu *the* N in sing

2 A **landing** is an act of bringing an aircraft or spacecraft down to the ground. *I had to make a controlled landing into the sea... The plane had been cleared for landing at Brunswick's Glynco Airport.* N-VAR =touchdown

3 A **landing** is an act of unloading troops in a place as part of a military invasion or other operation. *American forces have begun a big landing.* N-COUNT

4 A **landing** is the same as a **landing stage**. N-COUNT

landing craft; landing craft is both the singular and the plural form. A **landing craft** is a small boat designed for the landing of troops and equipment on the shore. *The engine of one landing craft was still running.* N-COUNT

landing stage, landing stages; also spelled **landing-stage.** A **landing stage** or a **landing** is a platform built over water where boats stop to let people get off, or to load or unload goods; used mainly in British English. N-COUNT =jetty

landing strip, landing strips. A **landing strip** is a long flat piece of land from which aircraft can take off and land, especially one used only by private or military aircraft. N-COUNT

landlady /lændleɪdi/ **landladies** ◆◇◇◇◇

1 Someone's **landlady** is the woman who allows them to live or work in a building which she owns, in return for payment of rent. *We had been made homeless by our landlady.* N-COUNT

2 The **landlady** of a pub is the woman who owns or runs it, or the wife of the man who owns or runs it; used mainly in British English. *...Bet, the landlady of the Rovers Return.* N-COUNT

landless /lændləs/. Someone who is **landless** is prevented from owning the land that they farm, usually by large landowners or by the economic system. *...landless peasants. ...the struggle of the landless poor.* ► **The landless** are people who are landless. *We are giving an equal area of land to the landless.* ADJ; N-PLURAL: *the* N

landlocked /lændlɒkt/; also spelled **land-locked.** A **landlocked** country is surrounded by other countries and does not have its own ports. *...the landlocked West African nation of Mali.* ADJ: usu ADJ n

landlord /lændlɔːʳd/ **landlords** ◆◆◇◇◇

1 Someone's **landlord** is the man who allows them to live or work in a building which he owns, in return for payment of rent. *His landlord doubled the rent.* N-COUNT

2 The **landlord** of a pub is the man who owns or runs it, or the husband of the woman who owns or runs it; used mainly in British English. *The landlord refused to serve him because he considered him too drunk.* N-COUNT

landlubber /lændlʌbəʳ/ **landlubbers.** A **landlubber** is a person who is not used to or does not like travelling by boat or ship, and is not knowledgeable about the sea; an old-fashioned word. N-COUNT

landmark /lændmɑːʳk/ **landmarks** ◆◆◇◇◇

1 A **landmark** is a building or feature which is easily noticed and can be used to judge your position or the position of other buildings or features. *The Ambassador Hotel is a Los Angeles landmark.* N-COUNT

2 You can refer to an important stage in the development of something as a **landmark**. *...a landmark arms control treaty... The baby was one of the big landmarks in our relationship.* N-COUNT: oft N n, N *in* n

land mass, land masses; also spelled **landmass.** A **land mass** is a very large area of land such as a continent. *...the Antarctic landmass. ...the country's large land mass of 768 million hectares.* N-COUNT

landmine /lændmaɪn/ **landmines;** also spelled **land mine.** A **landmine** is an explosive device which is placed on or under the ground and explodes when a person or vehicle touches it. N-COUNT

landowner /lændoʊnəʳ/ **landowners.** A **landowner** is a person who owns land, especially a large amount of land. *...rural communities involved in conflicts with large landowners.* ◆◇◇◇◇ N-COUNT

landowning /lændoʊnɪŋ/. **Landowning** is used to describe people who own a lot of land, especially when they are considered as a group within society. *...a wealthy Scottish landowning family. ...the Anglo-Irish landowning class.* ADJ: ADJ n

land reform, land reforms. Land reform is a change in the system of land ownership, especially when it involves giving land to the people who actually farm it and taking it away from people who own large areas for profit. *...the new land reform policy under which thousands of peasant families are to be resettled.* N-VAR

land registry, land registries. In Britain, a **land registry** is a government office where records are kept about each area of land in a country or region, its exact size and location, and its owner. N-COUNT

landscape /lændskeɪp/ **landscapes, landscaping, landscaped** ◆◆◆◇◇

1 The **landscape** is everything you can see when you look across an area of land, including hills, rivers, buildings, trees, and plants. *...Arizona's desert landscape... We moved to Northamptonshire and a new landscape of hedges and fields.* N-VAR: oft supp N

2 A **landscape** is all the features that are important in a particular situation, and which give it a unique character. *Mr Yeltsin's victory in the referendum has transformed Russia's political landscape. ...a landscape of unparalleled ignorance.* N-COUNT: with supp

3 A **landscape** is a painting which shows a scene in the countryside. N-COUNT

4 If an area of land **is landscaped**, it is redesigned and then altered to create a pleasing artistic effect, for example by adding streams or ponds, and planting trees and bushes. *The gravel pits have been landscaped and planted to make them attractive to wildfowl... They had landscaped their property with trees, shrubs, and lawns. ...a smart suburb of landscaped gardens and wide streets.* VERB *be* V-ed V n *with* n V-ed Also V n

♦ **landscaping** *The landowner insisted on a high standard of landscaping.* N-UNCOUNT

landscape architect, landscape architects. A **landscape architect** is the same as a **landscape gardener.** N-COUNT

landscape gardener, landscape gardeners. A **landscape gardener** is a person who designs gardens or parks so that they look attractive. N-COUNT =landscape architect

landslide /lændslaɪd/ **landslides** ◆◇◇◇◇

1 A **landslide** is a victory in an election in which a person or political party gets far more votes or seats than their opponents. *He won last month's* N-COUNT

presidential election by a landslide... The NLD won a landslide victory in the elections five months ago.

2 A **landslide** is a large amount of earth and rocks falling down a cliff or the side of a mountain. *The storm caused landslides and flooding in Savona.* N-COUNT

landslip /lændslɪp/ **landslips.** A **landslip** is a small movement of soil and rocks down a slope; used mainly in British English. *Roads were flooded or blocked by landslips.* N-COUNT

landward /lændwəʳd/. The **landward** side of something is the side nearest to the land or facing the land, rather than the sea. *Rebels surrounded the city's landward sides.* ADJ: ADJ n

lane /leɪn/ **lanes** ◆◆◆◇◇

1 A **lane** is a narrow road, especially in the country. *...a quiet country lane... Follow the lane to the river. ...The Dorchester Hotel, Park Lane.* N-COUNT: oft in names after n

2 A **lane** is a part of a main road which is marked by the edge of the road and a painted line, or by two painted lines. *The lorry was travelling at 20mph in the slow lane... I pulled out into the eastbound lane of Route 2.* N-COUNT: usu adj N

3 At a swimming pool or athletic track, a **lane** is a long narrow section which is marked by lines or ropes. *The pool is divided into three sections with a crawler lane for beginners... Drawn in lane three, she had all her rivals in sight.* N-COUNT

4 A **lane** is a route that is frequently used by aircraft or ships. *The collision took place in the busiest shipping lanes in the world.* N-COUNT: usu n N

language /læŋgwɪdʒ/ **languages** ◆◆◆◆◇

1 A **language** is a system of communication which consists of a set of sounds and written symbols which are used by the people of a particular country or region for talking or writing. *...the English language... Students are expected to master a second language... Holidays are for seeing the sights, hearing the language and savouring the smells.* N-COUNT

2 **Language** is the use of a system of communication which consists of a set of sounds or written symbols. *Students examined how children acquire language... Language is not art but both are forms of human behavior.* N-UNCOUNT

3 You can refer to the words used in connection with a particular subject as the **language** of that subject. *...the language of business.* N-UNCOUNT: *the* N *of* n, supp N

4 You can refer to someone's use of rude words or swearing as **bad language** when you find it offensive. *Television companies tend to censor bad language in feature films... There's a girl gonna be in the club, so you guys watch your language.* N-UNCOUNT: adj N, poss N

5 The **language** of a piece of writing or speech is the style in which it is written or spoken. *...a booklet summarising it in plain language... The tone of his language was diplomatic and polite... Mr Harris has not been afraid to use language that many in his party despise.* N-UNCOUNT: with supp

6 You can use **language** to refer to various means of communication involving recognizable symbols, non-verbal sounds, or actions. *Some sign languages are very sophisticated means of communication. ...the digital language of computers.* N-VAR: supp N, N *of* n

language laboratory, language laboratories. A **language laboratory** is a classroom equipped with tape recorders and headphones where people can improve their foreign language skills. N-COUNT

languid /læŋgwɪd/. If you describe someone as **languid**, you mean that they show little energy or interest and are very slow and casual in their movements; a literary word. *He's a large, languid man with a round and impassive face... Time spent at Jumby Bay can be as energetic or as languid as you wish.* ◆◇◇◇◇ ADJ-GRADED
♦ **languidly** *We sat about languidly after dinner... A tanned blonde in a bikini swims languidly in the clear swimming pool.* ADV-GRADED: usu ADV with v, also ADV adj

languish /læŋgwɪʃ/ **languishes, languishing, languished** ◆◇◇◇◇

1 If someone **languishes** somewhere, they are forced to remain and suffer in an unpleasant situation. *Pollard continues to languish in prison... No one knows for certain how many refugees wander the world today, or languish in camps without a permanent place of settlement.* VERB V prep/adv

2 If something **languishes**, it is not successful, often because of a lack of effort or because of a lot of difficulties. *Without the founder's drive and direction, the company gradually languished... New products languish on the drawing board.* VERB V

languor /læŋgəʳ/. **Languor** is a pleasant feeling of being relaxed and not having any energy or interest in anything; a literary word. *She, in her languor, had not troubled to eat much.* N-UNCOUNT

languorous /læŋgərəs/. If you describe an activity as **languorous**, you mean that it is lazy, relaxed, and not energetic, usually in a pleasant way; a literary word. *...languorous morning coffees on the terrace.* ADJ-GRADED: usu ADJ n

lank /læŋk/. If someone's hair is **lank** it is long and perhaps rather greasy and it lies or hangs in a dull and unattractive way. *She ran her fingers through her hair; it felt lank and dirty.* ADJ-GRADED

lanky /læŋki/ **lankier, lankiest.** If you describe someone as **lanky**, you mean that they are tall and thin and move rather awkwardly. *He was six feet four, all lanky and leggy.* ADJ-GRADED

lantern /læntəʳn/ **lanterns.** A **lantern** is a lamp in a metal frame with glass sides and with a handle on top so you can carry it. ◆◇◇◇◇ N-COUNT

Laotian /leɪoʊʃən/ **Laotians**

1 **Laotian** means belonging or relating to Laos, or its people, language, or culture. *...the Laotian border.* ADJ

2 A **Laotian** is a Laotian citizen, or a person of Laotian origin. *Four-fifths of Laotians are farmers.* N-COUNT

3 **Laotian** is the language spoken by people who live in Laos. N-UNCOUNT

lap /læp/ **laps, lapping, lapped** ◆◆◆◇◇

1 If you have something on your **lap**, it is on the flat area formed between your stomach and your thighs when you are sitting down. *She waited quietly with her hands in her lap... Hugh glanced at the child on her mother's lap.* N-COUNT: poss N

2 In a race, a competitor completes a **lap** when he or she has gone round a course once. *...that last lap of the race... On lap two, Baker edged forward.* N-COUNT: usu ord/adj N, N num

3 In a race, if you **lap** another competitor, you go past them while they are still on the previous lap. *He was caught out while lapping a slower rider.* VERB V n

4 A **lap** of a long journey is one part of it, between two points where you stop. *I had thought we might travel as far as Oak Valley, but we only managed the first lap of the journey.* N-COUNT: N *of* n, ord/adj N =leg

5 When water **laps** against something such as the shore or the side of a boat, it touches it gently and makes a soft sound; used in written English. *...the water that lapped against the pillars of the boathouse... With a rising tide the water was lapping at his chin before rescuers arrived... The building was right on the river and the water lapped the walls.* VERB V prep/adv, V n
♦ **lapping** *The only sound was the lapping of the waves.* N-UNCOUNT: *the* N *of* n

6 When an animal **laps** a drink, it uses short quick movements of its tongue to flick liquid up into its mouth. *It lapped milk from a dish.* VERB V n
▶ **Lap up** means the same as **lap**. *She poured some water into a plastic bowl. Faust, her Great Dane, lapped it up with relish.* PHRASAL VERB V n P

7 If you say that a situation is **in the lap of the gods**, you mean that its success or failure depends entirely on luck or on things that are outside your control. *They had to stop the operation, so at that stage my life was in the lap of the gods.* PHRASES v-link PHR

8 If you say that someone lives **in the lap of luxury**, you mean that they live in conditions of great comfort and wealth. *We don't live in the lap of luxury, but we're comfortable.* usu PHR after v, v-link PHR

lap up. If you say that someone **laps up** something such as information or attention, you mean that they accept it eagerly, usually when you think they are being foolish for believing that it is sincere. *Their audience will lap up whatever they throw at them... He lapped up the attention and the opportunity to voice his thoughts... They just* PHRASAL VERB V P n (not pron), V n P *haven't been to school before. They're so eager to learn, they lap it up.* • See **lap** 6

lapel /ləpel/ **lapels.** The **lapels** of a jacket or coat are the two top parts at the front that are folded back on each side and join on to the collar. ◆◇◇◇◇ N-COUNT

lapis lazuli /læpɪs læzjʊlaɪ, AM -liː/. **Lapis lazuli** is a bright blue semi-precious stone, used especially in making jewellery. N-UNCOUNT

lap of honour, laps of honour. If the winner of a race or game does a **lap of honour**, they run or drive slowly around a race track or sports field in order to receive the applause of the crowd; used mainly in British English. N-COUNT

lapse /læps/ **lapses, lapsing, lapsed** ◆◇◇◇◇

1 A **lapse** is a moment or instance of bad behaviour by someone who usually behaves well. *On Friday he showed neither decency nor dignity. It was an uncommon lapse.* N-COUNT: usu adj N, N *in* n

2 A **lapse** of something such as concentration or judgement is a temporary lack of that thing, which can often cause you to make a mistake. *I had a little lapse of concentration in the middle of the race... He was a genius and because of it you could accept lapses of taste... The incident was being seen as a serious security lapse.* N-COUNT: N *of* n, supp N

3 If you **lapse** into a quiet or inactive state, you stop talking or being active. *She muttered something unintelligible and lapsed into silence... Doris Brown closed her eyes and lapsed into sleep.* VERB V *into* n

4 If you say that someone **lapses** into a particular way of speaking, a particular language, or a way behaving, you mean they start speaking or behaving in a way. *She lapsed into a little girl voice to deliver a nursery rhyme... Teenagers occasionally find it all too much to cope with and lapse into bad behaviour.* ► Also a noun. *Her lapse into German didn't seem peculiar. After all, it was her native tongue.* VERB =slip V *into* n; N-COUNT: usu N *into* n

5 A **lapse** of time is a period that is long enough for a situation to change or for people to have a different opinion about it. *...the restoration of diplomatic relations after a lapse of 24 years... There is usually a time lapse between receipt of new information and its publication.* N-SING: usu N *of* n, supp N =interval

6 If a period of time **lapses**, it passes. *New products and production processes are transferred to the developing countries only after a substantial amount of time has lapsed.* VERB =pass V

7 If a situation or legal contract **lapses**, it is allowed to end or to become invalid rather than being continued, renewed, or extended. *Her membership of the Labour Party has lapsed... Ford allowed the name and trademark to lapse during the Eighties.* VERB ≠continue V

8 If a member of a particular religion **lapses**, he or she no longer believes in it or follows its rules and practices. *I lapsed in my 20s, returned to it, then lapsed again, while writing the life of historical Jesus... She calls herself a lapsed Catholic.* VERB V V-ed

laptop /læptɒp/ **laptops.** A **laptop** or a **laptop computer** is a small portable computer. *She used to work at her laptop until four in the morning. ...a laptop computer he called Magic Slate.* N-COUNT

lapwing /læpwɪŋ/ **lapwings.** A **lapwing** is a small bird with dark green feathers, a white breast, and a tuft of feathers on its head. N-COUNT

larceny /lɑːʳsəni/. **Larceny** is the crime of theft; a legal term. *Haggerman now faces two to 20 years in prison on grand larceny charges.* N-UNCOUNT

larch /lɑːʳtʃ/ **larches.** A **larch** is a tree with needle-shaped leaves. N-VAR

lard /lɑːʳd/ **lards, larding, larded**

1 **Lard** is soft white fat obtained from pigs. It is used in cooking. *...lard or beef fat.* N-UNCOUNT

2 If you **lard** meat, you insert small pieces of lard, pork, or seasoning into it before cooking. *He larded the lamb with cloves of garlic... The fish had been larded with pieces of ham.* VERB V n *with* n

3 If speech or writing **is larded** with particular types of words, there is a very large and sometimes excessive quantity of them. *Official speeches in recent days have been larded with promises of democracy. ...a long phone call, larded with 'darlings' and a sickening amount of baby-talk.* VERB be V-ed *with* n V-ed Also V n *with* n

larder /lɑːʳdəʳ/ **larders.** A **larder** is a room or cupboard in a house in which food is kept; used mainly in British English. N-COUNT =pantry

large /lɑːʳdʒ/ **larger, largest** ◆◆◆◆◆

1 A **large** thing or person is greater in size than usual or average. *The Pike lives mainly in large rivers and lakes... In the largest room about a dozen children and seven adults are sitting on the carpet... He was a large man with a thick square head.* ADJ-GRADED =big ≠small

2 A **large** amount or number of people or things is more than the average amount or number. *The gang finally fled with a large amount of cash and jewellery... There are a large number of centres where you can take full-time courses... The figures involved are truly very large.* ADJ-GRADED ≠small

3 A **large** organization or business does a lot of work or commercial activity and employs a lot of people. *...a large company in Chicago... Many large organizations run courses for their employees.* ADJ-GRADED =big ≠small

4 **Large** is used to indicate that a problem or issue which is being discussed is very important or serious. *...the already large problem of under-age drinking... There's a very large question about the viability of the newspaper.* ADJ-GRADED: usu ADJ n =serious

5 You use **at large** to indicate that you are talking in a general way about most of the people mentioned. *I think the chances of getting reforms accepted by the community at large remain extremely remote... Amongst the population at large the support for the present regime is virtually zero.* PHRASES n PHR

6 If you say that a dangerous person, thing, or animal is **at large**, you mean that they have not been captured or made safe. *The man who tried to have her killed is still at large.* v-link PHR =free

7 You use **by and large** to indicate that a statement is mostly but not completely true. *By and large, the papers greet the government's new policy document with a certain amount of scepticism.* PHR with cl =on the whole

8 • **to a large extent**: see **extent**. • **larger than life**: see **life**. • **to loom large**: see **loom**. • **in large measure**: see **measure**.

largely /lɑːʳdʒli/ ◆◆◆◆◇

1 You use **largely** to say that a statement is not completely true but is mostly true. *The fund is largely financed through government borrowing... I largely work with people who already are motivated... Their weapons have been largely stones.* ADV-GRADED: ADV with v, ADV with cl/group =mainly

2 **Largely** is used to introduce the main reason for a particular event or situation. *Retail sales dipped 6/10ths of a percent last month, largely because Americans were buying fewer cars... The French empire had expanded largely through military conquest.* ADV: ADV prep =mainly

large-scale; also spelled **large scale.** ◆◆◇◇◇

1 A **large-scale** action or event happens over a very wide area or involves a lot of people or things. *...a large scale military operation.* ADJ-GRADED: ADJ n

2 A **large-scale** map or diagram represents a small area of land or a building or machine on a scale that is large enough for small details to be shown. *...a large-scale map of the county.* ADJ-GRADED: ADJ n

largesse /lɑːʒes/; also spelled **largess** in American English. **Largesse** is kindness or generosity, especially when this involves giving more money than was expected or asked for; a formal word. *...grateful recipients of their largesse. ...his most recent act of largesse.* N-UNCOUNT

largish /lɑːʳdʒɪʃ/. **Largish** means fairly large. *The symphony does require a largish group of players. ...a largish modern city.* ADJ: usu ADJ n =biggish

largo /lɑːʳgoʊ/ **largos**

1 **Largo** written above a piece of music means that it should be played slowly. ADV-GRADED: ADV after v

2 A **largo** is a piece of music, especially part of a longer piece, that is played slowly. N-COUNT

lark /lɑːʳk/ **larks, larking, larked** ◆◇◇◇◇

1 A **lark** is a small brown bird which makes a pleasant sound. N-COUNT

2 If you say that doing something is a **lark**, you mean it is naughty or daring, but also fun; used N-COUNT mainly in British English. *The children thought it was a great lark... The chances are that the thief will be under 21 and doing it for a lark... He'd made it seem rather a lark, to be visiting a supposedly haunted house.*

3 In British English, you can use **lark** in expressions such as **this acting lark** and **the writing lark** to indicate humorously that you think an activity or job is amusing, foolish, or unnecessary. *He got the part, and eventually decided the acting lark wasn't half bad.* N-COUNT: *the/this* n N

lark around or **lark about.** If you **lark around** or **lark about**, you behave in a playful, childish, and silly way, often in order to make people laugh; used mainly in informal British English. *The other actors complained about me larking about when they were trying to concentrate.* PHRASAL VERB =muck around, fool around VP

larva /lɑːʳvə/ **larvae** /lɑːʳviː/. A **larva** is an insect at the stage of its life after it has developed from an egg and before it changes into its adult form. *The eggs quickly hatch into larvae. ...a dragonfly larva.* ◆◇◇◇◇ N-COUNT

larval /lɑːʳvəl/. **Larval** means concerning insect larvae or in the state of being an insect larva. ADJ: ADJ n

laryngitis /lærɪndʒaɪtɪs/. **Laryngitis** is an infection of the throat in which your larynx becomes swollen and painful, making it difficult to speak. N-UNCOUNT

larynx /lærɪŋks/ **larynxes.** Your **larynx** is the top part of the passage that leads from your throat to your lungs and contains your vocal cords; a technical term in anatomy and medicine. N-COUNT =voice box

lasagne /ləsænjə/ **lasagnes;** also spelled **lasagna. Lasagne** is a food dish that consists of layers of pasta, sauce, and a filling such as meat or cheese, baked in an oven. N-VAR

lascivious /ləsɪviəs/. If you describe someone as **lascivious**, you disapprove of them because you think they show an unnaturally strong interest in sex. *The man was lascivious, sexually perverted and insatiable. ...their lewd and lascivious talk.* ADJ-GRADED PRAGMATICS

laser /leɪzəʳ/ **lasers** ◆◆◇◇◇

1 A **laser** is a narrow beam of concentrated light produced by a special machine. It is used for cutting very hard materials, and in many technical fields such as surgery and telecommunications. *...new laser technology... Researchers realised that a tunable laser beam might be useful in surgery.* N-COUNT

2 A **laser** is a machine that produces a laser beam. *...the first-ever laser, built in 1960.* N-COUNT

laser disc, laser discs. A **laser disc** is a shiny flat disc which can be played on a machine which uses lasers to convert signals on the disc into television pictures and sound of a very high quality. *Getting Hollywood's latest films released on laser-disc has also helped... They've just lent me a laser disc player.* N-COUNT: oft N n, also *on* N

laser printer, laser printers. A **laser printer** is a computer printer that produces clear words and pictures by using laser beams. N-COUNT

lash /læʃ/ **lashes, lashing, lashed** ◆◆◇◇◇

1 Your **lashes** are the hairs that grow on the edge of your upper and lower eyelids. *...sombre grey eyes, with unusually long lashes... Joanna studied him through her lashes.* N-COUNT: usu pl =eyelash

2 If you **lash** something somewhere, you tie it firmly to something. If you **lash** two or more things together, you tie one of them firmly to the other. *Secure the anchor by lashing it to the rail... The shelter is built by lashing poles together to form a small dome... Cindy lashed her motorboat alongside... We were worried about the lifeboat which was not lashed down.* VERB =tie V n *to* n V pl-n with *together* V n with adv Also V n

3 If wind, rain, or water **lashes** someone or something, it hits them violently; used in written English. *The worst winter storms of the century lashed the east coast of North America... Suddenly rain lashed against the windows... The rain was absolutely lashing down. ...gales of lashing rain.* VERB V n V prep/adv V-ing

4 If someone **lashes** you or **lashes** into you, they speak very angrily to them, criticizing them or scolding them. *She went quiet for a moment while she summoned up the words to lash him... The report lashes into police commanders for failing to act on intelligence information.* ► Also a noun. *Never before had he felt the full lash of John's temper.* VERB V n V *into* n N-SING: det N

5 A **lash** is a thin strip of leather at the end of a whip. N-COUNT

6 A **lash** is a blow with a whip, especially a blow on someone's back as a punishment. *The villagers sentenced one man to five lashes for stealing a ham from his neighbor.* N-COUNT

7 If someone **lashes** another person, they hit that person with a whip. *They snatched up whips and lashed the backs of those who had fallen.* VERB =whip V n

8 If an animal **lashes** its tail, or if its tail **lashes**, it moves its tail very fast and violently. *When in danger, the anteater lashes its tail round a branch... They tried to get the harpoon into the ray before the sting tail came lashing over to retaliate... Don't go near that lashing tail.* V-ERG V n prep V adv/prep V-ing Also V n, V

lash out PHRASAL VERB

1 If you **lash out**, you attempt to hit someone quickly and violently with a weapon or with your hands or feet. *Riot police fired in the air and lashed out with clubs to disperse hundreds of demonstrators... Her husband has a terrible temper and lashes out at her for no good reason.* VP VP *at* n

2 If you **lash out** at someone or something, you speak about them very angrily or cruelly, criticizing or scolding them. *As a politician Jefferson frequently lashed out at the press... The Cuban leader lashed out against the policy of the US President.* VP *at/against* n Also VP

lashing /læʃɪŋ/ **lashings**

1 **Lashings of** something means a large quantity or amount of it; used mainly in informal British English. *Serve by cutting the scones in half and spreading with jam and lashings of clotted cream. ...lashings of slapstick comedy.* QUANT: QUANT *of* n-uncount

2 **Lashings** are ropes or cables used to tie one thing to another. *We made a tour of the yacht, checking lashings and emergency gear.* N-COUNT: usu pl

3 If you refer to someone's comments as a **lashing**, you mean that they are very cruel and angry, criticizing or scolding someone or something. *He never grew used to the lashings he got from the critics.* N-COUNT

4 A **lashing** is a punishment in which a person is hit with a whip. N-COUNT

lass /læs/ **lasses.** A **lass** is a young woman or girl; used mainly in Scottish and Northern English. *Anne is a Lancashire lass from Longton, near Preston... 'What is it, lass?' Finlay cried.* ◆◇◇◇◇ N-COUNT; N-VOC

lassie /læsi/ **lassies.** In Scottish English, a **lassie** is a young woman or girl; an informal word. N-COUNT; N-VOC

lassitude /læsɪtjuːd, AM -tuːd/. **Lassitude** is a state of tiredness, laziness, or lack of interest; a formal word. *Symptoms of anaemia include general fatigue and lassitude. ...periods of lassitude and inactivity.* N-UNCOUNT

lasso /læsuː, AM læsoʊ/ **lassoes, lassoing, lassoed**

1 A **lasso** is a long rope with a loop at one end, used especially by cowboys for catching cattle. N-COUNT

2 If you **lasso** an animal, you catch it by throwing a lasso round its neck and pulling it tight. *Cowboys drove covered wagons and rode horses, lassoing cattle.* VERB V n

last /lɑːst, læst/ **lasts, lasting, lasted** ◆◆◆◆◆

1 You use **last** in expressions such as **last Friday last night**, and **last year** to refer, for example, to the most recent Friday, night, or year. *I got married last July... He never made it home at all last night... Last month a shopkeeper's nephew was shot dead... It is not surprising they did so badly in last year's elections.* DET

2 The **last** event, person, thing, or period of time is the most recent one. *Much has changed since my last visit... At the last count inflation was 10.9 per cent... I split up with my last boyfriend three years ago... The last few weeks have been hectic.* ► Also a pronoun. *The next tide, it was announced, would be even higher than the last.* ADJ: det ADJ PRON

3 If something **last** happened on a particular occasion, that is the most recent occasion on which it ADV: ADV with v

happened. *When were you there last?... The house is a little more dilapidated than when I last saw it... Hunting on the trust's 625,000 acres was last debated two years ago.*
4 The **last** thing, person, event, or period of time is the one that happens or comes after all the others of the same kind. *This is his last chance as prime minister. ...the last three pages of the chapter... She said it was the very last house on the road... They didn't come last in their league.* ► Also a pronoun. *It wasn't the first time that this particular difference had divided them and it wouldn't be the last... The trickiest bits are the last on the list.* ORD ≠first PRON
5 If you do something **last**, you do it after everyone else does, or after you do everything else. *I testified last... I was always picked last for the football team at school... The foreground, nearest the viewer, is painted last.* ADV: ADV after v
6 If you are the **last** to do or know something, everyone else does or knows it before you. *She was the last to go to bed... Riccardo and I are always the last to know what's going on.* PRON: PRON to-inf
7 Last is used to refer to the only thing, person, or part of something that remains. *Jed nodded, finishing off the last piece of pizza. ...the freeing of the last hostage. ...tiny Albania, the last Stalinist bastion in Europe.* ► Also a noun. *He finished off the last of the wine... The last of the ten inmates gave themselves up after twenty eight hours on the roof of the prison.* ADJ: det ADJ N-SING: *the* N *of* n
8 You use **last** before numbers to refer to a position that someone has reached in a competition after other competitors have been knocked out. For example, if you reach the last four, you are one of four people remaining in a competition. *Sampras reached the last four at Wimbledon. ...the only woman among the authors making it through to the last six.* ADJ: det ADJ
9 You can use **last** to indicate for example that you definitely do not want to do something or that someone is extremely unlikely to have done something. *The last thing I wanted to do was teach... He would be the last person who would do such a thing.* ► Also a pronoun. *I would be the last to say that science has explained everything.* ADJ: det ADJ PRAGMATICS PRON: PRON to-inf
10 The last you see of someone or **the last** you hear of them is the final time that you see them or talk to them. *She disappeared shouting, 'To the river, to the river!' And that was the last we saw of her... I had a feeling it would be the last I heard of him.* PRON: *the* PRON that ≠first
11 If an event, situation, or problem **lasts** for a particular length of time, it continues to exist or happen for that length of time. *The marriage had lasted for less than two years... The games lasted only half the normal time... Enjoy it because it won't last.* VERB V *for* n V n V Also V adv
12 If something **lasts** for a particular length of time, it continues to be able to be used for that time, for example because there is some of it left or because it is in good enough condition. *You only need a very small blob of glue, so one tube lasts for ages... The repaired sail lasted less than 24 hours... The implication is that this battery lasts twice as long as batteries made by other battery makers... If you build more plastics into cars, the car lasts longer.* VERB V *for* n V n V adv Also V
13 You can use **last** in expressions such as **last the game**, **last the course**, and **last the week**, to indicate that someone manages to take part in an event or situation right to the end, especially when this is very difficult for them. *They wouldn't have lasted the full game... I almost lasted the two weeks. I only had a couple of days to do.* ► To **last out** means the same as to **last**. *It'll be a miracle if the band lasts out the tour... A breakfast will be served to those who last out til dawn!* VERB =get through V n PHRASAL VERB =get through V P n (not pron) V P
14 See also **lasting**.
15 If you say that something has happened **at last** or **at long last** you mean it has happened after you have been hoping for it for a long time. *I'm so glad that we've found you at last!... Here, at long last, was the moment he had waited for... At last the train arrived in the station... 'All right', he said at last. 'You may go.'* PHRASES PHR with cl =finally
16 You use expressions such as **the night before last**, **the election before last**, and **the leader before last**, to refer to the period of time, event, or person that happened or came immediately before the most recent one in a series. *It was the dog he'd heard the night before last... In the budget before last a tax penalty on the mobile phone was introduced.*
17 If someone **breathes** their **last**, they die; a literary expression. V inflects
18 You can use phrases such as the **last but one**, the **last but two**, or **last but three**, to refer to the thing or person that is, for example, one, two, or three before the final person or thing in a group or series. *It's the last but one day in the athletics programme... The British team finished last but one.* PHR n, PHR after v
19 You use **every last** to emphasize that you are talking about all the people or things in a group without exception or all the parts of something. *I'd spent all I had, every last penny... You'll never quite get rid of every last bit of grit... My tape recorder did not catch every last word.* PHR n PRAGMATICS
20 The expression **last in, first out** is used to say that the last person who started work in an organization should be the first person to leave it, if fewer people are needed. *Workers will go on a 'last in, first out' basis.*
21 You can use expressions such as **the last I heard** and **the last she heard** to introduce a piece of information that is the most recent that you have on a particular subject. *The last I heard, Joe and Irene were still happily married.* PHR with cl PRAGMATICS
22 If you **leave** something or someone **until last**, you delay using, choosing, or dealing with them until you have used, chosen, or dealt with all the others. *I have left my best wine until last... I picked first all the people who usually were left till last.* V inflects
23 If you **see the last of someone**, you do not expect to see them or deal with them again. *I honestly thought I'd seen the last of you.* V inflects
24 If you say that something goes on happening **to the last**, you mean that it happens throughout a book, film, or event. *...a highly readable political thriller with plenty of twists of plot to keep you guessing to the last.* PHR after v
25 If you say that someone is a particular kind of person **to the last**, you are emphasizing that they are that kind of person. *A gentleman to the last, he did not run, but merely attempted to stroll away... Armstrong was tall and handsome to the last.* group PHR PRAGMATICS
26 You use expressions such as **to the last detail** and **to the last man** to indicate that a plan, situation, or activity includes every single person, thing, or part involved. *Every movement, no matter how casual and spontaneous, needs to be worked out to the last detail... Our troops are being used up to the last man.* PHR after v
27 • **last breath**: see **breath**. • **to have the last laugh**: see **laugh**. • **last minute**: see **minute**. • someone's **last stand**: see **stand**. • **the last straw**: see **straw**. • **last thing**: see **thing**.
last out. See **last** 13. PHRASAL VERB

last-ditch. A **last-ditch** action is done only because there are no other ways left to achieve something or to prevent something happening. It is often done without much hope that it will succeed. *...a last-ditch attempt to prevent civil war. ...a desperate, last-ditch counterattack.* ◆◇◇◇◇ ADJ: ADJ n

lasting /lɑːstɪŋ, læst-/. You can use **lasting** to describe a situation, result, or agreement that continues to exist or have an effect for a very long time. *We are well on our way to a lasting peace... She left a lasting impression on him. ...but there was no lasting damage.* • See also **last**. ◆◆◇◇◇ ADJ: usu ADJ n

Last Judgement; also spelled **Last Judgment**. In the Christian religion, **the Last Judgement** is the last day of the world when God will judge everyone who has died and decide whether they will go to Heaven or Hell. N-PROPER: *the* N

lastly /lɑːstli, læst-/ ◆◇◇◇◇
1 You use **lastly** when you want to make a final point, ask a final question, or mention a final item ADV: ADV with cl/group

that is connected with the other ones you have already asked or mentioned. *Lastly, I would like to ask about your future plans... Thank you to Jim Sheppe for drawing the maps. And lastly, a very big thank-you to Tony, William, Deborah and Bethan.* PRAGMATICS =finally

2 You use **lastly** when you are saying what happens after everything else in a series of actions or events. *Spot all the differences between the two pictures opposite, then circle them in red. Lastly, complete the tiebreaker in no more than 25 words.* ADV: ADV cl =finally

last-minute. See **minute**.

last rites. **The last rites** are a religious ceremony performed by a Christian priest for a dying person. *Father Stephen Lea administered the last rites to the dead men.* N-PLURAL: *the* N

latch /lætʃ/ **latches, latching, latched** ◆◇◇◇◇

1 A **latch** is a fastening on a door or gate. It consists of a metal bar which is held in place to lock the door and which you lift in order to open the door. *You left the latch off the gate and the dog escaped.* N-COUNT

2 A **latch** is a lock on a door which locks automatically when you shut the door, so that you need a key in order to open it from the outside. *...a key clicked in the latch of the front door.* N-COUNT ● If a door is **on the latch** or **off the latch**, the latch has been set so that it will not lock when you shut the door. *Let yourself in; the door's on the latch... They leave their back door off the latch when they're at home so that friends can pop in.* PHRASE: v-link PHR, PHR after v

3 If you **latch** a door or gate, you fasten it by means of a latch. *He latched the door, tested it, and turned around to speak to Frank.* VERB V n

latch onto or **latch on** PHRASAL VERB

1 If someone **latches onto** a person or an idea or **latches on**, they become very interested in the person or idea, often finding them so useful that they do not want to abandon them; an informal expression. *Rob had latched onto me. He followed me around, sat beside me at, and usually ended up working with me... Other trades have been quick to latch on.* V P n, V P

2 In sports such as football or rugby, if a player **latches onto** a pass or another player's mistake, or if they **latch on**, they use the opportunity to do something such as score a goal; an informal expression, used mainly in British English. *Kanchelskis latched onto a superb through ball, before blasting a shot past Southall.* V P n, Also V P

3 If one thing **latches onto** another, or if it **latches on**, it attaches itself to it and becomes part of it. *These are substances which specifically latch onto the protein on the cell membrane.* V P n, Also V P

latchkey /lætʃkiː/; also spelled **latch-key**. If you refer to a child as a **latchkey** kid, you disapprove of the fact that they have to let themselves into their home when returning from school because their parents are out at work. ADJ: ADJ n PRAGMATICS

late /leɪt/ **later, latest** ◆◆◆◆◆

1 **Late** means near the end of a day, week, year, or other period of time. *It was late in the afternoon... She had to work late at night... His autobiography was written late in life... The case is expected to end late next week... Since late last year the border area has been the scene of heavy fighting.* ADV-GRADED: ADV with cl, ADV prep/n ≠early ► Also an adjective. *The talks eventually broke down in late spring... He was in his late 20s. ...the late 1960's.* ADJ-GRADED: ADJ n

2 If it is **late**, it is near the end of the day or it is past the time that you feel something should have been done. *It was very late and the streets were deserted... We've got to go now. It's getting late.* ADJ-GRADED: v-link ADJ ♦ **lateness** *A large crowd had gathered despite the lateness of the hour.* N-UNCOUNT

3 **Late** means after the time that was arranged or expected. *Steve arrived late... The talks began some fifteen minutes late... We got up late.* ADV-GRADED: ADV after v, oft amount ADV ► Also an adjective. *His campaign got off to a late start... We were a little late... The train was 40 minutes late... He's a half hour late.* ADJ-GRADED: oft amount ADJ ♦ **lateness** *He apologised for his lateness.* N-UNCOUNT

4 **Late** means after the usual time that a particular event or activity happens. *We went to bed very late... He married late.* ADV-GRADED: ADV after v ► Also an adjective. *They had a late lunch in a cafe... He was a very late developer.* ADJ-GRADED: ADJ n

5 You use **late** when you are talking about someone who is dead, especially someone who has died recently. *...my late husband. ...the late Mr Parkin.* ADJ: det ADJ

6 Someone who is **late of** a particular place or institution lived or worked there until recently; a formal expression. *...Cousin Zachary, late of Bellevue Avenue. ...Strobe Talbott, late of Time magazine.* ADJ: v-link ADJ *of* n

7 See also **later, latest**.

8 If you say **better late than never** when someone has done something, you think they should have done it earlier. *It's been a long time coming but better late than never.* PHRASES CONVENTION

9 If you say that someone is doing something **late in the day**, you mean that their action or behaviour may not be fully effective because they have waited too long before doing it. *I'd left it all too late in the day to get anywhere with these strategies.* PHR after v, PHR with cl

10 You use **of late** to refer to an event or state of affairs that happened or began to exist a short time ago; a formal expression. *His life has changed of late... The dollar has been stronger of late.* PHR with cl =recently

11 If an action or event is **too late** or happens **too late**, it is useless or ineffective because it occurs at a time after the proper or best time for it. *It was too late to turn back... We realized too late that we were caught like rats in a trap.* v-link PHR, PHR with v

12 ● **a late night**: see **night**.

latecomer /leɪtkʌməʳ/ **latecomers.** A **latecomer** is someone who arrives after the time that they should have done, or later than others. *The latecomers stood just outside at door and window.* N-COUNT

lately /leɪtli/ ◆◆◇◇◇

1 You use **lately** to describe events in the recent past, or situations that started not long ago. *Dad's health hasn't been too good lately... Lord Tomas had lately been appointed Chairman of the Centre for Policy Studies... 'Have you talked to her lately?—Not lately, really.' ...optimism about the US economy, a rare commodity lately.* ADV: ADV with v, ADV with cl =recently

2 You can use **lately** to refer to the job a person has been doing until recently; a formal use. *...Timothy Jean Geoffrey Pratt, lately deputy treasury solicitor... I spoke to Sir Robert Mark, lately retired as Commissioner of Metropolitan Police.* ADV: ADV n/-ed

late-night ◆◇◇◇◇

1 **Late-night** is used to describe events, especially entertainments, that happen late in the evening or late at night. *...John Peel's late-night show on BBC Radio One. ...late-night drinking parties.* ADJ: ADJ n

2 **Late-night** is used to describe services that are available late at night and do not shut when most commercial activities finish. *Saturday night was a late-night shopping night. ...late-night trains.* ADJ: ADJ n

latent /leɪtᵊnt/. **Latent** is used to describe something which is hidden and not obvious at the moment, but which may develop further in the future. *Advertisements attempt to project a latent meaning behind an overt message.* ◆◇◇◇◇ ADJ: usu ADJ n ≠overt

later /leɪtəʳ/ ◆◆◆◆◆

1 **Later** is the comparative of **late**.

2 You use **later** to refer to a time or situation that is after the one that you have been talking about or after the present one. *He resigned ten years later... I'll join you later... Burke later admitted he had lied.* ADV: ADV with cl, oft amount ADV ● You use **later on** to refer to a time or situation that is after the one that you have been talking about or after the present one. *Later on I'll be speaking to Patty Davis... This is only going to cause me more problems later on.* PHRASE: PHR with cl

3 You use **later** to refer to an event, period of time, or other thing which comes after the one that you have been talking about or after the present one. *At a later news conference, he said differences should not be dramatized... The competition should have been re-scheduled for a later date... A later report said the oil fire on the sea was out.* ADJ-COMPAR: ADJ n, *the* ADJ, *the* ADJ *of* n

4 You use **later** to refer to the last part of someone's life or career or of a period of history. *He found happiness in later life... In his later years he wrote very little... Her later career is best known for her* ADJ-COMPAR: ADJ n

partnership with Rudolf Nureyev. ...the later part of the 20th century.
5 See also **late**.
6 • **sooner or later**: see **sooner**.

lateral /lætərəl/. **Lateral** means relating to the sides of something, or moving in a sideways direction. *McKinnon estimated the lateral movement of the bridge to be between four and six inches.* ◆◇◇◇◇ ADJ: usu ADJ n
♦ **laterally** *Shafts were sunk, with tunnels dug laterally.* ADV: usu ADV after v

lateral thinking. **Lateral thinking** is a method of solving problems by using your imagination to help you think of solutions that are not at first obvious, rather than by using logic or other conventional ways of thinking; used mainly in British English. *The holiday romance can last – it just requires a bit of lateral thinking.* N-UNCOUNT

latest /leɪtɪst/ ◆◆◆◆◇
1 **Latest** is the superlative of **late**.
2 You use **latest** to describe something that is the most recent thing of its kind. *...her latest book... Latest reports say another five people have been killed... The resignations are the latest in a series of blows to Mr Amato's government.* ADJ-SUPERL: oft v-link ADJ *in/of* n
3 You can use **latest** to describe something that is extremely modern and up-to-date, and is therefore better than the other things of its type. *Crooks are using the latest laser photocopiers to produce millions of fake banknotes... I got to drive the latest model... Computers have always represented the latest in technology.* ADJ-SUPERL: oft v-link ADJ *in/of* n
4 See also **late**.
5 You use **at the latest** in order to indicate that something must happen at or before a particular time and not after that time. *She should be back by ten o'clock at the latest.* PHRASE: amount PHR PRAGMATICS

latex /leɪteks/. **Latex** is a substance obtained from some kinds of trees, which is used to make products like rubber and glue. N-UNCOUNT

lathe /leɪð/ **lathes.** A **lathe** is a machine which is used for shaping wood or metal. ◆◇◇◇◇ N-COUNT

lather /lɑːðəʳ, læðəʳ/ **lathers, lathering, lathered**
1 A **lather** is a white mass of bubbles which is produced by mixing a substance such as soap or washing powder with water. *...the sort of water that easily makes a lather with soap... He wiped off the remains of the lather with a towel.* N-SING
2 When a substance such as soap or washing powder **lathers**, it produces a white mass of bubbles because it has been mixed with water. *The shampoo lathers and foams so much it's very hard to rinse it all out.* VERB V
3 If you **lather** something, you rub a substance such as soap or washing powder on it until a lather is produced, in order to clean it. *Lather your hair as normal... For super-soft skin, lather on a light body lotion before you bathe.* VERB V n, V n with adv, Also V n prep
4 If you say that someone **works** themselves **up into a lather** or **gets in a lather** about something, you think that they are getting upset, angry, or agitated about it when there is no need to do so. *You have spent the past six months working yourself up into a lather over situations which are really none of your business... 'I'm not going to get into a lather over this defeat,' said the manager.* PHRASE: V inflects

Latin /lætɪn/ **Latins** ◆◆◆◇◇
1 **Latin** is the language which the ancient Romans used to speak. N-UNCOUNT
2 **Latin** countries are countries where Spanish, or perhaps Portuguese, Italian, or French, is spoken. You can also use **Latin** to refer to things and people that come from these countries. *Cuba was one of the least Catholic of the Latin countries... The enthusiasm for Latin music is worldwide.* ADJ: usu ADJ n
3 **Latins** are people who come from countries where Spanish, or perhaps Portuguese, Italian, or French, are spoken or whose families come from one of these countries. *They are role models for thousands of young Latins.* N-COUNT: usu pl

Latin American, Latin Americans ◆◆◇◇◇
1 **Latin American** means belonging or relating to the countries of South America, Central America, and Mexico. **Latin American** also means belonging or relating to the people of culture of these countries. *Leaders of eight Latin American countries are meeting in Caracas, Venezuela, today. ...Latin American art.* ADJ: usu ADJ n
2 A **Latin American** is someone who lives in or comes from South America, Central America, or Mexico. N-COUNT

Latino /lætiːnoʊ/ **Latinos.** A **Latino** is a citizen of the United States who originally came from Latin America, or whose family originally came from Latin America. *He was a champion for Latinos and blacks within the educational system. ...the city's office of Latino Affairs.* ◆◇◇◇◇ N-COUNT: oft N n

latitude /lætɪtjuːd, AM -tuːd/ **latitudes** ◆◇◇◇◇
1 The **latitude** of a place is its distance from the equator. Compare **longitude**. *In the middle to high latitudes rainfall has risen steadily over the last 20-30 years.* N-VAR
► Also an adjective. *The army must cease military operations above 36 degrees latitude north.* ADJ: usu amount ADJ
2 **Latitude** is freedom to choose the way in which you do something; a formal use. *He would be given every latitude in forming a new government... His status at the studio afforded him all the artistic latitude he could ask for.* N-UNCOUNT =freedom

latrine /lətriːn/ **latrines.** A **latrine** is a structure, usually consisting of a hole in the ground, that is used as a toilet for example in a military camp. *There were no proper toilets, but only an outdoor latrine... They made me clean out the latrines.* N-COUNT

latter /lætəʳ/ ◆◆◆◇◇
1 When two people, things, or groups have just been mentioned, you can refer to the second of them as **the latter**. *He tracked down his cousin and uncle. The latter was sick.* PRON: *the* PRON
► Also an adjective. *There are the people who speak after they think and the people who think while they're speaking. Mike definitely belongs in the latter category.* ADJ: ADJ n
2 You use **latter** to describe the later part of a period of time or event. *He is getting into the latter years of his career... The latter part of the debate concentrated on abortion.* ADJ: ADJ n =later

latter-day. **Latter-day** is used to describe something or someone that is a modern equivalent of something or someone in the past. *He holds the belief that he is a latter-day prophet.* ◆◇◇◇◇ ADJ: ADJ n

latterly /lætəʳli/. You can use **latterly** to indicate that a situation or event is the most recent one. *He was to remain active in the association, latterly as vice president, for the rest of his life... City centres were abandoned first by residents, then by shops, and latterly by businesses... Latterly, he has written extensively about alternative medicine.* ADV: ADV with cl/group =lately, recently

lattice /lætɪs/ **lattices.** A **lattice** is a pattern or structure made of strips of wood or another material which cross over each other diagonally leaving holes in between. *We were crawling along the narrow steel lattice of the bridge.* N-COUNT: usu sing

latticed /lætɪst/. Something that is **latticed** is decorated with or is in the form of a lattice. *...latticed doors... The surface of the brain is pinky-grey and latticed with tiny blood vessels.* ADJ: usu ADJ n, also v-link ADJ *with* n

latticework /lætɪswɜːʳk/. **Latticework** is any structure that is made in the form of a lattice. *...balconies shaded with latticework which lets in air but not light. ...latticework chairs.* N-UNCOUNT

laud /lɔːd/ **lauds, lauding, lauded.** If people **laud** someone, they praise and admire them; used in journalism. *He lauded the work of the UN High Commissioner for Refugees... They lauded the former president as a hero... The company also lauded Mr. Bush for his intention to correct market distortions through an international agreement.* ◆◇◇◇◇ VERB V n, V n *as* n, V n *for* n
♦ **lauded** *...the most lauded actress in New York.* ADJ-GRADED

laudable /lɔːdəbᵊl/. Something that is **laudable** deserves to be praised or admired; a formal word. *One of Diana's less laudable characteristics is her jealousy... These may be laudable aims, but* ADJ-GRADED =admirable *by enforcing them at gunpoint another vitally important principle is lost.*

laudatory /lɔːdətri, AM -tɔːri/. A **laudatory** piece of writing or speech expresses praise or admiration for someone; a formal word. *The New York Times has this very laudatory article about your retirement... Beth spoke of Dr. Hammer in laudatory terms.* — ADJ-GRADED: usu ADJ n =complimentary

laugh /lɑːf, læf/ **laughs, laughing, laughed** ◆◆◆◆◆

1 When you **laugh**, you make a sound with your throat while smiling and show that you are happy or amused. People also sometimes laugh when they feel nervous or are being unfriendly. *He was about to offer an explanation, but she was beginning to laugh... He laughed with pleasure when people said he looked like his dad... The British don't laugh at the same jokes as the French... 'They'll carry me away on a stretcher if I win on Sunday,' laughed Lyle.* ▶ Also a noun. *Lysenko gave a deep rumbling laugh at his own joke.* — VERB; V; V with n; V at n; V with quote; N-COUNT

2 If people **laugh at** someone or something, they mock them or make jokes about them. *I thought they were laughing at me because I was ugly... She wanted to laugh at the melodramatic way he was acting.* — VERB; V at n

3 If you do or say something **for a laugh** or **for laughs**, you do or say it as a joke or for fun rather than for any other reason. *They were persuaded onstage for a laugh by their mates... It's a project she's doing for laughs.* — PHRASES; PHR with v

4 If a person or their comments **get a laugh** or **raise a laugh**, they make the people listening to them laugh; used mainly in British English. *If you can get a laugh by wearing a silly hat, you must have been born a comic... The joke got a big laugh, which encouraged me to continue.* — V inflects

5 If you describe a situation as **a laugh**, **a good laugh**, or **a bit of a laugh**, you think that it is fun and do not take it too seriously. *Working there's great. It's quite a good laugh actually... It was a good laugh there!* — v-link PHR

6 If you describe someone as **a laugh** or **a good laugh**, you like them because they are amusing and fun to be with; used mainly in British English. *Mickey was a good laugh and great to have in the dressing room.* — v-link PHR

7 If you **have a good laugh about** something, you find it amusing and realize that it is funny, especially when the situation was at first rather upsetting. *We've both had a good laugh about the accident despite what's happened.* — V inflects, PHR n

8 If you say that you **have the last laugh**, you mean that you make your critics or opponents look foolish or wrong, by being successful when you were not expected to be. *Des O'Connor is expecting to have the last laugh on his critics by soaring to the top of the Christmas hit parade.* — V inflects

9 Some people reply to other people's comments or opinions by saying **'Don't make me laugh'** when they disagree with them and think they are foolish or inaccurate; an informal expression. *Claire, a poisoner? Don't make me laugh – She was just a lousy cook.* — CONVENTION; PRAGMATICS

10 If you say **'you've got to laugh'** or **'you have to laugh'**, you are trying to see the amusing side of a difficult or disappointing situation rather than being sad or angry about it; an informal expression. *The bikers have shown enough contempt of the law to ride their machines over police cars. 'You've got to laugh at their audacity,' said Mr Starkey.* — CONVENTION

11 • to **laugh someone out of court**: see **court**. • to **laugh in** someone's **face**: see **face** • to **laugh your head off**: see **head**. • **no laughing matter**: see **matter**. • to **laugh all the way to** something: see **way**.

laugh off. If you **laugh off** a difficult or serious situation, you try to suggest that it is amusing and unimportant, for example by making a joke about it. *The couple laughed off rumours that their marriage was in trouble... Whilst I used to laugh it off, I'm now getting irritated by it.* — PHRASAL VERB; V P n (not pron); V n P

laughable /lɑːfəb^{ə}l, læf-/. If you say that something such as an idea or suggestion is **laughable**, you mean that it is so stupid as to be funny and not worth serious consideration. *The idea that TV shows like 'Dallas' or 'Dynasty' represent typical American life is laughable... He has denied suggestions that he hates all English people, claiming the allegations are 'laughable'.* — ◆◇◇◇◇ ADJ-GRADED: usu v-link ADJ =ludicrous

♦ **laughably** *To an outsider, the issues that we fight about would seem almost laughably petty.* — ADV: usu ADV adj

laughing gas. **Laughing gas** is a type of anaesthetic gas which sometimes has the effect of making people laugh uncontrollably. — N-UNCOUNT

laughingly /lɑːfɪŋli, læf-/. If you **laughingly** refer to something with a particular name or description, the description is not appropriate and you think that this is either amusing or annoying. *I spent much of what I laughingly call 'the holidays' working through 621 pages of typescript... What I laughingly refer to as my garden is a corner lot by our postage-stamp size house.* — ADV: ADV with v

laughing stock, laughing stocks; also spelled **laughing-stock**. If you say that a person or an institution has become a **laughing stock**, you mean that they are supposed to be important or serious but have been made to seem ridiculous. *The truth must never get out. If it did she would be a laughing-stock. ...his policies became the laughing stock of the financial community.* — N-COUNT

laughter /lɑːftə^{r}, læf-/ ◆◆◆◇◇

1 **Laughter** is the sound of people laughing, for example because they are amused or happy. *Their laughter filled the corridor... He delivered the line perfectly, and everybody roared with laughter. ...hysterical laughter.* — N-UNCOUNT

2 **Laughter** is the fact of laughing, or the feeling of fun and amusement that you have when you are laughing. *Pantomime is about bringing laughter to thousands... My interests: eating out, fun nights in, music and laughter.* — N-UNCOUNT =fun, amusement

launch /lɔːntʃ/ **launches, launching, launched** ◆◆◆◆◇

1 To **launch** a rocket, missile, or satellite means to send it into the air or into space. *NASA plans to launch a satellite to study cosmic rays... A Delta II rocket was launched from Cape Canaveral early this morning.* ▶ Also a noun. *This morning's launch of the space shuttle Columbia has been delayed.* — VERB; V n; N-VAR

2 To **launch** a ship or a lifeboat means to put it into water, often for the first time after it has been built. *Coastguards launched three lifeboats off Great Ormes.* ▶ Also a noun. *The launch of a ship was a big occasion.* — VERB; V n; N-COUNT: usu with poss

3 To **launch** a large and important activity, for example a military attack, means to start it. *Heavy fighting has been going on after the guerrillas had launched their offensive... The police have launched an investigation into the incident... Mr Gorbachev was on holiday when the coup was launched.* ▶ Also a noun. *...the launch of a campaign to restore law and order.* — VERB =start; V n; N-COUNT: oft N of n

4 If a company **launches** a new product, it makes it available to the public. *Crabtree & Evelyn has just launched a new jam, Worcesterberry Preserve... Marks & Spencer recently hired model Linda Evangelista to launch its new range.* ▶ Also a noun. *British Airways has broken new ground with the launch of a new service to Taipei.* — VERB; V n; N-COUNT: oft N of n

5 A **launch** is a large motorboat that is used for carrying people on rivers and lakes and in harbours. *The captain was on the deck of the launch, steadying the boat for the pilot... We'll make a trip by launch to White Island.* — N-COUNT: also by N

launch into. If you **launch into** something such as a speech, task, or fight, you enthusiastically start it. *Horrigan launched into a speech about the importance of new projects... Geoff has launched himself into fatherhood with great enthusiasm.* — PHRASAL VERB; V P n; V pron-refl P n

launching pad, launching pads. A **launching pad** is the same as a **launch pad**. — N-COUNT

la̲unch pad, launch pads
1 A **launch pad** or **launching pad** is a platform from which rockets, missiles, or satellites are launched. *...the launch pad at Cape Canaveral.* N-COUNT
2 A **launch pad** or **launching pad** is a situation, for example a job, which you can use in order to go forward to something better or more important. *Wimbledon has been a launch pad for so many players... It was the launching pad for a media career that has made her one of the highest-paid people on British TV.* N-COUNT =stepping stone

launder /lɔːndəʳ/ **launders, laundering, laundered** ◆◇◇◇◇
1 When you **launder** clothes, bed linen, and towels, you wash and iron them; an old-fashioned use. *How many guests who expect clean towels every day in an hotel launder their own every day at home?... She wore a freshly laundered and starched white shirt.* VERB V n V-ed
2 To **launder** money that has been obtained illegally means to process it through a legitimate business or to send it abroad to a foreign bank, so that when it comes back nobody knows that it was illegally obtained. *The House voted today to crack down on banks that launder drug money.* VERB V n
♦ **launderer** *...a businessman and self-described money launderer.* N-COUNT

launderette /lɔːndret/ **launderettes;** also spelled **laundrette**. In British English, a **launderette** is a shop in which there are washing machines and dryers which people can use to wash and dry their clothes. The American word is **laundromat**. N-COUNT

laundromat /lɔːndrəmæt/ **laundromats.** In American English, a **laundromat** is a **laundrette**. N-COUNT

laundry /lɔːndri/ **laundries** ◆◇◇◇◇
1 **Laundry** is used to refer to clothes, sheets, and towels that are about to be washed, are being washed, or have just been washed. *I'll do your laundry. ...the room where I hang the laundry... He'd put his dirty laundry in the clothes basket.* N-UNCOUNT =washing
2 A **laundry** is a firm that washes and irons clothes, sheets, and towels for people. *We had to have the washing done at the laundry.* N-COUNT
3 A **laundry** or a **laundry room** is a room in a house, hotel, or institution where clothes, sheets, and towels are washed. *He worked in the laundry at Oxford prison.* N-COUNT: usu sing
4 • to **wash** your **dirty laundry in public**: see **dirty**.

la̲undry list, laundry lists. If you describe something as a **laundry list** of things, you mean that it is a long list of them. *...a laundry list of reasons why shareholders should reject the bid.* N-COUNT: usu N *of* n

laurel /lɒrᵊl, AM lɔːr-/ **laurels** ◆◇◇◇◇
1 A **laurel** or a **laurel tree** is a small evergreen tree with shiny leaves. The leaves are sometimes used to make ornaments such as wreaths. N-VAR
2 If someone is **resting on** their **laurels**, they appear to be satisfied with the things they have achieved and have stopped putting effort into what they are doing; used showing disapproval. *The committee's chairman accused NASA of resting on its laurels after making it to the moon... The government couldn't rest on its laurels and must press ahead with major policy changes.* PHRASE: V inflects PRAGMATICS =sit back

lava /lɑːvə/ **lavas. Lava** is the very hot molten rock that comes out of a volcano. ◆◇◇◇◇ N-MASS

lavatorial /lævətɔːriəl/. **Lavatorial** jokes or stories involve childish references to urine or faeces; used mainly in British English. ADJ-GRADED: usu ADJ n

lavatory /lævətri, AM -tɔːri/ **lavatories.** A **lavatory** is the same as a **toilet**; used mainly in British English. *...the ladies' lavatory at the University of London. ...a public lavatory.* ◆◇◇◇◇ N-COUNT =toilet

la̲vatory paper. Lavatory paper is thin absorbent paper that you use to clean yourself after you have got rid of urine or faeces from your body; used mainly in British English. N-UNCOUNT =toilet paper

lavender /lævɪndəʳ/ **lavenders** ◆◇◇◇◇
1 **Lavender** is a garden plant with sweet-smelling, bluish-purple flowers. N-UNCOUNT: also N in pl
2 **Lavender** is used to describe things that are pale bluish-purple in colour. COLOUR

lavish /lævɪʃ/ **lavishes, lavishing, lavished** ◆◆◇◇◇
1 If you describe something as **lavish**, you mean that a lot of time, effort, or money has been spent on it to make it as impressive as possible. *...a lavish party to celebrate Bryan's fiftieth birthday... He staged the most lavish productions of Mozart... The sets and costumes are lavish.* ADJ-GRADED =grand
♦ **lavishly** *...the train's lavishly furnished carriages... IBM spent lavishly on their workers' education and training.* ADV-GRADED: ADV with v
2 If you say that something is **lavish**, you mean it is extravagant and excessively wasteful. *...stealing antique jewellery and paintings to finance a lavish lifestyle... Entertainment expenses are not deductible when they are lavish.* ADJ-GRADED =extravagant
3 If you **lavish** something such as money, affection, or time on someone or something, you spend a lot of money on them or give them a lot of affection or attention. *Prince Sadruddin lavished praise on Britain's contributions to world diplomacy... The emperor promoted the general and lavished him with gifts.* VERB V n *on/upon* n V n *with* n

law /lɔː/ **laws** ◆◆◆◆◆
1 **The law** is a system of rules that a society or government develops in order to deal with crime, business agreements, and social relationships. You can also use the **law** to refer to the people who work in this system. *Obscene and threatening phone calls are against the law... They are seeking permission to begin criminal proceedings against him for breaking the law on financing political parties... There must be changes in the law quickly to stop this sort of thing ever happening to anyone else... The book analyses why women kill and how the law treats them.* N-SING: *the* N
2 **Law** is used to refer to a particular branch of the law, such as **criminal law** or **company law**. *He was a professor of criminal law at Harvard University law school... Under international law, diplomats living in foreign countries are exempt from criminal prosecution... Important questions of constitutional law were involved.* N-UNCOUNT: usu adj N
3 A **law** is one of the rules in a system of law which deals with a particular type of agreement, relationship, or crime. *...the country's liberal political asylum law... The law was passed on a second vote.* N-COUNT: oft n N
4 The **laws** of an organization or activity are its rules, which are used to organize and control it. *...the laws of the Church of England... Match officials should not tolerate such behaviour but instead enforce the laws of the game.* N-PLURAL: *the* N *of* n, supp N =rule
5 A **law** is a rule or set of rules for good behaviour which is considered right and important by the majority of people for moral, religious, or emotional reasons. *...inflexible moral laws.* N-COUNT =code
6 A **law** is a natural process in which a particular event or thing always leads to a particular result. *The laws of nature are absolute.* N-COUNT: with supp
7 A **law** is a scientific rule that someone has invented to explain a particular natural process. *...the law of gravity.* N-COUNT: with supp
8 **Law** or **the law** is all the professions which deal with advising people about the law, representing people in court, or giving decisions and punishments. *A career in law is becoming increasingly attractive to young people... Nearly 100 law firms are being referred to the Solicitors' Disciplinary Tribunal.* N-UNCOUNT
9 **Law** is the study of systems of law and how laws work. *He came to Oxford and studied law... He holds a law degree from Bristol University.* N-UNCOUNT
10 See also **court of law, rule of law**.
11 If you accuse someone of thinking they are **above the law**, you criticize them for thinking that they are so clever or important that they do not need to obey the law. *One opposition member of parliament accuses the government of wanting to be above the law... He considered himself above the law.* PHRASES v-link PHR PRAGMATICS
12 **The law of averages** is the idea that something is sure to happen at some time, considering the

number of times it generally happens or is expected to happen. *On the law of averages we just can't go on losing and losing and losing.*
13 If you have to do something **by law** or if you are not allowed to do something **by law**, the law states that you have to do it or that you are not allowed to do it. *By law all restaurants must display their prices outside... Minicabs are prohibited by law from touting passers-by for business.* PHR with cl
14 If you **go to law**, you go to court in order to get a dispute legally decided; used mainly in British English. *American Indians are going to law to reclaim land.* V inflects
15 If you say that someone **lays down the law**, you are critical of them because they give other people orders and they think that they are always right. *...traditional parents, who believed in laying down the law for their offspring.* V inflects PRAGMATICS
16 If someone **takes the law into** their **own hands**, they punish someone according to their own ideas of justice, often when this involves breaking the law. *The speeding motorist was pinned to the ground by angry locals who took the law into their own hands until police arrived.* V inflects
17 If you say that someone is **a law unto** himself or herself, you think that they behave in an independent way, ignoring laws, rules, or conventional ways of doing things. *Some of the landowners were a law unto themselves. There was nobody to check their excesses and they exploited the people.* v-link PHR PRAGMATICS
18 ● **Sod's law**: see **sod**.

law-abiding. A **law-abiding** person always obeys the law and is considered to be good and honest because of this. *The Prime Minister said: 'I am anxious that the law should protect decent law-abiding citizens and their property'... Gun ownership by law-abiding people was not a problem.* ◆◇◇◇◇ ADJ-GRADED: usu ADJ n

law and order. When there is **law and order** in a country, the laws are generally accepted and obeyed, so that society there functions normally. *If there were a breakdown of law and order, the army might be tempted to intervene. ...people who had no respect for law and order.* ◆◆◇◇◇ N-UNCOUNT

law-breaker, law-breakers; also spelled **law-breaker**. A **law-breaker** is someone who breaks the law. *The money spent on prisons could be better spent on training first-time law-breakers to earn an honest living.* N-COUNT

law-breaking. also spelled **law breaking**. **Law-breaking** is any kind of illegal activity. *Civil disobedience, violent or non-violent, is intentional law breaking.* N-UNCOUNT

law court, law courts. A **law court** is a place where legal matters are decided by a judge and jury or by a magistrate. *She would never resort to the law courts to resolve her marital problems.* N-COUNT

law-enforcement. **Law-enforcement** agencies or officials are responsible for catching people who break the law; a formal word used mainly in American English. *We need to restore respect for the law and for bodies such as the army and the law-enforcement agencies.* ◆◇◇◇◇ N-UNCOUNT: usu N n

lawful /lɔːfʊl/. If an activity, organization, or product is **lawful**, it is allowed by law; a formal word. *It was lawful for the doctors to treat her in whatever way they considered was in her best interests... Hunting is a lawful activity.* ♦ **lawfully** *Amnesty International is trying to establish whether the police acted lawfully in shooting him.* ◆◇◇◇◇ ADJ-GRADED =legal ≠unlawful, illegal; ADV: ADV with v ≠unlawfully

lawless /lɔːləs/ ◆◇◇◇◇
1 **Lawless** actions break the law, especially in a wild and violent way. *The government recognised there were problems in urban areas but these could never be an excuse for lawless behaviour.* ADJ: usu ADJ n
♦ **lawlessness** *Lawlessness is a major problem.* N-UNCOUNT
2 A **lawless** place or time is one where people do not respect the law. *...lawless inner-city streets plagued by muggings, thefts, assaults and even murder. ...people struggling to restore moral values in an increasingly lawless and godless age.* ADJ-GRADED: usu ADJ n

lawmaker /lɔːmeɪkəʳ/ **lawmakers.** In American English, a **lawmaker** is someone such as a politician who is responsible for proposing and passing new laws. ◆◆◇◇◇ N-COUNT

lawman /lɔːmæn/ **lawmen.** When journalists talk about **lawmen**, they are referring to men such as policemen or lawyers whose work involves the law. *...the 61-year-old lawman who headed the enquiry.* N-COUNT

lawn /lɔːn/ **lawns.** A **lawn** is an area of grass that is kept cut short and is usually part of someone's garden or part of a park. *They were sitting on the lawn under a large beech tree.* ◆◆◇◇◇ N-VAR

lawnmower /lɔːnmoʊəʳ/ **lawnmowers;** also spelled **lawn mower**. A **lawnmower** is a machine for cutting grass on lawns. N-COUNT

lawn tennis. **Lawn tennis** is the official name for **tennis**. N-UNCOUNT

lawsuit /lɔːsuːt/ **lawsuits.** A **lawsuit** is a case in a court of law which concerns a dispute between two people or organizations; a formal word. *The dispute culminated last week in a lawsuit against the government. ...a lawsuit brought by Barclays Bank.* ◆◆◇◇◇ N-COUNT

lawyer /lɔɪəʳ/ **lawyers.** A **lawyer** is a person who is qualified to advise people about the law and represent them in court. *Prosecution and defense lawyers are expected to deliver closing arguments next week.* ◆◆◆◆◇ N-COUNT

lax /læks/ **laxer, laxest.** If you say that a person's behaviour or a system is **lax**, you mean they are not careful or strict in making or obeying rules or maintaining high standards. *One of the problem areas is lax security for airport personnel... There have been allegations from survivors that safety standards had been lax... I was lax in my duties.* ♦ **laxity** *The laxity of export control authorities has made a significant contribution to the problem.* ◆◇◇◇◇ ADJ-GRADED; N-UNCOUNT

laxative /læksətɪv/ **laxatives** ◆◇◇◇◇
1 A **laxative** is something which you eat or drink that stops you being constipated. *Foods that ferment quickly in the stomach are excellent natural laxatives.* N-MASS
2 A **laxative** food or medicine stops you being constipated. *The artificial sweetener sorbitol has a laxative effect... Molasses are mildly laxative and something of a general tonic.* ADJ-GRADED

lay 1 verb and noun uses

lay /leɪ/ **lays, laying, laid** ◆◆◆◆◇
In standard English, the form **lay** is also the past tense of the verb **lie** in some meanings. In informal English, people sometimes use the word **lay** instead of **lie** in those meanings.
1 If you **lay** something somewhere, you put it there in a careful, gentle, or neat way. *Lay a sheet of newspaper on the floor... My father's working bench was covered with a cloth and his coffin was laid there... Mothers routinely lay babies on their backs to sleep.* VERB V n prep/adv
2 If you **lay** the table or **lay** the places at a table, you arrange the knives, forks, and other things that people need on the table before a meal; used mainly in British English. The usual American expression is **set the table**. *The butler always laid the table.* VERB V n
3 If you **lay** something such as carpets, cables, or foundations, you put them into their permanent position. *A man came to lay the saloon carpet... Public utilities dig up roads to lay pipes.* VERB V n
4 When someone **lays** a trap, they prepare it to catch someone or something. *They were laying a trap for the kidnapper.* VERB V n
5 When a female bird **lays** an egg, it produces an egg by pushing it out of its body. *My canary has laid an egg... Freezing weather in spring hampered the hens' ability to lay.* VERB V n V
6 **Lay** is used with some nouns to talk about making official preparations for something. For example, if you **lay the basis** for something or **lay plans** for it, you prepare it carefully so that you can continue with it, develop it, or benefit from it later. *Diplomats meeting in Chile have laid the ground-* VERB V n

work for far-reaching environmental regulations... The organisers meet in March to lay plans.

7 **Lay** is used with some nouns in expressions about accusing or blaming someone. For example, if you **lay the blame** for a mistake on someone, you say it is their fault, or if the police **lay charges** against someone, they officially accuse that person of a crime. *She refused to lay the blame on any one party... He could not bear to lay too much responsibility for the unhappiness of his later years on his own shoulders... Police have decided not to lay charges over allegations of a telephone tapping operation.* VERB V n prep V n

8 If you say that you would **lay** bets, odds, or money on something happening, you mean that you are very confident that it will happen; an informal use. *I wouldn't lay bets on his still remaining manager after the spring... I'll lay odds that Dean is at your office right now.* VERB V n on n/-ing V n that

9 To **lay** someone means to have sex with them; an offensive use. VERB: V n

10 **Lay** is used in expressions such a **good lay** or an **easy lay** to describe what someone is like as a sexual partner; an offensive use. N-COUNT: usu adj N

11 If someone **is laying it on thick** or is **laying it on**, they are exaggerating a statement, experience, or emotion in order to try to impress people; an informal expression. *Don't lay it on too thick, but make sure they are flattered... I may have spoken a bit too freely, been a bit extreme, even laid it on a little.* PHRASES V inflects

12 If you **lay** yourself **open to** criticism or attack, or if something **lays** you **open to** it, something you do makes it possible or likely that other people will criticize or attack you. *The party thereby lays itself open to charges of conflict of interest... Such a statement could lay her open to ridicule.* V inflects, PHR n

13 • to **lay** something **bare**: see **bare.** • to **lay claim to** something: see **claim.** • to **lay** something **at** someone's **door**: see **door.** • to **lay eyes on** something: see **eye.** • to **lay a finger on** someone: see **finger.** • to **lay** your **hands on** something: see **hand.** • to **lay down the law**: see **law.** • to **lay down** your **life**: see **life.** • to **lay** something **to rest**: see **rest.** • to **lay siege to** something: see **siege.** • to **lay waste**: see **waste.**

lay aside PHRASAL VERB

1 If you **lay** something **aside**, you put it down, usually because you have finished using it or want to save it to use later. *He finished the tea and laid the cup aside... This allowed Ms. Kelley to lay aside money to start her business.* V n P V P n (not pron)

2 If you **lay aside** a feeling or belief, you reject it or give it up in order to progress with something. *Perhaps the opposed parties will lay aside their sectional interests and rise to this challenge... All animosities were laid aside for the moment.* V P n (not pron) Also V n P

lay before. If you **lay** an idea or piece of information **before** someone, you present it to them in detail, usually in order to obtain their approval or advice; a formal expression. *Mr Patten laid regulations before Parliament giving himself wide general powers... Will Mr Gorbachev be able to lay before them an agreed plan for economic reform?* PHRASAL VERB V n P n V P n n

lay down PHRASAL VERB

1 If you **lay** something **down**, you put it down, usually because you have finished using it. *Daniel finished the article and laid the newspaper down on his desk... She laid down her knife and fork and pushed her plate away.* V n P V P n (not pron)

2 If rules or people in authority **lay down** what people should do or must do, they officially state what they should or must do. *The Companies Act lays down a set of minimum requirements... Taxis must conform to the rigorous standards laid down by the police.* V P n (not pron)

3 If someone **lays down** their weapons, they stop fighting a battle or war and make peace. *The drug-traffickers have offered to lay down their arms.* V P n (not pron)

lay in. If you **lay in** an amount of something, you buy it and store it to be used later. *They began to lay in extensive stores of food supplies.* PHRASAL VERB V P n (not pron)

lay into. To **lay into** someone or something means to start attacking them with physical violence or severe criticism; an informal expression. *A mob of women laid into him with handbags and pointed shoes... She used to lay into Gareth about how much he spent.* PHRASAL VERB V P n

lay off PHRASAL VERB

1 If workers **are laid off**, they are told by their employers to leave their job, usually because there is no more work for them to do. *100,000 federal workers will be laid off to reduce the deficit... They did not sell a single car for a month and had to lay off workers.* • See also **layoff**. be V-ed P V P n (not pron) Also V n P

2 If you tell someone to **lay off**, you mean that they should stop touching or criticizing you or someone else, or stop touching something; an informal expression. *He went on attacking her until other passengers arrived and told him to lay off.* PRAGMATICS V P

lay on. If you **lay on** something such as food, entertainment, or a service, you provide or supply it, especially in a generous or grand way; used mainly in British English. *They laid on a superb evening... Every facility was laid on to ease their homecoming.* PHRASAL VERB V P n (not pron) Also V n P

lay out PHRASAL VERB

1 If you **lay out** a group of things, you spread them out and arrange them neatly, for example so that they can all be seen clearly. *Grace laid out the knives and forks at the lunch-table... She took a deck of cards and began to lay them out.* V P n (not pron) V n P

2 To **lay out** ideas, principles, or plans means to explain or present them clearly, for example in a document or a meeting. *Maxwell listened closely as Johnson laid out his plan... Cuomo laid it out in simple language.* V P n (not pron) V n P

3 To **lay out** an area of land or a building means to plan and design how its different parts should be arranged. *When we laid out the car parks, we reckoned on one car per four families... Only people that use a kitchen all the time understand the best way to lay it out.* V P n (not pron) V n P

4 To **lay out** a dead person means to clean their body and dress them for people to see before the funeral. *Friends laid out the body.* V P n (not pron) Also V n P

5 If you **lay out** money on something, you spend a large amount of money on it; an informal expression. *You won't have to lay out a fortune for this dining table.* V P n (not pron)

6 To **lay** someone **out** means to knock them to the ground, especially by hitting them hard; an informal expression. *Andy turned round, marched over to Chris and just laid him out.* V n P Also V P n

7 See also **layout**.

lay up. If someone **is laid up** with an illness, the illness makes it necessary for them to stay in bed; an informal expression. *I was laid up in bed with acute rheumatism... Powell ruptured a disc in his back and was laid up for a year.* PHRASAL VERB usu passive be V-ed P with n be V-ed P

lay 2 adjective uses

lay /leɪ/

1 You use **lay** to describe people who are involved with a Christian church but are not members of the clergy or are not monks or nuns. *Edwards is a Methodist lay preacher and social worker.* ADJ: ADJ n

2 You use **lay** to describe people who are not experts or professionals in a particular subject or activity. *It is difficult for a lay person to gain access to medical libraries... It is not just a textbook for professional diplomats. The lay reader will enjoy the anecdotes.* ADJ: ADJ n

layabout /leɪəbaʊt/ **layabouts.** If you say that someone is a **layabout**, you disapprove of them because you think they are idle and lazy; used mainly in British English. *The plaintiff's sole witness, a gambler and layabout, was easily discredited.* N-COUNT PRAGMATICS

lay-by, lay-bys. A **lay-by** is a short strip of road by the side of a main road, where cars can stop for a while; used mainly in British English. *I left my car in a lay-by and set off on foot.* N-COUNT

layer /leɪəʳ/ **layers, layering, layered** ◆◆◆◇◇

1 A **layer** of a material or substance is a quantity or piece of it that covers a surface or that is between two other things. *A fresh layer of snow covered the* N-COUNT: usu with supp, oft N of n

street. ...the depletion of the ozone layer... Arrange all the vegetables except the potatoes in layers.

2 If something such as a system or an idea has many **layers**, it has many different levels or parts. *...an astounding ten layers of staff between the factory worker and the chief executive... Critics and the public puzzle out the layers of meaning in his photos.* N-COUNT

3 If you **layer** something, you arrange it in layers. *Layer the potatoes, asparagus and salmon in the tin... By lifting and layering her hair, Michael created a lighter frame for her face.* VERB V n

layered /leɪəʳd/. Something that is **layered** is made or exists in layers. *Maria wore a layered white dress that rustled when she moved.* ◆◇◇◇◇ ADJ

layman /leɪmən/ **laymen** ◆◇◇◇◇

1 A **layman** is a person who is not trained, qualified, or experienced in a particular subject or activity. *The mere mention of the words 'heart failure', can conjure up, to the layman, the prospect of imminent death... There are basically two types called, in layman's terms, blue and white asbestos.* N-COUNT

2 A **layman** is a man who is involved with the Christian church but is not a member of the clergy or a monk. *Alexander Ogorodnikov, a Russian Orthodox layman, is a founder of the Christian Democratic Union.* N-COUNT

layoff /leɪɒf, AM -ɔːf/ **layoffs** ◆◇◇◇◇

1 When there are **layoffs** in a company, people are made unemployed because there is no more work for them in the company. *It will close more than 200 stores nationwide resulting in the layoffs of an estimated 2,000 employees.* N-COUNT: usu pl

2 A **layoff** is a period of time in which people do not work or take part in their normal activities, often because they are resting or are injured. *They both made full recoveries after lengthy injury layoffs.* N-COUNT

layout /leɪaʊt/ **layouts.** The **layout** of a garden, building, or piece of writing is the way in which the parts of it are arranged. *He tried to recall the layout of the farmhouse... This boat has a good deck layout making everything easy to operate.* ◆◇◇◇◇ N-COUNT: usu with supp, oft N *of* n

layperson /leɪpɜːʳsᵊn/ **laypersons** or **laypeople.** A **layperson** is a person who is not trained, qualified, or experienced in a particular subject or activity. N-COUNT ≠expert

laze /leɪz/ **lazes, lazing, lazed.** If you **laze** somewhere for a period of time, you relax and enjoy yourself, not doing any work or anything else that requires effort. *Fred lazed in an easy chair... They used the swimming-pool, rode, lazed in the deep shade of the oaks in the heat of the day.* VERB V, V prep

► **Laze around** or **laze about** means the same as **laze.** *He went to Spain for nine months, to laze around and visit relations... I was happy enough to laze about on the beach.* PHRASAL VERB V P

lazy /leɪzi/ **lazier, laziest** ◆◆◇◇◇

1 If someone is **lazy**, they do not want to work or make any effort to do anything. *Lazy and incompetent police officers are letting the public down... I was too lazy to learn how to read music.* ♦ **laziness** *Current employment laws will be changed to reward effort and punish laziness.* ADJ-GRADED ≠hardworking; N-UNCOUNT

2 You can use **lazy** to describe an activity or event in which you are very relaxed and which you do or take part in without making much effort. *Her latest novel is perfect for a lazy summer's afternoon reading... We would have a lazy lunch and then lie on the beach in the sun.* ♦ **lazily** /leɪzɪli/ *Liz went back into the kitchen, stretching lazily.* ADJ-GRADED: ADJ n =relaxed; ADV-GRADED: ADV with v

3 If you describe something as **lazy**, you mean that it moves or flows slowly and gently; a literary use. *...a valley of rolling farms spread out along a lazy river. ...the lazy, loose grace of the born athlete.* ♦ **lazily** *The Salzach river threaded its way lazily between the old city and the new.* ADJ: ADJ n; ADV: ADV with v

lb. **lb** is a written abbreviation for **pound**, when 'pound' refers to weight. *The baby was born three months early at 3 lb 5oz.* ◆◆◇◇◇ =pound

LCD /el siː diː/ **LCDs.** An **LCD** is a display of information on a screen, which uses liquid crystals that become visible when electricity is passed through them. LCD is an abbreviation for **liquid crystal display**. ◆◇◇◇◇ N-COUNT

lead 1 being ahead or taking someone somewhere

lead /liːd/ **leads, leading, led** ◆◆◆◆◆

1 If you **lead** a group of moving people, you walk or ride in front of them. *John Major and the Duke of Edinburgh led the mourners... He walks with a stick but still leads his soldiers into battle... Tom was leading, a rifle slung over his back.* VERB V n, V n prep/adv, V

2 If you **lead** someone to a particular place or thing, you take them there. *He took Dickon by the hand to lead him into the house... She confessed to the killing and led police to his remains... Leading the horse, Evandar walked to the door.* VERB V n prep/adv, V n

3 If a road, gate, or door **leads** to a place or **leads** in a particular direction, you can get to that place or go in that direction by following the road or going through the gate or door. *...the doors that led to the yard. ...a short roadway leading to the car park... Hundreds of people are said to have blocked a main highway leading north.* VERB V prep/adv

4 If you **are leading** at a particular point in a race or competition, you are winning at that point. *He's leading in the presidential race... So far Fischer leads by five wins to two... Aston Villa last led the League in March 1990.* VERB V, V *by* amount, V n

5 If you have the **lead** or are in the **lead** in a race or competition, you are winning. *England took the lead after 31 minutes with a goal by Peter Nail... Labour are still in the lead in the opinion polls.* N-SING: *the* N, oft *in/into the* N

6 Someone's **lead** over a competitor at a particular point in a race or competition is the distance, amount of time, or number of points by which they are ahead of them. *Opinion polls give him a clear lead over Mr Stanislaw Tyminski... His goal gave Forest a two-goal lead against Southampton... Sainz now has a lead of 28 points.* N-SING: with supp, oft N *over* n

7 If one company or country **leads** others in a particular activity such as scientific research or business, it is more successful or advanced than they are in that activity. *When it comes to pop music we not only lead Europe, we lead the world. ...foodstores such as Marks & Spencer, which led the market in microwavable meals.* VERB V n, V n *in* n

8 If you **lead** a group of people, an organization, or an activity, you are in control or in charge of the people or the activity. *He led the country between 1949 and 1984... Mr Mendes was leading a campaign to save Brazil's rainforest from exploitation.* VERB V n

9 If you give a **lead**, you do something new or develop new ideas or methods that other people consider to be a good example or model to follow. *...the need for the president to give a moral lead... The American and Japanese navies took the lead in the development of naval aviation... Over the next 150 years, many others followed his lead.* N-COUNT: usu supp N

10 You can use **lead** when you are saying what kind of life someone has. For example, if you **lead** a busy life, your life is busy. *She led a normal, happy life with her sister and brother... Most of the women in here are not people who have led a life of crime.* VERB V n

11 If something **leads** to a situation or event, usually an unpleasant one, it begins a process which causes that situation or event to happen. *Ethnic tensions among the republics could lead to civil war... He warned yesterday that a pay rise for teachers would lead to job cuts.* VERB V *to* n

12 If something **leads** you to do something, it influences or affects you in such a way that you do it. *His abhorrence of racism led him to write The Algiers Motel Incident... What was it ultimately that led you to leave Sarajevo for Zagreb?* VERB V n to-inf

13 If you say that someone or something **led** you to think or expect something, you mean they caused you to think or expect it, although it was not true or did not happen. *Mother had led me to believe the new baby was a kind of present for me... It was not as straightforward as we were led to believe.* VERB V n to-inf

14 If you **lead** a conversation or discussion, you control the way that it develops so that you can introduce a particular subject. *After a while I led the conversation around to her job... He planned to* VERB V n adv/prep, V n

lead the conversation and keep Matt from changing the subject.

15 You can say that one point or topic in a discussion or piece of writing **leads** you to another in order to introduce a new point or topic that is linked with the previous one. *Well, I think that leads me to the real point.* VERB PRAGMATICS =bring V n to n

16 A **lead** is a piece of information or an idea which may help people to discover the facts in a situation where many facts are not known, for example in the investigation of a crime or in a scientific experiment. *The inquiry team is also following up possible leads after receiving 400 calls from the public.* N-COUNT

17 The **lead** in a play, film, or show is the most important part in it. The person who plays this part can also be called the **lead**. *Nina Ananiashvili and Alexei Fadeyechev from the Bolshoi Ballet dance the leads... The leads are Jack Hawkins and Glynis Johns.* N-COUNT

18 A dog's **lead** is a long, thin chain or piece of leather which you attach to the dog's collar so that you can control the dog. *An older man came out with a little dog on a lead.* N-COUNT =leash

19 A **lead** in a piece of equipment is a piece of wire covered in plastic which supplies electricity to the equipment or carries it from one part of the equipment to another. N-COUNT

20 The **lead** in a newspaper is the most important story in it; used mainly in British English. *The Turkish situation makes the lead in tomorrow's Guardian... Cossiga's reaction is the lead story in the Italian press.* N-SING: oft N n

21 See also **leading**, **-led**. • to **lead** someone **astray**: see **astray**. • **one thing led to another**: see **thing**. • to **lead the way**: see **way**.

lead off PHRASAL VERB

1 If a door, room, or path **leads off** a place or **leads off** from a place, you can go directly from that place through that door, into that room, or along that path. *There were two doors leading off the central room... The treatment rooms lead off from the swimming pool... A corridor led off to the left.* V P n, V P from n, V P prep

2 If someone **leads off** in an activity, meeting, or conversation, they start it. *Whenever there was a dance he and I led off... Boren surprisingly led off the most intensive line of questioning today.* =start off V P, V P n (not pron)

lead on. If someone **leads** you **on**, they encourage you to do something, especially by giving you false information or behaving in a misleading way. *I bet she led him on – but how could he be so weak?* PHRASAL VERB V n P

lead on to PHRASAL VERB

1 If one event or action **leads on to** another, it causes it or makes it possible; used mainly in British English. *It is often the case that early interests lead on to a career... This discovery led on to studies of the immune system.* V P P n

2 If a door, gate, or bridge **leads on to** a place, the place is on the other side of it. *There were glass doors leading on to this balcony.* V P P n

lead up to PHRASAL VERB

1 The events that **led up to** a particular event happened one after the other until that event occurred. *Alan Tomlinson has reconstructed the events that led up to the deaths... They had a series of arguments, leading up to a decision to separate.* • See also **lead-up**. V P P n

2 The period of time **leading up to** an event is the period of time immediately before it happens. *...the weeks leading up to Christmas.* usu cont V P P n

3 If someone **leads up to** a particular subject, they gradually guide a conversation to a point where they can introduce it. *I'm leading up to something quite important.* V P P n

lead 2 substances

lead /led/ **leads** ◆◆◇◇◇

1 **Lead** is a soft, grey, heavy metal. *...drinking water supplied by old-fashioned lead pipes.* N-UNCOUNT

2 **Lead** is sometimes used to refer to bullets; an informal use. *Eventually Bogart pumps him full of lead.* N-UNCOUNT =bullets

3 The **lead** in a pencil is the centre part of it which makes a mark on paper. N-COUNT

leaded /ledɪd/

1 **Leaded** petrol has had lead added to it. *Japanese refiners stopped producing leaded petrol in December 1987.* ADJ: ADJ n

2 **Leaded** windows are made of small pieces of glass held together in by strips of lead. ADJ: ADJ n

leaden /ledᵊn/

1 A **leaden** sky or sea is dark grey and has no movement of clouds or waves; a literary use. *The weather was at its worst; bitterly cold, with leaden skies that gave minimum visibility.* ADJ

2 A **leaden** piece of writing or a conversation is not very interesting. *...a leaden English translation from the Latin.* ADJ =dull

3 If your movements are **leaden**, you move slowly and heavily, usually because you are tired; a literary use. *He heard the father's leaden footsteps move down the stairs.* ADJ =heavy

leader /liːdəʳ/ **leaders** ◆◆◆◆◆

1 The **leader** of a group of people or an organization is the person who is in control of it or in charge of it. *...the leader of Poland's Solidarity movement, Mr Lech Walesa... The Republican Party's leader, Mr Franz Schoenhuber, has resigned.* N-COUNT: usu N of n, n N

2 The **leader** at a particular point in a race or competition is the person who is winning at that point. *The leaders came in two minutes clear of the field... The world drivers' championship leader crossed the line ahead of Sweden's Ingvar Carlsson.* N-COUNT

3 The **leader** among a range of products or companies is the one that is most successful. *Procter & Gamble is the leader in the mass market cosmetics industry.* N-COUNT

4 In British English, the **leader** of an orchestra is the most senior violin player, who acts as a deputy to the conductor. N-COUNT

5 In American English, the **leader** of an orchestra is the conductor. N-COUNT

6 In a newspaper, the **leader** is the main article, usually expressing the editor's opinion on the most important news items of the day; used mainly in British English. *...an editorial leader in the Financial Times.* N-COUNT

leadership /liːdəʳʃɪp/ **leaderships** ◆◆◆◆◇

1 You refer to people who are in control of a group or organization as the **leadership**. *Reunification is close to the hearts of both the Chinese and Taiwanese leaderships. ...the Labour leadership of Haringey council in north London.* N-COUNT

2 Someone's **leadership** is their position or state of being in control of a group of people. *He praised her leadership during the crisis... We find the leftists assuming leadership and becoming the spokesmen for an ideal of international revolution.* N-UNCOUNT: oft with poss

3 **Leadership** refers to the qualities that make someone a good leader, or the methods a leader uses to do his or her job. *What most people want to see is determined, decisive action and firm leadership.* N-UNCOUNT

lead-free /led friː/. Something such as petrol or paint which is **lead-free**, is made without lead, or has no lead added to it. ADJ

lead-in /liːd ɪn/ **lead-ins.** A **lead-in** is something that is said or done as an introduction before the main subject or event, especially before a radio or television programme. *They were thrilled, finally, to have a decent lead-in for their 9 a.m. local programs.* ◆◆◇◇◇ N-COUNT

leading /liːdɪŋ/ ◆◆◆◆◇

1 The **leading** person or thing in a particular area is the one which is most important or successful. *...a leading member of Bristol's Sikh community... Britain's future as a leading industrial nation depends on investment.* ADJ: ADJ n

2 The **leading** part or role in a play or film is the main part or role. A **leading** lady or man is an actor who plays this role. ADJ: ADJ n

3 The **leading** group, vehicle, or participant in a race or procession is the one that is at the front. ADJ: ADJ n

leading article, leading articles. The **leading article** in a newspaper is the main article in it, usually expressing the editor's opinion on the ◆◇◇◇◇ N-COUNT most important news item of the day. *The Guardian has a leading article on the Labour Party conference's decision to look at alternative systems for electing Members of Parliament.*

leading edge. The **leading edge** of a particular area of research or development is the area of it that seems most advanced or sophisticated. *I think Israel tends to be at the leading edge of technological development.* N-SING: usu *the* N *of* n

leading light, leading lights. If you say that someone is a **leading light** in an organization or campaign, you mean that they are considered to be one of the most important, active, enthusiastic, and successful people in it; used mainly in British English. N-COUNT

leading question, leading questions. A **leading question** is expressed in such a way that it suggests what the answer should be. N-COUNT

lead singer /liːd sɪŋəʳ/ **lead singers.** The **lead singer** of a pop group is the person who sings most of the songs. *...Mick Hucknall, lead singer of Simply Red... I was the lead singer in the band that became the Prefects.* ◆◇◇◇◇ N-COUNT

lead-up /liːd ʌp/. The **lead-up** to an event is things connected to that event that happen before it does. *The lead-up to the wedding was extremely interesting.* N-SING: usu *the* N *to* n

leaf /liːf/ **leaves; leafs, leafing, leafed** ◆◆◆◇◇

1 The **leaves** of a tree or plant are the parts that are flat, thin, and usually green. Many trees and plants lose their leaves in the winter and grow new leaves in the spring. *In the garden, the leaves of the horse chestnut had already fallen... The Japanese maple that stands across the drive had just come into leaf.* N-COUNT: usu pl, also *in/into* N

• See also **-leaved.**

2 A **leaf** is one of the pieces of paper of which a book is made. *He flattened the wrappers and put them between the leaves of his book.* N-COUNT =page

3 If you **take a leaf from** someone's **book** you behave in the same way as them because you want to be like that person or as successful as they are. *Kylie Minogue took a leaf from Madonna's book and hit the stage in a black g-string and bra.* PHRASES V inflects

4 If you say that are going to **turn over a new leaf**, you mean that you are going to start to behave in a better or more acceptable way. *He realized he was in the wrong and promised to turn over a new leaf.* V inflects

5 If you say that someone **is shaking like a leaf**, you mean that their body is shaking a lot for some reason, for instance because they are very cold or frightened. *I didn't think about the danger at the time. Afterwards I was shaking like a leaf.* V inflects

leaf through. If you **leaf through** something such as a book or magazine, you turn the pages without reading or looking at them very carefully. *Most patients derive enjoyment from leafing through old picture albums.* PHRASAL VERB =flip through V P n

leafless /liːfləs/. If a tree or plant is **leafless**, it has no leaves. *A beautiful fig tree that had stood in their yard was leafless and barren.* ADJ =bare

leaflet /liːflət/ **leaflets, leafleting, leafleted** ◆◆◇◇◇

1 A **leaflet** is a little book or a piece of paper containing information about a particular subject. *Campaigners handed out leaflets on passive smoking. ...a leaflet called 'Sexual Harassment at Work'.* N-COUNT

2 If you **leaflet** a place, you distribute leaflets there, for example by handing them to people, or by putting them through letter boxes. *We've leafleted the university today to try to drum up some support... The only reason we leafleted on the Jewish New Year was because more people than usual go to the synagogue on that day.* VERB V n V

leaf mould; spelled **leaf mold** in American English. **Leaf mould** is a substance consisting of decayed leaves that is used as a fertilizer. N-UNCOUNT

leafy /liːfi/ ◆◇◇◇◇

1 Leafy trees and plants have lots of leaves on them. *His two-story brick home was graced with a patio and surrounded by tall, leafy trees.* ADJ-GRADED

2 You say that a place is **leafy** when there are lots of trees and plants there. *...semi-detached homes with gardens in leafy suburban areas.* ADJ-GRADED

league /liːg/ **leagues** ◆◆◆◆◇

1 A **league** is a group of people, clubs, or countries that have joined together for a particular purpose, or because they share a common interest. *...the League of Nations. ...the World Muslim League.* N-COUNT: oft in names

2 A **league** is a group of clubs which play the same sport or activity in competition with each other. *The club are on the brink of promotion to the Premier League.* N-COUNT

3 You use the word **league** to make comparisons between different people or things, especially in terms of their quality. *Her success has taken her out of my league... Their record sales would put them in the same league as The Rolling Stones.* N-COUNT: with supp

4 If you say that someone is **in league** with someone else to do something bad, they are working together to do that thing. *He accused the President of being in league with terrorists... Williams operated the smuggling scheme in league with his brother.* PHRASE: usu v-link PHR, oft PHR *with* n

leak /liːk/ **leaks, leaking, leaked** ◆◆◆◇◇

1 If a container or other object **leaks**, or **leaks** a substance such as a liquid or gas, there is a hole or crack in the container which lets the substance escape. You can also say that a substance such as a liquid or gas **leaks** from a container. *The roof leaked... The gas had apparently leaked from a cylinder... The pool's fiberglass sides had cracked and the water had leaked out... A large diesel tank mysteriously leaked its contents into the river.* ► Also a noun. *It's thought a gas leak may have caused the blast.* V-ERG V V prep/adv V n *into* n Also V n N-COUNT

2 A **leak** is a crack, hole, or other fault that a substance such as a liquid or gas can pass through. *...a leak in the radiator... In May engineers found a leak in a hydrogen fuel line.* N-COUNT: oft N *in* n

3 If a secret document or piece of information **leaks** or **is leaked**, someone lets the public know about it. *Last year, a civil servant was imprisoned for leaking a document to the press... He revealed who leaked a confidential police report... We don't know how the transcript leaked. ...a leaked report.* ► Also a noun. *More serious leaks, possibly involving national security, are likely to be investigated by the police.* ► **Leak out** means the same as **leak**. *More details are now beginning to leak out... He said it would leak out to the newspapers and cause a scandal.* V-ERG V n *to* n V n V V-ed N-COUNT PHRASAL VERB ERG V P V P *to* n

leakage /liːkɪdʒ/ **leakages.** A **leakage** is an amount of liquid or gas that is escaping from a pipe or container by means of a crack, hole, or other fault. *A leakage of kerosene has polluted water supplies... It should be possible to reduce leakage from pipes.* N-VAR

leaker /liːkəʳ/ **leakers.** A **leaker** is someone who lets people know secret information; used by journalists. *He found no direct evidence to identify a leaker.* N-COUNT

leaky /liːki/ **leakiest.** Something that is **leaky** has holes, cracks, or other faults which allow liquids and gases to pass through. *...the cost of repairing the leaky roof.* ADJ-GRADED

lean /liːn/ **leans, leaning, leaned, leant; leaner, leanest.** The form **leant** can be used as the past tense and past participle in British English. ◆◆◆◇◇

1 When you **lean** in a particular direction, you bend your body in that direction. *Eileen leaned across and opened the passenger door... He leaned forward to give her a kiss... They stopped to lean over a gate.* VERB V adv/prep

2 If you **lean** on or against someone or something, you rest against them so that they partly support your weight. If you **lean** an object on or against something, you place the object so that it is partly supported by the thing it is resting against. *She was feeling tired and was glad to lean against him... Lean the plants against a wall and cover the roots with peat... The table lurched as a young man leant his weight on it.* VERB V adv V n adv/prep

3 If you describe someone as **lean**, you approve of the fact that they are thin but look strong and healthy. *Like most athletes, she was lean and* ADJ-GRADED PRAGMATICS ≠flabby *muscular... She watched the tall, lean figure step into the car.*

4 If meat is **lean**, it does not have very much fat. *It is a beautiful meat, very lean and tender. ...the leanest ground beef you can get.* ADJ-GRADED ≠fatty

5 If you describe an organization as **lean**, you mean that it has become stronger and more competitive by getting rid of staff or projects which were unprofitable. *The value of the pound will force British companies to be leaner and fitter. ...cutting corporate flab and building leaner companies.* ADJ-GRADED

6 If you describe periods of time as **lean**, you mean that people have less of something such as money or are less successful than they used to be. *...the lean years of the 1930s... With fewer tourists in town, the taxi trade is going through its leanest patch for 30 years.* ADJ-GRADED: usu ADJ n

lean on or **lean upon** PHRASAL VERB

1 If you **lean on** someone or **lean upon** them, you depend on them for support and encouragement. *She leaned on him to help her to solve her problems.* V P n

2 If you **lean on** someone, you try to influence them, especially by threatening them; an informal expression. *He told us to get stuffed so we leaned on his kid... Colin was being leaned on by his bankers.* V P n

lean towards. If you **lean towards** or **lean toward** a particular idea, belief, or type of behaviour, you have a tendency to think or act in a particular way. *Politically, I lean towards the right... Most scientists would probably lean toward this viewpoint.* PHRASAL VERB; V P n

leaning /liːnɪŋ/ **leanings.** Your particular **leanings** are the beliefs, ideas, or aims you hold or a tendency you have towards them. *Many companies are wary of their socialist leanings... I always had a leaning towards sport.* N-COUNT: usu pl, with supp, oft N *towards* n =tendency

leant /lent/. **Leant** is one of the forms of the past tense and past participle of **lean**.

lean-to, lean-tos. A **lean-to** is a building such as a shed or garage which is attached to one wall of a larger building. N-COUNT

leap /liːp/ **leaps, leaping, leaped, leapt** ◆◆◆◇◇

1 If you **leap**, you jump high in the air or jump a long distance. *He had leapt from a window in the building and escaped... The newsreels show him leaping into the air... The man threw his arms out as he leapt.* ► Also a noun. *Smith took Britain's fifth medal of the championships with a leap of 2.37 metres.* VERB; V prep/adv; V; N-COUNT

2 If you **leap** somewhere, you move there suddenly and quickly. *The two men leaped into the jeep and roared off... With a terrible howl, he leapt forward and threw himself into the water.* VERB; V prep/adv

3 If a vehicle **leaps** somewhere, it moves there in a short sudden movement. *The car leapt forward.* VERB; V adv/prep

4 A **leap** is a large and important change, increase, or advance; used mainly in journalism. *The result has been a giant leap in productivity. ...the leap in the unemployed from 35,000 to 75,000... Contemporary art has taken a huge leap forward in the last five or six years.* N-COUNT: oft N *in* n

5 If you **leap** to a particular place or position, you make a large and important change, increase, or advance. *Warwicks leap to third in the table, 31 points behind leaders Essex.* VERB; V prep

6 If your heart **leaps**, you experience a sudden, very strong feeling of surprise, fear, or happiness. *My heart leaped at the sight of her.* VERB; V

7 If you **leap** at a chance or opportunity, you accept it quickly and eagerly. *The post of principal of the theatre school became vacant and he leapt at the chance.* VERB =jump; V *at* n

8 You can use **in leaps and bounds** or **by leaps and bounds** to emphasize that someone or something is improving or increasing quickly and greatly. *He's improved in leaps and bounds this season... The total number of species on the planet appears to be growing by leaps and bounds.* PHRASES; usu PHR after v; PRAGMATICS

9 If you take **a leap in the dark** or **a leap into the unknown**, you do something without having any previous experience in or knowledge of that activity. *Prudent people are not going to take a leap in the dark... Once more he's making a leap into the unknown without a plan.* usu PHR after v

leapfrog /liːpfrɒg, AM -frɔːg/ **leapfrogs, leapfrogging, leapfrogged**

1 **Leapfrog** is a game which children play, in which a child bends over, while others jump over their back. *...children engaged in activities such as riding, playing leapfrog, or football.* N-UNCOUNT

2 If one group of people **leapfrogs** into a particular position or **leapfrogs** someone else, they use the achievements of another person or group in order to make advances of their own. *It is already obvious that all four American systems have leapfrogged over the European versions... American researchers have now leapfrogged the Japanese and are going to produce a digital system within a year or two.* VERB; V prep; V n

leap of faith, leaps of faith. A **leap of faith** is a deliberate decision to accept or believe something that you initially find difficult to accept or believe. *Take a leap of faith and trust them.* N-COUNT: a N in sing

leapt /lept/. **Leapt** is a past tense and past participle of **leap**.

leap year, leap years. A **leap year** is a year which has 366 days. The extra day is the 29th February. There is a leap year every four years. N-COUNT

learn /lɜːʳn/ **learns, learning, learned, learnt.** ◆◆◆◆◆ In British English, the forms **learned** and **learnt** can both be used for the past tense and past participle.

1 If you **learn** something, you obtain knowledge or a skill through studying or training. *Their children were going to learn English... He is learning to play the piano. ...learning how to use new computer systems... Experienced teachers help you learn quickly.* ♦ **learning** *...a bilingual approach to the learning of English.* VERB; V n; V to-inf; V wh; V; Also V *about* n; N-UNCOUNT

2 If you **learn** of something, you find out about it. *It was only after his death that she learned of his affair with Betty... It didn't come as a shock to learn that the fuel and cooling systems are the most common causes of breakdown... The Admiral, who, on learning who I was, wanted to meet me.* VERB =find out; V *of* n; V that; V wh

3 If people **learn** to behave or react in a particular way, they gradually start to behave in that way as a result of a change in attitudes. *You have to learn to face your problem... We are learning how to confront death instead of avoiding its reality.* VERB; V to-inf; V wh-to-inf

4 If you **learn** from an unpleasant experience, you change the way you behave so that it does not happen again or so that if it happens again, you can deal with it more easily. *I am convinced that he has learned from his mistakes... The company failed to learn any lessons from this experience.* VERB; V *from* n; V n *from* n

5 If you **learn** something such as a poem or the script of a play, you study or repeat the words so that you can remember them. *He learned this song as an inmate at a Texas prison.* VERB; V n

6 See also **learned, learning.**

7 ● to **learn** something **the hard way**: see **way**. ● to **learn the ropes**: see **rope**.

learned. Pronounced /lɜːʳnɪd/ for meanings 1 and 2, and /lɜːʳnd/ for meaning 3. ◆◇◇◇◇

1 A **learned** person has gained a lot of knowledge by studying. *He is a serious scholar, a genuinely learned man.* ADJ-GRADED: usu ADJ n

2 **Learned** books or papers have been written by someone who has gained a lot of knowledge by studying. *This learned book should start a real debate on Western policy towards the Baltics.* ADJ-GRADED: usu ADJ n

3 A **learned** reaction, response, or ability is one that you acquire from experience or from your environment, not one that you were born with. *Your anxiety is a learned reaction, and it is nurtured and sustained by the events of your everyday life.* ADJ: usu ADJ n ≠instinctive

4 See also **learn**.

learner /lɜːʳnəʳ/ **learners.**  A **learner** is someone who is learning about a particular subject or how to do something. *...a new aid for younger children or slow learners... Learner drivers must be supervised by adults who are at least 21 years old.* N-COUNT

learner-centred; spelled **learner-centered** in American English. In teaching, if you describe a ADJ =student-centred curriculum or activity as **learner-centred**, you mean that it is based on the needs or interests of the learner. *...a decentralized needs-based learner-centred curriculum.*

learning /lɜːʳnɪŋ/. **Learning** is the process of gaining knowledge through studying. *The brochure described the library as the focal point of learning on the campus.* • See also **learn, seat of learning**. ◆◆◇◇◇ N-UNCOUNT

learning curve, learning curves. A **learning curve** is a process where people develop a skill by learning from their mistakes. A steep learning curve involves learning very quickly. *Both he and the crew are on a steep learning curve... There is a learning curve in the process of seeking employment.* N-COUNT: usu sing

learnt /lɜːʳnt/. In British English, **learnt** is a past tense and past participle of **learn**.

lease /liːs/ **leases, leasing, leased** ◆◆◆◇◇

1 A **lease** is a legal agreement by which the owner of a building, a piece of land, or something such as a car allows someone else to use it for a period of time in return for money. *He took up a 10 year lease on the house at Rossie Priory.* N-COUNT

2 If you **lease** property or something such as a car from someone or if they **lease** it to you, they allow you to use it in return for regular payments of money. *He went to Toronto, where he leased an apartment... She hopes to lease the building to students... He will need more grazing land and perhaps La Prade could lease him a few acres.* VERB V n V n *to* n V n n

3 If you say that someone or something has been given **a new lease of life**, you are emphasizing that they are much more lively or successful than they have been in the past. *The operation has given me a new lease of life... The success of the group's products has given a whole new lease of life to Cobol.* PHRASE: PHR after v

leasehold /liːshould/ **leaseholds**

1 In British English, if a building or land is described as **leasehold**, it is allowed to be used in return for payment of money as arranged according to a lease. *I went into a leasehold property at four hundred and fifty pounds rent per year.* ADJ

2 If you have the **leasehold** of a building or piece of land, you have the legal right to use it for a period of time as arranged according to a lease; used mainly in British English. N-COUNT

leaseholder /liːshouldəʳ/ **leaseholders.** A **leaseholder** is a person who is allowed to use a property according to the terms of a lease; used mainly in British English. N-COUNT

leash /liːʃ/ **leashes.** A dog's **leash** is a long thin piece of leather or a chain, which you attach to the dog's collar so that you can keep the dog under control. *All dogs in public places should be on a leash.* N-COUNT =lead

least /liːst/ ◆◆◆◆◆

Least is often considered to be the superlative form of **little.**

1 You use **at least** to say that a number or amount is the smallest that is possible or likely and that the actual number or amount may be greater. The forms **at the least** and **at the very least** are also used. *...a dinner menu featuring at least 15 different sorts of fish... Aim to have at least half a pint of milk each day... About two-thirds of adults consult their doctor at least once a year... Normally it has only had eleven or twelve members in all. Now it will have seventeen at the very least.* PHRASE: PHR amount, amount PHR

2 You use **at least** to say that something is the minimum that is the case or should be done, although you think that more than this might be possible in the circumstances. The forms **at the least** and **at the very least** are also used. *She could take a nice holiday at least... He is at least content that there will be no immediate use of force... At the least, I needed some sleep... His possession of classified documents in his home was, at the very least, a violation of Navy security regulations.* PHRASE: PHR with cl/group

3 You use **at least** to indicate an advantage that exists in spite of the disadvantage or bad situation that has just been mentioned. *We've no idea what his state of health is but at least we know he is still alive... If something awful happens to you at least you can write about it.* PHRASE: PHR with cl

4 You use **at least** to indicate that you are correcting or changing something that you have just said. The forms **at the least** and **at the very least** are also used. *It's not difficult to get money for research or at least it's not always difficult... The police say his death was an accident, officially at least... They didn't actually like the magazine very much, but they bought it or, at the least, borrowed it from each other.* PHRASE: PHR with cl/group PRAGMATICS

5 You use **the least** to mean a smaller amount than anyone or anything else, or the smallest amount possible. *I try to offend the least amount of people possible... If you like cheese, go for the ones with the least fat.* ► Also a pronoun. *On education funding, Japan performs best but spends the least per student.* ► Also an adverb. *Damming the river may end up benefitting those who need it the least.* ADJ-SUPERL: *the* ADJ n ≠most PRON: *the* PRON ≠most ADV-SUPERL: *the* ADV after v

6 You use **least** to indicate that someone or something has less of a particular quality than most other things of its kind. *The least experienced athletes had caused a great many false-starts through the day's proceedings... He was one of the least warm human beings I had ever met. ...the least technically accomplished car in Europe.* ADV-SUPERL: ADV adj/adv ≠most

7 You use **the least** to emphasize the smallness of something, especially when it hardly exists at all. *I don't have the least idea of what you're talking about... They neglect their duty at the least hint of fun elsewhere... The bosses paid less than they had promised and at the least complaint went to the police.* ADJ-SUPERL: *the* ADJ n PRAGMATICS

8 You use **least** to indicate that something is true or happens to a smaller degree or extent than anything else or at any other time. *He had a way of throwing her off guard with his charm when she least expected it.* ADV-SUPERL: ADV with v ≠most

9 You use **least** in structures where you are emphasizing that a particular situation or event is much less important or serious than other possible or actual ones. *Having to get up at three o'clock every morning was the least of her worries... Although three days isn't very long, shortage of time was the least of his problems... At that moment, they were among the least of the concerns of the government.* ADJ-SUPERL: ADJ *of* def-n PRAGMATICS

10 You use **the least** in structures where you are stating the minimum that should be done in a situation, and suggesting that more should really be done. *Well, the least you can do, if you won't help me yourself, is to tell me where to go instead... The least they could have given me was half a day to rest... The least his hotel could do is provide a little privacy.* • You use expressions like **'that's the least that I can do'** to mean that you are very willing to do it, or to acknowledge someone's thanks. *Why not relax and let me teach you how to windsurf? It's the least I can do... I want to help – it's the least I can do for the girl who saved my brother... 'Right,' she said, chuckling. 'Thanks, anyway.' 'It was the least I could do'.* PRON: *the* PRON cl PRAGMATICS PHRASE PRAGMATICS

11 You can use **in the least** and **the least bit** to emphasize a negative. *I'm not like that at all. Not in the least... I'm not in the least bit touched by the Marilyn Monroe kind of beauty... Alice wasn't the least bit frightened.* PHRASES with brd-neg, PHR with cl, PHR adj PRAGMATICS

12 You use **last but not least** to say that the last person or thing to be mentioned is as important as all the others. *...her four sons, Christopher, twins Daniel and Nicholas, and last but not least 2-year-old Jack.* PHR with cl/group

13 You can use **least of all** after a negative statement to emphasize that it applies especially to the person or thing mentioned. *No one ever reads these articles, least of all me... Such a speech should never have been made, least of all by a so called responsible politician.* with brd-neg, PHR cl/group PRAGMATICS

14 You can use **not least** to emphasize a particularly important example or reason. *Dieting itself can be bad for you, not least because it is a cause of chronic stress... What is somewhat more curious is* PHR cl/group PRAGMATICS

the grip football has had on some Europeans, not least the British.

15 You can use **to say the least** to suggest that a situation is actually much more extreme or serious than you say it is. *Accommodation was basic to say the least... Some members of the public can be a bit abusive to say the least.* PHR with cl PRAGMATICS

leather /leðəʳ/ **leathers** ◆◆◆◇◇

1 **Leather** is treated animal skin which is used for making shoes, clothes, bags, and furniture. *He wore a leather jacket and dark trousers. ...an impressive range of upholstered furniture, in a choice of fabrics and leathers.* N-MASS

2 **Leathers** are leather clothes such as jackets and trousers, especially those worn by motorcyclists; used mainly in British English. *...a couple of youths in motorcyclists' black leathers.* N-PLURAL

leathery /leðəri/. If the texture of something, for example someone's skin, is **leathery**, it is tough and hard, like leather. *His hair and beard are both untidy and his skin is quite leathery.* ADJ-GRADED

leave /liːv/ **leaves, leaving, left** ◆◆◆◆◆

1 If you **leave** a place or person, you go away from that place or person. *He would not be allowed to leave the country... I simply couldn't bear to leave my little girl... My flight leaves in less than an hour... The last of the older children had left for school.* VERB V n V V for n

2 If you **leave** an institution, group, or job, you permanently stop attending that institution, being a member of that group, or doing that job. *He left school with no qualifications... I am leaving to concentrate on writing fiction. ...a leaving present.* VERB V n V V-ing

3 If you **leave** your husband, wife, or some other person with whom you have had a close relationship, you stop living with them or you finish the relationship. *He'll never leave you. You need have no worry... I would be insanely jealous if Bill left me for another woman.* VERB V n V n for n Also V

4 If you **leave** something or someone in a particular place, you let them remain there when you go away, deliberately or because you forget to take them with you. If you **leave** something or someone with a person, you let them remain with that person so they are safe while you are away. *I left my bags in the car... Don't leave your truck there... From the moment that Philippe had left her in the bedroom at the hotel, she had heard nothing of him... Leave your key with a neighbour in case you lock yourself out one day.* VERB V n prep/adv V n with n

5 If you **leave** a message or an answer, you write it, record it, or give it to someone so that it can be found or passed on. *You can leave a message on our answering machine... Decide whether the ball is in square A, B, C, or D, then call and leave your answer... I left my phone number with several people.* VERB V n prep/adv V n V n with n

6 If you **leave** someone doing something, they are doing that thing when you go away from them. *Salter drove off, leaving Callendar surveying the scene.* VERB V n -ing

7 If you **leave** someone to do something, you go away from them so that they do it on their own. If you **leave** someone to himself or herself, you go away from them and allow them to be alone. *I'd better leave you to get on with it, then... Diana took the hint and left them to it... One of the advantages of a department store is that you are left to yourself to try things on... He quietly slipped away and left me to my tears.* VERB V n to-inf V n to it be V-ed to pron-refl V n to n Also V n to pron-refl

8 If someone or something **leaves** an amount of something, they do not use it and it remains available after the rest has been used or taken away. *He always left a little food for the next day... Double rooms at any of the following hotels should leave you some change from £150.* VERB V n for n V n n

9 To **leave** someone with something, especially something that is difficult to deal with or that is unpleasant, means to make them have it or make them responsible for it. *...a crash which left him with a broken collar-bone... He left me with a child to support.* VERB V n with n

10 If an event **leaves** people or things in a particular state, they are in that state when the event has finished. *...violent disturbances which have left at least ten people dead... The documentary left me in a state of shock... So where does that leave me?* VERB V n adj V n prep/adv

11 If you **leave** food or drink, you do not eat or drink it, often because you do not like it. *If you don't like the cocktail you ordered, just leave it and try a different one.* VERB V n

12 If something **leaves** a mark, effect, or sign, it causes that mark, effect, or sign to remain as a result. *A muscle tear will leave a scar after healing... She left a lasting impression on him.* VERB V n

13 If you **leave** something in a particular state, position, or condition, you let it remain in that state, position, or condition. *He left the album open on the table... I've left the car lights on... I left the engine running.* VERB V n adj V n adv/prep V n -ing

14 If you **leave** a space or gap in something, you deliberately make that space or gap. *Leave a gap at the top and bottom so air can circulate.* VERB V n

15 If you **leave** a job, decision, or choice to someone, you give them the responsibility for dealing with it or making it. *Affix the blue airmail label and leave the rest to us... The judge should not have left it to the jury to decide... For the moment, I leave you to take all decisions.* VERB V n to n V it to n to-inf V n to-inf

16 If you say that something such as an arrangement or an agreement **leaves** a lot to another thing or person, you are critical of it because it is not adequate and its success depends on the other thing or person. *The ceasefire leaves a lot to the goodwill of the forces involved... It's a vague formulation that leaves much to the discretion of local authorities.* VERB PRAGMATICS V amount to n

17 To **leave** someone a particular course of action or the opportunity to do something means to let it be available to them, while restricting them in other ways. *He would have preferred not to have a fitted kitchen but the limited space left him no option.* VERB V n n

18 If you **leave** something until a particular time, you delay doing it or dealing with it until then. *Don't leave it all until the last minute.* • If you **leave** something **too late**, you delay doing it so that when you eventually do it, it is useless or ineffective. *I hope I haven't left it too late.* VERB V n until/to n PHRASE: V inflects

19 If you **leave** a particular subject, you stop talking about it and start discussing something else. *I think we'd better leave the subject of Nationalism... He suggested we get together for a drink sometime. I said I'd like that, and we left it there.* VERB V n V n prep/adv

20 If you **leave** property or money to someone, you arrange for it to be given to them after you have died. *He died two and a half years later, leaving everything to his wife.* VERB V n to n

21 If you say that someone **leaves** a wife, husband, or a particular number of children, you mean that the wife, husband, or children remain alive after that person has died; a formal use. *A charity worker killed trying to save Bosnian orphans has left a wife and six children.* VB: no cont V n

22 **Leave** is a period of time when you are not working at your job, because you are on holiday or for some other reason. If you are **on leave**, you are not working at your job. *Why don't you take a few days' leave? ...maternity leave... He is home on leave from the Navy.* N-UNCOUNT: oft on N

23 If you ask for **leave** to do something, you ask for permission to do it; a formal use. *...an application for leave to appeal against the judge's order.* N-UNCOUNT: N to-inf =permission

24 See also **left**.

25 If you **leave** someone or something **alone**, or if you **leave** them **be**, you do not pay them any attention or bother them. *Some people need to confront a traumatic past; others find it better to leave it alone... Why can't you leave him be?* PHRASES V inflects

26 You use the phrase **leaving aside** or **leaving to one side** when mentioning a fact or detail that you want to ignore when making a general statement. *Leaving aside the question of privacy, constant surveillance can be remarkably convenient.* PREP: PREP n PRAGMATICS

27 When you **take** your **leave** or **take leave of** someone, you say goodbye and go; a formal expression. *He thanked them for the pleasure of their company and took his leave.* V inflects

28 If someone tells you to **leave well alone**, they are telling you not to interfere in something, because it is all right as it is and you might only make it worse. *He knew when to leave well alone and when to interfere.* V inflects

29 If something continues from **where** it **left off**, it starts happening again at the point where it had previously stopped. *As soon as the police disappear the violence will take up from where it left off.* PHR after v, oft *from* PHR

30 • to **leave a lot to be desired**: see **desire.** • to **leave** someone **to** their **own devices**: see **device.** • to **take leave of** your **senses**: see **sense.** • **take it or leave it**: see **take.**

leave behind PHRASAL VERB

1 If you **leave** someone or something **behind**, you go away permanently from them. *Many of the women had left their husbands behind and they told of their fears that they may never see them again... We hear of women who run away, leaving behind their homes and families.* V n P; V P n (not pron)

2 If you **leave behind** an object or a situation, it remains after you have left a place. *I don't want to leave anything behind... A misty rain in the morning had left behind a coolness that would stay for hours.* V n P; V P n (not pron)

3 If a person, country, or organization **is left behind**, they remain at a lower level than others because they are not as quick at understanding things or developing. *We're going to be left behind by the rest of the world... I got left behind at school with the maths... Inflation has left them way behind.* be V-ed P; get V-ed P; V n P

leave off PHRASAL VERB

1 If someone or something **is left off** a list, they are not included on that list. *She has been deliberately left off the guest list... The judge left Walsh's name off the list of those he wanted arrested.* be V-ed P n; V n P n; Also V n P

2 If someone **leaves off** doing something, they stop doing it. *We all left off eating and stood about with bowed heads... The film takes up where the original left off and plots the final demise of Billy the Kid... Some of the patients left off treatment.* =stop; V P -ing; V P; V P n (not pron)

leave out. If you **leave** someone or something **out** of an activity, collection, discussion, or group, you do not include them in it. *Some would question the wisdom of leaving her out of the team... If you prefer mild flavours reduce or leave out the chilli... Now have we left any country out?* • If someone **feels left out**, they feel sad because they are not included in a group or activity. PHRASAL VERB; V n P *of* n; V P n (not pron); V n P; V inflects

-leaved /-liːvd/; also spelled **-leafed**. **-leaved** or **-leafed** combines with adjectives to form other adjectives which describe the type of leaves a tree or plant has. *...broad-leaved trees. ...very dense and small-leafed maples.* COMB in ADJ

leaven /lev^ə^n/ **leavens, leavening, leavened**

1 If a situation or activity **is leavened** by something, it is made more interesting or cheerful. *His mood of deep pessimism cannot have been leavened by his mode of transport — a black cab... He found congenial officers who knew how to leaven war's rigours with riotous enjoyment.* VERB; be V-ed *by/with* n; V n *by/with* n; Also V n

2 **Leaven** is the same as **yeast**; an old-fashioned use. N-UNCOUNT =yeast

leavened /levənd/. **Leavened** bread or dough has had yeast added to it. *...a sort of leavened scone which they baked in the ashes.* ADJ: usu ADJ n ≠unleavened

leave of absence, leaves of absence. If you have **leave of absence** you have permission to be away from work for a certain period. N-VAR

leaves /liːvz/. **Leaves** is the plural form of **leaf**, and the third person singular form of **leave**.

Lebanese /lebəniːz/. **Lebanese** is both the singular and plural form. ◆◆◆◆◇

1 **Lebanese** means belonging or relating to Lebanon, or to its people or culture. *...talks with the Lebanese government.* ADJ

2 A **Lebanese** is a Lebanese citizen, or a person of Lebanese origin. N-COUNT

lecher /letʃə^r^/ **lechers.** If you describe a man as a **lecher**, you disapprove of him because you think he behaves towards women in a way which shows he is only interested in them sexually; an informal word. N-COUNT PRAGMATICS

lecherous /letʃərəs/. If you describe a man as **lecherous**, you disapprove of him because he behaves towards women in a way which shows he is only interested in them sexually. *...lecherous old men offering sweets at the school gate.* ADJ-GRADED: usu ADJ n PRAGMATICS

lechery /letʃəri/. **Lechery** is the behaviour of men who are only interested in women sexually; used showing disapproval. *His lechery made him the enemy of every self-respecting husband and father in the county.* N-UNCOUNT PRAGMATICS

lectern /lektə^r^n/ **lecterns.** A **lectern** is a high sloping desk on which someone puts their notes when they are standing up and giving a lecture. N-COUNT

lecture /lektʃə^r^/ **lectures, lecturing, lectured** ◆◆◆◇◇

1 A **lecture** is a talk someone gives in order to teach people about a particular subject, usually at a university or college. *...a series of lectures by Professor Eric Robinson... In his lecture Riemann covered an enormous variety of topics.* N-COUNT

2 If you **lecture** on a particular subject, you give a lecture or a series of lectures about it. *She then invited him to Atlanta to lecture on the history of art... She has danced, choreographed, lectured and taught all over the world... Wendy Rigby was recently invited to lecture a group of doctors on the benefits of aromatherapy.* VERB; V *on/in* n; V; V n *on* n

3 If someone **lectures** you about something, they criticize you or tell you how they think you should behave. *He used to lecture me about getting too much sun... Chuck would lecture me, telling me to get a haircut... She was no longer interrogating but lecturing.* ► Also a noun. *Our captain gave us a stern lecture on safety.* VERB; V n *about/on* n; V n; Also V n to-inf; N-COUNT

lecturer /lektʃərə^r^/ **lecturers.** A **lecturer** is a teacher at a university or college. *...a lecturer in law at Southampton University.* ◆◆◇◇◇ N-COUNT

lectureship /lektʃə^r^ʃɪp/ **lectureships.** A **lectureship** is the position of a lecturer at a university or college. N-COUNT

led /led/. **Led** is the past tense and past participle of **lead**.

-led /-led/

1 **-led** combines with nouns to form adjectives which indicate that something is organized, directed, or controlled by a particular person or group. *...the student-led democracy movement. ...a German-led European consortium.* COMB in ADJ: usu ADJ n

2 **-led** combines with nouns to form adjectives which indicate that something is mainly caused or influenced by a particular factor. *Their prosperity depends on export-led growth. ...a market-led economy.* COMB in ADJ-GRADED

ledge /ledʒ/ **ledges** ◆◇◇◇◇

1 A **ledge** is a piece of rock on the side of a cliff or mountain, which is in the shape of a narrow shelf. N-COUNT

2 A **ledge** is a narrow shelf along the bottom edge of a window. *She had climbed onto the ledge outside his window.* N-COUNT

ledger /ledʒə^r^/ **ledgers.** A **ledger** is a book in which a company or organization writes down the amounts of money it spends and receives. N-COUNT

lee /liː/ **lees** ◆◆◆◇◇

1 The **lee** of a place is the shelter that it gives from the wind or bad weather. *...the cathedral, which nestles in the lee of a hill beneath the town... The sea started to ease as we came under Cuba's lee.* N-SING: with poss

2 The **lee** side of a ship is the one that is away from the wind; a technical use in sailing. ADJ: ADJ n

3 The **lees** are the sediment that collects at the bottom of a bottle or barrel of wine. *...a glass-fronted barrel showing the wine resting on its lees.* N-PLURAL

leech /liːtʃ/ **leeches** ◆◇◇◇◇

1 A **leech** is a small animal which looks like a worm and lives in water. Leeches feed by attaching themselves to other animals and sucking their blood. N-COUNT

2 If you describe someone as a **leech**, you disapprove of them because they deliberately depend on other people, often making money out of them. *They're just a bunch of leeches cadging off others!* N-COUNT PRAGMATICS

leek /liːk/ **leeks.** **Leeks** are long thin vegetables which smell similar to onions. They are white at one end, have long light green leaves, and are eaten cooked.
◆◇◇◇◇ N-VAR

leer /lɪə^{r}/ **leers, leering, leered.** If someone **leers** at you, they smile in an unpleasant way, usually because they are sexually interested in you; used showing disapproval. *...men standing around, swilling beer and occasionally leering at passing females... He looked back at Kenworthy and leered.* ▸ Also a noun. *When I asked the clerk for my room key, he gave it to me with a leer.*
◆◇◇◇◇ VERB PRAGMATICS; V prep/adv; V; N-COUNT

leery /lɪəri/. If you are **leery** of something, you are cautious and suspicious about it and try to avoid it; an informal word. *Executives say they are leery of the proposed system... They were leery about investing in a company controlled by a single individual.*
ADJ-GRADED: usu v-link ADJ, oft ADJ *of/about* n =wary

leeway /liːweɪ/
◆◇◇◇◇

1 **Leeway** is the flexibility that someone has to change their plans, for example by taking more time or spending more money than they had originally intended to. *Rarely do schoolteachers have leeway to teach classes the way they want... The President said that he wanted to give states more leeway to pursue their own health-care reforms.*
N-UNCOUNT

2 If you have **leeway** to make up, you have to work hard because you do not have much time to reach a particular goal; used mainly in British English. *He just could not make up the leeway from the earlier stages in which Ryan scored well.*
N-UNCOUNT

left 1 remaining

left /left/
◆◆◆◇◇

1 **Left** is the past tense and past participle of **leave**.

2 If there is a certain amount of something **left**, or if you have a certain amount of it **left**, it remains when the rest has gone or been used. *Is there any gin left?... He's got plenty of money left... They still have six games left to play.* • If there is a certain amount of something **left over**, or if you have it **left over**, it remains when the rest has gone or been used. *So much income is devoted to monthly mortgage payments that nothing is left over. ...a large bucket of cut flowers left over from the wedding.*
ADJ: v-link ADJ, v n ADJ; PHRASE: usu v-link PHR

left 2 direction and political groupings

left /left/; also written **Left** for meanings 3 and 4.
◆◆◆◆◆

1 The **left** is one of two opposite directions, sides, or positions. If you are facing north and you turn to the left, you will be facing west. In the word 'to', the 't' is to the left of the 'o'. *In Britain cars drive on the left. ...the brick wall to the left of the conservatory... Beaufort Castle is on your left.* ▸ Also an adverb. *Turn left at the crossroads into Clay Lane.*
N-SING: usu *the* N ≠right; ADV: ADV after v

2 Your **left** arm, leg, or ear, for example, is the one which is on the left side of your body. Your **left** shoe or glove is the one which is intended to be worn on your left foot or hand.
ADJ: ADJ n ≠right

3 You can refer to people who support the political ideals of socialism as **the left**. They are often contrasted with **the right**, who support the political ideals of capitalism and conservatism. *...the traditional parties of the Left... The government's industrial policy has been fiercely attacked by the left.*
N-SING-COLL: *the* N ≠right

4 If you say that a person or political party has moved to the **left**, you mean that their political beliefs have become more left-wing. *After Mrs Thatcher's first election victory in 1979, Labour moved sharply to the left... There will be a radical swing to the right or the left.*
N-SING: *the* N, usu *to the* N ≠right

left-field. **Left-field** means slightly odd or unusual; an informal use. *...a left-field cabaret act... Her parents were creative and left-field and wanted Polly to become a singer or a truck driver.*
ADJ-GRADED: usu ADJ n

left-hand. **Left-hand** describes the position of something when it is on the left side. *They drive on the left-hand side of the road... The keys are in the back left-hand corner of the drawer.*
◆◆◇◇◇ ADJ: ADJ n ≠right-hand

left-hand drive. A **left-hand drive** car, van, or lorry has the steering wheel on the left side, and is designed to be used in countries where people drive on the right-hand side of the road.
ADJ: usu ADJ n

left-handed. Someone who is **left-handed** finds it easier to use their left hand rather than their right hand for activities such as writing and throwing a ball. *I noticed she was left-handed... There is a place in London that supplies practically everything for left-handed people.* ▸ Also an adverb. *My father thought that I'd be at a disadvantage if I wrote left-handed.*
◆◇◇◇◇ ADJ ≠right-handed; ADV: ADV after v

left-hander, **left-handers.** A **left-hander** is someone who finds it easier to use their left hand rather than their right hand for activities such as writing and throwing a ball. *Left-handers have trouble using can-openers, scissors, and potato peelers.*
◆◇◇◇◇ N-COUNT ≠right-hander

leftism /leftɪzəm/. **Leftism** refers to the beliefs and behaviour of people who support socialist ideals. *...changes which would move the party away from the dreamy leftism that alienated so many people.*
N-UNCOUNT

leftist /leftɪst/ **leftists**
◆◇◇◇◇

1 Socialists and Communists are sometimes referred to as **leftists**. *Two of the men were leftists and two were centrists. ...Chilean leftists.*
N-COUNT

2 If you describe someone, their ideals or their activities as **leftist**, you mean that they support the ideas of socialism or communism. *...an alliance of seven leftist parties... They make no secret of their leftist sympathies. ...extreme leftist ideas.*
ADJ: ADJ n

left luggage. **Left luggage** is used to refer to luggage that people leave at a special place in a railway station or an airport, and which they collect later; used mainly in British English. *...a left luggage locker at Victoria Station.*
N-UNCOUNT: usu N n

left-of-centre; spelled **left of center** in American English. **Left-of-centre** people or political parties support political ideas which are closer to socialism than to capitalism. *...representatives of four new left-of-centre opposition parties.*
ADJ: usu ADJ n

leftover /leftoʊvə^{r}/ **leftovers;** also spelled **left-over.**
◆◇◇◇◇

1 You can refer to food that remains uneaten after a meal as **leftovers**. *Refrigerate any leftovers... The only food I ever got was the family's leftovers.*
N-PLURAL

2 You use **leftover** to describe an amount of something that remains after the rest of it has been used or eaten. *...leftover pieces of wallpaper... Leftover chicken makes a wonderful salad.*
ADJ: ADJ n

3 If you say that something is a **leftover from** a past period of time or from something that happened in the past, you mean that it has its origin there and still exists even though most other things connected to that time or event have disappeared. *...a leftover from the time our planet was first formed... He dragged a foot when he walked, a leftover from polio.*
N-COUNT: N *from* n

leftward /leftwə^{r}d/. The form **leftwards** is also used. **Leftward** or **leftwards** means on or towards a political position that is closer to socialism than to capitalism. *Their success does not necessarily reflect a leftward shift in politics.* ▸ Also an adverb. *He seemed to move leftwards as he grew older.*
ADJ: ADJ n; ADV: ADV after v

left-wing; also spelled **left wing.**
◆◆◇◇◇

1 **Left-wing** people have political ideas that are based on socialism. *They said they would not be voting for him because he was too left-wing.*
ADJ-GRADED ≠right-wing

2 The **left wing** of a group of people, especially a political party, consists of the members of it whose beliefs are closer to socialism than are those of its other members. *The left-wing of the party is confident that the motion will be carried.*
N-SING: usu *the* N ≠right wing

left-winger, **left-wingers.** A **left-winger** is a person whose political beliefs are close to socialism, or closer to them than most of the other people in the same group or party. *We were accused of being militant left-wingers.*
◆◇◇◇◇ N-COUNT ≠right-winger

lefty /lefti/ **lefties;** also spelled **leftie.**

1 If you refer to someone as a **lefty**, you mean that they have socialist beliefs and you disapprove of this; used mainly in informal British English. *...a large group of students and trendy lefties.*
N-COUNT: oft N n PRAGMATICS

2 A **lefty** is someone, especially a sports player,
N-COUNT

who is left-handed; used mainly in informal American English. *The fact that Goran is a lefty just makes his serve that little bit better.*

leg /leg/ **legs, legging, legged.** ◆◆◆◆◇

1 A person or animal's **legs** are the long parts of their body that they use to stand on. *He was tapping his walking stick against his leg.* ♦ **-legged** /-legɪd/ *Her name was Sheila, a long-legged blonde. ...a large four-legged animal.*
N-COUNT: usu poss N
COMB in ADJs

2 The **legs** of a pair of trousers are the parts that cover your legs. *He moved on through wet grass that soaked his trouser legs.*
N-COUNT: usu pl

3 A **leg** of lamb, pork, chicken, or other meat is a piece of meat that consists of the animal's or bird's leg, especially the thigh. *...a chicken leg. ...a leg of mutton.*
N-COUNT: n N, N of n

4 The **legs** of a table, chair, or other piece of furniture are the parts that rest on the floor and support the furniture's weight. *His ankles were tied to the legs of the chair... The teak table has fluted legs.* ♦ **-legged** *...a three-legged stool. ...an ancient Guatemalan bow-legged table.*
N-COUNT: usu with supp, oft n N, N of n
COMB in ADJ-GRADED

5 A **leg** of a long journey is one part of it, usually between two points where you stop. *The first leg of the journey was by boat to Lake Naivasha in Kenya.*
N-COUNT: usu ord N, N of n

6 A **leg** of a sports competition is one of a series of games that are played to decide an overall winner; used mainly in British English. *The first round of the cup was decided over two legs... They will televise both legs of Leeds' European Cup clash with Rangers.*
N-COUNT

7 If you **leg it**, you run somewhere very quickly, usually in order to escape from someone or something; an informal expression. *We saw some kids shinning up a drainpipe before legging it clutching a TV and hi-fi... He was now to be seen legging it across the field.*
PHRASES
V inflects

8 If you say that something or someone is **on** their **last legs**, you mean that the period of time when they were successful or strong is ending; an informal expression. *By the mid-1980s, the copper industry in the US was on its last legs.*
usu v-link PHR

9 If you **are pulling** someone's **leg**, you are teasing them by telling them something shocking or worrying as a joke; an informal expression. *Of course I won't tell them; I was only pulling your leg.*
V inflects
=joking

10 If you say that someone does not **have a leg to stand on**, or **hasn't got a leg to stand on**, you mean that a statement or claim they have made cannot be justified or proved; an informal expression. *It's only my word against his, I know. So I don't have a leg to stand on.*
with brd-neg

11 • **an arm and a leg**: see **arm**. • **with your tail between your legs**: see **tail**.

legacy /legəsi/ **legacies** ◆◆◇◇◇

1 A **legacy** is money or property which someone leaves to you when they die. *You could make a real difference to someone's life by leaving them a generous legacy.*
N-COUNT

2 A **legacy** of an event or period of history is something which is a direct result of it and which continues to exist after it is over. *...a programme to overcome the legacy of inequality and injustice created by Apartheid... Communism has left a mixed legacy.*
N-COUNT: with supp, usu N of n, n N

legal /liːgəl/ ◆◆◆◆◇

1 Legal is used to describe things that relate to the law. *He vowed to take legal action. ...the British legal system... I sought legal advice on this. ...the legal profession.* ♦ **legally** *There are reasons to doubt that a second trial is morally, legally or politically justified... It could be a bit problematic, legally speaking.*
ADJ: ADJ n
ADV: ADV with v, ADV adj, ADV with cl

2 An action or situation that is **legal** is allowed or required by law. *What I did was perfectly legal. ...drivers who have more than the legal limit of alcohol.* ♦ **legally** *The school is legally responsible for your child's safety... A lorry driver can legally work eighty-two hours a week.*
ADJ
≠illegal
ADV: ADV adj, ADV with v

legal aid. **Legal aid** is financial assistance given by the government or another organization to people who cannot afford to pay for a lawyer. ◆◇◇◇◇
N-UNCOUNT

legalise /liːgəlaɪz/. See **legalize**.

legalistic /liːgəlɪstɪk/. If you say that someone's language or ideas are **legalistic**, you are criticizing them for paying too much attention to legal details. *...complicated legalistic language. ...his fussily legalistic mind.*
ADJ-GRADED: usu ADJ n
PRAGMATICS

legality /ligælɪti/. If you talk about the **legality** of an action or situation, you are talking about whether it is legal or not. *The auditor has questioned the legality of the contracts.* ◆◇◇◇◇
N-UNCOUNT: usu the N of n

legalize /liːgəlaɪz/ **legalizes, legalizing, legalized;** also spelled **legalise** in British English. If something **is legalized**, a law is passed that makes it legal. *Divorce was legalized in 1981. ...the decision of the Georgian government to legalise multi-party elections.* ♦ **legalization** /liːgəlaɪzeɪʃən/ *She ruled out the legalisation of drugs.* ◆◇◇◇◇
VERB
be V-ed
V n
N-UNCOUNT: usu the N of n

legal tender. **Legal tender** is money, especially a particular coin or banknote, which is officially part of a country's currency at a particular time.
N-UNCOUNT

legate /legɪt/ **legates.** A **legate** is a person who is the official representative of another person, especially the Pope's official representative in a particular country; a formal word. *...Pope Innocent VI's legate, Cardinal Albornoz.*
N-COUNT
=representative

legation /lɪgeɪʃən/ **legations**

1 A **legation** is a group of government officials and diplomats who work in a foreign country and represent their government in that country. *...a member of the US legation.*
N-COUNT: usu supp N

2 A **legation** is the building in which a legation works. *We were still at the legation at Eaton Place.*
N-COUNT

legend /ledʒənd/ **legends** ◆◆◇◇◇

1 A **legend** is a very old and popular story that may be true. *...the legends of ancient Greece. ...the Robin Hood legend... The play was based on Irish legend.*
N-VAR

2 If you refer to someone as a **legend**, you mean that they are very famous and admired by a lot of people. *...blues legends John Lee Hooker and B.B. King.*
N-COUNT

3 A **legend** is a story that people talk about, concerning people, places, or events that exist or are famous at the present time. *The incident has since become a family legend... His frequent brushes with death are the stuff of legend among the press.*
N-VAR

legendary /ledʒəndri, AM -deri/ ◆◆◇◇◇

1 If you describe someone or something as **legendary**, you mean that they are very famous and that many stories are told about them. *...the legendary Jazz singer Adelaide Hall... His political skill is legendary.*
ADJ-GRADED

2 A **legendary** person, place, or event is mentioned or described in an old legend. *The hill is supposed to be the resting place of the legendary King Lud.*
ADJ: usu ADJ n

-legged /-legɪd/. See **leg**.

leggings /legɪŋz/ ◆◇◇◇◇

1 Leggings are close-fitting trousers, usually made out of a stretchy fabric, that are worn by women and girls. *She is wearing tight, black leggings and a baggy green jersey.*
N-PLURAL: also a pair of N

2 Leggings are an outer covering of leather or other strong material, often in the form of trousers, that you wear over your normal trousers in order to protect them. *...a pair of leggings to slip on over your other clothes.*
N-PLURAL: also a pair of N

leggy /legi/. If you describe someone, usually a woman, as **leggy**, you mean that they have very long legs and usually that you find this attractive. *The leggy beauty was none other than our own Naomi Campbell.*
ADJ-GRADED

legible /ledʒɪbəl/. **Legible** writing is clear enough to read. *My handwriting isn't very legible. ...a barely legible sign.*
ADJ-GRADED
≠illegible

legion /liːdʒən/ **legions** ◆◇◇◇◇

1 A **legion** is a large group of soldiers who form one section of an army. *...the Sudan-based troops of the Libyan Islamic Legion... The last of the Roman legions left Britain in AD 410.*
N-COUNT: oft in names after n

2 A **legion** of people or things is a great number of them; used in written English. *His delightful sense*
N-COUNT: usu N of n

of humour won him a legion of friends. ...a legion of stories about noisy neighbours.

3 If you say that things of a particular kind are **legion**, you mean that there are a great number of them; a formal use. *Books on the subject of Tarot Cards are legion... The number of women who become pregnant after adopting children is legion.*
ADJ: v-link ADJ

legislate /ledʒɪsleɪt/ **legislates, legislating, legislated.** When a government or state **legislates**, it passes a new law; a formal word. *Most member countries have already legislated against excessive overtime... You cannot legislate to change attitudes. ...attempts to legislate a national energy strategy.*
◆◇◇◇◇ VERB; V against/for/on n; V to-inf; V n; Also V

legislation /ledʒɪsleɪʃən/. **Legislation** consists of a law or laws passed by a government; a formal word. *...a letter calling for legislation to protect women's rights.*
◆◆◆◇◇ N-UNCOUNT

legislative /ledʒɪslətɪv, AM -leɪ-/. **Legislative** means involving or relating to the process of making and passing laws; a formal word. *Today's hearing was just the first step in the legislative process. ...the country's highest legislative body.*
◆◆◇◇◇ ADJ: ADJ n

legislator /ledʒɪsleɪtəʳ/ **legislators.** A **legislator** is a person who is involved in making or passing laws; a formal word. *...an attempt to get US legislators to change the system.*
◆◇◇◇◇ N-COUNT

legislature /ledʒɪslətʃəʳ, AM -leɪ-/ **legislatures.** The **legislature** of a particular state or country is the group of people in it who have the power to make and pass laws; a formal word. *The proposals before the legislature include the creation of two special courts to deal exclusively with violent crimes.*
◆◆◇◇◇ N-COUNT: usu *the* N in sing

legit /lədʒɪt/. If you describe a person or thing as **legit**, you mean that they are in accordance with the law or with a particular set of rules and regulations; an informal word. *I checked him out, he's legit... What is the point of going legit and getting married?*
ADJ-GRADED: usu v-link ADJ

legitimate, legitimates, legitimating, legitimated. The adjective is pronounced /lɪdʒɪtɪmət/. The verb is pronounced /lɪdʒɪtɪmeɪt/.
◆◆◇◇◇

1 Something that is **legitimate** is acceptable according to the law. *The French government has condemned the coup in Haiti and has demanded the restoration of the legitimate government... The government will not seek to disrupt the legitimate business activities of the defendant.* ♦ **legitimacy** /lɪdʒɪtɪmɪsi/ *The opposition parties do not recognise the political legitimacy of his government.* ♦ **legitimately** *The government has been legitimately elected by the people.*
ADJ-GRADED; N-UNCOUNT: usu with supp; ADV-GRADED: ADV with v

2 If you say that something such as a feeling or claim is **legitimate**, you think that it is reasonable and justified. *That's a perfectly legitimate fear... The New York Times has a legitimate claim to be a national newspaper.* ♦ **legitimacy** *Sampras beat Carl-Uwe Steeb by 6-1, 6-2, 6-1 to underline the legitimacy of his challenge for the title.* ♦ **legitimately** *They could quarrel quite legitimately with some of my choices.*
ADJ-GRADED; N-UNCOUNT: usu with supp; ADV-GRADED: ADV with v

3 A **legitimate** child is one whose parents were married before he or she was born. *We only married in order that the child should be legitimate.*
ADJ ≠illegitimate

4 To **legitimate** something means the same as to **legitimize** it; a formal use. *We want to legitimate this process by passing a law.* ♦ **legitimation** /lɪdʒɪtɪmeɪʃən/ *...the legitimation of state constitutions.*
VERB; V n; N-UNCOUNT

legitimize /lɪdʒɪtɪmaɪz/ **legitimizes, legitimizing, legitimized;** also spelled **legitimise** in British English. To **legitimize** something, especially something bad, means to officially allow it, approve it, or to make it seem acceptable; a formal word. *They will accept no agreement that legitimizes the ethnic division of the country... Images which glorify violence and cruelty, serve to legitimise such behaviour.*
◆◇◇◇◇ VERB =sanction; V n

legless /legləs/

1 A **legless** person or animal has no legs, for example as the result of an accident. *...Douglas Bader, the legless wartime fighter pilot... The slow-worm is in fact not a snake but a legless lizard.*
ADJ: ADJ n

2 In British English, if you say that someone is **legless**, you mean that they are extremely drunk; an informal use. *They found the locals getting legless on tequila.*
ADJ-GRADED: usu v-link ADJ

leg room. **Leg room** is the amount of space, especially in a car or other vehicle, that is available in front of your legs. *Tall drivers won't have enough leg room.*
N-UNCOUNT

legume /legjuːm/ **legumes.** People sometimes use **legumes** to refer to peas, beans, and other related vegetables; a technical word. *Legumes are an excellent source of protein.*
N-COUNT =pulse

leisure /leʒəʳ, AM liːʒ-/
◆◆◇◇◇

1 **Leisure** is the time when you are not working and you can relax and do things that you enjoy. *...a relaxing way to fill my leisure time. ...one of Britain's most popular leisure activities.*
N-UNCOUNT: usu N n

2 If someone does something **at leisure** or **at** their **leisure**, they enjoy themselves by doing it when they want to, without hurrying. *You will be able to stroll at leisure through the gardens... He could read all the national papers at his leisure.*
PHRASE: PHR after v

leisure centre, leisure centres. In British English, a **leisure centre** is a large public building containing different facilities for leisure activities, such as a sports hall, a swimming pool, and rooms for meetings. *The hour-long sessions take place at Bloxwich Leisure Centre.*
◆◇◇◇◇ N-COUNT: oft in names

leisured /leʒəʳd, AM liːʒ-/

1 **Leisured** people are people who do not work, usually because they are rich. *Bronzed skin became a symbol of wealth, health and beauty, a sign that the owner belonged to the leisured classes.*
ADJ: ADJ n

2 **Leisured** activities are done in a relaxed way or do not involve work. *...this leisured life of reading and writing.*
ADJ-GRADED =relaxed

leisurely /leʒəʳli, AM liːʒ-/. A **leisurely** action is done in a relaxed and unhurried way. *Lunch was a leisurely affair... Tweed walked at a leisurely pace.* ► Also an adverb. *We walked leisurely into the hotel.*
◆◇◇◇◇ ADJ-GRADED: usu ADJ n; ADV-GRADED: ADV with v

leisurewear /leʒəʳweəʳ, AM liːʒ-/. **Leisurewear** is informal clothing which you wear when you are not working, for example at weekends or on holiday; a formal word. *Their range of leisurewear is aimed at fashion-conscious 13 to 25 year-olds.*
N-UNCOUNT

leitmotif /laɪtmoutiːf/ **leitmotifs;** also spelled **leitmotiv**. A **leitmotif** in something such as a book or film or in a person's life is an idea or an object which occurs again and again; a formal word. *The title of one of Dietrich's best-known songs could serve as the leitmotif for her life.*
N-COUNT

lemming /lemɪŋ/ **lemmings**

1 A **lemming** is an animal that looks like a large rat with thick fur. Lemmings live in cold northern regions and sometimes migrate in very large numbers.
N-COUNT

2 If you say that a large group of people are acting like **lemmings**, you are critical of them because they all follow each other into an action without thinking about it. *The French crowds pour like lemmings down the motorway to Paris.*
N-COUNT: usu pl PRAGMATICS

lemon /lemən/ **lemons**
◆◆◇◇◇

1 A **lemon** is a bright yellow fruit with very sour juice. Lemons grow on trees in tropical countries. *...a slice of lemon. ...oranges, lemons and other citrus fruits. ...lemon juice.*
N-VAR

2 **Lemon** is a drink that tastes of lemons.
N-UNCOUNT

3 **Lemon** is the same as **lemon yellow**.
COLOUR

4 If you think that something is a failure, or not as good or as useful as it should be, you can say it is a **lemon**; an informal use. *He took a little test drive and agreed the car was a lemon.*
N-COUNT PRAGMATICS

5 If you think someone looks foolish, because they are shy or unassertive, you can say that they are like a **lemon**; used in informal British English. *I just stood there like a lemon.*
N-COUNT PRAGMATICS

lemonade /lemənеɪd/ **lemonades.** **Lemonade** is a colourless sweet fizzy drink. A drink that is
◆◇◇◇◇ N-UNCOUNT

made from lemons, sugar, and water can also be referred to as **lemonade**. *He was pouring ice and lemonade into tall glasses.* ▸ A glass of lemonade can be referred to as a **lemonade**. *I'm going to get you a lemonade.* N-COUNT

lemon curd. **Lemon curd** is a thick yellow food made from lemons. You spread it on bread or put it in tarts; used mainly in British English. N-UNCOUNT

lemongrass /lemənɡrɑːs, -ɡræs/; also spelled **lemon grass**. **Lemongrass** is a type of grass that grows in tropical countries. It is used as a flavouring in food. N-UNCOUNT

lemon squeezer, lemon squeezers. A **lemon squeezer** is an object used for squeezing juice out of lemons and oranges. N-COUNT

lemony /leməni/. Something that smells or tastes of lemons can be described as **lemony**. *The salad dressing was too lemony.* ADJ-GRADED

lemon yellow; also spelled **lemon-yellow**. **Lemon yellow** or **lemon** is used to describe things that are pale yellow in colour. *...a lovely shade of lemon yellow. ...lemon coloured trousers.* COLOUR

lemur /liːmə^{r}/ **lemurs.** A **lemur** is an animal that looks like a small monkey and has a long tail and a face similar to that of a fox. N-COUNT

lend /lend/ **lends, lending, lent** ◆◆◆◇◇

1 When people or organizations such as banks **lend** you money, they give it to you and you agree to pay it back at a future date, often with an extra amount as interest. *The bank is reassessing its criteria for lending money... I had to lend him ten pounds to take his children to the pictures. ...financial de-regulation that led to institutions being more willing to lend.* ♦ **lending** *...a financial institution that specializes in the lending of money. ...a slump in bank lending.* VERB; V n; V n n; V; Also V n *to*n, V *to*n; N-UNCOUNT: usu with supp

2 If you **lend** something that you own, you allow someone to have or to use it for a period of time. *Will you lend me your jacket for a little while?... He had lent the bungalow to the Conrads for a couple of weeks.* VERB; V n n; V n *to*n

3 If you **lend** your support to someone or something, you help them with something they are doing or with a problem that they have. *He was approached by the organisers to lend support to a benefit concert... Stipe attended yesterday's news conference to lend his support.* VERB =give; V n *to*n; V n; Also V n n

4 If something **lends** itself to a particular activity or result, it is easy for it to be used for that activity or to achieve that result. *The room lends itself well to summer eating with its light, airy atmosphere.* VERB; V pron-refl *to*n

5 If something **lends** a particular quality to something else, it adds that quality to it. *Enthusiastic applause lent a sense of occasion to the proceedings... A more relaxed regime and regular work lends the inmates a dignity not seen in other prisons.* VERB; V n *to*n; V n n; Also V n

6 See also **lent**.

7 • to **lend an ear**: see **ear**. • to **lend a hand**: see **hand**. • to **lend** your **name to** something: see **name**.

lender /lendə^{r}/ **lenders.** A **lender** is a person or an institution that lends money to people. *...the six leading mortgage lenders.* ◆◆◇◇◇ N-COUNT

lending library, lending libraries. A **lending library** is a public library from which people are allowed to borrow books. N-COUNT

lending rate, lending rates. The **lending rate** is the rate of interest that you have to pay when you are repaying a loan. *The bank left its lending rates unchanged.* ◆◇◇◇◇ N-COUNT

length /leŋθ/ **lengths** ◆◆◆◆◇

1 The **length** of something is the amount that it measures from one end to the other along the longest side. *It is about a metre in length. ...the length of the fish... The plane had a wing span of 34ft and a length of 22ft.* N-VAR: oft with poss, oft amount *in*N, N *of*amount

2 The **length** of something such as a piece of writing is the amount of writing that is contained in it. *...a book of at least 100 pages in length... The length of a paragraph depends on the amount of information that it conveys.* N-VAR: oft with poss, oft amount *in*N

3 The **length** of an event, activity, or situation is the period of time from beginning to end for which something lasts or during which something happens. *The exact length of each period may vary... His film, over two hours in length, is a subtle if slightly ponderous dissection of family life.* N-VAR: oft with poss, oft amount *in*N

4 A **length** of rope, cloth, wood, or other material is a piece of it that is intended to be used for a particular purpose or that exists in a particular situation. *...a 30ft length of rope... You can hang lengths of fabric behind the glass.* N-COUNT: with supp, oft N *of*n

5 The **length** of something is its quality of being long. *Many have been surprised at the length of time it has taken him to make up his mind... I noticed, too, the length of her fingers.* N-UNCOUNT: usu with supp, oft N *of*n

6 If you swim a **length** in a swimming pool, you swim the distance between the ends that are furthest from each other. *I swim 40 lengths a day.* N-COUNT: usu num N

7 In boat racing or horse racing, a **length** is the distance from the front to the back of the boat or horse. You can talk about one boat or horse being one or more **lengths** in front of or behind another. *Harvard won by four lengths.* N-COUNT: usu num N

8 If something happens or exists along **the length of** something, it happens or exists for the whole way along it. *I looked along the length of the building... The inspiration stemming from his travels lasted the length of his career.* N-SING: *the*N *of*n

9 See also **full-length**.

10 If someone does something **at length**, they do it after a long period of time; a literary expression. *At length my father went into the house.* PHRASES; PHR cl

11 If someone does something **at length**, they do it for a long time or in great detail. *They spoke at length, reviewing the entire incident.* PHR after v

12 If you say that someone **goes to great lengths** to achieve something, you mean that they try very hard and perhaps do extreme things in order to achieve it. *Greta Garbo went to great lengths to hide from reporters and photographers.* V inflects

13 • **at arm's length**: see **arm**. • **the length and breadth of**: see **breadth**.

-length /-leŋθ/. **-length** combines with nouns to form adjectives that describe something that is of a certain length, or long enough to reach the point indicated by the noun. *...shoulder-length hair. ...knee-length boots. ...a feature-length film.* • See also **full-length**. COMB in ADJ

lengthen /leŋθən/ **lengthens, lengthening, lengthened** ◆◇◇◇◇

1 When something **lengthens** or when you **lengthen** it, it increases in length. *The evening shadows were lengthening... She began to walk faster, but he lengthened his stride to keep up with her... The runway had to be lengthened.* V-ERG ≠shorten; V; V n

2 When something **lengthens** or when you **lengthen** it, it lasts for a longer time than it did previously. *Vacations have lengthened and the work week has shortened... The council does not support lengthening the school day to fit in other activities.* V-ERG ≠shorten; V; V n

lengthways /leŋθweɪz/ or **lengthwise** /leŋθwaɪz/. **Lengthways** or **lengthwise** means in a direction or position along the length of something. *Cut the aubergines in half lengthways... She tore off two sections of paper towel and folded them lengthwise.* ADV: ADV after v

lengthwise /leŋθwaɪz/. **Lengthwise** means the same as **lengthways**. *Peel the onion and cut it in half lengthwise.* ADV: ADV after v

lengthy /leŋθi/ **lengthier, lengthiest** ◆◆◇◇◇

1 You use **lengthy** to describe an event or process which lasts for a long time. *...a lengthy meeting. ...the lengthy process of filling out passport application forms.* ADJ-GRADED: usu ADJ n

2 A **lengthy** report, article, book, or document contains a lot of speech, writing, or other material. *...a lengthy report from the Council of Ministers... There is a lengthy article on Spike Milligan in the Observer newspaper.* ADJ-GRADED: usu ADJ n

leniency /liːniənsi/. **Leniency** is a lenient attitude or lenient behaviour. *The judge rejected pleas for leniency and sentenced him to six* N-UNCOUNT: oft N *to/towards*n *months in prison... He said he would show no leniency towards those who stirred up trouble between Muslims and Christians.*

lenient /liːniənt/. When someone in authority is **lenient**, they are not as strict or severe as expected. *He believes the government already is lenient with drug traffickers... Professor Oswald takes a sightly more lenient view of the matter.* ◆◇◇◇◇ ADJ-GRADED: oft ADJ *with* n
♦ **leniently** *Many people believe reckless drivers are treated too leniently.* ADV-GRADED: ADV after v

lens /lenz/ **lenses** ◆◆◆◇◇
1 A **lens** is a thin curved piece of glass or plastic used in things such as cameras, telescopes, and pairs of glasses. You look through a lens in order to make things look larger, smaller, or clearer. *...a camera lens... I packed your sunglasses with the green lenses.* N-COUNT
2 In your eye, the **lens** is the part behind the pupil that focuses light and helps you to see clearly. N-COUNT: usu sing
3 See also **contact lens, telephoto lens, wide-angle lens, zoom lens.**

lent /lent/. **Lent** is the past tense and past participle of **lend.**

Lent. **Lent** is the period of forty days before Easter, during which some Christians give up something that they enjoy. *It was a favourite meal on Fridays and fast days, particularly during Lent.* N-UNCOUNT

lentil /lentɪl/ **lentils.** **Lentils** are the seeds of a lentil plant. They can be dried and used to make soups and stews. ◆◇◇◇◇ N-COUNT: usu pl

Leo /liːoʊ/ **Leos** ◆◆◇◇◇
1 **Leo** is one of the twelve signs of the zodiac. Its symbol is a lion. People who are born approximately between the 23rd of July and the 22nd of August come under this sign. N-UNCOUNT
2 A **Leo** is a person whose sign of the zodiac is Leo. N-COUNT

leonine /liːənaɪn/. **Leonine** means like a lion, and is used especially to describe men with a lot of hair on their head, or with big beards; a literary word. *...a tall leonine grey-haired man.* ADJ: usu ADJ n

leopard /lepərd/ **leopards** ◆◇◇◇◇
1 A **leopard** is a type of large, wild cat. Leopards have yellow fur and black spots, and live in Africa and Asia. N-COUNT
2 If you say that **a leopard cannot change its spots,** you mean that people or things are not able to change their basic characteristics, especially when you are critical of those characteristics. *This only goes to show how this racist leopard has in no way changed his spots.* PHRASE: V inflects

leotard /liːətɑːrd/ **leotards.** A **leotard** is a tight-fitting piece of clothing, covering the body but not the legs, that some people wear when they practise dancing or do exercise. N-COUNT

leper /lepər/ **lepers**
1 A **leper** is a person who has leprosy. N-COUNT
2 If you refer to someone as a **leper,** you mean that people in their community avoid them because they have done something that has shocked or offended people. *The newspaper article had branded her a social leper not fit to be seen in company.* N-COUNT

leprosy /leprəsi/. **Leprosy** is an infectious disease that damages people's flesh. N-UNCOUNT

lesbian /lezbiən/ **lesbians** ◆◆◆◇◇
1 **Lesbian** is used to describe homosexual women. *Many of her best friends were lesbian.* ► A **lesbian** is a woman who is lesbian. *...a youth group for lesbians, gays and bisexuals.* ADJ / N-COUNT
2 **Lesbian** is used to describe the relationships and activities of homosexual women, and the organizations or publications intended for them or created by them. *...a long-term lesbian relationship.* ADJ

lesbianism /lezbiənɪzəm/. **Lesbianism** refers to homosexual relationships between women or the preference that a woman shows for sexual relationships with women. *...today's increased public awareness of lesbianism.* N-UNCOUNT

lesion /liːʒən/ **lesions.** A **lesion** is an injury or wound to someone's body; a technical word in medicine. *...skin lesions. ...a lesion of the spinal cord.* ◆◇◇◇◇ N-COUNT

less /les/ ◆◆◆◆◆
Less is often considered to be the comparative form of **little.**
1 You use **less** to indicate that there is a smaller number of things or a smaller amount of something than before or than average, or than something else. You can use 'a little', 'a lot', 'a bit', 'far', and 'much' in front of **less.** *People should eat less fat to reduce the risk of heart disease. ...a dishwasher that uses less water and electricity than older machines... Children of very low ability should not be permitted to pay less attention to the sciences.* DET: DET n-uncount ≠more
► Also a pronoun. *Borrowers are striving to ease their financial position by spending less and saving more.* PRON ≠more
► Also a quantifier. *Last year less of the money went into high-technology companies... The other option would be to for me to own less of the house but that would be stupid.* QUANT: QUANT *of* def-n-uncount/sing ≠more
2 You use **less than** before a number or amount to say that the actual number or amount is smaller than this. *Motorways actually cover less than 0.1 percent of the countryside... Less than a half hour later he returned upstairs.* PHR-PREP: PREP amount
3 You use **less** to indicate that something or someone has a smaller amount of a quality than they used to or than is average or usual. *I often think about those less fortunate than me... Other amenities, less commonly available, include a library and exercise room... Poverty is less of a problem now than it used to be.* ADV-COMPAR: ADV adj/adv, ADV *of* a n ≠more
4 If you say that something is **less** one thing **than** another, you mean that it is like the second thing rather than the first. *At first sight it looked less like a capital city than a mining camp... Trades union leadership in those days was less a career than a vocation.* ADV-COMPAR: ADV group *than* group/cl
5 If you do something **less** than before or **less** than someone else, you do it to a smaller extent or not as often. *We are eating more and exercising less... I see less of any of my friends than I used to.* ADV-COMPAR: ADV with v ≠more
6 In formal English, you use the expressions **still less, much less,** and **even less** after a negative statement in order to introduce and emphasize a further statement, and to make it negative too. *I never talked about it, still less about her... The boy didn't have a girlfriend, much less a wife.* PHR-CONJ-COORD PRAGMATICS
7 When you are referring to amounts, you use **less** in front of a number or quantity to indicate that it is to be subtracted from another number or quantity already mentioned. *...Boyton Financial Services Fees: £750, less £400... Company car drivers will pay between ten and twenty five percent, less tax.* PREP =minus ≠plus
8 You use **less and less** to say that something is becoming smaller all the time in degree or amount. *The couple seem to spend less and less time together... She sounded less and less eager to return to Ireland... Many basic goods are now rationed. Less and less is available.* PHRASES usu PHR group/cl, PHR with v ≠more and more
9 You use **less than** to say that something does not have a particular quality. For example, if you describe something as **less than** perfect, you mean that it is not perfect at all. *Her greeting was less than enthusiastic... Her advice has frequently been less than wholly helpful.* PHR adj/adv PRAGMATICS ≠more than
10 You can use **no less** as an emphatic way of expressing surprise or admiration at the importance of something or someone. *He had returned to England in an aircraft carrier no less... Who wrote the screenplay from Patricia Highsmith's book? Raymond Chandler, no less.* cl/group PHR PRAGMATICS
11 You use **no less than** before an amount to indicate that the amount is larger than you expected. *No less than 35 per cent of the country is protected in the form of parks and nature sanctuaries... He is lined up for no less than four US television interviews.* PHR amount =as many as
12 • **couldn't care less**: see **care.** • **more or less**: see **more.** • **nothing less than**: see **nothing.**

-less /-ləs/. **-less** is added to nouns in order to form adjectives that indicate that someone or something does not have the thing that the noun refers to. *...drink and talk and meaningless* SUFFIX ≠-full *laughter... He is not as friendless as he appeared to be.*

lessee /lesiː/ **lessees.** A **lessee** is a person who has taken out a lease on something such as a house or a piece of land; a legal term. N-COUNT

lessen /lesᵊn/ **lessens, lessening, lessened.** If something **lessens** or you **lessen** it, it becomes smaller in size, amount, degree, or importance. *He is used to a lot of attention from his wife, which will inevitably lessen when the baby is born... Make sure that your immunisations are up to date to lessen the risk of serious illness.* ◆◇◇◇◇ V-ERG ≠increase V V n
♦ **lessening** *...increased trade and a lessening of tension on the border.* N-UNCOUNT: usu N *of/in* n

lesser /lesəʳ/ ◆◆◇◇◇
1 You use **lesser** in order to indicate that something is smaller in extent, degree, or amount than another thing that has been mentioned. *No medication works in isolation but is affected to a greater or lesser extent by many other factors... The more obvious potential allies are Ireland, Denmark and, to a lesser degree, the Netherlands.* ► Also an adverb. *...lesser known works by famous artists.* ADJ-COMPAR: ADJ n, the ADJ *of* n ≠greater; ADV-COMPAR: ADV -ed
2 You can use **lesser** to refer to something or someone that is less important than other things or people of the same type. *They pleaded guilty to lesser charges of criminal damage... He was feared by other, lesser, men.* ADJ-COMPAR: ADJ n, the ADJ *of* n
3 Lesser is used in the names of some species of birds, animals, and plants. *...the lesser spotted woodpecker.* N-IN-NAMES
4 ● **the lesser of two evils**: see **evil**.

lesson /lesᵊn/ **lessons** ◆◆◆◇◇
1 A **lesson** is a fixed period of time when people are taught about a particular subject or taught how to do something. *It would be his last French lesson for months... Johanna took piano lessons.* N-COUNT
2 You use **lesson** to refer to an experience which acts as a warning to you or an example from which you should learn. *There's still one lesson to be learned from the crisis – we all need to better understand the thinking of the other side.* ● If you say that you are going to **teach** someone **a lesson**, you mean that you are going to punish them for something that they have done so that they do not do it again. N-COUNT: usu sing; PHRASE: V inflects
3 In a church service, the **lesson** is a short piece of text which is read aloud from the bible. *The Rev. Nicola Judd read the lesson.* N-COUNT: usu sing

lest /lest/. If you do something **lest** something unpleasant should happen, you do it to try to prevent the unpleasant thing from happening; a formal word. *I was afraid to open the door lest he should follow me... The president has gone along with the hardliners lest they be tempted to oust him... And, lest we forget, Einstein wrote his most influential papers while working as a clerk.* ◆◇◇◇◇ CONJ-SUBORD =in case

let /let/ **lets, letting;** the form **let** is used in the present tense and is the past tense and past participle. ◆◆◆◆◆
1 If you **let** something happen, you allow it to happen without doing anything to stop or prevent it. *People said we were interfering with nature, and that we should just let the animals die... Thorne let him talk... She let the door slam... I can't let myself be distracted by those things.* VERB V n inf V pron-refl inf
2 If you **let** someone do something, you give them your permission to do it. *I love sweets but Mum doesn't let me have them very often... The Americans won't let her leave the country... Visa or no visa, they won't let you into the country.* VERB V n inf V n prep/adv
3 If you **let** someone into, out of, or through a place, you allow them to enter, leave, or go through it, for example by opening a door or making room for them. *Cantrell had a key and let them into a small bedsitter... I let myself into the flat... I'd better go and let the dog out... The guards were removing a section of fencing to let it through.* VERB V n prep/adv
4 You use **let me** when you are introducing something you want to say. *Let me say it again. I despised Wade's life... Let me tell you what I saw last night... Let me explain why... Let me give you one quick example.* VB: only imper PRAGMATICS V *me* inf
5 You use **let me** when you are offering politely to do something. *Let me take your coat... Let me get you something to drink.* VB: only imper PRAGMATICS V *me* inf
6 You say **let's** or, in more formal English, **let us**, to direct the attention of the people you are talking to towards the subject that you want to consider next. *Let's consider ways of making it easier... Let us look at these views in more detail.* VB: only imper PRAGMATICS V *us* inf
7 You say **let's** or, in formal English, **let us** when you are making a suggestion that involves both you and the person you are talking to, or when you are agreeing to a suggestion of this kind. *I'm bored. Let's go home... 'Shall we go in and have some supper?'—'Yes, let's.'* VB: only imper PRAGMATICS V *us* inf V *'s*
8 Someone in authority, such as a teacher, can use **let's** or, in more formal English, **let us**, in order to give a polite instruction to another person or group of people. *Let's have some hush, please... 'Let us pray,' said the Methodist chaplain.* VB: only imper PRAGMATICS V *us* inf
9 People often use **let** in expressions like **let me see** or **let me think** when they are hesitating or thinking of what to say next. *Now, let's see. Where did I leave my bag?... 'How long you been living together then?'—'Erm, let me think. It's about four years now.'* VERB PRAGMATICS V pron inf
10 You can use **let** to say that you do not care if someone does something, although you think it is unpleasant or wrong. *If he wants to do that, let him do it... Let them talk about me; I'll be dead, anyway... 'She'll kill you.'—'Let her try.'* VB: only imper PRAGMATICS V n inf
11 You can use **let** when you are saying what you think someone should do, usually when they are behaving in a way that you think is unreasonable or wrong. *Let him get his own cup of tea... If they value these data, let them pay for them.* VB: only imper PRAGMATICS V n inf
12 You can use **let** when you are praying for something to happen or when you want it very much to happen. You can use **let** in this way when you are talking to yourself. *Please God, let him telephone me.* VB: only imper V n inf
13 You can use **let** to introduce an assumption on which you are going to base a theory, calculation, or story. *Let us assume that two golfers, Golfer A and Golfer B, are in contention for a club championship... The new man in my life (let's call him Dave) had a very jealous ex-girlfriend.* VB: only imper PRAGMATICS V n inf
14 If you **let** your house or land to someone, you allow them to use it in exchange for money that they pay you regularly; used mainly in British English. *She is thinking of letting her house to an American serviceman... The reasons for letting a house, or part of one, are varied.* ► **Let out** means the same as **let.** *I couldn't sell the London flat, so I let it out to pay the mortgage... Home owners who have extra space available may want to let out a room.* VERB =rent V n *to* n V n; PHRASAL VERB =rent out V n P V P n (not pron)
15 In tennis or badminton, if you serve a **let**, the ball or shuttlecock touches the net but is in the correct part of the court. You then serve again. N-COUNT
16 Let alone is used after a statement, usually a negative one, to indicate that the statement is even more true of the person, thing, or situation that you are going to mention next. *It is incredible that the 12-year-old managed to even reach the pedals, let alone drive the car.* PHRASES CONJ-COORD PRAGMATICS =never mind
17 To **let** someone **be** means to leave them alone and not interfere in what they are doing. *If your child is really sick and needs sleep and quiet, let him be.* *let* inflects
18 If you **let go** of someone or something, you stop holding them. *She let go of Mona's hand and took a sip of her drink... She held the photos with the determined grip of a small child and wouldn't let go.* *let* inflects, oft PHR *of* n
19 If you **let go** of a feeling, attitude, or the control that you have over something, you accept that you should give it up or that it should no longer influence you. *In therapy, she began to let go of her obsession with Mike... The work should focus on helping parents to let go of their children.* *let* inflects, oft PHR *of* n
20 If you **let** someone **go**, you allow them to leave or to escape. *They held him for three hours and they let him go... I'm quite happy really to net a fish and then let it go.* *let* inflects

21 When someone leaves a job, either because they have been sacked or because they want to, the employer sometimes says that they are **letting** that person **go**. *I've assured him I have no plans to let him go... Peterson was let go after less than two years.* *let* inflects

22 If someone says or does something that you think is annoying or stupid and you **let it go**, you do not react to it or say anything about it. *Let it go, he thought. He didn't feel like arguing.* *let* inflects

23 If you **let** yourself **go**, you relax, lose your inhibitions, and behave much more freely than usual. *Stop worrying about what you're feeling. Let yourself go.* *let* inflects

24 If someone **lets** themselves **go**, they pay less attention to themselves or their appearance than they used to, so that they look untidy or unattractive. *If you have let yourself go, you should consider doing something about it for the sake of your health.* *let* inflects

25 If you say that you did not know what you were **letting** yourself **in for** when you decided to do something, you mean you did not realize how difficult, unpleasant, or expensive it was going to be. *He got the impression that Miss Hawes had no idea of what she was letting herself in for... I realized I'd let myself in for something from which there was no turning back.* V inflects, usu with brd-neg, PHR n

26 If you **let** someone **know** something, you tell them about it or make sure that they know about it. *They want to let them know that they are safe... If you do want to go, please let me know.* *let* inflects, oft PHR that/wh, PHR n, PHR *about* n

27 If you **let drop**, **let fall**, or **let slip** information, you reveal it casually or by accident, during a conversation about something else. *How could she know about that? He'd certainly never let drop any hint... He might have let something slip in a moment of weakness.* *let* inflects

28 If you say that someone has **been let loose** in a place or situation, you mean that they have been given complete freedom to do what they like in that place or situation, and you suggest that this may be risky. *She has all the glee of a little girl let loose in a sweetie shop... Trainees go through a four-hour lesson before they are let loose on the controls.* V inflects, oft PHR *in/on* n

29 If someone **lets loose** a sound or remark, they make it, often suddenly. *He let loose a long, deep sigh... Hill let loose a torrent of abuse against those who prosecuted his case.* V inflects, PHR n

30 • to **let fly**: see **fly**. • to **let** your **hair down**: see **hair**. • to **let** someone **off the hook**: see **hook**. • to **let it be known**: see **known**. • to **live and let live**: see **live**. • to **let the side down**: see **side**. • to **let off steam**: see **steam**.

let down PHRASAL VERB

1 If you **let** someone **down** you disappoint them, by not doing something that you have said you will do or that they expected you to do. *Don't worry, Xiao, I won't let you down... When such advisers fail in their duty, they let down the whole system.* V n P, V P n (not pron) ♦ **let down** *The company now has a large number of workers who feel badly let down.* ADJ-GRADED: v-link ADJ

2 If something **lets** you **down**, it is the reason you are not as successful as you could have been. *Many believe it was his shyness and insecurity which let him down... Sadly, the film is let down by an excessively simple plot.* V n P, Also V P n (not pron)

3 If you **let down** something such as a tyre, hot-air balloon, or rubber dinghy, you allow air to escape from it; used mainly in British English. *I let the tyres down on his car... Remove wheelnuts, let down tyre, put on spare.* V n P, V P n (not pron)

let in. If an object **lets in** something such as air, light, or water, it allows air, light, or water to get into it or pass through it, for example because the object has a hole or crack. *...balconies shaded with lattice-work which lets in air but not light.* PHRASAL VERB, V P n (not pron), Also V n P

let in on. If you **let** someone **in on** something that is a secret from most people, you allow them to know about it. *I'm going to let you in on a little secret... He has not yet been let in on the bad news.* PHRASAL VERB, V n P P n

let into. If you **let** someone **into** a secret, you allow them to know it. *I'll let you into a little showbiz secret.* PHRASAL VERB, V n P n

let off PHRASAL VERB

1 If someone in authority **lets** you **off** a task or duty, they give you permission not to do it; used mainly in British English. *The theatre management kindly let me off a couple of performances to go to Yorkshire... I realised that having a new baby lets you off going to boring dinner-parties.* V n P n/-ing

2 If you **let** someone **off**, you give them a lighter punishment than they expect or no punishment at all. *Because he was a Christian, the judge let him off... When police realised who he was, they asked for an autograph and let him off with a warning.* V n P, V n P prep/adv

3 If you **let off** an explosive or a gun, you explode or fire it. *A resident of his neighbourhood had let off fireworks to celebrate the Revolution.* V P n (not pron), Also V n P

let on. If you do not **let on** that something is true, you do not tell anyone that it is true, and you keep it a secret; an informal expression. *She never let on that anything was wrong... I didn't let on to the staff what my conversation was... He knows the culprit but is not letting on.* PHRASAL VERB usu with brd-neg, V P that/wh, V P *to* n that/wh, V P

let out PHRASAL VERB

1 If something or someone **lets** water, air, or breath **out**, they allow it to flow out or escape. *It lets sunlight in but doesn't let heat out... Meer let out his breath in a long sigh.* V n P, V P n (not pron)

2 If you **let out** a particular sound, you make that sound; used in written English. *When she saw him, she let out a cry of horror.* V P n (not pron), Also V n P

3 See also **let** 14.

let up. If an unpleasant, continuous process **lets up**, it stops or its intensity is reduced. *The traffic in this city never lets up, even at night... The rain had let up.* • See also **let-up**. PHRASAL VERB oft with brd-neg =ease off, V P

let-down, let-downs; also spelled **letdown**. A **let-down** is a disappointment that you suffer, usually because something has not happened in the way in which you expected it to happen. *The flat was really very nice, but compared with what we'd been used to, it was a terrible let-down... The sense of let-down today is all the greater because in the past doctors have been over-confident about these treatments.* N-VAR =disappointment

lethal /liːθəl/ ◆◆◇◇◇

1 A substance that is **lethal** can kill people or animals. *...a lethal dose of sleeping pills. ...chemicals lethal to fish and aquatic mammals.* ADJ-GRADED

2 If you describe something as **lethal**, you mean that it is capable of causing a lot of damage. *High-powered cars are lethal weapons in the hands of inexperienced drivers... Shearer was the most lethal striker in British football.* ADJ-GRADED

lethargic /lɪθɑːrdʒɪk/. If you are **lethargic**, you do not have much energy or enthusiasm. *He felt too miserable and lethargic to get dressed.* ◆◇◇◇◇ ADJ-GRADED ≠energetic

lethargy /leθərdʒi/. **Lethargy** is the condition or state of being lethargic. *Symptoms include tiredness, paleness, and lethargy. ...the lethargy that plagued this project from its outset.* ◆◇◇◇◇ N-UNCOUNT

let's /lets/. In informal English, **let us** is usually said or written as **let's**. ◆◆◆◆◇

letter /letər/ **letters** ◆◆◆◆◆

1 If you write a **letter** to someone, you write a message on paper and send it to them, usually by post. *I had received a letter from a very close friend. ...a letter of resignation... Our long courtship had been conducted mostly by letter.* N-COUNT: also *by* N

2 **Letters** are written symbols which represent one of the sounds in a language. *...the letters of the alphabet. ...the letter E.* N-COUNT

3 See also **capital letter**, **covering letter**, **dead letter**, **love letter**, **newsletter**, **poison-pen letter**.

4 If you say that someone keeps to **the letter of the law** , you mean that they act according to what is actually written in the law, rather than according to the general principles of it, especially when you disapprove of this. *They had stuck to the letter of the law and in my view they should be ashamed.* PHRASES prep PHR, PHR after v ≠spirit of the law

5 If you say that someone carries out instructions **to the letter**, you mean that they do exactly what PHR after v they are told to do, paying great attention to every detail. *She obeyed his instructions to the letter.*

letter bomb, letter bombs. A **letter bomb** is a small bomb which is disguised as a letter or parcel and sent to someone through the post. It is designed to explode when it is opened. N-COUNT

letterbox /letəʳbɒks/ **letterboxes;** also spelled **letter box.** A **letterbox** is a rectangular hole in a door or a small box at the entrance to a building into which letters and small parcels are delivered. Compare **post box**, used mainly in British English. *A video tape arrived through my letterbox the other day.* N-COUNT

lettered /letəʳd/. Something that is **lettered** is covered or decorated with letters or words. *...a crudely lettered cardboard sign.* ADJ

letterhead /letəʳhed/ **letterheads.** A **letterhead** is the name and address of a person, company, or organization which is printed at the top of their writing paper. *Colleagues at work enjoy having a letterhead with their name at the top.* N-COUNT

lettering /letərɪŋ/. **Lettering** is writing, especially when you are describing the type of letters used. *...a small blue sign with white lettering.* N-UNCOUNT: usu supp N

lettuce /letɪs/ **lettuces.** A **lettuce** is a plant with large green leaves that is the basic ingredient of many salads. ◆◇◇◇◇ N-VAR

let-up. If there is no **let-up** in something, usually something unpleasant, there is no reduction in the intensity of it. *There was no let-up in the battle on the money markets yesterday... There were no signs of any let-up in job-shedding.* N-UNCOUNT: also *a* N, usu with brd-neg

leukaemia /luki:miə/; spelled **leukemia** in American English. **Leukaemia** is a disease of the blood in which the body produces too many white blood cells. ◆◇◇◇◇ N-UNCOUNT

level /levəl/ **levels, levelling, levelled;** spelled **leveling, leveled** in American English. ◆◆◆◆◆

1 A **level** is a point on a scale, for example a scale of amount, quality, or difficulty. *If you don't know your cholesterol level, it's a good idea to have it checked... Michael's roommate had been pleasant on a superficial level... We do have the lowest level of inflation for some years... The exercises are marked according to their level of difficulty.* N-COUNT: with supp

2 The **level** of a river, lake, or ocean or the **level** of liquid in a container is the height of its surface. *The water level of the Mississippi River is already 6.5 feet below normal... The gauge relies upon a sensor in the tank to relay the fuel level.* ● see also **sea level.** N-SING: *the* N

3 In cookery, a **level** spoonful of a substance such as flour or sugar is an amount that fills the spoon exactly, without going above the top edge. *Stir in 1 level teaspoon of yeast.* ADJ: ADJ n ≠heaped

4 If something is at a particular **level**, it is at that height. *Liz sank down until the water came up to her chin and the bubbles were at eye level.* N-SING: usu supp N

5 If one thing is **level** with another thing, it is at the same height as it. *He leaned over the counter so his face was almost level with the boy's... Amy knelt down so that their eyes were level.* ADJ: v-link ADJ, oft ADJ *with* n

6 When something is **level**, it is completely flat with no part higher than any other. *The floor was level, but the ceiling sloped toward his head. ...a plateau of fairly level ground.* ADJ-GRADED

7 If you draw **level** with someone or something, you get closer to them until you are by their side; used mainly in British English. *Just before we drew level with the gates, he slipped out of the jeep and disappeared into the crowd... When the car had pulled level with him, he had spoken into the lowered passenger window.* ► Also an adjective. *He waited until they were level with the door before he pivoted around sharply and punched Graham hard on the side of the head.* ADV: ADV after v; ADJ: v-link ADJ, oft ADJ *with* n

8 If you draw **level** with someone, you manage to improve your performance until it is the same as their's, by scoring the same number of points or goals as them. *Napoli have drawn level with AC Milan at the top of the Italian league.* ► Also an adjective. *The teams were level at the end of extra time.* ADV: ADV after v; ADJ: usu v-link ADJ

9 In sport, if a player or team **levels** the score, they score a goal or achieve some points so that their team has the same number of points or goals as the opposing team. *Iglesias scored twice to level the score... The Cincinnati Reds have levelled the score in the National League play-off against the Pittsburgh Pirates.* VERB; V n

10 If you keep your voice **level**, you speak in a deliberately calm and unemotional way; used in written English. *He forced his voice to remain level... When Julie speaks of her disability, she talks in the same calm, level tones she uses to discuss her A level prospects.* ADJ-GRADED

11 If someone or something such as a violent storm **levels** a building or area of land, they flatten or demolish it completely. *Further tremors could level more buildings... The storm was the most powerful to hit Hawaii this century. It leveled sugar plantations and destroyed homes.* VERB; V n

12 If an accusation or criticism is **levelled** at someone, they are criticized for something they have done or are accused of doing something wrong. *Allegations of corruption were levelled at him and his family... He leveled bitter criticism against the US.* VERB; be V-ed *at/against* n; V n *at/against* n; Also V n

13 If you **level** an object at someone or something, you lift it and point it in their direction. *He said thousands of Koreans still levelled guns at one another along the demilitarised zone between them.* VERB; V n *at* n; Also V n

14 If you **level** with someone, you tell them the truth and do not keep anything secret; an informal expression. *I'll level with you. I'm no great detective. I've no training or anything... He has leveled with the American people about his role in the affair.* VERB; V *with* n

15 See also **A level, O level.**

16 If you say that you will **do** your **level best** to do something, you are emphasizing that you will try as hard as you can to do it, often when the situation makes it very difficult. *The President told American troops that he would do his level best to bring them home soon.* PHRASES; V inflects, usu PHR to-inf; PRAGMATICS

17 If you say that someone or something is **on the level**, you mean they are sincere or honest, and are not attempting to deceive people; an informal expression. *There were probably moments when you wondered if anyone spoke the truth or was on the level.* v-link PHR

18 ● **a level playing field**: see **playing field.**

level off or **level out** PHRASAL VERB

1 If something that is progressing or developing **levels off** or **levels out**, it stops growing or diminishing at such a fast speed. *The figures show evidence that murders in the nation's capital are beginning to level off... Inflation is finally levelling out at around 11% a month.* V P; V P prep

2 If an aircraft **levels off** or **levels out**, it travels horizontally after having been travelling in an upwards or downwards direction. *The aircraft levelled out at about 30,000 feet.* V P

level out. See **level off.** PHRASAL VERB

level crossing, level crossings. In British English, a **level crossing** is a place where a railway line crosses a road. The usual American term is **grade crossing** or **railroad crossing.** N-COUNT

level-headed. If you describe a person as **level-headed**, you mean that they are calm and sensible even in difficult situations. *Simon is level-headed and practical... His level-headed approach suggests he will do what is necessary.* ADJ-GRADED =sensible

leveller /levələʳ/ **levellers;** spelled **leveler** in American English. If you describe something as a **leveller**, you mean that it makes all people seem the same, regardless of factors such as age, race, and social status. *The computer is a leveller, making information available to everyone... Violence is a dangerous leveller.* N-COUNT: usu sing, oft adj N

level pegging; also spelled **level-pegging.** If two opponents in a competition or contest are **level pegging**, they are equal with each other; used mainly in British English. *An opinion poll published in May showed Mrs Yardley was level-pegging with Mr Simpson.* ADJ: v-link ADJ, oft ADJ *with* n

lever /liːvəʳ, AM lev-/ **levers, levering, levered** ◆◇◇◇◇

1 A **lever** is a handle or bar that is attached to a piece of machinery which you push or pull in order to operate the machinery. *Push the tiny lever on the lock and let the door lock itself... The taps have a lever to control the mix of hot and cold water.* ● See also **gear lever**. N-COUNT

2 A **lever** is a long bar, one end of which is placed under a heavy object so that when you press down on the other end you can move the object. N-COUNT

3 If you **lever** something in a particular direction, you move it there, especially by using a lot of effort. *Neighbours eventually levered open the door with a crowbar... Insert the fork about 6in. from the root and simultaneously lever it backwards... Alex levered himself up from the sofa.* VERB V n with adj V n adv/prep V pron-refl adv/prep Also V, V n

4 A **lever** is an idea or action that you can use to make people do what you want them to do, rather than what they want to do. *Radical, militant factions want to continue using the hostages as a lever to gain concessions fron the west.* N-COUNT

leverage /liːvərɪdʒ, AM lev-/ **leverages, leveraging, leveraged** ◆◆◇◇◇

1 **Leverage** is the ability to influence situations or people so that you can control what happens to them. *His function as a Mayor affords him the leverage to get things done through attending committee meetings.* N-UNCOUNT

2 **Leverage** is the force that is applied to an object when something such as a lever is used. *The spade and fork have longer shafts, providing better leverage.* N-UNCOUNT

3 In business, to **leverage** a company or investment means to use borrowed money in order to buy it or pay for it. *Traditional criticisms of leveraging an airline no longer bar transactions.* VERB V n
♦ **leveraged** *The committee voted to limit tax refunds for corporations involved in leveraged buyouts.* ADJ-GRADED: usu ADJ n

leviathan /lɪvaɪəθən/ **leviathans.** A **leviathan** is something which is extremely large and difficult to control, and which you find rather frightening; a literary word. *Democracy survived the Civil War and the developing industrial leviathan and struggled on into the twentieth century.* N-COUNT: usu sing

Levi's /liːvaɪz/; also spelled **Levis**. **Levi's** are jeans. **Levi's** is a trademark. N-PLURAL: also *a pair of* N

levitate /levɪteɪt/ **levitates, levitating, levitated.** If someone **levitates**, they rise and float in the air without any support from other people or objects, usually through meditation. If someone appears to **levitate** something, they appear to make it rise into the air without touching or supporting it, by using magic. *The film shows the shaman levitating into the air and then floating across the room... They've managed to levitate a goldfish bowl, hardly perhaps the most useful thing to want to do.* ♦ **levitation** /levɪteɪʃən/ *...such magical powers as levitation, prophecy, and healing.* ◆◇◇◇◇ VERB V V n N-UNCOUNT

levity /levɪti/. **Levity** is behaviour that shows a tendency to treat serious matters in a non-serious way; a literary word. *At the time, Arnold had disapproved of such levity.* N-UNCOUNT =frivolity

levy /levi/ **levies, levying, levied** ◆◆◇◇◇

1 A **levy** is a sum of money that you have to pay, for example as a tax to the government. *...an annual motorway levy on all drivers.* N-COUNT

2 If a government or organization **levies** a tax or other sum of money, it demands it from people or organizations. *They levied religious taxes on Christian commercial transactions... Taxes should not be levied without the authority of Parliament.* VERB V n *on* n V n

lewd /ljuːd, AM luːd/. If you describe someone's behaviour as **lewd**, you are critical of them because you think they are interested in sex in a crude and unpleasant way. *Drew spends all day eyeing up the women and making lewd comments.* ♦ **lewdness** *The critics condemned the play for lewdness.* ADJ-GRADED PRAGMATICS N-UNCOUNT

lexical /leksɪkəl/. **Lexical** means relating to the words of a language. *We chose a few of the commonest lexical items in the languages.* ADJ: usu ADJ n

lexicography /leksɪkɒgrəfi/. **Lexicography** is the activity or profession of writing and editing dictionaries. ♦ **lexicographer, lexicographers** *A lexicographer's job is to describe the language.* N-UNCOUNT N-COUNT

lexicon /leksɪkən/ **lexicons**

1 The **lexicon** of a particular subject is all the terms associated with it. The **lexicon** of a person or group is all the words they commonly use. *...the lexicon of management... Chocolate equals sin in most people's lexicon.* N-SING: with supp

2 A **lexicon** is an alphabetical list of words of a language or of a particular subject. N-COUNT

3 A **lexicon** is a dictionary, especially of a very old language such as Greek or Hebrew; an old-fashioned use. N-COUNT

lexis /leksɪs/. In linguistics, the words of a language can be referred to as the **lexis** of that language. N-UNCOUNT =vocabulary

liability /laɪəbɪlɪti/ **liabilities** ◆◆◇◇◇

1 If you say that someone or something is a **liability**, you mean that they cause a lot of problems or embarrassment. *As the president's prestige continues to fall, they're clearly beginning to consider him a liability... Many commentators see the new local tax as the Conservatives' biggest political liability.* N-COUNT: usu sing

2 A company or organization's **liabilities** are the sums of money which it owes; a technical use in economics, finance, and law. *The company had assets of $138 million and liabilities of $120.5 million.* N-COUNT: usu pl ≠asset

3 See also **liable**.

liable /laɪəbəl/ ◆◆◇◇◇

1 When something **is liable to** happen, it is very likely to happen. *Only a small minority of the mentally ill are liable to harm themselves or others.* PHR-MODAL =be likely to

2 If people or things are **liable to** something unpleasant, they are likely to experience it or do it. *She will grow into a woman particularly liable to depression... Steroids are used to reduce the inflammation, which makes the muscles of the airways liable to constriction.* ADJ-GRADED: v-link ADJ *to* n =prone

3 If you are **liable** for something such as a debt, you are legally responsible for it. *The airline's insurer is liable for damages to the victims' families... As the killings took place outside British jurisdiction, the Ministry of Defence could not be held liable.* ADJ: v-link ADJ, usu ADJ *for* n
♦ **liability** /laɪəbɪlɪti/ *He is claiming damages from London Underground, which has admitted liability but dispute the amount of his claim.* N-UNCOUNT

liaise /lieɪz/ **liaises, liaising, liaised.** When organizations or people **liaise**, or when one organization **liaises** with another, they work together and keep each other fully informed about what is happening; used mainly in British English. *Detectives are liaising with Derbyshire police following the bomb explosion early today... The three groups will all liaise with each other to help the child... Social services and health workers liaise closely.* ◆◇◇◇◇ V-RECIP V *with* n pl-n V *with* pron-recip pl-n V Also V *between* pl-n

liaison /lieɪzɒn, AM liːeɪz-/ **liaisons** ◆◇◇◇◇

1 **Liaison** is cooperation and the exchange of information between different organizations or between different sections of an organization. *Liaison between police forces and the art world is vital to combat art crime. ...those who work in close liaison with alcoholics.* N-UNCOUNT

2 If someone acts as **liaison** between two or more groups, their job is to encourage cooperation and the exchange of information between those groups. *I have a professor on my staff here as liaison with our higher education institutions... She acts as a liaison between patients and staff.* N-UNCOUNT: also *a* N, oft N *with* n

3 You can refer to a sexual or romantic relationship between two people as a **liaison**. *She embarked on a series of sexual liaisons with society figures.* N-COUNT =affair

liar /laɪəʳ/ **liars.** If you say that someone is a **liar**, you mean that they tell lies. *He was a liar and a cheat... 'She seems at times an accomplished liar,' he said.* ◆◇◇◇◇ N-COUNT

lib /lɪb/. **Lib** is an abbreviation for 'liberation'. It is used in the names of some political movements that are concerned with freeing people from governments or traditional ideas which the members believe to be oppressive. *...Women's Lib.* ● See also **ad-lib**. ◆◇◇◇◇ N-UNCOUNT

libation /laɪbeɪʃən/ **libations.** In ancient Greece and Rome, a **libation** was an alcoholic drink that was offered to the gods; a literary word. *At the shrine of the god there were offerings, libations and incense.* N-COUNT

Lib Dem /lɪb dem/ **Lib Dems.** In Britain, you can refer to the Liberal Democrat Party or its members as **the Lib Dems**. *Three published polls all revealed the Lib Dems gaining ground at the Tories' expense. ...Lib-Dem councillors.* ◆◇◇◇◇ N-PROPER: the N, N n

libel /laɪbəl/ **libels, libelling, libelled;** spelled **libeling, libeled** in American English. ◆◆◇◇◇

1 Libel is something in writing which wrongly accuses someone of something, and which is therefore against the law; a legal use. Compare **slander**. *Warren sued him for libel over the remarks... If the jury decided there was a libel, it would have to consider its effect on Miss Smith's position. ...a libel action against the paper.* N-VAR

2 To **libel** someone means to write or print something in a book or a newspaper which wrongly damages that person's reputation and is therefore against the law; a legal use. *The newspaper which libelled him had already offered compensation.* VERB V n

libellous /laɪbələs/; spelled **libelous** in American English. If something in a book, newspaper, or magazine is **libellous**, it wrongly accuses someone of something, and is therefore against the law. *He claimed the articles were libellous and damaging to the interests of the team.* ADJ-GRADED

liberal /lɪbərəl/ **liberals** ◆◆◆◆◇

1 Someone who has **liberal** views is tolerant of different behaviour or opinions, and believes people should be free to do or think as they like. *She is known to have liberal views on divorce and contraception.* ► Also a noun. *...a nation of free-thinking liberals.* ADJ-GRADED: usu ADJ n; N-COUNT

2 A **liberal** system allows people or organizations a lot of political or economic freedom. *...a liberal democracy with a multiparty political system... They favour liberal free-market policies.* ► Also a noun. *These kinds of price controls go against all the financial principles of the free market liberals.* ADJ-GRADED: usu ADJ n; N-COUNT

3 A **Liberal** politician or voter is a member of a Liberal Party or votes for a Liberal Party. *The Liberal leader has announced his party's withdrawal from the ruling coalition.* ► Also a noun. *The Liberals hold twenty-three seats in parliament.* ADJ: ADJ n; N-COUNT

4 Liberal means giving, using, or taking a lot of something, or existing in large quantities. *As always he is liberal with his jokes... She made liberal use of her elder sister's make-up and clothes.* ♦ **liberally** *Chemical products were used liberally over agricultural land.* ADJ-GRADED: oft ADJ with n =generous; ADV-GRADED: ADV with v

Liberal Democrat, Liberal Democrats. In Britain, a **Liberal Democrat** is a member of the Liberal Democrat Party. ◆◆◇◇◇ N-PROPER

Liberal Democrat Party. **The Liberal Democrat Party** is the third largest political party in Britain and the main centre party. It believes in reforming the constitution and establishing proportional representation in British elections. N-PROPER: the N, N n

liberalism /lɪbərəlɪzəm/ ◆◇◇◇◇

1 Liberalism is a belief in gradual social progress by reform and by changing laws, rather than by revolution. *...a democrat who has decided that economic liberalism is the best way to secure change. ...the tradition of nineteenth-century liberalism.* N-UNCOUNT

2 Liberalism is the belief that people should have a lot of political and individual freedom. *He was concerned over growing liberalism in the Church.* N-UNCOUNT

liberalize /lɪbrəlaɪz/ **liberalizes, liberalizing, liberalized;** also spelled **liberalise** in British English. When a country or government **liberalizes**, or **liberalizes** its laws or its attitudes, it becomes less strict and allows people more freedom in their actions. *...authoritarian states that have only now begun to liberalise. ...the decision to liberalize travel restrictions.* ♦ **liberalization** /lɪbrəlaɪzeɪʃən/ *...the liberalization of divorce laws in the late 1960s.* ◆◆◇◇◇ VERB V; V n; N-UNCOUNT: oft N of n =relaxation

Liberal Party. In Britain, **the Liberal Party** was a political party which believed in limited controls on industry, the provision of welfare services, and more local government and individual freedom. **Liberal Party** is also used to refer to similar parties in some other countries. ◆◇◇◇◇ N-PROPER: the N, N n

liberate /lɪbəreɪt/ **liberates, liberating, liberated** ◆◆◆◇◇

1 To **liberate** a place or the people in it means to free them from the political or military control of another country, area, or group of people. *They planned to march on and liberate the city... They made a triumphal march into their liberated city.* ♦ **liberation** /lɪbəreɪʃən/ *...a mass liberation movement.* VERB V n; V-ed; N-UNCOUNT

2 To **liberate** someone from something means to help them escape from it or overcome it, and lead a better way of life. *He asked how committed the leadership was to liberating its people from poverty.* ♦ **liberating** *If you have the chance to spill your problems out to a therapist it can be a very liberating experience.* ♦ **liberation** *...the women's liberation movement.* VERB =free; V n from n; Also V n; ADJ-GRADED; N-UNCOUNT

3 To **liberate** a prisoner or hostage means to set them free. *The government is devising a plan to liberate prisoners held in detention camps.* VERB V n

liberated /lɪbəreɪtɪd/. If you describe someone as **liberated**, you mean that they do not accept their society's traditional values or restrictive way of behaving. *She was determined that she would become a liberated businesswoman.* ADJ-GRADED =emancipated

liberation theology. **Liberation theology** is a belief based on radical interpretations of the Scriptures which says that the Church should become actively involved in politics in order to bring about social change. N-UNCOUNT

liberator /lɪbəreɪtər/ **liberators.** A **liberator** is someone who sets people free from a system, situation, or set of ideas that restricts them in some way; a formal word. *We were the people's liberators from the Bolsheviks.* N-COUNT

Liberian /laɪbɪəriən/ **Liberians** ◆◆◆◆◇

1 Liberian means belonging or relating to Liberia, its people, or its culture. ADJ

2 A **Liberian** is a person who comes from Liberia, or a person of Liberian origin. N-COUNT

libertarian /lɪbəteəriən/ **libertarians.** If someone is **libertarian** or has **libertarian** attitudes, they believe in or support the idea that people should be free to think and behave in the way that they want; a formal word. *...the libertarian argument that people should be allowed to choose... The town's political climate was libertarian.* ► A **libertarian** is someone who with libertarian views. *Libertarians argue that nothing should be censored.* ◆◇◇◇◇ ADJ =liberal; N-COUNT =liberal

libertine /lɪbətiːn/ **libertines.** If you refer to someone as a **libertine**, you think they are immoral and unscrupulous in their sexual activities and do not care about the effect their behaviour has on other people; a literary word. *...a self-confessed coward, libertine, and scoundrel.* N-COUNT

liberty /lɪbəti/ **liberties** ◆◆◆◇◇

1 Liberty is the freedom to live your life in the way that you want, without interference from other people or the authorities. *...the ideal of equality and the appreciation of liberty... Such a system would be a fundamental blow to the rights and liberties of the English people.* ● See also **civil liberties**. N-VAR =freedom

2 Liberty is the freedom to go wherever you want, which you lose when you are a prisoner. *Why not say that three convictions before court for stealing cars means three months' loss of liberty... There is no formal confirmation so far that he is at liberty.* N-UNCOUNT: oft at N

3 If someone is **at liberty** to do something, they have been given permission to do it. *The island's in* PHRASES PHR to-inf, usu v-link PHR *the Pacific Ocean; I'm not at liberty to say exactly where, because we're still negotiating for its purchase.* =able

4 If you say that you have **taken the liberty of** doing something, you are saying that you have done it without asking permission. People say this when they do not think that anyone will mind what they have done. *I took the liberty of going into Assunta's wardrobe, as it was open; I was looking for a towel.* V inflects, PHR -ing PRAGMATICS

5 If you **take liberties** or **take a liberty** with someone or something, you act without caution or without concern for that thing or person, for example because you know the person well and think they will not mind. *You had to try and retain the excitement of the event in your writing, without taking liberties with the truth... She knew she was taking a big liberty in developing Mick's photos without his knowledge.* V and N inflect, oft PHR *with* n

libidinous /lɪbɪdɪnəs/. People who are **libidinous** have strong sexual feelings and express them in their behaviour; a literary word. *Powell let his libidinous imagination run away with him.* ADJ-GRADED =lustful

libido /lɪbiːdoʊ/ **libidos.** A person's **libido** is the part of their personality that is considered to cause their emotional, especially sexual, desires. *A flagging libido and a drop in sexual performance are all part of the ageing process... Lack of sleep is a major factor in loss of libido.* N-VAR

Libra /liːbrə/ **Libras** ◆◆◇◇◇

1 **Libra** is one of the twelve signs of the zodiac. Its symbol is a pair of scales. People who are born approximately between the 23rd of September and the 22nd of October come under this sign. N-UNCOUNT

2 A **Libra** is a person whose sign of the zodiac is Libra. N-COUNT

librarian /laɪbreəriən/ **librarians.** A **librarian** is a person who is in charge of a library or who has been specially trained to work in a library. ◆◇◇◇◇ N-COUNT

library /laɪbrəri, AM -breri/ **libraries** ◆◆◆◇◇

1 A public **library** is a building where things such as books, newspapers, videos, and music are kept for people to read, use, or borrow. *...the local library... She issued them library cards.* N-COUNT

2 A private **library** is a collection of things such as books or music, that is normally only used with the permission of the owner. *My thanks go to the British School of Osteopathy, for the use of their library.* N-COUNT

3 In some large houses the **library** is the room where most of the books are kept. *Guests were rarely entertained in the library.* N-COUNT

librettist /lɪbretɪst/ **librettists.** A **librettist** is a person who writes the words that are used in an opera or musical play. N-COUNT

libretto /lɪbretoʊ/ **librettos** or **libretti.** The **libretto** of an opera is the words that are sung in it. *...the author of one or two opera librettos.* N-COUNT

Libyan /lɪbiən/ **Libyans** ◆◆◆◆◇

1 **Libyan** means belonging or relating to Libya, or to its people or culture. *...the Libyan desert.* ADJ

2 A **Libyan** is a Libyan citizen, or a person of Libyan origin. N-COUNT

lice /laɪs/. **Lice** is the plural of **louse.**

licence /laɪsᵊns/ **licences;** spelled **license** in American English. ◆◆◆◇◇

1 A **licence** is an official document which gives you permission to do, use, or own something. *Smith, who did not have a licence, admitted driving without due care and attention... The painting was returned to Spain on a temporary import licence... It gained a licence to operate as a bank from the Bank of England in 1981.* N-COUNT =permit

2 If you say that something gives someone **licence** or a **licence** to act in a particular way, you disapprove of the fact that it gives them an excuse to behave in an irresponsible or excessive way. *The ANC claimed the curfew gave licence to the police to hunt people as if they were animals... 'Dropping the charges has given racists a licence to kill,' said Jim's aunt.* N-UNCOUNT: also a N, N to-inf PRAGMATICS

3 See also **poetic licence.**

4 If you describe a commercial activity as **a licence to print money**, you disapprove of the fact that it allows people to gain a lot of money with little effort or responsibility. *Running a television company may no longer be a licence to print money, but it is still highly rewarding.* PHRASES v-link PHR PRAGMATICS

5 If someone does something **under licence**, they do it by special permission from a government or other authority. *...a company which made the Mig-21 jet fighter under licence from Russia.* PHR after v

license /laɪsᵊns/ **licenses, licensing, licensed.** ◆◆◇◇◇ VERB If a government or other authority **licenses** a person, organization, or activity, they officially give permission for the person or organization to do something, or for the activity to take place. *...a proposal that would require the state to license guns... Under the agreement, the council can license a U.S. company to produce the drug.* V n, V n to-inf, Also V n *to* n

licensed /laɪsᵊnst/ ◆◇◇◇◇

1 If you are **licensed** to do something, you have official permission from the government or from the authorities to do it. *There were about 250 people on board, about 100 more than the ferry was licensed to carry. ...a licensed doctor.* ADJ: oft ADJ to-inf

2 If something that you own or use is **licensed** you have official permission to own it or use it. *While searching the house they discovered an unlicensed shotgun and a licensed rifle.* ADJ

3 If a place such as a restaurant, hotel, or casino is **licensed**, it has been given a licence to sell alcoholic drinks; used mainly in British English. *...licensed premises... The restaurant is licensed, offering draught beers, wines, spirits and soft drinks.* ADJ

licensee /laɪsᵊnsiː/ **licensees**

1 A **licensee** is a person or organization that has been given a licence; a formal use. N-COUNT

2 In British English, a **licensee** is someone who has been given a licence to sell alcoholic drinks, for example in a pub. N-COUNT

license number, license numbers. In American English, the **license number** of a car or other road vehicle is the series of letters and numbers that are shown at the front and back of it. The British term is **registration number.** N-COUNT

license plate, license plates. In American English, a **license plate** is a sign on the front and back of a vehicle that shows its registration number. The British expression is **number plate.** N-COUNT

licensing laws. In Britain, **licensing laws** are the laws which control the selling of alcoholic drinks. N-PLURAL

licentious /laɪsenʃəs/. If you describe a person as **licentious**, you disapprove of them because you think they are very immoral, especially in their sexual behaviour; a formal word. *...alarming stories of licentious behaviour.* ADJ-GRADED PRAGMATICS ♦ **licentiousness** *...moral licentiousness.* N-UNCOUNT

lichen /laɪkən/ **lichens. Lichen** is a cluster of tiny plants that looks like moss and grows on the surface of things such as rocks, trees, and walls. ◆◇◇◇◇ N-MASS

lick /lɪk/ **licks, licking, licked** ◆◇◇◇◇

1 When people or animals **lick** something, they move your tongue across its surface. *She folded up her letter, licking the envelope flap with relish... The dog rose awkwardly to his feet and licked the man's hand excitedly.* ► Also a noun. *He wouldn't lend the lollipop he was licking. Kevin, who was a year older, wanted a lick.* VERB V n; N-COUNT: usu sing

2 If you **lick** someone or something, you easily defeat them in a fight or competition; an informal use. *He might be able to lick us all in a fair fight... The Chancellor's upbeat message that the Government had licked inflation for good was marred by more job losses.* VERB =beat V n

3 When flames of a large fire **lick** somewhere or something, the fire begins to reach that place or thing and the flames touch it lightly and briefly; a literary use. *The fire came roaring through the kitchen ceiling and sent its red tongues licking into the entrance hall... The apex of the flames licked the crimson sky.* VERB V prep/adv V n

4 A **lick** of something is a small amount of it; an N-COUNT:

informal use. *It could do with a lick of paint to brighten up its premises.* usu N of n =spot

5 A **lick** is a short piece of music which is part of a song and played on a guitar; an informal use. *...the screeching licks of heavy metal guitar.* N-COUNT

6 • to **lick** your **lips**: see **lip.** • to **lick into shape**: see **shape.** • to **lick** your **wounds**: see **wound.**

licking /lɪkɪŋ/ **lickings.** A **licking** is a severe defeat by someone in a fight, battle, or competition. *They gave us a hell of a licking.* N-COUNT: usu sing =thrashing

licorice /lɪkərɪʃ, -ɪs/. See **liquorice.**

lid /lɪd/ **lids** ◆◆◇◇◇

1 A **lid** is the top of a box or other container which can be removed or raised when you want to open the container. N-COUNT =top

2 Your **lids** are the pieces of skin which cover your eyes when you close them. *A dull pain began to throb behind his lids.* N-COUNT: usu pl =eyelid

3 If you say that someone is keeping the **lid** on an activity or a piece of information, you mean that they are restricting the activity or are keeping the information secret; an informal use. *The soldiers' presence seemed to keep a lid on the violence... Their finance ministry is still trying to put a lid on the long-simmering securities scandal.* N-SING

4 If you say that you want to keep a **lid** on the cost of doing something, you mean that you want to prevent it costing you more than you feel is reasonable. *If our industry is to remain competitive it must mean keeping a lid on prices.* N-SING =limit

lidded /lɪdɪd/

1 **Lidded** is used to describe a container that has a lid. *...a lidded saucepan.* ADJ: ADJ n

2 When someone has **lidded** eyes, their eyelids are partly or fully closed; a literary use. *Julie squinted at her through lidded eyes... My own eyes had felt heavy-lidded, but now I was wide awake.* ADJ

lido /liːdoʊ/ **lidos.** A **lido** is an open-air swimming pool, or a part of a beach, which is used by the public for swimming or water sports; used mainly in British English. N-COUNT

lie 1 position or situation

lie /laɪ/ **lies, lying, lay, lain** ◆◆◆◆◇

1 If you **are lying** somewhere, you are in a horizontal position and are not standing or sitting. *There was a child lying on the ground... The injured man was lying motionless on his back... He lay awake watching her for a long time.* VERB V prep/adv V adj

2 If an object **lies** in a particular place, it is in a flat position in that place. *...a newspaper lying on a nearby couch... Broken glass lay scattered on the carpet. ...a two-page memo lying unread on his desk.* VERB V prep/adv V adj

3 If you say that a place **lies** in a particular position or direction, you mean that it is situated there. *The islands lie at the southern end of the Kurile chain.* VERB =sit V prep/adv

4 You can use **lie** to say that something is or remains in a particular state or condition. For example, if something **lies forgotten**, it has been and remains forgotten. *She turned back to the Bible lying open in her lap... The picture lay hidden in the archives for over 40 years... His country's economy lies in ruins.* V-LINK =sit V adj V prep

5 You can use **lie** to say what position a competitor or team is in during a competition; used mainly in British English. *I was going well and was lying fourth... Blyth Tait is lying in second place.* VERB V ord V in n

6 You can talk about where something such as a problem, solution, or fault **lies** to say what you think it consists of, involves, or is caused by. *The problem lay in the large amounts spent on defence... They will only assume that, as a woman, the fault lies with me... He realised his future lay elsewhere... We must be clear about where the responsibility lies.* VERB =rest V prep/adv

7 You use **lie** in expressions such as **lie ahead, lie in store**, and **lie in wait** when you are talking about what someone is going to experience or face in the future, especially when it is something unpleasant or difficult. *She'd need all her strength and bravery to cope with what lay in store... The President's most serious challenges lie ahead.* VERB V prep/adv

8 **Lie** is used in formal English, especially on gravestones and memorials, to say that a dead person is buried in a particular place. *The inscription reads: Here lies Catin, the son of Magarus... My father lies in the small cemetery a few miles up this road.* VERB V prep/adv

9 If you say that light, clouds, or fog **lie** somewhere, you mean that they exist there or are spread over the area mentioned; a literary use. *It had been wet overnight, and a morning mist lay on the field.* VERB V prep/adv

10 The **lie** of an object or area is its position or the way that it is arranged. *The actual site of a city is determined by the natural lie of the land.* N-SING: with supp, oft N of n

11 • to **let sleeping dogs lie**: see **dog.** • to **lie in state**: see **state.** • to **take** something **lying down**: see **take.**

lie around; the form **lie about** is also used in British English. PHRASAL VERB

1 If things are left **lying around** or **lying about**, they are not tidied away but left casually somewhere where they can be seen. *People should be careful about their possessions and not leave them lying around... My dad had a couple of Bob Dylan and Beatles songbooks lying around the house.* V P V P n

2 If you **lie around** or **lie about**, you spend your time relaxing and being lazy; used in informal English. *I'll just lie around in the sun... On Sunday Cohen lay around the house all day.* =laze around V P V P n

lie back. If you **lie back**, you relax and lower yourself from a sitting position so that you are resting on your back. *He lay back and closed his eyes.* PHRASAL VERB V P

lie behind. If you refer to what **lies behind** a situation or event, you are referring to the reason the situation exists or the event happened. *It seems that what lay behind the clashes was disagreement over the list of candidates.* PHRASAL VERB V P n

lie down. When you **lie down**, you move into a horizontal position, usually in order to rest or sleep. *Why don't you go upstairs and lie down for a bit?* PHRASAL VERB V P

lie 2 things that are not true

lie /laɪ/ **lies, lying, lied** ◆◆◆◇◇

1 A **lie** is something that someone says or writes which they know is untrue. *'Who else do you work for?'—'No one.'—'That's a lie.'... I've had enough of your lies... All the boys told lies about their adventures.* • See also **white lie.** N-COUNT

2 If someone **is lying**, they are saying something which they know is not true. *I know he's lying... If asked, he lies about his age... She lied to her husband so she could meet her lover... He reportedly called her 'a lying little twit'.* ♦ **lying** *Lying is something that I will not tolerate.* VERB V V about n V to n V-ing N-UNCOUNT

3 If you say that something **lies**, you mean that it does not express or represent something exactly as it is in reality. *The camera sometimes lies.* VERB V

4 See also **lying.**

5 If something **gives the lie to** a statement, claim, or theory, it suggests or proves that it is not true. *This survey gives the lie to the idea that Britain is moving towards economic recovery.* PHRASES V inflects, PHR n

6 If you say that someone **is living a lie**, you mean that in every part of their life they are hiding the truth about themselves from other people. *My mother never told my father the truth about me. We've been living a lie all this time.* V inflects, usu cont

7 People sometimes say **'I tell a lie'** when they have just made a mistake in something that they are saying and immediately correct it; used mainly in British English. *It is the first scene of the play chronologically. I tell a lie, it's actually strictly speaking the second scene.* CONVENTION PRAGMATICS =sorry

lie detector, lie detectors. A **lie detector** is an electronic machine used mainly by the police to find out whether a suspect is telling the truth. It is attached to the suspect's body and records any changes in blood pressure, temperature, or breathing which might indicate that he or she is lying. *...the results of a lie detector test which he said proved his client's innocence.* N-COUNT: oft N n =polygraph

lie-down. If you have a **lie-down**, you have a short rest, usually in bed; used mainly in informal British English. *She had departed upstairs for a lie-down.* ◆◇◇◇◇ N-SING

lie-in, lie-ins. If you have a **lie-in**, you rest by staying in bed later than usual in the morning; used mainly in informal British English. *I have a lie-in on Sundays.* ◆◇◇◇◇ N-COUNT: usu sing

lieu /ljuː, AM luː/ ◆◇◇◇◇

1 If you do, get, or give one thing **in lieu of** another, you do, get, or give it instead of the other thing, because the two things are considered to be of the same value or importance; a formal use. *He left what little furniture he owned to his landlord in lieu of rent.* PHR-PREP =in place of

2 If you do, get, or give something **in lieu**, you do, get, or give it instead of something else, because the two things are considered to be of the same value or importance; a formal use. *...an increased salary or time off in lieu.* PHRASE

Lieut. **Lieut.** is a written abbreviation for **lieutenant** when 'lieutenant' is a person's title. *...Lieut. J. J. Doughty.* =Lt

lieutenant /leftenənt, AM luː-/ **lieutenants** ◆◆◇◇◇

1 A **lieutenant** is a person who holds a junior officer's rank in the army, navy, or air force, or in the American police force. *Lieutenant Campbell ordered the man at the wheel to steer for the gunboat.* N-COUNT; N-TITLE
► Also a combining form. *...Lieutenant Colonel Gale Carter.* COMB in N-TITLE

2 If you refer to someone as a person's **lieutenant**, you mean they are that person's assistant, especially their main assistant, in an organization or activity. *He was my right-hand man, my lieutenant on the field, a cool, calculated footballer.* N-COUNT: usu poss N =second-in-command

life /laɪf/ **lives** /laɪvz/ ◆◆◆◆◆

1 **Life** is the quality which people, animals, and plants have when they are not dead, and which objects and substances do not have. *...a baby's first minutes of life... Amnesty International opposes the death penalty as a violation of the right to life. ...the earth's supply of life-giving oxygen.* N-UNCOUNT

2 You can use **life** to refer to things or groups of things which are alive. *Is there life on Mars?... The book includes some useful facts about animal and plant life.* N-UNCOUNT: with supp

3 If you refer to someone's **life**, you mean their state of being alive, especially when there is a risk or danger of them dying. *Your life is in danger... A nurse began to try to save his life... The intense fighting is reported to have claimed many lives.* N-COUNT: usu poss N

4 Someone's **life** is the period of time during which they are alive. *He spent the last fourteen years of his life in retirement... For the first time in his life he regretted that he had no faith.* N-COUNT: poss N

5 You can use **life** to refer to a period of someone's life when they are in a particular situation or job. *Interior designers spend their working lives keeping up to date with the latest trends... That was the beginning of my life in the television business.* N-COUNT: with supp, usu poss N

6 You can use **life** to refer to particular activities which people regularly do during their lives. *My personal life has had to take second place to my career... Most diabetics have a normal sex life.* N-COUNT: supp N

7 You can use **life** to refer to the events and experiences that happen to people while they are alive. *Life won't be dull!... It's the people with insecurities who make life difficult. ...the sort of life we can only fantasise about living.* N-UNCOUNT

8 If you know a lot about **life**, you have gained many varied experiences, for example by travelling a lot and meeting different kinds of people. *I was 19 and too young to know much about life... I needed some time off from education to experience life.* N-UNCOUNT

9 You can use **life** to refer to the things that people do and experience that are characteristic of a particular place, group, or activity. *How did you adjust to college life?... Margaret Thatcher had dominated political life in Britain for over a decade. ...the culture and life of north Africa.* N-UNCOUNT: usu supp N

10 A person, place, or something such as a book, or film that is full of **life** gives an impression of excitement, energy, or cheerfulness. *The town itself was full of life and character... The rejection of the Jewish theme meant the rejection of everything that gave the script passion and life... He's sucked the life out of her.* N-UNCOUNT

11 A **life** of a person is a book or film which tells the story of their life. *A life of John Paul Jones had long interested him.* N-COUNT: oft N *of* n =biography

12 If someone is sentenced to **life**, they are sentenced to stay in prison for the rest of their life or for a very long period of time; an informal use. *He could get life in prison, if convicted.* N-UNCOUNT =life imprisonment

13 The **life** of something such as a machine, organization, or project is the period of time that it lasts for. *The repairs did not increase the value or the life of the equipment.* N-COUNT: with poss

14 In art, **life** refers to the producing of drawings, paintings, or sculptures that represent actual people, objects, or landscapes, rather than images from the artist's imagination. *...learning to draw from life... She had once posed for Life classes when she was an art student.* N-UNCOUNT

15 If you say that something or someone **is** your **life**, you are emphasizing that they are extremely important to you. *The Church is my life.* PHRASES V inflects PRAGMATICS

16 If you **bring** something **to life** or if it **comes to life**, it becomes interesting or exciting. *The cold, hard cruelty of two young men is vividly brought to life in this true story... Poems which had seemed dull and boring suddenly came to life.* V inflects

17 If something or someone **comes to life**, they become active. *The volcano came to life a week ago.* V inflects

18 If you talk about **life after death**, you are discussing the possibility that people may continue to exist in some form after they die. *I believe in life after death.*

19 If you say that someone **is fighting for** their **life**, you mean they are in a very serious condition and may die as a result of an accident or illness; used mainly in journalism. *He was in a critical condition, fighting for his life in hospital.* V inflects

20 **For life** means for the rest of a person's life. *He was jailed for life in 1966 for the murder of three policemen... She may have been scarred for life... There can be no jobs for life.* PHR after v, n PHR

21 If you say that you cannot understand or remember something **for the life of** you, you are emphasizing that you cannot understand or remember it, however hard you try; an informal expression. *I can't for the life of me understand why you didn't think of it.* with brd-neg, usu PHR before v, PHR with cl PRAGMATICS

22 If you say that someone does something **for dear life** or **for** their **life**, you mean that they do it using all their strength and effort because they are in a dangerous or urgent situation; an informal expression. *I made for the life raft and hung on for dear life.* PHR after v

23 If you say that someone **lives life to the full**, you mean that they make a deliberate effort to gain a lot from life by being always busy and trying new activities. V inflects

24 If you tell someone to **get a life**, you are expressing frustration with them because they do not have any interests or activities which you think would make their life interesting or worthwhile. PRAGMATICS

25 You can say **'Life goes on'** after mentioning something very sad to indicate that although people are very upset or affected by it, they have to carry on living normally. *I can't spend the rest of my life wishing it hadn't happened. Life goes on.* CONVENTION PRAGMATICS

26 If you say that you **have a life**, you mean that you have interests and activities, particularly outside your work, which make your life enjoyable and worthwhile. V and N inflect

27 If you talk about the man or woman **in** someone**'s life**, you mean the person they are having a relationship with, especially a sexual relationship. *There is a new man in her life.* usu n PHR

28 You can use **in all my life** or **in my life** to emphasize that you have never previously experienced something to such a degree. *I have never been so scared in all my life... I have never seen such a shambles in my life.* usu with brd-neg, usu PHR after v PRAGMATICS

29 You can use expressions such as **the fright of** your **life** or **the race of** your **life** to emphasize, for N inflects PRAGMATICS

example, that something has made you more frightened than you have ever been before or that you have run faster than you have ever run before. *A top reggae singer gave a young fan the thrill of her life when he serenaded her.*

30 If you say that someone or something is **larger than life**, you mean that they appear or behave in a way that seems more exaggerated or important than usual. *...not that we should expect all good publishers to be larger than life... Nobody takes seriously the improbable storylines and larger than life characters.* v-link PHR, PHR n

31 If someone **lays down** their **life** for another person, they die so that the other person can live; a literary expression. *Man can have no greater love than to lay down his life for his friends.* V inflects, usu PHR *for* n

32 If someone **risks life and limb**, they do something very dangerous in order to achieve something, usually in a very brave way. *Viewers will remember the dashing hero, Dirk, risking life and limb to rescue Daphne from the dragons.* V inflects

33 If you start **a new life**, you move to another place or country, or change your career, usually to try and recover from an unpleasant experience. *He had gone as far away as possible to build a new life.* N inflects

34 If someone says **'Not on your life'**, they are totally rejecting a suggestion that has been made; an informal expression. *'You should have given him a lift.'—'In that condition? Not on your life!'* CONVENTION PRAGMATICS =no way

35 If you **live** your **own life**, you live in the way that you want to and accept responsibility for your actions and decisions, without other people's advice or interference. *Adults need to live their own lives and that's difficult with children.* V and N inflect

36 If you say that something **rules** someone's **life**, you mean that it affects everything they do, usually in a negative way. *I'm going to stop letting drugs and drink rule my life.* V and N inflect

37 If you say that someone cannot do something **to save** their **life**, you are emphasizing that they do it very badly; an informal expression. *Winston could not have read the road signs to save his life.* N inflects, PHR after v PRAGMATICS

38 If you refer to someone as **the life and soul of the party** or as **the life and soul**, you mean that they are very lively and entertaining on social occasions, and are good at mixing with people; used mainly in British English. usu v-link PHR

39 If something **starts life** or **begins life** as a particular thing, it is that thing when it first starts to exist. *Herr's book started life as a dramatic screenplay.* V inflects, usu PHR *as* n

40 If someone **takes** another person's **life**, they kill them. If someone **takes** their own **life**, they kill themselves; a formal expression. *Before execution, he admitted to taking the lives of at least 35 more women... He helped his first wife take her life when she was dying of cancer.* V and N inflect

41 People say **'That's life'** after an unlucky, unpleasant, or surprising event to show that they realize such events happen occasionally and must be accepted. *'It never would have happened if Florette had not gone back for the book.'—'That's life.'* CONVENTION PRAGMATICS

42 You can use expressions such as **to come to life**, **to spring to life**, and **to roar into life** to indicate that a machine or vehicle suddenly starts working or moving; a literary use. *To his great relief the engine came to life... In the garden of the Savoy Hotel the sprinklers suddenly burst into life.* V inflects

43 People say **'What a life'** to indicate that they are very dissatisfied or are having great difficulties. *Here I am at a crummy hotel with no clean clothes, no money and suffering from shock. What a life!* CONVENTION PRAGMATICS

44 If you say that **life isn't worth living** without someone or something, or that someone or something **makes life worth living**, you mean that you cannot enjoy life without them. *Life is not worth living without food you can look forward to and enjoy!... Those are the moments which make life worth living.* V inflects

45 • See also **fact of life, kiss of life.** • **a matter of life and death**: see **death.** • **a new lease of life**: see **lease.** • to **have the time of** your **life**: see **time.** • **true to life**: see **true.**

life-and-death. See **death.**

life assurance. In British English, **life assurance** is the same as **life insurance.** *...a life assurance policy.* ◆◇◇◇◇ N-UNCOUNT

lifebelt /laɪfbelt/ **lifebelts.** A **lifebelt** is a large ring used to keep a person afloat and prevent them from drowning when they fall into the sea or other deep water. N-COUNT

lifeblood /laɪfblʌd/; also spelled **life-blood.** The **lifeblood** of an organization, area, or person is the most important thing that they need in order to exist, develop, or be successful. *Small businesses are the lifeblood of the economy... Coal and steel were the region's lifeblood.* N-SING: usu with poss

lifeboat /laɪfbout/ **lifeboats** ◆◇◇◇◇

1 A **lifeboat** is a medium-sized boat that is sent out from a port or harbour in order to rescue people who are in danger at sea. N-COUNT

2 A **lifeboat** is a small boat that is carried on a ship, which people on the ship use to escape when the ship is in danger of sinking. *The captain ordered all passengers and crew into lifeboats.* N-COUNT

life cycle, life cycles ◆◇◇◇◇

1 The **life cycle** of an animal or plant is the series of changes and developments that it passes through from the beginning of its life until its death. *The dormant period is another stage in the life cycle of the plant.* N-COUNT: usu with poss

2 The **life cycle** of something such as an idea, product, or organization is the series of developments that take place in it from its beginning until the end of its usefulness. *...the stages of the familial and economic life cycle... Each new product would have a relatively long life cycle.* N-COUNT

life-enhancing. If you describe something as **life-enhancing**, you mean that it makes you feel happier and more content. *...a life-enhancing and exciting trip... His letters, like his poetry, are life-enhancing and a delight.* ADJ-GRADED

life expectancy, life expectancies. The **life expectancy** of a person, animal, or plant is the length of time that they are normally likely to live. *The average life expectancy was 40... Smoking reduces life expectancy.* ◆◇◇◇◇ N-UNCOUNT: also N in pl =lifespan

life form, life forms. A **life form** is any living thing such as an animal or plant. N-COUNT: with supp

lifeguard /laɪfgɑːʳd/ **lifeguards.** A **lifeguard** is a person who works at a beach or swimming pool and rescues people when they are in danger of drowning. N-COUNT

life imprisonment. If someone is sentenced to **life imprisonment**, they are sentenced to stay in prison for the rest of their life, or for a very long period of time. ◆◇◇◇◇ N-UNCOUNT =life

life insurance. **Life insurance** is a form of insurance in which a person makes regular payments to an insurance company, in return for a sum of money to be paid to them when they reach a certain age, or to a person they have nominated, usually their spouse or children, when they die. *I have also taken out a life insurance policy on him just in case.* ◆◇◇◇◇ N-UNCOUNT =life assurance

life jacket, life jackets; also spelled **lifejacket.** In British English, a **life jacket** is a sleeveless jacket which keeps you afloat in water. The American word is **life preserver.** N-COUNT

lifeless /laɪfləs/ ◆◇◇◇◇

1 If a person or animal is **lifeless**, they are dead, or are so still that they appear to be dead. *Their cold-blooded killers had then dragged their lifeless bodies upstairs to the bathroom... There was no breathing or pulse and he was lifeless.* ADJ

2 If you describe an object or a machine as **lifeless**, you mean that they are not living things, even though they may resemble living things. *It was made of plaster, hard and white and lifeless, bearing no resemblance to human flesh.* ADJ =inanimate

3 A **lifeless** place or area does not have anything living or growing there at all. *Dry stone walls may* ADJ-GRADED *appear stark and lifeless, but they provide a valuable habitat for plants and animals.*

4 If you describe a person, or something such as an artistic performance or a town as **lifeless**, you mean they lack any lively or exciting qualities. *With one exception his novels are shallow and lifeless things. ...a lifeless portrait of an elderly woman.* ADJ-GRADED

lifelike /laɪflaɪk/

1 Something that is **lifelike** has the appearance of being alive. *...a lifelike doll.* ADJ-GRADED

2 A **lifelike** work of art is so skilfully done that it appears very like the person or thing that it is supposed to represent. *The painting depicted a hall so lifelike that a casual observer might believe himself to be looking through an open door.* ADJ-GRADED =realistic

lifeline /laɪflaɪn/ **lifelines.** A **lifeline** is something that enables an organization or group to survive or to continue with an activity. *Information about the job market can be a lifeline for those who are out of work... The orders will throw a lifeline to Britain's shipyards.* ◆◇◇◇◇ N-COUNT: oft N *for/to* n

lifelong /laɪflɒŋ, AM -lɔːŋ/. **Lifelong** means existing or happening for the whole of a person's life. *...her lifelong friendship with Naomi.* ◆◇◇◇◇ ADJ: ADJ n

life member, life members. If you are a **life member** of a club or organization, your membership will last for the rest of your life. N-COUNT: oft N *of* n

life peer, life peers. In Britain, a **life peer** is a person who is given a title such as 'Lord' or 'Lady' which they can use for the rest of their life but which they cannot pass on to their eldest child when they die. Life peers have the right to a seat in the House of Lords in the British parliament. *He was made a life peer in 1991.* N-COUNT

life preserver, life preservers. In American English, a **life-preserver** is a sleeveless jacket which keeps you afloat in water. The British term is **life jacket**. N-COUNT

lifer /laɪfəʳ/ **lifers.** A **lifer** is a criminal who has been given a life sentence; an informal word. N-COUNT

life raft, life rafts; also spelled **life-raft**. A **life raft** is a small boat which is carried on aeroplanes, helicopters, and large boats to be used in emergencies. Life rafts are usually inflatable. N-COUNT

lifesaver /laɪfseɪvəʳ/ **lifesavers.** If you say that something is a **lifesaver**, you mean that it helps people in a very important way, often in a way that is important to their health. *The cervical smear test is a lifesaver.* N-COUNT

life-saving. ◆◇◇◇◇

1 A **life-saving** drug, operation, or action is one that saves someone's life or is likely to save their life. *...life-saving drugs such as antibiotics... She decided her child should go to America for life-saving treatment.* ADJ: usu ADJ n

2 You use **life-saving** to refer to the skills and activities connected with rescuing people, especially people who are drowning. *She teaches swimming, lifesaving and water aerobics.* N-UNCOUNT

life science, life sciences. The **life sciences** are sciences such as zoology, botany, and anthropology, which are concerned with human beings, animals, and plants. N-COUNT: usu pl

life sentence, life sentences. If someone receives a **life sentence**, they are sentenced to stay in prison for the rest of their life, or for a very long period of time. *Some were serving life sentences for murder.* ◆◇◇◇◇ N-COUNT

life-size. A **life-size** representation of someone or something, for example a painting or sculpture, is the same size as the person or thing that they represent. *...a life-sized statue of an Indian boy.* ADJ

life-sized. **Life-sized** means the same as **life-size.** ADJ

lifespan /laɪfspæn/ **lifespans;** also spelled **life span.**

1 The **lifespan** of a person, animal, or plant is the period of time for which they live or are normally expected to live. *A 15-year lifespan is not uncommon for a dog... They have extended the potential life span of humanity everywhere.* N-VAR: oft with poss

2 The **lifespan** of a product, organization, or idea is the period of time for which it is expected to work properly or to last. *Most boilers have a lifespan of 15 to 20 years.* N-COUNT: oft with poss

lifestyle /laɪfstaɪl/ **lifestyles;** also spelled **life style** or **life-style.** The **lifestyle** of a particular person or group of people is the living conditions, behaviour, and habits that are typical of them or are chosen by them. *They enjoyed an income and lifestyle that many people would envy. ...the change of lifestyle occasioned by the baby's arrival.* 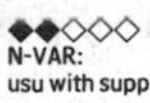 N-VAR: usu with supp

life-support machine, life-support machines. A **life-support machine** is the equipment that is used to keep a person alive when they are very ill and incapable of breathing without help; used mainly in British English. *He is in a coma and on a life-support machine.* N-COUNT

life-support system, life-support systems. A **life-support system** is the same as a **life-support machine.** N-COUNT

life's work. Someone's **life's work** or **life work** is the main activity that they have been involved in during their life, or their most important achievement. *An exhibition of his life's work is being shown in the garden of his home... My father's life work was devoted to the conservation of the Longleat estate.* N-SING: usu poss N

life-threatening. If someone has a **life-threatening** illness or is in a **life-threatening** situation, there is a strong possibility that the illness or the situation will kill them. *Anything but a rigorous approach is potentially life-threatening to patients.* ◆◇◇◇◇ ADJ: oft adv ADJ

lifetime /laɪftaɪm/ **lifetimes** ◆◆◇◇◇

1 A **lifetime** is the length of time that someone is alive. *During my lifetime I haven't got around to much travelling. ...a trust fund to be administered throughout his wife's lifetime. ...an extraordinary lifetime of achievement.* N-COUNT: usu sing, oft poss N

2 The **lifetime** of a particular thing is the period of time that it lasts. *...the lifetime of a parliament. ...a satellite's lifetime.* N-SING: with poss

3 If you describe something such as an opportunity or an experience as that particular thing **of a lifetime**, you are emphasizing that it is the most memorable or important thing of its type that you are ever likely to have. *This could be not just the trip of a lifetime but the experience of a lifetime.* PHRASE: n PHR PRAGMATICS

lift /lɪft/ **lifts, lifting, lifted** ◆◆◆◆◇

1 If you **lift** something, you move it to another position, especially upwards. *The Colonel lifted the phone and dialed his superior... She lifted the last of her drink to her lips.* VERB V n V n prep/adv ▸ **Lift up** means the same as **lift**. *She put her arms around him and lifted him up... Curious shoppers lifted up their children to take a closer look at the parade.* PHRASAL VERB V n P V P n (not pron)

2 If you **lift** a part of your body, you move it to a higher position. *Amy lifted her arm to wave. 'Goodbye,' she called... She lifted her foot and squashed the wasp into the ground.* VERB =raise V n ▸ **Lift up** means the same as **lift**. *Tom took his seat again and lifted his feet up on to the railing... The boys lifted up their legs, indicating they wanted to climb in.* PHRASAL VERB V n P V P n (not pron)

3 If you **lift** your eyes or your head, you look up, for example when you have been reading and someone comes into the room. *When he finished he lifted his eyes and looked out the window.* VERB =raise V n

4 If people in authority **lift** a law or rule that prevents people from doing something, they end it. *Mr Bush said he'd never been enthusiastic about sanctions in the first place and would lift them.* VERB V n

5 If something **lifts** your spirits or your mood, or if they **lift**, you start feeling more cheerful. *He used his incredible sense of humour to lift my spirits... A brisk walk in the fresh air can lift your mood and dissolve a winter depression... As soon as she heard the telephone ring her spirits lifted.* V-ERG V n V

6 If something gives you a **lift**, it gives you a feeling of greater confidence, energy, or enthusiasm; an informal use. *My selection for the team has given me a tremendous lift.* N-SING: usu *a* N =boost

7 In British English, a **lift** is a device that carries people or goods up and down inside tall buildings. The American word is **elevator**. *They took the lift to the fourth floor.* N-COUNT

8 If you give someone a **lift** somewhere, you take them there in your car as a favour to them. *He had a car and often gave me a lift home.* N-COUNT =ride

9 If a government or organization **lifts** people or goods in or out of a country or area, it transports them there by aeroplane, especially in special circumstances such as a war. *The army lifted people off rooftops where they had climbed to escape the flooding... The Apaches are designed to quickly lift soldiers and equipment to the battlefield.* VERB =fly V n prep/adv

10 To **lift** something means to increase its amount or to increase the level or the rate at which it happens. *The bank lifted its basic home loans rate to 10.99% from 10.75%... A barrage would halt the flow upstream and lift the water level.* VERB =increase V n to/from/by amount V n

11 If fog, cloud, or mist **lifts**, it reduces, for example by moving upwards or by becoming less thick. *The fog had lifted and revealed a warm, sunny day.* VERB V

12 If you **lift** root vegetables or bulbs, you dig them out of the ground. *Lift carrots on a dry day and pack them horizontally in boxes of damp sand.* VERB =dig up V n

13 • to **lift a finger**: see **finger**.

lift off. When an aircraft or rocket **lifts off**, it leaves the ground and rises into the air. *The plane lifted off and climbed steeply into the night sky.* PHRASAL VERB =take off V P

lift up. See **lift** 1, 2. PHRASAL VERB

lift-off, lift-offs. Lift-off is the act of launching a rocket into space, when it leaves the ground and rises into the air. *The lift-off was delayed about seven minutes... The rocket tumbled out of control shortly after lift-off.* ◆◇◇◇◇ N-VAR =takeoff

ligament /lɪgəmənt/ **ligaments.** A **ligament** is a band of strong tissue in a person's body which connects bones. *He suffered torn ligaments in his knee.* ◆◇◇◇◇ N-COUNT

light 1 brightness or illumination

light /laɪt/ **lights, lighting, lit, lighted; lighter, lightest.** The form **lit** is the usual past tense and past participle, but the form **lighted** is also used. ◆◆◆◆◇

1 **Light** is the brightness that lets you see things. Light comes from sources such as the sun, moon, lamps, and fire. *Cracks of light filtered through the shutters... Light and water in embassy buildings were cut off... It was difficult to see in the dim light. ...ultraviolet light.* N-UNCOUNT: also *the* N ≠darkness

2 A **light** is something such as an electric lamp which produces light. *The janitor comes round to turn the lights out... You get into the music, the lights and the people around you. ...street lights.* N-COUNT

3 You can use **lights** to refer to a set of traffic lights. *...the heavy city traffic with its endless delays at lights and crossings.* N-PLURAL

4 If a place or object **is lit** by something, it has light shining on it. *It was dark and a giant moon lit the road so brightly you could see the landscape clearly... The room was lit by only the one light... The low sun lit the fortress walls with yellow light. ...the little lighted space at the bottom of the stairwell.* VERB =illuminate V n V n with n V-ed

5 If it is **light**, there is enough natural daylight left to see by even though it is the evening. *It was still light when we arrived at Lalong Creek. ...light summer evenings.* ADJ-GRADED ≠dark

6 If a room or building is **light**, it has a lot of natural light in it, for example because it has large windows. *It is a light room with tall windows... Her house is light and airy, crisp and clean.* ♦ **lightness** *The dark green spare bedroom is in total contrast to the lightness of the large main bedroom.* ADJ-GRADED =bright ≠dark N-UNCOUNT: usu with supp

7 If you **light** something such as a cigarette or fire, or if it **lights**, it starts burning. *Stephen hunched down to light a cigarette... If the charcoal does fail to light, use a special liquid spray and light it with a long taper. ...a lighted candle.* V-ERG V n V V-ed

8 If someone asks you for **a light**, they want a match or cigarette lighter so they can start smoking; an informal use. *Have you got a light anybody?* N-SING: *a* N

9 If something is presented in a particular **light**, it is presented so that you think about it in a particular way or so that it appears to be of a particular nature. *He has worked hard in recent months to portray New York in a better light.* N-COUNT: with supp

10 You can refer to the type of influence that something has on situations, people, or things as **the light of** that situation, person, or thing; used mainly in written English. *...the harsh light of reality.* N-SING: *the* N *of* n

11 You say that something is done or is acceptable according to someone's **lights** when you mean that it is done or is acceptable according to their own ideas and standards; a formal use. *They can get on with running the school system according to their own lights and in their own interests.* N-PLURAL: prep poss N

12 If there is a **light** in someone's eyes, there is an expression in their eyes that shows you the mood they are in or what they are thinking about; a literary use. *I remembered the curious expectant light in his eyes.* N-SING: usu N *in* n =glint

13 See also **lighter, lighting; bright lights, night light, pilot light, red light.**

14 If something **comes to light** or **is brought to light**, it becomes obvious or is made known to a lot of people. *Nothing about this sum has come to light... The truth is unlikely to be brought to light by the promised enquiry.* PHRASES V inflects

15 If **light dawns** on you, you begin to understand something after a period of not being able to understand it. *At last the light dawned. He was going to marry Phylis!* V inflects

16 **First light** is the time in the early morning when light first appears and before the sun rises; a literary expression. *Three hours before first light Fuentes gave orders for the evacuation of the camp.* =daybreak

17 If someone in authority gives you **a green light**, they give you permission to do something. *The food industry was given a green light to extend the use of these chemicals... Other countries are eagerly awaiting an American green light to lift the sanctions altogether.* PHR after v, v-link PHR

18 If something is possible or if you make a decision **in the light of** particular information or knowledge, something is possible or you make a decision because you have this information or knowledge. *In the light of this information it is now possible to identify a number of key issues.* PREP

19 If someone goes **out like a light**, they fall asleep or become unconscious very quickly or immediately; an informal expression. *'Why didn't somebody come and tell me?'—'Because you were out like a light.'* v-link PHR, PHR after v

20 If you say that an object **sees the light of day** or **sees the light**, you mean that it is taken out of the place where it is stored. *Museum basements are stacked full of objects which never see the light of day.* V inflects

21 If something **sees the light of day** at a particular time, it comes into existence or is made known to the public at that time. *This extraordinary document first saw the light of day in 1966.* V inflects

22 If someone **sees the light**, they finally understand something after having thought about it for some time, or after having misunderstood it. *Mother made him see the light.* V inflects

23 If you **set light to** something, you make it start burning; used mainly in British English. The usual American expression is **set fire to**. *They had poured fuel through the door of the flat and had then set light to it.* V inflects: PHR n

24 If someone or something **sheds light on, throws light on**, or **casts light on** something, it makes it easier to understand, because more information is known about it. *A new approach offers an answer, and may shed light on an even bigger question.* V inflects, PHR n =clarify

25 When you talk about **the light at the end of the tunnel**, you are referring to a pleasant situation in the future which gives you a lot of hope and optimism, especially because you are in a difficult or unpleasant situation at the moment. *All I can do is tell her to hold on, that there's light at the end of the tunnel.*

26 • **all sweetness and light**: see **sweetness**.

light on or **light upon.** If you **light on** something PHRASAL VERB or **light upon** it, you suddenly notice it or find it. *Her eyes lit on the brandy bottle that Atanas had dropped on the floor.* V P n

light up PHRASAL VERB

1 If you **light** something **up** or if it **lights up**, it becomes bright, usually when you shine light on it. *...a keypad that lights up when you pick up the handset... It isn't possible to heat one half of a bedroom or only to light up one half of a sitting room!* ERG =illuminate V P V P n (not pron) Also V n P

2 If your face or your eyes **light up** you suddenly look very surprised or happy. *Sue's face lit up with surprise... When I said I'd like this baby to live in a nuclear free environment her eyes lit up.* V P *with* n V P

3 If you **light up**, you make a cigarette, cigar, or pipe start burning and you start smoking it; an informal expression. *He held a match while she lit up... He takes his time lighting up a cigarette, all the while moving with the rhythm.* V P V P n (not pron) Also V n P

light upon. See **light on.** PHRASAL VERB

light 2 not great in weight, amount, or intensity

light /laɪt/ **lighter, lightest** ◆◆◆◇◇

1 Something that is **light** does not weigh very much, or weighs less than you would expect it to. *Modern tennis rackets are now apparently 20 per cent lighter. ...weight training with light weights... Try to wear light, loose clothes.* ♦ **lightness** *The toughness, lightness, strength, and elasticity of whalebone gave it a wide variety of uses.* ADJ-GRADED ≠heavy N-UNCOUNT: usu with supp

2 Something that is **light** is not very great in amount, degree, or intensity. *It's a Sunday like any other with the usual light traffic in the city... Trading was very light ahead of yesterday's auction. ...a light breeze.* ♦ **lightly** *Put the onions in the pan and cook until lightly browned. ...the small and lightly armed UN contingent.* ADJ-GRADED ADV-GRADED: usu ADV -ed, also ADV after v

3 **Light** equipment and machines are small and easily moved, especially because they are not heavy. *...a convoy of light armoured vehicles... They used light machine guns and AK forty-sevens.* ADJ: ADJ n

4 Soil that is **light** is easy to dig, because it has a loose texture and is not sticky or solid. *Less chemical gets into the sub-soil which is particularly important with the light, tropical soils.* ADJ-GRADED

5 Something that is **light** is very pale in colour. *The walls are light in colour and covered in paper... He is light haired with gray eyes.* ► Also a combining form. *We know he has a light green van. ...a light blue box.* ADJ-GRADED =pale COMB in COLOUR

6 A **light** sleep is one that is easily disturbed and in which you are often aware of the things around you. If you are a **light** sleeper, you are easily woken when you are asleep. *She had drifted into a light sleep... She was usually a light sleeper.* ♦ **lightly** *He was dozing lightly in his chair.* ADJ-GRADED: ADJ n ≠heavy ADV-GRADED: ADV after v

7 A **light** sound, for example someone's voice, is pleasantly quiet. *The voice was sweet and light.* ADJ-GRADED

8 A **light** meal is small in quantity. *...a light, healthy lunch. ...wine and cheese or other light refreshment.* ♦ **lightly** *She found it nearly impossible to eat lightly.* ADJ-GRADED ADV-GRADED: ADV after v

9 Food that is **light** has a delicate flavour and is easy to digest. *Berti's clear tomato soup is deliciously light... Bake salmon in foil or poach in a light stock for 8-10 minutes. ...light table wines.* ADJ-GRADED

10 **Light** work does not involve much physical effort. *He was on the training field for some light work yesterday.* ADJ-GRADED: usu ADJ n

11 If you describe the result of an action or a punishment as **light**, you mean that it is less serious or severe than you expected. *She confessed her astonishment at her light sentence when her father visited her at the jail.* ♦ **lightly** *One of the accused got off lightly in exchange for pleading guilty to withholding information from Congress.* ADJ-GRADED =lenient ADV-GRADED: ADV after v

12 Movements and actions that are **light** are graceful or gentle and are done with very little force or effort. *Use a light touch when applying cream or make-up... There was a light knock at the door.* ♦ **lightly** *He kissed her lightly on the mouth... Knead the dough very lightly.* ♦ **lightness** *She danced with a grace and lightness that were breathtaking.* ADJ-GRADED ADV-GRADED: ADV with v N-UNCOUNT

13 See also **lighter.**

light 3 unimportant or not serious

light /laɪt/ **lighter, lightest** ◆◆◆◇◇

1 If you describe things such as books, music, and films as **light**, you mean that they entertain you without making you think very deeply. *He doesn't like me reading light novels. ...light classical music. ...a light entertainment programme.* ADJ-GRADED: usu ADJ n ≠deep

2 If you say something in a **light** way, you sound as if you think that something is not important or serious. *Talk to him in a friendly, light way about the relationship. ...to finish on a lighter note.* ♦ **lightly** *'Once a detective, always a detective,' he said lightly.* ♦ **lightness** *'I'm not an authority on them,' Jessica said with forced lightness.* ADJ-GRADED: usu ADJ n ≠serious ADV-GRADED: ADV after v N-UNCOUNT

3 If you say that something is not a **light** matter, you mean that it should be treated or considered as being important and serious. *It can be no light matter for the Home Office that so many young prisoners should have wanted to kill or injure themselves.* ♦ **lightly** *His allegations cannot be lightly dismissed.* ADJ-GRADED: usu with brd-neg ADV-GRADED: ADV with v

4 If you **make light of** something, you treat it as though it is not serious or important, when in fact it is. *Roberts attempted to make light of his discomfort.* ● to **make light work of**: see **work.** PHRASE: V inflects =play down

5 See also **lighter.**

light aircraft. **Light aircraft** is both the singular and plural form. A **light aircraft** is a small aeroplane that is designed to carry a small number of passengers or a small amount of goods. N-COUNT

light bulb, light bulbs. A **light bulb** or **bulb** is the round glass part of an electric light or lamp which light shines from. ◆◇◇◇◇ N-COUNT =bulb

lighten /laɪtᵊn/ **lightens, lightening, lightened** ◆◇◇◇◇

1 When something **lightens** or when you **lighten** it, it becomes less dark in colour. *The sky began to lighten... Leslie lightens her hair and has now had it cut into a short, feathered style.* V-ERG ≠darken V V n

2 If someone **lightens** a situation, they make it less serious or less boring. *Anthony felt the need to lighten the atmosphere... He managed to lighten the generally lifeless debate at times... Her existence was lightened by bits of gossip.* VERB V n

3 If your attitude, or mood **lightens**, or if someone or something **lightens** it, they make you feel more cheerful, happy, and relaxed. *As they approached the outskirts of the city, Ella's mood visibly lightened... The sun was streaming in through the window, yet it did nothing to lighten his mood.* V-ERG V V n

4 If you **lighten** something, you make it less heavy. *It is a good idea to blend it in a food processor as this lightens the mixture... He pulled the lightened sled with all his strength.* VERB V n V-ed

5 If someone or something **lightens** your **burden** or your **load**, they do something to make a bad or difficult situation better for you. *The minister has persuaded the banks to lighten the burden of the foreign debt... In sharing this secret you lighten your burden... If you are responsible for children, lighten the load by asking others to help.* PHRASE: V inflects

lighten up. If someone tells you to **lighten up**, they think you should be less serious and make an effort to be more relaxed and happy. *Come on, this is a party. Lighten up.* PHRASAL VERB V P

lighter /laɪtəʳ/ **lighters.** A **lighter** is a small device that produces a flame which you can use to light cigarettes, cigars, and pipes. ◆◇◇◇◇ N-COUNT

light-fingered. If you say that someone is **light-fingered**, you mean that they steal things; an informal word. ADJ-GRADED

light-headed. If you are **light-headed**, you feel rather dizzy and faint, for example because you are ill or because you have drunk too much alcohol. *If you skip breakfast, your blood sugar level will drop and you will probably feel light-headed.* ADJ-GRADED: usu v-link ADJ

light-hearted ◆◇◇◇◇

1 Someone who is **light-hearted** is cheerful and happy. *They were light-hearted and prepared to enjoy life.* ADJ-GRADED

2 Something that is **light-hearted** is intended to be entertaining or amusing, and not at all serious. ADJ-GRADED

There have been many attempts, both light-hearted and serious, to locate the Loch Ness Monster.

lighthouse /laɪthaʊs/ **lighthouses.** A **lighthouse** is a tower containing a powerful flashing lamp that is built on the coast or on a small island in the sea. Lighthouses are used to guide ships or to warn them of danger. ◆◇◇◇◇ N-COUNT

light industry, light industries. Light industry is industry in which only small items are made, for example household goods and clothes. N-VAR

lighting /laɪtɪŋ/ ◆◆◇◇◇

1 The **lighting** in a place is the way that it is lit, for example by electric lights, by candles, or by windows, or the quality of the light in it. *...the bright fluorescent lighting of the laboratory... The whole room is bathed in soft lighting. ...street lighting.* N-UNCOUNT

2 The **lighting** in a film or play is the use of different electric lights to give a particular effect. *Peter Mumford's lighting and David Freeman's direction make a crucial contribution to the success of the staging.* N-UNCOUNT

lightning /laɪtnɪŋ/ ◆◆◇◇◇

1 **Lightning** is the very bright flashes of light in the sky that happen during thunderstorms. *One man died when he was struck by lightning... Another flash of lightning lit up the cave. ...thunder and lightning.* • See also **forked lightning**. N-UNCOUNT

2 **Lightning** describes things that happen very quickly or last for only a short time. *Driving today demands lightning reflexes.* ADJ: ADJ n

lightning conductor, lightning conductors In British English, a **lightning conductor** is a long thin piece of metal on top of a building that attracts lightning and allows it to reach the ground safely. The American expression is **lightning rod**. N-COUNT

lightning rod, lightning rods

1 In American English, a **lightning rod** is a long thin piece of metal on top of a building that attracts lightning and allows it to reach the ground safely. The British expression is **lightning conductor**. N-COUNT

2 In American English, if you say that someone **is a lightning rod for** something, you mean that they attract that thing to themselves. *He is a lightning rod for controversy.* PHRASE: PHR n

lightning strike, lightning strikes. A **lightning strike** is a strike in which workers stop work suddenly and without any warning, in order to protest about something. *Bank staff are to stage a series of lightning strikes in a dispute over staffing.* N-COUNT

lightship /laɪtʃɪp/ **lightships.** A **lightship** is a small ship that stays in one place and that has a powerful flashing lamp like a lighthouse. It is used to guide ships or to warn them of danger. N-COUNT

lightweight /laɪtweɪt/ **lightweights;** also spelled **light-weight**. ◆◆◇◇◇

1 Something that is **lightweight** weighs less than most other things of the same type. *...lightweight denim... The company manufactures a range of innovative light-weight cycles.* ADJ-GRADED: usu ADJ n

2 **Lightweight** is a category in some sports, such as boxing, judo, or rowing, based on the weight of the athlete. *By the age of sixteen he was the junior lightweight champion of Poland... He changed from lightweight (under 71kg) to light middleweight (under 78kg).* N-UNCOUNT: usu N n ► A **lightweight** is a person who is in the lightweight category in a particular sport. N-COUNT

3 If you describe someone as a **lightweight**, you are critical of them because you think that they are not very important or skilful in a particular area of activity. *Hill considered Sam a lightweight, a real amateur.* N-COUNT PRAGMATICS ≠heavyweight ► Also an adjective. *Some of the discussion in the book is lightweight and unconvincing.* ADJ-GRADED

light year, light years ◆◇◇◇◇

1 A **light year** is the distance that light travels in a year. *...a star system millions of light years away.* N-COUNT

2 You can say that two things are **light years** apart to emphasize a very great difference or a very long distance or period of time between them; an informal use. *She says the French education system is light years ahead of the English one... I had not eaten anything hot since my last dinner with Sean. It seemed light-years away.* N-COUNT: usu pl, N prep/adv PRAGMATICS

likable /laɪkəbᵊl/. See **likeable**.

like 1 preposition and conjunction uses

like /laɪk, laɪk/ **likes** ◆◆◆◆◆

1 If you say that one person or thing is **like** another, you mean that the two people or things are similar or share some of the same qualities, features, or characteristics. *He looks like Father Christmas... Kathy is a great mate, we are like sisters... It's a bit like going to the dentist; it's never as bad as you fear... It's nothing like what happened in the mid-Seventies... This is just like old times. ...a mountain shaped like a reclining woman.* PREP

2 If you ask or talk about what something or someone is **like**, you are asking or talking about their qualities, features, or characteristics. *What was Bulgaria like?... What did she look like?... What was it like growing up in Hillsborough?... Joe still has no concept of what it's like to be the sole parent.* PREP

3 You can use **like** to introduce an example of the set of things or people that you have just mentioned. *The neglect that large cities like New York have received over the past 12 years is tremendous... He could say things like, 'Let's go to the car' or 'Let us go for a walk' in French.* PREP: n PREP n/-ing =such as

4 You can use **like** to say that someone or something is in the same situation as another person or thing. *It also moved those who, like me, are too young to have lived through the war... Like many cities in Germany, it had to re-create itself after the second world war.* PREP

5 If you say that someone is behaving or doing something **like** something or someone else, you mean that they are behaving in a way or doing something that is typical of that kind of thing or person. **Like** is used in this way in many fixed expressions, for example **to cry like a baby** and **to watch someone like a hawk**. *I was shaking all over, trembling like a leaf... Greenfield was behaving like an irresponsible idiot.* PREP: v PREP n

6 You can use **like** in expressions such as **that's just like her** and **it wasn't like him** to indicate that the person's behaviour is or is not typical of their character. *You should have told us. But it's just like you not to share... Why does he want to do a mad thing like that? It's not like him.* PREP: v-link PREP n

7 **Like** is sometimes used as a conjunction in order to say that something appears to be the case when it is not. Some people consider this use to be incorrect. *His arms look like they might snap under the weight of his gloves... On the train up to Waterloo, I felt like I was going on an adventure.* CONJ-SUBORD =as if, as though

8 **Like** is sometimes used as a conjunction in order to indicate that something happens or is done in the same way as something else. Some people consider this use to be incorrect. *People are strolling, buying ice cream for their children, just like they do every Sunday... He spoke exactly like I did... We really were afraid, not like in the cinema.* CONJ-SUBORD PRAGMATICS

9 You can use **like** in negative expressions such as **nothing like it** and **no place like it** to emphasize that there is nothing as good as the situation, thing, or person mentioned. *There's nothing like candlelight for creating a romantic mood... There was no feeling like it in the world.* PREP: with neg PRAGMATICS

10 You can use **like** in expressions such as **nothing like** to make an emphatic negative statement. *Three hundred million dollars will be nothing like enough... It's really not anything like as bad as it looks.* PREP: with neg PRAGMATICS

11 In informal spoken English, some people say **like** when they are thinking about what to say next or because it has become their habit to say it. Some people do not like this use. *I decided that I'd go and, like, take a picture of him while he was in the shower.* CONVENTION PRAGMATICS =you know

12 You can use **like** in expressions such as **like attracts like**, when you are referring to two or more people or things that have the same or similar characteristics. *You have to make sure you're* N-UNCOUNT

comparing like with like... Homeopathic treatment is based on the 'like cures like' principle.

13 If you mention particular things or people and then add **and the like**, you are indicating that there are other similar things or people that can be included in what you are saying. *Many students are also keeping fit through jogging, aerobics, weight training, and the like.*
PHRASES · n PHR · =and so on

14 In informal English, you can use the expressions **like anything**, **like crazy**, or **like mad** to emphasize that someone is doing something or something is happening in a very intense or noticeable way. *He's working like mad at the moment.*
PHR after v · PRAGMATICS

15 You can talk about **the likes of** someone or something to refer to people or things of a particular type; an informal use. *Why would somebody like her want to spend an evening with the likes of me?... She went to Cambridge and rubbed shoulders with the likes of George Bernard Shaw.*
PHR n

16 If you say **that's more like it**, you mean that the thing that you are referring to is more satisfactory than it was on earlier occasions. *That's more like it, you're getting into the swing of things now.*
CONVENTION

17 You use the expression **more like** when mentioning an amount, name, or description that in your opinion is more accurate than one that has already been mentioned. *It's on company advice – well, orders, more like.*
PHR n/-ing, n PHR

18 If you say that something will happen **like as not** or **as like as not**, you mean that it will probably happen. *They'd come and bring their neighbours, like as not.*
PHR with cl

19 You use the expression **something like** with an amount, number, or description to indicate that it is approximately accurate. *They can get something like £3,000 a year... 'When roughly would this be? Monday?'—'Something like that.'*
PHR n · =about

20 You say **like this**, **like that**, or **like so** when you are showing someone how something is done. *It opens and closes, like this.*
usu PHR with cl

21 You use **like this** or **like that** when you are drawing attention to something that you are doing or that someone else is doing. *I'm sorry to intrude on you like this... Stop pacing like that.*
PHR after v

22 If you refer to something **the like of which** or **the likes of which** has never been seen before, you are emphasizing how important, great, or noticeable the thing is. *...technological advances the like of which the world had previously only dreamed of... We are dealing with an epidemic the likes of which we have never seen in this century.*
n PHR cl · PRAGMATICS · =such as

like 2 verb uses

like /laɪk/ **likes, liking, liked** ◆◆◆◆◆

1 If you **like** something or someone, you think they are interesting, enjoyable, or attractive. *He likes baseball... I can't think why Grace doesn't like me... What music do you like best?... I just didn't like being in crowds... Do you like to go swimming?... I like my whisky neat... That's one of the things I like about you. You're strong.*
VB: no cont · V n · V -ing · V to-inf · V n adj/prep · V n *about* n/-ing

2 If you ask someone how they **like** something, you are asking them for their opinion of it and whether they enjoy it or find it pleasant. *How do you like America?... How did you like the trip?*
VB: no cont, no passive · =find · V n/-ing

3 If you **like** something such as a particular course of action or way of behaving, you approve of it. *I've been looking at the cookery book. I like the way it is set out... The US administration would like to see a negotiated settlement to the war... Opal, his wife, didn't really like him drinking so much... I don't like relying on the judges' decisions.*
VB: no cont · V n · V to-inf · V n -ing · V -ing · Also V n *about* n/-ing

4 If you say that you **like** to do something or that you **like** something to be done, you mean that you prefer to do it or prefer it to be done as part of your normal life or routine. *I like to get to airports in good time... I hear Mary's husband likes her to be home no later than six o'clock.*
VB: no cont, no passive · =prefer · V to-inf · V n to-inf

5 If you say that you would **like** something or would **like** to do something, you are indicating a wish or desire that you have. *I'd like a bath... If you don't mind, I think I'd like to go home.*
VB: no cont, no passive · PRAGMATICS · V n · V to-inf

6 You can say that you **would like** to say something to indicate that you are about to say it. *I'd like to apologize... I would like to take this opportunity of telling you about a new service which we are offering.*
VB: no cont, no passive · PRAGMATICS · V to-inf

7 If you ask someone if they **would like** something or **would like** to do something, you are politely offering them something or inviting them to do something. *Here's your change. Would you like a bag?... Perhaps while you wait you would like a drink at the bar... Would you like to come back for coffee?*
VB: no cont, no passive · PRAGMATICS · V n · V to-inf

8 If you say to someone that you **would like** something or you **would like** them to do something, or ask them if they **would like** to do it, you are politely telling them what you want or what you want them to do. *I'd like an explanation... We'd like you to look around and tell us if anything is missing... Would you like to tell me what happened?*
VB: no cont, no passive · PRAGMATICS · V n · V n to-inf · V to-inf

9 Someone's **likes** are the things that they enjoy or find pleasant. *I thought that I knew everything about Jemma: her likes and dislikes, her political viewpoints.*
N-PLURAL: usu poss N · ≠dislikes

10 See also **liking**.

11 You say **if you like** when you are making or agreeing to an offer or suggestion in a casual way. *You can stay here if you like... 'Shall we stop talking about her?'—'If you like.'*
PHRASES · PHR with cl · PRAGMATICS · =if you want

12 You say **if you like** when you are expressing something in a different way, or in a way that you think some people might disagree with or find strange. *This is more like a downpayment, or a deposit, if you like.*
PHR with cl/group · PRAGMATICS · =let's say

13 If you say that something will happen or is true **like it or not**, or **whether** someone **likes it or not**, you mean that although the situation may be unpleasant or unwelcome, it has to be faced and cannot be changed. *Like it or not, our families shape our lives and make us what we are... We're going to have to spend the night here whether we like it or not.*
PHR with cl

-like /-laɪk/. **-like** combines with nouns to form adjectives which describe something as being similar to the thing referred to by the noun. *...beautiful purple-red petunia-like flowers. ...a tiny worm-like creature. ...snake-like undulations.*
COMB in ADJs: usu ADJ n

likeable /laɪkəbᵊl/; also spelled **likable**. Someone or something that is **likeable** is pleasant and easy to like. *He was an immensely likeable chap.*
◆◇◇◇◇ · ADJ-GRADED · =pleasant

likelihood /laɪklihʊd/ ◆◆◇◇◇

1 The **likelihood** of something happening is how likely it is to happen. *The likelihood of infection is minimal... There didn't seem much likelihood of it happening... There is every likelihood that sanctions will work.*
N-UNCOUNT: usu N of n/-ing, N that · =probability

2 If something is a **likelihood**, it is likely to happen. *The likelihood is that, if the Republicans lose, Mr Baker will retire... That, as we all know, is not only a possibility but a likelihood.*
N-SING · =probability

3 If you say that something will happen **in all likelihood**, you mean that it will probably happen. *In all likelihood, the congress will try to impeach President Yeltsin.*
PHRASE: PHR with cl · =in all probability

likely /laɪkli/ **likelier, likeliest** ◆◆◆◆◆

1 You use **likely** to indicate that something is probably the case or will probably happen in a particular situation. *Experts say a 'yes' vote is still the likely outcome... If this is your first baby, it's far more likely that you'll get to the hospital too early... Francis thought it likely John still loved her.* ► Also an adverb. *Profit will most likely have risen by about £25 million... Very likely he'd told them he had American business interests.*
ADJ-GRADED: oft *it* v-link ADJ that · =probable · ≠unlikely · ADV-GRADED: ADV with cl/group · =probably

2 If someone or something is **likely** to do something, they will very probably do it. *Economists say this trend is likely to continue throughout the '90s... Once people have seen that something actually works, they are much more likely to accept change.*
ADJ-GRADED: v-link ADJ to-inf · ≠unlikely

3 A **likely** person, place, or thing is one that will probably be suitable for a particular purpose. *At one point he had seemed a likely candidate to*
ADJ-GRADED: ADJ n

become Prime Minister... We aimed the microscope at a likely looking target.
4 You can say **not likely** as an emphatic way of saying 'no', especially when someone asks you whether you are going to do something; an informal expression. *'How about having a phone out here?'—'Not likely!'* CONVENTION PRAGMATICS =no way

like-minded. **Like-minded** people have similar opinions, ideas, attitudes, or interests. *...the opportunity to mix with hundreds of like-minded people.* ◆◇◇◇◇ ADJ: usu ADJ n

liken /laɪkən/ **likens, likening, likened.** If you **liken** one thing or person **to** another thing or person, you say that they are similar. *She likens marriage to slavery... The pain is often likened to being drilled through the side of the head.* ◆◇◇◇◇ VERB =compare V n *to* n/-ing

likeness /laɪknəs/ **likenesses** ◆◇◇◇◇
1 If two things or people have a **likeness** to each other, they are similar to each other. *These myths have a startling likeness to one another... There might be a likeness between their features, but their eyes were totally dissimilar.* N-SING: oft N *to/between* n =similarity
2 A **likeness** of someone is a picture or sculpture of them. *The museum displays wax likenesses of every US president.* N-COUNT: with poss
3 If you say that a picture of someone is a good **likeness** of them, you mean that it looks just like them. *She says the artist's impression is an excellent likeness of her abductor.* N-COUNT: usu sing, usu adj N

likewise /laɪkwaɪz/ ◆◆◇◇◇
1 You use **likewise** when you are comparing two methods, states, or situations and saying that they are similar. *All attempts by the Socialists to woo him back were spurned. Similar overtures from the right have likewise been rejected... The V2 was not an ordinary weapon: it could only be used against cities. Likewise the atom bomb.* ADV: ADV with v, ADV with cl/group =similarly
2 If you do something and someone else does **likewise**, they do the same or a similar thing. *He lent money, made donations and encouraged others to do likewise.* ADV: ADV after v

liking /laɪkɪŋ/ ◆◇◇◇◇
1 If you have a **liking** for something or someone, you like them. *She had a liking for good clothes... He bought me records to encourage my liking for music... Mrs Jermyn took a great liking to him.* N-SING: with supp, oft N *for* n
2 If something is, for example, too fast **for** your **liking**, you would prefer it to be slower. If it is not fast enough **for** your **liking**, you would prefer it to be faster. *He had become too powerful for their liking... She's asking far too many personal questions for my liking.* PHRASES with *too/not enough*, usu group PHR
3 If something is **to** your **liking**, it suits your interests, tastes, or wishes. *London was more to his liking than Rome... Simmer over a very low flame until the rice is cooked to your liking.* v-link PHR, PHR after v

lilac /laɪlək/ **lilacs; lilac** can also be used as the plural form. ◆◇◇◇◇
1 A **lilac** or a **lilac tree** is a small tree which has pleasant-smelling purple, pink, or white flowers in large, cone-shaped clusters. *Lilacs grew against the side wall. ...a twig of lilac.* ► **Lilacs** are the flowers which grow on this tree. *...a vase of tulips, lilies, lilacs and primroses... Her hair smelt of lilac.* N-VAR; N-VAR
2 Something that is **lilac** is pale pinkish-purple in colour. *All shades of mauve, lilac, lavender and purple were fashionable.* COLOUR

lilt /lɪlt/. If someone's voice has a **lilt** in it, the pitch of their voice rises and falls in a pleasant way, as if they were singing. *Her voice is childlike, with a West Country lilt.* N-SING

lilting /lɪltɪŋ/. A **lilting** voice or song rises and falls in pitch in a pleasant way. *He had a pleasant, lilting northern accent.* ADJ: usu ADJ n

lily /lɪli/ **lilies.** A **lily** is a plant with large flowers that are often white. ◆◆◇◇◇ N-VAR

lily of the valley, lilies of the valley; lily of the valley can also be used as the plural. **Lily of the valley** are small plants with large leaves and small, white, bell-shaped flowers. N-VAR

lima bean /liːmə biːn/ **lima beans. Lima beans** are flat round beans that are light green in colour and are eaten as a vegetable. They are the seeds of a plant that grows in tropical parts of America. N-COUNT: usu pl

limb /lɪm/ **limbs** ◆◆◇◇◇
1 Your **limbs** are your arms and legs. *She would be able to stretch out her cramped limbs and rest for a few hours.* N-COUNT: usu pl
2 The **limbs** of a tree are its branches; a literary use. *This entire rickety structure was hanging from the limb of an enormous leafy tree.* N-COUNT
3 If someone goes **out on a limb**, they do something they strongly believe in even though it is risky or extreme, and is likely to fail or be criticized by other people. *They can see themselves going out on a limb, voting for a very controversial energy bill.* PHRASES PHR after v, v-link PHR
4 If someone **risks life and limb**, they do something very dangerous that may cause them to die or be seriously injured. *Aid workers have risked life and limb and we have had to hire our own protection to safeguard workers at our centres.* V inflects
5 If someone threatens to **tear** you **limb from limb**, they mean that they are extremely angry with you, and may use violence against you. *The police were lucky they found him before I did. I would have torn him limb from limb.* V inflects

-limbed /-lɪmd/. **-limbed** combines with adjectives to form other adjectives which indicate that a person or animal has limbs of a particular type or appearance. *He was long-limbed and dark-eyed.* COMB in ADJ-GRADED

limber /lɪmbəʳ/ **limbers, limbering, limbered**
limber up. If you **limber up**, you prepare for a physical activity such as a sport by exercising your muscles and limbs. *Next door, 200 girls are limbering up for their ballet exams... She ran a little way, limbering up... A short walk will limber up the legs.* PHRASAL VERB =warm up V P; V P n (not pron)

limbo /lɪmboʊ/ ◆◇◇◇◇
1 If you say that someone or something is in **limbo**, you mean that they are in a situation where they seem to be caught between two stages and it is unclear what will happen next. *I didn't know whether my family was alive or dead. I felt as if I was in limbo... The negotiations have been in limbo since mid-December.* N-UNCOUNT: usu *in/into* N
2 **The limbo** is a West Indian dance in which you have to pass under a low bar while leaning backwards. The bar is moved nearer to the floor each time you go under it. N-SING: *the* N, N n

lime /laɪm/ **limes** ◆◆◇◇◇
1 A **lime** is a green fruit that tastes like a lemon. Limes grow on trees in tropical countries. *...peeled slices of lime... Oranges, lemons and limes were found to cure scurvy... Add a few drops of lime juice.* N-VAR
2 **Lime** is a drink that tastes of limes. *...a pint of lager and lime.* N-UNCOUNT
3 A **lime** is a large tree with pale green leaves. It is often planted in parks in towns and cities. *...dilapidated avenues of limes.* N-COUNT =linden
4 **Lime** is a substance containing calcium. It is found in soil and water. *If your soil is very acid, add lime.* ► Also a combining form. *...lime-rich sand. ...old lime-stained baths.* N-UNCOUNT; COMB in ADJ

lime green; also spelled **lime-green**. Something that is **lime green** is light yellowish-green in colour. *She wore a lime-green trouser suit... Diana looked chic in lime green and navy.* COLOUR

limelight /laɪmlaɪt/. If someone is in the **limelight**, a lot of attention is being paid to them, because they are famous or because they have done something very unusual or exciting. *Tony has now been thrust into the limelight, with a high-profile job.* ◆◇◇◇◇ N-UNCOUNT: usu prep *the* N

limerick /lɪmərɪk/ **limericks.** A **limerick** is a humorous poem which has five lines. ◆◇◇◇◇ N-COUNT

limestone /laɪmstoʊn/ **limestones. Limestone** is a white-coloured rock which is used for building and making cement. *...high limestone cliffs... The local limestone is very porous. ...marine limestones.* ◆◇◇◇◇ N-MASS: oft N n

limey /laɪmi/ **limeys.** Some Americans refer to British people as **limeys**; an informal word. N-COUNT

limit /lɪmɪt/ **limits, limiting, limited** ◆◆◆◆◇
1 A **limit** is the greatest amount, extent, or degree N-COUNT:

of something that is possible. *Her love for him was being tested to its limits... There is no limit to how much fresh fruit you can eat in a day... Firefighters are being stretched to the limit as fire sweeps through the drought-stricken state.* usu sing, usu with supp

2 A **limit** of a particular kind is the largest or smallest amount of something such as time or money that is allowed because of a rule, law, or decision. *The three month time limit will be up in mid-June.... The economic affairs minister announced limits on petrol sales.* N-COUNT: usu with supp

3 The **limit** of an area is its boundary or edge. *...the city limits of Baghdad.* N-COUNT: with supp

4 The **limits** of a situation are the facts involved in it which make only some actions or results possible. *She has to work within the limits of a fairly tight budget... He outlined the limits of British power.* N-PLURAL: usu N *of* n =confines

5 If you **limit** something, you prevent it from becoming greater than a particular amount or degree. *He limited payments on the country's foreign debt... The view was that the economy would grow by 2.25 per cent. This would limit unemployment to around 2.5 million.* VERB =restrict; V n; V n *to* n

6 If you **limit** yourself to something, or if someone or something **limits** you, the number of things that you have or do is reduced. *It is now accepted that men should limit themselves to 20 units of alcohol a week... They have the best record in the Premier League. But we limited them to just a couple of chances.* ♦ **limiting** *The conditions laid down to me were not too limiting.* VERB; V pron-refl *to* n/-ing; V n *to* n/-ing; Also V pron-refl; ADJ-GRADED

7 If something **is limited** to a particular place or group of people, it exists only in that place, or is had or done only by that group. *The protests were not limited to New York... Entry to this prize draw is limited to UK residents.* VB: usu passive; be V-ed *to* n/-ing

8 See also **age limit**, **limited**.

9 If an area or a place is **off limits**, you are not allowed to go there. *A one-mile area around the wreck is still off limits... These establishments are off limits to ordinary citizens.* PHRASES; v-link PHR, oft PHR *to* n =out of bounds

10 If you say that something is **off limits**, you mean that you are not allowed to do it. *Smoking was off limits everywhere.* v-link PHR, PHR after v

11 In British English, If someone **is over the limit**, they have drunk more alcohol than they are legally allowed to when driving a vehicle. *If police breathalyse me and find I am over the limit I face a long ban and a crippling fine... He was found to be three times over the limit.* usu v-link PHR

12 If you say **the sky is the limit**, you mean that there is nothing to prevent someone or something from being very successful. *They have found that, in terms of both salary and career success, the sky is the limit.* V inflects

13 If you add **within limits** to a statement, you mean that it is true or applies only when talking about reasonable or normal situations. *In the circumstances we'll tell you what we can, within limits, of course, and in confidence.* PHR with cl =within reason

limitation /lɪmɪteɪʃən/ **limitations** ◆◆◇◇◇

1 The **limitation** of something is the act or process of controlling or reducing it. *All the talk had been about the limitation of nuclear weapons. ...damage limitation.* N-UNCOUNT: usu with supp, oft N *of* n

2 A **limitation** on something is a rule or decision which prevents that thing from growing or extending beyond certain limits. *...a limitation on the tax deductions for people who make more than $100,000 a year... There is to be no limitation on the number of opposition parties.* N-VAR: usu N *on* n

3 If you talk about the **limitations** of someone or something, you mean that they can only do some things and not others, or that they can only achieve a fairly low degree of success or excellence. *I realized how possible it was to overcome your limitations, to achieve well beyond what you believe yourself capable of... Parents are too likely to blame schools for the educational limitations of their children.* N-PLURAL: usu with poss =shortcomings

4 A **limitation** is a fact or situation that allows only some actions and makes others impossible. *This drug has one important limitation. Its effects only last six hours. ...an acute disc collapse in the spine, causing limitation of movement.* N-VAR: usu with supp

limited /lɪmɪtɪd/ ◆◆◆◇◇

1 Something that is **limited** is not very great in amount, range, or degree. *They may only have a limited amount of time to get their points across... Shops have a very limited selection.* ADJ-GRADED: usu ADJ n =small

2 A **limited** company is one in which the shareholders are legally responsible for only a part of any money that it may owe if it goes bankrupt; used mainly in British English. *They had plans to turn the club into a limited company... He is the founder of International Sports Management Limited.* ADJ: ADJ n, n ADJ

limited edition, **limited editions.** A **limited edition** is a work of art, such as a book which is only produced in very small numbers, so that each one will be valuable in the future. ◆◇◇◇◇ N-COUNT

limitless /lɪmɪtləs/. If you describe something as **limitless**, you mean that there is or appears to be so much of it that it will never be exhausted. *...a cheap and potentially limitless supply of energy... The opportunities are limitless.* ◆◇◇◇◇ ADJ =endless

limousine /lɪməziːn/ **limousines.** A **limousine** is a large and very comfortable car. Limousines are usually driven by a chauffeur and are used by very rich or important people. ◆◇◇◇◇ N-COUNT

limp /lɪmp/ **limps, limping, limped; limper, limpest** ◆◆◇◇◇

1 If a person or animal **limps**, they walk with difficulty or in an uneven way because one of their legs or feet is hurt. *I wasn't badly hurt, but I injured my thigh and had to limp... He had to limp off with a leg injury.* ► Also a noun. *A stiff knee following surgery forced her to walk with a limp.* VERB; V; V adv/prep; N-COUNT: usu *a* N in sing

2 If you say that something such as an organization, process, or vehicle **limps** along, you mean that it continues slowly or with difficulty, for example because it has been weakened or damaged. *In recent years the newspaper had been limping along on limited resources... A British battleship, which had been damaged severely in the battle of Crete, came limping into Pearl Harbor.* VERB; V adv/prep

3 If you describe something as **limp**, you mean that it is soft or weak when it should be firm or strong. *She was told to reject applicants with limp handshakes... A residue can build up on the hair shaft, leaving the hair limp and dull looking.* ♦ **limply** *Flags and bunting hung limply in the still, warm air.* ADJ-GRADED; ADV-GRADED: ADV with v

4 If someone is **limp**, their body has no strength and is not moving, for example because they are asleep or unconscious. *He carried her limp body into the room and laid her on the bed... He hit his head against a rock and went limp.* ADJ-GRADED

limpet /lɪmpɪt/ **limpets.** A **limpet** is a small sea animal with a cone-shaped shell which attaches itself tightly to rocks. N-COUNT

limpid /lɪmpɪd/

1 If you say that something is **limpid**, you mean that it is very clear and transparent; a literary use. *...limpid blue eyes. ...limpid rock-pools.* ADJ-GRADED =translucent

2 If you describe speech, writing, or music as **limpid**, you like it because it is clear, simple and flowing; a literary use. *He thought the speech a model of its kind, limpid and unaffected.* ADJ-GRADED

linchpin /lɪntʃpɪn/ **linchpins;** also spelled **lynchpin.** If you refer to a person or thing as the **linchpin** of something, you mean that they are the most important person or thing involved in it. *He's the lynchpin of our team and crucial to my long-term plans.* N-COUNT: with supp, usu N *of* n =mainstay

linden /lɪndən/ **lindens.** A **linden** or a **linden tree** is a large tree with pale green leaves which is often planted in parks in towns and cities. ◆◇◇◇◇ N-VAR =lime

line /laɪn/ **lines, lining, lined** 

1 A **line** is a long thin mark which is drawn or painted on a surface. Lines are often used to divide one part of a surface from another. *Draw a line down* N-COUNT

that page's center. ...a dotted line... The ball had clearly crossed the line.

2 The **lines** on someone's skin, especially on their face, are long thin marks that appear there as they grow older. *He has a large, generous face with deep lines. ...fine lines and wrinkles.* N-COUNT: usu pl =wrinkle

3 A **line** of people or things is a number of them arranged one behind the other or side by side. *The sparse line of spectators noticed nothing unusual.* N-COUNT: oft N *of* n =row

4 A **line** of people or vehicles is a number of them that are waiting one behind another, for example in order to buy something or to go in a particular direction. *Children clutching empty bowls form a line... The farmers sat in their trucks waiting in line to unload their grain.* N-COUNT: also *in* N =queue

5 A **line** of a piece of writing is one of the rows of words, numbers, or other symbols in it. *The next line should read: Five days, 23.5 hours... Tina wouldn't have read more than three lines.* N-COUNT

6 In school, if a child is given **lines**, he or she is punished by being made to write out a sentence many times or to write out a passage from a book; used mainly in British English. N-PLURAL

7 A **line** of a poem, song, or play is a group of words that are spoken or sung together. If an actor **learns** his or her **lines** for a play or film, they learn what they have to say and when they have to say it. *He lived by a line from one of his plays: Nothing succeeds like excess... Every time I sing that line, I have to compete with that bloody trombone!... Learning lines is very easy. Acting is very difficult.* N-COUNT

8 A particular type of **line** in a conversation is a remark that is intended to have a particular effect. *'In time perhaps you'll marry again'. 'That's a great line, coming from you!'. ...chat-up lines like 'You've got beautiful eyes'.* N-COUNT: with supp

9 You can refer to a long piece of wire, string, or cable as a **line** when it is used for a particular purpose. *She put her washing on the line. ...a piece of fishing-line... The winds downed power lines.* N-VAR: usu with supp

10 A **line** is a connection which makes it possible for two people to speak to each other on the telephone. *The telephone lines went dead... It's not a very good line. Shall we call you back Susan?... She's on the line from her home in Boston.* N-COUNT: oft *on the* N

11 You can use **line** to refer to a telephone number which you can ring in order to get information or advice. *...the 24-hours information line. ...details from Lesbian Line.* N-COUNT: oft in names after n

12 A **line** is a route, especially a dangerous or secret one, along which people move or send messages or supplies. *The American continent's geography severely limited the lines of attack... Negotiators say they're keeping communication lines open. ...the guerrillas' main supply lines.* N-COUNT: usu pl, usu with supp =channel

13 The **line** in which something or someone moves is the particular route that they take, especially when they take a straight path and do not deviate from it. *Walk in a straight line... The wings were at right angles to the line of flight.* N-COUNT

14 A **line** is a particular route, involving the same stations, roads, or stops along which a train or bus service regularly operates. *They've got to ride all the way to the end of the line... Fires broke out at three railway stations, halting service on two commuter lines for several hours... I would be able to stay on the Piccadilly Line and get off the tube at South Kensington.* N-COUNT: usu with supp, oft in names after n

15 A railway **line** consists of the pieces of metal and wood which form the track that the trains travel along. *Leaves on the line are an expensive problem for the railways.* N-COUNT =track

16 A shipping, air, or bus **line** is a company which provides services for transporting people or goods by sea, air, or bus. *The Foreign Office offered to pay the shipping line all the costs of diverting the ship to Bermuda.* N-COUNT: usu supp N =company

17 You can use **line** to refer to the edge, outline, or shape of an object or a person's body; a literary use. *The garden has an informal feel to soften the architectural lines of the conservatory. ...a sculptured evening dress that follows the lines of the body.* N-COUNT: with supp

18 A state or county **line** is a boundary between two states or counties; used mainly in American English. *...the California state line.* N-COUNT: usu sing, with supp =border

19 You can use **lines** to refer to the set of physical defences or the soldiers that have been established along the boundary of an area occupied by an army. *Their unit was shelling the German lines only seven miles away. ...the stupendous fortification they called the Maginot Line.* N-COUNT

20 The particular **line** that a person or group has towards a problem or topic is the attitude or policy that they have towards it. For example, if someone takes a **hard line** on something, they have a firm strict policy which they refuse to change. *Forty members of the governing Conservative party rebelled, voting against the government line... The government has taken a hard line against the continuing influx of Albanian boat people.* N-COUNT: usu sing, with supp

21 You can use **line** to refer to the way in which someone's thoughts or activities develop, particularly if this is logical or systematic. *Our discussion in the previous chapter continues this line of thinking... What are some of the practical benefits likely to be of this line of research?* N-COUNT: usu N *of* n/-ing

22 If you say that something happens along particular **lines**, or on particular **lines**, you are giving a general summary or approximate account of what happens, which may not be correct in every detail. *There followed an assortment of praise for the coffee along the lines of 'Hey, this coffee is fantastic!'... He'd said something on those lines already... Our forecast for 1990 was on the right lines... The main lines of the plan were a reduction in expenditure and the rationalization of government controls.* N-PLURAL: usu *along/on* N with supp

23 If something is organized on particular **lines**, or along particular **lines**, it is organized according to that method or principle. *...so-called autonomous republics based on ethnic lines. ...reorganising old factories to work along Japanese lines.* N-PLURAL: *on/alogg* N with supp

24 Your **line** of business or work is the kind of work that you do. *So what was your father's line of business?... In my line of work I often get home too late for dinner.* N-COUNT: usu N *of* n

25 If someone says that something is your **line**, or that it is **in your line**, they mean that it is the sort of thing that you often do because you enjoy doing it; an informal use. *Wild guesses aren't much in my line... Perhaps doing voluntary work is more your line?* N-SING: poss N

26 A **line** is a particular type of product that a company makes or sells. *His best selling line is the cheapest lager at £1.99.* N-COUNT

27 You can use **line** to refer to something connected with a particular activity. For example, something **in the sports line** is connected with sports. *Most kids can do something in the art line.* N-SING: *the* n N

28 In a factory, a **line** is an arrangement of workers or machines where a product passes from one worker to another until it is finished. *...a production line capable of producing three different products.* N-COUNT

29 You can use **line** to refer to all the generations of a family, especially when you are considering the social status or the physical characteristics that the various members inherit. *...the old Welsh royal line descended from Arthur and Uther Pendragon... This title will only pass down through the male line.* N-COUNT: with supp

30 You can use **line** when you are referring to a number of people who are ranked according to status or seniority. *Nicholas Paul Patrick was seventh in the line of succession to the throne... The line of command went from head office in Chicago to a regional boss and then down to a country boss and finally to a local-office managing-partner. ...the man who stands next in line for the presidency.* N-COUNT: usu sing, oft N *of* n, ord *in* N

31 A particular **line** of people or things is a series of them that has existed over a period of time, when they have all been similar in some way, or done similar things. *We were part of a long line of artists... It's the latest in a long line of tragedies.* N-COUNT: usu sing, usu N *of* n

32 If people or things **line** a road, room, or other place, they are present in large numbers along its edges or sides. *Thousands of cheering Albanians lined the streets of the capital. ...a square lined with pubs and clubs.* ♦ **-lined** *...a long tree-lined drive.* VERB V n V-ed COMB in ADJ

33 If you **line** a wall, container, or other object, you put a layer of something such as leaves or paper on the inside surface of it in order to make it stronger, warmer, or cleaner. *Scoop the blanket weed out and use it to line hanging baskets... Female bears tend to line their dens with leaves or grass.* ♦ **-lined** *...a dark, suede-lined case.* VERB V n V n *with* n COMB in ADJ

34 If something **lines** a container or area, especially an area inside a person, animal, or plant, it forms a layer on the inside surface. *...the muscles that line the intestines.* VERB V n

35 See also **lined**, **lining**; **battle lines**, **bottom line**, **branch line**, **dividing line**, **front line**, **party line**, **picket line**, **yellow line**.

36 If something happens somewhere **along the line** or somewhere **down the line**, it happens during the course of a situation or activity, often at a point that cannot be exactly identified. *Somewhere along the line he picked up an engineering degree... It would depend how far down the line the relationship was.* PHRASES

37 If you say that something happens all **down the line**, or right **down the line**, you mean that it happens in every case, or that your remark includes all the people or things involved in a particular situation or activity; an informal expression. *Excellent acting all down the line captures the sound and feeling of that semi-feudal age... Democrats and Republicans differed right down the line on what the proper responses were.* n PHR, PHR after v, oft adv PHR

38 If you **draw the line** at a particular activity, you refuse to do it, because you disapprove of it or because it is more extreme than what you normally do. *Letters have come from prisoners, declaring that they would draw the line at hitting an old lady.* V inflects, oft PHR *at* n/-ing

39 If you **draw a line** between two things, you make a distinction between them. *It is, however, not possible to draw a distinct line between the two categories.* V inflects =distinguish

40 If you **drop** someone **a line**, you write to them; an informal expression. *My phone doesn't work, so drop me a line.* V inflects

41 If you do something or if it happens to you **in the line of duty**, you do it or it happens as part of your regular work or as a result of it. *More than 3,000 police officers were wounded in the line of duty last year.* PHR after v, v-link PHR

42 If you refer to a method as **the first line of**, for example, defence or treatment, you mean that it is the first or most important method to be used in dealing with a problem. *Passport checks will remain the first line of defence against terrorists... The first line of treatment is to help the affected skin by moisturising it regularly.* PHR n

43 If you are **in line** for something, it is likely to happen to you or you are likely to obtain it. If something is **in line** to happen, it is likely to happen. *He must be in line for a place in the Guinness Book of Records... Public sector pay is also in line to be hit hard.* PHR *for* n, PHR to-inf =due

44 If one object is **in line** with others, or moves **into line** with others, they are arranged in a line. You can also say that a number of objects are **in line** or move **into line**. *The device itself was right under the vehicle, almost in line with the gear lever... Venus, the Sun and Earth all moved into line.* v-link PHR, PHR after v, oft PHR *with* n

45 If one thing is **in line** with another, or is brought **into line** with it, the first thing is, or becomes, similar to the second, especially in a way that has been agreed, planned, or expected. You can also say that two things are brought **into line**. *The structure of our schools is now broadly in line with the major countries of the world... This brings the law into line with most medical opinion. ...the economic discipline required to bring currencies into line.* usu PHR after v, v-link PHR, oft PHR *with* n

46 If you keep someone **in line** or bring them **into line**, you make them obey you, or you make them behave in the way you want them to. *All this was just designed to frighten me and keep me in line. ...if the Prime Minister fails to bring rebellious Tories into line.* PHR after v

47 If something such as a machine, power station, or defence system comes **on line**, or someone brings it **on line**, it starts operating. *The Energy Secretary hopes to bring on line a safer new tritium production reactor... The new machine will go on line in June 1992.* usu PHR after v

48 If you do something **on line**, you do it using a computer or a computer network. If an organization or person goes **on line**, they start to do their work on computer. *They can order their requirements on line. ...on-line transaction processing.* PHR after v, v-link PHR, PHR n

49 If something such as your job, career, or reputation is **on the line**, you may lose or harm it as a result of what you are doing or of the situation you are in; an informal expression. *He wouldn't put his career on the line to help a friend.* usu PHR after v, v-link PHR =at risk, at stake

50 In a row or group of objects, if one of them is **out of line**, it is not in its correct position. *You can see that her nose has been drawn slightly out of line.* PHR after v, v-link PHR

51 If one thing is **out of line** with another, the first thing is different from the second in a way that was not agreed, planned, or expected. *...if one set of figures is sharply out of line with a trend.* usu v-link PHR, oft PHR *with* n

52 If someone steps **out of line**, they disobey someone or behave in an unacceptable way. *Any one of my players who steps out of line will be in trouble with me as well... You're way out of line, lady.* v PHR, v-link PHR

53 If you **read between the lines**, you understand what someone really means, or what is really happening in a situation, even though it is not said openly. *Reading between the lines she sensed a certain lack of sympathy for the deceased.* V inflects

54 • to **sign on the dotted line**: see **dotted**. • to **line** your **pockets**: see **pocket**. • **the line of least resistance**: see **resistance**. • to **toe the line**: see **toe**.

line up PHRASAL VERB

1 If people **line up** or if you **line** them **up**, they move so that they are stand in a row or form a queue. *The senior leaders lined up behind him in orderly rows... The gym teachers lined us up against the cement walls... Four members of a family were lined up and shot... When he came back the sergeant had lined up the terrorists.* ERG V P V n P V P n (not pron)

2 If you **line** things **up**, you move them into a straight row. *I would line up my toys on this windowsill and play... He finished polishing the cocktail glasses and lined them up behind the bar.* V P n (not pron) V n P

3 If you **line** one thing **up** with another, or one thing **lines up** with another, the first thing is moved into its correct position in relation to the second. You can also say that two things **line up**, or **are lined up**. *You have to line the car up with the ones beside you... I just couldn't get it to line up with the surrounding body panels... Mahoney had lined up two of the crates... When the images line up exactly, the projectors should be fixed in place... All we have to do is to get the two pieces lined up properly.* RECIP-ERG V n P *with* n V P *with* n V P pl-n pl-n V P V-ed P Also V P n *with* n, V pl-n P

4 If you **line up** an event or activity, you arrange for it to happen. If you **line** someone **up** for an event or activity, you arrange for them to be available for that event or activity. *She lined up executives, politicians and educators to serve on the board of directors... Bob Dylan is lining up a two-week UK tour for the New Year.* V P n to-inf V P n (not pron) Also V n P, V n P to-inf

5 If you **line up** with, behind, or alongside a person or group, you support them. If you **line up** against a person or group, you oppose them. *Some surprising names have lined up behind the idea... It did give some indication of the forces lined up against Yeltsin.* V P prep V-ed P

6 See also **line-up**.

lineage /lɪniɪdʒ/ **lineages.** Someone's **lineage** is the series of families from which they are directly descended; a formal word. *They can trace their lineage directly back to the 18th century. ...a respectable family of ancient lineage.* N-VAR =ancestry

lineal /lɪniəl/. A **lineal** descendant of a particular person or family is someone in a later generation who is directly related to them; a formal word. ADJ: ADJ n =direct

linear /lɪniər/ ◆◇◇◇◇

1 A **linear** process or development is one in which something changes or progresses straight from one stage to another, and has a starting point and an ending point. *Her novel subverts the conventions of linear narrative. It has no neat chronology and no tidy denouement. ...the linear view of time, with the idea that the past is moving into the present and the present into the future.* ADJ: usu ADJ n ≠non-linear

2 A **linear** shape or form consists of straight lines. *...the sharp, linear designs of the Seventies and Eighties.* ADJ: usu ADJ n

3 **Linear** movement or force occurs in a straight line rather than in a curve. ADJ: usu ADJ n

lined /laɪnd/

1 If someone's face or skin is **lined**, it has wrinkles or lines on it as a result of old age, tiredness, worry, or illness. *His lined face was that of an old man.* ADJ-GRADED

2 **Lined** paper has lines printed across it to help you write neatly. ADJ

3 See also **line**.

line drawing, line drawings. A **line drawing** is a drawing which consists only of lines, in which darker or lighter areas are shown by the spacing and thickness of the lines. N-COUNT

line manager, line managers. Your **line manager** is the person at work who is in charge of the department, shift, or project you are working on; used mainly in British English. N-COUNT

linen /lɪnɪn/ **linens** ◆◆◇◇◇

1 **Linen** is a kind of cloth that is made from a plant called flax. It is used especially for making tea-towels, tablecloths, and sheets. *...a white linen suit. ...cottons, woolens, silks and linens.* N-MASS

2 **Linen** is tablecloths, napkins, sheets, pillowcases, and similar things made of cloth that are used in the house. *...embroidered bed linen... All linens and towels are provided.* • to **wash** your **dirty linen in public**: see **dirty**. N-UNCOUNT: also N in pl

line of sight, lines of sight. Your **line of sight** is an imaginary line that stretches between your eye and the object that you are looking at. *He was trying to keep out of the bird's line of sight.* N-COUNT: usu sing, oft with poss =line of vision

line of vision. Your **line of vision** is the same as your **line of sight**. *Any crack in a car windscreen always seems to be right in the driver's line of vision.* N-SING: usu with poss

liner /laɪnər/ **liners.** A **liner** is a large ship in which people travel long distances or go on holiday cruises. *...luxury ocean liners. ...the cruise liner, the QE2.* • See also **bin liner**. ◆◆◇◇◇ N-COUNT: oft n N

liner note, liner notes. In American English, the **liner notes** on record jackets are short pieces of writing that tell you something about the record or the musicians playing on the record. The British term is **sleeve notes**. N-COUNT: usu pl

linesman /laɪnzmən/ **linesmen.** A **linesman** is an official who assists the referee or umpire in games such as football and tennis by watching the boundary line of the field or court and indicating when the ball goes outside it. ◆◇◇◇◇ N-COUNT

line-up, line-ups ◆◆◇◇◇

1 A **line-up** is a group of people or a series of things that are assembled to take part in a particular activity or event. *Ryan Giggs is likely to be in Wales's starting line-up for their World Cup qualifying match... The programme is back for a new series with a great line-up of musicians and comedy acts.* N-COUNT

2 When the police organize a **line-up**, a witness to a crime walks past a line of people in order to see if they recognize the person who committed the crime among the people in the line. *He failed to identify Graham from photographs, but later picked him out of a police line-up.* N-COUNT =identity parade

linger /lɪŋgər/ **lingers, lingering, lingered** ◆◆◇◇◇

1 When something such as an idea, feeling, or illness **lingers**, it continues to exist for a long time, often much longer than expected. *The scent of her perfume lingered on in the room... A guerrilla war has lingered into its fourth decade... He was ashamed. That feeling lingered, and he was never comfortable in church after that... He would rather be killed in a race than die a lingering death in hospital.* VERB V adv/prep V V-ing

2 If you **linger** somewhere, you stay there for a longer time than is necessary, for example because you are enjoying yourself. *Customers are welcome to linger over coffee until around midnight... I lingered on in Atlanta for a few days, spending much of my time with an artist friend... It is a dreary little town where few would choose to linger.* VERB V adv/prep V

lingerie /lænʒəri, AM -reɪ/. **Lingerie** is women's underwear and nightclothes. ◆◇◇◇◇ N-UNCOUNT

lingo /lɪŋgoʊ/ **lingos**

1 In informal English, people sometimes refer to a foreign language, especially one that they do not speak or understand, as a **lingo**. *I don't speak the lingo.* N-COUNT: usu sing

2 A **lingo** is a range of vocabulary or a style of language which is used in a special context or by a small group of people; an informal use. *In record-business lingo, that means he wanted to buy the rights to the song and market it. ...an author who writes in a lurid lingo, freely punctuated with crude expletives.* N-UNCOUNT: also a N, usu with supp

lingua franca /lɪŋgwə fræŋkə/. A **lingua franca** is a language or way of communicating which is used between people who do not speak one another's native language; a formal term. *English is rapidly becoming the lingua franca of Asia.* N-SING

linguist /lɪŋgwɪst/ **linguists** ◆◇◇◇◇

1 A **linguist** is someone who is good at speaking or learning foreign languages. *Her brother was an accomplished linguist.* N-COUNT

2 A **linguist** is someone who studies or teaches linguistics. N-COUNT

linguistics /lɪŋgwɪstɪks/; the form **linguistic** is used as a modifier. ◆◇◇◇◇

1 **Linguistics** is the study of the way in which language works. *Modern linguistics emerged as a distinct field in the nineteenth century. ...applied linguistics.* N-UNCOUNT

2 **Linguistic** abilities or ideas relate to language or linguistics. *...linguistic skills. ...linguistic theory.* ♦ **linguistically** /lɪŋgwɪstɪkli/ *Somalia is an ethnically and linguistically homogeneous nation.* ADJ: usu ADJ n; ADV: usu ADV adj/-ed

liniment /lɪnɪmənt/ **liniments. Liniment** is a liquid that you rub into your skin in order to reduce pain or stiffness. N-MASS

lining /laɪnɪŋ/ **linings** ◆◆◇◇◇

1 The **lining** of something such as a piece of clothing or a curtain is a layer of cloth attached to the inside of it in order to make it thicker or warmer, or in order to make it hang better. *...a padded satin jacket with quilted lining.* N-VAR

2 You can use **lining** to refer to a layer of paper, plastic, metal, or other substance that is attached to the inside of something in order to insulate or protect it. *...brake linings... Moss makes an attractive lining to wire baskets.* N-VAR

3 The **lining** of your stomach or other organ is a layer of tissue on the inside of it. *...a bacterium that attacks the lining of the stomach. ...the uterine lining.* N-COUNT: usu with supp

4 See also **line**.

link /lɪŋk/ **links, linking, linked** ◆◆◆◆◇

1 If there is a **link** between two things or situations, there is a logical relationship between them, for example because one thing causes the other to exist or happen. *...the link between smoking and lung cancer.* N-COUNT: usu N *between/with* n =connection

2 If someone or something **links** two things or situations or if they **are linked**, there is a logical relationship between them, for example because one thing causes the other to exist or happen. *The UN Security Council has linked any lifting of sanctions to compliance with the ceasefire terms... The study further strengthens the evidence linking smoking with early death... Liver cancer is linked to the hepatitis B virus... The detention raised two distinct* VERB V n *to/with* n V-ed

but closely linked questions. • See also **index-linked.**

3 A **link** between two things or places is a physical connection between them. *...the high-speed rail link between London and the Channel Tunnel... The new road schemes include a link between Chelmsford and the M25... Stalin insisted that the radio link with the German Foreign Ministry should remain open.* — N-COUNT: oft supp N, usu N between/with n =connection

4 If two places or objects **are linked** or something **links** them, there is a physical connection between them. *...the Rama Road, which links the capital, Managua, with the Caribbean coast... The campus is linked by regular bus services to Coventry. ...the Channel Tunnel linking Britain and France.* — VERB =connect; V n with/to n; V pl-n

5 A **link** between two people, organizations, or places is a friendly or business connection between them. *Kiev hopes to cement close links with Bonn... In 1984 the long link between AC Cars and the Hurlock family was severed... A cabinet minister came under investigation for links to the Mafia.* — N-COUNT: usu N with/between/to n

6 A **link** to another person or organization is something that allows you to communicate with them or have contact with them. *She was my only link with the past... The Red Cross was created to provide a link between soldiers in battle and their families at home... These projects will provide vital links between companies and universities.* — N-COUNT: N with/between/to n

7 If you **link** one person or thing to another, you claim that there is a relationship or connection between them. *Criminologist Dr Ann Jones has linked the crime to social circumstances... They've linked her with various men, including magnate Donald Trump. ...a report in The Sunday Times linking him with Chinese Triad gangs.* — VERB; V n to/with n; Also V pl-n

8 A **link** is one of the rings in a chain. — N-COUNT

9 If you **link** one thing with another, you join them by putting one thing through the other. *She linked her arm through his... He linked the fingers of his hands together on his gross stomach.* • If two or more people **link arms**, or if one person **links arms** with another, they stand next to each other, and each person puts their arm round the arm of the person next to them. *It was so slippery that some of the walkers linked arms and proceeded very carefully... She stayed with them, linking arms with the two girls, joking with the boys.* — VERB; V n prep/adv; Also V n; PHR-RECIP: pl-n PHR, PHR with n

10 See also **link-up**.

link up — PHRASAL VERB

1 If you **link up** with someone, you join them for a particular purpose. *They linked up with a series of local anti-nuclear and anti-apartheid groups... The Russian and American armies linked up for the first time on the banks of the river Elbe.* — RECIP =join; V P with n; pl-n V P

2 If one thing **is linked up to** another, the two things are connected to each other. *The television screens of the next century will be linked up to an emerging world telecommunications grid.* — usu passive =connect; be V-ed P to n; Also be V-ed P

linkage /lɪŋkɪdʒ/ **linkages** ◆◇◇◇◇

1 A **linkage** between two things is a link or connection between them. The **linkage** of two things is the act of linking or connecting them. *No one disputes the direct linkage between the unemployment rate and crime... We're trying to establish linkages between these groups and financial institutions. ...the creation of new research materials by the linkage of previously existing sources.* — N-VAR: oft N between/with/of n

2 **Linkage** is a process in international diplomacy where one country agrees to do something only if another country agrees to do something in return. *There is no formal linkage between the two agreements... He insisted that there could be no linkage with other Mideast problems... Western diplomats firmly reject any linkage.* — N-UNCOUNT: oft N between/with n

linking word, linking words. A **linking word**, or in British English a **link word**, is a word which shows a connection between clauses or sentences. 'However', 'the former', and 'so' are linking words. — N-COUNT

link-up, link-ups ◆◇◇◇◇

1 A **link-up** is a connection between two machines or communication systems. *...a live satellite link-up with Bonn. ...computer link-ups with banks in Spain, Portugal, and France.* — N-COUNT: oft N with/between n

2 A **link-up** is a relationship or partnership between two organizations. *...new link-ups between school and commerce... The US airline has just announced a formal link-up with British Airways.* — N-COUNT: oft N with/between n

lino /laɪnoʊ/. **Lino** is the same as **linoleum**; used mainly in British English. *...lino floors. ...the dirty lino on the floor of the kitchen.* — N-UNCOUNT: oft N n

linoleum /lɪnoʊliəm/. **Linoleum** is a floor covering which is made of cloth covered with a hard shiny substance. *...a gray linoleum floor. ...black-and-white squares of linoleum.* — N-UNCOUNT: oft N n =lino

linseed oil /lɪnsiːd ɔɪl/. **Linseed oil** is an oil made from seeds of the flax plant. It is used to make paints and inks, or to rub into wooden surfaces to protect them. — N-UNCOUNT

lint /lɪnt/

1 **Lint** is cotton or linen fabric which you can put on your skin if you have a cut. — N-UNCOUNT

2 **Lint** is small unwanted particles of fluff that collects on clothes; used mainly in American English. — N-UNCOUNT

lintel /lɪntəl/ **lintels.** A **lintel** is a piece of stone or wood over a door or window which supports the bricks above the door or window. — N-COUNT

lion /laɪən/ **lions.** A **lion** is a large wild member of the cat family that is found in Africa. Lions have yellowish fur, and male lions have long hair on their head and neck. — ◆◆◇◇◇ N-COUNT

lioness /laɪənɪs/ **lionesses.** A **lioness** is a female lion. — N-COUNT

lionize /laɪənaɪz/ **lionizes, lionizing, lionized;** also spelled **lionise** in British English. If someone **is lionized**, they are treated as if they are very important or special by a particular group of people, often when they do not really deserve to be; a formal word. *By the 1920's, he was lionised by literary London... The press began to lionize him enthusiastically... In 1936, Max Schmeling had been lionised as boxing's great hope.* — VERB =fete; be V-ed; V n; be V-ed as n

lion's share. If a person, group, or project gets the **lion's share** of something, they get the largest part of it, leaving very little for other people. *Military and nuclear research have received the lion's share of public funding.* — ◆◇◇◇◇ N-SING: usu the N of n

lip /lɪp/ **lips** ◆◆◆◇◇

1 Your **lips** are the two outer parts of the edge of your mouth. *Wade stuck the cigarette between his lips.* — N-COUNT: usu pl, oft poss N

2 The **lip** of something such as a container or a high area of land is its edge. *...the lip of the jug. ...the lip of Mount Etna's smouldering crater.* — N-COUNT: usu with supp, oft N of n =rim

3 If you **bite your lip**, you try very hard not to show the anger or distress that you are feeling. *She bit her lip as she recalled the words he'd thrown at her.* — PHRASES V inflects

4 If you say that something is **on everyone's lips**, you mean that a lot of people seem to be interested in it and are talking about it. *A reporter asks the president the question on everyone's lips: 'Do you anticipate being re-appointed?'... He is the guy whose name is on everyone's lips at the moment.* — v-link PHR

5 If you **lick** your **lips**, you move your tongue across your lips as you think about or taste something pleasant. *They licked their lips in anticipation... We swallowed the chocolates in one gulp, licking our lips.* — V inflects

6 If you tell someone that your **lips are sealed**, you are promising them that you will keep a secret that they have told you. *As for anything told to me in confidence, well, my lips are sealed.* — PRAGMATICS

7 If you say that someone is keeping a **stiff upper lip**, you mean that they are not showing any emotion even though it is difficult for them not to. — usu v PHR, v-link PHR

liposuction /lɪpoʊsʌkʃən/. **Liposuction** is a form of cosmetic surgery where fat is removed from a particular area of the body by dissolving it with special chemicals and then sucking it out with a tube. — N-UNCOUNT

-lipped /-lɪpt/. **-lipped** combines with adjectives to form other adjectives which describe the sort of lips that someone has. *A thin-lipped smile* — COMB in ADJ-GRADED *spread over the captain's face. ...his full-lipped mouth.* • See also **tightlipped**.

lip-read, lip-reads, lip-reading. The form **lip-read** is pronounced /lɪpriːd/ when it is the present tense, and /lɪpred/ when it is the past tense and past participle. If someone can **lip-read**, they are able to understand what someone else is saying by looking at the way the other person's lips move as they speak, without actually hearing any of the words. *They are not given hearing aids or taught to lip-read.* ♦ **lip reading** *The teacher should not move around too much as this makes lip reading more difficult.* VERB V N-UNCOUNT

lip service. If you say that someone pays **lip service** to an idea, you are critical of them because they say they are in favour of it, but they do not do anything to support it. *Unhappily, he had done no more than pay lip service to their views.* ◆◇◇◇◇ N-UNCOUNT: usu N *to* n/-ing PRAGMATICS

lipstick /lɪpstɪk/ **lipsticks. Lipstick** is a coloured substance in the form of a stick which women put on their lips. *She was wearing red lipstick. ...glossy lipsticks made from natural oils and waxes.* ► A **lipstick** is a small tube containing this substance. ◆◆◇◇◇ N-MASS N-COUNT

liquefy /lɪkwɪfaɪ/ **liquefies, liquefying, liquefied.** When a gas or solid substance **liquefies** or **is liquefied**, it changes its form and becomes liquid. *Heat the jam until it liquefies... You can liquefy the carbon dioxide to separate it from the other constituents. ...a truck carrying liquefied petroleum gas.* V-ERG V V n V-ed

liqueur /lɪkjʊəʳ, AM -kɜːr/ **liqueurs** ◆◇◇◇◇

1 A **liqueur** is a strong alcoholic drink with a sweet taste. You drink it after a meal. *...liqueurs such as Grand Marnier and Kirsch. ...small glasses of liqueur.* ► A **liqueur** is a glass of liqueur. *'What about a liqueur with your coffee?' suggested the waitress.* N-MASS N-COUNT

2 **Liqueurs** are a type of chocolate. They contain a sweet substance that has the flavour of an alcoholic liqueur. *...two boxes of liqueurs.* N-COUNT

liquid /lɪkwɪd/ **liquids** ◆◆◇◇◇

1 A **liquid** is a substance which is not solid but which flows and can be poured, for example water. *Drink plenty of liquid... Boil for 20 minutes until the liquid has reduced by half... Solids turn to liquids at certain temperatures.* N-MASS

2 A **liquid** substance is in the form of a liquid rather than being solid or a gas. *Wash in warm water with liquid detergent. ...liquid nitrogen... Fats are solid at room temperature, and oil is liquid at room temperature.* ADJ

3 **Liquid** assets are the things that a person or company owns which can be quickly turned into cash if necessary; a technical term in finance. *The bank had sufficient liquid assets to continue operations.* ADJ

liquidate /lɪkwɪdeɪt/ **liquidates, liquidating, liquidated** ◆◇◇◇◇

1 To **liquidate** a company is to close it down and sell all its assets, usually because it is in debt; a technical term in finance. *A unanimous vote was taken to liquidate the company.* ♦ **liquidation** /lɪkwɪdeɪʃᵊn/ **liquidations** *The company went into liquidation... The number of company liquidations rose 11 per cent.* VERB V n N-VAR

2 If a company **liquidates** its assets, its property such as buildings or machinery is sold in order to get money; a technical term in finance. *The company closed down operations and began liquidating its assets in January.* VERB V n

3 If someone in a position of power **liquidates** people who are causing problems, they get rid of them, usually by killing them. *They have not hesitated in the past to liquidate their rivals.* VERB =eliminate V n

liquidator /lɪkwɪdeɪtəʳ/ **liquidators.** A **liquidator** is a person who is responsible for settling the affairs of a company that is being liquidated. ◆◇◇◇◇ N-COUNT

liquid crystal, liquid crystals. A **liquid crystal** is a liquid that has some of the qualities of crystals, for example reflecting light from different directions in different ways. N-COUNT

liquid crystal display, liquid crystal displays. A **liquid crystal display** is a display of information on a screen, which uses liquid crystals that become visible when electricity is passed through them. N-COUNT =LCD

liquidity /lɪkwɪdɪti/. A company's **liquidity** is the amount of cash or liquid assets it has easily available; a technical term in finance. *The company maintains a high degree of liquidity. ...serious liquidity problems.* ◆◇◇◇◇ N-UNCOUNT: oft N n

liquidize /lɪkwɪdaɪz/ **liquidizes, liquidizing, liquidized;** also spelled **liquidise** in British English. If you **liquidize** food, you process it using an electrical appliance in order to make it liquid. *Liquidize the mixture and then pass it through a sieve.* VERB V n

liquidizer /lɪkwɪdaɪzəʳ/ **liquidizers;** also spelled **liquidiser**. A **liquidizer** is an electric machine that you use to liquidize food; used mainly in British English. The usual American word is **blender**. N-COUNT

liquor /lɪkəʳ/ **liquors.** In American English, alcoholic drink such as whisky, vodka, and gin can be referred to as **liquor**. The British term is **spirits**. *The room was filled with cases of liquor. ...a liquor store. ...intoxicating liquors.* ◆◇◇◇◇ N-MASS

liquorice /lɪkərɪʃ, -ɪs/; also spelled **licorice**, especially in American English. **Liquorice** is a firm black substance with a strong taste. It is used for making sweets. N-UNCOUNT

lira /lɪərə/ **lire** /lɪərə/. The **lira** is the unit of money that is used in Italy. Turkey and Syria also have a unit of money called a **lira**. *It only cost me 400,000 lire... New coin-operated telephones take 100, 200 and 500 lire coins.* ► **The lira** is also used to refer to the Italian currency system, and sometimes to the currency system of other countries which use the lira. *The franc has been under no pressure compared with the lira and the pound.* ◆◇◇◇◇ N-COUNT: usu num N N-SING: *the* N

lisp /lɪsp/ **lisps, lisping, lisped**

1 If someone has a **lisp**, they pronounce the sounds 's' and 'z' as if they were 'th'. For example, they say 'thing' instead of 'sing'. *He has a slight lisp.* N-COUNT: usu sing

2 If someone **lisps** or if they **lisp** something, they say something with a lisp. *The little man, upset, was lisping badly... Bochmann lisped his congratulations. ...her low, lisping voice.* VERB V V n V-ing

list /lɪst/ **lists, listing, listed** ◆◆◆◆◆

1 A **list** of things such as names or addresses is a set of them which all belong to a particular category, written down one below the other. *We are making a list of the top ten men we would not want to be married to... There were six names on the list. ...fine wine from the hotel's exhaustive wine list.* • See also **civil list, hit list, honours list, laundry list, mailing list, shopping list, waiting list.** N-COUNT: oft N *of* n

2 A **list** of things such as events or priorities is a set of them that you think of as being in the same category and as being in a particular order. *High on the list of public demands is to end military control of broadcasting... I would have thought if they were looking for redundancies I would be last on the list... 'First City' joined a long list of failed banks.* N-COUNT: oft N *of* n

3 To **list** several things such as reasons or names means to write or say them one after another, usually in a particular order. *The pupils were asked to list the sports they loved most and hated most... Ingredients are listed in order of the amount used.* VERB V n

4 To **list** something in a particular way means to include it in that way in a list or report. *A medical examiner has listed the deaths as homicides... He was not listed under his real name on the residents panel. ...Margaret Thatcher, listed in Who's Who as 'daughter of the late Alfred Roberts'.* VERB V n prep V-ed

5 If something, especially a ship, **lists**, it leans over to one side; a technical use in sailing. *The ship listed again, and she was thrown back across the bunk.* ► Also a noun. *The ship's list was so strong now that almost at once she stumbled.* VERB V N-SING

6 See also **listed, listing.**

listed /lɪstɪd/. In Britain, a **listed** building is protected by law against being demolished or altered because it is historically or architecturally important. ...*a Grade II Listed 17th century farmhouse.* ADJ: usu ADJ n

listen /lɪsᵊn/ **listens, listening, listened** ◆◆◆◆◇

1 If you **listen** to someone who is talking or to a sound, you give your attention to them or it. *He spent his time listening to the radio... Sonia was not listening.* ♦ **listener, listeners** *One or two listeners had fallen asleep while the President was speaking.* VERB V to n V; N-COUNT

2 If you **listen** for a sound, you keep alert and are ready to hear it if it occurs. *We listen for footsteps approaching... They're both asleep upstairs, but you don't mind listening just in case of trouble, do you?* VERB V for n V

▸ **Listen out** means the same as **listen**; used mainly in British English. *I didn't really listen out for the lyrics.* PHRASAL VERB V P for n Also V P

3 If you **listen** to someone, you do what they advise you to do, or you believe them. *Anne, you need to listen to me this time... When I asked him to stop, he would not listen.* VERB V to n V

4 You say **listen** when you want someone to pay attention to you because you are going to say something important. *Listen, I finish at one.* CONVENTION PRAGMATICS =look

5 You say **listen here** when you are going to say something important to someone, especially when you are angry at something they have done or said. *Listen here, young lady. Don't you call me that!* CONVENTION PRAGMATICS =look here

listen in. If you **listen in** to a private conversation, you secretly listen to it. *He assigned federal agents to listen in on Martin Luther King's phone calls.* PHRASAL VERB =eavesdrop V P to/on n Also V P

listener /lɪsnəʳ/ **listeners** ◆◆◇◇◇

1 A **listener** is a person who listens to the radio or to a particular radio programme. *I'm a regular listener to her show... Each week Dr Buczacki chooses a listener's question and gives a detailed answer.* N-COUNT

2 If you describe someone as a good **listener**, you mean that they listen carefully and sympathetically to you when you talk, for example about your problems. *Dr Brian was a good listener... If you can be a sympathetic listener, it may put your own problems in perspective.* N-COUNT: adj N

3 See also **listen**.

listing /lɪstɪŋ/ **listings.** A **listing** is a published list, or an item in a published list. *A full listing of the companies will be published quarterly... For details of the nearest performance look in the local listings magazines.* ◆◆◇◇◇ N-COUNT

listless /lɪstləs/. Someone who is **listless** has no energy or enthusiasm. *He was listless and pale and wouldn't eat much.* ♦ **listlessly** *Usually, you would just sit listlessly, too hot to do anything else.* ♦ **listlessness** *Amy was distressed by Helen's listlessness.* ◆◇◇◇◇ ADJ-GRADED; ADV-GRADED: ADV with v; N-UNCOUNT

list price, list prices. The **list price** of an item is the price which the manufacturer suggests that a shopkeeper should charge for it. N-COUNT

lit /lɪt/. **Lit** is a past tense and past participle of **light**.

litany /lɪtəni/ **litanies** ◆◇◇◇◇

1 If you describe what someone says, especially when it is a long list of things, as a **litany**, you mean that you have often heard it repeated, and you think it is boring or insincere. *She remained in the doorway, listening to his litany of complaints against her client.* N-COUNT: usu with supp, oft N of n PRAGMATICS

2 A **litany** is part of a church service in which the priest says a set group of words and the people reply, also using a set group of words. N-COUNT

liter /liːtəʳ/. See **litre**.

literacy /lɪtərəsi/. **Literacy** is the ability to read and write. *Many adults have some problems with literacy and numeracy... The literacy rate there is the highest in Central America.* ◆◇◇◇◇ N-UNCOUNT

literal /lɪtərəl/ ◆◇◇◇◇

1 The **literal** sense of a word or phrase is its most basic sense. *In many cases, the people there are fighting, in a literal sense, for their homes.* ADJ: usu ADJ n

2 A **literal** translation is one in which you translate each word of the original work rather than giving the meaning of each expression or sentence using words that sound natural. *A literal translation of the name Tapies is 'walls.'* ADJ: usu ADJ n

3 You use **literal** to describe someone who uses or understands words in a plain and simple way. *Dennis is a very literal person.* ADJ-GRADED

4 If you describe something as the **literal** truth or a **literal** fact, you are emphasizing that it is true. *He was saying no more than the literal truth.* ADJ: usu ADJ n PRAGMATICS

literally /lɪtərəli/ ◆◆◇◇◇

1 You can use **literally** to emphasize a word or expression which is being used in a creative way to exaggerate a situation. Some careful speakers of English think that this use is incorrect. *We've got to get the economy under control or it will literally eat us up... The views are literally breath-taking.* ADV: ADV with cl/group (not last in cl), ADV before v PRAGMATICS

2 You use **literally** to emphasize that what you are saying is true, even though it seems exaggerated or surprising. *Putting on an opera is a tremendous enterprise involving literally hundreds of people... I literally crawled to the car.* ADV: ADV with cl/group (not last in cl), ADV before v PRAGMATICS

3 If a word or expression is translated **literally**, its most simple or basic meaning is translated. *The word 'volk' translates literally as 'folk'... A stanza is, literally, a room.* ADV: ADV with v, ADV with cl

4 If you **take** something **literally**, you think that a word or expression is being used with its most simple or basic meaning. *If you tell a person to 'step on it' or 'throw on your coat,' they may take you literally, with disastrous consequences.* PHRASE: V inflects

literary /lɪtərəri, AM -reri/ ◆◆◆◇◇

1 **Literary** means concerned with or connected with the writing, study, or appreciation of literature. *Her literary criticism focuses on the way great literature suggests ideas... She's the literary editor of the 'Sunday Review'. ...a literary masterpiece.* ADJ: usu ADJ n

2 **Literary** words and expressions are often unusual in some way and are used to create a special effect in a piece of writing such as a poem, speech, or novel. ADJ-GRADED

literate /lɪtərət/ ◆◇◇◇◇

1 Someone who is **literate** is able to read and write. *Over one-quarter of the adult population are not fully literate.* ADJ ≠illiterate

2 If you describe someone as **literate**, you mean that they are intelligent and well-educated, especially about literature and the arts. *Scientists should be literate and articulate as well as able to handle figures... His lyrics are highly literate. He even quotes Voltaire.* ADJ-GRADED ≠illiterate

3 If you describe someone as **literate** in a particular subject, especially one that many people do not know anything about, you mean that they have a good knowledge and understanding of that subject. *Head teachers need to be financially literate... We want to have more scientifically literate people running our television stations.* • See also **computer-literate**. ADJ-GRADED: usu adv ADJ

literati /lɪtərɑːti/. **Literati** are well-educated people who are interested in literature; often used showing disapproval. *That Walter Scott was a fervent Tory is something of an embarrassment to the leftist literati.* N-PLURAL

literature /lɪtrətʃəʳ, AM -tərətʃʊr/ **literatures** ◆◆◆◇◇

1 Novels, plays, and poetry are referred to as **literature**, especially when they are considered to have artistic merit. *...classic works of literature. ...a Professor of English Literature... It may not be great literature but it certainly had me riveted!... I have spent my life getting to know diverse literatures of different epochs.* N-VAR

2 The **literature** on a particular subject of study are the books and articles that have been published about it. *The literature on immigration policy is almost unrelievedly critical of the state... This work is documented in the scientific literature.* N-UNCOUNT: usu with supp

3 **Literature** is written information produced by people who want to sell you something or give you advice. *I am sending you literature from two other companies that provide a similar service... Some companies have toned down the claims on their promotional literature.* N-UNCOUNT: usu with supp

lithe /laɪð/. A **lithe** person is able to move and bend their body easily and gracefully. *...a lithe young gymnast... His walk was lithe and graceful.* ADJ-GRADED =agile

lithograph /lɪθəgrɑːf, -græf/ **lithographs.** A **lithograph** is a printed picture made by the method of lithography. N-COUNT

lithography /lɪθɒgrəfi/. **Lithography** is a method of printing in which a piece of stone or metal is specially treated so that ink sticks to some parts of it and not to others. N-UNCOUNT ♦ **lithographic** *The book's 85 colour lithographic plates look staggeringly fresh and bold.* ADJ: ADJ n

Lithuanian /lɪθjueɪniən/ **Lithuanians** ◆◆◆◆◇

1 **Lithuanian** means belonging or relating to Lithuania, or to its people, language, or culture. *...the Lithuanian parliament.* ADJ

2 A **Lithuanian** is a Lithuanian citizen, or a person of Lithuanian origin. N-COUNT

3 **Lithuanian** is the language spoken by people who live in Lithuania. N-UNCOUNT

litigant /lɪtɪgənt/ **litigants.** A **litigant** is a person who is involved in a civil lawsuit, either because they are making a formal complaint to the court about someone, or because a complaint is being made about them; a legal term. N-COUNT

litigate /lɪtɪgeɪt/ **litigates, litigating, litigated.** To **litigate** means to take legal action; a legal term. *...the cost of litigating personal injury claims in the county court... If we have to litigate, we will.* VERB V n V

litigation /lɪtɪgeɪʃən/. **Litigation** is the process of fighting or defending a case in a civil court of law. *The settlement ends more than four years of litigation on behalf of the residents.* ◆◇◇◇◇ N-UNCOUNT

litigator /lɪtɪgeɪtəʳ/ **litigators.** A **litigator** is a lawyer who helps someone take legal action; a legal term. N-COUNT

litigious /lɪtɪdʒəs/. Someone who is **litigious** often makes formal complaints about people to a civil court of law; a formal word. ADJ-GRADED

litmus test /lɪtməs test/ **litmus tests.** If you say that something is a **litmus test** of something such as the quality or success of a particular thing, you mean that it is an effective and conclusive way of proving it or measuring it. *Ending the fighting must be the absolute priority, the litmus test of the agreements' validity... The success of wind power represents a litmus test for renewable energy.* N-COUNT: usu sing, usu N *of/for* n

litre /liːtəʳ/ **litres;** spelled **liter** in American English. A **litre** is a metric unit of volume that is a thousand cubic centimetres. It is equal to 1.76 British pints or 2.11 American pints. *...15 litres of water... This tax would raise petrol prices by about 3.5p per litre. ...a Ford Escort with a 1.9-litre engine.* ◆◆◇◇◇ N-COUNT: num N, oft N *of* n

litter /lɪtəʳ/ **litters, littering, littered** ◆◆◇◇◇

1 **Litter** is rubbish that is left lying around outside. *If you see litter in the corridor, pick it up... On Wednesday we cleared a beach and woodland of litter.* N-UNCOUNT =rubbish

2 A **litter** of things is a quantity of them that are lying around in a disorganized way. *He pushed aside the litter of books and papers and laid two places at the table.* N-UNCOUNT: usu N *of* n

3 If a number of things **litter** a place, they are scattered around untidily on or in it. *Glass from broken bottles litters the pavement.* VERB V n ♦ **littered** *The entrance hall is littered with toys and wellington boots... Concrete purpose-built resorts are littered across the mountainsides.* ADJ: v-link ADJ prep

4 If you say that something such as history or someone's speech is **littered with** something, you mean that there are many examples of the second thing in the first. *History is littered with men and women spurred into achievement by a father's disregard... Charles' speech is littered with lots of marketing buzzwords like 'package' and 'product'.* ADJ: v-link ADJ *with* n =full of

5 A **litter** is a group of animals born to the same mother at the same time. *...a litter of pups.* N-COUNT

6 **Litter** is a dry substance that you put in the container where you want your cat to defecate and urinate. N-UNCOUNT

litter bin, litter bins. A **litter bin** is a container, usually in a street, park, or public building, into which people can put rubbish; used mainly in British English. N-COUNT =rubbish bin

little 1 determiner, quantifier, and adverb uses

little /lɪtəl/ ◆◆◆◆◆

1 You use **little** to indicate that there is only a very small amount of something. You can use 'so', 'too', and 'very' in front of **little**. *I had little money and little free time... I find that I need very little sleep these days... There is little doubt that a diet high in fibre is more satisfying... So far little progress has been made towards ending the fighting... The pudding is quick and easy and needs little attention once in the oven.* DET: DET n-uncount =a lot of ► Also a quantifier. *Little of the existing housing is of good enough quality... They claim that little of the $16.5 million dollars in aid sent by the US government has reached them.* QUANT: QUANT *of* def-n ≠much ► Also a pronoun. *He ate little, and drank less... In general, employers do little to help the single working mother... Little is known about his childhood.* PRON

2 **Little** means not very often or to only a small extent. *On their way back to Marseille they spoke very little... Only Africa is at present little affected by hard drugs.* ADV-GRADED: ADV with v

3 **A little** of something is a small amount of it, but not very much. You can also say **a very little**. *Mrs Caan needs a little help getting her groceries home... A little food would do us all some good. ...a little light reading... I shall be only a very little time.* DET: DET n-uncount ► Also a pronoun. *They get paid for it. Not much. Just a little.* PRON ► Also a quantifier. *Pour a little of the sauce over the chicken... I'm sure she won't mind sparing us a little of her time.* QUANT: QUANT *of* def-n-uncount/sing ≠a lot

4 If you do something **a little**, you do it for a short time. *He walked a little by himself in the garden.* ADV-GRADED: ADV after v

5 **A little** or **a little bit** means to a small extent or degree. *He complained a little of a nagging pain between his shoulder blades... He was a little bit afraid of his father's reaction... If you have to drive when you are tired, go a little more slowly than you would normally... He wanted to have someone to whom he could talk a little about himself.* ADV-GRADED: ADV after v, ADV adj/adv

6 If something happens **little by little**, it happens very gradually. *In the beginning he had felt well, but little by little he was becoming weaker... I would have to learn, little by little, to exist alone.* PHRASE: PHR with cl =gradually

little 2 adjective uses

little /lɪtəl/ **littler, littlest** ◆◆◆◆◆

The comparative **littler** and the superlative **littlest** are sometimes used in spoken English for meanings 1, 3, and 4, but otherwise the comparative and superlative forms of the adjective **little** are not used.

1 **Little** things are small in size. **Little** is slightly more informal than **small**. *We sat around a little table, eating and drinking wine. ...the little group of art students.* ADJ-GRADED: usu ADJ n =small ≠big

2 You use **little** to indicate that someone or something is small, in a pleasant and attractive way. *She's got the nicest little house not far from the library. ...a little old lady... James usually drives a little Citroen hatchback.* ADJ: ADJ n PRAGMATICS

3 A **little** child is young. *I have a little boy of 8... When I was little I was very hyper-active.* ADJ-GRADED

4 Your **little** sister or brother is younger than you are. *Whenever Daniel's little sister was asked to do something she always had a naughty reply.* ADJ: ADJ n =younger ≠big

5 A **little** distance, period of time, or event is short in length. *Just go down the road a little way, turn left, and cross the bridge... Why don't we just wait a little while and see what happens... I've been wanting to have a little talk with you.* ADJ-GRADED: ADJ n ≠long

6 A **little** sound or gesture is quick. *I had a little laugh to myself... She stood up quickly, giving a little cry of astonishment... He turned with a little nod and I watched him walk away.* ADJ-GRADED: ADJ n ≠big

7 You use **little** to indicate that something is not serious or important. *...irritating little habits... Harry* ADJ: ADJ n

found himself getting angry over little things that had never bothered him before.

little finger, little fingers. Your **little finger** is the smallest finger on your hand. ◆◇◇◇◇ N-COUNT

littoral /lɪtərəl/ **littorals.** The **littoral** means the coast; a technical term in geography. *...the countries of the north African littoral. ...the littoral countries of the Persian Gulf.* N-COUNT: usu sing, usu *the* N, N n

liturgical /lɪtɜːʳdʒɪkᵊl/. **Liturgical** things are used in or relate to church services; a formal word. ADJ: usu ADJ n

liturgy /lɪtəʳdʒi/ **liturgies.** A **liturgy** is a particular form of religious service, usually one that is set and approved by a branch of the Christian Church. *A clergyman read the liturgy from the prayer-book. ...the many similarities in ministry, liturgy and style between the two churches.* N-VAR

live 1 verb uses

live /lɪv/ **lives, living, lived** ◆◆◆◆◆

1 If someone **lives** in a particular place or with a particular person, their home is in that place or with that person. *She has lived here for 10 years... She always said I ought to live alone... Where do you live?... He still lives with his parents.* VERB V adv/prep

2 If you say that someone **lives** in particular circumstances or that they **live** a particular kind of life, you mean that they are in those circumstances or that they have that kind of life. *We lived quite grandly... Compared to people living only a few generations ago, we have greater opportunities to have a good time... We can start living a normal life again now. ...the local support group for people living with HIV and AIDS.* VERB V adv/prep V n V-ing

3 If you say that someone **lives for** a particular thing, you mean that it is the most important thing in their life. *He lived for his work.* VERB V *for* n

4 To **live** means to be alive, especially after a particular event or point in time. If you say that someone **lives** to a particular age, or to see a particular event, you mean that they stay alive until they are that age or until that event happens. *He's got a terrible disease and will not live long... A perennial is a plant that lives indefinitely... He lived to be 103... My father died nigh on ten years ago, but he lived to see his first grandson... Matilda was born in northern Italy in 1046 and apparently lived to a ripe old age... The blue whale is the largest living thing on the planet... Ian was her only living relative.* VERB V adv V to-inf V *to* n V-ing

5 If people **live by** doing a particular activity, they get the money, food, or clothing they need by doing that activity. *...the last indigenous people to live by hunting... These crimes were committed largely by professional criminals who lived by crime.* VB: no cont V *by*-ing/n

6 If a person or occasion **lives** in someone's mind or in history, they are remembered for ever or for a long time because they are significant or important. *The memory of that will live with me for many years to come... He will live in history as an entrepreneur who made co-operation with the Soviet Union possible.* ▸ **Live on** means the same as **live**. *Lenin lives on in the minds and hearts of millions of people.* VB: no cont V *with* n V *in* n PHRASAL VERB VP *in* n Also VP

7 See also **living**.

8 If you say that someone **lives and breathes** a particular subject or activity, you are emphasizing that they are extremely enthusiastic about it. *He has lived and breathed polo since he was seven.* PHRASES Vs inflect, PHR n PRAGMATICS

9 If you tell someone that they **haven't lived** unless they experience a particular thing, you are telling them that thing is extremely good and should be experienced. *If you have never been to an opera, you haven't lived... You haven't lived until you've used their new micro system.* *have* inflects, usu PHR with cl

10 You can use expressions such as **to live in fear** and **to live in terror** to indicate that someone is always thinking about an unpleasant or frightening event, because they think that it might happen. *One in 10 Californians is unemployed and thousands more live in fear of losing their jobs.* V inflects, usu PHR *of* -ing/n

11 You say **live and let live** as a way of saying that you should let other people behave in the way that they want to and not criticize them for behaving differently from you. CONVENTION PRAGMATICS

12 If you **live it up**, you have a very enjoyable and exciting time, for example by going to lots of parties or going out drinking with friends; an informal expression. *There is no reason why you couldn't live it up once in a while.* V inflects

13 • to **live hand to mouth**: see **hand.** • to **live a lie**: see **lie.** • to **live beyond** your **means**: see **means.** • to **live in sin**: see **sin.**

live down. If you are unable to **live down** a mistake, failure, or bad reputation, you are unable to make people forget about it. *Labor was also unable to live down its reputation as the party of high taxes... I thought I'd never live it down.* PHRASAL VERB V P n (not pron) V n P

live off. If you **live off** another person, you rely on them to provide you with money. *...a man who all his life had lived off his father.* PHRASAL VERB V P n

live on or **live off** PHRASAL VERB

1 If you **live on** or **live off** a particular amount of money, you have that amount of money to buy things. *Even with efficient budgeting, most students are unable to live on £3000 per year... You'll have enough to live on... She had to live off £46 a week.* V P amount

2 If you **live on** or **live off** a particular source of income, that is where you get the money that you need. *The proportion of Americans living on welfare rose... He's been living off state benefits.* V P n

3 If an animal, plant, or bacterium **lives on** or **lives off** a particular food, this is the kind of food that it eats to stay alive. *The fish live on the plankton... Most species live off aquatic snails.* V P n

4 If you say that a person **lives on** or **lives off** a particular kind of food, you mean that it is, or seems to be, the only thing that they eat, for example because they like it a lot or because they do not have enough money to buy other foods. *The children live on chips... Their room was bare of furniture and they lived off porridge.* V P n

live on PHRASAL VERB

1 See **live** 6.

2 If someone **lives on**, they continue to be alive for a long time after a particular point in time or after a particular event. *I know my life has been cut short by this terrible virus but Daniel will live on after me.* V P

live out PHRASAL VERB

1 If you **live out** your life in a particular place or in particular circumstances, you stay in that place or in those circumstances until the end of your life or until the end of a particular period of your life. *Gein did not stand trial but lived out his days in a mental asylum... I couldn't live my life out on tour like he does.* V P n (not pron) V n P

2 If you **live out** a dream, fantasy, or idea, you do the things that you have thought about. *He began living out his rock 'n' roll fantasy during his last year in law school... I suppose some people create an idea of who they want to be, and then they live it out.* V P n (not pron) V n P

live through. If you **live through** an unpleasant event or change, you experience it and survive. *We are too young to have lived through the war... It's been like living through a nightmare.* PHRASAL VERB V P n

live together. If two people are not married but live in the same house and have a sexual relationship, you can say that they **live together**. *The couple had been living together for 16 years.* PHRASAL VERB V P

live up to. If someone or something **lives up to** what they were expected or desired to be or do, they are as good as they were expected or desired to be. *Sales have not lived up to expectations this year... Had he lived up to his promise, he would have made a fortune in sponsorship money.* PHRASAL VERB V P P n

live 2 adjective uses

live /laɪv/ ◆◆◆◇◇

1 **Live** animals or plants are alive, rather than being dead or artificial. *...a protest against the company's tests on live animals. ...baskets of live chickens.* ADJ: ADJ n =dead

2 A **live** television or radio programme is one in which an event or performance is broadcast at exactly the same time as it happens, rather than being recorded first. *Murray was a guest on a live ra-* ADJ ≠pre-recorded *dio show... Last night Mr Rushdie appeared on live TV... They watch all the live matches... A broadcast of the speech was heard in San Francisco, but it is not known if this was live.* ► Also an adverb. *It was broadcast live in 50 countries... We'll be going live to Nottingham later in this bulletin.* ADV: ADV after v

3 A **live** performance is given in front of an audience, rather than being recorded and then broadcast or shown in a film. *The Rainbow has not hosted live music since the end of 1981... A live audience will pose the questions... The band was forced to cancel a string of live dates.* ► Also an adverb. *Kat Bjelland has been playing live with her new band.* ADJ: usu ADJ n ≠recorded; ADV: ADV after v

4 A **live** album is an album which has on it a recording of a band playing in a concert, rather than in a recording studio. *This is my favourite live album of all time... The LP features live recordings from the 'Great Xpectations' all-day show.* ADJ: usu ADJ n

5 A **live** wire or piece of electrical equipment is directly connected to a source of electricity. *The plug broke, exposing live wires... He warned others about the live electric cables as they climbed to safety.* ADJ: usu ADJ n

6 **Live** bullets are made of metal, rather than rubber or plastic, and are intended to kill people rather than injure them. *They trained in the jungle using live ammunition.* ADJ: usu ADJ n

7 A **live** bomb or missile is one which has not yet exploded. *A live bomb had earlier been defused.* ADJ: usu ADJ n

8 If a system, campaign, or other course of action **goes live**, it starts to be used; used mainly in British English. *The new system went live earlier this year... The service should go live this summer.* PHRASES V inflects

9 You use **real live** to say that someone or something is present or exists, when you want to indicate that you think this is exciting and unusual or unexpected; an informal expression. *He had never met a real live admiral... She has the best pet of all – a real live tiger.* PHR n

live-in /lɪv ɪn/ ◆◆◆◇◇

1 A **live-in** partner is someone who lives in the same house as the person they are having a sexual relationship with, but is not married to them. *She shared the apartment with her live-in partner.* ADJ: ADJ n

2 A **live-in** nanny, servant, or other domestic worker sleeps and eats in the house where they work. *I have a live-in nanny for my youngest daughter.* ADJ: ADJ n

livelihood /laɪvlihʊd/ **livelihoods.** Your **livelihood** is the job or other source of income which gives you the money to buy the things that you need in your daily life. *...fishermen who depend on the seas for their livelihood... As a result of this conflict he lost both his home and his means of livelihood.* ◆◇◇◇◇ N-VAR

lively /laɪvli/ **livelier, liveliest** ◆◆◇◇◇

1 You can describe someone as **lively** when they behave in an enthusiastic and cheerful way. *She had a sweet, lively personality... Josephine was bright, lively and cheerful.* ♦ **liveliness** *Amy could sense his liveliness even from where she stood.* ADJ-GRADED; N-UNCOUNT

2 A **lively** event or a **lively** discussion, for example, has lots of interesting and exciting things happening or being said in it. *It turned out to be a very interesting session with a lively debate... Their 4-1 win in Honduras was a particularly lively affair.* ♦ **liveliness** *Some may enjoy the liveliness of such a restaurant for a few hours a day or week.* ADJ-GRADED: usu ADJ n; N-UNCOUNT

3 Someone who has a **lively** mind is intelligent and interested in a lot of different things. *She was a very well educated girl with a lively mind, a girl with ambition. ...her very lively imagination.* ADJ-GRADED: usu ADJ n

4 A **lively** feeling or awareness is a strong and enthusiastic one. *The papers also show a lively interest in European developments.* ADJ-GRADED: ADJ n

liven /laɪvᵊn/ **livens, livening, livened**

liven up PHRASAL VERB

1 If a place or event **livens up**, or if something **livens it up**, it becomes more interesting and exciting. *How could we decorate the room to liven it up?... The multicoloured rag rug was chosen to liven up the grey carpet... The arena livens up only on Saturdays and Sundays when a flea market is open there.* ERG; V n P; V P n (not pron); V P

2 If people **liven up**, or if something **livens** them **up**, they become more cheerful and energetic. *Talking about her daughters livens her up... George livens up after midnight, relaxing a little.* ERG; V n P; V P

liver /lɪvəʳ/ **livers** ◆◆◇◇◇

1 Your **liver** is a large organ in your body which processes your blood and helps to clean unwanted substances out of it. N-COUNT

2 **Liver** is the liver of some animals, especially lambs, pigs, and cows, which is cooked and eaten. *...grilled calves' liver.* N-VAR

liveried /lɪvərid/. A **liveried** servant is one who wears a special uniform. *The tea was served to guests by liveried footmen.* ADJ: ADJ n

livery /lɪvəri/ **liveries** ◆◇◇◇◇

1 A servant's **livery** is the special uniform that he or she wears. *She was attended by servants in splendid livery and powdered wigs.* N-VAR

2 The **livery** of a particular company is the special design or set of colours associated with it that is put on its products and possessions. *Buffet cars in the company's bright red and yellow livery could soon be rattling along the tracks.* N-COUNT: usu with poss

lives

1 **Lives**, pronounced /laɪvz/, is the plural of **life**.

2 **Lives**, pronounced /lɪvz/, is the third person singular form of **live**.

livestock /laɪvstɒk/. Animals such as cattle and sheep which are kept on a farm are referred to as **livestock**. *The heavy rains and flooding killed scores of livestock.* ◆◇◇◇◇ N-UNCOUNT-COLL

live wire /laɪv waɪəʳ/ **live wires.** If you describe someone as a **live wire**, you mean that they are lively and energetic; an informal expression. N-COUNT

livid /lɪvɪd/

1 Someone who is **livid** is extremely angry; an informal use. *I am absolutely livid about it... She is livid that I have invited Dick.* ADJ-GRADED: usu v-link ADJ =furious

2 Something that is **livid** is an unpleasant dark colour. *The scarred side of his face was a livid red.* ADJ-GRADED

living /lɪvɪŋ/ **livings** ◆◆◆◇◇

1 The work that you do for a **living** is the work that you do in order to earn the money that you need. *Father never talked about what he did for a living... He earns his living doing all kinds of things.* N-COUNT: usu sing

2 You use **living** when you are talking about the quality of people's daily lives. *Olivia has always been a model of healthy living. ...the stresses of urban living.* N-UNCOUNT: with supp

3 You use **living** to talk about the places where people relax when they are not working. *The spacious living quarters were on the second floor... The study links the main living area to the kitchen.* ADJ: ADJ n

4 **The living** are people who are alive, rather than people who have died. *The young man is dead. We have only to consider the living.* N-PLURAL: the N ≠dead

5 If you say that someone **scrapes a living** or **scratches a living**, you mean that they just manage to earn enough to live on, but it is very difficult. *He almost manages to scrape a living as an artist.* PHRASE: V inflects =get by

6 • **living proof**: see **proof**. • **in living memory**: see **memory**. • **the world owes** them **a living**: see **world**.

living room, living rooms; also spelled **living-room**. The **living room** in a house is the room where people sit and relax. *We were sitting on the couch in the living room watching TV.* ◆◆◇◇◇ N-COUNT =sitting room, lounge

living standard, living standards. Living standards or **living standard** is used to refer to the level of comfort in which people live, which usually depends on how much money they have. *Cheaper housing would vastly improve the living standards of ordinary people... Critics say his reforms have caused the fall in living standards.* ◆◇◇◇◇ N-COUNT: usu pl

living wage. A **living wage** is a wage which is just sufficient to enable you to buy food, clothing, and other necessary things. *Many farmers have to depend on subsidies to make a living wage.* N-SING: usu a N

lizard /lɪzəʳd/ **lizards.** A **lizard** is a reptile with short legs and a long tail. ◆◇◇◇◇ N-COUNT

-'ll /-əl/. In spoken English and informal written English, **'ll** is the shortened form of 'will' that is added to the end of the pronoun or noun which is the subject of the verb. For example, 'you will' can be shortened to 'you'll'.

llama /lɑːmə/ **llamas.** A **llama** is a South American animal with thick hair, which looks like a small camel without a hump. N-COUNT

lo /loʊ/. **Lo and behold** or **lo** is used to emphasize a surprising event that is about to be mentioned, or to emphasize in an ironic way that something is not surprising at all; a literary or humorous use. *He called the minister of the interior and, lo and behold, within about an hour, the prisoners were released... I looked and lo! every one of the fifteen men who had been standing with me had disappeared.* ◆◇◇◇◇ CONVENTION PRAGMATICS

load /loʊd/ **loads, loading, loaded** ◆◆◆◇◇

1 If you **load** a vehicle or a container, or if you **load** things into or onto it, you put a large quantity of things or heavy things into or onto it. *The three men seemed to have finished loading the truck... Mr. Dambar had loaded his plate with lasagne... Soldiers were loaded with blankets and supplies... They load all their equipment into backpacks... She deposited the loaded tray.* ▶ **Load up** means the same as **load**. *I've just loaded my truck up... The giggling couple loaded up their red sports car and drove off... We loaded up carts with all the blankets, bandages, medication, water we could spare... She loaded up his collection of vintage wines into crates.* ♦ **loading** *...the loading of baggage onto international flights.* VERB V n V n *with* n V n *into/onto* n V-ed PHRASAL VERB V n P V P n (not pron) V P n *with* n V P n *into/onto* n Also V n P *with/into/onto* n N-SING: usu *the* N *of* n

2 A **load** is something, usually a large quantity or heavy object, which is being carried. *He drove by with a big load of hay... He was carrying a very heavy load.* N-COUNT

3 A **load** is a quantity of clothes or sheets which need washing and which are washed together in a washing machine. *I put another load in the washing machine.* N-COUNT

4 If you refer to **a load of** something or **loads of** it, you are emphasizing that there is a large amount of it. If you refer to **a load of** people or things or **loads of** them, you are emphasizing that there are a lot of them; an informal use. *I've got loads of money... His people came up with a load of embarrassing information... I used to read loads of Asterix books. ...a load of kids.* ● In informal English, you can use **a load of** to refer to a thing or a group of things or people which you do not like. For example, if you say that something is **a load of rubbish**, you are emphasizing that you think is no good at all or not true at all. *I've never heard such a load of nonsense... Personally, I think that's a load of garbage!* QUANT: QUANT *of* n-uncount/pl-n PRAGMATICS =a lot of, lots of PHRASE: usu PHR after v, v-link PHR PRAGMATICS

5 When someone **loads** a weapon such as a gun, they put a bullet or missile in it so that it is ready to use. *I knew how to load and handle a gun... He carried a loaded gun... They were quite safe because they weren't loaded.* VERB V n V-ed

6 When someone **loads** a camera or other piece of equipment or when they **load** film, tape, or data into it, they put film, tape, or data into it so that it is ready to use. *A photographer from the newspaper was loading his camera with film... A technician loads a video tape into one of the machines... The data can subsequently be loaded on a computer for processing.* VERB V n *with* n V n *into/onto/on* n

7 You can refer to the amount of work you have to do as a **load**. *She's taking some of the load off the secretaries.* N-COUNT

8 The **load** of a system or piece of equipment, especially a system supplying electricity or a computer, is the extent to which it is being used at a particular time. *An efficient bulb may lighten the load of power stations... Several processors can share the load of handling data in a single program.* N-COUNT

9 The **load** on something is the amount of weight that is pressing down on it or the amount of strain that it is under. *Some of these chairs have flattened feet which spread the load on the ground... High blood pressure imposes an extra load on the heart.* N-SING

10 See also **loaded**; ● **a load off your mind**: see **mind**.

load down. If you **load** someone **down** with things, especially heavy things, you give them a large number of them or put a large number of them on them. *She loaded me down with around a dozen cassettes... They had come up from London loaded down with six suitcases.* PHRASAL VERB V n P *with* n V-ed P Also V P

load up. See **load** 1. PHRASAL VERB

-load /-loʊd/ **-loads. -load** combines with nouns referring to a vehicle or container to form nouns that refer to the total amount of something that the vehicle or container mentioned can hold or carry. *The first plane-loads of food, children's clothing and medical supplies began arriving. ...a lorry-load of sheep on their way across Europe.* COMB in N-COUNT

loaded /loʊdɪd/ ◆◆◇◇◇

1 A **loaded** question or word has more meaning or purpose than it appears to have, because the person who uses it hopes it will cause people to respond in a particular way. *That's a loaded question. ...the loaded word 'sexist'.* ADJ-GRADED

2 If something is **loaded** with a particular characteristic, it has that characteristic to a very great degree. *The President's visit is loaded with symbolic significance... The phrase is loaded with irony.* ADJ-GRADED: usu v-link ADJ, usu ADJ *with* n

3 If you say that something is **loaded** in favour of someone or something, you mean it works unfairly to their advantage. If you say it is **loaded** against them, you mean it works unfairly to their disadvantage. *The press is loaded in favour of this present government... The article was heavily loaded against Morrissey. ...very loaded experiments carried out by General Bobby Marshall.* ADJ-GRADED: usu v-link ADJ *in favour of/against* n PRAGMATICS =biased

loaf /loʊf/ **loaves; loafs, loafing, loafed.** **Loaves** is the plural of the noun. **Loafs** is the 3rd person singular present tense of the verb. ◆◇◇◇◇

1 A **loaf** of bread is bread which has been shaped and baked in one piece. It is usually large enough for more than one person and can be cut into slices. *...a loaf of crusty bread. ...freshly baked loaves.* N-COUNT: oft N *of* n

2 If you **loaf**, you stand or wait in a place, not doing anything interesting or useful. *Soldiers loafed at street corners.* ▶ **Loaf around** means the same as **loaf**. *We had been at Cambridge together, she studying medicine and me loafing around.* VERB =hang around V PHRASAL VERB V P

loafer /loʊfəʳ/ **loafers. Loafers** are flat slip-on shoes, usually made of leather; used mainly in American English. N-COUNT

loam /loʊm/. **Loam** is soil that is good for growing crops and plants in because it contains a lot of decayed vegetable matter and does not contain too much sand or clay. N-UNCOUNT

loan /loʊn/ **loans, loaning, loaned** ◆◆◆◆◇

1 A **loan** is a sum of money that you borrow. *The country has no access to foreign loans or financial aid... The president wants to make it easier for small businesses to get bank loans. ...loan repayments.* ● See also **bridging loan, soft loan.** N-COUNT

2 If someone gives you a **loan of** something, you borrow it from them. *I am in need of a loan of a bike for a few weeks... He had offered the loan of his small villa at Cap Ferrat.* N-SING: N *of* n

3 If you **loan** something to someone, you lend it to them. *He had kindly offered to loan us all the plants required for the exhibit... We were approached by the Royal Yachting Association to see if we would loan our boat to them.* ▶ **Loan out** means the same as **loan**. *It is common practice for clubs to loan out players to sides in the lower divisions... The ground was loaned out for numerous events including pop concerts.* VERB =lend V n n V n *to* n Also V n PHRASAL VERB V P n (not pron) *to* n *be* V-ed *out* Also V n P, V P n

4 If something is **on loan**, it has been borrowed. *...impressionist paintings on loan from the National Gallery... Many of these are on display in the Museum, but some have been sent out on loan to other museums.* PHRASES v-link PHR, PHR after v

5 If a person is **on loan** from one organization to another, they are temporarily working for the second organization while still employed by the first. *David Speedie, on loan from Southampton, scored his first goal for Birmingham... She's on loan to us from the CIA.* usu v-link PHR

loan shark, loan sharks. If you describe someone as a **loan shark**, you disapprove of them because they lend money to people and charge them very high rates of interest on the loan. N-COUNT PRAGMATICS

loath /loʊθ/; also spelled **loth**. If you are **loath** to do something, you do not want to do it. *She is loath to give up her hard-earned liberty... The new finance minister seems loth to cut income tax.* ADJ-GRADED: v-link ADJ to-inf =reluctant

loathe /loʊð/ **loathes, loathing, loathed.** If you **loathe** something or someone, you dislike them very much. *The two men loathe each other... She loathed being the child of impoverished labourers.* ◆◇◇◇◇ VERB =detest V n V -ing

loathing /loʊðɪŋ/. **Loathing** is a feeling of great dislike and disgust. *Deacon made no secret of his loathing of Bayldon... She looked at him with loathing.* ◆◇◇◇◇ N-UNCOUNT

loathsome /loʊðsəm/. If you describe someone or something as **loathsome**, you are indicating how much you dislike them or how much they disgust you. *...the loathsome spectacle we were obliged to witness.* ADJ-GRADED

loaves /loʊvz/. **Loaves** is the plural of **loaf**.

lob /lɒb/ **lobs, lobbing, lobbed** ◆◇◇◇◇

1 If you **lob** something, you throw it or launch it so that it goes quite high in the air. *Enemy forces lobbed a series of artillery shells onto the city... A group of protesters gathered outside, chanting and lobbing firebombs.* VERB V n prep/adv V n

2 In sport, if you **lob** the ball, you hit or kick it high into the air so that it lands behind your opponent. *Brown lobbed the ball over the Australian goalkeeper.* ► Also a noun. *...long, high lobs that fell precisely on the baseline.* VERB V n prep Also V n, V N-COUNT

lobby /lɒbi/ **lobbies, lobbying, lobbied** ◆◆◆◇◇

1 If you **lobby** someone such as a member of a government or council, you try to persuade them that a particular law should be changed or that a particular thing should be done. *Carers from all over the UK lobbied Parliament last week to demand a better financial deal... Gun control advocates are lobbying hard for new laws... The union has attacked the plan and threatened to lobby against it... It must be terribly frustrating to lobby and get absolutely nowhere.* ♦ **lobbying** *The aid was frozen in June after intense lobbying by conservative Republicans.* VERB V n V for/against n V N-UNCOUNT

2 A **lobby** is a group of people who represent a particular organization or campaign, and try to persuade a government or council to change the laws or take action in favour of that organization or campaign. *Agricultural interests are some of the most powerful lobbies in Washington... He set up this lobby of independent producers. ...the Lawyers' Committee for Civil Rights, a housing lobby group.* N-COUNT: usu with supp, oft supp N, N of n

3 A **lobby** is the area near the entrance to a hotel or other large building that has corridors and staircases leading off it. *I met her in the lobby of the museum.* N-COUNT

lobbyist /lɒbiɪst/ **lobbyists.** A **lobbyist** is someone who tries actively to persuade a government or council that a particular law should be changed or that a particular thing should be done. ◆◇◇◇◇ N-COUNT

lobe /loʊb/ **lobes** ◆◇◇◇◇

1 The **lobe** of your ear is the soft, fleshy part at the bottom. N-COUNT =earlobe

2 A **lobe** is a rounded part of something, for example one of the sections of your brain or lungs, or one of the rounded sections along the edges of some leaves. *...damage to the temporal lobe of the brain.* ♦ **-lobed** *...a plant with large three-lobed leaves.* N-COUNT: usu with supp COMB in ADJ

lobotomy /ləbɒtəmi/ **lobotomies.** A **lobotomy** is a surgical operation in which some of the nerves in the brain are cut in order to treat severe mental illness; a medical term. N-VAR

lobster /lɒbstəʳ/ **lobsters.** A **lobster** is a sea creature that has a hard shell, two large claws, and eight legs. *She sold me a couple of live lobsters.* ► **Lobster** is the flesh of a lobster eaten as food. *...lobster on a bed of fresh vegetables.* ◆◇◇◇◇ N-VAR N-UNCOUNT

lobster pot, lobster pots. A **lobster pot** is a trap used for catching lobsters. It is in the shape of a basket. N-COUNT

local /loʊkəl/ **locals** ◆◆◆◆◆

1 **Local** means existing in or belonging to the area where you live, or to the area that you are talking about. *We'd better check on the match in the local paper... Some local residents joined the students' protest... I was going to pop up to the local library.* ► The **locals** are local people. *That's what the locals call the place.* ♦ **locally** *We've got cards which are drawn and printed and designed by someone locally.* ADJ: ADJ n N-COUNT: usu pl, oft the N ADV-GRADED: ADV after v, ADV -ed

2 **Local** government is elected by people in one area of a country and controls aspects such as education, housing, and transport within that area. *...commuter networks run with the help of subsidies from local authorities... Education comprises two-thirds of all local council spending. ...the controversial system of local taxation known as the poll tax.* ♦ **locally** *The curriculum was to be decided locally.* ADJ: usu ADJ n ≠national ADV

3 In British English, your **local** is a pub which is near where you live and where you often go for a drink; an informal use. *The Black Horse is my local.* N-COUNT: usu sing, usu poss N

4 A **local** anaesthetic or condition affects only a small area of your body; a medical use. *An injection of local anaesthetic is usually given first to numb the area.* ADJ

local authority, local authorities. In Britain, a **local authority** is an organization that is officially responsible for all the public services and facilities in a particular area. ◆◆◆◇◇ N-COUNT

local colour. **Local colour** is used to refer to customs, traditions, dress, and other things which give a place or period of history its own particular character. *The fishing boat harbour was usually bustling with lots of local colour.* N-UNCOUNT

locale /loʊkɑːl/ **locales.** A **locale** is a small area, for example the place where something happens or where the action of a book or film is set; a formal word. *An amusement park is the perfect locale for a bunch of irrepressible youngsters to have all sorts of adventures.* N-COUNT =setting

local government, local governments ◆◆◇◇◇

1 **Local government** is the system of electing representatives to be responsible for the administration of public services and facilities in a particular area. N-UNCOUNT

2 In the United States, a **local government** is an organization that is officially responsible for all the public services and facilities in a particular area. N-COUNT

locality /loʊkælɪti/ **localities.** A **locality** is a small area of a country or city; a formal word. *Following the discovery of the explosives the president cancelled his visit to the locality... Details of the drinking water quality in your locality can be obtained from the public register.* ◆◇◇◇◇ N-COUNT =area

localize /loʊkəlaɪz/ **localizes, localizing, localized**; also spelled **localise** in British English.

1 If you **localize** something, you identify precisely where it is. *Examine the painful area carefully in an effort to localize the most tender point.* VERB =identify V n

2 If you **localize** something, you limit the size of the area that it affects and prevent it from spreading. *There may be some attempt to localise the benefits of the university's output in its host region.* VERB =limit V n

localized /loʊkəlaɪzd/; also spelled **localised.** Something that is **localized** remains within a small area and does not spread; a formal word. *She had localized breast cancer and both of her doctors had advised surgery... Community radio is a concept which is much more localised.* ◆◇◇◇◇ ADJ-GRADED

local time. **Local time** is the official time in a particular region or country. *It was around 10.15 pm local time, 3.15 am at home.*  N-UNCOUNT

locate /loʊkeɪt, AM loʊkeɪt/ **locates, locating, located** 

1 If you **locate** something or someone, you find out where they are; a formal use. *The scientists want to* VERB =find V n

locate the position of the gene on a chromosome... We've simply been unable to locate him.

2 If you **locate** something in a particular place, you put it there or build it there; a formal use. *Atlanta was voted the best city in which to locate a business by more than 400 chief executives... Tudor Court represents your opportunity to locate at the heart of the new Birmingham.* VERB V n prep/adv V prep/adv

located. /loʊkeɪtɪd, AM loʊkeɪt-/ If something is **located** in a particular place, it is present or has been built there; a formal word. *The restaurant is located near the cathedral... A boutique and beauty salon are conveniently located within the grounds. ...well-located buildings.* ◆◆◇◇◇ ADJ: v-link ADJ prep, adv ADJ =situated

location /loʊkeɪʃᵊn/ **locations** ◆◆◆◇◇

1 A **location** is the place where something happens or is situated. *The first thing he looked at was his office's location... Macau's newest small luxury hotel has a beautiful location.* N-COUNT: usu with supp =setting

2 The **location** of someone or something is their exact position. *She knew the exact location of The Eagle's headquarters.* N-COUNT: with poss =position

3 A **location** is a place away from a studio where a film or part of a film is made. *...an art movie with dozens of exotic locations... We're shooting on location.* N-VAR: oft *on* N

loch /lɒx, lɒk/ **lochs.** A **loch** is a large area of water in Scotland that is completely or almost completely surrounded by land. *...twenty miles north of Loch Ness.* ◆◇◇◇◇ N-COUNT: oft in names before n

loci /loʊsaɪ, loʊkaɪ/. **Loci** is the plural of **locus.**

lock /lɒk/ **locks, locking, locked** ◆◆◆◇◇

1 When you **lock** something such as a door, drawer, or case, you fasten it, usually with a key, so that other people cannot open it. *Are you sure you locked the front door?... Wolfgang moved along the corridor towards the locked door at the end.* VERB V n V-ed

2 The **lock** on something such as a door or a drawer is the device which is used to keep it shut and prevent other people from opening it. Locks are opened with a key. *At that moment he heard Gill's key turning in the lock of the door... An intruder forced open a lock on french windows at the house.* N-COUNT

3 If you **lock** something or someone in a place, room, or container, you put them there and fasten the lock. *Her maid locked the case in the safe... They beat them up and locked them in a cell.* VERB V n *in/into* n

4 When you **lock** something in a particular position or place or when it **locks** there, it is held or fitted firmly in that position or place. *He leaned back in the swivel chair and locked his fingers behind his head... There was a whine of hydraulics as the undercarriage locked into position.* V-ERG V n prep/adv V prep/adv

5 On a canal or river, a **lock** is a place where walls have been built with gates at each end so that boats can move to a higher or lower section of the canal or river, by gradually changing the water level inside the gates. N-COUNT

6 A **lock** of hair is a small bunch of hairs on your head that grow together and curl or curve in the same direction. *She brushed a lock of hair off his forehead.* N-COUNT: usu N *of* n

7 Your **locks** are your hair; a literary use. *...women with long, wavy locks.* N-PLURAL: usu supp N

8 If something or someone is kept **under lock and key**, they are in a container or room which has been securely locked. *The books were normally kept under lock and key in the library vault... He is currently under lock and key at Eastmoor secure unit in Leeds.* ● **lock, stock, and barrel**: see **barrel.** PHRASE: PHR after v

lock away PHRASAL VERB

1 If you **lock** something **away** in a place or container, you put or hide it there and fasten the lock. *She meticulously cleaned the gun and locked it away in its case... He had even locked away all the videos of his previous exploits.* V n P V P n (not pron)

2 To **lock** someone **away** means to put them in prison or a secure psychiatric hospital. *Locking them away is not sufficient, you have to give them treatment.* V n P Also V P n (not pron)

3 If you **lock** yourself **away**, you go somewhere where you can be alone, and do not come out or see anyone for some time. *I locked myself away with books and magazines.* =hide away V pron-refl P

lock in. If you **lock** someone **in**, you put them in a room and lock the door so that they cannot get out. *Manda cried out that Mr Hoelt had no right to lock her in.* PHRASAL VERB V n P

lock out PHRASAL VERB

1 If someone **locks** you **out** of a place, they prevent you entering it by locking the doors. *They had had a row, and she had locked him out of the apartment... My husband's locked me out.* V n P *of* n V n P

2 If you **lock** yourself **out** of a place, such as your house, you cannot get in because the door is locked and you do not have your keys. *The new tenants locked themselves out of their apartment and had to break in... There had been a knock at the door and when she opened it she locked herself out... The wind had made the door swing closed, and she was now locked out.* V pron-refl P *of* n V pron-refl P V-ed P

3 In an industrial dispute, if a company **locks** its workers **out**, it closes the factory or office in order to prevent the employees coming to work. *The company locked out the workers, and then the rest of the work force went on strike.* V P n (not pron) Also V n P

lock up PHRASAL VERB

1 If you **lock** something **up** in a place or container, you put or hide it there and fasten the lock. *Give away any food you have on hand, or lock it up and give the key to the neighbours... Control of materials could be maintained by locking up bombs.* V n P V P n (not pron)

2 To **lock** someone **up** means to put them in prison or a secure psychiatric hospital. *Mr Milner persuaded the federal prosecutors not to lock up his client... You are mad, Isabel. You should be locked up.* V P n (not pron) Also V n P

3 When you **lock up** a building or car or **lock up**, you make sure that all the doors and windows are locked so that nobody can get in. *Don't forget to lock up... Leave your car here and lock it up.* V P V n P

locked /lɒkt/. If you say that people are **locked in** conflict or in battle, you mean they are arguing or fighting in a fierce or determined way, and neither side seems likely to stop. ◆◆◇◇◇ ADJ: v-link ADJ *in* n

locker /lɒkəʳ/ **lockers.** A **locker** is a small metal or wooden cupboard with a lock, where you can put your personal belongings temporarily, for example in a school, a place of work, or in a sports club. ◆◇◇◇◇ N-COUNT

locker room, locker rooms. A **locker room** is a room in which there are a lot of lockers, for example in a school, place of work, or a sports club. ◆◇◇◇◇ N-COUNT

locket /lɒkɪt/ **lockets.** A **locket** is a piece of jewellery containing something such as a picture, which a woman wears on a chain around her neck. N-COUNT

lock-out, lock-outs; spelled **lockout** in American English. A **lock-out** is a situation in which employers close a place of work and prevent workers from entering it until the workers accept the employer's new proposals on pay or conditions of work. N-COUNT

lock-up, lock-ups; also spelled **lockup.**

1 A **lock-up** is the same as a **jail**; an informal word, used in American English. *...the 450 inmates at the maximum-security lock-up in Lucasville.* N-COUNT

2 A **lock-up** is a garage that is not part of someone's main premises; used mainly in British English. *25lb of Semtex explosive was found in the lock-up she had rented to Mr Henderson.* ► Also an adjective. *A massive arms cache had been hidden in a lock-up garage near the couple's home.* N-COUNT ADJ: ADJ n

locomotion /loʊkəmoʊʃᵊn/. **Locomotion** is the ability to move and the act of moving from one place to another; a formal word. *Flight is the form of locomotion that puts the greatest demands on muscles... He specialises in the mechanics of locomotion.* N-UNCOUNT

locomotive /loʊkəmoʊtɪv/ **locomotives.** A **locomotive** is the same as a **railway engine**; a formal word. *Steam locomotives pumped out clouds of white smoke.* ◆◆◇◇◇ N-COUNT

locum /lo͟ʊkəm/ **locums.** A **locum** is a doctor or priest who does the work for another doctor or priest who is ill or on holiday; used mainly in British English. N-COUNT

locus /lo͟ʊkəs/ **loci.** The **locus of** something is the place where it happens or the most important area or point with which it is associated; a formal word. *Barcelona is the locus of Spanish industry... Thereafter, the military remained the locus of real power.* N-COUNT: usu sing, N *of* n

locust /lo͟ʊkəst/ **locusts. Locusts** are large insects that are similar to grasshoppers and live mainly in hot countries. They fly in large groups and eat crops. ◆◇◇◇◇ N-COUNT

lodge /lɒ̱dʒ/ **lodges, lodging, lodged** ◆◆◇◇◇

1 A **lodge** is a house or hut in the country or in the mountains where people stay on holiday, especially when they want to shoot or fish. *...a Victorian hunting lodge. ...a ski lodge.* N-COUNT: usu supp N

2 A **lodge** is a small house at the entrance to the grounds of a large house. *I drove out of the gates, past the keeper's lodge.* N-COUNT

3 In some organizations, a **lodge** is a local branch or meeting place of the organization. *My father would occasionally go to his Masonic lodge.* N-COUNT: usu supp N

4 If you **lodge** a complaint, protest, accusation, or claim, you officially make it. *He has four weeks in which to lodge an appeal.* VERB =make V n

5 If you **lodge** somewhere, such as in someone else's house or if you **are lodged** there, you live there, usually paying rent. *...the story of the farming family she lodged with as a young teacher... The building he was lodged in turned out to be a church.* VERB V prep/adv *be* V-ed prep/adv

6 If someone **lodges** you somewhere, they give you somewhere to stay, for example because they are responsible for your safety or comfort. *They took me into custody, questioned me, then lodged me in a children's home... Rebel and government delegates are lodged in different hotels.* VERB V n prep/adv

7 If an object **lodges** somewhere, it becomes stuck there. *The bullet lodged in the sergeant's leg, shattering his thigh bone... His car has a bullet lodged in the passenger door.* VERB V prep/adv V-ed

8 If a fact or feeling **lodges** in your mind or **is lodged** there, you remember it for a long time. *It just lodged in my mind as a very sentimental song... If you've got something to say it's got to be lodged in their brains at the end... The festival has lodged itself in the public mind.* VERB V *in* n *be* V-ed *in* n V pron-refl *in* n

9 See also **lodging.**

lodger /lɒ̱dʒəʳ/ **lodgers.** A **lodger** is a person who pays money to live in a part of someone else's house; used mainly in British English. *Jennie took in a lodger to help with the mortgage.* ◆◇◇◇◇ N-COUNT

lodging /lɒ̱dʒɪŋ/ **lodgings** ◆◇◇◇◇

1 If you are provided with **lodging** or **lodgings**, you are provided with a place to stay for a period of time. You can use **lodgings** to refer to one or more of these places. *He was given free lodging in a three-room flat. ...travel expenses including meals and lodgings while traveling away from home.* N-UNCOUNT: also N in pl

2 If you live in **lodgings**, you live in a room or rooms in someone's house and you pay them for this. *David had changed his lodgings, leaving no address behind... Many of the single men found lodgings in the surrounding villages.* N-COUNT: usu pl

3 See also **board and lodging.**

lo̱dging house, lodging houses. In British English, a **lodging house** is a house where people can rent rooms to live in or stay in. The usual American expression is **rooming house.** N-COUNT

loft /lɒ̱ft, AM lɔ̱ːft/ **lofts, lofting, lofted** ◆◇◇◇◇

1 A **loft** is the space inside the sloping roof of a house or other building, where things are sometimes stored. *We would like to convert the loft into another bedroom... A loft conversion can add considerably to the value of a house.* N-COUNT =attic

2 When someone such as a cricketer, golfer, or footballer **lofts** a ball, they hit it or send it high into the air. *From the kick-off he lofted the ball 60 yards into the top corner of the net.* VERB V n

lofty /lɒ̱fti, AM lɔ̱ːf-/ **loftier, loftiest** ◆◇◇◇◇

1 A **lofty** ideal or ambition is noble, important, and admirable. *It was a bank that started out with grand ideas and lofty ideals... Amid the chaos, he had lofty aims.* ADJ-GRADED: usu ADJ n

2 A **lofty** building or room is very high; a formal use. *...a light, lofty apartment in the suburbs of Salzburg... Victorian houses can seem cold with their lofty ceilings and rambling rooms.* ADJ-GRADED: usu ADJ n

3 If you say that someone behaves in a **lofty** way, you are critical of them for behaving in a proud and rather unpleasant way, as if they think they are very important. *...the lofty disdain he often expresses for his profession. ...lofty contempt.* ADJ-GRADED: usu ADJ n PRAGMATICS

♦ **loftily** /lɒ̱ftɪli, AM lɔ̱ːf-/ *'We supply financial information to selected clients,' Crook said loftily. ...loftily indifferent to the world outside.* ADV-GRADED: usu ADV with v, ADV adj

log /lɒ̱g, AM lɔ̱ːg/ **logs, logging, logged** ◆◆◇◇◇

1 A **log** is a piece of a thick branch or of the trunk of a tree that has been cut so that it can be used for fuel or for making things. *He dumped the logs on the big stone hearth. ...the original log cabin where Lincoln was born.* N-COUNT: oft N n

2 A **log** is an official written account of what happens each day, for example on board a ship. *The family made an official complaint to a ship's officer, which was recorded in the log.* N-COUNT

3 If you **log** an event or fact, you record it officially in writing or on a computer. *They log everyone and everything that comes in and out of here... Details of the crime are then logged in the computer.* VERB =record V n

4 See also **logging.**

log in or **log on.** When someone **logs in** or **logs on**, or **logs into** a computer system, they gain access to the system, usually by typing their name or identity code and a password. *Customers pay to log on and gossip with other users... They would log into their account and take a look at prices and decide what they'd like to do.* PHRASAL VERB V P V P n

log out or **log off.** When someone who is using a computer system **logs out** or **logs off**, they finish using the system by typing a particular command. *If a computer user fails to log off, the system is accessible to all.* PHRASAL VERB V P

loganberry /lo͟ʊgənbəri, AM -beri/ **loganberries.** A **loganberry** is a purplish red fruit that is similar to a raspberry. N-COUNT

logarithm /lɒ̱gərɪðəm, AM lɔ̱ːg-/ **logarithms.** In mathematics, the **logarithm** of a number is a number that it can be represented by in order to make a difficult multiplication or division sum simpler. Mathematics books often contain a list of logarithms. N-COUNT

lo̱g book, log books. A **log book** is a book in which someone records details and events relating to something, especially to their car. N-COUNT

logger /lɒ̱gəʳ, AM lɔ̱ːg-/ **loggers.** In American English, a **logger** is a man whose job is to cut down trees. The usual British word is **lumberjack.** ◆◇◇◇◇ N-COUNT

loggerheads /lɒ̱gəʳhed, AM lɔ̱ːg-/. If two or more people or groups are **at loggerheads**, they disagree very strongly with each other. *For months dentists and the health department have been at loggerheads over fees... The European Community is at loggerheads with the rest of the world over its agricultural subsidies.* PHRASE: usu v-link PHR, oft PHR *with* n

loggia /lɒ̱dʒə/ **loggias.** A **loggia** is a roofed area attached to a house; a formal word. N-COUNT =porch

logging /lɒ̱gɪŋ, AM lɔ̱ːg-/. **Logging** is the activity of cutting down trees in order to sell the wood. *Logging companies would have to leave a central area of the forest before the end of the year.* ◆◇◇◇◇ N-UNCOUNT: oft N n

logic /lɒ̱dʒɪk/ ◆◆◇◇◇

1 **Logic** is a method of reasoning that involves a series of statements, each of which must be true if the statement before it is true. *Apart from criminal investigation techniques, students learn forensic medicine, philosophy and logic.* N-UNCOUNT

2 The **logic** of a conclusion or an argument is its quality of being correct and reasonable. *I don't* N-UNCOUNT: oft N *of* n

follow the logic of your argument... There would be no logic in upsetting the agreements.

3 A particular kind of **logic** is the way of thinking and reasoning about things that is characteristic of a particular type of person or particular field of activity. *The plan was based on sound commercial logic.* N-UNCOUNT: with supp, oft adj N

logical /lɒdʒɪkəl/ ◆◆◇◇◇

1 In a **logical** argument or analysis, each step or point must be true if the step before it is true. *Only when each logical step has been checked by other mathematicians will the proof be accepted.* ADJ: usu ADJ n
♦ **logically** /lɒdʒɪkli/ *My professional training has taught me to look at things logically.* ADV: usu ADV with v

2 The **logical** conclusion or outcome of a series of facts or events is the one which can reasonably result from it, according to the rules of logic. *If the climate gets drier, then the logical conclusion is that even more drought will occur... He was reluctant to concede that the logical outcome could be a Soviet Union reduced in size. ...a society that dismisses God as a logical impossibility.* ADJ: usu ADJ n ♦ **logically** *From that it followed logically that he would not be meeting Hildegarde.* ADV: ADV with v

3 Something that is **logical** seems reasonable or sensible in the circumstances. *Connie suddenly struck her as a logical candidate... There was a logical explanation... It is logical to take precautions.* ADJ-GRADED: oft *it* v-link ADJ to-inf/that =sensible
♦ **logically** *This was the one possibility I hadn't taken into consideration, though logically I should have done.* ADV: ADV with cl, ADV with v

-logical. See **-ological**.

logician /lədʒɪʃən/ **logicians.** A **logician** is a person who is a specialist in logic. N-COUNT

-logist. See **-ologist**.

logistic /lədʒɪstɪk/ or **logistical** /lədʒɪstɪkəl/. ◆◇◇◇◇ **Logistic** or **logistical** means relating to the organization of something complicated. *Logistical problems may be causing the delay... She described the distribution of food and medical supplies as a logistical nightmare. ...logistic difficulties.* ADJ: ADJ n ♦ **logistically** /lədʒɪstɪkli/ *Organised junior football was either restricted or logistically impossible to operate... It is about time that the UN considers logistically deploying additional military resources... Logistically it is very difficult to value unit-linked policies.* ADV: ADV adj, ADV with v, ADV with cl

logistics /lədʒɪstɪks/. If you refer to the **logistics** of doing something complicated that involves a lot of people or equipment, you are referring to the skilful organization of it so that it can be done successfully and efficiently. *The skills and logistics of getting such a big show on the road pose enormous practical problems... Logistics is now more important in our industry than technology.* N-UNCOUNT-COLL

logjam /lɒgdʒæm/ **logjams.** If journalist talk about someone or something breaking the **logjam**, they mean that that person or thing may be able to change a situation which has been impossible to change for a long time, especially because people cannot agree about something. *A new initiative was needed to break the logjam.* N-COUNT: usu sing

logo /loʊgoʊ/ **logos.** The **logo** of a company or organization is the special design or way of writing its name that it puts on all its products, notepaper, or advertisements. ◆◆◇◇◇ N-COUNT

-logy. See **-ology**.

loin /lɔɪn/ **loins** ◆◇◇◇◇

1 Someone's **loins** are the front part of their body between their waist and thighs, especially their sexual parts; a literary or old-fashioned use. N-PLURAL

2 **Loin** or a **loin** is a piece of meat which comes from the back or sides of an animal, quite near the tail end. *Heat the honey and brush it on to the outside of the loin. ...roast loin of venison.* N-VAR

3 If you say that someone has to **gird** their **loins**, you are saying in a humorous way that they have to prepare themselves for a very difficult task. PHRASE: V inflects

loincloth /lɔɪnklɒθ, AM -klɔːθ/ **loincloths.** A **loincloth** is a piece of cloth sometimes worn by men in order to cover their sexual parts, especially in countries when it is too hot to wear anything else. N-COUNT

loiter /lɔɪtər/ **loiters, loitering, loitered.** If you **loiter** somewhere, you remain there or walk up and down without any real purpose. *Unemployed young men loiter at the entrance of the factory.* VERB =hang around V

loll /lɒl/ **lolls, lolling, lolled**

1 If you **loll** somewhere, you sit or lie in a very relaxed position. *He was lolling on the sofa in the shadows near the fire... He lolled back in his comfortable chair.* VERB =lounge, sprawl V prep/adv

2 If something fairly heavy, especially someone's head or tongue, **lolls**, it hangs down in a loose, uncontrolled way. *When he let go the head lolled sideways. ...his tongue lolling out of the side of his mouth... Tongue lolling, the dog came lolloping back from the forest.* VERB =flop V adv/prep V

loll about or **loll around.** The form **loll about** is mainly used in British English. If you **loll about** or **loll around**, you enjoy yourself by sitting or lying in a relaxed way. *Her husband dreams about lolling about on the deck and taking long snoozes in the afternoon sun. ...spending afternoons lolling around a swimming pool.* PHRASAL VERB =lounge around V P prep V P n

lollipop /lɒlipɒp/ **lollipops.** A **lollipop** is a sweet consisting of a hard disc or ball of a sugary substance on the end of a stick. N-COUNT =lolly

lollop /lɒləp/ **lollops, lolloping, lolloped.** When an animal or a person **lollops** along, they run along awkwardly and not very fast; a literary word. *A herd of elephants lolloped across the plains towards a watering hole.* VERB =lope V prep/adv

lolly /lɒli/ **lollies.** A **lolly** is the same as a **lollipop**; used mainly in British English. ● See also **ice lolly**. N-COUNT

lone /loʊn/ ◆◆◇◇◇

1 If you talk about a **lone** person or thing, you mean that they are alone. *A lone woman motorist waited for six hours for the RAC yesterday because of a name mix-up... He was shot by a lone gunman.* ADJ: ADJ n

2 A **lone** parent is a parent who is looking after her or his child or children and who is not married or living with a partner; used mainly in British English. *Ninety per cent of lone parent families are headed by mothers.* ADJ: ADJ n =single

loneliness /loʊnlinəs/. **Loneliness** is the unhappiness that is felt by someone because they do not have any friends or do not have anyone to talk to. *I have so many friends, but deep down, underneath, I have a fear of loneliness.* ◆◇◇◇◇ N-UNCOUNT

lonely /loʊnli/ **lonelier, loneliest** ◆◆◇◇◇

1 Someone who is **lonely** is unhappy because they are alone or do not have anyone they can talk to. *...lonely people who just want to talk... I feel lonelier in the middle of London than I do on my boat in the middle of nowhere.* ▶ **The lonely** are people who are lonely. *He looks for the lonely, the lost, the unloved.* ADJ-GRADED; N-PLURAL: *the* N

2 A **lonely** situation or period of time is one in which you feel unhappy because you are alone or do not have anyone to talk to. *I desperately needed something to occupy me during those long, lonely nights. ...her lonely childhood.* ADJ-GRADED

3 A **lonely** place is one where very few people come. *It felt like the loneliest place in the world. ...dark, lonely streets.* ADJ-GRADED

lonely hearts. A **lonely hearts** section in a newspaper or a **lonely hearts** club is used by people who are trying to find a lover or friend. ADJ: ADJ n

loner /loʊnər/ **loners.** If you describe someone as a **loner**, you mean they prefer to be alone rather than with a group of people. *I'm very much a loner – I never go out.* ◆◇◇◇◇ N-COUNT

lonesome /loʊnsəm/

1 In American English, someone who is **lonesome** is unhappy because they do not have any friends or do not have anyone to talk to. *I've grown so lonesome, thinking of you.* ADJ-GRADED: usu v-link ADJ =lonely

2 In American English, a **lonesome** place is one which very few people come to and which is a long way from places where people live. *He was finding the river lonesome.* ADJ-GRADED =lonely

long 1 time

long /lɒŋ/, AM /lɔːŋ/ **longer** /lɒŋgəʳ/, AM /lɔːŋgər/ **longest** /lɒŋgɪst/, AM /lɔːŋgɪst/ ◆◆◆◆◆

1 **Long** means a great amount of time or for a great amount of time. *Repairs to the cable did not take too long... Have you known her parents long?... I learned long ago to avoid these invitations... The railway had obviously been built long after the house... Chess has long been regarded as a measure of intellect. ...long-established social traditions.* [ADV-GRADED: ADV with v, oft ADV adv/prep]
• The expression **for long** is used to mean 'for a great amount of time'. *'Did you live there?'—'Not for long.'... Developing countries won't put up with the situation for much longer... For too long there was a huge gap in the market.* [PHRASE: PHR after v]

2 A **long** event or period of time lasts for a great amount of time or takes a great amount of time. *We had a long meeting with the attorney general... She is planning a long holiday in Egypt and America... They sat looking at each other for a long while... He must have started writing his book a long time ago.* [ADJ-GRADED: usu ADJ n ≠short]

3 You use **long** to ask or talk about amounts of time. *How long have you lived around here?... He has been on a diet for as long as any of his friends can remember... She reflected no longer than a second before she decisively slit the envelope.* [ADV-GRADED: *how* ADV, *as* ADV *as*, ADV-compar *than*] ► Also an adjective. *How long is the usual stay in hospital?... The average commuter journey there is five hours long.* [ADJ-GRADED: *how* ADJ, amount ADJ] ► Also a combining form. *She'd just returned from a month-long visit to Egypt.* [COMB in ADJ]

4 A **long** speech, book, film, or list contains a lot of information or a lot of items and takes a lot of time to listen to, read, watch, or deal with. *He was making quite a long speech... This is a long film, three hours and seven minutes.* [ADJ-GRADED: usu ADJ n ≠short]

5 If you describe a period of time or work as **long**, you mean it lasts for more hours or days than is usual, or seems to last for more time than it actually does. *Go to sleep. I've got a long day tomorrow... She was a TV reporter and worked long hours... This has been the longest week of my life.* [ADJ-GRADED: usu ADJ n ≠short]

6 If someone has a **long** memory, they are able to remember things that happened far back in the past. [ADJ-GRADED: usu ADJ n ≠short]

7 **Long** is used in expressions such as **all year long**, **the whole day long**, and **your whole life long** to say and emphasize that something happens for the whole of a particular period of time. *We played that record all night long... Snow is sometimes found all summer long upon the highest peaks.* [ADV: n ADV PRAGMATICS]

long 2 distance and size

long /lɒŋ/, AM /lɔːŋ/ **longer** /lɒŋgəʳ/, AM /lɔːŋgər/ **longest** /lɒŋgɪst/, AM /lɔːŋgɪst/ ◆◆◆◆◆

1 Something that is **long** measures a great distance from one end to the other. *...a long table... A long line of people formed outside the doctor's office... Lucy was 27, with long dark hair... Her legs were long and thin.* [ADJ-GRADED ≠short]

2 A **long** distance is a great distance. A **long** journey or route covers a great distance. *His destination was Chobham Common, a long way from his Cotswold home... The long journey tired him... I went for a long walk.* [ADJ-GRADED: usu ADJ n ≠short]

3 A **long** piece of clothing covers the whole of someone's legs or more of their legs than usual. Clothes with **long** sleeves cover the whole of someone's arms. *She is wearing a long black dress. ...a long-sleeved blouse.* [ADJ: ADJ n ≠short]

4 You use **long** to talk or ask about the distance something measures from one end to the other. *An eight-week-old embryo is only an inch long... How long is the tunnel?... In the roots of the olives, you could find centipedes as long as a pencil.* ► Also a combining form. *...a three-foot-long gash in the tanker's side.* [ADJ-GRADED: amount ADJ, *how* ADJ, *as* ADJ *as*, ADJ-compar *than*; COMB in ADJ]

5 If you describe a distance as **long**, you mean it seems to be greater than it actually is. *It was five long miles to the nearest pub.* [ADJ-GRADED: ADJ n ≠short]

long 3 phrases

long /lɒŋ/, AM /lɔːŋ/ **longer** /lɒŋgəʳ/, AM /lɔːŋgər/ ◆◆◆◆◆

1 If you say that something is the case **as long as** or **so long as** something else is the case, you mean that it is only the case if the second thing is the case. *The interior minister said he would still support them, as long as they didn't break the rules... The president need not step down so long as the elections are held under international supervision.* [PHRASES CONJ-SUBORD]

2 If you say that someone **won't be long**, you mean that you think they will arrive or be back soon. If you say that it **won't be long** before something happens, you mean that you think it will happen soon. *'What's happened to her?'—'I'm sure she won't be long.'... The Health Spokesman said it wouldn't be long before those with the money would also get better nursing.* [oft *it* PHR *before* cl]

3 If you say that something will happen or happened **before long**, you mean that it will happen or happened soon. *German interest rates will come down before long... Before long he took over the editing of the magazine.* [PHR after v, PHR with cl]

4 You use **long live** and **long may** in expressions such as **'long live the Queen'** and **'long may it continue'** to express your support for someone or something and your hope that they will live or last a long time. *Long live freedom!... It is a free world where we are all entitled to our opinions. Long may it remain so.* [PRAGMATICS]

5 Something that is **no longer** the case used to be the case but is not the case now. You can also say that something is not the case **any longer**. *Food shortages are no longer a problem... She could no longer afford to keep him at school... I noticed that he wasn't sitting by the door any longer.* [PHR group/cl, PHR with v]

6 You can say **so long** as an informal way of saying goodbye. *Well, so long, pal, see you around.* [CONVENTION PRAGMATICS =bye]

7 • **as long as your arm**: see **arm**. • **by a long chalk**: see **chalk**. • **a long face**: see **face**. • **at long last**: see **last**. • **in the long run**: see **run**. • **a long shot**: see **shot**. • **in the long term**: see **term**. • **long in the tooth**: see **tooth**. • **to take the long view**: see **view**. • **to go a long way**: see **way**.

long 4 verb uses

long /lɒŋ/, AM /lɔːŋ/ **longs, longing, longed.** If you **long** for something, you want it very much. *Steve longed for the good old days... I'm longing to meet her... He longed for the winter to be over.* • See also **longing**. ◆◆◇◇◇ [VERB: V *for* n, V to-inf, V *for* n to-inf]

long-awaited. A **long-awaited** event or thing is one that someone has been waiting for a long time. *...the long-awaited signing of a peace agreement. ...his long awaited autobiography.* ◆◇◇◇◇ [ADJ: ADJ n]

long-distance ◆◇◇◇◇

1 **Long-distance** is used to describe travel between places that are far apart. *Trains are reliable, cheap and best for long-distance journeys. ...the first long-distance sea voyages made by Portuguese navigators at the end of the 15th century.* [ADJ: ADJ n]

2 **Long-distance** is used to describe communication that takes place between people who are far apart. *He received a long-distance phone call from his girlfriend in Colorado.* ► Also an adverb. *I phoned Nicola long distance to suggest it.* [ADJ: usu ADJ n ≠local; ADV: ADV after v]

long drawn out; also spelled **long-drawn-out**. A **long drawn out** process or conflict lasts an unnecessarily long time or an unpleasantly long time. *A long drawn out war would likely deepen and prolong the recession. ...a long drawn out election campaign.* [ADJ-GRADED: usu ADJ n]

longed-for. A **longed-for** thing or event is one that someone wants very much. *...the wet weather that prevents your longed-for picnic.* ◆◇◇◇◇ [ADJ: ADJ n]

longevity /lɒndʒevɪti/. **Longevity** is long life; a formal word. *Human longevity runs in families... The main characteristic of the strike has been its longevity.* ◆◇◇◇◇ [N-UNCOUNT]

longhand /lɒŋhænd/, AM /lɔːŋ-/. If you write something down in **longhand**, you write it by hand using complete words and normal letters rather than typing it or using shortened forms or special symbols. [N-UNCOUNT: usu *in* N]

long-haul. **Long-haul** is used to describe things that involve transporting passengers or goods over long distances. *...learning how to* ◆◇◇◇◇ [ADJ: ADJ n ≠short-haul] *avoid the unpleasant side-effects of long-haul flights.*

longing /lɒŋɪŋ, AM lɔ:ŋ-/ **longings.** If you feel **longing** or a **longing** for something, you have a rather sad feeling because you want it very much. *He felt a longing for the familiar... Imelda spoke of her longing to return home... I was overwhelmed with longing for those innocent days of early childhood.* ◆◇◇◇◇ N-VAR: oft N for n, N to-inf

longingly /lɒŋɪŋli, AM lɔ:ŋ-/. If you look **longingly** at something you want, or think **longingly** about it, you look at it or think about it with a feeling of desire. *Claire looked longingly at the sunlit gardens outside the window.* ADV-GRADED: ADV with v =yearningly

longish /lɒŋɪʃ, AM lɔ:ŋ-/. **Longish** means fairly long. *She's about my age, with longish hair.* ADJ: usu ADJ n

longitude /lɒndʒɪtju:d, AM -tu:d/ **longitudes.** The **longitude** of a place is its distance to the west or east of a line passing through Greenwich. Compare **latitude**. *He noted the latitude and longitude, then made a mark on the admiralty chart.* N-VAR ▸ Also an adjective. *A similar feature is found at 13 degrees North between 230 degrees and 250 degrees longitude.* ADJ: usu amount ADJ

longitudinal /lɒndʒɪtju:dɪnəl, AM -tu:-/. A **longitudinal** measurement, axis, or cross-section goes from one end of an object to the other rather than across it from side to side. ADJ: ADJ n

long johns. **Long johns** are warm underpants with long legs. N-PLURAL: also *a pair of* N

long jump. **The long jump** is an athletics contest which involves jumping as far as you can from a marker which you run up to. N-SING: *the* N

long-lasting, longer-lasting; also spelled **long lasting.** Something that is **long-lasting** lasts for a long time. *One of the long-lasting effects of the infection is damage to a valve in the heart... Civil aircraft engines must be quiet, non-polluting, reliable and long-lasting.* ◆◇◇◇◇ ADJ-GRADED

long-life. **Long-life** milk, fruit juice, or batteries are treated so that they last a longer time than ordinary kinds. ADJ: ADJ n

long-lived; also spelled **long lived.** Something that is **long-lived** lives or lasts for a long time. *The flowers may only last a day but the plants are long-lived. ...huge piles of long-lived radioactive material.* ADJ-GRADED

long-lost. You use **long-lost** to describe someone or something that you have not seen for a long time. *A number of Albanian tourists are reported to have come to Turkey to visit long-lost relatives. ...finding a long-lost sixth century manuscript.* ADJ: ADJ n

long-range ◆◆◇◇◇

1 A **long-range** piece of military equipment or vehicle is able to hit or detect a target a long way away or to travel a long way in order to do something. *He is very keen to reach agreement with the US on reducing long-range nuclear missiles. ...the growing use on the North Atlantic routes of long-range twin-engined aircraft.* ADJ-GRADED: usu ADJ n

2 A **long-range** plan or prediction relates to a period extending a long time into the future. *Eisenhower was intensely aware of the need for long-range planning. ...a bold, complex, and long-range strategy for improving US education.* ADJ-GRADED: usu ADJ n

long-running, longest-running. Something that is **long-running** has been in existence, or has been performed, for a long time. *...efforts to find a peaceful solution to this long-running war. ...a long-running trade dispute... He was best-known for his role in the long-running television series.* ◆◇◇◇◇ ADJ-GRADED: ADJ n

longshoreman /lɒŋʃɔ:ʳmən, AM lɔ:ŋ-/ **longshoremen.** In American English, a **longshoreman** is a person who works in the docks, loading and unloading ships. The British word is **docker**. N-COUNT

long-sighted. In British English, **long-sighted** people cannot see things clearly that are close to them, and therefore need to wear glasses. The American word is **far-sighted**. *My husband is extremely long-sighted while I am very short-sighted.* ADJ-GRADED ≠short-sighted

long-standing. A **long-standing** situation has existed for a long time. *They are on the brink of resolving their long-standing dispute over money. ...long-standing economic links between Europe and much of Africa.* ◆◆◇◇◇ ADJ-GRADED: usu ADJ n

long-suffering. Someone who is **long-suffering** patiently bears continual trouble or unhappiness, especially unhappiness caused by someone else. *He went back to Yorkshire to join his loyal, long-suffering wife.* ◆◇◇◇◇ ADJ-GRADED: usu ADJ n

long-term, longer-term ◆◆◆◆◇

1 Something that is **long-term** has continued for a long time or will continue for a long time in the future. *A new training scheme to help the long-term unemployed is expected... The association believes new technology will provide a long-term solution to credit card fraud.* ADJ-GRADED: usu ADJ n ≠short-term

2 When you talk about what happens in **the long term**, you are talking about what happens over a long period of time, either in the future or after a particular event. *In the long term the company hopes to open in Moscow and other major cities... Over the long term, such measures may only make the underlying situation worse.* N-SING: *the* N ≠the short term

long-time. You use **long-time** to describe something that has existed or been a particular thing for a long time. *...newcomers had to pay far more in taxes than long-time land owners... She married her long-time boyfriend. ...a long-time member of the pro-democracy movement.* ◆◆◆◇◇ ADJ: ADJ n

long wave. **Long wave** is a range of radio waves which are used for broadcasting. *...broadcasting on long wave. ...1500m on long wave.* N-UNCOUNT

long-winded. If you describe something that is written or said as **long-winded**, you are critical of it because it is longer than necessary. *The manifesto is long-winded, repetitious and often ambiguous or poorly drafted... I hope I'm not being too long-winded.* ADJ-GRADED: usu v-link ADJ PRAGMATICS =verbose

loo /lu:/ **loos.** In British English, a **loo** is a toilet; an informal word. *I asked if I could go to the loo. ...public loos.* ◆◇◇◇◇ N-COUNT: usu *the* N in sing

loofah /lu:fə/ **loofahs.** A **loofah** is a long rough sponge which you use to wash yourself in the bath. N-COUNT

look 1 using your eyes or your mind

look /lʊk/ **looks, looking, looked** ◆◆◆◆◆

1 If you **look** in a particular direction, you direct your eyes in that direction, especially so that you can see what is there or see what something is like. *I looked down the hallway to room number nine... She turned to look at him... He looked away, apparently enraged... If you look, you'll see what was a lake.* VERB V prep/adv V ▸ Also a noun. *Lucille took a last look in the mirror... Assisi has a couple of churches that are worth a look if you have time.* N-SING

2 If you **look at** a book, newspaper, or magazine, you read it fairly quickly or read part of it. *You've just got to look at the last bit of Act Three.* VERB V at n ▸ Also a noun. *A quick look at Monday's British newspapers shows that there's plenty of interest in foreign news.* N-SING: oft N at n

3 If someone, especially an expert, **looks** at something, they examine it, and then deal with it or say how it should be dealt with. *Can you look at my back? I think something's wrong.* VERB V at n Also V ▸ Also a noun. *The car has not been running very well and a mechanic had to come over to have a look at it.* N-SING: usu N at n

4 If you **look at** someone in a particular way, you look at them with your expression showing what you are feeling or thinking. *She looked at him earnestly. 'You don't mind?'* VERB V at n adv/prep ▸ Also a noun. *He gave her a blank look, as if he had no idea who she was... Sally spun round, a feigned look of surprise on her face.* N-COUNT: usu with supp, oft adj N, N of n

5 If you **look** for something, for example something that you have lost or something that you want or need, you try to find it. *I'm looking for a child. I believe your husband can help me find her... I had gone to Maine looking for a place to work... I looked everywhere for ideas... Have you looked on* VERB =search V for n V prep/adv for n V prep/adv *the piano?* ▶ Also a noun. *Go and have another look.* N-SING

6 If you are **looking for** something such as the solution to a problem or a new method, you want it and are trying to obtain it or think of it. *The working group will be looking for practical solutions to the problems faced by doctors... He's looking for a way out from this conflict.* VERB =seek V *for* n

7 If you **look at** a subject, problem, or situation, you think about it or study it, so that you know all about it and can perhaps consider what should be done in relation to it. *Next term we'll be looking at the Second World War period... Anne Holker looks at the pros and cons of making changes to your property... He visited Florida a few years ago looking at the potential of the area to stage a big match.* VERB =examine, consider V *at* n

▶ Also a noun. *They're taking a close look at President Bill Clinton's economic proposal.* N-SING: oft N *at* n

8 If you **look at** a person, situation, or subject from a particular point of view, you judge them or consider them from that point of view. *Brian had learned to look at her with new respect... It depends how you look at it.* VERB V *at* n prep/adv

9 You say **look** when you want someone to pay attention to you because you are going to say something important. *Look, I'm sorry. I didn't mean it... Now, look, here is how things stand.* CONVENTION PRAGMATICS

10 You can use **look** to draw attention to a particular situation, person, or thing, for example because you find it very surprising, significant, or annoying. *Hey, look at the time! We'll talk about it tonight. All right?... I mean, look at how many people watch television and how few read books... Look what a mess you've made of your life.* VB: only imper PRAGMATICS V *at* n V wh

11 If something such as a building or window **looks** somewhere, it has a view of a particular place. *The castle looks over private parkland... Each front door looks across a narrow alley to the front door opposite.* ▶ **Look out** means the same as **look**. *Nine windows looked out over the sculpture gardens... We sit on the terrace, which looks out on the sea.* VERB V prep PHRASAL VERB V P prep

12 If you say that someone did something and then **never looked back**, you mean that they were very successful from that time on. *I went freelance when my son Adam was born, and have never looked back.* PHRASES

13 If you **look** someone **in the eye** or **look** them **in the face**, you look straight at their eyes in a bold and open way, for example in order to make them realize that you are not afraid of them or that you are telling the truth. *He could not look her in the eye.* V inflects

14 If you say that someone **looks the other way**, you are critical of them because they pay no attention to something unpleasant that is happening, when they should be dealing with it properly. *Judges and politicians routinely looked the other way while people were tortured or killed by police.* V inflects PRAGMATICS

15 You say **look here** when you are going to say something important to someone, especially when you are angry at something they have done or said. *Now look here, Tim, there really is no need for that kind of reaction.* CONVENTION PRAGMATICS

16 If you say or shout **'look out!'** to someone, you are warning them that they are in danger. *'Look out!' somebody shouted, as the truck started to roll toward the sea.* EXCLAM PRAGMATICS

17 If someone **looks** you **up and down**, they direct their eyes from your head to your feet, in a rude and superior way and often as though they disapprove of you. *The sales assistant looked me up and down and told me not to try the dress on because she didn't think I would get into it.* V inflects

18 • to **look down** your **nose at someone**: see **nose**.

look after PHRASAL VERB

1 If you **look after** someone or something, you do what is necessary to keep them healthy, safe, or in good condition. *I love looking after the children... People don't look after other people's property in the same way as they look after their own.* =take care of V P n

2 If you **look after** something, you are responsible for it and deal with it or make sure it is all right, especially because it is your job to do so. *...the farm manager who looks after the day-to-day organization... We'll help you look after your finances.* =attend to V P n

look ahead. If you **look ahead**, you think about what is going to happen in the future and perhaps make plans for the future. *I'm trying to look ahead at what might happen and be ready to handle it.* PHRASAL VERB V P

look around. See **look round.** PHRASAL VERB

look back. If you **look back**, you think about things that happened in the past. *Looking back, I am staggered how easily it was all arranged.* PHRASAL VERB V P

look down on. If you say that someone **looks down on** someone or something, you mean that they consider that person or thing to be inferior or unimportant, usually when this is not the case. *I wasn't successful, so they looked down on me.* PHRASAL VERB V P P n

look forward to PHRASAL VERB

1 If you **look forward to** something that is going to happen, you want it to happen because you think you will enjoy it. *He was looking forward to working with the new Prime Minister.* V P P -ing/n

2 If you say that someone **is looking forward** to something useful or positive, you mean they expect it to happen. *Motor traders are looking forward to a further increase in vehicle sales.* V P P n

look in. If you **look in** on a person or place, you visit them for a short time, usually when you are on your way somewhere else. *I looked in on Louisa. She was sleeping.* PHRASAL VERB V P *on* n Also V P

look into. If a person or organization **is looking into** a possible course of action, a problem, or a situation, they are finding out about it and examining the facts relating to it. *He had once looked into buying his own island off Nova Scotia... It should also look into the possibilities of wind-generated electricity.* PHRASAL VERB =investigate V P -ing/n

look on. If you **look on** while something happens, you watch it happening without taking part yourself. *About 150 local people looked on in silence as the two coffins were taken into the church.* PHRASAL VERB =watch V P

look on or **look upon.** If you **look on** or **look upon** someone or something as a particular type of person or thing, you think of them as that thing. If you **look on** or **look upon** them in a particular way, you think of them in that way. *A lot of people looked on him as a healer... A lot of people look on it like that... Employers look favourably on applicants who have work experience.* PHRASAL VERB =consider V P n *as* n V P n prep/adv V adv P n

look out. See **look** 11. PHRASAL VERB

look out for PHRASAL VERB

1 If you **look out for** something, you pay attention to things so that you notice it if or when it occurs. *Look out for special deals... What are the symptoms to look out for?* =watch for V P P n

2 If you **look out for** someone, you make sure that they have all the advantages that they can. *I'm just trying to look out for you... I felt that I had to look out for myself, because I didn't see that anyone else was going to.* V P P n V P P pron-refl

look over. If you **look** something **over**, you examine it quite quickly in order to get a general idea of what it is like. *They presented their draft to the president, who looked it over, nodded and signed it... He could have looked over the papers in less than ten minutes.* PHRASAL VERB V n P V P n (not pron)

look round or **look around.** If you **look round** or **look around** a building or place, you walk round it and look at the different parts of it. *We went to look round the show homes... I'm going to look around and see what I can find.* PHRASAL VERB V P n V P

look through PHRASAL VERB

1 If you **look through** a group of things, you examine each one so that you can find or choose the one that you want. *Peter starts looking through the mail as soon as the door shuts.* V P n

2 If you **look through** something that has been written or printed, you read it. *He happened to be looking through the medical book 'Gray's Anatomy' at the time.* V P n

3 If you say that someone **looks through** another

person, you mean that they look at that person without seeming to see them or recognize them, for example because they are angry with them or are thinking deeply about something else. *As for doctors, when you go to see them they just look right through you.* VPn

look to PHRASAL VERB

1 If you **look to** someone or something for a particular thing that you want, you expect or hope that they will provide it. *The difficulties women encounter with their doctors partly explain why so many of us are looking to alternative therapies.* VPn

2 If you **look to** something that will happen in the future, you think about it. *Looking to the future, though, we asked him what the prospects are for a vaccine to prevent infection in the first place.* VPn

look up PHRASAL VERB

1 If you **look up** a fact or a piece of information, you find it out by looking in something such as a reference book or a list. *I looked your address up in the personnel file... Many people have to look up the meaning of this word in the dictionary.* VnP / VPn (not pron)

2 If you **look** someone **up**, you visit them after not having seen them for a long time. *I'll try to look him up, ask him a few questions... She looked up some friends of bygone years.* =visit / VnP / VPn (not pron)

3 If a situation **is looking up**, it is improving; an informal expression. *Things could be looking up in the computer industry.* usu cont / =improve / VP

look upon. See **look on.** PHRASAL VERB

look up to. If you **look up to** someone, especially someone older than you, you respect and admire them. *You're a popular girl, Grace, and a lot of the younger ones look up to you.* PHRASAL VERB / =admire / VPPn

look 2 appearance

look /lʊk/ **looks, looking, looked** ◆◆◆◆◆

1 You use **look** when describing the appearance of a person or thing or the impression that they give. *Sheila was looking miserable... I shall use the money to make my home look lovely... You don't look 15 years old... He does not look the most reliable of animals... They look like stars to the naked eye... He looked as if he was going to smile.* ♦ **-looking** *She was a very peculiar-looking woman.* V-LINK / V adj / V n / V *like* n / V like/as if / COMB in ADJ-GRADED

2 If someone or something has a particular **look**, they have a particular appearance or expression. *She had the look of someone deserted and betrayed... When he came to decorate the kitchen, Kenneth opted for a friendly rustic look... To soften a formal look, Caroline recommends ethnic blouses.* N-SING: with supp / =appearance

3 When you refer to someone's **looks**, you are referring to how beautiful or ugly they are, especially how beautiful they are. *I never chose people just because of their looks. ...a young woman with wholesome good looks.* N-PLURAL

4 You use **look** when indicating what you think will happen in the future or how a situation seems to you. *He had lots of time to think about the future, and it didn't look good... Britain looks set to send a major force of over 100 tanks and supporting equipment... So far it looks like Warner Brothers' gamble is paying off... The Europeans had hoped to win, and, indeed, had looked like winning.* V-LINK / V adj / it V like/as if / V *like* -ing/n

5 You use expressions such as **by the look of him** and **by the looks of it** when you want to indicate that you are giving an opinion based on the appearance of someone or something. *He was not a well man by the look of him... By the look of things, Mr Stone and company will stay busy.* PHRASES

6 If you **don't like the look of** something or someone, you feel that they may be dangerous or result in something harmful or unpleasant. *I don't like the look of those clouds.* V inflects, PHR n

7 If you ask **what** someone or something **looks like**, you are asking for a description of them. V inflects

look-alike, look-alikes. A **look-alike** is someone who has a very similar appearance to another person, especially a famous person. *...a Marilyn Monroe look-alike.* N-COUNT: usu n-proper N

looker /lʊkəʳ/ **lookers.** In informal English, you can refer to an attractive man or woman as a **looker** or a **good looker.** *She was quite a looker before this happened.* N-COUNT

look-in. If you are trying to take part in an activity and you do not get a **look-in**, you do not get the chance to take part because too many other people are doing it; used mainly in informal British English. *They want to make sure the newcomers don't get a look-in.* N-SING: usu with brd-neg, a N

looking glass, looking glasses; also spelled **looking-glass.** A **looking glass** is a mirror; an old-fashioned word. N-COUNT

lookout /lʊkaʊt/ **lookouts** ◆◇◇◇◇

1 A **lookout** is a place from which you can see clearly in all directions. *Troops tried to set up a lookout post inside a refugee camp.* N-COUNT

2 A **lookout** is someone who is watching for danger in order to warn other people about it. N-COUNT / =sentry

3 If someone **keeps a lookout**, especially on a boat, they look around all the time in order to make sure there is no danger. *He denied that he'd failed to keep a proper lookout that night.* PHRASES / V inflects

4 If you are **keeping a lookout** for something or **are on the lookout** for it, you are alert and careful about it, either because you do not want to miss it or because it will be unpleasant or harmful and you need to avoid it. *Keep a lookout for a nasty little organization calling itself Defence Through Strength... Nature lovers will be on the lookout for eagles, cormorants, and the occasional whale.* V inflects, usu PHR *for* n

loom /luːm/ **looms, looming, loomed** ◆◆◇◇◇

1 If something **looms** over you, it appears as a large or unclear shape, often in a frightening way. *Vincent loomed over me, as pale and grey as a tombstone. ...the bleak mountains that loomed out of the blackness and towered around us.* VERB / V prep/adv / Also V

2 If a worrying or threatening situation or event **is looming**, it seems likely to happen soon; used by journalists. *Another government spending crisis is looming in the United States... The threat of renewed civil war looms ahead. ...the looming threat of recession.* VERB / V / V adv/prep / V-ing

3 If a problem or event **looms large**, it occupies a lot of your thoughts and seems to be a frightening prospect that you cannot avoid. *...the terrible problem of armed crime now looming large in our society... As such tensions increase, they loom larger in Russia's domestic politics.* PHRASE: V inflects

4 A **loom** is a machine that is used for weaving thread into cloth. N-COUNT

loom up. If something **looms up**, it comes into sight as a tall, unclear shape, often in a frightening way. *The great house loomed up ahead of them.* PHRASAL VERB / VP

loony /luːni/ **loonies; loonier, looniest** ◆◇◇◇◇

1 If you describe someone's behaviour or ideas as **loony**, you mean that they seem mad, strange, or eccentric; an informal word. *What's she up to? She's as loony as her brother! ...loony feminist nonsense.* ADJ-GRADED

2 If you refer to someone as a **loony**, you mean that they behave in a way that seems mad, strange, or eccentric; an informal word. *At first they all thought I was a loony.* N-COUNT / =nutter

loop /luːp/ **loops, looping, looped** ◆◆◇◇◇

1 A **loop** is a curved or circular shape in something long, for example in a piece of string. *Mrs. Morrell reached for a loop of garden hose.* N-COUNT: usu with supp

2 If you **loop** something such as a piece of rope around an object, you tie a length of it in a loop around the object, for example in order to fasten it to the object. *He looped the rope over the wood... He wore the watch and chain looped round his neck like a medallion.* VERB / V n prep / V-ed

3 If something **loops** somewhere, it goes there in a circular direction that makes the shape of a loop. *The enemy was looping around the south side... The helicopter took off and headed north. Then it looped west, heading for the hills.* VERB / V prep/adv

loophole /luːphoʊl/ **loopholes.** A **loophole** in the law is a small mistake or omission which allows some people to avoid doing something that the law intended them to do. *It is estimated that 60,000 shops open every Sunday and trade by*  N-COUNT: oft N *in* n

exploiting some loophole in the law to avoid prosecution.

loose /luːs/ **looser, loosest; looses, loosing, loosed** ◆◆◆◇◇

1 Something that is **loose** is not firmly held or fixed in place. *If a tooth feels very loose, your dentist may recommend that it's taken out... Two wooden beams had come loose from the ceiling... His tie was pulled loose and his collar hung open... She idly pulled at a loose thread on her skirt.* ♦ **loosely** *Tim clasped his hands together and held them loosely in front of his belly.* ADJ-GRADED; ADV-GRADED: ADV with v

2 Something that is **loose** is not attached to anything, or held or contained in anything. *Two young men were racing motorcycles on the loose gravel... Frank emptied a handful of loose change on the table... A page came loose and floated onto the tiles.* ADJ: usu ADJ n

3 If people or animals break **loose** or are set **loose**, they are freed after they have been restrained. *She broke loose from his embrace and crossed to the window... Why didn't you tell me she'd been set loose?... Jack was chased by a loose dog.* ADJ: ADJ after v, ADJ n, v-link ADJ

4 Clothes that are **loose** are rather large and do not fit closely. *A pistol wasn't that hard to hide under a loose shirt... Wear loose clothes as they're more comfortable.* ♦ **loosely** *His shirt hung loosely over his thin shoulders.* ADJ-GRADED =baggy ≠tight; ADV-GRADED: ADV after v, ADV -ed

5 If your hair is **loose**, it hangs freely round your shoulders and is not tied back. *She was still in her nightdress, with her hair hanging loose over her shoulders.* ADJ =unfastened

6 Something that is **loose** is not compact or dense in texture. *She gathered loose soil and let it filter slowly through her fingers.* ADJ

7 A **loose** grouping, arrangement, or organization is flexible rather than strictly controlled or organized. *Murray and Alison came to some sort of loose arrangement before he went home... He wants a loose coalition of leftwing forces.* ♦ **loosely** *The investigation had aimed at a loosely organised group of criminals.* ADJ-GRADED: usu ADJ n ≠rigid; ADV-GRADED: ADV with v

8 **Loose** words or expressions are not exact but rather vague. *...a loose translation... He despised loose thinking.* ♦ **loosely** *The book follows four characters, loosely based on my uncles.* ADJ-GRADED =imprecise; ADV-GRADED: ADV -ed, ADV after v

9 If someone describes a woman or someone's behaviour as **loose**, they disapprove of that person because they think she or he has sexual relationships with too many people; an old-fashioned use. *Is an actress who strips off in public necessarily a loose woman in private?... Lust now seems to be associated with casual sex and loose morals.* ADJ-GRADED: usu ADJ n PRAGMATICS

10 To **loose** something such as ammunition means to release a large amount of it suddenly. *He trained his gun down and loosed a brief burst.* ▸ **Loose off** means the same as **loose**; used mainly in British English. *He loosed off two shots at the oncoming car.* VERB V n; PHRASAL VERB V P n (not pron) Also V n P

11 If you **loose** something, you hold it less tightly or unfasten it slightly. *He gave a grunt and loosed his grip on the rifle... The guards loosed his arms.* VERB V n

12 If a person or an animal is **on the loose**, they are free because they have escaped from a person or place. *Up to a thousand prisoners may be on the loose inside the jail... A man-eating lion is on the loose somewhere in England.* PHRASES v-link PHR

13 • a **loose cannon**: see **cannon**. • to **cut loose**: see **cut**. • **all hell breaks loose**: see **hell**. • to **let** someone **loose**: see **let**. • to **play fast and loose**: see **fast**.

loose off. See **loose** 10. PHRASAL VERB

loose end, loose ends ◆◇◇◇◇

1 A **loose end** is part of a story, situation, or crime that has not yet been explained. *There are some annoying loose ends in the plot.* N-COUNT

2 If you are **at a loose end**, you are bored because you do not have anything to do and cannot think of anything that you want to do; an informal expression. *Adolescents are most likely to get into trouble when they're at a loose end.* PHRASE: v-link PHR

loose-fitting; also spelled **loose fitting**. **Loose-fitting** clothes are rather large and do not fit tightly on your body. ADJ-GRADED: usu ADJ n

loosen /luːsᵊn/ **loosens, loosening, loosened** ◆◆◇◇◇

1 If someone **loosens** restrictions or laws, for example, they make them less strict or severe. *Many business groups have been pressing the Federal Reserve to loosen interest rates... Drilling regulations, too, have been loosened to speed the development of the fields.* ♦ **loosening** *Domestic conditions did not justify a loosening of monetary policy.* VERB V n; N-SING: usu N of n

2 If someone or something **loosens** the ties between people or groups of people, or if the ties **loosen**, they become weaker. *The Federal Republic must loosen its ties with the United States... The deputy leader is cautious about loosening the links with the unions... The ties that bind them together are loosening.* V-ERG V n V

3 If you **loosen** your clothing or something that is tied or fastened, or if it **loosens**, you move it or undo it slightly so that it less tight or less firmly held in place. *He reached up to loosen the scarf around his neck... Loosen the bolt so the bars can be turned... Her hair had loosened and was tangled around her shoulders.* V-ERG ≠tighten V n V

4 If you **loosen** something that is stretched across something else, you make it less stretched or tight. *Insert a small knife into the top of the chicken breast to loosen the skin.* VERB V n

5 If you **loosen** your grip on something, or if your grip **loosens**, you hold it less tightly. *Harry loosened his grip momentarily and Anna wriggled free... When his grip loosened she eased herself away.* V-ERG V n V

6 If a government or organization **loosens** its grip on a group of people or an activity, or if its grip **loosens**, it begins to have less control over it. *There is no sign that the Party will loosen its tight grip on the country... The Soviet Union's grip on Eastern Europe loosened.* V-ERG =relax V n V

7 If you say that something **has loosened** someone's **tongue**, you mean that it has made them talk about something, often when they should have remained silent. *The wine had loosened his tongue.* PHRASE: V inflects

loosen up PHRASAL VERB

1 If a person or situation **loosens up**, they become more relaxed and less tense. *Relax, smile; loosen up in mind and body and behaviour... Things loosened up, in politics and the economy... I think people have loosened up their standards.* V P; V P n

2 If you **loosen up** your body, or if it **loosens up**, you do simple exercises to get your muscles ready for a difficult physical activity, such as running or playing football. *Squeeze the foot with both hands, again to loosen up tight muscles... Close your eyes. Relax. Let your body loosen up.* ERG V P n (not pron) V P Also V n P

loot /luːt/ **loots, looting, looted** ◆◆◇◇◇

1 If people **loot** shops or houses, they steal things from them during a battle, riot, or other disturbance. *The trouble began when gangs began breaking windows and looting shops... There have been reports of youths taking advantage of the general confusion to loot and steal.* ♦ **looting** *In the country's largest cities there has been rioting and looting.* VERB =plunder V n V; N-UNCOUNT

2 If someone **loots** money or goods, they steal them during a battle, riot, or other disturbance. *The town has been plagued by armed thugs who have looted food supplies and terrorized the population. ...lists of looted material ranging from tanks to office fittings.* VERB V n V-ed

3 **Loot** is stolen money and goods; an informal use. *Most criminals steal in order to sell their loot for cash on the black market.* N-UNCOUNT =plunder, spoils

looter /luːtəʳ/ **looters.** A **looter** is a person who steals things or takes things by force while there is a riot, war, or other disturbance going on. ◆◇◇◇◇ N-COUNT

lop /lɒp/ **lops, lopping, lopped**

lop off PHRASAL VERB

1 If you **lop** something **off**, you cut it away from what it was attached to, usually with a quick, strong stroke. *Somebody lopped the heads off our* =chop V n P *tulips. ...men with axes, lopping off branches... His ponytail had been lopped off.* V P n (not pron)

2 If you **lop** an amount of money or time **off** something such as a budget or a schedule, you reduce the budget or schedule by that amount; an informal use. *The Air France plane lopped over four hours off the previous best time... More than 100 million pounds will be lopped off the prison building programme.* V n P n; Also V P n (not pron), V n P

lope /lo͟ʊp/ **lopes, loping, loped.** If a person or animal **lopes** somewhere, they run in an easy and relaxed way, taking long steps. *He was loping across the sand toward Nancy... Matty saw him go loping off, running low.* ♦ **loping** *She turned and walked away with long, loping steps.* VERB =lollop; V prep/adv; Also V; ADJ: ADJ n

lopsided /lɒpsa͟ɪdɪd/; also spelled **lop-sided.**

1 Something that is **lopsided** is uneven because one side is lower or heavier than the other. *His suit had shoulders that made him look lopsided. ...a friendly, lopsided grin.* ADJ-GRADED

2 If you say that a situation is **lopsided**, you mean that one element is much stronger, bigger, or more important than another element. *In 1916, Georgia Tech beat Cumberland 222-0. No game since has been that lopsided. ...lopsided economic relations.* ADJ-GRADED

loquacious /ləkwe͟ɪʃəs/. If you describe someone as **loquacious**, you mean that they talk a lot; a formal word. *The normally loquacious Mr O'Reilly has said little.* ADJ-GRADED =talkative

lord /lɔ͟ːʳd/ **lords, lording, lorded** ♦♦♦♦◇

1 In Britain, a **lord** is a man who has a high rank in the nobility, for example an earl, a viscount, or a marquess. *She married a lord and lives in this huge house in the Cotswolds... A few days earlier he had received a telegram from Lord Lloyd.* N-COUNT; N-TITLE

2 In Britain, judges, bishops, and some male members of the nobility are addressed as **'my Lord'**. *My lord, I am instructed by my client to claim that the evidence has been tampered with.* N-VOC: my N PRAGMATICS

3 In Britain, **Lord** is used in the titles of some officials of very high rank. *He was Lord Chancellor from 1970 until 1974. ...Sir Brian Hutton, the Lord Chief Justice for Northern Ireland.*

4 **The Lords** is the same as the **House of Lords**. *It's very likely the bill will be defeated in the Lords.* N-PROPER-COLL: the N

5 In former times, especially in medieval times, a **lord** was a man who owned land or property and who had power and authority over people. *It was the home of the powerful lords of Baux.* N-COUNT

6 In the Christian church, people refer to God and to Jesus Christ as the **Lord**. *I know the Lord will look after him... She prayed now. 'Lord, help me to find courage.' ...the birth of the Lord Jesus Christ.* N-PROPER: usu the N; N-VOC

• See also **Our Lord**.

7 If you describe a man as the **lord** of a particular area, industry, or thing, you mean that they have total authority and power over it. *A century ago the aristocracy were truly lords of the earth. ...the lords of the black market.* N-COUNT: usu with supp, usu N of n

8 **Lord** is used in exclamations such as **'good Lord!'** and **'oh Lord!'** to express surprise, amusement, shock, frustration, or worry about something. *'Good lord, that's what he is: he's a policeman.'... 'They didn't fire you for drinking, did they?'—'Lord, no! I only drink beer, nowadays.'* PHRASES EXCLAM =heavens

9 You can say **'Lord knows'** to emphasize something that you feel or believe very strongly. *I've got to go home, but Lord knows I dread it.* usu PHR that PRAGMATICS

10 You can say **'Lord knows'** to emphasize that you do not know something. *He would turn up at meetings, but Lord knows where he came from.* usu PHR wh PRAGMATICS

11 If someone **lords it over** you, they act in a way that shows that they think they are better than you, especially by giving lots of orders; used showing disapproval. *Alex seemed to enjoy lording it over the three girls.* V inflects PRAGMATICS

lordly /lɔ͟ːʳdli/

1 If you say that someone's behaviour is **lordly**, you are critical of them because they treat other people in a proud and arrogant way. *...their usual lordly indifference to patients. ...the lordly elder brother.* ADJ-GRADED: usu ADJ n PRAGMATICS

2 **Lordly** means magnificent, impressive, and suitable for a lord. *...the site of a lordly mansion.* ADJ: ADJ n

Lordship /lɔ͟ːʳdʃɪp/ **Lordships.** You use the expressions **Your Lordship, His Lordship,** or **Their Lordships** when you are addressing or referring to a judge, bishop, or male member of the nobility. *My name is Richard Savage, your Lordship... His Lordship expressed the hope that the Law Commission might look at the subject.* ♦◇◇◇◇ N-VOC; N-PROPER: det-poss N PRAGMATICS

Lord's Prayer. **The Lord's Prayer** is a very important Christian prayer that was originally taught by Jesus Christ to his disciples. N-PROPER: the N

lore /lɔ͟ːʳ/. The **lore** of a particular country or culture is its traditional stories and history. *...the Book of the Sea, which was stuffed with sailors' lore. ...ancient Catalan lore.* ♦◇◇◇◇ N-UNCOUNT: with supp

lorry /lɒri, AM lɔ͟ːri/ **lorries** ♦♦◇◇◇

1 In British English, a **lorry** is a large vehicle that is used to transport goods by road. The American word is **truck**. *...a seven-ton lorry.* N-COUNT

2 In British English, if someone says that something has fallen **off the back of a lorry**, or that they got something **off the back of a lorry**, they mean that they bought something that they knew was stolen; an informal expression. *He gets caviare that has fallen off the back of a lorry... Pete once bought the boys a bicycle cheap off the back of a lorry.* PHRASE: PHR after v

lose /lu͟ːz/ **loses, losing, lost** ♦♦♦♦♦

1 If you **lose** a contest, a fight, or an argument, you do not succeed because someone does better than you and defeats you. *A C Milan lost the Italian Cup Final... The government lost the argument over the pace of reform... The Vietnam conflict ultimately was lost... No one likes to be on the losing side.* VERB; V n; V-ing

2 If you **lose** something, you do not know where it is, for example because you have forgotten where you put it. *I lost my keys... I had to go back for my checkup; they'd lost my X-rays.* VERB =mislay; V n

3 You say that you **lose** something when you no longer have it because it has been taken away from you or destroyed. *Mr Chirac subsequently lost his job as prime minister... He lost his licence for six months... She was terrified they'd lose their home.* VERB; V n

4 If someone **loses** a quality, characteristic, attitude, or belief, they no longer have it. *He lost all sense of reason... The government had lost all credibility... He had lost his desire to live.* VERB; V n

5 If you **lose** an ability, you stop having that ability because of something such as an accident. *They lost their ability to hear... He had lost the use of his legs.* VERB; V n

6 If someone or something **loses** heat, their temperature becomes lower. *Babies lose heat much faster than adults... A lot of body heat is lost through the scalp.* VERB; V n

7 If you **lose** blood or fluid from your body, it leaves your body so that you have less of it. *The victim suffered a dreadful injury and lost a lot of blood... During fever a large quantity of fluid is lost in perspiration.* VERB; V n

8 If you **lose** weight, you become less heavy, and usually look thinner. *I have lost a lot of weight... Martha was able to lose 25 pounds.* VERB; V n

9 If you **lose** a part of your body, it is cut off in an operation or in a violent accident. *He lost a foot when he was struck by a train.* VERB; V n

10 If someone **loses** their life, they die. *...the ferry disaster in 1987, in which 192 people lost their lives... Hundreds of lives were lost in fighting.* VERB; V n

11 If you **lose** a close relative or friend, they die. *My Grandma lost her brother in the war.* VERB; V n

12 If things **are lost**, they are destroyed in a disaster. *...the famous Nankin pottery that was lost in a shipwreck off the coast of China.* VB: usu passive; be V-ed

13 If you **lose** time, you waste it. *They claim that police lost valuable time in the early part of the investigation... Six hours were lost in all.* VERB; V n

14 If you **lose** an opportunity, you do not take advantage of it. *If you don't do it soon you're going to lose the opportunity... They did not lose the opportunity to say what they thought of events. ...a lost opportunity.* VERB; V n; V n to-inf; V-ed

15 If you **lose** yourself in something or if you **are lost** in it, you give a lot of attention to it and do not think about anything else. *Michael held on to her arm, losing himself in the music... He was lost in the contemplation of the landscape.* VERB =absorb V pron-refl *in* n *be* V-ed *in* n

16 If a business **loses** money, it earns less money than it spends, and is therefore in debt. *His shops stand to lose millions of pounds... $1 billion a year may be lost.* VERB V n

17 If something **loses** you a contest or **loses** you something that you had, it causes you to fail or to no longer have what you had. *My own stupidity lost me the match... His economic mismanagement has lost him the support of the general public.* VERB V n n

18 See also **lost**.

19 If say that you **have nothing to lose**, you mean that you will not suffer if you do something unsuccessfully. If you say that you **have much to lose**, you mean that you may suffer if you do something unsuccessfully. *They say they have nothing to lose and will continue protesting until the government vetos the agreement... Both countries have much to lose if there is a war.* PHRASES V inflects

20 If you say that someone **loses no opportunity** to do or say a particular thing, especially something that they will benefit from or that will harm someone else, you are emphasizing that they do it or say it whenever it is possible. *The President has lost no opportunity to capitalise on his new position... He said some sections of the press had lost no opportunity to create the impression that she was guilty.* V inflects, oft PHR to-inf PRAGMATICS

21 If you say that someone **loses no time** in doing something, you are emphasizing that they act quickly in order to benefit from a situation. *Officials have lost no time in expressing their concern and grief over this incident... Francine lost no time in defending herself.* V inflects, usu PHR *in*-ing PRAGMATICS

22 If you **lose** your **way**, you become lost when you are trying to go somewhere. *The men lost their way in a sandstorm.* V inflects

23 If you say that someone **loses** their **way**, you think they no longer have a clear idea of what they want to do or achieve. *For a while the artist completely lost his way. The famous humour gave way to sentimental nonsense... If we cannot understand that there's an issue of principle here, then we have lost our way.* V inflects

24 • to **lose** your **balance**: see **balance**. • to **lose contact**: see **contact**. • to **lose** your **cool**: see **cool**. • to **lose face**: see **face**. • to **lose** your **grip**: see **grip**. • to **lose** your **head**: see **head**. • to **lose heart**: see **heart**. • to **lose** your **mind**: see **mind**. • to **lose** your **nerve**: see **nerve**. • to **lose sight of**: see **sight**. • to **lose** your **temper**: see **temper**. • to **lose touch**: see **touch**. • to **lose track of**: see **track**.

lose out. If you **lose out**, you suffer a loss or disadvantage because you have not succeeded in what you were doing. *We both lost out... Laura lost out to Tom... Women have lost out in this new pay flexibility... Egypt has lost out on revenues from the Suez Canal.* PHRASAL VERB V P V P *to* n V P *in* n V P *on* n

loser /lu̲ːzəʳ/ **losers** ◆◆◇◇◇

1 The **losers** of a game, contest, or struggle are the people who are defeated or beaten. *...the Dallas Cowboys and Buffalo Bills, the winners and losers of this year's Super Bowl.* • If you say that someone is a **good loser**, you approve of the fact that they accept that they have lost a game or contest without complaining. If you say that someone is a **bad loser**, you are critical of them because they hate losing and complain a lot about it. *I'm sure the prime minister will turn out to be a good loser... You are a very bad loser Lou, aren't you?* N-COUNT: usu pl ≠winner PHRASE: usu v-link PHR PRAGMATICS

2 If you refer to someone as a **loser**, you have a low opinion of them because you think they are always unsuccessful; an informal use. *They've only been trained to compete with other men, so a successful woman can make them feel like a real loser.* N-COUNT PRAGMATICS =failure

3 People who are **losers** as the result of an action or event, are in a worse situation because of it or do not benefit from it. *Some of Britain's top business leaders of the 1980s have become the country's greatest losers in the recession.* N-COUNT: usu pl ≠beneficiary

loss /lɒ̲s, AM lɔ̲ːs/ **losses** ◆◆◆◆◇

1 **Loss** is the fact of no longer having something or having less of it than before. *...loss of sight... The loss of income for the government is about $250 million a month. ...hair loss... The job losses will reduce the total workforce to 7,000.* N-VAR: usu with supp

2 **Loss** of life occurs when people die. *...a terrible loss of human life... The allies suffered less than 20 casualties while enemy losses were said to be high.* N-VAR: usu with supp

3 The **loss** of a relative or friend is their death. *They took the time to talk about the loss of Thomas and how their grief was affecting them. ...the loss of his mother.* N-UNCOUNT: with supp, usu *the* N *of* n =death

4 If a business makes a **loss**, it earns less than it spends. *In 1986 Rover made a loss of nine hundred million pounds... The company said it will stop producing fertilizer in 1990 because of continued losses. ...profit and loss.* N-VAR ≠profit

5 **Loss** is the feeling of sadness you experience when someone or something you like is taken away from you. *Talk to others about your feelings of loss and grief... He always woke with a sense of deep sorrow and depressing loss.* N-UNCOUNT

6 A **loss** is the disadvantage you suffer when a valuable and useful person or thing leaves or is taken away. *She said his death was a great loss to herself.* N-COUNT: usu sing

7 The **loss** of something such as heat, blood, or fluid is the gradual reduction of it or of its level in a system or in someone's body. *...blood loss. ...weight loss. ...a rapid loss of heat from the body.* N-UNCOUNT: with supp

8 If a business produces something **at a loss**, they sell it at a price which is less than it cost them to produce it or buy it. *Timber owners have often produced lumber at a loss and survived these down cycles in demand.* PHRASES PHR after v

9 If you say that you are **at a loss**, you mean that you do not know what to do in a particular situation. *I was at a loss for what to do next... The government is at a loss to know how to tackle the violence.* usu v-link PHR, usu PHR *for* n, PHR to-inf

10 If you **cut** your **losses**, you stop doing what you were doing in order to prevent the bad situation that you are in becoming worse. *Directors are right to cut their losses, admit they chose the wrong man and make a change.* V inflects

11 If you say that someone or something is a **dead loss**, you have a low opinion of them because you think they are completely useless or unsuccessful; an informal British expression. *I'd had no experience of organizing anything of that sort. I think I was largely a dead loss.* usu v-link PHR PRAGMATICS

lo̲ss leader, loss leaders; also spelled **loss-leader**. A **loss leader** is an item that is sold at such a low price that it makes a loss in the hope that customers will be attracted by it and buy other goods at the same shop. N-COUNT

lost /lɒ̲st, AM lɔ̲ːst/ ◆◆◆◇◇

1 **Lost** is the past tense and past participle of **lose**.

2 If you are **lost** or if you get **lost**, you do not know where you are or are unable to find your way. *Barely had I set foot in the street when I realised I was lost... I took a wrong turn and we got lost in the mountains.* ADJ: usu v-link ADJ

3 If something is **lost**, or gets **lost**, you cannot find it, for example because you have forgotten where you put it. *...a lost book... My paper got lost... He was scrabbling for his pen, which had got lost somewhere under the sheets of paper.* ADJ =mislaid

4 If you feel **lost**, you feel very uncomfortable because you are in an unfamiliar situation. *Of the funeral he remembered only the cold, the waiting, and feeling very lost... I feel lost and lonely in a strange town alone.* ADJ-GRADED: usu v-link ADJ

5 If you describe a person or group of people as **lost**, you think that they do not have a clear idea of what they want to do or achieve. *They are a lost generation in search of an identity.* ADJ

6 If you describe something as **lost**, you mean that you no longer have it or it no longer exists. *...their lost homeland. ...a lost job or promotion... The* ADJ *sense of community is lost... The riots will also mean lost income for Los Angeles County.*

7 You use **lost** to refer to a period or state of affairs that existed in the past and no longer exists. *He seemed to pine for his lost youth... They are links to a lost age. ...the relics of a lost civilisation.* ADJ: ADJ n =past

8 If something is **lost**, it is not used properly and is considered wasted. *Fox is not bitter about the lost opportunity to compete in the Games... The advantage is lost.* ADJ: usu v-link ADJ =wasted

9 If you tell someone to **get lost**, you are telling them in a very rude way to go away. PHRASES PRAGMATICS

10 If advice or a comment **is lost on** someone, they do not understand it or they pay no attention to it. *The meaning of that was lost on me... This was a neighborhood where clearly you could be murdered for a pack of cigarettes, a fact that was not lost on me.* V inflects, PHR n

11 If you **are lost in thought**, you give all your attention to what you are thinking about and do not notice what is going on around you. *She was silent for a while, lost in thought, staring at the books littering the room.* V inflects

12 If you say that you **would be lost without** someone or something, you mean that you would be unhappy or unable to work properly without them. *I'd be lost without you here... I love the game and I'd be lost without golf now.* V inflects

lost cause, lost causes. If you refer to something or someone as a **lost cause**, you mean that people's attempts to change or influence them have no chance of succeeding. *They do not want to expend energy in what, to them, is a lost cause.* N-COUNT

lost property

1 **Lost property** consists of things that people have lost or accidentally left in a public place, for example on a train or in a school. *Lost property should be handed to the driver.* N-UNCOUNT

2 **Lost property** is a place where lost property is kept. *I was enquiring in Lost Property at Derby.* N-UNCOUNT

lost soul, lost souls. If you call someone a **lost soul**, you mean that they seem unhappy, and unable to fit in with any particular group of people in society. *They just clung to each other like two lost souls.* N-COUNT

lot /lɒt/ **lots** ◆◆◆◆◆

1 **A lot of** something or **lots of** it is a large amount of it. **A lot of** people or things, or **lots of** them, is a large number of them. *A lot of our land is used to grow crops for export... I remember a lot of things... 'You'll find that everybody will try and help their colleague.'—'Yeah. There's a lot of that.'... Lots of pubs like to deck themselves out with flowers in summer... He drank lots of milk... A lot of the play is very funny.* ▶ Also a pronoun. *There's lots going on at Selfridges this month... I learned a lot from him about how to run a band... I know a lot has been said about my sister's role in my career.* QUANT: QUANT of n =a great deal; PRON

2 **A lot** means to a great extent or degree. *Matthew's out quite a lot doing his research... I like you, a lot... If I went out and accepted a job at a lot less money, I'd jeopardize a good career.* ADV: ADV after v, oft ADV compar

3 If you do something **a lot**, you do it often or for a long time. *They went out a lot, to the Cafe Royal or the The Ivy... He talks a lot about his own children.* ADV: ADV after v

4 You can use **lot** to refer to a set or group of things or people. *He bought two lots of 1,000 shares in the company during August and September... We've just sacked one lot of builders.* N-COUNT: num N, oft N of n

5 You can refer to a specific group of people as a particular **lot**; an informal use. *Future generations are going to think that we were a pretty boring lot.* N-SING: adj N =bunch

6 In informal English, you can use **the lot** to refer to the whole of an amount that you have just mentioned. *Instead of paying his rent, he went to a betting shop and lost the lot in half an hour.* N-SING: the N

7 Your **lot** is the kind of life you have or the things that you have or experience. *She tried to accept her marriage as her lot in life but could not... Young people are usually less contented with their lot.* N-SING: usu with poss

8 A **lot** is a small area of land that belongs to a person or company; used mainly in American English. *If oil or gold are discovered under your lot, you can sell the mineral rights.* ● See also **parking lot**. N-COUNT

9 A **lot** in an auction is one of the objects or groups of objects that are being sold. *The receivers are keen to sell the stores as one lot... The two lots have made just over £5 million.* N-COUNT

10 If people **draw lots** to decide who will do something, they each take a piece of paper from a container. One or more pieces of paper is marked, and the people who take marked pieces are chosen. *Two names were selected by drawing lots... For the first time in a World Cup finals, lots had to be drawn to decide who would finish second and third.* PHRASES V inflects

11 If you **throw in** your **lot with** a particular person or group, you decide to work with them and support them from then on, whatever happens. *He has decided to throw in his lot with the far-right groups in parliament.* V inflects, PHR n =join forces with

loth /loʊθ/. See **loath**.

lotion /loʊʃᵊn/ **lotions.** A **lotion** is a liquid that you use to clean, improve, or protect your skin or hair. *...suntan lotion. ...cleansing lotions.* ◆◇◇◇◇ N-MASS: usu n N =cream

lottery /lɒtəri/ **lotteries** ◆◇◇◇◇

1 A **lottery** is a type of gambling game in which people buy numbered tickets. Several numbers are then chosen, and the people who have those numbers on their tickets win a prize. *...the national lottery.* N-COUNT

2 If you describe something as **a lottery**, you mean that what happens depends entirely on luck or chance. *The stockmarket is a lottery... Which judges are assigned to a case is always a bit of a lottery.* N-SING: a N

lotus /loʊtəs/ **lotuses.** A **lotus** or a **lotus flower** is a type of water-lily that grows in Africa and Asia. N-COUNT

lotus position. If someone is sitting in the **lotus position**, they are sitting with their legs crossed and each foot resting on top of the opposite thigh. If people are sitting like this, they are usually doing meditation or yoga. N-SING: usu the N

louche /luːʃ/. If you describe a person or place as **louche**, you mean that they are unconventional and not respectable, but often in a way that people find rather attractive; used in written English. *...that section of London society which somehow managed to be louche and fashionable at the same time.* ADJ-GRADED =disreputable

loud /laʊd/ **louder, loudest** ◆◆◆◇◇

1 If a noise is **loud**, the level of sound is very high and it can be easily heard. Someone or something that is **loud** produces a lot of noise. *Suddenly there was a loud bang... His voice became harsh and loud... The band was starting to play a fast, loud number. ...amazingly loud discos.* ▶ Also an adverb. *She wonders whether Paul's hearing is OK because he turns the television up very loud.* ♦ **loudly** *His footsteps echoed loudly in the tiled hall.* ♦ **loudness** *The students began to enter the classroom and Anna was startled at their loudness.* ADJ-GRADED; ADV-GRADED: ADV after v; ADV-GRADED: ADV with v; N-UNCOUNT

2 If someone is **loud** in their support for or criticism of something, they express their opinion very often and in a very strong way. *Mr Scargill's speech yesterday was very loud in condemnation of the media... Mr Jones received loud support from his local community.* ♦ **loudly** *Mac talked loudly in favour of the good works done by the Church.* ADJ-GRADED: oft ADJ in n/-ing =vociferous; ADV-GRADED: ADV with v

3 If you describe something, especially a piece of clothing, as **loud**, you dislike it because it has very bright colours or very large, bold patterns which look unpleasant. *He liked to shock with his gold chains and loud clothes... I once paid £120 for an extremely loud shirt which I've yet to wear.* ADJ-GRADED PRAGMATICS =garish

4 If you tell someone something **loud and clear**, you are very easily understood, either because your voice is very clear or because you express yourself very clearly. *Lisa's voice comes through loud and clear... The message is a powerful one, and I hope it will be heard loud and clear by the tobacco industry.* PHRASES usu PHR after v

5 If you say or read something **out loud**, you say it or read it so that it can be heard, rather than just usu PHR after v thinking it. *Even Ford, who seldom smiled, laughed out loud a few times... He began to read out loud.*

6 • for crying out loud: see **cry**.

loudhailer /laʊdheɪləʳ/ **loudhailers;** also spelled **loud-hailer**. In British English, a **loudhailer** is a portable device with a microphone at one end and a cone-shaped speaker at the other end. You use it when you want people to be able to hear you from a long way away, especially outdoors. The usual American word is **bullhorn**. N-COUNT =megaphone

loudmouth /laʊdmaʊθ/ **loudmouths** /laʊdmaʊðz/. If you describe someone as a **loudmouth**, you are critical of them because they talk a lot, especially in an unpleasant, offensive, or stupid way. N-COUNT PRAGMATICS

loud-mouthed. If you describe someone as **loud-mouthed**, you are critical of them because they talk a lot, especially in an unpleasant, offensive, or stupid way. *...a loud-mouthed oaf with very little respect for women.* ADJ-GRADED: usu ADJ n PRAGMATICS

loudspeaker /laʊdspiːkəʳ/ **loudspeakers;** also spelled **loud speaker**. A **loudspeaker** is a piece of equipment, for example part of a radio or hi-fi system, through which sound comes out. ◆◇◇◇◇ N-COUNT =speaker

lounge /laʊndʒ/ **lounges, lounging, lounged** ◆◆◇◇◇

1 A **lounge** is a room in a house where people sit and relax. *The Holmbergs were sitting before a roaring fire in the lounge, sipping their cocoa.* N-COUNT =living room, sitting room

2 A **lounge** is a room in a hotel or club where people can sit and relax. *I spoke to her in the lounge of a big Johannesburg hotel where she was attending a union meeting.* N-COUNT

3 A **lounge** is a very large room in an airport where people can sit and wait for aircraft to arrive or depart. *Instead of taking me to the departure lounge they took me right to my seat on the plane.* N-COUNT: usu supp N

4 If you **lounge** somewhere, you lean against something or lie somewhere in a relaxed or lazy way. *They ate and drank and lounged in the shade... If you don't want to lounge on the beach, you can go on a guided walk along the nature trail.* VERB =laze V prep

lounge about or **lounge around.** The form **lounge about** is mainly used in British English. If you **lounge about** or **lounge around**, you spend your time in a relaxed and lazy way, sometimes when you should be doing something useful. *It gives him a reason for lounging around doing nothing... He remembered mowing the lawn, lounging around the swimming pool.* PHRASAL VERB =loll about V P V P n

louse /laʊs/ **lice. Lice** are small insects that live on the bodies of people or animals and bite them in order to drink their blood. ◆◇◇◇◇ N-COUNT: usu pl

lousy /laʊzi/ **lousier, lousiest** ◆◇◇◇◇

1 If you describe something as **lousy**, you mean that it is of very bad quality or that you do not like it; an informal use. *He blamed Fiona for a lousy weekend... At Billy's Cafe, the menu is limited and the food is lousy... It's lousy to be the new kid.* ADJ-GRADED =rotten

2 If you describe someone as **lousy**, you mean that they are very bad at something they do; an informal use. *I was a lousy secretary... There can be no argument about how lousy he is at public relations.* ADJ-GRADED: oft ADJ *at* n =awful, terrible

3 If you describe the number or amount of something as **lousy**, you mean it is smaller than you think it should be; an informal use. *The pay is lousy.* ADJ PRAGMATICS =mingy

4 If you feel **lousy**, you feel very ill; an informal use. *I wasn't actually sick but I felt lousy.* ADJ-GRADED: *feel/look* ADJ

lout /laʊt/ **louts.** If you describe a man or boy as a **lout**, you are critical of them because they behave in an impolite or aggressive way. *...a drunken lout.* N-COUNT PRAGMATICS

loutish /laʊtɪʃ/. If you describe a man or a boy as **loutish**, you are critical of them because their behaviour is impolite and aggressive. *I was appalled by the loutish behaviour.* ADJ-GRADED: usu ADJ n PRAGMATICS

louvre /luːvəʳ/ **louvres;** spelled **louver** in American English. A **louvre** is a door or window with narrow, flat, sloping pieces of wood or glass across its frame. N-COUNT: oft N n

lovable /lʌvəbᵊl/. If you describe someone as **lovable**, you mean that they have attractive qualities, and are easy to like. *His vulnerability makes him even more lovable.* ◆◇◇◇◇ ADJ-GRADED =endearing

love /lʌv/ **loves, loving, loved** ◆◆◆◆◆

1 If you **love** someone, you feel romantically or sexually attracted to them, and they are very important to you. *Oh, Amy, I love you... We love each other. We want to spend our lives together.* VERB V n

2 Love is a very strong feeling of affection towards someone who you are romantically or sexually attracted to. *Our love for each other has been increased by what we've been through together. ...a old fashioned love story. ...an album of love songs.* N-UNCOUNT

3 You say that you **love** someone when their happiness is very important to you, so that you behave in a kind and caring way towards them. *You'll never love anyone the way you love your baby.* VERB V n

4 Love is the feeling that a person's happiness is very important to you, and the way you show this feeling in your behaviour towards them. *My love for all my children is unconditional... She's got a great capacity for love.* N-UNCOUNT

5 If you **love** something, you like it very much. *We loved the food so much, especially the fish dishes... I loved reading. ...one of these people that loves to be in the outdoors... I love it when I hear you laugh.* VERB V n/-ing V to-inf V *it* wh

6 You can say that you **love** something when you consider that it is important and want to protect or support it. *I love my country as you love yours.* VERB V n

7 Love is a strong liking for something, or a belief that it is important. *This is no way to encourage a love of literature... Much of Mr Chretien's speech was of his love of Canada.* N-UNCOUNT: oft N *of* n =passion

8 Your **love** is someone or something that you love. *'She is the love of my life,' he said... Music's one of my great loves.* N-COUNT: usu with poss

9 If you would **love** to have or do something, you very much want to have it or do it. *I would love to play for England again... I would love a hot bath and clean clothes... His wife would love him to give up his job.* VERB V to-inf V n V n to-inf

10 Some people use **love** as an affectionate way of addressing someone; an informal use. *Well, I'll take your word for it then, love... Don't cry, my love.* N-VOC =dear

11 In tennis, **love** is a score of zero. *He beat Thomas Muster of Austria three sets to love.* NUM

12 You can use expressions such as **'love'**, **'love from'**, and **'all my love'**, followed by your name, as an informal way of ending a letter to a friend or relation. *...with love from Grandma and Grandpa.* CONVENTION

13 If you send someone your **love**, you ask another person, who will soon be speaking or writing to them, to tell them that you are thinking about them with affection. *Please give her my love.* N-UNCOUNT: poss N

14 See also **-loved, loving; free love, peace-loving, tug-of-love.**

15 If you **fall in love** with someone, you start to be in love with them. *I fell in love with him because of his kind nature... We fell madly in love.* PHRASES V inflects, oft PHR *with* n

16 If you **fall in love** with something, you start to like it very much. *Working with Ford closely, I fell in love with the cinema.* V inflects, usu PHR *with* n

17 If you **are in love** with someone, you feel romantically or sexually attracted to them, and they are very important to you. *Laura had never before been in love... I've never really been in love with anyone... We were madly in love for about two years.* V inflects, oft PHR *with* n

18 If you are **in love** with something, you like it very much. *He had always been in love with the enchanted landscape of the West.* V inflects, usu PHR *with* n

19 If you say that there is **no love lost** between two people or groups or there is **little love lost** between them, you mean that they do not like each other at all. *Garry Kasparov and Anatoly Karpov may be fellow countrymen but there's no love lost between them.* usu v-link PHR *between* pl-n

20 When two people **make love**, they have sex. *Have you ever made love to a girl before?... One night, after 18 months of friendship, they made love for the first and last time.* RECIP: V inflects, oft pl-n PHR, PHR *to/with* n

21 If you cannot or will not do something **for love or money**, you are completely unable to do it or with brd-neg, PHR after v you do not intend to do it. *Replacement parts couldn't be found for love or money... I'm not coming back up here. Never, for love nor money.*

22 Love at first sight is the experience of starting to be in love with someone as soon as you see them for the first time. *It was love at first sight, and he proposed to me six weeks later.* usu *it be* PHR

23 ● labour of love: see **labour**.

love affair, love affairs ◆◇◇◇◇

1 A **love affair** is a romantic and usually sexual relationship between two people who love each other but who are not married or living together. *...a stressful love affair with a married man.* N-COUNT: oft N *with/between* n =relationship

2 If you refer to someone's **love affair** with something, you mean that they like it a lot and are very enthusiastic about it. *...the American love affair with firearms... Tom's love affair with France and most things French knew no bounds.* N-SING: with supp, usu N *with* n

lovebirds /lʌvbɜːʳdz/. You can refer in a humorous way to two people as **lovebirds** when they are obviously very much in love. *Jack and his missis are as happy as two lovebirds now.* N-PLURAL

love bite, love bites; also spelled **lovebite**. A **love bite** is a mark which someone has on their body as a result of being bitten by their partner when they were kissing or making love. N-COUNT

love child, love children; also spelled **lovechild**. If journalists refer to someone as a **love child**, they mean that the person was born as a result of a love affair between two people who have never been married to each other. *Eric has a secret love child.* N-COUNT

-loved /-lʌvd/. **-loved** combines with adverbs to form adjectives that describe how much someone or something is loved. *The similarities between the much-loved father and his son are remarkable. ...two of Mendelssohn's best-loved works.* COMB in ADJ-GRADED: usu ADJ n

love-hate relationship, love-hate relationships. If you have a **love-hate relationship** with someone or something, your feelings towards them change suddenly and often from love to hate. *...a book about the close love-hate relationship between two boys.* N-COUNT: usu sing

loveless /lʌvləs/. A **loveless** relationship or situation is one where there is no love. *She is in a loveless relationship.* ADJ: usu ADJ n

love letter, love letters. A **love letter** is a letter that you write to someone in order to tell them that you love them. N-COUNT

love life, love lives. Someone's **love life** is the part of their life that consists of their romantic and sexual relationships. *His love life was complicated, and involved intense relationships.* ◆◇◇◇◇ N-COUNT

lovelorn /lʌvlɔːʳn/. **Lovelorn** means the same as **lovesick**. *He was acting liking a lovelorn teenager.* ADJ-GRADED: usu ADJ n

lovely /lʌvli/ **lovelier, loveliest** ◆◆◆◇◇

1 If you describe someone or something as **lovely**, you mean that they are very beautiful and therefore pleasing to look at or listen to. *You look lovely, Marcia... He had a lovely voice... It was just one of those lovely old English gardens.* ♦ **loveliness** *You are a vision of loveliness.* ADJ-GRADED; N-UNCOUNT =beauty

2 If you describe something as **lovely**, you mean that it gives you pleasure. *Mary! How lovely to see you!... It's a lovely day... What a lovely surprise!* ADJ-GRADED =marvellous, wonderful

3 If you describe someone as **lovely**, you mean that they are friendly, kind, or generous. *Diana is a lovely young woman... She's a lovely child.* ADJ-GRADED =delightful

love-making. **Love-making** refers to sexual activities that take place between two people who love each other. *Their love-making became less and less frequent.* N-UNCOUNT

love nest, love nests; also spelled **love-nest**. A **love nest** is a house or flat where two people who are having a love affair live or meet; used in journalism. N-COUNT: usu sing

lover /lʌvəʳ/ **lovers** ◆◆◆◇◇

1 Someone's **lover** is someone who they are having a sexual relationship with but are not married to. *Every Thursday she would meet her lover Leon... He and Liz became lovers soon after they first met.* N-COUNT: oft poss N

2 If you are a **lover** of something such as animals or the arts, you enjoy them very much and take great pleasure in them. *She is a great lover of horses and horse racing... Are you an opera lover?* N-COUNT: with supp

lovesick /lʌvsɪk/. If you describe someone as **lovesick**, you mean that they are so in love with someone, usually someone who does not love them, that they are behaving in a strange and foolish way. *...a lovesick boy consumed with self-pity.* ADJ-GRADED: usu ADJ n =lovelorn

love story, love stories. A **love story** is something such as a novel or film about a love affair. ◆◇◇◇◇ N-COUNT

love triangle, love triangles. A **love triangle** is a situation which involves a group of three people who are each in love with at least one other person in the group, for example, a woman who is in love with two men and cannot decide which one to choose, or someone who is married but is also having a love affair; used in journalism. N-COUNT: usu sing

lovey-dovey /lʌvi dʌvi/. You can use **lovey-dovey** to describe, in a humorous or slightly disapproving way, lovers who show their affection for each other very openly; an informal expression. *All my friends were either lovey-dovey couples or wild, single girls.* ADJ-GRADED PRAGMATICS

loving /lʌvɪŋ/ ◆◆◇◇◇

1 Someone who is **loving** feels or shows love to other people. *Jim was a most loving husband and father... The children there were very loving to me.* ♦ **lovingly** *Brian gazed lovingly at MaryAnn.* ADJ-GRADED =affectionate; ADV-GRADED

2 **Loving** actions are done with great enjoyment and care. *The house has been restored with loving care.* ♦ **lovingly** *I lifted the box and ran my fingers lovingly over the top.* ADJ-GRADED: usu ADJ n; ADV-GRADED: ADV after v, ADV -ed

3 See also **peace-loving**.

low /loʊ/ **lower, lowest; lows** ◆◆◆◆◆

1 Something that is **low** measures only a short distance from the bottom to the top, or from the ground to the top. *...the low garden wall that separated the front garden from next door... She put it down on the low table... The country, with its low, rolling hills was beautiful... The Leisure Center is a long and low modern building.* ADJ-GRADED

2 If something is **low**, it is close to the ground, to sea level, or to the bottom of something. *He bumped his head on the low beams... It was late afternoon and the sun was low in the sky... They saw a government war plane make a series of low-level bombing raids. ...nagging low back pain.* ADJ-GRADED

3 When a river is **low**, it contains less water than usual. *...pumps that guarantee a constant depth of water even when the supplying river is low.* ADJ-GRADED: usu v-link ADJ ≠high

4 You can use **low** to indicate that something is small in amount or degree or that it is at the bottom of a particular scale. You can use phrases such as **in the low 80s** to indicate that, for example, a number or level is less than 85 but not as little as 80. *British casualties remained remarkably low... They are still having to live on very low incomes... The temperature's in the low 40s.* ADJ-GRADED ≠high

5 **Low** is used to describe people who are not considered to be very important because they are near the bottom of a particular scale or system. *She refused to promote Colin above the low rank of 'legal adviser'.* ADJ-GRADED: usu ADJ n ≠high

6 If something reaches a **low** of a particular amount or degree, that is the smallest it has ever been. *Eventually my weight stabilised at seven and a half stone after dropping to a low of five and a half stone... The dollar fell to a new low.* N-COUNT: usu sing, oft N *of* amount ≠high

7 If you drive or ride in a **low** gear, you select a gear which gives you the most control over your car or bike, usually first or second gear. *She selected a low gear and started down the track carefully.* ADJ-GRADED

8 If the quality or standard of something is **low**, it is very poor. *A school would not accept low-quality work from any student... The inquiry team criticises staff at the psychiatric hospital for the low standard of care. ...low-grade coal.* ADJ-GRADED =poor ≠high

9 If a food or other substance is **low in** a particular ingredient, it contains only a small amount of that ingredient. *They look for foods that are low in* ADJ-GRADED: v-link ADJ *in* n ≠high *calories.* ► Also a combining form. *...low-sodium tomato sauce... Low-odour paints help make decorating so much easier.* COMB in ADJ-GRADED: usu ADJ n

10 If you describe someone such as a student or a worker as a **low** achiever, you mean that they are not very good at their work, and do not achieve or produce as much as others. *Low achievers in schools will receive priority. ...if there are strikes by unrewarded low performers.* ADJ-GRADED: ADJ n

11 If you have a **low** opinion of someone or something, you disapprove of them or dislike them. *The majority of sex offenders have a low opinion of themselves... I have an extremely low opinion of the British tabloid newspapers.* ADJ-GRADED ≠high

12 You can use **low** to describe negative feelings and attitudes. *We are all very tired and morale is low... People had very low expectations.* ADJ-GRADED

13 If a sound or noise is **low**, it is deep. *Then suddenly she gave a low, choking moan and began to tremble violently... My voice has got so low now I was mistaken for a man the other day on the phone.* ADJ-GRADED =deep ≠high

14 If someone's voice is **low**, it is quiet or soft. *Her voice was so low he had to strain to catch it.* ADJ-GRADED

15 A light that is **low** is dim and not bright or strong. *Their eyesight is poor in low light.* ADJ-GRADED

16 If a radio, oven, or light is on **low**, it has been adjusted so that only a small amount of sound, heat, or light is produced. *She turned her little kitchen radio on low... Buy a dimmer switch and keep the light on low, or switch it off altogether... Cook the sauce over a low heat until it boils and thickens.* ADJ-GRADED

17 If you are **low** on something or if a supply of it is **low**, there is not much of it left. *We're a bit low on bed linen... World stocks of wheat were getting very low.* ADJ-GRADED: v-link ADJ, usu ADJ *on* n

18 If you are **low**, you are depressed; an informal use. *'I didn't ask for this job, you know,' he tells friends when he is low.* ADJ-GRADED =down

19 See also **lower**.

20 If a disease or illness **lays** you **low**, it makes you weak or ill. *...an undiagnosed medical condition that laid him low for months.* PHRASES V inflects

21 If you **are lying low**, you are hiding or not drawing attention to yourself; an informal expression. *Far from lying low, Kuti became more outspoken than ever.* V inflects

22 • to **look look high and low**: see **high**. • **low profile**: see **profile**. • to **be running low**: see **run**.

lowbrow /loubrau/; also spelled **low-brow**. If you say that something is **lowbrow**, you mean that it is simple and undemanding rather than being intellectual or complicated as is therefore sometimes regarded as being of inferior quality. *His choice of subject matter has been regarded as lowbrow. ...low-brow novels.* ADJ-GRADED ≠highbrow

low-cal. **Low-cal** food is food that contains only a few calories. People who are trying to lose weight eat low-cal food. *...low-cal, high-fiber recipes.* ADJ: usu ADJ n

low-cut. **Low-cut** dresses and blouses leave a woman's neck and the top part of her chest bare. *Her daringly low-cut dress scandalised audiences.* ADJ-GRADED: usu ADJ n

low-down; also spelled **lowdown**.

1 If someone gives you **the low-down** on something or someone, they tell you all the important information about them that they think you want or need to know; an informal use. *We want you to give us the low-down on your team-mates.* N-SING: *the* N, oft N *on* n =gen

2 You can use **low-down** to emphasize how bad, dishonest, or unfair you consider a particular person or their behaviour to be; an informal use. *...a lowdown, evil drunkard... They will stoop to every low-down trick.* ADJ-GRADED: ADJ n PRAGMATICS =despicable

lower /louə/ **lowers, lowering, lowered** ◆◆◆◇◇

1 You can use **lower** to refer to the bottom one of a pair of things. *She bit her lower lip. ...the lower deck of the bus... The upper layer of felt should overlap the lower. ...the lower of the two holes.* ADJ-COMPAR: ADJ n, *the* ADJ, *the* ADJ *of* n ≠upper

2 You can use **lower** to refer to the bottom part of something. *Use a small cushion to help give support to the lower back. ...fires which started in the lower part of a tower block.* ADJ-COMPAR: ADJ n ≠upper

3 You can use **lower** to refer to people or things that are less important than similar people or things. *Already the awards are causing resentment in the lower ranks of council officers... The nation's highest court reversed the lower court's decision... The higher orders of society must rule the lower.* ADJ-COMPAR: ADJ n, *the* ADJ ≠higher

4 If you **lower** something, you move it slowly downwards. *Two reporters had to help lower the coffin into the grave... Sokolowski lowered himself into the black leather chair... 'No movies of me getting out of the pool, boys.' They dutifully lowered their cameras.* ♦ **lowering** *...the extinguishing of the Olympic flame and the lowering of the flag.* VERB V n prep/adv V pron-refl prep/adv V n N-UNCOUNT: usu N *of* n

5 If you **lower** something, you make it less in amount, degree, value, or quality. *The Central Bank has lowered interest rates by 2 percent... This drug lowers cholesterol levels by binding fats in the intestine.* ♦ **lowering** *...a package of social measures which included the lowering of the retirement age.* VERB V n N-UNCOUNT: usu N *of* n

6 If someone **lowers** their head, eyes, or gaze, they move their head or eyes so that they look downwards, for example because they are sad or embarrassed. *She lowered her head and brushed past photographers as she went back inside... She lowered her gaze to the hands in her lap.* VERB ≠raise V n

7 If you say that you would not **lower** yourself by doing something, you mean that you would not behave in a way that would make you or other people respect you less. *Don't lower yourself, don't be the way they are... I've got no qualms about lowering myself to Lemmer's level to get what I want.* VB: oft with brd-neg V pron-refl V pron-refl *to* n

8 If you **lower** your voice or if your voice **lowers**, you speak more quietly. *The man moved closer, lowering his voice... His voice lowers confidentially.* V-ERG V n V

9 See also **low**.

lower case; also spelled **lower-case**. **Lower-case** letters are small letters, not capital letters. *It was printed in lower case... We did the logo in lower-case letters instead of capitals.* N-UNCOUNT: oft N n ≠upper case

lower class, lower classes; also spelled **lower-class**. Some people use the **lower class** or the **lower classes** to refer to the division of society that they consider to have the lowest social status. *Education now offers the lower classes access to job opportunities... The black middle class must now reach out with more empathy and concern to the lower class.* ► Also an adjective. *...lower-class families... Horse-racing was once considered vulgar and lower class in Japan.* N-COUNT-COLL: usu pl ADJ

lowest common denominator, lowest common denominators

1 If you describe a plan, idea, or policy as the **lowest common denominator**, you are critical of it because it has been deliberately reduced to its most basic and simple aspects so that it will appeal to or be understood by the greatest number of people. *Although the plan received unanimous approval, this does not mean that it represents the lowest common denominator.* N-COUNT: usu sing PRAGMATICS

2 **Lowest common denominator** is used to refer critically to opinions or tastes which appeal to the majority of people. *Tabloid newspapers pander to the lowest common denominator.* N-COUNT: usu sing PRAGMATICS

3 In mathematics, the **lowest common denominator** is the smallest number that all the numbers on the bottom of a particular group of fractions can be divided into; a technical use in mathematics. N-COUNT

low-flying. **Low-flying** aircraft or birds are flying very close to the ground, or lower than normal. *There is a complete ban on low-flying aircraft.* ADJ: ADJ n

low-key. If you say that something is **low-key**, you mean that it is controlled and restrained rather than being showy, impressive, or intense as it could be. *The wedding will be a very low-key affair... He wanted to keep the meetings low-key.* ◆◇◇◇◇ ADJ-GRADED =muted, understated

lowlands /louləndz/; the form **lowland** is used as a modifier. **Lowlands** are an area of low, flat land. *...wherever you travel in the lowlands of the United Kingdom. ...lowland areas.* N-PLURAL: usu *the* N ≠uplands

low life; also spelled **low-life.** People sometimes use **low life** to refer critically to people who they find extremely unpleasant and disturbing, especially people who are involved in crime and violence. *...observations on London low life. ...the sort of low-life characters who populate this film.* N-UNCOUNT: oft N n PRAGMATICS

lowly /lo͟ʊli/ **lowlier, lowliest.** ◆◇◇◇◇ If you describe someone or something as **lowly**, you mean that they are low in rank, status, or importance. *...lowly bureaucrats pretending to be senators... He was irked by his lowly status.* ADJ-GRADED

low-lying. **Low-lying** land is at, near, or below sea level. *Sea walls collapsed, and low-lying areas were flooded.* ADJ-GRADED: usu ADJ n

low-paid. ◆◇◇◇◇ If you describe someone or their job as **low-paid**, you mean that their work earns them very little money. *...low-paid workers... The majority of working women are in low-paid jobs.* ADJ-GRADED ≠highly-paid
► **The low-paid** are people who are low-paid. N-PLURAL: the N

low-pitched
1 A sound that is **low-pitched** is deep. *With a low-pitched rumbling noise, the propeller began to rotate.* ADJ-GRADED
2 A voice that is **low-pitched** is very soft and quiet. *He kept his voice low-pitched in case someone was listening.* ADJ-GRADED

low season. **The low season** is the time of year when a holiday resort, hotel, or tourist attraction receives the fewest visitors, and fares and holiday accommodation are often cheaper; used mainly in British English. The usual American term is **off season.** *Prices drop to £315 in the low season.* N-SING: the N

low-slung. **Low-slung** chairs or cars are very low, so that you are close to the ground when you are sitting in them. *...a low-slung chintz-armchair.* ADJ-GRADED: usu ADJ n

low-tech. **Low-tech** machines or systems are ones that do not use modern or sophisticated technology. *...a simple form of low-tech electric propulsion.* ADJ-GRADED: usu ADJ n ≠hi-tech

low tide, low tides. At the coast, **low tide** is the time when the sea is at its lowest level because the tide is out. *The causeway to the island is only accessible at low tide.* N-VAR: oft at N ≠high tide

low water. **Low water** is the same as **low tide.** N-UNCOUNT

loyal /lɔ͟ɪəl/. ◆◆◇◇◇ If you describe someone as **loyal**, you mean they remain firm in their friendship or support for someone or something. *They had remained loyal to the president... He'd always been such a loyal friend to us all.* ADJ-GRADED: oft ADJ to n =faithful ≠disloyal ♦ **loyally** *They have loyally supported their party and their leader.* ADV-GRADED: ADV with v

loyalist /lɔ͟ɪəlɪst/ **loyalists.** ◆◇◇◇◇ A **loyalist** is a person who remains firm in their support for a government or ruler. *Party loyalists responded as they always do, waving flags and carrying placards.* N-COUNT

loyalty /lɔ͟ɪəlti/ **loyalties** ◆◆◇◇◇
1 **Loyalty** is the quality of staying firm in your friendship or support for someone or something. *I have sworn an oath of loyalty to the monarchy... This is seen as a reward for the army's loyalty during a barracks revolt earlier this month.* N-UNCOUNT: oft N to n
2 **Loyalties** are feelings of friendship, support, or duty towards someone or something. *She had developed strong loyalties to the Manet family.* N-COUNT: usu pl, oft N to n

lozenge /lɒzɪndʒ/ **lozenges**
1 **Lozenges** are sweets which you can suck to soothe a cough or sore throat. *...throat lozenges.* N-COUNT
2 A **lozenge** is a shape with four corners. The two corners that point up and down are further apart than the two pointing sideways. N-COUNT =diamond

LP /e͟l pi͟ː/ **LPs.** ◆◆◇◇◇ An **LP** is a record which usually has about 25 minutes of music or speech on each side; **LP** is an abbreviation for 'long-playing record'. *...his first LP since 1986.* N-COUNT

L-plate, L-plates. In Britain, **L-plates** are signs with a red 'L' on them which you attach to a car to warn other drivers that you are a learner. N-COUNT: usu pl

LSD /e͟l es di͟ː/. ◆◇◇◇◇ **LSD** is a very powerful illegal drug which causes hallucinations. N-UNCOUNT

Lt. ◆◇◇◇◇ **Lt** is a written abbreviation for **lieutenant.** *He was replaced by Lt Frank Fraser.*

Ltd. ◆◆◆◇◇ In British English, **Ltd** is a written abbreviation for **limited**; it is used after the name of a company. Compare **plc.**

lubricant /lu͟ːbrɪkənt/ **lubricants** ◆◇◇◇◇
1 A **lubricant** is a substance which you put on the surfaces or parts of something, especially something mechanical, to make the parts move smoothly. *Its nozzle was smeared with some kind of lubricant. ...industrial lubricants.* N-MASS
2 If you refer to something as a **lubricant** in a particular situation, you mean that it helps to make things happen without any problems. *I think humor is a great lubricant for life.* N-COUNT: usu supp N

lubricate /lu͟ːbrɪkeɪt/ **lubricates, lubricating, lubricated** ◆◇◇◇◇
1 If you **lubricate** something such as a part of a machine, you put a substance such as oil on it so that it moves smoothly; a formal use. *Mineral oils are used to lubricate machinery. ...lubricating oil.* VERB: V n, V-ing, Also V ♦ **lubrication** /lu͟ːbrɪke͟ɪʃən/ *Use a touch of linseed oil for lubrication.* N-UNCOUNT
2 If you say that something **lubricates** a particular situation, you mean that it helps things to happen without any problems. *Franklin's task was to lubricate the discussions with the French.* VERB: V n

lucerne /luːsɜ͟ːʳn/. In British English, **lucerne** is a plant that is grown for animals to eat and in order to improve the soil. The usual American word is **alfalfa.** N-UNCOUNT =alfalfa

lucid /lu͟ːsɪd/ ◆◇◇◇◇
1 **Lucid** writing or speech is clear and easy to understand. *...a lucid account of the history of mankind... His prose as always lucid and compelling.* ADJ-GRADED =clear ♦ **lucidly** *Both of them had the ability to present complex matters lucidly.* ADV-GRADED: ADV with v ♦ **lucidity** /luːsɪ͟dɪti/ *His writings were marked by an extraordinary lucidity and elegance of style.* N-UNCOUNT
2 If someone is **lucid**, they are thinking clearly again after a period of illness or confusion; a formal use. *He wasn't very lucid, he didn't quite know where he was.* ADJ-GRADED =clear-headed ♦ **lucidity** *The pain had lessened in the night, but so had his lucidity.* N-UNCOUNT

luck /lʌ͟k/ **lucks, lucking, lucked** ◆◆◆◇◇
1 **Luck** or **good luck** is success or good things that happen to you, that do not come from your own abilities or efforts. *I knew I needed a bit of luck to win... The Sri Lankans have been having no luck with the weather... The goal, when it came, owed more to good luck than good planning.* N-UNCOUNT
2 **Bad luck** is lack of success or bad things that happen to you, that have not been caused by yourself or other people. *I had a lot of bad luck during the first half of this season... Randall's illness was only bad luck.* N-UNCOUNT
3 In informal English, if you **luck out** or **luck into** something, you get some advantage or are successful because you have good luck. *...a working-class lad who fell into pop music and lucked out in a big way... They've lucked into the best of all possible jobs.* VERB: V out, V into n
4 See also **hard luck, pot luck.**
5 If you ask someone the question **'Any luck?'** or **'No luck?'**, you want to know if they have been successful in something they were trying to do; an informal expression. *'Any luck?'—'No.'* PHRASES CONVENTION
6 You can say **'Bad luck'**, **'Hard luck'**, or **'Tough luck'** to someone when you want to express sympathy to them; an informal expression. *Well, hard luck, mate.* CONVENTION PRAGMATICS
7 If you say that something **brings bad luck** or **brings** someone **good luck**, you believe that it has an influence on whether good or bad things happen to them. *Jean was extremely superstitious and believed the colour green brought bad luck.* V inflects
8 If you describe someone as **down on their luck**, you mean that they have had bad experiences, often because they do not have enough money. usu v-link PHR
9 If you say that something is **the luck of the draw**, you mean that it is the result of chance and you cannot do anything about it. *The luck of the draw meant the young lad had to face one of America's best players.*

10 If you say **'Good luck'** or **'Best of luck'** to someone, you are telling them that you hope they will be successful in something they are trying to do; an informal expression. *He kissed her on the cheek. 'Best of luck!'* CONVENTION PRAGMATICS

11 You can say someone **is in luck** when they are in a situation where they can have what they want or need. *You're in luck. The doctor's still in.* V inflects

12 If you say it **is just** your **luck** that something unpleasant has happened to you, you mean that this is quite normal because unpleasant things are always happening to you; an informal expression. *It would be just his luck to miss the last boat.* V inflects

13 If you say that someone **is out of luck**, you mean that they cannot have something which they can normally have. *'What do you want, Roy? If it's money, you're out of luck.'* V inflects

14 You can say **'No such luck'** when you want to express your disappointment over something; an informal expression. *He must have been hoping for a relaxed time. No such luck.* CONVENTION

15 If you say that someone **is pushing** their **luck**, you think they are taking a bigger risk than is sensible, and may get into trouble. *I didn't dare push my luck too far and did not ask them to sign statements.* V inflects

16 If you say that **luck was on** someone's **side**, you mean that they succeeded in something by chance as well as by their own efforts or ability. *Rick seems to have had luck on his side during his 12-year acting career.* V inflects

17 If someone **tries their luck** at something, they try to succeed at it, often when it is very difficult or there is little chance of success. *She was going to try her luck at the Las Vegas casinos.* V inflects

18 You can add **with luck** or **with any luck** to a statement to indicate that you hope that a particular thing will happen; an informal expression. *We'll have a long talk and a good cry and then with any luck we'll both feel better.* PHR with cl PRAGMATICS

luckily /lʌkɪli/. You add **luckily** to a statement to indicate that it is fortunate that something happened or is the case because otherwise the situation would have been difficult or unpleasant. *Luckily, we both love football. ...but luckily for me, he talked very good English.* ◆◇◇◇◇ ADV-GRADED: ADV with cl =fortunately

luckless /lʌkləs/. If you describe someone or something as **luckless**, you mean that they are unsuccessful or unfortunate; a literary word. *...the luckless parent of an extremely difficult child. ...the President's luckless tour of the East.* ADJ-GRADED: usu ADJ n

lucky /lʌki/ **luckier, luckiest** ◆◆◆◇◇

1 You say that someone is **lucky** when they have something that is very desirable or when they are in a very desirable situation. *I am luckier than most. I have a job... I consider myself the luckiest man on the face of the Earth... He is incredibly lucky to be alive... Those who are lucky enough to be wealthy have a duty to give to the hungry.* ADJ-GRADED: oft ADJ to-inf =fortunate

2 Someone who is **lucky** seems to always have good luck. *Some people are born lucky aren't they?... He had always been lucky at cards.* ADJ-GRADED

3 If you describe a situation or event as **lucky**, you mean that it was fortunate or successful, and that it happened by chance and not as a result of planning or preparation. *They admit they are now desperate for a lucky break... He was lucky that it was only a can of beer that knocked him on the head.* ADJ-GRADED

4 A **lucky** object is something that people believe helps them to be successful. *He did not have on his other lucky charm, a pair of green socks.* ADJ: usu ADJ n

5 See also **happy-go-lucky**.

6 If you say that someone **will be lucky** to do or get something, you mean that they are very unlikely to be able to do or get it, and certainly will not do or get any more than that. *You'll be lucky if you get any breakfast... Those remaining in work will be lucky to get the smallest of pay increases... You'll be lucky to have change out of £750.* PHRASES V inflects, usu PHR if, PHR to-inf

7 If you say that someone can **count** themselves **lucky**, you mean that the situation they are in or the thing that has happened to them is better than it might have been or than they might have expected. *She counted herself lucky to get a job in one of Edinburgh's department stores... At the end of two days, you may count yourself lucky that you don't have to live here.* V inflects, oft PHR to-inf/that

8 You can use **lucky** in expressions such as **'Lucky you'** and **'Lucky devil'** when you are slightly jealous of someone else's good fortune or success, or surprised at it; an informal expression. *'The thing about Mr Kemp is that he always treats me like a lady.' 'Lucky old you.'* CONVENTION

9 If you **strike lucky** or **strike it lucky**, you have some good luck; used mainly in informal British English. *You may strike lucky and find a sympathetic and helpful clerk, but, there again, you might not.* V inflects

10 If you say that it is **third time lucky** for someone, you mean that they have tried to do a particular thing twice before and that this time they will succeed. *I've had two runners-up medals with Monaco and AC Milan, but I hope it will be third time lucky and I get a winners' medal with Rangers.* usu v-link PHR

11 ● to **thank one's lucky stars**: see **star**.

lucky dip, lucky dips. In Britain, a **lucky dip** is a game in which you take a prize out of a container full of hidden prizes and then find out what you have chosen. N-COUNT

lucrative /luːkrətɪv/. A **lucrative** activity, job, or business deal is very profitable. *Thousands of ex-army officers have found lucrative jobs in private security firms.* ◆◆◇◇◇ ADJ-GRADED

lucre /luːkəʳ/. People sometimes refer to money or profit as **lucre**, especially when they think that it has been obtained by dishonest means; an old-fashioned word. *...so they can feel less guilty about their piles of filthy lucre.* N-UNCOUNT PRAGMATICS

Luddite /lʌdaɪt/ **Luddites.** If you refer to someone as a **Luddite**, you are criticizing them for opposing changes in industrial methods, especially the introduction of new machines and modern methods. *The majority have a built-in Luddite mentality; they are resistant to change.* N-COUNT: oft N n PRAGMATICS

ludicrous /luːdɪkrəs/. If you describe something as **ludicrous**, you are emphasizing that you think it is foolish, unreasonable, or unsuitable. *It was ludicrous to suggest that the visit could be kept secret... It's a completely ludicrous idea.* ◆◇◇◇◇ ADJ-GRADED: oft *it* v-link ADJ to-inf PRAGMATICS =ridiculous
♦ **ludicrously** *By Western standards the prices are ludicrously low.* ADV-GRADED

lug /lʌg/ **lugs, lugging, lugged.** If you **lug** a heavy or awkward object somewhere, you carry it there with difficulty; an informal word. *Nobody wants to lug around huge suitcases full of clothes... I hastily packed the hamper and lugged it to the car.* ◆◇◇◇◇ VERB =drag V n with adv V n prep Also V n

luggage /lʌgɪdʒ/. **Luggage** is the suitcases and bags that you take with you when travel. *Leave your luggage in the hotel... Each passenger was allowed two 30-kg pieces of luggage.* ● See also **left luggage**. ◆◇◇◇◇ N-UNCOUNT

lugubrious /luːguːbriəs/. If you say that someone or something is **lugubrious**, you mean that they are sad and gloomy rather than lively or cheerful; a literary word. *...a tall, thin man with a long and lugubrious face... He plays some passages so slowly that they become lugubrious.* ADJ-GRADED =melancholy, morose
♦ **lugubriously** *The dog gazed at us lugubriously for a few minutes.* ADV-GRADED: ADV with v, ADV adj

lukewarm /luːkwɔːm/ ◆◇◇◇◇

1 Something, especially a liquid, that is **lukewarm** is only slightly warm. *Wash your face with lukewarm water... The coffee was weak and lukewarm.* ADJ-GRADED =tepid

2 If you describe a person or their attitude as **lukewarm**, you mean that they are not showing much enthusiasm or interest. *Economists have never been more than lukewarm towards him... The study received a lukewarm response from the Home Secretary.* ADJ-GRADED: oft ADJ *towards* n

lull /lʌl/ **lulls, lulling, lulled** ◆◇◇◇◇

1 A **lull** is a period of quiet or calm in a longer period of activity or excitement. *There was a lull in* N-COUNT: oft N *in* n *political violence after the election of the current president. ...a lull in the conversation.*

2 If you **are lulled** into feeling safe, someone or something causes you to feel safe at a time when you are not safe. *It is easy to be lulled into a false sense of security... I had been lulled into thinking the publicity would be a trivial matter... Lulled by almost uninterrupted economic growth, too many European firms assumed that this would last for ever.* VERB be V-ed into n/-ing V-ed Also V n into n/-ing

3 If someone or something **lulls** you, they cause you to feel calm or sleepy. *With the shutters half-closed and the calm airy height of the room to lull me, I soon fell into a doze... The swish of the tyres lulled him into a light doze... Before he knew it, the heat and hum of the forest had lulled him to sleep.* VERB V n V n into/to n

4 If you describe a situation as the **lull before the storm**, you mean that although it is calm now, there is going to be trouble in the future. PHRASE: v-link PHR

lullaby /lʌləbaɪ/ **lullabies.** A **lullaby** is a quiet song which is intended to be sung to babies and young children to help them go to sleep. N-COUNT

lumbago /lʌmbeɪgoʊ/. If someone has **lumbago**, they have pains in the lower part of their back. N-UNCOUNT

lumbar /lʌmbəʳ/. **Lumbar** means relating to the lower part of your back; a medical term. *Lumbar support is very important if you're driving a long way.* ADJ: ADJ n

lumber /lʌmbəʳ/ **lumbers, lumbering, lumbered** ◆◇◇◇◇

1 Lumber consists of trees and large pieces of wood that have been roughly cut up; used mainly in American English. *It was made of soft lumber, spruce by the look of it... He was going to have to purchase all his lumber at full retail price.* N-UNCOUNT

2 If someone or something **lumbers** from one place to another, they move there very slowly and clumsily. *He turned and lumbered back to his chair... The truck lumbered across the parking lot toward the road... He looked straight ahead and overtook a lumbering lorry.* VERB V adv/prep V-ing

lumber with. If you **are lumbered with** someone or something, you have to deal with them or take care of them even though you do not want to and this annoys you; an informal British expression. *I was lumbered with the job of taking charge of all the money... She was lumbered with a bill for about ninety pounds.* PHRASAL VERB usu passive PRAGMATICS be V-ed P n

lumberjack /lʌmbəʳdʒæk/ **lumberjacks.** A **lumberjack** is a person whose job is to cut down trees. N-COUNT

lumberyard /lʌmbəʳjɑːʳd/ **lumberyards;** also spelled **lumber yard.** In American English, a **lumberyard** is a place where timber is stored and sold. The usual British word is **timber yard.** N-COUNT

luminary /luːmɪnəri, AM -neri/ **luminaries.** If you refer to someone as a **luminary**, you mean that they are an expert in a particular subject or activity; a literary word. *...the political opinions of such luminaries as Sartre or de Beauvoir.* ◆◇◇◇◇ N-COUNT =expert

luminescence /luːmɪnesᵊns/. **Luminescence** is a soft, glowing light; a literary word. *Lights reflected off dust-covered walls creating a ghostly luminescence.* N-UNCOUNT

luminosity /luːmɪnɒsɪti/

1 The **luminosity** of a star or sun is how bright it is; a technical use in astrology. *For a few years its luminosity flared up to about 10,000 times the present-day luminosity of the Sun.* N-UNCOUNT

2 You can talk about the **luminosity** of someone's skin when it has a healthy glow. *Ultrafine powder with a rosy tinge gives the skin warmth and luminosity.* N-UNCOUNT

luminous /luːmɪnəs/. Something that is **luminous** shines or glows in the dark. *The luminous dial on the clock showed five minutes to seven. ...one of the most luminous and unstable stars in our Galaxy.* ◆◇◇◇◇ ADJ-GRADED: usu ADJ n

lump /lʌmp/ **lumps, lumping, lumped** ◆◆◇◇◇

1 A **lump** of something is a solid piece of it. *The potter shaped and squeezed the lump of clay into a graceful shape. ...a lump of wood... They used to buy ten kilos of beef in one lump.* N-COUNT: oft N of n

2 A **lump** on or in someone's body is a small, hard swelling that has been caused by an injury or an illness. *I've got a lump on my shoulder... Howard had to have cancer surgery for a lump in his chest.* N-COUNT

3 A **lump** of sugar is a small cube of it. *...a nugget of rough gold about the size of a lump of sugar... 'No sugar,' I said, and Jim asked for two lumps.* • See also **sugar lump.** N-COUNT: oft N of n

4 See also **lump sum.**

5 If you say that someone **will have to lump it**, you mean that they must accept a situation or decision whether they like it or not; used mainly in informal British English. *The crew will be sleeping in the hull and will have to lump it... William was going to kick up a fuss, but he realized he'd have to lump it.* PHRASES *have* inflects

6 If you say that you have a **lump in** your **throat**, you mean that you have a tight feeling in your throat because of a strong emotion such as sorrow or gratitude. *I stood there with a lump in my throat and tried to fight back tears... It was a great reception and it brought a lump to my throat.* Ns inflect, usu PHR after v

lump together. If a number of different people or things **are lumped together**, they are considered as a group rather than separately. *Policemen and prostitutes, bankers and butchers are all lumped together in the service sector... Because she was lumped together with alcoholics and hard-drug users, Claire felt out of place.* PHRASAL VERB usu passive =join be V-ed P be V-ed P with n

lumpectomy /lʌmpektəmi/ **lumpectomies.** A **lumpectomy** is an operation in which a woman has a lump such as a tumour removed from one of her breasts, rather than having the entire breast removed. N-COUNT

lumpen /lʌmpən/

1 A **lumpen** object is large, heavy, and lumpy; mainly used in literary British English. *She was kneading a lumpen mass of dough... Lumpen shapes began to appear out of the shadows.* ADJ-GRADED: usu ADJ n

2 If you describe people as **lumpen**, you think they are dull and clumsy; used mainly in British English. *The people seemed lumpen and boring.* ADJ-GRADED: usu ADJ n

lump sum, lump sums. A **lump sum** is an amount of money that is paid as a large amount on a single occasion rather than as smaller amounts on several separate occasions. *...a tax-free lump sum of £50,000 at retirement age.* ◆◇◇◇◇ N-COUNT

lumpy /lʌmpi/ **lumpier, lumpiest.** Something that is **lumpy** contains lumps or is covered with lumps. *When the rice isn't cooked properly it goes lumpy and gooey... Many women, especially as they get older, develop lumpy veins in their legs.* ◆◇◇◇◇ ADJ-GRADED

lunacy /luːnəsi/

1 If you describe someone's behaviour as **lunacy**, you mean that it seems very strange or foolish. *...while trying to explain to them the lunacy of the tax system... It remains lunacy to produce yet more coal to add to power stations' stockpiles.* N-UNCOUNT PRAGMATICS

2 Lunacy is severe mental illness; an old-fashioned use. N-UNCOUNT

lunar /luːnəʳ/. **Lunar** means relating to the moon. *The vast volcanic slope was eerily reminiscent of a lunar landscape. ...a magazine article celebrating the 25th anniversary of man's first lunar landing.* ◆◇◇◇◇ ADJ: ADJ n

lunatic /luːnətɪk/ **lunatics** ◆◇◇◇◇

1 If you describe someone as a **lunatic**, you think they behave in a dangerous, stupid, or annoying way; an informal use. *Her son thinks she's an absolute raving lunatic.* N-COUNT PRAGMATICS

2 If you describe someone's behaviour or ideas as **lunatic**, you think they are very foolish and possibly dangerous. *...the operation of the market taken to lunatic extremes. ...a country spurned until now by all except the more lunatic of journalists and adventurers.* ADJ-GRADED PRAGMATICS =mad, insane

3 If you describe a place or situation as **lunatic**, you mean that it is confused and seems out of control. *He pleads for sanity in a lunatic world.* ADJ-GRADED: ADJ n

4 People who were mentally ill used to be called N-COUNT

lunatics; an old-fashioned use which some people find offensive.

lunatic asylum, lunatic asylums. A **lunatic asylum** was a place where mentally disturbed people used to be locked up. N-COUNT

lunatic fringe. If you refer to a group of people as the **lunatic fringe**, you mean that they are very extreme in their opinions or behaviour. *Demands for a separate Siberia are confined for now to the lunatic fringe.* N-SING: usu *the* N

lunch /lʌntʃ/ **lunches, lunching, lunched** ◆◆◆◆◇
1 **Lunch** is the meal that you have in the middle of the day. *Shall we meet somewhere for lunch?... He did not enjoy business lunches... If anyone wants me, I'm at lunch with a client.* N-VAR
2 When you **lunch**, you have lunch, especially at a restaurant; a formal use. *Only the extremely rich could afford to lunch at the Mirabelle... Having not yet lunched, we went to the refreshment bar for ham sandwiches.* VERB V adv/prep V
3 If you say there's no such thing as a **free lunch**, you are saying that most things that are worth having need to be paid for or worked for, and that you cannot expect to get things for nothing. *The book includes 25 Lessons for Life: Lesson 1: There is no free lunch. Don't feel entitled to anything you don't sweat and struggle for... But, even in Hollywood, there is no such thing as a free lunch.* PHRASE: v-link PHR, PHR after v

lunch box, lunch boxes; also spelled **lunchbox**. A **lunch box** is a small container with a lid. You put food such as sandwiches in it to eat for lunch at work or at school. N-COUNT

lunch break, lunch breaks; also spelled **lunchbreak**. Your **lunch break** is the period in the middle of the day when you stop work in order to have a meal. N-COUNT: usu poss N

lunch counter, lunch counters. In American English, a **lunch counter** is an informal café or a counter in a shop where people can buy and eat meals. N-COUNT

luncheon /lʌntʃən/ **luncheons** ◆◇◇◇◇
1 A **luncheon** is a formal lunch. People are often invited to luncheons to celebrate an important event or to raise money for charity. *Earlier this month, a luncheon for former UN staff was held in Vienna.* N-COUNT
2 **Luncheon** is the meal that you eat in the middle of the day; a formal use. *Promptly at one, luncheon was served... I have a luncheon engagement.* N-VAR

luncheon meat, luncheon meats. In British English, **luncheon meat** is a type of cooked meat that is often sold in tins. It is a mixture of pork and cereal. ◆◇◇◇◇ N-MASS

lunch hour, lunch hours. Your **lunch hour** is the period in the middle of the day when you stop working, usually for one hour, in order to have a meal. N-COUNT: usu poss N

lunchroom /lʌntʃruːm/ **lunchrooms;** also spelled **lunch room**. In American English, a **lunchroom** is the room in a school or company where you buy and eat your lunch. N-COUNT

lunchtime /lʌntʃtaɪm/ **lunchtimes;** also spelled **lunch time. Lunchtime** is the period of the day when people have their lunch. *Could we meet at lunchtime? ...a lunchtime meeting.* ◆◆◇◇◇ N-VAR

lung /lʌŋ/ **lungs.** Your **lungs** are the two organs inside your chest which fill with air when you breathe in. ◆◆◇◇◇ N-COUNT: usu pl

lunge /lʌndʒ/ **lunges, lunging, lunged.** If you **lunge** in a particular direction, you move in that direction suddenly and clumsily. *He lunged at me, grabbing me violently... I lunged forward to try to hit him.* ► Also a noun. *The attacker knocked on their door and made a lunge for Wendy when she answered.* ◆◇◇◇◇ VERB V prep/adv N-COUNT: usu sing

lungful /lʌŋfʊl/ **lungfuls.** If someone takes a **lungful** of something such as fresh air or smoke, they breathe in deeply so that their lungs feel as if they are full of that thing. *I bobbed to the surface and gasped a lungful of air.* N-COUNT: usu N *of* n

lurch /lɜːʳtʃ/ **lurches, lurching, lurched** ◆◇◇◇◇
1 To **lurch** means to make a sudden, unintentional, jerky movement, especially forwards. *As the car sped over a pothole she lurched forward... Henry looked, stared, and lurched to his feet... More and more frequently the vessel lurched into a sudden roll.* ► Also a noun. *The car took a lurch forward but grounded in a deep rut.* VERB V adv/prep Also V N-COUNT
2 If you say that a person or organization **lurches** from one thing to another, you mean they move suddenly from one course of action or attitude to another in an uncontrolled way. *The state government has lurched from one budget crisis to another... The first round of multilateral trade talks has lurched between hope and despair.* ► Also a noun. *The property sector was another casualty of the lurch towards higher interest rates.* VERB V *from* n *to* n V prep/adv N-COUNT: usu N prep
3 If someone **leaves** you **in the lurch**, they go away or stop helping you at a very difficult time; an informal expression. *You wouldn't leave an old friend in the lurch, surely?* PHRASE: V inflects

lure /ljʊəʳ, AM lʊr/ **lures, luring, lured** ◆◆◇◇◇
1 To **lure** someone means to trick them into a particular place or to trick them into doing something that they should not do. *He lured her to his home and shot her with his father's gun... They did not realise that they were being lured into a trap... The company aims to lure smokers back to cigarettes.* VERB =trick V n prep/adv
2 A **lure** is something such as bait which is used to attract prey to a certain place so that they can be caught. N-COUNT
3 A **lure** is an attractive quality that something has, or something that you find attractive. *The excitement of hunting big game in Africa has been a lure to Europeans for 200 years... The lure of rural life is proving as strong as ever.* N-COUNT: usu sing

lurid /ljʊərɪd, AM lʊrɪd/ ◆◇◇◇◇
1 If you say that something is **lurid**, you are critical of it because it involves a lot of violence, sex, or shocking detail. *...lurid accounts of Claire's sexual exploits... Some reports have contained lurid accounts of deaths and mutilations.* ♦ **luridly** *His cousin was soon cursing luridly.* ADJ-GRADED: usu ADJ n PRAGMATICS =explicit ADV: ADV with v
2 If you describe something as **lurid**, you do not like it because it is very brightly coloured. *She took care to paint her toe nails a lurid red or orange.* ♦ **luridly** *It had a high ceiling and a luridly coloured square of carpet on the floor.* ADJ-GRADED: usu ADJ n PRAGMATICS ADV-GRADED: usu ADV adj/-ed

lurk /lɜːʳk/ **lurks, lurking, lurked** ◆◇◇◇◇
1 If someone **lurks** somewhere, they wait there secretly so that they cannot be seen, usually because they intend to do something bad. *He thought he saw someone lurking above the chamber during the address.* VERB V
2 If something such as a bad memory, suspicion, or danger **lurks**, it exists, but you are only slightly aware of it. *Hidden dangers lurk in every family saloon car... Around every corner lurked doubt and uncertainty.* VERB V

luscious /lʌʃəs/ ◆◇◇◇◇
1 If you describe a woman or something about her as **luscious**, you mean that you find them sexually attractive. *...a luscious young blonde... What I like most about Gabby is her luscious lips!* ADJ-GRADED: usu ADJ n
2 **Luscious** food is juicy and delicious. *A small apricot tree which bore luscious fruit.* ADJ-GRADED

lush /lʌʃ/ **lusher, lushest** ◆◇◇◇◇
1 **Lush** fields or gardens have a lot of very healthy grass or plants. *...the lush green meadows bordering the river... The beautifully landscaped gardens sprawl with lush vegetation.* ♦ **lushness** *...a tropical lushness.* ADJ-GRADED =verdant N-UNCOUNT
2 If you describe a place or thing as **lush**, you mean that it is very luxurious. *The Carlton-intercontinental hotel is lush, plush, and very non-backpacker... The fabrics were lush.* ADJ-GRADED: v-link ADJ =luxurious

lust /lʌst/ **lusts, lusting, lusted** ◆◇◇◇◇
1 **Lust** is a feeling of strong sexual desire for someone. *His relationship with Angie was the first which combined lust with friendship... His lust for her grew until it was overpowering.* N-UNCOUNT
2 A **lust** for something is a very strong and eager desire to have it. *It was Fred's lust for glitz and glamour that was driving them apart.* N-UNCOUNT: oft N *for* n =desire

lust after or **lust for** PHRASAL VERB
1 If you **lust after** someone or **lust for** them, you feel a very strong sexual desire for them. *From what I hear, half the campus is lusting after her.* V P n
2 If you **lust after** or **lust for** something, you have a very strong desire to possess it. *Sheard lusted after the Directorship.* V P n

lustful /lʌstfʊl/. **Lustful** means feeling or expressing strong sexual desire. *He can't stop himself from having lustful thoughts.* ADJ: usu ADJ n

lustre /lʌstəʳ/; spelled **luster** in American English.
1 **Lustre** is gentle shining light that is reflected from a surface, for example from polished metal. *Gold retains its lustre for far longer than other metals... It is softer than cotton and nylon and has a similar lustre to silk.* N-UNCOUNT
2 **Lustre** is the qualities that something has that make it interesting and exciting. *What do you do if your relationship is beginning to lose its lustre?* N-UNCOUNT

lustrous /lʌstrəs/. Something that is **lustrous** shines brightly and gently, because it has a smooth or shiny surface. *Joe stood up, and carefully removed his hat, revealing a head of thick, lustrous, wavy brown hair.* ADJ-GRADED

lusty /lʌsti/ **lustier, lustiest.** If you say that something is **lusty**, you mean that it is healthy and full of strength and energy. *...plants with large, lusty roots. ...remembering his lusty singing in the open park.* ADJ-GRADED: usu ADJ n ♦ **lustily** *Andrew asserted himself from the moment of his birth, crying lustily when he was hungry... Bob ate lustily.* ADV-GRADED: ADV with v

lute /luːt/ **lutes.** A **lute** is a stringed instrument that looks quite like a guitar. You play the lute by plucking the strings. N-VAR: oft *the*N

luv /lʌv/. In British English, **luv** is an informal written form of the word 'love', when it is being used as a way of addressing someone. *You'll have to be quick, luv; we've a plane to catch.* N-VOC PRAGMATICS

luvvie /lʌvi/ **luvvies.** In informal British English, people sometimes refer to actors and actresses as **luvvies** as a humorous way of criticizing their behaviour, attitudes, and pretentiousness. N-COUNT PRAGMATICS

luxuriance /lʌgʒʊəriəns/. You use **luxuriance** to describe plants or gardens which are healthy and produce a lot of foliage. *...a landscape of almost tropical luxuriance.* N-UNCOUNT

luxuriant /lʌgʒʊəriənt/
1 **Luxuriant** plants, trees, and gardens are large, healthy, and growing well. *There were two very large oak trees in front of our house with wide spreading branches and luxuriant foliage.* ADJ-GRADED: usu ADJ n
2 If you describe someone's hair as **luxuriant**, you mean that it is very thick and healthy. *Hair that's thick and luxuriant needs regular trimming.* ADJ-GRADED =healthy

luxuriate /lʌgʒʊərieɪt/ **luxuriates, luxuriating, luxuriated.** If you **luxuriate in** something, you relax in it and enjoy it very much, especially because you find it comfortable and luxurious. *Lie back and luxuriate in the scented oil... Ralph was luxuriating in the first real holiday he'd had in years.* VERB V in n

luxurious /lʌgʒʊəriəs/ ♦◇◇◇◇
1 If you describe something as **luxurious**, you mean that it is very comfortable and expensive. *Our honeymoon was two days in Las Vegas at a luxurious hotel called Le Mirage... She had come to enjoy Roberto's luxurious life-style.* ADJ-GRADED ♦ **luxuriously** *The lounge is luxuriously furnished and carpeted.* ADV-GRADED
2 **Luxurious** means feeling or expressing great pleasure and comfort. *Amy tilted her wine in her glass with a luxurious sigh.* ADJ-GRADED ♦ **luxuriously** *Liz laughed, stretching luxuriously.* ADV-GRADED: ADV after v

luxury /lʌkʃəri/ **luxuries** ♦♦♦◇◇
1 **Luxury** is very great comfort, especially among beautiful and expensive surroundings. *By all accounts he leads a life of considerable luxury... She was brought up in an atmosphere of luxury and wealth.* N-UNCOUNT =extravagance ≠penury
2 A **luxury** is something expensive which is not necessary but which gives you pleasure. *A week by the sea is a luxury they can no longer afford... Telephones are still a luxury in some parts of Spain, Portugal, and Greece.* N-COUNT =extravagance
3 A **luxury** item is something expensive which is not necessary but which gives you pleasure. *He could not afford luxury food on his pay... He rode on the president's luxury train through his own state.* ADJ: ADJ n
4 A **luxury** is a pleasure which you do not often have the opportunity to enjoy. *Hot baths and warm towels are my favourite luxury... We were going to have the luxury of a free weekend, to rest and do whatever we pleased.* N-SING: with supp

luxury goods. **Luxury goods** are things which are not necessary, but which give you pleasure or make your life more comfortable. *...increased taxes on luxury goods, such as boats, fur coats and expensive cars.* N-PLURAL

LW. **LW** is an abbreviation for **long wave.**

-ly /-li/ **-lier, -liest**
1 **-ly** is added to adjectives to form adverbs that indicate the manner or nature of something. *I saw Louise walking slowly to the bus stop... They were badly injured... Sarah has typically British fair skin.* SUFFIX
2 **-ly** is added to nouns to form adjectives that describe someone or something as being like or typical of a particular kind of person or thing. *The staff are very friendly... This was a cowardly thing to do.* SUFFIX
3 **-ly** is added to nouns referring to periods of time to form adjectives or adverbs that say how often something happens or is done. *...a weekly newspaper. ...monthly payments. ...the language that we use daily.* SUFFIX

lychee /laɪtʃiː, AM liːtsiː/ **lychees.** **Lychees** are Chinese fruit which have white flesh and large stones inside and a pinkish-brown skin. N-VAR

Lycra /laɪkrə/. **Lycra** is a type of stretchy fabric, similar to elastic, which is used to make tight-fitting garments such as tights and swimming costumes. **Lycra** is a trademark. ♦◇◇◇◇ N-UNCOUNT

lying /laɪɪŋ/. **Lying** is the present participle of **lie.**

lymph gland /lɪmf glænd/ **lymph glands.** A **lymph gland** is a small mass of tissue in your body where white blood cells are formed. N-COUNT

lynch /lɪntʃ/ **lynchs, lynching, lynched.** If an angry crowd of people **lynch** someone, they kill that person by hanging them, without letting them have a trial, because they believe that that person has committed a crime. *They were about to lynch him when reinforcements from the army burst into the room and rescued him.* ♦♦◇◇◇ VERB V n ♦ **lynching, lynchings** *Some towns found that lynching was the only way to drive away bands of outlaws.* N-VAR

lynchpin /lɪntʃpɪn/. See **linchpin.**

lynx /lɪŋks/ **lynxes.** A **lynx** is a wild animal similar to a large cat. N-COUNT

lyre /laɪəʳ/ **lyres.** A **lyre** is a stringed instrument that looks like a small harp. N-COUNT

lyric /lɪrɪk/ **lyrics** ♦♦◇◇◇
1 **Lyric** poetry is written in a simple and direct style, and usually expresses personal emotions such as love. *...Lawrence's splendid short stories and lyric poetry.* ADJ: ADJ n
2 The **lyrics** of a song are its words. *...Kurt Weill's Broadway opera with lyrics by Langston Hughes.* N-COUNT: usu pl

lyrical /lɪrɪkᵊl/. Something that is **lyrical** is poetic and romantic. *His paintings became more lyrical. ...its remarkable free-flowing and often lyrical style.* ♦◇◇◇◇ ADJ-GRADED ♦ **lyrically** *I'm trying to show children that it's lyrically beautiful out there, wherever you live.* ADV-GRADED: ADV adj/-ed, ADV after v ● to **wax lyrical**: see **wax.**

lyricism /lɪrɪsɪzəm/. **Lyricism** is gentle and romantic emotion, often expressed in writing, poetry, or music. *...a natural lyricism which can be expressed through dance and music.* N-UNCOUNT

lyricist /lɪrɪsɪst/ **lyricists.** A **lyricist** is someone who writes the words for modern songs or for musicals. N-COUNT

Mm

M, m /em/ **M's, m's**
1 **M** is the thirteenth letter of the English alphabet. N-VAR
2 **m** is a written abbreviation for 'metres' or 'metre'. *The isthmus is only 200m wide at its narrowest point.*
3 **m** is a written abbreviation for the number 'million'. *Last year exports reached $150m in value... The acting oil minister has estimated this year's output at 500m tonnes.*
4 **M** or **m** is used as an abbreviation for words beginning with m, such as 'minutes', 'married', 'male', and 'masculine'.

-'m /-m/. In spoken English and in informal written English, **'m** is a short form of 'am' that is used after the pronoun 'I'.

ma /mɑː/ **mas.** Some people refer to or address their mother as **ma**; an informal word. *Ma was still at work when I got back.* ◆◇◇◇◇ N-FAMILY =mum

MA /em eɪ/ **MAs** ◆◇◇◇◇
1 An **MA** is a master's degree in an arts or social science subject. **MA** is an abbreviation for **Master of Arts**. *She then went on to university where she got a BA and then an MA.* N-COUNT
2 **MA** is written after someone's name to indicate that they have an MA. *...Clive W Heaton, MA.*

ma'am /mæm, mɑːm/. People sometimes say **ma'am** as a very formal and polite way of addressing a woman whose name they do not know or a woman of superior rank; used mainly in American English. *Would you repeat that please, ma'am?* ◆◇◇◇◇ N-VOC PRAGMATICS =madam

mac /mæk/ **macs.** In British English, a **mac** is a raincoat, especially one made from a particular kind of waterproof cloth. N-COUNT

macabre /məkɑːbrə/. You describe something such as an event or story as **macabre** when it is strange and horrible or upsetting, usually because it involves death or injury. *Police have made a macabre discovery... Mr Dahl was well-known for his macabre adult stories called 'Tales of the Unexpected'.* ◆◇◇◇◇ ADJ-GRADED: usu ADJ n =chilling

macaroni /mækəroʊni/. **Macaroni** is a kind of pasta made in the shape of short hollow tubes. N-UNCOUNT

macaroni cheese. **Macaroni cheese**, or in American English **macaroni and cheese**, is a dish made from macaroni and cheese sauce. N-UNCOUNT

macaroon /mækəruːn/ **macaroons.** **Macaroons** are sweet biscuits flavoured with coconut or almond. N-COUNT

mace /meɪs/ **maces**
1 A **mace** is an ornamental stick carried by an official or placed somewhere as a symbol of authority. N-COUNT
2 **Mace** is a spice, usually in the form of a powder, made from the shell of nutmegs. N-UNCOUNT
3 **Mace** is a substance that causes tears and sickness, and that is used in sprays as a defence against rioters or attackers. **Mace** is a trademark. N-UNCOUNT

macerate /mæsəreɪt/ **macerates, macerating, macerated.** If you **macerate** food, or if it **macerates**, you soak it in a liquid for a period of time so that it absorb the liquid. *I like to macerate the food in liqueur for a few minutes before serving... Cognac is also used to macerate and flavour ingredients and casseroles... Seal tightly then leave for four to five days to macerate.* V-ERG =soak V n *in* n V n V

Mach /mɑːk/. **Mach** is used as a unit of measurement in stating the speed of a moving object in relation to the speed of sound. For example, if an aircraft is travelling at Mach 1, it is travelling at exactly the speed of sound; a technical term in physics and engineering. *The hot air permitted higher speeds before the critical Mach number was exceeded... The aim is to fly at about Mach 2, twice the speed of sound.* N-UNCOUNT: N n/num

machete /məʃeti/ **machetes.** A **machete** is a large knife with a broad blade. N-COUNT

Machiavellian /mækiəveliən/. If you describe someone as **Machiavellian**, you are critical of them because they use cleverness and trickery to get what they want, and they do not care about morals, conventions, or other people. *...Machiavellian republicans plotting to destabilise the throne. ...the Machiavellian and devious way decisions were made... A Machiavellian plot was suspected.* ADJ-GRADED: usu ADJ n PRAGMATICS =devious

machinations /mækɪneɪʃənz, mæʃ-/. You use **machinations** to describe disapprovingly someone's secret and complicated plans to gain power, especially by harming other people. *...the political machinations that brought him to power. ...the machinations of the currency speculators.* N-PLURAL: usu with supp PRAGMATICS

machine /məʃiːn/ **machines, machining, machined** ◆◆◆◆◇
1 A **machine** is a piece of equipment which uses electricity or an engine in order to do a particular kind of work. *I put the coin in the machine and pulled the lever... The machine can be remotely operated and monitored. ...a color photograph of the sort taken by machine to be pasted in passports.* N-COUNT: also *by* N
2 If you **machine** something, you make it or work on it using a machine. *The material is machined in a factory... All parts are machined from top grade, high tensile aluminium. ...machined brass zinc alloy gears.* ♦ **machining** *...our machining, fabrication and finishing processes.* VB: usu passive *be* V-ed *be* V-ed *from* n V-ed N-UNCOUNT
3 You can use **machine** to refer to a large and well-controlled system or organization. *...Nazi Germany's military machine... He has put the party publicity machine behind another candidate.* N-COUNT: usu supp N
4 If you say that someone is a **machine**, you mean that they are so tired or bored that they do their work without thinking. *I think I have got to stop or I might turn into a machine... He has dedicated himself to his work and become just a writing machine.* N-COUNT =automaton
5 See also **fruit machine**, **sewing machine**, **slot machine**, **vending machine**.

machine code. **Machine code** is a way of expressing instructions and information in a numerical form which can be understood by a computer or microchip; a technical term in computing. N-UNCOUNT

machine gun, **machine guns.** also spelled **machine-gun**. A **machine gun** is a gun which fires a lot of bullets one after the other very quickly. *The two sides joined battle once again using artillery, mortars and heavy machine guns. ...a burst of machine-gun fire.* ● See also **sub-machine gun**. ◆◆◇◇◇ N-COUNT

machinery /məʃiːnəri/ ◆◆◇◇◇
1 You can use **machinery** to refer to machines in general, or machines that are used in a factory or on a farm. *...quality tools and machinery. ...your local garden machinery specialist... Farmers import most of their machinery and materials.* N-UNCOUNT
2 The **machinery** of a government or organization is the system and all the procedures that it uses to deal with things. *The machinery of democracy could be created quickly. ...the government machinery and administrative procedures concerned with social provision... The full state and police machinery ground into action.* N-SING: *the* N, oft N *of* n

machine tool, machine tools. A **machine tool** is a machine driven by power that cuts, shapes, or finishes metal or other materials. ◆◇◇◇◇ N-COUNT

machinist /məʃiːnɪst/ **machinists.** A **machinist** is a person whose job is to operate a machine, especially in a factory. ◆◇◇◇◇ N-COUNT

machismo /mætʃɪzmoʊ, AM mɑːtʃiːz-/. You use **machismo** to refer to men's behaviour or attitudes when they are very conscious and proud of their masculinity. *Hooky, naturally, has to prove his machismo by going on the scariest rides twice.* N-UNCOUNT

macho /mætʃoʊ, AM mɑː-/. You use **macho** to describe men who are very conscious and proud of their masculinity; an informal use. *He was an extremely macho man. ...displays of macho bravado... Body building - that's a bit macho, isn't it?* ◆◇◇◇◇ ADJ-GRADED

macintosh /mækɪntɒʃ/. See **mackintosh.**

mackerel /mækərəl/; **mackerel** is both the singular and the plural. A **mackerel** is a sea fish with a greeny-blue skin. *Almiro's boat had sailed out to the middle of the bay to fish for mackerel.* ► **Mackerel** is this fish eaten as food. *Bay leaf is an excellent herb for mackerel.* ◆◇◇◇◇ N-VAR; N-UNCOUNT

mackintosh /mækɪntɒʃ/ **mackintoshes.** In British English, a **mackintosh** is a raincoat, especially one made from a particular kind of waterproof cloth. N-COUNT

macro /mækroʊ/ **macros** ◆◇◇◇◇

1 You use **macro** to indicate that something relates to a general area, rather than being detailed or specific, especially when talking about business, finance, and management. *...coordinated programmes of regulation of the economy both at the macro level and at the micro level.* ADJ: usu ADJ n =global ≠micro

2 **Macro** lenses and other devices are used for photographing or filming things at very close range; used in photography and film. *He photographed this using a macro lens... Zooming is not possible while in macro mode.* ADJ: usu ADJ n

3 A **macro** is a shortened version of a computer command which makes the computer carry out a set of actions; a technical use in computing. N-COUNT

macro- /mækroʊ-/. **Macro-** is added to words in order to form new words that are technical and that refer to things which are large in size or broad in scope. *...the cornerstone of macro-economic policy. ...the macro-relationship between unemployment and imprisonment.* PREFIX ≠micro-

macrobiotic /mækroʊbaɪɒtɪk/. **Macrobiotic** food consists of whole grains and vegetables that are grown without chemicals; a technical term in nutrition. *John's a vegetarian, and his girlfriend's on a strict macrobiotic diet.* ADJ: usu ADJ n =wholefood

macrobiotics /mækroʊbaɪɒtɪks/; the form **macrobiotic** is used as a modifier. **Macrobiotics** is an area of study concerned with diet that contains only macrobiotic food; a technical term in nutrition. *...Michio Kushi, father of modern macrobiotics... A macrobiotic diet rules out all artificially coloured or chemically treated foods.* N-UNCOUNT

macrocosm /mækroʊkɒzəm/. A **macrocosm** is a complex organized system such as the universe or a society, considered as a single unit; a formal word. *The macrocosm of the universe is mirrored in the microcosm of the mind.* N-SING: usu *the* N ≠microcosm

macroeconomic /mækroʊiːkənɒmɪk, -ek-/; also spelled **macro-economic. Macroeconomic** means relating to the major, general features of a country's economy, such as the level of inflation, unemployment, or interest rates; a technical term. *...the attempt to substitute low inflation for full employment as a goal of macro-economic policy.* ◆◇◇◇◇ ADJ: usu ADJ n

mad /mæd/ **madder, maddest** ◆◆◆◇◇

1 Someone who is **mad** has a mind that does not work in a normal way, with the result that their behaviour is very strange. *She was afraid of going mad. ...the mad old lady from down the street.* ♦ **madness** *He was driven to the brink of madness.* ADJ =insane; N-UNCOUNT

2 You use **mad** to describe people or things that you think are very foolish. *You'd be mad to work with him again... Isn't that a rather mad idea?* ♦ **madness** *It is political madness.* ADJ-GRADED PRAGMATICS =crazy; N-UNCOUNT

3 If you say that someone is **mad**, you mean that they are very angry; an informal use. *You're just mad at me because I don't want to go... I'm pretty mad about it, I can tell you.* ADJ-GRADED: usu v-link ADJ, oft ADJ *at/about* n

4 If you are **mad about** or **mad on** something or someone, you like them very much indeed; an informal use. *She's not as mad about sport as I am... He's mad about you... He's mad on trains.* ► Also a combining form. *...his football-mad son... He's not power-mad.* ADJ-GRADED: v-link ADJ *about/on* n; COMB in ADJ-GRADED

5 **Mad** behaviour is wild and uncontrolled. *You only have an hour to complete the game so it's a mad dash against the clock... The audience went mad.* ♦ **madly** *Down in the streets people were waving madly.* ADJ =frantic; ADV: ADV with v

6 If you say that someone or something **drives** you **mad**, you mean that you find them extremely annoying; an informal expression. *There are certain things he does that drive me mad... This itching is driving me mad.* PHRASES V inflects

7 If you do something **like mad**, you do it very energetically or enthusiastically; an informal expression. *He was weight training like mad.* PHR after v

8 ● See also **madly.** ● **mad keen**: see **keen.**

madam /mædəm/ **madams** ◆◇◇◇◇

1 People sometimes say **Madam** as a very formal and polite way of addressing a woman whose name they do not know or a woman of superior rank. For example, a shop assistant might address a woman customer as **Madam**. *Try them on, madam.* N-VOC PRAGMATICS

2 You use the expression '**Dear madam**' at the beginning of a formal letter or a business letter when you are writing to a woman. *Dear Madam, Thank you for your interest in our Memorial Scheme.* N-VOC PRAGMATICS

3 **Madam** is sometimes used in front of words such as 'Chairman' to address the woman who holds the position mentioned. *I have to say this, Madam Chairman.* N-VOC: N n PRAGMATICS

4 You can call a little girl a **madam** if you are annoyed because she is being naughty and behaving as if she expects other people to do what she wants; used mainly in spoken British English. *Sue is a thoroughly precocious little madam if ever there was one... Wait till I get you home, young madam.* N-COUNT; N-VOC PRAGMATICS

madcap /mædkæp/. A **madcap** plan or scheme is very foolish and not likely to succeed; an informal word. *The politicians simply flitted from one madcap scheme to another... His fast-paced novels are full of bizarre situations and madcap antics.* ADJ-GRADED: usu ADJ n

mad cow disease. Mad cow disease is a fatal disease which affects the nervous system of cattle; used mainly in British English. ◆◇◇◇◇ N-UNCOUNT =BSE

madden /mædᵊn/ **maddens, maddening, maddened.** To **madden** a person or animal means to make them very angry. *The swine were maddening farmers by guzzling their lettuces... He is calmed by a lullaby, but maddened by any sudden loud noise. ...the maddened dogs.* ◆◇◇◇◇ VERB =infuriate V n V-ed

maddening /mædənɪŋ/. If you describe something as **maddening**, you mean that it makes you feel angry, irritated, or frustrated. *Shopping in the January sales can be maddening... It is, in its way, a maddening biography.* ♦ **maddeningly** *The service is maddeningly slow... 'Aha!' Dave nodded maddeningly... Slowly, maddeningly, a smile surfaced on his face.* ADJ-GRADED =infuriating; ADV-GRADED: ADV adj, ADV after v, ADV with cl

made /meɪd/ ◆◆◇◇◇

1 **Made** is the past tense and past participle of **make.**

2 If something is **made of** or **made out of** a particular substance or material, that substance or material was used to build or construct it. *The top of the table is made of glass... What is the statue made out of?* ADJ: v-link ADJ *of/out of* n

3 If you say that someone **has it made** or **has got it made**, you mean that they are certain to be rich or successful; an informal expression. *When I was at school, I thought I had it made.* PHRASE: V inflects

-made /-meɪd/. **-made** combines with words such as 'factory' to make adjectives that indicate that something has been made or produced in a particular place or in a particular way. *...a British-made car. ...specially-made footwear.* COMB in ADJ: usu ADJ n

made-to-measure. A **made-to-measure** suit, shirt, or other item of clothing is one that is made by a tailor to fit you exactly, rather than one that you buy already made in a shop. ADJ: usu ADJ n

made-up; also spelled **made up.** ◆◆◆◇◇

1 If you are **made-up**, you are wearing make-up such as powder or eye shadow. *She was made-up and ready to go... She was beautifully made-up, beautifully groomed... Very dark glossy lips look wrong with heavily made-up eyes.* ADJ-GRADED: v-link ADJ, adv ADJ n

2 A **made-up** word, name, or story is invented, rather than really existing or being true. *It looks like a made-up word.* ADJ: usu ADJ n ≠real

madhouse /mædhaʊs/ **madhouses**

1 If you describe a place or situation as a **madhouse**, you mean that it is full of confusion and noise. *That place is a madhouse.* N-COUNT: usu sing

2 A **madhouse** is a mental hospital; an old-fashioned use. N-COUNT =asylum

madly /mædli/ ◆◇◇◇◇

1 You can use **madly** to indicate that one person loves another a great deal. *She has fallen madly in love with him... She was devoted to him, but she no longer loved him madly.* ADV: ADV prep, ADV after v =completely

2 You can use **madly** in front of an adjective in order to emphasize the quality expressed by the adjective. *Inside it is madly busy... This seemed madly dangerous.* ADV: ADV adj PRAGMATICS =wildly

madman /mædmən/ **madmen.** A **madman** is a man who is insane. *He wanted to jump up and run outside, screaming like a madman.* ◆◇◇◇◇ N-COUNT

Madonna /mədɒnə/. Catholics and other Christians sometimes call Mary, the mother of Jesus Christ, **the Madonna**. ◆◇◇◇◇ N-PROPER: *the* N

madras /mədræs, -drɑːs/. A **madras** curry is a rather hot spicy curry. *...Madras curry powder.* ◆◇◇◇◇ ADJ: ADJ n

madrigal /mædrɪgəl/ **madrigals.** A **madrigal** is a song sung by several singers without any musical instruments. Madrigals were popular in England in the sixteenth century. N-COUNT

madwoman /mædwʊmən/ **madwomen.** A **madwoman** is a woman who is insane; an informal word. N-COUNT

maelstrom /meɪlstrɒm/ **maelstroms.** If you describe a situation as a **maelstrom**, you mean that it is very confused, violent, or destructive; mainly used in written English. *...the maelstrom of ethnic hatreds and vendetta politics... Inside, she was a maelstrom of churning emotions.* N-COUNT: usu sing, usu with supp, oft N *of* n

maestro /maɪstroʊ/ **maestros.** A **maestro** is a skilled and well-known musician or conductor. *...the urbane maestro's delightful first show.* ◆◇◇◇◇ N-COUNT; N-VOC

mafia /mæfiə, AM mɑːf-/ **mafias** ◆◆◇◇◇

1 **The Mafia** is a criminal organization that gets money illegally, especially by threatening people, dealing in drugs, and prostitution. *The Mafia is by no means ignored by Italian television.* N-COUNT-COLL: *the* N

2 You can use **mafia** to refer to an organized group of people who you disapprove of because they use unfair or illegal means in order to get what they want. *They are well-connected with the south-based education-reform mafia.* N-COUNT: usu with supp PRAGMATICS

mag /mæg/ **mags.** In British English, a **mag** is the same as a magazine; an informal word. *...a well-known glossy mag.* ◆◇◇◇◇ N-COUNT

magazine /mægəziːn, AM -ziːn/ **magazines** ◆◆◆◆◇

1 A **magazine** is a publication with a paper cover which is issued regularly, usually weekly or monthly, and which contains articles, stories, photographs, and advertisements. *Her face is on the cover of a dozen or more magazines.* N-COUNT

2 On radio or television, a **magazine** or a **magazine programme** is a programme consisting of several items about different topics, people, and events. *...a live arts magazine. ...'Science In Action', a weekly science magazine programme.* N-COUNT: usu supp N

3 In a gun, the **magazine** is the compartment for the cartridges. N-COUNT

4 A **magazine** is a building in which ammunition and explosives are kept. N-COUNT

magenta /mədʒentə/ **magentas. Magenta** is used to describe things that are dark reddish-purple in colour. *...magenta cotton trousers.* COLOUR

maggot /mægət/ **maggots. Maggots** are tiny creatures that look like very small worms. Maggots turn into flies. ◆◆◇◇◇ N-COUNT

magic /mædʒɪk/ ◆◆◆◇◇

1 **Magic** is the power to use supernatural forces to make impossible things happen, such as making people disappear or controlling events in nature. *They believe in magic. ...the use of magic to combat any adverse powers or influences... Older legends say that Merlin raised the stones by magic.* N-UNCOUNT

2 You can use **magic** when you are referring to an event or change that is so wonderful, strange, quick, or unexpected that it seems as if supernatural powers have caused it. You can also say that something happens **as if by magic** or **like magic**. *All this was supposed to work magic... The picture will now appear, as if by magic!... The fog disappeared like magic.* N-UNCOUNT

3 You use **magic** to describe something that does things, or appears to do things, by magic. *So it's a magic potion? ...the magic ingredient that helps to keep skin looking smooth.* ADJ: ADJ n

4 **Magic** is the art and skill of performing mysterious tricks to entertain people, for example by making things appear and disappear. *His secret hobby: performing magic tricks.* N-UNCOUNT: oft N n

5 If you refer to the **magic** of something, you mean that it has a special mysterious quality which makes it seem wonderful and exciting to you and which makes you feel happy. *It infected them with some of the magic of a lost age... There can be a magic about love that defies all explanation... There were also moments of pure magic.* ► Also an adjective. *Then came those magic moments in the rose-garden.* N-UNCOUNT: usu with supp; ADJ-GRADED

6 If you refer to a person's **magic**, you mean a special talent or ability that they have, which you admire or consider very impressive. *The 32-year-old Jamaican-born fighter believes he can still regain some of his old magic.* N-UNCOUNT: usu with poss

7 You can use expressions such as **the magic number** and **the magic word** to indicate that a number or word is the one which is significant or desirable in a particular situation. *...their quest to gain the magic number of 270 electoral votes on Election Day. ...the magic word that opened doors onto private worlds.* ADJ: *the* ADJ n

8 **Magic** is used in expressions such as **there is no magic formula** and **there is no magic solution** in say that someone will have to make an effort to solve a problem, because it will not solve itself. *There is no magic formula that will carry Labour to effortless victory... There is no magic cure.* ADJ: ADJ n, with neg

9 If you say that something is **magic**, you think it is very good or enjoyable; an informal use, used mainly in British English. *It was magic – one of the best days of my life.* ADJ-GRADED PRAGMATICS =great

magical /mædʒɪkəl/ ◆◆◇◇◇

1 Something that is **magical** seems to use magic or to be able to produce magic. *...the story of Sin-Sin, a little boy who has magical powers.* ♦ **magically** /mædʒɪkli/ *...the story of a young boy's adventures after he is magically transported through the cinema screen.* N-UNCOUNT; ADV: ADV with v

2 You can say that a place or object is **magical** when it has a special mysterious quality that makes it seem wonderful and exciting. *The beautiful island of Cyprus is a magical place to get married.* ADJ-GRADED

magic carpet, magic carpets. In stories, a **magic carpet** is a special carpet that can carry people through the air. N-COUNT

magician /mədʒɪʃən/ **magicians** ◆◇◇◇◇

1 A **magician** is a person who entertains people by doing magic tricks. N-COUNT =conjurer

2 In fairy stories, a **magician** is a person, usually a man, who has magic powers. N-COUNT

3 If you call someone a **magician**, you admire the skilful and exciting way they do something. *Bevan was a magician with words. ...a magician of the keyboard.* N-COUNT: oft N *of/with* n PRAGMATICS

magic wand, magic wands

1 A **magic wand** or a **wand** is a long thin rod that magicians and fairies wave when they are performing tricks and magic. N-COUNT =wand

2 You use **magic wand**, especially in the expression **there is no magic wand**, to indicate that someone is dealing with a difficult problem which cannot be solved quickly and easily. *There is no magic wand to secure a just peace... People can't expect him to wave a magic wand.* N-COUNT: usu with brd-neg

magisterial /mædʒɪstɪəriəl/. If you describe someone's behaviour or work as **magisterial**, you mean that they show great authority or ability; a formal word. *...his magisterial voice and bearing... The Cambridge World History of Human Disease is a magisterial work.* ADJ-GRADED: usu ADJ n

magistrate /mædʒɪstreɪt/ **magistrates.** A **magistrate** is an official who acts as a judge in law courts which deal with minor crimes or disputes. ◆◆◇◇◇ N-COUNT

magnanimity /mægnənɪmɪti/. **Magnanimity** is kindness, fairness, and generosity towards someone, especially after being involved in a contest with them or being treated badly by them; a formal word. *Churchill took his defeat with good humour and magnanimity. ...the father of one victims spoke with remarkable magnanimity.* N-UNCOUNT ≠vindictiveness

magnanimous /mægnænɪməs/. If you are **magnanimous**, you behave well and generously towards other people, especially people who are weaker than you; a fairly formal word. *I was prepared to be magnanimous, prepared to feel compassion for him... He was a man capable of magnanimous gestures.* ♦ **magnanimously** *'You were right, and we were wrong,' he said magnanimously.* ADJ-GRADED =generous; ADV-GRADED: usu ADV with v

magnate /mægneɪt/ **magnates.** A **magnate** is someone who has earned a lot of money from a particular business or industry. *...a multimillionaire shipping magnate.* ◆◇◇◇◇ N-COUNT: usu supp N =tycoon

magnesium /mægniːziəm/. **Magnesium** is a metallic element which is light and silvery-white, and burns with a bright white flame. ◆◇◇◇◇ N-UNCOUNT

magnet /mægnɪt/ **magnets** ◆◇◇◇◇

1 If you say that something is a **magnet** or is like a **magnet**, you mean that people are very attracted by it and want to go to it or look at it. *...Prospect Park, with its vast lake is a magnet for all health freaks... Lower interest rates are acting like a magnet, dragging consumers back to the shops.* N-COUNT: usu *a* N in sing, oft N *for* n

2 A **magnet** is a piece of iron or other material which attracts iron towards it. *It's possible to hang a nail from a magnet and then use that nail to pick up another nail.* N-COUNT

magnetic /mægnetɪk/ ◆◆◇◇◇

1 If something is **magnetic**, it has the power of a magnet or functions like a magnet. *...magnetic particles.* ADJ-GRADED: usu ADJ n

2 You use **magnetic** to describe something that is caused by or relates to the force of magnetism. *The electrically charged gas particles are affected by magnetic forces.* ♦ **magnetically** /mægnetɪkli/ *...metal fragments held together magnetically.* ADJ; ADV: ADV after v

3 You use **magnetic** to describe tapes, parts of devices, and objects which have a coating of a magnetic substance and which contain coded information that can be read or written on by computers and other electronic machines. *...her magnetic strip ID card. ...magnetic recording tape.* ADJ: usu ADJ n

4 If you describe something as **magnetic**, you mean that it is very attractive to people because it has unusual, powerful, and exciting qualities. *...the magnetic effect of the prosperous German economy on would-be immigrants. ...the magnetic pull of his looks and her personality.* ADJ-GRADED: usu ADJ n

magnetic field, magnetic fields. A **magnetic field** is an area around a magnet, or something functioning as a magnet, in which the magnet's power to attract things is felt. ◆◇◇◇◇ N-COUNT

magnetic tape, magnetic tapes. Magnetic tape is plastic tape covered with iron oxide or a similar magnetic substance. It is used for recording sounds, film, or computer information. N-VAR

magnetism /mægnɪtɪzəm/

1 Someone or something that has **magnetism** has unusual, powerful, and exciting qualities which attract people to them. *There was no doubting the animal magnetism of the man... Later, she would describe his magnetism as irresistible. ...the extraordinary magnetism the music seemed to have.* N-UNCOUNT: usu with supp

2 **Magnetism** is the natural power of some objects and substances, especially iron, to attract other objects towards them. N-UNCOUNT

magnetize /mægnɪtaɪz/ **magnetizes, magnetizing, magnetized;** also spelled **magnetise** in British English.

1 If you **magnetize** something, you make it magnetic. *Make a Mobius strip out of a ribbon of mild steel and magnetise it. ...a small metal chessboard with magnetized playing pieces.* VERB V n V-ed

2 If one thing **is magnetised** towards another, it is attracted to it by magnetic forces. *Volcanic lava is magnetised in the direction of the Earth's magnetic field.* VB: usu passive *be* V-ed prep/adv

magnification /mægnɪfɪkeɪʃən/ **magnifications**

1 **Magnification** is the act or process of magnifying something. *The man was tall, his figure shortened by the magnification of Lenny's binoculars... I find England strange and unique and beautiful. And for me, London is the magnification of all that.* N-UNCOUNT

2 **Magnification** is the degree to which a lens, mirror, or other device can magnify an object, or the degree to which the object is magnified. *The electron microscope uses a beam of electrons to produce images at high magnifications... The magnification is 833,333 times the original size.* N-VAR

magnificent /mægnɪfɪsənt/. If you say that something or someone is **magnificent**, you mean that you think they are extremely good, beautiful, or impressive. *...a magnificent country house in wooded grounds. ...magnificent views over the San Fernando Valley... She is magnificent at making you feel you can talk quite naturally to her.* ♦ **magnificence** *I shall never forget the magnificence of the Swiss mountains and the beauty of the lakes.* ♦ **magnificently** *The team played magnificently throughout the competition. ...a magnificently elaborate head-dress.* ◆◆◇◇◇ ADJ-GRADED =splendid; N-UNCOUNT: oft N *of* n =splendour; ADV-GRADED: ADV after v, ADV adj/-ed =splendidly

magnify /mægnɪfaɪ/ **magnifies, magnifying, magnified** ◆◇◇◇◇

1 To **magnify** an object means to make it appear larger than it really is, by means of a special lens or mirror. *This version of the Digges telescope magnifies images 11 times... A lens would magnify the picture so it would be like looking at a large TV screen. ...magnifying lenses.* VERB =enlarge V n n V n V-ing

2 To **magnify** something means to increase its effect, size, loudness, or intensity. *Poverty and human folly magnify natural disasters... Their noises were magnified in the still, wet air. ...using bank loans to magnify his buying power.* VERB V n

3 If you **magnify** something, you make it seem more important or serious than it really is. *They do not grasp the broad situation and spend their time magnifying ridiculous details... Any signs of discontent tend to be magnified and overanalyzed.* VERB =exaggerate V n

magnifying glass, magnifying glasses. A **magnifying glass** is a piece of glass which makes objects appear bigger than they actually are. N-COUNT

magnitude /mægnɪtjuːd, AM -tuːd/ **magnitudes** ◆◇◇◇◇

1 If you talk about the **magnitude** of something, you are talking about its great size, scale, or importance. *An operation of this magnitude is going to be difficult... These are issues of great magnitude... No one seems to realise the magnitude of this problem.* N-UNCOUNT: usu with supp

2 **Magnitude** is used in stating the size or extent of something such as a star, earthquake, or explosion; a technical use in science. *...the 1.2 magnitude star* N-VAR: with supp, oft num N, N *of* num,

Fomalhaut... The San Francisco earthquake of 1906 had a magnitude of 8.3. N num

3 You can use **order of magnitude** when you are giving an approximate idea of the amount or importance of something. *America and Russia do not face a problem of the same order of magnitude as Japan.* PHRASES *order* inflects =scale

4 If one amount is an **order of magnitude** larger than another, it is ten times larger than the other. If it is two **orders of magnitude** larger, it is a hundred times larger; a technical expression in mathematics. *The time delay would be smaller by eight orders of magnitude.* *order* inflects

magnolia /mægnoʊliə/ **magnolias** ◆◇◇◇◇

1 A **magnolia** is a kind of tree with white, pink, yellow, or purple flowers. N-COUNT

2 You can use **magnolia** to describe things that are creamish-white in colour. COLOUR

magnum /mægnəm/ **magnums.** A **magnum** is a wine bottle holding the equivalent of two normal bottles, approximately 1.5 litres. *...a magnum of champagne.* N-COUNT: oft N *of* n

magnum opus. A **magnum opus** is the greatest or most important work produced by a writer, artist, musician, or scholar. *...Gadamer's magnum opus 'Truth and Method'.* N-SING: oft poss N

magpie /mægpaɪ/ **magpies** ◆◇◇◇◇

1 A **magpie** is a bird with black and white markings and a long tail. N-COUNT

2 If you describe someone as a **magpie**, you mean that they like collecting and keeping things, often things that have little value; an informal use. *A born magpie, Mandy collects any object that catches her eye.* N-COUNT =hoarder

maharaja /mɑːhərɑːdʒə/ **maharajas;** also spelled **maharajah**. A **maharaja** is the head of one of the royal families that used to rule parts of India. N-COUNT

mahogany /məhɒgəni/. **Mahogany** is a dark reddish-brown wood that is used to make furniture. *...mahogany tables and chairs.* ◆◇◇◇◇ N-UNCOUNT: oft N n

maid /meɪd/ **maids.** A **maid** is a woman who works as a servant in a hotel or private house. *A maid brought me breakfast at half past eight.* • See also **old maid**. ◆◆◇◇◇ N-COUNT

maiden /meɪdᵊn/ **maidens** ◆◇◇◇◇

1 A **maiden** is a young girl or woman; a literary use. *...stories of noble princes and their brave deeds on behalf of beautiful maidens.* N-COUNT =damsel

2 The **maiden** voyage or flight of a ship or aircraft is the first official journey that it makes. *In 1912, the Titanic sank on her maiden voyage.* ADJ: ADJ n

maiden aunt, maiden aunts. A **maiden aunt** is an aunt who is not married; an old-fashioned expression. N-COUNT

maiden name, maiden names. A married woman's **maiden name** is her parents' surname, which she used before she got married and started using her husband's surname. N-COUNT: usu poss N ≠married name

maiden speech, maiden speeches. A politician's **maiden speech** is the first speech that he or she makes in parliament after becoming a member of it. N-COUNT

maid of honour, maids of honour. In American English, a **maid of honour** is the chief bridesmaid at a wedding. N-COUNT

mail /meɪl/ **mails, mailing, mailed** ◆◆◆◇◇

1 **The mail** is the public service or system by which letters and parcels are collected and delivered. *Your check is in the mail... People had to renew their motor vehicle registrations through the mail... The firm has offices in several large cities, but does most of its business by mail.* N-SING: *the* N, also *by* N =post

2 You can refer to letters and parcels that are delivered to you as **mail**. *There was no mail except the usual junk addressed to the occupier... Nora looked through the mail.* N-UNCOUNT: also *the* N =post

3 If you **mail** a letter or parcel to someone, or you **mail** them with it, you send it to them by putting it in a post-box or by taking it to a post office; used mainly in American English. *Last year, he mailed the documents to French journalists... He mailed me the contract... The Government has already mailed some 18 million households with details of the public offer.* VERB V n to n, V n n, V n *with* n, Also V n

4 To **mail** a message to someone means to send it to them by means of electronic mail or a computer network. *...if a report must be electronically mailed to an office by 9 am the next day.* ► Also a noun. *If you have any problems then send me some mail.* VERB be V-ed prep, Also V n, N-UNCOUNT

5 See also **mailing**; **chain mail**, **email**, **electronic mail**, **hate mail**, **junk mail**, **surface mail**.

mail out. If someone **mails out** things such as letters, leaflets, or bills, they send them to a large number of people at the same time; used mainly in American English. *This week, the company mailed out its annual report.* PHRASAL VERB =send out, V P n (not pron), Also V n P

mailbag /meɪlbæg/ **mailbags;** also spelled **mail bag**. A **mailbag** is a large bag that is used by postal workers for carrying mail. N-COUNT

mailbox /meɪlbɒks/ **mailboxes.** In the United States, a **mailbox** is a box outside your house where letters are delivered. ◆◇◇◇◇ N-COUNT

mailing /meɪlɪŋ/ **mailings**

1 **Mailing** is the activity of sending things to people through the postal service. *The newsletter was printed towards the end of June in readiness for mailing... The owners of the store have stepped up customer mailings.* N-UNCOUNT: also N in pl

2 A **mailing** is something that is sent to people through the postal service. *The seniors organizations sent out mailings to their constituencies.* N-COUNT

mailing list, mailing lists. A **mailing list** is a list of names and addresses that a company or organization keeps, so that they can send people information or advertisements. N-COUNT

mailman /meɪlmæn/ **mailmen.** In American English, a **mailman** is a man whose job is to collect and deliver letters and parcels that are sent by post. The usual British word is **postman**. N-COUNT

mail order, mail orders. ◆◆◇◇◇

1 **Mail order** is a system of buying and selling goods. You choose the goods you want from a company by looking at their catalogue, and the company sends them to you by post. *The toys are available by mail order from Opi Toys... Many of them also offer a mail-order service.* N-UNCOUNT: oft *by* N, N n

2 **Mail orders** are goods that have been ordered by mail order; used mainly in American English. *I supervise the packing of all mail orders.* N-COUNT: usu pl

mailshot /meɪlʃɒt/ **mailshots.** In British English, a **mailshot** is a letter advertising something or appealing for money for a particular charity. Mailshots are sent out to a large number of people at once. N-COUNT

maim /meɪm/ **maims, maiming, maimed.** To **maim** someone means to injure them so badly that part of their body is permanently damaged. *Mines have been scattered in rice paddies and jungles, maiming and killing civilians... One man has lost his life, another has been maimed.* ◆◇◇◇◇ VERB =injure, V n

main /meɪn/ **mains** ◆◆◆◆◆

1 The **main** thing is the most important one of several similar things in a particular situation. *One of the main tourist areas of Amsterdam... My main concern now is to protect the children... What are the main differences and similarities between them?* ADJ: det ADJ =chief

2 If you say that something is true **in the main**, you mean that it is generally true, although there may be exceptions. *Tourists are, in the main, sympathetic people... In the main, children are taboo in the workplace.* PHRASE: PHR with cl, PRAGMATICS, =in general, on the whole

3 The **mains** are the pipes which supply gas or water to buildings, or which take sewage away from them. *...the water supply from the mains... The capital has been without mains water since Wednesday night.* N-COUNT: usu pl, usu with supp

4 **The mains** are the wires which supply electricity to buildings, or the place where the wires end inside the building; used mainly in British English. *...amplifiers which plug into the mains... Make sure plugs are disconnected from the mains... It is mains or battery powered.* N-PLURAL: usu *the* N

main clause, main clauses. A **main clause** is a clause that can stand alone as a complete sentence. Compare **subordinate clause**.
N-COUNT

main drag. **The main drag** in a town or city is its main street; an informal expression used mainly in American English. *...just two blocks off the main drag in Aberdeen, South Dakota.*
N-SING: *the*N

mainframe /meɪnfreɪm/ **mainframes.** A **mainframe** or **mainframe computer** is a large powerful computer which can be used by many people at the same time and which can do very large or complicated tasks.
◆◇◇◇◇ N-COUNT

mainland /meɪnlænd/. You can refer to the large principal part of a country or continent as **the mainland**, especially when this is being contrasted with the islands around it. *She was going to Nanaimo to catch the ferry to the mainland. ...the islands that lie off the coast of mainland Britain.*
◆◆◇◇◇ N-SING: *the*N, N n

mainline /meɪnlaɪn/ **mainlines, mainlining, mainlined**

1 A **mainline** railway or route is the principal railway between two places. A **mainline** station is situated on a mainline railway. *...the first mainline railway to be built in Britain for almost a hundred years... All of London's mainline stations were shut down after the explosion.*
ADJ: ADJ n

2 You can use **mainline** to describe people, ideas, and activities that belong to the most central, conventional, and normal part of a tradition, institution, or business. *We observe a striking shift away from a labor theory among all mainline economists... Mainline feminism was arguing for the inherent beauty of the natural woman.*
ADJ: ADJ n =mainstream

3 If people **mainline** a drug or if they **mainline**, they inject an illegal drug into themselves; an informal use. *We see him snorting and mainlining cocaine.*
VB: usu cont =inject V n Also V

mainly /meɪnli/
◆◆◆◆◇

1 You use **mainly** to indicate that your statement is broadly true or that it is a generalization. *The stockmarket scandal is refusing to go away, mainly because there's still no consensus over how it should be dealt with... The birds live mainly on nectar.*
ADV: ADV with cl/group, ADV with v =primarily

2 You use **mainly** when you are referring to a group and stating something that is true of most of it. *The African half of the audience was mainly from Senegal or Mali... The spacious main bedroom is mainly blue.*
ADV: ADV with group =mostly

main road, main roads. A **main road** is an important road that leads from one town or city to another. *Webb turned off the main road and drove round to the car park.*
◆◇◇◇◇ N-COUNT

mainspring /meɪnsprɪŋ/ **mainsprings.** If you say that an idea, emotion, or other factor is the **mainspring** of something, you mean that it is the most important reason or motive for that thing; used mainly in written English. *My life has been music, and a constant search for it has been the mainspring of my life... You begin to understand what actions were the mainspring of the story.*
N-COUNT: usu sing, usu *the*N *of*n

mainstay /meɪnsteɪ/ **mainstays.** If you describe something as the **mainstay** of a particular thing, you mean that it is the most basic part of it. *Fish and rice were the mainstays of the country's diet... This principle of collective bargaining has been a mainstay in labor relations in this country.*
◆◇◇◇◇ N-COUNT: usu *the*N *of*n

mainstream /meɪnstriːm/ **mainstreams.** People, activities, or ideas that are part of the **mainstream** are regarded as the most typical, normal, and conventional because they belong to the same group or system as most others of their kind. *...people outside the economic mainstream... This was the company's first step into the mainstream of scientific and commercial computing... The show wanted to attract a mainstream audience.*
◆◆◇◇◇ N-COUNT: usu sing, usu with supp

maintain /meɪnteɪn/ **maintains, maintaining, maintained**
◆◆◆◆◇

1 If you **maintain** something, you continue to have it, and do not let it stop or grow weaker. *The Department maintains many close contacts with the chemical industry... Push yourself to make friends and to maintain the friendships... The emergency powers to try to maintain law and order.*
VERB =preserve V n

2 If you say that someone **maintains** that something is true, you mean that they have stated their opinion strongly but not everyone agrees with them or believes them. *He has maintained that the money was donated for international purposes... Prosecutors maintain no deal was made... 'Not all feminism has to be like this,' Jo maintains... He had always maintained his innocence.*
VERB =claim V that V with quote V n

3 If you **maintain** something at a particular rate or level, you keep it at that rate or level. *The government was right to maintain interest rates at a high level. ...action is required to ensure standards are maintained at as high a level as possible... Iraq would like to see oil prices maintained at the $18 a barrel average for which OPEC strives.*
VERB =keep V n *at*n

4 If you **maintain** a road, building, vehicle, or machine, you keep it in good condition by regularly checking it and repairing it when necessary. *...a tough campaign to force authorities to maintain roads properly... The house costs a fortune to maintain... The cars are getting older and less well-maintained.*
VERB =look after V n V-ed

5 If you **maintain** someone, you provide them with money and other things that they need. *He should pay and maintain you as well. ...the basic costs of maintaining a child.*
VERB =provide for, keep V n

maintenance /meɪntɪnəns/
◆◆◇◇◇

1 The **maintenance** of a building, vehicle, road, or machine is the process of keeping it in good condition by regularly checking it and repairing it when necessary. *...maintenance work on government buildings... The window had been replaced last week during routine maintenance. ...car maintenance lessons.*
N-UNCOUNT

2 **Maintenance** is money that someone gives regularly to another person to pay for the things that the person needs. *...the government's plan to make absent fathers pay maintenance for their children.*
N-UNCOUNT

3 If you ensure the **maintenance** of a state or process, you make sure that it continues. *...the maintenance of peace and stability in Asia. ...the importance of natural food to the maintenance of health.*
N-UNCOUNT: usu N *of*n

maisonette /meɪzənet/ **maisonettes.** In Britain, a **maisonette** is a flat that usually has a separate door to the outside from the other flats in the same building. Most maisonettes have two storeys. *He lived in a ground floor maisonette.*
N-COUNT

maize /meɪz/. **Maize** is a tall plant which produces large cobs of sweetcorn. It is grown as the basic food crop in many parts of the world. *...vast fields of maize.*
◆◇◇◇◇ N-UNCOUNT =Indian corn

Maj. **Maj** is a written abbreviation for 'Major' when it is used as a title. *...Maj D B Lee.*
◆◇◇◇◇ N-TITLE

majestic /mədʒestɪk/. If you describe something or someone as **majestic**, you think they are very beautiful, dignified, and impressive. *...a majestic country home that once belonged to the Astor family... Anna looked tanned and majestic in her linen caftan.* ♦ **majestically** /mədʒestɪkli/ *She rose majestically to her feet... Fuji is a majestically beautiful mountain.*
◆◇◇◇◇ ADJ-GRADED =grand; ADV-GRADED: usu ADV with v, also ADV adj

majesty /mædʒɪsti/ **majesties**
◆◆◇◇◇

1 You use majesty in expressions such as **Your Majesty** or **Her Majesty** when you are addressing or referring to a King or Queen. *I quite agree, Your Majesty... His Majesty requests your presence in the royal chambers... Their Majesties celebrated our arrival by giving us each a little silver spoon.*
N-VOC: poss N; PRON: poss PRON PRAGMATICS =highness

2 **Majesty** is the quality of being beautiful, dignified, and impressive. *...the majesty of the mainland mountains.*
N-UNCOUNT

major /meɪdʒəʳ/ **majors, majoring, majored**

1 You use **major** when you want to describe something that is more important, serious, or significant than other things in a group or situation. *The major factor in the decision to stay or to leave was usually professional... Drug abuse has long been a major problem for the authorities there... Exercise has a*
ADJ-GRADED: ADJ n =significant

major part to play in preventing and combating disease.

2 A **major** is an army officer one rank above captain. *I was a major in the war, you know. ...Major Alan Bulman.* N-COUNT; N-TITLE; N-VOC

3 In American English, **an economics major** or **an English major**, for example, is a university student whose main subject is economics or English. *English majors would be asked to explore the roots of language.* N-COUNT: supp N

4 A student's **major** is the main subject that he or she is studying at university; used mainly in American English. *He switched his major in college to business.* N-COUNT: oft poss N

5 In American English, if someone **majors** in a particular subject, they study it as their main subject at university. *He majored in finance at Claremont Men's College in California.* VERB V in n

6 In European music, a **major** scale is one in which the third note is two tones higher than the first. *...Mozart's Symphony No 35 in D Major.* ADJ: n ADJ, ADJ n ≠minor

majorette /meɪdʒəre̲t/ **majorettes.** A **majorette** is one of a group of girls or young women who march at the front of a musical band in a procession. N-COUNT

ma̲jor ge̲neral, major generals; also spelled **major-general**. A **major general** is a senior officer in the army, one rank above a brigadier. ◆◇◇◇◇ N-COUNT; N-TITLE; N-VOC

majority /mədʒɒ̲rɪti, AM -dʒɔ̲ːr-/ **majorities** ◆◆◆◆◇

1 The **majority** of people or things in a group is more than half of them. *The majority of my patients come to me from out of town... The vast majority of our cheeses are made with pasteurised milk... As a fuel it is preferred by top chefs and is used in the majority of British homes... Still, a majority continue to support the treaty.* N-SING-COLL: usu sing, usu N of n ≠minority • If a group is **in a majority** or **in the majority**, they form more than half of a larger group. *The Albanians now constitute some 15 per cent of its total population and are in the majority in many Western areas.* PHRASE: v-link PHR

2 A **majority** is the difference between the number of votes or parliamentary seats that the winner gets in an election or vote and the number of votes or parliamentary seats that the next person or party gets. *Members of parliament approved the move by a majority of ninety-nine... According to most opinion polls, he is set to win a clear majority in the elections on Sunday... The Trust's annual meeting has decided by a narrow majority to ban deer hunting.* N-COUNT: usu with supp

3 **Majority** is used to describe opinions, decisions, and systems of government that are supported by more than half the people involved. *...her continuing disagreement with the majority view... A majority vote of 75% is required from shareholders for the plan to go ahead.* ADJ: ADJ n

4 **Majority** is the state of legally being an adult. In Britain, people reach their majority at the age of eighteen. *The age of majority in Romania is eighteen... Once you reach your majority, you may do what you damned well please.* N-UNCOUNT: oft with poss

5 See also **absolute majority**, **moral majority**

make 1 carrying out an action

make /meɪ̲k/ **makes, making, made** ◆◆◆◆◆

1 You can use **make** with a wide range of nouns to indicate that someone performs an action or says something. For example, if someone **makes** a suggestion, they suggest something. *I'd just like to make a comment... I made a few phone calls... I think you're making a serious mistake... The Pope said the world had made some progress towards peace in 1991... Science and technology have made major changes to the way we live... She had made us an offer too good to refuse.* VERB V n, V n n

2 You can use **make** with certain nouns to indicate that someone does something well or badly. For example, if you **make** a success of something, you do it successfully, and if you **make** a mess of something, you do it very badly. *Apparently he made a mess of his audition... Are you really going to make a better job of it this time?* VERB V n of n

3 If you **make** as if to do something or **make** to do something, you behave in a way that makes it seem that you are just about to do it; used in written English. *Mary made as if to protest, then hesitated... He made to chase Davey, who ran back laughing.* VERB V as if to-inf, V to-inf

4 In cricket, if a player **makes** a particular number of runs, they score that number of runs. In baseball or American football, if a player **makes** a particular score, they achieve that score. *He made 1,972 runs for the county.* VERB =score V amount

5 If you **make do** with something, you use or have it instead of something else that you do not have, although it is not as good. *Why make do with a copy if you can afford the genuine article?... We're a bit low on bed linen. You'll have to make do.* PHRASES *make* inflects, oft PHR *with* n

6 If you **make like** you are doing something, you act as if you are doing it, and if you **make like** someone, you act as if you are that person; an informal expression. *Bob makes like he's a fish blowing bubbles.* V inflects, PHR cl, PHR n

7 **Make** is used in a large number of expressions which are explained under other words in this dictionary. For example, the expression 'to make sense' is explained at 'sense'.

make 2 causing or changing

make /meɪ̲k/ **makes, making, made** ◆◆◆◆◆

1 If something **makes** you do something, it causes you to do it. *Grit from the highway made him cough... The white tips of his shirt collar made him look like a choirboy... I was made to feel guilty and irresponsible.* VERB V n inf, be V-ed to-inf

2 If you **make** someone do something, you force them to do it. *Mama made him clean up the plate... You can't make me do anything... All non-payers of poll tax will be traced and made to pay.* VERB V n inf, be V-ed to-inf

3 You use **make** to talk about causing someone or something to be a particular thing or to have a particular quality. For example, to **make** someone a star means to cause them to become a star, and to **make** someone angry means to cause them to become angry. *...James Bond, the role that made him a star... He returned to Chicago, and made it his base for the rest of his life... She made life very difficult for me... She's made it obvious that she's appalled by me... Rationing has made it easier to find some products like eggs, butter and meat... Does your film make a hero of Jim Garrison?* VERB V n n, V n adj, V it adj that, V it adj to-inf, V n of n

4 If you say that one thing or person **makes** another seem, for example, small, stupid, or good, you mean that they cause them to seem small, stupid, or good in comparison, even though they are not. *They live in fantasy worlds which make Euro Disney seem uninventive... Since he came to live with me, we have been subject to a campaign of spite and revenge which makes Lady Sarah appear angelic by comparison.* VERB V n inf adj/prep/n

5 If you **make** yourself understood, heard, or known, you succeed in getting people to understand you, hear you, or know that you are there. *Aron couldn't speak Polish. I made myself understood with difficulty... He almost had to shout to make himself heard above the music.* VERB V pron-refl -ed

6 If you **make** someone something, you appoint them to a particular job, role, or position. *Mr Major made him transport minister... If I am made chairman, I hope Simon will stay on as my trusted lieutenant.* VERB V n n

7 If you **make** something into something else, you change it in some way so that it becomes that other thing. *We made it into a beautiful home... Her bestseller 'Peachtree Road' is soon to be made into a television mini-series.* VERB V n into n

8 To **make** a total or score a particular amount means to increase it to that amount. *This makes the total cost of the bulb and energy £27... Lupescu scored from 20 yards and then Balint made it 4-0.* VERB V n amount

9 When someone **makes** a friend or an enemy, someone becomes their friend or their enemy, often because of a particular thing they have done. *Lorenzo was a natural leader who made friends easily... He was unruly in class and made an enemy of most of his teachers.* • to **make friends**: see **friend**. VERB V n, V n of n

make 3 creating or producing

make /meɪk/ **makes, making, made** ◆◆◆◆◆

1 To **make** something means to produce, construct, or create it. *She made her own bread... Nissan now makes cars at two plants in Europe... Having curtains made professionally can be costly... They make compost out of all kinds of waste.* VERB V n; have n V-ed; V n *from/out of* n

2 If someone **makes** a film or television programme, they are involved in creating or producing it. *We are making a film about wildlife. ...the film 'Queen Christina', made in 1934.* VERB V n; V-ed

3 If you **make** a meal or a drink, you prepare it. *You wash while I make some lunch... Would you like me to make us all a coffee?* VERB V n; V n n

4 If you **make** a note or list, you write something down in that form. *Mr Perry made a note in his book... Make a list of your questions beforehand.* VERB =write V n

5 If you **make** rules or laws, you decide what these should be. *The police don't make the laws, they merely enforce them... The only person who makes rules in this house is me.* VERB V n

6 If you **make** money, you get it by working for it, by selling something, or by winning it. *I think every business's goal is to make money... How much did we make?... Can it be moral to make so much money out of a commodity which is essential to life?.* VERB V n; V n *out of/from* n

7 If something **makes** something else, it is responsible for the success of that thing. *What really makes the book are the beautiful designs.* VERB V n

8 The **make** of something such as a car or radio is the name of the company that made it. *The only car parked outside is a black Saab – a different make. ...a certain make of wristwatch.* N-COUNT: supp N, N *of* n =brand

9 If you say that someone is **on the make**, you disapprove of them because they are trying to get a lot of money or power, possibly by illegal or immoral methods. PHRASE: v-link PHR PRAGMATICS

make 4 link verb uses

make /meɪk/ **makes, making, made** ◆◆◆◆◆

1 You can use **make** to say that someone or something has the right qualities for a particular task or role. For example, if you say that someone will **make** a good politician, you mean that they have the right qualities to be a good politician. *She'll make a good actress, if she gets the right training... You've a very good idea there. It will make a good book... I decided he would never make a pilot... I'm very fond of Ian and I'd make him a good wife.* V-LINK V n; V n n

2 If people **make** a particular pattern such as a line or a circle, they arrange themselves in this way. *A group of people made a circle around the Pentagon.* V-LINK =form V n

3 You can use **make** to say what two numbers add up to. *Four twos make eight... He is adding three aircraft carriers – that makes six in all.* V-LINK V amount

make 5 achieving or reaching

make /meɪk/ **makes, making, made** ◆◆◆◆◆

1 If someone **makes** a particular team or **makes** a particular high position, they do so well that they are put in that team or get that position. *The athletes are just happy to make the British team... He knew he was never going to make director.* VERB V n

2 If you **make** a place in or by a particular time, you get there in or by that time, often with some difficulty. *The engine is gulping two tons of fuel an hour in order to make New Orleans by nightfall.* VERB V n prep

3 If you **make it** somewhere, you succeed in getting there, especially in time to do something. *So you did make it to America, after all. ...the hostages who never made it home... I just made it!* PHRASES V inflects, oft PHR prep/adv

4 If you **make it**, you are successful in achieving something difficult, or in surviving through a very difficult period. *I believe I have the talent to make it... You're brave and courageous. You can make it.* V inflects

5 If you cannot **make it**, you are unable to attend an event that you have been invited to. *'I can't make it,' she said. 'That's Mother's Day.'... He hadn't been able to make it to our dinner.* V inflects, usu with brd-neg, oft PHR *to* n

make 6 stating an amount or time

make /meɪk/ **makes, making, made** ◆◆◆◆◆

1 You use **make** when saying what you calculate or guess an amount to be. *All I want to know is how many T-shirts Jim Martin has got. I make it three... I make the total for the year £69,599.* VERB V *it* amount; V n amount

2 You use **make** when saying what time your watch says it is. *I make it nearly 9.30... 'What time d'you make it?'—'Thirteen past.'* VERB V *it* n; Also V n n

make 7 phrasal verbs

make /meɪk/ **makes, making, made** ◆◆◆◆◆

make for PHRASAL VERB

1 If you **make for** a place, you move towards it. *He rose from his seat and made for the door.* =head for V P n

2 If something **makes for** another thing, it causes or helps to cause that thing to happen or exist; an informal expression. *A happy parent makes for a happy child.* V P n

make of. If you ask a person what they **make of** something, you want to know what their impression, opinion, or understanding of it is. *Well, what did you make of her?... Nancy wasn't sure what to make of Mick's apology.* PHRASAL VERB V P n

make off. If you **make off**, you leave somewhere as quickly as possible, often in order to escape. *They broke free and made off in a stolen car.* PHRASAL VERB =leave V P

make off with. If you **make off with** something, you steal it and take it away with you. *Masked robbers broke in and made off with $8,000.* PHRASAL VERB V P P n

make out PHRASAL VERB

1 If you **make** something **out**, you manage with difficulty to see or hear it. *I could just make out a tall, pale, shadowy figure tramping through the undergrowth... She thought she heard a name. She couldn't make it out, though... I heard the voices, but couldn't make out what they were saying.* V P n (not pron); V n P; V P wh

2 If you try to **make** something **out**, you try to understand it or decide whether or not it is true. *I couldn't make it out at all... It is hard to make out what criteria are used... At first I thought it was an accident, but as far as I can make out, the police consider that's unlikely.* =understand V n P; V P wh; V P

3 If you **make out** that something is the case or **make** something **out** to be the case, you try to cause people to believe that it is the case. *They were trying to make out that I'd actually done it... I don't think it was as glorious as everybody made it out to be... He's more business-minded than he makes himself out to be... He was never half as bad as his teachers made out.* V P that; V n P to-inf; V P

4 If you **make out** a case for something, you try to establish or prove that it is the best thing to do. *You could certainly make out a case for this point of view... Alice continued making out her case.* V P n (not pron) *for/against* n; V P n (not pron); Also V n P

5 When you **make out** a cheque, receipt, or order form, you write all the necessary information on it. *If you would like to send a donation, you can make a cheque out to Feed the Children... All cheques should be made out to 'EF International Language Schools'... I'm going to make out a receipt for you.* V n P *to* n; V P n (not pron)

6 If you ask how someone **is making out**, you are asking how well they are doing with a particular task, or in their life in general; an informal expression. *Who is making out better right now?... Bob turned over to sleep again, wondering how Jupiter and Pete were making out.* =get on V P adv

7 If two people **are making out**, they are engaged in sexual activity; an informal expression, used mainly in American English. *...pictures of the couple making out in their underwear on the beach.* RECIP pl-n V P; Also V P *with* n

make over. If you **make** something **over** to someone, you legally transfer the ownership of it to them. *Hampton Court was made over to Henry VIII as a present... John had made over to him most of the land... They moved on to a larger farm and in time made it over to Francis.* PHRASAL VERB be V-ed P *to* n; V P *to* n n; V n P *to* n

make up PHRASAL VERB

1 The people or things that **make up** something are the members or parts that form that thing. *Who exactly makes up the opposition in Kuwait?... Women officers make up 13 per cent of the police force... Insects are made up of tens of thousands of proteins.* =form V P n (not pron); be V-ed P *of* n; Also V n P

2 If you **make up** something such as a story or excuse, you invent it, sometimes in order to deceive people. *I think it's very unkind of you to make up* V P n (not pron)

stories about him... I'm not making it up. The character exists in real life. VnP

3 If you **make** yourself **up** or **make** your face **up**, or if someone else **makes** you **up**, make-up such as powder or lipstick is put on your face. *She spent too much time making herself up... She chose Maggie to make her up for her engagement photographs... I can't be bothered to make up my face.* VnP VPn (not pron)

4 If you **make up** an amount, you add something to it so that it is as large as it should be. *Less than half of the money that students receive is in the form of grants, and loans have made up the difference... The team had six professionals and made the number up with five amateurs... For every £100 you invest into a pension plan the Inland Revenue makes it up to £125.* VPn (not pron) VnP VnP *to* amount

5 If you **make up** time or hours, you work some extra hours to compensate for some time you have taken off work. *They'll have to make up time lost during the strike.* VPn (not pron) Also VnP

6 If two people **make up** or **make it up** after a quarrel or disagreement, they become friends again. *She came back and they made up... They never made up the quarrel... They should make up with their ex-enemy in the West... I'll make it up with him again.* RECIP pl-n VP pl-n VPn VP *with* n V *it* P *with* n Also pl-n V *it* P

7 If you **make up** something such as food or medicine, you prepare it by mixing or putting different things together. *Prepare the souffle dish before making up the souffle mixture.* VPn (not pron) Also VnP

8 If you **make up** a bed or couch, you put sheets and blankets onto it so that someone can sleep there. *Her mother made up a bed in her old room.* VPn (not pron)

make up for. To **make up for** something that is lost, missing, or damaged means to replace it or compensate for it. *Ask for an extra compensation payment to make up for the stress you have been caused... A conservatory would make up for the fact that we were refused planning permission for a roof terrace... The semi-finalists had to play twice in the day to make up for time lost to bad weather.* PHRASAL VERB =compensate VPPn

make up to. If you say that you will **make it up to** someone for something, you are promising that you will do something for them to compensate for the fact that they have been upset or disappointed, especially by you. *I'll make it up to you, I promise... I must make it up to him for the awful intrusion of last night.* PHRASAL VERB PRAGMATICS V *it* PPn V *it* PPn *for* n/-ing Also VnPPn

make-believe

1 If you say that someone is living in a **make-believe** world or is living in a world of **make-believe**, you mean that they are pretending that things are better or more exciting than they really are and that they are not facing up to reality; used showing disapproval. *The man lived in a 'make-believe' world surrounded by bizarre props including a pilot's raincoat and a microlite aircraft that he had never flown... She squandered millions on a life of make-believe.* N-UNCOUNT PRAGMATICS

2 When a child plays a game in which they pretend something, for example that they are someone else, you can refer to this activity as **make-believe**. *She used to play games of make-believe with her elder sister. ...his make-believe playmate.* N-UNCOUNT

3 You use **make-believe** to describe things, for example in a play or film, that imitate or copy something real, but which are not what they appear to be. *In the video, Michael Jackson danced down a make-believe street protesting that 'the kid is not my son'... The violence in those films was too unreal, it was make-believe... 'But, why?' he asked in make-believe astonishment.* ADJ

makeover /meɪkoʊvəʳ/ **makeovers.** If someone has a **makeover**, they have their make-up done by a beautician and their hair styled by a hair stylist, so that they feel they look as good as they possibly can. *She received a cosmetic makeover at a beauty salon as a birthday gift.* N-COUNT

maker /meɪkəʳ/ **makers** ◆◆◆◆◇

1 The **maker** of a product is the firm that manufactures it. *...Japan's two largest car makers. ...the makers of chocolates, sweets and biscuits.* N-COUNT: usu with supp =manufacturer

2 You can refer to the person who makes something as its **maker**. *...the makers of news and current affairs programmes.* N-COUNT: usu with supp

3 See also **peacemaker**.

makeshift /meɪkʃɪft/. **Makeshift** things are temporary and usually of poor quality, but they are used because there is nothing better available. *...the cardboard boxes and makeshift shelters of the homeless. ...a makeshift coffee table.* ◆◇◇◇◇ ADJ-GRADED: usu ADJ n

make-up; also spelled **makeup.** ◆◆◆◇◇

1 Make-up consists of things such as lipstick, eyeshadow, or powder which some women put on their faces to make themselves look more attractive or which actors use so that their faces can be clearly seen. *Normally she wore little make-up, but this evening was clearly an exception... She checked her makeup one last time, and then walked out with a spring in her step.* N-UNCOUNT

2 Someone's **make-up** is their nature and the various qualities in their character. *There was some fatal flaw in his makeup, and as time went on he lapsed into long silences or became off-hand.* N-UNCOUNT: with supp, usu poss N =personality

3 The **make-up** of something consists of its different parts and the way these parts are arranged. *The ideological make-up of the unions is now radically different from what it had been. ...the chemical make-up of the oceans and atmosphere.* N-UNCOUNT: with supp

makeweight /meɪkweɪt/ **makeweights.** If you describe someone or something as a **makeweight**, you think that they are not good or valuable and that they have been included in an activity in order to fill up a gap. *He has not been signed to the club as a makeweight to fill out the numbers.* N-COUNT PRAGMATICS

making /meɪkɪŋ/ **makings** ◆◆◇◇◇

1 The **making** of something is the act or process of producing or creating it. *...Salamon's book about the making of this movie... Ducks' eggs are particularly prized for cake making.* N-UNCOUNT: *the* N *of* n, n N

2 If you describe a person or thing as something **in the making**, you mean that they are going to become known or recognized as that thing. *Her drama teacher is confident Julie is a star in the making... I think it's a disaster in the making.* PHRASES usu n PHR

3 If something **is the making of** a person or thing, it is the reason that they become successful or become very much better than they used to be. *This discovery may yet be the making of him.* V inflects, PHR n

4 If you say that a person or thing has **the makings of** something, you mean it seems possible or likely that they will become that thing, as they have the necessary qualities. *Godfrey had the makings of a successful journalist.* V inflects, PHR n

5 If you say that something such as a problem you have is **of** your **own making**, you mean you have caused or created it yourself. *Some of the university's financial troubles are of its own making... The Prime Minister, however, is now caught in a trap of her own making.* v-link PHR

mal- /mæl-/. **Mal-** is added to words in order to form new words which describe things that are bad or unpleasant, or that are unsuccessful or imperfect. *Forty per cent of the population is suffering from malnutrition... The animals were seriously maltreated.* PREFIX

maladjusted /mælədʒʌstɪd/. If you describe a child as **maladjusted**, you mean that they have psychological problems and behave in a way which is not acceptable to society. *...a school for maladjusted children.* ADJ-GRADED

maladministration /mælædmɪnɪstreɪʃᵊn/. **Maladministration** is the act or process of administering a system or organization incorrectly; a formal word. *... a request to investigate a claim about maladministration.* N-UNCOUNT

maladroit /mælədrɔɪt/. If you describe someone as **maladroit**, you mean that they are clumsy, awkward, or tactless; a formal word. *Billings was a clumsy, maladroit man.* ADJ-GRADED

malady /mælədi/ **maladies**

1 A **malady** is an illness or disease; an old- N-COUNT fashioned use. *He was stricken at twenty-one with a crippling malady.* =illness

2 In written English, people sometimes use **maladies** to refer to serious problems in a society or situation. *When apartheid is over the maladies will linger on. ...the maladies of love.* N-COUNT =ill

malaise /mæleɪz/ ◆◇◇◇◇

1 **Malaise** is a state in which there is something wrong with a society or group, for which there does not seem to be a quick or easy solution; a formal use. *There is no easy short-term solution to Britain's chronic economic malaise... Unification has brought soaring unemployment and social malaise.* N-UNCOUNT

2 **Malaise** is a state in which people feel dissatisfied or unhappy but feel unable to change, usually because they do not know what is wrong; a formal use. *He complained of depression, headaches and malaise.* N-UNCOUNT

malaria /məleəriə/. **Malaria** is a serious disease carried by mosquitoes and which causes periods of fever. ◆◇◇◇◇ N-UNCOUNT

malarial /məleəriəl/. You can use **malarial** to refer to things that are connected with the transmission or treatment of malaria or to areas which are affected by malaria. *...malarial parasites.* ADJ: usu ADJ n

Malay /məleɪ/ **Malays** ◆◇◇◇◇

1 **Malay** means belonging or relating to the people, language, or culture of the largest ethnic group in Malaysia. *...the Malay community.* ADJ: usu ADJ n

2 A **Malay** is a member of the largest ethnic group in Malaysia. *...the three main racial groups in Malaysia – the Malays, the Indians and the Chinese.* N-COUNT

3 **Malay** is a language that is spoken in Malaysia and in parts of Indonesia. N-UNCOUNT

Malaysian /məleɪʒən/ **Malaysians.** Something that is **Malaysian** belongs or relates to Malaysia or to its people. *...the Malaysian coast. ...a Malaysian student.* ▶ **Malaysians** are people who are Malaysian. *I've got two Malaysians coming to see me at eleven thirty.* ◆◆◆◆◇ ADJ N-COUNT

malcontent /mælkəntent/ **malcontents.** You describe people as **malcontents** when you disapprove of the way in which they are dissatisfied with a situation and want it to change; a formal word. *Five years ago a band of malcontents, mainly half-educated communists, seized power.* N-COUNT: usu pl PRAGMATICS

male /meɪl/ **males** ◆◆◆◆◇

1 Someone who is **male** is a man or a boy. *Many women achievers appear to pose a threat to their male colleagues... The London City Ballet has engaged two male dancers from the Bolshoi... Most of the demonstrators were white and male.* ADJ ≠female

♦ **maleness** *...the small part of the Y chromosome which is responsible for maleness. ...the solidarity among men which is part of maleness.* N-UNCOUNT

2 Men and boys are sometimes referred to as **males** when they are being considered as a type. *...the remains of a Caucasian male, aged 65-70... He was very anxious to prove he was a red-blooded male... A high proportion of crime is perpetrated by young males in their teens and twenties.* N-COUNT =man ≠female

3 **Male** means relating, belonging, or affecting men rather than women. *The rate of male unemployment in Britain is now the third worst in Europe. ...male violence. ...a deep male voice.* ADJ: ADJ n ≠female

4 You can refer to any creature that belongs to the sex that cannot lay eggs or have babies as a **male**. *Males and females take turns brooding the eggs.* ▶ Also an adjective. *After mating the male wasps tunnel through the sides of their nursery.* N-COUNT ≠female ADJ ≠female

5 A **male** flower or plant fertilizes the part that will become the fruit; a technical use in biology. ADJ: usu ADJ n

male chauvinism. If you accuse a man of **male chauvinism**, you disapprove of him because his beliefs and behaviour show that he thinks men are naturally superior to women. N-UNCOUNT PRAGMATICS

male chauvinist, male chauvinists. If you describe an attitude or remark as **male chauvinist**, you are critical of it because you think it is based on the belief that men are naturally superior to women. *The male chauvinist attitude of some people in the company could get you down. ...the male chauvinist pig who wants women in the home and in their place.* ▶ A **male chauvinist** is a man who has male chauvinist views. *I'm not a male chauvinist.* ADJ-GRADED: usu ADJ n PRAGMATICS N-COUNT

male-dominated. A **male-dominated** society, organization, or area of activity is one in which men have most of the power and influence. *...the male-dominated world of journalism.* ◆◇◇◇◇ ADJ: usu ADJ n

malefactor /mælɪfæktər/ **malefactors.** A **malefactor** is someone who has done something bad or illegal; a formal word. *...a well-known criminal lawyer who had saved many a malefactor from going to jail.* N-COUNT =wrongdoer

malevolent /mælevələnt/. A **malevolent** person deliberately tries to cause harm or evil; a formal word. *Her stare was malevolent, her mouth a thin line, her eyes bright and glittering.* ◆◇◇◇◇ ADJ-GRADED ≠benevolent

♦ **malevolence** *...a rare streak of malevolence.* N-UNCOUNT ≠benevolence

♦ **malevolently** *Mark watched him malevolently.* ADV-GRADED

malformation /mælfɔːrmeɪʃən/ **malformations.** A **malformation** in a person's body is a part which does not have the proper shape or form, especially when it has been like this since birth; a technical term in medicine. *...babies with a high incidence of congenital malformations.* N-COUNT =deformity

malformed /mælfɔːrmd/. If people or parts of their body are **malformed**, they do not have the shape or form that they are supposed to, especially when they have been like this since birth; a technical term in medicine. *The deficiency can cause still births, premature births, malformed babies and mentally retarded babies... More rarely, the tubes have been malformed from birth.* ADJ-GRADED =deformed

malfunction /mælfʌŋkʃən/ **malfunctions, malfunctioning, malfunctioned.** If a machine or part of the body **malfunctions**, it fails to work properly; a formal use. *The radiation can damage microprocessors and computer memories, causing them to malfunction... Early physicians removed the malfunctioning organs.* ▶ Also a noun. *There must have been a computer malfunction.* ◆◇◇◇◇ VERB V V-ing N-COUNT

malice /mælɪs/. **Malice** is behaviour that is intended to harm people or their reputations, or cause them embarrassment and upset. *There was a strong current of malice in many of his portraits... There was no malice on his part.* ◆◇◇◇◇ N-UNCOUNT

malicious /məlɪʃəs/. If you describe someone's words or actions as **malicious**, you mean that they are intended to harm people or their reputation, or cause them embarrassment and upset. *That might merely have been malicious gossip... She described the charges as malicious.* ◆◇◇◇◇ ADJ-GRADED

♦ **maliciously** *'Oh, I stopped in at the club for a drink,' she said maliciously. ...his maliciously accurate imitation of Hubert de Burgh.* ADV-GRADED: usu ADV with v, also ADV adj

malign /məlaɪn/ **maligns, maligning, maligned** ◆◇◇◇◇

1 If you **malign** someone, you say unpleasant and untrue things about them; a formal use. *We maligned him dreadfully when you come to think of it. We assumed the very worst about him... Either the managers have been maligned or they are not telling the truth.* VERB =slander V n

2 If something is **malign**, it causes harm; a formal use. *...the malign influence jealousy had on their lives... Reliance on sponsorship can have a malign effect on theatre groups.* ADJ-GRADED: ADJ n =harmful ≠benign

3 See also **much-maligned.**

malignancy /məlɪgnənsi/ **malignancies.** A tumour or disease in a state of **malignancy** is out of control and is likely to cause death; a medical term. *Tissue that is removed during the operation is checked for signs of malignancy. ...cancerous malignancies of the skin.* N-VAR

malignant /məlɪgnənt/ ◆◇◇◇◇

1 A **malignant** tumour or disease is out of control and likely to cause death; a medical term. *She developed a malignant breast tumour.* ADJ: usu ADJ n ≠benign

2 If you say that someone is **malignant**, you think they are cruel and like to cause harm. *He said that we were evil, malignant and mean. ...a community* ADJ-GRADED =evil

over-run by a malignant minority indulging in crime and violence.

malinger /məlɪŋgəʳ/ **malingers, malingering, malingered.** If someone **is malingering**, they pretend to be ill in order to avoid working; used showing disapproval. *She was told by her doctor that she was malingering.* VB: usu cont PRAGMATICS V

mall /mɔːl, mæl/ **malls.** A **mall** is a very large enclosed shopping area. ◆◇◇◇◇ N-COUNT

mallard /mælɑːʳd/ **mallards.** A **mallard** is a kind of wild duck which is very common. N-COUNT

malleable /mæliəbᵊl/

1 If you say that someone is **malleable**, you mean that they are easily influenced or controlled by other people; a fairly formal word. *The malleable mayor of New York was under his control... She was young enough to be malleable.* ADJ-GRADED

2 A substance that is **malleable** is soft and can easily be made into different shapes. *Silver is the most malleable of all metals. ...using clay, plasticine or another malleable material.* ADJ-GRADED =supple ≠rigid

mallet /mælɪt/ **mallets.** A **mallet** is a wooden hammer with a square head. N-COUNT

malnourished /mælnʌrɪʃt/. If someone is **malnourished**, they are physically weak because they do not eat enough food or do not eat the right kind of food. *About thirty per-cent of the country's children were malnourished.* ADJ-GRADED: usu v-link ADJ =undernourished, underfed

malnutrition /mælnjuːtrɪʃᵊn, AM -nuːt-/. If someone is suffering from **malnutrition**, they are physically weak and extremely thin because they have not eaten enough food. *Infections are more likely in those suffering from malnutrition.* ◆◇◇◇◇ N-UNCOUNT

malodorous /mæloʊdərəs/. Something that is **malodorous** has an unpleasant smell; a literary word. *...tons of malodorous garbage bags. ...living in a malodorous London street.* ADJ-GRADED: usu ADJ n

malpractice /mælpræktɪs/ **malpractices.** If you accuse someone of **malpractice**, you are accusing them of breaking the law or the rules of their profession in order to gain some advantage for themselves; a formal word. *There were only one or two serious allegations of malpractice. ...alleged financial malpractices. ...medical malpractice suits.* ◆◇◇◇◇ N-VAR: oft N n

malt /mɔːlt/ **malts** ◆◇◇◇◇

1 **Malt** is a substance made from grain that has been soaked in water and then dried in a hot oven. Malt is used in the production of whisky, beer, and other alcoholic drinks. *German beer has traditionally been made from just four ingredients - hops, malt, yeast and water.* N-UNCOUNT

2 **Malt** is the same as **malt whisky**. N-MASS

malted /mɔːltɪd/. **Malted** barley has been soaked in water and then dried in a hot oven. It is used in the production of whisky, beer, and other alcoholic drinks. ADJ: ADJ n

Maltese /mɒltiːz/. **Maltese** is both the singular and the plural. ◆◆◆◆◇

1 **Maltese** means belonging or relating to Malta, or to its people, language, or culture. *...the Maltese writer Francis Ebejer.* ADJ: usu ADJ n

2 A **Maltese** is a Maltese citizen, or a person of Maltese origin. N-COUNT

3 **Maltese** is a language spoken by people who live in Malta. N-UNCOUNT

maltreat /mæltriːt/ **maltreats, maltreating, maltreated.** If a person or animal **is maltreated**, they are treated badly, especially by being hurt. *He said that he was not tortured or maltreated during his detention... Only when the animals were seriously maltreated was any inspection or prosecution called for.* VB: usu passive =mistreat be V-ed

maltreatment /mæltriːtmənt/. **Maltreatment** is cruel behaviour, especially involving hurting a person or animal. *2,000 prisoners died as a result of torture and maltreatment. ...the sexual maltreatment of women and children.* N-UNCOUNT: oft N of n =mistreatment

malt whisky, malt whiskies. Malt whisky or **malt** is whisky that is made from malt. *...a miniature bottle of malt whisky... I got a bottle of my best malt out of the sideboard.* ► A **malt whisky** is a glass of malt whisky. N-MASS N-COUNT

mam /mæm/ **mams.** In some dialects of British English, **mam** is used to mean mother; an informal word. *You sit here and rest, Mam.* ◆◇◇◇◇ N-FAMILY =mum

mama /məmɑː, AM mɑːmə/ **mamas. Mama** means the same as **mother**; an old-fashioned word. ◆◇◇◇◇ N-FAMILY

mamma /mɑːmə/ **mammas. Mamma** means the same as **mother**; an informal word used in American English. N-FAMILY =mommy

mammal /mæmᵊl/ **mammals. Mammals** are animals such as humans, dogs, lions, and whales. In general, female mammals give birth to babies rather than laying eggs, and feed their young with milk. ◆◇◇◇◇ N-COUNT

mammalian /mæmeɪliən/. **Mammalian** means relating to mammals; a technical term in zoology. *The disease can spread from one mammalian species to another.* ADJ: ADJ n

mammary /mæməri/. **Mammary** means relating to the breasts; a technical term in anatomy. *This stimulates the mammary glands after childbirth to produce milk.* ADJ: ADJ n

mammogram /mæməgræm/ **mammograms.** A **mammogram** is a test used to check whether women have breast cancer, using x-rays. N-COUNT

Mammon /mæmən/. You can use **Mammon** to refer to money and business activities if you want to show your disapproval of people who think that becoming rich is the most important thing in life. *It is not every day that one meets a business-person who is not obsessed with Mammon.* N-UNCOUNT PRAGMATICS

mammoth /mæməθ/ **mammoths** ◆◇◇◇◇

1 You can use **mammoth** to emphasize that a task or change is very large and needs a lot of effort to achieve. *...the mammoth task of relocating the library... You can only undertake mammoth changes if the finances are there... This mammoth undertaking was completed in 18 months.* ADJ-GRADED: usu ADJ n PRAGMATICS =enormous

2 A **mammoth** was an animal like an elephant, with very long tusks and long hair, that lived a long time ago but no longer exists. N-COUNT

mammy /mæmi/ **mammies.** In some dialects of English, **mammy** is used to mean mother; an informal word. N-FAMILY

man /mæn/ **men, mans, manning, manned** ◆◆◆◆◆

1 A **man** is an adult male human being. *He had not expected the young man to reappear before evening... I have always regarded him as a man of integrity. ...the thousands of men, women and children who are facing starvation.* N-COUNT

2 **Man** and **men** are sometimes used to refer to all human beings, including both males and females. Some people dislike this use. *The chick initially has no fear of man... Anxiety is modern man's natural state. ...a possible first step to sending a man back to the moon or to Mars.* N-VAR

3 If you say that a man is, for example, **a gambling man** or **an outdoors man**, you mean that he likes gambling or outdoor activities. *Are you a gambling man, Mr Graham?... He is a keen outdoors man with a great interest in photography and walking.* N-COUNT: supp N

4 If you say that a man is, for example, **a London man** or **an Oxford man**, you mean that he comes from London or Oxford, or went to university there. *...as the Stockport man collected his winnings... Bill Clinton, he's an Oxford man.* N-COUNT: n-proper N

5 If you refer to a particular company's or organization's **man**, you mean a man who works for or represents that company or organization; used in journalism. *...the Daily Telegraph's man in Abu Dhabi. ...America's man at the United Nations.* N-COUNT: poss N

6 If you say that a man is someone's **man**, you mean that he always supports that person or does what they want. *At the time he was said to be very much Rajiv Gandhi's man.* N-COUNT: poss N

7 Some people refer to a woman's husband, lover, or boyfriend as her **man**; an informal use. *...if they see your man cuddle you in the kitchen or living room.* N-SING: poss N

8 In the armed forces, the **men** are the ordinary soldiers, sailors, or airmen, but not the officers. *150 officers and men had to be taken straight to hospital. ...a drill sergeant who would work with the men at least one hour every morning.* N-PLURAL

9 Male workers are sometimes referred to as **men**, especially if they do physical work or work for a more senior person. *The men voted by a four-to-one majority to accept the pay offer... After the talks, the leader of the Workers' Council said his men would be going back down the mines.* N-PLURAL: oft poss N

10 One man sometimes addresses another as **'man'** when he is angry or impatient with him; an old-fashioned use. *I told you, man! It'll be some-time after eight o'clock.* N-VOC PRAGMATICS

11 In very informal social situations, **man** is sometimes used as a greeting or form of address to a man. *Hey wow, man! Where d'you get those boots?* N-VOC PRAGMATICS

12 If you **man** something such as a place or machine, you operate it or are in charge of it. *French soldiers manned roadblocks in the capital city. ...the person manning the phone at the complaints department... The station is seldom manned in the evening.* VERB V n

13 See also **manned; ladies' man, no-man's land.**

14 If you say that a man is **man enough** to do something, you mean that he has the necessary courage or ability to do it. *I told him that he should be man enough to admit he had done wrong... You can search me if you think you're man enough.* PHRASES v-link PHR

15 If you describe a man as **a man's man**, you mean that he has qualities which make him popular with other men rather than with women. v-link PHR

16 In American English, people sometimes address a man as **my man**; an informal expression. *'Get the guy in the purple shirt.'—'All right, my man.'* CONVENTION PRAGMATICS

17 In British English, people sometimes address a man as **my man, my dear man,** or **my good man.** This form of address is often friendly, but can also suggest that the speaker feels superior to the person being addressed. An old-fashioned expression. *My dear man, you are welcome to stay... It's not for you to say so, my man!* CONVENTION PRAGMATICS

18 If you say that a man **is** his **own man**, you approve of the fact that he makes his decisions and his plans himself, and does not depend on other people. *Be your own man. Make up your own mind... He'll be his own man and won't be dictated to.* V inflects PRAGMATICS

19 If you say that a group of men are, do, or think something **to a man**, you are emphasizing that every one of them is, does, or thinks that thing. *To a man, the surveyors blamed the government... They died, to a man, when they tried to break out... Economists, almost to a man, were sceptical.* PHR with v PRAGMATICS

20 A **man-to-man** conversation or meeting takes place between two men, especially two men who meet to discuss a serious personal matter. *He called me to his office for a man-to-man talk... Me and Ben should sort this out man to man.* PHR n, PHR after v

21 • **the man in the street**: see **street.** • **man about town**: see **town.** • **man of the world**: see **world.**

-man /-mæn/. **-man** combines with numbers to make adjectives which indicate that something involves or is intended for that number of people. *The four-man crew on board the fishing trawler... He set up a three-man panel to advise him. ...a two-man tent.* COMB in ADJ: ADJ n =-person

manacle /mænəkəl/ **manacles, manacling, manacled**

1 Manacles are metal devices attached to a prisoner's wrists or legs in order to prevent him or her from moving or escaping. N-COUNT: usu pl

2 If a prisoner **is manacled**, their wrists or legs are put in manacles in order to prevent them from moving or escaping. *His hands were manacled behind his back... He was manacled by the police.* VB: usu passive *be* V-ed prep/adv *be* V-ed

manage /mænɪdʒ/ **manages, managing, managed** ◆◆◆◆◇

1 If you **manage** an organization, business, or system, or the people who work in it, you are responsible for controlling them. *Within two years he was managing the store... Most factories in the area are obsolete and badly managed... There is a lack of confidence in the government's ability to manage the economy... Professors are notoriously difficult to manage.* VERB =run V n

2 If you **manage** time, money, or other resources, you deal with them carefully and do not waste them. *In a busy world, managing your time is increasingly important... Josh expects me to manage all the household expenses on very little.* VERB V n

3 If you **manage** to do something, especially something difficult, you succeed in doing it. *Somehow, he'd managed to persuade Kay to buy one for him... I managed to pull myself up onto a wet, sloping ledge... Over the past 12 months the company has managed a 10 per cent improvement.* VERB V to-inf V n

4 If you **manage**, you succeed in coping with a difficult situation. *She had managed perfectly well without medication for three years... I am managing, but I could not possibly give up work... How did your mother manage when your father left?* VERB =cope V

5 If you say that you can **manage** an amount of time or money for something, you mean that you can afford to spend that time or money on it. *This makes it ideal for those who can only manage a few hours in the morning or evening... 'All right, I can manage a fiver,' McMinn said with reluctance.* VERB =spare V n

6 If you say that someone **managed** a particular response, such as a laugh or a greeting, you mean that it was difficult for them to do it because they were feeling sad or upset. *He looked dazed as he spoke to reporters, managing only a weak smile... He managed a few sentences about his visit to the prison... Now is the time to forge ahead with all the enthusiasm and optimism that you can manage.* VERB V n

7 You say **'I can manage'** or **'I'll manage'** as a way of refusing someone's offer of help and insisting on doing something by yourself. *I know you mean well, but I can manage by myself... 'I'll do it, Eleanor,' Angus said, quickly jumping up. But this time she only shook her head. 'I'll manage,' she said firmly.* CONVENTION PRAGMATICS

manageable /mænɪdʒəbəl/. Something that is **manageable** is of a size, quantity, or level of difficulty that people are able to deal with. *He will now try to cut down the task to a manageable size... The present flow of refugees was manageable... Keep your spending on luxuries down to manageable proportions.* ◆◇◇◇◇ ADJ-GRADED

management /mænɪdʒmənt/ **managements** ◆◆◆◆◇

1 Management is the control and organizing of a business or other organization. *The zoo needed better management rather than more money... The dispute is about wages, working conditions and the management of the mining industry. ...the responsibility for its day to day management. ...having just completed a management studies course.* N-UNCOUNT

2 You can refer to the people who control and organize a business or other organization as the **management**. *The management is doing its best to improve the situation... We need to get more women into top management... A change of management would help.* N-VAR-COLL

3 Management is the way people control different parts of their lives. *...her management of her professional life. ...intelligent money management, for example paying big bills monthly where possible. ...the secret of time management.* N-UNCOUNT: usu with supp

manager /mænɪdʒər/ **managers** ◆◆◆◆◇

1 A **manager** is a person who is responsible for running part of or the whole of a business organization. *The chef, staff and managers are all Chinese. ...Linda Emery, marketing manager for Wall's sausages. ...a retired bank manager.* N-COUNT

2 The **manager** of a pop star or other entertainer is the person who looks after their business interests. N-COUNT

3 The **manager** of a sports team is the person responsible for training the players and organizing the way they play. N-COUNT

manageress /mænɪdʒəres/ **manageresses.** N-COUNT The **manageress** of a shop, restaurant, or other small business is the woman who is responsible for running it. Some women object to this word and prefer to be called a 'manager'. *...the manageress of a betting shop. ...a widowed restaurant manageress.*

managerial /mænɪdʒɪəriəl/. **Managerial** means ◆◇◇◇◇ relating to the work of a manager. ADJ: usu ADJ n *...his managerial skills. ...a managerial career... Some see themselves as the provider of ideas, while others view their role as essentially managerial.*

managing director, managing directors. ◆◆◇◇◇ N-COUNT The **managing director** of a company is the most important working director, and is in charge of the way the company is managed; used mainly in British English.

mandarin /mændərɪn/ **mandarins** ◆◇◇◇◇

1 British journalists sometimes use **mandarin** to N-COUNT: usu supp N refer to someone who has an important job in the Civil Service. *...Foreign Office mandarins. ...the latest evidence of the mandarins' power over their ministers.*

2 Mandarin is the official language of China. N-UNCOUNT

3 A **mandarin** or a **mandarin orange** is a small orange which is easy to peel. N-COUNT

4 A **mandarin** was, in former times, an important government official in China. N-COUNT

mandate /mændeɪt/ **mandates, mandating, mandated** ◆◆◇◇◇

1 If a government or other elected body has a **mandate** to carry out a particular policy or task, they have the authority to carry it out as a result of winning an election or vote. N-COUNT: oft N for n, N to-inf *The President and his supporters are almost certain to read this vote as a mandate for continued economic reform... The union already has a mandate from its conference to ballot for a strike.*

2 If someone is given a **mandate** to carry out a particular policy or task, they are given the official authority to do it or are instructed to do it. N-COUNT: oft N to-inf *How much longer does the independent prosecutor have a mandate to pursue this investigation?... A mandate from the UN would be needed before any plans could be implemented.*

3 You can refer to the fixed length of time that a country's leader or government remains in office as their **mandate**; a formal use. N-COUNT: usu with poss *...his intention to leave politics once his mandate ends.*

4 When someone **is mandated** to carry out a particular policy or task, they are given the official authority to do it or are instructed to do it. VB: usu passive, be V-ed to-inf, be V-ed *He'd now been mandated by the West African Economic Community to go in and to enforce a ceasefire... The elections are mandated by a peace accord signed by the government last May.*

5 In American English, to **mandate** something means to make it mandatory. VERB, V n, V that, V-ed *The proposed initiative would mandate a reduction of carbon dioxide of 40%... Sixteen years ago, Quebec mandated that all immigrants send their children to French schools. ...constitutionally mandated civil rights.*

mandatory /mændətri AM -tɔːri/ ◆◇◇◇◇

1 If an action or procedure is **mandatory**, people have to do it, because it is a rule or a law; a formal use. ADJ =obligatory *...the mandatory retirement age of 65... Attendance is mandatory.*

2 If a crime carries a **mandatory** punishment, that punishment is fixed by law for all cases, in contrast to crimes for which the judge or magistrate has to decide the punishment for each particular case; a formal use. ADJ ≠discretionary *...the mandatory life sentence for murder. ...the four-year ban which is mandatory.*

mandible /mændɪbəl/ **mandibles.** A **mandible** is N-COUNT a jawbone; a technical term in anatomy.

mandolin /mændəlɪn, -lɪn/ **mandolins.** A **mandolin** is a musical instrument that looks like a small guitar and has four pairs of strings. N-VAR: oft the N

mane /meɪn/ **manes** ◆◇◇◇◇

1 The **mane** on a horse or lion is the long thick hair that grows from its neck. N-COUNT

2 If you refer to a person's hair as their **mane**, you N-COUNT mean that they have a lot of hair; a literary use. *He had a great mane of white hair.*

man-eating. A **man-eating** animal is one that ADJ: ADJ n has killed and eaten human beings, or that people think might do so. *...lakes that contain man-eating sharks. ...man-eating lions.*

maneuver /mənuːvər/. See **manoeuvre.**

manfully /mænfəli/. If you say that someone, especially a man, does something **manfully**, you mean that they do it in a very determined or brave way. ADV-GRADED: ADV with v *They stuck to their task manfully. ...simple people who manfully bear the deprivations that are their lot.*

manganese /mæŋgəniːz/. **Manganese** is a N-UNCOUNT greyish-white metal that is used in making steel.

manger /meɪndʒər/ **mangers.** A **manger** is a low N-COUNT open container which cows, horses, and other animals feed from in a stable or barn; an old-fashioned word.

mangle /mæŋgəl/ **mangles, mangling, mangled** ◆◇◇◇◇

1 If a physical object **is mangled**, it is crushed or twisted very forcefully, so that it is difficult to see what its original shape was. VB: usu passive, be V-ed, V-ed *His body was crushed and mangled beyond recognition. ...the mangled wreckage.*

2 If you say that someone **mangles** words or information, you are criticizing them for not speaking or writing clearly or correctly. VERB PRAGMATICS V n *There is almost no phrase so simple that he cannot mangle it... They don't know what they're talking about and mangle scientific information.*

3 A **mangle** is an old-fashioned device for removing water from wet clothes after washing them. N-COUNT You put the clothes between two wooden rollers and turn a handle, and the water is squeezed out.

mango /mæŋgoʊ/ **mangoes** or **mangos.** A ◆◇◇◇◇ N-VAR **mango** is a large sweet yellowish fruit which grows on a tree in hot countries. *Peel, stone and dice the mango. ...mango chutney.* ► A **mango** is the tree that this fruit grows on. N-COUNT: oft N n *...orchards of lime and mango trees.*

mangrove /mæŋgroʊv/ **mangroves.** A **mangrove** or **mangrove tree** is a tree with roots which are above the ground and that grows along coasts or on the banks of large rivers in hot countries. N-COUNT: oft N n *...mangrove swamps.*

mangy /meɪndʒi/ **mangier, mangiest.** A **mangy** animal looks dirty, uncared for or ill. ADJ-GRADED: usu ADJ n *...mangy old dogs.*

manhandle /mænhændəl/ **manhandles, manhandling, manhandled**

1 If someone **is manhandled**, they are physically held or pushed, for example when they are being taken somewhere. VERB, be V-ed, V n prep/adv, Also V n *Foreign journalists were manhandled by armed police, and told to leave... They manhandled the old man along the corridor.*

2 If you **manhandle** something big or heavy somewhere, you move it there by hand. VERB, V n prep/adv *The three of us manhandled the uncovered dinghy out of the shed.*

manhole /mænhoʊl/ **manholes.** A **manhole** is a N-COUNT large hole in a road or path, usually covered by a metal plate that can be removed. Workers climb through manholes when they want to inspect or clean drains or sewers.

manhood /mænhʊd/ ◆◇◇◇◇

1 Manhood is the state of being a man rather than a boy. N-UNCOUNT *They were failing lamentably to help their sons grow from boyhood to manhood.*

2 Manhood is the period of a man's life during which he is a man rather than a boy. N-UNCOUNT *His handwriting, from earliest young manhood, was flowing and graceful.*

3 If you refer to **American manhood** or **French manhood** for example, you are referring to American men or French men considered as a group. N-UNCOUNT: supp N *Italian manhood was appalled.*

man-hour, man-hours; also spelled **man hour.** N-COUNT: usu pl A **man-hour** is the average amount of work that one person can do in an hour. **Man-hours** are used to estimate how long jobs take, or how many people are needed to do a job in a particular time. Some people disapprove of this expression because it seems to exclude women. *The restoration took almost 4,000 man-hours over four years. ...when output per man-hour is raised.*

manhunt /mænhʌnt/ **manhunts.** A **manhunt** is a major search for someone who has escaped or disappeared. [N-COUNT: oft N for n]

mania /meɪniə/ **manias** ◆◇◇◇◇

1 If you say that a person or group has a **mania** for something, you mean that they enjoy it very much or devote a lot of time to it. *It seemed to some observers that the English had a mania for travelling... The media have a mania about rugby union... The end of the year has seen an increase in Mozart mania.* [N-COUNT: usu sing, oft N for n/-ing, n N]

2 **Mania** is a mental illness which causes the sufferer to become very worried or concerned about something. *...the treatment of mania... He almost wouldn't eat at all and had the oddest manias.* [N-UNCOUNT: also N in pl]

maniac /meɪniæk/ **maniacs** ◆◇◇◇◇

1 A **maniac** is a mad person who is violent and dangerous. *The cabin looked as if a maniac had been let loose there. ...a drug-crazed maniac.* [N-COUNT =madman]

2 If you describe someone's behaviour as **maniac**, you are emphasizing that it is extremely foolish and reckless. *A maniac driver sped 35 miles along the wrong side of a motorway at 110 mph. ...a maniac cyclist.* [ADJ: ADJ n PRAGMATICS =lunatic]

3 If you call someone, for example, a religious **maniac** or a sports **maniac**, you are critical of them because they have an unnaturally strong and obsessive interest in religion or sport. *My mum is turning into a religious maniac. ...football maniacs.* [N-COUNT: supp N =freak]

maniacal /mənaɪəkəl/. If you describe someone's behaviour as **maniacal**, you mean that it is extreme, violent, or very determined, as if the person were insane. *He was almost maniacal in his pursuit of sporting records... She is hunched forward over the wheel with a maniacal expression.* [ADJ PRAGMATICS] ♦ **maniacally** /mənaɪəkli/ *He was last seen striding maniacally to the hotel reception. ...maniacally abrasive guitar pop.* [ADV: usu ADV with v, also ADV adj]

manic /mænɪk/ ◆◇◇◇◇

1 If you describe someone as **manic**, you mean that they do things extremely quickly or energetically, often because they are very excited or anxious about something. *He was really manic... Possessed by an almost manic energy, he seemed to be everywhere, inspiring and bullying his troops forward.* [ADJ-GRADED] ♦ **manically** /mænɪkli/ *We cleaned the house manically over the weekend... Hers is a manically full life.* [ADV: usu ADV with v, also ADV adj]

2 If you describe someone's smile, laughter, or sense of humour as **manic**, you mean that it seems excessive or strange, as if they were insane. *...a manic grin.* [ADJ-GRADED]

manic-depressive, manic-depressives; also spelled **manic depressive**. If someone is **manic-depressive**, they have a medical condition in which they sometimes feel excited and confident and at other times very depressed. *She told them that her daughter-in-law was manic-depressive... Manic depressive illness affects men and women equally.* [ADJ] ► A **manic-depressive** is someone who is manic-depressive. *Her mother is a manic depressive.* [N-COUNT]

manicure /mænɪkjʊəʳ/ **manicures, manicuring, manicured.** ◆◇◇◇◇ If you **manicure** your hands or nails, you care for them by softening your skin and cutting and polishing your nails. *He was surprised to see how carefully she had manicured her broad hands.* [VERB: V n] ► Also a noun. *I have a manicure occasionally.* [N-COUNT]

manicured /mænɪkjʊəʳd/. A **manicured** garden or lawn has very short neatly cut grass; used mainly in written English. *She stared out at the impeccably manicured garden. ...the manicured lawns of Government House.* [ADJ: oft adv ADJ]

manicurist /mænɪkjʊərɪst/ **manicurists.** A **manicurist** is a person whose job is manicuring people's hands and nails. [N-COUNT]

manifest /mænɪfest/ **manifests, manifesting, manifested** ◆◆◇◇◇

1 If you say that something is **manifest**, you mean that it is clearly true and that nobody would disagree with it if they saw it or considered it; a formal use. *...the manifest failure of the policies... There may be unrecognised cases of manifest injustice of which we are unaware.* [ADJ-GRADED: usu ADJ n =patent] ♦ **manifestly** *She manifestly failed to last the mile and a half of the race. ...the manifestly obvious health and social advantages of chastity.* [ADV-GRADED: ADV with v, ADV with cl/group =patently]

2 If you **manifest** a particular quality, feeling, or illness, or if it **manifests** itself, it becomes visible or obvious; a formal use. *He manifested a pleasing personality on stage... The virus needs two weeks to manifest itself. ...and so their frustration and anger will manifest itself in crying and screaming... He's only convincing when that inner fury manifests itself.* [V-ERG =show; V n; V pron-refl; V pron-refl in n/-ing; V] ► Also an adjective. *The same alarm is manifest everywhere... Some of her social aspirations were made manifest.* [ADJ-GRADED: usu v-link ADJ]

manifestation /mænɪfesteɪʃən/ **manifestations.** ◆◇◇◇◇ A **manifestation** of something is one of the different ways in which it can appear; a formal word. *Different animals in the colony had different manifestations of the disease... New York is the ultimate manifestation of American values.* [N-COUNT: with supp, oft N of n]

manifesto /mænɪfestoʊ/ **manifestos** or **manifestoes.** ◆◆◇◇◇ A **manifesto** is a statement published by a person or group of people, especially a political party, in which they say what their aims and policies are. *The Tories are currently drawing up their election manifesto... His manifesto promised measures to protect them.* [N-COUNT: usu sing, usu with poss]

manifold /mænɪfoʊld/. Things that are **manifold** are of many different kinds; a literary word. *Gaelic can be heard here in manifold forms... The difficulties are manifold.* [ADJ-GRADED]

manila /mənɪlə/; also spelled **manilla**. A **manila** envelope or folder is made from a strong paper that is usually light brown. [ADJ: ADJ n]

manipulate /mənɪpjʊleɪt/ **manipulates, manipulating, manipulated** ◆◆◇◇◇

1 If you say that someone **manipulates** people, you disapprove of them because they skilfully force or persuade people to do what they want. *He is a very difficult character. He manipulates people... She's always borrowing my clothes and manipulating me to give her vast sums of money... They'll have kids who are two, three, who are manipulating them into buying toys.* [VERB PRAGMATICS; V n; V n to-inf; V n into -ing] ♦ **manipulation** /mənɪpjʊleɪʃən/ **manipulations** *...repeated criticism or manipulation of our mind... I don't like manipulations or lies.* [N-VAR]

2 If you say that someone **manipulates** an event or situation, you disapprove of them because they use or control it for their own benefit, or cause it to develop in the way they want. *She was unable, for once, to control and manipulate events... They felt he had been cowardly in manipulating the system to avoid the draft.* [VERB PRAGMATICS =manoeuvre; V n] ♦ **manipulation, manipulations** *...accusations of political manipulation.* [N-VAR]

3 If you **manipulate** something that requires skill, such as a complicated piece of equipment or a difficult idea, you operate it or process it. *The technology uses a pen to manipulate a computer... The puppets are expertly manipulated by Liz Walker... His mind moves in quantum leaps, manipulating ideas and jumping on to new ones as soon as he can.* [VERB; V n] ♦ **manipulation, manipulations** *...science that requires only the simplest of mathematical manipulations.* [N-VAR]

4 If someone **manipulates** your bones or muscles, they skilfully move and press them with their hands in order to remove tension or push the bones into their correct position. *The way he can manipulate my leg has helped my arthritis so much.* [VERB; V n] ♦ **manipulation, manipulations** *A permanent cure will only be effected by acupuncture, chiropractic or manipulation.* [N-VAR]

manipulative /mənɪpjʊlətɪv/. If you describe someone as **manipulative**, you disapprove of [ADJ-GRADED PRAGMATICS] ◆◇◇◇◇

them because they skilfully force or persuade people to act in the way that they want. *He described Mr Long as cold, calculating and manipulative... The worker was promoted despite aggressive and manipulative behaviour.*

manipulator /mənɪpjʊleɪtəʳ/ **manipulators.** If you describe someone as a **manipulator**, you mean that they skilfully control events, situations, or people, often in a way that other people disapprove of. *Jean Brodie is a manipulator. She cons everybody. ...some of the best PR manipulators in the business.* N-COUNT

mankind /mænkaɪnd/. You can refer to all human beings as **mankind** when considering them as a group. Some people dislike this use. *...the evolution of mankind.* ◆◇◇◇◇ N-UNCOUNT =humankind

manly /mænli/ **manlier, manliest.** If you describe a man's behaviour or appearance as **manly**, you approve of it because it shows qualities that are considered typical of a man, such as strength or courage. *He set himself manly tasks and expected others to follow his example... He was the ideal of manly beauty.* ♦ **manliness** *He has no doubts about his manliness.* ◆◇◇◇◇ ADJ-GRADED: usu ADJ n PRAGMATICS =masculine; N-UNCOUNT: poss N

man-made. **Man-made** things are created or caused by people, rather than occurring naturally. *Man-made and natural disasters have disrupted the Government's economic plans. ...man-made lakes. ...a variety of materials, both natural and man-made.* ◆◇◇◇◇ ADJ ≠natural

manna /mænə/. If you say that something unexpected is **manna from heaven** or **manna**, you mean that it is good and happened just at the time that it was needed. *Ex-forces personnel could be the manna from heaven employers are seeking... The revealed documents were manna for journalists.* PHRASE: oft v-link PHR

manned /mænd/. A **manned** vehicle such as a spacecraft has people in it who are operating its controls. *In thirty years from now the United States should have a manned spacecraft on Mars. ...the history of manned flight. ...manned exploration of the solar system.* ● See also **man**. ADJ ≠unmanned

mannequin /mænɪkɪn/ **mannequins**

1 A **mannequin** is a life-sized model of a person which is used to display clothes, hats, or shoes, especially in shop windows; an old-fashioned use. N-COUNT

2 A **mannequin** is a person who displays clothes, hats, or shoes by wearing them, especially in fashion shows or in fashion photographs; an old-fashioned use. N-COUNT =model

manner /mænəʳ/ **manners** ◆◆◆◇◇

1 The **manner** in which you do something is the way that you do it. *She smiled again in a friendly manner... I'm a professional and I have to conduct myself in a professional manner... The manner in which young children are spoken to varies depending on who is present.* N-SING: with supp =way

2 If something is done in the **manner** of something else, it is done in the style of that thing. *It's a satire somewhat in the manner of Dickens... We kissed each other's cheeks in the European manner.* N-SING: with supp =style

3 Someone's **manner** is the way in which they behave and talk when they are with other people, for example whether they are polite, confident, or bad-tempered. *His manner was self-assured and brusque... Her manner offstage, like her manner on, is somewhat surly.* ♦ **-mannered** *Forrest was normally mild-mannered, affable, and untalkative... The British are considered ill-mannered, badly dressed and unsophisticated.* N-SING: usu poss N; COMB in ADJ-GRADED

4 If someone has **good manners**, they are polite and observe social customs. If someone has **bad manners**, they are impolite and do not observe these customs. *He dressed well and had impeccable manners... The manners of many doctors were appalling... They taught him his manners.* N-PLURAL

5 See also **bedside manner, table manners.**

6 If you refer to **all manner of** objects or people, you are talking about objects or people of many different kinds. *Mr Winchester is impressively knowledgeable about all manner of things. ...her pictures of all manner of wildlife.* PHRASES PHR n

7 You say **in a manner of speaking** to indicate that what you have just said is not absolutely or literally true, but is true in a general way. *An attorney is your employee, in a manner of speaking... 'You said she was a poor widow lady' – 'In a manner of speaking she is,' Alison said.* PHR with cl PRAGMATICS =in a way

8 You use **what manner of** to suggest that the person or thing you are about to mention is of an unusual or unknown kind; a literary expression. *There was much curiosity about what manner of man he was... What manner of place is this?* PHR n

mannered /mænəʳd/ ◆◇◇◇◇

1 If you describe someone's behaviour or a work of art as **mannered**, you dislike it because it is elaborate or formal, and therefore seems false or artificial. *...Naomi's mannered voice... If you arrange your picture too systematically the results can look very mannered and artificial.* ADJ-GRADED: usu ADJ n PRAGMATICS

2 **Mannered** behaviour is polite and observes social customs. *...its intention to restore pride in the past and create a more mannered society... They are always perfectly polite and beautifully mannered.* ADJ-GRADED

mannerism /mænərɪzəm/ **mannerisms.** Someone's **mannerisms** are the gestures or ways of speaking which are very characteristic of them, and which they often use. *His mannerisms are more those of a preoccupied math professor... In accent and mannerism he appeared to be completely Eastern European.* N-COUNT

mannish /mænɪʃ/. If you describe a woman's appearance or behaviour as **mannish**, you mean it is more like a man's appearance or behaviour than a woman's. *She shook hands in a mannish way, her grip dry and firm. ...a mannish trouser suit.* ADJ-GRADED: usu ADJ n

manoeuvrable /mənuːvərəbᵊl/; spelled **maneuverable** in American English. Something that is **manoeuvrable** can be easily moved into different positions. *Ferries are very powerful and manoeuvrable compared to cargo ships. ...the light, manoeuvrable cart.* ADJ-GRADED

manoeuvre /mənuːvəʳ/ **manoeuvres, manoeuvring, manoeuvred;** spelled **maneuver** in American English. ◆◆◇◇◇

1 If you **manoeuvre** something into or out of an awkward position, you skilfully move it there. *We attempted to manoeuvre the canoe closer to him... I manoeuvred my way among the tables to the back corner of the place... The pilot instinctively maneuvered to avoid them.* ► Also a noun. *...a ship capable of high speed and rapid manoeuvre.* VERB V n adv/prep V way prep/adv V; N-VAR

2 If you **manoeuvre** a situation, you change it in a clever and skilful way so that you can benefit from it. *The authorities have to manoeuvre the markets into demanding a cut in interest rates... He brilliantly manoeuvred himself back to power... He manoeuvres to foster recovery.* ► Also a noun. *...manoeuvres to block the electoral process.* ♦ **manoeuvring, manoeuvrings** *...his unrivalled skill in political manoeuvring. ...his manoeuvrings on the matter of free trade.* VERB =manipulate V n prep/adv V; N-COUNT =ploy; N-VAR

3 Military **manoeuvres** are training exercises which involve the movement of soldiers and equipment over a large area. *Allied troops begin maneuvers tomorrow to show how quickly forces could be mobilized in case of a new invasion... The camp was used for military manoeuvres.* N-PLURAL =exercises

4 ● **room for manoeuvre**: see **room**.

manor /mænəʳ/ **manors** ◆◆◇◇◇

1 A **manor** is a large private house in the country, usually built in the Middle Ages, and the land and smaller buildings around it. *Thieves broke into the manor at night. ...Bawdsey Manor on the Suffolk coast.* N-COUNT: oft in names after n

2 In British English, some people, especially police officers, refer to the area where they work as their **manor**; an informal use. *The Chief Constable deeply resented any intrusions into his manor... Thank God they're not on my manor any more.* N-SING: usu poss N =patch, turf

manor house, manor houses. A **manor house** is the main house that is or was on a medieval manor. ♦◇◇◇◇ N-COUNT

manpower /mænpaʊəʳ/. Workers are sometimes referred to as **manpower** when they are being considered as a part of the process of producing goods or providing services. *...the shortage of skilled manpower in the industry... These people do not have the equipment or the manpower to cut down the trees.* ♦◇◇◇◇ N-UNCOUNT

manqué /mɒŋkeɪ, AM -keɪ/. You use **manqué** to describe someone who has never succeeded in becoming the kind of person mentioned, although they tried to or had the potential to. *...his inescapable feeling that he is a great actor manqué... He was, in a sense, an academic manqué.* ADJ: n ADJ

manse /mæns/ **manses.** In some Christian churches, a **manse** is the house provided for a clergyman to live in; used mainly in British English. *...a Baptist manse in Monmouth.* N-COUNT

manservant /mænsɜːʳvᵊnt/ **manservants.** In British English, a **manservant** is a man who works as a servant in a private house; an old-fashioned word. The American word is **houseman**. *They were waited on by a manservant.* N-COUNT

mansion /mænʃᵊn/ **mansions** ♦♦◇◇◇

1 A **mansion** is a very large house. *...an eighteenth century mansion in Hampshire... The very best properties, however, the colonial mansions and villas, were reserved for the government.* N-COUNT

2 In Britain, **Mansions** is often used in the names of blocks of flats. *...Delaware Mansions, a block of 167 flats opposite the BBC Radio studios.* N-IN-NAMES

manslaughter /mænslɔːtəʳ/. **Manslaughter** is the unlawful killing of a person by someone who did not intend to kill them; a legal term. *A judge accepted her plea that she was guilty of manslaughter, not murder.* ♦◇◇◇◇ N-UNCOUNT

mantel /mæntᵊl/ **mantels.** A **mantel** is a mantelpiece; an old-fashioned word. *On the mantel were photographs of a man and a woman.* N-COUNT

mantelpiece /mæntᵊlpiːs/ **mantelpieces;** also spelled **mantlepiece**. A **mantelpiece** is a wood or stone shelf which is the top part of a border round a fireplace. *On the mantelpiece are a pair of bronze Ming vases.* N-COUNT: usu sing =mantelshelf

mantelshelf /mæntᵊlʃelf/ **mantelshelves;** also spelled **mantleshelf**. A **mantelshelf** is a mantelpiece; an old-fashioned word. *Beneath this, on the mantelshelf, is displayed a collection of seventeenth-century tulip vases.* N-COUNT: usu sing =mantelpiece

mantle /mæntᵊl/ **mantles** ♦◇◇◇◇

1 If you take on the **mantle** of something such as a profession or an important job, you take on the responsibilities and duties which must be fulfilled by anyone who has this profession or job; used in written English. *Glasgow has broadened its appeal since taking on the mantle of European City of Culture in 1990... She has the intellectual form to take up the mantle of leadership.* N-SING: the N of n

2 A **mantle** of something is a layer of it covering a surface, for example a layer of snow on the ground; used in written English. *The parks and squares looked grim under a mantle of soot and ash.* N-COUNT: with supp =layer

3 A **mantle** is a piece of clothing without sleeves that people used to wear over their other clothes in former times. N-COUNT =cloak

4 See also **mantel**.

mantlepiece /mæntᵊlpiːs/. See **mantelpiece**.

man-to-man. See **man**.

mantra /mæntrə/ **mantras.** A **mantra** is a chant used by Buddhists and Hindus when they meditate, or to help them feel calm and deal with problems. ♦◇◇◇◇ N-COUNT

manual /mænjuəl/ **manuals** ♦♦◇◇◇

1 **Manual** work is work in which you use your hands or your physical strength rather than your mind. *...skilled manual workers... They have no reservations about taking factory or manual jobs.* ADJ: usu ADJ n =blue-collar

2 **Manual** is used to talk about movements which are made by someone's hands; a formal use. *...toys designed to help develop manual dexterity.* ADJ: ADJ n

3 **Manual** means operated by hand, rather than by electricity or a motor. *There is a manual pump to get rid of the water.* ♦ **manually** *The device is manually operated, using a simple handle.* ADJ: ADJ n; ADV: ADV with v

4 A **manual** is a book which tells you how to do something or how a piece of machinery works. *...the instruction manual.* N-COUNT

manufacture /mænjʊfæktʃəʳ/ **manufactures, manufacturing, manufactured** ♦♦♦◇◇

1 To **manufacture** something means to make it in a factory, usually in large quantities. *They manufacture the class of plastics known as thermoplastic materials... The first three models are being manufactured to ICL's specification at the factory in Ashton-under-Lyne... We import foreign manufactured goods.* ▶ Also a noun. *...the manufacture of nuclear weapons. ...celebrating 90 years of car manufacture.* ♦ **manufacturing** *...management headquarters for manufacturing in China. ...the manufacturing of a luxury type automobile.* VERB =produce V n V-ed; N-UNCOUNT: with supp; N-UNCOUNT =production

2 **Manufactures** are goods or products which have been made in a factory; a technical use in economics. *...a long-term rise in the share of manufactures in non-oil exports.* N-COUNT: usu pl =product

3 If you say that someone **manufactures** information, you are criticising them because they invent information that is not true. *According to the prosecution, the officers manufactured an elaborate story... He said the allegations were manufactured on the flimsiest evidence.* VERB PRAGMATICS =fabricate V n

manufacturer /mænjʊfæktʃərəʳ/ **manufacturers.** A **manufacturer** is a business or company which makes goods in large quantities to sell. *...the world's largest doll manufacturer.* ♦♦♦◇◇ N-COUNT: oft supp N

manure /mənjʊəʳ, AM -nʊr/ **manures. Manure** is animal faeces, sometimes mixed with chemicals, that is spread on the ground in order to make plants grow healthy and strong. *...bags of manure. ...organic manures.* ♦◇◇◇◇ N-MASS

manuscript /mænjʊskrɪpt/ **manuscripts** ♦♦◇◇◇

1 A **manuscript** is a handwritten or typed document, especially a writer's first version of a book before it is published. *He had seen a manuscript of the book. ...discovering an original manuscript of the song in Paris... I am grateful to him for letting me read his early chapters in manuscript.* N-COUNT: also in N

2 A **manuscript** is an old document that was written by hand on paper or parchment before printing was invented. *...early printed books and rare manuscripts.* N-COUNT

Manx /mæŋks/. **Manx** is used to describe people or things that belong to or concern the Isle of Man and the people who live there. ♦◇◇◇◇ ADJ

many /meni/ ♦♦♦♦♦

1 You use **many** to indicate that you are talking about a large number of people or things. *I don't think many people would argue with that... Not many films are made in Finland... Do you keep many books and papers and memorabilia?... Many holidaymakers had avoided the worst of the delays by consulting tourist offices... Acting is definitely a young person's profession in many ways.* ▶ Also a pronoun. *We stood up, thinking through the possibilities. There weren't many.* ▶ Also a quantifier. *So, once we have cohabited, why do many of us feel the need to get married?... It seems there are not very many of them left in the sea... In many of these neighborhoods a lot of people don't have telephones.* ▶ Also an adjective. *Among his many hobbies was the breeding of fine horses... The possibilities are many.* DET: DET pl-n, oft with brd-neg =a lot of ≠few; PRON ≠few; QUANT: QUANT of def-pl-n; ADJ-GRADED: det ADJ, v-link ADJ

2 You use **many** in expressions such as 'not many', 'not very many', and 'too many' when replying to questions about numbers of things or people. *'How many of the songs that dealt with this theme became hit songs?'—'Not very many.'... How many years is it since we've seen each other? Too many, anyway.* ADV-GRADED: ADV as reply

3 You use **many** followed by 'a' and a noun to emphasize that there are a lot of people or things involved in something. *Many a mother tries to act out her unrealized dreams through her daughter... I* PREDET PRAGMATICS

have spent many a morning with my wife gathering mussels along the rocky beaches of Little Compton.

4 You use **many** after 'how' to ask questions about numbers or quantities. You use **many** after 'how' in reported clauses to talk about numbers or quantities. *How many years have you been here?... No-one knows how many people have been killed since the war began.* ▶ Also a pronoun. *How many do you smoke a day?* [DET: *how* DET pl-n] [PRON: *how* PRON]

5 You use **many** with 'as' when you are comparing numbers of things or people. *I've always entered as many photo competitions as I can... We produced ten times as many tractors as the United States.* ▶ Also a pronoun. *Let the child try on as many as she likes.* [DET: *as* DET pl-n, usu *as* DET pl-n *as* cl/group] [PRON: *as* PRON]

6 You use **many** to mean 'many people'. *Not many expected Ferdinand to be such a success this season... Iris Murdoch is regarded by many as a supremely good and serious writer.* [PRON]

7 **The many** means a large group of people considered as separate from a small minority, especially because they share a particular quality or disadvantage that the minority do not have. *The printing press gave power to a few to change the world for the many... He wanted to create a society of opportunity where benefits became available to the many.* [PRON: *the* PRON]

8 You use **as many as** before a number to suggest that it is surprisingly large. *New York City police say that as many as four and a half million people watched today's parade.* [PHRASES] [PHR num] [PRAGMATICS]

9 You use **a good many** or **a great many** to emphasize that you are referring to a large number of things or people. *We've both had a good many beers... For a great many men and women, romance can be a most important part of marriage.* [PHR pl-n] [PRAGMATICS]

10 ● **many happy returns**: see **return**. ● **in so many words**: see **word**.

Maori /maʊri/ **Maoris**

1 **Maori** means belonging to or relating to the race of people descended from those who lived in New Zealand and the Cook Islands before the European settlers arrived. *In New Zealand, the Maori people maintain a strong cultural tradition. ...Maori values.* [ADJ]

2 The **Maori** or the **Maoris** are people who are Maori. [N-COUNT]

map /mæp/ **maps, mapping, mapped** [◆◆◆◇◇]

1 A **map** is a drawing of a particular area such as a city, a country, or a continent, showing its main features as they would appear if you looked at them from above. *He unfolded the map and set it on the floor... Have you got a map of the city centre?* [N-COUNT: oft N *of* n]

2 A **map** is a drawing that gives special information about an area. *...geological maps, books and atlases. ...weather maps on television.* [N-COUNT: usu supp N =chart]

3 To **map** an area means to make a map of it. *...a spacecraft which is using radar to map the surface of Venus. ...better mapping of the ocean floor.* [VERB =chart] [V n] [V-ing]

4 If you say that someone or something **put** a person, thing, or place **on the map**, you approve of the fact that they made it become well-known and important. *...the attempts of the Edinburgh Festival's organisers to put C.P. Taylor firmly on the map... This could put cider back on the map as one of our great national drinks.* [PHRASE: V inflects] [PRAGMATICS]

map out. If you **map out** something that you are intending to do, you work out in detail how you will do it. *I went home and mapped out my strategy... I cannot conceive of anybody writing a play by sitting down and mapping it out... This whole plan has been most carefully mapped out.* [PHRASAL VERB] [V P n (not pron)] [V n P] [*be* V-ed P]

maple /meɪpəl/ **maples.** A **maple** or a **maple tree** is a tree with five-pointed leaves which turn bright red or gold in autumn. ▶ **Maple** is the wood of this tree. *It's made of maple. ...a solid maple worktop.* [◆◇◇◇◇] [N-VAR] [N-UNCOUNT]

maple syrup. **Maple syrup** is a sweet, sticky, brown liquid made from the sap of maple trees, that can be eaten with pancakes or used to make puddings. [N-UNCOUNT]

mar /mɑːr/ **mars, marring, marred.** To **mar** something means to spoil or damage it. *A number of problems marred the smooth running of this event... That election was marred by massive cheating.* [◆◆◇◇◇] [VERB =ruin] [V n]

Mar. **Mar.** is a written abbreviation for **March.** [◆◆◇◇◇]

marathon /mærəθən, AM -θɒn/ **marathons** [◆◆◇◇◇]

1 A **marathon** is a race in which people run a distance of 26 miles (about 42 km). *...running in his first marathon... Rodgers can also claim four victories in the New York Marathon.* ▶ **The marathon** is the sport of running marathon races. *...when I took up the marathon.* [N-COUNT] [N-SING: *the* N]

2 If you use **marathon** to describe an event or task, you are emphasizing that it takes a long time and is very tiring. *People make marathon journeys to buy glass here. ...a marathon session of talks with government representatives. ...the medical team which successfully carried out the marathon operation.* [ADJ: ADJ n] [PRAGMATICS]

marauder /mərɔːdər/ **marauders.** If you describe a group of people or animals as **marauders**, you mean they are unpleasant and dangerous, because they wander around looking for opportunities to steal or kill; a literary word. *Numb with terror, she stared at the departing marauders... They were raided by roaming bands of marauders.* [N-COUNT]

marauding /mərɔːdɪŋ/. If you talk about **marauding** groups of people or animals, you mean they are unpleasant and dangerous, because they wander around looking for opportunities to steal or kill; a literary word. *Marauding gangs of armed men have been looting food relief supplies. ...safe from danger, such as marauding wild animals.* [ADJ: ADJ n]

marble /mɑːrbəl/ **marbles** [◆◆◇◇◇]

1 **Marble** is a type of very hard rock which feels cold when you touch it and which shines when it is cut and polished. Statues and parts of buildings are sometimes made of marble. *The house has a superb staircase made from oak and marble... The entrance-hall was paved with black and white marble tiles... He collected classical marble busts of Caesar.* [N-UNCOUNT: oft N n]

2 **Marbles** are sculptures made of marble; a technical use in art. *...marbles and bronzes from the Golden Age of Athens.* [N-COUNT: usu pl]

3 **Marbles** is a children's game played with small balls, usually made of coloured glass. You roll a ball along the ground and try to hit an opponent's ball with it. *On the far side of the street, two boys were playing marbles.* [N-UNCOUNT]

4 A **marble** is one of the small balls used in the game of marbles. [N-COUNT]

5 If you say that someone **has lost** their **marbles**, you mean that their ideas or behaviour are very strange, as if they have become insane; an informal expression. *I'll tell it to you, although you'll probably think I've lost my marbles.* [PHRASE: V inflects =go mad]

marbled /mɑːrbəld/. Something that is **marbled** has a pattern or colouring like that of marble. *...green marbled soap... If the meat is marbled with fat it should be tender.* [ADJ: usu ADJ n, also v-link ADJ *with/in* n]

march /mɑːrtʃ/ **marches, marching, marched** [◆◆◆◇◇]

1 When soldiers **march** somewhere, or when a commanding officer **marches** them somewhere, they walk there with very regular steps, as a group. *A Scottish battalion was marching down the street... Captain Ramirez called them to attention and marched them off to the main camp... We marched fifteen miles to Yadkin River... The ice was not thick enough to bear the weight of marching men.* ▶ Also a noun. *After a short march, the column entered the village.* ● **A day's march** is the distance that a group of soldiers can march in one day. *The Colonel and his forces were camped on the plain of Tuna, a day's march north of Phari.* ● If a group of soldiers are **on the march**, they are marching somewhere. *Tarleton's men had been on the march for much of the night.* [V-ERG] [V prep/adv] [V n adv/prep] [V amount/n] [V-ing] [Also V] [N-COUNT] [PHRASE: usu PHR prep/adv] [PHRASE: oft v-link PHR]

2 When a large group of people **march** for a cause, they walk somewhere together in order to express their ideas or to protest about something. *The demonstrators then marched through the capital chanting slogans and demanding free elections...* [VERB] [V prep/adv] [Also V]

Hundreds of activists marked the holy day by marching for peace and disarmament. ▶ Also a noun. *Organisers expect up to 300,000 protesters to join the march.* N-COUNT ♦ **marcher, marchers** *Fights between police and marchers lasted for three hours.* N-COUNT

3 If you say that someone **marches** somewhere, you mean that they walk there quickly and in a determined way, for example because you are angry. *He marched into the kitchen without knocking.* VERB V prep/adv

4 If you **march** someone somewhere, you force them to walk there with you, for example by holding their arm tightly. *They were marched through a crocodile-infested area and, if they slowed down, were beaten with sticks... I marched him across the room, down the hall and out onto the doorstep.* VERB be V-ed prep/adv V n prep/adv

5 The **march** of something is its steady development or progress. *It is easy to feel trampled by the relentless march of technology... Society's march toward ever-increasing materialism was continuing.* N-SING: usu the N of n

6 A **march** is a piece of music with a regular rhythm that you can march to. *A military band played Russian marches and folk tunes.* N-COUNT: usu with supp

7 If you give someone their **marching orders**, you tell them that you no longer want or need them, for example as your employee or as your lover. *They've had their marching orders... What does it take for a woman to say 'that's enough' and give her man his marching orders?* PHRASES PHR after v

8 If you **steal a march** on someone, you start doing something before they do it in order to gain an advantage over them. *If its strategy succeeds, Mexico could even steal a march on its northern neighbour.* V inflects, oft PHR on n

March, Marches. March is the third month of the year in the Western calendar. *I flew to Milan in early March... She was born in Austria on March 6, 1920... The election could be held as early as next March.* ◆◆◆◆◇ N-VAR

marchioness /mɑːʳʃənes/ **marchionesses.** A **marchioness** is the wife or widow of a marquis, or a woman with the same rank as a marquis. N-COUNT; N-TITLE

march-past, march-pasts; also spelled **march past**. When soldiers take part in a **march-past**, they march in front of an important person as part of a ceremonial occasion. N-COUNT

mare /meəʳ/ **mares.** A **mare** is an adult female horse. ◆◆◇◇◇ N-COUNT

margarine /mɑːʳdʒəriːn, AM -rɪn/ **margarines. Margarine** is a yellow substance made from vegetable oil and animal fats that is similar to butter. You spread it on bread or use it for cooking. ◆◇◇◇◇ N-MASS

marge /mɑːʳdʒ/; also spelled **marg. Marge** is the same as margarine; an informal word. N-UNCOUNT

margin /mɑːʳdʒɪn/ **margins** ◆◆◆◇◇

1 A **margin** is the difference between two amounts, especially the difference in the number of votes or points between the winner and the loser in an election or other contest. *They could end up with a 50-point winning margin... The Sunday Times remains the brand leader by a huge margin... The margin in favor was 280-to-153.* N-COUNT: with supp

2 The **margin** of a written or printed page is the blank space at the side of the page. *She added her comments in the margin.* N-COUNT

3 If there is a **margin** for something in a situation, there is some freedom to choose what to do or decide how to do it. *The money is collected in a straightforward way with little margin for error... These charges can carry prison terms of up to five years, though there's a wide margin of discretion... Out in front, Clarke had built up such a sizeable safety margin that he eased the pace and started cruising.* N-VAR: with supp =scope, leeway

4 The **margin** of a place or area is the extreme edge of it. *...the low coastal plain along the western margin... These islands are on the margins of human habitation.* N-COUNT: with supp =edge, periphery

5 If you say that a person or thing is on the **margins** of a group, an idea, or a situation, you mean that the person or thing is among the least typical, least important, or least powerful parts of it. *Students have played an important role in the past, but for the moment, they're on the margins. ...signs of the party's rapid retreat to the political margins.* N-PLURAL: with supp =fringes

6 See also **profit margin.**

marginal /mɑːʳdʒɪnəl/ **marginals** ◆◆◇◇◇

1 If you describe something as **marginal**, you mean that it is small or not very important. *This is a marginal improvement on October... The role of the Communist Party proved marginal.* ADJ-GRADED

2 If you describe people as **marginal**, you mean that they are not involved in the main events or developments in society because they are poor or have no power. *The tribunals were established for the well-integrated members of society and not for marginal individuals... I don't want to call him marginal, but he's not a major character.* ADJ-GRADED ≠mainstream

3 In political elections, a **marginal** seat or constituency is one which is usually won or lost by a few votes, and is therefore of great interest to politicians and journalists. *...the views of voters in five marginal seats. ...marginal constituencies.* ADJ-GRADED: usu ADJ n ▶ A **marginal** is a marginal seat; used mainly in British English. *The votes in the marginals are those that really count... These are the key marginals which Labour must win.* N-COUNT

4 **Marginal** activities, costs, or taxes are not the main part of a business or an economic system, but often make the difference between its success or failure, and are therefore important to control; a technical term in economics. *The analysts applaud the cuts in marginal businesses, but insist the company must make deeper sacrifices... For low-paid workers, the marginal tax rate is at least 75%.* ADJ: usu ADJ n

5 **Marginal** land is not very fertile, and therefore not suitable for growing crops or grazing animals; a technical term. *The poor are forced to farm in more marginal lands higher up the mountains. ...helping farmers, so they do not have to exploit marginal lands.* ADJ-GRADED: ADJ n

marginalize /mɑːʳdʒɪnəlaɪz/ **marginalizes, marginalizing, marginalized;** also spelled **marginalise** in British English. To **marginalize** a group of people means to make them feel isolated and unimportant. *The effect of this has been to increasingly marginalize the local authority sector... We've always been marginalized, exploited, and constantly threatened.* ◆◇◇◇◇ VERB =isolate V n ♦ **marginalization** *He spoke of his fears of the marginalization of Africa.* N-UNCOUNT: usu N of n

marginally /mɑːʳdʒɪnəli/. **Marginally** means to only a small extent. *Sales last year were marginally higher than in 1991... The Christian Democrats did marginally worse than expected... These cameras have increased only marginally in value over the past decade.* ◆◇◇◇◇ ADV: ADV adv/adj/prep, ADV with v =slightly

marigold /mærɪgoʊld/ **marigolds.** A **marigold** is a type of yellow or orange flower. ◆◇◇◇◇ N-VAR

marijuana /mærɪwɑːnə/. **Marijuana** is a drug which is made from the dried leaves and flowers of the hemp plant, and which can be smoked in cigarettes. ◆◇◇◇◇ N-UNCOUNT =cannabis

marina /məriːnə/ **marinas.** A **marina** is a small harbour for yachts and other small boats. ◆◇◇◇◇ N-COUNT

marinade /mærɪneɪd/ **marinades, marinading, marinaded** ◆◇◇◇◇

1 A **marinade** is a sauce of oil, vinegar, spices, and herbs, which you pour over meat or fish before you cook it, in order to add flavour, or to make the meat or fish softer. N-COUNT

2 To **marinade** means the same as to **marinate**. *Marinade the chicken breasts in the tandoori paste... Leave to marinade for 24 hours.* V-ERG V n V

marinate /mærɪneɪt/ **marinates, marinating, marinated.** If you **marinate** meat or fish, or if it **marinates**, you keep it in a mixture of oil, vinegar, spices, and herbs, before cooking it, so that it can develop a special flavour. *Marinate the chicken for at least 4 hours... Put it in a screw-top jar with French dressing and leave to marinate.* ◆◇◇◇◇ V-ERG V n V

marine /məriːn/ **marines** ◆◆◆◇◇

1 A **marine** is a soldier, for example in the US Marine Corps or the Royal Marines, who is specially trained for military duties at sea as well as on land. N-COUNT

2 **Marine** is used to describe things relating to the ADJ:

sea or to the animals and plants that live in the sea. *...breeding grounds for marine life. ...research in marine biology.* ADJ n

3 Marine is used to describe things relating to ships and their movement at sea. *...a solicitor specialising in marine law. ...marine insurance claims.* ADJ: ADJ n =maritime

mariner /mærɪnər/ **mariners.** A **mariner** is a sailor; literary word or a technical word in naval contexts. ◆◇◇◇◇ N-COUNT =seafarer

marionette /mæriənet/ **marionettes.** A **marionette** is a puppet which you control by strings or wires. N-COUNT =puppet

marital /mærɪtəl/. **Marital** is used to describe things relating to marriage. *Caroline was keen to make her marital home in London to be near her family... Her son had no marital problems.* ◆◇◇◇◇ ADJ: ADJ n

marital status. Your **marital status** is whether you are married, single, or divorced; a formal word. *How well off you are in old age is largely determined by race, sex, and marital status.* N-UNCOUNT

maritime /mærɪtaɪm/. **Maritime** is used to describe things relating to the sea and to ships. *...the largest maritime museum of its kind.* ◆◇◇◇◇ ADJ: ADJ n

marjoram /mɑːrdʒərəm/. **Marjoram** is a kind of herb. N-UNCOUNT

mark /mɑːrk/ **marks, marking, marked** ◆◆◆◆◇

1 A **mark** is a small part of a surface which has become a different colour, for example because something has been spilled on it. *The dogs are always rubbing against the wall and making dirty marks... A properly fitting bra should never leave red marks.* N-COUNT

2 If something **marks** a surface, or the surface **marks**, the surface is damaged by marks or a mark. *Leather overshoes were put on the horses' hooves to stop them marking the turf... I have to be more careful with the work tops, as wood marks easily.* V-ERG V n V

3 A **mark** is a written or printed symbol, for example a letter of the alphabet. *He made marks with a pencil.* N-COUNT

4 If you **mark** something with a particular word or symbol, you write that word or symbol on it. *The bank marks the check 'certified'... Mark the frame with your postcode... For more details about these products, send a postcard marked HB/FF.* VERB V n quote V n *with* n V-ed

5 A **mark** is a point that is given for a correct answer or for doing something well in an exam or competition. A **mark** can also be a written symbol such as a letter that indicates how good a student's or competitor's work or performance is. *...a simple scoring device of marks out of 10, where '1' equates to 'Very poor performance'... Candidates who answered 'b' could be awarded half marks for demonstrating some understanding of the process... He did well to get such a good mark.* N-COUNT: oft supp N =score

6 If you say that someone gets good or high **marks** for doing something, you mean that they have done it well or deserve to be praised for doing it. If you say that they get poor or low **marks**, you mean that they have done it badly or do not deserve to be praised. *You have to give her top marks for moral guts... His administration has earned low marks for its economic policies.* N-PLURAL: supp N

7 When a teacher **marks** a student's work, he or she decides how good it is and writes a number or letter on it to indicate this opinion. *He was marking essays in his small study.* ♦ **marking** *For the rest of the lunchbreak I do my marking.* VERB V n N-UNCOUNT

8 A particular **mark** is a particular number, point, or stage which has been reached or might be reached, especially a significant one. *Unemployment is rapidly approaching the one million mark.* N-COUNT: usu *the* supp N

9 The **mark** of something is the characteristic feature that enables you to recognize it. *The mark of a civilized society is that it looks after its weakest members.* N-COUNT: N *of* n/-ing =sign

10 If you say that a type of behaviour or an event is a **mark** of a particular quality, feeling, or situation, you mean it shows that that quality, feeling, or situation exists. *It was a mark of his unfamiliarity with Hollywood that he didn't understand that an agent was paid out of his client's share... Shopkeepers closed their shutters as a mark of respect.* N-SING: a N *of* n =indication, sign

11 If something **marks** a place or position, it shows where something else is or where it used to be. *A huge crater marks the spot where the explosion happened. ...the river which marks the border with Thailand.* VERB V n

12 An event that **marks** a particular stage or point is a sign that something different is about to happen. *The announcement marks the end of an extraordinary period in European history... That programme received critical acclaim and marked a turning point in Sonita's career.* VERB V n

13 If you do something to **mark** an event or occasion, you do it to show that you are aware of the importance of the event or occasion. *The four new stamps mark the 100th anniversary of the British Astronomical Association... Hundreds of thousands of people took to the streets to mark the occasion.* VERB V n

14 If a particular quality or feature **marks** something, it is a quality or feature which that thing often or typically has or shows. *Tragedy has marked Wilmette's life... The style is marked by simplicity, clarity, and candor.* VERB V n

15 Something that **marks** someone as a particular type of person indicates that they are that type of person. *Her opposition to abortion and feminism mark her as a convinced traditionalist.* VERB V n *as* n

16 In a team game, when a defender **is marking** an attacker, the defender is responsible for staying close to the attacker in order to try and prevent them from getting the ball and scoring goals. *...Aston Villa defender Kent Nielsen, who so effectively marked Gary Lineker.* ♦ **marking** *They had stopped Ecuador from building up attacks with good marking.* VERB V n N-UNCOUNT

17 The **mark** is the unit of money that is used in Germany. *The government gave 30 million marks for new school books.* ► **The mark** is also used to refer to the German currency system. *Since the beginning of May, the mark has appreciated 12 per cent against the dollar.* N-COUNT: usu num N N-SING: *the* N

18 Mark is used before a number to indicate a particular temperature level in a gas oven. *Set the oven at gas mark 4.* N-UNCOUNT: N num

19 Mark is used before a number to indicate a particular version or model of a vehicle, machine, or device. *...his Mark II Ford Cortina.* N-UNCOUNT: N num

20 See also **marked, marking; black mark, exclamation mark, full marks, high-water mark, punctuation mark, question mark, scuff mark, stretch marks.**

21 If something or someone **leaves** their **mark** or **leaves a mark**, they have a lasting effect on something or someone else. *Years of conditioning had left their mark on her, and she never felt inclined to talk to strange men.* PHRASES V inflects, oft PHR *on* n

22 If you **make** your **mark** or **make a mark**, you become noticed or famous by doing something impressive or unusual. *She made her mark in the film industry in the 1960s.* V inflects, oft PHR *on/in* n

23 If you are **quick off the mark**, you are quick to understand or respond to something, or to take advantage of an opportunity. If you are **slow off the mark**, you are slow to understand or respond to something, or to take advantage of an opportunity. usu v-link PHR

24 On your marks is a command given to runners at the beginning of a race in order to get them into the correct position to start. *On your marks – get set – go!* CONVENTION PRAGMATICS

25 If something is **off the mark**, it is inaccurate or incorrect. If it is **on the mark**, it is accurate or correct. *Robinson didn't think the story was so far off the mark... He's right on the mark about movies being out of step with American culture.* usu v-link PHR

26 If something is **up to the mark**, it is good enough. *The workers get rid of those whose work is not up to the mark.* usu v-link PHR =up to scratch

27 If something such as a claim or estimate is **wide of the mark**, it is incorrect or inaccurate. *That comparison isn't as wide of the mark as it seems.* usu v-link PHR

28 You can say **mark you** to emphasize and draw PHR with cl attention to something you have just said; an old-fashioned expression. *We're not extremists, mark you.* PRAGMATICS =mind you

29 • to **overstep the mark**: see **overstep**. • **mark my words**: see **word**.

mark down PHRASAL VERB

1 If you **mark** something **down**, you write it down. *I tend to forget things unless I mark them down... As he marks down the prices, he stops now and then to pack things into a large bag.* V n P, V P n (not pron)

2 If you **mark** someone **down** as a particular type of person, especially a type that you do not like, you consider that they have the qualities which make them that type of person. *If he'd taken that five pounds, I would have marked him down as a greedy fool... In those days if you asked 'why?' about anything you were marked down as a militant.* V n P as n

3 To **mark** an item **down** or **mark** its price **down** means to reduce its price. *A toy store has marked down the Sonic Hedgehog computer game... Retailers will have to mark down prices sharply to bring in sales... Clothes are the best bargain, with many items marked down.* =reduce ≠mark up, V P n (not pron), V-ed P, Also V n P

4 If a teacher **marks** a student **down**, he or she puts a lower grade on the student's work because of a mistake that has been made. *If he'd marked them down when I thought they were good, then I would argue the case.* V n P

mark off PHRASAL VERB

1 If you **mark off** a piece or length of something, you make it separate, for example by putting a line on it or around it. *He used a rope to mark off the circle... Read the text through and mark off the sections you find particularly applicable.* V P n (not pron)

2 If a particular quality or feature **marks** someone or something **off** from other people or things, it is unusual or special and makes them seem noticeably different. *Her clothes, of course, marked her off from a great number of the delegates at the conference... The traditionalist influences within the navy marked it off as a rather old-fashioned institution.* V n P from n, V n P as n

3 If you **mark off** a date on a calendar or an item on a list, you put a line through it or next to it, in order to show that it has been completed or dealt with. *He marked off the days on a calendar... Miss Hoare called out names and marked them off.* V P n (not pron), V n P

mark out PHRASAL VERB

1 To **mark out** an area or shape means to show where it begins and ends. *When planting seedlings I prefer to mark out the rows in advance.* V P n (not pron), Also V n P

2 If a particular quality or feature **marks** someone or something **out**, it is unusual or special and makes them seem noticeably different from other people or things. *There were several things about that evening that marked it out as very unusual... It does not appear to possess any of the obvious signs that would mark it out as a restaurant... Her independence of spirit marked her out from her male fellow officers.* V n P as adj/n, V n P from n, Also V P n (not pron)

mark up. If you **mark** something **up**, you increase its price. *You can sell it to them at a set wholesale price, allowing them to mark it up for retail... A typical warehouse club marks up its goods by only 10 to 15 percent.* • See also **mark-up**. PHRASAL VERB =increase ≠mark down, V n P, V P n (not pron)

marked /mɑːʳkt/ ◆◆◆◇◇

1 A **marked** change or difference is very obvious and easily noticed. *There has been a marked increase in crimes against property... He was a man of austere habits, in marked contrast to his more flamboyant wife... The trends since the 1950s have become even more marked.* ♦ **markedly** /mɑːʳkɪdli/ *America's current economic downturn is markedly different from previous recessions... The quality of their relationship improved markedly.* ADJ-GRADED =noticeable; ADV-GRADED: ADV adj, ADV with v =noticeably

2 If you describe someone as a **marked** man or woman, you mean that they are in danger from someone who wants to harm or kill them. *All he needs to do is make one phone call and I'm a marked man.* ADJ: ADJ n

marker /mɑːʳkəʳ/ **markers** ◆◇◇◇◇

1 A **marker** is an object which is used to show the position of something, or is used to help somebody remember something. *He put a marker in his book and followed her out. ...lines of weathered stone markers sticking up from the desert.* N-COUNT

2 If you refer to something as a **marker** for a particular quality or feature, you mean that it demonstrates the existence or presence of that quality or feature. *Vitamin C is a good marker for the presence of other vitamins and nutrients in frozen food.* N-COUNT: oft N for n

3 A **marker** or a **marker pen** is a pen with a thick tip made of felt, which is used for drawing and for colouring things. *Draw your child's outline with a heavy black marker or crayon.* N-COUNT

market /mɑːʳkɪt/ **markets, marketing, marketed** ◆◆◆◆◆

1 A **market** is a place where goods are bought and sold, usually in the open air. *He sold boots on a market stall. ...a small market town.* N-COUNT

2 The **market** for a particular commodity or product is the number of people who want to buy it, or the area in the world in which it is sold. *The foreign market was increasingly crucial. ...the Russian market for personal computers... But there is no youth market in cars.* N-COUNT: usu sing, with supp, oft N for/in n

3 The **market** refers to the total amount of a product that is sold each year, especially when you are talking about the competition between the companies who sell that product. *The two big companies control 72% of the market.* N-SING: the N

4 If you talk about a **market** economy, or the **market** price of something, you are referring to an economic system in which the prices of things depend on how many are available and how many people want to buy them, rather than prices being fixed by governments. *Their ultimate aim was a market economy for Hungary... He must sell the house for the current market value. ...the market price of cocoa.* ADJ: ADJ n

5 To **market** a product means to organize its sale, by deciding on its price, where it should be sold, and how it should be advertised. *...if you marketed our music the way you market pop music... Touchtone telephones have been marketed in America since 1963. ...if a soap is marketed as an anti-acne product.* VERB V n, be V-ed as n

6 **The job market** or **the labour market** refers to the people who are looking for work and the jobs available for them to do. *Every year, 250,000 people enter the job market. ...the changes in the labour market during the 1980s.* N-SING: the n N

7 The stock market is sometimes referred to as **the market**. *The market collapsed last October.* N-SING: the N

8 See also **black market**, **market forces**, **open market**.

9 If you say that it is **a buyer's market**, you mean that it is a good time to buy something, because there is a lot of it available, and therefore its price is low. If you say that it is **a seller's market**, you mean that very little of it is available, so its price is high. *Don't be afraid to haggle: for the moment, it's a buyer's market... Housing became a seller's market, and prices zoomed up.* PHRASES v-link PHR

10 If you are **in the market for** something, you are interested in buying it. *...motorists in the market for a £10,000 car.* v-link PHR, PHR n

11 If something is **on the market**, it is available for people to buy. If it comes **onto the market**, it becomes available for people to buy. *...putting more empty offices on the market. ...new medicines that have just come onto the market.* v-link PHR, PHR after v

12 If you **price** yourself **out of the market**, you try to sell goods or services at a higher price than other people, with the result that no one buys them from you. *At £50,000 for a season, he really is pricing himself out of the market.* V inflects

marketable /mɑːʳkɪtəbᵊl/. Something that is **marketable** is able to be sold because people want to buy it. *What began as an attempt at artistic creation has turned into a marketable commodity... These are marketable skills and will allow these women to be professional therapists in their own right.* ♦ **marketability** /mɑːʳkɪtəbɪlɪti/ ◆◇◇◇◇ ADJ-GRADED; N-UNCOUNT

...a product that has sufficient marketability to enable them to recover their investment costs.

marketeer /mɑːʳkɪtɪəʳ/ **marketeers.** A **marketeer** is the same as a **marketer.** • See also **black marketeer, free-marketeer.** ◆◇◇◇◇ N-COUNT

marketer /mɑːʳkɪtəʳ/ **marketers.** A **marketer** is someone whose job involves marketing. ◆◇◇◇◇ N-COUNT

market forces. When politicians and economists talk about **market forces**, they mean the economic factors that affect the availability of goods and the demand for them, without any help or control by governments. *...opening the economy to market forces and increasing the role of private enterprise. ...saying that the prices of most commodities should be determined by market forces.* ◆◇◇◇◇ N-PLURAL

market garden, market gardens. A **market garden** is a small farm where vegetables and fruit are grown for sale; used mainly in British English. N-COUNT

marketing /mɑːʳkɪtɪŋ/. **Marketing** is the organization of the sale of a product, for example, deciding on its price, the areas it should be supplied to, and how it should be advertised. *...expert advice on production and marketing. ...a marketing campaign. ...Renault's marketing department. ...their sales and marketing director.* ◆◆◇◇◇ N-UNCOUNT: oft N n

marketplace /mɑːʳkɪtpleɪs/ **marketplaces;** also spelled **market place.** ◆◇◇◇◇
1 In business, the **marketplace** refers to the activity of buying and selling products. *It's our hope that we will play an increasingly greater role in the marketplace and, therefore, supply more jobs.* N-COUNT: usu *the* N in sing
2 A **marketplace** is a small area in a town or city where goods are bought and sold, often in the open air. *The marketplace was jammed with a noisy crowd of buyers and sellers.* N-COUNT

market research. **Market research** is the activity of collecting and studying information about what people want, need, and buy. *A new all-woman market research company has been set up to find out what women think about major news and issues.* ◆◇◇◇◇ N-UNCOUNT

market share, market shares. A company's **market share** in a product is the proportion of the total sales of that product that is produced by that company; a business term. *Ford has been gaining market share this year at the expense of GM and some Japanese car manufacturers.* ◆◆◇◇◇ N-VAR: oft with poss

marking /mɑːʳkɪŋ/ **markings. Markings** are coloured lines, shapes, or patterns on the surface of something, which help to identify it. *A plane with Danish markings was over-flying his vessel... The animal may have some white markings.* • See also **mark.** ◆◇◇◇◇ N-COUNT: usu pl

marksman /mɑːʳksmən/ **marksmen.** ◆◇◇◇◇
1 A **marksman** is a person who can shoot very accurately. *He was hit in the head and arm when police marksmen opened fire.* N-COUNT
2 In sports journalism, a **marksman** is a football player who scores a lot of goals. *City's principal marksman was Joe Harvey who scored seventeen goals.* N-COUNT

marksmanship /mɑːʳksmənʃɪp/. **Marksmanship** is the ability to shoot accurately. N-UNCOUNT

mark-up, mark-ups. A **mark-up** is an increase in the price of something, for example the difference between its cost and the price that you sell it for. N-COUNT

marmalade /mɑːʳməleɪd/ **marmalades. Marmalade** is a food made from oranges, lemons, or grapefruit that is similar to jam. It is eaten on bread or toast at breakfast. ◆◇◇◇◇ N-MASS

marmoset /mɑːʳməzet/ **marmosets.** A **marmoset** is a type of small monkey. N-COUNT

maroon /məruːn/ **maroons, marooning, marooned** ◆◇◇◇◇
1 Something that is **maroon** is dark reddish-purple in colour. *...maroon velvet curtains.* COLOUR
2 If someone **is marooned** somewhere, they are left in a place that is difficult for them to escape from. *Five couples were marooned in their caravans when the River Avon broke its banks. ...after years of being marooned on a desert island.* VB: usu passive =stranded be V-ed prep/adv V-ed

marooned /məruːnd/. If you say that you are **marooned**, you mean that you feel alone and helpless, because you are in an unpleasant situation that you cannot change. *I'm left feeling lonely, sad and marooned. ...families marooned in decaying inner-city areas. ...temporarily marooned at home by my injured knee.* ADJ: usu v-link ADJ, oft ADJ prep =isolated

marque /mɑːʳk/ **marques.** A **marque** is a famous make or brand of a particular product. *...a marque long-associated with motor racing success, Alfa Romeo.* ◆◇◇◇◇ N-COUNT

marquee /mɑːʳkiː/ **marquees** ◆◇◇◇◇
1 A **marquee** is a large tent which is used at a fair, garden party, or other outdoor event, usually for eating and drinking in. N-COUNT
2 In American English, a **marquee** is a cover over the entrance of a building, for example, a hotel or a theatre. *...the marquees of Broadway.* N-COUNT

marquis /mɑːʳkwɪs/ **marquises;** also spelled **marquess.** A **marquis** is a male member of the nobility who has the rank between duke and earl. ◆◇◇◇◇ N-COUNT; N-TITLE

marriage /mærɪdʒ/ **marriages** ◆◆◆◆◇
1 A **marriage** is the relationship between a husband and wife. *In a good marriage, both husband and wife work hard to solve any problems that arise... When I was 35 my marriage broke up... His son by his second marriage lives in Paris.* N-COUNT
2 A **marriage** is the act of marrying someone, or the ceremony at which this is done. *I opposed her marriage to Darryl.* N-VAR
3 **Marriage** is the state of being married. *Marriage might not suit you... In twenty years of marriage he has only taken two proper vacations.* N-UNCOUNT
4 See also **arranged marriage.**

marriageable /mærɪdʒəbᵊl/. If you describe someone as **marriageable**, you mean that they are suitable for marriage, especially that they are the right age to marry; an old-fashioned word. *Even girls of marriageable age were often ignorant of the basic facts of life. ...a marriageable daughter.* ADJ: usu ADJ n =eligible

married /mærid/ ◆◆◆◇◇
1 If you are **married**, you have a husband or wife. *We have been married for 14 years... She is married to an Englishman. ...a married man with two children.* ADJ: oft ADJ *to* n
2 **Married** means relating to marriage or to people who are married. *For the first ten years of our married life we lived in a farmhouse.* ADJ: ADJ n
3 If you say that someone is **married to** their work or another activity, you mean they are very involved with it and have little time or interest for anything else. *She was a very strict Christian who was married to her job... I have little time for women because I'm married to my cricket, so I'm leaving the arrangements to my sister.* ADJ: v-link ADJ *to* n

marrow /mærəʊ/ **marrows** ◆◇◇◇◇
1 In British English, a **marrow** is a long, thick, green vegetable with soft white flesh that is eaten cooked. The American term is 'vegetable marrow'. N-VAR
2 **Marrow** is the same as **bone marrow.** *The marrow donor is her 14-month-old sister.* N-UNCOUNT
3 The **marrow** of something is the most important and basic part of it. *We're getting into the marrow of the film.* N-SING: *the* N, usu N *of* n =crux
4 If you say that you are chilled **to the marrow**, you are emphasizing that you are extremely cold or extremely frightened. *When I got back at about ten a.m. I was frozen to the marrow... The very thought of it chilled me to the marrow.* PHRASE: usu PHR after v PRAGMATICS

marrow bone, marrow bones; also spelled **marrowbone. Marrow bones** are the bones of certain animals, especially cows, that contain a lot of bone marrow. They are used in cooking and in dog food. *Ask the butcher for soup bones (marrow bones are best). ...marrowbone jelly.* N-VAR

marry /mæri/ **marries, marrying, married** ◆◆◆◆◇
1 When two people **get married** or **marry**, they legally become husband and wife in a special ceremony. **Get married** is less formal and more com- V-RECIP

monly used than **marry**. *I thought he would change after we got married... They married a month after they met... He wants to marry her... Laura just got married to Jake and took it for granted that they and their kids would then live happily ever after... I am getting married on Monday... She ought to marry again, don't you think?*
pl-n get V-ed / pl-n V / V n / get V-ed to n / get V-ed (non-recip) / V (non-recip)

2 When a priest or registrar **marries** two people, he or she conducts the ceremony in which the two people legally become husband and wife. *The local vicar has agreed to marry us in the chapel on the estate... In July 1957, we were married in New York.*
VERB / V n

3 If a parent **marries** their child to someone, the parent chooses who their child will marry and arranges it. *He married his three daughters to princes of the ruling house.*
VERB / V n to n

marry off. If you **marry** someone **off**, you find a suitable person for them to marry. *They advised her mother to marry her off to the old man as he was very rich... He had the good fortune to marry off his daughter to the local chief... The poor are taking advantage of this edict to marry off their daughters without enormous expenditure while they can... Tradition dictates that girls should be married off early.*
PHRASAL VERB / V n P to n / V P n (not pron) to n / V P n (not pron) / be V-ed P / Also V n P

marsh /mɑːʳʃ/ **marshes.** A **marsh** is a wet, muddy, area of land.
◆◇◇◇◇ N-VAR

marshal /mɑːʳʃəl/ **marshals, marshalling, marshalled;** spelled **marshaling, marshaled** in American English.
◆◆◇◇◇

1 If you **marshal** people or things, you gather them together and arrange them for a particular purpose. *Richard was marshalling the doctors and nurses, showing them where to go. ...the way in which Britain marshalled its economic and political resources to protect its security interests.*
VERB =organize / V n

2 A **marshal** is an official who helps to supervise a public event, especially a sports event. *The grand prix is controlled by well-trained marshals... During the demonstration, marshals handed over to the police a young man caught breaking shop windows.*
N-COUNT

3 In the United States and some other countries, a **marshal** is a police officer, often one who is responsible for a particular area. *A federal marshal was killed in a shoot-out.*
N-COUNT

4 A **marshal** is an officer who has the highest rank in an army or air force. *A marshal of the Soviet Union was put in overall control. ...Air Chief Marshal Sir Kenneth Cross.*
N-COUNT; N-TITLE

marshland /mɑːʳʃlænd/ **marshlands.** **Marshland** is land that is covered in marshes.
N-UNCOUNT: also N in pl

marshmallow /mɑːʳʃmæloʊ, AM -mel-/ **marshmallows**

1 Marshmallow is a soft, sweet, spongy food that is used in some cakes, puddings, and sweets.
N-UNCOUNT

2 Marshmallows are sweets made from marshmallow. *...a snack of marshmallows and chocolate.*
N-COUNT

marshy /mɑːʳʃi/. **Marshy** land is covered in marshes. *...the broad, marshy plain of the River Spey.*
ADJ-GRADED: usu ADJ n

marsupial /mɑːʳsuːpiəl/ **marsupials.** A **marsupial** is an animal such as a kangaroo or an opossum. Female marsupials carry their babies in a pouch on their stomachs.
N-COUNT

mart /mɑːʳt/ **marts.** In American English, a **mart** is a place, such as a market, where things are bought and sold. *...the flower mart.*
N-COUNT: oft n N

martial /mɑːʳʃəl/. **Martial** is used to describe things relating to soldiers or war; a formal word. *The paper was actually twice banned under the martial regime.* • See also **court-martial**.
◆◆◇◇◇ ADJ: usu ADJ n

martial art, martial arts. A **martial art** is one of the philosophies and techniques of self-defence that come from the Far East, for example kung fu, karate, or judo.
◆◇◇◇◇ N-COUNT

martial law. **Martial law** is control of an area that is established and maintained by soldiers instead of civilians. *The military leadership have lifted martial law in several more towns.*
◆◇◇◇◇ N-UNCOUNT

Martian /mɑːʳʃən/ **Martians**

1 A **Martian** is an imaginary creature from the planet Mars. *Orson Welles managed to convince many Americans that they were being invaded by Martians.*
N-COUNT

2 Something that is **Martian** exists on or relates to the planet Mars. *The Martian atmosphere contains only tiny amounts of water.*
ADJ: usu ADJ n

martin /mɑːʳtɪn/ **martins.** A **martin** is a kind of small bird with a forked tail.
N-COUNT

martinet /mɑːʳtɪnet/ **martinets.** If you say that someone is a **martinet**, you are criticizing them because they believe in strict discipline and they expect their orders to be obeyed immediately and not questioned; a formal word. *He's a retired Lieutenant Colonel and a bit of a martinet.*
N-COUNT PRAGMATICS =disciplinarian

martyr /mɑːʳtəʳ/ **martyrs, martyring, martyred**
◆◇◇◇◇

1 A **martyr** is a person who is killed or made to suffer greatly, as a direct result of his or her religious or political beliefs, and therefore gives strength to people who share those beliefs. *...a glorious martyr to the cause of liberty. ...a Christian martyr... The dead student is now being regarded as a martyr.*
N-COUNT: oft N to n

2 If someone **is martyred**, they are killed or made to suffer very greatly, because of their religious or political beliefs. *St Pancras was martyred in 304 AD. ...whether its martyred leader is released or not.*
VB: usu passive / be V-ed / V-ed

3 If you refer to someone as a **martyr**, you disapprove of the fact that they pretend to suffer, or exaggerate their suffering, in order to get sympathy or praise from other people. *When are you going to quit acting like a martyr?... Jennifer responded with anger and played the martyr role.*
N-COUNT PRAGMATICS

4 If you say that someone is a **martyr** to something, you mean that they suffer as a result of it. *Ellsworth was a martyr to his sense of honour and responsibility... He said that he was a martyr to his back.*
N-COUNT: usu N to n

5 See also **martyred**.

martyrdom /mɑːʳtəʳdəm/

1 If someone suffers **martyrdom**, they are killed, tortured, or made to suffer because of their religious or political beliefs. *...the martyrdom of Bishop Feliciano... He suffered martyrdom by stoning.*
N-UNCOUNT

2 If you describe someone's behaviour as **martyrdom**, you are critical of them because they are showing that they are suffering in an exaggerated way, in order to gain sympathy or praise. *The air of patient martyrdom with which she greeted him when he got back made her feelings clear.*
N-UNCOUNT PRAGMATICS

martyred /mɑːʳtəʳd/. If you describe a person or their behaviour as **martyred**, you mean that they often exaggerate their suffering in order to get sympathy or praise from other people; a literary use. *'As usual,' muttered his martyred wife... You put on your martyred expression, sigh and say, 'If you really want to...'. ...with a lot of sighs, moans and a martyred air.*
ADJ: ADJ n PRAGMATICS =long-suffering

marvel /mɑːʳvəl/ **marvels, marvelling, marvelled;** spelled **marveling, marveled** in American English.
◆◇◇◇◇

1 If you **marvel** at something, you express your great surprise, wonder, or admiration. *Her fellow members marveled at her seemingly infinite energy... Sara and I read the story and marveled... 'That's the weirdest thing I've ever seen,' marveled Carl... He marvelled that a man in such intense pain could be so coherent.*
VERB / V at n / V / V with quote / V that

2 You can describe something or someone as a **marvel** to indicate that you think that they are wonderful. *The whale, like the dolphin, has become a symbol of the marvels of creation... A new technological marvel was invented at Cambridge University in England, the scanning electron microscope.*
N-COUNT: oft N of n =wonder

3 Marvels are things that people have done, or that have happened, which are very unexpected or surprising. *She almost died, but the hospital's skill achieved great marvels... He's done marvels with the team... It was a marvel that the floor never gave way.*
N-COUNT: usu pl =wonders

marvellous /mɑːʳvələs/; spelled **marvelous** in American English. If you describe someone or something as **marvellous**, you are emphasizing that they are very good. *He certainly is a marvellous actor... She made marvellous fish pie... He*

ADJ-GRADED PRAGMATICS =splendid

looked marvellous. ♦ **marvellously** *He always painted marvellously... Isabel gave me a marvellously funny birthday card.* ADV-GRADED: ADV with v, ADV adj/adv

Marxism /mɑːʳksɪzəm/. **Marxism** is a political philosophy based on the writings of Karl Marx which stresses the importance of the struggle between different social classes. ◆◇◇◇◇ N-UNCOUNT

Marxist /mɑːʳksɪst/ **Marxists** ◆◆◇◇◇
1 **Marxist** means based on Marxism or relating to Marxism. *...a Marxist state. ...Marxist ideology.* ADJ
2 A **Marxist** is a person who believes in Marxism or who is a member of a Marxist party. N-COUNT

marzipan /mɑːʳzɪpæn/. **Marzipan** is a paste made of almonds, sugar, and egg which is sometimes put on top of cakes. N-UNCOUNT

masc. **Masc.** is a written abbreviation of **masculine**.

mascara /mæskɑːrə, AM -kær-/ **mascaras.** **Mascara** is a substance used mainly by women, to colour their eyelashes. *...water-resistant mascaras.* ◆◇◇◇◇ N-MASS

mascot /mæskɒt/ **mascots.** A **mascot** is an animal, toy, or symbol which is associated with a particular organization or event, and which is thought to bring good luck. *Our school had a mascot known as Freddy Bird. ...the official mascot of the Barcelona Games.* ◆◇◇◇◇ N-COUNT: usu with supp

masculine /mæskjʊlɪn/ ◆◇◇◇◇
1 **Masculine** qualities and things relate to or are considered typical of men, in contrast to women. *...masculine characteristics like a husky voice and facial hair... Perhaps some kind of masculine pride was involved.* ADJ: usu ADJ n =male
2 If you say that someone or something is **masculine**, you mean that they have qualities such as strength or confidence which are considered typical of men. *...her aggressive, masculine image... The Duke's study was very masculine, with deep red wall-covering and dark oak shelving.* ADJ-GRADED ≠feminine
3 In some languages, a **masculine** noun, pronoun, or adjective has a different form from a feminine or neuter one, or behaves in a different way. ADJ

masculinity /mæskjʊlɪnɪti/ ◆◇◇◇◇
1 A man's **masculinity** is the fact that he is a man. *...a project on the link between masculinity and violence.* N-UNCOUNT ≠femininity
2 **Masculinity** means the qualities, especially sexual qualities, which are considered to be typical of men. *The old ideas of masculinity do not work for most men. ...being unable to prove his masculinity to society by getting his partner pregnant.* N-UNCOUNT =manhood ≠femininity

masculinize /mæskjʊlɪnaɪz/ **masculinizes, masculinizing, masculinized;** also spelled **masculinise** in British English. To **masculinize** something means to make it into something that involves mainly men or is thought suitable for or typical of men; a formal word. *Not all plantation work has been masculinized.* VB: usu passive, be V-ed

mash /mæʃ/ **mashes, mashing, mashed** ◆◇◇◇◇
1 If you **mash** food that is solid but soft, you crush it so that it forms a soft mass. *Mash the bananas with a fork. ...mashed potatoes.* VERB V n V-ed
2 In informal British English, **mash** is mashed potato. N-UNCOUNT
3 A **mash** of food is a soft mass of food. It is often a mixture of several ingredients. *They ate a mash of 2 potatoes, 2 carrots & cabbage... I'm feeding our horses the same mash the O'Briens used to win Gold Cups.* N-SING: usu N *of* n

mask /mɑːsk, mæsk/ **masks, masking, masked** ◆◆◆◇◇
1 A **mask** is a piece of cloth or other material, which you wear over your face so that people cannot see who you are, or so that you look like someone or something else. *The gunman, whose mask had slipped, fled. ...actors wearing masks.* N-COUNT
2 A **mask** is a piece of cloth or other material that you wear over all or part of your face to protect you from germs or harmful substances. *You must wear goggles and a mask that will protect you against the fumes... She wore a surgical mask and rubber gloves while she worked with the samples.* N-COUNT: oft supp N
3 If you describe someone's behaviour as a **mask**, you mean that they do not show their real feelings or character. *His mask of detachment cracked, and she saw for an instant an angry and violent man.* N-COUNT: oft N *of* n =front
4 A **mask** is a thick cream or paste made of various substances, which you spread over your face and leave for some time in order to improve your skin. *This mask leaves your complexion feeling soft and supple.* N-COUNT =face pack
5 If you **mask** your feelings, you deliberately do not show them in your behaviour, so that people cannot know what you really feel. *Dena lit a cigarette, trying to mask her agitation.* VERB =conceal, hide V n
6 If one thing **masks** another, it prevents people from noticing or recognizing the other thing. *A thick grey cloud masked the sun... Too much salt masks the true flavour of the food... The healthy trade figures mask a much gloomier picture.* VERB V n
7 See also **death mask, gas mask, oxygen mask.**

masked /mɑːskt, mæskt/. If someone is **masked**, they are wearing a mask. *Masked youths threw stones and fire-bombs.* ◆◇◇◇◇ ADJ

masking tape. **Masking tape** is plastic or paper tape which is sticky on one side and is used, for example, to protect part of a surface that you are painting. N-UNCOUNT

masochism /mæsəkɪzəm/ ◆◇◇◇◇
1 **Masochism** is behaviour in which someone gets sexual pleasure from their own pain or suffering. *The tendency towards masochism is however always linked with elements of sadism.* ♦ **masochist, masochists** *...consensual sexual masochists.* N-UNCOUNT N-COUNT
2 If you describe someone's behaviour as **masochism**, you mean that they seem to be trying to get into a situation which causes them suffering or great difficulty. *Once you have tasted life in southern California, it takes a peculiar kind of masochism to return to a British winter.* ♦ **masochist** *Anybody who enjoys this is a masochist.* N-UNCOUNT N-COUNT
3 See also **sado-masochism.**

masochistic /mæsəkɪstɪk/
1 **Masochistic** behaviour involves a person getting sexual pleasure from their own pain or suffering. *...his masochistic tendencies.* ADJ
2 If you describe someone's behaviour as **masochistic**, you mean that they seem to be trying to get into a situation which causes them suffering or great difficulty. *It seems masochistic, somehow.* ADJ-GRADED
3 See also **sado-masochistic.**

mason /meɪsᵊn/ **masons** ◆◇◇◇◇
1 A **mason** is a person who is skilled at making things or building things with stone. N-COUNT
2 A **Mason** is the same as a **Freemason.** N-COUNT

Masonic /məsɒnɪk/. **Masonic** is used to describe things relating to the beliefs, traditions, or organization of Freemasons. *...a Masonic lodge on Broughton Street.* ADJ: ADJ n

masonry /meɪsənri/. **Masonry** is bricks or pieces of stone which have been stuck together with cement as part of a wall or building. N-UNCOUNT

masquerade /mæskəreɪd/ **masquerades, masquerading, masqueraded** ◆◇◇◇◇
1 If someone or something **masquerades as** someone or something else, they pretend to be that person or thing, particularly in order to deceive other people. *He masqueraded as a doctor and fooled everyone. ...vices masquerading as virtues.* VERB =pretend V *as* n
2 A **masquerade** is an attempt to deceive people about the true nature or identity of something. *He told a news conference that the elections would be a masquerade.* N-COUNT =pretence
3 A **masquerade** is an event such as a party or dance where people dress up in disguise and wear masks. *...a masquerade ball.* N-COUNT

mass /mæs/ **masses, massing, massed** ◆◆◆◆◇
1 A **mass** of things is a large number of them grouped together. *On his desk is a mass of books and papers.* N-SING: N *of* n
2 A **mass** of something is a large amount of it. *She had a mass of auburn hair.* N-SING: N *of* n
3 **Masses** of something means a great deal of it; an QUANT:

informal use. *There's masses of work for her to do... It has masses of flowers each year.* QUANT of n-uncount/pl-n

4 Mass is used to describe something which involves or affects a very large number of people. *...ideas on combating mass unemployment... All the lights went off, and mass hysteria broke out. ...weapons of mass destruction. ...the harm caused by mass tourism.* ADJ: ADJ n

5 A **mass** of a solid substance, a liquid, or a gas is an amount of it, especially a large amount which has no definite shape. *...before it cools and sets into a solid mass... The fourteenth century cathedral was reduced to a mass of rubble. ...the strong temperature difference between the two masses of air.* N-COUNT: oft N of n

6 If you talk about **the masses**, you mean the ordinary people in society, in contrast to the leaders or the highly educated people. *His music is commercial. It is aimed at the masses. ...linking the Soviet leadership with the masses. ...appealing to the middle class and business as well as the masses.* N-PLURAL: the N

7 The **mass** of people are most of the people in a country, society, or group. *The 1939-45 world war involved the mass of the population... Schools allowed the mass of children to leave school at 16 with poor qualifications.* N-SING: the N of n =bulk, majority

8 A **mass** of people is a large crowd of them. *...masses of excited people clogged the streets. ...a mass of grinning teenage faces.* N-COUNT: N of n

9 When people or things **mass**, or when you **mass** them, they gather together into a large crowd or group. *Shortly after the workers went on strike, police began to mass at the shipyard... The clouds massed, whipped up by the wind... The General was massing his troops for a counterattack.* V-ERG =gather; V; V n

10 If you say that something is a **mass of** things, you mean that it is covered with them or full of them. *His body was a mass of sores... In the spring, the meadow is a mass of daffodils.* N-SING: N of n

11 The **mass** of an object is the amount of physical matter that it has; a technical term in physics. *Astronomers know that Pluto and Triton have nearly the same size, mass, and density.* N-VAR

12 Mass is a Christian church ceremony, especially in a Roman Catholic or Orthodox church, during which people eat bread and drink wine in order to remember the last meal of Jesus Christ. *She attended a convent school and went to Mass each day.* N-VAR

13 A **Mass** is a piece of music which uses the prayers from the Christian ceremony of Mass as the words that are sung. N-COUNT

14 See also **massed**; **critical mass, land mass.**

massacre /mæsəkəʳ/ **massacres, massacring, massacred** ◆◆◇◇◇

1 A **massacre** is the killing of a large number of people at the same time in a violent and cruel way. *Maria lost her 62-year-old mother in the massacre. ...reports of massacre, torture and starvation.* N-VAR

2 If people **are massacred**, a large number of them are attacked and killed in a violent and cruel way. *300 civilians are believed to have been massacred by the rebels... Troops indiscriminately massacred the defenceless population.* VERB be V-ed; V n

massage /mæsɑːʒ, AM məsɑ̲ːʒ/ **massages, massaging, massaged** ◆◆◇◇◇

1 Massage is the action of squeezing and rubbing someone's body, as a way of making them relax or reducing their pain. *Alex asked me if I wanted a massage... Massage isn't a long-term cure for stress.* N-VAR

2 If you **massage** someone or a part of their body, you squeeze and rub their body, in order to make them relax or reduce their pain. *She continued massaging her right foot, which was bruised and aching. ...if you wish to massage your family and friends yourself.* VERB; V n

3 If you say that someone **massages** statistics, figures, or evidence, you are criticizing them for changing or rearranging the facts in such a way that other people are deceived. *Their governments have no reason to 'massage' the statistics. ...efforts to massage the unemployment figures for electoral purposes.* VERB PRAGMATICS =doctor; V n

masse. See **en masse.**

massed /mæst/. **Massed** is used to describe a large number of people who have been brought together for a particular purpose. *He could not escape the massed ranks of newsmen who spotted him crossing the lawn.* ADJ: ADJ n

masseur /mæsɜ̲ːʳ/ **masseurs.** A **masseur** is a person whose job is to give massage. N-COUNT

masseuse /mæsɜ̲ːz/ **masseuses.** A **masseuse** is a woman whose job is to give massage. N-COUNT

massif /mæsi̲ːf/ **massifs.** A **massif** is a group of mountains that form part of a mountain range. N-COUNT: oft in names

massive /mæsɪv/ ◆◆◆◇◇

1 Something that is **massive** is very large in size, quantity, or extent. *There was evidence of massive fraud. ...massive air attacks... The scale of the problem is massive. ...a massive steam boat.* ADJ-GRADED =huge
♦ **massively** *...a massively popular game... Interest rates will rise massively.* ADV-GRADED

2 If you describe a medical condition as **massive**, you mean that it is extremely serious. *He died six weeks later of a massive heart attack.* ADJ: ADJ n

ma̲ss me̲dia. You can use **mass media** to refer to the various ways, especially television, radio, newspapers, and magazines, by which information and news is given to large numbers of people. *...the development of the mass media. ...mass media coverage of the issue.* ◆◇◇◇◇ N-SING-COLL: usu the N

ma̲ss noun, mass nouns

1 A **mass noun** is a noun such as 'wine' which is usually uncount, but is used with an indefinite article or in the plural form when it refers to types or brands of a substance, as in 'a range of Australian wines'. N-COUNT

2 In some descriptions of grammar, a **mass noun** is the same as an **uncount noun.** N-COUNT

ma̲ss-produ̲ce, mass-produces, mass-producing, mass-produced. If someone **mass-produces** something, they make it in large quantities, usually by machine. This means that the product can be sold cheaply. *...the invention of machinery to mass-produce footwear.* ◆◇◇◇◇ VERB; V n
♦ **mass-produced** *In 1981 it launched the first mass-produced mountain bike.* ADJ: ADJ n

ma̲ss produ̲ction; also spelled **mass-production. Mass production** is the production of something in large quantities, especially by machine. *...equipment that would allow the mass production of baby food.* N-UNCOUNT: oft N of n

mast /mɑːst, mæst/ **masts** ◆◇◇◇◇

1 The **masts** of a boat are the tall upright poles that support its sails. N-COUNT

2 A **mast** is a long vertical pole that is used as an aerial to transmit sound or television pictures. *...a 30ft high radio mast.* N-COUNT

3 • to **nail** your **colours to the mast**: see **colour**. • to **nail** your **colours to** someone's **mast**: see **colour.**

mastectomy /mæste̲ktəmi/ **mastectomies.** A **mastectomy** is a surgical operation to remove a woman's breast. N-VAR

master /mɑ̲ːstəʳ, mæ̲s-/ **masters, mastering, mastered** ◆◆◆◆◇

1 A servant's **master** is the man that he or she works for. *My master ordered me not to deliver the message except in private... In 1777 several northern states encouraged white masters to free their slaves for military service.* N-COUNT

2 A dog's **master** is the man or boy who owns it. *The dog yelped excitedly when his master opened a desk drawer and produced his leash.* N-COUNT: usu poss N

3 If you say that someone is a **master** of a particular activity, you mean that they are extremely skilled at it. *She was a master of the English language... He is a master at blocking progress... They appear masters in the art of making regulations work their way.* N-COUNT: usu N of/at/in n/-ing
• See also **past master.** ► Also an adjective. *...a master craftsman. ...a master criminal.* ADJ: ADJ n

4 If you are **master** of a situation, you have complete control over it. *Jackson remained calm and always master of his passions... He was under no illusions as to who was master in his house.* N-UNCOUNT: also N in pl, usu N of n

5 If you **master** something, you learn how to do it properly or you succeed in understanding it completely. *Duff soon mastered the skills of radio production... Students are expected to master a second language.* VERB Vn

6 If you **master** a difficult situation, you succeed in controlling it. *When you have mastered one situation you have to go on to the next... His genius alone has mastered every crisis.* VERB Vn

7 A **master** is a male teacher, especially one in a British public school. *Mr Palmer was a retired maths master.* • See also **headmaster**, **housemaster.** N-COUNT: usu n N

8 A famous male painter of the past is often called a **master**. *...a portrait by the Dutch master, Vincent Van Gogh.* • See also **old master.** N-COUNT

9 A **master** copy of something such as a film or a tape recording is an original copy that can be used to produce other copies. *Keep one as a master copy for your own reference and circulate the others.* ADJ: ADJ n

10 The **master** of a ship that carries passengers or goods is its captain. *...the Royal Pacific's master.* N-COUNT: usu with poss

11 A master's degree can be referred to as a **master's**. *I've a master's in economics.* N-SING

12 **Master** is sometimes used by the followers of a male religious teacher or leader as a way of referring to him or addressing him. *She believed that she had been selected by the Master to reveal forgotten wisdom.* N-COUNT: oft *the* N; N-VOC

13 In the past, **Master** was used before a boy's name as a polite way of referring to him or addressing him. Nowadays, **Master** can be written before a boy's name when addressing a letter to him; used mainly in British English. *Nice to see you, Master Simon.* N-TITLE

14 If you say that you **are** your **own master**, you mean that your decisions are not controlled by other people and you are free to do what you want. *It was no place for a man who liked to be his own master.* PHRASE: V and N inflect

master bedroom, master bedrooms. The **master bedroom** in a large house is the largest bedroom. N-COUNT

masterclass /mɑːstərklɑːs, mæstərklæs/ **masterclasses.** A **masterclass** is a lesson where someone who is an expert at something such as dancing or music gives advice to very talented students. Masterclasses usually take place in public or are broadcast on television. N-COUNT

masterful /mɑːstərfəl, mæs-/

1 If you describe a man as **masterful**, you approve of him because he behaves in a way which shows that he is in control of a situation and can tell other people what to do. *Big, successful moves need bold, masterful managers.* ADJ-GRADED PRAGMATICS

2 If you describe someone's behaviour or actions as **masterful**, you mean that they show great skill. *...a masterful performance of boxing and punching skills.* ADJ-GRADED =skilful

master key, master keys. A **master key** is a key which will open all the locks in a set, even though each lock has its own different key. N-COUNT

masterly /mɑːstərli, mæs-/. If you describe something as **masterly**, you admire it because it has been done extremely well or shows the highest level of ability and skill. *Malcolm Hebden gives a masterly performance... Attlee was extremely intelligent and his grasp of the situation was masterly.* ADJ-GRADED PRAGMATICS =excellent

mastermind /mɑːstərmaɪnd, mæs-/ **masterminds, masterminding, masterminded** ◆◇◇◇◇

1 If you **mastermind** a difficult or complicated activity, you plan it in detail and then make sure that it happens successfully. *The finance minister will continue to mastermind Poland's economic reform... The bombings were masterminded by a known drugs smuggler.* VERB Vn

2 The **mastermind** behind a difficult or complicated plan, often a criminal one, is the person who is responsible for planning and organizing it. *He was the mastermind behind the plan to acquire the explosives.* N-COUNT: usu sing, usu with supp, oft N *behind/of* n

Master of Arts. A **Master of Arts** degree is the same as an **MA** degree. N-SING =MA

master of ceremonies, masters of ceremonies. At events such as formal dinners, award ceremonies, and variety shows, the **master of ceremonies** is the person who introduces the speakers or performers, and who announces what is going to happen next. N-COUNT

Master of Science. A **Master of Science** degree is the same an **MSc** or **MS** degree. N-SING =MSc

masterpiece /mɑːstərpiːs, mæs-/ **masterpieces** ◆◆◇◇◇

1 A **masterpiece** is an extremely good painting, novel, film, or other work of art. *His book, I must add, is a masterpiece. ...masterpieces by artists like Rembrandt, Raphael and Ingres.* N-COUNT

2 An artist's, writer's, or composer's **masterpiece** is the best work that they have ever produced. *'Man's Fate,' translated into sixteen languages, is probably his masterpiece.* N-COUNT: with poss

3 A **masterpiece** is an extremely clever or skilful example of something. *The whole thing was a masterpiece of crowd management.* N-COUNT: oft N *of* n

master plan, master plans. A **master plan** is a clever plan that is intended to help someone succeed in a very difficult or important task. *...the master plan for the reform of the economy.* N-COUNT

master's degree, master's degrees; also spelled **Master's degree**. A **master's degree** is a university degree which is of a higher level than a first degree. A master's degree, for example, an MA or an MSc, usually takes one or two years to complete. N-COUNT

masterstroke /mɑːstərstroʊk, mæs-/ **masterstrokes.** A **masterstroke** is something you do which is unexpected but very clever and which helps you to achieve something. *To have convinced Hillsden that he would be justified in killing Calder was a masterstroke.* N-COUNT: usu sing

masterwork /mɑːstərwɜːrk, mæs-/ **masterworks.** If you describe something such as a book or a painting as a **masterwork**, it is your opinion that it is an excellent example of its type. *They endure as masterworks of American musical theatre.* N-COUNT: oft poss N, N *of* n

mastery /mɑːstəri, mæs-/ ◆◇◇◇◇

1 If you show **mastery** of a particular skill or language, you show you have learnt or understood it completely and have no difficulty using it. *He doesn't have mastery of the basic rules of grammar... He demonstrated his mastery of political manoeuvring.* N-UNCOUNT: oft N *of* n

2 **Mastery** is power or control over something. *Mesopotamia was probably the first region of the world where humans gained mastery over major rivers.* N-UNCOUNT: oft N *of/over* n

masthead /mɑːsthed, mæst-/ **mastheads**

1 A ship's **masthead** is the highest part of its mast. N-COUNT

2 A newspaper's **masthead** is the part at the top of the front page where its name appears in big letters. *We carry illustrations of these medals on our masthead.* N-COUNT: usu sing, usu with poss

masticate /mæstɪkeɪt/ **masticates, masticating, masticated.** When you **masticate** food, you chew it; a formal word. *Her mouth was working, as if she was masticating some tasty titbit... Don't gulp everything down without masticating.* VERB Vn V

♦ **mastication** /mæstɪkeɪʃən/ *Poor digestion can be caused by defective mastication of the food in the mouth.* N-UNCOUNT

mastiff /mæstɪf/ **mastiffs.** A **mastiff** is a large, powerful, short-haired dog. N-COUNT

masturbate /mæstərbeɪt/ **masturbates, masturbating, masturbated.** If someone **masturbates**, they stroke or rub their own genitals in order to get sexual pleasure. ◆◇◇◇◇ VERB: V

♦ **masturbation** /mæstərbeɪʃən/ N-UNCOUNT

mat /mæt/ **mats** ◆◇◇◇◇

1 A **mat** is a small piece of something such as cloth, card, or plastic which you put on a table to protect the table against heat or spillages. *The food is served on polished tables with mats.* N-COUNT

2 A **mat** is a small piece of carpet or other thick material which is put on the floor for protection, decoration, or comfort. *There was a letter on the mat... Bring a sleeping bag and foam mat.* N-COUNT

3 A **mat** of something such as grass or moss is a thick untidy layer of it. *The houses are well spaced out, each on its own plot of ground and mat of coarse grass... She touched the thick mat of sandy hair on his chest.* N-COUNT: with supp, usu N of n =tangle

4 See also **matt, place mat**.

matador /mætədɔːʳ/ **matadors.** A **matador** is the person in a bullfight who is supposed to kill the bull. N-COUNT =bullfighter

match /mætʃ/ **matches, matching, matched** ◆◆◆◆◆

1 A **match** is an organized game of football, tennis, cricket, or other sport; used mainly in British English. *He was watching a football match... France won the match 28-19.* N-COUNT =game

2 A **match** is a small wooden stick with a substance on one end that produces a flame when you rub it along the rough side of a matchbox. *...a packet of cigarettes and a box of matches.* N-COUNT

3 If something of a particular colour or design **matches** another, or if the two things **match**, they have the same colour or design, or have a pleasing appearance when they are used together. If you **match** two things, you choose them because they look pleasing together. *'The shoes are too tight.'—'Well, they do match your dress.'... All the chairs matched... You don't have to match your lipstick exactly to your outfit... Mix and match your tableware and textiles from the new Design House collection.* V-RECIP-ERG; V n; pl-n V; V n to/with n; V pl-n
▶ **Match up** means the same as **match**. *The pillow cover can match up with the sheets... Because false eyelashes come in various lengths and shades, it's so easy to match them up with your own.* PHRASAL VERB ERG; V P with/to n; V n P with/to n

4 If something such as an amount or a quality **matches** with another, or if the two things **match**, they are both the same or equal. If you **match** two things, or **match** one thing with another, you make them the same or equal. *Their strengths in memory and spatial skills matched... Our value system does not match with their value system. ...efforts to match demand with supply by building new schools.* V-RECIP-ERG; pl-n V; V with n; V n with n; Also V pl-n

5 If one thing **matches** another, or if the two things **match**, they are connected or suit each other in some way. If you **match** two things, or **match** one thing with another, you find the connection between them, or decide that they suit each other. *The students are asked to match the books with the authors... We will try to match you to employers with the vacancies you are looking for... It can take time and effort to match buyers and sellers... The sale would only go ahead if the name and number matched... If the figure matches with the target dividend declared in the paper you win or share the prize money.* ▶ **Match up** means the same as **match**. *The consultant seeks to match up jobless professionals with small companies in need of expertise... They compared the fat intake of groups of vegetarians and meat eaters, and matched their diets up with levels of harmful blood fats... My sister and I never really matched up... I'm sure that yellow lead matched up to that yellow socket.* V-RECIP-ERG; V n with/to n; V pl-n; pl-n V; V with n; PHRASAL VERB RECIP-ERG; V P n (not pron) with n; V n P with n; pl-n V P; V P to/with n; Also V P pl-n

6 If a combination of things or people is a good **match**, they have a pleasing effect when placed or used together. *Helen's choice of lipstick was a good match for her skin-tone... Moina was a perfect match for him.* N-SING: adj N

7 If you **match** something, you are as good as it or equal to it, for example in speed, size, or quality. *They played some fine attacking football, but I think we matched them in every department... His record has never been matched.* VERB =equal; V n

8 If you **match** one person or team against another, in sports or other contests, you make them compete with each other to see which one is better. *The finals of the Championship begin today, matching the United States against France... Lewis is matched against the WBO's heavyweight champion, Tommy Morrison.* VERB; V n with/against n

9 See also **matched, matching**.

10 If you **meet** your **match**, you find that you are competing or fighting against someone or something that you cannot beat. *I had finally met my match in power and intellect.* PHRASES; V inflects

11 If one person or thing is **no match for** another, they are unable to compete successfully with the other person or thing. *I was no match for a man with such power... Hand-held guns proved no match for heavy armor.* v-link PHR, PHR n

match up. See **match** 3 and 5. PHRASAL VERB

match up to. If someone or something does not **match up to** what was expected, they are smaller, less impressive, or of poorer quality. *Her career never quite matched up to its promise. ...a father's inability to match up to the expectations of his son... The other stories don't quite match up to the high standard of the first.* PHRASAL VERB; V P P n

matchbox /mætʃbɒks/ **matchboxes.** A **matchbox** is a small box that you buy with matches in it. N-COUNT

matched /mætʃt/ ◆◇◇◇◇

1 If you say that two people are well **matched**, you mean that they have qualities that will enable them to have a good relationship. *They were well matched, I thought... My parents were not very well matched... They couldn't be more perfectly matched.* ADJ: adv ADJ

2 In sports and other competitions, if the two opponents or teams are well **matched**, they are both of the same standard in strength or ability. *Two well-matched sides conjured up an entertaining game... The teams are evenly matched.* ADJ: adv ADJ

matching /mætʃɪŋ/. **Matching** is used to describe things which are of the same colour or design. *She bought more fabric in the same design so she could make matching curtains and cushions. ...a coat and a matching handbag.* ◆◇◇◇◇ ADJ: ADJ n

matchless /mætʃləs/. You can use **matchless** to emphasize that you think something is extremely good. *A timeless comic actor - his simplicity and his apparent ease are matchless... The Savoy provides a matchless hotel experience.* ADJ: usu ADJ n PRAGMATICS =unparalleled

matchmaker /mætʃmeɪkəʳ/ **matchmakers.** A **matchmaker** is someone who tries to encourage people they know to form relationships or to get married. *The matchmaker has been an important member of Jewish communities for centuries.* N-COUNT

matchmaking /mætʃmeɪkɪŋ/. **Matchmaking** is the activity of encouraging people you know to form relationships or get married. N-UNCOUNT

match point, match points. In a game of tennis, **match point** is the situation when the player who is in the lead can win the whole match if they win the next point. N-VAR

matchstick /mætʃstɪk/ **matchsticks**

1 A **matchstick** is the wooden part of a match. *Use a pointed object such as a broken matchstick.* N-COUNT

2 You can refer to something very small or thin as a **matchstick**. *Cut the cucumber into matchsticks. ...children with matchstick legs.* N-COUNT: oft N n

mate /meɪt/ **mates, mating, mated** ◆◆◆◇◇

1 You can refer to someone's friends as their **mates**, especially when you are talking about a man and his male friends; an informal British use. *He's off drinking with his mates... A mate of mine used to play soccer for Liverpool.* N-COUNT: usu with poss =friend

2 Some men use **mate** as a way of addressing other men when they are talking to them; an informal British use. *Come on mate, things aren't that bad.* N-VOC PRAGMATICS =pal

3 Someone's wife, husband, or sexual partner can be referred to as their **mate**. *He has found his ideal mate. ...as women do become as powerful in the marketplace as their mates.* N-COUNT: usu sing, oft poss N =partner

4 An animal's **mate** is its sexual partner. *The males guard their mates zealously.* N-COUNT: usu poss N

5 When animals **mate**, a male and a female have sex in order to produce young. *This allows the pair to mate properly and stops the hen staying in the nest-box... They want the males to mate with wild females... It is easy to tell when a female is ready to mate. ...the mating season.* V-RECIP; pl-n V; V with n; V (non-recip); V-ing

6 On a commercial ship, **the mate** or **first mate** is the most important officer except for the captain. *...the mate of a fishing trawler.* N-COUNT: usu sing

7 A **mate** is an officer on a merchant ship. *He was a mate on merchant ships when he was only 16.* N-COUNT

8 In chess, **mate** is the same as **checkmate**. N-UNCOUNT

9 See also **cellmate**, **classmate**, **flatmate**, **playmate**, **roommate**, **running mate**, **schoolmate**, **shipmate**, **soul mate**.

material /mətɪəriəl/ **materials** ◆◆◆◆◇

1 A **material** is a solid substance. *...electrons in a conducting material such as a metal. ...the design of new absorbent materials. ...recycling of all materials.* N-VAR

2 **Material** is cloth. *...the thick material of her skirt... The materials are soft and comfortable to wear.* N-MASS

3 **Materials** are the things that you need for a particular activity. *The builders ran out of materials. ...sewing materials.* N-PLURAL: usu supp N

4 Ideas or information that are used as a basis for a book, play, or film can be referred to as **material**. *In my version of the story, I added some new material. ...the film producer's debt to the author of original screen material.* N-UNCOUNT

5 **Material** things are related to possessions or money, rather than to more abstract things such as ideas or values. *Every room must have been stuffed with material things. ...the material world. ...his descriptions of their poor material conditions.* ADJ: usu ADJ n ≠spiritual
♦ **materially** *He has tried to help this child materially and spiritually... They believe that a tough, materially poor childhood is character-building... The object has no real value, materially or emotionally.* ADV: ADV with v, ADV adj/-ed, ADV with cl

6 If you say that someone is a particular kind of **material**, you mean that they have the qualities or abilities to do a particular job or task. *She was not university material... His message has changed little since he became presidential material.* N-UNCOUNT: supp N

7 **Material** evidence or information is directly relevant and important in a legal or academic argument; a formal word. *The nature and availability of material evidence was not to be discussed... They contend that the company failed to disclose material information.* ADJ: ADJ n

materialise /mətɪəriəlaɪz/. See **materialize**.

materialism /mətɪəriəlɪzəm/ ◆◇◇◇◇

1 **Materialism** is the attitude of someone who attaches a lot of importance to money and wants to possess a lot of material things. *...the rising consumer materialism in society at large.* N-UNCOUNT
♦ **materialist, materialists** *Leo is a materialist, living for life's little luxuries.* N-COUNT

2 **Materialism** is the belief that only physical matter exists, and that there is no spiritual world. N-UNCOUNT

materialist /mətɪəriəlɪst/. **Materialist** is used to describe things relating to the philosophy of materialism. *...the materialist view of nature and society.* ◆◇◇◇◇ ADJ: usu ADJ n

materialistic /mətɪəriəlɪstɪk/. If you describe a person or society as **materialistic**, you are critical of them because they attach too much importance to money and material possessions. *During the 1980s Britain became a very materialistic society.* ADJ-GRADED PRAGMATICS

materialize /mətɪəriəlaɪz/ **materializes, materializing, materialized;** also spelled **materialise** in British English. ◆◇◇◇◇

1 If a possible or expected event does not **materialize**, it does not happen. *A rebellion by radicals failed to materialize... None of the anticipated difficulties materialized.* VB: usu with brd-neg V

2 If a person or thing **materializes**, they suddenly appear, after they have been invisible or in another place. *Tamsin materialized at her side, notebook at the ready... A moment or two later champagne in an ice-bucket materialized beside them.* VERB =appear V

maternal /mətɜːʳnəl/ ◆◇◇◇◇

1 **Maternal** is used to describe feelings or actions which are typical of those of a kind mother towards her child. *She had little maternal instinct... Her feelings towards him were almost maternal.* ADJ-GRADED: usu ADJ n

2 **Maternal** is used to describe things that relate to the mother of a baby. *Maternal smoking can damage the unborn child.* ADJ: ADJ n

3 A **maternal** relative is one who is related through a person's mother rather than their father. *Her maternal grandfather was Mayor of Karachi.* ADJ: ADJ n

maternity /mətɜːʳnɪti/ ◆◇◇◇◇

1 **Maternity** is used to describe things relating to the help and medical care given to a woman when she is pregnant and when she gives birth. *Your job will be kept open for your return after maternity leave... The boy was born at the city's maternity hospital. ...maternity clothes.* ADJ: ADJ n

2 **Maternity** is the state of being a mother. *Morisot had experienced maternity herself.* N-UNCOUNT =motherhood

matey /meɪti/

1 If someone uses **matey** words or behaviour, they are being very friendly, usually insincerely; used mainly in informal British English. *Frost had displayed his usual matey charm as the pair sipped orange juice on national TV. ...her irritatingly matey tone.* ADJ-GRADED

2 In informal British English, you can address someone as **matey** when you are being friendly towards them. People sometimes also use **matey** when they are annoyed with someone. *No problem, matey.* N-VOC PRAGMATICS

math /mæθ/. In American English, **math** is the same as **mathematics**. The usual British word is **maths**. *He studied math in college.* ◆◇◇◇◇ N-UNCOUNT

mathematical /mæθəmætɪkəl/ ◆◆◇◇◇

1 Something that is **mathematical** involves numbers and calculations. *...mathematical calculations... Given the sheer number of stars that exist it's a mathematical certainty that there is life on other planets.* ADJ: ADJ n
♦ **mathematically** /mæθəmætɪkli/ *...a mathematically complicated formula... Mathematically, it made sense.* ADV: ADV with v, ADV adj, ADV with cl

2 If you have **mathematical** abilities or a **mathematical** mind, you are clever at doing calculations or understanding problems that involve numbers. *...children who display extraordinary mathematical ability. ...a mathematical genius.* ADJ-GRADED: usu ADJ n
♦ **mathematically** *Anyone can be an astrologer as long as they are mathematically minded.* ADV: ADV -ed/adj

mathematician /mæθəmətɪʃən/ **mathematicians** ◆◇◇◇◇

1 A **mathematician** is a person who is trained in the study of numbers and calculations. *The risks can be so complex that banks hire mathematicians to puzzle them out.* N-COUNT

2 A **mathematician** is a person who is good at doing calculations and using numbers. *I'm not a very good mathematician.* N-COUNT

mathematics /mæθəmætɪks/ ◆◆◇◇◇

1 **Mathematics** is the study of numbers, quantities, or shapes. *Elizabeth studied mathematics and classics. ...a professor of mathematics at Boston College.* N-UNCOUNT

2 The **mathematics** of a problem is the calculations that are involved in it. *Once you understand the mathematics of debt you can work your way out of it.* N-UNCOUNT

maths /mæθs/. In British English, **maths** is the same as **mathematics**. The usual American word is **math**. *He taught science and maths.* ◆◇◇◇◇ N-UNCOUNT

matinee /mætɪneɪ, AM -neɪ/ **matinees;** also spelled **matinée**. A **matinee** is a performance of a play or a showing of a film which takes place in the afternoon. N-COUNT

matriarch /meɪtriɑːʳk/ **matriarchs**

1 A **matriarch** is a woman who rules in a society in which power passes from mother to daughter. N-COUNT

2 A **matriarch** is an old and powerful female member of a family, for example a grandmother. N-COUNT

matriarchal /meɪtriɑːʳkəl/

1 A **matriarchal** society, family, or system is one in which the rulers are female and power or property is passed from mother to daughter. *...the 3,000 years of the matriarchal Sumerian society.* ADJ ≠patriarchal

2 A **matriarchal** family or group is one in which women are more powerful or prominent than ADJ-GRADED ≠patriarchal

men. *He was raised in a matriarchal family and was always closer to his mother than his father.*
3 If you describe a woman as **matriarchal**, you mean that she has authority and power within her family or group. *...the matriarchal figure of his grandmother.* ADJ: usu ADJ n

matriarchy /meɪtriɑːʳki/ **matriarchies**
1 **Matriarchy** is a system of government in which the ruler is female and the power is passed from mother to daughter. N-VAR ≠patriarchy
2 A **matriarchy** is a system of inheritance in which family property is traditionally inherited from women and not from men. N-VAR ≠patriarchy

matrices /meɪtrɪsiːz/. **Matrices** is the plural of **matrix**.

matriculate /mətrɪkjʊleɪt/ **matriculates, matriculating, matriculated.** In some countries, if you **matriculate**, you register formally as a student at a university, or you satisfy the academic requirements necessary for registration for a course. *I had to matriculate if I wanted to do a degree.* ♦ **matriculation** /mətrɪkjʊleɪʃᵊn/ *The head decided I should have another go at matriculation.* VERB V N-UNCOUNT

matrimonial /mætrɪmoʊniəl/. **Matrimonial** means concerning marriage or married people; a formal word. *...the matrimonial home.* ADJ: usu ADJ n

matrimony /mætrɪməni, AM -moʊni/. **Matrimony** is marriage; a formal word. *...the bonds of matrimony. ...holy matrimony.* N-UNCOUNT

matrix /meɪtrɪks/ **matrices** ◆◇◇◇◇
1 A **matrix** is the environment or context in which something such as a society develops and grows; a formal use. *...the matrix of their culture.* N-COUNT: with supp
2 A **matrix** is a rectangular arrangement of numbers, symbols, or letters written in rows and columns and used in solving certain mathematical problems; a technical term in mathematics. N-COUNT

matron /meɪtrən/ **matrons** ◆◇◇◇◇
1 In British English, the **matron** in a nursing home is the woman who is in charge of all the nurses. In the past, the woman in charge of the nurses in a hospital was also called a **matron**. *The Matron at the nursing home expressed a wish to attend... Have you told Matron?* N-COUNT; N-TITLE
2 In British boarding schools, the **matron** is the woman who looks after the health and hygiene of the children. *Matron was quite kind but brisk and hurried. ...a prep school matron.* N-TITLE; N-COUNT
3 In American English, the **matron** in a hospital or other institution is the woman who is in charge of domestic matters. **Matron** is also used to refer to a female officer in a prison; a fairly old-fashioned use. N-COUNT
4 People sometimes refer to middle-aged women as **matrons**, especially if they are rather fat. *Inside the changing-room was a middle-aged matron wriggling into a corset.* ♦ **matronly** *...a matronly woman with an air of authority.* N-COUNT ADJ-GRADED

matt /mæt/; also spelled **matte**. American English also uses the spelling **mat**. A **matt** colour, paint, or surface is dull rather than shiny. *...a creamy white matt emulsion. ...matt black.* ◆◇◇◇◇ ADJ

matted /mætɪd/. If you describe someone's hair as **matted**, you mean that it has become a thick untidy mass, often because it is wet or dirty. *She had matted hair and torn dusty clothes.* ADJ-GRADED

matter /mætəʳ/ **matters, mattering, mattered** ◆◆◆◆◆
1 A **matter** is a task, situation, or event which you have to deal with or think about, especially one that involves problems. *It was clear that she wanted to discuss some private matter... Until the matter is resolved the athletes will be ineligible to compete... Don't you think this is now a matter for the police?... Business matters drew him to Paris.* N-COUNT: usu with supp =affair
2 You use **matters** to refer to the situation you are talking about, especially when something is affecting the situation in some way. *If your ordinary life is out of control, then retreating into a cosy ritual will not improve matters... If it would facilitate matters, I would be happy to come to New York... Matters took an unexpected turn.* N-PLURAL: without det =things
3 If you say that a situation is a **matter** of a particular thing, you mean that that is the most important thing to be done or considered when you are involved in the situation or explaining it. *History is always a matter of interpretation... Observance of the law is a matter of principle for us... After that, life became a matter of defying school rules... Jack had attended these meetings as a matter of routine for years.* N-SING: a N of n/-ing =question
4 Printed **matter** consists of books, newspapers, and other texts that are printed. Reading **matter** consists of things that are suitable for reading, such as books and newspapers. *...the Government's plans to levy VAT on printed matter... Many of the papers have magazine supplements, providing a rich variety of reading matter.* N-UNCOUNT: supp N
5 **Matter** is the physical part of the universe consisting of solids, liquids, and gases. *A proton is an elementary particle of matter that possesses a positive charge... He has spent his career studying how matter behaves at the fine edge between order and disorder.* N-UNCOUNT
6 You use **matter** to refer to a particular type of substance. *They feed mostly on decaying vegetable matter. ...waste matter from industries.* N-UNCOUNT: with supp
7 You use **matter** in expressions such as **'What's the matter?'** or **'Is anything the matter?'** when you think that someone has a problem and you want to know what it is. *Carole, what's the matter? You don't seem happy... What's the matter with your office?... She told him there was nothing the matter.* N-SING: the N, oft N with n
8 You use **matter** in expressions such as **'a matter of weeks'** when you are emphasizing how small an amount is or how short a period of time is. *Within a matter of days she was back at work... He expected to be at East Grinstead station in a matter of hours... This time the journey was short, a matter of four or five miles up into the hills.* N-SING: a N of pl-n PRAGMATICS
9 If you say that something does not **matter**, you mean that it is not important to you because it does not have an effect on you or on a particular situation. *A lot of the food goes on the floor but that doesn't matter... As for Laura and me, the colour of our skin has never mattered... As long as staff are smart, it does not matter how long their hair is... Does it matter that people don't know this?... Money is the only thing that matters to them.* VB: no cont, usu with brd-neg V it V wh it V that V to n Also it V
10 See also **subject matter**.
11 If you say that something is **another matter** or a **different matter**, you mean that it is very different from the situation that you have just discussed or is an exception to a rule or general statement that you have just made. *Being responsible for one's own health is one thing, but being responsible for another person's health is quite a different matter... You have no business going into such places all by yourselves. If your parents take you, of course, that's another matter.* PHRASES v-link PHR
12 If you are going to do something **as a matter of** urgency or priority, you are going to do it as soon as possible, because it is important. *Your doctor and health visitor can help a great deal and you need to talk about it with them as a matter of urgency.* PHR n
13 If something is **no easy matter**, it is difficult to do it. *Choosing the colour for the drawing-room walls was no easy matter.* v-link PHR
14 If a person in authority says **that's the end of the matter** or **that's an end to the matter**, they mean that a decision that has been taken must not be changed or discussed any more. *'He's moving in here,' Maria said. 'So that's the end of the matter.'* PRAGMATICS =that's final
15 You use **the fact of the matter is** or **the truth of the matter is** to introduce a fact which supports what you are saying or which is not widely known, for example because it is a secret. *The fact of the matter is that most people consume far more protein than they actually need... The truth of the matter is that he was having an identity crisis when he met Carina.* V inflects, PHR that PRAGMATICS =the truth is
16 You can use **for that matter** to emphasize that the remark you are making is true in the same way as your previous, similar remark. *The irony was* PHR with cl PRAGMATICS =come to that

that Shawn had not seen her. Nor for that matter had anyone else... A great deal of hard work was done and, for that matter, is continuing.

17 You say **'it doesn't matter'** to tell someone who is apologizing to you that you are not angry or upset, and that they should not worry. *'Did I wake you?'—'Yes, but it doesn't matter.'* CONVENTION PRAGMATICS =never mind

18 You say **'it doesn't matter'** when someone offers you a choice between two or more things and you do not mind which is chosen. *'Steve, what do you want?'—'Coke, Pepsi, it doesn't matter.'* CONVENTION

19 If you say that something is **no laughing matter**, you mean that it is very serious and not something that you should laugh or joke about. *Their behaviour is an offence. It's no laughing matter.* V-link PHR =no joke, serious

20 If you say that something **makes matters worse**, you mean that it makes a difficult situation even more difficult. *Don't let yourself despair; this will only make matters worse... To make matters worse, it started to rain again.* V inflects, oft PHR with cl

21 You say **'no matter'** after you have just asked a question or mentioned an idea or doubt and you have decided that it is not really important, interesting, or worth discussing. *'Didn't you ever read the book?' Keating shook his head. 'Well, no matter.'... 'Shoddy workmanship these days,' he remarked. 'No matter, it will still bear my weight.'* CONVENTION PRAGMATICS =never mind

22 You use **no matter** in expressions like **'no matter how'** and **'no matter what'** to say that something is true or happens in all circumstances. *No matter what your age, you can lose weight by following this program... No matter how often they were urged, they could not bring themselves to join in... Jenkins would reward all investors, no matter when they made their investment.* PHR wh =never mind

23 If you say that you are going to do something **no matter what**, you are emphasizing that you are definitely going to do it, whatever obstacles or difficulties you may face. *He had decided to publish the manuscript no matter what... I vowed then, no matter what, I would never be like those people.* PHR with cl PRAGMATICS =regardless

24 If you say that a statement is **a matter of opinion**, you mean that it is not a fact, and that other people, including yourself, do not agree with it. *'We're not that contrived. We're not that theatrical.'—'That's a matter of opinion.'* V-link PHR =debatable

25 If you say that something is just **a matter of time**, you mean that it is certain to happen at some time in the future. *It would be only a matter of time before he went through with it.* V-link PHR

26 • **a matter of life and death**: see **death.** • **as a matter of course**: see **course.** • **as a matter of fact**: see **fact.** • **mind over matter**: see **mind.**

matter-of-fact. If you describe a person as **matter-of-fact**, you mean that they show no emotions such as enthusiasm, anger, or surprise, especially in a situation where you would expect them to be emotional. *John was doing his best to give Francis the news in a matter-of-fact way... He sounded matter-of-fact and unemotional.* ◆◇◇◇◇ ADJ-GRADED
♦ **matter-of-factly** *'She thinks you're a spy,' Scott said matter-of-factly.* ADV-GRADED: ADV after v

matting /mætɪŋ/. **Matting** is strong thick material, usually made from a material like rope, straw, or rushes, which is used as a floor covering. *There was rush matting on the floor.* N-UNCOUNT

mattress /mætrəs/ **mattresses.** A **mattress** is the large, flat layer of padding which is put on a bed to make it comfortable to sleep on. ◆◇◇◇◇ N-COUNT

maturation /mætjʊreɪʃən/

1 The **maturation** of something such as wine or cheese is the process of its being left for a time to become mature; a formal word. *The period of maturation is determined by the cellar master.* N-UNCOUNT

2 The **maturation** of a young person's body is the process of it becoming like an adult's; a formal use. N-UNCOUNT =development

mature /mətjʊəʳ/ **matures, maturing, matured; maturer, maturest** ◆◆◇◇◇

1 When a child or young animal **matures**, it becomes an adult. *You will learn what to expect as your child matures physically... The eggs hatched and the chicks matured. ...young girls who'd not yet matured.* VERB =grow up V

2 When something **matures**, it reaches a state of complete development. *When the trees matured they were cut in certain areas... Their songwriting has matured.* VERB =develop V

3 If someone **matures**, they become more fully developed in their personality and emotional behaviour. *Hopefully after three years at university I will have matured... I thought you had matured enough not to be giggly and silly about serious art.* VERB =develop V

4 If you describe someone as **mature**, you think that they are fully developed and balanced in their personality and emotional behaviour. *They are emotionally mature and should behave responsibly... You and I are mature, freethinking adults.* ADJ-GRADED PRAGMATICS

5 If you describe someone's work of art or fiction as **mature**, you mean they have created it thoughtfully and carefully and they have fully developed their abilities and potential. *It is his most mature comedy yet.* ADJ-GRADED: ADJ n PRAGMATICS

6 If something such as wine or cheese **matures** or **is matured**, it is left for a time to allow its full flavour or strength to develop. *Unlike wine, brandy matures only in wood, not glass. ...the cellars where the cheeses are matured. ...our best selling matured cheddar.* V-ERG V be V-ed V-ed

7 **Mature** cheese or wine has been left for a time to allow its full flavour or strength to develop. *Grate some mature cheddar cheese. ...the best place to enjoy fine, mature wines.* ADJ-GRADED: usu ADJ n

8 When an investment such as a savings policy or pension plan **matures**, the time comes when you stop paying money, and the bank, savings, or insurance company pays you back the money you have saved plus the interest. *These bonuses will be paid when your savings plan matures in ten years' time. ...an endowment policy that matured on September 1.* VERB V

9 If you say that someone is **mature** or of **mature** years, you are saying politely that they are middle-aged or old. *...a man of mature years who had been in the job for longer than most of the members could remember.* ADJ PRAGMATICS

mature student, mature students. In British English, a **mature student** is a person who begins their studies at university or college a number of years after leaving school, so that they are older than most of the people they are studying with. N-COUNT

maturity /mətjʊərɪti/ **maturities** ◆◆◇◇◇

1 **Maturity** is the state of being fully developed or adult. *Humans experience a delayed maturity; we arrive at all stages of life later than other mammals.* N-UNCOUNT

2 Someone's **maturity** is their quality of being fully developed in their personality and emotional behaviour. *Her speech showed great maturity and humanity... Lacking self-confidence and maturity, many teenagers are left feeling very vulnerable.* N-UNCOUNT

3 When an investment such as a savings policy or pension plan reaches **maturity**, the time comes when you stop paying money, and the bank, savings, or insurance company pays you back the money you have saved plus the interest. *Customers are told what their policies will be worth on maturity, not what they are worth today... Treasury bonds have maturities that extend out as far as 25 years or more.* N-COUNT

maudlin /mɔːdlɪn/

1 If you describe someone as **maudlin**, you mean that they are being sad and sentimental in a foolish way, perhaps because of drinking alcohol. *Jimmy turned maudlin after three drinks. ...maudlin self-pity.* ADJ-GRADED

2 If you describe a song, book, or film as **maudlin**, you are criticizing it for being very sentimental. *...the most maudlin song of all time. ...a hugely entertaining (if over-long and maudlin) movie.* ADJ-GRADED PRAGMATICS =soppy, mawkish

maul /mɔːl/ **mauls, mauling, mauled** ◆◇◇◇◇

1 If you **are mauled** by an animal, you are savagely attacked by it and badly injured. *He had been* VERB =attack be V-ed by n

mauled by a bear... The dog went berserk and mauled one of the girls. V n

2 If someone **is mauled**, they are attacked fiercely and aggressively, and often harmed in some way. *The troops were severely mauled and lost a quarter of their strength before evacuating the island... The cable-TV and health-care industries are both being mauled by government.* VB: usu passive =assault *be* V-ed

Maundy Thursday /mɔːndi θɜːʳzdeɪ/. **Maundy Thursday** is the Thursday before Easter Sunday. N-UNCOUNT

Mauritian /mərɪʃᵊn, AM mɔːr-/ **Mauritians**

1 **Mauritian** means belonging or relating to Mauritius, or to its people or culture. ADJ

2 A **Mauritian** is a Mauritian citizen, or a person of Mauritian origin. N-COUNT

mausoleum /mɔːzəliːəm/ **mausoleums.** A **mausoleum** is a building which contains the grave of a famous person or the graves of a rich family. N-COUNT =tomb

mauve /moʊv/ **mauves.** Something that is **mauve** is of a pale purple colour. *It bears clusters of mauve flowers in early summer.* ◆◇◇◇◇ COLOUR

maverick /mævərɪk/ **mavericks.** If you describe someone as a **maverick**, you mean that they are unconventional and independent, and do not think or behave in the same way as other people. *He was too much of a maverick ever to hold high office.* ◆◇◇◇◇ N-COUNT =outsider ► Also an adjective. *...a maverick group of scientists, who oppose the prevailing medical opinion on the disease... Her independence and maverick behaviour precluded any chance of promotion.* ADJ: ADJ n

maw /mɔː/ **maws.** If you describe something as a **maw**, you mean that it is like a huge mouth which swallows, consumes, or absorbs everything around it; a literary word. *Cale's best work has plunged fearlessly into the dripping maw of emotional extremes.* N-COUNT: usu sing, usu with supp

mawkish /mɔːkɪʃ/. You can describe something as **mawkish** when it is sentimental and silly, and you dislike it a lot. *A sordid, sentimental plot unwinds, with an inevitable mawkish ending.* ADJ-GRADED PRAGMATICS =nauseating, soppy

max /mæks/.

1 **Max.** is an abbreviation for 'maximum'; often used with numbers or amounts when you are giving measurements or ratings. *'Start small,' the man advised, 'Ten gallons, max.'... I'll give him eight out of 10, max... He twisted the throttle control to max power.* ADJ: num ADJ, ADJ n

2 If you do something **to the max**, you do it to the greatest degree possible; an informal use. *Everyone involved is enjoying himself to the max.* PHRASE: PHR after v =to the full

maxim /mæksɪm/ **maxims.** A **maxim** is a rule for good or sensible behaviour, especially one in the form of a saying or proverb. *I believe in the maxim 'if it ain't broke, don't fix it'.* ◆◇◇◇◇ N-COUNT

maximize /mæksɪmaɪz/ **maximizes, maximizing, maximized;** also spelled **maximise** in British English. If you **maximize** something, you make it as great in amount or importance as you can; a fairly formal word. *In order to maximize profit the firm would seek to maximize output... They were looking for suitable ways of maximising their electoral support.* ◆◇◇◇◇ VERB =increase ≠minimize V n ♦ **maximization** /mæksɪmaɪzeɪʃᵊn/ *...a pricing policy that was aimed at profit maximisation.* N-UNCOUNT: usu N *of* n

maximum /mæksɪməm/ ◆◆◆◇◇

1 You use **maximum** to describe an amount which is the largest that is possible, allowed, or required. *Under planning law the maximum height for a fence or hedge is 2 metres... China headed the table with maximum points.* ADJ: ADJ n ≠minimum ► Also a noun. *The law provides for a maximum of two years in prison... Twelve hours is the minimum, sixty hours the maximum.* N-SING: oft *a* N *of* amount ≠minimum

2 You use **maximum** to indicate how great an amount is. *...the maximum amount of information... It was achieved with minimum fuss and maximum efficiency... He is expected to be transferred to a maximum security prison.* ADJ: ADJ n ≠minimum

3 If you say that something is a particular amount **maximum**, you mean that this is the greatest amount it should be or could possibly be, although a smaller amount is acceptable or very possible. *We need an extra 6g a day maximum.* ADV: amount ADV ≠minimum

4 If you say that someone does something **to the maximum**, you are emphasizing that they do it to the greatest degree possible. *You have to develop your capabilities to the maximum.* PHRASE: PHR after v PRAGMATICS =to the full

may /meɪ/ ◆◆◆◆◆

May is a modal verb. It is used with the base form of a verb.

1 You use **may** to indicate that something will possibly happen or be true in the future, but you cannot be certain. *We may have some rain today... Rates may rise, but it won't be by much and it won't be for long... I may be back next year... I don't know if they'll publish it or not. They may... Scientists know that cancer may not show up for many years.* MODAL PRAGMATICS =might

2 You use **may** to indicate that there is a possibility that something is true, but you cannot be certain. *Civil rights officials say there may be hundreds of other cases of racial violence... Throwing good money after bad may not be a good idea, they say.* MODAL PRAGMATICS =might

3 You use **may** to indicate that something is sometimes true or is true in some circumstances. *A vegetarian diet may not provide enough calories for a child's normal growth... Up to five inches of snow may cover the mountains. ...families that may have both parents working.* MODAL =might

4 You use **may have** with a past participle when suggesting that it is possible that something happened or was true, or when giving a possible explanation for something. *He may have been to some of those places... The chaos may have contributed to the deaths of up to 20 people... Investigators say that a fuel explosion may have caused the crash... The events may or may not have been connected.* MODAL PRAGMATICS =might have

5 You use **may** in statements where you are accepting the truth of a situation, but contrasting it with something that is more important. *I may be almost 50, but there's not a lot of things I've forgotten... The elderly man may not be typical, but he speaks for a significant body of opinion... Walking exercise may be boring at times but early on a clear sunny morning there can be nothing finer.* MODAL PRAGMATICS

6 You use **may** when you are mentioning a quality or fact about something that people can make use of if they want to. *The bag has narrow straps, so it may be worn over the shoulder or carried in the hand... Some of the diseases of middle age may be prevented by improving nutrition.* MODAL =can

7 You use **may** to indicate that someone is allowed to do something or has the choice of doing something, usually because of a rule or law. You use **may not** to indicate that someone is not allowed to do something. *Any two persons may marry in Scotland provided that both persons are at least 16 years of age on the day of their marriage... Adolescents under the age of 18 may not work in jobs that require them to drive.* MODAL PRAGMATICS

8 You use **may** when you are giving permission to someone to do something, or when asking for permission to do something; a formal use. *Mr Hobbs? May we come in?... If you wish, you may now have a glass of milk... 'You may leave.'—'Yes, sir.'* MODAL PRAGMATICS =can

9 You use **may** when you are making polite requests. *I'd like the use of your living room, if I may... May I come with you to Southampton?... Ah, Julia, my dear, here is our guest. May we have some tea?* MODAL PRAGMATICS =can

10 You use **may**, usually in questions, when you are politely making suggestions or offering to do something; a formal use. *May we suggest you try one of our guest houses... May we recommend a weekend in Stockholm?... Do sit down. And may we offer you something to drink?... May I help you?* MODAL PRAGMATICS =can

11 In formal spoken English, you use **may** as a polite way of interrupting someone, asking a question, or introducing what you are going to say next. *'If I may interrupt for a moment,' Kenneth said... Anyway, may I just ask you one other thing?... If I may return to what we were talking about earlier..* MODAL PRAGMATICS =can

12 You use **may** when you are mentioning the reaction or attitude that you think someone is likely MODAL PRAGMATICS

to have to something you are about to say. *You know, Brian, whatever you may think, I work hard for a living... You may consider it useless, but for our customers it's an all-important sign of good service.*

13 You use **may** in expressions such as **I may add** and **I may say** in order to emphasize a statement that you are making. *However, I may add, as a Muslim, that the Muslims in this country are rather frustrated and disunited... Both of them, I may say, are thoroughly reliable men.* MODAL PRAGMATICS

14 If you do something so that a particular thing **may** happen, you do it so that there is an opportunity for it. *...the need for an increase in the numbers of surgeons so that patients may be treated as soon as possible... The door is shut so that no one may overhear what is said.* MODAL =can

15 In formal English, people use **may** to express hopes and wishes. *Courage seems now to have deserted him. May it quickly reappear.* MODAL: MODAL n v PRAGMATICS

16 • **be that as it may**: see **be**. • **may as well**: see **well**.

May /meɪ/ **Mays.** **May** is the fifth month of the year in the Western calendar. ◆◆◆◆◇ N-VAR

maybe /meɪbi/ ◆◆◆◆◇

1 You use **maybe** to express uncertainty, for example when you do not know that something is definitely true, or when you are mentioning something that may possibly happen in the future in the way you describe. *Maybe she is in love... Maybe he sincerely wanted to help his country... I do think about having children, maybe when I'm 40... Things are maybe not as good as they should be... Bill will come on then maybe Ralph, then Bobby and Johnny doing their hits.* ADV: ADV with cl/group PRAGMATICS =perhaps

2 You use **maybe** when you are making suggestions or giving advice. **Maybe** is also used to introduce polite requests. *Maybe we can go to the movies or something... Maybe you'd better tell me what this is all about... Maybe you shouldn't eat in that restaurant anymore... Maybe if you tell me a little about her?... Wait a while, maybe a few days.* ADV: ADV with cl/group PRAGMATICS =perhaps

3 You use **maybe** to indicate that, although a comment is partly true, there is also another point of view that should be considered. *Maybe there is jealousy, but I think the envy is more powerful... OK, maybe I am a failure, but, in my opinion, no more than the rest of this country.* ADV: ADV cl PRAGMATICS =perhaps

4 You can say **maybe** as a response to a question or remark, when you do not want to agree or disagree. *'Do you think that China and Japan will step in to become the dominant military powers in the region?'—'Maybe.'... 'Is she coming back?'—'Maybe. No one hears from her.'* ADV: ADV as reply PRAGMATICS =perhaps

5 You use **maybe** when you are making a rough guess at a number, quantity, or value, rather than stating it exactly. *The men were maybe a hundred feet away and coming closer.* ADV: ADV amount PRAGMATICS =about

6 People often use **maybe** to mean 'sometimes', particularly in a series of general statements about what someone does, or about something that regularly happens. *They'll come to the bar for a year, or maybe even two, then they'll find another favourite spot.* ADV: ADV with cl/group

Mayday /meɪdeɪ/ **Maydays**

1 If someone in a plane or ship sends out a **Mayday** or a **Mayday** message, they send out a radio message calling for help because they are in serious difficulty. *He raced to pick up the lifejackets while his stepmother sent out a Mayday call.* N-COUNT

2 **'Mayday! Mayday!'** is the phrase that is used in Mayday messages to indicate that help is needed. CONVENTION

May Day. **May Day** is the 1st of May, which in many countries is celebrated as a public holiday, especially as one in honour of working people. ◆◇◇◇◇ N-UNCOUNT

mayfly /meɪflaɪ/ **mayflies.** A **mayfly** is an insect which lives near water and only lives for a very short time as an adult. N-COUNT

mayhem /meɪhem/. You use **mayhem** to refer to a situation that is not controlled or ordered, when people are behaving in a disorganized, confused, and often violent way. *Their arrival caused mayhem as crowds of refugees rushed towards them. ...the economic mayhem that this country's going through now.* ◆◇◇◇◇ N-UNCOUNT =chaos

mayn't /meɪənt/. **Mayn't** is a spoken form of **may not**.

mayo /meɪoʊ/. **Mayo** is the same as **mayonnaise**; an informal word. N-UNCOUNT

mayonnaise /meɪəneɪz/. **Mayonnaise** is a thick pale sauce made from egg yolks and oil. It is put on salad to give it more taste. ◆◇◇◇◇ N-UNCOUNT

mayor /meəʳ, meɪəʳ/ **mayors.** The **mayor** of a town or city is the person who has been elected to represent it for a fixed period of time. ◆◆◆◇◇ N-COUNT: oft *the* N *of* n

mayoress /meəres, meɪəres/ **mayoresses**

1 In British English, a woman who holds the office of mayor is sometimes referred to as a **mayoress**. N-COUNT

2 In British English, a **mayoress** is the wife of a mayor. N-COUNT

may've /meɪəv/. **May've** is a spoken form of **may have**, especially when 'have' is an auxiliary verb.

maze /meɪz/ **mazes** ◆◇◇◇◇

1 A **maze** is a complex system of passages or paths separated by walls or hedges, which is designed to confuse people who try to find their way through it as a form of amusement. *The palace has extensive gardens, a maze, and tennis courts.* N-COUNT

2 A **maze** of streets, rooms, or tunnels is a large number of them that are connected in a complicated way, so that it is difficult to find your way through them. *The children lead me through the maze of alleys to the edge of the city. ...a maze of dimly-lighted, brown-carpeted corridors.* N-COUNT: usu N *of* n =labyrinth

3 You can refer to a set of ideas, topics, or rules as a **maze** when a large number of them are related to each other in a complicated way that makes them difficult to understand. *The book tries to steer you through the maze of alternative therapies. ...the maze of rules and regulations.* N-COUNT: usu N *of* n

MBA /em biː eɪ/ **MBAs** ◆◇◇◇◇

1 An **MBA** is a master's degree in business administration. You can also refer to a person who has this degree as an **MBA**. **MBA** is an abbreviation for 'Master of Business Administration'. N-COUNT

2 **MBA** is written after someone's name to indicate that they have an MBA.

MBE /em biː iː/ **MBEs.** An **MBE** is a British honour granted to a person by the King or Queen for a particular achievement. It is an abbreviation for 'Member of the Order of the British Empire'. The letters are used after the name of the person who has been awarded the honour. *He had to go to Buckingham Palace to accept an MBE from the Queen. ...Olympic gold medallist Sally Gunnell, MBE.* N-COUNT: usu sing

MC /em siː/ **MCs.** An **MC** is the same as a **master of ceremonies**. ◆◇◇◇◇ N-COUNT; N-TITLE

McCoy /məkɔɪ/. If you describe someone or something as **the real McCoy**, you mean that they are the genuine person or thing and not an imitation or fake; an informal expression. PHRASE: v-link PHR, PHR after v =genuine

MD /em diː/ **MDs** ◆◇◇◇◇

1 **MD** is written after someone's name to indicate that they have been awarded a degree in medicine and are qualified to practise as a doctor.

2 **MD** is an abbreviation for **managing director**; used mainly in British English. *He's going to be the MD of the Park Lane company.* N-COUNT

me /mi, STRONG miː/. A speaker or writer uses **me** to refer to himself or herself. **Me** is a first person singular pronoun. **Me** is used as the object of a verb or a preposition. *I had to make important decisions that would affect me for the rest of my life... He asked me to go to Cambridge with him... Give me a few hours to think about it... She looked up at me, smiling.* ◆◆◆◆◆ PRON-SING: v PRON, prep PRON

mead /miːd/. In former times, **mead** was an alcoholic drink made of honey, spices, and water. N-UNCOUNT

meadow /medoʊ/ **meadows.** A **meadow** is a field which has grass and flowers growing in it. ◆◇◇◇◇ N-COUNT

meagre /miːgəʳ/; spelled **meager** in American English. If you describe an amount or quantity of something as **meagre**, you are critical of it be-

ADJ-GRADED PRAGMATICS

cause it is very small or not enough. *The bank's staff were already angered by a meagre 3.1% pay rise... Their food supply is meager.*

meal /miːl/ **meals** ◆◆◆◇◇

1 A **meal** is an occasion when people eat, at breakfast time, lunchtime, or dinnertime. *She sat next to him throughout the meal... It's rare that I have an evening meal with my children.* N-COUNT

2 A **meal** is the food you eat at breakfast time, lunchtime, or dinnertime. *The waiter offered him red wine or white wine with his meal... Fresh fish makes a delicious meal.* N-COUNT

3 Meal is a rough powder made of crushed grain. It is used to make flour or animal food. N-UNCOUNT: usu n N

4 See also **bone meal**.

5 If you think someone is taking more time and energy to do something than is necessary, you can say they are **making a meal of** it; an informal expression. *Lawyers always make such a meal of the simplest little thing.* PHRASES V inflects PRAGMATICS

6 If you have a **square meal**, you have a large healthy meal. N inflects

meals on wheels; also spelled **Meals on Wheels. Meals on wheels** is a service provided by the local authority that delivers hot meals to people who are too old or too sick to cook for themselves. N-UNCOUNT

meal ticket; also spelled **meal-ticket.** If you say that something or someone is a **meal ticket**, you mean that they enable someone to have money or a rich lifestyle which they would not otherwise have. *His chosen field was unlikely to be a meal ticket for life... I don't intend to be a meal-ticket for anyone.* N-SING: usu *a* N

mealtime /miːltaɪm/ **mealtimes;** also spelled **meal time. Mealtimes** are occasions when you eat breakfast, lunch, or dinner. *At mealtimes he would watch her eat... The bell rings 10 minutes before mealtime.* N-VAR: usu pl

mealy /miːli/. Food that is dry and powdery can be described as **mealy**. *...the mealy stodge of pulse, grain and potato dishes.* ADJ-GRADED

mealy-mouthed /miːlimaʊðd/. If you say that someone is being **mealy-mouthed**, you are critical of them for being unwilling to speak in a simple or open way because they want to avoid talking directly about something unpleasant. *He repeated that he did not intend to be mealy-mouthed with the country's leaders.* ADJ-GRADED PRAGMATICS

mean 1 verb uses

mean /miːn/ **means, meaning, meant** ◆◆◆◆◆

1 If you want to know what a word, code, signal, or gesture **means**, you want to know what it refers to or what message it conveys. *In modern Welsh, 'glas' means 'blue'... What does 'evidence' mean?... The red signal means you can shoot.* VB: no cont =signify V n V that

2 If you ask someone what they **mean**, you are asking them to explain exactly what or who they are referring to or what they are intending to say. *Do you mean me?... Let me illustrate what I mean with an old story... What do you think he means by that?... I think he means that he does not want this marriage to turn out like his friend's.* VB: no cont V n V that

3 If something **means** something to you, it is important to you in some way. *The idea that she witnessed this shameful incident meant nothing to him... It would mean a lot to them to win.* VB: no cont V amount *to* n *it* V amount to-inf Also V amount

4 If one thing **means** another, it shows that the second thing exists or is true. *An enlarged prostate does not necessarily mean cancer... Just because he has a beard doesn't necessarily mean he's a hippy.* VB: no cont =prove V n V that

5 If one thing **means** another, it inevitably leads to the second thing happening. *It would almost certainly mean the end of NATO... Trade and product discounts can also mean big savings... The change will mean that Taiwan no longer has full diplomatic relations with any Middle Eastern state.* VB: no cont V n V that

6 If doing one thing **means** doing another, it involves doing the second thing. *Children universally prefer to live in peace and security, even if that means living with only one parent... Managing well means communicating well.* VERB =involve V -ing

7 If you say that you **mean** what you are saying, you are telling someone that you are serious about it and are not joking, exaggerating, or just being polite. *He says you're fired if you're not back at work on Friday. And I think he meant it... He could see I meant what I said. So he took his fur coat and left.* VB: no cont V n

8 If you say that someone **meant** to do something, you are saying that they did it quite deliberately. *I didn't mean to hurt you... If that sounds harsh, it is meant to... Did you mean to leave your dog here?... I can see why you believed my letters were threatening but I never meant them to be.* VB: no cont =intend V to-inf V n to-inf

9 If you say that someone did not **mean** any harm, offence, or disrespect, you are saying that they did not intend to upset or offend people or to cause problems, even though they may in fact have done so. *I'm sure he didn't mean any harm... I didn't mean any offence. It was a flippant, off-the-cuff remark.* VB: no cont, with brd-neg =intend V n

10 If you **mean** to do something, you intend or plan to do it. *Summer is the perfect time to catch up on the new books you meant to read... You know very well what I meant to say... I mean to look after my body.* VB: no cont =intend V to-inf

11 If you say that something **was meant** to happen, you believe it was made to happen by God or fate, and was not simply a coincidence or an accident. *John was constantly reassuring me that we were meant to be together.* VB: usu passive, no cont =destined *be* V-ed to-inf

12 You say **'I mean'** when making what you have just said clearer. *It was his idea. Gordon's, I mean... Is something upsetting you – I mean, apart from this business?* PHRASES PHR with cl PRAGMATICS

13 You can use **'I mean'** to introduce a statement, especially one that justifies something you have just said. *I'm sure he wouldn't mind. I mean, I was the one who asked him... They were filled with racial stereotypes, I mean, it looked like something from the 1930s.* PHR with cl PRAGMATICS

14 You say **I mean** when correcting something that you have just said. *It was law or classics – I mean English or classics.* PHR with cl PRAGMATICS =sorry

15 If you say that you **know what it means** to do something, or that you **know what** something **means**, you mean that you know everything that is involved in a particular activity or experience, especially the effect that it has on you. *I know what it means to lose a child under such tragic circumstances.* Vs inflect, oft PHR to-inf

16 If a name, word, or phrase **means something to** you, you have heard it before and you know what it refers to. *'Oh, Gairdner,' he said, as if that meant something to him... Does the word 'Fareham' mean anything to anyone?* V inflects, PHR n

17 If you say that someone **means well**, you mean they are trying to be kind and helpful, even though they might be causing someone problems or upsetting them. *I know you mean well, but I can manage by myself.* V inflects

18 You use **'you mean'** in a question to check that you have understood properly what someone has said. *What accident? You mean Christina's?... 'What if I had said no?' 'About the apartment, you mean?'* PHR with cl PRAGMATICS

19 ● to **mean business**: see **business**. ● **if you know what I mean**: see **know**. ● See also **meaning**, **meant**.

mean 2 adjective uses

mean /miːn/ **meaner, meanest** ◆◆◇◇◇

1 If you describe someone as **mean**, you are being critical of them because they are unwilling to spend much money or to use very much of a particular thing; used mainly in British English. *Don't be mean with fabric, otherwise curtains will end up looking skimpy.* ♦ **meanness** *This very careful attitude to money can sometimes border on meanness.* ADJ-GRADED PRAGMATICS =stingy N-UNCOUNT

2 In British English, if you describe an amount as **mean**, you are saying it is very small; used showing disapproval. *...the meanest grant possible from the local council.* ADJ-GRADED PRAGMATICS

3 If you say that someone is being **mean**, you are saying they are being unkind to someone, for ex- ADJ-GRADED: usu v-link ADJ, oft ADJ *to* n

ample by not allowing them to do something. *The little girls had locked themselves in upstairs because Mack had been mean to them... I'd feel mean saying no.* ♦ **meanly** *He had been behaving very meanly to his girlfriend.*
=unkind
ADV-GRADED: usu ADV with v, also ADV adj

4 If you describe a person or animal as **mean**, you are saying they are very bad-tempered and cruel; used mainly in American English. *The state's former commissioner of prisons once called Leonard the meanest man he'd ever seen.*
ADJ-GRADED

5 If you describe a place as **mean**, you think it looks poor and dirty. *He was raised on the mean streets of the central market district of Panama City.*
ADJ-GRADED: usu ADJ n

6 You can use **mean** in expressions such as **'He plays a mean trumpet'** and **'She mixes a mean cocktail'** to indicate that someone does something extremely well; an informal use. *He cooks a mean salmon... Marge played a mean game of tennis.*
ADJ: ADJ n

7 You can use **no mean** in expressions such as **'no mean writer'** and **'no mean golfer'** to indicate that someone does something well, often when comparing them with someone else who also does it well; an informal expression. *She was no mean performer on a variety of other instruments... Moreover, Ramsay was no mean thinker himself.*
PHRASES
PHR n

8 You can use **no mean** in expressions such as **'no mean achievement'** and **'no mean task'** to indicate that someone has done something they deserve to be proud of. *To destroy 121 enemy aircraft is no mean record... Repton reached the final, and since around 1,500 schools entered the competition, that was no mean achievement.*
PHR n

mean 3 noun use

mean
/miːn/. **The mean** is a number that is the average of a set of numbers. *Take a hundred and twenty values and calculate the mean. ...the mean score for 26-year-olds.* ● See also **means**.
N-SING: *the* N, oft N n
=average

meander
/miændəʳ/ **meanders, meandering, meandered** ◆◇◇◇◇

1 If a river or road **meanders**, it has a lot of bends, rather than going in a straight line from one place to another. *...roads that meandered round the edges of the fields... A rural single railway track meanders through the valley... The small river meandered in lazy curves down the centre... We crossed a small iron bridge over a meandering stream.*
VERB
V prep/adv
V-ing
Also V

2 A **meander** is a large bend in a river.
N-COUNT

3 If you **meander** somewhere, you move slowly and not in a straight line. *We meandered through a landscape of mountains, rivers, and vineyards... It's so restful to meander along Irish country roads.*
VERB
V prep/adv
Also V

4 If a speech, account, or piece of writing **meanders**, it seems to move from one topic to another without any order or purpose. *His sensitive and considerate talk appears to meander but by the end is seen to do so in order to focus attention on the true state of affairs. ...a rich and meandering novel.*
VERB
V
V-ing

meaning
/miːnɪŋ/ **meanings** ◆◆◆◇◇

1 The **meaning** of a word, expression, or gesture is the thing or idea that it refers to or represents and which can be explained using other words. *I hadn't a clue to the meaning of 'activism'... I became more aware of the symbols and their meanings.*
N-VAR

2 The **meaning** of what someone says or of something such as a book or film is the thoughts or ideas that are intended to be expressed by it. *Unsure of the meaning of this remark, Ryle chose to remain silent... Her book is not without autobiographical meaning.*
N-VAR
=significance

3 If an activity or action has **meaning**, it has a purpose and is worthwhile. *Art has real meaning when it helps people to understand themselves. ...a challenge that gives meaning to life.*
N-UNCOUNT
=purpose

4 If you mention something and say that someone **doesn't know the meaning of the word**, you are emphasizing that they have never experienced the thing mentioned or do not have the quality mentioned. *Don't mention failure when Kevin is around. He doesn't know the meaning of the word.*
PHRASE: V inflects
PRAGMATICS

meaningful
/miːnɪŋfʊl/ ◆◆◇◇◇

1 If you describe something as **meaningful**, you mean that it is serious, important, or useful in some way. *She believes these talks will be the start of a constructive and meaningful dialogue... He asked people to tell him about a meaningful event or period in their lives.* ♦ **meaningfully** *Marxist Yugoslavia thus contributed meaningfully to the formation of an international doctrine.*
ADJ-GRADED
=significant
ADV-GRADED: ADV with v
=significantly

2 A **meaningful** look or gesture is one that is intended to express something, usually to a particular person, without anything being said. *Upon the utterance of this word, Dan and Harry exchanged a quick, meaningful look.* ♦ **meaningfully** *He glanced meaningfully at the other policeman, then he went up the stairs... 'Who's your publisher?'—'Lockett Press,' she said, and she raised an eyebrow meaningfully.*
ADJ: ADJ n
ADV-GRADED: usu ADV after v, also ADV -ed

3 See also **meaningfully**.

meaningfully
/miːnɪŋfʊli/. You use **meaningfully** to indicate that someone has deliberately chosen their words in order to express something in a way which is not obvious but which is understood by the person they are talking to. *'I have a knack for making friends, you know,' she added meaningfully... 'I was once as bewildered as you are,' she said meaningfully.* ● See also **meaningful**.
ADV-GRADED: ADV after v

meaningless
/miːnɪŋləs/ ◆◇◇◇◇

1 If something that someone says or writes is **meaningless**, it has no meaning, or appears to have no meaning. *The sentence 'kicked the ball the man' is meaningless... She is fascinated by algebra while he considers it meaningless nonsense.*
ADJ-GRADED

2 Something that is **meaningless** is of no importance or relevance. *Widespread political and economic disarray threatens to make the constitution meaningless... Fines are meaningless to guys earning millions.*
ADJ-GRADED

3 If something that you do is **meaningless**, it has no purpose and is not at all worthwhile. *They seek strong sensations to dull their sense of a meaningless existence... She said it would have been meaningless for her to have made specific requests for assistance.*
ADJ-GRADED
=futile

means
/miːnz/ ◆◆◆◆◇

1 A **means** of doing something is a method, instrument, or process which can be used to do it. **Means** is both the singular and the plural form for this use. *The move is a means to fight crime... The army had perfected the use of terror as a means of controlling the population... Business managers are focused on increasing their personal wealth by any available means.*
N-COUNT: with supp

2 You can refer to the money that someone has as their **means**; a formal use. *...a person of means... He did not have the means to compensate her.*
N-PLURAL

3 If someone is living **beyond** their **means**, they are spending more money than they can afford. If someone is living **within** their **means**, they are not spending more money than they can afford. *The more gifts she received, the more she craved, until he was living beyond his means... It is far better to pay off old debts steadily by living within your means.*
PHRASES
v PHR,
v-link PHR

4 If you do something **by means of** a particular method, instrument, or process, you do it using that method, instrument, or process. *This is a two year course taught by means of lectures and seminars... The trailer was connected to the car by means of a complicated system of hoses, pipes and rods.*
PREP

5 You can say **'by all means'** to tell someone that you are very willing to allow them to do something. *'Can I come and have a look at your house?'—'Yes by all means'.*
CONVENTION
PRAGMATICS

6 You use expressions such as **'by no means'**, **'not by any means'**, and **'by no manner of means'** to emphasize that something is not true. *This is by no means out of the ordinary... They were not finished, however, not by any means.*
PHR with cl/group,
PHR before v
PRAGMATICS

7 If you say that something is **a means to an end**, you mean it enables you to achieve what you want, and is not enjoyable or important itself. *We seem to have lost sight of the fact that marketing is only a means to an end.*
usu v-link PHR

means test, means tests. A **means test** is a test in which your income is assessed in order to see if you are eligible for certain state grants or benefits. If your income is above a certain amount, you are not eligible. N-COUNT: usu sing

means-tested. A grant or benefit that is **means-tested** varies in amount depending on a means test; used mainly in British English. *...means-tested benefits.* ADJ

meant /ment/ ◆◆◇◇◇

1 **Meant** is the past tense and past participle of **mean**.

2 If you say that something or someone **is meant to** be or do a particular thing, you mean that they are intended to be or do that thing, often when they have failed to be or do it. *I can't say any more, it's meant to be a big secret... The decor was meant to keep the mind concentrated on the making of money... I'm meant to be on holiday.* ADJ: v-link ADJ to-inf =be supposed to

3 If something **is meant for** particular people or for a particular situation, it is intended for those people or for that situation. *Fairy tales weren't just meant for children... The seeds were not meant for human consumption... The letter might not have been meant for me at all.* ADJ: v-link ADJ for n =intended

4 If you say that something **is meant to** happen, you mean it is expected to happen or it ought to happen. *The peculiar thing about getting engaged is that you're meant to announce it to everyone... Parties are meant to be fun.* PHR-MODAL =be supposed to

5 If you say that something **is meant to** have a particular quality or characteristic, you mean it has a reputation for being like that. *Spurs are meant to be one of the top teams in the world.* PHR-MODAL PRAGMATICS =be thought to

meantime /miːntaɪm/ ◆◆◇◇◇

1 **In the meantime** or **meantime** means in the period of time between two events. *Eventually your child will leave home to lead her own life as a fully independent adult, but in the meantime she relies on your support... It now hopes to hold elections in February. Meantime, the state will continue to be run from Delhi.* PHR with cl =meanwhile

2 **For the meantime** means for a period of time from now until something else happens. *The Prime Minister has, for the meantime, seen off the challenge of the opposition... For the meantime, the opinion polls have to be taken on trust.* PHR with cl =for the moment

meanwhile /miːnʰwaɪl/ ◆◆◆◆◇

1 **Meanwhile** means while a particular thing is happening. *Brush the aubergines with oil, add salt and pepper, and bake till soft. Meanwhile, heat the remaining oil in a heavy pan... Kate turned to beckon Peter across from the car, but Bill waved him back, meanwhile pushing Kate inside.* ADV: ADV with cl

2 **Meanwhile** means in the period of time between two events. *You needn't worry; I'll be ready to greet them. Meanwhile I'm off to discuss the Fowler's party with Felix.* • **In the meanwhile** means the same as **meanwhile**. *'I can very easily explain my dealings with them.'—'I am sure you can, sir. But in the meanwhile I must ask you to come with me.'* ADV: ADV with cl =in the meantime PHRASE: PHR with cl

3 You use **meanwhile** to introduce a different aspect of a particular situation, especially one that is completely opposite to the one previously mentioned. *Personally, he had always found his wife's mother a bit annoying. The mother-daughter relationship, meanwhile, was close, and he understandably felt like an outsider.* ADV: ADV with cl PRAGMATICS

measles /miːzᵊlz/. **Measles** is an infectious illness that gives you a high temperature and red spots on your skin. ◆◇◇◇◇ N-UNCOUNT: also the N

measly /miːzli/. If you describe an amount, quantity, or size as **measly**, you are critical of it because it is very small or inadequate; an informal word. *The average British bathroom measures a measly 3.5 square metres. ...a measly twelve-year-old like me.* ADJ-GRADED: usu ADJ n, oft a ADJ amount PRAGMATICS

measurable /meʒərəbᵊl/ ◆◇◇◇◇

1 If you describe something as **measurable**, you mean that it is large enough to be noticed or to be significant; a formal word. *Both leaders seemed to expect measurable progress.* ♦ **measurably** *The old man's voice was measurably weaker than the last time they'd talked... After this, the pace of events quickened measurably.* ADJ: usu ADJ n ADV-GRADED: ADV adj/adv, ADV with v

2 Something that is **measurable** can be measured. *Economists emphasize measurable quantities – the number of jobs, the per capita income... So far the effect is barely measurable.* ADJ-GRADED

measure /meʒəʳ/ **measures, measuring, measured** ◆◆◆◆◇

1 If you **measure** the quality, value, or effect of something, you decide how great it is, by making observations or following particular procedures. *I continued to measure his progress against the charts in the doctor's office... A grammar school's success was measured in terms of the number of pupils who got into university... It was difficult to measure the precise impact of the labor action.* VERB =assess V n prep V n

2 If you **measure** a quantity that can be expressed in numbers, such as the length of something, you discover it using a particular instrument or device, for example a ruler. *Measure the length and width of the gap... He measured the speed at which ultrasonic waves travel along the bone.* VERB V n

3 If something **measures** a particular length, width, or amount, that is its size or intensity, expressed in numbers. *The house is more than twenty metres long and measures six metres in width... This hand-decorated plate measures 30cm across... Their paddock measures 24 metres square.* VB: no cont =be V amount

4 A **measure of** a particular quality, feeling, or activity is a fairly large amount of it; a formal use. *With the exception of Juan, each attained a measure of success... The colonies were claiming a larger measure of self-government.* N-SING: N of n =degree

5 If you say that one aspect of a situation is a **measure of** that situation, you mean that it shows that the situation is very serious or has developed to a very great extent. *It is a measure of their plight that few of them have anywhere to go to... That is a measure of how bad things have become at the bank.* N-SING: N of n/wh

6 When someone, usually a government or other authority, takes **measures** to do something, they carry out particular actions in order to achieve a particular result; a formal use. *The government warned that police would take tougher measures to contain the trouble... He said stern measures would be taken against the killers... As a precautionary measure repeat the medication.* N-COUNT: oft N to-inf, N against n =step

7 A **measure** of a strong alcoholic drink such as brandy or whisky is an amount of it in a glass. In pubs and bars, a **measure** is an official standard amount. *He poured himself another generous measure of malt. ...a pub measure of spirits.* N-COUNT: usu N of n

8 See also **measured**, **measuring**; **countermeasure**, **half measure**, **tape measure**.

9 If you say that something has changed or that it has affected you **beyond measure**, you are emphasizing that it has done this to a great extent. *Mankind's knowledge of the universe has increased beyond measure... She irritated him beyond measure.* PHRASES PHR after v PRAGMATICS =beyond belief

10 If you say that something is done **for good measure**, you mean that it is done in addition to a number of other things. *I repeated my question for good measure... For good measure, a few details of hotels were included.* PHR after v, PHR with cl

11 If you **get** or **take the measure of** someone or something, you discover what they are like, so that you are able to control them or deal with them. If you **have the measure of** someone or something, you have succeeded in doing this. Used in formal English. *The governments of the industrialized world had failed to get the measure of the crisis... Has he taken the measure of us and concluded that we're not willing to risk a life?... Lili was the only person I knew who had the measure of her brother.* V inflects, PHR n

12 If something is true **in some measure** or **in large measure**, it is true in a partial or general way, although it is not completely true; a formal expression. *Power is in some measure an act of will... In* PHR with cl

Britain, we have so far escaped, in large measure, either of these afflictions.

measure out. If you **measure out** a certain amount of something, you measure that amount and take it or mark it because it is the amount that you want or need. *I'd already measured out the ingredients... He was on the front lawn, measuring out two circles.* PHRASAL VERB VP n (not pron) Also V n P

measure up. If you do not **measure up** to a standard or to someone's expectations, you are not good enough to achieve the standard or fulfil the person's expectations. *It was fatiguing sometimes to try to measure up to her standard of perfection... She's always comparing me to other people, and somehow I never measure up.* PHRASAL VERB usu with brd-neg VP to n VP

measured /meʒəʳd/. You use **measured** to describe something that is careful and deliberate. *The men spoke in soft, measured tones... Her more measured response will appeal to voters... They have to proceed at a measured pace.* ADJ-GRADED: usu ADJ n

measurement /meʒəʳmənt/ **measurements** ◆◆◇◇◇

1 A **measurement** is a result, usually expressed in numbers, that you obtain by measuring something. *We took lots of measurements... The measurements are extraordinarily accurate.* N-COUNT

2 **Measurement** of something is the process of measuring it in order to obtain a result expressed in numbers. *Measurement of blood pressure can be undertaken by practice nurses.* N-VAR: oft N of n

3 The **measurement** of the quality, value, or effect of something is the activity of deciding how great it is. *...the measurement of output in the non-market sector.* N-VAR: oft N of n

4 Your **measurements** are the size of your waist, chest, hips, and other parts of your body, which you need to know when you are buying clothes. N-PLURAL: with poss

measuring /meʒərɪŋ/. A **measuring** jug or spoon is specially designed for measuring quantities, especially in cooking. ADJ: ADJ n

meat /miːt/ **meats** ◆◆◆◇◇

1 **Meat** is flesh taken from a dead animal that people cook and eat. *Meat and fish are relatively expensive. ...imported meat products. ...a buffet of cold meats and salads.* N-MASS

2 See also **luncheon meat, red meat, white meat.**

3 If you say something is **meat and drink** to someone, you mean that they enjoy it very much. *What normal people considered pressure was meat and drink to him.* PHRASE: usu v-link PHR to n

meatball /miːtbɔːl/ **meatballs. Meatballs** are small balls of chopped meat, breadcrumbs, and herbs. They are usually eaten with a sauce. N-COUNT: usu pl

meat loaf, meat loaves; also spelled **meatloaf. Meat loaf** is chopped meat and herbs cooked in the form of a loaf. N-VAR

meaty /miːti/ **meatier, meatiest**

1 Food that is **meaty** contains a lot of meat. *...a pleasant lasagne with a meaty sauce.* ADJ-GRADED

2 You can describe something such as a piece of writing or a part in a film as **meaty** if it contains a lot of interesting or important material. *The short, meaty reports are those he likes best... Famous for playing dizzy blondes, this time she has been given a more meaty role.* ADJ-GRADED: usu ADJ n

3 You can describe a part of someone's body as **meaty** if it is big and strong. *He looked up and down the corridor, meaty hands resting on his thighs. ...a pleasant lady with meaty arms.* ADJ-GRADED: usu ADJ n

mecca /mekə/ **meccas** ◆◇◇◇◇

1 **Mecca** is a city in Saudi Arabia, which is the holiest city in Islam because the Prophet Mohammed was born there. All Muslims face towards Mecca when they pray. N-PROPER

2 If you describe a place as a **mecca** or **Mecca** for a particular thing or activity, you mean that many people who are interested in it go there. *His Batley Variety Club became a mecca for high-class acts and mass audiences... Thailand has become the tourist mecca of Asia.* N-COUNT: usu sing, with supp

mechanic /mɪkænɪk/ **mechanics** ◆◆◇◇◇

1 A **mechanic** is someone whose job is to repair and maintain machines and engines, especially car engines. *If you smell something unusual (gas fumes or burning, for instance), take the car to your mechanic... An elevator mechanic can work the machinery directly by turning this lever.* N-COUNT

2 The **mechanics** of a process, system, or activity are the way in which it works or the way in which it is done. *What are the mechanics of this new process?... The mechanics of the job, however, have changed little since then.* N-PLURAL: usu the N of n

3 **Mechanics** is the part of physics that deals with the natural forces that act on moving or stationary objects. *...the other great theory of 20th-century physics, quantum mechanics... He has not studied mechanics or engineering.* N-UNCOUNT

mechanical /mɪkænɪkᵊl/ ◆◆◇◇◇

1 A **mechanical** device has parts that move when it is working, often using power from an engine or from electricity. *...a small mechanical device that taps out the numbers. ...the oldest working mechanical clock in the world... Most mechanical devices require oil as a lubricant.* ♦ **mechanically** /mɪkænɪkli/ *The air was circulated mechanically.* ADJ: usu ADJ n; ADV: ADV with v

2 **Mechanical** means relating to machines and engines and the way they work. *...mechanical engineering... The company undertakes mechanical work on all types of cars... The train had stopped due to a mechanical problem.* ♦ **mechanically** *The car was mechanically sound, he decided.* ADJ: ADJ n; ADV: ADV adj/-ed

3 If you describe a person as **mechanical**, you mean they are naturally good at understanding how machines work. *He was a very mechanical person, who knew a lot about sound... I'm not mechanical like my father; I have to follow the instructions.* ♦ **mechanically** *I'm not mechanically minded.* ADJ-GRADED; ADV-GRADED: ADV -ed

4 If you describe someone's action as **mechanical**, you mean that they do it automatically, without thinking about it. *It is real prayer, and not mechanical repetition... Many girls have a kind of mechanical attitude towards sex... Her retort was mechanical.* ♦ **mechanically** *He nodded mechanically, his eyes fixed on the girl.* ADJ-GRADED; ADV-GRADED: ADV with v

mechanise /mekənaɪz/. See **mechanize.**

mechanism /mekənɪzəm/ **mechanisms** ◆◆◆◇◇

1 In a machine or piece of equipment, a **mechanism** is a part, often consisting of a set of smaller parts, which performs a particular function. *...the locking mechanism. ...a terrorist bomb has been detonated by a special mechanism.* N-COUNT: usu sing, with supp

2 A **mechanism** is a special way of getting something done within a particular system. *There's no mechanism for punishing arms exporters who break the rules. ...the clumsy and ineffective mechanism of price controls.* N-COUNT: with supp

3 A **mechanism** is a part of your behaviour that is automatic and that helps you to survive or to cope with a difficult situation. *...a survival mechanism, a means of coping with intolerable stress.* N-COUNT: with supp

4 See also **defence mechanism.**

mechanistic /mekənɪstɪk/. If you describe a view or explanation of something as **mechanistic**, you are criticizing it because it describes a natural or social process as if it were a machine. *...a mechanistic view of things that ignores the emotional realities in people's lives... Most of my colleagues in biology are still very mechanistic in their thinking.* ADJ-GRADED PRAGMATICS

mechanize /mekənaɪz/ **mechanizes, mechanizing, mechanized;** also spelled **mechanise** in British English. If someone **mechanizes** a process, they cause it to be done by a machine or machines, when it was previously done by people. *Only gradually are technologies being developed to mechanize the task... Perhaps, in time, this treatment will be mechanised.* ♦ **mechanized** *...highly mechanised production methods.* ♦ **mechanization** /mekənaɪzeɪʃᵊn/ *Mechanization happened years ago on the farms of Islay.* ◆◇◇◇◇ VERB V n; ADJ-GRADED; N-UNCOUNT

medal /medᵊl/ **medals.** A **medal** is a small metal disc which is given as an award for bravery or as a prize in a sporting event. ◆◆◆◇◇ N-COUNT

medallion /mɪdæliən/ **medallions.** A **medallion** is a round metal disc which some people wear as an ornament, especially on a chain round their neck. N-COUNT

medallist /medəlɪst/ **medallists.** A **medallist** is a person who has won a medal in sport; used mainly in journalism. *...the Olympic gold medallists.* ◆◇◇◇◇ N-COUNT: usu supp N

meddle /medᵊl/ **meddles, meddling, meddled.** If you say that someone **meddles** in something, you are criticizing the fact they try to influence or change it without being asked. *Already some people are asking whether scientists have any right to meddle in such matters... If only you hadn't felt compelled to meddle. ...the inept and meddling bureaucrats.* ◆◇◇◇◇ VERB PRAGMATICS =interfere V in/with n V V-ing ♦ **meddler, meddlers** *They view activists as little more than meddlers.* N-COUNT

meddlesome /medᵊlsəm/. If you describe a person as **meddlesome**, you are criticizing them because they try to influence or change things that do not concern them. *...a meddlesome member of the public.* ADJ-GRADED PRAGMATICS =interfering

media /miːdiə/ ◆◆◆◆◇

1 You can refer to television, radio, newspapers, and magazines as **the media**. *It is hard work and not a glamorous job as portrayed by the media... They are wondering whether bias in the news media contributed to the president's defeat... Media coverage of cycling in July was pretty impressive.* ● See also **mass media, multimedia.** N-SING-COLL: the N

2 **Media** is a plural of **medium.**

mediaeval /mediiːvᵊl, AM miːd-/. See **medieval.**

median /miːdiən/. The **median** value of a set of values is the middle one when they are arranged in order; a technical term in mathematics. For example, if a group of five students take a test and their marks are 5, 7, 7, 8, and 10, the median mark is 7. ◆◇◇◇◇ ADJ: ADJ n

mediate /miːdieɪt/ **mediates, mediating, mediated** ◆◆◇◇◇

1 If someone **mediates** between two groups of people, or **mediates** an agreement between them, they try to settle an argument between them by talking to both groups and trying to find things that they can both agree to. *My mom was the one who mediated between Zelda and her mom... United Nations officials have mediated a series of peace meetings between the two sides... The Vatican successfully mediated in a territorial dispute between Argentina and Chile in 1984... UN peacekeepers mediated a new cease-fire.* VERB V between pl-n V n between pl-n V V n ♦ **mediation** /miːdieɪʃᵊn/ *The agreement provides for United Nations mediation between the two sides... She was released from prison through the mediation of President Kenneth Kaunda.* N-UNCOUNT ♦ **mediator, mediators** *An archbishop has been acting as mediator between the rebels and the authorities.* N-COUNT

2 If something **mediates** a particular process or event, it allows that process or event to happen and influences the way in which it happens; a formal use. *...the thymus, the organ which mediates the response of the white blood cells... People's responses to us have been mediated by their past experience of life.* VERB V n ♦ **mediation** *This works through the mediation of the central nervous system.* N-UNCOUNT

medic /medɪk/ **medics.** A **medic** is a doctor or medical student; an informal word. ◆◇◇◇◇ N-COUNT

medical /medɪkᵊl/ **medicals** ◆◆◆◆◇

1 **Medical** means relating to illness and injuries and to their treatment or prevention. *Several police officers received medical treatment for cuts and bruises. ...the medical profession.* ADJ: ADJ n ♦ **medically** /medɪkli/ *Therapists cannot prescribe drugs as they are not necessarily medically qualified.* ADV: ADV with v, ADV adj, ADV with cl

2 A **medical** is a thorough examination of your body by a doctor, for example before you start a new job. N-COUNT

medical examiner, medical examiners. In the United States, a **medical examiner** is a medical expert who is responsible for investigating the deaths of people who have died in a sudden, violent, or unusual way. N-COUNT

medicated /medɪkeɪtɪd/. A **medicated** soap or shampoo contains substances which are intended to kill bacteria and therefore make your skin or hair healthier. ADJ: usu ADJ n

medication /medɪkeɪʃᵊn/ **medications. Medication** is medicine that is used to treat and cure illness. *She stopped taking the prescribed medications... When somebody comes for treatment I always ask them if they are on any medication.* ◆◆◇◇◇ N-VAR

medicinal /medɪsənᵊl/. **Medicinal** substances or substances with **medicinal** effects can be used to treat and cure illnesses. *...medicinal plants.* ◆◇◇◇◇ ADJ ♦ **medicinally** *Root ginger has been used medicinally for centuries.* ADV: ADV after v

medicine /medsᵊn, AM medɪsɪn/ **medicines** ◆◆◆◇◇

1 **Medicine** is the treatment of illness and injuries by doctors and nurses. *He pursued a career in medicine... I was interested in alternative medicine and becoming an aromatherapist... Psychiatry is an accepted branch of medicine.* N-UNCOUNT

2 **Medicine** is a substance, usually a liquid, tablets, or a powder, that you drink or swallow in order to cure an illness. *People in hospitals are dying because of shortage of medicine. ...herbal medicines.* N-MASS

medieval /mediiːvᵊl, AM miːd-/; also spelled **mediaeval**. Something that is **medieval** relates to or dates from the period in European history between the end of the Roman Empire in 476AD and about 1500AD. *...a medieval castle. ...the medieval chroniclers.* ◆◆◇◇◇ ADJ: usu ADJ n

mediocre /miːdioʊkəʳ/. If you describe something as **mediocre**, you mean that it is of average quality but you think it should be better. *His school record was mediocre. ...mediocre music.* ◆◇◇◇◇ ADJ-GRADED PRAGMATICS =second rate

mediocrity /miːdiɒkrɪti, med-/ **mediocrities** ◆◇◇◇◇

1 If you refer to the **mediocrity** of something, you mean that it is of average quality but you think it should be better. *...the mediocrity of most contemporary literature... Fashion today is sloppy mediocrity.* N-UNCOUNT PRAGMATICS

2 If you refer to someone as a **mediocrity**, you think that they are not very good at what they do. *Surrounded by mediocrities, he can seem a towering intellectual.* N-COUNT PRAGMATICS

meditate /medɪteɪt/ **meditates, meditating, meditated** ◆◇◇◇◇

1 If you **meditate on** something, you think about it very carefully and deeply for a long time. *He meditated on the problem... On the day her son began school, she meditated on the uncertainties of his future.* VERB =reflect V on n

2 If you **meditate** you remain in a silent and calm state for a period of time, as part of a religious training or so that you are more able to deal with the problems and difficulties of everyday life. *I was meditating, and reached a higher state of consciousness.* VERB V

meditation /medɪteɪʃᵊn/ **meditations** ◆◆◇◇◇

1 **Meditation** is the act of remaining in a silent and calm state for a period of time, as part of a religious training, or so that you are more able to deal with the problems of everyday life. *Many busy executives have begun to practice yoga and meditation.* ● See also **transcendental meditation.** N-UNCOUNT ► A **meditation** is a particular exercise that is used in meditation. *Having chosen a meditation it is important that you stick to that meditation for, at the very least, a fortnight.* N-COUNT

2 **Meditation** is the act of thinking about something very carefully and deeply for a long time. *...the man, lost in meditation, walking with slow steps along the shore... In his lonely meditations Antony had been forced to the conclusion that there had been rumours.* N-UNCOUNT: also N in pl =contemplation

3 A **meditation** on a particular subject is something such as a piece of writing or a speech which expresses deep thoughts about that subject. *In fact, the entire novel is a long meditation on childbearing and mortality... The title track is a pointed meditation on a continent gone wrong.* N-COUNT: usu N on/upon n

meditative /medɪtətɪv, AM -teɪt-/. **Meditative** describes things that are related to the act of ADJ-GRADED: ADJ n meditating or the act of thinking very deeply about something. *Music can induce a meditative state in the listener... Yogis trained in Eastern meditative techniques can change their heart rate. ...moments of meditative silence.* ♦ **meditatively** ADV: ADV after v *Martin rubbed his chin meditatively.*

Mediterranean /meditəreiniən/ ◆◆◇◇◇

1 **The Mediterranean** is the sea which is between southern Europe and North Africa from north to south and the Straits of Gibraltar and western Asia from east to west. N-PROPER: the N

2 **The Mediterranean** refers to the southern part of Europe which borders the Mediterranean Sea. N-PROPER: the N *Barcelona has become one of the most dynamic and prosperous cities in the Mediterranean.*

3 Something that is **Mediterranean** is characteristic of or belongs to the people or region around the Mediterranean Sea. ADJ *There was very little meat in the classic Mediterranean diet.*

medium /miːdiəm/ **mediums, media.** ◆◆◆◇◇ The plural of the noun can be either **mediums** or **media** for meanings 4 and 5. The form **mediums** is the plural for meaning 6.

1 If something is of **medium** size, it is neither large nor small, but approximately half way between the two. ADJ: usu ADJ n *A medium dose produces severe nausea within hours... He was of medium height with blond hair and light blue eyes.*

2 You use **medium** to describe something which is average in degree or amount, or approximately half way along a scale between two extremes. ADJ: usu ADJ n *Foods that contain only medium levels of sodium are bread, cakes, milk, butter and margarine. ...a sweetish, medium-strength beer.* ► Also an adverb. ADV: ADV adj *Cook under a medium-hot grill.*

3 If something is of a **medium** colour, it is neither light nor dark, but approximately half way between the two. COMB in COLOUR *Andrea has medium brown hair, grey eyes and very pale skin... When violet is added to the medium blue a particularly striking, warm coloration is created.*

4 A **medium** is a way or means of expressing your ideas or of communicating with people. N-COUNT *In Sierra Leone, English is used as the medium of instruction for all primary education... But Artaud was increasingly dissatisfied with film as a medium.*

5 A **medium** is a substance or material which is used for a particular purpose or in order to produce a particular effect. N-COUNT *Blood is the medium in which oxygen is carried to all parts of the body... Hyatt has found a way of creating these qualities using the more permanent medium of oil paint.*

6 A **medium** is a person who claims to be able to contact and speak to people who are dead, and to pass messages between them and people who are still alive. N-COUNT

7 See also **media**.

8 If you strike or find a **happy medium** between two extreme and opposite courses of action, you find a sensible way of behaving that is somewhere between the two extremes. PHRASE: PHR after v *I still aim to strike a happy medium between producing football that's worth watching and getting results... It's very difficult to strike a happy medium and make it right for everybody.*

medium-dry; also spelled **medium dry.** ADJ **Medium-dry** wine or sherry is not very sweet.

medium-sized. ◆◇◇◇◇ The form **medium size** is also used. **Medium-sized** means neither large nor small, but approximately half way between the two. ADJ: usu ADJ n *Bring the milk to the boil in a medium-sized saucepan... Small and medium-sized accountancy firms are having an especially tough time.*

medium-term. ◆◇◇◇◇ The **medium-term** is the period of time which lasts a few months or years beyond the present time, in contrast with the short term or the long term. N-SING: usu N n *Economists had been arguing that the medium-term economic prospects remained poor... If a woman gives up her job to look after her baby, she will not only risk losing her salary in the medium-term, she may seriously damage her long-term career prospects.*

medium wave. **Medium wave** is a range of radio waves which are used for broadcasting. N-UNCOUNT: usu on N *...a station broadcasting pop music on medium wave.*

medley /medli/ **medleys** ◆◇◇◇◇

1 In music, a **medley** is a collection of different tunes or songs that are played one after the other as a single piece of music. N-COUNT: oft N of n *...a medley of traditional songs.*

2 In sport, a **medley** is a swimming race in which the four main strokes are used one after the other. N-COUNT: oft supp N *Japan won the Men's 200 metres Individual Medley.*

3 A **medley** of different foods or other things is a mixture of them. N-COUNT: usu N of n =mixture *...a medley of four fish in a cream sauce... We communicated in a medley of foreign words and universal gestures.*

meek /miːk/ **meeker, meekest.** ◆◇◇◇◇ If you describe a person as **meek**, you think that they are gentle and quiet, and likely to do what other people say. ADJ-GRADED *He was a meek, mild-mannered fellow. ...the meekest and most docile of people.* ► **The meek** are people who are meek. N-PLURAL: the N *The meek shall inherit the earth.* ♦ **meekly** ADV-GRADED: ADV with v *Most have meekly accepted such advice... 'Thank you, Peter', Amy said meekly.* ♦ **meekness** N-UNCOUNT *She maintained a kind of meekness.*

meet /miːt/ **meets, meeting, met** ◆◆◆◆◆

1 If you **meet** someone, you happen to be in the same place as them and start talking to them. V-RECIP You may know the other person, but be surprised to see them, or you may not know them at all. V n pl-n V *I have just met the man I want to spend the rest of my life with... He's the kindest and sincerest person I've ever met... We met by chance.* ► **Meet up** means the same as **meet**. PHRASAL VERB RECIP V P with n pl-n V P *Last night, when he was parking my automobile, he met up with a buddy he had at Oxford... They met up in 1956, when they were both young schoolboys.*

2 If two or more people **meet**, they go to the same place, which they have earlier arranged to do, so that they can talk or do something together. V-RECIP pl-n V V n *We could meet for a drink after work... Meet me down at the beach tomorrow, at 6am sharp.* ► **Meet up** means the same as **meet**. PHRASAL VERB RECIP pl-n V P V P with n *We tend to meet up for lunch once a week... My intention was to have a holiday and meet up with old friends.*

3 If you **meet** someone, you are introduced to them and begin talking to them and getting to know them. VERB V n *Hey, Terry, come and meet my Dad.*

4 You use **meet** in expressions such as **'Pleased to meet you'** and **'Nice to have met you'** when you want to politely say hello or goodbye to someone you have just met for the first time. VERB PRAGMATICS V n *'Jennifer,' Miss Mallory said, 'this is Leigh Van-Voreen.'—'Pleased to meet you,' Jennifer said... I have to leave. Nice to have met you.*

5 If you **meet** someone who is travelling, or if you **meet** someone off their train, plane, or bus, you go to the station, airport, or bus-stop in order to be there when they arrive. VERB You can also say that you **meet** someone's train, plane, or bus. V n prep/adv V n off n V n *Mama met me at the station... Lili and my father met me off the boat... Kurt's parents weren't able to meet our plane so we took a taxi.*

6 When a group of people such as a committee **meet**, they gather together for a particular purpose. VERB V *Officials from the two countries will meet again soon to resume negotiations... The commission met 14 times between 1988 and 1991.*

7 In American English, if you **meet with** someone, you have a meeting with them. VERB V with n *Most of the lawmakers who met with the president yesterday said they backed the mission.*

8 If something such as a suggestion, proposal, or new book **meets with** or **is met with** a particular reaction, it gets that reaction from people. V-ERG V with n V n with n *The idea met with a cool response from various quarters... We hope today's offer will meet with your approval too... Reagan's speech was met with incredulity in the US.*

9 If something **meets** a need, requirement, or condition, it is satisfactory or sufficiently large to fulfil it. VERB =satisfy V n *He suggested that the current arrangements for*

the care of severely mentally ill people are inadequate to meet their needs... Out of the original 23,000 applications, 16,000 candidates meet the entry requirements.

10 If you **meet** something such as a problem or challenge, you deal satisfactorily with it. *British manufacturing failed to meet the crisis of the 1970s... It is an enormous challenge but we hope to meet it within a year or 18 months... They had worked heroically to meet the deadline.* VERB V n

11 If you **meet** the cost of something, you provide the money that is needed for it. *The government said it will help meet some of the cost of the damage... As your income increases you will find less difficulty in finding the money to meet your monthly repayments.* VERB V n

12 If you **meet** a situation, attitude, or problem, you experience it or become aware of it. *I honestly don't know how I will react the next time I meet a potentially dangerous situation... Never had she met such spite and pettiness.* VERB =come across, encounter V n

13 You can say that someone **meets with** success or failure when they are successful or unsuccessful. *Attempts to find civilian volunteers have met with embarrassing failure... Efforts to commercialise the Russian space programme have met with little success.* VERB V with n

14 When a moving object **meets** another object, it hits or touches it. *You sense the stresses in the hull each time the keel meets the ground... Nick's head bent slowly over hers until their mouths met.* V-RECIP V n pl-n V

15 If your eyes **meet** someone else's, you both look at each other at the same time; used in written English. *Nina's eyes met her sisters' across the table... I found myself smiling back instinctively when our eyes met.* V-RECIP V n pl-n V

16 If two areas **meet**, especially two areas of land or sea, they are next to one another. *It is one of the rare places in the world where the desert meets the sea. ...the southernmost point of South America where the Pacific and Atlantic oceans meet.* V-RECIP V n pl-n V

17 The place where two lines **meet** is the place where they join together. *Parallel lines will never meet no matter how far extended... The track widened as it met the road.* V-RECIP pl-n V V n

18 If two sportsmen, teams, or armies **meet**, they compete or fight against one another. *The two women will meet tomorrow in the final... The unevenly matched armies met at Guilford on 15 March 1781... England last met the French in 1984 when they lost 2-0 in Paris.* V-RECIP pl-n V V n

19 A **meet** is an event in which athletes come to a particular place in order to take part in a race or races. *John Pennel became the first person to pole-vault 17 ft., at a meet in Miami, Florida.* N-COUNT

20 In Britain, a **meet** is when riders and hounds assemble at a place before they set off on a fox hunt. N-COUNT

21 If you do not **meet** someone's **eyes** or **meet** someone's **gaze**, you do not look at them although they are looking at you, for example because you are ashamed. *He hesitated, then shook his head, refusing to meet her eyes.* PHRASES V inflects

22 If someone **meets** their **death** or **meets** their **end** they die, especially in a violent or suspicious way; used in written English. *Jacob Sinclair met his death at the hands of a soldier... No one knows exactly how or where he met his end.* V inflects

23 • to **make ends meet**: see **end**. • **there's more to this than meets the eye**: see **eye**. • to **meet** someone's **eyes**: see **eye**. • to **meet** someone **halfway**: see **halfway**. • to **meet** your **match**: see **match**.

meet up. See **meet** 1, 2. PHRASAL VERB

meeting /miːtɪŋ/ **meetings** ◆◆◆◆◆

1 A **meeting** is an event in which a group of people come together to discuss things or make decisions. *Can we have a meeting to discuss that?... He still travels to London regularly for business meetings.* N-COUNT
▶ You can also refer to the people at a meeting as **the meeting**. *The meeting decided that further efforts were needed.* N-SING: the N

2 When you meet someone, either intentionally or accidentally, you can refer to this event as a **meeting**. *In January, 37 years after our first meeting, I was back in the studio with Denis... Her life was changed by a chance meeting with her former art master a few years ago.* N-COUNT: oft with poss =encounter

meeting house, meeting houses. A **meeting house** is a building in which a group of nonconformist Christians, for example Quakers, meet in order to worship together. N-COUNT

meeting place, meeting places. A **meeting place** is a place where people meet. ◆◇◇◇◇ N-COUNT

mega /megə/

1 Young people sometimes use **mega** in front of adjectives or adverbs in order to emphasize them; an informal use. *He has become mega rich... Roy was tremendously ugly, mega ugly.* ADV: usu ADV adj/adv PRAGMATICS =extremely

2 Young people sometimes use **mega** in front of nouns in order to emphasize that the thing they are talking about is very good, very large, or very impressive; an informal use. *...her newly acquired mega salary. ...the mega superstar Madonna.* ADJ: ADJ n PRAGMATICS

mega- /megə-/

1 **Mega-** is added to nouns that refer to units of measurement in order to form other nouns referring to units that are a million times bigger. *...a 100 megaton explosion. ...a two thousand megawatt surge in electricity.* PREFIX

2 **Mega-** combines with nouns and adjectives in order to emphasize the size, quality, or importance of something; an informal use. *Now he can begin to earn the sort of mega-bucks he has always dreamed about. ...a Hollywood mega-star.* PREFIX PRAGMATICS

megabyte /megəbaɪt/ **megabytes.** In computing, a **megabyte** is one million bytes of data. ◆◇◇◇◇ N-COUNT

megahertz /megəhɜːʳts/; **megahertz** is both the singular and the plural form. A **megahertz** is a unit of frequency, used especially for radio frequencies. One megahertz equals one million cycles per second. *...UHF frequencies of around 900 megahertz.* N-COUNT: num N

megalomania /megələmeɪniə/. **Megalomania** is the belief that you are more powerful and important than you really are. Megalomania is sometimes a mental illness. N-UNCOUNT

megalomaniac /megələmeɪniæk/ **megalomaniacs.** If you describe someone as a **megalomaniac**, you are criticizing them because they enjoy being powerful, or because they believe that they are more powerful or important than they really are. N-COUNT: oft N n PRAGMATICS

megaphone /megəfoʊn/ **megaphones.** A **megaphone** is a cone-shaped device for making your voice sound louder in the open air. N-COUNT

megaton /megətʌn/ **megatons.** You can use **megaton** to refer to the power of a nuclear weapon. A one megaton bomb has the same power as one million tons of TNT. N-COUNT: num N

megawatt /megəwɒt/ **megawatts.** A **megawatt** is a unit of power. One megawatt is a million watts. *The project is designed to generate around 30 megawatts of power for the national grid.* N-COUNT: num N, oft N of n

melancholia /melənkoʊliə/. **Melancholia** is a feeling of great melancholy or depression; a literary word. *He sank into deep melancholia.* N-UNCOUNT

melancholic /melənkɒlɪk/ **melancholics.** If you describe someone or something as **melancholic**, you mean that they are very sad; a literary word. *The night was as melancholic as his mood. ...his gentle, melancholic songs.* ADJ-GRADED
▶ A **melancholic** is someone who is melancholic. *...a self-made man, energetic and obsessively orderly, a histrionic exhibitionist and a melancholic.* N-COUNT

melancholy /melənkɒli/ ◆◇◇◇◇

1 You describe something that you see or hear as **melancholy** when it gives you an intense feeling of sadness. *...a painter of haunting melancholy canvases... The only sounds were the distant, melancholy cries of the sheep... The songs start soft and melancholy.* ADJ-GRADED

2 **Melancholy** is an intense feeling of sadness which lasts for a long time and which strongly affects your behaviour and attitudes; a literary use. *I* N-UNCOUNT

was deeply aware of his melancholy as he stood among the mourners... The general watched the process with an air of melancholy.

3 If someone feels or looks **melancholy**, they feel or look very sad; a literary use. *It was in these hours of the late afternoon that Tom Mulligan felt most melancholy... He fixed me with those luminous, empty eyes and his melancholy smile.* ADJ-GRADED =sad

melange /meɪlɒndʒ/ **melanges;** also spelled **mélange**. A **melange** of things is a mixture of them, especially when this is attractive or exciting; used mainly in written English. *...a successful melange of music styles, from soul and rhythm and blues to rap. ...a wonderful melange of flavours.* N-COUNT: with supp, oft N of n =blend, medley

melanin /melənɪn/. **Melanin** is a dark substance in the skin, eyes, and hair of people and animals, which gives them colour and can protect them against strong sunlight. N-UNCOUNT

melanoma /melənoʊmə/ **melanomas.** A **melanoma** is a tumour or type of cancer that usually forms in the skin and is caused by very strong sunlight. N-COUNT

melee /meleɪ, AM meɪ-/ **melees;** also spelled **mêlée**.

1 A **melee** is a noisy confusing fight between the people in a crowd; used mainly in written English. *A policeman was killed and scores of people were injured in the melee.* N-COUNT: usu sing =brawl

2 A **melee** of things is a large, confusing, disorganized group of them; used mainly in written English. *You may want to wander through the melee of streets around the waterfront.* N-SING: usu N of n =muddle

mellifluous /mɪlɪfluəs/. A **mellifluous** voice or piece of music is smooth and gentle and very pleasant to listen to; a formal word. *I grew up around people who had wonderful, mellifluous voices... Soon the room is filled with Bates' mellifluous tones.* ADJ-GRADED: usu ADJ n

mellow /meloʊ/ **mellower, mellowest; mellows, mellowing, mellowed** ◆◇◇◇◇

1 **Mellow** is used to describe things that have a pleasant, soft, rich colour, usually red, orange, yellow, or brown. *...a classic Queen Anne house of mellow red brick with a white portico. ...this mellow Cotswold manor house. ...the softer, mellower light of evening.* ADJ-GRADED: usu ADJ n/ colour

2 A **mellow** sound or flavour is pleasant, smooth, and rich. *His voice was deep and mellow and his speech had a soothing and comforting quality. ...the mellow background music. ...a delightfully mellow, soft and balanced wine.* ADJ-GRADED

3 If someone **mellows** or if something **mellows** them, they become kinder or less extreme in their behaviour, especially as a result of growing older. *He became a taciturn man, a man not easy to live with. Later, when the older children married and had children of their own, he mellowed a little... Marriage had not mellowed him.* ▶ Also an adjective. *Is she more mellow and tolerant?* V-ERG; V; V n; ADJ-GRADED

4 If someone is **mellow**, they feel very relaxed and cheerful, especially as the result of alcohol or good food; an informal use. *He'd had a few glasses of champagne himself and was fairly mellow... At the other tables couples were now in a mellow mood, chattering happily and drinking.* ADJ-GRADED

melodic /mɪlɒdɪk/ ◆◇◇◇◇

1 **Melodic** means relating to melody; a technical use in music. *...Schubert's effortless gift for melodic invention.* ♦ **melodically** /mɪlɒdɪkli/ *...the third of Tchaikovsky's ten operas, and melodically one of his richest scores.* ADJ: usu ADJ n; ADV

2 Music that is **melodic** has beautiful tunes in it. *Wonderfully melodic and tuneful, his songs have made me weep.* ♦ **melodically** *The leader has also learned to play more melodically.* ADJ-GRADED; ADV-GRADED: ADV after v

melodious /mɪloʊdiəs/. A **melodious** sound is pleasant to listen to; a formal word. *She spoke in a quietly melodious voice.* ADJ-GRADED =musical

melodrama /melədrɑːmə/ **melodramas.** A **melodrama** is a story or play in which there are a lot of exciting or sad events and in which people's emotions are very exaggerated. ◆◇◇◇◇ N-VAR

melodramatic /melədrəmætɪk/. **Melodramatic** behaviour is behaviour in which someone treats a situation as much more serious than it really is. *'Don't you think you're being rather melodramatic?' Jane asked... She'd flung herself in a pose of melodramatic exhaustion.* ♦ **melodramatically** /melədrəmætɪkli/ *'For God's sake,' Michael said melodramatically, 'Whatever you do, don't look down.'* ◆◇◇◇◇ ADJ-GRADED; ADV-GRADED: ADV with v

melody /melədi/ **melodies** ◆◆◇◇◇

1 A **melody** is a tune; a formal use. N-COUNT

2 **Melody** is the quality of being tuneful. *Her voice was full of melody.* N-UNCOUNT

melon /melən/ **melons.** A **melon** is a large fruit which is sweet and juicy inside and has a hard green or yellow skin. ◆◇◇◇◇ N-VAR

melt /melt/ **melts, melting, melted** ◆◆◇◇◇

1 When a solid substance **melts** or when you **melt** it, it changes to a liquid, usually because it has been heated. *The snow had melted, but the lake was still frozen solid... Meanwhile, melt the white chocolate in a bowl suspended over simmering water... Add the melted butter, molasses, salt, and flour.* V-ERG; V; V n; V-ed

2 If something such as your feelings **melt**, they suddenly disappear and you no longer feel them; a literary use. *His anxiety about the outcome melted, to return later but not yet... He would have struggled but his strength had melted.* ▶ **Melt away** means the same as **melt**. *When he heard these words, Shinran felt his inner doubts melt away.* VERB; V; PHRASAL VERB V P

3 If a person or thing **melts into** something such as darkness or a crowd of people, they become difficult to see, for example because they are moving away from you or are the same colour as the background; a literary use. *The youths dispersed and melted into the darkness... The squadron's armour is draped in sand-coloured nets that melt into the landscape.* VERB =disappear; V into n

4 If someone or something **melts** your heart, or if your heart **melts**, you start to feel loving or tender towards them. *When his lips break into a smile, it is enough to melt any woman's heart... When a bride walks down the aisle to a stirring tune, even the iciest of hearts melt.* V-ERG; V n; V

melt away. If a crowd of people **melts away**, members of the crowd gradually leave until there is no-one left. *The crowd around the bench began to melt away.* ● See also **melt** 2. PHRASAL VERB V P

melt down. If an object **is melted down**, it is heated until it melts, so that the material can be used to make something else. *Some of the guns were melted down and used to help build a statue... When Jefferson didn't like a pair of goblets given to him as a gift, he asked a local smith to melt them down and make eight new cups without stems and handles... Some thieves do not even bother to melt down stolen silver for its scrap value.* PHRASAL VERB be V-ed P; V n P; V P n (not pron)

meltdown /meltdaʊn/ **meltdowns**

1 If there is **meltdown** in a nuclear reactor, the fuel rods start melting because of a failure in the system, with the result that radiation starts to escape. *Scientists warned that emergency cooling systems could fail and a reactor meltdown could occur.* N-VAR

2 The **meltdown** of a company, organization, or system is its sudden and complete failure; used in journalism. *Urgent talks are going on to prevent the market going into financial meltdown during the summer.* N-UNCOUNT: with supp

melting point, melting points. The **melting point** of a substance is the temperature at which it melts when you heat it. N-COUNT: oft with poss

melting pot, melting pots

1 A **melting pot** is a place or situation in which people or ideas of different kinds gradually get mixed together. *The republic is a melting pot of different nationalities. ...the cultural melting pot... Marseilles has proved to be a better racial melting-pot than Lyons.* N-COUNT: usu sing

2 If someone or something is **in the melting pot**, PHRASE:

they are constantly changing, so that you don't know what will finally happen to them; used mainly in British English. *Fry's own future has been in the melting pot on many occasions... Their fate is still in the melting-pot.* v-link PHR, PHR after v

member /membəʳ/ **members** ◆◆◆◆◆
1 A **member** of a group is one of the people, animals, or things belonging to that group. *He refused to name the members of staff involved... Their lack of training could put members of the public at risk. ...a sunflower or a similar member of the daisy family. ...the brightest members of a dense cluster of stars at the Galaxy's centre.* N-COUNT: with supp, oft N *of*n
2 A **member** of an organization such as a club or a political party is a person who has officially joined the organization. *The support of our members is of great importance to the Association... Britain is a full member of NATO.* N-COUNT: usu with supp, oft N *of*n
3 A **member country** or **member state** is one of the countries that has joined an international organization or alliance. *...the member countries of the European Free Trade Association. ...a co-ordinated EC approach, with each member state doing what it could.* ADJ: ADJ n
4 A **member** is a Member of Parliament; used in British English. *He was elected to Parliament as the Member for Leeds. ...the Conservative member for Billericay.* N-COUNT: usu N *for*n

Member of Parliament, Members of Parliament. A **Member of Parliament** is a person who has been elected by people to represent them in a country's parliament. It is usually abbreviated to 'MP'. ◆◆◇◇◇ N-COUNT =MP

membership /membəʳʃɪp/ **memberships** ◆◆◆◇◇
1 **Membership** of an organization is the state of being a member of it. *...his membership of the Communist Party... He sent me a membership form... We have temporary memberships for visitors.* N-UNCOUNT: also N in pl
2 The **membership** of an organization is the people who belong to it, or the number of people who belong to it. *The European Builders Confederation has a membership of over 350,000 building companies. ...organizations with huge memberships. ...the recent fall in party membership.* N-VAR-COLL

membrane /membreɪn/ **membranes.** A **membrane** is a thin piece of skin which connects or covers parts of a person's or animal's body. ◆◇◇◇◇ N-COUNT

memento /mɪmentoʊ/ **mementos** or **mementoes.** A **memento** is an object which you keep because it reminds you of a person or a special occasion. *More anglers are taking cameras when they go fishing to provide a memento of catches.* ◆◇◇◇◇ N-COUNT: oft N *of*n =souvenir

memo /memoʊ/ **memos.** A **memo** is a short official note that is written from one person to another within the same company or organization. ◆◇◇◇◇ N-COUNT

memoir /memwɑːʳ/ **memoirs** ◆◇◇◇◇
1 A person's **memoirs** are a written account of the people who they have known and events that they remember. *If you've read my earlier memoirs you'll know all about it... In his memoirs, De Gaulle wrote that he had come to London determined to save the French nation.* N-PLURAL: usu with poss
2 A **memoir** is a book or article that you write about someone who you have known well; a formal use. *He has just published a memoir in honour of his captain.* N-COUNT

memorabilia /memərəbɪliə/. **Memorabilia** are things that you collect because they are connected with a person or organization in which you are interested. ◆◇◇◇◇ N-PLURAL

memorable /memərəbᵊl/. Something that is **memorable** is worth remembering or likely to be remembered, because it is special, enjoyable, or unique. *...the perfect setting for a nostalgic memorable day... Annette's performance as Eliza Doolittle in 'Pygmalion' was truly memorable.* ◆◆◇◇◇ ADJ-GRADED
♦ **memorably** *The National Theatre's production is memorably staged.* ADV-GRADED: usu ADV with v, also ADV adj

memorandum /memərændəm/ **memoranda** or **memorandums** ◆◇◇◇◇
1 A **memorandum** is a written report that is prepared for a person or committee in order to provide them with information about a particular matter. *...a memorandum from the Ministry of Defence on its role... The delegation submitted a memorandum to the Commons on the blatant violations of basic human rights.* N-COUNT
2 A **memorandum** is an informal diplomatic communication between governments which often summarizes a particular diplomatic purpose or point of view. *Bangladesh and China have signed a memorandum of understanding under which Chittagong and Shanghai will establish a closer relationship.* N-COUNT
3 A **memorandum** is a short official note that is written from one person to another within the same company or organization; a formal use. N-COUNT =memo

memorial /mɪmɔːriəl/ **memorials** ◆◆◇◇◇
1 A **memorial** is a structure built in order to remind people of a famous person or event. *Building a memorial to Columbus has been his lifelong dream... Every village had its war memorial.* N-COUNT: usu with supp
2 A **memorial** event, object, or prize is in honour of someone who has died, so that they will be remembered. *A memorial service is being held for her at St Paul's Church. ...memorial plaques to local regiments... He went on to win the James E. Sullivan Memorial Trophy as the outstanding amateur athlete of 1962.* ADJ: ADJ n
3 If you say that something will be **a memorial to** someone who has died, you mean that it will continue to exist and remind people of them. *The museum will serve as a memorial to the millions who passed through Ellis Island... The city's rather uncompromising bleakness is a permanent memorial to its dark and mysterious founders.* N-COUNT: usu sing, N *to*n

Memorial Day. In the United States, **Memorial Day** is a public holiday when people honour the memory of Americans who have died in wars. Memorial Day is celebrated in most states on the last Monday in May. N-UNCOUNT

memorialize /mɪmɔːriəlaɪz/ **memorializes, memorializing, memorialized;** also spelled **memorialise** in British English. If a person or event **is memorialized**, something is produced that will continue to exist and remind people of them. *He was praised in print and memorialized in stone throughout the South... Our affair was memorialized by those children... When she died in 1946, her friends wanted to memorialize her in some significant way.* VERB *be*V-ed V n

memorize /meməraɪz/ **memorizes, memorizing, memorized;** also spelled **memorise** in British English. If you **memorize** something, you learn it so that you can remember it exactly. *He studied his map, trying to memorize the way to Rose's street.* ◆◇◇◇◇ VERB =learn by heart V n

memory /meməri/ **memories** ◆◆◆◆◇
1 Your **memory** is your ability to remember things. *All the details of the meeting are fresh in my memory... He'd a good memory for faces, and he was sure he hadn't seen her before... But locals with long memories thought this was fair revenge for the injustice of 1961... Two major areas in which mentally retarded children require help are memory and attention.* N-VAR: oft poss N
2 A **memory** is something that you remember from the past. *She cannot bear to watch the film because of the bad memories it brings back... Her earliest memory is of singing at the age of four to wounded soldiers... He had happy memories of his father.* N-COUNT: usu with supp, oft N *of*n
3 A computer's **memory** is the part of the computer where information is stored, especially for a short time before it is transferred to disks or magnetic tapes. *The data are stored in the computer's memory. ...4-megabyte computer memory chips.* N-COUNT
4 If you talk about the **memory** of someone who has died, especially someone who was loved or respected, you are referring to the thoughts, actions, and ceremonies by which they are remembered. *She remained devoted to his memory... The congress opened with a minute's silence in memory of those who died in the struggle.* N-SING: usu with poss, also *in* N *of*n
5 If you do something **from memory**, for example PHRASES

recite a poem or play a piece of music, you do it without looking at anything written or printed. *Many members of the church sang from memory... Children write down the word, cover it up and then try to spell it from memory.* PHR after v

6 If you say that something is, for example, the best, worst, or first thing of its kind **in living memory** or **within living memory**, you are emphasizing that it is the best, worst, or only thing of that kind that people can remember happening. *The floods are the worst in living memory... No-one in living memory has come back from that place alive.* n/adj PHR, usu with adj-superl/brd-neg PRAGMATICS

7 If you **lose your memory**, you forget things that you used to know. *His illness caused him to lose his memory.* V inflects

8 • **commit something to memory**: see **commit**.

memsahib /mem̲sɑːb/ **memsahibs. Memsahib** was used to refer to or address white women in India, especially during the period of British rule, or sometimes to refer to or address upper-class Indian women; an old-fashioned word. N-COUNT; N-TITLE; N-VOC

men /me̲n/. **Men** is the plural of **man**.

menace /me̲nɪs/ **menaces, menacing, menaced** ◆◇◇◇◇

1 If you say that someone or something is a **menace** to other people or things, you mean that person or thing is likely to cause serious harm. *In my view you are a menace to the public. ...the menace of fascism... Excessive drinking is a social menace.* N-COUNT: usu sing, oft N *to* n, N *of* n =threat

2 You can refer to someone or something as a **menace** when you want to say that they cause you trouble or annoyance; an informal use. *You're a menace to my privacy, Kenworthy... As I have said earlier in this book, bad shoes are a menace.* N-COUNT: usu sing =nuisance

3 Menace is a quality or atmosphere that gives you the feeling that you are in danger or that someone wants to harm you. *There is a pervading sense of menace. ...a voice full of menace.* N-UNCOUNT

4 If you say that one thing **menaces** another, you mean that the first thing is likely to cause the second thing serious harm. *The European states retained a latent capability to menace Britain's own security.* VERB =threaten V n

5 If you **are menaced** by someone, they threaten to harm you. *She's being menaced by her sister's latest boyfriend.* VERB =threaten *be* V-ed Also V n

6 In British English, if someone commits the crime of demanding money **with menaces**, they threaten to cause harm unless they are given the money; a legal expression. *He also denies demanding £200,000 with menaces from British Rail in 1991.* PHRASE: usu PHR after v

menacing /me̲nɪsɪŋ/. If someone or something looks **menacing**, they give you a feeling that they are likely to cause you harm or put you in danger. *The strong dark eyebrows give his face an oddly menacing look... He moved his menacing bulk closer to the table... The wide river looked less menacing when flanked by the warm yellow houses.* ♦ **menacingly** *A group of men suddenly emerged from a doorway and moved menacingly forward to block her way.* ◆◇◇◇◇ ADJ-GRADED =threatening; ADV-GRADED: usu ADV after v, also ADV adj/-ed

menage /meɪnɑ̲ːʒ/; also spelled **ménage**. A **menage** is a group of people living together in one house; a formal word. N-SING: usu with supp

menage a trois /meɪnɑːʒ ɑː twɑ̲ː/ **menages a trois;** also spelled **ménage à trois**. A **menage a trois** is a situation where three people live together, especially when one of them is having a sexual relationship with both of the others. N-COUNT: usu sing

menagerie /mənæ̲dʒəri/ **menageries.** A **menagerie** is a collection of wild animals. N-COUNT

mend /me̲nd/ **mends, mending, mended** ◆◇◇◇◇

1 If you **mend** something that is broken or not working, you repair it, so that it works properly or can be used. *They took a long time to mend the roof... Somebody else lent me a pump and helped me mend the puncture... I should have had the catch mended, but never got round to it.* VERB =repair, fix V n *have* n V-ed

2 If a person or a part of their body **mends** or **is mended**, they get better after they have been ill or have had an injury. *You'll mend. The X-rays show that your arm will heal all right... I'm feeling a good bit better. The cut aches, but it's mending... He must have a major operation on his knee to mend severed ligaments.* V-ERG V V n

3 If you try to **mend** divisions between people, you try to end the disagreements or quarrels between them. *They will seek to mend divisions that were caused by the Gulf conflict... I felt that might well mend the rift between them.* VERB =heal V n

4 If a relationship or situation is **on the mend** after a difficult or unsuccessful period, it is improving; an informal expression. *More evidence that the economy was on the mend was needed.* PHRASES v-link PHR

5 If you are **on the mend** after an illness or injury, you are recovering from it; an informal expression. *The baby had been poorly but seemed on the mend.* v-link PHR

6 If someone who has been behaving badly **mends** their **ways**, they begin to behave well. *He has promised drastic disciplinary action if they do not mend their ways.* V inflects

7 • **to mend fences**: see **fence**.

mendacious /mende̲ɪʃəs/. A **mendacious** statement or remark is not truthful; a formal word. ADJ-GRADED

mendacity /mendæ̲sɪti/. **Mendacity** is the quality of lying, rather than being truthful; a formal word. *For a government minister it was an astonishing display of cowardice and mendacity.* N-UNCOUNT

mending /me̲ndɪŋ/. **Mending** is the sewing and repairing of clothes that have got holes in them; an old-fashioned word. *Who will then do the cooking, the washing, the mending?* • See also **mend**. N-UNCOUNT

menfolk /me̲nfoʊk/. When women refer to their **menfolk**, they mean the men in their family or society. N-PLURAL: usu poss N

menial /miː̲niəl/. **Menial** work is very boring and tiring, and the people who do it have a low status and are usually poorly paid. *...low paid menial jobs, such as cleaning and domestic work.* ADJ-GRADED

meningitis /me̲nɪndʒa̲ɪtɪs/. **Meningitis** is a serious infectious illness which affects your brain and spinal cord. ◆◇◇◇◇ N-UNCOUNT

menopause /me̲nəpɔːz/. The **menopause** is the time during which a woman gradually stops menstruating, usually when she is about fifty years old. ♦ **menopausal** *A menopausal woman of average build and height requires 1600 – 2400 calories daily.* ◆◇◇◇◇ N-SING: also no det; ADJ

me̲n's room, men's rooms. The **men's room** is a toilet for men; used mainly in American English. N-COUNT: usu *the* N in sing

menstrual /me̲nstruəl/. **Menstrual** means relating to menstruation. *...the menstrual cycle.* ◆◇◇◇◇ ADJ: ADJ n

menstruate /me̲nstrueɪt/ **menstruates, menstruating, menstruated.** When a woman **menstruates**, a flow of blood comes from her womb. Women who are fertile menstruate once a month unless they are pregnant; a formal word. *Lean hard-training women athletes may menstruate less frequently or not at all.* ♦ **menstruation** /me̲nstrue̲ɪʃən/ *Menstruation may cease when a woman is anywhere between forty-five and fifty years of age.* ◆◇◇◇◇ VERB V; N-UNCOUNT

menswear /me̲nzweəʳ/. **Menswear** is clothing for men; a formal word. *...the menswear industry.* N-UNCOUNT

-ment. **-ment** is added to some verbs to form nouns that refer to actions, processes, or states. *...shortly after the commencement of the service. ...the enrichment of uranium.* SUFFIX

mental /me̲ntəl/ ◆◆◆◇◇

1 Mental means relating to the process of thinking. *The intellectual environment has a significant influence on the mental development of the children. ...intensive mental effort.* ♦ **mentally** *I think you are mentally tired... I had never felt more mentally alive... Physically I might not have been overseas but mentally and spiritually I was with them.* ADJ: ADJ n; ADV: ADV adj/adv, ADV with v, ADV with cl

2 Mental means relating to the state or the health of a person's mind. *The mental state that had created her psychosis was no longer present... Most people know little about mental health problems.* ♦ **mentally** *...an inmate who is mentally disturbed.* ADJ: ADJ n; ADV:

...*the needs of the mentally ill and the mentally handicapped.* usu ADV with cl/group, also ADV after v

3 A **mental** act is one that involves only thinking and not physical action. *Practise mental arithmetic when you go out shopping... Graham made a quick mental calculation.* ♦ **mentally** *This technique will help people mentally organize information.* ADJ: ADJ n; ADV: ADV with v

4 If you say that someone is **mental**, you mean that you think they are mad; an informal British use which some people find offensive. *I just said to him 'you must be mental'.* ADJ-GRADED =crazy, mad

5 If you **make a mental note** of something, you make an effort to store it in your memory so that you will not forget it. *She made a mental note to have his prescription refilled.* PHRASE: V inflects, PHR of n, PHR to-inf

mental age, mental ages. A person's **mental age** is the age which they are considered to have reached in their thinking ability. This is worked out by comparing their ability with the average ability for people of various ages and is used especially when referring to people with learning difficulties. N-COUNT: usu sing

mental hospital, mental hospitals. A **mental hospital** is a hospital for people who are suffering from mental illness. N-COUNT

mentality /mentælɪti/ **mentalities.** Your **mentality** is your attitudes and your way of thinking. ...*a criminal mentality... Running a business requires a very different mentality from being a salaried employee.* ◆◇◇◇◇ N-COUNT: usu sing, with supp

menthol /menθɒl, AM -θɔːl/. **Menthol** is a substance that smells a bit like peppermint, and is used to flavour things such as cigarettes and toothpaste. It is also used in some medicinal products, especially for curing colds. N-UNCOUNT

mention /menʃᵊn/ **mentions, mentioning, mentioned** ◆◆◆◆◇

1 If you **mention** something, you say something about it, usually briefly. *She did not mention her mother's absence... I may not have mentioned it to her... I had mentioned that I didn't really like contemporary music... She shouldn't have mentioned how heavy the dress was... Elizabeth told of her love of archaeology and Clarice mentioned Turkey as a place of great antiquity.* VERB V n/-ing, V n to n, V that, V wh, V n as n

2 A **mention** is a reference to something or someone. *The statement made no mention of government casualties... At the community centre, mention of funds produces pained looks.* N-VAR: oft N of n

3 If someone **is mentioned** in writing, a reference is made to them by name, often to criticize or praise something that they have done. *I was absolutely outraged that I could be even mentioned in an article of this kind... As for your father, he won't be mentioned in my will. ...Brigadier Ferguson was mentioned in the report as being directly responsible.* VB: usu passive; be V-ed, be V-ed as n/adj

4 If someone **is mentioned** as a candidate for something such as a job, it is suggested that they might become a candidate. *His appointment is a complete surprise – he has never been mentioned as a front runner... He has been mentioned as a potential candidate for a top economic post in the Clinton administration.* VB: usu passive; be V-ed as n

5 A special or honourable **mention** is formal praise that is given for an achievement that is very good, although not usually the best of its kind. *Two of the losers deserve special mention: Caroline Swaithes, of Kings Norton, and Maria Pons, of Valencia.* N-VAR: with supp =commendation

6 People sometimes say **'don't mention it'** as a polite reply to someone who has just thanked them for doing something. PHRASES CONVENTION PRAGMATICS

7 You use **not to mention** when you want to add extra information which emphasizes the point that you are making. *The audience, not to mention the bewildered cast, were not amused... It was both deliberate and malicious, not to mention clever.* PHR group PRAGMATICS

8 • to be **mentioned in dispatches**: see **dispatch**.

mentor /mentɔːʳ/ **mentors.** A person's **mentor** is someone who teaches them and gives them a lot of advice over a period of time; a formal word. ◆◇◇◇◇ N-COUNT: usu poss N

menu /menjuː/ **menus** ◆◆◇◇◇

1 In a restaurant or café, or at a formal meal, the **menu** is a list of the meals and drinks that are available. *A waiter offered him the menu... Even the most elaborate dishes on the menu were quite low on calories.* N-COUNT: usu sing

2 A **menu** is the food that you serve at a meal. *Try out the menu on a few friends... The menu is all-important. Every component of every meal should create contrasts.* N-COUNT

3 On a computer, a **menu** is a list of choices. Each choice represents something you can do using the computer. N-COUNT

MEP /em iː piː/ **MEPs.** An **MEP** is a person who has been elected to the European Parliament. **MEP** is an abbreviation for 'Member of the European Parliament'. ◆◇◇◇◇ N-COUNT

mercantile /mɜːʳkəntaɪl/. **Mercantile** means relating to merchants or trading; a formal word. *The older noble families were eclipsed by the emergence of a new mercantile class.* ◆◇◇◇◇ ADJ: ADJ n

mercenary /mɜːʳsənri, AM -neri/ **mercenaries** ◆◇◇◇◇

1 A **mercenary** is a soldier who is paid to fight by a country or group that he or she does not belong to. N-COUNT

2 If you describe someone as a **mercenary** you are criticizing them because you think that they are only interested in the money that they can get from a particular person or situation. ADJ-GRADED

merchandise /mɜːʳtʃəndaɪz, -daɪs/. **Merchandise** is goods that are bought, sold, or traded; a formal word. ◆◇◇◇◇ N-UNCOUNT

merchandiser /mɜːʳtʃəndaɪzəʳ/ **merchandisers.** In American English, a **merchandiser** is a person or company that sells goods to the public. The British word is **retailer**. *In 1979, Liquor Barn thrived as a discount merchandiser.* N-COUNT: usu supp N =retailer

merchandising /mɜːʳtʃəndaɪzɪŋ/ ◆◇◇◇◇

1 **Merchandising** consists of goods such as toys and T-shirts that are produced in order to promote something such as a particular film, sports team, or pop group. *We are selling the full range of World Cup merchandising... The club says it will make increasing amounts from merchandising.* N-UNCOUNT

2 **Merchandising** is used to refer to the way shops and businesses organize the sale of their products, for example the way they are displayed and the prices that are chosen; used mainly in American English. *Company executives say revamped merchandising should help Macy's earnings to grow.* N-UNCOUNT

merchant /mɜːʳtʃənt/ **merchants** ◆◆◆◇◇

1 A **merchant** is a person who buys or sells goods in large quantities, especially one who imports and exports them. *Any knowledgeable wine merchant would be able to advise you.* N-COUNT

2 **Merchant** seamen or ships are involved in carrying goods for trade. *There's been a big reduction in the size of the British merchant fleet in recent years.* ADJ: ADJ n

merchant bank, merchant banks. A **merchant bank** is a bank that deals mainly with business firms, investment, and foreign trade. ◆◇◇◇◇ N-COUNT

merciful /mɜːʳsɪfʊl/

1 If you describe God or a person in a position of authority as **merciful**, you mean that they show kindness and forgiveness to people. ...*a merciful God... We can only hope the court is merciful.* ADJ-GRADED

2 If you describe an event or situation as **merciful**, you mean that it seems fortunate, especially because it stops someone's suffering or discomfort. *We were told when he was taken to hospital that his injuries were so severe death would be merciful... Eventually the session came to a merciful end.* ADJ-GRADED

mercifully /mɜːʳsɪfʊli/. You can use **mercifully** to show that you are glad that something good has happened, or that something which causes pain or discomfort has not happened or has stopped. *Mercifully, a friend came to the rescue... Bolivia has been mercifully free of large-scale, drug-related violence.* ◆◇◇◇◇ ADV: ADV with cl, ADV adj, ADV with v PRAGMATICS =thankfully

merciless /mɜːʳsɪləs/. If you describe someone as **merciless**, you mean that they are very cruel or determined and do not show any concern for the effect their actions have on other people. ◆◇◇◇◇ ADJ-GRADED =ruthless

Whistler, as always, was merciless. ...the merciless efficiency of a modern police state. ♦ **mercilessly** *We teased him mercilessly... The sun beat down mercilessly on the women's bare heads.*
ADV-GRADED: usu ADV with v, also ADV adj, ADV with cl

mercurial /mɜːʳkjʊəriəl/. If you describe someone as **mercurial**, you mean that they frequently change their mind or mood without warning; a literary word. *...his mercurial temperament.*
ADJ-GRADED =volatile

mercury /mɜːʳkjʊri/. **Mercury** is a silver-coloured liquid metal that is used especially in thermometers and barometers.
◆◇◇◇◇ N-UNCOUNT

mercy /mɜːʳsi/ **mercies** ◆◆◇◇◇

1 If someone in authority shows **mercy**, they choose not to harm someone they have power over, or they forgive someone they have the right to punish. *Neither side took prisoners or showed any mercy... They cried for mercy but their pleas were met with abuse and laughter... May God have mercy on your soul.*
N-UNCOUNT

2 **Mercy** is used to describe a special journey to help someone in great need, such as sick people or refugees; used in journalism. *...the man behind a daring mercy mission to bring back refugees from Bosnia... It's the first so-called mercy flight for a fortnight as the Americans have been waiting for enough people to fill a 747 jet.*
ADJ: ADJ n

3 If you refer to an event or situation as a **mercy**, it makes you feel happy or relieved, usually because it stops something unpleasant happening. *It really was a mercy that he'd gone so rapidly at the end... The two cars finished up in a run-off area, clear of the circuit, and that was a mercy.*
N-COUNT: usu a N =blessing

4 If one person or thing is **at the mercy** of another, the first person or thing is in a situation where they cannot prevent themselves being harmed or affected by the second. *Buildings are left to decay at the mercy of vandals and the weather... The Emperor must realize that he has us at his mercy.*
PHRASES with poss, usu PHR after v, v-link PHR

5 If you tell someone who is in an unpleasant situation that they should be **grateful** or **thankful for small mercies**, you mean that something relatively good or slightly less bad has happened to them, and that they should be happy about it, instead of complaining. *But so low has morale sunk that the team and the fans would have been grateful for small mercies.*
usu v-link PHR

6 If you say that you **are throwing** yourself **on** someone's **mercy**, you mean that you are deliberately putting yourself in a situation where they will have complete power to decide how to treat you, for example whether to punish or forgive you. *He's going to throw himself on the mercy of the court.*
V inflects

mercy killing, mercy killings. A **mercy killing** is an act of killing someone who is very ill, in order to stop them suffering any more pain.
N-VAR

mere /mɪəʳ/ **merest** ◆◆◆◇◇

Mere does not have a comparative form. The superlative form **merest** is used to emphasize how small something is, rather than in comparisons.

1 You use **mere** to emphasize how unimportant or inadequate something is, in comparison to the general situation you are describing. *...successful exhibitions which go beyond mere success... There is more to good health than the mere absence of disease... In Poland, the faith has always meant more than mere religion... She'd never received the merest hint of any communication from him.*
ADJ: ADJ n PRAGMATICS

2 You use **mere** to indicate that a quality or action that is usually unimportant has a very important or strong effect. *The mere mention of food had triggered off hunger pangs... Whenever there was a gap in the traffic the merest pressure on the accelerator was enough to close it... The mere suggestion that she might have to scrub the floor filled her with horror.*
ADJ: ADJ n

3 You use **mere** to emphasize how small a particular amount or number is. *Sixty per cent of teachers are women, but a mere 5 percent of women are heads and deputies... Tickets are a mere £7.50 at the door... For the past two decades, North Carolina taxed cigarettes at a mere 2 cents a packet.*
ADJ: a ADJ amount PRAGMATICS

merely /mɪəʳli/ ◆◆◆◇◇

1 You use **merely** to emphasize that something is only what you say and not better, more important, or more exciting. *Michael is now merely a good friend... Francis Watson was far from being merely a furniture expert... Merely because you believe a thing is right, it isn't automatically so... They are offering merely technical assistance.*
ADV: ADV with cl/group, ADV before v PRAGMATICS =just, simply

2 You use **merely** to emphasize that a particular amount or quantity is very small. *The brain accounts for merely three per cent of body weight.*
ADV: ADV amount PRAGMATICS =only

3 You use **not merely** before the less important of two contrasting statements, as a way of emphasizing the more important statement. *The team needs players who want to play cricket for England, not merely any country that will have them... His were not merely crimes of theft but of violence against elderly people.*
PHRASE: PHR with cl/group, PHR before v PRAGMATICS =not just

meretricious /merɪtrɪʃəs/. If you describe something as **meretricious**, you disapprove of it because although it looks attractive you think it is in fact of little value; a formal word. *...vulgar, meretricious and shabby souvenirs.*
ADJ-GRADED PRAGMATICS

merge /mɜːʳdʒ/ **merges, merging, merged** ◆◆◇◇◇

1 If one thing **merges** with another, or **is merged** with another, they combine or come together to make one whole thing. You can also say that two things **merge**, or **are merged**. *My life merged with his... Bank of America merged with a rival bank... The rivers merge just north of a vital irrigation system... The two countries merged into one... He sees sense in merging the two agencies while both are new... Then he showed me how to merge the graphic with text on the same screen.*
V-RECIP-ERG; V with n; pl-n V; pl-n V into n; V pl-n; V n with n; Also V pl-n into n

2 If one sound, colour, or object **merges** into another, the first changes so gradually into the second, or is so similar to it, that you do not notice the change or difference. You can also say that two sounds, colours, or objects **merge**. *Like a chameleon, he could merge unobtrusively into the background... His features merged with the darkness... Night and day begin to merge.*
V-RECIP; V into n; V with n; pl-n V

merger /mɜːʳdʒəʳ/ **mergers.** A **merger** is the joining together of two separate companies or organizations so that they become one. *...a merger between two of Britain's biggest trades unions. ...the proposed merger of two Japanese banks.*
◆◆◆◇◇ N-COUNT

meridian /mərɪdiən/ **meridians.** A **meridian** is an imaginary line from the North Pole to the South Pole. Meridians are drawn on maps to help you describe the position of a place.
N-COUNT

meringue /məræŋ/ **meringues.** A **meringue** is a very sweet cake that you make by whipping together sugar and the whites of eggs and then baking the mixture.
◆◇◇◇◇ N-VAR

merit /merɪt/ **merits, meriting, merited** ◆◆◇◇◇

1 If something has **merit**, it has good or worthwhile qualities. *The argument seemed to have considerable merit... Box-office success mattered more than artistic merit... Your feature has the merit of simply stating what has been achieved.*
N-UNCOUNT: usu with supp

2 The **merits** of something are its advantages or other good points. *They have been persuaded of the merits of peace. ...the technical merits of a film... It was obvious that, whatever its merits, their work would never be used.*
N-PLURAL: usu with poss

3 If someone or something **merits** a particular action or treatment, they are good, important, or serious enough for someone to treat them or act towards them in this way; a formal use. *He said he had done nothing wrong to merit a criminal investigation... Such ideas merit careful consideration.*
VERB =deserve; V n

4 If you judge something or someone **on merit** or **on** their **merits**, your judgement is based on what you notice when you look at or consider them, rather than on things that you know about them from other sources. *Everybody is selected on merit... Each case is judged on its merits.*
PHRASE: PHR after v

meritocracy /merɪtɒkrəsi/ **meritocracies.** A **meritocracy** is a society or social system in which people get status or rewards because of
N-VAR

what they achieve, rather than because of their wealth or social status.

meritocratic /merɪtəkrætɪk/. A **meritocratic** society or social system gives people status or rewards because of what they achieve, rather than because of their wealth or social position. *...a more meritocratic society.* ADJ-GRADED: usu ADJ n

meritorious /merɪtɔːriəs/. If you describe something as **meritorious**, you approve of it for its good or worthwhile qualities; a formal word. *I had been promoted for what was called gallant and meritorious service.* ADJ-GRADED PRAGMATICS

mermaid /mɜːʳmeɪd/ **mermaids.** In fairy stories and legends, a **mermaid** is a woman with a fish's tail instead of legs, who lives in the sea. ◆◇◇◇◇ N-COUNT

merrily /merɪli/

1 If you say that someone **merrily** does something, you are critical of the fact that they do it without realizing that there are a lot of problems which they have not thought about. *There they were, merrily describing their 16-hour working days while simultaneously claiming to be happily married... Both NATO and the Community knew they could not go merrily on as before.* ADV: ADV with v PRAGMATICS =blithely

2 If you say that something is happening **merrily**, you mean that it is happening fairly quickly, in a pleasant or satisfactory way. *The ferry cut merrily through the water... A pan of potatoes was boiling away merrily on the gas stove.* ADV: ADV with v

3 See also **merry**.

merriment /merɪmənt/. **Merriment** means laughter; an old-fashioned word. N-UNCOUNT

merry /meri/ **merrier, merriest** ◆◇◇◇◇

1 If you describe someone's character or behaviour as **merry**, you mean they are happy and cheerful; an old-fashioned use. *He was much loved for his merry nature... From the house come the bursts of merry laughter... Merry black eyes glinted at them.* ♦ **merrily** *Chris threw back his head and laughed merrily.* ADJ-GRADED =jolly, jovial; ADV-GRADED: ADV after v

2 A **merry** sound or sight makes you feel cheerful; an old-fashioned use. *...the merry sounds of a seven-piece brass band... She was humming a merry little tune.* ADJ-GRADED =cheerful

3 If you get **merry**, you get slightly drunk; used in informal British English. *They went off to Glengarriff to get merry.* ADJ-GRADED: v-link ADJ =tipsy

4 Some people use **merry** to emphasize something that they are saying, often when they want to express disapproval or humour. *It hasn't stopped the British Navy proceeding on its merry way... In the merry world of American lawyers it is the simplest thing in the world to start an action.* ADJ: ADJ n PRAGMATICS

5 See also **merrily**.

6 In the days just before Christmas and on Christmas Day, you say **'Merry Christmas'** to other people in order to show that you hope they will have a happy time. *Merry Christmas, everyone... I just wanted to wish you a merry Christmas... A merry Christmas to all our readers.* PHRASES CONVENTION =Happy Christmas

7 If people **make merry**, they enjoy themselves and have fun, for example by singing, dancing, and drinking together; an old-fashioned expression. *Neighbours approached their boundaries from opposite sides and made merry together.* V inflects

8 • to **lead** someone **a merry dance**: see **dance**. • to **play merry hell**: see **hell**.

merry-go-round, merry-go-rounds

1 A **merry-go-round** is a large circular rotating platform which is found at fairgrounds. It has model animals or vehicles on it which children can pretend to ride or drive when it turns round. N-COUNT

2 You can refer to a continuous series of activities as a **merry-go-round**. *...a merry-go-round of teas, fetes, musical events and the like.* N-COUNT: usu sing, oft N of n

merry-making. **Merry-making** is the activities of people who are enjoying themselves together in a lively way, for example by eating, drinking, or dancing. *...a time of merry-making, feasting and visiting friends.* N-UNCOUNT

mesa /meɪsə/ **mesas.** A **mesa** is a large hill with a flat top and steep sides; used mainly of hills like this in the south-western United States. N-COUNT

mesh /meʃ/ **meshes, meshing, meshed** ◆◇◇◇◇

1 **Mesh** is material like a net made from wire, thread, or plastic. *The ground-floor windows are obscured by wire mesh. ...a mesh small enough to exclude tiny insects.* N-VAR

2 If two things or ideas **mesh** or **are meshed**, they go together well or fit together closely. *Their senses of humor meshed perfectly... This of course meshes with the economic philosophy of those on the right... Meshing the research and marketing operations will be Mr. Furlaud's job as president of the new company.* V-RECIP-ERG pl-n V; V with n; V n-pl; Also V n with n

mesmerize /mezməraɪz/ **mesmerizes, mesmerizing, mesmerized;** also spelled **mesmerise** in British English. If you **are mesmerized** by something, you are so interested in it or so attracted to it that you cannot think about anything else. *He was absolutely mesmerised by Pavarotti on television... There was something about Pearl that mesmerised her.* ♦ **mesmerized** *I sat mesmerized long after the fairground closed and the folk had all gone.* ♦ **mesmerizing** *She has a mesmerising smile.* ◆◇◇◇◇ VERB =transfix; be V-ed; V n; ADJ-GRADED: usu v-link ADJ; ADJ-GRADED: ADJ n

mess /mes/ **messes, messing, messed** ◆◆◆◇◇

1 If you say that something is a **mess** or in a **mess**, you think that it is in an untidy state. *The roof was a mess of rusty corrugated steel, with leaks in four or five places... You always leave the bathroom in a mess... The wrong shampoo can leave curly hair in a tangled mess... Linda can't stand mess.* N-SING: also no det

2 If you say that a situation is a **mess**, you mean that it is full of trouble or problems. You can also say that something is in a **mess**. *I've made such a mess of my life. ...the many reasons why the economy is in such a mess... She'd got herself into a mess, of that he was certain.* N-VAR

3 A **mess** is something that has been spilt. *Finally, making a dreadful mess, they devour the fruit... I'll clear up the mess later.* N-VAR

4 The **mess** in an army barracks or on an airfield is the building in which members of the armed forces eat or relax. *...a party at the officers' mess... He hurried to the Mess to find the control officer.* N-COUNT: usu sing

mess about or **mess around.** The form **mess about** is mainly used in British English. PHRASAL VERB

1 If you **mess about** or **mess around**, you spend time doing things without any particular purpose or without achieving anything. *We were just messing around playing with paint... Stop messing about and go and buy one... Boys and girls will enjoy messing about with any kind of machine.* V P; V P with n

2 If you say that someone **is messing about with** or **messing around with** something, you mean that they are interfering with it in a harmful way. *I'd like to know who's been messing about with the pram.* V P with n

3 If someone **is messing about** or **messing around**, they are behaving in a joking or silly way. *I thought she was messing about.* =fool around; V P

4 If you **mess** someone **about** or **mess** them **around**, you treat them badly, for example by not being honest with them, or by continually changing plans which affect them; used mainly in British English. *Davison had pulled out of a move to his old club because they had 'messed him about'... I think they've been messed around far too much.* V n P

mess up PHRASAL VERB

1 If someone **messes** something **up**, or if they **mess up**, they cause something to fail or be spoiled; an informal use. *When politicians mess things up, it is the people who pay the price... He had messed up one career... If I messed up, I would probably be fired.* =spoil; V n P; V P n (not pron); V P

2 If you **mess up** a place or a thing, you make it untidy or dirty; an informal use. *I hope they haven't messed up your video tapes.* V P n (not pron); Also V n P

3 If something **messes** someone **up**, it causes them to be very confused or worried, or to have psychological problems; an informal expression. *That really messed them up, especially the boys.* V n P; Also V P n (not pron)

mess with. If you tell someone not to **mess with** someone or something, you are warning them not to get involved with that person or thing. *You are messing with people's religion and they don't like that... Do you know who you're messing with – do you know who I am?* PHRASAL VERB PRAGMATICS =fool with V P n

message /mesɪdʒ/ **messages** ◆◆◆◆◇
1 A **message** is a piece of information or a request that you send to someone or leave for them when you cannot speak to them directly. *I got a message you were trying to reach me... Would you like to leave a message?... A message taped by the President was broadcast to US troops around the world.* N-COUNT
2 The **message** that someone is trying to communicate, for example in a book or play, is the idea or point that they are trying to communicate. *The report's message was unequivocal... I no longer want to stay friendly with her but I don't know how to get the message across... I think they got the message that this is wrong.* N-COUNT: usu sing, usu with supp =idea

messenger /mesɪndʒəʳ/ **messengers.** A **messenger** takes a message to someone, or takes messages regularly as their job. *There will be a messenger at the Airport to collect the photographs from our courier... He gave the instruction for the document to be sent by messenger.* ◆◇◇◇◇ N-COUNT: also *by* N

messenger boy, messenger boys. A **messenger boy** is a boy who is employed to take messages to people. N-COUNT

messiah /mɪsaɪə/ **messiahs** ◆◇◇◇◇
1 For Jews, **the Messiah** is the King of the Jews, who will be sent to them by God. N-PROPER
2 For Christians, **the Messiah** is Jesus Christ. N-PROPER
3 If you refer to someone as a **messiah**, you mean that they are expected to do wonderful things, especially to rescue people from a very difficult or dangerous situation, or that they are thought to have done these things. *People see Mandela as their messiah... He was somehow destined to become a rock messiah.* N-COUNT: usu with supp

messianic /mesiænɪk/; also spelled **Messianic.**
1 **Messianic** means relating to the belief that a divine being has been born, or will be born, who will change the world. *The cult leader saw himself as a Messianic figure.* ADJ: ADJ n
2 **Messianic** means relating to the belief that there will be a complete change in the social order in a country or in the world. *The defeated radicals of the French Revolution were the first to have this messianic vision in 1794... He instilled a messianic vision in his followers.* ADJ-GRADED: usu ADJ n

Messrs /mesəʳz/ ◆◇◇◇◇
1 **Messrs** is used before the names of two or more men as part of the name of a business; used mainly in British English. *The repairs were hopefully to be put in hand by Messrs Clegg & Sons of Balham.* N-TITLE
2 In formal English, you use **Messrs** before the names of two or more men as the plural of **Mr.** *I cannot allow the remarks made by Messrs Fortt and Wyre to remain unchallenged.* N-TITLE

messy /mesi/ **messier, messiest** ◆◇◇◇◇
1 A **messy** person or activity makes things dirty or untidy. *She was a good, if messy, cook... As the work tends to be a bit messy you'll need to wear old clothes.* ♦ **messily** *She wrote it hastily and messily on a scrap of paper.* ADJ-GRADED; ADV-GRADED: usu ADV with v, also ADV adj
2 Something that is **messy** is dirty or untidy. *He had a very messy nappy... Don't worry if this first coat of paint looks messy.* ADJ-GRADED
3 If you describe a situation as **messy**, you are emphasizing that it is confused or complicated, and therefore unsatisfactory. *John had been through a messy divorce himself... Life is a messy and tangled business... Negotiations would be messy and time-consuming.* ADJ-GRADED PRAGMATICS

met /met/. **Met** is the past tense and past participle of **meet.**

metabolic /metəbɒlɪk/. **Metabolic** means relating to a person's or animal's metabolism; a technical term in biology. *People who have inherited a low metabolic rate will gain weight.* ◆◇◇◇◇ ADJ: ADJ n

metabolism /mɪtæbəlɪzəm/ **metabolisms.** Your **metabolism** is the way that chemical processes in your body cause food to be used in an efficient way, for example to make new cells and to give you energy. ◆◇◇◇◇ N-VAR: oft with poss

metabolize /mɪtæbəlaɪz/ **metabolizes, metabolizing, metabolized;** also spelled **metabolise** in British English. When you **metabolize** a substance, it is affected by chemical processes in your body, and, for example, it is broken down, absorbed, and used; a technical term in biology. *Diabetics cannot metabolise glucose properly.* VERB V n

metal /metᵊl/ **metals. Metal** is a hard substance such as iron, steel, copper, or lead. *...pieces of furniture in wood, metal and glass... He hit his head against a metal bar.* • See also **base metal.** ◆◆◆◇◇ N-MASS

metalanguage /metəlæŋgwɪdʒ/ **metalanguages;** also spelled **meta-language.** The words and expressions people use to describe or refer to language can be called **metalanguage**; a technical term in linguistics. N-VAR

metalled /metᵊld/. A **metalled** road has a level surface made of many small pieces of stone; used especially of country roads and tracks. *Take the metalled path running between the church and the fort.* ADJ: ADJ n

metallic /mətælɪk/ ◆◇◇◇◇
1 A **metallic** sound is like the sound of one piece of metal hitting another. *There was a metallic click and the gates swung open... It gave a metallic clang, like a cracked bell.* ADJ-GRADED: usu ADJ n
2 A **metallic** voice has a harsh unpleasant sound. *...that creaking metallic voice of hers.* ADJ-GRADED: usu ADJ n
3 **Metallic** paint or colours shine like metal. *He had painted all the wood with metallic silver paint... Metallic finishes are seen as upmarket.* ADJ: usu ADJ n
4 Something that tastes **metallic** has a bitter unpleasant taste. *There was a metallic taste at the back of his throat.* ADJ-GRADED
5 **Metallic** means consisting wholly or partly of metal. *Even the smallest metallic object, whether a nail file or cigarette lighter, is immediately confiscated... Place the salmon in a nonstick metallic dish.* ADJ: usu ADJ n =metal

metallurgist /metælərdʒɪst, AM metələ:ʳdʒɪst/ **metallurgists.** A **metallurgist** is an expert in metallurgy. N-COUNT

metallurgy /metælərdʒi, AM metələ:ʳdʒi/. **Metallurgy** is the scientific study of the properties and uses of metals. N-UNCOUNT

metalwork /metᵊlwɜ:ʳk/
1 **Metalwork** is the activity of making objects out of metal in a skilful way. *He was a craftsman in metalwork from Dresden... Many are employed in the prison's wood and metalwork factories.* N-UNCOUNT
2 The **metalwork** is the metal part of something. *Rust and flaking paint mean the metalwork is in poor condition. ...the surrounding metalwork.* N-UNCOUNT

metamorphose /metəmɔ:ʳfoʊz/ **metamorphoses, metamorphosing, metamorphosed.** To **metamorphose** or **be metamorphosed** means to develop and change into something completely different; a formal word. *...hysterical laughter which gradually metamorphoses into convulsive sobs... The group is having to metamorphose from a loose collection of businesses into a fully integrated multinational... I was going to metamorphose the movies into an art... The actors were metamorphosed into a living tapestry of color at the dress rehearsal... The tadpoles metamorphose and emerge onto land... She had been metamorphosed by the war.* • See also **metamorphosis.** V-ERG V *into/from* n, V n *into/from* n, V, *be* V-ed, Also V n

metamorphosis /metəmɔ:ʳfəsɪs/ **metamorphoses.** When a **metamorphosis** occurs, a person or thing develops and changes into something completely different; a formal word. *...his metamorphosis from Communist to nationalist... The employment department has undergone several metamorphoses.* N-VAR =transformation

metaphor /metəfɔ:r/ **metaphors** 
1 A **metaphor** is an imaginative way of describing N-VAR

something by referring to something else which has the qualities that you want to express. For example, if you want to say that someone is very shy and timid, you might say that they are a mouse. *He uses metaphors like, 'Well, we have to open up the hood of the car and see what's under it and fix it.' ...the writer's use of metaphor.*

2 If one thing is a **metaphor** for another, it is intended or regarded as a symbol of it. *The divided family remains a powerful metaphor for a society that continued to tear itself apart... The usual metaphor would be a bubble, which by its nature must collapse eventually.* N-VAR: oft N *for* n

3 If you **mix** your **metaphors**, you say something that consists of parts of two well-known phrases or sayings. People do this accidentally, or sometimes deliberately as a joke. *To mix yet more metaphors, you were trying to run before you could walk, and I've clipped your wings... Despite the mixed metaphor, there is some truth in this judgement.* PHRASE: V inflects

metaphorical /metəfɒrɪkəl, AM -fɔːr-/. You use the word **metaphorical** to indicate that you are not using words with their ordinary meaning, but are describing something by means of an image or symbol. *It turns out Levy is talking in metaphorical terms... The ship may be heading for the metaphorical rocks unless a buyer can be found.* ◆◇◇◇◇ ADJ-GRADED
♦ **metaphorically** *You're speaking metaphorically, I hope.* ADV: usu ADV with cl, ADV with v

metaphysical /metəfɪzɪkəl/. **Metaphysical** means relating to metaphysics. *...metaphysical questions like personal responsibility for violence.* ◆◇◇◇◇ ADJ: usu ADJ n

metaphysics /metəfɪzɪks/. **Metaphysics** is a part of philosophy which is concerned with understanding reality and developing theories about what exists and how we know that it exists. N-UNCOUNT

mete /miːt/ **metes, meting, meted** ◆◇◇◇◇
mete out. To **mete out** a punishment means to order that someone should be punished in a certain way; a formal word. *His father meted out punishment with a slipper. ...the two year sentence meted out to a convicted child molester.* PHRASAL VERB V P n (not pron) V-ed Also V n P

meteor /miːtiəʳ/ **meteors.** A **meteor** is a piece of rock or metal that burns very brightly when it enters the earth's atmosphere from space. ◆◇◇◇◇ N-COUNT

meteoric /miːtiɒrɪk, AM -ɔːr-/. If you use **meteoric** when you are describing someone's career, you mean that they achieved success very quickly. *Let's hope that the meteoric rise to fame and fortune does not adversely affect him... His early career had been meteoric.* ADJ-GRADED

meteorite /miːtiəraɪt/ **meteorites.** A **meteorite** is a large piece of rock or metal from space that has landed on Earth. ◆◇◇◇◇ N-COUNT

meteorological /miːtiərəlɒdʒɪkəl/. **Meteorological** means relating to meteorology. *...adverse meteorological conditions.* ◆◇◇◇◇ ADJ: ADJ n

meteorology /miːtiərɒlədʒi/. **Meteorology** is the study of the processes in the Earth's atmosphere that cause particular weather conditions. Meteorology is used especially for giving weather forecasts. ♦ **meteorologist** /miːtiərɒlədʒɪst/ **meteorologists** *Meteorologists have predicted mild rains for the next few days.* N-UNCOUNT N-COUNT

meter /miːtəʳ/ **meters, metering, metered** ◆◆◇◇◇
1 A **meter** is a device that measures and records something such as the amount of gas or electricity that you have used. *He was there to read the electricity meter... They have the right to come in and inspect the meter.* N-COUNT

2 To **meter** something such as gas or electricity means to use a meter to measure how much of it people use, usually in order to calculate how much they have to pay. *Only a third of these households thought it reasonable to meter water... Metered taxis are relatively inexpensive.* VERB V n V-ed

3 A **meter** is the same as a **parking meter**. N-COUNT

4 See also **metre**.

methane /miːθeɪn, AM meθ-/. **Methane** is a colourless gas that has no smell. Natural gas consists mostly of methane. ◆◇◇◇◇ N-UNCOUNT

method /meθəd/ **methods.** A **method** is a particular way of doing something. *The pill is the most efficient method of birth control. ...new teaching methods... The usual method of getting through the Amsterdam traffic is to cycle to your local railway station and take the train.* ◆◆◆◆◇ N-COUNT: oft N *of* n/-ing

methodical /məθɒdɪkəl/. If you describe someone as **methodical**, you mean that they do things carefully, thoroughly, and in order. *Da Vinci was methodical in his research, carefully recording his observations and theories... It seemed a sensible and methodical way of proceeding.* ◆◇◇◇◇ ADJ-GRADED
♦ **methodically** /məθɒdɪkli/ *She methodically put the things into her suitcase.* ADV-GRADED: ADV with v

Methodism /meθədɪzəm/. **Methodism** is the beliefs and practices of Methodists. N-UNCOUNT

Methodist /meθədɪst/ **Methodists. Methodists** are Christians who follow the teachings of John Wesley and who have their own branch of the Christian church and their own form of worship. ◆◇◇◇◇ N-COUNT

methodology /meθədɒlədʒi/ **methodologies.** A **methodology** is a system of methods and principles for doing something, for example for teaching or for carrying out research; a formal word. *Teaching methodologies vary according to the topic... In their own work they may have favored the use of methodology different from mine.* ◆◇◇◇◇ N-VAR
♦ **methodological** /meθədəlɒdʒɪkəl/ *...theoretical and methodological issues raised by the study of literary texts.* ADJ: usu ADJ n

meths /meθs/. **Meths** is the same as **methylated spirits**; used mainly in British English. N-UNCOUNT

methylated spirits /meθəleɪtɪd spɪrɪts/. **Methylated spirits** is a liquid made from alcohol and other chemicals. It is used for removing stains and as a fuel in small lamps and heaters; used mainly in British English. N-UNCOUNT

meticulous /mətɪkjʊləs/. If you describe someone as **meticulous**, you mean that they do things very carefully and with great attention to detail. *He was so meticulous about everything... The painting had been executed with meticulous attention to detail.* ♦ **meticulously** *The flat had been meticulously cleaned.* ◆◇◇◇◇ ADJ-GRADED ADV-GRADED: usu ADV with v, also ADV adj

metier /metieɪ, AM metjeɪ/ **metiers;** also spelled **métier**. Your **metier** is the type of work that you have a natural talent for and do well; a formal word. *It was as the magazine's business manager that he found his true metier.* N-COUNT: usu with poss

metre /miːtəʳ/ **metres;** spelled **meter** in American English. ◆◆◆◇◇
1 A **metre** is a metric unit of length equal to 100 centimetres. *Chris Boardman won the Olympic 4,000 metres pursuit... The scarves are 2.3 metres long and cost £125.* N-COUNT: num N, oft N *of* n

2 **Metre** is the regular and rhythmic arrangement of syllables in poetry; a technical use in literature. *They must each compose a poem in strict alliterative metre... All of the poems are written in traditional metres and rhyme schemes.* N-VAR

metric /metrɪk/. **Metric** means relating to the metric system. *Around 180,000 metric tons of food aid is required... Converting metric measurements to U.S. equivalents is easy.* ◆◇◇◇◇ ADJ: usu num ADJ n

metric system. The **metric system** is the system of measurement that uses metres, centimetres, grammes, and litres. N-SING: *the* N

metric ton, **metric tons.** A **metric ton** is 1,000 kilograms. *The Wall Street Journal uses 220,000 metric tons of newsprint each year... The Customs Service seized 27.2 metric tons of cocaine in 1986.* ◆◇◇◇◇ N-COUNT: num N, oft N *of* n

metro /metroʊ/ **metros;** also spelled **Metro**. The **metro** is the underground railway system in some cities, for example in Paris. ◆◇◇◇◇ N-COUNT: usu *the* N in sing

metronome /metrənoʊm/ **metronomes.** A **metronome** is a device which is used to indicate the speed of a piece of music. It makes a clicking sound and can be adjusted to make the sound at different speeds. N-COUNT

metronomic /metrənɒmɪk/. Something that happens in a **metronomic** way happens continually in a very regular way, like the ticking of a ADJ: ADJ n =monotonous metronome. *The tent was silent save for the metronomic ticking of the rain... Variety is the charm of tennis, which could otherwise become a metronomic bore.*

metropolis /mətrɒpəlɪs/ **metropolises** ◆◇◇◇◇

1 A **metropolis** is the principal city or capital of a country or region. *Shanghai aims to recapture its position as the metropolis of East Asia.* N-COUNT: usu sing

2 If you describe a city as a **metropolis**, you mean that it is an important centre of industrial or cultural activity, where lots of people live and work. *Anthony Cordova moved to this booming metropolis 17 months ago.* N-COUNT

metropolitan /metrəpɒlɪtən/ **metropolitans** ◆◆◇◇◇

1 **Metropolitan** means belonging to or typical of a large busy city. *...the metropolitan district of Miami. ...a dozen major metropolitan hospitals. ...metropolitan sophistication and rustic naivety.* ADJ: ADJ n

2 A **metropolitan** is an important priest in the Orthodox and Catholic Churches. He has authority over other priests and is in charge of a particular area. *...the Ukrainian Catholic representatives, Metropolitan Volodymyr and Bishop Sofron.* N-COUNT; N-TITLE

mettle /metəl/

1 Someone's **mettle** is their capability to do something well under difficult circumstances. *His first important chance to show his mettle came when he opened the new session of the Legislature... For both sides, it's the first real test of their mettle this season... It takes a man of mettle to keep a family safe and comfortable in this troubled world.* N-UNCOUNT: usu poss N

2 If you are **on** your **mettle**, you are ready to do something as well as you can, because you know that you are being tested or challenged. *The added competition keeps them on their mettle.* PHRASE: v-link PHR, PHR after v

mew /mjuː/ **mews, mewing, mewed.** When a cat **mews**, it makes a soft high-pitched noise. *From somewhere, the kitten mewed.* VERB V

mews /mjuːz/; **mews** is both the singular and the plural form. In British English, a **mews** is a yard or street surrounded by houses that were originally built as stables. *The house is in a secluded mews. ...her London mews house... his house in Stanhope Mews.* ◆◇◇◇◇ N-COUNT: oft in names

Mexican /meksɪkən/ **Mexicans** ◆◆◆◆◇

1 **Mexican** means belonging or relating to Mexico, or to its people or culture. *...the Mexican border town of Tijuana. ...Mexican officials.* ADJ

2 A **Mexican** is a Mexican citizen, or a person of Mexican origin. *He went down the bar to a group of Mexicans and talked to them in a low voice.* N-COUNT

Mexican wave, Mexican waves. In British English, if a crowd of people do a **Mexican wave**, each person in the crowd stands up and puts their arms in the air after the person to one side of them, creating a continuous rolling motion through the crowd. The usual American term is **wave**. N-COUNT

mezzanine /mezəniːn/ **mezzanines.** A **mezzanine** is a small floor which is built between two stories in a building. *...the dining room on the mezzanine. ...the mezzanine floor.* N-COUNT

mezzo /metsoʊ/ **mezzos.** A **mezzo** is the same as a **mezzo-soprano**. *...the American mezzo Catherine Keen. ...the fabulous mezzo voice of Phillida Bannister.* N-COUNT

mezzo-soprano, mezzo-sopranos. A **mezzo-soprano** is a female singer who sings with a higher range than a contralto but a lower range than a soprano. *She became a professional mezzo-soprano. ...her remarkable mezzo soprano voice.* N-COUNT

mg. **Mg** is a written abbreviation for **milligrams**. *...300 mg of calcium.* ◆◇◇◇◇

Mgr. **Mgr** is a written abbreviation for **Monsignor**.

MHz. **MHz** is a written abbreviation for **megahertz**.

miaow /miaʊ/ **miaows, miaowing, miaowed.** **Miaow** is used to represent the noise that a cat makes. *He made a frightened noise a little like the miaow of a cat.* ► Also a verb. *Cats miaow when they are unhappy, purr when they are happy.* N-COUNT; SOUND VERB: V

miasma /miæzmə/ **miasmas.** You can describe something bad or confused that seems to be in the air all around you as a **miasma**; a literary word. *He crouched back in his chair, a miasma of failure, stupidity, self-pity hovering all around him.* N-VAR

mica /maɪkə/ **micas.** **Mica** is a hard mineral which is found as small flat crystals in rocks. It has a great resistance to heat and electricity. N-MASS

mice /maɪs/. **Mice** is the plural of **mouse**.

mickey /mɪki/. In British English, if you **take the mickey** out of someone or something, you make fun of them, usually in an unkind way; an informal expression. *He started taking the mickey out of this poor man just because he is bald.* PHRASE: V inflects, oft PHR *out of* n =mock, tease

Mickey Mouse. You use **Mickey Mouse** to show that you think something is silly, childish, easy, or worthless. *This is not a Mickey Mouse course where every player has a chance... There's nothing Mickey Mouse about the 1993 version... The whole thing is somehow a bit Mickey Mouse.* ◆◇◇◇◇ ADJ-GRADED PRAGMATICS

micro- /maɪkroʊ-/. **Micro-** is used to form nouns that refer to something that is a very small example or fraction of a particular type of thing. *These are the cells that directly attack and kill micro-organisms... The pulse is usually timed in micro-seconds.* PREFIX

microbe /maɪkroʊb/ **microbes.** A **microbe** is a very small living thing, which you can only see if you use a microscope. N-COUNT =micro-organism

microbiological /maɪkroʊbaɪəlɒdʒɪkəl/. **Microbiological** refers to studies or tests involving micro-organisms and their effects on people. *...microbiological testing.* ADJ: ADJ n

microbiology /maɪkroʊbaiɒlədʒi/. **Microbiology** is the branch of biology which deals with the study of micro-organisms and their effects on people. *...a professor of microbiology and immunology.* ♦ **microbiologist, microbiologists** *...a microbiologist at Liverpool University.* N-UNCOUNT N-COUNT

microchip /maɪkroʊtʃɪp/ **microchips.** A **microchip** is a very small piece of silicon inside a computer. It has electronic circuits on it and can hold large quantities of information or perform mathematical and logical operations. ◆◇◇◇◇ N-COUNT

micro-computer, micro-computers. A **micro-computer** is a small computer, often used for word-processing. N-COUNT

microcosm /maɪkroʊkɒzəm/ **microcosms.** If you describe a place, society, or activity as a **microcosm** of a much larger place, society, or activity, you mean that it has all the typical features of the larger thing and so seems like a miniature version of it; a formal word. *Kitchell says the city was a microcosm of all American culture during the '60s... In many respects, Mahan's story is that of the Asian community in microcosm.* N-COUNT: oft N *of* n, also *in* N

microelectronics /maɪkroʊelektrɒnɪks/; the form **microelectronic** is used as a modifier. **Microelectronics** is the branch of electronics that deals with miniature electronic circuits. N-UNCOUNT

microfiche /maɪkroʊfiːʃ/ **microfiches.** A **microfiche** is a small sheet of film on which writing or other information is stored, greatly reduced in size. N-VAR

microfilm /maɪkroʊfɪlm/ **microfilms.** **Microfilm** is film that is used for photographing information and storing it in a reduced form. N-VAR

micro-organism, micro-organisms; also spelled **microorganism**. A **micro-organism** is a very small living thing which you can only see if you use a microscope; a technical term in biology. ◆◇◇◇◇ N-COUNT =microbe

microphone /maɪkrəfoʊn/ **microphones.** A **microphone** is a device that is used to make sounds louder or to record them on a tape recorder. ◆◆◇◇◇ N-COUNT

microprocessor /maɪkroʊproʊsesər/ **microprocessors.** A **microprocessor** is the central ◆◇◇◇◇ N-COUNT processing chip in a computer or other piece of equipment; a technical term in computing.

microscope /maɪkrəskoʊp/ **microscopes** ◆◇◇◇◇
1 A **microscope** is an instrument which magnifies very small objects so that you can look at them and study them. N-COUNT
2 If you say that something is **under the microscope**, you mean that it is being studied very closely, usually because it is believed that something is wrong with it. *The media put their every decision under the microscope.* PHRASE: PHR after v, v-link PHR

microscopic /maɪkrəskɒpɪk/ ◆◇◇◇◇
1 **Microscopic** objects are extremely small, and usually can be seen only through a microscope. *...microscopic fibres of protein.* ♦ **microscopically** *No living organisms, large or microscopically small, inhabited it.* ADJ: usu ADJ n; ADV: ADV adj
2 A **microscopic** examination is done using a microscope. *Microscopic examination of a cell's chromosomes can reveal the sex of the fetus.* ♦ **microscopically** *The tissue is examined microscopically to rule out or confirm cancer.* ADJ: ADJ n; ADV: ADV with v
3 If you say that something is done in **microscopic** detail, you are emphasizing that it is done in a very thorough, detailed way. *He carefully recounts the tale, the microscopic details of those crucial minutes.* ADJ: usu ADJ n PRAGMATICS

microsecond /maɪkroʊsekənd/ **microseconds.** A **microsecond** is one-millionth of a second. N-COUNT

microsurgery /maɪkroʊsɜːʳdʒəri/. **Microsurgery** is a form of surgery where doctors repair or remove parts of the body that are so small that they can only be seen clearly using a microscope. N-UNCOUNT

microwave /maɪkroʊweɪv/ **microwaves, microwaving, microwaved** ◆◆◇◇◇
1 A **microwave** or a **microwave oven** is an oven which cooks food very quickly by electromagnetic radiation rather than by heat. N-COUNT
2 To **microwave** food or drink means to cook or heat it in a microwave oven. *Steam or microwave the vegetables until tender. ...microwaved food.* VERB: V n, V-ed

mid- /mɪd-/. **Mid-** is used to form nouns or adjectives that refer to the middle part of a particular period of time, or the middle point of a particular place. *...the mid-eighteenth century... Davis is in her mid-thirties. ...the mid-west of America.* PREFIX

mid-air. If something happens in **mid-air**, it happens in the air, rather than on the ground. *The bird stopped and hovered in mid-air. ...a mid-air collision.* N-UNCOUNT

midday /mɪddeɪ/ ◆◇◇◇◇
1 **Midday** is twelve o'clock in the middle of the day. *At midday everyone would go down to Reg's Cafe... It's eight minutes after midday.* N-UNCOUNT: oft prep N
2 **Midday** is the middle part of the day, from late morning to early afternoon. *People were beginning to tire in the midday heat.* N-UNCOUNT: usu N n

middle /mɪdəl/ **middles** ◆◆◆◆◆
1 The **middle** of something is the part of it that is furthest from its edges, ends, or outside surface. *Howard stood in the middle of the room sipping a cup of coffee... Hyde accelerated away from the kerb, swerving out into the middle of the street... I was in the middle of the back row... Father told her to make sure the roast potatoes weren't raw in the middle.* N-COUNT: usu *the* N in sing, oft N *of* n =centre
• **the middle of nowhere**: see **nowhere**.
2 The **middle** object in a row of objects is the one that has an equal number of objects on each side. *The middle button of his uniform jacket was strained over his belly... Around the middle finger of her left hand, she wore a gold ring.* ADJ: ADJ n
3 Your **middle** is the part of your body around your stomach; an informal use. *At age fifty-three, he now has a few extra pounds around his middle... The cook's apron covered her middle.* N-COUNT: usu poss N =midriff
4 The **middle** of an event or period of time is the part that comes after the first part and before the last part. *I woke up in the middle of the night and could hear a tapping on the window... It was now the middle of November, cold and often foggy... By the middle of 1979, Jimmy Carter was in serious political trouble... She was born in the middle of a rain storm.* ► Also an adjective. *The month began and ended quite dry, but the middle fortnight saw nearly 100mm of rainfall nationwide.* N-SING: *the* N *of* n; ADJ: ADJ n
5 If someone is in their **middle** thirties, for example, they are aged somewhere approximately between thirty four and thirty six. *She knew he was in his middle fifties, although he looked much younger... I went on competing till I was in my middle forties.* ADJ: ADJ n
6 The **middle** child in a family has equal numbers of younger and older brothers and sisters. *His middle son died in a drowning accident five years back.* ADJ: ADJ n
7 The **middle** course or way is a moderate course of action that lies between two opposite and extreme courses. *He favoured a middle course between free enterprise and state intervention... The Mayor of Jerusalem has tried to minimise conflict by maintaining a middle way between the various religions.* ADJ: ADJ n ≠extreme
8 If you divide or split something **down the middle**, you divide or split it into two equal halves or groups. *After agreeing to split the bill down the middle, they ordered spaghetti and a bottle of red wine... If the conservatives are not removed, then the party will almost certainly split down the middle.* PHRASES: PHR after v =in half
9 If you are **in the middle of** doing something, you are busy doing it. *It's a bit hectic. I'm in the middle of cooking for nine people... He was always in the middle of a business transaction.* v-link PHR -ing/n

middle age; also spelled **middle-age. Middle age** is the period in your life when you are no longer young but have not yet become old. Middle age is usually considered to take place between the ages of 40 and 60. *Men tend to put on weight in middle age.* ◆◇◇◇◇ N-UNCOUNT

middle-aged ◆◆◇◇◇
1 If you describe someone as **middle-aged**, you mean that they are neither young nor old. People between the ages of 40 and 60 are usually considered to be middle-aged. *His sisters are grown up and his parents are middle-aged. ...middle-aged, married businessmen.* ► **The middle-aged** are people who are middle-aged. *...the perfect holiday for the middle-aged.* ADJ; N-PLURAL: *the* N
2 If you describe someone's activities or interests as **middle-aged**, you are critical of them because you think they are typical of a middle-aged person, for example by being conventional or old-fashioned. *Her novels are middle-aged and boring.* ADJ-GRADED PRAGMATICS

Middle Ages. In European history, **the Middle Ages** was the period between the end of the Roman Empire in 476 AD and about 1500 AD, especially the later part of this period. ◆◇◇◇◇ N-PLURAL: *the* N

middlebrow /mɪdəlbraʊ/; also spelled **middle-brow.** If you describe a piece of entertainment such as a book or film as **middlebrow**, you mean that although it may be interesting and enjoyable, it does not require much thought. *...such middlebrow fare as Poirot, Sherlock Holmes and Jeeves and Wooster.* ADJ-GRADED: usu ADJ n

middle class, middle classes ◆◆◆◇◇
1 The **middle class** or **middle classes** are the people in a society who are not working class or upper class. Business people, managers, doctors, lawyers, and teachers are usually regarded as middle class. *...the expansion of the middle class in the late 19th century... The President may have secured some support from the middle classes, despite the continued opposition she faces from the radical left.* ► Also an adjective. *He is rapidly losing the support of blue-collar voters and of middle-class conservatives... All the best revolutionaries have been middle class.* N-COUNT-COLL: usu *the* N; ADJ
2 People sometimes describe attitudes as **middle class** when they think that they are typical of middle class people, usually when they disapprove of these attitudes, for example because they are very conventional or attach too much importance to possessions. *...a very middle-class upbringing.* ADJ-GRADED PRAGMATICS =bourgeois

middle distance
1 If you are looking into the **middle distance**, you N-SING:

are looking at a place that is neither near nor far away. *He stares detachedly into the middle distance, towards nothing in particular.* the N, usu *into/in the* N

2 A **middle-distance** runner is someone who takes part in races that are longer than a sprint, but not as long as a marathon. *He was an Olympic, middle-distance runner.* ADJ: ADJ n

Middle East. The **Middle East** is the area around the eastern Mediterranean that includes Iran and all the countries in Asia that are to the west and south-west of Iran. *The two great rivers of the Middle East rise in the mountains of Turkey.* ◆◆◆◆◇ N-PROPER: *the* N

Middle Eastern. **Middle Eastern** means relating to the Middle East. *Most Middle Eastern countries have extremely high rates of population growth... The US economy depends on Middle Eastern oil.* ◆◇◇◇◇ ADJ: ADJ n

middleman /mɪdəlmæn/ **middlemen** ◆◇◇◇◇

1 A **middleman** is a person or company which buys things from the people who produce them and sells them to the people who want to buy them. *The CSO earns huge profits as the middleman... Why don't they cut out the middleman and let us do it ourselves?* N-COUNT

2 A **middleman** is a person who helps in negotiations between people who are unwilling to meet each other directly. *The two sides would only meet indirectly, through middlemen.* N-COUNT =go-between

middle name, middle names

1 Your **middle name** is the name that comes between your first name and your surname. *His middle name is Justin.* N-COUNT: usu poss N

2 You can use **middle name** in expressions such as **'discretion was her middle name'** and **'his middle name is loyalty'** to indicate humorously that someone always behaves with a great deal of a particular quality. *Geniality is my middle name. I rarely write a fierce word about any restaurant.* N-COUNT: usu poss N

middle-of-the-road

1 If you describe someone's opinions or policies as **middle-of-the-road**, you mean that they are neither left-wing nor right-wing, and not at all extreme. *Consensus need not be weak, nor need it result in middle-of-the-road policies. ...the Archbishop, who is middle-of-the-road in politics.* ADJ-GRADED =moderate

2 If you describe something or someone as **middle-of-the-road**, you mean that they have an ordinary or unadventurous nature or lifestyle. *I actually don't want to be a middle-of-the-road person, married with a mortgage.* ADJ-GRADED

middle-ranking. A **middle-ranking** person has a fairly important or responsible position in a particular organization, but is not one of the most important people in it. *...middle-ranking army officers.* ADJ: ADJ n

middle school, middle schools

1 In the United States, a **middle school** is a school that children go to between the ages of 6 and 11. *...Harlem Park Middle School... They recall the good buddies they used to have in middle school.* N-VAR: oft in names after n

2 In Britain, a **middle school** is a state school that children go to between the ages of 8 or 9 and 12 or 13. N-VAR: oft in names after n

Middle West. **The Middle West** is the central part of the United States of America. *...wheat farmers in the Middle West.* N-PROPER: *the* N =Midwest

middling /mɪdəlɪŋ/. If you describe a quality such as the size of something as **middling**, you mean that it is average. *The Beatles enjoyed only middling success until 1963. ...a man of middling height.* ADJ: usu ADJ n =average

midge /mɪdʒ/ **midges.** **Midges** are very small insects which fly in groups. N-COUNT

midget /mɪdʒɪt/ **midgets**

1 People who are very short are sometimes referred to as **midgets**; a use which some people find offensive. N-COUNT

2 **Midget** is used to describe something which is very small. *...midget submarines.* ADJ: ADJ n

Midlands /mɪdləndz/. **The Midlands** is the region or area in the central part of a country, in particular the central part of England. *...an engineering company in the Midlands.* ◆◆◇◇◇ N-PROPER-COLL: *the* N

midnight /mɪdnaɪt/ ◆◆◆◇◇

1 **Midnight** is twelve o'clock in the middle of the night. *It was well after midnight by the time Anne returned to her apartment... The entrance gates were locked at midnight.* N-UNCOUNT: usu prep N

2 **Midnight** is used to describe something which happens or appears at midnight or in the middle of the night. *It is totally out of the question to postpone the midnight deadline... Well we did have a midnight feast, me and my sister.* ADJ: ADJ n

3 If someone **is burning the midnight oil,** they are staying up very late in order to study or do some other work. *Chris is asleep after burning the midnight oil trying to finish his article.* PHRASE: V inflects

midnight blue. Something that is **midnight blue** is a very dark blue colour, almost black. *The sea was a deep midnight blue.* COLOUR

midpoint /mɪdpɔɪnt/; also spelled **mid-point.**

1 The **midpoint** between two things is the point that is the same distance from both things. *...the midpoint between Paris and Warsaw. ...the midpoint of the front of your house.* N-SING: oft N *between/of* n

2 The **midpoint** of an event is the time halfway between the beginning and the end of it. *She has not yet reached the midpoint of her life. ...the midpoint in the current fiscal year.* N-SING: oft N *of* n =middle

midriff /mɪdrɪf/ **midriffs.** Someone's **midriff** is the middle part of their body, between their waist and their chest. *...the girl with the bare midriff.* N-COUNT: usu sing

midsized /mɪdsaɪzd/; also spelled **mid-sized**. The form **midsize** is also used. You use **midsized** or **midsize** to describe products, cities, companies, and other things that are of average size, rather than being amongst the smallest or largest of their kind. *...a low-cost midsized car. ...a relatively small university in a mid-size city.* ADJ: ADJ n =medium-sized

midst /mɪdst/ ◆◆◇◇◇

1 If you are **in the midst of** doing something, you are doing it at the moment. *Congress is in the midst of rewriting the nation's banking laws... We are in the midst of one of the worst recessions for many, many years.* PHR-PREP: usu v-link PREP -ing/n =in the middle of

2 If something happens **in the midst of** an event, it happens during it. *Eleanor arrived in the midst of a blizzard.* PHR-PREP =during

3 If someone or something is **in the midst of** a group of people or things, they are among them or surrounded by them. *Many were surprised to see him exposed like this in the midst of a large crowd... Angelo laid the gun carefully on the table, in the midst of brochures and other papers.* PHR-PREP =amid

4 You say that someone is **in your midst** when you are drawing attention to the fact that they are in your group; a formal expression. *We're lucky to have such a man in our midst.* PHRASE: v-link PHR

midstream /mɪdstriːm/; also spelled **mid-stream.**

1 Someone or something that is in **midstream** is in the middle of a river, where the current is strongest. *Their boat had capsized in midstream.* ▶ Also an adverb. *Some of them got caught midstream by the tide.* N-UNCOUNT: oft *in* N; ADV: usu ADV after v, also n ADV

2 If someone who has been doing something such as talking stops or pauses in **midstream**, they stop doing it, often before continuing. *I was cut off in midstream.* ▶ Also an adverb. *The most difficult thing in a fast game of rugby is to change course midstream.* N-UNCOUNT: oft *in* N; ADV: ADV after v

midsummer /mɪdsʌməʳ/. **Midsummer** is the period in the middle of the summer. *In midsummer every town is impossibly crowded... It was a lovely midsummer morning.* ◆◇◇◇◇ N-UNCOUNT

Midsummer's Day. **Midsummer's Day** or **Midsummer Day** is the 24th of June. N-PROPER

midway /mɪdweɪ/; also spelled **mid-way.** ◆◇◇◇◇

1 If something is **midway** between two places, it is between them and the same distance from each of them. *The studio is midway between his aunt's old home and his cottage.* ▶ Also an adjective. *The* ADV: ADV prep =halfway; ADJ:

vineyard is close to the midway point between Gloucester, Hereford and Worcester. ADJ n =halfway

2 If something happens **midway** through a period of time, it happens during the middle part of it. *He crashed midway through the race... He returned midway through the afternoon.* ► Also an adjective. *They were denied an obvious penalty before the midway point of the first half.* ADV: ADV after v, usu ADV through n ADJ: ADJ n

midweek /mɪdwiːk/. **Midweek** describes something that happens in the middle of the week. *The package includes midweek flights from Gatwick.* ► Also an adverb. *They'll be able to go up to London midweek... By midweek officials were speaking hopefully of a 'compromise'.* ◆◇◇◇◇ ADJ: ADJ n ADV: ADV after v, prep ADV

Midwest /mɪdwest/. The **Midwest** is the region in the north of the central part of the USA. *...farmers in the Midwest. ...the Midwest states.* ◆◇◇◇◇ N-PROPER: usu *the* N

Midwestern /mɪdwestəʳn/. **Midwestern** means belonging or relating to the Midwest. *...the midwestern plains. ...traditional Midwestern values.* ADJ: usu ADJ n

midwife /mɪdwaɪf/ **midwives.** A **midwife** is a nurse who is trained to deliver babies and to advise pregnant women. ◆◇◇◇◇ N-COUNT

midwifery /mɪdwɪfəri/. **Midwifery** is the work of delivering babies and advising pregnant women. N-UNCOUNT

midwinter /mɪdwɪntəʳ/; also spelled **mid-winter.** **Midwinter** is the period in the middle of winter. *...the bleak midwinter. ...the cold midwinter weather.* N-UNCOUNT

mien /miːn/. Someone's **mien** is their general appearance and manner, especially the expression on their face, which shows what they are feeling or thinking; a literary word. *It was impossible to tell from his mien whether he was offended. ...his mild manner and aristocratic mien.* N-SING: usu poss N

miffed /mɪft/. If you are **miffed**, you are slightly annoyed and hurt because of something which someone has said or done to you; an informal word. *I was a bit miffed about that... Philip was pretty miffed at being cut out of his father's will.* ADJ-GRADED: usu v-link ADJ

might 1 modal uses

might /maɪt/ ◆◆◆◆◆

Might is a modal verb. It is used with the base form of a verb.

1 You use **might** to indicate that something will possibly happen or be true in the future, but you cannot be certain. *There's a report today that smoking might be banned totally in most buildings... The two countries might go to war... I might well regret it later... He said he might not be back until tonight.* MODAL PRAGMATICS =may

2 You use **might** to indicate that there is a possibility that something is true, but you cannot be certain. *She and Simon's father had not given up hope that he might be alive... You might be right... They haven't seen each other for five years; he might not be interested in her any more. ...a suit that looks as though it might contain polyester.* MODAL PRAGMATICS =may

3 You use **might** to indicate that something has the potential for happening or being true in particular circumstances. *America might sell more cars to the islands if they were made with the steering wheel on the right. ...the type of person who might appear in a fashion magazine.* MODAL PRAGMATICS =could

4 You use **might have** with a past participle to indicate that it is possible that something happened or was true, or when giving a possible explanation for something. *I heard what might have been an explosion... She thought the shooting might have been an accident... The equipment needed to clean up the spill might not have arrived yet... The letters might not have been meant for me at all.* MODAL PRAGMATICS =may have

5 You use **might have** with a past participle to indicate that something was a possibility in the past, although it did not actually happen. *If she had had to give up riding she might have taken up sailing competitively... Mrs Thatcher survived what might have been a parliamentary ordeal without injury... The report might have been better written... I didn't give my name because if I did I thought you might not have come.* MODAL PRAGMATICS

6 You use **might** in statements where you are accepting the truth of a situation, but contrasting it with something that is more important. *He might be a bore, but he was as quick-witted as a weasel... They might not have two cents to rub together, but at least they have a kind of lifestyle that is different.* MODAL PRAGMATICS =may

7 You use **might** when you are saying emphatically that someone ought to do the thing mentioned, especially when you are annoyed because they have not done it. *And while I'm out you might clean up the kitchen... You might have told me that before!* MODAL PRAGMATICS =could

8 You use **might** to make a suggestion or to give advice in a very polite way. *They might be wise to stop advertising on television... You might try the gas station down the street... You might want to consider cycling... I was just wondering if you might like to go feed the cat... I thought we might go for a drive on Sunday... It might be a good idea to tell your husband.* MODAL PRAGMATICS

9 In formal spoken English, you use **might** as a polite way of interrupting someone, asking a question, making a request, or introducing what you are going to say next. *Might I make a suggestion?... Might I ask what you're doing here?... Might I trouble you for a drop more tea?... I was wondering if I might talk to you for a moment... Might I draw your readers' attention to the dangers in the Government's proposal.* MODAL PRAGMATICS =could

10 You use **might** in expressions such as **as you might expect** and **as you might imagine** in order to indicate that the statement you are making is not surprising. *'How's Jan?' she asked.—'Bad. As you might expect.'... The drivers, as you might imagine, didn't care much for that.* MODAL PRAGMATICS =would

11 You use **might** in expressions such as **I might add** and **I might say** in order to emphasize a statement that you are making. *Relatives ring up constantly, not always for the best motives, I might add... It didn't come as a great surprise to me, I might say.* MODAL PRAGMATICS

12 You use **might** in expressions such as **I might have known** and **I might have guessed** to indicate that you are not surprised at a disappointing event or fact. *I might have known I'd find you with some little slut... 'I detest clutter, you know.'—'I didn't know, but I might have guessed.'* MODAL PRAGMATICS =should

13 ● **might as well**: see **well.**

might 2 noun uses

might /maɪt/ ◆◇◇◇◇

1 **Might** is power or strength; a formal use. *The might of the army could prove a decisive factor.* N-UNCOUNT: usu with supp

2 If you do something **with all** your **might**, you do it using all your strength and energy. *She swung the hammer at his head with all her might.* PHRASE: PHR with v

mightily /maɪtɪli/. **Mightily** means to a great extent or degree; an old-fashioned word. *He had given a mightily impressive performance... She strove mightily to put Mike from her thoughts.* ADV-GRADED: ADV adj/adv, ADV after v

mightn't /maɪtᵊnt/. **Mightn't** is a spoken form of **might not.**

might've /maɪtəv/. **Might've** is the usual spoken form of **might have**, especially when 'have' is an auxiliary verb.

mighty /maɪti/ **mightier, mightiest** ◆◆◇◇◇

1 **Mighty** is used to describe something that is very large or powerful; a literary use. *There was a flash and a mighty bang. ...a land marked with vast lakes and mighty rivers.* ADJ-GRADED: usu ADJ n

2 **Mighty** is used in front of adjectives and adverbs to emphasize the quality that they are describing; used mainly in informal American English. *It's something you'll be mighty proud of... Being paper money, it rotted away mighty fast.* ADV-GRADED: ADV adj/adv PRAGMATICS

3 See also **high and mighty.**

migraine /miːgreɪn, AM maɪ-/ **migraines.** A **migraine** is an extremely painful headache that makes you feel very ill. *Her mother suffered from migraines.* ◆◇◇◇◇ N-VAR

migrant /maɪgrənt/ **migrants** ◆◆◇◇◇

1 A **migrant** is a person who moves from one place to another, especially in order to find work. *The government divides asylum-seekers into economic migrants and genuine refugees. ...migrant workers following harvests northward.* N-COUNT

2 Migrants are birds, fish, or animals that migrate from one part of the world to another. *Migrant birds shelter in the reeds.* N-COUNT: oft N n

migrate /maɪgreɪt, AM maɪgreɪt/ **migrates, migrating, migrated** ◆◆◇◇◇

1 If people **migrate**, they move from one place to another, especially in order to find work or to live somewhere for a short time. *People migrate to cities like Jakarta in search of work... Farmers have learned that they have to migrate if they want to survive.* ♦ **migration** /maɪgreɪʃən/ **migrations** *...the migration of Soviet Jews to Israel.* VERB V prep/adv V N VAR

2 When birds, fish, or animals **migrate**, they move at a particular time or season from one part of the world or from one part of a country to another, usually in order to breed or to find new feeding grounds. *Most birds have to fly long distances to migrate. ...a dam system that kills the fish as they migrate from streams to the ocean.* ♦ **migration** *...the migration of animals in the Serengeti.* VERB V V prep/adv N-VAR

migratory /maɪgrətəri, AM -tɔːri/

1 A **migratory** bird, fish, or animal is one that migrates every year. ADJ: usu ADJ n

2 Migratory means relating to the migration of people, birds, fish, or animals. *...migratory farm labour.* ADJ: ADJ n

mike /maɪk/ **mikes.** A **mike** is the same as a **microphone**; an informal word. ◆◇◇◇◇ N-COUNT

mild /maɪld/ **milder, mildest** ◆◆◆◇◇

1 Mild is used to describe something such as a feeling, attitude, or illness that is not very strong or severe. *Teddy turned to Mona with a look of mild confusion... Anna put up a mild protest... If you have only mild symptoms, try an over-the-counter treatment.* ♦ **mildly** *I'm only mildly surprised... Josephine must have had the disease very mildly as she showed no symptoms.* ADJ-GRADED: usu ADJ n =slight ≠great ADV-GRADED: usu ADV adj/adv, also ADV after v

2 A **mild** person is gentle and does not get angry easily. *He is a mild man, who is reasonable almost to the point of blandness.* ♦ **mildly** *'I'm not meddling,' Kenworthy said mildly, 'I'm just curious.'* ADJ-GRADED: usu ADJ n ≠aggressive ADV-GRADED: ADV after v

3 Mild weather is pleasant because it is neither extremely hot nor extremely cold. *The area is famous for its very mild winter climate.* ADJ-GRADED ≠cold

4 You describe food as **mild** when it does not taste or smell strong, sharp, or bitter, especially when you like it because of this. *This cheese has a soft, mild flavour. ...a mild curry powder.* ADJ-GRADED ≠strong

5 Mild soap or washing-up liquid feels soft and pleasant on your skin and does not contain anything which might damage the things you want to wash. *Wash your face thoroughly with a mild soap and warm water.* ADJ-GRADED ≠harsh

6 In Britain, **mild** is a clear, dark-coloured beer. N-UNCOUNT

7 See also **mildly**.

mildew /mɪldjuː, AM -duː/. **Mildew** is a soft white fungus that grows in damp places. *The room smelled of mildew.* N-UNCOUNT

mildewed /mɪldjuːd, AM -duːd/. Something that is **mildewed** has mildew growing on it. ADJ

mildly /maɪldli/

1 See **mild**.

2 You use to **put it mildly** to indicate that you are describing something in language that is much less strong, direct, or critical than what you really think. *But not all the money, to put it mildly, has been used wisely... To say we are disappointed about this is putting it mildly.* PHRASE: V inflects

mild-mannered. If you describe someone as **mild-mannered**, you approve of them because they are gentle, kind, and polite. ADJ-GRADED PRAGMATICS =mild

mile /maɪl/ **miles** ◆◆◆◆◇

1 A **mile** is a unit of distance equal to 1760 yards or approximately 1.6 kilometres. *They drove 600 miles across the desert... The hurricane is moving to the west at about 18 miles per hour... She lives just half a mile away... There's a lake up there, about ten miles long. ...a 50-mile bike ride.* N-COUNT: num N

2 Miles is used, especially in the expression **miles away**, to refer to a long distance. *If you enrol at a gym that's miles away, you won't be visiting it as often as you should... I was miles and miles from anywhere... 'Shall I come to see you?'—'Are you kidding? It's miles.'* N-PLURAL

3 Miles or **a mile** is used with the meaning 'very much' in order to emphasize the difference between two things or qualities, or the difference between what you aimed to do and what you actually achieved; an informal use. *You're miles better than most of the performers we see nowadays... With a Labour candidate in place they won by a mile... The rehearsals were miles too slow and no work was getting done.* N-COUNT: usu pl PRAGMATICS =loads

4 If you say that someone is **miles away**, you mean that they are unaware of what is happening or of what someone is saying, because they are thinking deeply about something else; an informal expression. *What were you thinking about? You were miles away.* PHRASES v-link PHR

5 If you say that someone is willing to **go the extra mile**, you mean that they are willing to make a special effort to do or achieve something. *The President is determined 'to go the extra mile for peace'.* V inflects

6 If you say that you can see or recognize something **a mile off**, you are emphasizing that it is very obvious and easy to recognize; an informal expression. *You can spot undercover cops a mile off.* PHR after v PRAGMATICS

7 If you say that someone would **run a mile** when faced with a particular situation, you mean that they would be very frightened or unwilling to deal with it; an informal expression. *If anybody had told me when I first got married that I was going to have seven children, I would have run a mile... I'm very squeamish and when I see needles I run a mile.* V inflects

8 If you say that something or someone **sticks out a mile** or **stands out a mile**, you are emphasizing that they are very obvious and easy to recognize; an informal expression. *'How do you know he's Irish?'—'Sticks out a mile.'... We stood out a mile on that first day at school.* V inflects PRAGMATICS

mileage /maɪlɪdʒ/ **mileages** ◆◇◇◇◇

1 Mileage refers to the distance that you have travelled, measured in miles. *While most of their mileage may be in and around town, they still want motorways for longer trips.* N-UNCOUNT: also N in pl

2 The **mileage** of a vehicle is the number of miles that it can travel using one gallon of petrol. *They are willing to pay up to $500 more for cars that get better mileage.* N-UNCOUNT: also N in pl

3 The **mileage** in a particular course of action is its usefulness in getting you what you want. *It's obviously important to get as much mileage out of the convention as possible... The administration clearly decided there was no mileage in provoking a huge row with Congress.* N-UNCOUNT: usu N *out of/in* n/-ing

milestone /maɪlstoun/ **milestones** ◆◇◇◇◇

1 A **milestone** is an important event in the history or development of something or someone. *He said the launch of the party represented a milestone in Zambian history... Starting school is a milestone for both children and parents.* N-COUNT

2 A **milestone** is a stone by the side of a road showing the distances to particular places. N-COUNT

milieu /miːljɜː, AM mɪljuː/ **milieux** or **milieus.** Your **milieu** is the group of people or activities that you live among or are familiar with; a formal word. *They stayed, safe and happy, within their own social milieu... His natural milieu is that of the arts.* ◆◇◇◇◇ N-COUNT: usu supp N =setting

militant /mɪlɪtənt/ **militants.** You use **militant** to describe people who believe in something very strongly and are active in trying to bring about political or social change, often in extreme ways that other people find unacceptable. *Militant mineworkers in the Ukraine have voted for a one-day stoppage next month. ...one of the most active militant groups.* ▶ Also a noun. *According to the authorities, the militants were planning a series of terrorist acts.* ♦ **militancy** *...the rise of trade union militancy.* ♦ **militantly** *...Albania's militantly atheist authorities.* ◆◆◆◇◇ ADJ-GRADED N-COUNT: usu pl N-UNCOUNT ADV-GRADED: usu ADV adj

militarism /mɪlɪtərɪzəm/. **Militarism** is a country's desire to strengthen their armed forces in order to make themselves more powerful; N-UNCOUNT PRAGMATICS used showing disapproval. *The country slipped into a dangerous mixture of nationalism and militarism.*

militarist /mɪlɪtərɪst/ **militarists**
1 If you describe someone as a **militarist**, you mean that they are eager that their country's armed forces should be strengthened and used in order to make it more powerful; used showing disapproval. *They became overheated nationalists, militarists, and they were out to conquer.* N-COUNT: oft N n PRAGMATICS
2 **Militarist** means the same as **militaristic**. *...militarist policies.* ADJ-GRADED: usu ADJ n

militaristic /mɪlɪtərɪstɪk/. **Militaristic** is used to describe groups, ideas, or policies which support the strengthening and use of the armed forces of their country in order to make it more powerful; used showing disapproval. *...aggressive militaristic governments.* ADJ-GRADED PRAGMATICS

militarized /mɪlɪtəraɪzd/; also spelled **militarised** in British English.
1 A **militarized** area or region has members of the armed forces and military equipment in it. *...the militarized zone that separates the faction leaders' areas of control.* ADJ-GRADED: usu ADJ n
2 You can use **militarized** to show disapproval of something that has many military characteristics, for example the quality of being aggressive or strict. *...a militarized and confrontationist style of politics.* ADJ-GRADED PRAGMATICS

military /mɪlɪtri, AM -teri/ **militaries** ◆◆◆◆◆
1 **Military** means relating to the armed forces of a country. *Military action may become necessary... The president is sending in almost 20,000 military personnel to help with the relief efforts. ...last year's military coup.* ♦ **militarily** /mɪlɪteərɪli/ *They remain unwilling to intervene militarily in what could be an unending war... While that option would incur fewer casualties, it would not be militarily effective.* ADJ: usu ADJ n; ADV: ADV with v, ADV adj
2 **Military** means relating to or belonging to the army, rather than to the navy or the air force. *The attack has caused severe damage to American naval and military forces.* ADJ: ADJ n =army
3 **The military** are the armed forces of a country, especially officers of high rank. *The bombing has been far more widespread than the military will admit... Did you serve in the military?* N-COUNT-COLL: usu sing, the N =forces
4 If you do something in a **military** way, you do it in an exact and disciplined way, like a soldier. *Your working day will need to be organized with military precision.* ADJ-GRADED

military police ◆◇◇◇◇
1 The **military police** are the part of an army, navy, or air force that act as its police force. *The government has said it will reform the military police.* N-SING-COLL
2 **Military police** are men and women who are members of the part of an army, navy, or air force that act as its police force. *The camp is surrounded by razor-wire fences and guarded by military police.* N-PLURAL

military policeman, military policemen. A **military policeman** is a member of the military police. N-COUNT

military service. **Military service** is a period of compulsory service in the armed forces of a country. *Many conscripts resent having to do their military service.* ◆◇◇◇◇ N-UNCOUNT: oft with poss

militate /mɪlɪteɪt/ **militates, militating, militated.** If something **militates against** something or someone, it makes something less likely to happen or someone less likely to achieve something; a formal word. *Her background militates against her.* VERB V against n

militia /mɪlɪʃə/ **militias.** A **militia** is an organization that operates like an army but whose members are not professional soldiers. *The troops will not attempt to disarm the warring militias.* ◆◆◇◇◇ N-COUNT

militiaman /mɪlɪʃəmən/ **militiamen.** A **militiaman** is a member of a militia. ◆◇◇◇◇ N-COUNT

milk /mɪlk/ **milks, milking, milked** ◆◆◆◇◇
1 **Milk** is the white liquid produced by cows, goats, and some other animals. People drink milk, and use it to make butter, cheese, and yoghurt. *He popped out to buy a pint of milk. ...basic foods such as meat, bread and milk. ...empty milk bottles.* N-UNCOUNT
2 If someone **milks** a cow or goat, they get milk from it by pulling its udders, using either their hands or a special machine. *Farm-workers milked cows by hand.* ♦ **milking** *...an automatic milking machine... The evening milking is usually done at about 7.30pm.* VERB V n; N-UNCOUNT: oft N n
3 **Milk** is the white liquid produced by women to feed their babies. *Milk from the mother's breast is a perfect food for the human baby.* N-UNCOUNT =breast milk
4 Products used for cleansing or moisturising your skin which are in liquid form are sometimes referred to as **milks**. *Sales of cleansing milks, creams and gels have doubled over the past decade.* N-MASS =lotion
5 If you say that someone **milks** something, you mean that they get as much benefit or profit as they can from it, without caring about the effects this has on other people; used showing disapproval. *A few people tried to milk the insurance companies... The callous couple milked money from a hospital charity to fund a lavish lifestyle.* VERB PRAGMATICS V n V n *from* n
6 See also **coconut milk, condensed milk, evaporated milk, skimmed milk.**
7 In British English, if you think someone's suggestions or ideas are weak or sentimental, you can say they are **milk and water**. *Fryer dismisses the report as 'milk and water'.* PHRASE PRAGMATICS

milk chocolate. **Milk chocolate** is chocolate that has been made with milk. It is lighter in colour and has a creamier taste than plain chocolate. N-UNCOUNT

milk float, milk floats. In Britain, a **milk float** is a small van with a roof and no sides which is used to deliver milk to people's houses. Milk floats usually have an electric motor. N-COUNT

milkmaid /mɪlkmeɪd/ **milkmaids.** In former times, a **milkmaid** was a woman who worked in a dairy and who milked cows and made butter and cheese. N-COUNT

milkman /mɪlkmən, AM -mæn/ **milkmen.** A **milkman** is a person who delivers milk to people's homes. N-COUNT

milk product, milk products. **Milk products** are foods made from milk, for example butter, cheese, and yoghurt. *Milk products are an excellent source of calcium and protein.* N-COUNT: usu pl

milk round, milk rounds
1 In Britain, if someone has a **milk round**, they work as a milkman, going from house to house delivering milk. *Milk rounds are threatened as customers switch to buying from supermarkets.* N-COUNT
2 In Britain, **the milk round** is an annual event when employees from large companies visit colleges and universities and interview students who are interested in working for them. *He obtained his first job through the milk round.* N-SING: the N

milkshake /mɪlkʃeɪk/ **milkshakes;** also spelled **milk shake**. **Milkshake** is a cold drink made by mixing milk with a flavouring, and sometimes ice cream or fruit, and then whisking it. ► A **milkshake** is a glass of milkshake. N-MASS; N-COUNT

milk tooth, milk teeth. Your **milk teeth** are the first teeth that grow in your mouth, which later fall out and are replaced by a second set. N-COUNT: usu pl

milk white. You can use **milk white** to describe things that are a milky white colour. *Mist was rising, and trees and shrubs began to disappear in a milk-white haze.* COLOUR

milky /mɪlki/ ◆◇◇◇◇
1 If you describe something as **milky**, you mean it is pale white in colour. You can describe other colours as **milky** when they are very pale or have white streaks in them. *...milky white paint... A milky mist filled the valley.* ADJ
2 Drinks or food that are **milky** contain a lot of milk. *...a large bowl of milky coffee.* ADJ-GRADED

Milky Way. **The Milky Way** is the pale strip of light consisting of many stars that you can see stretched across the sky at night. ◆◇◇◇◇ N-PROPER: the N

mill /mɪl/ **mills, milling, milled** ◆◆◆◇◇

1 A **mill** is a building in which grain is crushed and ground to make flour. N-COUNT

2 A **mill** is a small device used for grinding something such as coffee beans or pepper into powder. *...a pepper mill.* N-COUNT: supp N =grinder

3 A **mill** is a factory used for making and processing materials such as steel, wool, or cotton. *...a steel mill. ...a textile mill.* N-COUNT: usu supp N

4 To **mill** something such as wheat or pepper means to grind it in a mill. *...small mills that ground corn. ...freshly milled black pepper.* VERB V n V-ed

5 • **grist to the mill**: see **grist**. See also **milling**; **rolling mill, run-of-the-mill, watermill.**

mill around; the form **mill about** is also used in British English. When a crowd of people **mill around** or **mill about**, they move around within a particular place or area, so that the movement of the whole crowd looks very confused. *Quite a few people were milling about, but nothing was happening... Dozens of people milled around Charing Cross Road and Denmark Street.* PHRASAL VERB V P V P n

millennium /mɪleniəm/ **millennia** or **millenniums** ◆◇◇◇◇

1 A **millennium** is a thousand years; a formal use. *Their creations survive half a millennium later... Techniques that were refined over millennia should not be ignored.* N-COUNT

2 A **millennium** is one of the periods of a thousand years before or after the birth of Jesus Christ. 1995 is in the second millennium A.D. A formal use. *Evidence exists that acupuncture was practised in China as long ago as the third millennium BC.* N-COUNT: usu *the* ord N in sing

3 According to the belief of some Christians, **the millennium** is a period of a thousand years during which Christ will rule on earth; a technical use in theology. N-SING: *the* N

miller /mɪləʳ/ **millers.** A **miller** is a person who owns or operates a mill in which grain is crushed and ground to make flour. ◆◇◇◇◇ N-COUNT

millet /mɪlɪt/ **millets. Millet** is a cereal crop that is grown for its seeds or for hay. ◆◇◇◇◇ N-MASS

milli- /mɪlɪ-/. **Milli-** is added to some nouns that refer to units of measurement in order to form other nouns referring to units a thousand times smaller. *...a small current, around 5 milliamps.* PREFIX

milligram /mɪlɪgræm/ **milligrams;** also spelled **milligramme** in British English. A **milligram** is a unit of weight that is equal to one thousandth of a gramme. *...0.5 milligrams of mercury.* ◆◇◇◇◇ N-COUNT: num N, oft N *of* n

millilitre /mɪlɪliːtəʳ/ **millilitres;** spelled **milliliter** in American English. A **millilitre** is a unit of volume for liquids and gases that is equal to a thousandth of a litre. *...100 millilitres of blood.* N-COUNT: num N, oft N *of* n

millimetre /mɪlɪmiːtəʳ/ **millimetres;** spelled **millimeter** in American English. A **millimetre** is a metric unit of length that is equal to a tenth of a centimetre or a thousandth of a metre. *...a tiny little transparent pill, about 20 millimetres long.* ◆◇◇◇◇ N-COUNT: num N, oft N *of* n

milliner /mɪlɪnəʳ/ **milliners.** A **milliner** is a person whose job is making or selling women's hats. N-COUNT

millinery /mɪlɪnəri, AM -neri/. **Millinery** is used to refer to hats made or sold by a milliner. *...her aunt's modest millinery shop.* N-UNCOUNT: oft N n

milling /mɪlɪŋ/. The people in a **milling** crowd move around within a particular place or area, so that the movement of the whole crowd looks very confused. *As they moved purposefully through the milling crowd, they spotted Billy Ford against a wall.* ADJ: ADJ n

million /mɪliən/ **millions.** The plural form is **million** after a number, or after a word or expression referring to a number, such as 'several' or 'a few'. ◆◆◆◆◆

1 A **million** or one **million** is the number 1,000,000. *Up to five million people a year visit the county... Profits for 1991 topped £100 million.* NUM

2 If you talk about **millions of** people or things, you mean that there is a very large number of them but you do not know or do not want to say exactly how many. *The programme was viewed on television in millions of homes.* ▶ Also a pronoun. *This wretched war has brought misery to millions.* QUANT-PL: QUANT *of* pl-n PRON

millionaire /mɪliəneəʳ/ **millionaires.** A **millionaire** is a very rich person who has money or property worth at least a million pounds or dollars. *By the time he died, he was a millionaire.* ◆◆◇◇◇ N-COUNT

millionairess /mɪliəneəres/ **millionairesses.** A **millionairess** is a woman who has money or property worth at least a million pounds or dollars. You can also refer to a woman who has this much money as a **millionaire**. N-COUNT

millionth /mɪliənθ/ **millionths** ◆◆◆◆◇

1 The **millionth** item in a series is the one you count as number one million. *Last year the millionth truck rolled off the assembly line.* ORD

2 A **millionth** of something is one of a million equal parts of it. *The bomb must explode within less than a millionth of a second.* FRACTION

millipede /mɪlɪpiːd/ **millipedes.** A **millipede** is a very small creature with a long, narrow body made of small segments, each with two pairs of legs. N-COUNT

millisecond /mɪlisekənd/ **milliseconds.** A **millisecond** is a unit of time equal to one thousandth of a second; a technical term. N-COUNT

millstone /mɪlstoʊn/ **millstones**

1 A **millstone** is a large, flat, round stone which is one of a pair of stones used to grind grain into flour. N-COUNT

2 If you describe something as **a millstone** or **a millstone around** your **neck**, you mean that it is a very unpleasant problem or responsibility that you cannot escape from. *For today's politicians, the treaty is becoming a millstone... That contract proved to be a millstone around his neck.* PHRASE: usu v-link PHR

mime /maɪm/ **mimes, miming, mimed** ◆◇◇◇◇

1 **Mime** is the use of movements and gestures in order to express something or tell a story without using speech. *Music, mime and strong visual imagery play a strong part in the productions... Pupils presented a mime and puppet show. ...a mime artist.* N-VAR

2 If you **mime** something, you describe or express it using mime rather than speech. *It featured a solo dance in which a woman in a short overall mimed a lot of dainty housework... I remember asking her to mime getting up in the morning.* VERB V n/-ing Also V

3 If you **mime**, you pretend to be singing or playing an instrument, although the music is in fact coming from a record or cassette. *Richey's not miming, he's playing very quiet guitar... In concerts, the group mime their songs... The waiters mime to records playing on the jukebox.* VERB V V n V *to* n

mimetic /mɪmetɪk/. **Mimetic** movements or activities are ones in which you imitate something; a formal word. *Both realism and naturalism are mimetic systems or practices of representation.* ADJ: usu ADJ n

mimic /mɪmɪk/ **mimics, mimicking, mimicked** ◆◇◇◇◇

1 If you **mimic** the actions or voice of a person or animal, you imitate it, usually in a way that is meant to be amusing or entertaining. *He could mimic anybody, and he often reduced Isabel to helpless laughter... He mimicked her upper-class accent.* VERB =imitate V n

2 If someone or something **mimics** another person or thing, they try to be like them or are like them, although they are not really that person or thing. *Don't try to mimic anybody. You have to be yourself if you are going to do your best... The computer doesn't mimic human thought; it reaches the same ends by different means.* VERB =imitate V n

3 A **mimic** is a person who is able to mimic people or animals. N-COUNT =impressionist, impersonator

mimicry /mɪmɪkri/. **Mimicry** is the action of mimicking someone or something. *One of his few strengths was his skill at mimicry.* N-UNCOUNT

min. **Min.** is a written abbreviation for **minimum**, or for **minutes** or **minute**. ◆◆◇◇◇

minaret /mɪnəret/ **minarets.** A **minaret** is a tall thin tower which is part of a mosque. N-COUNT

mince /mɪns/ **minces, mincing, minced** ◆◇◇◇◇

1 **Mince** is meat which has been cut into very small pieces by being forced through the small holes in a N-UNCOUNT =mincemeat

machine called a mincer; used mainly in British English. The usual American term is **hamburger meat**. *Brown the mince in a frying pan.*

2 If you **mince** food such as meat, you put it into a machine called a mincer which cuts it into very small pieces by forcing it through small holes. *Perhaps I'll buy lean meat and mince it myself. ...minced beef.* VERB V n V-ed

3 If you say that someone **minces** somewhere, you mean that they walk there with quick small steps; often used to say disapprovingly that a man walks in an exaggeratedly effeminate way. *They minced in, in beach costumes and make-up.* VERB V prep/adv

4 If you say someone does not **mince** their **words** or does not **mince words**, you mean they speak in a forceful direct way, especially when saying something unpleasant to someone. *The doctors didn't mince their words, and predicted the worst... Never one to mince words, Carlie told her daughter that her looks were fading.* PHRASE: V inflects, with brd-neg

mincemeat /mɪnsmiːt/

1 Mincemeat is a sticky mixture of small pieces of dried fruit. It is usually cooked in pastry to make mince pies. N-UNCOUNT

2 Mincemeat is meat which has been cut into very small pieces by being forced through the small holes in a machine called a mincer; used mainly in British English. The usual American term is **hamburger meat**. N-UNCOUNT =mince

3 If you **make mincemeat of** someone or **make mincemeat out of** them, you defeat them completely in an argument, fight, or competition. *I can imagine a defence lawyer making mincemeat of him if we ever put him up in court.* PHRASE: V inflects

mince pie, mince pies. Mince pies are small pies containing a sticky mixture of small pieces of dried fruit. Mince pies are usually eaten at Christmas. N-COUNT

mincer /mɪnsəʳ/ **mincers.** A **mincer** is a machine which cuts meat into very small pieces by forcing it through very small holes; used mainly in British English. N-COUNT

mind 1 noun uses

mind /maɪnd/ **minds** ◆◆◆◆◆

1 You refer to someone's **mind** when talking about their thoughts. For example, if you say that something is **in your mind**, you mean that you are thinking about it, and if you say that something is **at the back of your mind**, you mean that you are aware of it, although you are not thinking about it very much. *I'm trying to clear my mind of all this... There was no doubt in his mind that the man was serious... I put what happened during that game to the back of my mind... He spent the next hour going over the trial in his mind... She found herself thinking thoughts that would never have entered her mind until now.* N-COUNT: with poss =head

2 Your **mind** is your ability to think and reason. *You have a good mind... Studying stretched my mind and got me thinking about things. ...an excellent training for the young mind.* N-COUNT: supp N =intellect

3 If you have a particular type of **mind**, you have a particular way of thinking which is part of your character, or a result of your education or professional training. *Andrew, you have a very suspicious mind... The key to his success is his logical mind. ...an American writer who has researched the criminal mind.* N-COUNT: usu sing, with supp =mentality

4 You can refer to someone as a particular kind of **mind** as a way of saying that they are clever, intelligent, or imaginative. *She moved to London, meeting some of the best minds of her time.* N-COUNT: with supp =thinker

5 See also **minded, -minded; frame of mind, state of mind**.

6 If you tell someone to **bear** something **in mind** or to **keep** something **in mind**, you are reminding or warning them about something important which they should remember. *Bear in mind that petrol stations are scarce in the more remote areas... I should not be surprised about some of her comments, bearing in mind the party she belongs to.* PHRASES V inflects, oft PHR that, PHR n PRAGMATICS =remember

7 If something **brings** another thing **to mind** or **calls** another thing **to mind**, it makes you think of that other thing, usually because it is similar in some way. *That brings to mind a wonderful poem by Riokin... The fate of many British designers calls to mind the fable of the tortoise and the hare.* V inflects, usu PHR n =be reminiscent of

8 If you **cast** your **mind back** to a time in the past, you think about what happened then. *Cast your mind back to 1978, when Forest won the title.* V and N inflect, oft PHR *to* n

9 If you **close** your **mind** to something, you deliberately do not think about it or pay attention to it. *She has closed her mind to last year's traumas.* V and N inflect, usu PHR *to* n

10 If you **change** your **mind**, or if someone or something **changes** your **mind**, you change a decision you have made or an opinion that you had. *I was going to vote for him, but I changed my mind and voted for Reagan... She's very young. She might change her mind about what she wants to do... It would be impossible to change his mind.* V and N inflect

11 If something **comes to mind** or **springs to mind**, you think of it without making any effort. *Integrity and honesty are words that spring to mind when talking of the man.* V inflects

12 If you say that an idea or possibility never **crossed** your **mind**, you mean that you did not think of it. *It had never crossed his mind that there might be a problem... The possibility of failure did cross Haig's mind.* V and N inflect, oft with brd-neg, oft *it* PHR that =occur to you

13 If you see something **in your mind's eye**, you imagine it and have a clear picture of it in your mind. *In his mind's eye, he can imagine the effect he's having.* PHR after v, PHR with cl

14 If you **have a mind to** do something, you want, intend, or choose to do it. *The captain of guard looked as if he had a mind to challenge them... They could interpret it that way if they'd a mind to.* V inflects, oft PHR inf

15 If you say that you **have a good mind to** do something or **have half a mind to** do it, you are threatening or announcing that you have a strong desire to do it, although you probably will not do it. *He raged on about how he had a good mind to resign.* V inflects, usu PHR inf PRAGMATICS

16 If you ask someone what they **have in mind**, you want to know in more detail about an idea or wish they have. *'Maybe we could celebrate tonight.'—'What did you have in mind?'* V inflects =be thinking of

17 If you **have it in mind to** do something, you intend or want to do it. *Collins Harvill had it in mind to publish a short volume about Pasternak.* V inflects, usu PHR inf

18 If you do something **with** a particular thing **in mind**, you do it with that thing as your aim or as the reason or basis for your action. *These families need support. With this in mind a group of 35 specialists met last weekend.* PHR after v, PHR with cl

19 If you say that something such as an illness is all **in the mind**, you mean that it relates to someone's feelings or attitude, rather than having any physical cause. *It could be a virus, or it could be all in the mind.* v-link PHR

20 If you **know** your **own mind**, you are sure about your opinions, and are not easily influenced by other people. V and N inflect

21 If you say that someone **is losing** their **mind**, you mean that they are becoming mad. *Sometimes I feel I'm losing my mind.* V and N inflect

22 If you **make up** your **mind** or **make** your **mind up**, you decide which of a number of possible things you will have or do. *Once he made up his mind to do something, there was no stopping him... He simply can't make his mind up... She said her mind was made up.* V and N inflect, oft PHR to-inf =decide

23 You can use the expression **mind over matter** to describe situations in which a person seems to be able to control events, physical objects, or the condition of their own body using their mind. *Good health is simply a case of mind over matter.* oft n prep PHR

24 If a number of people are **of one mind**, **of like mind**, or **of the same mind**, they all agree about something. *He said that he and Mr Bush were entirely of one mind about the need for the use of force... Contact with other disabled yachtsmen of like mind would be helpful.* v-link PHR

25 If you say that something that happens is **a load** *mind* inflects,

off your **mind** or **a weight off** your **mind**, you mean that it causes you to stop worrying, for example because it solves a problem that you had. v-link PHR =relief

26 If something is **on** your **mind**, you are worried or concerned about it and think about it a lot. *This game has been on my mind all week... I just forgot. I've had a lot on my mind.* N inflects, v-link PHR, PHR after v

27 If your **mind is on** something or you **have** your **mind on** something, you are thinking about that thing rather than something else. *At school I was always in trouble – my mind was never on my work.* V and N inflect, PHR n/-ing

28 If you have **an open mind**, you avoid forming an opinion or making a decision until you know all the facts. *It's hard to see it any other way, though I'm trying to keep an open mind.* N inflects, PHR after v

29 If something **opens** your **mind** to new ideas or experiences, it makes you more willing to accept them or try them. *She also stimulated his curiosity and opened his mind to other cultures.* V and N inflect, usu PHR *to* n

30 If you say that someone is **out of their mind**, you mean that they are mad or very foolish; an informal expression. *What are you doing? Are you out of your mind?* N inflects, v-link PHR PRAGMATICS =crazy

31 If you say that you have been **out of your mind** with a feeling such as worry, jealousy, or frustration, you are emphasizing that you have been extremely worried, jealous, or frustrated; an informal expression. N inflects, v-link PHR, usu PHR *with* n PRAGMATICS

32 If you say that someone is, for example, **bored out of** their **mind**, **scared out of** their **mind**, or **stoned out of** their **mind**, you are emphasizing that they are extremely bored, scared, or affected by drugs; an informal expression. N inflects, v-link PHR PRAGMATICS

33 If you **put** your **mind to** something, you devote a lot of energy, effort, or attention to it. *You could do fine in the world if you put your mind to it.* V and N inflect, PHR n

34 If something **puts** you **in mind of** something else, it reminds you of it because it is similar to it or is associated with it. *This put me in mind of something Patrick said many years ago.* V inflects, PHR n =remind

35 If you can **read** someone's **mind**, you know what they are thinking without them saying anything. *Don't expect others to read your mind.* V and N inflect

36 To **put** someone's **mind at rest** or **set** their **mind at rest** means to stop them worrying about something. *It may be advisable to have a blood test to put your mind at rest... She could set your mind at rest by giving you the facts.* V and N inflect =reassure

37 If you say that nobody **in** their **right mind** would do a particular thing, you are emphasizing that it is an irrational thing to do and you would be surprised if anyone did it. *No one in her right mind would make such a major purchase without asking questions.* with brd-neg, n PHR PRAGMATICS

38 If you **set** your **mind on** something or **have** your **mind set on** it, you are determined to do it or obtain it. *When my wife sets her mind on something, she invariably finds a way to achieve it.* V and N inflect, PHR n

39 If something **slips** your **mind**, you forget it. *I was going to mention it, but it slipped my mind.* V and N inflect

40 If you **speak** your **mind**, you say firmly and honestly what you think about a situation, even if this may offend or upset people. *Martina Navratilova has never been afraid to speak her mind.* V and N inflect

41 If something **sticks in** your **mind**, it remains firmly in your memory. *I've always been fond of poetry and one piece has always stuck in my mind.* V and N inflect

42 If something **takes** your **mind off** a problem or unpleasant situation, it helps you to forget about it for a while. *'How about a game of tennis?' suggested Alan. 'That'll take your mind off things.'* V and N inflect, PHR n

43 You say or write **to my mind** to indicate that the statement you are making is your own opinion. *There are scenes in this play which to my mind are incredibly violent.* PHR with cl

44 If you are **in two minds** or **of two minds**, you are uncertain about what to do, especially when you have to choose between two courses of action. *Like many parents, I am in two minds about school uniforms... Roche was in two minds whether to make the trip to Oslo.* usu v-link PHR, oft PHR *about* n, PHR whether =unsure

45 • to **give** someone **a piece of** your **mind**: see piece. • **presence of mind**: see **presence**. • **out of sight, out of mind**: see **sight**.

mind 2 verb uses

mind /maɪnd/ **minds, minding, minded** ◆◆◆◇◇

1 If you do not **mind** something, you are not annoyed or bothered by it. *I don't mind the noise during the day... Do you mind being alone?... I hope you don't mind me calling in like this, without an appointment... It involved a little extra work, but nobody seemed to mind.* VB: usu with brd-neg =object to V n/-ing V n -ing V

2 You use **mind** in the expressions **'do you mind?'** and **'would you mind?'** as a polite way of asking permission or asking someone to do something. *Do you mind if I ask you one more thing?... You don't mind if they take a look round, do you?... Would you mind waiting outside for a moment?... 'Would you like me to read that for you?'—'If you wouldn't mind, please.'* VERB PRAGMATICS V if V -ing V

3 If someone does not **mind** what happens or what something is like, they do not have a strong preference for any particular thing. *I don't mind what we play, really... I want to play for a top club and I don't mind where it is... They don't mind what you do.* VB: with brd-neg V wh

4 If you tell someone to **mind** something, you are warning them to be careful so that they do not hurt themselves or other people, or damage something. *Mind that bike!* VB: usu imper PRAGMATICS =watch V n

5 You use **mind** when you are reminding someone that they must do something or telling them to be careful not to do something. *Mind you don't burn those sausages.* VB: only imper PRAGMATICS =make sure V that

6 If you **mind** a child or something such as a shop or luggage, you look after it, usually while the person who owns it or is usually responsible for it is elsewhere. *Jim Coulters will mind the store while I'm away.* VERB =keep an eye on V n

7 If you are offered something or offered a choice and you say **'I don't mind'**, you are saying politely that you will be happy with any of the things offered. *'Which one of these do you want?'—'I don't mind.'* PHRASES CONVENTION PRAGMATICS =I'm not bothered

8 You can say **'I don't mind if I do'** as a way of accepting something that someone has offered you, especially food or drink; an old-fashioned expression. CONVENTION PRAGMATICS

9 You say **'Don't mind me'** to apologize for your presence when you think that it might embarrass someone, and to tell them to carry on with what they were doing or about to do. CONVENTION PRAGMATICS

10 You use **don't mind** in expressions such as **don't mind him** or **don't mind them** to apologize for someone else's behaviour when you think it might have offended the person you are speaking to. *Don't mind the old lady. She's getting senile.* PHR n PRAGMATICS

11 Some people say **'Mind how you go'** when they are saying goodbye to someone who is leaving; an informal expression. CONVENTION PRAGMATICS =take care

12 People use the expression **if you don't mind** when they are rejecting an offer or saying that they do not want to do something, especially when they are annoyed. *'Sit down.'—'I prefer standing for a while, if you don't mind.'... If you don't mind, we won't talk about it any more.* PHR with cl PRAGMATICS

13 You use **mind you** to emphasize a piece of information that you are adding, especially when the new information explains what you have said or contrasts with it. Some people use **mind** in a similar way. *They pay full rates. Mind you, they can afford it... I got substantial damages. It took two years, mind you... You need a bit of cold water in there to make it comfortable. Not too cold, mind.* PHR with cl PRAGMATICS

14 If you tell someone, especially a child, to **mind** their **language**, **mind** their **tongue**, or **mind** their **manners**, you are telling them to speak or behave properly and politely. PRAGMATICS =watch

15 You say **never mind** to someone to try and make them feel better when they have failed to do something or done something wrong, or when something unpleasant has happened to them. CONVENTION PRAGMATICS

16 You use **never mind** to tell someone that they need not do something or worry about something, because it is not important or because you will do oft PHR n/wh PRAGMATICS it yourself. *'I'll go up in one second, I promise.'—'Never mind,' I said with a sigh. 'I'll do it.'... 'Was his name David?'—'No I don't think it was, but never mind, go on.'... Dorothy, come on. Never mind your shoes. They'll soon dry off... 'Fewter didn't seem to think so.'—'Never mind what Fewter said.'*

17 You use **never mind** after a statement, often a negative one, to indicate that the statement is even more true of the person, thing, or situation that you are going to mention next. *I'm not going to believe it myself, never mind convince anyone else... Many of the potholes are a danger even to motor vehicles, never mind cyclists.* CONJ-COORD PRAGMATICS =let alone

18 You use **never you mind** to tell someone not to ask about something because it is not their concern or they should not know about it; used in spoken English. *'Where is it?'—'Never you mind.'* CONVENTION PRAGMATICS

19 You can say **'I don't mind telling you'** to emphasize the statement you are making. *I don't mind telling you I was absolutely terrified.* PHR with cl PRAGMATICS

20 If you say that you **wouldn't mind** something, you mean that you would quite like it. *I wouldn't mind a coffee... Anne wouldn't mind going to Italy or France to live.* PHR n/-ing =fancy

21 • to **mind** your **own business**: see **business**. • to **mind** your **Ps and Qs**: see **p**.

mind-blowing; also spelled **mind blowing**. If you describe something as **mind-blowing**, you mean that it is extremely impressive or surprising; an informal word. *...a mind-blowing array of treatments... It must have been mind-blowing.* ADJ-GRADED =incredible

mind-boggling; also spelled **mind boggling**. If you say that something is **mind-boggling**, you mean that it is so enormous, complicated, or extreme that it is very hard to imagine; an informal word. *The amount of paperwork involved is mind-boggling.* ADJ-GRADED =incredible

minded /maɪndɪd/. If someone is **minded** to do something, they want or intend to do it; a formal word. *The Home Office said at that time that it was minded to reject his application for political asylum... If the Americans were so minded then they could take sanctions against them.* ADJ: v-link ADJ, ADJ to-inf, *so* ADJ =inclined

-minded /-maɪndɪd/

1 **-minded** combines with adjectives to form adjectives that describe someone's character, attitude, opinions, or intellect. *These are evil-minded people... He is famous for his tough-minded professionalism.* COMB in ADJ-GRADED

2 **-minded** combines with adverbs to form adjectives that indicate that someone is interested in a particular subject or is able to think in a particular way. *I am not an academically-minded person... He was not mechanically-minded.* COMB in ADJ-GRADED

3 **-minded** combines with nouns to form adjectives that indicate that someone has a particular aim, priority, or interest. *He is seen as more business-minded than his predecessor... We weren't career-minded like girls are today.* COMB in ADJ-GRADED =-oriented

minder /maɪndəʳ/ **minders** ◆◇◇◇◇

1 A **minder** is a person whose job is to protect someone such as a celebrity or businessman and make sure they do not get into any trouble. N-COUNT =bodyguard

2 A **minder** is the same as a **childminder**; used mainly in British English. N-COUNT

mindful /maɪndfʊl/. If you are **mindful** of something, you think about it and consider it when taking action; a formal word. *We must be mindful of the consequences of selfishness... Mindful of the needs of its students, Cardiff has invested heavily in providing new and improved residences.* ◆◇◇◇◇ ADJ-GRADED: v-link ADJ, usu ADJ *of* n =conscious

mindless /maɪndləs/ ◆◇◇◇◇

1 In British English, if you describe a destructive action as **mindless**, you mean it is not at all sensible and is done for no good reason. *...a plot that mixes blackmail, extortion and mindless violence.* ADJ: usu ADJ n =senseless

2 If you describe a person or group as **mindless**, you mean that they are stupid or do not think about what they are doing. *She wasn't at all the mindless little wife so many people perceived her to be.* ♦ **mindlessly** *I was annoyed with myself for having so quickly and mindlessly lost thirty dollars.* ADJ-GRADED; ADV: ADV with v

3 If you describe an activity as **mindless**, you mean that it is so dull that people do it or take part in it without thinking. *...the mindless repetitiveness of some tasks.* ♦ **mindlessly** *I spent many hours in it mindlessly banging a tennis ball against the wall.* ADJ-GRADED =tedious; ADV: ADV with v

mind-numbing. If you describe an event or experience as **mind-numbing**, you mean that it is so bad, boring, or great in extent that you are unable to think about it clearly. *It was another day of mind-numbing tedium.* ♦ **mind-numbingly** *...a mind-numbingly boring sport.* ADJ-GRADED; ADV-GRADED: ADV adj

mindset /maɪndset/ **mindsets.** If you refer to someone's **mindset**, you mean their general attitudes and the way they typically think about things. *The greatest challenge for the Americans is understanding the mindset of Eastern Europeans.* N-COUNT: oft with poss, adj N =attitude

mine 1 pronoun use

mine /maɪn/. **Mine** is the first person singular possessive pronoun. A speaker or writer uses **mine** to indicate that something belongs or relates to himself or herself. *Her right hand is inches from mine... That wasn't his fault, it was mine... I'm looking for a friend of mine who lives here.* ◆◆◆◆◆ PRON-POSS: oft n *of* PRON

mine 2 noun and verb uses

mine /maɪn/ **mines, mining, mined** ◆◆◇◇◇

1 A **mine** is a place where deep holes and tunnels are dug under the ground in order to obtain a mineral such as coal, diamonds, or gold. *...coal mines.* N-COUNT: oft n N

2 When a mineral such as coal, diamonds, or gold **is mined**, it is obtained from the ground by digging deep holes and tunnels. *The pit is being shut down because it no longer has enough coal that can be mined economically. ...the finest gems, mined from all corners of the world.* VB: usu passive *be* V-ed V-ed

3 A **mine** is a bomb which is hidden in the ground or in water and which explodes when people or things touch it. N-COUNT

4 If an area of land or water **is mined**, mines are placed there which will explode when people or things touch them. *The approaches to the garrison have been heavily mined.* VERB *be* V-ed Also V n

5 If you say that someone is a **mine of information**, you mean that they know a great deal about something. PHRASE: *mine* inflects, usu v-link PHR

6 See also **mining**.

minefield /maɪnfi:ld/ **minefields** ◆◇◇◇◇

1 A **minefield** is an area of land or water where explosive mines have been hidden. N-COUNT

2 If you describe a situation as a **minefield**, you are emphasizing that there are a lot of hidden dangers or problems, and where people need to behave with care because things could easily go wrong. *The whole subject is a political minefield... The kitchen is a minefield of potential hazards.* N-COUNT: oft adj N, N *of* n PRAGMATICS

miner /maɪnəʳ/ **miners.** A **miner** is a person who works underground in mines in order to obtain minerals such as coal, diamonds, or gold. ◆◆◆◇◇ N-COUNT

mineral /mɪnərəl/ **minerals.** A **mineral** is a substance such as tin, salt, uranium, or sulphur that is formed naturally in rocks and in the earth. Minerals are also found in small quantities in food and drink. ◆◆◇◇◇ N-COUNT

mineral water, mineral waters. Mineral water is water that comes out of the ground naturally and is considered healthy to drink. ◆◇◇◇◇ N-MASS

minestrone /mɪnɪstroʊni/. **Minestrone** soup is a type of soup made from meat stock that contains small pieces of vegetable and pasta. N-UNCOUNT

minesweeper /maɪnswi:pəʳ/ **minesweepers;** also spelled **mine sweeper**. A **minesweeper** is a ship that is used to clear away explosive mines in the sea. N-COUNT

mingle /mɪŋgəl/ **mingles, mingling, mingled** ◆◇◇◇◇

1 If things such as sounds, smells, or feelings **mingle**, they become mixed together but are usually still recognizable. *Now the cheers and applause mingled in a single sustained roar... Foreboding mingled with his excitement.* V-RECIP pl-n V V *with* n

2 At a party, if you **mingle** with other people, you V-RECIP

move around and chat to them. *Go out of your way to mingle with others at the wedding... Guests ate and mingled... Alison mingled for a while and then went to where Douglas stood with John.* =mix V with pl-n pl-n V V (non-recip)

mini /mɪni/ **minis.** A **mini** is the same as a **mini-skirt.** N-COUNT

mini- /mɪni-/. **Mini-** is used before nouns to form nouns which refer to something which is a smaller version of something else. *Provisions may be purchased from the mini-market... We were playing mini-golf.* PREFIX

miniature /mɪnɪtʃəʳ, AM mɪniətʃʊr/ **miniatures** ◆◆◇◇◇

1 **Miniature** is used to describe something which is very small, especially a smaller version of something which is normally much bigger. *Rosehill Farm has been selling miniature roses since 1979... He looked like a miniature version of his handsome and elegant big brother.* ADJ: ADJ n

2 If you describe one thing as another thing **in miniature**, you mean that it is much smaller in size or scale than the other thing, but is otherwise exactly the same. *Ecuador provides a perfect introduction to South America; it's a continent in miniature... If it can be done full-size, I can do it in miniature.* PHRASE: usu n PHR, PHR after v

3 A **miniature** is a very small detailed painting, often of a person. N-COUNT

4 A **miniature** is a very small bottle of alcoholic drink, usually containing enough for one or two servings. N-COUNT

miniaturize /mɪnɪtʃəraɪz/ **miniaturizes, miniaturizing, miniaturized;** also spelled **miniaturise** in British English. If you **miniaturize** something such as a machine, you produce a very small version of it. *...the problems of further miniaturizing the available technologies. ...miniaturized amplifiers and receivers.* ♦ **miniaturization** /mɪnɪtʃəraɪzeɪʃən/ *...increasing miniaturization in the computer industry.* VERB V n V-ed N-UNCOUNT

minibar /mɪnibɑːʳ/ **minibars.** In a hotel room, a **minibar** is a small fridge containing a selection of alcoholic drinks. N-COUNT

minibus /mɪnibʌs/ **minibuses;** also spelled **mini-bus**. A **minibus** is a large van which has seats in the back for passengers to sit on, and windows along its sides. *He was then taken by minibus to the military base.* ◆◇◇◇◇ N-COUNT: also by N

minicab /mɪnikæb/ **minicabs;** also spelled **mini-cab**. In Britain, a **minicab** is a taxi which you have to arrange to pick you up by telephone. *If you want a cheap ride, take a minicab.* N-COUNT =taxi

minim /mɪnɪm/ **minims.** A **minim** is a musical note that has a time value equal to two crotchets; used mainly in British English. N-COUNT =half-note

minimal /mɪnɪməl/. Something that is **minimal** is very small in quantity, value, or degree. *The co-operation between the two is minimal... One aim of these reforms is effective defence with minimal expenditure.* ♦ **minimally** *He was paid, but only minimally... I was minimally successful.* ◆◆◇◇◇ ADJ =negligible ADV: ADV with v, ADV adj

minimalism /mɪnɪməlɪzəm/. **Minimalism** is a style in which a small number of very simple things are used to create a particular effect. *In her own home, she replaced austere minimalism with cosy warmth and colour.* N-UNCOUNT

minimalist /mɪnɪməlɪst/ **minimalists** ◆◇◇◇◇

1 A **minimalist** is an artist or designer who uses minimalism. *He was influenced by the minimalists in the 1970s.* N-COUNT

2 **Minimalist** is used to describe ideas, artists, or designers that are influenced by minimalism. *The two designers settled upon a minimalist approach.* ADJ-GRADED

minimize /mɪnɪmaɪz/ **minimizes, minimizing, minimized;** also spelled **minimise** in British English. ◆◆◇◇◇

1 If you **minimize** a risk, problem, or unpleasant situation, you reduce it to the lowest possible level, or prevent it increasing beyond that level. *Concerned people want to minimize the risk of developing cancer... Many of these problems can be minimised by sensible planning.* VERB =reduce ≠maximize V n

2 If you **minimize** something, you make it seem smaller or less significant than it really is. *Some have minimized the importance of ideological factors... At his trial, he tried to minimize his behavior.* VERB =play down ≠maximize V n

minimum /mɪnɪməm/ ◆◆◆◇◇

1 You use **minimum** to describe an amount which is the smallest that is possible, allowed, or required. *He was only five feet nine, the minimum height for a policeman. ...a rise in the minimum wage.* ► Also a noun. *This will take a minimum of one hour... Four foot should be seen as an absolute minimum.* ADJ: ADJ n ≠maximum N-SING: oft a N of amount

2 You use **minimum** to state how small an amount is. *The basic needs of life are available with minimum effort... Neil and Chris try to spend the minimum amount of time on the garden.* ► Also a noun. *With a minimum of fuss, she produced the grandson he had so desperately wished for.* ADJ: ADJ n N-SING: a N of n

3 If you say that something is a particular amount **minimum**, you mean that this is the smallest amount it should be or could possibly be, although a larger amount is acceptable or very possible. *You're talking over a thousand pounds minimum for one course.* ADV: amount ADV ≠maximum

4 You use **at a minimum**, or **at the minimum**, when you want to indicate that something is the very least which could or should happen. *This would take three months at a minimum... At the minimum, they must be guaranteed against any form of further attack.* PHRASES amount PHR, PHR with cl, PHR after v ≠at the maximum

5 If you say that someone keeps something **to a minimum**, or **to the minimum**, you mean that they keep the amount of it as small as possible. *Office machinery is kept to a minimum... She has now cut her teaching hours to the minimum.* PHR after v

mining /maɪnɪŋ/. **Mining** is the industry and activities connected with getting valuable or useful minerals from the ground, for example coal, diamonds, or gold. *...traditional industries such as coal mining and steel making... He was born at Aberdare in South Wales, the son of a mining engineer.* ◆◆◇◇◇ N-UNCOUNT

minion /mɪnjən/ **minions.** If you refer to someone's **minions**, you are referring to people who carry out unimportant or unrewarding jobs for them. *She delegated the job to one of her minions.* N-COUNT: usu pl, usu poss N =underling

mini-skirt, mini-skirts; also spelled **miniskirt**. A **mini-skirt** is a very short skirt. N-COUNT =mini

minister /mɪnɪstəʳ/ **ministers, ministering, ministered** ◆◆◆◆◆

1 A **minister** is a person who is in charge of a particular government department. *When the government had come to power, he had been named minister of culture... The new Defence Minister is Senator Robert Ray.* N-COUNT: oft N of n, n N

2 A **minister** is a person who officially represents their government in a foreign country and has a lower rank than an ambassador. *He concluded a deal with the Danish minister in Washington.* N-COUNT: usu supp N

3 A **minister** is a member of the clergy, especially in Protestant churches. *His father was a Baptist minister.* N-COUNT

4 If you **minister to** people or **to** their needs, you serve them or help them, for example by making sure that they have everything they need or want; a formal use. *For 44 years he had ministered to the poor, the sick, the neglected and the deprived.* VERB V to n

ministerial /mɪnɪstɪəriəl/. You use **ministerial** to refer to people, events, or jobs that are connected with government ministers. *The prime minister's initial ministerial appointments haven't pleased all his supporters. ...the recent ministerial meeting.* ◆◆◇◇◇ ADJ: ADJ n

ministrations /mɪnɪstreɪʃənz/. A person's **ministrations** are the things they do to help or care for someone in a particular situation, especially someone who is weak or ill; a literary word which is often used humorously. *...the tender ministrations of the buxom woman who cut his hair.* N-PLURAL: usu with poss

ministry /mɪnɪstri/ **ministries** ◆◆◆◆◇

1 A **ministry** is a government department that deals with a particular area of administration with- N-COUNT: oft N of n, n N

in a country, for example employment, defence, or transport. *...the Ministry of Justice. ...a spokesman for the Agriculture Ministry.*

2 The **ministry** of a religious person is the work that they do that is based on or inspired by their religious beliefs. *His ministry is among the poor.* N-COUNT: usu sing, usu with poss

3 Members of the clergy belonging to some branches of the Christian church are referred to as **the ministry**. *So what prompted him to enter the ministry?* N-SING-COLL: *the*N

mink /mɪŋk/ **minks.** **Mink** can also be used as the plural form. ◆◇◇◇◇

1 A **mink** is a small furry animal with highly valued fur. *...a proposal for a ban on the hunting of foxes, mink and hares.* N-COUNT ► **Mink** is the fur of a mink. *...cashmere coats lined with mink. ...a mink coat.* N-UNCOUNT: oft N n

2 A **mink** is a coat or other garment made from the fur of a mink. *Some people like to dress up in minks and diamonds.* N-COUNT

minnow /mɪnoʊ/ **minnows.** A **minnow** is a very small freshwater fish. N-COUNT

minor /maɪnəʳ/ **minors** ◆◆◆◇◇

1 You use **minor** when you want to describe something that is less important, serious, or significant than other things in a group or situation. *She is known in Italy for a number of minor roles in films... Western officials say the problem is minor, and should be quickly overcome.* ADJ-GRADED ≠major

2 A **minor** illness or operation is not likely to be dangerous to someone's life or health. *Sarah had been plagued continually by a series of minor illnesses since her mid teens... His mother had to go to the hospital for minor surgery.* ADJ-GRADED: usu ADJ n ≠major

3 In European music, a **minor** scale is one in which the third note is three semitones higher than the first. *...the unfinished sonata movement in F minor.* ADJ: n ADJ, ADJ n ≠major

4 A **minor** is a person who is still legally a child. In Britain, people are minors until they reach the age of eighteen. *The approach has virtually ended cigarette sales to minors.* N-COUNT

minority /mɪnɒrɪti, AM -nɔːr-/ **minorities** ◆◆◆◆◇

1 If you talk about a **minority** of people or things in a larger group, you are referring to a number of them that forms less than half of the larger group, usually much less than half. *Local authority nursery provision covers only a tiny minority of working mothers... These children are only a small minority. ...minority shareholders.* N-SING: oft N *of* n ≠majority ● If people are **in a minority** or **in the minority**, they belong to a group of people or things that form less than half of a larger group. *Even in the 1960s, politically active students and academics were in a minority... In the past conservatives have been in the minority.* PHRASE: usu v-link PHR

2 A **minority** is a group of people of the same race, culture, or religion who live in a place where most of the people around them are of a different race, culture, or religion. *...the region's ethnic minorities... Students have called for greater numbers of women and minorities on the faculty... A final settlement must respect minority rights.* N-COUNT

minstrel /mɪnstrəl/ **minstrels.** In medieval times, a **minstrel** was a singer and musician who travelled around and performed for noble families. ◆◇◇◇◇ N-COUNT

mint /mɪnt/ **mints, minting, minted** ◆◆◇◇◇

1 **Mint** is a herb. *Garnish with mint sprigs.* N-UNCOUNT

2 A **mint** is a sweet with a peppermint flavour. Some people suck mints in order to make their breath smell fresher. N-COUNT

3 The **mint** is the place where the official coins of a country are made. *In 1965 the mint stopped putting silver in dimes.* N-COUNT: usu sing, usu *the* N

4 To **mint** coins or medals means to make them in a mint. *...the right to mint coins. ...its collection of locally minted Saxon coins.* ♦ **minting** *...the minting of new gold coins.* VERB V n V-ed N-UNCOUNT

5 If you say that someone makes a **mint**, you mean that they make a very large amount of money; an informal use. *Everybody thinks I'm making a mint... They were worth a mint.* N-SING: usu *a* N =pile

6 If you say that something is **in mint condition**, you mean that it is in perfect condition. PHRASE: usu v-link PHR

minted /mɪntɪd/. If you describe something as **newly minted** or **freshly minted**, you mean that it is very new, and that it has only just been produced or completed. *He seemed to be pleased by this newly minted vehicle. ...the movie's freshly minted script.* ADJ: usu ADJ n, adv ADJ

mint sauce. **Mint sauce** is a sauce made from mint leaves, vinegar, and sugar, which is often eaten with lamb in Britain. N-UNCOUNT

minuet /mɪnjuet/ **minuets**

1 In the music of the seventeenth and eighteenth centuries, a **minuet** is a section of a longer piece. Minuets are played at moderate speed and have three beats in a bar. N-COUNT

2 A **minuet** is a fairly slow and formal dance which was popular in the seventeenth and eighteenth centuries. N-COUNT

minus /maɪnəs/ **minuses** ◆◆◇◇◇

1 You use **minus** to show that one number or quantity is being subtracted from another. *One minus one is zero... They've been promised their full July salary minus the hardship payment.* CONJ-COORD =less ≠plus

2 **Minus** before a number or quantity means that the number or quantity is less than zero. *The aircraft was subjected to temperatures of minus 65 degrees and plus 120 degrees.* ADJ: ADJ amount ≠plus

3 Teachers use **minus** in grading work in schools and colleges. 'B minus' is not as good as 'B', but is a better grade than 'C'. *I'm giving him a B minus.* ≠plus

4 If someone or something is **minus** something, they do not have that thing. *The film company collapsed, leaving Chris jobless and minus his life savings.* PREP =without

5 A **minus** is a disadvantage; an informal use. *The minuses far outweigh that possible gain... The plusses and minuses were about equal... None of these minus points will have been mentioned.* N-COUNT =drawback ≠plus

6 You use **plus or minus** to give the amount by which a particular number may vary. *The poll has a margin of error of plus or minus 5 per cent.* PHRASE: PHR amount

minuscule /mɪnɪskjuːl/. If you describe something as **minuscule**, you mean that it is very small. *The film was shot in 17 days, a minuscule amount of time.* ADJ

minus sign, minus signs. A **minus sign** is the sign (−) which is put between two numbers in order to show that the second number is being subtracted from the first one. It is also put before a number to show that the number is less than zero. N-COUNT

minute 1 noun and verb uses

minute /mɪnɪt/ **minutes, minuting, minuted** ◆◆◆◆◆

1 A **minute** is one of the sixty parts that an hour is divided into. People often say **'a minute'** or **'minutes'** when they mean a short length of time. *The pizza will then take about twenty minutes to cook... Bye mum, see you in a minute... Half a minute later she came in the front door... Within minutes we realized our mistake.* N-COUNT: oft num N

2 The **minutes** of a meeting are the written records of the things that are discussed or decided at it. *He'd been reading the minutes of the last meeting.* N-PLURAL: oft N *of* n

3 When someone **minutes** something that is discussed or decided at a meeting, they make a written record of it. *You don't need to minute that.* VERB V n

4 See also **up-to-the-minute**.

5 People often use expressions such as **wait a minute** or **just a minute** when they want to stop you doing or saying something. *Wait a minute, folks, something is wrong here... Hey, just a minute!* PHRASES CONVENTION PRAGMATICS =hang on

6 If you say that something will or may happen **at any minute** or **any minute now**, you are emphasizing that it is likely to happen very soon. *It looked as though it might rain at any minute... He ought to be back any minute... Any minute now, that phone is going to ring.* PRAGMATICS

7 If you say that you do **not** believe **for a minute** or **for one minute** that something is true, you are emphasizing that you do not believe that it is true. *I don't believe for one minute she would have been scared... I don't believe him for a minute.* with brd-neg, PHR with v PRAGMATICS =for a moment

8 A **last-minute** action is one that is done at the lat- PHR n,

est time possible. *She was doing some last-minute revision for her exams... The location has been changed at the last minute... He will probably wait until the last minute.* prep PHR

9 You use the expression **the next minute** or expressions such as '**one minute** he was there, **the next** he was gone' to emphasize that something happens suddenly, especially when it is very different from what was happening before. *The next minute my father came in... Jobs are there one minute, gone the next.* PRAGMATICS =the next moment

10 If you say that something happens **the minute** something else happens, you are emphasizing that it happens immediately after the other thing. *The minute you do this, you'll lose control... The minute that the war started, everybody was glued to the television.* PHR that PRAGMATICS =the moment

11 If you say that something must be done **this minute**, you are emphasizing that it must be done immediately. *I need to speak with her right this minute... Anna, stop that. Sit down this minute.* PRAGMATICS =now, immediately

minute 2 adjective use

minute /maɪnjuːt, AM -nuːt/ **minutest.** If you say that something is **minute**, you mean that it is very small. *Only a minute amount is needed... The party was planned in the minutest detail.* ◆◇◇◇◇ ADJ-GRADED =tiny

minutely /maɪnjuːtli, AM -nuːt-/

1 You use **minutely** to indicate that something is done in great detail. *The metal is then minutely examined to ensure there are no cracks... They follow minutely the news from abroad on Cable News Network.* ADV-GRADED: ADV with v =meticulously

2 You use **minutely** to indicate that the size or extent of something is very small. *The benefit of an x-ray far outweighs the minutely increased risk of cancer.* ADV-GRADED: usu ADV adj/-ed

minutiae /maɪnjuːʃiiː, AM mɪnuːʃ-/. The **minutiae** of something such as someone's job or life are the very small details of it; a formal word. *Much of his early work is concerned with the minutiae of rural life.* N-PLURAL: usu *the* N *of* n =fine details

miracle /mɪrəkəl/ **miracles** ◆◆◇◇◇

1 If you say that an event, discovery, or invention is a **miracle**, you mean that it is very surprising and fortunate. *It is a miracle no one was killed... The Italian economic miracle has always been a mystery... Few teachers have any miracle cures for bad spelling.* N-COUNT

2 A **miracle** is a wonderful and surprising event that is believed to be caused by God. *...the miracle of the Virgin Birth. ...Jesus's ability to perform miracles.* N-COUNT

miraculous /mɪrækjʊləs/ ◆◇◇◇◇

1 If you describe something as **miraculous**, you mean that it is very surprising and fortunate. *The horse made a miraculous recovery to finish a close third. ...a miraculous escape... The change in Felicity was miraculous.* ♦ **miraculously** *Miraculously, the guards escaped death or serious injury... We miraculously survived the crossing to Muscat.* ADJ-GRADED =amazing; ADV-GRADED: usu ADV with cl, ADV with v, also ADV adj

2 If someone describes a wonderful event as **miraculous**, they believe the event has been caused by God. *...miraculous healing. ...miraculous powers.* ♦ **miraculously** *He was miraculously healed of a severe fever.* ADJ; ADV: usu ADV with v

mirage /mɪrɑːʒ/ **mirages**

1 A **mirage** is something which you see when it is extremely hot, for example in the desert, and which appears to be quite near but is actually a long way away or does not really exist. *Through my half-closed eyelids I began to see mirages... It hovered before his eyes like the mirage of an oasis.* N-COUNT

2 If you describe something as a **mirage**, you mean that it is an illusion although it may seem real. *The girl was a mirage, cast up by his troubled mind... The objectivity of science is a mirage.* N-COUNT: usu sing =illusion

mire /maɪəʳ/

1 You can refer to an unpleasant or difficult situation as a **mire** of some kind; a literary use. *...a mire of poverty and ignorance.* N-SING: oft N *of* n =quagmire

2 **Mire** is dirt or mud; a literary use. *...the muck and mire of sewers and farmyards.* N-UNCOUNT =muck

mirror /mɪrəʳ/ **mirrors, mirroring, mirrored** ◆◆◆◇◇

1 A **mirror** is a flat piece of glass which reflects light, so that when you look at it you can see yourself reflected in it. *He went into the bathroom absent-mindedly and looked at himself in the mirror... He checked his mirror and saw that a dark coloured van was immediately behind him.* ♦ **mirrored** *...a mirrored ceiling.* N-COUNT; ADJ

2 If something **mirrors** something else, it has similar features to it, and therefore seems like a copy or representation of it. *Despite the fact that I have tried to be objective, the book inevitably mirrors my own interests and experiences... His own shock was mirrored on her face.* VERB =reflect V n

3 If you see something reflected in water, you can say that the water **mirrors** it; a literary use. *...the sudden glitter where a newly-flooded field mirrors the sky... The ship would lie there mirrored in a perfectly unmoving glossy sea.* VERB =reflect V n V-ed

mirror image, mirror images; also spelled **mirror-image.** If something is a **mirror image** of something else, it is like a reflection of it, either because it is exactly the same or because it is the same but reversed. *I saw in him a mirror image of my younger self... This is almost the mirror image of the situation in Scotland.* ◆◇◇◇◇ N-COUNT: oft N *of* n

mirth /mɜːʳθ/. **Mirth** is amusement which you express by laughing; a literary word. *That caused considerable mirth amongst pupils and sports masters alike... It was all he could do to stop tears of mirth falling down his cheeks.* N-UNCOUNT =hilarity

mirthless /mɜːʳθləs/. If someone gives a **mirthless** laugh or smile, it is obvious that they are not really amused; used in written English. *He permitted himself a small mirthless smile.* ADJ: usu ADJ n

mis- /mɪs-/. **Mis-** is added to some verbs and nouns to form new verbs and nouns which indicate that something is done badly or wrongly. *The local newspaper misreported the story by claiming the premises were rented... He was eventually convicted for the misuse of official funds.* PREFIX

misadventure /mɪsədventʃəʳ/ **misadventures.** A **misadventure** is an unfortunate incident; a formal word. *...a series of misadventures... A verdict of death by misadventure was recorded.* N-VAR

misanthrope /mɪzənθroʊp/ **misanthropes.** A **misanthrope** is a person who does not like other people; a formal word. N-COUNT

misanthropic /mɪzənθrɒpik/. If you describe a person or their feelings as **misanthropic**, you mean that they do not like other people; a formal word. *His father was a misanthropic but successful businessman.* ADJ-GRADED

misanthropy /mɪzænθrəpi/. **Misanthropy** is a general dislike of people; a formal word. N-UNCOUNT

misapplication /mɪsæplɪkeɪʃən/ **misapplications.** If you talk about the **misapplication** of something, you mean it is used for a purpose it was not intended for. *He's charged with conspiracy, misapplication of funds and other crimes. ...a common misapplication of the law.* N-VAR: usu N *of* n =misuse

misapply /mɪsəplaɪ/ **misapplies, misapplying, misapplied.** If something **is misapplied**, it is used for a purpose for which it is not intended or not suitable. *Many lines from Shakespeare's plays are misquoted and misapplied... The law had been misapplied.* VB: usu passive =misused *be* V-ed

misapprehension /mɪsæprɪhenʃən/ **misapprehensions.** A **misapprehension** is a wrong idea or impression that you have about something. *Men still appear to be labouring under the misapprehension that women want hairy, muscular men... We were by now under no misapprehension about the extent of the problem.* N-VAR: oft N that, *under* N =misunderstanding

misappropriate /mɪsəproʊprieɪt/ **misappropriates, misappropriating, misappropriated.** If someone **misappropriates** money which does not belong to them, they take it without permission and use it for their own purposes. *I took no money for personal use and have not misappropriated any funds whatsoever... A total of $500 million is alleged to have been misappropriated.* VERB =embezzle V n

♦ **misappropriation** /mɪsəproʊprieɪʃən/ *He pleaded guilty to charges of misappropriation of bank funds.* N-UNCOUNT: usu N of n

misbehave /mɪsbɪheɪv/ **misbehaves, misbehaving, misbehaved.** If someone, especially a child, **misbehaves**, they behave in a way that is not acceptable to other people. *When the children misbehaved she was unable to cope.* VERB; V

misbehaviour /mɪsbɪheɪvjə^r/; spelled **misbehavior** in American English. **Misbehaviour** is behaviour that is not acceptable to other people; a formal word. *If the toddler had been dealt with properly at first, the rest of his misbehaviour would have been avoided.* N-UNCOUNT =misconduct

miscalculate /mɪskælkjʊleɪt/ **miscalculates, miscalculating, miscalculated.** If you **miscalculate**, you make a mistake in judging a situation or in making a calculation. *It's clear that he has badly miscalculated the mood of the people... The government appears to have miscalculated and bills are higher as a result.* ♦ **miscalculation** /mɪskælkjʊleɪʃən/ **miscalculations** *The coup failed because of miscalculations by the plotters... Southwark council admitted making serious miscalculations in this year's budget.* ◆◇◇◇◇ VERB; V n; V; N-VAR

miscarriage /mɪskærɪdʒ, -kær-/ **miscarriages.** If a woman has a **miscarriage**, she gives birth to a foetus before it is properly formed and it dies. ◆◆◇◇◇ N-VAR

miscarriage of justice, miscarriages of justice. A **miscarriage of justice** is a wrong decision made by a court, as a result of which an innocent person is punished. *I can imagine no greater miscarriage of justice than the execution of an innocent man. ...a report whose conclusions were that no miscarriage of justice had taken place.* ◆◇◇◇◇ N-VAR

miscarry /mɪskæri, -kæri/ **miscarries, miscarrying, miscarried.** If a woman **miscarries**, she has a miscarriage. *Many women who miscarry eventually have healthy babies.* VERB; V; Also V n

miscast /mɪskɑːst, -kæst/. If someone who is acting in a play or film is **miscast**, the role that they have is not suitable for them, so that they appear silly or unconvincing to the audience. ADJ-GRADED: usu v-link ADJ

miscellaneous /mɪsəleɪniəs/. A **miscellaneous** group consists of many different kinds of things or people that are difficult to put into a particular category. *...a hoard of miscellaneous junk... They eat a lot of meats and dairy foods, along with a lot of miscellaneous items that don't fall into any group.* ◆◇◇◇◇ ADJ-GRADED: ADJ n =assorted

miscellany /mɪseləni, AM mɪsəleɪni/ **miscellanies.** A **miscellany** of things is a collection or group of many different kinds of things; used in written English. *...glass cases filled with a miscellany of objects... The top drawer held a miscellany of foreign coins and banknotes.* N-COUNT: oft N of n =assortment

mischief /mɪstʃɪf/ ◆◇◇◇◇

1 **Mischief** is eagerness to have fun, especially by embarrassing people or by playing harmless tricks. *His eyes were full of mischief... She radiated health and mischief... The little lad was a real handful. He was always up to mischief.* N-UNCOUNT

2 **Mischief** is behaviour that is intended to cause trouble for people. *...a play about the mischief that young people get up to when they're not employed... They withdrew their support after the President described the conference as a platform to cause political mischief.* N-UNCOUNT

3 **Mischief** is the harm that someone or something does. *Voters have wisely never given him an overall parliamentary majority. There is no knowing what mischief he might have caused if they had.* N-UNCOUNT =harm

mischief-maker, mischief-makers. If you say that someone is a **mischief-maker**, you are criticising them for saying or doing things which are intended to cause trouble between people. *The letter had come from an unknown mischief-maker.* N-COUNT PRAGMATICS =stirrer

mischievous /mɪstʃɪvəs/ ◆◇◇◇◇

1 A **mischievous** person likes to have fun by playing harmless tricks or embarrassing people. *She rocks back and forth on her chair like a mischievous child... He's a little mischievous.* ♦ **mischievously** *Kathryn winked mischievously.* ADJ-GRADED =impish; ADV-GRADED: usu ADV with v

2 A **mischievous** act or suggestion is intended to cause trouble. *A statement issued after the meeting speaks of a mischievous campaign by the press to divide the ANC... The Foreign Office dismissed the story as mischievous and false.* ♦ **mischievously** *That does not require 'massive' military intervention, as some have mischievously claimed.* ADJ-GRADED =malicious; ADV-GRADED: usu ADV with v

misconceived /mɪskənsiːvd/. If you describe a plan or method as **misconceived**, you mean it is not the right one for dealing with a particular problem or situation. *The teachers say the tests for 14-year-olds are misconceived. ...Lawrence's worthy but misconceived idea.* ADJ-GRADED PRAGMATICS =misguided

misconception /mɪskənsepʃən/ **misconceptions.** A **misconception** is an idea that is not correct or which has been misunderstood. *It is a misconception that Peggy was fabulously wealthy... There are many fears and misconceptions about cancer.* ◆◇◇◇◇ N-COUNT =fallacy

misconduct /mɪskɒndʌkt/. **Misconduct** is bad or unacceptable behaviour, especially by a professional person. *He was dismissed from his job for gross misconduct after handing over confidential documents to the press... Dr Lee was cleared of serious professional misconduct.* ◆◇◇◇◇ N-UNCOUNT

misconstrue /mɪskənstruː/ **misconstrues, misconstruing, misconstrued.** If you **misconstrue** something that has been said or something that happens, you interpret it wrongly; a formal word. *An outsider might misconstrue the nature of the relationship... Jordan's policy has been misconstrued.* VERB =misinterpret; V n

miscreant /mɪskriənt/ **miscreants.** A **miscreant** is someone who has done something illegal or behaved badly; a literary word. *Local people demanded that the District Magistrate apprehend the miscreants.* N-COUNT =wrongdoer

misdeed /mɪsdiːd/ **misdeeds.** A **misdeed** is a bad or evil act; a formal word. *...the alleged financial misdeeds of his government.* N-COUNT

misdemeanour /mɪsdɪmiːnə^r/ **misdemeanours;** spelled **misdemeanor** in American English.

1 A **misdemeanour** is an act that some people consider to be wrong or unacceptable; a formal use. *Emily knew nothing about her husband's misdemeanours. ...his financial misdemeanours.* N-COUNT

2 In countries where the legal system distinguishes between very serious crimes and less serious ones, a **misdemeanour** is a less serious crime; a legal use. *She was charged with a misdemeanour, that of carrying a concealed weapon.* N-COUNT

misdirect /mɪsdɪrekt, -daɪr-/ **misdirects, misdirecting, misdirected**

1 If resources or efforts **are misdirected**, they are used for or based upon wrong or inappropriate goals. *Many of the aid projects in the developing world have been misdirected in the past.* ♦ **misdirected** *...a misdirected effort to mollify the bishop.* VB: usu passive; be V-ed; ADJ-GRADED

2 If you **misdirect** someone, you send them in the wrong direction. *He had deliberately misdirected the reporters.* VERB; V n

miser /maɪzə^r/ **misers.** If you say that someone is a **miser**, you disapprove of them because they are very mean and hate spending money. *I'm married to a miser.* N-COUNT PRAGMATICS =skinflint

miserable /mɪzərəbəl/ ◆◆◇◇◇

1 If you are **miserable**, you are very unhappy. *I took a series of badly paid secretarial jobs which made me really miserable... She went to bed, miserable and depressed.* ♦ **miserably** /mɪzərəbli/ *He looked miserably down at his plate.* ADJ-GRADED: usu v-link ADJ; ADV-GRADED: usu ADV after v

2 If you describe a place or situation as **miserable,** you mean that it makes you feel unhappy or depressed. *There was nothing at all in this miserable place to distract him.* ADJ-GRADED: usu ADJ n =depressing

3 If you describe the weather as **miserable**, you mean that it makes you feel depressed, because it is raining or dull. *On a grey, wet, miserable day our* ADJ-GRADED =depressing

teams congregated in Port Hamble... It was very cold, damp and miserable.

4 If you describe someone as **miserable**, you mean that you do not like them because they are bad-tempered or unfriendly. *He always was a miserable man. He never spoke to me nor anybody else, not even to pass the time of day.* [ADJ-GRADED: ADJ n =grumpy]

5 You can describe a quantity as **miserable** when you think that it is much smaller than it ought to be. *Our speed over the ground was a miserable 2.2 knots... It has so far accepted a miserable 1,100 refugees from the former Yugoslavia.* ♦ **miserably** *...the miserably inadequate supply of books now provided for schools.* [ADJ: usu a ADJ amount PRAGMATICS =paltry, measly] [ADV: ADV adj]

6 A **miserable** failure is very disappointing or humiliating. *The film was a miserable commercial failure both in Italy and in the United States.* ♦ **miserably** *Some manage it. Some fail miserably.* [ADJ: ADJ n] [ADV: ADV with v]

miserly /maɪzəʳli/

1 If you describe someone as **miserly**, you disapprove of them because they are very mean and hate spending money. *He is miserly with both his time and his money.* [ADJ-GRADED PRAGMATICS =mean]

2 If you describe an amount of something as **miserly**, you are critical of it because it is very small. *Being a student today with miserly grants and limited career prospects is difficult.* [ADJ-GRADED: usu ADJ n PRAGMATICS =measly]

misery /mɪzəri/ **miseries** ◆◆◇◇◇

1 **Misery** is great unhappiness. *All that money brought nothing but sadness and misery and tragedy. ...the miseries of his youth.* [N-VAR]

2 **Misery** is the way of life and unpleasant living conditions of people who are very poor. *A tiny, educated elite profited from the misery of their two million fellow countrymen.* [N-UNCOUNT =deprivation]

3 If you say that someone is a **misery**, you are critical of them because they are always complaining; used mainly in informal British English. *I'm not such a misery now! I gave up drink a few years back and that has changed things a lot.* [N-COUNT PRAGMATICS]

4 If someone **makes** your **life a misery**, they behave in an unpleasant way towards you over a period of time and make you very unhappy. *I would really like living here if it wasn't for the gangs of kids who make our lives a misery.* [PHRASES V and *life* inflect =make your life hell]

5 If you **put** someone **out of** their **misery**, you tell them something that they are very anxious to know; an informal use. *Please put me out of my misery. How do you do it?* [V inflects]

6 If you **put** an animal **out of** its **misery**, you kill it because it is ill or injured and cannot be cured or healed. [V inflects =put down]

misfire /mɪsfaɪəʳ/ **misfires, misfiring, misfired**

1 If a plan **misfires**, it goes wrong and does not have the results that you intend it to have. *Some of their policies had misfired.* [VERB V]

2 If an engine **misfires**, it fails to ignite when it should. *The boat's engine misfired after he tried to start it up.* [VERB V]

3 If a gun **misfires**, the bullet is not sent out as it should be when the gun is fired. *The gun misfired after one shot and jammed.* [VERB V]

misfit /mɪsfɪt/ **misfits.** A **misfit** is a person who is not easily accepted by other people, often because their behaviour is very different from that of everyone else. *I have been made to feel a social and psychological misfit for not wanting children.* [◆◇◇◇◇ N-COUNT]

misfortune /mɪsfɔːʳtʃuːn/ **misfortunes.** A **misfortune** is something unpleasant or unlucky that happens to someone. *She seemed to enjoy the misfortunes of others... He had his full share of misfortune.* [◆◇◇◇◇ N-VAR]

misgiving /mɪsgɪvɪŋ/ **misgivings.** If you have **misgivings** about something that is being proposed or done, you feel that it is not quite right, and you are worried that it may have undesirable consequences. *She had some misgivings about what she was about to do... The first words of the text filled us with misgiving.* [◆◇◇◇◇ N-VAR =doubt]

misguided /mɪsgaɪdɪd/. If you describe an opinion or plan as **misguided**, you are critical of it because you think it is based on a mistake or misunderstanding. *In a misguided attempt to be funny, he manages only offensiveness... He is misguided in expecting honesty from her.* [◆◇◇◇◇ ADJ-GRADED PRAGMATICS]

mishandle /mɪshændəl/ **mishandles, mishandling, mishandled.** If you say that someone **has mishandled** something, you are critical of them because you think they have dealt with it badly or inefficiently. *She completely mishandled an important project purely through lack of attention... The judge said the police had mishandled the siege.* ♦ **mishandling** *...the Government's mishandling of the economy.* [VERB PRAGMATICS =mismanage] [V n] [N-UNCOUNT: usu poss N of n]

mishap /mɪshæp/ **mishaps.** A **mishap** is an unfortunate but not very serious event that happens to someone. *After a number of mishaps she did manage to get back to Germany... The plot passed off without mishap.* [◆◇◇◇◇ N-VAR =incident]

mishear /mɪshɪəʳ/ **mishears, mishearing, misheard.** If you **mishear** what someone says, you hear it incorrectly, so that you think that they said something different. *You misheard me, Frank... She must have misheard.* [VERB] [V n] [V]

mishmash /mɪʃmæʃ/; also spelled **mish-mash**. If you say that something is a **mishmash**, you are criticizing it because it is a confused mixture of different types of things. *The letter was a mishmash of ill-fitting proposals taken from two different reform plans. ...a bizarre mishmash of colours and patterns.* [N-SING: usu a N of n PRAGMATICS =hotch-potch, hodgepodge]

misinform /mɪsɪnfɔːʳm/ **misinforms, misinforming, misinformed.** If you **are misinformed**, you are told something that is wrong or inaccurate. *He has been misinformed by members of his own party... We were clearly misinformed... The president defended the news blackout, accusing the media of misinforming the people.* [VERB =mislead] [be V-ed] [V n]

misinformation /mɪsɪnfəʳmeɪʃən/. **Misinformation** is wrong information which is given to someone, often in a deliberate attempt to make them believe something which is not true. *This was a deliberate piece of misinformation.* [N-UNCOUNT]

misinterpret /mɪsɪntɜːʳprɪt/ **misinterprets, misinterpreting, misinterpreted.** If you **misinterpret** something, you understand it wrongly. *He was amazed that he'd misinterpreted the situation so completely... The Prince's words had been misinterpreted.* ♦ **misinterpretation** /mɪsɪntɜːʳprɪteɪʃən/ **misinterpretations** *The message left no room for misinterpretation. ...a misinterpretation of the aims and ends of socialism.* [◆◇◇◇◇ VERB =misread] [V n] [N-VAR]

misjudge /mɪsdʒʌdʒ/ **misjudges, misjudging, misjudged.** If you say that someone **has misjudged** a person or situation, you mean that they have formed an incorrect idea or opinion about them, and often that they have made a wrong decision as a result of this. *Perhaps I had misjudged him, and he was not so predictable after all... As I swung down from out of my bunk, I got dizzy and misjudged the distance.* [◆◇◇◇◇ VERB] [V n]

misjudgement /mɪsdʒʌdʒmənt/ **misjudgements**; also spelled **misjudgment**. A **misjudgement** is an incorrect idea or opinion that is formed about someone or something, especially when a wrong decision is made as a result of this. *...a misjudgement in British foreign policy which had far-reaching consequences... Many accidents were due to pilot misjudgement.* [N-VAR]

mislay /mɪsleɪ/ **mislays, mislaying, mislaid.** If you **mislay** something, you put it somewhere and then forget where you have put it. *I appear to have mislaid my jumper.* [VERB =misplace] [V n]

mislead /mɪsliːd/ **misleads, misleading, misled.** If you say that someone **has misled** you, you mean that they have made you believe something which is not true, either by telling you a lie or by giving you a wrong idea or impression. *Jack was furious with his London doctors for having misled him... Mr Kinnock accused him of misleading Parliament.* [◆◇◇◇◇ VERB =misinform] [V n]

misleading /mɪsliːdɪŋ/. If you describe something as **misleading**, you mean that it gives you a [◆◆◇◇◇ ADJ-GRADED: oft *it* v-link ADJ] wrong idea or impression. *It would be misleading to say that we were friends... The article contains several misleading statements.* to-inf ♦ **misleadingly** ADV-GRADED: usu ADV with v, also ADV adj *The data had been presented misleadingly.*

misled /mɪsle̲d/. **Misled** is the past tense and past participle of **mislead**.

mismanage /mɪsmæ̲nɪdʒ/ **mismanages, mismanaging, mismanaged.** VERB =mishandle To **mismanage** something means to manage it badly. Vn *75% of voters think the President has mismanaged the economy.*

mismanagement /mɪsmæ̲nɪdʒmənt/. ◆◇◇◇◇ N-UNCOUNT: oft poss N, N of n =mishandling Someone's **mismanagement** of a system or organization is the bad or incompetent way they deal with or organize it. *...the Government's economic mismanagement... His gross mismanagement left the company desperately in need of restructuring.*

mismatch, mismatches, mismatching, mismatched. The noun is pronounced /mɪ̲smætʃ/. The verb is pronounced /mɪsmæ̲tʃ/.

1 If there is a **mismatch** between two or more things or people, they do not go together well or are not suitable for each other. N-COUNT: oft N *between*/*of* pl-n, N *of* pl-n *There is a mismatch between the skills offered by people and the skills needed by industry. ...an unfortunate mismatch of styles.*

2 To **mismatch** things or people means to put them together although they do not go together well or are not suitable for each other. VERB V pl-n *She was deliberately mismatching articles of clothing.* ♦ **mismatched** ADJ-GRADED *The two opponents are mismatched.*

misnamed /mɪsne̲ɪmd/. V-PASSIVE If you say that something or someone **is misnamed**, you mean that they have a name that describes them badly or incorrectly. *...a high school teacher who was misnamed Mr. Witty.* be V-ed n *...the misnamed Grand Hotel...* V-ed *The truth is that junk bonds were misnamed, and therefore misunderstood.* be V-ed

misnomer /mɪsno̲ʊmə^r/ **misnomers.** N-COUNT: usu a N in sing If you say that something is a **misnomer**, you mean that it is a word or name that describes something wrongly or inaccurately. *Herbal 'tea' is something of a misnomer because these drinks contain no tea at all.*

misogynist /mɪsɒ̲dʒɪnɪst, maɪs-/ **misogynists**

1 A **misogynist** is a man who hates women. N-COUNT

2 **Misogynist** attitudes or actions are ones that are inspired by or express a hatred of women. ADJ: usu ADJ n

misogyny /mɪsɒ̲dʒɪni/. N-UNCOUNT **Misogyny** is a strong and irrational dislike of women.

misplace /mɪsple̲ɪs/ **misplaces, misplacing, misplaced.** VERB =mislay If you **misplace** something, you lose it, usually only temporarily. Vn *He misplaces his reading glasses with such regularity that aides carry extras... Somehow the suitcase with my clothes was misplaced.*

misplaced /mɪsple̲ɪst/. ◆◇◇◇◇ ADJ-GRADED PRAGMATICS If you describe a feeling or action as **misplaced**, you are critical of it because you think it is inappropriate, or directed towards the wrong thing or person. *A telling sign of misplaced priorities is the concentration on health not environmental issues... I think your concern is misplaced. Ackroyd is no threat to anyone.*

misprint /mɪ̲sprɪnt/ **misprints.** N-COUNT A **misprint** is a mistake in the way something is printed, for example a spelling mistake.

mispronounce /mɪsprəna̲ʊns/ **mispronounces, mispronouncing, mispronounced.** VERB If you **mispronounce** a word, you pronounce it wrongly. Vn *He repeatedly mispronounced words and slurred his speech.*

misquote /mɪskwo̲ʊt/ **misquotes, misquoting, misquoted.** VERB If someone **is misquoted**, something that they have said or written is repeated inaccurately. *Mr Hurd denied the news story, and insists that he was misquoted...* be V-ed *The case was brought by a psychoanalyst who says a journalist misquoted him in a series of magazine articles.* Vn

misread /mɪsri̲ːd/ **misreads, misreading.** The form **misread** is used in the present tense, and is the past tense and past participle, when it is pronounced /mɪsre̲d/.

1 If you **misread** a situation or someone's behaviour, you do not understand it properly. VERB =misinterpret Vn *The government largely misread the mood of the electorate... Mothers may also misread signals and think the baby is crying because he is hungry.* ♦ **misreading, misreadings** N-COUNT *...a misreading of opinion in France.*

2 If you **misread** something that has been written or printed, you look at it and think that it says something that it does not say. VERB Vn *His chauffeur misread his route and took a wrong turning.*

misrepresent /mɪsreprɪze̲nt/ **misrepresents, misrepresenting, misrepresented.** ◆◇◇◇◇ VERB If someone **misrepresents** a person or situation, they give a wrong or inaccurate account of what the person or situation is like. *He said that the press had misrepresented him as arrogant and bullying...* V n as adj, V n as n *Hollywood films misrepresented us as terrorists and drunks, maniacs and murderers...* Vn *Keynes deliberately misrepresented the views of his opponents... The spokesman said that the extent of the current strike is being misrepresented.* ♦ **misrepresentation** /mɪsreprɪzente̲ɪʃ^ən/ **misrepresentations** N-VAR *I wish to point out your misrepresentation of the facts... The programme's researchers are guilty of bias and misrepresentation.*

misrule /mɪsru̲ːl/. N-UNCOUNT PRAGMATICS If you refer to someone's government of a country as **misrule**, you are critical of them for governing their country unfairly or inefficiently. *He was arrested last December, accused of corruption and misrule... In the 17 years of his misrule, famines intensified and rebellions multiplied.*

miss 1 used as a title or a form of address

Miss /mɪs/ **Misses** ◆◆◆◆◇

1 You use **Miss** in front of the name of a girl or unmarried woman when you are speaking to her or referring to her. N-TITLE PRAGMATICS *It was nice talking to you, Miss Giroux... Miss Singleton didn't call back, did she?... The club was run by Miss Ivy Streeter.*

2 In some schools, children address their women teachers as **Miss**. N-VOC PRAGMATICS *'Chivers!'—'Yes, Miss?'*

3 People sometimes address young women as **Miss**; an old-fashioned use. N-VOC PRAGMATICS *'I wouldn't know about that, Miss,' the woman said, backing away.*

4 **Miss** is used in front of the name of a place or region to refer to the young woman who has been chosen in a competition as the most beautiful woman there. N-TITLE *Kappy was named Miss Hawaii in 1954. ...two former Miss Scotlands.*

miss 2 verb and noun uses

miss /mɪs/ **misses, missing, missed** ◆◆◆◆◇

1 If you **miss** something, you fail to hit it, for example when you have thrown something at it or you have shot a bullet at it. VERB ≠hit *She hurled the ashtray across the room, narrowly missing my head...* Vn *When I'd missed a few times, he suggested I rest the rifle on a rock to steady it.* V ► Also a noun. N-COUNT *After more misses, they finally put two arrows into the lion's chest.*

2 In sport, if you **miss** a shot, you fail to get the ball in the goal, net, or hole. VERB Vn *He scored four of the goals but missed a penalty.* Also V ► Also a noun. N-COUNT *Striker Alan Smith was guilty of two glaring misses.*

3 If you **miss** something, you fail to notice it. VERB ≠spot Vn *From this vantage point he watched, his searching eye never missing a detail... It's the first thing you see as you come round the corner. You can't miss it... Sergeant Cobbins was an experienced officer and didn't miss much.*

4 If you **miss** the meaning or importance of something, you fail to understand or appreciate it. VERB ≠get Vn *Tambov had slightly missed the point... She seems to have missed the joke.*

5 If you **miss** a chance or opportunity, you fail to take advantage of it. VERB ≠seize Vn *Capriati knew that she had missed her chance of victory... It was too good an opportunity to miss.*

6 If you **miss** someone who is no longer with you or VERB

who has died, you feel sad and wish that they were still with you. *Your mama and I are gonna miss you at Christmas... He was a gentle, sensitive, lovable man who will be missed by a host of friends.* Vn

7 If you **miss** something, you feel sad because you no longer have it or are no longer doing or experiencing it. *I could happily move back into a flat if it wasn't for the fact that I'd miss my garden... He missed having good friends.* VERB Vn/-ing

8 If you **miss** something such as a plane or train, you arrive too late to catch it. *I had already missed my flight, and the next one wasn't until the following morning... He missed the last bus home.* VERB ≠catch Vn

9 If you **miss** something such as a meeting, a show, or an activity, you do not go to it, see it, or take part in it, because you are unable to or have forgotten to, or because you do not want to. *It's a pity Makku and I had to miss our lesson last week... You won't be missing much on TV tonight apart from the usual repeats... 'Are you coming to the show?'—'I wouldn't miss it for the world.'* VERB Vn

10 If you **give** something **a miss**, you decide not to do it or not to go to it; an informal expression. *Do you mind if I give it a miss?* PHRASE: V inflects =skip

11 See also **missing**; **hit and miss**, **near miss**. • to **miss the boat**: see **boat**. • to **not miss a trick**: see **trick**.

miss out PHRASAL VERB

1 If you **miss out** on something that would be beneficial or interesting to you, you are not involved in it or do not take part in it. *We're missing out on a tremendous opportunity... Well, I'm glad you could make it. I didn't want you to miss out.* =lose out VP *on*n VP

2 If you **miss out** something or someone, you fail to include them in something; used mainly in British English. *There should be an apostrophe here, and look, you've missed out the word 'men' altogether!... What about Sally? You've missed her out.* =leave out VP n (not pron) VnP

misshapen /mɪsʃeɪpən/. If you describe something as **misshapen**, you think that it does not have a normal or natural shape. *...misshapen vegetables... Her hands were weary and misshapen by arthritis.* ADJ-GRADED

missile /mɪsaɪl, AM -səl/ **missiles** ◆◆◆◇◇

1 A **missile** is a tube-shaped weapon that moves long distances through the air and explodes when it reaches its target. *The authorities offered to stop firing missiles if the rebels agreed to stop attacking civilian targets. ...nuclear missiles.* N-COUNT

2 Anything that is thrown as a weapon can be called a **missile**. *The football supporters began throwing missiles, one of which hit the referee.* N-COUNT

3 See also **cruise missile**, **guided missile**.

missing /mɪsɪŋ/ ◆◆◆◇◇

1 If something is **missing**, it is not in its usual place, and you cannot find it. *It was only an hour or so later that I discovered that my gun was missing... The playing cards had gone missing.* ADJ: usu v-link ADJ

2 If a part of something is **missing**, it has been removed or has come off, and has not been replaced. *Three buttons were missing from his shirt.* ADJ

3 If you say that something is **missing**, you mean that it has not been included, and you think that it should have been. *What is missing, however, is an internal, artistic cohesion... She had given me an incomplete list. One name was missing from it.* ADJ: usu v-link ADJ, oft ADJ *from* n

4 Someone who is **missing** cannot be found, and it is not known whether they are alive or dead. *Five people died in the explosion and more than one thousand were injured. One person is still missing.* ADJ

• If a member of the armed forces is **missing in action**, they have not returned from a battle, their body has not been found, and they are not thought to have been captured. PHRASE: usu v-link PHR

missing link, missing links. The **missing link** in a situation is the piece of information or evidence that you need in order to make your knowledge or understanding of something complete. *Here was the missing link between the claims that he had murdered his wife and the reason why he had murdered her.* N-COUNT: usu sing

missing person, missing persons. A **missing person** has suddenly left their home without telling their family where they are going, and it is not known whether they are alive or dead. *She's tracked down over two hundred missing persons, in many cases after the police have given up.* N-COUNT

mission /mɪʃən/ **missions** ◆◆◆◆◇

1 A **mission** is an important task that people are given to do, especially one that involves travelling to another country. *Salisbury sent him on a diplomatic mission to North America... He has been on a mission to help end Lebanon's political crisis. ...the most crucial stage of his latest peace mission.* N-COUNT: usu with supp

2 A **mission** is a group of people who have been sent to a foreign country to carry out an official task. *The head of the mission in South Africa. ...a senior member of a diplomatic mission.* N-COUNT: usu with supp =delegation

3 A **mission** is a special journey made by a military aeroplane or space rocket. *...a bomber that crashed during a training mission in the west Texas mountains. ...the first shuttle mission.* N-COUNT: usu supp N

4 If you say that you have a **mission**, you mean that you have a strong commitment and sense of duty to do or achieve something. *He viewed his mission in life as protecting the weak from the evil... There is an enormous sense of mission in his speech and gesture.* N-SING: usu poss N, also n *of* N =calling

5 A **mission** is the activities of a group of Christians who have been sent to a place to teach people about Christianity. *They say God spoke to them and told them to go on a mission to the poorest country in the Western Hemisphere.* N-COUNT

6 A **mission** is a building or group of buildings in which missionary work is carried out. *I reside at the mission at St Michael's. ...schools, monasteries and other mission buildings.* N-COUNT

missionary /mɪʃənri, -neri/ **missionaries** ◆◇◇◇◇

1 A **missionary** is a Christian who has been sent to a foreign country to teach people about Christianity. N-COUNT

2 **Missionary** is used to describe the activities of missionaries. *You should be in missionary work.* ADJ: ADJ n

3 If you refer to someone's enthusiasm for an activity or belief as **missionary** zeal, you are emphasizing that they are very enthusiastic about it. *She had a kind of missionary zeal about bringing culture to the masses.* ADJ: ADJ n PRAGMATICS

missive /mɪsɪv/ **missives.** A **missive** is a letter or other message that someone sends; a literary word that is often used humorously. *...the customary missive from your dear mother.* N-COUNT =epistle

misspell /mɪsspel/ **misspells, misspelling, misspelled** or **misspelt.** If someone **misspells** a word, they spell it wrongly. *Sorry I misspelled your last name.* ♦ **misspelling, misspellings** *...a misspelling of the writer's name.* VERB Vn N-COUNT

misspend /mɪsspend/ **misspends, misspending, misspent.** If you say that time or money **has been misspent**, you disapprove of the way in which it has been spent. *Much of the money was grossly misspent... Ruby recalled getting stoned during her misspent youth.* VERB PRAGMATICS =waste *be*V-ed V-ed

missus /mɪsɪz/

1 Some people refer to a man's wife as his **missus**; an informal use. *That's what bugs my missus more than anything... I do a bit of shopping for the missus.* N-SING: poss/*the* N =old lady

2 In some parts of Britain, people use **missus** as a very informal way of addressing a woman who they do not know. *Thanks, missus.* N-VOC PRAGMATICS

mist /mɪst/ **mists, misting, misted** ◆◆◇◇◇

1 **Mist** consists of a large number of tiny drops of water in the air, which make it difficult to see very far. *Thick mist made flying impossible... A bluish mist hung in the air... Mists and fog swirled about the road.* N-VAR

2 If a piece of glass **mists** or **is misted**, it becomes covered with tiny drops of moisture, so that you cannot see through it easily. *The windows misted, blurring the stark streetlight... The temperature in the car was misting the window.* ▶ **Mist over** and **mist up** mean the same as **mist**. *The front wind-* V-ERG V Vn PHRASAL VERB ERG VP

shield was misting over... She stood in front of the misted-up mirror. V-ed P

3 If someone's eyes **mist**, they cannot see easily because there are tears in their eyes. *Her eyes misted with tears.* ► **Mist over** means the same as **mist**. *His eyes misted over and he started to shake.* VERB V PHRASAL VERB V P

mist over. See **mist** 2 and 3. PHRASAL VERB

mist up. See **mist** 2. PHRASAL VERB

mistake /mɪsteɪk/ **mistakes, mistaking, mistook, mistaken** ◆◆◆◆◇

1 If you make a **mistake**, you do something which you did not intend to do, or which produces a result that you do not want. *They made the big mistake of thinking they could seize its border with a relatively small force... I think it's a serious mistake to confuse books with life... Jonathan says it was his mistake... There must be some mistake... He has been arrested by mistake.* N-COUNT: oft N *of*-ing, also *by* N =error

2 A **mistake** is something or part of something which is incorrect or not right. *Her mother sighed and rubbed out another mistake in the crossword puzzle... Spelling mistakes are often just the result of haste.* N-COUNT =error

3 If you **mistake** one person or thing **for** another, you wrongly think that they are the other person or thing. *I mistook you for Carlos... When hay fever first occurs it is often mistaken for a summer cold.* VERB V n *for* n

4 If you **mistake** something, you fail to recognize or understand it. *The government completely mistook the feeling of the country... No one should mistake how serious the issue is.* VERB =misjudge V n V wh

5 You can say **there is no mistaking** something when you are emphasizing that you cannot fail to recognize or understand it. *There's no mistaking the eastern flavour of the food... There was no mistaking Magda's sincerity, or her pain.* PHRASE: V inflects, PHR n PRAGMATICS

mistaken /mɪsteɪkən/ ◆◆◇◇◇

1 If you are **mistaken** about something, you are wrong about it. *I see I was mistaken about you... You couldn't be more mistaken, Alex. You've utterly misread the situation.* • You use expressions such as **if I'm not mistaken** and **unless I'm very much mistaken** as a polite way of emphasizing the statement you are making, especially when you are confident that it is correct. *I think he wanted to marry her, if I am not mistaken... Unless I'm mistaken, he didn't specify what time.* ADJ-GRADED: v-link ADJ, oft ADJ *about* n =wrong PHRASE: PHR with cl PRAGMATICS

2 A **mistaken** belief or opinion is incorrect. *I had a mistaken view of what was happening. ...a limited understanding of addiction and mistaken beliefs about how it can be overcome.* ♦ **mistakenly** *He says they mistakenly believed the standard licenses they held were sufficient.* ADJ: ADJ n ADV: ADV with v

mistaken identity. When someone incorrectly thinks that they have found or recognized a person who they have been looking for or who they know, you refer to this as a case of **mistaken identity**. *The dead men could have been the victims of mistaken identity. Their attackers may have wrongly believed them to be soldiers.* N-UNCOUNT

mister /mɪstəʳ/. Men are sometimes addressed as **mister**, especially by children and especially when the person talking to them does not know their name; an informal use. *Look, Mister, we know our job, so don't try to tell us what to do.* ◆◇◇◇◇ N-VOC PRAGMATICS

mistime /mɪstaɪm/ **mistimes, mistiming, mistimed.** If you **mistime** something, you do it at the wrong time, so that it is not successful. *You're bound to mistime a tackle every so often. ...a certain mistimed comment.* VERB V n V-ed

mistletoe /mɪsəltoʊ/. **Mistletoe** is a plant with white berries that grows on the branches of some trees. Mistletoe is used in Britain as a Christmas decoration. N-UNCOUNT

mistook /mɪstʊk/. **Mistook** is the past tense and past participle of **mistake**.

mistreat /mɪstriːt/ **mistreats, mistreating, mistreated.** If someone **mistreats** a person or an animal, they treat them badly, especially by making them suffer physically. *...a lad who mistreats a horse... She has been mistreated by men in the past.* VERB =ill-treat V n

mistreatment /mɪstriːtmənt/. **Mistreatment** of a person or animal is cruel behaviour towards them, especially by making them suffer physically. *...issues like police brutality and mistreatment of people in prisons.* N-UNCOUNT =maltreatment

mistress /mɪstrəs/ **mistresses** ◆◆◇◇◇

1 A married man's **mistress** is a woman who is not his wife with whom he is having a sexual relationship. Some people find this use offensive. *She was his mistress for three years... He has a wife and a mistress.* N-COUNT: usu with poss

2 A **mistress** is a female teacher, especially one in a British public school; an old-fashioned use. *My history mistress was extremely helpful.* N-COUNT: usu n N =teacher

3 A servant's **mistress** is the woman that he or she works for; an old-fashioned use. *It must be really bad, for her to ignore a summons from her mistress!* N-COUNT: usu with poss

4 A dog's **mistress** is the woman or girl who owns it. *The huge wolfhound danced in circles around his mistress.* N-COUNT: usu poss N

5 If a woman is **mistress** of a situation, she has complete control over it. *She had always been mistress of her own destiny.* N-UNCOUNT: also N in pl, usu N *of* n

6 If you say that a woman is a **mistress of** a particular activity, you mean that she is very skilled at it. *She is a mistress of disguise. ...another winner from the mistress of historical romance.* N-COUNT: N *of* n =queen

mistrial /mɪstraɪəl, AM -traɪ-/ **mistrials**

1 In British English, a **mistrial** is a legal trial that is conducted unfairly, for example because not all the evidence available is given, and therefore the trial must be conducted again. *The past has been scarred by countless mistrials and perversions of justice.* N-COUNT

2 In American English, a **mistrial** is a legal trial which ends without a verdict, for example because the jury cannot agree on one. *The judge said he would declare a mistrial if the jury did not reach its verdict today.* N-COUNT

mistrust /mɪstrʌst/ **mistrusts, mistrusting, mistrusted** ◆◇◇◇◇

1 **Mistrust** is the feeling that you have towards someone who you do not trust. *There was mutual mistrust between the two men. ...a deep mistrust of state banks.* N-UNCOUNT =distrust

2 If you **mistrust** someone or something, you do not trust them. *It frequently appears that Bell mistrusts all journalists.* VERB =distrust V n

mistrustful /mɪstrʌstfʊl/. If you are **mistrustful** of someone, you do not trust them. *He had always been mistrustful of women.* ADJ-GRADED: oft ADJ *of* n =distrustful

misty /mɪsti/. On a **misty** day, there is a lot of mist in the air. *It's a bit misty this morning... The air was cold and misty.* ◆◇◇◇◇ ADJ-GRADED: oft *it* v-link ADJ

misty-eyed. If you say that something makes you **misty-eyed**, you mean that it makes you feel so happy, sentimental, or nostalgic that you feel as if you are going to cry. *They got misty-eyed listening to records of Ruby Murray singing 'Danny Boy'.* ADJ-GRADED: usu v-link ADJ =soppy, gooey

misunderstand /mɪsʌndəʳstænd/ **misunderstands, misunderstanding, misunderstood.** If you **misunderstand** someone or something, you do not understand them properly. *They have simply misunderstood what rock and roll is... Maybe I misunderstood you.* • See also **misunderstood.** • You can say **don't misunderstand me** when you want to correct a wrong impression that you think someone may have got about what you are saying. *I'm not saying what he did was good, don't misunderstand me.* ◆◇◇◇◇ VERB =misinterpret V wh V n CONVENTION PRAGMATICS

misunderstanding /mɪsʌndəʳstændɪŋ/ **misunderstandings** ◆◇◇◇◇

1 A **misunderstanding** is a failure to understand something properly, for example a situation or a person's remarks. *There has been some misunderstanding of our publishing aims... Tell your midwife what you want so she can make a note of it and avoid misunderstandings.* N-VAR

2 You can refer to a disagreement or slight quarrel as a **misunderstanding**; a formal use. *...a little mis-* N-COUNT =disagreement *understanding with the police. ...a misunderstanding between friends.*

misunderstood /mɪsʌndəʳstʊd/ ◆◇◇◇◇

1 Misunderstood is the past tense and past participle of **misunderstand**.

2 If you describe someone or something as **misunderstood**, you mean that people do not understand them and have a wrong impression or idea of them. *Eric is very badly misunderstood... The cost of capital is widely misunderstood. ...a misunderstood genius.* ADJ-GRADED

misuse, misuses, misusing, misused. The noun is pronounced /mɪsjuːs/. The verb is pronounced /mɪsjuːz/. ◆◇◇◇◇

1 The **misuse** of something is incorrect, careless, or dishonest use of it. *...the misuse of power and privilege. ...a misuse of public funds... The effectiveness of this class of drug has, however, lead to their misuse.* N-VAR: usu with supp, oft N *of* n

2 If someone **misuses** something, they use it incorrectly, carelessly, or dishonestly. *You are protected instantly if a thief misuses your credit card... She misused her position in the appointment of 26,000 party supporters to government jobs.* VERB V n

mite /maɪt/ **mites** ◆◇◇◇◇

1 A mite means to a small extent or degree. It is sometimes used to make a statement less extreme. *I can't help feeling just a mite uneasy about it... 'I've got a copy,' I said, a mite shamefacedly.* PHRASE: PHR adj/adv =a bit, a touch

2 Mites are very tiny creatures that live on plants, for example, or in animals' fur. *...an itching skin disorder caused by parasitic mites.* N-COUNT: usu pl

3 If you refer to a small child as a poor little **mite**, you mean that you feel sorry for him or her; an informal use. *The poor mite was so ill.* N-COUNT: adj N

mitigate /mɪtɪgeɪt/ **mitigates, mitigating, mitigated.** To **mitigate** something means to make it less unpleasant, serious, or painful; a formal word. *...ways of mitigating the effects of an explosion... The cost of getting there is mitigated by Sydney's offer of a subsidy.* ◆◇◇◇◇ VERB =alleviate V n

mitigating /mɪtɪgeɪtɪŋ/. **Mitigating** circumstances or factors make a bad action, especially a crime, easier to understand and excuse, and may result in the person responsible being punished less severely; a formal or legal word. *The judge found that in her case there were mitigating circumstances... There are various mitigating factors.* ADJ: ADJ n

mitigation /mɪtɪgeɪʃᵊn/

1 If someone, especially someone in a court, is told something **in mitigation**, they are told something that makes a crime or fault easier to understand and excuse; a formal expression. *Kieran Coonan QC told the judge in mitigation that the offences had been at the lower end of the scale... In mitigation, it should be pointed out that there wasn't much incentive to make world-beating wine.* PHRASE: PHR with cl

2 Mitigation is a reduction in the unpleasantness, seriousness, or painfulness of something; a formal use. *...the mitigation or cure of a physical or mental condition.* N-UNCOUNT =alleviation

mitt /mɪt/ **mitts**

1 Mitts are the same as **mittens**; an informal use. N-COUNT

2 You can refer to a person's hands as their **mitts**; an informal use. *I pressed a dime into his grubby mitt.* N-COUNT =paw

3 In baseball, a **mitt** is a glove worn by a catcher or first baseman. *I bought myself a baseball mitt.* N-COUNT: usu supp N =glove

mitten /mɪtᵊn/ **mittens. Mittens** are gloves which have one section that covers your thumb and another section that covers your four fingers together. N-COUNT: usu pl

mix /mɪks/ **mixes, mixing, mixed** ◆◆◆◆◇

1 If two substances **mix** or if you **mix** one substance with another, you stir or shake them together, or combine them in some other way, so that they become a single substance. *Oil and water don't mix... It mixes easily with cold or hot water to make a tasty, filling drink... A quick stir will mix them thoroughly... Mix the cinnamon with the rest of the sugar... Mix the ingredients together slowly.* V-RECIP-ERG pl-n V V *with* n V pl-n V n *with* n V n with adv

♦ **mixing** *This final part of the mixing is done slowly and delicately.* N-UNCOUNT

2 If you **mix** something, you prepare it by mixing other things together. *He had spent several hours mixing cement... Are you sure I can't mix you a drink?* VERB V n V n n

3 A **mix** is a powder containing all the substances that you need in order to make something such as a cake or a sauce. When you want to use it, you add liquid. *For speed we used packets of pizza dough mix... It was a packet mix.* N-VAR: usu supp N

4 A **mix** of different things or people is two or more of them together. *The story is a magical mix of fantasy and reality... We get a very representative mix of people.* N-COUNT: usu sing, with supp =mixture

5 If you say that two things or activities do not **mix** or that you cannot **mix** one thing or activity with another, you mean that it is not a good idea to have them or do them together, because the result would be unpleasant or dangerous. *Politics and sport don't mix. ...some of these pills that don't mix with drink... Ted managed to mix business with pleasure... The military has accused the clergy of mixing religion and politics.* V-RECIP-ERG: usu with brd-neg pl-n V V *with* n V n *with* n V pl-n

6 If you **mix** with other people, you meet them and talk to them. You can also say that people **mix**. *I ventured the idea that the secret of staying young was to mix with older people... People are supposed to mix, do you understand?... When you came away you made a definite effort to mix.* V-RECIP =socialize V *with* n pl-n V V (non-recip)

7 When a record producer **mixes** a piece of music, he or she puts together the individual instrumental and vocal parts that have been recorded in order to make the finished sound. *They've been mixing tracks for a new album due out later this year.* VERB V n

♦ **mixing** *Final mixing should be completed by the end of this week.* N-UNCOUNT

8 In informal British English, if you say that someone **mixes it**, you mean that they often fight or argue strongly about things. The usual American expression is **mix it up**. *Stewart has developed a tendency to mix it verbally with the opposition.* PHRASE: V inflects, oft PHR *with* n

9 See also **mixed**; **cake mix**. • to **mix** your **metaphors**: see **metaphor**.

mix up PHRASAL VERB

1 If you **mix up** two things or people, you confuse them, so that you think that one of them is the other one. *People often mix me up with other actors... Depressed people may mix up their words... Any time you told one of them something, they'd swear you'd mixed them up and told the other.* =muddle up, confuse V n P *with* n V P pl-n (not pron) V pl-n P

2 If you **mix up** a number of things, you put them together in a random way so that they are not in any particular order. *I like to mix up designer clothes... Part of the plan was that the town should not fall into office, industrial and residential zones, but mix the three up together... This is music from a different era. I've taken those sounds from childhood and mixed them up with other things.* V P pl-n (not pron) V pl-n P V n P *with* n

3 See also **mixed up**, **mix-up**.

mixed /mɪkst/ ◆◆◆◇◇

1 If you have **mixed** feelings about something or someone, you feel uncertain about them because you can see both good and bad points about them. *I came home from the meeting with mixed feelings... There has been a very mixed reaction to the decision.* ADJ-GRADED: usu ADJ n

2 A **mixed** group of people consists of people of many different types. *I found a very mixed group of individuals some of whom I could relate to and others with whom I had very little in common... The community is very mixed, not least because there are plenty of small industrial enterprises.* ADJ-GRADED

3 Mixed is used to describe something that involves people from two or more different races. *...a woman of mixed race... She had attended a racially mixed school. ...mixed marriages.* ADJ: usu ADJ n

4 Mixed education or accommodation is intended for both males and females. *Girls who have always been at a mixed school know how to stand up for themselves... The spa has 6 indoor pools, 2 for women only, 2 for men only, and 2 for mixed bathing.* ADJ: usu ADJ n =co-ed

5 Mixed is used to describe something which includes or consists of different things of the same general kind. *...a small mixed salad... The mixed forest is cut commercially but is also carefully conserved to look good. ...a teaspoon of mixed herbs.* ADJ: ADJ n

6 • a mixed blessing: see **blessing**.

mixed ability. A **mixed ability** class or teaching system is one in which pupils are taught a subject together in the same class, even though their abilities are different. *In nearly all British state junior schools, children learn in mixed ability classes. ...mixed ability teaching.* ADJ: usu ADJ n

mixed bag. If you describe a situation or a group of things or people as a **mixed bag**, you mean that it contains some good items, features, or people and some bad ones. *Research on athletes and ordinary human subjects has yielded a mixed bag of results... This autumn's collections are a very mixed bag.* N-SING: usu *a* N, oft N *of* n

mixed doubles. In some sports, such as tennis and badminton, **mixed doubles** is a match in which a man and a woman play as partners against another man and woman. *Vic Seixas and Doris Hart won the mixed doubles. ...the mixed doubles final.* N-UNCOUNT: also *the* N

mixed economy, mixed economies. A **mixed economy** is an economic system in a country in which some companies are owned by the state and some are owned privately. N-COUNT

mixed up ◆◇◇◇◇

1 If you are **mixed up**, you are confused, often because of emotional or social problems. *I think he's a rather mixed up kid... I get mixed up about times and places.* ADJ-GRADED =confused, muddled

2 If you say that someone is **mixed up** in something bad or with someone you disapprove of, you mean they are involved in it or with them. *How could David be mixed up in a murder?... Why did I ever get mixed up with you?* ADJ: v-link ADJ *in/with* n =involved

mixer /mɪksəʳ/ **mixers** ◆◇◇◇◇

1 A **mixer** is a machine used for mixing things together. *...an electric mixer.* • See also **cement mixer, food mixer.** N-COUNT: usu supp N

2 A **mixer** is a non-alcoholic drink such as fruit juice that you mix with strong alcohol such as gin. N-COUNT

mixing bowl, mixing bowls. A **mixing bowl** is a large bowl used for mixing ingredients. N-COUNT

mixture /mɪkstʃəʳ/ **mixtures** ◆◆◆◇◇

1 A **mixture** of things consists of several different things together. *They looked at him with a mixture of horror, envy, and awe. ...a mixture of spiced, grilled vegetables served cold.* N-SING: usu N *of* pl-n =combination

2 A **mixture** is a substance that consists of other substances which have been stirred or shaken together. *Prepare the gravy mixture. ...a mixture of water and sugar and salt.* • See also **cough mixture.** N-COUNT: oft supp N, N *of* n =mix

mix-up, mix-ups. A **mix-up** is a mistake or a failure in something that was planned; an informal word. *I'm sure it was just some sort of mix-up. ...a mix-up over travel arrangements.* N-COUNT

Mk. **Mk** is a written abbreviation for **mark. Mk** is used to refer to a particular model or design of something such as a car or machine. *...a 1974 white MG Midget Mk 3.* ◆◇◇◇◇

ml. **ml** is a written abbreviation for **millilitre** or **millilitres.** *Boil the sugar and 100 ml of water.* ◆◇◇◇◇

mm. **mm** is an abbreviation for **millimetre** or **millimetres.** *...a 135mm lens. ...0.25mm of rain.* ◆◆◆◇◇

mnemonic /nɪmɒnɪk/ **mnemonics.** A **mnemonic** is a word, short poem, or sentence that is intended to help you remember things such as scientific rules or spelling rules. For example, 'i before e, except after c' is a mnemonic to help people remember how to spell words like 'believe' and 'receive'. *Like many mnemonic devices these depend for effect upon their bizarreness.* N-COUNT: oft N n =memory aid

mo /moʊ/. In spoken English, a **mo** is a very short length of time; an informal word. *Hang on a mo.* N-SING: *a* N =sec, tick

moan /moʊn/ **moans, moaning, moaned** ◆◆◇◇◇

1 If you **moan**, you make a low sound, usually because you are unhappy or in pain. *Tony moaned in his sleep and then turned over on his side... 'My head, my head,' he moaned. 'I can't see.'* ► Also a noun. *Suddenly she gave a low, choking moan and began to tremble violently. ...her moan of sorrow.* VERB =groan V V with quote N-COUNT

2 To **moan** means to complain or speak in a way which shows that you are very unhappy. *I used to moan if I didn't get at least six hours' sleep at night. ...moaning about the weather... They moan on a lot about money... Meg moans, 'I hated it!'... The gardener was moaning that he had another garden to do later that morning.* VERB =complain, whinge V V prep/adv V with quote V that

3 A **moan** is a complaint; an informal use. *They have been listening to people's gripes, moans and praise.* N-COUNT

4 If you **have a moan**, you complain about something; an informal expression. *You can go see him and have a good old moan.* PHRASE: V inflects

5 A **moan** is a low noise; a literary use. *...the occasional moan of the wind round the corners of the house. ...the moan of distant traffic.* N-COUNT: usu with supp

moaner /moʊnəʳ/ **moaners.** If you refer to someone as a **moaner**, you are critical of them because they often complain about things; an informal word. *Film critics are dreadful moaners.* N-COUNT PRAGMATICS =whinger

moat /moʊt/ **moats.** A **moat** is a deep and wide ditch which people used to dig round a hill or castle and then fill with water, in order to protect the place from people attacking it. ◆◇◇◇◇ N-COUNT

mob /mɒb/ **mobs, mobbing, mobbed** ◆◆◇◇◇

1 A **mob** is a large, disorganized, and often violent crowd of people. *Bottles and cans were hurled on the terraces by the mob... The inspectors watched a growing mob of demonstrators gathering.* N-COUNT

2 People sometimes use **the mob** to refer disapprovingly to the mass of people, especially when they are behaving in a violent or threatening way. *If they continue like this there is a danger of the mob taking over... They have been exercising what amounts to mob rule.* N-SING: *the* N, N n PRAGMATICS

3 You can refer to the people involved in organized crime as the **Mob**; an informal use. *...casinos that the Mob had operated. ...it was a Mob killing.* N-SING: usu *the* N, N n

4 If you say that someone **is being mobbed** by a crowd of people, you mean that the crowd are gathering around them, often in a disorderly or threatening way. *Her car was mobbed by the media... They found themselves being mobbed in the street for autographs.* VB: usu passive *be* V-ed

mobile /moʊbaɪl, AM -bəl/ **mobiles** ◆◆◆◇◇

1 You use **mobile** to describe something that is able to move freely or be moved easily from place to place. *Mobile units have been set up to get police quickly to an incident. ...the four hundred seat mobile theatre.* ADJ: usu ADJ n

2 If you are **mobile**, you can move or travel easily from place to place, for example because you are not physically disabled or because you have your own transport. *I'm still very mobile... For the first time in her life, 29-year-old Natasha is mobile.* ♦ **mobility** /moʊbɪlɪti/ *Two cars gave them the freedom and mobility to go their separate ways.* ADJ-GRADED: usu v-link ADJ; N-UNCOUNT

3 In a **mobile** society, people move easily from one job, home, or social class to another. *We're a very mobile society, and people move after they get divorced. ...young, mobile professionals.* ♦ **mobility** *Prior to the nineteenth century, there were almost no channels of social mobility.* ADJ-GRADED; N-UNCOUNT

4 If someone has a **mobile** face, the expression on their face changes quickly as their feelings change. *Robyn had the more mobile, more expressive face.* ADJ-GRADED

5 A **mobile** is a decoration which you hang from a ceiling. It usually consists of several small objects which move as the air around them moves. N-COUNT

6 A **mobile** is the same as a **mobile phone.** N-COUNT

7 See also **upwardly mobile.**

mobile home, mobile homes. A **mobile home** is a large caravan that people live in and that usually remains in the same place, but which can be pulled to another place using a car or van. ◆◇◇◇◇ N-COUNT =trailer

mobile phone, mobile phones. A **mobile phone** or a **mobile** is a telephone that you can ◆◇◇◇◇ N-COUNT =cellular phone carry with you and use to make or receive calls wherever you are.

mobilize /moʊbɪlaɪz/ **mobilizes, mobilizing, mobilized;** also spelled **mobilise** in British English. ◆◆◇◇◇

1 If you **mobilize** support or **mobilize** people to do something, you succeed in encouraging people to take action, especially political action. If people **mobilize**, they prepare to take action. A formal use. *The best hope is that we will mobilize international support and get down to action... The purpose of the journey is to mobilise public opinion on the controversial issue... Faced with crisis, people mobilized.* V-ERG V n V

♦ **mobilization** /moʊbɪlaɪzeɪʃən/ *...the rapid mobilization of international opinion in support of the revolution.* N-UNCOUNT: oft N *of* n

2 If you **mobilize** resources, you start to use them or make them available for use; a formal use. *If you could mobilize the resources, you could get it done.* VERB =marshal V n

♦ **mobilization** *...the mobilisation of resources for education.* N-UNCOUNT: oft N *of* n

3 If a country **mobilizes** or **mobilizes** its armed forces, or if its armed forces mobilize, they are given orders to prepare for a conflict; a formal use. *Sudan even threatened to mobilize in response to the ultimatums... India is now in a better position to mobilise its forces... It means that their whole army will mobilize.* ♦ **mobilization** *...a demand for full-scale mobilisation to defend the republic.* V-ERG V V n V N-UNCOUNT

mobster /mɒbstəʳ/ **mobsters.** A **mobster** is someone who is a member of an organized group of violent criminals. N-COUNT =gangster

moccasin /mɒkəsɪn/ **moccasins. Moccasins** are soft leather shoes which have a low heel and a raised seam at the front. N-COUNT

mock /mɒk/ **mocks, mocking, mocked** ◆◆◇◇◇

1 If someone **mocks** you, they show or pretend that they think you are foolish or inferior, for example by saying something funny about you, or by imitating your behaviour. *I thought you were mocking me... I distinctly remember mocking the idea... 'I'm astonished, Benjamin,' she mocked.* VERB V n V with quote

2 You use **mock** to describe something which is not real or genuine, but which is intended to be very similar to the real thing. *'It's tragic!' swoons Jeffrey in mock horror... One of them was subjected to a mock execution. ...a mock Tudor mansion.* ADJ: ADJ n

3 In British English, **mocks** are practice exams that you take as part of your preparation for real exams; an informal use. *She went from a D in her mocks to a B in the real thing.* N-COUNT: usu pl

mockery /mɒkəri/ ◆◇◇◇◇

1 If someone mocks you, you can refer to their behaviour or attitude as **mockery**. *Was there a glint of mockery in his eyes?... There should be no snobbish mockery of catering or fashion design as university subjects.* N-UNCOUNT =ridicule

2 If something makes a **mockery** of something, it makes it appear worthless and foolish. *This action makes a mockery of the Government's continuing protestations of concern... The present system is a mockery of justice.* N-SING

mocking /mɒkɪŋ/. A **mocking** expression or **mocking** behaviour indicates that someone thinks someone or something is stupid or inferior. *She gave a mocking smile... Behind the mocking laughter lurks a growing sense of unease.* ◆◇◇◇◇ ADJ-GRADED =scornful, derisive

♦ **mockingly** *'Isn't that sweet?' he says mockingly.* ADV-GRADED

mock-up, mock-ups. A **mock-up** of something such as a machine or building is a model of it which is made to do tests on or to show people what it will look like. *There's a mock up of the high street where the Goodwins go shopping.* N-COUNT: oft N *of* n =model

mod /mɒd/ **mods. Mods** are young people who wear a special kind of neat clothes, ride motor-scooters, and like soul music. Many young people were mods in the early 1960s. ◆◇◇◇◇ N-COUNT

modal /moʊdəl/ **modals.** A **modal** or a **modal auxiliary** is a word such as 'can' or 'would' which is used with a main verb to express ideas such as possibility, intention, or necessity; a technical term in grammar. N-COUNT

mod cons. In informal British English, **mod cons** are the modern facilities in a house that make it easy and pleasant to live in. *The house is spacious with all mod cons, handy for the station and has a garden.* N-PLURAL

mode /moʊd/ **modes** ◆◆◇◇◇

1 A **mode** of life or behaviour is a particular way of living or behaving; a formal use. *...the capitalist mode of production... He switched automatically into interview mode.* N-COUNT: usu N *of* n

2 A **mode** is also a particular style in art, literature, or dress. *...a slightly more elegant and formal mode of dress... Levi is best known for work in a very different mode from what is to be found here.* N-COUNT: usu with supp =style

3 On some cameras or electronic devices, the different **modes** available are the different programs or options that you can choose when you use them. *...when the camera is in manual mode.* N-COUNT: usu supp N

model /mɒdəl/ **models, modelling, modelled;** spelled **modeling, modeled** in American English. ◆◆◆◆◇

1 A **model** of an object is a physical representation that shows what it looks like or how it works. The model is often smaller than the object it represents. *...an architect's model of a wooden house. ...a working scale model of the whole Bay Area... I made a model out of paper and glue.* ► Also an adjective. *I had made a model aeroplane. ...a model railway.* N-COUNT: oft N *of* n =replica, mock-up ADJ: ADJ n

2 A **model** is a system that is being used and that people might want to copy in order to achieve similar results; a formal use. *We believe that this is a general model of managerial activity. ...the Chinese model of economic reform.* N-COUNT: with supp

3 A **model** of a system or process is a theoretical description that can help you understand how the system or process works, or how it might work; a technical use in science. *Darwin eventually put forward a model of biological evolution... He proposed a model of stress reaction in the body.* N-COUNT: usu with supp

4 If someone such as a scientist **models** a system or process, they make an accurate theoretical description of it in order to understand or explain how it works. *...the mathematics needed to model a nonlinear system like an atmosphere.* VERB V n

5 If you say that someone or something is a **model** of a particular quality, you are showing approval of them because they have that quality to a large degree. *A model of good manners, he has conquered any inward fury... His marriage and family life is a model of propriety.* N-COUNT: N *of* n PRAGMATICS

6 You use **model** to express approval of someone when you think that they give an excellent example by fulfilling their function very well. *As a girl she had been a model pupil... Hospital staff say he is a model patient.* ADJ: ADJ n PRAGMATICS =exemplary

7 If one thing **is modelled** on another, the first thing is made so that it is like the second thing in some way. *The quota system was modelled on those operated in America and continental Europe... The program will be modeled after a popular BBC series called 'The Archers'... She asked the author if she had modelled her hero on anybody in particular.* VERB be V-ed *on/after* n V n *on/after* n

8 If you **model** yourself **on** someone, you copy the way that they do things, because you admire them and want to be like them. *There's absolutely nothing wrong in modelling yourself on an older woman... They will tend to model their behaviour on the teacher's behaviour.* VERB V pron-refl *on/after* n V n *on/after* n

9 A particular **model** of a machine is a particular version of it. *To keep the cost down, opt for a basic model... The model number is 1870/285.* N-COUNT: usu supp N =version

10 An artist's **model** is a person who is painted, drawn, or sculpted by them. N-COUNT =sitter

11 If someone **models** for an artist, they stay in a particular position so that the artist can paint, draw, or sculpt them. *Tullio has been modelling for Sandra for eleven years.* VERB =pose V *for* n Also V

12 A fashion **model** is a person whose job is to display clothes by wearing them. *...Paris's top photographic fashion model.* N-COUNT

13 If someone **models** clothes, they display them by wearing them. *I wasn't here to model clothes...* VERB V n

She began modelling in Paris when she was only 15. ♦ **modelling** *She was being offered a modelling contract.* V / N-UNCOUNT: oft N n

14 If you **model** shapes or figures, you make them out of a substance such as clay or wood. *There she began to model in clay... Sometimes she carved wood and sometimes stone; sometimes she modelled clay... The artist recorded interviews on a variety of topics and modelled an appropriate animal for each voice.* VERB / V / V n

15 See also **role model**.

modeller /mɒdələʳ/ **modellers;** spelled **modeler** in American English.

1 A **modeller** is someone who makes shapes or figures out of substances such as wood or clay. N-COUNT

2 A **modeller** is someone who makes theoretical descriptions of systems or processes in order to understand them and be able to predict how they will develop. *This is definitely something that climate modellers need to take into account.* N-COUNT: usu supp N

modem /moʊdem/ **modems.** A **modem** is a device which uses a telephone line to connect computers or computer systems. *He sent his work to his publishers by modem.* N-COUNT: also by N

moderate, moderates, moderating, moderated. The adjective and noun are pronounced /mɒdərət/. The verb is pronounced /mɒdəreɪt/. ♦♦♦◇◇

1 **Moderate** political opinions or policies are not extreme. *He was an easygoing man of very moderate views... Both countries have called for a moderate approach to the use of force.* ADJ-GRADED ≠extreme

2 You use **moderate** to describe people or groups who have moderate political opinions or policies. *...a moderate Democrat. ...the moderate wing of the army.* ► A **moderate** is someone with moderate political opinions. *If he presents himself as a radical he risks scaring off the moderates whose votes he so desperately needs.* ADJ-GRADED / N-COUNT ≠extremist, hardliner

3 You use **moderate** to describe something that is neither large nor small in amount or degree. *While a moderate amount of stress can be beneficial, too much stress can exhaust you. ...moderate exercise.* ♦ **moderately** *Both are moderately large insects, with a wingspan of around four centimetres. ...a moderately attractive woman... I don't smoke and I drink only moderately.* ADJ-GRADED: usu ADJ n =reasonable ≠excessive / ADV-GRADED: usu ADV adj/-ed, also ADV after v =reasonably

4 A **moderate** change in something is a change that is not great. *Most drugs offer either no real improvement or, at best, only moderate improvements.* ♦ **moderately** *Share prices on the Tokyo Exchange declined moderately.* ADJ =slight / ADV: ADV after v

5 If you **moderate** something or if it **moderates**, it becomes less extreme or violent and more manageable or acceptable. *They are hoping that once in office he can be persuaded to moderate his views... Amongst relief workers, the immediate sense of crisis has moderated somewhat... Without Westcott's moderating influence, Mathers's autocratic manner became unbearable.* ♦ **moderation** /mɒdəreɪʃən/ *A moderation in food prices helped to offset the first increase in energy prices.* V-ERG =attenuate / V n / V / V-ing / N-UNCOUNT: oft N of/in n

moderation /mɒdəreɪʃən/. ♦◇◇◇◇

1 If you say that someone's behaviour shows **moderation**, you approve of them because they act in a way that you think is reasonable and not extreme. *The United Nations Secretary General called on all parties to show moderation. ...the moderation and deep sense of responsibility which characterized their thinking.* ● If you say that someone does something such as eat, drink, or smoke **in moderation**, you mean that they do not eat, smoke, or drink too much or more than is reasonable. *Many adults are able to drink in moderation, but others become dependent on alcohol... Fats and oils can be used in moderation.* N-UNCOUNT PRAGMATICS =restraint / PHRASE: PHR after v ≠to excess

2 See also **moderate**.

moderator /mɒdəreɪtəʳ/ **moderators**

1 In Protestant churches, a **moderator** is a senior member of the clergy who is in charge at large and important meetings. *...a former moderator of the General Assembly of the Church of Scotland.* N-COUNT

2 In some debates and negotiations, the **moderator** is a neutral person who presides over the discussion and makes sure that it is conducted in an orderly way; a formal use. N-COUNT =chair

modern /mɒdəʳn/ **moderns** ♦♦♦♦◇

1 **Modern** means relating to the present time, for example the present decade or present century. *We had a long talk about the problem of materialism in modern society. ...the risks facing every modern marriage... It's the sort of thing that would be very difficult to prove in any modern court of law.* ADJ: ADJ n =contemporary

2 Something that is **modern** is new and involves the latest ideas or equipment. *Modern technology has opened our eyes to many things... In many ways, it was a very modern school for its time... As China's economy prospered, it was bound to want a modern army.* ♦ **modernity** /mɒdɜːʳnɪti/ *...an office block that astonished the city with its modernity.* ADJ-GRADED =up-to-date ≠old-fashioned / N-UNCOUNT =innovation

3 People are sometimes described as **modern** when they have opinions or ways of behaviour that have not yet been accepted by most people in a society. *They were very modern Tories in almost every sense... She is very modern in outlook.* ADJ-GRADED =progressive ≠traditional

4 **Modern** is used to describe styles of art, dance, music, and architecture that have developed in recent times, in contrast to classical styles. *She'd been a professional dancer with a modern dance company in New York. ...the Museum of Modern Art.* ► The **moderns** are artists who follow modern styles. *I don't have much time for the moderns. Chaucer's my favourite.* ADJ: ADJ n ≠classical / N-COUNT: usu pl

modern-day. **Modern-day** is used to refer to the new or modern aspects of a place, an activity, or a society. *...modern-day America. ...the by-products of modern-day living.* ♦◇◇◇◇ ADJ: ADJ n =present-day, contemporary

modernise /mɒdənaɪz/. See **modernize**.

modernism /mɒdəʳnɪzəm/. In the first half of the 20th century, **modernism** was a tendency in the arts which was concerned with artistic form and language, and how these could be used to express mental and emotional states, rather than with realistic description and narrative. ● See also **post-modernism**. ♦◇◇◇◇ N-UNCOUNT

modernist /mɒdəʳnɪst/ **modernists.** **Modernist** means relating to the ideas and methods of modern art. *...modernist architecture. ...modernist art... The building is impeccably modernist: glass, aluminium and grey.* ● See also **post-modernist**. ► A **modernist** is an artist who uses modernist ideas and methods. ♦◇◇◇◇ ADJ: usu ADJ n / N-COUNT

modernistic /mɒdəʳnɪstɪk/. A **modernistic** building or piece of furniture has been designed or constructed in a noticeably modern way. *...the modernistic building that housed the city offices.* ADJ-GRADED ≠traditional

modernize /mɒdəʳnaɪz/ **modernizes, modernizing, modernized;** also spelled **modernise** in British English. To **modernize** something such as a system or a factory means to change it by replacing old equipment or methods with new ones. *...plans to modernize the refinery... There is a pressing need to modernise our electoral system.* ♦ **modernization** /mɒdəʳnaɪzeɪʃən/ *...the modernization of the region. ...a five-year modernization programme.* ♦♦◇◇◇ VERB / V n / N-UNCOUNT

modern languages. **Modern languages** refers to the modern European languages, for example French, German, and Russian, especially when considered as a subject of study at school or university. *...head of modern languages at a London grammar school.* N-PLURAL

modest /mɒdɪst/ ♦♦♦◇◇

1 A **modest** house or other building is not large or expensive. *...the modest home of a family who lived off the land... A one-night stay in a modest hotel costs around £35.* ADJ-GRADED =unassuming

2 You use **modest** to describe something such as an amount, rate, or improvement which is relatively small. *Swiss unemployment rose to the still modest rate of 0.7%... She let him place two modest bets on the last two races for her... The democratic reforms have been modest and they've occurred in only a few countries.* ♦ **modestly** *Most of us want to* ADJ-GRADED / ADV-GRADED:

drink modestly but well... Britain's balance of payments improved modestly last month. ADV after v, ADV adj/-ed/ adv

3 A **modest** income or success is not large, but is considered to be sufficient or satisfactory. *You don't get rich, but you can get a modest living out of it... Despite these limitations the interviews were a modest success and reported widely in the press.* ADJ: usu ADJ n =moderate

4 If you say that someone is **modest**, you approve of them because they do not talk much about their abilities, qualities, or possessions. *He's modest, as well as being a great player... Lord Carrington is modest about his achievements.* ♦ **modestly** *'You really must be very good at what you do.'—'I suppose I am,' Kate said modestly.* ADJ-GRADED PRAGMATICS =unassuming ≠arrogant; ADV-GRADED: ADV with v

5 You can describe a woman as **modest** when she avoids doing or wearing anything that might cause men to have sexual feelings towards her. You can also describe her clothes or behaviour as **modest**. *Asian women are more modest and shy, yet they tend to have an inner force... Last year, she forsook her old skin-tight jeans for the more modest clothes of a devout Muslim.* ♦ **modestly** *She sat down cautiously on the red canvas cushions, knees modestly together.* ADJ-GRADED; ADV-GRADED: ADV with v, ADV adj/adv

modesty /mɒdɪsti/ ♦◇◇◇◇

1 Someone who shows **modesty** does not talk much about their abilities, achievements, or possessions; used showing approval. *His modesty does him credit, for the food he produces speaks for itself... He plays the character with tremendous concentration combined with a pleasing modesty.* N-UNCOUNT PRAGMATICS ≠arrogance

2 You can refer to the **modesty** of something such as a place, an amount, or a plan when it is relatively small or unambitious. *The modesty of the town itself comes as something of a surprise. ...the modesty of their prices.* N-UNCOUNT: usu N *of* n

3 If someone, especially a woman, shows **modesty**, they are cautious about the way they dress and behave because they are aware that other people may view them in a sexual way. *There were shrieks of embarrassment, mingled with giggles, from some of the girls as they struggled to protect their modesty.* N-UNCOUNT: usu with supp

modicum /mɒdɪkəm/. A **modicum** of something, especially something that is good or desirable, is a reasonable but not large amount of it; a formal word. *I'd like to think I've had a modicum of success. ...a modicum of privacy.* QUANT: QUANT *of* n-uncount =degree

modifier /mɒdɪfaɪəʳ/ **modifiers.** A **modifier** is a word or group of words that modifies another word or group. In some descriptions of grammar, only words that are used before a noun are called **modifiers**. N-COUNT

modify /mɒdɪfaɪ/ **modifies, modifying, modified** ♦♦◇◇◇

1 If you **modify** something, you change it slightly, often in order to improve it. *The club members did agree to modify their recruitment policy... The plane was a modified version of the C-130.* ♦ **modification** /mɒdɪfɪkeɪʃᵊn/ **modifications** *Relatively minor modifications were required. ...behaviour modification techniques.* VERB =adapt; V n; V-ed; N-VAR

2 A word or group of words that **modifies** another word describes or classifies something, or restricts the meaning of the word. *It is a rule of English that adjectives generally precede the noun they modify: we say 'a good cry', not 'a cry good'.* VERB; V n

modish /moʊdɪʃ/. Something that is **modish** is fashionable; a literary word. *...a short checklist of much that is modish at the moment. ...modish young women from London society.* ADJ-GRADED =fashionable

modular /mɒdʒʊləʳ/

1 In building, **modular** means relating to the construction of buildings in parts called modules; a technical use. *They ended up buying a prebuilt modular home on a two-acre lot.* ADJ

2 **Modular** means relating to the teaching of courses at college or university in units called modules; used mainly in British English. *The course is modular in structure.* ADJ

modulate /mɒdʒʊleɪt/ **modulates, modulating, modulated**

1 If you **modulate** your voice or a sound, you change or vary the way that it sounds, for example its loudness, pitch, or tone, according to the effect you are trying to create. *He carefully modulated his voice.* ♦ **modulated** *'Who's this?' asked a well-modulated voice.* VERB; V n; Also V; ADJ-GRADED: usu ADJ n

2 To **modulate** an activity or process means to alter or adjust it in order to make it more suitable for a particular set of circumstances; a formal use. *These chemicals modulate the effect of potassium.* ♦ **modulation** /mɒdʒʊleɪʃᵊn/ **modulations** *The famine turned the normal modulation of climate into disaster.* VERB =modify; V n; N-VAR

module /mɒdʒuːl/ **modules** ♦◇◇◇◇

1 A **module** is one of the units of a course taught in units at a college or university; used mainly in British English. *These courses cover a twelve week period and are organised into three four week modules.* N-COUNT =component

2 A **module** is part of a spacecraft which can operate independently of the other parts, often away from the spacecraft. *A rescue plan could be achieved by sending an unmanned module to the space station.* N-COUNT

3 A **module** is one of a set of parts from which some buildings are made. Each module is made separately, and the completed modules are then joined together to form the building; a technical use in building. N-COUNT

4 A **module** is a part of a machine, especially a computer, which performs a particular function; a technical use in computing. N-COUNT

modus operandi /moʊdəs ɒpərændiː, -daɪ/. A **modus operandi** is a particular way of doing something; a formal expression. *An example of her modus operandi was provided during a terse exchange with the defendant.* N-SING

modus vivendi /moʊdəs vɪvendiː, -daɪ/. A **modus vivendi** is an arrangement which allows people who have different attitudes to live or work together; a formal expression. *After 1940, a modus vivendi between church and state was achieved.* N-SING =compromise

moggy /mɒgi/ **moggies;** also spelled **moggie**. In informal British English, a **moggy** is a **cat**. N-COUNT

mogul /moʊgᵊl/ **moguls** ♦◇◇◇◇

1 A **Mogul** was a Muslim ruler in India in the sixteenth to eighteenth centuries. N-COUNT

2 A **mogul** is an important, rich, and powerful businessman, especially one in the news, film, or television industry. *...an international media mogul. ...Hollywood movie moguls.* N-COUNT: usu supp N

mohair /moʊheəʳ/. **Mohair** is a type of very soft wool. *She was wearing a brown mohair dress.* N-UNCOUNT: oft N n

moist /mɔɪst/ **moister, moistest.** Something that is **moist** is slightly wet. *Wipe off any excess make-up with a clean, moist cotton flannel... The soil is reasonably moist after the September rain.* ♦◇◇◇◇ ADJ-GRADED ≠dry

moisten /mɔɪsᵊn/ **moistens, moistening, moistened.** To **moisten** something means to make it slightly wet. *She took a sip of water to moisten her dry throat. ...a moistened flannel.* VERB; V n; V-ed

moisture /mɔɪstʃəʳ/. **Moisture** is tiny drops of water in the air, on a surface, or in the ground. *When the soil is dry, more moisture is lost from the plant... Rainfall effects the moisture content of the atmosphere.* ♦♦◇◇◇ N-UNCOUNT

moisturize /mɔɪstʃəraɪz/ **moisturizes, moisturizing, moisturized;** also spelled **moisturise** in British English. If you **moisturize** your skin, you rub cream into it to make it softer. If a cream **moisturizes** your skin, it makes it softer. *...products to moisturise, protect and firm your skin... The lotion moisturizes while it cleanses. ...a pot of moisturising cream.* ♦◇◇◇◇ VERB; V n; V; V-ing

moisturizer /mɔɪstʃəraɪzəʳ/ **moisturizers;** also spelled **moisturiser**. A **moisturizer** is a cream that you put on your skin to make it feel softer and smoother. ♦◇◇◇◇ N-MASS

molar /moʊləʳ/ **molars.** Your **molars** are the large, flat teeth towards the back of your mouth that you use for chewing food. N-COUNT

molasses /məlæsɪz/. **Molasses** is a thick, dark brown syrup which is produced when sugar is refined. It is used in cooking. N-UNCOUNT

mold /mould/. See **mould**.

molding /mouldɪŋ/. See **moulding**.

moldy /mouldi/. See **mouldy**.

mole /moul/ **moles** ◆◇◇◇◇

1 A **mole** is a natural dark spot or small dark lump on someone's skin. N-COUNT

2 A **mole** is a small animal with black fur that lives underground. N-COUNT

3 A **mole** is a member of a government, administration, or other organization who secretly reveals confidential information to the press or to a rival organization. *He had been recruited by the Russians as a mole and trained in Moscow.* N-COUNT

molecular /məlekjʊlər/. **Molecular** means relating to or involving molecules. *...the molecular structure of fuel.* ◆◇◇◇◇ ADJ: ADJ n

molecular biology. **Molecular biology** is the study of the structure and function of the complex chemicals that are found in living things. ◆◇◇◇◇ N-UNCOUNT

♦ **molecular biologist, molecular biologists** *This substance has now been cloned by molecular biologists.* N-COUNT

molecule /mɒlɪkju:l/ **molecules.** A **molecule** is the smallest amount of a chemical substance which can exist by itself. *...the hydrogen bonds between water molecules.* ◆◆◇◇◇ N-COUNT: usu with supp, oft supp N

molehill /moulhɪl/ **molehills**

1 A **molehill** is a small pile of earth made by a mole digging a tunnel. N-COUNT

2 If you say that someone is **making a mountain out of a molehill**, you are critical of them for making an unimportant fact or difficulty seem like a serious one. *The British press, making a mountain out of a molehill, precipitated an unnecessary economic crisis.* PHRASE: V and Ns inflect PRAGMATICS

molest /məlest/ **molests, molesting, molested.** A person who **molests** someone, especially a woman or a child, interferes with them in a sexual way against their will. *He was accused of sexually molesting a female colleague.* ◆◇◇◇◇ VERB =abuse V n

♦ **molestation** /mɒlesteɪʃən, AM moul-/ *Any case of sexual molestation of a child should be reported to the police.* N-UNCOUNT =abuse ♦ **molester, molesters** *He'd been publicly labeled a child molester.* N-COUNT =abuser

mollify /mɒlɪfaɪ/ **mollifies, mollifying, mollified.** If you **mollify** someone, you do or say something to make them less upset or angry; a formal word. *The investigation was undertaken primarily to mollify pressure groups.* VERB =placate V n ♦ **mollified** *He looked first mollified and then relieved as it occurred to him his plight could be worse.* ADJ-GRADED: v-link ADJ

mollusc /mɒləsk/ **molluscs.** A **mollusc** is an animal such as a snail, slug, clam, or octopus, which has a soft body and no backbone. Many types of mollusc have hard shells to protect them. N-COUNT

mollycoddle /mɒlikɒdəl/ **mollycoddles, mollycoddling, mollycoddled.** If you accuse someone of **mollycoddling** someone else, you are critical of them for doing too many things for the other person and protecting them too much from unpleasant experiences. *Christopher accused me of mollycoddling Andrew.* VERB PRAGMATICS =pamper V n

Molotov cocktail /mɒlətɒv kɒkteɪl/ **Molotov cocktails.** A **Molotov cocktail** is a simple bomb made by putting petrol and cloth into a bottle. It is exploded by setting fire to the cloth. N-COUNT

molten /moultən/. **Molten** rock, metal, or glass has been heated to a very high temperature and has become a hot thick liquid. *The molten metal is poured into the mould.* ◆◇◇◇◇ ADJ: usu ADJ n

mom /mɒm/ **moms.** In American English, some people refer to or address their mother as **mom**; an informal word. The usual British word is **mum**. *We waited for Mom and Dad to get home... Mom, can you tell me how to do it?* ◆◆◇◇◇ N-FAMILY

moment /moumənt/ **moments** ◆◆◆◆◆

1 A **moment** or **moments** are a very short period of time, for example a few seconds. *In a moment he was gone... She stared at him a moment, then turned away... Stop for one moment and think about it!... In moments, I was asleep once more.* N-COUNT =minute, second

2 A particular **moment** is the point in time at which something happens. *At this moment a car stopped at the house... Many people still remember the moment when they heard that President Kennedy had been assassinated. ...a decision that may have been made in a moment of panic.* N-COUNT: with supp =instant

3 If you say that something will or may happen **at any moment** or **any moment now**, you are emphasizing that it is likely to happen very soon. *They ran the risk of being shot at any moment... He'll be here to see you any moment now.* PHRASES PRAGMATICS =at any minute

4 You use expressions such as **at the moment**, **at this moment**, and **at the present moment** to indicate that a particular situation exists at the time when you are speaking. *At the moment, no one is talking to me... This is being planned at the present moment... He's touring South America at this moment in time.* =now, currently

5 If you say that you do not believe **for a moment** or **for one moment** that something is true, you are emphasizing that you do not believe that it could possible be true. *I don't for a moment think there'll be a divorce.* with brd-neg, PHR with v PRAGMATICS =for a minute

6 You use **for the moment** to indicate that something is true now, even if it will not be true later or in the future. *For the moment, however, the government is happy to live with it.* PHR with cl =for now

7 If you say that someone or something **has** their **moments**, you are indicating that there are times when they are successful or interesting, but that this does not happen very often. *The film has its moments... He's not the thoroughly outgoing character you'd predict, although he has his moments.* V inflects

8 If someone does something at **the last moment**, they do it at the latest time possible. *They changed their minds at the last moment and refused to go.* prep PHR =the last minute

9 You use the expression **the next moment** or expressions such as **'one moment** he was there, **the next** he was gone' to emphasize that something happens suddenly, especially when it is very different from what was happening before. *The next moment there was an almighty crash... He is unpredictable, weeping one moment, laughing the next.* PRAGMATICS =the next minute

10 You use **of the moment** to describe someone or something that is or was especially popular at a particular time, especially when you want to suggest that their popularity is unlikely to last long or did not last long. *He's the man of the moment, isn't he?... He calls it a 'contraption', using his favourite word of the moment.* n PHR PRAGMATICS

11 If you say that something happens **the moment** something else happens, you are emphasizing that it happens immediately after the other thing. *The moment I closed my eyes, I fell asleep.* PHR that PRAGMATICS =the minute, as soon as

12 ● **spur of the moment**: see **spur**.

momentarily /moumənteərɪli/

1 **Momentarily** means for a short time. *She paused momentarily when she saw them.* ADV: usu ADV with v =briefly

2 In American English, **momentarily** means very soon. Some speakers think this use is incorrect. *The younger hunters stand up, all eyes turned towards the woods, towards the exact spot from which the pack will momentarily appear.* ADV: usu ADV after v =imminently

momentary /mouməntəri, AM -teri/. Something that is **momentary** lasts for a very short period of time, for example for a few seconds or less. *...a momentary lapse of concentration... His hesitation was only momentary.* ◆◇◇◇◇ ADJ =brief

moment of truth, moments of truth. If you refer to a time or event as the **moment of truth**, you mean that it is an important time when you must make a decision quickly, and whatever you decide will have important consequences in the future. *Both men knew the moment of truth had arrived.* N-COUNT =crunch

momentous /mouməntəs/. If you refer to a decision, event, or change as **momentous**, you mean that it is very important, often because of the effects that it will have in the future. *...the* ◆◇◇◇◇ ADJ-GRADED *momentous decision to send in the troops... The past three years have been among the most momentous in world history.*

momentum /moʊme̲ntəm/ ◆◆◇◇◇

1 If a process or movement gains **momentum**, it develops or progresses increasingly quickly, and becomes increasingly less likely to stop. *This campaign is really gaining momentum... They are each anxious to maintain the momentum of the search for a solution.* N-UNCOUNT =impetus

2 **Momentum** is the mass of a moving object multiplied by its velocity; a technical use in physics. N-UNCOUNT

momma /mɒ̲mə/ **mommas.** In American English, **momma** means the same as **mommy**; an informal word. ◆◇◇◇◇ N-FAMILY

mommy /mɒ̲mi/ **mommies.** In American English, some people refer to or address their mother as **mommy**; an informal word. The usual British word is **mummy**. *Mommy and I went in an aeroplane.* N-FAMILY

Mon. **Mon.** is a written abbreviation for **Monday**. *...Mon Oct 19.* ◆◆◇◇◇

monarch /mɒ̲nəʳk/ **monarchs.** The **monarch** of a country or an empire is the king, queen, or other hereditary ruler who reigns over the country or empire. ◆◆◇◇◇ N-COUNT

monarchical /mɒnɑ̲ːʳkɪkəl/. **Monarchical** means relating to a monarch or monarchs. *...a monarchical system of government.* ADJ: usu ADJ n

monarchist /mɒ̲nəʳkɪst/ **monarchists.** If someone has **monarchist** beliefs or views, they believe that their country should have a hereditary ruler such as a king or queen. *...the tiny monarchist party.* ► A **monarchist** is someone with monarchist views. ADJ-GRADED =royalist ≠republican; N-COUNT

monarchy /mɒ̲nəʳki/ **monarchies** ◆◆◇◇◇

1 A **monarchy** is a system in which a monarch reigns over a country. *In a few years we may no longer have a monarchy. ...a serious debate on the future of the monarchy.* N-VAR ≠republic

2 A **monarchy** is a country that is ruled by a monarch. N-COUNT ≠republic

3 The **monarchy** is used to refer to the monarch and his or her family. *The monarchy has to create a balance between its public and private lives.* N-COUNT: usu *the* N =royal family

monastery /mɒ̲nəstri, AM -teri/ **monasteries.** A **monastery** is a building or collection of buildings in which monks live. ◆◇◇◇◇ N-COUNT

monastic /mənæ̲stɪk/. **Monastic** means relating to monks or to a monastery. *He was drawn to the monastic life. ...monastic orders.* ADJ: usu ADJ n

Monday /mʌ̲ndeɪ, -di/ **Mondays.** **Monday** is the day after Sunday and before Tuesday. *I went back to work on Monday... The attack took place last Monday... I'm usually here on Mondays and Fridays.* ◆◆◆◆◇ N-VAR

monetarism /mʌ̲nɪtərɪzəm, AM mɑ̲ːn-/. **Monetarism** is the control of a country's economy by regulating the total amount of money that is available and in use at any one time; a technical term in economics. N-UNCOUNT

monetarist /mʌ̲nɪtərɪst, AM mɑ̲ːn-/ **monetarists.** **Monetarist** policies or beliefs are based on the theory that a country's economy should be controlled by regulating the total amount of money that is available and in use at any one time; a technical term in economics. *...tough monetarist policies.* ► A **monetarist** is someone with monetarist views. ADJ-GRADED; N-COUNT

monetary /mʌ̲nɪtri, AM mɑ̲ːnɪteri/. **Monetary** means relating to money, especially the total amount of money in a country. *Some countries tighten monetary policy to avoid inflation... The courts will be asked to place a monetary value on his unfinished career.* ◆◆◆◇◇ ADJ: ADJ n

money /mʌ̲ni/ **monies** or **moneys** ◆◆◆◆◆

1 **Money** is the coins or bank notes that you use to buy things, or the sum that you have in a bank account. *A lot of the money that you pay at the cinema goes back to the film distributors... Players should be allowed to earn money from advertising... She probably had more money but she didn't spend it. ...discounts and money saving offers.* N-UNCOUNT

2 **Monies** is used to refer to several separate sums of money that form part of a larger amount that is received or spent; a formal use. *We drew up a schedule of payments for the rest of the monies owed. ...the investment and management of monies by pension funds.* N-PLURAL

3 See also **blood money**, **pocket money**.

4 If you say that someone **has money to burn**, you mean that they have more money than they need or that they spend their money on things that you think are unnecessary. *He was a high-earning broker with money to burn.* PHRASES V inflects

5 If you are **in the money**, you have a lot of money to spend; an informal expression. *If you are one of the lucky callers chosen to play, you could be in the money.* usu v-link PHR =rolling in it

6 If you **make money**, you obtain money by earning it or by making a profit. *They couldn't find work or make money in the cities. ...the only bit of the firm that consistently made money.* V inflects

7 If you say that you want someone to **put** their **money where their mouth is**, you want them to spend money to improve a bad situation, instead of just talking about improving it. *The government might be obliged to put its money where its mouth is to prove its commitment.* V inflects

8 If a government or a central bank **prints money**, it provides the money for public spending by producing more banknotes, rather than by earning or borrowing what it needs. *He warned that they should not print money to spend their way out of the economic hole.* V inflects

9 If you say that the **smart money** is on a particular person or thing, you mean that people who know a lot about it think that this person will be successful, or this thing will happen; used in journalism. *With England not playing, the smart money was on the Germans... A lot of smart money in Washington says that peace is nearly at hand.*

10 If you say that **money talks**, you mean that if someone has a lot of money, they also have a lot of power. *The formula in Hollywood is simple – money talks.*

11 If you say that someone is **throwing money at** a problem, you are critical of them for trying to improve it by spending money on it, instead of doing more thoughtful and practical things to improve it. *The Australian government's answer to the problem has been to throw money at it.* V inflects, PHR n PRAGMATICS

12 If you say that someone is **throwing good money after bad**, you are critical of them for trying to improve a bad situation by spending more money on it, instead of doing more thoughtful or practical things to improve it. *Further heavy intervention would be throwing good money after bad.* V inflects PRAGMATICS

13 If you get your **money's worth**, you get something which is worth the money that it costs or the effort you have put in. *The fans get their money's worth.* PHR after v =value for money

14 • to **see the colour of someone's money**: see **colour**. • **a licence to print money**: see **licence**. • to **be rolling in money**: see **rolling**. • **money for old rope**: see **rope**. • **give someone a run for** their **money**: see **run**. • **value for money**: see **value**.

mo̲ney box, money boxes. A **money box** is a small box with an opening at the top, into which a child puts coins as a way of saving money; used mainly in British English. N-COUNT

moneyed /mʌ̲nid/; also spelled **monied**. A **moneyed** person has a lot of money; a formal word. *Fear of crime among Japan's new monied classes is rising rapidly.* ADJ =affluent

moneylender /mʌ̲nilendəʳ/ **moneylenders;** also spelled **money-lender**. A **moneylender** is a person who lends money which has to be paid back at a high rate of interest; an old-fashioned word. N-COUNT

mo̲ney-maker, money-makers; also spelled **moneymaker**. If you say that a business, product, or investment is a **money-maker**, you mean that it makes a big profit. N-COUNT =money-spinner

money market, money markets. A country's **money market** consists of all the institutions such as the government and commercial banks that deal with short-term loans, capital, and foreign exchange. *On the money markets the dollar was weaker against European currencies.* ◆◇◇◇◇ N-COUNT

money order, money orders. In the United States, a **money order** is a piece of paper representing a sum of money which you can buy at a post office and send to someone as a way of sending them money by post. The usual British term is **postal order**. N-COUNT

money-spinner, money-spinners; also spelled **moneyspinner**. If you say that something is a **money-spinner**, you mean that it earns a lot of money for someone; an informal word. *The films have been fantastic money-spinners.* N-COUNT: usu adj N =money-maker

money supply. The **money supply** is the amount of money in circulation in a country's economy; a technical term in economics. *They believed that controlling the money supply would reduce inflation.* ◆◇◇◇◇ N-UNCOUNT: usu *the* N

Mongol /mɒŋgᵊl/ **Mongols**
1 The **Mongols** were a nomadic Asiatic people who conquered large areas of China and Central Asia under the leadership of Genghis Khan and Kublai Khan in the 12th and 13th centuries A.D. N-COUNT
2 **Mongol** means belonging or relating to the Mongols. *...the Mongol conquest of China.* ADJ: ADJ n

Mongolian /mɒŋgoʊliən/ **Mongolians** ◆◆◆◆◇
1 **Mongolian** means belonging or relating to Mongolia, or to its people, language, or culture. *...the Mongolian capital, Ulan Bator.* ADJ
2 A **Mongolian** is a Mongolian citizen, or a person of Mongolian origin. N-COUNT
3 **Mongolian** is the language that is spoken in Mongolia. *Until August of this year there was no complete translation of the New Testament in Mongolian.* N-UNCOUNT

mongrel /mʌŋgrəl/ **mongrels.** A **mongrel** is a dog which is not a pedigree but a mixture of different breeds. N-COUNT

monied /mʌnid/. See **moneyed**.

monitor /mɒnɪtəʳ/ **monitors, monitoring, monitored** ◆◆◆◇◇
1 If you **monitor** something, you regularly check its development or progress, and sometimes comment on it. *Officials had not been allowed to monitor the voting... You need feedback to monitor progress.* VERB Vn ♦ **monitoring** *...analysis and monitoring of the global environment.* N-UNCOUNT
2 If someone **monitors** radio broadcasts from other countries, they record them or listen carefully to them in order to obtain information. *Peter Murray is in London and has been monitoring reports out of Monrovia.* VERB Vn
3 A **monitor** is a machine that is used to check or record things, for example processes or substances inside a person's body. *The heart monitor shows low levels of consciousness.* N-COUNT: usu n N
4 A **monitor** is a screen which is used to display certain kinds of information, for example in airports or television studios. *He was watching the test on the television monitor.* N-COUNT: oft N n =screen
5 You can refer to a person who checks that something is done correctly, or that it is fair, as a **monitor**. *Government monitors will continue to accompany reporters. ...UN monitors overseeing Namibian independence.* N-COUNT: usu supp N =screen

monk /mʌŋk/ **monks.** A **monk** is a member of a male religious community that is usually separated from the outside world. *...saffron-robed Buddhist monks.* ◆◆◇◇◇ N-COUNT

monkey /mʌŋki/ **monkeys** ◆◆◇◇◇
1 A **monkey** is an animal with a long tail which lives in hot countries. Monkeys climb trees, and belong to the same family as gorillas and chimpanzees. N-COUNT
2 If you refer to a child as a **monkey**, you are saying in an affectionate way that he or she is very lively and naughty. *She's such a little monkey.* N-COUNT: usu adj N PRAGMATICS =scamp

monkey wrench, monkey wrenches. See **wrench**.

mono /mɒnoʊ/. **Mono** is used to describe a system of playing music in which all the sound is directed through one speaker only. Compare **stereo**. *This model has a mono soundtrack.* ◆◇◇◇◇ ADJ

mono- /mɒnoʊ-/. **Mono-** is used at the beginning of nouns and adjectives that have 'one' or 'single' as part of their meanings. *...high in mono-unsaturated fats. ...interaction between bilingual parents and monolingual teachers.* PREFIX

monochrome /mɒnəkroʊm/
1 A **monochrome** film, photograph, or television shows black, white, and shades of grey, but no other colours. *...color and monochrome monitors. ...scratchy monochrome movies.* ADJ: usu ADJ n =black and white
2 A **monochrome** picture uses only one colour in various shades. *...an old monochrome etching of a brewery.* ADJ: usu ADJ n

monocle /mɒnəkᵊl/ **monocles.** A **monocle** is a glass lens which people wore in former times in front of one of their eyes to improve their ability to see with that eye. N-COUNT

monogamous /mənɒgəməs/
1 Someone who is **monogamous** or who has a **monogamous** relationship has a sexual relationship with only one partner. *Do you believe that men are not naturally monogamous?... She wouldn't want to be in a monogamous relationship.* ADJ
2 **Monogamous** animals have only one mate during their lives or during one mating season. ADJ

monogamy /mənɒgəmi/
1 **Monogamy** is used to refer to the state or custom of having a sexual relationship with only one partner. *People still opt for monogamy and marriage.* N-UNCOUNT
2 **Monogamy** is the state or custom of being married to only one person at a particular time. *In many non-Western societies, however, monogamy has never dominated.* N-UNCOUNT ≠polygamy

monogram /mɒnəgræm/ **monograms.** A **monogram** is a design based on someone's initials, which is usually marked on things they own such as their clothes. N-COUNT

monogrammed /mɒnəgræmd/. **Monogrammed** means marked with a design that includes a person's initials. *...a monogrammed handkerchief.* ADJ

monograph /mɒnəgrɑːf, -græf/ **monographs.** A **monograph** is a book which is a detailed study of only one subject; a formal word. *...a monograph on her favourite author, John Masefield.* N-COUNT: oft N *on* n

monolingual /mɒnoʊlɪŋgwəl/. **Monolingual** means involving, using, or speaking one language. *Even as a largely monolingual country, Great Britain holds the potential to be culturally pluralistic.* ADJ: usu ADJ n

monolith /mɒnəlɪθ/ **monoliths**
1 A **monolith** is a very large, upright piece of stone, often one that was erected in ancient times. N-COUNT
2 If you refer to an organization or system as a **monolith**, you are critical of it because it is very large and very slow to change, and it does not seem to have different parts with different characters. *In the past the USSR was a monolith under the control of the Communist Party.* N-COUNT PRAGMATICS

monolithic /mɒnəlɪθɪk/
1 If you refer to an organization or system as **monolithic**, you are critical of it because it is very large and very slow to change, and does not seem to have different parts with different characters. *...an authoritarian and monolithic system.* ADJ-GRADED PRAGMATICS
2 If you describe something such as a building as **monolithic**, you do not like it because it is very large and plain with no character. *...a huge monolithic concrete building.* ADJ-GRADED: usu ADJ n PRAGMATICS

monologue /mɒnəlɒg, AM -lɔːg/ **monologues** ◆◇◇◇◇
1 If you refer to a long speech by one person during a conversation as a **monologue**, you mean it prevents other people from talking or expressing their opinions. *Morris ignored the question and continued his monologue.* N-COUNT
2 A **monologue** is a long speech which is spoken by one person as an entertainment, or as part of an entertainment such as a play. *...a monologue based on the writing of Quentin Crisp.* N-VAR =dialogue

monopolistic /mənɒpəlɪstɪk/. If you refer to a business or its practices as **monopolistic**, you mean that it tries to control as much of an industry as it can and does not allow fair competition. ADJ-GRADED: usu ADJ n

monopolize /mənɒpəlaɪz/ **monopolizes, monopolizing, monopolized;** also spelled **monopolise** in British English. ◆◇◇◇◇

1 If you say that someone **monopolizes** something, you mean that they have a very large share of it and prevent other people from having a share. *They are controlling so much cocoa that they are virtually monopolizing the market... Johnson, as usual, monopolized the conversation.* VERB V n

♦ **monopolization** /mənɒpəlaɪzeɪʃᵊn/ *...the monopolization of a market by a single supplier.* N-UNCOUNT: oft N *of* n

2 If something or someone **monopolizes** you, they demand a lot of your time and attention, so that there is very little time left for anything or anyone else. *He would monopolize her totally, to the exclusion of her brothers and sisters.* VERB V n

monopoly /mənɒpəli/ **monopolies** ◆◆◇◇◇

1 If a company, person, or state has a **monopoly** on something such as an industry, they have complete control over it, so that it is impossible for others to become involved in it. *...Russian moves to end a state monopoly on land ownership. ...the governing party's monopoly over the media. ...an inquiry by the Monopolies Commission.* N-VAR: oft with poss, oft N *on/over* n/-ing

2 A **monopoly** is a company which is the only provider of a particular product or service and which therefore has complete control over an industry, so that it is impossible for other companies to compete with it. *...a state-owned monopoly.* N-COUNT

3 If you say that someone does not have a **monopoly** on something, you mean that they are not the only person who has that thing. *Women do not have a monopoly on feelings of betrayal.* N-SING: with brd-neg, usu N *on* n

monorail /mɒnoʊreɪl/ **monorails.** A **monorail** is a system of transport in which small trains travel along a single rail which is usually high above the ground. N-COUNT: also *by* N

monosodium glutamate /mɒnəsoʊdiəm gluːtəmeɪt/. **Monosodium glutamate** is a substance which is sometimes added to food in order to make it taste better. Monosodium glutamate is used in some ready-made foods. The abbreviation **MSG** is also used. N-UNCOUNT

monosyllabic /mɒnoʊsɪlæbɪk/. If you refer to someone or the way they speak as **monosyllabic**, you mean that they say very little, usually because they do not want to have a conversation. *He could be gruff and monosyllabic.* ADJ-GRADED

monosyllable /mɒnoʊsɪləbᵊl/ **monosyllables.** If you say that someone speaks in **monosyllables** you mean that they speak very little, usually because they do not want to have a conversation. *A taciturn man, he replied to my questions in monosyllables.* N-COUNT: usu *in* N in pl

monotone /mɒnətoʊn/ **monotones**

1 If someone speaks in a **monotone**, their voice does not vary at all in tone or loudness and so it is not interesting to listen to. *The evidence was read out to the court in a dull monotone.* N-COUNT: usu sing, also *in* N =drone

2 **Monotone** sounds and colours do not have any variations or shades. *He was seen on TV delivering platitudes about the crisis in a monotone voice.* ADJ: usu ADJ n

monotonous /mənɒtənəs/. Something that is **monotonous** is very boring because it has a regular, repeated pattern which never changes. *It's monotonous work, like most factory jobs... The food may get a bit monotonous, but there'll be enough of it.* ♦ **monotonously** *The rain dripped monotonously from the trees.* ◆◇◇◇◇ ADJ-GRADED =repetitive ≠varied ADV-GRADED

monotony /mənɒtəni/. The **monotony** of something is the fact that it never changes and is repetitive and boring. *A night on the town may help to break the monotony of the week. ...a life of secure monotony.* N-UNCOUNT: oft N *of* n

monoxide /mənɒksaɪd/. See **carbon monoxide**.

Monsignor /mɒnsiːnjɔːʳ/ **Monsignors. Monsignor** is the title of a priest of high rank in the Catholic Church. *Monsignor Jaime Goncalves was also there... The Monsignor gave him a slow, expressionless nod.* ◆◇◇◇◇ N-TITLE; N-COUNT: usu sing

monsoon /mɒnsuːn/ **monsoons** ◆◇◇◇◇

1 The **monsoon** is the season in Southern Asia when there is a lot of very heavy rain. *...the end of the monsoon. ...monsoon flooding.* N-COUNT: oft *the* N

2 Monsoon rains are sometimes referred to as the **monsoons**. *In Bangladesh, the monsoons have started.* N-PLURAL: oft *the* N

monster /mɒnstəʳ/ **monsters** ◆◆◇◇◇

1 A **monster** is a large imaginary creature that looks very ugly and frightening. N-COUNT

2 A **monster** is something which is extremely large, especially something which is difficult to manage or which is unpleasant. *...the monster which is now the London marathon. ...the monster of apartheid.* N-COUNT

3 **Monster** means extremely and surprisingly large; an informal use. *...a monster weapon... The film will be a monster hit.* ADJ: ADJ n PRAGMATICS =giant

4 If you describe someone as a **monster**, you mean that they are cruel, frightening, or evil. N-COUNT =fiend

monstrosity /mɒnstrɒsɪti/ **monstrosities.** If you describe something, especially something large, as a **monstrosity**, you mean that you think it is extremely ugly. *Most of the older buildings have been torn down and replaced by modern monstrosities.* N-COUNT PRAGMATICS

monstrous /mɒnstrəs/ ◆◇◇◇◇

1 If you describe a situation or event as **monstrous**, you mean that it is extremely shocking or unfair. *She endured the monstrous behaviour for years... I just hope the people who committed this monstrous evil will be able to live with themselves.* ♦ **monstrously** *Your husband's family has behaved monstrously.* ADJ-GRADED: usu ADJ n PRAGMATICS =atrocious ADV-GRADED: ADV after v

2 If you describe an unpleasant thing as **monstrous**, you mean that it is extremely large in size or extent. *A group of men are erecting a monstrous copper edifice... It was blowing a monstrous gale.* ♦ **monstrously** *It would be monstrously unfair... Monstrously inflated prices are designed to keep people like us at bay.* ADJ-GRADED: usu ADJ n PRAGMATICS ADV-GRADED: ADV adj/-ed =hugely

3 If you describe something as **monstrous**, you mean that it is extremely frightening because it appears unnatural or ugly. *...the film's monstrous fantasy figure.* ADJ-GRADED: usu ADJ n =hideous

montage /mɒntɑːʒ, mɒntɑːʒ/ **montages.** A **montage** is a picture, film, or piece of music which consists of several different items that are put together, often in an unusual combination or sequence. *...a photo montage of some of Italy's top television stars.* N-COUNT

month /mʌnθ/ **months** ◆◆◆◆◆

1 A **month** is one of the twelve periods of time that a year is divided into, for example January or February. *The trial is due to begin next month. ...an exhibition which opens this month at London's Design Museum... I send him fifteen dollars a month.* N-COUNT

2 A **month** is a period of about four weeks. *She was here for a month... Over the next several months I met most of her family... They had all spent £180 for a month's unlimited train travel around Europe.* N-COUNT

monthly /mʌnθli/ **monthlies** ◆◆◆◇◇

1 A **monthly** event or publication happens or appears every month. *Many people are now having trouble making their monthly house payments... Kidscape runs monthly workshops for teachers. ...Young Guard, a monthly journal founded in 1922.* ► Also an adverb. *In some areas the property price can rise monthly.* ADJ: ADJ n ADV: ADV after v

2 You can refer to a publication that is published monthly as a **monthly**. *...Scallywag, a London satirical monthly. ...the Nairobi Law Monthly.* N-COUNT: oft in names

3 **Monthly** quantities or rates relate to a period of one month. *The monthly rent for a two-bedroom flat would be £953.33... Monthly interest costs vary.* ADJ: ADJ n

monument /mɒnjʊmənt/ **monuments** ◆◆◇◇◇

1 A **monument** is a large structure, usually made of stone, which is built to remind people of an event in history or of a famous person. N-COUNT

2 A **monument** is something such as a castle or bridge which was built a very long time ago and is N-COUNT

regarded as an important part of a country's history. *...the ancient monuments of England, Scotland and Wales.*

3 If you describe something as a **monument** to someone's qualities, you mean that it is a very good example of the results or effects of those qualities. *By his international achievements he leaves a fitting monument to his beliefs.* N-COUNT: N to n

monumental /mɒnjʊmentᵊl/ ◆◇◇◇◇

1 You can use **monumental** to emphasize the size or extent of something. *It had been a monumental blunder to give him the assignment. ...a series of monumental disappointments.* ♦ **monumentally** *Suddenly it was monumentally successful... That was the most monumentally hideous night of my life!* ADJ-GRADED: usu ADJ n PRAGMATICS =huge ADV-GRADED: usu ADV adj/-ed, also ADV after v

2 If you describe a book or musical work as **monumental**, you are emphasizing that it is very large and impressive, and is likely to be important for a long time. *...his monumental work on Chinese astronomy.* ADJ-GRADED: usu ADJ n PRAGMATICS

3 A **monumental** building or sculpture is very large and historically or artistically important. *I take no real interest in monumental sculpture.* ADJ: ADJ n

moo /muː/ **moos, mooing, mooed.** When cattle, especially cows, **moo**, they make the long low sound that cattle typically make. *...a sound like a cow mooing.* ► Also a noun. *The cow says 'moo-moo'.* VERB =low V N-COUNT; SOUND

mooch /muːtʃ/ **mooches, mooching, mooched**

mooch around; the form **mooch about** is also used in British English. If you **mooch around** or **mooch about** a place, you move around there slowly with no particular purpose. *Andrew was left to mooch around the house on his own... He was awake at 3am, mooching about in the darkness.* PHRASAL VERB =wander around V P n V P

mood /muːd/ **moods** ◆◆◆◇◇

1 Your **mood** is the way you are feeling at a particular time. If you are in a good **mood**, you feel cheerful. If you are in a bad **mood**, you feel angry and impatient. *He is clearly in a good mood today... When he came back, he was in a foul mood... Lily was in one of her aggressive moods... His moods swing alarmingly.* • If you say that you are **in the mood** for something, you mean that you want to do it or have it. If you say that you are **in no mood** to do something, you mean that you do not want to do it or have it. *After a day of air and activity, you should be in the mood for a good meal... He was in no mood to celebrate.* N-COUNT: with supp, oft adj N, oft *in* N PHRASE: v-link PHR, PHR after v, oft PHR *for* n/-ing, PHR to-inf

2 If someone is in a **mood**, the way they are behaving shows that they are feeling angry and impatient. *She was obviously in a mood.* N-COUNT: oft *in a* N =temper

3 The **mood** of a group of people is the way that they think and feel about an idea, event, or question at a particular time. *The government seemed to be in tune with the popular mood... They largely misread the mood of the electorate.* N-SING: usu with supp, oft with poss

4 The **mood** of a place is the general impression that you get of it. *First set the mood with music... I wanted different moods in each room.* N-COUNT =atmosphere

5 In grammar, the **mood** of a clause is the way in which the verb forms are used to show whether the clause is, for example, a statement, a question, or an instruction. N-VAR

moody /muːdi/ **moodier, moodiest** ◆◆◇◇◇

1 If you describe someone as **moody**, you mean that their feelings and behaviour change frequently, and in particular that they often become depressed or angry without any warning. *David's mother was unstable and moody... Ray is a complicated, moody man behind the joking front.* ♦ **moodily** /muːdɪli/ *He sat and stared moodily out the window.* ♦ **moodiness** *His moodiness may have been caused by his poor health.* ADJ-GRADED =temperamental ADV-GRADED: usu ADV with v N-UNCOUNT

2 If you describe a picture, film, or piece of music as **moody**, you mean that it suggests particular emotions, especially sad ones. *...moody black and white photographs. ...a blend of melancholy guitars and moody lyrics.* ADJ-GRADED: usu ADJ n =atmospheric

moon /muːn/ **moons, mooning, mooned** ◆◆◆◇◇

1 The **moon** is the object in the sky that goes round the Earth once every four weeks and that you can often see at night as a circle or part of a circle. You also talk about the **moon** when you are referring to the fact that the moon can be seen or when you are describing what it looks like. *...the first man on the moon... There will be no moon. ...the light of a full moon.* • See also **new moon**. N-SING: usu *the* N, also *full/new* N

2 A **moon** is an object like a small planet that travels around a planet. *...Neptune's large moon.* N-COUNT: usu poss N

3 If you **are mooning** around, you are spending time doing nothing in particular, for example because you feel unhappy or lazy, or are worried about something. *Lettie was mooning around all morning, doing nothing... My working days were spent mooning round his department, trying to sneak a chance encounter.* VB: usu cont =mope V adv/prep

4 If you say that something happens **once in a blue moon**, you are emphasizing that it does not happen very often at all. *Once in a blue moon you get some problems.* PHRASES PHR with cl PRAGMATICS

5 If you say that you are **over the moon**, you mean that you are very pleased about something; an informal expression, used mainly in British English. v-link PHR =overjoyed

moonbeam /muːnbiːm/ **moonbeams.** A **moonbeam** is a ray of light from the moon. N-COUNT

moonless /muːnləs/. A **moonless** sky or night is dark because there is no moon. ADJ

moonlight /muːnlaɪt/ **moonlights, moonlighting, moonlighted** ◆◇◇◇◇

1 **Moonlight** is the light that comes from the moon at night. *They walked along the road in the moonlight... We went to the temple of Atlantis and saw it by moonlight.* N-UNCOUNT

2 If someone **moonlights**, they have a second job in addition to their main job, often without informing their main employers or the tax office. *...an engineer who was moonlighting as a taxi driver... Workers in state enterprises were permitted to moonlight.* VERB V as n V

moonlit /muːnlɪt/. Something that is **moonlit** is lit by moonlight. *...a beautiful moonlit night.* ADJ: usu ADJ n

moonshine /muːnʃaɪn/

1 In American English, **moonshine** is whisky that is made illegally. N-UNCOUNT

2 If you say that someone's thoughts, ideas, or comments are **moonshine**, you think they are foolish and not based on reality. *As Morison remarks, the story is pure moonshine.* N-UNCOUNT PRAGMATICS =fantasy

moor /mʊəʳ/ **moors, mooring, moored** ◆◆◇◇◇

1 A **moor** is an area of open, uncultivated, and usually high land with poor soil that is covered mainly with grass and heather; used mainly in British English. *Colliford is higher, right up on the moors... Exmoor National Park stretches over 265 square miles of moor.* N-VAR

2 If you **moor** a boat or if you **moor**, you stop in a place and attach the boat to the land with a rope or cable so that it cannot drift away. *She had moored her barge on the right bank of the river... I decided to moor near some tourist boats.* VERB =tie up V n V

3 The **Moors** were a dark-skinned Muslim people who established a civilization in North Africa and Spain between the 8th and the 15th century A.D. N-COUNT: usu pl

4 See also **mooring**.

mooring /mʊərɪŋ/ **moorings** ◆◇◇◇◇

1 A **mooring** is the place on land or the particular object such as a metal ring to which a boat is tied so that it cannot drift away. *Free moorings will be available. ...mooring fees.* N-COUNT

2 **Moorings** are the rope, anchors, or chains used to moor a boat or ship. *He cut the engine and grabbed the mooring lines... Emergency workers fear that the burning ship could slip its moorings.* N-PLURAL: oft N n

Moorish /mʊərɪʃ/. Something that is **Moorish** dates back to or is characteristic of Muslim civilization in North Africa and Spain between the 8th and the 15th century A.D. *...a medieval Moorish palace.* ADJ: usu ADJ n

moorland /mʊəʳlænd/ **moorlands.** **Moorland** is land which consists of moors. *...rugged Yorkshire moorland.* ◆◇◇◇◇ N-UNCOUNT: also N in pl

moose /muːs/; **moose** is both the singular and the plural form. A **moose** is a large North American deer. ◆◇◇◇◇ N-COUNT =elk

moot /muːt/ **moots, mooting, mooted** ◆◇◇◇◇
1 If a plan, idea, or subject **is mooted**, it is suggested or introduced for discussion; a formal word. *Plans have been mooted for a 450,000-strong Ukrainian army... When the theatre idea was first mooted I had my doubts.* VB: usu passive =propose, put forward *be* V-ed
2 If something is a **moot** point or question, people cannot agree about it. *How long he'll be able to do so is a moot point.* ADJ-GRADED

mop /mɒp/ **mops, mopping, mopped** ◆◇◇◇◇
1 A **mop** is a piece of equipment for washing floors. It consists of a sponge or many pieces of string attached to a long handle. N-COUNT
2 If you **mop** a surface such as a floor, you clean it with a mop. *There was a woman mopping the stairs.* VERB V n
3 If you **mop** sweat from your forehead, or if you **mop** your forehead, you wipe it with a handkerchief. *He mopped perspiration from his forehead... The Inspector took out a handkerchief and mopped his brow.* VERB =wipe V n *from* n V n
4 If someone has a **mop** of hair, they have a lot of hair and it looks rather untidy. *He was long-limbed and dark-eyed, with a mop of tight, dark curls.* N-COUNT: usu N *of* n

mop up PHRASAL VERB
1 If you **mop up** a liquid, you clean it with a cloth so that the liquid is absorbed. *A waiter mopped up the mess as best he could... When the washing machine spurts out water at least we can mop it up... Michael mopped up quickly with his napkin.* =wipe up V P n (not pron) V n P V P
2 If you **mop up** something that you think is undesirable or dangerous, you remove it or deal with it so that it is no longer a problem. *The infantry divisions mopped up remaining centres of resistance... These reactive molecules are mopped up and made harmless by Vitamin E.* V P n (not pron) Also V n P

mope /moʊp/ **mopes, moping, moped.** If you **mope**, you feel miserable and do not feel interested in doing anything. *Get on with life and don't sit back and mope.* VERB V

mope around; the form **mope about** is also used in British English. If you **mope around** or **mope about** a place, you wander around there not doing anything, looking and feeling unhappy. *He moped around the office for a while, feeling bored... He mopes about all day.* PHRASAL VERB V P n V P

moped /moʊped/ **mopeds.** A **moped** is a small motorcycle which you can also pedal like a bicycle; used mainly in British English. N-COUNT

moral /mɒrᵊl, AM mɔːr-/ **morals** ◆◆◆◇◇
1 **Morals** are principles and beliefs concerning right and wrong behaviour. *...Western ideas and morals... They have no morals.* N-PLURAL =ethics
2 **Moral** means relating to beliefs about what is right or wrong. *She describes her own moral dilemma in making the film. ...matters of church doctrine and moral teaching. ...the moral issues involved in 'playing God'.* ♦ **morally** *When, if ever, is it morally justifiable to allow a patient to die?... Is there really morally any difference between slaughtering a cow for food and a horse for food?* ADJ: ADJ n =ethical ADV-GRADED: ADV adj/adv, ADV after v, ADV with cl
3 **Moral** courage or duty is based on what you believe is right or acceptable, rather than on what the law says should be done. *The Government had a moral, if not a legal duty to pay compensation. ...his moral courage and sane defence of his philosophy.* ADJ: ADJ n
4 A **moral** person behaves in a way that is believed by most people to be good and right. *The people who will be on the committee are moral, cultured, competent people.* ♦ **morally** *Art is not there to improve you morally.* ADJ-GRADED: usu ADJ n =ethical ADV: ADV with v
5 If you give someone **moral** support, you encourage them in what they are doing by expressing approval. *Moral as well as financial support was what the West should provide.* ADJ: ADJ n
6 The **moral** of a story or event is what you learn from it about how you should or should not behave. *I think the moral of the story is let the buyer beware... The moral is that, once cooked, they look the same and taste every bit as good.* N-COUNT: usu *the* N in sing =message
7 ● **moral victory**: see **victory**.

morale /mərɑːl, -ræl/. **Morale** is the amount of confidence and optimism that people have. *Many pilots are suffering from low morale... They hope to boost the morale of their troops.* ◆◆◇◇◇ N-UNCOUNT: oft with poss

moral fibre; spelled **moral fiber** in American English. **Moral fibre** is the quality of being determined to do what you think is right. *...a man of stern moral fibre. ...the destruction of the moral fibre of the nation.* N-UNCOUNT

moralise /mɒrəlaɪz, AM mɔːr-/. See **moralize**.

moralist /mɒrəlɪst, AM mɔːr-/ **moralists.** A **moralist** is someone who has strong ideas about right and wrong behaviour, and who tries to make other people behave according to these ideas. N-COUNT

moralistic /mɒrəlɪstɪk, AM mɔːr-/. If you describe someone or something as **moralistic**, you are critical of them for making harsh judgements of other people on the basis of their own ideas about what is right and wrong. *He has become more moralistic... To me moralistic films are just unbearable.* ADJ-GRADED PRAGMATICS =self-righteous

morality /məræləti/ **moralities** ◆◆◇◇◇
1 **Morality** is the belief that some behaviour is right and acceptable and that other behaviour is wrong. *...standards of morality and justice in society. ...an effort to preserve traditional morality.* N-UNCOUNT =ethics
2 A **morality** is a system of principles and values concerning people's behaviour, which is generally accepted by a society or by a particular group of people. *...a morality that is sexist. ...communities and their shared moralities.* N-COUNT =ethic
3 The **morality** of something is how right or acceptable it is. *...the arguments about the morality of blood sports.* N-UNCOUNT: usu *the* N *of* n

moralize /mɒrəlaɪz, AM mɔːr-/ **moralizes, moralizing, moralized;** also spelled **moralise** in British English. If you say that someone **is moralizing**, you are critical of them for telling people what they think is right or wrong, especially when they have not been asked their opinion. *As a dramatist I hate to moralize... Society in general moralized about 'loose women'.* ♦ **moralizing** *We have tried to avoid any moralising.* VERB PRAGMATICS =preach V N-UNCOUNT

moral majority. If there is a large group in society that holds strong, conservative opinions on matters of morality and religion, you can refer to these people as the **moral majority**. In the United States, there is an organized group called **the Moral Majority**. *...unless the writers begin to write decent comedy and stop pandering to the moral majority.* N-SING-COLL; N-PROPER-COLL: *the* N

morass /məræs/ **morasses.** If you describe an unpleasant or confused situation as a **morass**, you mean that it seems impossible to escape from or resolve, because it has become so serious or so complicated. *I tried to drag myself out of the morass of despair. ...the economic morass.* N-COUNT: usu sing, with supp, oft N *of* n =quagmire

moratorium /mɒrətɔːriəm, AM mɔːr-/ **moratoriums** or **moratoria.** A **moratorium** on a particular activity or process is the stopping of it for a fixed period of time, usually as a result of an official agreement. *The House voted to impose a one-year moratorium on nuclear testing.* ◆◇◇◇◇ N-COUNT: usu sing, oft N *on* n

morbid /mɔːʳbɪd/. If you describe a person or their interest in something as **morbid**, you mean that they are very interested in unpleasant things, especially death, and you find this strange or unwise. *Some people have a morbid fascination with crime. ...morbid curiosity about the convicted murderer.* ♦ **morbidly** *There's something morbidly fascinating about the thought.* ◆◇◇◇◇ ADJ-GRADED =ghoulish ADV-GRADED: usu ADV adj

mordant /mɔːʳdᵊnt/. **Mordant** humour or wit is sarcastic, sharp, and critical, but also very funny; a formal word. *...his mordant wit. ...a mordant sense of humour.* ADJ-GRADED: usu ADJ n =biting

more /mɔːʳ/ ◆◆◆◆◆
More is often considered to be the comparative form of **much** and **many**.

1 You use **more** to indicate that there is a greater number of things or a greater amount of something than before or than average, or than something else. You can use 'a little', 'a lot', 'a bit', 'far', 'much' in front of **more**. *More and more people are surviving heart attacks... He spent more time perfecting his dance moves instead of gym work. ...teaching more children foreign languages other than English... It's a good idea to give adolescents a little more information than they ask for.* ► Also a pronoun. *As the level of work increased from light to heavy, workers ate more... He had four hundred dollars in his pocket. Billy had more.* ► Also a quantifier. *Employees may face increasing pressure to take on more of their own medical costs in retirement... The urgent need to bolster the reforms is beginning to demand more of his attention.*
DET: DET pl-n/n-uncount ≠less
PRON
QUANT: QUANT *of* def-n

2 You use **more than** before a number or amount to say that the actual number or amount is even greater. *The Afghan authorities say the airport had been closed for more than a year. ...classy leather and silk jackets at more than £250. ...a survey of more than 1,500 schools.*
PHR-PREP: PREP amount =over ≠less than

3 You use **more** to indicate that something or someone has a greater amount of a quality than they used to or than is average or usual. *Prison conditions have become more brutal... We can satisfy our basic wants more easily than in the past.*
ADV-COMPAR: ADV adj/adv ≠less

4 If you say that something is **more** one thing than another, you mean that it is like the first thing rather than the second. *The exhibition at Boston's Museum of Fine Arts is more a production than it is a museum display... He's more like a film star than a life-guard, really... She looked more sad than in pain... Sue screamed, not loudly, more in surprise than terror... She's more of a social animal than me.*
ADV-COMPAR: ADV group *than* group/cl, ADV *of a* n ≠less

5 If you do something **more** than before or **more** than someone else, you do it to a greater extent or more often. *When we are tired, tense, depressed or unwell, we feel pain much more... What impressed me more was that she knew Tennessee Williams.*
ADV-COMPAR: ADV with v ≠less

6 You can use **more** to indicate that something continues to happen for a further period of time. *Things might have been different if I'd talked a bit more.* ● You can use **some more** to indicate that something continues to happen for a further period of time. *We walked some more.*
ADV-COMPAR: ADV after v
PHRASE: PHR after v

7 You use **more** to indicate that something is repeated. For example, if you do something 'once more', you do it again once. *This train would stop twice more in the suburbs before rolling southeast toward Munich... The breathing exercises should be repeated several times more.*
ADV-COMPAR: adv ADV, n ADV

8 You use **more** to refer to an additional thing or amount. You can use 'a little', 'a lot', 'a bit', 'far', 'much' in front of **more**. *They needed more time to consider whether to hold an inquiry.* ► Also an adjective. *We stayed in Danville two more days... Are you sure you wouldn't like some more wine?* ► Also a pronoun. *Oxfam has appealed to western nations to do more to help the refugees... 'None of them are very nice folks.'—'Tell me more.'*
DET: DET pl-n/n-uncount
ADJ-COMPAR: ADJ n
PRON

9 You can use **more** in expressions like 'no more, no less' and 'neither more nor less' to indicate that what you are saying is exactly true or correct. *I told him the truth. No more, no less... I'm sixty-two. I feel sixty-two, neither more nor less.*
PRON PRAGMATICS

10 You use **more** in conversations when you want to draw someone's attention to something interesting or important that you are about to say. *Over the past few decades, continental Europe's economies have converged in several areas. More interestingly, there has been convergence in economic growth rates... More seriously for him, there are members who say he is wrong on this issue.*
ADV-COMPAR: ADV adv/adj PRAGMATICS ≠less

11 You can use **more and more** to indicate that something is becoming greater in amount, extent, or degree all the time. *Her life was heading more and more where she wanted it to go... Bob became more and more furious... More and more women are wearing men's fragrances.*
PHRASES usu PHR with v, PHR group/cl =less and less

12 If something is **more or less** true, it is true in a general way, but is not completely true. *The Conference is more or less over... He more or less started the firm... I was meeting these chaps who were mostly more or less my own age.*
PHR with group/cl, PHR before v PRAGMATICS

13 If something is **more than** a particular thing, it has greater value or importance than this thing. *He's more than a coach, he's a friend.*
v-link PHR n =less than

14 You use **more than** to say that something is true to a greater degree than is necessary or than average. *Lithuania produces more than enough food to feed itself. ...accommodation which is roomy and offers more than generous stowage.*
PHR n, PHR adj =less than

15 You use **no more than** or **not more than** when you want to emphasize how small a number or amount is. *Each box requires no more than a few hours of labor to build... He was a kid really, not more than eighteen or nineteen.*
PHR amount PRAGMATICS ≠no less than

16 If you say that someone or something is **nothing more than** a particular thing, you are emphasizing that they are only that thing, and nothing more interesting or important. *The newly discovered notes are nothing more than Lang's personal journal.*
v-link PHR n PRAGMATICS

17 You can use **what is more** or **what's more** to introduce an extra piece of information which supports or emphasizes the point you are making. *Many more institutions, especially banks, were allowed to lend money for mortgages, and what was more, banks could lend out more money than they actually held... You should remember it, and what's more, you should get it right.*
V inflects, PHR cl PRAGMATICS =moreover, furthermore

18 ● **all the more**: see **all**. ● **any more**: see **any**.

moreover /mɔːroʊvəʳ/. You use **moreover** to introduce a piece of information that adds to or supports the previous statement; a formal word. *She saw that there was indeed a man immediately behind her. Moreover, he was observing her strangely... The young find everything so simple. The young, moreover, see it as their duty to be happy and do their best to be so.*
◆◆◆◇◇ ADV: ADV with cl (not last in cl) PRAGMATICS =furthermore, what is more

mores /mɔːreɪz/. The **mores** of a particular place or group of people are the customs and behaviour that are typically found in that place or group; a formal word. *...the accepted mores of British society. ...profound changes in social and sexual mores.*
N-PLURAL: usu with supp

morgue /mɔːʳg/ **morgues**

1 A **morgue** is a building or room where dead bodies are kept before being cremated or buried.
N-COUNT =mortuary

2 In the United States, a **morgue** is a building or room where dead bodies are kept before being identified or examined by the medical examiner.
N-COUNT

moribund /mɒrɪbʌnd, AM mɔːr-/. If you describe something as **moribund**, you mean that it is in a very bad condition; a formal word. *...the moribund economy. ...the moribund housing market... The British music scene is nostalgic, decrepit and moribund.*
◆◇◇◇◇ ADJ-GRADED

Mormon /mɔːʳmən/ **Mormons. Mormon** means relating to the Christian religious group founded by Joseph Smith in the United States. *...the Mormon church. ...a Mormon family.* ► **Mormons** are people who are Mormon.
◆◇◇◇◇ ADJ
N-COUNT

morn /mɔːʳn/. **Morn** means the same as morning; a literary word. *...one cold February morn.*
N-SING: also no det

morning /mɔːʳnɪŋ/ **mornings** ◆◆◆◆◆

1 The **morning** is the part of each day between the time that people usually wake up and noon or lunchtime. *During the morning your guide will take you around the city... On Sunday morning Bill was woken by the telephone... He read about it in his morning paper.*
N-VAR

2 If you refer to a particular time in the **morning**, you mean a time during the part of a day between midnight and noon. *I often stayed up until two or three in the morning... The attack happened in the early hours of the morning.*
N-SING: *the* N

3 If you say that something will happen **in the morning**, you mean that it will happen during the
PHRASES =tomorrow morning

morning of the following day. *I'll fly it to London in the morning... Melanie promised that she would call them in the morning.*
4 If you say that something happens **morning, noon and night**, you mean that it happens all the time. *You get fit by playing the game, day in, day out, morning, noon and night.* PHR after v

morning dress. **Morning dress** is a suit of clothes that is worn by men for very formal or special occasions such as weddings. It consists of a grey or black coat that is longer at the back than the front, grey or grey striped trousers, a white shirt, a grey tie, and often a top hat. N-UNCOUNT

morning room, morning rooms; also spelled **morning-room**. In some large, old houses, the **morning room** is a sitting-room which gets the sun in the morning; an old-fashioned word. N-COUNT

morning sickness. **Morning sickness** is a feeling of sickness that some women have, often in the morning, when they are pregnant. N-UNCOUNT

morning star. The **morning star** is the planet Venus, which can be seen shining in the sky just after sunrise. N-SING: *the* N

Moroccan /mərɒkən/ **Moroccans** ◆◆◆◆◇
1 **Moroccan** means belonging or relating to Morocco or to its people or culture. ADJ
2 A **Moroccan** is a Moroccan citizen, or a person of Moroccan origin. N-COUNT

moron /mɔːrɒn/ **morons.** If you refer to someone as a **moron**, you think that they are very stupid; an offensive word. *I used to think that Gordon was a moron... You moron!* N-COUNT PRAGMATICS =idiot

moronic /mɔːrɒnɪk/. If you say that a person or their behaviour is **moronic**, you think that they are very stupid. *Most of them are just moronic... It was wanton, moronic vandalism.* ADJ-GRADED PRAGMATICS =idiotic

morose /mərous/. Someone who is **morose** is miserable, bad-tempered, and not willing to talk very much to other people. *She was morose, pale, and reticent.* ♦ **morosely** *One elderly man sat morosely at the bar.* ADJ-GRADED; ADV-GRADED: usu ADV with v

morpheme /mɔːʳfiːm/ **morphemes.** A **morpheme** is the smallest unit of meaning in a language. The words 'the', 'in', and 'girl' consist of one morpheme. The word 'girls' consists of two morphemes: 'girl' and 's'. N-COUNT

morphine /mɔːʳfiːn/. **Morphine** is a drug used to relieve pain. ◆◇◇◇◇ N-UNCOUNT

morphology /mɔːʳfɒlədʒi/. The **morphology** of something is its form and structure. In linguistics, **morphology** refers to the way words are constructed with stems, prefixes, and suffixes; a technical term. N-UNCOUNT

morris dancer /mɒrɪs dɑːnsəʳ, - dæns-/ **morris dancers.** A **morris dancer** is a person who takes part in morris dancing. N-COUNT

morris dancing /mɒrɪs dɑːnsɪŋ, - dæns-/. **Morris dancing** is a type of old English country dancing which is performed by people wearing special costumes. N-UNCOUNT

morrow /mɒrou, AM mɔːr-/
1 In old-fashioned English, the **morrow** means tomorrow or the next day. *We do depart for Wales on the morrow.* N-SING: *the* N, oft *on the* N
2 In old-fashioned English, **good morrow** means the same as 'good morning'. *Good morrow to you, my lord.* CONVENTION

morse code /mɔːʳs koud/; also spelled **Morse code**. **Morse code** or **morse** is an international code which is used for sending messages. It uses a system of written dots and dashes, or short and long sounds, to represent each letter of the alphabet. N-UNCOUNT

morsel /mɔːʳsəl/ **morsels.** A **morsel** is a very small amount of something, especially a very small piece of food. *...a delicious little morsel of meat.* N-COUNT: usu with supp, oft N *of* n =scrap

mortal /mɔːʳtəl/ **mortals** ◆◆◇◇◇
1 If you refer to the fact that people are **mortal**, you mean that they have to die and cannot live forever. *A man is deliberately designed to be mortal. He grows, he ages, and he dies.* ♦ **mortality** /mɔːʳtælɪti/ *She has suddenly come face to face with her own mortality.* ADJ ≠immortal; N-UNCOUNT: usu poss N
2 You can describe someone as a **mortal** when you want to say that they are an ordinary person, rather than someone who has power or has achieved something. *Tickets seem unobtainable to the ordinary mortal. ...impossible needs for any mere mortal to meet.* N-COUNT =human
3 You can use **mortal** to show that something is very serious or may cause death. *The police were defending themselves and others against mortal danger... Broadcasting was regarded at the time as the mortal enemy of live music-making.* ♦ **mortally** *He falls, mortally wounded.* ADJ-GRADED: ADJ n; ADV: usu ADV -ed/adj/adv
4 You can use **mortal** to emphasize that a feeling is extremely great or severe. *When self-esteem is high, we lose our mortal fear of jealousy.* ♦ **mortally** *Candida admits to having been 'mortally embarrassed'.* ADJ: ADJ n PRAGMATICS; ADV

mortality /mɔːʳtælɪti/. The **mortality** in a particular place or situation is the number of people who die. *...the relationships between mortality and unemployment... The nation's infant mortality rate has reached a record low.* N-UNCOUNT: oft N n =death rate

mortal sin, mortal sins. According to the Roman Catholic Church, a **mortal sin** is an extremely serious sin which will result in damnation unless the person who has committed it confesses, repents, and obtains forgiveness. *Adultery is a mortal sin.* N-VAR

mortar /mɔːʳtəʳ/ **mortars** ◆◆◇◇◇
1 A **mortar** is a short cannon which fires missiles high into the air for a short distance. *The two sides exchanged fire with artillery, mortars and small arms... He was killed in a mortar attack.* N-COUNT
2 **Mortar** is a mixture of sand, water, and cement or lime, which is put between bricks to make them stay firmly together when you are building walls. N-UNCOUNT
3 A **mortar** is a bowl in which you can crush or grind things such as herbs, spices, or grain using a special rod called a pestle. N-COUNT
4 ● **bricks and mortar**: see **brick**.

mortar board, mortar boards; also spelled **mortarboard**. A **mortar board** is a stiff black cap with a flat square top and a tassel hanging from it. Mortar boards are sometimes worn on formal occasions by university students and teachers. N-COUNT

mortgage /mɔːʳgɪdʒ/ **mortgages, mortgaging, mortgaged** ◆◆◆◆◇
1 A **mortgage** is a loan of money which you get from a bank or building society in order to buy a house. *...an increase in mortgage rates.* N-COUNT: oft N n
2 If you **mortgage** your house or land, you use it as a guarantee to a company in order to borrow money from them. *They had to mortgage their home to pay the bills. ...mortgaged homes.* VERB V n V-ed

mortice lock /mɔːʳtɪs lɒk/ **mortice locks.** A **mortice lock** is a type of lock which fits into a hole cut into the edge of a door rather than being fixed to one side of it. N-COUNT

mortician /mɔːʳtɪʃən/ **morticians.** A **mortician** is a person whose job is to deal with the bodies of people who have died and to arrange funerals; used mainly in American English. N-COUNT =undertaker

mortification /mɔːʳtɪfɪkeɪʃən/. **Mortification** is a strong feeling of shame and embarrassment. *The chairman tried to disguise his mortification.* N-UNCOUNT: oft poss N =embarrassment

mortified /mɔːʳtɪfaɪd/. If you say that someone is **mortified**, you mean that they feel extremely offended, ashamed, or embarrassed. *If I reduced somebody to tears I'd be mortified... I was so embarrassed and mortified and overwhelmed.* ADJ-GRADED: usu v-link ADJ =horrified

mortify /mɔːʳtɪfaɪ/ **mortifies, mortifying, mortified.** If you say that something **mortifies** you, you mean that it offends, ashames, or embarrasses you a great deal. *Jane mortified her family by leaving her husband.* VB: no cont =horrify V n

mortifying /mɔːʳtɪfaɪɪŋ/. If you say that something is **mortifying**, you mean that it makes you feel extremely ashamed or embarrassed. *She felt it would be utterly mortifying to be seen in such company as his by anyone.* ADJ-GRADED =embarrassing

mortuary /mɔːrtʃuəri, AM -eri/ **mortuaries.** A **mortuary** is a special building or a room in a hospital where dead bodies are kept before they are buried or cremated. N-COUNT

mosaic /mouzeɪɪk/ **mosaics.** A **mosaic** is a design which consists of small pieces of coloured glass, tiles, or stone set in concrete or plaster. ...*a Roman villa which once housed a fine collection of mosaics... He has used a mixture of mosaic, collage and felt-tip pen.* ◆◇◇◇◇ N-VAR

mosey /mouzi/ **moseys, moseying, moseyed.** If you **mosey** somewhere, you go there slowly, often without any particular purpose; an informal word. *He usually moseys into town for no special reason.* VERB =wander V adv/prep

Moslem /mɒzləm, muzlɪm/. See **Muslim.**

mosque /mɒsk/ **mosques.** A **mosque** is a building where Muslims go to worship. ◆◆◇◇◇ N-COUNT

mosquito /mɒskiːtou/ **mosquitoes** or **mosquitos. Mosquitos** are small flying insects which bite people and animals in order to suck their blood. ◆◇◇◇◇ N-COUNT

mosquito net, mosquito nets. A **mosquito net** is a curtain made of very fine cloth which is hung round a bed in order to keep mosquitoes and other insects away from a person while they are sleeping. N-COUNT

moss /mɒs, AM mɔːs/ **mosses. Moss** is a very small soft green plant which grows on damp soil, or on wood or stone. ...*ground covered over with moss.* ◆◇◇◇◇ N-MASS

mossy /mɒsi, AM mɔːsi/. A **mossy** surface is covered with moss. ...*a mossy wall.* ADJ-GRADED

most /moust/ ◆◆◆◆◆

Most is often considered to be the superlative form of **much** and **many**.

1 You use **most** to refer to the majority of a group of things or people or the largest part of something. *Most of the houses in the capital don't have piped water... By stopping smoking you are undoing most of the damage smoking has caused... Sadly, most of the house was destroyed by fire in 1828.* QUANT: QUANT of def-n =the majority ► Also a determiner. *Most people think the Queen has done a good job over the last 40 years... Most companies are looking to sponsor students on specific courses.* DET: DET pl-n ► Also a pronoun. *Seventeen civilians were hurt. Most are students who had been attending a twenty-first birthday party... All of the rooms have private baths, and most have radios and TV.* PRON =the majority

2 You use **the most** to mean a larger amount than anyone or anything else, or the largest amount possible. *The President himself won the most votes... The skippers get the most money, and after them the cooks... Tom had the most authority of all.* ADJ-SUPERL: the ADJ n ≠the least ► Also a pronoun. *The most they earn in a day is ten roubles.* PRON

3 You use **most** to indicate that something is true or happens to a greater degree or extent than anything else. *What she feared most was becoming like her mother... What they wanted most from the president was a leader who at least would try to educate the country. ...Professor Morris, the person he most hated.* ADV-SUPERL: ADV with v ≠least ● You use **most of all** to indicate that something happens or is true to a greater extent than anything else. *She said she wanted most of all to be fair.* PHRASE: PHR with v

4 You use **most** to indicate that someone or something has a greater amount of a particular quality than most other things of its kind. *Her children had the best, most elaborate birthday parties in the neighborhood... He was one of the most influential performers of modern jazz... If anything, swimming will appeal to her most strongly... Keeping pace with the litter during summer, when the park is most heavily used, is also a huge task. ...the most junior of the New York Times music critics.* ADV-SUPERL: ADV adj/adv ≠least

5 If you do something **the most**, you do it to the greatest extent possible or with the greatest frequency. *What question are you asked the most?... Inevitably those who suffer the most are the mothers and children... Among the subjects for which the pass rate has risen the most are art and design, business studies, and music.* ADV-SUPERL: the ADV after v ≠the least

6 You use **most** in conversations when you want to draw someone's attention to something very interesting or important that you are about to say. *Most surprisingly, quite a few said they don't intend to vote at all... Most interestingly, they are demanding that a national working party on crimes against women and children be established.* ADV-SUPERL: ADV adv/adj PRAGMATICS

7 You use **most** to emphasize an adjective or adverb; a rather formal use. *From tomorrow evening onwards I'll be most pleased to speak to them... I believe he is most painfully anxious about Diana.* ADV-SUPERL: ADV adj/adv PRAGMATICS

8 You use **at most** or **at the most** to say that a number or amount is the maximum that is possible or likely and that the actual number or amount may be smaller. *Poach the pears in apple juice or water and sugar for perhaps ten minutes at most. ...staying on at school for two extra years to study only three, or at the most four subjects... Many companies are expecting flat sales or at most a 1 to 2 per cent increase over last year.* PHRASES amount PHR, PHR with cl ≠at least, at the least

9 If you **make the most of** something, you get the maximum use or advantage from it. *Happiness is the ability to make the most of what you have... Making the most of your hair means getting the cut and shape right.* V inflects

10 ● **for the most part**: see **part**.

-most /-moust/. **-most** is added to adjectives in order to form other adjectives that describe something as being further in a particular direction than other things of the same kind. ...*the topmost branches of the trees... Many patients have told me their innermost thoughts. ...the northernmost suburbs of Chicago.* SUFFIX

mostly /moustli/. You use **mostly** to indicate that a statement is generally true, for example true about the majority of a group of things or people, true most of the time, or true in most respects. *I am working with mostly highly motivated people... Cars are mostly metal. ...men and women, mostly in their 30s... Her own twelve pictures sold fairly well, mostly to friends and family... They have mostly invested their money in expensive real estate.* ◆◆◆◇◇ ADV: ADV with cl/group =mainly

MOT /em ou tiː/ **MOTs.** In Britain, an **MOT** is a test which, by law, must be made each year on all road vehicles that are more than 3 years old, in order to check that they are safe to drive. *My car is due for its MOT in two days' time.* ◆◇◇◇◇ N-COUNT

motel /moutel/ **motels.** A **motel** is a hotel intended for people who are travelling by car. ◆◇◇◇◇ N-COUNT

moth /mɒθ, AM mɔːθ/ **moths.** A **moth** is an insect like a butterfly which usually flies about at night. ◆◇◇◇◇ N-COUNT

mothball /mɒθbɔːl, AM mɔːθ-/ **mothballs, mothballing, mothballed**

1 A **mothball** is a small white ball made of a special chemical, which you can put amongst clothes or blankets in order to keep moths away. N-COUNT

2 If someone in authority **mothballs** a plan, factory, or piece of equipment, they decide to stop developing or using it, perhaps temporarily; used mainly in journalism. ...*her decision in 1986 to mothball the Bataan Nuclear Power Plant, for safety and political reasons... The shuttle programme has now been mothballed to save money.* VERB V n

moth-eaten

1 **Moth-eaten** clothes look very old and ragged and have holes in them. ...*a moth-eaten leopardskin jacket.* ADJ-GRADED

2 If you describe something as **moth-eaten**, you mean that it seems unattractive or useless because it is old or has been used too much. *We drove through a somewhat moth-eaten deer park... This strategy looks increasingly moth-eaten.* ADJ-GRADED PRAGMATICS

mother /mʌðəʳ/ **mothers, mothering, mothered** ◆◆◆◆◆

1 Your **mother** is the woman who gave birth to you. You can also call someone your **mother** if she brings you up as if she was this woman. *She sat on the edge of her mother's bed... She's an English* N-FAMILY

teacher and a mother of two children... Mother and child form a close attachment... I'm here, Mother.

2 If a woman **mothers** a child, she looks after it and brings it up, usually because she is its mother. *Colleen had dreamed of mothering a large family.* VERB V n

♦ **mothering** *The reality of mothering is frequently very different from the romantic ideal.* N-UNCOUNT

3 If you **mother** someone, you treat them with great care and affection, as if they were a small child. *She felt a great need to mother him... Stop mothering me.* VERB V n

mother country, mother countries; also spelled **Mother Country.**

1 Someone's **mother country** is the country in which they were born or which their ancestors came from and to which they still feel emotionally linked, wherever they might live. *Dr Kengerli looks to Turkey as his mother country.* N-COUNT: oft with poss =motherland

2 If you refer to **the mother country** of a particular state or country, you are referring to the very powerful country that used to control its affairs. *Australia, New Zealand, and Canada, had no colonial conflict with the mother country.* N-SING: usu *the* N

mother figure, mother figures; also spelled **mother-figure**. If you regard someone as a **mother figure**, you think of them as having the role of a mother and being the person you can turn to for help, advice, or support. N-COUNT

motherfucker /mʌðəʳfʌkəʳ/ **motherfuckers.** If someone calls a person, usually a man, a **motherfucker**, they are insulting him in a very unpleasant way; a very rude and offensive word used mainly in American English. N-COUNT PRAGMATICS

motherhood /mʌðəʳhʊd/. **Motherhood** is the state of being a mother. *...women who try to combine work and motherhood.* ◆◇◇◇◇ N-UNCOUNT

Mothering Sunday. In British English, **Mothering Sunday** is a slightly old-fashioned name for **Mother's Day**. N-UNCOUNT

mother-in-law, mothers-in-law. Someone's **mother-in-law** is the mother of their husband or wife. ◆◇◇◇◇ N-COUNT: oft poss N

motherland /mʌðəʳlænd/; also spelled **Motherland.** The **motherland** is the country in which you were born and to which you still feel emotionally linked. *Central to our belief is love for the motherland and a desire to serve.* ◆◇◇◇◇ N-SING: usu *the* N =mother country

motherless /mʌðəʳləs/. You describe children as **motherless** if their mother has died or does not live with them. *...Michael's seven motherless children.* ADJ

motherly /mʌðəʳli/. **Motherly** feelings or actions are like those of a kind mother. *It was an incredible display of motherly love and forgiveness. ...a plump, motherly woman.* ADJ-GRADED: usu ADJ n =maternal

Mother Nature. Mother Nature is sometimes used to refer to nature, especially when it is being considered as a force that affects human beings. *The gardener is convinced he can improve on Mother Nature's rather casual attitude to the plant kingdom.* N-UNCOUNT

Mother of God. In Christianity, **Mother of God** is another name for the Virgin Mary, the mother of Jesus Christ. N-PROPER

mother-of-pearl; also spelled **mother of pearl. Mother-of-pearl** is the shiny layer on the inside of some shells. It is used to make buttons or to decorate things. N-UNCOUNT

Mother's Day. Mother's Day is a special day on which children give cards and presents to their mothers as a sign of their love for them. In Britain, Mother's Day is the fourth Sunday in Lent. In the United States, it is the second Sunday in May. N-UNCOUNT

Mother Superior, Mother Superiors. A **Mother Superior** is a nun who is in charge of the other nuns in a convent. N-COUNT

mother-to-be, mothers-to-be. A **mother-to-be** is a woman who is pregnant, especially for the first time. N-COUNT

mother tongue, mother tongues; also spelled **mother-tongue.** Your **mother tongue** is the language that you learn from your parents when you are a baby. N-COUNT: oft poss N =native tongue

motif /moʊtiːf/ **motifs** ◆◇◇◇◇

1 A **motif** is a design which is used as a decoration or as part of an artistic pattern. *...a rose motif.* N-COUNT: usu with supp

2 A **motif** is a theme or idea that is frequently repeated throughout a piece of literature or music. *The motif of these volumes is that 'solitude is the richness of the soul, loneliness is its poverty.'* N-COUNT =theme

motion /moʊʃəⁿn/ **motions, motioning, motioned** ◆◆◆◇◇

1 Motion is the activity or process of continually changing position or moving from one place to another. *...the laws governing light, sound, and motion... One group of muscles sets the next group in motion... The wind from the car's motion whipped her hair around her head.* N-UNCOUNT =movement

2 A **motion** is an action, gesture, or movement. *Cover each part of the body with long sweeping strokes or circular motions... He made a neat chopping motion with his hand.* N-COUNT: usu with supp =movement

3 A **motion** is a formal proposal or statement in a meeting, debate, or trial, which is discussed and then voted on or decided on. *The conference is now debating the motion and will vote on it shortly... Opposition parties are likely to bring a no-confidence motion against the government... He is eligible now to file a motion for a new trial.* N-COUNT

4 If you **motion** to someone, you move your hand or head as a way of telling them to do something or telling them where to go. *She motioned for the locked front doors to be opened... He stood aside and motioned Don to the door... I motioned him to join us... He motioned to her to go behind the screen.* VERB =signal V *for* n to-inf V n prep/adv V n to-inf V *to* n to-inf

5 In British English, some people, especially doctors or nurses, use **motion** as a polite way of referring to a person's act of defecation or the faeces produced. *Try to make sure your bowel motions are regular and that you avoid any constipation.* N-COUNT =movement

6 See also **slow motion, time and motion.**

7 If you say that someone **is going through the motions**, you think they are only saying or doing something because it is expected of them without being interested, enthusiastic, or sympathetic. *'You really don't care, do you?' she said quietly. 'You're just going through the motions.'* PHRASES V inflects PRAGMATICS

8 If you **go through the motions**, you pretend to do something by making the movements associated with a particular action. *The sailor went through all the motions smartly... Actors go through the motions of different types of labor.* V inflects

9 If a process or event is **in motion**, it is happening. If it is set **in motion**, it is happening or beginning to happen. *His job as England manager begins in earnest now his World Cup campaign is in motion... Her sharp, aggressive tone set in motion the events that led to her downfall.* usu v-link PHR, PHR after v =under way

10 If someone **sets the wheels in motion**, they take the necessary action to make something start happening. *I have set the wheels in motion to sell Endsleigh Court.* V inflects

motionless /moʊʃəⁿnləs/. Someone or something that is **motionless** is not moving at all. *He has this ability of being able to remain as motionless as a statue, for hours on end... Her hands were motionless... He stood there motionless.*  ADJ-GRADED: usu v-link ADJ =still

motion picture, motion pictures. A **motion picture** is a film made for cinema; used mainly in American English. *It was there that I saw my first motion picture. ...the motion picture industry.* 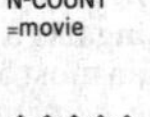 N-COUNT =movie

motivate /moʊtɪveɪt/ **motivates, motivating, motivated** 

1 If you **are motivated** by something, especially an emotion, it causes you to behave in a particular way. *They are motivated by a need to achieve... The crime was not politically motivated... I don't want to be missing out. And that motivates me to get up and do something every day.* VERB be V-ed V n to-inf Also V n

♦ **motivated** *...highly motivated employees.* ADJ-GRADED

♦ **motivation** /moʊtɪveɪʃəⁿn/ *His poor performance may be attributed to lack of motivation rather than to reading difficulties.* N-UNCOUNT

2 If someone **motivates** you to do something, they VERB make you feel determined to do it. *How do you motivate people to work hard and efficiently?... Never let it be said that the manager doesn't know how to motivate his players.* ♦ **motivation** *Given parental motivation we are optimistic about the ability of people to change.* =inspire V n to-inf V n N-UNCOUNT

motivation /moʊtɪveɪʃən/ **motivations.** Your **motivation** for doing something is what causes you to want to do it. *Money is my motivation... The timing of the attack, and its motivations, are unknown.* ◆◆◇◇◇ N-COUNT: usu with poss

motive /moʊtɪv/ **motives.** Your **motive** for doing something is your reason for doing it. *Police have ruled out robbery as a motive for the killing. ...the motives and objectives of British foreign policy... The doctor's motive was to bring an end to his patient's suffering.* ◆◆◇◇◇ N-COUNT: oft N prep

motley /mɒtli/. You can describe a group of things as a **motley** collection if you think they seem strange together because they are all very different. *...a motley collection of vans, old buses, cattle-trucks, and even a fire engine... The volunteers seem a motley crew.* ◆◇◇◇◇ ADJ-GRADED: ADJ n

motor /moʊtəʳ/ **motors, motoring, motored** ◆◆◆◆◇

1 The **motor** in a machine, vehicle, or boat is the part that uses electricity or fuel to produce movement, so that the machine, vehicle, or boat can work. *She got in and started the motor.* N-COUNT =engine

2 Motor vehicles and boats have a petrol or diesel engine. *Theft of motor vehicles is up by 15.9%.* ADJ: ADJ n

3 Motor is used to describe activities relating to vehicles such as cars and buses which have a petrol or diesel engine. *...the future of the British motor industry... He worked as a motor mechanic.* ADJ: ADJ n

4 In informal British English, some people refer to a car as a **motor.** N-COUNT =car

5 If you **motor** somewhere, you travel there in a car, usually for pleasure; an old-fashioned use. *I had motored down from Cheshire.* VERB =drive V adv/prep

6 If the crew of a small sailing boat **motor** somewhere, they use the boat's motor rather than the power of the wind to get the boat there. *Restarting the engine, we motored downriver.* VERB V adv/prep

7 See also **motoring, outboard motor.**

motorbike /moʊtəʳbaɪk/ **motorbikes;** also spelled **motor-bike.** A **motorbike** is the same as a **motorcycle.** ◆◇◇◇◇ N-COUNT

motorboat /moʊtəʳboʊt/ **motorboats;** also spelled **motor boat.** A **motorboat** is a boat that is driven by an engine. N-COUNT

motorcade /moʊtəʳkeɪd/ **motorcades.** A **motorcade** is a line of slowly-moving cars carrying important people, usually as part of a public ceremony. *At times the president's motorcade slowed to a crawl.* N-COUNT

motor car, motor cars; also spelled **motorcar.** A **motor car** is the same as a **car**; an old-fashioned expression. ◆◇◇◇◇ N-COUNT

motorcycle /moʊtəʳsaɪkəl/ **motorcycles.** A **motorcycle** is a two-wheeled vehicle which is driven by an engine. ◆◇◇◇◇ N-COUNT =motorbike

motorcyclist /moʊtəʳsaɪklɪst/ **motorcyclists.** A **motorcyclist** is a person who rides a motorcycle. N-COUNT

motoring /moʊtərɪŋ/. **Motoring** means relating to cars and driving. *...a three-month sentence for motoring offences... Police and motoring organizations said the roads were slightly busier than normal.* ◆◇◇◇◇ ADJ: ADJ n

motorised /moʊtəraɪzd/. See **motorized.**

motorist /moʊtərɪst/ **motorists.** A **motorist** is a person who drives a car. ◆◆◇◇◇ N-COUNT

motorized /moʊtəraɪzd/; also spelled **motorised.**

1 A **motorized** vehicle has an engine. *Around 1910 motorized carriages were beginning to replace horse-drawn cabs.* ADJ: usu ADJ n

2 A **motorized** group of soldiers is equipped with motor vehicles. *...motorized infantry and artillery.* ADJ: usu ADJ n

motor neurone disease. Motor neurone disease is a disease which destroys the part of a person's nervous system that controls movement. N-UNCOUNT

motorway /moʊtəʳweɪ/ **motorways.** In British English, a **motorway** is a major road that has been specially built for fast travel over long distances. Motorways have several lanes and special places where traffic gets on and leaves. The usual American word is **freeway.** *...the M1 motorway. ...the national motorway network.* ◆◆◇◇◇ N-VAR

mottled /mɒtəld/. Something that is **mottled** is covered with patches of different colours which do not form a regular pattern. *...mottled green and yellow leaves.* ADJ-GRADED

motto /mɒtoʊ/ **mottoes** or **mottos.** A **motto** is a short sentence or phrase that expresses a rule for sensible behaviour, especially a way of behaving in a particular situation. *The regiment's motto is 'Nemo nos impune lacessit' (No one provokes us with impunity).* ◆◇◇◇◇ N-COUNT: oft with poss

mould /moʊld/ **moulds, moulding, moulded;** spelled **mold** in American English. ◆◆◇◇◇

1 A **mould** is a container that you use to make something into a particular shape. You pour a soft or liquid substance such as melted metal or jelly into the mould, and when the metal or jelly becomes solid you take it out and it has the same shape as the mould. *Spoon the mixture carefully into the mould... The moulds for the foundry are made in the toolroom area. ...jelly moulds.* N-COUNT

2 If a person fits into or is cast in a **mould** of a particular kind, they have the characteristics, attitudes, behaviour, or lifestyle that are typical of that particular type of person. *At first sight, Joe Pesci is not exactly cast in the leading man mould... He was from the same mould as the men she had gazed at worshipfully when a child: rich, handsome, of impeccable social standing.* N-COUNT: usu with supp • If you say that someone **breaks the mould**, you mean that they do completely different things from what has been done before or from what is usually done. *Memorial services have become tedious and expected. I would like to help break the mould... When they first started, they said they were going to break the mould of British politics.* PHRASE: V inflects

3 If you **mould** a soft substance such as plastic or clay, you make it into a particular shape or into an object. *Using 2 spoons, mould the cheese mixture into small balls or ovals... Before we left the camp, my twin brother and I moulded a chair out of mud.* VERB V n into n V n

4 To **mould** someone or something means to change or influence them over a period of time so that they develop in a particular way. *She was only 17 at the time and the experience moulded her personality... Here we outline some of the sometimes conflicting forces moulding the debate... Too often we try to mold our children into something they do not wish to be.* VERB =form V n V n into n

5 When something **moulds** to an object or when you **mould** it there, it fits round the object tightly so that the shape of the object can still be seen. *You need a malleable pillow that will mould to the curves of your neck... She stepped onto the catwalk and stood there, the wind moulding the smock around her.* V-ERG V to/around/round n V n around/round/to n

6 Mould is a soft grey, green, or blue substance that sometimes forms in spots on old food or on damp walls or clothes. • See also **leaf mould.** N-MASS

moulder /moʊldəʳ/ **moulders, mouldering, mouldered;** spelled **molder** in American English. If something **is mouldering**, it is decaying slowly where it has been left. *...one of your scripts that's been mouldering under the bed for ages... It is clear that such ideas will be left to moulder. ...the empty, mouldering old house.* VB: usu cont V V-ing

moulding /moʊldɪŋ/ **mouldings;** spelled **molding** in American English. A **moulding** is a strip of plaster or wood along the top of a wall or round a door, which has been made into an ornamental shape or decorated with a pattern. ◆◇◇◇◇ N-COUNT

mouldy /moʊldi/; spelled **moldy** in American English. Something that is **mouldy** is covered with mould. *...mouldy bread... Oranges can be kept for a long time without going mouldy.* ADJ-GRADED

moult /moʊlt/ **moults, moulting, moulted;** spelled **molt** in American English. When an animal or bird **moults**, it gradually loses its coat or ◆◇◇◇◇ VERB feathers so that a new coat or feathers can grow. *Finches start to moult at around twelve weeks of age.* V

mound /maʊnd/ **mounds.** You can use **mound** to refer to a large heap or pile of a substance or of things. *The bulldozers piled up huge mounds of dirt... The table was a mound of paper and books.* ◆◇◇◇◇ N-COUNT: usu N *of* n =pile

mount /maʊnt/ **mounts, mounting, mounted** ◆◆◆◇◇

1 If you **mount** a campaign or event, you organize it and make it take place. *The ANC announced it was mounting a major campaign of mass political protests. ...a security operation mounted by the army.* VERB =launch, organize V n

2 If something **mounts**, it increases in intensity. *For several hours, tension mounted... The decibel level was mounting... There was mounting concern in her voice. ...the mounting heat of the stadium.* VERB =rise, increase V V-ing

3 If something **mounts**, it increases in quantity. *The uncollected garbage mounts in city streets... He ignored his mounting debts.* ▸ To **mount up** means the same as to **mount**. *If you hide away your problems and pretend that they don't exist they will just continue to mount up... Her medical bills mounted up.* VERB V V-ing PHRASAL VERB V P

4 If you **mount** the stairs or a platform, you go up the stairs or go up onto the platform; a formal use. *Llewelyn was mounting the stairs up into the keep... The vehicle mounted the pavement.* VERB =go up V n

5 If you **mount** a horse or cycle, you climb on to it so that you can ride it. *He mounted his horse and rode away... A man in a crash helmet was mounting a motorbike... He went to the small stable where his horse was, harnessed it, mounted, and rode out to the beach.* VERB =climb on, get on V n V

6 A **mount** is a horse; a formal use. *The number of owners who care for older mounts.* N-COUNT =horse

7 If you **mount** an object on something, you fix it there firmly. *Her husband mounts the work on velour paper and makes the frame... The support for the fence is mounted on an extension to the table. ...a specially mounted horse shoe.* ♦ **-mounted** *...a wall-mounted electric fan. ...pickup trucks with side-mounted fuel tanks.* VERB V n *on* n V-ed Also V n COMB in ADJ

8 If you **mount** an exhibition or display, you organize and present it. *The gallery has mounted an exhibition of art by Irish women painters.* VERB =put on V n

9 Mount is used as part of the name of a mountain. *...Mount Everest.* N-IN-NAMES

10 See also **mounted**.

mount up. See **mount** 3 PHRASAL VERB

mountain /maʊntɪn, AM -tᵊn/ **mountains** ◆◆◆◆◇

1 A **mountain** is a very high area of land with steep sides. *Ben Nevis, in Scotland, is Britain's highest mountain. ...a lovely little mountain village.* N-COUNT

2 If you talk about a **mountain** of something, or **mountains** of something, you are emphasizing that there is a large amount of it; an informal use. *They are faced with a mountain of bureaucracy... They have mountains of coffee to sell.* QUANT: QUANT *of* pl-n/n-uncount PRAGMATICS =pile, heap

3 If you say that someone has **a mountain to climb**, you mean that it will be difficult for them to achieve what they want to achieve; used mainly in journalism. *'We had a mountain to climb after the second goal went in,' said Crosby.* ● to **make a mountain out of a molehill**: see **molehill**. PHRASE: usu v PHR

mountain bike, mountain bikes. A **mountain bike** is a type of bicycle suitable for riding over rough ground. It has a strong frame, straight handlebars, and thick tyres with a deep tread. ◆◇◇◇◇ N-COUNT

mountaineer /maʊntɪnɪə^r/ **mountaineers.** A **mountaineer** is a person who is skilful at climbing the steep sides of mountains. N-COUNT

mountaineering /maʊntɪnɪərɪŋ/. **Mountaineering** is the activity of climbing the steep sides of mountains as a hobby or sport. N-UNCOUNT

mountainous /maʊntɪnəs/ ◆◇◇◇◇

1 A **mountainous** place has a lot of mountains. *...the mountainous region of Campania.* ADJ-GRADED

2 If you refer to **mountainous** seas, you are emphasizing that the sea is very rough. *The fishermen set off in mountainous seas.* ADJ PRAGMATICS

3 You use **mountainous** to emphasize that something is great in size, quantity, or degree. *In the lighted doorway stood the mountainous figure of a woman... The plan is designed to reduce some of the company's mountainous debt.* ADJ: ADJ n PRAGMATICS =huge

mountainside /maʊntɪnsaɪd/ **mountainsides.** A **mountainside** is one of the steep sides of a mountain. *The couple trudged up the dark mountainside.* ◆◇◇◇◇ N-COUNT

mounted /maʊntɪd/. **Mounted** police or soldiers ride horses when they are on duty. *A dozen mounted police rode into the square.* ● See also **mount**. ◆◆◇◇◇ ADJ: ADJ n

mourn /mɔːʳn/ **mourns, mourning, mourned** ◆◇◇◇◇

1 If you **mourn** someone who has died or **mourn** for them, you are very sad that they have died and show your sorrow in the way that you behave. *Joan still mourns her father... The whole nation had mourned the death of their great leader... He mourned for his valiant men... I buried him on the top of the hill and mourned.* VERB =grieve for V n V *for* n V

2 If you **mourn** something or **mourn** for it, you regret that you no longer have it and show your regret in the way that you behave. *We mourned the loss of our cities... She mourned for the beloved past.* VERB =grieve for V n V *for* n

3 See also **mourning**.

mourner /mɔːʳnəʳ/ **mourners.** A **mourner** is a person who attends a funeral, especially as a relative or friend of the dead person. ◆◇◇◇◇ N-COUNT

mournful /mɔːʳnfʊl/ ◆◇◇◇◇

1 If you are **mournful**, you are very sad. *He looked mournful, even near to tears... Miss Dickerman was tall and somewhat mournful-looking.* ♦ **mournfully** *He stood mournfully at the gate waving bye bye.* ADJ-GRADED =sorrowful ADV-GRADED: usu ADV with v

2 A **mournful** sound seems very sad. *...the mournful wail of bagpipes.* ADJ-GRADED =sorrowful

mourning /mɔːʳnɪŋ/ ◆◇◇◇◇

1 Mourning is behaviour in which you show sadness about a person's death. *The period of mourning and bereavement may be long... Expect to feel angry, depressed and confused. It's all part of the mourning process... Human rights groups declared what they called a day of mourning and protest.* N-UNCOUNT

2 If you are **in mourning**, you are dressed or behaving in a particular way because someone you love or respect has died. *Yesterday the whole of Greece was in mourning... The boys wore black tail coats in mourning for George III.* PHRASE: usu v-link PHR

mouse /maʊs/ **mice** ◆◆◇◇◇

1 A **mouse** is a small furry animal with a long tail. *...a mouse running in a wheel in its cage. ...the problem of rats and mice.* N-COUNT

2 A **mouse** is a hand-held device that you use with a computer system. By moving it over a flat surface and pressing its buttons, you can move the cursor around the screen and perform certain operations without using the keyboard. N-COUNT

3 ● **game of cat and mouse**: see **cat**.

mousetrap /maʊstræp/ **mousetraps.** A **mousetrap** is a small device that catches or kills mice. N-COUNT

mousey /maʊsi/. See **mousy**.

moussaka /mʊsɑːkə/ **moussakas. Moussaka** is a Greek dish consisting of layers of meat and aubergine. N-VAR

mousse /muːs/ **mousses** ◆◇◇◇◇

1 Mousse is a sweet light food made from eggs and cream. It is often flavoured with fruit or chocolate. N-VAR

2 Mousse is a white foamy substance that you can put in your hair to make it easier to shape into a particular style. N-MASS

moustache /məstɑːʃ, AM mʌstæʃ/ **moustaches;** also spelled **mustache**. A man's **moustache** is the hair that grows on his upper lip. If it is very long, it is sometimes referred to as his **moustaches**. *He was short and bald and had a moustache. ...a heavy man with drooping moustaches.* ♦ **moustached** *...three burly, moustached middle-aged men.* ◆◇◇◇◇ N-COUNT ADJ =moustachioed

moustachioed /məstæʃiəʊd, AM -tæʃəʊd/; also spelled **mustachioed**. A **moustachioed** man has ADJ =moustached a moustache, especially a thick, curly, or fancy moustache; a literary word.

mousy /maʊsi/; also spelled **mousey**.

1 **Mousy** hair is a dull light brown colour. *He was aged between 25 and 30, with a medium build and collar-length mousy hair.* ADJ-GRADED: usu ADJ n

2 If you describe someone as **mousy**, you mean that they are quiet and shy and that people do not notice them. *The Inspector remembered her as a small, mousy woman, invariably worried.* ADJ-GRADED: usu ADJ n

mouth, mouths, mouthing, mouthed. The noun is pronounced /maʊθ/. The verb is pronounced /maʊð/. The plural of the noun and the third person singular of the verb are both pronounced /maʊðz/. ◆◆◆◆◇

1 Your **mouth** is the area of your face where your lips are or the space behind your lips where your teeth and tongue are. *She clamped her hand against her mouth... His mouth was full of peas. ...an inflammation of the mouth.* ♦ **-mouthed** /-maʊðd/ *He straightened up and looked at me, open-mouthed. ...a wide-mouthed, gray-haired policeman.* N-COUNT: oft poss N; COMB in ADJ

2 You can say that someone has a particular kind of **mouth** to indicate that they speak in a particular kind of way or that they say particular kinds of things. *I've always had a loud mouth, I refuse to be silenced... You've got such a crude mouth!* ♦ **-mouthed** *...Simon, their smart-mouthed teenage son. ...mean-mouthed heavies with the sly sadistic eyes of professional bullies.* N-COUNT: with supp, oft adj N; COMB in ADJ-GRADED

3 The **mouth** of a cave, hole, or bottle is its entrance or opening. *By the mouth of the tunnel he bent to retie his lace.* ♦ **-mouthed** *He put the flowers in a wide-mouthed blue vase.* N-COUNT: usu with supp, oft N *of* n =entrance; COMB in ADJ

4 The **mouth** of a river is the place where it flows into the sea. *...the town at the mouth of the River Dart.* N-COUNT: usu with supp

5 If you **mouth** something, you form words with your lips without making any sound. *I mouthed a goodbye and hurried in behind Momma... She winked broadly at him and silently mouthed something... 'It's for you,' he mouthed.* VERB V n V with quote

6 If you **mouth** something, you say it, especially without believing it or without understanding it. *I mouthed some sympathetic platitudes... They mouthed the values of family, religion and charity, but demonstrated the opposite in their private lives.* VERB V n

7 If you have a number of **mouths to feed**, you have the responsibility of earning enough money to feed and look after that number of people. *He had to feed his family on the equivalent of four hundred pounds a month and, with five mouths to feed, he found this very hard.* PHRASES N inflects

8 If you say that someone does not **open** their **mouth**, you are emphasizing that they never say anything at all. *Sometimes I hardly dare open my mouth... He hasn't opened his mouth since he's been there.* V and N inflect, with brd-neg PRAGMATICS

9 If you **keep** your **mouth shut** about something, you do not talk about it, especially because it is a secret. *You wouldn't be here now if she'd kept her mouth shut.* V and N inflect =keep quiet

10 • **live hand to mouth**: see **hand**. • **heart in** your **mouth**: see **heart**. • **from the horse's mouth**: see **horse**. • to **put** your **money where** your **mouth is**: see **money**. • **shut** your **mouth**: see **shut**. • **born with a silver spoon in** your **mouth**: see **spoon**. • **word of mouth**: see **word**. • **put words into** someone's **mouth**: see **word**.

mouthful /maʊθfʊl/ **mouthfuls** ◆◇◇◇◇

1 A **mouthful** of drink or food is the amount that you put or have in your mouth. *She gulped down a mouthful of coffee... Chew each mouthful fully before the next bite.* N-COUNT: oft N *of* n

2 If you describe a long word or phrase as **a mouthful**, you mean that it is difficult to say; an informal use. *It's called the Pan-Caribbean Disaster Preparedness and Prevention Project, which is quite a mouthful.* N-SING: a N

mouth organ, mouth organs. A **mouth organ** is the same as a **harmonica**; used mainly in British English. N-COUNT

mouthpiece /maʊθpiːs/ **mouthpieces** ◆◇◇◇◇

1 The **mouthpiece** of a telephone is the part that you speak into. *He shouted into the mouthpiece.* N-COUNT

2 The **mouthpiece** of a musical instrument or other device is the part that you put into your mouth. *He showed him how to blow into the ivory mouthpiece. ...clamping the mouthpiece of my snorkel tightly between my teeth.* N-COUNT

3 The **mouthpiece** of an organization or person is someone who informs other people of the opinions and policies of that organization or person. *Their mouthpiece is the vice-president... He might be considered little more than a convenient mouthpiece for the Prime Minister's own economic views.* N-COUNT: usu with poss

mouthwash /maʊθwɒʃ/ **mouthwashes.** **Mouthwash** is a liquid that you rinse your mouth with, in order to clean and freshen it. N-MASS

mouth-watering; also spelled **mouthwatering**.

1 **Mouth-watering** food looks or smells extremely delicious. *...hundreds of cheeses, in a mouth-watering variety of shapes, textures and tastes. ...more than 150 mouthwatering recipes.* ADJ-GRADED

2 If you describe something as **mouth-watering**, you are emphasizing that it is very attractive; used mainly in journalism. *Prizes worth a mouth-watering £9.6 million are unclaimed.* ADJ-GRADED PRAGMATICS

movable /muːvəbᵊl/; also spelled **moveable**. Something that is **movable** can be moved from one place or position to another. *It's a vinyl doll with movable arms and legs... The wooden fence is movable.* ADJ

move /muːv/ **moves, moving, moved** ◆◆◆◆◆

1 When you **move** something or when it **moves**, its position changes and it does not remain still. *She moved the sheaf of papers into position... You can move the camera both vertically and horizontally... A traffic warden asked him to move his car... I could see the branches of the trees moving back and forth... The train began to move.* V-ERG V n prep/adv V n V prep/adv V

2 When you **move**, you change your position or go to a different place. *She waited for him to get up, but he didn't move... There was so much furniture you could hardly move without bumping into something... He moved around the room, putting his possessions together... She moved away from the window.* ► Also a noun. *The doctor made a move towards the door... Daniel's eyes followed her every move.* VERB V V prep/adv; N-COUNT: usu sing =movement

3 If you **move**, you act or you begin to do something. *Industrialists must move fast to take advantage of new opportunities in Eastern Europe.* VERB =act V

4 A **move** is an action that you take in order to achieve something. *The one point cut in interest rates was a wise move... It may also be a good move to suggest she talks things over... The thirty-five member nations agreed to the move... Her latest disappearing act may be no more than a stunt, or a smart career move.* N-COUNT: usu sing

5 If a person or company **moves**, they leave the building where they have been living or working, and they go to live or work in a different place, taking their possessions with them. *My family home is in Yorkshire and they don't want to move... She had often considered moving to London... They move house fairly frequently... The London Evening Standard moved offices a few years ago.* ► Also a noun. *Modigliani announced his move to Montparnasse in 1909.* VERB V V *to* n V n; N-COUNT

6 If people in authority **move** someone, they make that person go from one place or job to another one. *His superiors moved him to another parish... Ms Clark is still in position and there are no plans to move her... The family had to be moved because of an attack on their home.* VERB =transfer V n prep/adv V n

7 If you **move** from one job or interest to another, you change to it. *He moved from being an extramural tutor to being a lecturer in social history... In the early days Christina moved jobs to get experience.* ► Also a noun. *His move to the chairmanship* VERB V *from/to* n/-ing V n; N-COUNT *means he will take a less active role in day-to-day management.*

8 If you **move** to a new topic in a conversation, you start talking about something different. *Let's move to another subject, Dan.* VERB V from/to n/-ing

9 If you **move** an event or the date of an event, you change the time at which it happens. *The club has moved its meeting to Saturday, January 22nd... The band have moved forward their Leeds date to October 27.* VERB V n to n V n with adv Also V n

10 If you **move** towards a particular state, activity, or opinion, you start to be in that state, do that activity, or have that opinion. *The Labor Party has moved to the right and become like your Democrat Party... It is already possible to start moving toward the elimination of nuclear weapons... Since the Convention was drawn up international opinion has begun to move against it.* ▶ Also a noun. *His move to the left was not a sudden leap but a natural working out of ideas.* VERB =shift V prep/adv N-COUNT =shift

11 If a situation or process **is moving**, it is developing or progressing, rather than staying still. *Events are moving fast... Someone has got to get things moving.* VB: usu cont

12 If you say that you will not **be moved**, you mean that you have come to a decision and nothing will change your mind. *Everyone thought I was mad to go back, but I wouldn't be moved.* VB: usu passive, with neg =budge be V-ed

13 If something **moves** you to do something, it influences you and causes you to do it. *It was punk that first moved him to join a band seriously... The president was moved to come up with these suggestions after the hearings.* VERB =prompts V n to-inf

14 If something **moves** you, it has an effect on your emotions and causes you to feel sadness or sympathy for another person. *These stories surprised and moved me... His prayer moved me to tears.* ♦ **moved** *Walesa himself appeared to be deeply moved.* VERB V n V n to n ADJ-GRADED: v-link ADJ

15 You say that someone **moves in** a particular society, circle, or world when you mean that they know people in a particular social class or group and spend most of their time with them. *She moves in high-society circles in London... They moved in a world where hostility to racists was natural.* VERB V in n

16 If you **move** a motion or amendment, you formally propose it at a meeting so that everyone present can vote for or against it. *Labour quickly moved a closure motion to end the debate... I move that the case be dismissed.* VERB =put forward V n V that

17 A **move** is an act of putting a chess piece or other counter in a different position on a board when it is your turn to do so in a game. *With no idea of what to do for my next move, my hand hovered over the board.* N-COUNT

18 If you say that one **false move** will cause a disaster, you mean that you or someone else must not make even one mistake because the situation is so tricky or dangerous. *He knew one false move would end in death.* PHRASES

19 If you tell someone to **get a move on**, you are telling them to hurry; an informal expression. PRAGMATICS =hurry up

20 If you **make a move**, you prepare or begin to leave one place and go somewhere else. *He glanced at his wristwatch. 'I suppose we'd better make a move.'... He made a move to leave.* V inflects, oft PHR to-inf

21 If you **make a move**, you take a course of action. *The week before the deal was supposed to close, fifteen Japanese banks made a move to pull out... Don't wait for others to make the first move: invite friends to visit you.* V inflects, oft PHR to-inf

22 If you are **on the move**, you are going from one place to another. *Jack never wanted to stay in one place for very long, so they were always on the move.* usu PHR after v, v-link PHR

23 • to **move the goalposts**: see **goalpost**. • to **move heaven and earth**: see **heaven**. • to **move a muscle**: see **muscle**. • to **move with the times**: see **time**.

move about or **move around.** The form **move about** is mainly used in British English. If you **move about** or **move around**, or if you **move about** or **move around** a country, you keep changing your job or keep changing the place where you live. *I was born in Fort Worth but we moved around a lot and I was reared in east Texas... He moved around the country working in orange groves.* PHRASAL VERB V P V P n

move along PHRASAL VERB

1 If someone, especially a police officer, tells you to **move along**, or if they **move** you **along**, they tell you to stop standing in a particular place and to go somewhere else. *Curious pedestrians were ordered to move along... Our officers are moving them along and not allowing them to gather in large groups.* ERG V P V n P Also V P n (not pron)

2 If a process **moves along** or if something **moves** it **along**, it progresses. *Research tends to move along at a slow but orderly pace... Delay is part of the normal process, but I hope we can move things along.* ERG V P V n P

move away. If you **move away**, you go and live in a different town or area of a country. *He moved away and broke off relations with the family.* PHRASAL VERB V P

move down. If someone or something **moves down**, they go to a lower level, grade, or class. *Gold prices moved down.* PHRASAL VERB V P Also V P n

move in PHRASAL VERB

1 When you **move in** somewhere, you begin to live in a different house or place. *Her house was in perfect order when she moved in... Her husband had moved in with a younger woman... We'd been seeing each other for a year when he suggested we should move in together.* ≠move out V P V P with n V P together

2 If police, soldiers, or attackers **move in**, they go towards a place or person in order to deal with or attack them. *There were violent and chaotic scenes when police moved in to disperse the crowd... Forces were moving in on the town of Knin.* V P V P on n

3 If someone **moves in** on an area of activity which was previously only done by a particular group of people, they start becoming involved with it for the first time. *These black models are moving in on what was previously white territory: the lucrative cosmetic contracts.* V P on n Also V P

move into. If you **move into** a new house, you start living there. *I want you to move into my apartment. We've a spare room.* PHRASAL VERB V P n

move off. When you **move off**, you start moving away from a place. *Gil waved his hand and the car moved off.* PHRASAL VERB =set off V P

move on PHRASAL VERB

1 When you **move on** somewhere, you leave the place where you have been staying or waiting and go or travel there. *Mr Li moves on to Jordan later today... What's wrong with his wanting to sell his land and move on?* V P prep/adv V P

2 If someone such as a policeman **moves** you **on**, they order or cause you to leave a particular place and go somewhere else. *Eventually the police were called to move them on.* V n P Also V P n (not pron)

3 If you **move on**, you finish or stop one activity and start doing something new. *She ran this shop for ten years before deciding to move on to fresh challenges... His mother, Julia, soon moved on to a new relationship... Now, can we move on and discuss the vital business of the day.* =go on V P to n V P

move out. If you **move out**, you stop living in a particular house or place and you go to live somewhere else. *The harassment had become too much to tolerate and he decided to move out... They had a huge row and Sally moved out of the house.* PHRASAL VERB ≠move in V P V P of n

move over PHRASAL VERB

1 If you **move over** to a new system or way of doing something, you change to it. *The government is having to introduce some difficult changes, particularly in moving over to a market economy.* =change to V P to n Also V P

2 If someone **moves over**, they leave their job or position in order to let someone else have it. *They said Mr Morar should make balanced programmes about the Black community or move over and let someone else who can.* V P

3 If you **move over**, you change your position in order to make room for someone else. *Move over and let me drive.* V P

move up PHRASAL VERB

1 If you **move up**, you change your position, especially in order to be nearer someone or to make

room for someone else. *Move up, John, and let the lady sit down.* VP

2 If someone or something **moves up**, they go to a higher level, grade, or class. *Share prices moved up... In nearly all British schools, children learn in mixed ability classes and move up a class each year.* =go up VP VPn

moveable /muːvəbəl/. See **movable**.

movement /muːvmənt/ **movements** ◆◆◆◆◇

1 A **movement** is a group of people who share the same beliefs, ideas, or aims. *It's part of a broader Hindu nationalist movement that's gaining strength throughout the country. ...the women's movement.* N-COUNT: usu supp N

2 **Movement** involves changing position or going from one place to another. *They actually monitor the movement of the fish going up river. ...the plan for free movement of people, goods, capital and services across internal Community borders... There was movement behind the window in the back door... A tall, thin man was waving his arms in an effort to direct the movements of a large removal van... Her hand movements are becoming more animated.* N-VAR

3 A **movement** is a planned change in position that an army makes during a battle or military exercise. *There are reports of fresh troop movements towards China.* N-VAR

4 **Movement** is a gradual development or change of an attitude, opinion, or policy. *...the movement towards democracy in Latin America... There was a very good atmosphere at the talks and the participants believed movement forward was possible.* N-VAR: with supp, usu N towards/away from n

5 Your **movements** are everything which you do or plan to do during a period of time. *I want a full account of your movements the night Mr Gower was killed.* N-PLURAL: poss N

6 A **movement** of a piece of classical music is one of its main sections. *...the first movement of Beethoven's 7th symphony.* N-COUNT: usu with supp

mover /muːvəʳ/ **movers.** If you describe a person or animal as a particular kind of **mover**, you mean that they move at that speed or in that way. *We found him a nice horse – a good mover who could gallop.* • See also **prime mover**. ◆◇◇◇◇ N-COUNT: adj N

movie /muːvi/ **movies** ◆◆◆◆◇

1 A **movie** is a film; used mainly in American English. *In the first movie Tony Curtis ever made he played a grocery clerk. ...a horror movie.* N-COUNT =film

2 In American English, you can talk about **the movies** when you are talking about seeing a movie in a movie theater. The British term is **the cinema**. *He took her to the movies.* N-PLURAL: the N

moviegoer /muːvigoʊəʳ/ **moviegoers.** A **moviegoer** is a person who often goes to the cinema; used mainly in American English. N-COUNT

movie house, movie houses. In American English, a **movie house** is the same as a **movie theater**. N-COUNT

movie theater, movie theaters. In American English, a **movie theater** is a place where people go to watch films for entertainment. The British word is **cinema**. N-COUNT

moving /muːvɪŋ/ ◆◆◇◇◇

1 If something is **moving**, it makes you feel strongly an emotion such as sadness, pity, or sympathy. *It is very moving to see how much strangers can care for each other... It was a moving moment for Marianne.* ♦ **movingly** *You write very movingly of your sister Diana's suicide.* ADJ-GRADED =touching ADV-GRADED: ADV with v

2 A **moving** model or part of a machine moves or is able to move. ADJ: ADJ n

3 The **moving spirit** or **moving force** behind something is a person or thing that caused it to start and to keep going, or that influenced people to take part in it. *She alone must have been the moving spirit behind the lawsuit that lost me my position... Professor Krauss has been a moving force in the world of academic art criticism.* PHRASE: oft PHR behind/in n

moving picture, moving pictures. A **moving picture** is a film; an old-fashioned word. N-COUNT

mow /moʊ/ **mows, mowing, mowed, mown.** The past participle can be either **mowed** or **mown**. If you **mow** an area of grass, you cut it using a lawn mower. *He continued to mow the lawn and do other routine chores.* ◆◇◇◇◇ VERB Vn Also V

mow down. If someone **is mown down**, they are killed violently by a vehicle or gunfire. *She was mown down on a pedestrian crossing... Gunmen mowed down 10 people in one attack.* PHRASAL VERB beV ed P VPn (not pron) Also VnP

mower /moʊəʳ/ **mowers** ◆◇◇◇◇

1 A **mower** is the same as a **lawnmower**. N-COUNT

2 A **mower** is a machine that has sharp blades for cutting something such as corn or wheat. N-COUNT

MP /em piː/ **MPs** ◆◆◆◆◇

1 In Britain, an **MP** is a person who has been elected to represent the people from a particular area in the House of Commons. **MP** is an abbreviation for 'Member of Parliament'. *...Colin Pickthall, MP for West Lancashire... Several Conservative MPs have voted against the government.* N-COUNT

2 **MP** is written after someone's name to indicate that they have been elected as an MP. *...Margaret Beckett MP.*

mpg /em piː dʒiː/. **mpg** is an abbreviation for 'miles per gallon'; it is written after a number to indicate how many miles a vehicle can travel using one gallon of fuel. *Fuel consumption is 38 mpg around town, 55 mpg on the open road.*

mph. **mph** is a written abbreviation for 'miles per hour'; it is written after a number to indicate the speed of something such as a vehicle. *Inside these zones, traffic speeds are restricted to 20 mph.* ◆◇◇◇◇

Mr /mɪstəʳ/; this abbreviation is usually followed by a full stop in American English. ◆◆◆◆◆

1 **Mr** is used before a man's name when you are speaking or referring to him. *...Mr Grant. ...Mr Bob Price. ...Mr and Mrs Daniels.* N-TITLE

2 **Mr** is sometimes used in front of words such as 'President' and 'Chairman' to address the man who holds the position mentioned. *Mr. President, you're aware of the system.* N-VOC: N n

3 See also **Messrs**.

Mrs /mɪsɪz/; this abbreviation is usually followed by a full stop in American English. **Mrs** is used before the name of a married woman when you are speaking or referring to her. *Hello, Mrs Miles. ...Mrs Anne Pritchard. ...Mr and Mrs D H Alderson.* ◆◆◆◆◆ N-TITLE

Ms /məz, mɪz/. **Ms** is used, especially in written English, before a woman's name when you are speaking to her or referring to her. If you use **Ms**, you are not specifying if the woman is married or not. *...Ms Brown. ...Ms Elizabeth Harman.* ◆◆◆◆◆ N-TITLE

ms., mss. ms. is a written abbreviation for **manuscript**.

MS /em es/.

1 **MS** is a serious disease of the nervous system, which gradually makes a person weaker, and sometimes affects their sight or speech. **MS** is an abbreviation for **multiple sclerosis**. N-UNCOUNT

2 In American English, an **MS** is the same as an **MSc**.

MSc /em es siː/ **MScs** ◆◇◇◇◇

1 An **MSc** is a master's degree in a science subject. **MSc** is an abbreviation for 'Master of Science'. N-COUNT

2 **MSc** is written after someone's name to indicate that they have an MSc. *...A. A. Mattick BSc, MSc.*

MSG /em es dʒiː/. **MSG** is an abbreviation for **monosodium glutamate**. N-UNCOUNT

Msgr. **Msgr** is a written abbreviation for **Monsignor**. =Monsignor

Mt, Mts. **Mt** is a written abbreviation for **mount** or **mountain**. It is used as part of the name of a particular mountain or range of mountains. *...Mt Everest. ...the Rocky Mts.* ◆◇◇◇◇

much /mʌtʃ/ ◆◆◆◆◆

1 You use **much** to indicate the great intensity, extent, or degree of something such as an action, feeling, or change. **Much** is usually used with 'so', 'too', and 'very', and in negative clauses with this meaning. *She laughs too much... Thank you very much... My hairstyle hasn't changed much since I was five.* ADV-GRADED: ADV with v

2 If something does not happen **much**, it does not ADV-GRADED:

happen very often. *He said that his father never talked much about the war... Gwen had not seen her Daddy all that much, because mostly he worked on the ships... Do you get back East much?* oft with brd-neg, ADV after v =often

3 You use **much** in front of 'too' or comparative adjectives and adverbs in order to emphasize that there is a large amount of a particular quality. *The skin is much too delicate... You'd be so much happier if you could see yourself the way I see you... He had written to The Times and then, much more unacceptably, allowed himself to be interviewed on television.* ADV-GRADED: ADV compar, ADV *too* PRAGMATICS =far

4 If one thing is **much** the same as another thing, it is very similar to it. *The day ended much as it began... Sheep's milk is produced in much the same way as goat's milk.* ADV: ADV *as/like* cl, ADV *like* n, ADV n *as* n, ADV n

5 You use **much** to indicate that you are referring to a large amount of a substance, or of something else referred to by an uncount noun. *They are grown on the hillsides in full sun, without much water... Japan has been reluctant to offer much aid to Russia... The Home Office acknowledges that much crime goes unreported... Furniture is so bulky, it takes so much room.* ► Also a pronoun. *...eating too much and drinking too much... There was so much to talk about.* ► Also a quantifier. *Much of the time we do not notice that we are solving problems... She does much of her work abroad... Her father had been a merchant seaman, absent for much of her childhood.* DET: DET n-uncount, oft with brd-neg ≠little; PRON ≠little; QUANT: QUANT *of* def-n-uncount/def-sing-n =a lot of

6 You use **much** in expressions such as **not much**, **not very much**, and **too much** when replying to questions about amounts. *'Can you hear it where you live?' He shook his head. 'Not much.'... 'Do you care very much about what other people think?'—'Too much.'* ADV-GRADED: ADV as reply

7 If you do not see **much of** someone, you do not see them very often. *I don't see much of Tony nowadays... We won't be seeing much of each other for a while.* QUANT: with brd-neg, QUANT *of* n-proper/pron

8 You use **much** in the expression **how much** to ask questions about amount or degree, and also in reported clauses and statements to give information about the amount or degree of something. *How much money can I afford?... See just how much fat and cholesterol you're eating... I'm always very aware of how much work there is still to be done... Krock told this story to McCauley and asked him how much truth there was in it.* ► Also an adverb. *She knows how much this upsets me but she persists in doing it... How much cooler will it get?* ► Also a pronoun. *How much do you earn?... Greg made a vague gesture to indicate how much.* DET: *how* DET PRAGMATICS; ADV-GRADED: *how* ADV, ADV with cl, ADV compar; PRON: *how* PRON

9 You use **much** in the expression **as much** when you are comparing amounts. *I shall try, with as much patience as is possible, to explain yet again... Their aim will be to produce as much milk as possible ... With an 18-watt fluorescent bulb you get as much light but use 75% less electricity.* DET: *as* DET n, usu *as* DET n *as* cl/group

10 You use **much as** to introduce a fact which makes something else you have just said or will say rather surprising. *Much as they hope to go home tomorrow, they're resigned to staying on until the end of the year.* PHR-CONJ-SUBORD PRAGMATICS

11 You use **as much** in expressions such as **'I thought as much'** and **'I guessed as much'** after you have just been told something and you want to say that you already believed or expected it to be true. *You're waiting for a woman – I thought as much.* PHRASES v PHR PRAGMATICS

12 You use **as much as** before an amount to suggest that it is surprisingly large. *The organisers hope to raise as much as £6m for charity.* PHR amount PRAGMATICS

13 You use **much less** after a statement, often a negative one, to indicate that the statement is more true of the person, thing, or situation that you are going to mention next. *They are always short of water to drink, much less to bathe in... But we must not think of Chekhov as a leftist, much less a revolutionary.* PHR cl/group, PHR before v PRAGMATICS

14 You say **nothing much** to refer to something that is not very interesting or important. *'What was stolen?'—'Oh, nothing much.'... Nothing much interesting seemed to be happening.*

15 If you describe something as **not much of a** particular type of thing, you mean that it is small or of poor quality. *It hasn't been much of a holiday... It's not much of a career, you may think.* PHR n

16 **So much for** is used to indicate that you have finished talking about a subject; used mainly in spoken English. *Well, so much for the producers. But what of the consumers?* PHR n PRAGMATICS

17 If you say **so much for** a particular thing, you mean that it has not been successful or helpful; an informal expression. *He had panicked. And panic was fear. So much for all his damn theories!* PHR n

18 If you say that something is not **so much** one thing **as** another, you mean that it is more like the second thing than the first. *I don't really think of her as a daughter so much as a very good friend... She told me she was not so much leaving her job as it was leaving her.* with brd-neg, PHR group, PHR before v

19 If you say that someone did not do **so much as** perform a particular action, you are emphasizing that they did not even do that, when you were expecting them to do more. *I didn't so much as catch sight of him all day long... Laura had not reproached him, never so much as mentioned it... She auctioned off the car without so much as taking a ride in it.* with brd-neg, PHR before v PRAGMATICS =even

20 You use **so much so** to indicate that your previous statement is true to a very great extent, and therefore it has the result mentioned. *He himself believed in freedom, so much so that he would rather die than live without it.* PHR that PRAGMATICS

21 If a situation or action is **too much** for you, it is so difficult, tiring, or upsetting that you cannot cope with it. *His inability to stay at one job for long had finally proved too much for her.* v-link PHR, oft PHR *for* n

22 You use **very much** to emphasize that someone or something has a lot of a particular quality, or that the description you are about to give is particularly accurate. *...a man very much in charge of himself... Yorkshire is still very much a farming community with good meat, good dairy produce and eggs... Something was very much the matter.* oft PHR n PRAGMATICS

23 ● **a bit much**: see **bit**. ● **not up to much**: see **up**.

much- /mʌtʃ-/. **Much-** combines with past participles to form adjectives which emphasize the intensity of the specified state or action. *That means cutting or shelving some of our spending plans, including much-needed public works... The author of the computer game expects to have finished a much-improved program next year.* COMB in ADJ PRAGMATICS

much-maligned. If you describe someone or something as **much-maligned**, you mean that they are often criticized by people, but you think the criticism is unfair or exaggerated because they have good qualities too. *Let us not forget that the much-maligned British Rail has a major expertise in electronic communications... I'm happy for James. He's a much-maligned player but has tremendous spirit.* ADJ-GRADED: usu ADJ n PRAGMATICS

much-travelled; spelled **much-traveled** in American English. A **much-travelled** person has travelled a lot in foreign countries. ADJ =well-travelled

muck /mʌk/ **mucks, mucking, mucked** ◆◇◇◇◇

1 **Muck** is dirt or some other unpleasant substance; an informal use. *This congealed muck was interfering with the filter and causing the flooding.* N-UNCOUNT

2 **Muck** is manure. *He could smell muck and clean fresh hay. ...pigs foraging about in the muck.* N-UNCOUNT

3 If you refer to something as **muck**, you are emphasizing that you think it is very poor; an informal use. *He hasn't eaten anything for days. And are you surprised, when this muck is all I have to give him?... The script is utterly banal. It is incredible that human minds can put such muck on to paper.* N-UNCOUNT PRAGMATICS =rubbish

muck about or **muck around.** The form **muck about** is mainly used in British English. PHRASAL VERB

1 If you **muck about** or **muck around**, you behave in a childish or silly way, often so that you waste your time and fail to achieve anything; an informal expression, used mainly in British English. *We do* =mess about V P *not want people of his age mucking around risking people's lives... He'd spent his boyhood summers mucking about in boats... The last I saw of him though he was mucking about with the nurses and really enjoying himself.* — V P prep/adv

2 If you **muck about with** or **muck around with** something, you alter it, often making it worse than it already was; an informal expression. *The president's wife doesn't muck around with policy or sit in on Cabinet meetings.* — =mess around; V P with n

3 If you **muck** someone **about** or **muck** them **around**, you treat them badly, for example by not being honest with them or by continually changing plans which affect them; an informal expression, used mainly in British English. *He does not tolerate anyone who mucks him about.* — =mess about; V n P

muck in. If someone **mucks in**, they join in with an activity or help other people with a job and do not consider themselves to be too important to do it; an informal expression, used mainly in British English. *Course residents are expected to muck in and be prepared to share rooms... She mucked in with the chores and did her own washing and ironing... Ian was never afraid to take his coat off and muck in with everybody else.* — PHRASAL VERB; V P; V P with n; Also V P together

muck out. In British English, if you **muck out** a stable, pigsty, or other farm animal's home, you clean out all the manure and old hay. *He stamped off to muck out the pigsty... Here's how to muck out.* — PHRASAL VERB; V P n (not pron); V P; Also V n P

muck up. If you **muck up** or **muck** something **up**, you do something very badly so that you fail to achieve what you wanted to; an informal expression. *I mucked up at the 13th hole and told myself that this was getting stupid... Scientists should figure out how to keep the natural world from mucking up the affairs of people.* — PHRASAL VERB; =mess up; V P; V P n (not pron); Also V n P

muck-raking; also spelled **muckraking**. If you accuse someone of **muck-raking**, you are criticising them for finding and spreading scandal about someone, especially a public figure. *The Prime Minister accused opposition leaders of muck-raking.* — N-UNCOUNT; PRAGMATICS

mucky /mʌki/ **muckier, muckiest.** Something that is **mucky** is very dirty; an informal word. — ADJ-GRADED

mucous membrane /mjuːkəs membreɪn/ **mucous membranes.** A **mucous membrane** is a thin piece of skin that produces mucus to prevent itself from becoming dry. It covers delicate parts of the body such as the inside of your nose; a technical term in biology. — N-COUNT

mucus /mjuːkəs/. **Mucus** is a clear slimy liquid that is produced in some parts of your body, for example the inside of your nose; a formal word. — ◆◇◇◇◇ N-UNCOUNT

mud /mʌd/. **Mud** is a sticky mixture of earth and water. *His uniform was crumpled, untidy, splashed with mud... Their lorry got stuck in the mud.* — ◆◆◇◇◇ N-UNCOUNT

muddle /mʌdᵊl/ **muddles, muddling, muddled** ◆◇◇◇◇

1 If people or things are in a **muddle**, they are in a state of confusion or disorder. *My thoughts are all in a muddle... We are going to get into a hopeless muddle. ...a general muddle of pencils and boxes... The laws led to confusion, muddle and years of delay. ...domestic muddles and family tensions.* — N-VAR: oft in/into a N; =mess, confusion

2 If you **muddle** things or people, you get them mixed up, so that you do not know which is which. *Already, one or two critics have begun to muddle the two names... We are beginning to muddle the extended royal family and the monarchy.* — VERB; =mix up, confuse; V n

▸ **Muddle up** means the same as **muddle**. *The question muddles up three separate issues... He sometimes muddles me up with other patients.* — PHRASAL VERB; V P pl-n (not pron); V n P with n; Also V pl-n P

♦ **muddled up** *I know that I am getting my words muddled up.* — ADJ-GRADED

muddle along. If you **muddle along**, you live or exist without a proper plan or purpose in your life. *I've started going to evening classes to learn how to do things properly, rather than just muddling along.* — PHRASAL VERB; V P

muddle through. If you **muddle through**, you manage to do something even though you do not have the proper equipment or do not really know how to do it. *We will muddle through and just play it day by day... The BBC may be able to muddle through the next five years like this... Somehow or other, we muddled our way through.* — PHRASAL VERB; V P; V P n; V way P

muddle up. See **muddle** 2 — PHRASAL VERB

muddled /mʌdᵊld/. If someone is **muddled**, they are confused about something. *I'm afraid I'm a little muddled. I'm not exactly sure where to begin. ...the muddled thinking of the Government's transport policy in recent years.* — ◆◇◇◇◇ ADJ-GRADED; =confused

muddy /mʌdi/ **muddier, muddiest; muddies, muddying, muddied** ◆◇◇◇◇

1 Something that is **muddy** contains mud or is covered in mud. *...a muddy track... The ground was still very muddy. ...his muddy boots.* — ADJ-GRADED

2 If you **muddy** something, you cause it to be muddy. *The ground still smelled of rain and they muddied their shoes... His new grey jacket was torn and muddied.* — VERB; V n; V-ed

3 Muddy is used to describe a colour which is dull and brownish. *The paper has turned a muddy colour.* — ADJ-GRADED: ADJ n

4 If someone or something **muddies** a situation or issue, they cause it to seem less clear and less easy to understand. *It's difficult enough without muddying the issue with religion. ...the mixed motives that muddied Mr Crane's efforts.* — VERB; V n

♦ **muddied** *Overseas the legal issues are more muddied.* — ADJ-GRADED

• If someone or something **muddies the waters**, they cause a situation or issue to seem less clear and less easy to understand. *They keep on muddying the waters by raising other political issues.* — PHRASE: V inflects

mudflats /mʌdflæts/. **Mudflats** are areas of flat empty land at the coast which are covered by the sea only when the tide is in. — N-PLURAL

mudguard /mʌdgɑːʳd/ **mudguards.** The **mudguards** on a bicycle or other vehicle are curved pieces of metal or plastic above the tyres, which stop the rider or vehicle from being splashed with mud. — N-COUNT: usu pl

mudslide /mʌdslaɪd/ **mudslides.** A **mudslide** is a large amount of mud sliding down a mountain, usually causing damage or destruction. — N-COUNT

mud-slinging. If you accuse someone of **mud-slinging**, you are accusing them of making insulting, unfair, and damaging remarks about their opponents. *There will be no mudslinging, they promise... Voters are disillusioned with the mud-slinging campaigns run by many candidates in recent years.* — N-UNCOUNT; PRAGMATICS

muesli /mjuːzli/ **mueslis. Muesli** is a breakfast cereal made from chopped nuts, dried fruit, and grains. — N-MASS

muezzin /muezɪn/ **muezzins.** In a mosque, a **muezzin** is an official who calls from its tower when it is the time of day for Muslims to say their prayers. — N-COUNT

muff /mʌf/ **muffs, muffing, muffed**

1 If you **muff** something, you do it badly or you make a mistake while you are doing it, so that it is not successful; an informal use. *He muffed his opening speech. ...a muffed opportunity.* — VERB; V n; V-ed

2 A **muff** is a piece of fur or thick cloth shaped like a short hollow cylinder. You wear a muff on your hands to keep them warm in cold weather. — N-COUNT

3 Muffs are the same as **earmuffs**. — N-PLURAL

muffin /mʌfɪn/ **muffins. Muffins** are small, flat, sweet bread rolls that you eat hot with butter. — ◆◇◇◇◇ N-COUNT

muffle /mʌfᵊl/ **muffles, muffling, muffled.** If something **muffles** a sound, it makes it quieter and more difficult to hear. *Blake held his handkerchief over the mouthpiece to muffle his voice... She heard a muffled cough behind her.* — ◆◇◇◇◇ VERB; V n; V-ed

muffled /mʌfᵊld/. If you are **muffled**, you are wearing a lot of heavy clothes so that very little of your body or face is visible. *Children muffled in scarves and woolly hats were slipping and sliding on the ice.* — ADJ: usu v-link ADJ

• If you are **muffled up**, you are wearing a lot of heavy clothes so that very little of your body or face is visible. *All the women were muffled up in several layers of clothing.* — PHRASE: usu v-link PHR

muffler /mʌflə^r/ **mufflers**
1 A **muffler** is the same as a **scarf**; an old-fashioned use. N-COUNT
2 In American English, a **muffler** is a device on a car exhaust that makes it quieter. The usual British word is **silencer**. N-COUNT

mug /mʌg/ **mugs, mugging, mugged** ◆◆◇◇◇
1 A **mug** is a large deep cup with straight sides and a handle, used for hot drinks. *He spooned instant coffee into two of the mugs.* ▶ A **mug** of something is the amount of it contained in a mug. *He had been drinking mugs of coffee to keep himself awake.* N-COUNT; N-COUNT: usu N *of* n
2 If someone **mugs** you, they attack you in order to steal your money. *I was walking out to my car when this guy tried to mug me... He has been mugged more than once.* ♦ **mugging, muggings** *Bank robberies, burglaries and muggings are reported almost daily in the press... We usually think of a victim of mugging as being someone elderly.* VERB V n; N-VAR
3 In informal British English, if you say that someone is a **mug**, you mean that they are stupid and easily deceived or misled by other people. *He's a mug as far as women are concerned... I feel such a mug for signing the agreement.* N-COUNT PRAGMATICS
4 In informal British English, if you say that something is **a mug's game**, you mean that it is an activity that is not worth doing because it doesn't give the person who is doing it any benefit or satisfaction. *I used to be a very heavy gambler, but not any more. It's a mug's game... Dieting is a mug's game.* PHRASE: v-link PHR
5 Someone's **mug** is their face; an informal use. *He managed to get his ugly mug on the telly.* N-COUNT: usu poss N

mug up. In British English, if you **mug up** a subject or **mug up** on it, you study it quickly, so that you can remember the main facts about it; an informal expression. *...visitors who want to mug up their knowledge in the shortest possible time... It is advisable to mug up on your Spanish, too, as few locals speak English.* PHRASAL VERB =swot up; V P n (not pron); V P *on* n; Also V P

mugger /mʌgə^r/ **muggers.** A **mugger** is a person who attacks someone violently in a street in order to steal money from them. N-COUNT

muggy /mʌgi/. **Muggy** weather is unpleasantly warm and damp. *It was muggy and overcast.* ADJ-GRADED: oft *it* v-link ADJ =humid

mug shot, mug shots. A **mug shot** is a photograph of someone, especially a photograph of a criminal which has been taken by the police; an informal word. *...mug-shots of the five terrorists.* N-COUNT

mulberry /mʌlbəri, AM -beri/ **mulberries.** A **mulberry** or a **mulberry tree** is a tree which has small purple berries which you can eat. ▶ **Mulberries** are the fruit of a mulberry tree. N-VAR; N-COUNT

mulch /mʌltʃ/ **mulches, mulching, mulched** ◆◇◇◇◇
1 A **mulch** is a mixture of rotting leaves and twigs or manure which you put round the roots of plants in order to protect them and to help them to grow. N-MASS
2 To **mulch** plants means to put rotting leaves and twigs or manure round them to protect them and to make them grow. *In May, mulch the bed with garden compost.* VERB V n *with* n; Also V n

mule /mjuːl/ **mules** ◆◇◇◇◇
1 A **mule** is an animal whose parents are a horse and a donkey. N-COUNT
2 A **mule** is a shoe or slipper which is open around the heel. N-COUNT: usu pl

mull /mʌl/ **mulls, mulling, mulled.** In American English, if you **mull** something, you think about it for a long time before deciding what to do. *Last month, a federal grand jury began mulling evidence in the case... Do you know why he was mulling and hesitating?* ◆◇◇◇◇ VERB V n; V

mull over. If you **mull** something **over**, you think about it for a long time before deciding what to do. *Mclaren had been mulling over an idea to make a movie... I'll leave you alone here so you can mull it over.* PHRASAL VERB =consider; V P n (not pron); V n P

mullah /mʊlə, mʌlə/ **mullahs.** A **mullah** is a Muslim who is a teacher, scholar, or religious leader. N-COUNT; N-TITLE

mulled /mʌld/. **Mulled** wine has sugar and spice added to it and is then heated. ADJ: ADJ n

mullet, /mʌlɪt/ **mullets; mullet** can also be used as the plural form. A **mullet** is a small sea fish that people cook and eat. ▶ **Mullet** is this fish eaten as food. ◆◇◇◇◇ N-VAR; N-UNCOUNT

multi- /mʌlti-/. **Multi-** is used to form adjectives indicating that something consists of many things of a particular kind. *...the introduction of multi-party democracy. ...a multi-million-dollar outfit.* PREFIX

multicoloured /mʌltikʌlə^{r}d/; also spelled **multi coloured**, and spelled **multicolored** in American English. A **multicoloured** object has many different colours. *...a sea of multicoloured umbrellas.* ADJ: usu ADJ n

multicultural /mʌltikʌltʃərəl/; also spelled **multi-cultural**. **Multicultural** means consisting of or relating to people of many different nationalities and cultures. *...children growing up in a multicultural society... The school has been attempting to bring a multicultural perspective to its curriculum.* ADJ-GRADED: usu ADJ n

multiculturalism /mʌltikʌltʃərəlɪzəm/. **Multiculturalism** is the belief that all the different cultural or racial groups that make up a society should be given equal representation in areas such as education, the arts, and the workplace. N-UNCOUNT

multi-faceted. **Multi-faceted** means having a variety of different and important features or elements. *Webb is a multi-faceted performer... Her job is multi-faceted.* ADJ-GRADED: usu ADJ n

multifarious /mʌltɪfeəriəs/. If you describe things as **multifarious**, you mean that they are many in number and of many different kinds; a literary word. *Spain is a composite of multifarious traditions and people... The reasons for closure are multifarious.* ADJ-GRADED

multilateral /mʌltilætərəl/. **Multilateral** means involving at least three different groups of people or nations. *Many want to abandon the multilateral trade talks in Geneva.* ◆◇◇◇◇ ADJ: usu ADJ n

multilingual /mʌltilɪŋgwəl/; also spelled **multilingual.**
1 **Multilingual** means involving several different languages. *...a multilingual country. ...multilingual dictionaries.* ADJ: usu ADJ n
2 A **multilingual** person is able to speak more than two languages very well. *He recruited two multilingual engineers.* ADJ

multimedia /mʌltimiːdiə/ ◆◇◇◇◇
1 In computing, you use **multimedia** to refer to programs and products which involve the use of sound, pictures, and film, as well as ordinary text, to convey information. *...the case of an insurance company using multimedia to improve customer service in its branches. ...the next generation of computers, which will be 'multimedia machines' that allow users to control and manipulate sound, video, text and graphics.* N-UNCOUNT: usu N n
2 In education, **multimedia** is the use of television and other different media in a lesson, instead of only textbooks. N-UNCOUNT
3 In art, **multimedia** is the use of different kinds of material in a painting or sculpture. N-UNCOUNT

multi-millionaire, multi-millionaires; also spelled **multimillionaire**. A **multi-millionaire** is a very rich person who has money or property worth several million pounds or dollars. ◆◇◇◇◇ N-COUNT

multinational /mʌltinæʃənəl/ **multinationals;** also spelled **multi-national**. ◆◆◇◇◇
1 A **multinational** company has branches or subsidiary companies in many different countries. ▶ Also a noun. *...multinationals such as Ford and IBM.* ADJ: usu ADJ n; N-COUNT
2 **Multinational** armies, organizations, or other groups involve people from several different countries. *The US troops would be part of a multinational force.* ADJ: usu ADJ n
3 **Multinational** countries or regions have a population that is made up of people of several different nationalities. ADJ: usu ADJ n

multiple /mʌltɪpəl/ **multiples** ◆◆◇◇◇
1 You use **multiple** to describe things that consist ADJ:

of many parts, involve many people, or have many uses. *He died of multiple injuries... The most common multiple births are twins, two babies born at the same time.* usu ADJ n

2 If one number is a **multiple of** a smaller number, it can be exactly divided by that smaller number. *Their numerical system, derived from the Babylonians, was based on multiples of the number six.* N-COUNT: N *of* n

3 In British English, a **multiple** or a **multiple store** is a shop with a lot of branches in different towns; a technical term in business. *It made it almost impossible for the smaller retailer to compete against the multiples.* N-COUNT

multiple choice; also spelled **multiple-choice.** In a **multiple choice** test or question, you have to choose the answer that you think is right from several possible answers that are listed on the question paper. ADJ: usu ADJ n

multiple sclerosis /mʌltɪpəl sklərəʊsɪs/. ◆◇◇◇◇ **Multiple sclerosis** is a serious disease of the nervous system, which gradually makes a person weaker, and sometimes affects their sight or speech. The abbreviation 'MS' is also used. N-UNCOUNT

multiplex, multiplexes /mʌltipleks/. A **multiplex** is a cinema complex with six or more screens. N-COUNT

multiplication /mʌltɪplɪkeɪʃən/

1 **Multiplication** is the process of calculating the total of one number multiplied by another. *There will be simple tests in addition, subtraction, multiplication and division.* N-UNCOUNT

2 The **multiplication** of things of a particular kind is the process or fact of them increasing in number or amount. *Increasing gravity is known to speed up the multiplication of cells.* N-UNCOUNT: usu N *of* n

multiplication sign, multiplication signs. A **multiplication sign** is the sign (×) which is put between two numbers to show that they are being multiplied. N-COUNT

multiplication table, multiplication tables. A **multiplication table** is a list of the multiplications of numbers between one and twelve. Children often have to learn multiplication tables at school. N-COUNT =table

multiplicity /mʌltɪplɪsɪti/. A **multiplicity of** things is a large number or a large variety of them; a formal word. *...a writer who uses a multiplicity of styles. ...the multiplicity of tasks this machine can perform.* QUANT: QUANT *of* pl-n =host of

multiply /mʌltɪplaɪ/ **multiplies, multiplying, multiplied** ◆◆◇◇◇

1 When something **multiplies** or when you **multiply** it, it increases greatly in number or amount. *Such disputes multiplied in the eighteenth and nineteenth centuries... Her husband multiplied his demands on her time.* V-ERG; V; V n

2 When animals and insects **multiply**, they increase in number by giving birth to large numbers of young. *These creatures can multiply quickly.* VERB; V

3 If you **multiply** one number by another, you calculate the total which you get when you add the first number to itself as many times as is indicated by the second number. For example 2 multiplied by 3 is equal to 2 plus 2 plus 2, which equals 6. *What do you get if you multiply six by nine? ...the remarkable ability to multiply huge numbers correctly without pen or paper.* VERB; V n *by* n; V pl-n

multiracial /mʌltireɪʃəl/; also spelled **multi-racial. Multiracial** means consisting of or involving people of many different nationalities and cultures. *We live in a multiracial society.* ADJ-GRADED: usu ADJ n =multicultural

multi-storey. A **multi-storey** building has several floors at different levels above the ground. *...multi-storey hotels. ...a multi-storey car park.* ADJ: usu ADJ n

multi-tasking. Multi-tasking is the ability of some computers to do several tasks at the same time, usually with each task being shown in a different window. N-UNCOUNT

multitude /mʌltɪtjuːd, AM -tuːd/ **multitudes** ◆◇◇◇◇

1 A **multitude of** things or people, is a very large number of them. *There are a multitude of small quiet roads to cycle along... Addiction to drugs can bring a multitude of other problems.* QUANT: QUANT *of* pl-n ● If you say that something covers or hides **a multitude of sins**, you mean that it deliberately conceals things by appearing to be much better than it really is. *'Strong, centralized government' is a term that can cover a multitude of sins.* PHRASE: PHR after v

2 You can refer to a very large number of people as a **multitude**; used in written English. *...surrounded by a noisy multitude. ...the multitudes that throng around the Pope.* N-COUNT =crowd

3 **The multitude** or **the multitudes** are the great majority of people in a particular country or situation. *The hideous truth was hidden from the multitude... It is our task to convince the multitudes that we are pursuing a lawful hobby in a lawful way.* N-COUNT-COLL: *the* N

mum /mʌm/ **mums** ◆◆◆◇◇

1 Your **mum** is your mother; an informal use. *He misses his mum... Mum and Dad are coming for lunch... Don't worry, Mum... You're about to become a mum.* N-FAMILY =mom

2 If you **keep mum** or **stay mum** about something, you do not tell anyone about it; an informal expression. *I'd be in trouble if I let on. So I kept mum.* PHRASE: V inflects =keep quiet

mumble /mʌmbəl/ **mumbles, mumbling, mumbled.** ◆◇◇◇◇ If you **mumble** something or **mumble**, you speak very quietly and indistinctly so that the words are difficult to understand. *Her grandmother mumbled in her sleep... He mumbled a few words... 'Today of all days,' she mumbled.* VERB =mutter; V; V n; V with quote ► Also a noun. *He could hear the low mumble of Navarro's voice.* N-COUNT =mutter

mumbo jumbo /mʌmboʊ dʒʌmboʊ/; also spelled **mumbo-jumbo**. If you describe an idea or belief as **mumbo jumbo**, you are critical of it because you think it is unrealistic or nonsensical; an informal expression. *It's all full of psychoanalytic mumbo-jumbo.* N-UNCOUNT PRAGMATICS

mummify /mʌmɪfaɪ/ **mummifies, mummifying, mummified.** If a dead body **is mummified**, it is preserved, for example by rubbing it with special oils and wrapping it in cloth. *In America, people are paying up to $150,000 to be mummified after death. ...the mummified pharaoh.* VB: usu passive =embalm; be V-ed; V-ed

mummy /mʌmi/ **mummies** ◆◇◇◇◇

1 Some people, especially children, call their mother **mummy**; an informal use. *I want my mummy... Mummy, I'm tired!... Mummy says I can play out in the garden.* N-FAMILY

2 A **mummy** is a dead body which was preserved long ago by being rubbed with special oils and wrapped in cloth. *...an Egyptian mummy.* N-COUNT

mumps /mʌmps/. **Mumps** is a disease usually caught by children. It causes a mild fever and painful swelling of the glands in the neck. N-UNCOUNT

munch /mʌntʃ/ **munches, munching, munched.** ◆◇◇◇◇ If you **munch** food, you eat it by chewing it steadily, thoroughly, and rather noisily. *Luke munched the chicken sandwiches... Across the table, his son Benjie munched appreciatively... Sheep were munching their way through a yellow carpet of leaves.* VERB =chomp; V n; V; V *way through* n; Also V *away at/on* n

mundane /mʌndeɪn/. ◆◇◇◇◇ Something that is **mundane** is very ordinary and not at all interesting or unusual. *Be willing to do mundane tasks with good grace. ...the mundane realities of life.* ADJ-GRADED =boring ► You can refer to mundane things as **the mundane**. *It's an attitude that turns the mundane into something rather more interesting and exciting.* N-SING: *the* N

municipal /mjuːnɪsɪpəl/.  **Municipal** means associated with or belonging to a city or town that has its own local government. *The municipal authorities gave the go-ahead for the march. ...next month's municipal elections. ...the municipal library.* ADJ: ADJ n

municipality /mjuːnɪsɪpælɪti/ **municipalities.**  A **municipality** is a city or town which has authority to appoint a local council and local officials to administer its internal affairs. You can also refer to that city or town's local government as a **municipality**. N-COUNT

munificent /mjuːnɪfɪsənt/. A **munificent** person is very generous; a formal word. *...one of the* ADJ-GRADED *country's most munificent artistic benefactors. ...a munificent donation.*

munitions /mjuːnɪʃənz/. **Munitions** are military equipment and supplies, especially bombs, shells, and guns. *...the shortage of men and munitions. ...a munitions factory.* ◆◇◇◇◇ N-PLURAL

mural /mjʊərəl/ **murals.** A **mural** is a picture painted on a wall. *...a mural of Tangier bay.* ◆◇◇◇◇ N-COUNT =fresco

murder /mɜːʳdəʳ/ **murders, murdering, murdered** ◆◆◆◆◇

1 **Murder** is the deliberate and unlawful killing of a person. *The three accused, aged between 19 and 20, are charged with attempted murder... The murder charge was dismissed in 1969. ...brutal murders.* N-VAR

2 To **murder** someone means to commit the crime of killing them deliberately. *...a thriller about two men who murder a third to see if they can get away with it. ...the body of a murdered religious and political leader.* VERB V n V-ed Also V

3 If you say that someone **gets away with murder**, you are complaining that they can do whatever they like without anyone trying to control them or punish them; an informal expression. *His charm and the fact that he is so likeable often allows him to get away with murder.* PHRASES V inflects PRAGMATICS

4 If you say that someone **screams blue murder** or **screams bloody murder**, you are emphasizing that they make a lot of noise and fuss because something is happening or has happened that they do not like; an informal expression. *People are screaming blue murder about the amount of traffic going through their town.* V inflects PRAGMATICS

murderer /mɜːʳdərəʳ/ **murderers.** A **murderer** is someone who deliberately and unlawfully kills another person. *One of these men may have been the murderer. ...a notorious mass murderer.* ◆◆◇◇◇ N-COUNT

murderess /mɜːʳdərɪs/ **murderesses.** A **murderess** is a woman who deliberately and unlawfully kills another person. N-COUNT =murderer

murderous /mɜːʳdərəs/ ◆◇◇◇◇

1 Someone who is **murderous** is likely to murder someone and may already be guilty of murder. *This murderous lunatic could kill them both without a second thought.* ADJ: usu ADJ n

2 A **murderous** attack or other action is very violent and intended to result in someone's death. *He made a murderous attack on his wife that evening.* ADJ-GRADED: usu ADJ n

murderously /mɜːʳdərəsli/. You use **murderously** to indicate that something is extremely unpleasant or threatening. *The bags were murderously heavy... Beauchamp glared at her murderously, then held out the letter and dropped it.* ADV: ADV adj, ADV with v

murk /mɜːʳk/. The **murk** is darkness, dark water, or thick mist that is very difficult to see through. *All of a sudden a tall old man in a black cloak loomed out of the murk.* N-SING: usu *the* N

murky /mɜːʳki/ **murkier, murkiest** ◆◇◇◇◇

1 A **murky** place or time of day is dark and rather unpleasant because there is not enough light. *The large lamplit room was murky with woodsmoke... It happened at Stamford Bridge one murky November afternoon.* ADJ-GRADED

2 **Murky** water or fog is so dark and dirty that you cannot see through it. *...the deep, murky waters of Loch Ness.* ADJ-GRADED

3 If you describe an activity or situation as **murky**, you suspect that it is dishonest or morally wrong; used mainly in British English. *There has been a murky conspiracy to keep them out of power.* ADJ-GRADED =shady

4 If you describe something as **murky**, you mean that the details of it are not clear or that it is difficult to understand. *The law here is a little bit murky... The origins of bull-riding, which serves no practical purpose, are murkier.* ADJ-GRADED =obscure

murmur /mɜːʳməʳ/ **murmurs, murmuring, murmured** ◆◆◇◇◇

1 If you **murmur** or if you **murmur** something, you say it very quietly, so that not many people can hear what you are saying. *He turned and murmured something to the professor... She murmured a few words of support... 'How lovely,' she murmured... Murmuring softly that they must go somewhere to talk, he led her from the garden.* VERB V n *to* n V n V with quote V that

2 A **murmur** is a statement or utterance which can hardly be heard. *They spoke in low murmurs... She gave a little murmur.* N-COUNT: usu adj N

3 A **murmur** is a continuous low sound, like the noise of a river or of voices far away. *The piano music mixes with the murmur of conversation... I could hear the murmur of the sea... The clamor of traffic has receded to a distant murmur.* N-SING: with supp =hum

4 A **murmur** of a particular emotion is a quiet expression of that emotion. *The promise of some basic working rights draws murmurs of approval... Already there are murmurs of discontent.* N-COUNT: with supp

5 A **murmur** is an abnormal sound which is made by the heart and which shows that there is probably something wrong with it. *The doctor said James had now developed a heart murmur.* N-COUNT: usu sing

6 If someone does something **without a murmur**, they do it without complaining. PHRASE: PHR after v

murmurings /mɜːʳmərɪŋz/. If there are **murmurings**, people are expressing their opinions about something in a quiet and unforceful way. *For some time there have been murmurings of discontent over the government policy on inflation... At this point there were murmurings of approval from the experts.* N-PLURAL: usu N *of* n

muscle /mʌsəl/ **muscles, muscling, muscled** ◆◆◆◇◇

1 A **muscle** is a piece of tissue inside your body which connects two bones and which you use when you make a movement. *Keeping your muscles strong and in tone helps you to avoid back problems... He is likely to be out for the rest of the season because of a strained thigh muscle... There are three types of muscle in the body.* N-VAR

2 **Muscles** are the bulges that appear in someone's arms, legs, or other parts of their body when they make a movement or tense a part of their body. *...a body-builder flexing to display his muscles.* N-COUNT: usu pl

3 If you say that someone has **muscle**, you mean that they have power and influence, which enables them to do difficult things. *Eisenhower used his muscle to persuade Congress to change the law... In one town, all the women were urged to remove their money from the banks on an allotted day, to demonstrate women's financial muscle.* N-UNCOUNT =clout

4 If a group, organisation, or country **flexes** its **muscles**, it behaves in a way designed to show people that it has power and is considering using it. *The Japanese Fair Trade Commission has of late been flexing its muscles, cracking down on cases of corruption.* PHRASES V inflects

5 If you say that someone did not **move a muscle**, you mean that they stayed absolutely still. *He stood without moving a muscle, unable to believe what his eyes saw so plainly.* V inflects, with brd-neg

muscle in. If someone **muscles in** on something, they force their way into a situation where they have no right to be and where they are not welcome, in order to gain some advantage for themselves; used showing disapproval. *Cohen complained that Kravis was muscling in on his deal... It would be surprising were the Mafia not to have muscled in.* PHRASAL VERB PRAGMATICS V P *on* n V P

muscle-bound. If you describe someone as **muscle-bound**, you mean that their muscles are strongly developed, often in an exaggerated or unattractive way. *...a cartoon of a muscle-bound woman standing victorious astride a prone male.* ADJ-GRADED

muscular /mʌskjʊləʳ/ ◆◆◇◇◇

1 **Muscular** means involving or affecting your muscles. *As a general rule, all muscular effort is enhanced by breathing in as the effort is made... Early symptoms include anorexia, muscular weakness and fatigue.* ADJ: ADJ n

2 If a person or their body is **muscular**, they are very fit and strong, and have firm muscles which are not covered with a lot of fat. *Like most female athletes, she was lean and muscular. ...his tanned muscular legs.* ADJ-GRADED

muscular dystrophy /mʌskjʊləʳ dɪstrəfi/. N-UNCOUNT **Muscular dystrophy** is a serious disease in which your muscles gradually weaken.

musculature /mʌskjʊlətʃəʳ/. N-UNCOUNT: oft with poss **Musculature** is used to refer to all the muscles in your body, or to a system of muscles that you use to perform a particular type of action; a formal word.

muse /mjuːz/ **muses, musing, mused** ◆◆◇◇◇

1 If you **muse** on something, you think about it, usually saying or writing what you are thinking at the same time; used in written English. VERB =ponder V on/about/over n V with quote V that *Many of the papers muse on the fate of the President... 'As a whole,' she muses, 'the 'organized church' turns me off'... He once mused that he would have voted Labour in 1964 had he been old enough.* ♦ **musing, musings** N-COUNT *His musings were interrupted by Montagu who came and sat down next to him.*

2 A **muse** is a person, usually a woman, who is believed to give people inspiration and creative ideas, especially for art, poetry, or music. N-COUNT *Once she was a nude model and muse to French artist Henri Matisse. ...the muses who fuel his inspiration.*

museum /mjuːziːəm/ **museums.** ◆◆◆◆◇ N-COUNT A **museum** is a building where a large number of interesting and valuable objects, such as works of art or historical items, are kept, studied, and displayed to the public. *For months Malcolm had wanted to visit the Parisian art museums. ...the American Museum of Natural History.*

museum piece, museum pieces. N-COUNT If you describe an object or building as a **museum piece**, you mean that it is old and unusual. *It is virtually a flying museum piece, a descendant of the World War Two Lancaster bomber.*

mush /mʌʃ/. N-UNCOUNT: also a N **Mush** is a thick, soft paste. *Over-ripe bananas will collapse into a mush in the following recipe, so use only firm fruit.*

mushroom /mʌʃruːm/ **mushrooms, mushrooming, mushroomed** ◆◆◇◇◇

1 **Mushrooms** are fungi that you can eat. N-VAR They have short stems and round tops. *There are many types of wild mushrooms. ...eggs, bacon, sausage, and mushrooms. ...mushroom omelette.* • See also **button mushroom.**

2 If something such as an industry or a place **mushrooms**, it grows or comes into existence very quickly. VERB V V to/into n *The media training industry has mushroomed over the past decade... A sleepy capital of a few hundred thousand people has mushroomed to a crowded city of 2 million.* ♦ **mushrooming** N-UNCOUNT *...the mushrooming of commercial art galleries in Barcelona and Madrid.*

mushroom cloud, mushroom clouds. N-COUNT A **mushroom cloud** is an extremely large cloud caused by a nuclear explosion. *The blast sent a huge mushroom cloud of toxic gas into the air.*

mushy /mʌʃi/

1 Vegetables and fruit that are **mushy** are soft and have lost most of their shape. ADJ-GRADED *When the fruit is mushy and cooked, remove from the heat.*

2 If you describe someone or something as **mushy**, you dislike them because they are very sentimental. ADJ-GRADED PRAGMATICS *Don't go getting all mushy and sentimental.*

music /mjuːzɪk/ ◆◆◆◆◆

1 **Music** is the pattern of sounds produced by people singing or playing instruments. N-UNCOUNT *...classical music. ...the music of George Gershwin. ...a mixture of music, dance, cabaret and children's theatre. ...a music critic for the New York Times.*

2 **Music** is the art of creating or performing music. N-UNCOUNT *He went on to study music, specialising in the clarinet. ...a music lesson.*

3 **Music** is the symbols written on paper which represent musical sounds. N-UNCOUNT *He's never been able to read music.* • See also **sheet music.**

4 If something that you hear is **music to your ears**, it makes you feel very happy. PHRASES v-link PHR *Popular support – it's music to the ears of any politician.*

5 If you **face the music**, you put yourself in a position where you will be criticized or punished for something you have done. V inflects *Sooner or later, I'm going to have to face the music.*

musical /mjuːzɪkᵊl/ **musicals** ◆◆◆◇◇

1 You use **musical** to indicate that something is connected with playing or studying music. ADJ: ADJ n *We have a wealth of musical talent in this region... Stan Getz's musical career spanned five decades... London's musical life might become as exciting as Berlin's.* ♦ **musically** /mjuːzɪkli/ ADV: ADV with cl/group, ADV after v *Musically there is a lot to enjoy. ...trying to communicate verbally what he can only communicate musically.*

2 A **musical** is a play or film that uses singing and dancing in the story. N-COUNT *...London's smash hit musical Miss Saigon.*

3 Someone who is **musical** has a natural ability and interest in music. ADJ-GRADED *I came from a musical family.* ♦ **musicality** /mjuːzɪkælɪti/ N-UNCOUNT *...a people of extraordinary musicality.*

4 Sounds that are **musical** are light and pleasant to hear. ADJ-GRADED *He had a soft, almost musical voice.* ♦ **musically** ADV-GRADED *The voice was as musically soft as ever.*

musical box, musical boxes. N-COUNT A **musical box** is the same as a **music box**.

musical chairs

1 **Musical chairs** is a game that children play at parties. N-UNCOUNT They run round a row of chairs while music plays and try to sit down on one when the music stops.

2 If you describe the situation within a particular organization or area of activity as **musical chairs**, you are critical of the fact that people in that organization or area exchange jobs or positions very often. N-UNCOUNT PRAGMATICS *It was musical chairs. Creative people would switch jobs just to get more money.*

musical comedy, musical comedies. N-VAR **Musical comedy** is a type of play or film that has singing and dancing as part of the story, especially one written before the middle of the twentieth century; used especially in American English. *After failing a singing audition at the Metropolitan Opera, she turned to musical comedy.*

musical director, musical directors. N-COUNT A **musical director** is the same as a **music director**.

musical instrument, musical instruments. ◆◇◇◇◇ N-COUNT =instrument A **musical instrument** is an object such as a piano, guitar, or violin which you play in order to produce music. *The drum is one of the oldest musical instruments.*

music box, music boxes. N-COUNT =musical box A **music box** is a box that contains a clockwork mechanism which plays a tune when you open the lid.

music director, music directors. N-COUNT =musical director The **music director** of an orchestra or other group of musicians is the person who decides what they will play and where, and usually conducts them as well.

music hall, music halls; also spelled **musichall.** ◆◇◇◇◇

1 **Music hall** was a popular form of entertainment in the theatre in the nineteenth and early twentieth century. N-UNCOUNT: oft N n =vaudeville It consisted of a series of performances by comedians, singers, and dancers; used mainly in British English. *...an old music hall song.*

2 A **music hall** was a theatre that presented popular entertainment; used mainly in British English. N-COUNT

musician /mjuːzɪʃᵊn/ **musicians.** ◆◆◆◇◇ N-COUNT A **musician** is a person who plays a musical instrument as their job or hobby. *He was a brilliant musician. ...one of Britain's best known rock musicians.*

musicianship /mjuːzɪʃᵊnʃɪp/. N-UNCOUNT **Musicianship** is the skill involved in performing music. *Her musicianship is excellent.*

music stand, music stands. N-COUNT A **music stand** is a device that holds pages of music in position while you play a musical instrument.

musk /mʌsk/. N-UNCOUNT **Musk** is a substance with a strong smell which is used in making perfume.

musket /mʌskɪt/ **muskets.** ◆◇◇◇◇ N-COUNT A **musket** was an early type of gun with a long barrel, which was used before rifles were invented.

musky /mʌski/. ADJ-GRADED A **musky** smell is strong, warm, and sweet. *She dabbed a drop of the musky perfume behind each ear.*

Muslim /mʊzlɪm, muːs-, AM mʌz-/ **Muslims** ◆◆◆◆◇
1 A **Muslim** is someone who believes in Islam and lives according to its rules. N-COUNT
2 **Muslim** means relating to Islam or Muslims. *He also said Poland wanted closer ties with Iran and other Muslim countries.* ADJ

muslin /mʌzlɪn/ **muslins. Muslin** is very thin cotton cloth. *...white muslin curtains.* N-MASS

mussel /mʌsəl/ **mussels. Mussels** are a kind of shellfish that you can eat from their shells. ◆◇◇◇◇ N-COUNT

must /məst, STRONG mʌst/ **musts.** The noun is pronounced /mʌst/. ◆◆◆◆◆
Must is a modal verb. It is followed by the base form of a verb.
1 You use **must** to indicate that you think it is very important or necessary for something to happen. You use **must not** or **mustn't** to indicate that you think it is very important or necessary for something not to happen. *What you wear should be stylish and clean, and must definitely fit well... You are going to have to take a certain amount of criticism, but you must cope with it... The doctor must not allow the patient to be put at risk... The soil must not be overwatered, especially during the first few weeks... We must not forget your birthday.* MODAL PRAGMATICS
2 You use **must** to indicate that it is necessary for something to happen, usually because of a rule or law. *Candidates must satisfy the general conditions for admission... Mr Allen must pay Mr Farnham's legal costs... Equipment must be supervised if children are in the house.* MODAL PRAGMATICS
3 You use **must** to indicate that you are fairly sure that something is the case. *At 29 Russell must be one of the youngest ever Wembley referees... Reggae must be the only music that's got its own country - Jamaica... I'm sure he must feel he has lost a close family friend, because I know I do... I must have been a bore.* MODAL PRAGMATICS
4 You use **must**, or **must have** with a past participle, to indicate that you believe that something is the case, because of the available evidence. *'You must be Emma,' said the visitor... Miss Holloway had a weak heart. She must have had a heart attack... His only explanation was that he must have brought them home in order to continue his work... The medical reports really must have suggested that he was really seriously hurt.* MODAL PRAGMATICS
5 If you say that one thing **must have** happened in order for something else to happen, you mean that it is necessary for the first thing to have happened before the second thing can happen. *In order to take that job, you must have left another job... In order to start reading this book you must have had some idea that the physical symptoms you were experiencing were due to anxiety.* MODAL PRAGMATICS
6 You use **must** to express your intention to do something. *I must be getting back... I must have a whiskey... I must telephone my parents... I must speak to Tania at once... He told the Prime Minister that he felt he must now leave.* MODAL PRAGMATICS
7 You use **must** to make suggestions or invitations very forcefully. *You must see a doctor, Frederick... You must see the painting Paul has given me as a wedding present... You must come to lunch with us... You must visit me. Come to dinner.* MODAL PRAGMATICS
8 You use **must** in remarks and comments where you are expressing sympathy. *This must be a very difficult job for you... You must be very worried by now... Now sit down and make yourself comfortable. You must be very tired.* MODAL PRAGMATICS
9 You use **must** in conversation in expressions such as **'I must say'** and **'I must admit'** in order to emphasize a point that you are making. *This came as a surprise, I must say... I must admit I like looking feminine... They were very polite, I must confess.* MODAL PRAGMATICS
10 You use **must** in expressions such as **'it must be noted'** and **'it must be remembered'** in order to draw the reader's or listener's attention to what you are about to say. *It must be noted, however, that not all British and American officers carried out orders... It must be stated that this illness is one of the most complex conditions known to man.* MODAL PRAGMATICS
11 You use **must** in questions to express your anger or irritation about something that someone has done, usually because you do not understand their behaviour. *Why must you do everything as if you have to win?... Why must she interrupt?... Must you always run when the pressure gets too much?* MODAL PRAGMATICS
12 You use **must** in exclamations to express surprise or shock. *'Go! Please go.'—'You must be joking!'... I really must be quite mad!... You must have gone out of your mind!* MODAL PRAGMATICS
13 If you refer to something as a **must** you mean that it is absolutely necessary; an informal use. *The new 37th issue of National Savings Certificates is a must for any taxpayer... A must is a visit to the fascinating and world-renowned Motor Museum.* N-COUNT: usu a N in sing
14 You say **'if you must'** when you know that you cannot stop someone doing something that you think is wrong or stupid. *If you must be in the sunlight, use the strongest filter cream you can get... 'Could I have a word?'—'Oh dear, if you must.'... If you must have a cigarette, choose a seat in the first row of the smoking section.* PHRASES usu PHR inf PRAGMATICS
15 You say **'if you must know'** when you tell someone something that you did not want them to know and you want to suggest that you think they were wrong to ask you about it. *'Why don't you wear your jogging shorts Mum?'—'Well, my legs are too skinny, if you must know.'... 'You told him you'd been there that night.'—'If you must know, yes.'* PHR with cl PRAGMATICS

must- /mʌst-/. In informal English and in journalism, **must-** is added to verbs such as 'see', 'do', or 'read' to form adjectives and nouns which describe things that you consider that people must see, do, or read. For example, a **must-have** is something which you think people should get or which is very fashionable, and a **must-win** game is one which a team needs to win. *Leather jeans are the must-have fashion item of the season. ...a list of must-see movies... The Tugboat Saloon and Eatery is a must-visit.* COMB in ADJ and N-COUNT

mustache /məstɑːʃ, AM mʌstæʃ/. See **moustache**.

mustard /mʌstərd/ **mustards** ◆◇◇◇◇
1 **Mustard** is a yellow or brown paste usually eaten with meat. It tastes hot and spicy. *...a pot of mustard... Thinly paint the lamb with Dijon mustard.* N-MASS
2 **Mustard** is a small plant with yellow flowers and long seed pods. The seeds can be used to make mustard. N-UNCOUNT
3 **Mustard** is used to describe things that are brownish yellow in colour. *...a mustard coloured jumper.* COLOUR
4 If someone does not **cut the mustard**, their work or their performance is not as good as it should be or as good as it is expected to be; an informal expression. PHRASES V inflects, usu with neg PRAGMATICS
5 If you are **as keen as mustard** or **mustard keen**, you are very keen indeed. *I have a pupil who scored very low in assessments but is keen as mustard.* usu v-link PHR

mustard and cress. The seedlings of mustard and cress seeds that are eaten in salad are referred to as **mustard and cress**. N-UNCOUNT

mustard gas. Mustard gas is a gas used in chemical warfare. It burns and blisters the skin. N-UNCOUNT

mustard powder. Mustard powder is a yellow powder. You add hot water to it in order to make mustard. N-UNCOUNT

muster /mʌstər/ **musters, mustering, mustered** ◆◇◇◇◇
1 If you **muster** something such as support, strength, or energy, you gather as much of it as you can in order to do something. *He travelled around West Africa trying to muster support for his movement... Mustering all her strength, Nancy pulled hard on both oars.* VERB =summon V n
2 When soldiers **muster** or **are mustered**, they gather together in one place in order to take part in a military action. *The men mustered before their clan chiefs... The general had mustered his troops north of the Hindu Kush.* V-ERG =gather V V n
3 If someone or something **passes muster**, they are good enough for the thing they are needed for. *I* PHRASE: V inflects

could not pass muster in his language... If it doesn't pass muster, a radio station could have its license challenged.

mustn't /mʌsᵊnt/. **Mustn't** is the usual spoken form of **must not.**

must've /mʌstəv/. **Must've** is the usual spoken form of **must have**, especially when 'have' is an auxiliary verb.

musty /mʌsti/. Something that is **musty** smells stale and damp. *There are racks of musty clothing and piles of junk. ...that terrible musty smell.* ADJ-GRADED =fusty

mutant /mjuːtᵊnt/ **mutants.** A **mutant** is an animal or plant that is physically different from others of the same species as the result of a change in its genetic structure. ◆◇◇◇◇ N-COUNT =mutation

mutate /mjuːteɪt, AM mjuːteɪt/ **mutates, mutating, mutated** ◆◇◇◇◇

1 If an animal or plant **mutates**, or something **mutates** it, it develops different characteristics as the result of a change in its genes. *The virus mutates in the carrier's body... A newer anti-HIV drug called pyridnone caused HIV to mutate into a form which could not reproduce or infect new cells... The technique has been to mutate the genes by irradiation or chemicals... He found evidence of mutated forms of the gene.* ♦ **mutation** /mjuːteɪʃᵊn/ **mutations** *Scientists have found a genetic mutation that appears to be the cause of Huntington's disease.* V-ERG V V into n V n V-ed Also V n into n N-VAR

2 If something **mutates into** a very different thing, it changes into it. *Overnight, the gossip begins to mutate into headlines.* VERB V into n

mute /mjuːt/ **mutes, muting, muted** ◆◆◇◇◇

1 Someone who is **mute** is silent for some reason and does not speak. *He was mute, distant, and indifferent... I threw a mute look of appeal at Paula.* ▶ Also an adverb. *He could watch her standing mute by the phone... He sat mute, speechless with ecstasy, gazing into the sky.* ♦ **mutely** *I crouched by him and grasped his hand, mutely offering what comfort I could.* ADJ ADV: ADV after v ADV: ADV with v

2 Someone who is **mute** is unable to speak; an old-fashioned use. *Marianna, the duke's daughter, became mute after a shock.* ADJ

3 If someone **mutes** something such as their feelings or their activities, they reduce the strength or intensity of them. *It accuses the Bush administration of muting its criticism of repression... The corruption does not seem to have muted the country's prolonged economic boom.* ♦ **muted** *Reaction to the news was muted... The financial markets gave a muted response to the Democrats' triumph.* VERB V n ADJ-GRADED =subdued

4 If you **mute** a noise or sound, you lower its volume or make it less distinct. *They begin to mute their voices, not be as assertive... At first the wooded hillsides muted the sounds.* ♦ **muted** *'Yes,' he muttered, his voice so muted I hardly heard his reply... There were muted cheers from the public gallery.* VERB V n ADJ-GRADED

muted /mjuːtɪd/. **Muted** colours are soft and gentle, not bright and strong. *He likes sombre, muted colours – she likes bright colours... The muted greens of the far pasture.* ADJ-GRADED: usu ADJ n

mutilate /mjuːtɪleɪt/ **mutilates, mutilating, mutilated** ◆◇◇◇◇

1 If a person or animal **is mutilated**, their body is severely damaged, usually by someone who physically attacks them. *More than 30 horses have been mutilated in the last nine months... He tortured and mutilated six young men... The mutilated bodies of seven men have been found beside a railway line.* ♦ **mutilation** /mjuːtɪleɪʃᵊn/ **mutilations** *Amnesty International chronicles cases of torture and mutilation... She had suffered severe facial mutilations after an accident.* VERB =maim be V-ed V n V-ed N-VAR

2 If something **is mutilated**, it is deliberately damaged or spoiled. *Brecht's verdict was that his screenplay had been mutilated... I discovered a mutilated cassette stuffed in a wastebasket.* VERB be V-ed V-ed Also V n

mutineer /mjuːtɪnɪəʳ/ **mutineers.** A **mutineer** is a person who takes part in a mutiny. N-COUNT

mutinous /mjuːtɪnəs/. If someone is **mutinous**, they are strongly dissatisfied with a person's authority and are likely to rebel against it. *His own army, stung by defeats, is mutinous.* ADJ-GRADED

mutiny /mjuːtɪni/ **mutinies, mutinying, mutinied** ◆◇◇◇◇

1 A **mutiny** is a rebellion by a group of people, usually soldiers or sailors, against a person in authority. *A series of coup attempts and mutinies within the armed forces destabilized the regime... They were shot yesterday after being convicted of mutiny and high treason.* N-VAR

2 If a group of people, especially soldiers or sailors, **mutiny**, they refuse to obey the person who has authority over them. *Units stationed around the capital mutinied because they had received no pay for nine months... Radio stations said sailors at a naval base had mutinied against their officers.* VERB V V against n

mutt /mʌt/ **mutts.** A **mutt** is the same as a **mongrel**; an informal word. N-COUNT

mutter /mʌtəʳ/ **mutters, muttering, muttered.** ◆◆◇◇◇ If you **mutter**, you speak very quietly so that you cannot easily be heard, often because you are complaining about something. *'God knows,' she muttered, 'what's happening in that madman's mind.'... She can hear the old woman muttering about consideration... He sat there shaking his head, muttering to himself... She was staring into the fire muttering.* ▶ Also a noun. *They make no more than a mutter of protest.* ♦ **muttering, mutterings** *He heard muttering from the front of the crowd... He will lead the party into the election, in spite of the mutterings about his leadership.* VERB =mumble V with quote V about n V to n V N-COUNT N-VAR

mutton /mʌtᵊn/

1 **Mutton** is meat from an adult sheep that is eaten as food. *...a leg of mutton. ...mutton stew.* N-UNCOUNT

2 If you think a woman is trying to look younger than she really is by wearing a lot of make-up and fancy clothes, you can say she is **mutton dressed as lamb** or **mutton dressed up as lamb**; an informal Britishexpression used showing disapproval. PHRASE: usu v-link PHR PRAGMATICS

mutual /mjuːtʃuəl/ ◆◆◆◇◇

1 You use **mutual** to describe a situation, feeling, or action that is experienced, felt, or done by both of two people mentioned. *The East and the West can work together for their mutual benefit and progress... It's plain that he adores his daughter, and the feeling is mutual.* ♦ **mutually** *Attempts to reach a mutually agreed solution had been fruitless... A meeting would take place at a mutually convenient time.* ● **mutually exclusive**: see **exclusive**. ADJ ADV: ADV adj/adv, ADV before v

2 You use **mutual** to describe something such as an interest which two or more people share. *They do, however, share a mutual interest in design... We were introduced by a mutual friend who felt that we might like to go out together.* ADJ: usu ADJ n

mutual fund, mutual funds. In American English, a **mutual fund** is an organization which invests money in many different kinds of business and which offers units for sale to the public as an investment. The British expression is **unit trust**. ◆◇◇◇◇ N-COUNT

muzak /mjuːzæk/

1 **Muzak** is recorded music that is played as background music in shops or restaurants. **Muzak** is a trademark. N-UNCOUNT

2 If you describe music as **muzak**, you dislike it because you think it is dull or unnecessary. N-UNCOUNT PRAGMATICS

muzzle /mʌzᵊl/ **muzzles, muzzling, muzzled** ◆◇◇◇◇

1 The **muzzle** of an animal such as a dog is its nose and mouth. *The mongrel presented his muzzle for scratching.* N-COUNT

2 A **muzzle** is a device that is put over a dog's nose and mouth so that it cannot bite people or bark. *...dogs like pit bulls which have to wear a muzzle.* N-COUNT

3 If you **muzzle** a dog or other animal, you put a muzzle over its nose and mouth. *He was convicted of failing to muzzle a pit bull.* VERB V n

4 If you say that someone **is muzzled**, you are complaining that they are prevented from expressing their views freely. *He complained of being muzzled by the chairman... She was opposed to new laws to muzzle the press.* VERB PRAGMATICS ≠gag be V-ed V n

5 The **muzzle** of a gun is the end where the bullets come out when it is fired. N-COUNT: usu N of n

muzzy /mʌzi/
1 If someone feels **muzzy**, they are confused and unable to think clearly, usually because they are ill or have drunk too much alcohol; used mainly in informal British English. ADJ-GRADED =groggy
2 If a picture is **muzzy**, it is blurred and unclear; used mainly in informal British English. ADJ-GRADED =fuzzy

MW
1 **MW** is a written abbreviation for **medium wave**.
2 **MW** is a written abbreviation for **megawatt**.

my /maɪ/ ◆◆◆◆◆
My is the first person singular possessive determiner.
1 A speaker or writer uses **my** to indicate that something belongs or relates to himself or herself. *I invited him back to my flat for a coffee... John's my best friend... I received a bill for the car rental from my credit card company... My understanding was that we'd meet at her place.* DET-POSS
2 In conversations or in letters, **my** is used in front of a name or a word like 'darling' to show affection. *My sweet Freda... Yes, of course, my darling.* DET-POSS PRAGMATICS
3 In spoken English, **my** is used in phrases such as '**My God**' and '**My goodness**' to express surprise or shock. *My God, I've never seen you so nervous... My goodness, Tim, you have changed!* DET-POSS PRAGMATICS

myopia /maɪoʊpiə/. **Myopia** is the inability to see things properly when they are far away, because there is something wrong with your eyes; a formal word. N-UNCOUNT =short-sightedness

myopic /maɪɒpɪk/
1 If you describe someone as **myopic**, you are critical of them because they seem unable to realize that their actions might have negative consequences. *The Government still has a myopic attitude to spending.* ADJ-GRADED PRAGMATICS =short-sighted
2 If someone is **myopic**, they are unable to see things which are far away from them; a formal use. ADJ-GRADED =short-sighted

myriad /mɪriəd/; also spelled **myriads**. ◆◇◇◇◇
1 **A myriad** or **myriads** of people or things is a very large number or great variety of them. *They face a myriad of problems bringing up children... These myriads of fish would be enough to keep any swimmer entranced for hours.* QUANT: QUANT of pl-n
2 **Myriad** means having a large number or great variety. *The magazine has been celebrating British pop and culture in all its myriad forms. ...the myriad tiny animals and plants living in the ice.* ADJ: ADJ n =many

myself /maɪself/ ◆◆◆◆◇
Myself is the first person singular reflexive pronoun.
1 A speaker or writer uses **myself** to refer to himself or herself. **Myself** is used as the object of a verb or preposition when the subject refers to the same person. *I asked myself what I would have done in such a situation... I looked at myself in the mirror... I felt ashamed of myself.* PRON-REFL: v PRON, prep PRON
2 You use **myself** to emphasize a first person singular subject. In more formal English, **myself** is sometimes used instead of 'me' as the object of a verb or preposition, for emphasis. *I myself enjoy cinema, poetry, eating out and long walks... I'm fond of cake myself... He was roughly the same age as myself. ...a complete beginner like myself.* PRON-REFL-EMPH PRAGMATICS
3 If you say something such as 'I did it **myself**', you are emphasizing that you did it, rather than anyone else. *'Where did you get that embroidery?'—'I made it myself.'* PRON-REFL-EMPH PRAGMATICS
4 • **by myself**: see **by**.

mysterious /mɪstɪəriəs/ ◆◆◇◇◇
1 Someone or something that is **mysterious** is strange and is not known about or understood. *He died in mysterious circumstances... A mysterious illness confined him to bed for over a month... The whole thing seems very mysterious... He began to feel sympathy for this slightly mysterious man.* ADJ-GRADED
♦ **mysteriously** *A couple of messages had mysteriously disappeared.* ADV-GRADED: usu ADV with v
2 If someone is **mysterious** about something, they deliberately do not talk much about it, usually because they want people to be curious about it. *As for his job—well, he was very mysterious about it.* ADJ-GRADED: v-link ADJ, oft ADJ *about* n =enigmatic
♦ **mysteriously** *Asked what she meant, she said mysteriously: 'Work it out for yourself'.* ADV-GRADED: ADV after v =enigmatically

mystery /mɪstəri/ **mysteries** ◆◆◆◇◇
1 A **mystery** is something that is not understood or known about. *The source of the gunshots still remains a mystery. ...the mysteries of mental breakdown.* N-COUNT
2 If you talk about the **mystery** of someone or something, you are talking about how difficult they are to understand or know about, especially when this gives them a rather strange or magical quality. *She's a lady of mystery... It is an elaborate ceremony, shrouded in mystery.* N-UNCOUNT
3 A **mystery** person or thing is one whose identity or nature is not known. *The mystery hero immediately alerted police after spotting a bomb. ...a mystery prize of up to £1,000.* ADJ: ADJ n
4 A **mystery** is a story in which strange things happen that are not explained until the end. *His fourth novel is a murder mystery set in London.* N-COUNT

mystic /mɪstɪk/ **mystics** ◆◇◇◇◇
1 A **mystic** is a person who practises or believes in religious mysticism. *...an Indian mystic known as Bhagwan Shree Rajneesh.* N-COUNT
2 **Mystic** means the same as **mystical**. *...mystic union with God.* ADJ-GRADED: ADJ n

mystical /mɪstɪkəl/. Something that is **mystical** involves spiritual powers and influences that most people do not understand. *That was clearly a deep mystical experience. ...ancient Egyptian magical and mystical beliefs.* ◆◇◇◇◇ ADJ-GRADED: usu ADJ n =mystic

mysticism /mɪstɪsɪzəm/. **Mysticism** is a religious practice in which people search for truth, knowledge, and unity with God through meditation and prayer. ◆◇◇◇◇ N-UNCOUNT

mystify /mɪstɪfaɪ/ **mystifies, mystifying, mystified.** If you **are mystified** by something, you find it impossible to explain or understand. *The audience must have been totally mystified by the plot... There was something strange in her attitude which mystified me.* ◆◇◇◇◇ VERB =baffle be V-ed V n
♦ **mystification** /mɪstɪfɪkeɪʃən/ *Some minerals, Pough explained to my mystification, are not truly black but only look so.* N-UNCOUNT
♦ **mystifying** *I find your attitude a little mystifying, Moira.* ADJ-GRADED =puzzling

mystique /mɪstiːk/. **Mystique** is a sense or atmosphere of mystery and secrecy which is associated with a particular person or thing. *His book destroyed the mystique of monarchy. ...the mystique that surrounds fine art.* ◆◇◇◇◇ N-UNCOUNT: oft with poss

myth /mɪθ/ **myths** ◆◆◆◇◇
1 A **myth** is a well-known story which was made up in the past to explain natural events or to justify religious beliefs or social customs. *There is a famous Greek myth in which Icarus flew too near to the Sun. ...the world of magic and of myth.* N-VAR
2 If you describe a belief or explanation as a **myth**, you mean that many people believe it but it is actually untrue. *Contrary to the popular myth, women are not reckless spendthrifts.* N-VAR =fallacy

mythic /mɪθɪk/
1 Someone or something that is **mythic** exists only in a myth and is therefore imaginary; a literary use. *In the earlier Celtic texts, the mythic figure of King Arthur is more clearly defined.* ADJ: usu ADJ n =mythical ≠real
2 If you describe someone or something as **mythic**, you mean that they have become very famous or important. *...a team whose reputation has achieved mythic proportions... His rapid rise to power has given him a near-mythic status in the industry.* ADJ-GRADED: usu ADJ n

mythical /mɪθɪkəl/ ◆◇◇◇◇
1 Something that is **mythical** exists only in myths and is therefore imaginary. *...the Hydra, the mythical beast that had seven or more heads. ...traditional stories woven around a pantheon of gods and mythical figures.* ADJ-GRADED: usu ADJ n =mythic ≠real
2 If you describe something as **mythical**, you think it is untrue or does not exist. *...the American West, not the mythical, romanticized West of cowboys and gunslingers, but the real West. ...trying to preserve a mythical sense of nationhood.* ADJ-GRADED: usu ADJ n

mythology /mɪθɒlədʒi/ **mythologies** ◆◇◇◇◇
1 **Mythology** is a group of myths, especially all the myths from a particular country, religion, or culture. *In Greek mythology, the god Zeus took the form of a swan to seduce Leda... This is well illustrated in the mythologies of many cultures.* [N-VAR]
♦ **mythological** /mɪθəlɒdʒɪkəl/ *...the mythological beast that was part lion and part goat.* [ADJ: usu ADJ n]
2 You can use **mythology** to refer to the beliefs or opinions that people have about something, when you think that they are false or untrue. *Altman strips away the pretence and mythology to expose the film industry as a business like any other, dedicated to the pursuit of profit.* [N-VAR]

Nn

N, n /en/ **N's, n's**
1 **N** is the fourteenth letter of the English alphabet. [N-VAR]
2 **N** or **n** is used as an abbreviation for words beginning with N or n, such as 'north', 'northern', or 'noun'.

'n' /ən/. In informal writing, the word 'and' is sometimes written as **'n'** between certain pairs of words, as in 'rock 'n' roll'. *...a country 'n' western song. ...a fish 'n' chips restaurant.* [CONJ-COORD =and]

N.A.; also spelled **n/a**. **N.A.** is a written abbreviation for 'not applicable'. You use it when you are filling in a questionnaire when a question or category is not relevant to you. ◆◇◇◇◇ [CONVENTION]

naan, naans /nɑːn/; also spelled **nan**. **Naan** or **naan bread** is a type of bread that comes in a large, round, flat piece and is usually eaten with Indian food. *...traditional dishes, such as rogan josh, served with rice or naan.* [N-VAR]

nab /næb/ **nabs, nabbing, nabbed.** If people in authority such as the police **nab** someone who they think has done something wrong, they catch them or arrest them; an informal use. *He killed 12 people before the authorities finally nabbed him... After a short spell in the masonry business he was back in the armed robbery business. Again, he got nabbed.* ◆◇◇◇◇ [VERB =collar] [V n] [get V-ed]

nadir /neɪdɪəʳ, AM -dər/ ◆◆◇◇◇
1 The **nadir** of something such as someone's career or the history of an organization is its worst time; a literary use. *1945 to 1946 was the nadir of Truman's presidency.* [N-SING: usu with poss ≠zenith]
2 In astronomy, **the nadir** is the point at which the sun or moon is directly below you, on the other side of the earth. Compare **zenith.** [N-SING: the N]

naff /næf/ **naffer, naffest**
1 If you say that something is **naff**, you mean it is very unfashionable or unsophisticated; used in informal British English. *The music's really naff. ...naff 'his and hers' matching outfits.* [ADJ-GRADED]
2 If someone tells you to **naff off**, they are rudely telling you to go away; an informal expression, used in British English. *She didn't hesitate to tell intrusive photographers to 'naff off'.* [CONVENTION] [PRAGMATICS]

nag /næg/ **nags, nagging, nagged** ◆◇◇◇◇
1 If you say that someone **nags** you, you dislike them continuously asking you to do something, often something you do not want to do. *The more Sarah nagged her, the more stubborn Cissie became... My girlfriend nagged me to cut my hair... She had stopped nagging him about never being home. ...children nagging their parents into buying things.* [VERB] [PRAGMATICS] [V n] [V n to-inf] [V n about n] [V n into -ing] [Also V]
► A **nag** is someone who nags. *Aunt Molly is a nag about regular meals.* [N-COUNT]
♦ **nagging** *Her endless nagging drove him away from home.* [N-UNCOUNT =moaning]
2 If something such as a doubt or worry **nags** at you, or **nags** you, it keeps worrying you. *He could be wrong about her. The feeling nagged at him. ...the anxiety that had nagged Amy all through lunch... Something was nagging in the back of his mind.* [VERB =niggle] [V at n] [V n] [V]
3 People sometimes refer to a horse as a **nag**; an informal use. [N-COUNT]

nagging /nægɪŋ/. A **nagging** pain is not very severe but is difficult to cure. *He complained of a nagging pain between his shoulder blades. ...nagging headaches.* ● See also **nag.** [ADJ: ADJ n]

nail /neɪl/ **nails, nailing, nailed** ◆◆◇◇◇
1 A **nail** is a thin piece of metal with one pointed end and one flat end. You hit the flat end with a hammer in order to push the nail into something such as a wall. *A mirror hung on a nail above the washstand... He hammered the nail into the branch.* [N-COUNT]
2 If you **nail** something somewhere, you fix it there using one or more nails. *Frank put the first plank down and nailed it in place... They nail shut the front door... The windows were all nailed shut.* [VERB] [V n prep/adv] [V n with adj] [V-ed]
3 Your **nails** are the thin hard parts that grow at the ends of your fingers and toes. *Keep your nails short and your hands clean.* [N-COUNT: usu poss N in pl]
4 To **nail** someone means to catch them and prove that they have been breaking the law; an informal use. *The prosecution still managed to nail him for robberies at the homes of leading industrialists.* [VERB =nab] [V n]
5 If you say that someone is **as hard as nails** or **hard as nails**, you mean that they are extremely tough and aggressive, either physically or in their attitude towards other people or other situations. *He's a shrewd businessman and hard as nails... He simply looked mean and hard as nails.* [PHRASES] [v-link PHR]
6 If you say that someone **has hit the nail on the head**, you mean that you think their opinion about something is exactly right. *'I think it would civilize people a bit more if they had decent conditions.'—'I think you've hit the nail on the head.'* [V inflects]
7 ● **a nail in someone's coffin**: see **coffin.** ● **to nail your colours to the mast**: see **colour.** ● **to fight tooth and nail**: see **tooth.**

nail down [PHRASAL VERB]
1 If you **nail down** something unknown or uncertain, you find out exactly what it is. *It would be useful if you could nail down the source of this tension.* [=pin down] [V P n (not pron)] [Also V n P]
2 If you **nail down** an agreement, you manage to reach a firm agreement with a definite result. *The Secretary of State and his Russian counterpart met to try to nail down the elusive accord.* [V P n (not pron)] [Also V n P]
3 If you **nail** something **down**, you fix it firmly onto something. *Lay strips of 4mm ply over the mesh and nail these down with panel pins.* [V n P] [Also V P n (not pron)]

nail up [PHRASAL VERB]
1 If you **nail** something **up**, you fix it to a wall, post, or tree using nails. *He fished and nailed up his catch to dry on the wall of the byre.* [=fix] [V P n]
2 If you **nail up** a wooden container, you secure the lid with nails. *He took a hammer from his boot and nailed up the lid.* [V P n (not pron)] [Also V n P]

nail-biting
1 If you describe something such as a story or a sports match as **nail-biting**, you mean that it makes you feel very excited or nervous because you do not know how it is going to end. *...England's magnificent nail-biting 75-71 win over Russia. ...the nail-biting legal thriller, 'The Pelican Brief'.* [ADJ-GRADED]

2 Nail-biting is the activity of biting the ends of one's fingernails. This habit is usually associated with being tense or nervous. *...negative behaviour patterns such as nail-biting or thumb-sucking.*
N-UNCOUNT

nail bomb, nail bombs. A **nail bomb** is a bomb which contains nails that are intended to cause a lot of damage and injury when the bomb goes off.
N-COUNT

nail brush, nail brushes; also spelled **nailbrush**. A **nail brush** is a small brush that you use to clean your nails when washing your hands.
N-COUNT

nail file, nail files; also spelled **nailfile**. A **nail file** is a small strip of metal or sandpaper that you rub on the ends of your nails to shorten them or shape them.
N-COUNT

nail polish, nail polishes /neɪl pɒlɪʃ/. **Nail polish** is the same as **nail varnish**.
N-MASS

nail scissors; also spelled **nail-scissors**. **Nail scissors** are small scissors that you use for cutting your nails. *Mishka got some nail scissors and started carefully trimming his fingernails. ...an old pair of nail scissors.*
N-PLURAL: also *a pair of* N

nail varnish, nail varnishes. Nail varnish is a thick liquid that women paint on their nails; used mainly in British English. The usual American term is **nail polish**.
N-MASS =nail polish

naive /naɪiːv, AM nɑː-/; also spelled **naïve**. If you describe someone as **naive**, you think they lack experience, causing them to expect things to be uncomplicated or easy, or people to be honest or kind when they are not. *It's naive to think that teachers are always tolerant... I must have been naive to think we would get my parents' blessing. ...naive idealists... Their view was that he had been politically naive.* ♦ **naively** *...naively applying Western solutions to Eastern problems... I thought, naively, that this would be a nine-to five job.* ♦ **naivety** /naɪiːvɪti/ *I was alarmed by his naivety and ignorance of international affairs.*
◆◆◇◇◇ ADJ-GRADED: oft *it* v-link ADJ to-inf, ADJ to-inf =unrealistic
ADV-GRADED: usu ADV with v
N-UNCOUNT

naked /neɪkɪd/
◆◆◇◇◇

1 Someone who is **naked** is not wearing any clothes. *Her naked body was found wrapped in a sheet in a field... The hot paving stones scorched my naked feet... They stripped me naked... He stood naked in front of me.* ♦ **nakedness** *He had pulled the blanket over his body to hide his nakedness.* • See also **stark naked**.
ADJ: ADJ n, ADJ after v, v-link ADJ =bare
N-UNCOUNT: oft poss N

2 If an animal or part of an animal is **naked**, it has no fur or feathers on it. *The nest contained eight little mice that were naked and blind.*
ADJ

3 If you say that someone is **naked** or feels **naked**, you mean they are helpless, unprotected, or powerless. *If the reports are accurate, the deal leaves the authorities and the President virtually naked. ...Bevan's appeal against going 'naked into the conference chamber'.*
ADJ: ADJ after v, v-link ADJ, ADJ n =defenceless

4 You can describe an object as **naked** when it does not have its normal covering. *...a naked bulb dangling in a bare room... The water was heated by a naked gas flame.*
ADJ: usu ADJ n

5 **Naked** emotions are easy to recognize, because they are very strongly felt; used in written English. *The naked hatred in the woman's face shocked me... There had been naked misery in her voice when she'd spoken about the letter.* ♦ **nakedly** *She was embarrassed at showing her fear so nakedly.*
ADJ: ADJ n ≠veiled
ADV-GRADED

6 You can use **naked** to describe unpleasant or violent actions and behaviour which are not disguised or hidden in any way; used in journalism. *Naked aggression and an attempt to change frontiers by force could not go unchallenged. ...violence and the naked pursuit of power. ...naked greed.*
ADJ: ADJ n =blatant

7 If you say that something cannot be seen by **the naked eye**, you mean that it cannot be seen without the help of equipment such as a telescope or microscope. *The worms cannot be seen by the naked eye... The planet Mars will be visible to the naked eye all week... There's so much going on that you can't see with the naked eye.*
PHRASE: usu *to/with/by* PHR

name /neɪm/ **names, naming, named**
◆◆◆◆◆

1 The **name** of a person, place, or thing is the word or group of words that is used to identify them. *'What's his name?'—'Peter.'... I don't even know if Sullivan's his real name... They changed the name of the street.*
N-COUNT: usu with poss

2 When you **name** someone or something, you give them a name, usually at the beginning of their life. *My mother insisted on naming me Horace. ...a man named John T. Benson... He won his first Derby on the aptly named 'Never Say Die'.*
VERB
V n n
V-ed

3 If you **name** someone or something after another person or thing, you give them the same name as that person or thing. *Why have you not named any of your sons after yourself?*
VERB
V n *after* n
Also V n *for* n

4 If you **name** someone, you identify them by stating their name. *It's nearly thirty years since a journalist was jailed for refusing to name a source... One of the victims of the weekend's snowstorm has been named as twenty-year-old John Barr.*
VERB =identify
V n
V n *as* n

5 If you **name** something such as a price, time, or place, you say what you want it to be. *Call Marty, tell him to name his price.*
VERB =state
V n

6 If you **name** the person for a particular job, you say who you want to have the job. *The England manager will be naming a new captain, to replace the injured Bryan Robson... When the chairman of Campbell's retired, McGovern was named as his successor... Early in 1941 he was named commander of the Afrika Korps.*
VERB =nominate
V n
be V-ed *as* n
be V-ed n
Also V n *as* n, V n n

7 You can refer to the reputation of a person or thing as their **name**. *He had a name for good judgement... She's never had any drug problems or done anything to give jazz a bad name.*
N-COUNT: usu sing =reputation

8 You can refer to someone as, for example, a famous **name** or a great **name** when they are well-known; used in journalism. *...some of the most famous names in modelling and show business. ...top names such as Jimmy Connors, Tim Mayotte, and Yannick Noah.*
N-COUNT: usu with supp, oft adj N =star

9 See also **assumed name, big name, brand name, Christian name, code name, first name, given name, maiden name, middle name, pet name**.

10 If something is **in** someone's **name**, it officially belongs to them or is reserved for them. *The house is in my husband's name... A double room had been reserved for him in the name of Muller.*
PHRASES v-link PHR, PHR after v

11 If someone does something **in the name of** a group of people, they do it as the representative of that group. *In the United States the majority governs in the name of the people... She accepted the gift in the name of the Save the Children Fund.*
PHR n, usu PHR after v =on behalf of

12 If you do something **in the name of** an ideal or an abstract thing, you do it in order to preserve or promote that thing. *...one of those rare occasions in history when a political leader risked his own power in the name of the greater public good... There had been times when she had felt sickened by the things people did in the name of business.*
PHR n/-ing, usu PHR after v

13 People sometimes use expressions such as **'in the name of** heaven' or **'in the name of** humanity' to add emphasis to a question or request. *What in the name of heaven's going on?... In the name of humanity I ask the government to reappraise this important issue.*
PHR n, PHR with cl PRAGMATICS

14 If you say that a situation exists **in all but name**, you mean that it is not officially recognized but that it actually exists. *...the group, which is now a political party in all but name... It's the end of communism in all but name.*
usu n/adj PHR, PHR with cl

15 When you mention someone or something **by name**, or address someone **by name**, you use their name. *He greets customers by name and enquires about their health.*
PHR after v

16 You can use **by name** or **by the name of** when you are saying what someone is called; a formal use. *In 1911 he met up with a young Australian by the name of Harry Busteed... This guy, Jack Smith, does he go by the name of Jackal?*

17 If someone **calls** you **names**, they insult you by saying unpleasant things to you or about you. *At my last school they called me names because I was so slow... They had called her rude names.*
V inflects

18 If you say that something is **the name of the**

game, you mean that it is the most important aspect of a situation; an informal expression. *Family values are suddenly the name of the game... The name of the game is survival.*

19 If you **lend** your **name to** something such as a cause or project, you support it. *He had political points of view and lent his name to a lot of causes.* — V inflects, PHR n

20 If you **make a name for** yourself or **make** your **name** as something, you become well-known for that thing. *She was beginning to make a name for herself as a portrait photographer... He made his name with several collections of short stories.* — V inflects, oft PHR *as* n

21 If you **name names**, you identify the people who have done something, often something wrong. *Nobody was prepared to risk prosecution by actually naming names.* — V inflects

22 If you say that a situation exists **in name only**, you mean that it does not have the status or position that it claims to have. *Many of the groups exist in name only... He is commander-in-chief in name only.* — =nominally

23 You say **you name it**, usually after or before a list, to indicate that you are talking about a very wide range of things. *Pickled cucumbers, jam, pickled berries, tomatoes; you name it, they've got it... I also enjoy windsurfing, tennis, racquetball, swimming, you name it.*

24 • **a name to conjure with**: see **conjure**.

name-drop, name-drops, name-dropping, name-dropped. If you say that someone **name-drops**, you disapprove of them referring to famous people they have met in order to impress people. *The assistant carried on talking to his mate, name-dropping all the famous riders he knew... I must stop saying everyone famous is a good friend. It sounds as if I'm name-dropping.* — VERB, PRAGMATICS, V n, V

♦ **name-dropper, name-droppers** *Press agents are notorious name-droppers.* — N-COUNT ♦ **name-dropping** *One can do a lot of name-dropping with names of the school's parents. President Nixon sent his daughters there.* — N-UNCOUNT

nameless /neɪmləs/

1 You describe people or things as **nameless** when you do not know their name or when they do not have a name. *They can have their cases rejected, without reasons being given, by nameless officials.* — ADJ: usu ADJ n

2 If you say that someone or something will remain **nameless**, you mean that you will not mention their name, often because you do not want to embarrass them. *A local friend who shall be nameless warned me that I was in for trouble soon.* — ADJ: v-link ADJ =anonymous ≠named

namely /neɪmli/. You use **namely** to introduce detailed information about the subject you are discussing, or a particular aspect of it. *One group of people seems to be forgotten, namely pensioners... This shows how little they were aware of the challenge facing them, namely, to re-establish prosperity and the rule of law.* — ♦♦◇◇◇ ADV: ADV n, ADV cl, PRAGMATICS =that is

nameplate /neɪmpleɪt/ **nameplates;** also spelled **name-plate**. A **nameplate** is a sign on a door or wall which shows the name of the person or organization that occupies that particular room or building. — N-COUNT

namesake /neɪmseɪk/ **namesakes.** Someone's or something's **namesake** has the same name as they do; used in written English. *He is putting together a four-man team, including his son and namesake Tony O'Reilly Jnr... Cathedral Notre-Dame in Senlis is less famous than its namesake in Paris.* — N-COUNT: usu poss N

nan /næn/ **nans**

1 In British English, some people refer to their grandmother as their **nan**; an informal use. *I was brought up by my nan.* — ♦◇◇◇◇ N-COUNT; N-VOC =gran

2 See also **naan**.

nanny /næni/ **nannies.** A **nanny** is a woman who is paid by parents to look after their child or children. — ♦♦◇◇◇ N-COUNT

nannying /næniɪŋ/

1 Nannying is the job of being a nanny. *...low-paid jobs such as nannying.* — N-UNCOUNT

2 If you refer to activities such as helping and advising people as **nannying**, you disapprove of them because you think that they are over protective and therefore undesirable. *...governmental nannying and interference in markets.* — N-UNCOUNT, PRAGMATICS =mollycoddling

nanny state. If you refer to a government as the **nanny state**, you disapprove of its system of providing certain social services which you think makes people rely on the state rather than wanting to do things for themselves; used mainly in British English. *The tussle to free the individual from the nanny state is still far from won.* — N-SING: usu *the* N, PRAGMATICS

nap /næp/ **naps, napping, napped** — ♦◇◇◇◇

1 If you have a **nap**, you have a short sleep, usually during the day. *Use your lunch hour to have a nap in your chair... I might take a little nap.* — N-COUNT =snooze

2 If you **nap**, you sleep for a short period of time, usually during the day. *An elderly person may nap during the day and then sleep only five hours a night.* — VERB =doze V

3 The **nap** of a carpet or of a cloth such as velvet is the top layer of short threads, which usually lie smoothly in one direction. — N-SING

4 If someone **is caught napping**, something happens when they are not prepared for it, although they should have been; an informal expression. *The security services were clearly caught napping.* — PHRASE: V inflects

napalm /neɪpɑːm/ **napalms, napalming, napalmed**

1 Napalm is a substance containing petrol which is used to make bombs that burn people, buildings, and plants. *The government has consistently denied using napalm.* — N-UNCOUNT

2 If people **napalm** other people or places, they attack and burn them using napalm. *Why napalm a village now?* — VERB V n

nape /neɪp/ **napes.** The **nape** of your neck is the back of it. *...the way that his hair grew at the nape of his neck.* — N-COUNT: usu sing, usu *the* N *of* n

napkin /næpkɪn/ **napkins.** A **napkin** is a square of cloth or paper that you use when you are eating to protect your clothes, or to wipe your mouth or hands. *...taking tiny bites of a hot dog and daintily wiping my lips with a napkin.* — ♦◇◇◇◇ N-COUNT =serviette

nappy /næpi/ **nappies.** In British English, a **nappy** is a piece of soft thick cloth or paper which is fastened round a baby's bottom in order to soak up its urine and faeces. The usual American word is **diaper**. — ♦◇◇◇◇ N-COUNT =diaper

narcissi /nɑːˈsɪsaɪ/. **Narcissi** is a plural form of **narcissus**.

narcissism /nɑːˈsɪsɪzəm/. **Narcissism** is the habit of always thinking about yourself and admiring yourself; a formal word, used showing disapproval. *Those who suffer from narcissism become self-absorbed or chronic show-offs.* — N-UNCOUNT, PRAGMATICS =self-love

narcissistic /nɑːˈsɪsɪstɪk/. If you describe someone as **narcissistic**, you disapprove of them because they think about themselves a lot and admire themselves too much; a formal word. *He was insufferable at times – self-centred and narcissistic. ...the image of the vain, narcissistic man.* — ADJ-GRADED, PRAGMATICS

narcissus /nɑːˈsɪsəs/ **narcissi;** the plural can be either **narcissi** or **narcissus**. **Narcissi** are yellow, white, or orange trumpet-shaped flowers that bloom in the spring. — N-COUNT: usu pl

narcolepsy /nɑːˈkəlepsi/. **Narcolepsy** is a rare medical condition. It causes people who suffer from it to fall into a deep sleep at any time without any warning. *...an attack of narcolepsy.* — N-UNCOUNT

narcotic /nɑːˈkɒtɪk/ **narcotics** — ♦◇◇◇◇

1 Narcotics are drugs such as opium or heroin which make you sleepy and stop you feeling pain. *He was indicted for dealing in narcotics... He appears to be high on some sort of narcotic.* — N-COUNT

2 If something, especially a drug, has a **narcotic** effect, it makes the person who uses it feel sleepy and dazed. *...hormones that have a narcotic effect on the immune system.* — ADJ

narked /nɑːˈkt/. In informal British English, someone who is **narked** is annoyed about something. *He's probably narked because he didn't see the ad himself.* — ADJ-GRADED: v-link ADJ =annoyed

narrate /nərei̱t, AM næreɪt/ **narrates, narrating, narrated** ◆◇◇◇◇

1 If you **narrate** a story, you tell it from your own point of view; a formal use. *The three of them narrate the same events from three perspectives... The book is narrated by Richard Papen, a Californian boy.* ♦ **narration** /nərei̱ʃᵊn/ *Its story-within-a-story method of narration is confusing.* ♦ **narrator** /nərei̱təʳ, AM næreɪt-/ **narrators** *Jules, the story's narrator, is an actress in her late thirties.* VERB =relate, recount V n; N-UNCOUNT; N-COUNT

2 The person who **narrates** a documentary film or programme speaks the words which accompany the pictures, but does not appear in it. *She also narrated a documentary about the Kirov Ballet School.* ♦ **narration** *As the crew gets back from lunch, we can put your narration on it right away.* ♦ **narrator** /nərei̱təʳ, AM næreɪt-/ **narrators** *Famous actors were narrators of some of the early shows.* VERB V n Also V; N-UNCOUNT; N-COUNT

narrative /nærətɪv/ **narratives** ◆◆◇◇◇

1 A **narrative** is a story or an account of a series of events. *...a fast-moving narrative... Sloan began his narrative with the day of the murder.* N-COUNT

2 **Narrative** is the description of a series of events, usually in a novel. *Neither author was very strong on narrative. ...Nye's simple narrative style.* N-UNCOUNT

narrow /næroʊ/ **narrower, narrowest; narrows, narrowing, narrowed** ◆◆◆◆◇

1 Something that is **narrow** measures a very small distance from one side to the other, especially compared to its length or height. *...through the town's narrow streets... She had long, narrow feet. ...the narrow strip of land joining the peninsula to the rest of the island.* ♦ **narrowness** *...the narrowness of the river mouth.* ADJ-GRADED ≠wide; N-UNCOUNT: usu N *of* n

2 If something **narrows**, it becomes less wide. *The wide track narrows before crossing another stream.* VERB V

3 If your eyes **narrow** or if you **narrow** your eyes, you almost close them, for example because you are angry or because you are trying to concentrate on something; used in written English. *Coggins' eyes narrowed angrily. 'You think I'd tell you?'... He paused and narrowed his eyes in concentration.* V-ERG ≠widen V; V n

4 If you describe someone's ideas, attitudes, or beliefs as **narrow**, you disapprove of them because they are restricted in some way, and often ignore the more important aspects of an argument or situation. *...a narrow and outdated view of family life... I would have preferred somebody who had wider ideas, and he was rather narrow.* ♦ **narrowly** *The present A-level system requires schoolchildren to specialise far too early and too narrowly... They're making judgments based on a narrowly focused vision of the world.* ♦ **narrowness** *...the narrowness of their mental and spiritual outlook.* ADJ-GRADED PRAGMATICS =limited ≠broad; ADV-GRADED: ADV after v, ADV -ed/adj; N-UNCOUNT: usu N *of* n

5 If something **narrows** or if you **narrow** it, its extent, range, or scope becomes smaller. *Most recent opinion polls suggest that the gap between the two main parties has narrowed... The European Community and America had narrowed their differences over farm subsidies.* ♦ **narrowing** *...a narrowing of the gap between rich members and poor.* V-ERG ≠widen V; V n; N-SING

6 If you have a **narrow** victory, you succeed in winning but only by a small margin. *Delegates have voted by a narrow majority in favour of considering electoral reform.* ♦ **narrowly** *She narrowly failed to win enough votes... The People's Party is narrowly behind the Socialists in the polls.* ♦ **narrowness** *The narrowness of the government's victory reflected deep division within the Conservative Party.* ADJ-GRADED: usu ADJ n; ADV; N-UNCOUNT: usu N *of* n

7 If you have a **narrow** escape, something unpleasant nearly happens to you. *Two police officers had a narrow escape when separatists attacked their vehicles.* ♦ **narrowly** *Five firemen narrowly escaped death when a staircase collapsed beneath their feet.* ♦ **narrowness** *If he was shaken by the narrowness of his recent escape he showed no signs of it.* ADJ-GRADED: ADJ n; ADV-GRADED: ADV with v; N-UNCOUNT: usu N *of* n

8 ● **on the straight and narrow**: see **straight**.

narrow down. If you **narrow down** a range of things, you reduce the number of things included in it. *What's happened is that the new results narrow down the possibilities... I've managed to narrow the list down to twenty-three.* PHRASAL VERB V P n (not pron) V n P *to* n Also V n P

narrow boat, narrow boats; also spelled **narrowboat.** A **narrow boat** is a long, low boat used on canals; used in British English. N-COUNT =barge

narrowly /næroʊli/. If you look at someone **narrowly**, you look at them in a concentrated way, often because you think they are not giving you full information about something. *He grimaced and looked narrowly at his colleague.* ● See also **narrow**. ADV: ADV after v =closely

narrow-minded. If you describe someone as **narrow-minded**, you are criticizing them because they are unwilling to consider new ideas or other people's opinion. *...a narrow-minded bigot.* ♦ **narrow-mindedness** *It is unbelievable that as a result of this narrow-mindedness a group of people should suffer.* ADJ-GRADED PRAGMATICS ≠broad-minded; N-UNCOUNT

NASA /næsə/. **NASA** is the American government organization concerned with the exploration of space. **NASA** is an abbreviation for 'National Aeronautics and Space Administration'. ◆◆◇◇◇ N-PROPER

nasal /nei̱zᵊl/ ◆◇◇◇◇

1 **Nasal** is used to describe things relating to the nose and the functions it performs. *...inflamed nasal passages. ...nasal decongestant sprays.* ADJ: ADJ n

2 If someone's voice is **nasal**, it sounds as if air is passing through their nose as well as their mouth while they are speaking. *Her voice was nasal and penetrating... She talked in a deep nasal monotone.* ADJ

nascent /næsᵊnt/. **Nascent** things or processes are just beginning, and are expected to become stronger or to grow bigger; a formal word. *Kenya's nascent democracy was threatened by conflict yesterday. ...the still nascent science of psychology.* ADJ: ADJ n =budding

nasturtium /næst3ːʳʃəm/ **nasturtiums. Nasturtiums** are low plants which trail along the ground. They have orange, red, and yellow trumpet-shaped flowers. N-COUNT

nasty /nɑ̱ːsti, næsti/ **nasties; nastier, nastiest** ◆◆◇◇◇

1 Something that is **nasty** is very unpleasant to see, experience, or feel. *...an extremely nasty murder... This divorce could turn nasty.* ♦ **nastiness** *...the nastiness of war.* ADJ-GRADED =horrible; N-UNCOUNT =unpleasantness

2 If you describe a person or their behaviour as **nasty**, you mean that they behave in an unkind and unpleasant way. *What nasty little snobs you all are... The guards looked really nasty... Mummy is so nasty to me when Daddy isn't here.* ♦ **nastily** *She took the money and eyed me nastily... Nikki laughed nastily.* ♦ **nastiness** *As the years went by his nastiness began to annoy his readers.* ADJ-GRADED =disagreeable ≠nice, kind; ADV-GRADED: ADV after v; N-UNCOUNT

3 If you describe something as **nasty**, you mean it is unattractive, undesirable, or in bad taste. *...Emily's nasty little house in Balham... That damned Farrel made some nasty jokes here about Mr. Lane.* ADJ-GRADED =unpleasant ≠nice

4 A **nasty** problem or situation is very worrying and difficult to deal with. *A spokesman said this firm action had defused a very nasty situation.* ADJ-GRADED: usu ADJ n =tricky

5 If you describe an injury or a disease as **nasty**, you mean that it is serious or looks unpleasant. *My little granddaughter caught her heel in the spokes of her bicycle—it was a very nasty wound... Lili had a nasty chest infection.* ADJ-GRADED

6 **Nasties** are unpleasant or harmful people or things; an informal use. *...evil organisations, peopled with nasties... Decaffeinated coffee still contains some stimulants and other nasties linked with cancer.* N-PLURAL

7 See also **video nasty**.

natch /nætʃ/. In informal English, especially journalism, **natch** is used to indicate that something such as an idea or story is very obvious and predictable. *...a bizarre, dreamy (but sarcastic, natch) ballad... Ina is a bad girl so, natch, ends up in prison.* ADV: ADV with cl/group =naturally

nation /nei̱ʃᵊn/ **nations** ◆◆◆◆◆

1 A **nation** is an individual country considered together with its social and political structures. *Such policies would require unprecedented cooperation between nations... The Arab nations agreed to meet in Baghdad.* N-COUNT

2 The **nation** is sometimes used to refer to all the N-SING

people who live in a particular country; used in journalism. *It was a story that touched the nation's heart.*

national /næʃənᵊl/ **nationals** ◆◆◆◆◆

1 National means relating to the whole of a country or nation rather than to part of it or to other nations. *Ruling parties have lost ground in national and local elections. ...major national and international issues.* ♦ **nationally** *...a nationally televised speech... Duncan Campbell is nationally known for his investigative work.* ADJ: usu ADJ n; ADV: ADV with v, ADV adj

2 National means typical of the people or customs of a particular country or nation. *...the national characteristics and history of the country... Baseball is the national pastime.* ADJ: ADJ n

3 You can refer to someone who has citizenship of a country as a **national** of that country. *...a Sri Lankan-born British national.* N-COUNT: usu adj N =citizen

national anthem, national anthems. A **national anthem** is a nation's official song which is played or sung on public occasions. ◆◇◇◇◇ N-COUNT: usu sing

National Curriculum. **The National Curriculum** is the course of study that most school pupils in England and Wales are meant to follow between the ages of 5 and 16. ◆◆◇◇◇ N-PROPER: *the* N

national government, national governments. A **national government** is a coalition government, especially one that is formed during a crisis. ◆◇◇◇◇ N-COUNT: usu sing

National Health Service. In Britain, the **National Health Service** is the state system for providing medical care. It is paid for by taxes. *An increasing number of these treatments are now available on the National Health Service.* ◆◇◇◇◇ N-PROPER: *the* N

national insurance. In Britain, **national insurance** is the state system of paying money to people who are ill, unemployed, or retired. It is financed by money that the government collects from people in employment and their employers. ◆◇◇◇◇ N-UNCOUNT

nationalise /næʃənəlaɪz/. See **nationalize**.

nationalism /næʃənəlɪzəm/ ◆◆◇◇◇

1 Nationalism is the desire for political independence by people who have the same language, religion, or culture. *The rising tide of Slovak nationalism may also help the SNP to win representation in parliament.* N-UNCOUNT: oft supp N

2 You can refer to a person's great love for their nation as **nationalism**. It is often associated with the belief that a particular nation is better than any other nation, and in this case is often used showing disapproval. *This kind of fierce nationalism is a powerful and potentially volatile force.* N-UNCOUNT: oft supp N =jingoism

nationalist /næʃənəlɪst/ **nationalists** ◆◆◆◇◇

1 Nationalist means connected with the desire for political independence for a particular group of people. *The crisis has set off a wave of nationalist feelings in Quebec.* ► A **nationalist** is someone with nationalist views. *...demands by Slovak nationalists for an independent state.* ADJ: ADJ n; N-COUNT

2 Nationalist means connected with a person's great love for their nation. It is often associated with the belief that their nation is better than any other nation, and in this case is often used showing disapproval. *Political life has been infected by growing nationalist sentiment.* ► A **nationalist** is someone with nationalist views. *Some nationalists would like to depict the British monarchy as a purely English institution.* ADJ: ADJ n; N-COUNT

nationalistic /næʃənəlɪstɪk/. If you describe someone as **nationalistic**, you mean they are very proud of their nation, and believe that it is better than any other nation; often used showing disapproval. *...Barcelona, a team who are a monument to the nationalistic pride of the Catalan people.* ◆◇◇◇◇ ADJ-GRADED

nationality /næʃənælɪti/ **nationalities** ◆◆◇◇◇

1 If you have the **nationality** of a particular country, you were born there or have the legal right to be a citizen. *Asked his nationality, he said British... The crew are of different nationalities and have no common language.* N-VAR

2 You can refer to people who have the same racial origins as a **nationality**, especially when they do not have their own independent country. *...the many nationalities that comprise Ethiopia.* N-COUNT =race

nationalize /næʃənəlaɪz/ **nationalizes, nationalizing, nationalized;** also spelled **nationalise** in British English. If the government **nationalizes** a private company or industry, that company or industry becomes owned by the state and controlled by the government. *In 1987, Garcia introduced legislation to nationalize Peru's banking and financial systems... The coffee industry was nationalised at the time of independence.* ♦ **nationalization** /næʃənəlaɪzeɪʃᵊn/ **nationalizations** *...the campaign for the nationalization of the coal mines... The steel workers were relatively indifferent to the issue of nationalization.* ◆◇◇◇◇ VERB ≠privatise; V n; N-UNCOUNT: also N in pl ≠privatization

national park, national parks. A **national park** is a large area of land which is protected by the government because of its natural beauty, plants, or animals, and which the public can usually visit. *...the Masai Mara game reserve and Amboseli national park.* ◆◆◇◇◇ N-COUNT: oft in names after n

national service. **National service** is service in the armed forces, which young people in certain countries have to do by law. *Banks spent his national service in the Royal Navy.* ◆◇◇◇◇ N-UNCOUNT =military service

nationhood /neɪʃᵊnhʊd/. A country's **nationhood** is its status as a nation. *To them, the monarchy is the special symbol of nationhood.* N-UNCOUNT

nation state, nation states. A **nation state** is an independent state which consists of people from one particular national group. *Albania is a small nation state of around 3 million people.* ◆◇◇◇◇ N-COUNT

nationwide /neɪʃᵊnwaɪd/. **Nationwide** activities or situations happen or exist in all parts of a country. *The rising number of car crimes is a nationwide problem. ...the strike by teachers which is nationwide.* ► Also an adverb. *The figures show unemployment falling nationwide last month.* ◆◆◇◇◇ ADJ: usu ADJ n =national; ADV =nationally

native /neɪtɪv/ **natives** ◆◆◆◇◇

1 Your **native** country or area is the country or area where you were born and brought up. *It was his first visit to his native country since 1948... Mother Teresa visited her native Albania.* ADJ: ADJ n

2 A **native of** a particular country or region is someone who was born in that country or region. *Dr Aubin is a native of St Blaise. ...two Dutch volunteer workmen, natives of Tilburg.* ► Also an adjective. *Joshua Halpern is a native Northern Californian. ...men and women native to countries such as Japan.* N-COUNT: N *of* n; ADJ: ADJ n, v-link ADJ *to* n

3 Some European people use **native** to refer to a person who was born in or lives in a non-Western country and who belongs to the race or tribe that forms the majority of its inhabitants; some people consider this use offensive. *They used force to banish the natives from the more fertile land.* ► Also an adjective. *Native people were allowed to retain some sense of their traditional culture and religion.* N-COUNT; ADJ: ADJ n =indigenous

4 Your **native** language or tongue is the first language that you learned to speak when you were a child. *She spoke not only her native language, Swedish, but also English and French... French is not my native tongue.* ADJ: ADJ n

5 Plants or animals that are **native to** a particular region live or grow there naturally rather than being brought there. *...a project to create a 50 acre forest of native Caledonian pines... Many of the plants are native to Brazil.* ► Also a noun. *The coconut palm is a native of Malaysia.* ADJ: ADJ n, v-link ADJ *to* n =indigenous; N-COUNT: N *of* n

6 A **native** ability or quality is one that you possess naturally without having to learn it. *We have our native inborn talent, yet we hardly use it.* ADJ: ADJ n =innate

7 If you say that someone who is living away from their own country **goes native**, you mean that they try to live and dress like the local people; used showing disapproval. *You don't think he's gone native, do you? Perhaps he has married out there and decided he can't come home.* PHRASE: V inflects PRAGMATICS

Native American, Native Americans. **Native Americans** are people from any one of the many ◆◇◇◇◇ N-COUNT =American tribes which were already living in North America before the Europeans arrived there. *The eagle is the animal most sacred to the Native Americans.* ► Also an adjective. *...a gathering of Native American elders.* Indian ADJ: ADJ n

native speaker, native speakers. A **native speaker** of a language is someone who speaks that language as their first language rather than having learnt it as a foreign language. *Our programme ensures daily opportunities to practice your study language with native speakers.* N-COUNT

Nativity /nətɪvɪti/. **The Nativity** is the birth of Jesus, which is celebrated by Christians at Christmas. *They admired the tableau of the Nativity. ...the Nativity story.* N-SING: the N

nativity play, nativity plays. A **nativity play** is a play about the birth of Jesus, usually one performed by children at Christmas time. N-COUNT

NATO /neɪtoʊ/. **NATO** is an international organization which consists of the USA, Canada, the UK, and other European countries who have agreed to support one another if they are attacked. It is an abbreviation for 'North Atlantic Treaty Organization'. *NATO says it will keep a reduced number of modern nuclear weapons to guarantee peace.* ◆◆◆◇◇ N-PROPER

natter /nætəʳ/ **natters, nattering, nattered.** When people **natter**, they talk casually for a long time about unimportant things; an informal word. *If something dramatic has happened during the day, we'll sit and natter about it... Susan and the girl were still nattering away in German... Ahead of you is a day of nattering with fellow farmers at the local market... You natter all day long at the hospital... His mother would natter to anyone.* ► Also a noun. *What's the topic of conversation when a group of new mums get together for a natter?* V-RECIP =chat, gossip; pl-n V; pl-n V *away/on*; V *with* n; NON-RECIP: V; V *to* n; N-SING: *a* N =chinwag

natty /næti/ **nattier, nattiest**

1 If you describe a man as **natty**, you think that he dresses smartly and neatly; an informal use. *Cliff was a natty dresser. ...a natty pin stripe suit.* ADJ-GRADED: usu ADJ n

2 If you describe something as **natty**, you think it is smart and cleverly designed; an informal use. *...natty little houses.* ADJ-GRADED: usu ADJ n =nifty

natural /nætʃərəl/ **naturals** ◆◆◆◆◇

1 If you say that it is **natural** for someone to act in a particular way or for something to happen in that way, you mean that it is reasonable in the circumstances. *It is only natural for youngsters to crave the excitement of driving a fast car... It is only natural that he should resent you... A period of depression can be a perfectly natural response to certain aspects of life.* ADJ-GRADED: oft *it* v-link ADJ to-inf/that ≠unnatural, surprising

2 **Natural** behaviour is instinctive and has not been learned. *...the insect's natural instinct to feed... Anger is the natural reaction we experience when we feel threatened or frustrated.* ADJ =inborn ≠abnormal

3 Someone with a **natural** ability or skill was born with that ability and did not have to learn it. *She has a natural ability to understand the motives of others... He had a natural flair for business.* ADJ: usu ADJ n =instinctive

4 If you say that someone is a **natural**, you mean that they do something very well and very easily. *He's a natural with any kind of engine... She proved to be a natural on camera.* N-COUNT: usu *a* N in sing

5 If someone's behaviour is **natural**, they appear to be relaxed and are not trying to hide anything. *Bethan's sister was as friendly and natural as the rest of the family... Hannah's natural manner reassured her, and she relaxed.* ♦ **naturally** *For pictures of people behaving naturally, not posing for the camera, it is essential to shoot unnoticed... She is magnificent at making you feel you can talk quite naturally to her.* ♦ **naturalness** *The critics praised the reality of the scenery and the naturalness of the acting.* ADJ-GRADED =genuine ≠contrived; ADV-GRADED: ADV after v; N-UNCOUNT

6 **Natural** things exist or occur in nature and are not made or caused by people. *It has called the typhoon the worst natural disaster in South Korea in four years... The gigantic natural harbour of Poole is a haven for boats.* ♦ **naturally** *Nitrates are chemicals that occur naturally in water and the soil... Honey is a naturally acidic substance.* ADJ: ADJ n ≠artificial, man-made; ADV: ADV with v, ADV adj

7 Someone's **natural** parent is their actual parent, as opposed to one who has adopted or fostered them. Someone's **natural** child is their actual child, rather than one they have adopted or fostered. *She has been reunited with her natural mother... His commitments to the stepchildren will not reduce his obligation to his natural children.* ADJ: ADJ n

8 In music, a **natural** note is the ordinary note, not its sharp or flat form. *...B natural.* ► Also a noun. *Is that F a natural or a sharp?* ADJ: n ADJ; N-COUNT

9 If someone dies of **natural causes**, they die because they are ill or old rather than because of an accident, murder, or suicide. *According to the Home Office, your brother died of natural causes... A prisoner collapsed and died yesterday, apparently from natural causes.* PHRASE: usu prep PHR

natural childbirth. If a woman gives birth by **natural childbirth**, she is not given any drugs to relieve her pain or to send her to sleep. N-UNCOUNT

natural gas. **Natural gas** is gas which is found underground or under the sea. It is collected and stored, and piped into people's homes to be used for cooking and heating. ◆◇◇◇◇ N-UNCOUNT =methane

natural history. **Natural history** is the study of animals and plants and other living things. *Schools regularly bring children to the beach for natural history lessons.* ◆◇◇◇◇ N-UNCOUNT: usu N n

naturalise /nætʃərəlaɪz/. See **naturalize**.

naturalism /nætʃərəlɪzəm/. **Naturalism** is a theory in art and literature which states that people and objects should be shown as they actually are, rather than in an idealistic or unnatural way. N-UNCOUNT

naturalist /nætʃərəlɪst/ **naturalists.** A **naturalist** is a person who studies plants, animals, insects, and other living things. ◆◇◇◇◇ N-COUNT

naturalistic /nætʃərəlɪstɪk/

1 **Naturalistic** is used to describe the work of artists and writers who believe in and practice the theory of naturalism in their work. *These drawings are among his most naturalistic.* ADJ-GRADED

2 **Naturalistic** means simulating the effects or characteristics of nature. *Further research is needed under rather more naturalistic conditions.* ADJ-GRADED

naturalize /nætʃərəlaɪz/ **naturalizes, naturalizing, naturalized;** also spelled **naturalise** in British English.

1 To **naturalize** a species of plant means to replant it in an area where it is not usually found. If a plant **naturalizes** in an area where it was not found before, it starts to grow there naturally. *A friend sent me a root from Mexico, and I hope to naturalize it... The plant naturalises well in grass.* V-ERG; V n; V

2 If the government of a country **naturalizes** someone, they allow a person who was not born in that country to become a citizen of it. *No one expects the Baltic states to naturalise young Russian soldiers, but army pensioners can be given citizenship.* ♦ **naturalization** /nætʃərəlaɪzeɪʃᵊn/ *They swore their allegiance to the USA and received their naturalization papers.* VERB; V n; N-UNCOUNT

naturalized /nætʃərəlaɪzd/; also spelled **naturalised.** A **naturalized** citizen of a particular country is someone who has legally become a citizen of that country, although they were not born there. ADJ: ADJ n

naturally /nætʃərəli/ ◆◆◆◇◇

1 You use **naturally** to indicate that you think something is very obvious and not at all surprising in the circumstances. *When things go wrong, all of us naturally feel disappointed and frustrated... Naturally these comings and goings excited some curiosity... He had been stunned and, naturally, deeply upset... We are naturally concerned about the future.* ADV: ADV before v, ADV with cl, ADV adj =obviously

2 If one thing develops **naturally** from another, it develops as a normal consequence or result of it. *A study of yoga leads naturally to meditation.* ADV: ADV after v =logically

3 You can use **naturally** to talk about the characteristics of someone's personality when it is the way that they normally act. *He has a lively sense of humour and appears naturally confident.* ADV: ADV adj

4 If someone is **naturally** good at something, they learn it easily and quickly and do it very well. *Some individuals are naturally good communicators.* ADV: ADV adj

5 If something **comes naturally** to you, you find it easy to do and quickly become good at it. *With football, it was just something that came naturally to me.* PHRASE: V inflects, usu PHR *to* n

natural resources. **Natural resources** are all the land, forests, energy sources and minerals existing naturally in a place that can be used by people. *Angola was a country rich in natural resources... They are looking at ways of reducing the waste of natural resources.* ◆◇◇◇◇ N-PLURAL

natural selection. **Natural selection** is a process by which species of animals and plants that are best adapted to their environment survive and reproduce, while those that are less well adapted die out. *Natural selection ensures only the fittest survive to pass their genes on to the next generation.* N-UNCOUNT

natural wastage. **Natural wastage** is the process of employees leaving their jobs to retire or move to other jobs, rather than being sacked or made redundant; used mainly in British English. The usual American word is **attrition**. *The company hopes the job cuts will be made through natural wastage and voluntary redundancy.* N-UNCOUNT

nature /neɪtʃəʳ/ **natures** ◆◆◆◆◇

1 **Nature** is all the animals, plants, and other things in the world that are not made by people, and all the events and processes that are not caused by people. *The most amazing thing about nature is its infinite variety. ...grasses that grow wild in nature. ...the ecological balance of nature.* N-UNCOUNT

2 The **nature** of something is its basic quality or character. *Mr Sharp would not comment on the nature of the issues being investigated. ...the ambitious nature of the programme... The protests had been non-political by nature... The rise of a major power is both economic and military in nature.* N-SING: with supp, oft n N, also *by/in* N

3 Someone's **nature** is their character, which they show by the way they behave. *Jeya feels that her ambitious nature made her unsuitable for an arranged marriage... She trusted people. That was her nature... He was by nature affectionate.* • See also **human nature**, **Mother Nature**. N-SING: with poss, also *by* N

4 If you say that something is **against nature**, you think that it is unnatural. *All these activities are against nature.* PHRASES v-link PHR =unnatural

5 If you want to get **back to nature**, you want to return to a simpler way of living. *She was very anxious to get away from cities and back to nature.* PHR after v

6 If you say that something has a particular characteristic **by** its **nature** or **by** its **very nature**, you mean that things of that type always have that characteristic. *Peacekeeping, by its nature, makes pre-planning difficult... One could argue that smoking, by its very nature, is addictive.* N inflects, PHR with cl

7 Some people talk about a **call of nature** when referring politely to the need to go to the toilet. *I'm afraid I have to answer a call of nature.* PHR after v PRAGMATICS

8 If you say that something is **in the nature of things,** you mean that you would expect it to happen in the circumstances mentioned. *Of course, in the nature of things, and with a lot of drinking going on, people failed to notice... Many have already died, and in the nature of things many more will die.* PHR with cl

9 If you say that one thing is **in the nature of** another, you mean that you think it is like the other thing. *There is movement towards, I think, something in the nature of a pluralistic system... It was in the nature of a debate rather than an argument.* PHR n, usu v-link PHR, pron-indef PHR

10 If a way of behaving is **second nature** to you, you do it almost without thinking because it is easy or obvious to you. *Planning ahead had always come as second nature to her... It's not easy at first, but it soon becomes second nature.* v-link PHR, oft PHR *to* n

nature study. **Nature study** is the study of animals and plants at a very basic level by looking at them directly, for example as it is taught to young children. *They drove into the mountains for a weekend of nature study.* N-UNCOUNT

nature trail, nature trails. A **nature trail** is a route through an area of countryside which is signposted, pointing out things like animals, plants, and rocks. N-COUNT

naturism /neɪtʃərɪzəm/. **Naturism** is the same as **nudism**; used mainly in British English. N-UNCOUNT
♦ **naturist, naturists** *...a naturist beach.* N-COUNT: oft N n

naught /nɔːt/. See **nought**.

naughty /nɔːti/ **naughtier, naughtiest** ◆◇◇◇◇

1 If you say that a child is **naughty**, you think that he or she is behaving badly or is disobedient. *Girls, you're being very naughty... You naughty boy, you gave me such a fright.* ♦ **naughtiness** *When he poked his tongue at the press it was just a young boy's natural naughtiness.* ADJ-GRADED =bad ≠good; N-UNCOUNT

2 You can describe books, pictures, or words, as **naughty** when they are slightly rude or related to sex. *You know what little boys are like with naughty words. ...saucy TV shows, crammed full of naughty innuendo.* ♦ **naughtiness** *...a writer who shocked the bourgeosie with his sexual naughtiness.* ADJ-GRADED; N-UNCOUNT

nausea /nɔːziə/. **Nausea** is the condition of feeling sick and the feeling that you are going to vomit. *I was overcome with a feeling of nausea.* ◆◇◇◇◇ N-UNCOUNT

nauseam /nɔːziæm/. See **ad nauseam**.

nauseate /nɔːzieɪt/ **nauseates, nauseating, nauseated.** If something **nauseates** you, it makes you feel as if you are going to vomit. *The smell of frying nauseated her... She could not eat anything without feeling nauseated.* VERB =sicken; V n; V-ed

nauseating /nɔːzieɪtɪŋ/. If you describe someone's attitude or their behaviour as **nauseating**, you mean that you find it extremely unpleasant and feel disgusted by it. *The judge described the offences as nauseating and unspeakable... For them to attack the Liberals for racism is not just nauseating hypocrisy, it is pure, cynical opportunism.* ADJ-GRADED =sickening

nauseous /nɔːziəs, AM -ʃəs/. If you feel **nauseous**, you feel as if you want to vomit. *If the patient is poorly nourished, the drugs make them feel nauseous... A nauseous wave of pain broke over her.* ADJ-GRADED =queasy

nautical /nɔːtɪkᵊl/. **Nautical** means relating to ships and sailing. *...a nautical chart of the region you sail.* ◆◇◇◇◇ ADJ: usu ADJ n

nautical mile, nautical miles. A **nautical mile** is a unit of measurement used at sea. It is equal to 1852 metres. N-COUNT

naval /neɪvᵊl/. **Naval** means belonging to, relating to, or involving a country's navy. *He was the senior serving naval officer. ...the US naval base at Guantanamo Bay.* ◆◆◆◇◇ ADJ: ADJ n

nave /neɪv/ **naves.** The **nave** of a church or cathedral is the long central part where people gather to worship. N-COUNT

navel /neɪvᵊl/ **navels.** Your **navel** is the small hollow just below your waist at the front of your body. ◆◇◇◇◇ N-COUNT

navel-gazing. If you refer to an activity as **navel-gazing**, you are critical of it because people are thinking about something for a long time but take no action on it. *She dismisses the reform process as an exercise in collective navel gazing.* N-UNCOUNT PRAGMATICS

navigable /nævɪgəbᵊl/. **Navigable** rivers or waterways are wide and deep enough for a boat to travel along safely; a formal word. *...the navigable portion of the Nile. ...the Tiber, which was then still navigable.* ADJ

navigate /nævɪgeɪt/ **navigates, navigating, navigated** ◆◇◇◇◇

1 When someone **navigates** a ship or an aircraft somewhere or if a ship or aircraft **navigates** there, it is steered in the direction that has been decided upon by the navigator. *Captain Cook was responsible for safely navigating his ship without accident for 100 voyages... The purpose of the visit was to navigate into an ice-filled fiord. ...the new navigation system which will enable aircraft to navigate with total pinpoint accuracy.* ♦ **navigation** V-ERG; V n; V prep/adv; V; N-VAR

/nævɪɡeɪʃən/ **navigations** *The expedition was wrecked by bad planning and poor navigation. ...the boat's navigation system.*

2 When a ship or boat **navigates** an area of water, it sails on or across it. *...a lock system to allow sea-going craft to navigate the upper reaches of the river... Such boats can be built locally and, because they have a shallow draught, can navigate on the Nile.* VERB =sail V n V prep

3 When someone in a car **navigates**, they decide what roads the car should be driven along in order to get somewhere. *When travelling on fast roads at night it is impossible to drive and navigate at the same time. ...the relief at successfully navigating across the Golden Gate Bridge to arrive here... They had just navigated their way through Maidstone on their way to the coast.* VERB V V prep/adv V *way* prep Also V n

4 When fish, animals, or insects **navigate** somewhere, they find the right direction to go and travel there. *In tests, the bees navigate back home after being placed in a field a mile away.* VERB V adv/prep Also V

5 If you **navigate** an obstacle, you move carefully in order to avoid hitting the obstacle or hurting yourself. *He was not able to walk without a cane and could only navigate steps backwards... In the corridors he let her navigate her own way round the trolleys and other obstacles... If guests wished to use the sofa, they had first to navigate around chairs in the middle of the room.* VERB =negotiate V n V *way* prep V prep/adv

6 If you manage to **navigate** a difficult situation, you deal with it successfully. *During childhood each of us has to navigate a pathway through a series of developmental stages... This outlook helped her to navigate through her later years with success.* VERB V n V *through* n

navigation /nævɪɡeɪʃən/. You can refer to the movement of ships as **navigation**. *Pack ice around Iceland was becoming a threat to navigation.* • See also **navigate**. ◆◇◇◇◇ N-UNCOUNT

navigational /nævɪɡeɪʃənəl/. **Navigational** means relating to the act of navigating a ship or an aeroplane. *The pilot said the crash was a direct result of inadequate navigational aids.* ADJ: usu ADJ n

navigator /nævɪɡeɪtəʳ/ **navigators** ◆◇◇◇◇

1 The **navigator** on an aircraft or ship is the person whose job is to work out the direction in which the aircraft or ship should be travelling. *He became an RAF navigator during the war.* N-COUNT

2 In the past, a **navigator** was someone who explored unknown seas or travelled by sea to unknown areas of land. N-COUNT

navvy /nævi/ **navvies.** A **navvy** is a person who is employed to do hard physical work, for example building roads or canals; an old-fashioned word, used mainly in British English. *...a blackened young navvy, swinging a pickaxe in the sweating tunnel.* N-COUNT

navy /neɪvi/ **navies** ◆◆◆◇◇

1 A country's **navy** consists of the people it employs to fight at sea, and the ships they use. *The government announced an order for three Type 23 frigates for the Royal Navy yesterday... Her own son was also in the Navy. ...a United States navy ship.* N-COUNT: usu *the* N

2 Something that is **navy** or **navy-blue** is very dark blue. *When I was a fashion editor, I mostly wore white shirts and black or navy trousers. ...a navy-blue blazer.* COLOUR

nay /neɪ/

1 You use **nay** in front of a stronger word or phrase which you feel is more correct than the one you have just used and helps to emphasize the point you are making; a formal use. *He was grateful for and proud of his son's remarkable, nay, unique performance... Long essays, nay, whole books have been written on this.* ADV: ADV with cl/group PRAGMATICS =indeed

2 **Nay** is sometimes used to mean 'no' when people are talking about voting for or giving their consent for something. *The House of Commons can merely say yea or nay to the executive judgment.* CONVENTION

3 **Nay** is an old-fashioned, poetic, or religious word for 'no'. *'A doctor, fetch a doctor!'—'Nay, we do need a priest.'* CONVENTION =no

Nazi /nɑːtsi/ **Nazis** ◆◆◆◇◇

1 The **Nazis** were members of the right-wing political party, led by Adolf Hitler, which held power in Germany from 1933 to 1945. N-COUNT

2 You use **Nazi** to say that something relates to the Nazis. *...the rise of the Nazi Party. ...the Nazi occupation of the Channel Islands.* ADJ

Nazism /nɑːtsɪzəm/. **Nazism** was the political ideas and activities of the German Nazi Party. ◆◇◇◇◇ N-UNCOUNT

NB /en biː/. You write **NB** to draw someone's attention to what you are about to say or write. *NB The opinions stated in this essay do not necessarily represent those of the Church of God Missionary Society.* ◆◇◇◇◇ PRAGMATICS

NCO /en siː oʊ/ **NCOs.** An **NCO** is a soldier who has a rank such as sergeant or corporal. **NCO** is an abbreviation for 'non-commissioned officer'. *Food for the ordinary Soviet troops and NCOs was very poor.* N-COUNT

-nd. **-nd** is added to written numbers ending in 2 (except for numbers ending in 12) in order to form ordinal numbers. *...22nd February. ...2nd edition.* SUFFIX

NE. **NE** is a written abbreviation for **north-east**. *...on the NE outskirts of Bath.*

neanderthal /niændəʳtɑːl, -θɔːl/ **neanderthals**

1 **Neanderthal** people lived in Europe between 35,000 and 70,000 years ago. *Neanderthal man was able to kill woolly mammoths and bears. ...the late Neanderthal age.* ► You can refer to people from the Neanderthal period as **Neanderthals**. *The Neanderthals were very robust and quite different from us.* ADJ: ADJ n N-COUNT: usu pl

2 If you describe people's, especially men's, ideas or ways of behaving as **Neanderthal**, you disapprove of them because they are very old-fashioned and uncivilized. *Let us deal with the question of his notoriously Neanderthal attitude to women.* ADJ-GRADED: usu ADJ n PRAGMATICS =uncouth

3 If you call a man a **neanderthal**, you disapprove of him because you think he behaves in a very uncivilized way. *In fact, many sympathized with me for having to put up with such a neanderthal of a boss. ...drunken neanderthals.* N-COUNT PRAGMATICS

near /nɪəʳ/ **nearer, nearest; nears, nearing, neared** ◆◆◆◆◆

1 If something is **near** a place, thing, or person, it is a short distance from them. *Don't come near me... Her children went back every year to stay in a farmhouse near the cottage... He drew his chair nearer the fire... Some of the houses nearest the bridge were on fire.* ► Also an adverb. *He crouched as near to the door as he could... She took a step nearer to the barrier... As we drew near, I saw that the boot lid was up.* ► Also an adjective. *He collapsed into the nearest chair... Where's the nearest telephone?... He went back into the bedroom, slipped into the nearer bed, and said goodnight... The nearer of the two barges was perhaps a mile away.* ♦ **nearness** *He was suddenly aware of his nearness.* PREP ADV-GRADED: ADV after v, *be* ADV, oft ADV *to* n ADJ-SUPERL; ADJ-COMPAR: ADJ n, *the* ADJ *of* n N-UNCOUNT: usu with poss

2 If someone or something is **near to** a particular state, they have almost reached it. *After the war, The House of Hardie came near to bankruptcy... The repairs to the Hafner machine were near to completion... Apart from anything else, he comes near to contradicting himself.* ► **Near** means the same as **near to**. *He was near tears... For almost a month he lay near death... We are no nearer agreement now than in the past.* PHR-PREP: PREP n/-ing =close PREP =close to

3 If something is similar to something else, you can say that it is **near to** it. *It combined with the resinous cedar smell of the logs to produce a sickening sensation that was near to nausea.* ► **Near** means the same as **near to**. *Often her feelings were nearer hatred than love.* PHR-PREP =similar PREP

4 You describe the thing most similar to something as the **nearest** thing **to** it when there is no example of the thing itself. *It would appear that the legal profession is the nearest thing to a recession-proof industry... He is the nearest to a dead cert that Britain has in Albertville.* ADJ-SUPERL: *the* ADJ n *to* n, *the* ADJ *to* n

5 If a time or event draws **near**, it will happen soon; ADV-GRADED:

used in written English. *The time for my departure from Japan was drawing nearer every day.* ADV after v, *be* ADV

6 If something happens **near** a particular time, it happens just before or just after that time. *Performance is lowest between 3 a.m. and 5 a.m. and reaches a peak near midday... 'Since I retired to this place,' he wrote near the end of his life, 'I have never been out of these mountains.'... I'll tell you nearer the day.* PREP

7 You use **near** to say that something is a little more or less than an amount or number stated. *...to increase manufacturing from about 2.5 million cars a year to nearer 4.75 million... The pound, which ended last year near its annual low, is expected to come under renewed pressure today.* PREP

8 You can say that someone will not go **near** something or someone when you are emphasizing that they will not go somewhere, do something, or see someone. *He will absolutely not go near a hospital... I'm so annoyed with her that I haven't been near her for a week.* PREP: with brd-neg PRAGMATICS

9 The **near** one of two things is the one that is closer. *...a mighty beech tree on the near side of the little clearing... Jane put one foot in the near stirrup and turned to look at the stranger.* ADJ-GRADED: det ADJ n ≠far

10 You use **near** to indicate that something is almost the thing mentioned; used in written English. *She was believed to have died in near poverty on the French Riviera. ...the 48-year-old who was brought in to rescue the bank from near collapse.* ADJ: ADJ n ► Also an adverb. *...his near fatal accident two years ago... The picture beneath was near lifesize.* ADV: ADV adj

11 In a contest, your **nearest** rival or challenger is the one that is most likely to defeat you. *Mr Denktash is reported to have won twice as many votes as his nearest rival, Mr Ismail Bozkurt... That victory put the Ukrainians beyond the reach of their nearest challengers, Dynamo Moscow.* ADJ-SUPERL: ADJ n

12 When you **near** a place, you get quite near to it; used in written English. *As he neared the stable, he slowed the horse and patted it on the neck... We were nearing the top of the pass to Tsagochen Thang when the van spluttered and died.* VB: no passive =approach V n

13 When someone or something **nears** a particular stage or point, they will soon reach that stage or point. *His age was hard to guess – he must have been nearing fifty... You are nearing the end of your training and you haven't attempted any assessments yet... The project is taking a long time but is now nearing completion.* VB: no passive =approach V n

14 You say that an important time or event **nears** when it is going to occur quite soon. *As half time neared, Hardyman almost scored twice... This factor will come increasingly to the fore as election day nears.* VERB =approach V

15 People sometimes refer to their close relatives and friends as their **nearest and dearest**. *...that English convention of not showing your feelings, even to your nearest and dearest.* PHRASES =kith and kin

16 You use **near and far** to indicate that you are referring to a very large area or distance. *People would gather from near and far... Within months his reputation spread near and far.*

17 If you say that something will happen **in the near future**, you mean that it will happen quite soon. *The controversy regarding vitamin C is unlikely to be resolved in the near future.*

18 You use **nowhere near** and **not anywhere near** to emphasize that something is not the case. *They are nowhere near good enough... It was nowhere near as painful as David had expected... The state pension is nowhere near enough.* usu PHR adj, PHR n PRAGMATICS =not nearly

19 In informal English, if you want to indicate that something is almost true, you can use the expressions **near enough** and **damned near**. In British English, you can also say **as near as dammit**. *I bought them for a pound apiece, near enough... They are as near as dammit new... As a second lieutenant, he had to salute damned near everybody.*

20 In informal English, if you want to indicate that something almost happened, you can use the expression **damned near**. In British English, you can also say **as near as dammit**. *He damned near fooled me... As he was to tell Miranda later, he as near as dammit left it there.* PHR before v

nearby /nɪə^{r}baɪ/; also spelled **near by** or **nearby**. If something is **nearby**, it is only a short distance away. *He might easily have been seen by someone who lived nearby... He spoke softly to a couple standing nearby... There is less expensive accommodation nearby... There were one or two suspicious looks from nearby.* ◆◆◆◇◇ ADV: ADV after v, n ADV, *from* ADV ► Also an adjective. *At a nearby table a man was complaining in a loud voice... Arthur had some connection with the nearby village of Crowthorne.* ADJ: ADJ n ≠distant

near death experience, near death experiences. A **near death experience** is a strange experience that some people who have nearly died say they had when they were unconscious. *A recent Gallup poll revealed that 20 million Americans claimed to have had near-death experiences.* N-COUNT

Near East. The **Near East** is the same as the **Middle East**. N-PROPER: *the* N

nearly /nɪə^{r}li/ ◆◆◆◆◇

1 **Nearly** is used to indicate that something is not quite the case, or not completely the case. *Goldsworth stared at me in silence for nearly twenty seconds... Hunter knew nearly all of this already... Several times Thorne nearly fell... I nearly had a heart attack when she told me... The beach was nearly empty... They nearly always ate outside.* ADV-GRADED: ADV group, ADV before v =almost, practically

2 **Nearly** is used to indicate that something will soon be the case. *It was already nearly eight o'clock... I was nearly asleep... The voyage is nearly over... You're nearly there... I've nearly finished the words for your song.* ADV-GRADED: ADV group, ADV before v =almost

3 You use **not nearly** to emphasize that something is not the case. *Father's flat in Paris wasn't nearly as grand as this... Minerals in general are not nearly so well absorbed as other nutrients... British car workers did not earn nearly enough money to buy the products they were turning out.* PHRASE: PHR adj/adv, PHR n PRAGMATICS =nowhere near

near miss, near misses; also spelled **near-miss.**

1 A **near miss** is a bomb or shot that comes close to its target but misses it. *We've had a few near misses in the raids, as I expect you've noticed.* N-COUNT

2 You can say there is a **near miss** when a collision or accident nearly occurs. *Details have been given of a near miss between two airliners over southern England earlier this week. ...the near miss I had last week when an old man suddenly stepped into the middle of the road.* N-COUNT =narrow escape

3 A **near miss** is an attempt to do something which fails by a very small margin. *Last Saturday's near miss against Ireland has very nearly settled the Test team.* N-COUNT

nearside /nɪə^{r}saɪd/

1 The **nearside** wheels, lights, or doors of a vehicle are those nearest the edge of the road when the vehicle is being driven normally; used mainly in British English. *The nearside front tyre had been slashed.* ADJ: ADJ n ≠offside

2 **The nearside** of a vehicle is the side that is nearest the edge of the road when the vehicle is being driven normally; used mainly in British English. *It hit the kerb on the nearside and seemed to ricochet across the road on two wheels.* N-SING: *the* N ≠offside

near-sighted; also spelled **nearsighted**. Someone who is **near-sighted** cannot see distant things clearly; an old-fashioned word. *The girl squinted at the photograph. She seemed to be nearsighted.* ADJ-GRADED =short-sighted ≠long-sighted

neat /niːt/ **neater, neatest** ◆◆◆◇◇

1 A **neat** place, thing, or person is tidy and smart, with everything arranged in an orderly way. *So they left her in the neat little house, alone with her memories... She undressed and put her wet clothes in a neat pile in the corner. ...a girl in a neat grey flannel suit... Everything was neat and tidy and gleamingly clean.* ADJ-GRADED: usu ADJ n ≠shabby, scruffy ♦ **neatly** *He folded his paper neatly and sipped his coffee... At the door was a neatly dressed, dignified man... His hair was neatly* ADV-GRADED: ADV with v =tidily *brushed.* ♦ **neatness** *The grounds were a perfect balance between neatness and natural wildness.* N-UNCOUNT =tidiness

2 Someone who is **neat** keeps their home or possessions tidy, with everything arranged in an orderly way. *'That's not like Alf,' he said, 'leaving papers muddled like that. He's always so neat.'* ♦ **neatly** *I followed her into that room which her mother had maintained so neatly... He had maybe a thousand tapes, all neatly labelled and catalogued.* ♦ **neatness** *...a paragon of neatness, efficiency and reliability.* ADJ-GRADED =tidy ≠untidy, slovenly ADV-GRADED: ADV with v =tidily N-UNCOUNT =tidiness

3 A **neat** object, part of the body, or shape is quite small and has a smooth outline. *...a faded woman with neat features. ...neat handwriting.* ♦ **neatly** *She was a small woman, slender and neatly made.* ADJ-GRADED: usu ADJ n ≠irregular ADV-GRADED: ADV -ed

4 A **neat** movement or action is done accurately and skilfully, with no unnecessary movements. *A neat move between Black and Keane left Nigel Clough in the clear, but his shot skimmed wide of the far post.* ♦ **neatly** *He watched her peel and dissect a pear neatly, no mess, no sticky fingers. ...watching a solitary car backing out neatly.* ADJ-GRADED: usu ADJ n =nifty ≠clumsy ADV-GRADED: ADV with v ≠clumsily

5 A **neat** way of organizing, achieving, explaining, or expressing something is clever and convenient. *It had been such a neat, clever plan... Neat solutions are not easily found to these issues... 'Make the punishment fit the crime.' How neat and tidy it sounded.* ♦ **neatly** *Real people do not fit neatly into these categories... The theory that personality is determined by our biology neatly lets everyone off the hook.* ♦ **neatness** *He knew full well he had been outflanked, and he appreciated the neatness of it.* ADJ-GRADED =nice ADV-GRADED: ADV with v =nicely N-UNCOUNT

6 In informal American English, if you say that something is **neat** , you mean that you think it is very good. *'Oh, those new apartments are really neat,' the girl babbled on... It'll be neat to have a father and son playing on the same team... He thought Mick was a really neat guy.* ADJ-GRADED =great

7 When someone drinks strong alcohol **neat**, they do not add anything such as tonic or water to it; used mainly in British English. *He poured himself a brandy and swallowed it neat... He took a mouthful of neat whisky, and coughed.* ADJ: v n ADJ, ADJ n =straight

nebula /nebjələ/ **nebulae.** A **nebula** is a cloud of dust and gas in space. New stars are produced from nebulae. *...the Great Nebula.* N-COUNT: oft in names

nebulous /nebjələs/. If you describe something as **nebulous**, you mean that it is vague and not clearly defined or not easy to describe. *The notions we children were able to form of the great world beyond were exceedingly nebulous... Music is such a nebulous thing.* ADJ-GRADED =vague

necessarily /nesɪserɪli, -srɪli/ ◆◆◆◇◇

1 If you say that something is not **necessarily** the case, you mean that it may not be the case or is not always the case. *Anger is not necessarily the most useful or acceptable reaction to such events... Speed and safety are not necessarily incompatible... A higher fee does not necessarily mean a better course.* ● If you reply **'Not necessarily'**, you mean that what has just been said or suggested may not be true. *'He was lying, of course.'—'Not necessarily.'... 'So we're trapped.'—'Not necessarily.'* ADV: with neg, ADV group, ADV before v =automatically CONVENTION PRAGMATICS

2 If you say that something **necessarily** happens or is the case, you mean that it has to happen or be the case and cannot be any different. *Brookman & Langdon were said to manufacture the most desirable pens and these necessarily command astonishingly high prices... Tourism is an industry that has a necessarily close connection with governments.* ADV: ADV before v, ADV group =inevitably

necessary /nesɪsəri/ **necessaries** ◆◆◆◆◇

1 Something that is **necessary** is needed in order for something to happen, especially something you want to happen. *I kept the engine running because it might be necessary to leave fast... We will do whatever is necessary to stop them... Is that really necessary?... Make the necessary arrangements.* ADJ-GRADED: oft *it* v-link ADJ to-inf =required ≠unnecessary

2 A **necessary** consequence or connection must happen or exist, because of the nature of the things or events involved. *Wastage was no doubt a necessary consequence of war... Scientific work is differentiated from art by its necessary connection with the idea of progress.* ADJ: ADJ n

3 **Necessaries** are things, such as food or clothing, that you need to have in order to live; an old-fashioned use. *...a small parcel of necessaries tied up in a handkerchief and carried on a stick.* N-PLURAL =necessities ≠luxuries

4 If you say **'That won't be necessary'** when someone has offered to do something for you, you are refusing their offer in a very definite way, often showing that you do not value their offer. *I offered to show him the video tape. 'Oh, that won't be necessary,' he said with a slight flutter of his fingers.* PHRASES CONVENTION PRAGMATICS

5 If you say that something will happen **if necessary**, **when necessary**, or **where necessary**, you mean that it will happen if it is necessary, when it is necessary, or where it is necessary. *If necessary, the airship can stay up there for days to keep out of danger... The army needs men who are willing to fight, when necessary... All the rigging had been examined, and renewed where necessary.* PHR with cl

6 ● **a necessary evil**: see **evil**.

necessitate /nɪsesɪteɪt/ **necessitates, necessitating, necessitated.** If something **necessitates** an event, action, or situation, it makes it necessary; a formal word. *A prolonged drought had necessitated the introduction of water rationing... Frank was carrying out fuel-system tests which necessitated turning the booster pumps off.* ◆◇◇◇◇ VERB =require V n/-ing

necessity /nɪsesɪti/ **necessities** ◆◆◇◇◇

1 The **necessity** of something is the fact that it must happen or exist. *There is agreement on the necessity of reforms... As soon as the necessity for action is over the troops must be withdrawn... Most women, like men, work from economic necessity... Some people have to lead stressful lifestyles out of necessity.* ● If you say that something is **of necessity** the case, you mean that it is the case because nothing else is possible or practical in the circumstances; a formal expression. *The assembly line of necessity kept moving... Negotiations between the enemies are of necessity indirect.* N-UNCOUNT: usu with supp PHRASE: usu PHR before v, PHR n/adj/adv =inevitably

2 A **necessity** is something that you must have in order to live properly or do something. *Water is a basic necessity of life. ...food, fuel and other daily necessities. ...stockists of agricultural necessities.* N-COUNT =essential ≠luxury

3 A situation or action that is a **necessity** is necessary and cannot be avoided. *The President pleaded that strong rule from the centre was a regrettable, but temporary necessity.* N-COUNT: usu sing

neck /nek/ **necks, necking, necked** ◆◆◆◇◇

1 Your **neck** is the part of your body which joins your head to the rest of your body. *She threw her arms round his neck and hugged him warmly... He was short and stocky, and had a thick neck.* N-COUNT: usu poss N

2 The **neck** of an article of clothing such as a shirt, dress, jumper is the part which surrounds your neck. *...the low, ruffled neck of her blouse... He wore a blue shirt open at the neck.* N-COUNT: usu sing

3 The **neck** of something such as a bottle or a guitar is the long narrow part at one end of it. *Catherine gripped the broken neck of the bottle. ...cancer of the neck of the womb.* N-COUNT: usu *the* N *of* n

4 If two people **are necking**, or if one person **necks** with another, they are kissing each other passionately; an informal use. *They sat talking and necking in the car for another ten minutes... I found myself behind a curtain, necking with my best friend's wife.* V-RECIP: usu cont =snog pl-n V V *with* n Also V n (non-recip)

5 If a racehorse wins **by a neck**, it wins by a very small distance. *Cee En Cee went on to win by a neck from Leigh Crofter.* N-SING: usu *by a* N

6 If you say that someone **is breathing down** your **neck**, you mean that they are watching you very closely and checking everything you do. *Most farmers have bank managers breathing down their necks.* PHRASES V and N inflect

7 In a competition, especially an election, if two or more competitors are **neck and neck**, they are level with each other and have an equal chance of winning. *The latest polls indicate that the two main parties are neck and neck... The Communists are* usu v-link PHR, oft PHR *with* n

running absolutely neck-and-neck with the Christian Democrats.

8 If you say that someone **is risking** their **neck**, you mean they are doing something very dangerous, often in order to try to achieve an objective. *I won't have him risking his neck on that motorcycle.* V and N inflect

9 To **save** someone's **neck** means to prevent them from losing their job or their reputation. *He had enough friends in the right places to save his neck and cover up for him... He said the President was making a last ditch attempt to save his own neck.* V and N inflect

10 If you **stick** your **neck out**, you bravely say or do something that might be criticized or might turn out to be wrong; an informal expression. *During my political life I've earned myself a reputation as someone who'll stick his neck out, a bit of a rebel.* V and N inflect

11 If you say that you have something **round** your **neck**, or **around** your **neck**, you mean that it is your responsibility and it causes you a lot of worry. *No-one should start working life with a debt round their neck... It's a legacy which will hang around the country's neck for some time to come.* N inflects

12 If you say that someone is in some sort of trouble or criminal activity **up to** their **neck**, you mean that they are deeply involved in it; an informal expression. *The black market was flourishing, everybody was corrupt, in it up to their necks... He is probably up to his neck in debt.* N inflects

13 Someone or something that is from your **neck of the woods** is from the same part of the country as you are; an informal expression. *It's so good to see you. What brings you to this neck of the woods?* usu *in* PHR

14 • to **put your neck on the block**: see **block**. • to **have a millstone round your neck**: see **millstone**. • **the scruff of your neck**: see **scruff**.

neckerchief /nekərtʃiːf, -tʃif/ **neckerchiefs.** A **neckerchief** is a piece of cloth which is folded diagonally to form a triangle and worn round someone's neck. N-COUNT

necklace /neklɪs/ **necklaces, necklacing, necklaced** ◆◇◇◇◇

1 A **necklace** is a piece of jewellery such as a chain or a string of beads which someone, usually a woman, wears round their neck. *...a diamond necklace and matching earrings.* N-COUNT

2 To **necklace** someone means to kill them by putting a tyre soaked in petrol around their neck and then setting fire to it. *Alleged strike breakers had their houses petrol-bombed or were hacked to death or necklaced.* ♦ **necklacing, necklacings** *...the gruesome practice of necklacing.* VERB; *be* V-ed, Also V n; N-VAR

neckline /neklaɪn/ **necklines.** The **neckline** of a dress, blouse, or other piece of clothing is the edge that goes around the wearer's neck, especially the front part of it. *...a short brown dress with a plunging neckline. ...a dress with pale pink roses around the neckline.* N-COUNT: oft supp N =neck

necktie /nektaɪ/ **neckties.** A **necktie** is a narrow piece of cloth that someone, usually a man, puts under his shirt collar and ties so that the ends hang down in front. N-COUNT =tie

necromancy /nekrəmænsi/. **Necromancy** is magic that some people believe brings a dead person back to this world so that you can talk to them; a formal word. N-UNCOUNT

necrophilia /nekrəfɪliə/. **Necrophilia** is the act of having sexual intercourse with a dead body, or the desire for it. N-UNCOUNT

necropolis /nekrɒpəlɪs/ **necropolises.** A **necropolis** is a place where dead people are buried; a formal word. *...a small Etruscan museum and necropolis 3 km east of the village.* N-COUNT

necrosis /nekroʊsɪs/. **Necrosis** is the death of part of someone's body, for example because it is not getting enough blood; a medical term. *Disseminated clotting cuts off the blood supply to tissues, causing focal necrosis.* N-UNCOUNT: usu supp N

nectar /nektər/ **nectars** ◆◇◇◇◇

1 **Nectar** is a sweet liquid produced by flowers, which bees and other insects collect. N-UNCOUNT: also N in pl

2 If you refer to a drink, especially a gold-coloured alcoholic drink, as **nectar**, you think it is delicious; a literary use. *Tony sipped from his glass. 'Mmm. Ambrosia. Nectar of the gods. Divine. Wonderful.'* N-UNCOUNT

nectarine /nektəriːn, -rɪn/ **nectarines.** A **nectarine** is a kind of peach which has a smooth skin. N-COUNT

née /neɪ/. You use **née** after a married woman's name just before you mention the family surname she had before she got married; a formal word. *Lady Helen Taylor (née Windsor) chose a Catherine Walker gown for her wedding last year.* =born

need /niːd/ **needs, needing, needed** ◆◆◆◆◆

Need sometimes behaves like an ordinary verb, for example 'She needs to know' and 'She doesn't need to know' and sometimes like a modal, for example 'She need know', 'She needn't know', or, in more formal English, 'She need not know.'

1 If you **need** something, or **need** to do something, you cannot successfully achieve what you want or live properly without it. *He desperately needed money... These diets provide everything your body needs... I need to make a phone call... A baby does not need to wear shoes until he starts to walk... I need you to do something for me... I need you here, Wally... I need you sane and sober.* ► Also a noun. *Charles has never felt the need to compete with anyone. ...the child who never had his need for attention and importance satisfied. ...the special nutritional needs of the elderly, babies and children.* VB: no cont; V n, V to-inf, V n to-inf, V n adv/prep, V n adj; N-COUNT: usu with supp, oft N to-inf, N *for* n

2 If an object or place **needs** something doing to it, that action must or should be done to improve the object or place, or to improve a situation. If a task **needs** doing, it must or should be done to improve a situation. *The building needs quite a few repairs. ...a garden that needs tidying... The taste of vitamins is not too nice so the flavour sometimes needs to be disguised.* VB: no cont; V n/-ing, V to-inf

3 If there is a **need** for something, that thing would improve a situation or something cannot happen without it. *Mr Forrest believes there is a need for other similar schools throughout Britain... 'I think we should see a specialist.'—'I don't think there's any need for that.'... There's no need for you to stay.* N-SING: usu with supp, oft N *for* n, N to-inf

4 If you say that someone **needn't** do something, you are telling them not to do it, or advising or suggesting that they should not do it. *'I'll put the key in the window.'—'You needn't bother,' he said gruffly... Look, you needn't shout... She need not know I'm here.* ► Also a verb. *Well, for Heaven's sake, you don't need to apologize... Come along, Mother, we don't need to take up any more of Mr Kemp's time.* MODAL: with neg PRAGMATICS; VB: no cont, with neg, V to-inf

5 If you tell someone that they **needn't** do something, or that something **needn't** happen, you are reassuring them that it is not necessary or inevitable, because a situation is not as bad as they might think. *You needn't worry... This needn't take long, Simon... Buying budget-priced furniture needn't mean compromising on quality or style... Loneliness can be horrible, but it need not remain that way... He need never drink again if he doesn't want to... All he need fear is a general postponement of Britain's economic recovery.* ► Also a verb. *He replied, with a reassuring smile, 'Oh, you don't need to worry about them.'... You don't need to be a millionaire to consider having a bank account in Switzerland.* MODAL: with brd-neg PRAGMATICS; VB: no cont, with neg, V to-inf

6 You use **needn't** when you are giving someone permission not to do something. *You needn't come again, if you don't want to... Well, you needn't tell me anything if you don't want to.* ► Also a verb. *You don't need to wait for me... Mommy, you don't need to stay while we talk.* MODAL: with neg PRAGMATICS; VB: no cont, V to-inf

7 If something **need not** be true, it is not necessarily true or not always true; a formal use. *What is right for us need not be right for others... Freedom need not mean independence.* MODAL: with neg

8 If someone **needn't** have done something, it was not necessary or useful for them to do it, although they did it. *She could have made the sandwich herself; her mum needn't have bothered to do anything... I was a little nervous when I announced my engagement to Grace, but I needn't have worried...* MODAL: with neg

We spent a hell of a lot of money that we needn't have spent. ▶ If someone **didn't need to** do something, they needn't have done it. *You didn't need to give me any more money you know, but thank you.* VB: no cont, with neg V to-inf

9 You use **need** in expressions such as **I need hardly say** and **I needn't add** to emphasize to the person you are talking to that they should not be surprised by what you are about to say, because it is a natural consequence of what you have just said. *I needn't add that if you fail to do as I ask, you will suffer the consequences.* ▶ Also a verb. *I hardly need to say that I have never lost contact with him.* MODAL: oft with brd-neg PRAGMATICS VB: no cont V to-inf

10 You can use **need** in expressions such as **'Need I say more'** and **'Need I go on'** when you want to avoid stating an obvious consequence of something you have just said. *Mid-fifties, short black hair, grey moustache, distinctive Russian accent. Need I go on?* MODAL PRAGMATICS

11 People **in need** do not have enough of essential things such as money, food, or good health. *The new Children Act places an enhanced duty on education authorities to provide for children in need... Remember that when both of you were in need, I was the one who loaned you money.* PHRASES usu v-link PHR =needy

12 If someone or something is **in need of** something, they need it or ought to have it. *I was all right but in need of rest... He was badly in need of a shave... Prices start at £15,000 for a small terrace house in need of some modernisation.* PHR n

13 If you say that you will do something, especially an extreme action, **if need be**, or **if needs be**, you mean that you will do if it is necessary. *They will now seek permission to take their case to the House of Lords, and, if need be, to the European Court of Human Rights.* PHR with cl =if necessary

14 You can tell someone that **there's no need** for them to do something as a way of telling them not to do it or telling them to stop doing it, for example because it is unnecessary or unjustified; used in spoken English. *There's no need to call a doctor... There's no need for that kind of language in this magazine... 'I'm going to come with you.'—'Now look, Sue, there's no need.'* oft PHR to-inf, PHR *for* n PRAGMATICS

15 You can say **'Who needs** something?' as a way of emphasizing that you think that this thing is unnecessary or not useful; an informal expression. *With apologies to my old history teacher, who needs history lessons?... Cigarettes, who needs them?* PHR n PRAGMATICS

needful /niːdfʊl/. **Needful** means necessary; an old-fashioned word. *The section of society most needful of such guidance is the young male. ...stoppages for needful rest and recreation.* ADJ-GRADED =required

needle /niːdᵊl/ **needles, needling, needled** ◆◆◇◇◇

1 A **needle** is a small, very thin piece of polished metal which is used for sewing. It has a sharp point at one end and a hole in the other for a thread to go through. N-COUNT

2 Knitting **needles** are thin sticks that are used for knitting. They are usually made of plastic or metal and have a point at one end. N-COUNT: usu supp N

3 A **needle** is a thin hollow metal rod with a sharp point, which forms part of a syringe. It is used to inject a drug into someone's body. N-COUNT

4 A **needle** is a thin solid metal rod with a point which is put into a patient's body during acupuncture. N-COUNT

5 On a record player, the **needle** is the small pointed device that touches the record and picks up the sound signals. *She took the needle off the record and turned the lights out.* N-COUNT =stylus

6 On an instrument which measures something such as speed or weight, the **needle** is the long strip of metal or plastic on the dial that moves backwards and forwards, showing the measurement. *She kept looking at the dial on the boiler. The needle had reached 250 degrees.* N-COUNT

7 The **needles** of a fir or pine tree are its thin, hard, pointed leaves. *The carpet of pine needles was soft underfoot.* N-COUNT: usu pl

8 If someone **needles** you, they annoy you continually, especially by criticizing you. *Blake could see he had needled Jerrold, which might be unwise.* VERB =niggle V n

9 ● **like looking for a needle in a haystack**: see **haystack**. See also **pins and needles**.

needle exchange, needle exchanges; also spelled **needle-exchange**. A **needle exchange** is a place where drug addicts are able to obtain new hypodermic needles in exchange for used ones. Needle exchanges were started in an effort to reduce the spread of HIV and AIDS. *Measures such as needle exchanges and health education schemes had worked extremely successfully. ...needle exchange schemes* N-COUNT

needless /niːdləs/ ◆◇◇◇◇

1 Something that is **needless** is completely unnecessary. *But his death was so needless... 'I have never knowingly exposed any patient to needless risks,' he said.* ♦ **needlessly** *Half a million women die needlessly each year during childbirth... He said something to me so mean, so needlessly cruel.* ADJ-GRADED ADV-GRADED: ADV with v, ADV adj

2 You use **needless to say** when you want to emphasize that what you are about to say is obvious and to be expected in the circumstances. *Our budgie got out of its cage while our cat was in the room. Needless to say, the cat moved quicker than me and caught it.* PHRASE: PHR with cl PRAGMATICS =of course

needlework /niːdᵊlwɜːʳk/

1 **Needlework** is sewing or embroidery that is done by hand. *She did beautiful needlework and she embroidered table napkins.* N-UNCOUNT

2 **Needlework** is the activity of sewing or embroidering. *...watching my mother and grandmothers doing needlework.* N-UNCOUNT =sewing

needn't /niːdᵊnt/. **Needn't** is the usual spoken form of **need not**.

needy /niːdi/ **needier, neediest. Needy** people do not have enough food, medicine, or clothing or an adequate house to live in. *...a multinational force aimed at ensuring that food and medicine get to needy Somalis.* ▶ **The needy** are people who are needy. *There will be efforts to get larger amounts of food to the needy.* ◆◇◇◇◇ ADJ-GRADED: usu ADJ n =impoverished N-PLURAL: *the* N

nefarious /nɪfeəriəs/. If you describe an activity as **nefarious**, you mean that it is wicked and immoral; a literary word. *Why make a whole village prisoner if it was not to some nefarious purpose?* ADJ-GRADED: usu ADJ n =heinous

neg. **Neg.** is a written abbreviation for 'negative'. =negative

negate /nɪgeɪt/ **negates, negating, negated** ◆◇◇◇◇

1 If one thing **negates** another, it causes that other thing to lose the effect or value that it had; a formal use. *These weaknesses negated his otherwise progressive attitude towards the staff.* VERB =nullify ≠confirm V n

2 If someone **negates** something, they say that it does not exist; a formal use. *He warned that to negate the results of elections would only make things worse.* VERB =repudiate ≠affirm V n

negation /nɪgeɪʃᵊn/

1 **Negation** is the act of causing something not to exist, or the state of not existing; a formal use. *It was, in the final analysis, an act of negation rather than creation.* N-UNCOUNT =denial

2 The **negation of** a quality or ideal is its complete opposite or its complete absence; a formal use. *To do nothing would seem to be a negation of what we stand for.* N-SING: N *of* n =denial

3 **Negation** is a person's disagreement with someone or refusal of something; a formal use. *The editor grimaced, gesturing in negation... Irena shook her head, but in bewilderment, not negation.* N-UNCOUNT =contradiction ≠affirmation

negative /negətɪv/ **negatives** ◆◆◆◇◇

1 A fact, situation, or experience that is **negative** is unpleasant, depressing, or harmful. *The news from China is overwhelmingly negative... All this had an extremely negative effect on the criminal justice system.* ♦ **negatively** *This will negatively affect the result over the first half of the year.* ADJ-GRADED ≠positive ADV-GRADED: ADV with v

2 If someone is **negative** or has a **negative** attitude, they consider only the bad aspects of a situation, rather than the good ones. *When asked for your views about your current job, on no account must you be negative about it... Why does the media present such a negative view of this splendid city?* ♦ **negatively** *A few weeks later he said that maybe he viewed all his relationships rather negatively.* ADJ-GRADED ≠constructive ADV-GRADED: usu ADV after v

♦ **negativity** /negətɪvɪti/ *I loathe the negativity. I can't stand people who moan.* N-UNCOUNT

3 A **negative** reply or decision indicates the answer 'no'. *Dr Velayati gave a vague but negative response... Upon a negative decision, the applicant loses the protection offered by Belgian law... The Tory response to that was negative.* ♦ **negatively** *60 percent of the sample answered negatively... Stein shook his head slowly, negatively.* ADJ ≠affirmative; ADV: ADV after v

4 A **negative** is a word, expression, or gesture that means 'no' or 'not'. *In the past we have heard only negatives when it came to following a healthy diet.* N-COUNT

5 In grammar, a **negative** clause contains a word such as 'not', 'never', or 'no-one'. ADJ

6 If a medical test or scientific test is **negative**, it shows no evidence of the medical condition or substance that you are looking for. *So far 57 have taken the test and all have been negative. ...negative test results.* ADJ ≠positive

7 In photography, a **negative** is the image that is first produced when you use a camera, from which the final photograph is developed. The negative of a black-and-white photograph is dark in the places where the photograph is light, and light where the photograph is dark. N-COUNT

8 A **negative** charge or current has the same electrical charge as an electron. *Stimulate the injury or site of greatest pain with a small negative current.* ♦ **negatively** *As these electrons are negatively charged they will attempt to repel each other.* ADJ ≠positive; ADV: ADV -ed

9 A **negative** number, quantity, or measurement is less than zero. *Difficult texts record a positive score and simple ones score negative numbers.* ADJ: usu ADJ n =minus

10 If an answer is **in the negative**, it is 'no' or means 'no'. *The Council answered those questions in the negative... Seventy-nine voted in the affirmative, and none in the negative.* PHRASES PHR after v

11 If a sentence is **in the negative**, it contains a word such as 'not', 'never', or 'no-one'. *'I went' in the negative is 'I did not go'.* v-link PHR

negative equity. If a person with a mortgage on their home has **negative equity**, the amount of money they owe to the mortgage company is greater than the value of their home. N-UNCOUNT

neglect /nɪglekt/ **neglects, neglecting, neglected** ◆◆◇◇◇

1 If you **neglect** someone or something, you fail to look after them properly. *The woman denied that she had neglected her child... Feed plants and they grow, neglect them and they suffer. ...an ancient and neglected church.* ▸ Also a noun. *The town's old quayside is collapsing after years of neglect... Niwano's business began to suffer from neglect.* VERB V n V-ed; N-UNCOUNT ≠attention

2 If you **neglect** someone or something, you fail to give them the degree of attention, recognition, or consideration that they deserve. *He'd given too much to his career, worked long hours, neglected her... If you are not careful, children tend to neglect their homework.* ♦ **neglected** *The fact that she is not coming today makes her grandmother feel lonely and neglected. ... a neglected aspect of London's forgotten history... The journal she had begun lay neglected on her bedside table.* VERB =overlook V n; ADJ-GRADED: v-link ADJ, ADJ n, ADJ after v =uncared-for

3 If you **neglect** to do something you ought to do or **neglect** your duty, you fail to do it. *We often neglect to make proper use of our bodies... They never neglect their duties, and they care for their children conscientiously.* VERB V to-inf V n

4 • **benign neglect**: see **benign**.

neglectful /nɪglektfʊl/

1 If you describe someone as **neglectful**, you think they fail to do everything they should do to look after someone or something properly. *Children who are neglected tend to become neglectful parents.* ADJ-GRADED =uncaring

2 If someone is **neglectful** of something, they do not give it the attention or consideration that it should be given. *Have I been neglectful of my friend, taking him for granted?* ADJ-GRADED: oft v-link ADJ *of* n =careless

negligee /neglɪʒeɪ, AM -ʒeɪ/ **negligees;** also spelled **négligée**. A **negligee** is a woman's dressing gown which is made of very thin fabric. *...a pink satin negligee.* N-COUNT

negligence /neglɪdʒəns/. If someone is guilty of **negligence**, they have failed to do something which they ought to do; a formal word. *The soldiers were ordered to appear before a disciplinary council on charges of negligence.* ◆◇◇◇◇ N-UNCOUNT

negligent /neglɪdʒənt/ ◆◇◇◇◇

1 If someone in a position of responsibility is **negligent**, they do not do something which they ought to do or they fail to provide the care for someone or something they are responsible for. *The jury determined that the airline was negligent in training and supervising the crew... The Council had acted in a negligent manner.* ♦ **negligently** *A manufacturer negligently made and marketed a car with defective brakes.* ADJ-GRADED =neglectful; ADV: ADV with v

2 If you describe a person's movements or manner as **negligent**, you mean they look relaxed and informal; a literary use. *Laura acknowledged this compliment with a negligent wave of her left hand... She stood in the doorway, one hand above her head in a negligent pose.* ♦ **negligently** *He had not moved from his chair at the desk where he slouched, arms negligently spread over his papers.* ADJ-GRADED: usu ADJ n =nonchalant; ADV-GRADED: ADV with v =nonchalantly

negligible /neglɪdʒɪbəl/. An amount or effect that is **negligible** is so small that it is not worth considering or worrying about. *The pay that the soldiers received was negligible... Senior managers are convinced that the strike will have a negligible impact.* ◆◇◇◇◇ ADJ-GRADED =insignificant ≠significant

negotiable /nɪgoʊʃəbəl/ ◆◇◇◇◇

1 Something that is **negotiable** can be changed or agreed when people discuss it. *He warned that his economic programme for the country was not negotiable... The Manor is for sale at a negotiable price.* ADJ ≠fixed

2 Contracts or assets that are **negotiable** can be transferred to another person in exchange for money. *The bonds may no longer be negotiable. ...negotiable bearer bonds.* ADJ

3 An area of land that is **negotiable** is easy to travel across. *Parts of the road had been washed away by streams, but it was negotiable.* ADJ: usu v-link ADJ

negotiate /nɪgoʊʃieɪt/ **negotiates, negotiating, negotiated** ◆◆◆◆◇

1 If people **negotiate** with each other or **negotiate** an agreement, they talk about a problem or a situation such as a business arrangement in order to solve the problem or complete the arrangement. *It is not clear whether the president is willing to negotiate with the democrats... When you have two adversaries negotiating, you need to be on neutral territory... The local government and the army negotiated a truce... Western governments have this week urged him to negotiate and avoid force... The South African president has negotiated an end to white-minority rule... His publishing house had just begun negotiating for her next books... There were reports that three companies were negotiating to market the drug.* V-RECIP V *with* n pl-n V pl-n V n NON-RECIP: V V n V *for* n V to-inf Also V n *with* n

2 If you **negotiate** an area of land, a place, or an obstacle, you successfully travel across it or around it. *Frank Mariano negotiates the desert terrain in his battered pickup... I negotiated the corner on my motorbike and pulled to a stop... I negotiated my way out of the airport and joined the flow of cars.* VERB =navigate V n V *way* prep/adv

negotiating table. If you say that people are at the **negotiating table**, you mean that they are having discussions in order to settle a dispute or reach an agreement. *'We want to settle all matters at the negotiating table,' he said... The decision to return to the negotiating table marks an early victory for trade unions.*  N-SING: usu *the* N

negotiation /nɪgoʊʃieɪʃən/ **negotiations. Negotiations** are formal discussions between people who have different aims or intentions, especially in business or politics, during which they try to reach an agreement. *Warren said, 'We have had meaningful negotiations and I believe we are very close to a deal.'... After 10 years of negotiation, the Senate has ratified the strategic arms reduction treaty.* ◆◆◆◆◇ N-VAR =discussion

negotiator /nɪgoʊʃieɪtər/ **negotiators. Negotiators** are people who take part in political and  N-COUNT

financial negotiations. *American and Soviet arms negotiators have begun meetings at the State Department... Mr Clarke was a tough negotiator with the unions.*

Negress /niːgrəs/ **Negresses.** A **Negress** is a woman with dark skin who comes from Africa or whose ancestors came from Africa; an old-fashioned word that some people find offensive. N-COUNT =black woman

Negro /niːgroʊ/ **Negroes.** A **Negro** is someone with dark skin who comes from Africa or whose ancestors came from Africa; an old fashioned word which some people find offensive. ◆◇◇◇◇ N-COUNT

negroid /niːgrɔɪd/. **Negroid** physical features are those that are typical of black people who come from African countries below the Sahara desert. *...negroid hair.* ADJ: usu ADJ n

neigh /neɪ/ **neighs, neighing, neighed.** When a horse **neighs**, it makes a loud sound with its mouth. *The mare neighed once more, turned and disappeared amongst the trees.* ► Also a noun. *The horse gave a loud neigh.* VERB =whinny V N-COUNT =whinny

neighbour /neɪbəʳ/ **neighbours;** spelled **neighbor** in American English. ◆◆◆◇◇

1 Your **neighbour** is someone who lives near you. *I got chatting with my neighbour in the garden.* N-COUNT: oft poss N

2 You can refer to the person who is standing or sitting next to you as your **neighbour**. *The woman prodded her neighbour and whispered urgently in his ear.* N-COUNT: oft poss N

3 You can refer to something which stands next to something else of the same kind as its **neighbour**. *Each house was packed close behind its neighbour.* N-COUNT: usu poss N

4 A country's **neighbour** is a country that is next to it. *Malaysia, unlike some of its neighbours, is a democracy.* N-COUNT: usu poss N

neighbourhood /neɪbəʳhʊd/ **neighbourhoods;** spelled **neighborhood** in American English. ◆◆◇◇◇

1 A **neighbourhood** is one of the parts of a town where people live. *It seemed like a good neighbourhood to raise my children.* N-COUNT =area

2 The **neighbourhood** of a place or person is the area or the people around them. *He was born and grew up in the Flatbush neighbourhood of Brooklyn... I feel a part of my immediate neighbourhood.* N-COUNT =vicinity

3 **In the neighbourhood of** a number means approximately that number. *He's won in the neighbourhood of four million dollars... Its speed is probably in the neighbourhood of 380mph or even more.* PHRASES PREP: PREP amount =roughly, about

4 A place **in the neighbourhood of** another place is near it. *...the loss of woodlands in the neighbourhood of large towns.* PHR n =close to, by

neighbouring /neɪbərɪŋ/; spelled **neighboring** in American English. **Neighbouring** places or things are near other things of the same kind. *Rwanda is to hold talks with leaders of neighbouring countries next week. ...the hotel's boutique and neighboring shops.* ◆◆◇◇◇ ADJ: ADJ n

neighbourly /neɪbəʳli/; spelled **neighborly** in American English. If the people who live near you are **neighbourly**, they are friendly and helpful. If you live in a **neighbourly** place, it has a friendly atmosphere. *The noise would have provoked alarm and neighbourly concern... The older people had stopped being neighbourly to each other. ...a small, neighbourly seaside resort.* ADJ-GRADED
♦ **neighbourliness** *The head of state said his country had always attached great importance to good neighbourliness.* N-UNCOUNT

neither /naɪðəʳ, niːðəʳ/ ◆◆◆◆◇

1 You use **neither** in front of the first of two or more words or expressions when you are linking two or more things which are not true or do not happen. The other thing, or the last of the other things, is introduced by 'nor'. *Professor Hisamatsu spoke neither English nor German... The play is neither as funny nor as disturbing as Tabori thinks it is.* CONJ-COORD-NEG PRAGMATICS

2 You use **neither** to refer to each of two things or people, when you are making a negative statement that includes both of them. *At first, neither man could speak.* ► Also a quantifier. *Neither of us felt like going out.* ► Also a pronoun. *They both smiled; neither seemed likely to be aware of my absence for long.* DET-NEG QUANT-NEG PRON-NEG

3 If you say that one person or thing does not do something and **neither** does another, what you say is true of all the people or things that you are mentioning. *I never learned to swim and neither did they... Britain does not agree and neither do Denmark, Portugal and Ireland.* CONJ-COORD-NEG PRAGMATICS =nor

4 You use **neither** after a negative statement to emphasize that you are introducing another negative statement; a formal use. *I can't ever recall Dad hugging me. Neither did I sit on his knee.* CONJ-COORD-NEG PRAGMATICS =nor

5 If you say that something is **neither here nor there**, you mean that it does not matter because it is not a relevant point. *'I'd never heard of her before I came here.'—'That is neither here nor there.'... Whether or not he realised the fact was neither here nor there.* PHRASE: v-link PHR

nemesis /nemɪsɪs/. The **nemesis** of a person or thing is a situation, event, or person which causes it to be seriously harmed or destroyed, especially as a punishment or judgement. *He believes AIDS is our collective nemesis... Yet the imminent crisis in its balance of payments may be the President's nemesis.* N-UNCOUNT: oft with poss

neo- /niːoʊ-/. **Neo-** is used with nouns to form adjectives and nouns that refer to modern versions of styles and political groups that existed in the past. *...10ft high neo-Victorian gates... The neo Socialists were a small right wing group.* PREFIX

neoclassical /niːoʊklæsɪkəl/; also spelled **neo-classical**. **Neoclassical** architecture or art dates from the late 18th century and uses designs from Roman and Greek architecture and art. *The building was erected between 1798 and 1802 in the neoclassical style of the time.* ◆◇◇◇◇ ADJ

neolithic /niːəlɪθɪk/. **Neolithic** is used to describe things relating to the period of prehistory when people had started farming but still used stone for their weapons and tools. *...neolithic culture. ...the monument was Stone Age or Neolithic.* ADJ

neologism /niːələdʒɪzəm, niɒl-/ **neologisms.** A **neologism** is a new word or expression in a language, or a new meaning for an existing word or expression; a formal word. *The newspaper used the neologism 'dinks', Double Income No Kids.* N-COUNT =new word

neon /niːɒn/ ◆◇◇◇◇

1 **Neon** lights or signs are made from glass tubes filled with neon gas which produce a bright electric light. *In the city squares the neon lights flashed in turn. ...neon slogans which light up the city by night.* ADJ: ADJ n =fluorescent

2 **Neon** is a gas which occurs in very small amounts in the atmosphere. It is used in glass tubes for lights and illuminated signs. *Inert gases like neon and argon have eight electrons in their outer shell.* N-UNCOUNT

neonatal /niːoʊneɪtəl/. **Neonatal** means relating to the first few days of life of a new born baby. *...the neonatal intensive care unit.* ADJ: ADJ n

neophyte /niːəfaɪt/ **neophytes.** A **neophyte** is someone who is new to a particular activity; a formal word. *...the self-proclaimed political neophyte Ross Perot.* N-COUNT =novice

nephew /nefjuː, nev-/ **nephews.** Someone's **nephew** is the son of their sister or brother. *I am planning a 25th birthday party for my nephew.* ◆◇◇◇◇ N-COUNT: oft poss N

nepotism /nepətɪzəm/. **Nepotism** is using power unfairly in order to get jobs or other benefits for your family or friends; used showing disapproval. *Many will regard his appointment as the kind of nepotism British banking ought to avoid.* N-UNCOUNT PRAGMATICS

nerd /nɜːʳd/ **nerds.** If you say that someone is a **nerd**, you are saying in an unkind way that they are stupid or foolish, especially because they wear unstylish clothes and behave awkwardly in social situations; an informal word. *Mark claimed he was made to look a nerd.* N-COUNT PRAGMATICS

nerve /nɜːʳv/ **nerves, nerving, nerved** ◆◆◆◇◇

1 **Nerves** are long thin fibres that transmit messages between your brain and other parts of your body. *...spinal nerves. ...in cases where the nerve fibres are severed.* N-COUNT

2 If you refer to someone's **nerves**, you mean their ability to cope with problems such as emotional stress, tension, and danger. *Jill's nerves are stretched to breaking point... I can be very patient, and then I can burst if my nerves are worn out.* N-PLURAL: usu poss N

3 You can refer to someone's feelings of anxiety or tension as **nerves**. *I just played badly. It wasn't nerves.* N-PLURAL =nervousness

4 Nerve is the courage that you need in order to do something difficult or dangerous. *The brandy made him choke, but it restored his nerve... He never got up enough nerve to meet me.* N-UNCOUNT =courage

5 If you **nerve** yourself to do something difficult or frightening, you prepare yourself for it by trying to be brave; used in written English. *I nerved myself to face the pain.* VERB =steel V pron-refl to-inf

6 If someone or something **gets on** your **nerves**, they annoy or irritate you; an informal expression. *Lately he's not done a bloody thing and it's getting on my nerves.* PHRASES V inflects

7 If you say that someone **has a nerve** or **has the nerve** to do something, you are criticizing them for doing something which you feel they had no right to do; an informal expression. *He told his critics they had a nerve complaining about Lithuania... He had the nerve to ask me to prove who I was.* V inflects PRAGMATICS

8 If you **hold** your **nerve** or **keep** your **nerve**, you remain calm and determined in a difficult situation. *He held his nerve to beat Australian Sandon Stolle in a five-set thriller on Court One... We need to keep our nerve now.* V inflects =keep your cool

9 If someone **is living on** their **nerves**, they are continually worried and anxious about the circumstances that they are in; used mainly in British English. *Eileen, mother of three, had been living on her nerves for some considerable time.* V inflects

10 If you **lose** your **nerve**, you suddenly panic and become too afraid to do something that you were about to do. *The bomber had lost his nerve and fled.* V inflects =go to pieces, lose your cool

11 If you say that you have **touched a nerve** or **touched a raw nerve**, you mean that you have accidentally upset someone by talking about something that they feel strongly about or are very sensitive about. *Alistair saw Henry shrink, as if the words had touched a nerve... The mere mention of John had touched a very raw nerve indeed.* V inflects

nerve centre, nerve centres; spelled **nerve center** in American English. The **nerve centre** of an organization is the place from where its activities are controlled and where its leaders meet. *...the building that was once the nerve centre of the Communist party. ...the corporation's election night nerve centre.* N-COUNT: usu with poss

nerve ending, nerve endings. Your **nerve endings** are the millions of points on the surface of your body and inside it which send messages to your brain when you feel sensations such as heat, cold, and pain. N-COUNT: usu pl

nerve gas, nerve gases. Nerve gas is a poisonous gas that paralyses or kills people. N-MASS

nerve-racking; also spelled **nerve-wracking**. A **nerve-racking** situation or experience makes you feel very tense and worried. *The women and children spent a nerve-racking day outside waiting while fighting continued around them... It was more nerve-wracking than taking a World Cup penalty.* ADJ-GRADED

nervosa /nɜːʳvoʊsə/. See **anorexia** and **bulimia**.

nervous /nɜːʳvəs/ ◆◆◆◇◇

1 If someone is **nervous**, they are frightened or worried about something that is happening or might happen, and show this in their behaviour. *The party has become deeply nervous about its prospects of winning the next election... She described Mr Hutchinson as nervous and jumpy after his wife's disappearance.* ♦ **nervously** *Brunhilde stood up nervously as the men came into the room... Nervously clutching our glasses of chilled wine, we gathered on the terrace.* ♦ **nervousness** *I smiled warmly so he wouldn't see my nervousness.* ADJ-GRADED: usu v-link ADJ, oft ADJ *about/of*n =jittery ≠calm; ADV-GRADED: ADV with v =uneasily; N-UNCOUNT

2 A **nervous** person is very tense and easily upset. *She was apparently a very nervous woman, and that affected her career.* ADJ-GRADED: usu ADJ n =tense ≠confident

3 A **nervous** illness or condition is one that affects your emotions and your mental state. *The number of nervous disorders was rising in the region... He developed nervous problems after people began repeatedly correcting him.* ADJ: ADJ n

nervous breakdown, nervous breakdowns. A **nervous breakdown** is an illness caused by mental stress. Sufferers become extremely depressed and anxious, and have to be treated by a psychiatrist. *His wife would not be able to cope and might suffer a nervous breakdown.* ◆◇◇◇◇ N-COUNT

nervous system, nervous systems. Your **nervous system** consists of all the nerves in your body together with your brain and spinal cord. It controls your movements and reflexes as well as your thoughts and feelings. ◆◇◇◇◇ N-COUNT

nervous wreck, nervous wrecks. If you say that someone is a **nervous wreck**, you mean that they are extremely nervous or worried about something. *She was a nervous wreck, crying when anyone asked her about her experience.* N-COUNT

nervy /nɜːʳvi/. If someone is **nervy**, their behaviour shows that they are very tense or anxious, or they are the type of person who is easily upset. *Sometimes dad was nice to us, but sometimes he was bad-tempered and nervy... Alan was irritable, and very evidently in a nervy state.* ADJ-GRADED

-ness /-nəs/. **-ness** is added to adjectives to form nouns which often refer to a state or quality. For example, 'sadness' is the state of being sad and 'kindness' is the quality of being kind. *'You're a good lad, Hardcastle,' the doctor said with great seriousness.* SUFFIX

nest /nest/ **nests, nesting, nested** ◆◆◇◇◇

1 A bird's **nest** is the home that it makes to lay its eggs in. *I can see an eagle's nest on the rocks.* N-COUNT: oft poss N

2 When a bird **nests** somewhere, it builds a nest and settles there to lay its eggs. *Some species may nest in close proximity to each other. ...nesting sites.* VERB V V-ing

3 A **nest** is a home that a group of insects or other creatures make in order to live in and give birth to their young in. *Some solitary bees make their nests in burrows in the soil. ...a rat's nest.* N-COUNT: usu poss N

4 You can refer to a place as your **nest** when it is your home or where you feel comfortable and relaxed. *My wife seems to be building a nest of her own at Osborne House... The baby had been asleep in her nest of pink and white blankets.* N-COUNT: usu with poss

5 You can use **nest** to refer to a place where something bad is happening, or to the people there who are behaving in a bad or unpeasant way. *...Biarritz, notorious in those days as a nest of spies... Are you telling me that you've got your own little nest of informers in the Police Department?* N-COUNT: N *of*n

6 See also **crow's nest, love nest.**

7 If you say that someone **is feathering their nest**, you mean they are getting a lot of money out of something, so they can lead a comfortable life. *Mary's much more interested in doing things for other people than feathering her own nest.* PHRASES V and N inflec

8 When children **fly the nest**, they leave their parents' home to live on their own. *When their children had flown the nest, he and his wife moved to a thatched cottage in Dorset.* ● **a hornet's nest**: see **hornet.** V inflects =leave home

nest egg, nest eggs; also spelled **nest-egg**. A **nest egg** is a sum of money that you are saving for a particular purpose; an informal expression. *They have a little nest egg tucked away somewhere for a rainy day.* N-COUNT: usu sing

nestle /nesᵊl/ **nestles, nestling, nestled** ◆◇◇◇◇

1 If you **nestle** or **are nestled** somewhere, you move into a comfortable position, usually by pressing against someone or against something soft. *John took one child into the crook of each arm and let them nestle against him... Jade nestled her first child in her arms.* V-ERG =snuggle V prep V n prep

2 If a building, place, or thing **nestles** or **is nestled** somewhere, it is in that place or position and seems safe or sheltered. *Nearby, nestling in the* V-ERG V prep *hills, was the children's home... She nestled eggs safely in the straw in Jim's basket.* — V n prep

nestling /nestlɪŋ/ **nestlings.** A **nestling** is a young bird that has not yet learnt to fly. *She fluttered around me like a mother bird at her nestlings. ...nestling cuckoos.* — N-COUNT =fledgling

net 1 noun and verb uses

net /net/ **nets, netting, netted** ◆◆◆◇◇

1 **Net** is a kind of cloth that you can see through. It is made of very fine threads woven together so that there are small equal spaces between them. — N-UNCOUNT =netting

2 A **net** is a piece of netting which is used as a protective covering for something, for example to protect vegetables from birds. *I threw aside my mosquito net, jumped out of bed and drew up the blind.* — N-COUNT

3 A **net** is a piece of netting which is used for catching fish, insects, or animals. *Several fishermen sat on wooden barrels, tending their nets.* — N-COUNT

4 If you **net** a fish or other animal, you catch it in a net. *I'm quite happy to net a fish and then let it go... Poachers have been netting salmon to supply the black market.* — VERB =land V n

5 In games such as tennis, the **net** is the piece of netting across the centre of the court which the ball has to go over. — N-COUNT: usu *the* N in sing

6 The **net** on a football or hockey pitch is the framework with netting over it which is attached to the back of the goal. *He let the ball slip through his grasp and into the net.* — N-COUNT: usu *the* N in sing =goal

7 When a football player **nets** a goal, he scores a goal; used in journalism. *Centre half Tiler netted his first goal for the club.* — VERB =score V n Also V

8 If you **net** something, you manage to get it, especially by using skill. *They took to the water intent on netting the £250,000 reward offered for conclusive proof of the monster's existence.* — VERB =get V n

9 When a police operation **nets** a number of people or things, they catch those people or find those things. *Secret investigations have netted ninety staff suspected of fraud and theft... The anti-drug sweep had netted nearly 900 kilogrammes of cocaine.* — VERB V n

10 If you **net** a particular amount of money, you gain it as profit after all expenses have been paid. *Last year he netted a cool 3 million pounds by selling his holdings... Mr Yeltsin's book has already netted a quarter of a million pounds in Western sales.* — VERB =bring in, take V n

11 **The net** is the same as the **Internet**. — N-SING: *the* N

12 See also **netting; safety net.**

13 If you **cast** your **net wider**, you look for or consider a greater variety of things. *The security forces are casting their net wider.* — PHRASES V and N inflect

14 If criminals **slip through the net**, they avoid being caught by the system or trap that was meant to catch them. *Officials fear some of the thugs identified by British police may have slipped through the net.* — V inflects

15 You use **slip through the net** or **fall through the net** to describe a situation where people are not properly cared for by the system that is intended to help them. *And a number of African countries, too, are slipping through the net... The existence of more than one agency with power to intervene can lead to children falling through the net.* — V inflects

net 2 adjective and adverb uses

net /net/; also spelled **nett** in British English. ◆◆◆◇◇

1 A **net** amount is one which remains when everything that should be subtracted from it has been subtracted. *...arise in sales and net profit... At the year end, net assets were £18 million... What you actually receive is net of deductions for the airfare and administration.* ▶ Also an adverb. *Balances of £5,000 and above will earn 11 per cent gross, 8.25 per cent net. ...a first year profit of around £50,0000 net... All bank and building society interest is paid net.* — ADJ: ADJ n, v-link ADJ *of* n ≠gross; ADV: amount ADV, ADV after v

2 The **net** weight of something is its weight without its container or the material that has been used to wrap it. *...350 mg net weight.* — ADJ: ADJ n

3 A **net** result is a final result after all the details have been considered or included. *We have a net gain of nearly 50 seats, the biggest for any party in Scotland... We will be a net exporter of motor cars in just a few years' time.* — ADJ: ADJ n =overall

netball /netbɔːl/. In Britain and some other countries, **netball** is a game played by two teams of seven players, usually women. Each team tries to score goals by throwing a ball through a net on the top of a pole at each end of the court. — N-UNCOUNT

net curtain, net curtains. In British English, **net curtains** are pieces of lacy material that people hang in their windows. They allow you to see out but others can not see through them into your house. — N-COUNT: usu pl

nether /neðəʳ/. **Nether** means the lower part of a thing or place; an old-fashioned word. *He was escorted back to the nether regions of Main Street.* — ADJ: ADJ n

netherworld /neðəʳwɜːʳld/. If you refer to a place as a **netherworld**, you mean that it is gloomy and dangerous and full of poverty and deprivation. *...a London netherworld of criminals... Waits sang about the boozy netherworld of urban America.* — N-SING: usu with supp

nett /net/. See **net**.

netting /netɪŋ/. **Netting** is a kind of material made of pieces of thread or metal wires. These are woven together to create so that there are equal spaces between them. *...mosquito netting. ...wire netting.* — N-UNCOUNT: oft supp N

nettle /netᵊl/ **nettles, nettling, nettled** ◆◇◇◇◇

1 **Nettles** are wild plants with spiky leaves covered with fine hairs, that often sting you when you touch them. *The nettles stung their legs. ...numerous clumps of stinging nettles dotted across the meadow.* — N-COUNT

2 If you **are nettled** by something, you are annoyed or offended by it. *He was nettled by her manner... It was the suggestion that he might alter course to win an election that really nettled him.* — VERB *be* V-ed V n

3 If you **grasp the nettle**, you deal with a problem, or do something that is unpleasant, quickly and in a determined way; used mainly in British English. *Some industrialists believe the government should grasp the nettle of devaluation before the referendum takes place.* — PHRASE: V inflects, oft PHR *of* n/-ing

network /netwɜːʳk/ **networks, networking, networked** ◆◆◆◆◇

1 A **network** of lines, roads, veins, or other long thin things is a large number of them which cross each other or meet at many points. *...Strasbourg, with its rambling network of medieval streets... The uterus is supplied with a rich network of blood vessels and nerves.* — N-COUNT: usu N *of* n

2 A **network** of people or institutions is a large number of them that have a connection with each other and work together as a system. *Distribution of the food is going ahead using a network of local church people and other volunteers... He is keen to point out the benefits which the family network can provide.* • See also **old-boy network**. — N-COUNT: usu supp N, N *of* n

3 A particular **network** is a system of things which are connected and which operate together. For example, a **computer network** consists of a number of computers that are part of the same system. *...a computer network with 154 terminals... Huge sections of the rail network are out of action.* • See also **neural network**. — N-COUNT: oft n N =system

4 A radio or television **network** is a company or group of companies that broadcast radio or television programmes throughout an area. *An American network says it has obtained the recordings. ...Fuji Television Network, a highly successful commercial station.* — N-COUNT: usu supp N =station

5 When a television or radio programme **is networked**, it is broadcast at the same time by several different television companies. *Lumsdon would like to see his programme sold and networked... He had once had his own networked chat show.* — VB: usu passive =broadcast *be* V-ed V-ed

networking /netwɜːʳkɪŋ/ ◆◇◇◇◇

1 **Networking** is the process of establishing business contacts, often through social activities. *If executives fail to exploit the opportunities of networking they risk being left behind.* — N-UNCOUNT

2 You can refer to the things associated with a computer system or the process of establishing such a system as **networking**. *Managers have learned to grapple with networking, artificial intelligence, computer-aided engineering and manufacturing. ...computer and networking equipment.* N-UNCOUNT =interconnection

neural /njʊərəl, AM nʊr-/. **Neural** means relating to a nerve or to the nervous system; a technical term in biology. *It handles information about colour, form and motion using separate neural pathways in the brain.* ◆◇◇◇◇ ADJ

neuralgia /njʊəræld͡ʒə, AM nʊr-/. **Neuralgia** is very severe pain along the whole length of a nerve caused when the nerve is damaged or not working properly; a medical term. *The plant acts as a sedative in treating neuralgia.* N-UNCOUNT

neural network, neural networks. In computing, a **neural network** is a program or system which is modelled on the human brain and is designed to imitate the brain's method of functioning, particularly the process of learning. N-COUNT

neuro- /njʊəroʊ-, AM nʊroʊ-/. **Neuro** is used to form words that refer or relate to a nerve or the nervous system. *...Karl Pribram, the well-known neuro-scientist. ...disorders of the neuromuscular system.* PREFIX

neurological /njʊərəlɒd͡ʒɪkᵊl, AM nʊr-/. **Neurological** means related to the nervous system; a medical term. *...neurological disorders such as Parkinson's disease.* ◆◇◇◇◇ ADJ: ADJ n =nervous

neurology /njʊərɒləd͡ʒi, AM nʊr-/. **Neurology** is the study of the structure, function, and diseases of the nervous system; a medical term. *He trained in neurology at the National Hospital for Nervous Diseases.* ♦ **neurologist, neurologists** *...Dr Simon Shorvon, consultant neurologist of the Chalfont Centre for Epilepsy.* N-UNCOUNT; N-COUNT

neuron /njʊərɒn, AM nʊr-/ **neurons;** also spelled **neurone**. A **neuron** is a cell which is part of the nervous system. Neurons send messages to and from the brain; a technical term in biology. *Information is transferred along each neuron by means of an electrical impulse.* • See also **motor neurone disease**. ◆◇◇◇◇ N-COUNT

neurosis /njʊəroʊsɪs, AM nʊr-/ **neuroses** /njʊəroʊsiːz, AM nʊr-/. **Neurosis** is a mental condition which causes people to have unreasonable fears and worries over a long period of time. *He was anxious to the point of neurosis... She got a neurosis about chemicals and imagined them everywhere doing her harm.* ◆◇◇◇◇ N-VAR

neurotic /njʊərɒtɪk, AM nʊr-/ **neurotics.** If you say that someone is **neurotic**, you mean that they are always unreasonably frightened or worried about something that you consider unimportant. *He was almost neurotic about being followed... There are also unpleasant brain effects such as anxiety and neurotic behaviour.* ► A **neurotic** is someone who is neurotic. *These patients are not neurotics.* ◆◇◇◇◇ ADJ-GRADED =paranoid; N-COUNT

neuter /njuːtəʳ, AM nuːt-/ **neuters, neutering, neutered**

1 When an animal **is neutered**, its reproductive organs are removed. *We ask the public to have their dogs neutered and keep them under close supervision.* VB: usu passive have n V-ed

2 To **neuter** an organization, group, or person means to make them powerless and ineffective; used mainly in journalism, especially British journalism. *...the Government's 'hidden agenda' to neuter local authorities... Their air force had been neutered before the work began.* VERB Vn

3 In some languages, a **neuter** noun, pronoun, or adjective has a different form from a masculine or feminine one, or behaves in a different way. ADJ

neutral /njuːtrəl, AM nuːt-/ **neutrals** ◆◆◇◇◇

1 If a person or country adopts a **neutral** position or remains **neutral**, they do not support anyone in a disagreement, war, or contest. *Let's meet on neutral territory... Those who had decided to remain neutral in the struggle now found themselves required to take sides.* ► A **neutral** is someone who is neutral. *It was a good game to watch for the neutrals.* ♦ **neutrality** /njuːtrælɪti, AM nuːt-/ *...a reputation for political neutrality and impartiality.* ADJ-GRADED; N-COUNT; N-UNCOUNT

2 If someone speaks in a **neutral** voice or if their facial expression is **neutral**, they do not show what they are thinking or feeling. *Isabel put her magazine down and said in a neutral voice, 'You're very late, darling.'... He told her about the death, describing the events in as neutral a manner as he could.* ♦ **neutrality** *I noticed, behind the neutrality of his gaze, a deep weariness.* ADJ-GRADED: usu ADJ n; N-UNCOUNT

3 If you say that something is **neutral**, you mean it does not have any effect on other things because it lacks any significant qualities of its own, or it is an equal balance of two or more different qualities, amounts, or ideas. *Three in every five interviewed felt that the Budget was neutral and they would be no better off... Labour's tax and benefit plans, while neutral on the surface, are likely to be deflationary.* ADJ-GRADED

4 If someone uses **neutral** language, they choose words which do not indicate that they approve or disapprove of something. *Both sides had agreed to use neutral terms in their references to each other, avoiding controversial ones... He had departed from his prepared testimony, which was considered to be neutral.* ADJ-GRADED

5 **Neutral** is the position between the gears of a vehicle such as car, in which the gears are not connected to the engine. *Graham put the van in neutral and jumped out into the road.* N-UNCOUNT: oft *into/in* N

6 In an electrical device or system, the **neutral** wire is one of the three wires needed to complete the circuit so that the current can flow. The other two wires are called the earth wire and the live or positive wire. ADJ

7 **Neutral** is used to describe things that are a pale, indistinct colour such as light grey or beige, or things that contain no colour at all. *At the horizon the land mass becomes a continuous pale neutral grey, almost blending with the sky... Mary suggests using a neutral lip pencil.* COLOUR

8 In physics, **neutral** is used to describe things such as atomic particles that have neither a positive nor a negative charge. *A neutron is simply a neutral particle in the nucleus of an atom.* ADJ

9 In chemistry, **neutral** is used to describe things that are neither acidic nor alkaline. *Pure water is neutral with a pH of 7.* ADJ-GRADED

neutralize /njuːtrəlaɪz, AM nuːt-/ **neutralizes, neutralizing, neutralized;** also spelled **neutralise** in British English. ◆◇◇◇◇

1 To **neutralize** something means to prevent it from having any effect or from working properly. *The US is trying to neutralize the resolution in the UN Security Council... The intruder smashed a window to get in and then neutralized the alarm system.* ♦ **neutralization** /njuːtrəlaɪzeɪʃᵊn, AM nuːt-/ *...the sale or neutralization of the suspected nuclear site.* VERB =incapacitate Vn; N-UNCOUNT: usu N *of* n

2 When a chemical substance **neutralizes** an acid, it reduces the acidic level; a technical use. *Antacids are alkaline and they relieve pain by neutralizing acid in the contents of the stomach.* VERB Vn

neutron /njuːtrɒn, AM nuːt-/ **neutrons.** A **neutron** is an atomic particle that has no electrical charge. *Each atomic cluster is made up of neutrons and protons.* ◆◇◇◇◇ N-COUNT

neutron bomb, neutron bombs. A **neutron bomb** is a nuclear weapon that is designed to kill people and animals without a large explosion and without destroying buildings or causing serious radioactive pollution. N-COUNT

neutron star, neutron stars. A **neutron star** is a star that has collapsed under the weight of its own gravity. N-COUNT

never /nevəʳ/ ◆◆◆◆◆

1 **Never** means at no time in the past or at no time in the future. *I have never lost the weight I put on in my teens... Never had he been so free of worry... That was a mistake. We'll never do it again... Never say that. Never, do you hear?... He was never really healthy... This is never to happen again.* ADV-NEG: ADV before v, ADV group/to-inf

2 **Never** means not in any circumstances at all. *I would never do anything to hurt him... Even if you are desperate to get married, never let it show... Divorce is never easy for children... The golden rule is never to clean a valuable coin.* ADV-NEG: ADV before v, ADV group/to-inf

3 **Never ever** is an emphatic expression for 'never'; used mainly in spoken English. *I never, ever sit around thinking, 'What shall I do next?'... He's vowed never ever to talk about anything personal in public, ever again.* PHRASE: PHR before v, *be* PHR group PRAGMATICS

4 **Never** is used to refer to the past and means 'not'; used mainly in spoken English. *He never achieved anything... He waited until all the luggage was cleared, but Paula's never appeared... I never knew the lad... I'd never have dreamt of doing such a thing.* ADV-NEG

5 You say **'never!'** to indicate how surprised or shocked you are by something that someone has just said. EXCLAM PRAGMATICS

6 If you say **'Well, I never'**, you are indicating that you are very surprised about something that you have just seen or found out; an informal expression. *'What were you up to there?'—'I was head of the information department.'—'Well I never!'* EXCLAM PRAGMATICS =blow me

7 If you say that something **will never do** or **would never do**, you are saying, often humorously, that you think it is not appropriate or not suitable in some way. *It would never do to have Henry there in her apartment... I don't think it is an example of bad writing myself, otherwise I'd be agreeing with Leavis, and that would never do.* PHRASE: oft *it* PHR to-inf

8 • **never fear**: see **fear**. • **never mind**: see **mind**.

never-ending. If you describe something bad or unpleasant as **never-ending**, you are emphasizing that it seems to last a very long time. *...a never-ending series of scandals rocking the House of Windsor... The spiral of terrorism becomes never-ending.* ◆◇◇◇◇ ADJ PRAGMATICS =interminable

never-never land. If you refer to a place or way of life as **never-never land**, you mean that it is not like anything that exists in the real world. In the imaginary never-never land, everything is pleasant and people do not have any problems. An informal expression. *We became suspended in some stately never-never land of pleasure, luxury and idleness.* N-UNCOUNT: also *a* N

nevertheless /nevəʳðəles/. You use **nevertheless** when saying something that contrasts with what has just been said; a formal word. *Although the market has been flattened, residential property costs remain high. Nevertheless, the fall-off in demand has had an impact on resale values... There had been no indication of any loss of mental faculties. His whole life had nevertheless been clouded with a series of illnesses.* ◆◆◆◇◇ ADV: ADV with cl PRAGMATICS =nonetheless

new /njuː, AM nuː/ **newer, newest** ◆◆◆◆◆

1 Something that is **new** has been recently created, built, or invented or is in the process of being created, built, or invented. *They've just opened a new hotel in the Stoke area... The new invention ensures the beer keeps a full, frothy head. ...the introduction of new drugs to suppress the immune system... Their epic fight is the subject of a new film... These ideas are nothing new in America.* ♦ **newness** *The board acknowledges problems which arise from the newness of the approach.* ADJ-GRADED; N-UNCOUNT

2 Something that is **new** has not been used or owned by anyone. *That afternoon she went out and bought a new dress... There are many boats, new and used, for sale... They cost nine pounds new, three pounds secondhand.* ADJ

3 You use **new** to describe something which has replaced another thing, for example because you no longer have the old one, or it no longer exists, or it is no longer useful. *Under the new rules, some factories will cut emissions by as much as 90 percent... I had been in my new job only a few days... I had to find somewhere new to live... Rachel has a new boyfriend... They told me I needed a new battery.* ADJ

4 **New** is used to describe something that has only recently been discovered or noticed. *The new planet is about ten times the size of the earth.* ADJ: usu ADJ n

5 A **new** day or year is the beginning of the next day or year. *The start of a new year is a good time to reflect on the many achievements of the past... The next election is for the government to take us into the new century.* ADJ: ADJ n

6 **New** is used to describe someone or something that has recently acquired a particular status or position. *...the usual exhaustion of a new mother... The Association gives a free handbook to all new members.* ADJ: ADJ n

7 If you are **new** to a situation or place, or if the situation or place is **new** to you, you have not previously seen it or had any experience of it. *She wasn't new to the company... His name was new to me then and it stayed in my mind... I'm new here and all I did was follow orders.* ADJ-GRADED: v-link ADJ, oft ADJ *to* n

8 **New** potatoes, carrots, or peas are produced early in the season for such vegetables and are usually small with a sweet flavour. ADJ: ADJ n

9 See also **brand-new**. • **as good as new**: see **good**. • to **turn over a new leaf**: see **leaf**. • **a new lease of life**: see **lease**. • **pastures new**: see **pasture**.

new- /njuː-, AM nuː-/. **New-** combines with the past participle of some verbs to form adjectives which indicate that an action has been done or completed very recently. *He loved the smell of new-mown grass... Gerald treasures his new-won independence.* COMB in ADJ: usu ADJ n

New Age. **New Age** is used to refer to activities such as meditation, astrology, and alternative medicine, or to describe the people who are involved in these activities. *She was involved in many New Age activities such as yoga and healing... In the US, New Age is big business.* ◆◇◇◇◇ N-UNCOUNT: usu N n

New Age traveller, New Age travellers. In Britain, **New Age travellers** are people who live in tents and caravans and travel from place to place, and who reject many of the values of modern society. N-COUNT: usu pl

new blood. If people talk about bringing **new blood** into an organization or sports team, they are referring to new people who are likely to improve the organization or team. *There should be major changes in the government to bring in new blood... That's what we need, some new blood in the team.* N-UNCOUNT

newborn /njuːbɔːʳn, AM nuː-/ **newborns;** also spelled **new-born** or **new born.** ◆◇◇◇◇

1 A **newborn** baby or animal is one that has just been born. *This equipment has saved the lives of a number of new born children. ...new born lambs.* ▸ **The newborn** are babies or animals who are newborn. *Mild jaundice in the newborn is common and often clears without treatment.* ADJ: usu ADJ n; N-PLURAL: *the* N

2 A **newborn** is a baby that has just been born; a medical term. *...an instrument for taking a sample of blood from a newborn.* N-COUNT

3 Writers sometimes use **newborn** to describe things that have just come into existence. *The soft wind breathed their names to the newborn grass... Microbiology was a newborn science.* ADJ: ADJ n

new broom, new brooms. Someone who has just started a new job and who is expected to make a lot of changes can be referred to as a **new broom**; used mainly in journalism. *The company seemed set to make a fresh start under a new broom.* N-COUNT: usu sing

newcomer /njuːkʌməʳ, AM nuː-/ **newcomers** ◆◆◇◇◇

1 A **newcomer** is a person who has recently arrived in a place, joined an organization, or started a new activity. *He must be a newcomer to town and he obviously didn't understand our local customs... The candidates are both relative newcomers to politics.* N-COUNT

2 A **newcomer** is something which has not existed before or been available before. *The company's latest newcomer is a 4 x 4 estate with a 2.2 litre petrol engine. ...last year's aggressive price slashing by campsite newcomer, Airtours.* N-COUNT

new face, new faces. Someone who is new in a particular public role can be referred to as a **new face**; used mainly in journalism. *All together there are six new faces in the cabinet.* ◆◇◇◇◇ N-COUNT

new-fangled /njuː fæŋgəld, AM nuː -/; also spelled **newfangled**. If someone describes an idea or a piece of equipment as **new-fangled**, they dislike it because they find it too complicated or think it is unnecessary; an old-fashioned and informal word. *Mr Goss does not believe in any of this 'new-fangled nonsense' about lean meat. ...a newfangled tax structure.* — ADJ: ADJ n; PRAGMATICS

new-found; also spelled **newfound**. A **new-found** quality, ability, or attribute is one that you have discovered recently. *Juliana was brimming over with new-found confidence... The fall of the Ceausescu government brought newfound freedom to millions in Romania.* — ◆◇◇◇◇ ADJ: ADJ n

newly /njuːli, AM nuːli/. **Newly** is used before a past participle or an adjective to indicate that a particular action is very recent, or that a particular state of affairs has very recently begun to exist. *She was young at the time, and newly married. ...the newly independent countries of Africa and Asia.* — ◆◆◆◇◇ ADV: ADV -ed/adj =recently

newlywed /njuːliwed, AM nuː-/ **newlyweds;** also spelled **newly-wed**. **Newlyweds** are a man and woman who have very recently got married to each other. *Lavalais raised his glass to propose a toast to the newlyweds.* — N-COUNT: usu pl

new man, new men. If you describe someone as a **new man**, you are saying, often humorously, that he has modern ideas about the relations between men and women, and believes that men should share in domestic tasks and caring for children; used mainly in British English. *Sarah says I only change nappies when we have visitors. It is easy to be a new man in public; in private it's hard work.* — N-COUNT

new moon, new moons. A **new moon** is the moon when it appears as a thin crescent shape at the start of its four-week cycle of appearing to become larger and then smaller. The **new moon** is also the time of the month when the moon appears in this way. *...the pale crescent of a new moon... The new moon was the occasion of festivals of rejoicing in Egypt.* — N-COUNT: usu sing

news /njuːz, AM nuːz/ — ◆◆◆◆◆

1 **News** is information about a recently changed situation or a recent event. *We waited and waited for news of him... They still haven't had any news about when they'll be able to go home... I wish I had better news for you... He's thrilled to bits at the news.* — N-UNCOUNT: oft N prep

2 **News** is information that is published in newspapers and broadcast on radio and television about recent events in the country or world or in a particular area of activity. *Foreign News is on Page 16... We'll also have the latest sports news... The announcement was made at a news conference... Those are some of the top stories in the news.* — N-UNCOUNT: also the N

3 **The news** is a television or radio broadcast which consists of information about recent events in the country or the world. *I heard all about the bombs on the news. ...the six o'clock news.* — N-SING: the N

4 **News** is sometimes used in the names of newspapers. *...the New York Daily News.* — N-IN-NAMES

5 If you say that someone or something is **news**, you mean that they are considered to be interesting and important at the moment, and that people want to hear about them on the radio and television and in newspapers; an informal use. *A murder was big news... For the first time since 1959, Tibet was headline news again.* — N-UNCOUNT: usu supp N

6 If you say that something is **bad news**, you mean that it will cause you trouble or problems. If you say that something is **good news**, you mean that it will be useful or helpful to you. *The drop in travel is bad news for the airline industry... This new attitude is good news to AIDS activists.* — PHRASES: usu v-link PHR, usu PHR *for/to* n

7 If you say that something **is news to** you, you mean that you did not previously know what you have just been told, especially when you are surprised or annoyed about it. *I'd certainly tell you if I knew anything, but I don't. What you're saying is news to me.* — V inflects, PHR n

news agency, news agencies. A **news agency** is an organization that gathers news stories from a particular country or from all over the world and supplies them to journalists. *A correspondent for Reuters news agency says he saw a number of demonstrators being beaten.* — ◆◆◇◇◇ N-COUNT =press agency

newsagent /njuːzeɪdʒənt, AM nuːz-/ **newsagents** — ◆◇◇◇◇

1 In Britain, a **newsagent** or a **newsagent's** is a shop where newspapers and magazines, as well as sweets, cigarettes, and stationery, are sold. *I went into our local newsagent's.* — N-COUNT: oft *the* N =paper shop

2 In Britain, a **newsagent** is a shopkeeper who sells newspapers and magazines, as well as sweets, cigarettes, and stationery. *The newsagent said, 'Bye, Keith! See you later.'* — N-COUNT

newscast /njuːzkɑːst, AM nuːzkæst/ **newscasts.** A **newscast** is a news programme that is broadcast on the radio or on television; used mainly in American English. — ◆◇◇◇◇ N-COUNT

newscaster /njuːzkɑːstəʳ, AM nuːzkæstəʳ/ **newscasters.** A **newscaster** is a person who reads the news on the radio or on television. — ◆◆◆◆◆ N-COUNT =newsreader

news conference, news conferences. A **news conference** is a meeting held by a famous or important person in which they answer journalists' questions. — ◆◆◇◇◇ N-COUNT =press conference

newsflash /njuːzflæʃ, AM nuːz-/ **newsflashes;** also spelled **news flash**. A **newsflash** an important item of news that television or radio companies broadcast as soon as they receive it, often interrupting other programmes to do so. *We interrupt our programmes for a newsflash.* — N-COUNT

newsletter /njuːzletəʳ, AM nuːz-/ **newsletters;** also spelled **news letter**. A **newsletter** is one or more printed sheets of paper containing information about an organization that is sent regularly to its members. *HDRA now has around 18,000 members who receive a quarterly newsletter.* — ◆◇◇◇◇ N-COUNT =bulletin

newsman /njuːzmən, AM nuːz-/ **newsmen.** A **newsman** is a reporter for a newspaper or a television or radio news programme. *As the pictures flashed on the screen, the newsman continued talking.* — N-COUNT

newspaper /njuːspeɪpəʳ, AM nuːz-/ **newspapers** — ◆◆◆◆◇

1 A **newspaper** is a publication consisting of a number of large sheets of folded paper, on which news, advertisements, and other information is printed. *He was carrying a newspaper... They read their daughter's allegations in the newspaper. ...a Sunday newspaper feature about AIDS in America.* — N-COUNT

2 A **newspaper** is an organization that produces a newspaper. *It is Britain's fastest growing national daily newspaper... Alexander Lazarus is a food critic for the newspaper.* — N-COUNT

3 **Newspaper** consists of pieces of old newspapers, especially when they are being used for another purpose such as wrapping things up. *He found two pots, each wrapped in newspaper.* — N-UNCOUNT

newspaperman /njuːspeɪpəʳmæn, AM nuːz-/ **newspapermen.** A **newspaperman** is a reporter, especially a man, who works for a newspaper. — N-COUNT =newsman

newsprint /njuːzprɪnt, AM nuːz-/

1 **Newsprint** is the cheap fairly rough paper on which newspapers are printed. — N-UNCOUNT

2 **Newsprint** is the text that is printed in newspapers. *The papers are still devoting pages of newsprint to the Gulf Crisis.* — N-UNCOUNT

3 **Newsprint** is the ink which is used to print newspapers and magazines. *They get their hands covered in newsprint.* — N-UNCOUNT

newsreader /njuːzriːdəʳ, AM nuːz-/ **newsreaders.** A **newsreader** is a person who reads the news on the radio or on television; used mainly in British English. — N-COUNT =newscaster

newsreel /njuːzriːl, AM nuːz-/ **newsreels.** A **newsreel** is a short film of national or international news events. In the past newsreels were made for showing in cinemas. —  N-COUNT: oft N n

news release, news releases. A **news release** is a written statement about a matter of public interest which is given to the press by an organization concerned with the matter; used mainly in American English. *In a news release, the company said it had experienced severe financial problems.* N-COUNT =press release

newsroom /njuːzruːm, AM nuːz-/ **newsrooms.** A **newsroom** is an office in a newspaper, radio, or television organization, where news reports are written and edited before they are printed or broadcast. ◆◇◇◇◇ N-COUNT

news-sheet, news-sheets. A **news-sheet** is a small newspaper that is usually printed and distributed in small quantities by a local political or social organization. *...a copy of an illicit Communist news-sheet.* N-COUNT

newsstand /njuːzstænd, AM nuːz-/ **newsstands;** also spelled **news-stand**. A **newsstand** is a movable stall in the street, or a stall at a railway station, at which newspapers and magazines are sold. *Eight new national newspapers have appeared on the newsstands since 1981.* N-COUNT

newsworthy /njuːzwɜːʳði, AM nuːz-/. An event, fact, or person that is **newsworthy**, is considered to be interesting enough to be reported in newspapers or on the radio or television. *The number of deaths makes the story newsworthy... This situation might develop into an even more newsworthy item if the police were involved.* ADJ-GRADED

newt /njuːt, AM nuːt/ **newts.** A **newt** is a small creature which looks like a lizard and lives partly on land and partly in water. *This wet area also attracts frogs, toads and newts.* N-COUNT

New Testament. **The New Testament** is the part of the Bible that deals with the life and teachings of Jesus Christ and with Christianity in the early Church. ◆◇◇◇◇ N-PROPER: *the* N

new town, new towns. A **new town** is a town that has been planned and built as a single project, including houses, shops, and factories, rather than one that has developed gradually; used mainly in British English. *...Basildon New Town.* ◆◇◇◇◇ N-COUNT: oft in names

new wave, new waves. In the arts or in politics, a **new wave** is a group or movement that deliberately introduces new or unconventional ideas instead of using traditional ones. *...the new wave of satirical comedy... Tatum's friend asked Kevin if he liked New Wave music.* ◆◇◇◇◇ N-COUNT

New World. **The New World** is used to refer to the continents of North and South America. *...the massive growth in imports of good wines from the New World and Australasia.* ◆◆◇◇◇ N-PROPER: *the* N

New Year ◆◆◇◇◇

1 **New Year** or **the New Year** is the time when people celebrate the start of a year. *Happy New Year, everyone... The restaurant was closed over the New Year... He returned home each year to celebrate Christmas and New Year with his family.* N-UNCOUNT: also *the* N

2 **The New Year** is the first few weeks of a year. *Isabel was expecting their baby in the New Year... The oil shortages could lead the government to raise prices before the New Year.* N-SING: *the* N

New Year's. In American English, **New Year's** is another name for **New Year's Day** or **New Year's Eve**; an informal expression. ◆◇◇◇◇ N-UNCOUNT

New Year's Day. **New Year's Day** is the first day of the year. In Western countries this is the 1st of January. *On New Year's Day in 1974, I started keeping a journal.* ◆◇◇◇◇ N-UNCOUNT

New Year's Eve. **New Year's Eve** is the last day of the year, the day before New Year's Day. *On New Year's Eve I usually give a party, which is always chaotic.* ◆◇◇◇◇ N-UNCOUNT

New Year's resolution, New Year's resolutions; also spelled **New Year resolution**. If you make a **New Year's resolution**, you make a decision at the beginning of a year to start doing something or to stop doing something. *She made a New Year's resolution to get fit.* N-COUNT

New Zealander /njuː ziːləndəʳ, AM nuː -/ **New Zealanders.** A **New Zealander** is a citizen of New Zealand, or a person of New Zealand origin. ◆◆◆◆◇ N-COUNT

next /nekst/ ◆◆◆◆◆

1 The **next** period of time, event, person, or thing is the one that comes immediately after the present one or after the previous one. *I got up early the next morning. ...the next available flight... Who will be the next prime minister?... I want my next child born at home... Many senior citizens have very few visitors from one week to the next... And then Captain Charles sings, 'Don't ever laugh when a hearse goes by or you will be the next to die.'* ORD

2 You use **next** in expressions such as **next Friday**, **next day** and **next year** to refer, for example, to the Friday, day, or year which follows immediately after the present one or after the previous one. *Let's plan a big night next week... He retires next January... Next day the European Community summit strengthened their ultimatum.* ► Also an adjective. *I shall be 26 years old on Friday next.* ► Also a pronoun. *He predicted that the region's economy would grow by about six per cent both this year and next.* DET; ADJ: n ADJ; PRON

3 The **next** place or person is the one that is nearest to you or that is the first one that you come to. *Grace sighed so heavily that Trish could hear it in the next room... The man in the next chair was asleep... Stop at the next corner. I'm getting out.* ADJ: det ADJ

4 The thing that happens **next** is the thing that happens immediately after something else. *Next, close your eyes then screw them up tight... I don't know what to do next... The news is next.* ADV: ADV with cl, ADV after v, *be* ADV

5 When you **next** do something, you do it for the first time since you last did it. *I next saw him at his house in Berkshire... Maserati's engineers asked me some penetrating questions when we next met.* ADV: ADV before v

6 You use **next** to say that something has more of a particular quality than all other things except one. For example, the thing that is **next** best is the one that is the best except for one other thing. *The one thing he didn't have was a son. I think he's felt that a grandson is the next best thing... At least three times more daffodils are grown than in Holland, the next largest grower.* ADV: ADV adj-superl =second

7 You use **after next** in expressions such as **the week after next** to refer to a period of time after the next one. For example, when it is May, the month after next is July. *...the party's annual conference, to be held in Bournemouth the week after next.* PHRASES n PHR

8 If you say that you do something or experience something as much **as the next** person, you mean that you are no different from anyone else in the respect mentioned. *I enjoy pleasure as much as the next person... I'm as ambitious as the next man. I'd like to manage at the very highest level.* *as* group PHR

9 In spoken English, you can say **the next thing** I **knew** to suggest that a new situation which you are describing was surprising because it happened very suddenly; an informal use. *I had leaned over to pick up some change, and the next thing I know I felt this terrible pain in my ankle.* V inflects

10 If one thing is **next to** another thing, it is at the other side of it. *She sat down next to him on the sofa. ...at the southern end of the Gaza Strip next to the Egyptian border... The car was parked in the small weedy lot next to the hotel.* PREP =beside

11 You use **next to** in order to give the most important aspect of something when comparing it with another aspect. *Her children were the number two priority in her life next to her career... Next to the expense of cashiers, pricing items is one of the costliest labor costs of grocery retailers.* PREP =after

12 You use **next to** before a negative, or a word that suggests something negative, to mean almost, but not completely. *Johnson still knew next to nothing about tobacco... Last year a Food Commission report revealed that most pre-prepared weight loss products are next to useless.* PHR after v, v-link PHR, PHR *nothing*/adj =almost

next door ◆◆◇◇◇

1 If a room or building is **next door**, it is the next one to the right or left. *I went next door to the bathroom... She was next door at the time. ...the old lady who lived next door... The flat next door was empty.* ► Also an adjective. *She wandered back into the* ADV: ADV after v, *be* ADV, n ADV; ADJ: ADJ n

next door room... The wires trailed through other parts of the HQ into a next door building. ► If a room or building is **next door to** another one, it is the next one to the left or right. *The kitchen is right next door to the dining room.* PHR-PREP

2 The people **next door** are the people who live in the house to the right or left of yours. *The neighbors thought the family next door had moved.* ► Also an adjective. *Our next door neighbour knocked on the door to say that our car had been stolen.* ADV: n ADV; ADJ: ADJ n

3 If you refer to someone as **the boy next door** or **the girl next door**, you mean that they are respectable and dependable but rather dull and boring. *He was dependable, straightforward, the boy next door... She was the girl next door type.* PHRASE

next door's. You can use **next door's** to indicate that something belongs to the person or people who live in the house to the right or left of your own. *That's next door's alarm. ...next door's dog.* DET-POSS

next of kin. **Next of kin** is sometimes used to refer to the person who is your closest relative, especially in official or legal documents; a formal word. *We have notified the next of kin.* N-UNCOUNT-COLL

nexus /neksəs/; **nexus** is both the singular and plural. A **nexus** is a connection or series of connections within a particular situation or system; a formal word. *The Prayer Book has provided a flexible enough nexus of beliefs to hold together the different church parties. ...the nexus between the dominant class and the State.* N-COUNT: usu with supp

NHS /en eɪ ʃes/. **NHS** is an abbreviation for **National Health Service**. *This vaccine is not normally provided free under the NHS... Three out of four NHS patients were given an appointment within three months.* ◆◆◇◇◇ N-SING: the N, N n

niacin /naɪəsɪn/. **Niacin** is a vitamin that occurs in milk, liver, yeast, and some other foods. ◆◇◇◇◇ N-UNCOUNT

nib /nɪb/ **nibs.** A **nib** is a small pointed piece of metal at the end of a fountain pen, which controls the flow of ink as you write. N-COUNT

nibble /nɪbəl/ **nibbles, nibbling, nibbled** ◆◇◇◇◇

1 If you **nibble** food, you eat it by biting very small pieces of it, for example because you are not very hungry. *He started to nibble his biscuit... She nibbled at the corner of a piece of dry toast.* ► Also a noun. *We each took a nibble.* VERB: V n, V at/on n, Also V; N-COUNT

2 If you **nibble** something, you bite it very gently. *John found he was kissing and nibbling her ear... Daniel Winter nibbled on his pen.* VERB: V n, V on/at n

3 When an animal **nibbles** something, it takes small bites of it quickly and repeatedly. *A herd of goats was nibbling the turf around the base of the tower... The birds cling to the wall and nibble at the brickwork.* ► **Nibble away** means the same as **nibble**. *The rabbits nibbled away on the herbaceous plants.* VERB: V n, V at/on n, Also V; PHRASAL VERB: V P on/at n

4 If one thing **nibbles** at another, it gradually affects, harms, or destroys it. *It was all going to plan, yet small doubts kept nibbling at the edges of his mind.* ► **Nibble away** means the same as **nibble**. *Several manufacturers are also nibbling away at Ford's traditional customer base.* VERB: V at n; PHRASAL VERB: V P at n

5 **Nibbles** are small snacks such as biscuits, crisps, and peanuts, that are usually offered to you at parties; used mainly in British English. *Nibbles go down well with any age group.* N-COUNT: usu pl

nice /naɪs/ **nicer, nicest** ◆◆◆◆◇

1 If you say that something is **nice**, you mean that you find it attractive, pleasant, or enjoyable. *I think silk ties can be quite nice... It's nice to be here together again... We had a nice meal with a bottle of champagne.* ♦ **nicely** *He's just written a book, nicely illustrated and not too technical... The horse jumps nicely.* ADJ-GRADED: oft it v-link ADJ to-inf; ADV-GRADED: ADV after v, ADV -ed/adj ≠poorly

2 If you say that it is **nice of** someone to say or do something, you are saying that they are being kind and thoughtful. This is often used as a way of thanking someone. *It's awfully nice of you to come all this way to see me... 'How are your boys?' — 'How nice of you to ask.'... This has been so nice, so terribly kind of you.* ADJ-GRADED: it v-link ADJ of n to-inf, v-link ADJ of n PRAGMATICS =kind

3 If you say that someone is **nice**, you mean that you like them because they are friendly and pleasant. *I've met your father and he's rather nice... He was a nice fellow, very quiet and courteous.* ♦ **niceness** *Mr Major quietly warned them not to mistake his niceness for weakness.* ADJ-GRADED ≠unpleasant; N-UNCOUNT

4 If you are **nice** to people, you are friendly, pleasant, or polite towards them. *She met Mr and Mrs Ricciardi, who were very nice to her.* ♦ **nicely** *He treated you very nicely and acted like a decent guy.* ADJ-GRADED: v-link ADJ, oft ADJ to n; ADV-GRADED: ADV after v

5 When the weather is **nice**, it is warm and pleasant. *He nodded to us and said, 'Nice weather we're having.'* ADJ-GRADED =fine

6 You can use **nice** to emphasize a particular quality that you like. *With a nice dark colour, the wine is medium to full bodied... People have got used to nice glossy magazines... Add the oats to thicken the mixture and stir until it is nice and creamy... I'll explain it nice and simply so you can understand.* ADJ: ADJ adj n, v-link ADJ and adj, ADJ and adv after v PRAGMATICS

7 A **nice** point or distinction is very clear, precise, and based on good reasoning. *Those are nice academic arguments, but what about the immediate future?* ♦ **nicely** *I think this puts the problem very nicely.* ADJ; ADV-GRADED: ADV after v

8 You can use **nice** when you are greeting people. For example, you can say **Nice to meet you** when you meet someone for the first time and **Nice to have met you** when you are saying goodbye to them. You can also say **Nice to see you** when you meet someone you already know. *Good morning. Nice to meet you and thanks for being with us this weekend... 'It's so nice to see you,' said Charles.* ADJ: it v-link ADJ to-inf PRAGMATICS

9 If someone says **nice one**, they are showing their approval of something clever or funny that they have just seen or heard; an informal expression. *Knowles became Torquay's manager. Nice one.* CONVENTION

10 See also **nicely**.

nice-looking. Someone who is **nice-looking** is physically attractive. *I saw this nice-looking man in a gray suit... We got on very well and she was very nice-looking.* ADJ-GRADED =good-looking, attractive

nicely /naɪsli/ ◆◆◇◇◇

1 If something is happening or working **nicely**, is happening or working in a satisfactory way or in the way that you want it to. *She has a bit of private money, so they manage quite nicely... The crowds had been soaked and were now nicely drying out.* • See also **nice**. ADV-GRADED: ADV with v =satisfactorily

2 If someone or something **is doing nicely**, they are being successful. *...another hotel owner who is doing very nicely.* PHRASES: V inflects, usu cont

3 If you say that something will **do nicely**, you mean that it is adequate or satisfactory for the situation. *A shirt and jersey and an ordinary pair of trousers will do nicely, thank you... A quick nod of approval would have done nicely.* V inflects =do fine

nicety /naɪsɪti/ **niceties.** The **niceties** of a situation are its details, especially with regard to good manners or the appropriate behaviour for that situation. *By the end of term, girls will have learnt the niceties of dinner party conversation... He wasted no time with social niceties. ...the language of diplomatic niceties.* N-COUNT: usu pl, oft the N of n, adj N =subtlety

niche /niːʃ, AM nɪtʃ/ **niches** ◆◇◇◇◇

1 In business, a **niche** in the market is a specific area which has its own particular requirements, customers, and products. *I think we have found a niche in the toy market... Small companies can do extremely well if they can fill a specific market niche.* N-COUNT: usu with supp

2 In business, **niche** marketing is the practice of dividing the market into specialized areas for which particular products are produced. A **niche** market is one of these specialized areas. *Many media experts see such all-news channels as part of a general move towards niche marketing... The Japanese are able to supply niche markets because of their flexible production methods.* ADJ: ADJ n

3 A **niche** is a hollow area in a wall which has been made to hold a statue, or a natural hollow part in a hillside or cliff. *Above him, in a niche on the wall,* N-COUNT *sat a tiny veiled Ganesh, the elephant god... There was a niche in the rock where the path ended.*

4 Your **niche** is the job or activity which is exactly suitable for you. *Simon Lane quickly found his niche as a busy freelance model maker.* N-COUNT: usu poss N =slot

5 If you **carve a niche** for yourself, you organize your work to create a secure position. *...a firm of solicitors that has carved a niche for itself in handling claims for investor compensation... The new superconductors look set to carve themselves a useful niche in the world's electrical industries.* PHRASE: V inflects, oft PHR *for* pron-refl

nick /nɪk/ **nicks, nicking, nicked** ◆◆◇◇◇

1 In British English, if someone **nicks** something, they steal it; an informal use. *He smashed a window to get in and nicked a load of silver cups... We used to nick biscuits from the kitchen.* VERB =pinch V n

2 In British English, if the police **nick** someone, they arrest them; an informal use. *The police nicked me for carrying an offensive weapon... Keep quiet or we'll all get nicked.* VERB =pick up V n *get/be* V-ed

3 In British English, **the nick** is a prison, or a police station; an informal use. *After several years banged up in the nick, even you might start to go mad.* N-COUNT: usu sing, usu *the* N

4 If you **nick** something or **nick** yourself, you accidentally make a small cut or scratch in the surface of the object or your skin. *When I pulled out of the space, I nicked the rear bumper of the car in front of me... A sharp blade is likely to nick the skin and draw blood... He dropped a bottle in the kitchen and nicked himself on broken glass.* VERB V n V pron-refl

5 A **nick** is a small cut made in the surface of something, usually in someone's skin. *The barbed wire had left only the tiniest nick just below my right eye.* N-COUNT

6 **Nick** is used in expressions such as '**in good nick**' or '**in bad nick**' to describe the physical condition of someone or something. *His ribs were damaged, but other than that he's in good nick... Tom's house is actually in better nick than mine.* PHRASES v-link PHR

7 If you say that something happens **in the nick of time**, you are emphasizing that it happens at the last possible moment; an informal expression. *Seems we got here just in the nick of time... News of interest cuts came in the nick of time for borrowers.* usu PHR after v PRAGMATICS =just in time

nickel /nɪkəl/ **nickels** ◆◇◇◇◇

1 **Nickel** is a silver-coloured metal that is used in making steel. N-UNCOUNT

2 In the United States and Canada, a **nickel** is a coin worth five cents. N-COUNT

nickname /nɪkneɪm/ **nicknames, nicknaming, nicknamed** ◆◆◇◇◇

1 A **nickname** is an informal name for someone or something. *Red got his nickname for his red hair.* N-COUNT

2 If you **nickname** someone or something, you give them an informal name. *When he got older I nicknamed him Little Alf... Which newspaper was once nicknamed The Thunderer?* VERB V n n

nicotine /nɪkɪtiːn/. **Nicotine** is an addictive substance contained in tobacco. *Nicotine produces a feeling of well being in the smoker... Nicotine marks stained his chin and fingers.* ◆◇◇◇◇ N-UNCOUNT

niece /niːs/ **nieces.** Someone's **niece** is the daughter of their sister or brother. *...his niece from America, the daughter of his eldest sister.* ◆◇◇◇◇ N-COUNT: oft poss N

nifty /nɪfti/ **niftier, niftiest.** If you describe something as **nifty**, you think it is neat and pleasing or cleverly done; an informal word. *Bridgeport was a pretty nifty place... It was a nifty arrangement, a perfect partnership.* ADJ-GRADED: usu ADJ n =slick

Nigerian /naɪdʒɪəriən/ **Nigerians** ◆◆◆◆◇

1 **Nigerian** means belonging or relating to Nigeria, its people, or its culture. *...the Nigerian government. ...a Nigerian accent.* ADJ

2 A **Nigerian** is a Nigerian citizen, or a person of Nigerian origin. N-COUNT

niggardly /nɪgəʳdli/. If you describe someone or something as **niggardly**, you are critical of their meanness or lack of generosity. *Officials say the EU, which is supposed to provide most of the food needs, is being particularly niggardly. ...a niggardly supply of hot water.* ADJ-GRADED PRAGMATICS ≠generous

nigger /nɪgəʳ/ **niggers. Nigger** is an extremely offensive word for a black person. ◆◇◇◇◇ N-COUNT

niggle /nɪgəl/ **niggles, niggling, niggled**

1 If something **niggles** you, it causes you to worry slightly over a long period of time. *I realise now that the things which used to niggle and annoy me just don't really matter... It's been niggling at my mind ever since I met Neville in Nice... The puzzle niggled away in Arnold's mind.* ► Also a noun. *So why is there a little niggle at the back of my mind?* VERB =bother V n V *at* n V *away* Also V; N-COUNT

2 If someone **niggles** you, they annoy you by continually criticizing you for what you think are small or insignificant details. *I don't react anymore when opponents try to niggle me... You tend to niggle at your partner, and get hurt when he doesn't hug you.* ► Also a noun. *The life we have built together is more important than any minor niggle either of us might have.* VERB =nag V n V *at* n Also V, V n that; N-COUNT

niggling /nɪgəlɪŋ/. A **niggling** injury or worry is small but bothers you over a long period of time. *Both players have been suffering from niggling injuries. ...a niggling worry that the cheap car is also the one that will cause endless trouble.* ADJ-GRADED: usu ADJ n

nigh /naɪ/ ◆◇◇◇◇

1 If an event **is nigh**, it will happen very soon; an old-fashioned use. *The end of the world may be nigh, but do we really care?... The storm must still be nigh, she thought.* ● See also **well-nigh**. ADV: *be* ADV =close, near

2 **Nigh on** an amount, number, or age means almost that amount, number, or age; an old-fashioned expression. *I've been one of your number one fans for nigh on three years now... I had to pay nigh on forty pounds for him.* PHRASE: PHR amount =nearly

night /naɪt/ **nights** ◆◆◆◆◆

1 The **night** is the part of each day when the sun has set and it is dark outside, especially the time when people are sleeping. *He didn't leave the house all night, not until his regular time to go to work in the morning... The fighting began in the late afternoon and continued all night... Our reporter spent the night crossing the border from Austria into Slovenia... Finally night fell.* N-VAR

2 The **night** is the period of time between the end of the afternoon and the time that you go to bed, especially the time when you relax before going to bed. *So whose party was it last night?... Demiris took Catherine to dinner the following night.* N-COUNT

3 A particular **night** is a particular evening when a special event takes place, such as a show or a play. *The first night crowd packed the building. ...election night.* N-COUNT: supp N

4 If it is a particular time **at night**, it is during the time when it gets dark and before midnight. *It's eleven o'clock at night in Moscow... He works obsessively from 7.15 am to 9 or 10 at night.* PHRASES num PHR

5 If something happens **at night**, it happens regularly during the evening or night. *He was going to college at night, in order to become an accountant... The veranda was equipped with heavy wooden rain doors that were kept closed at night.* PHR after v

6 If something happens **day and night** or **night and day**, it happens all the time without stopping. *Dozens of doctors and nurses have been working day and night for weeks... He was at my door night and day, demanding my attention.* usu PHR after v

7 If you have **an early night**, you go to bed early. If you have **a late night**, you go to bed late. *I've had a hell of a day, and all I want is an early night... In spite of the travelling and the late night, she did not feel tired.* N inflects

8 ● **morning, noon and night**: see **morning**.

nightcap /naɪtkæp/ **nightcaps.** A **nightcap** is a drink that you have just before you go to bed, usually an alcoholic drink. *Perhaps you would join me for a nightcap?* N-COUNT

nightclothes /naɪtkloʊðz/. **Nightclothes** are clothes that you wear in bed. N-PLURAL

nightclub /naɪtklʌb/ **nightclubs;** also spelled **night club.** A **nightclub** is a place where people go late in the evening to drink and dance. ◆◆◇◇◇ N-COUNT

nightclubbing /naɪtklʌbɪŋ/. **Nightclubbing** is the activity of going to nightclubs. N-UNCOUNT =clubbing

nightdress /naɪtdres/ **nightdresses.** In British English, a **nightdress** is a sort of loose dress that N-COUNT a woman or girl wears in bed. The usual American word is **nightgown**.

nightfall /naɪtfɔːl/. **Nightfall** is the time of day when it starts to get dark. *I need to get to Lyon by nightfall... I started work at dawn and returned only at nightfall.* N-UNCOUNT =dusk

nightgown /naɪtgaʊn/ **nightgowns.** In American English, a **nightgown** is a **nightdress**. N-COUNT

nightie /naɪti/ **nighties.** A **nightie** is a nightdress; an informal word. N-COUNT

nightingale /naɪtɪŋgeɪl, AM -tᵊn-/ **nightingales.** A **nightingale** is a small brown bird. The male's song, which can be heard at night, is very melodic. *In May, if it's warm, we hear nightingales.* N-COUNT

nightlife /naɪtlaɪf/; also spelled **night-life**. **Nightlife** is all the entertainment and social activities that are available at night in towns and cities, such as nightclubs and theatres. *Hamburg's energetic nightlife is second to none... There are free buses around the resort and plenty of nightlife.* N-UNCOUNT

nightly /naɪtli/. A **nightly** event happens every night. *I'm sure we watched the nightly news, and then we turned on the movie... For months at a time, air raids were a nightly occurrence.* ▶ Also an adverb. *She appears nightly on the television news... A new and younger crowd filled the bar nightly.* ◆◇◇◇◇ ADJ: ADJ n; ADV: usu ADV after v

nightmare /naɪtmeəʳ/ **nightmares** ◆◆◆◇◇

1 A **nightmare** is a very frightening dream. *All the victims still suffered nightmares... Jane did not eat cheese because it gives her nightmares.* N-COUNT

2 If you refer to a situation as a **nightmare**, you mean that it is very frightening and unpleasant. *The years in prison were a nightmare.* N-COUNT

3 If you refer to a situation as a **nightmare**, you are saying in a very emphatic way that it is irritating because it causes you a lot of trouble. *Taking my son Peter to a restaurant was a nightmare... In practice a graduate tax is an administrative nightmare.* N-COUNT PRAGMATICS

nightmarish /naɪtmeərɪʃ/. If you describe something as **nightmarish**, you mean that it is extremely frightening and unpleasant. *She described a nightmarish scene of dead bodies lying in the streets.* ADJ-GRADED =terrifying

night owl, night owls. A **night owl** is someone who regularly stays up late at night, or who prefers to work at night; an informal expression. *The late-night parties make the hotel a haven for night owls and a hell for anyone with children.* N-COUNT

night porter, night porters. A **night porter** is a person whose job is to be on duty at the main reception desk of a hotel throughout the night. N-COUNT

night school, night schools. Someone who goes to **night school** does an educational course in the evenings. *People can go out to work in the daylight hours and then come to night school in the evening.* N-VAR =evening classes

nightshirt /naɪtʃɜːʳt/ **nightshirts.** A **nightshirt** is a long, loose shirt worn in bed. N-COUNT

nightspot /naɪtspɒt/ **nightspots.** A **nightspot** is a nightclub; an informal word. *...Harlem's most famous nightspot, the Cotton Club.* N-COUNT

nightstick /naɪtstɪk/ **nightsticks.** A **nightstick** is a short thick club that is carried by policemen in the United States. N-COUNT

night-time; also spelled **night time. Night-time** is the period of time between when it gets dark and when the sun rises. *They wanted someone responsible to look after the place at night-time... A twelve hour night time curfew is in force.* ◆◇◇◇◇ N-UNCOUNT: oft N n =night ≠daytime

nightwatchman /naɪtwɒtʃmən/ **nightwatchmen;** also spelled **night-watchman.** A **nightwatchman** is a person whose job is to guard buildings at night. N-COUNT

nightwear /naɪtweəʳ/. **Nightwear** is clothing that you wear in bed. N-UNCOUNT

nihilism /naɪɪlɪzəm/. **Nihilism** is a belief which rejects all political and religious authority and current ideas in favour of the individual. *Why should a great community like a university be afraid of nihilism?.* ♦ **nihilist, nihilists** *Why wasn't Weber a nihilist?* N-UNCOUNT; N-COUNT

nihilistic /naɪɪlɪstɪk/. If you describe someone as **nihilistic**, you mean they do not trust political and religious authority and place their faith in the individual. *She exhibited none of the narcissistic and nihilistic tendencies of her peers.* ADJ-GRADED

Nikkei average /nɪkeɪ ævrɪdʒ/. The **Nikkei average** or the **Nikkei index** is an index of share prices which is based on the average price of shares in 225 Japanese companies on the Japanese Stock Exchange. It is used by shareholders and investors to check changes in share prices. *The Nikkei average was down 654 points.* ◆◇◇◇◇ N-SING: usu *the* N

nil /nɪl/ ◆◆◇◇◇

1 **Nil** means the same as nought or zero. It is usually used to say what the score is in sports such as rugby or football. *They beat the defending champions, Argentina, one-nil in the final.* NUM =zero

2 If you say that something is **nil**, you mean that it does not exist at all. *Their legal rights are virtually nil... The heating in winter was almost nil.* N-UNCOUNT =non-existent

nimble /nɪmbᵊl/ **nimbler, nimblest** ◆◇◇◇◇

1 Someone who is **nimble** is able to move their fingers, hands, or legs quickly and easily. *Everything had been stitched by Molly's nimble fingers... Val, who was light and nimble on her feet, learnt to dance the tango.* ♦ **nimbly** *Sabrina jumped nimbly out of the van... Uncle George quickly descended the ladder and nimbly stepped aboard.* ADJ-GRADED =sprightly; ADV-GRADED: ADV with v =smartly

2 If you say that someone has a **nimble** mind, you mean they are clever and can think very quickly. *A nimble mind backed by a degree in economics gave him a firm grasp of financial matters... Elderly people are told that if they want to keep their minds nimble, they must use them.* ADJ-GRADED =alert

nimbus /nɪmbəs/. A **nimbus** is a large dark grey cloud that brings rain or snow; a technical term in meteorology. *...layers of cold nimbus clouds.* N-SING: usu N n

nimby /nɪmbi/; also spelled **Nimby**. If you say that someone has a **nimby** attitude, you are criticizing them because they do not want any new developments such as housing or roads near to where they live. **Nimby** is an abbreviation for 'not in my backyard'. An informal word. *...the usual nimby protests from local residents.* ADJ: usu ADJ n PRAGMATICS

nine /naɪn/ **nines** ◆◆◆◆◆

1 **Nine** is the number 9. *We still sighted nine yachts. ...nine hundred pounds.* NUM

2 If you say that someone **is dressed up to the nines** or **dressed to the nines**, you mean that they are wearing very smart or glamorous clothes; an informal expression. ● **nine times out of ten**: see **time**. PHRASE

ninepins /naɪnpɪnz/. If you say that people are going down **like ninepins**, you mean that large numbers of them are becoming ill within a short period of time. You can also say that things such as organizations are going down **like ninepins** when large numbers of them are doing very badly; used mainly in British English. *There was a time when Liverpool players never seemed to get injured, but now they are going down like ninepins... The credit ratings of other New York commercial banks have been falling like ninepins.* PHRASE: PHR after v

nineteen /naɪntiːn/. **Nineteen** is the number 19. *They have nineteen days to make up their minds.* ◆◆◆◆◆ NUM

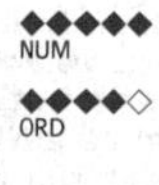

nineteenth /naɪntiːnθ/. The **nineteenth** item in a series is the one that you count as number nineteen. *...my nineteenth birthday. ...the nineteenth century.* ◆◆◆◆◇ ORD

ninetieth /naɪntiəθ/. The **ninetieth** item in a series is the one that you count as number ninety. *He celebrates his ninetieth birthday on Friday.* ◆◆◆◆◇ ORD

ninety /naɪnti/ **nineties.** ◆◆◆◆◆

1 **Ninety** is the number 90. *It was decided she had to stay another ninety days.* NUM

2 When you talk about the **nineties**, you are referring to numbers between 90 and 99. For example, if you are **in your nineties**, you are aged between 90 and 99. If the temperature is **in the nineties**, the temperature is between 90 and 99 degrees. *By this time she was in her nineties and needed help more and more frequently.* N-PLURAL

3 **The nineties** is the decade between 1990 and 1999. *These trends only got worse as we moved into the nineties.* N-PLURAL: the N

ninny /nɪni/ **ninnies.** If you refer to someone as a **ninny**, you think that they are foolish or silly; an informal, old-fashioned word. N-COUNT PRAGMATICS =twit

ninth /naɪnθ/ **ninths** ◆◆◆◆◇

1 The **ninth** item in a series is the one that you count as number nine. *...January the ninth. ...students in the ninth grade. ...ninth century illustrated manuscripts.* ORD

2 A **ninth** is one of nine equal parts of something. *In Brussels the dollar rose by a ninth of a cent... What you see is only the tip. Eight ninths of it is under the sea.* FRACTION

nip /nɪp/ **nips, nipping, nipped** ◆◇◇◇◇

1 If you **nip** somewhere, usually somewhere nearby, you go there quickly or for a short time; an informal British use. *Should I nip out and get some groceries?... Wayne is always nipping down to the corner shop for him... Beasley told me he'd seen you, so I nipped straight home.* VB: no passive =pop V adv/prep

2 If a person or an animal **nips** you, they pinch or bite you lightly. *He nipped Billy's cheek with two rough fingers... I have known cases where dogs have nipped babies.* ▶ Also a noun. *Incidents range from a petty nip, which fails to break the skin or draw blood, to serious injuries.* VERB V n Also V at n, V N-COUNT

3 A **nip** is a small sip or amount of strong alcoholic drink. *She had a habit of taking an occasional nip from a flask of cognac.* N-COUNT =tot

4 **Nip** is an extremely offensive word for a Japanese or oriental person. N-COUNT

5 ● to **nip** something **in the bud**: see **bud**.

nipper /nɪpəʳ/ **nippers.** A **nipper** is a child; used mainly in informal British English. *I'm not ever going to forget what you've done for the nippers.* N-COUNT =kid

nipple /nɪpᵊl/ **nipples** ◆◇◇◇◇

1 The **nipples** on someone's body are the two small pieces of slightly hard flesh on their chest. Babies suck milk from their mothers' breasts through their mothers' nipples. *Sore nipples can inhibit the milk supply.* N-COUNT

2 A **nipple** is a piece of rubber or plastic which is fitted to the top of a baby's bottle. *...a white plastic bottle with a rubber nipple.* N-COUNT =teat

nippy /nɪpi/

1 If the weather is **nippy**, it is rather cold. *It could get suddenly nippy in the evenings, and then you'd be glad of a fire.* ADJ-GRADED: usu v-link ADJ =chilly

2 If you describe something or someone as **nippy**, you mean they can move very quickly over short distances; used mainly in British English. *This nippy new car has fold down rear seats... Barnaby may be 15, but he's nippy and suited to badminton.* ADJ-GRADED

nirvana /nɪəʳvɑːnə, nɜːʳ-/

1 In the Hindu and Buddhist religions, **Nirvana** is the ultimate state of spiritual enlightenment that can possibly be achieved. *Entering the realm of Nirvana is only possible for those who have become pure.* N-UNCOUNT

2 People sometimes refer to a state of complete happiness and peace as **nirvana**. *Many businessmen think that a world where relative prices never varied would be nirvana.* N-UNCOUNT =paradise

Nissen hut /nɪsᵊn hʌt/ **Nissen huts.** In British English, a **Nissen hut** is a military hut made of metal. The walls and roof form the shape of a semi-circle. The American term is **Quonset hut**. N-COUNT

nit /nɪt/ **nits**

1 If someone has lice in their hair, the eggs of this insect are referred to as **nits**. *Borrowed combs were said to be the cause of spreading nits from one to another.* N-PLURAL

2 In informal British English, if you refer to someone as a **nit**, you think they are a stupid or silly. *I'd rather leave the business than work with such a nit.* N-COUNT PRAGMATICS =nitwit, twit

nitpicking /nɪtpɪkɪŋ/; also spelled **nit-picking**. If you refer to someone's opinion as **nitpicking**, you disapprove of the fact that it concentrates on small and unimportant details, especially to try and find fault with something. *A lot of nit-picking was going on about irrelevant things... I can get down to nitpicking detail, I am pretty fussy about certain things.* N-UNCOUNT PRAGMATICS =quibbling

nitrate /naɪtreɪt/ **nitrates. Nitrate** is a chemical compound that includes nitrogen and oxygen. Nitrates are used as fertilizers in agriculture. *High levels of nitrate occur in Eastern England because of the heavy use of fertilizers.* ◆◇◇◇◇ N-MASS

nitric /naɪtrɪk/. **Nitric** means relating to or containing nitrogen; a technical term in chemistry. *Nitric oxide gobbles up ozone.* ADJ: ADJ n

nitric acid. Nitric acid is a strong colourless acid containing nitrogen, hydrogen, and oxygen. N-UNCOUNT

nitro- /naɪtroʊ-/. **Nitro** combines with nouns to form other nouns referring to things which contain nitrogen and oxygen. *...highly corrosive substances such as nitro-phosphates.* COMB in N

nitrogen /naɪtrədʒən/. **Nitrogen** is a colourless element that has no smell and is usually found as a gas. It forms about 78% of the earth's atmosphere, and is found in all living things. ◆◇◇◇◇ N-UNCOUNT

nitroglycerin /naɪtroʊglɪsərɪn/; also spelled **nitroglycerine**. **Nitroglycerin** is an explosive liquid that is used in making dynamite and also in some medicines. N-UNCOUNT

nitrous /naɪtrəs/. **Nitrous** means coming from, relating to, or containing nitrogen; a technical term in chemistry. *Another group of gases like carbon monoxide are nitrous oxides. ...one waterhole where the water was nitrous.* ADJ: ADJ n

nitty-gritty /nɪti grɪti/; also spelled **nitty gritty**. If people get down to the **nitty-gritty** of a matter, situation, or activity, they discuss the most important, basic parts of it or facts about it; an informal word. *Peking's newspapers still attempt to get down to the nitty gritty of investigative journalism. ...the nitty gritty of everyday politics.* N-SING: usu the N =nuts and bolts

nitwit /nɪtwɪt/ **nitwits.** If you refer to someone as a **nitwit**, you think that they are a stupid or silly person; an informal word. *You great nitwit!... Hollywood was full of 'nitwits'.* N-COUNT PRAGMATICS =nit, twit

no /noʊ/ **noes** or **no's** ◆◆◆◆◆

1 You use **no** to give a negative response to a question. *'Any problems?'—'No, I'm O.K.'... 'Haven't you got your driver's licence?'—'No.'* CONVENTION PRAGMATICS ≠yes

2 You use **no** to say that something that someone has just said is not true. *'We thought you'd emigrated.'—'No, no.'... 'You're getting worse than me.'—'No I'm not.'* CONVENTION PRAGMATICS ≠yes

3 You use **no** to refuse an offer or a request, or to refuse permission. *'Here, have mine.'—'No, this is fine.'... 'Can you just get the message through to Pete for me?'—'No, no I can't.'... After all, the worst the boss can do is say no if you ask him.* CONVENTION PRAGMATICS ≠O.K.

4 You use **no** to indicate that you do not want someone to do something. *No. I forbid it. You cannot... She put up a hand to stop him. 'No. It's not right. We mustn't.'* EXCLAM PRAGMATICS

5 You use **no** to acknowledge a negative statement or to show that you accept and understand it. *'We're not on the main campus.'—'No.'... 'It's not one of my favourite forms of music.'—'No.'... 'I don't know him, do I?'—'No, you don't.'... 'Nobody's happy, are they?'—'No.'* CONVENTION PRAGMATICS =true, right

6 You use **no** as a way of introducing a correction to what you have just said. *'Everything?' Eleanor asked herself. 'No, not everything.' ...500 grams, no, a little less than that.* CONVENTION PRAGMATICS

7 You use **no** to express shock or disappointment at something you have just been told. *'John phoned to say that his computer wasn't working.'—'Oh God no.'... 'We went with Sarah and the married man that she's currently seeing.'—'Oh no.'* EXCLAM PRAGMATICS

8 You use **no** to mean not any or not one person or thing. *He had no intention of paying the cash... No job has more influence on the future of the world... No letters survive from this early period.* DET-NEG

9 You use **no** to emphasize that someone or something definitely does not have the characteristic or identity mentioned. *He is no singer... I make it no secret that our worst consultants earn nothing... Kathryn was no beauty at the best of times.* DET-NEG: DET n-sing PRAGMATICS

10 You use **no** when saying that something does not exceed a particular amount or number, or does not have more of a particular quality than something else. *It is to start broadcasting no later than the end of 1994... Yesterday no fewer than thirty climbers reached the summit... It would be unfair to suggest that he will be no more effective than his predecessors... He liked the Secretary no better than his assistant.* ADV: ADV compar

11 You use **no** in front of an adjective and noun to make the noun group mean its opposite. *Sometimes a bit of selfishness, if it leads to greater self-knowledge, is no bad thing... Today's elections in Peking are of no great importance in themselves.* DET-NEG: DET adj n

12 No is used in notices or instructions to say that a particular activity or thing is forbidden. *The captain turned out the 'no smoking' signs... No talking after lights out. ...a notice saying 'No Dogs'.* DET-NEG PRAGMATICS

13 A **no** is a person who has answered 'no' to a question or who has voted against something. **No** is also used to refer to their answer or vote. *According to the latest opinion polls, the noes have 50 percent, the yeses 35 percent... French officials say the government has made contingency plans in the event that the no's win.* N-COUNT ≠yes

14 If you say **there is no** doing a particular thing, you mean that it is very difficult or impossible to do that thing. *There is no going back to the life she had... There is no doubting them now.* PHRASE: PHR -ing

15 • to not **take no for an answer**: see **answer**. • **no doubt**: see **doubt**. • **no less**: see **less**. • **no less than**: see **less**. • **no longer**: see **long**. • **in no way**: see **way**. • **there's no way**: see **way**. • **no way**: see **way**.

No., Nos. No. is a written abbreviation for 'number'. *Mansell had two cars at his disposal and was the official No. 1... Columbia Law Review, vol. no. 698 p1317.* ◆◇◇◇◇ =number

nob /nɒb/ **nobs.** If you refer to a group of people as the **nobs**, you mean they are rich or come from a much higher social class than you do; an old-fashioned, informal British word. *...the nobs who live in the Big House... I'm not tellin' you. Not now you're in with the nobs.* N-COUNT: usu pl

no-ball, no-balls. In cricket, a **no-ball** is a ball that is bowled in a way that is not allowed by the rules. It results in an extra run being given to the side that is batting. *In the nine matches up to the final, England bowled 48 wides and 29 no-balls.* N-COUNT

nobble /nɒbᵊl/ **nobbles, nobbling, nobbled**

1 If someone **nobbles** an important group of people such as a committee, they bribe or threaten them in order to make them do something; used in informal British English. *The trial was stopped before Christmas after allegations of attempts to nobble the jury... Sir Gerald had been nobbled.* VERB Vn

2 If someone **nobbles** a racehorse, they deliberately harm it, often using drugs, in order to prevent it from winning a race; used in informal British English. *Jockey Club officials have identified the drug used to nobble two horses at Doncaster last week.* VERB Vn

3 If someone **nobbles** your plans or chances of succeeding, they prevent you from achieving what you want; used in informal British English. *...an attempt to nobble Mr Heseltine's political progress... His opportunity to re-establish himself had been nobbled by the manager's tactics.* VERB =thwart Vn

nobility /noʊbɪlɪti/ ◆◇◇◇◇

1 The nobility of a society are all the people who have titles and belong to a high social class. *They married into the nobility and entered the highest ranks of state administration... Despite its lack of formal power the nobility was not powerless.* N-SING-COLL: the N =aristocracy

2 A person's **nobility** is the noble and admirable quality of their behaviour and character; a formal use. *...his nobility of character, and his devotion to his country... She is not without some instincts of nobility and generosity.* N-UNCOUNT: usu with supp =dignity

noble /noʊbᵊl/ **nobles; nobler, noblest** ◆◆◇◇◇

1 If you say that someone is a **noble** person, you admire and respect their honesty, bravery, and unselfishness. *He was an upright and noble man who was always willing to help in any way he could... I wanted so much to believe he was pure and noble.* ♦ **nobly** *Eric's sister had nobly volunteered to help with the gardening... They have supported us nobly in this war.* ADJ-GRADED PRAGMATICS; ADV-GRADED: ADV with v

2 If you say that something is a **noble** idea, goal, or action, you admire it because it is based on high moral principles. *He had implicit faith in the noble intentions of the Emperor... We'll always justify our actions with noble sounding theories... Their cause was noble.* ADJ-GRADED PRAGMATICS =virtuous

3 If you describe something as **noble**, you think that its appearance or quality is very impressive, making it superior to other things of its type. *...the great parks with their noble trees. ...a noble and pure wine.* ADJ-GRADED =fine

4 Noble means belonging to a high social class and having a title. *...rich and noble families... Although he was of noble birth he lived as a poor man.* ADJ-GRADED: usu ADJ n =aristocratic

5 In former times, people who belonged to a high social class and had titles such as 'Baron' or 'Duke' were referred to as **nobles**. *More and more nobles made Moscow their home during Catherine's reign.* N-COUNT: usu pl =aristocrat

nobleman /noʊbᵊlmən/ **noblemen.** In former times, a **nobleman** was a man who was a member of the nobility. *It had once been the home of a wealthy nobleman.* N-COUNT =aristocrat

noblesse oblige /noʊbles əbliːʒ/. **Noblesse oblige** is the idea that privileged people, for example those of a high social class, should act honourably and use their privileges to help other people; a formal word. *They did so without hope of further profit and out of a sense of noblesse oblige.* N-UNCOUNT

noblewoman /noʊbᵊlwʊmən/ **noblewomen.** In former times, a **noblewoman** was a woman who was a member of the nobility. *...a religious retreat for Russian noblewomen and members of royalty.* N-COUNT =aristocrat

nobody /noʊbɒdi/ **nobodies** ◆◆◆◆◇

1 Nobody means not a single person, or not a single member of a particular group or set. *They were shut away in a little room where nobody could overhear... Nobody realizes how bad things are... Nobody ever spoke to me at press conferences... Nobody else in the neighbourhood can help.* PRON-INDEF-NEG: usu PRON v =no-one

2 If someone says that a person is a **nobody**, they are saying in an unkind way that the person is not at all important. *A man in my position has nothing to fear from a nobody like you.* N-COUNT: usu a N in sing =nonentity

no claims; also spelled **no-claims**. A **no claims** discount or bonus is a discount or bonus that you get on an insurance policy when you have not made any claims on it in the previous year. *Motorists could lose their no-claims discount, even if they are not at fault in an accident.* ADJ: ADJ n

no-confidence ◆◇◇◇◇

1 If members of an organization pass a vote or motion of **no-confidence** in someone, they take a vote which shows that they no longer support that person or their ideas. *A call for a vote of no-confidence in the president was rejected... The students passed a motion of no-confidence in the college principal. ...a no-confidence motion.* N-UNCOUNT: usu n of N, N n ≠confidence

2 You can refer to something people say or do as **a vote of no-confidence** when it shows that they no longer support a particular person or organization. *Many police officers view this action as a vote of no-confidence in their service.* N-UNCOUNT: usu n of N ≠confidence

nocturnal /nɒktɜːʳnᵊl/ ◆◇◇◇◇

1 Nocturnal means occurring at night. *The dog's main duties will be to accompany me on long nocturnal walks. ...the immensity of the nocturnal sky.* ADJ: usu ADJ n =night-time

2 Nocturnal creatures are active mostly at night. *When there is a full Moon, this nocturnal rodent is careful to stay in its burrow.* ADJ

nocturne /nɒktɜːʳn/ **nocturnes.** A **nocturne** is a short gentle piece of music, often one written to be played on the piano. *...Chopin's Piano Nocturne in B flat.* N-COUNT: usu with supp

nod /nɒd/ **nods, nodding, nodded** ◆◆◆◇◇

1 If you **nod**, you move your head downwards and upwards to show that you are answering 'yes' to a VB: no passive question, or to show agreement, understanding, or approval. *'Are you okay?' I asked. She nodded and smiled... David said nothing, but simply nodded, as if understanding perfectly... Jacques tasted one and nodded his approval... 'Oh, yes,' she nodded. 'I understand you very well.'* ► Also a noun. *She gave a nod and said, 'I see'... 'Probably,' agreed Hunter, with a slow nod of his head... He gave Sabrina a quick nod of acknowledgement.* V / V n / V with quote / N-COUNT: usu a N

2 If you **nod** in particular direction, you bend your head once in a that direction in order to indicate something or to give someone a signal to do something. *'Does it work?' he asked, nodding at the piano... She nodded towards the drawing room. 'He's in there.'... He lifted the end of the canoe, nodding to me to take up mine.* VB: no passive / V prep / V to n to-inf

3 If you **nod**, you bend your head once, as a way of saying hello or goodbye. *All the girls nodded and said 'Hi'... Tom nodded a greeting but didn't say anything... Both of them smiled and nodded at friends... They nodded goodnight to the security man.* VB: no passive / V / V n / V at/to n / V n to n

4 In football, if a player **nods** the ball in a particular direction, they hit the ball there with their head. *Taylor leapt up to nod the ball home... Brian McClair pulled United level, nodding in his twenty-third goal of the season.* VERB =head / V n adv/prep / V adv

5 If you **give** someone **the nod** or if you **give the nod** to someone, you give them permission to do something; an informal expression. *'Keep him outside till I give you the nod.'* PHRASES / V inflects

6 In informal British English, if a proposal is accepted **on the nod**, it is accepted without being questioned or argued about. *He has always argued that the party cannot be seen to let the treaty through on the nod... Big issues are going through on the nod.* PHR after v

nod off. If you **nod off**, you fall asleep, especially when you had not intended to; an informal expression. *The judge appeared to nod off yesterday while a witness was being cross-examined... He was nodding off to sleep in an armchair.* PHRASAL VERB =doze off / V P / V P to n

node /noʊd/ **nodes.** A **node** is a point, especially in the form of lump or swelling, where one thing joins another. *Cut them off cleanly through the stem just below the node. ...nerve nodes.* ◆◇◇◇◇ N-COUNT

nodule /nɒdjuːl, AM -dʒuːl/ **nodules**

1 A **nodule** is a small round lump that can appear on your body and is a sign of an illness; a medical use. *In a typical case, there is a small inflamed nodule just under the skin.* N-COUNT

2 A **nodule** is a small round lump which is found on the roots of certain plants. *...bacteria that live in root nodules on certain plants.* N-COUNT: oft n N

Noel /noʊel/. **Noel** is sometimes printed on Christmas cards and Christmas wrapping paper to mean 'Christmas'. N-PROPER

no-go area, no-go areas

1 If you refer to a place as a **no-go area**, you mean it has a reputation for violence and crime which makes people frightened to go there; used mainly in British English. *...a subway system whose reputation for violence and lawlessness makes it a no-go area for many natives of the city.* N-COUNT

2 A **no-go area** is a place which is controlled by a group of people who use force to prevent other people from entering it; used mainly in British English. *The area of the President's residence is a no-go area after six p.m... The security forces entered the IRA's no-go areas.* N-COUNT

noise /nɔɪz/ **noises** ◆◆◆◇◇

1 **Noise** is a loud or unpleasant sound. *There was too much noise in the room and he needed peace... The noise of bombs and guns was incessant... The baby, filled with alarm at the darkness and the noise, began to yell.* N-UNCOUNT =racket

2 A **noise** is a sound that someone or something makes. *Sir Gerald made a small noise in his throat. ...birdsong and other animal noises... She'd been working in her room till a noise had disturbed her.* N-COUNT =sound

3 If someone **makes noises** of a particular kind about something, they say things that indicate their attitude to it in a rather indirect or vague way. *The President took care to make encouraging noises about the future... His mother had also started making noises about it being time for him to leave home.* N-PLURAL: usu with supp

4 If you say that someone **makes the right noises** or **makes all the right noises**, you think that they are showing concern or enthusiasm about something because they feel they ought to rather than because they really want to. *But at the annual party conference he always made the right noises... He was making all the right noises about multi-party democracy and human rights.* PHRASE: V inflects

5 See also **big noise**.

noiseless /nɔɪzləs/. Something or someone that is **noiseless** does not make any sound. *The snow was light and noiseless as it floated down.* ♦ **noiselessly** *I shut the door noiselessly behind me.* ADJ-GRADED =silent ≠loud / ADV-GRADED: ADV with v

noisome /nɔɪsəm/. If you describe something or someone as **noisome**, you mean that you find them extremely unpleasant; a literary word. *Noisome vapours arise from the mud left in the docks... His noisome reputation for corruption had already begun to spread.* ADJ-GRADED: usu ADJ n =noxious

noisy /nɔɪzi/ **noisier, noisiest** ◆◆◇◇◇

1 A **noisy** person or thing makes a lot of loud or unpleasant noise. *...my noisy old typewriter... His daughter was very active and noisy in the mornings.* ♦ **noisily** *The students on the grass bank cheered noisily... She sat by the window, noisily gulping her morning coffee.* ADJ-GRADED ≠quiet / ADV-GRADED: usu ADV with v, also ADV adj =loudly

2 A **noisy** place is full of a lot of loud or unpleasant noise. *...the crowded and noisy terrace of the cafe... It's twelve years since Hong Kong was named the noisiest city in the world... The baggage hall was crowded and noisy.* ADJ-GRADED ≠quiet, peaceful

3 If you describe someone as **noisy**, you are critical of them for trying to attract attention to their views by frequently and forcefully discussing them. *It might, at last, silence the small but noisy intellectual clique. ...the noisy and unpopular fringe groups that are attempting to change the culture of their society.* ADJ-GRADED PRAGMATICS =strident

nomad /noʊmæd/ **nomads.** A **nomad** is a member of a tribe which travels from place to place rather than living in one place all the time. *...a country of nomads who raise cattle and camels.* ◆◇◇◇◇ N-COUNT

nomadic /noʊmædɪk/ ◆◇◇◇◇

1 **Nomadic** people travel from place to place rather than living in one place all the time. *...the great nomadic tribes of the Western Sahara.* ADJ

2 If someone has a **nomadic** way of life, they travel from place to place and do not have a settled home. *The daughter of a railway engineer, she at first had a somewhat nomadic childhood.* ADJ-GRADED

no-man's land ◆◇◇◇◇

1 **No-man's land** is an area of land that is not owned or controlled by anyone, for example the area of land between two opposing armies. *A mournful howl came drifting across no-man's land. ...the no-man's land between the Jordanian and Iraqi frontier posts.* N-UNCOUNT: also a N

2 If you refer to a situation as a **no-man's land** between different things, you mean that it seems unclear because it does not fit into any of the categories. *The play is set in the dangerous no-man's land between youth and adolescence... The failure has helped to drive Labour even further into a no-man's land of ideological muddle.* N-SING =grey area

nom de guerre /nɒm də geəʳ/ **noms de guerre.** A **nom de guerre** is a false name which is sometimes used by people who belong to an unofficial military organization; a formal expression. *...a Serb militia leader who goes by the nom de guerre Arkan.* N-COUNT

nom de plume /nɒm də pluːm/ **noms de plume.** An author's **nom de plume** is a name that he or she uses instead of their real name; a formal expression. *She writes under the nom de plume of Alison Cooper.* N-COUNT =pen name, pseudonym

nomenclature /nəmeŋklətʃəʳ, AM noʊmənkleɪtʃər/ **nomenclatures.** The **nomenclature** of a particular set of things is the system of naming those things; a formal word. *...mistakes arising from ignorance of the nomenclature of woody plants. ...the internationally agreed rules of chemical nomenclature.* N-UNCOUNT: also N in pl, usu supp N

nomenklatura /noʊmenklɑtʊərə/. In former communist countries, **the nomenklatura** were the people the communist party approved of and appointed to positions of authority. *Ordinary people have always resented the nomenklatura's privileges.* N-SING: the N

nominal /nɒmɪnəl/ ◆◆◇◇◇

1 You use **nominal** to indicate that someone or something is supposed to have a particular identity or status, but in reality does not have it. *As he was still not allowed to run a company, his wife became its nominal head... I was brought up a nominal Christian.* ♦ **nominally** *The Sultan was still nominally the Chief of Staff. ...South Africa's nominally independent homeland of Transkei... Nominally at least, Britain is committed to the first stage of European Monetary Union.* ADJ: usu ADJ n =in name only; ADV: ADV with cl/group, ADV before v =technically

2 A **nominal** price or sum of money is very small in comparison with the real cost or value of the thing that is being bought or sold. *I am prepared to sell my shares at a nominal price... All the ferries carry bicycles free or for a nominal charge.* ADJ: ADJ n =token

3 In economics, the **nominal** value, rate, or level of something is the one expressed in terms of current prices or figures, without taking into account the effects of changes in the level of prices over time. *Inflation would be lower and so nominal rates would be rather more attractive in real terms... In 1990 personal incomes grew a nominal 6.8 per cent.* ADJ: ADJ n ≠real

nominal group, nominal groups. A **nominal group** is the same as a **noun group**. N-COUNT

nominate /nɒmɪneɪt/ **nominates, nominating, nominated** ◆◆◇◇◇

1 If someone **is nominated** for a job or position, their name is formally suggested as a candidate for it. *Under party rules each candidate has to be nominated by 55 Labour MPs... The public will be able to nominate candidates for awards such as the MBE... The UN Secretary General has nominated Mrs Ogata as its next High Commissioner for Refugees.* VERB =propose, put forward; be V-ed; V n for n; V n as n; Also V n, V n to-inf

2 If you **nominate** someone to a job or position, you formally choose them to hold that job or position. *Voters will choose fifty of the seventy five deputies. The Emir will nominate the rest... The European Community would nominate two members to the committee... He was nominated by the African National Congress as one of its team at the Groote Sehuur talks... Mr Gorbachev must nominate someone to receive the award on his behalf.* VERB =appoint; V n; V n to n; be V-ed as n; V n to-inf; Also V n as n, V n n

3 If someone or something such as a book or film **is nominated** for an award, someone formally suggests that person or thing should be given that award. *Practically every movie he made was nominated for an Oscar. ...a campaign to nominate the twice World Champion as Sports Personality of the Year.* VERB =put forward; be V-ed for n; V n as n; Also V n for n

nomination /nɒmɪneɪʃən/ **nominations** ◆◆◇◇◇

1 A **nomination** is an official suggestion of someone as a candidate in an election or for a job. *Clinton emerged as the overwhelming favourite to win the Democratic presidential nomination. ...a list of nominations for senior lectureships.* N-COUNT: oft N for n

2 A **nomination** for an award is an official suggestion that someone or something should be given that award. *They say he's certain to get a nomination for best supporting actor... Alan Parker's film 'The Commitments' has six nominations.* N-COUNT: usu N for n

3 The **nomination** of someone to a particular job or position is their appointment to that job or position. *They opposed the nomination of a junior officer to the position of Inspector General of Police... On the death of Leo there were two main candidates for nomination as his replacement.* N-VAR: usu with supp =appointment

nominative /nɒmɪnətɪv/. In the grammar of some languages, **the nominative**, or **the nominative case** is the case used for a noun when it is the subject of a verb. In English, only the pronouns 'I', 'he', 'she', 'we', and 'they' are in the nominative. Compare **accusative**. N-SING: the N

nominee /nɒmɪniː/ **nominees.** A **nominee** is someone who is nominated for a job or position, or who is nominated for an award. *His nominee for vice president was elected only after a second ballot... Nelson Mandela is among nominees for the 1992 Nobel Peace Prize.* ◆◆◇◇◇ N-COUNT: oft N for n

non- /nɒn-/

1 **Non-** is used in front of adjectives and nouns to form adjectives that describe something as not having a particular quality or feature. *It is the first such treaty to put effective controls on non-nuclear weapons... Culture plays an important part in non-verbal communication.* PREFIX

2 **Non-** is used in front of nouns to form nouns which refer to situations where a particular action has not or will not take place. *He was disqualified from the council for non-attendance... Both countries agreed that normal relations would be based on non-interference in each other's internal affairs.* PREFIX

3 **Non-** is used in front of nouns to form nouns which refer to people who do not belong to a particular group or category. *How did these people, Chinese and non-Chinese, create the economic miracle Hong Kong is today?* PREFIX

non-aggression. If a country adopts a policy of **non-aggression**, it declares that it will not attack or try to harm a particular country in any way. *The agreement includes a pledge of non-aggression... A non-aggression pact will be signed between the two countries.* N-UNCOUNT: usu with supp

non-alcoholic. A **non-alcoholic** drink does not contain alcohol. *...bottles of non-alcoholic beer.* ADJ: usu ADJ n ≠alcoholic

non-aligned. **Non-aligned** countries did not support or were in no way linked to groups of countries headed by the United States or the former Soviet Union. *...a meeting of foreign ministers from non-aligned countries. ...India's role as the most influential member of the non-aligned movement.* ◆◇◇◇◇ ADJ: usu ADJ n ≠aligned

non-alignment. **Non-alignment** is the state or policy of being non-aligned. *The Afro-Asian nations had approved the basic general principles of non-alignment.* N-UNCOUNT ≠alignment

nonchalant /nɒnʃələnt, AM -lɑːnt/. If you describe someone as **nonchalant**, you mean that they appear not to worry or care about things and that they seem very calm. *Clark's mother is nonchalant about her role in her son's latest work... Denis tried to look nonchalant and uninterested... It merely underlines our rather more nonchalant attitude to life.* ♦ **nonchalance** /nɒnʃələns, AM -lɑːns/ *Affecting nonchalance, I handed her two hundred dollar bills.* ♦ **nonchalantly** *'Does Will intend to return with us?' Joanna asked as nonchalantly as she could.* ◆◇◇◇◇ ADJ-GRADED =casual; N-UNCOUNT; ADV-GRADED: usu ADV with v, also ADV adj =casually

non-combatant, non-combatants

1 **Non-combatant** troops are members of the armed forces whose duties do not include fighting. *The General does not like non-combatant personnel near a scene of action.* N-COUNT: usu N n ≠combatant

2 In a war, **non-combatants** are people who are not members of the armed forces. *The Red Cross has arranged two local ceasefires, allowing non-combatants to receive medical help.* N-COUNT: usu pl =civilian ≠combatant

noncommittal /nɒnkəmɪtəl/; also spelled **non-committal**. You can describe someone as **noncommittal** when they deliberately do not express their opinion or intentions clearly. *Mr Hall is non-committal about the number of jobs that the development corporation has created... Sylvia's face was noncommittal... I've got a nasty feeling that I shall get a very bland non-committal answer.* ♦ **noncommittally** *'I like some of his novels better than others,' I said noncommittally.* ADJ-GRADED: usu v-link ADJ; ADV-GRADED: ADV after v

nonconformist /nɒnkənfɔːʳmɪst/ **nonconformists;** also spelled **non-conformist**.

1 If you say that someone's way of life or views are **nonconformist**, you mean that they behave or ADJ-GRADED =unconventional ≠conventional

think in an unusual, original, or rebellious way, and not in the way that people in their society usually behave or think. *Their views are non-conformist and their political opinions are extreme... Your non-conformist ways will probably get you into trouble. ...a nonconformist lifestyle.*
► A **nonconformist** is someone who is nonconformist. *Nureyev remained a rebel and a non-conformist.* N-COUNT
2 In Britain, **nonconformist** churches are Protestant churches which are not part of the Church of England. *His father was a Nonconformist minister.* ADJ: ADJ n
► A **nonconformist** is a member of a nonconformist church. *Although he seems to be an old-fashioned non-conformist, he is in fact a very devout Catholic.* N-COUNT

nonconformity /nɒnkənfɔːʳmɪti/; also spelled **non-conformity**. **Nonconformity** is behaviour or thinking which is unusual, original, or rebellious. *You're deliberately unconventional. Even your choice of clothes is a statement of your non-conformity... Lovelock's principled nonconformity can be traced to his childhood.* N-UNCOUNT

nondescript /nɒndɪskrɪpt/. If you describe something or someone as **nondescript**, you mean that their appearance is rather dull, and not at all interesting or attractive. *Europa House is one of those hundreds of nondescript buildings along the Bath Road. ...a nondescript woman of uncertain age... Her clothes told me nothing: they were about as nondescript and lacking in chic as it was possible to be.* ADJ-GRADED: usu ADJ n

none /nʌn/ ◆◆◆◆◇
1 **None of** something means not even a small amount of it. **None of** a group of people or things means not even one of them. *She did none of the maintenance on the vehicle itself... The New York Times will soon carry colour advertisements. None of this will matter if newspapers eventually disappear... None of us knew how to treat her.* QUANT: QUANT of def-n ► Also a pronoun. *I turned to bookshops and libraries seeking information and found none... He searched for a sign of recognition on her face, but there was none... No one could imagine a great woman painter. None had existed yet... With none was he specially friendly... Only two cars produced by Austin-Morris could reach 100 mph and none could pass the 10-second acceleration test.* PRON-INDEF-NEG
2 If you say that someone **will have none of** something, **would have none of** something, or **is having none of** something, you mean that you refuse to tolerate it; an informal expression. *He knew his own mind and was having none of their attempts to keep him at home.* PHRASES be inflects, PHR n
3 **None but** means only; a formal expression. *None but God will ever know what I suffered... He whispered so softly that none but Julie heard him.* PHR n
4 You use **none too** in front of an adjective or adverb in order to emphasize that the quality mentioned is not present; a formal use. *He was none too thrilled to hear from me at that hour... Her hand grasped my shoulder, none too gently.* PHR adj/adv PRAGMATICS
5 You use **none the** to say that someone or something does not have any more of a particular quality than they did before. *You could end up committed to yet another savings scheme and none the wiser about managing your finances... He became convinced that his illness was purely imaginary: that made it none the better.* PHR compar =no
6 • **none of** your **business**: see **business**. • **none other than**: see **other**. • **second to none**: see **second**.

nonentity /nɒnentɪti/ **nonentities.** If you refer to someone as a **nonentity**, you mean that they are not special or important in any way. *Amidst the current bunch of nonentities, he is a towering figure... She was written off then as a political nonentity.* N-COUNT =nobody

non-essential, non-essentials
1 **Non-essential** means not absolutely necessary. *The crisis has led to the closure of a number of non-essential government services. ...non-essential goods.* ADJ: usu ADJ n ≠essential
2 **Non-essentials** are things that are not absolutely necessary. *In a recession, consumers could be expected to cut down on non-essentials like toys.* N-PLURAL ≠necessities

nonetheless /nʌnðəles/. **Nonetheless** means the same as **nevertheless**; a formal word. *There was still a long way to go. Nonetheless, some progress had been made... His face is serious but nonetheless very friendly.* ◆◆◇◇◇ ADV: ADV with cl PRAGMATICS =nevertheless

non-event, non-events. If you say that something was a **non-event**, you mean that it was disappointing or unexciting, especially when this was not what you had expected. *Unfortunately, the entire evening was not so much a disaster as a total non-event.* N-COUNT =anticlimax

non-existence. **Non-existence** is the fact of not existing. *I was left with puzzlement as to the existence or non-existence of God... The applause from the delegates was thin to the point of non-existence.* N-UNCOUNT ≠existence

non-existent. If you say that something is **non-existent**, you mean that it does not exist when you feel that it should. *Hygiene was non-existent: no running water, no bathroom... You'll take everything you're offered yet your own generosity is virtually non-existent.* ◆◇◇◇◇ ADJ

non-fat. **Non-fat** foods have very low amounts of fat in them. *...plain non-fat yogurt... Non-fat dairy products supply the needed nutrients without excessive calories.* ADJ =fat-free

non-fiction; also spelled **nonfiction**. **Non-fiction** is writing that gives information or describes real events, rather than telling a story. *The series will include both fiction and non-fiction... Lewis is the author of thirteen novels and ten non-fiction books.* N-UNCOUNT: oft N n ≠fiction

non-finite. A **non-finite** clause is a clause which is based on an infinitive or a participle and has no tense. Compare **finite**. ADJ: usu ADJ n

non-human. **Non-human** means not human or not produced by humans. *Hostility towards outsiders is characteristic of both human and non-human animals.* ADJ ≠human

non-intervention. **Non-intervention** is the practice or policy of not becoming involved in a dispute or disagreement between other people and of not helping either side. *Generally, I think the policy of non-intervention is the correct one.* N-UNCOUNT ≠intervention

non-linear; also spelled **nonlinear**. If you describe something as **non-linear**, you mean that it does not progress or develop smoothly from one stage to the next in a logical way. Instead, it makes sudden changes, or seems to develop in different directions at the same time. *...a non-linear narrative structure. ...a computer program that could help detect non-linear trends in currency markets.* ADJ ≠linear

non-member, non-members. **Non-members** of a club or organization people who are not members of it. *The scheme is also open to non-members... Spain imposed levies on farm imports from non-member states.* N-COUNT: usu pl =guest ≠member

non-nuclear. **Non-nuclear** means not using or involving nuclear weapons or nuclear power. *The agreement is the first postwar treaty to reduce non-nuclear weapons in Europe.* ADJ

no-no. If you say that something is **a no-no**, you think it is undesirable or unacceptable; an informal word. *We all know that cheating on our taxes is a no-no.* N-SING: a N

no-nonsense. If you describe someone as a **no-nonsense** person or something as a **no-nonsense** thing, you approve of the fact that they are efficient and concentrate on important matters rather than trivial things. *She saw herself as a direct, no-nonsense modern woman... The decor is straightforward and no-nonsense.* ◆◇◇◇◇ ADJ-GRADED: usu ADJ n PRAGMATICS =straightforward

non-payment. **Non-payment** is a failure to pay a sum of money that you owe. *She has received an eviction order from the council for non-payment of rent.* ◆◇◇◇◇ N-UNCOUNT: usu N of n ≠payment

nonplussed /nɒnplʌst/. If you are **nonplussed**, you feel confused and unsure how to react. *She expected him to ask for a scotch and was rather nonplussed when he asked her to mix him a martini and lemonade.* ADJ-GRADED: usu v-link ADJ =at a loss

non-profit. A **non-profit** organization is one which is not run with the aim of making a profit. *Her center is typical of many across the country – a non-profit organization that cares for about 50 children.* ◆◇◇◇◇ ADJ: usu ADJ n

non-profit-making. A **non-profit-making** organization or charity is not run with the intention of making a profit. *...the Film Theatre Foundation, a non-profit-making company which raises money for the arts.* ADJ: usu ADJ n

non-proliferation. **Non-proliferation** is the limiting of the production and spread of something such as nuclear or chemical weapons. *France today announced its plans to join the Nuclear Non-Proliferation Treaty... The declaration deals with disarmament and the non-proliferation of nuclear weapons.* ◆◇◇◇◇ N-UNCOUNT: usu N n

non-resident, non-residents. A **non-resident** person is someone who is visiting a particular place but who does not live or stay there permanently. *The paper said that 100,000 non-resident workers would have to be sent back to their home villages. ...non-resident voters.* ADJ ≠resident ► A **non-resident** is someone who is non-resident. *Both hotels have gardens and restaurants open to non-residents.* N-COUNT ≠resident

nonsense /nɒnsəns/ ◆◆◇◇◇

1 If you say that something spoken or written is **nonsense**, you mean that you consider it to be untrue or silly. *Most orthodox doctors however dismiss this as complete nonsense. ...all that poetic nonsense about love... 'I'm putting on weight.'—'Nonsense my dear.'* N-UNCOUNT =rubbish

2 You can use **nonsense** to refer to something that you think is foolish or that you disapprove of. *Surely it is an economic nonsense to deplete the world of natural resources... I think there is a limit to how much of this nonsense people are going to put up with.* N-UNCOUNT: also a N, usu supp N =rubbish

3 You can refer to spoken or written words that do not mean anything because they do not make sense as **nonsense**. *...a children's nonsense poem by Charles E Carryl.* N-UNCOUNT

4 See also **no-nonsense**.

5 To **make a nonsense of** something or to **make nonsense of** it means to make it seem ridiculous or pointless. *The fighting made a nonsense of peace pledges made in London last week... It makes nonsense of our own rules governing laws of adoption in this country.* PHRASE: V inflects, PHR n

nonsensical /nɒnsensɪkəl/. If you say that something is **nonsensical**, you think it is stupid, ridiculous, or untrue. *It seemed to me that Sir Robert's arguments were nonsensical... There were no nonsensical promises about reviving the economy.* ADJ-GRADED: usu v-link ADJ PRAGMATICS =absurd

non sequitur /nɒn sekwɪtəʳ/ **non sequiturs.** A **non sequitur** is a statement, remark, or conclusion that does not follow naturally or logically from what has just been said; a formal word. *Had she missed something important, or was this just a non sequitur?* N-VAR

non-smoker, non-smokers. A **non-smoker** is someone who does not smoke. *Nobody will be allowed to smoke in an office if there are non-smokers present.* ◆◇◇◇◇ N-COUNT

non-smoking; also spelled **nonsmoking**.

1 A **non-smoking** area in a public place is an area in which people are not allowed to smoke. *More and more restaurants are providing non-smoking areas.* ADJ ≠smoking

2 A **non-smoking** person is a person who does not smoke. *The fertility of women who smoke is half that of non-smoking women.* ADJ

non-specific; also spelled **nonspecific**.

1 **Non-specific** diseases or symptoms have more than one particular cause or diagnosis. *She was a 37 year old woman with a nine month history of non-specific headaches.* ADJ: usu ADJ n

2 Something that is **non-specific** is general rather than precise or exact. *I intend to use these terms in a deliberately non-specific and all-embracing way.* ADJ: usu ADJ n

non-standard. **Non-standard** things are different from the usual version or type of that thing. *...non-standard window shapes... The shop is completely out of non-standard sizes.* ADJ: usu ADJ n

non-starter, non-starters. If you describe a plan or idea as a **non-starter**, you mean that it has no chance of success; an informal word. *The United States is certain to reject the proposal as a non-starter... Some of the points that she put were indeed non-starters but some of them were really quite reasonable.* N-COUNT

non-stick; also spelled **nonstick**. **Non-stick** cooking equipment such as saucepans, frying-pans, or baking tins has a special coating on the inside, which prevents food from sticking to it. *Heat a non-stick frying pan over a medium heat until hot.* ◆◇◇◇◇ ADJ: usu ADJ n

non-stop; also spelled **nonstop**. Something that is **non-stop** continues without any pauses or interruptions. *Many US cities now have non-stop flights to Aspen. ...80 minutes of non-stop music... The training was non-stop and continued for three days.* ◆◇◇◇◇ ADJ ► Also an adverb. *Amy and her group had driven non-stop through Spain... The snow fell non-stop for 24 hours.* ADV: ADV after v

non-union; spelled **nonunion** in American English. **Non-union** workers do not belong to a trade union. A **non-union** company or organization does not employ workers who belong to a trade union. *The company originally intended to re-open the factory with non-union workers... Management hostility is apparent in about a third of non-union workplaces.* ADJ: usu ADJ n

non-verbal; also spelled **nonverbal**. **Non-verbal** communication consists of things such as your facial expressions, arm movements, or tone of voice which show how you feel about a particular situation, as opposed to the words which you actually speak. *Culture plays a large part in non-verbal communication... According to psychologist Martin Lloyd-Elliott, 90 per cent of communication between people is non-verbal.* ADJ: usu ADJ n ≠verbal

non-violent; also spelled **nonviolent**. ◆◇◇◇◇

1 **Non-violent** methods of bringing about change do not involve hurting people or causing damage. *King was a worldwide symbol of non-violent protest against racial injustice... I would only belong to an environmental movement if it was explicitly non-violent.* ADJ-GRADED ≠violent ♦ **non-violence** *The Albanian opposition has made a firm public commitment to non-violence.* N-UNCOUNT

2 You can refer to someone or something such as a crime as **non-violent** when that person or thing does not hurt or injure people. *The judiciary must think very hard before jailing non-violent offenders... The signs suggest that the elections will be non-violent and fair.* ADJ-GRADED ≠violent

non-white, non-whites. A **non-white** person is a member of a race of people who are not of European origin. *Non-white people are effectively excluded from certain jobs even though such a bar isn't explicit... 60 percent of the population is non-white.* ◆◇◇◇◇ ADJ ≠white ► Also a noun. *Not one non-white has ever been selected to play for the team.* N-COUNT

noodle /nuːdəl/ **noodles.** **Noodles** are long, thin, curly strips of pasta. They are used in Chinese and Italian cooking. ◆◇◇◇◇ N-COUNT: usu pl

nook /nʊk/ **nooks.** A **nook** is a small and sheltered place. *We found a seat in a little nook, and had some lunch.* N-COUNT =corner ● If you talk about every **nook and cranny** of a place or situation, you mean every part or every aspect of it. *Boxes are stacked in every nook and cranny at the factory. ...Cole's vast knowledge of the nooks and crannies of British politics.* PHRASE: Ns inflect PRAGMATICS =corner

nookie /nʊki/; also spelled **nooky**. You can refer to sexual intercourse as **nookie**; an informal N-UNCOUNT word. *...the fearful Hollywood sin of pre-marital nookie.*

noon /nuːn/ 

1 Noon is twelve o'clock in the middle of the day. *The long day of meetings started at noon... Our branches are open from 9am to 5pm during the week and until 12 noon on Saturdays.* • See also **high noon**. — N-UNCOUNT: oft prep N =midday

2 Noon means happening or appearing in the middle part of the day. *The noon sun was fierce... He confirmed that he expected the transfer to go through by today's noon deadline.* — ADJ: ADJ n =midday

3 • morning, noon, and night: see **morning**.

noonday /nuːndeɪ/. **Noonday** means happening or appearing in the middle part of the day. *It was hot, nearly 90 degrees in the noonday sun.* — ADJ: ADJ n =midday

no one; also spelled **no-one. No one** or **nobody** means not a single person, or not a single member of a particular group or set. *Everyone wants to be a hero, but no one wants to die... No one can open mail except the person to whom it has been addressed.* — ◆◆◆◆◇ PRON-INDEF-NEG: usu PRON v

noose /nuːs/ **nooses** ◆◇◇◇◇

1 A **noose** is a circular loop at the end of a piece of rope or wire. A noose is tied with a knot that allows it to be tightened, and it is usually used to trap animals or hang people. — N-COUNT

2 You can refer to something that traps people in a difficult situation as a **noose**. *The rebels are tighteninging the noose around the capital... Too often women find their jobs turning into nooses around their neck.* — N-COUNT: usu with supp

nope /noʊp/. **Nope** is sometimes used instead of 'no' as a response in informal spoken English. *'Is she supposed to work today?'—'Nope, tomorrow.'* — ◆◇◇◇◇ CONVENTION PRAGMATICS

nor /nɔːʳ/ ◆◆◆◆◇

1 You use **nor** after 'neither' in order to introduce the second alternative or the last of a number of alternatives in a negative statement. *Neither Mr Rose nor Mr Woodhead was available for comment yesterday... I can give you neither an opinion nor any advice... They can neither read nor write, nor can they comprehend such concepts.* — CONJ-COORD-NEG PRAGMATICS

2 You use **nor** after a negative statement in order to indicate that the negative statement also applies to you or to someone or something else. *'None of us has any idea how long we're going to be here.'—'Nor do I.'... 'If my husband has no future,' she said, 'then nor do my children.'... He doesn't want to live in the country when he grows up, nor does he want to live in the city.* — CONJ-COORD-NEG PRAGMATICS

3 You use **nor** after a negative statement in order to introduce another negative statement which adds information to the previous one. *Cooking up a quick dish doesn't mean you have to sacrifice flavour. Nor does fast food have to be junk food.* — CONJ-COORD-NEG PRAGMATICS

Nordic /nɔːʳdɪk/ ◆◇◇◇◇

1 Nordic means relating to the countries of northern Europe, especially Scandinavia. *The Nordic countries have been quick to assert their interest in the development of the Baltic States.* — ADJ: ADJ n

2 Someone who looks **Nordic** has blond hair, blue eyes, fair skin, and is fairly tall. *He was a handsome blond Nordic type.* — ADJ: ADJ n

norm /nɔːʳm/ **norms** ◆◆◇◇◇

1 Norms are ways of behaving that are considered normal in a particular society. *The actions taken depart from what she called the commonly accepted norms of democracy. ...a social norm that says drunkenness is inappropriate behaviour.* — N-COUNT: usu pl, usu with supp

2 If you say that a situation is **the norm**, you mean that it is usual and expected. *Families of six or seven are the norm in Borough Park... The changes will lead to more flexible leases, and leases nearer to 15 years than the present norm of 25 years.* — N-SING: the N, oft N for/of/in n

3 A **norm** is an official standard or level of achievement that you are expected to reach or conform to. *...a Europe-wide environmental protection agency which would establish European norms and co-ordinate national policies to halt pollution.* — N-COUNT: usu with supp

normal /nɔːʳməl/ ◆◆◆◆◇

1 Something that is **normal** is usual and ordinary, in accordance with what people expect. *He has occasional injections to maintain his good health but otherwise he lives a normal life... The two countries resumed normal diplomatic relations... Some of the shops were closed but that's quite normal for a Thursday afternoon... In November, Clean's bakery produced 50 percent more bread than normal... Life in Israel will continue as normal.* — ADJ-GRADED ≠abnormal

2 A **normal** person is generally healthy in body and mind, without any major defects or problems. *Statistics indicate that depressed patients are more likely to become ill than are normal people... Henry is a very normal kid... Will the baby be normal?.* — ADJ-GRADED =healthy

normalcy /nɔːʳməlsi/. **Normalcy** is a situation in which everything is normal. *He said that the government was committed to restore normalcy and hold elections in the Punjab... Underneath this image of normalcy, addiction threatened to rip this family apart.* — N-UNCOUNT =normality

normality /nɔːʳmælɪti/. **Normality** is a situation in which everything is normal. *A semblance of normality has returned with people going to work and shops re-opening.* — ◆◇◇◇◇ N-UNCOUNT: oft N of n

normalize /nɔːʳməlaɪz/ **normalizes, normalizing, normalized;** also spelled **normalise** in British English. ◆◇◇◇◇

1 When you **normalize** a situation or when it **normalizes,** it becomes normal. *Meditation tends to lower or normalize blood pressure... There may be some deep-seated emotional reason which has to be dealt with before your eating habits normalize.* — V-ERG V n V

2 If people, groups, or governments **normalize** relations or ties or when relations or ties **normalize,** they become normal or return to normal. *The two governments were close to normalizing relations... The United States says they are not prepared to join the EC in normalizing ties with Peking... If relations between Hanoi and Washington begin to normalise, anything is possible.* ♦ **normalization** /nɔːʳməlaɪzeɪʃən/ *What's not in doubt is that the two sides would like to see the normalisation of diplomatic relations.* — V-RECIP-ERG pl-n V n V n with n V; N-UNCOUNT

normally /nɔːʳməli/ ◆◆◆◇◇

1 If you say that something **normally** happens or that you **normally** do a particular thing, you mean that it is what usually happens or what you usually do. *All airports in the country are working normally today... Social progress is normally a matter of struggles and conflicts... Normally, the transportation system in Paris carries 950,000 passengers a day.* — ADV: ADV with v, ADV with cl/group

2 If you do something **normally**, you do it in the usual or conventional way. *She would apparently eat normally and then make herself sick. ...failure of the blood to clot normally.* — ADV: ADV after v

Norman /nɔːʳmən/ **Normans** ◆◇◇◇◇

1 The **Normans** were the people who came from northern France and conquered England in 1066, or their descendants. *The Normans built the castle which was reduced to ruins under Cromwell.* — N-COUNT

2 Norman is used to refer to the period of history in Britain from 1066 until around 1300, and in particular to the style of architecture of that period. *In Norman England, the greyhound was a symbol of nobility. ...a Norman castle.* — ADJ

normative /nɔːʳmətɪv/. **Normative** means creating or stating particular rules of behaviour; a formal word. *Normative sexual behaviour in our society remains heterosexual. ...a normative model of teaching.* — ◆◇◇◇◇ ADJ: usu ADJ n

Norse /nɔːʳs/

1 Norse means belonging or relating to medieval Scandinavia. *In Norse mythology the moon is personified as male.* — ADJ

2 Norse is the language that was spoken in medieval Scandinavia. *Norse had even more sounds than Old English.* — N-UNCOUNT

Norseman /nɔːʳsmən/ **Norsemen. Norsemen** were people who lived in Scandinavia during the medieval period. — N-COUNT

north /nɔːʳθ/; also spelled **North.** ◆◆◆◆◆

1 The **north** is the direction which is on your left — N-UNCOUNT:

when you are looking towards the direction where the sun rises. *In the north the ground becomes very cold as the winter snow and ice covers the ground... Birds usually migrate from north to south.* also *the*N

2 The **north** of a place, country, or region is the part which is in the north. *The scheme mostly benefits people in the North and Midlands where rateable values were lowest. ...a tiny house in a village in the north of France.* N-SING: usu *the*N, oft N *of*n

3 If you go **north**, you travel towards the north. *Anita drove north up Pacific Highway.* ADV: ADV after v

4 Something that is **north** of a place is positioned to the north of it. *That's a little village a few miles north of Portsmouth, off the old London Road.* ADV: usu ADV *of*n

5 The **north** edge, corner, or part of a place or country is the part which is towards the north. *...the north side of the mountain... They were coming in to land on the north coast of Crete.* ADJ: ADJ n

6 **'North'** is used in the names of some countries, states, and regions in the north of a larger area. *There were demonstrations this weekend in cities throughout North America, Asia and Europe.* ADJ: ADJ n

7 A **north** wind is a wind that blows from the north. *...a bitterly cold north wind.* ADJ: ADJ n

northbound /nɔːʳθbaʊnd/. **Northbound** roads, cars, and trains lead or are travelling towards the north. *A 25 mile traffic jam clogged the northbound carriageway of the M6... Traffic was already very congested by six thirty this morning, particularly on the M1 northbound.* ADJ: ADJ n, n ADJ

north-east; also spelled **North-East**. ◆◆◆◆◇

1 The **north-east** is the direction which is halfway between north and east. *The land to the north-east fell away into meadows.* N-UNCOUNT: also *the*N

2 **The north-east** of a place, country, or region is the part which is in the north-east. *The north-east, with 60 million people, is the most densely populated part of the United States... They're all from Newcastle in the North East of England.* N-SING: *the*N, oft N *of*n

3 If you go **north-east**, you travel towards the north-east. *The streets were jammed with slow moving traffic, army convoys moving north-east.* ADV: ADV after v

4 Something that is **north-east of** a place is positioned to the north-east of it. *This latest attack was at Careysburg, twenty miles north-east of the capital, Monrovia.* ADV: ADV *of*n

5 The **north-east** edge, corner, or part of a place is the part which is towards the north-east. *These islands of the north-east coast can only be reached in small boats. ...Waltham Abbey on the north-east outskirts of London.* ADJ: ADJ n =north-eastern

6 A **north-east** wind is a wind that blows from the north-east. *By 9.15 a bitter north-east wind was blowing.* ADJ: ADJ n

north-easterly; also spelled **north easterly**.

1 A **north-easterly** point, area, or direction is to the north-east or towards the north-east. ADJ: usu ADJ n

2 A **north-easterly** wind is a wind that blows from the north-east. ADJ: ADJ n

north-eastern; also spelled **north eastern**. ◆◇◇◇◇ **North-eastern** means in or from the north-east of a region or country. *...the north-eastern coast of the United States.* ADJ-GRADED: usu ADJ n

northerly /nɔːʳðəʳli/

1 A **northerly** point, area, or direction is to the north or towards the north. *Fetlaw is the most northerly island in the British Isles... I wanted to go a more northerly route across Montana.* ADJ-GRADED: usu ADJ n =northern

2 A **northerly** wind is a wind that blows from the north. ADJ

northern /nɔːʳðəʳn/; also spelled **Northern**. ◆◆◆◆◇ **Northern** means in or from the north of a region or country. *Their two children were immigrants to Northern Ireland from Pennsylvania... Prices at three-star hotels fell furthest in several northern cities.* ADJ: ADJ n

northerner /nɔːʳðəʳnəʳ/ **northerners.** A **northerner** is a person who was born in or who lives in the north of a place or country. *I like the openness and directness of northerners.* N-COUNT

northernmost /nɔːʳðəʳnmoʊst/. The **northernmost** part of an area or the **northernmost** place is the one that is further towards the north than any other. *...the northernmost tip of the British Isles... The Chablis vineyard is the northernmost in Burgundy.* ADJ-SUPERL: usu ADJ n

North Pole. The **North Pole** is the place on the surface of the earth which is farthest towards the north. N-PROPER: usu *the*N

northward /nɔːʳθwəʳd/; also spelled **northwards**. **Northward** or **northwards** means towards the north. *Tropical storm Marco is pushing northward up Florida's coast. ...the flow of immigrants northward.* ▶ Also an adjective. *The northward journey from Jalalabad was no more than 120 miles.* ADV: usu ADV after v, also n ADV; ADJ: ADJ n

north-west; also spelled **North-West**. ◆◆◆◆◇

1 The **north-west** is the direction which is halfway between north and west. *...Ushant, five miles out to the north-west.* N-UNCOUNT: also *the*N =direction

2 The **north-west** of a place, country, or region is the part which is towards the north-west. *Labour took its pre-election campaign to the North-West. ...the extreme north-west of South America.* N-SING: *the*N, oft N *of*n

3 If you go **north-west**, you travel towards the north-west. *Take the narrow lane going north-west parallel with the railway line.* ADV: ADV after v

4 Something that is **north-west of** a place is positioned to the north-west of it. *This was situated to the north-west of the town, a short walk from the railway station.* ADV: ADV *of*n

5 The **north-west** part of a place, country, or region is the part which is towards the north-west. *...the North-West Regional Health Authority. ...the north-west coast of the United States. ...Sydney's north-west suburbs.* ADJ-GRADED: ADJ n =north-western

6 A **north-west** wind is a wind that blows from the north-west. *A brisk north-west wind swept across the region.* ADJ: ADJ n

north-westerly; also spelled **north westerly**.

1 A **north-westerly** point, area, or direction is to the north-west or towards the north-west. ADJ: usu ADJ n

2 A **north-westerly** wind is a wind that blows from the north-west. ADJ

north-western; also spelled **north western**. ◆◇◇◇◇ **North-western** means in or from the north-west of a region or country. *He was from north-western Russia.* ADJ: usu ADJ n

Norwegian /nɔːʳwiːdʒən/ **Norwegians** ◆◆◆◆◇

1 **Norwegian** means belonging or relating to Norway, or to its people, language, or culture. *The main road from Murmansk to the Norwegian border is still closed to foreigners... I stood there breathing in the fresh Norwegian air.* ▶ A **Norwegian** is a Norwegian citizen, or a person of Norwegian origin. *Many Norwegians feel that Norway is a culturally young country.* ADJ; N-COUNT

2 **Norwegian** is the language spoken by people who live in Norway. *It is interesting that Grainger spoke Norwegian.* N-UNCOUNT

nose /noʊz/ **noses, nosing, nosed** ◆◆◆◇◇

1 Your **nose** is the part of your face which sticks out above your mouth. You use it for smelling and breathing. *She wiped her nose with a tissue... She's got funny eyes and a big nose.* N-COUNT: oft poss N

2 The **nose** of vehicle such as a car or aeroplane is the front part of it. *Sue parked off the main street, with the van's nose pointing away from the street.* N-COUNT: oft poss N

3 You can refer to your sense of smell as your **nose**. *The river that runs through Middlesbrough became ugly on the eye and hard on the nose.* N-COUNT

4 If a racehorse wins a race by a **nose**, it wins by the smallest possible distance. *Chirkpar rattled past him on the right to snatch the prize by a nose.* N-SING: usu *by a* N

5 If a vehicle **noses** in a certain direction or if you **nose** it there, you move it slowly and carefully in that direction. *He could not see the driver as the car nosed forward... A motorboat nosed out of the mist and nudged into the branches of a tree... Ben drove past them, nosing his car into the garage.* V-ERG; V adv/prep; V n prep/adv

6 See also **hard-nosed, toffee-nosed.**

7 If you say that someone should **keep** their **nose clean**, you mean that they should behave well and keep out of trouble; an informal expression. *The* PHRASES: V and N inflect

best advice I can give is tell you to keep your nose clean.

8 If you **follow** your **nose**, you make decisions and behave in a particular way because you feel instinctively that this is what you should do, rather than because you are following any guidelines or rules. *You won't have to think, just follow your nose.* V and N inflect

9 If you say that someone **has a nose for** something, you mean that they have an instinctive ability to find it or recognize it. *He had a nose for trouble and a brilliant tactical mind... Gergen had a great sense of news, a good nose for trends, and a wide range of contacts.* V inflects, PHR n

10 If you say that someone or something **gets up** your **nose**, you mean that they annoy you; an informal expression. *He's just getting up my nose so much at the moment.* V and N inflect

11 If you say that someone **looks down** their **nose** at something or someone else, you mean that the first person believes they are superior to the other thing or person and treats them with disrespect; used showing disapproval. *I don't look down my nose at comedy... They rather looked down their noses at the poor old French and especially the poor old Italians.* V and N inflect, usu PHR *at* n PRAGMATICS

12 If you say that you **paid through the nose** for something, you are emphasizing that you had to pay what you consider too high a price for it; an informal expression. *We don't like paying through the nose for our wine when eating out.* V inflects, oft PHR *for* n

13 If someone **pokes** their **nose into** something or **sticks** their **nose into** something, they try to interfere with it even though it does not concern them; an informal expression used showing disapproval. *We don't like strangers who poke their noses into our affairs... Why did you have to stick your nose in?* V and N inflect, PHR n PRAGMATICS =meddle

14 To **rub** someone's **nose in** something that they do not want to think about, such as a failing or a mistake they have made, means to remind them repeatedly about it; an informal expression. *His enemies will attempt to rub his nose in past policy statements.* V and N inflect, PHR n

15 If you say that someone **is cutting off** their **nose to spite** their **face**, you mean they do something that they think will hurt someone, without realizing or caring that it will hurt them as well. *There is evidence that the industry's greed means that it is cutting off its nose to spite its face.* V inflects PRAGMATICS

16 If vehicles are **nose to tail**, the front of one vehicle is close behind the back of another. *...a line of about twenty fast-moving trucks driving nose to tail.* v-link PHR, PHR after v

17 If you **thumb** your **nose at** someone, you behave in a way that shows that you do not care what they think. *He has always thumbed his nose at the media.* V and N inflect, usu PHR *at* n

18 If you **turn up** your **nose** at something, you reject it because you think that it is not good enough for you. *I'm not in a financial position to turn up my nose at several hundred thousand pounds.* V and N inflect, usu PHR *at* n

19 If you do something **under** someone's **nose**, you do it right in front of them, without trying to hide it from them. *We've been married 25 years and this carrying on under my nose was the last straw.* N inflects

20 • to **put sb's nose out of joint**: see **joint**.

nose around; the form **nose about** is also used in British English. If you **nose around** or **nose about**, you look around a place that belongs to someone else, to see if you can find something interesting; an informal expression. *Accountants are nosing around the BBC at the moment, conducting an efficiency study... Security people were nosing around, and Cortez joined them.* PHRASAL VERB V P n V P

nosebleed /nouzbli:d/ **nosebleeds;** also spelled **nose bleed**. If someone has a **nosebleed**, blood comes out from inside their nose. *Whenever I have a cold I get a nosebleed.* N-COUNT

nosedive /nouzdaɪv/ **nosedives, nosediving, nosedived;** also spelled **nose-dive**.

1 If prices, profits, or exchange rates **nosedive**, they fall very suddenly; used mainly in journalism. *The market suffered from a knock on effect, causing the value of other shares to nosedive by £2.6 billion.* VERB =plummet V ► Also a noun. *The bank yesterday revealed a 30 per cent nosedive in profits.* N-SING

2 If something such as someone's reputation or a particular situation **nosedives**, it gets worse very suddenly and dramatically; used mainly in journalism. *Since the US invasion the president's reputation has nosedived.* ► Also a noun. *He told the tribunal his career had 'taken a nosedive' since his dismissal last year.* VERB V N-SING

nose job, nose jobs. A **nose job** is surgical operation that some people have to improve the shape of their nose; an informal word. *I've never had plastic surgery, though people always think I've had a nose job.* N-COUNT

nosey /nouzi/. See **nosy**.

nosh /nɒʃ/ **noshes, noshing, noshed**

1 In informal British English, food can be referred to as **nosh**. *Fancy some nosh?* N-UNCOUNT =grub

2 If you **nosh**, you eat; used mainly in informal British English. *She sprinkled pepper on my grub, watching me nosh. ...a big-bellied bird noshing some heather.* VERB V V n

nostalgia /nɒstældʒə/. **Nostalgia** is an affectionate feeling you have for the past, especially for a particularly happy time. *He might be influenced by nostalgia for the surroundings of his happy youth... He discerned in the novel an air of Sixties nostalgia.* ◆◇◇◇◇ N-UNCOUNT: oft N *for* n

nostalgic /nɒstældʒɪk/ ◆◇◇◇◇

1 **Nostalgic** things cause you to think affectionately about the past. *Although we still depict nostalgic snow scenes on Christmas cards, winters are now very much warmer... Somehow the place even smelt wonderfully nostalgic.* ADJ-GRADED

2 If you feel **nostalgic**, you think affectionately about experiences you had in the past. *Many people were nostalgic for the good old days... You tend to be nostalgic, and like things to be as they have always been.* ♦ **nostalgically** /nɒstældʒɪkli/ *People look back nostalgically on the war period, simply because everyone pulled together.* ADJ-GRADED: usu v-link ADJ, oft ADJ *for/about* n =sentimental ADV: ADV with v, ADV adj

nostril /nɒstrɪl/ **nostrils.** Your **nostrils** are the two openings at the end of your nose. ◆◇◇◇◇ N-COUNT

nostrum /nɒstrəm/ **nostrums**

1 You can refer to ideas or theories which are intended to solve a particular problem as **nostrums**, especially when you think that they are untrue, simplistic, or outdated. *It is clear that the old nostrums of the classical state system and its framework of international law are being swiftly and thoroughly undermined.* N-COUNT: usu pl, oft N *of* n =cure-all

2 If you refer to a medicine as a **nostrum**, you mean that it is not effective or has not been tested in a proper scientific way. *Supermarket and pharmacy shelves are lined with pills, tablets, and other nostrums claiming to be magic potions.* N-COUNT =elixir

nosy /nouzi/ **nosier, nosiest;** also spelled **nosey**. If you describe someone as **nosy**, you mean that they are interested in things which do not concern them; used showing disapproval. *He was having to whisper in order to avoid being overheard by their nosy neighbours... I agree that the press is often too nosy about a candidate's personal history.* ADJ-GRADED PRAGMATICS =inquisitive

not /nɒt/ ◆◆◆◆◆

In spoken English and informal written English, **not** is often contracted to **n't** and added to the auxiliary or modal verb. For example, 'did not' is often contracted to 'didn't'.

1 You use **not** with verbs to form negative statements. *The sanctions are not working the way they were intended... I was not in Britain at the time... There are many things you won't understand here... I don't trust my father anymore.* NEG

2 You use **not** to form questions to which you expect the answer 'yes'. *Haven't they got enough problems there already?... Didn't I see you at the party last week?... Didn't you just love the Waltons?* NEG PRAGMATICS

3 You use **not**, usually in the form **n't**, in questions which imply that someone should have done NEG PRAGMATICS

something or should do something, or to express surprise that something is not the case. *Why didn't you do it months ago?... Why couldn't he listen to her?... Hasn't anyone ever kissed you before?... Shouldn't you have gone further?... Didn't I tell you to put some slippers on?*

4 You use **not**, usually in the form **n't**, in question tags after a positive statement. *'It's a nice piece of jewellery though, isn't it?'... I've been a great husband, haven't I?... You will take me tomorrow, won't you?* NEG

5 You use **not**, usually in the form **n't**, in polite suggestions. *Actually we do have a position in mind. Why don't you fill out our application?... Couldn't they send it by train?* NEG PRAGMATICS

6 You use **not** to represent the negative of a word, group, or clause that has just been used. *'Have you found Paula?'—'I'm afraid not, Kate.'... At first I really didn't care whether he came or not.* NEG

7 You can use **not** in front of 'all' or 'every' when you want to say something that applies only to some members of the group that you are talking about. *Not all the money, to put it mildly, has been used wisely... Not every applicant had a degree.* NEG

8 If something is **not** always the case, you mean that sometimes it is the case and sometimes it is not. *He didn't always win the arguments, but he often was right... She couldn't always afford a babysitter... The life of an FBI agent wasn't always as glamorous as people thought.* NEG

9 You can use **not** or **not even** in front of 'a' or 'one' to emphasize that there is none at all of what is being mentioned. *The houses are beautiful, but there's no shop, not even a pub to go into... I sent report after report. But not one word was published... 'Did he have any enemies?'—'Not a one. Not a damn one!'* NEG PRAGMATICS ≠lots, a lot

10 You can use **not** in front of a word referring to a distance, length of time, or other amount to say that the actual distance, time, or amount is less than the one mentioned. *The tug crossed our stern not fifty yards away. ...a large crowd not ten yards away waiting for a bus... They were here not five minutes ago!* NEG: NEG amount

11 You use **not** when you are contrasting something that is true with something that is untrue. You use this especially to indicate that people might think that the untrue statement is true. *He has his place in the Asian team not because he is white but because he is good... Training is an investment not a cost... There came an explosion, not so much a bang as a shaking like an earthquake.* NEG PRAGMATICS

12 You use **not** in expressions such as 'not only', 'not just', 'not simply', and 'not merely' to emphasize that something is true, but it is not the whole truth. *These movies were not only making money; they were also perceived to be original... There is always a 'black market' not just in Britain but in Europe as a whole... Hoffman did not simply oppose the system; he used the system against itself.* NEG PRAGMATICS

13 You use **not that** to introduce a negative clause that contradicts something that the previous statement implies. *His death took me a year to get over; not that you're ever really over it... It occurred to Tom to wonder whether Jane was quite trustworthy. Not that he thought she was in any way politically active.* PHR-CONJ-SUBORD PRAGMATICS

14 **Not at all** is an emphatic way of saying 'No' or of agreeing that the answer to a question is 'No'. *'Sorry. I sound like Abby, don't I?'—'No. Not at all.'... 'You don't think that you've betrayed your country.'—'No I don't. No, not at all.'* CONVENTION PRAGMATICS

15 **Not at all** is a polite way of acknowledging a person's thanks. *'Thank you very much for speaking with us.'—'Not at all.'* CONVENTION PRAGMATICS

16 • **not half**: see **half**. • **if not**: see **if**. • **not least**: see **least**. • **not to mention**: see **mention**. • **nothing if not**: see **nothing**. • **not for nothing**: see **nothing**. • **more often than not**: see **often**.

notable /nəʊtəbəl/ **notables** ◆◆◇◇◇

1 Someone or something that is **notable** is important or interesting. *The proposed new structure is notable not only for its height, but for its shape... Mo did not want to be ruled by anyone and it is notable that she never allowed the men in her life to eclipse her... With a few notable exceptions, doctors are a pretty sensible lot.* ADJ-GRADED: oft ADJ *for* n =noteworthy

2 **Notables** are important or powerful people; a formal use. *Elected by local notables for nine years Senators lack the democratic legitimacy of members of the National Assembly... The notables include five Senators, two Supreme Court judges and three State Governors.* N-COUNT: usu pl =VIP

notably /nəʊtəbli/ ◆◆◇◇◇

1 You use **notably** to specify an important or typical example of something that you are talking about. *The divorce would be granted when more important problems, notably the fate of the children, had been decided... It was a question of making sure certain needs were addressed, notably in the pensions area.* ADV-GRADED: ADV group/cl PRAGMATICS =particularly

2 You can use **notably** to emphasize a particular quality that someone or something has. *Old established friends are notably absent, so it's a good opportunity to make new contacts... A notably short, silver-haired man, he plays basketball with his staff several times a week.* ADV: ADV adj/adv PRAGMATICS =remarkably

notary /nəʊtəri/ **notaries.** A **notary** or a **notary public** is a person, usually a lawyer, who has legal authority to witness the signing of documents in order to make them legally valid. *She is the town clerk and a certified public accountant and notary public.* N-COUNT

notation /nəʊteɪʃən/ **notations.** A **notation** is a set of written symbols that are used to represent a system such as music, logic, or mathematics. *Musical notation was conceived for the C major scale and each line and space represents a note in this scale. ...some other abstract notation system like a computer language.* N-VAR: usu supp N

notch /nɒtʃ/ **notches, notching, notched** ◆◇◇◇◇

1 You can refer to a step on a scale of measurement or achievement as a **notch**; used mainly in journalism. *Average earnings in the economy moved up another notch in August... In this country the good players are pulled down a notch or two... On the third day, General Zhang raised the temperature of the assembly a few notches.* N-COUNT

2 If you **notch** a success, especially in sport, you achieve it; used mainly in journalism. *Steve Bull notched his 200th goal for Wolves as they beat Leicester 3-0... The President is keen to notch a political triumph that would foster freer world trade and faster economic growth.* VERB V n

3 A **notch** is a small V-shaped or circular cut in the surface or edge of something. *It is a myth that gunslingers in the American west cut notches in the handle of their pistol for each man they shot.* N-COUNT =nick

4 See also **top-notch**.

notch up. If you **notch up** something such as a score or total, you achieve it; an informal expression used mainly in journalism. *He had notched up more than 25 victories worldwide... The economy is expanding, notching up high growth rates.* PHRASAL VERB V P n (not pron) Also V n P

note /nəʊt/ **notes, noting, noted** ◆◆◆◆◇

1 A **note** is a short letter. *Stevens wrote him a note asking him to come to his apartment... I'll have to leave a note for Karen.* N-COUNT =message

2 A **note** is something that you write down to remind yourself of something. *I knew that if I didn't make a note I would lose the thought so I asked to borrow a pen or pencil... Take notes during the consultation as the final written report is very concise.* N-COUNT

3 In a book or article, a **note** is a short piece of additional information. *See Note 16 on page p. 223. ...'Exiles' by James Joyce, edited with an Introduction and notes by J C C Mays.* N-COUNT =annotation

4 A **note** is a short document that has to be signed by someone and that gives official information about something. *Since Mr Bennett was going to need some time off work, he asked for a sick note... I've got half a ton of gravel in the lorry but he won't sign my delivery note.* N-COUNT: with supp

5 In British English, you can refer to a banknote as N-COUNT a **note**. The usual American word is **bill**. *They exchange travellers cheques at a different rates from notes. ...a five pound note.*

6 In music, a **note** is the sound of a particular pitch, or a written symbol representing this sound. *She has a deep voice and doesn't even try for the high notes... If the note of D is sounded on a harp, all the corresponding D strings of other octaves will likewise resonate.* N-COUNT: usu with supp

7 You can use **note** to refer to a particular quality in someone's voice that shows how they are feeling. *There is an unmistakable note of nostalgia in his voice when he looks back on the early years of the family business... It was not difficult for him to catch the note of bitterness in my voice.* N-SING: with supp, usu N *of* n =tone

8 You can use **note** to refer to a particular feeling, impression, or atmosphere. *Yesterday's testimony began on a note of passionate but civilized disagreement... Somehow he tells these stories without a note of horror... The furniture strikes a traditional note which is appropriate to its Edwardian setting.* N-SING: with supp

9 If you **note** a fact, you become aware of it. *The White House has noted his promise to support any attack that was designed to enforce the UN resolutions... Suddenly, I noted that the rain had stopped... At every stage people noted how painstaking he was about personal relations with constituents, party workers and civil servants.* VERB =notice V n V that V wh

10 If you **note** something, you mention it in order to draw people's attention to it. *Note the statue to Sallustio Bandini, a prominent Sienese... The report notes that export and import volumes picked up in leading economies... Please note that there are a limited number of tickets.* VERB =observe, remark V n V that

11 When you **note** something, you write it down as a record of what has happened. *'He has had his tonsils out and has been ill, too,' she noted in her diary... One policeman was clearly visible noting the number plates of passing cars... A guard came and took our names and noted where each of us was sitting.* VERB =log V with quote V n V wh Also V that

12 See also **noted**, **promissory note**, **sleeve note**.

13 If you **compare notes** with someone on a particular subject, you talk to them and find out whether their opinion, information, or experience is the same as yours. You can also say that two people **compare notes**. *The women were busily comparing notes on the queen's outfit... They exchanged greetings, compared notes on their wives and families, and finally got down to business.* PHRASES RECIP: V inflects, oft PHR *on* n, PHR *with* n =discuss

14 Someone or something that is **of note** is important, worth mentioning, or well-known. *...politicians of note... He has published nothing of note in the last ten years.* n PHR =of consequence

15 If someone or something **strikes** a particular **note** or **sounds** a particular **note**, they create a particular feeling, impression, or atmosphere. *Before his first round of discussions, Mr Baker sounded an optimistic note... Plants growing out of cracks in paving strike the right note up a cottage-garden path.* V inflects

16 If you **take note** of something, you pay attention to it because you think that it is important or significant. *Take note of the weather conditions... They took note that she showed no surprise at the news of the murder.* V inflects, oft PHR *of* n, PHR that

17 • to **make a mental note**: see **mental**.

note down. If you **note down** something, you write it down quickly, so that you have a record of it. *She had noted down the names and she told me the story simply and factually... If you find a name that's on the list I've given you, note it down... Please note down what I'm about to say.* PHRASAL VERB V P n (not pron) V n P V P wh

notebook /noutbuk/ **notebooks** ◆◆◇◇◇

1 A **notebook** is a small book for writing notes in. *He brought out a notebook and pen from his pocket. ...her reporter's notebook.* N-COUNT =notepad

2 A **notebook** computer is a small personal computer. *...a range of notebook computers which allows all your important information to travel safely with you.* N-COUNT: usu N n

noted /noutɪd/. Someone or something that is **noted** for something they do or have is well-known and admired for it. *...a television programme noted for its attacks on organised crime... Lawyers are not noted for rushing into change.* ◆◆◆◇◇ ADJ-GRADED: oft ADJ *for* n/-ing =renowned

notepad /noutpæd/ **notepads.** A **notepad** is a pad of paper that you use for writing notes or letters on. *Have a pencil and notepad ready.* N-COUNT =notebook

notepaper /noutpeɪpəʳ/. **Notepaper** is paper that you use for writing letters on. *He had written letters on official notepaper to promote a relative's company.* • See also **headed notepaper.** N-UNCOUNT: oft supp N

noteworthy /noutwɜːʳði/. A fact or event that is **noteworthy** is interesting, remarkable, or significant in some way; a formal word. *It is noteworthy that the programme has been shifted from its original August slot to July... I found nothing particularly noteworthy to report... The most noteworthy event in the region was the February coup in Thailand.* ADJ-GRADED: oft *it* v-link ADJ that =notable, striking

nothing /nʌθɪŋ/ **nothings** ◆◆◆◆◆

1 **Nothing** means not a single thing, or not a single part of something. *I've done nothing much since coffee time... Mr Pearson said he knew nothing of his wife's daytime habits... He was dressed in jeans and nothing else... There's nothing else I can do for you.* PRON-INDEF-NEG

2 You use **nothing** to indicate that something or someone is not important or significant. *Because he had always had money it meant nothing to him... While the increase in homicides is alarming, it is nothing compared to what is to come in the rest of the decade... She kept bursting into tears over nothing at work... Do our years together mean nothing?* ▶ Also a noun. *It is the picture itself that is the problem; so small, so dull. It's a nothing, really... All it took was a word here, a word there, to convince him that he was a nothing.* PRON-INDEF-NEG; N-COUNT: usu sing

3 If you say that something cost **nothing** or is worth **nothing** you are indicating that it cost or is worth a surprisingly small amount of money. *The furniture was threadbare; he'd obviously picked it up for nothing... Homes in this corner of Mantua that once went for $350,000 are now worth nothing.* PRON-INDEF-NEG

4 You use **nothing** before an adjective or 'to'-infinitive to mean that a situation, event, or activity does not have the particular quality mentioned. *Around the lake the countryside generally is nothing special... There is nothing wrong with the car... All kids her age do silly things; it's nothing to worry about.* PRON-INDEF-NEG: PRON adj, PRON to-inf

5 You can use **nothing** before 'so' and an adjective or adverb, or before a comparative, to emphasize how strong or great a particular quality is. *Youngsters learn nothing so fast as how to beat the system... I consider nothing more important in my life than songwriting... There's nothing better than a good cup of hot coffee.* PRON-INDEF-NEG: PRON *so* adj/adv, PRON compar PRAGMATICS

6 You can use **all or nothing** to say that either something must be done fully and completely or else it cannot be done at all. *Either he went through with this thing or he did not; it was all or nothing.* PHRASES v-link PHR

7 If you say that something is **better than nothing**, you mean that it is not what is required, but that it is better to have that thing than to have nothing at all. *After all, 15 minutes of exercise is better than nothing.* v-link PHR

8 You use **nothing but** in front of a noun, an infinitive without 'to', or an '-ing' form to mean 'only'. *All that money brought nothing but sadness and misery and tragedy... It did nothing but make us ridiculous... They care for nothing but fighting.* PHR n/inf/-ing

9 In informal English, you can say **'Nothing doing'** when you want to say that something is not happening or cannot be done. *Pay now, or nothing doing... 'I could take the subway and have David pick me up at the station.'—'Nothing doing.'* CONVENTION PRAGMATICS

10 In British English, if you say that **there is nothing for it** but to take a particular action, you mean that it is the only possible course of action that you can take, even though it might be unpleasant. *Much depends on which individual ingredients you* V inflects, PHR *but* to-inf, PHR *but* n

choose. There is nothing for it but to taste and to experiment for yourself... He wished he was not in a room so far from the bathroom. There was nothing for it but a long trudge through the house.

11 You use **nothing if not** in front of an adjective to indicate that someone or something clearly has a lot of the particular quality mentioned. *Professor Fish has been nothing if not professional... Hollywood is nothing if not creative, especially if someone else will pick up the bills.* v-link PHR adj

12 People sometimes say **'It's nothing'** as a polite response after someone has thanked them for something they have done. *'Thank you for the wonderful dinner.'—'It's nothing,' Sarah said... 'I'll be on my way. I can't thank you enough, Alan.'—'It was nothing, but take care.'* CONVENTION PRAGMATICS

13 If you say about a story or report that there is **nothing in it** or **nothing to it**, you mean that it is untrue. *It's all rubbish and superstition, and there's nothing in it.* *there* v-link PHR

14 If you say about an activity that there is **nothing to it** or **nothing in it**, you mean that it is extremely easy. *This device has a gripper that electrically twists off the jar top. Nothing to it... If you've shied away from making pancakes in the past, don't be put off – there's really nothing in it!* *there* v-link PHR

15 You can use **nothing less than** to emphasize your next words, often indicating that something seems very surprising or important. *What he had in mind amounted to nothing less than a total reversal of the traditional role of the executive... You're nothing less than a murderer!* PHR n/adj PRAGMATICS =nothing short of

16 If you say that it was **not for nothing** that something happened, you are emphasizing that there was a very good reason for it to happen. *Not for nothing was the plane called 'The widow-maker'... It's not for nothing that interior decorators the world over look to the English country garden for glorious inspiration.* PHR cl, *it* v-link PHR that PRAGMATICS

17 If you say that someone is getting **something for nothing**, you disapprove of the fact that they are getting something that they want without having to give anything or do anything in return. *What's wrong with you is that you think you can get something for nothing.* PHR after v PRAGMATICS

18 Nothing of the sort is used as an emphatic way of refusing permission or of denying something that someone has said. *'We're going to talk this over in my office.'—'We're going to do nothing of the sort.'... Mrs Adamson said that she was extremely sorry, in tones that made it clear that she was nothing of the sort.* PHR after v, v-link PHR PRAGMATICS =no such thing

19 • See also **sweet nothings.** • **nothing to write home about**: see **home.** • to **say nothing of**: see **say.** • **nothing short of**: see **short.** • to **stop at nothing**: see **stop.** • to **think nothing of**: see **think.**

nothingness /nʌθɪŋnəs/

1 Nothingness is the fact of not existing. *There might be something beyond the grave, you know, and not nothingness.* N-UNCOUNT

2 Nothingness can refer to complete emptiness or a complete absence of things or feelings. *Her eyes, glazed with the drug, stared with half closed lids at nothingness. ...my never-ending search for love, always followed by nothingness.* N-UNCOUNT

notice /noʊtɪs/ **notices, noticing, noticed** ◆◆◆◆◇

1 If you **notice** something or someone, you become aware of them. *He stressed that people should not hesitate to contact the police if they've noticed any strangers in Hankham recently... I noticed that most academics were writing papers during the summer... Luckily, I'd noticed where you left the car... Mrs Shedden noticed a bird sitting on the garage roof... She needn't worry that he'll think she looks a mess. He won't notice.* VERB V n V that V wh V n -ing V Also V n inf

2 A **notice** is a written announcement in a place where everyone can read it. *Notices in the waiting room requested that you neither smoke nor spit... A few guest houses had 'No Vacancies' notices in their windows. ...a notice which said 'Beware Flooding'.* N-COUNT =announcement

3 If you give **notice** about something that is going to happen, you give a warning in advance that it is going to happen. *Interest is paid monthly. Three months' notice is required for withdrawals... Unions are required to give 7 days' notice of industrial action... She was transferred without notice.* N-UNCOUNT: usu with supp

4 A **notice** is a formal announcement in a newspaper or magazine about something that has happened or is going to happen. *I rang The Globe with news of Blake's death, and put notices in the personal column of The Times... The request is published in notices in today's national newspapers.* N-COUNT =announcement

5 A **notice** is one of a number of similar or identical letters that an organization sends to a number of people giving them some information or asking them to do something. *Bonus notices were issued each year from head office to local agents... There will be a creditors meeting on June 15 and notices will be circulated to all known creditors.* N-COUNT: usu supp N

6 A **notice** is a written article in a newspaper or magazine in which someone gives their opinion of a play, film, or concert. *Nevertheless, it's good to know you've had good notices, even if you don't read them.* N-COUNT =review

7 Notice is used in expressions such as **'at short notice'**, **'at a moment's notice'** or **'at twenty-four hours' notice'**, to indicate that something can or must be done within a short period of time. *There's no one available at such short notice to take her class... All our things stayed in our suitcase, as if we had to leave at a moment's notice.* PHRASES usu PHR after v

8 If you **bring** something **to** someone's **notice**, you make them aware of it. *I am so glad that you have brought this to my notice... It was in 1982 that his name was first brought to our notice.* V inflects

9 If something **comes to** your **notice**, you become aware of it. *Her work also came to the notice of the French actor-producer Louis Jouvet... As I write, a very interesting case has come to my notice.* V inflects

10 If something **escapes** your **notice**, you fail to recognize it or realize it. *It hasn't escaped our notice that the hospital has come out of all the proposed changes really quite nicely... From the smallest to the largest production unit, no one escaped notice.* V inflects, oft PHR that

11 If a situation is said to exist **until further notice**, it will continue for an uncertain length of time until someone changes it. *The bad news was that all flights to Lanchow had been cancelled until further notice.* PHR after v

12 If an employer **gives** an employee **notice**, the employer tells the employee that he or she must leave his or her job within a fixed period of time. *The next morning I telephoned him and gave him his notice.* V inflects =sack, fire

13 If you **hand in** your **notice** or **give in** your **notice**, you tell your employer that you intend to leave your job soon within a set period of time. *He handed in his notice at the bank and ruined his promising career.* V inflects =quit

14 If you **take notice** of a particular fact or situation, you behave in a way that shows that you are aware of it. *We want the government to take notice of what we think they should do for single parents... Michael Forsyth's publication of Scottish schools' exam results has made some people sit up and take notice.* V inflects, oft PHR *of* n =pay attention to

15 If you **take no notice** of someone or something, you do not consider them to be important enough to affect what you think or what you do. *They took no notice of him, he did not stand out, he was in no way remarkable... I tried not to take any notice at first but then I was offended by it.* V inflects, usu PHR *of* n =ignore

noticeable /noʊtɪsəbᵊl/. Something that is **noticeable** is very obvious, so that it is easy to see, hear, or recognize. *It is noticeable that women do not have the rivalry that men have... The most noticeable effect of these changes is in the way people are now working together.* ◆◆◇◇◇ ADJ-GRADED: oft *it* v-link ADJ that =conspicuous

♦ **noticeably** *Standards of living were deteriorating rather noticeably... There are also many physical signs, most noticeably a change in facial features.* ADV-GRADED: ADV with v, ADV group =perceptibly

noticeboard /noʊtɪsbɔːʳd/ **noticeboards.** In British English, a **noticeboard** is a board which is usually attached to a wall in order to display N-COUNT notices giving information about something. The usual American word is **bulletin board**. *She added her name to the list on the noticeboard.*

notifiable /noʊtɪfaɪəbᵊl/. A **notifiable** disease or crime is one that must be reported to the authorities whenever it occurs, because it is considered to be dangerous to the community. *Many doctors fail to report cases, even though food poisoning is a notifiable disease.* ADJ

notification /noʊtɪfɪkeɪʃᵊn/ **notifications.** If you are given **notification** of something, you are officially informed of it. *Names of the dead and injured are being withheld pending notification of relatives... Payments should be sent with the written notification.* ◆◇◇◇◇ N-VAR: oft N of n

notify /noʊtɪfaɪ/ **notifies, notifying, notified.** If you **notify** someone of something, you officially inform them about it; a formal word. *The skipper notified the coastguard of the tragedy... Earlier this year they were notified that their homes were to be cleared away... She confirmed that she would notify the police and the hospital.* ◆◇◇◇◇ VERB =inform V n of/about n be V-ed that V n Also V n that

notion /noʊʃᵊn/ **notions.** A **notion** is an idea or belief about something. *We each have a notion of just what kind of person we'd like to be... I reject absolutely the notion that privatisation of our industry is now inevitable... I'd had a few notions about being a journalist.* ◆◆◆◇◇ N-COUNT: oft N of n/-ing/wh, N that =idea

notional /noʊʃənᵊl/. Something that is **notional** exists only in theory or as a suggestion or idea, but not in reality; a formal word. *...the notional value of state assets.* ♦ **notionally** *Mr Deng, who is notionally retired, has not appeared in public for three months now... That meant that he, notionally at least, outranked them all.* ADJ =theoretical ADV: ADV with cl/group, ADV with v =theoretically

notoriety /noʊtəraɪɪti/. If someone or something achieves **notoriety**, they become well-known for something bad. *He achieved notoriety as chief counsel to President Nixon in the Watergate break-in. ...Christian Lacroix, who gained notoriety as one of Paris's most flamboyant dress designers in the 1980s.* ◆◇◇◇◇ N-UNCOUNT

notorious /noʊtɔːriəs/. Someone or something that is **notorious** is well-known for something bad. *West Berlin has long been notorious for its street violence... She told us the story of one of Britain's most notorious country house murders.* ♦ **notoriously** *The train company is overstaffed and notoriously inefficient... He worked mainly in New York City where living space is notoriously at a premium... Doctors notoriously neglect their own health and fail to seek help when they should.* ◆◆◇◇◇ ADJ-GRADED: oft ADJ for n/-ing =infamous ADV: usu ADV group, also ADV before v

notwithstanding /nɒtwɪðstændɪŋ/. If something is true **notwithstanding** something else, it is true in spite of that other thing; a formal word. *He despised William Pitt, notwithstanding the similar views they both held.* ▶ Also an adverb. *His relations with colleagues, differences of opinion notwithstanding, were unfailingly friendly.* ◆◇◇◇◇ PREP ADV: n ADV

nougat /nuːgɑː, AM -gət/. **Nougat** is a kind of hard chewy sweet, containing nuts and sometimes fruit. N-UNCOUNT

nought /nɔːt/ **noughts;** also spelled **naught** for meaning 2. ◆◇◇◇◇

1 **Nought** is the number 0; used mainly in British English. *Sales rose by nought point four per cent last month... Houses are graded from nought to ten for energy efficiency... When you write down in figures the number one million, how many noughts are there?* NUM =zero

2 If you try to do something but your efforts are not successful, you can say that your efforts **come to naught**; a formal expression. *Numerous attempts to persuade him to write his memoirs came to nought.* PHRASE: V inflects

noun /naʊn/ **nouns.** A **noun** is a word such as 'woman', 'guilt', or 'Harry' which is used to refer to a person or thing. • See also **collective noun, count noun, mass noun, proper noun, singular noun, uncount noun.** ◆◇◇◇◇ N-COUNT

noun group, noun groups. A **noun group** is a noun or pronoun, or a group of words based on a noun or pronoun. Noun groups can be the subject, object, or complement in a clause, or the object of a preposition. In the sentence, 'He put the bottle of wine on the kitchen table', 'He', 'the bottle of wine', and 'the kitchen table' are all noun groups. N-COUNT =noun phrase

noun phrase, noun phrases. A **noun phrase** is the same as a **noun group**. N-COUNT

nourish /nʌrɪʃ, AM nɜːrɪʃ/ **nourishes, nourishing, nourished** ◆◇◇◇◇

1 To **nourish** a person, animal, or plant means to provide them with the food that is necessary for life, growth, and good health. *The food she eats nourishes both her and the baby. ...microbes in the soil which nourish the plant.* ♦ **nourishing** *Most of these nourishing substances are in the yolk of the egg. ...sensible, nourishing food.* VERB V n ADJ-GRADED

2 To **nourish** something such as a feeling or belief means to allow or encourage it to grow. *Journalists on the whole don't create public opinion. They can help to nourish it. ...a current of thought which has been nourished by historical tradition.* VERB V n

3 See also **-nourished**.

-nourished /-nʌrɪʃt, AM -nɜːr-/. **-nourished** is used with adverbs such as 'well' or 'under' to indicate how much food someone eats or whether it is the right kind of food. *To make sure the children are well-nourished, vitamin drops are usually recommended. ...under-nourished and poorly dressed orphans.* COMB in ADJ-GRADED

nourishment /nʌrɪʃmənt, AM nɜːr-/ ◆◇◇◇◇

1 If something provides a person, animal, or plant with **nourishment**, it provides them with the food that is necessary for life, growth, and good health. *The mother provides the embryo with nourishment and a place to grow... He was unable to take nourishment for several days.* N-UNCOUNT

2 The action of nourishing someone or something, or the experience of being nourished, can be referred to as **nourishment**. *Sugar gives quick relief to hunger but provides no lasting nourishment.* N-UNCOUNT

nous /naʊs/. In British English, **nous** is intelligence or common sense. *I wonder which university will have the nous to appoint him professor of poetry... She may not be an intellectual, she may not have much political nous.* N-UNCOUNT: usu with supp =shrewdness

nouveau-riche /nuːvoʊ riːʃ/ **nouveaux-riches.** The plural can be either **nouveau-riche** or **nouveaux-riches.**

1 The **nouveaux-riches** are people who have only recently become rich and who have tastes and manners that some people consider vulgar; used showing disapproval. *The nouveau riche have to find a way to be accepted... As for India's nouveaux riches, they will now have to pay still higher duties on luxury goods.* N-PLURAL: usu the N PRAGMATICS =newly-rich

2 **Nouveau-riche** means belonging or relating to the nouveaux-riches. *He hit back at critics who did not appreciate his nouveau-riche taste.* ADJ-GRADED PRAGMATICS =newly-rich

nouvelle cuisine /nuːvel kwɪziːn/. **Nouvelle cuisine** is a style of cooking in which very fresh foods are lightly cooked and served in unusual combinations. You can also refer to food that has been cooked in this way as **nouvelle cuisine**. *More restaurants are favouring simple, healthy Mediterranean-style seafood dishes instead of fussy nouvelle cuisine.* N-UNCOUNT

Nov. **Nov.** is a written abbreviation for **November**. *The first ballot is on Tuesday Nov 20.* ◆◆◇◇◇

novel /nɒvᵊl/ **novels** ◆◆◆◆◇

1 A **novel** is a long written story about imaginary people and events. *...a novel by Herman Hesse... His first works of fiction were historical novels set in the time of the Pharaohs.* N-COUNT

2 **Novel** things are unlike anything that has been done, experienced, or created before. *Protesters found a novel way of demonstrating against steeply rising oil prices... The very idea of a sixth form college was novel in 1962.* ADJ-GRADED =original

novelist /nɒvəlɪst/ **novelists.** A **novelist** is a person who writes novels. *The key to success as a romantic novelist is absolute belief in your story.* ◆◆◇◇◇ N-COUNT

novella /noʊvelə/ **novellas.** A **novella** is a short novel or a long short story. *The story is based on an autobiographical novella from French writer Marguerite Duras.* N-COUNT

novelty /nɒvəlti/ **novelties** ◆◇◇◇◇

1 **Novelty** is the quality of being different, new, and unusual. *In the contemporary western world, rapidly changing styles cater to a desire for novelty and individualism.* N-UNCOUNT: oft *the* N *of* n

2 A **novelty** is something that is new and therefore interesting. *Seeing people queuing for food was a novelty... It came from the days when a motor car was a novelty.* N-COUNT

3 **Novelties** are cheap, unusual objects that are sold as gifts or souvenirs. *At Easter, we give them plastic eggs filled with small toys, novelties and coins.* N-COUNT

November /noʊvembəʳ/ **Novembers. November** is the eleventh month of the year in the Western calendar. *He arrived in London in November 1939... There's no telling what the voters will do next November.* ◆◆◆◆◇ N-VAR

novice /nɒvɪs/ **novices** ◆◆◇◇◇

1 A **novice** is someone who has been doing a job or other activity for only a short time and so is not experienced at it. *I'm a novice at these things, Lieutenant. You're the professional... As a novice writer, this is something I'm interested in.* N-COUNT: oft N *at* n, N n ≠old hand

2 In a monastery or convent, a **novice** is a person who is preparing to become a monk or nun. N-COUNT

now /naʊ/ ◆◆◆◆◆

1 You use **now** to refer to the present time, often in contrast to a time in the past or the future. *She's a widow now... But we are now a much more fragmented society... Beef now costs well over 30 roubles a pound... She should know that by now.* ADV: ADV with cl, oft prep ADV ► Also a pronoun. *Now is the time when we must all live as economically as possible.* PRON

2 If you do something **now**, you do it immediately. *I'm sorry, but I must go now... I fear that if I don't write now I shall never have another opportunity to do so.* ADV: ADV after v ► Also a pronoun. *Now is your chance to talk to him.* PRON

3 You use **now** or **now that** to indicate that an event has occurred and as a result something else may or will happen. *Now you're settled, why don't you take up some serious study?... Now that she was retired she lived with her sister.* CONJ-SUBORD PRAGMATICS

4 You use **now** to indicate that a particular situation is the result of something that has recently happened. *Mrs Chandra has received one sweater for each of her five children and says that the winter will not be so hard now... She told me not to repeat it, but now I don't suppose it matters... Diplomats now expect the mission to be much less ambitious.* ADV: ADV with cl, ADV before v

5 In stories and accounts of past events, **now** is used to refer to the particular time that is being written or spoken about. *She felt a little better now... It was too late now for Blake to lock his room door... By now it was completely dark outside.* ADV: ADV with cl, oft prep ADV

6 You use **now** in statements which specify the length of time up to the present that something has lasted. *They've been married now for 30 years... They have been missing for a long time now... It's some days now since I heard anything.* ADV: ADV with v, n ADV

7 In spoken English, you say **'Now'** or **'Now then'** to indicate to the person or people you are with that you want their attention, or that you are about to change the subject. *'Now then,' Max said, 'to get back to the point.'... She stays at school for drama and doesn't get back till nine. Now, what's everyone drinking?... Now then, laddie, what's the trouble?... Now, can we move on and discuss the vital business of the day, please.* ADV: ADV cl PRAGMATICS

8 In informal English, some people say **'Now'** when they are thinking of what to say next. *Now, er, dogs can live to fifteen... Now, erm, obviously some of our listeners may have some ideas.* ADV: ADV cl PRAGMATICS

9 In spoken English, you use **now** to give a slight emphasis to a request or command. *Come on now. You know you must be hungry... Come and sit down here, now... Now don't talk so loud and bother him, honey.* ADV: ADV with cl PRAGMATICS

10 In spoken English, you can say **'Now'** to introduce information which is relevant to the part of a story or account that you have reached, and which needs to be known before you can continue. *My son went to Almeria in Southern Spain. Now he and his wife are people who love a quiet holiday... Now, I hadn't told him these details, so he must have done some research on his own.* ADV: ADV cl PRAGMATICS

11 In spoken English, you say **'Now'** to introduce something which contrasts with what you have just said before. *Now, if it was me, I'd want to do more than just change the locks... Now, as for the Democrats, they've been able to use this issue quite effectively to portray the president as insensitive.* ADV: ADV cl PRAGMATICS =however

12 If you say that something happens **now and then** or **every now and again**, you mean that it happens sometimes but not very often or regularly. *My father has a collection of magazines to which I return every now and then... Now and again he'd join in when we were playing video games.* PHRASES PHR with cl =every so often

13 If you say that something will happen **any day now**, **any moment now**, or **any time now**, you mean that it will happen very soon. *Jim expects to be sent to Europe any day now... Any moment now the silence will be broken.* PHR with cl

14 People such as television presenters and entertainers sometimes use **now for** when they are going to start talking about a different subject or presenting a new activity. *And now for something completely different... Now for a quick look at some of the other stories in the news.* PHR n PRAGMATICS

15 **Just now** means a very short time ago. *You looked pretty upset just now... I spoke just now of being in love... Just now I thought I saw someone.* PHR with cl

16 You use **just now** when you want to say that a particular situation exists at the time when you are speaking, although it may change in the future. *I'm pretty busy just now... Mr Goldsworth is not available just now.* cl PHR =at the moment

17 If you say **'It's now or never'**, you mean that something must be done immediately, because if it is not done immediately there will not be another chance to do it. *It's now or never, so make up your mind... Much as I hate to go, it's now or never.* V inflects

18 You can say **'now, now'** as a friendly way of trying to comfort someone who is upset or distressed; used in spoken English. *'I figure it's all over.'—'Now, now. You did just fine.'... 'I want to go with you, Daddy.'—'Now, now, sweetheart.'* CONVENTION PRAGMATICS =there there

19 You can say **'Now, then'** or **'Now, now'** when you want to give someone you know well a friendly warning not to behave in a particular way; used in spoken English. *Now then, no unpleasantness, please... Now, now Roger, I'm sure you didn't mean it but that remark was in very poor taste.* CONVENTION PRAGMATICS =come come

nowadays /naʊədeɪz/. **Nowadays** means at the present time, in contrast with the past. *Nowadays it's acceptable for women to be ambitious. But it wasn't then... I don't see much of Tony nowadays.* ◆◆◇◇◇ ADV: ADV with cl =these days

nowhere /noʊʰweəʳ/ ◆◆◆◇◇

1 You use **nowhere** to emphasize that a place has more of a particular quality than any other places, or that it is the only place where something happens or exists. *Nowhere is language a more serious issue than in Hawaii... This kind of forest exists nowhere else in the world... If you are extremely rich, you could stay nowhere better than the Ruislip Court Hotel.* ADV-INDEF-NEG: ADV with *be*, ADV after v, oft ADV cl/group PRAGMATICS

2 You use **nowhere** when making negative statements to say that a suitable place of the specified kind does not exist. *There was nowhere to hide and nowhere to run... I have nowhere else to go, nowhere in the world... He had nowhere to call home.* ADV-INDEF-NEG: *be* ADV, ADV after v, usu ADV to-inf, ADV adj/-ed to-inf

3 You use **nowhere** to indicate that something or someone cannot be seen or found. *Michael glanced anxiously down the corridor, but Wilfred was nowhere to be seen... The escaped prisoner was* ADV: *be* ADV, oft ADV to-inf, ADV adv/prep

nowhere in sight... He had gone out to get the gin. The cigarettes were nowhere.

4 You can use **nowhere** to refer in a general way to small, unimportant, or uninteresting places. *...endless paths that led nowhere in particular. ...country roads that go from nowhere to nowhere.* ADV: ADV after v, *from/to* ADV

5 If you say that something or someone appears **from nowhere** or **out of nowhere**, you mean that they appear suddenly and unexpectedly. *A car came from nowhere, and I had to jump back into the hedge just in time... Houses had sprung up out of nowhere on the hills.* ADV: *from/out of* ADV =out of the blue

6 You use **nowhere** to mean not in any part of a text, speech, or argument. *He nowhere offers concrete historical background to support his arguments... Point taken, but nowhere did we suggest that this yacht's features were unique... The most important issue for most ordinary people was nowhere on the proposed agenda.* ADV: ADV before v, *be* ADV, oft ADV prep

7 If you say that a place is **in the middle of nowhere**, you mean it is a long way from other places. *At dusk we pitched camp in the middle of nowhere. ...a farmhouse in the middle of nowhere.* PHRASES usu PHR after v, v-link PHR =in the sticks

8 If you say that you **are getting nowhere**, or **getting nowhere fast**, or that something **is getting** you **nowhere**, you mean that you are not achieving anything or having any success. *My mind won't stop going round and round on the same subject and I seem to be getting nowhere... 'Getting nowhere fast,' pronounced Crosby, 'that's what we're doing.'... Oh, stop it! This is getting us nowhere.* V inflects

9 If you use **nowhere near** in front of a word or expression, you are emphasizing that the real situation is very different from, or has not yet reached, the state which that word or expression suggests. *He's nowhere near recovered yet from his experiences... The chair he sat in was nowhere near as comfortable as the custom-designed one behind his desk.* PRAGMATICS

no-win situation, no-win situations. If you are in a **no-win situation**, any action you take will fail to benefit you in any way. *It was a no-win situation. Either she pretended she hated Ned and felt awful or admitted she loved him and felt even worse!* N-COUNT

nowt /naʊt/. In some dialects of British English, **nowt** is used to mean the same as 'nothing'. *I'd got nowt to worry about... You could never do nowt right for him but he wasn't a bad chap.* PRON-INDEF-NEG =nothing

noxious /nɒkʃəs/

1 A **noxious** gas or substance is poisonous or very harmful. *Many household products give off noxious fumes. ...carbon monoxide and other noxious gases.* ADJ-GRADED: usu ADJ n

2 If you refer to someone or something as **noxious**, you mean that they are extremely unpleasant; a formal use. *...the heavy, noxious smell of burning sugar, butter, fats, and flour... Their behaviour was noxious.* ADJ-GRADED: usu ADJ n =nasty

nozzle /nɒzᵊl/ **nozzles.** The **nozzle** of a hose or pipe is a narrow piece fitted to the end to control the flow of liquid or gas. *If he put his finger over the nozzle he could produce a forceful spray.* ◆◇◇◇◇ N-COUNT

nr. In addresses, **nr** is used as a written abbreviation for **near**. *Brackhurst Agricultural College, Nr Southwell, Notts.* ◆◇◇◇◇ =near

-n't /-ᵊnt/. See **not**.

nth /enθ/

1 If you refer to the most recent item in a series of things as the **nth** item, you are emphasizing the number of times something has happened. *The story was raised with me for the nth time two days before the article appeared.* ADJ: ADJ n PRAGMATICS =umpteenth

2 If something is done **to the nth degree**, it is done to an extreme degree. *Ned and I discussed everything to the nth degree... You're a risk-taker to the nth degree.* PHRASE: PHR after v, n PHR

nuance /njuːɑːns, AM nuː-/ **nuances.** A **nuance** is a small and subtle difference in sound, feeling, appearance, or meaning. *We can use our eyes and facial expressions to communicate virtually every subtle nuance of emotion there is.* ◆◇◇◇◇ N-VAR

nub /nʌb/. **The nub** of a situation, problem, or argument is the central and most basic part of it. *That, I think, is the nub of the problem... Here we reach the nub of the argument: Williams refutes the idea that humour is escapist.* N-SING: *the* N, usu N *of* n =crux

nubile /njuːbaɪl, AM nuːbɪl/. A **nubile** woman is young, physically mature, and sexually attractive. *What is this current television obsession with older men and nubile young women?* ADJ-GRADED: usu ADJ n

nuclear /njuːkliəʳ, AM nuːk-/ ◆◆◆◆◇

1 **Nuclear** means relating to the nuclei of atoms, or to the energy released when these nuclei are split or combined. *...a nuclear power station. ...nuclear energy. ...nuclear physics.* ADJ: ADJ n

2 **Nuclear** means relating to weapons that explode by using the energy released when the nuclei of atoms are split or combined. *They rejected a demand for the removal of all nuclear weapons from UK soil. ...nuclear testing.* ADJ: ADJ n =atomic

nuclear family, nuclear families. A **nuclear family** is a family unit that consists of father, mother, and children. N-COUNT

nuclear-free. A **nuclear-free** place is a place where nuclear energy or nuclear weapons are forbidden. *Strathclyde council has declared itself a nuclear-free zone. ...proposals for a nuclear-free Korean peninsular.* ADJ: usu ADJ n

nuclear reactor, nuclear reactors. A **nuclear reactor** is a machine which is used to produce nuclear energy or the place where this machine and other related machinery and equipment is kept. *Germany has decided to shut its last Soviet-designed nuclear reactor this weekend for safety reasons.* ◆◇◇◇◇ N-COUNT

nuclear winter. **Nuclear winter** refers to the possible effects on the environment of a war in which large numbers of nuclear weapons are used. It is thought that there would be very low temperatures and very little light during a nuclear winter. N-UNCOUNT: also *a* N

nucleic acid /njuːkleɪɪk æsɪd, AM nuː-/ **nucleic acids.** **Nucleic acids** are complex chemical substances, such as DNA, which are found in living cells; a technical term in biochemistry. N-MASS

nucleus /njuːkliəs, AM nuː-/ **nuclei** /njuːkliaɪ, AM nuː-/ ◆◇◇◇◇

1 The **nucleus** of an atom or cell is the central part of it. *Neutrons and protons are bound together in the nucleus of an atom.* N-COUNT: usu with supp

2 The **nucleus** of a group of people or things is the small number of members which form the most important part of the group. *The Civic Movement could be the nucleus of a centrist party of the future.* N-COUNT: usu *the* N *of* n =core

nude /njuːd, AM nuːd/ **nudes** ◆◇◇◇◇

1 A **nude** person is not wearing any clothes. *The occasional nude bather comes here... 'We are not allowed to perform nude,' said the Chinese director... In the reproduced bronze she is completely nude.* ADJ: ADJ n, ADJ after v, v-link ADJ =naked

• If you do something **in the nude**, you are not wearing any clothes. If you paint or draw someone **in the nude**, they are not wearing any clothes. *Sleeping in the nude, if it suits you, is not a bad idea... The film mainly consists of M. Piccoli painting Mlle. Beart in the nude.* PHRASE: usu PHR after v =naked ≠fully clothed

2 A **nude** is a picture or statue of a person who is not wearing any clothes. A **nude** is also a person in a picture who is not wearing any clothes. *He was one of Australia's most distinguished artists, renowned for his portraits, landscapes and nudes.* N-COUNT

nudge /nʌdʒ/ **nudges, nudging, nudged** ◆◇◇◇◇

1 If you **nudge** someone, you push them gently, usually with your elbow, in order to draw their attention to something or to show them that you want them to do something. *I nudged Stan and pointed again... 'Stop it,' he said, and nudged the boy lightly with his knee.* ▶ Also a noun. *She slipped her arm under his and gave him a nudge.* VERB V n N-COUNT: usu sing

2 If you **nudge** someone or something into a place or position, you gently push them there. *Edna Swinson nudged him into the sitting room... The civil servant nudged him forward.* ▶ Also a noun. VERB V n prep/adv N-COUNT:

McKinnon gave the wheel another slight nudge to starboard. usu sing

3 If you **nudge** someone into doing something, you gently persuade them to do it. *Bit by bit Bob had nudged Fritz into selling his controlling interest... Foreigners must use their power not simply to punish the country but to nudge it towards greater tolerance... British tour companies are nudging clients to travel further afield.* ▶ Also a noun. *I had a feeling that the challenge appealed to him. All he needed was a nudge.*
VERB V n *into*-ing/n V n *towards* n V n to-inf; N-COUNT: usu sing

4 If someone or something **is nudging** a particular amount, level, or state, they have almost reached it. *...a little-known stage play writer and actress who was nudging 40 and going nowhere... The temperature when we were there was nudging 80°F.*
VB: usu cont =approach V n

5 If you refer to **a nudge and a wink** or to **nudge-nudge wink-wink**, you mean that the person who is writing or saying something is suggesting sexual misbehaviour without stating it openly; used mainly in journalism. *The article then listed a series of nudge-nudge, wink-wink rumors that have appeared in newspapers over the last two years.*
PHRASE: oft PHR n

nudism /njuːdɪzəm, AM nuː-/. **Nudism** is the practice of not wearing any clothes on beaches and other areas specially set aside for this purpose. *Nudism, the council decided, was doing the resort more harm than good.* ♦ **nudist, nudists** *There are no nudist areas and topless sunbathing is only allowed on a few beaches.*
N-UNCOUNT =naturism; N-COUNT: oft N n =naturist

nudity /njuːdɪti, AM nuː-/. **Nudity** is the state of wearing no clothes. *...constant nudity and bad language on TV.*
◆◇◇◇◇ N-UNCOUNT =nakedness

nugget /nʌgɪt/ **nuggets**

1 A **nugget** is a small lump of something, especially gold. *...pure high-grade gold nuggets. ...a small nugget of butter.*
N-COUNT: oft n N, N *of* n

2 A **nugget** of information is an interesting or useful piece of information. *He had felt on the telephone that Jordan had a little nugget of information tucked away somewhere.*
N-COUNT: usu N *of* n

nuisance /njuːsᵊns, AM nuː-/ **nuisances.** If you say that someone or something is a **nuisance**, you mean that they annoy you or cause you a lot of problems. *He could be a bit of a nuisance when he was drunk... Sorry to be a nuisance.* ● If someone **makes a nuisance of** themselves, they behave in a way that annoys other people. *He spent three days making an absolute nuisance of himself.*
◆◇◇◇◇ N-COUNT: usu sing =pain; PHRASE: V and N inflect

nuke /njuːk, AM nuːk/ **nukes, nuking, nuked**

1 A **nuke** is a nuclear weapon; an informal use. *They have nukes, and if they're sufficiently pushed, they'll use them.*
N-COUNT

2 If one country **nukes** another, it attacks it using nuclear weapons; an informal use. *A deterrent must still be maintained against any small country that puts together a bomb and threatens to nuke an American city.*
VERB V n

null /nʌl/. If an agreement, a declaration, or the result of an election is **null and void**, it is not legally valid. *A Chinese foreign spokeswoman said the agreement had been declared null and void... The declaration was null and void as it was proclaimed in completely illegal circumstances.*
PHRASE: PHR after v

nullify /nʌlɪfaɪ/ **nullifies, nullifying, nullified**

1 To **nullify** a legal decision or procedure means to declare that it is not legally valid; a formal use. *He used his broad executive powers to nullify decisions by local governments... It is worth remembering that previous wills are nullified automatically upon marriage.*
VERB =invalidate V n

2 To **nullify** something means to make it have no effect; a formal use. *He may be able to nullify that disadvantage by offering a wider variety of produce... This, of course, would nullify the effect of the move and merely accelerate inflation.*
VERB =negate V n

numb /nʌm/ **numbs, numbing, numbed**

1 If a part of your body is **numb**, you cannot feel anything there. *He could feel his fingers growing numb at their tips... My legs felt numb and my toes ached.* ♦ **numbness** *I have recently been suffering from pain and numbness in my hands.*
◆◇◇◇◇ ADJ-GRADED: usu v-link ADJ; N-UNCOUNT: oft N *in* n

2 If you are **numb** with shock, fear, or grief, you are so shocked, frightened, or upset that you cannot think clearly or feel any emotion. *The mother, numb with grief, has trouble speaking... I was so shocked I went numb.* ♦ **numbness** *Many men become more aware of emotional numbness in their 40s.* ♦ **numbly** /nʌmli/ *He walked numbly into the cemetery.*
ADJ-GRADED: usu v-link ADJ, oft ADJ *with* n; N-UNCOUNT: oft adj N; ADV: ADV with v

3 If an event or experience **numbs** you, you can no longer think clearly or feel any emotion. *For a while the shock of Philippe's letter numbed her... The horror of my experience has numbed my senses.* ● See also **mind-numbing**. ♦ **numbed** *I'm so numbed with shock that I can hardly think. ...the sort of numbed hush which usually follows an automobile accident.*
VERB =stun V n; ADJ-GRADED: usu v-link ADJ =stunned

4 If cold weather, a drug, or a blow **numbs** a part of your body, you can no longer feel anything in it. *The cold numbed my fingers... An injection of local anaesthetic is usually given first to numb the area... She awoke with a numbed feeling in her left leg.*
VERB =deaden V n V-ed

number /nʌmbəʳ/ **numbers, numbering, numbered**
◆◆◆◆◆

1 A **number** is a word such as 'two', 'nine', or 'twelve', or a symbol such as 1, 3, or 47. You use numbers to say how many things you are referring to or where something comes in a series. *No, I don't know the room number... Stan Laurel was born at number 3, Argyll Street... The number 47 bus leaves in 10 minutes.*
N-COUNT: usu with supp

2 You use **number** with words such as 'large' or 'small' to say approximately how many things or people there are. *Quite a considerable number of interviews are going on... I have had an enormous number of letters from single parents... Growing numbers of people in the rural areas are too frightened to vote.*
N-COUNT: adj N, usu N *of* n

3 If there are a **number** of things or people, there are several of them. If there are any **number** of things or people, there is a large quantity of them. *I seem to remember that Sam told a number of lies... There must be any number of people in my position.*
N-SING: *a/any* N, usu N *of* n

4 You can refer to someone's or something's position in a list of the most successful or most popular of a particular type of thing as, for example, **number** one or **number** two. *Martin now faces the world number one, Jansher Khan of Pakistan... Before you knew it, the single was at Number 90 in the US singles charts... Vikram Seth's 'A Suitable Boy' is number two in the best-seller lists.*
N-UNCOUNT: N num

5 If a group of people or things **numbers** a particular total, that is how many there are. *They told me that their village numbered 100... This time the dead were numbered in hundreds, not dozens.*
VERB =add up to V num *be* V-ed *in* num Also V n *in* num

6 A **number** is the series of digits that you dial when you are making a telephone call. *Sarah sat down and dialled a number. ...a list of names and telephone numbers... My number is 414-3925... 'You must have a wrong number,' she said. 'There's no one of that name here.'*
N-COUNT

7 You can refer to a short piece of music, a song, or a dance as a **number**. *...'Unforgettable', a number that was written and performed in 1951... Responsibility for the dance numbers was split between Robert Alton and the young George Balanchine.*
N-COUNT

8 If someone or something **is numbered** among a particular group, they are believed to belong in that group; a formal use. *The Leicester Swannington Railway is numbered among Britain's railway pioneers... He numbered several Americans among his friends.*
VERB *be* V-ed *among* n V n *among* n

9 If you **number** something, you mark it with a number, usually starting at 1. *He cut his paper up into tiny squares, and he numbered each one... Each factor has been numbered.*
VERB V n

10 See also **opposite number**, **prime number**, **serial number**.

11 If you say that someone's or something's **days are numbered**, you mean that they will not survive
PHRASES V inflects, with poss

or be successful for much longer. *The party is convinced that the Communists' days are numbered.*
12 One of your **number** is a member of your group. *Scientists like the idea that one of their number is close to the seat of power... One of our number has made a very interesting design of flooring, which has won a prize.*
13 • safety in numbers: see **safety**.

number cruncher, number crunchers. If you refer to **number crunchers**, you mean people whose jobs involve dealing with numbers or mathematical calculations, for example in finance or statistics; an informal expression. *Even if the recovery is under way, it may be some time before the official number crunchers confirm it.* N-COUNT: usu pl

number crunching. If you refer to **number crunching**, you mean activities or processes concerned with numbers or mathematical calculation, for example in finance, statistics, or computing; an informal expression. *The computer does most of the number crunching.* N-UNCOUNT: oft N n

numberless /nʌmbəʳləs/. If there are **numberless** things, there are too many to be counted; a literary word. *...numberless acts of personal bravery by firefighters and rescue workers.* ADJ: usu ADJ n =countless

number one, number ones ◆◆◇◇◇
1 Number one means better, more important, or more popular than anything else of its kind; an informal expression. *The economy is the number one issue by far... By the way, I'm your number-one fan.* ADJ: ADJ n
2 In popular music, the **number one** is the best selling record in any one week, or the group or person who has made that record; an informal expression. *Paula is the only artist to achieve four number ones from a debut album.* N-COUNT
3 If you are **looking out for number one**, you are thinking of yourself rather than considering other people; an informal expression. *My priority is to look after number one – to create a lifestyle I am happy with.* PHRASE: V inflects

number plate, number plates; also spelled **numberplate**. In British English, a **number plate** is a sign on the front and back of a vehicle that shows its registration number. The American term is **license plate**. *He drove a Rolls-Royce with a personalised number plate.* ◆◇◇◇◇ N-COUNT

numbers game. If you say that someone is playing the **numbers game**, you are criticizing them because, when considering a particular situation, they mention only those aspects of it that can be expressed in numbers, which may be misleading or dishonest. *Regrettably, he resorts to the familiar numbers game when he boasts that fewer than 300 state enterprises currently remain in the public sector.* N-SING

Number Ten. **Number Ten** is often used to refer to 10 Downing Street, London, the official home of the British Prime Minister. It is also used to refer to the political activity that takes place there. *John Major emerged from Number Ten a few hours later... Is such a man fit for Number Ten?* N-PROPER

numbskull /nʌmskʌl/ **numbskulls.** If you refer to someone as a **numbskull**, you mean that they are very stupid; an old-fashioned, informal word. *How were we to know that he was a numbskull?* N-COUNT

numeracy /njuːmərəsi, AM nuː-/. **Numeracy** is the ability to do arithmetic. *Six months later John had developed literacy and numeracy skills, plus confidence.* N-UNCOUNT: oft N n

numeral /njuːmərəl, AM nuː-/ **numerals.** **Numerals** are written symbols used to represent numbers. *...a flat, square wristwatch with classic Roman numerals. ...the numeral six.* N-COUNT

numerate /njuːmərət, AM nuː-/. Someone who is **numerate** is able to do arithmetic. *Your children should be literate and numerate.* ADJ-GRADED ≠innumerate

numerical /njuːmerɪkᵊl, AM nuː-/. **Numerical** means expressed in numbers or relating to numbers. *Your job is to group them by letter and put them in numerical order.* ◆◇◇◇◇ ADJ: usu ADJ n
♦ **numerically** *...a numerically coded colour chart... Numerically, there are a lot of young people involved in crime.* ADV

numerology /njuːmərɒlədʒi, AM nuː-/. **Numerology** is the study of particular numbers, such as a person's date of birth, in the belief that they may have special significance in a person's life. *The number eighty-eight is very lucky in Chinese numerology.* N-UNCOUNT

numerous /njuːmərəs, AM nuːm-/. If people or things are **numerous**, they exist or are present in large numbers. *Sex crimes were just as numerous as they are today... Despite numerous attempts to diet, her weight soared.* ◆◆◆◇◇ ADJ-GRADED ≠rare, scarce

numinous /njuːmɪnəs, AM nuːm-/. Things that are **numinous** are holy, awe-inspiring, and mysterious; a literary word. *This garment was beautifully numinous after being touched and blessed by so many loving hands.* ADJ-GRADED

nun /nʌn/ **nuns.** A **nun** is a member of a female religious community. Nuns take religious vows and promise to spend their lives serving God. *Mr Thomas was taught by the Catholic nuns whose school he attended, to work and study hard.* ◆◆◇◇◇ N-COUNT

nuncio /nʌnsioʊ/ **nuncios.** In the Roman Catholic church, a **nuncio** is an official who represents the Pope in a foreign country. *Ties were broken in 1949 when the papal nuncio was refused entry into Belgium.* N-COUNT

nunnery /nʌnəri/ **nunneries.** A **nunnery** is a group of buildings in which a community of nuns live together; an old-fashioned word. N-COUNT =convent

nuptial /nʌpʃᵊl/ **nuptials**
1 Nuptial is used to refer to things relating to a wedding or to marriage; an old-fashioned use. *I went to the room which he had called the nuptial chamber.* ADJ: usu ADJ n =marital
2 Someone's **nuptials** are their wedding celebrations; an old-fashioned use. *I've heard of your impending nuptials, my dear.* N-PLURAL: usu with poss =wedding

nurse /nɜːʳs/ **nurses, nursing, nursed** ◆◆◆◇◇
1 A **nurse** is a person whose job is to care for people who are ill. *She had spent 29 years as a nurse... Patients were dying because of an acute shortage of nurses.* N-COUNT; N-TITLE; N-VOC
2 If you **nurse** someone, you care for them when they are ill. *All the years he was sick my mother had nursed him... She rushed home to nurse her daughter back to health.* VERB V n V n *back to* n
3 If you **nurse** an illness or injury, you allow it to get better by resting as much as possible. *Botham continues to nurse a strained groin.* VERB V n
4 If you **nurse** an emotion or desire, you feel it strongly for a long time. *Jane still nurses the pain of rejection... Davidson has long nursed an ambition to win the world's premier three day event.* VERB =harbour V n
5 A **nurse** is a person who is trained to look after young children; an old-fashioned use. *Every morning she got up early with the children and the nurse.* N-COUNT =nanny
6 When a baby **nurses** or when its mother **nurses** it, it feeds by sucking milk from its mother's breast; an old-fashioned use. *Most authorities recommend letting the baby nurse whenever it wants. ...young women nursing babies... Young people and nursing mothers are exempted from charges.* V-ERG =suckle V V n V-ing
7 See also **nursery nurse, nursing, wet nurse.**

nursemaid /nɜːʳsmeɪd/ **nursemaids.** A **nursemaid** is a woman or girl who is paid to look after young children; an old-fashioned word. N-COUNT =nurse, nanny

nursery /nɜːʳsəri/ **nurseries** ◆◆◇◇◇
1 A **nursery** is a place where children who are not old enough to go to school are looked after. *This nursery will be able to cater for 29 children... Her company ran its own workplace nursery.* • See also **day nursery**. N-COUNT: also *at/from/to* N
2 Nursery is a school for young children who are not yet old enough to go to primary school. *An affordable nursery education service is an essential basic amenity. ...a nursery teacher.* N-VAR: oft N n
3 A **nursery** is a room in a family home in which the young children of the family sleep or play. *He has painted murals in his children's nursery.* N-COUNT
4 A **nursery** is a place where plants are grown in or- N-COUNT

der to be sold. *The garden, developed over the past 35 years, includes a nursery.*

nurseryman /nɜːʳsərimən/ **nurserymen.** A **nurseryman** is a man who works in a place where young plants are grown in order to be sold. N-COUNT

nursery nurse, nursery nurses. A **nursery nurse** is a person who has been trained to look after very young children. N-COUNT

nursery rhyme, nursery rhymes. A **nursery rhyme** is a poem or song for young children, especially one that is old or well known. N-COUNT

nursery school, nursery schools. A **nursery school** or a **nursery** is a school for young children who not yet old enough to go to primary school. *The availability of nursery school places varies widely across London.* ◆◇◇◇◇ N-VAR =kindergarten

nursing /nɜːʳsɪŋ/. **Nursing** is the profession of looking after people who are ill. *She had no aptitude for nursing... Does the nursing staff seem to care?* ◆◆◇◇◇ N-UNCOUNT

nursing home, nursing homes. A **nursing home** is a private hospital, especially one for old people. *Isaac Binger has died in a nursing home in Florida at the age of 87.* ◆◇◇◇◇ N-COUNT

nurture /nɜːʳtʃəʳ/ **nurtures, nurturing, nurtured** ◆◆◇◇◇

1 If you **nurture** something such as a young child or a young plant, you care for it while it is growing and developing; a formal use. *Parents want to know the best way to nurture and raise their child to adulthood... The modern conservatory is not an environment for nurturing plants.* ♦ **nurturing** *She was not receiving warm nurturing care.* ♦ **nurturing** *Which adult in these children's lives will provide the nurturing they need?* VERB V n ADJ-GRADED N-UNCOUNT

2 If you **nurture** plans, ideas, or people, you actively encourage their development and success; a formal use. *She had always nurtured great ambitions for her son. ...parents whose political views were nurtured in the sixties... Charlie Nelson has nurtured fine sprinters.* ♦ **nurturing** *The decision to cut back on film-making had a catastrophic effect on the nurturing of new talent.* VERB =cultivate V n N-UNCOUNT

3 **Nurture** is care and encouragement that is given to someone while they are growing and developing. *The human organism learns partly by nature, partly by nurture.* N-UNCOUNT

nut /nʌt/ **nuts** ◆◆◇◇◇

1 The firm shelled fruit of some trees and bushes are called **nuts**. Some nuts can be eaten. *Nuts and seeds are good sources of vitamin E.* • See also **groundnut, hazelnut.** N-COUNT

2 A **nut** is a small piece of metal with a hole through which you put a bolt. Nuts and bolts are used to hold things together such as pieces of machinery. *If you want to repair the wheels you just undo the four nuts. ...nuts and bolts that haven't been tightened up.* N-COUNT

3 If you think someone is extremely enthusiastic about a subject or activity, you can say they are a **nut** on it; an informal use. *I was a nut on records and statistics. ...a football nut who spends thousands of pounds travelling to watch games.* N-COUNT: usu with supp

4 If someone is **nuts** about something or someone, they like that thing or person very much; an informal use. *They're nuts about the car... She's nuts about you.* ADJ: v-link ADJ *about* n

5 If you refer to someone as a **nut**, you mean they are mad; an informal use. *There's some nut out there with a gun.* N-COUNT

6 If you say that someone is **nuts**, you think they are mad or very foolish; an informal use. *You guys are nuts... A number of the French players went nuts, completely out of control.* ADJ: v-link ADJ PRAGMATICS

7 A man's testicles can be referred to as his **nuts**; an informal use. N-PLURAL

8 Your head can be referred to as your **nut**; an informal use. N-COUNT: usu poss N

9 If someone **does** their **nut**, they become extremely angry; used in informal British English. *We heard your sister doing her nut.* PHRASES V inflects

10 If you talk about the **nuts and bolts** of a subject or an activity, you are referring to the detailed practical aspects of it rather than abstract ideas about it. *He's more concerned about the nuts and bolts of location work.* usu *the* PHR *of* n

11 If you think someone is difficult to deal with, you can say they are a **tough nut** or a **hard nut**; an informal expression. *The Daily Express describes Dr Carey as a pretty tough nut.* usu v-link PHR

12 If you say that something is **a hard nut to crack** or a **tough nut to crack**, you mean that it is difficult to do or to understand; an informal expression. *Getting out there is in many ways the hardest nut to crack.* usu v-link PHR

nut-brown. **Nut-brown** is used to describe things that are dark reddish brown in colour. *...a tiny, nut-brown monkey.* COLOUR

nutcase /nʌtkeɪs/ **nutcases;** also spelled **nut case.** If you think that someone is mad or that their behaviour is very strange, you can say they are a **nutcase**; an informal word. *The woman's a nutcase. She needs locking up.* N-COUNT

nutcracker /nʌtkrækəʳ/ **nutcrackers.** A **nutcracker** is a device used to crack the shell of a nut. **Nutcrackers** can be used to refer to one or more of these devices. N-COUNT

nutmeg /nʌtmeg/. **Nutmeg** is a spice made from the large dried fruit of a tree that grows in the tropics, especially in the Far East. Nutmeg is used to flavour sweet food. ◆◇◇◇◇ N-UNCOUNT

nutrasweet /njuːtrəswiːt, AM nuː-/. **Nutrasweet** is a low-calorie substance that is used instead of sugar to sweeten food. **Nutrasweet** is a trademark. N-UNCOUNT

nutrient /njuːtriənt, AM nuː-/ **nutrients.** **Nutrients** are substances that help plants and animals to grow. *In her first book she explained the role of vegetable fibres, vitamins, minerals and other essential nutrients.* ◆◆◇◇◇ N-COUNT: usu pl

nutrition /njuːtrɪʃəⁿn, AM nuː-/. **Nutrition** is the process of taking food into the body and absorbing the nutrients in those foods. *There are alternative sources of nutrition to animal meat... As in all experimental sciences, we still do not know everything about nutrition.* ◆◆◇◇◇ N-UNCOUNT

nutritional /njuːtrɪʃənəl, AM nuː-/. The **nutritional** content of food is all the proteins, vitamins, and minerals that are in it which help you to remain healthy. *It does sometimes help to know the nutritional content of foods... Cooking vegetables reduces their nutritional value.* ♦ **nutritionally** *...a nutritionally balanced diet.* ◆◇◇◇◇ ADJ: usu ADJ n =nutritive ADV

nutritionist /njuːtrɪʃənɪst, AM nuː-/ **nutritionists.** A **nutritionist** is a person whose job is to give advice on what you should eat to remain healthy. *Nutritionists say only 33% of our calorie intake should be from fat.* ◆◇◇◇◇ N-COUNT

nutritious /njuːtrɪʃəs, AM nuː-/. **Nutritious** food contains the proteins, vitamins, and minerals which help your body to be healthy. *It is always important to choose enjoyable, nutritious foods... Some ready made meals are nutritious and very easy to prepare.* ◆◇◇◇◇ ADJ-GRADED =nourishing

nutritive /njuːtrɪtɪv, AM nuː-/. The **nutritive** content of food is all the proteins, vitamins, and minerals that are in it which help you to remain healthy. *Coconut milk has little nutritive value.* ADJ: ADJ n =nutritional

nutshell /nʌtʃel/. You can use **in a nutshell** to indicate that what you are saying summarizes your opinions or thoughts in a very brief and concise way. *In a nutshell, the owners thought they knew best... This, in a nutshell, is what Richard Chaplin appears to have done.* PHRASE: usu PHR with cl PRAGMATICS =in a word

nutter /nʌtəʳ/ **nutters.** If you refer to someone as a **nutter**, you think they are mad, or that their behaviour is very strange; used in informal British English. *Is he a nutter, or is he a genius?... He was a bit of a nutter.* N-COUNT PRAGMATICS =nut, nutcase

nutty /nʌti/ **nuttier, nuttiest** ◆◇◇◇◇

1 If you describe food as **nutty**, you mean it tastes of nuts, has the texture of nuts, or is made with ADJ-GRADED

nuts. ...*nutty butter cookies... Chick peas have a distinctive, delicious and nutty flavour.*
2 If you describe someone as **nutty**, you think their behaviour is very strange or foolish; an informal use. *He looked like a nutty professor... That's a nutty idea.* ADJ-GRADED PRAGMATICS

nuzzle /nʌzᵊl/ **nuzzles, nuzzling, nuzzled.** If you **nuzzle** someone or something, you gently rub your nose and mouth against them to show affection. *She nuzzled me and I cuddled her... The dog came and nuzzled up against me in the most friendly manner.* VERB V n V adv/prep

NW. NW is a written abbreviation for **northwest**. ...*Ivor Place, London NW 1.*

nylon /naɪlɒn/ **nylons** ◆◇◇◇◇
1 **Nylon** is a strong, flexible artificial fibre. *Europe's largest producer of nylon is based in Belgium... I put on a new pair of nylon socks.* N-UNCOUNT: oft N n
2 **Nylons** are stockings made of nylon; an old-fashioned use. *This woman wore seamed nylons and kept smoothing her skirt.* N-PLURAL

nymph /nɪmf/ **nymphs** ◆◇◇◇◇
1 In Greek and Roman mythology, **nymphs** were spirits of nature who took the form of young women. N-COUNT
2 A **nymph** is the larva of an insect such as a dragonfly. It develops into an adult without going through the stage of being a pupa. N-COUNT

nymphomaniac /nɪmfəmeɪniæk/ **nymphomaniacs.** If someone refers to a woman as a **nymphomaniac**, they mean that she has sex or wants to have sex much more often than they consider normal or acceptable; used showing disapproval. *Lucia was a known nymphomaniac in Paris in the Thirties.* N-COUNT PRAGMATICS

Oo

O, o /oʊ/ **O's, o's**
1 **O** is the fifteenth letter of the English alphabet. N-VAR
2 In spoken English, **O** is used to mean nought or zero, for example when you are telling someone a telephone number, or the number of a year such as '1908'. NUM
3 **O** is used in exclamations, especially when you are expressing strong feelings; a literary use. *O how mistaken you are!... O God, I want to go home.* ● See also **oh**. EXCLAM PRAGMATICS
4 **O** is used as an abbreviation for words beginning with o, such as 'old' or 'organization'.

o' /ə/. **O'** is used in written English to represent the word 'of' pronounced in a particular way. *I lost a lot o' blood... Can we have a cup o' coffee, please?* ● See also **o'clock**. PREP

oaf /oʊf/ **oafs.** If you refer to someone, especially a man or boy, as an **oaf**, you think that they are impolite, clumsy, or aggressive. *Leave the lady alone, you drunken oaf.* N-COUNT: oft adj N PRAGMATICS =lout

oafish /oʊfɪʃ/. If you describe someone, especially a man or a boy, as **oafish**, you disapprove of their behaviour because you think that it is impolite, clumsy, or aggressive. *The bodyguards, as usual, were brave but oafish. ...oafish humour.* ADJ-GRADED PRAGMATICS =loutish

oak /oʊk/ **oaks.** An **oak** or an **oak tree** is a large tree that often grows in woods and forests and has strong, hard wood. *Many large oaks were felled during the war. ...forests of beech, chestnut, and oak.* ▶ **Oak** is the wood of this tree. *The cabinet was made of oak and was hand-carved.* ◆◆◇◇◇ N-VAR N-UNCOUNT

oaken /oʊkən/. **Oaken** means made of the wood from an oak tree; a literary word. *She went up the path and opened the oaken door.* ADJ: ADJ n

OAP /oʊ eɪ piː/ **OAPs.** In British English, **OAP** is an abbreviation for 'old age pensioner'. An **OAP** is a person who is old enough to receive an old age pension from the government. *In 11 years I will be 60 and an OAP. ...tickets only £6 each and half that for OAPs and kids.* N-COUNT =senior citizen

oar /ɔːʳ/ **oars. Oars** are long poles with a wide, flat blade at one end which are used for rowing a boat. ◆◇◇◇◇ N-COUNT

oasis /oʊeɪsɪs/ **oases** /oʊeɪsiːz/ ◆◇◇◇◇
1 An **oasis** is a small area in a desert where water and plants are found. N-COUNT
2 You can refer to a pleasant place or situation as an **oasis** when it is surrounded by unpleasant ones. *The immaculately tended gardens are an oasis in the midst of Cairo's urban sprawl.* N-COUNT =haven

oath /oʊθ/ **oaths** ◆◇◇◇◇
1 An **oath** is a formal promise, especially a promise to be loyal to a person or country. *He took an oath of loyalty to the government... He swore an oath promising to uphold and protect the country's laws and constitution.* ● See also **Hippocratic oath**. N-COUNT: oft N *of* n =pledge
2 In a court of law, if someone takes the **oath**, they formally promise to tell the truth, and are then legally bound to do so. You can say that someone is **on oath** or **under oath** when they have made this promise. *His girlfriend had gone into the witness box and taken the oath... Under oath, Aston finally admitted that he had lied... Three officers gave evidence on oath against him.* N-SING: *the*N, also *on/under* N
3 An **oath** is an offensive expression or a swearword; used in written English. *Wellor let out a foul oath and hurled himself upon him.* N-COUNT =curse

oatmeal /oʊtmiːl/ ◆◇◇◇◇
1 **Oatmeal** is a coarse flour made by crushing oats. ...*oatmeal biscuits.* N-UNCOUNT: oft N n
2 Something that is **oatmeal** is a pale creamy brown colour. ...*an oatmeal tweed jacket.* COLOUR

oats /oʊts/; the form **oat** is used as a modifier. ◆◇◇◇◇
1 **Oats** are a cereal crop or its grains, used for making porridge or feeding animals. *Oats provide good, nutritious food for horses. ...oat bran.* N-PLURAL
2 If you say that someone **sows** their **wild oats**, you mean they behave in a rather uncontrolled and irresponsible way, especially in their sexual activity. This behaviour is considered characteristic of young people before they settle down to family life. *The kids need to sow a few wild oats.* PHRASE: V inflects

obduracy /ɒbdjʊrəsi, AM -dʊr-/. If you accuse someone of **obduracy**, you think their refusal to alter their decision about something is motivated by stubbornness; a formal word. *MPs have accused the government of obduracy and called on ministers to reverse their decision.* N-UNCOUNT =obstinacy

obdurate /ɒbdjʊrət, AM -dʊr-/. If you describe someone as **obdurate**, you think that they are being stubborn in their refusal to change their mind about something; a formal word. *Parts of the administration may be changing but others have been obdurate defenders of the status quo.* ADJ-GRADED =obstinate

obedient /oʊbiːdiənt/. A person or animal who is **obedient** does what they are told to do. *He was very respectful at home and obedient to his parents... What a sweet, obedient little girl she was in the sixth grade.* ♦ **obedience** ...*unquestioning obedience to the law... They command the respect and obedience of the armed forces.* ♦ **obediently** *He was looking obediently at Keith, waiting for orders.* ◆◇◇◇◇ ADJ-GRADED ≠disobedient N-UNCOUNT: oft N *to* n ADV-GRADED: ADV with v

obeisance /oʊbeɪsəns/ **obeisances**
1 **Obeisance** to someone or something is respect for them and obedience towards them; a formal N-UNCOUNT: usu N *to* n

use. *While he was still young and strong all paid obeisance to him.*

2 An **obeisance** is a physical gesture, especially a bow, that you make in order to show your respect for someone or something; a formal use. *One by one they came forward, mumbled grudging words of welcome, made awkward obeisances.* [N-VAR]

obelisk /ɒbəlɪsk/ **obelisks.** An **obelisk** is a tall stone pillar that has been built in honour of a person or an important event. [N-COUNT]

obese /oʊbiːs/. If someone is **obese**, they are extremely overweight or extremely fat. *The tendency to become obese is at least in part hereditary... Obese people tend to have higher blood pressure than lean people.* ♦ **obesity** /oʊbiːsɪti/ *...the excessive consumption of sugar that leads to problems of obesity.* [◆◇◇◇◇ ADJ-GRADED =fat; N-UNCOUNT]

obey /oʊbeɪ/ **obeys, obeying, obeyed.** If you **obey** a person, a command, or an instruction, you do what you are told to do. *Cissie obeyed her mother without question... Most people obey the law... It was still Baker's duty to obey.* [◆◆◇◇◇ VERB =follow; V n; V]

obfuscate /ɒbfʌskeɪt/ **obfuscates, obfuscating, obfuscated.** To **obfuscate** something means to deliberately make it seem confusing and difficult to understand; a formal word. *They are obfuscating the issue, as only insurance companies can... There are still some forces in Russia who do not want to cooperate on this matter, who want to obfuscate.* ♦ **obfuscation** /ɒbfʌskeɪʃᵊn/ **obfuscations** *He gave a more lucid exposition of the party's strategy than Bush has managed in months of obfuscation.* [VERB; V n; V; N-UNCOUNT: also N in pl ≠elucidation]

obituary /oʊbɪtʃuəri, AM -ʃueri/ **obituaries.** Someone's **obituary** is an account of their character and achievements which is published or broadcast shortly after they have died. *I read your brother's obituary in the Times.* [◆◆◇◇◇ N-COUNT: oft poss N]

object, **objects, objecting, objected.** The noun is pronounced /ɒbdʒɪkt/. The verb is pronounced /əbdʒekt/. [◆◆◆◆◇]

1 An **object** is anything that has a fixed shape or form, that you can touch or see, and that is not alive. *He squinted his eyes as though he were studying an object on the horizon. ...an object the shape of a coconut... In the cosy consulting room the children are surrounded by familiar objects.* [N-COUNT =article]

2 The **object** of what someone is doing is their aim or purpose. *The object of the exercise is to raise money for the charity... He made it his object in life to find the island... My object was to publish a scholarly work on Peter Mourne.* [N-COUNT: usu with poss =objective, aim]

3 The **object of** a particular feeling or reaction is the person or thing it is directed towards, or the person or thing that causes it. *The object of her hatred was 24-year-old model Ros French... The object of great interest at the Temple was a large marble tower built in memory of Buddha... She knew that she was an object of pity among her friends.* • See also **sex object**. [N-COUNT: N *of* n]

4 In grammar, the **object** of a verb or a preposition is the word or phrase which completes the structure begun by the verb or preposition. • See also **direct object**, **indirect object**. [N-COUNT]

5 If you **object** to something, you express your dislike or disapproval of it. *A lot of people will object to the book... Cullen objected that his small staff would be unable to handle the added work... We objected strongly but were outvoted... 'Hey, I don't know what you're talking about,' Russo objected.* [VERB; V *to* n; V that; V; V with quote]

6 If you say that **money is no object** or **distance is no object**, you are emphasizing that you are willing or able to spend as much money as necessary or travel whatever distance is required. *Hugh Johnson's shop in London has a range of superb Swedish crystal glasses that I would have if money were no object... Although he was based in Wales, distance was no object.* [PHRASE: V inflects; PRAGMATICS =irrelevant]

objection /əbdʒekʃᵊn/ **objections** [◆◆◇◇◇]

1 If you make or raise an **objection** to something, you say that you do not like it or agree with it. *Some managers have recently raised objection to the PFA handling these negotiations... Despite objections by the White House, the Senate voted today to cut off aid to Jordan.* [N-VAR ≠approval]

2 If you say that you have no **objection** to something, you mean that you are not annoyed or bothered by it. *I have no objection to banks making money... I no longer have any objection to your going to see her.* [N-UNCOUNT: with brd-neg]

objectionable /əbdʒekʃənəbᵊl/. If you describe someone or something as **objectionable**, you consider them to be extremely offensive and unacceptable; a formal word. *I don't like your tone young woman, in fact I find it highly objectionable... Such power is politically dangerous and morally objectionable.* [ADJ-GRADED =offensive]

objective /əbdʒektɪv/ **objectives** [◆◆◆◇◇]

1 Your **objective** is what you are trying to achieve. *Our main objective was the recovery of the child safe and well... His objective was to play golf and win.* [N-COUNT: usu with poss =aim, goal]

2 **Objective** information is based on facts. *He had no objective evidence that anything extraordinary was happening.* ♦ **objectively** *We simply want to inform people objectively about events all over Yugoslavia.* ♦ **objectivity** /ɒbdʒektɪvɪti/ *The poll, whose objectivity is open to question, gave the communist party a 39% share of the vote.* [ADJ: ADJ n =factual; ADV-GRADED: usu ADV with v; N-UNCOUNT]

3 If someone is **objective**, they base their opinions on facts rather than on their personal feelings. *I believe that a journalist should be completely objective... I would really like to have your objective opinion on this.* ♦ **objectively** *Try to view situations more objectively, especially with regard to work.* ♦ **objectivity** *The psychiatrist must learn to maintain an unusual degree of objectivity.* [ADJ-GRADED =impartial ≠subjective; ADV-GRADED: usu ADV with v; N-UNCOUNT]

object lesson, object lessons. If you describe an action, event, or situation as an **object lesson**, you think that it demonstrates the correct way to do something, or that it demonstrates the truth of a particular principle. *It was an object lesson in how to use television as a means of persuasion.* [N-COUNT: oft N *on/in* n =example]

objector /əbdʒektəʳ/ **objectors.** An **objector** is someone who states or shows that they oppose or disapprove of something. *The district council agreed with the objectors and turned down the application.* • See also **conscientious objector**. [N-COUNT ≠supporter]

objet d'art /ɒbʒeɪ dɑːʳ/ **objets d'art. Objet d'arts** are a small ornaments or objects that are considered to have artistic merit. [N-COUNT: usu pl]

obligate /ɒblɪgeɪt/ **obligates, obligating, obligated.** If something **obligates** you to do a particular thing, it creates a situation where you have to do it. *The ruling obligates airlines to release information about their flight delays... Under a separation agreement, he was obligated to pay his ex-wife £20,000 a year for life.* [VERB; V n to-inf]

obligated /ɒblɪgeɪtɪd/. If you feel **obligated** to do something, you feel that it is your duty to do it. If you are **obligated to** someone, you feel that it is your duty to look after them. *I felt obligated to let him read the letter... He had got a girl pregnant and felt obligated to her and the child.* [ADJ: v-link ADJ, oft ADJ to-inf, ADJ *to* n]

obligation /ɒblɪgeɪʃᵊn/ **obligations** [◆◆◇◇◇]

1 If you have an **obligation** to do something, it is your duty to do that thing. *When teachers assign homework, students usually feel an obligation to do it... Ministers are under no obligation to follow the committee's recommendations.* [N-VAR: usu N to-inf =duty]

2 If you have an **obligation** to a person, it is your duty to look after them or protect their interests. *The United States will do that which is necessary to meet its obligations to its own citizens... I have an ethical and a moral obligation to my client.* [N-VAR: usu N *to* n =responsibility]

3 In advertisements, if a product or a service is available **without obligation**, you do not have to pay for that product or service until you have tried it and are satisfied with it. *If you are selling your property, why not call us for a free valuation without obligation... You can review your policy in detail for a full 15 days without obligation.* [PHRASE]

obligatory /əblɪgətri, AM -tɔːri/ [◆◇◇◇◇]

1 If something is **obligatory**, you must do it be- [ADJ]

cause of a rule or a law. *Most women will be offered an ultrasound scan during pregnancy, although it's not obligatory... These rates do not include the charge for obligatory medical consultations.*
=compulsory ≠optional

2 If you describe something as **obligatory**, you mean that it is done from habit or custom rather than any sense of enthusiasm. *His lips curved up in the obligatory smile, acknowledging the compliment... She was wearing the obligatory sweater and pearl necklace.*
ADJ: ADJ n =customary

oblige /əbla͟ɪdʒ/ **obliges, obliging, obliged** ◆◆◇◇◇

1 If you **are obliged** to do something, a situation, rule, or law makes it necessary for you to do that thing. *The storm got worse and worse. Finally, I was obliged to abandon the car and continue on foot... This decree obliges unions to delay strikes.*
VERB =compel; be V-ed to-inf; V n to-inf

2 To **oblige** someone means to be helpful to them by doing what they have asked you to do. *If you ever need help with the babysitting, I'd be glad to oblige... We called up three economists to ask how to eliminate the deficit and they obliged with very straightforward answers... Mr Oakley always has been ready to oblige journalists with information.*
VERB; V; V with n; V n with n; Also V n

3 People sometimes use **obliged** in expressions such as '**much obliged**' or '**I am obliged to you**' when they want to indicate that they are very grateful for something. *Much obliged for your assistance... Thank you very much indeed, Doctor, I am extremely obliged to you.*
PHRASES; CONVENTION; PRAGMATICS

4 If you tell someone that you **would be obliged** or **should be obliged** if they would do something, you are telling them in a polite but firm way that you want them to do it; a formal expression. *I would be obliged if you could read it to us.*
CONVENTION; PRAGMATICS

obliging /əbla͟ɪdʒɪŋ/. If you describe someone as **obliging**, you think that they are willing and eager to be helpful. *He is an extremely pleasant and obliging man.* ♦ **obligingly** *He swung round and strode towards the door. Benedict obligingly held it open.*
◆◇◇◇◇ ADJ-GRADED =accommodating; ADV-GRADED: ADV with v

oblique /oʊbli͟ːk/ ◆◇◇◇◇

1 If you describe a statement as **oblique**, you mean that is not expressed directly or openly, making it difficult to understand. *It was an oblique reference to his mother... Mr Golding delivered an oblique warning, talking of the danger of sudden action.* ♦ **obliquely** *He obliquely referred to the US, Britain and Saudi Arabia.*
ADJ-GRADED =indirect; ADV: ADV with v =indirectly

2 An **oblique** line is a straight line that is not horizontal or vertical. An **oblique** angle is any angle other than a right angle. *It lies between the plain and the sea at an oblique angle to the coastline.* ♦ **obliquely** *This muscle runs obliquely downwards inside the abdominal cavity.*
ADJ: usu ADJ n; ADV: ADV after v

obliterate /əblɪ͟təreɪt/ **obliterates, obliterating, obliterated** ◆◇◇◇◇

1 If something **obliterates** an object or place, it destroys it completely. *Their warheads are enough to obliterate the world several times over... Whole villages were obliterated by fire.* ♦ **obliteration** /əblɪ͟təre͟ɪʃ^ən/ *...the obliteration of three isolated rainforests.*
VERB; V n; N-UNCOUNT: oft N of n

2 If you **obliterate** something such as a memory, emotion, or thought, you remove it completely from your mind; a literary use. *There was time enough to obliterate memories of how things once were for him.*
VERB =eradicate; V n

oblivion /əblɪ͟viən/ ◆◇◇◇◇

1 **Oblivion** is the state of not being aware of what is happening around you, for example because you are asleep or unconscious. *He just drank himself jovially into oblivion... Within the hour he had slipped once again into deep and dreamless oblivion.*
N-UNCOUNT: usu into N =unconsciousness

2 **Oblivion** is also the state of having been forgotten or of no longer being considered important. *The Marxist-Leninist wing of the party looks set to sink into oblivion.*
N-UNCOUNT: usu into N =obscurity

3 If you say that something is bombed or blasted **into oblivion**, you are emphasizing that it is completely destroyed, so that it is unrecognizable and seems never to have existed. *An entire poor section of town was bombed into oblivion.*
N-UNCOUNT: into N; PRAGMATICS

oblivious /əblɪ͟viəs/. If you are **oblivious** to something or oblivious of it, you are not aware of it. *She lay motionless where she was, oblivious to pain... Llewelyn appeared oblivious of his surroundings.* ♦ **obliviously** *Burke was asleep, sprawled obliviously against the window.* ♦ **obliviousness** *Her obliviousness of what was happening in Germany seems extraordinary.*
◆◇◇◇◇ ADJ-GRADED: usu v-link ADJ, oft ADJ to/of n ≠conscious; ADV-GRADED: ADV with v; N-UNCOUNT =ignorance

oblong /ɒ͟blɒŋ, AM -lɔːŋ/ **oblongs.** An **oblong** is a shape which has two long sides and two short sides and in which all the angles are right angles. *...an oblong table.*
N-COUNT: oft N n =rectangle

obnoxious /ɒbnɒ͟kʃəs/. If you describe someone as **obnoxious**, you think that they are very unpleasant. *One of the parents was a most obnoxious character. No-one liked him... The people at my table were so obnoxious I simply had to change my seat.*
◆◇◇◇◇ ADJ-GRADED =loathsome

oboe /o͟ʊboʊ/ **oboes.** An **oboe** is a wooden orchestral instrument that is shaped like a tube and played by blowing through a reed inserted at its top.
N-VAR: oft the N

oboist /o͟ʊboʊɪst/ **oboists.** An **oboist** is someone who plays the oboe.
N-COUNT

obscene /ɒbsi͟ːn/ ◆◇◇◇◇

1 If you describe something as **obscene**, you mean it offends you because it relates to sex or violence in a way that you think is unpleasant and shocking. *I'm not prudish but I think these photographs are obscene... He continued to use obscene language and also to make threats.*
ADJ-GRADED

2 In law, books, pictures, or films which are judged **obscene** are illegal because they deal with sex or violence in a way that is offensive to the general public. *A city magistrate ruled that the novel was obscene and copies should be destroyed... The bill leaves it up to the courts to decide what is obscene. ...the Obscene Publications Act.*
ADJ

3 If you describe something as **obscene**, you disapprove of it very strongly and consider it to be offensive or immoral. *It was obscene to spend millions producing unwanted food... His salary was obscene for three 40-minute shows a week.*
ADJ-GRADED: oft it v-link ADJ to-inf/that; PRAGMATICS =offensive

obscenity /ɒbse͟nɪti/ **obscenities** ◆◇◇◇◇

1 **Obscenity** is behaviour that offends people because it relates to sex in an unpleasant or indecent way. *He insisted these photographs were not art but obscenity... James Joyce justified his use of 'obscenity' on the grounds that it was a natural part of life.*
N-UNCOUNT

2 An **obscenity** is a very offensive word or expression. *They shouted obscenities at us and smashed bottles on the floor.*
N-VAR

3 If you refer to an action or event as an **obscenity**, you disapprove of it very strongly and consider it to be offensive or immoral. *Bosnia is not the only place experiencing the obscenities of civil war.*
N-COUNT; PRAGMATICS =atrocity

obscurantism /ɒ͟bskjʊræ͟ntɪzəm, AM ɒbskjʊ͟rənt-/. **Obscurantism** is the practice or policy of deliberately making something vague and difficult to understand, especially in order to prevent people from finding out the truth. *...legalistic obscurantism.*
N-UNCOUNT =obfuscation

obscurantist /ɒ͟bskjʊræ͟ntɪst, AM ɒbskjʊ͟rənt-/. If you describe something as **obscurantist**, you mean that it is deliberately vague and difficult to understand, so that it prevents people from finding out the truth about it. *Their brutality was an integral part of the obscurantist communism they practised.*
ADJ-GRADED

obscure /ɒbskjʊ͟əʳ/ **obscurer, obscurest; obscures, obscuring, obscured** ◆◆◇◇◇

1 If something or someone is **obscure**, they are unknown, or are known by only a few people. *The origin of the custom is obscure... The hymn was written by an obscure Greek composer for the 1896 Athens Olympics.*
ADJ-GRADED =unknown

2 Something that is **obscure** is difficult to understand or deal with, usually because it involves so many parts or details. *The contracts are written in*
ADJ-GRADED ≠straightforward

obscure language... Richard's statement was disgracefully obscure.
3 If one thing **obscures** another, it prevents it from being seen or heard properly. *Trees obscured his vision; he couldn't see much of the Square's southern half... One wall of the parliament building is now almost completely obscured by a huge banner.* VERB =hide V n
4 To **obscure** something means to make it difficult to understand. *...the jargon that frequently obscures educational writing... This issue has been obscured by recent events.* VERB V n

obscurity /ɒbskjʊ̲ərɪti/ ◆◇◇◇◇
1 **Obscurity** is the state of being known by only a few people. *For the lucky few, there's the chance of being plucked from obscurity and thrown into the glamorous world of modelling... The latter half of his life was spent in obscurity and loneliness.* N-UNCOUNT ≠fame
2 **Obscurity** is the quality of being difficult to understand. *'How can that be?' asked Hunt, irritated by the obscurity of Henry's reply.* N-UNCOUNT ≠clarity

obsequious /ɒbsi̲ːkwiəs/. If you describe someone as **obsequious**, you think their eagerness to help or agree with someone is based on how important they consider that person to be; used showing disapproval. *Barrow was positively obsequious to me until he learnt that I too was the son of a labouring man. ...a weak and obsequious officer.* ♦ **obsequiously** *He smiled and bowed obsequiously to Winger.* ♦ **obsequiousness** *I told him to get lost and leave me alone and his tone quickly changed from obsequiousness to outright anger.* ADJ-GRADED PRAGMATICS =servile ADV: ADV with v N-UNCOUNT

observable /əbzɜ̲ːʳvəbᵊl/. Something that is **observable** can be seen. *If lifelong personality characteristics are observable in the womb, where do they come from?* ADJ =noticeable

observance /əbzɜ̲ːʳvᵊns/ **observances.** The **observance** of something such as a law or custom is the practice of obeying or following it. *Local councils should use their powers to ensure strict observance of laws.* ◆◇◇◇◇ N-VAR

observant /əbzɜ̲ːʳvᵊnt/
1 Someone who is **observant** pays a lot of attention to things and notices more about them than most people do. *That's a marvellous description, Mrs Drummond. You're unusually observant... An observant doctor can often detect depression from expression, posture, and movement.* ADJ-GRADED
2 An **observant** follower of a religion performs all the duties that his or her religion requires. *...a profoundly observant Islamic country.* ADJ: ADJ n

observation /ɒ̲bzəʳve͟ɪʃᵊn/ **observations** ◆◆◇◇◇
1 **Observation** is the action or process of carefully watching someone or something. *...careful observation of the movement of the planets... In hospital she'll be under observation all the time.* N-UNCOUNT
2 An **observation** is something that you have learned by seeing or watching something and thinking about it. *This book contains observations about the causes of addictions.* N-COUNT
3 If a person makes an **observation**, they make a comment about something or someone, usually as a result of watching how they behave. *'You're an obstinate man,' she said. 'Is that a criticism,' I said, 'or just an observation?'.* N-COUNT
4 **Observation** is the ability to pay a lot of attention to things and to notice more about them than most people do. *She has good powers of observation.* N-UNCOUNT =perception

observational /ɒ̲bzəʳve͟ɪʃənᵊl/. **Observational** means relating to the watching of people or things, especially in order to learn something new; a formal word. *...observational humour... The observational work is carried out on a range of telescopes.* ADJ

observatory /əbzɜ̲ːʳvətri, AM -tɔːri/ **observatories.** An **observatory** is a building with a large telescope from which scientists study things such as the planets by watching them. ◆◇◇◇◇ N-COUNT

observe /əbzɜ̲ːʳv/ **observes, observing, observed** ◆◆◆◇◇
1 If you **observe** someone or something, you watch them carefully, especially in order to learn something about them. *Stern also studies and observes the behaviour of babies... Are there any classes I could observe?... Our sniper teams observed them manning an anti-aircraft gun.* VERB =watch, study V n V n -ing Also V, V n inf
2 If you **observe** someone or something, you see or notice them; a formal use. *In 1664 Hooke observed a reddish spot on the surface of the planet.* VERB =notice V n
3 If you **observe** that something is the case, you make a remark or comment about it, especially when it is something you have noticed and thought about a lot; a formal use. *We observe that the first calls for radical transformation did not begin until the period of the industrial revolution... 'He is a fine young man,' observed Stephen.* VERB V that V with quote
4 If you **observe** something such as a law or custom, you obey it or follow it. *Imposing speed restrictions is easy, but forcing motorists to observe them is trickier... The army was observing a ceasefire... American forces are observing Christmas quietly.* VERB =honour V n

observer /əbzɜ̲ːʳvəʳ/ **observers** ◆◆◆◇◇
1 You can refer to someone who sees or notices something as an **observer**. *A casual observer would have taken them to be three men out for an evening stroll... Observers say the woman pulled a knife out of the bunch of flowers and stabbed him in the neck.* N-COUNT =witness
2 An **observer** is someone who studies current events and situations, especially in order to comment on them and predict what will happen next; used in newspapers and broadcast news. *Observers say the events of the weekend seem to have increased support for the opposition... Political observers believe that a new cabinet may be formed shortly.* N-COUNT: oft supp N
3 An **observer** is a person who is sent to observe an important event or situation, especially in order to make sure it happens as it should, or so that they can tell other people about it. *The president suggested that a UN observer should attend the conference.* N-COUNT: oft supp N

obsess /əbse̲s/ **obsesses, obsessing, obsessed.** If something **obsesses** you or you **obsess** about something, you keep thinking about it and find it difficult to think about anything else. *I must admit that maps obsess me... A string of scandals is obsessing America... She stopped drinking but began obsessing about her weight... I started obsessing that Trish might die.* ◆◆◇◇◇ V-ERG V n V *about/over* n V that

obsessed /əbse̲st/. If you say that someone is **obsessed**, or is **obsessed** with something or someone, you mean that they keep thinking about them and find it difficult to think about anything else. *He was obsessed with American gangster movies... She wasn't in love with Steve, she was obsessed by him physically. ...letters from all these really obsessed people.* ◆◇◇◇◇ ADJ-GRADED: oft ADJ *with/by* n

obsession /əbse̲ʃᵊn/ **obsessions.** If you say that someone has an **obsession** with someone or something, you feel they are spending too much of their time thinking about that person or thing. *She would try to forget her obsession with Chistopher... 95% of patients know their obsessions are irrational.* ◆◆◇◇◇ N-VAR: oft N *with* n =fixation

obsessional /əbse̲ʃənᵊl/. **Obsessional** means the same as **obsessive**. *She became almost obsessional about the way she looked.* ADJ-GRADED =obsessive

obsessive /əbse̲sɪv/ **obsessives** ◆◇◇◇◇
1 If someone's behaviour is **obsessive**, they cannot stop doing something or thinking about something. *Williams is obsessive about motor racing... You were suffering from a period of obsessive depression after losing your job.* ♦ **obsessively** *He couldn't help worrying obsessively about what would happen... The Ministry is being obsessively secretive about the issue.* ADJ-GRADED: oft ADJ *about* n =obsessional ADV: ADV with v, ADV adj
2 An **obsessive** is someone who is obsessive about something or who behaves in an obsessive way. *It has something to please everyone from Genesis obsessives to Napalm Death disciples... I am not an obsessive. Not at all.* N-COUNT

obsolescence /ɒ̲bsəle̲sᵊns/. **Obsolescence** is the state of being no longer needed because something newer or more efficient has been N-UNCOUNT =redundancy invented. *The aircraft was nearing obsolescence by early 1942.*

obsolescent /ɒbsəlesənt/. If something is **obsolescent**, it is no longer needed because something better has been invented. *...outmoded, obsolescent equipment.* ADJ =outdated

obsolete /ɒbsəliːt/. Something that is **obsolete** is no longer needed because something better has been invented. *So much equipment becomes obsolete almost as soon as it's made.* ◆◇◇◇◇ ADJ-GRADED =outdated

obstacle /ɒbstəkəl/ **obstacles** ◆◆◇◇◇

1 An **obstacle** is an object that makes it difficult for you to go where you want to go, because it is in your way. *Most competition cars will only roll over if they hit an obstacle... He left her to navigate her own way round the trolleys and other obstacles.* N-COUNT

2 You can refer to anything that makes it difficult for you to do something as an **obstacle**. *Overcrowding remains a large obstacle to improving conditions... To succeed, you must learn to overcome obstacles.* N-COUNT: oft N to n/-ing =hindrance

obstetrician /ɒbstətrɪʃən/ **obstetricians.** An **obstetrician** is a doctor who is specially trained to deal with childbirth and the care of pregnant women; a medical term. N-COUNT

obstetrics /ɒbstetrɪks/; the form **obstetric** is used as a modifier.

1 **Obstetrics** is the branch of medicine that is concerned with pregnancy and childbirth; a medical use. *The training covers extended periods in obstetrics and gynaecology.* N-UNCOUNT

2 **Obstetric** medicine and care is concerned with pregnancy and childbirth; a medical use. *For a child to be born with this disability indicates a defect in obstetric care.* ADJ: ADJ n

obstinate /ɒbstɪnət/ ◆◇◇◇◇

1 If you describe someone as **obstinate**, you are being critical of them because they are very determined to do what they want, and refuse to change their mind or be persuaded to do something else. *He is obstinate and determined and will not give up... She was a wicked and obstinate child.* ADJ-GRADED PRAGMATICS =stubborn ♦ **obstinately** *I stayed obstinately in my room, sitting by the telephone... Smith obstinately refused to carry out the order.* ADV-GRADED: ADV with v =stubbornly ♦ **obstinacy** *I might have become a dangerous man with all that stubbornness and obstinacy built into me.* N-UNCOUNT =stubbornness

2 You can describe things as **obstinate** when they are difficult to move, change, or destroy. *...rusted farm equipment strewn among the obstinate weeds.* ADJ-GRADED ♦ **obstinately** *...the door of the shop which obstinately stayed closed when he tried to push it open.* ADV-GRADED: ADV with v

obstreperous /ɒbstrepərəs/. If you say that someone is **obstreperous**, you think that they are noisy and difficult to control. *You know I have no intention of being awkward and obstreperous.* ADJ-GRADED PRAGMATICS

obstruct /ɒbstrʌkt/ **obstructs, obstructing, obstructed** ◆◇◇◇◇

1 If something **obstructs** a road or path, it blocks it, stopping people or vehicles getting past. *Tractors and container lorries have completely obstructed the road.* VERB =block V n

2 To **obstruct** someone or something, means to make it difficult for them to move forward by blocking their path. *A number of local people have been arrested for trying to obstruct lorries loaded with logs... Drivers who park their cars illegally, particularly obstructing traffic flow, deserve to be punished.* VERB =block V n

3 To **obstruct** something such as justice or progress means to prevent it from happening properly or from developing. *The authorities are obstructing a United Nations investigation.* VERB V n

4 If someone or something **obstructs** your view, they are positioned between you and the thing you are trying to look at, stopping you from seeing it properly. *Claire positioned herself so as not to obstruct David's line of sight.* VERB =block V n

obstruction /ɒbstrʌkʃən/ **obstructions** ◆◇◇◇◇

1 An **obstruction** is something that blocks a road or path. *John was irritated by drivers parking near his house and causing an obstruction.* N-COUNT

2 An **obstruction** is something that blocks a passage in your body. *The boy was suffering from a bowel obstruction and he died.* N-VAR

3 **Obstruction** is the act of deliberately delaying something or preventing something from happening, usually in business, law, or government. *Mr Guest refused to let them in and now faces a criminal charge of obstruction.* N-UNCOUNT

obstructionism /ɒbstrʌkʃənɪzəm/. **Obstructionism** is the practice of deliberately delaying or preventing legal, business, or parliamentary operations. *Obstructionism is generally most evident at the stage of implementing a law.* N-UNCOUNT

obstructive /ɒbstrʌktɪv/. If you say that someone is being **obstructive**, you think that they are intentionally causing difficulties for other people. *Mr Smith was obstructive and refused to follow correct procedure.* ADJ-GRADED

obtain /ɒbteɪn/ **obtains, obtaining, obtained** ◆◆◆◇◇

1 To **obtain** something means to get it or achieve it; a formal use. *Evans was trying to obtain a false passport and other documents... The perfect body has always been difficult to obtain.* VERB V n

2 If a situation **obtains**, it exists; a formal use. *The longer this situation obtains, the more extensive the problems become.* VERB V

obtainable /ɒbteɪnəbəl/. If something is **obtainable**, it is possible to get or achieve it. *The dried herb is obtainable from health shops. ...delicious cheeses which are obtainable anywhere in France.* ADJ: usu v-link ADJ, oft ADJ prep

obtrude /ɒbtruːd/ **obtrudes, obtruding, obtruded.** When something **obtrudes** or when you **obtrude** it, it becomes noticeable in an undesirable way; a literary word. *A 40 watt bulb would be quite sufficient and would not obtrude... Gertrude now clearly felt that she had obtruded her sorrow... He didn't want to obtrude on her privacy.* V-ERG =impose V V n V on n

obtrusive /ɒbtruːsɪv/. If you say that someone or something is **obtrusive**, you think they are noticeable in an unpleasant way. *'You are rude and obtrusive, Mr Galbraith,' said Tommy... These heaters are less obtrusive and are easy to store away in the summer.* ADJ-GRADED ♦ **obtrusively** *Hawke got up and walked obtrusively out of the building.* ADV-GRADED: ADV with v

obtuse /əbtjuːs, AM -tuːs/

1 Someone who is **obtuse** has difficulty understanding things, or makes no effort to understand them; a formal word. *I've really been very obtuse and stupid... I'm a limited and obtuse clergyman while you're the expert.* ADJ-GRADED ♦ **obtuseness** *Naivety bordering on obtuseness helped sustain his faith.* N-UNCOUNT =slowness

2 An **obtuse** angle is between 90° and 180°; a technical term in mathematics. Compare **acute angle**. ADJ ≠acute

obverse /ɒbvɜːʳs/. The **obverse** of an opinion, situation, or argument is its opposite; a formal word. *The obverse of rising unemployment is continued gains in productivity.* N-SING: the N, oft N of n =reverse

obviate /ɒbvieɪt/ **obviates, obviating, obviated.** To **obviate** something such as a problem or a need means to remove it or make it unnecessary; a formal word. *The use of a solicitor trained as a mediator would obviate the need for independent legal advice... This deferral would obviate pressure on the rouble exchange rate.* VERB =avert V n

obvious /ɒbviəs/ ◆◆◆◆◇

1 If something is **obvious**, it is easy to see or understand. *...the need to rectify what is an obvious injustice... Determining how the Democratic challenger would conduct his presidency isn't quite so obvious.* ADJ-GRADED =clear

2 If you describe something that someone says as **obvious**, you are being critical of it because you think it is unnecessary or shows lack of imagination. *There are some very obvious phrases that we all know or certainly should know better than to use.* ADJ-GRADED PRAGMATICS ♦ **obviousness** *Francis smiled agreement, irritated by the obviousness of his answer.* N-UNCOUNT ● If you say that someone **is stating the obvious**, you mean that they are saying something that everyone already knows and understands. *It may be stating the obvious, but most teleworking at present is connected with computers.* PHRASE: V inflects

obviously /ɒbviəsli/ ◆◆◆◆◇
1 You use **obviously** when you are stating something that you expect your listener to know already. *Obviously, they've had sponsorship from some big companies... There are obviously exceptions to this.* ADV: ADV with cl =clearly
2 You use **obviously** to indicate that something is easily noticed, seen, or recognized. *They obviously appreciate you very much... She's so obviously cleverer and prettier than I am.* ADV-GRADED: ADV with cl/group =plainly

occasion /əkeɪʒən/ **occasions, occasioning, occasioned** ◆◆◆◆◇
1 An **occasion** is a time when something happens, or a case of it happening. *I often think fondly of an occasion some years ago at Covent Garden... Mr Davis has been asked on a number of occasions.* N-COUNT
2 An **occasion** is an important event, ceremony, or celebration. *Taking her with me on official occasions has been a challenge... It will be a unique family occasion.* N-COUNT: usu supp N =function
3 An **occasion for** doing something is an opportunity for doing it; a formal use. *It is an occasion for all the family to celebrate... It is always an important occasion for setting out government policy.* N-COUNT: N *for* n/-ing =opportunity
4 To **occasion** something means to cause it; a formal use. *He argued that the release of hostages should not occasion a change in policy.* VERB V n
5 See also **sense of occasion**.
6 If you **have occasion** to do something, it is necessary for you to do it. *We have had occasion to deal with members of the group on a variety of charges.* PHRASES V inflects, PHR to-inf
7 If something happens **on occasion**, it happens sometimes, but not very often. *He treated them seriously and, on occasion, entertained them hilariously... He translated not only from the French but also, on occasion, from the Polish.* N inflects, PHR with cl =occasionally
8 If you say that someone **rose to the occasion**, you mean that they did what was necessary to successfully overcome a difficult situation. *Agassi rose to the occasion and crushed Novacek in three sets to give his country a 3-2 victory.* V inflects

occasional /əkeɪʒənəl/. **Occasional** means happening sometimes, but not regularly or often. *I've had occasional mild headaches all my life... Esther used to visit him for the occasional days and weekends.* ♦ **occasionally** *He still misbehaves occasionally... I'll occasionally go to a local jazz evening with a friend.* ◆◆◆◇◇ ADJ-GRADED: usu ADJ n; ADV-GRADED: ADV with cl/group, ADV with v

occidental /ɒksɪdentəl/. **Occidental** means relating to the countries of Europe and America; a formal word. *In some respects the African mind works rather differently from the occidental one.* ◆◇◇◇◇ ADJ: ADJ n =western

occult /ɒkʌlt, ɒkʌlt/. **The occult** is the knowledge and study of supernatural or magical forces. *However, interest in the occult tended more towards ceremonial magic rather than witchcraft. ...books dealing with the occult.* ► Also an adjective. *...organisations which campaign against paganism and occult practice.* ◆◇◇◇◇ N-SING: *the* N; ADJ: ADJ n

occultist /ɒkʌltɪst/ **occultists.** An **occultist** is a person who believes in the supernatural and the power of magic. N-COUNT

occupancy /ɒkjʊpənsi/. **Occupancy** is the act of using a room, building, or area of land, usually for a fixed period of time; a formal word. *Hotel occupancy has been as low as 40%... Tour operators report low occupancy rates.* ◆◇◇◇◇ N-UNCOUNT: usu with supp =occupation

occupant /ɒkjʊpənt/ **occupants** ◆◇◇◇◇
1 The **occupants** of a building or room are the people who live or work there. *Most of the occupants had left before the fire broke out... The filing cabinets had all gone with the previous occupants.* N-COUNT =occupier
2 You can refer to the people who are in a place such as a room, vehicle, or bed at a particular time as the **occupants**. *He wanted the occupants of the vehicle to get out... The lifeboat capsized, throwing the occupants into the water.* N-PLURAL

occupation /ɒkjʊpeɪʃən/ **occupations** ◆◆◆◇◇
1 Your **occupation** is your job or profession. *I suppose I was looking for an occupation which was going to be an adventure... Occupation: administrative assistant.* N-COUNT
2 An **occupation** is something that you do for pleasure or as part of your daily life. *Parachuting is a dangerous occupation.* N-COUNT =pursuit
3 The **occupation** of a country is its invasion and control by a foreign army. *Prii had become fluent in German during the Wehrmacht's occupation of Estonia in 1942... The communist regime was established in Romania during the Soviet occupation.* N-UNCOUNT =invasion
4 The **occupation** of a building is the act or fact of someone living or working in it. *...people who sell their home and buy another one for their own occupation.* N-UNCOUNT =occupancy

occupational /ɒkjʊpeɪʃənəl/. **Occupational** means relating to a person's job or profession. *Some received substantial occupational assistance in the form of low-interest loans.* ♦ **occupationally** *You might be having an occupationally related skin problem.* ◆◇◇◇◇ ADJ-GRADED: usu ADJ n =job-related; ADV: usu ADV adj/-ed

occupational hazard, occupational hazards. An **occupational hazard** is something unpleasant that you may suffer or experience as a result of doing your job or hobby. *Catching colds is unfortunately an occupational hazard in this profession.* N-COUNT

occupational therapist, occupational therapists. An **occupational therapist** is someone whose job involves helping people by means of occupational therapy. N-COUNT

occupational therapy. Occupational therapy is a method of helping people who have been ill or injured to develop or regain skills by giving them certain activities to do. *She will now begin occupational therapy to regain the use of her hands.* N-UNCOUNT

occupier /ɒkjʊpaɪəʳ/ **occupiers.** The **occupier** of a house, flat, or piece of land is the person who lives or works there; a formal word. • See also **owner-occupier.**. ◆◇◇◇◇ N-COUNT =occupant

occupy /ɒkjʊpaɪ/ **occupies, occupying, occupied** ◆◆◆◆◇
1 The people who **occupy** a building or a place are the people who live or work there. *There were over 40 tenants, all occupying one wing of the hospital... Land is, in most instances, purchased by those who occupy it.* VERB =inhabit V n
2 If a room or something such as a seat **is occupied**, someone is using it, so that it is not available for anyone else. *The hospital bed is no longer occupied by his wife... I saw three camp beds, two of which were occupied.* V-PASSIVE ≠vacant *be* V-ed
3 If a group of people or an army **occupies** a place or country, they move into it, using force in order to gain control of it. *U.S. forces now occupy a part of the country... Alexandretta had been occupied by the French in 1918 after the defeat of Turkey. ...the occupied territories.* VERB V n V-ed
4 If someone or something **occupies** a particular place in a system, process, or plan, they have that place. *We occupy a quality position in the market place... Many men still occupy more positions of power than women.* VERB =hold V n
5 If something **occupies** you, or if you **occupy** yourself, your time, or your mind with it, you are busy doing that thing or thinking about it. *Her parliamentary career has occupied all of her time... He hurried to take the suitcases and occupy himself with packing the car... I would deserve to be pitied if I couldn't occupy myself.* ♦ **occupied** *Keep the brain occupied... I had forgotten all about it because I had been so occupied with other things.* VERB V n V pron-refl *with* n V pron-refl Also V n *with* n; ADJ-GRADED: v-link ADJ, oft ADJ *with* n
6 If something **occupies** you, it requires your efforts, attention, or time. *I had other matters to occupy me, during the day at least... This challenge will occupy Europe for a generation or more.* VERB V n
7 If something **occupies** a particular area or place, it fills or covers it, or exists there. *Even quite small aircraft occupy a lot of space... Bookshelves occupied most of the living room walls.* VERB =take up V n
8 If something such as a journey **occupies** a particular period of time, it takes that amount of time to complete. *She reached Karachi on Monday* VERB =last V n

evening, the journey having occupied three days and nine hours.

occur /əkɜ͟ːʳ/ **occurs, occurring, occurred** ◆◆◆◆◇

1 When something **occurs**, it happens. *If headaches only occur at night, lack of fresh air and oxygen is often the cause... The crash occurred when the crew shut down the wrong engine... In March 1770, there occurred what became known as the Boston Massacre.* VERB =take place V there V n

2 When something **occurs** in a particular place, it exists or is present there. *The cattle disease occurs more or less anywhere in Africa where the fly occurs... These snails do not occur on low-lying coral islands or atolls.* VERB =exist V adv/prep

3 If a thought or idea **occurs** to you, you suddenly think of it or realize it. *It did not occur to me to check my insurance policy... It occurred to me that I could have the book sent to me... The same idea had occurred to Elizabeth.* VB: no passive, no cont it V to n to-inf it V to n that V to n

occurrence /əkʌ͟rəns, AM -kɜ͟ːr-/ **occurrences** ◆◇◇◇◇

1 An **occurrence** is something that happens; a formal use. *Complaints seemed to be an everyday occurrence... The food queues have become a daily occurrence across the country.* N-COUNT

2 **The occurrence of** something is the fact that it happens or is present. *The greatest occurrence of coronary heart disease is in those over 65.* N-COUNT: the N of n =instance

ocean /o͟ʊʃᵊn/ **oceans** ◆◆◆◇◇

1 **The ocean** is the sea. *There were few sights as beautiful as the calm ocean on a warm night.* N-SING: the N

2 An **ocean** is one of the five very large areas of sea on the Earth's surface. *They spent many days cruising the northern Pacific Ocean. ...the Indian Ocean.* N-COUNT: with supp

3 If you say that there is an **ocean of** something, you are emphasizing that there is a very large amount of it; an informal use. *I had cried oceans of tears... I've got oceans of loyal fans out there.* N-COUNT: N of n PRAGMATICS =no end

4 If you say that something is **a drop in the ocean**, you mean that it is a very small amount which is unimportant compared to the cost of other things or is so small that it has very little effect on something. *His fee is a drop in the ocean compared with the real cost of broadcasting.* PHRASE: usu v-link PHR

o͟cean-going. Ocean-going ships are designed for travelling on the sea rather than on rivers, canals, or lakes. *At the height of his shipping career he owned about 60 ocean-going vessels.* ADJ: usu ADJ n =seafaring

oceanic /o͟ʊʃiæ͟nɪk/. **Oceanic** means belonging or relating to an ocean or to the sea. *Many oceanic islands are volcanic. ...oceanic plants.* ADJ: ADJ n

oceanography /o͟ʊʃənɒ͟grəfi/. **Oceanography** is the scientific study of sea currents, the sea bed, and the fish and animals that live in the sea. *The latest techniques in oceanography are now available to many more scientists.* N-UNCOUNT ♦ **oceanographer, oceanographers** *...an oceanographer working on an environmental protection programme.* N-COUNT ♦ **oceanographic** /o͟ʊʃənəgræ͟fɪk/ *...oceanographic research.* ADJ: ADJ n

och /ɒ͟x/. In Scottish and Irish English, **och** is used to express surprise at something, or to emphasize agreement or disagreement with what has just been said. *'Och be quiet then,' Shawn said... Och aye. I always liked him.* CONVENTION PRAGMATICS =O, Oh

ochre /o͟ʊkəʳ/; also spelled **ocher**.

1 Something that is **ochre** is a yellowish orange colour. *For our dining room I have chosen ochre yellow walls.* COLOUR

2 **Ochre** is coloured earth, usually red or yellow, that is used to make dyes and paints. N-UNCOUNT

o'clock /əklɒ͟k/. You use **o'clock** after numbers from one to twelve to say what time it is. For example, if you say that it is 9 o'clock, you mean that it is nine hours after midnight or nine hours after midday. *The trouble began just after ten o'clock last night... I went to sleep, and at two o'clock in the morning I woke up.* ◆◆◆◇◇ ADV: num ADV

Oct. Oct. is a written abbreviation for **October**. *...Tuesday Oct. 25th.* ◆◆◇◇◇

octagon /ɒ͟ktəgən/ **octagons.** An **octagon** is a geometrical shape that has eight straight sides. N-COUNT

octagonal /ɒktæ͟gənᵊl/. Something that is **octagonal** has eight straight sides. *...a white octagonal box... The room was octagonal.* ADJ

octane /ɒ͟kteɪn/. **Octane** is a chemical substance that exists in petrol and that is used to measure the quality of petrol. *Your engine can run happily on 76 octane petrol. ...high octane fuel for cars.* N-UNCOUNT: usu with supp

octave /ɒ͟ktɪv/ **octaves.** An **octave** is the musical interval between the first note and the eighth note of a scale. N-COUNT

octet /ɒkte͟t/ **octets.** An **octet** is a group of eight singers or musicians. *...the Stan Tracey Octet.* N-COUNT: oft in names

October /ɒkto͟ʊbəʳ/ **Octobers. October** is the tenth month of the year in the Western calendar. *Most seasonal hiring is done in early October... The first plane is due to leave on October 2... My grandson has been away since last October.* ◆◆◆◆◇ N-VAR

octogenarian /ɒ͟ktoʊdʒɪne͟əriən/ **octogenarians.** An **octogenarian** is a person who is between eighty and eighty-nine years old. N-COUNT

octopus /ɒ͟ktəpəs/ **octopuses.** An **octopus** is a sea creature with eight tentacles which it uses to catch food. ► **Octopus** is this fish eaten as food. N-VAR; N-UNCOUNT

ocular /ɒ͟kjələʳ/. **Ocular** means relating to or concerned with the eyes or eyesight: a medical word. *Other ocular signs include involuntary rhythmic movement of the eyeball.* ADJ: ADJ n

OD /o͟ʊ di͟ː/ **OD's, OD'ing, OD'd.** To **OD** means the same as to **overdose**; an informal word. *His son was a junkie, the kid OD'd a year ago.* ► Also a noun. *'I had a friend died of an OD,' she said.* VERB V; N-COUNT

odd /ɒ͟d/ **odder, oddest** ◆◆◆◆◇

1 If you describe someone or something as **odd**, you think that they are strange or unusual. *He'd always been odd, but not to this extent... What an odd coincidence that he should have known your family... Something odd began to happen.* • See also **odd-looking**. ♦ **oddly** *...an oddly shaped hill... His own boss was behaving rather oddly.* ♦ **oddness** *Perhaps it was that very oddness that attracted me to Glen's music.* ADJ-GRADED =peculiar, queer; ADV-GRADED: ADV with v; N-UNCOUNT =strangeness

2 You use **odd** before a noun to indicate that you are not mentioning the type, size, or quality of something because it is not important. *...moving from place to place where she could find the odd bit of work... He had various odd cleaning jobs around the place... I knew that Alan liked the odd drink.* ADJ: det ADJ =occasional

3 You use **odd** after a number to indicate that it is only approximate; an informal use. *How many pages was it, 500 odd?... He has now appeared in sixty odd films... 'How long have you lived here?'—'Twenty odd years.'* ADV: num ADV

4 **Odd** numbers, such as 3 and 17, are those which cannot be divided exactly by the number two. *The odd numbers are on the left as you walk up the street... There's an odd number of candidates.* ADJ: usu ADJ n ≠even

5 You say that two things are **odd** when they do not belong to the same set or pair. *I'm wearing odd socks today by the way.* ADJ ≠matching

6 **The odd man out, the odd woman out**, or **the odd one out** in a particular situation is a person who is different from the other people in it. *Azerbaijan has been the odd man out, the one republic not to hold democratic elections... Mark and Rick were the odd ones out in claiming to like this cherry beer.* PHRASE: N inflects, usu v-link PHR

7 See also **odds, odds and ends**.

oddball /ɒ͟dbɔːl/ **oddballs.** If you refer to someone as an **oddball**, you think they behave in a strange or peculiar way; an informal word. *His mother and father thought Jim was a bit of an oddball too.* ► Also an adjective. *I came from a family that was decidedly oddball you know.* N-COUNT =eccentric; ADJ-GRADED =peculiar

oddity /ɒ͟dɪti/ **oddities** ◆◇◇◇◇

1 An **oddity** is someone or something that is very strange. *Losing my hair made me feel an oddity... Carlson noticed another oddity; his plant had bloomed twice.* N-COUNT =curiosity

2 The **oddity** of something is the fact that it is very strange. *...the oddities of the Welsh legal system.* N-COUNT: usu the N of n =peculiarity

o͟dd-jo͟b man, odd-job men. An **odd-job man** is a man who is paid to do various manual jobs, N-COUNT usually in somebody's home, for example clearing drains or cleaning windows.

odd-looking. If you describe someone or something as **odd-looking**, you think that they look unusual or peculiar. *They were an odd-looking couple... One of the waitresses arrived with a very odd-looking dish.* ADJ-GRADED

oddly /ɒdli/. You use **oddly** to indicate that what you are saying is true, but that it is not what you expected. *He said no and seemed oddly reluctant to talk about it... Oddly, Emma says she never considered her face was attractive... There were, oddly, few other Britons living in this northern part.* • See also **odd**. ◆◇◇◇◇ ADV: ADV adj, ADV with cl PRAGMATICS =strangely

oddment /ɒdmənt/ **oddments. Oddments** are unimportant objects of any kind, usually ones that are old or left over from a larger group of things. *...searching street markets for interesting jewellery and oddments.* N-COUNT =bit, scrap

odds /ɒdz/ ◆◆◇◇◇

1 You refer to the probability of something happening as the **odds** that it will happen. In gambling, if you bet one pound on a horse whose odds are '10 to 1', you will receive ten pounds if the horse wins. *What are the odds of finding a parking space right outside the door?... Gavin Jones, who put £25 on Eugene, at odds of 50 to 1, has won £1,250 pounds... The odds are that you are going to fail.* • See also **odds-on**. N-PLURAL: usu *the* N =chances

2 If someone is **at odds** with someone else, or if two people are **at odds**, they are disagreeing or quarrelling with each other. *He was at odds with his Prime Minister... An adviser said there was no reason why the two countries should remain at odds.* PHRASES usu v-link PHR, oft PHR *with* n

3 If you say that **the odds are against** something or someone, you mean that they are unlikely to succeed. *He reckoned the odds are against the scheme going ahead... I'm sorry. I just feel as if the odds are stacked up against me.* V inflects, PHR n

4 If something happens **against** all **odds**, it happens or succeeds although it seemed impossible or very unlikely. *Some women do manage to achieve business success against all odds... Finally, late in life and against considerable odds, she became a nun.* PHR with cl

5 If you say that **the odds are in** someone's **favour**, you mean that they are likely to succeed in what they are doing. *His troops will only engage in a ground battle when all the odds are in their favour.* V inflects

6 To **shorten the odds** on something happening means to make it more likely to happen. To **lengthen the odds** means to make it less likely to happen. You can also say that **the odds are shortening** or **lengthening**. *His reception there shortened the odds that he might be the next Tory leader.* ERG: V inflects

odds and ends. You can refer to a disorganized group of things of various kinds as **odds and ends**; an informal word. *She put in some clothes, odds and ends, and make-up... He sweeps up and does a few odds and ends.* N-PLURAL =bits and pieces

odds-on; also spelled **odds on**. If there is an **odds-on** chance that something will happen, it is very likely that it will happen; an informal word. *Gerald was no longer the odds-on favourite to win the contest... It was odds-on that there was no killer.* ◆◇◇◇◇ ADJ

ode /oʊd/ **odes.** An **ode** is a poem that is usually written in praise of a particular person, thing, or event; a literary word. *...Keats' Ode to a Nightingale.* N-COUNT

odious /oʊdiəs/. If you describe people or things as **odious**, you think that they are extremely unpleasant. *Herr Schmidt is certainly the most odious man I have ever met... The judge described the crime as odious.* ADJ-GRADED

odium /oʊdiəm/. **Odium** is the dislike, disapproval, or hatred that people feel for a particular person, usually because of something that the person has done; a formal word. *The complainant has been exposed to public odium, scandal and contempt.* N-UNCOUNT =abhorrence

odor /oʊdər/. See **odour**.

odour /oʊdər/ **odours;** spelled **odor** in American English. An **odour** is a particular and distinctive smell. *The whole herb has a characteristic taste and odour... The taste is only slightly bitter, and there is little odour.* • See also **body odour**. ◆◇◇◇◇ N-VAR =aroma, scent

odourless /oʊdərləs/; spelled **odorless** in American English. An **odourless** substance has no smell. *...a completely odourless, colourless, transparent liquid... The gases are odourless.* ADJ-GRADED

odyssey /ɒdɪsi/ **odysseys.** An **odyssey** is a long exciting journey on which a lot of things happen; a literary word. *The march to Travnik was the final stretch of a 16-hour odyssey.* ◆◇◇◇◇ N-COUNT

Oedipus complex /iːdɪpəs kɒmpleks/. If a boy or man has an **Oedipus complex**, he feels sexual desire for his mother and is jealous of his father. N-SING

o'er /ɔːr/. **O'er** means the same as 'over'; an old-fashioned word, used mainly in poetry. *As long as mist hangs o'er the mountains, The deeds of the brave will be remembered.* PREP =over

oesophagus /iːsɒfəgəs/ **oesophaguses;** also spelled **esophagus**. Your **oesophagus** is the part of your body that carries the food from the throat to the stomach. N-COUNT =gullet

oestrogen /iːstrədʒən, AM e-/; also spelled **estrogen. Oestrogen** is a hormone produced in the ovaries of female animals. Oestrogen controls the reproductive cycle and prepares the body for pregnancy. *As ovulation gets nearer, oestrogen levels rise.* ◆◇◇◇◇ N-UNCOUNT

of /əv, STRONG ɒv, AM ʌv/ ◆◆◆◆◆

In addition to the uses shown below, **of** is used after some verbs, nouns, and adjectives in order to introduce extra information. **Of** is also used in phrasal prepositions such as 'because of', 'instead of' and 'in spite of', and in phrasal verbs such as 'make of' and 'dispose of'.

1 You use **of** to combine two nouns when the first noun identifies the feature of the second noun that you want to talk about. *The average age of the women interviewed was only 21.5. ...the population of this town... The aim of the course is to help students to comprehend the structure of contemporary political and social systems.* PREP: n PREP n

2 You use **of** to combine two nouns, or a noun and a present participle, when the second noun or present participle defines or gives more information about the first noun. *Would you say what you felt was a feeling of betrayal?... She let out a little cry of pain. ...the problem of a national shortage of teachers. ...an idealized but hazy notion of world socialism. ...the recession of 1974-75... This has been a good chance of meeting up with everyone again.* PREP: n PREP n/-ing

3 You use **of** after nouns referring to actions to specify the person or thing that is affected by the action or that performs the action. For example, 'the kidnapping of the child' refers to an action affecting a child; 'the arrival of the next train' refers to an action performed by a train. *...the reduction of trade union power inside the party. ...the assessment of future senior managers. ...the death of their father. ...the Marriage of Figaro.* PREP: n PREP n

4 You use **of** after words and phrases referring to quantities or groups of things to indicate the substance or thing that is being measured. *...7.6 litres of pure alcohol. ...a few kilometres of new roads. ...dozens of people. ...billions of dollars. ...groups of protestors. ...a collection of short stories... A flock of birds flew towards us slowly from far away.* PREP: quant PREP n, n PREP n

5 You use **of** after the name of someone or something to introduce the institution or place they belong to or are connected with. *...the Prince of Wales. ...the Finance Minister of Bangladesh. ...the superb rock-hewn Cave Temples of Badami.* PREP: n PREP n

6 You use **of** after a noun referring to a container to form an expression referring to the container and its contents. *We could all do with a cup of tea... Conder opened another bottle of wine... Marta drank a glass of juice. ...a box of tissues. ...a packet of cigarettes. ...a roomful of people.* PREP: n PREP n

7 You use **of** after a count noun and before an PREP:

uncount noun when you want to talk about individual instances of something that is normally considered as a whole. *...a blade of grass... Marina ate only one slice of bread... With a stick of chalk he wrote her order on a blackboard.* n PREP n

8 You use **of** to indicate the materials or things that form something. *...local decorations of wood and straw. ...loose-fitting garments of linen. ...a mixture of paint-thinner and petrol.* PREP: n PREP n

9 You use **of** after a noun which specifies a particular part of something, to introduce the thing that it is a part of. *...the other side of the square... We had almost reached the end of the street. ...the beginning of the year... Edward disappeared around 9.30pm on the 23rd of July. ...the core of the problem.* PREP: n PREP n

10 You use **of** after some verbs to indicate someone or something else involved in the action. *He'd been dreaming of her... Listen, I shall be thinking of you always... Her parents did not approve of her decision... The Americans cannot accuse him of ignoring the problem... The elderly relative had died of old age.* PREP: v PREP n/-ing, v n PREP n/-ing

11 You use **of** after some adjectives to indicate the thing that a feeling or quality relates to. *I have grown very fond of Alec... His father was quite naturally very proud of him... I think everyone was scared of her... She would be guilty of betraying her own mother.* PREP: adj PREP n/-ing

12 You use **of** before a word referring to the person who performed an action when saying what you think about the action. *This has been so nice, so terribly kind of you... I suppose it's stupid of us not to be able to make up our own minds... That's certainly very generous of you Tony.* PREP: adj PREP pron/n-proper

13 You use **of** after a noun which describes someone or something, to introduce the person or thing you are talking about. *...an awkward, slow-moving giant of a man.* PREP: a n PREP a n

14 If something is **more** or **less of** a particular thing, it is that thing to a greater or lesser degree. *Your extra fat may be more of a health risk than you realize... As time goes by, sleeping becomes less of a problem.* PREP: *more/less* PREP a n

15 You use **of** to indicate a characteristic or quality that someone or something has or to introduce a person or thing that has a particular quality. *...the worth of their music. ...the creaminess of her skin... She is a woman of enviable beauty. ...a matter of overwhelming importance... The new deal was considered to be the most generous of its kind.* PREP: n PREP n, adj-superl PREP n

16 You use **of** after the verb 'be' to indicate in a formal way a characteristic or quality that someone or something has. *The crisis faced over the next few months is of an entirely different scale... Both world wars were of unquestionable importance as economic events.* PREP: *be* PREP n

17 You use **of** to specify an amount, value, or age. *Last Thursday, Nick announced record revenues of $3.4 billion... He has been sentenced to a total of 21 years in prison since 1973... The last figures so far this year indicate a rise of 13.8%. ...young people under the age of 16 years... I feel like a girl of 18.* PREP: n PREP amount

18 You use **of** after a noun such as 'month' or 'year' to indicate the length of time that some state or activity continues. *...eight bruising years of war... The project has gone through nearly a dozen years of planning.* PREP: n PREP n/-ing

19 In American English, you use **of** to say what time it is by indicating how many minutes there are before the hour mentioned. *At about a quarter of eight in the evening Joe Urber calls... We got to the beach at five of one in the afternoon.* PREP

of course ◆◆◆◆◆

1 You say **of course** to suggest that something is normal, obvious, or well-known, and should therefore not surprise the person you are talking to. *Of course there were lots of other interesting things at the exhibition... 'I have read about you in the newspapers of course,' Charlie said... The only honest answer is, of course, yes.* ADV: ADV with cl, PRAGMATICS =naturally

2 You use **of course** as a polite way of giving permission; used in spoken English. *'Can I just say something about the cup game on Saturday?'—'Yes of course you can.'... 'Could I see these documents?'—'Of course.'* CONVENTION PRAGMATICS

3 You use **of course** in order to emphasize a statement that you are making, especially when you are agreeing or disagreeing with someone; used in spoken English. *'I expect you're right.'—'Of course I'm right.'... Of course I'm not afraid!... 'You will strictly observe your diet: no wine or spirits, very little meat.'—'Of course.'... 'She doesn't have to know how things work.'—'Of course she does.'* ADV: ADV with cl, ADV as reply, PRAGMATICS

4 **Of course not** is an emphatic way of saying no; used in spoken English. *'You're not really seriously considering this thing, are you?'—'No, of course not.'... 'I'd like to talk to the lads if you don't mind.'—'Of course not, Chief.'* CONVENTION PRAGMATICS

off. The preposition is pronounced /ɒf, AM ɔːf/. ◆◆◆◆◆ The adverb is pronounced /ɒf, AM ɔːf/

In addition to the uses shown below, **off** is used after some verbs and nouns in order to introduce extra information. **Off** is also used in phrasal verbs such as 'get off', 'pair off', and 'sleep off'.

1 If something is taken **off** something else or moves **off** it, it is no longer touching that thing. *He took his feet off the desk... I took the key for the room off a rack above her head... Hugh wiped the rest of the blood off his face with his handkerchief.* PREP =from ► Also an adverb. *Lee broke off a small piece of orange and held it out to him... His exhaust fell off six laps from the finish.* ADV: ADV after v

2 When you get **off** a bus, train, or plane, you come out of it or leave it after you have been travelling on it. *Don't try to get on or off a moving train!... As he stepped off the aeroplane, he was shot dead.* PREP ≠on ► Also an adverb. *At the next stop the man got off too and introduced himself.* ADV: ADV after v

3 If you keep **off** a street or piece of land, you do not step on it or go there. *Locking up men does nothing more than keep them off the streets... The local police had warned visitors to keep off the beach at night.* PREP ► Also an adverb. *...a sign saying 'Keep Off'.* ADV

4 If something is situated **off** a place such as a coast, room, or road, it is near to it or next to it, but not exactly in it. *The boat was anchored off the northern coast of the peninsula... Lily lives in a penthouse just off Park Avenue... The Princess's sitting-room leads off the drawing room... Tiny secluded beaches can be found off the beaten track.* PREP

5 If you go **off**, you leave a place. *He was just about to drive off when the secretary came running out... She gave a hurried wave and set off across the grass... She was off again. Last year she had been to Kenya. This year it was Goa... When his master's off traveling, Caleb stays with Pierre's parents.* ADV: ADV after v, *be* ADV, oft ADV -ing

6 **Off** is used in a number of informal and offensive phrasal verbs, such as **buzz off**, **clear off**, or **bugger off**, which are used to tell someone angrily to go away. ADV: ADV after v

7 When you take **off** clothing or jewellery that you are wearing, you remove it from your body. *He took off his spectacles and rubbed frantically at the lens... He hastily stripped off his old uniform and began pulling on the new one.* ADV: ADV after v

8 If you have time **off** or a particular day **off**, you do not go to work or school, for example because you are ill or it is a day when you do not usually work. *The rest of the men had the day off... You can even snatch a few hours off, and perhaps negotiate the occasional night off too... She was sacked for demanding Saturdays off... I'm off tomorrow... The average Swede was off sick 27 days last year.* ADV: usu n ADV, also *be* ADV ► Also a preposition. *He could not get time off work to go on holiday.* PREP

9 If you keep **off** a subject, you deliberately avoid talking about it. *Keep off the subject of politics... Keep the conversation off linguistic matters.* PREP =away from

10 If something such as an agreement or a sporting event is **off**, it is cancelled. *Until Pointon is completely happy, however, the deal's off... The vacant W.B.C. junior-lightweight title has been called off... Greenpeace refused to call off the event.* ADV: *be* ADV, ADV after v =cancelled

11 If someone is **off** something harmful such as a PREP drug, they have stopped taking or using it. *She felt better and the psychiatrist took her off drug therapy... Most pregnant women remain off cigarettes while carrying the child.*

12 If you are **off** something, you have stopped liking it. *I'm off coffee at the moment... Diarrhoea can make you feel weak, as well as putting you off your food.* PREP

13 When something such as a machine or electric light is **off**, it is not functioning or in use. When you switch it **off**, you stop it functioning. *As he pulled into the driveway, he saw her bedroom light was off... We used sail power and turned the engine off to save our fuel... The microphones had been switched off.* ADV: *be* ADV, ADV after v ≠on

14 If there is money **off** something, its price is reduced by the amount specified. *...Simons Leatherwear, 37 Old Christchurch Road. 20 per cent off all jackets this Saturday. ...discounts offering thousands of pounds off the normal price of a car.* PREP: amount PREP n
▸ Also an adverb. *I'm prepared to knock five hundred pounds off but no more.* ADV: ADV after v, v-link ADV, amount ADV

15 If something is a long way **off**, it is a long distance away from you. *Florida was a long way off. ...animals that from a long way off look like flies... Below you, though still 50 miles off, is the most treeless stretch of land imaginable.* ADV: n/amount ADV =away

16 If something is a long time **off**, it will not happen for a long time. *An end to the crisis seems a long way off... The required technology is probably still two years off.* ADV: n/amount ADV

17 If you get something **off** someone, you obtain it from them; used in spoken English. *I don't really get a lot of information, and if I do I get it off Mark... I can't find the boys' shampoo. I can't think where I put it when I took it off them... 'Telmex' was bought off the government by a group of investors.* PREP =from

18 **Off** combines with adverbs such as 'well', 'badly', and 'worse' to form adjectives that indicate how poor or rich someone is. *Most of these people aren't very well off... Surely you can't be that badly off?... He's very comfortably off.* COMB in ADJ-GRADED

19 If food has gone **off**, it tastes and smells bad because it is no longer fresh enough to be eaten; used mainly in British English. *Food can be something of a problem. It goes off, and when it's gone off it smells.* ADJ-GRADED: v-link ADJ =bad

20 If you live **off** a particular kind of food, you eat it in order to live. If you live **off** a particular source of money, you use it to live. *Her husband's memories are of living off roast chicken and drinking whisky... Antony had been living off the sale of his own paintings.* PREP: v PREP n =on

21 If a machine runs **off** a particular kind of fuel or power, it uses that power in order to function. *The Auto Compact Disc Cleaner can run off batteries or mains.* PREP: v PREP n

22 If you say that someone's behaviour is a bit **off**, you mean that you find it unacceptable or wrong; an informal use. *...coming home with make-up all over his clothes – it's a bit off isn't it... Some of the dialogue is slightly off.* ADJ-GRADED: v-link adv ADJ

23 If something happens **on and off**, or **off and on**, it happens occasionally, or only for part of a period of time, not in a regular or continuous way. *I was still working on and off as a waitress to support myself... We lived together, off and on, for two years.* PHRASE: PHR after v, PHR with cl =now and again

off-air; also spelled **off air**. In radio or television, when a programme goes **off-air** or when something happens **off-air**, it is not broadcast. *When I get off air around 2am my neck and shoulders are locked with tension... The argument continued off air.* ADV: ADV after v, *be* ADV
▸ Also an adjective. *...a special off-air advice line.* ADJ: ADJ n

offal /ɒfᵊl, AM ɔːfᵊl/. **Offal** is the internal organs of animals, for example their hearts and livers, when they are cooked and eaten. N-UNCOUNT

off-balance; also spelled **off balance**. ◆◇◇◇◇
1 If someone or something is **off-balance**, they can easily fall or be knocked over because they are not standing firmly. *He tried to use his own weight to push his attacker off but he was off balance... The lunge had thrown him off-balance and he spun, trying to regain his centre of gravity.* ADJ-GRADED: v n ADJ, v-link ADJ
2 If someone is caught **off-balance**, they are extremely surprised or upset by a particular event or piece of news they are not expecting. *Mullins knocked me off-balance with his abrupt change of subject... The Communist Party was thrown off-balance by the attempted coup.* ADJ-GRADED: usu v n ADJ

off balance sheet; also spelled **off-balance-sheet**. In finance, an **off balance sheet** transaction is one that is not recorded in a company's balance sheets. ADJ: usu ADJ n

off-beam; also spelled **off beam**. If you describe something or someone as **off-beam**, you mean that they are wrong, mistaken, or inaccurate; an informal expression. *Everything she says is a little off beam.* ADJ-GRADED: usu v-link ADJ

offbeat /ɒfbiːt, AM ɔːf-/; also spelled **off-beat**. If you describe something or someone as **offbeat**, you think that they are different from normal. *She adores old, offbeat antiques. ...a wickedly offbeat imagination.* ADJ-GRADED: usu ADJ n =unorthodox

off-Broadway /ɒf brɔːdweɪ, AM ɔːf -/
1 An **off-Broadway** theatre is located away from Broadway, the main theatre district in New York. *...the city's most famous off-Broadway theater.* ADJ: ADJ n
2 An **off-Broadway** play is less commercial and often more experimental than those usually staged in Broadway, the main theatre district in New York. *...adapted from the off-Broadway stage show of the same name. ...the avant-garde and off-Broadway theater community.* ADJ: ADJ n

off-centre; spelled **off-center** in American English.
1 If something is **off-centre**, it is not exactly in the middle of a space or surface. *The pedals seem a bit off-centre and the clutch is rather stiff... If the blocks are placed off-centre, they will fall down.* ADJ-GRADED: usu v-link ADJ
2 If you describe someone or something as **off-centre**, you mean that they are less conventional than other people or things. *Davies's writing is far too off-centre to be commercial.* ADJ-GRADED: usu v-link ADJ =unorthodox

off-chance; also spelled **offchance**. If you do something **on the off-chance**, you do it because you hope that it will succeed, although you think that this is unlikely. *He had taken a flight to Paris on the off-chance that he might be able to meet Francesca. ...an American visitor who had turned up on the off-chance of catching a glimpse of the princess.* PHRASE: PHR after v, oft PHR that, PHR *of* n/-ing

off-colour; spelled **off-color** in American English.
1 In British English, if you say that you are feeling **off-colour**, you mean that you are slightly ill. *For three weeks Maurice felt off-colour but did not have any dramatic symptoms.* ADJ-GRADED: v-link ADJ =out of sorts
2 If you say that someone's performance is **off-colour**, you mean that they are not performing as well as they usually do; used in British journalism. *Milan looked off-colour but eventually took the lead in the 82nd minute.* ADJ-GRADED
3 An **off-colour** joke or remark is rude, improper, or offensive. *He denies making off-color remarks about women.* ADJ-GRADED =rude

off day, off days; also spelled **off-day**. If someone, especially an athlete, has an **off day**, they do not perform as well as usual; an informal word. *Whittingham, the League's top scorer, had an off day, missing three good chances.* N-COUNT

off-duty; also spelled **off duty**. When someone such as a soldier or policeman is **off-duty**, they are not working. *The place is the haunt of off-duty policemen.* ◆◇◇◇◇ ADJ ≠on duty

offence /əfens/ **offences**; spelled **offense** in American English. The pronunciation /ɔːfens/ is used for meaning 3. ◆◆◆◇◇
1 An **offence** is a crime that breaks a particular law and requires a particular punishment. *Thirteen people have been charged with treason – an offence which can carry the death penalty... In Britain the Consumer Protection Act makes it a criminal offence to sell goods that are unsafe.* N-COUNT

2 **Offence** or an **offence** is behaviour which causes people to be upset or embarrassed. *The book might be published without creating offense... Privilege determined by birth is an offence to any modern sense of justice.*
N-VAR =outrage

3 In American English, in sports such as American football, ice hockey, or basketball, **the offense** is the team which has possession of the ball and is trying to score. *Between plays the coach was talking to the offense in the huddle.*
N-SING: *the* N

4 If you **cause offence** or **give offence** to someone, you upset or embarrass them, for example by being rude or tactless. *It says the photograph is likely cause distress and offence to the public... 'We have had our differences and I'm sorry if it has caused offence.'*
PHRASES V inflects

5 Some people say **'no offence'** to reassure you that they do not want to upset you, although what they are saying may seem rude. *'Yes I think it's the equivalent of Welsh, it's practically unpronounceable. No offence to the Welsh, of course.'*
CONVENTION PRAGMATICS

6 If someone **takes offence** at something you say or do, they feel upset, often unnecessarily, because they think you are being rude to them. *She never takes offence at anything.'... Never had she seen him so tense, so quick to take offence as he had been in recent weeks.*
V inflects

offend /əfe̲nd/ **offends, offending, offended** ◆◆◇◇◇

1 If you **offend** someone, you upset or embarrass them by doing something rude or tactless. *He apologizes for his comments and says he had no intention of offending the community... The survey found almost 90 percent of people were offended by strong swearwords... Television censors are cutting out scenes which they claim may offend.*
VERB =insult, upset; V n; V
♦ **offended** *She is terribly offended, angered and hurt by this.*
ADJ-GRADED: v-link ADJ

2 To **offend** against a law, rule, or principle means to break it; a formal use. *This bill offends against good sense and against justice... In showing contempt for the heavyweight championship Douglas offended a stern code.*
VERB; V *against* n; V n

3 If someone **offends**, they commit a crime; a formal use. *In Western countries girls are far less likely to offend than boys.*
VB: no cont =break the law; V

offender /əfe̲ndəʳ/ **offenders** ◆◆◇◇◇

1 An **offender** is a person who has committed a crime. *The authorities often know that sex offenders will attack again when they are released.*
N-COUNT: oft supp N

2 You can refer to someone or something which you think is causing a problem as an **offender**. *The contraceptive pill is the worst offender, but it is not the only drug to deplete the body's vitamin levels.*
N-COUNT =culprit

offending /əfe̲ndɪŋ/ ◆◇◇◇◇

1 You can use **offending** to describe something that is causing a problem that needs to be dealt with. *The book was withdrawn for the offending passages to be deleted... The dentist commenced to dig, drill and finally fill the offending tooth.*
ADJ-GRADED: *the* ADJ n

2 **Offending** is the act of committing a crime. *Ms Mann is working with young offenders and trying to break cycles of offending.*
N-UNCOUNT

offense /əfe̲ns, ɒ̲fens/. See **offence**.

offensive /əfe̲nsɪv/ **offensives** ◆◆◆◇◇

1 If you say that something is **offensive**, you mean that it upsets or embarrasses you because it is rude or insulting. *Some friends of his found the play horribly offensive. ...offensive remarks which called into question the integrity of my firm.*
ADJ-GRADED =objectionable
♦ **offensively** *The group who had been shouting offensively opened to let her through... I thought his glance at me had been offensively bold.*
ADV-GRADED: ADV after v, ADV adj

2 A military **offensive** is a carefully planned attack made by a large group of soldiers. *Its latest military offensive against rebel forces is aimed at re-opening important trade routes... The armed forces have launched offensives to recapture lost ground.*
N-COUNT: oft supp N

3 If you conduct an **offensive**, you take strong action to show how angry you are about something or how much you disapprove of something. *Republicans acknowledged that they had little choice but to mount an all-out offensive on the Democratic nominee. ...a diplomatic offensive.* ● See also **charm offensive**.
N-COUNT: usu supp N

4 If you **go on the offensive, go over to the offensive**, or **take the offensive**, you begin to take strong action against people who have been attacking you. *The West African forces went on the offensive in response to attacks on them... The Foreign Secretary has decided to take the offensive in the discussion on the future of the community.*
PHRASE: V inflects

offer /ɒ̲fəʳ, AM ɔ̲ːfər/ **offers, offering, offered** ◆◆◆◆◆

1 If you **offer** something to someone, you ask them if they would like to have it or use it. *He has offered seats at the conference table to the Russian leader and the president of Kazakhstan... The number of companies offering them work increased... Rhys offered him an apple... Western governments have offered aid.*
VERB; V n *to* n; V n n; V n

2 If you **offer** to do something, you say that you are willing to do it. *Peter offered to teach them water-skiing... 'Can I get you a drink,' she offered.*
VERB; V to-inf; V with quote

3 An **offer** is something that someone says they will give you or do for you. *The offer of talks with Moscow marks a significant change from the previous western position... 'I ought to reconsider her offer to move in,' he mused... He had refused several excellent job offers.*
N-COUNT

4 If you **offer** someone information, advice, or praise, you give it to them, usually because you feel that they need it or deserve it. *They manage a company offering advice on mergers and acquisitions... Western leaders, who had been offering Yeltsin moral support, now rang to congratulate him... They are offered very little counselling or support.*
VERB; V n; V n n; Also V n *to* n

5 If you **offer** someone something such as love or friendship, you show them that you feel that way towards them. *The President has offered his sympathy to the Georgian people... It must be better to be able to offer them love and security... John's mother and sister rallied round offering comfort.*
VERB; V n *to* n; V n n; V n

6 If people **offer** prayers, praise, or a sacrifice to God or a god, they worship their god in one of those ways. *Church leaders offered prayers and condemned the bloodshed... He will offer the first harvest of rice to the sun goddess.* ▶ **Offer up** means the same as **offer**. *He should consider offering up a prayer to St Lambert.*
VERB; V n; V n *to* n; Also V n n; PHRASAL VERB V P n (not pron)

7 If an organization **offers** something such as a service or product, it provides it. *We have been successful because we are offering a quality service... Sainsbury's is offering customers 1p for each shopping bag re-used... Eagle Star offers a 10% discount to the over-55s.*
VERB =provide; V n; V n n; V n *to* n

8 An **offer** in a shop is a specially low price for a specific product or something extra that you get if you buy a certain product. *This month's offers include a shirt, trousers and bed covers... Today's special offer gives you a choice of three destinations... Weight watchers can save at Gateway with Special K on offer at £1.59, down 26p.*
N-COUNT: oft supp N, also *on* N =reduction

9 If you **offer** a particular amount of money for something, you say that you will pay that much to buy it. *Whitney has offered $21.50 a share in cash for 49.5 million Prime shares... They are offering farmers $2.15 a bushel for corn... He will write Rachel a note and offer her a fair price for the land... It was his custom in buying real estate to offer a rather low price.*
VERB; V amount; V n amount; V n n; V n; Also V n *to* n

10 An **offer** is the amount of money that someone says they will pay to buy something. *The lawyers say no one else will make me an offer... He has dismissed an offer of compensation.*
N-COUNT =bid

11 If someone or something **has something to offer**, they have a particular quality or ability that makes them important, attractive, or useful. *In your free time, explore all that this incredible city has to offer.*
PHRASES V inflects

12 If there is something **on offer**, it is available to be used or bought. *Savings schemes are the best retail investment products on offer. ...country cottages on offer at bargain prices.*
v-link PHR

13 If you are **open to offers**, you are willing to sell something or do something if someone will pay
v-link PHR

you an amount of money that you think is reasonable. *It seems that while the Kiwis are keen to have him, he is still open to offers.*

offer up. See **offer** 6. PHRASAL VERB

offering /ɒfərɪŋ, AM ɔːf-/ **offerings** ◆◆◆◇◇

1 An **offering** is something that is specially produced to be sold. *Dishes of the day include Provencal offerings such as aioli with salt cod.* N-COUNT

2 An **offering** is something that people offer to their God or gods as a sacrifice. *...the holiest of the Shinto rituals, where offerings are made at night to the great Sun.* N-COUNT

offertory /ɒfəʳtri, AM ɔːfərtɔːri/ **offertories.** In the Christian Mass, the **offertory** is the part of the service where the bread and wine of the Eucharist is offered to God by the priest. N-COUNT

off-guard. If someone is caught **off-guard**, they are not expecting a surprise or danger that suddenly occurs. *The question caught her completely off-guard.* ADJ-GRADED: v n ADJ, v-link ADJ =unawares

off-hand; also spelled **off hand.**

1 If you say that someone is being **off-hand**, you are critical of them for being unfriendly or impolite, and not showing any interest in what other people are doing or saying. *He lapsed into long silences or became offensively off-hand... Consumers found the attitude of its staff off-hand and generally offensive to the paying customer.* ADJ-GRADED: usu v-link ADJ PRAGMATICS

2 If you say something **off-hand**, you say it without checking the details or facts of it. *'Have you done the repairs?'—'Can't say off-hand, but I doubt it.'... 'Were they at home or away, do you know offhand?'* ADV: ADV after v

office /ɒfɪs, AM ɔːf-/ **offices** ◆◆◆◆◆

1 An **office** is a room or a part of a building where people work sitting at desks. *He had an office big enough for his desk and chair, plus his VDU... At about 4.30 p.m. Audrey arrived at the office... Telephone their head office for more details. ...an office block.* N-COUNT

2 An **office** is a department of an organization, especially the government, where people deal with a particular kind of administrative work. *Thousands have registered with unemployment offices. ...Downing Street's press office. ...the Congressional Budget Office.* N-COUNT: usu n N, oft in names

3 An **office** is a small building or room where people can go for information, tickets, or a service of some kind. *The tourist office operates a useful room-finding service. ...the airline ticket offices.* N-COUNT: usu supp N

4 If someone holds **office** in a government, they have an important job or position of authority. *The events to mark the President's ten years in office went ahead as planned... They are fed up with the politicians and want to vote them out of office... The president shall hold office for five years... The Vietnam War dashed President Johnson's hopes of a second term of office... He ran for office.* N-UNCOUNT: oft *in/out of*N

5 Someone's **good offices** are the help that they give to other people who are trying to achieve something; a formal expression. *She sought the good offices of the President for the smooth passage of the Bill.* PHRASE: usu with poss =support

6 See also **booking office, box office, post office, register office, registry office.**

office boy, office boys. An **office boy** is a young man, especially one who has just left school, who is employed in an office to do simple tasks; an old-fashioned word. N-COUNT

office-holder, office-holders; also spelled **office holder.** An **office-holder** is a person who has an important official position in an organization; a formal word. *They appear to be in a mood to vote against office-holders in the elections.* N-COUNT

office hours. Office hours are the times when an office or similar place of work is open for business. In Britain, office hours are usually between 9 o'clock and 5 o'clock on weekdays. *If you have any queries, please call Anne Fisher on 0121-414-6203 during office hours.* N-PLURAL: usu prep N

officer /ɒfɪsəʳ, AM ɔːf-/ **officers** ◆◆◆◆◆

1 In the armed forces, an **officer** is a person in a position of authority. *...a retired British army officer... Her husband served during the Civil War as an officer in the White Army.* N-COUNT

2 An **officer** is a person who has a responsible position in an organization, especially a government organization. *...a local authority education officer.* N-COUNT: usu supp N

3 Members of the police force can be referred to as **officers.** *...senior officers in the West Midlands police force... Thank you, Officer.* N-COUNT: usu with supp; N-VOC

4 See also **commanding officer, petty officer, pilot officer, police officer, probation officer, returning officer, warrant officer.**

official /əfɪʃəl/ **officials** ◆◆◆◆◆

1 **Official** means approved by the government or by someone in authority. *According to the official figures, over one thousand people died during the revolution... An official announcement is expected in the next few days... A report in the official police newspaper gave no reason for the move.* ♦ **officially** *The election results have still not been officially announced... The nine-year civil war is officially over.* ADJ: usu ADJ n ≠unofficial; ADV: usu ADV -ed, also ADV group, ADV after v

2 **Official** activities are carried out by a person in authority as part of their job. *The President is in Brazil for an official two-day visit.* ADJ: ADJ n ≠private

3 **Official** things are used by a person in authority as part of their job. *...the official residence of the Head of State.* ADJ: ADJ n

4 If you describe someone's explanation or reason for something as the **official** explanation, you are suggesting that it is probably not true, but is used because the real explanation is embarrassing. *The official explanation for the cancellation of the party conference is that there are no premises available... The official reason given for the President's absence was sickness.* ♦ **officially** *Officially, the guard was to protect us. In fact, they were there to report on our movements.* ADJ: ADJ n PRAGMATICS ≠actual, real; ADV: ADV with cl/group

5 An **official** is a person who holds a position of authority in an organization. *A senior UN official hopes to visit Baghdad this month.* N-COUNT: oft n N

officialdom /əfɪʃəldəm/. **Officialdom** is used to refer to government officials or officials in other organizations, especially when you think that their rules and regulations make them very slow and unhelpful. *Officialdom has been against us from the start.* N-UNCOUNT

officiate /əfɪʃieɪt/ **officiates, officiating, officiated**

1 When someone **officiates** at a ceremony or formal occasion, he or she is in charge and performs the official part of the ceremony. *Bishop Silvester officiated at the funeral... A memorial service was held yesterday at Wadhurst Parish Church. The Rev Michael Inch officiated.* VERB: V at n, V

2 When someone **officiates** at a sports match or competition, he or she acts as the referee or umpire. *Mr Ellis was selected to officiate at a cup game between Grimsby and Rotherham... Frik Burger will officiate when the Pumas play Scotland.* VERB: V at n, V, Also V *in* n

officious /əfɪʃəs/. If you describe someone as **officious**, you are critical of them because they are eager to tell people what to do when you think they should not. *They wouldn't welcome any officious interference from the police... When people put on uniforms, their attitude becomes more confident and their manner more officious.* ♦ **officiously** *Lance Corporal Williams officiously ordered them out.* ADJ-GRADED PRAGMATICS =interfering; ADV: ADV with v

offing /ɒfɪŋ, AM ɔːf-/. If you say that something is **in the offing**, you mean that it is likely to happen soon. *A general amnesty for political prisoners may be in the offing.* PHRASE: v-link PHR =imminent

off-key. When music is **off-key**, it is not in tune. *...wailing, off-key vocals and strangled guitars... No, no, no. This won't do. Someone is off-key.* ► Also an adverb. *Laura couldn't sing off-key if she tried.* ADJ-GRADED; ADV-GRADED: ADV after v =out of tune

off-licence, off-licences. In British English, an **off-licence** is a shop which sells beer, wine, and other alcoholic drinks, as well as cigarettes. The usual American expression is **liquor store**. *I'm going to the off-licence to buy some whisky.* N-COUNT: oft *the* N

off limits; also spelled **off-limits.**
1 If a place is **off limits** to someone, they are not allowed to go there. *Downing Street has been off limits to the general public since 1982... Certain areas have been declared off limits to servicemen.* ADJ: usu v-link ADJ, oft ADJ *to* n =out of bounds
2 If you say that an activity or a substance is **off limits** for someone, you mean that they are not allowed to do it or have it. *Fraternizing with the customers is off-limits... Cream cleansers are totally off limits for oily skin.* ADJ-GRADED: v-link ADJ, oft ADJ *for* n

offload /ɒfloʊd, AM ɔːf-/ **offloads, offloading, offloaded**
1 If you **offload** something that you do not want, you get rid of it by giving it or selling it to someone else. *Prices have been cut by developers anxious to offload unsold apartments... Already in financial difficulties, Turner offloaded the painting on to the Getty Museum.* VERB V n V n *onto* n
2 When goods **are offloaded**, they are removed from a container or vehicle and put somewhere else. *The supplies need to be offloaded and put on helicopters... The cargo was due to be offloaded in Singapore three days later.* VERB =unload ≠load be V-ed Also V n

off-peak. You use **off-peak** to describe something that happens or that is used at times when there is least demand for it. Prices at off-peak times are often lower than at other times. *The price for indoor courts is £10 per hour at peak times and £7 per hour at off-peak times. ...off-peak electricity.* ► Also an adverb. *Each tape lasts three minutes and costs 36p per minute off-peak and 48p at all other times.* ADJ: ADJ n ≠peak ADV: ADV after v

off-putting. If you describe someone as **off-putting**, you mean that they make you feel uneasy or uncomfortable. If you describe something as **off-putting**, you mean that it makes you dislike that thing. *I hope that neither of you will find my presence off-putting... You couldn't really get a more off-putting name for an island than Foulness.* ADJ-GRADED

off-screen; also spelled **offscreen.** You use **off-screen** to refer to the real lives of film or television actors, in contrast with the lives of the characters they play. *He was immensely attractive to women, onscreen and offscreen... Off-screen, Kathy is under the watchful eye of her father Terry.* ► Also an adjective. *They were quick to dismiss rumours of an off-screen romance.* ADV: ADV with cl =in real life ≠on-screen ADJ: ADJ n ≠on-screen

off season; also spelled **off-season.**
1 The **off season** is the time of the year when not many people go on holiday and when things such as hotels and plane tickets are often cheaper. *It is possible to vacation at some of the more expensive resorts if you go in the off-season... Although it was off-season, the hotel was fully occupied. ...off-season prices.* ► Also an adverb. *Times become more flexible off-season, especially in the smaller provincial museums.* N-SING: also no det, oft N n =low season ≠high season ADV: usu ADV with cl, also ADV after v
2 The **off season** is the time of the year when a particular sport is not played. *He has coached and played in Italy during the Australian off-season. ...intensive off-season training.* ► Also an adverb. *To stay fit off season, I play tennis or football.* N-SING: oft N n ≠season ADV: usu ADV with cl, also ADV after v

offset /ɒfset, AM ɔːf-/ **offsets, offsetting.** The form **offset** is used in the present tense and is the past tense and past participle of the verb. If one thing **is offset** by another, the effect of the first thing is reduced by the second, so that any advantage or disadvantage is cancelled out. *The increase in pay costs was more than offset by higher productivity... There'll be a large shipment of food to the former Soviet Union to help offset winter shortages.* ◆◆◇◇◇ VERB be V-ed V n

offshoot /ɒfʃuːt, AM ɔːf-/ **offshoots.** If one thing is an **offshoot** of another, it has developed from that other thing. *Psychology began as a purely academic offshoot of natural philosophy... Firstdirect, Midland Bank's telephone banking offshoot, has cut its Visa card rate to APR 22.2%.* ◆◇◇◇◇ N-COUNT: usu with poss =spin-off

offshore /ɒfʃɔːʳ, AM ɔːf-/; also spelled **off-shore.** ◆◆◇◇◇
1 **Offshore** means situated or happening in the sea, near to the coast. *...Britain's offshore oil industry. ...offshore islands.* ► Also an adverb. *One day a larger ship anchored offshore... When they hit the rocks, they were just 500 yards offshore.* ADJ: ADJ n ADV: ADV after v, be ADV, oft amount ADV
2 An **offshore** wind blows from the land towards the sea. *...a strong off-shore wind.* ADJ: ADJ n
3 **Offshore** investments or companies are located in a place, usually an island, which has fewer tax regulations than most other countries. *The island offers a wide range of offshore banking facilities.* ADJ: ADJ n

offside /ɒfsaɪd, AM ɔːf-/; also spelled **off-side.** ◆◇◇◇◇
1 In games such as football or hockey, when an attacking player is **offside**, they have broken the rules by being nearer to the goal than a defending player when the ball is passed to them. *The goal was disallowed because Wark was offside.* ► Also an adverb. *Wise was standing at least ten yards offside.* ► Also a noun. *Rush had a 45th-minute goal disallowed for offside.* ADJ: usu v-link ADJ ≠onside ADV: ADV after v N-UNCOUNT
2 The **offside** of a vehicle is the side that is furthest from the edge of the road when you are driving; used mainly in British English. *The driver of the car lowered his offside front window.* N-SING: usu N n ≠nearside

offspring /ɒfsprɪŋ, AM ɔːf-/; **offspring** is both the singular and the plural form. You can refer to a person's children or to an animal's young as their **offspring**; a formal word. *Eleanor was now less anxious about her offspring than she had once been.* ◆◇◇◇◇ N-COUNT: oft with poss

offstage /ɒfsteɪdʒ, AM ɔːf-/; also spelled **off-stage.**
1 When an actor or entertainer goes **offstage**, they go into the area behind or to the side of the stage, so that the audience no longer sees them. *She ran offstage in tears... There was a lot of noise offstage.* ADV: ADV after v, n ADV ≠onstage
2 In a theatre, **offstage** sounds are produced behind or to the side of the stage, so that the audience hears them but does not see them produced. *'It's almost one o'clock!' lamented the off-stage voice.* ADJ: ADJ n ≠onstage
3 **Offstage** is used to describe the behaviour of actors or entertainers in real life, when they are not performing. *...the tragedies of their off-stage lives.* ► Also an adverb. *Despite their bitter screen rivalry, off-stage they are close friends.* ADJ: ADJ n ≠onstage ADV: ADV with cl ≠onstage

off-the-cuff. See **cuff.**
off-the-peg. See **peg.**
off-the-record. See **record.**
off-the-shelf. See **shelf.**

off-the-wall ◆◇◇◇◇
1 If you describe something as **off-the-wall**, you mean that it is unusual and rather strange but in an amusing or interesting way: an informal word. *...surreal off-the-wall humor.* ADJ-GRADED: usu ADJ n
2 If you say that a person, their ideas, or their ways of doing something are **off-the-wall**, you are critical of them because you think they are mad or very foolish. *It can be done without following some absurd, off-the-wall investment strategy.* ADJ-GRADED PRAGMATICS

off-white. Something that is **off-white** is not pure white, but slightly grey or yellow. *...an off-white shirt.* COLOUR

oft- /ɒft-, AM ɔːft-/. **Oft** combines with past participles to form adjectives that mean that something happens or is done often; a literary form. *The Foreign Secretary's views on the treaty are well-documented and oft-repeated... It turns out to be a far more irritating poem than its oft-quoted lines suggest.* COMB in ADJ

often /ɒfᵊn, AM ɔːf-/ ◆◆◆◆◆
Often is usually used before the verb, but it may be used after the verb when it has a word like 'less' or 'more' before it, or when the clause is negative.
1 If something **often** happens, it happens many times or much of the time. *They often spent Christmas at Prescott Hill... Early American weathervanes were most often cut from flat wooden boards... They used these words freely, often in front of their parents too... It was often hard to work and do the course at the same time... That doesn't happen very often.* ADV-GRADED: ADV before v, ADV with cl/group =frequently ≠rarely
2 You use **often** after 'how' to ask questions about frequency. You also use **often** in reported clauses and other statements to give information about ADV: *how* ADV, *as* ADV *as* n/cl =frequently

the frequency of something. *How often do you brush your teeth?... I don't know how often I heard the same awful jokes... They jog, play tennis and water ski nearly twice as often as the general population.*

3 If something happens **every so often**, it happens regularly, but with fairly long intervals between each occasion. *She's going to come back every so often... Every so often he would turn and look at her.* PHRASES PHR with cl =occasionally

4 If you say that something happens **as often as not**, or **more often than not**, you mean that it happens fairly frequently, and that this can be considered as typical of the kind of situation you are talking about. *Yet, as often as not, they find themselves the target of persecution rather than praise... Although sometimes I feel like bothering, as often as not I don't... Behind many successful men there is, more often than not, a woman who makes this success possible.* PHR with cl

oftentimes /ɒfᵊntaɪmz, AM ɔːf-/. In American English, if something **oftentimes** happens, it happens many times or much of the time. The usual British word is **often**. *Oftentimes, these fossils are not made available to science at all... Oftentimes, I wouldn't even return the calls... It was oftentimes difficult to discuss certain issues while he was in the room.* ADV: ADV with cl, ADV with v, be ADV group =often

ogle /oʊgᵊl/ **ogles, ogling, ogled.** If you say that one person is **ogling** another, you disapprove of them continually staring at that person in a way that indicates a strong sexual interest. *All she did was hang around ogling the men in the factory... Paula is not used to everyone ogling at her while she undresses backstage.* VERB PRAGMATICS V n V at n Also V

ogre /oʊgəʳ/ **ogres**

1 If you refer to someone as an **ogre**, you are saying in a humorous way that they are very frightening. *Bank managers -- like tax inspectors -- do not really like being thought of as ogres.* N-COUNT

2 In legends and fairy stories, an **ogre** is a cruel, frightening giant who often eats people. N-COUNT

oh /oʊ/ ◆◆◆◆◆

1 You use **oh** to introduce a response or a comment on something that has just been said; used mainly in spoken English. *'Had you seen the car before?'—'Oh yes, it was always in the drive.'... 'Would you like me to phone and explain the situation?'—'Oh, would you?'... 'You don't understand!'—'Oh, I think I do, Grace.'* CONVENTION PRAGMATICS

2 You use **oh** to express a feeling such as surprise, pain, annoyance, or joy; used mainly in spoken English. *'Oh!' Kenny blinked. 'Has everyone gone?'... 'Oh, my God,' Korontzis moaned... Oh, I'm so glad you're here.* • See also **o**. EXCLAM PRAGMATICS

3 You use **'oh'** when you are hesitating while speaking, for example because you are trying to estimate something, or because you are searching for the right word; used in spoken English. *I've been here, oh, since the end of June... The invaders have destroyed the, oh, I don't know what the right word is – the atmosphere, the ambience.* CONVENTION PRAGMATICS =er, erm

ohm /oʊm/ **ohms.** An **ohm** is a unit which is used to measure electrical resistance; a technical term in physics. *...a resistance of 40 ohms.* N-COUNT

OHMS /oʊ eɪtʃ em es/. **OHMS** is the abbreviation for 'On Her Majesty's Service' or 'On His Majesty's Service'. It is used on official letters from British or Commonwealth government offices.

OHP /oʊ eɪtʃ piː/ **OHPs.** An **OHP** is the same as an **overhead projector**. N-COUNT

oik /ɔɪk/ **oiks.** In British English, if you refer to someone as an **oik**, you think that they behave in a rude or uncivilized way, especially in a way that you believe to be typical of their social class; an informal word. *She has to live cheek by jowl with oiks, people with tattoos and stolen videos. ...a dozen public school oiks standing and screeching at each other.* N-COUNT PRAGMATICS

oil /ɔɪl/ **oils, oiling, oiled** ◆◆◆◆◆

1 **Oil** is a smooth, thick liquid that is used as a fuel and for lubricating machines. Oil is found underground. *The company buys and sells about 600,000 barrels of oil a day. ...the rapid rise in prices for oil and petrol. ...a small oil lamp.* N-MASS

2 If you **oil** something, you put oil onto or into it, for example to make it work smoothly or to protect it. *A crew of assistants oiled and adjusted the release mechanism until it worked perfectly... The leather may need to be oiled every two to three weeks in order to retain its suppleness.* VERB =lubricate V n

3 **Oil** is a smooth, thick liquid that is made from plants or fish. Oils are often used for cooking. *Combine the beans, chopped mint and olive oil in a large bowl... Drop the slices into the oil and fry until golden brown.* N-MASS: usu n N

4 **Oil** is a smooth, thick liquid that is often scented and that you rub into your skin or add to your bath. You use oils to improve or protect your skin, or to help you relax. *Try a hot bath with some relaxing bath oil... My sister smeared herself with suntan oil and slept by the swimming pool all day.* N-MASS: usu supp N

5 **Oils** are **oil paintings**. *Her colourful oils and works on paper have a naive, dreamlike quality.* N-COUNT: usu pl

6 When an artist paints in **oils** he or she uses oil paints. *When she paints in oils she always uses the same range of colours.* N-PLURAL

7 See also **castor oil, crude oil, olive oil**.

8 If you **pour oil on troubled waters**, you try to calm down a difficult situation. PHRASES V inflects

9 If someone or something **oils the wheels** of a process or system, they help things to run smoothly and successfully. *On all such occasions, the king stands in the wings, oiling the wheels of diplomacy.* V inflects

10 • to **burn the midnight oil**: see **midnight**.

oilcloth /ɔɪlklɒθ, AM -klɔːθ/ **oilcloths**

1 **Oilcloth** is a cotton fabric with a shiny waterproof surface. *He wrapped the painting in a big square of oilcloth.* N-UNCOUNT

2 An **oilcloth** is a covering such as a tablecloth which has been made from oilcloth. N-COUNT

oiled /ɔɪld/. Something that is **oiled** has had oil put into or onto it, for example to make it work smoothly or to protect it. *Oiled wood is water-resistant and won't flake.* • See also **well-oiled**. ◆◇◇◇◇ ADJ-GRADED: usu ADJ n

oilfield /ɔɪlfiːld/ **oilfields;** also spelled **oil field**. An **oilfield** is an area of land or seabed under which there is oil. ◆◇◇◇◇ N-COUNT

oil-fired. Oil-fired heating systems and power stations use oil as a fuel. *The hot air is provided by an oil-fired furnace.* ADJ: ADJ n

oilman /ɔɪlmæn/ **oilmen;** also spelled **oil man**. An **oilman** is a man who owns an oil company or who works in the oil business, for example on an oil rig. *Five oilmen were injured when a gas explosion shook a North Sea oil rig yesterday.* N-COUNT

oil paint, oil paints. Oil paint is a thick paint used by artists. It is made from coloured powder and linseed oil. N-UNCOUNT: also N in pl

oil painting, oil paintings. An **oil painting** is a picture which has been painted using oil paints. *Several magnificent oil paintings adorn the walls.* N-COUNT

oil platform, oil platforms. An **oil platform** is a structure that is used as a base when drilling for and extracting oil from the sea. N-COUNT

oil rig, oil rigs. An **oil rig** is a structure on land or in the sea that is used as a base when drilling for or extracting oil. N-COUNT

oilseed rape /ɔɪlsiːd reɪp/. **Oilseed rape** is a plant with yellow flowers which is grown as a crop. Its seeds are crushed to make cooking oil. N-UNCOUNT

oilskins /ɔɪlskɪnz/. **Oilskins** are a coat and a pair of trousers made from thick waterproof cotton cloth. *It was cold and wet, and I had left all our precious oilskins at home.* N-PLURAL

oil slick, oil slicks. An **oil slick** is a layer of oil that is floating on the sea or on a lake. It is formed when oil accidentally spills out of a ship or container. *The oil slick is now 35 miles long.* ◆◇◇◇◇ N-COUNT

oil tanker, oil tankers. An **oil tanker** is a ship that is used for transporting oil. ◆◇◇◇◇ N-COUNT

oil well, oil wells. An **oil well** is a hole which is drilled into the ground or the seabed in order to extract oil.  N-COUNT

oily /ɔɪli/ **oilier, oiliest** ◆◇◇◇◇

1 Something that is **oily** is covered with oil or contains oil. *He was wiping his hands on an oily rag... When she was younger, she had very oily skin... Paul found the sauce too oily.* ADJ-GRADED

2 **Oily** means looking, feeling, tasting, or smelling like oil. *...traces of an oily substance. ...a medium dry wine with an oily, spicy flavour.* ADJ-GRADED: usu ADJ n

3 If you describe someone as **oily**, you dislike them because you think they flatter people too much or are excessively but insincerely polite. *He had behaved with undue and oily familiarity... The older man asked in his oily voice what he could do for them today.* ADJ-GRADED PRAGMATICS =smarmy, unctuous

ointment /ɔɪntmənt/ **ointments** ◆◇◇◇◇

1 An **ointment** is a smooth thick substance that is put on sore skin or a wound to help it heal. *A range of ointments and creams is available for the treatment of eczema... I saw his legs being bathed and new bandages and ointment being put on to bring a measure of relief.* N-MASS =salve

2 If you describe someone or something as a **fly in the ointment**, you think they spoil a situation and prevent it being as successful as you had hoped. *Rachel seems to be the one fly in the ointment of Caroline's smooth life.* PHRASE: v-link PHR

OK /oʊ keɪ/. See **okay**.

okay /oʊkeɪ/ **okays, okaying, okayed;** also spelled **OK**. ◆◆◆◆◇

1 If you say that something is **okay**, you find it satisfactory or acceptable; an informal use. *...a shooting range where it's OK to use weapons... Is it okay if I come by myself?... I guess for a fashionable restaurant like this the prices are OK.* ▶ Also an adverb. *We seemed to manage okay for the first year or so after David was born.* ADJ: usu v-link ADJ, oft *it* v-link ADJ to-inf, *it* v-link ADJ if =all right ADV: ADV after v =all right

2 If you say that someone is **okay**, you mean that they are safe and well; an informal use. *Check that the baby's okay... 'Don't worry about me,' I said. 'I'll be okay.'* ADJ: v-link ADJ =all right

3 You can say **'Okay'** to show that you agree to something; an informal use. *'Just tell him Sir Kenneth would like to talk to him.'—'OK.'... 'Shall I give you a ring on Friday?'—'Yeah okay.'* CONVENTION PRAGMATICS =all right

4 You can say **'Okay?'** to check whether the person you are talking to understands what you have said and accepts it; an informal use. *Add them together, divide by five, and you've got the average. Okay?... We'll get together next week, OK?* CONVENTION PRAGMATICS =all right

5 You can use **okay** to indicate to someone that you want to start talking about something else or doing something else; an informal use. *OK. Now, let's talk some business... Tim jumped to his feet. 'Okay, let's go.'* CONVENTION PRAGMATICS =right

6 You can use **okay** to stop someone arguing with you by showing that you accept the point they are making, though you do not necessarily regard it as very important; an informal use. *Okay, there is a slight difference... Okay, so I'm forty-two.* CONVENTION PRAGMATICS

7 If someone in authority **okays** something, they officially agree to it or allow it to happen; an informal use. *His doctor wouldn't OK the trip... We are all wondering why the government is suddenly okaying a brand new school on the island.* ▶ Also a noun. *He gave the okay to issue a new press release... We are ready to start flying to Britain as soon as we get the okay.* VERB V n N-SING: *the* N

okra /oʊkrə/. **Okra** is a vegetable that consists of long green pods. N-UNCOUNT

old /oʊld/ **older, oldest** ◆◆◆◆◆

1 Someone who is **old** has lived for many years and is no longer young. *...a white-haired old man... He was considered too old for the job.* ▶ **The old** are people who are old. *...providing a caring response for the needs of the old and the handicapped.* ADJ-GRADED =elderly ≠young N-PLURAL: *the* N =elderly

2 You use **old** to talk or ask about how many days, weeks, months, or years someone or something has lived or existed. *He was abandoned by his father when he was three months old... The paintings in the chapel were perhaps a thousand years old... How old are you now?... These weren't young kids, they were as old as I was... Bill was six years older than David.* ADJ: amount ADJ, *how* ADJ, *as* ADJ *as*, ADJ-compar *than*

3 Something that is **old** has existed for a long time. *She loved the big old house... These books must be very old. ...an old Arab proverb. ...her old habit of criticizing his speech... Ethnic tensions are an old problem here.* ADJ-GRADED ≠new

4 Something that is **old** is no longer in good condition because of its age or because it has been used a lot. *He took a bunch of keys from the pocket of his old corduroy trousers. ...an old toothbrush.* ADJ-GRADED: usu ADJ n ≠new

5 You use **old** to refer to something that is no longer used, that no longer exists, or that has been replaced by something else. *The old road had disappeared under grass and heather... Although the old secret police have been abolished, the military police still exist... In the old Liberal party the peace movement was a powerful voice.* ADJ: ADJ n

6 You use **old** to refer to something that used to belong to you, or to a person or thing that used to have a particular role in your life. *I'll make up the bed in your old room... I still have affection for my old school... Mark was heartbroken when Jane returned to her old boyfriend.* ADJ: poss ADJ n

7 An **old** friend, enemy, or rival is someone who has been your friend, enemy, or rival for a long time. *I called my old friend John Horner... Mr Brownson, I assure you King's an old enemy of mine... The French and English are old rivals.* ADJ-GRADED: ADJ n

8 You can use **old** to express affection or familiarity when talking to or about someone you know; an informal use. *Are you all right, old chap?... Good old Bergen would do him the favor.* ADJ: ADJ n PRAGMATICS

9 You use **any old** to emphasize that the quality or type of something is not important. If you say that a particular thing is not **any old** thing, you are emphasizing how special or famous it is; an informal expression. *Any old paper will do... The portraits and sumptuous ornaments, and the gold clock, show that this is not just any old front room.* PHRASES PHR n PRAGMATICS

10 **In the old days** means in the past, before things changed. *In the old days we got a visit from the vet maybe once a year.* PHR with cl

11 When people refer to **the good old days**, they are referring to a time in the past when they think that life was better than it is now. *He remembers the good old days when everyone in his village knew him and you could leave your door open at night.*

12 If you talk about people or things **of old**, you are referring to people or things that existed long ago but which no longer exist, or no longer exist in the same form; a literary expression. *...the warrior knights of old. ...a programme of work to recreate the Sherwood Forest of old.* n PHR

13 ● **you can't teach an old dog new tricks**: see **dog**. ● **good old**: see **good**. ● **of the old school**: see **school**. ● **to settle an old score**: see **score**. ● **up to one's old tricks**: see **trick**.

old age ◆◇◇◇◇

1 Your **old age** is the period of years towards the end of your life. *They worry about how they will support themselves in their old age... In old age the two men wrote each other wistful letters.* N-UNCOUNT: oft poss N ≠youth

2 **Old age** is the quality or state of being old and near the end of one's life. *In Britain today we tend to consider old age as a social problem... He is unable to travel much because of old age.* N-UNCOUNT ≠youth

old age pension, old age pensions; also spelled **old-age pension**. An **old age pension** is a regular amount of money that people receive from the government when they have retired from work. N-COUNT =state pension

old age pensioner, old age pensioners; also spelled **old-age pensioner**. An **old age pensioner** is a person who is old enough to receive an pension from their employer or the government. N-COUNT =senior citizen

old bat, old bats. If someone refers to an elderly person as an **old bat**, they think that person is silly, annoying or unpleasant; an informal, offensive expression. N-COUNT: usu sing PRAGMATICS

old boy, old boys ◆◆◇◇◇

1 In British English, you can refer to a man who N-COUNT

used to be a pupil at a particular school or university as an **old boy**. *...Eton College, with all its traditions and long list of famous old boys. ...Cardiff High School Old Boys rugby team.*

2 In informal British English, if you refer to an old or middle-aged man as an **old boy**, you are referring to him in a disrespectful way. *Outside, two old boys lingered on the street corner discussing cattle.* — N-COUNT

old-boy network, old-boy networks; also spelled **old boy network**. When people talk about the **old-boy network**, they are referring to a situation in which people who went to the same public school or university use their positions of influence to help each other; used showing disapproval. *The majority obtained their positions through the old boy network.* — N-COUNT: usu *the* N in sing; PRAGMATICS

olde /oʊld/. **Olde** is used in names of places and in advertising to make people think that something is very old and interesting. *I always feel at home at Ye Olde Starre Inn.* — ADJ: ADJ n

olden /oʊldən/. If you refer to a period in the past as the **olden** days, you are thinking or talking about it affectionately. *We had a delightful time talking about the olden days on his farm. ...the nicely painted old railways of olden times.* — ADJ: ADJ n
• **In the olden days** or **in olden days** means in the past. *In the olden days the girls were married young... In olden days, of course, a flag-lieutenant was in charge of the Admiral's signal flags.* — PHRASE: PHR with cl

old-fashioned ◆◆◇◇◇

1 Something such as a style, method, or device that is **old-fashioned** is no longer used, done, or admired by most people, because it has been replaced by something that is more modern. *The house was dull, old-fashioned and in bad condition... There are some traditional farmers left who still make cheese the old-fashioned way.* — ADJ-GRADED ≠modern

2 **Old-fashioned** ideas, customs, or values are the ideas, customs, and values of the past. *She has some old-fashioned values and can be a strict disciplinarian. ...good old-fashioned English cooking.* — ADJ-GRADED =traditional

old flame, old flames. An **old flame** is someone with whom you once had a romantic relationship. *Sue was seen dating an old flame... Julia Samuel was one of Prince Andrew's old flames.* — N-COUNT

old girl, old girls ◆◇◇◇◇

1 In British English, you can refer to a woman who used to be a pupil at a particular school or university as an **old girl**. *...the St Mary's Ascot Old Girls' Reunion Lunch.* — N-COUNT

2 In informal British English, if you refer to an old or middle-aged woman as an **old girl**, you are referring to her in a disrespectful way. *The old girl in there runs the saloon bar at the pub in the evenings.* — N-COUNT

old guard. If you refer to a group of people as the **old guard**, you mean that they have worked in a particular organization for a very long time and are unwilling to accept new ideas or practices; used showing disapproval. *The old guard did not like the changes that Brewer introduced... He belongs to the ruling Nationalist Party's old guard.* — ◆◇◇◇◇ N-SING-COLL: usu *the*/poss N; PRAGMATICS

old hand, old hands. If someone is an **old hand** at something, they are very skilled at it because they have been doing it for a long time. *An old hand at photography, Tim has been shooting wildlife as a hobby for the last 13 years.* — N-COUNT: oft N *at* n =veteran ≠novice

old hat. See **hat**.

oldie /oʊldi/ **oldies.** In informal English, you can use **oldie** to refer affectionately to an old song, film, or person, especially when they are unfashionable or outdated but still seem interesting or relevant. *Radio Aire only plays Top 40 stuff and oldies. ...a lush English fairy tale that many oldies will remember from their youth.* ► Also an adjective. *During the festival, we'll be showing 13 classic oldie films.* — ◆◇◇◇◇ N-COUNT; ADJ-GRADED: ADJ n

old lady. Some men refer to their wife, girlfriend, or mother as their **old lady**; an informal expression. *He had met his old lady when he was a house painter and she was a waitress.* —  N-SING: usu poss N

old maid, old maids. People sometimes refer to an old or middle-aged woman as an **old maid** when she has never married and they think that it is unlikely that she ever will marry; an offensive expression. *Alex is too young to be already thinking of herself as an old maid.* — N-COUNT =spinster

old man. Some people refer to their father, husband, or boyfriend as their **old man**; an informal expression. *Her old man left her a few millions when he died... Hey, Ma. It's the old man.* — ◆◇◇◇◇ N-SING: *the*/poss N

old master, old masters. An **old master** is a painting by one of the famous European painters of the 16th, 17th, and 18th centuries. These painters can also be referred to as the **Old Masters**. *...his collection of old masters and modern art. ...portraits by Gainsborough, Rubens and other Old Masters.* — ◆◇◇◇◇ N-COUNT

old people's home, old people's homes. An **old people's home** is a place where old people live and are cared for when they are too old to look after themselves. — N-COUNT

old school. • **of the old school**: see **school**.

old school tie. In British English, when people talk about **the old school tie**, they are referring to the situation in which people who attended the same public school use their positions of influence to help each other. *Of course, the old school tie has been a help.* — N-SING: *the* N

old-style. You use **old-style** to describe something or someone of a type that was common in the past but is not common now. *...a proper barber shop with real old-style barber chairs.* — ◆◇◇◇◇ ADJ: ADJ n =old-fashioned

Old Testament. **The Old Testament** is the first part of the Bible. It deals especially with the relationship between God and the Jewish people. — ◆◇◇◇◇ N-PROPER: *the* N

old-time ◆◇◇◇◇

1 If you describe something as **old-time**, you mean that it was common in the past but is not common now. *...an old-time dance hall which still has a tea dance on Monday afternoons.* — ADJ: ADJ n =old-fashioned

2 You can use **old-time** before the name of someone's job to show that they do their job in the way it was done in the past. *The effect of that singing, as the old-time reporters used to say, was electrical. ...like an old-time sailor climbing the rigging.* — ADJ: ADJ n

old-timer, old-timers

1 If you refer to someone as an **old-timer**, you mean that he or she has been living in a particular place or doing a particular job for a long time; an informal use. *The old-timers and established families clutched the reins of power.* — N-COUNT =veteran ≠newcomer

2 In informal American English, an old man is sometimes referred to as an **old-timer**. *The old-timers used to recall how hot 1886 was.* — N-COUNT =old man ≠youngster

old wives' tale, old wives' tales. An **old wives' tale** is a commonly held belief that is based on traditional ideas which have been proved to be incorrect. *Ann Bradley dispels the old-wives' tales and gives the medical facts.* — N-COUNT

old woman, old women. If you refer to someone, especially a man, as an **old woman**, you are critical of them because you think that they are very fussy or very timid; an informal expression. — N-COUNT; PRAGMATICS

ole /oʊl/. **Ole** is used in written English to represent the word 'old' pronounced in a particular way. *'I started fixin' up ole bicycles fer poor kids.'* — ADJ: ADJ n

oleander /oʊliændəʳ/ **oleanders.** An **oleander** is an evergreen tree or shrub that has white, pink, or purple flowers. Oleanders grow in Mediterranean countries and in some parts of Asia and Australia. — N-VAR

O level, O levels. O levels are British educational qualifications which schoolchildren used to take at the age of fifteen or sixteen. In 1988, O levels, together with CSEs, were replaced by GCSEs. *She left after taking nine O levels... She acquired seven O level passes... He had studied maths to O-level at a Norwich comprehensive.* — ◆◇◇◇◇ N-VAR

olfactory /ɒlfæktəri/. **Olfactory** means concerned with the sense of smell; a formal use. *This olfactory sense develops in the womb.* — ADJ: ADJ n

oligarchy /ɒlɪgɑːʳki/ **oligarchies**
1 An **oligarchy** is a small group of people who control and run a particular country or organization. You can also refer to a country which is governed in this way as an **oligarchy**. *Athens was suffering under the rule of an oligarchy that had no concern for the people's welfare.* N-COUNT
2 **Oligarchy** is a situation in which a country or organization is run by an oligarchy. *...a protest against imperialism and oligarchy in the region.* N-UNCOUNT

olive /ɒlɪv/ **olives** ◆◆◇◇◇
1 **Olives** are small green or black fruit with a bitter taste. Olives are often pressed to make olive oil. *...bowls of black and green olives. ...market stores, where more than 20 types of olive are sold by weight.* N-VAR
2 An **olive tree** or an **olive** is a tree on which olives grow. *Olives look romantic on a hillside in Provence. ...an olive grove.* N-VAR
3 Something that is **olive** is yellowish-green in colour. *...glowing colours such as deep red, olive, saffron and ochre.* ► Also a combining form. *She wore an olive-green T-shirt.* COLOUR; COMB in COLOUR
4 If someone has **olive** skin, the colour of their skin is light brown. *They are handsome with dark, shining hair, olive skin and fine brown eyes.* ADJ: usu ADJ n

olive branch, olive branches; also spelled **olive-branch**. If you offer an **olive branch** to someone, you say or do something in order to show or symbolize that you want to end a disagreement or quarrel. *Clarke also offered an olive branch to critics in his party.* N-COUNT: usu sing

olive oil, olive oils. **Olive oil** is oil that is obtained by pressing olives. It is used for putting on salads or in cooking. *Pour in about 4-6 tablespoons of olive oil. ...a range of virgin olive oils.* ◆◆◇◇◇ N-MASS

-ological /-əlɒdʒɪkəl/. **-ological** is used to replace '-ology' at the end of nouns in order to form adjectives. These adjectives describe something as relating to a particular science or subject. For example, 'biological' means relating to biology. Adjectives formed in this way are not usually defined in this dictionary, but may be found at the entry for the related noun. SUFFIX

-ologist /-ɒlədʒɪst/. **-ologist** is used to replace '-ology' at the end of nouns in order to form other nouns that refer to people who are concerned with a particular science or subject. For example, a 'biologist' is concerned with biology. Nouns formed in this way are not usually defined in this dictionary, but may be found at the entry for the noun ending in '-ology'. SUFFIX

-ology /-ɒlədʒi/. **-ology** is used at the end of some nouns that refer to a particular science or subject, for example 'geology' or 'sociology'. SUFFIX

Olympian /əlɪmpiən/ **Olympians.**
1 **Olympian** means very powerful, large, or impressive; a formal use. *Getting his book into print has been an Olympian task in itself.* ADJ: usu ADJ n
2 An **Olympian** is a competitor in the Olympic Games. *The importance of being an Olympian will vary from athlete to athlete.* N-COUNT

Olympic /əlɪmpɪk/ **Olympics** ◆◆◆◆◇
1 **Olympic** means relating to the Olympic Games. *...Gao, the reigning Olympic champion.* ADJ: ADJ n
2 **The Olympics** are the Olympic Games. *I will be in Atlanta for the next Olympics... She won the individual gold medal at the Winter Olympics.* N-PROPER: the N

Olympic Games. **The Olympic Games** are a set of international sports competitions which take place every four years, each time in a different country. *At the 1968 Olympic Games she had won gold medals in races at 200, 400, and 800m.* ◆◆◇◇◇ N-PROPER-COLL: the N =Olympics

ombudsman /ɒmbʊdzmən/ **ombudsmen.** The **ombudsman** is an independent official who has been appointed to investigate complaints that people make against the government or public organizations. *The leaflet explains how to complain to the banking ombudsman.* ◆◇◇◇◇ N-COUNT: usu the N, supp N

omelette /ɒmlət/ **omelettes;** spelled **omelet** in American English. An **omelette** is a type of food made by beating eggs and cooking them in a flat pan. *...a cheese omelette.* ◆◇◇◇◇ N-COUNT

omen /oʊmen/ **omens.** If you say that something is an **omen**, you think it indicates what is likely to happen in the future and whether it will be good or bad. *Her appearance at this moment is an omen of disaster... Could this at last be a good omen for peace?* ◆◇◇◇◇ N-COUNT =portent

ominous /ɒmɪnəs/. If you describe something as **ominous**, you mean that it worries you because it makes you think that something unpleasant is going to happen. *There was an ominous silence at the other end of the phone... The rolls of distant thunder were growing more ominous.* ♦ **ominously** *The bar seemed ominously quiet... Ominously, car sales slumped in August... King Hussein talked ominously of an impending threat against his country.* ◆◇◇◇◇ ADJ-GRADED =menacing; ADV-GRADED: ADV adj, ADV with cl, ADV with v

omission /oʊmɪʃən/ **omissions** ◆◇◇◇◇
1 An **omission** is something that has not been included or has not been done, either deliberately or accidentally. *The duke was surprised by his wife's omission from the guest list.* N-COUNT ≠inclusion
2 **Omission** is the act of not including someone or something or of not doing something. *...the prosecution's seemingly malicious omission of recorded evidence.* N-VAR

omit /oʊmɪt/ **omits, omitting, omitted** ◆◆◇◇◇
1 If you **omit** something, you do not include it in an activity or piece or work, deliberately or accidentally. *Omit the salt in this recipe... Our apologies to David Pannick for omitting his name from last week's article.* VERB =leave out; V n; V n *from* n
2 If you **omit** to do something, you do not do it; a formal use. *His new girlfriend had omitted to tell him she was married.* VERB =fail; V to-inf

omnibus /ɒmnɪbʌs/ **omnibuses**
1 In British English, an **omnibus** edition of a radio or television programme contains two or more similar programmes that were originally broadcast separately. *I enjoy the omnibus edition of Eastenders on Sunday.* N-COUNT: usu N n
2 An **omnibus** is a book which contains a large collection of stories or articles, often by a particular person or about a particular subject. *...a new omnibus edition of three Ruth Rendell chillers.* N-COUNT =anthology
3 An **omnibus** is a **bus**; an old-fashioned use. N-COUNT

omnipotence /ɒmnɪpətəns/. **Omnipotence** is the state of having total authority or power; a formal word. *...the omnipotence of God.* N-UNCOUNT

omnipotent /ɒmnɪpətənt/. Someone or something that is **omnipotent** has complete power over things or people; a formal word. *Doug lived in the shadow of his seemingly omnipotent father. ...the omnipotent power of an author.* ADJ =all-powerful

omnipresent /ɒmnɪprezənt/. Something that is **omnipresent** is present everywhere or seems to be always present; a formal word. *The sound of sirens was an omnipresent background noise in New York... The obsessive thoughts became so omnipresent that her memory was affected.* ADJ-GRADED =pervasive

omniscient /ɒmnɪsiənt, AM -nɪʃənt/. If you describe someone as **omniscient**, you mean they know or seem to know everything; a formal word. *...a benevolent and omniscient deity... We all, long ago, expected teachers to be omniscient.* ♦ **omniscience** *...the divine attributes of omnipotence, benevolence and omniscience.* ADJ; N-UNCOUNT

omnivorous /ɒmnɪvərəs/
1 An **omnivorous** person or animal eats all kinds of food, including both meat and plants; a technical or formal use. *Brown bears are omnivorous, eating anything that they can get their paws on.* ADJ
2 **Omnivorous** means liking a wide variety of things of a particular type; a formal use. *As a child, Coleridge seems to have developed omnivorous reading habits.* ADJ =wide-ranging

on. The preposition is pronounced /ɒn/. The adverb and the adjective are pronounced /ɒn/. ◆◆◆◆◆
In addition to the uses shown below, **on** is used after some verbs, nouns, and adjectives in order to introduce extra information. **On** is also used in phrasal verbs such as 'keep on', 'cotton on', and 'sign on'.

1 If someone or something is **on** a surface or object, the surface or object is immediately below them and is supporting their weight. *He is sitting beside her on the sofa... On top of the cupboards are vast straw baskets which Pat uses for dried flower arrangements... On the table were dishes piled high with sweets... The cushions were soft blue to match the Chinese rug on the floor.* PREP

2 If something is **on** a surface or object, it is stuck to it or attached to it. *I admired the peeling paint on the ceiling... The clock on the wall showed one minute to twelve... There was a smear of gravy on his chin.* ► Also an adverb. *I know how to darn, and how to sew a button on.* PREP; ADV: ADV after v

3 If you put, throw, or drop something **on** a surface, you move it or drop it so that it is then supported by the surface. *He got his winter jacket from the closet and dropped it on the sofa... He threw a folded dollar on the counter.* PREP =onto

4 You use **on** to say what part of your body is supporting your weight. *He continued to lie on his back and look at clouds... He raised himself on his elbows, squinting into the sun... She was on her hands and knees in the bathroom.* PREP

5 You use **on** to say that someone or something is touching a part of someone's body. *He leaned down and kissed her lightly on the mouth... His jaw was broken after he was hit on the head.* PREP

6 If someone has a particular expression **on** their face, their face has that expression. *The maid looked at him, a nervous smile on her face... She looked at him with a hurt expression on her face.* PREP: n PREP n

7 When you put a piece of clothing **on**, you place it over part of your body in order to wear it. If you have it **on**, you are wearing it. *He put his coat on while she opened the front door... I had a hat on.* ADV: ADV after v

8 You can say that you have something **on** you if you are carrying it in your pocket or in a bag. *I didn't have any money on me... I have those numbers, but not on me at the moment, they're at home.* PREP: PREP pron

9 If someone's eyes are **on** you, they are looking or staring at you. *Everyone's eyes were fixed on him... It's as if all eyes are focused on me... Ellen is eating, her eyes on her food.* PREP

10 If you hurt yourself **on** something, you accidentally hit a part of your body against it and that thing causes damage to you. *Mr Pendle hit his head on a wall as he fell... One day when my wife was doing the dishes she cut her hand on a broken glass.* PREP

11 If you are **on** an area of land, you are there. *He was able to spend only a few days at a time on the island... You lived on the farm until you came back to America? ...a tall tree on a mountain. ...their winter retreat on Barbados... I've eaten ostrich meat on the continent.* PREP

12 If something is situated **on** a place such as road or coast, it forms part of it or is by the side of it. *Bergdorf Goodman has opened a men's store on Fifth Avenue... The hotel is on the coast... He visited relatives at their summer house on the river.* PREP

13 If you get **on** a bus, train, or plane, you go into it in order to travel somewhere. If you are **on** it, you are travelling in it. *We waited till twelve and we finally got on the plane... I never go on the bus into the town... His son came up with me to Birmingham every day on the train.* ► Also an adverb. *He showed his ticket to the conductor and got on.* PREP; ADV: ADV after v

14 If there is something **on** a piece of paper, it has been written or printed there. *The writing on the back of the card was cramped but scrupulously neat... The numbers she put on the chart were 98.4, 64, and 105... How does a poem change when you read it out loud as opposed to it being on the page?* PREP

15 If something is **on** a list, it is included in it. *I've seen your name on the list of deportees... The Queen now doesn't even appear on the list of the 40 richest people in Britain... The range of topics on the agenda for their talks includes the future of Germany.* PREP

16 Books, discussions, or ideas **on** a particular subject are concerned with that subject. *The longest chapter in almost any book on baby care is on feeding... They offer a free counselling service which can offer help and advice on legal matters... He declined to give any information on the Presidential election... China's comments on the US decision were relatively restrained.* PREP

17 You use **on** to introduce the method, principle, or system which is used to do something. *...a television that we bought on credit two months ago. ...a levelling system which acts on the same principle as a spirit level... They want all groups to be treated on an equal basis.* PREP

18 If something is done **on** an instrument or a machine, it is done using that instrument or machine. *...songs that I could just sit down and play on the piano... I could do all my work on the computer... She sewed the dresses on the sewing machine.* PREP

19 If information is, for example, **on** tape or **on** computer, that is the way that it is stored. *'I thought it was a load of rubbish.'—'Right we've got that on tape.'... Descriptions of the pieces have been logged on computer by the Art Loss Register... A special version of 'Casablanca' is being released on video to commemorate the film's 50th birthday.* PREP

20 If something is being broadcast, you can say that it is **on** the radio or television. *Every sporting event on television and satellite over the next seven days is listed... Here, listen, they're talking about it on Radio-Paris right now.* ► Also an adjective. *...teenagers complaining there's nothing good on.* PREP; ADJ: v-link ADJ

21 When an activity is taking place, you can say that it is **on**. *There's a marvellous match on at Wimbledon at the moment... Every year they put a play on at Saint Holy Cross Church... We in Berlin hardly knew a war was on during the early part of 1941.* ADJ: v-link ADJ

22 You use **on** in expressions such as **'have a lot on'** and **'not have very much on'** to indicate how busy someone is; used in spoken English. *I have a lot on in the next week.* ADV: ADV after v, amount ADV

23 You use **on** to introduce an activity that someone is doing, particularly travelling. *I've always wanted to go on a cruise... They look happy and relaxed as they stroll in the sunshine on a shopping trip... Students on the full-time course of study are usually sponsored... President Bush and James Baker are on a fishing holiday.* PREP

24 When something such as a machine or an electric light is **on**, it is functioning or in use. When you switch it **on**, it starts functioning. *The light was on and the door was open... The central heating's been turned off. I've turned it on again... The light had been left on... He didn't bother to switch on the light.* ADV: be ADV, ADV after v ≠off

25 If you are **on** a committee or council, you are a member of it. *Claire and Beryl were on the organizing committee... He was on the Council of Foreign Relations.* PREP

26 You can indicate when something happens by saying that it happens **on** a particular day or date. *This year's event will take place on June 19th, a week earlier than usual... She travels to Korea on Monday... I was born on Christmas day... I took some photos with her camera on my birthday... Dr. Keen arrived about seven on Sunday morning.* PREP

27 You use **on** when mentioning an event that was followed by another one. *She waited in her hotel to welcome her children on their arrival from London... On reaching Dubai the evacuees are taken straight to Dubai international airport.* PREP: PREP n/-ing

28 You use **on** to say that someone is continuing to do something. *They walked on in silence for a while... If the examination shows your company enjoys basically good health, read on... He happened to be in England when the war broke out and he just stayed on.* ADV: ADV after v

29 If you say that someone goes **on** at you, you mean that they continually criticize you, complain to you, or ask you to do something. *She's been on at me for weeks to show her round the stables... He used to keep on at me about the need to win... He'll go on at me for telling... She hadn't learned to drive, but she had kept going on at him to let her try.* ADV: be ADV, ADV after v, usu ADV at n

30 You use **on** in expressions such as **from now on** and **from then on** to indicate that something starts to happen at the time mentioned and continues to ADV: from n ADV =onwards

happen afterwards. *Perhaps it would be best not to see much of you from now on... We can expect trouble from this moment on... Morrison took the news badly and from then on his spirits noticeably sagged.*

31 You often use **on** after the adverbs 'early', 'late', 'far', and their comparative forms, especially at the beginning or end of a sentence, or before a preposition. *The market square is a riot of colour and animation from early on in the morning... Later on I learned how to read music... The pub where I had arranged to meet Nobby was a good five minutes walk further on.* ADV: adv ADV

32 Someone who is **on** a drug takes it regularly. *She was on antibiotics for an eye infection that wouldn't go away... Many of the elderly are on medication.* PREP

33 If you live **on** a particular kind of food, you eat it. If a machine runs **on** a particular kind of power or fuel, it uses it in order to function. *The caterpillars feed on a wide range of trees, shrubs and plants... He lived on a diet of water and tinned fish... The system could be used to ensure that cars are converted to run on unleaded petrol. ...making and selling vehicles that run on batteries or fuel-cells.* PREP: v PREP n =off

34 If you are **on** a particular income, that is the income that you have. *...young people who are unemployed or on low wages... He's on three hundred a week... You won't be rich as an MP, but you'll have enough to live on.* PREP

35 Taxes or profits that are obtained from something are referred to as taxes or profits **on** it. *...a general strike to protest a tax on food and medicine last week... The Church was to receive a cut of the profits on every record sold... Loans were extended to help pay the interest on the old ones.* PREP: n PREP n

36 When you buy something or pay for something, you spend money **on** it. *I resolved not to waste money on a hotel... He spent more on feeding the dog than he spent on feeding himself... More money should be spent on education and housing.* PREP: PREP n/-ing

37 When you spend time or energy **on** a particular activity, you spend time or energy doing it. *People complain about how children spend so much time on computer games... You all know why I am here. So I won't waste time on preliminaries. ...the opportunity to concentrate more time and energy on America's domestic agenda.* PREP: PREP n/-ing

38 If you say that something is **not on** or is **just not on**, you mean that it is unacceptable or impossible; used mainly in informal British English. *I'm not having children who don't like cheese. It's not on... We shouldn't use the police in that way. It's just not on.* PHRASES v-link PHR

39 If you say that something happens **on and on**, you mean that it continues to happen for a very long time. *...designers, builders, fitters – the list goes on and on... Lobell drove on and on through the dense and blowing snow. ...a desert of ice stretching on and on.* usu PHR after v

40 If you ask someone **what** they **are on about** or **what** they **are going on about**, you are puzzled because you cannot understand what they are talking about; an informal expression. *What on earth are you going on about?... Honest, Kate, I don't know what you're on about.* V inflects

41 If you say that someone **knows what** they **are on about**, you are confident that what they are saying is true or makes sense, for example because they are an expert; an informal expression. *It looks like he knows what he's on about.* Vs inflect

42 • **on behalf of**: see **behalf**. • **on and off**: see **off**. • **and so on**: see **so**. • **on top of**: see **top**.

once /wʌns/ ◆◆◆◆◆

1 If something happens **once**, it happens one time only. *I met Wilma once, briefly... I only saw it once at the cinema and it's a good film... Since that I haven't once slept through the night... Mary had only been to Manchester once before.* ► Also a pronoun. *'Have they been to visit you yet?'—'Just the once yeah.'... Listen to us, if only this once.* ADV: ADV with v; PRON: the/this PRON

2 You use **once** with 'a' and words like 'day', 'week', and 'month' to indicate that something happens regularly, one time in each day, week, or month. *Lung cells die and are replaced about once a week... We arranged a special social event once a year to which we invited our major customers.* ADV: ADV a n

3 You use **once** with 'every' and words like 'day', 'week', and 'year' to indicate that something happens a specified number of times and on a regular basis. *The patient was seen for follow-up visits once every three months... My daughter comes to visit me once every fortnight.* ADV: ADV every n, ADV every num n

4 If something was **once true**, it was true at some time in the past, but is no longer true. *The culture minister once ran a theatre... I lived there once myself, before I got married... The house where she lives was once the village post office... My memory isn't as good as it once was. ...an undulating park, once lovely but now ruined by new buildings.* ADV: ADV with v, ADV with be, ADV with group/cl

5 If someone **once** did something, they did it at an unspecified time in the past. *I once went camping at Lake Darling with a friend... We once walked across London at two in the morning... Diana had taken that path once.* ADV: ADV with v

6 If something happens **once** another thing has happened, it happens immediately afterwards. *The decision had taken about 10 seconds once he'd read a market research study... Once customers come to rely on these systems they almost never take their business elsewhere... Once inside her apartment she felt an urge to brush her teeth.* CONJ-SUBORD

7 If something happens **all at once**, it happens suddenly, often when you are not expecting it to happen. *I feel terribly sleepy all at once... All at once there was someone knocking on the door.* PHRASES PHR with cl =all of a sudden

8 If you do something **at once**, you do it immediately. *I have to go, I really must, at once... Remove from the heat, add the parsley, toss and serve at once... The audience at once greeted it warmly.* PHR with v =immediately

9 If a number of different things happen **at once** or **all at once**, they all happen at the same time. *You can't be doing two things at once... No bank could ever pay off its creditors if they all demanded their money at once... She seems at once feminine and able to cope in a man's world.* PHR after v, PHR adj/n *and* adj/n

10 **For once** is used to emphasize that something happens on this particular occasion, especially if it has never happened before, and may never happen again. *For once, dad is not complaining... His smile, for once, was genuine.* PHR with cl

11 If something happens **once again** or **once more**, it happens again. *Amy picked up the hairbrush and smoothed her hair once more... Once again an official inquiry has spoken of weak management and ill-trained workers.* PHR with v, PHR with cl

12 If something happens **once and for all**, it happens completely or finally. *We have to resolve this matter once and for all... If we act fast, we can once and for all prevent wild animals in Britain from suffering terrible cruelty.* PHR with v

13 If something happens **once in a while**, it happens sometimes, but not very often. *Your body, like any other machine, needs a full service once in a while... Once in a while she phoned him.* PHR with cl =now and again

14 If you have done something **once or twice**, you have done it a few times, but not very often. *I popped my head round the door once or twice... Once or twice she had caught a flash of interest in William's eyes... She gazed up at him, blinking once or twice, apparently surprised at his cleverness.* PHR with cl, PHR with v =occasionally

15 **Once upon a time** is used to indicate that something happened or existed a long time ago or in an imaginary world. It is often used at the beginning of children's stories. *'Once upon a time,' he began, 'there was a man who had everything.'... Once upon a time, asking a woman if she has a job was quite a straightforward question.* PHR with cl

16 • **once in a blue moon**: see **moon**.

once-over. If you **give** something or someone **the once-over**, you quickly look at or inspect them; an informal expression. *She gave the apartment a once-over.* PHRASE: V inflects, PHR after v

oncoming /ɒnkʌmɪŋ/. **Oncoming** means moving towards you. *She was thrown from his car* ADJ: ADJ n *after it skidded into the path of an oncoming car. ...the oncoming cold of winter.*

one /wʌn/ **ones** ◆◆◆◆◆

1 One is the number 1. *They had three sons and one daughter. ...one thousand years ago... Czechoslovakia beat the United States five-one. ...one of the children killed in the crash.* NUM

2 If you say that someone or something is the **one** person or thing of a particular kind, you are emphasizing that they are the only person or thing of that kind. *They had alienated the one man who knew the business... His one regret is that he has never learned a language.* ADJ: det ADJ PRAGMATICS =only

3 One can be used instead of 'a' to emphasize the following noun. *There is one thing I would like to know – What is it about Tim that you find so irresistible?... One person I hate is Russ.* DET: DET sing-n PRAGMATICS

4 You can use **one** instead of 'a' to emphasize the following adjective or expression; an informal use. *If we ever get married we'll have one terrific wedding... It's like one enormous street carnival here.* DET: DET adj sing-n PRAGMATICS

5 You can use **one** in front of someone's name to indicate that you have not met them or heard of them before; a formal use. *It seems that the fifth man is one John Cairncross.* DET: DET n-proper =a certain

6 You can use **one** to refer to the first of two or more things that you are comparing. *Prices vary from one shop to another... The road hugs the coast for hundreds of miles, the South China sea on one side, jungle on the other.* ► Also an adjective. *We ask why peace should have an apparent chance in the one territory and not the other.* ► Also a pronoun. *The twins were dressed differently and one was thinner than the other.* DET: DET sing-n; ADJ: det ADJ; PRON

7 You can use **one** or **ones** instead of a noun when it is clear what type of thing or person you are referring to and you are describing them or giving more information about them. *They are selling their house to move to a smaller one... We test each one to see that it flies well.* PRON

8 You use **ones** to refer to people in general. *We are the only ones who know.* PRON

9 You can use **one** instead of a noun group when you have just mentioned something and you want to describe it or give more information about it. *His response is one of anger and frustration... The issue of land reform was one that dominated Hungary's parliamentary elections.* PRON: PRON *of*n, PRON that

10 You can use **one** when you have been talking or writing about a group of people or things and you want to say something about a particular member of the group. *'A college degree isn't enough', said one honors student.* ► Also a pronoun. *Some of them couldn't eat a thing. One couldn't even drink.* DET: DET sing-n; PRON

11 You use **one** in expressions such as '**one of the biggest airports**' or '**one of the most experienced players**' to indicate that something or someone is bigger or more experienced than most other things or people of the same kind. *Subaru is one of the smallest Japanese car makers.* QUANT: QUANT *of* adj-superl

12 You can use **one** when referring to a time in the past or in the future. For example, if you say that you did something **one day**, you mean that you did it on a day in the past. *How would you like to have dinner one night, just you and me?... Then one evening Harry phoned, asking me to come to their flat as soon as possible.* ● **one day**: see **day**. DET: DET sing-n

13 You can use **one** to refer to a question, joke, remark, or subject of discussion. *This is a tricky one to answer... Have you heard the one about the Irishman, the Englishman and the American?... I told him I'd have to think about that one.* PRON: with supp

14 You can use **one** to refer to an alcoholic drink; an informal use. *Other members of the committee drifted in for a quick one before closing time.* PRON

15 You use **one** to make statements about people in general which also apply to themselves. **One** can be used as the subject or object of a sentence; a formal use. *If one looks at the longer run, a lot of positive things are happening... Where does one go from there?... Shares and bonds can bring one quite a considerable additional income.* PRON

16 If a group of people does something **as one**, all the people do the same thing at the same time or in the same way; used in written English. *The 40,000 crowd rose as one.* PHRASES PHR after v

17 If you say that someone is **one for** or is **a one for** something, you mean that they like or approve of it or enjoy doing it. *I'm not one for political discussions... She was a real one for flirting with the boys.* oft with brd-neg, v-link PHR n/-ing

18 You can use **for one** to emphasize that a particular person is definitely reacting or behaving in a particular way, even if other people are not. *I, for one, hope you don't get the job.* PHR before v PRAGMATICS

19 You can use expressions such as **a hundred and one, a thousand and one**, and **a million and one** to emphasize that you are talking about a large number of things or people. *There are a hundred and one ways in which you can raise money.* usu PHR pl-n PRAGMATICS

20 You can use **in one** to indicate that something is a single unit, but is made up of several different parts or has several different functions. *...a love story and an adventure all in one... This cream moisturises and repairs in one.* pl-n PHR, PHR after v

21 You can use **in ones and twos** to indicate that people do things or something happens gradually and in small groups. *They lose interest and start drifting away in ones and twos.* PHR with cl

22 You use **one after the other** or **one after another** to say that actions or events happen with very little time between them. *My three guitars broke one after the other... One after another, people described how hard it is for them to get medical care.* PHR with cl

23 The one and only can be used in front of the name of an actor, singer, or other famous person when they are being introduced on a show. *...one of the greatest ever rock performers, the one and only Tina Turner.* PHR n-proper

24 You can use **one by one** to indicate that people do things or that things happen in sequence, not all at the same time. *We went into the room one by one... One by one the houses burst into flames.* PHR with cl

25 You use **one or other** to refer to one or more things or people in a group, when it does not matter which particular one or ones are thought of or chosen. *One or other of the two women was wrong.* usu PHR *of* pl-n

26 One or two means a few. *We may make one or two changes... I've also sold one or two to an American publisher... I asked one or two of the stallholders about it.* oft PHR pl-n, PHR *of* pl-n =a few

27 If you say that someone is **not one** to do something, you think that it is very unlikely that they would do it because it is not their normal behaviour. *I'm not one to waste time on just anyone.* PHR to-inf, usu v-link PHR

28 If you try to get **one up on** someone, you try to gain an advantage over them, usually by doing something they have not done or knowing something they do not know. *...the competitive kind who will see this as the opportunity to be one up on you.* PHR n, usu v-link PHR, PHR after v

29 ● **one and all**: see **all**. ● **one another**: see **another**. ● **one thing after another**: see **another**. ● to **pull a fast one**: see **fast**. ● **of one mind**: see **mind**. ● **in one piece**: see **piece**. ● **put one over on**: see **put**.

one-armed bandit, one-armed bandits. A **one-armed bandit** is the same as a **fruit machine**. N-COUNT

one-horse

1 If someone describes a town as a **one-horse** town, they mean it is very small, dull, and old-fashioned. *Would you want to live in a small, one horse town for your whole life?* ADJ: ADJ n

2 If a contest is described as a **one-horse** race, it is thought that one person or thing will obviously win it. *He described the referendum as a one-horse race... Last season looked to be a one-horse race for much of the time, with the reigning champions coasting to an 11-point lead.* ADJ: ADJ n

one-liner, one-liners. A **one-liner** is a funny remark or a joke told in one sentence, for example in a play or comedy programme; an informal word. *The book is witty and peppered with good one-liners.* N-COUNT

one-man ◆◇◇◇◇
1 A **one-man** performance is given by only one man rather than by several people. *I saw him do his one-man show in London, which I loved.* ADJ: ADJ n
2 A **one-man** organization, such as a business or type of government is controlled by one person, rather than by several people. *...a one-man cottage industry... He established one-man rule in his country seven months ago.* ADJ: ADJ n

one-man band, one-man bands. A **one-man band** is a street entertainer who wears and plays a lot of different instruments at the same time. N-COUNT

one-night stand, one-night stands. A **one-night stand** is a very brief sexual relationship, usually involving having sex with a particular person on only one occasion. N-COUNT

one-of-a-kind. You use **one-of-a-kind** to describe something that is special because there is nothing else exactly like it; used mainly in American English. *...a small one-of-a-kind publishing house.* ADJ: ADJ n

one-off, one-offs ◆◆◇◇◇
1 You can refer to something as a **one-off** when it is made or happens only once; used mainly in British English. *Our survey revealed that these allergies were mainly one-offs.* N-COUNT
2 A **one-off** thing is made or happens only once; used mainly in British English. *...one-off cash benefits.* ADJ: ADJ n

one-parent family, one-parent families. A **one-parent family** is a family that consists of one parent and his or her children living together. This happens, for example, when one parent has died or the parents are divorced. *I have been brought up in a one-parent family by my mother.* N-COUNT

one-piece, one-pieces ◆◇◇◇◇
1 A **one-piece** article of clothing consists of one piece only, rather than two or more separate parts. *...a blue one-piece bathing suit.* ADJ: ADJ n
2 A **one-piece** is a type of woman's swimming costume that consists of one piece of material and which covers her chest. *A one-piece is more flattering than a bikini.* N-COUNT

onerous /oʊnərəs, AM ɑːn-/. If you describe a task as **onerous**, you dislike having to do it because you find it difficult or unpleasant; a formal word. *...parents who have had the onerous task of bringing up a very difficult child.* ◆◇◇◇◇ ADJ-GRADED =burdensome

one's /wʌnz/ ◆◆◆◇◇
1 Speakers and writers use **one's** to indicate that something belongs or relates to people in general, or to themselves in particular; a formal use. *...a feeling of responsibility for the welfare of others in one's community... It seems to me a fatal illusion to expect one's children simply to reproduce one's own views.* DET-POSS =your
2 **One's** can be used in informal written English or in spoken English as a form of **one is** or **one has**, especially when 'has' is an auxiliary verb. See **one**. *No one's going to hurt you. No one. Not any more.*

oneself /wʌnself/ ◆◇◇◇◇
Oneself is a third person singular reflexive pronoun.
1 A speaker or writer uses **oneself** as the object of a verb or preposition in a clause where 'oneself' meaning 'me' or 'any person in general' refers to the same person as the subject of the verb. *One must apply oneself to the present and keep one's eyes firmly fixed on one's future goals... To work one must have time to oneself.* PRON-REFL
2 **Oneself** can be used as the object of a verb or preposition, when 'one' is not present but is understood to be the subject of the verb. *The historic feeling of the town makes it a pleasant place to base oneself for summer vacations... The only guarantee of having a cabin to oneself is by travelling first class... It's so easy to feel sorry for oneself... The doll-like figures in these stories are unlike anybody, let alone oneself.* PRON-REFL
3 In formal English, to do something **oneself** means to do it without any help or interference from anyone else. *It is a very rewarding exercise to work this out oneself... Some things one must do oneself.* PRON-REFL-EMPH
4 In formal English, you use **oneself** to emphasize that something happens to you rather than to people in general. *It is better to die oneself than to kill.* PRON-REFL-EMPH
5 • **by oneself**: see **by**.

one-sided ◆◇◇◇◇
1 If you say that an activity or relationship is **one-sided**, you think that one of the people or groups involved does much more than the other or is much stronger than the other. *The negotiating was completely one-sided... Muster needed just 72 minutes to win the one-sided match, 6-2, 6-3.* ADJ-GRADED
2 If you describe someone as **one-sided**, you are critical of what they say or do because you think it shows that they have considered only one side of an issue or event. *The organisation still believes the government is being one sided... There has been a very one-sided account of her problems with Ted.* ADJ-GRADED PRAGMATICS =biased

one-time; also spelled **onetime**. **One-time** can be used to describe something such as a job, position, or role which someone used to have, or something which happened or existed in the past; used in journalism. *She's 87 years old, and a one-time member of the Ziegfeld Follies... The legislative body had voted to oust the country's onetime rulers.* ◆◆◇◇◇ ADJ: ADJ n =former

one-to-one ◆◇◇◇◇
1 In a **one-to-one** relationship, one person deals directly with only one other person. *...one-to-one training. ...negotiating on a one-to-one basis.* ► Also an adverb. *She would like to talk to people one to one.* ADJ: ADJ n =individual ADV: ADV after v
2 In a **one-to-one** comparison, one thing is compared with another thing that is broadly equivalent or similar to it. *All bearers would be compensated in Iraqi dinars on a one-to-one basis.* ADJ: ADJ n

one-upmanship /wʌn ʌpmənʃɪp/. If you refer to someone's behaviour as **one-upmanship**, you disapprove of them trying to make other people feel inferior in order to make themselves appear more important. *It was the expression of a man who'd won a trifling game of one-upmanship. ...political one-upmanship.* N-UNCOUNT: oft supp N PRAGMATICS

one-way ◆◇◇◇◇
1 In **one-way** streets or traffic systems, vehicles can only travel along in one direction. *...Gotham's maze of no-thoroughfares and one-way streets.* ADJ: ADJ n
2 **One-way** describes journeys or tickets which go to just one place, rather than to that place and then back again. *The trailers will be rented for one-way trips... Charlie's ticket was one way, Park's a return.* ADJ: usu ADJ n
3 **One-way** glass or a **one-way** mirror is a device which acts as a mirror when looked at from one side, but acts as a window when looked through from the other side. They are used for watching people without their knowledge or consent. *From the observation booth, we watched Ted and his therapist through the one-way glass.* ADJ: usu ADJ n

one-woman. A **one-woman** performance or business is done by only one woman, rather than by several people. *She has already presented a one-woman show of her paintings.* ADJ: ADJ n

ongoing /ɒngoʊɪŋ/. An **ongoing** situation has been happening for quite a long time and seems likely to continue for some time in the future. *There is an ongoing debate on the issue... That research is ongoing.* ◆◆◇◇◇ ADJ

onion /ʌnjən/ **onions.** An **onion** is a small round vegetable with a brown skin that grows underground. It has many white layers on its inside which have a strong, sharp smell and taste. *Will you chop an onion up for me?... It is made with fresh minced meat, cooked with onion and a rich tomato sauce. ...onion soup.* ◆◆◇◇◇ N-VAR

online /ɒnlaɪn/; also spelled **on-line**. See **line**.

onlooker /ɒnlʊkə^r/ **onlookers.** An **onlooker** is someone who watches an event take place but does not take part in it. *A small crowd of onlookers were there to watch Mrs Thatcher.* ◆◇◇◇◇ N-COUNT =spectator

only /oʊnli/ ◆◆◆◆◆
In written English, **only** is usually placed immedi-

ately before the word it qualifies. In spoken English, however, you can use stress to indicate what **only** qualifies, so its position is not so important.

1 You use **only** to indicate the one thing that is true, appropriate, or necessary in a particular situation, in contrast to all the other things that are not true, appropriate, or necessary. *Only the President could authorize the use of the atomic bomb. ...the guidance and discipline that can be provided only by a strong male... Only here were the police visible in any strength at all... 44-year-old woman seeks caring, honest male of similar age for friendship and fun. Genuine replies only... A business can only be built and expanded on a sound financial base... It's true that I seem to have forgotten you, but it only seems that way.* ADV: ADV with group, ADV before v

2 You use **only** to introduce the thing which must happen before the thing mentioned in the main part of the sentence can happen. *The lawyer is paid only if he wins... The Bank of England insists that it will cut interest rates only when it is ready... Dark matter gives out no light and is detectable only because of its gravitational effect on visible matter.* ADV: ADV cl/prep PRAGMATICS

3 If you talk about the **only** person or thing involved in a particular situation, you mean there are no others involved in it. *She was the only woman in Shell's legal department... The only thing I have is television and these four walls... That left Mr Dertliev as the only candidate.* ADJ: det ADJ

4 An **only** child is a child who has no brothers or sisters. ADJ: ADJ n

5 You use **only** to indicate that something is no more important, interesting, or difficult, for example, than you say it is, especially when you want to correct a wrong idea that someone may get or has already got. *At the moment it is only a theory... 'I'm only a sergeant,' said Clements... Don't get defensive, Charlie. I was only joking.* ADV: ADV group, ADV before v =just

6 You use **only** to emphasize how small an amount is or how short a length of time is. *Child car seats only cost about £10 a week to hire. ...spacecraft guidance systems weighing only a few grams... My father allowed me only a sip or two of wine with each meal... I've only recently met him.* ADV: ADV n/adv PRAGMATICS =just

7 You use **only** to indicate that you are talking about a small part or sample, not the whole of an amount. *These are only a few of the possibilities... Teenagers typically earn only half the adult wage... Only a minority of the people supported the Revolution.* ADV: ADV n =just

8 Only is used after 'can' or 'could' to emphasize that it is impossible to do anything except the rather inadequate or limited action that is mentioned. *For a moment I could say nothing. I could only stand and look... The police can only guess at the scale of the problem.* ADV: modal ADV inf PRAGMATICS

9 You can use **only** in the expressions **I only wish** or **I only hope** in order to emphasize what you are hoping or wishing. *I only wish he were here now that things are getting better for me... We can only hope that the elephants can recover.* ADV: ADV before v PRAGMATICS =just

10 Only can be used to add a comment which slightly changes or limits what you have just said; an informal use. *It's just as dramatic as a film, only it's real... It's a bit like my house, only nicer... Drop in and see me when you're ready. Only don't take too long about it.* CONJ-SUBORD PRAGMATICS =but, except

11 Only can be used after a clause with 'would' to indicate why something is not done; used in spoken English. *I'd invite you to come with me, only it's such a long way... I'd be quite happy to go. Only I don't know what my kids would say about living there.* CONJ-SUBORD =but

12 You can use **only** before an infinitive to introduce an event which happens immediately after one you have just mentioned, and which is rather surprising or unfortunate. *Ryle tried the Embassy, only to be told that Hugh was in a meeting... He raced through the living room, only to find the front door closed.* ADV: ADV to-inf PRAGMATICS

13 You can use **only** to emphasize how appropriate a certain course of action or type of behaviour is. *It's only fair to let her know that you intend to apply... She appeared to have changed considerably, which was only to be expected.* ADV: usu ADV adj, also ADV to-inf PRAGMATICS

14 You can use **only** in front of a verb to indicate that the result of something is unfortunate or undesirable and is likely to make the situation worse rather than better. *The embargo would only hurt innocent civilians... She says that legalising prostitution will only cause problems.* ADV: ADV before v =just, merely

15 If you say you **only have to** or **have only to** do one thing in order to achieve or prove a second thing, you are emphasizing how easily the second thing can be achieved or proved. *Any time you want a babysitter, dear, you only have to ask... We have only to read the labels to know what ingredients are in foods.* PHRASES V inflects, PHR inf PRAGMATICS

16 You can say that something has **only just** happened when you want to emphasize that it happened a very short time ago. *I've only just arrived... The signs of an economic revival are only just beginning... You're only just back from leave.* PHR before v, PHR adv PRAGMATICS

17 You use **only just** to emphasize that something is true, but by such a small degree that it is almost not true at all. *For centuries farmers there have only just managed to survive... I am old enough to remember the Blitz, but only just... 'I think we could agree on that one.'—'Only just.'* usu PHR before v, PHR with cl/group PRAGMATICS =barely

18 You can use **only too** to emphasize that something is true or exists to a much greater extent than you would expect or like. *I know only too well that plans can easily go wrong... When the new baby comes along it is only too easy to shut out the others.* PHR adv/adj PRAGMATICS =all too

19 You can say that you are **only too** happy to do something to emphasize how willing you are to do it. *I'll be only too pleased to help them out with any queries.* PHR adj PRAGMATICS =more than

20 • **if only**: see **if**. • **not only**: see **not**. • **the one and only**: see **one**.

o.n.o. In British English, **o.n.o.** is a written abbreviation for 'or near offer'. It is used after a price in an advertisement to indicate that the person who is selling something is willing to accept slightly less money than the sum they have mentioned.

onomatopoeia /ɒnəmætəpiːə/. **Onomatopoeia** refers to the use of words which have been formed to sound like the noise of the thing that they are describing or representing. 'Hiss', 'buzz', and 'rat-a-tat-tat' are examples of onomatopoeia. N-UNCOUNT

onomatopoeic /ɒnəmætəpiːɪk/. **Onomatopoeic** words use onomatopoeia. ADJ

onrush /ɒnrʌʃ/. The **onrush** of something is its sudden development, which happens so quickly and forcefully that you are unable to control it. *The onrush of tears took me by surprise... She was screwing up her eyes against the onrush of air.* N-SING: usu N of n =surge

onrushing /ɒnrʌʃɪŋ/. **Onrushing** describes something such as a vehicle that is moving forward so quickly or forcefully that it would be very difficult to stop. *He was killed by an onrushing locomotive. ...the roar of the onrushing water.* ADJ: ADJ n

on-screen; also spelled **onscreen**. ◆◇◇◇◇

1 On-screen means appearing on the screen of a television, cinema, or computer. *...a clear and easy-to-follow menu-driven on-screen display... Read the on-screen lyrics and sing along.* ADJ: ADJ n

2 On-screen means relating to the roles being played by film or television actors, in contrast with their real life. *Producers decided to end her on-screen romance with Pierce Lawton. ...an onscreen kiss.* ► Also an adverb. *He was immensely attractive to women, onscreen and offscreen... Onscreen, she lacks the vitality or charisma to pass this performance off.* ADJ: ADJ n ≠off-screen; ADV: ADV with cl ≠off-screen

onset /ɒnset/. The **onset** of something is the beginning of it, used especially to refer to something unpleasant. *Most of the passes have been closed with the onset of winter... With the onset of war, oil prices climbed past $30 a barrel.* ◆◇◇◇◇ N-SING: usu the N of n, also no det

onshore /ɒnʃɔːʳ/

1 Onshore means happening on or near land, ADJ:

rather than at sea. ...*Western Europe's biggest onshore oilfield.* ► Also an adverb. *They missed the ferry and remained onshore.*
usu ADJ n ≠offshore ADV: ADV after v

2 **Onshore** means happening or moving towards the land. *The onshore wind blew steadily past him.* ► Also an adverb. *There was a bit of a wind and it was blowing onshore. ...the gas comes onshore in great quantities.*
ADJ-GRADED: usu ADJ n ADV: ADV after v

onslaught /ɒnslɔːt/ **onslaughts** ◆◇◇◇◇

1 An **onslaught** on someone or something is a very violent, forceful attack against them. *The attackers launched another vicious onslaught on their victim. ...their relentless onslaught against Labour's tax and spending plans. ...a media onslaught.*
N-COUNT: usu with supp, oft N *on/against* n, N *by* n =assault

2 If you refer to an **onslaught** of something, you mean that there is a large amount of it, often so that it is very difficult to deal with. *The onslaught of orders should keep aircraft manufacturers busy for some time. ...the constant onslaught of ads on American TV.*
N-COUNT: usu N *of* n =barrage

onstage /ɒnsteɪdʒ/. When someone such as an actor or musician goes **onstage**, they go onto the stage in a theatre to give a performance. *When she walked onstage she was given a standing ovation... You have to be onstage at eight o'clock... Onstage, the musicians are actually sitting behind the loudspeakers.*
◆◇◇◇◇ ADV: ADV after v, *be* ADV, ADV with cl ≠off-stage

on-the-job. See **job**.

on-the-spot. **On-the-spot** things are done at the place that you are in at the time that you are there. *Rail travellers who try to avoid paying their fares could face on the spot fines.*
◆◇◇◇◇ ADJ: ADJ n

onto /ɒntu/; also spelled **on to.** ◆◆◆◇◇

In addition to the uses shown below, **onto** is used in phrasal verbs such as 'hold onto' and 'latch onto'.

1 If someone or something moves **onto** an object or surface, or is put there, it is then on that object or surface. *I took my bags inside, lowered myself onto the bed and switched on the TV... Smear Vaseline on to your baby's skin to prevent soreness.*
PREP

2 You can sometimes use **onto** to introduce the place that someone moves into or towards. When someone is already in that place, you would normally use the preposition 'on'. *The players emerged onto the field. ...when the photographer sets off onto the moors... Alex turned his car on to the Albert Quay and drove along until he found a parking place.*
PREP

3 You can use **onto** to introduce the place towards which a light or someone's look is directed. ...*the metal part of the door onto which the sun had been shining... The colours rotated round on a disc and were reflected onto the wall behind. ...the house with its leafy garden and its view on to Regent's Park.*
PREP

4 You can use **onto** to introduce a place that you would immediately come to after leaving another place that you have just mentioned, because they are next to each other. ...*windows opening onto carved black-wood balconies... The door opened onto a lighted hallway. ...a two-hundred-yard-wide strip of land that backs onto a large lake.*
PREP: v PREP n

5 When you change the position of your body, you use **onto** to introduce the part your body which is now supporting you. *As he stepped backwards she fell onto her knees, then onto her face... Puffing a little, Mabel shifted her weight onto her feet... I willed my eyes to open and heaved myself over on to my back.*
PREP

6 When you get **onto** a bus, train, or plane, you enter it in order to travel somewhere. *As he got on to the plane, he asked me how I was feeling... Who can fold up a pushchair, toddler and shopping and then get them all onto the bus?... 'I'll see you onto the train.'—'Thank you.'*
PREP ≠off

7 **Onto** is used after verbs such as 'hold', 'hang', and 'cling' to indicate what someone is holding firmly or where something is being held firmly. *The reflector is held onto the sides of the spacecraft with a frame... She was conscious of a second man hanging on to the rail... She had to cling onto the doorhandle until the pain passed.*
PREP

8 If people who are talking get **onto** a different subject, they begin talking about it. *Let's get on to more important matters... So, if we could just move onto something else?*
PREP

9 You can sometimes use **onto** to indicate that something or someone becomes included as a part of a list or system. When they are already included in this list or system, you would normally use the preposition 'on'. *The Macedonian question had failed to get on to the agenda... The pill itself has changed a lot since it first came onto the market... Twelve-thousand workers will go onto a four-day week at their factory in Birmingham.*
PREP

10 If someone **is onto** something, they are about to make a discovery; an informal use. *He leaned across the table and whispered to me, 'I'm really onto something.'... Archaeologists knew they were onto something big when they started digging.*
PREP: *be* PREP n

11 If someone **is onto** you, they have discovered that you are doing something illegal or wrong; an informal use. *He did not want Pollard to become suspicious that he was now onto him... I had told people what he had been doing, so now the police were onto him.*
PREP: *be* PREP n

ontology /ɒntɒlədʒi/. **Ontology** is the branch of philosophy that deals with the nature of existence. *Kant's work on the critique of experience became ultimately indistinguishable from ontology and metaphysics.* ♦ **ontological** /ɒntəlɒdʒɪkəl/. ...*the ontological question of the relationship between mind and body.*
N-UNCOUNT; ADJ: usu ADJ n

onus /oʊnəs/. If you say that the **onus** is on someone to do something, you mean it is their duty or responsibility to do it; a formal word. *The onus is on the shopkeeper to provide goods which live up to the quality of their description... The onus of proof is reversed in libel actions and placed firmly on the defender.*
◆◇◇◇◇ N-SING: usu *the* N, oft N *of* n/-ing

onward /ɒnwəʳd/; also spelled **onwards.** ◆◇◇◇◇

In British English, **onwards** is an adverb and **onward** is an adjective. In American English and sometimes in formal British English, **onward** may also be an adverb.

1 **Onward** means moving forward or continuing a journey. *British Airways have two flights a day to Bangkok, and there are onward flights to Phnom Penh.* ► Also an adverb. *The bus continued onward... He measured the distance to the nearest Antarctic coast, and onwards to the South Pole.*
ADJ: usu ADJ n ADV: ADV after v =forwards, on

2 **Onward** means developing, progressing, or becoming more important over a period of time. ...*the onward march of progress in the British aircraft industry.* ► Also an adverb. *I can see things just going onwards and upwards for us now... The most important thing now is to move onwards.*
ADJ: usu ADJ n ADV: ADV after v =forwards, on

3 If something happens from a particular time **onwards** or **onward**, it begins to happen at that time and continues to happen afterwards. *From the turn of the century onward, she shared the life of the aborigines.*
ADV: *from* n ADV =from then on

onyx /ɒnɪks/. **Onyx** is a semi-precious stone which can be various colours. It is used for making ornaments, jewellery, or furniture.
N-UNCOUNT

oo /uː/. See **ooh**.

oodles /uːdəlz/. If you say that there is **oodles of** something, you are emphasizing that there is a very large quantity of it; an informal word. *The recipe calls for oodles of melted chocolate.*
QUANT: QUANT *of* n-uncount/pl-n PRAGMATICS =lots

ooh /uː/; also spelled **oo**. People say '**ooh**' when they are surprised, looking forward to something, or find something pleasant or unpleasant; an informal word. *'Ooh dear me, that's a bit of a racist comment isn't it.'... 'Red? Ooh how nice.'*
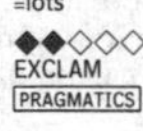
EXCLAM PRAGMATICS

oomph /ʊmf/. If you say that someone or something has **oomph**, you mean that they are energetic and exciting; an informal word. *'There's no buzz, there's no oomph about the place,' he complained.*
N-UNCOUNT =vitality

oops /ʊps, uːps/. You say '**oops**' to indicate that there has been a slight accident or mistake, or to
EXCLAM PRAGMATICS =whoops

apologize to someone for it; an informal word. *Today they're saying, 'Oops, we made a mistake.'*

ooze /uːz/ **oozes, oozing, oozed** ◆◇◇◇◇

1 When a thick or sticky liquid **oozes** from something or when something **oozes** it, the liquid flows slowly and in small quantities. *He put a plaster on a graze behind Ken's ear that was still oozing... The lava will just ooze gently out of the crater... The wounds may heal cleanly or they may ooze a clear liquid.* V-ERG =trickle, seep; V; V adv; V n

2 If you say that someone or something **oozes** a quality or characteristic, or **oozes** with it, you mean that they show it very strongly. *Outwardly, Graham will ooze all his old confidence... The Elizabethan house oozes charm... Manchester United were by now oozing with confidence.* VERB; V n; V *with* n

3 You can refer to any thick, sticky, liquid substance as **ooze**, especially the mud at the bottom of a river, lake, or the sea. *...a primeval ooze... He grabbed into the ooze and came up clutching a large toad.* N-UNCOUNT =sludge

op /ɒp/ **ops** ◆◆◇◇◇

1 An **op** is a medical operation; an informal word. *...breast cancer ops.* N-COUNT

2 Ops are military operations. *Flt Lt Beamont had completed a 200 hour tour of ops in December 1941... Fusilier Jones ran towards the Ops Room to find his lieutenant.* N-COUNT: usu pl

op. In music, **op.** is a written abbreviation for **opus**. *...Beethoven's Op. 101 and 111 sonatas.*

opacity /oʊpæsɪti/

1 Opacity is the quality of being difficult to see through; a formal use. *Opacity of the eye lens can be induced by deficiency of certain vitamins... He insisted that the mineral content of the water determined the opacity.* N-UNCOUNT

2 If you refer to something's **opacity**, you mean that it is difficult to understand; a formal use. *Its dramatic nuances were often generalised to the point of opacity.* N-UNCOUNT =obscurity ≠clarity

opal /oʊpəl/ **opals.** An **opal** is a precious stone. They are colourless or milky white, but other colours are reflected in them. N-VAR

opalescent /oʊpəlesənt/. **Opalescent** means colourless or milky white like an opal, or changing colour like an opal; a literary word. *Elaine turned her opalescent eyes on him. ...a sky which was still faintly opalescent.* ♦ **opalescence** *The sunset was making great splashes of fiery opalescence across the sky.* ADJ-GRADED =iridescent; N-UNCOUNT

opaque /oʊpeɪk/ ◆◇◇◇◇

1 If an object or substance is **opaque**, you cannot see through it. *You can always use opaque glass if you need to block a street view.* ADJ-GRADED ≠transparent

2 If you say that something is **opaque**, you mean that it is difficult to understand. *...the opaque language of the inspector's reports.* ADJ-GRADED

op. cit. /ɒp sɪt/. In reference books, **op. cit.** is used after an author's name to refer to a book of theirs which has already been mentioned; a formal expression. *...quoted in Iyer, op. cit., p. 332.* ◆◇◇◇◇

OPEC /oʊpek/. **OPEC** is an organization of countries that produce oil. It tries to develop a common policy and system of prices. **OPEC** is an abbreviation for 'Organization of Petroleum-Exporting Countries'. *Each member of OPEC would seek to maximize its own production.* ◆◆◇◇◇ N-PROPER

open /oʊpən/ **opens, opening, opened** ◆◆◆◆◆

1 If you **open** something such as a door, window, or lid, or if it **opens**, its position is changed so that it no longer covers a hole or gap. *He opened the window and looked out... The church doors would open and the crowd would surge out.* ► Also an adjective. *...an open window... A door had been forced open.* V-ERG ≠close, shut; V n; V; ADJ ≠closed, shut

2 If you **open** something such as a bottle, box, parcel, or envelope, you move, remove, or cut part of it so you can take out what is inside. *The Inspector opened the packet of cigarettes... The capsules are fiddly to open.* ► Also an adjective. *...an open bottle of milk... I tore the letter open.* ► **Open up** means the same as **open**. *He opened up a cage and lifted out a 6ft python.* VERB; V n; ADJ; PHRASAL VERB; V P n (not pron) Also V n P

3 If you **open** something such as a book, an umbrella, or your hand, or if it **opens**, the different parts of it move away from each other so that the inside of it can be seen. *He opened the heavy Bible... She opens her umbrella, and walks up River Street... The flower opens to reveal a Queen Bee... The officer's mouth opened, showing white, even teeth.* ► Also an adjective. *Without warning, Bardo smacked his fist into his open hand... His mouth was a little open, as if he'd started to scream.* ► **Open out** means the same as **open**. *Keith took a map from the dashboard and opened it out on his knees. ...oval tables which open out to become circular.* V-ERG; V n; V; ADJ-GRADED; PHRASAL VERB ERG; V n P; V P; Also V P n (not pron)

4 When you **open** your eyes or your eyes **open**, you move your eyelids upwards, for example when you wake up, so that you can see. *When I opened my eyes I saw a man with an axe standing at the end of my bed... His eyes were opening wide.* ► Also an adjective. *As soon as he saw that her eyes were open he sat up.* V-ERG; V n; V; ADJ

5 If you **open** your arms, you stretch them wide apart in front of you, usually in order to hug someone. *She opened her arms and gave me a big hug.* VERB; V n

6 If you stand or sit in an **open** way, the front of your body is fully exposed and you are not hunched or at an angle to someone. *Good listeners even sit in an open way: relaxed, arms loose... I play normal bunker shots with an open stance.* ADJ-GRADED: usu ADJ n

7 If you describe a person or their character as **open**, you mean they are honest and do not want or try to hide anything or to deceive anyone. *He had always been open with her and she always felt she would know if he lied... She has an open, trusting nature.* ♦ **openness** *...a relationship based on honesty and openness.* ADJ-GRADED; N-UNCOUNT

8 If you describe a situation, attitude, or way of behaving as **open**, you mean it is not kept hidden or secret. *The action is an open violation of the Vienna Convention... President Menem also wants suspect officials to be tried in open court.* ♦ **openness** *...the new climate of political openness.* ADJ: ADJ n; N-UNCOUNT

9 If you are **open to** suggestions or ideas, you are ready and willing to consider or accept them. *They are open to suggestions on how working conditions might be improved.* ADJ-GRADED: v-link ADJ *to* n =receptive

10 If you say that a system, person, or idea is **open to** something such as abuse or criticism, you mean they might receive it because of the qualities they possess or the effects they have had. *The system, though well-meaning, is open to abuse... They left themselves wide open to accusations of double standards and hypocrisy.* ADJ: v-link ADJ *to* n =susceptible

11 If you say that a fact or question is **open** to debate, interpretation, or discussion, you mean that people are uncertain whether it is true, what it means, or what the answer is. *The truth of the facts produced may be open to doubt... It is an open question how long that commitment can last.* ADJ: oft v-link ADJ *to* n

12 If people **open** something such as a blocked road or a border, or if it **opens**, people can then pass along it or through it. *The rebels have opened the road from Monrovia to the Ivory Coast... The solid rank of carabinieri lining the courtroom opened to let them pass.* ► Also an adjective. *We were part of an entire regiment that had nothing else to do but to keep that highway open.* ► **Open up** means the same as **open**. *As rescue workers opened up roads today, it became apparent that some small towns were totally devastated... When the Berlin Wall came down it wasn't just the roads that opened up but the waterways too.* V-ERG ≠close; V n; V; ADJ; PHRASAL VERB ERG; V P n (not pron); V P; Also V n P

13 If a place **opens** into another, larger place, you can move from one directly into the other. *The corridor opened into a low smoky room.* ► **Open out** means the same as **open**. *...narrow streets opening out into charming squares.* VERB; V *into/onto/to* n; PHRASAL VERB; V P *into/onto/to* n

14 An **open** area is a large area that does not have many structures or obstructions in it. *Officers will also continue their search of nearby open ground.* ADJ: usu ADJ n

15 An **open** structure or object is not covered or enclosed. *Don't leave a child alone in a room with an open fire. ...open sandwiches.* ADJ: ADJ n

16 An **open** wound is one from which blood or pus is coming out. ADJ: usu ADJ n

17 If you **open** your shirt or coat, you unfasten or unzip it. *I opened my coat and let him see the belt.* VERB V n ► Also an adjective. *The top can be worn buttoned up or open over a T-shirt. ...dressing informally in open shirt and cowboy boots.* ADJ: ADJ n, v-link ADJ =undone

18 When a shop, office, or public building **opens** or when someone **opens** it, its doors are unlocked, the people in it start working, and customers or clients can use it. *Banks closed on Friday afternoon and did not open again until Monday morning....a gang of three who'd apparently been lying in wait for him to open the shop. ...opening and closing times.* V-ERG V V n V-ing ► Also an adjective. *His shop is open Monday through Friday, 9am to 6pm.* ADJ

19 When a public building, factory, or company **opens** or when someone **opens** it, it starts operating for the first time. *The original station opened in 1754... The complex opens to the public tomorrow... They are planning to open a factory in Eastern Europe... The Savoy Theatre was opened in 1881 by Richard D'Oyly Carte.* V-ERG ≠close V V to n V n ► Also an adjective. *...any operating subsidy required to keep the pits open.* ADJ: v-link ADJ ♦ **opening, openings** *He was there, though, for the official opening.* N-COUNT: usu sing

20 If something such as a meeting or series of talks **opens**, or if someone **opens** it, it begins. *...an emergency session of the Russian Parliament due to open later this morning... They are now ready to open negotiations.* V-ERG V V n ♦ **opening** *...a communique issued at the opening of the talks.* N-SING: the N of n

21 If an event such as a meeting or discussion **opens** or **is opened** with a particular activity or topic, that activity or topic is the first thing that happens or is dealt with. You can also say that someone such as a speaker or singer **opens** in a particular way. *The service opened with a hymn... She opened with an impressive version of 'I Still Haven't Found What I'm Looking For'... I opened by saying, 'Honey, you look sensational.'... Pollard opened the conversation with some small talk.* V-ERG =begin ≠end V with n V by-ing V n with n Also V n by-ing

22 On the stock exchange, the price at which currencies, shares, or commodities **open** is their value at the start of that day's trading. *Gold declined $2 in Zurich to open at 385.50... In Paris and Milan, the dollar opened almost unchanged.* VERB ≠close V prep/adv V adj

23 When a film, play, or other public event **opens**, it begins to be shown, be performed, or take place for a limited period of time. *A photographic exhibition opens at the Royal College of Art on Wednesday... This show, too, was virtually sold out before it opened.* VERB V ♦ **opening** *He is due to attend the opening of the Asian Games on Saturday.* N-SING: the N of n

24 If you **open** an account with a bank or a commercial organization, you begin to use their services. *He tried to open an account at the branch of his bank nearest to his workplace.* VERB V n

25 If an opportunity or choice **is open to** you, you are able to do a particular thing if you choose to. *There are a wide range of career opportunities open to young people.* ADJ: v-link ADJ to n

26 To **open** opportunities or possibilities means the same as to **open** them **up**. *The chief of naval operations wants to open opportunities for women in the Navy.* V-ERG V n Also V

27 You can use **open** to describe something that anyone is allowed to take part in or accept. *A recent open meeting of College members revealed widespread dissatisfaction... A portfolio approach would keep entry into the managerial profession open and flexible. ...an open invitation.* ADJ

28 If something such as an offer or vacancy is **open**, it is available for someone to accept or apply for. *The offer will remain open until further notice.* ADJ: v-link ADJ

29 See also **opening**.

30 If you do something **in the open**, you do it out of doors rather than in a house or other building. *Many are sleeping in the open because they have no shelter.* PHRASES PHR after v =outside

31 If an attitude or situation is **in the open** or **out in the open**, people know about it and it is no longer kept secret. *The medical service had advised us to keep it a secret, but we wanted it in the open.* usu v-link PHR

32 If something is **wide open**, it is open to its full extent. *The child had left the inner door wide open.* PHR after v, v-link PHR

33 If you say that a competition, race, or election is **wide open**, you mean that anyone could win it, because there is no competitor who seems to be much better than the others. *The competition has been thrown wide open by the absence of the world champion.* v-link PHR, PHR after v

34 • **with open arms**: see **arm**. • **to open the door**: see **door**. • **to keep** your **eyes open**: see **eye**. • **with** your **eyes open**: see **eye**. • to **open** your **eyes**: see **eye**. • to **open fire**: see **fire**. • to **open** your **heart**: see **heart**. • **the heavens open**: see **heaven**. • **an open mind**: see **mind**. • to **open** your **mind**: see **mind**. • to **keep** your **options open**: see **option**.

open out. See **open** 3, 13, **open up**. PHRASAL VERB

open up PHRASAL VERB

1 See **open** 2, 12.

2 If a place, economy, or area of interest **opens up**, or if someone **opens** it **up**, it becomes accessible to more people. *As the market opens up, I think people are going to be able to spend more money on consumer goods... He said he wanted to see how Albania was opening up to the world... If this agreement's going to succeed, the European Community must dramatically open up its markets... The money could open up music to more children.* ERG V P V P to n V P n (not pron) V P n to n Also V n P, V n P to n

3 If something **opens up** opportunities or possibilities, or if opportunities or possibilities **open up**, they are able to arise or develop. *It was also felt that the collapse of communism in Eastern Europe opened up new possibilities... New opportunities are opening up for investors who want a more direct stake in overseas companies.* ERG V P n (not pron) V P Also V n P

4 If you **open up** a lead in a race or competition, you get yourself into a position where you are leading, usually by quite a long way. *The Chinese quartet had opened up a lead of more than two minutes.* V P n (not pron)

5 When you **open up** a building, you unlock and open the door so that people can get in. *Three armed men were waiting when the postmaster and his wife arrived to open up the shop... Open up, or I break in!* V P n (not pron) V P

open up or **open out.** If someone **opens up**, or in British English **opens out**, they start to say exactly what they think or feel about something or someone. *Lorna found that people were willing to open up to her... It will be difficult for her to open out and discuss her problems freely with you.* PHRASAL VERB V P to n V P

open-air; also spelled **open air**. ◆◇◇◇◇

1 An **open-air** place or event is outside rather than in a building. *...the Open Air Theatre in Regents Park. ...an open air concert in brilliant sunshine.* ADJ: usu ADJ n =outdoor

2 If you are in the **open air**, you are outside rather than in a building. *We sleep out under the stars, and eat our meals in the open air.* N-SING: the N, usu in the N

open-and-shut. If you describe a dispute or a legal case as **open-and-shut**, you mean that is easily decided or solved because the facts are very clear. *It's an open and shut case. The hospital is at fault. ...an open-and-shut murder charge.* ADJ: usu ADJ n =straightforward

opencast /oʊpənkɑːst, -kæst/; also spelled **open-cast**. At an **opencast** mine, the coal, metal, or minerals are near the surface and underground passages are not used; used mainly in British English. American English uses expressions such as **strip mine** and **strip mining**. ADJ: ADJ n

open day, open days. At a school, university, or other institution, an **open day** is a specific day when the members of the public are encouraged to visit the campus; used in British English. N-COUNT

open-door; also spelled **open door**. If a country or organization has an **open-door** policy towards people or goods, it allows them to come there freely, without any restrictions. *...reformers who have advocated an open door economic policy.* ◆◇◇◇◇ ADJ: ADJ n

▸ Also a noun. *...an open door to further foreign investment.* N-SING

open-ended. When people begin an **open-ended** discussion or activity, they do not start with any intention of achieving a particular decision or result. *...an open-ended commitment to the security of the Gulf. ...open-ended questions about what passengers expect of an airline.* ◆◇◇◇◇ ADJ: usu ADJ n

opener /oʊpənər/ **openers.** An **opener** is a tool which is used to open containers such as tins or bottles. *...a tin opener.* • See also **eye-opener.** ◆◇◇◇◇ N-COUNT: usu n N

open house. If you say that someone keeps **open house**, you mean that they welcome friends or visitors to their house whenever they arrive and allow them to stay for as long as they want to. *Father Illtyd kept open house and the boys would congregate in his study during their recreation time, playing cards or games.* N-UNCOUNT

opening /oʊpənɪŋ/ **openings** ◆◆◆◇◇

1 The **opening** event, item, day, or week in a series is the first one. *They returned to take part in the season's opening game. ...the opening day of the fifth General Synod.* ADJ: ADJ n =first

2 The **opening** of something such as a book, play, or concert is the first part of it. *The opening of the scene depicts Akhnaten and his family in a moment of intimacy.* N-COUNT: usu N *of*n

3 An **opening** is a hole or empty space through which things or people can pass. *He squeezed through a narrow opening in the fence.* N-COUNT

4 An **opening** is a good opportunity to do something, for example to show people how good you are. *Her capabilities were always there; all she needed was an opening to show them.* N-COUNT =opportunity

5 An **opening** is a job that is available. *We don't have any openings now, but we'll call you if something comes up.* N-COUNT

6 See also **open.**

opening hours. **Opening hours** are the times during which a shop, bank, library, or pub is open for business. *Opening hours are 9.30am--5.45pm, Mon--Fri.* N-PLURAL =opening times

opening night, opening nights. The **opening night** of a play or an opera is the first night on which a particular production is performed. ◆◇◇◇◇ N-COUNT =premier, first night

opening time, opening times

1 You can refer to the time that a shop, bank, library, or pub opens for business as its **opening time**. *Shoppers began arriving long before the 10am opening time.* N-UNCOUNT: also *the* N

2 The **opening times** of a place such as a shop, a restaurant, or a museum is the period during which it is open. *Ask the local tourist office about opening times.* N-PLURAL =opening hours

open letter, open letters. An **open letter** is a letter that is published in a newspaper or magazine. It is addressed to a particular person but is intended for the general reader, usually in order to protest or give an opinion about something. *They set out their case in an open letter to a leading Soviet newspaper.* ◆◇◇◇◇ N-COUNT

openly /oʊpənli/. If you do something **openly**, you do it without hiding any facts or hiding your feelings. *We can now talk openly about AIDS which we couldn't before... Some officials openly criticized US decisions concerning the Persian Gulf... She hung around with a pair of nurses who were openly gay.* ◆◆◇◇◇ ADV-GRADED: ADV with v, ADV adj ≠secretly

open market. Goods that are bought and sold on **the open market** are advertised and sold publicly rather than privately. Compare **black market.** *The Central Bank is authorized to sell government bonds on the open market.* ◆◇◇◇◇ N-SING: *the* N

open-minded. If you describe someone as **open-minded**, you approve of them because they are willing to listen to and consider other people's ideas and suggestions. *He was very open-minded about other people's work.* ♦ **open-mindedness** *He was praised for his enthusiasm and his open-mindedness.* ◆◇◇◇◇ ADJ-GRADED: oft ADJ *about*n PRAGMATICS ≠narrow-minded; N-UNCOUNT ≠narrow-mindedness

open-mouthed. If someone is looking **open-mouthed**, they are staring at something with their mouth wide open because it has shocked, frightened, or excited them. *They watched almost open-mouthed as the two men came towards them... The finale had 50,000 adults standing in open-mouthed wonderment.* ADJ: usu ADJ after v, ADJ n

open-necked or **open-neck.** If you are wearing an **open-necked** shirt or blouse, you are wearing a shirt or blouse with the top button unfastened and no tie. *He was wearing cotton pants and an open-necked shirt.* ADJ: ADJ n

open-plan. An **open-plan** building or room has no internal walls dividing it into smaller areas. *The firm's top managers share the same open-plan office.* ADJ

open question, open questions. If something is an **open question**, people have different opinions about it and nobody can say which opinion is correct. *A British official said he thought it was an open question whether sanctions would do any good.* N-COUNT

open secret, open secrets. If you refer to something an **open secret**, you mean that it is supposed to be a secret, but many people know about it. *It's an open secret that the security service bugged telephones.* N-COUNT

Open University. In Britain, **the Open University** is a university that runs degree courses on the radio and television for students who do not have the qualifications necessary for ordinary universities, or who want to study part-time or mainly at home. Students send their work by post to their tutors. *She was holding down a job she was enjoying and studying at the Open University.* ◆◇◇◇◇ N-PROPER: *the* N

opera /ɒpərə/ **operas.** An **opera** is a musical entertainment. It is like a play but most of the words are sung. *...a one-act opera about contemporary women in America. ...Donizetti's opera 'Lucia di Lammermoor'. ...an opera singer... He was also learned in classical music with a great love of opera.* • See also **soap opera.** ◆◆◆◇◇ N-VAR

opera house, opera houses. An **opera house** is a theatre that is specially designed for the performance of operas. *...Sydney Opera House.* ◆◇◇◇◇ N-COUNT: oft in names

operandi /ɒpərændaɪ/. See **modus operandi.**

operate /ɒpəreɪt/ **operates, operating, operated** ◆◆◆◆◆

1 If you **operate** a business or organization, you work to keep it running properly. If a business or organization **operates,** it carries out its work. *Until his death in 1986 Greenwood owned and operated an enormous pear orchard. ...allowing commercial banks to operate in the country... Operating costs jumped from £85.3m to £95m.* ♦ **operation** /ɒpəreɪʃən/ *Company finance is to provide funds for the everyday operation of the business.* V-ERG V n V V-ing; N-UNCOUNT

2 The way that something **operates** is the way that it works or has a particular effect. *Ceiling and wall lights can operate independently... How do accounting records operate?... The world of work doesn't operate that way.* ♦ **operation** *Mrs Thatcher said the operation of the new tax was being studied.* VERB =function V adv/prep V n; N-UNCOUNT: oft N *of*n =functioning

3 When you **operate** a machine or device, or when it **operates**, you make it work. *A massive rock fall trapped the men as they operated a tunnelling machine... The number of fax machines operating around the world has now reached ten million.* ♦ **operation** *...over 1,000 dials monitoring every aspect of the operation of the aeroplane.* V-ERG V n V; N-UNCOUNT

4 When surgeons **operate** on a patient in a hospital, they cut open a patient's body in order to remove, replace, or repair a diseased or damaged part. *The surgeon who operated on the King released new details of his injuries... You examine a patient and then you decide whether or not to operate.* VERB V *on*n V

5 If military forces **are operating** in a particular region, they are in that place in order to carry out their orders. *Up to ten thousand Zimbabwean soldiers are operating in Mozambique... This freed the Austrian army to operate against the French.* VERB V prep

operatic /ɒpəræ̱tɪk/. **Operatic** means relating to opera. *...the local amateur operatic society.* ◆◇◇◇◇ ADJ

o̱perating system, operating systems. The **operating system** of a computer is its most basic program, which it needs in order to function and run other programs. ◆◇◇◇◇ N-COUNT

o̱perating table, operating tables. An **operating table** is a table which a patient in a hospital lies on during a surgical operation. N-COUNT

o̱perating theatre, operating theatres; spelled **operating theater** in American English. An **operating theatre** is a special room in a hospital where surgeons carry out medical operations; used mainly in British English. The usual American term is **operating room**. N-COUNT =theatre

operation /ɒpəre̱ɪʃᵊn/ **operations** ◆◆◆◆◆

1 An **operation** is a highly organized activity that involves many people doing different things. *The rescue operation began on Friday afternoon... The soldiers were engaged in a military operation close to the Ugandan border. ...a big operation against the drugs trade.* N-COUNT: usu supp N

2 A business or company can be referred to as an **operation**. *Thorn's electronic's operation employs around 5,000 people... The two parent groups now run their business as a single combined operation.* N-COUNT =enterprise

3 When a patient has an **operation**, a surgeon cuts open their body in order to remove, replace, or repair a diseased or damaged part. *Charles was at the clinic recovering from an operation on his arm.* N-COUNT

4 If a system is in **operation**, it is being used. *Until the rail links are in operation, passengers can only travel through the tunnel by coach. ...the free banking system that has been in operation since the early eighties.* N-UNCOUNT: *in/out of*N =in use

5 If a machine or device is in **operation**, it is working. *There are three ski lifts in operation.* N-UNCOUNT: *in/out of*N

6 When a rule, system, or plan **comes into operation** or you **put it into operation**, you begin to use it. *The Financial Services Act came into operation four years ago... Cheaper energy conservation techniques have been put into operation in the developed world.* PHRASE: V inflects

operational /ɒpəre̱ɪʃənᵊl/ ◆◆◇◇◇

1 A machine or piece of equipment that is **operational** is in use or is ready for use. *The whole system will be fully operational by December 1995.* ADJ: usu v-link ADJ

2 **Operational** factors or problems relate to the working of a system, device, or plan. *The nuclear industry was required to prove that every operational and safety aspect had been fully researched.* ADJ: usu ADJ n
♦ **operationally** *An all-female political section would have been operationally ineffective... The device had been used operationally some months previously.* ADV: ADV adj, ADV after v

operative /ɒpərətɪv/ **operatives** ◆◆◇◇◇

1 A system or service that is **operative** is working or having an effect; a formal use. *The commercial telephone service was no longer operative... The Youth Training Scheme was operative by the end of 1983.* ADJ: usu v-link ADJ =in operation

2 An **operative** is a worker, especially one with a manual skill; a formal use. *In an automated car plant there is not a human operative to be seen.* N-COUNT

3 An **operative** is someone who works for a government agency such as the intelligence service; used mainly in American English. *Naturally the CIA wants to protect its operatives.* N-COUNT

4 If you describe a word as **the operative word**, you want to draw attention to it because you think it is important or exactly true in a particular situation. *As long as the operative word is 'greed', you can't count on people keeping the costs down... A small dram of whisky may be prescribed by doctors for those over 60 to help them sleep. It is vital though to emphasize that 'small' is the operative word.* PHRASE: N inflects

operator /ɒpəreɪtəʳ/ **operators** ◆◆◆◇◇

1 An **operator** is a person who works at a telephone exchange or at the switchboard of an office or hotel. *He dialled the operator and put in a call for Rome.* N-COUNT

2 An **operator** is a person who is employed to operate or control a machine. *...computer operators.* N-COUNT: usu n N

3 An **operator** is a person or a company that runs a business. *...'Tele-Communications', the nation's largest cable TV operator.* N-COUNT: usu with supp

4 If you call someone a good **operator**, you mean that they are skilful at achieving what they want, often in a slightly dishonest way; an informal use. *He was a smart operator. Don't underestimate him. ...one of the shrewdest political operators in the Arab World.* N-COUNT: usu adj N

5 See also **tour operator**.

operetta /ɒpərე̱tə/ **operettas.** An **operetta** is a light-hearted and often comic opera which has some of the words spoken rather than sung. N VAR

ophthalmic /ɒfθæ̱lmɪk/. **Ophthalmic** means relating to or concerned with the medical care of people's eyes and eyesight; a formal word. *Ophthalmic surgeons are now performing laser surgery to correct myopia.* ADJ: ADJ n

ophthalmologist /ɒfθælmɒ̱lədʒɪst/ **ophthalmologists.** An **ophthalmologist** is a medical doctor who specializes in diseases and problems affecting people's eyes and eyesight. N-COUNT

ophthalmology /ɒfθælmɒ̱lədʒi/. **Ophthalmology** is branch of medicine concerned with people's eyes and eyesight and the problems that affect them. N-UNCOUNT

opiate /o̱ʊpiət/ **opiates**

1 An **opiate** is a drug that contains opium. Opiates are used to reduce pain or to help people to sleep. *One woman suffered such severe pain she had to take opiates to control it.* N-COUNT

2 If you call something an **opiate**, you disapprove of it because it makes people think less or spend less time on important activities. *...the opiate of mass entertainment... It was Karl Marx who said, 'Religion is the opiate of the people'.* N-COUNT PRAGMATICS =drug

opine /oʊpa̱ɪn/ **opines, opining, opined.** To **opine** means to express your opinion; a formal word. *'She's probably had a row with her boyfriend,' Charles opined... He opined that the navy would have to start again from the beginning.* VERB V with quote V that Also V *on/about*n

opinion /əpɪ̱njən/ **opinions** ◆◆◆◆◇

1 Your **opinion** about something is what you think or believe about it. *I wasn't asking for your opinion, Dick... He held the opinion that a government should think before introducing a tax... Most who expressed an opinion spoke favorably of Thomas.* N-COUNT: oft poss N, N that

2 Your **opinion** of someone is your judgement of their character or ability. *That improved Mrs Goole's already favourable opinion of him.* N-SING: usu supp N, N *of*n =estimation

3 You can refer to the beliefs or views that people have as **opinion**. *Some, I suppose, might even be in positions to influence opinion... There is a broad consensus of opinion about the policies which should be pursued.* N-UNCOUNT

4 An **opinion** from an expert is the advice or judgement that they give you in the subject that they know a lot about. *Even if you have had a regular physical check-up recently, you should still seek a medical opinion.* N-COUNT: usu sing

5 See also **public opinion, second opinion**.

6 You add expressions such as **'in my opinion'** or **'in their opinion'** to a statement in order to emphasize that it is what you or someone else thinks, and is not necessarily a fact. *The book is, in Henry's opinion, the best book on the subject... Well he's not making a very good job of it in my opinion.* PHRASES PHR with cl PRAGMATICS

7 If someone is **of the opinion** that something is the case, that is what they believe; a formal expression. *Frank is of the opinion that the 1934 yacht should have won.* v-link PHR that

8 ● **a matter of opinion**: see **matter**.

opinionated /əpɪ̱njəneɪtɪd/. If you describe someone as **opinionated**, you mean that they have very strong opinions and refuse to accept that they may be wrong. *She seemed frail but as strongly opinionated and prone to arguments as ever... Your article is full of some of the most opinionated rubbish I have ever read.* ● See also **self-opinionated**. ADJ-GRADED

opi̱nion poll, opinion polls. An **opinion poll** involves asking people's opinions on a particular ◆◆◇◇◇ N-COUNT =poll subject, especially one concerning politics. *Nearly three-quarters of people questioned in an opinion poll agreed with the government's decision.*

opium /oupiəm/. **Opium** is a powerful drug made from the seeds of a type of poppy. Opium is used in medicines that relieve pain or help someone sleep. ◆◇◇◇◇ N-UNCOUNT

opossum /əpɒsəm/ **opossums.** An **opossum** is a small animal that lives in America. It carries its young in a pouch on its body, and has thick fur and a long tail. N-VAR

opponent /əpounənt/ **opponents** ◆◆◆◇◇

1 A politician's **opponents** are other politicians who belong to a different party or who have different aims or policies. *...Mr Gorbachev's opponent in the leadership contest... He described the detention without trial of political opponents as a cowardly act.* N-COUNT: usu with poss

2 In a sporting contest, your **opponent** is the person who is playing against you. *Norris twice knocked down his opponent in the early rounds of the fight... He's the best opponent I've come across this season, a great player.* N-COUNT: usu poss N

3 The **opponents** of an idea or policy do not agree with it and do not want it to be carried out. *...opponents of the spread of nuclear weapons... He became an outspoken opponent of the old Soviet system.* N-COUNT: usu N *of* n ≠supporter

opportune /ɒpəʳtjuːn, AM -tuːn/. If something happens at an **opportune** time or is **opportune**, it happens at the time that is most convenient for someone or most likely to lead to success; a formal word. *I believe that I have arrived at a very opportune moment... The timing of the meetings was opportune.* ADJ-GRADED =providential

opportunism /ɒpəʳtjuːnɪzəm, AM -tuːn-/. If you refer to someone's behaviour as **opportunism**, you are criticizing them for taking advantage of any opportunity that occurs in order to gain money or power, without thinking about whether their actions are right or wrong. *The Energy Minister responded by saying that the opposition's concern for the environment was political opportunism.* N-UNCOUNT PRAGMATICS

opportunist /ɒpəʳtjuːnɪst, AM -tuːn-/ **opportunists** ◆◇◇◇◇

1 If you describe someone as **opportunist**, you are critical of them because they take advantage of any situation in order to gain money or power, without considering whether their actions are right or wrong. *...corrupt and opportunist politicians.* ▶ An **opportunist** is someone who is opportunist. *Like most successful politicians, Sinclair was an opportunist... Car thieves are opportunists.* ADJ-GRADED: usu ADJ n PRAGMATICS; N-COUNT

2 **Opportunist** actions are not planned, but are carried out in order to take advantage of the immediate situation. *Eric Cantona made the game safe with a brilliant opportunist goal.* ADJ: usu ADJ n

opportunistic /ɒpəʳtjuːnɪstɪk, AM -tuːn-/. If you describe someone's behaviour as **opportunistic**, you are critical of them because they take advantage of situations in order to gain money or power, without thinking about whether their actions are right or wrong. *Many of the party's members joined only for opportunistic reasons.* ◆◇◇◇◇ ADJ-GRADED PRAGMATICS

♦ **opportunistically** *This nationalist feeling has been exploited opportunistically by several important politicians.* ADV-GRADED: ADV with v

opportunity /ɒpəʳtjuːnɪti, AM -tuːn-/ **opportunities.** An **opportunity** is a situation in which it is possible for you to do something that you want to do. *I had an opportunity to go to New York and study... The best reason for a trip to London is the super opportunity for shopping... I want to see more opportunities for young people. ...equal opportunities in employment.* • See also **photo opportunity.** ◆◆◆◆◇ N-VAR: oft N to-inf, N *for* n/-ing

oppose /əpouz/ **opposes, opposing, opposed.** If you **oppose** someone or **oppose** their plans or ideas, you disagree with what they want to do and try to prevent them from doing it. *Mr Taylor was not bitter towards those who had opposed him... Many parents oppose bilingual education in schools.* ◆◆◆◇◇ VERB =be against V n

opposed /əpouzd/ ◆◆◆◇◇

1 If you **are opposed to** something, you disagree with it or disapprove of it. *I am utterly opposed to any form of terrorism... We are strongly opposed to the presence of America in this region.* ADJ-GRADED: v-link ADJ *to* n/-ing =against

2 You say that two ideas or systems are **opposed** when they are opposite to each other or very different from each other. *...people with policies almost diametrically opposed to his own... This was a straight conflict of directly opposed aims.* ADJ: oft ADJ *to* n =opposite

3 You use **as opposed to** when you want to make it clear that you are talking about one particular thing and not something else. *We ate in the restaurant, as opposed to the bistro.* PHRASE: PHR group =rather than

opposing /əpouzɪŋ/ ◆◇◇◇◇

1 **Opposing** ideas or tendencies are totally different from each other. *I have a friend who has the opposing view and felt that the war was immoral... Water is the opposing force to fire.* ADJ: ADJ n =opposite

2 **Opposing** groups of people disagree about something or are in competition with one another. *The Georgian leader said in a radio address that he still favoured dialogue between the opposing sides... The opposing team must in turn try to keep the ball in the air before hitting it back over the net.* ADJ: ADJ n

opposite /ɒpəzɪt/ **opposites** ◆◆◆◇◇

1 If one thing is **opposite** another, it is on the other side of a space from it. *Jennie had sat opposite her at breakfast.* ▶ Also an adverb. *He looked up at the buildings opposite, but could see no open window... Melissa slid in beside Paula, and her husband sat opposite.* PREP; ADV: usu n ADV, ADV after v

2 The **opposite** side or part of something is the side or part that is furthest away from you. *...the opposite corner of the room.* ADJ: ADJ n =far

3 **Opposite** is used to describe things of the same kind which are completely different in a particular way. For example, north and south are opposite directions, and winning and losing are opposite results in a game. *All the cars driving in the opposite direction had their headlights on... I should have written the notes in the opposite order... In fact everything he does is opposite to what is considered normal behaviour.* ADJ: usu ADJ n, also v-link ADJ *to* n, v-link ADJ

4 The **opposite** of someone or something is the person or thing that is most different from them. *Ritter was a very complex man but Marius was the opposite, a simple farmer... Well, whatever he says you can bet he's thinking the opposite... What's the opposite of white?* N-COUNT: usu *the* N, oft *the* N *of* n =reverse

opposite number, opposite numbers. Your **opposite number** is a person who has the same job or rank as you, but works in a different department, firm, or organization; used mainly in journalism. *The French Defence Minister is to visit Japan later this month for talks with his Japanese opposite number... Mr Burlatsky had been invited by his European parliament opposite number, Mr Ken Coates.* ◆◇◇◇◇ N-COUNT: usu poss N =counterpart

opposite sex. If you are talking about men and refer to **the opposite sex**, you mean women. If you are talking about women and refer to **the opposite sex**, you mean men. *These people, usually men, seem unable to relate to the opposite sex... Body language can also be used to attract members of the opposite sex.* ◆◇◇◇◇ N-SING: *the* N

opposition /ɒpəzɪʃᵊn/ **oppositions** ◆◆◆◆◇

1 **Opposition** is strong, angry, or violent disagreement and disapproval. *The government is facing a new wave of opposition in the form of a student strike... Much of the opposition to this plan has come from the media.* N-UNCOUNT: oft N *to* n

2 The **opposition** is the political parties or groups that are opposed to a government. *The main opposition parties boycotted the election, saying it would not be conducted fairly.* N-COUNT-COLL: usu sing, oft N n

3 In a country's parliament, the **opposition** refers to the politicians or political parties that form part of the parliament but are not in the government. *...the Leader of the Opposition.* N-COUNT-COLL: usu sing, oft *the* N

4 The **opposition** is the person or team you are competing against in a sports event. *Poland provide the opposition for the Scots' last warm-up match at home.* N-SING-COLL

oppress /əpres/ **oppresses, oppressing, oppressed**

1 To **oppress** people means to treat them cruelly, or to prevent them from having the same opportunities, freedom, and benefits as others. *These people often are oppressed by the governments of the countries they find themselves in... We are not normal like everybody else. If we were they wouldn't be oppressing us.* VERB be V-ed V n Also V, V n with n

2 If something **oppresses** you, it makes you feel depressed, anxious, and uncomfortable; a literary use. *The place oppressed Aubrey even before his eyes adjusted to the dark... It was not just the weather which oppressed her.* VERB =depressed V n

oppressed /əprest/. People who are **oppressed** are treated cruelly or are prevented from having the same opportunities, freedom, and benefits as others. *Before they took power, they felt oppressed by the white English speakers who controlled things... The socialist standpoint is that there should be no division between any oppressed group.* ▶ **The oppressed** are people who are oppressed. *...a sense of community with the poor and oppressed.* ◆◇◇◇◇ ADJ-GRADED N-PLURAL: the N =downtrodden

oppression /əpreʃən/ **oppressions. Oppression** is the cruel or unfair treatment of a group of people. *...an attempt to escape political oppression. ...the oppression of the 19th-century poor by the rich.* ◆◇◇◇◇ N-UNCOUNT: also N in pl, oft N of n

oppressive /əpresɪv/ ◆◇◇◇◇

1 If you describe a society, its laws, or customs as **oppressive**, you think they treat people cruelly and unfairly. *The new laws will be just as oppressive as those they replace. ...refugees from the oppressive regime.* ADJ-GRADED =repressive

2 If you describe the weather or the atmosphere in a room as **oppressive**, you mean that it is uncomfortably hot and humid. *The oppressive afternoon heat had quite tired him out... The little room was windowless and oppressive.* ADJ-GRADED =stifling

3 An **oppressive** situation makes you feel depressed and uncomfortable. *...the oppressive sadness that weighed upon him like a physical pain.* ADJ-GRADED: usu ADJ n

oppressor /əpresəʳ/ **oppressors.** An **oppressor** is a person or group of people that is treating another person or group of people cruelly or unfairly. *Lacking sovereignty, they could organise no defence against their oppressors.* N-COUNT: oft with poss

opprobrium /əproubriəm/. **Opprobrium** is open criticism or disapproval of something that someone has done; a formal word. *His political opinions have attracted the opprobrium of the Left. ...public opprobrium.* N-UNCOUNT =censure

opt /ɒpt/ **opts, opting, opted.** If you **opt** for something, or **opt** to do something, you choose it or decide to do it in preference to anything else. *Depending on your circumstances you may wish to opt for one method or the other... Our students can also opt to stay in residence.* ◆◆◆◇◇ VERB V for n V to-inf

opt in. If you can **opt in**, you are able to choose to be part of an agreement or system. *He proposed that only those countries which were willing and able should opt in to phase three... He didn't exactly opt out because he never opted in.* PHRASAL VERB V P to n V P

opt out. If you **opt out** of something, you choose to be no longer involved in it. *...schools that opt out of local authority control... Under the agreement the Vietnamese can opt out at any time... The elderly and infirm are proving unattractive customers to opted-out hospitals.* PHRASAL VERB V P of n V P V-ed P

optic /ɒptɪk/. **Optic** means relating to the eyes or to sight. *The reason for this is that the optic nerve is a part of the brain.* • See also **optics**. ◆◇◇◇◇ ADJ: ADJ n

optical /ɒptɪkəl/ ◆◇◇◇◇

1 **Optical** instruments, devices, or processes are concerned with vision, light, or images. *...optical telescopes.* ADJ: usu ADJ n

2 **Optical** means relating to how people see things. *...the optical effects of volcanic dust in the stratosphere.* ADJ: ADJ n =visual

optical fibre, optical fibres; spelled **optical fiber** in American English. An **optical fibre** is a very thin strand of glass inside a protective coating. Optical fibres are used to transmit information in the form of light, for example in telecommunications. *Nearly every long-distance call made in Britain now travels on optical fibre instead of cable. ...an optical fibre network to which every home and office can be connected.* N-VAR

optical illusion, optical illusions. An **optical illusion** is something that tricks your eyes so that what you think you see is different from what is really there. *Sloping walls on the bulk of the building create an optical illusion.* N-COUNT

optician /ɒptɪʃən/ **opticians**

1 An **optician** is someone whose job involves testing people's eyesight, and making and selling glasses and contact lenses. N-COUNT

2 An **optician** or an **optician's** is a shop where you can have your eyes tested and buy glasses and contact lenses. *Some may need specialist treatment at the optician's.* N-COUNT: oft the N

optics /ɒptɪks/. **Optics** is the branch of science concerned with vision, sight, and light. • See also **fibre optics**. ◆◇◇◇◇ N-UNCOUNT

optimal /ɒptɪməl/. See **optimum**.

optimism /ɒptɪmɪzəm/. **Optimism** is the feeling of being hopeful about the future or about the success of something in particular. *The Indian Prime Minister has expressed optimism about India's future relations with the USA. ...a mood of cautious optimism.* ◆◆◇◇◇ N-UNCOUNT =confidence ≠pessimism

optimist /ɒptɪmɪst/ **optimists.** An **optimist** is someone who is hopeful about the future. *He has the upbeat manner of an eternal optimist.* ◆◇◇◇◇ N-COUNT ≠pessimist

optimistic /ɒptɪmɪstɪk/. Someone who is **optimistic** is hopeful about the future or the success of something in particular. *The President says she is optimistic that an agreement can be worked out soon... Michael was in a jovial and optimistic mood.* ♦ **optimistically** *Both sides have spoken optimistically about the talks.* ◆◆◆◇◇ ADJ-GRADED: oft ADJ about n, ADJ that =confident ≠pessimistic ADV-GRADED: ADV with v ≠pessimistically

optimize /ɒptɪmaɪz/ **optimizes, optimizing, optimized;** also spelled **optimise** in British English.

1 To **optimize** a plan, system, or machine means to arrange or design it so that it operates as smoothly and efficiently as possible; a formal use. *Doctors are concentrating on understanding the disease better, and on optimizing the treatment... The new systems have been optimised for running Microsoft Windows.* VERB V n

2 To **optimize** a situation or opportunity means to get as much advantage or benefit from it as you can; a formal use. *What can you do to optimize your family situation?* VERB V n

optimum /ɒptɪməm/ or **optimal.** The **optimum** or **optimal** level or state of something is the best level or state that it could achieve; a formal word. *Aim to do some physical activity three times a week for optimum health. ...regions in which optimal conditions for farming can be created.* ◆◇◇◇◇ ADJ: usu ADJ n =ideal

option /ɒpʃən/ **options** ◆◆◆◆◇

1 An **option** is something that you can choose to do in preference to one or more alternatives. *He's argued from the start that America and its allies are putting too much emphasis on the military option... What other options do you have?* N-COUNT =choice

2 If you have the **option** to do something, you can choose whether to do it or not. *Criminals are given the option of going to jail or facing public humiliation... We had no option but to abandon the meeting.* N-SING: oft N of n/-ing, N to-inf =choice

3 In business, an **option** is an agreement or contract that gives someone the right to buy or sell something such as property or shares at a future date. *Each bank has granted the other an option on 19.9% of its shares.* N-COUNT

4 An **option** is one of a number of subjects which a student can choose to study as a part of his or her N-COUNT

course. *Several options are offered for the student's senior year.*

5 If you **keep** your **options open** or **leave** your **options open**, you avoid making an immediate decision about something. *I am keeping my options open. I have not made a decision on either matter.* PHRASES V inflects ≠commit yourself

6 If you say that someone has taken a **soft option**, you mean that they have taken a course of action because it is the easiest thing to do or least likely to produce conflict rather than because it is the best thing to do in the circumstances. *We take the soft option. I like to keep the crowd happy because that's what they pay for... The job of chairman can no longer be regarded as a convenient soft option.* N inflects =easy option

optional /ɒpʃənᵊl/. If something is **optional**, you can choose whether or not you do it or have it. *A holiday isn't an optional extra. In this stressful, frantic world it's a must... Sex education is a sensitive area for some parents, and thus it should remain optional.* ◆◇◇◇◇ ADJ ≠mandatory, compulsory

opt-out, opt-outs ◆◇◇◇◇

1 In Britain, an **opt-out** school or hospital has chosen to leave local government control and manage itself using national government money. *...teachers at opt-out schools.* ADJ: ADJ n

2 In Britain, you can refer to the action taken by a school or hospital in which they choose not to be controlled by a local government authority as an **opt-out**. *More freedom and choice will be given to parents, and the school opt-outs will be stepped up.* N-COUNT

3 An **opt-out** clause in an agreement gives participants the choice not to be involved in one part of that agreement; used mainly in British English. *...an opt-out clause on a single Euro-currency.* ADJ: ADJ n

4 You can refer to the action of choosing not to be involved in a particular part of an agreement as an **opt-out**. *...a list of demands, such as opt-outs from some parts of the treaty.* N-COUNT

opulent /ɒpjʊlənt/ ◆◇◇◇◇

1 **Opulent** things or places look grand and expensive; a formal use. *...an opulent office on Wimpole Street in London's West End.* ♦ **opulence** *...the elegant opulence of the German embassy.* ADJ-GRADED =sumptuous N-UNCOUNT: oft N *of* n

2 **Opulent** people are very wealthy and spend a lot of money; a formal use. *Most of the cash went on supporting his opulent lifestyle.* ADJ-GRADED: usu ADJ n =affluent

opus /oʊpəs, ɒpəs/ **opuses** or **opera** ◆◇◇◇◇

1 An **opus** is a musical composition. **Opus** is usually followed by a number which indicates when the composition was written. The abbreviation 'op.' is also used. *...Beethoven's Piano Sonata in E minor, Opus 90.* N-COUNT: usu N num

2 You can refer to an artistic work such as a piece of music or writing or a painting as an **opus**. *...the new opus from Peter Gabriel.* • See also **magnum opus**. N-COUNT =work

or /əʳ, STRONG ɔːʳ/ ◆◆◆◆◆

1 You use **or** to link two or more alternatives. *'Tea or coffee?' John asked... Was she blonde or brunette?... Spread the inside of the loaf with olive paste or pesto sauce for extra flavour... He said he would try to write or call as soon as he reached the Canary Islands... Students are asked to take another course in English, or science, or mathematics.* CONJ-COORD PRAGMATICS

2 You use **or** to give another alternative, when the first alternative is introduced by 'either' or 'whether'. *Items like bread, milk and meat were either unavailable or could be obtained only on the black market... Either you can talk to him, or I will... I don't know whether people will buy it or not... I am not sure whether I was knocked over by the blast or whether I just fell... The bathroom has taken a lot longer to get right than either Elaine or Dennis had envisaged.* CONJ-COORD PRAGMATICS

3 You use **or** between two numbers to indicate that you are giving an approximate amount. *Everyone benefited from limiting their intake of tea to just three or four cups a day... When I was nine or ten someone explained to me that when you are grown up you have to work... Normally he asked questions, and had a humorous remark or two.* CONJ-COORD

4 You use **or** to introduce a comment which corrects or modifies what you have just said. *The man was a fool, he thought, or at least incompetent... There was nothing more he wanted, or so he thought... That was sporting of him. Or should I say cowardly... She was aware of tension between them. Or had it been there from the beginning?* CONJ-COORD PRAGMATICS

5 If you say that someone should do something **or** something unpleasant will happen, you are warning them that if they do not do it, the unpleasant thing will happen. *She had to have the operation, or she would die.* CONJ-COORD PRAGMATICS =otherwise

6 You use **or** to introduce something which is an explanation or justification for a statement you have just made. *He must have thought Jane was worth it or he wouldn't have wasted time on her, I suppose.* CONJ-COORD PRAGMATICS =otherwise

7 You use **or no** or **or not** to emphasize that a particular thing makes no difference to what is going to happen. *Chairman or no, if I want to stop the project, I can... The first difficulty is that, old-fashioned or not, it is very good.* PHRASES group PHR PRAGMATICS

8 You use **or no** between two occurrences of the same noun in order to say that whether something is true or not makes no difference to a situation. *The next day, rain or no rain, it was business as usual... Oil or no oil, Serbia has troubles.* n PHR n

9 • **or else**: see **else**. • **or other**: see **other**. • **or so**: see **so**. • **or something**: see **something**.

-or /-əʳ/. **-or** is used at the end of nouns that refer to people or things which perform a particular action. *...a major investor. ...the translator. ...an electric generator.* SUFFIX

oracle /ɒrəkᵊl, AM ɔːr-/ **oracles.** In ancient Greece, an **oracle** was a priest or priestess who made statements about future events or about the truth. N-COUNT

oral /ɔːrəl/ **orals** ◆◆◇◇◇

1 **Oral** communication is spoken rather than written. *...the written and oral traditions of ancient cultures. ...an oral agreement.* ♦ **orally** *...their ability to present ideas orally and in writing.* ADJ: usu ADJ n ADV: ADV after v

2 An **oral** is an examination, especially in a foreign language, that is spoken rather than written. *I spoke privately to the candidate after the oral.* N-COUNT

3 You use **oral** to indicate that something is done with a person's mouth or relates to a person's mouth. *...good oral hygiene.* ADJ: usu ADJ n

4 **Oral** medicines are taken by mouth. *...oral contraceptives.* ♦ **orally** *...antibiotic tablets taken orally.* ADJ: ADJ n ADV: usu ADV after v

oral sex. **Oral sex** is sexual activity involving contact between a person's mouth and their partner's genitals. N-UNCOUNT

orange /ɒrɪndʒ, AM ɔːr-/ **oranges** ◆◆◆◇◇

1 Something that is **orange** is of a colour between red and yellow. *...men in bright orange uniforms.* COLOUR

2 An **orange** is a round juicy fruit with a thick, orange coloured skin. *An orange a day will give you all the vitamin C you need. ...orange trees. ...fresh orange juice.* N-VAR: oft N n

3 **Orange** is a drink that is made from or tastes of oranges. *...vodka and orange.* N-UNCOUNT

orange blossom. The flowers of the orange tree are called **orange blossom**. Orange blossom is white and is traditionally associated with weddings in Europe and America. N-UNCOUNT

orangery /ɒrɪndʒri, AM ɔːr-/ **orangeries.** An **orangery** is a building with glass walls and roof which is used for growing orange trees and other plants which need to be kept warm. N-COUNT

orangey /ɒrɪndʒi, AM ɔːr-/. **Orangey** means slightly orange in colour. *He used to have orangey coloured hair.* ► Also a combining form. *The hall is decorated in bright orangey-red with black and gold woodwork.* ADJ-GRADED COMB in COLOUR

orang-outan /ɔːræŋuːtæn/ **orang-outans;** also spelled **orang-utang**. An **orang-outan** is an ape with long reddish hair that comes from Borneo and Sumatra. N-COUNT

oration /əreɪʃən, AM ɔːr-/ **orations.** An **oration** is a formal speech made in public; a formal word. *...a brief funeral oration.* N-COUNT: oft supp N =address

orator /ɒrətəʳ, AM ɔːr-/ **orators.** An **orator** is someone who is skilled at making formal speeches in public which strongly affect people's feelings and beliefs. *Lenin was the great orator of the Russian Revolution.* N-COUNT: oft adj N =public speaker

oratorical /ɒrətɒrɪkəl, AM ɔːrətɔːr-/. **Oratorical** means relating to or using oratory; a formal word. *He reached oratorical heights which left him and some of his players in tears.* ADJ: ADJ n =rhetorical

oratorio /ɒrətɔːrioʊ, AM ɔːr-/ **oratorios.** An **oratorio** is a long piece of music with a religious theme which is written for singers and an orchestra. *...Handel's oratorio 'Samson'.* N-COUNT

oratory /ɒrətəri, AM ɔːrətɔːri/ **oratories**
1 **Oratory** is the art of making formal speeches; a formal use. *He displayed determination as well as powerful oratory.* N-UNCOUNT =rhetoric
2 An **oratory** is a room or building where Christians go to pray. *The wedding will be at the Brompton Oratory next month.* N-COUNT: oft in names

orb /ɔːʳb/ **orbs**
1 An **orb** is something that is shaped like a ball, for example the sun or moon; a literary use. *The moon's round orb would shine high in the sky, casting its velvety light on everything.* N-COUNT =sphere
2 An **orb** is a small, ornamental ball with a cross on top that is carried by a king or queen at important ceremonies. N-COUNT

orbit /ɔːʳbɪt/ **orbits, orbiting, orbited** ◆◆◇◇◇
1 An **orbit** is the curved path in space that is followed by an object going round and round a planet, moon, or star. *Mars and Earth have orbits which change with time... The planet is probably in orbit around a small star.* N-COUNT: also *in/into* N
2 If something such as a satellite **orbits** a planet, moon, or sun, it moves around it in a continuous, curving path. *In 1957 the Soviet Union launched the first satellite to orbit the earth.* VERB =circle V n
3 The **orbit** of a particular person, group, or institution is the area over which they have influence. *In the late 1970s Laos fell within the orbit of Vietnam and the Soviet Union.* N-SING: with supp, oft with poss

orbital /ɔːʳbɪtəl/ ◆◇◇◇◇
1 An **orbital** road goes all the way round a large city. *...a new orbital road round Paris.* ADJ: ADJ n
2 **Orbital** describes things relating to the orbit of an object in space. *The newly discovered world followed an orbital path unlike that of any other planet.* ADJ: ADJ n

orchard /ɔːʳtʃəʳd/ **orchards.** An **orchard** is an area of land on which fruit trees are grown. ◆◇◇◇◇ N-COUNT

orchestra /ɔːʳkɪstrə/ **orchestras.** An **orchestra** is a large group of musicians who play a variety of different instruments together. Orchestras usually play classical music. *...the Royal Liverpool Philharmonic Orchestra.* • See also **chamber orchestra, symphony orchestra.** ◆◆◇◇◇ N-COUNT: oft in names

orchestral /ɔːʳkestrəl/. **Orchestral** means relating to an orchestra and the music it plays. *...an orchestral concert.* ◆◇◇◇◇ ADJ: ADJ n

orchestra pit. In a theatre, the **orchestra pit** is the space reserved for the musicians playing the music for an opera, musical, or ballet, immediately in front of or below the stage. N-SING

orchestrate /ɔːʳkɪstreɪt/ **orchestrates, orchestrating, orchestrated** ◆◇◇◇◇
1 If you say that someone **orchestrates** an event or situation, you mean that they carefully organise it in a way that will produce the particular result that they want. *The colonel was able to orchestrate a rebellion from inside an army jail. ...a carefully orchestrated campaign.* ♦ **orchestration** *...his skilful orchestration of latent nationalist feeling.* VERB =stage-manage V n V-ed N-UNCOUNT
2 When someone **orchestrates** a piece of music, they write the individual parts to be played by the different instruments of an orchestra. *He was orchestrating the second act of his opera.* ♦ **orchestration** *...my first lessons in orchestration.* VERB =arrange V n N-UNCOUNT

orchestration /ɔːʳkɪstreɪʃən/ **orchestrations.** An **orchestration** is a piece of music that has been rewritten so that it can be played by an orchestra. *Mahler's own imaginative orchestration was heard in the same concert.* N-COUNT =arrangement

orchid /ɔːʳkɪd/ **orchids. Orchids** are plants with brightly coloured, unusually shaped flowers. N-COUNT

ordain /ɔʳdeɪn/ **ordains, ordaining, ordained** ◆◇◇◇◇
1 When someone **is ordained**, they are made a member of the clergy in a religious ceremony. *He was ordained a Catholic priest in 1982... Women have been ordained for many years in the Church of Scotland... He ordained his own priests, and threatened to ordain bishops... The church's ruling body voted to ordain women as priests. ...plans to ordain women to the priesthood... He became a fully ordained monk at the age of 20.* VERB be V-ed n be V-ed V n V n as n V n to n V-ed
2 If some authority or power **ordains** something, they decide that it should happen or be in existence; a formal use. *Nehru ordained that socialism should rule... His rule was ordained by heaven... The recession may already be severe enough to ordain structural change.* VERB =decree V that be V-ed V n

ordeal /ɔʳdiːl/ **ordeals.** If you describe an experience or situation as an **ordeal**, you think it is difficult and unpleasant. *...the painful ordeal of the last eight months... She described her agonising ordeal.* ◆◆◇◇◇ N-COUNT: usu sing, oft with poss

order 1 subordinating conjunction uses

order /ɔːʳdəʳ/ ◆◆◆◆◇
1 If you do something **in order to** achieve a particular thing or **in order that** something can happen, you do it because you want to achieve that thing. *Most schools are extremely unwilling to cut down on staff in order to cut costs. ...asking them to risk their lives in order that the rest of us can sleep better.* PHR-CONJ-SUBORD
2 If someone must be in a particular situation **in order to** achieve something they want, they cannot achieve that thing if they are not in that situation. *We need to get rid of the idea that we must be liked all the time in order to be worthwhile... They need hostages in order to bargain with the government.* PHR-CONJ-SUBORD
3 If something must happen **in order for** something else to happen, the second thing cannot happen if the first thing does not happen. *In order for their computers to trace a person's records, they need both the name and address of the individual.* PHR-CONJ-SUBORD: CONJ n to-inf

order 2 commands and requests

order /ɔːʳdəʳ/ **orders, ordering, ordered** ◆◆◆◆◆
1 If someone in authority **orders** someone to do something, they tell them to do it. *Williams ordered him to leave... He ordered the women out of the car... 'Let him go!' he ordered... 'Go up to your room. Now,' he ordered him.* VERB =command V n to-inf V n prep/adv V with quote V n with quote
2 If someone in authority **orders** something, they give instructions that it should be done. *The President has ordered a full investigation... The radio said that the prime minister had ordered price controls to be introduced... He ordered that all party property be confiscated... The President ordered him moved because of fears that his comrades would try to free him.* VERB V n V n to-inf V that V n -ed
3 If someone in authority gives you an **order**, they tell you to do something. *The activists were shot when they refused to obey an order to halt... As darkness fell, Clinton gave orders for his men to rest... I don't take orders from him any more... They were later arrested and executed on the orders of Stalin.* N-COUNT =instruction
4 A court **order** is a legal instruction stating that something must be done. *She has decided not to appeal against a court order banning her from keeping animals... He was placed under a two-year supervision order.* N-COUNT: usu supp N
5 When you **order** something that you are going to pay for, you ask for it to be brought to you, sent to you, or obtained for you. *Atanas ordered a shrimp cocktail and a salad... Iris finally ordered coffees for herself and Tania... The waitress appeared. 'Are you ready to order?'... We ordered him a beer.* VERB V n V n for n V V n n
6 An **order** is a request for something to be brought, made, or obtained for you in return for N-COUNT: oft N for n

money. *British Rail are going to place an order for a hundred and eighty-eight trains.*

7 Someone's **order** is what they have asked to be brought, made, or obtained for them in return for money. *The waiter returned with their order and Graham signed the bill... They can't supply our order.* N-COUNT: poss N

8 See also **holy orders**, **mail order**, **postal order**, **standing order**.

9 Something that is **on order** at a shop or factory has been asked for but has not yet been supplied. *The airlines still have 2,500 new aeroplanes on order.* PHRASES PHR after v, v-link PHR

10 If you do something **to order**, you do it whenever you are asked to do it. *She now makes wonderful dried flower arrangements to order... Cars are stolen to order for clients.* PHR after v

11 If you are **under orders** to do something, you have been told to do it by someone in authority. *I am under orders not to discuss his mission or his location with anyone.* v-link PHR to-inf

12 • your **marching orders**: see **march**. • **a tall order**: see **tall**.

order around or **order about.** The form **order about** is mainly used in British English. If you say that someone **is ordering you around** or **is ordering you about**, you mean they are telling you what to do as if they have authority over you, and you dislike this. *When we're out he gets really bossy and starts ordering me around... Grandmother felt free to order her about just as she wished.* PHRASAL VERB PRAGMATICS =boss around V n P Also V P n (not pron)

order 3 arrangements, situations, and groupings

order /ɔːʳdəʳ/ **orders, ordering, ordered** ◆◆◆◆◇

1 If a set of things are arranged or done in a particular **order**, they are arranged or done so one thing follows another, often according to a particular factor such as importance. *Write down (in order of priority) the qualities you'd like to have... Music shops should arrange their recordings in simple alphabetical order, rather than by category... List the key headings and sort them into a logical order... The chairman has re-arranged the order of the speakers.* N-UNCOUNT: also a N, usu with supp, oft *in/into* N =sequence

2 **Order** is the situation that exists when everything is in a correct or predictable place, or happens at a correct or predictable time. *The wish to impose order upon confusion is a kind of intellectual instinct... Making lists can create order and control.* N-UNCOUNT ≠confusion, chaos

3 **Order** is the situation that exists when people obey the law and do things peacefully, rather than fighting or rioting. *Troops were sent to the islands to restore order last November... He has the power to use force to maintain public order.* N-UNCOUNT

4 When people talk about a particular **order**, they mean the way society is organized at a particular time. *The end of the Cold War has produced the prospect of a new world order based on international co-operation... Some feminists sought reforms within the existing social order.* N-SING: with supp =system

5 The way that something **is ordered** is the way that it is organized and structured. *...a society which is ordered by hierarchy... We know the French order things differently. ...a carefully ordered system in which everyone has his place.* VERB be V-ed V n V-ed

6 If you refer to something of a particular **order**, you mean something of a particular kind; a formal use. *Another unexpected event, though of quite a different order, occurred one evening in 1973... Our commitment will be of the highest order.* N-COUNT: with supp, usu *of* supp N =type

7 A religious **order** is a group of monks or nuns who live according to a particular set of rules. *...the Benedictine order of monks.* N-COUNT

8 People who belong to a particular **order** have been given a particular honour or rank by the head of their country as a reward for their services or achievements. *The highest Order of Knighthood is the Order of the Garter.* N-COUNT

9 The chairman or chairwoman of a meeting or tribunal can say **'Order!'** to tell people to stop causing a disturbance. CONVENTION PRAGMATICS

10 See also **ordered**; **law and order**, **pecking order**, **point of order**.

11 If you put or keep something **in order**, you make sure that it is tidy or properly organized. *Now he has a chance to put his life back in order... It was her job to keep the room in order... Someone comes in every day to check all is in order.* PHRASES PHR after v, v-link PHR

12 If you think something is **in order**, you think it should happen or be provided. *Reforms are clearly in order... It's great to have you back. Congratulations are surely in order!* v-link PHR

13 You use **in the order of** or **of the order of** when mentioning an approximate figure. *They borrowed something in the order of £10 million... At other times the discrepancy was of the order of 20%.* PREP: PREP amount

14 If something is **in good order**, it is in good condition. *The vessel's safety equipment was not in good order.* v-link PHR

15 A machine or device that is **in working order** is functioning properly and is not broken. *Only half of the spacecraft's six science instruments are still in working order.* v-link PHR

16 If a particular way of behaving or doing something is **the order of the day**, it is very common. *These are strange times in which we live, and strange arrangements appear to be the order of the day.* v-link PHR

17 A machine or device that is **out of order** is broken and does not work. *Their phone's out of order.* v-link PHR ≠working

18 If you say that someone or their behaviour is **out of order**, you mean that their behaviour is unacceptable or unfair; an informal use. *You don't think the paper's a bit out of order in publishing it?* v-link PHR PRAGMATICS

19 • to **put your house in order**: see **house**. • **order of magnitude**: see **magnitude**.

order book, order books. When you talk about the state of a company's **order book** or **order books**, you are talking about how many orders for their goods the company has; used mainly in British English. *He has a full order book for his boat-building yard on the Thames.* N-COUNT

ordered /ɔːʳdəʳd/. An **ordered** society or system is well-organized and has a clear structure. *An objective set of rules which we all agree to accept is necessary for any ordered society.* ADJ-GRADED: usu ADJ n ≠chaotic

orderly /ɔːʳdəʳli/ **orderlies** ◆◇◇◇◇

1 If something is done in an **orderly** fashion or manner, it is done in a well organized and controlled way. *The organizers guided them in orderly fashion out of the building... Despite the violence that preceded the elections, reports say that polling was orderly and peaceful.* ADJ-GRADED ≠chaotic

2 Something that is **orderly** is neat and well-arranged. *It's a beautiful, clean and orderly city... Their vehicles were parked in orderly rows.* ♦ **orderliness** *A balance is achieved in the painting between orderliness and unpredictability.* ADJ-GRADED N-UNCOUNT

3 An **orderly** is a person who works in a hospital and does jobs that do not require any special training. N-COUNT: oft supp N

ordinal number /ɔːʳdɪnəl nʌmbəʳ/ **ordinal numbers.** An **ordinal number** or an **ordinal** is a word such as 'first', 'third', and 'tenth' that tells you where a particular thing occurs in a sequence of things. Compare **cardinal number**. N-COUNT

ordinance /ɔːʳdɪnəns/ **ordinances.** An **ordinance** is an official rule or order; a formal word. *...ordinances that restrict building development.* ◆◇◇◇◇ N-COUNT =regulation

ordinand /ɔːʳdɪnænd/ **ordinands.** An **ordinand** is someone who is being trained to be a priest. N-COUNT

ordinarily /ɔːʳdɪnərəli, AM -nerɪli/. If you say what is **ordinarily** the case, you are saying what is normally the case. *The streets would ordinarily have been full of people. There was no one... Similar arrangements apply to students who are ordinarily resident in Scotland. ...places where the patient does not ordinarily go.* ◆◇◇◇◇ ADV: usu ADV with cl, also ADV adj, ADV before v =normally

ordinary /ɔːʳdɪnri, AM -neri/ ◆◆◆◇◇

1 **Ordinary** people or things are normal and not special or different in any way. *I strongly suspect that most ordinary people would agree with me... It has 25 calories less than ordinary ice cream... It was just an ordinary weekend for us.* ADJ-GRADED: usu ADJ n =normal ≠unusual

2 If you describe someone or something as ADJ-GRADED

ordinary, you mean they are not special or interesting in any way and may be rather dull. *I'm just a very ordinary, boring normal guy... Your life since then must have seemed very ordinary. ...very ordinary, if very well made, drinking glasses, lamps and tableware.*

3 Something that is **out of the ordinary** is unusual or different. *The boy's knowledge was out of the ordinary... I've noticed nothing out of the ordinary.* PHRASE: usu v-link PHR =unusual

ordination /ɔːʳdɪneɪʃᵊn/ **ordinations.** When someone's **ordination** takes place, they are made a member of the clergy. *...supporters of the ordination of women. ...the process of selecting candidates for ordination.* ◆◇◇◇◇ N-VAR

ordnance /ɔːʳdnəns/. **Ordnance** refers to military supplies, especially weapons. *...a team clearing an area littered with unexploded ordnance. ...the Royal Ordnance factory at Chorley.* ◆◇◇◇◇ N-UNCOUNT =munitions

Ordnance Survey map, Ordnance Survey maps. An **Ordnance Survey map** is a map produced by the British or Irish government map-making organization. Ordnance Survey maps are usually very detailed. N-COUNT

ore /ɔːʳ/ **ores. Ore** is rock or earth from which metal can be obtained. *...a huge iron ore mine.* ◆◇◇◇◇ N-MASS

oregano /ɒrɪgɑːnoʊ, AM ərегənoʊ/. **Oregano** is a herb that is used in cooking. N-UNCOUNT

organ /ɔːʳgən/ **organs** ◆◆◇◇◇

1 An **organ** is a part of your body that has a particular purpose or function, for example your heart or lungs. *...damage to the muscles and internal organs. ...the reproductive organs. ...organ transplants.* • See also **sense organ.** N-COUNT

2 An **organ** is a large musical instrument with pipes of different lengths through which air is forced. It has keys and pedals rather like a piano. • See also **barrel organ, mouth organ.** N-COUNT

3 You refer to a newspaper or organization as the **organ** of the government or another group when it is used by them as a means of giving information or getting things done. *...according to the People's Daily, the official organ of the Chinese communist party... The most powerful organ of government in Scotland is the Scottish Office.* N-COUNT: usu with supp =mouthpiece

organdie /ɔːʳgəndi/; also spelled **organdy**. **Organdie** is a thin, slightly stiff cotton fabric. N-UNCOUNT: oft N n

organ grinder, organ grinders; also spelled **organ-grinder**. An **organ grinder** was an entertainer who played a barrel organ in the streets. N-COUNT

organic /ɔːʳgænɪk/ ◆◆◇◇◇

1 **Organic** methods of farming and gardening use only natural animal and plant products to fertilize the land and control pests and diseases, rather than using chemicals. *Organic farming is expanding everywhere. ...organic fruit and vegetables.* ♦ **organically** *...organically grown vegetables.* ADJ: usu ADJ n; ADV

2 **Organic** substances are of the sort produced by or found in living things. *Incorporating organic material into chalky soils will reduce the alkalinity.* ADJ: usu ADJ n ≠inorganic

3 **Organic** change or development happens gradually and naturally rather than suddenly; a formal use. *...to manage the company and supervise its organic growth.* ADJ: usu ADJ n

4 If a community or structure is an **organic** whole, each part of it is necessary and is in harmony with the other parts; a formal use. *City planning treats the city as a unit, as an organic whole.* ADJ: ADJ n

organisation /ɔːʳgənaɪzeɪʃᵊn/. See **organization.**

organisational /ɔːʳgənaɪzeɪʃənᵊl/. See **organizational.**

organise /ɔːʳgənaɪz/. See **organize.**

organiser /ɔːʳgənaɪzəʳ/. See **organizer.**

organism /ɔːʳgənɪzəm/ **organisms.** An **organism** is an animal or plant, especially one that is so small that you cannot see it without using a microscope. *Not all chemicals normally present in living organisms are harmless. ...the insect-borne organisms that cause sleeping sickness.* ◆◆◇◇◇ N-COUNT

organist /ɔːʳgənɪst/ **organists.** An **organist** is someone who plays the organ. N-COUNT

organization /ɔːʳgənaɪzeɪʃᵊn/ **organizations;** also spelled **organisation.** ◆◆◆◆◇

1 An **organization** is an official group of people, for example a political party, a business, a charity, or a club. *Most of these specialized schools are provided by voluntary organizations. ...a report by the International Labour Organisation.* N-COUNT: oft in names

2 The **organization** of an event or activity involves making all the necessary arrangements for it. *...the exceptional attention to detail that goes into the organisation of this event... Several projects have been delayed by poor organisation.* N-UNCOUNT

3 The **organization** of something is the way in which its different parts are arranged or relate to each other. *I am aware that the organization of the book leaves something to be desired.* N-UNCOUNT: usu with supp, oft N of n

organizational /ɔːʳgənaɪzeɪʃənᵊl/; also spelled **organisational.** ◆◇◇◇◇

1 **Organizational** abilities and methods relate to the way that work, activities, or events are planned and arranged. *Evelyn's excellent organisational skills were soon spotted by her employers... Because we took the whole class for a complete afternoon session, organisational problems were minimal.* ADJ: ADJ n

2 **Organizational** means relating to the structure of an organization. *The police now recognise that big organisational changes are needed. ...the organizational structure of British trade unions.* ADJ: ADJ n

3 **Organizational** means relating to organizations, rather than individuals. *This problem needs to be dealt with at an organizational level... There was no strong organizational base on which to build.* ADJ: ADJ n

organize /ɔːʳgənaɪz/ **organizes, organizing, organized;** also spelled **organise** in British English. ◆◆◆◆◇

1 If you **organize** an event or activity, you make sure that the necessary arrangements are made. *In the end, we all decided to organize a concert for Easter. ...a two-day meeting organised by the United Nations... The initial mobilisation was well organised.* VERB =arrange V n

2 If you **organize** something that someone wants or needs, you make sure that it is provided. *I will organize transport... He rang his wife and asked her to organize coffee and sandwiches.* VERB V n

3 If you **organize** a set of things, you arrange them in an ordered way or give them a structure. *He began to organize his materials... She took a hasty cup of coffee and tried to organize her scattered thoughts. ...the way in which the Army is organised.* VERB V n

4 If you **organize** yourself, you plan your work and activities in an ordered, efficient way. *...changing the way you organize yourself... Go right ahead, I'm sure you don't need me to organize you... Get organised and get going.* VERB V pron-refl V n V-ed

5 If someone **organizes** workers or if workers **organize**, they form a group or society such as a trade union in order to have more power. *...helping to organize women working abroad... It's the first time farmers have decided to organize. ...organised labour.* V-ERG V n V V-ed

organized /ɔːʳgənaɪzd/; also spelled **organised.** ◆◆◆◇◇

1 An **organized** activity or group involves a number of people doing something together in a structured way, rather than doing it by themselves. *...organised groups of art thieves. ...organised religion. ...years of steadfast, organized resistance.* ADJ: ADJ n

2 Someone who is **organized** plans their work and activities efficiently. *These people are very efficient, very organized and excellent time managers.* ADJ-GRADED ≠disorganized

-organized /-ɔːʳgənaɪzd/

-organized is added to nouns to form adjectives which indicate who organizes something. *...student-organized seminars.* COMB in ADJ: ADJ n

organized crime; also spelled **organised crime**. **Organized crime** refers to criminal activity such as the production and sale of illegal drugs which involves large numbers of people and is centrally organized. *...the battle being waged against organised crime.* ◆◇◇◇◇ N-UNCOUNT

organizer /ɔːʳgənaɪzəʳ/ **organizers;** also spelled **organiser**. The **organizer** of an event or activity ◆◆◇◇◇ N-COUNT

is the person who makes sure that the necessary arrangements are made. *The organisers of the demonstration concede that they hadn't sought permission for it. ...Jack Cunningham, Labour's campaign organiser... She was a good organiser.*
• See also **personal organizer**.

organza /ɔːˈgænzə/. **Organza** is a thin, stiff fabric made of silk, cotton, or an artificial fibre. N-UNCOUNT: oft N n

orgasm /ɔːˈgæzəm/ **orgasms.** An **orgasm** is the moment of greatest pleasure and excitement in sexual activity. ◆◇◇◇◇ N-VAR

orgasmic /ɔːˈgæzmɪk/
1 **Orgasmic** means relating to a sexual orgasm. *Testosterone does not increase their erectile or orgasmic ability.* ADJ: usu ADJ n
2 Some people refer to things they find extremely enjoyable or exciting as **orgasmic**; used especially in informal journalism. *...jerking the neck of his guitar in orgasmic fits of ecstasy.* ADJ: usu ADJ n

orgiastic /ɔːdʒiˈæstɪk/. An **orgiastic** event is one in which people enjoy themselves in an extreme, uncontrolled way. *...an orgiastic party.* ADJ: ADJ n =riotous

orgy /ɔːdʒi/ **orgies** ◆◇◇◇◇
1 An **orgy** is a party in which people behave in a very uncontrolled way, especially one involving sexual activity. *It was reminiscent of a scene from a Roman orgy. ...a drunken orgy.* N-COUNT
2 You can refer to an activity as an **orgy** of that activity to emphasize that it is done to an excessive extent. *One eye-witness said the rioters were engaged in an orgy of destruction... He blew £43,000 in an 18-month orgy of spending.* N-COUNT: with supp, usu N of n PRAGMATICS =frenzy

orient /ɔːrient/ **orients, orienting, oriented;** the form **orientate** is also used. ◆◇◇◇◇
1 When you **orient** yourself to a new situation or course of action, you learn about it and prepare to deal with it; a formal use. *You will need the time to orient yourself to your new way of eating. ...orienting students to new ways of thinking about their participation in classroom learning... Anxiety comes from not being able to orient yourself in your own existence.* VERB =accustom V pron-refl towards/to n/-ing V n towards/to n/-ing V pron-refl
2 When you **orient** yourself, you find out exactly where you are and which direction you are facing in. *She lay still for a few seconds, trying to orient herself.* VERB V pron-refl
3 See also **oriented**.

Orient /ɔːriənt/. The eastern part of Asia is sometimes referred to as **the Orient**; a literary or old-fashioned word. ◆◇◇◇◇ N-PROPER: the N =East

oriental /ɔːrientəl/ **orientals** ◆◆◇◇◇
1 **Oriental** means coming from or associated with eastern Asia, especially China and Japan. *There were Oriental carpets on the floors. ...oriental food.* ADJ: usu ADJ n =eastern ≠western
2 Some people refer to people from eastern Asia, especially China or Japan as **Orientals**; a use which some people find offensive. *The Orientals use no butter. They prefer the very healthful peanut oil.* N-COUNT

orientalist /ɔːrientəlɪst/ **orientalists.** An **orientalist** is someone from the West who studies the language, culture, history, or customs of countries in eastern Asia. N-COUNT

orientate /ɔːrianteɪt/. See **orient**.

orientated /ɔːrianteɪtɪd/. See **oriented**.

-orientated /-ɔːrianteɪtɪd/. **-orientated** means the same as **-oriented**. COMB in ADJ-GRADED

orientation /ɔːrianteɪʃən/ **orientations** ◆◆◇◇◇
1 If you talk about the **orientation** of an organization or country, you are talking about the kinds of aims and interests it has. *...a marketing orientation... To a society which has lost its orientation he has much to offer... The movement is liberal and social democratic in orientation.* N-VAR: with supp =inclination
2 Someone's **orientation** is their basic beliefs or preferences. *...legislation that would have made discrimination on the basis of sexual orientation illegal.* N-VAR: supp N =inclination
3 **Orientation** is basic information or training that is given to people starting a new job or course. *They give their new employees a day or two of perfunctory orientation. ...a one-day orientation session.* N-UNCOUNT: oft N n =induction
4 The **orientation** of a structure or object is the direction it faces. *Farnese had the orientation of the church changed so that the front would face a square.* N-COUNT: usu with poss

oriented /ɔːrientɪd/; the form **orientated** is also used. If someone **is oriented towards** or **oriented to** a particular thing or person, they are mainly concerned with that thing or person. *It seems almost inevitable that North African economies will still be primarily oriented towards Europe... Most students here are oriented to computers.* ◆◆◇◇◇ ADJ-GRADED: v-link ADJ towards/to n

-oriented /-ɔːrientɪd/; the form **-orientated** is also used. **-oriented** is added to nouns and adverbs to form adjectives which describe what someone or something is primarily interested or concerned with. *...a market-oriented economy. ...family oriented holidays. ...politically-oriented music.* COMB in ADJ-GRADED

orienteering /ɔːrientɪərɪŋ/. **Orienteering** is a sport in which people run from one place to another, using a compass and a map to guide them between points that are marked along the route. N-UNCOUNT

orifice /ɒrɪfɪs, AM ɔːr-/ **orifices.** An **orifice** is an opening or hole, especially one in your body such as your mouth; a formal word. *After a massive heart attack, he was strapped to a bed, with tubes in every orifice.* N-COUNT

origami /ɒrɪgɑːmi, AM ɔːr-/. **Origami** is the craft of folding paper to make models of animals, people, and objects. N-UNCOUNT

origin /ɒrɪdʒɪn, AM ɔːr-/ **origins** ◆◆◆◇◇
1 You can refer to the beginning, cause, or source of something as its **origin** or **origins**. *...theories about the origin of life... The disorder in military policy had its origins in Truman's first term... Their medical problems are basically physical in origin... Most of the thickeners are of plant origin.* N-COUNT: usu with poss, also in/of N
2 When you talk about a person's **origin** or **origins**, you are referring to the country, race, or social class of their parents or ancestors. *Thomas has not forgotten his humble origins. ...people of Asian origin... They are forced to return to their country of origin.* N-COUNT: usu poss N, also of/in N

original /ərɪdʒɪnəl/ **originals** ◆◆◆◆◇
1 You use **original** when referring to something that existed at the beginning of a process or activity, or the characteristics that something had when it began or was made. *The original plan was to hold an indefinite stoppage... The inhabitants have voted overwhelmingly to restore the city's original name of Chemnitz.* ADJ: det ADJ
2 If something such as a document, a work of art, or a piece of writing is an **original**, it is not a copy or a later version. *When you have filled in the questionnaire, copy it and send the original to your employer... For once the sequel is as good as the original.* N-COUNT ≠copy
3 An **original** document or work of art is not a copy. *...an original movie poster.* ADJ: usu ADJ n =genuine
4 An **original** piece of writing or music was written recently and has not been published or performed before. *...its policy of commissioning original work. ...with catchy original songs by Richard Warner.* ADJ: usu ADJ n
5 If you describe someone or their work as **original**, you mean that they are very imaginative and have new ideas. *It is one of the most original works of imagination in the language. ...an original writer. ...a chef with an original touch and a measure of inspiration.* ♦ **originality** /ərɪdʒɪnælɪti/ *He was capable of writing things of startling originality.* ADJ-GRADED =creative N-UNCOUNT =inventiveness
6 If you read or sing something **in the original** or, for example, **in the original French**, you read or sing it in the language it was written in, rather than a translation. *He read every book or author it deals with, often in the original... The texts were sung in the original Italian.* PHRASE: PHR after v

originally /ərɪdʒɪnəli/. When you say what happened or was the case **originally**, you are saying what happened or was the case when something began or came into existence, often to contrast it with what happened later. *The plane has been kept in service far longer than originally intended... France originally refused to sign the treaty...* ◆◆◆◇◇ ADV: ADV with v, ADV with cl/group =initially

The castle was originally surrounded by a triple wall, only one of which remains.

original sin. According to some Christians, **original sin** is the wickedness that all human beings are born with, because the first human beings, Adam and Eve, disobeyed God. N-UNCOUNT

originate /ərɪdʒɪneɪt/ **originates, originating, originated.** ◆◆◇◇◇ V-ERG When something **originates** or when someone **originates** it, it begins to happen or exist; a formal word. *The disease originated in Africa... All carbohydrates originate from plants... I suppose no one has any idea who originated the story?* V prep/adv; V n

originator /ərɪdʒɪneɪtə/ **originators.** The **originator** of something such as an idea or scheme is the person who first thought of it or began it; a formal word. *...the originator of the theory of relativity.* N-COUNT: usu with poss =author

ornament /ɔːʳnəmənt/ **ornaments** ◆◇◇◇◇

1 An **ornament** is an attractive object that you display in your home, or your garden. *...a shelf containing a few photographs and ornaments. ...Christmas tree ornaments.* N-COUNT

2 Pieces of jewellery are sometimes referred to as **ornaments**; a formal use. *I guessed he was the chief because he wore more gold ornaments than the others.* N-COUNT: usu with supp =jewellery

3 Decorations and patterns on a building or a piece of furniture can be referred to as **ornament**; a formal use. *...walls of glass overlaid with ornament.* N-UNCOUNT

ornamental /ɔːʳnəmentᵊl/ ◆◇◇◇◇

1 **Ornamental** things have no practical function but are put in a place because they look attractive. *...ornamental trees.* ADJ: usu ADJ n =decorative

2 Something that is **ornamental** is attractive and decorative. *...ornamental plaster mouldings.* ADJ-GRADED

ornamentation /ɔːʳnəmenteɪʃᵊn/. Decorations and patterns can be referred to as **ornamentation**; a formal word. *The chairs were comfortable, functional and free of ornamentation.* N-UNCOUNT =decoration

ornamented /ɔːʳnəmentɪd/. If something is **ornamented** with attractive objects or patterns, it is decorated with them. *It had a high ceiling, ornamented with plaster fruits and flowers.* ADJ-GRADED: oft ADJ *with* n

ornate /ɔʳneɪt/. ◆◇◇◇◇ An **ornate** building, piece of furniture, or object is decorated with complicated patterns or carvings. *...an ornate iron staircase. ...the big dining-room with its massive fireplace and ornate ceiling.* ADJ-GRADED =elaborate ≠plain ♦ **ornately** *...the ornately carved doors.* ADV-GRADED: usu ADV -ed =elaborately

ornery /ɔːʳnəri/. In informal American English, if you describe someone as **ornery**, you mean that they are bad-tempered, difficult, and often do mean things. *The old lady was still being ornery, but at least she had consented to this visit.* ADJ-GRADED PRAGMATICS =mean, cantankerous

ornithology /ɔːʳnɪθɒlədʒi/. **Ornithology** is the study of birds; a formal word. N-UNCOUNT ♦ **ornithological** /ɔːʳnɪθəlɒdʒɪkᵊl/ *...the Hampshire Ornithological Society.* ADJ: ADJ n ♦ **ornithologist, ornithologists** *That area is an ornithologist's paradise.* N-COUNT

orphan /ɔːʳfən/ **orphans, orphaned** ◆◇◇◇◇

1 An **orphan** is a child whose parents are dead. *I'm an orphan and pretty much grew up on my own. ...the orphan girl he smuggled out of Bosnia.* N-COUNT

2 If a child **is orphaned**, their parents die, or their remaining parent dies. *Jones was orphaned at the age of ten, and taken in by next-door neighbours... By the end of the decade, some ten million children are expected to have been orphaned by the disease. ...a fifteen-year-old boy left orphaned by the recent disaster.* V-PASSIVE: no cont; *be* V-ed; V-ed

orphanage /ɔːʳfənɪdʒ/ **orphanages.** ◆◇◇◇◇ An **orphanage** is a place where orphans live and are looked after. N-COUNT

orthodontist /ɔːʳθədɒntɪst/ **orthodontists.** An **orthodontist** is a dentist who corrects the position of people's teeth. N-COUNT

orthodox /ɔːʳθədɒks/; also spelled **Orthodox** for meaning 3. ◆◆◇◇◇

1 **Orthodox** beliefs, methods, or systems are ones which are accepted or used by most people. *Payne gained a reputation for sound, if orthodox, views... Many of these ideas are now being incorporated into orthodox medical treatment. ...orthodox police methods.* ADJ-GRADED =conventional ≠unorthodox

2 If you describe someone as **orthodox**, you mean that they hold the older and more traditional ideas of their religion or party. *...orthodox Jews. ...orthodox communists.* ADJ: usu ADJ n =traditional

3 The **Orthodox** churches are Christian churches in Eastern Europe which separated from the western church in the eleventh century. *...the Greek Orthodox Church.* ADJ

orthodoxy /ɔːʳθədɒksi/ **orthodoxies** ◆◇◇◇◇

1 An **orthodoxy** is an accepted view about something. *These ideas rapidly became the new orthodoxy in linguistics... He broke from prevailing orthodoxies and asked the awkward questions... What was once a novel approach had become orthodoxy.* N-VAR

2 The old, traditional beliefs of a religion, political party, or philosophy can be referred to as **orthodoxy**. *...the latest step in a purge of liberals and a return to Marxist orthodoxy. ...a conflict between Nat's religious orthodoxy and Rube's belief that his mission is to make money.* N-UNCOUNT: also N in pl =traditionalism

orthopaedic /ɔːʳθəpiːdɪk/; also spelled **orthopedic**. **Orthopaedic** means relating to problems affecting people's joints and spines; a medical term. *...an orthopaedic surgeon. ...orthopedic shoes.* ADJ: ADJ n

-ory /-əri/

1 **-ory** is added in place of the '-e' at the end of some verbs and nouns in order to form adjectives. For example, advise -- advisory, sense -- sensory. SUFFIX

2 **-ory** is added in place of the '-ion' at the end of some uncountable nouns in order to form adjectives. For example, illusion -- illusory, exploration -- exploratory. SUFFIX

oscillate /ɒsɪleɪt/ **oscillates, oscillating, oscillated** ◆◇◇◇◇

1 If an object **oscillates**, it moves repeatedly from one position to another and back again, or keeps getting bigger and smaller; a technical use in physics. *I checked to see if the needle indicating volume was oscillating.* VERB; V ♦ **oscillation** /ɒsɪleɪʃᵊn/ **oscillations** *Some oscillation of the fuselage had been noticed on early flights.* N-VAR

2 If something **oscillates** between one amount or value and another, there is a frequent or regular increase or decrease in it or in its value; a technical use in physics, statistics, or economics. *The lira oscillated between 840 and 850 lire to the mark... Oil markets oscillated on the day's reports from Geneva. ...an oscillating signal of microwave frequency.* VB: no passive =fluctuate; V *between* pl-amount; V; V-ing ♦ **oscillation, oscillations** *There have always been slight oscillations in world temperature.* N-VAR

3 If you **oscillate** between two moods, attitudes, or types of behaviour, you keep changing from one to the other and back again; a formal use. *The president of the Republic oscillated between a certain audacity and a prudent realism.* VB: no passive; V *between* n *and* n ♦ **oscillation** *...that perpetual oscillation between despair and distracted joy.* N-UNCOUNT =variation

osmosis /ɒsmoʊsɪs/

1 **Osmosis** is the process by which a liquid passes through a thin piece of solid substance such as the roots of a plant; a technical use in science. *...the processes of diffusion and osmosis.* N-UNCOUNT

2 If you say that people influence each other by **osmosis**, or that skills are gained by **osmosis**, you mean that this is done gradually and without any obvious effort. *She allowed her life to be absorbed by his, taking on as if by osmosis his likes and dislikes.* N-UNCOUNT: usu *by/through* N

ossify /ɒsɪfaɪ/ **ossifies, ossifying, ossified.** If an idea, system, or organization **ossifies** or if something **ossifies** it, it becomes fixed and difficult to change; a formal word, used showing disapproval. *It reckons that rationing would ossify the farm industry... Mary kept the old man from ossifying by stimulating his natural rebelliousness. ...an ossified institution.* V-ERG PRAGMATICS =fossilize; V n; V; V-ed; Also V *into* n

ostensible /ɒstensɪbəl/. **Ostensible** is used to describe something that seems to be true or is officially stated to be true, but about which you or other people have doubts; a formal word. *The ostensible purpose of these meetings was to gather information on financial strategies.* ♦ **ostensibly** /ɒstensɪbli/ *...ostensibly independent organisations... A bachelor farmer began to call, ostensibly to talk to her father, but really to see her.* ◆◇◇◇◇ ADJ: ADJ n =alleged; ADV: usu ADV with cl/group

ostentation /ɒstenteɪʃən/. If you describe someone's behaviour as **ostentation**, you are criticizing them for doing things or buying things purely in order to impress people; a formal word. *Consumers are abandoning the excess and ostentation of the 1980s... On the whole she had lived modestly, with a notable lack of ostentation.* N-UNCOUNT PRAGMATICS

ostentatious /ɒstenteɪʃəs/ ◆◇◇◇◇

1 If you describe something as **ostentatious**, you disapprove of it because it is expensive and is intended to impress people; a formal use. *...his house, which, however elaborate, is less ostentatious than the preserves of other Dallas tycoons. ...an ostentatious wedding reception.* ADJ-GRADED PRAGMATICS

2 If you describe someone as **ostentatious**, you disapprove of them because they want to impress people with their wealth or importance; a formal use. *Obviously he had plenty of money and was generous in its use without being ostentatious... She's got a lovely way with language without ever sounding ostentatious.* ♦ **ostentatiously** *Her servants were similarly, if less ostentatiously attired.* ADJ-GRADED; ADV-GRADED

3 You can describe an action or behaviour as **ostentatious** when it is done in an exaggerated way to attract people's attention. *His wife was fairly quiet but she is not an ostentatious person anyway.* ♦ **ostentatiously** *Harry stopped under a street lamp and ostentatiously began inspecting the contents of his bag.* ADJ-GRADED: usu ADJ n =conspicuous; ADV-GRADED: usu ADV with v

osteopath /ɒstiəpæθ/ **osteopaths.** An **osteopath** is a person who treats illnesses by massaging people's bodies and bending them in different ways, especially in order to reduce pain or stiffness. N-COUNT

osteoporosis /ɒstioupərousɪs/. **Osteoporosis** is a condition in which your bones lose calcium and become more likely to break. ◆◇◇◇◇ N-UNCOUNT

ostracism /ɒstrəsɪzəm/. **Ostracism** is the state of being ostracized or the act of ostracizing someone; a formal word. *...those who have decided to risk social ostracism and stay on the wrong side of town. ...denunciation, tougher sanctions and ostracism from the civilised world.* N-UNCOUNT

ostracize /ɒstrəsaɪz/ **ostracizes, ostracizing, ostracized;** also spelled **ostracise** in British English. If someone **is ostracized**, people deliberately behave in an unfriendly way towards them and do not allow them to take part in any of their social activities; a formal word. *She claims she's being ostracized by some members of her local community.* VB: usu passive; be V-ed

ostrich /ɒstrɪtʃ, AM ɔːst-/ **ostriches.** An **ostrich** is a very large African bird that cannot fly. ◆◇◇◇◇ N-COUNT

other /ʌðər/ **others** ◆◆◆◆◆

When **other** follows the determiner **an**, it is written as one word: see **another**.

1 You use **other** to refer to an additional thing or person of the same type as one that has been mentioned or is known about. *They were just like any other young couple... The communique gave no other details.* ► Also a pronoun. *Four crewmen were killed, one other was injured... In 1914 he (like so many others) lied about his age so that he could join the war effort.* ADJ: det ADJ, ADJ n; PRON

2 You use **other** when you want to indicate that something or someone is not the thing or person already mentioned, but something or someone else. *The authorities insist that the discussions must not be linked to any other issue... Calls cost 36p per minute cheap rate and 48p per minute at all other times... He would have to accept it; there was no other way... They will then have more money to spend on other things.* ► Also a pronoun. *This issue, more than any other, has divided her cabinet... Some of these methods will work. Others will not.* ADJ: det ADJ, ADJ n; PRON

3 You use **other** to refer to the second of two things or people when the identity of the first is already known or understood, or has already been mentioned. *The Captain was at the other end of the room... You deliberately went in the other direction... Half of PML's scientists have first degrees, the other half have Phds.* ► Also a pronoun. *Almost everybody had a cigarette in one hand and a martini in the other... While one of them tried to put his hand in my pocket, the other held me from behind.* ADJ: det ADJ; PRON: the PRON

4 You use **other** at the end of a list or a group of examples, to refer generally to people or things like the ones just mentioned. *Queensway Quay will incorporate shops, restaurants and other amenities... Place them in a jam jar, porcelain bowl, or other similar container.* ► Also a pronoun. *Descartes received his stimulus from the new physics and astronomy of Copernicus, Galileo, and others.* ADJ: det ADJ, ADJ n; PRON

5 You use **other** to refer to the rest of the people or things in a group, when you are talking about one particular person or thing. *When the other pupils were taken to an exhibition, he was left behind... The United States, in company with other nations, was urging the Burmese military leadership to respond to the election results.* ► Also a pronoun. *Aubrey's on his way here, with the others.* ADJ: det ADJ, ADJ n; PRON: the PRON

6 **Other** people are people in general, excluding yourself or the particular person you have mentioned. *The suffering of other people appals me... She likes to be with other people.* ► **Others** means the same as **other people**. *His humour depended on contempt for others.* ADJ: ADJ n; PRON

7 You use **other** in informal expressions of time such as **the other day**, **the other evening**, or **the other week** to refer to a day, evening, or week in the recent past. *I rang her the other day and she said she'd like to come round... The other evening we had a party.* ADJ: the ADJ n

8 You use expressions like **among other** things or **among others** to indicate that there are several more facts, things, or people like the one or ones mentioned, but that you do not intend to mention them all. *He moved to England in 1980 where, among other things, he worked as a journalist... His travels took him to Dublin, among other places... He is expected to be supported at the meeting by Dennis Skinner and Tony Benn among others.* PHRASES PHR with cl, oft PHR n PRAGMATICS

9 If something happens, for example, **every other day** or **every other month**, it does not happen every day or month, but on one day or in one month and then every second day or month after that. *Their food is adequate. It includes meat at least every other day, vegetables and fruit... Now that their children have grown up she joins Paddy in London every other week.* usu PHR after v

10 You use **every other** to emphasize that you are referring to all the rest of the people or things in a group. *The same will apply in every other country.* PHR n PRAGMATICS

11 You use **none other than** and **no other than** to emphasize the name of a person or thing when something about that person or thing is surprising in a particular situation. *He called together all his employees and announced that the manager was none other than his son.* PHR n PRAGMATICS

12 You use **nothing other than** and **no other than** when you are going to mention a course of action, decision, or description and emphasize that it is the only one possible in the situation. *Nothing other than an immediate custodial sentence could be justified... The rebels would not be happy with anything other than the complete removal of the current regime... They have left us with no other choice than to take formal action.* PHR n PRAGMATICS

13 You use **or other** in expressions like **somehow or other** and **someone or other** to indicate that you cannot or do not want to be more precise about the information that you are giving. *I was going to have him called away from the house on some pretext or other... The Foundation is holding a* n/adv PHR

dinner in honour of something or other... Somehow or other he's involved.

14 You use **other than** after a negative statement to say that the person, item, or thing that follows is the only exception to the statement. *She makes no reference to any feminist work other than her own... The journey by road to Wolverhampton is not recommended to anyone other than the most experienced cyclist.*
with brd-neg, PHR n/-ing =apart from, except

15 • **each other**: see **each**. • your **other half**: see **half.** • **one after the other**: see **one.** • **one or other**: see **one.** • **this, that and the other**: see **this.** • **in other words**: see **word.**

otherness /ʌðəʳnəs/. **Otherness** is the quality that someone or something has which is different from yourself or from the things that you have experienced. *I like the otherness of men's minds and bodies.*
N-UNCOUNT

otherwise /ʌðəʳwaɪz/ ◆◆◆◆◇

1 You use **otherwise** after stating a situation or fact, in order to say what the result or consequence would be if this situation or fact was not the case. *Make a note of the questions you want to ask. You will invariably forget some of them otherwise... I'm lucky that I'm interested in school work, otherwise I'd go mad. ...men who want to provide positive role models for kids who might otherwise be out on the streets.*
ADV: ADV with cl

2 You use **otherwise** before stating the general condition or quality of something, when you are also mentioning an exception to this general condition or quality. *The decorations for the games have lent a splash of colour to an otherwise drab city. ...a blue and gold caravan, slightly travel-stained but otherwise in good condition.*
ADV: ADV group

3 You use **otherwise** to refer in a general way to actions or situations that are very different from, or the opposite to, your main statement; used in written English. *Take approximately 60mg up to four times a day, unless advised otherwise by a doctor... There is no way anything would ever happen between us, and believe me I've tried to convince myself otherwise... All photographs are by the author unless otherwise stated.*
ADV: ADV with v

4 You use **otherwise** to indicate that other ways of doing something are possible in addition to the way already mentioned. *The studio could punish its players by keeping them out of work, and otherwise controlling their lives.*
ADV: ADV before v

5 You use **or otherwise** or **and otherwise** to refer to something which contrasts with the preceding word. *It was for the police to assess the validity or otherwise of the evidence... He didn't want company, talkative or otherwise... Many thousands of foreigners, diplomats and otherwise are still being held against their will.*
PHRASE: n/adj PHR

other-worldly. **Other-worldly** means more concerned with spiritual matters than with daily life. *They encourage an image of Tibet as an other-worldly sort of place.*
ADJ-GRADED: usu ADJ n ≠worldly

OTT /oʊ tiː tiː/. In informal English, if you describe something as **OTT**, you mean that it is exaggerated and extreme. **OTT** is an abbreviation for 'over the top'. *...an OTT comedy cabaret revue... Some of the designs are subtle, some gloriously OTT.*
ADJ-GRADED ≠understated

otter /ɒtəʳ/ **otters.** An **otter** is a small animal with brown fur, short legs, and a long tail. Otters swim well and eat fish.
◆◇◇◇◇ N-COUNT

ouch /aʊtʃ/. People say **ouch** when they suddenly feel pain. *She was barefoot and stones dug into her feet. 'Ouch, ouch,' she cried.*
EXCLAM =ow

ought /ɔːt/ ◆◆◆◇◇

Ought to is a phrasal modal verb. It is used with the base form of a verb. The negative form of **ought to** is **ought not to**, which is sometimes shortened to **oughtn't to.**

1 You use **ought to** to say that you think that it is morally right to do a particular thing or behave in a particular way or that it is morally right for a situation to exist, especially when giving or asking for advice or opinions. *Mark, you've got a good wife. You ought to take care of her... The people who already own a bit of money or land ought to have a voice in saying where it goes... You ought to be ashamed of yourselves. You've created this problem.*
PHR-MODAL PRAGMATICS =should

2 You use **ought to** when saying that you think it is a good idea and important for you or someone else to do a particular thing, especially when giving or asking for advice or opinions. *You don't have to be alone with him and I don't think you ought to be... You ought to ask a lawyer's advice... She wondered if she ought to take some coffee out to Alfred... We ought not to be quarrelling now.*
PHR-MODAL PRAGMATICS =should

3 You use **ought to** to indicate that you expect something to be the case or you expect something to happen. You use **ought to have** to indicate that you expect something to have happened already. *'This ought to be fun,' he told Alex, eyes gleaming.*
PHR-MODAL =should

4 You use **ought to** to indicate that you think that something should be the case, but might not be. *This ought to be the perfect time for opponents of Mrs Thatcher to strike... This news ought to send a shiver down John Major's spine.*
PHR-MODAL =should

5 You use **ought to** to indicate that you think that something has happened because of what you know about the situation, but you are not certain. *He ought to have reached the house some time ago.*
PHR-MODAL =should

6 You use **ought to have** with a past participle to indicate that something was expected to happen or be the case, but it did not happen or was not the case. *Basically the system ought to have worked... The money to build the power station ought to have been sufficient.*
PHR-MODAL =should have

7 You use **ought to have** with a past participle to indicate that although it was best or correct for someone to do something in the past, they did not actually do it. *I realize I ought to have told you about it... Perhaps we ought to have trusted people more... I ought not to have asked you a thing like that. I'm sorry... I'm beginning to feel now we oughtn't to have let her go away like that.*
PHR-MODAL =should have

8 You use **ought to** when politely telling someone that you must do something, for example that you must leave. *I really ought to be getting back now... I think I ought to go.*
PHR-MODAL PRAGMATICS =should

oughtn't /ɔːtᵊnt/. **Oughtn't** is a spoken form of **ought not.**
=shouldn't

ounce /aʊns/ **ounces** ◆◆◇◇◇

1 An **ounce** is a unit of weight used in Britain and the USA. There are sixteen ounces in a pound and one ounce is equal to 28.35 grams. *...four ounces of sugar.*
N-COUNT: num N, oft N of n

2 You can refer to a very small amount of something, such as a quality or characteristic, as an **ounce.** *If only my father had possessed an ounce of business sense... I spent every ounce of energy trying to hide.*
N-SING: usu N of n

3 See also **fluid ounce.**

our /aʊəʳ/ ◆◆◆◆◆

Our is the first person plural possessive determiner.

1 A speaker or writer uses **our** to indicate that something belongs or relates both to himself or herself and to one or more other people. *We're expecting our first baby... I locked myself out of our apartment and had to break in... Clear it away so we can put our mugs down.*
DET-POSS

2 A speaker or writer sometimes uses **our** to indicate that something belongs or relates to people in general. *The quality of our life depends on keeping well... We are all entirely responsible for our actions, and for our reactions.*
DET-POSS

3 In non-standard spoken English, speakers sometimes use **our** with the name of a member of their family or a very close friend. *Our Barry had a habit of doing that sort of thing.*
DET-POSS

Our Lady. Some Christians, especially Catholics, refer to Mary, the mother of Jesus Christ, as **Our Lady.** *Will you pray to Our Lady for me?*
◆◇◇◇◇ N-PROPER =the Virgin Mary

Our Lord. Christians refer to Jesus Christ as **Our Lord.** *Let us remember the words of Our Lord from the gospel of Mark.*
N-PROPER =Jesus Christ, Jesus

ours /aʊəʳz/ ◆◆◇◇◇
Ours is the first person plural possessive pronoun. A speaker or writer uses **ours** to refer to something that belongs or relates both to himself or herself and to one or more other people. *Japanese democracy is certainly different from ours... There are few strangers in a town like ours... Half the houses had been fitted with alarms and ours hadn't.* PRON-POSS

ourself /aʊəʳself/. **Ourself** is sometimes used instead of 'ourselves' when it clearly refers to a singular subject. Some people consider this use to be incorrect. *...the way we think of ourself and others.* PRON-REFL: v PRON, prep PRON

ourselves /aʊəʳselvz/ ◆◆◆◇◇
Ourselves is the first person plural reflexive pronoun.

1 A speaker or writer uses **ourselves** to refer to himself or herself and one or more other people as a group. **Ourselves** is used as the object of a verb or preposition when the subject refers to the same people. *We sat round the fire to keep ourselves warm... It was the first time we admitted to ourselves that we were tired.* PRON-REFL: v PRON, prep PRON

2 A speaker or writer sometimes uses **ourselves** to refer to people in general. **Ourselves** is used as the object of a verb or preposition when the subject refers to the same people. *We all know that when we exert ourselves our heart rate increases.* PRON-REFL: v PRON, prep PRON

3 You use **ourselves** to emphasize a first person plural subject. In more formal English, **ourselves** is sometimes used instead of 'us' as the object of a verb or preposition, for emphasis. *Others are feeling just the way we ourselves would feel in the same situation... The people who will suffer won't be people like ourselves.* PRON-REFL-EMPH PRAGMATICS

4 If you say something such as 'We did it **ourselves**', you are indicating that the people you are referring to did it, rather than anyone else. *We villagers built that ourselves, we had no help from anyone.* PRON-REFL-EMPH

5 ● **by ourselves**: see **by**.

oust /aʊst/ **ousts, ousting, ousted.** ◆◆◇◇◇ VERB
If someone **is ousted** from a position of power, job, or place, you force them to leave it; a formal word. *The leaders have been ousted from power by nationalists... Last week they tried to oust him in a parliamentary vote of no confidence. ...the ousted government.* ♦ **ousting** *The ousting of his predecessor was one of the most dramatic coups the business world had seen in years.* be V-ed; V n; V-ed; N-UNCOUNT =removal

out 1 adverb uses

out /aʊt/ ◆◆◆◆◆
Out is often used with verbs of movement, such as 'walk' and 'pull', and also in phrasal verbs such as 'give out' and 'run out'.

1 When something is in a particular place and you take it **out**, you remove it from that place. *Carefully pull out the centre pages... He took out his notebook and flipped the pages... They paid in that cheque a couple of days ago, and drew out around two thousand in cash.* ADV: ADV after v

2 You can use **out** to indicate that you are talking about the situation outside, rather than inside buildings. *It's hot out – very hot, very humid.* ADV: ADV after v =outside

3 If you are **out**, you are not at home or not at your usual place of work. *I tried to get in touch with you yesterday evening, but I think you were out... She had to go out.* ADV: be ADV, ADV after v ≠in

4 If you say that someone is **out** in a particular place, you mean that they are in a different place, usually one far away. *The police tell me they've finished their investigations out there... Rosie's husband was now out East.* ADV: ADV adv/prep

5 When the sea or tide goes **out**, the sea moves away from the shore. *The tide was out and they walked among the rock pools.* ADV: ADV after v, be ADV ≠in

out 2 adjective uses

out /aʊt/ ◆◆◆◆◆
1 If a light or fire is **out** or goes **out**, it is no longer shining or burning. *All the lights were out in the house... Several of the lights went out, one after another.* ADJ: v-link ADJ

2 If flowers are **out**, their petals have opened. *Well, the daffodils are out in the gardens and they're always a beautiful show.* ► Also an adverb. *I usually put it in my diary when I see the wild flowers coming out.* ADJ: v-link ADJ; ADV: ADV after v

3 If something such as a book or record is **out**, it is available for people to buy. *...cover versions of 40 British Number Ones – out now.* ► Also an adverb. *The HMSO edition came out a week later, priced £13.30.* ADJ: v-link ADJ; ADV: ADV after v

4 If workers are **out**, they are on strike; an informal use. *We've been out for two and a half months and we're not going back until we get what we're asking for.* ► Also an adverb. *In June last year, 26 people came out on strike protesting against a compulsory 65-hour week.* ADJ: v-link ADJ =on strike; ADV: ADV after v

5 In a game or sport, if someone is **out**, they can no longer take part either because they are unable to or because they have been defeated. ADJ: v-link ADJ

6 If you say that a proposal or suggestion is **out**, you mean that it is unacceptable. *That's right out, I'm afraid.* ADJ: v-link ADJ

7 If you say that a particular fashion or method is **out**, you mean that it is unfashionable. *Romance is making a comeback. Reality is out.* ADJ: v-link ADJ ≠in

8 If you say that a calculation or measurement is **out**, you mean that it is incorrect. *When the two ends of the tunnel met in the middle they were only a few inches out.* ADJ-GRADED: v-link ADJ, oft amount ADJ

9 If someone is **out** to do something, they intend to do it; an informal use. *Most companies these days are just out to make a quick profit.* ADJ: v-link ADJ to-inf

out 3 verb use

out /aʊt/ **outs, outing, outed.** If a group of people **out** a public figure or famous person, they reveal that person's homosexuality against their wishes. *The New York gay action group 'Queer Nation' recently outed an American Congressman.* ♦ **outing** *The gay and lesbian rights group, Stonewall, sees outing as completely unhelpful.* VERB; V n; N-UNCOUNT

out 4 preposition uses

out of ◆◆◆◆◆
Out of is used with verbs of movement, such as 'walk' and 'pull', and also in phrasal verbs such as 'do out of' and 'grow out of'. In American English and informal British English, **out** is often used instead of **out of**.

1 If you go **out of** a place, you leave it. *She let him out of the house.* PHR-PREP ≠into

2 If you take something **out of** the container or place where it has been, you remove it so that it is no longer there. *I always took my key out of my bag and put it in my pocket.* PHR-PREP

3 If you look or shout **out of** a window, you look or shout away from the room where you are towards the outside. *He went on staring out of the window... He looked out the window at the car on the street below.* PHR-PREP

4 If you are **out of** the sun, the rain, or the wind, you are sheltered from it. *People can keep out of the sun to avoid skin cancer.* PHR-PREP

5 If someone or something gets **out of** a situation, especially an unpleasant one, they are then no longer in it. If they keep **out of** it, they do not start being in it. *In the past army troops have relied heavily on air support to get them out of trouble... The economy is starting to climb out of recession... The Salvation Army has worked in the big cities to keep endangered young people out of a life of crime.* PHR-PREP

6 You can use **out of** to say that someone leaves an institution. *You come out of university and find there are no jobs available... Doctors should be able to decide who they can safely let out of hospital early.* PHR-PREP

7 If you are **out of** range of something, you are beyond the limits of that range. *Shaun was in the bedroom, out of earshot, watching television... He turned to look back, but by then she was out of sight.* PHR-PREP

8 You use **out of** to say what emotion or motive causes someone to do something. For example, if you do something **out of** pity, you do it because you pity someone. *He took up office out of a sense of* PHR-PREP

duty... Some people have left out of embarrassment at what's happened to them.

9 If you get something such as information or work **out of** someone, you manage to make them give it to you, usually when they are unwilling to give it. *'Where is she being held prisoner?' I asked. 'Did you get it out of him?'... We knew we could get better work out of them.* PHR-PREP

10 If you get pleasure or an advantage **out of** something, you get it as a result of being involved with that thing or making use of it. *We all had a lot of fun out of him... To get the most out of your money, you have to invest.* PHR-PREP =from

11 If you are **out of** something, you no longer have any of it. *I can't find the sugar – and we're out of milk.* PHR-PREP

12 If something is made **out of** a particular material, it consists of that material because it has been formed or constructed from it. *Would you advise people to make a building out of wood or stone?* PHR-PREP =from

13 You use **out of** to indicate what proportion of a group of things something is true of. For example, if something is true of one **out of** five things, it is true of one fifth of all things of that kind. *Two out of five thought the business would be sold privately on their retirement or death... In 99 cases out of a hundred this will be done more effectively by the army.* PHR-PREP: num PREP num =in

out- /aʊt-/. You can use **out-** to form verbs that describe an action as being done better by one person than by another. For example, if you can outswim someone, you can swim further or faster than they can. *European investors may outspend the Japanese this year. ...a younger brother who always outperformed him.* PREFIX

outage /aʊtɪdʒ/ **outages.** In American English, an **outage** is a period of time when the electricity supply to a building or area is interrupted, for example because of damage to the cables. The British term is **power failure**. *A windstorm in Washington is causing power outages throughout the region.* N-COUNT

out-and-out. You use **out-and-out** to emphasize that someone or something has all the characteristics of a particular type of person or thing. *The Olympic theme tune 'Amigos para Siempre' (Friends for Life) proved an out-and-out success.* ADJ: ADJ n =absolute, thorough

outback /aʊtbæk/. The remote parts of Australia where very few people live are referred to as **the outback**. N-SING: the N

outbid /aʊtbɪd/ **outbids, outbidding.** The form **outbid** is used in the present tense and is the past tense and past participle. If you **outbid** someone, you offer more money than they do for something that you both want to buy. *You could spend a lot of money on house surveys and end up with nothing if somebody outbids you... Last year, Cray failed to take over the software company, when it was outbid by Electronic Data Systems.* VERB =top V n

outboard /aʊtbɔːʳd/. An **outboard** motor is one that you can fix to the back of a small boat. ◆◇◇◇◇ ADJ: ADJ n

outbound /aʊtbaʊnd/. An **outbound** flight is one that is leaving or is due to leave its place of departure. ADJ: usu ADJ n ≠inbound

outbreak /aʊtbreɪk/ **outbreaks.** If there is an **outbreak** of something unpleasant, such as violence or a disease, it suddenly starts to happen. *The four-day festival ended a day early after an outbreak of violence involving hundreds of youths. ...the outbreak of war in the Middle East... In Peru, a cholera outbreak continues to spread.* ◆◆◇◇◇ N-COUNT: usu sing, usu with supp

outbuilding /aʊtbɪldɪŋ/ **outbuildings.** **Outbuildings** are small buildings such as barns or stables that are part of a larger property. N-COUNT: usu pl

outburst /aʊtbɜːʳst/ **outbursts** ◆◇◇◇◇

1 An **outburst** of an emotion, especially anger, is a sudden strong expression of that emotion. *...an outburst of anger. ...a spontaneous outburst of cheers and applause... There has been another angry outburst against the new local tax introduced today.* N-COUNT: usu with supp, oft N of n =explosion

2 An **outburst** of violent activity is a sudden period of this activity. *Five people were reported killed today in a fresh outburst of violence. ...this first great outburst of nationalist student protest.* N-COUNT: usu N of n =eruption

outcast /aʊtkɑːst, -kæst/ **outcasts.** An **outcast** is someone who is not accepted by a group of people or by society. *He had always been an outcast, unwanted and alone... All of us felt like social outcasts.* ◆◇◇◇◇ N-COUNT =pariah

outclass /aʊtklɑːs, -klæs/ **outclasses, outclassing, outclassed**

1 If you **are outclassed** by someone, they are a lot better than you are at a particular activity. *Mason was outclassed by Lennox Lewis in his tragic last fight at Wembley... Few city hotels can outclass the Hotel de Crillon. ...the hopelessly outclassed French champion.* VERB be V-ed V n V-ed

2 If one thing **outclasses** another thing, the first thing is of a much higher quality than the second thing. *These planes are outclassed by the most recent designs from the former Soviet Union... The story outclasses anything written by Frederick Forsyth.* VERB =outshine be V-ed V n

outcome /aʊtkʌm/ **outcomes.** The **outcome** of an activity, process, or situation is the situation that exists at the end of it. *Mr. Singh said he was pleased with the outcome... It's too early to know the outcome of her illness. ...a successful outcome.* ◆◆◆◇◇ N-COUNT: usu sing, oft the N of n =result

outcrop /aʊtkrɒp/ **outcrops;** spelled **outcropping** in American English. An **outcrop** is a large area of rock sticking out of the ground. *...an outcrop of rugged granite. ...rocky outcrops, covered in trees and bushes.* N-COUNT: usu with supp, oft N of n

outcry /aʊtkraɪ/ **outcries.** An **outcry** is a reaction of strong disapproval and anger shown by the public or media about a recent event. *The killing caused an international outcry... There was public outcry from those opposed to abortion.* ◆◇◇◇◇ N-VAR: usu with supp =protest

outdated /aʊtdeɪtɪd/. If you describe something as **outdated**, you mean that you think it is old-fashioned and no longer useful or relevant to modern life. *...outdated and inefficient factories. ...outdated attitudes... Caryl Churchill's play about Romania is already outdated.*  ADJ-GRADED =outmoded

outdid /aʊtdɪd/. **Outdid** is the past tense of **outdo**.

outdistance /aʊtdɪstəns/ **outdistances, outdistancing, outdistanced**

1 If you **outdistance** someone, you are a lot better and more successful than they are at a particular activity over a period of time. *It didn't matter that Ingrid had outdistanced them as a movie star.* VERB =outstrip V n

2 If you **outdistance** your opponents in contest of some kind, you beat them easily. *...a millionaire businessman who easily outdistanced his major rivals for the nomination.* VERB =outstrip V n

outdo /aʊtduː/ **outdoes, outdoing, outdid, outdone** ◆◇◇◇◇

1 If you **outdo** someone, you are a lot more successful than they are at a particular activity. *It was important for me to outdo them, to feel better than they were... Both sides have tried to outdo each other to show how tough they can be.* VERB V n

2 You use **not to be outdone** to introduce an action which someone takes in response to a previous action. *Not to be outdone, the Croats came up with a peacekeeping proposal of their own... She wore a lovely tiara but the groom, not to be outdone, had on a very smart embroidered waistcoat.* PHRASE: PHR with cl

outdoor /aʊtdɔːʳ/. **Outdoor** activities or things happen or are used outside and not in a building. *If you enjoy outdoor activities, this is the trip for you... There were outdoor cafes on almost every block.* ◆◆◇◇◇ ADJ: ADJ n ≠indoor

outdoors /aʊtdɔːʳz/ ◆◇◇◇◇

1 If something happens **outdoors**, it happens outside in the fresh air rather than in a building. *It was warm enough to be outdoors all afternoon... The ceremony was being held outdoors.* ADV: be ADV, ADV after v =out of doors ≠indoors

2 You refer to **the outdoors** when talking about work or leisure activities which take place outside away from buildings. *I'm a lover of the outdoors... Life in the great outdoors isn't supposed to be luxurious.* N-SING: the N

outer /aʊtəʳ/. The **outer** parts of something are the parts which contain or enclose the other parts, and which are furthest from the centre. *He heard a voice in the outer room. ...the outer suburbs of the city.* ◆◆◇◇◇ ADJ: ADJ n ≠inner

outermost /aʊtəʳmoʊst/. The **outermost** thing in a group is the one that is furthest from the centre. *...the outermost corners of each room. ...Pluto, the outermost known planet.* ADJ: ADJ n ≠innermost

outer space. **Outer space** is the area outside the earth's atmosphere where the other planets and stars are situated. *In 1957, the Soviets launched Sputnik 1 into outer space.* ◆◇◇◇◇ N-UNCOUNT

outerwear /aʊtəʳweəʳ/. **Outerwear** is clothing that is not worn underneath other clothing. *The latest in sports bras are colorful tops designed as outerwear.* N-UNCOUNT

outfall /aʊtfɔːl/ **outfalls.** An **outfall** is a place where water or waste flows out of a drain, often into the sea. *During the winter months, great flocks of gulls gather at rubbish tips and sewage outfalls.* N-COUNT

outfield /aʊtfiːld/. In baseball and cricket, the **outfield** is the part of the field that is furthest from the batting area. N-SING: the N

outfielder /aʊtfiːldəʳ/ **outfielders.** In baseball and cricket, the **outfielders** are the players in the part of the field that is furthest from the batting area. N-COUNT

outfit /aʊtfɪt/ **outfits, outfitting, outfitted** ◆◆◇◇◇
1 An **outfit** is a set of clothes. *She was wearing an outfit she'd bought the previous day... I spent lots of money on smart new outfits for work.* N-COUNT
2 You can refer to an organization as an **outfit**; used in journalism. *He works for a private security outfit... We are a professional outfit and we do require payment for our services.* N-COUNT: oft supp N =organization
3 To **outfit** someone or something means to provide them with equipment for a particular purpose; used mainly in American English. *They outfitted him with artificial legs... I outfitted an attic bedroom as a studio.* VERB =fit out V n with/as n Also V n

outfitter /aʊtfɪtəʳ/ **outfitters;** also spelled **outfitters**. An **outfitter** or an **outfitters** is a shop that sells clothes and equipment for a specific purpose; used mainly in British English. *...J. Hepworth, the men's outfitter... He went into a sports outfitters and made a few purchases.* N-COUNT: oft supp N

outflank /aʊtflæŋk/ **outflanks, outflanking, outflanked**
1 In a battle, when one group of soldiers **outflanks** another, it succeeds in moving past the other group in order to be able to attack it from the side. *...plans designed by General Schwarzkopf to outflank them from the west.* VERB V n
2 If you **outflank** someone, you succeed in getting into a position where you can defeat them, for example in an argument. *He had tried to outflank them... His own ideas were outflanked by those of more radical reformers.* VERB =outdo V n

outflow /aʊtfloʊ/ **outflows.** When there is an **outflow** of money or people, a large amount of money or people move from one place to another. *There was a net outflow of about £650m in short-term capital. ...an increasing outflow of refugees.* ◆◇◇◇◇ N-COUNT: usu N of n ≠inflow

outfox /aʊtfɒks/ **outfoxes, outfoxing, outfoxed.** If you **outfox** someone, you defeat them in some way because you are cleverer or more cunning than they are. *There is no greater thrill than to bluff a man, trap him and outfox him.* VERB =outwit, outsmart V n

outgoing /aʊtgoʊɪŋ/ ◆◇◇◇◇
1 An **outgoing** president, chairman, or minister is one who is going to leave. *...the outgoing director of the Edinburgh International Festival.* ADJ: ADJ n =retiring
2 **Outgoing** things such as planes, mail, and passengers are leaving or being sent somewhere. *All outgoing flights were grounded.* ADJ: ADJ n ≠incoming
3 Someone who is **outgoing** is very friendly and likes meeting and talking to people. *She's very outgoing. ...his outgoing behaviour.* ADJ-GRADED =extrovert

outgoings /aʊtgoʊɪŋz/. Your **outgoings** are the regular amounts of money which you have to spend every week or every month, for example in order to pay your rent or bills; used mainly in British English. *She suggests you first assess your income and outgoings. ...monthly outgoings.* N-PLURAL =expenses

outgrow /aʊtgroʊ/ **outgrows, outgrowing, outgrew, outgrown** ◆◇◇◇◇
1 If you **outgrow** a piece of clothing, you can no longer wear it because you have grown and are now too big for it. *She outgrew her clothes so rapidly that Patsy was always having to buy new ones. ...outgrown baby clothes.* VERB =grow out of V n V-ed
2 If you **outgrow** a particular way of behaving or thinking, you change and become more mature, so that you no longer behave or think in that way. *The girl may or may not outgrow her interest in fashion.* VERB =grow out of V n

outgrowth /aʊtgroʊθ/ **outgrowths.** Something that is an **outgrowth** of another thing has developed naturally as a result of it. *Her first book is an outgrowth of an art project she began in 1988.* N-COUNT: usu N of n =consequence

outguess /aʊtges/ **outguesses, outguessing, outguessed.** If you **outguess** someone, you try to predict what they are going to do in order to gain some advantage. *Only by being him can you hope to out-guess him... A very good investor will outguess the market.* VERB V n

outgun /aʊtgʌn/ **outguns, outgunning, outgunned**
1 In a battle, if one army **is outgunned**, they are in a very weak position because the opposing army has more or better weapons. *First Airborne Division was heavily outgunned by German forces... The outgunned Bosnian forces had lost 100 men.* VB: usu passive be V-ed V-ed
2 If you **are outgunned** in a contest, you are beaten because your rival is stronger or better than you. *Clearly, the BBC is being outgunned by ITV's original drama... He soon hit top speed to outgun all his rivals in the opening qualifying session.* VERB be V-ed V n

outhouse /aʊthaʊs/ **outhouses**
1 An **outhouse** is a small building attached to a house or very close to the house, used, for example, for storing things in. N-COUNT
2 In American English, an **outhouse** is an outside toilet. N-COUNT

outing /aʊtɪŋ/ **outings** ◆◆◇◇◇
1 An **outing** is a short enjoyable trip, usually with a group of people, away from your home, school, or place of work. *One evening, she made a rare outing to the local discotheque. ...families on a Sunday afternoon outing.* N-COUNT =excursion
2 In sport, an **outing** is an occasion when a player competes in a particular contest or competition. *Playing against Zebre in England's first outing, he suffered a whiplash injury to his neck.* N-COUNT
3 See also **out** section 3.

outlandish /aʊtlændɪʃ/. If you describe something as **outlandish**, you disapprove of it because you think it is very unusual, strange, or unreasonable. *They appeared at parties in outlandish clothes... This idea is not as outlandish as it sounds.* ◆◇◇◇◇ ADJ-GRADED =bizarre

outlast /aʊtlɑːst, -læst/ **outlasts, outlasting, outlasted.** If one thing **outlasts** another thing, the first thing lives or exists longer than the second. *These naturally dried flowers will outlast a bouquet of fresh blooms... People should listen to his music – it will outlast us all.* VB: no passive V n

outlaw /aʊtlɔː/ **outlaws, outlawing, outlawed** ◆◆◇◇◇
1 When something **is outlawed**, it is made illegal. *In 1975 gambling was outlawed... The German government has outlawed some fascist groups. ...the outlawed political parties.* VERB =ban be V-ed V n V-ed
2 An **outlaw** is a criminal who is hiding from the authorities; an old-fashioned use. *Jesse was an outlaw, a bandit, a criminal.* N-COUNT =fugitive

outlay /aʊtleɪ/ **outlays. Outlay** is the amount of money that you have to spend in order to buy something or start a project. *Apart from the capital outlay of buying the machine, dishwashers can actually save you money... A beginner could really* ◆◇◇◇◇ N-VAR: usu with supp *enjoy the hobby for an outlay of between £5 or £10 a month.*

outlet /aʊtlet/ **outlets** ◆◆◇◇◇

1 An **outlet** is a shop or organization which sells the goods made by a particular manufacturer. *...the largest retail outlet in the city.* N-COUNT: usu supp N

2 If someone has an **outlet** for their feelings or ideas, they have a means of expressing and releasing them. *Her father had found an outlet for his ambition in his work.* N-COUNT: oft N *for* n =channel

3 An **outlet** is a hole or pipe through which liquid or air can flow away. *...a warm air outlet. ...an underwater outlet pipe discharging waste into the sea.* N-COUNT

4 An **outlet** is a place, usually in a wall, where you can connect electrical devices to the electricity supply; used especially in American English. N-COUNT =power point

outline /aʊtlaɪn/ **outlines, outlining, outlined** ◆◆◆◇◇

1 If you **outline** an idea or a plan, you explain it in a general way. *The mayor outlined his plan to clean up the town's image... The methods outlined in this book are only suggestions.* VERB =sketch out V n

2 An **outline** is a general explanation or description of something. *Following is an outline of the survey findings... The proposals were given in outline by the Secretary of State.* N-COUNT: also *in* N =sketch

3 You say that an object **is outlined** when you can see its general shape because there is light behind it. *The Ritz was outlined against the lights up there... It was a beautiful sight outlined above the starry sky.* V-PASSIVE *be* V-ed V-ed

4 The **outline** of something is its general shape, especially when it cannot be clearly seen. *He could see only the hazy outline of the goalposts.* N-COUNT: usu N *of* n

outlive /aʊtlɪv/ **outlives, outliving, outlived.** If one person **outlives** another, they are still alive after the second person has died. If one thing **outlives** another thing, the first thing continues to exist after the second has disappeared or been replaced. *I'm sure Rose will outlive many of us... Khrushchev predicted that Communism would outlive Capitalism... By the early 1980s, the power station had outlived its purpose.* ◆◇◇◇◇ VERB V n

outlook /aʊtlʊk/ **outlooks** ◆◆◇◇◇

1 Your **outlook** is your general attitude towards life. *The illness had a profound effect on his outlook... I adopted a positive outlook on life... We were quite different in outlook, Philip and I.* N-COUNT: usu sing, with supp, also *in* N =perspective

2 The **outlook** for something is whether or not it is going to be prosperous, successful, or safe. *The economic outlook is one of rising unemployment... Has motherhood changed your career outlook? ...the uncertain outlook for the motor industry.* N-SING: oft supp N =prospect

outlying /aʊtlaɪɪŋ/. **Outlying** places are far away from the main cities of a country. *Tourists can visit outlying areas like the Napa Valley Wine Country... The main industry on the outlying islands is farming.* ◆◇◇◇◇ ADJ: ADJ n =remote

outmanoeuvre /aʊtmənuːvəʳ/ **outmanoeuvres, outmanoeuvring, outmanoeuvred;** spelled **outmaneuver** in American English. When you **outmanoeuvre** someone, you gain an advantage over them in a particular situation by behaving in a clever and skilful way. *He has shown once again that he's able to outmanoeuvre the military... Great Britain's hockey players were outmanoeuvred by Germany.* VERB V n

outmoded /aʊtmoʊdɪd/. If you describe something as **outmoded**, you mean that you think it is old-fashioned and no longer useful or relevant to modern life. *Romania badly needs aid to modernise its outmoded industries... What hope is there, if people in positions of power continue to promote outmoded attitudes?... The political system has become thoroughly outmoded.* ADJ-GRADED =outdated

outnumber /aʊtnʌmbəʳ/ **outnumbers, outnumbering, outnumbered.** If one group of people or things **outnumbers** another, the first group has more people or things in it than the second group. *...a town where men outnumber women four to one... Donkeys outnumber cars in this landscape of tiny stone-walled fields.* ◆◇◇◇◇ VERB V n

out of. See **out.**

out-of-body. An **out-of-body** experience is one in which you feel as if you are outside your own body, watching it and what is going on around it. ADJ: usu ADJ n

out of date; also spelled **out-of-date.** Something that is **out of date** is old-fashioned and no longer useful. *Think how rapidly medical knowledge has gone out of date in recent years. ...out-of-date nuclear power stations.* ◆◇◇◇◇ ADJ-GRADED

out of doors; also spelled **out-of-doors.** If you are **out of doors**, you are outside a building rather than inside it. *Sometimes we eat out of doors... Don't you worry about them when they're out of doors?* ADV: ADV after v, *be* ADV =outdoors ≠indoors

out-of-pocket. Out-of-pocket expenses are those which you pay out of your own money on behalf of someone else, and which are often paid back to you later. *I charge twenty dollars an hour plus out-of-pocket expenses.* • See also **pocket.** ADJ: ADJ n

out-of-the-way; also spelled **out of the way. Out-of-the-way** places are difficult to reach and are therefore not often visited. *...an out-of-the-way spot. ...the difficulty of travelling anywhere out of the way.* ◆◇◇◇◇ ADJ-GRADED =remote

out of touch ◆◇◇◇◇

1 Someone who is **out of touch** with a situation is not aware of recent changes in it. *Washington politicians are out of touch with the American people... If they really believe in this then they must be completely out of touch.* ADJ-GRADED: v-link ADJ, oft ADJ *with* n

2 If you are **out of touch** with someone, you have not been in contact with them recently and are not familiar with their present situation. *James wasn't invited. We've been out of touch for years. But I did invite Caleb.* ADJ: v-link ADJ, oft ADJ *with* n =in touch

out-of-town ◆◇◇◇◇

1 **Out-of-town** shops or facilities are situated away from the centre of a town or city. *...shopping at cheaper, out-of-town supermarkets.* ADJ: ADJ n

2 **Out-of-town** is used to describe people who do not live in a particular town or city, but have travelled there for a particular purpose. *...a deluxe hotel for out-of-town visitors.* ADJ: ADJ n

out of work; also spelled **out-of-work.** Someone who is **out of work** does not have a job. *...a town where half the men are usually out of work. ...an out of work actor.* ◆◇◇◇◇ ADJ =unemployed

outpace /aʊtpeɪs/ **outpaces, outpacing, outpaced.** To **outpace** someone or something means to perform a particular action faster or better than they can. *These hovercraft can easily outpace most boats... The Japanese economy will continue to outpace its foreign rivals for years to come... She outpaced the former Olympic champion Evelyn Ashford.* ◆◇◇◇◇ VERB =outstrip V n

outpatient /aʊtpeɪʃənt/ **outpatients;** also spelled **out-patient.** An **outpatient** is someone who receives treatment at a hospital but does not stay there overnight. *...the outpatient clinic... She received psychiatric care as an outpatient.* ◆◇◇◇◇ N-COUNT: oft N n ≠in-patient

outperform /aʊtpəʳfɔːʳm/ **outperforms, outperforming, outperformed.** If one thing **outperforms** another, the first is more successful or efficient than the second; used mainly in journalism. *In recent years the Austrian economy has outperformed most other industrial economies... It was yet another case where the human eye outperformed radar.* ◆◇◇◇◇ VERB V n

outplacement /aʊtpleɪsmənt/. An **outplacement** agency gives advice to managers and other professional people who have recently become unemployed, and helps them find new jobs. N-UNCOUNT: usu N n

outplay /aʊtpleɪ/ **outplays, outplaying, outplayed.** In sport, if one person or team **outplays** an opposing person or team, they play much better than their opponents. *We outplayed the Australians... He was outplayed by the Swedish 21-year-old.* VERB V n

outpoint /aʊtpɔɪnt/ **outpoints, outpointing, outpointed.** In boxing, if one boxer **outpoints** another, they win the match by getting more VERB points then their opponent. *Kane won the world title in 1938 when he outpointed Jackie Durich.* [V n]

outpost /aʊtpoʊst/ **outposts.** An **outpost** is a small settlement in a foreign country or a distant part of your own country which is used for trading or military purposes. *...a remote mountain outpost, linked to the outside world by the poorest of roads.* [◆◇◇◇◇ N-COUNT: usu with supp, oft supp N, N of n]

outpouring /aʊtpɔːrɪŋ/ **outpourings.** An **outpouring** of something such as an emotion or a reaction is the expression of it in an uncontrolled way. *The news of his death produced an instant outpouring of grief. ...an outpouring of anti-Western feeling.* [N-COUNT: usu sing, usu N of n =flood]

output /aʊtpʊt/ **outputs** [◆◆◆◇◇]

1 Output is used to refer to the amount of something that a person or thing produces. *Manual workers need a good breakfast for high-energy output... Government statistics show the largest drop in industrial output for ten-years.* [N-VAR: usu supp N]

2 The **output** of a computer or word processor is the information that it displays on a screen or prints on paper as a result of a particular program. *You run the software, you look at the output, you make modifications.* [N-VAR]

outrage, outrages, outraging, outraged. The verb is pronounced /aʊtreɪdʒ/. The noun is pronounced /aʊtreɪdʒ/. [◆◆◇◇◇]

1 If you **are outraged** by something, it makes you extremely shocked and angry. *Many people have been outraged by some of the things that have been said... Reports of torture and mass executions in Serbia's detention camps have outraged the world's religious leaders.* [VERB: be V-ed, V n] ♦ **outraged** *He is truly outraged about what's happened to him... Some outraged readers said the story was extremely offensive and distressing.* [ADJ-GRADED: oft ADJ at/about n =appalled]

2 Outrage is an intense feeling of anger and shock. *The decision provoked outrage from women and human rights groups... The Treaty has failed to arouse genuine public outrage.* [N-UNCOUNT: usu with supp =indignation]

3 You can refer to an act or event which you find very shocking as an **outrage**. *The latest outrage was to have been a co-ordinated gun and bomb attack on the station... Tom, this is an outrage!* [N-COUNT]

outrageous /aʊtreɪdʒəs/. If you describe something as **outrageous**, you are emphasizing that it is unacceptable or very shocking. *I must apologise for my outrageous behaviour... Charges for local telephone calls are particularly outrageous.* [◆◆◇◇◇ ADJ-GRADED PRAGMATICS =scandalous] ♦ **outrageously** *Car-parks are few, crammed, and outrageously expensive... She flirted with him outrageously at times.* [ADV: usu ADV adj]

outran /aʊtræn/. **Outran** is the past tense of **outrun.**

outrank /aʊtræŋk/ **outranks, outranking, outranked.** If one person **outranks** another person, he or she has a higher position or grade within an organization than the other person. *The most junior executive officer outranked the senior engineer officer aboard ship.* [VERB: V n]

outré /uːtreɪ, AM uːtreɪ/. Something that is **outré** is very unusual and strange; a formal word. *...outré outfits designed by students at the Royal College of Art.* [ADJ-GRADED =way-out]

outreach /aʊtriːtʃ/. **Outreach** programmes and schemes try to find people who need help or advice rather than waiting for those people to come and ask for help. *Their brief is to undertake outreach work essentially aimed at the young African Caribbeans on the South Acton Estate.* [N-UNCOUNT: usu N n]

outrider /aʊtraɪdə^r/ **outriders. Outriders** are people such as policemen who ride on motorcycles or horses beside or in front of an official vehicle, in order to protect the people in the vehicle. *...a black Mercedes with motorcycle outriders provided by the city's police.* [N-COUNT: usu n N]

outright. The adjective is pronounced /aʊtraɪt/. The adverb is pronounced /aʊtraɪt/. [◆◆◇◇◇]

1 You use **outright** to describe behaviour and actions that are open and direct, rather than indirect. *Kawaguchi finally resorted to an outright lie. ...outright condemnation.* [ADJ: ADJ n] ► Also an adverb. *Why are you so mysterious? Why don't you tell me outright?... Sharon laughed outright.* [ADV: ADV after v =openly]

2 Outright means complete and total. *She had failed to win an outright victory... The response of the audience varied from outright rejection to warm hospitality.* [ADJ: ADJ n =absolute] ► Also an adverb. *The peace plan wasn't rejected outright.* [ADV: ADV after v =completely] ● If someone **is killed outright**, they die immediately, for example in an accident. *My driver was killed outright.* [PHRASE: V inflects]

outrun /aʊtrʌn/ **outruns, outrunning, outran.** The form **outrun** is used in the present tense and is also the past participle of the verb.

1 If you **outrun** someone, you run faster than they do, and therefore are able to escape from them or to arrive somewhere before they do. *There are not many players who can outrun me.* [VERB =outstrip, V n]

2 If one thing **outruns** another thing, the first thing develops faster than the second thing. *Spending could outrun the capacity of businesses to produce the goods.* [VERB =exceed, V n]

outsell /aʊtsel/ **outsells, outselling, outsold.** If one product **outsells** another product, the first product is sold more quickly or in larger quantities than the second. *The team's products easily outsell those of other American baseball clubs overseas... Armani consistently outsells all other European designers.* [VERB: V n]

outset /aʊtset/. If something happens **at the outset** of an event, process, or period of time, it happens at the beginning of it. If something happens **from the outset** it happens from the beginning and continues to happen. *Decide at the outset what kind of learning programme you want to follow... From the outset he had put his trust in me, the son of his old friend.* [◆◆◇◇◇ PHRASE: PHR after v, PHR cl]

outshine /aʊtʃaɪn/ **outshines, outshining, outshone.** If you **outshine** someone at a particular activity, you are much better at it than they are. *Jesse has begun to outshine me in sports.* [VERB =outclass, V n]

outside /aʊtsaɪd/ **outsides** [◆◆◆◆◆]

The form **outside of** can also be used as a preposition. This form is more usual in American English.

1 The **outside** of something is the part which surrounds or encloses the rest of it. *...the outside of the building... Cook over a fairly high heat until the outsides are browned.* [N-COUNT: usu the N, oft N of n ≠inside] ► Also an adjective. *...high up on the outside wall.* [ADJ: ADJ n]

2 If you are **outside**, you are not inside a building but are quite close to it. *'Was the car inside the garage?'—'No, it was still outside.'... I stepped outside and pulled up my collar against the cold mist... Outside, the light was fading rapidly... The shouting outside grew louder.* [ADV: be ADV, ADV after v, n ADV, ADV with cl ≠inside] ► Also a preposition. *The victim was outside a shop when he was attacked.* [PREP ≠inside] ► Also an adjective. *...the outside temperature. ...an outside toilet.* [ADJ: ADJ n]

3 If you are **outside** a room, you are not in it but are in the hall or corridor next to it. *She'd sent him outside the classroom... He stood in the narrow hallway just outside the door.* [PREP ≠inside] ► Also an adverb. *They heard voices coming from outside in the corridor... She heard the dog on the landing outside.* [ADV: ADV after v, n ADV ≠inside]

4 When you talk about the **outside** world, you are referring to things that happen or exist in places other than your own home or community. *...a side of Morris's character she hid carefully from the outside world... It's important to have outside interests.* [ADJ: ADJ n] ► Also an adverb. *The scheme was good for the prisoners because it brought them outside into the community.* [ADV: ADV after v]

5 People or things **outside** a country, town, or region are not in it. *...an old castle outside Budapest... The number of warships stationed outside European waters roughly doubled. ...theatres both in and outside London.* [PREP: n/-ed PREP n ≠in] ► Also a noun. *Peace cannot be imposed from the outside by the United States or anyone else.* [N-SING: the N]

6 On a wide road, the **outside** lanes are the ones which are closest to its centre. *...driving in the outside lane of a dual carriageway.* [ADJ: ADJ n ≠inside] ► Also a noun. *...coming up on the outside.* [N-SING: the N]

7 **Outside** people or organizations are not part of a particular organization or group. *The company now makes much greater use of outside consultants. ...church services given on Sundays by outside chaplains.* ► Also a preposition. *He is hoping to recruit a chairman from outside the company.*
ADJ: ADJ n — PREP

8 **Outside** a particular institution or field of activity means in other fields of activity or in general life. *The condition is practically unknown outside psychiatry clinics. ...the largest merger ever to take place outside the oil industry.*
PREP

9 Something that is **outside** a particular range of things is not included within it. *She is a beautiful boat, but way, way outside my price range... When Cathy sings about love, you feel that she's singing about something outside her experience.*
PREP =beyond ≠within

10 Something that happens **outside** a particular period of time happens at a different time from the one mentioned. *They are open outside normal daily banking hours. ...nor does it help if your job involves working outside normal office hours.*
PREP ≠in, within

11 **Outside of** is used to introduce the only thing or person that prevents your main statement from being completely true. *Every single relationship I've had with a man, outside of my husband, has ended in disaster.*
PHR-PREP: PREP n/-ing PRAGMATICS =apart from

12 You use **at the outside** to say that you think that a particular amount is the largest possible in a particular situation, or that a particular time is the latest possible time for something to happen. *Give yourself forty minutes at the outside.*
PHRASE: PHR with cl, amount PHR

outside broadcast, outside broadcasts. An **outside broadcast** is a radio or television programme that is not recorded or filmed in a studio, but in another building or in the open air.
N-COUNT

outsider /aʊtsaɪdəʳ/ **outsiders** ◆◆◇◇◇

1 An **outsider** is someone who does not belong to a particular group or organization. *The most likely outcome may be to subcontract much of the work to an outsider.*
N-COUNT

2 An **outsider** is someone who is not accepted by a particular group, or who feels that they do not belong in it. *Malone, a cop, felt as much an outsider as any of them.*
N-COUNT =odd man out

3 In a competition, an **outsider** is a competitor who is unlikely to win. *Mr Yeltsin entered the elections as something of an outsider.*
N-COUNT ≠favourite

outsize /aʊtsaɪz/ or **outsized**

1 **Outsize** or **outsized** things are much larger than usual or much larger than you would expect; used mainly in British English. *...an outsize pair of scissors... An outsized photograph hung above her bedroom fireplace.*
ADJ: usu ADJ n

2 **Outsize** clothes are clothes for very large people; used in British English. *Often outsize clothes are made from cheap fabric and look like ugly tents.*
ADJ: usu ADJ n

outskirts /aʊtskɜːʳts/. **The outskirts** of a city or town are the parts of it that are farthest away from its centre. *Hours later we reached the outskirts of New York.*
◆◆◇◇◇ N-PLURAL: *the*N, oft N *of* n

outsmart /aʊtsmɑːʳt/ **outsmarts, outsmarting, outsmarted.** If you **outsmart** someone, you defeat them or gain an advantage over them in a clever and sometimes dishonest way. *Troy was very clever for his age and had already figured out ways to outsmart her.*
VERB =outwit — V n

outsold /aʊtsoʊld/. **Outsold** is the past tense and past participle of **outsell**.

outspoken /aʊtspoʊkən/. Someone who is **outspoken** gives their opinions about things openly and honestly, even if they are likely to shock or offend people. *Some church leaders have been outspoken in their support for political reform in Kenya... He was an outspoken critic of apartheid. ...his outspoken criticism of the prime minister.*
◆◇◇◇◇ ADJ-GRADED =forthright

♦ **outspokenness** *His outspokenness has ensured that he has at least one senior enemy within the BBC hierarchy.*
N-UNCOUNT

outstanding /aʊtstændɪŋ/ ◆◆◆◇◇

1 If you describe someone or something as **outstanding**, you think that they are very remarkable and impressive. *Derartu is an outstanding athlete and deserved to win. ...an area of outstanding natural beauty... He was outstanding at tennis and golf.*
ADJ-GRADED

2 Money that is **outstanding** has not yet been paid and is still owed to someone. *The total debt outstanding is $70 billion... You have to pay your outstanding bill before joining the scheme.*
ADJ

3 **Outstanding** issues or problems have not yet been resolved. *We still have some outstanding issues to resolve before we'll have a treaty that is ready to sign.*
ADJ: usu ADJ n =remaining

4 **Outstanding** means very important or obvious. *The company is an outstanding example of a small business that grew into a big one... His mother, whose influence on his development was outstanding, came of a distinguished American family.*
ADJ =notable

outstandingly /aʊtstændɪŋli/. You use **outstandingly** to emphasize how good, or occasionally how bad, something is. *Salzburg is an outstandingly beautiful place to visit... All his novels were outstandingly well written.*
ADV-GRADED: ADV adj/adv PRAGMATICS =exceptionally

outstay /aʊtsteɪ/ **outstays, outstaying, outstayed.** • to **outstay** your **welcome**: see **welcome**.

outstretched /aʊtstretʃt/. If a part of the body of a person or animal is **outstretched**, it is stretched out as far as possible. *She was staring into the fire muttering, and holding her arms outstretched to warm her hands. ...an eagle with outstretched wings.*
◆◇◇◇◇ ADJ

outstrip /aʊtstrɪp/ **outstrips, outstripping, outstripped.** If one thing **outstrips** another, the first thing becomes larger in amount, or more successful or important, than the second thing. *In the mid-eighteenth century the production of food far outstripped the rise in population... In 1989 and 1990 demand outstripped supply, and prices went up by more than a third.*
◆◇◇◇◇ VERB =surpass — V n

out-take, out-takes; also spelled **outtake**. An **out-take** is a song on an album or part of a film or programme that is removed before the album is released or the film or programme is shown. *...an exclusive showing of hilarious out-takes from the show.*
N-COUNT

out tray, out trays; also spelled **out-tray**. An **out tray** is a tray or shallow basket used in offices to put letters and documents in when they have been dealt with and are ready to be sent out of the office.
N-COUNT ≠in tray

outvote /aʊtvoʊt/ **outvotes, outvoting, outvoted.** If you **are outvoted**, more people vote against what you are proposing than vote for it, so that your proposal is defeated. *They walked out in protest after being outvoted by the National Salvation Front majority... Twice his colleagues have outvoted him.*
VERB =vote down — be V-ed — V n

outward /aʊtwəʳd/ ◆◇◇◇◇

1 An **outward** journey is a journey that you make away from a place that you are intending to return to later. *Tickets must be bought seven days in advance, with outward and return journey dates specified.*
ADJ: ADJ n ≠return

2 The **outward** feelings, qualities, or attitudes of someone or something are the ones they appear to have rather than the ones that they actually have. *In spite of my outward calm I was very shaken... What the military rulers have done is to restore the outward appearance of order.*
ADJ: ADJ n

3 The **outward** features of something are the ones that you can see from the outside. *Mark was lying unconscious but with no outward sign of injury.*
ADJ: ADJ n

4 See also **outwards**.

outwardly /aʊtwəʳdli/. You use **outwardly** to indicate the feelings or qualities that a person or situation may appear to have, rather than the ones that they actually have. *They may feel tired and though outwardly calm, can be irritable... Outwardly this looked like the beginning of a terrific programme but the stage was actually set for a major disaster.*
◆◇◇◇◇ ADV: ADV adj/adv, ADV with cl =on the surface

outwards /aʊtwəʳdz/; the form **outward** is also used. In American English, **outward** is more usual.
◆◇◇◇◇

1 If something moves or faces **outwards**, it moves or faces away from the place you are in or the place you are talking about. *The top door opened outwards... The idea is to spread social democracy and economics outwards from Europe.* ADV: ADV after v ≠inwards

2 If you say that a person or a group of people, such as a government, looks **outwards**, you mean that they turn their attention to another group that they are interested in or would like greater involvement with. *Other poor countries looked outward, strengthening their ties to the economic superpowers... His belief is that the future of the Community lies in looking outwards.* ADV: ADV after v

outweigh /aʊtweɪ/ **outweighs, outweighing, outweighed.** If one thing **outweighs** another, the first thing is of greater importance, benefit, or significance than the second thing; a formal word. *The medical benefits of x-rays far outweigh the risk of having them... The advantages of this deal largely outweigh the disadvantages.* ◆◇◇◇◇ VERB V n

outwit /aʊtwɪt/ **outwits, outwitting, outwitted.** If you **outwit** someone, you use your intelligence or a clever trick to defeat them or to gain an advantage over them. *To win the presidency he had first to outwit his rivals within the Socialist Party... Seeing how cleverly he had been outwitted he made no complaint.* VERB =outsmart V n

outworn /aʊtwɔːʳn/. If you describe a belief or custom as **outworn**, you mean that it is old-fashioned and no longer has any meaning or usefulness. *...an ancient nation irretrievably sunk in an outworn culture.* ADJ

ouzo /uːzoʊ/ **ouzos. Ouzo** is a strong aniseed-flavoured alcoholic drink that is made in Greece. ► A glass of ouzo can be referred to as an **ouzo**. N-UNCOUNT N-COUNT

ova /oʊvə/. **Ova** is the plural of **ovum**.

oval /oʊvəl/ **ovals. Oval** things have a shape that is like a circle but is wider in one direction than the other. *He was a man in his late thirties, with fine, dark hair and a pale oval face. ...the small oval framed picture of a little boy.* ► Also a noun. *Using 2 spoons, mould the cheese into small balls or ovals.* ◆◆◇◇◇ ADJ: usu ADJ n N-COUNT: usu sing

ovarian /oʊveəriən/. **Ovarian** means relating to or coming from the ovaries. *...a new treatment for ovarian cancer.* ◆◇◇◇◇ ADJ: ADJ n

ovary /oʊvəri/ **ovaries.** A woman's **ovaries** are the two organs in her body that produce eggs. ◆◇◇◇◇ N-COUNT

ovation /oʊveɪʃən/ **ovations.** An **ovation** is a long burst of applause from an audience for a particular performer or speaker; a formal word. *They became civic heroes and received a tumultuous ovation on their appearance in New York City.* • See also **standing ovation**. ◆◇◇◇◇ N-COUNT

oven /ʌvən/ **ovens.** An **oven** is a cooker or part of a cooker that is like a box with a door. You cook food inside an oven. *Put the onions and ginger in the oven and let them roast for thirty minutes.* ◆◆◇◇◇ N-COUNT

ovenproof /ʌvənpruːf/. An **ovenproof** dish is one that has been specially made to be used in an oven without being damaged by the heat. ADJ: usu ADJ n

over 1 position and movement

over /oʊvəʳ/ ◆◆◆◆◆

In addition to the uses shown below, **over** is used after some verbs, nouns, and adjectives in order to introduce extra information. **Over** is also used in phrasal verbs such as 'hand over' and 'glaze over'.

1 If one thing is **over** another thing or is moving **over** it, the first thing is directly above the second, either resting on it, or with a space between them. *He looked at himself in the mirror over the table. ...a bridge over the river Danube. ...helicopters flying low over the crowd.* ► Also an adverb. *...planes flying over every 10 or 15 minutes.* PREP ADV: ADV after v

2 If one thing is **over** another thing, it is supported by it and its ends are hanging down on each side of it. *A grey mackintosh was folded over her arm... Joe's clothing was flung over the back of a chair.* PREP: usu -ed PREP n

3 If one thing is **over** another thing, it covers part or all of it. *His hair fell over his brow instead of being brushed straight back... Mix the ingredients and pour over the mushrooms... He was wearing a light-grey suit over a shirt... He pulled the cap halfway over his ears.* ► Also an adverb. *Heat this syrup and pour it over.* PREP ADV: ADV after v

4 If you lean **over** an object, you bend your body so that the top part of it is above the object. *They stopped to lean over a gate... Everyone in the room was bent over her desk.* ► Also an adverb. *Sam leant over to open the door of the car.* PREP: v PREP n ADV: ADV after v

5 If you look **over** or talk **over** an object, you look or talk across the top of it. *I went and stood beside him, looking over his shoulder. ...conversing over the fence with your friend... I heard various scraps of conversation over the dinner table.* PREP: usu v PREP n

6 If a window has a view **over** an area of land or water, you can see the land or water through the window. *...a light and airy bar with a wonderful view over the River Amstel... His rooms looked out over a narrow lane behind the college.* PREP: n PREP n, v PREP n =onto

7 If someone or something goes **over** a barrier, obstacle, or boundary, they get to the other side of it by going across it, or across the top of it. *Policemen jumped over the wall of the Spanish Embassy in pursuit... I stepped over a broken piece of wood... Nearly one million people crossed over the river into Moldavia... He'd just come over the border.* ► Also an adverb. *I climbed over into the back seat.* PREP: v PREP n ADV: ADV after v

8 If someone or something moves **over** an area or surface, they move across it, from one side to the other. *She ran swiftly over the lawn to the gate... Joe passed his hand over his face and looked puzzled.* PREP =across

9 If something is on the opposite side of a road or river, you can say that it is **over** the road or river. *...Richard Garrick, who lived in the house over the road. ...a fashionable neighbourhood, just over the river from Manhattan.* PREP =across

10 If you go **over** to a place, you go to that place. *I got out the car and drove over to Dervaig... I thought you might have invited her over.* ADV: ADV after v, oft ADV *to* n

11 You can use **over** to indicate a particular position or place a short distance away from someone or something. *He noticed Rolfe standing silently over by the window... John reached over and took Joanna's hand... He tossed over a cigarette.* ADV: ADV after v, oft ADV prep

12 You use **over** to say that someone or something falls towards or onto the ground, often suddenly or violently. *If he drinks more than two glasses of wine he falls over... He was knocked over by a bus and broke his leg... The truck had gone off the road and toppled over.* ADV: ADV after v

13 If something rolls **over** or is turned **over**, its position changes so that the part that was facing upwards is now facing downwards. *His car rolled over after a tyre was punctured... The alarm did go off but all I did was yawn, turn over and go back to sleep.* ADV: ADV after v

14 **All over** a place means in every part of it. *...doctors who work all over the country. ...the letters she received from people all over the world.* PHRASES PREP

15 **Over here** means near you, or in the country you are in. *Why don't you come over here tomorrow evening... My father was in the U.S. army over here.* usu PHR after v, v-link PHR

16 **Over there** means in a place a short distance away from you, or in another country. *The cafe is just across the road over there... She'd married some American and settled down over there.* usu PHR after v, v-link PHR

17 • **the world over**: see **world**.

over 2 amounts and occurrences

over /oʊvəʳ/ ◆◆◆◆◆

1 If something is **over** a particular amount, measurement, or age, it is more than that amount, measurement, or age. *Cigarettes kill over a hundred thousand Britains every year... I met George well over a year ago. ...equipment costs of over £100m.* ► Also an adverb. *...people aged 65 and over.* PREP: PREP amount =more than ADV: amount *and* ADV

2 **Over and above** an amount, especially a normal amount, means more than that amount or in addition to it. *Expenditure on education has gone up by seven point eight per cent over and above inflation... Consider supplements over and above this healthy diet.* PHR-PREP =in addition to

3 If you say that you have some food or money **over**, you mean that it remains after you have used all that you need. *Larsons pay me well enough, but there's not much over for luxuries when there's two of you to live on it... Primrose was given an apple, left over from our picnic lunch.* ADV: *be* ADV, n ADV, ADV after v

4 In American English, if you do something **over**, you do it again or start doing it again from the beginning. *She said if she had the chance to do it over, she would have hired a press secretary... Dave, the pianist, played it over a couple of times.* ADV: ADV after v =again

5 If you say that something happened **twice over**, **three times over** and so on, you are stating the number of times that it happened and emphasizing that it happened more than once. *He had to have everything spelled out twice over for him.* PHRASES PHR after v PRAGMATICS

6 If you say that something is happening **all over again**, you are emphasizing that it is happening again, and you are suggesting that it is tiring, boring, or unpleasant. *He doesn't want the hassle all over again... The whole process started all over again... He had to prove himself all over again.* PHR after v PRAGMATICS

7 If you say that something happened **over and over** or **over and over again**, you are emphasizing that it happened many times. *He plays the same songs over and over... 'I don't understand it,' he said, over and over again.* PHR after v PRAGMATICS =again and again, repeatedly

over 3 other uses

over /oʊvəʳ/ **overs** ◆◆◆◆◆

1 If an activity is **over** or all **over**, it is completely finished. *Warplanes that have landed there will be kept until the war is over... The bad times were over... I am glad it's all over.* ADJ: v-link ADJ =finished

2 If you are **over** an illness or an experience, it has finished and you have recovered from its effects. *I'm glad that you're over the flu... She was still getting over the shock of what she had been told.* PREP

3 If you have control or influence **over** someone or something, you are able to control them or influence them. *He's never had any influence over her... For two decades she has sought complete control over her film career... The oil companies have lost their power over oil price and oil production.* PREP: n PREP n

4 You use **over** to indicate what a disagreement or feeling relates to or is caused by. *The women were making a fuss over nothing. ...concern over recent events in Burma... Staff at some air and sea ports are beginning to protest over pay... They had already begun fighting over her.* PREP: n PREP n, v PREP n =about

5 If something happens **over** a period of time or **over** a meal or a drink, it happens during that time or during that meal or drink. *The number of attacks on the capital had gone down over the past week... Many strikes over the last few years have not ended successfully... Over breakfast we discussed plans for the day. ...discussing the problem over a glass of wine.* PREP

6 You use **over** to indicate that you give or receive information using a telephone, radio, or other piece of electrical equipment. *I'm not prepared to discuss this over the telephone... The head of state addressed the nation over the radio... Announcements were made over the loudspeaker system.* PREP =on

7 The presenter of a radio or television programme says '**over to** someone' to indicate the person who will speak next. *With the rest of the sports news, over to Colin Maitland.* PHR-PREP

8 When people such as the police or the army are using a radio to communicate, they say **'Over'** to indicate that they have finished speaking and are waiting for a reply. CONVENTION PRAGMATICS

9 In cricket, an **over** consists of six correctly bowled balls. *At the start of the last over, bowled by Chris Lewis, the Welsh county were favourites.* N-COUNT

over- /oʊvəʳ-/. You can add **over-** to an adjective or verb to indicate that a quality exists or an action is done to too great an extent. For example, if you say that someone is being over-cautious, you mean that they are being too cautious. *Tony looked tired and over-anxious... They generally ate a lot and over-indulged.* PREFIX

overact /oʊvərækt/ **overacts, overacting, overacted.** If you say that someone **overacts**, you mean they exaggerate their emotions and movements, usually when acting in a play. *Sometimes he had overacted in his role as Prince.* VERB V

overall, overalls. The adjective and adverb are pronounced /oʊvərɔːl/. The noun is pronounced /oʊvərɔːl/. ◆◆◆◆◇

1 You use **overall** to indicate that you are talking about a situation in general or about the whole of something. *...the overall rise in unemployment... Cut down your overall amount of physical activity... It is usually the woman who assumes overall care of the baby.* ► Also an adverb. *Overall, I like Connie. I think she's great... Overall I was disappointed... The college has few ways to assess the quality of education overall.* ADJ: ADJ n; ADV: ADV with cl

2 **Overalls** consist of a single piece of clothing that combines trousers and a jacket. You wear overalls over your clothes in order to protect them from dirt while you are working. *...workers in blue overalls.* N-PLURAL: also *a pair of* N

3 In American English, **overalls** are trousers that are attached to a piece of cloth which covers your chest and which has straps going over your shoulders. The British word is **dungarees**. *An elderly man dressed in faded overalls took the witness stand.* N-PLURAL: also *a pair of* N

4 An **overall** is a piece of clothing shaped like a coat that you wear over your clothes in order to protect them from dirt while you are working; used mainly in British English. N-COUNT

overall majority, overall majorities. If a political party wins an **overall majority** in an election or vote, they get more votes than the total number of votes or seats won by all their opponents. ◆◇◇◇◇ N-COUNT: usu sing

overarching /oʊvərɑːʳtʃɪŋ/. You use **overarching** to indicate that you are talking about something that includes or affects everything or everyone. *The overarching question seems to be what happens when the US pulls out?... Home ownership has been an overarching and innate desire of the British.* ADJ: ADJ n

overarm /oʊvərɑːʳm/. You use **overarm** to describe actions, such as throwing a ball, in which you stretch your arm over your shoulder. *...a single overarm stroke.* ADJ: ADJ n ≠underarm

overawe /oʊvərɔː/ **overawes, overawing, overawed.** If you **are overawed** by something or someone, you are very impressed by them and a little afraid of them. *Don't be overawed by people in authority, however important they are... He's never been overawed or intimidated by big occasions.* ♦ **overawed** *Benjamin said that he had been rather overawed to meet one of the Billington family.* VB: usu passive =intimidate; *be* V-ed; ADJ-GRADED: usu v-link ADJ =intimidated

overbalance /oʊvəʳbæləns/ **overbalances, overbalancing, overbalanced.** If you **overbalance**, you fall over or nearly fall over, because you are not standing properly. *He overbalanced and fell head first, his towel flying and his modesty shattered.* VERB V

overbearing /oʊvəʳbeərɪŋ/. An **overbearing** person tries to make other people do what he or she wants in an unpleasant and forceful way. *My husband can be quite overbearing with our son.* ADJ-GRADED =domineering

overblown /oʊvəʳbloʊn/. Something that is **overblown** makes something seem larger, more important, or more significant than it really is. *Warnings of disaster may be overblown... The reporting of the hostage story was fair, if sometimes overblown. ...overblown dreams.* ADJ-GRADED

overboard /oʊvəʳbɔːʳd/ ◆◇◇◇◇

1 If you fall **overboard**, you fall over the side of a boat into the water. *His sailing instructor fell overboard and drowned during a lesson... He had jumped overboard in New York harbor and swum to shore.* ADV: ADV after v

2 If you say that someone **goes overboard**, you mean that they do something to a greater extent than is necessary or reasonable; an informal use. *Women sometimes damage their skin by going* PHRASES V inflects =go over the top *overboard with abrasive cleansers... What do you think causes the police to go overboard, to use excessive violence?*

3 If you **throw** something **overboard**, for example an idea or suggestion, you reject it completely. *They had thrown their neutrality overboard in the crisis.* V inflects

overbook /oʊvəʳbʊk/ **overbooks, overbooking, overbooked.** If an organization such as an airline or a theatre company **overbooks**, they sell more tickets than they have places for. *Planes are crowded, airlines overbook, and departures are almost never on time.* VERB V Also V n

overbooked /oʊvəʳbʊkt/. If something such as a hotel or a coach is **overbooked**, more people have booked than the number of places that are available. *Sorry, the plane is overbooked.* ADJ-GRADED: usu v-link ADJ

overburdened /oʊvəʳbɜːʳdənd/

1 If a system or organization is **overburdened**, it has too many people or things to deal with and so does not function properly. *The city's hospitals are overburdened by casualties. ...an overburdened air traffic control system.* ADJ-GRADED: oft ADJ *with/by* n

2 If you are **overburdened** with something such as work or problems, you have more of it than you can cope with. *The Chief Inspector disliked being overburdened with insignificant detail. ...overburdened teachers.* ADJ-GRADED: oft ADJ *with/by* n

overcame /oʊvəʳkeɪm/. **Overcame** is the past tense of **overcome**.

overcast /oʊvəʳkɑːst, -kæst/. If it is **overcast**, or if the sky or the day is **overcast**, the sky is completely covered with cloud and there is not much light. *For three days it was overcast... The weather forecast is for showers and overcast skies... It was a cold, windy, overcast afternoon in Washington.* ADJ

overcharge /oʊvəʳtʃɑːʳdʒ/ **overcharges, overcharging, overcharged.** If someone **overcharges** you, they charge you too much for their goods or services. *If you feel a taxi driver has overcharged you, say so... She claims she was overcharged by £7,000.* ♦ **overcharging** *...protests of overcharging and harsh treatment of small businesses.* ◆◇◇◇◇ VERB V n N-UNCOUNT

overcoat /oʊvəʳkoʊt/ **overcoats.** An **overcoat** is a thick warm coat that you wear in winter. ◆◇◇◇◇ N-COUNT

overcome /oʊvəʳkʌm/ **overcomes, overcoming, overcame.** The form **overcome** is used in the present tense and is also the past participle. ◆◆◆◇◇

1 If you **overcome** a problem or a feeling, you successfully deal with it and control it. *Molly had fought and overcome her fear of flying... Find a way to overcome your difficulties.* VERB V n

2 If you **are overcome** by something, it makes you feel so helpless, surprised, or embarrassed that you cannot think clearly. *The night before the test I was overcome by fear and despair... The blinding headache overcame him.* VERB =overwhelm *be* V-ed V n

3 If you **are overcome** by smoke or a poisonous gas, you become very ill or die from breathing it in. *The residents were trying to escape from the fire but were overcome by smoke.* VB: usu passive *be* V-ed

overcrowded /oʊvəʳkraʊdɪd/. An **overcrowded** place has too many things or people in it. *...one of the most overcrowded prisons in the country. ...a windswept, overcrowded, unattractive beach... Morocco's capital, until independence, was badly overcrowded.* ◆◇◇◇◇ ADJ-GRADED: usu ADJ n

overcrowding /oʊvəʳkraʊdɪŋ/. If there is a problem of **overcrowding**, there are more people living in a place than it was designed for. *Students were protesting at overcrowding in the university hostels. ...overcrowding and lack of facilities for patients.* ◆◇◇◇◇ N-UNCOUNT

overdo /oʊvəʳduː/ **overdoes, overdoing, overdid, overdone** ◆◇◇◇◇

1 If someone **overdoes** something, they behave in an exaggerated or extreme way. *Do you think the West has overdone its enthusiasm for Mr Yeltsin?... He wants to give up working and stay home to look after the children. She feels, however, that this is overdoing it a bit.* VERB V n V it

2 If you **overdo** an activity, you try to do more than you can physically manage. *It is important never to overdo new exercises... The taxi drivers' association is urging its members, who can work as many hours as they want, not to overdo it.* VERB V n V it

overdone /oʊvəʳdʌn/

1 If food is **overdone**, it has been spoiled by being cooked for too long. *The meat was overdone and the vegetables disappointing.* ADJ-GRADED =overcooked ≠underdone

2 If you say that something is **overdone**, you mean that you think it is excessive or exaggerated. *In fact, the panic is overdone. As the map shows, the drought has been confined to the south and east of Britain.* ADJ-GRADED: usu v-link ADJ

overdose /oʊvəʳdoʊs/ **overdoses, overdosing, overdosed** ◆◇◇◇◇

1 If someone takes an **overdose** of a drug, they take more of it than is safe. *Each year, one in 100 girls aged 15-19 takes an overdose... In 1970, guitarist Jimi Hendrix died of a drug overdose.* N-COUNT: usu sing

2 If someone **overdoses** on a drug, they take more of it than is safe. *He'd overdosed on heroin... Medical opinion varies on how many tablets it takes to overdose.* VERB V on n V

3 You can refer to an excess of something, especially something harmful, as an **overdose**. *An overdose of sun, sea, sand and chlorine can give lighter hair a green tinge.* N-COUNT: usu sing, oft N *of* n

4 You can say that someone **overdoses** on something if they have or do too much of it. *The city, he concluded, had overdosed on design. ...tourists that tend to overdose on the regional specialities of goose, duck and Armagnac.* VERB V on n Also V

overdraft /oʊvəʳdrɑːft, -dræft/ **overdrafts.** If you have an **overdraft**, you have spent more money than you have in your bank account, and so you are in debt to the bank. *When I left Cambridge I had a £600 overdraft... Her bank warned that unless she repaid the overdraft she could face legal action.* ◆◇◇◇◇ N-COUNT

overdrawn /oʊvəʳdrɔːn/. If you are **overdrawn** or if your bank account is **overdrawn**, you have spent more money than you have in your account, and so you are in debt to the bank. *Nick's bank sent him a letter saying he was £100 overdrawn... Talk to the bank before you go overdrawn.* ADJ-GRADED: usu v-link ADJ

overdressed /oʊvəʳdrest/. If you say that someone is **overdressed**, you are criticizing them for wearing clothes that are not appropriate for the occasion because they are too formal or too smart. ADJ-GRADED PRAGMATICS

overdrive /oʊvəʳdraɪv/ **overdrives**

1 The **overdrive** in a vehicle is a very high gear that is used when you are driving at high speeds. *The overdrive switch was on the steering column.* N-COUNT: usu sing, oft N n

2 If you go **into overdrive**, you begin to work very hard or perform a particular activity in a very intense way. *I have a peculiar response to crises. I either become immobile or go into overdrive.* PHRASE: PHR after v

overdue /oʊvəʳdjuː, -duː/ ◆◇◇◇◇

1 If you say that a change or an event is **overdue**, you mean that you think it should have happened before now. *This debate is long overdue... I'll go home and pay an overdue visit to my mother.* ADJ-GRADED: usu v-link ADJ

2 **Overdue** sums of money have not been paid, even though it is later than the date on which they should have been paid. *Teachers have joined a strike aimed at forcing the government to pay overdue salaries and allowances.* ADJ-GRADED

3 An **overdue** library book has not been returned to the library, even though the date on which it should have been returned has passed. ADJ-GRADED

overeat /oʊvəʳiːt/ **overeats, overeating, overate, overeaten.** If you say that someone **overeats**, you mean they eat more than they need to or more than is healthy. *If you tend to overeat because of depression, first take steps to recognize the source of your sadness. ...people who overeat spicy foods.* ♦ **overeater, overeaters** *She eats in secret like most compulsive overeaters.* ♦ **overeating** *If you have a serious problem with* ◆◇◇◇◇ VERB V V n N-COUNT N-UNCOUNT *overeating you should get together with others who share this problem.*

overemphasis /oʊvəremfəsɪs/. If you say that there is an **overemphasis** on a particular thing, you mean that more importance or attention is given to it than is necessary. *He attributed the party's lack of success to an overemphasis on ideology and ideas.* N-SING: also no det, usu N *on* n

overemphasize /oʊvəremfəsaɪz/ **overemphasizes, overemphasizing, overemphasized;** also spelled **overemphasise** in British English.

1 If you say that someone **overemphasizes** something, you mean that they give it more importance than it deserves or than you consider appropriate. *In the public discussion of nuclear policies, technology has usually been overemphasized and morality neglected... Democrats will complain he overemphasizes punishment at the expense of prevention and treatment.* VERB *be* V-ed V n

2 If you say that something cannot **be overemphasized**, you are emphasizing that you think it is very important. *The importance of education cannot be overemphasised... I can't overemphasize the cleanliness of this place.* VB: with brd-neg PRAGMATICS *be* V-ed V n

overestimate, overestimates, overestimating, overestimated. ◆◇◇◇◇ The verb is pronounced /oʊvərestɪmeɪt/. The noun is pronounced /oʊvərestɪmət/.

1 If you say that someone **overestimates** something, you mean that they think it is greater in amount or importance than it really is. *With hindsight, he was overestimating their desire for peace.* VERB ≠underestimate V n Also V
► Also a noun. *Average earnings in the South East were about £59,000, although that may be an overestimate.* N-COUNT ♦ **overestimation** /oʊvərestɪmeɪʃən/ *This led to an overestimation of what conceptual thinking could contribute to practical life. ...excessive overestimation of one's own importance.* N-SING: also no det, usu N *of* n ≠underestimation

2 If you say that something cannot **be overestimated**, you are emphasizing that you think it is very important. *The importance of participating in the life of the country cannot be overestimated... It is hard to overestimate the potential gains from this process.* VB: with brd-neg PRAGMATICS *be* V-ed V n

3 If you **overestimate** someone, you think that they have more of a skill or quality than they really have. *I think you overestimate me, Fred.* VERB ≠underestimate V n

over-excited; also spelled **overexcited**. If you say that someone is **over-excited**, you mean that they are more excited than you think is desirable. *You'll need to provide continuous, organised entertainment or children may get over-excited.* ADJ-GRADED: usu v-link ADJ

overexposed /oʊvərɪkspoʊzd/. An **overexposed** photograph is of poor quality because the film has been exposed to too much light, either when the photograph was taken or during the developing process. ADJ-GRADED ≠underexposed

overextended /oʊvərɪkstendɪd/. If a person or organization is **overextended**, they have become involved in more activities than they can financially or physically manage. *The British East India Tea Company was overextended and faced bankruptcy... The overworked, overextended parent may be seen as unloving, but may simply be exhausted.* ADJ-GRADED =overstretched

overflight /oʊvərflaɪt/ **overflights.** An **overflight** is the passage of an aircraft from one country over another country's territory. *Nations react strongly to unauthorized overflights.* N-VAR

overflow, overflows, overflowing, overflowed. ◆◇◇◇◇ The verb is pronounced /oʊvərfloʊ/. The noun is pronounced /oʊvərfloʊ/.

1 If a liquid or a river **overflows**, it flows over the edges of the container or place it is in. *Pour in some of the syrup, but not all of it, as it will probably overflow... Rivers and streams have overflowed their banks in countless places.* VB: no passive V V n

2 If a place or container **is overflowing** with people or things, it is too full of them. *The great hall was overflowing with people... Jails and temporary detention camps are overflowing... He emptied a few overflowing ashtrays.* VB: usu cont V *with* n V V-ing

3 If someone **is overflowing** with a feeling or if the feeling **overflows**, the person is experiencing it very strongly and shows this in their behaviour. *Kenneth overflowed with friendliness and hospitality... Ridley's anger finally overflowed.* VERB V *with* n V

4 The **overflow** is the extra people or things that something cannot contain or deal with because it is not large enough. *Tents have been set up next to hospitals to handle the overflow... The loch's overflow cascades into the waterfalls of a Japanese water garden.* N-COUNT: usu *the* N in sing

5 An **overflow** is a hole or pipe through which liquid can flow out of a container when it gets too full. *...the overflow pipe.* N-COUNT

6 If a place or container is filled **to overflowing**, it is so full of people or things that no more can fit in. *The kitchen garden was full to overflowing with fresh vegetables... He was one of the few teachers who always filled the lecture room to overflowing.* PHRASE: adj PHR, PHR after v

overfly /oʊvərflaɪ/ **overflies, overflying, overflew, overflown.** When an aircraft **overflies** an area, it flies over it. *Permission has not yet been granted for the airline to overfly Tanzania.* VERB =fly over V n

overground. The adjective is pronounced /oʊvərgraʊnd/. The adverb is pronounced /oʊvərgraʊnd/. In an **overground** transport system, vehicles run on the surface of the ground, rather than below it. *Bus routes and railways, both overground and underground, converged on the station. ...the overground section of the Metropolitan line.* ADJ: ADJ n ≠underground
► Also an adverb. *There are plans to run the line overground close to the village of Boxley.* ADV: ADV after v

overgrown /oʊvərgroʊn/ ◆◇◇◇◇

1 If a place is **overgrown**, it is thickly covered with plants because it has not been looked after. *We hurried on until we reached a courtyard overgrown with weeds... As the equipment was unpacked, I led Lee around the overgrown garden.* ADJ-GRADED

2 If you describe an adult as an **overgrown** child, you mean that their behaviour and attitudes are like those of a child, and that you dislike this. *...a bunch of overgrown kids... Daphne Farlow, at forty-five, still looked and spoke like an overgrown schoolgirl.* ADJ: ADJ n PRAGMATICS

overhang, overhangs, overhanging, overhung. ◆◇◇◇◇ The verb is pronounced /oʊvərhæŋ/. The noun is pronounced /oʊvərhæŋ/.

1 If one thing **overhangs** another, it sticks out over and above it. *Part of the rock wall overhung the path at one point... These restored houses overhang a system of quiet canals. ...the low, overhanging branches of a giant pine tree.* VERB V n V-ing

2 An **overhang** is the part of something that sticks out over and above something else. *A sharp overhang of rock gave them cover... There is a wide veranda under the overhang of the roof.* N-COUNT

3 If one thing **overhangs** another, it is supported by it and hangs down its sides. *Let the pastry overhang the rim and brush between the layers with the melted butter.* VERB V n

overhaul, overhauls, overhauling, overhauled. ◆◇◇◇◇ The verb is pronounced /oʊvərhɔːl/. The noun is pronounced /oʊvərhɔːl/.

1 If a piece of equipment **is overhauled**, it is cleaned, checked thoroughly, and repaired if necessary. *They had ensured the plumbing was overhauled a year ago... Our mud-encrusted Citroen was towed away to have its suspension overhauled.* VB: usu passive =service *be* V-ed *have* n V-ed
► Also a noun. *...the overhaul of aero engines.* N-COUNT

2 If you **overhaul** a system or method, you examine it carefully and make many changes in it in order to improve it. *The government said it wanted to overhaul the employment training scheme to make it cost effective... The legal system needs to be overhauled.* ► Also a noun. *The study says there must be a complete overhaul of air traffic control systems.* VERB V n N-COUNT: usu N *of* n

3 If one person or vehicle **overhauls** another, especially in a sports competition, they overtake them. *The win kept alive Becker's challenge to overhaul Stefan Edberg as the world No. 1... Beattie led for several laps before he was overhauled by Itoh.* VERB =overtake V n

overhead. The adjective is pronounced /oʊvəʳhed/. The adverb is pronounced /oʊvəʳhed/. You use **overhead** to indicate that something is above you or above the place that you are talking about. *She turned on the overhead light and looked around the little room. ...people who live under or near overhead cables.* ► Also an adverb. *...planes passing overhead... Now there were only the stars overhead.* ◆◆◇◇◇ ADJ: ADJ n; ADV: ADV after v, be ADV

overhead projector, overhead projectors. An **overhead projector** is a machine that projects writing or pictures from a transparency onto a screen or wall. The abbreviation 'OHP' is also used. N-COUNT =OHP

overheads /oʊvəʳhedz/. The **overheads** of a business are its regular and essential expenses, such as salaries, rent, electricity, and telephone bills. *We are having to cut our costs to reduce overheads and remain competitive.* ◆◇◇◇◇ N-PLURAL

overhear /oʊvəʳhɪəʳ/ **overhears, overhearing, overheard.** If you **overhear** someone, you hear what they are saying when they are not talking to you and they do not know that you are listening. *I overheard two doctors discussing my case. ...snatches of overheard conversation.* ◆◇◇◇◇ VERB; V n; V-ed

overheat /oʊvəʳhiːt/ **overheats, overheating, overheated** ◆◇◇◇◇

1 If something **overheats** or if you **overheat** it, it becomes hotter than is necessary or desirable. *The engine was overheating and the car was not handling well... Why do we pay to overheat pubs and hotels?* ♦ **overheated** *...that stuffy, overheated apartment.* V-ERG; V; V n; ADJ-GRADED

2 If a country's economy **overheats** or if conditions **overheat** it, it grows so rapidly that inflation and interest rates rise very quickly. *The private sector is increasing its spending so sharply that the economy is overheating... Their prime consideration has been not to overheat the economy.* ♦ **overheated** *...the disastrous consequences of an overheated market.* V-ERG; V; V n; ADJ-GRADED

overheated /oʊvəʳhiːtɪd/. Someone who is **overheated** is very angry about something. *I think the reaction has been a little overheated... In America, overheated drivers have been known to shoot each other.* ADJ-GRADED

overhung /oʊvəʳhʌŋ/. **Overhung** is the past tense and past participle of **overhang**.

overindulge /oʊvərɪndʌldʒ/ **overindulges, overindulging, overindulged.** If you **overindulge**, or **overindulge** in something that you like very much, usually food or drink, you allow yourself to have more of it than is good for you. *We all overindulge occasionally... Don't abuse your body by overindulging in alcohol.* VERB; V; V in n

overjoyed /oʊvəʳdʒɔɪd/. If you are **overjoyed**, you are extremely pleased about something. *Shelley was overjoyed to see me... He was overjoyed at his son's return.* ADJ-GRADED: v-link ADJ, oft ADJ to-inf, ADJ at n =delighted

overkill /oʊvəʳkɪl/. You can say that something is **overkill** when you think that there is more of it than is necessary or appropriate. *Every time I switch on the TV, there's football. It's overkill... Such security measures may well be overkill.* N-UNCOUNT

overland /oʊvəʳlænd/. An **overland** journey is made across land rather than by ship or aeroplane. *...an overland journey through Iraq, Turkey, Iran and Pakistan... The overland route is across some really tough mountains... Militia leaders had halted overland food convoys in the region.* ► Also an adverb. *They're travelling to Baghdad overland.* ◆◇◇◇◇ ADJ: ADJ n; ADV: ADV after v

overlap, overlaps, overlapping, overlapped. The verb is pronounced /oʊvəʳlæp/. The noun is pronounced /oʊvəʳlæp/. ◆◆◇◇◇

1 If one thing **overlaps** another, or if you **overlap** them, a part of the first thing occupies the same area as a part of the other thing. You can also say that two things **overlap**. *When the bag is folded flat, the bag bottom overlaps one side of the bag... Overlap the slices carefully so there are no gaps... Use vinyl seam adhesive where vinyls overlap... The edges must overlap each other or weeds will push through the gaps. ...neat overlapping circles.* V-RECIP-ERG; V n; V pl-n; pl-n V; pl-n V n; V-ing

2 If one idea or activity **overlaps** another, or **overlaps** with another, they involve some of the same subjects, people, or periods of time. You can also say that two ideas or activities **overlap**. *Elizabeth met other Oxford intellectuals some of whom overlapped Naomi's world... Christian holy week overlaps with the beginning of the Jewish holiday of Passover... The needs of patients invariably overlap... Their life-spans overlapped by six years.* ► Also a noun. *...the overlap between civil and military technology... We may begin to discover overlaps.* V-RECIP; V n; V with n; pl-n V; N-VAR: oft N between pl-n

overlay, overlays, overlaying, overlaid. The verb is pronounced /oʊvəʳleɪ/. The noun is pronounced /oʊvəʳleɪ/. ◆◇◇◇◇

1 If something **is overlaid** with something else, it is covered by it. *The floor was overlaid with rugs of oriental design. ...woollen cloth, overlaid with gold and silver embroidery.* VB: usu passive; be V-ed with n; V-ed

2 You can use **overlay** to refer to a substance which covers the surface of something. *Silver overlay is bonded to the entire surface. ...an overlay of snow on the tops of the iron fences.* N-VAR: usu with supp

3 If something **is overlaid** with a feeling or quality, that feeling or quality is the most noticeable one, but there may be deeper and more important ones involved. *The party had been overlaid with a certain nervousness. ...a surge of feeling which at this moment overlaid all others.* ► Also a noun. *There can be an emotional overlay to the frustration of solving real problems. ...the thin overlay of success.* VERB; be V-ed with n; V n; N-COUNT: usu with supp

overleaf /oʊvəʳliːf/. **Overleaf** is used in books and magazines to say that something is on the other side of the page you are reading. *Answer the questionnaire overleaf... There are two types of contraceptive pill available and these are described overleaf.* ADV: n ADV, ADV after v, ADV with cl

overload, overloads, overloading, overloaded. The verb is pronounced /oʊvəʳloʊd/. The noun is pronounced /oʊvəʳloʊd/. ◆◇◇◇◇

1 If you **overload** something such as a vehicle, you put more things or people into it than it was designed to carry. *Don't overload the boat or it will sink... Large meals overload the digestive system.* ♦ **overloaded** *Some trains were so overloaded that their suspension collapsed.* VERB; V n; ADJ-GRADED

2 To **overload** someone **with** work, problems, or information means to give them more work, problems, or information than they can cope with. *...an effective method that will not overload staff with yet more paperwork.* ► Also a noun. *57 per cent complained of work overload... The greatest danger is that we simply create information overload for our executives.* ♦ **overloaded** *The bar waiter was already overloaded with orders.* VERB; V n with n; N-UNCOUNT: usu supp N; ADJ-GRADED

3 If you **overload** an electrical system, you cause too much electricity to flow through it, and so damage it. *Never overload an electrical socket.* VERB; V n

overlook /oʊvəʳlʊk/ **overlooks, overlooking, overlooked** ◆◆◇◇◇

1 If a building or window **overlooks** a place, you can see the place clearly from the building or window. *Pretty and comfortable rooms overlook a flower-filled garden... Jack Aldwych lived in a huge, old two-storeyed house overlooking Harbord.* VERB =look over; V n; V-ing

2 If you **overlook** a fact or problem, you do not notice it, or do not realize how important it is. *We overlook all sorts of warning signals about our own health. ...a fact that we all tend to overlook.* VERB; V n

3 If you **overlook** someone's faults or bad behaviour, you forgive them and take no action. *...satisfying relationships that enable them to overlook each other's faults.* VERB =excuse; V n

overlord /oʊvəʳlɔːʳd/ **overlords**

1 If you refer to someone as an **overlord**, you mean that they have great power which they exercise in an unjust way. *We really don't want to be the overlords of the Palestinian population... The running of Welsh rugby was left in chaos yesterday after a vote of no confidence in the game's overlords.* N-COUNT: usu with supp

2 In former times, an **overlord** was someone who had power over many people. *Henry II was the first king to be recognized as overlord of Ireland.* N-COUNT

overly /oʊvəʳli/. **Overly** means more than is normal, necessary, or reasonable. *Employers may become overly cautious about taking on new staff.* ◆◇◇◇◇ ADV: ADV adj/adv/-ed

overmanned /oʊvəʳmænd/. If you say that a place or an industry is **overmanned**, you mean that you think there are more people working there or doing the work than is necessary. *Many factories were chronically overmanned.* ADJ-GRADED =overstaffed ≠undermanned

overmanning /oʊvəʳmænɪŋ/. If there is a problem of **overmanning** in an industry, there are more people working there or doing the work than is necessary. N-UNCOUNT

overmuch /oʊvəʳmʌtʃ/. If something happens **overmuch**, it happens too much or very much; a formal word. *He was not a man who thought overmuch about clothes.* ADV: usu ADV after v, also ADV -ed =unduly

overnight /oʊvəʳnaɪt/ ◆◆◆◇◇

1 If something happens **overnight**, it happens throughout the night or at some point during the night. *The weather remained calm overnight... The decision was reached overnight... Overnight a man died after being shot and wounded yesterday.* ▶ Also an adjective. *Travel and overnight accommodation are included... Overnight buying in the Far East also helped the dollar.* ADV: ADV after v; ADJ: ADJ n

2 You can say that something happens **overnight** when it happens very quickly and unexpectedly. *The rules are not going to change overnight... He's realistic enough to know he's not going to succeed overnight... Almost overnight, she had aged ten years and become fat.* ▶ Also an adjective. *In 1970 he became an overnight success in America.* ADV: ADV after v; ADJ: ADJ n

3 **Overnight** bags or clothes are ones that you take when you go and stay somewhere for one or two nights. *He realized he'd left his overnight bag at Mary's house.* ADJ: ADJ n

overpaid /oʊvəʳpeɪd/. If you say that someone is **overpaid**, you mean that you think they are paid more than they deserve for the work they do. *...grossly overpaid corporate lawyers.* • See also **overpay**. ADJ-GRADED

overpass /oʊvəʳpɑːs, -pæs/ **overpasses.** In American English, an **overpass** is a structure which carries one road over the top of another one. The British word is **flyover**. *...a $16 million highway overpass over Route 1.* N-COUNT

overpay /oʊvəʳpeɪ/ **overpays, overpaying, overpaid.** If you **overpay** someone, or if you **overpay** for something, you pay more than is necessary or reasonable. *Absurdly, the EC makes shoppers overpay farmers to grow too much food... The council is said to have been overpaying for repairs made by its housing department... The scheme will overpay some lawyers and underpay others.* • See also **overpaid**. VERB; V n to-inf; V for n; V n; Also V

overplay /oʊvəʳpleɪ/ **overplays, overplaying, overplayed**

1 If you say that someone **is overplaying** something such as a problem, you mean that they are making it seem more important than it really is. *...overplaying the depth of the economic crisis... I think the historical factor is overplayed, that it really doesn't mean much.* VERB =exaggerate ≠underplay V n

2 If someone **overplays** their **hand**, they act more confidently than they should because they believe that they are in a stronger position than they actually are. *The United States has to be careful it doesn't overplay its hand.* PHRASE: V inflects

overpopulated /oʊvəʳpɒpjʊleɪtɪd/. If an area is **overpopulated**, there are problems because it has too many people living there. *Environmentalists say Australia is already overpopulated. ...the overpopulated valleys of the north Omah region.* ADJ-GRADED =overcrowded

overpopulation /oʊvəʳpɒpjʊleɪʃᵊn/. If there is a problem of **overpopulation** in an area, there are more people living there than can be supported properly. *...young persons who are concerned about overpopulation in the world.* N-UNCOUNT =overcrowding

overpower /oʊvəʳpaʊəʳ/ **overpowers, overpowering, overpowered** ◆◇◇◇◇

1 If you **overpower** someone, you seize them despite their struggles because you are stronger than they are. *It took ten guardsmen to overpower him... The rebels were overpowered and arrested.* VERB =overwhelm V n

2 If a feeling **overpowers** you, it suddenly affects you very strongly. *A sudden dizziness overpowered him... I was so overpowered by my guilt and my shame that I was unable to speak.* VERB V n

3 In a sports match, when one team or player **overpowers** the other, they play much better than them and beat them easily. *Britain's tennis No 1 yesterday overpowered American Brian Garrow 7-6, 6-3.* VERB V n

4 If something such as a colour or flavour **overpowers** another colour or flavour, it is so strong that it makes the second one less noticeable. *On fair skin, pale shades are delicate enough not to overpower your colouring... Vegetables such as peppers can overpower the flavor of the stock.* VERB =overwhelm V n

overpowering /oʊvəʳpaʊərɪŋ/ ◆◇◇◇◇

1 An **overpowering** feeling is so strong that you cannot resist it. *...hard, cold, overpowering anger... The desire for revenge can be overpowering.* ADJ-GRADED =overwhelming

2 An **overpowering** smell or sound is so strong that you cannot smell or hear anything else. *There was an overpowering smell of alcohol... The noise was overpowering.* ADJ-GRADED =overwhelming

3 An **overpowering** person makes other people feel uncomfortable because they have such a strong personality. *Mrs Winter was large and somewhat overpowering. ...an overpowering manner.* ADJ-GRADED =overwhelming

overpriced /oʊvəʳpraɪst/. If you say that something is **overpriced**, you mean that you think it costs much more than it should. *I went and had an overpriced cup of coffee in the hotel cafeteria... Any property which does not sell within six weeks is overpriced.* ADJ-GRADED

overran /oʊvəʳræn/; also spelled **over-ran. Overran** is the past tense of **overrun**.

overrate /oʊvəʳreɪt/ **overrates, overrating, overrated;** also spelled **over-rate.** If you say that something or someone **is overrated**, you mean that people have a higher opinion of them than they deserve. *More men are finding out that the joys of work have been overrated... If you consider him a miracle man, you're overrating him.* VERB =overvalue ≠underrate be V-ed; V n

♦ **overrated** *Success in the eyes of others is an overrated achievement... Life in the wild is vastly overrated.* ADJ-GRADED ≠underrated

overreach /oʊvəʳriːtʃ/ **overreaches, overreaching, overreached;** also spelled **over-reach.** If you say that someone **overreaches** themselves, you mean that they fail at something because they are trying to do more than they are able to. *He overreached himself and lost much of his fortune... The company had overreached itself and made unwise investments... The people who sustain the worst losses are usually those who overreach.* VERB =overstretch V pron-refl; V

overreact /oʊvəʳriækt/ **overreacts, overreacting, overreacted;** also spelled **over-react.** If you say that someone **overreacts** to something, you mean that they have and show more of an emotion than is necessary or appropriate. *Is the council right to be concerned, or is it overreacting?... The market appeared to overreact, but this is not the case... I overreact to anything sad.* VERB V; V to n

♦ **overreaction** /oʊvəʳriækʃᵊn/ **overreactions** *This is actually an outrageous overreaction.* N-VAR

override, overrides, overriding, overrode, overridden; also spelled **over-ride.** The verb is pronounced /oʊvəʳraɪd/. The noun is pronounced /oʊvəʳraɪd/. ◆◇◇◇◇

1 If one thing in a situation **overrides** other things, it is more important than them. *The welfare of a child should always override the wishes of its parents... Their work is frequently an obsession that overrides all other considerations.* VERB V n

2 If someone in authority **overrides** a person or their decisions, they cancel their decisions. *The president vetoed the bill, and the Senate failed by a* VERB =overrule V n

single vote to override his veto... I'm applying in advance for the authority to override him... Big companies think they can sometimes override local opinion.

3 An **override** is an attempt to cancel someone's decisions by using your authority over them or by gaining more votes than them in an election or contest; used mainly in American English. *The bill now goes to the House where an override vote is expected to fail... An override of the veto appears unlikely.* N-COUNT

overriding /oʊvəʳraɪdɪŋ/; also spelled **overriding**. In a particular situation, the **overriding** factor is the one that is the most important. *My overriding concern is to raise the standards of state education... Given the overriding need to cut the budget deficit, the administration will ask congress for only $15 million this summer.* ◆◇◇◇◇ ADJ: usu ADJ n

overrule /oʊvəʳruːl/ **overrules, overruling, overruled;** also spelled **over-rule**. If someone in authority **overrules** a person or their decision, they officially decide that the decision is incorrect or not valid. *In 1991, the Court of Appeal overruled this decision... I told them it was a lousy idea, but I was overruled.* ◆◇◇◇◇ VERB =override V n

overrun /oʊvəʳrʌn/ **overruns, overrunning, overran;** also spelled **over-run**.

1 If an army or an armed force **overruns** a place, area, or country, it succeeds in occupying it very quickly. *A group of rebels overran the port area and most of the northern suburbs... The centre of New Delhi was overrun by an armed mob which attacked government buildings.* ◆◇◇◇◇ VERB V n

2 If you say that a place is **overrun** with things that you consider undesirable, you mean that there are a large number of them there. *The flower beds were overrun with grasses... The Hotel has been ordered to close because it is overrun by mice and rats... Padua and Vicenza are prosperous, well-preserved cities, not overrun by tourists.* ADJ-GRADED: v-link ADJ, usu ADJ *with/by* n

3 If an event or meeting **overruns** by, for example, ten minutes, it continues for ten minutes longer than it was intended to. *Tuesday's lunch overran by three-quarters of an hour... The talks overran their allotted time.* VERB V *by* n V n Also V

4 If costs **overrun**, they are higher than was planned or expected. *We should stop the nonsense of taxpayers trying to finance joint weapons whose costs always overrun hugely... Costs overran the budget by about 30%.* ▶ Also a noun. *He was stunned to discover cost overruns of at least $1 billion.* VERB V V n N-COUNT: usu n N

overseas /oʊvəʳsiːz/ ◆◆◆◇◇

1 You use **overseas** to describe things that happen or exist abroad. *He has returned to South Africa from his long overseas trip. ...overseas trade figures.* ▶ Also an adverb. *If you're staying for more than three months or working overseas, a full 10-year passport is required... Much of the investment was overseas.* ADJ: ADJ n =foreign ADV: ADV after v, *be* ADV =abroad

2 An **overseas** student or visitor comes from abroad. *Every year nine million overseas visitors come to London.* ADJ: ADJ n =foreign

oversee /oʊvəʳsiː/ **oversees, overseeing, oversaw, overseen.** If someone in authority **oversees** a job or an activity, they make sure that it is done properly. *Use a surveyor or architect to oversee and inspect the different stages of the work. ...the agreement to set up a commission to oversee the peace process.* ◆◆◇◇◇ VERB =supervise V n

overseer /oʊvəʳsiːəʳ/ **overseers**

1 An **overseer** is someone whose job is to make sure that employees are working properly. *I was put in the tailor shop, and I loved it, I really did. I was promoted to overseer.* N-COUNT =supervisor

2 If a person or organization is the **overseer** of a particular system or activity, they are responsible for making sure that the system or activity works properly and is successful. *...the department's dual role as overseer of oil production and safety.* N-COUNT: usu with poss

oversell /oʊvəʳsel/ **oversells, overselling, oversold.** If you say that something or someone **is oversold**, you mean that people say they are better or more useful than they really are. *The couple idea is certainly oversold. There's so much pressure to become a couple that people feel failure if they don't conform... I think the reformers have at times oversold the reforms.* VERB ≠undersell *be* V-ed V n

oversexed /oʊvəʳsekst/. If you describe someone as **oversexed**, you mean that they are more interested in sex or more involved in sexual activities than you think they should be; used showing disapproval. ADJ-GRADED PRAGMATICS

overshadow /oʊvəʳʃædoʊ/ **overshadows, overshadowing, overshadowed** ◆◇◇◇◇

1 If an unpleasant event or feeling **overshadows** something, it makes it less happy or enjoyable. *Fears for the President's safety could overshadow his peace-making mission... Her childhood was overshadowed by her mother's incarceration in a psychiatric hospital.* VERB =cloud V n

2 If someone or something **is overshadowed** by another person or thing, they are less successful, important, or impressive than the other person or thing. *Hester is overshadowed by her younger and more attractive sister.* VB: usu passive =eclipse *be* V-ed

3 If one building, tree, or large structure **overshadows** another, it stands near it, is much taller than it, and casts a shadow over it. *He also designed one of the Edinburgh University towers that overshadows George Square... She said stations should be in the open, near housing, not overshadowed by trees or walls.* VERB V n V-ed

overshoot, overshoots, overshooting, overshot. The verb is pronounced /oʊvəʳʃuːt/. The noun is pronounced /oʊvəʳʃuːt/.

1 If you **overshoot** a place that you want to get to, you go past it by mistake. *The plane apparently overshot the runway after landing... They had already overshot the corner once.* VERB V n Also V

2 If a government or organization **overshoots** its budget, it spends more than it had planned to. *The government usually overshot its original spending target.* ▶ Also a noun. *...the 100 million pounds overshoot in the cost of building the hospital.* VERB V n N-COUNT: usu supp N

oversight /oʊvəʳsaɪt/ **oversights** ◆◇◇◇◇

1 If there has been an **oversight**, someone has forgotten to do something which they should have done. *William was angered and embarrassed by his oversight... By an unfortunate oversight, full instructions do not come with the product.* N-COUNT

2 If someone has **oversight** of a process or system, they are responsible for making sure that it works efficiently and correctly. *Mr Yeltsin entrusted Mr Rutskoi with the oversight of agricultural reform... The UN will also be given a loose oversight role.* N-UNCOUNT: oft N *of* n

oversimplify /oʊvəʳsɪmplɪfaɪ/ **oversimplifies, oversimplifying, oversimplified.** If you say that someone is **oversimplifying** something, you mean that they are describing or explaining it so simply that what they say is no longer true or reasonable. *One should not oversimplify the situation... To judge trips as if they're successes or failures may be oversimplifying things.* VERB V n

♦ **oversimplified** *...an oversimplified view of mathematics and the sciences.* ADJ-GRADED: usu ADJ n

♦ **oversimplification** /oʊvəʳsɪmplɪfɪkeɪʃᵊn/ **oversimplifications** *There is an old saying that 'we are what we eat'. Obviously this is an oversimplification.* N-VAR

oversize /oʊvəʳsaɪz/ or **oversized. Oversize** or **oversized** things are too big, or much bigger than usual. *She brought out the oversize white sweater she had worn at school. ...an oversized bed.* ◆◇◇◇◇ ADJ-GRADED: usu ADJ n

oversleep /oʊvəʳsliːp/ **oversleeps, oversleeping, overslept.** If you **oversleep**, you sleep longer than you should have done. *I'm really sorry I'm late, Andrew. I forgot to set my alarm and I overslept.* VERB V

overspend, overspends, overspending, overspent. The verb is pronounced /oʊvəʳspend/. The noun is pronounced /oʊvəʳspend/.

1 If you **overspend**, you spend more money than you can afford to. *Don't overspend on your home* VERB V *on* n

and expect to get the money back when you sell... I overspent by £1 on your shopping so I'm afraid you owe me... He argued that local councils which overspend should be forced to face fresh elections. V by amount V

2 If an organization or business has an **overspend**, it spends more money than was planned or allowed in its budget; a business term, used mainly in British English. The usual American term is **overrun**. *Efforts are under way to avoid a £800,000 overspend.* N-COUNT: usu sing

overspill /oʊvəʳspɪl/

1 **Overspill** is used to refer to people who live near a city because there is no room in the city itself; used mainly in British English. *...new towns built to absorb overspill from nearby cities. ...overspill council housing.* N-UNCOUNT: also a N, oft N n

2 You can use **overspill** to refer to something or someone which is extra and cannot be accommodated in the usual place. *There is often overspill, with the office piled high with parts and the shop jammed full of goods waiting to be posted out... With the best seats taken, it was ruled that the overspill could stand at the back of the court.* N-UNCOUNT: also a N

overstaffed /oʊvəʳstɑːft, -stæft/. If you say that a place is **overstaffed**, you think there are more people working there than is necessary. *Many workers believe the factory is overstaffed.* ADJ-GRADED ≠understaffed

overstate /oʊvəʳsteɪt/ **overstates, overstating, overstated.** If you say that someone is **overstating** something, you mean they are describing it in a way that makes it seem more important or serious than it really is. *The authors no doubt overstated their case with a view to catching the public's attention... The importance of health education cannot be overstated.* ◆◇◇◇◇ VERB =exaggerate ≠understate V n

overstatement /oʊvəʳsteɪtmənt/ **overstatements.** If you refer to the way something is described is an **overstatement**, you mean it is described in a way that makes it seem more important or serious than it really is. *This may have been an improvement, but 'breakthrough' was an overstatement... True emotion ought not to require overstatement.* N-VAR =exaggeration ≠understatement

overstay /oʊvəʳsteɪ/ **overstays, overstaying, overstayed.** If you **overstay** your time, you stay somewhere for longer than you have permission to stay. *Up to forty per cent of the students had overstayed their visas.* • to **overstay** your **welcome**: see **welcome**. VB: no passive =outstay V n Also V

overstep /oʊvəʳstep/ **oversteps, overstepping, overstepped.** If you say that someone **oversteps** the limits of a system or situation, you mean that they do something that is not permissible or acceptable. *The Commission is sensitive to accusations that it is overstepping its authority... In male company, perhaps he did overstep the bounds of propriety.* • If someone **oversteps the mark**, they behave in a way that is considered unacceptable. *He overstepped the mark and we had no option but to suspend him.* VERB =go beyond V n PHRASE: V inflects =go too far

overstretch /oʊvəʳstretʃ/ **overstretches, overstretching, overstretched.** If you **overstretch** something or someone or if they **overstretch**, you force them to do something they are not really capable of, and may do them harm as a result. *Dr Boutros Ghali said the operation would overstretch resources... Do what you know you can do well and don't overstretch yourself... Never force your legs to overstretch, or you can cause injuries.* V-ERG V n V pron-refl V

overstretched /oʊvəʳstretʃt/. If a system or organization is **overstretched**, it is being forced to work more than it is supposed to. *The crime rate is rising rapidly at present and the police force is overstretched... Analysts fear the overstretched air traffic control system could reach breaking point.* ADJ-GRADED

oversubscribed /oʊvəʳsəbskraɪbd/. If something such as an event or a service is **oversubscribed**, too many people apply to attend the event or use the service. *The popular schools – the sort you really might drive across town for – tend to be heavily oversubscribed.* ADJ-GRADED: usu v-link ADJ ≠undersubscribed

overt /oʊvɜːʳt/. An **overt** action or attitude is done or shown in an open and obvious way. *His recent productions have been beautifully crafted works with little overt political content... Although there is no overt hostility, black and white students do not mix much.* ♦ **overtly** *He's written a few overtly political lyrics over the years.* ◆◇◇◇◇ ADJ-GRADED: usu ADJ n ≠covert ADV-GRADED: usu ADV adj

overtake /oʊvəʳteɪk/ **overtakes, overtaking, overtook, overtaken**

1 If you **overtake** a vehicle or a person that is ahead of you and moving in the same direction, you pass them. *When he eventually overtook the last truck he pulled over to the inside lane... The red car was pulling out ready to overtake.* ◆◆◇◇◇ VERB V n V

2 If someone or something **overtakes** a competitor, they become more successful than them. *It's the first time at these games that the Americans have overtaken the Cubans... Lung cancer has now overtaken breast cancer as a cause of death for women in the US... Labour has overtaken the Tories in popularity for the first time since the election.* VERB V n

3 If an event **overtakes** you, it happens unexpectedly or suddenly. *Tragedy was shortly to overtake him, however.* VERB =befall V n

4 If a feeling **overtakes** you, it affects you very strongly; a literary use. *Something like panic overtook me in a flood... From the moment Edward had told her of the escape attempt, she had been overtaken by a sense of impending doom.* VERB =engulf V n

overtax /oʊvəʳtæks/ **overtaxes, overtaxing, overtaxed**

1 If you **overtax** someone or something, you force them to work harder than they can really manage, and may do them harm as a result. *...a contralto who has overtaxed her voice.* VERB =overstretch V n

2 If you say that a government **is overtaxing** its people, you mean that it is making them pay more tax than you think they should pay. *You can't help Britain by overtaxing its people.* VERB ≠undertax V n

over-the-counter. See **counter**.

over-the-top. See **top**.

overthrow, overthrows, overthrowing, overthrew, overthrown. The verb is pronounced /oʊvəʳθroʊ/. The noun is pronounced /oʊvəʳθroʊ/. When a government or leader **is overthrown**, they are removed from power by force. *That government was overthrown in a military coup three years ago. ...an attempt to overthrow the president.* ► Also a noun. *Slovak national feeling has been gathering strength since the overthrow of the Communists.* ◆◆◇◇◇ VERB =topple be V-ed V n N-SING: oft N of n

overtime /oʊvəʳtaɪm/

1 **Overtime** is time that you spend doing your job in addition to your normal working hours. *He would work overtime, without pay, to finish a job... Union leaders had urged miners to vote in favour of an overtime ban.* ◆◇◇◇◇ N-UNCOUNT

2 If you say that someone **is working overtime** to do something, you mean that they are using a lot of energy, effort, or enthusiasm trying to do it; an informal expression. *We had to battle very hard and our defence worked overtime to keep us in the game... She works overtime with her vacuum cleaner to keep grit out of the kitchen.* PHRASE: V inflects, usu PHR to-inf

3 In American English, **overtime** is an additional period of time that is added to the end of a sports match in which the two teams are level, as a way of allowing the teams more time to produce a conclusive result. The British expression is **extra time**. *Denver had won the championship by defeating the Cleveland Browns 23-20 in overtime.* N-UNCOUNT

overtired /oʊvəʳtaɪəʳd/. If you are **overtired**, you are so tired that you feel unhappy or irritable, or feel that you cannot do things properly. *Make sure you avoid getting overtired or missing meals, when at all possible.* ADJ-GRADED: usu v-link ADJ

overtone /oʊvəʳtoʊn/ **overtones.** If something has **overtones** of a particular thing or quality, it suggests that thing or quality but does not openly express it. *The strike has taken on overtones of a civil rights campaign... It's a quite profound story, with powerful religious overtones.* ◆◇◇◇◇ N-COUNT: usu pl, with supp

overtook /oʊvəʳtʊk/. **Overtook** is the past tense of **overtake**.

overture /oʊvəʳtʃʊəʳ/ **overtures** ◆◇◇◇◇

1 An **overture** is a piece of music, often one that is the introduction to an opera or play. *...Wagner's Mastersingers Overture.* N-COUNT: oft in names

2 If you make **overtures** to someone, you behave in a friendly or romantic way towards them. *He had lately begun to make clumsy yet endearing overtures of friendship... If only the West had been more responsive to his peace overtures in the fifties.* N-COUNT: usu pl

overturn /oʊvəʳtɜːʳn/ **overturns, overturning, overturned** ◆◆◇◇◇

1 If something **overturns** or if you **overturn** it, it turns upside down or on its side. *The lorry veered out of control, overturned and smashed into a wall... Alex jumped up so violently that he overturned his glass of sherry... A dozen cartons of books had been overturned and strewn about the floor. ...a battered overturned boat.* V-ERG V Vn V-ed

2 If someone in authority **overturns** a legal decision, they officially decide that that decision is incorrect or not valid. *When the Russian parliament overturned his decision, he backed down... His nine-month sentence was overturned by Appeal Court judge Lord Justice Watkins.* VERB =overrule Vn

3 To **overturn** a government or system means to remove it or destroy it. *He accused his opponents of wanting to overturn the government. ...a society where all the old values had been overturned.* VERB =overthrow Vn

overuse, overuses, overusing, overused. The verb is pronounced /oʊvəʳjuːz/. The noun is pronounced /oʊvəʳjuːs/.

1 If someone **overuses** something, they use more of it than necessary, or use it more often than necessary. *A nasal spray or drops would ease your symptoms, but don't overuse them or further congestion could result... Don't overuse heated appliances on you hair.* ► Also a noun. *The record player packed up from overuse.* VERB Vn N-UNCOUNT

2 If you say that people **overuse** a word or idea, you mean that they use it so often that it no longer has any real meaning or effect. *Which words or phrases do you most overuse?* ♦ **overused** *'Just Do It' has become one of the most overused catch phrases in recent memory.* VERB Vn ADJ-GRADED =overworked

overvalue /oʊvəʳvæljuː/ **overvalues, overvaluing, overvalued.** To **overvalue** something such as a currency or a share means to fix its value at too high a level as compared to other similar things. *She attacked Mr Major's handling of the economy, saying he was wrong to overvalue sterling in the first place.* ♦ **overvaluation** /oʊvəʳvæljueɪʃᵊn/ *These problems were aggravated by the overvaluation of the pound.* ♦ **overvalued** *It still can be argued that Japanese shares are overvalued in terms of the return they offer.* ◆◇◇◇◇ VERB Vn N-UNCOUNT: oft N of n ADJ-GRADED ≠undervalued

overview /oʊvəʳvjuː/ **overviews.** An **overview** of a situation is a general understanding or description of it as a whole. *The central section of the book is a historical overview of drug use.* ◆◇◇◇◇ N-COUNT: usu sing, oft N of n

overweening /oʊvəʳwiːnɪŋ/. If you want to emphasize your disapproval of someone's very great ambition or arrogance, you can refer to their **overweening** ambition or their **overweening** arrogance; a formal word. *'Your modesty is a cover for your overweening conceit,' she said.* ADJ: usu ADJ n PRAGMATICS

overweight /əʊvəʳweɪt/. Someone who is **overweight** weighs more than is considered healthy or attractive. *Being even moderately overweight increases your risk of developing high blood pressure. ...a middle-aged, overweight farmer's wife.* ◆◇◇◇◇ ADJ-GRADED ≠underweight

overwhelm /oʊvəʳʰwelm/ **overwhelms, overwhelming, overwhelmed** ◆◆◇◇◇

1 If you **are overwhelmed** by a feeling or event, it affects you very strongly, and you do not know how to deal with it. *He was overwhelmed by a longing for times past... The need to talk to someone, anyone, overwhelmed her.* ♦ **overwhelmed** *Sightseers may be a little overwhelmed by the crowds and noise.* VERB be V-ed Vn ADJ-GRADED: usu v-link ADJ

2 If a group of people **overwhelm** a place or another group, they gain complete control or victory over them. *It was clear that one massive Allied offensive would overwhelm the weakened enemy.* VERB =overpower Vn

overwhelming /oʊvəʳʰwelmɪŋ/ ◆◆◆◇◇

1 If something is **overwhelming**, it affects you very strongly, and you do not know how to deal with it. *The task won't feel so overwhelming if you break it down into small, easy-to-accomplish steps... She felt an overwhelming desire to have another child.* ♦ **overwhelmingly** *Women of his own middle class found him overwhelmingly attractive. ...the overwhelmingly strange medieval city of Fès.* ADJ-GRADED =overpowering ADV-GRADED: ADV adj

2 You can use **overwhelming** to emphasize that an amount or quantity is much greater than other amounts or quantities. *The overwhelming majority of small businesses go broke within the first twenty-four months... The party won an overwhelming victory in Burma's general elections last May... The vote was overwhelming – 283 in favour, and only twenty-nine against.* ♦ **overwhelmingly** *The House of Commons has overwhelmingly rejected calls to bring back the death penalty for murder... Although things are changing the medical establishment is still overwhelmingly male.* ADJ-GRADED: usu ADJ n PRAGMATICS ADV: usu ADV with v, also ADV adj

overwork /oʊvəʳwɜːʳk/ **overworks, overworking, overworked.** If you **overwork** or if someone **overworks** you, you work too hard, and are likely to become very tired or ill. *He's overworking and has got a lot on his mind... He overworks and underpays the poor clerk whom he employs.* ► Also a noun. *He died of a heart attack brought on by overwork.* ♦ **overworked** *...an overworked doctor.* ◆◇◇◇◇ V-ERG V Vn N-UNCOUNT ADJ-GRADED

overworked /oʊvəʳwɜːʳkt/. If you describe a word, expression, or idea as **overworked**, you mean it has been used so often that it is no longer effective or meaningful. *'Ecological' has become one of the most overworked adjectives among manufacturers of garden supplies. ...an overworked simile.* ADJ-GRADED: usu ADJ n =overused

overwrought /oʊvəʳrɔːt/. Someone who is **overwrought** is very upset and is behaving in an uncontrolled way. *One overwrought member had to be restrained by friends.* ADJ-GRADED =distraught

ovulate /ɒvjʊleɪt/ **ovulates, ovulating, ovulated.** When a woman or female animal **ovulates**, she produces eggs from her ovary. *Some girls may first ovulate even before they menstruate.* ♦ **ovulation** /ɒvjʊleɪʃᵊn/ *By noticing these changes, the woman can tell when ovulation is about to occur.* ◆◇◇◇◇ VERB V N-UNCOUNT

ovum /oʊvəm/ **ova.** An **ovum** is one of the reproductive cells of a woman or female animal. It is fertilized by a male sperm to produce young. A technical term in biology. *Once the ovum is released it has a lifespan of 12 to 36 hours.* N-COUNT =egg

ow /aʊ/. **'Ow!'** is used in writing to represent the noise that people make when they suddenly feel pain. *Ow! Don't do that!* EXCLAM =ouch

owe /oʊ/ **owes, owing, owed** ◆◆◆◇◇

1 If you **owe** money to someone, they have lent it to you and you have not yet paid it back. You can also say that the money **is owing**. *The company owes money to more than 60 banks... Blake already owed him nearly £50... I'm broke, Livy, and I owe a couple of million dollars... He could take what was owing for the rent.* VERB Vn to n Vnn Vn V

2 If someone or something **owes** a particular quality, their success, or their existence to a person or thing, they only have it because of that person or thing. *I always suspected she owed her first job to her friendship with Roger... He owed his survival to his strength as a swimmer... The fruit owes its extraordinary aroma to a mixture of three main chemicals... The city essentially owes its fame and beauty to the Moors who transformed it into the Muslim capital of Spain... I owe him my life.* VB: no passive Vn to n Vnn

3 If you say that you **owe** a great deal to someone or something, you mean that they have helped you or influenced you a lot, and you feel very grateful to them. *As a professional composer I owe much to Radio 3... He's been fantastic. I owe him a lot.* VERB V amount to n Vn amount

4 If you say that something **owes** a great deal to VERB

someone or something, you mean that it exists, is successful, or has its particular form largely because of them. *The island's present economy owes a good deal to whisky distilling... Mrs Allen's style of cooking owes much to her mother-in-law.* [V amount to n]

5 If you say that you **owe** someone gratitude, respect, or loyalty, you mean that they deserve it from you; a formal use. *Perhaps we owe these people more respect... I owe you an apology. You must have found my attitude very annoying... I owe a big debt of gratitude to her.* [VERB: V n n, V n to n]

6 If you say that you **owe it to** someone to do something, you mean that you should do that thing because they deserve it. *I can't go. I owe it to him to stay... You owe it to yourself to get some professional help... Of course she would have to send a letter; she owed it to the family.* [VB: no passive; V it to n to-inf, V it to pron-refl to-inf, V it to n]

7 You use **owing to** when you are introducing the reason for something. *He was out of work owing to a physical injury... Owing to staff shortages, there was no restaurant car on the train.* [PHR-PREP: PREP n =due to]

8 ● **the world owes** someone **a living**: see **world**.

owl /aʊl/ **owls.** An **owl** is a bird with a flat face, large eyes, and a small sharp beak. Most owls obtain their food by hunting small animals at night. [◆◆◇◇◇ N-COUNT]
● See also **night owl**.

owlish /aʊlɪʃ/. An **owlish** person looks rather like an owl, especially because they wear glasses, and seem to be very serious and clever. *With his owlish face, it is easy to understand why he was called 'The Professor'.* [ADJ-GRADED: usu ADJ n]

own /oʊn/ **owns, owning, owned** [◆◆◆◆◆]

1 You use **own** to indicate that something belongs to a particular person or thing. *My wife decided I should have my own shop. ...another group of patients who were taught to change their own dressings... Why can't I live a normal life in my own country?... He could no longer trust his own judgement... His office had its own private entrance.* [ADJ: poss ADJ]
► Also a pronoun. *He saw the Major's face a few inches from his own.* [PRON: poss PRON]

2 You use **own** to indicate that something is used by, or is characteristic of, only one person, thing, or group. *Jennifer insisted on her own room... I let her tell me about it in her own way... Each nation has its own peculiarities when it comes to doing business.* [ADJ: poss ADJ]
► Also a pronoun. *This young lady has a sense of style that is very much her own.* [PRON: poss PRON]

3 You use **own** to indicate that someone does something without any help from other people. *They enjoy making their own decisions... Tony also built his own house from his own plans... He'll have to make his own arrangements.* [ADJ: poss ADJ] ► Also a pronoun. *There's no career structure, you have to create your own.* [PRON: poss PRON]

4 If you **own** something, it is your property. *His father owns a local pub... At least three British golf courses are now owned by the Japanese.* [VERB: V n]

5 If you say that someone has something they can **call** their **own**, you mean it belongs to them personally, rather than, for example, being controlled by or shared with someone else. *They don't yet have a country to call their own... I would like a place I could call my own.* [PHRASES]

6 If someone or something **comes into** their **own**, they become very successful or start to perform very well because the circumstances are right. *The goalkeeper came into his own with a series of brilliant saves... This is when geraniums and petunias come into their own.* [V inflects]

7 If you **get** your **own back** on someone, you have your revenge on them because of something bad that they have done to you; an informal expression. *Renshaw reveals 20 bizarre ways in which women have got their own back on former loved ones.* [V inflects, oft PHR on n]

8 If you **make** something your **own**, you become involved in it in such a way that people think of it as being related only to you or belonging only to you, rather than to anyone else. *Here again is the song that Pavarotti has made his own.* [V inflects]

9 If you say that someone has a particular thing **of** their **own**, you mean that that thing belongs or relates to them, rather than to other people. *You see, we have a problem of our own... He set out in search of ideas for starting a company of his own.* [n PHR]

10 If you say that someone or something has a particular quality or characteristic **of** their **own** or **all of** their **own**, you mean that that quality or characteristic is especially theirs, rather than being shared by other things or people of that type. *Groups have a personality of their own... The cries of the seagulls gave this part of the harbour a fascinating character all of its own.* [n PHR]

11 When you are **on** your **own**, you are alone. *He lives on his own... I told him how scared I was of being on my own... I need some time on my own.* [PHR after v, v-link PHR =alone]

12 If you do something **on** your **own**, you do it without any help from other people. *I work best on my own. ...the jobs your child can do on her own.* [PHR after v =by yourself]

13 If you say that someone does something **as if** they **own the place** or **like** they **own the place**, you are critical of them because they do it in a very arrogant way. *He struts around town like he owns the place.* [V inflects, PHR after v, PRAGMATICS]

14 ● to **hold** your **own**: see **hold**.

own up. If you **own up** to something wrong that you have done, you admit that you did it. *The headmaster is waiting for someone to own up... Last year my husband owned up to a secret affair with his secretary.* [PHRASAL VERB: V P, V P to n/-ing]

-owned /-oʊnd/. **-owned** combines with nouns, adjectives, and adverbs to form adjectives that indicate who owns something. *More than 50 state-owned companies have been sold since the early 1980s. ...the Japanese-owned Bel Air Hotel in Los Angeles... Most local radio stations are privately-owned.* [COMB in ADJ]

owner /oʊnəʳ/ **owners.** The **owner** of something is the person to whom it belongs. *The owner of the store was sweeping his floor when I walked in... Every pet owner knows their animal has its own personality... New owners will have to wait until September before moving in.* ● See also **home owner**, **landowner**. [◆◆◆◆◇ N-COUNT: usu with supp]

owner-occupier, owner-occupiers. In British English, an **owner-occupier** is a person who owns the house or flat that they live in. *The Northern Region has a lower proportion of owner-occupiers than any other English region.* [N-COUNT]

ownership /oʊnəʳʃɪp/. **Ownership** of something is the state of owning it. *On January 23rd, America decided to relax its rules on the foreign ownership of its airlines. ...the growth of home ownership in Britain... He said that anyone trying to export goods without proof of ownership would have them seized.* [◆◆◆◇◇ N-UNCOUNT: usu with supp]

own goal, own goals [◆◇◇◇◇]

1 In sport, if someone scores an **own goal**, they accidentally score a goal for the team they are playing against; used in British English. *Southampton took the lead through a Richard Shaw own goal after only 30 seconds.* [N-COUNT: usu sing]

2 If a course of action that someone takes harms their own interests, you can refer to it as an **own goal**; used in British English. *Because of the legislation I could not employ a woman. Women have made themselves unemployable. They have scored an own goal.* [N-COUNT: usu sing]

ox /ɒks/ **oxen** /ɒksən/. An **ox** is a bull that has been castrated. Oxen are used in some countries for pulling vehicles or carrying things. [◆◇◇◇◇ N-COUNT]

Oxbridge /ɒksbrɪdʒ/. In British English, **Oxbridge** is used to refer to the universities of Oxford and Cambridge together. *Last year Oxbridge graduates accounted for 41% of entrants to the civil service's fast stream to promotion. ...an offer of a place at Oxbridge.* [◆◇◇◇◇ N-PROPER]

oxcart /ɒkskɑːʳt/ **oxcarts;** also spelled **ox-cart**. An **oxcart** is a cart pulled by an ox or oxen. [N-COUNT]

oxidation /ɒksɪdeɪʃən/. **Oxidation** is a process in which a chemical substance changes because of the addition of oxygen. *Carbon dioxide is a* [N-UNCOUNT] *necessary result of the oxidation of carbon compounds.*

oxide /ɒksaɪd/ **oxides.** An **oxide** is a compound of oxygen and another chemical element. *Atoms of iron in the nail combine with atoms of oxygen from the air to form molecules of iron oxide, or rust.* ◆◇◇◇◇ N-MASS: usu supp N

oxidize /ɒksɪdaɪz/ **oxidizes, oxidizing, oxidized;** also spelled **oxidise** in British English. When a substance **is oxidized** or when it **oxidizes**, it changes chemically because of the effect of oxygen on it. *Aluminium is rapidly oxidized in air... The original white lead pigments have oxidized and turned black.* ◆◇◇◇◇ V-ERG be V-ed V

oxtail /ɒksteɪl/ **oxtails. Oxtail** is meat from the tail of a cow. It is used for making soups and stews. *...oxtail soup.* N-VAR

oxygen /ɒksɪdʒən/. **Oxygen** is a colourless gas that exists in large quantities in the air. All plants and animals need oxygen in order to live. *The human brain needs to be without oxygen for only four minutes before permanent damage occurs.* ◆◆◇◇◇ N-UNCOUNT

oxygenate /ɒksɪdʒɪneɪt/ **oxygenates, oxygenating, oxygenated.** To **oxygenate** something means to mix or dissolve oxygen into it. *Previous attempts at filtering and oxygenating aquarium water had failed... Vessels which carry freshly oxygenated blood are called arteries.* VERB V n V-ed

oxygen mask, oxygen masks. An **oxygen mask** is a device that is connected to a cylinder of oxygen by means of a tube. It is placed over the nose and mouth of someone who is having difficulty in breathing in order to help them breathe more easily. N-COUNT

oxymoron /ɒksimɔːrɒn/ **oxymorons.** If you describe a phrase as an **oxymoron**, you mean that what it refers to combines two contradictory qualities or ideas and therefore seems impossible. *This has made many Americans conclude that business ethics is an oxymoron.* N-COUNT

oyster /ɔɪstəʳ/ **oysters** ◆◇◇◇◇

1 An **oyster** is a large flat shellfish. Some oysters can be eaten and others produce pearls. *He had two dozen oysters and enjoyed every one of them.* N-COUNT

2 If you say that **the world is** someone's **oyster**, you mean that they can do anything or go anywhere that they want to. *You're young, you've got a lot of opportunity. The world is your oyster.* PHRASE: V inflects

oyster bed, oyster beds. An **oyster bed** is a place where oysters breed and grow naturally or are cultivated for food or pearls. N-COUNT

oystercatcher /ɔɪstəʳkætʃəʳ/ **oystercatchers.** An **oystercatcher** is a black and white wading bird with a long red beak. It lives near the sea and eats small shellfish. N-COUNT

oz. **Oz** is a written abbreviation for **ounce.** *Whisk 25g (1 oz) of butter into the sauce.* ◆◆◇◇◇

ozone /oʊzoʊn/. **Ozone** is a colourless gas which is a form of oxygen. There is a layer of ozone high above the earth's surface. *Ozone is best known for its role in screening the Earth from harmful ultraviolet rays from the Sun... What they find could provide clues to what might happen worldwide if ozone depletion continues.* ◆◆◇◇◇ N-UNCOUNT: oft N n

ozone layer. The **ozone layer** is the part of the Earth's atmosphere that has the highest number of ozone molecules. The ozone layer protects living things from the harmful radiation of the sun. ◆◇◇◇◇ N-SING: usu the N

Pp

P, p /piː/ **Ps, ps**

1 **P** is the sixteenth letter of the English alphabet. N-VAR

2 **p** is an abbreviation for 'pence' or 'penny'. *They cost 5p each. ...to increase income tax by 1p.* =pence, penny

3 You write **p.** before a number as an abbreviation for 'page'. The plural form is 'pp.'. *See p. 246 for Thom Bean's response. ...examined in Chapter 4 (pp. 109-13).*

4 **P** or **p** is used as an abbreviation for words beginning with p, such as 'per' or 'parking'.

pa /pɑː/ **pas.** Some people address or refer to their father as **pa**; an informal word. *'Pa,' he said, 'I don't feel well.'... Pa used to be in the army.* N-FAMILY =dad

p.a. **p.a.** is a written abbreviation for **per annum**. *...dentists with an average net income of £41,000 p.a. ... a yield of 10.5% p.a.*

PA /piː eɪ/ **PAs**

1 A **PA** is the same as a **personal assistant**. N-COUNT

2 If you refer to the **PA** or the **PA system** in a place, you are referring to the public address system. *A voice came booming over the PA... Elvis comes on the coffee shop PA system.* N-COUNT: usu the N in sing

pace /peɪs/ **paces, pacing, paced** ◆◆◆◇◇

1 The **pace** of something is the speed at which it happens or is done. *Many people were not satisfied with the pace of change. ...people who prefer to live at a slower pace... They could not stand the pace or the workload... Interest rates would come down as the recovery gathered pace.* N-SING: usu with supp =speed

2 Your **pace** is the speed at which you walk. *He moved at a brisk pace down the rue St Antoine... Their pace quickened as they approached their cars.* N-SING: usu with supp

3 A **pace** is the distance that you move when you take one step. *He'd only gone a few paces before he stopped again... I took a pace backwards.* N-COUNT: usu with supp

4 If you **pace** a small area, you keep walking up and down it, because you are anxious or impatient. *As they waited, Kravis paced the room nervously... He found John pacing around the flat, unable to sleep... She stared as he paced and yelled.* VERB V n V prep/adv V

5 If you **pace** yourself when doing something, you do it at a steady rate. *It was a tough race and I had to pace myself.* VERB V pron-refl

6 If something **keeps pace** with something else that is changing, it changes quickly in response to it. *Farmers are angry because the rise fails to keep pace with inflation. ...a world changing far too fast for her to keep pace.* PHRASES V inflects, oft PHR with n =keep up

7 If you **keep pace** with someone who is walking or running, you succeed in going as fast as them, so that you remain close to them. *With four laps to go, he kept pace with the leaders... Daisy strode alongside her, breathing heavily but keeping pace.* V inflects, oft PHR with n =keep up

8 If you do something **at your own pace**, you do it at a speed that is comfortable for you. *The computer will give students the opportunity to learn at their own pace... She was going too fast so I decided to keep riding at my own pace.* PHR after v =at your own speed

9 If you **put someone through** their **paces** or make them **go through** their **paces**, you get them to show you how well they can do something. *The eleven boxers are in the hands of the British coach, who is putting them through their paces... A group of the world's best waterskiers will be going through their paces.* V inflects

10 ● **at a snail's pace**: see **snail.**

pace out or **pace off.** If you **pace out** or **pace off** a distance, you measure it by walking from one end of it to the other. *Nash saw Colin pace out the length of the field in which he had landed to ensure that he could fly safely out of it... I marked the ground and then paced it out to be sure.* PHRASAL VERB V P n (not pron) V n P

paced /peɪst/. If you talk about the way that something such as a film or book is **paced**, you ADJ: adv ADJ are referring to the way in which the story is revealed and the speed at which the narrative moves along. *This excellent thriller is fast paced and believable. ...good special effects and well-paced action.*

pacemaker /peɪsmeɪkəʳ/ **pacemakers**
1 A **pacemaker** is a device that is placed inside someone's body in order to help their heart beat in the right way. *She was fitted with a pacemaker after suffering serious heart trouble.* N-COUNT
2 A **pacemaker** is a competitor in a race whose task is to start the race very quickly in order to help the other runners achieve a very fast time. Pacemakers usually stop before the race is finished. N-COUNT

pacesetter /peɪsetəʳ/ **pacesetters;** also spelled **pace-setter.**
1 A **pacesetter** is someone who is in the lead during part of a race or competition and therefore decides the speed or standard of the race or competition for that time. *Real's victory keeps them five points behind the pacesetters, Barcelona... Hammond was the early pace-setter.* N-COUNT
2 A **pacesetter** is a person or a company that is considered to be the leader in a particular field or activity. *Mongolia seemed an unlikely candidate as the pacesetter for political change in Asia.* N-COUNT

pachyderm /pækɪdɜːʳm/ **pachyderms.** A **pachyderm** is a large thick-skinned animal such as an elephant or rhinoceros; a technical term in zoology. N-COUNT

pacific /pəsɪfɪk/. A **pacific** person, country, or course of action is peaceful or has the aim of bringing about peace; a formal use. *The Liberals were traditionally seen as the more pacific party.* ADJ-GRADED: usu ADJ n =peaceable ≠belligerent

Pacific ◆◆◆◇◇
1 **The Pacific** or **the Pacific Ocean** is a very large sea to the west of North and South America, and to the east of Asia and Australia. *...an island in the Pacific.* N-PROPER: the N
2 **Pacific** is used to describe things that are in or that relate to the Pacific Ocean. *...the tiny Pacific island of Pohnpei.* ADJ: ADJ n

pacifier /pæsɪfaɪəʳ/ **pacifiers.** In American English, a **pacifier** is a rubber or plastic object that you give a baby to suck in order to comfort it. The British word is **dummy.** N-COUNT

pacifism /pæsɪfɪzəm/. **Pacifism** is the belief that war and violence are always wrong. N-UNCOUNT

pacifist /pæsɪfɪst/ **pacifists** ◆◇◇◇◇
1 A **pacifist** is someone who believes in pacifism and refuses to take part in wars. N-COUNT
2 If someone has **pacifist** views, they believe that war and violence are always wrong. ADJ-GRADED: usu ADJ n

pacify /pæsɪfaɪ/ **pacifies, pacifying, pacified** ◆◇◇◇◇
1 If you **pacify** someone who is angry, upset, or dissatisfied, you succeed in making them calm or satisfied. *Is this a serious step, or is this just something to pacify the critics?... She shrieked again, refusing to be pacified.* VERB =placate V n
2 If the army or the police **pacify** a group of people, they use force to overcome their resistance or protests. *Government forces have found it difficult to pacify the rebels... They were eventually pacified by officers of the local police.* ♦ **pacification** /pæsɪfɪkeɪʃən/ *...the pacification of the country.* VERB V n N-UNCOUNT

pack /pæk/ **packs, packing, packed** ◆◆◆◆◇
1 When you **pack** a bag, you put your belongings into it, because you are leaving a place or going on holiday. *When I was 17, I packed my bags and left home... I decided to pack a few things and take the kids to my Mum's... I packed and said goodbye to Charlie.* ♦ **packing** *She left Frances to finish her packing.* VERB V n V N-UNCOUNT
2 When people **pack** things, for example in a factory, they put them into containers or parcels so that they can be transported and sold. *They offered me a job packing goods in a warehouse... Machines now exist to pack olives in jars. ...sardines packed in oil.* ♦ **packing** *His onions cost 9p a lb wholesale; packing and transport costs 10p.* VERB V n V n in n V-ed N-UNCOUNT
3 If people or things **pack into** a place or if they **pack** a place, there are so many of them that the place is full. *Hundreds of thousands of people packed into the mosque... Seventy thousand people will pack the stadium.* VERB =cram V into n V n
4 A **pack** of things is a collection of them in one packet. *The club will send a free information pack. ...a pack of cigarettes... She read the back of the pack and said it had the same ingredients.* N-COUNT: oft N of n
5 A **pack** is a bag containing your belongings that you carry on your back when you are travelling. *I hid the money in my pack.* N-COUNT =rucksack, backpack
6 You can refer to a group of people who go around together as a **pack**, especially when it is a large group that you feel threatened by. *He thus avoided a pack of journalists eager to question him... Sal was the leader of the pack.* N-COUNT: usu N of n PRAGMATICS =gang
7 A **pack** of wolves or dogs is a group of them that hunt together. N-COUNT: oft N of n
8 A **pack** of playing cards is a complete set of playing cards; used mainly in British English. The usual American word is **deck.** *...a pack of cards. ...shuffle the pack.* N-COUNT: oft N of n
9 If someone **packs** a gun, they carry it; an informal use. *...eight bodyguards, at least one of them packing a pistol.* VERB =carry V n
10 If someone **packs** a jury, committee, or meeting, they make sure that it includes people who support them. *Opposition parties have boycotted the proceedings, saying the government has packed the conference with its own supporters... John Major will not try to pack the House of Lords.* VERB V n with n V n
11 See also **packed, packing.**
12 If you say that an account is **a pack of lies**, you mean that it is completely untrue. *You told me a pack of lies.* PHRASES PHR after v, v-link PHR
13 If something **packs a punch**, it has a very powerful effect. *W. Somerset Maugham's novel still packs an emotional punch. ...drinks that pack a punch.* V inflects
14 If you **send** someone **packing**, you make them go away; an informal expression. *I decided I wanted to live alone and I sent him packing.* V inflects
15 You can say that someone is **ahead of the pack** or **leading the pack** if they are ahead of everyone else in a race or competition. *The Socialists may still finish ahead of the pack... Europe has got used to following rather than leading the pack.*

pack in PHRASAL VERB
1 In British English, if you **pack** something **in**, you stop doing it; an informal expression. *I'd just packed in a job the day before... Pack it in. Stop being spiteful.* =give up V P n (not pron) V n P
2 If someone **packs in** things or people, they fit a lot of them into a limited space or time. *Prison authorities concentrate too much on packing in as many inmates as possible... It's kind of a referendum, though a lot of issues are packed in.* • If a play, film or event **packs them in**, lots of people go to see it; an informal expression. *'Blow your head!' is still packing them in at Camden's Jazz Café every Friday night.* =cram in V P n (not pron) Also V n P V inflects

pack into PHRASAL VERB
1 If someone **packs** a lot of something **into** a limited space or time, they fit a lot into it. *...packing more events or tasks into less time... I have tried to pack a good deal into a few words.* =cram into V n P n
2 If people or things **are packed into** a place, so many of them are put in there that the place becomes very full. *Some 700 people were packed into a hotel room.* usu passive =cram into be V-ed P n

pack off. If you **pack** someone **off** somewhere, you send them there to stay for a period of time; an informal expression. *Malcolm packed off Vivienne and the two children to stay in a caravan somewhere in Wales... I finally succeeded in packing her off to bed.* PHRASAL VERB V P n (not pron) to-inf V n P to n Also V n P

pack up PHRASAL VERB
1 If you **pack up** or if you **pack up** your belongings, you tidy everything away and put all your belongings in a case or bag, because you are leaving. *They packed up and went home... He began packing up his things.* V P V P n (not pron) Also V n P
2 In British English, if a machine or a part of the

body **packs up**, it stops working; an informal expression. *In the end it was his stomach and lungs that packed up... Our car packed up.* V P

package /pækɪdʒ/ **packages, packaging, packaged** ◆◆◆◆◇

1 A **package** is a small parcel. *I tore open the package. ...a package addressed to the Princess of Wales.* N-COUNT

2 In American English, a **package** is a small container in which a quantity of something is sold. Packages are either small boxes made of thin cardboard, or bags or envelopes made of paper or plastic. The usual British word is **packet**. *...a package of doughnuts... It is listed among the ingredients on the package.* N-COUNT

3 A **package** is a set of proposals that are made by a government or organization and which must be accepted or rejected as a group. *The government has announced a package of measures to help the British film industry... They are putting together a Western economic aid package for Moscow.* N-COUNT

4 When a product **is packaged**, it is put into packets to be sold. *The beans are then ground and packaged for sale as ground coffee... Most packaged foods have to show a list of ingredients in order of weight.* VB: usu passive be V-ed V-ed

5 If something such as an idea, place, or politician **is packaged**, advertisers try to make it seem attractive or interesting. *A city is like any product, it has to be packaged properly to be attractive to the consumer. ...entertainment packaged as information.* VB: usu passive be V-ed be V-ed as n

package deal, package deals. A **package deal** is a set of offers or proposals which is made by a government or an organization, and which must be accepted or rejected as a whole. N-COUNT: usu sing

package holiday, package holidays. A **package holiday** or a **package tour** is a holiday arranged by a travel company in which your travel and your accommodation are booked for you. *If you are on a package holiday, your travel company's rep should act on your behalf.* N-COUNT

packaging /pækɪdʒɪŋ/. **Packaging** is the container or wrappings that something is sold in. *It is selling very well, in part because the packaging is so attractive. ...layers of expensive, wasteful packaging.* ◆◆◇◇◇ N-UNCOUNT

pack animal, pack animals. A **pack animal** is an animal such as a horse or donkey that is used to carry things on journeys. N-COUNT

packed /pækt/ ◆◆◇◇◇

1 A place that is **packed** is very crowded. *From 3.30 until 7pm, the shop is packed. ...a packed meeting at Westminster... The streets were packed with men, women and children.* ADJ-GRADED

2 Something that is **packed with** things contains a very large number of them. *The Encyclopedia is packed with clear illustrations and over 250 recipes... Fish and chips are packed with protein.* ADJ-GRADED: v-link ADJ *with* n

packed lunch, packed lunches. In British English, a **packed lunch** is food, for example sandwiches, which you take to work, to school, or on an outing and eat as your lunch. N-COUNT

packed out. If a place is **packed out**, it is very full of people; an informal expression used in British English. *There are 350 cinemas in Paris and most are packed out.* ADJ: usu v-link ADJ

packer /pækəʳ/ **packers.** A **packer** is a worker whose job is to pack things into containers. *Norma Jones worked as a packer in a local chemical factory.* ◆◇◇◇◇ N-COUNT

packet /pækɪt/ **packets** ◆◆◇◇◇

1 A **packet** is a small container in which a quantity of something is sold. Packets are either small boxes made of thin cardboard, or bags or envelopes made of paper or plastic; used mainly in British English. *Cook the rice according to instructions on the packet... We gave her our phone number on the back of a cigarette packet.* ► A **packet** of something is an amount of it contained in a packet. *He had smoked half a packet of cigarettes... Elinor bought her a packet of biscuits.* N-COUNT =pack N-COUNT: usu N *of* n =pack

2 A **packet** is a small flat parcel; used mainly in British English. *...to send letters and packets abroad. ...a packet of photographs.* N-COUNT

3 In informal British English, you can refer to a lot of money as **a packet**. *It'll cost you a packet... You could save yourself a packet... Someone's making a packet out of it.* N-SING: a N =fortune

4 See also **pay packet, wage packet**.

pack ice. **Pack ice** is an area of ice that is floating on the sea. It is made up of pieces of ice that have been pushed together. N-UNCOUNT

packing /pækɪŋ/. **Packing** is the paper, plastic, or other material which is put round things that are being sent somewhere. • See also **pack**. ◆◆◇◇◇ N-UNCOUNT

packing case, packing cases. A **packing case** is a large wooden box in which things are put so that they can be stored or taken somewhere. N-COUNT =tea chest

pact /pækt/ **pacts.** A **pact** is a formal agreement between two or more people, organizations, or governments to do a particular thing or to help each other. *Last month he signed a new non-aggression pact with Germany... The other two opposition parties cannot agree on an electoral pact between themselves.* ◆◆◆◇◇ N-COUNT: oft supp N

pad /pæd/ **pads, padding, padded** ◆◆◇◇◇

1 A **pad** is a fairly thick, flat piece of a material such as cloth or rubber. Pads are used, for example, to clean things, to protect things, or to change their shape. *He withdrew the needle and placed a pad of cotton-wool over the spot. ...a scouring pad. ...a flowered dress with shoulder pads.* N-COUNT

2 A **pad** of paper is a number of pieces of paper which are fixed together along the top or the side, so that each piece can be torn off when it has been used. *She wrote on a pad of paper... Have a pad and pencil ready and jot down some of your thoughts... 'Here's your ticket,' he said, and he tore it off the pad.* N-COUNT

3 When someone **pads** somewhere, they walk there with steps that are fairly quick, light, and quiet. *Freddy speaks very quietly and pads around in soft velvet slippers. ...a dog padding through the streets... Kissinger rages as he pads the corridors.* VERB V prep/adv V n

4 A **pad** is a platform or an area of flat, hard ground where helicopters take off and land or rockets are launched. *...a little round helicopter pad. ...a landing pad on the back of the ship... Journalists report seeing a fire on the pad after the launch.* • See also **launch pad**. N-COUNT

5 People can refer to the place where they live as their **pad**, especially if it is a flat; an informal, old-fashioned use. *I moved on round the big house to reach my pad... It wouldn't have occurred to me to get myself a bachelor pad.* N-COUNT: usu sing, usu poss N

6 The **pads** of a person's fingers and toes or of an animal's paws are the soft, fleshy parts of them. *Tap your cheeks all over with the pads of your fingers.* N-COUNT: usu pl, usu N *of* n

7 If you **pad** something, you put something soft in it or over it in order to make it less hard, to protect it, or to give it a different shape. *Pad the back of a car seat with a pillow... Combatants padded themselves with deer hair as protection... I can tell you I always padded my bras.* ♦ **padded** *...a man in a padded jacket. ...a padded bra. ...back-rests padded with camel's wool.* VERB V n *with* n V n ADJ

8 See also **padding**.

pad out. If you **pad out** a piece of writing or a speech with unnecessary words or pieces of information, you include them in it to make it longer and hide the fact that you have not got very much to say. *The reviewer padded out his review with a lengthy biography of the author... If I wanted to pad out my sermon a little, I might offer my congregation one of my favourite quotations.* PHRASAL VERB V P n (not pron) *with* n V P n (not pron) Also V n P, V n P *with* n

padded cell, padded cells. A **padded cell** is a small room with padded walls in a psychiatric hospital or prison, where people can be put if it is thought that they might hurt themselves in an ordinary room. N-COUNT

padding /pædɪŋ/

1 **Padding** is soft material which is put on something or inside it in order to make it less hard, to N-UNCOUNT

protect it, or to give it a different shape. *...the foam rubber padding on the headphones... Players must wear padding to protect them from injury. ...the fat on our bodies, which acts as padding.*

2 **Padding** is unnecessary words or information used to make a piece of writing or a speech longer. *Of the sonnet eleven of the lines are mere padding and say nothing. ...the kind of subject that politicians put in their speeches for a bit of padding.* N-UNCOUNT

paddle /pædəl/ **paddles, paddling, paddled** ◆◇◇◇◇

1 A **paddle** is a short pole with a wide flat part at one end or at both ends. You hold it in your hands and use it as an oar to move a small boat through water. *We might be able to push ourselves across with the paddle. ...a piece of driftwood which he used as a paddle.* N-COUNT

2 If you **paddle** a boat, you move it through water using a paddle. *...the skills you will use to paddle the canoe. ...paddling around the South Pacific in a kayak.* VERB V n V prep/adv

3 If you **paddle**, you walk or stand in shallow water, for example at the edge of the sea, for pleasure. *Wear sandals when you paddle. ...a lovely little stream that you can paddle in.* ► Also a noun. *Ruth enjoyed her paddle.* VERB V V prep N-SING

paddle boat, paddle boats. A **paddle boat** or a **paddle steamer** is a large boat that is pushed through the water by the movement of large wheels that are attached to its sides. N-COUNT

paddling pool, paddling pools. In British English, a **paddling pool** is a shallow artificial pool for children to paddle in. The usual American terms is **wading pool.** N-COUNT

paddock /pædək/ **paddocks** ◆◇◇◇◇

1 A **paddock** is a small field where horses are kept. *The family kept horses in the paddock in front of the house.* N-COUNT

2 In horse racing or motor racing, the **paddock** is the place where the horses or cars are kept just before each race. N-COUNT

paddy /pædi/ **paddies** ◆◇◇◇◇

1 A **paddy** or a **paddy field** is a field that is kept flooded with water and is used for growing rice. *...the paddy fields of China.* N-COUNT

2 A **Paddy** is an Irishman; an informal use which some people find offensive. N-COUNT; N-VOC

padlock /pædlɒk/ **padlocks, padlocking, padlocked**

1 A **padlock** is a lock which is used for fastening two things or two parts of something together. It consists of a block of metal with a U-shaped bar attached to it. One end of the bar is released when the padlock is unlocked with a key. *They had put a padlock on the door of his flat.* N-COUNT

2 If you **padlock** something, you lock it or fasten it to something else using a padlock. *Eddie parked his cycle against a lamp post and padlocked it... An old mailbox has been padlocked shut.* VERB V n Also V n *to* n

padre /pɑːdreɪ/ **padres.** A **padre** is a Christian priest, especially a chaplain to the armed forces; an informal word. *Could I speak to you in private a moment, padre.* N-COUNT; N-VOC

paean /piːən/ **paeans.** A **paean** is a piece of music, writing, or film that expresses praise, admiration, or joy; a literary word. *...a paean to deep, passionate love.* N-COUNT: usu N *to* n =eulogy

paediatrician /piːdiətrɪʃən/ **paediatricians;** spelled **pediatrician** in American English. A **paediatrician** is a doctor who specializes in treating sick children. N-COUNT

paediatrics /piːdiætrɪks/; spelled **pediatrics** in American English. The form **paediatric** is used as a modifier. **Paediatrics** is the area of medicine that is concerned with the treatment of children's illnesses. N-UNCOUNT

paedophile /piːdəfaɪl/ **paedophiles;** spelled **pedophile** in American English. A **paedophile** is a person, usually a man, who is sexually attracted to children. N-COUNT

paedophilia /piːdəfɪliə/; spelled **pedophilia** in American English. **Paedophilia** is sexual activity with children or the condition of being sexually attracted to children. N-UNCOUNT

paella /paɪelə/ **paellas.** **Paella** is a dish cooked especially in Spain, which consists of rice mixed with small pieces of vegetables, fish, and chicken. N-VAR

paeony /piːəni/. See **peony.**

pagan /peɪgən/ **pagans** ◆◆◇◇◇

1 **Pagan** beliefs and activities do not belong to any of the main religions of the world and take nature and a belief in many gods as a basis. They are older, or are believed to be older, than other religions. ADJ: usu ADJ n

2 In former times, **pagans** were people who did not believe in Christianity and who many Christians considered to be inferior people. *The new religion was eager to convert the pagan world. ...female saints who took vows of virginity rather than submit to an undesired marriage with a pagan.* N-COUNT: oft N n =heathen ≠Christian

paganism /peɪgənɪzəm/. **Paganism** is the belief in pagan ideas and activities. *The country swayed precariously between Christianity and paganism.* N-UNCOUNT

page /peɪdʒ/ **pages, paging, paged** ◆◆◆◆◆

1 A **page** is one side of one of the pieces of paper in a book, magazine, or newspaper. Each page usually has a number printed at the top or bottom. *Where's your book? Take it out and turn to page 4. ...the front page of the Guardian. ...1,400 pages of top-secret information.* N-COUNT: oft N num

2 The **pages** of a book, magazine, or newspaper are the pieces of paper it consists of. *He turned the pages of his notebook... Over the page you can read all about the six great books on offer.* N-COUNT

3 You can refer to an important event or period of time as a **page** of history; a literary use. *...a new page in the country's political history.* N-COUNT: with supp

4 If someone who is in a public place **is paged**, they receive a message, often over a speaker, telling them that someone is trying to contact them. *He was paged repeatedly as the flight was boarding... I'll have them paged and tell them you're here.* VERB *be* V-ed *have* n V-ed

5 In American English, a **page** is a small boy who is one of the bride's attendants at a wedding. The British word is **pageboy.** N-COUNT

6 In former times, a **page** was a young boy who was a knight's servant and was learning to be a knight. N-COUNT: oft poss N

pageant /pædʒənt/ **pageants.** A **pageant** is a colourful public parade, show, or ceremony. Pageants are usually held out of doors and are often organized to celebrate a historic event. ◆◇◇◇◇ N-COUNT

pageantry /pædʒəntri/. **Pageantry** is the colour and formality associated with royal celebrations and other official occasions, for example, when people dress in special clothes and bands play. *He was greeted with all the pageantry of an official state visit.* N-UNCOUNT

pageboy /peɪdʒbɔɪ/ **pageboys;** also spelled **page-boy.**

1 In British English, a **pageboy** is a small boy who is one of the bride's attendants at a wedding. The American word is **page.** N-COUNT

2 A **pageboy** or a **pageboy** hairstyle is a hairstyle in which all the hair is smooth and the same medium length and the ends are curled under. N-SING

pager /peɪdʒəʳ/ **pagers.** A **pager** is a small electronic device which you can carry around with you and which can receive signals from a telephone. The pager gives you a number or a message when someone is trying to telephone you. N-COUNT

pagoda /pəgoʊdə/ **pagodas.** A **pagoda** is a tall building which is used for religious purposes, especially by Buddhists, in China, Japan, and South-East Asia. Pagodas are usually very highly decorated. N-COUNT

pah /pæ/. **Pah** is used in writing to represent the sound someone makes when they show their disgust or scorn at something. EXCLAM

paid /peɪd/ ◆◆◇◇◇

1 **Paid** is the past tense and past participle of **pay.**

2 **Paid** workers receive money for the work that they do. If you do **paid** work or are in **paid** employment, you receive money for the work that you do. *Apart from a small team of paid staff, the organisa-* ADJ: ADJ n ≠unpaid

tion consists of unpaid volunteers. ...tourist visas, which prohibit paid work.
3 If you are given **paid** holiday, you get your wages or salary even though you are not at work. *...10 day's paid holiday for house hunting... He has been placed on a paid leave of absence while investigations are made.* ADJ: ADJ n
4 If you are well **paid**, you receive a lot of money for the work that you do. If you are badly **paid**, you do not receive much money. *...a well-paid accountant... Travel and tourism employees in the UK are among the worst paid in the developed world... Fruit-picking is boring, badly paid and very hard work.* ADJ: adv ADJ
5 If an unexpected event **puts paid to** someone's hopes, chances, or plans, it completely ends or destroys them; used mainly in British English. *...a series of airforce strikes that put paid to the General's hopes of fighting on... Only six months ago I ran my own business. The recession put paid to that.* PHRASE: V inflects, PHR n

paid-up; also spelled **paid up**. ◆◇◇◇◇
1 If a person or country is a **paid-up** member of a group, they are an enthusiastic member or are recognized by most people as being a member of it. *...our future as an independent nation lies as a fully paid-up member of Europe.* ADJ: ADJ n
2 If someone is a **paid-up** member of a political party or other organization, they have paid the money needed to become an official member. *...a fully paid-up member of the Labour Party.* ADJ: ADJ n

pail /peɪl/ **pails.** A **pail** is a bucket, usually made of metal or wood; used mainly in American English or old-fashioned British English. N-COUNT

pain /peɪn/ **pains, pained** ◆◆◆◆◇
1 **Pain** is the feeling of great discomfort you have, for example when you have been hurt or when you are ill. *...back pain. ...a bone disease that caused excruciating pain... To help ease the pain, heat can be applied to the area with a hot water bottle... I felt a sharp pain in my lower back... The illness began with a nagging pain. ...chest pains.* N-VAR • If you are **in pain**, you feel pain in a part of your body, because you are injured or ill. *She was writhing in pain, bathed in perspiration.* PHRASE: PHR after v
2 **Pain** is the feeling of unhappiness that you have when something unpleasant or upsetting happens. *...grey eyes that seemed filled with pain.* N-UNCOUNT =anguish
3 If a fact or idea **pains** you, it makes you feel upset and disappointed. *This public acknowledgment of Ted's disability pained my mother... It pains me to think of you struggling all alone.* VB: no cont V n *it* V n to-inf Also *it* V n that
4 If you think that a person, job, or situation is very annoying or irritating, you can say that they are **a pain** or **a pain in the neck**; an informal expression. **A pain in the arse** and **a pain in the backside** are very informal rude variations of this expression. PHRASES *pain* inflects, v-link PHR, PHR to-inf PRAGMATICS
5 If someone **is at pains to** do something, they are very eager and anxious to do it, especially because they want to avoid a difficult situation; used in newspapers and broadcast news. *Mobil is at pains to point out that the chances of an explosion at the site are remote.* V inflects, usu PHR to-inf =anxious
6 You say that something was all you got **for** your **pains** when you are mentioning the disappointing result of situation into which you put a lot of work or effort. *All Corfield got for his pains was a bullet in the head... The Professor lavished his learning on the young visitor but gained little gratitude for his pains.* PHR with cl PRAGMATICS
7 If someone is ordered not to do something **on pain of** or **under pain of** death, imprisonment, or arrest, they must not do it and if they do it they will be killed, put in prison, or arrested. *We were forbidden, under pain of imprisonment, to use our native language.* PREP
8 If you **take pains** to do something or **go to great pains** to do something, you try hard to do it, because you think it is important to do it. *Social workers went to great pains to acknowledge men's domestic rights... I had taken great pains with my appearance.* V inflects, usu PHR to-inf =go to great lengths

pain barrier. If you say that a sports player has gone through **the pain barrier**, you mean that he or she is continuing to make a great effort in spite of being injured or exhausted; used in journalism. *England's World Cup hero is determined to play through the pain barrier.* N-SING: the N

pained /peɪnd/. If you have a **pained** expression or look, you look upset, worried, or slightly annoyed. ◆◇◇◇◇ ADJ-GRADED

painful /peɪnfʊl/ ◆◆◆◇◇
1 If a part of your body is **painful**, it hurts because it is injured or because there is something wrong with it. *Her glands were swollen and painful... Sampras awaits the results of a bone scan on a painful left shin.* ADJ-GRADED: oft ADJ to-inf =sore ♦ **painfully** *His tooth had started to throb painfully again.* ADV-GRADED: ADV with v
2 If something such as an illness, injury, or operation is **painful**, it causes you a lot of physical pain. *...a painful back injury... Sunburn is painful and potentially dangerous.* ADJ-GRADED ♦ **painfully** *...cracking his head painfully against the cupboard.* ADV-GRADED: ADV with v
3 Situations, memories, or experiences that are **painful** are difficult and unpleasant to deal with, and often make you feel sad and upset. *Remarks like that brought back painful memories. ...the painful transition to democracy... She finds it too painful to return there without him.* ADJ-GRADED: oft ADJ to-inf ♦ **painfully** *...their old relationship, which he had painfully broken off.* ADV-GRADED: ADV with v
4 If a performance or interview is **painful**, it is so bad that it makes you feel embarrassed for the people taking part in it; an informal use. *It was a joint interview with the BBC and ITV and was painful both to watch and to listen to.* ADJ-GRADED: oft ADJ to-inf =embarrassing

painfully /peɪnfʊli/. You use **painfully** to emphasize a quality or situation that is undesirable. *Things are moving painfully slowly. ...a painfully shy young man... I am painfully aware that staff have a heavy work schedule.* ◆◇◇◇◇ ADV: ADV adv/adj PRAGMATICS

painkiller /peɪnkɪləʳ/ **painkillers.** A **painkiller** is a pill or other form of drug which reduces or stops physical pain. ◆◇◇◇◇ N-COUNT =analgesic

painless /peɪnləs/ ◆◇◇◇◇
1 Something such as a treatment that is **painless** causes no physical pain. *Acupuncture treatment is gentle, painless, and, invariably, most relaxing... The operation itself is a brief, painless procedure. ...a quick and painless death.* ADJ-GRADED ≠painful ♦ **painlessly** *...a technique to eliminate unwanted facial hair quickly and painlessly.* ADV-GRADED: ADV with v ≠painfully
2 If a process or activity is **painless**, there are no difficulties involved, and you do not have to make a great effort or suffer in any way. *House-hunting is in fact relatively painless, in this region... There are no easy or painless solutions to the nation's economic ills.* ADJ-GRADED =easy, trouble-free ≠difficult ♦ **painlessly** *...a game for children which painlessly teaches essential pre-reading skills.* ADV-GRADED: ADV with v

painstaking /peɪnsteɪkɪŋ/. A **painstaking** search, examination, or investigation is done extremely carefully and thoroughly. *Forensic experts carried out a painstaking search of the debris.* ◆◇◇◇◇ ADJ-GRADED: usu ADJ n =careful, thorough ♦ **painstakingly** *Broken bones were painstakingly pieced together and reshaped.* ADV-GRADED: usu ADV before v

paint /peɪnt/ **paints, painting, painted** ◆◆◆◆◇
1 **Paint** is a coloured liquid that you put onto a surface with a brush in order to protect the surface or to make it look nice, or that you use to produce a picture. *...a pot of red paint... They saw some large letters in white paint. ...water-based artist's paints.* N-MASS
2 On a wall or object, **the paint** is the covering of dried paint on it. *The paint was peeling on the window frames... They'll probably scrape the paint off and make it look like a regular patrol car.* N-SING: the N
3 If you **paint** a wall or an object, you cover it with paint. *They started to mend the woodwork and paint the walls... I made a guitar and painted it red. ...painted furniture.* VERB V n V n colour V-ed Also V
4 If you **paint** something or **paint** a picture of it, you produce a picture of it using paint. *He is painting a huge volcano... Why do people paint pictures?... I had come here to paint.* VERB V n V

5 When you **paint** a design or message on a surface, you put it on the surface using paint. *...a machine for painting white lines down roads... They went around painting rude slogans on cars... The recesses are decorated with gold stars, with smaller stars painted along the edges.* VERB V n prep V-ed

6 If a woman **paints** her lips or nails, she puts lipstick or nail varnish on them. *She propped the mirror against her handbag and began to paint her lips... She painted her fingernails bright red.* VERB V n V n colour

7 If you **paint** a grim or vivid picture of something, you give a description of it that is grim or vivid. *The report paints a grim picture of life there... He went on to paint a rosy picture about how much has already been accomplished.* VERB V n

8 See also **painting; gloss paint, oil paint, poster paint, war paint.**

paintbox /peɪntbɒks/ **paintboxes.** A **paintbox** is a small flat tin containing a number of little blocks of paint which can be made wet and used to paint a picture. N-COUNT

paintbrush /peɪntbrʌʃ/ **paintbrushes;** also spelled **paint brush** or **paint-brush**. A **paintbrush** is a brush which you use for painting. N-COUNT

painter /peɪntəʳ/ **painters** ◆◆◇◇◇

1 A **painter** is an artist who paints pictures. N-COUNT

2 A **painter** is someone who paints walls, doors, and some other parts of buildings as their job. N-COUNT

painterly /peɪntəʳli/. **Painterly** means relating to or characteristic of painting or painters. *...his painterly talents... The film has a painterly eye.* ADJ: usu ADJ n

painting /peɪntɪŋ/ **paintings** ◆◆◆◆◇

1 A **painting** is a picture which someone has painted. *...a large oil-painting of Queen Victoria.* N-COUNT

2 **Painting** is the activity of painting pictures. *...two hobbies she really enjoyed, painting and gardening.* N-UNCOUNT

3 **Painting** is the activity of painting doors, walls, and some other parts of buildings. *...painting and decorating.* N-UNCOUNT

paint stripper, paint strippers. Paint stripper is a liquid which you use in order to remove old paint from things such as doors, woodwork, or pieces of furniture. N-MASS

paintwork /peɪntwɜːʳk/. The **paintwork** of a building, room, or vehicle is the covering of paint on it, or the parts of it that are painted. *The paintwork, the wardrobes and the bedside cupboards were coffee-cream.* N-UNCOUNT

pair /peəʳ/ **pairs, pairing, paired** ◆◆◆◆◇

1 A **pair** of things are two things of the same size and shape that are intended to be used together, for example shoes, earrings, or parts of the body. *...a pair of socks. ...trainers that cost up to 90 pounds a pair... 72,000 pairs of hands clapped in unison to the song.* N-COUNT: usu with supp

2 Some objects that have two main parts of the same size and shape are referred to as a **pair**, for example **a pair of trousers** or **a pair of scissors**. *...a pair of faded jeans. ...a pair of binoculars.* N-COUNT: usu with supp

3 You can refer to two people as a **pair** when they are standing or walking together or when they have some kind of relationship with each other. *A pair of teenage boys were smoking cigarettes... The pair admitted that their three-year-old marriage was going through 'a difficult time'... He and Paula made an unlikely pair.* N-SING

4 If one thing **is paired with** another, it is put with it or considered with it. *The trainees will then be paired with experienced managers.* ♦ **pairing** *...the pairing of these two fine musicians.* VB: usu passive be V-ed with n N-UNCOUNT: usu the N of n

5 See also **au pair**.

6 If you say that someone is or has **a safe pair of hands**, you mean that they are reliable and will not make any serious mistakes. *He has now held five cabinet posts and remains a safe pair of hands.* PHRASE: PHR after v

pair off. When people **pair off** or **are paired off**, they form a pair, often in order to become girlfriend and boyfriend. *I knew she wouldn't be able to resist pairing me off with someone... The squad members paired off to find places to eat and sleep.* PHRASAL VERB RECIP-ERG V n P with n pl-n V P Also V P with n

pair up. If people **pair up** or **are paired up**, they form a pair, especially in order to do something together. *They asked us to pair up with the person next to us and form teams... Men and teenage girls pair up to dance... Smokers and nonsmokers are paired up as roommates.* PHRASAL VERB RECIP-ERG V P with n pl-n V P pl-n be V-ed Also V n P with n

pairing /peərɪŋ/ **pairings.** Two people, especially sportspeople, actors, or musicians, who are working together as a pair can be referred to as a **pairing**. *In first place we now find the Belgian pairing of Nancy Feber and Laurence Courtois.* ◆◇◇◇◇ N-COUNT =pair

paisley /peɪzli/ **paisleys. Paisley** is a special pattern of curving shapes and colours, used especially on fabric. *He was elegantly dressed in a grey suit, blue shirt and paisley tie.* ◆◇◇◇◇ N-VAR

pajamas /pədʒɑːməz/. See **pyjamas**.

Pakistani /pɑːkɪstɑːni/ **Pakistanis** ◆◆◆◆◇

1 **Pakistani** means belonging or relating to Pakistan, or to its people or culture. *...the Pakistani city of Hyderabad. ...Pakistani cricketers.* ADJ

2 A **Pakistani** is a Pakistani citizen, or a person of Pakistani origin. N-COUNT: usu pl

pal /pæl/ **pals.** Your **pals** are your friends; an old-fashioned, informal word. ◆◇◇◇◇ N-COUNT

palace /pælɪs/ **palaces** ◆◆◆◇◇

1 A **palace** is a very large splendid house, especially one which is the home of a king, queen, or president. *...Buckingham Palace... They entered the palace courtyard.* N-COUNT: oft in names after n, N n

2 When the members of a royal palace make an announcement through an official spokesperson, journalists refer to them as **the Palace**. *'We couldn't possibly comment', is the palace's response to all questions about the family's private life.* N-SING: the N

3 You can refer to any large splendid house or other building as a **palace**. *...a barn Maxwell bought and turned into a palace.* N-COUNT

palaeontology /pæliɒntɒlədʒi, AM peɪl-/; also spelled **paleontology**. **Palaeontology** is the study of fossils as a guide to the history of life on earth. ♦ **palaeontologist, palaeontologists** N-UNCOUNT N-COUNT

palatable /pælətəbᵊl/ ◆◇◇◇◇

1 If you describe food or drink as **palatable**, you mean that it tastes pleasant; a formal use. *...flavourings and preservatives, designed to make the food look more palatable.* ADJ-GRADED =tasty ≠unpalatable

2 If you describe something such as an idea or method as **palatable**, you mean that people are willing to accept it. *...a palatable way of sacking staff... That option is not very palatable.* ADJ-GRADED =acceptable

palate /pælɪt/ **palates** ◆◇◇◇◇

1 Your **palate** is the top part of the inside of your mouth. N-COUNT: usu poss N

2 You can refer to someone's **palate** as a way of talking about their ability to judge good food or drink. *...fresh pasta sauces to tempt more demanding palates. ...a discerning palate.* N-COUNT: usu with supp

palatial /pəleɪʃᵊl/. A **palatial** house, hotel, or office building is large and splendid like a palace. *...a palatial Hollywood mansion. ...the academy's palatial headquarters in Moscow.* ADJ-GRADED: usu ADJ n

palaver /pəlɑːvəʳ, -læv-/. **Palaver** is unnecessary fuss and bother about the way something is done; an informal word. *We don't want all that palaver, do we?* N-UNCOUNT

pale /peɪl/ **paler, palest; pales, paling, paled** ◆◆◆◇◇

1 If something is **pale**, it is very light in colour or almost white. *Migrating birds filled the pale sky... As we age, our skin becomes paler. ...a circle of pale light.* ► Also a combining form. *...a pale blue sailor dress... In the background, dressed in pale green, stood Eunice.* ADJ-GRADED =light ≠dark COMB in COLOUR

2 If someone looks **pale**, their face looks a lighter colour than usual, usually because they are ill, frightened, or shocked. *She looked pale and tired... He went deathly pale.* ♦ **paleness** *...his paleness when he realized that he was bleeding.* ADJ-GRADED: usu v-link ADJ N-UNCOUNT: oft with poss

3 If one thing **pales** in comparison with another, it is made to seem much less important, serious, or good by it. *When someone you love has a life-threatening illness, everything else pales in comparison. ...a soap opera against which other soaps pale into insignificance.* VERB V V prep

4 If you think that someone's actions or behaviour PHRASE:

are not acceptable, you can say that they are **beyond the pale**. *This sort of thing really is quite beyond the pale. ...beyond the pale of acceptable human behaviour.* PHR after v, oft PHR of n =unacceptable

Palestinian /pælɪstɪniən/ **Palestinians** ◆◆◆◆◇
1 Something that is **Palestinian** comes from, belongs to or relates to the region between the River Jordan and the Mediterranean Sea which used to be called Palestine, or to the Arabs who come from this region. ADJ
2 A **Palestinian** is an Arab who comes from the region that used to be called Palestine. N-COUNT: usu pl

palette /pælɪt/ **palettes** ◆◇◇◇◇
1 A **palette** is a flat piece of wood or plastic on which an artist mixes paints. N-COUNT
2 You can refer to the range of colours that are used by a particular artist or group of artists as their **palette**. *David Fincher paints from a palette consisting almost exclusively of grey and mud brown.* N-COUNT: usu sing

palette knife, palette knives. A **palette knife** is a knife with a broad, flat, flexible blade, used in cookery and in oil painting. N-COUNT

palimony /pælɪmoʊni/. **Palimony** is money that a person pays to a partner they have lived with for a long time and are now separated from. Compare **alimony**. N-UNCOUNT

palindrome /pælɪndroʊm/ **palindromes.** A **palindrome** is a word or a phrase that is the same whether you read it backwards or forwards, for example the word 'refer'. N-COUNT

palisade /pælɪseɪd/ **palisades.** A **palisade** is a fence of wooden posts which are driven into the ground in order to protect people from attack. N-COUNT

pall /pɔːl/ **palls, palled** ◆◇◇◇◇
1 If something **palls**, it becomes less interesting or less enjoyable after a period of time. *Already the allure of meals in restaurants had begun to pall.* VB: no cont =wear off V
2 If a **pall** of smoke hangs over a place, there is a thick cloud of smoke above it. *A pall of oily black smoke drifted over the cliff-top.* N-COUNT: usu N of n =cloud
3 If something unpleasant **casts a pall over** an event or occasion, it makes it less enjoyable than it should be. *The unrest has cast a pall over what is usually a day of national rejoicing... We don't want to cast a pall over the festivities.* PHRASE: V inflects, PHR n =spoil

pallbearer /pɔːlbeərəʳ/ **pallbearers.** A **pallbearer** is a person who helps to carry the coffin or walks beside it at a funeral. N-COUNT

pallet /pælɪt/ **pallets**
1 A **pallet** is a narrow mattress filled with straw which is put on the floor for someone to sleep on. N-COUNT
2 A **pallet** is a hard, narrow bed. *He was given only a wooden pallet with a blanket.* N-COUNT
3 A **pallet** is a flat wooden or metal platform on which goods are stacked and stored so that they can be lifted and moved using a fork-lift truck. *The warehouse will hold more than 90,000 pallets storing 30 million Easter eggs.* N-COUNT

palliative /pæliətɪv, AM -eɪt-/ **palliatives**
1 A **palliative** is a drug or medical treatment that relieves suffering without treating the cause of the suffering. N-COUNT
2 A **palliative** is an action that is intended to make the effects of a problem less severe but does not actually solve the problem. *The society's board realised that the loan was a palliative, not a cure, for ever-increasing financial troubles... Marxist analysts see the welfare state merely as a palliative for the worst effects of the economic system.* N-COUNT

pallid /pælɪd/
1 Someone or something that is **pallid** is unattractively or unnaturally pale in appearance. *...helpless grief on pallid faces. ...pallid grey vapour.* ADJ-GRADED
2 You can describe something as **pallid** if it is weak and unexciting. *...a pallid account of the future of transport. ...a pallid unsuccessful romance.* ADJ-GRADED

pallor /pæləʳ/. If you refer to the **pallor** of someone's face or skin, you mean that it is pale and unhealthy. *The deathly pallor of her skin had been replaced by the faintest flush of color... My face had a greenish pallor.* N-SING: usu with supp

pally /pæli/. If you are **pally** with someone, you are friendly with them; an informal word. ADJ-GRADED: oft ADJ with n =friendly

palm /pɑːm/ **palms, palming, palmed** ◆◆◇◇◇
1 A **palm** or a **palm tree** is a tree that grows in hot countries. It has long leaves growing at the top, and no branches. N-COUNT
2 The **palm** of your hand is the inside part. *Dornberg slapped the table with the palm of his hand... He wiped his sweaty palm.* N-COUNT: usu poss N, N of n
3 If you have someone or something **in the palm of your hand**, you have control over them. *Johnson thought he had the board of directors in the palm of his hand... They held his fate in the palms of their ancient hands.* PHRASE: Ns inflect

palm off. If you say that someone **has palmed** something or someone **off** on you or that they **have palmed** you **off** with something, you feel annoyed because they have made you accept something which is not valuable or which is not your responsibility. *I couldn't keep palming her off on friends... Joseph Smith made sure that he was never palmed off with such inferior stuff.* PHRASAL VERB PRAGMATICS V n P on n be V-ed P with n

palm off with. If you say that you **are palmed off with** a lie or an excuse, you are annoyed because you are told something in order to stop you asking any more questions. *Mark was palmed off with a series of excuses.* PHRASAL VERB usu passive PRAGMATICS be V-ed P with n

palmcorder /pɑːmkɔːʳdəʳ/ **palmcorders.** A **palmcorder** is a small video-camera that you can hold in the palm of your hand. N-COUNT

palmistry /pɑːmɪstri/. **Palmistry** is the practice and art of trying to find out what people are like and what will happen in their future life by examining the lines on the palms of their hands. N-UNCOUNT

palm oil. **Palm oil** is a yellow oil which comes from the fruit of certain palm trees and is used in making soap and sometimes as a fat in cooking. N-UNCOUNT

Palm Sunday. **Palm Sunday** is the Sunday before Easter. It is the day when Christians remember Jesus Christ's entry into Jerusalem a few days before he was killed. N-UNCOUNT

palmtop /pɑːmtɒp/ **palmtops.** A **palmtop** is a small computer that you can hold in your hand. N-COUNT

palomino /pæləmiːnoʊ/ **palominos.** A **palomino** is a horse which is golden or cream in colour and has a white mane and tail. N-COUNT

palpable /pælpəbᵊl/. You describe something as **palpable** when it is obvious or intense and easily noticed. *The tension between Amy and Jim is palpable... There is an almost palpable feeling of hopelessness.* ♦ **palpably** /pælpəbli/ *The scene was palpably intense to watch.* ◆◇◇◇◇ ADJ-GRADED; ADV-GRADED: ADV with cl/group

palpitate /pælpɪteɪt/ **palpitates, palpitating, palpitated**
1 If someone's heart **palpitates**, it beats very fast and irregularly because they are frightened or anxious. *He felt suddenly faint, and his heart began to palpitate.* VERB =pound V
2 If something **palpitates**, it trembles or moves quickly backwards and forwards, or seems to move in this way; a literary use. *She lay on the bed her eyes closed and her bosom palpitating.* VERB V-ing Also V

palpitation /pælpɪteɪʃᵊn/ **palpitations.** When someone has **palpitations**, their heart beats very fast and with an irregular beat. *Caffeine can cause palpitations and headaches.* N-VAR

palsy /pɔːlzi/. **Palsy** is an illness which results in paralysis. • See also **cerebral palsy**. N-UNCOUNT

paltry /pɔːltri/ ◆◇◇◇◇
1 A **paltry** amount of money or something else is one that you consider to be very small. *...a paltry fine of £150... They suffered an electoral catastrophe, winning a paltry 3 seats.* ADJ-GRADED: usu ADJ n, oft a ADJ amount
2 You can use **paltry** to describe something or someone that you consider to be small or unimportant. *The parents had little interest in paltry domestic concerns.* ADJ-GRADED: usu ADJ n

pampas /pæmpəs, -əz/. **The pampas** is the large area of flat, grassy land in South America. N-SING: the N

pamper /pæmpəʳ/ **pampers, pampering, pampered.** If you **pamper** someone, you make them feel comfortable by doing things for them or giv- ◆◇◇◇◇ VERB ing them expensive or luxurious things, sometimes in a way which has a bad effect on their character. *Why don't you let your mother pamper you for a while?... Pamper yourself with our luxury gifts... The only son had been pampered and spoiled.* ♦ **pampered** *...today's pampered superstars... He felt pampered and at home.* Vn ADJ-GRADED

pamphlet /pæmflət/ **pamphlets.** A **pamphlet** is a very thin book, with a paper cover, which gives information about something. ◆◇◇◇◇ N-COUNT =booklet

pamphleteer /pæmflətɪə^r/ **pamphleteers.** A **pamphleteer** is a person who writes pamphlets, especially about political subjects. N-COUNT

pan /pæn/ **pans, panning, panned** ◆◆◆◇◇

1 A **pan** is a round metal container with a long handle, which is used for cooking things in, usually on top of a cooker. *Heat the butter and oil in a large pan.* N-COUNT =saucepan

2 In American English, a **pan** is a shallow metal container used for baking foods. The British term is **baking tin**. N-COUNT

3 If something such as a film or a book **is panned** by critics, they say it is very bad; an informal use. *His first high-budget movie, called 'Brain Donors', was panned by the critics.* VB: usu passive =slate be V-ed

4 If you **pan** a film or television camera or if it **pans** somewhere, it moves slowly across an area in a wide sweep. You can also say that you **pan** somewhere. *The camera panned along the line of players... A television camera panned the stadium... He panned the camera, giving a sense of motion... He panned over the crowd for a few minutes before swivelling back to the right.* V-ERG V prep/adv Vn Also V

5 If someone **pans** for gold or **pans** gold, they use a shallow pan to sift gold from a river. *People came westward in the 1800s to pan for gold in the stream beds of the Sierra Nevada... Every year they panned about a ton and a half of gold.* VERB V for n Vn

pan out. If something, for example a project or some information, **pans out**, it produces something useful or valuable; an informal expression. *None of Morgan's proposed financings panned out.* PHRASAL VERB VP

pan- /pæn-/. **pan-** is added to the beginning of adjectives and nouns to form other adjectives and nouns that describe something as being connected with all places or people of a particular kind. *...a pan-European defence system. ...the ideology of pan-Arabism.* PREFIX

panacea /pænəsiːə/ **panaceas.** If you say that something is not a **panacea** for a particular set of problems, you mean that it will not solve all those problems. *Membership of the ERM is not a panacea for Britain's economic problems... Western aid may help but will not be a panacea.* ◆◇◇◇◇ N-COUNT PRAGMATICS =cure-all

panache /pənæʃ/. If you do something with **panache**, you do it in a confident, stylish, and elegant way. *The BBC Symphony Orchestra played with great panache... Her panache at dealing with the world's media is quite astonishing.* ◆◇◇◇◇ N-UNCOUNT =flair

panama hat /pænəmɑː hæt/ **panama hats.** A **panama hat** or a **panama** is a hat, worn especially by men, that is made from the plaited leaves of a palm-like plant. It has a rounded crown and quite a wide brim. N-COUNT

pancake /pænkeɪk/ **pancakes.** A **pancake** is a thin, flat, circular piece of cooked batter made of milk, flour, and eggs. Pancakes are usually rolled up or folded and eaten hot with a sweet or savoury filling inside. ● **flat as a pancake**: see **flat**. ◆◇◇◇◇ N-COUNT =crepe

Pancake Day. In British English, **Pancake Day** is the popular name for **Shrove Tuesday**. N-UNCOUNT

pancake roll, pancake rolls. A **pancake roll** is an item of Chinese food consisting of a small roll of thin crisp pastry filled with vegetables and sometimes meat. N-COUNT =spring roll

pancreas /pæŋkriəs/ **pancreases.** Your **pancreas** is an organ in your body that is situated behind your stomach. It produces insulin and enzymes that help in the digestion of food. ◆◇◇◇◇ N-COUNT

pancreatic /pæŋkriætɪk/. **Pancreatic** means relating to or involving the pancreas. *Pancreatic juices dissolve proteins that were not digested in the stomach.* ADJ: ADJ n

panda /pændə/ **pandas.** A **panda** or a **giant panda** is a large animal rather like a bear, which has black and white fur and lives in the bamboo forests of China. ◆◇◇◇◇ N-COUNT

panda car, panda cars. In British English, a **panda car** is a small police patrol car. N-COUNT

pandemic /pændemɪk/ **pandemics.** A **pandemic** is an occurrence of a disease that affects many people over a very wide area; a formal word. *The AIDS pandemic has highlighted many deficiencies in public health care throughout the world... One pandemic of Spanish flu took nearly 22 million lives worldwide.* N-COUNT

pandemonium /pændɪmoʊniəm/. If there is **pandemonium** in a place, the people there are behaving in a very noisy and uncontrolled way. *There was pandemonium in court as the judge gave his summing up... Pandemonium broke out as they ran into the street shouting.* N-UNCOUNT

pander /pændə^r/ **panders, pandering, pandered.** If you **pander to** someone or to their wishes, you do everything that they want, often to get some advantage for yourself; used showing disapproval. *He said the government had pandered to the terrorists for too long. ...books which don't pander to popular taste.* ◆◇◇◇◇ VERB PRAGMATICS V to n

Pandora /pændɔːrə/. If someone or something **opens Pandora's box** or **opens** a **Pandora's box**, they take an action which unintentionally causes a lot of problems to appear that did not exist or were not known about before. PHRASE: V inflects

p & p; also spelled **p and p. p & p** is a written abbreviation for 'postage and packing'. It is used when stating the cost of packing goods in a parcel and sending them through the post to a customer. *They also publish an excellent cookery book called 'The Flavours Of Gujarat' (£6.95, plus £2.25 p & p)... The guide costs £9.95 (inc. p & p).*

pane /peɪn/ **panes.** A **pane** of glass is a flat sheet of glass in a window or door. ◆◇◇◇◇ N-COUNT

panegyric /pænɪdʒɪrɪk/ **panegyrics.** A **panegyric** is a speech or piece of writing that praises someone or something; a formal word. *...Prince Charles's panegyric on rural living.* N-COUNT =eulogy

panel /pænəl/ **panels** ◆◆◆◇◇

1 A **panel** is a small group of people who are chosen to do something, for example to discuss something in public or to make a decision. *He assembled a panel of scholars to advise him... All the writers on the panel agreed Quinn's book should be singled out for special praise... The advisory panel disagreed with the decision.* N-COUNT-COLL

2 A **panel** is a flat rectangular piece of wood or other material that forms part of a larger object such as a door. *...the frosted glass panel set in the centre of the door.* N-COUNT

3 A control **panel** or instrument **panel** is a board or surface which contains switches and controls to operate a machine or piece of equipment. *The equipment was extremely sophisticated and was monitored from a central control-panel... They had failed to recognise signs on their instrument panel indicating a serious problem.* N-COUNT: n N

panelled /pænəld/; spelled **paneled** in American English. ◆◇◇◇◇

1 A **panelled** room has decorative wooden panels covering its walls. *...a large, comfortable, panelled room... The cheerful room was panelled in pine.* ADJ: usu ADJ n
▸ **-panelled** combines with nouns to form adjectives that describe the way a room or wall is decorated or the way a door or window is made. *...a wood-panelled dining room... The walls are oak-panelled.* COMB in ADJ

2 A **panelled** wall, door, or window does not have a flat surface but has square or rectangular areas set into its surface. *The panelled walls were covered with portraits... The doors are panelled.* ADJ: usu ADJ n

panelling /pænəlɪŋ/; spelled **paneling** in American English. **Panelling** consists of boards or strips of wood covering a wall inside a building. ◆◇◇◇◇ N-UNCOUNT

It was a huge apartment with oak beams and rosewood panelling.

panellist /pænəlɪst/ **panellists;** spelled **panelist** in American English. A **panellist** is a person who is a member of a panel and speaks in public, especially on a radio or television programme. N-COUNT

pang /pæŋ/ **pangs.** A **pang** is a sudden strong feeling or emotion, for example of sadness or pain. *For a moment she felt a pang of guilt about the way she was treating him. ...hunger pangs.* ◆◇◇◇◇ N-COUNT: oft N *of*n, n N

panhandle /pænhændəl/ **panhandles, panhandling, panhandled**

1 In American English, a **panhandle** is a narrow strip of land joined to a larger area of land. *Thunderstorms caused flooding in the Texas panhandle early today.* N-COUNT

2 In American English, if someone **panhandles**, they stop people in the street and ask them for food or money; an informal use. The usual British word is **beg**. *Many of these street people seemed to support themselves by panhandling and doing odd jobs... There was also a guy panhandling for quarters.* ♦ **panhandling** *Sergeant Rivero says arrests for panhandling take place every day.* VERB V, V *for*n, Also V n; N-UNCOUNT

panhandler /pænhændləʳ/ **panhandlers.** In American English, a **panhandler** is a person who stops people in the street and asks them for food or money; an informal word. The usual British word is **beggar**. N-COUNT

panic /pænɪk/ **panics, panicking, panicked** ◆◆◆◇◇

1 **Panic** is a very strong feeling of anxiety or fear, which makes you act without thinking carefully. *An earthquake has hit the capital, causing damage to buildings and panic among the population... I phoned the doctor in a panic, crying that I'd lost the baby.* N-VAR

2 **Panic** or a **panic** is a situation in which people are affected by a strong feeling of anxiety. *There was a moment of panic in Britain as it became clear just how vulnerable the nation was. ...the Aids panic... Previous moral panics have centred on targets such as pornography.* N-VAR

3 If you **panic** or if someone **panics** you, you suddenly feel anxious or afraid, and act quickly and without thinking carefully. *Guests panicked and screamed when the bomb exploded... The unexpected and sudden memory briefly panicked her... The Government has been panicked into giving us a promise to abolish it.* V-ERG V, V n, *be* V-ed *into*n, Also V n *into*n

panicky /pænɪki/. A **panicky** feeling or **panicky** behaviour is characterized by panic. *Amy felt a moment of pure, panicky loneliness... Many women feel panicky travelling home at night alone. ...yesterday's panicky decision by the Bank of Ireland.* ADJ-GRADED

panic-stricken. If someone is **panic-stricken** or is behaving in a **panic-stricken** way, they are so anxious or afraid that they may act without thinking carefully. *Panic-stricken travellers fled for the borders... A wall collapsed and 39 people were killed in the panic-stricken stampede.* ADJ-GRADED

pannier /pæniəʳ/ **panniers**

1 A **pannier** is one of two bags or boxes for carrying things in, which are fixed on each side of the back wheel of a bicycle or motorbike. N-COUNT

2 A **pannier** is a large basket or bag, usually one of two that are put over an animal and used for carrying loads. N-COUNT

panoply /pænəpli/. A **panoply** of things is a wide range of them, especially one that is considered impressive; a formal word. *On a modern battlefield an infantryman can expect to be the target of the whole panoply of weaponry. ...the marvellous panoply of exhibitions laid on this year.* N-SING: usu N *of*n =array

panorama /pænərɑːmə, -ræmə/ **panoramas** ◆◇◇◇◇

1 A **panorama** is a view in which you can see a long way over a wide area of land, usually because you are on high ground. *Horton looked out over a panorama of fertile valleys and gentle hills.* N-COUNT: oft N *of*n =vista

2 A **panorama** is a broad view of a state of affairs or of a constantly changing series of events. *The play presents a panorama of the history of communism.* N-COUNT: usu N *of*n

panoramic /pænəræmɪk/. If you have a **panoramic** view, you can see a long way over a wide area. *The terrain's high points provide a panoramic view of Los Angeles.* ◆◇◇◇◇ ADJ-GRADED: usu ADJ n

pansy /pænzi/ **pansies**

1 A **pansy** is a small brightly coloured garden flower with large round petals. N-COUNT

2 If someone describes a man as a **pansy**, they mean that he is a homosexual; an offensive use. N-COUNT

pant /pænt/ **pants, panting, panted.** If you **pant**, you breathe quickly and loudly with your mouth open, because you have been doing something energetic. *She climbed rapidly until she was panting with the effort.* • See also **pants**. ◆◇◇◇◇ VERB =gasp V

pantaloons /pæntəluːnz/. **Pantaloons** are long trousers with very wide legs, gathered at the ankle. *Hallah wears the stylish tunic and pantaloons common in Kurdistan.* N-PLURAL

pantechnicon /pæntɛknɪkɒn, AM -kɑːn/ **pantechnicons.** In British English, a **pantechnicon** is a large covered lorry, especially one used for moving equipment or furniture from one place to another; a formal word. N-COUNT

pantheism /pænθiːɪzəm/

1 **Pantheism** is the religious belief that God is in everything in nature and the universe. N-UNCOUNT

2 **Pantheism** is a willingness to worship and believe in all gods. N-UNCOUNT

pantheistic /pænθiːɪstɪk/. **Pantheistic** religions involve the acceptance of the idea that God is in everything in nature and the universe. ADJ: usu ADJ n

pantheon /pænθiən/ **pantheons.** You can refer to a group of gods or a group of important people as a **pantheon**. *The gods of the Hindu pantheon occupy the heavens above the Tibetan peaks. ...the Communist Party's pantheon of Marx, Engels, Lenin and Stalin.* ◆◇◇◇◇ N-COUNT: oft N *of*n

panther /pænθəʳ/ **panthers.** A **panther** is a large wild animal that belongs to the cat family. Panthers are usually black. ◆◇◇◇◇ N-COUNT

panties /pæntiz/. In Britain, some people use the word **panties** to refer to the short, close-fitting underpants worn by women or girls. **Panties** is the usual American word for women's underpants. N-PLURAL: also *a pair of*N =knickers

panto /pæntoʊ/ **pantos.** A **panto** is the same as a **pantomime**; an informal British word. *...a Christmas panto... I had one of my most embarrassing moments in panto in Nottingham.* N-VAR

pantomime /pæntəmaɪm/ **pantomimes** ◆◇◇◇◇

1 In Britain, a **pantomime** is a funny musical play for children. Pantomimes are usually based on fairy stories and are performed at Christmas. N-COUNT =panto

2 **Pantomime** is the form of entertainment which involves producing a pantomime; used mainly in British English. *What she does very well is pantomime... He is currently starring in pantomime in Weston-super-Mare.* N-UNCOUNT

3 **Pantomime** is acting something out without speaking. *Chaplin feared that the art of pantomime was under threat.* N-UNCOUNT =mime

4 If you say that a situation or a person's behaviour is a **pantomime**, you mean that it is silly or exaggerated and that there is something false about it; used mainly in British English. *They were made welcome with the usual pantomime of exaggerated smiles and gestures... The rights of every American to good government have been damaged by the pantomime on Capitol Hill.* N-SING =farce

pantry /pæntri/ **pantries.** A **pantry** is a small room or large cupboard in a house, usually near the kitchen, where food is kept. N-COUNT =larder

pants /pænts/ ◆◆◇◇◇

1 In British English, **pants** are a piece of underwear which have two holes to put your legs through and elastic around the top to hold them up round your waist or hips. *I wash and dry myself and put on my bra and pants.* N-PLURAL: also *a pair of*N =knickers

2 In American English, **pants** are a piece of clothing that covers the lower part of your body and each leg. The British word is **trousers**. *She de-* N-PLURAL: also *a pair of*N

scribed him as wearing brown corduroy pants and a white cotton shirt.

3 If someone bores, charms, or scares **the pants off** you, for example, they bore, charm, or scare you a lot; an informal expression. *You'll bore the pants off your grandchildren... We all love to frighten the pants off ourselves by going on hair-raising rides at funfairs.* PHRASES V PHR

4 If you **fly by the seat of** your **pants** or do something **by the seat of** your **pants,** you use your instincts to tell you what to do in a new or difficult situation rather than following a plan or relying on equipment. V inflects

5 • to **be caught with one's pants down**: see **catch.**
• to **wear the pants**: see **wear.**

pantyhose /pæntihoʊz/; also spelled **panty hose.** In American English, **pantyhose** are nylon tights worn by women. The usual British word is **tights.** N-PLURAL: also *a pair of* N

pap /pæp/. If you describe something such as information, writing, or entertainment as **pap,** you mean that you consider it to be of no worth, value, or serious interest. N-UNCOUNT =drivel

papa /pəpɑː, AM pɑːpə/ **papas.** Some people refer to or address their father as **papa**; an old-fashioned word. *He was so much older than me, older even than my papa.* ◆◇◇◇◇ N-FAMILY

papacy /peɪpəsi/; also spelled **Papacy.** The **papacy** is the position, power, and authority of the Pope, including the period of time that a particular person holds this position. *Throughout his papacy, John Paul has called for a second evangelization of Europe.* N-SING: usu *the* N

papal /peɪpəl/. **Papal** is used to describe things relating to the Pope. *...the doctrine of papal infallibility.* ◆◇◇◇◇ ADJ: ADJ n

paparazzo /pæpərætsoʊ/ **paparazzi** /pæpərætsi/. The **paparazzi** are photographers who follow rich or famous people around, hoping to take interesting or shocking photographs of them that they can sell to a newspaper. *The paparazzi pursue Armani wherever he travels.* N-COUNT: usu pl

papaya /pəpaɪə/ **papayas.** A **papaya** is a fruit with a green skin, sweet yellow flesh, and small black seeds. Papayas grow on trees in hot countries such as the West Indies. N-COUNT =pawpaw

paper /peɪpəʳ/ **papers, papering, papered** ◆◆◆◆◆

1 **Paper** is a material that you write on or wrap things with. The pages of this book are made of paper. *He wrote his name down on a piece of paper for me... She sat at the table with pen and paper. ...a sheet of pretty wrapping paper. ...a paper bag.* N-UNCOUNT

2 A **paper** is a newspaper. *I might get a paper in the village... I'll cook and you read the paper.* N-COUNT

3 You can refer to newspapers in general as **the paper** or **the papers.** *You can't believe everything you read in the paper... There's been a lot in the papers about the problems facing stepchildren.* N-COUNT: *the* N =the press

4 Your **papers** are sheets of paper with writing or information on them, which you might keep in a safe place at home. *After her death, her papers – including unpublished articles and correspondence – were deposited at the library.* N-PLURAL: usu with poss =documents

5 Your **papers** are official documents, for example your passport or identity card, which prove who you are or which give you official permission to do something. *A young Moroccan stopped by police refused to show his papers... They have arrested four people who were trying to leave the country with forged papers.* N-PLURAL: usu poss N =identification

6 A **paper** is a long essay written on an academic subject. *He just published a paper in the journal Nature analyzing the fires.* N-COUNT

7 A **paper** prepared by a government or a committee is a report on a question they have been considering or a set of proposals for changes in the law. *...a new government paper on European policy.* N-COUNT
• See also **green paper, white paper.**

8 A **paper** is a part of a written examination in which you answer a number of questions in a particular period of time. *We sat each paper in the Hall... She finished the exam paper. ...the applied mathematics paper.* N-COUNT

9 **Paper** agreements, qualifications, or profits are ones that are stated by official documents to exist, although they may not really be effective or useful. *They expressed deep mistrust of the paper promises... We're looking for people who have experience rather than paper qualifications.* ADJ: ADJ n

10 If you **paper** a wall, you put wallpaper on it. *We papered all four bedrooms... We have papered this bedroom in softest grey... The room was strange, the walls half papered, half painted.* VERB V n V-ed

11 If you put your thoughts down **on paper,** you write them down. *It is important to get something down on paper... It was the first time I had put it all down on paper. I found it helped.* PHRASES PHR after v

12 If something seems to be the case **on paper,** it seems to be the case from what you read or hear about it, but it may not really be the case. *On paper, their country is a multi-party democracy... The family is estimated to have been worth, on paper at least, more than £1.1billion.* =in theory

13 If you say that a promise, an agreement, or a guarantee **is not worth the paper it's written on,** you mean that although it has been written down and seems to be official, it is in fact worthless because what has been promised, agreed, or guaranteed will not be done. Vs inflect

paper over. If people **paper over** a disagreement between them, they find a temporary solution to it in order to give the impression that things are going well. *...his determination to paper over the cracks in his party and avoid confrontation... Differences were papered over but by no means were they fully resolved.* PHRASAL VERB V P n

paperback /peɪpəʳbæk/ **paperbacks.** A **paperback** is a book with a thin cardboard or paper cover. Compare **hardback** and **softback.** *She said she would buy the book when it comes out in paperback.* ◆◆◇◇◇ N-COUNT: also *in* N

paperboy /peɪpəʳbɔɪ/ **paperboys;** also spelled **paper boy.** A **paperboy** is a boy who delivers newspapers to people's homes. N-COUNT

paper clip, paper clips; also spelled **paper-clip** or **paperclip.** A **paper clip** is a small piece of bent wire that is used to fasten papers together. N-COUNT

papergirl /peɪpəʳgɜːʳl/ **papergirls;** also spelled **paper girl.** A **papergirl** is a girl who delivers newspapers to people's homes. N-COUNT

paper knife, paper knives; also spelled **paper-knife.** A **paper knife** is a tool shaped like a blunt knife, which is used for opening envelopes. N-COUNT

paperless /peɪpəʳləs/. **Paperless** is used to describe transactions or office activities which are done by computer and telephone, rather than by writing things down and exchanging pieces of paper. *Paperless trading can save time and money. ...the paperless office.* ADJ: ADJ n

paper money. **Paper money** is money which is made of paper. Paper money is usually worth more than coins. N-UNCOUNT

paper round, paper rounds. A **paper round** is a job of delivering newspapers to houses along a certain route. Paper rounds are usually done by children before or after school. N-COUNT

paper shop, paper shops. In Britain, a **paper shop** is a shop that sells newspapers, tobacco, sweets, and stationery. N-COUNT =newsagent

paper-thin; also spelled **paper thin.** If something is **paper-thin,** it is very thin. *Cut the onion into paper-thin slices... The walls are paper thin; you can hear everything that goes on.* ADJ

paper tiger, paper tigers. If you say that an institution, a country, or a person is a **paper tiger,** you mean that although they seem powerful they do not really have any power. N-COUNT

paper trail. In American English, documentary evidence of someone's activities can be referred to as a **paper trail.** *Criminals are very reluctant to leave a paper trail.* N-SING

paperweight /peɪpəʳweɪt/ **paperweights.** A **paperweight** is a small heavy object which you place on papers to prevent them from being disturbed or blown away. N-COUNT

paperwork /peɪpəʳwɜːʳk/. **Paperwork** is the routine part of a job which involves writing or dealing with letters, reports, and records. *At every stage in the production there will be paperwork – forms to fill in, permissions to obtain, letters to write.* ◆◇◇◇◇ N-UNCOUNT

papery /peɪpəri/. Something that is **papery** is thin and dry like paper. *Leave each garlic clove in its papery skin.* ADJ

papier-mâché /pæpieɪ mæʃeɪ, AM peɪpəʳ məʃeɪ/. **Papier-mâché** is a mixture of pieces of paper and glue. It can be made, while still damp, into objects such as bowls, ornaments, and models. *Hannah Downes designs, makes and decorates papier mâché bowls, plates, mirror frames, shelves and wall plaques.* N-UNCOUNT: oft N n

papist /peɪpɪst/ **papists;** also spelled **Papist**. Some Protestants refer to Catholics as **Papists**; an offensive word. N-COUNT

paprika /pəpriːkə, pæprɪkə/. **Paprika** is a mild-tasting red powder that is used for flavouring food. N-UNCOUNT

papyrus /pəpaɪrəs/ **papyri**

1 **Papyrus** is a tall water plant that grows in Africa. N-UNCOUNT

2 **Papyrus** is a type of paper made from papyrus stems that was used in ancient Egypt, Rome, and Greece. N-UNCOUNT

3 A **papyrus** is an ancient document that is written on papyrus. N-COUNT

par /pɑːʳ/ ◆◆◇◇◇

1 If you say that someone or something is **on a par with** someone or something else, you mean that the two people or things are equally good or bad, or equally important. *Parts of Glasgow are on a par with the worst areas of London and Liverpool for burglaries.* PHRASE: PHR n/-ing, usu v-link PHR, PHR after v

2 In golf, **par** is the number of strokes that a good golfer should take to get the ball into a hole or into all the holes on a particular golf course. *He was five under par after the first round.* N-UNCOUNT: N with num, *under/over* N

3 If you say that someone or something is **below par** or **under par**, you are disappointed in them because they are below the standard you expected. *Duffy's primitive guitar playing is well below par... A teacher's job is relatively safe, even if they perform under par in the classroom. ...a below par effort.* PHRASES v-link PHR, PHR after v, PHR n ≠up to scratch

4 If you say that someone or something is not **up to par**, you are disappointed in them because they are below the standard you expected. *His performance was not up to par... It's a constant struggle to try to keep them up to par.* usu with neg, v-link PHR, PHR after v

5 If you **feel below par** or **under par**, you feel tired and unable to perform as well as you normally do. usu v-link PHR =under the weather

6 If you say that something that happens is **par for the course**, you mean that you are not pleased with it but it is what you expected to happen. *He said long hours are par for the course.* v-link PHR PRAGMATICS =typical

para /pærə/ **paras.** A **para** is a **paratrooper**; an informal word. *...some guys who had just come out of the paras.* N-COUNT: usu pl, usu *the* N

para. /pærə/ **paras. Para.** is a written abbreviation for **paragraph**. *See Chapter 9, para 1.2.* =paragraph

parable /pærəbəl/ **parables.** A **parable** is a short story, which is told in order to make a moral or religious point, like those in the Bible. *... the parable of the Good Samaritan... The story is a pleasing parable of the problems created by an excess of wealth.* ◆◇◇◇◇ N-COUNT: oft N *of* n

parabola /pəræbələ/ **parabolas.** A **parabola** is a type of curve such as the path of something that is thrown up into the air and comes down in a different place. N-COUNT =arc

parabolic /pærəbɒlɪk/. A **parabolic** object or curve is shaped like a parabola. *...a parabolic mirror.* ADJ: usu ADJ n

paracetamol /pærəsiːtəmɒl/; **paracetamol** is both the singular and the plural form. **Paracetamol** is a mild drug which reduces pain and fever. It is sold in the form of tablets. *I often take paracetamol at work if I get a bad headache... I took 2 paracetamol.* N-VAR

parachute /pærəʃuːt/ **parachutes, parachuting, parachuted** ◆◇◇◇◇

1 A **parachute** is a device which enables a person to jump from an aircraft and float safely to the ground. It consists of a large piece of thin cloth attached to your body by strings. *They fell 41,000 ft. before opening their parachutes... UN troops could be landed by helicopter or even by parachute.* N-COUNT: also *by* N

2 If a person **parachutes** or someone **parachutes** them somewhere, they jump from an aircraft using a parachute. *He was a courier for the Polish underground and parachuted into Warsaw... He was parachuted in.* V-ERG V prep/adv *be* V-ed prep/adv

3 If someone **parachutes** something, they drop it somewhere by parachute. *Planes parachuted food, clothing, blankets, medicine and water into the rugged mountainous border region... Supplies were parachuted into the mountains.* VERB =drop V n prep/adv

parachuting /pærəʃuːtɪŋ/. **Parachuting** is the activity or sport of jumping from an aircraft with a parachute. *His hobby is freefall parachuting.* N-UNCOUNT

parachutist /pærəʃuːtɪst/ **parachutists.** A **parachutist** is a person who jumps from an aircraft using a parachute. *He was an experienced parachutist who had done over 150 jumps.* N-COUNT

parade /pəreɪd/ **parades, parading, paraded** ◆◆◇◇◇

1 A **parade** is a procession of people or vehicles moving through a public place in order to celebrate an important day or event. *A military parade marched slowly and solemnly down Pennsylvania Avenue.* N-COUNT

2 When people **parade**, they walk together in a formal group or in a line, usually in front of spectators. *More than four thousand soldiers, sailors and airmen paraded down the Champs Elysee... Everybody was beginning to parade back to the village.* VERB V prep/adv

3 **Parade** is a formal occasion when soldiers stand in lines in order to be inspected, or march in formation. *He had them on parade at six o'clock in the morning... Morning parade was in progress on the parade ground.* N-VAR: oft *on* N

4 If flags or statues **are paraded**, they are carried in a procession. *Banners were paraded from church to church on feast days.* VB: usu passive *be* V-ed prep

5 If prisoners **are paraded** through the streets of a town or on television, their captors show them to the public in order to show their power. *Five leading Communist fighters have been captured and paraded before the media.* VB: usu passive *be* V-ed prep

6 If you say that someone **parades** a person, you mean that they show that person to others only in order to gain some advantage for themselves. *Every day in this election campaign children have been paraded alongside the party leaders to publicise the latest issue.* VB: usu passive *be* V-ed

7 If people **parade** something, they show it in public so that they can be admired or envied. *Valentino is keen to see celebrities parading his clothes at big occasions.* VERB =show off V n

8 If someone **parades**, they walk about somewhere in order to be seen and admired. *I love to put on a bathing suit and parade on the beach... They danced and paraded around.* VERB V prep/adv

9 If someone **parades** a real or pretended feeling or quality, they draw attention to themselves by displaying it. *They parade their virtuous beliefs and hide their vices... Women were not supposed to parade their ambition nakedly.* VERB =flaunt V n

10 If you say that something **parades as** or **is paraded as** a good or important thing, you mean that some people say that it is good or important but you think it probably is not. *The Chancellor will be able to parade his cut in interest rates as a small victory... She might have been paraded as a woman who was working hard to change her ways. ...all the fashions that parade as modern movements in art.* V-ERG PRAGMATICS V n *as* n V *as* n

11 If you talk about a **parade of** people or things, you mean that there is a series of them that seems never to end. *When I ask Nick about his childhood, he remembers a parade of baby-sitters. ...an endless parade of advertisements.* N-COUNT: N *of* n

12 A **parade** is a short row of shops, usually set back from the main street; used in British English. N-COUNT
13 **Parade** is used as part of the name of a street. *Queens Hotel, Clarence Parade, Southsea.* N-IN-NAMES
14 See also **hit parade, identity parade.**

parade ground, parade grounds. A **parade ground** is an area of ground where soldiers practise marching and where they hold parades. N-COUNT

paradigm /pærədaɪm/ **paradigms** ◆◇◇◇◇
1 A **paradigm** is a model for something which explains it or shows how it can be produced; a formal term. *...a new paradigm of production.* N-VAR: usu with supp =pattern
2 A **paradigm** is a clear and typical example of something. *By the time the war was over he had become the paradigm of the successful man.* N-COUNT: usu with supp

paradigmatic /pærədɪgmætɪk/. You can describe something as **paradigmatic** if it acts as a model or example for something; a formal word. *Their great academic success was paraded as paradigmatic.* ADJ

paradise /pærədaɪs/ **paradises** ◆◆◇◇◇
1 According to some religions, **paradise** is a wonderful place where people go after they die, if they have led good lives. *The Koran describes paradise as a place containing a garden of delight... If they were captured they wished to die, believing that they would go to paradise.* N-PROPER =heaven
2 You can refer to a place or situation that seems beautiful or perfect as **paradise** or **a paradise**. *...one of the world's great natural paradises... Scott is living and working at a mission for the homeless. He calls it a paradise compared to the camp.* N-VAR
3 You can also use **paradise** to say that a place is very attractive to a particular kind of person and has everything they need for a particular activity. *The Algarve is a golfer's paradise... Very few people have the money to take advantage of this consumer paradise.* • see also **fool's paradise**. N-COUNT: supp N

paradox /pærədɒks/ **paradoxes** ◆◇◇◇◇
1 You describe a situation as a **paradox** when it involves two or more facts or qualities which seem to contradict each other. *The paradox is that the region's most dynamic economies have the most primitive financial systems... The paradox of exercise is that while using a lot of energy it seems to generate more... Death itself is a paradox, the end yet the beginning.* N-COUNT =enigma
2 A **paradox** is a statement in which it seems that if one part of it is true, the other part of it cannot be true. *The story contains many levels of paradox... Although I'm so successful I'm really rather a failure. That's a paradox, isn't it?* N-VAR

paradoxical /pærədɒksɪkəl/. If something is **paradoxical**, it involves two facts or qualities which seem to contradict each other. *Some sedatives produce the paradoxical effect of making the person more anxious... We were a team of individuals – as paradoxical as that sounds.* ◆◇◇◇◇ ADJ-GRADED
♦ **paradoxically** /pærədɒksɪkli/ *Paradoxically, the less you have to do the more you may resent the work that does come your way. ...a growing up that paradoxically involves remaining a child, too.* ADV-GRADED: usu ADV with cl/group, ADV with v

paraffin /pærəfɪn/. **Paraffin** is a strong-smelling liquid which is used as a fuel in heaters, lamps, and engines. The usual American word is **kerosene**. *...a paraffin lamp.* N-UNCOUNT =kerosene

paraffin wax. **Paraffin wax** is a white wax obtained from petrol or coal. It is used to make candles and in beauty treatments. N-UNCOUNT

paragon /pærəgɒn/ **paragons.** If you refer to someone as a **paragon**, you mean that you think they are perfect. If you say that they are a **paragon** of virtue, or some other good quality, you mean that they have a lot of that quality. *We don't expect candidates to be paragons of virtue. ...a paragon of neatness, efficiency and reliability... He was not a paragon. He would never be perfect.* ◆◇◇◇◇ N-COUNT: oft N of n

paragraph /pærəgrɑːf, -græf/ **paragraphs.** A **paragraph** is a section of a piece of writing. A paragraph always begins on a new line and contains at least one sentence. *The length of a paragraph depends on the information it conveys... Paragraph 81 sets out the rules that should apply if a gift is accepted.* ◆◆◇◇◇ N-COUNT

parakeet /pærəkiːt/ **parakeets;** also spelled **parrakeet.** A **parakeet** is a small parrot with a long tail. N-COUNT

paralegal /pærəliːgəl/ **paralegals.** A **paralegal** is someone who works in the legal profession helping lawyers and solicitors, but who is not yet completely qualified; used mainly in American English. N-COUNT

parallax /pærəlæks/ **parallaxes. Parallax** is the effect whereby an object appears to change its position because the person or instrument observing it has changed their position; a technical term. N-VAR

parallel /pærəlel/ **parallels, parallelling, parallelled;** spelled **paralleling, paralleled** in American English. ◆◆◇◇◇
1 If something has a **parallel**, it is similar to something else, but exists or happens in a different place or at a different time. If it has **no parallel** or is **without parallel**, it is not similar to anything else. *Readers familiar with English history will find a vague parallel to the suppression of the monasteries... It's an ecological disaster with no parallel anywhere else in the world. ...an achievement without parallel in the modern era.* N-COUNT =equivalent
2 If there are **parallels** between two things, they are similar in some ways. *Detailed study of folk music from a variety of countries reveals many close parallels... There are significant parallels with the 1980s... Friends of the dead lawyer were quick to draw a parallel between the two murders.* N-COUNT: oft N *between/to/with* n
3 If one thing **parallels** another, they happen at the same time or are similar, and often seem to be connected. *Often there are emotional reasons paralleling the financial ones... The change in smoking is paralleled by a change in the incidence of lung cancer... His remarks paralleled those of the president.* VERB =echo V n
4 **Parallel** events or situations happen at the same time as one another, or are similar to one another. *...parallel talks between the two countries' Foreign Ministers... Their instincts do not always run parallel with ours... This is a real world, running parallel to our own.* ADJ: oft ADJ *with/to* n
5 If two lines, two objects, or two lines of movement are **parallel**, they are the same distance apart along their whole length. *...seventy-two ships, drawn up in two parallel lines... Farthing Lane's just above the High Street and parallel with it... This trail was roughly parallel to the border.* ADJ: oft ADJ *to/with* n
6 A **parallel** is an imaginary line round the earth that is parallel to the equator. Parallels are shown on maps. *...the area south of the 38th parallel.* N-COUNT: usu *the* ord N
7 Something that occurs **in parallel** with something else occurs at the same time as it. *Davies has managed to pursue his diverse interests in parallel with his fast-moving career... Progress on this issue must be made in parallel to any moves on the economic front.* PHRASE: PHR after v, usu PHR *with/to* n =in concurrence

parallel bars. **Parallel bars** consist of a pair of bars on posts which are used for doing gymnastic exercises. N-PLURAL

parallelism /pærəlelɪzəm/. When there is **parallelism** between two things, there are similarities between them; a formal word. *The commission sees growing parallelism between the priorities of the European Community and the United States.* N-UNCOUNT

parallelogram /pærəleləgræm/ **parallelograms.** A **parallelogram** is a four-sided geometrical figure in which every side is parallel to the side opposite it. N-COUNT

parallel processing. In computing, **parallel processing** is a system in which several instructions are carried out at the same time instead of one after the other. N-UNCOUNT

paralyse /pærəlaɪz/ **paralyses, paralysing, paralysed;** spelled **paralyze** in American English. ◆◇◇◇◇
1 If someone **is paralysed** by an accident or an ill- VERB

ness, they have no feeling in their body, or in part of their body, and are unable to move. *Her married sister had been paralysed in a road accident. ...a virus which paralysed his legs.* ♦ **paralysed** *The disease left him with a paralysed right arm. ...sports for people paralysed by illness or injury.* =immobilize; be V-ed; V n; ADJ

2 If a person, place, or organization **is paralysed** by something, they become unable to act or function properly. *For weeks now the government has been paralysed by indecision... He was suddenly paralysed by fear... The strike has virtually paralysed the island.* ♦ **paralysed** *He was absolutely paralysed with shock. ...an indefinite period of chaos, with disrupted air services and a paralysed civil service.* ♦ **paralysing** *...paralysing shyness. ...a wave of paralysing strikes.* VERB; be V-ed; V n; ADJ; ADJ-GRADED: ADJ n

paralysis /pərælәsɪs/ ♦◇◇◇◇
1 Paralysis is the loss of feeling in all or part of your body, and the inability to move. *...paralysis of the leg.* N-UNCOUNT
2 Paralysis is the state of being unable to act or function properly. *The paralysis of the leadership leaves the army without its supreme command. ...a kind of mental paralysis.* N-UNCOUNT

paralytic /pærəlɪtɪk/
1 Paralytic means suffering from or related to paralysis. *We were able to reverse paralytic disease in laboratory animals.* ADJ: usu ADJ n
2 In informal British English, someone who is **paralytic** is very drunk indeed. *By the end of the evening they were all absolutely paralytic.* ADJ-GRADED: usu v-link ADJ

paramedic /pærəmedɪk, AM -medɪk/ **paramedics.** A **paramedic** is a person whose training is similar to that of a nurse and who helps to do medical work. *We intend to have a paramedic on every ambulance within the next three years.* N-COUNT

paramedical /pærəmedɪkəl/. **Paramedical** workers and services help doctors and nurses in medical work. *...doctors and paramedical staff.* ADJ: ADJ n

parameter /pəræmɪtəʳ/ **parameters. Parameters** are factors or limits which affect the way that something can be done or made. *That would be enough to make sure we fell within the parameters of our loan agreement. ...some of the parameters that determine the taste of a wine.* ♦◇◇◇◇ N-COUNT: usu pl

paramilitary /pærəmɪlɪtri, AM -teri/ **paramilitaries** ♦◇◇◇◇
1 A **paramilitary** organization is organized like an army and performs either civil or military functions in a country. *Searches by the army and paramilitary forces have continued today... Paramilitary police units are taking part in rescue efforts.* ► **Paramilitaries** are members of a paramilitary organization. *Paramilitaries and army recruits patrolled the village... They had cropped heads and wore paramilitary uniforms.* ADJ: ADJ n; N-COUNT: usu pl
2 A **paramilitary** organization is an illegal group that is organized like an army. *...a law which said that all paramilitary groups must be disarmed... There are signs of paramilitary activity supported from abroad.* ► **Paramilitaries** are members of an illegal paramilitary organization. *Loyalist paramilitaries were blamed for the shooting.* ADJ: ADJ n; N-COUNT: usu pl

paramount /pærəmaʊnt/. Something that is **paramount** or of **paramount** importance is more important than anything else. *The child's welfare must be seen as paramount... Nitrogen is of paramount importance to life on earth. ...the paramount need for a peaceful solution to the crisis.* ♦◇◇◇◇ ADJ

paramour /pærəmʊəʳ/ **paramours.** Someone's **paramour** is their lover; an old-fashioned word. N-COUNT: oft poss N =beloved

paranoia /pærənɔɪə/ ♦◇◇◇◇
1 If you say that someone suffers from **paranoia**, you think that they are too suspicious, distrustful, and afraid of other people. *The mood is one of paranoia and expectation of war. ...the mounting paranoia with which he viewed the world around him.* N-UNCOUNT
2 If someone suffers from **paranoia**, they wrongly believe that other people are trying to harm them, or believe themselves to be much more important than they really are. N-UNCOUNT

paranoiac /pærənɔɪæk/. **Paranoiac** means the same as **paranoid**. ADJ-GRADED

paranoid /pærənɔɪd/ **paranoids** ♦◇◇◇◇
1 If you say that someone is **paranoid**, you mean that they are extremely suspicious, distrustful, and afraid of other people. *I'm not going to get paranoid about it. ...a paranoid politician who saw enemies all around him. ...an increasingly paranoid and fearful society.* ADJ-GRADED PRAGMATICS
2 Someone who is **paranoid** suffers from the mental illness of paranoia. *...paranoid delusions. ...a paranoid schizophrenic.* ► A **paranoid** is someone who is paranoid. ADJ; N-COUNT

paranormal /pærənɔːʳməl/. A **paranormal** event or power, for example the appearance of a ghost, cannot be explained by scientific laws and is thought to involve strange, unknown forces. *Science may be able to provide some explanations of paranormal phenomena.* ► You can refer to paranormal events and matters as **the paranormal**. *We have been looking at the shadowy world of the paranormal.* ADJ: usu ADJ n =supernatural; N-SING: the N =supernatural

parapet /pærəpɪt/ **parapets**
1 A **parapet** is a low wall along the edge of a bridge, roof, or balcony. N-COUNT
2 If you say that someone **puts their head above the parapet**, you mean they take a risk. If you say they **keep their head below the parapet**, you mean they avoid taking a risk; used mainly in British English. PHRASE: V and *head* inflect

paraphernalia /pærəfəʳneɪliə/ ♦◇◇◇◇
1 You can refer to a large number of objects that someone has with them or that are connected with a particular activity as **paraphernalia**. *...a large courtyard full of builders' paraphernalia... Get rid of all cigarettes and ashtrays and other paraphernalia associated with smoking.* N-UNCOUNT =stuff
2 If you disapprove of the things and events that are involved in a particular system or activity, and you think they are unnecessary, you can refer to them as **paraphernalia**. *The public don't necessarily want the paraphernalia of a full hearing.* N-UNCOUNT: usu with supp, oft N *of*n PRAGMATICS =trappings

paraphrase /pærəfreɪz/ **paraphrases, paraphrasing, paraphrased**
1 If you **paraphrase** someone or **paraphrase** something that they have said or written, you express what they have said or written in a different way. *Parents, to paraphrase Philip Larkin, can seriously damage your health... Baxter paraphrased the contents of the press release... I'm paraphrasing but this is honestly what he said.* VERB; V n; V
2 A **paraphrase** of something written or spoken is the same thing expressed in a different way. N-COUNT: oft N *of*n

paraplegia /pærəpliːdʒə/. **Paraplegia** is paralysis of the lower half of the body; a medical term. N-UNCOUNT

paraplegic /pærəpliːdʒɪk/ **paraplegics.** A **paraplegic** is someone whose lower body is paralysed, for example as a result of an injury to their spine. ► Also an adjective. *A passenger was injured so badly he will be paraplegic for the rest of his life.* N-COUNT; ADJ

parapsychology /pærəsaɪkɒlədʒi/. **Parapsychology** is the study of strange mental abilities that seem to exist but cannot be explained by accepted scientific theories. N-UNCOUNT

paraquat /pærəkwæt/. **Paraquat** is a very poisonous substance that is used to kill weeds. **Paraquat** is a trademark. N-UNCOUNT

parasite /pærəsaɪt/ **parasites** ♦◇◇◇◇
1 A **parasite** is a small animal or plant that lives on or inside a larger animal or plant, and gets its food from it. N-COUNT
2 If you disapprove of someone because you think that they get money or other things from other people but do not do anything in return, you can call them a **parasite**. N-COUNT PRAGMATICS =sponger

parasitic /pærəsɪtɪk/; also spelled **parasitical.** 
1 Parasitic diseases are caused by parasites. *Will global warming mean the spread of tropical parasitic diseases?* ADJ: usu ADJ n
2 Parasitic animals and plants live on or inside ADJ:

larger animals or plants and get their food from them. ...*tiny parasitic insects.* usu ADJ n

3 If you describe a person or organization as **parasitic**, you mean that they get money or other things from people without doing anything in return. ADJ PRAGMATICS

parasol /pærəsɒl, AM -sɔːl/ **parasols.** A **parasol** is an object like an umbrella that provides shade from the sun. N-COUNT =sunshade

paratrooper /pærətruːpəʳ/ **paratroopers. Paratroopers** are soldiers who are trained to be dropped by parachute into battle or into enemy territory. ◆◇◇◇◇ N-COUNT: usu pl =para

paratroops /pærətruːps/; the form **paratroop** is used as a modifier. **Paratroops** are soldiers who are trained to be dropped by parachute into battle or into enemy territory. *The airport is in the hands of French paratroops. ...special paratroop regiments.* N-PLURAL =paras

parboil /pɑːʳbɔɪl/ **parboils, parboiling, parboiled.** If you **parboil** food, especially vegetables, you boil it until it is partly cooked. *Roughly chop and parboil the potatoes, then sauté them in butter.* VERB V n

parcel /pɑːʳsᵊl/ **parcels, parcelling, parcelled;** spelled **parceling, parceled** in American English. ◆◆◇◇◇

1 A **parcel** is something wrapped in paper, usually so that it can be sent to someone by post. The more usual American word is **package**. *...parcels of food and clothing... He had a large brown paper parcel under his left arm.* N-COUNT

2 A **parcel of** land is a piece of land. *These small parcels of land were purchased for the most part by local people.* N-COUNT: N *of* n

3 A **parcel of** things or people is a quantity of them; used mainly in British English. *The woman who became his wife would be acquiring not just a husband but a run-down house and a parcel of financial worries.* N-COUNT: N *of* n

4 If you say that something is **part and parcel** of something else, you are emphasizing that it is involved or included in it. *Payment was part and parcel of carrying on insurance business within the UK... It's all part and parcel - just a day's work really you know.* PHRASE: v-link PHR, usu PHR *of* n

parcel out. If you **parcel out** something, you divide it into several parts or amounts and give them to different people. *They signed an agreement that parcelled out the Middle East into several spheres of influence.* PHRASAL VERB =divide V P n (not pron) Also V n P

parcel bomb, parcel bombs. In British English, a **parcel bomb** is a small bomb which is sent in a parcel through the post and which is designed to explode when the parcel is opened. N-COUNT

parched /pɑːʳtʃt/

1 If something, especially the ground or a plant, is **parched**, it is very dry, because there has been no rain. *The clouds gathered and showers poured down upon the parched earth. ...a hill of parched brown grass.* ADJ-GRADED

2 If your mouth, throat, or lips are **parched**, they are unpleasantly dry. ADJ-GRADED =dry

3 If you say that you are **parched**, you mean that you are very thirsty; an informal use. ADJ-GRADED: v-link ADJ

parchment /pɑːʳtʃmənt/ **parchments**

1 In former times, **parchment** was the skin of a sheep or goat that was used for writing on. *...old manuscripts written on parchment.* N-UNCOUNT

2 **Parchment** is a kind of thick yellowish paper. *...an old lamp with a parchment shade... Cover with a sheet of non-stick baking parchment.* N-UNCOUNT

3 A **parchment** is a document written on parchment. N-COUNT

pardon /pɑːʳdᵊn/ **pardons, pardoning, pardoned** ◆◆◇◇◇

1 You say **'Pardon?'** or **'I beg your pardon?'** or, in American English, **'Pardon me?'** when you want someone to repeat what they have just said because you have not heard or understood it. *'Will you let me open it?'—'Pardon?'—'Can I open it?'... 'Does it have wires coming out of it?'—'Pardon me?'—'Does it have wires coming out of it?'* CONVENTION PRAGMATICS

2 People say **'I beg your pardon?'** when they are surprised or offended by something that someone has just said. *'Would you get undressed, please?'—'I beg your pardon?'—'Will you get undressed?'* CONVENTION PRAGMATICS

3 You say **'I beg your pardon'** or **'I do beg your pardon'** as a way of apologizing for accidentally doing something wrong, such as disturbing someone or making a mistake. *I was impolite and I do beg your pardon... 'We're meant to do it quarterly actually.'—'Oh quarterly, I beg your pardon, I thought it was monthly.'* CONVENTION PRAGMATICS

4 Some people say **'Pardon me'** instead of 'Excuse me' when they want to politely get someone's attention or interrupt them. *Pardon me, are you finished, madam?* CONVENTION PRAGMATICS

5 You can say things like **'Pardon me for asking'** or **'Pardon my frankness'** as a way of showing you understand that what you are going to say may sound rude. *That, if you'll pardon my saying so, is neither here nor there.* CONVENTION PRAGMATICS

6 Some people say things like **'If you'll pardon the expression'** or **'Pardon my French'** just before or after saying something which they think might offend people. *It's enough to make you wet yourself, if you'll pardon the expression.* CONVENTION PRAGMATICS

7 If someone who has been found guilty of a crime **is pardoned**, they are officially allowed to go free and are not punished. *Hundreds of political prisoners were pardoned and released.* ► Also a noun. *They lobbied the government on his behalf and he was granted a presidential pardon.* VB: usu passive *be* V-ed N-COUNT

pardonable /pɑːʳdənəbᵊl/. You describe someone's action or attitude as **pardonable** if you think it is wrong but you understand why they did that action or have that attitude. *'I have', he remarked with pardonable pride, 'done what I set out to do.'* ADJ-GRADED

pare /peəʳ/ **pares, paring, pared** ◆◇◇◇◇

1 When you **pare** something, or **pare** part of it off or away, you cut off its skin or its outer layer. *Pare the brown skin from the meat with a very sharp knife... He took out a slab of cheese, pared off a slice and ate it hastily. ...thinly pared lemon rind.* ● See also **paring**. VERB V n *from* n V n with adv V-ed

2 If you **pare** something **down** or **back**, or if you **pare** it, you reduce it. *The number of Ministries has been pared down by a third... The luxury tax won't really do much to pare down the budget deficit... The United States can pare back its military presence in Asia as well... Local authorities must pare their budgets.* VERB *be* V-ed adv V n with adv V n

pared-down. If you describe something as **pared-down**, you mean that it has no unnecessary features, and has been reduced to a very simple form. *Her style is pared-down and simple... The new NATO will be a pared-down military organization.* ADJ-GRADED ≠elaborate

parent /peərənt/ **parents** ◆◆◆◆◆

1 Your **parents** are your mother and father. *Children need their parents... This is where a lot of parents go wrong... When you become a parent the things you once cared about seem to have less value.* ● See also **foster parent**; **one-parent family**, **single parent**. N-COUNT: usu pl

2 An organization's **parent** organization is the organization that created it and usually still controls it. *Each unit including the parent company has its own, local management. ...the zoo's parent body, the Zoological Society of London.* ADJ: ADJ n

3 The **parent** animal, plant, or organism of a particular animal, plant or organism is the one that it comes from or is produced by. *Parent birds began to hunt for food for their young.* ADJ: ADJ n

parentage /peərəntɪdʒ/. Your **parentage** is the identity and origins of your parents. For example, if you are of Greek **parentage**, your parents are Greek. *She's a Londoner of mixed parentage (English and Jamaican)... We are all the result of our parentage and up-bringing.* ◆◇◇◇◇ N-UNCOUNT: oft *of* adj N

parental /pərentᵊl/. **Parental** is used to describe something that relates to parents in general, or to one or both of the parents of a particular child. *Medical treatment was sometimes given to* ◆◇◇◇◇ ADJ: usu ADJ n *children without parental consent... Parental attitudes vary widely. ...the removal of children from the parental home.*

parenthesis /pərenθəsɪs/ **parentheses** /pərenθəsiːz/
1 **Parentheses** are brackets used in writing. (This sentence is in parentheses). N-COUNT: usu pl =bracket
2 A **parenthesis** is a remark that is made in the middle of a piece of speech or writing, and which gives a little more information about the subject being discussed. N-COUNT =aside
3 You say '**in parenthesis**' to indicate that you are about to add something before going back to the main topic. *In parenthesis, I'd say that there were two aspects to writing you must never lose sight of.* PHRASE: PHR cl PRAGMATICS

parenthetical /pærənθetɪkəl/. A **parenthetical** remark or section is put into something written or spoken but is not essential to it. *Fox was making a long parenthetical remark about his travels on the border of Tibet.* ADJ: usu ADJ n ♦ **parenthetically** *Well, parenthetically, I was trying to quit smoking at the time... And what, we may ask parenthetically, does it mean?* ADV: ADV with cl, ADV with v, ADV adj

parenthood /peərənthʊd/. **Parenthood** is the state of being a parent. *She may feel unready for the responsibilities of parenthood.* ◆◇◇◇◇ N-UNCOUNT

parenting /peərəntɪŋ/. **Parenting** is the activity of bringing up and looking after your child. *Parenting is not fully valued by society. ...parenting classes.* ◆◇◇◇◇ N-UNCOUNT: oft N n

parent-teacher association, parent-teacher associations. A **parent-teacher association** is the same as a **PTA**. N-COUNT

par excellence /pɑːʳ eksəlɑːns, AM - lɑːns/. You say that something is a particular kind of thing **par excellence** in order to emphasize that it is a very good example of that kind of thing. *Mr Yeltsin is the populist par excellence.* ADJ: n ADJ PRAGMATICS ► Also an adverb. *Bresson is par excellence the Catholic film-maker.* ADV: ADV after v

pariah /pəraɪə/ **pariahs.** If you describe someone as a **pariah**, you mean that other people dislike them so much that they refuse to associate with them. *His landlady had treated him like a dangerous criminal, a pariah.* N-COUNT =outcast

paring /peərɪŋ/ **parings. Parings** are thin pieces that have been cut off things such as a fingernails, fruit, or vegetables. *...nail parings. ...vegetable parings.* N-COUNT: usu pl

parish /pærɪʃ/ **parishes** ◆◆◇◇◇
1 A **parish** is a village or part of a town which has its own church and clergyman. *...the parish of St Mark's, Lakenham... Parish priests have referred to it in their sermons. ...a 13th century parish church.* N-COUNT: oft N n
2 A **parish** is a small country area in England which has its own elected council. *...a closely fought parish council election. ...elected representatives, such as County and Parish Councillors.* N-COUNT: usu N n

parishioner /pərɪʃənəʳ/ **parishioners.** A clergyman's **parishioners** are the people who live in his parish, especially the ones who go to his church. *He was greatly loved by his parishioners.* N-COUNT: usu pl

Parisian /pərɪziən/ **Parisians** ◆◇◇◇◇
1 **Parisian** means belonging or relating to Paris. *...a Parisian restaurant. ...Parisian fashion.* ADJ: usu ADJ n
2 A **Parisian** is a person who comes from Paris. N-COUNT

parity /pærɪti/ **parities.** ◆◇◇◇◇
1 If there is **parity** between two things, they are equal; a formal use. *Women have yet to achieve wage or occupational parity in many fields... Italy wanted naval parity with France.* N-UNCOUNT =equality
2 If there is **parity** between the units of currency of two countries, the exchange rate is such that the units are equal to each other; a technical use in economics. *The government was ready to let the pound sink to parity with the dollar if necessary.* N-VAR

park /pɑːʳk/ **parks, parking, parked** ◆◆◆◆◇
1 A **park** is a public area of land with grass and trees, usually in a town, where people go in order to relax and enjoy themselves. *...Regent's Park. ...a brisk walk with the dog around the park... They stopped and sat on a park bench.* N-COUNT
2 When you **park** a vehicle or **park** somewhere, you drive the vehicle into a position where it can stay for a period of time, and leave it there. *Greenfield turned into the next side street and parked... He found a place to park the car... Ben parked across the street. ...rows of parked cars.* • See also **double-park.** VERB V V n V prep/adv V-ed
3 You can refer to a place where a particular activity is carried out as a **park**. *...a science and technology park. ...a business park.* N-COUNT: supp N
4 In Britain, a private area of grass and trees around a large country house is referred to as a **park**. *...a 19th century manor house in six acres of park and woodland.* N-VAR
5 In British English, some people refer to a football or rugby field as **the park**; used in journalism. *Chris was also the best player on the park.* N-SING: usu *on the* N
6 See also **parked**; **amusement park, ballpark, car park, national park, safari park, theme park.**

parka /pɑːʳkə/ **parkas.** A **parka** is a jacket or coat which has a quilted lining and a hood with fur round the edge. N-COUNT =anorak

parked /pɑːʳkt/. If you are **parked** somewhere, you have parked your car there. *My sister was parked down the road... We're parked out front.* ◆◇◇◇◇ ADJ: v-link ADJ

parking /pɑːʳkɪŋ/ ◆◆◇◇◇
1 **Parking** is the action of moving a vehicle into a place in a car park or by the side of the road where it can be left. *In many towns parking is allowed only on one side of the street... I knew I'd never find a parking space in the Square.* N-UNCOUNT
2 **Parking** is space for parking a vehicle in. *Cars allowed, but parking is limited.* N-UNCOUNT

parking garage, parking garages. In American English, a **parking garage** is a building where people can leave their cars. The usual British term is **car park**. *...a multi-level parking garage.* N-COUNT

parking light, parking lights. In American English, the **parking lights** on a vehicle are the small lights at the front that help other drivers to notice the vehicle and to judge its width. The British word is **sidelights**. N-COUNT

parking lot, parking lots. In American English, a **parking lot** is an area of ground where people can leave their cars. The usual British word is **car park**. *A block up the street I found a parking lot.* ◆◇◇◇◇ N-COUNT

parking meter, parking meters. A **parking meter** is a device which you have to put money into when you park in a parking space. N-COUNT =meter

parking ticket, parking tickets. A **parking ticket** is a piece of paper with instructions to pay a fine which a traffic warden puts on your car when you have parked it somewhere illegally. *I've just got a parking ticket – my first in years.* N-COUNT

park-keeper, park-keepers; also spelled **park keeper.** A **park-keeper** is a person whose job is to look after a park; used mainly in British English. *We saw the Park Keeper telling a bunch of older boys to get off the swings.* N-COUNT

parkland /pɑːʳklænd/ **parklands. Parkland** is land with grass and trees on it. *Its beautiful gardens and parkland are also open to the public... The resort is surrounded by extensive national and regional parklands.* ◆◇◇◇◇ N-UNCOUNT: also N in pl

parkway /pɑːʳkweɪ/ **parkways.** In American English, a **parkway** is a wide road with trees and grass on both sides. N-COUNT

parlance /pɑːʳləns/. You use **parlance** when indicating that the expression you are using is normally used by a particular group of people; a formal word. *Under the Communists local councils became, in official parlance, 'agencies of the state authority'.* N-UNCOUNT: supp N, usu *in* N =phraseology

parley /pɑːʳli/ **parleys, parleying, parleyed**
1 **A parley** is a discussion between two opposing people or groups in which both sides try to come to an agreement; an old-fashioned use. N-VAR
2 When two opposing people or groups **parley**, they meet to discuss something in order to come to an agreement; an informal and humorous use. *...a* V-RECIP V

place where we meet and parley... I don't think you've ever tried parleying with Gleed, have you? V with n

parliament /pɑːʳləmənt/ **parliaments;** also spelled **Parliament.** ◆◆◆◆◇

1 The **parliament** of a country is the group of people who make or change its laws. *The Bangladesh Parliament today (Monday) approved the policy, but it has not yet become law.* • See also **Member of Parliament, Houses of Parliament.** N-COUNT; N-PROPER

2 A particular **parliament** is a particular period of time in which a parliament is doing its work, between two elections or between two periods of holiday. *The legislation is expected to be passed in the next parliament.* N-COUNT

parliamentarian /pɑːʳləmenteəriən/ **parliamentarians** ◆◇◇◇◇

1 **Parliamentarians** are Members of a Parliament; used especially to refer to a group of Members of Parliament who are dealing with a particular task. *A delegation of Iraqi parliamentarians is expected to visit Tokyo later this month.* N-COUNT

2 A **parliamentarian** is a Member of Parliament who is an expert on the rules and procedures of Parliament and takes an active part in debates. *He is a veteran parliamentarian whose views enjoy widespread respect.* N-COUNT

parliamentary /pɑːʳləmentəri/. **Parliamentary** is used to describe things that are connected with a parliament or with Members of Parliament. *He used his influence to make sure she was not selected as a parliamentary candidate.* ◆◆◆◇◇ ADJ: ADJ n

parlour /pɑːʳləʳ/ **parlours;** spelled **parlor** in American English. ◆◇◇◇◇

1 A **parlour** is a sitting-room; an old-fashioned word. N-COUNT

2 **Parlour** is used in the names of some types of shops which provide a service, rather than selling things. *...a funeral parlour. ...a notorious massage parlour.* N-COUNT: n N

parlour game, parlour games; spelled **parlor game** in American English. A **parlour game** is a game that is played indoors by families or at parties, for example a guessing game or word game. N-COUNT

parlourmaid /pɑːʳləʳmeɪd/ **parlourmaids.** In former times, a **parlourmaid** was a female servant in a private house whose job involved serving people at table. N-COUNT

parlous /pɑːʳləs/. If something is in a **parlous** state, it is in a bad or dangerous condition; a formal word. *...the parlous state of our economy.* ADJ-GRADED: usu ADJ n =dire

Parmesan /pɑːʳmɪzæn/; also spelled **parmesan.** **Parmesan** or **Parmesan cheese** is a hard cheese with a strong flavour. It is often grated and used in Italian cooking. ◆◇◇◇◇ N-UNCOUNT

parochial /pəroʊkiəl/. ◆◇◇◇◇

1 If you describe someone as **parochial**, you are critical of them because you think that they are too concerned with their own local affairs and interests and that they should be thinking about more important things. ADJ-GRADED PRAGMATICS =insular

2 **Parochial** is used to describe things that relate to the parish connected with a particular church. *She was a secretary on the local parochial church council.* ADJ: ADJ n

parochialism /pəroʊkiəlɪzəm/. **Parochialism** is the quality of being parochial and self-centred; used showing disapproval. *We have been guilty of parochialism, of resistance to change.* N-UNCOUNT PRAGMATICS

parody /pærədi/ **parodies, parodying, parodied** ◆◇◇◇◇

1 A **parody** is a humorous piece of writing, drama, or music which imitates the style of a well-known person or represents a familiar situation in an exaggerated way. *'The Scarlet Capsule' was a parody of the popular 1959 TV series 'The Quatermass Experiment'... Throughout the Twenties, Lardner tried in vain to write a hit song, so at last he turned to parody.* N-VAR: oft N of n

2 When someone **parodies** a particular work, thing, or person, they imitate it in an amusing or exaggerated way. *Mr Frost had previously done a brilliant job of parodying a number of television and film genres... Any style can be parodied.* VERB =mimic V n

3 When you say that something is a **parody** of a particular thing, you are criticizing it because you think it is a very poor example or bad imitation of that thing. *After the first trial, a parody of justice, defence lawyers are now allowed a bit of a say.* N-COUNT: usu N of n PRAGMATICS =travesty

parole /pəroʊl/ **paroles, paroling, paroled** ◆◇◇◇◇

1 When prisoners are given **parole**, they are released before their prison sentence is due to end, on condition that they behave well. *Although sentenced to life, he will become eligible for parole after serving 10 years.* • If someone is **on parole**, they will stay out of prison if they behave well. *If released, he will continue to be on parole for eight more years.* N-UNCOUNT PHRASE: usu v-link PHR

2 If a prisoner **is paroled**, they are released before their prison sentence is due to end, on condition that they behave well. *He faces at most 12 years in prison and could be paroled after eight years.* VB: usu passive be V-ed

paroxysm /pærəksɪzəm/ **paroxysms**

1 A **paroxysm** of emotion is a sudden, very strong occurrence of it. *Later the same day, he exploded in a paroxysm of rage which continued for half an hour. ...a paroxysm of grief.* N-COUNT: usu N of n =fit

2 A **paroxysm** is a series of sudden, violent, uncontrollable movements that your body makes because you are coughing, laughing, or in great pain. *If he lay on his right side, he broke into a paroxysm of coughing.* N-COUNT: usu N of n/-ing =spasm

parquet /pɑːʳkeɪ, AM -keɪ/. **Parquet** is a floor covering made of small rectangular blocks of wood fitted together in a pattern. *...expensive rugs and carpets on the polished parquet floors.* N-UNCOUNT: usu N n

parrakeet. See **parakeet.**

parrot /pærət/ **parrots, parroting, parroted** ◆◇◇◇◇

1 A **parrot** is a tropical bird with a curved beak and brightly-coloured or grey feathers. Parrots can be kept as pets. Some parrots are able to copy what people say. N-COUNT

2 If you disapprove of the fact that someone is just repeating what someone else has said, often without really understanding it, you can say that they are **parroting** it. *Generations of students have learnt to parrot the standard explanations.* VERB PRAGMATICS =repeat V n

3 If you say that you feel **as sick as a parrot**, you feel very disappointed about something; used in informal British English. PHRASE: v-link PHR

parrot-fashion; also spelled **parrot fashion.** If you learn or repeat something **parrot-fashion**, you do it accurately but without really understanding what it means. *Under the old system pupils often had to stand to attention and repeat lessons parrot fashion.* ADV: ADV after v =by rote

parry /pæri/ **parries, parrying, parried**

1 If you **parry** a question or argument, you cleverly avoid answering it or dealing with it. *Mr King had to endure an awkward press conference, in which he parried questions on the depth of the divisions between Britain and its allies.* VERB =counter V n

2 If you **parry** a blow from someone who is attacking you, you push aside their arm or weapon so that you are not hurt. *I did not want to wound him, but to restrict myself to defence, to parry his attacks... I parried, and that's when my sword broke.* VERB =deflect V n V

parse /pɑːʳz/ **parses, parsing, parsed.** In grammar, if you **parse** a sentence, you examine each word and clause in order to work out what grammatical type each one is. V n

parsimonious /pɑːʳsɪmoʊniəs/. Someone who is **parsimonious** is very unwilling to spend money; a formal word, used showing disapproval. ADJ-GRADED: usu ADJ n PRAGMATICS =stingy

parsimony /pɑːʳsɪməni, AM -moʊni/. **Parsimony** is extreme unwillingness to spend money; a formal word used showing disapproval. *Due to official parsimony only the one machine was built.* N-UNCOUNT PRAGMATICS

parsley /pɑːʳsli, AM -zli/. **Parsley** is a small plant with curly leaves that are used for flavouring or decorating savoury food. *...parsley sauce.* ◆◆◇◇◇ N-UNCOUNT

parsnip /pɑːʳsnɪp/ **parsnips.** A **parsnip** is a long cream-coloured root vegetable. N-COUNT

parson /pɑːʳsᵊn/ **parsons.** A **parson** is a vicar or parish priest in the Church of England, or any clergyman; an old-fashioned word. ◆◆◇◇◇ N-COUNT

parsonage /pɑːʳsənɪdʒ/ **parsonages.** A **parsonage** is the house where a parson lives; an old-fashioned word. N-COUNT

part 1 noun uses, quantifier uses, and phrases

part /pɑːʳt/ **parts** ◆◆◆◆◆

1 A **part of** something is one of the pieces, sections, or elements that it consists of. *I like that part of Cape Town... Respect is a very important part of any relationship.* N-COUNT: usu N *of* n =bit, piece

2 A **part** for a machine or vehicle is one of the smaller pieces that is used to make it. *...spare parts for military equipment... This engine has only got three moving parts.* N-COUNT =component

3 **Part of** something is some of it. *It was a very severe accident and he lost part of his foot... Mum and he were able to walk part of the way together... Woodhead spent part of his childhood in Rhodesia.* QUANT: QUANT *of* sing-n/n-uncount =some

4 If you say that something is **part** one thing, **part** another, you mean that it is to some extent the first thing and to some extent the second thing. *The television producer today has to be part news person, part educator... Several people looked over the part-Jacobean, part-Georgian building.* ADV: ADV n, ADV adj =half

5 You can use **part** when you are talking about the proportions of substances in a mixture. For example, if some instructions say that you should use two **parts** disinfectant to three **parts** water, you should mix two measures of disinfectant with three measures of water. *Use turpentine and linseed oil, three parts to two.* N-COUNT

6 A **part** in a play or film is one of the roles in it which an actor or actress can perform. *Alf Sjoberg offered her a large part in the play he was directing... He was just right for the part.* N-COUNT =role

7 Your **part in** something that happens is your involvement in it. *If only he could conceal his part in the accident... He felt a sense of relief that his part in this business was now over.* N-SING: poss N *in* n =involvement

8 If something or someone is **part of** a group or organization, they belong to it or are included in it. *...voting on whether to remain part of the Union or become independent... I was a part of the team and wanted to remain a part of the team.* • **part and parcel**: see **parcel**. N-UNCOUNT: also *a* N, N *of* n

9 See also **private parts**.

10 If something or someone **plays a** large or important **part** in something, they are very involved in it and have an important effect on what happens. *These days work plays an important part in a single woman's life... We believe she may have played a part in hiding the cash.* PHRASES V inflects, oft PHR *in* n/-ing

11 If you **take part in** an activity, you do it together with other people. *Thousands of students have taken part in demonstrations.* V inflects, usu PHR *in* n/-ing

12 If you say that you **want no part of** something, you mean that you do not want to be involved in it at all. *What some other clubs do is unfortunate, but we want no part of it.* V inflects, PHR n

13 When you are describing people's thoughts or actions, you can say **for** her **part** or **for** my **part**, for example, to introduce what a particular person thinks or does; a formal use. *For my part, I feel elated and close to tears... The soldiers, for their part, agreed not to disrupt the election campaign.* PHR with cl PRAGMATICS

14 If you talk about a feeling or action **on** someone's **part**, you are referring to something that they feel or do. *...techniques on their part to keep us from knowing exactly what's going on... There is no need for any further instructions on my part... There have been numerous instances of excessive force on the part of security police.* n PHR

15 **For the most part** means mostly or usually. *For the most part the Germans kept out of local disputes... Professors, for the most part, are firmly committed to teaching, not research.* PHR with cl =by and large

16 You use **in part** to indicate that something exists or happens to some extent but not completely; a formal use. *The levels of blood glucose depend in part on what you eat and when you eat... In part this attitude was due to fear of trade union and employee reactions.* PHR with cl/group =to some degree

17 If you say that something happened for **the best part** or **the better part of** a period of time, you mean that it happened for most of that time. *He had been in Israel for the best part of twenty-four hours... We spent the better part of an hour searching for her.* PHR n =most

part 2 verb uses

part /pɑːʳt/ **parts, parting, parted** ◆◆◆◇◇

1 If things that are next to each other **part** or if you **part** them, they move in opposite directions, so that there is a space between them. *Her lips parted as if she were about to take a deep breath... He crossed to the window of the sitting-room and parted the curtains.* V-ERG =open V, V n

2 If you **part** your hair in the middle or at one side, you comb it in two different directions so that there is a straight line running from the front of your head to the back. *Picking up a brush, Joanna parted her hair... His hair was slicked back and neatly parted.* VERB V n, V-ed

3 When two people **part**, or if one person **parts from** another, they leave each other; a formal use. *He gave me the envelope and we parted... He has confirmed he is parting from his Swedish-born wife Eva.* • **to part company**: see **company**. V-RECIP pl-n V, V *from* n

4 If you **are parted from** someone you love, you are prevented from being with them. *I don't believe Lotte and I will ever be parted... A stay in hospital may be the first time a child is ever parted from its parents.* V-RECIP =separate pl-n *be* V-ed, *be* V-ed *from* n, Also V n *from* n

5 See also **parting**.

part with. If you **part with** something that is valuable or that you would prefer to keep, you give it or sell it to someone else. *Buyers might require further assurances before parting with their cash... He parted with much of his collection to pay his gardening bills.* PHRASAL VERB =surrender V P n

part- /pɑːʳt-/. **Part-** combines with adjectives, nouns, and verbs to mean partly but not completely the thing mentioned. *...part-baked breads and rolls... Some associations provide homes to buy or part-buy.* PREFIX

partake /pɑːʳteɪk/ **partakes, partaking, partook, partaken**

1 If you **partake of** food or drink, you eat or drink some of it; a formal use. *They were happy to partake of our feast, but not to share our company.* VERB V *of* n

2 If you **partake in** an activity, you take part in it. *You will probably be asked about whether you partake in very vigorous sports; a formal use.* VERB =participate V *in* n

3 If something **partakes of** a particular quality, it has that quality to some extent; a formal use. *Miracles are not generally regarded as magical. Nevertheless, they do partake of the same nature.* VERB V *of* n

part exchange; also spelled **part-exchange.** If you give an old item in **part exchange** for something you are buying, the seller accepts the old item as a partial payment, so reducing the amount of money you have to pay; used mainly in British English. *Electrical retailers will often take away old appliances if you buy a new one, sometimes in part-exchange. ...part-exchange deals.* N-UNCOUNT: oft *in* N

partial /pɑːʳʃᵊl/ ◆◆◇◇◇

1 You use **partial** to refer to something that is not complete or whole. *He managed to reach a partial agreement with both republics. ...a partial ban on the use of cars in the city. ...partial blindness.* ADJ: usu ADJ n

2 If you are **partial to** something, you like it. *He's partial to sporty women with blue eyes... Mollie confesses she is rather partial to pink... I am partial to baking cookies.* ♦ **partiality** /pɑːʳʃiælɪti/ *He has a great partiality for chocolate biscuits.* ADJ-GRADED: v-link ADJ *to* n/-ing =fond of; N-UNCOUNT: oft N *for* n =fondness

3 Someone who is **partial** supports a particular person or thing, for example in a competition or dispute, when they should be completely fair and unbiased. *I might be accused of being partial... A newspaper criticized the president's proposal, saying that it was partial to Israel.* ♦ **partiality** *She is* ADJ: v-link ADJ ≠impartial; N-UNCOUNT *criticized by some others for her one-sidedness and partiality.* =bias ≠impartiality

partially /pɑːʳʃəli/. If something happens or exists **partially**, it happens or exists to some extent, but not completely. *Lisa is deaf in one ear and partially blind.* ◆◆◇◇◇ ADV: ADV with cl/group =partly

participant /pɑːʳtɪsɪpənt/ **participants.** The **participants** in an activity are the people who take part in it. *40 of the course participants are offered employment with the company... You are expected to be an active participant.* ◆◆◇◇◇ N-COUNT

participate /pɑːʳtɪsɪpeɪt/ **participates, participating, participated.** If you **participate** in an activity, you take part in it. *They expected him to participate in the ceremony... Over half the population of this country participate in sport. ...special contracts at lower rates for participating corporations.* ♦ **participation** /pɑːʳtɪsɪpeɪʃᵊn/ *...participation in religious activities.* ◆◆◆◇◇ VERB V in n V-ing N-UNCOUNT =involvement

participative /pɑːʳtɪsɪpətɪv/. **Participative** management or decision-making involves the participation of all the people engaged in an activity or affected by certain decisions; a formal word. *A participative management style has developed in Japan to induce better cooperation.* ADJ-GRADED: usu ADJ n

participatory /pɑːʳtɪsɪpeɪtəri, AM -tɔːri/. A **participatory** system, activity, or role involves a particular person or group of people taking part in it. *Fishing is said to be the most popular participatory sport in the U.K... Studies have shown that women tend to be more participatory in their management style.* ADJ: usu ADJ n

participial /pɑːʳtɪsɪpiəl/. In grammar, **participial** means relating to a participle. ADJ

participle /pɑːʳtɪsɪpᵊl/ **participles.** In grammar, a **participle** is a form of a verb that can be used in compound tenses of the verb. There are two participles in English: the past participle, which usually ends in '-ed', and the present participle, which usually ends in '-ing'. N-COUNT

particle /pɑːʳtɪkᵊl/ **particles** ◆◆◇◇◇

1 A **particle** of something is a very small piece or amount of it. *...a particle of hot metal... There is a particle of truth in his statement. ...food particles.* N-COUNT: oft N of n

2 In physics, a **particle** is a piece of matter smaller than an atom, for example an electron or a proton; a technical use. N-COUNT

3 In grammar, a **particle** is a preposition such as 'into' or an adverb such as 'out' which can combine with a verb to form a phrasal verb. N-COUNT

particle accelerator, particle accelerators. A **particle accelerator** is a machine used for research in nuclear physics which can make subatomic particles go very fast. N-COUNT

particle physics. **Particle physics** is the study of the qualities of atoms and molecules and the way they behave and react. *It's easy to forget that particle physics is still a very young science.* N-UNCOUNT

particular /pəʳtɪkjʊləʳ/ ◆◆◆◆◇

1 You use **particular** to emphasize that you are talking about one thing or one kind of thing rather than other similar ones. *I remembered a particular story about a postman who was a murderer... I have to know exactly why it is I'm doing a particular job. ...if there are particular things you're interested in.* ADJ: ADJ n =specific

2 If a person or thing has a **particular** quality or possession, it is distinct and belongs only to them. *I have a particular responsibility to ensure I make the right decision... Fatigue is a particular problem for women.* ADJ: ADJ n =special

3 You can use **particular** to emphasize that something is greater or more intense than usual. *Particular emphasis will be placed on oral language training.* ADJ: ADJ n =especial

4 If you say that someone is **particular**, you mean that they choose things and do things very carefully, and are not easily satisfied. *Ted was very particular about the colors he used.* ADJ-GRADED: usu v-link ADJ, oft ADJ about n =fussy

5 See also **particulars**.

6 You use **in particular** to indicate that what you are saying applies especially to one thing or person. *The situation in Ethiopia in particular is worrying... Why should he notice her car in particular?... In particular I admire Gary Lineker.* PHRASES PHR with cl/group =particularly

7 You use **nothing in particular** or **nobody in particular** to mean nothing or nobody important or special, or no one thing or person more than any other. *I went along thinking of nothing in particular only looking at things around me... Drew made some remarks to nobody in particular and said goodbye.*

particularity /pəʳtɪkjʊlærɪti/ **particularities**

1 **Particularity** is the quality of being unusual or unique. The **particularities** of something are the unusual features that characterize it; a formal use. *What is lacking is an insight into the particularity of our societal system... Time inevitably glosses over the particularities of each situation.* N-UNCOUNT, also N in pl

2 **Particularity** is attention to detail; a formal use. N-UNCOUNT

particularize /pəʳtɪkjʊləraɪz/ **particularizes, particularizing, particularized;** also spelled **particularise** in British English. If you **particularize** something that you have been talking about in a general way, you give details or specific examples of it. *Mr Johnson particularizes the general points he wants to make... A farmer is entitled to a certain particularized tax treatment.* VERB =detail V n V-ed Also V

particularly /pəʳtɪkjʊləʳli/ ◆◆◆◆◇

1 You use **particularly** to indicate that what you are saying applies especially to one thing or situation. *Keep your office space looking good, particularly your desk... More local employment will be created, particularly in service industries... I often do absent-minded things, particularly when I'm worried.* ADV: ADV with cl/group =especially

2 **Particularly** means more than usual or more than other things. *Progress has been particularly disappointing... I particularly liked the wooden chests and chairs.* ADV: ADV with cl/group =especially

particulars /pəʳtɪkjʊləz/. The **particulars** of something or someone are facts or details about them which are written down and kept as a record. *You will find all the particulars in Chapter 9... The nurses at the admission desk asked her for particulars. ...a written statement of particulars of employment.* N-PLURAL =details

parting /pɑːʳtɪŋ/ **partings** ◆◇◇◇◇

1 **Parting** is the act of leaving a particular person or place. A **parting** is an occasion when this happens. *Parting from any one of you for even a short time is hard... It was a dreadfully emotional parting.* N-VAR

2 Your **parting** words or actions are the things that you say or do as you are leaving a place or person. *Her parting words left him feeling empty and alone. ...his bold parting kiss.* ADJ: ADJ n =final

3 In British English, the **parting** in someone's hair is the line running from the front to the back of their head where their hair has been combed in opposite directions. N-COUNT

4 When there is **a parting of the ways**, two or more people or groups of people stop working together or travelling together. *...a negotiated parting of the ways for the three Baltic republics.* PHRASE

parting shot, parting shots. If someone makes a **parting shot**, they make an unpleasant or forceful remark at the end of a conversation, and then leave so that no-one has the chance to reply. *He turned to face her for his parting shot. 'You're one coldhearted woman, you know that?'* N-COUNT

partisan /pɑːʳtɪzæn, AM -zən/ **partisans** ◆◇◇◇◇

1 Someone who is **partisan** strongly supports a particular person or cause, often without thinking carefully about the matter. *He is clearly too partisan to be a referee.* ▶ A **partisan** is someone who is partisan. *At first the eager young poet was a partisan of the Revolution.* ADJ-GRADED: usu v-link ADJ =prejudiced N-COUNT: usu N of n =champion

2 **Partisans** are ordinary people, rather than soldiers, who join together to fight enemy soldiers who are occupying their country. *He was rescued by some Italian partisans. ...serving in resistance and partisan activities.* N-COUNT

partisanship /pɑːʳtɪzænʃɪp, AM -zən-/. **Partisanship** is support for a person or group without N-UNCOUNT =prejudice fair consideration of the facts and circumstances. *His politics were based on loyal partisanship.*

partition /pɑːʳtɪʃᵊn/ **partitions, partitioning, partitioned** ♦◇◇◇◇

1 A **partition** is a wall or screen that separates one part of a room or vehicle from another. *...new offices divided only by glass partitions... Her taxicab has a thick perspex partition between the passengers' seats and the driver.* N-COUNT

2 If you **partition** a room, you separate one part of it from another by means of a partition. *Bedrooms have again been created by partitioning a single larger room... He sat on the two-seater sofa in the partitioned office.* VERB V n V-ed

3 If a country **is partitioned**, it is divided into two or more independent countries. *Korea was partitioned in 1945... Britain was accused of trying to partition the country 'because of historic enmity'... The island has been partitioned since the mid-seventies.* ► Also a noun. *...areas ruled by the Russian Tsar during Poland's period of partition. ...fighting which followed the partition of India.* VERB be V-ed V n V-ed N-UNCOUNT: oft N of n

partly /pɑːʳtli/. You use **partly** to indicate that something happens or exists to some extent, but not completely. *It's partly my fault... He let out a long sigh, mainly of relief, partly of sadness... I have not worried so much this year, partly because I have had other things to think about... I feel partly responsible for the problems we're in.* ♦♦♦◇◇ ADV: ADV with cl/group =partially

partner /pɑːʳtnəʳ/ **partners, partnering, partnered** ♦♦♦♦◇

1 Your **partner** is the person you are married to or are having a romantic or sexual relationship with. *Wanting other friends doesn't mean you don't love your partner. ...his choice of marriage partner.* N-COUNT: oft poss N

2 Your **partner** is the person you are doing something with, for example dancing with or playing with in a game against two other people. *...to dance with a partner... My partner for the event was the marvellous American player. ...a partner in crime.* N-COUNT

3 The **partners** in a firm or business are the people who share the ownership of it. *He's a partner in a Chicago law firm. ...her business partner Max Hampshire.* N-COUNT =associates

4 The **partner** of a country or organization is another country or organization with which they have an alliance or agreement. *Spain has been one of Cuba's major trading partners. ...the main coalition partner in the Slovak government.* N-COUNT: usu with supp

5 If you **partner** someone, you are their partner in a game or in a dance. *He had partnered the famous Russian ballerina... He will be partnered by Ian Baker, the defending champion... He partnered Andre Agassi to victory.* VERB V n be V-ed by/with n V n to n

partnership /pɑːʳtnəʳʃɪp/ **partnerships.** **Partnership** or a **partnership** is a relationship in which two or more people, organizations, or countries work together as partners. *...the partnership between Germany's banks and its businesses... Alex and Mikhail were in partnership then: Mikhail handled the creative side; Alex was the financier.* ♦♦♦◇◇ N-VAR

part of speech, parts of speech. A **part of speech** is a particular grammatical class of word, for example noun, adjective, or verb. N-COUNT

partook /pɑːʳtʊk/. **Partook** is the past tense of **partake**.

partridge /pɑːʳtrɪdʒ/ **partridges.** A **partridge** is a wild bird with brown feathers, a round body, and a short tail. *...to shoot a partridge.* ► **Partridge** is the flesh of this bird eaten as food. *...a main course of partridge.* N-COUNT N-UNCOUNT

part-time. If someone is a **part-time** worker or has a **part-time** job, they work for only part of each day or week. *Many businesses are cutting back by employing lower-paid part-time workers... Part-time work is generally hard to find... I'm part-time. I work three days a week.* ► Also an adverb. *I want to work part-time.* ♦♦◇◇◇ ADJ ADV: ADV after v

part-timer, part-timers. A **part-timer** is a person who works part-time. *Customer service departments are often staffed by part-timers.* N-COUNT

part way; also spelled **part-way.** **Part way** means part of the way or partly. *Local authorities will run out of money part way through the financial year... She was on the hillside, part way up... It might go part way to repaying the debt.* ADV: ADV after v, ADV prep/adv

party /pɑːʳti/ **parties, partying, partied** ♦♦♦♦♦

1 A **party** is a political organization whose members have similar aims and beliefs. Usually the organization tries to get its members elected to the government of a country. *...a member of the Labour party. ...India's ruling party. ...opposition parties. ...her resignation as party leader.* N-COUNT

2 A **party** is a social event, often in someone's home, at which people enjoy themselves doing things such as eating, drinking, dancing, talking, or playing games. *The couple met at a party... We threw a huge birthday party... Most teenagers like to go to parties.* • See also **dinner party, garden party, hen party, stag party.** N-COUNT

3 If you **party**, you enjoy yourself doing things such as going out to parties, drinking, dancing, and talking to people. *They come to eat and drink, to swim, to party. Sometimes they never go to bed... After a long evening of partying he looked tired.* VERB V

4 A **party** of people is a group of people who are doing something together, for example travelling together. *They became separated from their party. ...a party of sightseers. ...a research party of scientists.* • See also **search party, working party.** N-COUNT: usu with supp

5 One of the people involved in a legal agreement or dispute can be referred to as a particular **party**; a legal use. *It has to be proved that they are the guilty party. ...he was the injured party. ...a court, the decision of which may not satisfy either party.* • See also **third party.** N-COUNT: usu supp N

6 Someone who **is a party to** or **is party to** an action or agreement is involved in it, and therefore partly responsible for it. *Crook had resigned his post rather than be party to such treachery.* PHRASE: V inflects, PHR n

partygoer /pɑːʳtigoʊəʳ/ **partygoers.** A **partygoer** is someone who likes going to parties or someone who is at a particular party. *Eleanor did her best to be the gay, enthusiastic partygoer her husband wished she were... At least half the partygoers were under 15.* N-COUNT

party line. The **party line** on a particular issue is the official view taken by a political party, which its members are expected to support. *They ignored the official party line.* ♦◇◇◇◇ N-SING

party piece, party pieces. Someone's **party piece** is something that they often do to entertain people, especially at parties, for example singing a particular song or reciting a particular poem; an informal word. N-COUNT: oft poss N

party political. **Party political** matters relate to political parties. *The debate is being conducted almost exclusively on party political lines.* ♦◇◇◇◇ ADJ: ADJ n

party political broadcast, party political broadcasts. A **party political broadcast** is a short broadcast on radio or television made by a political party, especially before an election, which explains their views and often criticizes other political parties. N-COUNT

party politics ♦◇◇◇◇

1 **Party politics** is political activity involving political parties. *Mr Pereira said he had decided to retire from party politics.* N-UNCOUNT

2 If politicians are accused of playing **party politics**, they are criticised for doing or saying something only because they are trying to improve people's opinion of their party, rather than because they believe it to be true. *Usually when Opposition MPs question Ministers they are just playing party politics.* N-UNCOUNT PRAGMATICS

party pooper /pɑːʳti puːpə/ **party poopers.** You describe someone as a **party pooper** when you think that they spoil other people's fun and their enjoyment of something; an informal word, used showing disapproval. *I hate to be a party pooper, but I am really tired.* N-COUNT PRAGMATICS

party spirit. If you talk about someone being in the **party spirit**, you mean that they are in the N-UNCOUNT =party mood

mood to enjoy a party or to have fun. *Sparkling wine can also put you in the party spirit.*

parvenu /pɑːʳvənjuː, AM -nuː/ **parvenus.** If you describe someone as a **parvenu**, you think that although they have acquired wealth or high status they are not very cultured or well-educated; a formal word.
N-COUNT PRAGMATICS =upstart

pas de deux. **Pas de deux** is both the singular and the plural form. Both forms are pronounced /pɑː də dɜː/; the plural form can also be pronounced /pɑː də dɜːz/. In ballet, a **pas de deux** is a dance sequence for two dancers.
N-COUNT

pass /pɑːs, pæs/ **passes, passing, passed** ◆◆◆◆◆

1 To **pass** someone or something means to go past them without stopping. *As she passed the library door, the telephone began to ring... Jane stood aside to let her pass... I sat in the garden and watched the passing cars.*
VERB V n V V-ing

2 When someone or something **passes** in a particular direction, they move in that direction. *He passed through the doorway into Ward B... He passed down the tunnel... The car passed over the body twice, once backward and then forward.*
VERB =go V prep/adv

3 If something such as a road or pipe **passes** along a particular route, it goes along that route. *After going over the Col de Vars, the route passes through St-Paul-sur-Ubaye... The road passes a farmyard.*
VERB V prep/adv V n

4 If you **pass** something through, over, or round something else, you move or push it through, over, or round that thing. *She passed the needle through the rough cloth, back and forth... 'I don't understand,' the Inspector mumbled, passing a hand through his hair... He passed a hand wearily over his eyes.*
VERB V n prep/adv

5 If you **pass** something to someone, you take it in your hand and give it to them. *Ken passed the books to Sergeant Parrott... Pass me that bottle.*
VERB =hand V n *to* n V n n

6 If something **passes** or **is passed** from one person to another, the second person then has it instead of the first. *His mother's small estate had passed to him after her death... These powers were eventually passed to municipalities. ...a genetic trait, which can be passed from one generation to the next.*
V-ERG V *to* n *be* V-ed *to* n *be* V-ed *from* n *to* n

7 If you **pass** information **to** someone, you give it to them because it concerns them. *Officials failed to pass vital information to their superiors... He passed the letters to the Department of Trade and Industry.* ► **Pass on** means the same as **pass**. *I do not know what to do with the information if I cannot pass it on... From time to time he passed on confidential information to him... He has written a note asking me to pass on his thanks.*
VERB V n *to* n
PHRASAL VERB V n P V P n (not pron) *to* n V P n (not pron) Also V n P *to* n

8 If you **pass** the ball to someone in your team in a game such as football, hockey, or rugby, you kick, hit, or throw it to them. *Your partner should then pass the ball back to you... Dodd passed back to Flowers.* ► Also a noun. *Hirst rolled a short pass to Merson.*
VERB V n adv/prep V prep/adv
N-COUNT

9 When a period of time **passes**, it happens and finishes. *He couldn't imagine why he had let so much time pass without contacting her... As the years passed he felt trapped by certain realities of marriage... Several minutes passed before the girls were noticed.*
VERB =go by V

10 If you **pass** a period of time in a particular way, you spend it in that way. *The children passed the time playing in the streets... To pass the time they sang songs and played cards.*
VERB V n -ing/adv V n

11 If you **pass through** a stage of development or a period of time, you experience it. *The country was passing through a grave crisis... 'Have you ever been at all religious?'—'No. I never passed through that phase.'*
VERB =go V *through* n

12 If an amount **passes** a particular total or level, it becomes greater than that total or level. *They became the first company in their field to pass the £2 billion turn-over mark.*
VERB =exceed V n

13 If someone or something **passes** a test, they are considered to be of an acceptable standard. *Kevin has just passed his driving test. ...new drugs which have passed early tests to show that they are safe... I didn't pass.*
VERB ≠fail V n V

14 A **pass** in an examination or test is a successful result in it. *An A-level pass in Biology is preferred for all courses... Passes are graded from 'A' down to 'E'.*
N-COUNT ≠fail

15 If an examiner or someone in authority **passes** something or someone, they declare that they are of an acceptable standard. *Several popular beaches were found unfit for bathing although the government passed them last year... The medical board would not pass him fit for General Service.*
VERB V n V n adj

16 When people in authority **pass** a new law or a proposal, they formally agree to it or approve it. *The Estonian parliament has passed a resolution declaring the republic fully independent... Race Relations Acts were passed in 1968 and 1976.*
VERB V n

17 When a judge **passes** sentence on someone, he or she says what their punishment will be. *Passing sentence, the judge said it all had the appearance of a con trick... Before sentence was passed, Mr Mills escaped from jail.*
VERB V n

18 If you **pass** comment or **pass** a comment, you say something. *I don't really know so I could not pass comment on that... We passed a few remarks about the weather.*
VERB V n

19 If something **passes** without comment, or **passes** unnoticed, nobody comments on it, reacts to it, or notices it. *This practice embarrassed Luther, but he let it pass without comment... The cocktails were so sweet that the strength of them might pass unnoticed until it was too late.*
VERB =go V *without* n V adj

20 If someone or something **passes for** or **passes as** something that they are not, they are accepted as that thing or mistaken for that thing. *Childrens' toy guns now look so realistic that they can often pass for the real thing... It is doubtful whether Ted, even with his fluent French, passed for one of the locals. ...a woman passing as a man.*
VERB V *for/as* n

21 If someone makes you an offer or asks you a question and you say that you will **pass** on it, you mean that you do not want to accept or answer it now; an informal use. *I think I'll pass on the hiking next time... 'You can join us if you like.' Brad shook his head. 'I'll pass, thanks.'*
VERB V *on* n V

22 If someone **passes** water or **passes** urine, they urinate. *A sensitive bladder can make you feel the need to pass water frequently.*
VERB V n

23 A **pass** is a document that allows you to do something. *I got myself a pass into the barracks... Malaysian Railways has a rail pass for foreign visitors: 10 days' unlimited travel costs around £43.*
N-COUNT =permit

24 A **pass** in a mountainous area is a narrow way between two mountains. *The monastery is in a remote mountain pass.*
N-COUNT: oft in names after n

25 See also **passing**.

26 If someone **makes a pass at** you, they try to begin a romantic or sexual relationship with you; an informal expression. *Nancy wasn't sure if Dirk was making a pass at her.*
PHRASE: V inflects, usu PHR *at* n

27 ● to **pass the buck**: see **buck**. ● to **pass judgement**: see **judgement**. ● to **pass the time of day**: see **time**.

pass around or **pass round.** If a group of people **pass** something **around** or **pass** it **round**, they each take it and then give it to the next person. *Serve the pudding, and pass around a bowl of yogurt to go with it... Just pass this round as I'm talking and take a little look at it... A bottle of whisky was passed around.*
PHRASAL VERB V P n (not pron) V n P *be* V-ed P

pass away. You can say that someone **passed away** to mean that they died, if you want to avoid using the word 'die' because you think it is too blunt. *He unfortunately passed away last year.*
PHRASAL VERB =pass on V P

pass by. If you **pass by** something, you go past it or near it on your way to another place. *I told him to drop in and spend a few days with us if he passed by here on his way back... They were injured when a parked car exploded as their convoy passed by.*
PHRASAL VERB V P n V P

pass off. If an event **passes off** without any trouble, it happens and ends without any trouble. *The main demonstration passed off peacefully... The event passed off without any major incidents.*
PHRASAL VERB V P adv/prep

pass off as. If you **pass** something **off as** another thing, you convince people that it is that other
PHRASAL VERB

thing. *He passed himself off as a senior psychologist... I've tried to pass off my accent as a convent school accent. ...horse meat being passed off as ground beef.* V n P P n, V P n (not pron), P n

pass on PHRASAL VERB

1 If you **pass** something **on** to someone, you give it to them so that they have it instead of you. *The Queen is passing the money on to a selection of her favourite charities... There is a risk of passing the virus on... The late Earl passed on much of his fortune to the Princess... Tenants remain liable if they pass on their lease.* V n P to n, V n P, V P n (not pron) to n, V P n (not pron)

2 If you **pass on** costs or savings to someone else, you make them pay for your costs or allow them to benefit from your savings. *They pass on their cost of borrowing and add to it their profit margin... I found we could make some saving and it is right to pass the savings on to the customer.* V P n (not pron), V n P to n, Also V n P, V P n (not pron) to n

3 You can say that someone **passed on** to mean that they died, if you want to avoid using the word 'die' because you think it is too blunt. *He passed on with a heart attack at the age of 72.* =pass away, V P

4 See also **pass** 7.

pass out PHRASAL VERB

1 If you **pass out**, you faint or collapse. *He felt sick and dizzy and then passed out... She passed out drunk.* V P

2 When a police, army, navy, or air force cadet **passes out**, he or she satisfactorily finishes his or her training; used mainly in British English. *He passed out in November 1924 and was posted to No 24 Squadron.* V P

pass over PHRASAL VERB

1 If someone **is passed over** for a job or position, they do not get the job or position and someone younger or less experienced is chosen instead. *She claimed she was repeatedly passed over for promotion while less experienced white male colleagues were given postings... They've been rejected, disappointed, ignored, passed over.* usu passive, be V-ed P for n, be V-ed P

2 If you **pass over** a topic in a conversation or speech, you do not talk about it. *He largely passed over the government's record... They seem to think her crimes should be passed over in silence.* V P n, be V-ed P

pass round. In British English, **pass round** means the same as **pass around**. PHRASAL VERB

pass up. If you **pass up** a chance or an opportunity, you do not take advantage of it. *The official urged the government not to pass up the opportunity that has now presented itself... 'I can't pass this up.' She waved the invitation.* PHRASAL VERB, V P n (not pron), V n P

passable /pɑːsəbᵊl, pæs-/

1 If something is a **passable** effort or of **passable** quality, it is satisfactory or quite good. *Stan puffed out his thin cheeks in a passable imitation of his dad... Ms Campbell speaks passable French.* ADJ-GRADED: usu ADJ n =adequate, fair

♦ **passably** /pɑːsəbli, pæs-/ *She has always been quick to pick things up, doing passably well in school without really trying.* ADV-GRADED: usu ADV adj/adv, also ADV after v

2 If a **road** is **passable**, it is not completely blocked, and people can still use it. *The airport road is passable today for the first time in a week. ...muddy mountain roads that are barely passable.* ADJ: usu v-link ADJ

passage /pæsɪdʒ/ **passages** ◆◆◆◇◇

1 A **passage** is a long narrow space with walls or fences on both sides, which connects one place or room with another. *Harry stepped into the passage, and closed the door behind him. ...up some stairs and along a narrow passage towards a door.* N-COUNT =passageway, corridor

2 A **passage** in a book, speech, or piece of music is a section of it that you are considering separately from the rest. *He reads a passage from Milton. ...the passage in which Blake spoke of the world of imagination... Compare the following passages.* N-COUNT: usu with supp =excerpt, extract

3 A **passage** is a long narrow hole or tube in your body, which air or liquid can pass along. *...cells that line the air passages. ...blocked nasal passages.* N-COUNT: usu supp N

4 A **passage** through a crowd of people or things is an empty space that allows you to move through them. *He cleared a passage for himself through the crammed streets... Two men suddenly elbowed a passage through the shoppers.* N-COUNT: oft N through n =way

5 The **passage** of someone or something is their movement from one place to another. *Yugoslavia would not permit the passage of German troops through its territory... The passage of heat through rock is extremely slow.* N-UNCOUNT: usu with poss =movement

6 The **passage** of someone or something is their progress from one situation or one stage in their development to another. *...to ease their passage from Socialist to market economies. ...the passage from school to college.* N-UNCOUNT: usu N from/to n, oft with poss =transition

7 The **passage** of a bill or act is the official acceptance of it by a parliament. *It's been 200 years since the passage of the Bill of Rights.* N-UNCOUNT: oft N of n =passing

8 **The passage of** a period of time is its passing. *An asset that increases in value with the passage of time. ...after the passage of eighteen months.* N-SING: the N of n =passing

9 A **passage** is a journey by ship. *We'd arrived the day before after a 10-hour passage from Swansea.* N-COUNT =crossing

10 If you are granted **passage** through a country or area of land, you are given permission to go through it. *Mr Thomas would be given safe passage to and from Jaffna... You may have free passage across our territory whenever you require it.* N-UNCOUNT: oft N prep

passageway /pæsɪdʒweɪ/ **passageways.** A **passageway** is a long narrow space with walls or fences on both sides, which connects one place or room with another. *Outside, in the passageway, I could hear people moving about... There's an underground passageway that connects the five buildings.* ◆◇◇◇◇ N-COUNT =passage

passbook /pɑːsbʊk, pæs-/ **passbooks.** A **passbook** is a small book recording the amount of money you pay in or take out of a savings account at a bank or building society. N-COUNT

passé /pæseɪ/. If someone describes something as **passé**, they think that it is no longer fashionable or that it is no longer effective. *Punk is passé... She has publicly proclaimed that the Socialist Party is passé and that it is time to create a new party.* ADJ-GRADED: usu v-link ADJ, PRAGMATICS =old hat, dated

passenger /pæsɪndʒəʳ/ **passengers** ◆◆◆◇◇

1 A **passenger** in a vehicle such as a bus, boat, or plane is a person who is travelling in it, but who is not driving it or working on it. *Mr Fullemann was a passenger in the car when it crashed. ...a flight from Milan with more than forty passengers on board.* N-COUNT

2 **Passenger** is used to describe something that is designed for travellers, rather than drivers or goods. *I sat in the passenger seat. ...a passenger train.* ADJ: ADJ n

passer-by, passers-by; also spelled **passerby.** A **passer-by** is a person who is walking past someone or something. *A passer-by described what he saw moments after the car bomb had exploded... I went and sat in a cafe and watched the passers-by.* ◆◇◇◇◇ N-COUNT

passim /pæsɪm/. In indexes and notes, **passim** indicates that a particular name or subject occurs frequently throughout a particular piece of writing or section of a book. *...The Theories of their Relation (London, 1873), p. 8 and passim.*

passing /pɑːsɪŋ, pæs-/ ◆◆◇◇◇

1 A **passing** fashion, activity, or feeling lasts for only a short period of time and is not worth taking very seriously. *Hamnett does not believe environmental concern is a passing fad... He had never taken more than a passing interest in the girl.* ADJ: ADJ n =fleeting ≠lasting

2 The **passing** of an empire, era, or custom is the fact of its coming to an end. *East Germany as a state is on the point of disappearing. Few will mourn its passing... He laments the passing of the good old days.* N-SING: with poss

3 Someone's **passing** is their death. *His passing will be mourned by many people. ...the passing of one of this century's great artists, Miles Davis.* N-SING: with poss =death

4 **The passing of** a period of time is the fact or process of its going by. *The passing of time brought a sense of emptiness... The passing of the years has been kind to Dan. He looks like a man of half his age.* N-SING: the N of n

5 A **passing** mention or reference is brief and is made while you are talking or writing about some- ADJ: ADJ n =casual

thing else. *It was just a passing comment, he didn't go on about it... The colonies received only a passing mention.*

6 See also **pass**.

7 If you mention something **in passing**, you mention it briefly while you are talking or writing about something else. *In passing, it should be noted that... The army is only mentioned in passing.* PHRASES PHR with cl, PHR after v =incidentally

8 If something changes **with each passing year** or **with every passing day**, it changes continuously. *His stomach had grown more prominent with every passing year... Work becomes harder with each passing day.*

passion /pæʃən/ **passions** ◆◆◆◇◇

1 **Passion** is a feeling of very strong sexual attraction for someone. *...my passion for a dark-haired, slender boy named James. ...the expression of love and passion. ...Maggy, the object of his passions.* N-UNCOUNT: also N in pl =desire

2 **Passion** is a very strong feeling about something or a strong belief in something. *He spoke with great passion. ...the passion and commitment of the Republican candidate.* N-UNCOUNT: also N in pl =feeling

3 If you have a **passion for** something, you have a very strong interest in it and like it very much. *She had a passion for gardening... His other great passion was Italy.* N-COUNT: usu with supp

passionate /pæʃənət/ ◆◆◇◇◇

1 A **passionate** person has very strong feelings about something or a strong belief in something. *...his passionate commitment to peace... I'm a passionate believer in public art... He is very passionate about the project. ...a passionate and combative speech.* ADJ-GRADED =fervent ♦ **passionately** *I am passionately opposed to the death penalty.* ADV-GRADED =fervently

2 A **passionate** person has strong romantic or sexual feelings and expresses them in their behaviour. *...a beautiful, passionate woman of twenty-six. ...the story of a passionate love affair... We were both very tender and passionate towards one another.* ADJ-GRADED ≠passionless ♦ **passionately** *He was passionately in love with her... She kissed him passionately.* ADV-GRADED

passion fruit; passion fruit is both the singular and the plural form. A **passion fruit** is a small, round, brown fruit that is produced by certain types of tropical flower. N-VAR

passionless /pæʃənləs/. If you describe someone or something as **passionless**, you mean that they lack passion and liveliness. *...a passionless academic. ...their late and apparently passionless marriage.* ADJ-GRADED ≠passionate

passive /pæsɪv/ ◆◆◇◇◇

1 If you describe someone as **passive**, you mean that they do not take action but instead lets things happen to them; used showing disapproval. *His passive attitude made things easier for me... Even passive acceptance of the regime was a kind of collaboration.* ADJ-GRADED PRAGMATICS =docile ≠active ♦ **passively** *He sat there passively, content to wait for his father to make the opening move.* ADV-GRADED: usu ADV with v ♦ **passivity** /pæsɪvɪti/ *...the passivity of the public under communism.* N-UNCOUNT

2 A **passive** activity involves watching, looking at, or listening to things rather than doing things. *They want less passive ways of filling their time. ...the passive enjoyment one gets from looking at a painting or sculpture.* ADJ: ADJ n ≠active

3 **Passive** resistance involves showing opposition to the people in power in your country by not cooperating with them and protesting in non-violent ways. *They made it clear that they would only exercise passive resistance in the event of a military takeover.* ADJ: ADJ n ≠active

4 In grammar, **the passive** or **the passive voice** is formed using 'be' and the past participle of a verb. The subject of a passive clause does not perform the action expressed by the verb but is affected by it. For example, in 'He's been murdered', the verb is in the passive. Compare **active**. N-SING: the N

passive smoking. Passive smoking involves breathing in the smoke from other people's cigarettes because you happen to be near them. *...the dangers of passive smoking.* N-UNCOUNT

passivize /pæsɪvaɪz/ **passivizes, passivizing, passivized;** also spelled **passivise** in British English. If you can **passivize** a verb or clause, or if it can **passivize**, you can put the verb in the passive voice. V-ERG: V n, V

Passover /pɑːsoʊvəʳ, pæs-/. **Passover** is a Jewish festival that begins in March or April and lasts for seven or eight days. Passover begins with a special symbolic meal that reminds Jewish people of how God freed their ancestors from slavery in Egypt. *Tomorrow night at sundown, the Jewish holiday of Passover begins... Kate had invited Alan to spend the Passover with her.* N-UNCOUNT: also the N

passport /pɑːspɔːʳt, pæs-/ **passports** ◆◆◇◇◇

1 Your **passport** is an official document containing your name, photograph, and personal details, which you need to show when you enter or leave a country. *You should take your passport with you when changing money. ...a South African businessman travelling on a British passport.* N-COUNT

2 If you say that a thing is a **passport to** success or happiness, you mean that this thing makes success or happiness possible. *Victory would give him a passport to the riches he craves... If the interview goes well it could be the passport to an exciting new career.* N-COUNT: N to n

password /pɑːswɜːʳd, pæs-/ **passwords.** A **password** is a secret word or phrase that you must know in order to be allowed to enter a place such as a military base, or to be allowed to use a computer system. *Advance and give the password... No-one could use the computer unless they had a password.* N-COUNT

past /pɑːst, pæst/ **pasts** ◆◆◆◆◆

In addition to the uses shown below, **past** is used in the phrasal verb 'run past'.

1 **The past** is the time before the present, and the things that have happened. *In the past, about a third of the babies born to women with diabetes were lost... It is a sign that Mr Gorbachev is learning from the mistakes of the past... We would like to put the past behind us.* N-SING: the N ≠future ● If you accuse someone of **living in the past**, you mean that they think too much about the past or believe that things are the same as they were in the past. *What was the point in living in the past, thinking about what had or had not happened?* PHRASE: V inflects

2 Your **past** consists of all the things that you have done or that have happened to you. *...revelations about his past. ...Germany's recent past.* N-COUNT: usu sing, usu with supp =history

3 **Past** events and things happened or existed before the present time. *I knew from past experience that alternative therapies could help. ...a return to the turbulence of past centuries... The list of past champions includes many British internationals.* ADJ: ADJ n =former ► used after periods of time; a literary use. *A South Korean newspaper said today the event will be smaller than in years past.*

4 You use **past** to talk about a period of time that has just finished. For example, if you talk about the **past five years**, you mean the period of five years that has just finished. *Mr Hammond said the trade union movement had changed over the past two years. ...the momentous events of the past few days.* ADJ: det ADJ n =last ≠next

5 If a situation is **past**, it has ended and no longer exists; a literary use. *Many economists believe the worst of the economic downturn is past... The time for loyalty is past. ...images from years long past.* ADJ: v-link ADJ =gone

6 The **past tenses** of a verb are the ones used to talk about things that happened at some time before the present. In English, the simple past tense is sometimes called the **past tense**. The past tense uses the past form of a verb, which for regular verbs ends in '-ed', as in 'They walked back to the car'. See also **past perfect**. ADJ: ADJ n

7 You use **past** when you are stating a time which is thirty minutes or less after a particular hour. For example, if it is **twenty past** six, it is twenty minutes after six o'clock. *It's ten past eleven... I arrived at half past ten.* PREP: num PREP num ≠to ► Also an adverb. *I have my lunch at half past.* ADV: num ADV ≠to

8 If it is **past** a particular time, it is later than that time. *It was past midnight... It's past your bedtime.* [PREP =gone, after]

9 If you go **past** someone or something, you go near them and keep moving, so that they are then behind you. *I dashed past him and out of the door... A steady procession of people filed past the coffin... He was never able to get past the border guards.* [PREP =by] ► Also an adverb. *An ambulance drove past.* [ADV =by]

10 If you look or point **past** someone or something, you look or point at something behind them. *She stared past Christine at the bed.* [PREP: v PREP n =beyond]

11 If something is **past** a place, it is on the other side of it. *Go north on I-15 to the exit just past Barstow... Just past the Barlby roundabout there's temporary traffic lights.* [PREP: v-link PREP n ≠before]

12 If someone or something is **past** a particular point or stage, they are no longer at that point or stage. *He was well past retirement age... They felt that, at 69 or so, Mr Peters was past his prime. ...a piece of cheese four weeks past its sell-by date... The situation is long past the stage when anyone's advice would help.* [PREP: usu v-link PREP n =beyond]

13 If you are **past** doing something, you are no longer able to do it, often because you have undergone so much. In particular, if you are **past caring**, you do not care about something because so many bad things have happened to you. *The aeroplane seats were somewhat narrow, but by that time she was past caring... Often by the time they do accept the truth they are past being able to put words to feelings.* [PREP: v-link PREP -ing =beyond] • If you say that someone or something is **past it**, they are no longer able to do what they used to do; an informal expression. *I suppose they're saying that I'm past it... We could do with a new car. The one we've got at the moment is getting a bit past it.* [PHRASE: v-link PHR PRAGMATICS]

14 If you say that you **would not put it past** someone to do something bad, you mean that you would not be surprised if they did it because you think their character is bad. *You know what she's like. I wouldn't put it past her to call the police and say I stole them.* [PHRASE: oft PHR to-inf]

pasta /pæstə, AM pɑːstə/ **pastas. Pasta** is a type of food made from a mixture of flour, eggs, and water that is formed into different shapes and then boiled. Spaghetti, macaroni, and noodles are types of pasta. [◆◆◇◇◇ N-MASS]

paste /peɪst/ **pastes, pasting, pasted** [◆◇◇◇◇]

1 Paste is a soft, wet, sticky mixture of a substance and a liquid, which can be spread easily. Some types of paste are used to stick things together. *He then sticks it back together with flour paste... Blend a little milk with the custard powder to form a paste. ...wallpaper paste.* [N-MASS]

2 Paste is a soft smooth mixture made of crushed meat, fruit, or vegetables. You can, for example, spread it onto bread or use it in cooking. *...tomato paste. ...fish paste sandwiches.* [N-MASS]

3 If you **paste** something on a surface, you put glue or paste on it and stick it on the surface. *...pasting labels on bottles... Activists pasted up posters criticizing the leftist leaders.* [VERB V n prep V n with adv Also V n *with* n]

4 Paste is a hard shiny glass that is used for making imitation jewellery. *...paste emeralds.* [N-UNCOUNT: oft N n]

5 See also **pasting**.

pastel /pæstᵊl, AM pæstel/ **pastels** [◆◇◇◇◇]

1 Pastel colours are pale rather than dark or bright. *...delicate pastel shades. ...pastel pink, blue, peach and green. ...pretty pastel-coloured houses.* [ADJ: ADJ n, ADJ colour] ► Also a noun. *The lobby is decorated in pastels.* [N-COUNT]

2 Pastels are also small sticks of different coloured chalks that are used for drawing pictures. *...pastels and charcoal. ...the portrait in pastels.* [N-COUNT: usu pl]

3 A **pastel** is a picture that has been done using pastels. *...Degas's paintings, pastels, and prints. ...a pastel by Toulouse-Lautrec. ...a pastel drawing.* [N-COUNT]

pasteurized /pɑːstʃəraɪzd, pæs-/; also spelled **pasteurised. Pasteurized** milk, cream, or cheese has had bacteria removed from it by a special heating process to make it safer to eat or drink. [ADJ: usu ADJ n]

pastiche /pæstiːʃ/ **pastiches.** A **pastiche** is something such as a piece of writing or music in which the style is copied from someone or something else, or which contains a mixture of different styles; a formal word. *Umberto Eco published an amusing seven-page pastiche of Nabokov's 'Lolita' entitled 'Granita'.* [◆◇◇◇◇ N-VAR]

pastille /pæstᵊl, AM pæstiːl/ **pastilles.** A **pastille** is a small, round sweet that has a fruit flavour. Some pastilles contain medicine and you can suck them if you have a sore throat or a cough. [N-COUNT]

pastime /pɑːstaɪm, pæs-/ **pastimes.** A **pastime** is something that you do in your spare time because you enjoy it or are interested in it. *His favourite pastime is golf.* [◆◇◇◇◇ N-COUNT =hobby]

pasting /peɪstɪŋ/

1 If something or someone takes a **pasting**, they are severely criticized; used mainly in informal British English. *The people who run Lloyd's of London took a pasting yesterday. ...the critical pasting that the film received.* [N-SING]

2 If a sports team or political party is given a **pasting**, they are heavily defeated; used mainly in informal British English. [N-SING =thrashing]

past master, past masters. If you are a **past master** at something, you are very skilful at it because you have had a lot of experience doing it. *He was a past-master at manipulating the media for his own ends... She is an adept rock-climber and a past master of the assault course.* [N-COUNT: usu N *at/in/of* n =expert]

pastor /pɑːstəʳ, pæstəʳ/ **pastors.** A **pastor** is a member of the Christian clergy in some Protestant churches. [◆◇◇◇◇ N-COUNT]

pastoral /pɑːstərəl, pæst-/ [◆◇◇◇◇]

1 The **pastoral** duties of a priest, rabbi, or other religious leader are his responsibilities to the members of his religious group, especially for their personal problems rather than their religious needs. *...the pastoral care of the sick... Many churches provide excellent pastoral counselling.* [ADJ: ADJ n]

2 If a school offers **pastoral** care, it is concerned with the personal needs and problems of its pupils, not just with their schoolwork. *A few schools now offer counselling sessions; all have some system of pastoral care.* [ADJ: ADJ n]

3 A **pastoral** place, atmosphere, or idea is characteristic of peaceful country life and scenery. *...the pastoral beauty of a park. ...a tranquil pastoral scene. ...the pastoral joys of rural districts.* [ADJ-GRADED: ADJ n =rustic, bucolic]

4 A **pastoral** way of life is one in which people keep animals such as cows and sheep that feed off the land. *...the Israelites, who were a pastoral people. ...a system of pastoral farming.* [ADJ: ADJ n]

past participle, past participles. The **past participle** of a verb is a form which is usually the same as the past form and so ends in '-ed'. A number of verbs have irregular past participles, for example 'break' (past participle 'broken') and 'come' ('come'). Past participles are used to form perfect tenses and the passive voice, and many of them can be used like an adjective in front of a noun. [N-COUNT]

past perfect. The **past perfect** tenses of a verb are the ones used to talk about things that happened at some time before a specific time. The simple past perfect tense uses 'had' and the past participle of the verb, as in 'She had seen him before'. It is sometimes called the **pluperfect**. [ADJ: ADJ n]

pastrami /pæstrɑːmi/. **Pastrami** is strongly seasoned smoked beef. [N-UNCOUNT]

pastry /peɪstri/ **pastries** [◆◆◇◇◇]

1 Pastry is a food made of flour, fat, and water that is mixed into a dough, rolled flat, and baked in the oven. It is used for making pies and flans. *...courgettes wrapped in pastry.* [N-UNCOUNT]

2 A **pastry** is a small cake made with sweet pastry. [N-COUNT]

pasture /pɑːstʃəʳ, pæs-/ **pastures** [◆◇◇◇◇]

1 Pasture is land that has grass growing on it and that is used for farm animals to graze on. *...clearing the land for pasture. ...three acres of pasture and woodland... The cows are out now, grazing in the pasture. ...mountain pastures.* [N-VAR]

2 If someone leaves for **greener pastures**, or in British English **pastures new**, they leave their job, [PHRASES prep PHR, v PHR] their home, or the situation they are in for something they think will be much better. *Michael decided he wanted to move on to pastures new for financial reasons. ...nurses seeking greener pastures overseas.*

3 If you **put** animals **out to pasture**, you move them out into the fields so they can eat the grass. V inflects

4 If you say that someone has been **put out to pasture**, you disapprove of the fact that they have been made to stop work because they are considered too old; an informal expression. *I'm retiring next month. They're putting me out to pasture.* V inflects PRAGMATICS =retire

pasty, pasties. The adjective is pronounced /peɪsti/. The noun is pronounced /pæsti/.

1 If you are **pasty** or if you have a **pasty face**, you look pale and unhealthy. *My complexion remained pale and pasty... Ron Freeman appeared pasty faced and nervous.* ADJ-GRADED =sallow

2 In Britain, a **pasty** is a small pie which consists of pastry folded around meat, vegetables, or cheese. *...meat pasties.* ● See also **Cornish pasty**. N-COUNT

pat /pæt/ **pats, patting, patted** ◆◆◇◇◇

1 If you **pat** something or someone, you tap them lightly, usually with your hand held flat. *'Don't you worry about any of this,' she said patting me on the knee... The landlady patted her hair nervously... Wash the lettuce and pat it dry.* ► Also a noun. *He gave her an encouraging pat on the shoulder.* VERB V n on n V n V n adj N-COUNT

2 A **pat** of butter or something else that is soft is a small lump of it. N-COUNT: usu N of n

3 If you say that an answer or explanation is **pat**, you disapprove of it because it is too simple and sounds as if it has been prepared in advance. *There's no pat answer to that... Despite the film's merits I felt it was too pat.* ADJ-GRADED PRAGMATICS =glib, facile

4 If you give someone **a pat on the back** or if you **pat** them **on the back**, you show them that you think they have done well and deserve to be praised. *The players deserve a pat on the back... If you do something well, give yourself a pat on the back.* PHRASES V inflects

5 If you **have** an answer or explanation **down pat** or **off pat**, you have prepared and learned it so you are ready to say it at any time. *I have my story down pat... He had his answer off pat.* V inflects

patch /pætʃ/ **patches, patching, patched** ◆◆◇◇◇

1 A **patch** on a surface is a part of it which is different in appearance from the area around it. *...the bald patch on the top of his head... There was a small patch of blue in the grey clouds. ...two big damp patches on the carpet.* N-COUNT: usu with supp

2 A **patch** of land is a small area of land where a particular plant or crop grows. *...a patch of land covered in forest. ...the little vegetable patch in her backyard. ...a patch of wild cornflowers.* N-COUNT: with supp, oft N of n

3 A **patch** is a piece of material which you use to cover a hole in something. *...jackets with patches on the elbows. ...trying to fix the flat tire by putting a patch on it.* N-COUNT

4 A **patch** is a small piece of material which you wear to cover an injured eye. *She went to the hospital and found him lying down with a patch over his eye.* ● See also **eye patch**. N-COUNT

5 If you **patch** something that has a hole in it, you mend it by fastening a patch over the hole. *He and Walker patched the barn roof... One of the mechanics took off the damaged tyre, and took it back to the station to be patched. ...their patched clothes.* VERB V n V-ed

6 If you have or go through **a bad patch** or **a rough patch**, you have a lot of problems for a time; used mainly in British English. *His marriage was going through a bad patch... The company I work for went through a rough patch.* PHRASES N inflects

7 If you say that someone or something is **not a patch on** someone or something else, you mean that they are not nearly as good as the other person or thing; an informal British expression. *He's not a patch on the rest of the Cabinet... Handsome, she thought, but not a patch on Alex.* v-link PHR, PHR n

patch together. If you **patch** something **together**, you form it from a number of parts in a quick, hurried way. *...to avoid an election by patching together a new government... A hasty deal was patched together. ...this patched-together Commonwealth.* PHRASAL VERB V P n (not pron) V-ed P Also V n P

patch up PHRASAL VERB

1 If you **patch up** a quarrel or relationship, you try to be friendly again and not to quarrel any more. *She has gone on holiday with her husband to try to patch up their marriage... He has now patched up his differences with the Minister... France patched things up with New Zealand... They managed to patch it up.* RECIP V P n (not pron) V P n (not pron) with n V n P with n V n P

2 If you **patch up** something which is damaged, you mend it or patch it. *We can patch up those holes... He did not have enough money to have the tire patched up, let alone buy a new one.* V P n (not pron) Also V n P

3 If doctors **patch** someone **up** or **patch** their wounds **up**, they treat their injuries, for example by putting bandages on them. *...the medical staff who patched her up after the accident... Emergency surgery patched up his face.* V n P V P n (not pron)

4 If people or countries **patch up** a deal, they manage to agree on it after difficult discussions. *Trade ministers patched up a compromise.* V P n (not pron) Also V n P

patchwork /pætʃwɜːʳk/ ◆◇◇◇◇

1 A **patchwork** quilt or cushion is made by sewing together small pieces of material of different colours. *...beds covered in patchwork quilts.* ► Also a noun. *For centuries, quilting and patchwork have been popular needlecrafts.* ADJ: ADJ n N-UNCOUNT

2 If you refer to something as a **patchwork**, you mean that it is made up of many different parts, pieces or colours. *The low mountains were a patchwork of green and brown. ...this complex republic, a patchwork of cultures, religions and nationalities.* N-SING: oft N of n

patchy /pætʃi/ ◆◇◇◇◇

1 A **patchy** substance or colour is not spread evenly, but is scattered around in small quantities. *Thick patchy fog and irresponsible driving were to blame... Bottle tans can make your legs, arms and face look a patchy orange colour. ...the brown, patchy grass.* ADJ-GRADED ≠even

2 If something is **patchy**, it is not completely reliable or satisfactory because it is not always good. *The evidence is patchy... Transport is difficult, communications are patchy... The rest of the acting is patchy at best.* ADJ-GRADED

pate /peɪt/ **pates.** Your **pate** is the top of your head; an old-fashioned word. *...Bryan's bald pate.* N-COUNT

pâté /pæteɪ, AM pɑːteɪ/ **pâtés. Pâté** is a mixture of meat, fish, or vegetables with various flavourings, which is blended into a paste and eaten cold. ◆◇◇◇◇ N-MASS

patent /peɪtᵊnt, AM pæt-/ **patents, patenting, patented.** The pronunciation /pætᵊnt/ is also used for meanings 1 and 2 in British English. ◆◆◇◇◇

1 A **patent** is an official right to be the only person or company allowed to make or sell a new product for a certain period of time. *P&G applied for a patent on its cookies... He held a number of patents for his many innovations... It sued Centrocorp for patent infringement.* N-COUNT

2 If you **patent** something, you obtain a patent for it. *He patented the idea that the atom could be split... The invention has been patented by the university. ...a patented machine called the VCR II.* VERB V n V-ed

3 If you use **patent** to describe something, especially something bad, you are emphatically indicating your opinion that its nature or existence is clear and obvious. *This was patent nonsense. ...a patent lie.* ♦ **patently** *He made his displeasure patently obvious... This is patently absurd.* ADJ-GRADED PRAGMATICS =obvious, clear ADV-GRADED =clearly

patent leather. **Patent leather** is leather or plastic which has a shiny surface. It is used to make shoes, handbags, and belts. *He wore patent leather shoes.* N-UNCOUNT: oft N n

paternal /pətɜːʳnᵊl/ ◆◇◇◇◇

1 **Paternal** is used to describe feelings or actions which are typical of those of a kind father towards his child. *...paternal love for his children... He put his hand under her chin in an almost paternal gesture.* ADJ-GRADED: usu ADJ n =fatherly

2 A **paternal** relative is one that is related through a ADJ:

person's father rather than their mother. *...my paternal grandparents.* ADJ n

paternalism /pətɜːʳnəlɪzəm/. **Paternalism** means taking all the decisions for the people you govern, employ, or are responsible for, thus taking away their own personal responsibility. *...Tory paternalism. ...the company's reputation for paternalism.* N-UNCOUNT

paternalist /pətɜːʳnəlɪst/ **paternalists**
1 A **paternalist** is a person who believes in the policy of paternalism or who acts in a paternalistic way. *Primo de Rivera himself was a benevolent and sincere paternalist.* N-COUNT ≠libertarian
2 **Paternalist** means the same as **paternalistic**. *The whole place was the romantic vision of the paternalist local squire. ...a paternalist policy of state welfare for the deserving poor.* ADJ-GRADED: usu ADJ n

paternalistic /pətɜːʳnəlɪstɪk/. Someone who is **paternalistic** takes all the decisions for the people they govern, employ, or are responsible for. *The doctor is being paternalistic. He's deciding what information the patient needs to know... IBM has always been a paternalistic employer.* ADJ-GRADED

paternity /pətɜːʳnɪti/. **Paternity** is the state or fact of being the father of a particular child; a formal word. *He was tricked into marriage by a false accusation of paternity.* N-UNCOUNT

paternity leave. If a man has **paternity leave**, his employer allows him some time off work because his child has just been born. *Paternity leave is rare and, where it does exist, it's unlikely to be for any longer than two weeks.* N-UNCOUNT

paternity suit, paternity suits. If a woman starts or takes out a **paternity suit**, she asks a court of law to help her to prove that a particular man is the father of her child, often in order to claim financial support from him. N-COUNT

path /pɑːθ, pæθ/ **paths** ◆◆◆◇◇
1 A **path** is a strip of ground which people walk on. Some paths have been made by many people walking, for example through a forest or up a mountain. Others are built in gardens or parks and covered with concrete or gravel. *We followed the path along the clifftops... Feet had worn a path in the rock... He went up the garden path to knock on the door.* N-COUNT
2 Your **path** is the space ahead of you as you move along. *A group of reporters blocked his path... She did not notice the man until he moved into her path.* N-COUNT: usu poss N
3 The **path** of something is the line which it moves along in a particular direction. *He stepped without looking into the path of a reversing car. ...people who live near airports or under the flight path of airplanes... The storm wrecked homes in its path.* N-COUNT: with poss
4 A **path** that you take is a particular course of action or way of achieving something. *The opposition appear to have chosen the path of cooperation rather than confrontation... He promised that within 100 days he would put the country on the path to economic recovery.* N-COUNT: oft N *of/to* n =way, road, route
5 You can say that something is in your **path** or blocking your **path** to mean that it is preventing you from doing or achieving what you want. *The Church of England put a serious obstacle in the path of women who want to become priests.* N-COUNT: usu with poss =way
6 If you **cross** someone's **path** or if your **paths cross**, you meet them by chance. *It was highly unlikely that their paths would cross again... Over the years, Yul and Kirk had crossed paths many times.* PHRASE: V inflects

pathetic /pəθetɪk/ ◆◆◇◇◇
1 If you describe a person or animal as **pathetic**, you mean that they are sad and weak or helpless, and they make you feel very sorry for them. *...a pathetic little dog with a curly tail... The small group of onlookers presented a pathetic sight... She now looked small, shrunken and pathetic.* ♦ **pathetically** /pəθetɪkli/ *She was pathetically thin.* ADJ-GRADED =pitiful; ADV-GRADED
2 If you describe someone or something as **pathetic**, you mean that they make you feel impatient or angry, often because they are very bad or weak. *What pathetic excuses... It's a pound for a small glass of wine which is pathetic. ...the pathetic attempts at public speaking made by members of all parties... Don't be so pathetic.* ♦ **pathetically** *Five women in a group of 18 people is a pathetically small number.* ADJ-GRADED; ADV-GRADED: ADV adj

pathfinder /pɑːθfaɪndəʳ, pæθ-/ **pathfinders.** A **pathfinder** is someone whose job is to find routes across areas. N-COUNT

pathogen /pæθədʒen/ **pathogens.** A **pathogen** is any organism which can cause disease in a person, animal, or plant; a technical term in science. *Much disease is caused by pathogens.* N-COUNT

pathogenic /pæθədʒenɪk/. A **pathogenic** organism can cause disease in a person, animal, or plant; a technical term in science. ADJ: usu ADJ n

pathological /pæθəlɒdʒɪkəl/ ◆◇◇◇◇
1 You describe a person or their behaviour as **pathological** when they behave in an extreme and unacceptable way, and have very powerful feelings which they cannot control. *He experiences chronic, almost pathological jealousy... He's a pathological liar. ...a pathological fear of snakes... The man is crazy, pathological.* ADJ-GRADED: usu ADJ n
2 **Pathological** also means relating to pathology; a medical use. *...pathological conditions in animals.* ADJ

pathologist /pəθɒlədʒɪst/ **pathologists.** A **pathologist** is someone who studies or investigates diseases and illnesses, and examines dead bodies in order to find out the cause of death. ◆◇◇◇◇ N-COUNT

pathology /pəθɒlədʒi/. **Pathology** is the study of the way diseases and illnesses develop; a medical term. ◆◇◇◇◇ N-UNCOUNT

pathos /peɪθɒs/. **Pathos** is a quality in a situation, film, or play that makes people feel sadness and pity. *...the pathos of man's isolation... With touching pathos he described the pangs of hunger.* ◆◇◇◇◇ N-UNCOUNT

pathway /pɑːθweɪ, pæθ-/ **pathways** ◆◇◇◇◇
1 A **pathway** is a path which you can walk along or a route which you can take. *Richard was coming up the pathway. ...a pathway leading towards the nearby river.* N-COUNT
2 A **pathway** is a particular course of action or a way of achieving something. *Diplomacy will smooth your pathway to success. ... the call to arms that opened the pathway to freedom for the Brazilian people.* N-COUNT: oft N *to* n =path

patience /peɪʃəns/ ◆◆◇◇◇
1 If you have **patience**, you are able to stay calm and not get annoyed, for example when something takes a long time, or when someone is not doing what you want them to do. *He doesn't have the patience to wait... It was exacting work and required all his patience.* N-UNCOUNT ≠impatience
2 In British English, **patience** is also a card game for only one player; the American word is **solitaire**. *He would often sit and play patience.* N-UNCOUNT
3 If someone **tries** your **patience** or **tests** your **patience**, they annoy you so much that it is very difficult for you to stay calm. *He tended to stutter whenever he spoke to her. It undermined her confidence in him and tried her patience... I feel that she would try the patience of a saint.* PHRASE: V inflects

patient /peɪʃənt/ **patients** ◆◆◆◆◇
1 A **patient** is a person who is receiving medical treatment from a doctor or hospital. A **patient** is also someone who is registered with a particular doctor. *The earlier the treatment is given, the better the patient's chances... She was tough but wonderful with her patients... He specialized in treatment of cancer patients.* N-COUNT
2 If you are **patient**, you stay calm and do not get annoyed, for example when something takes a long time, or when someone is not doing what you want them to do. *Please be patient – your cheque will arrive... He was endlessly kind and patient with children.* ♦ **patiently** *She waited patiently for Frances to finish.* ADJ-GRADED ≠impatient; ADV-GRADED: ADV with v

patina /pætɪnə/
1 A **patina** is a thin layer of something that has formed on the surface of something. *The trophy is very impressive and rather special because it has a* N-SING: with supp

beautiful green patina... He allowed a fine patina of old coffee to develop around the inside of the mug.
2 The **patina** on an antique or other old object is a soft shine that develops on its surface as it grows older. *...a mahogany door that is golden brown with the patina of age.* N-SING: with supp
3 If you say that someone has a **patina** of a quality or characteristic, you mean that they have a small but impressive amount of this quality or characteristic. *...a superficial patina of knowledge... Except for a patina of charisma, he was like a thousand other bright young men in Toronto.* N-SING: with supp, oft N of n

patio /pætiou/ **patios.** A **patio** is an area of paving or concrete in a garden close to a house, where people can sit to eat or relax. ◆◇◇◇◇ N-COUNT

patio door, patio doors. **Patio doors** are glass doors that lead onto a patio. N-COUNT

patisserie /pətiːsəri, AM -tɪs-/ **patisseries**
1 A **patisserie** is a shop where cakes and pastries are sold. *...real cakes from a patisserie.* N-COUNT
2 **Patisserie** is cakes and pastries. *Blois is famous for patisserie.* N-UNCOUNT: also N in pl

patois. **Patois** is both the singular and the plural form. The singular form is pronounced /pætwɑː/, the plural form is pronounced /pætwɑːz/.
1 A **patois** is an unwritten form of a language, especially French, that is spoken in a particular area of a country. *In France patois was spoken in rural, less developed regions.* N-VAR =dialect
2 A **patois** is a language that has developed from a mixture of other languages. *A substantial proportion of the population speak a French-based patois.* N-VAR =creole

patriarch /peɪtriɑːʳk/ **patriarchs** ◆◇◇◇◇
1 A **patriarch** is the male head of a family or tribe. *The patriarch of the house, Mr Jawad, rules it with a ferocity renowned throughout the neighbourhood... Joseph Kennedy, the clan's patriarch, communicated with Bobby in a series of notes.* N-COUNT
2 A **patriarch** is the head of one of a number of Eastern Christian Churches. *...the new head of the Russian Orthodox church, Patriarch Alexei the Second.* N-COUNT; N-TITLE

patriarchal /peɪtriɑːʳkəl/. A **patriarchal** society, family, or system is one in which the men have all or most of the power and importance. *To feminists she is a classic victim of the patriarchal society... I think marriage is used to uphold patriarchal control.* ◆◇◇◇◇ ADJ-GRADED: usu ADJ n

patriarchy /peɪtriɑːʳki/ **patriarchies** ◆◇◇◇◇
1 **Patriarchy** is a system in which men have all or most of the power and importance in a society or group. *The main cause of women's and children's oppression is patriarchy.* N-UNCOUNT
2 A **patriarchy** is a patriarchal society. N-COUNT

patrician /pətrɪʃən/ **patricians** ◆◇◇◇◇
1 A **patrician** is a person who comes from a family of high social rank; a formal word. *...the patrician banker Sir Charles Villiers.* N-COUNT ≠plebeian
2 If you describe someone as **patrician**, you mean that they behave in a sophisticated way, and look as though they are from a high social rank. *He was a lean, patrician gent in his early sixties. ...her crisp, patrician voice.* ADJ-GRADED =refined

patrimony /pætrɪməni, AM -mouni/
1 Someone's **patrimony** is the possessions that they have inherited from their father or ancestors; a formal use. *I left my parents' house, relinquished my estate and my patrimony.* N-SING
2 A country's **patrimony** is its national treasures and works of art; a formal use. *In the 1930's, The National Trust began its campaign to save Britain's patrimony of threatened country houses.* N-SING =heritage

patriot /pætriət, peɪt-/ **patriots.** Someone who is a **patriot** loves their country and feels very loyal towards it. *They were staunch British patriots and had portraits of the Queen in their flat.* ◆◆◇◇◇ N-COUNT: oft supp N

patriotic /pætriɒtɪk, peɪt-/. Someone who is **patriotic** loves their country and feels very loyal towards it. *Woosnam is fiercely patriotic... The crowd sang 'Land of Hope and Glory' and other patriotic songs.* ◆◆◇◇◇ ADJ-GRADED ≠unpatriotic

patriotism /pætriətɪzəm, peɪt-/. **Patriotism** is love for your country and loyalty towards it. *He was a country boy who had joined the army out of a sense of patriotism and adventure... We live in an age when patriotism is often sneered at.* ◆◇◇◇◇ N-UNCOUNT

patrol /pətroul/ **patrols, patrolling, patrolled** ◆◆◇◇◇
1 When soldiers, police, or guards **patrol** an area or building, they move around it in order to make sure that there is no trouble there. *Prison officers continued to patrol the grounds within the jail.* VERB V n
► Also a noun. *He failed to return from a patrol.* N-COUNT
2 Soldiers, police, or guards who are **on patrol** are patrolling an area. *The army is now on patrol in Srinagar and a curfew has been imposed... Security forces remained on patrol until late into the night.* PHRASE: usu v-link PHR
3 A **patrol** is a group of soldiers or vehicles that are patrolling an area. *Guerrillas attacked a patrol with hand grenades. ...a border patrol operating near the Burmese frontier... A few minutes later the car and van were spotted by a patrol car at Great Milton.* N-COUNT

patrol car, patrol cars. A **patrol car** is a police car used for patrolling streets and highways. N-COUNT =squad car

patrolman /pətroulmən/ **patrolmen**
1 In American English, a **patrolman** is a uniformed policeman who patrols a particular area. *In Petersburg, 30 patrolmen have died violently in the past five years.* N-COUNT
2 In British English, a **patrolman** is a person employed by a motorists' association who is based in a particular area and goes to help motorists when, for example, their cars break down. *Mal's car had broken down en route and the AA patrolman had taken an hour to arrive.* N-COUNT

patron /peɪtrən/ **patrons** ◆◆◇◇◇
1 A **patron** is a person who supports and gives money to artists, writers, or musicians. *Catherine the Great was a patron of the arts and sciences.* N-COUNT: with supp, oft N of n =sponsor
2 The **patron** of a charity, group, or campaign is an important person who allows his or her name to be used for publicity. *The Princess is patron of the National AIDS Trust.* N-COUNT: with supp, oft N of n
3 The **patrons** of a place such as a pub or a hotel are its customers; a formal use. *He spent the night at the Savoy: like so many of its patrons, he could not resist the exclusively English cooking.* N-COUNT =client

patronage /pætrənɪdʒ, peɪt-/. **Patronage** is the support and money given by someone to a person or a group such as a charity. *...government patronage of the arts in Europe... The Vevey Festival was founded 12 years ago under the patronage of Oona Chaplin.* ◆◇◇◇◇ N-UNCOUNT: oft with poss =sponsorship

patroness /peɪtrənes/ **patronesses.** A woman who is a patron of something can be described as a **patroness**. N-COUNT: usu with supp =sponsor

patronise /pætrənaɪz/. See **patronize**.

patronising /pætrənaɪzɪŋ/. See **patronizing**.

patronize /pætrənaɪz, AM peɪt-/ **patronizes, patronizing, patronized;** also spelled **patronise** in British English. ◆◇◇◇◇
1 If someone **patronizes** you, they speak or behave towards you in a way which seems friendly, but which shows that they think they are superior to you in some way; used showing disapproval. *Don't you patronize me!... Cornelia often felt patronised by her tutors.* VERB PRAGMATICS V n V-ed
2 Someone who **patronizes** artists, writers, or musicians supports them and gives them money; a formal use. *The Japanese Imperial family patronises the Japanese Art Association.* VERB =sponsor V n
3 If someone **patronizes** a place such as a pub or a hotel, they are one of its customers; a formal use. *The ladies of Berne liked to patronize the Palace for tea and little cakes.* VERB =frequent V n

patronizing /pætrənaɪzɪŋ, AM peɪt-/; also spelled **patronising**. If someone is **patronizing**, they speak or behave towards you in a way that seems friendly, but which shows that they think they are superior to you; used showing disapproval. *The tone of the interview was unnecessarily patronizing . ...his patronising attitude to the homeless.* ◆◇◇◇◇ ADJ-GRADED PRAGMATICS
♦ **patronizingly** *Schneider patted the girl patronizingly on the cheek.* ADV-GRADED =condescending

patron saint, patron saints. The **patron saint** of a place, an activity, or a group of people is a saint who is believed to give them special help and protection. *Chiswick church is dedicated to St Nicholas, patron saint of sailors.* N-COUNT: usu with poss

patsy /pætsi/ **patsies.** In American English, if you describe someone as a **patsy**, you mean that they are rather stupid and are easily cheated or misled by other people, or that they take the blame for other people's actions; an informal word. *Davis was nobody's patsy... He has long felt that Ray was set up, that he was a patsy.* N-COUNT PRAGMATICS =mug

patter /pætəʳ/ **patters, pattering, pattered** ◆◇◇◇◇

1 If something **patters** on a surface, it hits it quickly several times, making quiet, tapping sounds. *Rain pattered gently outside, dripping on to the roof from the pines.* VERB V adv/prep

2 A **patter** is a series of quick, quiet, tapping sounds. *...the patter of the driving rain on the roof.* N-SING: oft *the* N *of* n

3 Someone's **patter** is a series of things that they say quickly and easily, usually in order to entertain people or to persuade them to buy or do something. *There's no doubt women found him charming. It must have been his patter because he's certainly not at all good-looking... Fran began her automatic patter about how Jon had been unavoidably detained.* N-SING: usu poss N =spiel

pattern /pætəʳn/ **patterns** ◆◆◆◆◇

1 A **pattern** is the repeated or regular way in which something happens or is done. *All three attacks followed the same pattern... A change in the pattern of his breathing became apparent.* N-COUNT: oft *the* N *of* n

2 A **pattern** is an arrangement of lines or shapes, especially a design in which the same shape is repeated at regular intervals over a surface. *...a golden robe embroidered with red and purple thread stitched into a pattern of flames.* N-COUNT

3 A **pattern** is a diagram or shape that you can use as a guide when you are making something such as a model or a piece of clothing. *...cutting out a pattern for trousers... Send for our free patterns to knit yourself. ...sewing patterns.* N-COUNT

patterned /pætəʳnd/ ◆◇◇◇◇

1 Something that is **patterned** is covered with a pattern or design. *...a plain carpet with a patterned border. ...bone china patterned with flowers.* ADJ: oft ADJ *with* n

2 If something new **is patterned** on something else that already exists, it is deliberately made so that it has similar features; used mainly in American English. *New York City announced a 10-point policy patterned on the federal bill of rights for taxpayers... He says this contract should not be patterned after the Deere pact.* V-PASSIVE =is modelled *be* V-ed *on* n *be* V-ed *after* n

patterning /pætəʳnɪŋ/

1 **Patterning** is the forming of fixed ways of behaving or of doing things by constantly repeating or copying other people; a formal use. *...social patterning. ...the patterning of behaviour.* N-UNCOUNT: usu with supp

2 You can refer to lines, spots, or other patterns as **patterning**. *...geometric patterning. ...a jazzy patterning of lights.* N-UNCOUNT: usu with supp

patty /pæti/ **patties**

1 A **patty** is a small, round meat pie; used mainly in American English. N-COUNT

2 A **patty** is an amount of minced beef formed into a flat, round shape. *...the beef patties frying on the grill behind the counter.* N-COUNT

paucity /pɔːsɪti/. If you say that there is a **paucity of** something, you mean that there is an insufficient amount of it; a formal word. *Even the film's impressive finale can't hide the first hour's paucity of imagination. ...the paucity of good British women sprinters.* N-SING: N *of* n =lack

paunch /pɔːntʃ/ **paunches.** If a man has a **paunch**, he has a fat stomach. *He finished his dessert and patted his paunch... His once lean figure was developing a paunch.* N-COUNT =pot-belly

paunchy /pɔːntʃi/ **paunchier, paunchiest.** A man who is **paunchy** has a fat stomach. *He was a heavy man, paunchy, with a lined, kind face.* ADJ-GRADED: usu v-link ADJ =pot-bellied

pauper /pɔːpəʳ/ **paupers.** A **pauper** is a very poor person; a formal word. *He did die a pauper and is buried in an unmarked grave.* N-COUNT

pause /pɔːz/ **pauses, pausing, paused** ◆◆◆◇◇

1 If you **pause** while you are doing something, you stop for a short period and then continue. *'It's rather embarrassing,' he began, and paused... He had to pause to clear his throat... He worked steadily, and fast, pausing only to toss away clumps of grass roots... On leaving, she paused for a moment at the door... He talked for two hours without pausing for breath.* VERB V V *for* n

2 A **pause** is a short period when you stop doing something before continuing. *After a pause Alex said sharply: 'I'm sorry if I've upset you'... There was a pause while the barmaid set down two plates in front of us.* N-COUNT

3 If something **gives** you **pause for thought**, it makes you think carefully about something, especially in a different way than you have thought about it before. *An opposition spokesman said he hoped the agreement would give them pause for thought about the futility of violence.* PHRASE: V inflects

pave /peɪv/ **paves, paving, paved** ◆◆◇◇◇

1 If a road or an area of ground **has been paved**, it has been covered with blocks of stone or concrete, so that it is suitable for walking or driving on. *The avenue had never been paved, and deep mud made it impassable in winter... The cobblestone street was paved in 1987.* ♦ **paved** *...a small paved courtyard... The sidewalks were paved with brick and lined with trees.* VB: usu passive *be* V-ed ADJ: oft ADJ *with* n

2 If one thing **paves the way for** another, it creates a situation in which it is possible or more likely that the other thing will happen; used in journalism. *...a new proposal intended to pave the way for the signing of a chemical weapons reduction agreement... The discussions are aimed at paving the way for formal negotiations between the two countries.* PHRASE: V inflects

pavement /peɪvmənt/ **pavements** ◆◆◇◇◇

1 In British English, a **pavement** is a path with a hard surface, usually by the side of a road. The usual American word is **sidewalk**. *He was hurrying along the pavement.* N-COUNT: oft supp N

2 In American English, the **pavement** is the hard surface of a road. N-COUNT

pavilion /pəvɪliən/ **pavilions** ◆◇◇◇◇

1 In British English, a **pavilion** is a building on the edge of a sports field where players can change their clothes and wash. *...the cricket pavilion.* N-COUNT: oft supp N

2 A **pavilion** is a large temporary structure such as a tent, which is used at outdoor public events. *...heading across the beautiful green lawn towards the International Pavilion. ...the United States pavilion at the Expo '70 exhibition in Japan.* N-COUNT: oft supp N =marquee

3 A **pavilion** is an ornamental building in a garden or park. *...Humphrey Repton's design for a garden pavilion at Durham Park.* N-COUNT: usu with supp

paving /peɪvɪŋ/. **Paving** is a paved area or surface. *In the centre of the paving stood a statue. ...concrete paving.* N-UNCOUNT: oft supp N

paving stone, paving stones. Paving stones are flat pieces of stone, usually square in shape, that are used for making pavements. N-COUNT

pavlova /pævloʊvə/ **pavlovas.** A **pavlova** is a dessert that consists of a meringue base with fruit and whipped cream on top. N-VAR

paw /pɔː/ **paws, pawing, pawed** ◆◇◇◇◇

1 The **paws** of an animal such as a cat, dog, or bear are its feet, which have claws for gripping things and soft pads for walking on. *The kitten was black with white front paws and a white splotch on her chest... He removes a thorn from a lion's paw.* N-COUNT: oft with poss

2 You can describe someone's hand as their **paw**, especially if it is very large or if they are very clumsy. *He shook Keaton's hand with his big paw.* N-COUNT: oft poss N, adj N

3 If an animal **paws** something, it draws its paw or hoof over it or hits at it. *Madigan's horse pawed the ground... The dogs continued to paw and claw frantically at the chain mesh.* VERB V n V *at* n

4 If one person **paws** another, they touch or stroke them in a way that the other person finds offensive. VERB PRAGMATICS V n

Stop pawing me, Giles!... He pawed at my jacket with his free hand. V at n

pawn /pɔːn/ **pawns, pawning, pawned** ◆◇◇◇◇

1 If you **pawn** something that you own, you leave it with a pawnbroker, who gives you money for it and who can sell it if you do not pay back the money before a certain time. *He is contemplating pawning his watch... Every saleable piece of furniture had been pawned during their father's illness.* VERB V n

2 In chess, a **pawn** is the smallest and least valuable playing piece. Each player has eight pawns at the start of the game. *Anatoly Karpov picked up another pawn and placed it down on another square... Very quickly he moved his pawn one pace forward.* N-COUNT

3 If you say that someone is using you as a **pawn**, you mean that they are using you for their own advantage. *It looks as though he is being used as a political pawn by the President... They are the pawns in the power game played by their unseen captors.* N-COUNT: usu with supp, oft N *in* n =dupe

pawnbroker /pɔːnbroʊkəʳ/ **pawnbrokers.** A **pawnbroker** is a person who will lend you money if you give them something that you own. The pawnbroker can sell that thing if you do not pay back the money before a certain time. N-COUNT

pawn shop, pawn shops; also spelled **pawnshop**. A **pawn shop** is a pawnbroker's shop. N-COUNT

pawpaw /pɔːpɔː/ **pawpaws;** also spelled **paw-paw**. A **pawpaw** is a fruit with green skin, sweet yellow flesh, and black seeds that grows in the West Indies. N-VAR =papaya

pay /peɪ/ **pays, paying, paid** ◆◆◆◆◆

1 When you **pay** an amount of money to someone, you give it to them because you are buying something from them or because you owe it to them. When you **pay** something such as a bill or a debt, you pay the amount that you owe. *Accommodation is free – all you pay for is breakfast and dinner... She paid £300,000 for the 34-room mansion... The wealthier may have to pay a little more in taxes... He proposes that businesses should pay taxes to the federal government... You can pay by credit card.* VERB V *for* n, V n *for* n, V n, V n *to* n, V adv/prep, Also V to-inf, V n to-inf, V

2 When you are **paid**, you get your wages or salary from your employer. *The lawyer was paid a huge salary... I get paid monthly... They could wander where they wished and take jobs from who paid best.* VERB *be/get* V-ed n, *get/be* V-ed adv, V adv

3 Your **pay** is the money that you get from your employer as wages or salary. *...their complaints about their pay and conditions. ...the workers' demand for a twenty per cent pay rise.* N-UNCOUNT

4 If you **are paid** to do something, someone gives you some money so that you will help them or perform some service for them. *Students were paid substantial sums of money to do nothing all day but lie in bed... If you help me, I'll pay you anything.* VERB *be* V-ed to-inf, V n n

5 If a government or organization makes someone **pay** for something, it makes them responsible for providing the money for it, for example by increasing prices or taxes. *...a legally binding international treaty that establishes who must pay for environmental damage... If you don't subsidize things like ballet and opera it means that seat prices are going to have to go up to pay for it.* VERB V *for* n, Also V

6 If a job, deal, or investment **pays** a particular amount, it brings you that amount of money. *We're stuck in jobs that don't pay very well... The account does not pay interest on a credit balance.* VERB V adv, V n

7 If a job, deal, or investment **pays**, it brings you a profit or earns you some money. *There are some agencies now specialising in helping older people to find jobs which pay... They owned land; they made it pay.* VERB V

8 When you **pay** money into a bank account, you put the money in the account. *He paid £20 into his savings account... There is nothing more annoying than queueing when you only want to pay in a few cheques.* VERB V n *into* n, V n with adv

9 If a course of action **pays**, it results in some advantage or benefit for you. *It pays to invest in protective clothing... He talked of defending small nations, of ensuring that aggression does not pay.* VERB *it* V to-inf, V

10 If you **pay** for something that you do or have, you suffer as a result of it. *Britain was to pay dearly for its lack of resolve... Why should I pay the penalty for somebody else's mistake?... She feels it's a small price to pay for the pleasure of living in this delightful house.* VERB V *for* n, V n *for* n, Also V

11 You use **pay** with some nouns, for example in the expressions **pay a visit** and **pay attention**, to indicate that something is given or done. *Do pay us a visit next time you're in Birmingham... He felt a heavy bump, but paid no attention to it... He had nothing to do with arranging the funeral, but came along to pay his last respects.* VERB V n n, V n *to* n, V n

12 **Pay television** consists of programmes and channels which are not part of an ordinary public broadcasting system, and for which viewers have to pay a special fee or subscription. *The company has set up joint-venture pay-TV channels in Belgium, Spain, and Germany.* ADJ: ADJ n

13 See also **paid; sick pay**.

14 If something that you buy or invest in **pays for itself** after a period of time, the money you gain from it, or save because you have it, is greater than the amount you originally spent or invested. *...investments in energy efficiency that would pay for themselves within five years.* PHRASES V inflects

15 If you say that someone is **in the pay of** a certain person or group, you disapprove of the fact that they are being paid by and are working for that person or group, often secretly or illegally. *He was murdered at a presidential rally by gunmen in the pay of drug traffickers.* PHR n PRAGMATICS

16 If you **pay** your **way**, you have or earn enough money to pay for what you need, without needing other people to give or lend you money. *I went to college anyway, as a part-time student, paying my own way... The British film industry could not pay its way without a substantial export market.* V inflects

17 • to **pay dividends**: see **dividend**. • to **pay through the nose**: see **nose**. • **he who pays the piper calls the tune**: see **piper**.

pay back PHRASAL VERB

1 If you **pay back** some money that you have borrowed or taken from someone, you give them an equal sum of money at a later time. *He burst into tears, begging her to forgive him and swearing to pay back everything he had stolen... I'll pay you back that two quid tomorrow.* V P n (not pron), V n P n, Also V n P

2 If you **pay** someone **back** for doing something unpleasant to you, you take your revenge on them or make them suffer for what they did. *Some day I'll pay you back for this!* =get someone back, V n P *for* n, Also V n P

pay off PHRASAL VERB

1 If you **pay off** a debt, you give someone all the money that you owe them. *It would take him the rest of his life to pay off that loan.* V P n (not pron), Also V n P

2 If you **pay off** someone, you give them the amount of money that you owe them or that they are asking for, so that they will not take action against you or cause you any trouble. *...his bid to raise funds to pay off his creditors... In societies where corruption is endemic, decision-making is slowed as more politicians and officials have to be paid off.* V P n (not pron), Also V n P

3 If an action **pays off**, it is successful or profitable after a period of time. *Sandra was determined to become a doctor and her persistence paid off.* V P

4 See also **payoff**.

pay out PHRASAL VERB

1 If you **pay out** money, usually a large amount, you spend it on something. *...football clubs who pay out millions of pounds for players.* V P n *for/to* n, Also V P n

2 When an insurance policy **pays out**, the holder of the policy receives the money that he or she is entitled to receive. *Many policies pay out only after a period of weeks or months.* V P

3 See also **payout**.

pay up. If you **pay up**, you give someone the money that you owe them or that they are entitled to, even though you would prefer not to give it. *We claimed a refund from the association, but they would not pay up.* PHRASAL VERB V P

payable /peɪəbᵊl/ ◆◇◇◇◇
1 If an amount of money is **payable**, it has to be paid or it can be paid; a formal use. *Purchase tax was not payable on goods for export.* ADJ: v-link ADJ, oft ADJ *on/to* n
2 If a cheque or postal order is made **payable to** you, it has your name written on it to indicate that you are the person who will receive the money. *Write, enclosing a cheque made payable to Cobuild Limited.* ADJ: v n ADJ, n ADJ, ADJ *to* n

payback /peɪbæk/ **paybacks;** also spelled **pay-back.**
1 You can use **payback** to refer to the profit or benefit that you obtain from something that you have spent money, time, or effort on; used mainly in American English. *There is a substantial payback in terms of employee and union relations... They are prepared to wait longer for a pay-back from investment rather than concentrate on short-term profits.* N-COUNT: usu sing
2 The **payback** period of a loan is the time in which you are required or allowed to pay it back. ADJ: ADJ n

pay cheque, pay cheques; spelled **paycheck** in American English. Your **pay cheque** is a piece of paper that your employer gives you as your wages or salary, and which you can then cash at a bank. You can also use **pay cheque** as a way of referring to your wages or salary. *They've worked for about two weeks without a paycheck.* N-COUNT: oft poss N

pay day, pay days; also spelled **payday.**
1 **Pay day** is the day of the week or month on which you receive your wages or salary. *Until next payday, I was literally without any money.* N-UNCOUNT: also N in pl
2 If a sports player has a **big pay day**, he or she earns a lot of money from winning or taking part in a game or contest; used in newspapers and broadcast news. N-COUNT: oft adj N

paydirt /peɪdɜːʳt/; also spelled **pay dirt**. If you say that someone **has struck paydirt** or **has hit paydirt**, you mean that they have achieved sudden success or gained a lot of money very quickly; an informal expression. *Movies have not seen such a fixation with the same story since Howard Hawks hit paydirt with 'Rio Bravo'.* PHRASE: V inflects

PAYE /piː eɪ waɪ iː/. In Britain, **PAYE** is a system of paying income tax in which your employer pays your tax directly to the government, and then deducts this amount from your salary or wages; PAYE is an abbreviation for 'pay as you earn'. N-UNCOUNT

payee /peɪiː/ **payees.** The **payee** of a cheque, or of a document authorizing payment, is the person who receives the cheque or payment; a formal word. N-COUNT: usu sing ≠payer

payer /peɪəʳ/ **payers** ◆◇◇◇◇
1 You can refer to someone as a **payer** if they pay a particular kind of bill or fee. For example, a mortgage **payer** is someone who pays a mortgage. *Lower interest rates pleased millions of mortgage payers.* ● See also **ratepayer, taxpayer.** N-COUNT: usu with supp, oft n N ≠payee
2 A **good payer** pays you quickly or pays you a lot of money. A **bad payer** takes a long time to pay you, or does not pay you very much. *Small businesses, hit hard by the recession, blame the government, banks and late payers.* N-COUNT: adj N

paying guest, paying guests. A **paying guest** is a person who pays to stay with someone in their home, usually for a short time. *At that time my mother took in paying guests.* N-COUNT

payload /peɪloud/ **payloads**
1 The **payload** of an aircraft or spaceship is the amount of things or people that it is carrying; a technical use in aviation. *With these very large passenger payloads one question looms above all others – safety.* N-VAR =cargo
2 The **payload** of a missile or similar weapon is the quantity of explosives it contains; a technical military use. *...a hypervelocity gun capable of delivering substantial payloads to extreme ranges.* N-VAR

paymaster /peɪmɑːstəʳ, -mæst-/ **paymasters**
1 A **paymaster** is a person or organization that pays and therefore controls another person or organization; used showing disapproval. *...the ruling party's paymasters in business and banking... Germany is the European Community's biggest country, its most powerful economy and the paymaster of its budget.* N-COUNT: oft with poss PRAGMATICS
2 A **paymaster** is an official in the armed forces who is responsible for the payment of wages and salaries; a technical military use. N-COUNT

payment /peɪmənt/ **payments** ◆◆◆◆◇
1 A **payment** is an amount of money that is paid to someone, or the act of paying this money. *Thousands of its customers are in arrears with loans and mortgage payments... The fund will make payments of just over £1 billion next year.* N-COUNT: oft n N, N *to/of/on* n
2 **Payment** is the act of paying money to someone or of being paid. *He had sought to obtain payment of a sum which he had claimed was owed to him.* N-UNCOUNT: oft N *of/for* n
3 See also **balance of payments, down payment.**

payment card, payment cards. A **payment card** is a plastic card which you use like a credit card in order to pay for things, but which takes the money directly from your bank account. N-COUNT =debit card

payoff /peɪɒf/ **payoffs;** also spelled **pay-off.** ◆◇◇◇◇
1 The **payoff** from an action is the advantage or benefit that you get from it. *If such materials became generally available to the optics industry the payoffs from such a breakthrough would be enormous... You're doing what you really love to do, which is making music – that's the payoff.* N-COUNT: oft N *from* n
2 A **payoff** is a payment which is made to someone, often secretly or illegally, so that they will not cause trouble. *Soldiers in both countries supplement their incomes with payoffs from drugs exporters.* N-COUNT: oft N *from* n
3 A **payoff** is a payment made to someone when they have been dismissed from their job. *The ousted chairman received a £1.5 million payoff from the loss-making oil company.* N-COUNT

payola /peɪoulə/. In American English, **payola** is the illegal practice of paying radio broadcasters to play certain records, so that the records will become more popular and therefore make more profits for the record company. N-UNCOUNT

payout /peɪaut/ **payouts;** also spelled **pay-out.** ◆◇◇◇◇
A **payout** is a sum of money, especially a large one, that is paid to someone, for example by an insurance company or as a prize. *And there's time to win more, with a £10,000 payout still to play for over the next few days. ...long delays in receiving insurance payouts.* N-COUNT

pay packet, pay packets. In British English, your **pay packet** is the envelope containing your wages, which your employer gives you at the end of every week. **Pay packet** can also be used to refer to someone's wages or salary. N-COUNT: oft poss N =paycheck

pay-per-view. A **pay-per-view** television station charges viewers for each film or programme that they watch. ADJ: ADJ n

payphone /peɪfoun/ **payphones;** also spelled **pay phone.** A **payphone** is a telephone which you need to put coins or a card in before you can make a call. Payphones are usually in public places. N-COUNT

payroll /peɪroul/ **payrolls.** The people on the **payroll** of a company or an organization are the people who work for it and are paid by it. *They had 87,000 employees on the payroll.* ◆◇◇◇◇ N-COUNT: oft *on* N

payslip /peɪslɪp/ **payslips;** also spelled **pay slip.** In British English, a **payslip** is a piece of paper given to an employee at the end of each week or month, which states how much money he or she has earned and how much has been deducted for such things as tax and national insurance. N-COUNT

PC /piː siː/ **PCs** ◆◆◇◇◇
1 In Britain, a **PC** is a male police officer of the lowest rank. **PC** is an abbreviation for **police constable**. *The PCs took her to the local station... PC Keith Gate helped arrest the men.* N-COUNT; N-TITLE
2 A **PC** is a small computer that is usually used by one person in a small business, a school, or in their own home. **PC** is an abbreviation for **personal computer**. *The price of a PC has fallen by an average of 25% a year since 1982... Drawing offices may use PCs for computer-aided design.* N-COUNT
3 If you say that someone is **PC**, you mean that ADJ-GRADED

their attitudes and language are typical of people who hold left-wing or liberal views; used showing disapproval. **PC** is an abbreviation for 'politically correct'. *Sorry to be so PC, but that's the way I feel.* PRAGMATICS

pcm. **pcm** is used in advertisements for housing as a written abbreviation for 'per calendar month', when indicating how much the rent will be.

pd. **pd** is a written abbreviation for 'paid'. It is written on a bill to indicate that it has been paid.

PE /piː iː/. In schools, **PE** is a lesson in which pupils do physical exercises or sport. **PE** is an abbreviation for 'physical education'. ◆◇◇◇◇ N-UNCOUNT

pea /piː/ **peas.** **Peas** are small, round, green seeds which grow in pods and are eaten as a vegetable. ◆◆◇◇◇ N-COUNT: usu pl

peace /piːs/ ◆◆◆◆◆

1 If countries or groups involved in a war or violent conflict are discussing **peace**, they are talking to each other in order to try to end the conflict. *The agreement was reached during peace talks sponsored by the European Community... Leaders of some rival factions signed a peace agreement last week. ...a fresh attempt to negotiate peace in Bosnia-Herzegovina.* N-UNCOUNT: usu N n

2 If there is **peace** in a country or in the world, there are no wars or violent conflicts going on. *The President spoke of a shared commitment to world peace and economic development. ...the Nobel Peace Prize.* N-UNCOUNT: oft *at* N ≠war

3 If you approve of disarmament, especially nuclear disarmament, you can use **peace** to refer to campaigns and other activities designed to promote it. *...two peace campaigners accused of causing damage to an F1-11 nuclear bomber... He campaigned for peace and against the spread of nuclear weapons.* N-UNCOUNT: usu N n PRAGMATICS

4 If you have **peace**, you are not being disturbed, and you are in calm, quiet surroundings. *All I want is to have some peace and quiet and spend a couple of nice days with my grandchildren... One more question and I'll leave you in peace.* N-UNCOUNT: oft *in* N

5 If you have a feeling of **peace**, you feel contented and calm and not at all worried. You can also say that you are **at peace**. *I had a wonderful feeling of peace and serenity when I saw my husband... The peace of the Lord be always with you... I know you will never be at peace until you have discovered where your brother is.* N-UNCOUNT: oft *at* N

6 If there is **peace** among a group of people, they live or work together in a friendly way and do not quarrel. You can also say that people live or work **in peace with** each other. *...a period of relative peace in the country's industrial relations... If you can't live in peace with your little brother then get out of the house.* N-UNCOUNT: oft *in* N =harmony

7 The **Peace of** a particular place is a treaty or an agreement that was signed there, bringing an end to a war; an old-fashioned use. *The Peace of Ryswick was signed in September 1697.* N-IN-NAMES: *the* N *of* n

8 See also **breach of the peace**, **Justice of the Peace**.

9 If you **hold** or **keep your peace**, you do not speak, even though there is something you want or ought to say; a formal expression. *...people who knew about this evil man but held their peace... I felt it politic to keep my peace and play the part of the attentive listener.* PHRASES V inflects =keep quiet

10 If someone in authority, such as the army or the police, **keeps the peace**, they make sure that people behave in an orderly way and do not fight or quarrel with each other. *...the first UN contingent assigned to help keep the peace in Cambodia... How did your mother succeed in keeping the peace between these two very different men?* V inflects

11 If the law requires you **to keep the peace**, you must behave in an orderly way and not cause any trouble in public; a legal expression. *The demonstrators were bound over to keep the peace.*

12 If you **make peace** with someone or **make** your **peace** with them, you put an end to your quarrel with them, often by apologizing. You can also say that two or more people **make peace**. *The President ought to seize this opportunity to make his peace with political parties and negotiate a speedy return to democracy... All of a sudden she seemed to want to make peace and patch up our quarrel.* RECIP: V inflects, PHR *with* n, pl-n PHR

13 If something gives you **peace of mind**, it stops you from worrying about a particular problem or difficulty. *The main appeal these bonds hold for individual investors is the safety and peace of mind they offer... He began to insist upon a bullet-proof limousine, just for peace of mind.* PHR after v, *for* PHR

14 If you express the wish that a dead person may **rest in peace**, you are showing respect and sympathy for him or her. **'Rest in peace'** is also sometimes written on gravestones; a formal expression. usu PHR after modal PRAGMATICS

15 If you are **at peace with** yourself or **at peace with the world**, you feel calm and contented, and you have no emotional conflicts within yourself or with other people. *Once I knew I was forgiven I could be at peace with myself at last... They make you relax. They make you feel at peace with the world.* usu v-link PHR n

16 • to **disturb the peace**: see **disturb**.

peaceable /piːsəbᵊl/. Someone who is **peaceable** tries to avoid quarrelling or fighting with other people; used in written English. *...an attempt by ruthless people to impose their will on a peaceable majority... John was always so extraordinarily peaceable, one who invariably saw an opponent's point of view.* ADJ-GRADED

peaceably /piːsəbli/. If you do something **peaceably**, you do it quietly or peacefully, without violence or anger; used in written English. *The rival guerrilla groups had agreed to stop fighting and settle their differences peaceably... 'OK, whatever you say,' he had agreed peaceably.* ADV-GRADED: ADV with v ≠violently

Peace Corps; also spelled **peace corps.** **The Peace Corps** is an American organization that sends young people as volunteers to help with projects in developing countries. The British equivalent is **VSO**. ◆◇◇◇◇ N-PROPER: *the* N

peace dividend, peace dividends. The **peace dividend** is the economic benefit that was expected in the world after the end of the Cold War, as a result of money previously spent on defence and arms becoming available for other purposes. *The peace dividend has not materialised despite military spending going down in most countries.* N-COUNT: usu sing

peaceful /piːsfʊl/ ◆◆◆◇◇

1 **Peaceful** activities and situations do not involve war. *He has attempted to find a peaceful solution to the Ossetian conflict... They emphasised that their equipment was for peaceful and not military purposes.* ♦ **peacefully** *The US military expects the matter to be resolved peacefully.* ADJ-GRADED: usu ADJ n ≠violent; ADV-GRADED: ADV with v

2 **Peaceful** occasions happen without violence or serious disorder. *The farmers staged a noisy but peaceful protest outside the headquarters of the organization... Despite the violence that preceded the elections, reports say that polling was orderly and peaceful.* ♦ **peacefully** *Ten thousand people are reported to have taken part in the protest which passed off peacefully.* ADJ-GRADED ≠violent; ADV-GRADED: ADV with v

3 **Peaceful** people are not violent and try to avoid quarrelling or fighting with other people. *...warriors who killed or enslaved the peaceful farmers.* ♦ **peacefully** *They've been living and working peacefully with members of various ethnic groups.* ADJ-GRADED; ADV-GRADED: ADV with v

4 A **peaceful** place or time is quiet, calm, and free from disturbance. *...a peaceful Georgian house in the heart of Dorset... Mornings are usually quiet and peaceful in Hueytown.* ♦ **peacefully** *Except for traffic noise the night passed peacefully.* ADJ-GRADED; ADV-GRADED: ADV after v

5 Someone who **feels** or **looks peaceful** feels or looks calm and free from worry. *I feel relaxed and peaceful... The animals look peaceful and happy.* ♦ **peacefully** *Would she wake to find Gaston sleeping peacefully at her side?* ADJ-GRADED =worried, anxious; ADV-GRADED

peacefully /piːsfʊli/. If you say that someone died **peacefully**, you mean that they suffered no ◆◇◇◇◇ ADV: ADV after v pain or violence when they died. *He died peacefully on 10th December after a short illness.* PRAGMATICS

peacekeeper /piːskiːpəʳ/ **peacekeepers;** also spelled **peace-keeper.** ◆◇◇◇◇

1 **Peacekeepers** are soldiers who are members of a peacekeeping force. *United Nations peacekeepers have been in Croatia for four months now.* N-COUNT: usu pl, oft supp N

2 If you describe a country or an organization as a **peacekeeper**, you mean that it often uses its influence or armed forces to try to prevent wars or violent conflicts in the world. *They want the United Nations to play a bigger role as the world's peacekeeper... Russia's record as a peace-keeper is mixed.* N-COUNT: usu sing

peacekeeping /piːskiːpɪŋ/; also spelled **peace-keeping**. A **peacekeeping** force is a group of soldiers that is sent to a country where there is war or fighting, in order to try to prevent more violence. Peacekeeping forces are usually made up of troops from several different countries. *...the possibilities of a UN peacekeeping force monitoring the ceasefire in the country. ...Nigerian warplanes involved in peace-keeping operations in Liberia. ...Marrack Goulding, the UN's undersecretary-general in charge of peacekeeping.* ◆◆◇◇◇ N-UNCOUNT: usu N n

peace-loving. If you describe someone as **peace-loving**, you mean that they try to avoid quarrelling or fighting with other people. *By and large, these people are peace-loving, law-abiding citizens.* ADJ-GRADED: usu ADJ n

peacemaker /piːsmeɪkəʳ/ **peacemakers;** also spelled **peace-maker** or **peace maker**. You can describe an organization, a country or a person as a **peacemaker** when they try to persuade countries or people to stop fighting or quarrelling. *Is the Soviet Union trying to play the role of peacemaker in the Middle East?... She was a powerful peace-maker in local feuds.* N-COUNT

peacemaking /piːsmeɪkɪŋ/; also spelled **peace-making**. **Peacemaking** efforts are attempts to persuade countries or groups to stop fighting with each other. *...the failure of international peacemaking efforts... The United States is more than ever the prime mover in Middle East peacemaking.* N-UNCOUNT: usu N n

peacenik /piːsnɪk/ **peaceniks.** If you describe someone as a **peacenik**, you mean that they are strongly opposed to war and support such causes as nuclear disarmament; an informal word. *His campaign attracted the support of feminists, peaceniks and ecologists.* N-COUNT PRAGMATICS

peace offering, peace offerings. You can use **peace offering** to refer to something that is given or said to someone as a kind of apology in order to end a quarrel. *'A peace offering,' Roberts said as he handed the box of cigars to Cohen.* N-COUNT: usu sing

peacetime /piːstaɪm/; also spelled **peace-time.** **Peacetime** is a period of time during which a country is not at war. *The British could afford to reduce defence spending in peacetime without excessive risk... He served during peace-time as an intelligence officer in the Navy. ...one of the greatest peacetime Prime Ministers of this country.* ◆◇◇◇◇ N-UNCOUNT: oft *in* N

peach /piːtʃ/ **peaches** ◆◆◇◇◇

1 A **peach** is a soft, round, juicy fruit with sweet yellow flesh and pinky-orange skin. Peaches grow in warm countries. N-COUNT: oft N n

2 Something that is **peach** is pale pinky-orange in colour. *...the romantic Tower Suite, decorated throughout in peach and ivory. ...a peach silk blouse.* COLOUR

3 If you describe someone or something as a **peach**, you find them very pleasing or attractive; an informal use. *Frank was there and he is a perfect peach. ...a peach of a goal from Beardsley.* N-SING: oft *a* N *of* n

peaches and cream. If you say that a woman or a girl has a **peaches and cream complexion**, you mean that she has very clear, smooth, pale skin. *...pretty young things with peaches-and-cream complexions... What astonishes everyone she meets is her complexion—it is a typical. English peaches-and-cream.* ADJ: usu ADJ n

peachy /piːtʃi/

1 If you describe something as **peachy**, you mean that it tastes or smells like a peach or is similar in colour to a peach. *...a rich, peachy dessert wine. ...peachy pink.* ADJ-GRADED: usu ADJ n, ADJ colour

2 In American English, if you say that something is **peachy** or **peachy keen**, you mean that it is very nice; an informal use. *Everything in her life is just peachy.* ADJ-GRADED

peacock /piːkɒk/ **peacocks** ◆◇◇◇◇

1 A **peacock** is a large bird of the pheasant family. The male has a very large tail which it can spread out like a fan and which is marked with beautiful blue and green spots. *...peacocks strutting slowly across the garden. ...peacock feathers.* N-COUNT

2 If you describe someone as a **peacock**, you think that they behave in a vain and arrogant way. *He was a born peacock... He introduced himself as 'the leader' and strutted up and down like a peacock.* N-COUNT PRAGMATICS

peacock blue. Something that is **peacock blue** is a deep, bright, greeny-blue in colour. *...Lady Henrietta's peacock blue, silk cocktail frock.* COLOUR

peak /piːk/ **peaks, peaking, peaked** ◆◆◆◇◇

1 The **peak** of a process or an activity is the point at which it is at its strongest, most successful, or most fully developed. *The party's membership has fallen from a peak of fifty-thousand after the Second World War... The bomb went off in a concrete dustbin at the peak of the morning rush hour. ...a flourishing career that was at its peak at the time of his death... Economies have peaks and troughs.* N-COUNT: usu sing, usu with supp =height

2 When something **peaks**, it reaches its highest value or its highest level. *Temperatures have peaked at over thirty degrees Celsius... The crisis peaked in July 1974... His career peaked during the 1970's.* VERB V at n V

3 The **peak** level or value of something is its highest level or value. *Calls cost 36p (cheap rate) and 48p (peak rate) per minute... We bought it at the wrong time and paid the peak price.* ADJ: ADJ n

4 **Peak** times are the times when there is most demand for something or most use of something. *It's always crowded at peak times... During peak periods, reservations are difficult to make at some of the hotels.* • See also **peak time**. ADJ: ADJ n ≠off-peak

5 A **peak** is a mountain or the top of a mountain. *...the snow-covered peaks.* N-COUNT

6 The **peak** of a cap is the part at the front that sticks out above your eyes. *The man touched the peak of his cap.* N-COUNT

peaked /piːkt/. A **peaked cap** has a pointed or rounded part that sticks out above your eyes. *...a man in a blue-grey uniform and peaked cap.* ADJ: ADJ n

peak time. Programmes which are broadcast at **peak time** are broadcast when the greatest number of people are watching television or listening to the radio. *The news programme goes out four times a week at peak time. ...peak-time television drama.* N-UNCOUNT: oft *at/in* N, N n

peal /piːl/ **peals, pealing, pealed**

1 When **bells peal**, they ring one after another, making a musical sound. *Church bells pealed at the stroke of midnight.* ► Also a noun. *...the great peal of the Abbey bells.* VERB V N-COUNT

2 A **peal** of laughter or thunder consists of a long, loud series of sounds. *I heard a peal of merry laughter. ...great peals of thunder.* N-COUNT: oft N *of* n

peanut /piːnʌt/ **peanuts** ◆◇◇◇◇

1 **Peanuts** are small oval-shaped nuts that grow under the ground. Peanuts are often eaten as a snack, especially roasted and salted. *...a packet of peanuts... Add 2 tablespoons of peanut oil.* N-COUNT: usu pl, oft N n

2 If you say that a sum of money is **peanuts**, you mean that it is very small; an informal use. *The cost was peanuts compared to a new kitchen... The jobs they offer pay peanuts.* N-PLURAL PRAGMATICS

peanut butter. **Peanut butter** is a brown paste made out of crushed peanuts which you can spread on bread and eat. ◆◇◇◇◇ N-UNCOUNT

pear /peəʳ/ **pears.** A **pear** is a sweet, juicy fruit which is narrow near its stalk, and wider and ◆◇◇◇◇ N-COUNT rounded at the bottom. Pears have white flesh and thin green or yellow skin.

pearl /pɜːʳl/ **pearls** ◆◆◇◇◇

1 A **pearl** is a hard round object which is shiny and creamy white in colour. Pearls grow inside the shell of an oyster and are used for making expensive jewellery. *She wore a string of pearls at her throat... I put on the pearl earrings Daddy had bought me.* • See also **mother-of-pearl**. N-COUNT

2 **Pearl** is used to describe something which looks like a pearl. *...tiny pearl buttons.* ADJ: usu ADJ n

3 If you say that someone is **casting pearls before swine**, you mean that they are wasting their time by offering something that is helpful or valuable to someone who does not appreciate or understand it. *You do not value what should be valued, I see I was casting pearls before swine.* PHRASES V inflects

4 If you describe something that someone has said as **pearls of wisdom**, you mean that it sounds very wise or helpful. People usually use this expression in a way that shows that, in fact, that they mean the opposite of what they are saying. *And what is that pearl of wisdom supposed to mean?... Her advice includes perfectly true but rather fulsome pearls of wisdom.* N inflects PRAGMATICS

pearly /pɜːʳli/. Something that is **pearly** has a soft, smooth, shiny appearance, like a pearl. *...the pearly light of early morning.* ► Also a combining form. *...pearly pink lipstick... Her skin was pearly white.* ADJ: usu ADJ n; COMB in COLOUR

pear-shaped

1 Something that is **pear-shaped** has a shape like a pear. *...her pear-shaped diamond earrings.* ADJ

2 If one person describes another person, especially a woman as **pear-shaped**, they mean that they are wider around their hips than around the top half of their body. ADJ

peasant /pezᵊnt/ **peasants.** A **peasant** is a poor person of low social status who works on the land; used of people who live in countries where farming is still a common way of life. *...the peasants in the Peruvian highlands... Chinese peasants farm their own plots.* ◆◆◇◇◇ N-COUNT: oft supp N, N n

peasantry /pezᵊntri/. You can refer to all the peasants in a particular country as the **peasantry**. *The Communists may have won power largely through support among the peasantry.* ◆◇◇◇◇ N-SING-COLL: also no det, usu *the* N

peat /piːt/. **Peat** is decaying plant material which is found under the ground in some cool, wet regions. Peat can be added to soil to help plants grow, or can be burnt on fires instead of coal. ◆◇◇◇◇ N-UNCOUNT: oft N n

peaty /piːti/. **Peaty** soil or land contains a large quantity of peat. ADJ-GRADED: usu ADJ n

pebble /pebᵊl/ **pebbles.** A **pebble** is a small, smooth, round stone which is found on seashores and river beds. ◆◇◇◇◇ N-COUNT

pebbly /pebəli/. A **pebbly** beach or river bed is covered in pebbles. *...the lake's pebbly shore.* ADJ-GRADED: usu ADJ n

pec /pek/ **pecs.** Your **pecs** are the main muscles in your chest; an informal word. *Initially, I wanted Stallone to play the part because he has such marvelous pecs.* N-COUNT: usu pl =pectoral

pecan /piːkən, AM pɪkɑːn/ **pecans. Pecans** or **pecan nuts** are nuts with a thin, smooth shell that grow on trees in the southern United States and central America and that you can eat. N-COUNT

peccadillo /pekədɪloʊ/ **peccadilloes** or **peccadillos. Peccadilloes** are small, unimportant sins or faults; used in written English. *People are prepared to be tolerant of extra-marital peccadilloes by public figures.* N-COUNT: usu pl

peck /pek/ **pecks, pecking, pecked** ◆◇◇◇◇

1 If a bird **pecks at** something or **pecks** something, it moves its beak forward quickly and bites at it. *It was winter and the sparrows were pecking at whatever they could find... Chickens pecked in the dust... It pecked his leg... They turn on their own kind and peck each other to death... These birds peck off all the red flowers.* VERB V *at* n, V prep/adv, V n, V n prep, V n with adv, Also V

2 If you **peck** someone on the cheek, you give them a quick, light kiss. *Elizabeth walked up to him and pecked him on the cheek... She pecked his cheek.* ► Also a noun. *He gave me a little peck on the cheek.* VERB V n *on* n, V n; N-COUNT: usu *a* N

pecker /pekəʳ/ **peckers**

1 In informal British English, if you tell someone to **keep** their **pecker up**, you are encouraging them to be cheerful in a difficult situation. PHRASE =keep one's chin up

2 In American English, a man's **pecker** is his penis; a very informal use which some people may find offensive. N-COUNT

pecking order, pecking orders. The **pecking order** of a group is the order of seniority or power within the group. *He knew his place in the pecking order... They both came from families fairly far down the social pecking order.* N-COUNT: usu sing

peckish /pekɪʃ/. In informal British English, if you say that you are feeling **peckish**, you mean that you are slightly hungry. ADJ-GRADED: usu v-link ADJ

pectin /pektɪn/ **pectins. Pectin** is a substance that is found in ripe fruit. It is used in the manufacture of jam to help it set. N-MASS

pectoral /pektərəl/ **pectorals.** Your **pectorals** are the large chest muscles that help you to move your shoulders and your arms. *I was required to hold out my arms and flex my pectorals.* N-COUNT: usu pl

peculiar /pɪkjuːliəʳ/ ◆◆◇◇◇

1 If you describe someone or something as **peculiar**, you think that they are strange or unusual, sometimes in an unpleasant way. *Mr Kennet has a rather peculiar sense of humour... Rachel thought it tasted peculiar.* ♦ **peculiarly** *His face had become peculiarly expressionless.* ADJ-GRADED =odd, strange; ADV-GRADED

2 If something is **peculiar** to a particular thing, person, or situation, it belongs or relates only to that thing, person, or situation. *Punks, soldiers, hippies, and Sumo wrestlers all have distinct hair styles, peculiar to their group.* ♦ **peculiarly** *But cricket, surely, is so peculiarly English that the continentals will never catch on.* ADJ: oft ADJ *to* n =unique; ADV-GRADED

3 If you say that you **feel peculiar**, you mean that you feel slightly ill or dizzy. *All this has made me feel quite peculiar.* ADJ-GRADED: v-link ADJ

peculiarity /pɪkjuːliærɪti/ **peculiarities**

1 A **peculiarity** that someone or something has is a strange or unusual characteristic or habit. *Joe's other peculiarity was that he was constantly munching hard candy.* N-COUNT: with supp, oft N *of* n

2 A **peculiarity** is a characteristic or quality which belongs or relates only to one person or thing. *Each nation can have its own peculiarities when it comes to doing business. ...a strange peculiarity of the Soviet system.* N-COUNT: with supp, oft N *of* n

pecuniary /pɪkjuːniəri, AM -eri/. **Pecuniary** means concerning or involving money; a formal word. *She denies obtaining a pecuniary advantage by deception.* ADJ: usu ADJ n =monetary

pedagogic /pedəgɒdʒɪk/. • **Pedagogic** means the same as **pedagogical**.

pedagogical /pedəgɒdʒɪkᵊl/. **Pedagogical** means concerning the methods and theory of teaching; a formal word. *With a teacher like Mr Innes, the pedagogical method used in the classroom was by no means standardized.* ADJ: ADJ n

pedagogue /pedəgɒg/ **pedagogues.** If you describe someone as a **pedagogue**, you mean that they like to teach people things in a firm way as if they know more than anyone else; a formal word. *De Gaulle was a born pedagogue who used the public platform and the television screen to great effect.* N-COUNT

pedagogy /pedəgɒdʒi, AM -goʊdʒi/. **Pedagogy** is the study and theory of the methods and principles of teaching; a formal word. N-UNCOUNT

pedal /pedᵊl/ **pedals, pedalling, pedalled;** spelled **pedaling, pedaled** in American English. ◆◇◇◇◇

1 The **pedals** on a bicycle are the two parts that you push with your feet in order to make the bicycle move. N-COUNT

2 When you **pedal** a bicycle, you push the pedals around with your feet to make it move. *She climbed on her bike with a feeling of pride and pedalled the* VERB V n, V adv/prep

five miles home... She was too tired to pedal back. • See also **back-pedal**, **soft-pedal**.

3 A **pedal** in a car or on a machine is a lever that you press with your foot in order to control the car or machine. *...the brake or accelerator pedals.* N-COUNT

pedal bin, pedal bins. A **pedal bin** is a waste bin that has a lid controlled by a pedal and that you keep in the house. N-COUNT

pedant /pedᵊnt/ **pedants.** If you say that someone is a **pedant**, you mean that they are too concerned with unimportant details or traditional rules, especially in connection with academic subjects; used showing disapproval. *In last May's election, only a pedant could distinguish the Liberal from the Labour programme.* N-COUNT PRAGMATICS

pedantic /pɪdæntɪk/. If you think someone is **pedantic**, you mean that they are too concerned with unimportant details or traditional rules, especially in connection with academic subjects. *His lecture was so pedantic and uninteresting.* ADJ-GRADED

pedantry /pedᵊntri/. If you accuse someone of **pedantry**, you mean that you disapprove of them because they pay excessive attention to unimportant details or traditional rules, especially in connection with academic subjects. N-UNCOUNT PRAGMATICS

peddle /pedᵊl/ **peddles, peddling, peddled** ◆◇◇◇◇

1 Someone who **peddles** things goes from place to place trying to sell them; an old-fashioned use. *His attempts to peddle his paintings around London's tiny gallery scene proved unsuccessful.* VERB V n

2 Someone who **peddles drugs** sells illegal drugs. *When a drug pusher offered the Los Angeles youngster $100 to peddle drugs, Jack refused.* ♦ **peddling** *The war against drug peddling is all about cash.* VERB =push V n N-UNCOUNT

3 If someone **peddles** an idea or piece of information, they try very hard to get people to accept it. Used showing disapproval. *They even set up their own news agency to peddle anti-isolationist propaganda.* VERB PRAGMATICS V n

peddler /pedləʳ/ **peddlers.** British English also uses the spelling **pedlar** for meanings 1 and 3.

1 A **peddler** is someone who goes from place to place in order to sell something; used in American English and old-fashioned British English. N-COUNT

2 A **drug peddler** is a person who sells illegal drugs. N-COUNT

3 A **peddler** of information or ideas is someone who frequently expresses such ideas to other people; used showing disapproval. *...the peddlers of fear.* N-COUNT: usu N *of* n PRAGMATICS

pedestal /pedɪstᵊl/ **pedestals** ◆◇◇◇◇

1 A **pedestal** is the base on which something such as a statue stands. *...a larger than life sized bronze statue on a granite pedestal.* N-COUNT

2 If you **put** someone **on a pedestal**, you admire them very much and think that they cannot be criticized. If someone is knocked off a **pedestal** they are no longer admired. *Since childhood, I put my own parents on a pedestal. I felt they could do no wrong... That failure knocked me off my pedestal.* N-COUNT

pedestrian /pɪdestriən/ **pedestrians** ◆◇◇◇◇

1 A **pedestrian** is a person who is walking, especially in a town or city, rather than travelling in a vehicle. *Ingrid was a walker, even in Los Angeles, where a pedestrian is a rare spectacle... More than a third of all pedestrian injuries are to children.* N-COUNT: oft N n

2 If you describe something as **pedestrian**, you mean that it is ordinary and not at all interesting; used showing disapproval. *His style is so pedestrian that the book becomes a real bore... I drove home contemplating my own more pedestrian lifestyle.* ADJ-GRADED PRAGMATICS =dull

pedestrian crossing, pedestrian crossings. In British English, a **pedestrian crossing** is a place where pedestrians can cross a street and where motorists must stop to let them cross. The American word is **crosswalk**. *He was knocked down on a pedestrian crossing.* N-COUNT

pedestrianized /pɪdestriənaɪzd/; also spelled **pedestrianised**. A **pedestrianized** area has been made into an area that is intended for pedestrians, not vehicles. *You may want to spend a day here to go shopping in the pedestrianized streets... There's plans to make Birmingham city centre pedestrianized.* ADJ: usu ADJ n

pedestrian precinct, pedestrian precincts. A **pedestrian precinct** is a street or part of a town where vehicles are not allowed. N-COUNT

pediatrician /piːdiətrɪʃᵊn/. See **paediatrician**.

pediatrics /piːdiætrɪks/. See **paediatrics**.

pedicure /pedɪkjʊəʳ/ **pedicures.** If you have a **pedicure**, you have your toenails cut and the skin on your feet softened by a medical expert or by a beautician. *I have a manicure and a pedicure every week.* N-COUNT

pedigree /pedɪgriː/ **pedigrees** ◆◇◇◇◇

1 If a dog, cat, or other animal has a **pedigree**, its ancestors are known and recorded. An animal is considered to have a good pedigree when all its known ancestors are of the same type. *60 per cent of dogs and ten per cent of cats have pedigrees.* N-COUNT

2 A **pedigree** animal is descended from animals which have all been of a particular type, and is therefore considered to be of good quality. *...a pedigree dog. ...pedigree horses.* ADJ: usu ADJ n

3 Someone's **pedigree** is their background or ancestry. *Hammer's business pedigree almost guaranteed him the acquaintance of U.S. presidents... She had an impeccable aristocratic pedigree.* N-COUNT: oft poss N

pediment /pedɪmənt/ **pediments.** A **pediment** is a large triangular structure built over a doorway or window as a decoration. N-COUNT

pedlar /pedləʳ/ **pedlars.** See **peddler**.

pedophile /piːdəfaɪl/ **pedophiles.** See **paedophile**.

pedophilia /piːdəfɪliə/. See **paedophilia**.

pee /piː/ **pees, peeing, peed.** When someone **pees**, they urinate; an informal word which some people think is rude. *He needed to pee.* ► Also a noun. *The driver was probably having a pee.* ◆◇◇◇◇ VERB V N-SING: a N

peek /piːk/ **peeks, peeking, peeked.** If you **peek at** something or someone, you have a quick look at them, often secretly. *On two occasions she had peeked at him through a crack in the wall.* ► Also a noun. *American firms have been paying outrageous fees for a peek at the technical data.* ◆◇◇◇◇ VERB =peep V *at* n N-COUNT =peep

peekaboo /piːkəbuː/; also spelled **peek-a-boo**. **Peekaboo** is a game for young children where you cover your face with your hands or hide behind something and then suddenly take your hands away or peep out, saying 'peekaboo!' N-UNCOUNT, also EXCLAM =peepbo

peel /piːl/ **peels, peeling, peeled** ◆◆◇◇◇

1 The **peel** of a fruit such as a lemon or an apple is its skin. In American English, you can also refer to a **peel**. *...grated lemon peel. ...a banana peel.* N-UNCOUNT

2 When you **peel** fruit or vegetables, you remove their skins. *She sat down in the kitchen and began peeling potatoes.* VERB V n

3 If you **peel** off something that has been sticking to a surface or if it **peels** off, it comes away from the surface. *One of the kids was peeling plaster off the wall... It took me two days to peel off the labels... Paint was peeling off the walls... The wallpaper was peeling away close to the ceiling. ...an unrenovated bungalow with slightly peeling blue paint.* V-ERG V n *off/from* n V n with *off/away* V *off/from* n V *off/away* V-ing

4 If a surface **is peeling**, the paint on it is coming away. *Its once-elegant white pillars are peeling.* VB: usu cont V

5 If you **are peeling** or if your skin **is peeling**, small pieces of skin are coming off your body, usually because you are sunburnt. *His face, at the moment, was peeling from sunburn.* VB: usu cont V

6 • to **keep** your **eyes peeled**: see **eye**.

peel off. If you **peel off** a tight piece of clothing, you take it off, especially by turning it inside out. *She peeled off her gloves.* PHRASAL VERB V P n (not pron) Also V n P

peeler /piːləʳ/ **peelers.** A **peeler** is a special tool used for removing the skin from fruit and vegetables. *Peel the aubergines with a potato peeler.* N-COUNT

peelings /piːlɪŋz/. **Peelings** are pieces of skin peeled from vegetables and fruit. *...potato peelings. ...cabbage peelings.* N-PLURAL: usu supp N

peep /piːp/ **peeps, peeping, peeped** ◆◇◇◇◇

1 If you **peep**, or **peep at** something, you have a quick look at it, often secretly and quietly. *Children came to peep at him round the doorway... Now and* VERB =peek V *at* n V

then she peeped to see if he was noticing her. ► Also a noun. *'Fourteen minutes,' Chris said, taking a peep at his watch.* N-SING: a N =peek

2 If something **peeps** out from behind or under something, a small part of it is visible or becomes visible. *Purple and yellow flowers peeped up between rocks... Here and there a face peeped out from the shop doorway.* VERB V prep/adv

3 If you say that you **don't hear a peep** from someone, you mean that they do not say anything or made any noise. *You don't hear a peep from her once she's gone to bed.* PHRASE: V inflects

peepbo /piːpoʊ/. In British English, **peepbo** is a game you play with young children in which you cover your face with your hands or hide behind something and then suddenly take your hands away or peep out, saying 'peepbo'. The usual American word is **peekaboo**. N-UNCOUNT; EXCLAM =peekaboo

peephole /piːphoʊl/ **peepholes.** A **peephole** is small hole in a door or wall through which you can look secretly at what is happening on the other side. *The guards checked at the peephole before entering.* N-COUNT =spyhole

Peeping Tom, Peeping Toms. If you refer to someone as a **Peeping Tom**, you mean that they secretly watch other people, especially when those people are undressing; used showing disapproval. N-COUNT PRAGMATICS =voyeur

peepshow /piːpʃoʊ/ **peepshows.** A **peepshow** is box containing moving pictures which you can look at through a small hole. Peepshows used to be a form of entertainment at fairs. N-COUNT

peer /pɪəʳ/ **peers, peering, peered** ◆◆◆◇◇

1 If you **peer** at something, you look at it very hard, usually because it is difficult to see clearly. *I had been peering at a computer print-out that made no sense at all... He watched the Customs official peer into the driver's window.* VERB V prep

2 In Britain, a **peer** is a member of the nobility, either by being a child of aristocratic parents, or by being appointed by a King or Queen. *Lord Swan retired was made a life peer in 1981.* N-COUNT

3 Your **peers** are the people who are the same age as you or who have the same status as you. *...children who are much cleverer than their peers... His engaging personality made him popular with his peers.* N-COUNT: usu pl, poss N

peerage /pɪərɪdʒ/ **peerages** ◆◇◇◇◇

1 If someone has a **peerage**, they have the rank of a peer. *The Prime Minister offered him a peerage... It's thought she may eventually accept a peerage and move to the House of Lords.* N-COUNT

2 The peers of a particular country are referred to as **the peerage**. N-SING: the N

peeress /pɪəres/ **peeresses.** A **peeress** is a woman who is a member of the nobility. N-COUNT

peer group, peer groups. Your **peer group** is the group of people you know who are the same age as you or who have the same social status as you. *It is important for a manager to be able to get the support of his peer group. ...peer group pressure.* N-COUNT

peerless /pɪəʳləs/. Something that is **peerless** is so beautiful or wonderful that you feel that nothing can equal it; a formal word. *...two days of clear sunshine under peerless blue skies.* ADJ-GRADED: usu ADJ n =matchless

peer of the realm, peers of the realm. In Britain, a **peer of the realm** is a member of the nobility who has the right to sit in the House of Lords. N-COUNT

peeved /piːvd/. If you are **peeved** about something, you are annoyed about it; an informal word. *Susan couldn't help feeling a little peeved. ...complaints from peeved citizens who pay taxes.* ADJ-GRADED: usu v-link ADJ

peevish /piːvɪʃ/. Someone who is **peevish** is bad-tempered. *Aubrey had slept little and that always made him peevish... She glared down at me with a peevish expression on her face.* ADJ-GRADED =bad-tempered ♦ **peevishly** *Brian sighed peevishly... She had grown ever more peevishly dependent on him.* ADV-GRADED: ADV with v, ADV adj ♦ **peevishness** *He complained with characteristic peevishness.* N-UNCOUNT

peg /peg/ **pegs, pegging, pegged** ◆◆◆◇◇

1 A **peg** is a small hook or knob that is attached to a wall or door and is used for hanging things on. *His work jacket hung on the peg in the kitchen.* N-COUNT

2 In British English, a **peg** is a small device which you use to fasten clothes to a washing line. The usual American word is **clothespin**. N-COUNT =clothes peg

3 A **peg** is a small piece of wood or metal that is used for fastening something to something else. *He builds furniture using wooden pegs instead of nails. ...the noise of the hammer striking the steel pegs.* N-COUNT

4 If you **peg** something somewhere or **peg** it down, you fix it there with pegs; used mainly in British English. *...trying to peg a double sheet on a washing line on a blustery day... Peg down netting over the top to keep out leaves. ...a tent pegged to the ground nearby for the kids.* VERB V n prep/adv V n with adv V-ed prep

5 If a price or amount of something **is pegged** at a particular level, it is fixed at that level; used by journalists. *They'll have to set the rate at which the pound is pegged to the deutschmark... UK trading profits were pegged at £40million... The Bank wants to peg rates at 9%. ...a pegged European currency.* ● See also **level-pegging**. VERB be V-ed at n V n at amount V-ed

6 If you say that someone should **be brought down a peg** or **be taken down a peg**, you mean that they should be made to realize that they are not so important or wonderful as they think they are. *We thought it was time they were brought down a peg or two... We'd have liked to see her taken down a peg, but not this way.* PHRASES V inflects

7 **Off-the-peg** clothes are bought ready-made from a shop and not made specially for a particular person; used mainly in British English. *...an off-the-peg two-piece suit... Instead of dining in top restaurants and wearing expensive suits, he likes to eat hamburgers and buys clothes off the peg.* PHR n, PHR after v ≠made-to-measure

8 If you describe someone as **a square peg in a round hole**, you mean that they are in a situation or doing something that does not suit them at all. *Taylor is clearly the wrong man for the job – a square peg in a round hole... I've been something of a square peg in a round hole.* v-link PHR =misfit

peg out PHRASAL VERB

1 If someone **pegs out**, they are too exhausted to carry on with what they have been doing; used mainly in informal British English. *I nipped round the corner for a quick beer and nearly pegged out on the spot.* =flake out V P

2 If you say that someone **pegs out**, you mean that they die; used mainly in informal British English. *I thought the oldest were going to peg out.* V P

peg leg, peg legs. A **peg leg** is an artificial leg made out of wood; an old-fashioned, informal expression. N-COUNT =wooden leg

pejorative /pədʒɒrətɪv, AM -dʒɔːr-/. A **pejorative** word or expression is one that expresses criticism of someone or something; a formal word. *I agree I am ambitious, and I don't see that as a pejorative term... Isn't there a suggestion that 'poetess' is slightly pejorative?* ADJ-GRADED =derogatory, disparaging

pekinese /piːkɪniːz/ **pekineses;** also spelled **pekingese**. A **pekinese** is a type of small dog with long hair, short legs, and a short, flat nose. N-COUNT

pelican /pelɪkən/ **pelicans.** A **pelican** is a type of large water bird. It catches fish and keeps them in the bottom part of its beak which is shaped like a large bag. N-COUNT

pelican crossing, pelican crossings. In Britain, a **pelican crossing** is a place where pedestrians can cross a busy road. Pedestrians press a button at the side of the road, which operates traffic lights to stop the traffic. N-COUNT

pellagra /pəlægrə, -leɪg-/. **Pellagra** is a disease caused by poor diet. The symptoms of this disease are tiredness and disorders of the skin and central nervous system. N-UNCOUNT

pellet /pelɪt/ **pellets.** A **pellet** is a small ball of paper, mud, lead, or other material. *He was shot in the head by an air gun pellet... A beetle was rolling a pellet of dried dung up the hill.* ◆◇◇◇◇ N-COUNT: usu with supp

pell-mell /pel mel/. If you move **pell-mell** somewhere, you move there in a hurried, uncontrolled way. *All three of us rushed pell-mell into the kitchen.* ADV: ADV after v

pellucid /pelu:sɪd/. Something that is **pellucid** is extremely clear; a literary word. *...her pellucid blue eyes... The anchor chain had rattled out in that warm pellucid water.* ADJ =limpid

pelmet /pelmɪt/ **pelmets.** In British English, a **pelmet** is a long, narrow piece of wood or fabric which is fitted at the top of a window for decoration and to hide the curtain rail. The usual American word is **valance**. N-COUNT

pelota /peloʊtɑ/. **Pelota** is a game that is played in Spain, America, and the Philippines, in which the players hit a ball against a wall using a long basket tied to their wrist. N-UNCOUNT

pelt /pelt/ **pelts, pelting, pelted** ◆◇◇◇◇

1 The **pelt** of an animal is its skin which can be used to make clothing or rugs. *...a bed covered with beaver pelts. ...rapidly diminishing suppliers of furs and pelts.* N-COUNT: usu pl =hide

2 If you **pelt** someone **with** things, you throw things at them. *Some of the younger men began to pelt one another with snowballs... Crowds started to pelt police cars with stones.* VERB V n *with* n

3 If the rain **is pelting down**, or if it **is pelting with** rain, it is raining very hard; an informal use. *The rain now was pelting down... It's pelting with rain... We drove through pelting rain.* VB: usu cont =pouring V adv *it* V *with* n V-ing

4 If you **pelt** somewhere, you run there very fast; an informal use. *Without thinking, she pelted down the stairs in her nightgown.* VERB =dash V prep

5 If you do something **full pelt** or **at full pelt**, you do it very quickly indeed; an informal expression. *Alice leapt from the car and ran full pelt towards the emergency room... He drove his car through the gates at full pelt.* PHRASE: PHR after v

pelvic /pelvɪk/. **Pelvic** means near or relating to your pelvis. ◆◇◇◇◇ ADJ: ADJ n

pelvis /pelvɪs/ **pelvises.** Your **pelvis** is the wide, curved group of bones at the level of your hips. ◆◇◇◇◇ N-COUNT

pen /pen/ **pens, penning, penned** ◆◆◆◇◇

1 A **pen** is a long thin object which you use to write in ink. • **ballpoint pen**: see **ballpoint**. • **felt-tip pen**: see **felt-tip**. • See also **fountain pen**. N-COUNT

2 If someone **pens** a letter, article, or book, they write it; a formal use. *I really intended to pen this letter to you early this morning... She penned a short memo to his private secretary.* VERB =draft, write V n *to* n Also V n n

3 A **pen** is also a small area with a fence round it in which farm animals are kept for a short time. *...a holding pen for sheep... He wasn't sure exactly how a fox could have got into the sheep's pen.* • See also **playpen**. N-COUNT =enclosure

4 If people or animals **are penned** somewhere or **are penned up**, they are forced to remain in a very small area. *...to drive the cattle back to the house so they could be milked and penned for the night... The goats are penned in and fodder has to be cut and carried each day... I don't have to stay in my room penned up like a prisoner.* VB: usu passive *be* V-ed V-ed *up*

5 If you **put pen to paper**, you write something. *Whenever he put pen to paper he was at a loss for the right words to break the news.* PHRASE: V inflects

penal /pi:nəl/ ◆◇◇◇◇

1 **Penal** means relating to the punishment of criminals. *...director-general of penal affairs at the justice ministry. ...penal and legal systems.* ADJ: usu ADJ n

2 A **penal** institution or colony is one where criminals are imprisoned or kept. *...imprisoned on an island that has served as a penal colony since Roman times.* ADJ: ADJ n

penal code, penal codes. The **penal code** of a country consist of all the laws that are related to crime and punishment; a formal expression. N-COUNT

penalize /pi:nəlaɪz/ **penalizes, penalizing, penalized;** also spelled **penalise** in British English. If someone **is penalized** for something, they are made to suffer some disadvantage because of it. *Some of the players may, on occasion, break the rules and be penalized... Use of the car is penalized by increasing the fares of parking lots... Bad teaching is not penalized in a formal way.* ◆◇◇◇◇ VB: usu passive =punish *be* V-ed

penal servitude. **Penal servitude** is the punishment of being sent to prison and forced to do hard physical work; a formal expression. N-UNCOUNT =hard labour

penalty /penəlti/ **penalties** ◆◆◆◇◇

1 A **penalty** is a punishment that someone is given for doing something which is against a law or rule. *One of those arrested could face the death penalty... The maximum penalty is up to 7 years imprisonment or an unlimited fine.* N-COUNT: usu sing

2 In sports such as football, rugby, and hockey, a **penalty** is a free kick or hit at a goal, which is given to the attacking team if the defending team commit a foul near their own goal. *Referee Michael Reed had no hesitation in awarding a penalty... Jonathan Davies scored a penalty goal.* N-COUNT

3 The **penalty** that you pay for something you have done is something unpleasant that you experience as a result. *Why should I pay the penalty for somebody else's mistake?... It's a penalty of us being girls – sons have an easy time.* N-COUNT: usu *the* N in sing =price

penalty area, penalty areas. On a football pitch, the **penalty area** is the rectangular area in front of the goal. Inside this area, the goalkeeper is allowed to handle the ball and a penalty is given if a foul is committed by the defending team; used mainly in British English. ◆◇◇◇◇ N-COUNT =penalty box

penalty box, penalty boxes

1 In football, the **penalty box** is the same as the **penalty area**; used mainly in British English. N-COUNT: usu *the* N in sing

2 In ice hockey, the **penalty box** is an area in which players who have been penalized have to sit for the period of time of their penalty. N-COUNT

penalty shoot-out, penalty shoot-outs. In football, a **penalty shoot-out** is a way of deciding the results of a game that has ended in a draw. Each team takes penalty kicks in turn until one of them misses and loses the game; used mainly in British English. N-COUNT

penance /penəns/ **penances.** If you do **penance** for something wrong that you have done, you do something that you find unpleasant to show that you are sorry. *...the sacred month of Gunia a time of fasting, penance and pilgrimage... The Koran recommends fasting as a penance before pilgrimages.* N-VAR

pen and ink. A **pen and ink** drawing is done using a pen rather than a pencil. ADJ: usu ADJ n

pence /pens/. See **penny**.

penchant /pɒnʃɒn, pentʃənt/. If someone has a **penchant for** something, they have a special liking for it or a tendency to do it; a formal word. *...a stylish woman with a penchant for dark glasses... He had a penchant for playing jokes on people.* ◆◇◇◇◇ N-SING: N *for* n/-ing =fondness

pencil /pensəl/ **pencils, pencilling, pencilled** ◆◆◇◇◇

1 A **pencil** is an object that you write or draw with. It consists of a thin piece of wood with a rod of graphite in the middle. If you write or draw something in **pencil**, you do it using a pencil. *I found a pencil and some blank paper in her desk... He had written her a note in pencil.* N-COUNT: also *in* N

2 If you **pencil** a letter or a note, you write it using a pencil. *He pencilled a note to Joseph Daniels.* VERB V n *to* n

♦ **pencilled.** *...folded notepaper with the pencilled block letters on the outside.* ADJ

pencil in. If an event or appointment **is pencilled in**, it has been agreed that it should take place, but it will have to be confirmed later. *He told us that the tour was pencilled in for the following March.* PHRASAL VERB usu passive *be* V-ed P

pendant /pendənt/ **pendants.** A **pendant** is an ornament on a chain that you wear round your neck. N-COUNT

pending /pendɪŋ/ ◆◆◇◇◇

1 If something such as a legal procedure is **pending**, it is waiting to be dealt with or settled; a formal use. *The cause of death was listed as pending... In 1989, the court had 600 pending cases... She had a libel action against the magazine pending.* ADJ

2 If something is done **pending** a future event, it is done until that event happens; a formal use. PREP

Mendoza is here pending his request for political asylum... A judge has suspended a ban on the magazine pending a full inquiry.

3 Something that is **pending** is going to happen soon; a formal use. *A growing number of customers have been inquiring about the pending price rises.* ADJ =imminent

pendulous /pendʒʊləs/. Something that is **pendulous** hangs downwards and moves loosely, usually in an unattractive way. *...a stout, gloomy man with a pendulous lower lip. ...pendulous cheeks.* ADJ =sagging

pendulum /pendʒʊləm/ **pendulums** ◆◇◇◇◇

1 The **pendulum** of a clock is a rod with a weight at the end which swings from side to side in order to make the clock work. N-COUNT

2 You can use the idea of a **pendulum** and the way it swings regularly as a way of talking about regular changes in a situation or in people's opinions. *The pendulum has swung back and the American car companies have made dramatic advances in safety... Many people in Czechoslovakia fear a sort of pendulum effect.* N-SING: usu *the* N

penetrate /penɪtreɪt/ **penetrates, penetrating, penetrated** ◆◆◇◇◇

1 If something or someone **penetrates** a physical object or an area, they succeed in getting into it or passing through it. *X-rays can penetrate many objects... His men had been ordered to shoot on sight anyone trying to penetrate the area.* ♦ **penetration** /penɪtreɪʃən/ **penetrations** *The exterior walls are three to three and a half feet thick to prevent penetration by bombs. ...moves designed to block enemy penetrations.* VERB V n; N-UNCOUNT: also N in pl

2 If someone **penetrates** an organization, a group, or a profession, they succeed in entering it although it is difficult to do so. *...the continuing failure of women to penetrate the higher levels of engineering... The drugs industry is complex and hard to penetrate.* VERB =get into V n

3 If someone **penetrates** an enemy group or a rival organization, they succeed in joining it in order to get information or cause trouble. *The CIA had requested our help to penetrate a drugs ring operating out of Munich... The army was one of the few institutions the secret police were not encouraged to penetrate.* ♦ **penetration** *The successful penetration by the KGB of the French intelligence service.* VERB =infiltrate V n; N-UNCOUNT: with supp

4 If a company or country **penetrates** a market or area, they succeed in selling their products there. *There have been around 15 attempts from outside France to penetrate the market.* ♦ **penetration** *...import penetration across a broad range of heavy industries.* VERB V n; N-UNCOUNT: with supp

5 If you **penetrate** something that is difficult to understand, you succeed in understanding it; a formal use. *...long answers that were often difficult to penetrate.* VERB =grasp, fathom V n

penetrating /penɪtreɪtɪŋ/ ◆◇◇◇◇

1 A **penetrating** sound is loud and usually high-pitched. *Mary heard the penetrating bell of an ambulance... Her voice was nasal and penetrating.* ADJ-GRADED =piercing

2 If someone gives you a **penetrating** look, it makes you think that they know what you are thinking. *He gazed at me with a sharp, penetrating look that made my heart pound. ...dark penetrating eyes. ...a suspicious, penetrating stare.* ADJ-GRADED: usu ADJ n =piercing

3 Someone who has a **penetrating** mind understands and recognizes things quickly and thoroughly. *...a thoughtful, penetrating mind... He never stopped asking penetrating questions.* ADJ-GRADED: usu ADJ n =sharp, keen

penetrative /penɪtrətɪv, AM -treɪt-/. If a man has **penetrative** sex with someone, he inserts his penis into his partner's vagina or anus. ADJ: ADJ n

pen-friend, pen-friends; also spelled **penfriend**. In British English, a **pen-friend** is someone you write friendly letters to and receive letters from, although the two of you may never have met. The usual American word is **pen pal**. N-COUNT =pen pal

penguin /peŋgwɪn/ **penguins.** A **penguin** is a type of large black and white sea bird found mainly in the Antarctic. Penguins cannot fly but use their flipper-like wings for swimming. ◆◆◇◇◇ N-COUNT

penicillin /penɪsɪlɪn/. **Penicillin** is an antibiotic. N-UNCOUNT

penile /piːnaɪl/. **Penile** means relating to a penis; a formal word. *...penile cancer.* ADJ: ADJ n

peninsula /pənɪnsjʊlə/ **peninsulas.** A **peninsula** is a long narrow piece of land that is joined at one part to the mainland and is almost completely surrounded by water. *...the political situation in the Korean peninsula... I had walked around the entire peninsula.* ◆◆◇◇◇ N-COUNT: oft in names

penis /piːnɪs/ **penises.** A man's **penis** is the part of his body that he uses when urinating and when having sex. ◆◆◇◇◇ N-COUNT

penitence /penɪtəns/. **Penitence** is sincere regret for wrong or evil things that you have done. N-UNCOUNT =repentance

penitent /penɪtənt/. Someone who is **penitent** is very sorry for something wrong that they have done, and regrets their actions; a literary word. *Robert Gates sat before them, almost penitent about the past... She is deeply penitent. ...penitent criminals.* ♦ **penitently** *He sat penitently in his chair by the window.* ADJ-GRADED: usu v-link ADJ; ADV-GRADED: ADV after v

penitential /penɪtenʃəl/. **Penitential** means expressing deep sorrow and regret at having done something wrong; a formal word. *They made their way from church to church, singing penitential psalms.* ADJ-GRADED: usu ADJ n

penitentiary /penɪtenʃəri/ **penitentiaries.** In formal American English, a **penitentiary** is a prison. N-COUNT =jail

penknife /pennaɪf/ **penknives.** A **penknife** is a small knife with a blade that folds back into the handle. N-COUNT

penmanship /penmənʃɪp/. **Penmanship** is the art and skill of writing by hand; a formal word. N-UNCOUNT

pen name, pen names; also spelled **pen-name**. A writer's **pen name** is the name that he or she uses on books and articles instead of his or her real name. *...Baroness Blixen, also known by her pen-name Isak Dinesen.* N-COUNT =nom de plume, pseudonym

pennant /penənt/ **pennants** ◆◇◇◇◇

1 A **pennant** is a long, narrow, triangular flag. *The second car was flying the Ghanaian pennant.* N-COUNT =flag

2 In baseball, a **pennant** is a flag that is given to the team that wins a league championship; used in American English. *The Red Sox lost the pennant to Detroit by a single game.* N-COUNT

pennies /peniz/. **Pennies** is the plural of **penny**. In Britain, **pennies** is used to refer only to coins.

penniless /peniləs/. Someone who is **penniless** has hardly any money at all. *They'd soon be penniless and homeless if she couldn't find suitable work. ...a penniless refugee.* ◆◇◇◇◇ ADJ: usu v-link ADJ

penn'orth /penəθ/. During a discussion about something, if you have your **two penn'orth** or put in your **two penn'orth**, you add your own opinion, even when it is unwelcome; used in British English. *Please do be patient – I'm sure you want to have your two penn'orth.* PHRASE: det-poss PHR, usu PHR after v

penny /peni/ **pennies, pence.** The form **pence** is used for the plural of meaning 1. ◆◆◆◇◇

1 A **penny** is a British coin which is worth one hundredth of a pound. A **penny** is the amount of money which a penny is worth. *... a shiny newly minted penny... Cider also goes up by a penny a pint, while sparkling wine will cost another eight pence a bottle.* N-COUNT

2 A **penny** is a British coin used before 1971 that was worth one twelfth of a shilling. N-COUNT

3 In informal American English, a **penny** is a coin or an amount that is worth one cent. *Unleaded gasoline rose more than a penny a gallon.* N-COUNT

4 If you say, for example, that you do not have **a penny**, or that something does not cost **a penny**, you are emphasizing that you do not have any money at all, or that something did not cost you any money at all. *From the day you arrive at my house, you need not spend a single penny... The Brilliantons paid their rent on time and did not owe him a penny... I asked her if he had given her any money. 'Not a penny.'* N-SING: a N PRAGMATICS

5 If you say **the penny dropped**, you mean that someone suddenly understood or realized PHRASES V inflects

something. *'Did he know who you are?'—'I think so. I think the penny dropped.'*

6 In British English, if you say that you are going to **spend a penny**, you mean that you are going to the toilet; an old-fashioned expression, used especially when people are trying to be polite. *We were out sightseeing one afternoon when she decided she wanted to spend a penny.* V inflects

7 Things that are said to be **two a penny** or **ten a penny** are not valuable or interesting because they are very common and easy to find; used showing disapproval. *Leggy blondes are two a penny in Hollywood... Irish accents are ten a penny in those parts.* v-link PHR PRAGMATICS

8 If you say that something or someone is **worth every penny**, you mean that they are worth all the money that is spent on them. *The operation cost £100,000 and it was worth every penny... The directors of this company feel he's worth every penny.* v-link PHR

penny farthing, penny farthings. A **penny farthing** is an old-fashioned bicycle that had a very large front wheel and a small back wheel; used mainly in British English. N-COUNT

penny-pinching

1 **Penny-pinching** is the practice of trying to spend as little money as possible; used showing disapproval. *The bridges have not been painted regularly and this penny-pinching has exposed them to the corroding effects of salt and water.* N-UNCOUNT PRAGMATICS

2 **Penny-pinching** people spend as little money as possible; used showing disapproval. *...small-minded penny-pinching administrators.* ADJ PRAGMATICS =mean

pen pal; also spelled **pen-pal. pen pals.** In American English and informal British English, a **pen pal** is someone you write friendly letters to and receive letters from, although the two of you may never have met. ◆◇◇◇◇ N-COUNT =pen-friend

pen-pusher, pen-pushers; also spelled **pen-pusher.** In British English, if you call someone a **pen-pusher**, you mean that their work consists of writing or dealing with letters, reports, and records, and that it seems pointless to you; used showing disapproval. *As a result, industry was overmanned and pen-pushers were everywhere.* N-COUNT PRAGMATICS =bureaucrat

pension /pɛnʃᵊn/ **pensions, pensioning, pensioned.** Someone who has a **pension** receives a regular sum of money from the state or from a former employer because they have retired or because they are widowed or disabled. *...struggling by on a pension. ...if you are not a member cf a company pension scheme.* ◆◆◆◇◇ N-COUNT

pension off. If someone **is pensioned off**, they are made to retire from work and are given a pension. *Many successful women do not want to be pensioned off at 60... When his employees were no longer of use to him, he pensioned them off.* PHRASAL VERB be V-ed P V n P Also V P n (not pron)

pensionable /pɛnʃənəbᵊl/. **Pensionable** means relating to someone's right to receive a pension. *...civil servants who were nearing pensionable age. ...if his wife has no pensionable earnings.* ADJ: ADJ n

pension book, pension books. In Britain, a **pension book** is a small booklet containing payment slips, which is issued to pensioners by the government. Each week, one slip can be exchanged for money at a Post Office. N-COUNT

pensioner /pɛnʃənəʳ/ **pensioners.** A **pensioner** is someone who receives a pension, especially a pension paid by the state to retired people. ◆◆◇◇◇ N-COUNT =OAP

pensive /pɛnsɪv/. Someone who is **pensive** is thinking deeply about something, especially something that worries them slightly. *He looked suddenly sombre, pensive.* ♦ **pensively** *Angela stared pensively out of the window.* ADJ-GRADED =thoughtful ADV: ADV with v

pentagon /pɛntəgən, AM -gɑːn/ **pentagons.** A **pentagon** is a shape with five sides. N-COUNT

Pentagon. The **Pentagon** is the headquarters of the US Defense Department in Washington. The US Defense Department is often referred to as the **Pentagon.** *...a news conference at the Pentagon... The Pentagon says bad weather is hampering the allied air raids... A Pentagon spokesman refused to comment.* ◆◆◇◇◇ N-PROPER: the N, N n

pentameter /pentæmɪtəʳ/ **pentameters.** A **pentameter** is a line of poetry that has five strong beats in it; a technical term in literary criticism. N-COUNT

pentathlon /pentæθlɒn/ **pentathlons.** A **pentathlon** is an athletics competition in which each person must compete in five different events. N-COUNT: oft the N

Pentecost /pɛntɪkɒst, AM -kɔːst/

1 **Pentecost** is a Christian festival that takes place on the seventh Sunday after Easter and celebrates the sending of the Holy Spirit to the first apostles. N-UNCOUNT

2 **Pentecost** is a Jewish festival that takes place 50 days after Passover and celebrates the harvest. N-UNCOUNT

Pentecostal /pɛntɪkɒstᵊl, AM -kɔːst-/. **Pentecostal** churches are Christian churches that emphasize the inspiration of the Holy Spirit and the literal truth of the Bible. *...one of the fastest growing Pentecostal religious groups in the United States today.* ADJ: ADJ n

penthouse /pɛnthaʊs/ **penthouses.** A **penthouse** or a **penthouse** apartment or suite is a luxurious flat or set of rooms at the top of a tall building. *...her swish Manhattan penthouse. ...his penthouse flat in Chelsea.* N-COUNT: oft N n

pent-up /pɛnt ʌp/. **Pent-up** emotions, energies, or forces have been held back and not expressed, used, or released. *He still had a lot of pent-up anger to release.* ◆◇◇◇◇ ADJ: usu ADJ n

penultimate /penʌltɪmət/. The **penultimate** thing in a series of things is the last but one; a formal word. *...on the penultimate day of the Asian Games. ...in the penultimate chapter.* ◆◇◇◇◇ ADJ: det ADJ

penumbra /pɛnʌmbrə/ **penumbras.** A **penumbra** is an area of light shadow; a formal word. N-COUNT

penury /pɛnjʊri/. **Penury** is extreme poverty; a formal word. *He was brought up in penury, without education.* N-UNCOUNT

peony /piːəni/ **peonies;** also spelled **paeony.** A **peony** is a medium-sized garden plant which has large round flowers, usually pink, red, or white. N-COUNT

people /piːpᵊl/ **peoples, peopling, peopled** ◆◆◆◆◆

1 **People** are men, women, and children. **People** is normally used as the plural of **person**, instead of 'persons'. *Millions of people have lost their homes. ...the people of Angola. ...homeless young people... I don't think people should make promises they don't mean to keep... It is illegal and could endanger other people's lives.* N-PLURAL

2 **The people** is sometimes used to refer to ordinary men and women, in contrast to the government or the upper classes. *...the will of the people. ...a tremendous rift between the people and their leadership.* N-PLURAL: the N

3 A **people** is all the men, women, and children of a particular country or race. *...the native peoples of Central and South America... It's a triumph for the American people.* N-COUNT-COLL

4 If a place or country **is peopled by** a particular group of people, that group of people live there. *It was peopled by a fiercely independent race of peace-loving Buddhists. ...a small town peopled by lay workers and families.* VB: usu passive =populate be V-ed by/with n V-ed

5 If something such as a story or a time in history **is peopled** with people of a particular kind, those people occur or exist in it; a literary use. *Grass's novels are peopled with outlandish characters... British history of the 19th Century is peopled by energetic reformers... Other people had the gift of peopling their lives with friends and colleagues.* VERB be V-ed with/by n V n

pep /pɛp/ **peps, pepping, pepped. Pep** is liveliness and energy; an old-fashioned, informal word. *Many say that, given a choice, they would opt for a holiday to put the pep back in their lives.* ◆◇◇◇◇ N-UNCOUNT =sparkle

pep up. If you try to **pep** something **up**, you try to make it more lively, more interesting, or stronger; an informal expression. *The prime minister aired some ideas about pepping up trade in the region... How about pepping up plain tiles with transfers?.* PHRASAL VERB =perk up V P n (not pron) Also V n P

pepper /pɛpəʳ/ **peppers, peppering, peppered** ◆◆◆◇◇

1 **Pepper** is a hot-tasting spice which is used to flavour food. *Season with salt and pepper. ...freshly ground black pepper.* N-UNCOUNT

2 A **pepper** is a hollow green, red, or yellow vegetable with seeds. N-COUNT =capsicum

3 If something **is peppered with** small objects, a lot of those objects hit it. *He was wounded in both legs and severely peppered with shrapnel... Suddenly the garden was peppered with pellets.* VB: usu passive be V-ed with n

4 If something **is peppered** with things, it has a lot of those things in it or on it. *While her English was correct, it was peppered with French phrases... Outside, the road was peppered with glass... Yachts peppered the tranquil waters of Botafogo Bay.* VERB be V-ed with n V n

peppercorn /pepəʳkɔːʳn/ **peppercorns. Peppercorns** are the small berries which are dried and crushed to make pepper. They are sometimes used whole in cooking. N-COUNT

peppercorn rent, peppercorn rents. A **peppercorn rent** is an extremely low rent. N-COUNT

peppermill /pepəʳmɪl/ **peppermills.** A **peppermill** is a narrow container in which peppercorns are ground to make pepper. N-COUNT

peppermint /pepəʳmɪnt/ **peppermints** ◆◇◇◇◇

1 **Peppermint** is a strong, sharp flavouring that is obtained from the peppermint plant or that is made artificially. N-UNCOUNT

2 A **peppermint** is a peppermint-flavoured sweet. N-COUNT

pepperoni /pepərouni/. **Pepperoni** is a kind of spicy sausage which is often sliced and put on pizzas. N-UNCOUNT

pepperpot /pepəʳpɒt/ **pepperpots;** also spelled **pepper pot**. A **pepperpot** is a small container with holes in the top, used for shaking pepper onto food; used mainly in British English. The usual American word is **pepper shaker**. N-COUNT

peppery /pepəri/. Food that is **peppery** has a strong, hot taste like pepper. *...a crisp green salad with a few peppery radishes.* ADJ-GRADED

pep pill, pep pills. A **pep pill** is a pill that makes you feel more energetic or happier; an old-fashioned expression. N-COUNT

peppy /pepi/. Someone or something that is **peppy** is lively and full of energy; an informal word. *At the end of every day, jot down a brief note on how peppy or tired you felt. ...peppy dance-numbers.* ADJ-GRADED =lively

pep talk, pep talks; also spelled **pep-talk**. A **pep talk** is a speech which is intended to encourage someone to make more effort or feel more confident; an informal expression. *Powell and Cheney spent the day giving pep talks to the troops.* N-COUNT

peptic ulcer /peptɪk ʌlsəʳ/ **peptic ulcers.** A **peptic ulcer** is an ulcer that occurs in the digestive system. N-COUNT

per /pɜːʳ/ ◆◆◆◆◇

1 You use **per** to express rates and ratios. For example, if something costs £50 **per** year, you must pay £50 each year for it. If a vehicle is travelling at 40 miles **per** hour, it travels 40 miles each hour. *Social Security refused to pay her more than £17 per week... Buses and trains use much less fuel per person than cars.* • **per head**: see **head**. PREP: amount PREP n

2 If something happens or is done **as per** a particular plan or suggestion, it happens or is done in the way planned or suggested; a formal expression. *When they reach here they complain that they are not being paid as per the agreement... I approached an Intourist official, as per instructions.* PHR-PREP

perambulate /pəræmbjʊleɪt/ **perambulates, perambulating, perambulated.** When someone **perambulates**, they walk about for pleasure; an old-fashioned word. ♦ **perambulation** /pəræmbjʊleɪʃən/ **perambulations** *It was time now to end our perambulation round Paris.* VERB N-COUNT

per annum /pər ænəm/. A particular amount **per annum** means that amount each year. *...a fee of £35 per annum... Kenya's population is growing at 4.1 per cent per annum.* ◆◇◇◇◇ ADV: amount ADV

per capita /pəʳ kæpɪtə/. The **per capita** amount of something is the total amount of it in a country or area divided by the number of people in that country or area. *They have the world's largest per capita income... The per capita consumption of alcohol has dropped over the past two years.* ► Also an adverb. *Ethiopia has almost the lowest oil consumption per capita in the world... This year Americans will eat about 40% more fresh apples per capita than the Japanese.* ◆◇◇◇◇ ADJ: ADJ n; ADV: n ADV =per head

perceive /pəʳsiːv/ **perceives, perceiving, perceived** ◆◆◇◇◇

1 If you **perceive** something, you see, notice, or realize it, especially when it is not obvious. *A key task is to get pupils to perceive for themselves the relationship between success and effort... 'Precisely what other problems do you perceive?' she asked.* VERB V n

2 If you **perceive** someone or something **as** doing or being a particular thing, it is your opinion that they do this thing or that they are that thing. *Stress is widely perceived as contributing to coronary heart disease... They strangely perceive television as entertainment.* VERB V n as n/-ing

per cent /pəʳ sent/; also spelled **percent. Per cent** is both the singular and the plural form. You use **per cent** to talk about amounts. For example, if an amount is 10 per cent (10%) of a larger amount, it is equal to 10 hundredths of the larger amount. *20 to 40 per cent of the voters are undecided... We aim to increase sales by 10 per cent... The area has an unemployment level of 40 per cent.* ► Also an adjective. *There has been a ten per cent increase in the number of new students arriving at polytechnics this year.* ► Also an adverb. *...its prediction that house prices will fall 5 per cent over the year... It's 50 per cent wool, 50 per cent acrylic.* ◆◆◆◆◆ N-COUNT: num N, oft N of n; ADJ: ADJ n; ADV: ADV with v

percentage /pəʳsentɪdʒ/ **percentages.** A **percentage** is a fraction of an amount expressed as a particular number of hundredths of that amount. *Only a few vegetable-origin foods have such a high percentage of protein.* ◆◆◆◇◇ N-COUNT: usu N of n

perceptible /pəʳseptɪbəl/. Something that is **perceptible** can only just be seen or noticed. *Pasternak gave him a barely perceptible smile... There was a slight but perceptible air of neglect.* ♦ **perceptibly** /pəʳseptɪbli/ *The tension was mounting perceptibly.* ADJ-GRADED =discernible; ADV-GRADED: ADV with v

perception /pəʳsepʃən/ **perceptions** ◆◆◇◇◇

1 Your **perception** of something is the way that you think about it or the impression you have of it. *He is interested in is how our perceptions of death affect the way we live. ...their perception of foreigners.* N-COUNT: usu poss N, N of n

2 Someone who has **perception** realizes or notices things that are not obvious. *It did not require a great deal of perception to realise the interview was over.* N-UNCOUNT

3 **Perception** is the recognition of things using your senses, especially the sense of sight. N-COUNT: usu with supp

perceptive /pəʳseptɪv/. If you describe a person or their remarks or thoughts as **perceptive**, you think that they are good at noticing or realizing things, especially things that are not obvious. *He was one of the most perceptive US political commentators. ...a very perceptive critique of Wordsworth.* ♦ **perceptively** *The stages in her love affair with Harry are perceptively written.* ♦ **perceptiveness** *The task I have in mind requires little more than perceptiveness and a good memory.* ◆◇◇◇◇ ADJ-GRADED; ADV-GRADED: usu ADV with v, also ADV adj; N-UNCOUNT

perceptual /pəʳseptʃuəl/. Your **perceptual** skills are the mental abilities that you use in the process of learning in order to interpret and understand what you perceive; a formal word. *Some children come to school with more finely trained perceptual skills than others.* ADJ: ADJ n

perch /pɜːʳtʃ/ **perches, perching, perched** ◆◆◇◇◇

1 If you **perch on** something, you sit down lightly on the very edge or tip of it. *He lit a cigarette and perched on the corner of the desk... He perched himself on the side of the bed.* ♦ **perched** *She was perched on the edge of the sofa.* VERB V prep/adv V pron-refl prep/adv; ADJ: v-link ADJ

2 If something **perches** somewhere, it is on the top or edge of something. *...the vast slums that perch precariously on top of the hills around which the city was built.* ♦ **perched** *St. John's is a small* VERB V prep/adv ADJ:

college perched high up in the hills... Frank's tinted glasses are perched precariously on his head. — v-link ADJ prep/adv

3 If you **perch** something **on** something else, you put or balance it on the top or edge of that thing. *The use of steel and concrete has allowed the builders to perch a light concrete dome on eight slender columns.* — VERB; V n *on* n

4 When a bird **perches** on something such as a branch or a wall, it lands on it and stands there. *A blackbird flew down and perched on the parapet outside his window.* — VERB; V prep

5 A **perch** is a short rod for a bird to stand on. — N-COUNT

6 You can refer to a high place where someone is sitting as their **perch**. — N-COUNT: usu poss N

7 If someone is **knocked off** their **perch**, they are no longer admired or no longer thought of as important or clever. *There is a trend for knocking public-school headmasters and headmistresses off their perches.* — PHRASE: V inflects

8 A **perch** is an edible fish. There are several kinds of perch. The form **perch** is used for both singular and plural. — N-COUNT

perchance /pəʳtʃɑːns, -tʃæns/. **Perchance** means perhaps; an old-fashioned, literary word. — ADV: ADV with group/cl

percolate /pɜːʳkəleɪt/ **percolates, percolating, percolated**

1 If an idea, feeling, or piece of information **percolates** through a group of people or a thing, it spreads slowly through the group or thing. *New fashions took a long time to percolate down. ...all of these thoughts percolated through my mind.* — VERB =filter; V prep/adv

2 When you **percolate** coffee or when coffee **percolates**, you prepare it in a percolator. *She percolated the coffee and put croissants in the oven to warm. ...freshly percolated coffee.* — V-ERG; V n; V-ed; Also V

3 If something **percolates** somewhere, it passes slowly through something that has very small holes or gaps in it. *Rain water will only percolate through slowly.* — VERB; V prep/adv

percolator /pɜːʳkəleɪtəʳ/ **percolators.** A **percolator** is a special piece of equipment for making and serving coffee. — N-COUNT

percussion /pəʳkʌʃᵊn/. **Percussion** instruments are musical instruments that you hit, such as drums and cymbals. — ◆◇◇◇◇ N-UNCOUNT: oft N n

percussionist /pəʳkʌʃᵊnɪst/ **percussionists.** A **percussionist** is a person who plays percussion instruments such as drums. — N-COUNT

percussive /pəʳkʌsɪv/. **Percussive** sounds are like the sound of drums. *...using all manner of percussive effects.* — ADJ-GRADED: usu ADJ n

perdition /pɜːʳdɪʃᵊn/. If you say that someone is on the road to **perdition**, you mean that their behaviour is likely to lead them to failure and disaster; a literary word. — N-UNCOUNT: usu prep N

peregrine falcon /perɪgrɪn fɔːlkən/ **peregrine falcons.** A **peregrine falcon** or a **peregrine** is a large bird of prey, which has a dark-coloured back and is lighter coloured underneath. — N-COUNT

peremptory /pəremptəri/. Someone who does something in a **peremptory** way does it in a way that shows that they expect to be obeyed immediately; a formal word, used showing disapproval. *With a brief, almost peremptory gesture he pointed to a chair.* — ADJ-GRADED: usu ADJ n; PRAGMATICS ♦ **peremptorily** /pəremptərɪli/ *'Hello!' the voice said, more peremptorily. 'Who is it? Who do you want?'* — ADV-GRADED: ADV with v

perennial /pəreniəl/ **perennials** — ◆◆◇◇◇

1 You use **perennial** to describe situations or states that keep occurring or which seem to exist all the time; used especially to describe problems or difficulties. *...the perennial urban problems of drugs and homelessness... There's a perennial shortage of teachers with science qualifications.* — ADJ-GRADED: usu ADJ n =constant, continual ♦ **perennially** *Both services are perennially short of staff.* — ADV: usu ADV adj

2 A **perennial** plant lives for several years and has flowers each year. *...a perennial herb with greenish-yellow flowers.* — ADJ: usu ADJ n ▸ Also a noun. *...a low-growing perennial.* — N-COUNT

perestroika /perɪstrɔɪkə/. **Perestroika** is a term which was used to describe the changing political and social structure of the former Soviet Union during the late 1980s. — ◆◆◇◇◇ N-UNCOUNT

perfect, perfects, perfecting, perfected. The adjective is pronounced /pɜːʳfɪkt/. The verb is pronounced /pəʳfekt/ — ◆◆◆◆◇

1 Something that is **perfect** is as good as it could possibly be. *He spoke perfect English... Hiring a nanny has turned out to be the perfect solution... It's a perfect example of a house reflecting the person who lives there... Nobody is perfect.* • **practice makes perfect**: see **practice**. — ADJ-GRADED

2 If you say that something is **perfect** for a particular person, thing, or activity, you are emphasizing that it is very suitable for them or for that activity. *Carpet tiles are perfect for kitchens because they're easy to take up and wash... So this could be the perfect time to buy a home.* — ADJ-GRADED: oft ADJ *for* n =ideal

3 If an object or surface is **perfect**, it does not have any marks on it, or have any lumps, cracks, or dents in it. *Use only clean, Grade A, perfect eggs. ...their perfect white teeth.* — ADJ =flawless

4 You can use **perfect** to give emphasis to the noun following it. *She was a perfect fool... Some people are always coming up to perfect strangers and asking them what they do... What he had said to her made perfect sense.* — ADJ: ADJ n; PRAGMATICS =complete

5 If you **perfect** something, you improve it so that it becomes as good as it can possibly be. *We perfected a hand-signal system so that he could keep me informed of hazards... I removed the fibroid tumours, using the techniques that I have perfected. ...girls who needed to perfect their English.* — VERB; V n

6 The **perfect** tenses of a verb are the ones used to talk about things that happened or began before a particular time, as in 'He's already left' and 'They had always liked her'. The present perfect tense is sometimes called the **perfect** tense. • See also **future, present perfect, past perfect**. — ADJ: ADJ n

perfection /pəʳfekʃᵊn/ — ◆◆◇◇◇

1 **Perfection** is the quality of being as good as it is possible for something of a particular kind to be. *His quest for perfection is relentless... Physical perfection in a human being is exceedingly rare.* — N-UNCOUNT

2 If you say that something is **perfection**, you mean that you think it is as good as it could possibly be. *The house and garden were perfection.* — N-UNCOUNT

3 **The perfection of** something such as a skill, system, or product involves making it as good as it could possibly be. *Madame Clicquot is credited with the perfection of this technique.* — N-UNCOUNT: usu *the* N *of* n

4 If something is done **to perfection**, it is done so well that it could not be done any better. *Like the old trouper he is, he timed his entry to perfection. ...fresh fish, cooked to perfection.* — PHRASE: PHR after v

perfectionism /pəʳfekʃənɪzəm/. **Perfectionism** is the state or quality of being a perfectionist. — N-UNCOUNT

perfectionist /pəʳfekʃənɪst/ **perfectionists.** Someone who is a **perfectionist** refuses to do or accept anything that is not as good as it could possibly be. — 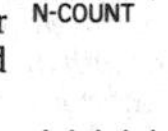 N-COUNT

perfectly /pɜːʳfɪktli/ — 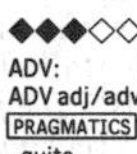

1 You can use **perfectly** to emphasize an adjective or adverb, especially when you think the person you are talking to might doubt what you are saying. *There's no reason why you can't have a perfectly normal child... They made it perfectly clear that it was pointless to go on... They are perfectly safe to eat... You know perfectly well what happened.* — ADV: ADV adj/adv; PRAGMATICS =quite

2 If something is done **perfectly**, it is done so well that it could not possibly be done better. *This ambitious adaptation perfectly captures the spirit of Kurt Vonnegut's acclaimed novel... The system worked perfectly.* — ADV-GRADED: ADV with v

3 If you describe something as **perfectly** good or acceptable, you are emphasizing that there is no reason to use or get something else, although someone else has a different opinion. *Bunbury, ignoring a perfectly good pedestrian crossing twenty yards further along, marched boldly out into the traffic.* — ADV: ADV adj/adv; PRAGMATICS

perfect pitch. Someone who has **perfect pitch** is able to identify or sing musical notes correctly. — N-UNCOUNT

perfidious /pəʳfɪdiəs/. If you describe someone as **perfidious**, you mean that you think they are treacherous or untrustworthy; a literary word. *Their feet will trample on the dead bodies of their perfidious aggressors.* ADJ-GRADED: usu ADJ n =treacherous

perfidy /pɜːʳfɪdi/. **Perfidy** is treacherous behaviour or actions; a literary word. N-UNCOUNT =treachery

perforate /pɜːʳfəreɪt/ **perforates, perforating, perforated.** To **perforate** something means to pierce it or cause it to have a hole or holes in it. *I refused to wear headphones because they can perforate your eardrums.* VERB V n ♦ **perforated** *Keep good apples in perforated polythene bags.* ADJ: ADJ n

perforation /pɜːʳfəreɪʃᵊn/ **perforations. Perforations** are small holes that are made in something, especially in paper. *From the perforations on the sides of the paper, she could tell the letter had been written on a computer... When held to the light the small oblong leaves are seen to possess tiny perforations.* N-COUNT: usu pl =holes

perforce /pəʳfɔːʳs/. **Perforce** is used to indicate that something happens or is the case because it is unavoidable or inevitable rather than because it is intended or desired; an old-fashioned word. *The war in 1939 perforce ushered in an era of more grime and drabness.* ADV: ADV with cl, ADV with v

perform /pəʳfɔːʳm/ **performs, performing, performed** ◆◆◆◆◇

1 When you **perform** a task or action, especially a complicated one, you do it. *We're looking for people of all ages who have performed outstanding acts of bravery, kindness or courage... His council had had to perform miracles on a tiny budget... Several grafts may be performed at one operation.* VERB V n

2 If something **performs** a particular function, it has that function. *A complex engine has many separate components, each performing a different function.* VERB V n

3 If you **perform** a play, a piece of music, or a dance, you do it in front of an audience. *Gardiner has pursued relentlessly high standards in performing classical music... This play was first performed in 411 BC... He began performing in the early fifties, singing and playing guitar.* VERB V n V

4 If someone or something **performs well**, they work well or achieve a good result. If they **perform badly**, they work badly or achieve a poor result. *He had not performed well in his exams... England performed so well against France at Wembley... 'State-owned industries will always perform poorly,' John Moore informed readers... When there's snow and ice, how's this car going to perform?* VERB V adv

performance /pəʳfɔːʳməns/ **performances** ◆◆◆◆◇

1 A **performance** involves entertaining an audience by doing something such as singing, dancing, or acting. *Inside the theatre, they were giving a performance of Bizet's Carmen. ...her performance as the betrayed Medea... The Festival Of Asian Arts & Music will include two days of live performances.* N-COUNT

2 Someone's or something's **performance** is how successful they are or how well they do something. *That study looked at the performance of 18 surgeons... The poor performance has been blamed on the recession and cheaper sports car imports... The job of the new director-general was to ensure that performance targets were met.* N-VAR: oft with poss

3 A car's **performance** is its ability to go fast and accelerate quickly. N-UNCOUNT

4 A **performance car** is one that can go very fast and accelerate very quickly. *...a sporty performance car.* ● See also **high-performance**. ADJ: ADJ n

5 The **performance** of a task is the fact or action of doing it. *He devoted in excess of seventy hours a week to the performance of his duties... The people believe that the performance of this ritual is the will of the Great Spirit.* N-SING: usu the N of n

6 You can describe something that is or looks complicated or difficult to do as **a performance**; an informal use. *The whole process is quite a performance... She made a big performance of sprinkling all the spices on.* N-SING: usu a N

7 ● **a repeat performance**: see **repeat**.

perf<u>o</u>rmance art. Performance art is a theatrical presentation that includes various art forms such as dance, music, painting, and sculpture. N-UNCOUNT

performer /pəʳfɔːʳməʳ/ **performers** ◆◆◇◇◇

1 A **performer** is a person who acts, sings, or does other entertainment in front of audiences. *A performer in evening dress plays classical selections on the violin.* N-COUNT

2 You can use **performer** when describing someone or something in a way that indicates how well they do a particular thing. *Until 1987, Canada's industry had been the star performer... He is a world class performer.* N-COUNT: supp N

perf<u>o</u>rming <u>a</u>rts. Dance, drama, music, and other forms of entertainment that are usually performed live in front of an audience are referred to as the **performing arts**. N-PLURAL: usu the N

perfume /pɜːʳfjuːm, pəʳfjuːm/ **perfumes, perfuming, perfumed** ◆◆◇◇◇

1 **Perfume** is a pleasant-smelling liquid which women put on their necks and wrists to make themselves smell nice. *The hall smelled of her mother's perfume. ...a bottle of perfume. ...the manufacture of soaps and perfumes.* N-MASS =scent

2 **Perfume** is the ingredient that is added to some products to make them smell nice. *...a delicate white soap without perfume. ...a perfume for skin creams.* N-MASS

3 The **perfume** of something is the pleasant smell it has; a literary use. *...the perfume of roses... There were two lemon trees and I paused to enjoy their perfume.* N-COUNT: with poss =fragrance

4 If the smell of something **perfumes** a place or area, it makes it smell nice; a literary use. *Flowers started to perfume the air... As they bake, they perfume the whole house with the aroma of apples and spices. ...gardens perfumed with jasmine.* VERB V n V n with n

5 If something is used to **perfume** a product, it is added to the product to make it smell nice. *The oil is used to flavour and perfume soaps, foam baths, and scents. ...shower gel perfumed with the popular Paris fragrance.* VERB V n be V-ed with n

perfumed /pɜːʳfjuːmd, pəʳfjuːmd/ ◆◇◇◇◇

1 Something such as fruit or wine that is **perfumed** has a sweet pleasant smell. *Champenois wines can be particularly fragrant and perfumed. ...sweetly perfumed, creamy yellow flowers.* ADJ-GRADED

2 **Perfumed** things have a sweet pleasant smell, either naturally or because perfume has been added to them. *She opened the perfumed envelope. ...perfumed roses.* ADJ: usu ADJ n =scented

perfumery /pəʳfjuːməri/ **perfumeries**

1 **Perfumery** is the activity or business of producing perfume. *...the perfumery trade... Provence is the home of perfumery.* N-UNCOUNT: oft N n

2 A **perfumery** is a shop or a department in a shop where perfume is the main product that is sold. *...a perfumery called Bayley's of Bond Street. ...the perfumery department.* N-COUNT

perfunctory /pəʳfʌŋktəri, AM -tɔːri/. A **perfunctory** action is done quickly and carelessly, and shows a lack of interest in what you are doing. *She gave the list only a perfunctory glance. ...a perfunctory handshake... Our interest was purely perfunctory.* ADJ-GRADED: usu ADJ n ♦ **perfunctorily** /pəʳfʌŋktərɪli, AM -tɔːr-/ *Melina was perfunctorily introduced to the men.* ADV-GRADED: ADV with v

pergola /pɜːʳgələ/ **pergolas.** In a garden, a **pergola** is an arch or a structure with a roof that has a framework over which climbing plants can be grown. N-COUNT

perhaps /pəʳhæps, præps/ ◆◆◆◆◆

1 You use **perhaps** to express uncertainty, for example, when you do not know that something is definitely true, or when you are mentioning something that may possibly happen in the future in the way you describe. *Millson regarded her thoughtfully. Perhaps she was right... In the end they lose millions, perhaps billions... He does not paint for very long on any one painting, perhaps for two and a half hours at a time... It was bulky, perhaps three feet long and almost as high... Perhaps, in time, the* ADV: ADV with cl/group PRAGMATICS =possibly, maybe ≠definitely

message will get through... They'd come soon, perhaps when the radio broadcast was over.

2 You use **perhaps** in opinions and remarks to make them appear less definite or more polite. *Perhaps the most important lesson to be learned is that you simply cannot please everyone... His very last paintings are perhaps the most puzzling... The lesson from all of this is perhaps a broader one... Do you perhaps disapprove of Agatha Christie and her Poirot and Miss Marple?... He was not perhaps physically the strongest in the class.* ADV: ADV with cl/group PRAGMATICS

3 You use **perhaps** when you are making suggestions or giving advice. **Perhaps** is also used in formal English to introduce requests. *Perhaps I may be permitted a few suggestions... Well, perhaps you'll come and see us at our place?... Perhaps if you rang me when you got back to your office?* ADV: ADV with cl PRAGMATICS

4 You can say **perhaps** as a response to a question or remark, when you do not want to agree or accept, but think that it would be rude to disagree or refuse. *'You know it doesn't make sense for you.'—'Perhaps. I don't know. Maybe it does maybe it doesn't.'... 'I'm sure we can make it,' he says. Perhaps, but it will not be easy.* ADV: ADV as reply PRAGMATICS

peril /perɪl/ **perils** ◆◇◇◇◇

1 **Perils** are great dangers; a formal use. *...the perils of the sea... In spite of great peril, I have survived.* N-VAR: with supp

2 The **perils** of a particular activity or course of action are the dangers or problems that can arise from doing it. *...the perils of starring in a television commercial.* N-PLURAL: with poss

3 If you say that someone does something **at** their **peril**, you are warning them that they will probably suffer as a result of doing it. *Ignore it at your peril... Anyone who breaks the law does so at their peril.* PHRASES PHR after v

4 If someone or something is **in peril**, they are in great danger. *We are in the gravest peril.* usu v-link PHR =in danger

perilous /perɪləs/. Something that is **perilous** is very dangerous; a literary use. *...a perilous journey across the war-zone... The road grew even steeper and more perilous. ...perilous cliffs.* ◆◇◇◇◇ ADJ-GRADED =dangerous ♦ **perilously** *The track snaked perilously upwards. ...a perilously narrow bridge.* ADV-GRADED: ADV after v, ADV adj

perimeter /pərɪmɪtəʳ/ **perimeters.** The **perimeter** of an area of land is the whole of its outer edge or boundary. *...the perimeter of the airport... Officers dressed in riot gear are surrounding the perimeter fence.* ◆◇◇◇◇ N-COUNT

perinatal /perineɪtᵊl/. **Perinatal** deaths, complications, or experiences happen at the time of birth or soon after the time of birth; a medical term. *Premature birth is the main cause of perinatal mortality.* ADJ: ADJ n

period /pɪəriəd/ **periods** ◆◆◆◆◇

1 A **period** is a length of time. *This crisis might last for a long period of time. ...a period of a few months. ...for a limited period only.* N-COUNT: usu with supp

2 A **period** in the life of a person, organization, or society is a length of time which is remembered for a particular situation or activity. *...a period of economic good health and expansion... He went through a period of wanting to be accepted... The South African years were his most creative period.* N-COUNT: with supp =phase

3 A particular length of time in history is sometimes called a **period**. For example, you can talk about the Victorian period or the Elizabethan period in Britain. *...the Roman period... No reference to their existence appears in any literature of the period. ...the most difficult periods of history.* N-COUNT: usu with supp

4 **Period** costumes, furniture, and instruments were made at an earlier time in history, or look as if they were made then. *...dressed in full period costume. ...replicas of period instruments.* ADJ: ADJ n

5 Exercise, training, or study **periods** are lengths of time that are set aside for exercise, training, or study. *They accompanied him during his exercise periods.* N-COUNT: usu n N

6 At a school or college, a **period** is one of the parts that the day is divided into during which lessons or private study take place. *...periods of private study. ...taking his scripts to school in order to learn the lines in free periods.* N-COUNT

7 When a woman has a **period**, she bleeds from her womb. This usually happens once a month, unless she is pregnant. N-COUNT

8 Some people say **period** after stating a fact or opinion when they want to emphasize that they are definite about something and do not want to discuss it further. *I don't want to do it, period.* ADV: cl ADV PRAGMATICS =full stop

9 In American English, a **period** is the punctuation mark (.) which you use at the end of a sentence when it is not a question or an explanation. The British expression is **full stop**. N-COUNT =full stop

periodic /pɪəriɒdɪk/. **Periodic** events or situations happen occasionally, at fairly regular intervals. *Periodic checks are taken to ensure that high standards are maintained. ...periodic bouts of illness.* ◆◇◇◇◇ ADJ: usu ADJ n =periodical

periodical /pɪəriɒdɪkəl/ **periodicals** ◆◇◇◇◇

1 **Periodicals** are magazines, especially serious or academic ones, that are published at regular intervals. *The walls would be lined with books and periodicals. ...a monthly periodical.* N-COUNT

2 **Periodical** events or situations happen occasionally, at fairly regular intervals. *She made periodical visits to her dentist. ...periodical screening for cancer.* ADJ: usu ADJ n =periodic ♦ **periodically** /pɪəriɒdɪkli/ *Meetings are held periodically to monitor progress on the case... Police were periodically patrolling the area.* ADV: ADV with v

periodic table. In chemistry, **the periodic table** is a table showing the chemical elements arranged according to their atomic numbers. N-SING: the N

periodontal /perioʊdɒntᵊl/. **Periodontal** disease is disease of the gums; a technical term in dentistry. ADJ: ADJ n

period piece, period pieces. A **period piece** is a play, book, or film that is set at a particular time in history and describes life at that time. N-COUNT

peripatetic /perɪpətetɪk/. If someone has a **peripatetic** life or career, they travel around a lot, living or working in places for short periods of time; a formal word. *Her father was in the army and the family led a peripatetic existence. ...a hectic, peripatetic life full of people and parties.* ADJ-GRADED: usu ADJ n

peripheral /pərɪfərəl/ **peripherals** ◆◇◇◇◇

1 A **peripheral** activity or issue is one which is not very important compared with other activities or issues. *Companies are increasingly keen to contract out peripheral activities like training. ...peripheral and boring information... Science is peripheral to that debate.* ADJ-GRADED ♦ **peripherally** *The Marshall Plan did not include Britain, except peripherally.* ADV-GRADED

2 **Peripheral** areas of land are ones which are on the edge of a larger area. *...peripheral regions beyond the reach of powerful rulers. ...urban development in the outer peripheral areas of large towns.* ADJ: usu ADJ n

3 **Peripherals** are devices that can be attached to computers; a technical use in computing. *...peripherals to expand the use of our computers. ... peripheral products for the basic computer.* N-COUNT: usu pl, oft N n

periphery /pərɪfəri/ **peripheries** ◆◇◇◇◇

1 If something is on the **periphery** of an area, place, or thing, it is on the edge of it; a formal word. *...the republics on the periphery of the Soviet Union... Taste buds are concentrated at the tip and rear of the tongue and around its periphery.* N-COUNT: usu with poss =edge

2 The **periphery** of a subject or area of interest is the part of it that is not considered to be as important or basic as the main part. *The sociological study of religion moved from the centre to the periphery of sociology.* N-COUNT: usu with poss

periscope /perɪskoʊp/ **periscopes.** A **periscope** is a vertical tube which people inside submarines can look through to see above the surface of the water. N-COUNT

perish /perɪʃ/ **perishes, perishing, perished** ◆◇◇◇◇

1 If people or animals **perish**, they die as a result of very harsh conditions or as the result of an accident; used in written English. *Most of the butterflies perish in the first frosts of autumn. ...the ferry disaster in which 193 passengers perished.* VERB =die V

2 If something **perishes**, it comes to an end or is destroyed for ever; used in written English. VERB =collapse

Buddhism had to adapt to the new world or perish... Civilizations do eventually decline and perish. V

3 If a substance or material **perishes** or **is perished**, it starts to fall to pieces and becomes useless. *Obviously the plaster's just perished and all fallen off. ...their tyres are slowly perishing.* ♦ **perished** *...tattered pieces of ancient, perished leather.* V-ERG =disintegrate V Also V n ADJ: usu ADJ n

4 If someone says **perish the thought**, they mean that they think that a suggestion or possibility is unpleasant or ridiculous. *Me a policeman! Perish the thought!... We don't have a computer (perish the thought) and have only recently bought an electric typewriter.* CONVENTION PRAGMATICS =God forbid

perishable /pe̲rɪʃəbᵊl/. Goods such as food that are **perishable** go bad after quite a short length of time. *...perishable food like fruit, vegetables and meat... Raw eggs are highly perishable and must be chilled before and after cooking.* ADJ

perished /pe̲rɪʃt/. If someone is **perished**, they are extremely cold; used in informal British English. *I was absolutely perished... I was perished. No jacket, no torch, wet through, exhausted.* ADJ: usu v-link ADJ

peritonitis /pe̲rɪtənaɪtɪs/. **Peritonitis** is a disease in which the inside wall of your abdomen becomes swollen and very painful; a medical term. N-UNCOUNT

periwinkle /pe̲riwɪŋkᵊl/ **periwinkles**

1 **Periwinkle** is a plant that grows along the ground and has blue flowers. N-VAR

2 **Periwinkles** are small creatures that are similar to snails and that live by the sea. N-COUNT: usu pl

perjure /pɜ̲ːʳdʒəʳ/ **perjures, perjuring, perjured.** If someone **perjures** themselves in a court of law, they lie, even though they have promised to tell the truth. *Witnesses lied and perjured themselves... She would rather perjure herself than admit to her sins.* VERB V pron-refl

perjured /pɜ̲ːʳdʒəʳd/. In a court of law **perjured evidence** or **perjured testimony** is a false statement of events. *The judgment depended on information that was based on perjured testimony.* ADJ: usu ADJ n

perjury /pɜ̲ːʳdʒəri/. If someone who is giving evidence in a court of law commits **perjury**, they lie; a legal term. *This witness has committed perjury and no reliance can be placed on her evidence. ...charges of perjury.* N-UNCOUNT

perk /pɜ̲ːʳk/ **perks, perking, perked. Perks** are special benefits that are given to people who have a particular job or belong to a particular group. *...a company car, private medical insurance and other perks... One of the perks of being a student is cheap travel.* ◆◇◇◇◇ N-COUNT: usu pl

perk up PHRASAL VERB

1 If something **perks** you **up** or if you **perk up**, you become cheerful and lively, after feeling tired, bored, or depressed. *He perks up and jokes with them. ...suggestions to make you smile and perk you up.* ERG V P V n P Also V P n (not pron)

2 If you **perk** something **up**, you make it more interesting. *To make the bland taste more interesting, the locals began perking it up with local produce... Psychological twists perk up an otherwise predictable story line.* V n P V P n

3 If sales, prices, or economies **perk up**, or if something **perks** them **up**, they begin to increase or improve; used mainly by journalists. *House prices could perk up during the autumn... Anything that could save the company money and perk up its cash flow was examined.* ERG V P V P n (not pron) Also V n P

perky /pɜ̲ːʳki/ **perkier, perkiest.** If someone is **perky**, they are cheerful and lively. *He wasn't quite as perky as normal... She had a perky, independent spirit.* ADJ-GRADED

perm /pɜ̲ːʳm/ **perms, perming, permed** ◆◇◇◇◇

1 In British English, if you have a **perm**, your hair is curled and treated with chemicals, so that it stays curly or wavy for several months. The usual American word is **permanent.** N-COUNT

2 When a hair stylist **perms** someone's hair, they curl it and treat it with chemicals so that it stays curly or wavy for several months. *Her cousin, a hairdresser, was perming her hair as a special treat... She had her hair permed.* ♦ **permed** *...dry, damaged or permed hair.* VERB V n have n V-ed ADJ

permafrost /pɜ̲ːʳməfrɒst/. **Permafrost** is land that is permanently frozen to a great depth. N-UNCOUNT

permanent /pɜ̲ːʳmənənt/ **permanents** ◆◆◆◇◇

1 Something that is **permanent** lasts for ever. *Heavy drinking can cause permanent damage to the brain. ...a permanent solution to the problem... The ban is intended to be permanent.* ♦ **permanently** *His reason had been permanently affected by what he had witnessed... The only way to lose weight permanently is to completely change your attitudes toward food.* ♦ **permanence** *Anything which threatens the permanence of the treaty is a threat to stability and to peace.* ♦ **permanency** *They gradually realized the permanency of their condition.* ADJ ≠temporary ADV: ADV with v, ADV adj ≠temporarily N-UNCOUNT N-UNCOUNT

2 You use **permanent** to describe situations or states that keep occurring or which seem to exist all the time; used especially to describe problems or difficulties. *...a permanent state of tension... They feel under permanent threat... There was a permanent 20-yard queue for the portable toilets.* ♦ **permanently** *...the heavy, permanently locked gate.* ADJ: usu ADJ n =constant ADV =constantly

3 A **permanent** employee is one who is employed for an unlimited length of time. *At the end of the probationary period you will become a permanent employee. ...a permanent job.* ♦ **permanently** *...permanently employed registered dockers.* ADJ: ADJ n ≠temporary ADV: ADV with v

4 Your **permanent home** or your **permanent address** is the one at which you spend most of your time or the one that you return to after having stayed in other places. *York Cottage was as near to a permanent home as the children knew... They had no permanent address.* ADJ: ADJ n

5 In American English, a **permanent** is a treatment where a hairstylist curls your hair and treats it with a chemical so that it stays curly or wavy for several months. The British word is a **perm.** N-COUNT

pe̲rmanent wa̲ve, permanent waves. A **permanant wave** is the same as a **perm**; an old-fashioned word. N-COUNT =perm

permeable /pɜ̲ːʳmiəbᵊl/. If a substance is **permeable**, something such as water or gas can pass through it or soak into it. *A number of products have been developed which are permeable to air and water.* ♦ **permeability** /pɜ̲ːʳmiəbɪ̲lɪti/ *...ingenious devices for adjusting the permeability of the exterior wall.* ADJ-GRADED =porous ≠impermeable N-UNCOUNT ≠impermeability

permeate /pɜ̲ːʳmieɪt/ **permeates, permeating, permeated** ◆◇◇◇◇

1 If an idea, feeling, or attitude **permeates** a system or **permeates** society, it affects every part of it or is present throughout it. *Bias against women permeates every level of the judicial system... An obvious change of attitude at the top will permeate through the system.* VERB V n V *through* n

2 If something **permeates** a place, it spreads throughout it. *The smell of roast beef permeated the air... Eventually, the water will permeate through the surrounding concrete.* VERB V n V *through* n

permissible /pəʳmɪ̲sɪbᵊl/. If something is **permissible**, it is considered to be acceptable because it does not break any laws or rules. *Religious practices are permissible under the Constitution... He said it was just not permissible to postpone the main issue by allowing business to carry on as usual.* ◆◇◇◇◇ ADJ: usu v-link ADJ ≠forbidden

permission /pəʳmɪ̲ʃᵊn/ **permissions** ◆◆◆◇◇

1 If someone who has authority over you gives you **permission** to do something, they say that they will allow you to do it. *He asked permission to leave the room... Finally his mother relented and gave permission for her youngest son to marry... Police said permission for the march had not been granted... They cannot leave the country without permission.* N-UNCOUNT: oft N to-inf, N *for* n to-inf, N *for* n

2 A **permission** is a formal, written statement from an official group or place allowing you to do something. *...oil exploration permissions.* ● see also **planning permission.** N-COUNT: usu pl

permissive /pəʳmɪsɪv/. A **permissive** person, society, or way of behaving allows or tolerates things which other people disapprove of. *The call for law and order replaced the 'permissive tolerance' of the 1960s... Single parents are more likely to be permissive.* ♦ **permissiveness** *Permissiveness and democracy go together.* ADJ-GRADED N-UNCOUNT

permit, permits, permitting, permitted. The verb is pronounced /pəʳmɪt/. The noun is pronounced /pɜːʳmɪt/. ◆◆◆◇◇

1 If someone **permits** something, they allow it to happen. If they **permit** you to do something, they allow you to do it. *He can let the court's decision stand and permit the execution... The guards permitted me to bring my camera and tape recorder... Employees are permitted to use the golf course during their free hours... No outside journalists have been permitted into the country... If they appear to be under 12, then the doorman is not allowed to permit them entry to the film.* VERB =allow V n V n to-inf be V-ed into n V n n

2 A **permit** is an official document which says that you may do something. For example you usually need a **permit** to work in a foreign country. *The majority of foreign nationals working here have work permits... He has to apply for a permit, and we have to find him a job.* N-COUNT

3 If a situation **permits** something, it makes it possible for that thing to exist, happen, or be done or it provides the opportunity for it; a formal use. *However, Vance said conditions do not yet permit the use of UN forces... Try to go out for a walk at lunchtime, if the weather permits... This method of cooking also permits heat to penetrate evenly from both sides.* VERB =allow V n V V n to-inf Also V of n

4 If you **permit** yourself something, you allow yourself to have or do something that you do not normally have or do or that you think you probably should not have or do. *Captain Bowen, permitted himself one cigar a day... Only once in his life had Douglas permitted himself to lose control of his emotions.* VERB =allow V pron-refl n V pron-refl to-inf

5 In formal English, you can use **permit me** when you are about to say something or to make a suggestion. *Permit me to give you some advice... Permit me to offer you my sincere congratulations.* PHRASE: PHR to-inf PRAGMATICS =allow me

permutation /pɜːʳmjuːteɪʃᵊn/ **permutations.** A **permutation** is one of the ways in which a number of things can be ordered or arranged. *The possibilities of variation among members of the human species are limited to the possible permutations of our genes.* N-COUNT: usu pl

pernicious /pəʳnɪʃəs/. If you describe something as **pernicious**, you mean that it is very harmful. *I did what I could, but her mother's influence was pernicious... There is a pernicious culture of excellence: everything has to be not merely good but the best.* ◆◇◇◇◇ ADJ-GRADED

pernicious anaemia; also spelled **pernicious anemia**. **Pernicious anaemia** is a very severe blood disease. N-UNCOUNT

pernickety /pəʳnɪkɪti/. If you describe someone as **pernickety**, you think that they pay too much attention to small, unimportant details; an informal word, used showing disapproval. *Customs officials can get extremely pernickety about things like that.* ADJ-GRADED PRAGMATICS =fussy

peroration /perəreɪʃᵊn/ **perorations**

1 A **peroration** is the last part of a speech, especially the part where the speaker sums up his or her argument; a formal use. N-COUNT

2 If someone describes a speech as a **peroration**, they mean that they dislike it because they think it is very long and not worth listening to; an informal use. N-COUNT PRAGMATICS

peroxide /pərɒksaɪd/ **peroxides. Peroxide** is a chemical that is often used for making hair lighter in colour. It can also be used as an antiseptic. • See also **hydrogen peroxide.** N-MASS =hydrogen peroxide

peroxide blonde, peroxide blondes. You can refer to a woman whose hair has been artificially been made lighter in colour as a **peroxide blonde**, especially when you want to show that you disapprove of this, or that you think her hair looks unnatural or unattractive. N-COUNT PRAGMATICS

perpendicular /pɜːʳpəndɪkjʊləʳ/

1 A **perpendicular** line or surface points straight up, rather than being sloping or horizontal. *We made two slits for the eyes and a perpendicular line for the nose... The sides of the loch are almost perpendicular.* ADJ-GRADED: usu ADJ n =vertical ≠horizontal

2 If one thing is **perpendicular** to another, it is at an angle of 90 degrees to it; a formal use. *The left wing dipped until it was perpendicular to the ground.* ADJ: usu v-link ADJ to n

perpetrate /pɜːʳpɪtreɪt/ **perpetrates, perpetrating, perpetrated.** If someone **perpetrates** a crime or any other immoral or harmful act, they do it. *A high proportion of crime in any country is perpetrated by young males in their teens and twenties... Tremendous wrongs were being perpetrated on the poorest and least privileged human beings... You begin to ask yourself what kind of person perpetrated this crime.* ♦ **perpetration** /pɜːʳpɪtreɪʃᵊn/ *...a very small minority who persist in the perpetration of these crimes.* ♦ **perpetrator, perpetrators** *It's time the death penalty was used for perpetrators of terrorist acts.* ◆◇◇◇◇ VERB =commit be V-ed be V-ed on/against n V n N-SING: usu N of n N-COUNT

perpetual /pəʳpetʃuəl/ ◆◇◇◇◇

1 A **perpetual** feeling, state, or quality is one that never ends or changes. *...the creation of a perpetual union.* ♦ **perpetually** *They were all perpetually starving... He and his wife would be compelled to live perpetually as second-class citizens.* ADJ: usu ADJ n =permanent ADV: ADV with v, ADV adj/prep =permanently

2 A **perpetual** act, situation, or state is one that happens again and again and so seems never to end. *I thought her perpetual complaints were going to prove too much for me.* ♦ **perpetually** *...a perpetually renewed miracle... He perpetually interferes in political affairs.* ADJ: usu ADJ n =continual ADV: ADV with v, ADV adj/prep =continually

perpetual motion; also spelled **perpetual-motion**. The idea of **perpetual motion** is the idea of something continuing to move for ever without getting energy from anything else. N-UNCOUNT

perpetuate /pəʳpetʃueɪt/ **perpetuates, perpetuating, perpetuated.** If someone or something **perpetuates** a situation, system, or belief, especially a bad one, they cause it to continue. *We must not perpetuate the religious divisions of the past... This image is a myth perpetuated by the media.* ♦ **perpetuation** /pəʳpetʃueɪʃᵊn/ *The perpetuation of nuclear deployments is morally unacceptable.* ◆◇◇◇◇ VERB V n V-ed N-SING: usu N of n

perpetuity /pɜːʳpɪtjuːɪti/. If something is done **in perpetuity**, it is intended to last for ever; a formal expression. *The US Government gave the land to the tribe in perpetuity.* PHRASE: PHR after v

perplex /pəʳpleks/ **perplexes, perplexing, perplexed.** If something **perplexes** you, it confuses and worries you because you do not understand it or because it causes you difficulty. *It perplexed him because he was tackling it the wrong way.* VERB =puzzle, bewilder V n

perplexed /pəʳplekst/. If you are **perplexed**, you feel confused and slightly worried by something because you do not understand it. *She is perplexed about what to do for her daughter... Japan's perplexed bankers need not worry.* ◆◇◇◇◇ ADJ-GRADED: usu v-link ADJ =puzzled

perplexing /pəʳpleksɪŋ/. If you find something **perplexing**, you do not understand it or do not know how to deal with it. *It took years to understand many perplexing diseases... British Parliamentary procedure is perplexing at the best of times.* ADJ-GRADED: usu ADJ n =puzzling

perplexity /pəʳpleksɪti/ **perplexities**

1 **Perplexity** is a feeling of being confused and frustrated because you don't completely understand something. *He began counting them and then, with growing perplexity, counted them a second time.* N-UNCOUNT =puzzlement, anxiety

2 The **perplexities** of something are those things about it which are difficult to understand because they are complicated. *...the perplexities of quantum mechanics.* N-COUNT: usu pl =difficulty, complexity

perquisite /pɜːʳkwɪzɪt/ **perquisites.** A **perquisite** is the same as a **perk**; a formal word. N-COUNT =perk

...*cost-free long-distance calls, a perquisite of her employment.*

persecute /pɜːʳsɪkjuːt/ **persecutes, persecuting, persecuted** ◆◇◇◇◇

1 If someone is **persecuted**, they are treated cruelly and unfairly, often because of their race or beliefs. *Mr Weaver and his family have been persecuted by the authorities for their beliefs... The Communists began by brutally persecuting the Catholic Church. ...a persecuted minority.* VERB: be V-ed, V n, V-ed

2 If you say that someone is **persecuting** you, you mean that they are deliberately making your life difficult. *He also described his first wife as persistently persecuting him and ruining his life with her unreasonable demands... Vic was bullied by his father and persecuted by his sisters.* VERB =harass, V n

persecution /pɜːʳsɪkjuːʃᵊn/ **persecutions.** **Persecution** is cruel and unfair treatment of a person or group, especially because of their religious or political beliefs, or their race. ...*the persecution of minorities. ...victims of political persecution... We had to leave the country because of the persecutions.* ◆◇◇◇◇ N-UNCOUNT: also N in pl

persecutor /pɜːʳsɪkjuːtəʳ/ **persecutors.** The **persecutors** of a person or group treats them cruelly and unfairly, especially because of their religious or political beliefs, or their race. N-COUNT: usu pl

perseverance /pɜːʳsɪvɪərəns/. **Perseverance** is the quality of continuing with something even though it is difficult. N-UNCOUNT =persistence

persevere /pɜːʳsɪvɪəʳ/ **perseveres, persevering, persevered.** If you **persevere** with something, you keep trying to do it and do not give up, even though it is difficult. *This ability to persevere despite obstacles and setbacks is the quality people most admire in others. ...a school with a reputation for persevering with difficult and disruptive children... She persevered in her idea despite obvious objections raised by friends.* ◆◇◇◇◇ VERB =persist, V, V with n, V prep
♦ **persevering** *He is a persevering, approachable family man.* ADJ-GRADED

Persian /pɜːʒᵊn/ **Persians** ◆◆◆◇◇

1 Something that is **Persian** belongs or relates to the ancient kingdom of Persia, or sometimes to the modern state of Iran. ...*the Persian Empire. ...Persian poetry.* ADJ

2 **Persians** were the people who came from the ancient kingdom of Persia. N-COUNT

3 **Persian** carpets and rugs traditionally come from Iran. They are made by hand from silk or wool and usually have geometric patterns in rich colours. ADJ

4 **Persian** is the language that is spoken in Iran, and was spoken in the ancient Persian empire. N-UNCOUNT

Persian cat, Persian cats. A **Persian cat** is a type of cat which has a round face and long hair. N-COUNT

Persian Gulf. The **Persian Gulf** is the area of sea between Saudi Arabia and Iran. ◆◆◆◇◇ N-PROPER: usu *the* N

persimmon /pɜːʳsɪmən/ **persimmons.** A **persimmon** is a soft, orange fruit that looks rather like a large tomato. **Persimmons** grow on trees in hot countries. N-COUNT

persist /pəʳsɪst/ **persists, persisting, persisted** ◆◆◇◇◇

1 If something undesirable **persists**, it continues to exist. *Contact your doctor if the cough persists... These problems persisted for much of the decade.* VERB =continue, V

2 If you **persist** in doing something, you continue to do it, even though it is difficult or other people are against it. *Why does Britain persist in running down its defence forces?... He urged the United States to persist with its efforts to bring about peace... 'You haven't answered me,' she persisted... When I set my mind to something, I persist.* VERB: V *in*-ing, V *with/in* n, V with quote, V

persistence /pəʳsɪstəns/ ◆◇◇◇◇

1 If you have **persistence**, you continue to do something even though it is difficult or other people are against it. *Skill comes only with practice, patience and persistence... Chandra was determined to become a doctor and her persistence paid off.* N-UNCOUNT =perseverance

2 The **persistence** of something, especially something bad, is the fact of its continuing to exist for a long time. ...*an expression of concern at the persistence of inflation and high interest rates.* N-UNCOUNT: usu *the* N *of* n

persistent /pəʳsɪstənt/ ◆◆◇◇◇

1 Something that is **persistent** continues to exist or happen for a long time; used especially about bad or undesirable states or situations. *Her position as national leader has been weakened by persistent fears of another coup attempt... His cough grew more persistent until it never stopped... Shoppers picked their way through puddles caused by persistent rain.* ADJ-GRADED

2 Someone who is **persistent** continues trying to do something, even though it is difficult or other people are against it. ...*a persistent critic of the government's transport policies... He phoned again this morning. He's very persistent.* ADJ-GRADED

persistently /pəʳsɪstəntli/ ◆◇◇◇◇

1 If something happens **persistently**, it happens again and again or for a long time. *The allegations have been persistently denied by ministers... People with rail season tickets will get refunds if trains are persistently late.* ADV-GRADED: ADV with v, ADV adj =continually

2 If someone does something **persistently**, they do it with determination even though it is difficult or other people are against it. *Rachel gently but persistently imposed her will upon Douglas... Slowly, persistently, patiently, we will end this conflict.* ADV-GRADED: ADV with v

person /pɜːʳsᵊn/ **people, persons.** The usual word for 'more than one person' is **people**. The form **persons** is used as the plural in formal or legal language. ◆◆◆◆◆

1 A **person** is a man or a woman. *At least one person died and several others were injured... Everyone knows he's the only person who can do the job... My great-grandfather was a person of some importance here... The amount of sleep we need varies from person to person... They were both lovely, friendly people... At least fifty four people have been killed. and a further fifty are missing.* N-COUNT

2 **Persons** is used as the plural of **person** in formal, legal, and technical writing. ...*removal of the right of accused persons to remain silent... Persons who wish to adopt a child may contact their local social services department. ...persons with neck problems.* N-PLURAL

3 If you talk about someone **as a person**, you are considering them from the point of view of their real nature. *I've a lot of time for him as a person now... Robin didn't feel good about herself as a person.* N-COUNT

4 If someone says, for example,**'I'm an outdoor person'** or **'I'm not a coffee person'**, they are saying whether or not they like that particular activity or thing. *I am not a country person at all. I prefer the cities.* N-COUNT: *a* supp N

5 If you do something **in person**, you do it yourself rather than letting someone else do it for you. *You must collect the mail in person and take along some form of identification... She went to New York to receive the award in person.* PHRASE: PHR after v

6 If you meet, hear, or see someone **in person**, you are in the same place as them, rather than, for example, speaking to them on the telephone, writing to them, or seeing them on television. *It was the first time she had seen him in person. ...a trip to Hollywood to meet his favorite actor in person... She wanted to hear him sing in person.* PHRASE: PHR after v

7 Your **person** is your body; a formal use. *The suspect had refused to give any details of his identity and had carried no documents on his person.* N-COUNT: poss N

8 You can use **in the person of** when mentioning the name of someone you have just referred to in a more general or indirect way. *We had a knowledgeable guide in the person of George Adams.* PHRASE: PHR n

9 In grammar, we use the term **first person** when referring to 'I' and 'we', **second person** when referring to 'you', and **third person** when referring to 'he', 'she', 'it', 'they', and all other noun groups. **Person** is also used like this when referring to the verb forms that go with these pronouns and noun groups. • See also **first person**, **second person**, **third person**. N-COUNT: usu supp N

-person /-pɜːʳsᵊn/ **-people** or **-persons**
1 **-person** is added to numbers to form adjectives which indicate how many people are involved in something or can use something. **People** is not used in this way. *...two-person households. ...the spa's 32-person staff. ...his 1971 one-person exhibition. ...two-person tents.* COMB in ADJ: ADJ n
2 **-person** is added to nouns to form nouns which refer to someone who does a particular job or is in a particular group. **-person** is used by people who do not want to use a term which indicates whether someone is a man or a woman. **-people** can also be used in this way. *...Mrs. Sahana Pradhan, chairperson of the United Leftist Front. ...Jessie Marshall, a contemporary craftsperson... He had a staff of six salespeople working for him.* COMB in N-COUNT

persona /pəʳsoʊnə/ **personas** or **personae** /pəʳsoʊnaɪ/. Someone's **persona** is the aspect of their character or nature that they present to other people, perhaps in contrast to their real character or nature; a formal word used especially in American English. *The contradictions between her private life and the public persona are not always fully explored... From time to time he will take on a new persona.* • See also **persona non grata**. ◆◇◇◇◇ N-COUNT =image

personable /pɜːʳsənəbᵊl/. Someone who is **personable** has a pleasant appearance and character. *The people I met were intelligent, mature, personable.* ADJ-GRADED

personage /pɜːʳsənɪdʒ/ **personages**
1 A **personage** is a famous or important person; a formal use. *...MPs, film stars and other important personages.* N-COUNT =person
2 A **personage** is also a character in a play or book, or in history; a formal use. *There is no evidence for such a historical personage. ...Shakespeare's famous personages.* N-COUNT =character

personal /pɜːʳsənᵊl/ ◆◆◆◆◇
1 A **personal** opinion, quality, or thing belongs or relates to one particular person rather than to other people. *He learned this lesson the hard way – from his own personal experience... That's my personal opinion. ...books, furniture, and other personal belongings... The President arrived, followed by his personal bodyguard. ...an estimated personal fortune of almost seventy million dollars.* ADJ: ADJ n
2 If you give something your **personal** care or attention, you deal with it yourself rather than letting someone else deal with it. *...a business that requires a great deal of personal contact. ...a personal letter from the President's secretary... People do not mind paying a bit extra for the personal touch.* ADJ: usu ADJ n
3 **Personal** matters relate to your feelings, relationships, and health. *...teaching young people about marriage and personal relationships... You never allow personal problems to affect your performance... We sacrifice our personal lives to our work... Mr Knight said that he had resigned for personal reasons.* ADJ
4 **Personal** comments refer to someone's appearance or character in an offensive way. *...newspapers resorted to personal abuse... Myra was attacking something I'd written, and her attack got a little personal.* ADJ-GRADED
5 **Personal** care involves looking after your body and appearance. *...the new breed of men who take as much time and trouble over personal hygiene as the women in their lives.* ADJ: ADJ n
6 A **personal** relationship is one that is not connected with your job or public life. *He was a great and valued personal friend whom I've known for many many years... Mr Gamsakhurdia said he had a good personal relationship with Boris Yeltsin.* ADJ

personal assistant, personal assistants. A **personal assistant** is a person who does secretarial and administrative work for someone. The abbreviation PA is also used. N-COUNT

personal best, personal bests. A sports player's **personal best** is the highest score or fastest time that they have ever achieved. *She ran a personal best of 13.01 sec in the 100m hurdles.* ◆◇◇◇◇ N-COUNT: usu sing

personal column, personal columns. The **personal column** in a newspaper or magazine contains messages for individual people and advertisements of a private nature. N-COUNT

personal computer, personal computers. A **personal computer** is a computer which is used by one person, normally independently. The abbreviation 'PC' is also used. ◆◆◇◇◇ N-COUNT

personality /pɜːʳsənælɪti/ **personalities** ◆◆◆◇◇
1 Your **personality** is your whole character and nature. *She has such a kind, friendly personality... Through sheer force of personality Hugh Trenchard had got his way... These personality traits get passed on from generation to generation... The contest was as much about personalities as it was about politics.* N-VAR: usu with supp
2 If someone has **personality** or is **a personality**, they have a strong and lively character. *...a woman of great personality... He is such a personality—he is so funny.* N-VAR: usu with supp =character
3 You can refer to a famous person, especially in entertainment, broadcasting, or sport, as a **personality**. *...the radio and television personality, Jimmy Saville.* N-COUNT

personalize /pɜːʳsənᵊlaɪz/ **personalizes, personalizing, personalized;** also spelled **personalise** in British English. ◆◇◇◇◇
1 If an object **is personalized**, it is marked with the name or initials of its owner. *The clock has easy-to-read numbers and is personalised with the child's name and birth date.* ♦ **personalized** *...a unique collection of personalised presents, colourful toys & games. ...a Rolls-Royce with a personalised number plate.* VB: usu passive be V-ed; ADJ: ADJ n
2 If you **personalize** something, you do or design it specially according to the needs of an individual or to your own needs. *Personalising your car has never been cheaper. ...an ideal centre for professional men or women who need intensive, personalised French courses.* VERB =customize V n V-ed
3 If you **personalize** an argument, discussion, idea, or issue, you consider it from the point of view of individual people and their characters or relationships, rather than considering the facts in a general or abstract way. *Women tend to personalise rejection more than men... I hope they won't make the mistake of personalising the issue... The contest has become personalised, if not bitter.* VERB V n V-ed Also V

personally /pɜːʳsənəli/ ◆◆◆◇◇
1 You use **personally** to emphasize that you are giving your own opinion. *Personally I think it's a waste of time... You can disagree about them, and I personally do, but they are great ideas that have made people think... I think it's going to cause chaos personally but never mind.* ADV: ADV with cl PRAGMATICS
2 If you do something **personally**, you do it yourself rather than letting someone else do it. *The minister is returning to Paris to answer the allegations personally... When the great man arrived, the club's manager personally escorted him upstairs... You'll deal with it personally? Good.* ADV: ADV with v
3 If you meet or know someone **personally**, you meet or know them in real life, rather than knowing about them or knowing their work. *He did not know them personally, but he was familiar with their reputation... I have orders to deliver it to Mr Demiris personally... It is important for us to meet personally although we have been in touch in various ways.* ADV: ADV with v
4 You can use **personally** to say that something refers to an individual person rather than to other people. *To a far greater degree than other communist leaders, he was personally responsible for all that Romanians had suffered under his rule... In order for me to spend three months on something it has to interest me personally.* ADV: ADV with v, ADV adj
5 You can use **personally** to show that you are talking about someone's private life rather than their professional or public life. *This has taken a great toll on me personally and professionally... Personally he was quiet, modest and unobtrusive... Parks has a tendency to become personally involved with his photographic subjects.* ADV: oft ADV with cl

6 If you **take** someone's remarks **personally**, you are upset because you think that they are criticizing you in particular. *I take everything too personally... Remember, stick to the issues and don't take it personally.* PHRASE: V inflects

personal organizer, personal organizers; also spelled **personal organiser**. A **personal organizer** is a kind of diary which you can add pages to or remove pages from to keep the information up to date. Small computers with a similar function are also called **personal organizers**. N-COUNT

personal pronoun, personal pronouns. A **personal pronoun** is a pronoun such as 'I', 'you', 'she', or 'they' which is used to refer to the speaker or the hearer, or to a person or thing whose identity is clear, usually because they have already been mentioned. N-COUNT

personal space

1 If someone invades your **personal space**, they stand or lean too close to you, so that you feel uncomfortable. *I felt my body involuntarily stiffen against her invasion of my personal space.* N-UNCOUNT: oft poss N

2 If you need your **personal space**, you need time on your own, with the freedom to do something that you want to do or to think about something. *Self-confidence means being relaxed enough to allow your lover their personal space.* N-UNCOUNT: oft poss N

personal stereo, personal stereos. A **personal stereo** is a small cassette player with very light headphones, which people carry round so that they can listen to music while doing something else. N-COUNT =Walkman

persona non grata /pəʳsoʊnə nɒn grɑːtə/ **personae non gratae.** If someone becomes or is declared **persona non grata**, they become unwelcome or unacceptable because of something they have said or done. *The government has declared the French ambassador persona non grata and ordered him to leave the country.* PHRASE: PHR after v, v-link PHR

personification /pəʳsɒnɪfɪkeɪʃᵊn/ **personifications**

1 If you say that someone is the **personification** of a particular thing or quality, you mean that they are a perfect example of that thing or that they have a lot of that quality. *Janis Joplin was the personification of the '60s female rock singer... He was usually the personification of kindness.* N-SING: usu *the* N *of* n

2 A **personification** of something abstract is its representation in the form of a person. *...personifications of the attributes of Justice, Prudence and Truth.* N-VAR: usu N *of* n

personify /pəʳsɒnɪfaɪ/ **personifies, personifying, personified.** If you say that someone **personifies** a particular thing or quality, you mean that they seem to be a perfect example of that thing, or to have that quality to a very large degree. *She seemed to personify goodness and nobility. ...the world of inter-war decency as personified by Stanley Baldwin... On other occasions she can be charm personified.* ◆◇◇◇◇ VERB V n V-ed

personnel /pɜːʳsənel/ ◆◆◆◇◇

1 The **personnel** of an organization are the people who work for it. *Since 1954 Japan has never dispatched military personnel abroad... There has been very little renewal of personnel in higher education... If you need help at work, your Personnel Manager should be able to help.* N-PLURAL: oft N n =staff

2 **Personnel** is the department in a large company or organization that deals with employees, keeps their records, and helps with any problems they might have. *Her first job was in personnel.* N-UNCOUNT =human resources

person-to-person. **Person-to-person** telephone calls are a service offered by some telephone companies. If you make a person-to-person call, you specify that you want to talk to one person in particular. If that person cannot come to the telephone, you do not have to pay for the call. ADJ

perspective /pəʳspektɪv/ **perspectives** ◆◆◆◇◇

1 A particular **perspective** is a particular way of thinking about something, especially one that is influenced by your beliefs or experiences. *He says the death of his father 18 months ago has given him a new perspective on life. ...two different perspectives on the nature of adolescent development... Most literature on the subject of immigrants in France has been written from the perspective of the French themselves... I would like to offer a historical perspective.* N-COUNT: usu with supp =view

2 If you get something **in perspective** or **into perspective**, you judge its real importance by considering it in relation to everything else. If you get something **out of perspective**, you fail to judge its real importance in relation to everything else. *Remember to keep things in perspective... It helps to put their personal problems into perspective... Labor economist Harley Shaekin argues the cost needs to be viewed in perspective... I let things get out of perspective.* PHRASE: PHR after v

3 **Perspective** is the art of making some objects or people in a picture look further away than others. N-UNCOUNT

perspex /pɜːʳspeks/; also spelled **Perspex**. In Britain, **perspex** is a strong clear plastic which is sometimes used instead of glass. **Perspex** is a trademark. N-UNCOUNT: usu N n

perspicacious /pɜːʳspɪkeɪʃəs/. Someone who is **perspicacious** notices, realizes, and understands things quickly; a formal word. *Ordinary British people become steadily more worldly, knowing, perspicacious and cynical.* ♦ **perspicacity** /pɜːʳspɪkæsɪti/ *Channel 4's overseas buyers have foreseen the audience demand with their usual perspicacity.* ADJ-GRADED =perceptive, astute N-UNCOUNT =astuteness

perspiration /pɜːʳspɪreɪʃᵊn/. **Perspiration** is the liquid which comes out on the surface of your skin when you are hot or frightened; a formal word. *His hands were wet with perspiration. ...night sweats and excessive perspiration.* N-UNCOUNT =sweat

perspire /pəʳspaɪəʳ/ **perspires, perspiring, perspired.** When you **perspire**, a liquid comes out on the surface of your skin, because you are hot or frightened; a formal word. *He began to perspire heavily. ...mopping their perspiring brows.* VERB =sweat V V-ing

persuade /pəʳsweɪd/ **persuades, persuading, persuaded** ◆◆◆◇◇

1 If you **persuade** someone to do something, you cause them to do it by giving them good reasons for doing it. *My husband persuaded me to come... We're trying to persuade manufacturers to sell them here... They were eventually persuaded by the police to give themselves up.* ♦ **persuader, persuaders** *All great persuaders and salesmen are the same.* VERB V n to-inf Also V n *into* n/-ing, V n N-COUNT

2 If something **persuades** someone to take a particular course of action, it causes them to take that course of action because it is a good reason for doing so. *The Conservative Party's victory in April's general election persuaded him to run for President again... It was the lack of privacy that eventually persuaded us to move after Ben was born.* VERB V n to-inf

3 If you **persuade** someone that something is true, you say things that eventually make them believe that it is true. *I've persuaded Mrs Tennant that it's time she retired... We had managed to persuade them that it was worth working with us... Derek persuaded me of the feasibility of the idea.* ♦ **persuaded** *He is not persuaded of the need for electoral reform... I remain persuaded that the decisions we made last year were broadly right.* VERB =convince V n that V n *of* n ADJ-GRADED: v-link ADJ, ADJ *of* n, ADJ that

persuasion /pəʳsweɪʒᵊn/ **persuasions** ◆◇◇◇◇

1 **Persuasion** is the act of persuading someone to do something or to believe that something is true. *Only after much persuasion from Ellis had she agreed to hold a show at all... She was using all her powers of persuasion to induce the Griffins to remain in Rollway.* N-UNCOUNT

2 If you are **of** a particular **persuasion**, you have a particular belief or set of beliefs; a formal use. *It is a national movement and has within it people of all political persuasions... Fortunately for me, my kids are of the persuasion that their failings are of their own making.* N-COUNT: usu with supp

persuasive /pəʳsweɪsɪv/. Someone or something that is **persuasive** is likely to persuade someone to believe or do a particular thing. ◆◇◇◇◇ ADJ-GRADED

What do you think were some of the more persuasive arguments on the other side?... I can be very persuasive when I want to be... Michael Grade's persuasive powers overcame their objections. ♦ **persuasively** *...a trained lawyer who can present arguments persuasively.* [ADV-GRADED: ADV with v] ♦ **persuasiveness** *He was convinced that his eloquence and persuasiveness would tip them into supporting him.* [N-UNCOUNT]

pert /pɜːʳt/

1 If someone describes a young woman as **pert**, they mean that they like her because she is lively and cheeky. Some women find this use offensive. *A pert redhead in uniform read off the printed schedule for him. ...pert replies by servant girls.* [ADJ-GRADED; PRAGMATICS; =saucy]

2 If you say that someone has, for example, a **pert** bottom or nose, you mean that it is quite small and neat, and you think it is attractive. *But there is more to Charles than his pert bottom and hairy chest. ...the tiny drops of rain gleaming on her wide forehead and her pert nose.* [ADJ; PRAGMATICS]

pertain /pəʳteɪn/ **pertains, pertaining, pertained.** If one thing **pertains** to another, it relates, belongs, or applies to it; a formal word. *The restrictions he imposed pertained to the type and height of buildings and the activities for which they could be used... I would much rather that you asked Mrs Zuckerman any questions pertaining to herself. ...matters pertaining to naval district defense.* [◆◇◇◇◇; VERB; =relate; V *to* n; Also V]

pertinacious /pɜːʳtɪneɪʃəs/. Someone who is **pertinacious** continues trying to do something difficult rather than giving up quickly; a formal word. [ADJ-GRADED; =persistent, tenacious]

pertinent /pɜːʳtɪnənt/. Something that is **pertinent** is relevant to a particular subject; a formal word. *She had asked some pertinent questions... Pertinent information will be forwarded to the appropriate party. ...knowledge and skills pertinent to classroom teaching.* [◆◇◇◇◇; ADJ-GRADED: oft ADJ *to* n; =relevant] ♦ **pertinently** *'If we pay players, how far do we go?' Gresson asked pertinently... Where had they learned all this, or, more pertinently, why had they remembered it?* [ADV-GRADED: ADV with v, ADV with cl] ♦ **pertinence** *I do not see the pertinence of most of this material.* [N-UNCOUNT]

perturb /pəʳtɜːʳb/ **perturbs, perturbing, perturbed.** If something **perturbs** you, it worries you quite a lot; a fairly formal word. *What perturbs me is that magazine articles are so much shorter nowadays.* • See also **perturbed.** [VERB; =alarm, worry; V n]

perturbation /pɜːʳtəʳbeɪʃᵊn/ **perturbations**

1 A **perturbation** is a small change in the movement, quality, or behaviour of something, especially an unusual change; a technical use in science. *...perturbations in Jupiter's gravitational field.* [N-VAR]

2 **Perturbation** is worry caused by some event; a formal use. *This message caused perturbation in the Middle East Headquarters.* [N-UNCOUNT; =alarm]

perturbed /pəʳtɜːʳbd/. If someone is **perturbed** by something, they are worried by it; a fairly formal word. *He apparently was not perturbed by the prospect of a policeman coming to call... She was really quite perturbed at the prospect.* [ADJ-GRADED: usu v-link ADJ, oft ADJ *by/at* n, ADJ that; =alarmed]

pertussis /pəʳtʌsɪs/. **Pertussis** is the medical term for **whooping cough**. [N-UNCOUNT]

perusal /pəruːzᵊl/. **Perusal** of something such as a letter, article, or document is the action of reading it; a formal use. *Peter Cooke undertook to send each of us a sample contract for perusal... A perusal of the letters which we have published has satisfied him of the reality of our claim. ...a casual perusal of this list.* [N-UNCOUNT: also *a* N]

peruse /pəʳuːz/ **peruses, perusing, perused.** If you **peruse** something such as a letter, article, or document, you read it; a formal word. *In making our decision we perused the company's financial statements for the past five years... She found the information while she was perusing a copy of Life magazine.* [VERB; =read; V n]

Peruvian /pəruːviən/ **Peruvians. Peruvian** means belonging or related to Peru, or to its people or culture. *...the high, fertile valleys of the Peruvian Andes.* [◆◆◆◆◇; ADJ] ▶ A **Peruvian** is someone who is Peruvian. *The disease has killed thousands of Peruvians this year.* [N-COUNT]

pervade /pəʳveɪd/ **pervades, pervading, pervaded.** If something **pervades** a place or thing, it is a noticeable feature throughout it; a formal word. *The smell of sawdust and glue pervaded the factory. ...the corruption that pervades every stratum of the country... Throughout the book there is a pervading sense of menace.* [◆◇◇◇◇; VERB; V n; V-ing]

pervasive /pəʳveɪsɪv/. Something, especially something bad, that is **pervasive** is present or felt throughout a place or thing; a formal word. *...the pervasive influence of the army in national life... She lives with a pervasive sense of guilt.* [◆◇◇◇◇; ADJ-GRADED; PRAGMATICS] ♦ **pervasively** *It is a pervasively religious school.* [ADV-GRADED] ♦ **pervasiveness** *...the pervasiveness of computer technology.* [N-UNCOUNT]

perverse /pəʳvɜːʳs/. Someone who is **perverse** deliberately does things that are unreasonable or that result in harm for themselves. *It would be perverse to stop this healthy trend... Psychotherapists often take a perverse delight in criticizing other psychotherapists... In some perverse way the ill-matched partners do actually need each other.* [◆◇◇◇◇; ADJ-GRADED: oft *it* v-link ADJ to-inf; PRAGMATICS] ♦ **perversely** *She was perversely pleased to be causing trouble... Some saw it, perversely, as a victory.* [ADV-GRADED: usu ADV with v] ♦ **perversity** /pəʳvɜːʳsɪti/ *It would be wrong to continue out of perversity.* [N-UNCOUNT]

perversion /pəʳvɜːʳʃᵊn, -ʒᵊn/ **perversions** [◆◇◇◇◇]

1 You can refer to a sexual desire or action that you consider to be abnormal and unacceptable as a **perversion**. [N-VAR]

2 A **perversion** of something is a form of it that is bad or wrong, or the changing of it into this form. *What monstrous perversion of the human spirit leads a sniper to open fire on a bus carrying children?... The past has been scarred by countless perversions of justice.* [N-VAR: usu with supp]

pervert, perverts, perverting, perverted. The verb is pronounced /pəʳvɜːʳt/. The noun is pronounced /pɜːʳvɜːʳt/. [◆◇◇◇◇]

1 If you **pervert** something such as a process or society, you interfere with it so that it is not as good as it used to be or as it should be; a formal use. *Any reform will destroy and pervert our constitution... He perverted her mind.* [VERB; V n]

2 If someone **perverts the course of justice**, they deliberately do something that will make it difficult to discover who really committed a particular crime, for example, destroying evidence or lying to the police; a legal expression. *He was charged with conspiring to pervert the course of justice.* [PHRASE: V inflects]

3 If you say that someone is a **pervert**, you mean that you consider their behaviour, especially their sexual behaviour, to be immoral or unacceptable. [N-COUNT; =deviant]

perverted /pəʳvɜːʳtɪd/

1 If you say that someone is **perverted**, you mean that you consider their behaviour, especially their sexual behaviour, to be immoral or unacceptable. *You've been protecting sick and perverted men... His actions, to his small perverted mind, were surely forgivable.* [ADJ-GRADED]

2 You can use **perverted** to describe actions or ideas which you think are wrong, unnatural, or harmful. *...a perverted form of knowledge. ...the assertion of a perverted patriotism.* [ADJ-GRADED]

peseta /pəseɪtə/ **pesetas.** The **peseta** is the unit of money that is used in Spain. [◆◇◇◇◇; N-COUNT]

pesky /peski/. **Pesky** means irritating; an informal word. *...as if he were a pesky tourist asking silly questions of a busy man.* [ADJ: ADJ n]

peso /peɪsoʊ/ **pesos.** The **peso** is the unit of money that is used in Argentina, Colombia, Cuba, the Dominican Republic, Mexico, the Philippines, and Uruguay. [N-COUNT]

pessary /pesəri/ **pessaries**

1 A **pessary** is a small block of a medicine or a contraceptive chemical that a woman puts in her vagina. [N-COUNT]

2 A **pessary** is a device that is put in a woman's vagina to support her womb. [N-COUNT]

pessimism /pesɪmɪzəm/. **Pessimism** is the belief that bad things are going to happen. *...universal pessimism about the economy... My first reaction was one of deep pessimism.* ◆◇◇◇◇ N-UNCOUNT: oft N *about*/*over* n ≠optimism

pessimist /pesɪmɪst/ **pessimists.** A **pessimist** is someone who thinks that bad things are going to happen. *I'm a natural pessimist; I usually expect the worst... It looks as if the pessimists are being proved right.* ◆◇◇◇◇ N-COUNT ≠optimist

pessimistic /pesɪmɪstɪk/. Someone who is **pessimistic** thinks that bad things are going to happen. *Not everyone is so pessimistic about the future... Hardy has often been criticised for an excessively pessimistic view of life. ...one of the most pessimistic forecasts for 1992.* ◆◇◇◇◇ ADJ-GRADED: oft ADJ *about* n ≠optimistic ♦ **pessimistically** /pesɪmɪstɪkli/ *'But it'll not happen,' she concluded pessimistically.* ADV-GRADED: ADV with v

pest /pest/ **pests** ◆◆◇◇◇
1 **Pests** are insects or small animals which damage crops or food supplies. *...crops which are resistant to some of the major insect pests and diseases... Each year ten percent of the crop is lost to a pest called corn rootworm. ...new and innovative methods of pest control.* N-COUNT
2 You can describe someone, especially a child, as a **pest** if they keep bothering you; an informal use. *He climbed on the table, pulled my hair, and was generally a pest.* N-COUNT PRAGMATICS =nuisance

pester /pestəʳ/ **pesters, pestering, pestered.** If you say that someone **is pestering** you, you mean that they keep asking you to do something, or keep talking to you, and you find this annoying. *I thought she'd stop pestering me, but it only seemed to make her worse... I know he gets fed up with people pestering him for money. ...that creep who's been pestering you to go out with him.* ◆◇◇◇◇ VERB PRAGMATICS =badger, nag V n V n prep V n to-inf Also V

pesticide /pestɪsaɪd/ **pesticides. Pesticides** are chemicals which farmers put on their crops to kill harmful insects. ◆◆◇◇◇ N-MASS

pestilence /pestɪləns/ **pestilences. Pestilence** is any disease that spreads quickly and kills large numbers of people; a literary word. N-VAR =plague

pestilential /pestɪlenʃəl/
1 **Pestilential** is used to refer to things that cause disease or are caused by disease; a formal use. *...people who were dependent for their water supply on this pestilential stream. ...a pestilential fever.* ADJ: ADJ n
2 **Pestilential** animals destroy crops or exist in such large numbers that they cause harm; a formal use. *...the robust and pestilential grey squirrel.* ADJ: ADJ n

pestle /pesəl/ **pestles.** A **pestle** is a short rod with a thick round end. It is used for crushing things such as herbs, spices, or grain in a bowl called a mortar. N-COUNT

pesto /pestoʊ/. **Pesto** is an Italian sauce made from basil, garlic, pine nuts, cheese, and olive oil. N-UNCOUNT

pet /pet/ **pets, petting, petted** ◆◆◆◇◇
1 A **pet** is an animal that you keep in your home to give you company and pleasure. *It is plainly cruel to keep turtles as pets. ...a bachelor living alone in a flat with his pet dog... They would sell the meat off as pet food.* N-COUNT
2 Someone's **pet** theory, project, or subject is one that they particularly support or like. *He would not stand by and let his pet project be killed off... The example is chosen solely for its aptness in illustrating the current pet theory of the critic.* ADJ
3 Some people call the person they are talking to **'pet'** to show affection or friendliness. *It's all right, pet, let me do it.* N-VOC PRAGMATICS =dear
4 If you **pet** a person or animal, you pat or stroke them affectionately. *The policeman reached down and petted the wolfhound... I petted and smoothed her hair.* VERB =fondle V n

petal /petəl/ **petals.** The **petals** of a flower are the thin coloured or white parts which together form the flower. *...bowls of dried rose petals.* ◆◇◇◇◇ N-COUNT

petard /petɑːʳd/ **petards.** If someone who has planned to harm someone else is **hoist with** their **own petard** or **hoist by** their **own petard**, their plan in fact results in harm to themselves. *The students were hoist by their own petards, however, as Granada decided to transmit the programme anyway.* PHRASE: N inflects

peter /piːtəʳ/ **peters, petering, petered** ◆◆◇◇◇
peter out. If something **peters out**, it gradually comes to an end. *The six-month strike seemed to be petering out. ...where the road petered out into a rutted track.* PHRASAL VERB V P

Peter. If you say that someone **is robbing Peter to pay Paul**, you mean that they are transferring money from one group of people or place to another, rather than providing extra money; used showing disapproval. *Sometimes he was moving money from one account to another, robbing Peter to pay Paul.* PHRASE: *rob* inflects PRAGMATICS

pethidine /peθɪdɪn/. **Pethidine** is a drug given to people to stop them feeling pain. Women who are giving birth are often given pethidine. N-UNCOUNT

petit bourgeois /peti bʊəʳʒwɑː/; also spelled **petty bourgeois**. Someone or something that is **petit bourgeois** belongs or relates to the lower middle class; a formal expression, used showing disapproval. *He had a petit bourgeois mentality.* ADJ PRAGMATICS

petit bourgeoisie /peti bʊəʳʒwɑːziː/; also spelled **petty bourgeoisie. The petit bourgeoisie** are people in the lower middle class; a formal expression, used showing disapproval. N-SING-COLL: *the* N PRAGMATICS

petite /pətiːt/. If you describe a woman as **petite**, you are politely saying that she is small and slim. ◆◇◇◇◇ ADJ-GRADED PRAGMATICS

petit four /peti fɔːʳ/ **petits fours** or **petit fours. Petits fours** are very small sweet cakes or biscuits. They are sometimes served in restaurants with coffee at the end of a meal. N-COUNT: usu pl

petition /pətɪʃən/ **petitions, petitioning, petitioned** ◆◆◇◇◇
1 A **petition** is a document signed by a lot of people which asks a government or other official group to do a particular thing. *People feel so strongly that we recently presented the government with a petition signed by 4,500 people.* N-COUNT: usu with supp
2 A **petition** is an application to a court of law for some legal action to be taken; a formal use. *His lawyers filed a petition for all charges to be dropped... The court rejected their petition.* N-COUNT
3 If you **petition** someone in authority, you make a formal request to them. *...couples petitioning for divorce... All the attempts to petition the Congress had failed... Twenty-five of his supporters petitioned him to restore the monarchy... She's petitioning to regain custody of the child.* VERB V *for* n V n V n to-inf V to-inf Also V *for* n to-inf, V n *for* n

petitioner /pətɪʃənəʳ/ **petitioners**
1 A **petitioner** is a person who presents or signs a petition. N-COUNT
2 A **petitioner** is a person who brings a legal case to a court of law. *The judge awarded the costs of the case to the petitioners.* N-COUNT
3 In Britain, a **petitioner** is someone who goes to a court of law to ask for a divorce. *Both the petitioner and respondent provide for the upkeep of the children.* N-COUNT

pet name, pet names. A **pet name** is a special name that you use for a close friend or a member of your family instead of using their real name. N-COUNT

petrel /petrəl/ **petrels.** A **petrel** is a type of seabird which often flies a long way out from land. There are many varieties of petrel. N-COUNT

petrified /petrɪfaɪd/ ◆◇◇◇◇
1 If you are **petrified**, you are extremely frightened, perhaps so frightened that you cannot think or move. *I've always been petrified of being alone... Most people seem to be petrified of snakes.* ADJ-GRADED: oft ADJ *of* n/-ing, ADJ that =terrified
2 A **petrified** plant or animal has died and has gradually turned into stone. *...a block of petrified wood.* ADJ: ADJ n

petrify /petrɪfaɪ/ **petrifies, petrifying, petrified**
1 If something **petrifies** you, it makes you feel very frightened indeed. *Prison petrifies me and I don't want to go there.* VERB =terrify V n ♦ **petrifying** *I have to say it's the funniest thing I've ever done, but it was absolutely petrifying.* ADJ =terrifying
2 If something such as a society or institution **petrifies**, or if something else **petrifies** it, it ceases to V-ERG

change and develop; a formal use. *...the fear that a political deadlock may petrify economic initiatives.* V n Also V

petrochemical /petroʊkemɪkᵊl/ **petrochemicals;** also spelled **petro-chemical. Petrochemicals** are chemicals that are obtained from petroleum or natural gas. ◆◇◇◇◇ N-COUNT: usu pl

petrodollars /petroʊdɒləʳz/; also spelled **petro-dollars. Petrodollars** are a unit of money used to calculate how much a country has earned by exporting petroleum or natural gas. N-PLURAL

petrol /petrəl/. In British English, **petrol** is a liquid which is used as a fuel for motor vehicles. The usual American word is **gas** or **gasoline**. ◆◆◇◇◇ N-UNCOUNT

petrol bomb, petrol bombs. A **petrol bomb** is a simple bomb consisting of a bottle full of petrol with a cloth in it that is lit just before the bottle is thrown; used mainly in British English. ◆◇◇◇◇ N-COUNT

petroleum /pətroʊliəm/. **Petroleum** is oil which is found under the surface of the earth or under the sea bed. Petrol and paraffin are obtained from petroleum. ◆◆◇◇◇ N-UNCOUNT

petroleum jelly. Petroleum jelly is a soft, clear, jelly-like substance which is obtained from petroleum. It is used to make ointments for your skin or to grease surfaces. N-UNCOUNT

petrol station, petrol stations. In British English, a **petrol station** is a garage by the side of the road where petrol is sold and put into vehicles. The usual American expression is **gas station**. ◆◇◇◇◇ N-COUNT

petrol tank, petrol tanks. In British English, the **petrol tank** In a motor vehicle is the container for petrol. The usual American word is **gas tank**. N-COUNT

petticoat /petikoʊt/ **petticoats.** A **petticoat** is a piece of clothing like a thin skirt, which is worn under a skirt or dress. N-COUNT =slip, underskirt

pettifogging /petifɒgɪŋ/. You can describe an action or situation as **pettifogging** when you think that unnecessary attention is being paid to unimportant, boring details; an old-fashioned word. *...pettifogging bureaucratic interference.* ADJ: ADJ n PRAGMATICS

petting /petɪŋ/. **Petting** is the activity of kissing and stroking another person in a sexual way, but without having sexual intercourse; used especially of teenagers. N-UNCOUNT

petty /peti/ **pettier, pettiest** ◆◆◇◇◇

1 You can use **petty** to describe things such as rules, problems, or arguments which you think are trivial or unimportant. *...endless rules and petty regulations... The meeting degenerated into petty squabbling.* ADJ-GRADED: usu ADJ n PRAGMATICS

2 If you describe someone's behaviour as **petty**, you mean that they care too much about small, unimportant things and perhaps that they are unnecessarily unkind; used showing disapproval. *He was petty-minded and obsessed with detail... I think that attitude is a bit petty.* ♦ **pettiness** *Never had she met such spite and pettiness.* ADJ-GRADED: usu v-link ADJ PRAGMATICS; N-UNCOUNT

3 **Petty** is used of people or actions that are comparatively low in importance, rank, seriousness, or scale. *Wilson was not a man who dealt with petty officials. ...petty crime, such as handbag-snatching and minor break-ins.* ADJ: ADJ n

petty bourgeois. See **petit bourgeois**.

petty bourgeoisie. See **petit bourgeoisie**.

petty cash. Petty cash is money that is kept in the office of a company, ready to be used for making small payments when necessary; used mainly in British English. N-UNCOUNT

petty officer, petty officers. A **petty officer** is a non-commissioned officer in the navy. *Petty officers are the backbone of a navy. ...Petty Officer Amy Gaskill.* N-COUNT; N-TITLE

petulance /petʃʊləns/. **Petulance** is unreasonable, childish bad temper over something unimportant. *His petulance made her impatient.* N-UNCOUNT

petulant /petʃʊlənt/. Someone who is **petulant** is unreasonably angry and upset in a childish way. *His critics say he's just being silly and petulant... He picked the pen up with a petulant gesture.* ♦ **petulantly** *'I don't need help.' he said petulantly.* ADJ-GRADED; ADV-GRADED: ADV with v

petunia /pɪtjuːniə, AM -tuː-/ **petunias.** A **petunia** is a type of garden plant with pink, white or purple trumpet-shaped flowers. N-COUNT

pew /pjuː/ **pews.** A **pew** is a long wooden seat with a back, which people sit on in church. *Claire sat in the front pew.* ◆◇◇◇◇ N-COUNT

pewter /pjuːtəʳ/. **Pewter** is a grey metal which is made by mixing tin and lead. Pewter was often used in former times to make ornaments or containers for eating and drinking. *...pewter plates. ...the best 18th century pewter.* ◆◇◇◇◇ N-UNCOUNT: oft N n

pfennig /fenɪg/ **pfennigs.** A **pfennig** is a small German coin worth one hundredth of a mark. ◆◇◇◇◇ N-COUNT

PG /piː dʒiː/. In Britain, films that are labelled **PG** are not considered suitable for younger children to see without an adult being with them. **PG** is an abbreviation for 'parental guidance'. ◆◇◇◇◇ ADJ

PGCE /piː dʒiː siː iː/ **PGCEs.** In Britain, a **PGCE** is a teaching qualification that qualifies someone to teach in a state school. PGCE courses usually last one year and are taken by people who already have a degree in a subject other than teaching. **PGCE** is an abbreviation of 'Postgraduate Certificate of Education'. Compare **BEd**. N-COUNT

pH /piː eɪtʃ/. The **pH** of a solution indicates how acid or alkali the solution is. A pH of less than 7 indicates that it is an acid, and a pH of more than 7 indicates that it is an alkali. *...the pH of sea water... Skin is naturally slightly acidic and has a pH of 5.5... The fluid that emerges from the vents is acidic (pH 3) and hot.* ◆◇◇◇◇ N-UNCOUNT: also *a* N, oft N *of* n, N num

phalanx /fælæŋks/ **phalanxes** or **phalanges** /fəlændʒiːz/

1 A **phalanx** is a group of soldiers or police who are standing or marching close together ready to fight; a formal word. N-COUNT

2 A **phalanx** of people is a large group who are brought together for a particular purpose; a formal word. *...a phalanx of waiters with silver dishes balanced at shoulder height.* N-COUNT: usu N *of* n

phallic /fælɪk/. Something that is **phallic** is shaped like an erect penis. It can also relate to male sexual powers. ADJ-GRADED: usu ADJ n

phallus /fæləs/ **phalluses** or **phalli** /fælaɪ/

1 A **phallus** is a model of an erect penis, especially one used as a symbol in ancient religions. N-COUNT

2 A **phallus** is a penis; a technical term used in psychology. N-COUNT

phantasmagorical /fæntæzməgɒrɪkᵊl, AM -gɔːr-/. **Phantasmagorical** means dream-like or bizarre; a literary word. ADJ-GRADED: usu ADJ n

phantasy /fæntəzi/ **phantasies.** See **fantasy**.

phantom /fæntəm/ **phantoms** ◆◇◇◇◇

1 A **phantom** is a ghost. *They vanished down the stairs like two phantoms... The phantom used to appear unexpectedly, but mostly during the winter.* N-COUNT =ghost

2 You use **phantom** to describe something which you think you experience but which is not real. *She was always taking regular days off for what her colleagues considered phantom illnesses. ...phantom pregnancies.* ADJ: ADJ n

3 **Phantom** can refer to something that is done by an unknown person, especially something criminal. *Up to 30 victims of alleged 'phantom' withdrawals from high-street cash machines are to issue a High Court writ against their banks and building societies.* ADJ: ADJ n

4 **Phantom** is used to describe business organizations, agreements, or goods which do not really exist, but which someone pretends do exist in order to cheat people. *Mrs Collor had handed out contracts worth hundreds of thousands of dollars to phantom companies run by her relations.* ADJ: ADJ n

pharaoh /feəroʊ/ **pharaohs.** A **pharaoh** was a king of ancient Egypt. *On becoming Pharaoh of Upper and Lower Egypt, he declared a new religion based upon Aten, associated with the sun... Rameses II, Pharaoh of All Egypt.* N-COUNT; N-PROPER

Pharisee /færɪsiː/ **Pharisees.** The **Pharisees** were a group of Jews, mentioned in the New Testament of the Bible, who believed in strictly obeying the laws of Judaism. N-PROPER-PLURAL

pharmaceutical /fɑːʳməsuːtɪkəl/ **pharmaceuticals** ◆◆◇◇◇

1 **Pharmaceutical** means connected with the industrial production of medicine. *...a Swiss pharmaceutical company.* — ADJ: ADJ n

2 **Pharmaceuticals** are medicines. *Antibiotics were of no use, neither were other pharmaceuticals.* — N-PLURAL

pharmacist /fɑːʳməsɪst/ **pharmacists** ◆◇◇◇◇

1 A **pharmacist** is a person who is qualified to prepare and sell medicines. — N-COUNT =chemist

2 A **pharmacist** or a **pharmacist's** is a shop in which drugs and medicines are sold by a pharmacist; used mainly in British English. — N-COUNT =chemist, chemist's

pharmacology /fɑːʳməkɒlədʒi/.
Pharmacology is the branch of science relating to drugs and medicines. — N-UNCOUNT ♦ **pharmacological** /fɑːʳməkəlɒdʒɪkəl/ *As little as 50mg of caffeine can produce pharmacological effects.* — ADJ: ADJ n
♦ **pharmacologist, pharmacologists** *...a pharmacologist from the University of California.* — N-COUNT

pharmacopoeia /fɑːʳməkoʊpiːə/ **pharmacopoeias.** A **pharmacopoeia** is an official book that lists all the drugs that can be used to treat people in a particular country, and describes how to use them. — N-COUNT

pharmacy /fɑːʳməsi/ **pharmacies** ◆◇◇◇◇

1 A **pharmacy** is a shop or a department in a shop where medicines are sold or given out. *Make sure you understand exactly how to take your medicines before you leave the pharmacy. ...the pharmacy section of the drugstore.* — N-COUNT

2 **Pharmacy** is the job or the science of preparing medicines. *He spent four years studying pharmacy.* — N-UNCOUNT

phase /feɪz/ **phases, phasing, phased** ◆◆◆◇◇

1 A **phase** is a particular stage in a process or in the gradual development of something. *This autumn, 6000 residents will participate in the first phase of the project... Eritrea's long civil war appears to have reached its most critical phase... Most kids will go through a phase of being faddy about what they eat.* — N-COUNT =period

2 If an action or change **is phased** over a period of time, it is done in stages. *The redundancies will be phased over two years... Both countries agree on the need for a phased withdrawal of American forces from the Philippines.* — VB: usu passive be V-ed V-ed

3 If one thing is **out of phase** with another, the two things are not working or happening together as they should be, or are not in harmony with each other. If two things are **in phase**, they are happening or working together as they should be, or are in harmony with each other. *Oligarchic liberalism was increasingly out of phase with a rapidly changing society. ...uncomfortable jet-lag symptoms of indigestion and out-of-phase sleeping and waking.* — PHRASE: usu PHR after v, v-link PHR

phase in. If a new way of doing something **is phased in**, it is introduced gradually. *The Health Secretary told Parliament that the reforms would be phased in over three years... The change is part of the government's policy of phasing in Arabic as the official academic language.* — PHRASAL VERB be V-ed P V P n (not pron) Also V n P

phase out. If something **is phased out**, people gradually stop using it. *They said the present system of military conscription should be phased out... They phased out my job in favor of a computer.* — PHRASAL VERB be V-ed P V P n (not pron) Also V n P

PhD /piː eɪtʃ diː/ **PhDs** 

1 A **PhD** is a degree awarded to people who have done advanced research into a particular subject. **PhD** is an abbreviation for 'Doctor of Philosophy'. *He is more highly educated, with a PhD in Chemistry. ...an unpublished PhD thesis.* — N-COUNT

2 **PhD** is written after someone's name to indicate that they have a PhD. *...R.D. Combes, PhD.*

pheasant /fezənt/ **pheasants; pheasant** can also be used as the plural form. A **pheasant** is a long-tailed bird. Pheasants are often shot as a sport and then eaten. — ◆◇◇◇◇ N-COUNT ► **Pheasant** is a piece of this bird eaten as food. *...roast pheasant.* — N-UNCOUNT

phenomena /fɪnɒmɪnə/. **Phenomena** is the plural of **phenomenon**. — N-COUNT

phenomenal /fɪnɒmɪnəl/. Something that is **phenomenal** is so great or good that it is very unusual indeed. *Exports of Australian wine are growing at a phenomenal rate... The performances have been absolutely phenomenal.* — ◆◇◇◇◇ ADJ-GRADED =incredible ♦ **phenomenally** *Scots-born Annie, 37, has recently re-launched her phenomenally successful singing career... Food production once again rose phenomenally, by 4 per cent or more a year.* — ADV-GRADED: ADV adj/adv, ADV after v

phenomenology /fɪnɒmɪnɒlədʒi/. **Phenomenology** is a branch of philosophy which deals with consciousness, thought, and experience. — N-UNCOUNT ♦ **phenomenological** /fɪnɒmɪnəlɒdʒɪkəl/ *...a phenomenological approach to the definition of 'reality'.* — ADJ: usu ADJ n

phenomenon /fɪnɒmɪnən, AM -nɑːn/ **phenomena.** A **phenomenon** is something that is observed to happen or exist; a formal word. *...scientific explanations of natural phenomena... This form of civil disobedience isn't a particularly new phenomenon.* — ◆◆◇◇◇ N-COUNT

pheromone /ferəmoʊn/ **pheromones.** Some animals and insects produce chemicals called **pheromones** which affect the behaviour of other animals and insects of the same type, for example by attracting them sexually; a technical term in biology. — ◆◇◇◇◇ N-COUNT

phew /fjuː/. **Phew** is used in writing to represent the soft whistling sound that you make when you breathe out quickly, for example when you are relieved or shocked about something or when you are very hot. *Phew, what a relief!* — EXCLAM

phial /faɪəl/ **phials.** A **phial** is a small tube-shaped glass bottle used, for example, to hold medicine; a formal word. — N-COUNT

philanderer /fɪlændərəʳ/ **philanderers.** If you say that a man is a **philanderer**, you mean that he flirts a lot or has a lot of casual love affairs with women; a formal word used showing disapproval. — N-COUNT PRAGMATICS =womanizer

philandering /fɪlændərɪŋ/ **philanderings**

1 A **philandering** man flirts a lot and has a lot of casual affairs with women; used showing disapproval. *...her philandering husband.* — ADJ: ADJ n PRAGMATICS

2 **Philandering** means having casual affairs with women; used showing disapproval. *She intended to leave her husband because of his philandering.* — N-UNCOUNT: also N in pl PRAGMATICS

philanthropic /fɪlənθrɒpɪk/. A **philanthropic** person or organization freely gives money or other help to people who need it. *Some of the best services for the ageing are sponsored by philanthropic organizations.* — ADJ-GRADED: usu ADJ n

philanthropist /fɪlænθrəpɪst/ **philanthropists.** A **philanthropist** is someone who freely gives money and help to people who need it. — N-COUNT

philanthropy /fɪlænθrəpi/. **Philanthropy** is the giving of money to people who need it, without wanting anything in return. *...a retired banker well known for his philanthropy.* — N-UNCOUNT

philatelist /fɪlætəlɪst/ **philatelists.** A **philatelist** is a person who collects and studies postage stamps; a formal word. — N-COUNT

philately /fɪlætəli/. **Philately** is the hobby of collecting and learning about postage stamps; a formal word. — N-UNCOUNT

-phile /-faɪl/ or **-ophile** /-əfaɪl/ **-philes** or **-ophiles.** **-phile** or **-ophile** occurs in words which refer to someone who has a very strong liking for people or things of a particular kind. *...the operaphile Hirotaro Higuchi, president of the tour's chief sponsors. ...essential reading for the culture-hungry Yankophile.* — SUFFIX

philharmonic /fɪlɑːʳmɒnɪk/. A **philharmonic** orchestra is a large orchestra which plays classical music. *The Lithuanian Philharmonic Orchestra played Beethoven's Ninth Symphony.* — ◆◇◇◇◇ ADJ: ADJ n ► Also a noun. *He will conduct the Vienna Philharmonic in the final concert of the season.* — N-IN-NAMES

Philippine /fɪlɪpiːn/. **Philippine** means belonging or relating to the Philippines, or to their people or culture. — ◆◇◇◇◇ ADJ

philistine /fɪlɪstaɪn, AM -stiːn/ **philistines**

1 If you call someone a **philistine**, you mean that they do not care about or understand good art, — N-COUNT PRAGMATICS

music, or literature, and do not think that they are important; used showing disapproval.
2 You can use **philistine** to describe people or organizations who you think do not care about or understand the value of good art, music, or theatre; used showing disapproval. *...a philistine government that is blamed for allowing the arts to decline. ...a philistine city lacking in elegance.* ADJ-GRADED: ADJ n PRAGMATICS

philistinism /fɪlɪstɪnɪzəm/. **Philistinism** is the attitude or quality of not caring about, understanding, or liking good music; used showing disapproval. N-UNCOUNT PRAGMATICS

philology /fɪlɒlədʒi/. **Philology** is the study of words, especially the history and development of the words in a particular language or group of languages. N-UNCOUNT ♦ **philologist, philologists** N-COUNT

philosopher /fɪlɒsəfəʳ/ **philosophers** ◆◆◇◇◇
1 A **philosopher** is a person studies or writes about philosophy. *...the Greek philosopher Plato.* N-COUNT
2 If you refer to someone as a **philosopher**, you mean that they think deeply and seriously about life and other basic matters. N-COUNT

philosophic /fɪləsɒfɪk/. **Philosophic** means the same as **philosophical**. ADJ-GRADED

philosophical /fɪləsɒfɪkəl/ ◆◆◇◇◇
1 **Philosophical** means concerned with or relating to philosophy. *He was more accustomed to cocktail party chatter than to political or philosophical discussions.* ADJ ♦ **philosophically** /fɪləsɒfɪkli/ *Wiggins says he's not a coward, but that he's philosophically opposed to war.* ADV: ADV with v, ADV adj, ADV with cl
2 Someone who is **philosophical** does not get upset when disappointing or disturbing things happen; used showing approval. *Lewis has grown philosophical about life.* ADJ-GRADED PRAGMATICS ♦ **philosophically** *She says philosophically: 'It could have been far worse.'* ADV-GRADED: ADV after v

philosophize /fɪlɒsəfaɪz/ **philosophizes, philosophizing, philosophized;** also spelled **philosophise** in British English. If you say that someone **is philosophizing**, you mean that they are talking or thinking about important subjects such as life, often in a boring or pointless way. *He philosophized, he admitted, not because he was certain of establishing the truth, but because it gave him pleasure. ...a tendency to philosophize about racial harmony.* VERB =theorize V V *about/on* n Also V with quote ♦ **philosophizing** *The General was anxious to cut short the philosophizing and get down to more urgent problems.* N-UNCOUNT

philosophy /fɪlɒsəfi/ **philosophies** ◆◆◆◇◇
1 **Philosophy** is the study or creation of theories about basic things such as the nature of existence, knowledge, thought, or about how people should live. *He studied philosophy and psychology at Cambridge. ...a very detailed discussion of traditional Chinese philosophy.* N-UNCOUNT
2 A **philosophy** is a particular set of ideas that a philosopher has. *...the philosophies of Socrates, Plato, and Aristotle. ...a whole spectrum of political philosophies.* N-COUNT: usu with supp =ideology
3 A **philosophy** is a particular theory that someone has about how to live or how to deal with a particular situation. *The best philosophy is to change your food habits to a low-sugar, high-fibre diet... When I interviewed Shakira I felt in tune with her philosophy of life... Annie's work reflects her philosophy that life is full of mysteries.* N-COUNT: usu with supp, oft N *of* n, N that

phlegm /flem/. **Phlegm** is the thick yellowish substance that develops in your throat and at the back of your nose when you have a cold. N-UNCOUNT =mucus

phlegmatic /flegmætɪk/. Someone who is **phlegmatic** stays calm even when upsetting or exciting things happen; a formal word. *...a most phlegmatic man, steadily working on as the rain splashed down.* ADJ-GRADED =stoic ≠nervous

-phobe /-foʊb/ or **-ophobe** /-əfoʊb/ **-phobes** or **-ophobes. -phobe** or **-ophobe** occurs in words which refer to someone who has a very strong, irrational fear or hatred of people or things of a particular kind. *Its design makes it suitable for the computerphobe who just wants to type and see something come out looking right.* SUFFIX

phobia /foʊbiə/ **phobias.** A **phobia** is a very strong irrational fear or hatred of something. *The man had a phobia about flying.* ◆◇◇◇◇ N-COUNT: oft N *about/of* n/-ing

-phobia /-foʊbiə/. **-phobia** occurs in words which refer to a very strong, irrational fear or hatred of people or things of a particular kind. *The place seethed with Europhobia... Technophobia increases with age.* SUFFIX

phobic /foʊbɪk/ **phobics**
1 A **phobic** feeling or reaction results from or is related to a strong, irrational fear or hatred of something. *Many children acquire a phobic horror of dogs.* ADJ
2 Someone who is **phobic** has a strong, irrational fear or hatred of something. *In Victorian times people were phobic about getting on trains. They weren't used to it.* ADJ-GRADED ► Also a noun. *Social phobics quake at the thought of meeting strangers.* N-COUNT

-phobic /-foʊbɪk/. **-phobic** occurs in words which describe something relating to a strong, irrational fear or hatred of people or things of a particular kind. *Curtiz seemed to have a particular taste for Anglophobic items.* SUFFIX

phoenix /fiːnɪks/ **phoenixes**
1 A **phoenix** is an imaginary bird which, according to ancient myths, burns itself to ashes every five hundred years and is then born again. N-COUNT: usu sing
2 If you describe someone or something as a **phoenix**, you mean that they return again after seeming to disappear or be destroyed. *Out of the ashes of the economic shambles, a phoenix of recovery can arise.* N-SING

phone /foʊn/ **phones, phoning, phoned** ◆◆◆◆◇
1 The **phone** is an electrical system that you use to talk to someone else in another place, by dialling a number on a piece of equipment and speaking into it. *'I didn't tell you over the phone,' she said. 'I didn't know who might be listening... She looked forward to talking to her daughter by phone... Do you have an address and phone number for him?* N-SING: usu *the* N, also *by* N =telephone
2 The **phone** is the piece of equipment that you use when you dial someone's phone number and talk to them. *Two minutes later the phone rang... Doug's 14-year-old son Jamie answered the phone.* N-COUNT: usu *the* N =telephone
● See also **mobile phone**.
3 If you say that someone picks up or puts down **the phone**, you mean that they lift or replace the receiver. *She picked up the phone, and began to dial Maurice Campbell's number... Trembling, she put the phone down. It rang again almost immediately.* N-SING: usu *the* N =receiver
4 When you **phone** someone, you dial their phone number and speak to them by phone. *He'd phoned Laura to see if she was better... I got more and more angry as I waited for her to phone.* VERB =telephone, ring V n V
5 If you say that someone is **on the phone**, you mean that they are speaking to someone else by phone. *She's always on the phone, wanting to know what I've been up to.* PHRASES v-link PHR, PHR after v
6 If you are **on the phone**, you have a phone in your home or place of work, so that you can be contacted by phone; used mainly in British English. *The Frosts were not on the phone.* v-link PHR

phone up. When you **phone** someone **up**, you dial their phone number and speak to them by phone. *Phone him up and tell him to come and have dinner with you one night.* PHRASAL VERB V n P Also V P n (not pron)

phone book, phone books. A **phone book** is a book that contains an alphabetical list of the names, addresses, and telephone numbers of the people in a town or area. N-COUNT =directory

phone booth, phone booths
1 A **phone booth** is a place in a station, hotel, or other public building where there is a public telephone. N-COUNT
2 In American English, a **phone booth** is a small shelter in the street in which there is a public telephone. The British term is **phone box** or **call box**. N-COUNT =call box, phone box

phone box, phone boxes. In British English, a **phone box** is a small shelter in the street in which there is a public telephone. The American term is **phone booth**. N-COUNT

phone call, phone calls. If you **make a phone call**, you dial somebody's phone number and speak to them by phone. *Wait there for a minute. I have to make a phone call.* ◆◆◇◇◇ N-COUNT

phone-in, phone-ins. A **phone-in** is a programme on radio or television in which people telephone with questions or opinions and their calls are broadcast; used mainly in British English. *She took part in a BBC radio phone-in programme.* ◆◇◇◇◇ N-COUNT

phoneme /founi:m/ **phonemes.** A **phoneme** is the smallest unit of sound which is significant in a language. N-COUNT

phone-tapping. Phone-tapping is the activity of listening secretly to someone's phone conversations using special electronic equipment. In most cases phone-tapping is illegal. *There have also been claims of continued phone-tapping and bugging.* ● See also **tap**. N-UNCOUNT

phonetics /fənetɪks/; the form **phonetic** is used as a modifier.

1 **Phonetics** is the study of speech sounds; a technical term in linguistics. N-UNCOUNT

2 **Phonetic** means relating to the sound of a word or to the sounds that are used in languages. *...the Japanese phonetic system, with its relatively few, simple sounds... I thought a phonetic spelling might aid in pronunciation.* ♦ **phonetically** /fənetɪkli/ *It's wonderful to watch her now going through things phonetically learning how to spell things.* ADJ: usu ADJ n; ADV: ADV with v

phoney /founi/ **phoneys;** also spelled **phony.** ◆◇◇◇◇

1 If you describe something as **phoney**, you disapprove of it because it is false rather than genuine; a fairly informal use. *He'd telephoned with some phoney excuse she didn't believe for a minute... He didn't really have that moustache. It was phoney... He used a phoney accent.* ADJ-GRADED PRAGMATICS

2 If you say that someone is **phoney**, you disapprove of them because they are pretending to be someone that they are not in order to deceive people; a fairly informal use. *He looks totally phoney to me. ...phoney 'experts'.* ► Also a noun. *'He's false, a phoney,' Harry muttered.* ADJ-GRADED PRAGMATICS; N-COUNT

phoney war. A **phoney war** is when two opposing groups are openly hostile towards each other or are in competition with each other, as if they were at war, but there is no real fighting; used mainly in British English. *There is a chance that the phoney war of the past three months will turn into real fighting.* N-SING

phonic /fɒnɪk/. **Phonic** means to do with the sounds of speech. *...the phonic system underlying a particular language.* ADJ: usu ADJ n

phonograph /founəgrɑ:f, -græf/ **phonographs.** A **phonograph** is a record player; mainly used in American English or in old-fashioned British English. *... old phonograph records.* N-COUNT

phonology /fənɒlədʒi/. **Phonology** is the study of speech sounds in a particular language; a technical term in linguistics. N-UNCOUNT

phony /founi/. See **phoney**.

phosphate /fɒsfeɪt/ **phosphates.** A **phosphate** is a chemical compound that contains phosphorus. Phosphates are often used in fertilizers. ◆◇◇◇◇ N-MASS

phosphorescence /fɒsfəresᵊns/. **Phosphorescence** is a glow or soft light which is produced in the dark without using heat. N-UNCOUNT

phosphorescent /fɒsfəresᵊnt/. A **phosphorescent** object or colour glows in the dark with a soft light, but gives out little or no heat. *...phosphorescent paint.* ADJ: usu ADJ n =luminescence

phosphoric acid /fɒsfɒrɪk æsɪd, AM -fɔ:r-/. **Phosphoric acid** is a type of acid which contains phosphorus. N-UNCOUNT

phosphorus /fɒsfərəs/. **Phosphorus** is a chemical element. It is yellow-white and poisonous, it glows faintly, and it burns on contact with air. ◆◇◇◇◇ N-UNCOUNT

photo /foutou/ **photos.** A **photo** is the same as a **photograph**. *We must take a photo!... I've got a photo of him on the wall.* ◆◆◆◆◆ N-COUNT

photo- /foutou-/. **Photo-** is added to nouns and adjectives in order to form other nouns and adjectives which refer or relate to photography or photographic processes, or to light. *...an eight-day photo-trip to northern Greece. ...a photo-sensitive detector system.* PREFIX

photocopier /foutoukɒpiəʳ/ **photocopiers.** A **photocopier** is a machine which quickly copies documents onto paper by photographing them. N-COUNT

photocopy /foutoukɒpi/ **photocopies, photocopying, photocopied** ◆◇◇◇◇

1 A **photocopy** is a copy of a document made using a photocopier. N-COUNT

2 If you **photocopy** a document, you make a copy of it using a photocopier. *Staff photocopied the cheque before cashing it.* VERB V n

photo-finish, photo-finishes. If the end of a race is a **photo-finish**, two or more of the competitors cross the finishing line so close together that a photograph of the finish has to be examined to decide who has won. *He was just beaten in a photo-finish.* N-COUNT

Photofit /foutoufɪt/ **Photofits.** In British English, a **Photofit** is a picture of someone wanted by the police which is made up of several photographs or drawings of different facial features. Photofit is a trademark. *The girl sat down with a police artist to compile a Photofit of the attacker.* N-COUNT

photogenic /foutədʒenɪk/. Someone who is **photogenic** looks nice in photographs. *I've got a million photos of my boy. He's very photogenic.* ADJ-GRADED

photograph /foutəgrɑ:f, -græf/ **photographs, photographing, photographed** ◆◆◆◆◇

1 A **photograph** is a picture that is made using a camera. *He wants to take some photographs of the house... Her photograph appeared on the front page of The New York Times.* N-COUNT

2 When you **photograph** someone or something, you use a camera to obtain a picture of them. *She photographed the children... I hate being photographed... They were photographed kissing on the platform.* VERB V n be V-ed -ing

photographer /fətɒgrəfəʳ/ **photographers.** A **photographer** is someone who takes photographs as a job or hobby. *...a group of TV cameramen and press photographers. ...a keen amateur photographer with a special interest in natural history subjects.* ◆◆◆◇◇ N-COUNT

photographic /foutəgræfɪk/ ◆◆◇◇◇

1 **Photographic** means connected with photographs or photography. *...photographic equipment... The bank is able to provide photographic evidence of who used the machine.* ♦ **photographically** /foutəgræfɪkli/ *...photographically reproduced copies of his notes.* ADJ: usu ADJ n; ADV

2 If you have a **photographic** memory, you are able to remember things in great detail after you have seen them. *He had a photographic memory for maps.* ADJ: usu ADJ n

photography /fətɒgrəfi/. **Photography** is the skill, job, or process of producing photographs. *Photography is one of her hobbies. ...some of the top names in fashion photography.* ◆◆◇◇◇ N-UNCOUNT

photojournalism /foutoudʒɜ:ʳnəlɪzəm/; also spelled **photo-journalism**. **Photojournalism** is a form of journalism in which stories are presented mainly through photographs rather than words. *...some of the finest photo-journalism of the Civil Rights era.* ♦ **photojournalist, photojournalists** *...the agency for many international photojournalists, Magnum Photos.* N-UNCOUNT; N-COUNT

photon /foutɒn/ **photons.** A **photon** is a particle of light; a technical term in physics. ◆◇◇◇◇ N-COUNT

photo opportunity, photo opportunities. If a politician or other public figure arranges a **photo opportunity**, they invite the newspapers and television to photograph them doing something which they think will interest or impress the public. N-COUNT

photostat /foutəstæt/ **photostats.** A **photostat** is a particular type of photocopy. **Photostat** is a trademark. *...a photostat of the actual script.* N-COUNT

photosynthesis /fo̱ʊθoʊ sɪ̱nθəsɪs/. **Photosynthesis** is the way that green plants make their food using sunlight; a technical term in biology. N-UNCOUNT

phrasal verb /fre̱ɪzᵊl vɜ:ʳb/ **phrasal verbs.** A **phrasal verb** is a combination of a verb and an adverb or preposition, for example 'shut up' or 'look after', which together have a particular meaning. N-COUNT

phrase /fre̱ɪz/ **phrases, phrasing, phrased** ♦♦♦◇◇

1 A **phrase** is a short group of words that people often use as a way of referring to something or saying something. The meaning of a phrase is often not obvious from the meaning of the individual words in it. In this dictionary phrases are labelled PHR in the grammar notes beside the entries. *He used a phrase I hate: 'You have to be cruel to be kind.' ...the American phrase 'laying an egg' meaning to fail at something.* N-COUNT

2 A **phrase** is a small group of words which forms a unit, either on its own or within a sentence. *A writer spends many hours going over and over a scene – changing a phrase here, a word there.* N-COUNT

3 If you **phrase** something in a particular way, you express it in words in that way. *I would have phrased it quite differently... The speech was carefully phrased... They phrased it as a question.* VERB =express, put V n adv V n *as* n

4 If someone has a particular **turn of phrase**, they have a particular way of expressing themselves in words. *Rose's stories weren't bad; she had a nice turn of phrase. ...Schwarzkopf's distinctive turn of phrase.* • **to coin a phrase**: see **coin**. PHRASE: N inflects

phra̱se book, phrase books. A **phrase book** is a book used by people travelling to a foreign country. It has lists of useful words and expressions, together with the translation of each word or expression in the language of that country. *We bought a Danish phrase book.* N-COUNT

phraseology /fre̱ɪziɒ̱lədʒi/. If something is expressed using a particular type of **phraseology**, it is expressed in words and expressions of that type. *This careful phraseology is clearly intended to appeal to various sides of the conflict.* N-UNCOUNT: usu with supp =terminology

phrasing /fre̱ɪzɪŋ/

1 The **phrasing** of something that is said or written is the exact words that are chosen to express the ideas in it. *The phrasing of the question was vague. ...a letter to the Pope, which necessitates careful phrasing.* N-UNCOUNT: oft N *of* n =wording

2 The **phrasing** of someone who is singing, playing a piece of music, acting, or reading something aloud is the way in which they divide up the work by pausing slightly in appropriate places. *...certain features that make a performance good or bad – the timing, the phrasing, and so on.* N-UNCOUNT

phrenology /frɪnɒ̱lədʒi/. **Phrenology** is the study of the size and shape of people's skulls in the belief that it can reveal what their characters and abilities are. *...the ancient science of phrenology.* ♦ **phrenologist, phrenologists** *Queen Victoria had her own personal phrenologist.* N-UNCOUNT N-COUNT

physical /fɪ̱zɪkᵊl/ **physicals** ♦♦♦♦◇

1 **Physical** qualities, actions, or things are connected with a person's body, rather than with their mind. *...the physical and mental problems caused by the illness... Physical activity promotes good health... The attraction between them is physical.* ♦ **physically** *You may be physically and mentally exhausted after a long flight. ...disabled people who cannot physically use a telephone.* ADJ-GRADED: usu ADJ n ADV: ADV adj, ADV with v

2 **Physical** things are real things that can be touched and seen, rather than ideas or concepts. *Physical and ideological barriers had come down in Eastern Europe. ...physical evidence to support the story. ...the physical similarities among the towns.* ♦ **physically** *...physically cut off from every other country.* ADJ: usu ADJ n ADV

3 **Physical** means relating to the structure, size, or shape of something that can be touched and seen. *...the physical characteristics of the terrain. ...the physical properties (weight, volume, hardness, etc.) of a substance.* ADJ: ADJ n

4 **Physical** means connected with physics or the laws of physics. *...the physical laws of combustion and thermodynamics.* ADJ: ADJ n

5 Someone who is **physical** touches people a lot, either in an affectionate way or in a rough way. *We decided that in the game we would be physical and aggressive.* ADJ-GRADED

6 **Physical** is used in expressions such as **physical love** and **physical relationships** to refer to sexual relationships between people. *the book celebrated the sublime joys of physical love... It had been years since they had shared any meaningful form of physical relationship.* ADJ: ADJ n

7 A **physical** is a medical examination, done in order to see if someone is fit and well enough to do a particular job or to join the army. *Bob failed his physical... Routine physicals are done by a nurse.* N-COUNT =medical

phy̱sical educa̱tion. **Physical education** is the school subject in which children do physical exercises or take part in physical games and sports. N-UNCOUNT =PE, games

phy̱sical sci̱ence, physical sciences. The **physical sciences** are branches of science such as physics, chemistry, and geology that are concerned with natural forces and with things that do not have life. *...the rapid growth of interest in both the natural and physical sciences.* N-COUNT: usu pl

physician /fɪzɪ̱ʃᵊn/ **physicians.** A **physician** is a doctor; mainly used in formal American English or in old-fashioned British English. ♦♦◇◇◇ N-COUNT

physicist /fɪ̱zɪsɪst/ **physicists.** A **physicist** is a person who does research connected with physics or who studies physics. *...a nuclear physicist.* ♦♦◇◇◇ N-COUNT

physics /fɪ̱zɪks/. **Physics** is the scientific study of forces such as heat, light, sound, pressure, gravity, and electricity, and the way that they affect objects. *...the laws of physics. ...experiments in particle physics.* ♦♦◇◇◇ N-UNCOUNT

physio /fɪ̱zioʊ/ **physios**

1 A **physio** is a **physiotherapist**; an informal use. *The athlete is checked by their physio or doctor.* N-COUNT =physiotherapist

2 **Physio** is **physiotherapy**; used mainly in informal British English. *I have been for some physio.* N-UNCOUNT =physiotherapy

physiognomy /fɪ̱ziɒ̱nəmi/ **physiognomies.** Your **physiognomy** is your face, especially when it is considered to show your real character; a formal word. *...an unmistakably Irish Celtic physiognomy.* N-COUNT =face

physiology /fɪ̱ziɒ̱lədʒi/ ♦◇◇◇◇

1 **Physiology** is the scientific study of how people's and animals' bodies function, and of how plants function. *...the Nobel Prize for Medicine and Physiology.* ♦ **physiologist, physiologists** *... a retired plant physiologist.* N-UNCOUNT N-COUNT

2 The **physiology** of a human or animal's body or of a plant is the way that it functions. *...the physiology of respiration. ...insect physiology.* ♦ **physiological** /fɪ̱ziəlɒ̱dʒɪkᵊl/ *...the physiological effects of stress.* ♦ **physiologically** *Camels are among the most physiologically resilient creatures on Earth.* N-UNCOUNT: usu with supp ADJ ADV: ADV adj, ADV with v

physiotherapist /fɪ̱zioʊθe̱rəpɪst/ **physiotherapists.** A **physiotherapist** is a person who treats people using physiotherapy. ♦◇◇◇◇ N-COUNT =physio

physiotherapy /fɪ̱zioʊθe̱rəpi/. **Physiotherapy** is medical treatment for problems of the joints, muscles, or nerves, which involves doing exercises or having part of your body massaged or warmed. *He'll need intensive physiotherapy.* N-UNCOUNT

physique /fɪzi̱:k/ **physiques.** Someone's **physique** is the shape and size of their body. *He has the physique and energy of a man half his age. ...men of powerful physique.* ♦◇◇◇◇ N-COUNT: usu sing, usu with supp =build

pi /pa̱ɪ/. **Pi** is a number, approximately 3.142, which is equal to the circumference of a circle divided by its diameter. It is usually represented by the Greek letter π. NUM

pianissimo /piæ̱nɪsɪmoʊ/. A piece of music that is played **pianissimo** is played very quietly; a technical term in music. ADV: ADV after v ≠fortissimo

pianist /pi̱:ənɪst, AM piæ̱n-/ **pianists.** A **pianist** is a person who plays the piano. *...the brilliant Romanian pianist Radu Lupu.* ♦◇◇◇◇ N-COUNT

piano, pianos. Pronounced /piænoʊ/ for meaning 1, and /piɑːnoʊ/ for meaning 2. ◆◆◇◇◇
1 A **piano** is a large musical instrument with a row of black and white keys. When you press these keys with your fingers, little hammers hit wire strings inside the piano which vibrate to produce musical notes. *I taught myself how to play the piano... He started piano lessons at the age of 7. ...sonatas for cello and piano. ...Rachmaninov's Fourth Piano Concerto.* • See also **grand piano, upright piano.** N-VAR: oft *the* N
2 A piece of music that is played **piano** is played quietly; a technical term in music. ADV; ADV after v
pianoforte /piænoʊfɔːʳteɪ/ **pianofortes.** A **pianoforte** is a piano; an old-fashioned word. N-COUNT
pianola /piːænoʊlə/ **pianolas.** In British English, a **pianola** is a type of mechanical piano. When you press the pedals, air is forced through holes in a roll of paper and presses the keys to play a tune. Pianola is a trademark. N-VAR: oft *the* N =player piano
piazza /piætsə/ **piazzas.** A **piazza** is a large open square in a town or city, especially in Italy. *They were seated at a table outside a pub in a pleasant piazza close by St Paul's... Turn south at Mulinello to reach Piazza Armerina.* ◆◇◇◇◇ N-COUNT: oft in names before n
pic /pɪk/ **pics** ◆◇◇◇◇
1 A **pic** is a film; an informal word. *'Angels with Dirty Faces' is a Cagney gangster pic.* N-COUNT =picture
2 A **pic** is a photograph; an informal word. *Photographer Weegee shot to fame with his shocking pics of New York crime in the 30s.* N-COUNT =picture
picador /pɪkədɔːʳ/ **picadors.** In bullfighting, a **picador** is a man on a horse who attacks the bull with a lance in the early stages of the fight in order to make it angry or weaken it. N-COUNT
picaresque /pɪkəresk/. A **picaresque** story is one in which a dishonest but likeable hero travels around and has lots of exciting adventures; a literary term. *...a picaresque novel about the life and crimes of Joey Blueglass.* ADJ: usu ADJ n
piccolo /pɪkəloʊ/ **piccolos.** A **piccolo** is a small musical instrument that is like a flute but produces higher notes. N-VAR
pick /pɪk/ **picks, picking, picked** ◆◆◆◆◇
1 If you **pick** a particular person or thing, you choose that one. *Mr Nowell had picked ten people to interview for six sales jobs in London... I had deliberately picked a city with a tropical climate.* VERB =choose V n
2 You can refer to the best things or people in a particular group as **the pick** of that group. *The boys here are the pick of the under-15 cricketers in the country... We had the pick of suits from the shop.* N-SING: *the* N, usu *the* N *of* n =cream
3 When you **pick** flowers, fruit, or leaves, you break them off the plant or tree and collect them. *She used to pick flowers in the Cromwell Road... He helps his mother pick fruit.* VERB V n
4 If you **pick** something from a place, you remove it from there with your fingers or your hand. *He picked the napkin from his lap and placed it alongside his plate... He picked the telephone off the wall bracket.* VERB V n prep
5 If you **pick your nose** or **teeth**, you remove dried mucus from your nostrils or food from your teeth. *Edgar, don't pick your nose, dear... He had just had a meal and was picking his teeth after it.* VERB V n
6 If you **pick** a fight or quarrel **with** someone, you deliberately cause one. *He picked a fight with a waiter and landed in jail... He was clearly in a mood to pick a quarrel with anybody.* VERB V n *with* n Also V n
7 If someone such as a thief **picks** a lock, they open it without a key, for example by using a piece of wire. *He picked each lock deftly, and rifled the papers within each drawer.* VERB V n
8 A **pick** is the same as a **pickaxe.** N-COUNT
9 See also **hand-pick, ice pick.**
10 If you **pick and choose,** you carefully choose only things that you really want and reject the others. *As a vocational teacher I could pretty much pick and choose my work... We, the patients, cannot pick and choose our doctors.* PHRASES Vs inflect, usu PHR n
11 If you **have** your **pick of** a group of things, you are able to choose any of them that you want. *Here is an actress who could have her pick of any part... Klein could have had his pick of the world's top models.* V inflects, PHR *of* n
12 If you are told to **take** your **pick**, you can choose any one that you like from a group of things. *Accountants can take their pick of company cars... Take your pick from ten luxury hotels... See our selection of autumn favourites and take your pick.* V inflects, oft PHR *of/from* n
13 If you **pick** your **way** across an area, you walk across it very carefully in order to avoid obstacles or dangerous things. *The girls were afraid of snakes and picked their way along with extreme caution... I moved away from the shack and picked my way among the rubble.* V inflects, PHR prep/adv
14 • to **pick** someone's **brains**: see **brains.** • to **pick holes in** something: see **hole.** • to **pick** someone's **pocket**: see **pocket.**
pick at. If you **pick at** the food that you are eating, you eat only very small amounts of it. *Sarah picked at a plate of cheese for supper, but she wasn't really hungry.* PHRASAL VERB =nibble V P n
pick off. If someone **picks off** people or aircraft, they shoot them down one by one, aiming carefully at them from a distance. *Both groups on either side are just picking off innocent bystanders... Any decent shot with telescopic sights could pick us off at random.* PHRASAL VERB V P n (not pron) V n P
pick on PHRASAL VERB
1 If someone **picks on** you, they repeatedly criticize you unfairly or treat you unkindly. *Bullies pick on younger children... Mr Adams was repeatedly bullied and picked on by manageress Elizabeth Archer.* =get at V P n
2 If someone **picks on** a particular person or thing, they choose them for special attention or treatment which is often unpleasant. *When you have made up your mind, pick on a day when you will not be under much stress... I picked on simple things – rice and peas, meat and bread.* =single out V P n
pick out PHRASAL VERB
1 If you **pick out** someone or something, you recognize them when it is difficult to see them, for example because they are among a large group. *The detective-constable picked out the words with difficulty... Steven describes himself as 'a regular guy – you couldn't pick me out of a crowd'.* =spot V P n (not pron) V n P
2 If you **pick out** someone or something, you choose them from a group of people or things. *I will pick out three new plays particularly... I have been picked out to represent the whole team... There are so many great newscasters it's difficult to pick one out.* =choose, select V P n (not pron) V n P
3 If part of something **is picked out** in a particular colour, it is painted in that colour so that it can be seen clearly beside the other parts. *The name is picked out in gold letters over the shop-front.* usu passive =highlight *be* V-ed P
pick over. If you **pick over** a quantity of things, you examine them carefully, for example to reject the ones you do not want. *Pick over the fruit and pile on top of the cream.* PHRASAL VERB V P n (not pron)
pick up PHRASAL VERB
1 When you **pick** something **up**, you lift it up. *He picked his cap up from the floor and stuck it back on his head... Ridley picked up a pencil and fiddled with it.* V n P V P n (not pron)
2 When you **pick** yourself **up** after you have fallen or been knocked down, you stand up rather slowly. *Anthony picked himself up and set off along the track.* V pron-refl P
3 When you **pick up** someone or something that is waiting to be collected, you go to the place where they are and take them away, often in a car. *We drove to the airport the next morning to pick up Susan... She was going over to her parents' house to pick up some clean clothes for Owen... I picked her up at Covent Garden to take her to lunch with my mother.* V P n (not pron) V n P
4 If someone **is picked up** by the police, they are arrested and taken to a police station. *Rawlings had been picked up by police at his office... The police picked him up within the hour.* *be* V-ed P V n P Also V P n (not pron)
5 If you **pick up** something such as a skill or an idea, you acquire it without effort over a period of

time; an informal use. *Where did you pick up your English?... Young people are picking up ideas about good drugs and bad drugs.* V P n (not pron) Also V n P

6 If you **pick up** someone you do not know, you talk to them and try to start a sexual relationship with them; an informal use. *He had picked her up at a nightclub on Kallari Street, where she worked as a singer.* V n P Also V P n (not pron)

7 If you **pick up** an illness, you get it from somewhere or something. *They've picked up a really nasty infection from something they've eaten.* =catch V P n (not pron) Also V n P

8 If a piece of equipment, for example a radio or a microphone, **picks up** a signal or sound, it receives it or detects it. *We can pick up Italian television... The crew of Philante picked up a distress signal from the yacht Sans Peur III.* =receive V P n (not pron)

9 If you **pick up** something, such as a feature or a pattern, you discover or identify it. *Consumers in Europe are slow to pick up trends in the use of information technology.* V P n (not pron)

10 If someone **picks up** a point or topic that has already been mentioned, or if they **pick up on** it, they refer to it or develop it. *Can I just pick up that gentleman's point?... I'll pick up on what I said a couple of minutes ago.* V P n (not pron) V P P n Also V n P

11 If trade or the economy of a country **picks up**, it improves. *Chinese officials hope that trade will pick up when the two countries switch to hard currency... Industrial production is beginning to pick up.* =improve V P

12 If someone **picks up**, or their health **picks up**, they get better. *A good dose of tonic will help you to pick up.* V P

13 If you **pick** someone **up on** something that they have said or done, you mention it and tell them that you think it is wrong. *If I may pick you up on that point... Don't pick me up on words.* V n P P n

14 See also **pick-up**.

15 When you **pick up the pieces** after a disaster, you do what you can to get the situation back to normal again. *Do we try and prevent problems or do we try and pick up the pieces afterwards?... She died, and somehow I never picked up the pieces and started again.* PHRASES V inflects

16 When a vehicle **picks up speed**, it begins to move more quickly. *Brian started the engine and pulled away slowly, but picked up speed once he entered Oakwood Drive.* V inflects =accelerate

pickaxe /pɪkæks/ **pickaxes;** also spelled **pickax** in American English. A **pickaxe** is a large tool consisting of a curved, pointed piece of metal with a long handle joined to the middle. Pickaxes are used for breaking up rocks or the ground. N-COUNT =pick

picker /pɪkəʳ/ **pickers.** A fruit **picker** or cotton **picker**, for example, is a person who picks fruit or cotton, usually for money. ◆◇◇◇◇ N-COUNT: usu supp N

picket /pɪkɪt/ **pickets, picketing, picketed** ◆◇◇◇◇

1 When a group of people, usually trade union members, **picket** a place of work, they stand outside it in order to protest about something, to prevent people from going in, or to persuade the workers to join a strike. *The miners went on strike and picketed the power stations... 100 union members and supporters picketed outside.* ► Also a noun. *...forty demonstrators who have set up a twenty four hour picket.* ♦ **picketing** *There was widespread picketing of mines where work was continuing.* VERB V n V N-COUNT N-UNCOUNT

2 Pickets are people who are picketing a place of work. *Ten hotels were damaged by pickets in the weekend strike of hotel workers... The strikers agreed to remove their pickets and hold talks with the government.* N-COUNT

picket fence, picket fences. A **picket fence** is a fence made of pointed wooden sticks fixed into the ground at regular intervals, supported by pieces of wood nailed horizontally across. N-COUNT

picket line, picket lines. A **picket line** is a group of pickets outside a place of work. *The miners are trying to get factory workers to join them on the picket line... No one tried to cross the picket lines.* ◆◇◇◇◇ N-COUNT

pickings /pɪkɪŋz/. You can refer to the money that can be made easily in a particular place or area of activity as the **pickings**. *Traditional hiding places are easy pickings for experienced burglars... Other rich pickings, including season ticket sales, are expected to exceed last year's £3m.* N-PLURAL: usu supp N

pickle /pɪkᵊl/ **pickles, pickling, pickled** ◆◇◇◇◇

1 Pickles are vegetables or fruit, sometimes cut into pieces, which have been kept in vinegar or salt water for a long time so that they have a strong, sharp taste. *Another strong Yorkshire country tradition is making pickles and chutneys.* N-PLURAL

2 Pickle is a spicy fruity sauce that is made by boiling chopped vegetables and fruit with spices for several hours and then left to cool. *...jars of pickle.* N-MASS

3 When you **pickle** food, you keep it in vinegar or salt water so that it does not go bad and it develops a strong, sharp taste. *Select your favourite fruit or veg and pickle them while they are still fresh... Herrings can be salted, smoked and pickled.* ♦ **pickling** *Small pickling onions can be used instead of sliced ones.* VERB V n N-UNCOUNT: oft N n

4 If you are in **a pickle**, you are in a difficult and awkward situation; an informal use. *Companies find themselves in a pickle when their markets change... Caroline had sure as hell got herself into a pickle this time.* N-SING: a N =mess, jam

pickled /pɪkᵊld/ ◆◇◇◇◇

1 Pickled food, such as vegetables, fruit, and fish, has been kept in vinegar or salt water to preserve them. *...a jar of pickled fruit. ...little tins of pickled herring.* ADJ: usu ADJ n

2 In British English, if you say that someone is **pickled**, you mean that they are drunk; an informal use. *She was already pickled.* ADJ-GRADED: usu v-link ADJ =plastered

pick-me-up, pick-me-ups. A **pick-me-up** is something that you have or do when you are tired or depressed in order to make you feel better; an informal word. *When you crave a pick-me-up, don't reach for chocolate or coffee – try peppermint oil instead... This is an ideal New Year pick-me-up – a five day holiday in the Bahamas.* N-COUNT =tonic

pick 'n' mix; also spelled **pick and mix. Pick 'n' mix** is used to describe a way of assembling a collection of things by choosing a lot of different elements and putting them together. *It is, as some senior officials conceded, a pick'n'mix approach to policy. ...a pick-and-mix selection of fabrics and wallpapers.* ADJ: ADJ n

pickpocket /pɪkpɒkɪt/ **pickpockets.** A **pickpocket** is a person who steals things from people's pockets or handbags in public places. N-COUNT

pick-up, pick-ups; also spelled **pickup.** ◆◆◆◇◇

1 A **pick-up** or a **pick-up truck** is a small truck with low sides that can be easily loaded and unloaded. N-COUNT

2 A **pick-up** in trade or in a country's economy is an improvement in it. *...a pick-up in the housing market... The economy remains deep in recession with few signs of a pick-up.* N-SING: usu N *in* n =improvement

3 A **pick-up** takes place when someone picks up a person or thing that is waiting to be collected. *The company had pick-up points in most cities... Trains will operate from Waterloo with a pick-up stop at Ashford.* N-COUNT: usu N n

4 When a **pick-up** takes place, someone talks to a person in a friendly way in the hope of having a casual sexual relationship with them; an informal use. *They had come to the world's most famous pick-up joint.* N-COUNT

picky /pɪki/. Someone who is **picky** is difficult to please and only likes a small range of things; an informal word. *Some people are very picky about who they choose to share their lives with... Everyone knows children are picky eaters.* ADJ-GRADED =fussy, choosy

picnic /pɪknɪk/ **picnics, picnicking, picnicked** ◆◆◇◇◇

1 When people have a **picnic**, they eat a meal out of doors, usually in a field or a forest, or at the beach. *We're going on a picnic tomorrow... We'll take a picnic lunch.* N-COUNT

2 When people **picnic** somewhere, they have a picnic. *Afterwards, we picnicked on the riverbank.* VERB V

...*such a perfect day for picnicking.* ♦ **picnicker, picnickers** ...*fires started by careless picnickers.* V-ing N-COUNT

3 If you say that an experience, task, or activity **is no picnic**, you mean that it is quite difficult or unpleasant; an informal expression. *Emigrating is no picnic.* PHRASE: V inflects

pictorial /pɪktɔːriəl/. **Pictorial** means using or relating to pictures. ...*a pictorial history of the Special Air Service.* ...*pictorial images.* ◆◇◇◇◇ ADJ: usu ADJ n
♦ **pictorially** *Each section is explained pictorially.* ADV

picture /pɪktʃəʳ/ **pictures, picturing, pictured** ◆◆◆◆◇

1 A **picture** consists of lines and shapes which are drawn, painted, or printed on a surface and show a person, thing, or scene. *A picture of Rory O'Moore hangs in the dining room at Kildangan.* ...*drawing a small picture with coloured chalks.* N-COUNT

2 A **picture** is a photograph. *The tourists have nothing to do but take pictures of each other... The Observer carries a big front-page picture of rioters in a litter-strewn street.* N-COUNT

3 **Television pictures** are the scenes which you see on a television screen. ...*heartrending television pictures of human suffering.* N-COUNT: usu pl

4 If someone or something **is pictured** somewhere, usually in a newspaper or magazine, they appear in a photograph or picture. *The golfer is pictured on many of the front pages, kissing his trophy as he holds it aloft.* ...*a woman who claimed she had been pictured dancing with a celebrity in Stringfellows nightclub... The rattan and wrought-iron chair pictured here costs £125.* VB: usu passive be V-ed be V-ed -ing V-ed

5 You can refer to a film as a **picture**. *Warner Communications Inc. has refused to distribute the picture in the United States.* ...*a director of epic action pictures.* N-COUNT =motion picture

6 In British English, if you go to **the pictures**, you go to a cinema to see a film. The American word is **movies**. *We're going to the pictures tonight... I'd rather see it at the pictures than on video anyway.* N-PLURAL: the N =cinema

7 If you have a **picture** of something in your mind, you have a clear idea or memory of it in your mind as if you were actually seeing it. *They have in their mind a picture of what an alcoholic should look like... We are just trying to get our picture of the whole afternoon straight... I tried to put the picture from my mind.* N-COUNT: oft N of n =image

8 If you **picture** something in your mind, you think of it and have such a clear memory or idea of it that you seem to be able to see it. *He pictured her with long black braided hair... I never would have pictured this as her home... He pictured Claire sitting out in the car, waiting for him... She pictured herself working with animals... I tried to picture the place, but could not.* VERB =imagine V n prep V n -ing V n Also V n adj

9 A **picture** of something is a description of it or an indication of what it is like. *I'll try and give you a better picture of what the boys do... Her book paints a bleak picture of the problems women now face... From the files that have now been released, a truer picture emerges.* N-COUNT: usu sing, with supp

10 When you refer to the **picture** in a particular place, you are referring to the situation there. *But as with other charitable bodies, these figures mask the true picture... It's a similar picture across the border in Ethiopia.* N-SING: oft the N =situation

11 If you **get the picture**, you understand the situation, especially one which someone is describing to you. *Luke never tells you the whole story, but you always get the picture.* PHRASES V inflects =get the idea

12 If you say that someone is **in the picture**, you mean that they are involved in the situation that you are talking about. If you say that they are **out of the picture**, you mean that they are not involved in the situation. *Some Cambodians don't believe it will ever be safe to go home as long as the Khmer Rouge are still in the picture... Sometimes security was so tight that people who might have had something important to offer were left out of the picture.* v-link PHR, PHR after v

13 You use **picture** to describe what someone looks like. For example, if you say that someone is **a picture of health** or **the picture of misery**, you mean that they look extremely healthy or extremely miserable. *We found her standing on a chair, the picture of terror, screaming hysterically.* v-link PHR

14 If you **put** someone **in the picture**, you tell them about a situation which they need to know about. *Has Inspector Fayard put you in the picture?* V inflects

picture book, picture books; also spelled **picture-book**. A **picture book** is a book with a lot of pictures in and not much writing. Many picture books are intended for children. N-COUNT

picture postcard, picture postcards; also spelled **picture-postcard** for meaning 2.

1 A **picture postcard** is a postcard with a photograph of a place on it. People often buy picture postcards of places they visit when on holiday. N-COUNT

2 You can use **picture postcard** to describe a place that is attractive and unspoiled. ...*picture-postcard Normandy villages.* ADJ: ADJ n =picturesque

picture rail, picture rails; also spelled **picture-rail**. A **picture rail** is a continuous narrow piece of wood which is fixed round a room just below the ceiling. Pictures can be hung from it using string and hooks. N-COUNT

picturesque /pɪktʃəresk/ ◆◇◇◇◇

1 A **picturesque** place is attractive, interesting, and unspoiled. *Sir Peter Terry and his family live in the picturesque village of Milford.* ► You can refer to picturesque things as **the picturesque**. ...*lovers of the picturesque.* ♦ **picturesquely** ...*the shantytowns perched picturesquely on the hillsides.* ADJ-GRADED N-SING: the N ADV-GRADED

2 **Picturesque** words and expressions are unusual or poetical. *Every inn had a quaint and picturesque name – the Black Locust Inn, the Blueberry Inn, the Old Cutter Inn.* ♦ **picturesquely** *The historian Yakut described it picturesquely as a 'mother of castles'.* ADJ-GRADED =colourful ADV-GRADED: ADV with v

picture window, picture windows. A **picture window** is a window containing one large sheet of glass, so that people have a good view of what is outside. N-COUNT

piddle /pɪdᵊl/ **piddles, piddling, piddled.** To **piddle** means to urinate; an informal word. V

piddling /pɪdəlɪŋ/. **Piddling** means small or unimportant; an informal word. ...*arguing over piddling amounts of money.* ADJ-GRADED: usu ADJ n =paltry

pidgin /pɪdʒɪn/

1 **Pidgin** is a language which is a mixture of two other languages. **Pidgin** is not anyone's native language but is used when people who speak different languages communicate with each other. *He's at ease speaking pidgin with the factory workers and guys on the docks.* N-UNCOUNT

2 If someone is speaking in, for example, **pidgin** English or **pidgin** Italian, they may be speaking in a mixture of two languages. Or, they may be speaking another language badly or their own language simply, in an attempt to communicate. *The restaurant owner could only speak pidgin English.* ADJ: ADJ n

pie /paɪ/ **pies** ◆◆◇◇◇

1 A **pie** consists of meat, vegetables, or fruit baked in pastry. ...*a pork pie.* ...*apple pie and custard.* N-VAR
• See also **cottage pie, shepherd's pie.**

2 If you describe an idea, plan, or promise of something good as **pie in the sky**, you mean that you think that it is very unlikely to happen. *The true regeneration of devastated Docklands seemed like pie in the sky... He can't help thinking it's all just 'pie in the sky' talk.* • to **eat humble pie**: see **humble.** PHRASE: usu v-link PHR

piebald /paɪbɔːld/. A **piebald** animal has patches of black and white on it. ...*a piebald pony.* ADJ

piece /piːs/ **pieces, piecing, pieced** ◆◆◆◆◇

1 A **piece of** something is an amount of it that has been broken off, torn off, or cut off. ...*a piece of cake.* ...*a piece of wood.* ...*a few words scrawled on a piece of paper... Cut the ham into pieces... Do you want another piece?* N-COUNT: usu N of n =bit

2 A **piece** of an object is one of the individual parts or sections which it is made of, especially a part that can be removed. ...*assembling objects out of standard pieces... The equipment was taken down the shaft in pieces.* N-COUNT =bit

3 A **piece of land** is an area of land. *People struggle to get the best piece of land.* N-COUNT: usu N of n

4 You can use **piece** with many uncount nouns to refer to an individual thing of a particular kind. For example, you can refer to some advice as a **piece of advice**. *When I produced this piece of work, my lecturers were very critical... It is a highly complex piece of legislation. ...an interesting piece of information. ...a sensitive piece of equipment used to detect radiation. ...a sturdy piece of furniture... What essential piece of clothing would you take?*
N-COUNT: N *of* n =bit

5 You can refer to an article in a newspaper or magazine, a musical composition, a broadcast, or a play as a **piece**. *I disagree with Andrew Russell over his piece on British Rail. ...a vaguely familiar orchestral piece... The day after his death there was a piece about him on television.*
N-COUNT

6 You can refer to a work of art or a high-quality decorative object as a **piece**; a formal use. *Each piece is unique, an exquisite painting of a real person, done on ivory... None of the pieces is insured.*
N-COUNT

7 You can refer to specific coins as **pieces**. For example, a 10p **piece** is a coin that is worth 10p.
N-COUNT: supp N

8 The **pieces** which you use when you play a board game such as chess or backgammon are the specially shaped objects which you move around on the board.
N-COUNT

9 In American English, **a piece of** something is part of it or a share of it. *They got a small piece of the net profits and a screen credit. ...the disclosure that Texas Air might sell a piece or all of Continental.*
QUANT: QUANT *of* def-n

10 See also **museum piece**, **party piece**, **set piece**.

11 If you **give** someone **a piece of** your **mind**, you tell them very clearly that you think they have behaved badly; an informal expression. *How very thoughtless. I'll give him a piece of my mind.*
PHRASES V inflects

12 If something with several different parts is **all of a piece**, each part is consistent with the others. If one thing is **of a piece with another**, it is consistent with it. *At its peak in the Thirties, Underground design and architecture was all of a piece... The essays that Parsons completed in the latter part of his life are of a piece with his earlier work.*
v-link PHR, oft PHR *with* n

13 If someone or something is still **in one piece** after a dangerous journey or experience, they are safe and not damaged or hurt. *...providing that my brother gets back alive and in one piece from his mission.*
v-link PHR, PHR after v =intact

14 If you **say** your **piece**, you say everything you want to say about a particular matter without being interrupted, although people may be wanting to express opposing views. *I'll answer your questions when I've said my piece.*
V inflects

15 If something is smashed to **pieces**, is taken **to pieces**, or falls **to pieces**, it is broken or comes apart so that it is in separate pieces. *If the shell had hit the boat, it would have blown it to pieces... He took it all to pieces, cleaned it inside and out and put it together again... Do you wear your old clothes until they fall to pieces?.*
PHR after v =to bits

16 If you **go to pieces**, you are so upset or nervous that you lose control of yourself and cannot do what you should do; an informal expression. *She's a strong woman, but she nearly went to pieces when Arnie died.*
V inflects

17 If someone **tears** you **to pieces**, **pulls** your work **to pieces**, or **picks** your work **to pieces**, they criticize you or your work very severely; an informal expression. *He made numerous errors of fact and was torn to pieces during the subsequent question time... In 1987, Labour's programme was picked to pieces by Nigel Lawson.*
V inflects

18 If you say that someone is **a nasty piece of work**, you mean that they are very unkind or unpleasant; used mainly in informal British English.
usu v-link PHR PRAGMATICS

19 • **a piece of the action**: see **action**. • **bits and pieces**: see **bit**. • **a piece of cake**: see **cake**. • **to pick up the pieces**: see **pick up**.

piece together
PHRASAL VERB

1 If you **piece together** the truth about something, you gradually discover it. *They've pieced together his movements for the last few days before his death... In the following days, Francis was able to piece together what had happened... Frank was beginning to piece things together.*
V P n (not pron) V P what V n P

2 If you **piece** something **together**, you gradually make it by joining several things or parts together. *This process is akin to piecing together a jigsaw puzzle... Doctors painstakingly pieced together the broken bones.*
=assemble V P n (not pron) Also V n P

-piece /-piːs/. **-piece** combines with numbers to form adjectives indicating that something consists of a particular number of items. *...his well-cut three-piece suit. ...a hundred-piece dinner service. ...a four-piece band from Belgium.*
COMB in ADJ: ADJ n

pièce de résistance /pies də reɪzɪstɒns, AM -zɪstɑːns/. The **pièce de résistance** of a collection or series of things is the most impressive thing in it; a formal word. *The pièce de résistance, however, was a gold evening gown.*
N-SING

piecemeal /piːsmiːl/. If describe a change or process as **piecemeal**, you disapprove of it because it happens gradually and usually at irregular intervals, although this may not be satisfactory. *Instead of the government's piecemeal approach, what is needed is a radical shake-up of 16-19 education. ...piecemeal changes to the constitution.* ► Also an adverb. *The government plans to sell the railways piecemeal to the private sector... It was built piecemeal over some 130 years.*
◆◇◇◇◇ ADJ-GRADED: usu ADJ n PRAGMATICS =sporadic
ADV: ADV after v

piecework /piːswɜːʳk/; also spelled **piece-work**. If you do **piecework**, you are paid according to the amount of work that you do rather than the length of time that you work. *All my men are on piece-work... The tobacco workers were paid on a piecework basis.*
N-UNCOUNT

pie chart, pie charts. A **pie chart** is a circle divided into sections to show the relative proportions of a set of things.
N-COUNT

pied-à-terre /pieɪd ɑː teəʳ/ **pieds-à-terre.** A **pied-à-terre** is a small house or flat, especially in a town, which you own or rent but only use occasionally. *...my London pied-à-terre.*
N-COUNT

pier /pɪəʳ/ **piers.** A **pier** is a platform sticking out into water, usually the sea, which people walk along or use when getting onto or off boats. *...Brighton Pier.*
◆◇◇◇◇ N-COUNT: oft in names after n

pierce /pɪəʳs/ **pierces, piercing, pierced**
◆◆◇◇◇

1 If a sharp object **pierces** something, or if you **pierce** something with a sharp object, the object goes into it and makes a hole in it. *One bullet pierced the left side of his chest... Pierce the skin of the potato with a fork.*
VERB V n

2 If you have your ears or some other part of your body **pierced**, you have a small hole made through them so that you can wear a piece of jewellery in them. *I'm having my ears pierced on Saturday. ...her pierced ears with their tiny gold studs.*
VERB *have* n V-ed V-ed Also V n

3 If a light or sound **pierces** something or **pierces through** it, it is suddenly seen or heard very strongly or clearly; a literary use. *A spotlight pierced the darkness... Then he spoke, in a voice that pierced the thick air... The clock striking the hour pierced through his thoughts.*
VERB =penetrate V n V *through* n

4 If a thought, feeling, or sound **pierces** someone's heart, it makes them experience a feeling, especially sadness, very strongly; a literary use. *This sound, like all music, pierced my heart like a dagger.*
VERB V n

5 If someone **pierces** something that acts as a barrier, they manage to get through it. *German armoured divisions pierced the Russian lines.*
VERB =penetrate V n

piercing /pɪəʳsɪŋ/
◆◇◇◇◇

1 A **piercing** sound or voice is high-pitched and very sharp and clear in an unpleasant way. *A piercing scream split the air. ...a piercing whistle.*
♦ **piercingly** *She screamed again, piercingly.*
ADJ-GRADED: usu ADJ n
ADV-GRADED

2 If someone has **piercing** eyes or a **piercing** stare, they seem to look at you very intensely; used in written English. *...his sandy blond hair and piercing blue eyes... He fixes you with a piercing stare.*
♦ **piercingly** *Ben looked at him piercingly.*
ADJ-GRADED: usu ADJ n =penetrating
ADV-GRADED

3 If you describe a quality or feeling as **piercing**, you mean that it makes you experience a feeling,
ADJ-GRADED: ADJ n

especially sadness, very strongly; a literary use. *She was aware of a sharp piercing regret.*

4 A **piercing** wind makes you feel very cold. ADJ-GRADED

pierrot /piːəroʊ/ **pierrots.** A **pierrot** is a clown who wears a white costume and a pointed hat, and whose face is covered with white make-up. N-COUNT

pieties /paɪɪtiz/. You refer to statements about what is morally right as **pieties** when you think they are insincere or unrealistic. *...politicians who constantly intone pieties about respect for the rule of law.* N-PLURAL PRAGMATICS

piety /paɪɪti/. **Piety** is strong religious belief, or religious or dutiful behaviour. *Her piety earned her a personal missive from Pope Gregory VII.* N-UNCOUNT

piffle /pɪfᵊl/. If you describe what someone says as **piffle**, you think that it is nonsense; an informal word. *He talks such a load of piffle.* N-UNCOUNT =rubbish

piffling /pɪfəlɪŋ/. If you describe something as **piffling**, you are critical of it because it is very small or unimportant; an informal word. *...some piffling dispute regarding visiting rights.* ADJ-GRADED: usu ADJ n PRAGMATICS =trifling

pig /pɪg/ **pigs, pigging, pigged** ◆◆◇◇◇

1 A **pig** is a pink or black animal with short legs and not much hair on its skin. Pigs are often kept on farms for their meat, which is called pork, ham, bacon, or gammon. *...the grunting of the pigs. ...a pig farmer.* • See also **guinea pig**. N-COUNT =hog

2 If you call someone a **pig**, you think that they are unpleasant in some way, especially that they are greedy or unkind; an offensive use. N-COUNT

3 In British English, if you say that something is, for example, **a pig of** a job, you mean it is very difficult; an informal use. *According to the British show jumping team manager, 'It's a pig of a course – much too big and also very technical.'* N-SING: a N, usu N *of* n

4 If you say that people **are pigging** themselves, you are criticizing them for eating a very large amount at one meal; used mainly in informal British English. *A vicar's wife accused them of 'pigging themselves' at the expense of churchgoers.* ► **Pig out** means the same as **pig**. *He had probably pigged out in a fast-food place beforehand.* VERB PRAGMATICS =gorge V pron-refl PHRASAL VERB V P

5 If you **make a pig's ear of** something you are doing, you do it very badly; used in informal British English. *...he and Dermott Reeve almost made a complete pig's ear of the final push for victory.* PHRASES V inflects =bungle, make a mess of

6 If you say **'pigs might fly'** after someone has said that something might happen, you are emphasizing that you think it is very unlikely; an informal expression. *'There's a chance he won't get involved in this, of course.'—'And pigs might fly.'* PRAGMATICS

7 If you say that someone is **making a pig of** themselves, you are criticizing them for eating a very large amount at one meal. *I'm afraid I made a pig of myself at dinner.* V and N inflect PRAGMATICS

pig out. See **pig** 4. PHRASAL VERB

pigeon /pɪdʒɪn/ **pigeons.** A **pigeon** is a bird, usually grey in colour, which has a fat body. Pigeons often live in towns. • See also **clay pigeon, homing pigeon.** • to **put the cat among the pigeons**: see **cat**. ◆◇◇◇◇ N-COUNT

pigeon-hole, pigeon-holes, pigeon-holing, pigeon-holed; also spelled **pigeonhole**.

1 A **pigeon-hole** is one of the sections in a frame on a wall where letters and messages can be left for someone, or one of the sections in a writing desk where you can keep documents. N-COUNT

2 To **pigeon-hole** someone or something means to decide that they belong to a particular class or category, often without considering all their qualities or characteristics. *He felt they had pigeonholed him... I don't want to be pigeonholed as a kids' presenter.* VERB =label V n be V-ed as n

3 If you put someone in a particular **pigeon-hole**, you decide that they belong in a particular category. *Because I had an unusual accent people were not able to put me into a pigeon-hole.* N-COUNT

pigeon-toed. Someone who is **pigeon-toed** walks with their toes pointing slightly inwards. ADJ-GRADED

pigged off. If you are feeling **pigged off**, you feel rather angry or unhappy; an informal British expression. ADJ-GRADED: v-link ADJ

piggery /pɪgəri/ **piggeries.** A **piggery** is a farm or building where pigs are kept. N-COUNT

piggy /pɪgi/ **piggies**

1 A **piggy** is a pig or a piglet; used by children. N-COUNT

2 If someone has **piggy** eyes, their eyes are small and unattractive. ADJ: ADJ n

piggyback /pɪgibæk/ **piggybacks, piggybacking, piggybacked;** also spelled **piggy-back**.

1 If you give someone a **piggyback**, you carry them high on your back, supporting them under their knees. *They give each other piggy-back rides.* ► Also an adverb. *My father carried me up the hill, piggy-back.* N-COUNT ADV: ADV after v

2 If you **piggyback on** something that someone else has thought of or done, you use it to your advantage. *I was just piggybacking on Stokes's idea... They are piggybacking onto developed technology.* VERB V on n V onto n Also V

piggy bank, piggy banks; also spelled **piggybank**. A **piggy bank** is a small container shaped like a pig, with a slot in it to put coins in. Children use piggy banks to save money in. N-COUNT

piggy-in-the-middle; also spelled **pig-in-the-middle**.

1 **Piggy-in-the-middle** or **pig-in-the-middle** is a game in which two children throw a ball to each other and a child standing between them tries to catch it. N-UNCOUNT

2 If someone is **piggy-in-the-middle** or **pig-in-the-middle**, they are unwillingly involved in a dispute between two other people or groups. N-SING: also no det

pig-headed. If you describe someone as **pig-headed**, you are critical of them because they refuse to change their mind about things, and you think they are unreasonable. *She, in her pig-headed way, insists that she is right and that everyone else is wrong.* ♦ **pig-headedness** *I am not sure whether this was courage or pig-headedness.* ADJ-GRADED PRAGMATICS =stubborn, obstinate N-UNCOUNT

pig iron; also spelled **pig-iron**. **Pig iron** is iron which has been produced from iron ore in a furnace and has not yet been processed further. N-UNCOUNT

piglet /pɪglət/ **piglets.** A **piglet** is a young pig. N-COUNT

pigment /pɪgmənt/ **pigments.** A **pigment** is a substance that gives something a particular colour; a formal word. *The Romans used natural pigments on their fabrics and walls. ...the brown pigment in the skin.* ◆◇◇◇◇ N-MASS

pigmentation /pɪgmenteɪʃᵊn/. The **pigmentation** of a person's or animal's skin is its natural colouring; a formal word. *I have a skin disorder, it destroys the pigmentation in my skin.* N-UNCOUNT

pigmented /pɪgmentɪd/. **Pigmented** skin has a lot of natural colouring; a formal word. *...deeply pigmented areas on the skin.* ADJ-GRADED

pigmy /pɪgmi/. See **pygmy**.

pigpen /pɪgpen/ **pigpens.** In American English, a **pigpen** is a hut with a yard where pigs are kept on a farm. N-COUNT =pigsty

pigskin /pɪgskɪn/. **Pigskin** is leather made from the skin of a pig. *...handmade pigskin luggage.* N-UNCOUNT: oft N n

pigsty /pɪgstaɪ/ **pigsties**

1 A **pigsty** is a hut with a yard where pigs are kept on a farm. N-COUNT =pigpen

2 If you describe a room or a house as a **pigsty**, you are criticizing the fact that it is very dirty and untidy; a informal use. *The office is a pigsty.* N-COUNT: usu sing PRAGMATICS =tip, dump

pigswill /pɪgswɪl/

1 **Pigswill** is waste food that is fed to pigs. N-UNCOUNT

2 If you describe food as **pigswill**, you are criticizing it because it is of very poor quality; an informal use. N-UNCOUNT PRAGMATICS

pigtail /pɪgteɪl/ **pigtails.** In British English, if someone has a **pigtail** or **pigtails**, their hair is tied into one or two bunches and then plaited. The usual American word is **braid**. *...a little girl with pigtails.* N-COUNT =plait

pike /paɪk/ **pikes;** the form **pike** can be used as the plural for meaning 1. ◆◇◇◇◇

1 A **pike** is a large fish that lives in rivers and lakes and eats other fish. ► **Pike** is a piece of this fish eaten as food. N-VAR N-UNCOUNT

2 In former times, a **pike** was a weapon consisting N-COUNT

of a pointed blade on the end of a long pole. *Some of them carried pikes with shrivelled heads on top.*

3 In American English, when something **comes down the pike**, it happens or occurs; an informal expression. *There have been threats to veto any legislation that comes down the pike.* PHRASE: V inflects =come up

pilaf /pɪlæf, AM pɪlɑːf/ **pilafs;** also spelled **pilaff.** **Pilaf** is the same as **pilau.** N-MASS

pilaster /pɪlɑːstəʳ/ **pilasters. Pilasters** are shallow decorative pillars attached to a wall. N-COUNT: usu pl

pilau /piːlaʊ, AM pɪloʊ/ **pilaus. Pilau** or **pilau rice** is rice flavoured with spices, often mixed with pieces of meat or fish. N-MASS

pilchard /pɪltʃəʳd/ **pilchards. Pilchards** are small fish that live in the sea. Pilchards can be eaten as food. *...tinned pilchards.* N-COUNT

pile /paɪl/ **piles, piling, piled** ◆◆◆◇◇

1 A **pile of** things is a mass of them that is high in the middle and has sloping sides. *...a pile of sand. ...a little pile of crumbs... The leaves had been swept into huge piles.* N-COUNT: usu N *of* n =heap, mound

2 A **pile of** things is a quantity of things that have been put neatly somewhere so that each thing is on top of the one below. *...a pile of boxes... We sat in Sam's study, among the piles of books... The clothes were folded in a neat pile.* N-COUNT: usu N *of* n =stack

3 If you **pile** things somewhere, you put them there so that they form a pile. *He was piling clothes into the suitcase... A few newspapers and magazines were piled on a table.* VERB =stack V n adv/prep

4 If something **is piled with** things, it is covered or filled with piles of things. *Tables were piled high with local produce. ...trucks piled with luggage.* VB: usu passive =heap, stack *be* V-ed *with* n

5 If you talk about a **pile** of something or **piles** of something, you mean a large amount of it; an informal word. *I've got a pile of questions afterwards for you. ...a whole pile of disasters.* QUANT: QUANT *of* pl-n/n-uncount =stacks, heaps

6 If a group of people **pile into** or **out of** a vehicle, they all get into it or out of it in a disorganized way. *They all piled into Jerrold's car... A fleet of police cars suddenly arrived. Dozens of officers piled out.* VERB V *into/out of* n V *in/out*

7 You can refer to a large impressive building as a **pile**, especially when it is the home of a rich important person. *...some stately pile in the country.* N-COUNT

8 Piles are wooden, concrete, or metal posts which are pushed into the ground and on which buildings or bridges are built. Piles are often used in very wet areas so that the buildings do not flood. *...settlements of wooden houses, set on piles along the shore.* N-COUNT: usu pl =piling

9 Piles are painful swellings that can appear in the veins inside a person's anus. N-PLURAL =haemorrhoids

10 The **pile** of a carpet or of a fabric such as velvet is its soft surface. It consists of a lot of little threads standing on end. *...the carpet's thick pile.* N-SING

11 Someone who is **at the bottom of the pile** is low down in society or low down in an organization. Someone who is **at the top of the pile** is high up in society or high up in an organization. These are informal expressions. PHRASE: oft v-link PHR

pile up PHRASAL VERB

1 If you **pile up** a quantity of things or if they **pile up**, they gradually form a pile. *Bulldozers piled up huge mounds of dirt... Mail was still piling up at the office.* ERG V P n (not pron) V P Also V n P

2 If you **pile up** work, problems, or losses or if they **pile up**, you get more and more of them. *Problems were piling up at work... He piled up huge debts.* ERG =mount up V P V P n (not pron)

pile-up, pile-ups; also spelled **pileup** in American English. A **pile-up** is a road accident in which a lot of vehicles crash into each other. *...a 54-car pile-up.* ◆◇◇◇◇ N-COUNT

pilfer /pɪlfəʳ/ **pilfers, pilfering, pilfered.** If someone **pilfers**, they steal things, usually small inexpensive things. *Staff were pilfering behind the bar... When food stores close, a they go to work, pilfering food for resale on the black market.* VERB V V n ♦ **pilfering** *Precautions had to be taken to prevent pilfering.* N-UNCOUNT

pilgrim /pɪlgrɪm/ **pilgrims. Pilgrims** are people who make a journey to a holy place for a religious reason. ◆◆◇◇◇ N-COUNT

pilgrimage /pɪlgrɪmɪdʒ/ **pilgrimages** ◆◇◇◇◇

1 If you make a **pilgrimage** to a holy place, you go there for a religious reason. *...the pilgrimage to Mecca.* N-COUNT

2 A **pilgrimage** is a journey that someone makes to a place that is very important to them. *...a private pilgrimage to family graves... His father took him on a sentimental pilgrimage to Ireland.* N-COUNT: usu with supp

piling /paɪlɪŋ/ **pilings. Pilings** are wooden, concrete, or metal posts which are pushed into the ground and on which buildings or bridges are built. Pilings are often used in very wet areas so that the buildings do not flood. *...bridges set on stone pilings.* N-COUNT: usu pl =piles

pill /pɪl/ **pills** ◆◆◆◇◇

1 Pills are small solid round masses of medicine or vitamins that you swallow without chewing. *Why do I have to take all these pills? ...sleeping pills.* N-COUNT =tablet

2 If a woman is on **the pill**, she takes a special pill that prevents her becoming pregnant. *She had been on the pill for three years. ...the contraceptive pill.* N-SING: *the* N

3 If a person or group has to accept a failure or an unpleasant piece of news, you can say that it was **a bitter pill** or **a bitter pill to swallow**. *You're too old to be given a job. That's a bitter pill to swallow.* PHRASES N inflects

4 If someone does something to **sweeten the pill** or **sugar the pill**, they do it to make some unpleasant news or an unpleasant measure more acceptable. *He sweetened the pill by increasing wages, although by slightly less than he raised prices.* V inflects

pillage /pɪlɪdʒ/ **pillages, pillaging, pillaged.** If a group of people **pillage** a place, they steal property from it using violent methods. *Soldiers went on a rampage, pillaging stores and shooting. ...the boldness to pillage and rape.* ◆◇◇◇◇ VERB =plunder V n V ► Also a noun. *There were no signs of violence or pillage.* N-UNCOUNT ♦ **pillaging** *...pillaging by people looking for something to eat.* N-UNCOUNT

pillar /pɪləʳ/ **pillars** ◆◆◇◇◇

1 A **pillar** is a tall solid structure, which is usually used to support part of a building. *...the pillars supporting the roof.* N-COUNT =column

2 If something is the **pillar** of a system or agreement, it is the most important part of it or what makes it strong and successful. *The pillar of her economic policy was keeping tight control over money supply. ...the last pillar of apartheid.* N-COUNT: usu N *of* n

3 If you describe someone as a **pillar of** society or as a **pillar** of the community, you approve of them because they play an important and active part in society or in the community. *My father had been a pillar of the community. ...well-respected pillars of society.* N-COUNT: N *of* n PRAGMATICS

pillar box, pillar boxes; also spelled **pillar-box.** In Britain, a **pillar box** is a tall red box in the street in which you put letters that you are sending by post. N-COUNT

pillared /pɪləʳd/. A **pillared** building is a building that is supported by pillars. ADJ: usu ADJ n

pillbox /pɪlbɒks/ **pillboxes;** also spelled **pill box.** A **pillbox** is a small tin or box in which you can keep pills. N-COUNT

pillion /pɪliən/ **pillions**

1 If someone rides **pillion** on a motorcycle or bicycle, they sit behind the person who is controlling it. *She rode pillion on her son's motor bike.* ADV: ADV after v

2 On a motorcycle, the **pillion** is the seat or part behind the rider. *As a learner rider you must not carry a pillion passenger.* N-COUNT: oft N n

pillock /pɪlək/ **pillocks.** If you call someone a **pillock**, you are showing that you think they are very stupid; an offensive word, used mainly in British English. *The guy you put in charge is a complete pillock.* N-COUNT PRAGMATICS =idiot

pillory /pɪləri/ **pillories, pillorying, pilloried**

1 If someone **is pilloried**, a lot of people, especially journalists, criticize them and make them look stupid. *A man has been forced to resign as a result of being pilloried by some of the press.* VB: usu passive =ridicule *be* V-ed

2 A **pillory** is a wooden frame with holes for the head and hands. In Europe in former times N-COUNT criminals were sometimes locked in a pillory as a form of punishment.

pillow /pɪloʊ/ **pillows.** A **pillow** is a rectangular cushion which you rest your head on when you are in bed. ◆◆◇◇◇ N-COUNT

pillowcase /pɪloʊkeɪs/ **pillowcases;** also spelled **pillow case.** A **pillowcase** is a cover for a pillow, which can be removed and washed. ◆◇◇◇◇ N-COUNT

pillow slip, pillow slips. A **pillow slip** is the same as a **pillowcase.** N-COUNT

pillow talk. Conversations that people have when they are in bed together can be referred to as **pillow talk.** These conversations are often about secret or intimate subjects. N-UNCOUNT

pilot /paɪlət/ **pilots, piloting, piloted** ◆◆◆◇◇

1 A **pilot** is a person who is trained to fly an aircraft. *He spent seventeen years as an airline pilot. ...fighter pilots of the British Royal Air Force.* N-COUNT

2 A **pilot** is a person who steers a ship through a difficult stretch of water, for example the entrance to a harbour. N-COUNT

3 If someone **pilots** an aircraft or ship, they act as its pilot. *He piloted his own plane part of the way to Washington.* VERB V n

4 A **pilot scheme** or a **pilot project** is one which is used to test an idea before deciding whether to introduce it on a larger scale. *The service is being expanded following the success of a pilot scheme. ...a ten-year pilot project backed by the trade and industry department.* N-COUNT: usu N n

5 If a government or organization **pilots a programme** or a **scheme**, they test it, before deciding whether to introduce it on a larger scale. *The trust is looking for 50 schools to pilot a programme aimed at teenage pupils preparing for work.* VERB V n

6 If a government minister **pilots** a new law or bill through parliament, he or she makes sure that it is introduced successfully. *...Mr Mellor's likely role in piloting possible privacy legislation through Parliament.* VERB V n *through* n Also V n

7 A **pilot** or a **pilot episode** is a single TV programme that is shown in order to find out whether a series of TV programmes is likely to be popular. *A pilot episode of Nothing's Impossible has already been filmed.* N-COUNT: oft N n

8 A **pilot** is the pilot light on a gas cooker, boiler, or fire. N-COUNT

9 See also **automatic pilot, test pilot.**

pilot light, pilot lights. A **pilot light** is a small gas flame in a cooker, boiler, or fire. It burns all the time and lights the main large flame when the gas is turned fully on. N-COUNT

pilot officer, pilot officers. In the British Royal Air Force, **a pilot officer** is someone who has the rank below Flying Officer. N-COUNT; N-TITLE

pimento /pɪmentoʊ/ **pimentos.** A **pimento** is a mild-tasting red pepper. N-VAR

pimp /pɪmp/ **pimps, pimping, pimped** ◆◇◇◇◇

1 A **pimp** is a man who gets clients for prostitutes and takes a large part of the money they earn. N-COUNT

2 Someone who **pimps** gets clients for prostitutes and takes a large part of the money they earn. *He stole, lied, deceived and pimped his way out of poverty.* ♦ **pimping** *...corruption, pimping and prostitution.* VERB V N-UNCOUNT

pimpernel /pɪmpəʳnel/ **pimpernels.** A **pimpernel** is a small wild plant that usually has red flowers. N-VAR

pimple /pɪmpəl/ **pimples. Pimples** are small red spots. They appear especially on the face. *...spots and pimples... His face was covered with pimples.* N-COUNT

pimply /pɪmpli/. If someone is **pimply** or has a **pimply** face, they have a lot of pimples on their face. *...pimply teenagers. ...an old man with a pimply nose.* ADJ-GRADED

pin /pɪn/ **pins, pinning, pinned** ◆◆◆◇◇

1 **Pins** are very small thin pieces of metal with points at one end. They are used in needlework to fasten pieces of material together. *...needles and pins... Use pins to keep the braid in place as you work.* N-COUNT

2 If you **pin** something on something or if you **pin** it to something, you attach it with a pin, a drawing pin, or a safety pin. *They pinned a notice to the door... Everyone was supposed to dance with the bride and pin money on her dress... He had pinned up a map of Finland.* VERB V n prep V n with adv

3 If someone **pins** you to something or **pins** you against something, they press you against a surface so that you cannot move. *I pinned him against the wall... I'd try to get away and he'd pin me down, saying he would kill me... She fought at the bulk that pinned her.* VERB V n adv/prep V n

4 You can refer to any long narrow piece of metal or wood with a blunt end, especially one that is used to fasten two things together, as a **pin.** *...the 18-inch steel pin holding his left leg together. ...a two-pin continental adaptor.* N-COUNT

5 If someone tries to **pin** something **on** you or to **pin the blame on** you, they say, often unfairly, that you were responsible for something bad or illegal. *They're trying to pin it on us... The trade unions are pinning the blame for the violence on the government.* VERB V n *on* n

6 If you **pin** your hopes **on** something or **pin** your faith **on** something, you hope very much that it will produce the result you want. *The Democrats are pinning their hopes on the next election.* VERB V n *on* n

7 If someone **pins their hair** up or **pins their hair** back, they arrange their hair away from their face using hair pins. *Cleanse your face thoroughly and pin back your hair... In an effort to look older she has pinned her fair hair into a French pleat.* VERB V n with adv V n prep

8 A **pin** is a small brooch or badge. *...necklaces, bracelets, and pins.* N-COUNT

9 A **pin** is the clip on a hand grenade that prevents it from exploding and that is pulled out when you want the grenade to explode. N-COUNT

10 See also **pins and needles, drawing pin, rolling pin, safety pin.**

11 You can say **you could have heard a pin drop** when a place is extremely quiet, especially because everyone is waiting for someone to say something or when someone has said something shocking. PHRASE

pin down PHRASAL VERB

1 If you try to **pin** something **down**, you try to discover exactly what, where, or when it is. *It has taken until now to pin down its exact location... I can only pin it down to between 1936 and 1942... If we cannot pin down exactly what we are supposed to be managing, how can we manage it?* V P n (not pron) V n P *to* n V P wh Also V n P

2 If you **pin** someone **down**, you force them to make a decision or to tell you what their decision is, when they have been trying to avoid doing this. *She couldn't pin him down to a date. ...their repeated efforts to pin him down on a number of topics... If you pin people down, they will tell you some puzzling things about stress.* V n P *to/on* n V n P Also V P n (not pron)

PIN /pɪn/. Someone's **PIN** or **PIN number** is the secret number they use with a bank card to withdraw money from a cash machine. **PIN** is an abbreviation for 'personal identification number'. N-SING: oft N n

pina colada /piːnə koʊlɑːdə, AM piːnjə -/ **pina coladas.** A **pina colada** is a cocktail made from rum, coconut juice, and pineapple juice. N-COUNT

pinafore /pɪnəfɔːʳ/ **pinafores.** In British English, a **pinafore** or a **pinafore dress** is a sleeveless dress. It is worn over a blouse or sweater. The usual American word is **jumper.** N-COUNT: oft N n

pinball /pɪnbɔːl/. **Pinball** is a game in which a player presses two buttons on each side of a pinball machine in order to flick a small ball to the top of the machine. The aim of the game is to prevent the ball reaching the bottom of the machine by pressing the buttons. N-UNCOUNT

pinball machine, pinball machines. A **pinball machine** is a games machine consisting of a sloping table with obstructions, on which pinball is played. The obstructions are often electrically wired so that they light up and a bell rings when the ball touches them. N-COUNT

pince-nez /pæns neɪ/. **Pince-nez** are an old-fashioned kind of spectacles that consist of two N-UNCOUNT: also *a* N lenses that fit tightly onto the top of the nose. *His secretary was a tall woman in pince-nez.*

pincer /pɪnsəʳ/ **pincers**
1 **Pincers** consist of two pieces of metal that are hinged in the middle. They are used as a tool for gripping things or for pulling things out. *His surgical instruments were a knife and a pair of pincers.* N-PLURAL: also *a pair of* N
2 The **pincers** of an animal such as a crab or a lobster are its front claws. N-COUNT: usu pl

pincer movement, pincer movements. A **pincer movement** is an attack by an army or other group in which they attack their enemies in two places at once with the aim of surrounding them. *They are moving in a pincer movement to cut the republic in two.* N-COUNT

pinch /pɪntʃ/ **pinches, pinching, pinched** ◆◆◇◇◇
1 If you **pinch** a part of someone's body, you take a piece of their skin between your thumb and first finger and give it a short squeeze. *She pinched his arm as hard as she could... We both kept pinching ourselves to prove that it wasn't all a dream.* VERB V n ► Also a noun. *She gave him a little pinch.* N-COUNT
2 A **pinch of** an ingredient such as salt is the amount of it that you can hold between your thumb and your first finger. *Put all the ingredients, including a pinch of salt, into a food processor. ...a pinch of nutmeg.* ● to **take something with a pinch of salt**: see **salt**. N-COUNT: usu N *of* n
3 If someone **pinches** something, especially something of little value, they steal it; an informal use. *Do you remember when I pinched your glasses? ...pickpockets who pinched his wallet.* VERB =steal V n
4 If something is possible **at a pinch** it would be possible if it was absolutely necessary and if there was no alternative. In American English the expression is **in a pinch**. *Six people, and more at a pinch, could be seated comfortably at the table.* PHRASES PHR with cl/group
5 If a person or company **is feeling the pinch**, they do not have as much money as they used to, and so they cannot buy the things they would like to buy. *Consumers are spending less and traders are feeling the pinch.* V inflects
6 If you are **in a pinch**, you are in a difficult situation. *I'd trust her in a pinch... Everyone knew he was in a pinch.* oft PHR with cl

pinched /pɪntʃt/. If someone's face is **pinched**, it looks thin and pale, usually because they are ill or old. *Her face was pinched and drawn... She was a small, silent woman with pinched features and thin hair.* ADJ-GRADED

pincushion /pɪnkʊʃᵊn/ **pincushions;** also spelled **pin-cushion**. A **pincushion** is a very small cushion that you stick pins and needles into so that you can get them easily when you need them. N-COUNT

pine /paɪn/ **pines, pining, pined** ◆◆◇◇◇
1 A **pine tree** or a **pine** is a tall tree which has needle-like leaves and a fresh smell. Pine trees keep their leaves all year round. *...high mountains covered in pine trees... They cut down all the pines.* N-VAR ► **Pine** is the wood of this tree. *...a big pine table.* N-UNCOUNT
2 If you **pine for** someone who has died or gone away, you want them to be with you very much and feel sad because they are not there. *She'd be sitting at home pining for her lost husband... Make sure your pet won't pine while you're away.* VERB V *for* n V
3 If you **pine for** something, you want it very much, especially when it is unlikely that you will be able to have it. *I pine for the countryside. ...the democracy they have pined for since 1939.* VERB =yearn for V *for* n

pineapple /paɪnæpᵊl/ **pineapples.** A **pineapple** is a large oval fruit that grows in hot countries. It is sweet, juicy, and yellow inside. It has a thick, brownish skin. ◆◇◇◇◇ N-VAR

pine cone, pine cones. A **pine cone** is the seed case produced by a pine tree. It is small, brown, and oval-shaped. N-COUNT

pine needle, pine needles. Pine needles are very thin, sharp leaves that grow on pine trees. N-COUNT: usu pl

pine nut, pine nuts. Pine nuts are small cream-coloured seeds that grow on pine trees. They can be used in salads and other dishes. N-COUNT: usu pl

pinewood /paɪnwʊd/ **pinewoods;** also spelled **pine wood** for meaning 1.
1 A **pinewood** is a wood which consists mainly of pine trees. *...the hilly pinewoods of northeast Georgia.* N-COUNT
2 **Pinewood** is wood that has come from a pine tree. *...Italian pinewood furniture.* N-UNCOUNT: usu N n

ping /pɪŋ/ **pings, pinging, pinged.** If a bell or a piece of metal **pings**, it makes a short, high-pitched noise. *The lift bell pinged at the fourth floor.* ► Also a noun. *...a metallic ping.* ◆◇◇◇◇ VERB V N-COUNT

ping-pong. Ping-pong is the game of **table tennis**; an informal expression. N-UNCOUNT

pinhead /pɪnhed/ **pinheads**
1 A **pinhead** is the small metal or plastic part on the top of a pin. *It may even be possible to make computers the size of a pinhead one day.* N-COUNT
2 If you think someone is very stupid, you can say they are a **pinhead**; an informal use. *...the pinheads with the money and connections.* N-COUNT PRAGMATICS

pinhole /pɪnhoʊl/ **pinholes.** A **pinhole** is a tiny hole. N-COUNT

pinion /pɪnjən/ **pinions, pinioning, pinioned.** If you **are pinioned**, someone prevents you from moving or escaping, especially by holding or tying your arms. *At nine the next morning Bentley was pinioned, hooded and hanged.* VERB *be* V-ed Also V n

pink /pɪŋk/ **pinker, pinkest; pinks** ◆◆◆◇◇
1 **Pink** is the colour between red and white. *...pink lipstick. ...white flowers edged in pink. ...sweaters in a variety of pinks and blues.* ♦ **pinkish** *Her nostrils and eyelids were always a little pinkish, as though she had a cold.* ♦ **pinkness** *Only eat meat which has been cooked thoroughly and shows no traces of blood or pinkness.* COLOUR ADJ N-UNCOUNT
2 If you **go pink**, your face turns a slightly redder colour than usual because you are embarrassed or angry, or because you are doing something energetic. *She went pink again as she remembered her mistake.* COLOUR: usu v-link COLOUR =flush
3 **Pinks** are small plants that people grow in their gardens. They have sweet-smelling pink, white, or red flowers. N-COUNT: usu pl
4 If you are **in the pink**, you are fit, healthy, and happy. *A glass of red wine keeps you in the pink.* PHRASES v-link PHR, PHR after v
5 ● be **tickled pink**: see **tickle**.

pinkie /pɪŋki/ **pinkies;** also spelled **pinky**. In American and Scottish English, your **pinkie** is the smallest finger on your hand; an informal word. *He pushes his glasses up his nose with his pinkie.* ◆◇◇◇◇ N-COUNT

pinko /pɪŋkoʊ/ **pinkos** or **pinkoes.** If someone says they are a Socialist, but you think that their beliefs are too moderate, you can call them a **pinko**; an offensive word. *...Conservatives who believe television is full of pinkoes.* N-COUNT

pinky /pɪŋki/. See **pinkie**.

pin money. Pin money is small amounts of extra money that someone earns or gets in order to buy things that they want but that they do not really need. *She'd do anything for a bit of pin money.* N-UNCOUNT

pinnace /pɪnɪs/ **pinnaces.** A **pinnace** is a small boat carried on a large ship. Pinnaces are used to carry goods and people from the ship to the shore. N-COUNT

pinnacle /pɪnɪkəl/ **pinnacles** ◆◇◇◇◇
1 A **pinnacle** is a pointed piece of stone or rock that is high above the ground. *A walker broke his arms, legs and pelvis yesterday when he plunged 80ft from a rocky pinnacle.* N-COUNT
2 If someone reaches the **pinnacle of** their career or the **pinnacle of** a particular area of life, they are at the highest point of it. *John Major has reached the pinnacle of British politics... She was still a screen goddess at the pinnacle of her career. ...trophies that represent the pinnacle of sporting achievement.* N-COUNT: usu sing, N *of* n

pinny /pɪni/ **pinnies.** In British English, a **pinny** is an apron; an informal word. N-COUNT

pinpoint /pɪnpɔɪnt/ **pinpoints, pinpointing, pinpointed** ◆◇◇◇◇
1 If you **pinpoint** the cause of something, you VERB

discover or explain the cause exactly. *It was almost impossible to pinpoint the cause of death. ...if you can pinpoint exactly what the anger is about... The commission pinpoints inadequate housing as a basic problem threatening village life.* =identify V n V wh V n as n

2 If you **pinpoint** something or its position, you discover or show exactly where it is. *I could pinpoint his precise location on a map... Computers pinpointed where the shells were coming from.* VERB =locate V n V wh

3 If something is placed with **pinpoint** accuracy, it is placed in exactly the right place or position. *...the pinpoint accuracy of the bombing campaigns.* ADJ: ADJ n

pinprick /pɪnprɪk/ **pinpricks;** also spelled **pin-prick** or **pin prick**. A very small spot of something can be described as a **pinprick**. *...a pinprick of light... She looked up at me with pinpricks of sweat along her hairline.* N-COUNT: with supp

pins and needles. If you have **pins and needles** in part of your body, you feel sharp tingling pains there for a short period of time. It usually happens when the part of your body has been in an awkward or uncomfortable position. *I had pins and needles in the tips of my fingers.* N-UNCOUNT

pinstripe /pɪnstraɪp/ **pinstripes;** also spelled **pin-stripe**. **Pinstripes** are very narrow vertical stripes found on certain types of clothing. Businessmen's suits often have pinstripes. *He wore an expensive, dark blue pinstripe suit.* N-COUNT: usu N n

pinstriped /pɪnstraɪpt/. A **pinstriped suit** is made of cloth that has very narrow vertical stripes. ADJ: usu ADJ n

pint /paɪnt/ **pints** ◆◆◇◇◇

1 A **pint** is a unit of measurement for liquids. In Britain, it is equal to 568 cubic centimetres or one eighth of an imperial gallon. In America, it is equal to 473 cubic centimetres or one eighth of an American gallon. *...a pint of milk... The military requested 6,000 pints of blood from the American Red Cross. ...glasses which can hold a full pint.* N-COUNT: usu N *of* n

2 In Britain, if you go for a **pint**, you go to the pub to drink a pint of beer or more. *He sits down and reads the paper, then goes out for a pint.* N-COUNT

pint-sized. If you describe someone or something as **pint-sized**, you think they are smaller than is normal or smaller than they should be; an informal expression. *Two pint-sized kids emerged from a doorway.* ADJ: usu ADJ n PRAGMATICS =diminutive

pin-up, pin-ups; also spelled **pinup**. A **pin-up** is an attractive man or woman who appears on posters, often wearing very few clothes. *...pin-up boys... She was already a famous model and pin-up by the time she made her film debut.* N-COUNT

pioneer /paɪənɪəʳ/ **pioneers, pioneering, pioneered** ◆◆◇◇◇

1 Someone who is referred to as a **pioneer** in a particular area of activity is one of the first people to be involved in it and develop it. *...one of the leading pioneers of British photo journalism... What they lacked in speed those pioneer pilots made up for by flying only a few feet above the ground.* N-COUNT: oft N *of/in* n, N n

2 Someone who **pioneers** a new activity, invention, or process is one of the first people to do it. *...Professor Alec Jeffreys, who invented and pioneered DNA tests... The campaigns are part of American-style innovations being pioneered by the new universities... In the end, the battle followed the pattern pioneered by the Russians themselves during World War II.* VERB V n V-ed Also V

3 **Pioneers** are people who leave their own country, go to a new one, and settle in a part of it that has not been settled in before. *...abandoned settlements of early European pioneers.* N-COUNT

pioneering /paɪənɪəʳɪŋ/. **Pioneering** work or a **pioneering** individual does something that has not been done before, for example by developing or using new methods or techniques. *The school has won awards for its pioneering work with the community... America has always retained her pioneering spirit.* ◆◇◇◇◇ ADJ: usu ADJ n =innovative

pious /paɪəs/ ◆◇◇◇◇

1 Someone who is **pious** is very religious and moral. *He was brought up by pious female relatives. ...pious acts of charity.* ♦ **piously** *Conti kneeled and crossed himself piously.* ADJ-GRADED =devout ADV-GRADED: ADV with v

2 If you describe a someone's words as **pious**, you disapprove of them because their words are full of good intentions but do not lead to anything useful being done. *What we need is not manifestos of pious intentions, but real action.* ♦ **piously** *The groups at the conference spoke piously of their fondness for democracy.* ADJ-GRADED: ADJ n PRAGMATICS ADV-GRADED: ADV with v

3 **Pious hopes** are unlikely to come true. *But with the Socialists still so deeply split, that seems to be little more than a pious hope.* ADJ: ADJ n

4 If you describe someone as **pious**, you disapprove of the fact that they pretend to be very religious without being sincere. *His attitude is compassionate without being pious. ...an expression of pious innocence.* ♦ **piously** *'Life,' said Dr Holly piously, 'is the only wealth, and I gave you life.'* ADJ-GRADED PRAGMATICS ADV-GRADED: ADV with v

pip /pɪp/ **pips, pipping, pipped** ◆◇◇◇◇

1 **Pips** are the small hard seeds in a fruit such as an apple, orange, or pear. N-COUNT: usu pl

2 If someone **is pipped** to something, such as a prize or an award, they are narrowly defeated; used mainly in informal British English. *It's still possible for the losers to be pipped by West Germany for a semi-final place... She pipped actress Meryl Streep to the part.* VERB *be* V-ed prep V n prep

3 In Britain, **the pips** on the radio are a series of short, high-pitched sounds that are used as a time signal. N-PLURAL: usu *the* N

4 In Britain, when you make a telephone call from a public telephone, **the pips** are a signal that you need to put in more money. N-PLURAL: usu *the* N

5 If someone **is pipped at the post** or **pipped to the post** they are just beaten in a competition or in a race to achieve something; ; used mainly in informal British English. *I didn't want us to be pipped to the post.* PHRASE

pipe /paɪp/ **pipes, piping, piped** ◆◆◆◇◇

1 A **pipe** is a long, round, hollow object, usually made of metal or plastic, through which a liquid or gas can flow. *The liquid can't escape into the air, because it's inside a pipe... The plant makes plastic covered steel pipes for the oil and gas industries.* N-COUNT

2 If liquid or gas **is piped** somewhere, it is transferred from one place to another through a pipe. *The heated gas is piped through a coil surrounded by water... The Communists brought electricity to his village and piped in drinking water from the reservoir... Most of the houses in the capital don't have piped water.* VERB *be* V-ed prep V n with adv V-ed

3 A **pipe** is an object which is used for smoking tobacco. You put the tobacco into the cup-shaped part at the end of the pipe, light it, and breathe in the smoke through a narrow tube. N-COUNT

4 If someone, especially a child, **pipes** something, they say it in a high-pitched voice. *'But I want to help,' Bessie piped.* VERB V with quote

5 An **organ pipe** is one of the long hollow tubes in which air vibrates and produces a musical note. N-COUNT

6 A **pipe** is a simple musical instrument in the shape of a tube with holes in it. You play a pipe by blowing into it while covering and uncovering the holes with your fingers. N-COUNT

7 **Pipes** are the same as **bagpipes**. N-PLURAL

8 See also **piping, piping hot**.

pipe down. If you tell someone who is talking a lot or talking too loudly to **pipe down**, you are telling them to stop talking; an informal expression. *Just pipe down and I'll tell you what I want.* PHRASAL VERB no cont, usu imper V P

pipe up. If someone who has been silent for a while **pipes up**, they say something, especially something surprising or strange. *'That's right, mister,' another child piped up... At which point I piped up and asked whether it might be at all possible to have some positive input.* PHRASAL VERB no cont V P with quote V P

pipe bomb, pipe bombs. A **pipe bomb** is a small, home-made bomb hidden in a narrow tube. N-COUNT

pipe cleaner, pipe cleaners. A **pipe cleaner** is a piece of wire covered with a soft woolly substance which is used to clean a tobacco pipe. N-COUNT

piped music. **Piped music** is music which is played through loudspeakers in some supermarkets, restaurants, and other public places. *The book lists over 400 restaurants, pubs and shops which do not play piped music.* N-UNCOUNT

pipe dream, pipe dreams; also spelled **pipe-dream**. A **pipe dream** is a hope or plan that you have which you know will never really happen. *You could waste your whole life on a pipe-dream.* N-COUNT

pipeline /paɪplaɪn/ **pipelines** ◆◆◇◇◇
1 A **pipeline** is a large pipe which is used for carrying oil or gas over a long distance, often underground. *A consortium plans to build a natural-gas pipeline from Russia to supply eastern Germany.* N-COUNT
2 If something is **in the pipeline**, it has already been planned or begun. *Mr Major said some changes and modifications were already in the pipeline, but it was probable that more needed to be done.* PHRASE: v-link PHR, PHR after v

piper /paɪpəʳ/ **pipers** ◆◇◇◇◇
1 A **piper** is a musician who plays the bagpipes. N-COUNT
2 If you say **'He who pays the piper calls the tune'**, you mean that the person who provides the money for something decides what will be done, or has a right to decide what will be done. PHRASE

pipework /paɪpwɜːʳk/. **Pipework** is the pipes that are part of a machine or construction. *The stainless steel pipework has been constructed, tested and inspected to very high standards.* N-UNCOUNT

piping /paɪpɪŋ/ ◆◇◇◇◇
1 **Piping** is metal, plastic, or another substance made in the shape of a pipe or tube. *...rolls of bright yellow plastic piping.* N-UNCOUNT
2 **Piping** is cloth made into a narrow tube. Piping is used to decorate the edges of clothing and things such as cushions. *The red dress had slim black piping around the neck.* N-UNCOUNT
3 A **piping** voice is high-pitched; used in written English. *As she was about to follow there came a piping voice from upstairs. 'Is that Daddy back?'* ADJ: ADJ n

piping hot; also spelled **piping-hot**. Food or water that is **piping hot** is very hot. *...large cups of piping-hot coffee... Serve piping hot, with herbs sprinkled on top.* ADJ

pipit /pɪpɪt/ **pipits.** A **pipit** is a small, brownish songbird. N-COUNT

piquant /piːkənt, -kɑːnt/
1 Food that is **piquant** has a pleasantly spicy taste; used mainly in written English. *...a crisp mixed salad with an unusually piquant dressing.* ADJ-GRADED
♦ **piquancy** /piːkənsi/ *A little mustard is served on the side to add further piquancy.* N-UNCOUNT
2 Something that is **piquant** is interesting and exciting; used mainly in written English. *There may well have been a piquant novelty about her books when they came out.* ADJ-GRADED ♦ **piquancy** *Piquancy was added to the situation because Dr Porter was then on the point of marrying Hugh Miller.* N-UNCOUNT

pique /piːk/ **piques, piquing, piqued**
1 **Pique** is the feeling of anger and resentment that you have when your pride is hurt. *Mimi had gotten over her pique at Susan's refusal to accept the job.* N-UNCOUNT
2 If something **piques** your interest or curiosity, it arouses your interest or curiosity. *This phenomenon piqued Dr Morris' interest... Their curiosity piqued, they stopped writing.* VERB =arouse V n V-ed
3 If someone does something **in a fit of pique**, they do it because they are angry and resentful that their pride has been hurt. *Lawrence, in a fit of pique, left the Army and took up a career in the City.* PHRASE

piqued /piːkt/. If someone is **piqued**, they are offended or annoyed, often by something that is not very important. *Granny was astounded and a little piqued, I think, because it had all been arranged without her knowledge... She wrinkled her nose, piqued by his total lack of enthusiasm.* ADJ-GRADED: usu v-link ADJ

piracy /paɪrəsi/
1 **Piracy** is robbery at sea carried out by pirates. *Seven of the fishermen have been formally charged with piracy.* N-UNCOUNT
2 You can refer to the illegal copying of things such as video tapes and computer programs as **piracy**. *...protection against piracy of books, films and other intellectual property.* N-UNCOUNT

piranha /pɪrɑːnə/ **piranhas; piranha** can also be used as the plural form. A **piranha** is a small, fierce fish which is found in South America. N-COUNT

pirate /paɪrət/ **pirates, pirating, pirated** ◆◆◇◇◇
1 **Pirates** are sailors who attack other ships and steal property from them. *In the nineteenth century pirates roamed the seas.* N-COUNT
2 You can refer to someone who behaves in an immoral or illegal way as a **pirate**. *Of course I knew Max was a rogue, a bit of a pirate.* N-COUNT
3 Someone who **pirates** video tapes, cassettes, books, or computer programs copies and sells them when they have no right to do so. *A school technician pirated anything from video nasties to computer games. ...American manufacturers who've seen their designs pirated in other countries.* VERB V n
♦ **pirated** *Pirated copies of music tapes are flooding the market... A pirated edition of the book was published in August 1986.* ADJ
4 A **pirate** version of something is an illegal copy of it. *Pirate copies of the video are already said to be in Britain.* ADJ: ADJ n

pirate radio, pirate radios. Pirate radio is the broadcasting of radio programmes illegally. *...a pirate radio station.* N-VAR

pirouette /pɪruet/ **pirouettes, pirouetting, pirouetted**
1 A **pirouette** is a movement in ballet dancing. The dancer stands on one foot and spins their body round fast. *Virginia Zucci of the Russian Ballet was famous for her pirouettes.* N-COUNT
2 If someone **pirouettes**, they perform one or more pirouettes. *She pirouetted in front of the glass.* VERB V

Pisces /paɪsiːz/ ◆◆◇◇◇
1 **Pisces** is one of the twelve signs of the zodiac. Its symbol is two fish. People who are born between the 19th of February and the 20th of March come under this sign. N-UNCOUNT
2 **A Pisces** is a person whose sign of the zodiac is Pisces. N-SING: a N

piss /pɪs/ **pisses, pissing, pissed** ◆◆◇◇◇
1 To **piss** means to urinate; a rude use which many people find offensive. VERB: V
2 If someone has **a piss**, they urinate; a rude use which many people find offensive. N-SING: a N
3 **Piss** is urine; a rude use which many people find offensive. N-UNCOUNT
4 If it is **pissing with** rain, it is raining very hard; an informal British use which some people find offensive. *It may be pissing with rain.* ▸ **Piss down** means the same as **piss**. *It was pissing down out there, but I just felt like a breath of air.* VB: usu cont V with n PHRASAL VERB V P
5 If someone **is pissing** themselves, or **is pissing** themselves laughing, they are laughing uncontrollably; an informal British use which many people find offensive. *I just pissed myself with laughter.* VERB V pron-refl
6 If you **take the piss out of** someone, you tease them and make fun of them; an informal British use which some people find offensive. PHRASE: V inflects

piss about or **piss around.** The form **piss about** is mainly used in British English. PHRASAL VERB
1 If you say that someone **pisses about** or **pisses around**, you mean they waste a lot of time doing things that do not really need doing, especially when there are more important things to be done; an informal use which some people find offensive. *Now, let's stop pissing about, shall we?* =muck about V P
2 If you say that someone **pisses about** or **pisses around**, you mean they behave in a silly, childish way; an informal British use which some people find offensive. *We just pissed about, laughing.* =muck about V P

piss down. See **piss** 4. PHRASAL VERB

piss off PHRASAL VERB
1 If someone or something **pisses** you **off**, they annoy you; an informal use which some people find offensive. *It pisses me off when they start moaning about going to war.* V n P ♦ **pissed off** *I was really pissed off.* ADJ-GRADED
2 If someone tells a person to **piss off**, they are V P

telling the person in a rude way to go away; a rude use which many people find offensive. PRAGMATICS

pissed /pɪst/ ◆◇◇◇◇
1 Someone who is **pissed** is drunk; an informal word which some people find offensive, and which is used mainly in British English. *He was just lying there completely pissed.* ADJ-GRADED
2 In American English, if you say that someone is **pissed**, you mean that they are annoyed; an informal use which some people find offensive. *You know Molly's pissed at you.* ADJ-GRADED: v-link ADJ, oft ADJ *at* n =annoyed

piss-take, piss-takes. In British English, a **piss-take** is an act of making fun of someone or something. N-COUNT: usu sing

piss-up, piss-ups. In British English, if a group of people have a **piss-up**, they drink a lot of alcohol; an informal expression which some people find offensive. N-COUNT: usu sing

pistachio /pɪstætʃioʊ/ **pistachios. Pistachios** or **pistachio nuts** are small, green, edible nuts. N-VAR

piste /piːst/ **pistes.** A **piste** is a track of firm snow for skiing on. N-COUNT

pistol /pɪstəl/ **pistols.** A **pistol** is a small handgun. ◆◆◇◇◇ N-COUNT

piston /pɪstən/ **pistons.** A **piston** is a cylinder or metal disc that is part of an engine. Pistons slide up and down inside tubes and cause various parts of the engine to move. ◆◇◇◇◇ N-COUNT

pit /pɪt/ **pits, pitting, pitted** ◆◆◆◇◇
1 A **pit** is a coal mine. *It was a better community then when all the pits were working.* N-COUNT
2 A **pit** is a large hole that is dug in the ground. *Eric lost his footing and began to slide into the pit.* N-COUNT
3 A **gravel pit** or **clay pit** is a very large hole that is left where gravel or clay has been dug from the ground. *This area of former farmland was worked as a gravel pit until 1964.* N-COUNT: supp N
4 If two opposing things or people **are pitted against** one another, they are in conflict. *You will be pitted against two, three, or four people who are every bit as good as you are... This was one man pitted against the universe.* VB: usu passive be V-ed *against* n V-ed
5 In motor racing, the **pits** are the areas at the side of the track where drivers stop to get more fuel and to repair their cars during races. *He moved quickly into the pits and climbed rapidly out of the car.* • See also **pit stop**. N-COUNT: usu pl
6 If you describe someone or something as **the pits**, you mean that it is really awful; used in spoken English. *Mary Ann asked him how dinner had been. 'The pits,' he replied.* N-PLURAL: *the* N
7 In American English, a **pit** is the stone of a fruit or vegetable. N-COUNT =stone
8 See also **pitted**; **fleapit**, **orchestra pit**, **sandpit**.
9 If you **pit** your **wits against** someone, you compete with them in a test of knowledge or intelligence. *I'd like to manage at the very highest level and pit my wits against the best.* PHRASES V inflects
10 If you have a feeling **in the pit of** your **stomach**, you have a tight or heavy feeling inside your body and maybe feel a bit sick, usually because you are afraid or anxious. *I had a funny feeling in the pit of my stomach.*
11 • **a bottomless pit**: see **bottomless**.

pita /piːtə/ **pitas.** See **pitta**.

pit bull terrier, pit bull terriers. A **pit bull terrier** or a **pit bull** is a very fierce kind of dog. Some people train pit bull terriers to fight other dogs. N-COUNT

pitch /pɪtʃ/ **pitches, pitching, pitched** ◆◆◆◇◇
1 A **pitch** is an area of ground that is marked out and used for playing a game such as football, cricket, or hockey; used mainly in British English. The more usual American word is **field**. *There was a swimming-pool, cricket pitches, playing fields... In their conduct, both on and off the pitch, the Danes were a credit to the game.* N-COUNT: oft n N
2 If you **pitch** something somewhere, you throw it with quite a lot of force, usually aiming it carefully. *Simon pitched the empty bottle into the lake.* VERB V n prep
3 If someone or something **pitches** somewhere, they fall forwards suddenly and with a lot of force. *The movement took him by surprise, and he pitched forward... Alan staggered sideways, pitched headfirst over the low wall and fell into the lake... I was pitched into the water and swam ashore.* VERB V adv be V-ed prep/adv
4 If someone **is pitched into** a new situation, they are suddenly forced into it. *They were being pitched into a new adventure in which they would have to fight the whole world... This could pitch the government into confrontation with the work-force.* VERB be V-ed prep V n prep
5 In the game of baseball or rounders, when you **pitch** the ball, you throw it to the batsman for him to hit. *We passed long, hot afternoons pitching a baseball.* ♦ **pitching** *His pitching was a legend among major league hitters.* VERB V n Also V prep N-UNCOUNT
6 The **pitch** of a sound is how high or low it is. *He raised his voice to an even higher pitch.* • See also **absolute pitch**, **perfect pitch**. N-UNCOUNT
7 If a sound **is pitched at** a particular level, it is produced at the level indicated. *His cry is pitched at a level that makes it impossible to ignore... His voice was pitched high, the words muffled by his crying... Her voice was well pitched and brisk.* • See also **high-pitched**, **low-pitched**. VB: usu passive be V-ed prep/adv V-ed
8 If something **is pitched** at a particular level or degree of difficulty, it is set at that level. *Whilst this is very important material I think it's probably pitched at rather too high a level for our purposes... The government has pitched High Street interest rates at a new level.* VERB be V-ed prep V n prep
9 If something such as a feeling or a situation rises to a high **pitch**, it rises to a high level. *I feel very sorry for the competitors who have all worked themselves up to a very high pitch for this first day... Tension has reached such a pitch that the armed forces say soldiers may have to use their weapons to defend themselves against local people.* • See also **fever pitch**. N-SING: usu with supp
10 If you **pitch your tent**, or **pitch camp**, you put up your tent in a place where you are going to stay. *He had pitched his tent in the yard... At dusk we pitched camp in the middle of nowhere.* VERB V n
11 If a boat **pitches**, it moves violently up and down with the movement of the waves when the sea is rough. *The ship is pitching and rolling in what looks like about fifteen foot seas.* VERB V
12 **Pitch** is a black substance that is sticky when it is hot and very hard when it is dry. Pitch is used on the bottoms of boats and on the roofs of houses to prevent water getting in. *The timbers of similar houses were painted with pitch.* • See also **pitch-black**. N-UNCOUNT
13 See also **pitched**.
14 If someone **makes a pitch** for something, they try to persuade people to do or buy that thing. *Mr. Bush used his remarks to make a pitch for further space exploration... Prue invited the magazine's editor to lunch and made her pitch.* • See also **sales pitch**. PHRASE: V inflects, oft PHR *for* n

pitch for. If someone is **pitching for** something, they are trying to persuade other people to give it to them. *...laws prohibiting the state's accountants from pitching for business... It was middle-class votes they were pitching for.* PHRASAL VERB usu cont V P n

pitch in. If you **pitch in**, you join in and help with an activity; an informal expression. *The agency says international relief agencies also have pitched in... Cartoonists have pitched in with their favourites from their own and other hands... The entire company pitched in to help.* PHRASAL VERB V P V P *with* n V P to-inf

pitch-black. If a place or the night is **pitch-black**, it is completely dark. *...a cold pitch-black winter morning.* ADJ =pitch-dark

pitch-dark; also spelled **pitch dark. Pitch-dark** means the same as **pitch-black**. *It was pitch-dark in the room and I couldn't see a thing.* ADJ =pitch-black

pitched /pɪtʃt/. A **pitched roof** is one that slopes quite steeply as opposed to one that is flat. *...a rather quaint lodge with a steeply-pitched roof.* • See also **high-pitched**, **low-pitched**. ADJ-GRADED =slanting

pitched battle, pitched battles. A **pitched battle** is a very fierce and violent fight involving a N-COUNT large number of people. *For the next three nights pitched battles were fought with the police.*

pitcher /pɪtʃəʳ/ **pitchers** ◆◇◇◇◇
1 A **pitcher** is a jug; used mainly in American English. *...a pitcher of iced water.* N-COUNT =ewer
2 A **pitcher** is a large container made of clay. Pitchers are usually round in shape and have a narrow neck and two handles shaped like ears. N-COUNT
3 In baseball, the **pitcher** is the person who throws the ball to the batsman, who tries to hit it. *Over the next five years, he became one of the greatest pitchers in baseball.* N-COUNT

pitchfork /pɪtʃfɔːʳk/ **pitchforks.** A **pitchfork** is a large fork with a long handle and two prongs that is used for lifting hay or cut grass. N-COUNT

pitch invasion, pitch invasions. If there is a **pitch invasion** during or after a football, rugby, or cricket match, fans run on to the pitch. *There was a peaceful pitch invasion after Milan's eighth goal.* N-COUNT

piteous /pɪtiəs/. Something that is **piteous** is so sad that you feel great pity for the person involved; used in written English. *As they pass by, a piteous wailing is heard.* ♦ **piteously** *'I can't bear to face anyone,' she said piteously.* ADJ-GRADED =pitiful; ADV-GRADED: ADV after v

pitfall /pɪtfɔːl/ **pitfalls.** The **pitfalls** involved in a particular activity or situation are the things that may go wrong or may cause problems. *The pitfalls of working abroad are numerous... He also points out that forward planning can help avoid stressful pitfalls.* ◆◇◇◇◇ N-COUNT: usu pl

pith /pɪθ/. The **pith** of an orange, lemon, or other citrus fruit is the white substance between the peel and the inside of the fruit. N-UNCOUNT: usu *the* N

pithead /pɪthed/ **pitheads.** The **pithead** at a coal mine is all the buildings and machinery which are above ground. *Across the river the railway track ran up to the pithead.* N-COUNT: usu *the* N in sing

pithy /pɪθi/ **pithier, pithiest.** A **pithy** comment or piece of writing is short, direct, sensible, and memorable; used in written English. *His pithy advice to young painters was, 'Above all, keep your colours fresh.'... Many of them made a point of praising the film's pithy dialogue.* ♦ **pithily** *Louis Armstrong defined jazz pithily as 'what I play for a living'.* ADJ-GRADED: usu ADJ n; ADV-GRADED: ADV with v

pitiable /pɪtiəbᵊl/. Someone who is **pitiable** is in such a sad or weak state that you feel pity for them; used in written English. *Her grandmother seemed to her a pitiable figure.* ♦ **pitiably** /pɪtiəbli/. *Their main grievance was that they had not received their pitiably low pay... She found Frances lying on the bed crying pitiably.* ADJ-GRADED =pitiful; ADV-GRADED: ADV with v, ADV adj =pitifully

pitiful /pɪtɪfʊl/ ◆◇◇◇◇
1 Someone or something that is **pitiful** is so sad, weak, or small that you feel pity for them. *He sounded both pitiful and eager to get what he wanted... It was the most pitiful sight I had ever seen.* ♦ **pitifully** *His legs were pitifully thin compared to the rest of his bulk.* ADJ-GRADED; ADV-GRADED
2 If you describe something as **pitiful**, you mean that it is completely inadequate. *The choice is pitiful and the quality of some of the products is very low... The farmers pay pitiful wages, often in the form of food and clothes.* ♦ **pitifully** *State help for the mentally handicapped is pitifully inadequate.* ADJ-GRADED =meagre; ADV-GRADED: ADV adj, ADV with v
3 If you describe something as **pitiful**, you mean that it does not deserve respect or consideration. *Mr Clinton said the attacks were 'pitiful' and riddled with 'distortions'... This argument seems to show a pitiful lack of confidence in the capabilities of our juries.* ADJ-GRADED =pathetic

pitiless /pɪtiləs/
1 Someone or something that is **pitiless** shows no feelings of pity or mercy. *He saw the pitiless eyes of his enemy... His judgements are immediate, pitiless.* ♦ **pitilessly** *She had scorned him pitilessly.* ADJ-GRADED =merciless; ADV-GRADED
2 If you describe something such as the weather or the heat as **pitiless**, you mean that it is very extreme. *John Steinbeck used the dust and the pitiless skies as the backcloth to his novel.* ADJ-GRADED

pitman /pɪtmən/ **pitmen. Pitmen** are coal-miners; used in British journalism. *Many of the older pitmen may never work again.* ◆◇◇◇◇ N-COUNT: usu pl

pit stop, pit stops
1 In motor racing, if a driver makes a **pit stop**, he stops in a special place at the side of the track to get more fuel and to make repairs. *He had to make four pit stops during the race.* N-COUNT
2 A **pit stop** is a brief stop for rest and refreshment, especially when you are on a journey. *They went around the world in a week without a pit stop.* N-COUNT

pitta /pɪtə/ **pittas;** spelled **pita** and pronounced /piːtə/ in American English. **Pitta** or **pitta bread** is a type of bread in the shape of a flat oval. It can be split open and filled with food such as meat and salad. *...pitta bread stuffed with slices of home-cooked ham.* N-VAR

pittance /pɪtᵊns/ **pittances.** If you say that you receive a **pittance**, you are emphasizing that you get only a very small amount of money, probably not as much as you think you deserve. *Her secretaries work tirelessly for a pittance.* N-COUNT: usu sing PRAGMATICS

pitted /pɪtɪd/
1 **Pitted** fruits have had their stones removed. *...green and black pitted olives.* ADJ: ADJ n
2 If the surface of something is **pitted**, it is covered with a lot of small, shallow holes. *Everywhere building facades are pitted with shell and bullet holes. ...the pitted surface of the moon.* ADJ: oft ADJ *with* n

pituitary gland /pɪtjuːɪtri glænd, AM -tuːɪteri -/ **pituitary glands.** The **pituitary gland** or the **pituitary** is a gland that is attached to the base of the brain. It produces hormones which affect growth, sexual development, and other functions of the body. N-COUNT: usu sing

pity /pɪti/ **pities, pitying, pitied** ◆◆◇◇◇
1 If you feel **pity** for someone, you feel very sorry for them. *He felt a sudden tender pity for her... She knew that she was an object of pity among her friends.* ● See also **self-pity**. N-UNCOUNT: oft N *for* n
2 If you **pity** someone, you feel very sorry for them. *I don't know whether to hate or pity him.* VERB V n
3 If you say that it is **a pity** that something is the case, you mean that you feel disappointment or regret about it. *It is a great pity that all pupils in the city cannot have the same chances... Pity you haven't got your car, isn't it... It seemed a pity to let it all go to waste.* N-SING: *a* N, oft *it* v-link N that/to-inf PRAGMATICS
4 If someone shows **pity**, they show mercy and forgiveness. If they show **no pity**, they do not show mercy and forgiveness. *Non-communist forces have some pity towards people here... She saw no pity in their faces.* N-UNCOUNT =mercy
5 If you add **more's the pity** to a comment, you are expressing your disappointment or regret about something. *But my world isn't your world, more's the pity.* PHRASES PHR with cl PRAGMATICS
6 You can say **for pity's sake** to add emphasis to what you are saying, especially when you are annoyed or upset. *'Run, Katherine. For pity's sake run!' he screamed.* usu PHR with cl PRAGMATICS
7 If you **take pity on** someone, you feel sorry for them and help them. *No woman had ever felt the need to take pity on him before.* V inflects
8 If you say **the pity is that**, or **the pity of it is that**, before a comment, you are emphasizing your disappointment or regret about something. *The pity is that it was all completely unnecessary... The pity of it was that the Americans didn't play cricket.* V inflects PRAGMATICS

pitying /pɪtiɪŋ/. A **pitying** look shows that someone feels pity and perhaps slight contempt. *She gave him a pitying look; that was the sort of excuse her father would use.* ♦ **pityingly** *Stasik looked at him pityingly and said nothing.* ADJ: usu ADJ n; ADV: ADV after v

pivot /pɪvət/ **pivots, pivoting, pivoted** ◆◇◇◇◇
1 **The pivot** in a situation is the most important thing which everything else is based on or arranged around. *Forming the pivot of the exhibition is a large group of watercolours.* N-COUNT: usu *the* N in sing, oft *the* N *of* n
2 If something **pivots**, it balances or turns on a central point. *The boat pivoted on its central axis and pointed straight at the harbour entrance... She* VERB V prep/adv V n prep

pivots gracefully on the stage... He pivoted his whole body through ninety degrees.

3 A **pivot** is the pin or the central point on which something balances or turns. *The pedal had sheared off at the pivot.* N-COUNT: usu sing

pivot on. If one thing **pivots on** another, it depends on it. *Peace brought no solution to the economic problems that pivoted on overseas trade.* PHRASAL VERB V P n

pivotal /pɪvətəl/. A **pivotal** role, point or figure in something is one that is very important and affects the success of that thing. *The Court of Appeal has a pivotal role in the English legal system... The elections may prove to be pivotal in Colombia's political history.* ◆◇◇◇◇ ADJ =critical

pixel /pɪksəl/ **pixels.** A **pixel** is the smallest size of spot on a computer screen which can be independently controlled by the computer; a technical term. N-COUNT

pixie /pɪksi/ **pixies.** A **pixie** is an imaginary little creature like a fairy. Pixies have pointed ears and wear pointed hats. N-COUNT

pizza /piːtsə/ **pizzas.** A **pizza** is a flat, round piece of dough covered with tomatoes, cheese, and other savoury food, and then baked in an oven. *...the last piece of pizza... We went for a pizza together at lunch-time.* ◆◆◇◇◇ N-VAR

pizzazz /pɪzæz/; also spelled **pzazz** or **pizazz.** If you say that someone or something has **pizzazz,** you approve of the fact that they are exceptionally exciting, energetic, and stylish; an informal word. *...a young woman with a lot of energy and pizazz.* N-UNCOUNT PRAGMATICS

pizzeria /piːtsəriːə/ **pizzerias.** A **pizzeria** is a place where pizza is made, sold, and eaten. N-COUNT

pizzicato /pɪtsɪkɑːtoʊ/ **pizzicatos.** If a stringed instrument is played **pizzicato,** it is played by plucking the strings with the fingers rather than by using the bow; a technical term in music. *...a piece designed to be played pizzicato.* ► Also a noun. *...an extended pizzicato section.* ADV: ADV after v; N-COUNT: oft N n

pkt. **Pkt** is used in recipes as a written abbreviation for **packet.**

pl ◆◇◇◇◇

1 In addresses and on maps and signs, **Pl** is often used as a written abbreviation for **Place.** *27 Queensdale Pl, London W11, England.*

2 In grammar, **pl** is often used as a written abbreviation for **plural.**

placard /plækɑːrd/ **placards.** A **placard** is a large notice that is carried in a march or demonstration or is displayed in a public place. *The protesters sang songs and waved placards.* ◆◇◇◇◇ N-COUNT

placate /pləkeɪt, AM pleɪkeɪt/ **placates, placating, placated.** If you **placate** someone, you stop them feeling angry or resentful by doing or saying things that will please them. *He smiled, and made a gesture intended to placate me... 'I didn't mean to upset you,' Agnew said in a placating voice.* ◆◇◇◇◇ VERB =appease, pacify V n V-ing Also V

placatory /pləkeɪtəri, AM pleɪkətɔːri/. A **placatory** remark or action is intended to stop someone feeling angry or resentful by doing or saying things that will please them. *When next he spoke he was more placatory... He raised a placatory hand. 'All right, we'll see what we can do.'* ADJ-GRADED =appeasing

place /pleɪs/ **places, placing, placed** ◆◆◆◆◆

1 A **place** is any point, building, area, town, or country. *...Temple Mount, the place where the Temple actually stood. ...a list of museums and places of interest... We're going to a place called Mont-St-Jean. ...the opportunity to visit new places... The best place to catch fish on a canal is close to a lock... The pain is always in the same place.* N-COUNT: usu with supp

2 You can use **the place** to refer to the point, building, area, town, or country that you have already mentioned. *Except for the remarkably tidy kitchen, the place was a mess... For a ruin it was in good condition, as though the place was still being used.* N-SING: the N

3 You can refer to somewhere that provides a service, such as a hotel, restaurant, or institution, as a particular kind of **place.** *He found a bed-and-breakfast place... My wife and I discovered some superb places to eat... My hospital is one of many places that benefited from the support of Queen Alexandra.* N-COUNT: usu with supp =establishment

4 When something **takes place,** it happens, especially in a controlled or organized way. *The discussion took place in a famous villa on the lake's shore... She wanted Hugh's wedding to take place quickly... Elections will now take place on November the twenty-fifth.* PHRASE: V inflects

5 In American English, **place** can be used after 'any', 'no', 'some', or 'every' to mean 'anywhere', 'nowhere', 'somewhere', or 'everywhere'; an informal use. *The poor guy obviously didn't have any place to go for Easter... Why not go out and see if there's some place we can dance?* N-SING: det N

6 In American English, if you go **places,** you visit pleasant or interesting places. *I don't have money to go places... People were talking to him, listening to him, taking him places.* ADV: ADV after v

7 You can refer to the position where something belongs, or where it is supposed to be, as its **place.** *He returned the album to its place on the shelf... He returned to his place on the sofa.* N-COUNT: poss N

8 A **place** is a seat or position that is available for someone to occupy. *He walked back to the table and sat at the nearest of two empty places... I found a place to park beside a station wagon.* N-COUNT: usu with supp

9 Someone's or something's **place** in a society, system, or situation is their position or role in relation to other people or things. *They want to see more women take their place higher up the corporate or professional ladder... It would be foolish to exclude Christianity from the curriculum, in view of its important place in our national culture.* N-COUNT: with poss

10 Your **place** in a race or competition is your position in relation to the other competitors. If you are in first place, you are ahead of all the other competitors. *Jane's goals helped Britain win third place in the Barcelona games... He has risen second place in the opinion polls.* N-COUNT: usu sing, usu ord N

11 If you get a **place** in a team, on a committee, on a course, or on a trip, for example, you are accepted as a member of the team or committee or as a participant on the course or trip. *He has found a place in the first team... All the candidates won places on the ruling council... I eventually got a place at York University... They should be in residential care but there are no places available... To book your place fill in the coupon on page 187 and return it by 1st October.* N-COUNT: usu with supp

12 A good **place** to do something in a situation or activity is a good time or stage at which to do it. *It seemed an appropriate place to end somehow... This is not the place for a lengthy discussion.* N-SING: with supp, oft N to-inf, N *for* n/-ing =time

13 Your **place** is the house or flat where you live; an informal use. *Let's all go back to my place!... He kept encouraging Rosie to find a place of her own.* N-COUNT: usu sing, usu poss N

14 Your **place** in a book or speech is the point you have reached in reading the book or making the speech. *...her finger marking her place in the book... He lost his place in his notes.* N-COUNT: usu sing, usu poss N

15 If you say how many decimal **places** there are in a number, you are saying how many numbers there are to the right of the decimal point. *A pocket calculator only works to eight decimal places.* N-COUNT: usu num N

16 If you **place** something somewhere, you put it in a particular position, especially in a careful, firm, or deliberate way. *Brand folded it in his handkerchief and placed it in the inside pocket of his jacket... Chairs were hastily placed in rows for the parents.* VERB =put V n prep/adv

17 To **place** a person or thing in a particular state means to cause them to be in it. *Widespread protests have placed the President under serious pressure... The crisis could well place the relationship at risk... The remaining 30 percent of each army will be placed under UN control.* VERB =put V n prep *be* V-ed prep

18 You can use **place** instead of 'put' or 'lay' in certain expressions where the meaning is carried by the associated noun. For example, if you **place emphasis** on something, you emphasize it; and if you **place the blame** on someone, you blame them. *We* VERB =put V n *on/upon* n

should teach the young by placing responsibility on them and by trusting them in real endeavors... He placed great emphasis on the importance of family life and ties... She seemed to be placing most of the blame on her mother... His government is placing its faith in international diplomacy. V n *in* n

19 If you **place** someone or something in a particular class or group, you classify them in that way. *The authorities have placed the drug in Class A, the same category as heroin and cocaine... Dr. Boris Sidis was a Russian-born psychiatrist who enjoyed considerable prestige; some placed him on a par with Pierre Janet and Morton Prince.* VERB =put, rank V n prep

20 If a competitor **is placed** first, second, or last, for example, that is their position at the end of a race or competition. *I had been placed 2nd and 3rd a few times but had never won... Second-placed Auxerre suffered a surprising 2-0 home defeat to Nantes.* VB: usu passive *be* V-ed ord ord V-ed

21 If you **place an order** for some goods or for a meal, you ask a company to send you the goods or a waiter to bring you the meal. *It is a good idea to place your order well in advance as delivery can often take months rather than weeks... Before placing your order for a meal, study the menu.* VERB V n

22 If you **place an advertisement** in a newspaper, you arrange for the advertisement to appear in the newspaper. *They placed an advertisement in the local paper for a secretary.* VERB =put V n *in* n Also V n

23 If you **place a telephone call** to a particular place, you give the operator the number of the person you want to speak to and ask them to connect you. *I'd like to place an overseas call.* VERB V n

24 If you **place a bet** with a bookmaker, you bet on the result of a future event. *For this race, though, he had already placed a bet on one of the horses.* VERB V n *on* n Also V n

25 If an agency or organization **places** someone, it finds them a job or somewhere to live. *In 1861, they managed to place fourteen women in paid positions in the colonies... In cases where it proves very difficult to place a child, the reception centre might end by providing relatively long-term care.* VERB V n *in* n V n

26 If you say that you cannot **place** someone, you mean that you recognize them but cannot remember exactly who they are or where you have met them before. *Something about the man was familiar, although Hillsden could not immediately place him... It was a voice he recognized, though he could not immediately place it.* VERB V n

27 See also **meeting place**.

28 If something is happening **all over the place**, it is happening in many different places. *Businesses are closing down all over the place... There are picket lines all over the place.* PHRASES PHR after v, v-link PHR

29 If things are **all over the place**, they are spread over a very large area, usually in a disorganised way. *Our fingerprints are probably all over the place... There was ammunition lying all over the place.* v-link PHR, PHR after v

30 If you say that someone is **all over the place**, you mean that they are confused or disorganized, and unable to think clearly or act properly. *He was careful and diligent. I was all over the place.* v-link PHR

31 If you **change places** with another person, you change situations or roles in life with them. *When he has tried to identify all the items, you can change places, and he can test you... With his door key in his hand, knowing Millie and the kids awaited him, he wouldn't change places with anyone.* RECIP: V inflects, pl-n PHR, PHR *with* n =swap

32 If you have been trying to understand something puzzling and then everything **falls into place** or **clicks into place**, you suddenly understand how different pieces of information are connected and everything becomes clearer. *When the reasons behind the decision were explained, of course, it all fell into place... But it wasn't until I saw the photograph in the paper that everything clicked into place.* V inflects

33 If things **fall into place**, events happen naturally to produce a situation you want. *Once the decision was made, things fell into place rapidly... Keep your options open and everything will fall into place.* V inflects

34 If you say that someone **is going places**, you mean that they are showing a lot of talent or ability and are likely to become very successful. *You always knew Barbara was going places, she was different.* V inflects, oft cont

35 People **in high places** are people who have powerful and influential positions in a government, society, or organization. *He had friends in high places... The discontent has been fuelled by allegations of corruption in high places.* usu n PHR

36 If something is **in place**, it is in its correct or usual position. If it is **out of place**, it is not in its correct or usual position. *Geoff hastily pushed the drawer back into place... Not a strand of her golden hair was out of place.* PHR after v, v-link PHR

37 If something such as a law, a policy, or an administrative structure is **in place**, it is working or able to be used. *Similar legislation is already in place in Wales... They're offended by the elaborate security measures the police have put in place.* v-link PHR, PHR after v

38 If one thing or person is used or appears **in place of** another or **in** another's **place**, they replace the other thing or person. *Cooked kidney beans can be used in place of French beans... Laurence Waters visited us in place of John Trethewy who was unfortunately ill... They're nice pictures and we've nothing to put in their place.*

39 If something has particular characteristics or features **in places**, it has them at several points within an area. *Even now the snow along the roadside was five or six feet deep in places... His face was scarred and oddly puffy in places.* PHR with cl/group

40 If you say what you would have done **in** someone else's **place**, you say what you would have done if you had been in their situation and had been experiencing what they were experiencing. *In her place I wouldn't have been able to resist it... What would you have done in my place, my dear?*

41 You say **in the first place** when you are talking about the beginning of a situation or about the situation as it was before a series of events. *What brought you to Washington in the first place?... The emphasis is swinging away from simply finding cures for illness to ways of preventing illness in the first place... I don't think we should have been there in the first place.* PHR after v PRAGMATICS

42 You say **in the first place** and **in the second place** to introduce the first and second in a series of points or reasons. **In the first place** can also be used to emphasize a very important point or reason. *In the first place you are not old, Norman. And in the second place, you are a very strong and appealing man... She could not have taken these massive doses orally. In the first place, she did not have enough pills.* PHR with cl PRAGMATICS =firstly

43 If you say that **it is not** your **place** to do something, you mean that it is not right or appropriate for you to do it, or that it is not your responsibility to do it. *He says that it is not his place to comment on government commitment to further funds... It's not my place to do their job.* V inflects, usu PHR to-inf

44 If someone or something seems **out of place** in a particular situation, they do not seem to belong there or to be suitable for that situation. *I felt out of place in my suit and tie... Her use of the word hate sounded strange and out of place. ...a noble building that would not have been out of place along the Grand Canal in Venice.* v-link PHR

45 If you say that someone has found their **place in the sun**, you mean that they are in a job or a situation where they will be happy, well-off, and have everything that they want. usu poss PHR

46 If you **place** one thing **above**, **before**, or **over** another, you think that the first thing is more important than the second and you show this in your behaviour. *Many provincial governments have taken advantage of this to place local interests above those of the central government... He continued to place security above all other objectives.* =put

47 If you **put** someone **in** their **place**, you show them that they are less important or clever than they think they are. *In a few words she had not only* V inflects =humble *put him in his place but delivered a precise and damning assessment of his movie.*

48 If you say that someone should **be shown** their **place** or **be kept in** their **place**, you mean that they should be made aware of their unimportance or low status; often used ironically. *...an uppity publican who needs to be shown his place. ...discrimination intended to keep women soldiers in their place.*

49 If one thing **takes second place** to another, it is considered to be less important and is given less attention than the other thing. *My personal life has had to take second place to my career.* V inflects, oft PHR *to* n

50 If one thing or person **takes the place of** another or **takes** another's **place**, they replace the other thing or person. *Optimism was gradually taking the place of pessimism... He eventually took Charlie's place in a popular Latin band.* V inflects =replace

51 • **pride of place**: see **pride**.

Place. **Place** is used as part of the name of a square or short street in a town. *...15 Portland Place, London W1A 4DD.* ◆◆◇◇◇ N-IN-NAMES

placebo /pləsiːboʊ/ **placebos.** A **placebo** is a harmless inactive substance that a doctor gives to a patient instead of a drug. Placebos are used when testing new drugs or when a patient has imagined their illness. ◆◇◇◇◇ N-COUNT

placebo effect, placebo effects. The **placebo effect** is the fact that some patients' health improves after taking what they believe is an effective drug but which is in fact only a placebo. *The placebo effect can be understood only if we acknowledge the unity of mind and body.* N-COUNT: usu *the* N in sing

place card, place cards. A **place card** is a small card with a person's name on it which is put on a table at a formal meal to indicate where that person is to sit. N-COUNT

-placed /-pleɪst/

1 **-placed** combines with adverbs to form adjectives which describe how well or badly someone is able to do a particular task. *A member of the Royal Commission on Criminal Justice, Miss Rafferty is well-placed to comment... I imagine he thought you were better-placed than most to know the truth... Fund managers are poorly placed to monitor firms.* COMB in ADJ-GRADED

2 **-placed** combines with adverbs to form adjectives which indicate how good or bad the position of a building or area is considered to be. *The hotel is wonderfully placed only a minute's walk from the city centre... Chicago is perfectly-placed for exploring the US by rail... In the absence of any well-placed pub, this was the perfect spot to flop down for a packed lunch.* COMB in ADJ-GRADED

placeman /pleɪsmən/ **placemen.** If you refer to a public official as a **placeman**, you disapprove of the fact that they use their position for their own personal benefit, or that they have been given their position because those who appointed them know that they can be relied upon to give political support. *...the party's programme to purify the Commons by the removal of placemen.* N-COUNT: usu pl PRAGMATICS

place mat, place mats; also spelled **placemat.** **Place mats** are mats that are put on a table before a meal for people to put their plates or bowls on. N-COUNT

placement /pleɪsmənt/ **placements** ◆◇◇◇◇

1 The **placement** of something or someone is the act of putting them in a particular place or position. *The treatment involves the placement of twenty-two electrodes in the inner ear.* N-UNCOUNT: with supp, usu *the* N *of* n

2 If someone who is training gets a **placement**, they get a job for a period of time which is intended to give them experience in the work they are training for. *He spent a year studying Japanese in Tokyo, followed by a six-month work placement with the Japanese government.* N-COUNT: usu supp N

3 The **placement** of someone in a job, home, or school is the act or process of finding them a job, home, or school. *The children were waiting for placement in a foster care home... A job placement program exists to help those who are unemployed.* N-UNCOUNT: with supp

4 You can refer to a home that is found for someone who is unable to look after themselves, for example a child, as a **placement**. *This home seemed like a good placement for Sarah.* N-COUNT

placenta /pləsentə/ **placentas.** The **placenta** is the mass of veins and tissue inside the womb of a pregnant woman or animal, which the foetus is attached to. *The drug can be transferred from the mother to the baby in the womb via the placenta.* N-COUNT: usu *the* N

place setting, place settings

1 A **place setting** is an arrangement of knives, forks, spoons, and glasses that has been laid out on a table for the use of one person at a meal. *He saw the note on the kitchen table, next to one of the two place settings.* N-COUNT

2 A **place setting** of cutlery or crockery is a complete set of all the cutlery or crockery that one person might use at a meal. *A seven-piece place setting costs about £45.* N-COUNT

placid /plæsɪd/ ◆◇◇◇◇

1 A **placid** person or animal is calm and does not easily become excited, angry, or upset. *She was a placid child who rarely cried... Marcus remained placid in the face of her outburst.* ADJ-GRADED =calm ♦ **placidly** *'No matter, we will pay the difference,' Helena said placidly... The cow in the nearby field was still chewing placidly on its cud.* ADV-GRADED: ADV with v =calmly

2 A **placid** place, area of water, or life is calm and peaceful. *...the placid waters of Lake Erie... He had been leading a placid life for the past eight years.* ADJ-GRADED: usu ADJ n =tranquil

placings /pleɪsɪŋz/. **The placings** in a competition are the relative positions of the competitors at the end or at a particular stage of the competition. *The placings remained unaltered... Northampton were third in the League placings.* ◆◇◇◇◇ N-PLURAL: usu *the* N, oft supp N

plagiarism /pleɪdʒərɪzəm/ **plagiarisms**

1 **Plagiarism** is the practice of using or copying someone else's idea or work and pretending that you thought of it or created it. *Now he's in real trouble. He's accused of plagiarism.* N-UNCOUNT ♦ **plagiarist, plagiarists** *Colleagues call Oates an unlikely plagiarist.* N-COUNT

2 A **plagiarism** is an idea or a piece of writing or music that has been secretly copied from someone else's work. *Most famous political quotes are plagiarisms and this was no exception.* N-COUNT

plagiarize /pleɪdʒəraɪz/ **plagiarizes, plagiarizing, plagiarized;** also spelled **plagiarise** in British English. If someone **plagiarizes** another person's idea or work, they use it or copy it and pretend that they thought of it or created it. *He has pointed out that moderates are plagiarizing his ideas in hopes of wooing voters... The poem employs as its first lines a verse plagiarized from a billboard.* VERB V n V *from* n Also V

plague /pleɪg/ **plagues, plaguing, plagued** ◆◆◇◇◇

1 A **plague** is a very infectious disease that spreads quickly and kills large numbers of people. *A cholera plague had been killing many prisoners of war at the time.* N-COUNT: oft supp N =epidemic

2 **Plague** or **the plague** is a very infectious and usually fatal disease, in which the patient has a severe fever and swellings on his or her body. *... a fresh outbreak of plague. ...illnesses such as smallpox, typhus and the plague.* N-UNCOUNT: also *the* N

3 A **plague of** unpleasant things is a large number of them that arrive or happen at the same time. *The city is under threat from a plague of rats... Last year there was a plague of robbery and housebreaking.* N-COUNT: N *of* n =epidemic

4 If you describe something as a **plague**, you mean that it causes a great deal of trouble or harm. *Inflation will remain a recurrent plague... Tim seems to have escaped the cynicism which is the absolute plague of our generation.* N-COUNT: usu sing =curse

5 If you are **plagued** by unpleasant things, they continually cause you a lot of trouble or suffering. *She was plagued by weakness, fatigue, and dizziness... Fears about job security plague nearly half the workforce.* VERB be V-ed *by* n V n

6 If someone **plagues** you, they keep bothering you or asking you for something. *I'm not going to plague you with a lot more questions, Miss Culver... Tommy Cook had been plaguing Pinner for months.* VERB =pester V n *with* n V n

7 If you say that you **avoid** someone or something **like the plague**, you are emphasizing that you deliberately avoid them completely. *I would avoid him like the plague when his wife and my parents were around... I normally avoid cheap wine like the plague.* PHRASES V inflects PRAGMATICS

8 You say **a plague on** a particular person or thing when you are very irritated by them and do not want to bother with them any more; an old-fashioned expression. *A plague on you and your damned percentages!* PHR n PRAGMATICS

plaice /pleɪs/; **plaice** is both the singular and the plural form. **Plaice** are a type of flat sea fish. ◆◇◇◇◇ N-VAR
▶ **Plaice** is this fish eaten as food. *...a fillet of plaice with sautéd rice and vegetables.* N-UNCOUNT

plaid /plæd/ **plaids** ◆◇◇◇◇

1 **Plaid** is material with a check design on it. **Plaid** is also the design itself. *Eddie wore blue jeans and a plaid shirt.* N-MASS: oft N n

2 A **plaid** is a long piece of tartan material that is worn over the shoulder as part of the Scottish Highland national dress. N-COUNT

plain /pleɪn/ **plainer, plainest; plains** ◆◆◆◇◇

1 A **plain** object, surface, or fabric is entirely in one colour and has no pattern, design, or writing on it. *In general, a plain carpet makes a room look bigger... He placed the paper in a plain envelope... He wore a plain blue shirt, open at the collar.* ADJ: usu ADJ n

2 Something that is **plain** is very simple in style. *Bronwen's dress was plain but it hung well on her... It was a plain, grey stone house, distinguished mainly by its largely unspoilt simplicity.* ♦ **plainly** *He was very tall and plainly dressed.* ADJ-GRADED ≠fancy, elaborate; ADV-GRADED: ADV -ed

3 If a fact, situation, or statement is **plain**, it is easy to recognize or understand. *It was plain to him that I was having a nervous breakdown... He's made it plain that he loves the game and wants to be involved still.* ● See also **plain-spoken**. ADJ-GRADED: usu v-link ADJ, oft *it* v-link ADJ that =clear

4 If you describe someone as **plain**, you think they look ordinary and not at all beautiful. *...a shy, rather plain girl with a pale complexion.* ADJ-GRADED

5 A **plain** is a large flat area of land with very few trees on it. *Once there were 70 million buffalo on the plains.* N-COUNT

6 You can use **plain** before an adjective in order to emphasize it. *The food was just plain terrible.* ▶ also used before a noun. *Is it love of publicity or plain stupidity on her part?* ADV: ADV adj PRAGMATICS; ADJ: ADJ n

7 You can use **plain** before a name to emphasize how simple and ordinary it is, especially when you are comparing it with another more unusual or impressive name. *Why couldn't they call you plain Ann or Alice like the rest?* ADJ: ADJ n-proper

8 If a police officer is **in plain clothes**, he or she is wearing ordinary clothes instead of a police uniform. *Three officers in plain clothes told me to get out of the car.* ● **plain sailing**: see **sailing**. PHRASE: v-link PHR, PHR after v ≠in uniform

plain chocolate. **Plain chocolate** is dark brown chocolate that has a stronger and less sweet taste than milk chocolate. N-UNCOUNT

plain-clothes; also spelled **plainclothes**. **Plain-clothes** police officers wear ordinary clothes instead of a police uniform. *He was arrested by plain-clothes detectives as he walked through the customs hall.* ● **in plain clothes**: see **plain**. ADJ: ADJ n ≠uniformed

plain flour. **Plain flour** is flour that does not make cakes and biscuits rise when they are cooked because it has no chemicals added to it. N-UNCOUNT

plainly /pleɪnli/ ◆◇◇◇◇

1 You use **plainly** when stating something that you believe cannot be doubted or denied. Plainly is often used when you are trying to convince someone else that what you are saying is true. *The judge's conclusion was plainly wrong... Plainly, a more objective method of description must be adopted... The administration plainly has some serious charges to answer.* ADV-GRADED: ADV with cl, not last in cl PRAGMATICS =undoubtedly

2 You use **plainly** to indicate that something is easily seen, noticed, or recognized. *He was plainly annoyed... I could plainly see him turning his head to the right and left... Loch plainly felt guilty about it.* ADV-GRADED: ADV with v, ADV adj =clearly

3 If you say something **plainly**, you say it in a direct and honest way, without trying to hide the facts. *'You're a coward,' Mark said very plainly and soberly... Few of our political leaders are willing to talk plainly and honestly about the emergency facing the country.* ADV-GRADED: ADV with v

plain-spoken; also spelled **plainspoken**. If you say that someone is **plain-spoken**, you mean that they say exactly what they think, even when they know that what they say may not please other people; used showing approval. *...a plain-spoken American full of scorn for pomp and pretense.* ADJ-GRADED PRAGMATICS =candid, frank

plaint /pleɪnt/ **plaints.** A **plaint** is a complaint or a sad cry; a literary word. *Somewhere a dog was howling, a forlorn, haunting plaint that echoed eerily upon the sea-misted air.* N-COUNT

plaintiff /pleɪntɪf/ **plaintiffs.** A **plaintiff** is a person who brings a legal case against someone in a court of law. ◆◇◇◇◇ N-COUNT

plaintive /pleɪntɪv/. A **plaintive** sound or voice is sad and mournful. *They lay on the firm sands, listening to the plaintive cry of the seagulls... Her voice was small and plaintive.* ♦ **plaintively** *'Why don't we do something?' Davis asked plaintively.* ◆◇◇◇◇ ADJ-GRADED =mournful; ADV-GRADED: usu ADV with v

plait /plæt, AM pleɪt/ **plaits, plaiting, plaited** ◆◇◇◇◇

1 If you **plait** three or more lengths of hair, rope, or other material together, you twist them over and under each other to make one thick length; used mainly in British English. *Joanna parted her hair, and then began to plait it into two thick braids. ...a plaited leather belt.* VERB =braid; V n; V-ed

2 A **plait** is a length of hair that has been plaited; used mainly in British English. N-COUNT =braid

plan /plæn/ **plans, planning, planned** ◆◆◆◆◆

1 A **plan** is a method of achieving something that you have worked out in detail beforehand. *The three leaders had worked out a peace plan... The project is part of a United Nations plan for refugees. ...a detailed plan of action for restructuring the group... He maintains that everything is going according to plan.* N-COUNT: usu with supp, also *according to* N =strategy

2 If you **plan** what you are going to do, you decide in detail what you are going to do, and you intend to do it. *If you plan what you're going to eat, you reduce your chances of overeating... He planned to leave Baghdad on Monday... It would be difficult for schools to plan for the future... I had been planning a trip to the West Coast... A planned demonstration in the capital later today has been called off by its organisers.* VERB; V wh; V to-inf; V *for* n; V n; V-ed

3 If you have **plans**, you are intending to do a particular thing. *'I'm sorry,' she said. 'I have plans for tonight.'... The Bonn government is making plans to evacuate more than two hundred of its citizens from the troubled area.* N-PLURAL: usu with supp, oft N *for* n/-ing, N to-inf =arrangements

4 When you **plan** something that you are going to make, build, or create, you decide what the main parts of it will be and do a drawing of how it should be made. *It is no use trying to plan an 18-hole golf course on a 120-acre site if you have to ruin the environment to do it.* VERB =design, think out; V n

5 A **plan** of something that is going to be built or made is a detailed diagram or drawing of it. *...when you have drawn a plan of the garden.* N-COUNT: oft N *of/for* n

6 See also **planning**.

plan on. If you **plan on** doing something, you intend to do it. *They were planning on getting married... They are planning on a trip to Guyana next month.* PHRASAL VERB V P -ing/n

plan out. If you **plan out** the future, you decide in detail what you are going to do. *Tony spent the next week with his marketing people planning out the production and sale of portrait dolls.* PHRASAL VERB V P n (not pron) Also V n P

plane /pleɪn/ **planes, planing, planed** ◆◆◆◆◇

1 A **plane** is a vehicle with wings and one or more engines, which can fly through the air. *He had plenty of time to catch his plane... Her mother was killed in a plane crash. ...fighter planes.* N-COUNT =aeroplane, airplane

2 A **plane** is a flat, level surface which may be slop- N-COUNT

ing at a particular angle; a technical use in geometry and science. ...*a building with angled planes.*

3 If a number of points are in the same **plane**, one line or one flat surface could pass through them all; a technical use. *All the planets orbit the Sun in roughly the same plane, round its equator.* N-SING

4 If you say that something is **on a higher plane**, you mean that it is more spiritual or less concerned with worldly things. ...*life on a higher plane of existence... We felt we were living life on several different planes.* N-COUNT: adj N =level

5 A **plane** is a tool that has a flat bottom with a sharp blade in it. You move the plane over a piece of wood in order to remove thin pieces of its surface. N-COUNT

6 If you **plane** a piece of wood, you make it smaller or smoother by using a plane. *She watches him plane the surface of a walnut board... Again I planed the surface flush.* VERB V n V n adj ► **Plane down** means the same as **plane**. *The piece was reduced in size by planing down the four corners.* PHRASAL VERB V P n (not pron) Also V n P

7 If something such as a boat **planes** across water, it moves quickly across the water, just touching the surface. *All four of the boats planed across the Solent with the greatest of ease.* VERB =skim V *across* n Also V

8 A **plane** or a **plane tree** is a large tree with broad leaves which often grows in towns. N-COUNT

plane down. See **plane** 6. PHRASAL VERB

planeload /pleɪnləʊd/ **planeloads.** A **planeload** of people or goods is as many people or goods as a plane can carry. *The British Red Cross has sent four planeloads of relief supplies to the stricken areas.* N-COUNT: usu N *of* n

planet /plænɪt/ **planets.** ◆◆◆◇◇ A **planet** is a large, round object in space that moves around a star. The Earth is a planet. *The picture shows six of the nine planets in the solar system.* N-COUNT

planetarium /plænɪteəriəm/ **planetariums.** A **planetarium** is a building where lights are shone on the ceiling to represent the planets and the stars and to show how they appear to move. N-COUNT

planetary /plænɪtri, AM -teri/. ◆◇◇◇◇ **Planetary** means relating to or belonging to planets. *Within our own galaxy there are probably tens of thousands of planetary systems.* ADJ: ADJ n

plangent /plændʒənt/. A **plangent** sound is a deep, loud sound, which may be sad; a literary word. ...*plangent violins supported by soft chords on viols.* ADJ-GRADED

plank /plæŋk/ **planks** ◆◇◇◇◇

1 A **plank** is a long, thin, rectangular piece of wood. *It was very strong, made of three solid planks of wood.* N-COUNT: oft N *of* n =board

2 The main **plank** of the policy of a particular group or political party is the main principle on which it bases its policy, or its main aim; used in journalism. *It was a defeat for Mr Lamont and a collapse of the main plank of the government's economic policy.* N-COUNT: with supp, usu N *of* n

planking /plæŋkɪŋ/. **Planking** is wood that has been cut into planks. It is used especially to make floors. N-UNCOUNT

plankton /plæŋktən/. **Plankton** is a mass of tiny animals and plants that live in the surface layer of the sea. ...*its usual diet of plankton and other small organisms.* N-UNCOUNT

planner /plænəʳ/ **planners.** ◆◆◇◇◇ **Planners** are people whose job is to make decisions about what is going to be done in the future. For example, town planners decide how land should be used and what new buildings should be built. ...*a panel that includes city planners, art experts and historians.* ...*a national meeting of economic planners.* N-COUNT: oft supp N

planning /plænɪŋ/ ◆◆◆◇◇

1 **Planning** is the process of deciding in detail how to do something before you actually start to do it. *The trip needs careful planning... The new system is still in the planning stages.* ● See also **family planning**. N-UNCOUNT

2 **Planning** is control by the local government of the way that land is used in an area and of what new buildings are built there. ...*a masterpiece of 18th-century town planning... He supported the planning authority in refusing the application because of pressures on the Green Belt.* N-UNCOUNT

planning permission, planning permissions. ◆◇◇◇◇ In Britain, **planning permission** is official permission that you must get from the local authority before a new building can be built or before an extension can be made to an existing building. N-COUNT

plant /plɑːnt, plænt/ **plants, planting, planted** ◆◆◆◆◆

1 A **plant** is a living thing that grows in the earth and has a stem, leaves, and roots. *Water each plant as often as required.* ...*exotic plants.* ● See also **bedding plant**, **pot plant**, **rubber plant**. N-COUNT

2 When you **plant** a seed, plant, or young tree, you put it into the ground so that it will grow there. *He says he plans to plant fruit trees and vegetables.* VERB V n ♦ **planting** *Extensive flooding in the country has delayed planting and many crops are still under water.* N-UNCOUNT

3 When someone **plants** land with a particular type of plant or crop, they put plants, seeds, or young trees into the land to grow them there. *They plan to plant the area with grass and trees... Recently much of their energy has gone into planting a large vegetable garden.* ...*newly planted fields.* VERB V n *with* n V n V-ed

4 A **plant** is a factory or a place where power is generated. ...*Ford's British car assembly plants... The plant provides forty per cent of the country's electricity.* N-COUNT

5 **Plant** is large machinery that is used in industrial processes. *Firms may start to invest in plant and equipment abroad where costs may be lower.* N-UNCOUNT =machinery

6 If you **plant** something somewhere, you put it there firmly. *She planted her feet wide and bent her knees slightly.* ...*with his enormous feet planted heavily apart.* VERB V n adv/prep

7 If someone **plants** something such as a bomb somewhere, they hide it in the place where they want it to function. *So far no one has admitted planting the bomb.* VERB V n

8 If something such as a weapon or drugs **is planted** on someone, it is put amongst their belongings or in their house or office so that they will be wrongly accused of a crime. *He always protested his innocence and claimed that the drugs had been planted to incriminate him.* VB: oft passive *be* V-ed

9 If an organization **plants** an informer or a spy somewhere, they send that person there so that they can do something secretly. *Journalists informed police who planted an undercover detective to trap Smith..* VERB V n

10 If you **plant a kiss** on someone, you give them a kiss. *She planted a kiss on each of his leathery cheeks.* VERB V n *on* n

11 If you **plant an idea** in someone's mind, they begin to accept the idea without realizing that it has originally come from you and not from them. *He hoped that he could plant the idea in such a way that Abramov would believe it was his own.* VERB V n

plant out. When you **plant out** young plants, you plant them in the ground in the place where they are to be left to grow. *Plant out the spring cabbage whenever opportunities arise.* PHRASAL VERB V P n (not pron) Also V n P

plantain /plæntɪn/ **plantains**

1 A **plantain** is a type of green banana which can be cooked and eaten as a vegetable. ...*fried plantain.* N-VAR

2 A **plantain** is a wild plant with broad leaves and a head of tiny green flowers on a long stem. N-VAR

plantation /plɑːnteɪʃən, plæn-/ **plantations.** ◆◆◇◇◇

1 A **plantation** is a large piece of land, especially in a tropical country, where crops such as rubber, coffee, tea, or sugar are grown. ...*banana plantations in Costa Rica.* N-COUNT

2 A **plantation** is a large number of trees that have been planted together. ...*a plantation of almond trees.* N-COUNT

planter /plɑːntəʳ, plæn-/ **planters** ◆◇◇◇◇

1 **Planters** are people who own or manage plantations in tropical countries. N-COUNT

2 A **planter** is a container for plants that people keep in their homes. N-COUNT

plant pot, plant pots. A **plant pot** is a container that is used for growing plants. N-COUNT =flowerpot

plaque /plæk, plɑːk/ **plaques** ◆◇◇◇◇
1 A **plaque** is a flat piece of metal, wood, or stone, which is fixed to a wall or monument in memory of a famous person or event. *After touring the hospital, Her Majesty unveiled a commemorative plaque.* N-COUNT
2 **Plaque** is a substance that forms on the surface of your teeth. It consists of saliva, bacteria, and food. *Deposits of plaque build up between the tooth and the gum.* N-UNCOUNT

plasma /plæzmə/. **Plasma** is the clear fluid part of blood which contains the corpuscles and cells. ◆◇◇◇◇ N-UNCOUNT

plaster /plɑːstəʳ, plæs-/ **plasters, plastering, plastered** ◆◇◇◇◇
1 **Plaster** is a smooth paste made of sand, lime, and water which dries and forms a hard layer. Plaster is used to cover walls and ceilings especially inside buildings and is also used to make sculptures. *There were huge cracks in the plaster, and the green shutters were faded... In the Musée d'Orsay in Paris is a sculpture in plaster by Rodin.* N-UNCOUNT
2 If you **plaster a wall** or **ceiling**, you cover it with a layer of plaster. *The ceiling he had just plastered fell in and knocked him off his ladder.* VERB V n
3 If you **plaster** a surface or a place with posters or pictures, you stick a lot of them all over it. *He has plastered the city with posters proclaiming his qualifications and experience... His room is plastered with pictures of Porsches and Ferraris.* VERB V n *with* n V-ed
4 If you **plaster** yourself in some kind of sticky substance, you cover yourself in it. *She gets sunburnt even when she plasters herself from head to toe in Factor 7 sun lotion.* VERB V pron-refl *in* n
5 In British English, a **plaster** is a strip of sticky material used for covering small cuts or sores on your body. The usual American word is **Band-Aid.** ● See also **sticking plaster**. N-COUNT
6 See also **plastered**.
7 If you have a leg or arm **in plaster**, you have a cast made of plaster of Paris around your leg or arm, in order to protect a broken bone and allow it to mend. PHRASE

plasterboard /plɑːstəʳbɔːʳd, plæs-/. **Plasterboard** is thin, rectangular sheets of board. It is made from sheets of cardboard which are held together with plaster, and is used for covering walls and ceilings instead of using plaster. N-UNCOUNT

plaster cast, plaster casts. A **plaster cast** is a case made of plaster of Paris, which is used for protecting broken bones by keeping part of the body stiff and rigid, and can also be used as a mould for sculptures. *A few years ago I broke my leg and had a plaster cast on up to my hip. ...a plaster cast of the Venus de Milo.* N-COUNT

plastered /plɑːstəʳd, plæs-/ ◆◇◇◇◇
1 If something is **plastered to** a surface, it is sticking to the surface. *His hair was plastered down to his scalp by the rain.* ADJ: v-link ADJ prep/adv
2 If something or someone is **plastered with** a sticky substance, they are covered with it. *My hands, boots and trousers were plastered with mud.* ADJ: v-link ADJ, usu ADJ *with/in* n
3 If a story or a set of photos is **plastered all over** the front page of a newspaper, it is given a lot of space on the page and is printed or displayed in a very prominent way. *His picture was plastered all over the newspapers on the weekend.* ADJ: v-link ADJ prep/adv
4 If someone gets **plastered**, they get very drunk; used in informal British English. *With gin at 9p a tot, getting plastered is cheap and easy.* ADJ: v-link ADJ =sloshed
5 If someone's arm or leg is **plastered**, it has a hard cast of plaster of Paris around it to protect the broken bone whilst it is mending. *She was sitting in a hospital bed, her plastered leg up in the air.* ADJ

plasterer /plɑːstərəʳ, plæs-/ **plasterers.** A **plasterer** is a person whose job it is to cover walls and ceilings with plaster. N-COUNT

plaster of Paris /plɑːstər əv pærɪs, plæs-/. **Plaster of Paris** is a type of plaster made from white powder and water which dries quickly. It is used to make plaster casts. N-UNCOUNT

plastic /plæstɪk/ **plastics** ◆◆◆◇◇
1 **Plastic** is a material which is produced by a chemical process and which is used to make many objects. It is light in weight and does not break easily. *...a wooden crate, sheltered from wetness by sheets of plastic... A lot of the plastics that carmakers are using cannot be recycled. ...a black plastic bag.* N-MASS: oft N n
2 If you describe something as **plastic**, you mean that you think it looks or tastes unnatural or false because it is man-made; used showing disapproval. *You wanted proper home-cooked meals, you said you had enough plastic hotel food and airline food... When girls put on too much eye-shadow, they look plastic.* ADJ-GRADED PRAGMATICS
3 If you use **plastic** or **plastic money** to pay for something, you pay for it with a credit card instead of using cash; an informal use. *Using plastic to pay for an order is simplicity itself. ...shopping with their plastic money.* N-UNCOUNT
4 Something that is **plastic** is soft and can easily be made into different shapes. *You can also enjoy mud packs with the natural mud, smooth, gray, soft, and plastic as butter.* ♦ **plasticity** /plæstɪsɪti/ *...the plasticity of the flesh.* ADJ =pliable, flexible N-UNCOUNT

plastic bullet, plastic bullets. A **plastic bullet** is a bullet made of plastic, which is intended to disperse crowds in riots, rather than to kill people. N-COUNT

plastic explosive, plastic explosives. Plastic explosive is a substance which explodes and which is used in making small bombs. N-MASS

Plasticine /plæstɪsiːn/. **Plasticine** is a soft coloured substance like clay which children use for making little models. **Plasticine** is a British trademark. N-UNCOUNT

plastic surgeon, plastic surgeons. A **plastic surgeon** is a doctor who performs operations to repair or replace skin which has been damaged, or to improve people's appearance. N-COUNT

plastic surgery. Plastic surgery is the practice of performing operations to repair or replace skin which has been damaged, or to improve people's appearance. *She even had plastic surgery to change the shape of her nose.* ◆◇◇◇◇ N-UNCOUNT

plate /pleɪt/ **plates** ◆◆◆◇◇
1 A **plate** is a round or oval flat dish that is used to hold food. *Anita pushed her plate away; she had eaten virtually nothing.* ► A **plate** of food is the amount of food on the plate. *...a huge plate of bacon and eggs.* N-COUNT N-COUNT: usu N *of* n
2 A **plate** is a flat piece of metal, especially on machinery or a building. N-COUNT
3 A **plate** is a small, flat piece of metal with someone's name written on it, which you usually find beside the front door of an office or house. N-COUNT
4 On a road vehicle, the **plates** are the panels at the front and back which display the license number in the United States, and the registration number in Britain. *...dusty-looking cars with New Jersey plates.* ● See also **number plate, license plate**. N-PLURAL
5 **Plate** is dishes, bowls, and cups that are made of precious metal, especially silver, gold, or pewter. *...gold and silver plate, jewellery, and roomfuls of antique furniture.* N-UNCOUNT
6 In printing, a **plate** is a sheet of metal which is carved or specially treated with chemicals so that it can be used to print text or pictures. N-COUNT
7 In photography, a **plate** is a thin sheet of glass that is covered with a layer of chemicals which react to the light and on which an image can be formed. N-COUNT
8 A **plate** in a book is a picture or photograph which takes up a whole page and is usually printed on better quality paper than the rest of the book. *Fermor's book has 55 colour plates.* N-COUNT =illustration
9 In a microscope, the **plate** is a small rectangular piece of glass onto which you put a small amount of the substance that you want to look at. You then slide the plate under the microscope to look at the substance. N-COUNT =slide
10 A dental **plate** is a piece of plastic which is N-COUNT

shaped to fit inside a person's mouth and which a set of false teeth is attached to.

11 In geology, a **plate** is a large piece of the earth's surface, perhaps as large as a continent, which moves very slowly; a technical use. *The United States Geological Survey has revealed that the earthquake was not caused by a simple horizontal movement of one plate past another.* N-COUNT

12 If you **have enough on** your **plate** or **have a lot on** your **plate**, you have a lot of work to do or a lot of things to deal with. *We have enough on our plate. There is plenty of work to be done on what we have.* PHRASES V inflects

13 If you say that someone has things **handed to them on a plate**, you disapprove of them because they get good things easily. *Even the presidency was handed to him on a plate.* V inflects PRAGMATICS

plateau /plætoʊ, AM plætoʊ/ **plateaus** or **plateaux** ◆◇◇◇◇

1 A **plateau** is a large area of high and fairly flat land. *A broad valley opened up leading to a high, flat plateau of cultivated land.* N-COUNT

2 If you say that an activity or process has reached a **plateau**, you mean that it has reached a stage where there is no further change or development. *The US heroin market now appears to have reached a plateau... I think the economy is stuck on a kind of plateau of slow growth.* N-COUNT

plated /pleɪtɪd/. If something made of metal is **plated with** a thin layer of another type of metal, it is covered with it. *...a range of jewellery, plated with 22-carat nickel-free gold.* ◆◇◇◇◇ ADJ: v-link ADJ *with* n

-plated /-pleɪtɪd/

1 Something made of metal that is **plated** is covered with a thin layer of another type of metal such as gold and silver. *...a gold-plated watch.* COMB in ADJ

2 See also **armour-plated**, **gold-plated**, **silver-plated**.

plateful /pleɪtfʊl/ **platefuls.** A **plateful** of food is an amount of food that is on a plate and fills it. *...a greasy plateful of bacon and eggs.* N-COUNT: usu N *of* n

plate glass; also spelled **plate-glass**. **Plate glass** is thick glass made in large, flat pieces, which is used especially to make large windows and doors. N-UNCOUNT

platelet /pleɪtlət/ **platelets. Platelets** are a kind of blood cell. If you cut yourself and you are bleeding, platelets help to stop the bleeding. A technical term in biology. N-COUNT: usu pl

plate tectonics. Plate tectonics is the way that large pieces of the earth's surface move slowly around and interact with each other; a technical term in geology. N-UNCOUNT

platform /plætfɔːʳm/ **platforms** ◆◆◆◇◇

1 A **platform** is a flat, raised structure, usually made of wood, which people stand on when they make speeches or give a performance. *Nick finished what he was saying and jumped down from the platform.* N-COUNT =stage, dais

2 A **platform** is a flat raised structure or area, usually one which something can stand on or land on. *Some of these flood shelters are on raised platforms, which have allowed government helicopters to land amid the continuing floods... They found a spot on a rocky platform where they could pitch their tents.* N-COUNT

3 A **platform** is a structure built for people to work and live on when drilling for oil or gas at sea, or when extracting it. N-COUNT

4 A **platform** in a railway station is the area beside the rails where you wait for or get off a train. *The train was about to leave and I was not even on the platform.* N-COUNT

5 The **platform** of a political party is what they say they will do if they are elected. *The party has announced a platform of political and economic reforms as it campaigns for the country's first multi-party elections next month... The Socialist Party won a landslide victory on a nationalist platform.* N-COUNT: with supp =programme

6 If someone has a **platform**, they have an opportunity to tell people what they think or want. *The demonstration provided a platform for a broad cross section of speakers.* N-COUNT =stage

7 In a bus, the **platform** is the area of floor at the front or back where you get on and off. *I stood on the crowded back platform of the seven o'clock bus as it lurched along the wet damp street.* N-SING: usu *the* N

plating /pleɪtɪŋ/. **Plating** is a thin layer of metal on something, or a covering of metal plates. *The tanker began spilling oil the moment her outer plating ruptured.* N-UNCOUNT

platinum /plætɪnəm/ ◆◇◇◇◇

1 **Platinum** is a very valuable, silvery-grey metal. It is often used for making jewellery. N-UNCOUNT

2 **Platinum** hair is very fair, almost white. *...a platinum blonde with thick eye shadow and scarlet lipstick.* COLOUR

platitude /plætɪtjuːd, AM -tuːd/ **platitudes.** A **platitude** is a statement which is considered meaningless and boring because it has been made many times before in similar situations. *Why couldn't he, for once, say something vital and original instead of just spouting the same old platitudes? ...a stream of platitudes, outlining many problems but offering few solutions.* N-COUNT

platonic /plətɒnɪk/; also spelled **Platonic.**

1 **Platonic** relationships or feelings of affection do not involve sex. *She values the platonic friendship she has had with Chris for ten years.* ADJ-GRADED ≠sexual

2 **Platonic** means relating to the ideas of the Greek philosopher Plato. *...the Platonic tradition of Greek philosophy.* ADJ: usu ADJ n

platoon /plətuːn/ **platoons.** A **platoon** is a small group of soldiers which is commanded by a lieutenant. ◆◇◇◇◇ N-COUNT

platter /plætəʳ/ **platters** ◆◇◇◇◇

1 A **platter** is a large, flat plate used for serving food; a word used mainly in American English. *The food was being served on silver platters. ...platters of ham and chicken sandwiches.* N-COUNT

2 A **platter** is a large flat plate which has different kinds of the same food on, especially cheese and fruit. *...a low-calorie fruit mousse or souffle for dessert, or a cheese platter.* N-COUNT

plaudits /plɔːdɪtz/. If a person or a thing receives **plaudits** from a group of people, those people express their admiration for or approval of that person or thing; a formal word. *They won plaudits and prizes for their accomplished films.* N-PLURAL =acclaim ≠criticism

plausible /plɔːzɪbᵊl/ ◆◇◇◇◇

1 An explanation or statement that is **plausible** seems likely to be true or valid. *A more plausible explanation would seem to be that people are fed up with the Communist Party... That explanation seems entirely plausible to me.* ♦ **plausibly** /plɔːzɪbli/ *Having bluffed his way in without paying, he could not plausibly demand his money back.* ♦ **plausibility** /plɔːzɪbɪlɪti/ *...the plausibility of the theory.* ADJ-GRADED =reasonable ≠implausible ADV-GRADED: ADV with v N-UNCOUNT =credibility

2 If you say that someone is **plausible**, you mean that although they seem to be telling the truth and they seem to be sincere and honest, they may be deceiving people. *All I can say is that he was so plausible it wasn't just me that he conned.* ADJ-GRADED =believable

play /pleɪ/ **plays, playing, played** ◆◆◆◆◆

1 When children, animals, or perhaps adults **play**, they spend time doing enjoyable things, such as using toys and taking part in games. *...invite the children round to play... They played in the little garden... Polly was playing with her teddy bear.* ► Also a noun. *...a few hours of play until the baby-sitter takes them off to bed.* VERB V V *with* n N-UNCOUNT

2 When you **play** a sport, game, or match, you take part in it. *While the twins played cards, Francis sat reading... Alain was playing cards with his friends... I used to play basketball... I want to play for my country... He captained the team but he didn't actually play.* ► Also a noun. *Both sides adopted the Continental style of play.* V-RECIP pl-n V n V n *with* n V n (non-recip) V *for* n (non-recip) V (non-recip) N-UNCOUNT

3 When one person or team **plays** another or **plays against** them, they compete against them in a sport or game. *Northern Ireland will play Latvia... I've played against him a few times.* ► Also a noun. *Fischer won after 5 hours and 41 minutes of play.* VERB V n V *against* n N-UNCOUNT

4 When you **play** the ball or **play** a shot or a stroke VERB

in a game or sport, you kick or hit the ball. *Think first before playing the ball... Sikander Bakht played a bad shot... I played the ball back slightly.*
V n / V n adv

5 If you **play a joke** or **a trick** on someone, you deceive them or give them a surprise in a way that you think is funny, but that often causes problems for them or annoys them. *Someone had played a trick on her, stretched a piece of string at the top of those steps... I thought: 'This cannot be happening, somebody must be playing a joke'.*
VERB / V n on n / V n

6 If you **play with** an object or with your hair, you keep moving it or touching it with your fingers, perhaps because you are bored or nervous. *She stared at the floor, idly playing with the strap of her handbag.*
VERB / =toy / V *with* n

7 A **play** is a piece of writing which is performed in a theatre, on the radio, or on television. *The company put on a play about the homeless... It's my favourite Shakespeare play.*
N-COUNT

8 If an actor **plays** a role or character in a play or film, he or she performs the part of that character. *...Dr Jekyll and Mr Hyde, in which he played Hyde... His ambition is to play the part of Dracula.*
VERB / V n

9 You can use **play** to describe how someone behaves, when they are deliberately behaving in a certain way or like a certain type of person. For example, if someone **plays the innocent**, they pretend to be innocent, and if someone **plays deaf**, they pretend not to hear something. *Hill tried to play the peacemaker... She was just playing the devoted mother... So you want to play nervous today?*
V-LINK / =act / V n / Also V adj

10 You can describe how someone deals with a situation by saying that they **play it** in a certain way. For example, if someone **plays it cool**, they keep calm and do not show much emotion, and if someone **plays it straight**, they behave in an honest and direct way. *Investors are playing it cautious, and they're playing it smart.*
VERB / V *it* adj/adv

11 If you **play** a musical instrument or **play** a tune on a musical instrument, or if a musical instrument **plays**, music is produced from it. *Nina had been playing the piano... Two people played jazz on a piano... He played for me... Place your baby in her seat and play her a lullaby... The guitars played.*
V-ERG / V n / V *for* n / V n n / V / Also V n *for* n

12 If you **play** a record, a compact disc, or a tape, you put it onto a record player or into a tape recorder and sound is produced. If a record or tape **is playing**, sound is being produced from it. *She played her records too loudly... Every evening in those days the BBC played 'God Save The King'... The records were played on the radio... There is classical music playing in the background.*
V-ERG / V n / V / Also V n n

13 If a musician or group of musicians **plays** or **plays** a concert, they perform music for people to listen or dance to. *A band was playing... He will play concerts in Amsterdam and Paris.*
VERB / =perform / V / V n

14 When light **plays** somewhere, it moves about on a surface in an unsteady way; a literary use. *The sun played on the frosty roofs.*
VERB / V prep

15 If you ask **what** someone **is playing at**, you are angry because you think they are doing something stupid or wrong; an informal expression. *What the hell are you playing at?.*
PHRASES / V inflects / PRAGMATICS

16 When something **comes into play** or **is brought into play**, it begins to be used or to have an effect. *The real existence of a military option will come into play... Breathing brings many muscles into play.*
V inflects

17 If something or someone **plays a part** or **plays a role** in a situation, they are involved in it and have an effect on it. *They played a part in the life of their community... The UN would play a major role in monitoring a ceasefire. ...the role played by diet in disease.*
V inflects, usu PHR *in* n

18 • to **play ball**: see **ball**. • to **play your cards right**: see **card**. • to **play it by ear**: see **ear**. • to **play fair**: see **fair**. • to **play fast and loose**: see **fast**. • to **play second fiddle**: see **fiddle**. • to **play the field**: see **field**. • to **play with fire**: see **fire**. • to **play the fool**: see **fool**. • to **play to the gallery**: see **gallery**. • to **play into** someone's **hands**: see **hand**. • to **play hard to get**: see **hard**. • to **play havoc**: see **havoc**. • to **play host**: see **host**. • to **play safe**: see **safe**. • to **play for time**: see **time**. • to **play truant**: see **truant**.

play along. If you **play along** with a person, with what they say, or with their plans, you appear to agree with them and do what they want, even though you are not sure whether they are right. *My mother has learnt to play along with the bizarre conversations begun by father... He turned and led the way to the lift. Fox played along, following him.*
PHRASAL VERB / no passive / V P with n / V P

play at
PHRASAL VERB

1 If you say that someone is **playing at** something, you disapprove of the fact that they are doing it casually and not very seriously. *We were still playing at war – dropping leaflets instead of bombs.*
no passive / V P n/-ing

2 If someone, especially a child, **plays at** being someone or doing something, they pretend to be that person or do that thing as a game. *Ed played at being a pirate.*
no passive / V P n/-ing

play around
PHRASAL VERB

1 If you **play around**, you behave in a silly way to amuse yourself or other people; an informal expression. *Stop playing around and eat!... There was no doubt he was serious, it wasn't just playing around... Had he taken the keys and played around with her car?*
=mess about, fool around / V P / V P *with* n

2 If you **play around with** a problem or an arrangement of objects, you try different ways of organizing it in order to find the best solution or arrangement; an informal expression. *I can play around with the pictures in all sorts of ways to make them more eye-catching.*
V P *with* n

3 If someone **plays around**, they have sex with people other than the person they are married to or having a serious relationship with; an informal expression. *Up to 75 per cent of married men may be playing around... Robert was playing around with another woman.*
=fool around / V P / V P *with* n

play back. When you **play back** a tape or film, you listen to the sounds or watch the pictures after recording them. *He bought an answering machine that plays back his messages when he calls... Ted might benefit from hearing his own voice recorded and played back... I played the tape back.* • See also **playback**.
PHRASAL VERB / V P n (not pron) / V-ed P / V n P

play down. If you **play down** something, you try to make people believe that it is not particularly important. *Western diplomats have played down the significance of the reports... He plays down rumours that he aims to become a Labour MP... Both London and Dublin are playing the matter down.*
PHRASAL VERB / =underplay / ≠play up / V P n (not pron) / V n P

play off against. If you **play** people **off against** each other, you make them compete or argue, so that you gain some advantage. *Gregory would interview them, and would play one off against the other.*
PHRASAL VERB / V n P P n / Also V P n (not pron) P n

play on. If you **play on** someone's fears, weaknesses, or faults, you deliberately use them in order to persuade that person to do something, or to achieve what you want. *...an election campaign which plays on the population's fear of change... I felt guilty saying that, playing on her generosity.*
PHRASAL VERB / =exploit / V P n

play out. If a tragic or dramatic event **is played out**, it gradually continues. *...a political power struggle being played out in Cambodia... The film has eerie parallels with the drama being played out in real life.*
PHRASAL VERB / usu passive / =unfold / *be* V-ed P / Also V P n

play up
PHRASAL VERB

1 If you **play up** something, you emphasize it and try to make people believe that it is important. *The media played up the prospects for a settlement... His Japanese ancestry has been played up by some of his opponents.*
=emphasize / ≠play down, underplay / V P n (not pron) / Also V n P

2 If something such as a machine or a part of your body **is playing up** or **is playing** you **up**, it is causing you problems because it is not working properly; used mainly in informal British English. *The engine had been playing up... It was his back playing him up.*
usu cont, no passive / V P / V n P

3 When children **play up**, they are naughty and difficult to control; used mainly in informal British

English. *Patrick often plays up when he knows I'm in a hurry.* V P

play upon. To **play upon** something means the same as to play on it; a formal expression. PHRASAL VERB

play-act, play-acts, play-acting, play-acted. VB: usu cont If someone **is play-acting**, they are pretending to have attitudes or feelings that they do not really have. *The 'victim' revealed he was only play acting.* V ► Also a noun. *It was just a piece of play-acting.* N-UNCOUNT

playback /pleɪbæk/ **playbacks.** The **playback** of a tape is the operation of playing it on a machine in order to listen to the sound or watch the pictures recorded on it. *I heard a playback of one of the tapes.* N-COUNT: usu sing

playboy /pleɪbɔɪ/ **playboys.** You can refer to a rich man who spends most of his time enjoying himself as a **playboy**. *Father was a rich playboy. ...the playboy millionaire.* N-COUNT

player /pleɪəʳ/ **players** ◆◆◆◆◆

1 A **player** in a sport or game is a person who takes part, either as a job or for fun. *...his greatness as a player... She was a good golfer and tennis player. ...top chess-players.* N-COUNT

2 You can use **player** to refer to a musician. For example, a **piano player** is someone who plays the piano. *...a professional trumpet player.* N-COUNT

3 If a person, country, or organization is a **player** in something, they are involved in it and important in it. *Big business has become a major player in the art market... America is not a party to the negotiations, yet it is a key player... Mr Lafontant has re-emerged as a player in Haiti's affairs.* N-COUNT: oft supp N, N inn

4 A **player** is an actor. *...a company of players... Oscar nominations went to all five leading players.* N-COUNT

5 See also **cassette player**, **CD player**, **record player**.

playful /pleɪfʊl/ ◆◇◇◇◇

1 A **playful** gesture or person is friendly and jokey. *...a playful kiss on the tip of his nose. ...a playful fight... Her manner is playful and girlish.* ADJ-GRADED ♦ **playfully** *She pushed him away playfully.* ADV-GRADED ♦ **playfulness** *...the child's natural playfulness.* N-UNCOUNT

2 A **playful** animal is lively and cheerful. *...a playful puppy.* ADJ-GRADED

playground /pleɪgraʊnd/ **playgrounds** ◆◇◇◇◇

1 A **playground** is a piece of land, at school or in a public area, where children can play. • See also **adventure playground.** N-COUNT

2 If you describe a place as a **playground** for a certain group of people, you mean that those people like to enjoy themselves there or go on holiday there. *...St Tropez, playground of the rich and famous.* N-COUNT: usu sing, oft N supp

playgroup /pleɪgruːp/ **playgroups.** A **playgroup** is an informal kind of school for very young children, where they learn things by playing. ◆◇◇◇◇ N-COUNT: also prep N =playschool

playhouse /pleɪhaʊs/ **playhouses** ◆◇◇◇◇

1 A **playhouse** is a theatre. *The Theatre Royal is one of the oldest playhouses in Britain.* N-COUNT =theatre

2 A **playhouse** is a small house made for children to play in. *My father built me a playhouse.* N-COUNT =wendy house

playing card, playing cards. Playing cards are thin pieces of cardboard with numbers or pictures printed on them, which are used to play various games. N-COUNT =card

playing field, playing fields ◆◇◇◇◇

1 A **playing field** is a large area of grass where people play sports. *...the playing fields of the girls' Grammar School.* N-COUNT

2 You talk about a **level playing field** to mean a situation that is fair, because no competitor or opponent in it has an advantage over another. *American businessmen ask for a level playing field when they compete with foreign companies.* PHRASE: N inflects

playmate /pleɪmeɪt/ **playmates.** A child's **playmate** is another child who often plays with him or her. *The young girl loved to play with her playmates.* N-COUNT

play-off, play-offs; also spelled **playoff**. A **playoff** is an extra game which is played to decide the winner of a sports competition when two or more people have got the same score. *Nick Faldo was beaten by Peter Baker in a play-off. ...a playoff game to determine who is the league winner.* ◆◇◇◇◇ N-COUNT

play on words, plays on words. A **play on words** is the same as a **pun.** N-COUNT: usu a N in sing

playpen /pleɪpen/ **playpens.** A **playpen** is a small structure which is designed for a baby or young child to play safely in. It has bars or a net round the sides and is open at the top. N-COUNT

playroom /pleɪruːm/ **playrooms.** A **playroom** is a room in a house for children to play in. N-COUNT

playschool /pleɪskuːl/ **playschools.** A **playschool** is an informal kind of school for very young children where they learn things by playing. N-COUNT: also prep N =playgroup

plaything /pleɪθɪŋ/ **playthings**

1 A **plaything** is a toy or other object that a child plays with. *...an untidy garden scattered with children's playthings.* N-COUNT =toy

2 If you say that someone is treating you as a **plaything**, you think that they are using you for their amusement or advantage, and do not care about you. *...an unfaithful husband who treated women as playthings... He would not allow anyone to make him into a political plaything for their own ends.* N-COUNT PRAGMATICS =toy

playtime /pleɪtaɪm/. In a school for young children **playtime** is the period of time between lessons when they can play outside. *Any child who is caught will be kept in at playtime.* N-UNCOUNT =break

playwright /pleɪraɪt/ **playwrights.** A **playwright** is a person who writes plays. ◆◆◇◇◇ N-COUNT =dramatist

plaza /plɑːzə, AM plæzə/ **plazas.** A **plaza** is an open square in a city. *Across the busy plaza, vendors sell hot dogs and croissant sandwiches.* ◆◇◇◇◇ N-COUNT

plc /piː el siː/ **plcs;** also spelled **PLC.** In Britain, **plc** is an abbreviation for 'public limited company', meaning a company whose shares can be bought by the public. It is usually used after the name of a company. *...British Telecommunications plc... This licence would not allow him to trade as a plc.* ◆◆◇◇◇ N-COUNT: usu sing, usu n N

plea /pliː/ **pleas** ◆◆◇◇◇

1 A **plea** is an appeal or request for something, made in an intense or emotional way; used by journalists. *Mr Nicholas made his emotional plea for help in solving the killing. ...an impassioned plea to mankind to act to save the planet.* N-COUNT: oft N for n, N to-inf =appeal

2 In a court of law, a person's **plea** is the answer that they give when they have been charged with a crime, saying whether or not they are guilty of that crime. *The judge questioned him about his guilty plea... We will enter a plea of not guilty... Her plea of guilty to manslaughter through provocation was rejected.* N-COUNT: usu adj N, N of adj

3 A **plea** is a reason which is given, to a court or to other people, as an excuse for doing something or for not doing something. *Phillips murdered his wife, but got off on a plea of insanity... Mr Dunn's pleas of poverty are only partly justified.* N-COUNT: usu N of n

plea bargain, plea bargains, plea bargaining, plea bargained

1 In some legal systems, a **plea bargain** is an agreement that, if the defendant pleads guilty, he or she will be charged with a less serious crime or receive a lighter punishment. *A plea bargain was offered by the state assuring her that she wouldn't have to serve time in prison.* N-COUNT

2 If a defendant **plea bargains**, they accept a plea bargain. *More and more criminals will agree to plea-bargain.* VERB V ♦ **plea bargaining** *...the introduction of a system of plea bargaining.* N-UNCOUNT

plead /pliːd/ **pleads, pleading, pleaded** ◆◆◇◇◇

1 If you **plead with** someone to do something, you ask them in an intense, emotional way to do it. *The lady pleaded with her daughter to come back home... He was kneeling on the floor pleading for mercy... 'Do not say that,' she pleaded... I pleaded to be allowed to go.* VERB =beg V with n to-inf V for n V with quote V to-inf-passive Also V, V that

2 When someone charged with a crime **pleads guilty** or **not guilty** in a court of law, they officially VERB

state that they are guilty or not guilty of the crime. *Morris had pleaded guilty to robbery.* V adj

3 If someone **pleads the case** or **cause** of someone or something, they speak out in their support or defence. *He appeared before the Committee to plead his case... He would plead the cause of Russian unity.* VERB V n

4 If you **plead** a particular thing as the reason for doing or not doing something, you give it as your excuse. *Mr Burke, pleading poverty, changed his mind... Mr Giles pleads ignorance as his excuse... It was no defence for the guards to plead that they were only obeying orders.* VERB V n V that

pleading /pliːdɪŋ/ **pleadings** ◆◇◇◇◇

1 A **pleading** expression or gesture shows someone that you want something very much. *...his pleading eyes. ...the pleading expression on her face... Her voice was pleading.* ♦ **pleadingly** *He looked at me pleadingly.* ADJ: usu ADJ n =beseeching ADV-GRADED: ADV after v

2 **Pleading** is asking someone for something you want very much, in an intense or emotional way. *He simply ignored Sid's pleading. ...the pleadings of the poorer countries.* ● See also **special pleading**. N-UNCOUNT: also N in pl =entreaty

pleasant /plezᵊnt/ **pleasanter, pleasantest** ◆◆◆◇◇

1 Something that is **pleasant** is nice, enjoyable, or attractive. *I've got a pleasant little apartment... It's always pleasant to do what you're good at doing.* ♦ **pleasantly** *We talked pleasantly of old times... The room was pleasantly warm.* ADJ-GRADED: oft *it* v-link ADJ to-inf, ADJ to-inf ADV-GRADED: ADV with v, ADV adj

2 Someone who is **pleasant** is friendly and likeable. *The woman had a pleasant face... Lloyd George was most anxious to be agreeable and pleasant.* ADJ-GRADED: oft ADJ to-inf ≠unpleasant

pleasantry /plezᵊntri/ **pleasantries. Pleasantries** are casual, friendly remarks which you make in order to be polite. *He exchanged pleasantries about his hotel and the weather.* N-COUNT: usu pl

please /pliːz/ **pleases, pleasing, pleased** ◆◆◆◆◇

1 You say **please** when you are politely asking or inviting someone to do something, or when you are asking someone for something. *Can you help us please?... Would you please open the door?... Please come in... 'May I sit here?' 'Please do.'... Can we have the bill please?* ADV: ADV with cl PRAGMATICS

2 You say **please** when you are accepting something politely. *'Tea?'—'Yes, please.'... 'You want an apple with your cheese?'—'Please.'* ADV: ADV with cl, ADV as reply PRAGMATICS

3 You can say **please** to indicate that you want someone to stop doing something or stop speaking. You would say this if, for example, what they are doing or saying makes you angry or upset. *Please, Mary, this is all so unnecessary... Isabella. Please. I don't have time for this.* CONVENTION PRAGMATICS

4 You can say **please** in order to attract someone's attention politely. Children in particular say '**please**' to attract the attention of a teacher or other adult. *Please sir, can we have some more?... Please, Miss Smith, a moment.* CONVENTION PRAGMATICS

5 If someone or something **pleases** you, they make you feel happy and satisfied. *More than anything, I want to please you... Much of the food pleases rather than excites... It pleased him to talk to her.* VERB V n V *it* V n to-inf

6 You use **please** in expressions such as **as she pleases**, **whatever you please**, and **anything he pleases** to indicate that someone can do or have whatever they want. *Women should be free to dress and act as they please... He does whatever he pleases... Isabel can live where she pleases.* PHRASES PHR after v

7 You can use **as you please** in expressions such as **bold as you please** or **casually as you please** or **charming as you please** in order to emphasize what you are saying; an informal use. *He walked by my table and, casually as you please, picked up my address book... Bold as you please, she grabbed me by the sleeve.* adj/adv PHR PRAGMATICS

8 **If you please** is sometimes used as a very polite and formal way of attracting someone's attention or of asking someone to do something; a literary use. *Ladies and gentlemen, if you please. Miss Taylor's going to play for us... Sir Harry! Stop, if you please!* CONVENTION PRAGMATICS

9 You can say **if you please** to indicate that a situation surprises or annoys you, or is difficult to believe. *She was pretty unforthcoming. Made Sally wait till she'd cooked Selby's lunch, if you please.* PHR with cl PRAGMATICS

10 You say '**please yourself**' to indicate in a rather rude way that you do not mind or care whether the person you are talking to does a particular thing or not; an informal use. *'Do you mind if I wait?' I asked. Melanie shrugged: 'Please yourself.'* CONVENTION PRAGMATICS

11 ● **please God**: see **God**.

pleased /pliːzd/ ◆◆◆◇◇

1 If you are **pleased**, you are happy about something or satisfied with something. *Felicity seemed pleased at the suggestion... I think he's going to be pleased that we identified the real problems... They're pleased to be going home... He glanced at her with a pleased smile.* ADJ-GRADED: usu v-link ADJ, usu ADJ prep/that/to-inf ≠displeased

2 If you say you will be **pleased** to do something, you are saying in a polite way that you are willing to do it. *We will be pleased to answer any questions you may have... I shall be very pleased to help you in every way I can.* ADJ-GRADED: v-link ADJ to-inf PRAGMATICS =happy, willing

3 You can tell someone that you are **pleased** with something they have done in order to express your approval. *I'm pleased with the way things have been going... I am very pleased about the result... We are pleased that the problems have been resolved... We were very pleased to hear this encouraging news.* ADJ-GRADED: v-link ADJ, usu ADJ prep/that/to-inf PRAGMATICS =happy

4 You can say that you are **not pleased** or **none too pleased**, in order to express the fact that you are annoyed about something or dissatisfied with something. *I was not too pleased with the record you sent me... He's not too pleased that I don't seem to be doing my bit... Marianne was none too pleased to find Simon seated beside her.* ADJ-GRADED: v-link ADJ, usu ADJ prep/that/to-inf PRAGMATICS

5 When you are about to give someone some news you know will please them you can say that you are **pleased** to tell them the news or that they will be **pleased** to hear it. *I'm pleased to say that he is now doing well... You'll be very pleased to know that we offered help immediately.* ADJ-GRADED: v-link ADJ to-inf PRAGMATICS =happy

6 In official letters, people often say they will be **pleased** to do something, as a polite way of introducing what they are going to do or inviting people to do something. *We will be pleased to delete the charge from the original invoice... We are always pleased to hear from our customers.* ADJ-GRADED: v-link ADJ to-inf PRAGMATICS

7 If someone seems very satisfied with something they have done, you can say that they are **pleased with** themselves, especially if you think they are more satisfied than they should be. *'I dare say Sophie was glad to see you,' he said, pleased with himself again for having remembered her name... He had reason to be pleased with himself, since he was one of only seven out of forty candidates who were successful.* PHRASES v-link PHR, PHR with cl

8 You can say '**Pleased to meet you**' as a polite way of greeting someone who you are meeting for the first time. CONVENTION PRAGMATICS

pleasing /pliːzɪŋ/. Something that is **pleasing** gives you pleasure and satisfaction. *This area of France has a pleasing climate in August... Such a view is pleasing... It's pleasing to listen to... It's pleasing to see some criminals have a conscience.* ♦ **pleasingly** *The interior design is pleasingly simple... He sets the atmosphere and shapes the scenes pleasingly.* ◆◇◇◇◇ ADJ-GRADED: oft ADJ *to* n, ADJ to-inf =agreeable ADV-GRADED: usu ADV adj

pleasurable /pleʒərəbᵊl/. **Pleasurable** experiences or sensations are pleasant and enjoyable. *The most pleasurable experience of the evening was the wonderful fireworks display... He found sailing more pleasurable than skiing.* ♦ **pleasurably** /pleʒərəbli/ *I will teach him, she thought pleasurably. I will show him how it is done.* ◆◇◇◇◇ ADJ-GRADED =enjoyable ≠unpleasurable ADV-GRADED: ADV with v, ADV adj

pleasure /pleʒəʳ/ **pleasures** ◆◆◆◇◇

1 If something gives you **pleasure**, you get a feeling of happiness, satisfaction, or enjoyment from it. *Watching sport gave him great pleasure... Everybody takes pleasure in eating... He gets huge pleasure from ballet and contemporary dance.* N-UNCOUNT: oft N *from/in* n/-ing

2 **Pleasure** is the activity of enjoying yourself, especially rather than working or doing what you have a N-UNCOUNT duty to do. *He mixed business and pleasure in a perfect and dynamic way... I read for pleasure.*

3 A **pleasure** is an activity, experience or aspect of something that you find very enjoyable or satisfying. *Watching TV is our only pleasure. ...the pleasure of seeing a smiling face. ...the conveniences and pleasures of modern life.* N-COUNT: oft N of n/-ing

4 If you meet someone for the first time, you can say, as a way of being polite, that it is **a pleasure to meet them**. You can also ask for **the pleasure of** someone's **company** as a polite and formal way of inviting them. *'A pleasure to meet you, sir,' he said... Mr and Mrs James Stephens request the pleasure of your company at the marriage of their daughter Caroline Mary to Mr David Smith.* PHRASES CONVENTION PRAGMATICS

5 You can say **'It's a pleasure'** or **'My pleasure'** as a polite way of replying to someone who has just thanked you for doing something. *'Thanks very much anyhow.'—'It's a pleasure.'... 'Thanks for your call.'—'My pleasure.'* CONVENTION PRAGMATICS

6 You can say **'With pleasure'** as a polite way of saying that you are very willing to do something; a formal use. *Could you photocopy the advert and put it in the post to us?'—'With pleasure John.'* CONVENTION PRAGMATICS

pleasure boat, pleasure boats. A **pleasure boat** is a large boat which takes people for trips on rivers, lakes, or on the sea for pleasure. N-COUNT

pleasure craft; pleasure craft is both the singular and the plural form. A **pleasure craft** is the same as a **pleasure boat**. N-COUNT

pleat /pliːt/ **pleats.** A **pleat** in a piece of clothing is a permanent fold that is made in the cloth by folding one part over the other and sewing across the top end of the fold. ◆◇◇◇◇ N-COUNT

pleated /pliːtɪd/. A **pleated** piece of clothing has pleats in it. *...a short white pleated skirt.* ADJ: usu ADJ n

pleb /pleb/ **plebs.** If someone refers to people as **plebs**, they think that they are ignorant and uncultured; an informal British word, used showing disapproval. N-COUNT: usu pl PRAGMATICS =prole

plebeian /pləbiːən/; also spelled **plebian**.

1 A person, especially one from an earlier period of history, who is **plebeian**, comes from a low social class. *In the 1790s Tom Paine taught plebeian radicals that mankind would live in harmony were it not for the vested interest which princes, diplomats and soldiers had in promoting wars to enrich themselves.* ADJ: usu ADJ n

2 If someone describes something as **plebeian**, they think that it is unsophisticated and connected with or typical of people from a low social class; an informal use. *...a philosophy professor with a cockney accent and an alarmingly plebeian manner... He spent all day playing rackets on the beach, a plebeian sport if there ever was one.* ADJ-GRADED: usu ADJ n PRAGMATICS =common ≠sophisticated, refined

plebiscite /plebɪsaɪt, -sɪt/ **plebiscites.** A **plebiscite** is a direct vote by the people of a country or region in which they say whether they agree or disagree with a particular policy, for example whether a region should become an independent state. ◆◇◇◇◇ N-COUNT =referendum

pledge /pledʒ/ **pledges, pledging, pledged** ◆◆◆◇◇

1 When someone makes a **pledge**, they make a solemn promise that they will do something or provide something. *The meeting ended with a pledge to step up cooperation between the six states of the region. ...a £1.1m pledge of support from the Spanish ministry of culture.* N-COUNT: usu N to-inf =promise

2 When someone **pledges** to do something, they promise solemnly that they will do it or provide it. *The Communists have pledged to support the opposition's motion... Britain pledged $36 million to the refugees... Both sides pledged that a nuclear war must never be fought.* VERB V to-inf V n V that

3 If you **pledge** yourself to something, you commit yourself to following a particular course of action or to supporting a particular person, group, or idea. *The President pledged himself to increase taxes for the rich but not the middle classes... Tony Cottee has pledged himself to Everton Football Club for another three years... The treaties renounce the use of force and pledge the two countries to cooperation.* VERB =commit V pron-refl to-inf V pron-refl to n V n to n

4 If you **pledge** something such as a valuable possession or a sum of money, you leave it with someone as a guarantee that you will repay money that you have borrowed. *He asked her to pledge the house as security for a loan.* VERB =guarantee V n

plenary /pliːnəri, plen-/ **plenaries.** A **plenary session** or **plenary meeting** is one that is attended by everyone who has the right to attend. *The programme was approved at a plenary session of the Central Committee last week.* ► Also a noun. *There'll be another plenary at the end of the afternoon after the workshop.* ADJ: ADJ n =plenum N-COUNT

plenipotentiary /plenɪpətenʃəri, AM -ʃieri/ **plenipotentiaries;** also spelled **Plenipotentiary.**

1 A **plenipotentiary** is a person who has full power to make decisions or take action on behalf of their government, especially in a foreign country; a formal use. *...the Polish government in exile's plenipotentiary in Warsaw. ...the British Plenipotentiary to the China Tibet Conference.* N-COUNT

2 An **ambassador plenipotentiary** or **minister plenipotentiary** has full power or authority to represent their country; a formal use. *She became Her Britannic Majesty's new ambassador plenipotentiary to the Republic of Lebanon... Edwin H. Conger was envoy extraordinary and Minister Plenipotentiary.* ADJ: n ADJ

3 If someone such as an ambassador has **plenipotentiary powers**, they have full power or authority to represent their country; a formal use. *The Constitution grants the president plenipotentiary powers to use military force to protect our national security.* ADJ: ADJ n

plenitude /plenɪtjuːd, AM -tuːd/

1 **Plenitude** is a feeling that an experience is satisfying because it is full or complete; a formal use. *The music brought him a feeling of plenitude and freedom. ...the safety and plenitude of their life.* N-UNCOUNT =fullness, completeness ≠emptiness

2 If there is a **plenitude of** something, there is a great quantity of it; a formal use. *What is the use of a book about interior design without a plenitude of pictures in color?* N-SING: usu N of n =abundance, plenty ≠dearth

plentiful /plentɪfʊl/. Things that are **plentiful** exist in such large amounts or numbers that there is enough for people's wants or needs. *Fish are plentiful in the lake. ...a plentiful supply of vegetables and salads and fruits.* ♦ **plentifully** *Nettle grows plentifully on any rich waste ground.* ◆◇◇◇◇ ADJ-GRADED: usu v-link ADJ ADV-GRADED

plenty /plenti/ ◆◆◆◇◇

1 If there is **plenty of** something, there is a large amount of it. If there are **plenty of** things, there are many of them. It is used especially to indicate that there is enough of something, or more than you need. *There was still plenty of time to take Jill out for pizza... Most businesses face plenty of competition... Taking plenty of exercise can be of great benefit... Are there plenty of fresh fruits and vegetables in your diet?* ► Also a pronoun. *I don't believe in long interviews. Fifteen minutes is plenty... She's got plenty to do these days.* QUANT: QUANT of n-uncount/pl-n =lots PRON =lots

2 **Plenty** is a situation in which people have a lot to eat or a lot of money to live on; a formal use, sometimes used in connection with the economic state of a country. *You are all fortunate to be growing up in a time of peace and plenty. ...an area that has become a symbol of despair in the midst of America's plenty.* N-UNCOUNT

3 You use **plenty** in front of adjectives or adverbs to emphasize the degree of the quality they are describing; an informal use. *The water looked plenty deep... The compartment is plenty big enough... Keep in mind you're going to be fighting lots of men who hit plenty hard.* ADV: ADV adj/adv PRAGMATICS

4 If there are things **in plenty**, those things exist or happen in large amounts or numbers. *There were thrills in plenty on Saturday at Terrassa, where Germany won the gold medal... School inspectors visit regularly, finding everything satisfactory, books in plenty and five computer terminals.* PHRASE: n PHR, PHR after v

plenum /pli̲ːnəm/ **plenums.** A **plenum** is a meeting that is attended by all the members of a committee or conference. ◆◇◇◇◇ N-COUNT =plenary

plethora /ple̲θərə/. A **plethora of** something is a large amount of it, especially an amount of it that is greater than you need, want, or can cope with; a formal word. *A plethora of new operators will be allowed to enter the market.* ◆◇◇◇◇ N-SING: N of n

pleurisy /plʊ̲ərɪsi/. **Pleurisy** is a serious illness in which a person's lungs are inflamed and breathing is difficult. N-SING

plexus /ple̲ksəs/. see **solar plexus.**

pliable /plaɪ̲əbᵊl/

1 If something is **pliable**, you can bend it easily without cracking or breaking it. *As your baby grows bigger, his bones become less pliable... The finely twined baskets are made with young, pliable spruce roots.* ADJ-GRADED =supple, pliant ≠rigid

2 Someone who is **pliable** can be easily influenced and controlled by other people. *If we go on expecting our daughters to be decorative and pliable and empty-headed, they'll be inadequately prepared for the future.* ADJ-GRADED =pliant, compliant

pliant /plaɪ̲ənt/

1 A **pliant** person can be easily influenced and controlled by other people. *She's proud and stubborn, you know, under that pliant exterior.* ADJ-GRADED =compliant, pliable

2 If something is **pliant**, you can bend it easily without breaking it. *...pliant young willows.* ADJ-GRADED =pliable

pliers /plaɪ̲əʳz/. **Pliers** are a tool with two handles at one end and two hard, flat, metal parts at the other. **Pliers** are used for holding or pulling out things such as nails, or for bending or cutting wire. N-PLURAL: also *a pair of* N

plight /plaɪ̲t/ **plights.** If you refer to someone's **plight**, you mean that they are in a difficult or distressing situation that is full of problems. *...the worsening plight of Third World countries plagued by debts, economic dependency, corruption and militarism.* ◆◆◇◇◇ N-COUNT: usu sing, with supp

plimsoll /plɪ̲msoʊl/ **plimsolls.** In British English, **plimsolls** are canvas shoes with flat rubber soles. People wear **plimsolls** for sports and leisure activities. N-COUNT: usu pl

plinth /plɪ̲nθ/ **plinths.** A **plinth** is a rectangular block of stone on which a statue or pillar stands. N-COUNT

plod /plɒ̲d/ **plods, plodding, plodded** ◆◇◇◇◇

1 If someone **plods**, they walk slowly and heavily. *Crowds of French and British families plodded around in yellow plastic macs.* VERB V adv/prep

2 If you say that someone **plods on** or **plods along** with a job, you mean that the job is taking a long time. *He is plodding on with negotiations... Aircraft production continued to plod along at an agonizingly slow pace.* ♦ **plodding** *The plot unfolds at a plodding pace.* VERB V adv ADJ-GRADED: usu ADJ n

plodder /plɒ̲dəʳ/ **plodders.** If you say that someone is a **plodder**, you have a low opinion of them because you think they work slowly and steadily but without enthusiasm or inspiration; an informal word. *He was quiet, conscientious, a bit of a plodder. The sort Ted used to like.* N-COUNT PRAGMATICS

plonk /plɒ̲ŋk/ **plonks, plonking, plonked**

1 If you **plonk** something somewhere, you put it or drop it there heavily and carelessly; used mainly in informal British English. *She plonked the beer on the counter.* VERB =plunk V n prep/adv

2 If you **plonk** yourself somewhere, you sit down carelessly without paying attention to the people around you; used mainly in informal British English. *Steve plonked himself down on a seat and stayed motionless as the bus moved away.* VERB V pron-refl adv/prep

3 **Plonk** is cheap or poor quality wine; used mainly in informal British English. N-MASS

4 A **plonk** is a heavy, hollow sound; used mainly in British English. *...the dry plonk of tennis balls... Then plonk, down went the fork.* N-SING; SOUND

plonker /plɒ̲ŋkəʳ/ **plonkers.** In British English if someone calls a person, especially a man, a **plonker**, they think that he is stupid and incompetent; an informal word which some people find offensive. N-COUNT PRAGMATICS

plop /plɒ̲p/ **plops, plopping, plopped**

1 A **plop** is a soft, gentle sound, like the sound made by something light dropping into water without a splash. *Another drop of water fell high above them with a soft plop... A football landed with a huge 'plop' in the water outside.* N-COUNT; SOUND

2 If something **plops** somewhere, it drops there with a soft, gentle sound. *The ice cream plopped to the ground.* VERB V prep

3 If you **plop** something somewhere, you drop it there gently and without making a loud noise; an informal use. *Just plop the noodles over the center of the sauce... She picked up the coffee pot, then plopped it down and went into the living room.* VERB =put down V n prep/adv

plop down. If you **plop down** or **plop** yourself **down** somewhere, you sit down quickly but gently; an informal expression. *I plopped down on one of the dark red sofas... He plopped himself down on the grass.* PHRASAL VERB =sit down V P V pron-refl P

plot /plɒ̲t/ **plots, plotting, plotted** ◆◆◆◇◇

1 A **plot** is a secret plan by a group of people to do something that is illegal or wrong, usually against a person or a government. *Security forces have uncovered a plot to overthrow the government... He was responding to reports of an assassination plot against him.* N-COUNT: usu N to-inf, N *against* n =conspiracy

2 If people **plot** to do something or **plot** something that is illegal or wrong, they plan secretly to do it. *Prosecutors in the trial allege the defendants plotted to overthrow the government... The military were plotting a coup... They are awaiting trial on charges of plotting against the state.* VERB =conspire V to-inf V n V *against* n

3 When people **plot** a strategy or a course of action, they carefully plan each step of it. *Yesterday's meeting was intended to plot a survival strategy for the party... For the next five years she plotted her career.* VERB V n

4 The **plot** of a film, novel, or play is the connected series of events which make up the story. • see also **sub-plot.** N-VAR

5 A **plot** of land is a small piece of land, especially one that has been measured or marked out for a special purpose, such as building houses or growing vegetables. *I thought that I'd buy myself a small plot of land and build a house on it... The bottom of the garden was given over to vegetable plots.* N-COUNT: usu with supp, oft N of n

6 When someone **plots** something on a graph, they mark certain points on it and then join the points up. *So we form the cumulative distribution in the usual way and plot about eight points on the graph.* VERB V n

7 When someone **plots** the position or course of a plane or ship, they mark it on a map using instruments to obtain accurate information. *We were trying to plot the course of the submarine.* VERB =chart, map V n

8 If someone **plots** the progress or development of something, they make a diagram or a plan which shows how it has developed in order to give some indication of how it will develop in the future. *They used a computer to plot the movements of everyone in the police station on December 24, 1990.* VERB =chart V n

plotless /plɒ̲tləs/. If someone describes a film, play or novel as **plotless**, they mean that the plot does not play an important part in the development of the story. *...a surprisingly plotless play.* ADJ-GRADED: usu ADJ n

plotter /plɒ̲təʳ/ **plotters** ◆◇◇◇◇

1 A **plotter** is a person who secretly plans with others to do something that is illegal or wrong, usually against a person or government. *Coup plotters tried to seize power in Moscow.* N-COUNT: usu pl =conspirator

2 A **plotter** is a person or instrument that marks the position of something such as a ship on a map or chart. N-COUNT

plough /plaʊ̲/ **ploughs, ploughing, ploughed;** spelled **plow** in American English. ◆◆◇◇◇

1 A **plough** is a large farming tool with sharp blades which is attached to a tractor or an animal such as a horse. A plough is pulled across the soil to turn it over, usually before seeds are planted. • See also **snowplough.** N-COUNT

2 When someone **ploughs** an area of land, they turn over the soil using a plough. *They ploughed nearly 100,000 acres of virgin moorland. ...a carefully ploughed field.* ♦ **ploughing** *In Roman times* VERB V n V-ed N-UNCOUNT

November was a month of hard work in ploughing and sowing.

3 If an area of land is **under the plough**, it is used for growing crops. If land is brought or put **under the plough**, it is ploughed for the first time and is then used for growing crops. *There was not one inch of soil that was not under the plough. ...as we put more and more wilderness under the plough.* PHRASE: v-link PHR, PHR after v

4 • **to plough a lonely furrow**: see **furrow**.

plough back. If profits **are ploughed back** into a business, they are invested in it in order to expand it or improve it. *About 70 per cent of its profits are being ploughed back into the investment programme.* PHRASAL VERB usu passive; be V-ed P into n

plough into PHRASAL VERB

1 If something, for example a car, **ploughs into** something else, it goes out of control and crashes violently into it. *A young girl and her little brother were seriously hurt when a car ploughed into them on a crossing.* V P n

2 If you say that money **is ploughed into** something such as a business or a service, you are emphasizing that the amount of money which is invested in it or spent on it in order to improve it is very large. *Huge sums of private capital will be ploughed into the ailing industries of the east... He claimed he ploughed all his money into his antique business.* PRAGMATICS; be V-ed P n/-ing; V n P n/-ing

plough on. If you **plough on**, you continue moving or trying to complete something, even though it takes a lot of effort to go on. *The King, however dispirited, ploughs on... The Chancellor has opted to plough on with policies that could run his coalition on to the rocks.* PHRASAL VERB no passive; V P; V P with n

plough through PHRASAL VERB

1 If you **plough through** something such as a large meal or a long piece of work, you finally finish it although it takes a lot of effort. *Researchers have ploughed through 16,000 different pieces of classical, rock and jazz music... He used to watch body building videos and plough through a daily diet of a dozen eggs and four pints of milk.* no passive; V P n

2 If someone **ploughs through** a place or if a ship **ploughs through** water, they move through it, especially with great effort. *Mr. Dambar watched her plough through the grass... The ship ploughed through the waves.* no passive; V P n

3 If a vehicle or a missile **ploughs through** something, it goes violently or carelessly through it as though it is out of control. *The car ploughed through three gardens and flattened a tree.* no passive; V P n

plough up. If someone **ploughs up** an area of land, they plough the land, usually in order to turn grassland into land used for growing crops. *It would pay farmers to plough up the scrub and plant wheat.* PHRASAL VERB; V P n

ploughman /plaʊmən/ **ploughmen.** A **ploughman** is a man whose job it is to plough the land, especially with a plough pulled by horses or oxen. N-COUNT

ploughman's lunch, ploughman's lunches. In Britain, a **ploughman's lunch** or a **ploughman's** is a meal consisting of bread, cheese, and pickle. It is usually bought and eaten in a pub. N-COUNT

ploughshare /plaʊʃeəʳ/ **ploughshares;** spelled **plowshare** in American English. If you say that **swords have been turned into ploughshares** or **beaten into ploughshares**, you mean that a state of conflict between two or more groups of people has ended and a period of peace has begun; used in journalism. *Swords have been turned into ploughshares: factories which in the past were devoted to military production have been making pianos, refrigerators and television sets.* PHRASE: V inflects

plover /plʌvəʳ/ **plovers.** A **plover** is a bird with a rounded body, a short tail, and a short beak. Plovers are often found by the seashore or in marshland. ◆◇◇◇◇ N-COUNT

plow /plaʊ/ **plows, plowing, plowed.** See **plough**.

plowshare /plaʊʃeəʳ/ **plowshares.** See **ploughshare.**

ploy /plɔɪ/ **ploys.** A **ploy** is a way of behaving that someone plans carefully and secretly in order to gain an advantage for themselves. *Christmas should be a time of excitement and wonder, not a cynical marketing ploy.* ◆◇◇◇◇ N-COUNT: oft adj N, N to-inf, N of-ing

pluck /plʌk/ **plucks, plucking, plucked** ◆◇◇◇◇

1 If you **pluck** a fruit, flower, or leaf, you take it between your fingers and pull it in order to remove it from its stalk where it is growing; used in written English. *I plucked a lemon from the tree... He plucked a stalk of dried fennel.* VERB; V n from n; V n

2 If you **pluck** something from somewhere, you take it between your fingers and pull it sharply from where it is. *He plucked the cigarette from his mouth and tossed it out into the street... He plucked the baby out of my arms... He plucks Brazil nuts off the ground and tosses them into the basket.* VERB; V n from/out of/off n

3 If you **pluck** a guitar or other musical instrument, you pull the strings with your fingers and let them go, so that they make a sound. *Nell was plucking a harp.* VERB; V n

4 If you **pluck** a chicken or other dead bird, you pull its feathers out to prepare it for cooking. *She looked relaxed as she plucked a chicken.* VERB; V n

5 If a woman **plucks her eyebrows**, she pulls out some of the hairs using tweezers. *You've plucked your eyebrows at last!* VERB; V n

6 If someone unknown is given an important job or role and quickly becomes famous because of it, you can say that they **have been plucked from obscurity** or **plucked** from an unimportant position; used in written English. *When Gorbachev appointed Shevardnadze as foreign minister in 1985, it seemed to many in the west that he had been plucked from obscurity... Brigitte Bardot was plucked from the cover of 'Elle' magazine.* VB: usu passive; be V-ed from n

7 If someone is rescued from a dangerous situation, you can say that they **are plucked from** it or **are plucked to safety**. *A workman was plucked from the roof of a burning power station by a police helicopter last night... Ten fishermen were plucked to safety from life-rafts yesterday.* VB: usu passive; be V-ed from n; be V-ed to n

8 If you say that someone has **pluck**, you mean that they show courage and determination when they are in a difficult or frightening situation. *Little companies are known for their pluck and perseverance, even in the face of a recession.* N-UNCOUNT =courage, spirit

9 If you **pluck up the courage** to do something that you feel nervous about, you make an effort to be brave enough to do it. *It took me about two hours to pluck up courage to call.* PHRASES; V inflects, oft PHR to-inf

10 If you say that someone **plucks** a figure, name, or date **out of the air**, you mean that they say it without thinking much about it before they speak. *Accurate valuations are becoming almost impossible to make. Numbers are simply being plucked out of the air.* V inflects

pluck at. If you **pluck at** something, you take it between your fingertips and pull it sharply but gently. *The boy plucked at Adam's sleeve.* PHRASAL VERB; V P n

plucky /plʌki/. If someone, for example a sick child, is described as **plucky**, it means that although they are weak, they face their difficulties with courage; used in journalism. *The plucky schoolgirl amazed doctors at Newcastle's Freeman Hospital by hanging on to life for nearly two months.* ADJ-GRADED: usu ADJ n

plug /plʌg/ **plugs, plugging, plugged** ◆◆◇◇◇

1 A **plug** on a piece of electrical equipment is a small plastic object with two or three metal pins which fit into the holes of an electric socket, usually in the wall of a room, in order to connect the equipment to the electrical supply. N-COUNT

2 A **plug** is an electric socket; an informal use. N-COUNT

3 A **plug** is a thick, circular piece of rubber or plastic that you use to block the hole in a bath or sink when it is filled with water. *She put the plug in the sink and filled it with cold water.* N-COUNT

4 A **plug** is a small, round piece of wood, plastic, or N-COUNT

wax which is used to block holes. *A plug had been inserted in the drill hole.*

5 If you **plug** a hole, a gap, or a leak, you block it with something. *Crews are working to plug a major oil leak.* VERB Vn

6 If someone **plugs** a commercial product, especially a book or a film, they praise it in order to encourage people to buy it or see it because they have an interest in it doing well. *We did not want people on the show who are purely interested in plugging a book or film.* ► Also a noun. *Let's do this show tonight and it'll be a great plug, a great promotion.* VERB =promote Vn N-COUNT

7 See also **earplug, spark plug.**

8 If someone in a position of power **pulls the plug on** a project or on someone's activities, they use their power to stop them continuing. *The banks have the power to pull the plug on the project.* PHRASE: V inflects, usu PHR *on* n

plug away. If you **plug away**, you keep trying very hard to do something or achieve something even though you find it difficult. *My confidence is still there and I'll just keep plugging away.* PHRASAL VERB VP

plug in/into PHRASAL VERB

1 If you **plug** a piece of electrical equipment **into** an electricity supply or if you **plug it in**, you push its plug into an electric socket so that it can work. *They plugged in their tape-recorders... I filled the kettle while she was talking and plugged it in... He took the machine from its bag and plugged it into the wall socket... Some barbecues can be plugged into a household electricity supply.* VP n (not pron) VnP VnPn

2 If you **plug** one piece of electrical equipment **into** another or if you **plug it in**, you make it work by connecting the two. *They plugged their guitars into amplifiers... He plugged in his guitar.* VnPn VP n (not pron)

3 If one piece of electrical equipment **plugs in** or **plugs into** another piece of electrical equipment, it works by being connected by an electrical lead to an electricity supply or to the other piece of equipment. *A CD-I deck looks like a video recorder and plugs into the home television and stereo system... They plug into the mains... They've found out where the other speaker plugs in.* VPn VP

4 If you **plug** something **into** a hole, you push it into the hole. *Her instructor plugged live bullets into the gun's chamber.* VnPn

plug into PHRASAL VERB

1 If you **plug into** a computer system, you get access to the information on it. *It is possible to plug into remote databases to pick up information.* VPn

2 If you **plug into** a group of people or their ideas, you find out about them and try to understand them; an informal use. *The Centre for European Policy Studies is plugged into the thinking of the people who matter.* VPn

plughole /plʌghoʊl/ **plugholes**

1 A **plughole** is a small hole in a bath or sink which allows the water to flow away and into which you can put a plug. N-COUNT

2 If you say that something has gone **down the plughole**, you mean that it has failed or has been lost or wasted. *Millions of pounds have gone down the plughole... Germans worry that their economy is going down the plughole.* PHRASE: V inflects =down the drain

plug-in. A **plug-in** machine is a piece of electrical equipment that is operated by being connected to an electricity supply or to another piece of electrical equipment by means of a plug. *...a plug-in radio.* ADJ: ADJ n

plum /plʌm/ **plums** ◆◇◇◇◇

1 A **plum** is a small, sweet fruit with a smooth red or yellow skin and a stone in the middle. N-COUNT

2 Something that is **plum** or **plum-coloured** is a dark reddish-purple colour. *...plum-coloured silk.* COLOUR

3 A **plum** job, contract, or role is a very good one that a lot of people would like; used mainly in journalism. *Laura landed a plum job with a smart art gallery.* ADJ: ADJ n

plumage /pluːmɪdʒ/. A bird's **plumage** is all the feathers on its body. ◆◇◇◇◇ N-UNCOUNT

plumb /plʌm/ **plumbs, plumbing, plumbed** ◆◇◇◇◇

1 If you **plumb** something mysterious or difficult to understand, you succeed in understanding it; a literary use. *She never abandoned her attempts to plumb my innermost emotions... Magda had plumbed her own heart for answers.* VERB =fathom Vn

2 If something is **plumb** in a particular place, it is exactly in that place; an informal use. *The hotel is set plumb in the middle of the high street... Grenville took another wallop plumb on the jaw.* ADV: ADV prep =right

3 When someone **plumbs** a building, they connect all the water and drainage pipes and make sure they are all working properly. *She learned to wire and plumb the house herself.* VERB Vn

4 If someone **plumbs the depths** of an unpleasant emotion or quality, they experience it or show it to an extreme degree. *They frequently plumb the depths of loneliness, humiliation and despair... Is this the first of many questions that will plumb the depths of stupidity?* PHRASES V inflects, oft PHR *of* n

5 If you say that something **plumbs new depths**, you mean that it is worse than all the things of its kind that have existed before, even though some of them have been very bad. *Relations between the two countries have plumbed new depths... Last night's harrowing television pictures plumbed new depths of depravity.* V inflects, oft PHR *of* n

plumb in. When someone **plumbs in** a device such as a washing machine, toilet, or bath, they connect it to the water and drainage pipes in a building. *Please come and plumb in my new central heating system... He had a washing machine plumbed in.* PHRASAL VERB VP n (not pron) *have* n V-ed P Also VnP

plumber /plʌməʳ/ **plumbers.** A **plumber** is a person whose job is to connect and repair things such as water and drainage pipes, baths, and toilets. ◆◇◇◇◇ N-COUNT

plumbing /plʌmɪŋ/ ◆◇◇◇◇

1 The **plumbing** in a building consists of the water and drainage pipes, baths, and toilets in it. *The electrics and the plumbing were sound but everything else had to be cleaned up.* N-UNCOUNT

2 **Plumbing** is the work of connecting and repairing things such as water and drainage pipes, baths, and toilets. *She learned the rudiments of bricklaying, wiring and plumbing.* N-UNCOUNT

plumb line, plumb lines. A **plumb line** is a piece of string with a weight attached to the end that is used to check that something such as a wall is vertical or that it slopes at the correct angle. N-COUNT

plume /pluːm/ **plumes** ◆◇◇◇◇

1 A **plume** of smoke, dust, fire, or water is a large quantity of it that rises into the air in a column. *The rising plume of black smoke could be seen all over Kabul. ...the volcano's towering ash plume.* N-COUNT: usu N *of* n

2 A **plume** is a large, soft bird's feather. *...broad straw hats decorated with ostrich plumes.* N-COUNT

3 A **plume** is a bunch of long, thin strands of material, tied at one end and flowing loosely at the other. Plumes are usually attached to soldiers' helmets and horses' heads as decoration. N-COUNT

plumed /pluːmd/. **Plumed** means decorated with a plume or plumes. *...a young man wearing a plumed hat... Three plumed horses entered.* ADJ: usu ADJ n

plummet /plʌmɪt/ **plummets, plummeting, plummeted.** If an amount, rate, or price **plummets**, it decreases quickly by a large amount; used mainly in journalism. *In Tokyo share prices have plummeted for the sixth successive day... The Prime Minister's popularity has plummeted to an all-time low in recent weeks... The shares have plummeted from 130p to 2.25p in the past year.* ◆◇◇◇◇ VERB =tumble, plunge V V *to* n V *from/to/by* n

plummy /plʌmi/. In British English, if you say that someone has a **plummy voice** or **accent**, you mean that they sound snobbish or upper-class. You usually use **plummy** to criticize the way someone speaks. *...those precious, plummy-voiced radio announcers. ...a plummy accent.* ADJ-GRADED PRAGMATICS

plump /plʌmp/ **plumper, plumpest; plumps, plumping, plumped** ◆◇◇◇◇

1 You can describe someone or something as **plump** to indicate, usually in an affectionate or appreciative way, that they are rather fat or rounded. *Maria was a pretty little thing, small and plump* ADJ-GRADED PRAGMATICS

with a mass of curly hair... He pushed a plump little hand towards me. ...red pears, ripe peaches and plump nectarines. ♦ **plumpness** *There was a sturdy plumpness about her hips.* N-UNCOUNT

2 If you **plump a pillow** or **cushion**, you shake and pat it so that it goes back into a rounded shape. *She panics when people pop in unexpectedly, rushing round plumping cushions.* ► **Plump up** means the same as **plump**. *'You need to rest,' she told her reassuringly as she moved to plump up her pillows.* VERB V n PHRASAL VERB V P n (not pron) Also V n P

3 If you **plump for** someone or something, you choose them, often after hesitating or thinking carefully. *I think Tessa should play it safe and plump for Malcolm, her long-suffering admirer.* VERB V for n

plum pudding, plum puddings. In Britain, **plum pudding** is a special pudding eaten at Christmas, which is made with dried fruit, spices, and suet; an old-fashioned expression. N-COUNT =Christmas pudding

plum tomato, plum tomatoes. Plum tomatoes are long egg-shaped tomatoes. N-VAR

plunder /plʌndəʳ/ **plunders, plundering, plundered** ◆◇◇◇◇

1 If someone **plunders** a place or **plunders** things from a place, they steal things from it; a literary use. *They plundered and burned the market town of Leominster... She faces charges of helping to plunder her country's treasury of billions of dollars... This has been done by plundering £4 billion from the Government reserves.* ► Also a noun. *...a guerrilla group infamous for torture and plunder.* VERB =loot V n V n of n V n from n N-UNCOUNT

2 **Plunder** is property that is stolen; a literary use. *The thieves are often armed and in some cases have killed for their plunder.* N-UNCOUNT

plunge /plʌndʒ/ **plunges, plunging, plunged** ◆◆◆◇◇

1 If something or someone **plunges** in a particular direction, especially into water, they fall, rush, or throw themselves in that direction. *At least 50 people died when a bus plunged into a river... He ran down the steps to the pool terrace and plunged in.* ► Also a noun. *...a plunge into cold water.* VERB V prep/adv N-COUNT

2 If you **plunge** an object into something, you push it quickly or violently into it. *A soldier plunged a bayonet into his body... She plunged her face into a bowl of cold water... I plunged in my knife and fork.* VERB =thrust V n into n V n with in

3 If something **plunges** someone or something into a particular state or situation, or if they **plunge into** it, they are suddenly in that state or situation. *The government's political and economic reforms threaten to plunge the country into chaos... 8,000 homes were plunged into darkness as electricity cables crashed down... Eddy finds himself plunged into a world of brutal violence... The economy is plunging into recession.* ► Also a noun. *That peace often looked like a brief truce before the next plunge into war.* V-ERG V n into n V-ed V into n N-COUNT: usu sing, N into n

4 If you **plunge into** an activity or **are plunged into** it, you suddenly get very involved in it. *The two men plunged into discussion... The prince should be plunged into work... Take the opportunity to plunge yourself into your career.* ► Also a noun. *His sudden plunge into the field of international diplomacy is a major surprise.* V-ERG V into n be V-ed into n V pron-refl into n N-COUNT: usu sing, N into n

5 If an amount or rate **plunges**, it decreases quickly and suddenly. *His weight began to plunge... The Pound plunged to a new low on the foreign exchange markets yesterday... Shares have plunged from £17 to £7.55... The bank's profits plunged by 87 per cent... Its net profits plunged 73% last year.* ► Also a noun. *Japan's banks are in trouble because of bad loans and the stock market plunge.* VERB =plummet V V to n V from/to amount V by amount V amount N-COUNT

6 See also **plunging**.

7 If you **take the plunge**, you decide to do something that you consider difficult or risky. *If you have been thinking about buying shares, now could be the time to take the plunge.* PHRASE: V inflects

plunger /plʌndʒəʳ/ **plungers.** A **plunger** is a device for unblocking pipes and sinks. It consists of a rubber cup on the end of a stick. You press it up and down over the pipe or the hole in the sink, and the suction moves the blockage. ◆◇◇◇◇ N-COUNT

plunging /plʌndʒɪŋ/. A dress or blouse with a **plunging** neckline is cut in a very low V-shape at the front. ADJ: ADJ n

plunk /plʌŋk/ **plunks, plunking, plunked**

1 If you **plunk** something down, you put it down without great care; an informal word used mainly in American English. *Melanie plunked her cosmetic case down on a chair... She swept up a hat from where it had fallen on the ground, and plunked it on her hair.* VERB =plonk V n with down V n on n

2 If you **plunk down**, you sit down heavily and clumsily; an informal word used mainly in American English. *I watched them go and plunked down on one of the small metal chairs.* VERB V down

pluperfect /pluːpɜːʳfɪkt/. **The pluperfect** is the same as **the past perfect.** N-SING: the N

plural /plʊərəl/ **plurals** ◆◇◇◇◇

1 The **plural** form of a word is the form that is used when referring to more than one person or thing. *'Data' is the Latin plural form of 'datum'. ...his use of the plural pronoun 'we'.* ADJ ≠singular

2 The **plural** of a noun is the form of it that is used to refer to more than one person or thing. *What is the plural of 'person'? ...irregular plurals.* N-COUNT

3 A **plural** society or system involves different kinds of people; a formal use. *Britain is a plural society in which the secular predominates... His government has pledged to move the country towards a plural democracy.* ADJ-GRADED: ADJ n

pluralism /plʊərəlɪzəm/. If there is **pluralism** within a society, it has many different groups and political parties; a formal word. *...as the country shifts towards political pluralism.* ◆◇◇◇◇ N-UNCOUNT

pluralist /plʊərəlɪst/. A **pluralist** society is one in which many different groups and political parties are allowed to exist; a formal word. *...an attempt to create a pluralist democracy.* ◆◇◇◇◇ ADJ-GRADED: usu ADJ n =pluralistic

pluralistic /plʊərəlɪstɪk/. **Pluralistic** means the same as **pluralist**; a formal word. *Our objective is a free, open and pluralistic society.* ADJ-GRADED: usu ADJ n

plurality /plʊəræl̲ɪti/

1 If there is a **plurality of** things, a number of them exist; a formal use. *Federalism implies a plurality of political authorities, each with its own powers.* QUANT-PL

2 If a candidate, political party, or idea has the support of a **plurality of** people, they have more support than any other candidate, party, or idea; a formal use. *The Conservative party retained a plurality of the votes... 35% of the population, a plurality, believed that the economic reforms would result in only insignificant change.* QUANT-PL

plus /plʌs/ **pluses** or **plusses** ◆◆◆◆◇

1 You say **plus** to show that one number or quantity is being added to another. *Send a cheque for £18.99 plus £2 for postage and packing... They will pay about $673 million plus interest.* CONJ-COORD ≠minus

2 **Plus** before a number or quantity means that the number or quantity is greater than zero. *The aircraft was subjected to temperatures of minus 65 degrees and plus 120 degrees.* • **plus or minus**: see **minus**. ADJ: ADJ amount ≠minus

3 You can use **plus** when mentioning an additional item or fact; an informal use. *There's easily enough room for two adults and three children, plus a dog in the boot... We had to have an actor who could generate real empathy. Plus he had to carry the audience through a lot of plot.* CONJ-COORD =and

4 You use **plus** after a number or quantity to indicate that the actual number or quantity is greater than the one mentioned. *There are only 35 staff to serve 30,000-plus customers... Among the guests were 16 high-flying executives, all on salaries of £50,000 a year plus.* ADJ: amount ADJ

5 Teachers use **plus** in grading work in schools and colleges. 'B plus' is a better grade than 'B', but it is not as good as 'A'. ≠minus

6 A **plus** is an advantage or benefit; an informal use. *Experience of any career in sales is a big plus... There are plenty of plus points about being an older first-time mum.* N-COUNT ≠drawback, minus

plus-fours; also spelled **plus fours**. In Britain, **plus-fours** are short baggy trousers fastened be- N-PLURAL: also a pair of N low the knees which people used to wear when hunting or playing golf; an old-fashioned word.

plush /plʌʃ/ **plusher, plushest** ◆◇◇◇◇

1 If you describe something as **plush**, you mean that it is very smart, comfortable, or expensive. *...a plush, four-storey, Georgian house in Mayfair. ...one of the plushest posts in US diplomacy.* ADJ-GRADED: usu ADJ n

2 **Plush** is a thick soft material like velvet, used especially for carpets and to cover furniture. *All the seats were in red plush.* N-UNCOUNT

plus sign, plus signs. A **plus sign** is the sign + which is put between two numbers in order to show that the second number is being added to the first. It can also be put before a number to show that the number is greater than zero (+3), and after a number to show that the real number is greater than the one mentioned (18+). N-COUNT

plutocracy /pluːtɒkrəsi/ **plutocracies.** A **plutocracy** is a country which is ruled by its wealthiest people, or a class of wealthy people who rule a country; a formal word. *Financial, not moral, considerations will prevail in a plutocracy.* N-COUNT

plutocrat /pluːtəkræt/ **plutocrats.** If you describe someone as a **plutocrat**, you disapprove of them because you believe they are powerful only because they are rich; a formal word. *He proclaimed his fellow-feeling with workers, and denounced plutocrats and the idle rich in terms which caused them alarm.* N-COUNT PRAGMATICS

plutonium /pluːtoʊniəm/. **Plutonium** is a radioactive element used especially in nuclear weapons and as a fuel in nuclear power stations. ◆◇◇◇◇ N-UNCOUNT

ply /plaɪ/ **plies, plying, plied** ◆◇◇◇◇

1 If you **ply** someone with food or drink, you keep giving them more of it in an insistent way. *Elsie, who had been told that Maria wasn't well, plied her with food... The poor priest was plied with drink at a dinner party.* VERB V n *with* n

2 If you **ply** someone with questions, you keep asking them questions in an insistent way. *Giovanni plied him with questions and comments with the deliberate intention of prolonging his stay.* VERB V n *with* n

3 If you **ply** a trade, you do a particular kind of work regularly as your job, especially a kind of work that involves trying to sell goods or services to passers-by. *...the market traders noisily plying their wares... It's illegal for unmarked mini-cabs to ply for hire.* VERB V n V *for* n

4 If a ship, aircraft, or vehicle **plies** a route, it makes regular journeys along that route. *Eighteen boats plied the 1,000 miles of river along a trading route... The brightly-coloured boats ply between the islands.* VERB V n V prep

-ply /-plaɪ/. You use **-ply** after a number to indicate how many strands a type of wool, thread, or rope is made from. *You need 3 balls of any 4-ply knitting wool.* COMB in ADJ: ADJ n

plywood /plaɪwʊd/. **Plywood** is wood that consists of thin layers of wood stuck together. *...a sheet of plywood.* ◆◇◇◇◇ N-UNCOUNT

PM /piː em/ **PMs. The PM** is an abbreviation for the **Prime Minister**; used mainly in informal British English. *Michael Heseltine said he welcomed the PM's decision.* ◆◆◆◇◇ N-COUNT: *the* N

p.m. /piː em/. also spelled **pm**. **p.m.** is used after a number to show that you are referring to a particular time between noon and midnight. *The spa is open from 7:00 am to 9:00 pm every day of the year.* ◆◆◇◇◇ ADV: num ADV

PMS /piː em es/. **PMS** is an abbreviation for **premenstrual syndrome**. ◆◇◇◇◇ N-UNCOUNT

PMT /piː em tiː/. **PMT** is an abbreviation for **premenstrual tension**. N-UNCOUNT

pneumatic /njuːmætɪk/

1 A **pneumatic drill** is operated by compressed air and is very powerful. Pneumatic drills are often used for digging up roads. *...the sound of a pneumatic drill hammering away.* ADJ: ADJ n

2 **Pneumatic** means filled with air. *Use a bicycle pump to keep the pneumatic tyres full of air.* ADJ: ADJ n

pneumonia /njuːmoʊniə/. **Pneumonia** is a serious disease which affects your lungs and makes it difficult for you to breathe. *She nearly died of pneumonia.* ◆◇◇◇◇ N-UNCOUNT: also *a* N

PO /piː oʊ/. **PO** is an abbreviation for **Post Office** or **postal order**.

poach /poʊtʃ/ **poaches, poaching, poached** ◆◇◇◇◇

1 If someone **poaches** fish, animals, or birds, they illegally catch them on someone else's property. *Many national parks set up to provide a refuge for wildlife are regularly invaded by people poaching game.* ♦ **poacher, poachers** *Security cameras have been installed to guard against poachers.* ♦ **poaching** *The poaching of elephants for their tusks could start to decline soon.* VERB V n Also V N-COUNT N-UNCOUNT

2 If an organization or team **poaches** members or customers from another organization or team, they secretly or dishonestly persuade them to join them or become their customers. *The company authorised its staff to poach customers and instigate dirty tricks against the opposition. ...allegations that it had poached members from other unions.* ♦ **poaching** *The union was accused of poaching.* VERB =steal V n V n *from* n N-UNCOUNT

3 If someone **poaches** an idea, they dishonestly or illegally use the idea. *The opposition parties have complained that the government has poached many of their ideas.* VERB =steal V n

4 When you **poach an egg**, you cook it gently in boiling water without its shell. *Poach the eggs for 4 minutes... He had a light breakfast of poached eggs and tea.* VERB V n V-ed

5 If you **poach** food such as fish, you cook it gently in boiling water, milk, or other liquid. *Poach the chicken until just cooked. ...a pear poached in red wine... The main course was to be a whole poached salmon.* ♦ **poaching** *You will need a pot of broth for poaching.* VERB V n V-ed N-UNCOUNT

PO Box /piː oʊ bɒks/. **PO Box** is used before a number as a kind of address. The Post Office keeps letters addressed to the PO Box until they are collected by the person who has paid for the service. ◆◆◇◇◇

pocked /pɒkt/. **Pocked** means the same as **pockmarked**. *...a bus pocked with bullet holes.* ADJ-GRADED: usu v-link ADJ, oft ADJ *with* n

pocket /pɒkɪt/ **pockets, pocketing, pocketed** ◆◆◆◇◇

1 A **pocket** is a kind of small bag which forms part of a piece of clothing, and which is used for carrying small things such as money or a handkerchief. *He took his flashlight from his jacket pocket and switched it on... The man stood with his hands in his pockets.* N-COUNT: oft poss N, n N

2 You can use **pocket** in a lot of different ways to refer to money that people have, get, or spend. For example, if someone gives or pays a lot of money, you can say that they **dig deep into their pocket**. If you approve of something because it is very cheap to buy, you can say that it **suits people's pockets**. *When you come to choosing a dining table, it really is worth digging deep into your pocket for the best you can afford. ...ladies' fashions to suit all shapes, sizes and pockets... You would be buying a piece of history as well as a boat, if you put your hand in your pocket for this one... We don't believe that they have the economic reforms in place which would justify putting huge sums of Western money into their pockets.* N-COUNT

3 You use **pocket** to describe something that is small enough to fit into a pocket, often something that is a smaller version of a larger item. *...a pocket calculator. ...my pocket edition of the Oxford English Dictionary.* ADJ: ADJ n

4 A **pocket** of something is a small area where something is happening, or a small area which has a particular quality, and which is different from the other areas around it. *Trapped in a pocket of air, they had only 40 minutes before the tide flooded the chamber... The newly established government controls the bulk of the city apart from a few pockets of resistance.* N-COUNT: usu N *of* n

5 If someone who is in possession of something valuable such as a sum of money **pockets** it, they steal it or take it for themselves, even though it does not belong to them. *Dishonest importers* VERB V n

would be able to pocket the VAT collected from customers.

6 If you say that someone **pockets** something such as a prize or sum of money, you mean that they win or obtain it, often without needing to make much effort or in a way that seems unfair; used in journalism. *He pocketed more money from this tournament than in his entire three years as a professional.* VERB V n

7 If someone **pockets** something, they put it in their pocket, for example because they want to steal it or hide it. *Anthony snatched his letters and pocketed them... He pocketed a wallet containing £40 cash from the bedside of a dead man.* VERB V n

8 If you say that some money **is burning a hole in** someone's **pocket**, you mean that they want to spend it as soon as possible. *It's Saturday, you're down the high street and you've got a few quid burning a hole in your pocket.* PHRASES V inflects

9 If you say that someone is **in** someone else's **pocket**, you disapprove of the fact that the first person is willing to do whatever the second person tells them, for example because the first person is weak or is being paid by the second person. *The board of directors must surely have been in Johnstone's pocket.* usu v-link PHR PRAGMATICS

10 If you say that someone **is lining** their own or someone else's **pockets**, you disapprove of them because they are making money dishonestly or unfairly for themselves or for someone else. *It is estimated that 5,000 bank staff could be lining their own pockets from customer accounts. ...a government that ignores the needs of the majority in order to line the pockets of the favoured few.* V inflects

11 If you are **out of pocket**, you have less money than you should have or than you intended, for example because you have spent too much or because of a mistake. *They were well out of pocket – they had spent far more in Hollywood than he had earned... Statements with errors could still be going out, but customers who notify us will not be left out of pocket.* • See also **out-of-pocket**. v-link PHR, PHR after v

12 If someone **picks** your **pocket**, they steal something from your pocket, usually without you noticing. *They were more in danger of having their pockets picked than being shot at.* V and N inflect

pocketbook /pɒkɪtbʊk/ **pocketbooks**

1 In American English, you can use **pocketbook** to refer to people's concerns about the money they have or hope to earn; used in journalism. *People feel pinched in their pocketbooks and insecure about their futures. ...the voters' concerns over pocketbook issues.* N-COUNT

2 In American English, a **pocketbook** is a small bag which a woman uses to carry things such as her money and keys in when she goes out. The usual British word is **handbag**. N-COUNT

3 In American English, a **pocketbook** is the same as a **wallet**. N-COUNT

pocket knife, pocket knives; also spelled **pocketknife**. A **pocket knife** is a small knife with several blades which fold into the handle so that you can carry it around with you safely. N-COUNT =penknife

pocket money; also spelled **pocket-money**. ◆◇◇◇◇

1 **Pocket money** is money which children are given by their parents, usually every week; used mainly in British English. *We agreed to give her £6 a week pocket money.* N-UNCOUNT

2 **Pocket money** is a small amount of money which you earn, and which you can use for buying the things that you want; used mainly in British English. *Volunteers receive £21 pocket money each week, accommodation and expenses.* N-UNCOUNT

pocket-sized; also spelled **pocket-size**. If you describe something as **pocket-sized**, you approve of it because it is small enough to fit in your pocket. *...a handy pocket-sized reference book.* ADJ: usu ADJ n PRAGMATICS

pockmark /pɒkmɑːʳk/ **pockmarks;** also spelled **pock mark**. **Pockmarks** are small hollows on the surface of something. *She has a poor complexion and pock marks on her forehead... The pockmarks made by her bullets are still on the wall.* N-COUNT: usu pl

pockmarked /pɒkmɑːʳkt/; also spelled **pock-marked**. If the surface of something is **pockmarked**, it has small hollow marks covering it. *He had a pockmarked face... The living room is pockmarked with bullet holes.* ADJ-GRADED: oft ADJ *with* n =pocked

pod /pɒd/ **pods.** A **pod** is a seed container that grows on plants such as peas or beans. *...fresh peas in the pod. ...hot red pepper pods.* ◆◇◇◇◇ N-COUNT

podgy /pɒdʒi/. In informal British English, if you describe someone as **podgy**, you think that they are a little overweight but not fat. The usual American word is **pudgy**. ADJ-GRADED

podiatrist, podiatrists. A **podiatrist** is a person whose job is to treat and care for people's feet. **Podiatrist** is a more modern term for **chiropodist**. N-COUNT

podiatry /pədaɪətri/. **Podiatry** is the professional care and treatment of people's feet. **Podiatry** is a more modern term for **chiropody** and also deals with correcting foot problems relating to the way people stand and walk. N-UNCOUNT =chiropody

podium /poʊdiəm/ **podiums.** A **podium** is a small platform on which someone stands in order to give a lecture or conduct an orchestra. ◆◇◇◇◇ N-COUNT: usu sing =dais

poem /poʊɪm/ **poems.** A **poem** is a piece of writing in which the words are chosen for their beauty and sound and are carefully arranged, often in short lines which rhyme. ◆◆◆◇◇ N-COUNT

poet /poʊɪt/ **poets.** A **poet** is a person who writes poems. *He was a painter and poet.* ◆◆◆◇◇ N-COUNT

poetess /poʊɪtes/ **poetesses.** A **poetess** is a female poet. Most female poets prefer to be called poets. N-COUNT PRAGMATICS

poetic /poʊetɪk/ ◆◇◇◇◇

1 Something that is **poetic** is very beautiful, expressive, and sensitive. *Nikolai Demidenko gave an exciting yet poetic performance.* ♦ **poetically** *The speech was as poetically written as any he'd ever heard.* ADJ-GRADED ADV-GRADED: ADV with v, ADV adj

2 **Poetic** means relating to poetry. *There's a very rich poetic tradition in Gaelic.* ADJ

poetical /poʊetɪkᵊl/. **Poetical** means the same as **poetic**. *...a work of real merit and genuine poetical feeling.* ADJ-GRADED

poetic justice. If you describe something bad that happens to someone as **poetic justice**, you mean that it is exactly what they deserve because of the things that that person has done. N-UNCOUNT

poetic licence. If writers use **poetic licence**, they do not obey the normal rules of language and truth. Poetic licence is often used in journalism and spoken English. *In his diary, Waite is both more precise and less inclined to poetic licence.* N-UNCOUNT

poet laureate /poʊɪt lɒriət, AM - lɔːr-/ **poet laureates** or **poets laureate.** The **poet laureate** is the poet who has been chosen to write poems for special occasions. In Britain the poet laureate is paid by the monarch or government for the rest of their lifetime. In the United States they are paid for a fixed term. N-COUNT: usu *the* N

poetry /poʊɪtri/ ◆◆◆◇◇

1 Poems, considered as a form of literature, are referred to as **poetry**. *...Russian poetry... Lawrence Durrell wrote a great deal of poetry... Since when have you been interested in poetry?* N-UNCOUNT

2 You can refer to the beauty or greatness that people see or experience in something as **poetry**. *His music is purer poetry than a poem in words.* N-UNCOUNT

po-faced /poʊ feɪst/. If you describe someone as **po-faced**, you think that they are being unnecessarily serious about something. *Coltrane took a rather po-faced view of this.* ADJ-GRADED PRAGMATICS

pogrom /pɒgrəm, AM pəgrɑːm/ **pogroms.** A **pogrom** is an organized, official persecution, for racial or religious reasons, which usually leads to mass killing of a group of people. *...a systematic and brutal pogrom against southern black Mauritanians.* N-COUNT =massacre

poignancy /pɔɪnjənsi/. **Poignancy** is the quality that something has when it affects you deeply and makes you feel very sad. *The fact that he had* N-UNCOUNT =pathos *been talking to the victims only minutes before their deaths gave the tragedy greater poignancy... There is a certain poignancy about Eric.*

poignant /pɔɪnjənt/. Something that is **poignant** makes you feel very sad because it reminds you of something that has happened in the past, or because something that you wanted to happen did not happen. *...a poignant combination of beautiful surroundings and tragic history. ...a poignant love story... Harry thought the sight of her was inexpressibly poignant.* ♦ **poignantly** *Naomi's mothering experiences are poignantly described in her fiction.* ◆◇◇◇◇ ADJ-GRADED =moving ADV-GRADED: ADV with v, ADV adj

poinsettia /pɔɪnsetiə/ **poinsettias.** A **poinsettia** is a plant with groups of bright red or pink leaves that grows in Central and South America. Poinsettias are very popular in Britain as house plants. N-COUNT

point /pɔɪnt/ **points, pointing, pointed** ◆◆◆◆◆

1 You use **point** to refer to something that someone has said or written. *We disagree with every point Mr Blunkett makes... Dave Hill's article makes the right point about the Taylor Report... The following tale will clearly illustrate this point.* N-COUNT

2 If you say that someone **has a point**, or if you **take their point**, you mean that you accept that what they have said is important and should be considered. *'If he'd already killed once, surely he'd have killed Sarah?' She had a point there... Oh I take your point, John, about that.* N-SING: a N, poss N

3 The point of what you are saying or discussing is the most important part that provides a reason or explanation for the rest. *'Did I ask you to talk to me?'—'That's not the point.'... The American Congress and media mostly missed the point about all this.* N-SING: the N

4 If you ask what the **point** of something is, or say that there is **no point** in it, you are indicating that a particular action has no purpose or would not be useful. *What was the point of thinking about him?... There was no point in staying any longer.* N-SING: usu N of/in n/-ing

5 A **point** is a detail, aspect, or quality of something or someone. *Many of the points in the report are correct... The most interesting point about the village was its religion... Science was never my strong point at school.* N-COUNT: usu with supp

6 A **point** is a particular place or position where something happens. *As a mark of respect the emperor met him at a point several weeks' march from the capital... The pain originated from a point in his right thigh.* N-COUNT =spot

7 You use **point** to refer to a particular time, or to a particular stage in the development of something. *We're all going to die at some point... At one point, around 70,000 members had failed to pay... At this point Diana arrived... It got to the point where he had to leave.* N-SING: with supp, oft at N =time

8 The **point** of something such as a pin, needle, or knife is the thin, sharp end of it. N-COUNT: oft N of n

9 In spoken English, you use **point** to refer to the dot or mark in a decimal number that separates the whole numbers from the fractions. *This is FM stereo one oh three point seven... Inflation at nine point four percent is the worst for eight years.*

10 In some sports, competitions, and games, a **point** is one of the single marks that are added together to give the total score. *They lost the 1977 World Cup final to Australia by a single point... Chamberlain scored 50 or more points four times in the season.* N-COUNT

11 The **points** of a compass are the marks on it that show the directions, such as North, South, East, and West. *...the four points of the compass.* N-COUNT: usu with supp

12 On a railway track, the **points** are the levers and rails at a place where two tracks join or separate. The points enable a train to move from one track to another; used mainly in British English. *...the rattle of the wheels across the points.* N-PLURAL

13 In British English, a **point** is an electric socket. *...too far away from the nearest electrical point.* N-COUNT: usu supp N

14 If you **point at** someone, you hold out your finger towards them in order to show someone else where they are. If you **point** at something, you hold out your finger towards it to make someone notice it. *I pointed at the boy sitting nearest me... He pointed at me with the stem of his pipe... He pointed to a chair, signalling for her to sit.* VERB V at n V to n

15 If you **point** something **at** someone, you aim the tip or end of it towards them. *David Khan pointed his finger at Mary... A man pointed a gun at them and pulled the trigger.* VERB V n at n

16 If something **points** to a place or **points** in a particular direction, it shows where that place is or it faces in that direction. *An arrow pointed to the toilets... You can go anywhere and still the compass points north or south... He controlled the car until it was pointing forwards again.* VERB V prep/adv

17 If something **points to** a particular situation, it suggests that the situation exists or is likely to occur. *Earlier reports pointed to pupils working harder, more continuously, and with enthusiasm... Private polls and embassy reports pointed to a no vote.* VERB =indicate V to n

18 If you **point to** something that has happened or that is happening, you are using it as proof that a particular situation exists. *George Fodor points to other weaknesses in the way the campaign has progressed... Gooch last night pointed to their bowling as the key to World Cup success.* VERB =call attention V to n

19 When builders **point** a wall, they put mortar or cement into the gaps between the bricks or stones so that the surface becomes sealed. VERB: V n

20 See also **pointed**; **breaking point**, **focal point**, **vantage point**, **power point**, **sticking point**.

21 If you say that something is **beside the point**, you mean that it is not relevant to the subject that you are discussing. *Brian didn't like it, but that was beside the point.* PHRASES v-link PHR =irrelevant

22 When someone **comes to the point** or **gets to the point**, they start talking about the thing that is most important to them. *He came to the point at once. 'You did a splendid job on this case.'... Was she ever going to get to the point?* V inflects

23 If you **make** your **point** or **prove** your **point**, you prove that something is true, either by arguing about it or by your actions or behaviour. *I think you've made your point, dear... Dr David McCleland, of Boston University, studied one-hundred people, aged eighteen to sixty, to prove the point... The tie-break proved the point.* V inflects

24 If you **make a point of** doing something, you do it in a very deliberate or obvious way. *She made a point of spending as much time as possible away from Osborne House.* V inflects, PHR -ing

25 If you are **on the point of** doing something, you are about to do it. *He was on the point of saying something when the phone rang... She looked on the point of tears.* v-link PHR n/-ing =on the verge of

26 Something that is **to the point** is relevant to the subject that you are discussing, or expressed neatly without wasting words or time. *Mr. Baker was smiling and to the point... The description which he had been given was brief and to the point.* v-link PHR

27 If you say that something is true **up to a point**, you mean that it is partly but not completely true. *'Was she good?'—'Mmm. Up to a point.'... It worked up to a point.* PHR with cl

28 • **a case in point**: see **case**. • **in point of fact**: see **fact**. • to **point the finger at** someone: see **finger**. • **a sore point**: see **sore**.

point out PHRASAL VERB

1 If you **point out** an object or place, you make people look at it or show them where it is. *They kept standing up to take pictures and point things out to each other... They'd already driven along the wharf so that she could point out her father's boat.* V n P V P n (not pron)

2 If you **point out** a fact or mistake, you tell someone about it or draw their attention to it. *Critics point out that the prince, on his income, should be paying tax... I should point out that these estimates cover just the hospital expenditures... We all too easily point out our mothers' failings.* V P that V P n (not pron) Also V n P

point-blank ◆◇◇◇◇

1 If you say something **point-blank**, you say it very directly or rudely, without explaining or ADV: ADV after v =outright apologizing. *The army apparently refused point blank to do what was required of them... Mr Mellor was asked point blank if he would resign.* ▶ Also an adjective. *...a point-blank refusal.* ADJ: ADJ n =outright

2 If someone or something is shot **point-blank**, they are shot when the gun is touching them or extremely close to them. *He put a gun through the open window of the car and fired point-blank at Bernadette.* ▶ Also an adjective. *He had been shot at point-blank range in the back of the head.* ADV: ADV after v; ADJ: ADJ n

pointed /pɔɪntɪd/ ◆◆◇◇◇

1 Something that is **pointed** has a point at one end. *...a pointed roof. ...pointed shoes.* ADJ-GRADED: usu ADJ n

2 Pointed comments or behaviour express criticism in a clear and direct way. *I couldn't help notice the pointed remarks slung in my direction... Her new book is a pointed look at life in a small community, and the position of women within it.* ADJ-GRADED: usu ADJ n ♦ **pointedly** *They were pointedly absent from the news conference... 'This is my house,' Blair said rather pointedly.* ADV-GRADED: usu ADV with v, also ADV adj

pointer /pɔɪntəʳ/ **pointers** ◆◇◇◇◇

1 A **pointer** is a piece of advice or information which helps you to understand a situation or to find a way of making progress. *I hope at least my daughter was able to offer you some useful pointers... Here are a few pointers to help you make a choice.* N-COUNT: with supp =tip

2 A **pointer** to something suggests that it exists or gives an indication of what it is like. *His victory in the first race here on Tuesday was a timely pointer to his chance of remaining unbeaten... Sunday's elections should be a pointer to the public mood.* N-COUNT: N *to/towards* n

3 A **pointer** is also a long thin stick that is used to point at something such as a chart on a wall. *She tapped on the world map with her pointer.* N-COUNT

4 The **pointer** on a measuring instrument is the long, thin piece of metal that points to the numbers on the dial. N-COUNT =needle

pointing /pɔɪntɪŋ/

1 Pointing is a way of filling in the gaps between the bricks or stones on the outside of a building so that the surface becomes sealed. *He did the pointing in the stonework himself.* N-UNCOUNT

2 Pointing is the cement between the bricks or stones in a wall. *Cracks, bulges, crumbling pointing and damp patches mean trouble.* N-UNCOUNT

pointless /pɔɪntləs/. If you say that something is **pointless**, you are criticizing it because it has no sense or purpose. *Violence is always pointless... Without an audience the performance is pointless. ...pointless arguments.* ◆◇◇◇◇ ADJ-GRADED: usu v-link ADJ PRAGMATICS =senseless ♦ **pointlessly** *Chemicals were pointlessly poisoning the soil. ...lying awake pointlessly going over and over again something we need to do.* ADV: usu ADV with v =senselessly ♦ **pointlessness** *You cannot help wondering about the pointlessness of it all.* N-UNCOUNT =senselessness

point of order, points of order. In a formal debate, a **point of order** is an objection that someone makes because the proper rules of behaviour or organization have been broken; a formal word. *A point of order was raised in parliament by Mr Ben Morris... The postponement was demanded and won on a point of order.* N-COUNT: usu sing

point of reference, points of reference. A **point of reference** is something which you use to help you understand a situation or communicate with someone. *Do we still have any fixed point of reference in the teaching of English?* N-COUNT

point of view, points of view ◆◆◆◇◇

1 You can refer to the opinions or attitudes that you have about something as your **point of view**. *Thanks for your point of view, John... Try to look at this from my point of view.* N-COUNT: oft with poss =viewpoint

2 If you consider something from a particular **point of view**, you are using one aspect of a situation in order to judge that situation. *Do you think that, from the point of view of results, this exercise was worth the cost?... The average man doing hard physical work has the best record, from the point of view of heart disease... Lennox has taken the point of view that money is not everything.* N-COUNT: usu sing, usu *from* N with poss

pointy /pɔɪnti/ **pointier, pointiest.** Something that is **pointy** has a point at one end; an informal word. *...a pointy little beard.* ADJ-GRADED: usu ADJ n =pointed

poise /pɔɪz/

1 If someone has **poise**, they are calm, dignified, and self-controlled. *What amazed him even more than her appearance was her poise... It took a moment for Mark to recover his poise.* N-UNCOUNT: oft poss N

2 Poise is a graceful, very controlled way of standing and moving. *Ballet classes are important for poise and grace... Even when he moved he did so without poise.* N-UNCOUNT

poised /pɔɪzd/ ◆◆◇◇◇

1 If a part of your body is **poised**, it is completely still but ready to move at any moment. *He studied the keyboard carefully, one finger poised.* ADJ

2 If someone is **poised** to do something, they are ready to take action at any moment. *Britain was poised to fly medical staff to the country at short notice... US forces are poised for a massive air, land and sea assault.* ADJ: v-link ADJ, usu ADJ to-inf, ADJ *for* n =all set

3 If you are **poised**, you are calm, dignified, and self-controlled. *She was self-assured, poised, almost self-satisfied... Rachel appeared poised and calm.* ADJ-GRADED: usu v-link ADJ =self-possessed

poison /pɔɪzᵊn/ **poisons, poisoning, poisoned** ◆◆◇◇◇

1 Poison is a substance that harms or kills people or animals if they swallow it or absorb it. *Poison from the weaver fish causes paralysis, swelling, and nausea... Mercury is a known poison.* N-MASS =toxin

2 If someone **poisons** another person, they kill the person or make them ill by giving them poison. *The rumours that she had poisoned him could never be proved.* VERB V n ♦ **poisoning** *She was sentenced to twenty years' imprisonment for poisoning and attempted murder.* N-UNCOUNT

3 If you **are poisoned** by a substance, it makes you very ill and sometimes kills you. *Employees were taken to hospital yesterday after being poisoned by fumes... Toxic waste could endanger lives and poison fish.* VERB *be* V-ed *by* n, V n ♦ **poisoning** *...acute alcohol poisoning... His illness was initially, but wrongly, diagnosed as food poisoning.* N-UNCOUNT: supp N

4 If someone **poisons** a food, drink, or weapon, they add poison to it so that it can be used to kill someone. *If I was your wife I would poison your coffee.* VERB V n ♦ **poisoned** *He was terrified to eat, suspecting that the food was poisoned. ...an umbrella tipped with a poisoned dart.* ADJ

5 To **poison** water, air, or land means to damage it with harmful substances such as chemicals. *...the textile and fibre industries that taint the air, poison the water and use vast amounts of natural resources... The land has been completely poisoned by chemicals. ...dying forests, poisoned rivers and lakes.* ADJ =contaminate V n V-ed

6 Something that **poisons** a good situation or relationship spoils it or destroys it. *The whole atmosphere has really been poisoned. ...ill-feeling that will poison further talk of a common foreign policy.* VERB =taint *be* V-ed V n

7 If someone **poisons** your **mind** against another person, they make you dislike that person, usually by telling you things that are not true. PHRASE: V inflects, usu PHR *against* n

poisoner /pɔɪzənəʳ/ **poisoners.** A **poisoner** is someone who has killed or harmed another person by using poison. *Soon they were dead, victims of a mysterious poisoner.* N-COUNT

poison gas. Poison gas is a gas that is poisonous and is usually used to kill people in war or to execute criminals. N-UNCOUNT

poisonous /pɔɪzᵊnəs/ ◆◇◇◇◇

1 Something that is **poisonous** will kill you or make you ill if you swallow or absorb it. *All parts of the yew tree are poisonous, including the berries. ...a large cloud of poisonous gas.* ADJ-GRADED =toxic

2 An animal that is **poisonous** produces a poison that will kill you or make you ill if the animal bites you. *There are hundreds of poisonous spiders and snakes.* ADJ-GRADED

3 If you describe something as **poisonous**, you mean that it is extremely unpleasant and likely to spoil or destroy a good relationship or situation. ADJ-GRADED: usu ADJ n =vicious

...poisonous comments. ...lying awake half the night tormented by poisonous suspicions. ...poisonous attacks on the state-run church.

poison-pen letter, poison-pen letters. A **poison-pen letter** is an anonymous letter which is sent in order to upset someone or to cause trouble. It says unpleasant things about the person who gets it or about someone close to him or her. N-COUNT

poke /pouk/ **pokes, poking, poked** ◆◇◇◇◇

1 If you **poke** someone or something, you quickly push them with your finger or with a sharp object. *Lindy poked him in the ribs.* ► Also a noun. *John smiled at them and gave Richard a playful poke.* VERB =jab V n N-COUNT =prod

2 If you **poke** one thing **into** another, you push the first thing into the second thing. *He poked his finger into the hole.* VERB V n into n

3 If something **pokes out of** or **through** another thing, you can see part of it appearing from behind or underneath the other thing. *He saw the dog's twitching nose poke out of the basket... His fingers poked through the worn tips of his gloves.* VERB =stick V out of n V through n

4 If you **poke** your head through an opening or if it **pokes** through an opening, you push it through, often so that you can see something more easily. *Julie tapped on my door and poked her head in... We hadn't been able to poke our heads out and see what was going on... Raymond's head poked through the doorway.* V-ERG V n adv/prep V prep/adv

5 • to **poke fun at**: see **fun**. • to **poke** your **nose into** something: see **nose**.

poke around; the form **poke about** is also used in British English. If you **poke around** or **poke about** for something, you search for it, usually by moving lots of objects around; an informal expression. *He poked around the top of his cupboard for the bottle of whisky... We opened up the car bonnet and he started poking around in my engine.* PHRASAL VERB =grope around VP n VP

poke at. If you **poke at** something, you make lots of little pushing movements at it with a sharp object. *She poked at her food with a fork... Reggie threw more wood on the fire and poked at it.* PHRASAL VERB =prod VP n

poker /poukə^r/ **pokers** ◆◇◇◇◇

1 **Poker** is a card game that people usually play in order to win money. *Lon and I play in the same weekly poker game.* N-UNCOUNT

2 A **poker** is a metal bar which you use to move coal or wood in a fire in order to make it burn better. *Mrs Malone took up the poker and stirred at the little fire burning beside her.* N-COUNT

poker face, poker faces. A **poker face** is an expression on your face that shows none of your feelings; an informal expression. *In business a poker face can be very useful... She managed to keep a poker face.* N-COUNT =straight face

poker-faced. If you are **poker-faced**, you have a calm expression on your face which shows none of your thoughts or feelings; an informal word. *His expressions varied from poker-faced to blank... The officer listened, poker-faced.* ADJ-GRADED

poky /pouki/ **pokier, pokiest.** A room or house that is **poky** is uncomfortably small; an informal word. *...apartments which were poky, dimly lit and poorly furnished. ...poky little rooms.* ADJ-GRADED =cramped

polar /poulə^r/ ◆◇◇◇◇

1 **Polar** means near the North and South Poles. *...the polar regions of the Soviet Union... There was a period of excessive warmth which melted some of the polar ice. ...polar explorers.* ADJ: ADJ n

2 **Polar** is used to describe things which are completely opposite in character, quality, or type; a formal use. *The nomads' lifestyle was the polar opposite of collectivization. ...economists at polar ends of the politico-economic spectrum.* ADJ: ADJ n

polar bear, polar bears. A **polar bear** is a large white bear which is found near the North Pole. N-COUNT

polarise /pouləraɪz/. See **polarize**.

polarity /poulærɪti/ **polarities.** If there is a **polarity** between two people or things, they are completely different from each other in some way; a formal word. *...the ideological polarity between nations. ...the polarities of good and evil... In him the polarities of life are resolved and balanced: male and female, strength and compassion, severity and mercy.* N-VAR

polarize /pouləraɪz/ **polarizes, polarizing, polarized;** also spelled **polarise** in British English. If something **polarizes** people or if something **polarizes**, two separate groups are formed with opposite opinions or positions. *Missile deployment did much to further polarize opinion in Britain... As the car rental industry polarizes, business will go to the bigger companies... The green debate tends to polarise into science-as-saviour versus science-as-devil camps.* ◆◇◇◇◇ V-ERG =divide V n V V into n

♦ **polarized** *Since Independence the electorate has been polarized equally between two parties.* ADJ-GRADED

♦ **polarization** /pouləraɪzeɪʃən/ *There is increasing polarization between the blacks and whites in the US.* N-UNCOUNT =division

Polaroid /poulərɔɪd/ **Polaroids** ◆◇◇◇◇

1 A **Polaroid** camera is a small camera that can take, develop, and print a photograph in a few seconds. **Polaroid** is a trademark. *He called the Polaroid camera a godsend to his work... Polaroid film is very sensitive.* ADJ: ADJ n

2 A **Polaroid** is a photograph taken with a Polaroid camera. *I took a Polaroid of them so I could remember them when they were gone.* N-COUNT

3 **Polaroid sunglasses** have been treated with a special substance in order to reduce the glare of the sun. ADJ: ADJ n

pole /poul/ **poles** ◆◆◆◇◇

1 A **pole** is a long thin piece of wood or metal, used especially for supporting things. *The truck crashed into a telegraph pole... He reached up with a hooked pole to roll down the metal shutter.* N-COUNT

2 The earth's **poles** are the two opposite ends of its axis. *For six months of the year, there is hardly any light at the poles.* • See also **North Pole**, **South Pole**. N-COUNT

3 The two **poles** of a range of qualities, opinions, or beliefs are the completely opposite qualities, opinions, or beliefs at either end of the range. *The two politicians represent opposite poles of the political spectrum.* N-COUNT

4 If you say that two people or things are **poles apart**, you mean that they have completely different beliefs, opinions, or qualities. PHRASE: v-link PHR

Pole, Poles. A **Pole** is a Polish citizen, or a person of Polish origin. ◆◆◆◇◇ N-COUNT

pole-axed; also spelled **poleaxed**. If someone is **pole-axed**, they are so surprised or shocked that they do not know what to say or do; an informal word. *Sitting pole-axed on the sofa, Mahoney stared in astonishment at the spectacle before him.* ADJ: usu v-link ADJ

polecat /poulkæt/ **polecats.** A **polecat** is a small, fierce, wild animal rather like a weasel. Polecats have a very unpleasant smell. N-COUNT

polemic /pəlemɪk/ **polemics** ◆◇◇◇◇

1 A **polemic** is a fierce written or spoken attack on, or defence of, a particular doctrine, belief, or opinion. *...a polemic against the danger of secret societies... The book is both a history and a passionate polemic for tolerance.* N-VAR =argument

2 **Polemics** is the skill or practice of arguing passionately for or against a doctrine, belief, or opinion. *He enjoys polemics, persuasion, and controversy.* N-UNCOUNT =debate

polemical /pəlemɪkəl/. **Polemical** means arguing fiercely and passionately for or against a doctrine, belief, or opinion. *Daniels is at his best when he's cool and direct, rather than combative and polemical. ...Kramer's biting polemical novel.* ADJ-GRADED

polemicist /pəlemɪsɪst/ **polemicists.** A **polemicist** is someone who is skilled at arguing passionately for or against a doctrine, opinion, or belief; a formal word. *The greatest polemicist of the 20th century must be Leon Trotsky.* N-COUNT =debater

pole position, pole positions. When a racing car is in **pole position**, it is in front of the other cars at the start of a race. *Gardner recorded the* ◆◇◇◇◇ N-UNCOUNT: also N in pl *fastest lap in qualifying to earn pole position for today's US Grand Prix.*

pole vault. **The pole vault** is an athletics event in which athletes jump over a high bar, using a long flexible pole to help lift themselves up. N-SING: *the* N

pole vaulter, pole vaulters. A **pole vaulter** is an athlete who performs the pole vault. N-COUNT

police /pəliːs/ **polices, policing, policed** ◆◆◆◆◆

1 The **police** are the official organization that is responsible for making sure that people obey the law. *The police are also looking for a second car... Police say they have arrested twenty people following the disturbances... I noticed a police car shadowing us.* N-SING-COLL

2 **Police** are men and women who are members of the official organization that is responsible for making sure that people obey the law. *More than one hundred police have ringed the area.* N-PLURAL

3 If the police or military forces **police** an area or event, they make sure that law and order is preserved in that area or at that event. *...the tiny UN observer force whose job it is to police the border... The march was well-organised, heavily policed and largely good-humoured.* ● See also **secret police.** ♦ **policing** *...the policing of public places.* ● See also **community policing**. VERB V n V-ed N-UNCOUNT

4 If a person or group in authority **polices** a law or an area of public life, they make sure that what is done is fair and legal. *...Imro, the self-regulatory body that polices the investment management business.* ♦ **policing** *Policing of business courses varies widely.* VERB V n N-UNCOUNT

police constable, police constables. In British English, a **police constable** is a policeman or policewoman of the lowest rank. The American term is **police officer**. *A police constable is handling all inquiries. ...Police Constable David Casey.* N-COUNT; N-TITLE

police dog, police dogs. A **police dog** is a working dog which is owned by the police. N-COUNT

police force, police forces. A **police force** is the police organization in a particular country or area. *...the South Wales police force.* ◆◆◇◇◇ N-COUNT: oft N n

policeman /pəliːsmən/ **policemen.** A **policeman** is a man who is a member of the police force. ◆◆◆◇◇ N-COUNT

police officer, police officers. A **police officer** is a member of the police force. *...a meeting of senior police officers.* ◆◆◆◇◇ N-COUNT

police state, police states. A **police state** is a country in which the government controls people's freedom by means of the police, especially secret police; used showing disapproval. *Their land has been turned into a police state.* N-COUNT PRAGMATICS

police station, police stations. A **police station** is the local office of a police force in a particular area. *Two police officers arrested him and took him to Kensington police station.* ◆◆◇◇◇ N-COUNT: oft in names

policewoman /pəliːswʊmən/ **policewomen.** A **policewoman** is a woman who is a member of the police force. ◆◇◇◇◇ N-COUNT

policy /pɒlɪsi/ **policies** ◆◆◆◆◆

1 A **policy** is a set of ideas or plans that is used as a basis for making decisions, especially in politics, economics, or business. *...the evolution of British foreign policy under Thatcher. ...the UN's policy-making body.* N-VAR

2 An official organization's **policy** on a particular issue or towards a country is their attitude and actions regarding that issue or country. *...the organisation's future policy towards South Africa. ...the government's policy on repatriation. ...the corporation's policy of forbidding building on common land.* N-COUNT: usu poss N =stance

3 An **insurance policy** is a document which shows the agreement that you have made with an insurance company. *You are advised to read the small print of household and motor insurance policies.* N-COUNT: usu N n

policyholder /pɒlɪsihoʊldə^r^/ **policyholders;** also spelled **policy-holder**. A **policyholder** is a person who has an insurance policy with an insurance company. *The first 10 per cent of legal fees will be paid by the policy-holder.* ◆◇◇◇◇ N-COUNT

policymaker /pɒlɪsimeɪkə^r^/ **policymakers;** also spelled **policy-maker**. In politics, **policymakers** are people who are involved in making policies and policy decisions. *...the top economic policymakers of the seven leading industrial nations.* N-COUNT: usu pl

policy-making; also spelled **policymaking. Policy-making** is the making of policies. *The Central Committee is the party's policymaking body... He will play a key background role in government policy-making.* ◆◇◇◇◇ N-UNCOUNT: oft N n

polio /poʊlioʊ/. **Polio** is a serious infectious disease caused by a virus. It often causes paralysis. *Gladys was crippled by polio at the age of 3.* ◆◇◇◇◇ N-UNCOUNT

poliomyelitis /poʊlioʊmaɪəlaɪtɪs/. **Poliomyelitis** is the same as **polio**; a medical term. N-UNCOUNT

polish /pɒlɪʃ/ **polishes, polishing, polished** ◆◆◇◇◇

1 **Polish** is a substance that you put on the surface of an object in order to clean it, protect it, and make it shine. *The still air smelt faintly of furniture polish. ...soap powders, detergents, and polishes.* N-MASS

2 If you **polish** something, you put polish on it or rub it with a cloth to make it shine. *Each morning he shaved and polished his shoes... He removed his glasses and began polishing them with his handkerchief.* ► Also a noun. *He gave his counter a polish with a soft duster.* ♦ **polished** *...a highly polished floor.* VERB V n Also V N-SING: a N ADJ-GRADED

3 If you say that someone has **polish**, you mean that they show confidence and sophistication. N-UNCOUNT

4 If you say that a performance or piece of work has **polish**, you mean that it is of a very high standard. *The opera lacks the polish of his later work.* N-UNCOUNT

5 If you **polish** your technique, performance, or skill at doing something, you work on improving it. *They just need to polish their technique.* ► **Polish up** means the same as **polish**. *Polish up your writing skills on a one-week professional course.* VERB V n PHRASAL VERB V P n (not pron) Also V n P

6 See also **polished; french polish, nail polish.**

polish off. If you **polish off** food or drink, you eat or drink all of it, or finish it; an informal expression. *No matter what he is offered to eat he polishes it off in an instant... He polished off his scotch and slammed the glass down.* PHRASAL VERB V n P V P n (not pron)

polish up. See **polish** 5. PHRASAL VERB

Polish /poʊlɪʃ/ ◆◆◆◆◇

1 **Polish** means belonging or relating to Poland, or to its people, language, or culture. *The press conference was broadcast live on Polish television. ...the new Polish government.* ADJ

2 **Polish** is the language spoken in Poland. N-UNCOUNT

polished /pɒlɪʃt/ ◆◇◇◇◇

1 Someone who is **polished** shows confidence and sophistication. *He is polished, charming, articulate and an excellent negotiator.* ADJ-GRADED: usu v-link ADJ

2 If you describe a performance, ability, or skill as **polished**, you mean that it is of a very high standard. *It was simply a very polished performance. ...polished promotional skills.* ADJ-GRADED

3 See also **polish**.

Politburo /pɒlɪtbjʊəroʊ/ **Politburos.** In communist countries the **Politburo** is the chief committee that formulates policy and makes decisions. *The Politburo has been meeting in Peking to discuss the situation.* ◆◇◇◇◇ N-COUNT: usu *the* N

polite /pəlaɪt/ **politer, politest** ◆◆◇◇◇

1 Someone who is **polite** has good manners and behaves in a way that is socially correct and not rude to other people. *Everyone around him was trying to be polite, but you could tell they were all bored... It's not polite to point or talk about strangers in public... Gately, a quiet and very polite young man, made a favourable impression... I hate having to make polite conversation.* ♦ **politely** *'Your home is beautiful,' I said politely... Learning difficulties, as they are politely called, make children a target for bullies.* ♦ **politeness** *She listened to him, but only out of politeness.* ADJ-GRADED =courteous ≠rude ADV-GRADED: usu ADV with v, also ADV adj =courteously ≠rudely N-UNCOUNT

2 You can refer to people who consider themselves to be socially superior and to set standards of ADJ: ADJ n

behaviour for everyone else as **polite society** or **polite company**. *Certain words are vulgar and not acceptable in polite society.*

politic /pɒlɪtɪk/. If it seems **politic** to do a particular thing, that seems to be the most sensible thing to do in the circumstances; a formal word. *Many towns often found it politic to change their allegiance.* • See also **politics**; **body politic**. ADJ-GRADED: usu *it* v-link ADJ to-inf =wise

political /pəlɪtɪkəl/ ◆◆◆◆◆

1 **Political** means relating to the way power is achieved and used in a country or society. *All other political parties there have been completely banned... The Canadian government is facing another political crisis. ...a democratic political system... Abortion is once again a controversial political and moral issue.* • See also **party political**. ADJ: usu ADJ n

♦ **politically** /pəlɪtɪkli/ *They do not believe the killings were politically motivated... Politically and economically this is an extremely difficult question.* ADV: ADV adj/adv, ADV with v, ADV with cl

2 Someone who is **political** is interested or involved in politics and holds strong beliefs about it. *Oh I'm not political, I take no interest in politics... This play is very political.* ADJ-GRADED

political asylum. **Political asylum** is the right to live in a country which is given by the government to foreigners who have to leave their own country for political reasons. *...a university teacher who is seeking political asylum in Britain... Fewer than 10 percent of applicants are granted political asylum by German courts.* ◆◇◇◇◇ N-UNCOUNT

political correctness. **Political correctness** is behaviour and beliefs that reflect the attitudes and language that are typical of people who hold left-wing or liberal views; often used showing disapproval. *In some sectors, where political correctness is a powerful force, I've been criticized for that.* ◆◇◇◇◇ N-UNCOUNT ≠political incorrectness

political economy. **Political economy** is the study of the way in which a government influences or organizes a nation's wealth. ◆◇◇◇◇ N-UNCOUNT

politically correct. If you say that someone or something is **politically correct**, you mean that they reflect the attitudes and language that are typical of people who hold left-wing or liberal views; often used showing disapproval. ▸ **The politically correct** are people who are politically correct. ◆◇◇◇◇ ADJ-GRADED =right-on; N-PLURAL: *the* N ≠politically incorrect

politically incorrect. If you say that someone or something is **politically incorrect**, you mean that they reflect old-fashioned ideas and beliefs about equality. *Gershwin's lyrics would today probably be deemed politically incorrect.* ADJ-GRADED PRAGMATICS ≠politically correct, right-on

political prisoner, political prisoners. A **political prisoner** is someone who has been imprisoned for criticizing or disagreeing with their own government. ◆◇◇◇◇ N-COUNT

political science. **Political science** is the study of the ways in which political power is acquired and used in a country. ◆◇◇◇◇ N-UNCOUNT

political scientist, political scientists. A **political scientist** is someone who studies, writes, or lectures about political science. ◆◇◇◇◇ N-COUNT

politician /pɒlɪtɪʃən/ **politicians.** A **politician** is a person whose job is in politics, especially a member of parliament. *They have arrested a number of leading opposition politicians.* ◆◆◆◆◇ N-COUNT

politicize /pəlɪtɪsaɪz/ **politicizes, politicizing, politicized;** also spelled **politicise** in British English. If you **politicize** someone or something, you make them more interested in politics or more involved with politics. *...ideas which might politicize the labouring classes and cause them to question the status quo... Some feminists had attempted to politicize personal life.* ♦ **politicized** *...the highly politicized nature of China's legal system.* ♦ **politicization** /pəlɪtɪsaɪzeɪʃən/ *There has been increasing politicization of the civil service.* ◆◇◇◇◇ VERB; V n; ADJ-GRADED; N-UNCOUNT

politicking /pɒlɪtɪkɪŋ/. If you describe someone's political activity as **politicking**, you think that they are engaged in it to gain votes or personal advantage for themselves; used showing disapproval. *The politicking at Westminster is extremely intense.* N-UNCOUNT PRAGMATICS

politico /pəlɪtɪkoʊ/ **politicos.** You can describe a politician as a **politico**, especially if you do not like them or approve of what they do. N-COUNT PRAGMATICS

politico- /pəlɪtɪkoʊ-/. **Politico-** is added to adjectives to form other adjectives that describe something as being both political and the other thing that is mentioned. *...the capitalist politico-economic system. ...the old politico-military struggle for supremacy.* COMB in ADJ: ADJ n

politics /pɒlɪtɪks/ ◆◆◆◆◇

1 **Politics** are the actions or activities concerned with achieving and using power in a country or society. The verb that follows **politics** may be either singular or plural. *The key question in British politics was how long the prime minister could survive... He quickly involved himself in local politics... The film takes no position on the politics of Northern Ireland... Politics is by no means the only arena in which women are excelling.* • See also **party politics**. N-PLURAL

2 Your **politics** are your beliefs about how a country ought to be governed. *My politics are well to the left of centre.* N-PLURAL: usu with poss

3 **Politics** is the study of the ways in which countries are governed. *He began studying politics and medieval history. ...young politics graduates.* N-UNCOUNT

4 **Politics** can be used to talk about the ways that power is shared in an organization and the ways it is affected by personal relationships between people who work together. The verb that follows **politics** may be either singular or plural. *You need to understand how office politics influence the working environment.* N-PLURAL

polity /pɒlɪti/ **polities.** A **polity** is an organized society, such as a nation, city, or church, together with its government and administration; a formal word. *In the United States, citizenship rested on choices by individuals about the polity in which they wished to participate.* N-COUNT

polka /pɒlkə, AM poʊlkə/ **polkas.** A **polka** is a fast lively dance that was popular in the nineteenth century. ◆◇◇◇◇ N-COUNT

polka dots; the form **polka-dot** is used as a modifier. The word **polka** is usually pronounced /poʊkə/ in American English when it is part of this compound. **Polka dots** are very small spots printed on a piece of cloth. *Bethany wore a yellow bikini with polka dots... She wore a tight-fitting polka dot blouse.* N-PLURAL: oft N n

poll /poʊl/ **polls, polling, polled** ◆◆◆◆◇

1 A **poll** is a survey in which people are asked their opinions about something, usually in order to find out how popular something is or what people intend to do in the future. *Polls show that the European treaty has gained support in Denmark... We are doing a weekly poll on the president, and clearly his popularity has declined... The Socialist Party, which won a convincing victory in elections in June, has been losing support in the polls recently.* • See also **opinion poll**, **straw poll**. N-COUNT

2 If you **are polled** on something, you are asked what you think about it as part of a survey. *More than 18,000 people were polled... Audiences were going to be polled on which of three pieces of contemporary music they liked best... More than 70 per cent of those polled said that they approved of his record as president.* VB: usu passive; *be* V-ed; *be* V-ed on wh/n; V-ed

3 **The polls** means an election for a country's government, or the place where people go to vote in an election. *In 1945, Winston Churchill was defeated at the polls... Voters are due to go to the polls on Sunday to elect a new president... The polls have closed in the Pakistan parliamentary elections.* N-PLURAL: *the* N

4 If a political party or a candidate **polls** a particular number or percentage of votes, they get that number or percentage of votes in an election. *It was a disappointing result for the Greens who polled three percent... The result showed he had polled enough votes to force a second ballot.* VERB =net, win; V n

5 See also **polling**; **deed poll**.

pollen /pɒlən/ **pollens.** **Pollen** is a fine powder produced by flowers. It fertilizes other flowers of the same species so that they produce seeds. ◆◇◇◇◇ N-MASS

pollen count, pollen counts. The **pollen count** is a measure of how much pollen is in the air at a particular place and time. Information about the pollen count is given to help people who are allergic to pollen. *Avoid trips to the country while the pollen count is high.* N-COUNT

pollinate /pɒlɪneɪt/ **pollinates, pollinating, pollinated.** To **pollinate** a plant or tree means to fertilize it with pollen. This is often done by insects. *Many of the indigenous insects are needed to pollinate the local plants.* ♦ **pollination** /pɒlɪneɪʃən/ *Without sufficient pollination, the growth of the corn is stunted.* VERB; V n; N-UNCOUNT

pollinator /pɒlɪneɪtəʳ/ **pollinators.** A **pollinator** is something which pollinates plants, especially a type of insect. N-COUNT

polling /poʊlɪŋ/. **Polling** is the act of voting in an election. *There has been a busy start to polling in today's local elections... Elections were postponed the day before polling was due to take place.* ◆◇◇◇◇ N-UNCOUNT =voting

polling booth, polling booths

1 **Polling booths** are the places where people go to vote in an election. *In Darlington, queues formed at some polling booths.* N-COUNT: usu pl =polling station

2 A **polling booth** is one of the compartments in a polling station where people can vote in private. *When you are there, in the polling booth, nobody can see where you put your cross.* N-COUNT

polling day. **Polling day** is the day on which people vote in an election. N-UNCOUNT

polling station, polling stations. A **polling station** is a place where people go to vote at an election. It is often a school or other public building. *The voting was said to be very brisk and queues formed even before polling stations opened.* ◆◇◇◇◇ N-COUNT

pollster /poʊlstəʳ/ **pollsters.** A **pollster** is a person or organization who conducts opinion polls. ◆◇◇◇◇ N-COUNT

poll tax. In Britain, many people refer to the **community charge** as the **poll tax**. *The aim is to replace the poll tax with a tax based on property.* ◆◆◇◇◇ N-UNCOUNT: also *the* N

pollutant /pəluːtənt/ **pollutants.** **Pollutants** are substances that pollute the environment, especially fumes from vehicles and poisonous chemicals that are produced as waste by industrial processes. *A steady stream of California traffic clogs the air with pollutants.* ◆◇◇◇◇ N-VAR

pollute /pəluːt/ **pollutes, polluting, polluted.** To **pollute** water, air, or land means to make it dirty and dangerous to live in or to use, especially with poisonous chemicals or sewage. *Heavy industry pollutes our rivers with noxious chemicals... A number of beaches in the region have been polluted by sewage pumped into the Irish Sea.* ♦ **polluted** *The police have warned the city's inhabitants not to bathe in the polluted river.* ◆◆◇◇◇ VERB =contaminate, poison; V n; ADJ-GRADED

polluter /pəluːtəʳ/ **polluters.** A **polluter** is someone or something that pollutes the environment. ◆◇◇◇◇ N-COUNT

pollution /pəluːʃən/ ◆◆◆◇◇

1 **Pollution** is the process of polluting water, air, or land, especially with poisonous chemicals. *The fine was for the company's pollution of the air near its plants... Recycling also helps control environmental pollution by reducing the need for waste dumps.* N-UNCOUNT =contamination

2 **Pollution** is poisonous or dirty substances that are polluting the water, air, or land somewhere. *The level of pollution in the river was falling.* N-UNCOUNT =contamination

polo /poʊloʊ/. **Polo** is a game played between two teams of players. The players ride horses and use wooden hammers with long handles to hit a ball. • See also **water polo**. ◆◇◇◇◇ N-UNCOUNT

polo neck, polo necks; also spelled **polo-neck**. A **polo neck** or a **polo neck sweater** is a sweater with a high neck which folds over. N-COUNT

polo shirt, polo shirts. A **polo shirt** is a T-shirt with a collar. N-COUNT

poltergeist /pɒltəʳgaɪst, AM poʊl-/ **poltergeists.** A **poltergeist** is a ghost or supernatural force which is believed to move furniture or throw objects around. N-COUNT

poly /pɒli/ **polys.** A **poly** is the same as a **polytechnic**; an informal word, used mainly in British English. *...theatre design students from Birmingham Poly.* ◆◇◇◇◇ N-COUNT: oft in names after n

poly- /pɒli-/. **Poly-** is used to form adjectives and nouns which indicate that many things or types of something are involved in something. For example, a polysyllabic word contains many syllables. *He portrays the psyche as polycentric. ...polyclinics that integrate primary and secondary health care.* PREFIX

polyester /pɒliestəʳ, AM -es-/ **polyesters.** **Polyester** is a type of synthetic cloth used especially to make clothes. *...a green polyester shirt.* ◆◇◇◇◇ N-MASS

polyethylene /pɒlieθɪliːn/. **Polyethylene** is the same as **polythene**. N-UNCOUNT

polygamous /pəlɪgəməs/. In a **polygamous** society, people can be legally married to more than one person at the same time. A **polygamous** person, especially a man, is married to more than one person. *Less than 1 percent of the men in any Muslim country are polygamous.* ADJ

polygamy /pəlɪgəmi/. **Polygamy** is the custom in some societies in which someone can be legally married to more than one person at the same time. N-UNCOUNT

polyglot /pɒliglɒt/ **polyglots**

1 **Polyglot** is used to describe something such as a book or society in which several different languages are used; a formal use. *...Chicago's polyglot population.* ADJ: usu ADJ n =multilingual

2 A **polyglot** is a person who speaks or understands many languages. *...a polyglot who speaks four languages.* N-COUNT

polygraph /pɒligrɑːf, -græf/ **polygraphs.** A **polygraph** or a **polygraph test** is a test in which someone asks you questions and a machine records any changes in your blood pressure, temperature, or breathing in order to find out if you are telling the truth when you answer. *Hill's lawyers announced she had taken and passed a polygraph test.* N-COUNT =lie detector

polymath /pɒlimæθ/ **polymaths.** A **polymath** is a person who is very knowledgeable in many different subjects; a formal word. N-COUNT

polymer /pɒlɪməʳ/ **polymers.** A **polymer** is a chemical compound with large molecules made of many smaller molecules of the same kind. Some polymers exist naturally and others are produced in laboratories and factories. ◆◇◇◇◇ N-COUNT

polyp /pɒlɪp/ **polyps**

1 A **polyp** is a small unhealthy growth on a surface inside your body, especially inside your nose. *It takes ten years or more for a benign polyp to turn malignant.* N-COUNT

2 A **polyp** is a small animal that lives in the sea. It has a hollow body like a tube and tentacles around its mouth. N-COUNT

polypropylene /pɒliprɒpɪliːn/. **Polypropylene** is a synthetic material that is very strong and flexible. It is used to make things such as rope, carpet, and pipes. N-UNCOUNT

polystyrene /pɒlɪstaɪriːn/. In British English, **polystyrene** is a very light, plastic substance used especially to make containers or as an insulating material. The usual American word is **styrofoam**. *...polystyrene cups.* N-UNCOUNT

polytechnic /pɒlɪteknɪk/ **polytechnics.** In Britain, a **polytechnic** is a college where you can go after leaving school in order to study academic subjects at various levels up to degree level or to train for particular jobs. In 1992, all the polytechnics in Britain became universities. ◆◆◇◇◇ N-VAR: oft in names =poly

polythene /pɒlɪθiːn/. **Polythene** is a type of plastic made into thin sheets or bags and used especially to keep food fresh or to keep things dry. *Simply put them into a polythene bag and store them in the freezer for a day.* ◆◇◇◇◇ N-UNCOUNT

polyunsaturate /pɒliʌnsætʃʊrət/ **polyunsaturates.** **Polyunsaturates** are types of animal or vegetable fats which are used to make cooking oil and margarine. They are thought to be less harmful to your body than other fats. N-COUNT: usu pl

polyunsaturated /pɒliʌnsætʃʊreɪtɪd/. **Polyunsaturated** oils and margarines are made mainly from vegetable fats and are considered healthier than those made from animal fats. *Use polyunsaturated spread instead of butter.* ◆◇◇◇◇ ADJ

polyurethane /pɒlijʊərəθeɪn/ **polyurethanes.** **Polyurethane** is a plastic material used especially to make paint or types of foam and rubber which prevent water or heat from passing through them. *...polyurethane varnish.* N-MASS

pom /pɒm/ **poms.** A **pom** is the same as a **pommy.** N-COUNT

pomegranate /pɒmɪgrænɪt/ **pomegranates.** A **pomegranate** is a round fruit with a thick reddish skin. It contains lots of small seeds with juicy flesh around them. N-VAR

pommel /pʌməl, pɒm-/ **pommels.** A **pommel** is the part of a saddle that rises up at the front, or a knob that is fixed there. N-COUNT

pommy /pɒmi/ **pommies;** also spelled **pommie.** In Australian English, a **pommy** is an English person; a slightly offensive word. N-COUNT PRAGMATICS

pomp /pɒmp/. **Pomp** is the use of a lot of ceremony, fine clothes, and decorations, especially on a special occasion. *They were treated to a display of pomp and power. ...the pomp and splendour of the English aristocracy.* ◆◇◇◇◇ N-UNCOUNT

pom-pom, pom-poms. A **pom-pom** is a small ball of wool or other material which is used to decorate things such as hats or furniture. In the United States, cheer-leaders carry large pom-poms at football matches. *...wide-brimmed hats with red pom-poms worn by the local girls.* N-COUNT

pomposity /pɒmpɒsɪti/ **pomposities.** **Pomposity** means speaking or behaving in a very serious manner which shows that you think you are more important than you really are; a formal word, used showing disapproval. *Einstein was a scientist who hated pomposity and disliked being called a genius.* N-UNCOUNT: also N in pl PRAGMATICS =self-importance

pompous /pɒmpəs/ ◆◇◇◇◇

1 If you describe someone as **pompous**, you mean that they behave or speak in a very serious way because they think they are more important than they really are; used showing disapproval. *He was somewhat pompous and had a high opinion of his own capabilities.* ♦ **pompously** *Robin told me firmly and pompously that he had an important business appointment.* ADJ-GRADED PRAGMATICS =grandiose; ADV-GRADED: usu ADV with v

2 A **pompous** building or ceremony is very grand and elaborate. *The service was grand without being pompous.* ADJ-GRADED

ponce /pɒns/ **ponces, poncing, ponced**

1 A **ponce** is the same as a **pimp**; used mainly in British English. N-COUNT

2 If you call a man a **ponce**, you are insulting him because you think that he is too fussy in the way he dresses and in his manners; used mainly in British English. *The younger ones as far as I am concerned are a bunch of ponces.* N-COUNT PRAGMATICS

ponce about or **ponce around.** In informal British English, if you say that someone **is poncing about** or **poncing around**, you mean that they are not doing something properly, quickly, or seriously; used showing disapproval. *I spent my working life poncing around on a beach instead of doing a proper job.* PHRASAL VERB; V P

poncho /pɒntʃoʊ/ **ponchos.** A **poncho** is a piece of clothing that consists of a long piece of material, usually wool, with a hole cut in the middle through which you put your head. Some ponchos have a hood. N-COUNT

pond /pɒnd/ **ponds.** A **pond** is a small area of water that is smaller than a lake. Ponds are often made artificially. *She chose a bench beside the duck pond and sat down... You can build a garden pond any size or shape you want.* ◆◆◇◇◇ N-COUNT: oft n N =pool

ponder /pɒndər/ **ponders, pondering, pondered.** If you **ponder** something, you think about it carefully. *I found myself constantly pondering the question: 'How could anyone do these things?'... The Prime Minister pondered on when to go to the polls... I'm continually pondering how to improve the team.* ◆◆◇◇◇ VERB =deliberate; V n; V on/over n; V wh; Also V

ponderous /pɒndərəs/ ◆◇◇◇◇

1 **Ponderous** writing or speech is very serious, uses more words than necessary, and is rather dull. *He had a dense, ponderous style.* ♦ **ponderously** *...the rather ponderously titled 'Recommendation for National Reconciliation and Salvation'.* ADJ-GRADED; ADV-GRADED: ADV with v

2 A movement or action that is **ponderous** is very slow or clumsy; used in written English. *His steps were heavy and ponderous.* ♦ **ponderously** *Wilson shifted ponderously in his chair.* ADJ-GRADED; ADV-GRADED: ADV with v

pong /pɒŋ, AM pɔːŋ/ **pongs.** In British English, a **pong** is an unpleasant smell; an informal word. *...the pong of milk and sick and nappies.* N-COUNT =smell

pontiff /pɒntɪf/ **pontiffs.** The **Pontiff** is the Pope; a formal word. *The Pontiff celebrated mass before a crowd of tens of thousands of worshippers in Mexico City.* N-COUNT: usu *the* N =Pope

pontificate, pontificates, pontificating, pontificated. The verb is pronounced /pɒntɪfɪkeɪt/. The noun is pronounced /pɒntɪfɪkət/.

1 If someone **pontificates** about something, they state their opinions as if they are the only correct ones and nobody could possibly argue against them. *Politicians like to pontificate about falling standards.* VERB =preach; V about/on n; Also V

2 The **pontificate** of a pope is the period of time during which he is pope. *Pope Formosus died of natural causes in 896 after a pontificate of four and a half years.* N-COUNT

pontoon /pɒntuːn/ **pontoons.** A **pontoon** is a floating platform, often one used to support a bridge. *...a pontoon bridge.* N-COUNT

pony /poʊni/ **ponies, ponying, ponied.** A **pony** is a type of small horse. ◆◆◇◇◇ N-COUNT

pony up. If you **pony up** a sum of money, you pay the money that is needed for something, often reluctantly; an informal expression, used in American English. *The IMF is not prepared to pony up the second half of the $4 billion... People can't even afford to pony up for movie tickets.* PHRASAL VERB =stump up; V n; V P for n

ponytail /poʊniteɪl/ **ponytails;** also spelled **pony-tail.** A **ponytail** is a hairstyle in which someone's hair is tied up at the back of the head and hangs down like a tail. *Her long, fine hair was swept back in a ponytail.* N-COUNT

poo /puː/ **poos.** **Poo** is excrement; an informal word, used by children. ◆◇◇◇◇ N-VAR

pooch /puːtʃ/ **pooches.** A **pooch** is a dog; an informal word used mainly in journalism. N-COUNT

poodle /puːdəl/ **poodles.** A **poodle** is a type of dog with thick curly hair. ◆◇◇◇◇ N-COUNT

poof /pʊf/ **poofs;** also spelled **pouf.**

1 A **poof** is a homosexual man; an offensive word, used in British English. N-COUNT

2 Some people say **poof** to indicate that something happened very suddenly. *They approach, embrace, and poof! they disappear in a blinding flash of light.* EXCLAM

poofter /pʊftər/ **poofters.** A **poofter** is the same as a **poof**; an offensive word, used in British English. N-COUNT

pooh-pooh /puː puː/ **pooh-poohs, pooh-poohing, pooh-poohed.** If someone **pooh-poohs** an idea or suggestion, they say or imply that it is foolish, impractical, or unnecessary; an informal word. *In the past he has pooh-poohed suggestions that he might succeed Isaacs.* VERB =scorn, dismiss; V n

pool /puːl/ **pools, pooling, pooled** ◆◆◆◇◇

1 A **pool** is the same as a **swimming pool**. *...a heated indoor pool... During winter, many people swim and the pool is crowded.* N-COUNT

2 A **pool** is a fairly small area of still water. *The pool had dried up and was full of bracken and reeds. ...beautiful gardens filled with pools, fountains and rare birds.* • See also **rock pool**. N-COUNT

3 A **pool of** liquid or light is a small area of it on the N-COUNT:

ground or on a surface. *She was found lying in a pool of blood... It was raining quietly and steadily and there were little pools of water on the gravel drive... The lamps on the side-tables threw warm pools of light on the polished wood.* N of n

4 A **pool** of people, money, or things is a quantity or number of them that is available for an organization or group to use. *The available pool of healthy manpower was not as large as military officials had expected... The new proposal would create a reserve pool of cash.* • See also **car pool**. N-COUNT: with supp, usu N of n

5 If a group of people or organizations **pool** their money, knowledge, or equipment, they share it or put it together so that it can be used for a particular purpose. *We pooled ideas and information... Philip and I pooled our savings to start up my business.* VERB V n

6 **Pool** is a game played on a large cloth-covered table. Players use a long stick called a cue to hit a white ball across the table so that it knocks coloured balls with numbers on them into six holes around the edge of the table. *We played pool together and were good mates... The Seaman was a bar for pool players and hard drinkers... He was shooting pool with two other men.* N-UNCOUNT

7 In British English, if you do **the pools**, you take part in a gambling competition in which people try to win money by guessing correctly the results of football matches. *The odds of winning the pools are about one in 20 million.* N-PLURAL: the N =football pools

poop /puːp/ **poops.** The **poop** of an old-fashioned sailing ship is the raised structure at the back end of it. *...the poop deck.* N-COUNT

pooped /puːpt/. In American English, if you are **pooped**, you are very tired; an informal word. ADJ-GRADED: v-link ADJ

poor /pʊəʳ, pɔːʳ/ **poorer, poorest** ◆◆◆◆◇

1 Someone who is **poor** has very little money and few possessions. *The reason our schools cannot afford better teachers is because people here are poor... He was one of thirteen children from a poor family.* ► **The poor** are people who are poor. *Even the poor have their pride.* ADJ-GRADED ≠rich; N-PLURAL: the N

2 A **poor** country or area is inhabited by people with very little money and few possessions. *Many countries in the Third World are as poor as they have ever been. ...a settlement house for children in a poor neighborhood.* ADJ-GRADED =impoverished ≠rich

3 You use **poor** to express your sympathy for someone. *I feel sorry for that poor child... Poor chap – he was killed in that air crash when a lot of our athletes were coming back from Paris... Poor Gordon!* ADJ: ADJ n

4 If you describe something as **poor**, you mean that it is of a low quality or standard or that it is in bad condition. *The flat was in a poor state of repair... The gap between the best and poorest childcare provision in the European Community has widened... The wine was poor.* ♦ **poorly** *Some are living in poorly built dormitories, even in tents... They were dressed and fed poorly.* ADJ-GRADED =bad; ADV-GRADED: ADV -ed, ADV after v

5 If you describe an amount, rate, or number as **poor**, you mean that it is less than expected or less than is considered reasonable. *...poor wages and working conditions.* ♦ **poorly** *During the first week, the evening meetings were poorly attended... For one of the top ten releases in rock history, the record sold poorly.* ADJ-GRADED =bad; ADV-GRADED: ADV -ed, ADV after v =badly

6 You use **poor** to describe someone who is not very skilful in a particular activity. *He was a poor actor... Hospitals are poor at collecting information.* ♦ **poorly** *That is the fact of Hungarian football – they can play very well or very poorly.* ADJ-GRADED: usu ADJ n, also v-link ADJ at -ing/n; ADV-GRADED: ADV after v

7 If something is **poor in** a particular quality or substance, it contains very little of the quality or substance. *Fats and sugar are very rich in energy but poor in vitamins, minerals and dietary fibre. ...soil that is poor in zinc.* ADJ-GRADED: v-link ADJ in n =low in

poorhouse /pʊəʳhaʊs, pɔːʳ-/ **poorhouses;** also spelled **poor-house**. In former times in Britain, a **poorhouse** was an institution in which poor people could live. It was paid for by the public. *I was certain I was on the brink of poverty, going to the poorhouse.* N-COUNT: usu the N =workhouse

poorly /pʊəʳli, pɔːʳ-/. In British English, if someone is **poorly**, they are ill; an informal word. The American word is **sick**. *I've just phoned Julie and she's still poorly.* • See also **poor**. ◆◇◇◇◇ ADJ-GRADED: usu v-link ADJ

poor relation, poor relations. If you describe one thing as a **poor relation** of another, you mean that it is similar to or part of the other thing, but is considered to be inferior to it. *Watercolour still seems somehow to be the poor relation of oil painting.* N-COUNT: usu N of n

pop /pɒp/ **pops, popping, popped** ◆◆◆◇◇

1 **Pop** is modern music that usually has a strong rhythm and uses electronic equipment. *...the perfect combination of Caribbean rhythms, European pop, and American soul... Which great British pop band had a hit with 'In the Army Now'? ...a life-size poster of a pop star... I know nothing about pop music.* N-UNCOUNT: oft N n

2 You can refer to fizzy drinks such as lemonade as **pop**; an informal use. *He still visits the village shop for buns and fizzy pop. ...glass pop bottles.* N-UNCOUNT

3 **Pop** is used to represent a short sharp sound, for example the sound made by bursting a balloon or by pulling a cork out of a bottle. *Each corn kernel will make a loud pop when cooked... His back tyre just went pop on a motorway.* N-COUNT; SOUND

4 If something **pops**, it makes a short sharp sound. *He untwisted the wire off the champagne bottle, and the cork popped and shot to the ceiling.* VERB V

5 If your **eyes pop**, you look very surprised or excited when you see something; an informal use. *My eyes popped at the sight of the rich variety of food on show.* VERB V

6 If you **pop** something somewhere, you put it there quickly; an informal use. *Marianne got a couple of mugs from the dresser and popped a teabag into each of them... He plucked a purple grape from the bunch and popped it in his mouth.* VERB V n prep/adv

7 If you **pop** somewhere, you go there for a short time; an informal use. *He does pop down to the pub, but he seldom stays longer than an hour... Wendy popped in for a quick bite to eat on Monday night.* VERB V adv/prep

8 In American English, some people call their father **Pop**; an informal use. *I looked at Pop and he had big tears in his eyes... Yes, Pop, I made a big mistake – you and Mark made me realize that.* N-FAMILY

9 • to **pop the question**: see **question**.

pop off PHRASAL VERB

1 When someone **pops off**, they die; an informal use. *None of Olive's relatives looked likely to pop off for the time being, thank God.* V P

2 If you **pop off**, you leave and go somewhere else; an informal use. *I'll make the tea and you pop off for a while... She should pop off back to Scotland.* V P; V P adv

pop up. If someone or something **pops up**, they appear in a place or situation unexpectedly; an informal expression. *She was startled when Lisa popped up at the door all smiles... You solved one problem and another would immediately pop up.* • See also **pop-up**. PHRASAL VERB =crop up, appear; V P

pop. /pɒp/. **pop.** is an abbreviation for 'population'. It is used before a number when indicating the total population of a city or country. *Somalia, pop. 7.9 million, income per head about £1.60 a week.*

pop art. **Pop art** is a style of modern art which began in the 1960s. It uses bright colours and takes a lot of its techniques and subject matter from everyday, modern life. *...a massive pop-art silk-screen of Buddy Holly.* N-UNCOUNT

popcorn /pɒpkɔːʳn/. **Popcorn** is a snack which consists of grains of maize that have been heated until they have burst and become large and light. It can be eaten with sugar or salt. ◆◇◇◇◇ N-UNCOUNT

pope /poʊp/ **popes.** The **Pope** is the head of the Roman Catholic Church. *The highlight of the Pope's visit will be his message to the people. ...Pope John Paul II.* ◆◆◇◇◇ N-COUNT: usu the N; N-TITLE =Pontiff

poplar /pɒpləʳ/ **poplars.** A **poplar** is a type of tall thin tree. ◆◇◇◇◇ N-VAR

poplin /pɒplɪn/. **Poplin** is a type of cotton material used to make clothes. N-UNCOUNT

poppadom /pɒpədɒm/ **poppadoms.** A **poppadom** is a very thin circular crisp made from a mixture of flour and water, which is fried in oil. Poppadoms are usually eaten with Indian food. N-COUNT

popper /pɒpəʳ/ **poppers.** In British English, a **popper** is a device for fastening clothes. It consists of two pieces of plastic or metal which you press together. N-COUNT

poppy /pɒpi/ **poppies** ◆◇◇◇◇
1 A **poppy** is a plant with a large, delicate flower, usually red in colour. Opium is obtained from one type of poppy. *...a field of poppies.* N-COUNT
2 In Britain, on a particular day in November, people wear an artificial **poppy** in memory of the people who died in the two world wars. *She pinned the poppy to his raincoat. ...a wreath of poppies.* N-COUNT

populace /pɒpjʊləs/. The **populace** of a country is its people, especially its working-class people; a formal word. *...a large proportion of the populace.* ◆◇◇◇◇ N-UNCOUNT: usu *the* N =population

popular /pɒpjʊləʳ/ ◆◆◆◆◇
1 Something that is **popular** is enjoyed or liked by a lot of people. *This is the most popular ball game ever devised... Chocolate sauce is always popular with youngsters.* ♦ **popularity** /pɒpjʊlærɪti/ *...the growing popularity of Australian wines among consumers... Walking and golf increased in popularity during the 1980s.* ADJ-GRADED ≠unpopular; N-UNCOUNT: oft with poss
2 Someone who is **popular** is liked by most people, or by most people in a particular group. *He remained the most popular politician in France... He was not only talented but immensely popular with his colleagues.* ♦ **popularity** *It is his popularity with ordinary people that sets him apart.* ADJ-GRADED ≠unpopular; N-UNCOUNT: oft with poss
3 **Popular** newspapers, television programmes, or forms of art are aimed at ordinary people and not at experts or intellectuals. *Once again the popular press in Britain has been rife with stories about their marriage. ...one of the classics of modern popular music. ...the popular culture of his native Mexico.* ADJ: ADJ n
4 **Popular** ideas, feelings, or attitudes are approved of or held by most people. *Contrary to popular belief, the oil companies can't control the price of crude... The military government has been unable to win popular support... Popular anger has been expressed in demonstrations.* ♦ **popularity** *Over time, though, Watson's views gained in popularity.* ADJ: usu ADJ n; N-UNCOUNT
5 **Popular** is used to describe political activities which involve the ordinary people of a country, and not just members of political parties. *The late President Ferdinand Marcos was overthrown by a popular uprising in 1986.* ADJ: ADJ n

popularize /pɒpjʊləraɪz/ **popularizes, popularizing, popularized;** also spelled **popularise** in British English. ◆◇◇◇◇
1 To **popularize** something means to make a lot of people interested in it and able to enjoy it. *Irving Brokaw, who had studied figure skating in Europe, returned to the US and popularized the new sport.* ♦ **popularization** /pɒpjʊləraɪzeɪʃən/ *...the popularisation of sport through television.* VERB V n; N-UNCOUNT: usu N *of* n
2 To **popularize** an academic subject or scientific idea means to make it more easily understandable to ordinary people. *It was Aristotle who proved the world is round. Plato popularized the concept.* ♦ **popularization** *He became world famous for his popularisation of science.* VERB V n; N-UNCOUNT: usu N *of* n

popularly /pɒpjʊləʳli/ ◆◇◇◇◇
1 If something or someone is **popularly** known as something, most people call them that, although it is not their official name or title. *...the Mesozoic era, more popularly known as the age of dinosaurs. ...an infection popularly called mad cow disease. ...Sir Lynden Pindling, the Bahamian prime minister known popularly as 'King Ping'.* ADV-GRADED: ADV with -ed =commonly
2 If something is **popularly** believed or supposed to be the case, most people believe or suppose it to be the case, although it may not be true. *Schizophrenia is not a 'split mind' as is popularly believed... She possessed the vibrant personality that is so often popularly associated with Spanish women.* ADV: ADV -ed =commonly
3 A **popularly elected** leader or government has been elected by a majority of the people in a country. *Walesa is Poland's first popularly elected President.* ADV: ADV -ed =democratically

populate /pɒpjʊleɪt/ **populates, populating, populated** ◆◇◇◇◇
1 If an area **is populated** by certain people or animals, those people or animals live there, often in large numbers. *Before all this the island was populated by native American Arawaks. ...native Sindhis, who populate the surrounding villages.* ♦ **populated** *The southeast is the most densely populated area... Rural areas are sparsely populated.* ♦ **-populated** *Shelling from federal army tanks razed half the houses in the Croat-populated part of Glina.* VERB =inhabit; *be* V-ed; V n; ADJ-GRADED: adv ADJ; COMB in ADJ-GRADED
2 To **populate** an area means to cause people to live there. *Successive regimes annexed the region and populated it with lowland people.* VERB V n *with* n Also V n
3 The people or characters who **populate** an area of public life or a piece of entertainment are the people or characters in it. *...the diligent and discreet technocrats who populate the upper reaches of French power. ...the sort of low-life characters who populate the film.* VERB V n

population /pɒpjʊleɪʃən/ **populations** ◆◆◆◆◇
1 The **population** of a country or area is all the people who live in it. *Bangladesh now has a population of about 110 million. ...the annual rate of population growth. ...the local population.* N-COUNT
2 If you refer to a particular type of **population** in a country or area, you are referring to all the people or animals of that type there; a formal use. *...75.6 per cent of the male population over sixteen. ...areas with a large black population. ...the elephant populations of Tanzania and Kenya.* N-COUNT: usu supp N

populism /pɒpjʊlɪzəm/. **Populism** refers to political activities or ideas that claim to promote the interests and opinions of ordinary people; a formal word. *...an artful blend of Russian nationalism and economic populism. ...a wave of populism.* N-UNCOUNT

populist /pɒpʊlɪst/ **populists.** If you describe a politician or an artist as **populist**, you mean that they claim to promote the interests and opinions of ordinary people rather than the interests and opinions of a political or artistic minority; a formal word. *...Jose Sarney, the current populist president... The city of Memphis is promoting a populist approach to culture.* ► A **populist** is someone who expresses populist views. ◆◇◇◇◇ ADJ-GRADED: usu ADJ n ≠élitist; N-COUNT ≠élitist

populous /pɒpjʊləs/. A **populous** country or area has a lot of people living in it; a formal word. *Indonesia, with 185 million people, is the fifth most populous country in the world.* ◆◇◇◇◇ ADJ-GRADED: usu ADJ n

pop-up ◆◇◇◇◇
1 A **pop-up book**, usually a children's book, has pictures that stand up when you open the pages. ADJ: ADJ n
2 A **pop-up toaster** has a mechanism that pushes slices of bread up when they are toasted. ADJ: ADJ n

porcelain /pɔːʳsəlɪn/ **porcelains** ◆◇◇◇◇
1 **Porcelain** is a hard, shiny substance made by heating clay. It is used to make delicate cups, plates, and ornaments. *There were lilies everywhere in tall white porcelain vases.* N-UNCOUNT
2 A **porcelain** is an ornament that is made of porcelain. You can refer to a number of such ornaments as **porcelain**. *...decorative 17th and 18th century porcelains. ...a priceless collection of English porcelain.* N-VAR

porch /pɔːʳtʃ/ **porches** ◆◇◇◇◇
1 A **porch** is a sheltered area at the entrance to a building. It has a roof and sometimes has walls. *Is there a light in the porch or garden?* N-COUNT
2 In American English, a **porch** is a raised platform built along the outside wall of a house and often covered with a roof. The usual British word is **veranda**. *We'd eat during the hot summer evenings on the front porch.* N-COUNT

porcine /pɔːʳsaɪn/. If you describe someone as **porcine**, you mean that they look like a pig; a literary word. *...a porcine countenance.* ADJ-GRADED: usu ADJ n

porcupine /pɔːʳkjʊpaɪn/ **porcupines.** A **porcupine** is an animal with many long, thin, sharp spikes on its back that stick out as protection when it is attacked. N-COUNT

pore /pɔːʳ/ **pores, poring, pored** ◆◇◇◇◇

1 Your **pores** are the tiny holes in your skin. *The size of your pores is determined by the amount of oil they produce.* N-COUNT: usu pl

2 The **pores** of a plant are the tiny holes on its surface. *A plant's lungs are the microscopic pores in its leaves.* N-COUNT: usu pl

3 If you **pore over** or **through** information, you look at it and study it very carefully. *We spent hours poring over travel brochures... It will take several more months to pore through the volumes of documents.* VERB V over/through n

4 You can say that someone has a certain quality or emotion coming from or in **every pore** to emphasize the degree or strength of that quality or emotion. *She oozes sexuality from every pore... Waves of misery penetrated every pore.* PHRASE

pork /pɔːʳk/. **Pork** is meat from a pig, usually fresh and not smoked or salted. *...fried pork chops. ...a packet of pork sausages.* ◆◆◇◇◇ N-UNCOUNT

pork barrel; also spelled **pork-barrel**. If you say that someone is using **pork barrel** politics, you mean that they are spending a lot of government money on a local project in order to win the votes of the people who live in that area; used showing disapproval. *Pork-barrel politicians hand out rents to win votes and influence people.* N-SING: usu N n PRAGMATICS

pork pie, pork pies. A **pork pie** is a round pie with cooked pork inside. N-VAR

porn /pɔːʳn/. **Porn** is the same as **pornography**; an informal word. *...a porn cinema.* ● See also **soft porn, hard porn.** ◆◇◇◇◇ N-UNCOUNT

porno /pɔːʳnoʊ/. **Porno** is the same as **pornographic**. *...porno mags.* ADJ

pornographer /pɔːʳnɒgrəfəʳ/ **pornographers.** A **pornographer** is a person who produces or sells pornography; used showing disapproval. N-COUNT PRAGMATICS

pornographic /pɔːʳnəgræfɪk/. **Pornographic** materials such as films, videos, and magazines are designed to cause sexual excitement by showing naked people or referring to sexual acts; used showing disapproval. *I found out he'd been watching pornographic videos.* ◆◇◇◇◇ ADJ-GRADED: usu ADJ n PRAGMATICS

pornography /pɔːʳnɒgrəfi/. **Pornography** refers to books, magazines, and films that are designed to cause sexual excitement by showing naked people or referring to sexual acts; used showing disapproval. *China's leading newspaper has called for a new campaign against pornography in China.* ◆◇◇◇◇ N-UNCOUNT PRAGMATICS

porosity /pɔːrɒsɪti/. **Porosity** is the state of being porous; a formal word. *...the porosity of the coal.* N-UNCOUNT

porous /pɔːrəs/. Something that is **porous** has many small holes in it, which water and air can pass through. *The local limestone is so porous that all the rainwater immediately sinks below ground.* ◆◇◇◇◇ ADJ-GRADED =permeable

porpoise /pɔːʳpəs/ **porpoises.** A **porpoise** is a sea animal that looks similar to a dolphin. Porpoises usually swim about in groups. N-COUNT

porridge /pɒrɪdʒ, AM pɔːr-/. **Porridge** is a thick sticky food made from oats cooked in water or milk and eaten hot, especially for breakfast. ◆◇◇◇◇ N-UNCOUNT

port /pɔːʳt/ **ports** ◆◆◆◇◇

1 A **port** is a town by the sea or on a river, which has a harbour. *Port-Louis is an attractive little fishing port. ...the Mediterranean port of Marseilles.* N-COUNT

2 A **port** is a harbour area with docks and warehouses, where ships load or unload goods or passengers. *...the bridges which link the port area to the city centre. ...the city's port authority.* N-COUNT: oft N n

3 The **port** side of a ship is the left side when you are on it and facing towards the front. *Her official number is carved on the port side of the forecabin.* ADJ ≠starboard ► Also a noun. *USS Ogden turned to port.* N-UNCOUNT: usu to N ≠starboard

4 **Port** is a type of strong, sweet red wine. *He asked for a glass of port after dinner.* N-UNCOUNT

portable /pɔːʳtəbᵊl/ **portables** ◆◆◇◇◇

1 A **portable** machine or device is designed to be easily carried or moved. *There was a little portable television switched on behind the bar... I always carry a portable computer with me.* ♦ **portability** /pɔːʳtəbɪlɪti/ *When it came to choosing photographic equipment portability was as important as reliability.* ADJ-GRADED: usu ADJ n N-UNCOUNT

2 A **portable** is something such as a television, radio, or computer which can be easily carried or moved. *We bought a colour portable for the bedroom.* N-COUNT

portal /pɔːʳtᵊl/ **portals.** A **portal** is a large impressive doorway at the entrance to a building; a literary word. *I went in through the royal portal.* N-COUNT

portcullis /pɔːʳtkʌlɪs/ **portcullises.** A **portcullis** is a strong gate above an entrance to a castle or fort, which used to be lowered to the ground in order to keep out enemies. N-COUNT

portend /pɔːʳtend/ **portends, portending, portended.** If something **portends** an event or occurrence, it indicates that it is likely to happen in the future; a formal word. *The change did not portend a basic improvement in social conditions.* VERB V n

portent /pɔːʳtent/ **portents.** A **portent** is something that indicates what is likely to happen in the future; a formal word. *The savage civil war there could be a portent of what's to come in the rest of the region... I hope this is a portent for the rest of the year... As for her engagement with Adam, I would say the portents are gloomy.* N-COUNT: oft N of n =indication, sign

portentous /pɔːʳtentəs/

1 If someone's way of speaking, writing, or behaving is **portentous**, they speak, write, or behave more seriously than necessary because they want to impress other people; a formal use, used showing disapproval. *There was nothing portentous or solemn about him. He was bubbling with humour. ...portentous prose.* ♦ **portentously** *'The difference is,' he said portentously, 'you are Anglo-Saxons, we are Latins.'* ADJ-GRADED PRAGMATICS =pompous ADV-GRADED: usu ADV with v

2 Something that is **portentous** is important in indicating or affecting future events; a formal use. *In social politics, too, the city's contribution to 20th century thought and culture was no less portentous... Portentous choices were forced on him by the dozen.* ADJ-GRADED

porter /pɔːʳtəʳ/ **porters** ◆◆◇◇◇

1 A **porter** is a person whose job is to be in charge of the entrance of a building such as a hotel; used mainly in British English. The usual American word is **doorman**. N-COUNT =concierge

2 A **porter** is a person whose job is to carry things, for example people's luggage at a railway station or in a hotel. N-COUNT

3 In a hospital, a **porter** is someone whose job is to move patients around. N-COUNT

portfolio /pɔːʳtfoʊlioʊ/ **portfolios** ◆◆◇◇◇

1 A **portfolio** is a set of pictures by someone, or photographs of examples of their work, which they use when entering competitions or applying for work. *After dinner that evening, Edith showed them a portfolio of her own political cartoons.* N-COUNT

2 In finance, a **portfolio** is the combination of shares or other investments that a particular investor or company has. *Short-term securities can also be held as part of an investment portfolio. ...Roger Early, a portfolio manager at Federated Investors Corp.* N-COUNT

3 In politics, a **portfolio** is a minister's responsibility for a particular area of a government's activities. *He has held the defence portfolio since the first free elections in 1990.* ● A **minister without portfolio** is a politician who is given the rank of minister without being given responsibility for any particular area of a government's activities; a formal expression. *He was appointed government leader in the senate, and minister without portfolio.* N-COUNT PHRASE: minister inflects

4 A company's **portfolio** of products or designs is their range of products or designs; a formal word. *The company has continued to invest heavily in a strong portfolio of products.* N-COUNT =range

porthole /pɔːʳthoul/ **portholes.** A **porthole** is a small round window in the side of a ship or aircraft. *Dan was in his cabin, staring out of a porthole.* N-COUNT

portico /pɔːʳtɪkou/ **porticoes** or **porticos.** A **portico** is a large covered area at the entrance to a building, with pillars supporting the roof; a formal word. N-COUNT

portion /pɔːʳʃᵊn/ **portions** ◆◆◇◇◇

1 A **portion of** something is a part of it. *Damage was confined to a small portion of the castle... I have spent a fairly considerable portion of my life here... I had learnt a portion of the Koran... Insurance can represent a significant portion of the total price of a holiday.* N-COUNT: N of n =part

2 A **portion** is the amount of food that is given to one person at a meal. *Desserts can be substituted by a portion of fresh fruit... The portions were generous. ...fish and chips at about £2.70 a portion.* N-COUNT =serving

portly /pɔːʳtli/ **portlier, portliest.** A **portly** person, especially a man, is rather fat; a formal word. *...a portly middle-aged man.* ADJ-GRADED: usu ADJ n =stout

port of call, ports of call

1 A **port of call** is a place where a ship stops during a journey. *Their first port of call will be Cape Town.* N-COUNT

2 A **port of call** is any place where you stop for a short time when you are visiting several places, shops, or people; an informal use. *The local tourist office should be your first port of call in any town.* N-COUNT

portrait /pɔːʳtreɪt/ **portraits.** A **portrait** is a painting, drawing, or photograph of a particular person. *Lucian Freud has been asked to paint a portrait of the Queen. ...the English portrait painter Augustus John.* ◆◆◆◇◇ N-COUNT

portraitist /pɔːʳtreɪtɪst/ **portraitists.** A **portraitist** is an artist who paints or draws people's portraits; a formal word. N-COUNT

portraiture /pɔːʳtrɪtʃəʳ/. **Portraiture** is the art of painting or drawing portraits; a formal word. N-UNCOUNT

portray /pɔːʳtreɪ/ **portrays, portraying, portrayed** ◆◆◇◇◇

1 When an actor or actress **portrays** someone, he or she plays that person in a play or film. *In 1975 he portrayed the king in a Los Angeles revival of 'Camelot'. ...the busty and rumbustious Mrs Hall, excellently portrayed by Toni Palmer.* VERB V n

2 When a writer or artist **portrays** something, he or she writes a description or produces a painting of it. *...this northern novelist, who accurately portrays provincial domestic life. ...the landscape as portrayed by painters such as Claude and Poussin.* VERB =depict V n

3 If a film, book, or television programme **portrays** someone in a certain way, it represents them in that way. *She says the programme portrayed her as a 'lady of easy virtue'. ...complaints about the way women are portrayed in adverts.* VERB =represent V n as n be V-ed

portrayal /pɔːʳtreɪəl/ **portrayals** ◆◇◇◇◇

1 An actor's **portrayal** of a character in a play or film is the way that he or she portrays the character. *Mr Ying is well-known for his portrayal of a prison guard in the film 'The Last Emperor'.* N-COUNT: usu sing, usu poss N of n

2 An artist's **portrayal** of something is a drawing, painting, or photograph of it. *'Scene with a Winding River' (1827) is a near-monochrome portrayal of a wood infused with silvery light. ...a moving portrayal of St John the Evangelist by Simone Martini.* N-COUNT: usu N of n =depiction, representation

3 The **portrayal** of something in a book or film is the act of describing it or showing it. *This is a sensitive and often funny portrayal of a friendship between two 11-year-old boys. ...Leigh's portrayal of English society.* N-COUNT: usu sing, usu N of n =depiction

4 The **portrayal** of something in a book, film, or programme is the way that it is made to appear. *The media persists in its portrayal of us as muggers, dope sellers and gangsters... I get criticized for the portrayal of women in that movie.* N-COUNT: usu N of n =depiction

Portuguese /pɔːʳtʃʊgiːz/ ◆◆◆◆◇

1 Something that is **Portuguese** belongs or relates to Portugal, its people, language, or culture. *...a former Portuguese colony. ...a Portuguese woman. ...the Portuguese Grand Prix.* ADJ

2 **The Portuguese** are the people of Portugal. *...a former palace built by the Portuguese.* N-PLURAL: the N

3 **Portuguese** is the language spoken in Portugal, Brazil, Angola, and Mozambique. *If you are intent on learning to speak Portuguese, there is no better place. ...the leading news agency in the Spanish and Portuguese-speaking world.* N-UNCOUNT

pos. Pos. is the written abbreviation for **positive.**

pose /pouz/ **poses, posing, posed** ◆◆◆◇◇

1 If something **poses** a problem or a danger, it is the cause of that problem or danger. *This could pose a threat to jobs in the coal industry... His ill health poses serious problems for the future.* VERB V n

2 If you **pose** a question, you ask it. If you **pose** an issue that needs considering, you mention the issue; a formal use. *When I finally posed the question, 'Why?' he merely shrugged. ...the moral issues posed by new technologies.* VERB =raise V n V-ed

3 If you **pose as** someone, you pretend to be that person in order to deceive people. *The team posed as drug dealers to trap the ringleaders.* VERB V as n

4 If you **pose for** a photograph or painting, you stay in a particular position so that someone can photograph you or paint you. *Before going into their meeting the six foreign ministers posed for photographs.* VERB V

5 You can say that people **are posing** when you think that they are behaving in an insincere or exaggerated way because they want to make a particular impression on other people; used showing disapproval. *He criticized them for dressing outrageously and posing pretentiously.* VB: usu cont PRAGMATICS V

6 A **pose** is a particular way that you stand, sit, or lie, for example when you are being photographed or painted. *We have had several preliminary sittings in various poses.* N-COUNT

7 A **pose** is an insincere or exaggerated way of behaving that is intended to make a particular impression on other people; used showing disapproval. *In many writers modesty is a pose, but in Ford it seems to have been genuine.* N-COUNT PRAGMATICS

poser /pouzəʳ/ **posers**

1 A **poser** is the same as a **poseur**. *He's such a poser.* N-COUNT

2 A **poser** is a difficult problem or puzzle; an old-fashioned, informal use. *Here is a little poser for you.* N-COUNT =puzzle

poseur /pouzɜːʳ/ **poseurs.** You can describe someone as a **poseur** when you think that they behave in an insincere or exaggerated way because they want to make a particular impression on other people; used showing disapproval. *I am sometimes accused of being an inveterate poseur.* N-COUNT PRAGMATICS =poser

posh /pɒʃ/ **posher, poshest** ◆◇◇◇◇

1 If you describe something as **posh**, you mean that it is smart, fashionable, and expensive; an informal use. *Celebrating a promotion, I took her to a posh hotel for a cocktail. ...a posh car. ...a posh dinner party.* ADJ-GRADED: usu ADJ n =swish, grand

2 If you describe a person as **posh**, you mean that they belong to or behave as if they belong to the upper classes; an informal use. *I wouldn't have thought she had such posh friends... He sounded so posh on the phone.* ADJ-GRADED =upper class

posit /pɒzɪt/ **posits, positing, posited.** If you **posit** something, you suggest or assume it as the basis for an argument or calculation; a formal word. *Several writers have posited the idea of a universal consciousness... Callahan goes further, positing that chemical elements radiate electromagnetic signals.* VERB =postulate V n V that

position /pəzɪʃᵊn/ **positions, positioning, positioned** ◆◆◆◆◆

1 The **position** of someone or something is the place where they are in relation to other things. *The ship was identified, and its name and position were reported to the coastguard... This conservatory enjoys an enviable position overlooking a leafy expanse.* N-COUNT =location

2 When someone or something is in a particular N-COUNT:

position, they are sitting, lying, or arranged in that way. *It is crucial that the upper back and neck are held in an erect position to give support for the head... Ensure the patient is turned into the recovery position... Mr. Dambar had raised himself to a sitting position.*
usu with supp

3 If you **position** something somewhere, you put it there carefully, so that it is in the right place or position. *Position trailing plants near the edges and in the sides of the basket to hang down... Place the pastry circles on to a baking sheet and position one apple on each circle.*
VERB =place V n prep Also V n prep

4 Your **position** in society is the role and the importance that you have in it. *Adjustment to their changing role and position in society can be painful for some old people.*
N-COUNT: usu with supp

5 A **position** in a company or organization is a job; a formal use. *He left a career in teaching to take up a position with the Arts Council... Hyundai said this week it is scaling back its U.S. operations by eliminating 50 positions.*
N-COUNT =post

6 Your **position** in a race or competition is how well you did in relation to the other competitors or how well you are doing. *Edberg and Becker resumed their battle for the world's No. 1 position, both winning their opening matches... By the ninth hour the car was running in eighth position.*
N-COUNT: usu supp N =place

7 You can describe your situation at a particular time by saying that you are in a particular **position**. *He's going to be in a very difficult position indeed if things go badly for him... Companies should be made to reveal more about their financial position... It was not the only time he found himself in this position.*
N-COUNT: usu sing, usu with supp =situation

8 Your **position** on a particular matter is your attitude towards it or your opinion of it; a formal use. *He could be depended on to take a moderate position on most of the key issues... The former Soviet Union has been reluctant to state a clear position on the crisis.*
N-COUNT: usu supp N =stance

9 If you are **in a position** to do something, you are able to do it. If you are **in no position** to do something, you are unable to do it. *The UN system will be in a position to support the extensive relief efforts needed... I am not in a position to comment.*
N-SING: N to-inf

10 If someone or something is **in position**, they are in their correct or usual place or arrangement. *This second door is an extra security measure and can be locked in position during the day... Some 28,000 US troops are moving into position.*
PHRASE: usu PHR after v

positive /pɒzɪtɪv/ ◆◆◆◆◇

1 If you are **positive** about things, you are hopeful and confident, and think of the good aspects of a situation rather than the bad ones. *Be positive about your future and get on with living a normal life... Her husband became much more positive and was soon back in full-time employment. ...a positive frame of mind.* ♦ **positively** *You really must try to start thinking positively.*
ADJ-GRADED: usu v-link ADJ, oft ADJ *about* n =optimistic ≠negative
ADV-GRADED: ADV after v

2 A **positive** fact, situation, or experience is pleasant and helpful to you in some way. *The parting from his sister had a positive effect on John... Working abroad should be an exciting and positive experience for all concerned.* ▸ **The positive** in a situation is the good and pleasant aspects of it. *Work on the positive, creating beautiful, loving and fulfilling relationships.*
ADJ-GRADED: usu ADJ n =constructive ≠negative
N-SING: *the* N ≠negative

3 If you make a **positive** decision or take **positive** action, you do something definite in order to deal with a task or problem. *There are positive changes that should be implemented in the rearing of animals... He was expected to make a very positive contribution to the 1996 Games organisation... Having a good diet gives me a sense that I'm doing something positive and that I'm in control.*
ADJ-GRADED: usu ADJ n ≠negative

4 A **positive** response to something indicates agreement, approval, or encouragement. *There's been a positive response to the UN Secretary-General's recent peace efforts.* ♦ **positively** *He responded positively and accepted the fee of £1000 I had offered.*
ADJ-GRADED: usu ADJ n ≠negative
ADV: ADV after v

5 If you are **positive** about something, you are completely sure about it. *I'm as positive as I can be about it... 'She's never late. You sure she said eight?'—'Positive.'*
ADJ-GRADED: v-link ADJ =certain

6 **Positive** evidence gives definite proof of the truth or identity of something. *There was no positive evidence that any birth defects had arisen as a result of Vitamin A intake.* ♦ **positively** *He has positively identified the body as that of his wife.*
ADJ: ADJ n =conclusive
ADV: ADV with v

7 If a medical or scientific test is **positive**, it shows that something has happened or is present. *If the test is positive, a course of antibiotics may be prescribed... He was stripped of his Olympic Hundred Metres gold medal after testing positive for steroids.*
ADJ ≠negative
● **HIV positive**: see **HIV**.

8 You can use **positive** to emphasize a noun; an old-fashioned use. *Good day to you, Bernard! It's a positive delight to see you... He was in a positive fury... The man was being a positive embarrassment.* ● See also **positively**.
ADJ: ADJ n PRAGMATICS =real

9 A **positive number** is greater than zero. *It's really a simple numbers game with negative and positive numbers.*
ADJ: ADJ n ≠negative

10 If something has a **positive** electrical **charge**, it has the same charge as a proton and the opposite charge to an electron; a technical use. ♦ **positively** *The atom was pictured as a small positively charged core or nucleus.*
ADJ: usu ADJ n ≠negative
ADV: ADV adj

11 ● **proof positive**: see **positive**.

positive discrimination. In British English, **positive discrimination** means making sure that members of disadvantaged groups, such as racial minorities or women, get an appropriate share of the opportunities available. The American term is **affirmative action**. *Mr Singh wanted to reserve places for low-caste Indians within the country's public sector, as a form of positive discrimination.*
N-UNCOUNT

positively /pɒzɪtɪvli/ ◆◇◇◇◇

1 You use **positively** to emphasize that you really mean what you are saying. *This is positively the worst thing that I can even imagine... This is positively the last chance for the industry to establish such a system.*
ADV: ADV adj-superl PRAGMATICS =definitely, absolutely

2 You use **positively** to emphasize that something really is the case, although it may sound surprising or extreme. *He's changed since he came back—he seems positively cheerful... Parents are positively encouraged to be at school whenever possible.*
ADV: ADV adj, ADV before v PRAGMATICS

positivism /pɒzɪtɪvɪsm/. **Positivism** is a philosophical system which accepts only things that can be seen or proved. ♦ **positivist, positivists** *By far the most popular idea is the positivist one that we should keep only the facts.*
N-UNCOUNT =empiricism
N-COUNT: usu N n =empiricist

poss /pɒs/

1 In British English, **'if poss'** means the same as 'if possible'; an informal use. *We'll rush it round today if poss.*
PHRASES PHR with cl

2 In British English, **'as poss'** means the same as 'as possible'; an informal use. *Tell them I'll be there as soon as poss.*
PHR with cl

posse /pɒsi/ **posses** ◆◇◇◇◇

1 A **posse of** people is a group of people with the same job or purpose; an informal use. *He refused to engage in conversation with a posse of reporters when leaving Belmont... A posse of Marsh's friends persuaded them that this was a bad idea.*
N-COUNT: N *of* n =group

2 In former times, in the United States, a **posse** was a group of men who were brought together by the local sheriff to help him chase and capture a criminal.
N-COUNT

possess /pəzes/ **possesses, possessing, possessed** ◆◆◇◇◇

1 If you **possess** something, you have it or own it. *He was then arrested and charged with possessing an offensive weapon... He is said to possess a fortune of more than two-and-a-half-thousand million dollars.*
VB: no passive, no cont V n

2 If someone or something **possesses** a particular quality, ability, or feature, they have it; a formal use. *...individuals who are deemed to possess the qualities of sense, loyalty and discretion... This figure has long been held to possess miraculous power.*
VB: no cont =have V n

3 If a feeling or belief **possesses** you, it strongly
VERB

influences your thinking or behaviour; a literary use. *Absolute terror possessed her... Tsvetayeva was possessed by a frenzied urge to get out of Moscow.* V n
4 See also **possessed.**
5 If you ask **what possessed** someone to do something, you are emphasising your great surprise that they have done something which you consider foolish or dangerous. *What on earth had possessed her to agree to marry him?.* PHRASE: V inflects PRAGMATICS

possessed /pəzest/ ◆◇◇◇◇
1 If someone is described as being **possessed** by the devil or by an evil spirit, it is believed that their mind and body are controlled by the devil or by the evil spirit. *She even claimed the couple's daughter was possessed by the devil... He behaved like someone possessed.* ADJ: v-link ADJ, oft ADJ *by* n
2 If someone or something is **possessed of** a particular quality, ability, or feature, they have that quality, ability, or feature. If someone is **possessed of** a particular feeling or belief, they have that feeling or belief. Used in formal English. *He is possessed of the most brilliant talents... She was possessed of a terrifying sensation that the life was being squeezed slowly out of her.* ADJ: v-link ADJ *of* n
3 See also **possess.**

possession /pəzeʃən/ **possessions** ◆◆◇◇◇
1 If you are in **possession** of something, you have it, because you have obtained it or because it belongs to you; a formal use. *Those documents are now in the possession of the Guardian... We should go up and take possession of the land... He was also charged with illegal possession of firearms... Religious pamphlets were found in their possession.* N-UNCOUNT: oft *in* N *of* n
2 Your **possessions** are the things that you own or have with you at a particular time. *People had lost their homes and all their possessions... She had tidied away her possessions.* N-COUNT: usu pl, poss N =belongings
3 A country's **possessions** are countries or territories that it controls; a formal use. *All of them were French possessions at one time or another. ...Britain's imperial possessions.* N-COUNT: usu pl, supp N =colonies
4 A belief in **possession** by the devil or by an evil spirit is the belief that a person's mind and body can be controlled or are being controlled by the devil or by an evil spirit. *They were convinced the girls' behaviour was due to possession by the devil.* N-UNCOUNT

possessive /pəzesɪv/ **possessives** ◆◇◇◇◇
1 Someone who is **possessive** about another person wants all that person's love and attention. *Danny could be very jealous and possessive about me... He used to ring his possessive mother several times a day.* ♦ **possessively** *Leaning over, he kissed her possessively on the mouth.* ADJ-GRADED: oft ADJ *about/of* n =jealous; ADV
♦ **possessiveness** *I've ruined every relationship with my possessiveness.* N-UNCOUNT =jealousy
2 Someone who is **possessive** about things that they own does not like other people to use them. *People were very possessive about their coupons.* ADJ-GRADED: usu v-link ADJ, usu ADJ *about* n
3 In grammar, a **possessive determiner** or **possessive adjective** is a word such as "my" or "his" which shows who or what something belongs to or is connected with. The **possessive** form of a name or noun has 's added to it, as in "Jenny's" or "cat's". ADJ: ADJ n
4 A **possessive** is a possessive determiner or the possessive form of a name or noun. N-COUNT

possessive pronoun, possessive pronouns. N-COUNT
A **possessive pronoun** is a pronoun such as 'mine', 'yours', or 'theirs' which is used to refer to the thing of a particular kind that belongs to someone, as in 'Can I borrow your pen? I've lost mine.'

possessor /pəzesəʳ/ **possessors.** The **possessor** of something is the person who has it; a formal word. *Ms Nova is the proud possessor of a truly incredible voice.* N-COUNT: usu N *of* n

possibility /pɒsɪbɪlɪti/ **possibilities** ◆◆◆◆◇
1 If you say there is a **possibility** that something is the case or that something will happen, you mean that it might be the case or it might happen. *We were not in the least worried about the possibility that sweets could rot the teeth... Tax on food has become a very real possibility.* N-COUNT: oft N that
2 A **possibility** is one of several different things that could be done. *The government now owns a lot of our land – one possibility would be to compensate us with other property... There were several possibilities open to each manufacturer.* N-COUNT =option
3 You can say **'It is not beyond the realms of possibility'** or **'It is not beyond the bounds of possibility'** when you are stating something that you believe is possibly true, but which other people might consider unlikely or impossible. *It's not beyond the realms of possibility that the security services do bug important public figures.* PHRASE: usu PHR that PRAGMATICS

possible /pɒsɪbəl/ **possibles** ◆◆◆◆◆
1 If it is **possible** to do something, it can be done. *If it is possible to find out where you brother is, we shall... Everything is possible if we want it enough... This morning he had tried every way possible to contact her... Live as you like, leave home if you want – that was never possible when I was young... It's been a beautiful evening and you have made it all possible.* ADJ: usu v-link ADJ, oft *it* v-link ADJ to-inf
2 A **possible** event is one that might happen. *Mr. Bush will meet with his advisers to discuss possible action... Her family is discussing a possible move to America... One possible solution, if all else fails, is to take legal action... Department officials have warned of possible terrorist attacks.* ADJ: usu ADJ n =likely ≠unlikely
3 If you say that it is **possible** that something is true or correct, you mean that although you do not know whether it is true or correct, you accept that it might be. *It is possible that there's an explanation for all this... It was possible that Harry himself did not know what he had intended to do.* ADJ-GRADED: v-link ADJ, oft *it* v-link ADJ that PRAGMATICS =conceivable ≠unlikely
4 If you do something **as** soon **as possible**, you do it as soon as you can. If you get **as** much **as possible** of something, you get as much of it as you can. *Please make your decision as soon as possible... Mrs. Pollard decided to learn as much as possible about the People's Republic of China... Michael sat down as far away from her as possible... Buy fresh produce as often as possible.* ADJ: *as* adv/pron *as* ADJ
5 You use **possible** with superlative adjectives to emphasize that something has more or less of a quality than anything else of its kind. *They have joined the job market at the worst possible time... We expressed in the clearest possible way our disappointment, hurt and anger... He is doing the best job possible.* ADJ: adj-superl ADJ n, adj-superl n ADJ PRAGMATICS
6 You use **possible** in expressions such as **'if possible'** and **'if at all possible'** when stating a wish or intention, to show that although this is what you really want, you may have to accept something less, or something slightly different. *I need to see you, right away if possible... It is wise to get insurance cover for this kind of care, if at all possible.* ADJ PRAGMATICS
7 If you describe someone as, for example, a **possible** Prime Minister, you mean that he or she may become the Prime Minister. *Mr Lukanov is thought of as a possible successor to the president... Bradley has been considered a possible presidential contender himself.* ► Also a noun. *Kennedy, who divorced wife Joan in 1982, was tipped as a presidential possible... He had been on the Nobel Prize committee's list of possibles.* ADJ: ADJ n =potential; N-COUNT
8 **The possible** is everything that can be done in a situation. *He is a democrat with the skill, nerve, and ingenuity to push the limits of the possible.* N-SING: *the* N

possibly /pɒsɪbli/ ◆◆◆◆◇
1 You use **possibly** to indicate that you are not sure whether something is true or might happen. *Exercise will not only lower blood pressure but possibly protect against heart attacks... They were smartly but casually dressed; possibly students... Do you think that he could possibly be right?.* ADV: ADV with cl/group, ADV with v PRAGMATICS =perhaps
2 You use **possibly** to emphasize that you are surprised, puzzled, or shocked by something that you have seen or heard. *It was the most unexpected piece of news one could possibly imagine... I mean, how could they possibly eat that stuff?... What could this possibly mean?* ADV: ADV before v PRAGMATICS =conceivably
3 You use **possibly** to emphasize that someone has tried their hardest to do something, or has done it ADV: ADV before v PRAGMATICS

as well as they can. *They've done everything they can possibly think of... It's one of the nicest feelings you can possibly have.*

4 You use **possibly** with a negative and a modal, to emphasize that something definitely cannot happen or definitely cannot be done. *No I really can't possibly answer that!... There's nothing more they can possibly do right... We cannot possibly risk so many innocent lives... That can't possibly be right.* ADV: with brd-neg, ADV before v PRAGMATICS

possum /pɒsəm/ **possums.** In American English, a **possum** is the same as an **opossum**; an informal word. N-COUNT =opossum

post 1 letters, parcels, and information

post /poʊst/ **posts, posting, posted** ◆◆◆◆◇

1 In British English, **the post** is the public service or system by which letters and parcels are collected and delivered. The American word is **mail**. *You'll receive your book through the post... The winner will be notified by post... The cheque is in the post.* N-SING: the N, also by N =mail

2 In British English, you can use **post** to refer to letters and parcels that are delivered to you. The American word is **mail**. *He flipped through the post without opening any of it... There has been no post in three weeks.* N-UNCOUNT =mail

3 In Britain, **post** is used to refer to a particular delivery of letters or parcels. For example, **first post** is the first delivery on a particular day. *Entries must arrive by first post next Wednesday... They just have to wait patiently for the next post.* N-UNCOUNT: supp N

4 In British English, if you **post** a letter or parcel, you send it to someone by putting it in a post-box or by taking it to a post office. The American word is **mail**. *If I write a letter, would you post it for me?... I'm posting you a cheque tonight... I posted a letter to Stanley saying I was an old Army friend.* ▶ **Post off** means the same as **post**. *He'd left me to pack up the mail and post it off... All you do is complete and post off a form.* VERB =mail V n V n n V n to n PHRASAL VERB V n P V P n (not pron)

5 If you **post** notices, signs, or other pieces of information somewhere, you fix them to a wall or noticeboard so that everyone can see them. *Officials began posting warning notices... She has posted photographs on bulletin boards.* ▶ **Post up** means the same as **post**. *He has posted a sign up that says 'No Fishing'... We post up a set of rules for the house.* VERB V n V n prep/adv PHRASAL VERB V n P V P n (not pron) Also V n P prep/adv

6 If you **keep** someone **posted**, you keep giving them the latest information about a situation that they are interested in. *Keep me posted on your progress.* PHRASE: keep inflects, oft PHR on/with n

post 2 jobs and places

post /poʊst/ **posts, posting, posted.** ◆◆◆◆◇

1 A **post** in a company or organization is a job or official position in it, usually one that involves responsibility; a formal use. *She had earlier resigned her post as President Menem's assistant... Sir Peter has held several senior military posts.* N-COUNT: usu with supp, oft N of/as n =position

2 If you **are posted** somewhere, you are sent there by the organization that you work for and usually work there for several years. *After training she was posted to Brixton... It is normal to spend two or three years working in this country before being posted overseas.* VB: usu passive be V-ed prep/adv

3 You can use **post** to refer to the place where a soldier, guard, or other person has been told to remain and to do his or her job. *Quick men, back to your post!* N-COUNT: usu poss N =station, position

4 If a soldier, guard, or other person **is posted** somewhere, they are told to stand there, in order to supervise an activity or guard a place. *Police have now been posted outside all temples... British Rail had to post a signalman at the entrance to the tunnel... We have guards posted near the windows.* VERB =position be V-ed prep/adv V n prep/adv V-ed Also be V-ed

5 See also **posting**; **staging post**.

post 3 poles

post /poʊst/ **posts** ◆◆◇◇◇

1 A **post** is a strong upright pole made of wood or metal that is fixed into the ground. *You have to get eight wooden posts, and drive them into the ground... The device is fixed to a post.* N-COUNT =pole

2 A **post** is the same as a **goalpost**. *Wimbledon were unlucky not to win after hitting the post twice.* N-COUNT =goalpost

3 On a horse-racing track, **the post** is a pole which marks the finishing point. N-SING: the N

4 See also **first-past-the-post**. • to **pip** someone **at the post**: see **pip**.

post- /poʊst-/. **Post-** is used to form words that indicate that something takes place after a particular date, period, or event. *For most of the post-1945 era defence policy was not a salient political issue. ...the transition from industrial to post-industrial society. ...post-election euphoria.* PREFIX ≠pre-

postage /poʊstɪdʒ/. **Postage** is the money that you pay for sending letters and parcels by post. ◆◇◇◇◇ N-UNCOUNT

postage stamp, postage stamps. A **postage stamp** is a small piece of gummed paper that you buy from the post office and stick on an envelope or parcel before you post it; a formal expression. N-COUNT =stamp

postal /poʊstəl/ ◆◆◇◇◇

1 **Postal** is used to describe things or people connected with the public service of carrying letters and parcels from one place to another. *Compensation for lost or damaged mail will be handled by the postal service... Include your full postal address. ...postal workers.* ADJ: ADJ n

2 **Postal** is used to describe activities that involve sending things by post. *Unions would elect their leadership by secret postal ballot. ...a postal course in freelance photography.* ADJ: ADJ n

postal order, postal orders. In Britain, a **postal order** is a piece of paper representing a sum of money which you can buy at a post office and send to someone as a way of sending them money by post. The usual American term is **money order**. N-COUNT

postbag /poʊstbæg/ **postbags;** also spelled **post-bag**. In Britain, the letters that are received by an important person, a newspaper, or a television or radio company can be referred to as the **postbag**; used mainly in journalism. *Here's another selection of recent letters from our postbag. ...Lady Thatcher's huge postbag.* N-COUNT: usu sing

post box, post boxes; also spelled **post-box**. In British English, a **post box** is a metal box with a hole in it, which you put letters into to be collected by a postman. The usual American word is **mailbox**. N-COUNT

postcard /poʊstkɑːʳd/ **postcards;** also spelled **post card**. A **postcard** is a piece of thin card, often with a picture on one side, which you can write on and send to people without using an envelope. • See also **picture postcard**. ◆◆◇◇◇ N-COUNT

postcode /poʊstkoʊd/ **postcodes.** In British English, your **postcode** is a short sequence of numbers and letters at the end of your address, which helps the post office to sort the mail. The American term is **zip code**. N-COUNT

post-dated. On a **post-dated** cheque the date is a later one than the date when the cheque was actually written. You write a post-dated cheque to allow yourself a period of time before the cheque can be cashed. ADJ: usu ADJ n

poster /poʊstəʳ/ **posters.** A **poster** is a large notice or picture that you stick on a wall or noticeboard, often in order to advertise something. ◆◆◇◇◇ N-COUNT

poste restante /poʊst restɑːnt, AM - restɑːnt/. **Poste restante** is a service operated by post offices by which letters and parcels that are sent to you are kept at a particular post office until you collect them; used mainly in British English. N-UNCOUNT: oft N n

posterior /pɒstɪəriəʳ/ **posteriors**

1 Someone's buttocks can be referred to as their **posterior**; often used humorously. N-COUNT =backside

2 **Posterior** describes something that is situated at the back of something else; a medical use. *...the posterior leg muscles.* ADJ: ADJ n =rear ≠anterior

posterity /pɒsterɪti/. You can refer to everyone who will be alive in the future as **posterity**; a formal word. *A photographer recorded the scene on video for posterity... Was he making these notes for the benefit of posterity?* ◆◇◇◇◇ N-UNCOUNT: oft for N

poster paint, poster paints. **Poster paint** is a type of brightly coloured paint which contains no oil and which is used for painting pictures and posters. N-MASS

postgrad /pəʊstgræd/ **postgrads;** also spelled **post-grad**. In British English, a **postgrad** is the same as a **postgraduate**; an informal use. N-COUNT

postgraduate /pəʊstgrædʒuət/ **postgraduates;** also spelled **post-graduate**. ◆◇◇◇◇

1 In British English, a **postgraduate** or a **postgraduate student** is a student with a first degree from a university who is studying or doing research at a more advanced level. N-COUNT

2 In British English, **postgraduate** study or research is done by a student who has a first degree and is studying or doing research at a more advanced level. The American term is **graduate**. *...postgraduate courses... Dr Hoffman did his postgraduate work at Leicester University.* ADJ: ADJ n

post-haste; also spelled **post haste**. If you go somewhere or do something **post-haste**, you go there or do it as quickly as you can; a formal expression. *The pilot wisely decided to return to Farnborough post haste.* ADV: ADV after v

posthumous /pɒstʃʊməs/. **Posthumous** is used to describe something that happens after someone's death but that relates to something that they did before they died. *They collected a posthumous award for the band's lead singer, who died of Aids last year. ...the posthumous publication of his first novel.* ◆◇◇◇◇ ADJ: usu ADJ n ♦ **posthumously** *After the war she was posthumously awarded the George Cross.* ADV: ADV with v

post-industrial. **Post-industrial** is used to describe the present state of many Western societies, whose economies are no longer based on heavy industry but are based on service industries and the production of consumer goods. ADJ: ADJ n ≠pre-industrial

posting /pəʊstɪŋ/ **postings.** If you get a **posting** to a different town or country, your employers send you to work there, usually for several years; used mainly in British English. *He was rewarded with a posting to New York... Relevant work experience is required for overseas postings.* ● See also **post**. ◆◇◇◇◇ N-COUNT: with supp, oft N *to* n

postman /pəʊstmən/ **postmen.** In British English, a **postman** is a man whose job is to collect and deliver letters and parcels that are sent by post. The usual American word is **mailman**. ◆◇◇◇◇ N-COUNT

postmark /pəʊstmɑːʳk/ **postmarks.** A **postmark** is a mark which is printed on letters and parcels at a post office. It shows the time and place at which something was posted. *The incendiary device was in a padded bag with a Scottish postmark.* N-COUNT

postmarked /pəʊstmɑːʳkt/. If a letter is **postmarked**, it has a printed mark on the envelope showing when and where the letter was posted. *The envelope was postmarked Helsinki.* ADJ: usu v-link ADJ

postmaster /pəʊstmɑːstəʳ, -mæs-/ **postmasters.** A **postmaster** is a man who is in charge of a local post office; a formal word. N-COUNT

postmistress /pəʊstmɪstrəs/ **postmistresses.** A **postmistress** is a woman who is in charge of a local post office; a formal word. N-COUNT

post-modern; also spelled **postmodern**. **Post-modern** is used to describe something or someone that is strongly influenced by post-modernism. *Ripe with in-jokes, self-references, and post-modern metaphor, the movie questions a too-civilized world. ...post-modern architecture.* ◆◇◇◇◇ ADJ: usu ADJ n =post-modernist

post-modernism; also spelled **postmodernism**. In late 20th-century culture, **post-modernism** is a general tendency in which there is an increased awareness of the artificial nature of all means of expression and systems of thought. The main characteristics of post-modernism are usually considered to be playfulness, irony, and a preference for things that are fragmented or incomplete. ◆◇◇◇◇ N-UNCOUNT

post-modernist, post-modernists; also spelled **postmodernist**. A **post-modernist** is a writer, artist, or architect who is strongly influenced by post-modernism. *Postmodernists say there is no objective truth. Why should anyone believe them?* ► Also an adjective. *...the post-modernist suspicion of grand ideological narratives.* ◆◇◇◇◇ N-COUNT; ADJ: usu ADJ n =post-modern

post-mortem /pəʊst mɔːʳtəm/ **post-mortems;** also spelled **post mortem** or **postmortem**. ◆◇◇◇◇

1 A **post-mortem** is a medical examination of a dead person's body in order to find out how they died. N-COUNT =autopsy

2 A **post-mortem** is an examination of something that has recently happened, especially something that has failed or gone wrong. *Almost every post-mortem on the Los Angeles riots lists unemployment among the urban poor as an underlying cause of the violence... Mr Major warned there must be no backbiting, no recriminations, no post mortems.* N-COUNT: oft N *on* n

postnatal /pəʊstneɪtəl/; also spelled **post-natal**. **Postnatal** means happening after and relating to the birth of a baby. *One study suggests that nearly 40 per cent of women suffer postnatal depression... After the birth, midwives on the postnatal ward will provide care until you go home.* ADJ: ADJ n ≠antenatal

post office, post offices ◆◆◇◇◇

1 The **Post Office** is the national organization that is responsible for postal services. *The Post Office has confirmed that up to fifteen thousand jobs could be lost in sorting offices over the next five years.* N-SING: usu *the* N

2 A **post office** is a building where you can buy stamps, post letters and parcels, and use other services provided by the national postal service. N-COUNT

post office box, post office boxes. A **post office box** is a numbered box in a post office where a person's mail is kept for them until they come to fetch it. N-COUNT =PO Box

postoperative /pəʊstɒpərətɪv/; also spelled **post-operative**. **Postoperative** means occurring after and relating to a medical operation. *Relaxation techniques can sometimes help to reduce post-operative pain.* ADJ: ADJ n

postpone /pəʊspəʊn/ **postpones, postponing, postponed.** If you **postpone** an event, you delay it or arrange for it to take place at a later time than was originally planned. *He decided to postpone the expedition until the following day... The visit has now been postponed indefinitely.* ◆◆◇◇◇ VERB =delay V n/-ing

postponement /pəʊspəʊnmənt/ **postponements.** The **postponement** of an event is the act of delaying it happening or arranging for it to take place at a later time than originally planned. *The postponement was due to a dispute over where the talks should be held.* ◆◇◇◇◇ N-VAR: oft N *of* n =deferral

post-prandial /pəʊst prændiəl/; also spelled **postprandial**. You use **post-prandial** to refer to things you do or have after a meal; a formal word. *He was taking a post-prandial nap in the hotel lounge. ...a post-prandial cigar.* ADJ: ADJ n

postscript /pəʊstskrɪpt/ **postscripts**

1 A **postscript** is something written at the end of a letter after you have signed your name. You usually write 'PS' in front of it. *A brief, hand-written postscript lay beneath his signature.* N-COUNT

2 A **postscript** is an addition to a finished story, account, or statement, which gives further information. *As the editor's postscript reminds the reader, she was to endure two more spells of mental illness before the book was published... I should like to add a postscript to your obituary for John Cage.* N-COUNT: oft N *to* n

postulate, postulates, postulating, postulated. The verb is pronounced /pɒstʃʊleɪt/. The noun is pronounced /pɒstʃʊlət/. ◆◇◇◇◇

1 If you **postulate** something, you suggest it as the basis for a theory, argument, or calculation, or assume that it is the basis; a formal use. *He dismissed arguments postulating differing standards for human rights in different cultures and regions... Freud postulated that we all have a death instinct as well as a life instinct.* VERB =posit V n V that

2 A **postulate** is an idea that is suggested as or assumed to be the basis for a theory, argument, or N-COUNT: oft N *of* n, N that calculation; a formal use. *Offe also challenges the postulate of an 'organized capitalism'.*

postural /pɒstʃərəl/. **Postural** means relating to the way a person stands or sits; a formal word. *Children can develop bad postural habits from quite an early age. ...postural exercises.* ADJ: ADJ n

posture /pɒstʃəʳ/ **postures, posturing, postured** ◆◆◇◇◇

1 Your **posture** is the position in which you stand or sit. *You can make your stomach look flatter instantly by improving your posture... Exercise, fresh air, and good posture are all helpful... Sit in a relaxed upright posture.* N-VAR

2 A **posture** is an attitude that you have towards something; a formal use. *The military machine is ready to change its defensive posture to one prepared for action... None of the banks changed their posture on the deal as a result of the inquiry.* N-COUNT: usu sing, usu adj N =position, stance

3 You can say that someone **is posturing** when you disapprove of their behaviour because you think they are trying to give a particular impression in order to deceive people; a formal use. *She says the President may just be posturing.* ♦ **posturing** *Any calls for a new UN resolution are largely political posturing... There's been a lot of posturing on both sides.* VB: usu cont PRAGMATICS V N-UNCOUNT

post-war; also spelled **postwar**. **Post-war** is used to describe things that happened, existed, or were made in the period immediately after a war, especially the Second World War (1939-45). *In the post-war years her writing regularly appeared in The New Journal... He really was one of the finest boxers in post-war Britain. ...postwar architecture.* ◆◆◇◇◇ ADJ: usu ADJ n ≠pre-war

posy /pouzi/ **posies.** A **posy** is a small bunch of flowers. N-COUNT: oft N *of* n

pot /pɒt/ **pots, potting, potted** ◆◆◆◇◇

1 A **pot** is a deep round container used for cooking stews, soups, and other food. *...metal cooking pots.* ► A **pot** of stew, soup, or other food is an amount of it contained in a pot. *He was stirring a pot of soup.* N-COUNT N-COUNT: usu N *of* n

2 You can use **pot** to refer to a teapot or coffee pot. *There's tea in the pot.* ► A **pot** of tea or coffee is an amount of it contained in a pot. *He spilt a pot of coffee.* N-COUNT N-COUNT: usu N *of* n

3 A **pot** is a cylindrical container for jam, paint, or some other thick liquid. *Hundreds of jam pots lined her scrubbed shelves.* ► A **pot** of jam, paint, or some other thick liquid is an amount of it contained in a pot. *...a pot of red paint.* N-COUNT: usu with supp, oft n N N-COUNT: usu N *of* n

4 A **pot** is the same as a **flowerpot**. N-COUNT

5 If you **pot** a young plant, or part of a plant, you put it into a flowerpot filled with soil, so it can grow there. *Pot the cuttings individually. ...potted plants.* VERB V n V-ed

6 Pot is sometimes used to refer to cannabis; an informal use. N-UNCOUNT =cannabis

7 If you have **pots of money**, you have a lot of it; an informal use. *He must have pots of money.* QUANT: QUANT *of* pl-n/n-uncount

8 In a card game, **the pot** is a sum of money to which each player has contributed and which the winner of the game takes as a prize. N-SING: *the* N =pool, kitty

9 In American English, you can refer to a fund of money to which several people contribute as **the pot**. *I've taken some money from the pot for wrapping paper.* N-SING: *the* N =kitty

10 In the games of snooker and billiards, if you **pot** a ball, you succeed in hitting it into one of the pockets. *He did not pot a ball for the next two frames.* VERB =pocket V n

11 See also **potted; chamber pot, chimney pot, coffee pot, lobster pot, melting pot, plant pot.**

12 If something **goes to pot**, it loses all its good qualities because nobody looks after it or works at it; an informal expression. *The neighbourhood really is going to pot.* PHRASES V inflects =deteriorate

13 If you take **pot luck**, you decide to do something even though you do not know what you will get as a result. *If you haven't made an appointment, take pot luck and knock on the door... He scorns the 'pot-luck' approach.* ● **pot of gold**: see **gold**. PHR after v, PHR n

potable /poutəbəl/. **Potable** water is clean and safe for drinking; used mainly in American English. ADJ: usu ADJ n =drinkable

potash /pɒtæʃ/. **Potash** is a white powdery substance, obtained from the ashes of burnt wood. It can be used as a fertilizer. N-UNCOUNT

potassium /pətæsiəm/. **Potassium** is a soft silvery-white chemical element, which occurs mainly in compounds. These compounds are used in making such things as glass, soap, detergents, and fertilizers. ◆◇◇◇◇ N-UNCOUNT

potato /pəteɪtou/ **potatoes** ◆◆◆◇◇

1 Potatoes are roundish vegetables with brown or red skins and white insides. They grow under the ground. ● See also **sweet potato.** N-VAR

2 You can refer to a difficult subject that people disagree on as a **hot potato.** *...a political hot potato such as abortion.* PHRASE: N inflects

potato chip, potato chips. In American English, **potato chips** are very thin slices of potato that have been fried until they are hard, dry, and crispy. The British word is **crisps.** N-COUNT: usu pl

potato crisp, potato crisps. Potato crisps are the same as **crisps**; a formal expression in British English. N-COUNT: usu pl

pot-bellied; also spelled **potbellied.** Someone, usually a man, who is **pot-bellied** has a pot belly. ADJ-GRADED

pot belly, pot bellies; also spelled **potbelly.** Someone who has a **pot belly** has a round, fat stomach which sticks out. A pot belly is caused either by eating or drinking too much or else by poor-quality food and starvation. N-COUNT

potboiler /pɒtbɔɪləʳ/ **potboilers;** also spelled **pot-boiler.** You can use a **potboiler** to describe something such as a book or film which has been created in order to earn money quickly and which may have no artistic merit. N-COUNT PRAGMATICS

potency /poutᵊnsi/ ◆◇◇◇◇

1 Potency is the power and influence that a person, action, or idea has to affect or change people's lives, feelings, or beliefs. *They testify to the extraordinary potency of his personality... All their songs have a lingering potency.* N-UNCOUNT: usu with supp =power

2 The **potency** of a drug, poison, or other chemical is its strength. *Sunscreen can lose its potency if left over winter in the bathroom cabinet.* N-UNCOUNT: usu with poss

3 Potency is the ability of a man to have sex. *Alcohol abuse in men can cause loss of sex drive and reduced potency.* N-UNCOUNT

potent /poutᵊnt/. Something that is **potent** is very effective and powerful. *Their most potent weapon was the Exocet missile... The drug is extremely potent, but causes unpleasant side effects.* ◆◆◇◇◇ ADJ-GRADED =effective

potentate /poutᵊnteɪt/ **potentates.** A **potentate** is a ruler who has absolute power over his people; a formal word. N-COUNT =autocrat

potential /pətenʃᵊl/ **potentials** ◆◆◆◆◇

1 You use **potential** to say that someone or something is capable of developing into the particular kind of person or thing mentioned. *The firm has identified 60 potential customers at home and abroad. ...potential party members... We are aware of the potential problems and have taken every precaution.* ♦ **potentially** *Clearly this is a potentially dangerous situation... Potentially this could damage the reputation of the whole industry.* ADJ: ADJ n =likely, possible ADV: ADV with cl/group

2 If you say that someone or something has **potential**, you mean that they have the necessary abilities or qualities to become successful or useful in the future. *The boy has great potential... The school strives to treat pupils as individuals and to help each one to achieve their full potential... Denmark recognised the potential of wind energy early. ...the economic potentials of Eastern and Western Europe.* N-UNCOUNT: also N in pl

3 If you say that someone or something has **potential** for doing something, you mean that it is possible that they may do it. If there is **the potential for** something, it may happen. *John seemed as horrified as I about his potential for violence... The meeting has the potential to be a watershed event... The potential for conflict is great... Death and* N-UNCOUNT: also N in pl, with supp, oft N *for* n/-ing

murder always lurk as potentials in very violent relationships.

potentiality /pətenʃiælɪti/ **potentialities.** If something has **potentialities** or **potentiality**, it is capable of being used or developed in particular ways; a formal word. *The breathtaking potentialities of mechanization set the minds of manufacturers and merchants on fire... All of these are quite useful breeds whose potentiality has not been realised.* N-VAR: usu with supp =potential

pothole /pɒthoʊl/ **potholes;** also spelled **pot-hole.**
1 A **pothole** is a large hole in the surface of a road, caused by traffic and bad weather. N-COUNT
2 A **pothole** is a deep hole in the ground in a limestone area. Potholes often lead to networks of underground caves and tunnels. N-COUNT

pot-holed; also spelled **potholed**. A **pot-holed road** has a lot of potholes in it. ADJ-GRADED: usu ADJ n

potholing /pɒthoʊlɪŋ/. **Potholing** is the leisure activity of exploring underground caves; used mainly in British English. N-UNCOUNT

potion /poʊʃᵊn/ **potions.** A **potion** is a drink that contains medicine, poison, or something that is supposed to have magic powers. ◆◇◇◇◇ N-COUNT

pot-luck. See **pot.**

pot plant, pot plants. In British English, a **pot plant** is a plant in a flowerpot which is grown indoors. The usual American term is **house plant**. N-COUNT

potpourri /poʊpʊəri, AM -pʊriː/ **potpourris;** also spelled **pot-pourri** or **pot pourri**.
1 **Potpourri** is a mixture of dried petals and leaves from different flowers. Potpourri is used to make rooms smell pleasant. N-MASS
2 A **potpourri of** things is a collection of various different items which were not originally intended to form a group. *Displaying a potpourri of architectural styles from all over the world, the village looks as outlandish as a colourful film set.* N-SING: usu N *of* n =miscellany

pot roast, pot roasts. A **pot roast** is a piece of meat that is cooked very slowly with a small amount of liquid in a covered pot. N-VAR

pot shot, pot shots; also spelled **pot-shot.**
1 If someone takes a **pot shot** at something or someone, they shoot at them without taking the time to aim carefully; an informal use. N-COUNT
2 A **pot shot** is a criticism of someone which may be unexpected and unfair; an informal use. *Their campaign was taking pot shots at Clinton's personal life.* N-COUNT

potted /pɒtɪd/
1 **Potted** meat or fish is cooked meat or fish, usually in the form of a paste, which has been put into a small sealed container. *...potted shrimps.* ADJ: ADJ n
2 A **potted** history or biography contains the main facts about someone or something in a short and simplified form. *The film is a potted history of the band... I would give them a potted version of a book I've just finished reading.* ADJ: ADJ n =condensed
3 See also **pot.**

potter /pɒtəʳ/ **potters, pottering, pottered.** A **potter** is someone who makes pottery. ◆◆◇◇◇ N-COUNT

potter around or **potter about.** In British English, if you **potter around** or **potter about**, you pass the time in a gentle, unhurried way, doing pleasant but unimportant things. The American term is **putter around**. *I was perfectly happy just pottering around doing up my flat... At weekends he would potter around the garden.* PHRASAL VERB PRAGMATICS V P V P n

potter's wheel, potter's wheels. A **potter's wheel** is a piece of equipment with a flat disc which spins round, on which a potter puts soft clay in order to shape it into a pot. N-COUNT

pottery /pɒtəri/ **potteries** ◆◇◇◇◇
1 You can use **pottery** to refer to pots, dishes, and other objects which are made from clay and then baked in an oven until they are hard. N-UNCOUNT
2 You can use **pottery** to refer to the hard clay that some pots, dishes, and other objects are made of. *Some bowls were made of pottery and wood.* N-UNCOUNT
3 **Pottery** is the craft or activity of making objects out of clay. N-UNCOUNT
4 A **pottery** is a factory or workshop where pottery is made. N-COUNT

potting compost, potting composts. Potting compost is soil that is specially prepared to help young plants to grow. N-MASS

potting shed, potting sheds. A **potting shed** is a shed in a garden, in which you can keep seeds or garden tools. N-COUNT

potty /pɒti/ **potties**
1 A **potty** is a deep bowl which a small child uses instead of a toilet. N-COUNT
2 In British English, if you say that someone is **potty**, you think that they are crazy or foolish; an informal use. ADJ-GRADED: usu v-link ADJ PRAGMATICS =crazy

potty trained; also spelled **potty-trained**. In British English, **potty trained** means the same as **toilet trained**. ADJ =toilet trained

potty training; also spelled **potty-training**. In British English, **potty training** is the same as **toilet training**. N-UNCOUNT =toilet training

pouch /paʊtʃ/ **pouches** ◆◇◇◇◇
1 A **pouch** is a flexible container like a small bag. N-COUNT
2 The **pouch** of an animal such as a kangaroo or a koala bear is the pocket of skin on its stomach in which its baby grows. N-COUNT

pouf /pʊf/. See **poof**.

poultice /poʊltɪs/ **poultices.** A **poultice** is a bandage with a soft substance such as clay or a mixture of herbs or plants on it. The substance is heated and the bandage is put over a painful or swollen part of someone's body in order to soothe the pain or reduce the swelling. N-COUNT

poultry /poʊltri/. You can refer to chickens, ducks, and other birds that are kept for their eggs and meat as **poultry**. *Dr Binger keeps poultry, pigs and goats... Most poultry farmers have to rely on commercially manufactured feeds.* ► Meat from these birds is also referred to as **poultry**. *The menu features roast meats and poultry.* ◆◇◇◇◇ N-PLURAL N-UNCOUNT

pounce /paʊns/ **pounces, pouncing, pounced** ◆◇◇◇◇
1 If someone **pounces** on you, they come up towards you suddenly and take hold of you. *He pounced on the photographer, beat him up and smashed his camera... Fraud squad officers had bugged the phone and were ready to pounce.* VERB V *on/upon* n V
2 If someone **pounces** on something such as a mistake, they draw attention to it, usually in order to gain an advantage for themselves or to prove that they are right about something. *The Democrats were ready to pounce on any Republican failings or mistakes... 'That's much too subtle, even for Sam.'—'Even for Sam!' He pounced on the phrase with a sound of triumph.* VERB V *on/upon* n Also V
3 When an animal or bird **pounces** on something, it leaps on it and grabs it, in order to kill it. *...like a tiger pouncing on its prey... Before I could get the pigeon the cat pounced.* VERB V *on/upon* n V

pound /paʊnd/ **pounds, pounding, pounded** ◆◆◆◆◆
1 The **pound** is the unit of money which is used in Britain. It is represented by the symbol £. One British pound is divided into a hundred pence. Some other countries, for example Egypt, also have a unit of money called a **pound**. *Beer cost three pounds a bottle... A thousand pounds worth of jewellery and silver has been stolen. ...multi-million pound profits. ...a pound coin.* N-COUNT: num N
2 **The pound** is used to refer to the British currency system, and sometimes to the currency systems of other countries which use pounds. *The pound is expected to continue to increase against most other currencies.* N-SING: *the* N
3 A **pound** is a unit of weight used mainly in Britain, America, and other countries where English is spoken. One pound is equal to 0.454 kilograms. A **pound of** something is a quantity of it that weighs one pound. *Her weight was under ninety pounds. ...a pound of cheese.* N-COUNT: num N, N *of* n
4 A **pound** is a place where stray dogs and cats are taken and kept until they are claimed by their owners. N-COUNT
5 A **pound** is a place where cars that have been N-COUNT

parked illegally are taken by the police and kept until they have been claimed by their owners.

6 If you **pound** something or **pound on** it, you hit it with great force, usually loudly and repeatedly. *He pounded the table with his fist... Somebody began pounding on the front door... She came at him, pounding her fists against his chest. ...the pounding waves.* VERB =hammer V n V prep/adv V n prep V-ing

7 If you **pound** something, you crush it into a paste or a powder or into very small pieces. *She paused as she pounded the maize grains.* VERB =pulverize V n

8 If your heart **is pounding**, it is beating with an unusually strong and fast rhythm, usually because you are afraid. *I'm sweating, my heart is pounding. I can't breathe.* ♦ **pounding** *...the fast pounding of her heart.* VERB V N-UNCOUNT: usu N *of* n

9 See also **pounding**.

10 If you say that someone demands their **pound of flesh**, you mean that they insist on getting something they are entitled to, even though they do not really need it and it may cause distress to the person it is demanded from; used showing disapproval. *Banks are quick to demand their pound of flesh when overdrafts run a little over the limit.* PHRASE: usu poss PHR PRAGMATICS

-pounder /-paʊndəʳ/ **-pounders**

1 **-pounder** can be added to numbers to form nouns that refer to animals or fish that weigh a particular number of pounds. *My fish average 2 lb 8 oz and I've had two eight-pounders.* COMB in N-COUNT

2 **-pounder** can be added to numbers to form nouns that refer to guns that fire shells weighing a particular number of pounds. *The guns were twelve-pounders.* COMB in N-COUNT

pounding /paʊndɪŋ/ **poundings**

1 In British English, if someone or something takes a **pounding**, they are severely injured or damaged; an informal use. *Sarajevo took one of its worst poundings in weeks.* N-COUNT: usu sing, usu supp N

2 In British English, if a person or team gets a **pounding**, they are severely defeated; an informal use. *The prospects are that he will give opponents a thorough pounding.* N-COUNT: usu sing, usu supp N

3 See also **pound**.

pour /pɔːʳ/ **pours, pouring, poured** ◆◆◆◇◇

1 If you **pour** a liquid or other substance, you make it flow steadily out of a container by holding the container at an angle. *Pour a pool of sauce on two plates and arrange the meat neatly... Francis poured a generous measure of the whisky into a fresh glass... Heat the oil in a non-stick frying-pan, then pour in the egg mixture.* VERB V n prep V n with adv

2 If you **pour** someone a drink, you put some of the drink in a cup or glass so that they can drink it. *He got up and poured himself another drink... She asked Tillie to pour her a cup of coffee... Quietly Mark poured and served drinks for all of them.* VERB V n n V n *for* n Also V n

3 When a liquid or other substance **pours** somewhere, for example through a hole, it flows quickly and in large quantities. *Blood was pouring from his broken nose... There was dense smoke pouring from all four engines... Tears poured down both our faces... The tide poured in from the south.* VERB V V adv

4 When it rains very heavily, you can say that **it is pouring**. *It has been pouring in Delhi almost non stop for the past three days, disrupting normal life... It has been pouring with rain all week... The rain was pouring down... We drove all the way through pouring rain.* VB: usu cont *it* V V *down* V-ing

5 If people **pour** into or out of a place, they go there quickly and in large numbers. *Any day now, the Northern forces may pour across the new border... Holidaymakers continued to pour down to the coast in search of surf and sun... At six p.m. large groups poured from the numerous offices.* VERB =stream V prep/adv

6 If information or correspondence **pours** into a place, a lot of it is obtained or given. *As the results poured in, Labour chiefs were forced to admit the scale of their defeat... The commission has invited interested parties to submit comments, and these are now pouring in.* VERB =flood V adv/prep

7 If someone **pours cold water on** a plan or idea, they criticize it so much that people lose their enthusiasm for it. *The education secretary poured cold water on the recommendations of a working party set up to look at physical education.* ● to **pour scorn on** something: see **scorn**. PHRASE: V inflects =dismiss

pour into. If you **pour** money or supplies **into** an activity or organization, or if it **pours in**, a lot of money or supplies are given in order to do the activity or help the organization. *The Government continues to pour billions of pounds into its massive road-building programme... Food donations have poured in from all over the country.* PHRASAL VERB ERG V n P n V P

pour out PHRASAL VERB

1 If you **pour out** a drink, you put some of it in a cup or glass. *Larry was pouring out four glasses of champagne... Carefully and slowly he poured the beer out.* V P n (not pron) V n P

2 If you **pour out** your thoughts, feelings, or experiences, you tell someone all about them. *They have started pouring out their hearts and expressing their hopes and fears about the present situation... I poured my thoughts out on paper in an attempt to rationalize my feelings.* V P n (not pron) V n P

pout /paʊt/ **pouts, pouting, pouted** ◆◇◇◇◇

1 If someone **pouts**, they stick out their lips, usually in order to show that they are annoyed or to make themselves sexually attractive. *Like one of the kids, he whined and pouted when he did not get what he wanted. ...gorgeous pouting models.* VERB V V-ing

► Also a noun. *She shot me a reproachful pout.* N-COUNT

2 If someone **pouts**, they say something with a pout. *'You're no fun,' she pouted.* VERB V with quote

poverty /pɒvəʳti/ ◆◆◆◇◇

1 **Poverty** is the state of being extremely poor. *According to World Bank figures, 41 per cent of Brazilians live in absolute poverty... Garvey died in loneliness and poverty.* N-UNCOUNT ≠wealth

2 You can use **poverty** to refer to any situation in which there is not enough of something or its quality is poor; a formal use. *Britain has suffered from a poverty of ambition. ...a poverty of ideas.* N-SING: also no det, N *of* n ≠wealth

poverty line. If someone is on **the poverty line**, they have just enough income to buy the things they need in order to live. *Thirteen per cent of the population live below the poverty line.* N-SING: *the* N

poverty-stricken. Poverty-stricken people or places are extremely poor. *...a teacher of poverty-stricken kids... The Pope is visiting some of the most poverty-stricken areas of the city.* ADJ: usu ADJ n =poor

poverty trap, poverty traps. If someone is in a **poverty trap**, they are in a situation where they are very poor, but cannot improve their income because they depend on government benefits which decrease as their earnings increase. N-COUNT

POW /piː oʊ dʌbəljuː/ **POWs.** A POW is the same as a **prisoner of war**. ◆◇◇◇◇ N-COUNT

powder /paʊdəʳ/ **powders, powdering, powdered** ◆◆◇◇◇

1 **Powder** consists of many tiny particles of a solid substance. *Put a small amount of the powder into a container and mix with water... The wood turns to powder in his fingers. ...a fine white powder. ...cocoa powder.* N-MASS

2 **Powder** is the same as **face powder**. N-MASS

3 If a woman **powders** her face or some other part of her body, she puts face powder or talcum powder on it. *She powdered her face and applied her lipstick and rouge. ...the old woman's powdered face.* VERB V n V-ed

4 **Powder** is the same as **gunpowder**; an old-fashioned use. *The smell of powder was in the air.* N-UNCOUNT =gunpowder

5 **Powder** is very fine snow. *...a day's powder skiing.* N-UNCOUNT: oft N n

6 See also **baking powder, chilli powder, curry powder, talcum powder, washing powder.**

powder blue; also spelled **powder-blue**. Something that is **powder blue** is a pale greyish-blue colour. *...a powder blue leisure suit.* COLOUR

powdered /paʊdəʳd/. A **powdered** substance is one which is in the form of a powder although it can come in a different form. *There are only two tins of powdered milk left. ...powdered gelatine.* ◆◇◇◇◇ ADJ: usu ADJ n

powder keg, powder kegs; also spelled **powder-keg**. If you describe a situation or a N-COUNT place as a **powder keg**, you mean that it could easily become very dangerous. *Unless these questions are solved, the region will remain a powder keg.*

powder room, powder rooms. N-COUNT A **powder room** is a room for women in a public building such as a hotel, where they can use the toilet, have a wash, or put on make-up; a formal expression.

powdery /paʊdəri/. ADJ-GRADED Something that is **powdery** looks or feels like powder. *A couple of inches of dry, powdery snow had fallen.*

power /paʊəʳ/ **powers, powering, powered** ◆◆◆◆◆

1 N-UNCOUNT If someone has **power**, they have a lot of control over people and activities. *She interviewed six women who have reached positions of great power and influence... In a democracy, power must be divided. ...a power struggle at the top of Albania's ruling Communist Party.*

2 N-UNCOUNT: usu N to-inf, N *of* n Your **power** to do something is your ability to do it. *Human societies have the power to solve the problems confronting them... Fathers have the power to dominate children and young people... He was so drunk that he had lost the power of speech.*

3 N-UNCOUNT: poss N If it is **in** or **within** your **power** to do something, you are able to do it or you have the resources to deal with it. *Your debt situation is only temporary, and it is within your power to resolve it... Although it is not in his power to do so, he said he would rebuild the Air Base... We must do everything in our power to ensure the success of the conference.*

4 N-UNCOUNT: also N in pl, oft *the* N to-inf If someone in authority has the **power** to do something, they have the legal right to do it. *The Prime Minister has the power to dismiss and appoint senior ministers... The police have the power of arrest... The legal powers of British Customs officers are laid out in the Customs and Excise Management Act of 1969.*

5 N-UNCOUNT: oft *in* N If people take **power** or come to **power**, they take charge of a country's affairs. If a group of people are **in power**, they are in charge of a country's affairs. *In 1964 Labour came into power... He first assumed power in 1970... The party has been in power since independence in 1964.*

6 N-COUNT: usu supp N You can use **power** to refer to a country that is very rich or important, or has strong military forces. *In Western eyes, Iraq is a major power in an area of great strategic importance. ...the emergence of the new major economic power, Japan.*

7 N-UNCOUNT: usu supp N The **power** of something is the physical strength or the electronic capability that it has to move or affect things. *The Roadrunner had better power, better tyres, and better brakes. ...massive computing power.*

8 N-UNCOUNT **Power** is energy, especially electricity, that is obtained in large quantities from a fuel source and used to operate lights, heating, and machinery. *Nuclear power is cleaner than coal... Power has been restored to most parts that were hit last night by high winds... There is enough power to run up to four lights.*

9 VERB =drive; V n The device or fuel that **powers** a machine provides the energy that the machine needs in order to work. *The 'flywheel' battery, it is said, could power an electric car for 600 miles on a single charge... The planes are powered by Rolls Royce engines.* ♦ **-powered** COMB in ADJ *...battery-powered radios. ...nuclear-powered submarines.* • See also **high-powered.**

10 ADJ: ADJ n ≠mechanical **Power** tools are operated by electricity. *...large power tools, such as chainsaws. ...a power drill.*

11 N-SING: *to the* N *of* num, *to the* ord N In mathematics, **power** is used in expressions such as **2 to the power of 4** or **2 to the 4th power** to indicate that 2 must be multiplied by itself 4 times. This is written in numbers as 2^4, or 2 x 2 x 2 x 2, which equals 16. *Any number to the power of nought is equal to one. ...10^{-35}m, or ten metres taken to the negative 35th power.*

12 PHRASE PRAGMATICS You can refer to people in authority as **the powers that be**, especially when you want to say that you disagree with them or do not understand what they say or do. *The powers that be, in this case the independent Television Association, banned the advertisement altogether... The powers that be may keep us from building a house just where we want to.*

power base, power bases; also spelled **power-base.** ◆◇◇◇◇ N-COUNT: oft with poss The **power base** of a politician or other leader is the area or the group of people from which they get most support, and which enables him or her to become powerful. *Milan was Mr Craxi's home town and his power base during his 16-year rule as party leader.*

powerboat /paʊəʳbəʊt/ **powerboats.** N-COUNT A **powerboat** is a very fast, powerful motorboat.

power breakfast, power breakfasts. N-COUNT If business people have a **power breakfast**, they go to a restaurant early in the morning so that they can have a meeting while they eat breakfast.

power cut, power cuts. N-COUNT A **power cut** is a period of time when the electricity supply to a particular building or area is interrupted, sometimes deliberately.

power failure, power failures. N-VAR A **power failure** is a period of time when the electricity supply to a particular building or area is interrupted, for example because of damage to the cables.

powerful /paʊəʳfʊl/ ◆◆◆◆◇

1 ADJ-GRADED =influential ≠powerless A **powerful** person or organization is able to control or influence people and events. *You're a powerful man – people will listen to you. ...Russia and India, two large, powerful countries. ...Hong Kong's powerful business community.* • See also **all powerful.**

2 ADJ-GRADED =strong ≠weak You say that someone's body is **powerful** when it is physically strong. *Hans flexed his powerful muscles... It's such a big powerful dog.* ♦ **powerfully** ADV-GRADED: ADV with v *He is described as a strong, powerfully-built man of 60... You can contract your muscles more powerfully by linking up your breathing to the exercise.*

3 ADJ-GRADED: usu ADJ n A **powerful** machine or substance is effective because it is very strong. *The more powerful the car the more difficult it is to handle. ...powerful computer systems... Alcohol is also a powerful and fast-acting drug.* ♦ **powerfully** ADV: ADV adj *Crack is a much cheaper, smokable form of cocaine which is powerfully addictive.*

4 ADJ-GRADED: usu ADJ n =strong A **powerful** smell is very strong. *There was a powerful smell of stale beer. ...tiny creamy flowers with a powerful scent.* ♦ **powerfully** ADV-GRADED: ADV after v *The railway station smelt powerfully of cats and drains.*

5 ADJ-GRADED =loud A **powerful** voice is loud and can be heard from a long way away. *At that moment Mrs. Jones's powerful voice interrupted them, announcing a visitor.*

6 ADJ-GRADED You describe a piece of writing, speech, or work of art as **powerful** when it has a strong effect on people's feelings or beliefs. *...Bleasdale's powerful 11-part drama about a corrupt city leader. ...one of the world's most powerful and moving operas, Verdi's 'Otello'. ...a powerful new style of dance-theatre.* ♦ **powerfully** ADV-GRADED: ADV -ed, ADV after v *It's a play – painful, funny and powerfully acted.*

power game, power games. N-COUNT: oft adj N PRAGMATICS You can refer to a situation in which different people or groups are competing for power as a **power game**, especially if you disapprove of the methods they are using in order to try to win power. *...the dangerous power games in the Kremlin following Stalin's death.*

powerhouse /paʊəʳhaʊs/ **powerhouses** ◆◇◇◇◇

1 N-COUNT A **powerhouse** is a country or organization that has a lot of power or influence. *...Shanghai, China's industrial powerhouse.*

2 N-COUNT If you say that someone is a **powerhouse**, you mean that they are very energetic; an informal use.

powerless /paʊəʳləs/ ◆◇◇◇◇

1 ADJ-GRADED =helpless ≠powerful, influential Someone who is **powerless** is unable to control or influence events. *If you don't have money, you're powerless. ...political and economic systems that keep women poor and powerless.* ♦ **powerlessness** N-UNCOUNT =impotence, helplessness *If we can't bring our problems under control, feelings of powerlessness and despair often ensue.*

2 ADJ-GRADED: ADJ to-inf =unable If you are **powerless** to do something, you are completely unable to do it. *People are being* *murdered every day and I am powerless to stop it... He was sympathetic, but powerless to help.* ≠able

power line, power lines. A **power line** is a cable, especially above ground, along which electricity is passes to an area or building. ◆◇◇◇◇ N-COUNT

power of attorney. **Power of attorney** is a legal document which allows you to appoint someone, for example a lawyer, to act on your behalf in specified matters. N-UNCOUNT

power plant, power plants. A **power plant** is a place where electricity is generated. ◆◇◇◇◇ N-COUNT =power station

power point, power points. In British English, a **power point** is a place in a wall where you can connect electrical devices such as televisions and fridges to the electricity supply. The American word is **socket** or **outlet**. N-COUNT

power-sharing; also spelled **power sharing.** **Power-sharing** is a type of political arrangement which allows different or opposing groups all to participate in government, so that the government can be seen as representing the whole of society. ◆◇◇◇◇ N-UNCOUNT

power station, power stations. A **power station** is a place where electricity is generated. ◆◆◇◇◇ N-COUNT =power plant

power steering. In a vehicle, **power steering** is a system for steering which uses power from the engine so that it is easier for the driver to steer the vehicle. N-UNCOUNT

pow-wow /paʊ waʊ/ **pow-wows;** also spelled **powwow.**

1 A **pow-wow** is a meeting or conference of Native Americans. N-COUNT

2 People sometimes refer to a meeting or discussion as a **pow-wow**; an informal use. *Every year my father would call a family powwow to discuss where we were going on vacation.* N-COUNT =meeting

pox /pɒks/. People sometimes refer to syphilis as **the pox**; an informal word. • See also **chickenpox, smallpox.** N-SING: the N

poxy /pɒksi/. In British English, if you describe something or someone as **poxy**, you think that they are pathetic and insignificant; an informal word which some people find offensive. *...some poxy band from Denver. ...a poxy one per cent of the transport budget.* ADJ: ADJ n PRAGMATICS =crummy

pp. **pp** is written before a person's name at the bottom of a formal or business letter in order to indicate that they have signed the letter on behalf of the person whose name appears before theirs. *...J.R. Adams, pp D. Philips.*

pp. **pp.** is the plural of 'p.' and means 'pages'. *See chapter 6, pp. 137-41.* ◆◆◆◇◇

PPS /piː piː es/ **PPS's.** In Britain, a **PPS** is an MP who is appointed by a more senior MP to help them with their duties. **PPS** is an abbreviation for 'parliamentary private secretary'. N-COUNT

PR /piː ɑːr/ ◆◆◇◇◇

1 **PR** is an abbreviation for **public relations.** *It will be good PR. ...a PR firm.* N-UNCOUNT

2 **PR** is an abbreviation for **proportional representation.** N-UNCOUNT

practicable /præktɪkəbəl/. If a task, plan, or idea is **practicable**, people are able to carry it out; a formal word. *It is not reasonably practicable to offer her the original job back... Teachers can only be expected to do what is reasonable and practicable.* ♦ **practicability** /præktɪkəbɪlɪti/ *Knotman and I first thought of the idea and discussed the practicability of it one night in March.* ADJ-GRADED: usu v-link ADJ =feasible ≠impracticable, unfeasible; N-UNCOUNT =feasibility

practical /præktɪkəl/ **practicals** ◆◆◆◇◇

1 The **practical** aspects of something involve real situations and events, rather than just ideas and theories. *We can offer you practical suggestions on how to increase the fibre in your daily diet... This practical guidebook teaches you about relaxation, coping skills, and time management.* ADJ: usu ADJ n ≠theoretical

2 You describe people as **practical** when they make sensible decisions and deal effectively with problems. *You were always so practical, Maria... How could she be so practical when he'd just told her something so shattering?... He lacked any of the practical common sense essential in management.* ADJ-GRADED: usu v-link ADJ =down-to-earth ≠impractical

3 **Practical** ideas and methods are likely to be effective or successful in a real situation. *Although the causes of cancer are being uncovered, we do not yet have any practical way to prevent it... It is not easy to make practical suggestions for helping her.* ADJ-GRADED: usu ADJ n

4 You can describe clothes and things in your house as **practical** when they are suitable for a particular purpose rather than just being fashionable or attractive. *Our clothes are lightweight, fashionable, practical for holidays.* ADJ-GRADED =useful ≠impractical

5 A **practical** is an examination or a lesson in which you make things or do experiments rather than simply writing answers to questions. N-COUNT

practicality /præktɪkælɪti/ **practicalities.** The **practicalities** of a situation are the practical aspects of it, as opposed to its theoretical aspects. *Decisions about your children should be based on the practicalities of everyday life.* ◆◇◇◇◇ N-VAR: usu with supp, oft N of n

practical joke, practical jokes. A **practical joke** is a trick that is intended to embarrass someone or make them look ridiculous. N-COUNT =prank

practically /præktɪkli/ ◆◆◇◇◇

1 **Practically** means almost, but not completely or exactly. *He'd known the old man practically all his life... I know people who find it practically impossible to give up smoking.* ADV: ADV with group/cl =almost

2 You use **practically** to describe something which involves real actions or events rather than ideas or theories. *The course is essentially more practically based than the Masters degree... The British are not famed for their philosophy and tend to be more practically minded.* ADV: ADV adj/-ed ≠theoretically

practice /præktɪs/ **practices** ◆◆◆◆◇

1 You can refer to something that people do regularly as a **practice**. *Some firms have reached agreements to cut workers' pay below the level set in their contract, a practice that is illegal in Germany... Gordon Brown has demanded a public inquiry into bank practices.* N-COUNT =procedure

2 **Practice** means doing something regularly in order to be able to do it better. A **practice** is a session of this. *She was taking all three of her daughters to basketball practice every day. ...the hard practice necessary to develop from a learner to an accomplished musician... The defending world racing champion recorded the fastest time in a final practice today.* N-VAR: usu supp N

3 The work done by doctors and lawyers is referred to as the **practice** of medicine and law. People's religious activities are referred to as the **practice** of a religion. *...maintaining or improving his skills in the practice of internal medicine... I eventually realized I had to change my attitude toward medical practice. ...a law guaranteeing the people freedom of conscience and religious practice.* N-UNCOUNT: with supp

4 A doctor's or lawyer's **practice** is his or her business, often shared with other doctors or lawyers. *The new doctor's practice was miles away from where I lived... My law practice isn't the most important thing in my life, you know.* N-COUNT

5 See also **practise**.

6 What happens **in practice** is what actually happens, in contrast to what is supposed to happen. *...the difference between foreign policy as presented to the public and foreign policy in actual practice... In practice, workers do not work to satisfy their needs.* PHRASES PHR with cl ≠in theory

7 If something such as a procedure is **normal practice** or **standard practice**, it is the usual thing that is done in a particular situation. *It is normal practice not to reveal details of a patient's condition... The transcript is full of codewords, which is standard practice in any army.* v-link PHR

8 If you are **out of practice** at doing something, you have not had much experience of it recently, although you used to do it a lot or be quite good at it. *'How's your German?'—'Not bad, but I'm out of practice.'* v-link PHR

9 If you say **'practice makes perfect'**, you mean that it is possible to learn something or develop a skill if you practise enough. People often say this to encourage someone to keep practising something. PRAGMATICS

10 If you **put** a belief or method **into practice**, you behave or act in accordance with it. *Now that he is back, the prime minister has another chance to put his new ideas into practice... We weren't allowed to put into practice in our daily lives the teachings we received.* V inflects

practise /præktɪs/ **practises, practising, practised;** spelled **practice** in American English. ◆◆◇◇◇

1 If you **practise** something, you keep doing it regularly in order to be able to do it better. *Lauren practises the piano every day... When she wanted to get something right, she would practise and practise and practise.* ● See also **practised**. VERB V n V

2 When people **practise** something such as a custom, craft, or religion, they take part in the activities associated with it. *It was suggested that American aid should be directed towards countries which practised multi-party politics... Acupuncture was practised in China as long ago as the third millennium BC... He was brought up in a family which practised traditional Judaism.* ♦ **practising** *The church has broken the agreement, by insisting all employees must be practising Christians.* VERB V n; ADJ: ADJ n

3 If something cruel is regularly done to people, you can say that it **is practised on** them. *There are consistent reports of electrical torture being practised on inmates.* VB: usu passive be V-ed on n

4 Someone who **practises** medicine or law works as a doctor or a lawyer. *In Belgium only qualified doctors may practise alternative medicine... He was born in Hong Kong where he subsequently practised as a lawyer until his retirement... The ways in which solicitors practise are varied... An art historian and collector, he was also a practising architect.* VERB V n V as n V V-ing

5 ● to **practise what** you **preach**: see **preach**.

practised /præktɪst/; spelled **practiced** in American English. Someone who is **practised** at doing something is good at it because they have had experience and have developed their skill at it. *Once you are practised at this sort of relaxation you will feel quite refreshed afterwards. ...a practised and experienced surgeon.* ADJ-GRADED: oft ADJ at n

practitioner /præktɪʃənə^r/ **practitioners.** Doctors are sometimes referred to as **practitioners** or **medical practitioners**; a formal word. ● See also **GP**. ◆◆◇◇◇ N-COUNT

praesidium /prɪsɪdiəm, praɪ-/. See **presidium**.

praetorian guard /prɪtɔːriən gɑːrd/. You can use **praetorian guard** to refer to a group of people who are close associates and loyal supporters of someone important; a formal expression. N-SING-COLL

pragmatic /prægmætɪk/. A **pragmatic** way of dealing with something is based on practical considerations, rather than theoretical ones. A **pragmatic** person deals with things in a practical way. *Robin took a pragmatic look at her situation. ...a pragmatic approach to the problems faced by Latin America.* ♦ **pragmatically** /prægmætɪkli/ *'I can't ever see us doing anything else,' states Brian pragmatically... Pragmatically, MTV's survival depends on selling the youth market to advertisers.* ◆◇◇◇◇ ADJ-GRADED: usu ADJ n =realistic, practical; ADV-GRADED: usu ADV with v, also ADV with cl, ADV adj

pragmatics /prægmætɪks/. **Pragmatics** is the branch of linguistics that deals with the meanings and effects which come from the use of language in particular situations. Compare **semantics**. In this dictionary, the word 'pragmatics' appears in the extra column to show that a word, meaning, or phrase is being used to convey a particular evaluation or to carry out a particular function. This use is explained in the introductory section of the dictionary. N-SING

pragmatism /prægmətɪzəm/. **Pragmatism** means thinking or of dealing with problems in a practical way, rather than by using theory or abstract principles; a formal word. *She had a reputation for clear thinking and pragmatism.* ♦ **pragmatist, pragmatists** *He is a political pragmatist, not an idealist.* ◆◇◇◇◇ N-UNCOUNT; N-COUNT

prairie /preəri/ **prairies.** A **prairie** is a large area of flat, grassy land in North America. Prairies have very few trees. ◆◇◇◇◇ N-VAR

prairie dog, prairie dogs. A **prairie dog** is a type of small furry animal that lives underground in the prairies of North America. N-COUNT

praise /preɪz/ **praises, praising, praised** ◆◆◆◇◇

1 If you **praise** someone or something, you express approval for their achievements or qualities. *The American president praised Turkey for its courage... Many others praised Sanford for taking a strong stand... He praised the excellent work of the UN weapons inspectors.* VERB =compliment V n for n/-ing V n

2 **Praise** is what you say or write about someone when you are praising them. *All the ladies are full of praise for the staff and service they received... I have nothing but praise for the police... That is high praise indeed.* N-UNCOUNT =commendation

3 If you **praise** God, you express your respect, honour, and thanks to God. *She asked the church to praise God.* VERB V n

4 **Praise** is the expression of respect, honour, and thanks to God. *Hindus were singing hymns in praise of the god Rama.* N-UNCOUNT: also N in pl

5 If someone **damns** something **with faint praise**, they say something about it which sounds quite nice but which shows that they do not have a high opinion of it. *...the belief that the US had signalled a policy shift by damning with faint praise the mediation efforts.* PHRASES

6 If you **sing** someone's **praises**, you praise them in an enthusiastic way. *Ottershaw's been singing your praises for years... Andy Sinton is not a man given to singing his own praises.* V inflects

praiseworthy /preɪzwɜːrði/. If you say that something is **praiseworthy**, you mean that you approve of it and it deserves to be praised; a formal use. *...the government's praiseworthy efforts to improve efficiency in health and education.* ADJ-GRADED PRAGMATICS

praline /prɑːliːn, preɪ-/. **Praline** is a sweet substance made from nuts cooked in boiling sugar. It is used in desserts and as a filling for chocolates. N-UNCOUNT

pram /præm/ **prams.** In British English, a **pram** is a baby's cot which has wheels so that you can push it along when you want to take a baby somewhere. The usual American term is **baby carriage**. ◆◇◇◇◇ N-COUNT

prance /prɑːns, præns/ **prances, prancing, pranced**

1 If someone **prances** around, they walk or move around with exaggerated movements, usually because they want people to look at them and admire them; used showing disapproval. *He was horrified at the thought of any son of his prancing about on a stage in tights.* VERB PRAGMATICS V adv/prep

2 When a horse **prances**, it moves with quick, high steps. *As they neared the corral, both their horses pranced and whinnied. ...as the carriage horses pranced through the bustling thoroughfares. ...a prancing light-footed mare named Princess.* VERB V V prep/adv V-ing

prank /præŋk/ **pranks.** A **prank** is a childish trick; an old-fashioned word. ◆◇◇◇◇ N-COUNT

prankster /præŋkstə^r/ **pranksters.** A **prankster** is someone who plays tricks and practical jokes on people; an old-fashioned word. N-COUNT =joker

prat /præt/ **prats.** In British English, if you describe someone as a **prat**, you are saying in an unkind way that you think that they are very stupid or foolish; an informal word. *What's that prat doing out there now?* N-COUNT PRAGMATICS =idiot

pratfall /prætfɔːl/ **pratfalls**

1 If someone takes a **pratfall**, they make an embarrassing mistake; used mainly in American English. *They're waiting for the poor little rich girl to take a pratfall.* N-COUNT

2 In American English, a **pratfall** is a fall on the buttocks. N-COUNT

prattle /prætᵊl/ **prattles, prattling, prattled.** If you say that someone **prattles on** about something, or that someone **prattles**, you are showing that you disapprove of them or are annoyed by them because they are talking a great deal without saying anything important; an informal word. *Lou prattled on about various trivialities* VERB PRAGMATICS =witter V on/away *till I wanted to scream... She prattled on as she drove out to the Highway... Archie, shut up. You're prattling.* ► Also a noun. *What a bore it was to listen to the woman's prattle!* — about n; V *on/away*; V; N-UNCOUNT

prawn /prɔːn/ **prawns.** In British English, a **prawn** is a small shellfish, similar to a shrimp, which can be eaten. The American word is **shrimp**. *...a prawn sandwich.* — ◆◇◇◇◇ N-COUNT

prawn cocktail, prawn cocktails. A **prawn cocktail** is a dish that consists of prawns, salad, and a sauce. It is usually eaten at the beginning of a meal. — N-VAR

pray /preɪ/ **prays, praying, prayed** — ◆◆◇◇◇

1 When people **pray**, they speak to God in order to give thanks or to ask for his help. *He spent his time in prison praying and studying... Now all we have to do is help ourselves and to pray to God. ...all those who work and pray for peace... Kelly prayed that God would judge her with mercy.* — VERB; V; V *to* n; V *for* n; V that; Also V with quote, V to-inf

2 When someone is hoping very much that something will happen, you can say that they **are praying** that it will happen. *I'm just praying that somebody in Congress will do something before it's too late... One can only pray that the team's manager learns something from it... By the time it came to vote, many of the centrists were secretly praying for a compromise.* — VB: usu cont =hope; V that; V *for* n

3 In old-fashioned English, **pray** was used to add sarcasm to a question. *'And what, pray, do you buy and sell, Major?'* — ADV: ADV with cl PRAGMATICS

4 In old-fashioned English, **pray** was used to add politeness to a command. *I beg your pardon, pray continue.* — ADV: ADV cl PRAGMATICS =please

prayer /preəʳ/ **prayers** — ◆◆◇◇◇

1 **Prayer** is the activity of speaking to God. *They had joined a religious order and dedicated their lives to prayer and good works... The night was spent in prayer.* — N-UNCOUNT

2 A **prayer** is the words a person says when they speak to God. *They should take a little time and say a prayer for the people on both sides. ...prayers of thanksgiving.* — N-COUNT

3 You can refer to a strong hope that you have as your **prayer**. *This drug could be the answer to our prayers.* — N-COUNT: poss N

4 A short religious service at which people gather to pray can be referred to as **prayers**. *He promised that the boy would be back at school in time for evening prayers. ...Muslims attending prayers in the main mosque.* — N-PLURAL

5 If you say that someone **hasn't got a prayer**, you mean that it is impossible for them to succeed in what they are trying to do; an informal use. *She'd been caught from behind and hadn't a prayer of freeing herself.* — PHRASE: V inflects, oft PHR *of*-ing

prayer book, prayer books. A **prayer book** is a book which contains the prayers which are used in church or at home. — N-COUNT

prayer meeting, prayer meetings. A **prayer meeting** is a religious meeting where people say prayers to God. — N-COUNT

pre- /priː-/. **Pre-** is used to form words that indicate that something takes place before a particular date, period, or event. *It was 1950 before he returned to his pre-war job at the British Museum... Last year the company offered to buy pre-1971 cars for $700 apiece. ...life in pre-industrial England.* — PREFIX ≠post-

preach /priːtʃ/ **preaches, preaching, preached** — ◆◆◇◇◇

1 When a member of the clergy **preaches** a sermon, he or she gives a talk on a religious or moral subject during a religious service. *At High Mass the priest preached a sermon on the devil... The bishop preached to a crowd of several hundred local people... He denounced the decision to invite his fellow archbishop to preach.* — VERB; V n; V *to* n; V; Also V *against/on* n

2 When people **preach** a belief or a course of action, they try to persuade other people to accept the belief or to take the course of action. *The Prime Minister said he was trying to preach peace and tolerance to his people... Health experts are now preaching that even a little exercise is far better than none at all... For many years I have preached against war.* — VERB =advocate; V n; V that; V *against/about* n

3 If someone gives you advice in a boring, pompous way, you can say that they **are preaching at** you; used showing disapproval. *'Don't preach at me,' he shouted.* — VERB PRAGMATICS; V *at* n

4 If you say that someone **practises what** they **preach**, you mean that they behave in the way that they encourage other people to behave in. *He ought to practise what he preaches.* — PHRASES; Vs inflect

5 If you say that someone **is preaching to the converted**, you mean that they are wasting their time because they are trying to persuade people to think or believe in things that they already think or believe in. — V inflects

preacher /priːtʃəʳ/ **preachers.** A **preacher** is a person, often a member of the clergy, who preaches sermons as part of a church service. — ◆◇◇◇◇ N-COUNT

preamble /priːæmbəl/ **preambles.** A **preamble** is an introduction that comes before something you say or write. *The controversy has arisen over the text of the preamble to the unification treaty... 'I would like you to return to the villa as soon as possible,' she said without preamble.* — N-VAR: oft N *to/of* n, *without* N

prearrange /priːəreɪndʒ/ **prearranges, prearranging, prearranged;** also spelled **pre-arrange**. If you **prearrange** something, you plan or arrange it before the time when it actually happens. *When you prearrange your funeral, you can pick your own flowers and music.* — VERB; V n

prearranged /priːəreɪndʒd/; also spelled **pre-arranged**. You use **prearranged** to indicate that something has been planned or arranged before the time when it actually happens. *Working to a prearranged plan, he rang the First Secretary and requested an appointment with the Ambassador.* — ADJ: ADJ n

precarious /prɪkeəriəs/ — ◆◇◇◇◇

1 If your situation is **precarious**, you are not in complete control of events and might fail in what you are doing at any moment. *Our financial situation had become precarious. ...the Government's precarious position.* ♦ **precariously** *We lived precariously. I suppose I wanted to squeeze as much pleasure from each day as I possibly could.* ♦ **precariousness** *Wells was well aware of the precariousness of human life.* — ADJ-GRADED =uncertain, unstable ≠stable, secure; ADV-GRADED: ADV with v, ADV adj/adv; N-UNCOUNT: usu N *of* n

2 Something that is **precarious** is not securely held in place and seems likely to fall or collapse at any moment. *They looked rather comical as they crawled up precarious ladders.* ♦ **precariously** *One of my grocery bags was still precariously perched on the car bumper.* — ADJ-GRADED; ADV-GRADED: ADV with v, ADV adj/adv

precaution /prɪkɔːʃən/ **precautions.** A **precaution** is an action that is intended to prevent something dangerous or unpleasant from happening. *Could he not, just as a precaution, move to a place of safety?... I had taken the precaution of doing a little research before I left London... Extra safety precautions are essential in homes where older people live.* — ◆◆◇◇◇ N-COUNT

precautionary /prɪkɔːʃənri, AM -neri/. **Precautionary** actions are taken in order to prevent something dangerous or unpleasant from happening; a formal word. *The local administration says the curfew is a precautionary measure.* — ADJ: usu ADJ n

precede /prɪsiːd/ **precedes, preceding, preceded** — ◆◆◇◇◇

1 If one event or period of time **precedes** another, it happens before it; a formal use. *Intensive negotiations between the main parties preceded the vote... The earthquake was preceded by a loud roar and lasted 20 seconds... Industrial orders had already fallen in the preceding months.* — VERB; V n; *be* V-ed *by* n; V-ing

2 If you **precede** someone somewhere, you go in front of them; a formal use. *He gestured to Alice to precede them from the room... They were preceded by mounted cowboys.* — VERB; V n; *be* V-ed *by* n

3 A sentence, paragraph, or chapter that **precedes** another one occurs just before it in, for example, a particular book, magazine, or article. *Look at the information that precedes the paragraph in* — VERB ≠follow; V n; V-ing

question... In the preceding chapter we traced the redefinition of Britain's global position in the years 1942-73.

precedence /presɪdəns/. If one thing takes **precedence** over another, it is regarded as more important than the other thing. *Have as much fun as possible at college, but don't let it take precedence over work... As the King's representative he took precedence over everyone else on the island.* ◆◇◇◇◇ N-UNCOUNT: usu N over n =priority

precedent /presɪdənt/ **precedents.** If there is a **precedent** for an action or event, it has happened before, and this can be regarded as an argument for doing it again; a formal word. *The trial could set an important precedent for dealing with large numbers of similar cases... There are plenty of precedents in Hollywood for letting people out of contracts.* ◆◆◇◇◇ N-VAR: oft N for n

precept /priːsept/ **precepts.** A **precept** is a general rule that helps you to decide how you should behave in particular circumstances; a formal word. *...an electoral process based on the central precept that all men are born equal regardless of race or colour. ...the precepts of Buddhism.* N-COUNT =maxim, principle

precinct /priːsɪŋkt/ **precincts** ◆◇◇◇◇

1 In British English, a shopping **precinct** is an area in the centre of a town in which cars are not allowed. *The Centre was a pedestrian precinct with a bandstand in the middle.* N-COUNT =shopping centre

2 In the United States, a **precinct** is a part of a city which has its own police force and fire service. *The shooting occurred in the 34th Precinct.* N-COUNT: usu ord N

3 The **precincts** of an institution are its buildings and land; a formal use. *No one carrying is allowed within the precincts of a temple.* N-PLURAL

precious /preʃəs/ ◆◆◇◇◇

1 If you say that something such as a resource is **precious**, you mean that it is valuable and should not be wasted or used badly. *After four months in foreign parts, every hour at home was precious... A family break allows you to spend precious time together... Water is becoming an increasingly precious resource.* ADJ-GRADED =valuable

2 **Precious** objects and materials are worth a lot of money because they are rare. *...jewellery and precious objects belonging to the Princess.* ADJ-GRADED =valuable

3 If something is **precious** to you, you regard it as important and do not want to lose it. *Her family's support is particularly precious to Josie... Mary left her most precious possession—a small bookcase—to her niece.* ADJ-GRADED

4 People sometimes use **precious** to express their dislike for things which other people think are important; an informal use. *You don't care about anything but yourself and your precious face.* ADJ: ADJ n PRAGMATICS

5 If you describe someone as **precious**, you mean that they behave in a formal and unnatural way. *Actors, he decided, were too precious and neurotic.* ADJ-GRADED =affected, mannered

6 If you say that there is **precious little** of something, you are emphasizing that there is very little of it, and that it would be better if there were more. **Precious few** has a similar meaning. *The battered banks of Japan have had precious little to celebrate recently... Precious few homebuyers will notice any reduction in their monthly repayments.* PHRASE PRAGMATICS

precious metal, precious metals. A **precious metal** is a valuable metal such as gold or silver. ◆◇◇◇◇ N-VAR

precious stone, precious stones. A **precious stone** is a valuable stone, such as a diamond or a ruby, that is used for making jewellery. N-COUNT =gem, jewel

precipice /presɪpɪs/ **precipices**

1 A **precipice** is a very steep cliff on a mountain. N-COUNT

2 If you say that someone is on the edge of a **precipice**, you mean that they are in a dangerous situation in which they are extremely close to disaster or failure. *I was beginning to admit to myself that our marriage was rolling toward the edge of a precipice... The King now stands on the brink of a political precipice.* N-COUNT

precipitate, precipitates, precipitating, precipitated. The verb is pronounced /prɪsɪpəteɪt/. The adjective is pronounced /prɪsɪpɪtət/. ◆◇◇◇◇

1 If something **precipitates** an event or situation, usually a bad one, it causes it to happen suddenly or sooner than normal; a formal use. *The killings in Vilnius have precipitated the worst crisis yet... A slight mistake could precipitate a disaster.* VERB =bring about, hasten V n

2 A **precipitate** action or decision happens or is made more quickly or suddenly than most people think is sensible; a formal use. *I don't think we should make precipitate decisions... Many of our current problems have been caused by precipitate policy making in the past.* ♦ **precipitately** *Somebody hired from another country is not likely to resign precipitately... He hurried precipitately away.* ADJ-GRADED: usu ADJ n =hasty; ADV-GRADED: ADV with v

precipitation /prɪsɪpɪteɪʃən/

1 **Precipitation** is rain, snow, or hail; a technical use in meteorology. N-UNCOUNT

2 **Precipitation** is a process in a chemical reaction which causes solid particles to become separated from a liquid; a technical use in chemistry. N-UNCOUNT

precipitous /prɪsɪpɪtəs/ ◆◇◇◇◇

1 A **precipitous** slope or drop is very steep and often dangerous. *The town is perched on the edge of a steep, precipitous cliff.* ♦ **precipitously** *The ground beyond the road fell away precipitously.* ADJ-GRADED: usu ADJ n; ADV-GRADED: usu ADV after v

2 A **precipitous** change is sudden and unpleasant. *The stock market's precipitous drop frightened foreign investors... Meryl's health started a precipitous decline.* ♦ **precipitously** *The company has seen its profits fall precipitously over the past few years.* ADJ-GRADED: usu ADJ n; ADV-GRADED: ADV with v

3 A **precipitous** action happens very quickly and often without being planned. *...a precipitous decision.* ♦ **precipitously** *They've got to act precipitously to make the deals.* ADJ-GRADED: usu ADJ n; ADV-GRADED: usu ADV with v

précis /preɪsi, AM preɪsiː/. The form **précis** is both the singular and the plural. It is pronounced /preɪsiz/ when it is the plural. A **précis** is a short written or spoken account of something, which gives the important points but not the details; a formal word. *A nine-page précis of the manuscript was sent to the Australian magazine New Idea.* N-COUNT: oft N of n =summary

precise /prɪsaɪs/ ◆◆◇◇◇

1 You use **precise** to emphasize that you are referring to an exact thing, rather than something vague. *I can remember the precise moment when my daughter came to see me and her new baby brother in hospital... The precise location of the wreck was discovered in 1988... He was not clear on the precise nature of his mission... We will never know the precise details of his death.* ADJ-GRADED: ADJ n =exact

2 Something that is **precise** is exact and accurate in all its details. *They speak very precise English... He does not talk too much and what he has to say is precise and to the point.* ADJ-GRADED

3 You say **'to be precise'** to indicate that you are giving more detailed or accurate information than you have just given. *More than a week ago, Thursday evening to be precise, Susanne was at her evening class... The restaurant in which we ate that night had more people in it at 11pm, 51 more to be precise, than it did at 10pm.* PHRASE: cl/group PHR

precisely /prɪsaɪsli/ ◆◆◆◇◇

1 **Precisely** means accurately and exactly. *Nobody knows precisely how many people are still living in the camp... The meeting began at precisely 4.00 p.m... Breakfast television arrived in British life precisely a decade ago.* ADV-GRADED: ADV with v, ADV with cl/group =exactly

2 You can use **precisely** to emphasize that a reason or fact is the only important one there is, or that it is obvious. *Children come to zoos precisely to see captive animals... That is precisely the result the system is designed to produce.* ADV-GRADED: ADV with cl/group PRAGMATICS

3 You can say **'precisely'** to confirm in an emphatic way that what someone has just said is true. *'So, you're trying to put trained, responsible people in every place where you think they might be able to help?'—'Precisely.'* ADV as reply PRAGMATICS =exactly

precision /prɪsɪʒən/. If you do something with **precision**, you do it exactly as it should be done. *The choir sang with precision... The interior is planned with a precision the military would be proud of.* ◆◆◇◇◇ N-UNCOUNT: oft with N

preclude /prɪkluːd/ **precludes, precluding, precluded** ◆◇◇◇◇
1 If something **precludes** an event or action, it prevents the event or action from happening; a formal use. *At 84, John feels his age precludes too much travel... He would rebuff enquiries in such a way as to preclude any further discussion.* (VERB =prevent; V n/-ing)
2 If something **precludes** you **from** doing something or going somewhere, it prevents you from doing it or going there; a formal use. *A constitutional amendment precludes any president from serving more than two terms... In some cases poor English precluded them from ever finding a job.* (VERB =prevent; V n *from* -ing/n)

precocious /prɪkoʊʃəs/. A **precocious** child is very clever, talented, or mature, often in a way that you usually only expect to find in an adult. *Margaret was always a precocious child... She burst on to the world tennis scene as a precocious 14-year old... Despite her precocious talent for music and art, she failed both subjects at school.* ◆◇◇◇◇ (ADJ-GRADED: usu ADJ n)
♦ **precociously** *He was a precociously bright school boy.* (ADV-GRADED: usu ADV adj, also ADV with v)

precocity /prɪkɒsɪti/. **Precocity** is the quality or state of being precocious; a formal word. (N-UNCOUNT)

preconceived /priːkənsiːvd/. If you have **preconceived** ideas about something, you have already formed an opinion about it before you have enough information or experience. *Five minutes after he had arrived for the interview, I had abandoned my preconceived ideas about boxers... We all start with preconceived notions of what we want from life.* (ADJ: ADJ n)

preconception /priːkənsepʃən/ **preconceptions.** Your **preconceptions** about something are beliefs formed about it before you have enough information or experience. *Did you have any preconceptions about the sort of people who did computing?... He did not allow his preconceptions to compromise his scientific work.* ◆◇◇◇◇ (N-COUNT: usu with supp)

precondition /priːkəndɪʃən/ **preconditions.** If one thing is a **precondition** for another, it must happen or be done before the second thing can happen or exist; a formal word. *They have been demanding the release of three of their colleagues from prison as a precondition for further negotiation.* ◆◇◇◇◇ (N-COUNT: oft N *for/of/to* n/-ing =prerequisite)

pre-cooked; also spelled **precooked**. **Precooked** food has been prepared and cooked in advance so that it only needs to be heated quickly before you eat it. *...pre-cooked baby food.* (ADJ: usu ADJ n)

precursor /priːkɜːʳsəʳ/ **precursors.** A **precursor** of something is a similar thing that happened or existed before it, often something which led to the existence or development of that thing. *Real tennis, an ancient precursor of the modern game, originated in the eleventh century... He said that the deal should not be seen as a precursor to a merger.* ◆◇◇◇◇ (N-COUNT: usu with supp, oft N *of/to* n =forerunner)

predate /priːdeɪt/ **predates, predating, predated.** If you say that one thing **predated** another, you mean that the first thing happened or existed some time before the second thing; a formal word. *His troubles predated the recession... The monument predates the arrival of the druids in Britain.* (VERB; V n)

predator /predətəʳ/ **predators** ◆◇◇◇◇
1 A **predator** is an animal that kills and eats other animals. (N-COUNT)
2 People sometimes refer to predatory people or organizations as **predators**. *Rumours of a takeover by Hanson are probably far-fetched, but the company is worried about other predators.* (N-COUNT)

predatory /predətri, AM -tɔːri/ ◆◇◇◇◇
1 **Predatory** animals live by killing other animals for food. *...predatory birds like the eagle.* (ADJ: usu ADJ n)
2 **Predatory** people or organizations are eager to gain something out of someone else's weakness or suffering. *People will not set up new businesses while they are frightened by the predatory behaviour of the banks.* (ADJ-GRADED: usu ADJ n)

predecease /priːdɪsiːs/ **predeceases, predeceasing, predeceased.** If one person **predeceases** another, they die before them; a formal word. *His wife of 63 years, Mary, predeceased him by 11 months.* (VERB; V n)

predecessor /priːdɪsesəʳ, AM pred-/ **predecessors** ◆◆◇◇◇
1 Your **predecessor** is the person who had your job before you. *He maintained that he learned everything he knew from his predecessor Kenneth Sisam.* (N-COUNT: usu poss N)
2 The **predecessor** of an object or machine is the object or machine that came before it in a sequence or process of development. *Although the car is some 40mm shorter than its predecessor, its boot is 20 per cent larger.* (N-COUNT: usu with poss =forerunner)

predestination /priːdestɪneɪʃən, AM priːdest-/. If you believe in **predestination**, you believe that people have no control over events because they have already been decided by God or by fate. (N-UNCOUNT)

predestined /priːdestɪnd/. If you say that something was **predestined**, you mean that it could not have been prevented or altered because it had already been decided by God or by fate. *His was not a political career predestined from birth... He wished that he could be like other children instead of pursuing his lonely predestined path.* (ADJ)

predetermined /priːdɪtɜːʳmɪnd/. If you say that something is **predetermined**, you mean that its form or nature was decided by previous events or by people rather than by chance. *The Prince's destiny was predetermined from the moment of his birth... The capsules can be made to release the pesticides at a predetermined time.* (ADJ)

predeterminer /priːdɪtɜːʳmɪnəʳ/ **predeterminers.** In grammar, a **predeterminer** is a word that is used before a determiner, but is still part of the noun group. For example, 'all' in 'all the time' and 'both' in 'both our children' are predeterminers. (N-COUNT)

predicament /prɪdɪkəmənt/ **predicaments.** If you are in a **predicament**, you are an unpleasant situation that is difficult to get out of. *Hank explained our predicament... The decision will leave her in a peculiar predicament.* ◆◇◇◇◇ (N-COUNT: usu with supp =dilemma)

predicate, predicates, predicating, predicated. The noun is pronounced /predɪkət/. The verb is pronounced /predɪkeɪt/.
1 In some systems of grammar, the **predicate** of a clause is the part of it that is not the subject. For example, in 'I decided what to do', 'decided what to do' is the predicate. (N-COUNT)
2 If you say that one idea or situation **is predicated on** another, you mean that the first idea or situation can be true or real only if the second one is true or real; a formal use. *Financial success is usually predicated on having money or being able to obtain it.* (VB: usu passive =be dependent upon; *be* V-ed *on* n/-ing)

predict /prɪdɪkt/ **predicts, predicting, predicted.** If you **predict** an event, you say that it will happen. *The latest opinion polls are predicting a very close contest... He predicted that my hair would grow back 'in no time'... It's hard to predict how a jury will react... 'The war will continue another two or three years,' he predicted.*  (VERB; V n; V that; V wh; V with quote)

predictable /prɪdɪktəbəl/. If you say that an event is **predictable**, you mean that it is obvious in advance that it will happen. *This was a predictable reaction, given the bitter hostility between the two countries... The result was entirely predictable.* ◆◆◇◇◇ (ADJ-GRADED ≠unpredictable)
♦ **predictably** *His article is, predictably, a scathing attack on communism... The central London hospitals have reacted predictably.* (ADV-GRADED: ADV with cl, ADV with v, ADV adj/adv)
♦ **predictability** /prɪdɪktəbɪlɪti/ *Your mother values the predictability of your Sunday calls.* (N-UNCOUNT)

prediction /prɪdɪkʃən/ **predictions.** If you make a **prediction** about something, you say what you think will happen. *He was unwilling to make a prediction for the coming year: 'It's hard to tell which of our books are going to sell.'... Predictions that the recession will be short are small comfort to those already affected... Weather prediction has never been a perfect science, and it isn't one now.*  (N-VAR)

predictive /prɪdɪktɪv/. You use **predictive** to describe something such as a test, science, or theory that is concerned with determining what will happen in the future; a formal word. *...the predictive branch of economics.* ADJ-GRADED: usu ADJ n

predictor /prɪdɪktəʳ/ **predictors.** You can refer to something that helps you predict something that will happen in the future as a **predictor** of that thing. *Opinion polls are an unreliable predictor of election outcomes... The child's reaction to the arrival of the new baby was a very good predictor of how they would get on during the year that followed.* N-COUNT: with supp, usu N *of* n =indication

predilection /priːdɪlekʃᵊn, AM pred-/ **predilections.** If you have a **predilection** for something, you have a strong liking for it; a formal word. *...his predilection for fast cars and fast horses.* N-COUNT: oft N *for* n/-ing =fondness

predispose /priːdɪspoʊz/ **predisposes, predisposing, predisposed**

1 If something **predisposes** you to think or behave in a particular way, it makes it likely that you will think or behave in that way; a formal use. *They take pains to hire people whose personalities predispose them to serve customers well... There is evidence to suggest that factors such as personality and attitude predispose some individuals to criminal behaviour.* VERB; V n to-inf; V n *to* n/-ing
♦ **predisposed** *Franklin was predisposed to believe him. ...people who are predisposed to violent crime.* ADJ-GRADED: v-link ADJ, usu ADJ to-inf, ADJ *to* n

2 If something **predisposes** you **to** a disease or illness, it makes it likely that you will suffer from that disease or illness; a formal use. *...a gene that predisposes people to alcoholism.* ♦ **predisposed** *Some people are genetically predisposed to diabetes.* VERB; V n *to* n; ADJ-GRADED: v-link ADJ, usu ADJ *to* n

predisposition /priːdɪspəzɪʃᵊn/ **predispositions**

1 If you have a **predisposition** to behave in a particular way, you tend to behave like that because of the kind of person that you are or the attitudes that you have; a formal use. *...a woman's predisposition to use the right side of her brain... There is a thin dividing line between educating the public and creating a predisposition to panic.* N-COUNT: usu with supp, oft N to-inf, N *to/towards* n/-ing

2 If you have a **predisposition** to a disease or illness, it is likely that you will suffer from that disease or illness; a formal use. *...a genetic predisposition to lung cancer.* N-COUNT: with supp, usu N *to/towards* n

predominance /prɪdɒmɪnəns/

1 If there is a **predominance** of one type of person or thing, there are many more of that type than of any other type; a formal use. *Another interesting note was the predominance of London club players.* N-SING: usu N *of* n =preponderance

2 If someone or something has **predominance**, they have the most power or importance among a group of people or things; a formal use. *Eventually even their economic predominance was to suffer.* N-UNCOUNT: usu with supp

predominant /prɪdɒmɪnənt/. If something is **predominant**, it is more important or noticeable than anything else in a set of people or things. *Amanda's predominant emotion was that of confusion.* ♦◇◇◇◇ ADJ-GRADED

predominantly /prɪdɒmɪnəntli/. You use **predominantly** to indicate which feature or quality is most noticeable in a situation. *The landscape has remained predominantly rural in appearance. ...a predominantly female profession... Although it is predominantly a teenage problem, acne can occur in early childhood... His audience consists predominantly of groups of rugby-club revellers.* ♦♦◇◇◇ ADV-GRADED: usu ADV group, also ADV after v =mainly

predominate /prɪdɒmɪneɪt/ **predominates, predominating, predominated** ♦◇◇◇◇

1 If one type of person or thing **predominates** in a group, there is more of that type of person or thing in the group than of any other; a formal use. *In older age groups women predominate because men tend to die younger... All nationalities were represented – but the English predominated.* VERB; V

2 When a feature or quality **predominates**, it is the most important or noticeable one in a situation; a formal use. *He wants to create a society where Islamic principles predominate.* VERB; V

predominately /prɪdɒmɪnətli/. **Predominately** means the same as **predominantly**. *...a predominately white, middle-class suburb.* ADV: usu ADV group, also ADV after v

pre-eminent. If someone or something is **pre-eminent** in a group, they are more important, powerful, or capable than other people or things in the group; a formal word. *...his fifty years as the pre-eminent political figure in the country... For a decade 'X' was the pre-eminent punk band in Los Angeles.* ♦ **pre-eminence** *...London's continuing pre-eminence among European financial centres... For those under 40 the pre-eminence of post-war US literature goes unquestioned.* ♦◇◇◇◇ ADJ-GRADED; N-UNCOUNT

pre-eminently. **Pre-eminently** means to a very great extent. *The party was pre-eminently the party of the landed interest.* ADV: ADV with v, ADV adj/adv, ADV n

pre-empt /priː empt/ **pre-empts, pre-empting, pre-empted.** If you **pre-empt** an action, you prevent it from happening by doing something which makes it pointless or impossible. *You can pre-empt pain by taking a painkiller at the first warning sign... He pre-empted any decision to sack him... The government pre-empted a threatened strike at the state-owned copper company.* ♦ **pre-emption** /priː empʃᵊn/ *...strategic plans which demanded pre-emption as the only method of averting defeat.* ♦◇◇◇◇ VERB; V n; N-UNCOUNT

pre-emptive /priː emptɪv/. A **pre-emptive** attack or strike is intended to weaken or damage an enemy or opponent, for example by destroying their weapons before they can do any harm. *Pitt wanted to cripple Spain's war-making ability by launching a pre-emptive strike against her South American treasure fleet... In a pre-emptive move the Interior Ministry arrested a number of suspected dissidents.* ADJ: usu ADJ n

preen /priːn/ **preens, preening, preened**

1 If someone **preens** themself, they spend a lot of time making themself look neat and attractive; used especially if you want to show that you disapprove of this behaviour or that you find it ridiculous and amusing. *50% of men under 35 spend at least 20 minutes preening themselves every morning in the bathroom... Bill turned to preen his beard and study his reflection in the dark mirror.* VERB PRAGMATICS; V pron-refl; V n

2 If someone **preens**, they think in a pleased way about how attractive, clever, or good at something they are; used showing disapproval. *She stood preening in their midst, delighted with the attention... He preened himself on the praise he had received... He disrobes like a preening prize fighter about to enter a ring.* VERB PRAGMATICS; V; V pron-refl *on* n; V-ing

3 When birds **preen** their feathers, they clean them and arrange them neatly using their beaks. *Rare birds, normally too shy to be seen, preen themselves right in front of your camera.* VERB; V pron-refl; Also V, V n

pre-existing; also spelled **preexisting.** A **pre-existing** situation or thing exists already or existed before something else. *...the pre-existing tensions between the two countries. ...people who have been infected in the course of their NHS treatment for a pre-existing illness.* ADJ: ADJ n

prefab /priːfæb/ **prefabs.** In British English, a **prefab** is a house built with parts which have been made in a factory and then quickly put together. *...some ugly Sixties prefabs.* N-COUNT

prefabricated /priːfæbrɪkeɪtɪd/. **Prefabricated** buildings are built with parts which have been made in a factory so that they can be easily carried and put together. *...high-quality, Scandinavian prefabricated wooden homes.* ADJ

preface /prefɪs/ **prefaces, prefacing, prefaced** ♦◇◇◇◇

1 A **preface** is an introduction at the beginning of a book, which explains what the book is about or why it was written. N-COUNT =foreword, introduction

2 If you **preface** an action or speech with something else, you do or say this other thing first. *I will preface what I am going to say with a few lines from Shakespeare... The president prefaced his remarks* VERB; V n *with* n; V n *by*-ing

by saying he has supported unemployment benefits all along.

prefect /priːfekt/ **prefects** ◆◇◇◇◇

1 In some British schools, a **prefect** is an older pupil who does special duties and helps the teachers to control the younger pupils. N-COUNT

2 In some countries, a **prefect** is the head of the local government administration or of a local government department. *...the prefect of the city. ...the police prefect for the district of Mehedinti.* N-COUNT

prefecture /priːfektʃəʳ/ **prefectures.** In some countries, administrative areas are called **prefectures**. *He was born in Yamagata prefecture, north of Tokyo.* N-COUNT: oft in names

prefer /prɪfɜːʳ/ **prefers, preferring, preferred.** If you **prefer** someone or something, you like that person or thing better than another, and so you are more likely to choose them if there is a choice. *Does he prefer a particular sort of music?... I became a teacher because I preferred books and people to politics... I prefer to go on self-catering holidays... I would prefer him to be with us next season... Bob prefers making original pieces rather than reproductions... The woodwork's green now. I preferred it blue... Her own preferred methods of exercise are hiking and long cycle rides.* ◆◆◆◆◇ VB: no cont; V n; V n to n; V to-inf; V n to-inf; V -ing; V n adj; V-ed; Also V that

preferable /prefrəbəl/. If you say that one thing is **preferable** to another, you mean that it is more desirable or suitable. *A big earthquake a long way off is preferable to a smaller one nearby... The hazards of the theatre seemed preferable to joining the family paint business... Was an evening with Peter in their company preferable to being left at home alone?* ♦ **preferably** /prefrəbli/ *Do something creative or take exercise, preferably in the fresh air.* ◆◆◇◇◇ ADJ-GRADED: usu v-link ADJ, usu ADJ to n/-ing, it v-link ADJ to-inf/that; ADV-GRADED: usu ADV with cl/group

preference /prefərəns/ **preferences** ◆◆◇◇◇

1 If you have a **preference** for something, you would like to have or do that thing rather than something else. *The Bill will allow parents the right to express a preference for the school their child attends... Many of these products were bought in preference to their own.* N-VAR: usu N for n

2 If you **give preference** to someone with a particular qualification or feature, you choose them rather than someone else. *The Pentagon has said it will give preference to companies with which it can do business electronically.* N-UNCOUNT: usu N to n =priority

preferential /prefərenʃəl/. If you get **preferential** treatment, you are treated better than other people and therefore have an advantage over them. *Despite her status, the Duchess will not be given preferential treatment.* ♦ **preferentially** *His face collapses when the baby preferentially reaches for the mother.* ◆◇◇◇◇ ADJ-GRADED: usu ADJ n =special; ADV-GRADED: ADV with v

preferment /prɪfɜːʳmənt/ **preferments. Preferment** is promotion to a better and more influential job; a formal word. *He was told by the governors that he could expect no further preferment.* N-VAR =advancement, promotion

prefigure /priːfɪgəʳ, AM -gjər/ **prefigures, prefiguring, prefigured.** If one thing **prefigures** another, it is a first indication which suggests or determines that the second thing will happen; a formal word. *The communist-built wall through Berlin was finally ruptured, prefiguring the disintegration of East Germany.* VERB; V n

prefix /priːfɪks/ **prefixes**

1 A **prefix** is a letter or group of letters, for example 'un-' or 'multi-', which is added to the beginning of a word in order to form a different word. For example, the prefix 'un-' is added to 'happy' to form 'unhappy'. Compare **affix** and **suffix**. N-COUNT

2 A **prefix** is one or more numbers or letters added to the beginning of a code number to indicate, for example, what area something belongs to. *To telephone from the US use the prefix 011 33 before the numbers given here... I soon learnt to read the licence plates' prefixes.* N-COUNT

prefixed /priːfɪkst/. A word or code number that **is prefixed** by one or more letters or numbers has those letters or numbers as its prefix. *Sulphur-containing compounds are often prefixed by the term 'thio', derived from the Greek word for sulphur... Calls to Dublin should now be prefixed with 010 3531.* V-PASSIVE; be V-ed by n; be V-ed with n

pregnancy /pregnənsi/ **pregnancies. Pregnancy** is the condition of being pregnant or the period of time during which a female is pregnant. *It would be wiser to cut out all alcohol during pregnancy... She was exhausted by eight pregnancies in 13 years.* ◆◆◆◇◇ N-VAR

pregnancy test, pregnancy tests. A **pregnancy test** is a medical test which women have to find out if they have become pregnant. N-COUNT

pregnant /pregnənt/ ◆◆◆◇◇

1 If a woman or female animal is **pregnant**, she has a baby or babies developing in her body. *Lena got pregnant and married... Tina was pregnant with their first daughter.* ADJ-GRADED

2 A **pregnant** silence or moment has a special meaning which is not obvious but which people are aware of. *There was a long, pregnant silence, which Mrs. Madrigal punctuated by reaching for the check. ...a deceptive peace, pregnant with invisible threats.* ADJ: ADJ n, v-link ADJ with n

preheat /priːhiːt/ **preheats, preheating, preheated.** If you **preheat** an oven, you switch it on and allow it to reach a certain temperature before you put food inside it. *Preheat the oven to 400 degrees... Bake in the preheated oven for 25 minutes or until golden brown.* ◆◇◇◇◇ VERB; V n; V-ed

prehistoric /priːhɪstɒrɪk, AM -tɔːr-/. **Prehistoric** people and things existed at a time before information was written down. *...the famous prehistoric cave paintings of Lascaux.* ◆◇◇◇◇ ADJ

prehistory /priːhɪstəri/. **Prehistory** is the time in history before any information was written down. N-UNCOUNT

pre-industrial. Pre-industrial refers to the time before machines were introduced to produce goods on a large scale. *...the transition from pre-industrial to industrial society.* ADJ: ADJ n =post-industrial

prejudge /priːdʒʌdʒ/ **prejudges, prejudging, prejudged.** If you **prejudge** a situation, you form an opinion about it before you know all the facts; a formal word. *They tried to prejudge the commission's findings.* VERB; V n; Also V

prejudice /predʒʊdɪs/ **prejudices, prejudicing, prejudiced** ◆◆◇◇◇

1 **Prejudice** is an unreasonable dislike of or preference for one group of people or thing over another. *There was a deep-rooted racial prejudice long before the two countries became rivals and went to war... There is widespread prejudice against workers over 45... He said he hoped the Swiss authorities would investigate the case thoroughly and without prejudice.* N-VAR: oft supp N, N against n =discrimination, bias

2 If you **prejudice** someone or something, you influence them in an unfair way. *I think your South American youth has prejudiced you... The report was held back for fear of prejudicing his trial... He claimed his case would be prejudiced if it became known he was refusing to answer questions.* VERB; V n

3 If someone **prejudices** another person's situation, they do something which makes it worse than it should be; a formal use. *Her study was not in any way intended to prejudice the future development of the college... They claim the council has prejudiced their health by failing to deal with asbestos.* VERB =damage, harm; V n

4 If you take an action **without prejudice to** an existing situation, your action does not change or harm that situation; a formal use. *I think we can say without prejudice to our position, let's get our arms around all the issues that'll be involved in autonomy.* PHRASE: PHR n

prejudiced /predʒʊdɪst/. A person who is **prejudiced** against someone has an unreasonable dislike of them. A person who is **prejudiced** in favour of someone has an unreasonable preference for them. *Some landlords and landladies are racially prejudiced... I like to think I'm not prejudiced.* ◆◇◇◇◇ ADJ-GRADED: usu v-link ADJ =biased

prejudicial /prẹdʒʊdɪʃəl/. If an action or situation is **prejudicial** to someone or something, it is harmful to them; a formal word. *You could face up to eight years in jail for spreading rumours considered prejudicial to security... The judge agreed with the prosecution that such information would be too prejudicial for the jury to hear.* ADJ-GRADED: usu v-link ADJ, oft ADJ *to* n

prelate /prẹlɪt/ **prelates.** A **prelate** is a clergyman of high rank, for example a bishop or an archbishop; a technical term. N-COUNT

preliminary /prɪlɪ̱mɪnri, AM -neri/ **preliminaries** ◆◆◇◇◇

1 **Preliminary** activities or discussions take place at the beginning of an event, often as a form of preparation. *Preliminary results show the Republican party with 11 percent of the vote... Preliminary talks on the future of the bases began yesterday.* ADJ: usu ADJ n

2 A **preliminary** is something that you do at the beginning of an activity, often as a form of preparation. *It had taken about ten minutes to cover the preliminaries... A background check is normally a preliminary to a presidential appointment.* N-COUNT: oft N *to* n/-ing

3 A **preliminary** is the first part of a competition to see who will go on to the main competition. *The winner of each preliminary goes through to the final.* N-COUNT

prelude /prẹlju:d, AM preɪlu:d/ **preludes** ◆◇◇◇◇

1 You can describe an event as a **prelude** to a more important event when it happens before it and acts as an introduction to it. *The protests in Brasov in 1987 are today seen as the prelude to last year's uprising against Ceausescu... The conference, which closed yesterday, was a prelude to a Communist Party Central Committee meeting.* N-COUNT: usu sing, usu N *to* n

2 A **prelude** is a short piece of music for the piano or organ. *...the famous E minor prelude of Chopin.* N-COUNT

premarital /pri:mæ̱rɪtəl/; also spelled **pre-marital**. **Premarital** means happening at some time before someone gets married. *I rejected the teaching that premarital sex was immoral.* ADJ: ADJ n

premature /prẹmətʃʊəʳ, AM pri̱:-/ ◆◆◇◇◇

1 Something that is **premature** happens earlier than usual or earlier than people expect. *Accidents are still the number one cause of premature death for Americans... His career was brought to a premature end by a succession of knee injuries. ...a twenty-four-year-old man who suffered from premature baldness.* ♦ **prematurely** *The war and the years in the harsh mountains had prematurely aged him... The heavy rain driving against the windows made the room prematurely dark.* ADJ-GRADED: usu ADJ n; ADV-GRADED: ADV with v, ADV adj

2 You can say that something is **premature** when it happens too early and is therefore inappropriate. *It now seems their optimism was premature... I think it's premature for restaurants to come out with that advice.* ♦ **prematurely** *Holmgren is careful not to celebrate prematurely.* ADJ-GRADED: usu v-link ADJ, oft *it* v-link ADJ to-inf; ADV-GRADED: usu ADV with v, also ADV adj

3 A **premature** baby is one that was born before the date when it was due to be born. *Even very young premature babies respond to their mother's presence... When my daughter Emma was born she was two and a half months premature.* ♦ **prematurely** *Danny was born prematurely, weighing only 3lb 3oz.* ADJ-GRADED; ADV-GRADED: ADV after v

premeditated /pri:mẹdɪteɪtɪd/. A **premeditated** crime is planned or thought about before it is done. *In a case of premeditated murder a life sentence is mandatory... The attack was premeditated and preplanned.* ADJ =deliberate, intentional ≠spontaneous

premeditation /pri:mẹdɪteɪʃən/. **Premeditation** is thinking about something or planning it before you actually do it; a formal word. *The judge finally concluded there was insufficient evidence of premeditation.* N-UNCOUNT

premenstrual /pri:mẹnstruəl/. **Premenstrual** is used to refer to the time immediately before menstruation and a woman's behaviour and feelings at this time. *...premenstrual symptoms.* ADJ: ADJ n

premenstrual syndrome. **Premenstrual syndrome** is used to refer to the problems, including strain and tiredness, that many women experience before menstruation. *About 70% of women suffer from premenstrual syndrome.* N-UNCOUNT =premenstrual tension, PMT

premenstrual tension. **Premenstrual tension** is the same as **premenstrual syndrome**. N-UNCOUNT =PMT

premier /prẹmiəʳ, AM prɪmɪ̱r/ **premiers** ◆◆◆◇◇

1 The leader of the government of a country is sometimes referred to as the country's **premier**. *...Australian premier Paul Keating.* N-COUNT

2 **Premier** is used to describe something that is considered to be the best or most important thing of a particular type. *...the country's premier opera company.* ADJ: ADJ n =principal

premiere /prẹmieəʳ, AM prɪmjẹr/ **premieres, premiering, premiered** ◆◆◇◇◇

1 The **premiere** of a new play or film is the first public performance of it. *A new Czechoslovak film has had its premiere at the Karlovy Vary film festival. ...a royal film premiere.* N-COUNT

2 When a film or show **premieres** or **is premiered**, it is shown to an audience for the first time. *The documentary premiered at the Jerusalem Film Festival... The opera is due to be premiered by ENO next year.* V-ERG: V; *be* V-ed

premiership /prẹmiəʳʃɪp, AM prɪmɪ̱r-/. The **premiership** of a leader of a government is the period of time during which they are the leader. *...the final years of Margaret Thatcher's premiership... So far, his premiership has been dominated by crisis-management.* ◆◇◇◇◇ N-SING

premise /prẹmɪs/ **premises;** also spelled **premiss** in British English for meaning 2. ◆◆◇◇◇

1 The **premises** of a business or an institution are all the buildings and land that it occupies on one site. *There is a kitchen on the premises... The business moved to premises in Brompton Road.* N-PLURAL: oft *on the* N

2 A **premise** is something that you suppose is true and that you use as a basis for developing an idea; a formal use. *The premise is that schools will work harder to improve if they must compete... The programme started from the premise that men and women are on equal terms in this society.* N-COUNT: oft N that =assumption, hypothesis

premised /prẹmɪst/. If a theory or attitude **is premised on** an idea or belief, that idea or belief has been used as the basis for it; a formal word. *All our activities are premised on the basis of 'Quality with Equality'.* V-PASSIVE: *be* V-ed *on* n

premiss /prẹmɪs/. See **premise**.

premium /pri̱:miəm/ **premiums** ◆◆◆◇◇

1 A **premium** is a sum of money that you pay regularly to an insurance company for an insurance policy. *It is too early to say whether insurance premiums will be affected.* N-COUNT

2 A **premium** is a sum of money that you have to pay for something in addition to the normal cost. *Even if customers want 'solutions', most are not willing to pay a premium for them... Callers are charged a premium rate of 48p a minute.* N-COUNT: usu sing, oft N n

3 **Premium** goods are of a higher than usual quality and are often expensive. *At the premium end of the market, business is booming. ...the most popular premium ice cream in this country.* ADJ: ADJ n =quality, luxury

4 If something is **at a premium**, it is wanted or needed, but is difficult to get or achieve. *If space is at a premium, choose adaptable furniture that won't fill the room.* PHRASES: usu v-link PHR =scarce

5 If you buy or sell something **at a premium**, you buy or sell it at a higher price than usual, for example because it is in short supply. *He eventually sold the shares back to the bank at a premium.* PHR after v

6 If you **place a high premium on** a quality or characteristic or **put a high premium on** it, you regard it as very important. *I place a high premium on what someone is like as a person... They put a high premium on prevention and primary care.* V inflects, PHR n

premium bond, premium bonds. In Britain, **premium bonds** are numbered tickets that are sold by the government. Each month, a computer randomly selects several numbers, and the people whose tickets have those numbers win money. N-COUNT

premonition /prẹmənɪʃən, AM pri:-/ **premonitions.** If you have a **premonition**, you have a ◆◇◇◇◇ N-COUNT feeling that something is going to happen, often something unpleasant. *He had an unshakable premonition that he would die. ...a real, genuine premonition of bad news.*

prenatal /priːneɪtᵊl/. **Prenatal** is used to describe things relating to the medical care of women during pregnancy. *I'd met her briefly in a prenatal class.* ADJ: usu ADJ n =antenatal ≠postnatal

preoccupation /priɒkjʊpeɪʃᵊn/ **preoccupations**
◆◇◇◇◇
1 If you have a **preoccupation with** something or someone, you keep thinking about them because they are important to you. *Karouzos's poetry shows a profound preoccupation with the Orthodox Church... In his preoccupation with Robyn, Crook had neglected everything.* N-COUNT: oft N with n
2 **Preoccupation** is a state of mind in which you think about something so much that you do not consider other things to be important. *It was hard for him to be aware of her; he kept sinking back into black preoccupation.* N-UNCOUNT =obsession

preoccupied /priɒkjʊpaɪd/. Someone who is **preoccupied** is thinking a lot about something or someone, and so hardly notices other things. *Tom Banbury was preoccupied with the missing Shepherd child and did not want to devote time to the new murder... She looked very preoccupied.* ◆◇◇◇◇ ADJ-GRADED: usu v-link ADJ, oft ADJ with/by n

preoccupy /priɒkjʊpaɪ/ **preoccupies, preoccupying, preoccupied.** If something **is preoccupying** you, you are thinking about it a lot. *The Persian Gulf crisis is preoccupying both American citizens and their leaders... Crime and the fear of crime preoccupy the community.* VERB V n

preordained /priːɔːʳdeɪnd/. If you say that something is **preordained**, you mean you believe it to be happening in the way that has been decided by God or by fate; a formal word. *...the belief that our actions are the unfolding of a preordained destiny.* ADJ =predestined

prep /prep/. In some British private schools, **prep** is the name given to school work that children do in the evening after school has finished. *Anne struggled to help Peter and Zara with their prep.* ◆◇◇◇◇ N-UNCOUNT =homework

pre-packaged. **Pre-packaged** foods have been prepared in advance and put in plastic or cardboard packages before they are sold. *...pre-packaged duck and orange sauce.* ADJ

pre-packed. **Pre-packed** goods are packed or wrapped before they are sent to the shop where they are sold. *...pre-packed bacon.* ADJ

prepaid /priːpeɪd/; also spelled **pre-paid**. **Prepaid** items are paid for in advance, before the time when you would normally pay for them. *Return the enclosed Donation Form today in the prepaid envelope provided. ...prepaid funerals.* ADJ: usu ADJ n

preparation /prepəreɪʃᵊn/ **preparations**
◆◆◆◇◇
1 **Preparation** is the process of getting something ready for use or for a particular purpose or making arrangements for something. *Rub the surface of the wood in preparation for the varnish... Few things distracted the Pastor from the preparation of his weekly sermons... Behind any successful event lay months of preparation.* N-UNCOUNT: usu with supp, oft N for/of n
2 **Preparations** are all the arrangements that are made for a future event. *The United States is making preparations for a large-scale airlift of 1,200 American citizens... Final preparations are under way for celebrations to mark German unification.* N-PLURAL
3 A **preparation** is a mixture that has been prepared for use as food, medicine, or a cosmetic; a formal use. *...anti-ageing creams and sensitive-skin preparations.* N-COUNT

preparatory /prɪpærətri, AM -tɔːri/
◆◇◇◇◇
1 **Preparatory** actions are done before doing something else as a form of preparation or as an introduction; a formal use. *At least a year's preparatory work will be necessary before building can start. ...preparatory talks for this week's summit in the Maldive Islands.* ADJ: usu ADJ n =preliminary
2 If one action is done **preparatory to** another, it is done before the other action, usually as preparation for it; a formal use. *Sloan cleared his throat preparatory to speaking... She lit the oven, preparatory to putting the pie into it.* PHR-PREP

preparatory school, preparatory schools. A **preparatory school** is the same as a **prep school**. N-VAR

prepare /prɪpeəʳ/ **prepares, preparing, prepared**
◆◆◆◆◇
1 If you **prepare** something, you make it ready for something that is going to happen. *Two technicians were preparing a videotape recording of last week's programme... On average each report requires 1,000 hours to prepare... The crew of the Iowa has been preparing the ship for storage.* VERB V n V n for n
2 If you **prepare** for an event or action that will happen soon, you get yourself ready for it or make the necessary arrangements. *He told the deputies that they needed to prepare for new elections for the Supreme Soviet... He had to go back to his hotel and prepare to catch a train for New York... His doctor had told him to prepare himself for surgery.* VERB =get V for n V to-inf V pron-refl for n Also V
3 When you **prepare** food, you get it ready to be eaten, for example by cooking it. *She made her way to the kitchen, hoping to find someone preparing dinner... The best way of preparing the nuts is to rehydrate them by soaking overnight.* VERB V n

prepared /prɪpeəʳd/
◆◆◆◆◇
1 If you are **prepared** to do something, you are willing to do it if necessary. *Are you prepared to take industrial action?... Members of the KGB service were only prepared to take orders from the President.* ADJ: v-link ADJ to-inf =willing
2 If you are **prepared for** something that you think is going to happen, you are ready for it. *Police are prepared for large numbers of demonstrators... I'm well prepared for a 12-round fight.* ADJ: v-link ADJ for n ≠unprepared
3 You can describe something as **prepared** when it has been done or made beforehand, so that it is ready when it is needed. *He ended his prepared statement by thanking the police.* ADJ: ADJ n

preparedness /prɪpeərɪdnəs/. **Preparedness** is the state of being ready for something to happen, especially for war or a disaster; a formal word. *The situation in the capital forced them to maintain military preparedness. ...red alert, the maximum state of preparedness.* N-UNCOUNT =readiness

preponderance /prɪpɒndərəns/. If there is a **preponderance of** one type of person or thing in a group, there is more of that type than of any other. *...a preponderance of bright, middle-class children in one group. ...Bath, with its preponderance of small businesses.* N-SING: usu N of n

preposition /prepəzɪʃᵊn/ **prepositions.** A **preposition** is a word such as 'by', 'for', 'into', or 'with' which usually has a noun group as its object. *There is nothing in the rules of grammar to suggest that ending a sentence with a preposition is wrong.* N-COUNT

prepositional phrase /prepəzɪʃənᵊl freɪz/ **prepositional phrases.** A **prepositional phrase** is a structure consisting of a preposition and its object. Examples are 'on the table' and 'by the sea'. N-COUNT

preposterous /prɪpɒstᵊrəs/. If you describe something as **preposterous**, you mean that it is extremely unreasonable and foolish. *The whole idea was preposterous. ...their preposterous claim that they had unearthed a plot.* ◆◇◇◇◇ ADJ-GRADED =absurd, ludicrous
♦ **preposterously** *Some prices are preposterously high.* ADV-GRADED: usu ADV adj/adv

preppy /prepi/ **preppies**
1 **Preppies** are young people, especially in America, who have often been to a prep school or Ivy League University, and who are conventional and conservative in their attitudes, behaviour, and style of dress. *...Rick Corse, a 30-year-old preppy.* N-COUNT
2 If you describe someone or their clothes, attitudes, or behaviour as **preppy**, you mean that they are like preppies, or trying to be like preppies. *I couldn't believe how straight-looking he was, how preppy. ...a preppy collar and tie.* ADJ-GRADED

pre-prandial /priː prændiəl/. You use **pre-prandial** to refer to things you do or have before a meal; a formal word. *The elegant Palm Terrace* ADJ: ADJ n ≠post-prandial

Lounge is perfect for cocktails or pre-prandial drinks.

prep school, prep schools ◆◇◇◇◇

1 In Britain, a **prep school** is a private school where children are educated until the age of 11 or 13. N-VAR: oft prep N

2 In the United States, a **prep school** is a private secondary school for students who intend to go to college after they leave. *...an exclusive prep school in Washington.* N-VAR

prepubescent /priːpjuːbesᵊnt/. **Prepubescent** means relating to the time just before someone reaches puberty; a formal word. *Prepubescent boys and girls look very similar in terms of size and the amount of muscle and fat that they carry.* ADJ: usu ADJ n

prequel /priːkwəl/ **prequels.** A **prequel** is a film that is made about an earlier stage of a story or a character's life when the later part of it has already been made into a successful film. *...'Fire Walk With Me', David Lynch's prequel to the overhyped TV series 'Twin Peaks'..* N-COUNT: oft N *to* n

Pre-Raphaelite /priː ræfəlaɪt/ **Pre-Raphaelites**

1 The **Pre-Raphaelites** were a group of British painters in the nineteenth century who concentrated on themes from medieval history, romantic myth, and folklore. N-COUNT

2 **Pre-Raphaelite** art was created by the Pre-Raphaelites. *...a number of pre-Raphaelite murals designed by Dante Gabriel Rossetti in 1857.* ADJ: ADJ n

3 If you say that a woman looks **Pre-Raphaelite**, you mean that she looks like a character in a Pre-Raphaelite painting, for example because she has long wavy hair. ADJ

pre-recorded. Something that is **pre-recorded** has been recorded in advance so that it can be broadcast or played later. *...a pre-recorded interview.* ADJ

prerequisite /priːrekwɪzɪt/ **prerequisites.** If one thing is a **prerequisite** for another, it must happen or exist before the other thing is possible. *Good self-esteem is a prerequisite for a happy life... Party membership was an essential prerequisite of a successful career.* ◆◇◇◇◇ N-COUNT: N *for/of* n =precondition

prerogative /prɪrɒgətɪv/ **prerogatives.** If something is the **prerogative** of a particular person or group, it is a privilege or a power that only they have; a formal word. *Constitutional changes are exclusively the prerogative of the parliament... It is your prerogative to stop seeing that particular therapist and find another one.* ◆◇◇◇◇ N-COUNT: usu with poss

presage /presɪdʒ/ **presages, presaging, presaged.** If something **presages** a situation or event, it is considered to be a warning or sign of what is about to happen; a formal word. *...the dawn's loud chorus that seemed to presage a bright hot summer's day.* VERB V n

Presbyterian /prezbɪtɪəriən/ **Presbyterians** ◆◇◇◇◇

1 **Presbyterian** means belonging or relating to a Protestant church, found especially in Scotland, which is governed by a body of official people all of equal rank. *...a Presbyterian minister. ...long Presbyterian sermons.* ADJ

2 A **Presbyterian** is a member of the Presbyterian church. N-COUNT

presbytery /prezbɪtri, AM -teri/ **presbyteries.** A **presbytery** is the house in which a Roman Catholic priest lives. N-COUNT

pre-school, pre-schools; also spelled **preschool.** Pronounced /priː skuːl/ for meaning 1, and /priː skuːl/ for meaning 2.

1 **Pre-school** is used to describe things relating to the care and education of children before they reach the age when they have to go to school; used in written English. *Looking after pre-school children is very tiring... The Halsey Report emphasized the value of a pre-school education.* ADJ: ADJ n

2 In the United States, a **pre-school** is a school for children between the ages of 2 and 5. *Children graduate to the kindergarten, then pre-school, and then school.* N-VAR

preschooler /priːskuːləʳ/ **preschoolers;** also spelled **pre-schooler.** Children who are no longer babies but are not yet old enough to go to school are sometimes referred to as **preschoolers**; used in written English. *...preschoolers and toddlers.* N-COUNT: usu pl

prescient /presiənt, AM preʃ-/. If you say that someone or something was **prescient**, you mean that they were able to know or predict what was going to happen in the future; a formal word. *...'Bob Roberts', an eerily prescient comedy about a populist multimillionaire political candidate.* ADJ-GRADED =prophetic

♦ **prescience** *Over the years he's demonstrated a certain prescience in foreign affairs.* N-UNCOUNT

prescribe /prɪskraɪb/ **prescribes, prescribing, prescribed** ◆◆◇◇◇

1 If a doctor **prescribes** medicine or treatment for you, he or she tells you what medicine or treatment to have. *Our doctor diagnosed a throat infection and prescribed antibiotic and junior aspirin... She took twice the prescribed dose of sleeping tablets... The law allows doctors to prescribe contraception to the under 16s.* VERB V n V-ed Also V n n

2 If a person or set of laws or rules **prescribes** an action or duty, they state that it must be carried out; a formal use. *...article II of the constitution, which prescribes the method of electing a president... Alliott told Singleton he was passing the sentence prescribed by law.* VERB V n V-ed

prescription /prɪskrɪpʃᵊn/ **prescriptions** ◆◆◇◇◇

1 A **prescription** is the piece of paper on which your doctor writes an order for medicine and which you give to a chemist in exchange for the medicine. *You will have to take your prescription to a chemist.* N-COUNT

2 A **prescription** is a medicine which a doctor has told you to take. *I'm not sleeping even with the prescription Ackerman gave me.* N-COUNT ● If a medicine is available **on prescription**, you can get it from a chemist if a doctor gives you a prescription for it. *The drug is available on prescription only.* PHRASE: usu PHR after v ≠over the counter

3 A **prescription** is a proposal or a plan which gives ideas about how to solve a problem or improve a situation. *There's not much difference in the economic prescriptions of Ireland's two main political parties... President Clinton's proposed prescription for reform may not be palatable to many.* N-COUNT

prescriptive /prɪskrɪptɪv/. A **prescriptive** approach to something involves telling people what they should do, rather than simply giving suggestions or describing what is done; a formal word. *...prescriptive attitudes to language on the part of teachers... The psychologists insist, however, that they are not being prescriptive.* ADJ-GRADED

presence /prezᵊns/ **presences** ◆◆◆◆◇

1 Someone's **presence** in a place is the fact that they are there; a formal use. *They argued that his presence in the village could only stir up trouble... Her Majesty later honoured the Headmaster with her presence at lunch.* N-SING: with poss ≠absence

2 If you say that someone has **presence**, you mean that they impress people by their appearance and manner. *They do not seem to have the vast, authoritative presence of those great men... Hendrix's stage presence appealed to thousands of teenage rebels.* N-UNCOUNT: oft supp N

3 A **presence** is a person or creature that you cannot see, but that you are aware of; a literary use. *The forest was dark and silent, haunted by shadows and unseen presences... She started to be affected by the ghostly presence she could feel in the house.* N-COUNT

4 If a country has a military **presence** in another country, it has some of its armed forces there. *The Philippine government wants the US to maintain a military presence in Southeast Asia.* N-SING: usu supp N

5 If you refer to the **presence** of a substance in another thing, you mean that it is in that thing. *The somewhat acid flavour is caused by the presence of lactic acid. ...the presence of a carcinogen in the water... Although the fluid presents no symptoms to the patient, its presence can be detected by a test.* N-UNCOUNT: with poss ≠absence

6 If someone or something **makes** their **presence felt**, they do something which forces people to pay attention to them. *Rather than politely lobbying politicians, Gay Dignity will be making its presence felt through demonstrations.* PHRASES *make* inflects

7 If you are **in** someone's **presence**, you are in the PHR after v,

same place as that person, and are close enough to them to be seen or heard. *The talks took place in the presence of a diplomatic observer.* v-link PHR

8 If you say that someone had the **presence of mind** to do something, you approve of them because they were able to think and act calmly in a difficult situation. *He had the presence of mind to put his emergency oxygen tube in his mouth.* usu PHR after v PRAGMATICS

present 1 existing or happening now

present /prezənt/ ◆◆◆◆◇

1 You use **present** to describe things and people that exist now, rather than those that existed in the past or those that may exist in the future. *He has brought much of the present crisis on himself. ...the government's present economic difficulties... It has been skilfully renovated by the present owners... No statement can be made at the present time.* ADJ: ADJ n =current

2 **The present** is the period of time that we are in now and the things that are happening now. *...his struggle to reconcile the past with the present. ...continuing right up to the present... Then her thoughts would switch to the present.* N-SING: the N

3 The **present** tenses of a verb are the ones used to talk about things that happen regularly or situations that exist at this time. In English, the simple present tense is sometimes called the **present tense**. The present tense uses the base form or the 's' form of a verb, as in 'I play tennis twice a week' and 'He works in a bank'. ADJ: ADJ n

4 A situation that exists **at present** exists now, although it may change. *There is no way at present of predicting which individuals will develop the disease... At present children under 14 are not permitted in bars.* PHRASES PHR with cl/group =at the moment

5 **The present day** is the period of history that we are in now. *...Western European art from the period of Giotto to the present day. ...monastic music of the present day.* prep PHR =today

6 Something that exists or will be done **for the present** exists now or will continue for a while, although the situation may change later. *The ministers had expressed the unanimous view that sanctions should remain in place for the present.* PHR with cl =for the time being

7 If you say **'There's no time like the present'**, you are suggesting to someone that they should do something now, not later. *Don't wait until New Year to resolve to organise your life. There's no time like the present.* PRAGMATICS

present 2 being somewhere

present /prezənt/ ◆◆◆◆◇

1 If someone is **present at** an event, they are there. *The president was not present at the meeting... Nearly 85 per cent of men are present at the birth of their children... The whole family was present.* ADJ: v-link ADJ, oft ADJ at n ≠absent

2 If something, especially a substance or disease, is **present in** something else, it exists within that thing. *This special form of vitamin D is naturally present in breast milk... One theory is that the infection has been present in humans for a very long time... If the gene is present, a human embryo will go on to develop as a male.* ADJ: v-link ADJ, oft ADJ in n ≠absent

present 3 gift

present /prezənt/ **presents.** A **present** is something that you give to someone, for example at Christmas or when you visit them. *The carpet was a wedding present from the Prime Minister... I bought a birthday present for my mother... This book would make a great Christmas present.* ◆◆◇◇◇ N-COUNT =gift

present 4 verb uses

present /prɪzent/ **presents, presenting, presented** ◆◆◆◆◇

1 If you **present** someone **with** something such as a prize or document, or if you **present** it to them, you formally give it to them. *President Reagan presented Ford with the Medal of Freedom... Prince Michael of Kent presented the prizes... The group intended to present this petition to China's parliament.* ♦ **presentation** *Then came the presentation of the awards by the Queen Mother.* VERB V n with n V n V n to n N-UNCOUNT: usu N of n

2 If something **presents** a difficulty, challenge, or opportunity, it causes it or provides it. *This presents a problem for many financial consumers... The future is going to be one that presents many challenges... This summer school presents an opportunity to experience all aspects of dance... Public policy on the family presents liberals with a dilemma.* VERB V n V n with n Also V n to n

3 If an opportunity or problem **presents** itself, it occurs, often when you do not expect it. *Their colleagues insulted them whenever the opportunity presented itself... A further obstacle has presented itself, however.* VERB V pron-refl

4 When you **present** information, you give it to people in a formal way. *We spend the time collating and presenting the information in a variety of chart forms... We presented three options to the unions for discussion... In effect, Parsons presents us with a beguilingly simple outline of social evolution.* ♦ **presentation, presentations** *...in his first presentation of the theory to the Berlin Academy. ...a fair presentation of the facts to a jury... No amount of slick presentation can disguise the gap between what the government promised and what it has delivered.* VERB V n V n to n V n with n N-VAR: oft N of n

5 If you **present** someone or something in a particular way, you describe them in that way. *The government has presented these changes as major reforms... The British like to present themselves as a nation of dog-lovers... In Europe, Aga Khan III presented himself in a completely different light.* VERB V n as n V n in n

6 The way you **present yourself** is the way you speak and act when meeting new people. *...all those tricks which would help him to present himself in a more confident way in public.* VERB V pron-refl prep/adv

7 If someone or something **presents** a particular appearance or image, that is how they appear or try to appear. *The small group of onlookers presented a pathetic sight... But some feel in presenting a more professional image the party risks losing its radical edge and its individuality. ...presenting a calm and dignified face to the world at large.* VERB V n V n to n

8 If you **present yourself** somewhere, you officially arrive there, for example for an appointment. *She was told to present herself at the Town Hall at 11.30 for the induction ceremony... We presented ourselves to the authorities promptly.* VERB V pron-refl prep/adv

9 If someone **presents** a programme on television or radio, they introduce each item in it. *She presents a monthly magazine programme on the BBC.* VERB V n

10 When someone **presents** something such as a production of a play or an exhibition, they organize it. *The Lyric Theatre is presenting a new production of 'Over the Bridge'.* VERB V n

11 If you **present** someone **to** someone else, often someone important, you formally introduce them. *Fox stepped forward, welcomed him in Malay, and presented him to Jack... Allow me to present my wife's cousin, Mr Zachary Colenso.* VERB =introduce V n to n V n

12 See also **presentation.**

presentable /prɪzentəbəl/

1 If you say that someone looks **presentable**, you mean that they look fairly tidy or attractive. *She managed to make herself presentable in time for work. ...wearing his most presentable suit.* ADJ-GRADED =respectable

2 If you describe something as **presentable**, you mean that it is acceptable or quite good. *His score of 29 had helped Leicestershire reach a presentable total... Sometimes when I performed in New Zealand, I was doing a very presentable job.* ADJ-GRADED =respectable

presentation /prezənteɪʃən, AM priːzen-/ **presentations** ◆◆◇◇◇

1 **Presentation** is the appearance of something, which someone has worked to create. *We serve traditional French food cooked in a lighter way, keeping the presentation simple... Check the presentation. Get it properly laid out with a title page.* N-UNCOUNT

2 A **presentation** is a formal event at which someone is given a prize or award. *...after receiving his award at a presentation in London yesterday. ...at the presentation ceremony.* N-COUNT

3 When someone gives a **presentation**, they give a formal talk, often in order to sell something or get support for a proposal. *James Watson, Philip Mayo and I gave a slide and video presentation... I always* N-COUNT

ask how much time I have to make my presentation. ...a business presentation.

4 A **presentation** is something that is performed in front of an audience, for example a play or a ballet; a formal use. *...Blackpool Opera House's presentation of Buddy, the musical.* N-COUNT: usu with supp =production

5 See also **present**.

present-day; also spelled **present day**. ◆◇◇◇◇ **Present-day** things, situations, and people exist at the time in history we are now in. *Even by present-day standards these were large aircraft. ...a huge area of northern India, stretching from present-day Afghanistan to Bengal. ...present-day champions of the cause.* ADJ: ADJ n

presenter /prɪzentəʳ/ **presenters.** ◆◆◇◇◇ A radio or television **presenter** is a person who introduces the items in a particular programme; used mainly in British English. The usual American word is **anchorman** or **anchorwoman**. *...the television presenter Esther Rantzen... Marcel Berlins is the presenter of the BBC radio programme Law in Action.* N-COUNT

presentiment /prɪzentɪmənt/ **presentiments.** A **presentiment** is a feeling that a particular event, for example someone's death, will soon take place; a formal word. *I had a presentiment that he represented a danger to me... He had a presentiment of disaster.* N-COUNT: usu N that, N of n

presently /prezəntli/ ◆◇◇◇◇

1 If you say that something is **presently** happening, you mean that it is happening now. *She is presently developing a number of projects... The island is presently uninhabited... He is presently the medical director for the Fellowship of World Christians.* ADV: ADV before v, ADV group =at present, currently

2 You use **presently** to indicate that something happened quite a short time after the time or event that you have just mentioned; used in written English. *He was shown to a small office. Presently, a young woman in a white coat came in... 'You're not looking too well, Thomas,' he said presently.* ADV: ADV with cl

3 If you say that something will happen **presently**, you mean that it will happen quite soon; a formal use. *'Who's Agnes?'—'You'll be meeting her presently.'... 'Just take it easy,' David said. 'You'll feel better presently.'* ADV: ADV after v =shortly

present participle, present participles. The **present participle** of a verb is the form which ends in '-ing'. Present participles are used to form continuous tenses, as in 'She was wearing a neat blue suit'. They are often nouns, as in 'I hate cooking' and 'Cooking can be fun'. Many of them can be used like an adjective in front of a noun, as in 'their smiling faces'. N-COUNT

present perfect. The **present perfect** tenses of a verb are the ones used to talk about things which happened before the time you are speaking or writing but are relevant to the present situation or are still happening. The simple present perfect tense uses 'have' or 'has' and the past participle of the verb, as in 'They have already decided what to do'. ADJ: ADJ n

preservationist /prezəʳveɪʃənɪst/ **preservationists.** A **preservationist** is someone who takes action to preserve something such as historic buildings or an area of countryside. *The house fell into disrepair but a group of preservationists have reconstructed the roofs.* N-COUNT

preservation order, preservation orders. In Britain, a **preservation order** is an official order that preserves the condition of something such as a historic building or an area of land and makes it illegal for anyone to alter its appearance or destroy it. *The entire city is under a preservation order. ...a tree preservation order.* N-COUNT

preservative /prɪzɜːʳvətɪv/ **preservatives.** ◆◇◇◇◇ A **preservative** is a chemical that prevents things from decaying. Some preservatives are added to food, and others are used to treat wood or metal. *Nitrates are used as preservatives in food manufacture... Though the panels come pre-treated, they needed a final sealing with two coats of preservative.* N-MASS

preserve /prɪzɜːʳv/ **preserves, preserving, preserved** ◆◆◆◇◇

1 If you **preserve** a situation or condition, you make sure that it remains as it is, and does not change or end. *We will do everything to preserve peace... The meeting will be about squeezing in more students while preserving standards.* VERB =maintain; V n ♦ **preservation** /prezəʳveɪʃən/ *...the preservation of the status quo.* N-UNCOUNT =maintenance

2 If you **preserve** something, you take action to save it or protect it from damage or decay. *We need to preserve the forest... Conservation is an issue which gets a lot of attention these days - whether it means preserving old buildings, or protecting the environment. ...perfectly preserved medieval houses.* VERB =conserve ≠destroy; V n; V-ed ♦ **preservation** *...the preservation of buildings of architectural or historic interest.* N-UNCOUNT

3 If you **preserve** food, you treat it in order to prevent it from decaying so that you can store it for a long time. *I like to make puree, using only enough sugar to preserve the plums. ...preserved ginger in syrup.* VERB; V n; V-ed

4 **Preserves** are foods such as jam and marmalade that are made by cooking fruit with a large amount of sugar so that they can be stored for a long time. N-PLURAL

5 If you say that a job or activity is the **preserve of** a particular person or group of people, you mean that they are the only ones who take part in it. *The making and conduct of foreign policy is largely the preserve of the president... With the menfolk away at war, women got their first crack at the male preserves of employment and sport.* N-COUNT: usu N of n =domain

6 A nature **preserve** is an area of land or water where animals are protected from hunters. *...Pantanal, one of the world's great wildlife preserves.* N-COUNT: usu supp N =reserve

preset /priːset/ **presets, presetting;** also spelled **pre-set**. The form **preset** is used in the present tense and is the past tense and past participle. If a piece of equipment **is preset**, its controls have been set in advance of the time you want it to work. *...a computerised timer that can be preset to a variety of programs... Bake the cake in a preset oven.* VB: usu passive; be V-ed; V-ed

preside /prɪzaɪd/ **presides, presiding, presided.** ◆◆◇◇◇ If you **preside over** a meeting or an event, you are in charge or act as the chairperson. *The PM returned to Downing Street to preside over a meeting of his inner Cabinet... He presided at the trial of the Maguire Seven... The presiding officer ruled that the motion was out of order.* VERB; V over/at n; V-ing

presidency /prezɪdənsi/ **presidencies.** ◆◆◆◇◇ The **presidency** of a country or organization is the position of being the president or the period of time during which someone is president. *Britain will support him as a candidate for the presidency of the organisation... Poverty had declined during his presidency.* N-COUNT: oft N of n, poss N

president /prezɪdənt/ **presidents** ◆◆◆◆◆

1 The **president** of a country that has no king or queen is the person who has the highest political position and is the leader of the country. *...President Mubarak... The White House says the president would veto the bill.* N-TITLE; N-COUNT: oft the N; N-VOC

2 The **president** of an organization is the person who has the highest position in it. *Research and marketing operations will be Mr. Furlaud's job as president of the new company. ...Alexandre de Merode, the president of the medical commission.* N-COUNT: usu N of n

president-elect. ◆◆◇◇◇ The **president-elect** is the person who has been elected as an organization or country's president, but who has not yet taken office. *...one of the president-elect's best proposals during the campaign.* N-SING

presidential /prezɪdenʃəl/. ◆◆◆◆◇ **Presidential** activities or things relate or belong to a president. *...campaigning for Peru's presidential election... There are several presidential candidates.* ADJ: ADJ n

presidium /prɪsɪdiəm/; also spelled **praesidium**. In Communist countries, a **presidium** is a committee which takes policy decisions on behalf of a larger group such as a parliament. N-SING

press /pres/ **presses, pressing, pressed** ◆◆◆◆◆

1 If you **press** something somewhere, you push it firmly against something else. *He pressed his back against the door... They pressed the silver knife into the cake.* VERB V n *against* n V n prep

2 If you **press** a button or switch, you push it with your finger in order to make a machine or device work. *Drago pressed a button and the door closed... There was no-one at the reception desk, so he pressed a bell for service.* ► Also a noun. *...a TV which rises from a table at the press of a button.* VERB V n N-COUNT: usu sing

3 If you **press** something or **press down on** it, you push hard against it with your foot or hand. *The engine stalled. He pressed the accelerator hard... She stood up and leaned forward with her hands pressing down on the desk.* VERB V n V adv Also V *on* n

4 If you **press for** something, you try hard to persuade someone to give it to you or to agree to it. *Police might now press for changes in the law... They had pressed for their children to be taught French.* VERB =push V *for* n V *for* n to-inf

5 If you **press** someone, you try hard to persuade them to do something or to tell you something. *Trade unions are pressing him to stand firm... Mr King seems certain to be pressed for further details... She smiles coyly when pressed about her private life.* VERB V n to-inf be V-ed *for/about* n Also V n *into* n/-ing

6 If someone **presses** their claim, demand, or point, they state it in a very forceful way. *The protest campaign has used mass strikes and demonstrations to press its demands... His officials have visited Washington to press their case for economic aid.* VERB V n

7 If an unpleasant feeling such as guilt, sadness, or anxiety **presses on** you, it worries you very much and you are always thinking about it. *The weight of irrational guilt pressed on her... Right now, I've got other problems that are pressing on me.* VERB V *on* n

8 If you **press** something **on** someone, you give it to them and insist that they take it. *All I had was money, which I pressed on her reluctant mother... Food and cigarettes were pressed on him.* VERB V n *on* n

9 If you **press** clothes, you iron them in order to get rid of the creases. *Vera pressed his shirt... There's a couple of dresses to be pressed. ...clean, neatly pressed, conservative clothes.* VERB =iron V n V-ed

10 If you **press** fruits or vegetables, you squeeze them or crush them, usually in order to extract the juice. *The grapes are hand-picked and pressed... I pressed the juice of half a lemon into a glass of water. ...1 clove fresh garlic, pressed or diced.* VERB be V-ed V n V-ed

11 Newspapers are referred to as **the press**. *Today the British press is full of articles on India's new prime minister. ...freedom of the Press... Press reports say the cargo was bound for Iran.* N-SING-COLL: *the* N

12 Journalists are referred to as **the press**. *Christie looked relaxed and calm as he faced the press afterwards... A meeting was promised, but the Press was not admitted.* N-SING-COLL: *the* N =reporters

13 A **press** or a **printing press** is a machine used for printing books, newspapers, and leaflets. *...the invention of the printing press... He was writing the book up to the moment the presses rolled.* N-COUNT

14 See also **pressed, pressing**.

15 If someone or something **gets a bad press**, they are criticized, especially in the newspapers, on television, or on radio. If they **get a good press**, they are praised. *...the bad press that career women consistently get in this country... Men get more bad press in her new novel.* PHRASES V inflects

16 If you **press charges** against someone, you make an official accusation against them which has to be decided in a court of law. *I could have pressed charges against him... Police have announced they will not be pressing charges.* V inflects, oft PHR *against* n

17 When a newspaper or magazine **goes to press**, an edition of it starts to be printed. *We check prices at the time of going to press... As this column went to press, I learnt that the man had died.* V inflects

18 If something or someone is **pressed into service** as something or to do something, they are used temporarily as that thing or to do that thing. *The local bar has been pressed into service as a school... Kenny had been pressed into service to guard the door.* V inflects

press ahead. See **press on** 1 PHRASAL VERB

press on or **press ahead** PHRASAL VERB

1 If you **press on** or **press ahead**, you continue with a task or activity in a determined way, and do not allow any problems or difficulties to delay you. *Organizers of the strike are determined to press on... He was persuaded by his advisers to press ahead... Poland pressed on with economic reform.* =continue V P V P *with* n

2 If you **press on**, you continue with a journey, even though it is becoming more difficult or more dangerous. *I considered turning back, but it was getting late, so I pressed on.* =go on V P

press agency, press agencies. A country's **press agency** is an organization that gathers news from that country and supplies it to journalists from all over the world. *The Saudi Press Agency reported that 29 people were injured.* N-COUNT

press agent, press agents. A **press agent** is a person who is employed by a famous person to give information about that person to the press. *The child actor's press agent says: 'He does not talk to the press on such matters.'* N-COUNT: oft with poss

press box, press boxes. The **press box** at a sports ground is a room or area which is reserved for journalists to watch sporting events. N-COUNT: usu *the* N in sing

press conference, press conferences. A **press conference** is a meeting held by a famous or important person in which they answer journalists' questions. *She gave her reaction to his release at a press conference... Botham called a Press conference and announced his resignation.* ◆◆◇◇◇ N-COUNT

press corps; press corps. is both the singular and plural form. In American English, the **press corps** is a group of reporters who are all working in the same place. *David McNeil is travelling with the White House press corps.* N-COUNT-COLL: usu *the* N

pressed /prest/. If you say that you are **pressed for time** or **pressed for money**, you mean that you do not have enough time or money at the moment. *Are you pressed for time, Mr Bayliss? If not, I suggest we have lunch.* • See also **hard-pressed**. ADJ-GRADED: v-link ADJ, usu ADJ *for* n

press gallery, press galleries. The **press gallery** is the area in a parliament which is reserved for journalists who report on the parliament's activities. N-COUNT: usu *the* N in sing

press-gang, press-gangs, press-ganging, press-ganged

1 If you **are press-ganged into** doing something, you are made or persuaded to do it, even though you do not really want to. *I was press-ganged into working in that business... She was a volunteer, she hadn't had to be press-ganged.* VB: usu passive =force be V-ed *into* -ing/n be V-ed

2 If civilians **are press-ganged**, they are captured and forced to join the army or navy. *They left their villages to evade being press-ganged into the army... The government denies that the women were press-ganged.* ♦ **press-ganging** *...the press-ganging of young people into the country's armed forces.* VB: usu passive be V-ed *into* n be V-ed N-SING: *the* N *of* n

3 In former times, a **press-gang** was a group of men who used to capture boys and men and force them to join the navy. *The navy resorted to the press-gang.* N-COUNT

pressing /presɪŋ/. ◆◇◇◇◇

1 A **pressing** problem, need, or issue has to be dealt with immediately. *It is one of the most pressing problems facing this country... There is a pressing need for more funds.* ADJ-GRADED: usu ADJ n =urgent

2 See also **press**.

pressman /presmæn/ **pressmen.** A **pressman** is a reporter, especially a man, who works for a newspaper or magazine. *There were television crews and pressmen from all around the world.* N-COUNT =reporter, newspaperman

press officer, press officers. A **press officer** is a person who is employed by an organization to give information about that organization to the press. *...the Press Officer of the Bavarian Government.* ◆◇◇◇◇ N-COUNT

press release, press releases. A **press release** is a written statement about a matter of public interest which is given to the press by an organization concerned with the matter. *The government had put out a press release naming the men.* ◆◇◇◇◇ N-COUNT

press stud, press studs. In British English, a **press stud** is a small metal fastener for clothes, made up of two parts which can be pressed together. The American term is **snap fastener** or **snap**. N-COUNT =popper

press-up, press-ups. In British English, **press-ups** are exercises to strengthen your arms and chest muscles. They are done by lying with your face towards the floor and pushing with your hands to raise your body until your arms are straight. *He made me do 30 press-ups.* N-COUNT: usu pl

pressure /preʃəʳ/ **pressures, pressuring, pressured** ◆◆◆◆◆

1 **Pressure** is force that you produce when you press hard on something. *She kicked at the door with her foot, and the pressure was enough to open it... The pressure of his fingers had relaxed... The best way to treat such bleeding is to apply firm pressure.* N-UNCOUNT

2 The **pressure** in a place or container is the force produced by the quantity of gas or liquid in that place or container. *The window in the cockpit had blown in and the pressure dropped dramatically... Warm air is now being drawn in from another high pressure area over the North Sea.* N-UNCOUNT: also N in pl

3 If there is **pressure** on someone to do something, someone is trying to persuade or force them to do it. *He may have put pressure on her to agree... Its government is under pressure from the European Commission... The political pressures to do something are pretty enormous.* N-UNCOUNT: also N in pl

4 If you are experiencing **pressure**, you feel that you must do a lot of tasks or make a lot of decisions in very little time, or that people expect a lot from you. *Can you work under pressure?... Even if I had the talent to play tennis I couldn't stand the pressure... The pressures of modern life are great.* N-UNCOUNT: also N in pl =stress

5 If you **pressure** someone to do something, you try forcefully to persuade them to do it. *He will never pressure you to get married... The Government should not be pressured into making hasty decisions... Don't pressure me... His boss did not pressure him for results.* ♦ **pressured** *You're likely to feel anxious and pressured.* VERB V n to-inf; be V-ed *into* -ing; V n; V n *for* n; ADJ-GRADED: usu v-link ADJ

6 See also **blood pressure**.

pressure cooker, pressure cookers. A **pressure cooker** is a large saucepan with a lid that fits tightly, in which you can cook food quickly using steam at high pressure. N-COUNT

pressure group, pressure groups. A **pressure group** is an organized group of people who are trying to persuade a government or other authority to do something, for example to change a law. *...the environmental pressure group Greenpeace.* ◆◇◇◇◇ N-COUNT

pressurize /preʃəraɪz/ **pressurizes, pressurizing, pressurized;** also spelled **pressurise** in British English. If you are **pressurized into** doing something, you are forcefully persuaded to do it. *Do not be pressurized into making your decision immediately... He thought she was trying to pressurize him.* • See also **pressurized.** VERB =pressure; be V-ed *into* -ing; V n; Also V n to-inf

pressurized /preʃəraɪzd/; also spelled **pressurised** in British English. In a **pressurized** container or area, the pressure inside is different from the pressure outside. *Supplementary oxygen is rarely needed in pressurized aircraft... Certain types of foods are also dispensed in pressurized canisters.* ◆◇◇◇◇ ADJ: usu ADJ n

prestige /prestiːʒ/ ◆◆◇◇◇

1 If a person, a country, or an organization has **prestige**, they are admired and respected because of the position they hold or the things they have achieved. *...efforts to build up the prestige of the United Nations... It was his responsibility for foreign affairs that gained him international prestige. ...high prestige jobs.* N-UNCOUNT =status

2 **Prestige** is used to describe products, places, or activities which people admire because they are associated with being rich or having a high social position. *...such prestige cars as Cadillac, Mercedes, Porsche and Jaguar.* ADJ: ADJ n =luxury

prestigious /prestɪdʒəs/. A **prestigious** institution, job, or activity is respected and admired by people. *It's one of the best equipped and most prestigious schools in the country.* ◆◆◇◇◇ ADJ-GRADED: usu ADJ n =reputable

presumably /prɪzjuːməbli, AM -zuːm-/. If you say that something is **presumably** the case, you mean that you think it is very likely to be the case, although you are not certain. *Presumably the front door was locked when you came down this morning?... The spear is presumably the murder weapon... He had gone to the reception desk, presumably to check out.* ◆◆◆◇◇ ADV: ADV with cl/group, ADV before v PRAGMATICS

presume /prɪzjuːm, AM -zuːm/ **presumes, presuming, presumed** ◆◆◇◇◇

1 If you **presume** that something is the case, you think that it is the case, although you are not certain. *I presume you're here on business... Dido's told you the whole sad story, I presume?... 'Had he been home all week?'—'I presume so.' ...areas that have been presumed to be safe... The missing person is presumed dead.* VERB =assume; V that; V *so*; be V-ed to-inf; be V-ed adj; Also *it be* V-ed that

2 If you say that someone **presumes** to do something, you mean that they do it even though they have no right to do it; a formal use. *They're resentful that outsiders presume to meddle in their affairs... I wouldn't presume to question your judgement.* VERB V to-inf

3 If an idea, theory, or plan **presumes** certain facts, it regards them as true so that they can be used as a basis for further ideas and theories; a formal use. *The legal definition of 'know' often presumes mental control... The arrangement presumes that both lenders and borrowers are rational.* VERB V n; V that

presumption /prɪzʌmpʃən/ **presumptions** ◆◇◇◇◇

1 A **presumption** is something that is accepted as true but is not certain to be true. *...the presumption that a defendant is innocent until proved guilty... I'm having to make a lot of presumptions since I don't really know anything about the case.* N-COUNT =assumption

2 If you describe someone's behaviour as **presumption**, you disapprove of it because they are doing something that they have no right to do; a formal use. *They were angered by his presumption.* N-UNCOUNT PRAGMATICS

presumptuous /prɪzʌmptʃuəs/. If you describe someone or their behaviour as **presumptuous**, you disapprove of them because they are doing something that they have no right or authority to do. *It would be presumptuous to judge what the outcome will be.* ADJ-GRADED: usu v-link ADJ PRAGMATICS

presuppose /priːsəpoʊz/ **presupposes, presupposing, presupposed.** If one thing **presupposes** another, the first thing cannot be true or exist unless the second thing is true or exists. *All your arguments presuppose that he's a rational, intelligent man... The end of an era presupposes the start of another.* VERB =assume; V that; V n

presupposition /priːsʌpəzɪʃən/ **presuppositions.** A **presupposition** is something that you assume to be true, especially something which you must assume is true in order to continue with what you are saying or thinking; a formal word. *...the presupposition within medical science that human life must be sustained for as long as possible.* N-COUNT =assumption

pre-tax; also spelled **pretax**. **Pre-tax** profits or losses are the total profits or losses made by a company before tax has been deducted. *Storehouse made pre-tax profits of £3.1m.* ► Also an adverb. *Last year it made £2.5m pre-tax.* ◆◆◇◇◇ ADJ: ADJ n; ADV: ADV after v

pre-teen, pre-teens; also spelled **preteen**. A **pre-teen** is a child who is not yet a teenager, usually a child aged between nine and thirteen. *Some preteens are able to handle a good deal of responsibility. ...a programme aimed at a pre-teen audience. ...pre-teen children.* N-COUNT: oft N n

pretence /prɪtens, AM priːtens/ **pretences;** ◆◇◇◇◇ spelled **pretense** in American English.
1 A **pretence** is an action or way of behaving that is intended to make people believe something that is not true. *Welland made a pretence of writing a note in his pad... We have to go along with the pretence that things are getting better... The government abandoned any pretence of reform.* N-VAR
2 If you do something under **false pretences**, you do it when people do not know the truth about you and your intentions. *I could not go on living with a man who had married me under false pretences... Conrad had been imprisoned for a year for gaining money by false pretences.* PHRASE: usu *under* PHR

pretend /prɪtend/ **pretends, pretending, pretended** ◆◆◇◇◇
1 If you **pretend** that something is the case, you act in a way that is intended to make people believe that it is the case, although in fact it is not. *I pretend that things are really okay when they're not... Sometimes the boy pretended to be asleep... I had no option but to pretend ignorance.* VERB V that V to-inf V n
2 If children or adults **pretend** that they are doing something, they imagine that they are doing it, for example as part of a game. *She can sunbathe and pretend she's in Spain... The children pretend to be different animals dancing to the music.* VERB V that V to-inf
3 If you **pretend** that something is the case, you claim that it is the case. *We do not pretend that the past six years have been without problems for us... Within this lecture I cannot pretend to deal adequately with dreams.* VB: with neg V that V to-inf

pretender /prɪtendəʳ/ **pretenders.** A **pretender** to a position is someone who claims the right to that position, and whose claim is disputed by others. *...the Comte de Paris, pretender to the French throne.* ◆◇◇◇◇ N-COUNT: usu N *to* n, adj N

pretension /prɪtenʃən/ **pretensions** ◆◇◇◇◇
1 If you say that someone has **pretensions**, you disapprove of them because they claim or pretend that they are more important than they really are. *Her wide-eyed innocence soon exposes the pretensions of the art world... We like him for his honesty, his lack of pretension.* N-VAR PRAGMATICS =pretentiousness
2 If someone has **pretensions to** something, they claim to be or do that thing. *The city has unrealistic pretensions to world-class status... It will remain as a pressure group, but no longer has any pretension to be a political party.* N-UNCOUNT: also N in pl, N *to* n/-ing, N to-inf =claim

pretentious /prɪtenʃəs/. If you say that someone or something is **pretentious**, you mean that they try to seem important or significant, but you do not think that they are; used showing disapproval. *His response was full of pretentious nonsense... This pub was of a very different type, smaller, less pretentious.* ♦ **pretentiousness** *He has a tendency towards pretentiousness.* ◆◇◇◇◇ ADJ-GRADED PRAGMATICS; N-UNCOUNT

preternatural /priːtəʳnætʃrəl/. **Preternatural** abilities, qualities, or events are unusual or exceptional in a way that might make you think that superhuman forces are involved. *Their parents had an almost preternatural ability to understand what was going on in their children's minds.* ♦ **preternaturally** *It was suddenly preternaturally quiet.* ADJ: ADJ n; ADV: ADV adj

pretext /priːtekst/ **pretexts.** A **pretext** is a reason which you pretend has caused you to do something. *They wanted a pretext for subduing the region by force... He excused himself on the pretext of a stomach upset... They would now find some dubious pretext to restart the war.* ◆◇◇◇◇ N-COUNT

prettify /prɪtɪfaɪ/ **prettifies, prettifying, prettified.** If someone **prettifies** something, especially something that is not beautiful or glamorous, they make it appear pretty; used showing disapproval. *...just a clever effort to prettify animal slaughter... It presented an intolerably prettified view of the countryside.* VERB PRAGMATICS V n V-ed

pretty /prɪti/ **prettier, prettiest** ◆◆◆◆◇
1 If you describe someone, especially a girl, as **pretty**, you mean that they look nice and are attractive in a delicate way. *She's a very charming and very pretty girl.* ♦ **prettily** /prɪtɪli/ *She was laughing prettily at me.* ♦ **prettiness** *Her prettiness had been much admired.* ADJ-GRADED =good-looking; ADV-GRADED; N-UNCOUNT
2 A place or a thing that is **pretty** is attractive and pleasant, in a charming but not particularly unusual way. *Whitstable is still a very pretty little town. ...comfortable sofas covered in a pretty floral print.* ♦ **prettily** *The living-room was prettily decorated.* ♦ **prettiness** *...shells of quite unbelievable prettiness.* ADJ-GRADED =charming; ADV-GRADED; N-UNCOUNT
3 You can use **pretty** before an adjective or adverb to mean 'quite' or 'rather'; an informal use. *I had a pretty good idea what she was going to do... Pretty soon after my arrival I found lodgings.* ADV: ADV adj/adv
4 **Pretty much** or **pretty well** means 'almost'; an informal expression. *His new government looks pretty much like the old one... I travel pretty well every week.* PHRASES =almost, practically
5 If you say that someone **is sitting pretty**, you mean that they are in a good, safe, or comfortable position; an informal expression. *When the war started, they thought they were sitting pretty, because they had all that extra grain.* V inflects
6 • **not a pretty sight**: see **sight**.

pretzel /pretsəl/ **pretzels.** A **pretzel** is a small, glazed, crisp biscuit, which has salt on the outside. Pretzels are usually shaped like knots or sticks. N-COUNT

prevail /prɪveɪl/ **prevails, prevailing, prevailed** ◆◆◇◇◇
1 If a proposal, principle, or opinion **prevails**, it gains influence or is accepted, often after a struggle or argument. *We hope that common sense would prevail... Rick still believes that justice will prevail... Political and personal ambitions are starting to prevail over economic interests.* VERB =triumph V V *over* n
2 If a situation, attitude, or custom **prevails** in a particular place at a particular time, it is normal or most common in that place at that time. *A similar situation prevails in America. ...the confusion which had prevailed at the time of the revolution... How people in a certain era bury their dead says much about the prevailing attitudes toward death.* VERB V V-ing
3 If one side in a battle, contest, or dispute **prevails**, it overcomes the other side and is victorious. *He appears to have the votes he needs to prevail... I do hope he will prevail over the rebels.* VERB =be victorious V V *over/against* n
4 If you **prevail upon** someone or **prevail on** someone to do something, you succeed in persuading them to do it; a formal use. *We must, each of us, prevail upon our congressman to act... Do you think she could be prevailed upon to do those things?* VERB V *upon/on* n to-inf

prevailing /prɪveɪlɪŋ/. The **prevailing wind** in an area is the type of wind that blows over that area most of the time. *The direction of the prevailing winds should be taken into account.* ADJ: ADJ n

prevalent /prevələnt/. A condition or belief that is **prevalent** is common. *This condition is more prevalent in women than in men... Smoking is becoming increasingly prevalent among younger women... The prevalent view is that interest rates will fall.* ♦ **prevalence** *Not much is known about the prevalence of AIDS in the general population.* ◆◇◇◇◇ ADJ-GRADED: usu v-link ADJ =common; N-UNCOUNT

prevaricate /prɪværɪkeɪt/ **prevaricates, prevaricating, prevaricated.** If you **prevaricate**, you avoid giving a direct answer or making a firm decision. *British ministers continued to prevaricate.* ♦ **prevarication** /prɪværɪkeɪʃən/ **prevarications** *After months of prevarication, the political decision had at last been made.* VERB V; N-UNCOUNT: also N in pl

prevent /prɪvent/ **prevents, preventing, prevented** ◆◆◆◆◇
1 To **prevent** something means to ensure that it does not happen. *These methods prevent pregnancy... Further treatment will prevent cancer from developing... We recognized the possibility and took steps to prevent it happening.* ♦ **prevention** *...the prevention of heart disease. ...crime prevention.* VERB =stop V n V n *from*-ing V n -ing; N-UNCOUNT
2 To **prevent** someone **from** doing something means to make it impossible for them to do it. *He said this would prevent companies from creating new jobs... Its nationals may be prevented from* VERB =stop V n *from*-ing V n -ing Also V n

leaving the country... The police have been trying to prevent them carrying weapons.

preventable /prɪventəbᵊl/. **Preventable** diseases, illnesses, or deaths could be stopped from occurring. *Forty-thousand children a day die from preventable diseases... Aids is totally preventable.* ADJ

preventative /prɪventətɪv/. **Preventative** means the same as **preventive**. ADJ: ADJ n

preventive /prɪventɪv/. **Preventive** actions are intended to help prevent things such as disease or crime. *Too much is spent on expensive curative medicine and too little on preventive medicine... People accused the ministry of failing to take adequate preventive measures.* ◆◇◇◇◇ ADJ: usu ADJ n =preventative

preview /priːvjuː/ **previews, previewing, previewed** ◆◆◇◇◇

1 A **preview** is an opportunity to see something such as a film, exhibition, or invention before it is open or available to the public. *He had gone to see the preview of a play. ...a sneak preview of the type of car that could be commonplace within ten years.* N-COUNT

2 If a journalist or critic **previews** something such as a film, exhibition, or invention, they see it and describe it to the public before the public see it for themselves. *He knew about the interview prior to its publication and had actually previewed the piece... Nick Sullivan previews this season's collections from Paris and Milan.* VERB V n

previous /priːviəs/ ◆◆◆◆◇

1 A **previous** event or thing is one that happened or came before the one that you are talking about. *She has a teenage daughter from a previous marriage... He has no previous convictions.* ADJ: ADJ n

2 You refer to the period of time or the thing immediately before the one that you are talking about as the **previous** one. *It was a surprisingly dry day after the rain of the previous week... He recalled exactly what Bob had told him the previous night.* ADJ: det ADJ =preceding

previously /priːviəsli/ ◆◆◆◇◇

1 Previously means at some time before the period that you are talking about. *Guyana's railways were previously owned by private companies... The contract was awarded to a previously unknown company... Previously she had very little time to work in her own garden.* ADV: usu ADV with v, also ADV adj, ADV with cl

2 You can use **previously** to say how much earlier one event was than another event. *He had first entered the House 12 years previously... She had rented the flat from the council some fourteen months previously.* ADV: n ADV =before

pre-war; also spelled **prewar**. **Pre-war** is used to describe things that happened, existed, or were made in the period immediately before a war, especially the Second World War (1939-45). *...Poland's pre-war leader.* ◆◇◇◇◇ ADJ: usu ADJ n ≠post-war

prey /preɪ/ **preys, preying, preyed** ◆◆◇◇◇

1 A creature's **prey** are the creatures that it hunts and eats in order to live. *Electric ray's stun their prey with huge electrical discharges... These animals were the prey of hyenas.* • See also **bird of prey**. N-UNCOUNT-COLL: usu with poss

2 A creature that **preys on** other creatures lives by catching and eating them. *The effect was to disrupt the food chain, starving many animals and those that preyed on them... The larvae prey upon small aphids.* VERB =feed V on/upon n

3 You can refer to people as someone's **prey** when they are the victims of criminals or other dishonest people. *Police officers lie in wait for the gangs who stalk their prey at night... This burglar thought old people are easy prey.* N-UNCOUNT: usu with poss

4 If someone **preys on** other people, especially people who are unable to protect themselves, they take advantage of them or harm them in some way. *Pam had never learned that there were men who preyed on young runaways... The survey claims loan companies prey on weak families already in debt.* VERB V on n

5 If something **preys on** your mind, you cannot stop thinking and worrying about it. *The absence of children at Christmas preyed on Liz's mind... It was a misunderstanding. Herr Kettner was unwise and it preyed on his conscience.* VERB =weigh V on n

6 If someone or something is **prey to** something bad, they have a tendency to let themselves be affected by it. *He was prey to a growing despair... You were both a prey to compulsions.* N-UNCOUNT: also a N, N to n

7 To **fall prey to** something bad means to be taken over or affected by it. *On the flight from Paris to Toulon, Mechiche fell prey to panic... Children in evacuation centres are falling prey to disease.* PHRASE: V inflects

price /praɪs/ **prices, pricing, priced** ◆◆◆◆◆

1 The **price** of something is the amount of money that you have to pay in order to buy it. *...a sharp increase in the price of petrol... They expected house prices to rise... They haven't come down in price.* N-COUNT: usu with supp, also in N

2 The **price** that you pay for something that you want is an unpleasant thing that you have to do or suffer in order to get it. *Slovenia will have to pay a high price for independence... There may be a price to pay for such relentless activity, perhaps ill health or even divorce... He's paying the price for working his body so hard.* N-SING: usu N for n/-ing =penalty

3 If something **is priced at** a particular amount, the price is set at that amount. *The shares are expected to be priced at about 330p... Analysts predict that Digital will price the new line at less than half the cost of comparable IBM mainframes... There is a very reasonably priced menu.* ♦ **pricing** *It's hard to maintain competitive pricing.* VERB be V-ed at n V n at n V-ed N-UNCOUNT

4 See also **retail price index**, **selling price**.

5 If you want something **at any price**, you are determined to get it, even if unpleasant things happen as a result. *If they wanted a deal at any price, they would have to face the consequences... We obviously want to see the hostages home, but not at any price.* PHRASES PHR after v =at any cost

6 If you can buy something that you want **at a price**, it is for sale, but it is extremely expensive. *Most goods are available, but at a price.* PHR with cl

7 If you get something that you want **at a price**, you get it but something unpleasant happens as a result. *Fame comes at a price... Theismann's precious information came at a price, however.* usu PHR after v

8 If there is a **price on** someone**'s head**, an amount of money has been offered for the capture or killing of that person. *He remains at large despite the high price put on his head by the authorities.* *head* inflects

9 If you say that you cannot **put a price on** something, you mean that it is very valuable. *You can't put a price on friendship... You can't put a price on the value of the work done by our nurses.* with brd-neg, PHR n

10 You use **what price** in front of a word or expression that refers to something happening when you want to ask how likely it is to happen. You usually do this to emphasize either that it is very likely or that it is very unlikely to happen. *What price a glorious repeat of last week's triumph?* PHR n PRAGMATICS

11 You use '**at what price**?' to comment on the fact that the consequences of doing something are unpleasant. *Yes, they are free of him, but at what price to themselves, their families, those left behind?... What price success!*

12 • to **price** yourself **out of the market**: see **market**.

priceless /praɪsləs/ ◆◇◇◇◇

1 If you say that something is **priceless**, you are emphasizing that it is worth a very large amount of money. *They are priceless, unique and irreplaceable. ...the priceless treasures of the Royal Collection.* ADJ-GRADED PRAGMATICS

2 If you say that something is **priceless**, you approve of it because it is extremely useful. *They are a priceless record of a brief period in British history... The influence of someone like David York will be priceless.* ADJ-GRADED PRAGMATICS

price tag, **price tags**; also spelled **price-tag**. ◆◇◇◇◇

1 If something has a **price tag** of a particular amount, that is the amount that you must pay in order to buy it; used in written English. *I can't say it justifies the price tag of £100... The price tag on the 34-room white Regency mansion is £17.5 million.* N-COUNT

2 In a shop, the **price tag** on an article for sale is a N-COUNT small piece of card or paper which is attached to the article and which has the price written on it.

price war, price wars. ◆◇◇◇◇ [N-COUNT] If competing companies are involved in a **price war**, they each try to gain an advantage by lowering their prices as much as possible in order to sell more of their products and damage their competitors financially. *Their loss was partly due to a vicious price war between manufacturers that has cut margins to the bone.*

pricey /praɪsi/ **pricier, priciest.** [ADJ-GRADED] If you say that something is **pricey**, you mean that it is expensive; an informal word. *Medical insurance is very pricey.*

prick /prɪk/ **pricks, pricking, pricked** ◆◇◇◇◇

1 [VERB] If you **prick** something or **prick** holes in it, you make small holes in it with a sharp object such as a pin. *Prick the potatoes and rub the skins with salt...* [V n] *He pricks holes in the foil with a pin.* [V n prep]

2 [VERB] If something sharp **pricks** you or if you **prick** yourself with something sharp, it sticks into you or presses your skin and causes you pain. *She had just pricked her finger with the needle.* [V n; Also V pron-refl]

3 [VERB] If **tears prick your eyes**, you feel as if you are about to cry; a literary use. *Davydd felt tears prick his eyes.* [V n]

4 [VERB] If something **pricks your conscience**, you are suddenly aware of your conscience. If you **are pricked** by an emotion, you suddenly experience the emotion. *Most were sympathetic once we pricked their consciences... I was pricked by the needle of curiosity.* [V n]

5 [N-COUNT] A **prick** is a small, sharp pain that you get when something pricks you. *At the same time she felt a prick on her neck.*

6 [N-COUNT; PRAGMATICS] If someone calls a man a **prick**, they are indicating that they do not like him and that they think he is stupid; a rude and offensive use which you should avoid.

7 [N-COUNT: poss N] A man's **prick** is his penis; a rude and offensive use which you should avoid.

prick up. [PHRASAL VERB ERG] If someone **pricks up their ears** or if **their ears prick up**, they listen eagerly when they suddenly hear an interesting sound or an important piece of information. *She stopped talking to prick up her ears...* [V P n (not pron)] *Ears which prick up at the mention of royalty are sure to be disappointed.* [V P]

prickle /prɪkəl/ **prickles, prickling, prickled**

1 [VERB] If your skin **prickles**, it feels as if a lot of small sharp points are being stuck into it, either because of something touching it or because you feel a strong emotion. *He paused, feeling his scalp prickling under his hat... Her skin prickled with apprehension.* [V] ► Also a noun. *I felt a prickle of disquiet.* [N-COUNT]

2 [N-COUNT: usu pl] **Prickles** are small sharp points that stick out from leaves or from the stalks of plants. *...an erect stem covered at the base with a few prickles.*

prickly /prɪkəli/ ◆◇◇◇◇

1 [ADJ-GRADED] Something that is **prickly** feels rough and uncomfortable, as if it has a lot of prickles. *The bunk mattress was hard, the blankets prickly and slightly damp... The grass was prickly and cold.*

2 [ADJ-GRADED =touchy] Someone who is **prickly** loses their temper or gets upset very easily. *You know how prickly she is.*

3 [ADJ-GRADED =thorny] A **prickly** issue or subject is one that is rather complicated and difficult to discuss or resolve. *The issue is likely to prove a prickly one.*

prickly heat. [N-UNCOUNT] **Prickly heat** is a condition caused by very hot weather, in which your skin becomes hot, itchy, and covered with tiny bumps.

prickly pear, prickly pears. [N-COUNT] A **prickly pear** is a kind of cactus that has round fruit with prickles on. The fruit from the cactus, which you can eat, is also called a **prickly pear**.

pride /praɪd/ **prides, priding, prided** ◆◆◆◇◇

1 [N-UNCOUNT: oft N *in* n/-ing] **Pride** is a feeling of satisfaction which you have because you or people close to you have done something good or possess something good. *...the sense of pride in a job well done... We take pride in offering you the highest standards... They can look back on their endeavours with pride.*

2 [N-UNCOUNT =self-esteem] **Pride** is a sense of dignity and self-respect. *Davis had to salvage his pride... It was a severe blow to Kendall's pride.*

3 [N-UNCOUNT; PRAGMATICS =arrogance] Someone's **pride** is the feeling that they have that they are better or more important than other people; used showing disapproval. *His pride may still be his downfall.*

4 [VERB] If you **pride** yourself **on** a quality or skill that you have, you are very proud of it. *Smith prides himself on being able to organise his own life... Doyle prides himself on his accuracy.* [V pron-refl *on* -ing/n]

5 [N-COUNT: usu N *of* n] A **pride of lions** is a group of lions that live together.

6 [PHRASES; v-link PHR] Someone or something that is your **pride and joy** is very important to you and makes you feel very happy. *The bike soon became his pride and joy.*

7 [PHR after v] If something takes **pride of place**, it is treated as the most important thing in a group of things. *A three-foot-high silver World Championship cup takes pride of place near a carved wooden chair... The manifesto gives pride of place to job creation.*

8 [V inflects] If you **swallow** your **pride**, you decide to do something even though you think it will cause you to lose some of your dignity and self-respect. *No doubt his old mother would now swallow her pride and go and live with Gladys.*

priest /priːst/ **priests** ◆◆◆◇◇

1 [N-COUNT] A **priest** is a member of the Christian clergy in the Catholic, Anglican, or Orthodox church. *He had trained to be a Catholic priest.*

2 [N-COUNT] In many non-Christian religions a **priest** is a man who has particular duties and responsibilities in a place where people worship.

3 See also **high priest**.

priestess /priːstes/ **priestesses.** ◆◇◇◇◇ [N-COUNT] A **priestess** is a woman in a non-Christian religion who has particular duties and responsibilities in a place where people worship. • See also **high priestess**.

priesthood /priːsthʊd/ ◆◇◇◇◇

1 [N-UNCOUNT] **Priesthood** is the position of being a priest or the period of time during which someone is a priest. *...the early rites of priesthood... He spent the first twenty-five years of his priesthood as an academic.*

2 [N-SING: *the* N] **The priesthood** is all the members of the Christian clergy, especially in a particular Church. *Should the General Synod vote women into the priesthood?*

priestly /priːstli/. [ADJ: usu ADJ n] **Priestly** is used to describe things that belong or relate to a priest. *Priestly robes hang on the walls. ...his priestly duties.*

prig /prɪg/ **prigs.** [N-COUNT; PRAGMATICS] If you call someone a **prig**, you disapprove of them because they behave in a very moral way and disapprove of other people's behaviour as though they are superior.

priggish /prɪgɪʃ/. [ADJ-GRADED; PRAGMATICS] If you describe someone as **priggish**, you think that they are a prig.

prim /prɪm/

1 [ADJ-GRADED; PRAGMATICS =prissy] If you describe someone as **prim**, you disapprove of them because they behave too correctly and are too easily shocked by anything rude or improper. *We tend to imagine that the Victorians were very prim and proper. ...a rather prim British spinster.* ♦ **primly** [ADV-GRADED: ADV with v] *We sat primly at either end of a long settee... She sipped her white wine primly.*

2 [ADJ-GRADED] If you describe something as **prim**, you mean that it is very neat, tidy, or sensible. *On her blonde wavy hair, the white hat looked nicely prim.*

primacy /praɪməsi/. ◆◇◇◇◇ [N-UNCOUNT: oft *the* N *of* n =supremacy] The **primacy** of something is the fact that it is the most important or most powerful thing in a particular situation; a formal word. *The political idea at the heart of this is the primacy of the individual. ...the primacy of experience over analysis.*

prima donna /priːmə dɒnə/ **prima donnas**

1 [N-COUNT] A **prima donna** is the main female singer in an opera. *Her career began as prima donna with the Royal Carl Rosa Opera Company.*

2 [N-COUNT; PRAGMATICS] If you describe someone as a **prima donna**, you disapprove of them because they think they can behave badly or get what they want because they have a particular talent. *Nobody who comes to this*

club is allowed to behave like a prima donna. ...prima donna behaviour.

primaeval /praɪmiːvəl/. See **primeval.**

prima facie /praɪmə feɪʃi/. **Prima facie** is used to describe something which appears to be true when you first consider it; a formal word. *There was a prima facie case that a contempt of court had been committed.* ADJ: usu ADJ n

primal /praɪməl/. **Primal** is used to describe something that relates to the origins of things or that is very basic; a formal word. *Jealousy is a primal emotion. ...the primal mysteries of the earth.* ◆◇◇◇◇ ADJ-GRADED

primarily /praɪmərɪli, AM praɪmeərɪli/. You use **primarily** to say what is mainly true in a particular situation. *...a book aimed primarily at high-energy physicists... Public order is primarily an urban problem... Investment remains tiny primarily because of the exorbitant cost of land.* ◆◆◇◇◇ ADV: ADV with v, ADV with cl/group =chiefly, essentially

primary /praɪməri, AM -meri/ **primaries** ◆◆◆◇◇

1 You use **primary** to describe something that is extremely important or most important for someone or something; a formal use. *That's the primary reason the company's share price has held up so well... I don't think young people's primary aim in life is to get drunk... His misunderstanding of language was the primary cause of his other problems... The family continues to be the primary source of care and comfort for people as they grow older.* ADJ: ADJ n =main

2 In Britain, **primary** education is given to pupils between the ages of 5 and 11. The American equivalent is **elementary** education. *Britain did not introduce compulsory primary education until 1880... Ninety-nine per cent of primary pupils now have hands-on experience of computers. ...primary teachers.* ADJ: ADJ n

3 Primary is used to describe something that occurs first. *It is not the primary tumour that kills, but secondary growths elsewhere in the body... They have been barred from primary bidding for clients.* ADJ: ADJ n

4 A **primary** or a **primary election** is an election in an American state in which people vote for someone to become a candidate for a political office. *...the 1968 New Hampshire primary... She won the Democratic primary... New York holds its primary election on Tuesday.* N-COUNT

primary colour, primary colours; spelled **primary color** in American English. **Primary colours** are basic colours that can be mixed together to produce other colours. They are usually considered to be red, yellow, blue, and sometimes green. *It comes in bright primary colours that kids will love.* N-COUNT: usu pl

primary school, primary schools. In Britain, a **primary school** is a school for children between the ages of 5 and 11. The American equivalent is an **elementary school**. *...eight- to nine-year-olds in their third year at primary school... Greenside Primary School.* ◆◆◇◇◇ N-VAR: oft in names

primate /praɪmət/ **primates.** The pronunciation /praɪmeɪt/ is also used for meaning 2. ◆◇◇◇◇

1 A **primate** is a member of the group of mammals which includes humans, monkeys, and apes. *The woolly spider monkey is the largest primate in the Americas.* N-COUNT

2 The Primate of a particular country or region is the archbishop of that country or region. *...the Roman Catholic Primate of All Ireland.* N-COUNT: usu *the* N of n

prime /praɪm/ **primes, priming, primed** ◆◆◆◇◇

1 You use **prime** to describe something that is most important in a situation. *Political stability, meanwhile, will be a prime concern... It could be a prime target for guerrilla attack... The police will see me as the prime suspect!... Prime candidate to take over his job is Margaret Ramsay.* ADJ: ADJ n

2 You use **prime** to describe something that is of the best possible quality. *It was one of the City's prime sites, giving a clear view of the Stock Exchange and the Bank of England.* ADJ: ADJ n =top

3 You use **prime** to describe an example of a particular kind of thing that is absolutely typical. *The prime example is Macy's, once the undisputed king of California retailers.* ADJ: ADJ n =classic

4 If someone or something is in their **prime**, they are at the stage in their existence when they are at their strongest, most active, or most successful. *Maybe I'm just coming into my prime now... She was in her intellectual prime... We've had a series of athletes trying to come back well past their prime. ...young persons in the prime of life.* N-UNCOUNT: usu poss N

5 If you **prime** someone to do something, you prepare them to do it, for example by giving them information about it beforehand. *Claire wished she'd primed Sarah beforehand... Marianne had not known until Arnold primed her for her duties that she was to be the sole female... The White House press corps has been primed to leap to the defense of the fired officials.* VERB =brief V n V n *for* n *be* V-ed to-inf

6 If someone **primes a bomb** or **a gun**, they prepare it so that it is ready to explode or fire. *He was priming the bomb to go off in an hour's time... Tom keeps a primed 10-foot shotgun in his office.* VERB V n to-inf V-ed Also V n

7 • to **prime the pump**: see **pump**.

Prime Minister, Prime Ministers. The leader of the government in some countries is called **the Prime Minister**. *...the former Prime Minister of Pakistan, Miss Benazir Bhutto... This had been a disastrous week for Prime Minister Major.* ◆◆◆◆◆ N-COUNT: usu *the* N; N-TITLE; N-VOC =PM, premier

prime mover, prime movers. The **prime mover** behind a plan, idea, or situation is someone who has an important influence in starting it. *He was the prime mover behind the coup... He has been named as the prime mover in the conspiracy to murder Carroll.* N-COUNT: usu N *behind/in* n =driving force

prime number, prime numbers. In mathematics, a **prime number** is a whole number greater than 1 that cannot be divided exactly by any whole number except itself and the number 1, for example 17. N-COUNT

primer /praɪmər/ **primers**

1 Primer is a type of paint that is put onto wood in order to prepare it for the main layer of paint. N-MASS

2 A **primer** is a book containing basic facts about a subject, which is used by someone who is beginning to study that subject; an old-fashioned use. N-COUNT

prime rate, prime rates. A bank's **prime rate** is the lowest rate of interest which it charges at a particular time and which is offered only to certain customers. *At least one bank cut its prime rate today.* ◆◇◇◇◇ N-COUNT

prime time; also spelled **primetime. Prime time** television or radio programmes are broadcast when the most viewers or listeners are watching television or listening to the radio. *...a prime-time television show. ...prime time viewing in mid-evening.* ◆◇◇◇◇ N-UNCOUNT: usu N n

primeval /praɪmiːvəl/; also spelled **primaeval** in British English.

1 You use **primeval** to describe things that belong to a very early period in the history of the world; a formal use. *...the dense primeval forests that once covered inland Brittany. ...a vast expanse of primeval swamp.* ADJ: usu ADJ n =primordial

2 You use **primeval** to describe feelings and emotions that are instinctive. *...a primeval urge to hit out at that which causes him pain.* ADJ: usu ADJ n

primitive /prɪmɪtɪv/ ◆◆◇◇◇

1 Primitive means belonging to a society in which people live in a very simple way, usually without industries or a writing system. *...studies of primitive societies. ...primitive tribes.* ADJ-GRADED: usu ADJ n

2 Primitive means belonging to a very early period in the development of an animal or plant. *...primitive whales... Primitive humans needed to be able to react like this to escape from dangerous animals... It is a primitive instinct to flee a place of danger.* ADJ-GRADED

3 If you describe something as **primitive**, you mean that it is very simple in style or very old-fashioned. *The conditions are primitive by any standards... The primitive surgery of those days left him virtually deaf in one ear... It's using some rather primitive technology.* ADJ-GRADED =crude ≠sophisticated

primordial /praɪmɔːʳdiəl/. You use **primordial** to describe things that belong to a very early time in the history of the world; a formal word. *Twenty million years ago, Idaho was populated by dense primordial forest. ...the original primordial explosion.* ADJ =primeval

primrose /prɪmrouz/ **primroses.** A **primrose** is a wild plant which has pale yellow flowers. ◆◇◇◇◇ N-VAR

primula /prɪmjʊlə/ **primulas.** A **primula** is a type of primrose with very brightly coloured flowers. N-VAR

Primus /praɪməs/. A **Primus** or a **Primus stove** is a small cooker that burns paraffin and is often used in camping; used mainly in British English. Primus is a trademark. N-SING

prince /prɪns/ **princes** ◆◆◆◆◇

1 A **prince** is a male member of a royal family, especially the son of the king or queen of a country. *...Prince Edward and other royal guests... The Prince won warm applause for his ideas.* N-TITLE; N-COUNT

2 A **prince** is the male royal ruler of a small country or state. *He was speaking without the prince's authority.* N-TITLE; N-COUNT

3 If someone describes a man as the **prince** of a particular type of work, they mean that he is the best man doing that type of work; a literary use. *To his 19th-century peers, Robert Brown was the prince of botany.* N-COUNT: usu N *of* n

Prince Charming. A woman's **Prince Charming** is a man who seems to her to be a perfect lover or boyfriend, because he is good-looking, kind, and considerate. *To begin with he was Prince Charming.* N-SING: also no det

princely /prɪnsli/

1 A **princely** sum of money is a large sum of money. *It'll cost them the princely sum of seventy-five pounds.* ADJ-GRADED: usu ADJ n =handsome

2 **Princely** means belonging to a prince or suitable for a prince. *It was the embodiment of princely magnificence.* ADJ: usu ADJ n

princess /prɪnses, AM -səs/ **princesses.** A **princess** is a female member of a royal family, usually the daughter of a king or queen or the wife of a prince. *Princess Anne topped the guest list. ...the Prince and Princess of Wales.* ◆◆◆◆◇ N-TITLE; N-COUNT

principal /prɪnsɪpᵊl/ **principals** ◆◆◆◇◇

1 **Principal** means first in order of importance. *The principal reason for my change of mind is this. ...the country's principal source of foreign exchange earnings... Their principal concern is bound to be that of winning the next general election.* ADJ: ADJ n =main

2 The **principal** of a school or college is the person in charge of it. *Donald King is the principal of Dartmouth High School.* N-COUNT =head, headteacher

principality /prɪnsɪpælɪti/ **principalities.** A **principality** is a country that is ruled by a prince. *...the tiny principality of Liechtenstein.* N-COUNT

principally /prɪnsɪpəli/. **Principally** means more than anything else. *This is principally because the major export markets are slowing... Embryonic development seems to be controlled principally by a very small number of master genes.* ◆◇◇◇◇ ADV: ADV with cl/group =chiefly, mainly

principle /prɪnsɪpᵊl/ **principles** ◆◆◆◆◇

1 A **principle** is a general belief that you have about the way you should behave, which influences your behaviour. *Buck never allowed himself to be bullied into doing anything that went against his principles. ...moral principles... It's not just a matter of principle. ...a man of principle.* N-VAR: usu poss N, adj N, prep N

2 The **principles** of a particular theory or philosophy are its basic rules or laws. *...a violation of the basic principles of Marxism... The doctrine was based on three fundamental principles.* N-COUNT: usu N *of* n, adj N

3 Scientific **principles** are general scientific laws which explain how something happens or works. *These people lack all understanding of scientific principles. ...the principles of quantum theory.* N-COUNT: usu adj N, N *of* n

4 If you agree with something **in principle**, you agree in general terms to the idea of it, although you do yet know the details or know if it will be possible. *I agree with it in principle but I doubt if it will happen in practice... The conference approved in principle a new policy-making process.* PHRASES usu PHR after v

5 If something is possible **in principle**, there is no known reason why it should not happen, even though it has not happened before. *Even assuming this to be in principle possible, it will not be achieved soon.* =in theory

6 If you refuse to do something **on principle**, you refuse to do it because of a particular belief that you have. *President Bush refused, on principle, to do so... He would vote against it on principle.* usu with brd-neg, PHR after v

principled /prɪnsɪpᵊld/. If you describe someone as **principled**, you approve of them because they have strong moral principles. *She was a strong, principled woman... You have to take a principled stand.* ADJ-GRADED: usu ADJ n PRAGMATICS

print /prɪnt/ **prints, printing, printed** ◆◆◆◆◇

1 If someone **prints** something such as a book, newspaper, or leaflet, they produce it in large quantities by a mechanical process. *He started to print his own posters to distribute abroad... The Slovene bank has printed a specimen bank note... Our brochure is printed on environmentally-friendly paper... We found that television and radio gave rise to far fewer complaints than did the printed media.* ▶ **Print up** means the same as **print**. *Community workers here are printing up pamphlets for peace demonstrations... Hey, I know what, I'll get a bumper sticker printed up.* ♦ **printing** *His brother ran a printing and publishing company. ...stocks of paper and printing ink.* VERB V n be V-ed prep/adv V-ed PHRASAL VERB V P n (not pron) *have/get* n V-ed P N-UNCOUNT: oft N n

2 If a newspaper or magazine **prints** a piece of writing, it includes it or publishes it. *We can only print letters which are accompanied by the writer's name and address. ...a questionnaire printed in the magazine recently.* VERB =published V n V-ed Also be V-ed *in* n

3 If numbers or letters **are printed** on an object, they appear on it and form part of the object itself. You can also say that an object **is printed** with letters or numbers. *...the number printed on the receipt. ...a clear glass bottle with CASTORIA plainly printed in raised letters on one side... The company has for some time printed its phone number on its products... Each photo is automatically printed with the date on which it was taken.* VERB V-ed V n *on* n be V-ed *with* n

4 If a text or a picture **is printed**, a copy of it is produced by means of a computer printer or some other type of equipment. *'Ecu' was printed in lower case rather than capital letters. ...machines that can print on both sides of a page... The printed page that comes out of the machine has a characteristic odor.* VERB be V-ed prep/adv V prep/adv V-ed Also V n

5 If material or clothing **is printed** with a pattern, or a pattern **is printed** on it, the pattern is reproduced on the material, usually by means of dye and special machinery. *The shirts were printed with a paisley pattern. ...motifs printed on chiffon dresses. ...printed cotton fabric. ...She hand-paints and prints scarves, ties and T-shirts.* VERB be V-ed *with* n V n

6 A **print** is a piece of clothing or material with a pattern printed on it. You can also refer to the pattern itself as a **print**. *Her mother wore one of her dark summer prints... In this living room we've mixed glorious floral prints that complement one another in scale and colour. ...multi-coloured print jackets.* N-COUNT

7 When you **print** a photograph, you produce it from a negative. *Printing a black-and-white negative on to colour paper produces a similar monochrome effect... I selected two negatives to print from.* VERB V n *onto/from* n Also V n

8 A **print** is a photograph from a film that has been developed. *...black and white prints of Margaret and Jean as children. ...35mm colour print films.* N-COUNT =photo

9 A **print** of a cinema film is a particular copy or set of copies of it. *First released in 1957, the movie now appears in a new print.* N-COUNT

10 A **print** is a picture that is copied from a painting by photography or made mechanically from specially prepared surfaces and dyes. Usually several copies of one print are made at the same time. N-COUNT

...*12 original copper plates engraved by William Hogarth for his famous series of prints.*

11 Print is used to refer to letters and numbers as they appear on the pages of a book, newspaper, or printed document. ...*columns of tiny print... Laser printers are popular because of their high quality print and silent working.* N-UNCOUNT

12 The **print** media consists of newspapers and magazines, but not television or radio. *I have been convinced that the print media are more accurate and more reliable than television. ...print journalists.* ADJ: ADJ n ≠broadcasting

13 If you **print** words, you write in letters that are not joined together and that look like the letters in a book or newspaper. *Print your name and address on a postcard and send it to us.* VERB =write V n

14 You can refer to a footprint as a **print**. *He crawled from print to print, sniffing at the earth, following the scent left in the tracks. ...boot prints.* N-COUNT

15 You can refer to someone's fingerprints as their **prints**. *Fresh prints of both girls were found in the flat.* N-COUNT: usu pl =fingerprint

16 See also **printing**.

17 If you or your words appear **in print**, or get **into print**, what you say or write is published in a book, newspaper, or other printed text. *Many of these poets appeared in print only long after their deaths... There was no immediate prospect of the diaries' getting into print.* PHRASES PHR after v, v-link PHR

18 If a book is **in print**, it is available from a publisher. *Many of their books have been in print for nearly 40 years.* usu v-link PHR ≠out of print

19 If a book is **out of print**, it is no longer available from a publisher. *I believe the book is now out of print, but it can easily be borrowed from libraries.* v-link PHR ≠in print

20 The **small print** or the **fine print** of something such as an advertisement or a contract consists of the technical details and legal conditions, which are often printed in much smaller letters than the rest of the text. *I'm looking at the small print; I don't want to sign anything that I shouldn't sign... The US embassy says the fine print needs to be worked out on the trade agreement between the United States and the European Community.*

21 • **a licence to print money**: see **license**. • **to print money**: see **money**.

print out. If a computer or a machine attached to a computer **prints** something **out**, it produces a copy of it on paper. *You measure yourself, enter measurements and the computer will print out the pattern... The images of the moon's surface were transmitted back to earth and printed out... I shall just print this out and put it in the post.* • See also **printout**. PHRASAL VERB V P n (not pron) V n P Also V P

print up. See **print** 1. PHRASAL VERB

printable /prɪntəbəl/. If you say that someone's words or remarks are not **printable**, you mean that they are likely to offend people, and are therefore not suitable to be repeated in writing or speech; used in journalism. *His team-mates opened hotel windows, shouting 'Jump!' and somewhat less printable banter.* ADJ-GRADED: usu with brd-neg

printed circuit board, printed circuit boards. A **printed circuit board** is an electronic circuit in which some of the components and connections are formed by fine metallic lines and shapes on a thin insulating board; a technical term in electronics. N-COUNT

printed word. **The printed word** is the same as **the written word**. N-SING: the N

printer /prɪntəʳ/ **printers** ◆◆◇◇◇

1 A **printer** is a machine that can be connected to a computer in order to make copies on paper of documents or other information held by the computer. • See also **laser printer**. N-COUNT

2 A **printer** is a person or firm whose job is printing books, leaflets, or similar material. *The manuscript had already been sent off to the printers.* N-COUNT

printing /prɪntɪŋ/ **printings.** If copies of a book are printed and published on a number of different occasions, you can refer to each of these occasions as a **printing**. *The American edition of 'Cloud Street' is already in its third printing.* • See also **print**. N-COUNT: oft ord N

printing press, printing presses. A **printing press** is a machine used for printing, especially one that can print books, newspapers, or leaflets in large numbers. N-COUNT

printmaking /prɪntmeɪkɪŋ/. **Printmaking** is an artistic technique which consists of making a series of pictures from an original, or from a specially prepared surface. N-UNCOUNT

printout /prɪntaʊt/ **printouts;** also spelled **print-out**. A **printout** is a piece of paper on which information from a computer or similar device has been printed. ...*a computer printout of various financial projections.* N-COUNT

print run, print runs. A **print run** of something such as a book or a newspaper is the number of copies of it that are printed and published at one time; a technical term in publishing. *It was launched last year in paperback with an initial print run of 7,000 copies.* N-COUNT: usu with supp, supp N, N of n

print shop, print shops. A **print shop** is a small business which prints and copies things such as documents, leaflets, and cards for customers. N-COUNT

prior /praɪəʳ/ **priors** ◆◆◆◇◇

1 You use **prior** to indicate that something has already happened, or must happen, before another event takes place. *He claimed he had no prior knowledge of the protest... The Constitution requires the president to seek the prior approval of Congress for military action... For the prior year, they reported net income of $1.1 million.* ADJ: ADJ n ≠subsequent

2 A **prior** claim or duty is more important than other claims or duties and needs to be dealt with first. *The firm I wanted to use had prior commitments.* ADJ: ADJ n

3 A **prior** is a monk who is in charge of a priory or a monk who is an abbot's deputy in a monastery. N-COUNT; N-TITLE

4 If something happens **prior to** a particular time or event, it happens before that time or event; a formal use. *In the car industry, the August sales will involve a build up of stocks prior to this date... A man seen hanging around the area prior to the shooting could have been involved.* PHR-PREP =before

prioress /praɪərəs/ **prioresses.** A **prioress** is a nun who is in charge of a convent. N-COUNT; N-TITLE

prioritize /praɪɒrɪtaɪz, AM -ɔːr-/ **prioritizes, prioritizing, prioritized;** also spelled **prioritise** in British English.

1 If you **prioritize** something, you treat it as more important than other things. *The government is prioritising the service sector, rather than investing in industry and production.* VERB V n

2 If you **prioritize** the tasks you have to do, you decide which are the most important and do them first. *Make lists of what to do and prioritize your tasks.* VERB V n Also V

priority /praɪɒrɪti, AM -ɔːr-/ **priorities** ◆◆◆◇◇

1 If something is a **priority**, it is the most important thing you have to do or deal with, or must be done or dealt with before everything else you have to do. *Being a parent is her first priority... The government's priority is to build more power plants... Getting your priorities in order is a good way to not waste energy on meaningless pursuits.* N-COUNT

2 If you **give priority** to something or someone, you treat them as more important than anything or anyone else. *The school will give priority to science, maths and modern languages... The proposals deserve support as they give priority to the needs of children.* PHRASES V inflects, usu PHR to n =give precedence

3 If something **takes priority** or **has priority** over other things, it is regarded as being more important than them and is dealt with first. *The fight against inflation took priority over measures to combat the deepening recession... I disagree with the premise that economic development has priority over the environment.* V inflects, usu PHR over n =take precedence

priory /praɪəri/ **priories.** A **priory** is a place where a small group of monks live and work together. ...*Lindisfarne Priory on Holy Island.* ◆◇◇◇◇ N-COUNT: oft in names after n

prise /praɪz/. See **prize**. ◆◇◇◇◇

prism /prɪzəm/ **prisms**
1 A **prism** is an object made of clear glass or plastic which has many straight sides. It separates the light which passes through it into the colours of the rainbow. N-COUNT
2 If you see something through a **prism of** something such as time or memory, your perception is distorted by that thing; a literary use. *Through the smoky prism of time, I could just barely make out my father as a young man.* N-COUNT: usu sing, N *of* n

prison /prɪzᵊn/ **prisons.** A **prison** is a building where criminals are kept in order to punish them or where people awaiting trial are kept. *The prison's inmates are being kept in their cells... He was sentenced to life in prison... They released Mr Mandela from prison in 1990. ...the gas chamber at San Quentin Prison.* ◆◆◆◆◇ N VAR: oft in names after n =jail

prison camp, prison camps. A **prison camp** is a guarded camp where prisoners of war or political prisoners are kept. *He was shot down over Denmark and spent three years in a prison camp.* N-COUNT

prisoner /prɪzənəʳ/ **prisoners** ◆◆◆◆◇
1 A **prisoner** is a person who is kept in a prison as a punishment for a crime that they have committed. *The committee is concerned about the large number of prisoners sharing cells.* N-COUNT =inmate
2 A **prisoner** is a person who has been captured by an enemy, for example in war. *...wartime hostages and concentration-camp prisoners... He was held prisoner in Vietnam from 1966 to 1973... He was taken prisoner in North Africa in 1942.* N-COUNT: also *hold/take* n N =captive
3 If you say that you are a **prisoner of** a situation, you mean that your are trapped by it. *We are all prisoners of our childhood and feel an obligation to it... She was a prisoner of her own ego.* N-COUNT: N *of* n

prisoner of conscience, prisoners of conscience. Prisoners of conscience are people who have been put into prison for their political or social beliefs or for breaking the law while protesting against a political or social system. *The boost to human rights came with the release of prisoners of conscience in Eastern Europe.* N-COUNT =political prisoner

prisoner of war, prisoners of war. Prisoners of war are soldiers who have been captured by their enemy during a war and kept as prisoners until the end of the war. ◆◇◇◇◇ N-COUNT

prissy /prɪsi/ **prissier, prissiest.** If you say that someone is **prissy**, you are critical of them because they are very easily shocked by anything rude or improper; an informal word. *I grew to dislike the people from my background – they were rather uptight and prissy.* ADJ-GRADED PRAGMATICS =prim

pristine /prɪstiːn/. **Pristine** things are extremely clean or new; a formal word. *Now the house is in pristine condition. ...pristine white shirts.* ◆◇◇◇◇ ADJ: usu ADJ n =immaculate

privacy /prɪvəsi, AM praɪ-/. ◆◆◇◇◇
1 If you have **privacy**, you are in a place or situation which allows you to do things without other people seeing you or disturbing you. *He greatly resented the publication of this book, which he saw as an embarrassing invasion of his privacy... Thatched pavilions provide shady retreats for relaxing and reading in privacy. ...a collection of over 60 designs to try on in the privacy of your own home.* N-UNCOUNT: oft poss N
2 If someone or something **invades your privacy**, they interfere in your life without your permission. *He said the press invaded people's privacy unfairly and unjustifiably every day.* PHRASE: V inflects

private /praɪvɪt/ **privates** ◆◆◆◆◇
1 **Private** industries and services are owned or controlled by an individual person or a commercial company, rather than by the state or an official organization. *...a joint venture with private industry... Bupa runs private hospitals in Britain... Brazil says its constitution forbids the private ownership of energy assets.* ♦ **privately** *No other European country had so much state ownership and so few privately owned businesses... She was privately educated at schools in Ireland and Paris.* ADJ: usu ADJ n; ADV: ADV with v
2 **Private** individuals are acting only for themselves, and are not representing any group, company, or organization. *...the law's insistence that private citizens are not permitted to have weapons... President Bush is expected on a private visit to Germany on Sunday... The family tried to bring a private prosecution against him for assault.* ADJ: ADJ n
3 Your **private** things belong only to you, or may only be used by you. *The landowners have had to sell their private aircraft. ...communists, who want more State control over private property... There are 76 individually furnished bedrooms, all with private bathrooms... I took the precaution of clearing out my desk before I left, and only my private secretary knows it.* ADJ: usu ADJ n
4 **Private** places or gatherings may be attended only by a particular group of people, rather than by the general public. *673 private golf clubs took part in a recent study... The door is marked 'Private'... Brian Epstein was buried in a private ceremony at Long Lane Cemetery, Liverpool.* ADJ: usu ADJ n ≠public
5 **Private** meetings, discussions, and other activities involve only a small number of people, and very little information about them is given to other people. *Don't bug private conversations, and don't buy papers that reprint them.* ♦ **privately** *Few senior figures have issued any public statements but privately the resignation's been welcomed... I had not talked to Winnette privately for weeks.* ADJ: usu ADJ n; ADV: usu ADV with cl, also ADV after v
6 Your **private** life is that part of your life that is concerned with your personal relationships and activities, rather than with your work or business. *I've always kept my private and professional life separate... My private affairs are no one's business but my own.* ADJ: usu ADJ n =personal
7 Your **private** thoughts or feelings are ones that you do not talk about to other people. *We all felt as if we were intruding on his private grief. ...the enactment of her private sexual fantasies... It's just that it's something very private, and I simply can't talk about it.* ♦ **privately** *Privately, she worries about whether she's really good enough... He had privately resolved he would buy her the dress.* ADJ-GRADED: usu ADJ n; ADV: ADV with cl, ADV with v
8 You can use **private** to describe situations or activities that are understood only by the people involved in them, and not by anybody else. *Chinese waiters stood in a cluster, sharing a private joke... As many as 40 per cent of twins have a private language that excludes the rest of the family.* ADJ: ADJ n
9 If you describe a place as **private**, or as somewhere where you can be **private**, you mean that it is a quiet place and you can be alone there without being disturbed. *It was the only reasonably private place they could find. ...a very attractive country house set within a uniquely beautiful and private position... We were alone, completely private, with not even Angela present.* ADJ-GRADED
10 If you describe someone as a **private** person, you mean that they are very quiet by nature and do not reveal their thoughts and feelings to other people. *She has always been a rather private person... Gould was an intensely private individual.* ADJ-GRADED: usu ADJ n
11 You can use **private** to describe lessons that are not part of ordinary school activity, and which are given by a teacher to an individual pupil or a small group, usually in return for payment. *Martial arts: Private lessons: £8 per hour. ...Donald Tovey, who took her as his private pupil for the piano.* ADJ: usu ADJ n
12 A **private** is a soldier of the lowest rank in an army. *One gunner in each battery was an NCO and the rest were privates. ...Private Martin Ferguson.* N-COUNT; N-TITLE
13 Your **privates** are your genitals; an informal use. *You should wash your feet and your privates every day.* N-PLURAL: usu poss N =private parts
14 See also **privately**.
15 If you do something **in private**, you do it without other people being present, often because it is something that you want to keep secret. *Some of what we're talking about might better be discussed in private.* PHRASE: usu PHR after v

private detective, private detectives. A **private detective** is a detective who is not in the police, and who you can hire to find missing people or do other kinds of investigation for you. *The* N-COUNT =private investigator *money enabled her to hire a private detective to search for evidence that would clear him.*

private enterprise. **Private enterprise** is industry and business which is owned by individual people or commercial companies, and not by the government or an official organization. *...the government's plans to sell state companies to private enterprise.* ◆◇◇◇◇ N-UNCOUNT

private eye, private eyes. You can refer to a private detective as a **private eye**, especially when he or she is a character in a film or story; an informal expression. *Harmon plays a private eye hired by Mimi Rogers to investigate her husband's disappearance.* ◆◇◇◇◇ N-COUNT

private investigator, private investigators. A **private investigator** is the same as a **private detective.** N-COUNT

privately /praɪvɪtli/. If you buy or sell something **privately**, you buy it from or sell it to another person directly, rather than, for example, going to a shop or asking a dealer to act for you. *The whole process makes buying a car privately as painless as buying from a garage... A great deal of food is distributed and sold privately without ever reaching the shops.* ● See also **private.** ◆◇◇◇◇ ADV: ADV after v

Private Member's Bill, Private Members' Bills. In Britain, a **Private Member's Bill** is a law that is proposed by a Member of Parliament acting as an individual rather than as a member of his or her political party. N-COUNT

private parts. Your **private parts** are your genitals; an informal word. N-PLURAL: usu poss N

private school, private schools. A **private school** is a school which is not supported financially by the government and which parents have to pay for their children to go to. *He attended Eton, the most exclusive private school in Britain.* ◆◇◇◇◇ N-VAR =public school ≠state school

private sector. **The private sector** is the part of a country's economy which consists of industries and commercial companies that are not owned or controlled by the government. *...small firms in the private sector. ...the gap between the salaries of public and private sector employees.* ◆◆◇◇◇ N-SING: the N, N n ≠public sector, state sector

private soldier, private soldiers. A **private soldier** is a soldier of the lowest rank in an army; a formal expression. *Sergeants and corporals outnumber private soldiers.* N-COUNT =private

privation /praɪveɪʃᵊn/ **privations.** If you suffer **privation** or **privations**, you have to live without many of the things that are thought to be necessary in life, such as food, clothing, or comfort; a formal word. *They endured five years of privation during the second world war... The privations of monastery life were evident in his appearance.* N-UNCOUNT: also N in pl =hardship

privatize /praɪvətaɪz/ **privatizes, privatizing, privatized;** also spelled **privatise** in British English. If a company, industry, or service that is owned or controlled by the state **is privatized**, the government sells it or transfers control of it to one or more private companies. *The water boards are about to be privatized. ...a pledge to privatise the rail and coal industries. ...the newly privatized FM radio stations.* ◆◆◆◇◇ VERB =denationalize ≠nationalize be V-ed V n V-ed ♦ **privatization** /praɪvətaɪzeɪʃᵊn/ **privatizations** *...the privatisation of British Rail. ...fresh rules governing the conduct of future privatizations.* N-VAR: oft N of n =denationalization ≠nationalization

privet /prɪvɪt/. **Privet** is a type of bush with small leaves that stay green all year round. It is often grown in gardens to form hedges. *The garden was enclosed by a privet hedge.* N-UNCOUNT

privilege /prɪvɪlɪdʒ/ **privileges, privileging, privileged** ◆◆◇◇◇
1 A **privilege** is a special right or advantage that only one person or group has. *The Russian Federation has issued a decree abolishing special privileges for government officials. ...the ancient powers and privileges of the House of Commons.* N-COUNT
2 If you talk about **privilege**, you are talking about the power and advantage that only a small group of people have, usually because of their wealth or their high social class. *Pironi was the son of privilege and wealth, and it showed... Having been born to privilege in old Hollywood, she was carrying on a family tradition by acting.* N-UNCOUNT
3 You can use **privilege** in expressions such as **be a privilege** or **have the privilege** when you want to show your appreciation of someone or something or to show your respect. *It must be a privilege to know such a man... I once had the privilege of meeting the late philosopher CLR James.* N-SING PRAGMATICS =honour
4 To **privilege** someone or something means to treat them better or differently than other people or things rather than treat them all equally. *We want to privilege them because without the top graduate students, we can't remain a top university... They are privileging a tiny number to the disadvantage of the rest.* VERB =favour V n

privileged /prɪvɪlɪdʒd/ ◆◆◇◇◇
1 Someone who is **privileged** has an advantage or opportunity that most other people do not have, often because of their wealth or high social class. *They were, by and large, a very wealthy, privileged elite. ...I felt very privileged to work at the university.* ADJ-GRADED ► Also a noun. *They are only interested in preserving the power of the privileged and the well off... Family problems are found in every class, he said, but were more common among the less privileged.* N-PLURAL: the N
2 **Privileged** information is known by only a small group of people who are not legally required to disclose it. *The data is privileged information, not to be shared with the general public... Mr Nixon argued the tapes were privileged.* ADJ: usu ADJ n =confidential

privy /prɪvi/ **privies** ◆◇◇◇◇
1 If you **are privy to** something secret, you have been allowed to know about it; a formal use. *Only three people, including a policeman, will be privy to the facts.* ADJ: v-link ADJ to n
2 A **privy** is a toilet, especially one that is in a small shed outside a house; an old-fashioned use. N-COUNT

Privy Council. In Britain, **the Privy Council** is a group of people who are appointed to advise the king or queen on political affairs. N-PROPER: the N

prize /praɪz/ **prizes, prizing, prized;** also spelled **prise** in British English for meanings 5 and 6. ◆◆◆◆◇
1 A **prize** is something valuable, for example money or a trophy, that is given to someone who has the best results in a competition or game, or as a reward for doing good work. *You must claim your prize by telephoning our claims line... He won first prize at the Leeds Piano Competition... He was awarded the Nobel Prize for Physics in 1985... They were going all out for the prize-money, £6,500 for the winning team.* N-COUNT
2 You use **prize** to describe things that are of such good quality that they win prizes or deserve to win prizes. *...a prize bull. ...prize blooms.* ADJ: ADJ n
3 You can refer to someone or something as a **prize** when people consider them to be of great value or importance. *With no lands of his own, he was no great matrimonial prize.* N-COUNT
4 Something that **is prized** is wanted and admired because it is considered to be very valuable or very good quality. *Military figures, made out of lead are prized by collectors... One of the gallery's most prized possessions is the portrait of Ginevra da Vinci.* VB: usu passive be V-ed V-ed
5 If you **prize** something open or **prize** it away from a surface, you force it to open or force it to come away from the surface. *He tried to prize the dog's mouth open... I prised off the metal rim surrounding one of the dials... Your dad would prise bullets out of old dead trees.* VERB V n with adj V n with adv V n out of/from n
6 If you **prize** something such as information **out of** someone, you persuade them to tell you although they may be very unwilling to. *Alison and I had to prize conversation out of him.* VERB V n out of n Also V n with out

prize fight, prize fights. A **prize fight** is a boxing match where the boxers are paid to fight, especially when this match is not authorized by an official boxing authority. *Banning boxing would achieve nothing, and may result in worse injuries from illegal prize fights.* N-COUNT

prize fighter, prize fighters. A **prize fighter** is a boxer who fights to win money. N-COUNT

prize-giving, prize-givings; also spelled **prizegiving**. In Britain, a **prize-giving** is a ceremony where prizes are awarded to people who have produced a very high standard of work. *Neil had been at a prize giving ceremony at a school in Birmingham. ...a prize-giving for cattle-breeding.* N-COUNT

pro /prou/ **pros** ◆◆◇◇◇

1 A **pro** is a professional; an informal use. *In the professional theater, there is a tremendous need to prove that you're a pro... I have enjoyed playing with some of the top pros from Europe and America.* N-COUNT =professional ≠amateur

2 In American English, a **pro** player is a professional sportsman or woman. You can also use **pro** to refer to sports that are played be professional sportsmen or women. *...a former college and pro basketball player... Corsin played pro football for nine years.* ADJ: ADJ n

3 If you are **pro** a particular course of action or belief, you agree with it or support it. *They're still very pro the Communist party.* PREP =for ≠against

4 The **pros and cons** of something are its advantages and disadvantages, which you consider carefully so that you can make a sensible decision. *They sat for hours debating the pros and cons of setting up their own firm... Motherhood has both its pros and cons.* PHRASE: PHR after v, oft PHR *of* -ing/n

pro- /prou-/. You can add **pro-** to adjectives and nouns in order to form adjectives that describe people who support or admire a particular person, system, or idea. *...pro-Yeltsin forces in the Russian Congress... He was at the forefront of the pro-democracy campaign in the country... Younger voters are strongly pro-European.* PREFIX

proactive /prouæktɪv/. **Proactive** actions are intended to cause changes, rather than just reacting to change. *In order to survive the competition a company should be proactive not reactive... Industry must adopt a much more proactive approach to formulating environmental policy.* ADJ-GRADED ≠reactive

pro-am, pro-ams; also spelled **pro am**. A **pro-am** is a tournament where professional and amateur players compete together in the same event. *...a sponsored pro-am golf tournament.* N-COUNT: oft N n

probabilistic /prɒbəbɪlɪstɪk/. **Probabilistic** actions, methods, or arguments are based on the idea that you cannot be certain about results or future events but you can judge whether or not they are probable, and act or formulate beliefs on the basis of this judgement. *...probabilistic exposure to risk.* ADJ: usu ADJ n

probability /prɒbəbɪlɪti/ **probabilities** ◆◇◇◇◇

1 The **probability** of something happening is how likely it is to happen, sometimes expressed as a fraction or a percentage. *Without a transfusion, the victim's probability of dying was 100%... The probabilities of crime or victimization are higher with some situations than with others... You cannot prove conclusively that Sellafield caused cancer. You can only work on the basis of probability.* N-VAR =likelihood

2 You say that there is a **probability** that something will happen when it is likely to happen. *There's an excellent probability that unless action is quickly taken, pipes will freeze... If you've owned property for several years, the probability is that values have increased... Formal talks are still said to be a possibility, not a probability... His story-telling can push the bounds of probability a bit far at times.* N-VAR PRAGMATICS

3 If you say that something will happen **in all probability**, you mean that you think it is very likely to happen. *The Republicans had better get used to the fact that in all probability, they are going to lose... In all probability, the final upturn in their fortunes is some months away yet.* PHRASE: PHR with cl PRAGMATICS

probable /prɒbəbᵊl/ ◆◇◇◇◇

1 If you say that something is **probable**, you mean that it is likely to be true or likely to happen. *It is probable that the medication will suppress the symptom without treating the condition... She does not want to be taken to an optician with the probable result of having to wear glasses... An airline official said a bomb was the incident's most probable cause.* ADJ-GRADED: oft *it* v-link ADJ that PRAGMATICS =likely ≠unlikely

2 You can use **probable** to describe a role or function that someone or something is likely to have. *The Socialists united behind their probable presidential candidate, Michel Rocard.* ADJ: ADJ n =likely

probably /prɒbəbli/ ◆◆◆◆◆

1 If you say that something is **probably** the case, you think that it is likely to be the case, although you are not sure. *The White House probably won't make this plan public until July... Van Gogh is probably the best-known painter in the world. ...a new and probably highly dangerous development in the area.* ADV-GRADED: ADV with cl/group PRAGMATICS

2 You can use **probably** when you want to make your opinion sound less forceful or definite, so that you do not offend people. *What would he think of their story. He'd probably think she and Lenny were both crazy!* ADV-GRADED: ADV with cl/group PRAGMATICS

probate /proubeɪt/. **Probate** is the act or process of officially proving a will to be valid. *Probate cases can go on for two years or more.* N-UNCOUNT: oft N n

probation /prəbeɪʃᵊn, AM prou-/ ◆◇◇◇◇

1 **Probation** is a period of time during which a person who has committed a crime has to obey the law and be supervised by a probation officer, rather than being sent to prison. *A young woman admitted three theft charges and was put on probation for two years.* N-UNCOUNT

2 **Probation** is a period of time during which someone is judging your character and ability while you work, in order to see if you are suitable for that type of work. *Employee appointment to the Council will be subject to a term of probation of 6 months... After a further four-month extension of her probation period, she was sacked.* N-UNCOUNT

probationary /prəbeɪʃənəri, AM proubeɪʃəneri/. A **probationary** period is a period during which someone is assessed at the beginning of their career before they are allowed to continue. *The National Union of Teachers said it wanted the probationary period extended to two years.* ADJ: ADJ n =trial

probationer /prəbeɪʃənəʳ, prou-/ **probationers**

1 A **probationer** is someone who has been found guilty of committing a crime but is on probation rather than in prison. N-COUNT

2 A **probationer** is someone who is still being trained to do a job and is on trial. *He was a probationer policeman before he decided to return to his job as security guard.* N-COUNT

probation officer, probation officers. A **probation officer** is a person whose job is to supervise and help people who have committed crimes and been put on probation. ◆◇◇◇◇ N-COUNT

probe /proub/ **probes, probing, probed** ◆◆◇◇◇

1 If you **probe** into something, you ask questions or make enquiries in order to discover facts about it. *The more they probed into his background, the more inflamed their suspicions would become... For three years, I have probed for understanding... The Office of Fair Trading has been probing banking practices... The form asks probing questions.* ► Also a noun. *...a federal grand-jury probe into corruption within the FDA.* ♦ **probing, probings** *If he remains here, he'll be away from the press and their probings.* VERB V *into* n V *for* n V n V-ing N-COUNT N-COUNT

2 If a doctor or dentist **probes**, he or she uses a special instrument to examine delicate parts of a patient's body. *The surgeon would pick up his instruments, probe, repair and stitch up again... Dr Amid probed around the sensitive area... A doctor probed deep in his shoulder wound for shrapnel.* VERB V V prep/adv

3 A **probe** is a long thin instrument that doctors and dentists use to examine delicate parts of the body. *...a fibre-optic probe.* N-COUNT

4 If you **probe** a place, you search it in order to find someone or something that you looking for. *A flashlight beam probed the underbrush only yards away from their hiding place... I probed around for some time in the bushes.* VERB V n V adv/prep

5 In a conflict such as a war, if one side **probes** another side's defences, they try to find their weak- VERB

nesses, for example by attacking them in specific areas using a small number of troops; used in journalism. *He probes the enemy's weak positions, ignoring his strongholds... Squads of prison officers have been probing the rioters' defences.* ► Also a noun. *Small probes would give the allied armies some combat experience before the main battle started.* — V n; N-COUNT

6 A **space probe** is an unmanned spacecraft which travels deep into space in order to study the planets and send information about them back to earth. *Its rings were discovered by telescope from Earth, but space probes later found that spectacular rings surround some other planets... The Pioneer probes have on board ultra-violet instruments which are measuring light that we can't measure on the earth.* — N-COUNT: usu n N

probity /proubɪti/. **Probity** is a high standard of correct moral behaviour; a formal word. *He asserted his innocence and his financial probity.* — N-UNCOUNT

problem /prɒbləm/ **problems** ◆◆◆◆◆

1 A **problem** is a situation that is unsatisfactory and causes difficulties for people. *...the economic problems of the inner city... The main problem is unemployment... He told Americans that solving the energy problem was very important... I do not have a simple solution to the drug problem.* — N-COUNT: usu with supp, oft N *of/with* n

2 A **problem** is a puzzle that requires logical thought or mathematics to solve it. *With mathematical problems, you can save time by approximating.* — N-COUNT

3 **Problem** children or **problem** families cause a lot of difficulties for themselves or for other people, often because they come from a deprived background or because they have had a lot of bad experiences. *In some cases a problem child is placed in a special school... She is afraid to contact the social services in case they are labelled a problem family.* — ADJ: ADJ n =difficult

4 **'No problem'** is an informal expression that people say to show their willingness to do what they have been asked. *'Can you repair it?' 'No problem. ... If the property needs a new dishwasher, no problem, just put it on a credit card.* — PHRASES CONVENTION PRAGMATICS

5 **'No problem'** is an informal expression that you can use to let someone else know that you do not mind them doing something they have said they are going to do; used in spoken English. *'I ought to think about going actually. If that's all right with you.' 'Yeah. No problem.'... If they don't want to speak to me, fine. No problem.* — CONVENTION PRAGMATICS

problematic /prɒbləmætɪk/. Something that is **problematic** involves problems and difficulties; a formal word. *Some places are more problematic than others for women traveling alone. ...the problematic business of running an economy.* — ◆◇◇◇◇ ADJ-GRADED =problematical

problematical /prɒbləmætɪkəl/. **Problematical** means the same as **problematic**; a formal word. — ADJ-GRADED

procedural /prəsiːdʒərəl/. **Procedural** means involving a formal procedure; a formal word. *A Spanish judge rejected the suit on procedural grounds... The Paris talks will mainly be about procedural matters.* — ◆◇◇◇◇ ADJ: usu ADJ n

procedure /prəsiːdʒər/ **procedures.** A **procedure** is a way of doing something, especially the usual or correct way. *A biopsy is usually a minor surgical procedure... Police insist that Michael did not follow the correct procedure in applying for a visa... The White House said there would be no change in procedure.* — ◆◆◆◇◇ N-VAR =practice

proceed, proceeds, proceeding, proceeded. ◆◆◆◇◇

The verb is pronounced /prəsiːd/. The plural noun in meaning 5 is pronounced /prousiːdz/.

1 If you **proceed** to do something, you do it, often after doing something else first. *He proceeded to tell me of my birth... He asked for ice for his whiskey and proceeded to get contentedly drunk.* — VERB V to-inf

2 If you **proceed with** a course of action, you continue with it; a formal use. *The group proceeded with a march they knew would lead to bloodshed... Charges has been delayed until November because the defence is not ready to proceed.* — VERB =continue V *with* n V

3 If an activity, process, or event **proceeds**, it goes on and does not stop. *The ideas were not new. Their development had proceeded steadily since the war... Efforts to reform the Interior Ministry have not yet proceeded very far.* — VERB V

4 If you **proceed** in a particular direction, you go in that direction; a formal use. *She climbed the steps and proceeded along the upstairs hallway... The freighter was allowed to proceed after satisfying them that it was not breaking sanctions.* — VERB =continue V prep/adv V

5 **The proceeds** of an event or activity are the money that has been obtained from it. *The proceeds of the arms sales were then funneled to Contra fighters in Central America... The proceeds from the concert will go towards famine relief.* — N-PLURAL: *the* N, oft *the* N *of/from* n

proceeding /prəsiːdɪŋ/ **proceedings** ◆◆◇◇◇

1 Legal **proceedings** are legal action taken against someone; a formal use. *...criminal proceedings against the former prime minister... The Council had brought proceedings to stop the store from trading on Sundays.* — N-COUNT: usu pl

2 **The proceedings** are an organized series of events that take place in a particular place; a formal use. *The proceedings of the enquiry will take place in private... He viewed the proceedings with doubt and alarm.* — N-COUNT: usu pl, usu *the* N

3 You can refer to a written record of the discussions at a meeting or conference as **the proceedings**. *The Department of Transport is to publish the conference proceedings.* — N-PLURAL: *the* N

process /prouses, AM prɑːses/ **processes, processing, processed** ◆◆◆◆◆

1 A **process** is a series of actions which are carried out in order to achieve a particular result. *There was total agreement to start the peace process as soon as possible... They decided to spread the building process over three years... The best way to proceed is by a process of elimination.* — N-COUNT: oft supp N, N of n

2 A **process** is a series of things which happen naturally and result in a biological or chemical change. *It occurs in elderly men, apparently as part of the ageing process... The regularity with which this occurs suggests that the process is genetically determined.* — N-COUNT

3 When raw materials or foods **are processed**, they are treated chemically or industrially before they are used or sold. *...fish which are processed by the best methods: from freezing to canning and smoking... The material will be processed into plastic pellets. ...diets high in refined and processed foods.* — VERB *be* V-ed *be* V-ed *into* n V-ed Also V n
► Also a noun. *...the cost of re-engineering the production process.* — N-COUNT
♦ **processing** *America sent cotton to England for processing. ...nuclear fuel processing plant.* — N-UNCOUNT: usu with supp

4 When people **process** information, they put it through a system or into a computer in order to deal with it. *...facilities to process the data, and the right to publish the results... The information gathered by the telescopes will be processed by computers.* — VERB V n
♦ **processing** *...data processing... The advances in communications altered the nature of information processing.* ● See also **word processing**. — N-UNCOUNT: supp N

5 When people **are processed** by officials, their case is dealt with in stages and they pass from one stage of the process to the next. *Patients took more than two and a half hours to be processed through the department.* — VB: usu passive *be* V-ed

6 If you are **in the process of** doing something, you have started to do it and are still doing it. *The administration is in the process of drawing up a peace plan... Her novel is in the process of being turned into a television series.* — PHRASES V inflects, usu v-link PHR

7 If you are doing something and you do something else **in the process**, you do the second thing as part of doing the first thing. *He finished ahead of the Spaniard, and in the process picked up his first time trial win as a pro... You have to let us struggle for ourselves, even if we must die in the process.* — PHR with cl

processed cheese, processed cheeses. **Processed cheese** is cheese that has been specially made so that it can be sold and stored in — N-MASS large quantities. It is sometimes sold in the form of thin individually wrapped slices.

procession /prəseʃən/ **processions.** A **procession** is a group of people who are walking, riding, or driving in a line as part of a public event. *...a funeral procession. ...religious processions.* ◆◆◇◇◇ N-COUNT

processional /prəseʃənəl/. **Processional** means used for or taking part in a ceremonial procession. *The processional route along the town's main streets was festooned with flowers.* ADJ: ADJ n

processor /prouseəsər, AM prɑːs-/ **processors** ◆◆◇◇◇
1 A **processor** is the part of a computer that interprets commands and performs the processes the user has requested; a technical use in computer science. N-COUNT =CPU
2 A **processor** is someone or something which carries out a process. *The frozen-food industry could be supplied entirely by growers and processors outside the country.* N-COUNT

proclaim /proʊkleɪm/ **proclaims, proclaiming, proclaimed** ◆◆◇◇◇
1 If people **proclaim** something, they formally make it known to the public. *The Boers rebelled against British rule, proclaiming their independence on 30 December 1880... Britain proudly proclaims that it is a nation of animal lovers... He still proclaims himself a believer in the Revolution.* VERB =declare, announce V n V that V pron-refl n Also V n n, V n *as* n
2 If you **proclaim** something such as an opinion, you state it emphatically. *'I think we have been heard today,' he proclaimed... He confidently proclaims that he is offering the best value in the market.* VERB V with quote V that

proclamation /prɒkləmeɪʃən/ **proclamations.** A **proclamation** is a public announcement about something important, often about something of national importance. *The proclamation of independence was broadcast over the radio.* ◆◇◇◇◇ N-COUNT: oft N *of* n =declaration, announcement

proclivity /prəklɪvɪti, AM proʊ-/ **proclivities.** A **proclivity** is a tendency to behave in a particular way or to like a particular thing, often a bad way or thing; a formal word. *He was indulging his own sexual proclivities. ...a proclivity to daydream.* N-COUNT =tendency

procrastinate /proʊkræstɪneɪt/ **procrastinates, procrastinating, procrastinated.** If you **procrastinate**, you keep postponing things that you should do, often because you do not want to do them; a formal word. *Most often we procrastinate when faced with something we do not want to do.* ♦ **procrastination** /proʊkræstɪneɪʃən/ *He hates delay and procrastination in all its forms.* VERB =stall V N-UNCOUNT

procreate /proʊkrieɪt/ **procreates, procreating, procreated.** When animals or people **procreate**, they produce young or babies; a formal word. *Most young women feel a biological need to procreate.* ♦ **procreation** /proʊkrieɪʃən/ *Early marriage and procreation are no longer discouraged there.* VERB =reproduce V N-UNCOUNT =reproduction

procurator /prɒkjʊreɪtər/ **procurators.** A **procurator** is an administrative official with legal powers, especially in the former Soviet Union, the Roman Catholic Church, or the ancient Roman Empire. N-COUNT

procurator fiscal, procurators fiscal. In the Scottish legal system, the **procurator fiscal** is an officer who performs the functions of a public prosecutor. N-COUNT: usu *the* N

procure /prəkjʊər/ **procures, procuring, procured** ◆◇◇◇◇
1 If you **procure** something, especially something that is difficult to get, you obtain it; a formal use. *It remained very difficult to procure food, fuel and other daily necessities.* VERB V n
2 If someone **procures** a prostitute, they introduce the prostitute to a client. *He procured girls of 16 and 17 to be mistresses for his influential friends.* VERB V n

procurement /prəkjʊərmənt/. **Procurement** is the act of obtaining something such as supplies for an army or other organization; a formal word. *Russia was cutting procurement of new weapons 'by about 80 per cent', he said.* ◆◇◇◇◇ N-UNCOUNT =acquisition

prod /prɒd/ **prods, prodding, prodded** ◆◇◇◇◇
1 If you **prod** someone or something, you give them a quick push with your finger or with a pointed object. *He prodded Murray with the shotgun... Prod the windowsills to check for signs of rot... Cathy was prodding at a boiled egg.* ► Also a noun. *He gave the donkey a mighty prod in the backside.* VERB =poke V n *with* n V n V *at* n N-COUNT =poke
2 If you **prod** someone **into** doing something, you remind or persuade them to do it. *The report was a shock tactic to prod the Government into spending more on the Health Service... 'I thought a nice cosy dinner for two,' he said. That prodded her to say: 'Where has Mora gone, then?'* ♦ **prodding** *She did her chores without prodding.* VERB =stimulate, stir V n *into* n/-ing V n to-inf N-UNCOUNT =prompting
3 See also **cattle prod.**

prodigal /prɒdɪgəl/ **prodigals**
1 You can describe someone as **prodigal** if they leave their family or friends but later return as a better person; a literary word. *...the parable of the prodigal son.* ► A **prodigal** is someone who is prodigal. *...the prodigal had returned.* ADJ: usu ADJ n N-COUNT
2 Someone who behaves in a **prodigal** way spends a lot of money carelessly without thinking about what will happen when they have none left; used showing disapproval. *Prodigal habits die hard.* ADJ: usu ADJ n PRAGMATICS

prodigious /prədɪdʒəs/. Something that is **prodigious** is very large or impressive; a literary word. *This business generates cash in prodigious amounts... He impressed all who met him with his prodigious memory.* ♦ **prodigiously** *She ate prodigiously.* ◆◇◇◇◇ ADJ-GRADED: usu ADJ n ADV-GRADED: ADV with v

prodigy /prɒdɪdʒi/ **prodigies.** A **prodigy** is someone who has a great natural talent for something such as music or mathematics which shows itself at an early age. *The Russian tennis prodigy is well on the way to becoming the youngest world champion of all time.* ◆◇◇◇◇ N-COUNT: usu supp N

produce, produces, producing, produced. ◆◆◆◆◆ The verb is pronounced /prədjuːs, AM -duːs/. The noun is pronounced /prɒdjuːs, AM -duːs/.
1 To **produce** something means to cause it to happen. *The drug is known to produce side-effects in women... Talks aimed at producing a new world trade treaty have been under way for six years.* VERB =bring about V n
2 If you **produce** something, you make or create it. *The company produced circuitry for communications systems... I'm quite pleased that we do have the capacity to produce that much food.* VERB V n
3 When things or people **produce** something, it comes from them or slowly forms from them, especially as the result of a biological or chemical process. *These plants are then pollinated and allowed to mature and produce seed... Acid rain forms when gases produced by burning coal and oil are dissolved in the atmosphere.* VERB V n V-ed
4 If you **produce** evidence or an argument, you show it or explain it to people in order to make them agree with you. *They challenged him to produce evidence to support his allegations... Scientists have produced powerful arguments against his ideas.* VERB =come up with V n
5 If you **produce** an object from somewhere, you show it or bring it out so that it can be seen. *To hire a car you must produce a passport and a current driving licence... She produced the knife during arguments with her friends.* VERB V n
6 If someone **produces** something such as a film, a magazine, or a record, they organize it and decide how it should be done. *He has produced his own sports magazine called Yes Sport... He produced 'A Chorus Line', Broadway's longest running show.* VERB V n
7 **Produce** is food or other things that are grown in large quantities to be sold. *We manage to get most of our produce in Britain... Winter produce will cost more for the next few weeks.* N-UNCOUNT

producer /prədjuːsər, AM -duːs-/ **producers** ◆◆◆◆◇
1 A **producer** is a person whose job is to produce plays, films, programmes, or records. *Vanya Kewley is a freelance film producer. ...Mike Morley, the producer of Central Television's Dennis Nilsen documentary.* N-COUNT
2 A **producer** of a food or material is a company or N-COUNT

country that grows or manufactures a large amount of it. *The estate is generally a producer of high quality wines. ...Saudi Arabia, the world's leading oil producer.*

product /prɒdʌkt/ **products** ◆◆◆◆◆

1 A **product** is something that is produced and sold in large quantities, often as a result of a manufacturing process. *Try to get the best product at the lowest price... South Korea's imports of consumer products jumped 33% in this year.* N-COUNT

2 If you say that someone or something is a **product of** a situation or process, you mean that the situation or process has had a significant effect in making that person or thing what they are. *We are all products of our time... The bank is the product of a 1971 merger of two Japanese banks.* N-COUNT: N *of* n

production /prədʌkʃᵊn/ **productions** ◆◆◆◆◇

1 Production is the process of manufacturing or growing something in large quantities. *That model won't go into production before late 1990. ...tax incentives to encourage domestic production of oil.* N-UNCOUNT: oft *into* N

2 Production is the amount of goods manufactured or grown by a company or country. *We needed to increase the volume of production... It expected to maintain production of cars at the same level as last year.* N-UNCOUNT =output

3 The **production of** something is its creation as the result of a natural process. *These proteins stimulate the production of blood cells.* N-UNCOUNT: oft N *of* n

4 Production is the process of organizing and preparing a play, film, programme, or record, in order to present it to the public. *During the film's production, the director wanted to shoot a riot scene but the filming was blocked... She is head of the production company.* N-UNCOUNT: usu with supp

5 A **production** is a play, opera, or other show that is performed in a theatre. *For this production she has learnt the role in Spanish. ...a critically proclaimed production of Othello.* N-COUNT

6 When you can do something **on production of** or **on the production of** documents, you need to show someone those documents in order to be able to do that thing. *Entry to the show is free to members on production of their membership cards.* PHRASE: PHR n =on presentation of

prod<u>u</u>ction line, production lines. A **production line** is an arrangement of machines in a factory where the products pass from machine to machine until they are finished. *Their first car rolls off the production line on December 16.* ◆◇◇◇◇ N-COUNT =assembly line

productive /prədʌktɪv/ ◆◆◇◇◇

1 Someone or something that is **productive** is very efficient at what they do, for example growing a large amount of food at a competitive cost. *Training makes workers highly productive... More productive farmers have been able to provide cheaper food. ...fertile and productive soils.* ADJ-GRADED ♦ **productively** *The company is certain to reinvest its profits productively.* ADV-GRADED: ADV with v

2 If you say that a relationship between people is **productive**, you mean that a lot of good or useful things happen as a result of it. *He was hopeful that the next round of talks would also be productive... I was sorry he had left, although I soon developed a productive relationship with his successors.* ADJ-GRADED =fruitful ♦ **productively** *They feel they are interacting productively with elderly patients.* ADV: ADV with v

3 Something that is **productive of** a situation or feeling creates it; a formal use. *Land, labor and capital are all productive of wealth.* ADJ-GRADED: v-link ADJ *of* n

productivity /prɒdʊktɪvɪti/. **Productivity** is the rate at which goods are produced. *The third-quarter results reflect continued improvements in productivity... His method of obtaining a high level of productivity is demanding.* ◆◆◇◇◇ N-UNCOUNT =output

Prof. /prɒf/ **Profs;** also spelled **prof.** ◆◇◇◇◇

1 Prof. is an abbreviation for **'professor'**. You write it in front of a professor's name. *...Prof. Richard Joyner of Liverpool University.* N-TITLE; N-COUNT

2 In conversations with other people, someone might refer to a professor as **prof**; an informal use. *Write a note to my prof and tell him why I missed an exam this morning.* N-VOC; N-COUNT PRAGMATICS

3 In newspaper advertisements for things such as flats that are for rent, **prof.** means **'professional'**. *Single room in lovely flat, roof terrace, non-smoking prof., woman pref.*

profane /prəfeɪn, AM proʊ-/ **profanes, profaning, profaned**

1 Profane behaviour shows disrespect for a religion or religious things, so that it is considered sinful; a formal use. *...profane language.* ADJ-GRADED

2 Something that is **profane** is concerned with everyday life rather than religion and spiritual things. *Cardinal Daly has said that churches should not be used for profane or secular purposes.* ADJ ≠spiritual

3 If someone **profanes** a religious belief or institution, they treat it with disrespect. *They have profaned the long upheld traditions of the Church.* VERB V n ♦ **profanation** /prɒfəneɪʃᵊn/ *They called for demonstrations to express revulsion at the profanation of a Jewish cemetery.* N-UNCOUNT: oft N *of* n =violation

profanity /prəfænɪti, AM proʊ-/ **profanities**

1 Profanity is an act that shows disrespect for a religion or religious beliefs; a formal use. *To desecrate a holy spring is considered profanity.* N-UNCOUNT =sacrilege

2 Profanities are swear words; a formal use. *We have grown accustomed to having our ears assailed by mindless cursing and profanities.* N-COUNT: usu pl =obscenities

profess /prəfes/ **professes, professing, professed** ◆◇◇◇◇

1 If you **profess** to do or have something, you claim that you do it or have it, often when you do not; a formal use. *She professed to hate her nickname... Why do organisations profess that they care?... 'I don't know,' Pollard replied, professing innocence. ...the Republicans' professed support for traditional family values.* VERB =claim V to-inf V that V n V-ed

2 If you **profess** a feeling, opinion, or belief, you express it; a formal use. *He professed to be content with the arrangement... Bacher professed himself pleased with the Indian tour. ...a right to profess their faith in Islam.* VERB =declare V to-inf V pron-refl adj V n

profession /prəfeʃᵊn/ **professions** ◆◆◆◇◇

1 A **profession** is a type of job that requires advanced education or training. *Harper was a teacher by profession... Only 20 per cent of jobs in the professions are held by women.* N-COUNT: also *by* N

2 You can use **profession** to refer to all the people who have the same profession. *The attitude of the medical profession is very much more liberal now.* N-COUNT-COLL: oft supp N

professional /prəfeʃənᵊl/ **professionals** ◆◆◆◆◇

1 Professional means relating to a person's work, especially work that requires special training. *His professional career started at Liverpool University.* ADJ: ADJ n ♦ **professionally** *...a professionally-qualified architect... The opening months of 1987 were difficult, personally and professionally.* ADV: ADV -ed/adj, ADV with cl

2 Professional people have jobs that require advanced education or training. *...highly qualified professional people like doctors and engineers.* ADJ: ADJ n ► Also a noun. *My father wanted me to become a professional and have more stability.* N-COUNT

3 You use **professional** to describe people who do a particular thing to earn money rather than as a hobby. *This has been my worst time for injuries since I started as a professional footballer... Jack Nicklaus has played in every Major Championship since he turned professional in 1961.* ADJ ≠amateur ► Also a noun. *He had been a professional since March 1985.* N-COUNT ♦ **professionally** *By age 16 he was playing professionally with bands in Greenwich Village.* ADV: ADV after v

4 Professional sports are played for money rather than as a hobby. *...an art student who had played professional football for a short time.* ADJ: ADJ n

5 If you say that something that someone does or produces is **professional**, you approve of it because you think that it is of a very high standard. *They run it with a truly professional but personal touch.* ADJ-GRADED PRAGMATICS ≠amateur ► Also a noun. *...a dedicated professional who worked harmoniously with the cast and crew.* N-COUNT ♦ **professionally** *These tickets have been produced very professionally.* ADV-GRADED: ADV with v

6 See also **semi-professional**.

professional foul, professional fouls. **N-COUNT** In football, if a player commits a **professional foul,** they deliberately do something which is against the rules in order to prevent another player from scoring a goal.

professionalism /prəfeʃənəlɪzəm/. ◆◇◇◇◇ **N-UNCOUNT** **PRAGMATICS** **Professionalism** in a job is a combination of skill and high standards; used showing approval. *American companies pride themselves on their professionalism... There was a lack of professionalism in their dealings.*

professionalize /prəfeʃənəlaɪz/ **professionalizes, professionalizing, professionalized;** **VERB** also spelled **professionalise** in British English. To **professionalize** an organization, an institution, or an activity means to make it more professional, for example by paying the people who are involved in it. **V n** *...the possibility of professionalising local government by offering salaries to senior councillors.*
♦ **professionalization** /prəfeʃənəlaɪzeɪʃən/ **N-UNCOUNT: oft N of n** *The professionalisation of politics is a major source of our ills.*

professor /prəfesəʳ/ **professors** ◆◆◆◆◇
1 **N-TITLE; N-COUNT; N-VOC** A **professor** in a British university is the most senior teacher in a department. *...Professor Cameron... In 1979, only 2% of British professors were female.*
2 **N-COUNT; N-TITLE; N-VOC** A **professor** in an American or Canadian university or college is a teacher there. *Robert Dunn is a professor of economics at George Washington University.*

professorial /prɒfɪsɔːriəl/
1 **ADJ-GRADED** If you describe someone as **professorial**, you mean that they look or behave like a professor. *His manner is not so much regal as professorial... I raised my voice to a professorial tone.*
2 **ADJ: ADJ n** **Professorial** means relating to the work of a professor. *...the cuts which have led to 36 per cent of professorial posts remaining unfilled.*

professorship /prəfesəʳʃɪp/ **professorships.** **N-COUNT** A **professorship** is the post of professor in a university. *He has accepted a research professorship at Cambridge University.*

proffer /prɒfəʳ/ **proffers, proffering, proffered** ◆◇◇◇◇
1 **VERB =offer** If you **proffer** something to someone, you hold it towards them so that they can take it or touch it; a formal use. **V n Also V n to n** *He rose and proffered a silver box full of cigarettes.*
2 **VERB =volunteer** If you **proffer** something such as advice to someone, you offer it to them; a formal use. **V n Also V n to n, V n n** *The army has not yet proffered an explanation of how and why the accident happened.*

proficiency /prəfɪʃənsi/. **N-UNCOUNT: oft N in n =ability** If you show **proficiency** in something, you show ability or skill at it. *Evidence of basic proficiency in English is part of the admission requirement.*

proficient /prəfɪʃənt/. **ADJ-GRADED: oft ADJ in/at n =competent** If you are **proficient** in something, you can do it well. *A great number of Egyptians are proficient in foreign languages.*

profile /proʊfaɪl/ **profiles, profiling, profiled** ◆◆◆◇◇
1 **N-COUNT** Your **profile** is the outline of your face as it is seen when someone is looking at you from the side. *His handsome profile was turned away from the company.*
2 **N-UNCOUNT: in N** If you see someone **in profile**, you see them from the side. *This picture shows the girl in profile.*
3 **N-COUNT: with supp, usu N of n** A **profile of** someone is a short article or programme in which their life and character are described. *A Washington newspaper published comparative profiles of the candidates' wives.*
4 **VERB** If a journalist **profiles** someone, they give an account of that person's life and character. **V n** *Tamar Golan, a Paris-based journalist, profiles the rebel leader.*
5 **PHRASE: PHR after v** If someone has a **high profile**, people notice them and what they do. If you keep a **low profile**, you avoid doing things that will make people notice you. *...a move that would give Egypt a much higher profile in the upcoming peace talks... Football is a high profile business... The police deliberately kept a low profile in most places.* ● See also **high-profile**.

profit /prɒfɪt/ **profits, profiting, profited** ◆◆◆◆◇
1 **N-VAR ≠loss** A **profit** is an amount of money that you gain when you are paid more for something than it cost you to make, get, or do it. *The bank made pre-tax profits of £3.5 million... You can improve your chances of profit by sensible planning... The profit motive is inherently at odds with principles of fairness and equity.*
2 **VERB** If you **profit** from something, you earn a profit from it. **V from/by n/-ing** *Footballers are accustomed to profiting handsomely from bonuses...* **V** *He has profited by selling his holdings to other investors... The dealers profited shamefully at the expense of my family.*
3 **V-ERG** If you **profit** from something, or it **profits** you, you gain some advantage or benefit from it; a formal use. **V from/by n** *Jennifer wasn't yet totally convinced that she'd profit from a more relaxed lifestyle...* **V n** *So far the French alliance had profited the rebels little...* **it V n to-inf** *Whom would it profit to terrify or to kill James Sinclair?* ► Also a noun. **N-UNCOUNT** *The artist found more to his profit in the sculpture collections of the Louvre and other museums.*

profitable /prɒfɪtəbəl/ ◆◆◇◇◇
1 **ADJ-GRADED: oft it v-link ADJ to-inf** A **profitable** organization or practice makes a profit. *Drug manufacturing is the most profitable business in America... It was profitable for them to produce large amounts of food.* ♦ **profitably** **ADV-GRADED: ADV with v** /prɒfɪtəbli/ *The 28 French stores are trading profitably.* ♦ **profitability** **N-UNCOUNT** /prɒfɪtəbɪlɪti/ *Changes were made in operating methods in an effort to increase profitability.*
2 **ADJ-GRADED: usu ADJ n** Something that is **profitable** results in some benefit for you. *...close collaboration with industry which leads to a profitable exchange of personnel and ideas.* ♦ **profitably** **ADV-GRADED: ADV with v** *In fact he could scarcely have spent his time more profitably.*

profiteer /prɒfɪtɪəʳ/ **profiteers.** **N-COUNT: usu pl** **PRAGMATICS** **=racketeer** If you describe someone as a **profiteer**, you are critical of them because they make large profits by charging high prices for goods that are hard to get. *...a new social class composed largely of war profiteers and gangsters.*

profiteering /prɒfɪtɪərɪŋ/. **N-UNCOUNT** **PRAGMATICS** **=racketeering** If someone makes large profits by charging high prices for goods that are hard to get, you can say that they are engaged in **profiteering**; used showing disapproval. *There's been a wave of profiteering and corruption.*

profit-making. **ADJ: usu ADJ n** A **profit-making** business or organization makes a profit. *He wants to set up a profit-making company, owned mostly by the university.* ● See also **non-profit-making**.

profit margin, profit margins. ◆◇◇◇◇ **N-COUNT** A **profit margin** is the difference between the selling price of a product and the cost of producing and marketing it. *The group had a net profit margin of 30% last year.*

profit-sharing. **N-UNCOUNT: oft N n** **Profit-sharing** is a system by which all the people who work in a company have a share in its profits.

profit-taking. ◆◇◇◇◇ **N-UNCOUNT** **Profit-taking** is the selling of stocks and shares at a profit after their value has risen or just before their value falls.

profligacy /prɒflɪgəsi/. **N-UNCOUNT =wastefulness** **Profligacy** is extravagance and wastefulness; a formal word. *...the continuing profligacy of certain states.*

profligate /prɒflɪgɪt/. **ADJ-GRADED =wasteful ≠careful** **Profligate** means extravagant and wasteful; a formal word. *...the most profligate consumer of energy in the world.*

pro forma /proʊ fɔːʳmə/; also spelled **pro-forma.** **ADJ: usu ADJ n** In banking, a company's **pro forma** balance or earnings are their expected balance or earnings.

profound /prəfaʊnd/ **profounder, profoundest** ◆◆◇◇◇
1 **ADJ-GRADED =great** You use **profound** to emphasize that something is very great or intense. *...discoveries which had a profound effect on many areas of medicine. ...profound disagreement... The overwhelming feeling is just deep, profound shock and anger... Anna's patriotism was profound.* ♦ **profoundly** **ADV-GRADED:** *This has pro-*

foundly affected my life... In politics, as in other areas, he is profoundly conservative. ADV with v, ADV adj/-ed

2 A **profound** idea, work, or person shows great intellectual depth and understanding. *This is a book full of profound, original and challenging insights. ...one of the country's most profound minds.* ADJ-GRADED =deep ≠shallow

profundity /prəfʌndɪti/ **profundities**

1 **Profundity** is great intellectual depth and understanding. *The profundity of this book is achieved with breathtaking lightness.* N-UNCOUNT =depth

2 If you refer to the **profundity of** a feeling, experience, or change, you mean that it is deep, powerful, or serious. *...the profundity of the structural problems besetting the country.* N-UNCOUNT: usu N *of*n

3 A **profundity** is a remark that shows great intellectual depth and understanding. *His work is full of profundities and asides concerning the human condition.* N-COUNT ≠banality

profuse /prəfjuːs/

1 **Profuse** sweating, bleeding, or vomiting is sweating, bleeding, or vomiting large amounts; a medical use. *...a remedy that produces profuse sweating.* ADJ-GRADED: usu ADJ n
♦ **profusely** *He was bleeding profusely... Profusely sweating and quivering with chills, he murmured his last words.* ADV-GRADED: ADV after v

2 If you offer **profuse** apologies or thanks, you apologize or thank someone a lot. *Then the policeman recognised me, breaking into profuse apologies.* ♦ **profusely** *They were very grateful to be put right and thanked me profusely.* ADJ: usu ADJ n; ADV-GRADED: ADV after v

profusion /prəfjuːʒən/. If there is a **profusion of** something or if it occurs **in profusion**, there is a very large quantity or variety of it; a formal word. *The Dart is a delightful river with a profusion of wild flowers along its banks... Olive groves, grapes, and citrus fruits grow in profusion.* ♦◇◇◇◇ N-SING-COLL: usu N *of*n, also *in*N =abundance

progenitor /proʊdʒenɪtəʳ/ **progenitors**

1 A **progenitor** of someone is a direct ancestor of theirs; a formal use. *He was also a progenitor of seven presidents of Nicaragua.* N-COUNT: usu with poss =forefather

2 The **progenitor** of an idea or invention is the person who first thought of it; a formal use. *...Clive Sinclair, progenitor of the C5 electric car.* N-COUNT: usu with poss =originator

progeny /prɒdʒəni/

1 You can refer to a person's children or to an animal's young as their **progeny**; a formal use. *Davis was never loquacious on the subject of his progeny.* N-PLURAL: usu with poss =offspring

2 The **progeny** of a particular thing are the things that develop from it. *Among its many progeny, the 1944 Education Act gave birth to the modern youth service.* N-PLURAL: usu with poss =offspring

progesterone /proʊdʒestəroʊn/. **Progesterone** is a hormone produced in the ovaries of women and female animals. Progesterone helps prepare the body for pregnancy. *If the egg is not fertilised oestrogen and progesterone decrease.* ♦◇◇◇◇ N-UNCOUNT

prognosis /prɒgnoʊsɪs/ **prognoses** /prɒgnoʊsiːz/. A **prognosis** is an estimate of the future of someone or something, especially about whether a patient will recover from an illness; a formal word. *The hospital physiotherapist's prognosis was that Laurence might walk within 12 months. ...a gloomy prognosis of the Scots' championship prospects.* ♦◇◇◇◇ N-COUNT

prognostication /prɒgnɒstɪkeɪʃən/ **prognostications.** A **prognostication** is a prediction about something; a formal word. *The country is currently obsessed with gloomy prognostications about its future.* N-VAR

program /proʊgræm/ **programs, programming, programmed** ♦♦♦♦◇

1 A **program** is a set of instructions that a computer follows in order to perform a particular task. *The chances of an error occurring in a computer program increase with the size of the program.* N-COUNT

2 When you **program** a computer, you give it a set of instructions to make it able to perform a particular task. *He programmed his computer to compare the 1431 possible combinations of pairs in this population. ...45 million people, about half of whom can program their own computers. ...a computer programmed to translate a story given to it in Chinese.* ♦ **programming** *...programming skills... Nicklaus Wirth designed Pascal to teach the concepts of programming.* VERB; V n to-inf, V n, V-ed; N-UNCOUNT: oft N n

3 See also **programme.**

programmable /proʊgræməbəl/. A **programmable** machine can be programmed, so that for example it will switch on and off automatically or do things in a particular order. *Most CD-players are programmable.* ADJ

programmatic /proʊgrəmætɪk/. **Programmatic** ideas or policies follow a particular programme. *He gave up on programmatic politics and turned his back on public life.* ADJ

programme /proʊgræm/ **programmes, programming, programmed;** spelled **program** in American English. ♦♦♦♦♦

1 A **programme** of actions or events is a series of actions or events that are planned to be done. *The general argued that the nuclear programme should still continue... The programme of sell-offs has been implemented by the new chief executive.* N-COUNT: usu with supp

2 A television or radio **programme** is something that is broadcast on television or radio. *...a series of TV programmes on global environment. ...local news programmes.* N-COUNT: oft n N

3 A theatre or concert **programme** is a booklet or sheet of paper which gives information about the play or concert you are attending. N-COUNT

4 When you **programme** a machine or system, you set its controls so that it will work in a particular way. *Parents can programme the machine not to turn on at certain times.* VERB; V n to-inf, Also V n

5 If a living creature **is programmed** to behave in a particular way, they are likely to behave in that way because of social or biological factors that they cannot control. *We are all genetically programmed to develop certain illnesses.* VB: usu passive; *be* V-ed to-inf, Also *be* V-ed

programmer /proʊgræməʳ/ **programmers.** A computer **programmer** is a person whose job involves writing programs for computers. ♦◇◇◇◇ N-COUNT

progress, **progresses, progressing, progressed.** The noun is pronounced /proʊgres, AM prɑː-/. The verb is pronounced /prəgres/. ♦♦♦♦◇

1 **Progress** is the process of gradually improving or getting nearer to achieving or completing something. *The medical community continues to make progress in the fight against cancer... The two sides made little if any progress towards agreement.* N-UNCOUNT

2 The **progress** of a situation or action is the way in which it develops. *The Chancellor is reported to have been delighted with the progress of the first day's talks... Ellen would keep me abreast of the progress by phone.* N-SING: *the*N, oft N *of*n

3 To **progress** means to move over a period of time to a stronger, more advanced, or more desirable state. *He will visit once a fortnight to see how his new staff are progressing... Were you surprised that his disease progressed so quickly?... He started only five years ago, sketching first and then progressing to painting.* VERB; V, V *to*n

4 If events **progress**, they continue to happen gradually over a period of time. *As the evening progressed, sadness turned to rage... Life was hard, and it became harder as the war progressed.* VERB; V

5 If something is **in progress**, it has started and is still continuing. *The game was already in progress when we took our seats... The diaries are a mixture of confession, work in progress and observation.* PHRASE

progression /prəgreʃən/ **progressions** ♦◇◇◇◇

1 A **progression** is a gradual development from one state to another. *Both drugs slow the progression of AIDS, but neither cures the disease... I think they saw it as a natural progression for me.* N-COUNT: usu sing, usu with supp =development

2 A **progression of** things is a number of things which come one after the other; a formal use. *There is a complete progression of habitats from dry meadows through marshes and reed-beds to open water.* N-COUNT: N *of*n

progressive /prəgresɪv/ **progressives** ♦♦◇◇◇

1 Someone who is **progressive** or has **progressive** ideas has modern ideas about how things should be done, rather than traditional ones. *...a progres-* ADJ-GRADED ≠conservative

sive businessman who had voted for Roosevelt in 1932 and 1936... Willan was able to point to the progressive changes he had already introduced... The children go to a progressive school. ► A **progressive** is someone who is progressive. *The Republicans were deeply split between progressives and conservatives.* N-COUNT ≠conservative

2 A **progressive** change happens gradually over a period of time. *One prominent symptom of the disease is progressive loss of memory. ...the progressive development of a common foreign and security policy.* ♦ **progressively** *Her symptoms became progressively worse... The amount of grant the council received from the Government was progressively reduced.* ADJ: usu ADJ n =gradual ≠sudden ADV: ADV compar, ADV with v =gradually

3 In grammar, **progressive** means the same as **continuous**. ADJ: ADJ n

prohibit /prəhɪbɪt, AM proʊ-/ **prohibits, prohibiting, prohibited.** If a law or someone in authority **prohibits** something, they forbid it or make it illegal; a formal word. *...a law that prohibits tobacco advertising in newspapers and magazines... Fishing is prohibited... Federal law prohibits foreign airlines from owning more than 25% of any U.S. airline.* ♦ **prohibition** *The Air Force and the Navy retain and codify their prohibition of women on air combat missions.* ◆◆◇◇◇ VERB =ban ≠allow V n V n *from* -ing N-UNCOUNT =banning

prohibition /proʊɪbɪʃən/ **prohibitions.** A **prohibition** is a law or rule forbidding something. *...a prohibition on discrimination. ...prohibitions against feeding birds at the airport.* ◆◇◇◇◇ N-COUNT

Prohibition. In the United States, **Prohibition** was the official banning of alcoholic drinks between 1920 and 1933. N-UNCOUNT

prohibitive /prəhɪbɪtɪv, AM proʊ-/. If the cost of something is **prohibitive**, it is so high that many people cannot afford it; a formal word. *The cost of private treatment can be prohibitive. ...the prohibitive prices charged for seats at the opera.* ♦ **prohibitively** *Meat and butter were prohibitively expensive.* ◆◇◇◇◇ ADJ-GRADED ADV: ADV adj

project, projects, projecting, projected. The noun is pronounced /prɒdʒekt/. The verb is pronounced /prədʒekt/. ◆◆◆◆◇

1 A **project** is a task that requires a lot of time and effort. *Money will also go into local development projects in Vietnam. ...an international science project... Besides film and record projects, I have continued to work in the theater.* N-COUNT: oft supp N =scheme

2 A **project** is a detailed study of a subject by a pupil or student. *Students complete projects for a personal tutor, working at home at their own pace.* N-COUNT

3 If something **is projected**, it is planned or expected. *Africa's mid-1993 population is projected to more than double by 2025... The government had been projecting a 5% consumer price increase for the entire year. ...a projected deficit of $1.5 million.* VERB *be* V-ed to-inf V n V-ed

4 If you **project** someone or something in a particular way, you try to make people see them in that way. If you **project** a particular feeling or quality, you show it in your behaviour. *Bradley projects a natural warmth and sincerity... He just hasn't been able to project himself as the strong leader... His first job will be to project Glasgow as a friendly city... The initial image projected was of a caring, effective president.* VERB V n V pron-refl *as* n V n *as* n V-ed

5 If you **project** feelings or ideas on to other people, you imagine that they have the same ideas or feelings as you. *He projects his own thoughts and ideas onto her.* VERB V n *on/onto/upon* n

6 If you **project** a film or picture onto a screen or wall, you make it appear there. *The team tried projecting the maps with two different projectors onto the same screen.* VERB V n

7 If something **projects**, it sticks out above or beyond a surface or edge; a formal use. *...the remains of a war-time defence which projected out from the shore. ...a piece of projecting metal.* VERB V prep/adv V-ing

8 See also **housing project**.

projectile /prədʒektaɪl, AM -təl/ **projectiles.** A **projectile** is an object that is fired from a gun or other weapon; a formal word. N-COUNT

projection /prədʒekʃən/ **projections** ◆◆◇◇◇

1 A **projection** is an estimate of a future amount. *...the company's projection of 11 million visitors for the first year. ...sales projections.* N-COUNT =forecast, estimate

2 The **projection** of a film or picture is the act of projecting it onto a screen or wall. *They took me into a projection room to see a picture.* N-UNCOUNT: usu N n

projectionist /prədʒekʃənɪst/ **projectionists.** A **projectionist** is someone whose job is to work a projector at a cinema. N-COUNT

projector /prədʒektər/ **projectors.** A **projector** is a machine that projects films or slides onto a screen or wall. *...a 35-millimetre slide projector.* • See also **overhead projector**. ◆◇◇◇◇ N-COUNT

prolapse /proʊlæps, AM proʊlæps/ **prolapses, prolapsing, prolapsed.** The verb is also pronounced /prəlæps/.

1 A **prolapse** is the sagging or falling of one of the organs in the body; a medical use. *One complication which can arise is a prolapse. ...the causes and treatment of uterine prolapse.* N-VAR

2 If an organ in someone's body **prolapses**, it sags or falls within the body; a medical use. *Sometimes the original abortion was done so badly that the uterus prolapses.* VERB V

prole /proʊl/ **proles.** In British English, a **prole** is a working-class person; an informal word which some people find offensive. *We had proles working alongside university types as equals.* N-COUNT PRAGMATICS =pleb

proletarian /proʊlɪteəriən/ **proletarians**

1 In socialist theory, **proletarian** means relating to the proletariat. *...a proletarian revolution.* ADJ

2 A **proletarian** is a member of the proletariat. N-COUNT

proletariat /proʊlɪteəriæt/. In socialist theory, **the proletariat** is a term used to refer to working-class people, especially industrial workers. *...a struggle between the bourgeoisie and the proletariat.* N-SING-COLL: *the* N =working class

pro-life. The **pro-life** movement consists of people who campaign against legalized abortion, euthanasia, and experiments using human embryos. *The pro-life movement remains vigilant about measures that expand abortion rights.* ◆◇◇◇◇ ADJ: usu ADJ n

proliferate /prəlɪfəreɪt/ **proliferates, proliferating, proliferated.** If things **proliferate**, they increase in number very quickly; a formal word. *Computerized data bases are proliferating fast... In recent years commercial, cultural, travel and other contacts have proliferated between Taiwan and China.* ♦ **proliferation** /prəlɪfəreɪʃən/ *...the proliferation of nuclear weapons... Smoking triggers off cell proliferation.* ◆◆◇◇◇ VERB =multiply V N-UNCOUNT: oft N *of* n, n N

prolific /prəlɪfɪk/ ◆◇◇◇◇

1 A **prolific** writer, artist, or composer produces a large number of works. *She is a prolific writer of novels and short stories... During the Seventies, Rundgren was astonishingly prolific.* ADJ-GRADED

2 A **prolific** sports player scores a lot of goals or wins a lot of matches or races. *Another prolific scorer is Dean Saunders. ...Ideal Key, the prolific winner from last season.* ADJ-GRADED: usu ADJ n

3 An animal, person, or plant that is **prolific** produces a large number of offspring, children, young plants, or fruit. *They are prolific breeders, with many hens laying up to six eggs. ...a prolific crop of creamy gold coloured pods.* ADJ-GRADED

4 If animals are **prolific** somewhere, there are a lot of them there; a formal use. *All the big game congregate here, and birdlife is particularly prolific.* ADJ-GRADED: usu v-link ADJ =numerous

prologue /proʊlɒg, AM -lɔːg/ **prologues** ◆◇◇◇◇

1 A **prologue** is a speech or section of text that introduces a play or book. *The prologue to the novel is written in the form of a newspaper account.* N-COUNT ≠epilogue

2 If one event is a **prologue to** another event, it leads to it; a formal use. *I am convinced that it was a prologue to today's bloodless revolution in the countries of Eastern Europe.* N-COUNT: usu N *to* n

prolong /prəlɒŋ, AM -lɔːŋ/ **prolongs, prolonging, prolonged.** If someone or something **prolongs** something, they make it last a longer period of time. *Mr Chesler said foreign military aid was prolonging the war... The actual action of the* ◆◇◇◇◇ VERB =extend ≠shorten V n *drug can be prolonged significantly.* ♦ **prolongation** /proʊlɒŋgeɪʃən, AM -lɔːŋ-/ **prolongations** *...the prolongation of productive human life.* N-VAR: usu N *of* n

prolonged /prəlɒŋd, AM -lɔːŋd/. A **prolonged** event or situation continues for a long time, or for longer than expected. *...a prolonged period of low interest rates. ...a prolonged drought.* ◆◆◇◇◇ ADJ-GRADED: usu ADJ n =lengthy

prom /prɒm/ **proms** ◆◇◇◇◇

1 In the United States, a **prom** is a formal dance at school or college which is usually held at the end of the academic year. *I didn't want to go to the prom with Craig. ...my senior prom.* N-COUNT

2 In Britain, **the prom** is the same as the promenade. N-SING: usu *the* N

promenade /prɒmənɑːd, AM -neɪd/ **promenades, promenading, promenaded** ◆◇◇◇◇

1 In a seaside town, the **promenade** is the road by the sea where people go for a walk. N-COUNT =sea-front

2 If someone **promenades** somewhere for example along a beach, a lake, or a main street, they go for a walk there; an old-fashioned use. *People came out in smarter clothes to promenade along the front.* VERB =stroll V prep

prominence /prɒmɪnəns/. If someone or something is in a position of **prominence**, they are well-known and important. *He came to prominence during the World Cup in Italy... Crime prevention had to be given more prominence.* ◆◇◇◇◇ N-UNCOUNT

prominent /prɒmɪnənt/ ◆◆◆◇◇

1 Someone who is **prominent** is important. *...a prominent member of the Law Society. ...the children of very prominent or successful parents.* ADJ-GRADED =well-known

2 Something that is **prominent** is very noticeable or is an important part of something else. *Here the window plays a prominent part in the design. ...Romania's most prominent independent newspaper.* ♦ **prominently** *Trade will figure prominently in the second day of talks in Washington... Entries will be prominently displayed in the exhibition hall.* ADJ-GRADED ADV-GRADED: ADV with v

promiscuous /prəmɪskjuəs/ ◆◇◇◇◇

1 Someone who is **promiscuous** has sex with many different people; used showing disapproval. *She is perceived as vain, spoilt and promiscuous... You know the risks of promiscuous sex.* ♦ **promiscuity** /prɒmɪskjuːɪti/ *Johnson's excuse for his promiscuity was that women would be waiting outside his hotel room.* ADJ-GRADED PRAGMATICS N-UNCOUNT

2 **Promiscuous** means including a wide range of different things; a formal use. *...the dazzling, promiscuous display of new styles. ...fifty years of promiscuous reading in pursuit of pleasure.* ADJ-GRADED: usu ADJ n =wide

promise /prɒmɪs/ **promises, promising, promised** ◆◆◆◆◇

1 If you **promise** that you will do something, you say to someone that you will definitely do it. *The post office has promised to resume first class mail delivery to the area on Friday... He had promised that the rich and privileged would no longer get preferential treatment... Promise me you will not waste your time... 'We'll be back next year,' he promised... 'You promise?'—'All right, I promise.'* VERB V to-inf V that V n that V with quote V Also V n

2 If you **promise** someone something, you tell them that you will definitely give it to them or make sure that they have it. *In 1920 the great powers promised them an independent state... The officers promise a return to multiparty rule.* VERB V n n V n

3 A **promise** is a statement which you make to someone in which you say that you will definitely do something or give them something. *If you make a promise, you should keep it... The program has lived up to its promise to promote family welfare.* N-COUNT: oft N to-inf, N that

4 If a situation or event **promises** to have a particular quality or to be a particular thing, it shows signs that it will have that quality or be that thing. *While it will be fun, the seminar also promises to be most instructive.* VERB V to-inf

5 If someone or something shows **promise**, they seem likely to be very good or successful. *The boy first showed promise as an athlete in grade school.* N-UNCOUNT =potential

promised land, promised lands. If you refer to a place or a state as a **promised land**, you mean that people desire it and expect to find happiness or success there. *Sweden has already reached the promised land of near-zero inflation.* N-COUNT: usu sing

promising /prɒmɪsɪŋ/. Someone or something that is **promising** seems likely to be very good or successful. *A school has honoured one of its brightest and most promising former pupils.* ◆◆◇◇◇ ADJ-GRADED

promisingly /prɒmɪsɪŋli/. If something or someone starts **promisingly**, they begin well but often fail in the end. *It all started so promisingly when Speed scored a tremendous first goal.* ADV-GRADED: usu ADV with v, also ADV adj

promissory note /prɒmɪsəri noʊt, AM -sɔːri/ **promissory notes.** A **promissory note** is a written promise that you make to pay a specific sum of money to a particular person; used mainly in American English. *...a $36.4 million, five-year promissory note.* N-COUNT

promo /proʊmoʊ/ **promos.** A **promo** is something such as a short video film which is used to promote a product; an informal word used mainly by journalists. *He races his cars, and hires them out for film, TV and promo videos.* ◆◆◇◇◇ N-COUNT: oft N n

promontory /prɒməntri, AM -tɔːri/ **promontories.** A **promontory** is a cliff that stretches out into the sea. *...a promontory jutting out into the bay.* N-COUNT

promote /prəmoʊt/ **promotes, promoting, promoted** ◆◆◆◆◇

1 If people **promote** something, they help or encourage it to happen, increase, or spread. *You don't have to sacrifice environmental protection to promote economic growth... In many ways, our society actively promotes alcoholism.* ♦ **promotion** *Clinton has pledged to give human rights and the promotion of democracy higher priority. ...disease prevention and health promotion.* VERB =encourage ≠discourage V n N-UNCOUNT: with supp, usu N *of* n

2 If a firm **promotes** a product, it tries to increase the sales or popularity of that product. *Paul Weller has announced a full British tour to promote his second solo album. ...a special St Lucia week where the island could be promoted as a tourist destination.* VERB V n *be* V-ed *as* n

3 If someone **is promoted**, they are given a more important job in the organization they work for. *I was promoted to editor and then editorial director... In fact, those people have been promoted.* VB: usu passive *be* V-ed *from*/*to* n *be* V-ed

4 If a team that competes in a league **is promoted**, it starts competing in a higher division in the next season because it was one of the most successful teams in the lower division. *Woodford Green won the Second Division title and are promoted to the First Division.* ♦ **promotion** *Fans of Leeds United football club have been celebrating their team's promotion to the first division.* VB: usu passive ≠relegate *be* V-ed *to* n Also *be* V-ed N-UNCOUNT ≠relegation

promoter /prəmoʊtəʳ/ **promoters** ◆◆◇◇◇

1 A **promoter** is a person who helps organize and finance an event, especially a sports event. *...one of the top boxing promoters in Britain.* N-COUNT

2 The **promoter of** a cause or idea tries to make it become popular. *Aaron Copeland was always the most energetic promoter of American music.* N-COUNT: usu N *of* n

promotion /prəmoʊʃən/ **promotions** ◆◆◆◇◇

1 If you are given **promotion** in your job, you are given more important things to do and you are paid more money. *Consider changing jobs or trying for promotion. ...rewarding outstanding employees with promotions to higher-paid posts.* N-VAR

2 A **promotion** is an attempt to make a product or event popular or successful, especially by advertising. *During 1984, Remington spent a lot of money on advertising and promotion... Ask about special promotions and weekend deals too.* N-COUNT

promotional /prəmoʊʃənəl/. **Promotional** material, events, or ideas are designed to increase the sales of a product or service. *'Jeans,' according to one company's promotional material, 'are designed and made to be worn hard'.* ◆◇◇◇◇ ADJ: usu ADJ n

prompt /prɒmpt/ **prompts, prompting, prompted** ◆◆◆◇◇

1 If something **prompts** someone to do something, VERB

it makes them decide to do it. *Japan's recession has prompted consumers to cut back on buying cars... The need for villagers to control their own destinities has prompted a new plan.* V n to-inf, V n

2 If you **prompt** someone when they stop speaking, you encourage or help them to continue. *'You wouldn't have wanted to bring those people to justice anyway, would you?' Brand prompted him... How exactly did he prompt her, Mr Markham?.* VERB: V with quote, V n
▶ Also a noun. *Her blushes were saved by a prompt from one of her hosts.* N-COUNT

3 A **prompt** action is done without any delay. *It is not too late, but prompt action is needed. ...an inflammation of the eyeball which needs prompt treatment.* ADJ-GRADED: usu ADJ n

4 If you are **prompt** to do something, you do it without delay or you are not late. *You have been so prompt in carrying out all these commissions... We didn't worry because they were always so prompt with their rental payment.* ADJ-GRADED: v-link ADJ

prompting /prɒmptɪŋ/ **promptings.** ◆◇◇◇◇ If you respond to **prompting**, you do what someone encourages or reminds you to do. *New York needed little prompting from their coach Bill Parcells. ...the promptings of your subconscious.* N-UNCOUNT: also N in pl

promptly /prɒmptli/ ◆◆◇◇◇

1 If you do something **promptly**, you do it immediately. *Sister Francesca entered the chapel, took her seat, and promptly fell asleep.* ADV-GRADED: ADV with v =immediately

2 If you do something **promptly at** a particular time, you do it at exactly that time. *Promptly at a quarter past seven, we left the hotel.* ADV: ADV with v, ADV *at/on* n =punctually

promulgate /prɒməlgeɪt/ **promulgates, promulgating, promulgated** ◆◇◇◇◇

1 If people **promulgate** a new law or a new idea, they make it widely known; a formal use. *The oil and shipping industries undertook to promulgate a voluntary code.* VERB: V n

2 If a new law or a country's constitution **is promulgated** by a government or national leader, it is publicly approved or made official; a formal use. *The constitution is expected to be promulgated by King Birendra before the end of September.* VB: usu passive, *be* V-ed
♦ **promulgation** /prɒməlgeɪʃən/ *...the promulgation of the constitution.* N-UNCOUNT

prone /proʊn/ ◆◆◇◇◇

1 If someone or something is **prone to** something, usually something bad, they have a tendency to be affected by it or to do it. *For all her experience as a television reporter, she was still prone to camera nerves... People with fair skin who sunburn easily are very prone to develop skin cancer.* ADJ-GRADED: v-link ADJ, ADJ *to* n, ADJ to-inf ▶ **-prone** combines with nouns to make adjectives that describe people who are frequently affected by something bad. *...the most injury-prone rider on the circuit.* COMB in ADJ-GRADED ● See also **accident prone**.

2 If you are lying **prone** or if you are in a **prone** position, you are lying flat with the front of your body facing downwards; a formal use. *Bob slid from his chair and lay prone on the floor.* ADJ: ADJ after v, ADJ n

prong /prɒŋ, AM prɔːŋ/ **prongs**

1 The **prongs** of something such as a fork are the long, thin pointed parts. *Mark the loaf with the prongs of a fork in a criss-cross pattern. ...a prong attached to the back of a rider's boot.* N-COUNT: usu pl

2 The **prongs** of something such as a policy or strategy are the separate stages or parts of it. *The shareholder rights movement has two prongs... The second prong of the strategy is the provision of basic social services for the poor.* N-COUNT

-pronged /-prɒŋd, AM -prɔːŋd/. A two-**pronged** or three-**pronged** attack or strategy has two or three parts or stages. *...a two-pronged attack on the recession... The bank has a three-pronged strategy for recovery.* COMB in ADJ: ADJ n

pronominal /proʊnɒmɪnəl/. **Pronominal** means relating to pronouns or like a pronoun. *...a pronominal use..* ADJ

pronoun /proʊnaʊn/ **pronouns.** A **pronoun** is a word that you use to refer to someone or something when you do not need or want to use a noun, often because the person or thing has been mentioned earlier. Examples are 'it', 'she', 'something', and 'myself'. ● See also **indefinite pronoun, personal pronoun, reflexive pronoun, relative pronoun.** N-COUNT

pronounce /prənaʊns/ **pronounces, pronouncing, pronounced** ◆◆◇◇◇

1 To **pronounce** a word means to say it by making sounds that are right or understandable. *Have I pronounced your name correctly?... He pronounced it Per-sha, the way the English do.* VERB: V n, V n n

2 If you **pronounce** something to be true, you state that it is the case; a formal use. *A specialist has now pronounced him fully fit... I now pronounce you man and wife.* VERB =declare, V n adj, V n n

3 If someone **pronounces** a verdict or opinion on something, they give their verdict or opinion; a formal use. *The Communist authorities took time to pronounce their verdicts... 'Too many families in our society,' pronounces Cardinal Hume, 'fail to become sources of love and stability.'... He walked around the garden and pronounced himself satisfied... Men feel perfectly free to pronounce on the way women should look.* VERB: V n, V with quote, V pron-refl adj, V *on* n, Also V that

pronounced /prənaʊnst/. Something that is **pronounced** is very noticeable. *Most of the art exhibitions have a pronounced Scottish theme. ...a pronounced Australian accent... Since then, the contrast between his two careers has become even more pronounced.* ◆◇◇◇◇ ADJ-GRADED =noticeable, distinct

pronouncement /prənaʊnsmənt/ **pronouncements. Pronouncements** are public or official statements on an important subject. *...the President's latest pronouncements about the protection of minorities.* ◆◇◇◇◇ N-COUNT: usu pl =statement

pronto /prɒntoʊ/. If you say that something must be done **pronto**, you mean that it must be done quickly and at once; an informal word. *Get down to the post office pronto!* ADV: ADV after v =sharpish, now

pronunciation /prənʌnsieɪʃən/ **pronunciations.** The **pronunciation** of a word or language is the way in which it is pronounced. *She gave the word its French pronunciation... You're going to have to forgive my pronunciation.* ◆◇◇◇◇ N-VAR

proof /pruːf/ **proofs** ◆◆◆◇◇

1 Proof is a fact, argument, or piece of evidence which shows that something is definitely true or definitely exists. *You have to have proof of residence in the state of Texas, such as a Texas ID card... This is not necessarily proof that he is wrong... Economists have been concerned with establishing proofs for their arguments.* N-VAR: oft N *of* n, N that

2 The **proofs** of a book, magazine, or article are a first copy of it that is printed so that mistakes can be corrected before more copies are printed and published; a technical use in publishing. *I'm correcting the proofs of the Spanish edition right now.* N-COUNT: usu pl, oft N *of* n
▶ Also an adjective. *Peter gave me an uncorrected proof copy of the book.* ADJ: ADJ n

3 Proof is used after a number of degrees or a percentage, when indicating the strength of a strong alcoholic drink such as whisky. *...a glass of Wild Turkey bourbon: 101 degrees proof.* ADJ: amount ADJ

4 If something or someone is **proof against** something, they cannot be damaged, harmed, or affected by that thing; used in written English. *The fortress was proof against the techniques of attack then in use... His papers were proof against all but the most expert of scrutinies.* ADJ: v-link ADJ *against* n

5 If you say that someone is **living proof** of something, you mean that their actions or personal qualities show that a particular fact is true or that a particular quality exists. *He is living proof that some players just get better with age.* PHRASES: usu v-link PHR, oft PHR that, PHR *of* n

6 If you say that something or someone is **proof positive** of a certain fact or quality, you mean that their existence or actions prove that it is true or that it exists. *The Windermere Golf Club is proof positive that golf and ecology can co-exist in perfect harmony.* usu v-link PHR, oft PHR that, PHR *of* n

7 ● **burden of proof**: see **burden.** ● **the proof of the pudding is in the eating**: see **pudding.**

-proof /-pruːf/ **-proofs, -proofing, -proofed**
1 **-proof** combines with nouns and verbs to form adjectives which indicate that something cannot be damaged or badly affected by the thing or action mentioned. *...a bomb-proof aircraft... In a large microwave-proof dish, melt butter for 20 seconds. ...tamper-proof medicine bottles.* COMB in ADJ
2 **-proof** combines with nouns to form verbs which refer to protecting something against being damaged or badly affected by the thing mentioned. *...home energy efficiency grants towards the cost of draught-proofing your home. ...inflation-proofed pensions.* COMB in VB; V n; V-ed
3 See also **bullet-proof**, **childproof**, **damp-proof course**, **fireproof**, **ovenproof**, **soundproof**, **waterproof**, **weatherproof**.

proofread /pruːfriːd/ **proofreads, proofreading;** also spelled **proof-read**. When someone **proofreads** something such as a book or an article, they read it before it is published in order to find and mark mistakes that need to be corrected; a technical term in publishing. *I didn't even have the chance to proofread my own report.* ◆◇◇◇◇ VERB; V n; Also V

prop /prɒp/ **props, propping, propped** ◆◆◇◇◇
1 If you **prop** an object **on** or **against** something, you support it by putting something underneath it or by resting it against something. *He rocked back in the chair and propped his feet on the desk... He propped his bike against the bus.* ► **Prop up** means the same as **prop**. *Sam slouched back and propped his elbows up on the bench behind him... If you have difficulty sitting like this, prop up your back against a wall.* VERB; V n on/against n; Also V n adv/prep; PHRASAL VERB; V n P prep; V P n (not pron) prep
2 A **prop** is a stick or other object that you use to support something. N-COUNT
3 Someone or something that is a **prop** for a system, institution, or person is the main thing that keeps that system or person strong or helps them survive. *The army is one of the main props of the government... I had two props in my life; one was alcohol, the other work.* N-COUNT
4 The **props** in a play or film are all the objects or pieces of furniture that are used in it. *...the backdrop and props for a stage show. ...stage props.* N-COUNT: usu pl
5 In rugby, a **prop** or **prop forward** is one of the two forward players who position themselves in the front row during a scrum. N-COUNT: usu sing
6 A **prop** is the same as a **propeller**; an informal use. N-COUNT

prop up PHRASAL VERB
1 To **prop up** something means to support it or help it to survive. *Investments in the U.S. money market have propped up the American dollar... On the Tokyo Stock Exchange, aggressive buying propped the market up after yesterday's slide.* V P n (not pron); V n P
2 See **prop** 1.

propaganda /prɒpəgændə/. **Propaganda** is information, often inaccurate or biased information, which a political organization publishes or broadcasts in order to influence people; used showing disapproval. *The Front adopted an aggressive propaganda campaign against its rivals. ...anti-communist propaganda movies.* ◆◆◇◇◇ N-UNCOUNT: oft N n; PRAGMATICS

propagandist /prɒpəgændɪst/ **propagandists.** A **propagandist** is a person who tries to persuade people to support a particular idea or group; often used showing disapproval. *He was in large part a journalist and propagandist... He was also a brilliant propagandist for free trade.* N-COUNT; PRAGMATICS

propagandize /prɒpəgændaɪz/ **propagandizes, propagandizing, propagandized;** also spelled **propagandise** in British English. If you say that a group of people **propagandize**, you think that they are dishonestly trying to persuade other people to share their views; used showing disapproval. *You can propagandize just by calling attention to something... This government shouldn't propagandize its own people.* VERB; PRAGMATICS; V; V n

propagate /prɒpəgeɪt/ **propagates, propagating, propagated** ◆◇◇◇◇
1 If people **propagate** an idea or piece of information, they spread it and try to make people believe it or support it; a formal use. *They propagated political doctrines which promised to tear apart the fabric of British society.* ♦ **propagation** /prɒpəgeɪʃᵊn/ *These two countries must work together towards the propagation of true Buddhism.* VERB =disseminate; V n; N-UNCOUNT: oft N of n
2 If you **propagate** plants, you grow more of them from the original ones; a technical term. *The easiest way to propagate a vine is to take hardwood cuttings... The pasque flower can be propagated from seed.* ♦ **propagation** *Few things give more pleasure in gardening than the successful propagation of a batch of plants.* VERB; V n; be V-ed from n; Also V n from n; N-UNCOUNT: oft N of n

propane /proupeɪn/. **Propane** is a gas that comes from petroleum and is used for cooking and heating. *...a propane gas cylinder.* N-UNCOUNT: oft N n

propel /prəpel/ **propels, propelling, propelled** ◆◇◇◇◇
1 To **propel** something in a particular direction means to cause it to move in that direction. *The tiny rocket is attached to the spacecraft and is designed to propel it toward Mars.* ► **-propelled** combines with nouns to form adjectives which indicate how something, especially a weapon, is propelled. *...rocket-propelled grenades. ...the first jet-propelled aeroplane.* VERB; V n prep; COMB in ADJ
2 If something **propels** you into a particular activity, it causes you to do it. *It was a shooting star that propelled me into astronomy in the first place... He is propelled by both guilt and the need to avenge his father.* VERB; V n prep; be V-ed

propellant /prəpelənt/ **propellants**
1 **Propellant** is a substance that causes something to move forwards. *...an enormous amount of propellant. ...a propellant for nuclear rockets.* N-MASS
2 **Propellant** is a gas that is used in aerosol cans to force the contents out of the can when you press the button. *By 1978, in the USA, the use of CFCs in aerosol propellants was banned.* N-MASS

propeller /prəpeləʳ/ **propellers.** A **propeller** is a device with blades which is attached to a boat or aircraft. The engine makes the propeller spin round and causes the boat or aircraft to move. *...a fixed three-bladed propeller.* ◆◇◇◇◇ N-COUNT

propensity /prəpensɪti/ **propensities.** A **propensity to** do something or a **propensity** for something is a natural tendency that you have to behave in a particular way; a formal word. *Mr Bint has a propensity to put off decisions to the last minute... She hasn't reckoned on his propensity for violence.* ◆◇◇◇◇ N-COUNT: oft N to-inf, N for n =tendency

proper /prɒpəʳ/ ◆◆◆◇◇
1 You use **proper** to describe things that you consider to be real and satisfactory rather than inadequate in some way. *Two out of five people lack a proper job... I always cook a proper evening meal.* ADJ: ADJ n
2 The **proper** thing is the one that is correct or most suitable. *The Supreme Court will ensure that the proper procedures have been followed... He helped to put things in their proper place.* ADJ: ADJ n =correct ≠incorrect
3 If you say that a way of behaving is **proper**, you mean that it is considered socially acceptable and right. *In those days it was not thought entirely proper for a woman to be on the stage... It is right and proper to do this.* ADJ-GRADED: usu v-link ADJ =fitting, decent ≠improper
4 You can add **proper** after a word to emphasize that you are referring to the main, central, and most important part of a place, event, or object in order to distinguish it from other things which are not regarded as being important or central to it. *A distinction must be made between archaeology proper and science-based archaeology.* ADJ: n ADJ

properly /prɒpəʳli/ ◆◆◆◇◇
1 If something is done **properly**, it is done correctly and satisfactorily. *You're too thin. You're not eating properly... There needs to be a properly informed public debate.* ADV: usu ADV with v, also ADV adj =correctly
2 If someone behaves **properly**, they behave in a way that is considered acceptable and not rude. *He's a spoilt brat and it's about time he learnt to behave properly... They will be concerned to do the right thing – to dress properly, for instance.* ADV: ADV after v =correctly ≠improperly

proper noun, proper nouns. A **proper noun** is the name of a particular person, place, organiza- N-COUNT tion, or thing. Proper nouns begin with a capital letter. Examples are 'Margaret', 'London', and 'the United Nations'.

propertied /prɒpəʳtid/. **Propertied** people own land or property; a formal word. *...the propertied classes.* ADJ: usu ADJ n

property /prɒpəʳti/ **properties** ◆◆◆◆◇

1 Someone's **property** is all the things that belong to them or something that belongs to them ; a formal use. *Richard could easily destroy her personal property to punish her for walking out on him... Security forces searched thousands of homes, confiscating weapons and stolen property.* N-UNCOUNT: usu with poss =belongings, possessions

2 A **property** is a building and the land belonging to it; a formal use. *Cecil inherited a family property near Stamford... This vehicle has been parked on private property.* N-VAR

3 The **properties** of a substance or object are the ways in which it behaves in particular conditions; a technical use in science. *A radio signal has both electrical and magnetic properties.* N-COUNT: usu pl

prophecy /prɒfɪsi/ **prophecies.** A **prophecy** is a statement in which someone says they strongly believe that a particular thing will happen. *The youth, too, fulfilled the prophecy. ...Biblical prophecy.* ◆◇◇◇◇ N-VAR

prophesy /prɒfɪsaɪ/ **prophesies, prophesying, prophesied.** If you **prophesy** that something will happen, you say that you strongly believe that it will happen. *He prophesied that within five years his opponent would either be dead or in prison... She prophesied a bad ending for the expedition.* VERB =predict ≠foretell V that V n Also V

prophet /prɒfɪt/ **prophets** ◆◇◇◇◇

1 A **prophet** is a person who is believed to be chosen by God to say the things that God wants to tell people. *...the sacred name of the Holy Prophet of Islam.* N-COUNT

2 A **prophet** is someone who predicts that something will happen in the future; a literary use. *I promised myself I'd defy all the prophets of doom and battle back to fitness.* N-COUNT: with supp, usu N of n

prophetic /prəfetɪk/ ◆◇◇◇◇

1 If something was **prophetic**, it described or suggested something that did actually happen later. *This ominous warning soon proved prophetic... Friends recalled Elisabeth's prophetic words of several years ago.* ADJ-GRADED

2 **Prophetic** means related to a prophecy or a prophet. *...a charming romance intermingled with scientific fact and prophetic vision.* ADJ: usu ADJ n

prophylactic /prɒfɪlæktɪk/ **prophylactics**

1 **Prophylactic** means concerned with preventing disease; a medical use. *Vaccination and other prophylactic measures can be carried out.* ADJ: usu ADJ n =preventive

2 A **prophylactic** is a substance or device used for preventing disease or pregnancy; a medical use. *The region began to use quinine successfully as a prophylactic... The prospect of teachers passing out prophylactics to their pupils has infuriated some parents.* N-COUNT

propitiate /prəpɪʃieɪt/ **propitiates, propitiating, propitiated.** If you **propitiate** someone, you stop them being angry or impatient by doing something to please them; a formal word. *I've never gone out of my way to propitiate people... These ancient ceremonies propitiate the spirits of the waters.* VERB =appease, placate V n

propitious /prəpɪʃəs/. If something is **propitious**, it is likely to lead to success; a formal word. *They should wait for the most propitious moment between now and the next election... The omens for the game are still not propitious.* ADJ-GRADED =favourable ≠unfavourable

proponent /prəpoʊnənt/ **proponents.** If you are a **proponent** of a particular idea or course of action, you actively support it; a formal word. *Halsey was identified as a leading proponent of the values of progressive education.* ◆◇◇◇◇ N-COUNT: with poss, usu N of n =advocate ≠critic

proportion /prəpɔːʳʃən/ **proportions** ◆◆◆◇◇

1 A **proportion of** a group or an amount is a part of it; a formal use. *A large proportion of the dolphins in that area will eventually die... A proportion of the rent is met by the city council.* N-COUNT: usu sing, usu N of n =percentage

2 The **proportion of** one kind of person or thing in a group is the number of people or things of that kind compared to the total number of people or things in the group. *The proportion of women in the profession had risen to 17.3%... The radio station has to include a substantial proportion of classical music.* N-COUNT: usu sing, usu N of n

3 The **proportion of** one amount **to** another is the relationship between the two amounts in terms of how much there is of each thing. *Women's bodies tend to have a higher proportion of fat to water.* N-COUNT: oft N of n to n =ratio

4 If you refer to the **proportions** of something, you are referring to its size, usually when this is extremely large; used in written English. *In the tropics plants grow to huge proportions. ...a fraud of breathtaking proportions.* N-PLURAL: usu supp N =dimensions

5 If you refer to the **proportions** in a work of art or design, you are referring to the relative sizes of its different parts. *You can vary the relative proportions of things in a picture very simply.* N-PLURAL =dimensions

6 If one thing increases or decreases **in proportion to** another thing, it increases or decreases to the same degree as that thing. *The pressure in the cylinders would go up in proportion to the boiler pressure.* PHRASES PREP

7 If something is small or large **in proportion to** something else, it is small or large when compared with that thing. *Children tend to have relatively larger heads than adults in proportion to the rest of their body.* PREP =in relation to

8 If you say that something is **out of all proportion to** something else, you think that it is far greater or more serious than it should be. *The punishment was out of all proportion to the crime.* PREP: usu v-link PREP ≠commensurate with

9 If you get something **out of proportion**, you think it is more important or worrying than it really is. If you keep something **in proportion**, you have a realistic view of how important it is. *Everything just got blown out of proportion... We've got to keep this in proportion.* PHR after v

10 If someone has a **sense of proportion**, they know what is really important and what is not. *We must not lose our sense of proportion.*

proportional /prəpɔːʳʃənəl/. If one amount is **proportional to** another, the two amounts increase and decrease at the same rate so there is always the same relationship between them; a formal use. *Loss of weight is directly proportional to the rate at which the disease is progressing. ...a proportional fee based on the final sale price.* ◆◇◇◇◇ ADJ: usu v-link ADJ to n

♦ **proportionally** *You have proportionally more fat on your thighs and hips than anywhere else on your body... Candidates would be elected proportionally.* ADV: ADV with v, ADV with cl/group

proportionality /prəpɔːʳʃənælɪti/. The principle of **proportionality** is the idea that an action should not be more severe than is necessary, especially in a war or when punishing someone for a crime; a formal word. *Nuclear weapons seem to violate the just war principle of proportionality... He said there was a need for proportionality in sentencing.* N-UNCOUNT

proportional representation. **Proportional representation** is a system of voting in which each political party is represented in parliament in proportion to the number of people who vote for it in an election. ◆◇◇◇◇ N-UNCOUNT

proportionate /prəpɔːʳʃənət/. **Proportionate** means the same as **proportional**. *Republics will have voting rights proportionate to the size of their economies... The extra field cultivated meant a proportionate increase in work.* ◆◇◇◇◇ ADJ: oft ADJ to n

♦ **proportionately** *We have significantly increased the number of people in education but the size of the classes hasn't changed proportionately... Proportionately more Americans get married nowadays than ever before.* ADV: ADV with v, ADV with cl/group

-proportioned /-prəpɔːʳʃənd/. **-proportioned** is added to adverbs to form adjectives that indicate that the proportions of the different parts of COMB in ADJ-GRADED something or someone are good or bad. *The flat has high ceilings and well-proportioned rooms. ...a perfectly-proportioned young woman.*

proposal /prəpoʊzᵊl/ **proposals** ◆◆◆◆◇

1 A **proposal** is a plan or an idea, often a formal or written one, which is suggested for people to think about and decide upon. *The President is to put forward new proposals for resolving the country's constitutional crisis. ...the government's proposals to abolish free health care... The Security Council has rejected the latest peace proposal.* N-COUNT: oft N *for* n, N to-inf =plan

2 A **proposal** is the act of asking someone to marry you. *After a three-weekend courtship, Pamela accepted Randolph's proposal of marriage.* N-COUNT

propose /prəpoʊz/ **proposes, proposing, proposed** ◆◆◆◆◇

1 If you **propose** something such as a plan or an idea, you suggest it for people to think about and decide upon. *Britain is about to propose changes to European Community institutions... It was George who first proposed that we dry clothes in that locker.* VERB =suggest V n/-ing V that

2 If you **propose** to do something, you intend to do it. *It's still far from clear what action the government proposes to take over the affair... And where do you propose building such a huge thing?* VERB V to-inf V -ing Also V n

3 If you **propose** a theory or an explanation, you state that it is possibly or probably true, because it fits in with the evidence that you have considered; a formal use. *This highlights a problem faced by people proposing theories of ball lightning... Newton proposed that heavenly and terrestrial motion could be unified with the idea of gravity.* VERB =propound, posit V n V that

4 If you **propose** a motion for debate, or a candidate for election, you begin the debate or the election procedure by formally stating your support for that motion or candidate. *A delegate from Siberia proposed a resolution that he stand down as party chairman... I asked Robert Balfour and Dawyck Haig to propose and second me.* ♦ **proposer, proposers** *...Mr Ian Murch, the proposer of the motion.* VERB V n Also V that N-COUNT

5 If you **propose a toast** to someone or something, you ask people to drink a toast to them. *Usually the bride's father proposes a toast to the health of the bride and groom.* VERB V n

6 If you **propose to** someone, or **propose marriage** to them, you ask them to marry you. *He had proposed to Isabel the day after taking his seat in Parliament.* VERB V *to* n Also V, V n, V n *to* n

proposition /prɒpəzɪʃᵊn/ **propositions, propositioning, propositioned** ◆◆◇◇◇

1 If you describe something such as a task or an activity as, for example, a difficult **proposition** or an attractive **proposition**, you mean that it is difficult or pleasant to do. *Making easy money has always been an attractive proposition... Even among seasoned mountaineers Pinnacle Ridge is considered quite a tough proposition.* N-COUNT: usu sing, adj N

2 A **proposition** is a statement or an idea which people can consider or discuss to decide whether it is true; a formal use. *The proposition that democracies do not fight each other is based on a tiny historical sample.* N-COUNT: oft N that =suggestion, theory

3 In the United States, a **proposition** is a question or statement which appears on a ballot paper, and which people can vote for or against, in order to decide an issue of public policy. *Vote Yes on Proposition 136, but No on Propositions 129, 133 and 134.* N-COUNT: oft N num

4 A **proposition** is an offer or a suggestion that someone makes to you, usually concerning some work or business that you might be able to do together. *You came to see me at my office the other day with a business proposition... I want to make you a proposition.* N-COUNT

5 If someone who you do not know very well **propositions** you, they suggest that you have sex with them. *Mr Whitfield had allegedly tried to proposition Miss Hawes.* ► Also a noun. *...unwanted sexual propositions.* VERB V n N-COUNT

6 A **proposition** is a statement in language or mathematics which can be analysed in terms of its meaning and logical structure; a technical use in philosophy. N-COUNT

propound /prəpaʊnd/ **propounds, propounding, propounded.** If someone **propounds** an idea or point of view they have, they suggest it for people to consider, a formal word. *Zoologist Eugene Morton has propounded a general theory of the vocal sounds that animals make.* VERB =put forward V n

proprietary /prəpraɪətri, AM -teri/ ◆◇◇◇◇

1 **Proprietary** substances or products are sold under a trade name; a formal use. *...some proprietary brands of dog food... We had to take action to protect the proprietary technology.* ADJ: ADJ n ≠generic

2 If someone has a **proprietary** attitude towards something, they act as though they own it; a formal use. *Directors weren't allowed any proprietary airs about the product they made.* ADJ-GRADED: usu ADJ n =proprietorial

proprieties /prəpraɪɪtiz/. The **proprieties** are the standards of social behaviour which most people consider socially or morally acceptable; an old-fashioned word. *...respectable couples who observe the proprieties but loathe each other.* N-PLURAL: usu *the* N =civilities

proprietor /prəpraɪətəʳ/ **proprietors.** The **proprietor** of a hotel, shop, newspaper, or other business is the person who owns it; a formal word. *...the proprietor of a local restaurant... He was the sole proprietor with total management control.* ◆◇◇◇◇ N-COUNT =owner

proprietorial /prəpraɪətɔːriəl/. If your behaviour is **proprietorial**, you are behaving in a proud way because you are, or feel like you are, the owner of something; a formal word. *The longer I live alone the more proprietorial I become about my home.* ADJ-GRADED =proprietary

proprietress /prəpraɪətrɪs/ **proprietresses.** The **proprietress** of a hotel, shop, or business is the woman who owns it. *The proprietress was alone in the bar.* N-COUNT =owner

propriety /prəpraɪɪti/. **Propriety** is the quality of being socially or morally acceptable; a formal word. *Their sense of social propriety is eroded.* N-UNCOUNT ≠impropriety

propulsion /prəpʌlʃᵊn/. **Propulsion** is the power that moves something, especially a vehicle, in a forward direction; a formal word. *Interest in jet propulsion was now growing at the Air Ministry. ...the submarine's propulsion system.* ◆◇◇◇◇ N-UNCOUNT: oft n N, N n

pro rata /proʊ rɑːtə, AM - reɪtə/; also spelled **pro-rata**. If something is distributed **pro rata**, it is distributed in proportion to the amount or size of something; a formal expression. *All part-timers should be paid the same, pro rata, as full-timers doing the same job.* ► Also an adjective. *They are paid their salaries and are entitled to fringe benefits on a pro-rata basis.* ADV: ADV after v ADJ: ADJ n

prosaic /proʊzeɪɪk/. Something that is **prosaic** is dull and uninteresting; a formal word. *His instructor offered a more prosaic explanation for the surge in interest... The truth is more prosaic.* ♦ **prosaically** /proʊzeɪɪkli/. *Arabian jam is also known as angels' hair preserve, or more prosaically as carrot jam... His father wrote briefly and prosaically.* ◆◇◇◇◇ ADJ-GRADED =mundane ≠interesting ADV-GRADED: ADV with cl, ADV with v

proscenium /proʊsiːniəm/ **prosceniums.** A **proscenium** or a **proscenium arch** is an arch in a theatre which separates the stage from the audience. N-COUNT: usu sing

proscribe /proʊskraɪb/ **proscribes, proscribing, proscribed.** If something **is proscribed** by people in authority, the existence or the use of that thing is forbidden; a formal word. *In some cultures surgery is proscribed... They are proscribed by federal law from owning guns.* VB: usu passive =prohibit ≠permit *be* V-ed *be* V-ed *from* -ing

proscription /proʊskrɪpʃᵊn/ **proscriptions.** The **proscription** of something is the official forbidding of its existence or use; a formal word. *...the proscription against any religious service. ...the proscription of his records.* N-VAR =prohibition

prose /proʊz/. **Prose** is ordinary written language, in contrast to poetry. *Shute's prose is stark and chillingly unsentimental... What he has to say is expressed in prose of exceptional lucidity and grace.* ◆◆◇◇◇ N-UNCOUNT: oft poss N, *in* N ≠poetry

prosecute /prɒsɪkjuːt/ **prosecutes, prosecuting, prosecuted** ◆◆◇◇◇

1 If the authorities **prosecute** someone, they charge them with a crime and put them on trial. *The police have decided not to prosecute because the evidence is not strong enough... He is being prosecuted for two criminal offences.* VERB V V n for n

2 When a lawyer **prosecutes** a case, he or she tries to prove that the person who is on trial is guilty. *The attorney who will prosecute the case says he cannot reveal how much money is involved. ...the prosecuting attorney.* VERB V n V-ing

prosecution /prɒsɪkjuːʃᵊn/ **prosecutions** ◆◆◆◇◇

1 Prosecution is the action of charging someone with a crime and putting them on trial. *Yesterday the head of government called for the prosecution of those responsible for the deaths.* N-VAR: usu N of n

2 The lawyers who try to prove that a person on trial is guilty are called **the prosecution**. *Colonel Pugh, for the prosecution, said that the offences occurred over a six-year period.* N-SING: the N

prosecutor /prɒsɪkjuːtəʳ/ **prosecutors.** In some countries, a **prosecutor** is a lawyer or official who brings charges against someone or tries to prove in a trial that they are guilty. ◆◆◇◇◇ N-COUNT

proselytize /prɒsɪlɪtaɪz/ **proselytizes, proselytizing, proselytized;** also spelled **proselytise** in British English. If you **proselytize**, you try to persuade someone to share your beliefs, especially religious or political beliefs; a formal word. *I assured him we didn't come here to proselytize... Christians were arrested for trying to convert people, to proselytise them.* VERB V V n

prospect, prospects, prospecting, prospected. The noun is pronounced /prɒspekt/. The verb is pronounced /prəspekt, AM prɑːspekt/. ◆◆◆◆◇

1 If there is some **prospect** of something happening, there is a possibility that it will happen. *Unfortunately, there is little prospect of seeing these big questions answered... The prospects for peace in the country's eight-year civil war are becoming brighter... There is a real prospect that the bill will be defeated in parliament.* N-VAR: with supp, oft N of n/-ing =possibility

2 A particular **prospect** is something that you expect or know is going to happen. *They now face the prospect of having to wear a cycling helmet by law... After supper he'd put his feet up and read. It was a pleasant prospect.* N-SING: usu with supp, oft N of n/-ing

3 Someone's **prospects** are their chances of being successful, especially in their career. *I chose to work abroad to improve my career prospects. ...a detailed review of the company's prospects.* N-PLURAL: usu supp N

4 When people **prospect for** oil, gold, or some other valuable substance, they look for it in the ground or under the sea. *He had prospected for minerals everywhere from the Gobi Desert to the Transvaal... In fact, the oil companies are already prospecting not far from here.* ♦ **prospecting** *He was involved in oil, zinc and lead prospecting.* ♦ **prospector, prospectors** *The discovery of gold and silver had brought a flood of prospectors into the Arizona and New Mexico Territories.* VERB V for n V N-UNCOUNT N-COUNT

prospective /prəspektɪv, AM prɑː-/ ◆◆◇◇◇

1 You use **prospective** to describe someone who wants to be the thing mentioned or who is likely to be the thing mentioned. *The story should act as a warning to other prospective buyers... When his prospective employers learned that he smoked, they said they wouldn't hire him.* ADJ: ADJ n =would-be

2 You use **prospective** to describe something that is likely to happen soon. *The terms of the prospective deal are most clearly spelt out in the Financial Times.* ADJ: ADJ n =forthcoming

prospectus /prəspektəs, AM prɑː-/ **prospectuses.** A **prospectus** is a detailed document produced by a college, school, or company, which gives details about it. ◆◇◇◇◇ N-COUNT

prosper /prɒspəʳ/ **prospers, prospering, prospered.** If people or businesses **prosper**, they are successful and do well; a formal word. *The high street banks continue to prosper... His teams have always prospered in cup competitions.* ◆◇◇◇◇ VERB =thrive V

prosperity /prɒsperɪti/. **Prosperity** is a condition in which a person or community is doing well financially. *...a new era of peace and prosperity. ...Japan's economic prosperity.* ◆◆◇◇◇ N-UNCOUNT =affluence

prosperous /prɒspərəs/. **Prosperous** people, places, and economies are rich and successful; a formal word. *...the youngest son of a relatively prosperous British family... The place looks more prosperous than ever.* ◆◇◇◇◇ ADJ-GRADED =wealthy, well-off

prostate /prɒsteɪt/ **prostates.** The **prostate** or the **prostate gland** is an organ in the body of male mammals which is situated at the neck of the bladder and produces a liquid which forms part of the semen. ◆◇◇◇◇ N-COUNT

prosthesis /prɒsθiːsɪs/ **prostheses.** A **prosthesis** is an artificial external body part; a medical term. *The woman whose leg had been amputated could get a prosthesis and learn to walk on it.* N-COUNT

prosthetic /prɒsθetɪk/. **Prosthetic** limbs or devices are artificial replacements for external parts of people's bodies; a medical term. ADJ: ADJ n =artificial

prostitute /prɒstɪtjuːt, AM -tuːt/ **prostitutes, prostituting, prostituted** ◆◆◇◇◇

1 A **prostitute** is a person, usually a woman, who has sex with men in exchange for money. *He admitted last week he paid for sex with a prostitute. ...male prostitutes.* N-COUNT

2 If someone **prostitutes** a woman or if a woman **prostitutes** herself, she has sex with men for money. *...this terrible story of famine and a woman who's forced to prostitute herself in order to get food. ...prostituting his beautiful daughters.* VERB V pron-refl V n

3 If you **prostitute** yourself or your talents, you use your talents for unworthy purposes, usually for money. *Higher education is being forced to prostitute itself to market forces. ...haunted by the idea of his friends whispering about his having prostituted his talent.* VERB V pron-refl V n

prostitution /prɒstɪtjuːʃᵊn, AM -tuː-/. **Prostitution** means having sex with people in exchange for money. *She eventually drifts into prostitution. ...the leader of a drugs and prostitution ring.* ◆◇◇◇◇ N-UNCOUNT

prostrate, prostrates, prostrating, prostrated. The verb is pronounced /prɒstreɪt, AM prɑːstreɪt/. The adjective is pronounced /prɒstreɪt/.

1 If you **prostrate** yourself, you lie down stretched out flat on the ground with your face downwards, usually as an act of worship or submission. *They reached the throne of their king, and prostrated themselves in awe and fear.* VERB V pron-refl

2 If you are lying **prostrate**, you are lying flat on the ground with your face downwards. *Percy was lying prostrate, his arms outstretched and his eyes closed.* ADJ: ADJ after v

3 If someone is **prostrate**, they are so distressed or affected by a very bad experience that they are unable to do anything at all; a formal use. *Immediately after my father's death my stepmother was prostrate... I was prostrate with grief. ...his country's prostrate economy.* ADJ: oft ADJ with n =devastated

protagonist /prətægənɪst, AM proʊ-/ **protagonists** ◆◇◇◇◇

1 Someone who is a **protagonist of** an idea or movement is a supporter of it; a formal use. *He was one of the most active protagonists of British membership of the EEC. ...the main protagonists of their countries' integration into the world market.* N-COUNT: oft N of n =proponent, champion ≠critic

2 A **protagonist** in a play, novel, or real event is one of the main people in it; a formal use. *...the protagonist of Fay Weldon's new novel, 'Life Force'. ...the leading protagonists in the Gulf crisis.* N-COUNT

protean /proʊtiən/. If you describe someone or something as **protean**, you mean that they have the ability to continually change their nature, appearance, or behaviour; a formal word. *He is a protean stylist who can move from blues to ballads and grand symphony.* ADJ-GRADED: usu ADJ n

protect /prətekt/ **protects, protecting, protected** ◆◆◆◆◇

1 To **protect** someone or something means to prevent them from being harmed or damaged. *So, what can women do to protect themselves from* VERB =defend V n from/against n *heart disease?... A long thin wool coat and a purple headscarf protected her against the wind... The government is committed to protecting the interests of tenants.* V n Also V *against* n

2 If an insurance policy **protects** you against a particular event such as death, injury, fire, or theft, it states that it will give money to you or your family if that event occurs. *Many manufacturers have policies to protect themselves against blackmailers.* VERB V n *against* n Also V *against* n

protected /prətektɪd/. **Protected** is used to describe animals, plants, and areas of land which are not allowed, by law, to be destroyed, harmed, or damaged. *In England, thrushes are a protected species so you will not find them on any menu. ...a protected zone of national forest.* ADJ

protection /prətekʃᵊn/ **protections** ◆◆◆◆◇

1 If something gives **protection** against something unpleasant, it prevents people or things from being harmed or damaged by it. *Such a diet is widely believed to offer protection against a number of cancers... It is clear that the primary duty of parents is to provide protection for our children.* N-VAR

2 If something or someone is **protection** against something unpleasant, they prevent you from being harmed or damaged by it. *Innocence and decent living are no protection from the evil elements within our society... The birch is still considered a protection against evil spirits by some people in northern Europe.* N-UNCOUNT: also *a* N

3 If an insurance policy gives you **protection** against a particular event such as death, injury, fire, or theft, it states that it will give money to you or your family if that event happens. *The new policy is believed to be the first scheme to offer protection against an illness.* N-UNCOUNT: oft N *against* n =security

4 Protections are laws and other official measures intended to protect people's rights and freedoms. *...civil rights bills providing a myriad of protections for gays, women and the disabled.* N-COUNT: usu pl =safeguard

5 If a government has a policy of **protection**, it helps its own industries by putting a tax on imported goods or by restricting imports in some other way. *Over the same period trade protection has increased in the rich countries.* N-UNCOUNT ≠free trade

6 If gangsters offer people **protection**, they demand money from them and in return promise not to hurt them or damage their property. *A businessman who refused to pay protection money was shot nine times. ...protection rackets.* N-UNCOUNT: usu N n

protectionism /prətekʃənɪzəm/. **Protectionism** is the policy some countries have of helping their own industries by putting a large tax on imported goods or by restricting imports in some other way. *The aim of the current round of talks is to promote free trade and to avert the threat of increasing protectionism.* ◆◇◇◇◇ N-UNCOUNT ≠free trade

protectionist /prətekʃənɪst/ **protectionists** ◆◇◇◇◇

1 A **protectionist** is someone who agrees with and supports protectionism. *Trade frictions between the two countries had been caused by trade protectionists.* N-COUNT

2 Protectionist policies, measures, and laws are based on protectionism, or help to create or support it. *...the European Community's protectionist agricultural policies.* ADJ-GRADED ≠free trade

protective /prətektɪv/ ◆◆◇◇◇

1 Protective means designed or intended to protect something or someone from harm. *Protective gloves reduce the absorption of chemicals through the skin... Protective measures are necessary if the city's monuments are to be preserved.* ADJ: usu ADJ n

2 If someone is **protective** towards you, they look after you and show a strong desire to keep you safe. *He is very protective towards his mother... Glynis was beside her, putting a protective arm around her shoulders.* ♦ **protectively** *Simon drove me to the airport, gave me a bear-hug and protectively told me to look after myself.* ♦ **protectiveness** *What she felt now was protectiveness towards her brothers, her sister and her new baby.* ADJ-GRADED: oft ADJ *towards/of* n ADV: ADV with v N-UNCOUNT

protective custody. If a witness in a court case is being held in **protective custody**, they are being kept in prison in order to prevent them from being harmed. *They might be doing me a good turn if they took me into protective custody.* N-UNCOUNT

protector /prətektəʳ/ **protectors** ◆◇◇◇◇

1 If you refer to someone as your **protector**, you mean that they protect you from being harmed. *Many mothers see their son as a potential protector and provider.* N-COUNT

2 A **protector** is a device that protects someone or something from physical harm. *He was the only National League umpire to wear an outside chest protector.* N-COUNT: usu n N

protectorate /prətektərət/ **protectorates.** A **protectorate** is a country that is controlled and protected by a more powerful country. *In 1914 the country became a British protectorate.* N-COUNT

protégé /prɒtɪʒeɪ, AM proʊt-/ **protégés;** sometimes spelled **protégée** when referring to a woman. The **protégé** of an older and more experienced person is a young person who is helped and guided by them over a period of time. *He had been a protégé of Captain James. ...Klimt's young protége, Egon Schiele.* ◆◇◇◇◇ N-COUNT

protein /proʊtiːn/ **proteins. Protein** is a substance found in food and drink such as meat, eggs, and milk. You need protein in order to grow and be healthy. *Fish was a major source of protein for the working man. ...a high protein diet.* ◆◆◆◇◇ N-MASS

pro tem /proʊ tem/. If someone has a particular position or job **pro tem**, they have it temporarily; a formal expression. *...the president pro tem of the California State Senate.* ADV: n ADV

protest, protests, protesting, protested. The verb is pronounced /prətest/. The noun is pronounced /proʊtest/. ◆◆◆◆◇

1 To **protest** means to say or show publicly that you object to something. In British English, you **protest about** something or **against** something. In American English, you **protest** something. *Groups of women took to the streets to protest against the arrests... The students were protesting at overcrowding in the university hostels... They were protesting soaring prices... He picked up the cat before Rosa could protest.* VERB V *about/against/at* n V n V

2 A **protest** is the act of saying or showing publicly that you object to something. *The opposition now seems too weak to stage any serious protests against the government... The unions called a two-hour strike in protest at the railway authority's announcement. ...a protest march.* N-VAR: oft N *against/at/about* n

3 If you **protest** that something is the case, you insist that it is the case, when other people think that it may not be. *When we tried to protest that Mo was beaten up they didn't believe us... 'I never said any of that to her,' he protested... He has always protested his innocence.* VERB V that V with quote V n

4 A **protest** that something is true is a strong declaration that it is true. *That was how she usually dealt with their protests that she was spoiling her grandchildren.* N-COUNT: usu N that =protestation

Protestant /prɒtɪstənt/ **Protestants** ◆◆◇◇◇

1 A **Protestant** is a Christian who belongs to the branch of the Christian church which separated from the Catholic church in the sixteenth century. N-COUNT

2 Protestant means relating to Protestants or their churches. *Most Protestant churches now have women ministers.* ADJ: usu ADJ n

Protestantism /prɒtɪstəntɪzəm/. **Protestantism** is the set of Christian beliefs that are held by Protestants. *...the spread of Protestantism.* N-UNCOUNT

protestation /prɒtɪsteɪʃᵊn/ **protestations.** A **protestation** is a strong declaration that something is true or not true; a formal word. *Despite his constant protestations of devotion and love, her doubts persisted.* N-COUNT: oft N *of* n =avowal

protester /prətestəʳ/ **protesters;** also spelled **protestor**. A **protester** is a person who protests publicly about an issue, for example by taking part in a demonstration. *The protesters say the government is corrupt and inefficient. ...anti-abortion protesters.* ◆◆◇◇◇ N-COUNT

proto- /proutou-/. **Proto-** is used to form adjectives and nouns which indicate that something is in the early stages of its development. *...the proto-fascist tendencies of some of its supporters. ...Albion, whose own legend stretches back to the mists of proto-history.* PREFIX

protocol /proutəkɒl, AM -kɔːl/ **protocols** ◆◇◇◇◇
1 **Protocol** is a system of rules about the correct way to act in formal situations. *He has become something of a stickler for the finer observances of royal protocol. ...minor breaches of protocol.* N-VAR
2 A **protocol** is a written record of a treaty or agreement that has been made by two or more countries; a formal use. *...the Montreal Protocol to phase out use and production of CFCs... There are also protocols on the testing of nuclear weapons.* N-COUNT =accord
3 In American English, a **protocol** is a course of medical treatment for someone who is ill or has an addiction; a medical use. *...the detoxification protocol.* N-COUNT

proton /proutɒn/ **protons.** A **proton** is an atomic particle that has a positive electrical charge; a technical term in physics. ◆◇◇◇◇ N-COUNT

prototype /proutətaɪp/ **prototypes** ◆◆◇◇◇
1 A **prototype** is an experimental model of something new which has not yet been produced commercially. *Chris Retzler has built a prototype of a machine called the wave rotor. ...the first prototype aircraft.* N-COUNT: oft N of n, N n
2 If you say that someone or something is a **prototype of** a type of person or thing, you mean that they are the first or most typical one of that type. *He was the prototype of the elder statesman.* N-COUNT: usu N of n

prototypical /proutətɪpɪkᵊl/. **Prototypical** is used to indicate that someone or something is a very typical example of a type of person or thing; a formal word. *Park Ridge is the prototypical American suburb. ...a prototypical socialist.* ADJ: usu ADJ n =typical

protozoan /proutəzouən/ **protozoa** or **protozoans. Protozoa** are very small life forms which often live inside larger animals; a technical term in biology. N-COUNT: usu pl

protracted /prətræktɪd, AM prou-/. Something, usually something unpleasant, that is **protracted** lasts a long time, especially longer than usual or longer than you hoped; a formal word. *However, after protracted negotiations Ogden got the deal he wanted. ...a protracted civil war... The struggle would be bitter and protracted.* ◆◇◇◇◇ ADJ-GRADED =lengthy, prolonged

protractor /prətræktəʳ, AM prou-/ **protractors.** A **protractor** is a flat, semicircular piece of plastic or metal which is used for measuring angles. N-COUNT

protrude /prətruːd, AM prou-/ **protrudes, protruding, protruded.** If something **protrudes** from somewhere, it sticks out; a formal word. *...a huge round mass of smooth rock protruding from the water... The tip of her tongue was protruding slightly.* ♦ **protruding** *...protruding ears.* ◆◇◇◇◇ VERB =stick out V prep V; ADJ-GRADED

protrusion /prətruːʒᵊn, AM prou-/ **protrusions.** A **protrusion** is something that sticks out from something; a formal word. *He grabbed at a protrusion of rock with his right hand.* N-COUNT =lump

protuberance /prətjuːbərəns, AM proutuːb-/ **protuberances.** A **protuberance** is a rounded part that sticks out from the surface of something; a formal word. *...a protuberance on the upper jawbone.* N-COUNT =lump

protuberant /prətjuːbərənt, AM proutuːb-/. **Protuberant** eyes, lips, noses, or teeth stick out more than usual from the face; a formal word. *...a high-beaked nose and large protuberant eyes.* ADJ-GRADED: usu ADJ n =protruding

proud /praud/ **prouder, proudest** ◆◆◆◇◇
1 If you feel **proud**, you feel glad about something good that you possess or have done, or about something that someone close to you possesses or has done. *I felt proud of his efforts... They are proud that she is doing well at school... I am proud to be a Canadian... Derek is now the proud father of a bouncing baby girl.* ♦ **proudly** *'That's the first part finished,' he said proudly.* ADJ-GRADED: oft ADJ of n, ADJ that/to-inf ≠ashamed; ADV-GRADED: ADV with v
2 Your **proudest** moments or achievements are the ones that you are most proud of. *This must have been one of the proudest moments of his busy and hard working life.* ADJ-GRADED: ADJ n, usu ADJ-superl
3 Someone who is **proud** has dignity and self-respect. *He was too proud to ask his family for help and support... We are a proud people. We are not used to begging or taking things.* ADJ-GRADED
4 Someone who is **proud** feels that they are better or more important than other people. *She was said to be proud and arrogant.* ADJ-GRADED =arrogant, vain ≠humble
5 In old-fashioned British English, if one object stands **proud** of another object that it is attached to or next to, it extends beyond it. *The handles stand proud of the doors of the car.* ADJ: ADJ after v
6 If someone **does you proud**, they treat you very well, for example by welcoming you and giving you good food and entertainment; an informal expression. *The hotel has indeed done them proud.* PHRASE: V inflects

prove /pruːv/ **proves, proving, proved, proven.** The forms **proved** and **proven** can both be used as a past participle. ◆◆◆◆◇
1 If something **proves** to be true or to have a particular quality, it becomes clear after a period of time that it is true or has that quality. *We have been accused of exaggerating before, but unfortunately all our reports proved to be true... In the past this process of transition has often proven difficult. ...an experiment which was to prove a source of inspiration for many years to come.* V-LINK =turn out; V to-inf; V adj; V n
2 If you **prove** that something is true, you show by means of argument or evidence that it is definitely true. *You brought this charge. You prove it! I have nothing to say... The results prove that regulation of the salmon farming industry is inadequate. ...trying to prove how groups of animals have evolved... That made me hopping mad and determined to prove him wrong... History will prove him to have been right all along. ...a proven cause of cancer.* VERB; V n; V that; V wh; V n adj; V n to-inf; V-ed
3 If you **prove** yourself to have a certain good quality, you show by your actions that you have it. *Margaret proved herself to be a good mother... As a composer he proved himself adept at large dramatic forms... A man needs time to prove himself... Few would argue that this team has experience and proven ability.* VERB; V pron-refl to-inf; V pron-refl adj; V pron-refl; V-ed; Also V pron-refl n, V that
4 If you **prove** a **point**, you do something which shows other people that you know something or can do something, although your action may have no other purpose. *It seemed pretty pointless to me to make a 3,000 mile detour simply to prove a point.* PHRASE: V inflects

proven /pruːvᵊn, prouvᵊn/. **Proven** is a past participle of **prove**. **Proven** is the usual form of the past participle when you are using it as an adjective.

provenance /prɒvɪnəns/ **provenances.** The **provenance** of something is the place that it comes from or that it originally came from; a formal word. *Kato was fully aware of the provenance of these treasures... He had no idea of its provenance.* N-VAR: usu with poss =origin, source

proverb /prɒvɜːʳb/ **proverbs.** A **proverb** is a short sentence that people often quote, which gives advice or tells you something about life. *An old Arab proverb says, 'The enemy of my enemy is my friend'.* N-COUNT =saying

proverbial /prəvɜːʳbiəl/ ◆◇◇◇◇
1 You use **proverbial** to show that you know the way you are describing something is one that is often used or is part of a popular saying. *The limousine sped off down the road in the proverbial cloud of dust... My audience certainly isn't the proverbial man in the street.* ADJ: ADJ n
2 Something that is **proverbial** is very well-known by a lot of people. *His mastery of the French language was proverbial.* ADJ

provide /prəvaɪd/ **provides, providing, provided** ◆◆◆◆◆
1 If you **provide** something that someone needs or wants, or if you **provide** them with it, you give it to them or make it available to them. *I'll be glad to provide a copy of this... They would not provide any details... The government was not in a position to* VERB =supply; V n; V n with n

provide them with food. ♦ **provider, providers** N-COUNT *They remain the main providers of sports facilities.*
2 If a law or agreement **provides** that something will happen, it states that it will happen; a formal use. *The treaty provides that, by the end of the century, the United States must have removed its bases... The Act provides that only the parents of a child have a responsibility for that child's financial support.* VERB =stipulate V that
3 See also **provided, providing.**

provide for PHRASAL VERB
1 If you **provide for** someone, you support them financially and make sure that they have the things that they need. *Elaine wouldn't let him provide for her... Her father always ensured she was well provided for.* V P n
2 If you **provide for** something that might happen or that might need to be done, you make arrangements to deal with it. *James had provided for just such an emergency.* V P n
3 If a law or agreement **provides for** something, it makes it possible; a formal use. *The bill also provides for the automatic review by the appeal court of all death sentences.* V P n

provided /prəvaɪdɪd/. If you say that something will happen **provided** or **provided that** something else happens, you mean that the first thing will happen only if the second thing also happens. *The other banks are going to be very eager to help, provided that they see that he has a specific plan... Provided they are fit I see no reason why they shouldn't go on playing for another four or five years.* ◆◆◇◇◇ CONJ-SUBORD =so long as, providing

providence /prɒvɪdəns/. **Providence** is God, or a force which is believed by some people to arrange the things that happen to us; a literary word. *The first Slav pope, John Paul, said that providence had chosen him to proclaim the spiritual unity of Europe... These women regard his death as an act of providence.* ◆◇◇◇◇ N-UNCOUNT =fate

providential /prɒvɪdenʃəl/. A **providential** event is lucky because it happens at exactly the right time; a formal word. *He explained the yellow fever epidemic as a providential act to discourage urban growth... The pistols were loaded so our escape is indeed providential.* ADJ-GRADED =fortunate
♦ **providentially** *Providentially, he had earlier made friends with a Russian Colonel.* ADV

providing /prəvaɪdɪŋ/. If you say that something will happen **providing** or **providing that** something else happens, you mean that the first thing will happen only if the second thing also happens. *I do believe in people being able to do what they want to do, providing they're not hurting someone else... Providing they do not panic, I believe that their chances of survival will be beyond 95 per cent.* ◆◇◇◇◇ CONJ-SUBORD =provided, so long as

province /prɒvɪns/ **provinces** ◆◆◆◇◇
1 A **province** is a large section of a country which has its own administration. *The Algarve, Portugal's southernmost province, has become one of the most popular destinations for British holidaymakers.* N-COUNT
2 The **provinces** are all the parts of a country except the part where the capital is situated. *The government plans to transfer some 30,000 government jobs from Paris to the provinces.* N-PLURAL: usu *the* N
3 If you say that a subject or activity is a particular person's **province**, you mean that this person has a special interest in it, a special knowledge of it, or a special responsibility for it. *Arvo avoided committing himself. 'I'm afraid that's not my province,' he replied... Industrial research is the province of the Department of Trade and Industry.* N-SING: with poss =area

provincial /prəvɪnʃəl/ **provincials** ◆◆◇◇◇
1 **Provincial** means connected with the parts of a country outside the capital. *Jeremy Styles, 34, was the house manager for a provincial theatre for ten years. ...in Rasht, the provincial capital of Gilan province.* ADJ: ADJ n
2 If you describe someone or something as **provincial**, you disapprove of them because you think that they are narrow-minded and unsophisticated. *He decided to revamp the company's provincial image... The audience was dull and very provincial.* ADJ-GRADED PRAGMATICS ≠sophisticated
► Also a noun. *Owen died an unknown provincial. ...uncouth provincials.* N-COUNT

provincialism /prəvɪnʃəlɪzəm/. **Provincialism** is a narrow outlook and lack of cultural sophistication which is some people think exists in the provinces. *...the stifling bourgeois provincialism of Buxton.* N-UNCOUNT PRAGMATICS

proving ground, proving grounds. If you describe a place as a **proving ground**, you mean that new things or ideas are tried out or tested there. *New York is a proving ground today for the Democratic presidential candidates.* N-COUNT

provision /prəvɪʒən/ **provisions** ◆◆◆◇◇
1 The **provision** of something is the act of giving it or making it available to people who need or want it. *The department is responsible for the provision of residential care services. ...nursery provision for children with special needs.* N-UNCOUNT: also *a* N, with supp, oft N *of* n
2 If you make **provision for** something that might happen or that might need to be done, you make arrangements to deal with it. *Mr King asked if it had ever occurred to her to make provision for her own pension... There is no provision for funding performance-related pay rises.* N-VAR: usu N *for* n/-ing
3 If you make **provision for** someone, you support them financially and make sure that they have the things that they need. *Special provision should be made for children... There are very generous provisions for the mother.* N-UNCOUNT: also N in pl, N *for* n
4 A **provision** in a law or an agreement is an arrangement which is included in it. *He backed a provision that would allow judges to delay granting a divorce decree in some cases... The bill's provision for the sale and purchase of land faces stiff opposition from conservatives.* N-COUNT
5 **Provisions** are supplies of food; an old-fashioned use. *On board were enough provisions for two weeks.* N-PLURAL =supplies

provisional /prəvɪʒənəl/. You use **provisional** to describe something that has been arranged or appointed for the present, but may be changed in the future. *...the possibility of setting up a provisional coalition government... If you have never held a driving licence before, you should apply for a provisional licence... It was announced that the times were provisional and subject to confirmation.* ♦ **provisionally** *The European Community has provisionally agreed to increase the quotas.* ◆◆◇◇◇ ADJ; ADV: ADV with v

proviso /prəvaɪzoʊ/ **provisos.** A **proviso** is a condition in an agreement. You agree to do something if this condition is fulfilled. *I told Norman I would invest in his venture as long as he agreed to one proviso... Okay, with the proviso that Jane agrees, I accept.* N-COUNT: oft N that =condition

provocateur /proʊvɒkətɜːʳ/ **provocateurs.** See **agent provocateur**.

provocation /prɒvəkeɪʃən/ **provocations.** If you describe something that someone does as **provocation** or a **provocation**, you mean that it is a reason for someone to react angrily, violently, or emotionally. *He denies murder on the grounds of provocation... The soldiers fired without provocation... The Deputy Commander has condemned this weekend's protest as deliberate provocation.* ◆◇◇◇◇ N-VAR: usu prep N

provocative /prəvɒkətɪv/ ◆◇◇◇◇
1 If you describe something as **provocative**, you mean that it is intended to make people react angrily or argue against it. *He has made a string of outspoken and sometimes provocative speeches in recent years... His behavior was called provocative and antisocial.* ♦ **provocatively** *The soldiers fired into the air when the demonstrators behaved provocatively.* ADJ-GRADED; ADV-GRADED: usu ADV with v
2 If you describe someone's clothing or behaviour as **provocative**, you mean that it is intended to make someone feel sexual desire. *Some adolescents might be more sexually mature and provocative than others.* ♦ **provocatively** *She smiled at him provocatively.* ADJ-GRADED; ADV-GRADED: usu ADV with v, also ADV adj

provoke /prəvouk/ **provokes, provoking, provoked** ◆◆◆◇◇
1 If you **provoke** someone, you deliberately annoy them and try to make them behave aggressively. *He started beating me when I was about fifteen but I didn't do anything to provoke him... I provoked him into doing something really stupid.* VERB =goad V n V n *into*-ing/n
2 If something **provokes** a reaction, it causes it. *His election success has provoked a shocked reaction... The destruction of the mosque has provoked anger throughout the Muslim world.* VERB V n

provost /prɒvəst, AM prouvoust/ **provosts**
1 A **provost** is the head of a university college in Britain. N-COUNT
2 A **provost** is the chief magistrate of a Scottish borough. N-COUNT
3 In the Roman Catholic and Anglican Churches, a **provost** is the person who is in charge of the administration of a cathedral. N-COUNT

prow /praʊ/ **prows.** The **prow** of a ship or boat is the front part of it. N-COUNT

prowess /praʊɪs/. Someone's **prowess** is their outstanding ability at doing a particular thing; a formal word. *He's always bragging about his prowess as a cricketer... Nureyev captivated audiences with his grace and athletic prowess.* ◆◇◇◇◇ N-UNCOUNT

prowl /praʊl/ **prowls, prowling, prowled** ◆◇◇◇◇
1 If an animal or a person **prowls** around, they move around quietly, for example when they are hunting. *He prowled around the room, not sure what he was looking for or even why he was there.* VERB V prep/adv Also V, V n
2 If an animal is **on the prowl**, it is hunting. If a person is **on the prowl**, they are hunting for something such as a sexual partner or a business deal. *Their fellow travellers are a mix of honeymooners, single girls on the prowl and elderly couples... The new administration are on the prowl for ways to reduce spending.* PHRASE: v-link PHR, oft PHR *for*n

prowler /praʊləʳ/ **prowlers.** A **prowler** is an unknown man who creeps around, especially at night, following women and children or hiding near their houses in order to steal something, frighten them, or perhaps harm them. N-COUNT

proximity /prɒksɪmɪti/. **Proximity** to a place or person is nearness to that place or person; a formal word. *Part of the attraction is Darwin's proximity to Asia... He became aware of the proximity of the Afghans... Families are no longer in close proximity to each other.* ◆◇◇◇◇ N-UNCOUNT: usu N *to/of*n, *in*N =closeness

proxy /prɒksi/ **proxies** ◆◇◇◇◇
1 If you do something **by proxy**, you arrange for someone else to do it for you. *Those not attending the meeting may vote by proxy.* N-UNCOUNT: usu *by*N
2 A **proxy** is a person or thing that is acting or being used in the place of someone or something else. *Price differences are used as a proxy for differences in quality.* N-COUNT: usu N *for*n

prude /pru:d/ **prudes.** If you call someone a **prude**, you think that they are easily shocked and embarrassed by things relating to nudity or sex; used showing disapproval. N-COUNT PRAGMATICS

prudence /pru:dᵊns/. **Prudence** is the care and wisdom that someone shows when they are making judgements or decisions; a formal word. *Western businessmen are showing remarkable prudence in investing in the region... A lack of prudence may lead to financial problems.* ◆◇◇◇◇ N-UNCOUNT =good sense ≠rashness, stupidity

prudent /pru:dᵊnt/. Someone who is **prudent** is sensible and careful. *It is always prudent to start any exercise programme gradually at first... Being a prudent and cautious person, you realise that the problem must be resolved.* ♦ **prudently** *I believe it is essential that we act prudently... Prudently, Joanna spoke none of this aloud.* ◆◇◇◇◇ ADJ-GRADED: oft *it* v-link ADJ to-inf =sensible ≠rash ADV-GRADED: usu ADV with v

prudery /pru:dəri/. **Prudery** is prudish behaviour or attitudes; used showing disapproval. N-UNCOUNT PRAGMATICS

prudish /pru:dɪʃ/. If you describe someone as **prudish**, you think that they are easily shocked by things relating to nudity or sex; used showing disapproval. *I'm not prudish but I think these photographs are obscene.* ♦ **prudishness** *Older people will have grown up in a time of greater sexual prudishness.* ADJ-GRADED PRAGMATICS N-UNCOUNT =prudery

prune /pru:n/ **prunes, pruning, pruned** ◆◆◇◇◇
1 A **prune** is a dried plum. N-COUNT
2 When you **prune** a tree or bush, you cut off some of the branches so that it will grow better the next year. *You have to prune a bush if you want fruit... There is no best way to prune, apart from making sure tools are sharp and every cut is clean.* ► **Prune back** means the same as **prune**. *Apples, pears and cherries can be pruned back when they've lost their leaves.* VERB V n V PHRASAL VERB V P n (not pron) Also V n P
3 If you **prune** something, you cut out all the parts that you do not need. *Firms are cutting investment and pruning their product ranges.* ► **Prune back** means the same as **prune**. *The company has pruned back its workforce by 20,000 since 1989.* VERB V n PHRASAL VERB V P n (not pron)

prune back. See **prune** 2 and 3. PHRASAL VERB

prurience /prʊəriəns/. **Prurience** is a strong interest that someone shows in sexual matters; a formal word, used showing disapproval. *Nobody ever lost money by overestimating the public's prurience.* N-UNCOUNT PRAGMATICS

prurient /prʊəriənt/. If you describe someone as **prurient**, you are criticizing them for showing too much interest in sexual matters; a formal word. *We read the gossip written about them with prurient interest.* ADJ-GRADED: usu ADJ n PRAGMATICS =salacious

pry /praɪ/ **pries, prying, pried** ◆◇◇◇◇
1 If someone **pries**, they try to find out about someone else's private affairs, or look at their personal possessions. *We do not want people prying into our affairs... Imelda might think she was prying... She thought she was safe from prying eyes and could do as she wished.* VERB =snoop V *into*n V V-ing
2 If you **pry** something **open** or **pry** it away from a surface, you force it open or away from a surface. *They pried open a sticky can of blue paint... I pried the top off a can of chilli... Prying off the plastic lid, she took out a small scoop.* VERB =prise V n with adj V n prep V n with adv

PS /pi: es/. You write **PS** to introduce something you add at the end of a letter after you have signed it. *PS. Please show your friends this letter and the enclosed leaflet.* ◆◇◇◇◇

psalm /sɑ:m/ **psalms.** The **Psalms** are the 150 songs, poems, and prayers which together form the Book of Psalms in the Bible. *He recited a verse of the twenty-third psalm.* N-COUNT

psephologist /sɪfɒlədʒɪst, AM si:-/ **psephologists.** A **psephologist** studies how people vote in elections. N-COUNT

pseud /sju:d/ **pseuds.** If you say that someone is a **pseud**, you mean that they are trying to appear very well-educated or artistic but you think that they are being pretentious; an informal British word, used showing disapproval. N-COUNT PRAGMATICS =poser

pseudo- /sju:doʊ-, AM su:doʊ-/. **Pseudo-** is used to form adjectives and nouns that indicate that something is not the thing it is claimed to be. For example, if you describe a country as a pseudo-democracy, you mean that it is not really a democracy, although its government claims that it is. *...pseudo-intellectual images.* PREFIX

pseudonym /sju:dənɪm, AM su:-/ **pseudonyms.** A **pseudonym** is a name which someone, usually a writer, uses instead of his or her real name. *Both plays were published under the pseudonym of Philip Dayre.* N-COUNT: oft N *of/for*n =alias

psoriasis /səraɪəsɪs/. **Psoriasis** is a skin disease that causes red scaly patches. N-UNCOUNT

psst /psst/. **Psst** is a sound that someone makes when they want to attract another person's attention secretly or quietly. *'Psst! Come over here!' one youth hissed furtively.*

psych /saɪk/ **psychs, psyching, psyched;** also spelled **psyche**.

psych up. If you **psych** yourself **up** before a contest or a difficult task, you prepare yourself for it mentally, especially by telling yourself that you can win or succeed; an informal expression. *After work, it is hard to psych yourself up for an hour at the* PHRASAL VERB V pron-refl P *get* V-ed P *gym... Before the game everyone gets psyched up and starts shouting.*

psych out. If you **psych out** your opponent in a contest, you try to make them feel less confident by behaving in a very confident or aggressive way; an informal expression. *They are like heavyweight boxers, trying to psych each other out and build themselves up.* PHRASAL VERB V n P Also V P n (not pron)

psyche /saɪki/ **psyches.** Your **psyche** is your mind and your deepest feelings and attitudes; a technical term in psychology. *'It probably shows up a deeply immature part of my psyche,' he confesses... His exploration of the myth brings insight into the American psyche.* ◆◇◇◇◇ N-COUNT

psychedelia /saɪkədiːliə/. **Psychedelia** refers to psychedelic objects, clothes, and music. N-UNCOUNT

psychedelic /saɪkədelɪk/ ◆◇◇◇◇

1 **Psychedelic** means relating to drugs such as LSD which have a strong effect on your mind, often producing hallucinations and visions. *Grof describes his research with psychedelic drugs and the experiences they triggered. ...his first real, full-blown psychedelic experience.* ADJ-GRADED: usu ADJ n =hallucinogenic

2 **Psychedelic** art has bright colours and strange patterns. *...psychedelic patterns.* ADJ-GRADED: usu ADJ n

3 **Psychedelic** music is pop music, especially of the late 1960s and early 1970s, which is closely associated with hallucinogenic drugs. *...at a time when, you know, everyone was doing kind of trippy, psychedelic music.* ADJ: usu ADJ n

psychiatric /saɪkiætrɪk/ ◆◆◇◇◇

1 **Psychiatric** means relating to psychiatry. *We finally insisted that he seek psychiatric help.* ADJ: ADJ n

2 **Psychiatric** means involving mental illness. *About 4% of the prison population have chronic psychiatric illnesses.* ADJ: ADJ n

psychiatrist /saɪkaɪətrɪst, AM sɪ-/ **psychiatrists.** A **psychiatrist** is a doctor who treats people suffering from mental illness. *Alex will probably be seeing a psychiatrist for many months or even years.* ◆◆◇◇◇ N-COUNT

psychiatry /saɪkaɪətri, AM sɪ-/. **Psychiatry** is the branch of medicine concerned with the treatment of mental illness. ◆◇◇◇◇ N-UNCOUNT

psychic /saɪkɪk/ **psychics** ◆◆◇◇◇

1 If you believe that someone is **psychic** or has **psychic powers**, you believe that they have strange mental powers, such as being able to read the minds of other people or to see into the future. *Trevor helped police by using his psychic powers.* ADJ-GRADED
► A **psychic** is someone who seems to be psychic. N-COUNT

2 **Psychic** means relating to ghosts and the spirits of the dead. *He declared his total disbelief in psychic phenomena.* ADJ

3 **Psychic** means relating to the mind rather than the body; a formal use. *These truths cause individuals much psychic pain.* ADJ

psychical /saɪkɪkəl/. **Psychical** means relating to ghosts and the spirits of the dead; a formal word. ADJ

psycho /saɪkoʊ/ **psychos.** A **psycho** is someone who has serious mental problems and who may act in a violent way without feeling sorry for what they have done; an informal word. *Some psycho picked her up, and killed her.* ◆◇◇◇◇ N-COUNT =psychopath

psycho- /saɪkoʊ-/. **Psycho-** is added to words in order to form other words which describe or refer to things connected with the mind or with mental processes. *...the psycho-social aspects of youth unemployment.* PREFIX

psychoactive /saɪkoʊæktɪv/. **Psychoactive** drugs or stimulants affect your mind. *Nicotine is a psychoactive drug.* ADJ

psychoanalyse /saɪkoʊænəlaɪz/ **psychoanalyses, psychoanalysing, psychoanalysed;** spelled **psychoanalyze** in American English. When a psychotherapist or psychiatrist **psychoanalyses** someone who has mental problems, he or she examines or treats them using psychoanalysis. *The movie sees Burton psychoanalysing Firth to cure him of his depression.* VERB V n

psychoanalysis /saɪkoʊənælɪsɪs/. **Psychoanalysis** is the treatment of someone who has mental problems by asking them about their feelings and their past in order to try to discover what may be causing their condition. ◆◇◇◇◇ N-UNCOUNT =analysis

psychoanalyst /saɪkoʊænəlɪst/ **psychoanalysts.** A **psychoanalyst** is someone who treats people who have mental problems using psychoanalysis. ◆◇◇◇◇ N-COUNT =analyst

psychoanalytic /saɪkoʊænəlɪtɪk/. **Psychoanalytic** means relating to psychoanalysis. *...psychoanalytic therapy... Much of her work is speculative, based on psychoanalytic theory rather than empirical data.* ADJ: ADJ n

psychoanalyze /saɪkoʊænəlaɪz/. See **psychoanalyse.**

psychobabble /saɪkoʊbæbəl/. You can use **psychobabble** to refer to complicated or pretentious language which is used in a meaningless way; an informal word. *Beneath the sentimental psychobabble, there's a likeable movie trying to get out.* N-UNCOUNT

psychokinesis /saɪkoʊkɪniːsɪs/. **Psychokinesis** is the ability to move solid objects by the power of your mind. N-UNCOUNT

psychological /saɪkəlɒdʒɪkəl/ ◆◆◆◇◇

1 **Psychological** means concerned with a person's mind and thoughts. *John received constant physical and psychological abuse from his father... Robyn's loss of memory is a psychological problem, rather than a physical one.* ♦ **psychologically** /saɪkəlɒdʒɪkli/ *It was very important psychologically for us to succeed. ...a psychologically disturbed person.* ADJ: usu ADJ n =mental ADV: ADV with cl, ADV adj/adv

2 **Psychological** also means relating to psychology. *...psychological testing.* ADJ: ADJ n

psychological warfare. **Psychological warfare** consists of attempts to make your enemy lose confidence, give up hope, or feel afraid, so that you can win. N-UNCOUNT

psychologist /saɪkɒlədʒɪst/ **psychologists.** A **psychologist** is a person who studies the human mind and tries to explain why people behave in the way that they do. *Psychologists tested a group of six-year-olds with a video.* ◆◆◇◇◇ N-COUNT

psychology /saɪkɒlədʒi/ ◆◆◇◇◇

1 **Psychology** is the scientific study of the human mind and the reasons for people's behaviour. *...Professor of Psychology at Bedford College.* N-UNCOUNT

2 The **psychology** of a person is the kind of mind that they have, which makes them think or behave in the way that they do. *...a fascination with the psychology of murderers.* N-UNCOUNT: usu N *of* n

psychometric /saɪkəmetrɪk/. **Psychometric** tests are designed to test a person's mental state, personality, and thought processes. *Psychometric testing is simply a way of measuring people's individual talents and capabilities.* ADJ: ADJ n

psychopath /saɪkoʊpæθ/ **psychopaths.** A **psychopath** is someone who has serious mental problems and who may act in a violent way without feeling sorry for what they have done. *She was abducted by a dangerous psychopath.* N-COUNT

psychopathic /saɪkoʊpæθɪk/. Someone who is **psychopathic** is a psychopath. *...a report labelling him psychopathic. ...a psychopathic killer.* ADJ

psychosis /saɪkoʊsɪs/ **psychoses.** **Psychosis** is mental illness of a severe kind which can make people lose contact with reality; a medical term. *He may have some kind of neurosis or psychosis later in life. ...senile psychoses.* ◆◇◇◇◇ N-VAR

psychosomatic /saɪkoʊsoʊmætɪk/. If someone has a **psychosomatic** illness, their symptoms are caused by worry or unhappiness rather than by a physical problem. *Doctors refused to treat her, claiming that her problems were all psychosomatic.* ADJ

psychotherapist /saɪkoʊθerəpɪst/ **psychotherapists.** A **psychotherapist** is a person who treats people who are mentally ill using psychotherapy. ◆◇◇◇◇ N-COUNT

psychotherapy /saɪkoʊθerəpi/. **Psychotherapy** is the use of psychological methods in treating people who are mentally ill, rather than using physical methods such as drugs or surgery. *For milder depressions, certain forms of psychotherapy do work well. ...monthly psychotherapy sessions.* ◆◇◇◇◇ N-UNCOUNT

psychotic /saɪkɒtɪk/ **psychotics.** Someone who is **psychotic** has a type of severe mental illness; a medical term. *The man, who police believe is psychotic, is thought to be responsible for eight attacks.* ▶ Also a noun. *A religious psychotic in Las Vegas has killed four people.* ◆◇◇◇◇ ADJ =schizophrenic N-COUNT

pt, pts ◆◇◇◇◇
1 **pt** is a written abbreviation for 'pint'. The plural is either 'pt' or 'pts'. *...1 pt single cream.*
2 **pt** is the written abbreviation for 'point'. *Here's how it works. 3 pts for a correct result 1 pt for the correct winning team.*

PTA /piː tiː eɪ/ **PTAs.** A **PTA** is a school association run by some of the parents and teachers to discuss matters that affect the children and to organize fund-raising and social events. **PTA** is an abbreviation for 'parent-teacher association'. N-COUNT

Pte /praɪvɪt/. **Pte** is used before a person's name as a written abbreviation for the military title 'Private'. *...Pte Owen Butler.* N-TITLE

pterodactyl /terədæktɪl/ **pterodactyls.** A **pterodactyl** was a flying reptile that existed in prehistoric times. N-COUNT

PTO /piː tiː oʊ/. **PTO** is a written abbreviation for 'please turn over'. You write it at the bottom of a page to indicate that there is more writing on the other side.

pub /pʌb/ **pubs.** A **pub** is a building where people can have drinks, especially alcoholic drinks, and talk to their friends; used mainly in British English. *He was in the pub until closing time... Richard used to run a pub.* ◆◆◆◇◇ N-COUNT

pub crawl, pub crawls. In British English, if people go on a **pub crawl**, they go from one pub to another having drinks in each one; an informal expression. *David had been on a pub crawl with pals from his rugby club.* N-COUNT

puberty /pjuːbərti/. **Puberty** is the stage in someone's life when their body starts to become physically mature. *Margaret had reached the age of puberty.* ◆◇◇◇◇ N-UNCOUNT

pubescent /pjuːbesənt/. A **pubescent** girl or boy has reached the stage in their life when their bodies are becoming physically like an adult; a formal term. *...a hoard of pubescent boys and girls who tug at his microphone.* ADJ

pubic /pjuːbɪk/. **Pubic** means relating to the area just above a person's genitals. *...pubic hair.* ADJ: ADJ n

public /pʌblɪk/ ◆◆◆◆◆
1 You can refer to people in general, or to all the people in a particular country or community, as **the public**. *Lauderdale House is now open to the public... Pure alcohol is not for sale to the general public... Trade unions are regarding the poll as a test of the public's confidence in the government.* N-SING-COLL: *the* N
2 You can refer to a set of people in a country who share a common interest, activity, or characteristic as a particular kind of **public**. *Market research showed that 93% of the viewing public wanted a hit film channel. ...the American voting public.* N-SING-COLL: supp N
3 **Public** means relating to all the people in a country or community. *The President is attempting to drum up public support for his economic program.* ADJ: ADJ n
4 **Public** means relating to the government or state, or things that are done by the state for the people. *The social services account for a substantial part of public spending.* ♦ **publicly** *...publicly funded legal services.* ADJ: ADJ n =government, state ADV: ADV -ed
5 **Public** buildings and services are provided for everyone to use. *...the New York Public Library... The new museum must be accessible by public transport. ...a public health service available to all.* ADJ: ADJ n ≠private
6 A **public** place is one where people can go about freely and where you can easily be seen and heard. *...the heavily congested public areas of international airports... I avoid working in places which are too public.* ADJ-GRADED ≠private
7 If someone is a **public figure** or in **public life**, many people know who they are because they are often mentioned in newspapers and on television. *The Archbishop of Canterbury yesterday hit out at public figures who commit adultery... I'd like to see more women in public life, especially Parliament.* ADJ: ADJ n
8 **Public** is used to describe statements, actions, and events that are made or done in such a way that any member of the public can see them or be aware of them. *The National Heritage Committee has conducted a public inquiry to find the answer... The comments were the ministry's first detailed public statement on the subject... Marilyn made her last public appearance at Madison Square Garden.* ♦ **publicly** *He never spoke publicly about the affair... Every move the President makes is publicly discussed as openly as possible.* ADJ: ADJ n ADV-GRADED: usu ADV with v
9 If a fact is **made public** or **becomes public**, it becomes known to everyone rather than being kept secret. *Blair wants any new evidence on IRA pub bombs made public... The facts could cause embarrassment if they ever became public.* ADJ: v-link ADJ
10 If someone is in **the public eye**, many people know who they are, because they are famous or because they are often mentioned on television or in the newspapers. *One expects people in the public eye to conduct their personal lives with a certain decorum... He has kept his wife and daughter out of the public eye.* PHRASES prep PHR
11 If a company **goes public**, it starts selling its shares on the stock exchange. *In 1951 AC went public, having achieved an average annual profit of more than £50,000.* V inflects
12 If you say or do something **in public**, you say or do it when a group of people are present. *By-laws are to make it illegal to smoke in public.* PHR after v =publicly
13 ● to **wash your dirty linen in public**: see **dirty**.

public address system, public address systems. A **public address system** is an electrical system including a microphone, amplifier, and loudspeakers which is used so that someone's voice, or music, can be heard by everyone in a large building or ship. The abbreviation 'PA' is also used. *The news was announced on the public address system at the high school.* N-COUNT

publican /pʌblɪkən/ **publicans.** In Britain, a **publican** is a person who owns or manages a pub; a formal word. N-COUNT =landlady, landlord

publication /pʌblɪkeɪʃən/ **publications** ◆◆◆◇◇
1 The **publication** of a book or magazine is the act of printing it and sending it to shops to be sold. *The guide is being translated into several languages for publication near Christmas... The publication of his collected poems was approaching the status of an event.* N-UNCOUNT
2 A **publication** is a book or magazine that has been published. *They have started legal proceedings against two publications which spoke of an affair.* N-COUNT
3 The **publication of** something such as information is the act of making it known to the public, for example by informing journalists or by publishing a government document. *A spokesman said: 'We have no comment regarding the publication of these photographs.'* N-UNCOUNT: usu N *of* n

public bar, public bars. In a British pub, a **public bar** is a room where the furniture is plain and the drinks are cheaper than in the pub's other bars. N-COUNT

public company, public companies. A **public company** is a company whose shares can be bought by the general public. ◆◇◇◇◇ N-COUNT

public convenience, public conveniences. In British English, a **public convenience** is a toilet in a public place for everyone to use; a formal word. N-COUNT

public domain. If information is **in the public domain**, it is not secret or copyright and can be used or discussed by anybody. *It is outrageous that the figures are not in the public domain...* N-SING: usu *in the* N

The state of their marriage has been put into the public domain.

public house, public houses. In British English, a **public house** is the same as a **pub**; a formal word. N-COUNT

publicise /pʌblɪsaɪz/. See **publicize.**

publicist /pʌblɪsɪst/ **publicists.** A **publicist** is a person who publicizes things, especially as part of a job in advertising or journalism. ◆◇◇◇◇ N-COUNT

publicity /pʌblɪsɪti/ ◆◆◆◇◇

1 **Publicity** is information or actions intended to attract the public's attention to someone or something. *Peking is to give unprecedented advance publicity to the talks. ...government publicity campaigns. ...publicity stunt.* N-UNCOUNT

2 When the news media and the public show a lot of interest in something, you can say that it is receiving **publicity**. *The case has generated enormous publicity in Brazil. ...the renewed publicity over the Casey affair.* N-UNCOUNT

publicity agent, publicity agents. A **publicity agent** is a person whose job is to make sure that a large number of people know about a person, show, or event so that they are successful. N-COUNT

publicize /pʌblɪsaɪz/ **publicizes, publicizing, publicized;** also spelled **publicise** in British English. If you **publicize** a fact or event, you make it widely known to the public. *The author appeared on television to publicize her latest book... He never publicized his plans. ...his highly publicized trial this summer.* ◆◆◇◇◇ VERB V n V-ed

public limited company, public limited companies. A **public limited company** is the same as a **public company**. The abbreviation 'plc' is used after such companies' names. N-COUNT

public nuisance, public nuisances. If something or someone is, or causes, a **public nuisance**, they break the law by harming or annoying members of the public; a legal term. *...the 45-day jail sentence he received for causing a public nuisance after taking part in a demonstration... Back in the 1980s drug users were a public nuisance in Zurich.* N-COUNT: usu sing

public opinion. **Public opinion** is the opinion or attitude of the public regarding a particular matter. *He mobilized public opinion all over the world against hydrogen-bomb tests.* ◆◆◇◇◇ N-UNCOUNT

public property

1 **Public property** is land and other assets that belong to the general public and not to a private owner. *...vandals who wrecked public property... Half of the north-west's timber land is public property.* N-UNCOUNT ≠private property

2 If you describe a person or thing as **public property**, you mean that all information about them is known and discussed by everybody. *He couldn't handle being public property... She complained that intimate aspects of her personal life had been made public property.* N-UNCOUNT

public prosecutor, public prosecutors. A **public prosecutor** is an official who carries out criminal prosecutions on behalf of the government and people of a particular country. N-COUNT

public relations ◆◆◇◇◇

1 **Public relations** is the part of an organization's work that is concerned with obtaining the public's approval for what it does. The abbreviation 'PR' is used. *His behaviour was not good for public relations... George is a public relations officer for The John Bennett Trust.* N-UNCOUNT =PR

2 **Public relations** are the state of the relationship between an organization and the public. *...improved public relations.* N-PLURAL

public school, public schools ◆◆◇◇◇

1 In Britain, a **public school** is a private school that provides secondary education which parents have to pay for. The pupils often live at the school during the school term. *He was headmaster of a public school in the West of England. ...the boy from the streets who went to public school.* N-VAR ≠state school

2 In the USA, Australia, and some other parts of the world, a **public school** is a school that is supported financially by the government and usually provides free education. *...Milwaukee's public school system.* N-VAR

public sector. **The public sector** is the part of a country's economy which is controlled or supported financially by the government. *...Carlos Menem's policy of reducing the public sector and opening up the economy to free-market forces... To keep economic reform on track, 60,000 public-sector jobs must be cut.* ◆◆◇◇◇ N-SING: the N ≠private sector

public servant, public servants. A **public servant** is a person who is appointed or elected to a public office, for example working for a local or state government. N-COUNT

public service, public services ◆◇◇◇◇

1 A **public service** is something such as health care, transport, or waste disposal which is organized by the government or an official body in order to benefit all the people in a particular society or community. *The money is used by local authorities to pay for public services. ...a strike by public service workers.* N-COUNT

2 **Public service** broadcasting consists of television and radio programmes supplied by an official or government organization, rather than by a commercial company. Such programmes often provide information or education, as well as entertainment. ADJ: ADJ n

3 **Public service** activities and types of work are concerned with helping people and providing them with what they need, rather than making a profit. *...the notion of public service and obligation which has been under such attack. ...an egalitarian society based on cooperation and public service.* N-UNCOUNT

4 If you perform a **public service**, you do something that helps or benefits the people in a particular community. *Sportsmen are performing a public service by bringing the joys of major-league baseball to their communities.* N-COUNT: usu sing

public-spirited. A **public-spirited** person tries to help the community that they belong to. *Thanks to a group of public-spirited citizens, the Krippendorf garden has been preserved.* ADJ-GRADED

public utility, public utilities. **Public utilities** are services provided by the state, such as the supply of electricity and gas, or the train network. *Officials said water supplies and other public utilities in the capital were badly affected.* N-COUNT =public service

public works. **Public works** are buildings, roads, and other projects that are built by the government for the public. ◆◇◇◇◇ N-PLURAL

publish /pʌblɪʃ/ **publishes, publishing, published** ◆◆◆◆◇

1 When a company **publishes** a book or magazine, it prints copies of it, which are sent to shops to be sold. *They publish reference books... His latest book of poetry will be published by Faber in May.* VERB V n

2 When the people in charge of a newspaper or magazine **publish** a piece of writing or a photograph, they print it in their newspaper or magazine. *The ban was imposed after the magazine published an article satirising the government... I don't encourage people to take photographs like this without permission, but by law we can publish.* VERB =print V n V

3 If someone **publishes** a book or an article that they have written, they arrange to have it published. *John Lennon found time to publish two books of his humorous prose.* VERB V n

4 If you **publish** information or an opinion, you make it known to the public by having it printed in a newspaper, magazine, or official document. *The demonstrators called on the government to publish a list of registered voters.* VERB V n

publisher /pʌblɪʃəʳ/ **publishers.** A **publisher** is a person or a company that publishes books, newspapers, or magazines. *The publishers planned to produce the journal on a weekly basis.* ◆◆◆◇◇ N-COUNT

publishing /pʌblɪʃɪŋ/. **Publishing** is the profession of publishing books. *I had a very high-powered job in publishing.* ◆◆◆◇◇ N-UNCOUNT

publishing house, publishing houses. A **publishing house** is a company which publishes books. ◆◇◇◇◇ N-COUNT =publishers

puce /pjuːs/. Something that is **puce** is a dark purple colour. *...Mrs Carstairs, a large, solid, round-faced woman in puce and black lace.* COLOUR

puck /pʌk/ **pucks.** In the game of ice hockey, the **puck** is the small rubber disc that is used instead of a ball. N-COUNT

pucker /pʌkəʳ/ **puckers, puckering, puckered.** When a part of your face **puckers** or when you **pucker** it, it becomes wrinkled, often because you are frowning or trying not to cry. *Toby's face puckered... She puckered her lips into a rosebud and kissed him on the nose.* ♦ **puckered** *...puckered lips... Across his upper arm there was a long puckered scar.* V-ERG; V; V n; ADJ-GRADED

puckish /pʌkɪʃ/. If you describe someone as **puckish**, you mean that they are mischievous and enjoy playing tricks on people; an old-fashioned term; used in written English. *He had a puckish sense of humour, but was just as ready to apply it to himself as to others.* ADJ: usu ADJ n =impish

pud /pʊd/ **puds.** In British English, **pud** is the same as **pudding**; an informal word. *...rice pud.* N-VAR

pudding /pʊdɪŋ/ **puddings** ◆◆◇◇◇

1 A **pudding** is a cooked sweet food made with flour, fat, and eggs, and usually served hot. *...a cherry sponge pudding with warm custard.* N-VAR

2 In British English, some people refer to the sweet course of a meal as the **pudding**. *...a menu featuring canapes, a starter, a main course and a pudding... I tend to stick to fresh fruit for pudding.* N-VAR =dessert, sweet

3 See also **Yorkshire pudding**.

4 If you say that **the proof of the pudding** is in the eating, you mean that something new can only be judged to be good or bad after it has been tried or used. PHRASE

pudding basin, pudding basins. In British English, a **pudding basin** is a deep round bowl that is used in the kitchen, especially for mixing or for cooking puddings. N-COUNT

puddle /pʌdᵊl/ **puddles.** A **puddle** is a small, shallow pool of liquid that has spread on the ground. *The road was shiny with puddles, but the rain was at an end. ...puddles of oil.* ◆◇◇◇◇ N-COUNT: oft N *of* n

pudgy /pʌdʒi/. If you describe someone as **pudgy**, you mean that they are unpleasantly plump. *He put a pudgy arm around Harry's shoulder.* ADJ-GRADED PRAGMATICS =podgy

puerile /pjʊəraɪl, AM -rᵊl/. If you describe someone or something as **puerile**, you mean that they are silly and childish. *Concert organisers branded the group's actions as puerile... The story is simple, even puerile. ...puerile, schoolboy humour.* ADJ-GRADED =juvenile

puff /pʌf/ **puffs, puffing, puffed** ◆◇◇◇◇

1 If someone **puffs** at a cigarette, cigar, or a pipe, they smoke it. *He lit a cigar and puffed at it twice... He nodded and puffed on a stubby pipe as he listened.* ► Also a noun. *She was taking quick puffs at her cigarette like a beginner.* VERB; V *at/on* n; Also V n, V; N-COUNT =drag

2 If you **puff** smoke or moisture from your mouth or if it **puffs** from your mouth, you breathe it out. *Richard lit another cigarette and puffed smoke towards the ceiling... The weather was dry and cold; wisps of steam puffed from their lips.* ► **Puff out** means the same as **puff**. *He drew heavily on his cigarette and puffed out a cloud of smoke.* V-ERG; V n; V prep; PHRASAL VERB; V P n (not pron); Also V n P

3 If an engine or a boiler **puffs smoke** or **steam**, it expels it through a pipe which has been designed for this purpose. *As I completed my 26th lap the Porsche puffed blue smoke. A valve had dropped.* VERB; V n

4 A **puff of** something such as air or smoke is a small amount of it that is blown out from somewhere. *Wind caught the sudden puff of dust and blew it inland.* N-COUNT: usu N *of* n

5 If you **are puffing**, you are breathing loudly and quickly with your mouth open because you are out of breath after a lot of physical effort. *I know nothing about boxing, but I could see he was unfit, because he was puffing.* VB: usu cont; V

6 A **puff** is the same as a **poof**. N-COUNT

7 See also **puffed**.

puff out. If you **puff out your cheeks**, you make them larger and rounder by filling them with air. *He puffed out his fat cheeks and let out a lungful of steamy breath.* ● See also **puff** 2. PHRASAL VERB; V P n (not pron); Also V n P

puff up. If part of your body **puffs up** as a result of an injury or illness, it becomes swollen. *Her body bloated and puffed up till pain seemed to burst out through her skin.* ● See also **puffed up**. PHRASAL VERB =swell; V P

puffball /pʌfbɔːl/ **puffballs;** also spelled **puff-ball.** A **puffball** is a fungus which bursts to release a cloud of spores when it is ripe. N-COUNT

puffed /pʌft/

1 If a part of your body **is puffed** or **puffed up**, it is swollen because of an injury or because you are unwell. *His face was a little puffed... His mouth was all puffed up where he had taken a rifle butt.* ADJ-GRADED: v-link ADJ =swollen, puffy

2 If you are **puffed** or **puffed out**, you are breathing with difficulty because you have been using a lot of energy; an informal use. *Do you get puffed out easily or can you run up and down the stairs without panting?* ADJ-GRADED: v-link ADJ =breathless

puffed up. If you describe someone as **puffed up**, you disapprove of them because they are very proud of themselves and think of themselves as being very important. *He was too puffed up with his own importance, too blinded by vanity to accept their verdict on him.* ● See also **puffed**. ADJ-GRADED: oft ADJ *with* n PRAGMATICS

puffin /pʌfɪn/ **puffins.** A **puffin** is a black and white seabird with a large, brightly-coloured beak. N-COUNT

puff pastry. **Puff pastry** is a type of pastry which is very light and flaky. N-UNCOUNT

puffy /pʌfi/ **puffier, puffiest**

1 If part of someone's body, especially their face, is **puffy**, it is has a round, swollen appearance. *Her cheeks were puffy with crying. ...dark-ringed puffy eyes.* ♦ **puffiness** *He noticed some slight puffiness beneath her eyes.* ADJ-GRADED =swollen; N-UNCOUNT

2 If you describe a cloud as **puffy**, you mean that it looks like a large ball of white cotton wool. **Puffy** clouds appear during fine weather; a literary use. *The sea was blue, and white puffy clouds sailed by.* ADJ-GRADED: usu ADJ n =fluffy

pug /pʌg/ **pugs.** A **pug** is a small, fat, short-haired dog with a flat nose. N-COUNT

pugilist /pjuːdʒɪlɪst/ **pugilists.** A **pugilist** is a boxer; an old-fashioned word. N-COUNT

pugnacious /pʌgneɪʃəs/. Someone who is **pugnacious** is always ready to quarrel or start a fight; a formal word. *The President was in a pugnacious mood when he spoke to journalists about the rebellion.* ADJ-GRADED =argumentative

pugnacity /pʌgnæsɪti/. **Pugnacity** is the quality of being pugnacious. *Many Hong Kong businessmen criticise the colonial government for the pugnacity of its approach.* N-UNCOUNT

puke /pjuːk/ **pukes, puking, puked.**

1 When someone **pukes**, they vomit; an informal word. *He's puked... They got drunk and puked out the window.* ► **Puke up** means the same as **puke**. *He peered at me like I'd just puked up on his jeans... I figured, why eat when I was going to puke it up again?* VERB; V; PHRASAL VERB; V P; V n P

2 **Puke** is the same as vomit; an informal word. *He was fully clothed and covered in puke and piss.* N-UNCOUNT

pukka /pʌkə/. In British English, if you describe something or someone as **pukka**, you mean that they are real or genuine, and of good quality; an old-fashioned word. *...a pukka English gentleman.* ADJ-GRADED

pull /pʊl/ **pulls, pulling, pulled** ◆◆◆◆◇

1 When you **pull** something, you hold it firmly and use force in order to move it towards you or away from its previous position. *They have pulled out patients' teeth unnecessarily... He pulled on a jersey... Erica was solemn, pulling at her blonde curls... I helped pull him out of the water... Someone pulled her hair... He knew he should pull the trigger, but he was suddenly paralysed by fear... Pull as hard as you can... I let myself out into the street and pulled the door shut.* ► Also a noun. *The feather must be removed with a straight, firm pull.* VERB; V n with adv; V prep; V n prep; V n; V; V n adj; N-COUNT: usu sing

2 When you **pull** an object from a bag, pocket, or cupboard, you put your hand in and bring the VERB =take out

object out. *Jack pulled the slip of paper from his shirt pocket... Wade walked quickly to the refrigerator and pulled out another beer.*
V n prep / V n with adv

3 When a vehicle, animal, or person **pulls** a cart or piece of machinery, they are attached to it or hold it, so that it moves along behind them when they move forward. *This is early-20th-century rural Sussex, when horses still pulled the plough... He pulls a rickshaw, probably the oldest form of human taxi service.*
VERB / V n

4 If you **pull yourself** or **pull** a part of your body in a particular direction, you move your body or a part of your body with effort or force. *Hughes pulled himself slowly to his feet... He pulled his arms out of the sleeves... She tried to pull her hand free... Lillian brushed his cheek with her fingertips. He pulled away and said, 'Don't!'*
VERB / V pron-refl prep/adv / V n prep/adv / V n adj / V adv

5 When a driver or vehicle **pulls to a stop** or **a halt**, the vehicle stops. *He pulled to a stop behind a pickup truck... The train pulled to a halt at the platform.*
VERB / V prep

6 In a race or contest, if you **pull ahead** of or **pull away from** an opponent, you gradually increase the margin by which you are ahead of them. *He pulled away, extending his lead to 15 seconds... The six states he won in 1988 are the same states in which he has yet to pull ahead of his opponent.*
VERB / V adv

7 If you **pull** something **apart**, you break or divide it into small pieces, often in order to put them back together again in a different way. *If I wanted to improve the car significantly I would have to pull it apart and start again.*
VERB / V n with adv

8 If someone **pulls a gun** or **a knife** on someone else, they take out a gun or knife and threaten the other person with it; an informal use. *They had a fight. One of them pulled a gun on the other... I pulled a knife and threatened her.*
VERB / V n *on* n / V n

9 To **pull** crowds, viewers, or voters means to attract them or attract their support; an informal use. *The organisers have to employ performers to pull a crowd.* ► **Pull in** means the same as **pull**. *They provided a far better news service and pulled in many more viewers... She is still beautiful, and still pulling them in at sixty.*
VERB / =attract / V n / PHRASAL VERB / V P n (not pron) / V n P

10 If something **pulls** you or **pulls** your thoughts or feelings in a particular direction, it strongly attracts you or influences you in a particular way. *Joe felt there was little he could do to help Betty, and his heart was pulling him elsewhere.* ► Also a noun. *No matter how much you feel the pull of the past, make a determined effort to look to the future.*
VERB / V n adv / N-COUNT: usu sing, with supp

11 A **pull** is a strong physical force which causes things to move in a particular direction. *...the pull of gravity.*
N-COUNT

12 If you **pull a muscle**, you injure it by straining it. *Dave pulled a back muscle and could barely kick the ball... He suffered a pulled calf muscle.*
VERB / V n / V-ed

13 If someone **pulls on a cigarette**, they take a deep breath with the cigarette in their mouth. *Jeff leaned back and pulled on his cigarette.* ► Also a noun. *He took a deep pull of his cigarette and exhaled the smoke.*
VERB / =draw / V *on* n / N-COUNT: usu sing

14 If someone **pulls a stunt** or **a trick** on someone, they do something dramatic or silly to fool them, or to get their attention; an informal use. *Everyone saw the stunt you pulled on me.*
VERB / PRAGMATICS / V n *on* n / Also V n

15 If someone **pulls** someone else, they succeed in attracting them sexually and in spending the rest of the evening or night with them; an informal British use.
VERB: V n, V

16 You can say to someone **'Pull the other one'** or **'Pull the other one, it's got bells on'** to tell them that you don't believe what they have told you and you think they must be joking; an informal British expression. *What! A big bloke like you, beaten by his wife! Pull the other one; it's got bells on.*
PHRASES / PRAGMATICS

17 • to **pull oneself up by one's bootstraps**: see **bootstrap**. • to **pull a face**: see **face**. • to **pull a fast one**: see **fast**. • to **pull** someone's **leg**: see **leg**. • to **pull** your **punches**: see **punch**. • to **pull rank**: see **rank**. • to **pull** your **socks up**: see **sock**. • to **pull out all the stops**: see **stop**. • to **pull strings**: see **string**. • to **pull** your **weight**: see **weight**. • to **pull the wool over** someone's **eyes**: see **wool**.

pull away
PHRASAL VERB

1 When a vehicle or driver **pulls away**, the vehicle starts moving forward. *I stood in the driveway and watched him back out and pull away.*
V P

2 If you **pull away from** someone that you have had close links with, you deliberately become less close to them. *Other daughters, faced with their mother's emotional hunger, pull away... The Soviet Union began pulling away from Cuba.*
V P / V P *from* n

pull back
PHRASAL VERB

1 If someone **pulls back from** an action, they decide not to continue or persist with it, because it could have bad consequences. *They will plead with him to pull back from confrontation... The British government threatened to make public its disquiet but then pulled back.*
=withdraw / V P *from* n / V P

2 If troops **pull back** or if a commander **pulls** them **back**, they retreat some or all of the way back to their own territory. *They were asked to pull back from their artillery positions around the city... He pulled back forces from Mongolia, and he withdrew from Afghanistan.*
ERG / =retreat / V P / V P n (not pron) / Also V n P

pull down. To **pull down** a building or statue means to deliberately destroy it. *They'd pulled the registry office down which then left an open space... A small crowd attempted to pull down a Communist statue.*
PHRASAL VERB / =demolish / V n P / V P n (not pron)

pull in
PHRASAL VERB

1 When a vehicle or driver **pulls in** somewhere, the vehicle stops there. *He pulled in at the side of the road... The van pulled in and waited.*
V P prep/adv / V P

2 In British English, if the police **pull** someone **in**, they arrest them and take them to the police station; an informal expression. *'Brady looks like a suspect.'—'I'd pull him in.'*
V n P / Also V P n (not pron)

3 If you **pull in** an amount of money, you earn or collect that amount; an informal expression. *I only pull in 15,000 a year as a social worker.*
V P amount

4 See **pull** 9.

pull into. When a vehicle or driver **pulls into** a road or driveway, the vehicle makes a turn into the road or driveway and stops there. *He pulled into the driveway in front of his garage... She pulled the car into a tight parking space on a side street.*
PHRASAL VERB / V P n / V n P n

pull off
PHRASAL VERB

1 If you **pull off** something very difficult, you manage to achieve it successfully. *The National League for Democracy pulled off a landslide victory... It will be a very, very fine piece of mountaineering if they pull it off.*
=carry off / V P n (not pron) / V n P

2 If a vehicle or driver **pulls off the road**, the vehicle stops by the side of the road. *I pulled off the road at a small village pub... One evening, crossing a small creek, he pulled the car off the road.*
V P n / V n P n

pull out
PHRASAL VERB

1 When a vehicle or driver **pulls out**, the vehicle moves out into the road or nearer the centre of the road. *She pulled out into the street... He was about to pull out to overtake the guy in front of him.*
V P prep / V P

2 If you **pull out of** an agreement, a contest, or an organization, you withdraw from it. *The World Bank should pull out of the project... France was going to pull out of NATO... A racing injury forced Stephen Roche to pull out.*
=withdraw / V P *of* n / V P

3 If troops **pull out of** a place or if a commander **pulls** them **out**, they leave it. *The militia in Lebanon has agreed to pull out of Beirut... Economic sanctions will be lifted once two-thirds of their forces have pulled out... His government decided to pull its troops out of Cuba.*
ERG / =withdraw / V P *of* n / V P / V n P *of* n / Also V n P, V P n (not pron)

4 If a country **pulls out of recession** or if someone **pulls it out**, it begins to recover from it. *Sterling has been hit by the economy's failure to pull out of recession... What we want to see today are policies to pull us out of this recession.*
ERG / V P *of* n / V n P *of* n / Also V P

5 See also **pull-out**.

pull over
PHRASAL VERB

1 When a vehicle or driver **pulls over**, the vehicle moves closer to the side of the road and stops there. *He noticed a man behind him in a blue Ford gesticulating to pull over.* V P

2 If the police **pull** someone **over**, they make them stop their car at the side of the road, usually because they have been driving dangerously. *The officers pulled him over after a high-speed chase... Police pulled over his Mercedes near Dieppe.* V n P / V P n (not pron)

3 See also **pullover**.

pull through. If someone with a serious illness or in a very difficult situation **pulls through**, or if someone or something **pulls** them **through**, they recover. *Everyone was very concerned whether he would pull through or not... It is only our determination to fight that has pulled us through... Finding ways of helping Russia pull through its upheavals will be the most pressing task.* PHRASAL VERB ERG V P V n P V P n

pull together PHRASAL VERB

1 If people **pull together**, they co-operate with each other in order to get through a difficult period. *The nation was urged to pull together to avoid a slide into complete chaos... They would be far better off, materially and emotionally, if they all pulled together.* =join forces V P

2 If you are upset or depressed and someone tells you to **pull** yourself **together**, they are telling you to control your feelings and behave calmly again. *Pull yourself together, you stupid woman!... He pulled himself together, as always, by throwing himself back into his work.* =get a grip on yourself V pron-refl P

3 If you **pull together** different facts or ideas, you link them to form a single theory, argument, or story. *Let me now pull together the threads of my argument... Data exists but it needs pulling together.* =draw together V P n (not pron) V P Also V n P

pull up PHRASAL VERB

1 When a vehicle or driver **pulls up**, the vehicle slows down and stops. *The cab pulled up and the driver jumped out.* =draw up V P

2 If you **pull up a chair**, you move it closer to something or someone and sit on it. *He pulled up a chair behind her and put his chin on her shoulder.* =draw up V P n (not pron) Also V n P

3 If you **pull up** or if something **pulls** you **up**, you suddenly stop what you are doing. *Suddenly, he pulled up sharply in his stride, and fell to the floor... She recognized at the same instant Rachel's presence. It pulled her up short.* ERG V P V n P

4 If someone **pulls** you **up** or if you **pull** yourself **up**, you improve your situation or your skill at something. *We had a very good mathematics mistress who pulled me up... He was made redundant and now he's trying to pull himself up again.* V n P V pron-refl P

pulley /pʊli/ **pulleys.** A **pulley** is a device which is used for lifting or lowering heavy objects. It consists of a wheel with a hollow rim which is fixed above the ground. You pass a rope over the rim, attach one end of the rope to the object, and pull or gradually release the other end. *The weights are moved via a cable and pulley system.* N-COUNT

Pullman /pʊlmən/ **Pullmans**

1 A **Pullman** is a type of train or railway carriage which is extremely comfortable and luxurious. You can also refer to a **Pullman train** or a **Pullman carriage**. Used mainly in British English. N-COUNT: oft N n

2 In American English, a **Pullman** or a **Pullman car** is a railway carriage that provides beds for passengers to sleep in. The usual British expression is **sleeping car**. N-COUNT: oft N n

pull-out, pull-outs

1 In a newspaper or magazine, a **pull-out** is a section which you can remove easily and keep. *...an eight-page pull-out supplement.* N-COUNT: usu N n

2 When there is a **pull-out** of armed forces from a place, troops which have occupied an area of land withdraw from it. *...a pull-out from the occupied territories... The pull-out of the army paves the way for independence.* N-SING: oft N *from/of* n

pullover /pʊloʊvəʳ/ **pullovers.** A **pullover** is a woollen piece of clothing that covers the upper part of your body and your arms. You put it on by pulling it over your head. Used mainly in British English. N-COUNT =jumper

pulmonary /pʌlmənəri, AM -neri/. **Pulmonary** means relating to your lungs; a medical term. *...respiratory and pulmonary disease.* ADJ: ADJ n

pulp /pʌlp/ **pulps, pulping, pulped** ◆◇◇◇◇

1 If an object is pressed into a **pulp**, it is crushed or beaten until it is soft, smooth, and wet. *The olives are crushed to a pulp by stone rollers.* N-SING: also no det

2 In fruit or vegetables, **the pulp** is the soft inner part. *Make maximum use of the whole fruit, including the pulp which is high in fibre.* N-SING: *the* N, also no det

3 **Wood pulp** is material made from crushed wood. It is used to make paper. N-UNCOUNT

4 People refer to books or magazines as **pulp** fiction when they consider them to be of poor quality because they are intentionally written to shock people or to be sensational. *...lurid '50s pulp novels.* ADJ: ADJ n

5 If paper, vegetables, or fruit **are pulped**, they are crushed into a smooth, wet paste. *Onions can be boiled and pulped to a puree. ...creamed or pulped tomatoes.* VB: usu passive *be* V-ed V-ed

6 If money or documents **are pulped**, they are destroyed. This is done to stop the money being used or to stop the documents being seen by the public. *25 million pounds worth of five pound notes have been pulped because the designers made a mistake.* VB: usu passive =shredded *be* V-ed

7 If someone **is beaten to a pulp** or **beaten to pulp**, they are hit repeatedly until they are very badly injured. *I tried to talk myself out of a fight and got beaten to a pulp instead by three other boys.* PHRASE: V inflects

pulpit /pʊlpɪt/ **pulpits.** A **pulpit** is a small raised platform in a church with a rail or barrier around it, where a member of the clergy stands to preach. ◆◇◇◇◇ N-COUNT

pulpy /pʌlpi/. Something that is **pulpy** is soft, smooth, and wet, often because it has been crushed or beaten. *The chutney should be a thick, pulpy consistency.* ADJ-GRADED

pulsar /pʌlsɑːʳ/ **pulsars.** A **pulsar** is a rapidly rotating star that cannot be seen but which is known to exist because of the regular radio signals it emits. ◆◇◇◇◇ N-COUNT

pulsate /pʌlseɪt, AM pʌlseɪt/ **pulsates, pulsating, pulsated.** If something **pulsates**, it beats, moves in and out, or shakes with strong, regular movements. *The Pole Star appears to be changing rapidly from a star that pulsates into one that is stable. ...a pulsating blood vessel.* ♦ **pulsation** /pʌlseɪʃən/ **pulsations** *Several astronomers noted that the star's pulsations seemed less pronounced.* ◆◇◇◇◇ VERB V V-ing N-VAR

pulse /pʌls/ **pulses, pulsing, pulsed** ◆◆◇◇◇

1 Your **pulse** is the regular beating of blood through your body, which you can feel when you touch particular parts of your body, especially your wrist. *Mahoney's pulse was racing, and he felt confused.* N-COUNT: usu sing

2 In music, a **pulse** is a regular beat, which is often produced by a drum. *...the repetitive pulse of the music.* N-COUNT =tempo beat

3 A **pulse** of electrical current, light, or sound is a temporary increase in its level. *The switch works by passing a pulse of current between the tip and the surface.* N-COUNT

4 If you refer to **the pulse of** a group in society, you mean the ideas, opinions, or feelings they have at that particular time. *The White House insists that the president is in touch with the pulse of the black community.* N-SING: *the* N *of* n

5 If something **pulses**, it has a strong regular tempo. *His temples pulsed a little, threatening a headache... It was a slow, pulsing rhythm that seemed to sway languidly in the air.* VERB =throb V V-ing

6 Some seeds which can be cooked and eaten are called **pulses**, for example peas, beans, and lentils. N-PLURAL

7 If you have your **finger on the pulse** of something, you know all the latest opinions or developments. *He claims to have his finger on the pulse of the industry... It's important to keep your finger on the pulse by reading all the right magazines.* PHRASES Ns inflect, usu PHR after v

8 When someone **takes** your **pulse** or **feels** your **pulse**, they find out the speed of your heartbeat by feeling the pulse in your wrist. V and N inflect

pulverize /pʌlvəraɪz/ **pulverizes, pulverizing, pulverized;** also spelled **pulverise** in British English.
1 To **pulverize** something means to do great damage to it or to destroy it completely. *...the economic policies which pulverised the economy during the 1980s... A factory making armaments had been bombed the night before and a residential area not far away had been pulverized.* VERB =destroy V n
2 If someone **pulverizes** an opponent in an election or competition, they thoroughly defeat them; an informal use. *He is set to pulverise his two opponents in the race for the presidency.* VERB =thrash V n
3 If you **pulverize** something, you make it into a powder by crushing it. *Using a pestle and mortar, pulverise the bran to a coarse powder... The fries are made from pellets of pulverised potato.* VERB =grind V n V-ed

puma /pjuːmə/ **pumas.** A **puma** is a wild animal that is a member of the cat family. Pumas are a similar size to lions. They have brownish-grey fur and live in mountain regions of North and South America. N-COUNT =cougar, mountain lion

pumice /pʌmɪs/. **Pumice** is a kind of grey volcanic stone that is very light in weight. You can use it to clean surfaces, or you can rub it over your skin in order to soften it or to remove stains. N-UNCOUNT =pumice stone

pumice stone, pumice stones
1 A **pumice stone** is a piece of pumice that you rub over your skin in order to soften it or to remove stains. N-COUNT
2 **Pumice stone** is the same as **pumice.** N-UNCOUNT

pummel /pʌməl/ **pummels, pummelling, pummelled;** spelled **pummeling, pummeled** in American English. If you **pummel** someone or something, you hit them again and again using your fists. *He trapped Conn in a corner and pummeled him ferociously for thirty seconds.* VERB V n

pump /pʌmp/ **pumps, pumping, pumped** ◆◆◆◇◇
1 A **pump** is a machine which is used to force a liquid or gas to flow in strong regular movements in a particular direction. *...pumps that circulate the fuel around in the engine.* N-COUNT
2 To **pump** a liquid or gas in a particular direction means to force it to flow in that direction, using a pump. *It's not enough to get rid of raw sewage by pumping it out to sea... The money raised will be used to dig bore holes to pump water into the dried-up lake... Heart failure results when the heart is unable to pump blood efficiently.* VERB V n with adv V n prep V n
3 A **pump** is a device for bringing water to the surface from below the ground. Pumps often have a handle that you push in order to force the water upwards. *There was no water in the building, just a pump in the courtyard.* N-COUNT
4 To **pump** water, oil, or gas means to get a supply of it from below the surface of the ground, using a pump. *She pumps drinking water from a well... The country is trying very hard to pump out more oil. ...drill rigs that are busy pumping natural gas.* VERB V n prep V n with adv V n
5 A **pump** is a device that you use to force air into something, for example a tyre. *...a bicycle pump.* N-COUNT
6 In garages, a **petrol pump** is a machine with a hose attached to it from which you can fill a car with petrol. *There are already long queues of vehicles at petrol pumps. ...gas pumps.* N-COUNT: oft n N
7 If someone has their stomach **pumped,** doctors use a special pump to remove the contents of their stomach, for example because they have swallowed poison or taken an overdose of drugs. *She was released from hospital yesterday after having her stomach pumped.* VB: usu passive *have* n V-ed Also *be* V-ed
8 If you **pump** money or other resources into something such as a project or an industry, you invest a lot of money or resources in it; an informal use. *West Germany is set to pump huge amounts of resources into East Germany.* VERB =pour V n *into* n
9 If you **pump** someone about something, you keep asking them questions in order to get information; an informal use. *He ran in every five minutes to pump me about the case... He must have pumped Janey for details... Stop trying to pump information out of me.* VERB =grill V n *about/for* n V n *out of/from* n
10 To **pump** bullets **into** someone means to fire a lot of bullets into them very quickly; used in written English. *A gunman burst in and pumped five bullets into her head.* VERB V n *into* n
11 **Pumps** are canvas shoes with flat rubber soles which people wear for sports and leisure; used mainly in British English. N-COUNT =plimsoll
12 In American English, **pumps** are ladies' shoes that do not cover the top part of the foot and are usually made of plain leather with no design. The British expression is **court shoes.** N-COUNT
13 In American English, if someone **primes the pump,** they do something to encourage the success or growth of something, especially the economy. *...the use of tax money to prime the pump of the state's economy.* PHRASE: V inflects
14 ● to **pump iron**: see **iron.**

pump out PHRASAL VERB
1 To **pump out** something means to produce or supply it continually and in large amounts. *Japanese companies have been pumping out plenty of innovative products... World Service Television is pumping out 24-hour news to 38 countries in Asia.* V P n (not pron) Also V n P
2 If pop music **pumps out,** it plays very loudly. *Teenage disco music pumped out at every station.* V P

pump up. If you **pump up** something such as a tyre, you fill it with air using a pump. *I tried to pump up my back tyre.* PHRASAL VERB V P n (not pron) Also V n P

pumpernickel /pʌmpəʳnɪkəl/. **Pumpernickel** is a dark brown, heavy bread made from rye, which is eaten especially in Germany. N-UNCOUNT

pumpkin /pʌmpkɪn/ **pumpkins.** A **pumpkin** is a large, round, orange-coloured vegetable with a thick skin. *Quarter the pumpkin and remove the seeds. ...pumpkin pie.* ◆◇◇◇◇ N-VAR

pun /pʌn/ **puns, punning, punned** ◆◇◇◇◇
1 A **pun** is a clever and amusing use of a word with more than one meaning, or a word that sounds like another word, so that what you say has two different meanings. For example, if someone says 'My pony's a little hoarse', this is a pun because it can be interpreted as meaning either that it was a small animal or that the pony has a throat infection. N-COUNT =play on words
2 If you **pun,** you try to amuse people by making a pun. *He is constantly punning, constantly playing with language.* ♦ **punning** *...his son's incorrigible punning.* VERB V N-UNCOUNT

punch /pʌntʃ/ **punches, punching, punched** ◆◆◆◇◇
1 If you **punch** someone or something, you hit them hard with your fist. *After punching him on the chin she wound up hitting him over the head... He punched the wall angrily, then spun round to face her.* ► In American English, **punch out** means the same as **punch.** *'I almost lost my job today.'—'What happened?'—'Oh, I punched out this guy.'... In the past, many kids would settle disputes by punching each other out.* ► Also a noun. *He was hurting Johansson with body punches in the fourth round.* ♦ **puncher, punchers** *...the awesome range of blows which have confirmed him as boxing's hardest puncher.* VERB V n PHRASAL VERB V P n (not pron) V n P N-COUNT N-COUNT: usu supp N
2 If you **punch the air,** you put one or both of your fists forcefully above your shoulders as a gesture of delight or victory. *At the end, Graf punched the air in delight, a huge grin on her face.* VERB V n
3 If you **punch** something such as the buttons on a keyboard, you touch them in order to store information on a machine such as a computer or to give the machine a command to do something. *Mrs. Baylor strode to the elevator and punched the button.* VERB =push V n
4 If you **punch holes** in something, you make holes in it by pushing or pressing it with something sharp. *I took a ballpoint pen and punched a hole in the carton.* VERB V n *in* n
5 A **punch** is a tool that you use for making holes in something. *Make two holes with a hole punch.* N-COUNT
6 If you say that something has **punch,** you mean that it has force or effectiveness. *My nervousness made me deliver the vital points of my address* N-UNCOUNT

without sufficient punch... Hurricane Andrew may be slowly losing its punch, but its winds are still around 100 miles an hour.

7 **Punch** is a drink made from wine or spirits mixed with things such as sugar, lemons, and spices. N-MASS

8 If you say that someone does not **pull** their **punches** when they are criticizing someone or something, you mean that they say exactly what they think and do not moderate their criticism in any way. *She has a reputation for getting at the guts of a subject and never pulling her punches.* • to **pack a punch**: see **pack**. PHRASE: V and N inflect, oft with brd-neg

punch in. If you **punch in** a number on a machine or **punch** numbers **into** it, you push the machine's numerical keys in order to give it a command to do something. *You can bank by phone in the USA, punching in account numbers on the phone. ...a code which allows them into the hotel once they punch the number into a special keyboard.* PHRASAL VERB V P n (not pron) V n P

Punch and Judy show /pʌntʃ ən dʒuːdi ʃoʊ/ **Punch and Judy shows.** A **Punch and Judy show** is a puppet show for children. Punch and Judy are the two main characters in the show and they are always fighting. These shows are usually performed in small booths at fairs or at the seaside. N-COUNT

punchbag /pʌntʃbæg/ **punchbags;** also spelled **punch bag**. In British English, a **punchbag** is a heavy leather bag, stuffed with horsehair or other material and hanging on a rope. Punchbags are punched hard by boxers and other sportsmen for training and exercise. The American term is **punching bag**. N-COUNT

punch bowl, punch bowls. A **punch bowl** is a large bowl in which drinks, especially punch, are mixed and served. N-COUNT

punch-drunk; also spelled **punch drunk**.

1 A **punch-drunk boxer** shows signs of brain damage, for example unsteadiness and the inability to think clearly, after suffering too many blows on their head. ADJ: usu ADJ n

2 If you say that someone **is punch-drunk**, you mean that they are dazed and confused, for example because they have been working too hard. *He was punch-drunk with fatigue and depressed by the rain.* ADJ-GRADED: usu v-link ADJ

punching bag, punching bags. A **punching bag** is the same as a **punchbag**; used mainly in American English. N-COUNT

punchline /pʌntʃlaɪn/ **punchlines;** also spelled **punch line** or **punch-line**. The **punchline** of a joke or funny story is its last sentence or phrase, which gives it its humour. N-COUNT

punch-up, punch-ups. In British English, a **punch-up** is a fight in which people hit each other; an informal word. *He was involved in a punch-up with Sarah's former lover.* N-COUNT =brawl

punchy /pʌntʃi/ **punchier, punchiest.** If you describe something as **punchy**, you mean it conveys a meaning or creates an effect in a forceful or effective way. *A good way to sound confident is to use short punchy sentences.* ADJ-GRADED =incisive

punctilious /pʌŋktɪliəs/. Someone who is **punctilious** is very careful to behave correctly; a formal word. *He was punctilious about being ready and waiting in the entrance hall exactly on time... He was a punctilious young man.* ADJ-GRADED =meticulous

♦ **punctiliously** *Given the circumstances, his behaviour to Laura had been punctiliously correct.* ADV-GRADED

punctual /pʌŋktʃuəl/. Someone who is **punctual** arrives somewhere or does something at the right time and is not late. *He's always very punctual. I'll see if he's here yet.* ♦ **punctually** *My guest arrived punctually.* ♦ **punctuality** /pʌŋktʃuælɪti/ *I'll have to have a word with them about punctuality.* ◆◇◇◇◇ ADJ-GRADED; ADV-GRADED: usu ADV with v; N-UNCOUNT

punctuate /pʌŋktʃueɪt/ **punctuates, punctuating, punctuated.** If an activity or situation **is punctuated** by particular things, it is interrupted by them at intervals. *The silence of the night was punctuated by the distant rumble of traffic.* ◆◇◇◇◇ VB: usu passive =intersperse be V-ed by/with n

punctuation /pʌŋktʃueɪʃən/

1 **Punctuation** is the use of signs such as full stops, commas, or question marks to divide words into sentences and clauses. *He was known for his poor grammar and punctuation.* N-UNCOUNT

2 **Punctuation** is the signs such as full stops, commas, or question marks that you use in writing to divide words into sentences and clauses. *Jessica had rapidly scanned the lines, none of which boasted a capital letter or any punctuation.* N-UNCOUNT =punctuation marks

punctuation mark, punctuation marks. A **punctuation mark** is a sign such as a full stop, comma, or question mark that you use in writing to divide words into sentences and clauses. N-COUNT

puncture /pʌŋktʃər/ **punctures, puncturing, punctured** ◆◇◇◇◇

1 A **puncture** is a small hole in a car tyre or bicycle tyre that has been made by a sharp object. *Somebody helped me mend the puncture. ...a tyre that has a slow puncture.* N-COUNT

2 A **puncture** is a small hole in someone's skin that has been made by or with a sharp object; a technical use in medicine. *An instrument called a trocar makes a puncture in the abdominal wall. ...people with puncture wounds.* N-COUNT

3 If a sharp object **punctures** something, it makes a hole in it. *The bullet punctured the skull.* VERB V n

4 If a car tyre or bicycle tyre **punctures** or something **punctures** it, a hole is made in the tyre. *The tyre is guaranteed never to puncture or go flat... Then the Englishman made a mistake, brushing a wall and apparently puncturing a tyre.* V-ERG V V n

5 If someone's feelings or beliefs **are punctured**, something happens which causes a sudden and complete change in their mood or their outlook. *He sat and watched, his tiny enthusiasm for fishing having been punctured by the sight of what he might catch.* VERB =deflate be V-ed Also V n

pundit /pʌndɪt/ **pundits.** A **pundit** is a person who knows a lot about a subject and is often asked to give information or opinions about it to the public. *...a well known political pundit.* ◆◇◇◇◇ N-COUNT: oft supp N =expert

pungent /pʌndʒənt/ ◆◇◇◇◇

1 Something that is **pungent** has a strong, sharp smell or taste which is often so strong that it is unpleasant. *The more herbs you use, the more pungent the sauce will be. ...the pungent smell of burning rubber.* ♦ **pungency** *...the spices that give Jamaican food its pungency.* ADJ-GRADED =powerful ≠delicate; N-UNCOUNT: usu with poss

2 If you describe something someone has said or written as **pungent**, you approve of it because it has a direct and powerful effect, often criticizes something very cleverly; a formal use. *He enjoyed the play's shrewd and pungent social analysis.* ADJ-GRADED PRAGMATICS =biting, pointed

punish /pʌnɪʃ/ **punishes, punishing, punished** ◆◆◇◇◇

1 To **punish** someone means to make them suffer in some way because they have done something wrong. *I don't believe that George ever had to punish the children... According to present law, the authorities can only punish smugglers with small fines... Don't punish your child for being honest.* VERB V n V n for n

2 To **punish** a crime means to punish anyone who commits that crime. *The government voted to punish corruption in sport with up to four years in jail... Such behaviour is unacceptable and will be punished.* VERB V n

punishable /pʌnɪʃəbəl/. If a crime is **punishable** in a particular way, anyone who commits it is punished in that way. *Treason in this country is still punishable by death... They called on the authorities to make slavery a punishable offence.* ADJ: usu v-link ADJ by/with n

punishing /pʌnɪʃɪŋ/. A **punishing** schedule, activity, or experience requires a lot of physical effort and makes you very tired or weak. *He claimed his punishing work schedule had made him resort to taking the drug... Besides diets, he devised punishing exercise routines.* ◆◇◇◇◇ ADJ-GRADED: usu ADJ n =crippling

punishment /pʌnɪʃmənt/ **punishments** ◆◆◇◇◇

1 **Punishment** is the act of punishing someone or of being punished. *...a group which campaigns against the physical punishment of children... I* N-UNCOUNT

have no doubt that the man is guilty and that he deserves punishment.

2 A **punishment** is a particular way of punishing someone. *The government is proposing tougher punishments for officials convicted of corruption... The usual punishment is a fine.* N-VAR

3 You can use **punishment** to refer to severe physical treatment of any kind. *Don't expect these types of boot to take the punishment that gardening will give them.* N-UNCOUNT

4 See also **capital punishment**, **corporal punishment**.

punitive /pjuːnɪtɪv/. **Punitive** actions are intended to punish people; a formal word. *...a punitive bombing raid... Other economists say any punitive measures against foreign companies would hurt US interests.* ◆◇◇◇◇ ADJ-GRADED: usu ADJ n

Punjabi /pʌndʒɑːbi/ **Punjabis** ◆◇◇◇◇

1 **Punjabi** means belonging or relating to the Punjab, its people, or its language. *He comes from a middle-class Punjabi family. ...Punjabi cuisine.* ADJ: usu ADJ n

2 A **Punjabi** is a person who comes from the Punjab. N-COUNT

3 **Punjabi** is the language spoken by people who live in the Punjab. N-UNCOUNT

punk /pʌŋk/ **punks** ◆◆◇◇◇

1 **Punk** or **punk rock** is rock music that is played in a fast, loud, and aggressive way and is often a protest against conventional attitudes and behaviour. Punk rock was particularly popular in the late 1970s. *I was never really into punk. ...a punk rock band.* N-UNCOUNT: oft N n

2 **Punk** clothes or styles are associated with punk music and are very noticeable and unconventional. *...a punk hairdo.* ADJ: ADJ n

3 A **punk** or a **punk rocker** is a young person who likes punk music and dresses in a very noticeable and unconventional way, for example by having brightly coloured hair and wearing metal chains. N-COUNT

4 In American English, a **punk** is a young person who behaves in an unruly, aggressive, or anti-social manner; an informal use. *He is fast getting a reputation as a young punk.* N-COUNT

punnet /pʌnɪt/ **punnets.** In British English, a **punnet** is a small, light, square box in which soft fruits such as strawberries or raspberries are often sold. ► In British English, a **punnet of** fruit is the amount of fruit that a punnet contains. *...a punnet of strawberries.* N-COUNT; N-COUNT: usu N *of* n

punt /pʌnt/ **punts, punting, punted** ◆◇◇◇◇

1 A **punt** is a long boat with a flat bottom. You move the boat along by standing at one end and pushing a long pole against the bottom of the river; used mainly in British English. N-COUNT

2 When you **punt**, you travel along a river in a punt; used mainly in British English. *We punted up towards Grantchester and had a picnic in a meadow.* ♦ **punting** *The one thing I look forward to is going punting in Cambridge.* VERB V prep/adv Also V; N-UNCOUNT

3 The **punt** is the unit of money used in the Irish Republic. *The round-trip fare to Havana is 410 Irish punts ($578).* ► **The punt** is also used to refer to the Irish currency system. *...the cost of defending the punt against speculators.* N-COUNT: num N; N-SING: the N

punter /pʌntəʳ/ **punters** ◆◇◇◇◇

1 A **punter** is a person who bets money, especially on horse races; used mainly in informal British English. *Punters are expected to gamble £50m on the Grand National.* N-COUNT

2 People sometimes refer to their customers or clients as **punters**; used mainly in informal British English. *Should anyone attack the stripper, the punters know that it is likely to be the end of the show... Despite the recession, he hopes 80,000 punters will be tempted to pay between £15 and £55 for seats to see the show.* N-COUNT

puny /pjuːni/ **punier, puniest.** Someone or something that is **puny** is very small or weak. *Our Kevin was a very puny lad, always dashing off to do weight-training exercises to build up his body... The resources at the central banks' disposal are simply too puny.* ADJ-GRADED =feeble

pup /pʌp/ **pups** ◆◇◇◇◇

1 A **pup** is a young dog. *I'll get you an Alsatian pup for Christmas.* N-COUNT =puppy

2 The young of some other animals, for example seals, are called **pups**. *Two thousand grey seal pups are born there every autumn.* N-COUNT: oft n N

pupa /pjuːpə/ **pupae** /pjuːpiː/. A **pupa** is an insect that is in the stage of development between a larva and a fully grown adult. It has a protective covering and does not move; a technical term in biology. *The pupae remain dormant in the soil until they emerge as adult moths in the winter.* N-COUNT

pupil /pjuːpɪl/ **pupils** ◆◆◆◇◇

1 The **pupils** of a school are the children who go to it. *Over a third of those now at secondary school in Wales attend schools with over 1,000 pupils... Eleanor was a reluctant, anxious pupil.* N-COUNT

2 A **pupil** of a painter, musician, or other expert is someone who studies under that expert and learns his or her skills. *After his education, Goldschmidt became a pupil of the composer Franz Schreker.* N-COUNT: with poss

3 The **pupils** of your eyes are the small, round, black holes in the centre of them. N-COUNT

puppet /pʌpɪt/ **puppets** ◆◇◇◇◇

1 A **puppet** is a doll that you can move, either by pulling strings which are attached to it or by putting your hand inside its body and moving your fingers. N-COUNT =marionette

2 You can refer to a person or country as a **puppet** when you mean their actions are controlled by a more powerful person or government, even though they may appear to be independent. *The radical students say Seoul is a puppet of the Washington government... He warned there would be a 'social explosion' if the army installed another puppet prime minister.* N-COUNT: oft N n PRAGMATICS

puppeteer /pʌpɪtɪəʳ/ **puppeteers.** A **puppeteer** is a person who gives shows using puppets. N-COUNT

puppy /pʌpi/ **puppies.** A **puppy** is a young dog. *One Sunday he began trying to teach the two puppies to walk on a leash.* ◆◇◇◇◇ N-COUNT =pup

puppy fat; also spelled **puppy-fat. Puppy fat** is fat that some children have on their bodies when they are young but that disappears when they grow older and taller. *Her face had already lost its puppy-fat.* N-UNCOUNT

purchase /pɜːʳtʃɪs/ **purchases, purchasing, purchased** ◆◆◆◆◇

1 When you **purchase** something, you buy it; a formal use. *He purchased a ticket and went up on the top deck... Most of those shares were purchased from brokers.* ♦ **purchaser, purchasers** *The broker will get 5% if he finds a purchaser... The group is the second largest purchaser of fresh fruit in the US.* VERB =buy V n; N-COUNT =buyer

2 The **purchase of** something is the act of buying it; a formal use. *This week he is to visit China to discuss the purchase of military supplies.* • See also **hire purchase.** N-UNCOUNT: oft N *of* n

3 A **purchase** is something that you buy; a formal use. *She opened the tie box and looked at her purchase. It was silk, with maroon stripes.* N-COUNT

4 If someone or something is able to get a **purchase** on something, they manage to get a firm grip on it; a formal use. *I got a purchase on the rope and pulled... I couldn't get any purchase with the screwdriver on the damn screws.* N-UNCOUNT: also a N =hold, grip

purdah /pɜːʳdə/. **Purdah** is a custom practised in some Muslim and Hindu societies, in which women keep apart from male strangers by remaining in a special part of a house or by covering their faces and the whole of their bodies to avoid being seen. If a woman is **in purdah**, she lives according to this custom. N-UNCOUNT: oft *in* N

pure /pjʊəʳ/ **purer, purest** ◆◆◆◇◇

1 A **pure** substance is not mixed with anything else. *...a carton of pure orange juice.* ADJ-GRADED: usu ADJ n

2 Something that is **pure** is clean and does not contain any harmful substances. *In remote regions, the air is pure and the crops are free of poisonous insecticides. ...demands for purer and cleaner river water.* ♦ **purity** /pjʊərɪti/ *They worried about the purity of tap water.* ADJ-GRADED ≠contaminated; N-UNCOUNT: with poss

3 If you describe something such as a colour, sound, or a type of light as **pure**, you mean that it is very clear and represents a perfect example of its type. *These flowers bring to the garden a whole family of blue colours with the occasional pure white.* ♦ **purity** *The soaring purity of her voice conjured up the frozen bleakness of the Far North.* ADJ-GRADED: usu ADJ n; N-UNCOUNT

4 If you describe a form of art or a philosophy as **pure**, you mean that it is produced or practised according to a standard or form that is expected of it; a formal use. *Nicholson never swerved from his aim of making pure and simple art.* ♦ **purity** *...verse of great purity, sonority of rhythm, and symphonic form.* ADJ-GRADED: usu ADJ n; N-UNCOUNT

5 **Pure** science or **pure** research is concerned only with theory and not with how this theory can be used in practical ways. *Physics isn't just about pure science with no immediate applications... They did not approach their subject solely as a matter of 'pure' theory.* ADJ: ADJ n ≠applied

6 **Pure** means complete and total. *The old man turned to give her a look of pure surprise... To sleep on my own and not hear the boys snore or grunt was pure bliss.* ADJ-GRADED PRAGMATICS =sheer

7 A person, especially a woman, who is described as **pure** is considered to be free from things which are sinful or bad, especially sex; a literary use. *She was baptized and she was pure and clean of sin.* ♦ **purity** *The American Female Reform Society promoted sexual purity.* ADJ-GRADED =unsullied; N-UNCOUNT: usu with supp

8 You use **pure and simple** to emphasize that the thing you are mentioning is the only thing that is involved or that should be considered. *It's blackmail, pure and simple.* PHRASE: n PHR, PHR n PRAGMATICS

pure-bred; also spelled **purebred**. A **pure-bred** animal is one whose parents and ancestors all belong to the same breed. *...pure-bred Arab horses.* ADJ: ADJ n

puree /pjʊəreɪ, AM pjʊreɪ/ **purees, pureeing, pureed** ♦◇◇◇◇

1 **Puree** is food which has been mashed, sieved, or blended so that it forms a thick, smooth sauce. *...a can of tomato puree... Push the potatoes through a sieve to make a puree.* N-VAR

2 If you **puree** food, you make it into a puree. *Puree the apricots in a liquidiser until completely smooth.* VERB Vn

purely /pjʊəʳli/ ♦♦◇◇◇

1 You use **purely** to emphasize that the thing you are mentioning is the most important feature or that it is the only thing which should be considered. *It is a racing machine, designed purely for speed... The government said the moves were purely defensive.* ADV: ADV with cl/group PRAGMATICS

2 You use **purely and simply** to emphasize that the thing you are mentioning is the only thing involved. *If Arthur was attracted here by the prospects of therapy, John came down purely and simply to make money... It was purely and simply a coup,' Mr Nabiyev said. 'I had no choice but to resign.'* PHRASE: PHR with cl PRAGMATICS

purgative /pɜːʳgətɪv/ **purgatives**

1 A **purgative** is a medicine that causes you to defecate and so to get rid of unwanted substances from your body; a formal use. *The doctors attempted to reduce his high fever by inducing diarrhea with a purgative.* N-COUNT =laxative

2 A **purgative** substance acts as a purgative; a formal use. *...purgative oils. ...a purgative tea.* ADJ: ADJ n

purgatory /pɜːʳgətri, AM -tɔːri/

1 **Purgatory** is the place where Roman Catholics believe the spirits of dead people are sent to suffer for their sins before they go to heaven. *Prayers were said for souls in Purgatory.* N-PROPER

2 You can describe a very unpleasant experience as **purgatory**. *Every step of the last three miles was purgatory. ...five years of economic purgatory.* N-UNCOUNT =hell

purge /pɜːʳdʒ/ **purges, purging, purged** ♦◇◇◇◇

1 To **purge** an organization of its unacceptable members means to remove them from it. You can also talk about **purging** people from an organization. *The leadership voted to purge the party of 'hostile and anti-party elements'... He recently purged the armed forces, sending hundreds of officers into retirement... They have purged thousands from the upper levels of the civil service.* ▶ Also a noun. *The army have called for a more thorough purge of people associated with the late President... His own father died during Stalin's purges.* VERB V n of n, V n, V n from n; N-COUNT: oft N of n

2 If you **purge** something **of** undesirable things, you get rid of them. *He closed his eyes and lay still, trying to purge his mind of anxiety... The only way to purge the economy of this new burst of inflation is a short, sharp recession.* VERB =rid V n of n Also V n

purifier /pjʊərɪfaɪəʳ/ **purifiers.** A **purifier** is a device or a substance that is used to purify something such as water, air, or blood. *I hope to see aromatic air purifiers being used in antenatal clinics.* N-COUNT: oft n N

purify /pjʊərɪfaɪ/ **purifies, purifying, purified.** ♦◇◇◇◇ If you **purify** a substance, you make it pure by removing any harmful, dirty, or inferior substances from it. *I take wheat and yeast tablets daily to purify the blood... Only purified water is used.* ♦ **purification** /pjʊərɪfɪkeɪʃᵊn/ *...a water purification plant.* VERB ≠contaminate V n V-ed; N-UNCOUNT

purism /pjʊərɪzəm/. You can refer to the attitudes of purists as **purism**. *The retreat to 'old school' purism means every record revolves around the same formula.* N-UNCOUNT

purist /pjʊərɪst/ **purists** ♦◇◇◇◇

1 A **purist** is a person who believes in absolute correctness, especially concerning a particular subject which they know a lot about. *This version of 'The Marriage Of Figaro' may not satisfy opera purists, but it is glorious fun for the less fastidious.* N-COUNT

2 **Purist** attitudes are the kind of attitudes that purists have. *Britain wanted a 'more purist' approach.* ADJ-GRADED: usu ADJ n

puritan /pjʊərɪtᵊn/ **puritans**

1 You describe someone as a **puritan** when they live according to strict moral or religious principles, especially by avoiding physical pleasures; used showing disapproval. *Bykov had forgotten that Malinin was something of a puritan... As for the subjects that so enrage puritans, they will continue to form the focus of her work.* N-COUNT PRAGMATICS

2 **Puritan** behaviour is based on strict moral or religious principles, especially on the avoidance of physical pleasures; often used showing disapproval. *Paul was someone who certainly had a puritan streak in him. ...puritan self-denial.* ADJ-GRADED: usu ADJ n PRAGMATICS

Puritan, Puritans. The **Puritans** were a group of English Protestants who lived in the sixteenth and seventeenth centuries. They lived in a very strict and religious way. N-COUNT

puritanical /pjʊərɪtænɪkᵊl/. If you describe someone as **puritanical**, you mean that they have very strict moral principles, which they often try to impose on other people; used showing disapproval. *...puritanical fathers... He has a puritanical attitude towards sex.* ADJ-GRADED PRAGMATICS

puritanism /pjʊərɪtənɪzəm/. **Puritanism** is behaviour or beliefs that are based on strict moral or religious principles, especially the principle that people should avoid physical pleasures; often used showing disapproval. *...the tight-lipped puritanism of the Scottish literary world.* N-UNCOUNT PRAGMATICS

Puritanism. **Puritanism** is the set of beliefs that were held by the Puritans. *Out of Puritanism came the intense work ethic.* N-UNCOUNT

purloin /pɜːʳlɔɪn/ **purloins, purloining, purloined.** If someone **purloins** something, they steal it or borrow it without asking permission; a formal word. *Each side purloins the other's private letters.* VERB V n

purple /pɜːʳpᵊl/ **purples.** Something that is **purple** is of a reddish-blue colour. *She wore purple and green silk. ...sinister dark greens and purples.* ♦♦◇◇◇ COLOUR

Purple Heart, Purple Hearts. The **Purple Heart** is a medal that is given to members of the US Armed Forces who have been wounded during battle. N-COUNT

purplish /pɜːʳplɪʃ/. **Purplish** means slightly purple in colour. *The large, purplish blue flowers appear in early June.* ADJ

purport /pəʳpɔːʳt/ **purports, purporting, purported.** If you say that someone or something **purports** to do or be a particular thing, you mean that they claim to do or be that thing, although you may not always believe that claim; a formal word. *...a book that purports to tell the whole truth.* ◆◇◇◇◇ VERB =claim V to-inf

purportedly /pəʳpɔːʳtɪdli/. If you say that something has **purportedly** been done, you mean that you think that it has been done but you cannot be sure; a formal word. *He was given a letter purportedly signed by the Prime Minister.* ADV: ADV with v, ADV cl/group =supposedly

purpose /pɜːʳpəs/ **purposes** ◆◆◆◆◇

1 The **purpose** of something is the reason for which it is made or done. *The purpose of the occasion was to raise money for medical supplies... Various insurance schemes already exist for this purpose. ...the use of nuclear energy for military purposes... He was asked about casualties, but said it would serve no purpose to count bodies... Most of them are destroyed because they've served their purpose.* N-COUNT: with supp =aim

2 Your **purpose** is the thing that you want to achieve. *They might well be prepared to do you harm in order to achieve their purpose... His purpose was to make a profit by improving the company's performance.* N-COUNT: with poss =aim, objective

3 **Purpose** is the feeling of having a definite aim and of being determined to achieve it. *The teachers are enthusiastic and have a sense of purpose.* N-UNCOUNT =resolve

4 See also **cross-purposes.**

5 You use **for all practical purposes** or **to all intents and purposes** to suggest that a situation is not exactly as you describe it, but the effect is the same as if it were. *For all practical purposes the treaty has already ceased to exist... To all intents and purposes the case was closed.* PHRASES PHR with cl =in effect, effectively

6 If you do something **on purpose**, you do it deliberately. *Was it an accident or did David do it on purpose?* PHR after v =intentionally ≠by mistake

purpose-built. A **purpose-built** building has been specially designed and built for a particular use. *The company has recently moved into a new purpose-built factory.* ◆◇◇◇◇ ADJ

purposeful /pɜːʳpəsfʊl/. If someone is **purposeful**, they show that they have a definite aim and a strong desire to achieve it. *She had a purposeful air, and it became evident that this was not a casual visit.* ♦ **purposefully** *He strode purposefully towards the barn.* ◆◇◇◇◇ ADJ-GRADED ≠aimless ADV-GRADED: usu ADV with v ≠aimlessly

purposeless /pɜːʳpəsləs/. If an action is **purposeless**, it does not seem to have a sensible purpose. *Time may also be wasted in purposeless meetings... Surely my existence cannot be so purposeless?* ADJ-GRADED =senseless, pointless

purposely /pɜːʳpəsli/. If you do something **purposely**, you do it deliberately; a formal word. *They are purposely withholding information.* ADV: usu ADV with v, also ADV adj =intentionally

purr /pɜːʳ/ **purrs, purring, purred** ◆◇◇◇◇

1 When a cat **purrs**, it makes a low vibrating sound with its throat because it is contented. *The plump ginger kitten had settled comfortably in her arms and was purring enthusiastically.* VERB V

2 When the engine of a machine such as a car **purrs**, it is working and making a quiet, continuous, vibrating sound. *Both boats purred out of the cave mouth and into open water... The Rolls Royce purred down the country road.* ► Also a noun. *Carmela heard the purr of a motor-cycle coming up the drive.* VERB V prep Also V N-SING

3 When someone **purrs**, they speak in a soft, gentle voice because they are pleased about something or because they want to persuade you to do something for them. *'You can tell me the truth,' she purred.* VERB V with quote

purse /pɜːʳs/ **purses, pursing, pursed** ◆◆◇◇◇

1 In British English, a **purse** is a very small bag that people, especially women, keep their money in. The usual American expression is **change purse.** N-COUNT =wallet

2 In American English, a **purse** is a small bag that women carry. The usual British word is **handbag.** *She looked at me and then reached in her purse for cigarettes.* N-COUNT

3 The word **purse** is used to refer to the total amount of money that a country, family, or group has. *The money could simply go into the public purse, helping to lower taxes.* N-SING: with supp

4 If you **purse your lips**, you move them into a small, rounded shape, usually because you disapprove of something or when you are thinking. *She pursed her lips in disapproval.* VERB V n

purser /pɜːʳsəʳ/ **pursers.** On a ship, the **purser** is an officer who deals with the accounts and official papers. On a passenger ship, the purser is also responsible for the welfare of the passengers. N-COUNT

purse strings. If you say that someone holds or controls **the purse strings**, you mean that they control the way that money is spent in a particular family, group, or country. *Women control the purse-strings of most families... The bank has been too slow in loosening the purse strings.* N-PLURAL: the N

pursuance /pəʳsjuːəns, AM -suː-/. If do something in **pursuance of** a particular activity, you do it as part of carrying out that activity; a formal word. *He ordered disclosure of a medical report to the Metropolitan Police in pursuance of an investigation of murder.* N-UNCOUNT: usu in N of n

pursuant /pəʳsjuːənt, AM -suː-/. If something is done **pursuant to** a law or regulation, it is done in agreement or conformity with it; a formal expression. *He should continue to act pursuant to the United Nations Security Council resolutions.* PHR-PREP

pursue /pəʳsjuː, -suː/ **pursues, pursuing, pursued** ◆◆◆◇◇

1 If you **pursue** an activity, interest, or plan, you carry it out or follow it; a formal use. *It became harder for women married to diplomats to pursue their own interests... He said Japan would continue to pursue the policies laid down at the London summit... She had come to England to pursue an acting career.* VERB =follow V n

2 If you **pursue** a particular aim or result, you make efforts to achieve it, often over a long period of time; a formal use. *The implication seems to be that it is impossible to pursue economic reform and democracy simultaneously... Mr. Menendez has aggressively pursued new business.* VERB =strive for V n

3 If you **pursue** a particular topic, you try to find out more about it by asking questions; a formal use. *If your original request is denied, don't be afraid to pursue the matter.* VERB =follow up ≠drop V n

4 If you **pursue** a person, vehicle, or animal, you follow them, usually in order to catch them; a formal use. *She pursued the man who had stolen a woman's bag.* VERB =follow V n

pursuer /pəʳsjuːəʳ, AM -suː-/ **pursuers.** Your **pursuers** are the people who are chasing or searching for you; a formal word. *They had shaken off their pursuers.* N-COUNT: oft poss N in pl

pursuit /pəʳsjuːt, AM -suːt/ **pursuits** ◆◆◇◇◇

1 Your **pursuit of** something is your attempts at achieving it. If you do something **in pursuit of** a particular result, you do it in order to achieve that result. *...a young man whose relentless pursuit of excellence is conducted with single-minded determination. ...individuals who impoverish their families in pursuit of some dream.* N-UNCOUNT: N of n, oft in N of n

2 The **pursuit of** an activity, interest, or plan consists of all the things that you do when you are carrying it out; a formal use. *The vigorous pursuit of policies is no guarantee of success.* N-UNCOUNT: N of n

3 Someone who is **in pursuit of** a person, vehicle, or animal is chasing them; a formal use. *...a police officer who drove a patrol car at more than 120mph in pursuit of a motor cycle.* N-UNCOUNT: usu in N of n

4 In cycling and skating, **the pursuit** is a race in which two competitors or teams start on opposite sides of the circuit and try to catch up with each other. *Moreau took gold in the five-kilometre individual pursuit competition.* N-SING: the N, oft N n

5 Your **pursuits** are your activities, usually activities that you enjoy when you are not working; a N-COUNT: usu pl, with supp

formal use. *They both love outdoor pursuits... His favourite childhood pursuits were sailing, swimming and cycling.*

6 If you are **in hot pursuit** of someone, you are chasing after them with great determination. *I rushed through with Sue in hot pursuit.* PHRASE

purvey /pəʳveɪ/ **purveys, purveying, purveyed**

1 If you **purvey** something such as information, you tell it to people; a formal use. *The Director of the Institute of Education, accused me of purveying 'silly gossip' about practices in schools.* VERB =transmit V n

2 If someone **purveys** goods or services, they provide them; a formal use. *They have two restaurants that purvey dumplings and chicken noodle soup.* VERB =supply, sell V n

purveyor /pəʳveɪəʳ/ **purveyors.** A **purveyor of** goods or services is a person or company that provides them. *...purveyors of gourmet foods.* N-COUNT: usu N *of* n =supplier

purview /pɜːʳvjuː/. The **purview of** an organization or operation is the scope of its powers or influence; a formal word. *That, however, was beyond the purview of the court; it was a diplomatic matter.* N-SING: usu N *of* n

pus /pʌs/. **Pus** is a thick yellowish liquid that forms in wounds when they are infected. N-UNCOUNT

push /pʊʃ/ **pushes, pushing, pushed** ◆◆◆◆◇

1 When you **push** something, you use force to make it move away from you or away from its previous position. *The woman pushed back her chair and stood up... They pushed him into the car. ...a woman pushing a pushchair... He put both hands flat on the door and pushed as hard as he could... When there was no reply, he pushed the door open.* ▶ Also a noun. *He gave me a sharp push... Information is called up at the push of a button.* VERB V n with adv, V n prep, V n, V, V n adj; N-COUNT: usu sing

2 If you **push through** things that are blocking your way or **push your way through** them, you use force in order to move past them. *I pushed through the crowds and on to the escalator... Dix pushed forward carrying a glass... He pushed his way towards her, laughing.* VERB V prep/adv, V *way* prep/adv

3 If an army **pushes into** a country or area that it is attacking or invading, it moves further into it. *One detachment pushed into the eastern suburbs towards the airfield... The army may push southwards into the Kurdish areas.* ▶ Also a noun. *...the allied push into occupied Kuwait. ...the final push to capture Berlin.* VERB =advance V *into* n, V adv *into* n; N-COUNT: usu sing

4 To **push** a value or amount **up** or **down** means to cause it to increase or decrease. *Any shortage could push up grain prices... The government had done everything it could to push down inflation... Interest had pushed the loan up to $27,000.* VERB V n with adv, V n prep

5 If someone or something **pushes** an idea or project in a particular direction, they cause it to develop or progress in a particular way. *China would use its influence to help push forward the peace process... The government seemed intent on pushing local and central government in opposite directions.* VERB V n with adv, V n prep

6 If you **push** someone to do something or **push** them **into** doing something, you urge, encourage, or force them to do it. *She thanks her parents for keeping her in school and pushing her to study... James did not push her into stealing the money... I knew he was pushing himself to the limit and felt rather anxious... There is no point in pushing them unless they are talented and they enjoy it.* ▶ Also a noun. *We need a push to take the first step.* VERB V n to-inf, V n *into*-ing, V n prep/adv, V n; N-COUNT: usu sing

7 If you **push for** something, you try very hard to achieve it or to persuade someone to do it. *Britain's health experts are pushing for a ban on all cigarette advertising... Germany is pushing for direct flights to be established.* ▶ Also a noun. *In its push for economic growth it has ignored projects that would improve living standards... They urged negotiators to make a final push to arrive at an agreement.* VERB =press for V *for* n, V *for* n to-inf; N-COUNT: usu sing

8 If someone **pushes** an idea, a point, or a product, they try in a forceful way to convince people to accept it or buy it. *Ministers will push the case for opening the plant... She knew enough about publishing to know that they could push a hundred thousand copies into the bookshops.* VERB V n

9 When someone **pushes** drugs, they sell them illegally; an informal expression. *She was sent for trial yesterday accused of pushing drugs.* VERB =deal V n

10 If you say that someone **is pushing it**, you mean that their actions or claims are rather excessive or risky; an informal use. *I think that he was pushing it a bit when he said it was the best stadium in the world.* VB: usu cont V *it*

11 See also **pushed, pushing**.

12 If you **get the push** or **are given the push**, you are told that you are not wanted any more, either in your job or by someone you are having a relationship with; used mainly in informal British English. *Two cabinet ministers also got the push.* PHRASES V inflects

13 ● to **push the boat out**: see **boat**. ● to **push** your **luck**: see **luck**.

push ahead or **push forward.** If you **push ahead** or **push forward** with something, you make progress with it. *The government intends to push ahead with its reform programme.* PHRASAL VERB =press forward V P *with* n, Also V P

push around. If someone **pushes** you **around**, they give you orders in a rude and insulting way; an informal expression. *We don't like somebody coming in with lots of money and trying to push people around.* PHRASAL VERB =bully V n P

push aside. If you **push** something **aside**, you ignore it or refuse to think about it. *By pushing aside unpleasant thoughts they merely repress these thoughts... For a moment her husband came to mind, but she pushed the guilt aside.* PHRASAL VERB =ignore V P n (not pron), V n P

push forward. See **push ahead**. PHRASAL VERB

push in. When someone **pushes in**, they join a queue in front of other people when they have no right to do so; used showing disapproval. *Nina pushed in next to Liddie.* PHRASAL VERB PRAGMATICS V P

push off. If you tell someone to **push off**, you are telling them rather rudely to go away; an informal expression. *Push off, Bob.* PHRASAL VERB usu imper PRAGMATICS V P

push on. When you **push on**, you continue with a journey or task. *Although the journey was a long and lonely one, Tumalo pushed on.* PHRASAL VERB =press on V P

push over. If you **push** someone or something **over**, you push them so that they fall onto the ground. *We have had trouble with people damaging hedges, uprooting trees and pushing over walls... Anna is always attacking other children, pushing them over.* ● See also **pushover**. PHRASAL VERB =knock over V P n (not pron), V n P

push through. If someone **pushes through** a law, reform, or policy, they succeed in getting it accepted, often despite opposition. *The vote will enable the Prime Minister to push through tough policies... He tried to push the amendment through Parliament.* PHRASAL VERB V P n (not pron), V n P n, Also V n P

push bike, push bikes. A **push bike** is a bicycle which you move by turning the pedals with your feet; an old-fashioned word used in British English. N-COUNT

push-button. A **push-button** machine or process is controlled by means of buttons or switches. *...push button phones.* ADJ: ADJ n

pushchair /pʊʃtʃeəʳ/ **pushchairs.** In British English, a **pushchair** is a small chair on wheels, in which a baby or small child can sit and be wheeled around. The usual American word is **stroller**. N-COUNT

pushed /pʊʃt/

1 If you are **pushed for** something such as time or money, you do not have enough of it; an informal use. *He's going to be a bit pushed for money.* ADJ-GRADED: v-link ADJ, usu ADJ *for* n

2 If you **are hard pushed to do** something, you find it very difficult to do it. *I'd be hard pushed to teach him anything.* PHRASE: V inflects

pusher /pʊʃəʳ/ **pushers.** A **pusher** is a person who sells illegal drugs; an informal word. *His father accused him of acting as a carrier for some drug pushers.* ◆◇◇◇◇ N-COUNT

pushing /pʊʃɪŋ/. If you say that someone is **pushing** a particular age, you mean that they are nearly that age; an informal word. *Pushing 40, he was an ageing rock star.* PREP =almost, going on

pushover /pʊʃoʊvəʳ/ **pushovers**

1 You say that someone is a **pushover** when you find it easy to persuade them to do what you want; N-COUNT

an informal word. *He is a tough negotiator. We did not expect to find him a pushover and he has not been one.*
2 You say that something is a **pushover** when it is easy to do or easy to get. *You might think Hungarian a pushover to learn. It is not.* N-COUNT: usu sing =doddle

push-up, push-ups. A **push-up** is the same as a **press-up**; used mainly in American English. ◆◇◇◇◇ N-COUNT

pushy /pʊʃi/ **pushier, pushiest.** If you describe someone as **pushy**, you mean that they try in a forceful way to get things done as they would like or to increase their status or influence; an informal word used showing disapproval. *She was a confident and pushy young woman... My mother encouraged us, but was never pushy.* ADJ-GRADED PRAGMATICS =forceful

pusillanimous /pjuːsɪlænɪməs/. If you say that someone is **pusillanimous**, you think that they are timid or cowardly; a formal word. *The authorities have been too pusillanimous in merely condemning the violence.* ADJ-GRADED =cowardly ≠brave

puss /pʊs/. People sometimes call a cat by saying **'Puss'**. N-VOC

pussy /pʊsi/ **pussies** ◆◇◇◇◇
1 Children or people talking to children often refer to a cat as a **pussy**. N-COUNT
2 Some people use the word **pussy** to refer to a woman's genitals; a rude and offensive word which you should avoid using. N-COUNT

pussycat /pʊsikæt/ **pussycats**
1 Children or people talking to children often refer to a cat as a **pussycat**. N-COUNT =pussy
2 If you describe someone as a **pussycat**, you think that they are kind and gentle. N-COUNT =sweetie

pussyfoot /pʊsifʊt/ **pussyfoots, pussyfooting, pussyfooted.** If you say that someone **is pussyfooting** around, you think that they are behaving in a cautious way because they are not sure what to do and are afraid to commit themselves. *Why don't they stop pussyfooting around and say what they really mean?* VERB =prevaricate V *around/about* Also V

pustule /pʌstʃuːl/ **pustules.** A **pustule** is a pimple on the skin which contains pus; a medical term. N-COUNT =boil

put /pʊt/ **puts, putting.** The form **put** is used in the present tense and is the past tense and past participle. ◆◆◆◆◆
1 When you **put** something in a particular place or position, you move it into that place or position. *Leaphorn put the photograph on the desk... She hesitated, then put her hand on Grace's arm... Mishka put down a heavy shopping bag.* VERB V n prep/adv V n with adv
2 If you **put** someone somewhere, you cause them to go there and to stay there for a period of time. *Rather than put him in the hospital, she had been caring for him at home... I'd put the children to bed.* VERB V n prep/adv
3 To **put** someone or something in a particular state or situation means to cause them to be in that state or situation. *This is going to put them out of business... He was putting himself at risk... My doctor put me in touch with a psychiatrist... The British people put us back in power.* VERB =place V n prep/adv
4 To **put** something **on** people or things means to cause them to have it, or to cause them to be affected by it. *Mr Wapenhans's comments put additional pressure on the Polish government... Be aware of the terrible strain it can put on a child when you expect the best reports... They will also force schools to put more emphasis on teaching basic subjects.* VERB =place V n *on* n
5 If you **put** your trust, faith, or confidence **in** someone or something, you trust them or have faith or confidence in them. *He had decided long ago that he would put his trust in socialism when the time came... How much faith should we put in anti-ageing products?* VERB =place V n *in* n
6 If you **put** time, strength, or energy **into** an activity, you use it in doing that activity. *We're not saying that activists should put all their effort and time into party politics... Eleanor did not put much energy into the discussion.* VERB V n *into* n/-ing
7 If you **put** money **into** a business or project, you invest money in it. *Investors should consider putting some money into an annuity... Put $10,000 into this investment and in 10 years, you'll have almost $18,000.* VERB =invest V n *into* n
8 When you **put** an idea or remark in a particular way, you express it in that way. You can use expressions like **to put it simply** and **to put it bluntly** before saying something to explain that you are going to express it in a simple way or in a blunt way. *I had already met Pete a couple of times through – how should I put it – friends in low places... He doesn't, to put it very bluntly, give a damn about the woman or the baby... If I was auditioning for a vocalist, let me put it this way, he wouldn't get to sing in my band... He admitted the security forces might have made some mistakes, as he put it... You can't put that sort of fear into words.* VERB =express V it adv/prep V it V n *into* n
9 When you **put a question** to someone, you ask them the question. *Is this fair? Well, I put that question today to Deputy Counsel Craig Gillen... The first questions put to Mr. Bush by reporters concerned Ross Perot... He thinks that some workers may be afraid to put questions publicly.* VERB V n *to* n V n adv
10 If you **put** a case, opinion, or proposal, you explain it and list the reasons why you support or believe it. *He always put his point of view with clarity and with courage... He put the case to the Saudi Foreign Minister... He sat there listening as we put suggestions to him.* VERB =present V n V n *to* n
11 If you **put** something **at** a particular value or **in** a particular category, or **put** a particular value or category label **on** it, you estimate it to have that value or to be in that category. *I would put her age at about 50 or so... All the more technically advanced countries put a high value on science... It is not easy to put the guilty and innocent into clear-cut categories.* VERB V n *at* amount V n *on* n V n *into* n Also V n adj-compar
12 If you **put** written information somewhere, you write, type, or print it there. *Mary's family were so pleased that they put an announcement in the local paper to thank them... I think what I put in that book is now pretty much the agenda for this country... He crossed out 'Screenplay' and put 'Written by' instead.* VERB V n prep/adv V n
13 If someone **puts one over on** you, they make you do or believe something by telling you things that are not true; an informal expression. *He considered himself a crafty man – a man would have to get up very early in the morning to put one over on Alf Tandy.* PHRASES V inflects =get the better of
14 If you **put it to** someone **that** something is true, you suggest that it is true, especially when you think that they will be unwilling to admit this. *But I put it to you that they're useless... I put this to Kenyon. 'Absolutely untrue,' he said.* V inflects
15 If you say that something is bigger or better than several other things **put together**, you mean that it is bigger or has more good qualities than all of those other things together. *...a huge Soviet tank park, consisting of more tanks than in the rest of the world put together.* n PHR
16 **Put** is used in a large number of expressions which are explained under other words in this dictionary. For example, the expression **to put someone in the picture** is explained at **picture**.

put about. If you **put** something **about**, you tell it to people that you meet and cause it to become well-known; used mainly in British English. *Senior US officials are now putting it about that President Bush has definitely decided to go for a quick strike... The King had been putting about lurid rumours for months.* PHRASAL VERB =put around V it P that V P n (not pron) Also V n P

put across or **put over.** When you **put** something **across** or **put it over**, you succeed in describing or explaining it to someone. *He has taken out a half-page advertisement in his local paper to put his point across... This is actually a very entertaining book putting over serious health messages... He really enjoys putting across a technical argument.* PHRASAL VERB =get across V n P V P n (not pron)

put aside PHRASAL VERB
1 If you **put** something **aside**, you keep it to be dealt with or used at a later time. *She took up a slice of bread, broke it nervously, then put it aside...* =put to one side V n P V P n (not pron)

Encourage children to put aside some of their pocket-money to buy Christmas presents.

2 If you **put** a feeling or disagreement **aside**, you forget about it or ignore it in order to solve a problem or argument. *We should put aside our differences and discuss the things we have in common... We admitted that the attraction was there, but decided that we would put the feelings aside.*
=forget; V P n (not pron); V n P

put away PHRASAL VERB

1 If you **put** something **away**, you put it into the place where it is normally kept when it is not being used, for example in a drawer. *She finished putting the milk away and turned around... 'Yes, Mum,' replied Cheryl as she slowly put away her doll... Her bed was crisply made, her clothes put away.*
V n P; V P n (not pron); V-ed P

2 If someone **is put away**, they are sent to prison or to a mental hospital for a long time; an informal expression. *He's an animal! He should be put away... His testimony could put Drago away for life.*
=lock up; *be* V-ed P; V n P

put back. To **put** something **back** means to delay it or postpone it. *There are always new projects which seem to put the reunion back further... News conferences due to be held by both men have been put back.*
PHRASAL VERB =delay; V n P; *be* V-ed P; Also V P n (not pron)

put by. If you **put** money **by**, you save it so that you can use it at a later time. *Dermot's putting his money by, in a Deposit Account... There was enough put by for her fare... Well we need to put by £400 for the pump valves to be renewed.*
PHRASAL VERB =save; V n P; V-ed P; V P n (not pron)

put down PHRASAL VERB

1 If you **put** something **down** somewhere, you write or type it there. *Never put anything down on paper which might be used in evidence against you at a later date... We've put down on our staff development plan for this year that we would like some technology courses... I had prepared for the meeting by putting down what I wanted from them.*
V n P *in/on* n; V P that; V P wh; Also V P n (not pron)

2 If you **put down** some money, you pay part of the price of something as a deposit. *He bought an investment property for $100,000 and put down $20,000... He's got to put cash down.*
V P n (not pron); V n P

3 When soldiers, police, or the government **put down** a riot or rebellion, they stop it by using force. *Soldiers went in to put down a rebellion.*
=crush; V P n (not pron); Also V n P

4 If someone **puts** you **down**, they treat you in an unpleasant way by criticizing you in front of other people or making you appear foolish; an informal expression. *I know that I do put people down occasionally... She learned to stop putting herself down and comparing herself to others... Racist jokes come from wanting to put down other kinds of people we feel threatened by.* • See also **put-down**.
=humiliate; V n P; V P n (not pron)

5 When an animal **is put down**, it is killed because it is dangerous or very ill; used mainly in British English. *Magistrates ordered his dog Samson to be put down immediately... They think that any legislation that involved putting down dogs was wrong.*
be V-ed P; V P n (not pron); Also V n P

put down as. If you **put** someone or something **down as** a particular type of person or thing, you consider that they are that thing. *I think they'll put her down as being one of our best Prime Ministers.*
PHRASAL VERB =classify as; V n P P n/-ing

put down for. If you **put** someone **down for** an activity, donation, or purchase, you record their name and the fact that they intend to do that activity or make that donation or purchase. *Put her down for a 'yes' vote.*
PHRASAL VERB; V n P P n

put down to. If you **put** something **down to** a particular thing, you believe that it is caused by that thing. *You may be a sceptic and put it down to life's inequalities.*
PHRASAL VERB =attribute; V n P P n

put forth. If someone **puts forth** a plan or proposal, they suggest it; a formal expression. *The rebels put forth a five-point plan.*
PHRASAL VERB; V P n

put forward. If you **put forward** a plan, proposal, or name, you suggest that it should be considered for a particular purpose or job. *He has put forward new peace proposals... Mr Ryzhkov put his name forward for the presidency.*
PHRASAL VERB =submit; V P n (not pron); V n P *for* n; Also V n P

put in PHRASAL VERB

1 If you **put in** an amount of time or effort doing something, you spend that time or effort doing it. *Wade was going to be paid a salary, instead of by the hour, whether he put in forty hours or not... They've put in time and effort to keep the strike going... If we don't put money in we will lose our investment.*
V P n (not pron); V n P

2 If you **put in a request** or **put in for** something, you make a formal request or application. *The ministry ordered 113 of these and later put in a request for 21 more... I decided to put in for a job as deputy secretary.*
V P n (not pron); V P *for* n

3 If you **put in** a remark, you interrupt someone or add to what they have said with the remark. *'He was a lawyer before that,' Mary Ann put in... 'Helen had something to eat before she left,' put in Cecil anxiously.*
=interject; V P with quote

4 When a ship **puts in** or **puts into** a port, it goes into the port for a short stop. *It's due to put in at Aden and some other ports before arriving in Basra... They had asked Hong Kong for permission to put into port there.*
V P adv/prep

put off PHRASAL VERB

1 If you **put** something **off**, you delay doing it. *Women who put off having a baby often make the best mothers... The Association has put the event off until October.*
=postpone; V P -ing/n (not pron); V n P

2 If you **put** someone **off**, you make them wait for something that they want. *The old priest tried to put them off, saying that the hour was late.*
V n P

3 If something **puts** you **off** something, it makes you dislike it, or decide not to do or have it. *The high divorce figures don't seem to be putting people off marriage... His personal habits put them off... The country's worsening reputation does not seem to be putting off the tourists... We tried to visit the Abbey but were put off by the queues.*
=deter; V n P n/-ing; V n P; V P n (not pron); *be* V-ed P

4 If someone or something **puts** you **off**, it distracts you from something you are trying to do and makes it more difficult for you to do it. *She asked me to be serious – said it put her off if I laughed... It put her off revising for her exams.*
=distract; V n P; V n P n/-ing; Also V P n (not pron)

put on PHRASAL VERB

1 When you **put on** clothing or make-up, you place it on your body in order to wear it. *She put on her coat and went out... Maximo put on a pair of glasses... I haven't even put any lipstick on.*
≠take off; V P n (not pron); V n P

2 When people **put on** a show, exhibition, or service, they perform it or organize it. *The band are hoping to put on a UK show before the end of the year... British Airways is putting on an extra flight to London tomorrow... We put it on and everybody said 'Oh it's a brilliant production'.*
V P n (not pron); V n P

3 If someone **puts on** weight, they become heavier. *I can eat what I want but I never put on weight... Luther's put on three stone.*
=gain; V P n (not pron); Also V n P

4 If you **put on** a piece of equipment or a device, you make it start working, for example by pressing a switch or turning a knob. *I put the radio on... I put on the light by the bed.*
V n P; V P n (not pron)

5 If you **put** a record, tape, or CD **on**, you place it in a record, tape, or CD player and listen to it. *She poured them drinks, and put a record on loud... Let's go into the study and put on some music.*
≠take off; V n P; V P n (not pron)

6 If you **put** something **on**, you begin to cook or heat it. *She immediately put the kettle on... Put some rice on now... Put on a pan of water to summer and gently poach the eggs.*
V n P; V P n (not pron)

7 If you **put** a sum of money **on** something, you make a bet about it. For example, if you put £10 on a racehorse, you bet £10 that it will win. *They each put £20 on Matthew scoring the first goal... He'll be back in an hour. I'd put money on it... I'll put a bet on for you.*
=lay; V n P n/-ing; V n P; Also V P n (not pron)

8 To **put** a particular amount **on** the cost or value of something means to add that amount to it. *The proposal could put 3p on a loaf of bread.*
≠take off; V n P n

9 If you **put on** a way of behaving, you behave in a way that is not natural to you or that does not express your real feelings. *Stop putting on an act and be yourself... She had hoped the couple would put on a show of unity... It was hard to believe she was ill, she was putting it on.*
V P n (not pron); V *it* P; Also V n P

put onto. If you **put** someone **onto** something useful, you tell them about it. *This elastic is a pow-*
PHRASAL VERB; V n P n

erful variety which a friend in the clothing trade put me onto.

put out PHRASAL VERB

1 If you **put out** an announcement or story, you make it known to a lot of people. *The French news agency put out a statement from the Trade Minister.* =broadcast V P n (not pron) Also V n P

2 If you **put out** a fire, candle, or cigarette, you make it stop burning. *Firemen tried to free the injured and put out the blaze... He lit a half-cigarette and almost immediately put it out again.* =extinguish V P n (not pron) V n P

3 If you **put out** an electric light, you make it stop shining by pressing a switch. *He crossed to the bedside table and put out the light.* =turn out V P n (not pron) Also V n P

4 If you **put out** things that will be needed, you place them somewhere ready to be used. *Paula had put out her luggage for the coach... I slowly unpacked the teapot and put it out on the table.* V P n (not pron) V n P

5 If you **put out your hand**, you move it forward, away from your body. *He put out his hand to Alfred... She put her hand out and tried to touch her mother's arm.* =stretch out V P n (not pron) V n P

6 If you **put** someone **out**, you cause them trouble or inconvenience because they have to do something for you. *It is a very sociable diet to follow because you don't have to put anyone out... I've always put myself out for others and I'm not doing it any more.* =inconvenience V n P

7 In a sporting competition, to **put out** a player or team means to defeat them and eliminate them from the competition. *Another Spaniard, Emilio Sanchez, put out Jens Woehrmann in three sets. ...the debatable goal that put Villa out of the UEFA Cup in Milan.* =knock out V P n (not pron) V n P *of* n Also V n P

8 See also **put out**.

put over. See **put across.** PHRASAL VERB

put through PHRASAL VERB

1 When someone **puts through** a telephone call or a caller, they make the connection that allows the caller to speak to the person they are phoning. *The operator will put you through... He asked to be put through to Charley Lunn.* =connect V n P Also V P n (not pron)

2 If someone **puts** you **through** an unpleasant experience, they make you experience it. *She wouldn't want to put them through the ordeal of a huge ceremony... Those two husbands put me through hell.* V n P n

put together PHRASAL VERB

1 If you **put** something **together**, you join its different parts to each other so that it can be used. *He took it apart brick by brick, and put it back together again... The factories no longer relied upon a mechanic to put together looms within the plant.* =assemble V n P V P n (not pron)

2 If you **put together** a group of people or things, you form them into a team or collection. *It will be able to put together a governing coalition... He is trying to put a team together for next season.* =form, assemble V P n (not pron) V n P

3 If you **put together** an agreement, plan, or product, you design and create it. *We wouldn't have time to put together an agreement... Reports speak of Bonn putting together an aid package for Moscow... We got to work on putting the book together.* V P n (not pron) V n P

put up PHRASAL VERB

1 If people **put up** a wall, building, tent, or other structure, they construct it so that it is upright. *Protesters have been putting up barricades across a number of major intersections... He was putting up a new fence at his home.* =erect ≠take down V P n (not pron) Also V n P

2 If you **put up** a poster or notice, you fix it to a wall or board. *They're putting new street signs up... The teacher training college put up a plaque to the college's founder.* ≠take down V n P

3 To **put up** resistance to something means to resist it. *In the end the Kurds surrendered without putting up any resistance... He'd put up a real fight to keep you there... The fish put up a spectacular 20 minute struggle before being netted.* V P n

4 If you **put up** money for something, you provide the money that is needed to pay for it. *The state agreed to put up $69,000 to start his company... The merchant banks raise capital for industry. They don't actually put it up themselves.* =provide V P n (not pron) V n P

5 To **put up** the price of something means to cause it to increase. *Their friends suggested they should put up their prices... They know he would put their taxes up.* =raise, increase V P n (not pron) V n P

6 If a person or hotel **puts** you **up** or if you **put up** somewhere, you stay at the person's home or at the hotel for one or more nights. *I wanted to know if she could put me up for a few days... Hundreds of junior civil servants have to be put up in hotel rooms and temporary hostels... He decided that he would drive back to town instead of putting up for the night at the hotel.* ERG V n P V P prep

7 If a political party **puts up** a candidate in an election or if the candidate **puts up**, the candidate fights the election. *They plan to put up a candidate against Kenneth Baker in Mole Valley... He put up as a candidate.* ERG V P n (not pron) V P *as* n

put up for. If you **put** something **up for** sale, review, or auction, you make it available to be sold, reviewed, or auctioned. *The company should put its claims up for review by an arbitrator... The old flower and fruit market has been put up for sale... She put up her daughter for adoption in 1967.* PHRASAL VERB V n P P n V P n P n

put up to. If you **put** someone **up to** something wrong or foolish or something that they would not normally do, you suggest that they do it and you encourage them to do it; used showing disapproval. *How do you know he asked me out? You put him up to it.* PHRASAL VERB PRAGMATICS V n P P n

put up with. If you **put up with** something, you tolerate or accept it, even though you find it unpleasant or unsatisfactory. *They had put up with behaviour from their son which they would not have tolerated from anyone else.* PHRASAL VERB =tolerate, endure V P P n

putative /pjuːtətɪv/. If you describe someone or something as **putative** you mean that they are generally thought to be the thing mentioned; a formal or legal word. *...a putative father.* ADJ: ADJ n

put-down, put-downs; also spelled **put down.** ◆◆◇◇◇ A **put-down** is something that you say or do to criticize someone or make them appear foolish; an informal expression. *I see the term as a put-down of women... She was getting very sick of Mick's put-downs.* N-COUNT

put out. If you feel **put out**, you feel rather annoyed or upset. *I did not blame him for feeling put out... He was plainly very put out at finding her there.* ◆◆◇◇◇ ADJ-GRADED: v-link ADJ =annoyed

putrefaction /pjuːtrɪfækʃᵊn/. **Putrefaction** is the process of rotting or decaying; a formal word. *...the lingering stench of putrefaction.* N-UNCOUNT =decay, decomposition

putrefy /pjuːtrɪfaɪ/ **putrefies, putrefying, putrefied.** When something **putrefies**, it rots and produces a disgusting smell; a formal word. *The meat in all of the open flasks putrefied. ...putrefying corpses.* VERB =rot V V-ing

putrid /pjuːtrɪd/. Something that is **putrid** is rotten and beginning to smell disgusting; a formal word. *...a foul, putrid stench.* ADJ-GRADED =rotten

putsch /pʊtʃ/ **putsches.** A **putsch** is a sudden attempt to get rid of a government by force. *Spectacular changes have taken place at the top since the failed putsch.* N-COUNT =coup

putt /pʌt/ **putts, putting, putted** ◆◆◇◇◇

1 A **putt** is a stroke in golf that you make when the ball has reached the green in an attempt to get the ball in the hole. *...a 5-foot putt.* N-COUNT

2 In golf, when you **putt** the ball, you hit a putt. *Turner, however, putted superbly, twice holing from 40 feet.* VERB V

putter /pʌtəʳ/ **putters, puttering, puttered** ◆◇◇◇◇

1 A **putter** is a club used for hitting a golf ball a short distance once it is on the green. N-COUNT

2 In American English, if you **putter** around, you pass the time in a gentle, unhurried way, doing pleasant but unimportant things. The usual British word is **potter.** *I started puttering around outside, not knowing what I was doing... She liked to putter in the kitchen.* VERB =potter V *around/about* V

putting green /pʌtɪŋ griːn/ **putting greens.** A **putting green** is a very small golf course on which the grass is kept very short and on which there are no obstacles. N-COUNT

putty /pʌti/. **Putty** is a stiff paste used to fix glass panes into frames. N-UNCOUNT

put-upon; also spelled **put upon**. If you are **put-upon**, you are treated badly by someone who takes advantage of your willingness to help them; an informal expression. *Volunteers from all walks of life are feeling put upon. ...Bernard's put-upon wife Maud.* ADJ-GRADED =used

puzzle /pʌzᵊl/ **puzzles, puzzling, puzzled** ◆◆◇◇◇

1 If something **puzzles** you, you do not understand it and feel confused. *My sister puzzles me and causes me anxiety.* ♦ **puzzling** *His letter poses a number of puzzling questions.* VERB Vn ADJ-GRADED

2 If you **puzzle over** something, you try hard to think of the answer to it or the explanation for it. *Researchers continue to puzzle over the relationship between HIV and AIDS.* VERB V over/about n

3 A **puzzle** is a question, game, or toy which you have to think about carefully in order to answer it correctly or put it together properly. *...a word puzzle.* ● See also **crossword puzzle**. N-COUNT: oft supp N

4 You can describe a person or thing that is hard to understand as **a puzzle**. *Data from Voyager II has presented astronomers with a puzzle about why our outermost planet exists... She was a puzzle.* N-SING: a N =mystery

puzzle out. If you **puzzle out** a problem, you find the answer to it by thinking hard about it. *He left for his summer cottage to puzzle out what he might try next... Nosenko puzzled out Kutya's surname... The risks can be so complex that banks hire mathematicians to puzzle them out.* PHRASAL VERB V P wh V P n (not pron) V n P

puzzled /pʌzᵊld/. Someone who is **puzzled** is confused because they do not understand something. *Critics remain puzzled by the British election results... Norman looked puzzled.* ◆◇◇◇◇ ADJ-GRADED: oft ADJ by/about/at n =mystified

puzzlement /pʌzᵊlmənt/. **Puzzlement** is the confusion that you feel when you do not understand something. *He frowned in puzzlement.* N-UNCOUNT =bafflement

PVC /piː viː siː/. **PVC** is a plastic material used for making things such as tiles, shoes, and items of clothing. **PVC** is an abbreviation for 'polyvinyl chloride'. N-UNCOUNT: oft N n

pw. **pw** is the written abbreviation for 'per week'. It is used especially when stating the weekly cost of something. *...single room-£40 pw.*

pygmy /pɪgmi/ **pygmies;** also spelled **pigmy**.

1 **Pygmy** means belonging to a species of animal which is the smallest of a group of related species. *Reaching a maximum height of 56cm the pygmy goat is essentially a pet.* ADJ: ADJ n

2 A **pygmy** is a member of a tribal group of very small people. *...the pygmy tribes of Papua New Guinea.* N-COUNT

pyjamas /pɪdʒɑːməz/; spelled **pajamas** in American English. The form **pyjama** is used as a modifier. A pair of **pyjamas** consists of loose trousers and a loose jacket that people, especially men, wear in bed. *My brother was still in his pyjamas. ...a pyjama jacket.* ◆◇◇◇◇ N-PLURAL: also a pair of N

pylon /paɪlɒn/ **pylons. Pylons** are very tall metal structures which hold electric cables high above the ground so that electricity can be transmitted over long distances. *...electricity pylons.* N-COUNT

pyramid /pɪrəmɪd/ **pyramids** ◆◇◇◇◇

1 **Pyramids** are ancient stone buildings four triangular sloping sides. The most famous pyramids are those built as royal tombs in ancient Egypt. *We set off to see the Pyramids and Sphinx.* N-COUNT

2 A **pyramid** is a shape, object, or pile of things with a flat base and sloping triangular sides that meet at a point. *On a plate in front of him was piled a pyramid of flat white biscuits.* N-COUNT: usu N of n

3 You can describe something as a **pyramid** when it is organized so that there are fewer people at each level as you go towards the top. *Traditionally, the Brahmins, or the priestly class, are set at the top of the social pyramid.* N-COUNT

pyramidal /pɪrəmɪdᵊl, pɪræm-/. Something that is **pyramidal** is shaped like a pyramid. *...a black pyramidal tent.* ADJ

pyre /paɪəʳ/ **pyres.** A **pyre** is a high pile of wood which is built outside to ceremonially burn dead bodies or religious offerings. N-COUNT

Pyrex /paɪreks/. **Pyrex** is a type of strong glass which is used for making bowls and dishes that do not break when you cook things in them. **Pyrex** is a trademark. N-UNCOUNT: oft N n

pyromaniac /paɪəroʊmeɪniæk/ **pyromaniacs.** A **pyromaniac** is a person who has an uncontrollable desire to start fires. N-COUNT

pyrotechnics /paɪroʊteknɪks/

1 **Pyrotechnics** is the making or displaying of fireworks. *The festival will feature pyrotechnics, live music, and sculptures.* N-UNCOUNT

2 Amazing displays of skill are sometimes referred to as **pyrotechnics**. *...the soaring pyrotechnics of the singer's voice.* N-PLURAL

pyrrhic victory /pɪrɪk vɪktəri/ **pyrrhic victories.** If you describe something as a **pyrrhic victory**, you mean that although someone has won or gained something, it was not worth the sacrifices that they had to make. N-COUNT

python /paɪθən/ **pythons.** A **python** is a large, snake that kills animals by squeezing them with its body. ◆◇◇◇◇ N-COUNT

Q q

Q, q /kjuː/ **Q's, q's**

1 **Q** is the seventeenth letter of the English alphabet. N-VAR

2 **Q** or **q** is used as an abbreviation for words beginning with q, such as 'question' or 'queen'. *Q: Should I dress up or dress down on the first date? A: It depends.*

QC /kjuː siː/ **QCs** ◆◆◇◇◇

1 In Britain, a **QC** is a senior barrister. **QC** is an abbreviation for 'Queen's Counsel'. *The Sun hired a top QC to defend Kay.* N-COUNT

2 **QC** is written after someone's name to indicate that they are qualified as a QC. *...Channel 4's counsel, George Carman QC.*

quack /kwæk/ **quacks, quacking, quacked**

1 If you call someone a **quack** or a **quack doctor**, you mean that they claim to be skilled in medicine but are not. *I went everywhere for treatment, tried all sorts of quacks.* N-COUNT: oft N n

2 **Quack** is used in expressions such as **quack remedies** or **quack cures** to talk about remedies or cures that you think are unlikely to work because they have been suggested by a quack doctor. *Why do intelligent people find quack remedies so appealing?* ADJ: ADJ n

3 When a duck **quacks**, it makes the noise that ducks typically make. *There are plenty of ducks and geese quacking on the lawn.* ► Also a noun. *Suddenly he heard a quack.* VERB V N-COUNT; SOUND

quackery /kwækəri/. If you refer to a form of medical treatment as **quackery**, you mean that the person who prescribes the treatment claims to be skilled in medicine but is not, and that the treatment will not have the effect it is supposed to have. *To some people, herbal remedies smell of quackery.* N-UNCOUNT

quad /kwɒd/ **quads**
1 **Quads** are the same as **quadruplets**. *...a 34-year-old mother of quads.* N-COUNT: usu pl
2 A **quad** is the same as a **quadrangle**; not used in formal English. *His rooms were on the left-hand side of the quad.* N-COUNT: usu the N

quadrangle /kwɒdræŋgəl/ **quadrangles.** A **quadrangle** is an open square area with buildings round it, especially in a college or school. N-COUNT: oft the N

quadrant /kwɒdrənt/ **quadrants.** A **quadrant** is one of four equal parts into which a circle or other shape has been divided. *The player appears in an upper quadrant of the screen, answering a question, while the game continues.* N-COUNT: usu with supp, adj N, N of n

quadraphonic /kwɒdrəfɒnɪk/. See **quadrophonic.**

quadriceps /kwɒdrɪseps/; **quadriceps** is both the singular and the plural form. Your **quadriceps** are the groups of four muscles at the front of your thighs. N-COUNT: usu pl

quadrille /kwɒdrɪ:l/ **quadrilles.** A **quadrille** is a type of old-fashioned dance for four or more couples. N-COUNT

quadriplegic /kwɒdrɪpli:dʒɪk/ **quadriplegics.** A **quadriplegic** is a person who is permanently unable to use their arms and legs. N-COUNT ► Also an adjective. *He is now quadriplegic and confined to a wheelchair.* ADJ

quadrophonic /kwɒdrəfɒnɪk/; also spelled **quadraphonic**. In a **quadrophonic** music system, sounds are recorded on four separate tracks and are replayed through four speakers. *...a top-of-the-range quadrophonic CD system.* ADJ: ADJ n

quadruped /kwɒdrʊped/ **quadrupeds.** A **quadruped** is any animal with four legs; a technical term in biology. N-COUNT

quadruple /kwɒdru:pəl/ **quadruples, quadrupling, quadrupled** ◆◇◇◇◇
1 If someone **quadruples** an amount or if it **quadruples**, it becomes four times bigger. *China seeks to quadruple its income in twenty years... The price has quadrupled in the last few years.* V-ERG: V n, V
2 If one amount is **quadruple** another amount, it is four times bigger. *Fifty-nine percent of its residents have attended graduate school – quadruple the national average.* PREDET: PREDET det n
3 You use **quadruple** to indicate that something has four parts or happens four times. *The quadruple murder has replaced property prices as the sole topic of interest.* ADJ: ADJ n

quadruplet /kwɒdrʊplət, kwɒdru:-/ **quadruplets. Quadruplets** are four children who are born to the same mother at the same time. N-COUNT: usu pl

quaff /kwɒf/ **quaffs, quaffing, quaffed.** If you **quaff** an alcoholic drink, you drink a lot of it in a short space of time; an old-fashioned word. *By the time he had quaffed his third, he was winking playfully at a plump woman who sat across from him.* VERB: V n

quagmire /kwægmaɪəʳ/ **quagmires** ◆◇◇◇◇
1 A **quagmire** is a difficult, complicated, or unpleasant situation which is not easy to avoid or escape from. *His people had fallen further and further into a quagmire of confusion... We have no intention of being drawn into a political quagmire.* N-COUNT: usu sing with supp
2 A **quagmire** is a soft, wet area of land which your feet sink into if you try to walk across it. *Overnight rain had turned the grass airstrip into a quagmire.* N-COUNT: usu sing

quail /kweɪl/ **quails, quailing, quailed; quail** can also be used as the plural form. ◆◇◇◇◇
1 A **quail** is a type of small bird which is often shot and eaten. *I've shot hundreds of quail with that gun.* N-COUNT ► **Quail** is the meat of this bird eaten as food. *They dined off salmon, quail, and fruit.* N-UNCOUNT
2 If someone or something makes you **quail**, they make you feel very afraid, often so that you hesitate; a literary use. *The very words make many of us quail... He told Naomi she was becoming just like Maya. Naomi quailed at the thought.* VERB: V, V at n

quaint /kweɪnt/ **quainter, quaintest.** Something that is **quaint** is attractive because it is unusual and rather old-fashioned. *...a small, quaint town with narrow streets and traditional half-timbered houses... That's how concepts like general welfare start to sound quaint in this age.* ◆◇◇◇◇ ADJ-GRADED ♦ **quaintly** *This may seem a quaintly old-fashioned idea.* ADV-GRADED: usu ADV adj ♦ **quaintness** *...the quaintness of the rural north.* N-UNCOUNT

quake /kweɪk/ **quakes, quaking, quaked** ◆◇◇◇◇
1 A **quake** is the same as an **earthquake**. *The quake destroyed mud buildings in many remote villages.* N-COUNT =earthquake
2 If you **quake**, you tremble or shake, usually because you are very afraid. *I just stood there quaking with fear... Her shoulders quaked.* VERB: V with n, V
3 If you **are quaking in your boots** or **quaking in your shoes**, you feel very nervous or afraid, and may be feeling slightly weak as a result. *If you stand up straight you'll give an impression of self-confidence even if you're quaking in your boots.* PHRASE: V inflects

Quaker /kweɪkəʳ/ **Quakers.** A **Quaker** is a person who belongs to a Christian group called the Society of Friends. ◆◇◇◇◇ N-COUNT

qualification /kwɒlɪfɪkeɪʃən/ **qualifications** ◆◆◇◇◇
1 Your **qualifications** are the examinations that you have passed. *They will be encouraged to mix academic A-levels with vocational qualifications... Lucy Thomson, 16, wants to study theatre but needs more qualifications.* N-COUNT: usu pl
2 **Qualification** is the act of passing the examinations you need to work in a particular profession. *Following qualification, he worked as a social worker.* N-UNCOUNT
3 The **qualifications** you need for an activity or task are the qualities and skills that you need to be able to do it. *Responsibility and reliability are necessary qualifications, as well as a friendly and outgoing personality... That time with him is my qualification to write this book.* N-COUNT
4 A **qualification** is a detail or explanation that you add to a statement to make it less strong or less generalized. *The empirical evidence considered here is subject to many qualifications... This statement requires qualification and clarification.* N-VAR ● If something is stated or accepted **without qualification**, it is stated or accepted as it is. *The government has also conceded, almost without qualification, to most of the students' other demands.* PHRASE: PHR with cl/group =without reservation

qualified /kwɒlɪfaɪd/ ◆◆◆◇◇
1 Someone who is **qualified** has passed the examinations that they need to pass in order to work in a particular profession. *Demand has far outstripped supply of qualified teachers... The reader should seek the services of a qualified professional for such advice.* ADJ: usu ADJ n
2 If you give someone or something **qualified** support, acceptance, or approval, you give support, acceptance, or approval that is not total and suggests that you have some doubts. *The government has in the past given qualified support to the idea of tightening the legislation... Mr Wade answers both questions with a qualified yes.* ADJ: ADJ n ≠unqualified
3 If you describe something as a **qualified success**, you mean that it is only partly successful. *Even as a humanitarian mission it has been only a qualified success.* PHRASE: v-link PHR

qualifier /kwɒlɪfaɪəʳ/ **qualifiers** ◆◆◇◇◇
1 A **qualifier** is an early round or match in some competitions. The players or teams who are successful are able to continue to the next round or to the main competition. *Last week Wales lost 5-1 to Romania in a World Cup qualifier.* N-COUNT
2 In grammar, a **qualifier** is a word or group of words that comes after a noun and gives more information about the person or thing that the noun refers to. N-COUNT
3 See also **qualify.**

qualify /kwɒlɪfaɪ/ **qualifies, qualifying, qualified** ◆◆◆◇◇
1 When someone **qualifies**, they pass the examinations that they need to be able to work in a particular profession. *But when I'd qualified and started teaching it was a different story... I qualified as a doctor from London University over 30 years ago.* VERB: V, V as/in n, Also V to-inf
2 If someone **qualifies** for something or if some- V-ERG

thing **qualifies** them for it, they have the right to do it or have it. *To qualify for maternity leave you must have worked for the same employer for two years... The basic course does not qualify you to practise as a therapist... A few useful skills – English-teaching, for example – qualified foreigners for work visas. ...highly trained staff who are well qualified to give unbiased, practical advice.* V for n / V n to-inf / V n for n / V-ed / Also V, V to-inf

3 To **qualify** as something or to **be qualified** as something means to have all the features that are needed to be that thing. *13 percent of American households qualify as poor, says Mr. Mishel... These people seem to think that reading a few books on old age qualifies them as experts.* V-ERG / V as n / V n as n / Also V

4 If you **qualify** in a competition, you are successful in one part of it and go on to the next stage. *Nottingham Forest qualified for the final by beating Tranmere on Tuesday... Cameroon have also qualified after beating Sierra Leone... Canada scored an unexpected victory in a World Cup qualifying match in Buenos Aires.* ♦ **qualifier, qualifiers** *Kenya's Robert Kibe was the fastest qualifier for the 800 metres final.* VERB / V for n / V / V-ing / N-COUNT

5 If you **qualify** a statement, you make it less strong or less general by adding a detail or explanation to it. *I would qualify that by putting it into context.* VERB / V n

6 See also **qualified**.

qualitative /kwɒlɪtətɪv, AM -teɪt-/. **Qualitative** means relating to the nature or standard of something, rather than to its quantity; a formal word. *There are qualitative differences in the way children of different ages and adults think... That's the whole difference between quantitative and qualitative research.* ♦ **qualitatively** *The new media are unlikely to prove qualitatively different from the old.* ◆◇◇◇◇ ADJ: usu ADJ n / ADV: ADV adj, ADV with v

quality /kwɒlɪti/ **qualities** ◆◆◆◆◇

1 The **quality** of something is how good or bad it is. *Everyone can greatly improve the quality of life... Other services vary dramatically in quality. ...high quality paper and plywood.* N-UNCOUNT: usu with supp

2 Something of **quality** is of a high standard. *...a college of quality... As a measure of our concern for quality, we took the decision to withdraw a quantity of stock from sale... We have been successful because we are offering a quality service.* N-UNCOUNT: usu with supp, oft N n

3 Someone's **qualities** are the good characteristics that they have which are part of their nature. *Sometimes you wonder where your kids get their good qualities... He wanted to introduce mature people with leadership qualities... A job analysis should also include what skills and personal qualities are required.* N-COUNT: usu pl, usu supp N

4 You can describe a particular characteristic of a person or thing as a **quality**. *...a childlike quality. ...the pretentious quality of the poetry... Thyme tea can be used by adults for its antiseptic qualities.* N-COUNT: oft adj N

5 In Britain, the **quality papers** or the **quality press** are the more serious newspapers which give detailed accounts of world events, as well as reports on business, culture, and society. *Even the quality papers agreed that it was a triumph.* ADJ: ADJ n

quality control. In an organization that produces goods or provides services, **quality control** is the activity of checking that the goods or services are of an acceptable standard. ◆◇◇◇◇ N-UNCOUNT

qualm /kwɑːm/ **qualms.** If you have no **qualms** about doing something, you are not worried that it may be wrong in some way. *I have no qualms about recommending the same approach to other doctors... Did she see her husband as capable of murder? She had used the word without a qualm.* ◆◇◇◇◇ N-COUNT

quandary /kwɒndəri/ **quandaries.** If you are in a **quandary**, you have to make a decision but cannot decide what to do. *The government appears to be in a quandary about what to do with so many people.* N-COUNT: usu sing =dilemma

quango /kwæŋgoʊ/ **quangos.** In Britain, a **quango** is a committee appointed by the government, but which works independently. A quango has responsibility for a particular area of activity, for exampled giving government grants to arts organizations. N-COUNT

quantifiable /kwɒntɪfaɪəbᵊl/. Something that is **quantifiable** can be measured or counted in a scientific way. *A clearly quantifiable measure of quality is not necessary.* ADJ-GRADED ≠unquantifiable

quantifier /kwɒntɪfaɪəʳ/ **quantifiers.** In grammar, a **quantifier** is a word or phrase like 'plenty' or 'a lot', which allows you to refer to the quantity of something without being absolutely precise. It is often followed by 'of', as in 'a lot of money'. N-COUNT

quantify /kwɒntɪfaɪ/ **quantifies, quantifying, quantified.** If you try to **quantify** something, you try to calculate how much of it there is. *It is difficult to quantify an exact figure as firms are reluctant to declare their losses.* ♦ **quantification** /kwɒntɪfɪkeɪʃᵊn/ *Others are more susceptible to attempts at quantification.* ◆◇◇◇◇ VB: usu with brd-neg / V n / N-UNCOUNT

quantitative /kwɒntɪtətɪv, AM -teɪt-/. **Quantitative** means relating to different sizes or amounts of things; a formal word. *...the advantages of quantitative and qualitative research. ...the quantitative analysis of migration.* ♦ **quantitatively** *We cannot predict quantitatively the value or the cost of a new technology.* ◆◇◇◇◇ ADJ: usu ADJ n / ADV

quantity /kwɒntɪti/ **quantities** ◆◆◆◇◇

1 A **quantity** is an amount that you can measure or count. *...a small quantity of water. ...vast quantities of food... The bowl needs to be re-frozen after each use, so it takes a long time to make a large quantity... Cheap goods are available, but not in sufficient quantities to satisfy demand... Uranium is available in considerable quantity from various areas of the world.* N-VAR =amount

2 Things that are produced or available in **quantity** are produced or available in large amounts. *After some initial problems, acetone was successfully produced in quantity... But even with those databases, the sheer quantity of data can still cause problems.* N-UNCOUNT

3 You can use **quantity** to refer to the amount of something that there is, especially when you want to contrast it with its quality. *...the less discerning drinker who prefers quantity to quality... In terms of quantity, production grew faster than ever before.* N-UNCOUNT =amount

4 If you say that someone or something is an **unknown quantity**, you mean that not much is known about what they are like or how they will behave. *She had known Max for some years now, but he was still pretty much an unknown quantity.* PHRASE: v-link PHR

quantity surveyor, quantity surveyors. A **quantity surveyor** is a person who calculates the costs and amounts of materials and labour needed for a job such as building a house or a road; used mainly in British English. N-COUNT

quantum /kwɒntəm/ ◆◆◇◇◇

1 In physics, **quantum** theory and **quantum** mechanics are concerned with the behaviour of atomic particles. *Both quantum mechanics and chaos theory suggest a world constantly in flux.* ADJ: ADJ n

2 You can use **quantum** in the expressions **quantum leap** and **quantum jump**, which mean a very great and sudden increase in size, amount, or quality. *A vaccine which can halt this suffering represents a quantum leap in healthcare in this country... The scale of migration took a quantum leap in the early 1970s.* ADJ: ADJ n

quarantine /kwɒrəntiːn, AM kwɔːr-/ **quarantines, quarantining, quarantined** ◆◇◇◇◇

1 If a person or animal is in **quarantine**, they are being kept separate from other people or animals for a set period of time, usually because they have or may have a disease. *She was sent home to Oxford and put in quarantine... No mammals other than people may enter the country without lengthy quarantine.* N-UNCOUNT: oft *in/into* n

2 If people or animals **are quarantined**, they are stopped from having contact with other people or animals. If a place **is quarantined**, people and animals are prevented from entering or leaving it. VB: usu passive

Dogs have to be quarantined for six months before they'll let them in. be V-ed

quark /kwɑːʳk, AM kwɔːrk/ **quarks.** In physics, a **quark** is one of the basic units of matter. ◆◇◇◇◇ N-COUNT

quarrel /kwɒrəl, AM kwɔːr-/ **quarrels, quarrelling, quarrelled;** spelled **quarreling, quarreled** in American English. ◆◆◇◇◇

1 A **quarrel** is an angry argument between two or more friends or family members. *I had a terrible quarrel with my other brothers... It could have happened during a quarrel between them over Naomi.* N-COUNT

2 **Quarrels** between countries or groups of people are disagreements which may be diplomatic or include fighting; used mainly in journalism. *New Zealand's quarrel with France over the Rainbow Warrior incident was formally ended... The quarrel between the Serbs and the Croats is old and bitter.* N-COUNT

3 When two or more people **quarrel**, they have an angry argument. *At one point we quarrelled, over something silly... My brother quarrelled with my father.* V-RECIP pl-n V, V with n

4 If you say that you have no **quarrel** with someone or something, you mean that you do not disagree with them. *We have no quarrel with the people of Spain or of any other country... She had no quarrel with much of what had been said at dinner.* N-SING: with neg

5 If you say that you would **quarrel** with someone or with something that they have said, you mean that you disagree with them. *I would quarrel with you on that figure... While some of his peers might quarrel with the title, his credentials remain impressive.* VERB V with n

quarrelsome /kwɒrəlsəm, AM kwɔːr-/. A **quarrelsome** person often gets involved in arguments. *Benedict had been a wild boy and a quarrelsome young man.* ADJ-GRADED: usu ADJ n =argumentative

quarry /kwɒri, AM kwɔːri/ **quarries, quarrying, quarried** ◆◇◇◇◇

1 A **quarry** is an area that is dug out from a piece of land or mountainside in order to extract stone, slate, or minerals. *...an old limestone quarry.* N-COUNT

2 When stone or minerals **are quarried** or when an area **is quarried** for them, they are removed from a the area by digging, drilling, or using explosives. *The large limestone caves are also quarried for cement. ...locally quarried stone.* ♦ **quarrying** *Farming, quarrying and other local industries have declined.* VERB be V-ed, V-ed; N-UNCOUNT

3 A person's or animal's **quarry** is the person or animal that they are hunting. N-SING

quart /kwɔːʳt/ **quarts.** A **quart** is a unit of volume that is equal to two pints. *Pick up a quart of milk or a loaf of bread.* N-COUNT: num N, oft N of n

quarter /kwɔːʳtəʳ/ **quarters, quartering, quartered** ◆◆◆◆◇

1 A **quarter** is one of four equal parts of something. *A quarter of the residents are over 55 years old... I've got to go and collect my son in about a quarter of an hour... Prices have fallen by a quarter since January... Cut the peppers into quarters.* ► Also a predeterminer. *The largest asteroid is Ceres which is about a quarter the size of the moon.* ► Also an adjective. *...the past quarter century... He closed his door and started the quarter-mile walk down the hill.* FRACTION; PREDET; ADJ: ADJ n

2 A **quarter** is a fixed period of three months. Companies often divide their financial year into four quarters. *The group said results for the third quarter are due on October 29.* N-COUNT: usu sing

3 When you are telling the time, you use **quarter** to talk about the fifteen minutes before or after the hour. For example, 8.15 is **quarter past** eight, and 8.45 is **quarter to** nine. In American English you can also say that 8.15 is a **quarter after** eight and 8.45 is a **quarter of** nine. *It was a quarter to six... See you about quarter to nine... I got a call at quarter of seven one night... Nobody else turned up till a quarter past ten... The time was recorded at a quarter after five.* N-UNCOUNT: also a N

4 If you **quarter** something such as a fruit or a vegetable, you cut it into four roughly equal parts. *Chop the mushrooms and quarter the tomatoes.* VERB V n

5 If the number or size of something **is quartered**, it is reduced to about 25 per cent of its previous number or size. *The doses I suggested for adults could be halved or quartered.* VB: usu passive be V-ed

6 A **quarter** is an American or Canadian coin that is worth 25 cents. *I dropped a quarter into the slot of the pay phone.* N-COUNT

7 A particular **quarter** of a town is a part of the town where a particular group of people traditionally live or work. *We wandered through the Chinese quarter.* N-COUNT: supp N

8 To refer to a person or group you may not want to name, you can talk about the reactions or actions from a particular **quarter**. *Help came from an unexpected quarter... There are fears in some quarters that the republic would have little chance of surviving on its own.* N-COUNT: usu supp N

9 The rooms provided for soldiers, sailors, or servants to live in are called their **quarters**. *Mckinnon went down from deck to the officers' quarters.* N-PLURAL: poss N

10 If people **are quartered** somewhere, they are provided with accommodation for a short time, usually while they are working away from home. *Our soldiers are quartered in Peredelkino.* VB: usu passive be V-ed prep/adv

11 If you do something **at close quarters**, you do it from a place that is very near to someone or something. *You can watch aircraft take off or land at close quarters.* PHRASES PHR after v, v-link PHR

12 If you say that someone was given **no quarter**, you mean that they were not shown any mercy or forgiveness by someone who has power or control over them. *This is not war as you learned it. It is brutal work, with no quarter given.* PHR with v

quarter-final, quarter-finals; spelled **quarterfinal** in American English. A **quarter-final** is one of the four matches in a competition which decides which four players or teams will compete in the semi-final. *The very least I'm looking for at Wimbledon is to reach the quarter-finals.* ◆◆◇◇◇ N-COUNT

quarterly /kwɔːʳtəʳli/ **quarterlies** ◆◆◇◇◇

1 A **quarterly** event happens four times a year, at intervals of three months. *...the latest Bank of Japan quarterly survey of 5,000 companies.* ► Also an adverb. *It makes no difference whether dividends are paid quarterly or annually.* ADJ; ADV: ADV after v

2 A **quarterly** is a magazine or journal that is published four times a year, at intervals of three months. *The quarterly had been a forum for sound academic debate. ...'Foreign Policy', a quarterly journal published in Paris.* N-COUNT: oft N n

quartet /kwɔːʳtet/ **quartets** ◆◆◇◇◇

1 A **quartet** is a group of four people who play musical instruments or sing together. *...a string quartet. ...a quartet of singers.* N-COUNT-COLL

2 A **quartet** is a piece of music for four instruments or four singers. N-COUNT

3 A **quartet** of people or things is a group or set of four people or things; used in written English. *...a quartet of books. ...a quartet of local women in their mid-forties.* N-COUNT: usu N of n

quartz /kwɔːʳts/. **Quartz** is a mineral in the form of a hard, shiny crystal. It is used in making electronic equipment and very accurate watches and clocks. *...a quartz crystal.* N-UNCOUNT: oft N n

quasar /kweɪzɑːʳ/ **quasars.** A **quasar** is a galaxy that has a very bright centre and is often a very strong source of radio waves; a technical term in astronomy. ◆◇◇◇◇ N-COUNT

quash /kwɒʃ/ **quashes, quashing, quashed** ◆◇◇◇◇

1 If a court or someone in authority **quashes** a decision or conviction, they officially reject it and make it no longer legally valid. *The Appeal Court has quashed the convictions of all eleven people.* VERB =overturn V n

2 If someone **quashes** rumours, they say or do something to demonstrate that the rumours are not true. *Graham attempted to quash rumours of growing discontent in the dressing room.* VERB V n

3 To **quash** rebellion or protest is to stop it, often in a violent way. *Troops were displaying an obvious reluctance to get involved in quashing demonstrations.* VERB =put down V n

quasi- /kweɪzaɪ-/. **Quasi-** is used to form adjectives and nouns that describe something as being in many ways like something else, without actually being that thing. *The flame is a quasi-religious emblem of immortality. ...a few key quasi-governmental institutions.* COMB in ADJ

quaver /kweɪvəʳ/ **quavers, quavering, quavered** ◆◇◇◇◇
1 If someone's voice **quavers**, it sounds unsteady, usually because they are nervous or uncertain. *Her voice quavered and she fell silent.* ► Also a noun. *There was a quaver in Beryl's voice.* VERB =tremble V; N-COUNT
2 In music, a **quaver** is a musical note that has half the time value of a crotchet; used mainly in British English. N-COUNT

quay /kiː/ **quays.** A **quay** is a long platform beside the sea or a river where boats can be tied up and loaded or unloaded. *Jack and Stephen were waiting for them on the quay.* ◆◇◇◇◇ N-COUNT

quayside /kiːsaɪd/ **quaysides.** A **quayside** is the same as a **quay**. *A large group had gathered on the quayside to see them off. ...an old quayside warehouse.* N-COUNT: oft N n

queasy /kwiːzi/ **queasier, queasiest**
1 If you feel **queasy** or if you have a **queasy** stomach, you feel rather ill, as if you are going to be sick; an informal use. *He was very prone to seasickness and already felt queasy.* ♦ **queasiness** *The food did nothing to stifle her queasiness.* ADJ-GRADED; N-UNCOUNT
2 If you feel **queasy** about something, you are a little worried about it; an informal use. *Some people feel queasy about how their names and addresses have been obtained.* ♦ **queasiness** *Despite their queasiness, if war comes, most MPs will back our lads.* ADJ-GRADED: usu v-link ADJ =uneasy; N-UNCOUNT =unease

queen /kwiːn/ **queens** ◆◆◆◆◇
1 A **queen** is a woman who rules a country as its monarch. *...Queen Victoria. ...the time she met the Queen.* N-TITLE; N-COUNT: oft *the* N
2 A **queen** is a woman who is married to a king. *The king and queen had fled.* N-TITLE; N-COUNT: oft *the* N
3 If you refer to a woman as the **queen** of a particular activity, you are referring to the fact that she is well-known for being very good at it. *...the queen of crime writing.* • See also **beauty queen.** N-COUNT: with supp, N *of* n, n N
4 A **queen** is a male homosexual who dresses and speaks rather like a woman; an informal use. N-COUNT
5 In chess, the **queen** is the most powerful piece. It can be moved in any direction. N-COUNT
6 A **queen** is a playing card with a picture of a queen on it. *...the queen of spades.* N-COUNT: oft *the* N *of* n
7 A **queen** or a **queen bee** is a large female bee which can lay eggs. N-COUNT

queenly /kwiːnli/. You use **queenly** to describe a woman's appearance or behaviour if she looks or behaves as if she is very important, refined, and wealthy. *She was a queenly, organizing type.* ADJ: usu ADJ n =regal

Queen Mother. **The Queen Mother** is the mother of a ruling king or queen. ◆◇◇◇◇ N-PROPER: *the* N

queer /kwɪəʳ/ **queerer, queerest; queers** ◆◇◇◇◇
1 Something that is **queer** is strange; an old-fashioned use. *If you ask me, there's something a bit queer going on.* ADJ-GRADED
2 People sometimes call homosexual men **queers**; an informal use which some people find offensive. N-COUNT
3 A man who is **queer** is homosexual; an informal use which some people find offensive. ADJ: usu v-link ADJ
4 **Queer** means relating to homosexual people; used by some homosexuals. *...contemporary queer culture. ...queer activism.* ADJ: ADJ n =gay

quell /kwel/ **quells, quelling, quelled** ◆◇◇◇◇
1 To **quell** opposition or violent behaviour means to put an end to it using persuasion or force. *Troops eventually quelled the unrest.* VERB V n
2 If you **quell** unpleasant feelings such as fear or grief, you stop yourself or other people having these feelings. *The Information Minister is trying to quell fears of a looming oil crisis.* VERB V n

quench /kwentʃ/ **quenches, quenching, quenched.** When you are thirsty, you can **quench** your thirst by having a drink. *He stopped to quench his thirst at a stream.* VERB V n

querulous /kwerʊləs/. Someone who is **querulous** often complains about things; a formal word used showing disapproval. *A querulous male voice said, 'Look, are you going to order, or what?'* ADJ-GRADED PRAGMATICS

query /kwɪəri/ **queries, querying, queried** ◆◆◇◇◇
1 A **query** is a question, especially one that you ask an organization, publication, or expert. *If you have any queries about this insurance, please contact Travel Insurance Services Limited.* N-COUNT: oft N *about* n =question
2 If you **query** something, you check it by asking about it because you are not sure if it is correct. *It's got a number you can ring to query your bill... No one queried my decision.* VERB =question V n
3 To **query** means to ask a question. *'Is there something else?' Ryle queried as Helen stopped speaking... One of the journalists queried whether sabotage could have been involved.* VERB V with quote V wh Also V n

quest /kwest/ **quests.** A **quest** is a long and difficult search for something. *My quest for a better bank continues. ...his quest to find true love... Waite spent his life on a spiritual quest.* • If you go **in quest of** something, you try to find or obtain it. *He went on to say that he was going to New York in quest of peace... The Puritans became fugitives in quest of liberty.* ◆◆◇◇◇ N-COUNT: oft N *for* n, N to-inf =search; PHRASE: PHR after v, v-link PHR, PHR n

questing /kwestɪŋ/. If you **are questing** for something, you are searching for it; a literary word. *The knights searching for the Holy Grail were questing for vision and wisdom. ...his questing mind and boundless enthusiasm.* VB: only cont V *for* n V-ing

question /kwestʃᵊn/ **questions, questioning, questioned** ◆◆◆◆◆
1 A **question** is something which you say or write in order to ask someone about something. *They asked a great many questions about England... The President refused to answer further questions on the subject... Right, next question... 'Do you feel that the British gamble more than they should?'—'Well, that's a very difficult question to answer.'* N-COUNT: oft N *about/on* n
2 If you **question** someone, you ask them a lot of questions about something. *This led the therapist to question Jim about his parents and their marriage... A man is being questioned by police in connection with an attack on a disabled woman.* ♦ **questioning** *The police have detained thirty-two people for questioning.* VERB V n; N-UNCOUNT
3 If you **question** something, you have or express doubts about whether it is true, reasonable, or worthwhile. *It never occurs to them to question the doctor's decisions... Weber is challenging his audience to question their own beliefs.* VERB V n
4 If you say that there is some **question** about something, you mean that there is doubt or uncertainty about it. If something is **in question** or has been called **into question**, doubt or uncertainty has been expressed about it. *There's no question about their success... There's some question as to whether he will sign this resolution... As a footballer, Le Saux's ability was beyond question... The paper says the President's move has called into question the whole basis of democracy in the country... Why Marlowe was killed may be open to question, but where he is buried is not... With the loyalty of key military units in question, that could prove an extraordinarily difficult task.* N-SING: with supp, also prep N
5 A **question** is a problem, matter, or point which needs to be considered. *But the whole question of aid is a tricky political one... The unrest raised questions about the timing of the pullout from Somalia... The question is: Is this what we really want? ...if the security question is not resolved... It was just a question of having the time to re-adjust.* N-COUNT: oft N *of* n/wh
6 The **questions** in an examination are the problems which are set in order to test your knowledge or ability. *He'd heard somewhere that the questions in economics examination papers stayed the same from year to year... That question did come up in the examination.* N-COUNT
7 See also **questioning; cross-question, leading question, trick question.**
8 If you say **'Good question'** in reply to a question, PHRASES

you mean that it is a difficult one to answer, or perhaps that you are embarrassed about the answer or do not know the answer. *'Why didn't you appoint Ron twelve months ago?'—'Good question.'* CONVENTION PRAGMATICS

9 The person, thing, or time **in question** is one which you have just been talking about or which is relevant. *The player in question is Mark Williams... Add up all the income you've received over the period in question.* n PHR =concerned

10 If you say that something is **out of the question**, you are emphasizing that it is completely impossible or unacceptable. *For the homeless, private medical care is simply out of the question... Is a tax increase still out of the question?* v-link PHR PRAGMATICS

11 If you **pop the question**, you ask someone to marry you; an informal expression used mainly in journalism. *Stuart got serious quickly and popped the question six months later.* V inflects =propose

12 If you say **there is no question of** something happening, you are emphasizing that it is not going to happen. *As far as he was concerned there was no question of betraying his own comrades... There is no question of the tax-payer picking up the bill for the party.* V inflects, PHR -ing, PHR n -ing PRAGMATICS

13 If you do something **without question**, you do it without arguing or asking why it is necessary. *...military formations, carrying out without question the battle orders of superior officers.* PHR after v

14 You use **without question** to emphasize the opinion you are expressing. *He was our greatest storyteller, without question.* PHR with cl PRAGMATICS

questionable /kwestʃənəbᵊl/. If you say that something is **questionable**, you do not consider it to be completely honest, reasonable, or acceptable; a formal word. *He has been dogged by allegations of questionable business practices... It is questionable whether the expenditure on this project is really justified... The film is a comedy in highly questionable taste.* ◆◇◇◇◇ ADJ-GRADED: oft *it* v-link ADJ wh =dubious

questioner /kwestʃənər/ **questioners.** A **questioner** is a person who is asking a question. *He agreed with the questioner that the debts now to be forgiven are only a drop in the ocean.* ◆◇◇◇◇ N-COUNT

questioning /kwestʃənɪŋ/. If someone has a **questioning** expression on their face, they look as if they want to know the answer to a question; used in written English. *He raised a questioning eyebrow.* • See also **question.** ♦ **questioningly** *Brenda looked questioningly at Daniel.* ADJ: ADJ n; ADV: ADV with v

question mark, question marks ◆◇◇◇◇

1 A **question mark** is the punctuation mark (?) which is used in writing at the end of a question. N-COUNT

2 If there is doubt or uncertainty about something, you can say that there is a **question mark** over it. *There are bound to be question marks over his future... There's now a huge question mark hanging over the success of the negotiations.* N-COUNT: oft N *over* n

questionnaire /kwestʃəneəʳ, kes-/ **questionnaires.** A **questionnaire** is a written list of questions which are answered by a lot of people in order to provide information for a report or a survey. *Headteachers will be asked to fill in a questionnaire.* ◆◇◇◇◇ N-COUNT

question tag, question tags. A **question tag** is a very short clause at the end of a statement which changes the statement into a question. For example, in 'She said half price, didn't she?', the words 'didn't she' are a question tag. N-COUNT

queue /kjuː/ **queues, queuing, queued; queueing** can also be used as the continuous form. ◆◆◇◇◇

1 A **queue** is a line of people or vehicles that are waiting for something; used mainly in British English. *I watched as he got a tray and joined the queue... She pondered on this as she waited in the bus queue... There was still a queue for tickets on the night... Behind him was a long queue of angry motorists.* N-COUNT: oft N *for* n, N *of* n

2 If you say there is a **queue** of people who want to do or have something, you mean that a lot of people are waiting for an opportunity to do it or have it; used mainly in British English. *Manchester United would be at the front of a queue of potential buyers... Single parents got priority in the housing queue... The queue for places at the school has never been longer.* N-COUNT: usu sing, oft N *of* n

3 When people **queue**, they stand in a line waiting for something; used mainly in British English. *I had to queue for quite a while. ...a line of women queueing for bread.* ► **Queue up** means the same as **queue.** *A mob of journalists are queuing up at the gate to photograph him... We all had to queue up for our ration books.* VERB V V *for* n; PHRASAL VERB V P V P *for* n

queue up. If you say that people **are queuing up** to do or have something, you mean that a lot of them want the opportunity to do it or have it; used mainly in British English. *People are queueing up to work for me!... There are a growing number of countries queueing up for membership.* • See also **queue** 3. PHRASAL VERB usu cont V P to-inf V P *for* n

queue-jumping. In British English, **queue-jumping** is getting to the front of a queue unfairly; used showing disapproval. *...queue-jumping within the National Health Service.* N-UNCOUNT PRAGMATICS

quibble /kwɪbᵊl/ **quibbles, quibbling, quibbled**

1 When people **quibble** over a small matter, they argue about it even though it is not important. *Council members spent the day quibbling over the final wording of the resolution... Let's not quibble.* VERB V *over/about/with* n V

2 A **quibble** is a small and unimportant objection to something. *These are minor quibbles.* N-COUNT

quiche /kiːʃ/ **quiches.** A **quiche** is a tart filled with a savoury mixture of eggs, cheese, and other foods or flavourings. N-VAR

quick /kwɪk/ **quicker, quickest** ◆◆◆◆◆

1 Someone or something that is **quick** moves or does things with great speed. *You'll have to be quick. The flight leaves in about three hours... I think I'm a reasonably quick learner... Europe has moved a long way since then at a very quick pace.* ♦ **quickly** *Cussane worked quickly and methodically... Stop me if I'm speaking too quickly.* ♦ **quickness** *...the natural quickness of his mind.* ADJ-GRADED ≠slow; ADV-GRADED: ADV with v ≠slowly; N-UNCOUNT

2 In informal English, **quicker** is used to mean 'at a greater speed' and **quickest** is used to mean 'at the greatest speed'. In non-standard English, **quick** is used to mean 'with great speed'. *Warm the sugar slightly first to make it dissolve quicker... Prost went quickest.* ADV-GRADED: ADV after v

3 Something that is **quick** takes or lasts only a short time. *He took one last quick look about the room... I just popped in for a quick drink... Although this recipe looks long, it is actually very quick to prepare... My father would have driven me to Cornwall, but we decided it would be quicker by train.* ♦ **quickly** *You can become fitter quite quickly and easily.* ADJ-GRADED; ADV-GRADED: ADV with v

4 **Quick** means happening without delay or with very little delay. *Officials played down any hope for a quick end to the bloodshed... These investors feel the need to make quick profits.* ♦ **quickly** *We need to get it back as quickly as possible... It quickly became the most popular men's fragrance in the world... 'Not me,' Robarts said quickly.* ADJ-GRADED: usu ADJ n =speedy; ADV-GRADED: ADV with v

5 In informal English, **quick** is sometimes used to mean 'with very little delay'. *I got away as quick as I could... Quick! John! It's Carmela. I think she's taken an overdose... The advantage in going faster is that you get there quicker.* ADV-GRADED: ADV after v

6 If you are **quick** to do something, you do not hesitate to do it. *Mark says the ideas are Katie's own, and is quick to praise her talent... Furthermore, as Gervaise was quick to point out, Mr Scully was not a detective.* ADJ-GRADED: v-link ADJ, usu ADJ to-inf

7 If someone has a **quick** temper, they are easily made angry. ADJ-GRADED: ADJ n

8 If someone **bites** their nails **to the quick**, they bite off so much of their fingernails that the flesh underneath them is exposed. *Her fingernails are bitten to the quick.* PHRASES V inflects

9 If something **cuts** you **to the quick**, it makes you feel very upset; a literary expression. *I once heard her weeping in her bedroom, which cut me to the quick.* V inflects

10 • **quick as a flash**: see **flash**. • **quick off the mark**: see **mark**. • **quick on the uptake**: see **uptake**.

quick- /kwɪk-/. **quick-** is added to words, especially present participles, to form adjectives which indicate that someone or something does something quickly. *Quick-thinking young Alice shut the cupboard, which prevented the fire from spreading. ...quick-drying paint.* COMB in ADJ-GRADED

quicken /kwɪkən/ **quickens, quickening, quickened.** ◆◇◇◇◇ If something **quickens** or if you **quicken** it, it becomes faster or moves at a greater speed. *Ainslie's pulse quickened in alarm... He quickened his pace a little.* V-ERG ≠slow V; V n

quickfire /kwɪkfaɪəʳ/; also spelled **quick-fire**. **Quickfire** speech or action is very fast with no pauses in it. *...that talent for quickfire response.* ADJ: ADJ n

quick fix, quick fixes. If you use **quick fix** to refer to an attempt to deal with a problem, you disapprove of it because, although it seems an easy solution, it is only temporary or inadequate. *Any tax measures enacted now as a quick fix would only be reversed in a few years when the economy picks up.* N-COUNT: oft with neg PRAGMATICS

quickie /kwɪki/ **quickies.** In informal English, you can refer to something as a **quickie** if it only takes a very short time. For example, sex that happens suddenly without being planned, and only takes a short time, is often called a **quickie**. *...a quickie divorce.* N-COUNT: oft N n

quicksand /kwɪksænd/ **quicksands**

1 **Quicksand** is deep, wet sand that you sink into if you try to walk on it. N-UNCOUNT: also N in pl

2 You can refer to a situation as **quicksand** when you want to suggest that it is dangerous or difficult to escape from, or does not provide a strong basis for what you are doing. *I was about to sink into the quicksand of sin... The research seemed founded on quicksand.* N-UNCOUNT, also N in pl

quicksilver /kwɪksɪlvəʳ/

1 **Quicksilver** is the same as **mercury**; an old-fashioned use. N-UNCOUNT

2 **Quicksilver** movements or changes are very fast and unpredictable. *...her quicksilver changes of mood.* ADJ: ADJ n

quick-tempered. Someone who is **quick-tempered** often gets angry without having a good reason. ADJ-GRADED

quick-witted. Someone who is **quick-witted** is intelligent and good at thinking quickly. ADJ-GRADED

quid /kwɪd/; **quid** is both the singular and the plural form. In informal British English, a **quid** is a pound in money. *It cost him five hundred quid.* ◆◇◇◇◇ N-COUNT

quid pro quo, quid pro quos. A **quid pro quo** is a gift or advantage that is given to someone in return for something that they have done; a formal expression. *The statement is emphatic in stating that there must be a quid pro quo... They share a great deal of information on a quid pro quo basis.* N-COUNT

quids /kwɪdz/. If you **are quids in**, you have more money left than you expected or get more for your money than you expected; used in informal British English. *Still, we were quids in, we didn't care!* PHRASE: V inflects

quiescent /kwiesᵊnt, AM kwaɪ-/. Someone or something that is **quiescent** is quiet and inactive; a literary word. *...a society which was politically quiescent and above all deferential. ...a quiescent Southern seaside town.* ♦ **quiescence** *...a long period of quiescence.* ADJ-GRADED; N-UNCOUNT

quiet /kwaɪət/ **quieter, quietest; quiets, quieting, quieted** ◆◆◆◆◇

1 Someone or something that is **quiet** makes only a small amount of noise. *Tania kept the children reasonably quiet and contented... A quiet murmur passed through the classroom... The airlines have invested enormous sums in new, quieter aircraft.* ♦ **quietly** *'This is goodbye, isn't it?' she said quietly... He closed the door quietly.* ♦ **quietness** *...the smoothness and quietness of the flight.* ADJ-GRADED ≠noisy; ADV-GRADED: ADV with v; N-UNCOUNT

2 If a place is **quiet**, there is very little noise there. *She was received in a small, quiet office... The street was unnaturally quiet.* ♦ **quietness** *I miss the quietness of the countryside.* ADJ-GRADED ≠noisy; N-UNCOUNT

3 If a place, situation, or time is **quiet**, there is no excitement, activity, disturbance, or trouble. *...a quiet rural backwater... It is very quiet without him... While he wanted Los Angeles and partying, she wanted a quiet life... The Bosnian capital is reported relatively quiet this morning.* ♦ **quietly** *His most prized time, though, will be spent quietly on his farm in Karklaaf, Durban.* ♦ **quietness** *I do very much appreciate the quietness and privacy here.* ADJ-GRADED; ADV-GRADED: ADV with v; N-UNCOUNT

4 **Quiet** is silence. *He called for quiet and announced that the next song was in our honor... Jeremy wants some peace and quiet before his big match.* N-UNCOUNT

5 If you are **quiet**, you are not saying anything. *I told them to be quiet and go to sleep... I just went quiet, embarrassed, and couldn't answer... They were both quiet for a while. Then Charlie said: 'I must go.'... Then a voice called out, 'Quiet, everybody, please!'* ♦ **quietly** *Amy stood quietly in the doorway watching him.* ADJ-GRADED: v-link ADJ =silent; ADV: ADV with v

6 If you refer, for example, to someone's **quiet** confidence or **quiet** despair, you mean that they do not say much about the way they are feeling. *The three candidates are going out of their way to present a picture of quiet confidence... All through his life he has shown a quiet determination to get things done.* ♦ **quietly** *Nigel Deering, the publisher, is quietly confident about the magazine's chances.* ADJ: ADJ n; ADV: ADV adj

7 You describe activities as **quiet** when they happen in secret or in such a way that people do not notice. *The Swedes had sought his freedom through quiet diplomacy... Then it was back to the house for a quiet celebration... Can I have a quiet word with you, son?* ♦ **quietly** *I slipped away quietly... The goal of shifting freight from road to rail has been quietly abandoned... Lee's body was flown to the US, where he was quietly buried in Seattle.* ADJ: ADJ n =discreet; ADV: usu ADV with v, also ADV adj

8 A **quiet** person behaves in a calm way and is not easily made angry or upset. *He's a nice quiet man.* ADJ-GRADED =placid

9 You describe colours or clothes as **quiet** when they are not bright or not very noticeable. *They dress in quiet colors so as not to call attention to themselves.* ADJ-GRADED =muted

10 In American English, if someone or something **quiets** or if you **quiet** them, they become less noisy, less active, or silent. The British word is **quieten**. *The wind dropped and the sea quieted... Estela started to say something but a gesture from her husband quieted her at once.* V-ERG V; V n

11 In American English, to **quiet** fears or complaints means to say or show that they are unjustified. The British word is **quieten**. *Supporters of the Constitution had to quiet fears that aristocrats plotted to steal the fruits of the Revolution.* VERB V n

12 If someone does not **go quietly**, they do not voluntarily leave a job or a place without complaining or resisting. *She's not going to go quietly.* PHRASES V inflects

13 If you **keep quiet about** something or **keep** something **quiet**, you do not say anything about it. *I told her to keep quiet about it... I think I found it easier than Nell to keep our engagement quiet.* V inflects

14 If something is done **on the quiet**, it is done secretly or in such a way that people do not notice. *She'd promised to give him driving lessons, on the quiet, when no one could see.* PHR after v =secretly

quiet down. In American English, if someone or something **quiets down** or if you **quiet** them **down**, they become less noisy or less active. The British term is **quieten down**. *Once the vote was taken, things quieted down quickly... Try gradually to quiet them down as bedtime approaches.* PHRASAL VERB ERG V P; V n P

quieten /kwaɪətᵊn/ **quietens, quietening, quietened**

1 If you **quieten** someone or something, or if they **quieten**, you make them become less noisy, less active, or silent; used mainly in British English. The usual American word is **quiet**. *She tried to quieten* V-ERG V n

her breathing... A man shouted and the dogs suddenly quietened. V

2 To **quieten** fears or complaints means to say or show that they are unjustified; used mainly in British English. The usual American word is **quiet**. *Soviet intelligence will take a long time to quieten the paranoia of the West.* VERB V n

quieten down. If someone or something **quietens down** or if you **quieten** them **down**, they become less noisy or less active; used mainly in British English. The usual American term is **quiet down**. *The labour unrest which swept the country last week has quietened down... Somehow I managed to quieten her down... Tom's words before the match might also have quietened down our own supporters.* PHRASAL VERB ERG =calm down V P V n P V P n (not pron)

quietude /kwaɪətjuːd, AM -tuːd/. **Quietude** is quietness and calm; a formal word. N-UNCOUNT =tranquillity

quiff /kwɪf/ **quiffs.** If a man has a **quiff**, he has his hair swept upwards and backwards from his forehead; used mainly in British English. *I attempted a classic rock and roll quiff.* N-COUNT

quill /kwɪl/ **quills**

1 A **quill** is a pen made from a bird's feather. *She dipped a quill in ink, then began to write.* N-COUNT

2 A bird's **quills** are large, stiff feathers on its wings and tail. N-COUNT

3 The **quills** of a porcupine are the stiff, sharp points on its body. N-COUNT

quilt /kwɪlt/ **quilts** ◆◇◇◇◇

1 A **quilt** is a thin cover filled with feathers or some other warm, soft material, which you put over your blankets when you are in bed. *...an old patchwork quilt.* N-COUNT

2 In Britain, a **quilt** is the same as a **duvet**. N-COUNT

quilted /kwɪltɪd/. Something that is **quilted** consists of two layers of fabric with a layer of thick material between them, often decorated with lines of stitching which form a pattern. *...a quilted bedspread.* ADJ

quince /kwɪns/ **quinces.** A **quince** is a hard yellow fruit that looks like a large pear. Quinces are used for making jelly or marmalade. N-VAR

quinine /kwɪniːn, AM kwaɪnaɪn/. **Quinine** is a drug that is used to treat fevers such as malaria. N-UNCOUNT

quintessence /kwɪntesᵊns/

1 The **quintessence** of something is the most perfect or typical example of it; a formal use. *He was the quintessence of all that Eva most deeply loathed.* N-UNCOUNT: with supp, usu *the* N *of* n

2 The **quintessence** of something is the aspect of it which seems to represent its central nature; a formal use. *According to this tradition, religious institutions represented the quintessence of civilized culture.* N-UNCOUNT: with supp, usu *the* N *of* n

quintessential /kwɪntɪsenʃᵊl/ ◆◇◇◇◇

1 **Quintessential** means representing a perfect or typical example of something; a formal use. *This was quintessential Midwestern farming country... Everybody thinks of him as the quintessential New Yorker.* ♦ **quintessentially** *It is a familiar, and quintessentially British, ritual.* ADJ-GRADED: usu ADJ n; ADV-GRADED: ADV adj

2 **Quintessential** means representing the central nature of something; a formal use. *...the quintessential charm of his songs.* ADJ: usu ADJ n

quintet /kwɪntet/ **quintets**

1 A **quintet** is a group of five singers or musicians singing or playing together. N-COUNT

2 A **quintet** is a piece of music written for five instruments or five singers. N-COUNT

quip /kwɪp/ **quips, quipping, quipped** ◆◇◇◇◇

1 A **quip** is a remark that is intended be amusing or clever; used in written English. *The commentators make endless quips about the female players' appearance.* N-COUNT

2 To **quip** means to say something that is intended to be amusing or clever; used in written English. *'He'll have to go on a diet,' Ballard quipped... The chairman of American Airlines quipped that he would rather sell his airline than his computer systems.* VERB V with quote V that

quirk /kwɜːʳk/ **quirks** ◆◇◇◇◇

1 A **quirk** is a strange accidental occurrence that is difficult to explain. *By a tantalising quirk of fate, the pair have been drawn to meet in the first round of the championship... The spate of storms and hurricanes in recent years could be a statistical quirk.* N-COUNT: usu with supp, N *of* n, adj N =fluke

2 A **quirk** is a habit or aspect of a person's character which is odd or unusual. *Brown was always fascinated by the quirks and foibles of people in everyday situations.* N-COUNT

quirky /kwɜːʳki/ **quirkier, quirkiest.** Something or someone that is **quirky** is rather odd or unpredictable in their appearance, character, or behaviour. *The judges liked her quirky and original style.* ♦ **quirkiness** *You will probably notice an element of quirkiness in his behaviour.* ◆◇◇◇◇ ADJ-GRADED; N-UNCOUNT

quisling /kwɪzlɪŋ/ **quislings.** A **quisling** is a traitor who helps the enemy army that has invaded his or her own country; an old-fashioned word. N-COUNT

quit /kwɪt/ **quits, quitting.** The form **quit** is used in the present tense and is the past tense and past participle. ◆◆◇◇◇

1 If you **quit** your job, you resign from it; an informal use. *He quit his job as an office boy in Athens... He figured he would quit before Johnson fired him.* VERB V n V

2 If you **quit** an activity or **quit** doing something, you stop doing it; used mainly in American English. *A nicotine spray can help smokers quit the habit without putting on weight... I was trying to quit smoking at the time.* VERB =give up V n/-ing

3 If you **quit** a place, you leave it completely and do not go back to it. *Science fiction writers have long dreamt that humans might one day quit the earth to colonise other planets... Police were called when he refused to quit the building.* VERB V n

4 If you say that you are going to **call it quits**, you mean that you have decided to stop doing something or being involved in something. *They raised $630,000 through listener donations, and then called it quits... You can decide whether there is hope in working for mutual happiness, or if you should call it quits.* PHRASE: V inflects

quite /kwaɪt/ ◆◆◆◆◆

1 You use **quite** to indicate that something is the case to a fairly great extent. **Quite** is less emphatic than 'very' and 'extremely'. *I felt quite bitter about it at the time... I was doing quite well, but I wasn't earning a lot of money... Well, actually it requires quite a bit of work and research... I was quite a long way away, on the terrace... I quite enjoy living here.* ADV: ADV adj/adv, ADV a n, ADV before v PRAGMATICS

2 You use **quite** to indicate certainty or to emphasize that something is definitely the case. *It is quite clear that we were firing in self defence... That's a general British failing. In the USA it's quite different... I can state quite definitely it will be terrible... This was a serious breach of trust quite apart from the gravity of any offence... It's difficult to know quite how much to tell them... I quite agree with you. That's a good way of looking at it.* ADV: ADV group, ADV before v PRAGMATICS

3 You use **quite** after a negative to weaken the force of your statement. *Something here is not quite right... It is still good after that, but not quite the same... We still can't quite believe he's here with us after all this time... And at the beginning, I didn't quite understand what all this was about... I can't quite decide which is best.* ADV: with brd-neg, ADV group, ADV before v PRAGMATICS =exactly

4 You use **quite** in front of a noun group to emphasize that a person or thing is very impressive or unusual. *'Oh, he's quite a character,' Sean replied... It's quite a city, Boston.* PREDET: PREDET *a* n PRAGMATICS

5 You can say **'quite'** to express your agreement with someone; used in formal or old-fashioned spoken English. *'And if you buy the record it's your choice isn't it.'—'Quite'... 'I won't say over the air who it is.'—'No, quite.'* ADV: ADV as reply PRAGMATICS

quitter /kwɪtəʳ/ **quitters.** If you say that someone is not a **quitter**, you mean that they continue doing something even though it is very difficult. *He won't resign because he's not a quitter.* N-COUNT: usu with brd-neg

quiver /kwɪvəʳ/ **quivers, quivering, quivered** ◆◇◇◇◇

1 If something **quivers**, it shakes with very small movements. *Her bottom lip quivered and big tears rolled down her cheeks.* VERB =tremble V

2 If you say that someone **is quivering** with an VERB

emotion such as rage or happiness, you mean that their appearance or voice clearly shows this emotion. *Cooper arrived, quivering with rage... Mack made his voice quiver with fear on these last two words.* ► Also a noun. *I recognized it instantly and felt a quiver of panic.* — V with n; N-COUNT: usu N *of* n

3 A **quiver** is a container for carrying arrows in. — N-COUNT

quixotic /kwɪksɒtɪk/. If you describe someone's ideas or plans as **quixotic**, you mean that they are imaginative or hopeful but unrealistic; a formal word. *He has always lived his life by a hopelessly quixotic code of honour.* — ADJ-GRADED

quiz /kwɪz/ **quizzes, quizzing, quizzed** ◆◇◇◇◇

1 A **quiz** is a game or competition in which someone tests your knowledge by asking you questions. *We'll have a quiz at the end of the show.* — N-COUNT

2 If you **are quizzed** by someone about something, they ask you questions because they want to get information from you. *He was quizzed about his income, debts and eligibility for state benefits... Sybil quizzed her about life as a working girl.* — VERB; be V-ed about n; V n about n

quizmaster /kwɪzmɑːstəʳ, -mæs-/ **quizmasters.** In British English, a **quizmaster** is the person who asks the questions in a game or quiz on the television or radio. — N-COUNT

quizzical /kwɪzɪkəl/. If you give someone a **quizzical** look or smile, you look at them in a way that shows that you are surprised or amused by their behaviour. *He gave Robin a mildly quizzical glance.* ♦ **quizzically** *She looked at him quizzically.* — ADJ-GRADED: usu ADJ n; ADV-GRADED: ADV after v

quo /kwoʊ/. See **quid pro quo, status quo.**

quoit /kɔɪt, AM kwɔɪt/ **quoits**

1 **Quoits** is a game which is played by throwing rings over a small post. Quoits is usually played on board ships. — N-UNCOUNT

2 A **quoit** is a ring used in the game of quoits. — N-COUNT

Quonset hut /kwɒnsɪt hʌt/ **Quonset huts.** In American English, a **Quonset hut** is a military hut made of metal. The walls and roof form the shape of a semi-circle. **Quonset hut** is a trademark. The British term is **Nissen hut.** — N-COUNT

quorate /kwɔːreɪt/. When a committee is **quorate**, there are enough people present for it to conduct official business and make decisions; used mainly in British English. *Saturday's session was still technically quorate.* — ADJ: v-link ADJ

quorum /kwɔːrəm/. A **quorum** is the minimum number of people that a committee needs in order to carry out its business officially. When a meeting has a quorum, there are at least that number of people present. *It's not certain enough deputies will show up to make a quorum.* — N-SING

quota /kwoʊtə/ **quotas** ◆◆◇◇◇

1 A **quota** is the limited number or quantity of something which is officially allowed. *The quota of four tickets per person had been reduced to two.* — N-COUNT: oft N *of* n

2 A **quota** is a fixed maximum or minimum proportion of people from a particular group who are permitted to do something, such as come and live in a country or work for the government. *The bill would force employers to adopt a quota system when recruiting workers.* — N-COUNT: oft N *of* n, N n

3 Someone's **quota** of something is their expected or deserved share of it. *They have the usual quota of human weaknesses, no doubt.* — N-COUNT: oft N *of* n =share

quotable /kwoʊtəbəl/. **Quotable** comments are written or spoken comments that people think are interesting and worth quoting. *'I deal in ends rather than means' was another of his more quotable sayings.* — ADJ-GRADED

quotation /kwoʊteɪʃən/ **quotations** ◆◇◇◇◇

1 A **quotation** is a sentence or phrase taken from a book, poem, or play, which is repeated by someone else. *He illustrated his argument with quotations from Pasternak... The second quotation is from an essay that D H Lawrence wrote in the nineteen-twenties.* — N-COUNT =quote

2 When someone gives you a **quotation**, they tell you how much they will charge to do a particular piece of work. *Get several written quotations and check exactly what's included in the cost.* — N-COUNT =quote

quotation mark, quotation marks. Quotation marks are punctuation marks that are used in writing to show where speech or a quotation begins and ends. They are usually written or printed as '...' and "...". — N-COUNT: usu pl =inverted commas

quote /kwoʊt/ **quotes, quoting, quoted** ◆◆◆◆◇

1 If you **quote** someone as saying something, you repeat what they have written or said. *He quoted Mr Polay as saying that peace negotiations were already underway... She was quoted in the Express by an unnamed source as saying: 'I won't bail out those two silly girls.'... She quoted a great line from a book by Romain Gary... Yesterday the Belgian newspaper Le Soir quoted a professor who said he witnessed the killings... I gave the letter to our local press and they quoted from it.* — VERB; V n as -ing; V n; V from n

2 A **quote** from a book, poem, play, or speech is a passage or phrase from it. *The paper starts its editorial comment with a quote from an unnamed member of the Cabinet... There is a Groucho Marx quote that he is fond of using.* — N-COUNT: oft N *from* n =quotation

3 If you **quote** something such as a law or a fact, you state it because it supports what you are saying. *Mr Meacher quoted statistics saying that the standard of living of the poorest people had fallen.* — VERB; V n

4 If someone **quotes** a price for doing something, they say how much money they would charge you for a service they are offering or a for a job that you want them to do. *British Telecom quoted him £50 to put in a telephone... He was quoted a very reasonable price... Lantz quoted a price for trucking in water... An independent CD manufacturer had quoted 58p to make a disc.* — VERB; V n n; V n

5 A **quote** for a piece of work is the price that someone says they will charge you to do the work. *Never agree to even the smallest extra job without getting a quote first.* — N-COUNT =quotation

6 If a company's shares, a substance, or a currency **is quoted** at a particular price, that is its current market price; a technical use in finance. *In early trading in Hong Kong yesterday, gold was quoted at $368.20 an ounce... Heron is a private company and is not quoted on the Stock Market.* — V-PASSIVE; be V-ed at amount; be V-ed on n

7 **Quotes** are the same as **quotation marks**. *The word 'remembered' is in quotes.* — N-PLURAL

8 In spoken English, you can say **'quote'** to show that you are about to quote someone's words. *William Schneider predicts the Democrats will have, quote, 'an awful lot of explaining to do.'* — CONVENTION PRAGMATICS

quoth /kwoʊθ/. **Quoth** is an old-fashioned word that means 'said'. **Quoth** comes before the subject of the verb, and is now mainly used for humorous effect. *'I blame the selectors,' quoth he.* — VERB; V with quote

quotidian /kwoʊtɪdiən/. **Quotidian** activities or experiences are basic, everyday activities or experiences; a formal word. *...the minutiae of their quotidian existence.* — ADJ-GRADED: ADJ n

quotient /kwoʊʃənt/ **quotients. Quotient** is used when indicating the presence or degree of a characteristic in someone or something. *Being rich doesn't actually increase your happiness quotient... The film had its own quotient of stylistic lapses.* • **intelligence quotient**: see **IQ.** — N-COUNT: usu sing, usu n N, N *of* n

Quran /kɔːrɑːn/; also spelled **Koran** or **Qur'an. The Quran** is the sacred book on which the religion of Islam is based. — N-PROPER: *the* N

Quranic /kɔːrænɪk/; also spelled **Koranic** or **Qur'anic. Quranic** is used to describe something which belongs or relates to the Quran. — ADJ: ADJ n

Qwerty /kwɜːʳti/. A **Qwerty** keyboard on a typewriter or computer is the standard English language keyboard, on which the top line of keys begins with the letters q, w, e, r, t, and y. — ADJ: ADJ n

Rr

R, r /ɑːʳ/ **R's, r's**
1 **R** is the eighteenth letter of the English alphabet. N-VAR
• See also **three Rs.**
2 **R** is a written abbreviation meaning king or queen. It is short for the Latin words 'rex' and 'regina'. ...*Elizabeth R.* N-TITLE: n N
3 **R** is used as an abbreviation for words beginning with r. For example, it is used on maps as a written abbreviation for 'river'.

rabbi /ræbaɪ/ **rabbis.** A **rabbi** is a Jewish religious leader, usually one who is in charge of a synagogue, one who is qualified to teach Judaism, or one who is an expert on Jewish law. ◆◇◇◇◇ N-COUNT; N-TITLE

rabbinical /ræbɪnɪkᵊl/ or **rabbinic** /ræbɪnɪk/. **Rabbinical** or **rabbinic** refers to the teachings of Jewish religious teachers and leaders. *The statements of earlier rabbinic scholars imply such a belief.* ADJ

rabbit /ræbɪt/ **rabbits, rabbiting, rabbited.** A **rabbit** is a small furry animal with long ears. Rabbits are sometimes kept as pets, or live wild in holes in the ground. ► **Rabbit** is the flesh of this animal eaten as food. ...*rabbit stew.* ◆◆◇◇◇ N-COUNT N-UNCOUNT

rabbit on. If you describe someone as **rabbiting on** about something, you do not like the way they keep talking for a long time about something that is not very interesting; an informal expression, used mainly in British English. *What are you rabbiting on about?* PHRASAL VERB usu cont PRAGMATICS V P about n

rabble /ræbᵊl/
1 A **rabble** is a crowd of noisy, disorderly people; used showing disapproval. *He seems to attract a rabble of supporters more loyal to the man than to the cause.* N-SING: usu with supp PRAGMATICS
2 People sometimes refer to ordinary people in general as **the rabble** to suggest that they are superior to them. *In 40 years, the Guards' Polo Club has changed, but it has managed to keep most of the rabble out.* N-SING: the N PRAGMATICS

rabble-rouser, rabble-rousers. A **rabble-rouser** is a clever speaker who can persuade a group of people to behave violently or aggressively, often for his or her own political advantage; used showing disapproval. N-COUNT PRAGMATICS

rabble-rousing. **Rabble-rousing** is encouragement that a person gives to a group of people to behave violently or aggressively, often for his or her own political advantage; used showing disapproval. *Critics have accused him of rabble-rousing and opportunism.* N-UNCOUNT PRAGMATICS

rabid /ræbɪd, reɪb-/
1 You can use **rabid** to describe someone who has very strong and unreasonable opinions or beliefs about a subject, especially in politics. *The party has distanced itself from the more rabid nationalist groups in the country.* ♦ **rabidly** *Mead calls the group 'rabidly right-wing'.* ADJ-GRADED: usu ADJ n PRAGMATICS ADV: ADV adj, ADV -ed
2 A **rabid** dog or other animal is infected with the disease of rabies. ADJ: usu ADJ n

rabies /reɪbiːz/. **Rabies** is a serious disease which causes people and animals to go mad and die. Rabies is particularly common in dogs. ◆◇◇◇◇ N-UNCOUNT

raccoon /rækuːn/ **raccoons;** also spelled **racoon.** **Raccoon** can also be used as the plural form. A **raccoon** is a small animal that has dark-coloured fur with white stripes on its face and on its long tail. Raccoons live in forests in North and Central America and the West Indies. N-COUNT

race /reɪs/ **races, racing, raced** ◆◆◆◆◆
1 A **race** is a competition to see who is the fastest, for example in running, swimming, or driving. *The women's race was won by the only American in the field, Patti Sue Plumer.* N-COUNT
2 If you **race**, you take part in a race. *In the 10 years I raced in Europe, 30 drivers were killed... They may even have raced each other – but not regularly.* VERB V V n Also V against n
3 **The races** are a series of horse races that are held at a racecourse on a particular day. People go to watch and to bet on which horse will win. *The high point of this trip was a day at the races.* N-PLURAL: the N
4 A **race** is a situation in which people or organizations compete with each other for power or control. *The race for the White House begins in earnest today... The race is on to build up membership fast.* N-COUNT: usu sing, usu with supp
• See also **arms race, rat race.**
5 A **race** is one of the major groups which human beings can be divided into according to their physical features, such as the colour of their skin. *The College welcomes students of all races, faiths, and nationalities... Discrimination by employers on the grounds of race and nationality was illegal.* N-VAR
• See also **human race, race relations.**
6 If you **race** somewhere, you go there as quickly as possible. *He raced across town to the State House building... The hares raced away out of sight.* VERB V adv/prep
7 If something **races** towards a particular state or position, it moves very fast towards that state or position. *Do they realize we are racing towards complete economic collapse?... American economic growth raced ahead.* VERB V prep/adv
8 If you **race** a vehicle or animal, you prepare it for races and make it take part in races. *He still raced sports cars as often as he could.* VERB V n
9 If your mind **races**, or thoughts **race** through your mind, you think very fast about something, especially when you are in a difficult or dangerous situation. *I made sure I sounded calm but my mind was racing... Already her mind was racing ahead to the hundred and one things she had to do... Bits and pieces of the past raced through her mind.* VERB V V adv/prep
10 If your heart **races**, it beats very quickly because you are excited or afraid. *Her heart raced uncontrollably.* VERB V
11 See also **racing.**
12 You describe a situation as a **race against time** when you have to work very fast in order to do something before a particular time, or before another thing happens. *An air force spokesman said the rescue operation was a race against time.* PHRASE

racecourse /reɪskɔːʳs/ **racecourses;** also spelled **race course.** In British English, a **racecourse** is a track on which horses race. The American word is **racetrack.** ◆◇◇◇◇ N-COUNT

racegoer /reɪsgoʊəʳ/ **racegoers;** also spelled **race-goer.** Journalists refer to people who regularly go to watch horse races as **racegoers**; used mainly in British English. N-COUNT: usu pl

racehorse /reɪshɔːʳs/ **racehorses;** also spelled **race horse.** A **racehorse** is a horse that is trained to run in races. ◆◇◇◇◇ N-COUNT

race meeting, race meetings. A **race meeting** is an occasion when a series of horse races are held at the same racecourse, often during a period of several days; used mainly in British English. N-COUNT

racer /reɪsəʳ/ **racers** ◆◇◇◇◇
1 A **racer** is a person or animal that takes part in races. *Tim Powell is a former champion powerboat racer.* N-COUNT
2 A **racer** is a vehicle such as a car or bicycle that is designed to be used in races and therefore travels fast. N-COUNT

race relations. **Race relations** are the ways in which people of different races living together in the same community behave towards one another. *In some communities there is a particular need to develop tolerance and improve race relations. ...the development of race relations legislation.* ◆◇◇◇◇ N-PLURAL: oft N n

race riot, race riots. **Race riots** are violent fights between people of different races living in the same community. N-COUNT: usu pl

racetrack /reɪstræk/ **racetracks;** also spelled **race track.**
1 A **racetrack** is a track for races, especially car or bicycle races. N-COUNT
2 In American English, a **racetrack** is a track on which horses race. The British word is **racecourse.** N-COUNT

racial /reɪʃəl/. **Racial** describes things relating to people's race. *...the protection of national and racial minorities. ...the elimination of racial discrimination and the promotion of equal opportunity between people of different racial groups.* ◆◆◆◇◇ ADJ: usu ADJ n
♦ **racially** *We are both children of racially mixed marriages... There are no indications that the killings were racially motivated.* ADV: ADV -ed/adj, ADV with cl

racialism /reɪʃəlɪzəm/. **Racialism** means the same as **racism**; used mainly in British English. *The cause of their beliefs, however, was not racialism pure and simple.* ♦ **racialist** *I felt that these racialist groups were getting more organised.* N-UNCOUNT =racism; ADJ: usu ADJ n

racing /reɪsɪŋ/. **Racing** refers to races between animals, especially horses, or between vehicles. *Mr Honda was himself a keen racing driver in his younger days... If he could play golf all day and watch horse racing at the same time life would be paradise for him... In that 2.7-litre form it really was a terrific racing car.* ◆◆◆◇◇ N-UNCOUNT: usu with supp, oft N n

racism /reɪsɪzəm/. **Racism** is the belief that people of some races are inferior to others, and the behaviour which is the result of this belief. *There is a feeling among some black people that the level of racism is declining.* ◆◆◇◇◇ N-UNCOUNT

racist /reɪsɪst/ **racists.** If you describe people, things, or behaviour as **racist**, you mean that they are influenced by the belief that some people are inferior because they belong to a particular race; used showing disapproval. *You have to acknowledge that we live in a racist society.* ◆◆◇◇◇ ADJ-GRADED PRAGMATICS
► Also a noun. *He has a hard core of support among white racists.* N-COUNT

rack /ræk/ **racks, racking, racked.** The verb is also spelled **wrack** in American English. ◆◆◇◇◇
1 A **rack** is a piece of equipment, usually with bars, hooks, or pegs, that is used for holding things or for hanging things on. *A luggage rack, which fits over the spare wheel, is a sensible option... You have to fight to reach the racks of clothes but the bargains are amazing.* ● See also **roof rack, toast rack.** N-COUNT: oft supp N
2 If someone **is racked** by something such as illness or anxiety, it causes them great suffering or pain. *His already infirm body was racked by high fever... The country is now racked by three violent separatist movements. ...a teenager racked with guilt and anxiety.* ● See also **racking.** VB: usu passive; be V-ed by/with n; V-ed
3 If you **rack** your **brains**, you try very hard to think of something. *She began to rack her brains to remember what had happened at the nursing home.* PHRASES V and N inflect
4 If you say that someone is **on the rack**, you mean that they are suffering either physically or mentally; used in journalism. *The price increases which have put the population on the rack came from Boris Yeltsin.* usu PHR after v
5 If you say that a place **is going to rack and ruin**, you are emphasizing that it is it slowly decaying and falling to pieces because no-one is bothering to look after it. V inflects PRAGMATICS

rack up. If a business **racks up** profits, losses, or sales, it makes a lot of them. If a sportsperson **racks up** wins, they win a lot of matches or races. Used in journalism. *Lower rates mean that firms are more likely to rack up profits in the coming months... India while not racking up such an impressive score beat Japan 3-0.* PHRASAL VERB no passive; V P n (not pron)

racket /rækɪt/ **rackets;** also spelled **racquet** for meanings 3 and 4. ◆◇◇◇◇
1 A **racket** is a loud unpleasant noise. *He makes such a racket I'm afraid he disturbs the neighbours... My dream was interrupted by the most awful racket coming through the walls... The racket of drills and electric saws went on past midnight.* N-SING PRAGMATICS =din
2 You can refer to an illegal activity used to make money as a **racket**; an informal use. *I'm sure he'll admit he was in the drugs racket in the end... Suspicious fans exposed the racket and police arrested a man in Nottingham.* N-COUNT: oft n N
3 A **racket** is an oval-shaped bat with strings across it. Rackets are used in tennis, squash, and badminton. *Tennis rackets and balls are provided.* N-COUNT: oft n N
4 **Rackets** is a game which is similar to squash but which is played with a hard ball. N-UNCOUNT

racketeer /rækɪtɪəʳ/ **racketeers.** A **racketeer** is someone who makes money from illegal activities such as threatening people or selling worthless, immoral, or illegal goods or services. N-COUNT

racketeering /rækɪtɪərɪŋ/. **Racketeering** is making money from illegal activities such as threatening people or selling worthless, immoral, or illegal goods or services. *Edwards was indicted on racketeering charges but never convicted.* ◆◇◇◇◇ N-UNCOUNT: oft N n

racking /rækɪŋ/. A **racking** pain or emotion is a distressing one which you feel very strongly. *She was now shaking with long, racking sobs.* ● See also **nerve-racking.** ADJ: ADJ n

raconteur /rækɒntɜːʳ/ **raconteurs.** A **raconteur** is someone, usually a man, who can tell stories in an interesting or amusing way. *He spoke eight languages and was a noted raconteur.* N-COUNT

racoon /rækuːn/. See **raccoon.**

racquet /rækɪt/. See **racket.**

racy /reɪsi/ **racier, raciest. Racy** writing or behaviour is lively, amusing, and slightly shocking; used showing approval. ADJ-GRADED

radar /reɪdɑːʳ/ **radars. Radar** is a way of discovering the position or speed of objects such as aircraft or ships when they cannot be seen, by using radio signals. *How far out into the Mediterranean could the Libyan radars go?... The aircraft was on a flight from Milan when it disappeared from radar screens.* ◆◆◇◇◇ N-VAR: oft N n

radial /reɪdiəl/ **radials** ◆◇◇◇◇
1 **Radial** refers to the pattern that you get when straight lines are drawn from the centre of a circle to a number of points round the edge. *The white marble floors were inlaid in a radial pattern of brass.* ADJ: usu ADJ n
2 A **radial** or a **radial tyre** is a tyre which is strengthened inside by cords that point towards the centre of the wheel. Radials look softer and are less likely to skid than other tyres. N-COUNT

radiance /reɪdiəns/
1 **Radiance** is great happiness which shows in someone's face and makes them look very attractive. *She has the vigour and radiance of someone young enough to be her grand-daughter... There was about her a new radiance.* N-UNCOUNT: also a N
2 **Radiance** is a glowing light shining from something. *The dim bulb of the bedside lamp cast a soft radiance over his face.* N-UNCOUNT: also a N

radiant /reɪdiənt/ ◆◇◇◇◇
1 Someone who is **radiant** is so happy that their joy shows in their face. *Kathy smiled at her daughter's radiant face... On her wedding day the bride looked truly radiant.* ♦ **radiantly** *He smiled radiantly and embraced her... She looks radiantly happy.* ADJ-GRADED; ADV-GRADED
2 Something that is **radiant** glows brightly. *The evening sun warms the old red brick wall to a radiant glow... Out on the bay the morning is radiant.* ADJ-GRADED
♦ **radiantly** *The sun was still shining radiantly.* ADV-GRADED
3 **Radiant** heat or energy is sent out in the form of rays. *The earth would be a frozen ball if it were not for the radiant heat of the sun.* ADJ: ADJ n

radiate /reɪdieɪt/ **radiates, radiating, radiated** ◆◇◇◇◇
1 If things **radiate** out from a place, they form a pattern that is like lines drawn from the centre of a circle to various points on its edge. *Many kinds of* VERB; V from n

woodland can be seen on the various walks which radiate from the Heritage Centre... From here, contaminated air radiates out to the open countryside. V prep/adv

2 If you **radiate** an emotion or quality or if it **radiates** from you, people can see it very clearly in your face and in your behaviour. *She radiates happiness and health... Her voice hadn't changed but I felt the anger that radiated from her.* VERB V n V *from* n

3 If something **radiates** heat or light, heat or light comes from it. *The metal plate behind my head radiated heat like a cooker's hotplate.* VERB V n

radiation /reɪdieɪʃᵊn/ ◆◆◇◇◇

1 **Radiation** is very small particles of a radioactive substance. Large amounts of radiation can cause illness and death. *They suffer from health problems and fear the long term effects of radiation... If the cancer returns, radiation therapy is successful in 90 per cent of cases.* N-UNCOUNT: also N in pl, oft N n

2 **Radiation** is energy, especially heat, that comes from a particular source. *The $617 million satellite will study energy radiation from the most violent stars in the universe.* N-UNCOUNT: also N in pl, usu with supp

radiation sickness. **Radiation sickness** is an illness that people get when they are exposed to too much radiation. N-UNCOUNT

radiator /reɪdieɪtəʳ/ **radiators** ◆◇◇◇◇

1 A **radiator** is a hollow metal device, usually connected by pipes to a central heating system, that is used to heat a room. N-COUNT

2 The **radiator** in a car is the part of the engine which is filled with water in order to cool the engine. N-COUNT

radical /rædɪkᵊl/ **radicals** ◆◆◆◆◇

1 **Radical** changes and differences are very important and great in degree. *The country needs a period of calm without more surges of radical change... He wants to continue the radical economic reforms begun under Mr Mazowiecki.* ♦ **radically** /rædɪkli/ *...two large groups of people with radically different beliefs and cultures.* ADJ-GRADED: usu ADJ n =fundamental ADV-GRADED =fundamentally

2 **Radical** people believe that there should be great changes in society and try to bring about these changes. *...threats by left-wing radical groups to disrupt the proceedings. ...political tension between radical and conservative politicians.* ▸ A **radical** is someone who has radical views. ADJ-GRADED: usu ADJ n ≠reactionary, conservative N-COUNT

radicalism /rædɪkəlɪzəm/. **Radicalism** is radical beliefs, ideas, or behaviour. *Williams himself was rather a curious mixture of radicalism and conservatism.* ◆◇◇◇◇ N-UNCOUNT ≠conservatism

radicalize /rædɪkəlaɪz/ **radicalizes, radicalizing, radicalized;** also spelled **radicalise** in British English. If something **radicalizes** a process, situation, or person, it makes them more radical. *He says the opposition will radicalize its demands if these conditions aren't met... Many women radicalized by feminism have maintained a quest for new forms of community... Whatever the trial's outcome, it was bound to be a radicalizing experience for her.* ♦ **radicalization** /rædɪkəlaɪzeɪʃᵊn/ *...the radicalization of the conservative right.* VERB V n V-ed V-ing N-UNCOUNT: oft N *of* n

radicchio /rædɪkioʊ, AM rɑːdiː-/. **Radicchio** is a vegetable with purple and white leaves that is usually eaten raw in salads. N-UNCOUNT

radii /reɪdiaɪ/. **Radii** is the plural of **radius**.

radio /reɪdioʊ/ **radios, radioing, radioed** ◆◆◆◆◆

1 **Radio** is the broadcasting of programmes for the public to listen to, by sending out signals from a transmitter. *The last 12 months have been difficult ones for local radio... The announcement was broadcast on radio and television. ...Britain's first national commercial radio station. ...BBC Radio 4.* N-UNCOUNT: oft N n

2 You can refer to the programmes broadcast by radio stations as **the radio**. *A lot of people tend to listen to the radio in the mornings... He's been on the radio a lot recently... They've been saying on the radio she was missing.* N-SING: *the* N

3 A **radio** is the piece of equipment that you use in order to listen to radio programmes. *He sat down in the armchair and turned on the radio.* N-COUNT

4 **Radio** is a system of sending sound over a distance by transmitting electrical signals. *They are in twice daily radio contact with the rebel leader. ...radio waves.* N-UNCOUNT: oft N n

5 A **radio** is a piece of equipment that is used for sending and receiving messages. *Judge Bruce Laughland praised the courage of the young constable, who managed to raise the alarm on his radio... The radio message was brief.* N-COUNT

6 If you **radio** someone, you send a message to them by radio. *The officer radioed for advice... A few minutes after take-off, the pilot radioed that a fire had broken out.* VERB V adv/prep V that Also V n, V

radioactive /reɪdioʊæktɪv/. Something that is **radioactive** contains a substance that produces energy in the form of powerful and harmful rays. *The government has been storing radioactive waste at Fernald for 50 years.* ♦ **radioactivity** /reɪdioʊæktɪvɪti/ *...the storage and disposal of solid waste which is contaminated with low levels of radioactivity.* ◆◆◇◇◇ ADJ-GRADED N-UNCOUNT

radio astronomy. **Radio astronomy** is a branch of astronomy in which a radio telescope is used to receive and analyse radio waves from space. N-UNCOUNT

radiocarbon /reɪdioʊkɑːʳbən/; also spelled **radio carbon**. **Radiocarbon** is a type of carbon which is radioactive, and which therefore breaks up slowly at a steady rate. Its presence in an object can be measured in order to find out how old the object is. *The most frequently used method is radiocarbon dating.* N-UNCOUNT: usu N n

radio cassette. A **radio cassette** is a radio and a cassette player together in a single machine; used mainly in British English. *...a radio cassette player.* N-SING: oft N n

radio-controlled. A **radio-controlled** device works by receiving radio signals which operate it. *...radio-controlled model planes.* ADJ: usu ADJ n

radiographer /reɪdiɒgrəfəʳ/ **radiographers.** A **radiographer** is a person who is trained to take X-rays; used in British English. N-COUNT

radiography /reɪdiɒgrəfi/. **Radiography** is the process of taking X-rays; used mainly in British English. N-UNCOUNT

radiological /reɪdiəlɒdʒɪkᵊl/

1 **Radiological** means relating to radiology. *Patients subjected to extensive radiological examinations can face a risk as high as one in a few hundred.* ADJ: ADJ n

2 **Radiological** means relating radioactive materials. *This is the limit set by the National Radiological Protection Board in guidelines for storing solid nuclear waste.* ADJ: ADJ n

radiologist /reɪdiɒlədʒɪst/ **radiologists.** A **radiologist** is a doctor who is trained in radiology. N-COUNT

radiology /reɪdiɒlədʒi/. **Radiology** is the branch of medical science that uses X-rays and radioactive substances to treat diseases. N-UNCOUNT

radio telephone, radio telephones. A **radio telephone** is a telephone which carries sound by sending radio signals rather than by using wires. Radio telephones are often used in cars. N-COUNT

radio telescope, radio telescopes. A **radio telescope** is an instrument that receives radio waves from space and finds the position of stars and other objects in space. N-COUNT

radiotherapist /reɪdioʊθerəpɪst/ **radiotherapists.** A **radiotherapist** is a person who treats diseases such as cancer by using radiation. N-COUNT

radiotherapy /reɪdioʊθerəpi/. **Radiotherapy** is the treatment of diseases such as cancer by using radiation. N-UNCOUNT

radish /rædɪʃ/ **radishes.** **Radishes** are small red or white vegetables that are the roots of a plant. They are eaten raw in salads. N-VAR

radium /reɪdiəm/. **Radium** is a radioactive element which is used in the treatment of cancer. N-UNCOUNT

radius /reɪdiəs/ **radii** /reɪdiaɪ/ ◆◇◇◇◇

1 The **radius** around a particular point is the distance from it in any direction. *Nigel has searched for work in a ten-mile radius around his home.* N-SING: with supp

2 The **radius** of a circle is the distance from its N-COUNT

centre to its outside edge. *He indicated a semicircle with a radius of about thirty miles.*

radon /reɪdɒn/. **Radon** is a radioactive element in the form of a gas. ◆◇◇◇◇ N-UNCOUNT

RAF /ɑːr eɪ ef, ræf/. **The RAF** is the air force of the United Kingdom. **RAF** is an abbreviation for 'Royal Air Force'. *An RAF helicopter rescued the men after the boat began taking in water.* ◆◆◇◇◇ N-PROPER: *the* N

raffia /ræfiə/. **Raffia** is a fibre made from palm leaves. It is used to make mats and baskets. *Some embroidered tablecloths or made raffia mats.* N-UNCOUNT: oft N n

raffish /ræfɪʃ/. **Raffish** people and places are not very respectable but are attractive and stylish nevertheless; used mainly in written English. *He was handsome in a raffish kind of way... The theatre's raffish auditorium recalls an earlier era.* ADJ-GRADED: usu ADJ n PRAGMATICS

raffle /ræfəl/ **raffles, raffling, raffled** ◆◇◇◇◇
1 A **raffle** is a competition in which you buy tickets with numbers on them. Afterwards some numbers are chosen, and if your ticket has one of these numbers on it, you win a prize. *Any more raffle tickets? Twenty-five pence each or five for a pound.* N-COUNT =lottery, draw
2 If someone **raffles** something, they give it as a prize in a raffle. *During each show we will be raffling a fabulous prize.* VERB V n

raft /rɑːft, ræft/ **rafts** ◆◇◇◇◇
1 A **raft** is a floating platform made from large pieces of wood or other materials tied together. *...a river trip on bamboo rafts through dense rainforest.* N-COUNT
2 A **raft** is a small inflatable rubber or plastic boat. *The crew spent two days and nights in their raft.* N-COUNT
• See also **life raft**.
3 A **raft of** people or things is a lot of them. *He has surrounded himself with a raft of advisers who are very radical... This is likely to revive consumer spending and a whole raft of consumer industries.* N-COUNT: usu sing, N *of* n =host of

rafter /rɑːftər, ræf-/ **rafters. Rafters** are the sloping pieces of wood that support a roof. *From the rafters of the thatched roofs hung strings of dried onions and garlic.* ◆◇◇◇◇ N-COUNT: usu pl

rafting /rɑːftɪŋ, ræf-/. **Rafting** is the sport of travelling down a river on a raft. *Winter Park offers innumerable opportunities for water sports such as boating, fishing, and rafting.* N-UNCOUNT

rag /ræg/ **rags, ragging, ragged** ◆◆◇◇◇
1 A **rag** is a piece of old cloth which you can use to clean or wipe things. *He was wiping his hands on an oily rag. ...a bundle of old rags... It looked like a piece of rag.* N-VAR
2 **Rags** are old torn clothes. *There were men, women and small children, some dressed in rags.* N-PLURAL
3 People refer to a newspaper as a **rag** when they have a low opinion of it; an informal use. *'This man Tom works for a local rag,' he said.* N-COUNT
4 In British English, to **rag** someone means to tease them unkindly. *She was about thirty, ten years older than the youngsters ragging her.* VERB =tease V n
5 See also **ragged**.
6 In informal British English, if you **lose** your **rag**, you suddenly become so angry that you are not in control of yourself. *I've only once seen him lose his rag.* PHRASES V inflects
7 You use **rags to riches** to describe the way in which someone quickly becomes very rich after they have been quite poor. *His was a rags-to-riches story and people admire that.*
8 If you describe something as **a red rag to a bull**, you mean that it is certain to make a particular person or group very angry; used mainly in British English. *This sort of information is like a red rag to a bull for the tobacco companies.* v-link PHR, *like* PHR

raga /rɑːgə/ **ragas.** A **raga** is a piece of Indian music based on a traditional pattern of notes which is also called a **raga**. N-COUNT

ragamuffin /rægəmʌfɪn/ **ragamuffins.** A **ragamuffin** is someone, especially a child, who is dirty and has torn clothes; an old-fashioned word. *...two small figures, black against the white snow, two ragamuffins with a torch.* N-COUNT

rag-and-bone man, rag-and-bone men. In British English, a **rag-and-bone man** is a person who goes from street to street in a van or with a horse and cart buying things such as old clothes and furniture. N-COUNT

ragbag /rægbæg/; also spelled **rag-bag.** A **ragbag** of things is a group of things which do not have much in common with each other, but which are being considered together at the same time. *The government was still in effect a ragbag of ex-Communists, Social Democrats and Liberals.* N-SING: usu N *of* n

rag doll, rag dolls. A **rag doll** is a soft doll made of cloth. N-COUNT

rage /reɪdʒ/ **rages, raging, raged** ◆◆◆◇◇
1 **Rage** is strong anger that is difficult to control. *He was red-cheeked with rage... I flew into a rage... He admitted shooting the man in a fit of rage.* N-VAR =fury
2 You say that something powerful or unpleasant **rages** when it continues with great force or violence. *Train services were halted as the fire raged for more than four hours. ...the fierce arguments raging over the future of the Holy City... The war rages on and the time has come to take sides.* VERB V V *on*
3 If you **rage** about something, you speak or think very angrily about it. *Monroe was on the phone, raging about her mistreatment by the brothers... Inside, Frannie was raging... 'I can't see it's any of your business,' he raged.* VERB V *about/against/at* n V V with quote
4 When something is popular and fashionable, you can say that it is **the rage**. *Badges are all the rage in France, Mr Toff explains.* N-SING: *the* N
5 See also **raging**.

ragged /rægɪd/ ◆◇◇◇◇
1 Someone who is **ragged** looks untidy and is wearing clothes that are old and torn. *The five survivors eventually reached safety, ragged, half-starved and exhausted.* ♦ **raggedly** *...a dismal London district of broken-down buildings and raggedly dressed children.* ADJ-GRADED ADV-GRADED: ADV -ed
2 **Ragged** clothes are old and torn. ADJ-GRADED
3 You can say that something is **ragged** when it is untidy or uneven. *She could hear his ragged breathing, as if he had been running... O'Brien formed the men into a ragged line.* ♦ **raggedly** *Some people tried to sing, but their voices soon died raggedly away.* ADJ-GRADED =uneven ADV-GRADED: ADV after v, ADV -ed
4 If someone **runs** you **ragged**, they make you do so much that you become exhausted; an informal expression. *They'd send me here, there and everywhere and I'd run myself ragged and get no place... Spain ran England ragged early on but goalkeeper Ian Walker proved a formidable barrier.* PHRASE: V inflects

raggedy /rægɪdi/. People and things that are **raggedy** are dirty and untidy. **Raggedy** clothes are old and torn. An informal use. *The people there, quite raggedy, stare at us. ...an old man in a raggedy topcoat.* ADJ-GRADED

raging /reɪdʒɪŋ/ ◆◇◇◇◇
1 **Raging** water moves very forcefully and violently. *The field trip involved crossing a raging torrent.* ADJ: ADJ n
2 **Raging** fire is very hot and fierce. *As he came closer he saw a gigantic wall of raging flame before him.* ADJ: ADJ n
3 **Raging** is used to describe things, especially bad things, that are very intense. *If raging inflation returns, then interest rates will shoot up... There may be the occasional criticism but it's clear there is no raging debate right now... He felt a raging thirst.* ADJ: ADJ n
4 See also **rage**.

ragout /rægu:/ **ragouts.** A **ragout** is a strongly flavoured stew of meat or vegetables or both. N-VAR

rag rug, rag rugs. A **rag rug** is a small carpet made of old pieces of cloth stitched or woven together. N-COUNT

ragtag /rægtæg/; also spelled **rag-tag.** If you want to say that a group of people or an organization is badly organized and not very respectable, you can describe it as a **ragtag** group or organization; an informal word. *We started out with that little rag-tag team of 30 people, and now we're up to 150.* ADJ: ADJ n

ragtime /rægtaɪm/. **Ragtime** is a kind of jazz piano music that was invented in America in the early 1900s. N-UNCOUNT

rag trade. **The rag trade** is the business and industry of making and selling clothes, especially N-SING: *the* N women's clothes. *The rag trade is extremely competitive, and one needs plenty of contacts in order to survive.*

raid /reɪd/ **raids, raiding, raided** ◆◆◆◇◇

1 When soldiers **raid** a place, they make a sudden armed attack against it, with the aim of causing damage rather than occupying any of the enemy's land. *Warplanes raided the capital of Croatia.* ► Also a noun. *The rebels attempted a surprise raid on a military camp... Its planes are carrying out heavy bombing raids against the guerrillas.* • See also **air raid**. VERB V n N-COUNT: oft N *on/against* n

2 If the police **raid** a building, they enter it suddenly and by force in order to look for dangerous criminals or for evidence of something illegal, such as drugs or weapons. *Fraud squad officers raided the firm's offices.* ► Also a noun. *They were arrested early this morning after a raid on a house by thirty armed police.* VERB V n N-COUNT: oft N *on* n

3 In British English, if someone **raids** a building or place, they enter it by force in order to steal something. *A 19-year-old man has been found guilty of raiding a bank.* ► Also a noun. *...an armed raid on a small Post Office... He carried out a series of bank raids.* VERB V n N-COUNT: oft N *on* n

4 If you **raid** the fridge or the larder, you take something from it to eat instead of a meal or in between meals; an informal use. *She made her way to the kitchen, hoping to find someone preparing dinner and if not, to raid the fridge.* VERB V n

raider /reɪdəʳ/ **raiders** ◆◇◇◇◇

1 In British English, **raiders** are people who enter a building or place by force in order to steal something. *The raiders escaped with cash and jewellery.* N-COUNT =robber, thief

2 Raiders are soldiers who make a sudden armed attack on a place, with the aim of causing damage or taking something, rather than occupying any of the enemy's land. *The raiders continued on their mission – to seek out and destroy American air and sea forces.* N-COUNT

3 See also **corporate raider**.

rail /reɪl/ **rails, railing, railed** ◆◆◆◇◇

1 A **rail** is a horizontal bar attached to posts or fixed round the edge of something as a fence or support. *They had to walk across an emergency footbridge, holding onto a rope that served as a rail... She gripped the hand rail in the lift.* N-COUNT: oft supp N

2 A **rail** is a horizontal bar that you hang things on. *...frocks hanging from a rail... This pair of curtains will fit a rail up to 7ft 6in wide.* N-COUNT

3 Rails are the steel bars which trains run on. *The train left the rails but somehow forced its way back onto the line.* N-COUNT: usu pl =track

4 If you travel or send something by **rail**, you travel or send it on a train. *The president traveled by rail to his home town. ...the electric rail link between Manchester and Sheffield.* N-UNCOUNT: oft N n

5 If you **rail** against something, you criticize it loudly and bitterly; used in written English. *He railed against hypocrisy and greed... I'd cursed him and railed at him.* VERB V *against/at* n

6 See also **railing**.

7 If something is **back on the rails**, it is beginning to be successful again after a period when it almost failed; used in journalism. *They are keen to get the negotiating process back on the rails... Her career is back on the rails.* PHRASES

8 If someone **goes off the rails**, they start to behave in a way that other people think is unacceptable or very strange, for example they start taking drugs or breaking the law. *They've got to do something about these children because clearly they've gone off the rails.* V inflects

railcard /reɪlkɑːʳd/ **railcards.** In Britain, a **railcard** is an identity card that allows people to buy train tickets cheaply. N-COUNT

railing /reɪlɪŋ/ **railings** ◆◇◇◇◇

1 A **railing** or **railings** are a fence made from metal bars. *He walked out on to the balcony where he rested his arms on the railing. ...the iron railings of the convent grounds.* N-COUNT

2 See also **rail**.

railroad /reɪlroʊd/ **railroads, railroading, railroaded** ◆◇◇◇◇

1 In American English, a **railroad** is the same as a **railway**. *...railroad tracks that led to nowhere... He came to Frankfurt in 1945 to work on the railroad.* N-COUNT

2 If you **railroad** someone into doing something, you make them do it although they do not really want to, by hurrying them and putting pressure on them. *He more or less railroaded the rest of Europe into recognising the new 'independent' states... He railroaded the reforms through.* VERB V n *into*/-ing V n *through*

railway /reɪlweɪ/ **railways** ◆◆◆◇◇

1 In British English, a **railway** is a route between two places along which trains travel on steel rails. The American word is **railroad**. *The road ran beside a railway. ...a disused railway line.* N-COUNT

2 In British English, a **railway** is a company or organization that operates railway routes. The American word is **railroad**. *...the state-owned French railway. ...the privatisation of the railways.* N-COUNT

railwayman /reɪlweɪmæn/ **railwaymen.** In British English, **railwaymen** are men who work for the railway. The usual American term is **rail workers** or **railroad workers**. N-COUNT

raiment /reɪmənt/ **raiments. Raiment** is clothing; a literary word. *I want nothing but raiment and daily bread.* N-UNCOUNT: also N in pl =clothing

rain /reɪn/ **rains, raining, rained** ◆◆◆◆◇

1 Rain is water that falls from the clouds in small drops. *I hope you didn't get soaked standing out in the rain... A spot of rain fell on her hand.* N-UNCOUNT: also *the* N

2 In countries where rain only falls in certain seasons, this rain is referred to as **the rains**. *...the spring, when the rains came... The rains have failed again in the Horn of Africa.* N-PLURAL: usu *the* N

3 When rain falls, you can say that **it is raining**. *It rained the whole weekend... It was raining hard, and she hadn't an umbrella.* VERB *it* V

4 If someone **rains** blows, kicks, or bombs **on** a person or place, or if they **rain on** a person or place, the person or place is heavily attacked. *The police, raining blows on rioters and spectators alike, cleared the park... Rockets, mortars and artillery rounds rained on buildings.* ► **Rain down** means the same as **rain**. *Fighter aircraft rained down high explosives... Grenades and mortars rained down on Dubrovnik.* V-ERG V n *on* n V *on* n PHRASAL VERB ERG V P n (not pron) V P *on* n

5 A **rain of** things is a large number of things that fall from the sky at the same time. *A rain of stones descended on the police.* N-SING: N *of* n

6 You can use the expression **it never rains but it pours** to mean that several unfortunate events often happen at the same time. PHRASES

7 If you say that someone is **as right as rain**, you mean that they are completely well or healthy again, for example when they have recovered from an illness or a shock; an informal expression. *You'll be as right as rain as soon as you are back in your own home with your baby.* v-link PHR

8 If you say that someone does something **rain or shine**, you mean that they do it regularly, without being affected by the weather or other circumstances. *Frances took her daughter walking every day, rain or shine.*

rain off. In British English, if a sports match **is rained off**, it has to stop, or it is not able to start, because of rain. The usual American expression is **be rained out**. *Most of the games have been rained off. ...a rained-off cricket match.* PHRASAL VERB PASSIVE *be* V-ed P V-ed P

rainbow /reɪnboʊ/ **rainbows** ◆◆◇◇◇

1 A **rainbow** is an arch of different colours that you can sometimes see in the sky when it is raining. *Oh look, a rainbow! ...silk brocade of every colour of the rainbow.* N-COUNT

2 A **rainbow** of colours is a wide range of bright colours. *...a rainbow of coloured cushions.* N-COUNT: usu N *of* n

3 If you say that something is at **the end of the rainbow**, you mean that people want it but it is almost impossible to obtain or achieve. *The promise of a cure – the pot of gold at the end of the rainbow – often makes sensible people do irrational things.* PHRASE

rain check. If you say you will take a **rain check** on an offer or suggestion, you mean that you do not want to accept it straight away, but you might accept it at another time. *I was planning to ask you in for a brandy, but if you want to take a rain check, that's fine... Can I take a rain check on that?* PHRASE: PHR after v

raincoat /reɪnkoʊt/ **raincoats.** A **raincoat** is a waterproof coat. ◆◇◇◇◇ N-COUNT

raindrop /reɪndrɒp/ **raindrops.** A **raindrop** is a single drop of rain. N-COUNT

rainfall /reɪnfɔːl/ **rainfalls. Rainfall** is the amount of rain that falls in a place during a particular period. *There have been four years of below average rainfall.* ◆◇◇◇◇ N-UNCOUNT: also N in pl

rainforest /reɪnfɒrɪst, AM -fɔːr-/ **rainforests.** A **rainforest** is a thick forest of tall trees which is found in tropical areas where there is a lot of rain. *There is worldwide concern about the destruction of the rainforests. ...a vast area of tropical rainforest.* ◆◇◇◇◇ N-VAR

rainstorm /reɪnstɔːʳm/ **rainstorms.** A **rainstorm** is a fall of very heavy rain. *His car collided with another car during a heavy rainstorm.* N-COUNT

rain-swept; also spelled **rainswept.** A **rain-swept** place is a place where it is raining heavily. *He looked up and down the rain-swept street. ...a cold and rainswept evening.* ADJ: ADJ n

rainwater /reɪnwɔːtəʳ/. **Rainwater** is water that has fallen as rain. N-UNCOUNT

rainy /reɪni/ **rainier, rainiest** ◆◇◇◇◇

1 During a **rainy** day, season, or period it rains a lot. *They walked along the promenade on a rainy night... The rainy season in the Andes normally starts in December.* ADJ-GRADED: usu ADJ n

2 If you say that you are saving something, especially money, **for a rainy day**, you mean that you are saving it until a time in the future when you might need it. *I'll put the rest in the bank for a rainy day.* PHRASE

raise /reɪz/ **raises, raising, raised** ◆◆◆◆◆

1 If you **raise** something, you move it so that it is in a higher position. *He raised his hand to wave... She went to the window and raised the blinds... Milton raised the glass to his lips. ...a small raised platform.* VERB =lift V n V n prep/adv V-ed

2 If you **raise** a flag or banner, you display it by moving it into a high place. *They had raised the white flag in surrender... At midnight, the German flag will be raised over the Reichstag.* VERB V n

3 If you **raise** yourself, you lift your body so that you are standing up straight, or so that you are no longer lying flat. *He raised himself into a sitting position... She raised herself on one elbow.* VERB =lift V pron-refl

4 If you **raise** the rate or level of something, you increase it. *The Republic of Ireland is expected to raise interest rates... Two incidents in recent days have raised the level of concern. ...a raised body temperature.* VERB =increase V n V-ed

5 To **raise** the standard of something means to improve it. *...a new drive to raise standards of literacy in Britain's schools.* VERB =improve V n

6 If you **raise** your voice, you speak more loudly, usually because you are angry. *Don't you raise your voice to me, Henry Rollins!... Anne raised her voice in order to be heard.* VERB V n

7 In American English, a **raise** is an increase in your wages or salary. The British word is **rise**. *Within two months Kelly got a raise.* N-COUNT

8 If you **raise** money for a charity or an institution, you ask people for money which you collect on its behalf. *...events held to raise money for Help the Aged... All funds raised will be used by Children With Leukaemia.* VERB V n *for* n V-ed

9 If a person or company **raises** money that they need, they manage to get it, for example by selling their property or by borrowing. *They raised the money to buy the house and two hundred acres of grounds.* VERB V n

10 If an event **raises** a particular emotion or question, it makes people feel the emotion or consider the question. *The agreement has raised hopes that the war may end soon... The accident again raises questions about the safety of the plant. ...a joke that raised a smile on everyone's lips.* VERB =provoke V n

11 If you **raise** a subject, an objection, or a question, you mention it or bring it to someone's attention. *In the meeting Mrs. Ashrawi raised the three main concerns that the Palestinians have... He had been consulted and had raised no objections.* VERB V n

12 Someone who **raises** a child looks after it until it is grown up. *My mother was an amazing woman. She raised four of us kids virtually singlehandedly. ...the house where she was raised.* VERB =bring up V n

13 If someone **raises** a particular type of animal or crop, they breed that type of animal or grow that type of crop. *He raises 2,000 acres of wheat and hay. ...a perfectly cooked farm-raised chicken.* VERB V n V-ed

14 • to **raise the alarm**: see **alarm.** • to **raise** your **eyebrows**: see **eyebrow.** • to **raise a finger**: see **finger.** • to **raise hell**: see **hell.** • to **raise a laugh**: see **laugh.** • to **raise the roof**: see **roof.**

raisin /reɪzᵊn/ **raisins. Raisins** are dried grapes. *For breakfast I have porridge made with water, to which I add raisins.* ◆◇◇◇◇ N-COUNT

raison d'etre /reɪzɒn detrə/; also spelled **raison d'être.** A person's or organization's **raison d'etre** is the most important reason for them existing in the way that they do. *The armed forces are caught up in a debate about their raison d'etre.* N-SING: usu with poss

Raj /rɑːʒ/. **The** British **Raj** was the period of British rule in India which ended in 1947. *...Indian living conditions under the Raj.* ◆◇◇◇◇ N-SING: *the* N

rake /reɪk/ **rakes, raking, raked** ◆◇◇◇◇

1 A **rake** is a garden tool consisting of a row of metal or wooden teeth attached to a long handle. You can use a rake to loosen the earth and make it level before you put plants in, or to gather leaves together. N-COUNT

2 If you **rake** a surface, you move a rake across it in order to make it smooth and level. *Rake the soil, press the seed into it, then cover it lightly... The beach is raked and cleaned daily.* VERB V n

3 If you **rake** leaves or ashes, you move them somewhere using a rake or a similar tool. *I watched the men rake leaves into heaps... She raked out the ashes from the boiler.* VERB V n adv/prep V prep

4 If someone **rakes** an area with gunfire or with light, they cover it thoroughly by moving the gun or the light across from one side of the area to another. *Planes dropped bombs and raked the beach with machine gun fire... The caravan was raked with bullets... The headlights raked across a painted sign.* VERB V n *with* n V prep

5 If fingernails or branches **rake** your skin, they scrape across it; a literary use. *Ragged fingernails raked her skin... He found the man's cheeks and raked them with his nails.* VERB =scrape V n V n *with* n

6 If you **rake through** a pile of objects or rubbish, you search through it thoroughly with your hands. *Many can survive only by raking through dustbins.* VERB =rummage through V *through* n

7 If you call a man a **rake**, you mean that he is rather immoral, for example because he gambles, drinks, or has sexual relationships with many women; an old-fashioned use. N-COUNT

rake in. If you say that someone **is raking in** money, you mean that they are making a lot of money very easily, more easily than you think they should; an informal expression. *The privatisation allowed companies to rake in huge profits.* PHRASAL VERB PRAGMATICS V P n (not pron) Also V n P

rake over. If you say that someone **is raking over** something that has been said, done, or written in the past, you mean they are examining and discussing it in detail, in a way that you do not think is very pleasant or useful. *...raking over lifestyles of victims and perpetrators in a manner that reeks of tabloid journalism.* PHRASAL VERB PRAGMATICS V P n (not pron)

rake up. If you say that someone **is raking up** something unpleasant or embarrassing that happened in the past, you mean they are talking about it or reminding someone about it, and you do not think they should. *Raking up the past won't help anyone.* PHRASAL VERB PRAGMATICS =drag up V P n (not pron) Also V n P

raked /reɪkt/. A **raked** stage or other surface is sloping, for example so that all the audience can ADJ: ADJ n see more clearly. *The action takes place on a steeply raked stage.*

rake-off, rake-offs. If someone who has helped to arrange a business deal takes or gets a **rake-off**, they illegally or unfairly take a share of the profits; an informal word. N-COUNT =cut

rakish /reɪkɪʃ/. A **rakish** person or appearance is stylish in a confident, daring way. *...a soft-brimmed hat which he wore at a rakish angle. ...rakish young gentlemen.* ADJ-GRADED: usu ADJ n ♦ **rakishly** *...a hat cocked rakishly over one eye.* ADV-GRADED

rally /ræli/ **rallies, rallying, rallied** ◆◆◆◇◇

1 A **rally** is a large public meeting that is held in order to show support for something such as a political party. *About three thousand people held a rally to mark international human rights day... Supporters of the policy are reported to be gathering in Dehli for a mass rally.* N-COUNT

2 When people **rally** to something or when something **rallies** them, they unite to support it. *Her cabinet colleagues have continued to rally to her support... He rallied his own supporters for a fight.* V-ERG V to n V n

3 When someone or something **rallies**, they begin to recover or improve after having been weak. *He rallied enough to thank his doctors... Markets began to rally worldwide.* VERB =recover V ▶ Also a noun. *After a brief rally the shares returned to 126p.* N-COUNT: usu sing

4 A **rally** is a competition in which vehicles are driven over public roads. *Carlos Sainz of Spain has won the New Zealand Motor Rally. ...an accomplished rally driver.* N-COUNT: usu with supp

5 A **rally** in tennis, badminton, or squash is a continuous series of shots that the players exchange without stopping. *...a long rally.* N-COUNT

rally around or **rally round.** When people **rally around** or **rally round**, they work as a group in order to support someone or something at a difficult time. *So many people have rallied round to help the family... Connie's friends rallied round her.* PHRASAL VERB V P V P n

rallying cry, rallying cries. A **rallying cry** or **rallying call** is something such as a slogan, event, or belief which inspires people to unite and to act in support of a group or ideal. *...an issue that is fast becoming a rallying cry for many Democrats: national health care.* N-COUNT

rallying point, rallying points. A **rallying point** is a place, event, or person that people are attracted to as a symbol of a political group or ideal. *Students used the death of political activists as a rallying point for anti-government protests.* N-COUNT =focus

ram /ræm/ **rams, ramming, rammed** ◆◇◇◇◇

1 If a vehicle **rams** something such as another vehicle, it crashes into it with a lot of force, usually deliberately. *The thieves fled, ramming the policeman's car... They used a lorry to ram the main gate.* VERB V n

2 If you **ram** something somewhere, you push it there with great force. *He rammed the key into the lock and kicked the front door open.* VERB V n adv/prep

3 A **ram** is an adult male sheep. N-COUNT

4 See also **battering ram**.

5 If something **rams home** a message or a point, it makes it clear in a way that is very forceful and that people are likely to listen to. *Railway lines are dangerous places and it is up to parents to ram home the dangers to their children... Hundreds of party workers were flooding the streets to ram the Tory message home.* PHRASE: V inflects ● to **ram** something **down** someone's **throat**: see **throat**.

RAM /ræm/. **RAM** is the part of a computer in which information is kept temporarily for immediate use. It is an abbreviation for 'Random Access Memory'. A technical term. *...an IBM PC with hard disk drive and 256k RAM minimum. For this application, 512k RAM is recommended and 640k RAM is preferred.* N-UNCOUNT

Ramadan /ræmədæn/. **Ramadan** is the ninth month of the Muslim year, when Muslims do not eat between sunrise and sunset. During Ramadan, Muslims celebrate the fact that it was in this month that God first revealed the words of the Quran to Mohammed. ◆◇◇◇◇ N-UNCOUNT

ramble /ræmbᵊl/ **rambles, rambling, rambled** ◆◇◇◇◇

1 A **ramble** is a long walk in the countryside. *...an hour's ramble through the woods.* N-COUNT =walk

2 If you **ramble**, you go on a long walk in the countryside. *...freedom to ramble across the moors.* VERB =walk V adv/prep

3 If you say that a person **rambles** in their speech or writing, you mean they do not make much sense because they keep going off the subject in a confused way. *Sometimes she spoke sensibly; sometimes she rambled... It would have been best written in a more concise way as it does tend to ramble.* VERB V

ramble on. If you say that someone **is rambling on**, you mean that they have been talking for a long time in a boring and rather confused way. *She only half-listened as Ella rambled on... He stood in my kitchen drinking beer, rambling on about Lillian.* PHRASAL VERB =rattle on V P V P *about* n

rambler /ræmbləʳ/ **ramblers.** A **rambler** is a person whose hobby is going on long walks in the countryside, often as part of an organized group; used mainly in British English. ◆◇◇◇◇ N-COUNT

rambling /ræmblɪŋ/ ◆◇◇◇◇

1 A **rambling** building is big and old with an irregular shape. *...that rambling house and its bizarre contents.* ADJ: usu ADJ n

2 If you describe a speech or piece of writing as **rambling**, you are criticizing it for being too long and very confused. *His actions were accompanied by a rambling monologue... Cameron wrote a rambling letter to his wife.* ADJ-GRADED: usu ADJ n

ramblings /ræmblɪŋz/. If you describe a speech or piece of writing as someone's **ramblings**, you are saying that it is meaningless or unimportant because the person who said or wrote it was very confused or perhaps even slightly insane. *The official dismissed the speech as the ramblings of a desperate lunatic.* N-PLURAL: usu with poss

rambunctious /ræmbʌŋkʃəs/. A **rambunctious** person is energetic in a cheerful, noisy way; used especially in American English. The usual British word is **rumbustious**. *...a very rambunctious and energetic class.* ADJ-GRADED: usu ADJ n =boisterous

ramekin /ræmɪkɪn/ **ramekins.** A **ramekin** or a **ramekin dish** is a small dish in which a portion of food for one person can be baked in the oven. N-COUNT

ramification /ræmɪfɪkeɪʃᵊn/ **ramifications.** The **ramifications** of a decision, plan, or event are all its consequences and effects, especially ones which are not obvious at first. *The book analyses the social and political ramifications of AIDS for the gay community.* ◆◇◇◇◇ N-COUNT: usu pl, oft with poss =consequence, effect

ramp /ræmp/ **ramps** ◆◇◇◇◇

1 A **ramp** is a sloping surface between two places that are at different levels. *Lillian was coming down the ramp from the museum. ...a ramp to facilitate entry into the pool from a wheelchair.* N-COUNT

2 In American English, an **entrance ramp** is a road which cars use to drive onto an expressway, and an **exit ramp** is a road which cars use to drive off a expressway. The usual British expression for both of these roads is **slip road**. N-COUNT

rampage, rampages, rampaging, rampaged. ◆◇◇◇◇ Pronounced /ræmpeɪdʒ/ for meaning 1, and /ræmpeɪdʒ/ for meaning 2.

1 When people or animals **rampage** through a place, they rush about there in a wild or violent way, causing damage or destruction. *Hundreds of youths rampaged through the town, shop windows were smashed and cars overturned... He used a sword to try to defend his shop from a rampaging mob.* VERB V adv/prep V-ing

2 If people go **on the rampage**, they rush about in a wild or violent way, causing damage or destruction. *The prisoners went on the rampage destroying everything in their way. ...a bull on the rampage.* PHRASE: v PHR, v-link PHR

rampant /ræmpənt/. If you describe something bad, such as a crime or disease, as **rampant**, you mean that it is very widespread and is growing in an uncontrolled way. *Inflation is rampant and industry in decline. ...the rampant corruption of the administration.* ◆◇◇◇◇ ADJ-GRADED

rampart /ræmpɑːʳt/ **ramparts.** The **ramparts** of a castle or city are the earth banks, often with N-COUNT: usu pl walls on them, that were built to protect it. *...a walk along the ramparts of the Old City.*

ram-raid, ram-raids, ram-raiding, ram-raided
1 In British English, a **ram-raid** is a robbery on a shop or other building in which the robbers use a car to smash their way into the building. *He was out to do a ram-raid.* N-COUNT
2 In British English, if people **ram-raid**, they carry out a robbery on a shop or other building using a car to smash their way into the building. *The kids who are joyriding and ramraiding are unemployed.* VERB V Also V n
♦ **ram-raider, ram-raiders** *Ram-raiders smashed their way into a high-class store.* N-COUNT

ramrod /ræmrɒd/ **ramrods**
1 A **ramrod** is a long, thin rod which can be used for pushing something into a narrow tube. Ramrods were used, for example, for forcing gunpowder down the barrels of old-fashioned guns, or for cleaning the barrel of a gun. N-COUNT
2 If someone sits or stands **like a ramrod** or **straight as a ramrod**, they have a very straight back and appear rather stiff and formal. *...a woman with iron grey hair, high cheekbones and a figure like a ramrod. ...his dashing military moustache and straight-as-a-ramrod back.* PHRASE
3 If someone has a **ramrod** back or posture, they have a very straight back and hold themselves in a rather stiff and formal way. *I don't have the ramrod posture I had when I was in the Navy.* ► Also an adverb. *At 75, she's still ramrod straight.* ADJ: ADJ n; ADV: ADV adj

ramshackle /ræmʃækəl/ ◆◇◇◇◇
1 A **ramshackle** building is badly made or in bad condition, and looks as if it is likely to fall down. *They entered the shop, which was a curious ramshackle building.* ADJ-GRADED: usu ADJ n =tumbledown
2 A **ramshackle** system, coalition, or collection has been put together without much thought and is not likely to work or last very well. *They joined with a ramshackle alliance of other rebels. ...the present tax system, which the opposition says is ramshackle and complicated.* ADJ-GRADED: usu ADJ n

ran /ræn/. **Ran** is the past tense of **run**.

ranch /rɑːntʃ, ræntʃ/ **ranches.** A **ranch** is a large farm used for raising animals, especially cattle, horses, or sheep. *He lives on a cattle ranch in Australia.* • See also **dude ranch**. ◆◇◇◇◇ N-COUNT

rancher /rɑːntʃəʳ, ræn-/ **ranchers.** A **rancher** is someone who owns or manages a large farm, especially one used for raising cattle, horses, or sheep. *...a cattle rancher.* ◆◇◇◇◇ N-COUNT

ranching /rɑːntʃɪŋ, ræn-/. **Ranching** is the activity of running a large farm, especially one used for raising cattle, horses, or sheep. N-UNCOUNT

rancid /rænsɪd/. If butter, bacon, or other fatty foods are **rancid**, they have gone bad and taste stale and unpleasant. *Butter is perishable and can go rancid. ...the odour of rancid milk.* ADJ-GRADED

rancor /ræŋkər/. See **rancour**.

rancorous /ræŋkərəs/. A **rancorous** argument or person is full of bitterness and resentment; a formal word. *The deal ended after a series of rancorous disputes.* ADJ-GRADED =bitter, acrimonious

rancour /ræŋkəʳ/; spelled **rancor** in American English. **Rancour** is a feeling of bitterness and resentment; a formal word. *'That's too bad,' Teddy said without rancour.* N-UNCOUNT =bitterness

rand /rænd/ **rands; rand** can also be used as the plural form. The **rand** is the unit of currency used in South Africa. *...12 million rand.* ► **The rand** is also used to refer to the South African currency system. *The rand slumped by 22% against the dollar.* N-COUNT: usu num N; N-SING: *the* N

R&B /ɑːr ən biː/. **R&B** is a style of popular music developed in the 1940's from blues music, but using electrically amplified instruments. **R&B** is an abbreviation for 'rhythm and blues'. ◆◇◇◇◇ N-UNCOUNT: oft N n

R&D /ɑːr ən diː/; also spelled **R and D**. **R&D** refers to the research and development work or department within a large company or organization. **R&D** is an abbreviation for 'Research and Development'. A technical term used in business. *Businesses need to train their workers better, and spend more on R&D. ...investment in R&D.* ◆◇◇◇◇ N-UNCOUNT: oft *in/on* N

random /rændəm/ ◆◆◇◇◇
1 A **random** sample or method is one in which all the people or things involved have an equal chance of being chosen. *The survey used a random sample of two thousand people across England and Wales... The competitors will be subject to random drug testing.* ♦ **randomly** *...interviews with a randomly selected sample of thirty girls aged between 13 and 18.* ADJ: usu ADJ n; ADV: ADV with v
2 If you describe events as **random**, you mean that they do not seem to follow a definite plan or pattern. *...random violence against innocent victims... Children's words and actions are often fairly random. ...random variations of the wind.* ♦ **randomly** *...drinks and magazines left scattered randomly around.* ♦ **randomness** *Isn't this a demand to control the randomness of life?* ADJ-GRADED: usu ADJ n; ADV-GRADED: ADV with v; N-UNCOUNT
3 If you choose people or things **at random**, you do not use any particular method, so they all have an equal chance of being chosen. *We received several answers, and we picked one at random.* PHRASES PHR after v
4 If something happens **at random**, it happens without a definite plan or pattern. *Three black people were killed by shots fired at random from a minibus.* PHR after v

randomize /rændəmaɪz/ **randomizes, randomizing, randomized;** also spelled **randomise** in British English. If you **randomize** the events or people in scientific experiments or academic research, you use a method that gives them all an equal chance of happening or being chosen; a technical term. *The wheel is designed with obstacles in the ball's path to randomise its movement... Properly randomized studies are only now being completed.* VERB ≠bias, skew; V n; V-ed

randy /rændi/ **randier, randiest.** In informal British English, someone who is **randy** is sexually excited and eager to have sex. *It was extremely hot and I was feeling rather randy.* ◆◇◇◇◇ ADJ-GRADED =horny

rang /ræŋ/. **Rang** is the past tense of **ring**.

range /reɪndʒ/ **ranges, ranging, ranged** ◆◆◆◆◇
1 A **range** of things is a number of different things of the same general kind. *A wide range of colours and patterns are available... The two men discussed a range of issues... The range includes chests of drawers, tables and wardrobes.* N-COUNT: usu with supp, oft N *of* n
2 A **range** is the complete group that is included between two points on a scale of measurement or quality. *The average age range is between 35 and 55. ...properties available in the price range they are looking for. ...top-of-the-range products for which people are prepared to pay a little bit more.* N-COUNT: usu with supp, oft n N
3 The **range** of something is the maximum area in which it can reach things or detect things. *The 120mm mortar has a range of 18,000 yards... The trees on the mountains within my range of vision had all been felled... Tactical nuclear weapons have shorter ranges.* N-COUNT: usu with supp
4 If things **range** between two points or **range** from one point to another, they vary within these points on a scale of measurement or quality. *They range in price from $3 to $15. ...offering merchandise ranging from the everyday to the esoteric. ...temperatures ranging between 5°C and 20°C.* VERB V *from* amount *to* amount; V *from* n *to* n; V *between* pl-amount
5 If a piece of writing or speech **ranges over** a group of topics, it includes all those topics. *The conversation ranged over the desirability of such restaurants, the shortcomings of men, and why it had only taken 15 minutes to cross a continent.* VERB V *over* n
6 If people or things **are ranged** somewhere, they are arranged in a row or in lines; a formal use. *Some 300 trees have been ranged along the perimeter hedge... More than 1,500 police and troops are ranged against them.* VB: usu passive *be* V-ed prep V-ed
7 If animals or people **range** somewhere, they move around in a place without having a particular destination in mind. *Feeding is not a problem because the birds range over such a large area... They range widely in search of carrion.* VERB =roam V prep/adv Also V n
8 A **range** of mountains or hills is a line of them. N-COUNT:

...the massive mountain ranges to the north. ...an impressive range of hills topped with trees. usu with supp

9 A rifle **range** or a shooting **range** is a place where people can practise shooting at targets. *It reminds me of my days on the rifle range preparing for duty in Vietnam. ...an Army firing range.* N-COUNT: usu supp N

10 A **range** is an old-fashioned metal cooking stove. *...if the kitchen has a gas range.* N-COUNT: usu with supp

11 See also **free-range**.

12 If something is **in range** or **within range**, it is near enough to be reached or detected. If it is **out of range**, it is too far away to be reached or detected. *Cars are driven through the mess, splashing everyone in range. ...within range of their aircraft. ...out of range of their rockets... The fish stayed 50 yards offshore, well out of range.* PHRASES v-link PHR, PHR after v

13 If you see or hit something **at close range**, or **from close range**, you are very close to it when you see it or hit it. If you do something **at a range of** half a mile, for example, you are half a mile away from it when you do it. *He was shot in the head at close range... McCoist knocked the ball in from close range. ...photographing wild animals from close range... The enemy opened fire at a range of only 20 yards.* PHR after v

rangefinder /reɪndʒfaɪndəʳ/ **rangefinders.** A **rangefinder** is an instrument, usually part of a camera or a piece of military equipment, that measures the distance between things that are far away from each other; a technical term. N-COUNT

ranger /reɪndʒəʳ/ **rangers.** A **ranger** is a person whose job is to look after a forest or large park. *Bill Justice is a park ranger at the Carlsbad Caverns National Park.* ◆◇◇◇◇ N-COUNT

rangy /reɪndʒi/. If you describe a person or animal as **rangy**, you mean that they have long, slim, powerful legs; used in written English. *...a tall, rangy, redheaded girl.* ADJ: usu ADJ n =long-legged

rank /ræŋk/ **ranks, ranking, ranked** ◆◆◆◇◇

1 Someone's **rank** is the position or grade that they have in an organization. *He eventually rose to the rank of captain... The former head of counter-intelligence had been stripped of his rank and privileges. ...officers of equivalent rank in the other branches.* N-VAR: with supp

2 Someone's **rank** is the social class, especially the high social class, that they belong to; a formal use. *Each rank of the peerage was represented... He must be treated as a hostage of high rank, not as a common prisoner.* N-VAR: usu with supp

3 If an official organization **ranks** someone or something 1st, 5th, or 50th, for example, they calculate that the person or thing has that position in their list or scale. *The report ranks the UK 20th out of 22 advanced nations... He was at the time ranked 10th in the world and had a regular place in the Swedish Davis Cup team... The United States ranks 20th in its infant mortality rate. ...the only British woman to be ranked in the top 50 of the women's world rankings... Mr Short does not even rank in the world's top ten.* V-ERG; V n ord *in/out of* n; V ord *in/out of* n; be V-ed *in* n; V *in/among* n

4 If you say that someone or something **ranks** high or low, or **ranks** as important, for example, you are saying how good, important, or useful you think they are. *His prices rank high among those of other contemporary photographers... Investors ranked South Korea high among Asian nations... St Petersburg's night life ranks as more exciting than the capital's... 18 per cent of women ranked sex as very important in their lives... The Ritz-Carlton in Aspen has to rank as one of the most extraordinary hotels I have ever been to... Since the 1930s, cancer has always been ranked as the disease people are most concerned about.* V-ERG; V adj *among* n; V n adj *among* n; V *as* adj; V n *as* adj; V *as* n; be V-ed *as* n; Also V n *among* n, V *among* n, V n *as* n

5 If you say that someone or something **ranks with** a group of famous people or things, you mean that they are extremely good and should be included in that group. *...a performance of heroic calibre that must rank with the most memorable in international rugby... As a novel, Nineteen Eighty-four hardly ranks with the greats.* VERB; V *with* n

6 The **ranks** of a group or organization are the people who belong to it. *There were some misgivings within the ranks of the media too... The General Assembly welcomed five new members to its ranks. ...the growing ranks of companies building personal computers.* N-PLURAL: with supp

7 **The ranks** are the ordinary members of an organization, especially of the armed forces. *Top military leaders say there have been reports of demoralization in the ranks... Most store managers have worked their way up through the ranks.* N-PLURAL: *the* N, oft prep N

8 A **rank** of people or things is a row of them. *Ranks of police in riot gear stood nervously by... She continued to smile at the ranks of cameras on their doorstep.* N-COUNT: usu N *of* n =row

9 A taxi **rank** is a part of a city street where taxis park when they are available for hire. *The man led the way to the taxi rank... He walked towards the first taxi on the rank.* N-COUNT

10 You can use **rank** to emphasize a bad or undesirable quality that exists in an extreme form; a formal use. *He called it 'rank hypocrisy' that the government was now promoting equal rights.* ADJ: ADJ n PRAGMATICS =sheer

11 You can describe something as **rank** when it has a strong and unpleasant smell; an old-fashioned, literary use. *The kitchen was rank with the smell of drying uniforms. ...the rank smell of unwashed clothes.* ADJ

12 If you say that a member of a group or organization **breaks ranks**, you mean that they disobey the instructions of their group or organization. *'Even the President's staunchest supporters have some issues where they simply must break ranks,' says Senator Lott... China appears unlikely to break ranks with other members of the United Nations Security Council.* PHRASES V inflects

13 If you say that the members of a group **close ranks**, you mean that they are supporting each other only because their group is being criticized; used showing disapproval. *Conservative MPs intend to put aside their differences over Europe and close ranks behind the Prime Minister... Institutions tend to close ranks when a member has been accused of misconduct.* V inflects PRAGMATICS

14 If you experience something, usually something bad, that other people have experienced, you can say that you have **joined** their **ranks**. *Last month, 370,000 Americans joined the ranks of the unemployed... Many have now joined Amnesty's growing ranks of prisoners of conscience.* V inflects

15 If one of the people in a competition is described as a **rank outsider**, they are considered to have very little chance of winning. *The rank outsiders, Cameroon, beat the defending champions, Argentina, by one goal to nil.* N inflects

16 If you say that someone in authority **pulls rank**, you mean that they unfairly force other people to do what they want because of their higher rank or position; used showing disapproval. *The Captain pulled rank and made his sergeant row the entire way.* V inflects PRAGMATICS

rank and file. The **rank and file** are the ordinary members of an organization or workers in a company, as opposed to its leaders or managers; used mainly in politics and journalism. *There was widespread support for him among the rank and file... Substantial numbers of rank and file members ignored their union's advice... It seems that the rank and file of the party hadn't been consulted.* ◆◇◇◇◇ N-SING: usu *the* N

-ranked /-ræŋkt/. **-ranked** is added to words, usually ordinal numbers, to form adjectives which indicate what position someone or something has in a list or scale. *...Cheryl Thibedeau, Canada's second-ranked sprinter. ...the world's ten highest-ranked players.* COMB in ADJ: ADJ n

ranking /ræŋkɪŋ/ **rankings** ◆◆◇◇◇

1 In many sports, the list of the best players made by an official organization is called **the rankings**. *...the 25 leading teams in the world rankings... Goellner has shot up the rankings.* N-PLURAL: *the* N

2 Someone's **ranking** is their position in an official N-COUNT:

list of the best players of a sport. *Agassi was playing well above his world ranking of 12.* usu with poss

3 In American English, the **ranking** member of a group, usually a political group, is the most senior person in it. *...the ranking Republican on the senate intelligence committee. ...the ranking American diplomat in Baghdad.* ADJ: ADJ n

-ranking /-ræŋkɪŋ/. **-ranking** is used to form adjectives which indicate what rank someone has in an organization. *...a colonel on trial with three lower-ranking officers... He was the third-ranking official of the CIA from 1984 to 1987.* COMB in ADJ: ADJ n

rankle /ræŋkəl/ **rankles, rankling, rankled.** If an event or situation **rankles**, it makes you feel angry or bitter afterwards, because you think it was unfair or wrong. *They paid him only £10 for it and it really rankled... Britain's refusal to sell Portugal arms in 1937 still rankled with him... The only thing that rankles me is what she says about Ireland.* VERB V V with n V n

ransack /rænsæk/ **ransacks, ransacking, ransacked.** If people **ransack** a building, they make a mess and damage things in it, often because they are looking for something. *Demonstrators ransacked and burned the house where he was staying... He returned from hospital to find thieves had ransacked his home. ...the wrecked schools and churches, the ransacked embassies and homes.* ♦ **ransacking** *Nor did he explicitly denounce the ransacking of the opposition parties' offices.* ◆◇◇◇◇ VERB V n V-ed N SING: the N of n

ransom /rænsəm/ **ransoms, ransoming, ransomed** ◆◇◇◇◇

1 A **ransom** is the money that has to be paid to someone so that they will set free a person they have kidnapped. *Her kidnapper successfully extorted a £175,000 ransom for her release... The president has said the United States will never pay ransom for the hostages... The ransom demand was made by telephone.* N-VAR

2 If you **ransom** someone who has been kidnapped, you pay the money to set them free. *The same system was used for ransoming or exchanging captives.* VERB V n

3 If a kidnapper **holds** a person **to ransom** or **for ransom**, or **holds** a person **ransom**, they keep that person prisoner until they are given what they want. *In Rio, nearly forty people have been held to ransom this year alone... A bus-load of schoolchildren were held ransom until the gang were given a plane.* PHRASES V inflects

4 If you say that someone **is holding** you **to ransom**, you mean that they are using their power to force you to do something you don't want to do; used showing disapproval. *He said terrorists would not be allowed to hold Britain to ransom.* V inflects PRAGMATICS

5 If you refer to a sum of money as **a king's ransom**, you are emphasizing that it is very large; an old-fashioned expression. *...clients happy to pay a king's ransom for a haircut.* usu v PHR

rant /rænt/ **rants, ranting, ranted** ◆◇◇◇◇

1 If you say that someone **rants**, you mean that they talk loudly or angrily, and exaggerate or say foolish things. *As the boss began to rant, I stood up and went out. ...the mentally ill patient we heard ranting about demons... Even their three dogs got bored and fell asleep as he ranted on... 'Let's get it over and done with, and to hell with them,' he ranted.* ► Also a noun. *Part I is a rant against organised religion.* ♦ **ranting, rantings** *He had been listening to Goldstone's rantings all night... There was no occasion for ranting.* VERB V V about/at/against n V on V with quote N-COUNT N-VAR

2 If you say that someone **rants and raves**, you mean that they talk loudly and angrily in an uncontrolled way; used showing disapproval. *I don't rant and rave or throw tea cups.* PHRASE: Vs inflect PRAGMATICS

rap /ræp/ **raps, rapping, rapped** ◆◆◇◇◇

1 **Rap** is a type of music in which the words are not sung but are spoken in a rapid, rhythmic way. *For some people, rap – the music of the hip-hop generation – is just so much noise... Her favorite music was by Run DMC, a rap group.* N-UNCOUNT: oft N n

2 Someone who **raps** performs rap music. *...the unexpected pleasure of hearing the Kids not only rap but even sing... New Yorkers rap about parties and clubs, I rap about car chases and guns.* VERB V V about n

3 A **rap** is a piece of music performed in rap style, or the words that are used in it. *Every member contributes to the rap, singing either solo or as part of a rap chorus.* N-COUNT

4 If you **rap** on something or **rap** it, you hit it with a series of quick blows. *Mary Ann turned and rapped on Simon's door. ...rapping the glass with the knuckles of his right hand... A guard raps his stick on a metal hand rail.* ► Also a noun. *There was a sharp rap on the door.* VERB V on n V n V n on n N-COUNT: usu N on n

5 In informal American English, a **rap** is a criminal conviction. *You'll be facing a Federal rap for aiding and abetting an escaped convict.* N-COUNT: oft adj N for n

6 A **rap** is an act of criticizing or blaming someone; used in journalism. *Paul Ringer faces a rap after playing for Penarth on Boxing Day... Timeshare companies also come in for a rap as they continue to flout the rules.* N-COUNT: usu sing

7 If you **rap** someone for something, you criticize or blame them for it; used in journalism. *Mr Kavanagh firmly rapped the DTP for its analysis... The minister rapped banks over their treatment of small businesses.* VERB =criticize V n for/over n

8 In informal American English, the **rap** about someone or something is their reputation, often a bad reputation which is based on gossip. *The rap against Conn was that he was far too reckless... The rap on this guy is that he doesn't really care... He said statisticians gave them a bad rap by 'lying with figures'.* N-SING: usu with supp

9 If someone in authority **raps** your **knuckles** or **raps** you **on the knuckles**, they criticize you or blame you for doing something they think is wrong; used especially in journalism. *We rap the manufacturers on their knuckles if the toy is shoddy... I joined the workers on strike and was rapped over the knuckles... Ms Tyson also had her knuckles rapped for doing this.* PHRASES V inflects

10 If someone in authority gives you **a rap on the knuckles**, they criticize you or blame you for doing something they think is wrong; used especially in journalism. *The remark earned him a rap on the knuckles... Britain gave them a diplomatic rap over the knuckles.* PHR after v

11 If you **take the rap**, you are blamed or punished for something, especially something that is not your fault or for which other people are equally guilty. *When the client was murdered, his wife took the rap, but did she really do it?* V inflects

rap out. If you **rap out** an order or a question, you say it quickly and sharply. *She kept rapping out orders: 'Up a bit, down a bit, do it like that.'... 'How do we know that?' rapped out Lester.* PHRASAL VERB V P n (not pron) V P with quote

rapacious /rəpeɪʃəs/. If you describe a person or their behaviour as **rapacious**, you disapprove of their greedy or uncaring behaviour; a formal word. *He had a rapacious appetite for bird's nest soup... The oil fields have been depleted by a rapacious exploitation policy.* ADJ-GRADED: usu ADJ n PRAGMATICS

rapacity /rəpæsɪti/. **Rapacity** is very greedy or uncaring behaviour; a formal word, used showing disapproval. *He argued that the overcrowded cities were the product of a system based on 'selfishness' and 'rapacity'. ...the rapacity of landlords and the misery of tenants. ...their sexual desire and rapacity.* N-UNCOUNT: oft with poss PRAGMATICS

rape /reɪp/ **rapes, raping, raped** ◆◆◆◇◇

1 If someone **is raped**, they are forced to have sex, usually by violence or threats of violence. *A young woman was brutally raped in her own home... They'd held him down and raped him.* VERB be V-ed V n

2 **Rape** is the crime of forcing someone to have sex. *Her party opposes abortion, except in cases of rape or incest... Almost ninety per cent of all rapes and violent assaults went unreported.* N-VAR

3 **The rape of** an area or of a country is the destruction or spoiling of it; a literary use. *As a result of the* N-SING: the N of n

rape of the forests, parts of the country are now short of water.

4 See also **date rape, gang rape, oil seed rape.**

rapid /ræpɪd/ ◆◆◆◆◇

1 A **rapid** change is one that happens very quickly. *...the country's rapid economic growth in the 1980's... This signals a rapid change of mind by the government. ...the rapid decline in the birth rate in Western Europe.* [ADJ-GRADED: usu ADJ n =fast] ♦ **rapidly** *...countries with rapidly growing populations... Try to rip it apart as rapidly as possible... 'Operating profit is rising more rapidly,' he said.* [ADV-GRADED: usu ADV with v, also ADV adj =quickly] ♦ **rapidity** /rəpɪdɪti/ *...the rapidity with which the weather can change.* [N-UNCOUNT =speed]

2 A **rapid** movement is one that is very fast. *He walked at a rapid pace along Charles Street. ...whether the Tunnel will provide more rapid car transport than ferries... Breathing becomes more rapid and sweating starts.* [ADJ-GRADED: usu ADJ n =fast] ♦ **rapidly** *He was moving rapidly around the room... They rapidly spread out over the field.* [ADV-GRADED: ADV with v =quickly] ♦ **rapidity** *The water rushed through the holes with great rapidity.* [N-UNCOUNT =speed]

rapid-fire

1 A **rapid-fire** gun is one that shoots a lot of bullets very quickly, one after the other. *In the back of the truck was a 12.7 millimeter rapid-fire machine gun.* [ADJ: ADJ n]

2 A **rapid-fire** conversation or speech is one in which people talk or reply very quickly. *Yul listened to their sophisticated, rapid-fire conversation. ...arguing a point in rapid-fire Spanish.* [ADJ: ADJ n]

3 A **rapid-fire** economic activity or development is one that takes place very quickly; used mainly in American journalism. *...the rapid-fire buying and selling of stocks... The company made a rapid-fire series of settlements with 25 States. ...Japan's rapid-fire industrialization.* [ADJ: ADJ n]

rapids /ræpɪdz/. **Rapids** are a section of a river where the water moves very fast, often over rocks. *His canoe was there, on the river below the rapids.* [◆◇◇◇◇ N-PLURAL]

rapid transit. A **rapid transit** system is a transport system in a city which allows people to travel quickly, using trains that run underground or above the streets. *...a rapid transit link with the City and London's underground system... Two rapid transit trains collided early this morning in Boston.* [ADJ: ADJ n]

rapier /reɪpiəʳ/ **rapiers**

1 A **rapier** is a very thin sword with a long sharp point. [N-COUNT]

2 If you say that someone has a **rapier** wit, you mean that they are very intelligent and quick at making clever comments or jokes in a conversation. *Julie Burchill is famous for her precocity and rapier wit.* [ADJ: ADJ n]

rapist /reɪpɪst/ **rapists.** A **rapist** is a man who has raped someone. *The convicted murderer and rapist is scheduled to be executed next Friday.* [◆◇◇◇◇ N-COUNT]

rapper /ræpəʳ/ **rappers.** A **rapper** is a person who performs rap music. *The British pop charts have been dominated by rappers like MC Hammer in recent months.* [◆◇◇◇◇ N-COUNT]

rapport /ræpɔːʳ/. If two people or groups have a **rapport**, they have a good relationship in which they are able to understand each other's ideas or feelings very well. *He said he wanted 'to establish a rapport with the Indian people'... The success depends on good rapport between interviewer and interviewee... You have an intellectual rapport, a kind of easy companionship that makes me really jealous.* [◆◇◇◇◇ N-SING: also no det, oft N *with*/*between* n]

rapporteur /ræpɔːʳtɜːʳ/ **rapporteurs.** A **rapporteur** is a person who is officially appointed by an organization to investigate a problem or attend a meeting and to report on it; a technical term. *...the United Nations special rapporteur on torture. ...UN human rights rapporteurs.* [N-COUNT: usu with supp]

rapprochement /ræprɒʃmɒn, AM -proʊʃ-/. A **rapprochement** is an increase in friendliness between two countries, groups, or people, especially after a period of unfriendliness; used mainly in journalism. *There have been growing signs of a rapprochement with Vietnam. ...the process of political rapprochement between the two former foes.* [◆◇◇◇◇ N-SING: also no det, oft N *with*/*between* n =reconciliation]

rapt /ræpt/. If someone watches or listens with **rapt** attention, they are extremely interested or fascinated; used in written English. *I noticed that everyone was watching me with rapt attention... Delegates sat in rapt silence as Mrs Fisher spoke... Phillips had a rapt expression on his face... He had held his audience rapt.* [ADJ-GRADED: usu ADJ n] ♦ **raptly** *...listening raptly to stories about fascinating people.* [ADV: ADV with v]

raptor /ræptəʳ/ **raptors. Raptors** are birds of prey, such as eagles and hawks; a technical term in zoology. [N-COUNT =bird of prey]

rapture /ræptʃəʳ/. **Rapture** is a feeling of extreme joy or pleasure; a literary word. *The film was shown to gasps of rapture at the Democratic Convention... His speech was received with rapture by his supporters... I stare in rapture at the ball... What joy, what rapture, what glory to see him again!* [N-UNCOUNT =delight]

raptures /ræptʃəʳz/. If you are **in raptures** or go **into raptures** about something, you are extremely impressed by it and enthusiastic about it; used mainly in written British English. *They will be in raptures over the French countryside... Davies goes into raptures over the brilliantly coloured paintwork... His goal sent the crowd into raptures.* [PHRASE: v-link PHR, PHR after v]

rapturous /ræptʃərəs/. A **rapturous** feeling or reaction is one of extreme happiness or enthusiasm; used mainly in journalism. *The students gave him a rapturous welcome... Pope John Paul received a rapturous reception when he visited East Timor... The conference greeted the speech with rapturous applause.* [ADJ: usu ADJ n] ♦ **rapturously** *He was rapturously received by the American Congress... They were kissing each other rapturously.* [ADV: ADV with v]

rare /reəʳ/ **rarer, rarest** ◆◆◆◇◇

1 Something that is **rare** is not common and is therefore interesting or valuable. *...the black-necked crane, one of the rarest species in the world... She collects rare plants... Do you want to know about a particular rare stamp or rare stamps in general?* [ADJ-GRADED =uncommon ≠common]

2 An event or situation that is **rare** does not occur very often. *...on those rare occasions when he did eat alone... Heart attacks were extremely rare in babies, he said... It's apparently rare for anyone to have two legs the same length... I think it's very rare to have big families nowadays.* [ADJ-GRADED: oft *it* v-link ADJ to-inf =uncommon ≠common]

3 You use **rare** to emphasize an extremely good or remarkable quality. *Ferris has a rare ability to record her observations on paper... It was a rare pleasure to see him in action. ...a leader of rare strength and instinct.* [ADJ: ADJ n PRAGMATICS =uncommon]

4 Meat that is **rare** is cooked very lightly so that the inside is still red. *Thick tuna steaks are eaten rare, like beef... Waiter, I specifically asked for this steak rare.* [ADJ-GRADED]

rarefied /reərɪfaɪd/

1 If you talk about the **rarefied** atmosphere of a place or institution, you are expressing your disapproval of it, because it has a special social or academic status that makes it very different from ordinary life. *...the fear and loneliness that working class students can feel when they are plunged into the rarefied atmosphere of university... It is important for the state's future administrators to get out of the rarefied air of the capital.* [ADJ-GRADED: usu ADJ n PRAGMATICS]

2 Rarefied air is air that does not contain much oxygen, for example in mountain areas. *Both animals and people were gasping for breath in the rarefied air. ...living at very high altitudes where the atmosphere is rarefied.* [ADJ-GRADED]

rarely /reəʳli/. If something **rarely** happens, it does not happen very often. *They battled against other Indian tribes, but rarely fought with the whites... I very rarely wear a raincoat because I spend most of my time in a car... Money was plentiful, and rarely did anyone seem very bothered about levels of expenditure... They were rarely seen together and certainly did not travel together... Adolescent suicide is rarely an impulsive* [◆◆◆◇◇ ADV-BRD-NEG: ADV before v, ADV with cl/group =seldom ≠often] *reaction to immediate distress... Rarely does a grand jury publicly disagree with a prosecutor.*

raring /reərɪŋ/
1 If you say that you **are raring to go**, you mean that you are very eager to start doing something. *After a good night's sleep, Paul said he was raring to go... Ferdinand, who has missed the last three games with an ankle injury, said last night: 'I'm raring to go'.* PHRASE: V inflects
2 If you are **raring** to do something or are **raring** for it, you are very eager to do it or very eager that it should happen; used mainly in American English. *Sarah's here and raring to meet you... He is raring to charge into the fray and lay down the law... Baker suggested the administration isn't raring for a fight.* ADJ: v-link ADJ, ADJ to-inf, ADJ for n =eager, keen

rarity /reərɪti/ **rarities** ◆◇◇◇◇
1 If someone or something is a **rarity**, they are interesting or valuable because they are so unusual; used especially in journalism. *Motorized wheelchairs are a rarity here... He was a rarity among Wall Street lawyers... Sontag has always been that rarity, a glamorous intellectual... Other rarities include an interview with Presley.* N-COUNT: usu sing, oft N in/among n PRAGMATICS
2 The **rarity** of something is the fact that it is very uncommon. *This indicates the rarity of such attacks... It was a real prize due to its rarity and good condition... 'Its rarity value is high,' Gibson announced gravely.* N-UNCOUNT: oft with poss

rascal /rɑːskəl, ræs-/ **rascals.** If you call a man or child a **rascal**, you mean that they are mischievous, rude, or dishonest; an old-fashioned word. *What's that old rascal been telling you?* N-COUNT =rogue

rascally /rɑːskəli, ræs-/. If you describe someone as a **rascally** person, you mean that they are mischievous, wicked, or dishonest; a literary word. *They stumble across a ghost town inhabited by a rascally gold prospector.* ADJ-GRADED: usu ADJ n

rash /ræʃ/ **rashes** ◆◆◇◇◇
1 If someone is **rash** or does **rash** things, they act without thinking carefully first, and therefore make mistakes or behave foolishly. *It would be rash to rely on such evidence... Mr. Major is making no rash promises... Don't do anything rash until the feelings subside.* ♦ **rashly** *I made quite a lot of money, but I rashly gave most of it away... My sister always said I acted rashly.* ♦ **rashness** *With characteristic rashness and valor, Peter plunged into the icy water. ...the rashness of youth.* ADJ-GRADED =hasty, impulsive ≠careful; ADV-GRADED: ADV with cl, ADV after v; N-UNCOUNT
2 A **rash** is an area of red spots that appear on your skin when you are ill or have an allergy. *I noticed a rash on my leg... He may break out in a rash when he eats these nuts... The symptoms include skin rashes, fever, and painful joints.* N-COUNT
3 If you talk about a **rash of** events or things, you mean a large number of unpleasant events or undesirable things, which have happened or appeared within a short period of time. *They believe this confusion is responsible for a rash of suicides this spring. ...one of the few major airlines left untouched by the industry's rash of takeovers... Now a rash of scruffy little shops bordered one side of the street.* N-SING: N of n PRAGMATICS =spate of

rasher /ræʃər/ **rashers.** In British English, a **rasher** of bacon is a slice of bacon. N-COUNT: oft N of n

rasp /rɑːsp, ræsp/ **rasps, rasping, rasped** ◆◇◇◇◇
1 If someone **rasps**, their voice or breathing is harsh and unpleasant to listen to. *'Where've you put it?' he rasped... He fell back into the water, his breath rasping in his heaving chest... In a rasping voice, she told of her long and agonising battle.* ▶ Also a noun. *He was still laughing when he heard the rasp of Rennie's voice.* VERB: V with quote, V, V-ing; N-SING: with supp
2 If something **rasps**, or if you **rasp** it on something, it makes a harsh, unpleasant sound as it rubs against something hard or rough. *Sabres rasped from scabbards and the horsemen spurred forward... Foden rasped a hand across his chin... He pulled the cloth and it came away with a rasping sound.* ▶ Also a noun. *...the rasp of something being drawn across the sand.* V-ERG: V prep, V n prep, V-ing; N-SING: with supp
3 A **rasp** is a long metal tool with rough surfaces, used to rub on solid objects and give them smooth surfaces. N-COUNT =file

raspberry /rɑːzbri, AM ræzberi/ **raspberries** ◆◇◇◇◇
1 **Raspberries** are small, soft, red fruit that grow on bushes. N-COUNT
2 In informal British English, if you blow a **raspberry**, you make a sound by putting your tongue out and blowing, in order to insult someone. *He blows a raspberry down the telephone line and hangs up... They're all making raspberry noises.* N-COUNT
3 If you blow a **raspberry** at someone or something, you reject them completely or criticize them severely; used mainly in British journalism. *...a time to blow a modest raspberry at politics... There should be no blowing of raspberries, therefore, over Leicester's choice of Mr Lineker.* N-COUNT

raspy /rɑːspi, ræs-/. If someone has a **raspy** voice, they make rough sounds as if they have a sore throat or have difficulty in breathing; a literary word. *Both men sang in a deep, raspy tone... Her voice was raspy with nicotine and whiskey.* ADJ =hoarse

Rasta /ræstə/ **Rastas**
1 A **Rasta** is the same as a **Rastafarian**; an informal use. *The LP was called Rastas Never Die.* N-COUNT
2 **Rasta** means the same as **Rastafarian**; an informal use. *...Rasta singer Pablo Moses.* ADJ: ADJ n

Rastafarian /ræstəfeəriən/ **Rastafarians**
1 A **Rastafarian** is a member of a Jamaican religious group which considers Haile Selassie, the former Emperor of Ethiopia, to be God. Rastafarians often have long, matted hair called dreadlocks. *He was one of the few thousand committed Rastafarians in South Africa.* N-COUNT =Rasta
2 **Rastafarian** is used to describe Rastafarians and their beliefs and lifestyle. *Rastafarian poet Benjamin Zephaniah is a special guest in the programme... He refused to cut his hair due to his Rastafarian beliefs.* ADJ: ADJ n =Rasta

rat /ræt/ **rats, ratting, ratted** ◆◆◇◇◇
1 A **rat** is an animal which has a long tail and looks like a large mouse. *This was demonstrated in a laboratory experiment with rats. ...a rat-infested derelict building.* N-COUNT
2 If you call someone a **rat**, you mean that you are angry with them or dislike them, often because they have cheated you or betrayed you; an offensive use. *What did you do with the gun you took from that little rat Turner?* N-COUNT
3 If someone **rats on** you, they tell someone in authority about things that you have done, especially bad things; an informal use. *They were both accused of encouraging children to rat on their parents.* VERB =grass on V on n
4 If someone **rats on** an agreement, they do not do what they said they would do; an informal use. *She claims he ratted on their divorce settlement.* VERB =renege on V on n
5 If you **smell a rat**, you begin to suspect or realize that something is wrong in a particular situation, for example that someone is trying to deceive you or harm you. *If I don't send a picture, he will smell a rat... Though Lloyd George's behaviour seemed curious, Haig still did not smell a rat.* PHRASE: V inflects

rata /rɑːtə/. See **pro rata**.

rat-a-tat. You use **rat-a-tat** to represent a series of sharp, repeated sounds, for example the sound of someone knocking at a door. *...the rat-a-tat at the door. ...the rat-a-tat of machine guns.* N-SING; SOUND

ratatouille /rætətuːi/. **Ratatouille** is a cooked vegetable dish, usually made with onions, tomatoes, aubergines, courgettes, and peppers. *You should have prepared something other than lamb and ratatouille. ...a delicious ratatouille.* N-UNCOUNT: also a N

ratbag /rætbæg/ **ratbags.** In British English, if you call someone a **ratbag**, you are insulting them; an offensive word. *Lying ratbags, that's what they are.* N-COUNT

ratchet /rætʃɪt/ **ratchets, ratcheting, ratcheted**
1 In a tool or machine, a **ratchet** is a wheel or bar with sloping teeth, which can move only in one direction, because a piece of metal stops the teeth from moving backwards. *The chair has a ratchet* N-COUNT

below it to adjust the height... A ratchet mechanism transfers the thread from spool to bobbin.

2 If a tool or machine **ratchets** or if you **ratchet** it, it makes a clicking noise as it operates, because it has a ratchet in it. *The rod bent double, the reel shrieked and ratcheted... She took up a sheet and ratcheted it into the typewriter.*
V-ERG; V; V n

3 If you describe a situation as a **ratchet**, you think that it is bad and can only become worse; used mainly in British journalism. *...another raising of the ratchet of violence in the conflict.*
N-SING: with supp; PRAGMATICS

ratchet up. If something that you disapprove of **ratchets up** or **is ratcheted up**, it increases by a fixed amount or degree, and will probably not decrease; used mainly in American journalism. *...an attempt to ratchet up the pressure on Israel... He fears inflation will ratchet up as the year ends... Audiences' expectations are ratcheted up as they are exposed to high-budget productions.*
PHRASAL VERB ERG; PRAGMATICS; =escalate; V P n (not pron); V P

rate /reɪt/ **rates, rating, rated** ◆◆◆◆◆

1 The **rate** at which something happens is the speed with which it happens. *The rate at which hair grows can be agonisingly slow... The world's tropical forests are disappearing at an even faster rate than experts had thought.*
N-COUNT: with supp

2 The **rate** at which something happens is the number of times it happens over a period of time. *New diet books appear at a rate of nearly one a week... His heart rate was 30 beats per minute slower... Britain held the unenviable record of having the highest divorce rate in Europe.*
N-COUNT: with supp

3 A **rate** is the amount of money that is charged for goods or services. *Calls cost 36p per minute cheap rate and 48p at all other times. ...specially reduced rates for travellers using Gatwick Airport... East German wages were converted at the rate of one old East mark for one Deutschmark.* • See also **exchange rate**.
N-COUNT: with supp

4 The **rate** of taxation or interest is the amount of tax or interest that needs to be paid. It is expressed as a percentage of the amount that is earned, gained as profit, or borrowed. *The government insisted that it would not be panicked into interest rate cuts.*
N-COUNT: with supp

5 In Britain, the **rates** were a local tax which you paid if you owned property or rented unfurnished property. *Soldiers were exempt from paying rates... The new council tax combines elements of both the community charge and the rates.*
N-PLURAL

6 If you **rate** someone or something as good or bad, you consider them to be good or bad. *Of all the men in the survey, they rate themselves the least fun-loving and the most responsible... The film was rated excellent by 90 per cent of children... Most rated it a hit... We rate him as one of the best... She rated the course highly... Reading books does not rate highly among Britons as a leisure activity. ...the most highly rated player in English football.*
V-ERG: no cont; V n adj; V n n; V n as n/adj; V n adv; V adv prep; V-ed

7 If you **rate** someone or something, you think that they are good; an informal use. *It's flattering to know that other clubs have shown interest and seem to rate me... Its artistic value failed to move Paddy Clegg. 'I don't know what all the fuss is about. I didn't rate it at all,' he said.*
VERB; V n

8 If someone or something **is rated** at a particular position or rank, they are calculated or estimated to be in that position in a table or list. *He is generally rated Italy's No. 3 industrialist... He came here rated 100th on the tennis computer.*
V-PASSIVE: no cont; =ranked; be V-ed n; be V-ed ord

9 If you say that someone or something **rates** a particular reaction, you mean that is the reaction you consider to be appropriate. *This is so extraordinary, it rates a medal and a phone call from the President... In those crowded streets her attire did not rate a second glance.*
VB: no cont; =merit; V n

10 See also **rating**.

11 You use **at any rate** to indicate that what you have just said might be incorrect or unclear in some way, and that you are now being more precise. *She modestly suggests that 'sex, or at any rate gender, may account for the difference'... He is the least appealing character, to me at any rate.*
PHRASES; PHR with cl; PRAGMATICS

12 You use **at any rate** to indicate that the important thing is what you are saying now, and not what was said before. *At any rate, Pankin said that relations between the two nations will be restored before the conference... Well, at any rate, let me thank you for all you did.*
PHR with cl; PRAGMATICS

13 If you say that **at this rate** something bad or extreme will happen, you mean that it will happen if things continue to develop as they have been doing. *At this rate, she would be almost seven feet tall by then... At this rate they'd be lucky to get home before eight-thirty or nine.*
PHR with cl; PRAGMATICS

rateable value /reɪtəbᵊl væljuː/ **rateable values.** In Britain, the **rateable value** of a building was a value based on its size and facilities, which was used in calculating local taxes called rates.
N-COUNT

rate-cap, rate-caps, rate-capping, rate-capped

1 In Britain, when a local council **was rate-capped**, the government prevented it from increasing local taxes called rates, in order to force the council to reduce its spending or improve its efficiency. *Notts County Council is to cut 200 jobs in a bid to escape being rate-capped.* ♦ **rate-capping** *The project is seriously threatened by rate-capping.*
VB: usu passive; be V-ed; N-UNCOUNT

2 In America, a **rate cap** is a limit placed by the government on the amount of interest that banks or credit card companies can charge their customers.
N-COUNT

rate of exchange, rates of exchange. A **rate of exchange** is the same as an **exchange rate**. *...four thousand dinars - about four hundred dollars at the official rate of exchange.*
N-COUNT; =exchange rate

ratepayer /reɪtpeɪəʳ/ **ratepayers**

1 In Britain, a **ratepayer** was a person who owned or rented property and therefore had to pay the local taxes called rates. The citizens of a district are sometimes still called the **ratepayers** when their interests and the use of local taxes are being considered. *The Conservatives see this as stopping the waste of ratepayers' money.*
N-COUNT

2 In the United States, a **ratepayer** is a person whose property is served by an electricity, water, or telephone company, and who pays for these services. *The new law could create a 'no lose' situation for the phone companies that could leave ratepayers worse off.*
N-COUNT

rather /rɑːðəʳ, ræð-/ ◆◆◆◆◆

1 You use **rather than** when you are contrasting two things or situations. **Rather than** introduces the thing or situation that is not the case or that you do not want or approve of. *The problem was psychological rather than physiological... Sedge is similar in appearance to grass but has a solid rather than a hollow stem... The dark star in Nova Muscae 1991 is a black hole rather than a neutron star... When I'm going out in the evening I use the bike if I can rather than the car.* ▶ Also a conjunction. *Rather than break her appointment and disappoint me, Katie again took the car... She made students think for themselves, rather than telling them what to think... I suggest that rather than the show season starting in June, it should be brought forward to April or May... Most of these will be fleeing cold and hunger, rather than fighting... She prefers to stay in detention rather than be released and go into exile.*
PHR-PREP; PHR-CONJ-SUBORD

2 You use **rather** when you are correcting the thing that you have just said, especially when you are describing the true situation after saying what it is not. *Twenty million years ago, Idaho was not the arid place it is now. Rather, it was warm and damp, populated by dense primordial forest... But there must be no talk of final victory; rather, the long, hard slog to a solution... The process is not a circle but rather a spiral... He explained what the Crux is, or rather, what it was.*
ADV: ADV with cl/group; PRAGMATICS

3 If you say that you **would rather** do something or you**'d rather** do it, you mean that you would prefer to do it. If you say you **would rather not** do something, you mean that you do not want to do it. *If it's all the same to you, I'd rather work at home... Which programme would you rather appear on?...*
PHR-MODAL; MODAL inf; MODAL inf *than* inf; MODAL that

Kids would rather play than study... I have no information one way or the other, but I would rather he do it than not do it... I would rather Lionel took it on... Sorry. I'd rather not talk about it... Would you like that? Don't hesitate to say no if you'd rather not. MODAL *not* inf, MODAL *not*

4 You use **rather** to indicate that something is true to a fairly great extent, especially when you are talking about something unpleasant or undesirable. *I grew up in rather unusual circumstances... It had made some rather bad mistakes which I thought should be corrected... He had had an excellent dinner at a rather good local hotel... The first speaker began to talk, very fast and rather loudly... We got along rather well... I'm afraid it's rather a long story... The reality is rather more complex... As you can see, he did rather better for himself than I did. ...a figure rather too good to be true... The fruit is rather like a sweet chestnut... Robbie was there with his family, keeping rather in the background.* ADV: ADV adj/adv, ADV *a* n, ADV compar, ADV *too* adj/adv, ADV prep

5 You use **rather** before verbs that introduce your thoughts and feelings, in order to express your opinion politely, especially when a different opinion has been expressed. *I rather think he was telling the truth... I rather like the decorative effect.* ADV: ADV before v, PRAGMATICS

6 In formal or old-fashioned British English, people sometimes say **rather** to express agreement or acceptance. *'Well, he did have a sort of family connection with it, didn't he.'—'Oh yes. Rather.'* CONVENTION

ratification /rætɪfɪkeɪʃən/ **ratifications.** The **ratification** of a treaty or written agreement is the process of ratifying it. *We believe we should proceed with the ratification of the Maastricht Treaty.* ◆◇◇◇◇ N-COUNT: usu sing, oft N *of* n

ratify /rætɪfaɪ/ **ratifies, ratifying, ratified.** When national leaders or organizations **ratify** a treaty or written agreement, they make it official by giving their formal approval to it, usually by signing it or voting for it. *The parliaments of Australia and Indonesia have yet to ratify the treaty.* ◆◆◇◇◇ VERB; V n

rating /reɪtɪŋ/ **ratings** ◆◆◆◇◇

1 A **rating** of something is a score or assessment of how good or popular it is. *...a value-for-money rating of ten out of ten... New public opinion polls show the president's approval rating at its lowest point since he took office.* • See also **credit rating.** N-COUNT: usu with supp

2 The **ratings** are the statistics published each week which show how popular each television programme is. *Eurocops was beaten in the ratings on Channel 4 by Kate and Allie, Hill Street Blues and St Elsewhere... CBS's ratings again showed huge improvement over the previous year.* N-PLURAL

3 **Ratings** are the sailors in national navies who are not officers or who have no rank; used mainly in British English. N-COUNT: usu pl

ratio /reɪʃioʊ, AM -ʃoʊ/ **ratios.** The **ratio** of something is the relationship between two things expressed in numbers or amounts, to show how much greater one is than the other. For example, if there are two boys and six girls in a room, the ratio of boys to girls is 1:3, or one to three. *In 1978 there were 884 students at a lecturer/student ratio of 1:15... The bottom chart shows the ratio of personal debt to personal income... The adult to child ratio is 1 to 6.* ◆◆◇◇◇ N-COUNT: usu sing, oft N *of* n *to* n, =proportion

ration /ræʃən/ **rations, rationing, rationed** ◆◇◇◇◇

1 When there is a shortage of something, your **ration** of it is the amount that you are allowed to have. *The meat ration was down to one pound per person per week... They have begun to issue ration cards for basic necessities such as rice and flour.* N-COUNT

2 When something **is rationed** by a person or government, you are only allowed to have a limited amount of it, usually because there is a shortage. *Staples such as bread, rice and tea are already being rationed... The decision to ration food comes as Muscovites have overrun bakeries... Motorists will be rationed to thirty litres of petrol a month... There's a black market in rationed goods.* VERB; *be* V-ed, V n, *be* V-ed *to* amount, V-ed, Also V n *to* amount

3 **Rations** are the food which is given to people with food shortages or to soldiers. *Aid officials said that the first emergency food rations of wheat and oil were handed out here last month... The Russian soldiers sampled the officers' rations and wolfed the superior food with delight.* N-PLURAL

4 Your **ration** of something is the amount of it that you normally have. *...after consuming his ration of junk food and two cigarettes.* N-COUNT: usu N *of* n

5 See also **rationing.**

rational /ræʃənəl/ ◆◆◇◇◇

1 **Rational** decisions and thoughts are based on reason rather than on emotion. *He's asking you to look at both sides of the case and come to a rational decision... Mary was able to short-circuit her stress response by keeping her thoughts calm and rational.* ♦ **rationally** *It can be very hard to think rationally when you're feeling so vulnerable and alone.* ♦ **rationality** /ræʃənælɪti/ *We live in an era of rationality.* ADJ-GRADED: usu ADJ n ≠irrational; ADV-GRADED: usu ADV with v ≠irrationally; N-UNCOUNT ≠irrationality

2 A **rational** person is someone who thinks clearly and is not emotionally or mentally unbalanced. *Did he come across as a sane rational person?... Rachel looked calmer and more rational now.* ADJ-GRADED ≠irrational

rationale /ræʃənɑːl, -næl/ **rationales.** The **rationale** for a course of action, practice, or belief is the set of reasons on which it is based; a formal word. *However, the rationale for such initiatives is not, of course, solely economic... The rationale of reprocessing spent nuclear fuel is inevitably being questioned.* ◆◇◇◇◇ N-COUNT: oft N *for* n/-ing

rationalism /ræʃənəlɪzəm/. **Rationalism** is the belief that your life should be based on reason and logic, rather than emotions or religious beliefs. *Coleridge was to spend the next thirty years attacking rationalism. ...the scientific rationalism of the West.* N-UNCOUNT

rationalist /ræʃənəlɪst/ **rationalists**

1 If you describe someone as **rationalist**, you mean that their beliefs are based on reason and logic rather than emotion or religion. *...the rationalist philosopher Lakatos. ...the rationalist and liberal ideas of the nineteenth century... White was both visionary and rationalist.* ADJ

2 If you describe someone as a **rationalist**, you mean that they base their life on rationalist beliefs. N-COUNT

3 See also **rationalism.**

rationalize /ræʃənəlaɪz/ **rationalizes, rationalizing, rationalized;** also spelled **rationalise** in British English. ◆◇◇◇◇

1 If you try to **rationalize** attitudes or actions that are difficult to accept, you think of reasons to justify or explain them. *He further rationalized his activity by convincing himself that he was actually promoting peace... I poured my thoughts out on paper in an attempt to rationalize my feelings.* ♦ **rationalization** /ræʃənəlaɪzeɪʃən/ **rationalizations** *...this rationalization of his bedside grief.* VERB; V n; N-VAR

2 When a company, system, or industry **is rationalized**, it is made more efficient, usually by getting rid of staff and equipment that are not essential. *The network of 366 local offices is being rationalised to leave the company with 150 to 200 larger branch offices.* ♦ **rationalization** *...the rationalization of the textile industry.* VB: usu passive =streamline; *be* V-ed; N-UNCOUNT

rationing /ræʃənɪŋ/. **Rationing** is the system of limiting the amount of food, water, petrol, or other necessary substances that each person is permitted to have or buy when there is a shortage of them. *The municipal authorities here are preparing for food rationing.* ◆◇◇◇◇ N-UNCOUNT: usu with supp

rat race. If you talk about getting out of **the rat race**, you mean leaving a job or way of life in which people compete aggressively with each other to be successful. *I had to get out of the rat race and take a look at the real world again.* N-SING: *the* N

rat run, rat runs. In informal British English, a **rat run** is a small residential street which drivers use during busy times in order to avoid heavy traffic on the main roads. N-COUNT

rattan /rætæn/. **Rattan** furniture is made from the woven strips of stems of a plant which grows in South East Asia. *...a light airy room set with cloth-covered tables and rattan chairs.* N-UNCOUNT: usu N n

rattle /rætəl/ **rattles, rattling, rattled** ◆◆◇◇◇

1 When something **rattles** or when you **rattle** it, it V-ERG

makes short sharp knocking sounds because it is being shaken or it keeps hitting against something hard. *She slams the kitchen door so hard I hear dishes rattle... He gently rattled the cage and whispered to the canary... Somewhere close at hand a train rattled by... The truck pulled away, and she listened to the rattling noises fade down the lane.* V / V n / V adv / V-ing
► Also a noun. *There was a rattle of rifle-fire.* N-COUNT
♦ **rattling** *At that moment, there was a rattling at the door.* N-SING

2 A **rattle** is a baby's toy with loose bits inside which make a noise when the baby shakes it. N-COUNT

3 A **rattle** is a wooden instrument that adults shake to make a loud rattling noise at football matches or tribal ceremonies. N-COUNT

4 If something or someone **rattles** you, they make you nervous. *The news from Body Shop rattled the rest of the retail sector... She refused to be rattled by his £3,000-a-day lawyer.* ♦ **rattled** *He swore in Spanish, another indication that he was rattled.* VERB =unnerve V n / ADJ-GRADED: usu v-link ADJ

5 You can say that a bus, train or car **rattles** somewhere when it moves noisily from one place to another. *The bus from Odense rattled into a dusty village called Pozo Almonte... Somewhere close at hand a train rattled by.* VERB / V prep/adv

rattle around. If you say that someone **rattles around** in a room or other space, you mean that the space is too large for them. *We don't want to move, but we're rattling around in our large house.* PHRASAL VERB / V P *in* n / Also V P n

rattle off. If you **rattle off** something, you say it or do it very quickly and without much effort. *Asked what English he knew, Mr Semko rattled off 'One, two, three'... Hendry, playing an afternoon match, rattled off a 6-1 win over the Englishman.* PHRASAL VERB =reel off / V P n (not pron) / Also V n P

rattle on. When you say that someone **rattles on** about something, you mean that they talk about it for a long time in a way that annoys you. *I heard my mother rattling on and on about the day I get married, what I must wear, how I must act, who I must invite... He listened in silence as Niccolini rattled on, emphasizing his remarks with one hand and steering with the other.* PHRASAL VERB =prattle on / V P *about* n / V P

rattle through. If you **rattle through** something, you deal with it quickly in order to finish it; used mainly in British English. *She rattled through a translation from Virgil's Aeneid.* PHRASAL VERB / V P n

rattler /rætlərʳ/ **rattlers.** In informal American English, a **rattler** is the same as a **rattlesnake**. N-COUNT

rattlesnake /rætəlsneɪk/ **rattlesnakes.** A **rattlesnake** is a poisonous American snake which can make a rattling noise with its tail. *He had been bitten by a rattlesnake.* N-COUNT

rattling good. In old-fashioned British English, if you describe a story as a **rattling good** yarn or tale, you mean that it is very good and very exciting. *He tells a rattling good yarn.* ADJ: ADJ n

ratty /ræti/ **rattier, rattiest**

1 In informal British English, if someone is **ratty**, they get angry and irritated easily. *I had spent too many hours there and was beginning to get a bit ratty and fed up.* ADJ-GRADED =grumpy, irritable

2 In American English, **ratty** clothes and objects are frayed or tattered, especially because they are old. *I towelled myself dry and slipped into my ratty old flannel pyjamas.* ADJ-GRADED

raucous /rɔːkəs/. A **raucous** sound is loud, harsh, and rather unpleasant. *They heard a bottle being smashed, then more raucous laughter. ...the raucous cries of the sea-birds. ...a raucous crowd of 25,000 delirious fans.* ♦ **raucously** *They laughed together raucously.* ◆◇◇◇◇ ADJ-GRADED: usu ADJ n PRAGMATICS / ADV-GRADED: usu ADV with v

raunchy /rɔːntʃi/ **raunchier, raunchiest.** If you describe a film, a person, or the way that someone is dressed as **raunchy**, you mean that they are sexually exciting or sexually explicit; an informal word. *...her raunchy new movie.* ◆◇◇◇◇ ADJ-GRADED =sexy

ravage /rævɪdʒ/ **ravages, ravaging, ravaged.** A town, country, or economy that **has been ravaged** is one that has been damaged so much that it is almost competely destroyed. *For two decades the country has been ravaged by civil war and foreign intervention. ...the ravaged streets of Sarajevo. ...Nicaragua's ravaged economy.* ◆◇◇◇◇ VB: usu passive / be V-ed / V-ed

ravages /rævɪdʒɪz/. The **ravages** of time, war, or the weather are the damaging effects that they have. *Carol Drinkwater is blessed with a fine bone structure that stands up better to the ravages of time. ...a hi-tech grass pitch that can survive the ravages of a cold, wet climate.* N-PLURAL: usu *the* N *of* n

rave /reɪv/ **raves, raving, raved** ◆◆◇◇◇

1 If someone **raves**, they talk in an excited and uncontrolled way. *She cried and raved for weeks, and people did not know what to do... 'What is wrong with you, acting like that,' she raved, pacing up and down frantically.* VERB / V / V with quote

2 If you **rave** about something, you speak or write about it with great enthusiasm. *Rachel raved about the new foods she ate while she was there... 'Such lovely clothes. I'd no idea Milan was so wonderful,' she raved.* VERB =enthuse / V *about* n / V with quote

3 In British English, a **rave** or a **rave party** is a large event at which young people dance to electronic music in a warehouse or in the open air. Raves are often associated with illegal drugs. *...an all-night rave at Castle Donington.* ► Also an adjective. *Old faces and new talents are making it big on the rave scene.* N-COUNT / ADJ: ADJ n

4 A **rave** is the same as a **rave review**; an informal use. *The resulting show, 'Only the Truth is Funny', has drawn raves from the critics.* N-COUNT =rave review

5 ● to **rant and rave**: see **rant**. See also **raving**.

raven /reɪvən/ **ravens** ◆◇◇◇◇

1 A **raven** is a large bird with shiny black feathers and a deep harsh call. N-COUNT

2 **Raven** hair is black, shiny, and smooth. *...a striking woman with long raven hair... The picture shows a dreamy, raven-haired young woman.* ADJ

ravenous /rævənəs/. If you are **ravenous**, you are extremely hungry. *Amy realized that she had eaten nothing since leaving Bruton Street, and she was ravenous. ...a pack of ravenous animals.* ♦ **ravenously** *She began to eat ravenously... She emerged looking ravenously hungry.* ADJ =starving / ADV

raver /reɪvəʳ/ **ravers.** In informal British English, a **raver** is a young person who has a busy social life and goes to a lot of parties, raves, or nightclubs. N-COUNT

rave review, rave reviews. When journalists write **rave reviews**, they praise something such as a play or book in a very enthusiastic way. *The play received rave reviews from the critics.* N-COUNT: usu pl

ravine /rəviːn/ **ravines.** A **ravine** is a very deep narrow valley with steep sides. *The bus is said to have overturned and fallen into a ravine.* ◆◇◇◇◇ N-COUNT =gorge, canyon

raving /reɪvɪŋ/ ◆◇◇◇◇

1 You use **raving** to describe someone who you think is completely mad; an informal word. *Malcolm looked at her as if she were a raving lunatic.* ► Also an adverb. *I'm afraid Jean-Paul has gone raving mad.* ADJ: usu ADJ n / ADV: ADV adj

2 See also **rave**.

ravings /reɪvɪŋz/. If you describe what someone says or writes as their **ravings**, you mean that it makes no sense because they are mad or very ill. *Haig and Robertson saw it as the lunatic ravings of a mad politician.* N-PLURAL: usu *the* N *of* n

ravioli /ræviəʊli/ **raviolis. Ravioli** is a type of pasta which is shaped like very small pillows and usually filled with minced meat or cheese and served in a sauce. N-MASS

ravish /rævɪʃ/ **ravishes, ravishing, ravished.** If a woman **is ravished** by a man, she is raped by him; a literary use. *She'll never know how close she came to being dragged off and ravished.* VB: usu passive =rape / be V-ed

ravishing /rævɪʃɪŋ/. If you describe someone or something as **ravishing**, you mean that they are very beautiful; a literary word. *She looked ravishing. ...driving through the ravishing scenery of Cumbria and Yorkshire.* ♦ **ravishingly** *The Beaujolais hills are ravishingly pretty.* ADJ-GRADED / ADV-GRADED: ADV adj

raw /rɔː/ **rawer, rawest** ◆◆◆◇◇

1 **Raw** materials or substances are in their natural state before being processed or used in ADJ: usu ADJ n manufacturing. *We import raw materials and energy and export mainly industrial products. ...two ships carrying raw sugar from Cuba.*

2 Raw food is food that is eaten uncooked, that has not yet been cooked, or that has not been cooked enough. *...a popular dish made of raw fish... This versatile vegetable can be eaten raw or cooked... Half of it is burned and half of it is raw.* ADJ ≠cooked

3 If a part of your body is **raw**, it is red and painful, perhaps because the skin has come off or has been burnt. *...the drag of the rope against the raw flesh of my shoulders... Her feet hurt and her hands were rubbed raw from unaccustomed work.* ADJ-GRADED

4 Raw emotions are strong basic feelings or responses which are not weakened by other influences. *...the raw passions of nationalism... Her grief was still raw and he did not know how to help her.* ♦ **rawness** *The rawness of his greed was frank and uninhibited.* ADJ-GRADED: usu ADJ n; N-SING

5 If you describe something as **raw**, you mean that it is simple, powerful, and real. *...the raw power of instinct. ...the raw vitality of his earlier painting.* ♦ **rawness** *Recorded almost live, there's a certain seductive rawness about the whole thing.* ADJ-GRADED: usu ADJ n; N-UNCOUNT

6 Raw data is facts or information that has not yet been sorted, analysed, or prepared for presentation. *Analyses were conducted on the raw data. ...a statistical model that fully adjusts the census's raw figures.* ADJ: usu ADJ n

7 If you describe someone in a new job as **raw**, or as a **raw** recruit, you mean that they lack experience in that job. *...replacing experienced men with raw recruits... Davies is still raw but his potential shows.* ADJ-GRADED: usu ADJ n =inexperienced ≠experienced

8 Raw weather feels unpleasantly cold. *Once they cleared the housetops, the wind was raw and biting. ...a raw December morning.* ADJ-GRADED =bitter

9 Raw sewage is sewage that has been disposed of without being treated. *...contamination of bathing water by raw sewage.* ADJ: ADJ n =untreated ≠treated

10 If you say that you are getting **a raw deal**, you mean that you are being treated unfairly; an informal expression. *They feel that Quebec is getting a raw deal... I think women have a raw deal.* PHRASES v PHR ≠a fair deal

11 You use **in the raw** to describe something in its true unsophisticated state. *This is nature in the raw... He also wanted to see Bangladesh in the raw... It exposes capitalism in the raw.* n PHR

12 If you say something **touches a raw nerve**, you mean that it upsets someone because it reminds them of something that they feel sad or angry about. *The programme has undoubtedly touched a very raw nerve.* V inflects

rawhide /rɔːhaɪd/. In American English, **rawhide** is stiff untreated leather from cows or buffalos. *At his belt he carried a rawhide whip.* N-UNCOUNT: usu N n

ray /reɪ/ **rays** ◆◆◆◇◇

1 Rays of light are narrow beams of light. *...the first rays of light spread over the horizon... It can be seen clearly in a ray of sunlight or under a lamp... The sun's rays can penetrate water up to 10 feet.* • See also **cosmic ray**, **gamma ray**, **X-ray**. N-COUNT

2 A **ray of** hope, comfort, or other positive quality is a small amount of it that you welcome because it makes a bad situation seem less bad. *They could provide a ray of hope amid the general business and economic gloom... The one ray of sunlight in this depressing history is her meeting and falling in love with Martin.* N-COUNT: N *of* n =glimmer

3 A **ray** is a fairly large sea fish which has a flat body, eyes on the top of its body, and a long tail. N-COUNT

rayon /reɪɒn/. **Rayon** is a smooth man-made fabric that is made from cellulose. *...the old woman's rayon dress.* N-UNCOUNT: oft N n

raze /reɪz/ **razes, razing, razed.** If buildings, villages or towns **are razed** or **razed** to the ground, they are completely destroyed. *Dozens of villages have been razed... Towns such as Mittelwihr and Bennwihr were virtually razed to the ground.* VB: usu passive *be* V-ed *be* V-ed *to* n

razor /reɪzəʳ/ **razors.** A **razor** is a tool that people use for shaving. ◆◇◇◇◇ N-COUNT

razor blade, razor blades. A **razor blade** is a small flat piece of metal with a very sharp edge that is put into a razor or a razor cartridge and used for shaving. *...an adequate supply of towels, soap, razor blades, toothpaste, etc. ...a pencil sharpened with a razor blade.* N-COUNT

razor-sharp

1 A cutting tool that is **razor-sharp** is extremely sharp. *...a razor sharp butcher's knife. ...razor-sharp teeth.* ADJ: usu ADJ n

2 If you describe someone or someone's mind as **razor-sharp**, you mean that they have a very accurate and clear understanding of things. *...his razor-sharp intelligence.* ADJ

razor wire. **Razor wire** is strong wire with sharp blades sticking out of it. In wars or civil conflict it is sometimes used to prevent people from entering or leaving buildings or areas of land. *...plans to use razor wire to seal off hostels for migrant workers.* N-UNCOUNT

razzamatazz /ræzəmətæz/. **Razzamatazz** is the same as **razzmatazz**. N-UNCOUNT

razzle-dazzle /ræzᵊl dæzᵊl/. **Razzle-dazzle** is the same as **razzmatazz**. *...a razzle-dazzle marketing man.* N-UNCOUNT: oft N n

razzmatazz /ræzmətæz/. **Razzmatazz** is a noisy and showy display. *...the colour and razzmatazz of a US election.* N-UNCOUNT

RC /ɑːʳ siː/. **RC** is an abbreviation for **Roman Catholic**. *...St Mary's RC Cathedral.* ◆◆◇◇◇ ADJ

Rd. **Rd** is a written abbreviation for 'road'. It is used especially in addresses and on maps or signs. *St Pancras Library, 100 Euston Rd, London, NW1.* ◆◆◇◇◇

-rd. **-rd** is added to numbers that end in 3, except those ending in 13. It is written in figures to form an ordinal number. 3rd is pronounced 'third'. *...September 3rd 1990. ...the 33rd Boston Marathon. ...Canada's 123rd birthday.*

re /riː/. You use **re** in business letters, faxes, or memos to introduce a subject or item which you are going to discuss or refer to in detail. *Dear Mrs Cox, Re: Household Insurance. We note from our files that.* =regarding, concerning

re-. Usually pronounced /riː-/ for meaning 1, and before an unstressed syllable for meanings 2 and 3. Otherwise the pronunciation is /ri-/ before a vowel sound and /rɪ-/ before a consonant sound.

1 Re- is added to verbs and nouns to form new verbs and nouns that refer to the repeating of an action or process. For example, to 're-read' something means to read it again, and someone's 're-election' is their being elected again. PREFIX

2 Re- is added to verbs and nouns to form new verbs and nouns that refer to a process opposite to one that has already taken place. For example, to 'reappear' means to appear after disappearing, and to 'regain' something means to gain it after you have lost it. PREFIX

3 Re- is added to verbs and nouns to form new verbs and nouns which describe a change in the position or state of something. For example, to 'relocate' something means to locate it in a different place and to 'rearrange' something means to arrange it in a different way. PREFIX

R.E. /ɑːr iː/. In British English, **R.E.** is a school subject in which children learn about religion and other social matters. R.E. is an abbreviation for 'religious education'. N-UNCOUNT

-'re /əʳ/. **-'re** is a shortened form of 'are'. In spoken or informal written English, it is added to the end of the pronoun or noun which is the subject of the verb. *We're not, are we?... They're not as good looking as we are... What're you going to do with all that money?*

reach /riːtʃ/ **reaches, reaching, reached** ◆◆◆◆◆

1 When someone or something **reaches** a place, they arrive there. *He did not stop until he reached the door... When the bus reached High Holborn, Tony rang the bell and they jumped off together... He reached Cambridge shortly before three o'clock.* VERB =get to V n

2 If someone or something has **reached** a certain VERB stage, level, or amount, they are at that stage, level, or amount. *The process of political change in South Africa has reached the stage where it is irreversible... The Belgian player Eduardo Masso has reached the final of the Dutch Open in Hilversum... We're told the figure could reach 100,000 next year.* =get to V n

3 If you **reach** somewhere, you move your arm and hand to take or touch something. *Judy reached into her handbag and handed me a small printed leaflet... I reached across the table and squeezed his hand... One day while he was bathing in a river, he reached up for an overhanging branch.* VERB =stretch V prep/adv

4 If you can **reach** something, you are able to touch it by stretching out your arm or leg. *Can you reach your toes with your fingertips?* VERB V n

5 If you try to **reach** someone, you try to contact them, usually by telephone. *Has the doctor told you how to reach him or her in emergencies?... If I see her, I'll tell her you've been trying to reach her.* VERB =contact V n

6 If something **reaches** a place, point, or level, it extends as far as that place, point, or level. *...a nightshirt which reached to his knees... The water level in Lake Taihu has reached record levels... Eventually those ideas should reach the capital city.* VERB V to n V n

7 When people **reach** an agreement, compromise, or settlement, they succeed in achieving it. *A meeting of agriculture ministers in Luxembourg today has so far failed to reach agreement over farm subsidies... They are meeting in Lusaka in an attempt to reach a compromise.* VERB V n

8 Someone's or something's **reach** is the distance or limit to which they can stretch, extend, or travel. *Isabelle placed a wine cup on the table within his reach. ...a heavyweight who possesses a longer reach and more strength. ...long-handled shears, secateurs and long-reach tree pruners.* N-UNCOUNT: oft poss N

9 If a place or thing is within **reach**, it is possible to have it or get to it because of its position or price. If it is beyond your **reach** or out of **reach**, you are not able to have it or get to it. *It is located within reach of many important Norman towns, including Bayeux... The clothes they model for Littlewoods are all within easy reach of every woman... These products are normally bought and stored carefully out of reach of children... The price is ten times what it normally is and totally beyond the reach of ordinary people.* N-UNCOUNT

reaches /riːtʃiz/ ◆◇◇◇◇

1 The upper, middle, or lower **reaches** of a river are parts of a river. The upper **reaches** are nearer to the river's source and the lower **reaches** are nearer to the sea into which it flows. *This year water levels in the middle and lower reaches of the Yangtze are unusually high.* N-PLURAL: usu *the* adj N *of* n

2 You can refer to the distant or outer parts of a place or area as the far, farthest, or outer **reaches**; a formal use. *...the outer reaches of the solar system. ...the farthest reaches of Cambodia.* N-PLURAL: usu *the* adj N *of* n

3 You can refer to the higher or lower levels of an organization as its upper or lower **reaches**; a formal use. *...the upper reaches of the legal profession. ...the lower reaches of the accounting world.* N-PLURAL: usu *the* adj N *of* n =levels, echelons

react /riækt/ **reacts, reacting, reacted** ◆◆◆◇◇

1 When you **react** to something that has happened to you, you behave in a particular way because of it. *They reacted violently to the news... It's natural to react with disbelief if your child is accused of bullying... 'How did he react?'—'Very calmly.'* VERB =respond V to n V adv/prep Also V

2 If you **react against** someone's way of behaving, you deliberately behave in a different way because you do not like the way they behave. *She reacted against the mindlessness and luxury of their lives... My father never saved and perhaps I reacted against that.* VERB =rebel V *against* n

3 If you **react** to a substance such as a drug that has got into your body, you are affected unpleasantly or made ill by it. *Someone allergic to milk is likely to react to cheese... He reacted very badly to the radiation therapy.* VERB V to n Also V

4 When one chemical substance **reacts** with another, or when two chemical substances **react**, they combine chemically to form another substance. *Calcium reacts with water but less violently than sodium and potassium do... Under normal circumstances, these two gases react readily to produce carbon dioxide and water.* V-RECIP V *with* n pl-n V

reaction /riækʃᵊn/ **reactions** ◆◆◆◆◇

1 Your **reaction** to something that has happened or something that you have experienced is what you feel, say, or do because of it. *Reaction to the visit is mixed... The initial reaction of most participants is fear... He was surprised that his answer should have caused such a strong reaction.* N-VAR: usu with supp =response

2 A **reaction against** something is a way of behaving or doing something that is deliberately different from what has been done before. *All new fashion starts out as a reaction against existing convention... Her three years of freedom seemed like a reaction against that childhood.* N-COUNT: N *against* n

3 If there is a **reaction against** something, it becomes unpopular. *Premature moves in this respect might well provoke a reaction against socialism... The government response seems to be the result of strong public reaction against the police apathy.* N-SING: also no det, N *against* n

4 Your **reactions** are your ability to move quickly in response to something, for example when you are in danger. *If his reactions are so slow, he shouldn't be in charge of a bus... The sport requires very fast reactions.* N-PLURAL: oft poss N =reflexes

5 **Reaction** is the belief that the political or social system of your country should not change; used showing disapproval. *Thus, he aided reaction and thwarted progress. ...their victory against the forces of reaction and censorship.* N-UNCOUNT

6 A chemical **reaction** is a process in which two substances combine together chemically to form another substance. *Ozone is produced by the reaction between oxygen and ultra-violet light... Catalysts are materials which greatly speed up chemical reactions.* N-COUNT

7 If you have an allergic **reaction** to a substance such as a drug that has got into your body, you are affected unpleasantly or made ill by it. *Every year, 5000 people have life-threatening reactions to anaesthetics... Common foods which cause this kind of reaction are fish, eggs, and shellfish.* N-COUNT: oft adj N *to* n

reactionary /riækʃənri, AM -neri/ **reactionaries.** A **reactionary** person or group tries to prevent changes in the political or social system of their country; used showing disapproval. *It grew ever more clear to everyone that the Minister was too reactionary, too blinkered... As long as I have strength, I shall be trying to remove the reactionary forces from the party. ...narrow and reactionary ideas about family life.* ▸ A **reactionary** is someone with reactionary views. *Critics viewed him as a reactionary, even a monarchist.* ◆◇◇◇◇ ADJ-GRADED PRAGMATICS ≠radical N-COUNT ≠radical

reactivate /riæktɪveɪt/ **reactivates, reactivating, reactivated.** If people **reactivate** a system or organization, they make it work again after a period in which it has not been working. *The government today is expected to announce a series of economic reforms to reactivate the economy... It was also agreed to reactivate two joint committees on negotiations.* VERB V n

reactive /riæktɪv/ ◆◇◇◇◇

1 Something that is **reactive** is able to react chemically with a lot of different substances. *Ozone is a highly reactive form of oxygen gas.* ADJ-GRADED

2 If someone is **reactive**, they behave in response to what happens to them, rather than deciding in advance how they want to behave. *I want our organization to be less reactive and more pro-active.* ADJ-GRADED: usu v-link ADJ ≠proactive

reactor /riæktəʳ/ **reactors.** A **reactor** is the same as a **nuclear reactor**. ◆◆◇◇◇ N-COUNT

read, reads, reading. The form **read** is pronounced /riːd/ when it is the present tense, and /red/ when it is the past tense and past participle. ◆◆◆◆◆

1 When you **read** something such as a book or article, you look at and understand the words that are written there. *Have you read this book?... I read about it in the paper... He read through the pages slowly and carefully... It was nice to read that the Duke will not be sending his son off to boarding* VERB V n V *about* n V *through* n V that V *school... She spends her days reading and watching television.* ▶ Also a noun. *I settled down to have a good read.* N-SING: a N

2 When you **read** a piece of writing to someone, you say the words aloud. *Jay reads poetry so beautifully... I like it when she reads to us... I sing to the boys or read them a story before tucking them in.* VERB; V n; V to n; V n n; Also V n to n

3 People who can **read** have the ability to look at and understand written words. *He couldn't read or write... He could read words at 18 months.* VERB; V; V n

4 If you can **read** music, you have the ability to look at and understand the symbols that are used in written music to represent musical sounds. *Later on I learned how to read music.* VERB; V n

5 You can use **read** when saying what is written on something or in something. For example, if a notice **reads** 'Exit', the word 'Exit' is written on it. *The sign on the bus read 'Private: Not In Service'.* VB: no cont; V with quote

6 If you refer to how a piece of writing **reads**, you are referring to its style. *The book reads like a ballad... It reads very awkwardly.* VERB; V prep/adv

7 If you say that a book or magazine is a good **read**, you mean that it is very enjoyable to read. *Ben Okri's latest novel is a good read.* N-COUNT: adj N

8 If something **is read** in a particular way, it is understood or interpreted in that way. *The play is being widely read as an allegory of imperialist conquest... South Africans were praying last night that he has read the situation correctly... Now how do you read his remarks on that subject?* VERB; =interpret; be V-ed as n; V n adv/prep

9 If you **read** someone's mind or thoughts, you know exactly what they are thinking without them telling you. *From behind her, as if he could read her thoughts, Benny said, 'You're free to go any time you like, Madame.'* VERB; V n

10 If you can **read** someone or you can **read** their gestures, you can understand what they are thinking or feeling by the way they behave or the things they say. *If you have to work in a team you must learn to read people... Under the shaded light her expression was difficult to read.* VERB; V n

11 If someone who is trying to talk to you with a radio transmitter says, 'Do you **read** me?', they are asking you if you can hear them. *Alpha-Bravo-Zulu 643 to Saltezar, do you read me? Over... We read you loud and clear. Over.* VERB; =hear; V n

12 When you **read** a measuring device, you look at it to see what the figure or measurement on it is. *When officials like gas and electricity men call to read the meter, ask for identification... It is essential that you are able to read a thermometer.* VERB; V n

13 If a measuring device **reads** a particular amount, it shows that amount. *The thermometer read 105 degrees Fahrenheit... The fuel gauge reads below zero.* VERB; V amount

14 In formal British English, if you **read** a subject at university, you study it. *She read French and German at Cambridge University... He is now reading for a maths degree at Surrey University.* VERB; =study; V n; V for n

15 If you **take** something **as read**, you accept it as being true or right and therefore feel that it does not need to be discussed or proved. *We took it as read that he must have been a KGB agent... The case for aid to eastern Europe is taken as read.* PHRASE: V inflects

16 See also **reading.** • to **read between the lines**: see **line**.

read into. If you **read** a meaning **into** something, you think it is there although it may not actually be there. *The addict often misinterprets the signals coming to him, reading disapproval into people's reactions to him even where it does not exist... It would be wrong to try to read too much into such a light-hearted production.* PHRASAL VERB; V n P n; V amount P n; Also V P n n

read out. If you **read out** a piece of writing, you say it aloud. *He's obliged to take his turn at reading out the announcements... Shall I read them out?* PHRASAL VERB; V P n (not pron); V n P

read up on. If you **read up on** a subject, you read a lot about it so that you become informed on it. *I've read up on the dangers of all these drugs.* PHRASAL VERB; V P P n

readable /riːdəbəl/ ◆◇◇◇◇

1 If you say that a book or article is **readable**, you mean that it is enjoyable and easy to read. *This is an impeccably researched and very readable book.* ADJ-GRADED

2 A piece of writing that is **readable** is written or printed clearly and can be read easily. *My secretary worked long hours translating my almost illegible writing into a typewritten and readable script.* ADJ-GRADED; =legible

reader /riːdər/ **readers** ◆◆◆◆◇

1 The **readers** of a newspaper, magazine, or book are the people who read it. *If you are a regular reader of Homes & Gardens you will know what an invaluable source of inspiration it is... These texts give the reader an insight into the Chinese mind.* N-COUNT

2 A **reader** is a person who reads, especially one who reads for pleasure. *Thanks to that job I became an avid reader... Their books are loved by young readers the world over.* N-COUNT: usu with supp

3 A **reader** is a person who reads books for a publisher in order to give an opinion on whether they should be published or not. N-COUNT

4 In Britain, a **reader** is a senior lecturer at a university, with a rank just below that of a professor. *John Stevenson is Reader in History at the University of Sheffield.* N-COUNT

5 A **reader** is a book of simplified literature, selected passages, and exercises used for teaching at school. N-COUNT

readership /riːdərʃɪp/ **readerships** ◆◇◇◇◇

1 The **readership** of a book, newspaper, or magazine is the number or type of people who read it. *Its readership has grown to over 15,000 subscribers... A new format would alienate its ageing readership without attracting young readers.* N-COUNT: usu sing, usu with supp

2 In Britain, a **readership** is the post of a reader at a university. N-COUNT

readily /redɪli/ ◆◆◇◇◇

1 If you do something **readily**, you do it in a way which shows that you are very willing to do it. *I asked her if she would allow me to interview her, and she readily agreed... When I was invited to the party, I readily accepted.* ADV-GRADED: ADV with v; =willingly

2 You also use **readily** to say that something can be done or obtained quickly and easily. For example, if you say that something can be readily understood, you mean that people can understand it quickly and easily. *The components are readily available in hardware shops... I don't readily make friends.* ADV-GRADED: ADV adj, ADV with v; =easily

reading /riːdɪŋ/ **readings** ◆◆◆◇◇

1 Reading is the activity of reading books. *I have always loved reading. ...young people who find reading and writing difficult.* N-UNCOUNT

2 A **reading** is an event at which poetry or extracts from books are read to an audience. *This year's event consisted of readings, lectures and workshops. ...a poetry reading.* N-COUNT

3 Your **reading** of a word, text, or situation is the way in which you understand or interpret it. *My reading of her character makes me feel that she was too responsible a person to do those things... Local public housing authorities disagree with this reading of the law.* N-COUNT: with supp, usu N of n

4 The **reading** on a measuring device is the figure or measurement that it shows. *Once you have recorded the reading, shake the thermometer down to below 36 degrees... The gauge must be giving a faulty reading.* N-COUNT

5 In the British Parliament or the US Congress, a **reading** is one of the three stages of presentation and discussion of a new bill before it can be passed as law. *The bill is expected to pass its second reading with a comfortable majority.* N-COUNT: usu ord N

6 If you say that a book or an article **makes** interesting **reading** or **makes for** interesting **reading**, you mean that it is interesting to read. *The list of drinks, a dozen pages long, makes fascinating reading... The report, called 'Child Poverty and Deprivation in the UK', makes for depressing reading.* PHRASE: V inflects

reading glasses. Reading glasses are spectacles that are worn by people who cannot see things close to them very well, when they want to see properly, for example when they are reading. N-PLURAL: also a pair of N

reading lamp, reading lamps. A **reading lamp** is a small lamp that you keep on a desk or table. You can move its lampshade in order to direct the light to where you need it for reading. N-COUNT

reading room, reading rooms. A **reading room** is a quiet room in a library or museum where you can read and study. N-COUNT

readjust /riːədʒʌst/ **readjusts, readjusting, readjusted**

1 When you **readjust** to a new situation, usually one you have been in before, you adapt to it. *I can understand why astronauts find it difficult to readjust to life on earth... They are bound to take time to readjust after a holiday.* VERB V to n V

2 If you **readjust** the way you do something, your attitude to something, or the level of something, you change it so that it is more effective or appropriate. *The rebel army has readjusted its strategy... In the end you have to readjust your expectations... We are simply going to readjust her medication and see how things are.* VERB V n

3 If you **readjust** something such as a piece of clothing or a mechanical device, you correct or alter its position or setting. *Michael groaned and readjusted his shorts... Readjust your watch. You are now on Moscow time.* VERB V n

readjustment /riːədʒʌstmənt/ **readjustments**

1 **Readjustment** is the process of adapting to a new situation, usually one that you have been in before. *The next few weeks will be a period of readjustment, and will probably not be easy... The readjustment to peace and home is slow and painful.* N-VAR: usu with supp

2 A **readjustment** of something is an alteration to it so that it is more effective or appropriate. *The organization denies that it is seeking any readjustment of state borders. ...the effects of economic readjustment.* N-VAR: usu with supp

readout /riːdaʊt/ **readouts.** If an electronic measuring device gives you a **readout**, it displays information about the level of something such as a speed, height, or sound. *The system provides a digital readout of the vehicle's speed... The visibility readout is .019.* N-COUNT

ready /redi/ **readier, readiest; readies, readying, readied** ◆◆◆◆◇

1 If someone is **ready**, they are properly prepared for something. If something is **ready**, it has been properly prepared and is now able to be used. *It took her a long time to get ready for church... The cocaine was ready for distribution... Are you ready to board, Mr. Daly?... In a few days time the sprouts will be ready to eat... Tomorrow he would tell his pilot to get the aircraft ready... It's eight-fifteen, dear, and your breakfast's ready.* ADJ: v-link ADJ, oft ADJ for n, ADJ to-inf

2 If you are **ready** for something or **ready** to do something, you have enough experience to do it or you are old enough and sensible enough to do it. *She says she's not ready for marriage... You'll have no trouble getting him into a normal school when you feel he's ready to go.* ADJ: v-link ADJ, usu ADJ for n, ADJ to-inf

3 If you are **ready** to do something, you are willing to do it. *They were ready to die for their beliefs... She was always ready to give interviews.* ADJ-GRADED: v-link ADJ to-inf =willing

4 If you are **ready for** something, you need it or want it. *I don't know about you, but I'm ready for bed... After five days in the heat of Bangkok, we were ready for the beach.* ADJ: v-link ADJ for n

5 If someone or something is **ready** to do something, they are about to do it or likely to do it. *She looked ready to cry... Just as we were ready to sit down to dinner, a little boy came running in... He says it's like a volcano ready to erupt.* ADJ: v-link ADJ to-inf

6 You use **ready** to describe things that are able to be used very quickly and easily. *I didn't have a ready answer for this dilemma... 'But not quite yet,' he says quickly, with that ready smile of his... Why does German industry enjoy such a ready supply of well-trained and well-motivated workers?* ADJ-GRADED: ADJ n

7 **Ready** money is in the form of notes and coins rather than cheques or credit cards, and so it can be used immediately. *I'm afraid I don't have enough ready cash, but I'll call a colleague from another store.* ADJ: ADJ n ► In informal British English, ready money is sometimes referred to as **the readies**; an informal use. *She was a bit short of the readies.* N-PLURAL: usu the N

8 When you **ready** something, you prepare it for a particular purpose; a formal use. *John's soldiers were readying themselves for the final assault... In Egypt, two new camps were readied for the absorption of refugees... Cameramen readied tripods.* VERB =prepare V n for n V n Also V n to-inf

9 **Ready** combines with past participles to indicate that something has already been done, and that therefore you do not have to do it yourself. *You can buy ready-printed forms for wills at stationery shops... If you buy the fish ready filleted, make sure the flesh is firm and springy.* COMB in ADJ

10 If you have something **at the ready**, you have it in a position where it can be quickly and easily used. *Soldiers came charging through the forest, guns at the ready.* PHRASES usu n PHR

11 If you want to emphasize that someone is properly prepared for something, or that something is now able to be used, you can say that they are **ready and waiting**. *She liked to be ready and waiting at home when Bernard returned from work... The chalet was kept ready and waiting for them at all times.* v-link PHR PRAGMATICS

12 If you say to someone **'Ready when you are'**, you are telling them that you are now ready to do something and that as soon as they are ready, you will do it. *'Are you ready to pull out?'—'I'm ready when you are, Captain.'* CONVENTION

ready-made ◆◇◇◇◇

1 If something that you buy is **ready-made**, you can use it immediately, because the work you would normally have to do has been done by the producer of the product. *We rely quite a bit on ready-made meals – they are so convenient... You can buy it ready-made at Chinese groceries... The ready-made bedcovers cost from £200.* ADJ

2 **Ready-made** means extremely convenient or useful for a particular purpose. *Those wishing to study urban development have a ready-made example on their doorstep... It provides perfect strangers with a ready-made and infinitely adaptable topic of conversation.* ADJ: usu ADJ n

ready meal, ready meals. Ready meals are complete meals that are sold in shops. They are already prepared and you need only heat them before eating them. N-COUNT

ready-to-wear. Ready-to-wear clothes are bought ready-made from a shop and not made specially for a particular person. *In 1978 he launched his first major ready-to-wear collection for the Austin Reed stores.* ADJ: ADJ n =off-the-peg

reaffirm /riːəfɜːm/ **reaffirms, reaffirming, reaffirmed.** If you **reaffirm** something, you state it again clearly and firmly; a formal word. *He reaffirmed his commitment to the country's economic reform programme... The government has reaffirmed that it will take any steps necessary to maintain law and order.* ◆◇◇◇◇ VERB V n V that

reafforestation /riːəfɒrɪsteɪʃən, AM -fɔːr-/. **Reafforestation** is the same as **reforestation**; used mainly in British English. N-UNCOUNT

reagent /rieɪdʒənt/ **reagents.** A **reagent** is a substance that is used to cause a chemical reaction. Reagents are often used in order to indicate the presence of another substance. A technical term in chemistry. N-COUNT

real /riːl/ ◆◆◆◆◆

1 Something that is **real** actually exists and is not imagined, invented, or theoretical. *No, it wasn't a dream. It was real... Legends grew up around a great many figures, both real and fictitious.* ADJ =genuine ≠imaginary

2 If something is **real** to someone, they experience it as though it really exists or happens, even though it does not. *Whitechild's life becomes increasingly real to the reader.* ADJ-GRADED: usu v-link ADJ, oft ADJ to n

3 A material or object that is **real** is natural or functioning, and not artificial or an imitation. *...the smell of real leather... Who's to know if they're real guns or not?... Desmond did not believe the diamond was real.* ADJ: usu ADJ n =genuine ≠fake, imitation

ADJ: ADJ n =proper 4 You can use **real** to describe someone or something that has all the characteristics or qualities that such a person or thing typically has. *...his first real girlfriend... He's not a real alcoholic... The only real job I'd ever had was as manager of the local cafe.*

ADJ: ADJ n =true 5 You can use **real** to describe something that is the true or original thing of its kind, in contrast to one that someone wants you to believe is true. *This was the real reason for her call... Her real name had been Miriam Pinckus.*

ADJ: ADJ n =true 6 You can use **real** to describe something that is the most important or typical part of a thing. *When he talks, he only gives glimpses of his real self... The smart executive has people he can trust doing all the real work. ...a solo journey to discover the real America.*

ADJ-GRADED: usu ADJ n PRAGMATICS 7 You can use **real** when you are talking about a situation or feeling to emphasize that it exists and is important or serious. *Global warming is a real problem... The prospect of civil war is very real... There was never any real danger of the children being affected... Political defeat seemed a real possibility at the end of 1981... At least they have a real chance to find work.*

ADJ-GRADED: ADJ n PRAGMATICS 8 You can use **real** to emphasize a quality that is genuine and sincere. *You've been drifting from job to job without any real commitment... Germany has shown real determination to come to terms with the anti-Semitism of its past.*

ADJ: ADJ n PRAGMATICS 9 You can use **real** before nouns to emphasize your description of something or someone; used in spoken English. *'It's a fabulous deal, a real bargain.'... 'You must think I'm a real idiot.'*

ADJ: ADJ n =actual, net 10 The **real** cost or value of something is its cost or value after other amounts have been added or subtracted and when factors such as the level of inflation have been considered. *...the real cost of borrowing.*

ADV: ADV adj/adv PRAGMATICS =really 11 In informal American English, you can use **real** to emphasize an adjective or adverb. *He is finding prison life 'real tough'... I don't think you are trying real hard.*

PHRASES usu PHR after v 12 If you say that someone does something **for real**, you mean that they actually do it and do not just pretend to do it. *The sex scenes were just good acting. We didn't do it for real.*

v-link PHR 13 In informal American English, if you think someone or something is very surprising, you can ask if they are **for real.** *Is this guy for real?*

PHR with cl 14 The cost or value of something **in real terms** is the same as its real cost. *In real terms the cost of driving is cheaper than a decade ago... Pensions have increased in real terms over the last twenty years.*

15 If you say that a thing or event is **the real thing**, you mean that it is the actual thing or event, and not an imitation or rehearsal. *The counterfeits sell for about $20 less than the real thing... The Blairgowrie Highland Games, on the other hand, are the real thing rather than a media event.*

real ale, real ales.

N-MASS **Real ale** is beer which is stored in a barrel and is pumped from it without the use of carbon dioxide; used mainly in British English.

real estate ◆◆◇◇◇

N-UNCOUNT =property 1 **Real estate** is property in the form of land and buildings, rather than personal possessions; used mainly in American English. *By investing in real estate, he was one of the richest men in the United States. ...the most spectacular piece of real estate he had ever imagined.*

N-UNCOUNT: usu N n 2 In American English, **real estate** businesses or **real estate** agents sell houses, buildings, and land. In British English, real estate agents are called **estate agents.** *...the real estate agent who sold you your house. ...the real estate industry... He had a long career in real estate.*

realign /riːəlaɪn/ realigns, realigning, realigned

VERB =restructure, V n, Also V 1 If you **realign** your ideas, policies, or plans, you organize them in a different way in order to take account of new circumstances. *She has, almost single-handedly, realigned British politics.*

VERB =re-position, V n 2 If you **realign** objects, you move some or all of them in order to make them into a particular pattern. *I turned aside to realign the photographs of my children on the shelf.*

realignment /riːəlaɪnmənt/ realignments. ◆◇◇◇◇

N-VAR: usu N of n =restructuring If a company, economy, or system undergoes a **realignment**, it is organized or arranged in a new way. *...a realignment of the existing political structure.*

realise /riːəlaɪz/. See realize.

realism /riːəlɪzəm/ ◆◇◇◇◇

N-UNCOUNT PRAGMATICS 1 When people show **realism** in their behaviour, they recognize and accept the true nature of a situation and try to deal with it in a practical way; used showing approval. *It was time now to show more political realism... The early ambitions of youthful enthusiasm soon become tempered with realism.*

N-UNCOUNT PRAGMATICS 2 If things and people are presented with **realism** in painting, novels, or films, they are presented in a way that is like real life; used showing approval. *Greene's stories had an edge of realism that made it easy to forget they were fiction... Sincere performances and gritty Boston settings add to the film's realism.*

realist /riːəlɪst/ realists ◆◇◇◇◇

N-COUNT PRAGMATICS 1 A **realist** is someone who recognizes and accepts the true nature of a situation and tries to deal with it in a practical way; used showing approval. *I see myself not as a cynic but as a realist... Realists would agree with many of these criticisms.*

ADJ: ADJ n 2 A **realist** painter or writer is one who represents things and people in a way that is like real life. *...perhaps the foremost realist painter of our times.*

realistic /riːəlɪstɪk/ ◆◆◇◇◇

ADJ-GRADED: usu v-link ADJ, oft ADJ about n, it v-link ADJ to-inf 1 If you are **realistic** about a situation, you recognize and accept its true nature and try to deal with it in a practical way. *Police have to be realistic about violent crime... It's only realistic to acknowledge that something, some time, will go wrong. ...a realistic view of what we can afford.* ♦ **realistically** **ADV-GRADED: usu ADV with v, also ADV adj** *As an adult, you can assess the situation realistically.*

ADJ-GRADED: usu ADJ n =sensible 2 Something such as a goal, target, or deadline that is **realistic** is one which you can sensibly expect to achieve. *Is EC membership a realistic goal for Eastern European countries?... A more realistic figure is eleven million... Establish deadlines that are more realistic.*

ADJ-GRADED 3 You say that a painting, story, or film is **realistic** when the people and things in it are like people and things in real life. *...extraordinarily realistic paintings of Indians... The language is foul and the violence horribly realistic.* ♦ **realistically** **ADV-GRADED: usu ADV with v** *The film starts off realistically and then develops into a ridiculous fantasy.*

realistically /riːəlɪstɪkəli/. ◆◇◇◇◇

ADV: ADV with cl PRAGMATICS =frankly You use **realistically** when you want to emphasize that what you are saying is true, even though you would prefer it not to be true. *Realistically, there is never one right answer.* • See also **realistic.**

reality /riælɪti/ realities ◆◆◆◆◇

N-UNCOUNT ≠fiction 1 You use **reality** to refer to real things or the real nature of things rather than imagined, invented, or theoretical ideas. *Fiction and reality were increasingly blurred... Psychiatrists become too caught up in their theories to deal adequately with reality.* • See also **virtual reality.**

N-COUNT: usu the N of n 2 The **reality** of a situation is the truth about it, especially when it is unpleasant or difficult to deal with. *...the harsh reality of top international competition... Other psychoanalysts do accept the reality of child sexual abuse.*

N-SING 3 You say that something has become a **reality** when it actually exists or is actually happening. *...the whole procedure that made this book become a reality... The reality is that they are poor.*

PHRASE: PHR with cl =in fact 4 You can use **in reality** to introduce a statement about the real nature of something, when it contrasts with something incorrect that has just been described. *He came across as streetwise, but in reality he was not.*

realizable /riːəlaɪzəbᵊl/; also spelled **realisable** in British English.

1 If your hopes or aims are **realizable,** there is a possibility that the things that you want to happen will happen; a formal use. *...the reasonless assumption that one's dreams and desires were realizable.* ADJ =attainable

2 **Realizable** wealth can be easily obtained by selling something; a technical use in finance. *In many cases this realizable wealth is not realized during the lifetime of the home owner... They must prove they own £250,000 of realisable assets.* ADJ

realize /riːəlaɪz/ **realizes, realizing, realized;** also spelled **realise** in British English. ◆◆◆◆◇

1 If you **realize** that something is true, you become aware of that fact or understand it. *As soon as we realised something was wrong, we moved the children away... People don't realize how serious this recession has actually been... Once they realised their mistake the phone was reconnected again... 'That's my brother.'—'Oh, I hadn't realized.'* VERB V that V wh V n V
♦ **realization** /riːəlaɪzeɪʃᵊn/ **realizations.** *There is now a growing realisation that things cannot go on like this for much longer... He nearly cried out at the sudden realization of how much Randall looked like him.* N-VAR: usu N that, N *of*n

2 If your hopes, desires, or fears **are realized**, the things that you hope for, desire, or fear actually happen. *Straightaway our worst fears were realised... Those are our hopes; we are starting this clinical trial to investigate whether those hopes will be realised.* ♦ **realization** *In Kravis's venomous tone he recognized the realization of his worst fears.* VB: usu passive *be* V-ed; N-UNCOUNT: oft *the* N *of*n

3 When someone **realizes** a design or an idea, they make or organize something based on that design or idea; a formal use. *Various textile techniques will be explored to realise design possibilities... The kaleidoscopic quality of the book is brilliantly realised on stage.* VERB V n

4 If someone or something **realizes** their potential, they do everything they are capable of doing, because they have been given the opportunity to do so. *The support systems to enable women to realize their potential at work are seriously inadequate... I think probably that the laser has not realised the potential that was expected of it in that domain.* VERB =achieve V n

5 If something **realizes** a particular amount of money when it is sold, that amount of money is paid for it; a technical term in finance. *A selection of correspondence from P G Wodehouse realised £1,232.* ♦ **realization** *I have taken this course solely to assist the realisation of my assets for the benefit of all my creditors.* VERB =make, raise V n; N-VAR

real life. If something happens in **real life**, it actually happens and is not just in a story or in someone's imagination. *In real life men like Richard Gere don't marry street girls... Children use fantasy to explore worrying aspects of real life.* ◆◆◇◇◇ N-UNCOUNT: usu *in* N ≠fiction, fantasy

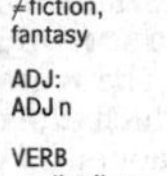

► Also an adjective. *...a real-life horror story.* ADJ: ADJ n

reallocate /riː æləkeɪt/ **reallocates, reallocating, reallocated.** When organizations **reallocate** money or resources, they decide to change the way they spend the money or use the resources. *...a cost-cutting program to reallocate people and resources within the company... Other areas are to lose aid so that money can be reallocated to towns devastated by pit closures.* VERB =redistribute V n V n to n

really /riːəli/ ◆◆◆◆◆

1 You can use **really** to emphasize a statement; used mainly in spoken English. *I'm very sorry. I really am... It really is best to manage without any medication if you possibly can... I really do feel that some people are being unfair... You know, we really ought to get another car... I'm fine, really I'm fine.* ADV: usu ADV with v PRAGMATICS

2 You can use **really** to emphasize an adjective or adverb; used mainly in spoken English. *It was really good... They were really nice people... I know her really well.* ADV: ADV adj/adv PRAGMATICS =very

3 You use **really** when you are discussing the real facts about something, in contrast to the ones someone wants you to believe. *My father didn't really love her... What was really going on?... You make them feel that it was their decision when it wasn't really.* ADV: usu ADV with v, also ADV adj

4 People use **really** in questions and negative statements when they want you to answer 'no'; used mainly in spoken English. *Do you really think he would be that stupid?... You can't really expect me to believe you didn't know him.* ADV: ADV before v PRAGMATICS =honestly, actually

5 If you say when something **really** begins to happen, you are emphasizing that it starts to happen then to a much greater extent and much more seriously than before. *That's when the pressure really started... He only really started going out with girls at college.* ADV: ADV before v PRAGMATICS

6 People sometimes use the word **really** to slightly reduce the force of a negative statement; used in spoken English. *I'm not really surprised... 'Did they hurt you?'—'Not really'... I didn't really notice what I was eating... I don't think that's very fair really.* ADV: ADV after neg, usu ADV with v, also ADV with cl PRAGMATICS

7 People sometimes add **really** to statements in order to make them less definite and more hesitant; used in spoken English. *She is a quiet girl really... I'm happy most of the time, really.* ADV: ADV with cl PRAGMATICS

8 People use the word **really** to show they are surprised or that the speaker may be surprised about something; used mainly in spoken British English. *Actually it was quite good really... I was really rather fond of Arthur.* ADV: ADV with cl PRAGMATICS

9 You can say **really** to express surprise or disbelief at what someone has said. *'We discovered it was totally the wrong decision.'—'Really?'... 'We saw a very bright shooting star.'—'Did you really?'* CONVENTION PRAGMATICS

10 You can say **'really'** in a conversation to show that you are interested in what someone is saying. *'We had a very interesting chat.'—'Really? About what?'* CONVENTION PRAGMATICS

11 Some people say **really** when they are slightly annoyed or offended by something someone has said or done; used mainly in spoken British English. *Really, Mr Riss, I expected better of you.* EXCLAM PRAGMATICS

realm /relm/ **realms** ◆◆◇◇◇

1 In formal English, you can use the word **realm** to refer to any area of activity, interest, or thought. *...the realm of politics... Students' interests are mostly limited to the academic realm.* N-COUNT: usu with supp, oft N *of*n, adj N

2 A **realm** is a country that has a king or queen; a formal use. *Defence of the realm is crucial.* N-COUNT: usu sing

3 If you say that something is not beyond **the realms of possibility**, you mean that it is possible. *A fall of 50 per cent or more on prices is not beyond the realms of possibility... This is a target which is surely within the realm of possibility.* PHRASE: *realm* inflects, v-link prep PHR

real property. In American English, **real property** is property in the form of land and buildings, rather than personal possessions. N-UNCOUNT =real estate

real time. If something is done in **real time**, there is no noticeable delay between the action and its effect or consequence. *...umpires, who have to make every decision in real time.* N-UNCOUNT: oft *in* N

real-time. Real-time processing is a type of computer programming or data processing in which the information received is processed by the computer almost immediately. *...real-time language translations.* ADJ: ADJ n

realtor /riːəltɔːr/ **realtors.** In American English, a **realtor** is a person whose job is to sell houses, buildings, and land. The usual British term is **estate agent.** N-COUNT

real world. If you talk about the **real world**, you are referring to the world and life in general, in contrast to a particular person's own life, experience, and ideas, which may seem untypical and unrealistic. *When they eventually leave the school they will be totally ill-equipped to deal with the real world... I was Olympic champion but I had to go out into the real world and work for a living.* ◆◆◇◇◇ N-SING: *the* N

ream /riːm/ **reams.** If you say that there are **reams** of paper or **reams** of writing, you mean that there are large amounts of it; an informal word. *Their specific task is to sort through the reams of information and try to determine what it* ◆◇◇◇◇ N-COUNT: usu pl, usu N *of*n

may mean... Kelly spent three hours going through reams of paper.

reap /riːp/ **reaps, reaping, reaped** ◆◇◇◇◇

1 If you **reap** the benefits or the rewards of something, you enjoy the good things that happen as a result of it. *You'll soon begin to reap the benefits of being fitter... We are not in this to reap immense financial rewards.* VERB; V n

2 To **reap** crops means to cut them down and gather them. *The painting depicted a group of peasants reaping a harvest of fruits and vegetables.* VERB; V n

reaper /riːpəʳ/ **reapers.** A **reaper** is a machine used to cut and gather crops. • See also **Grim Reaper.** N-COUNT

reappear /riːəpɪəʳ/ **reappears, reappearing, reappeared.** When people or things **reappear**, they return again after they have been away or out of sight for some time. *Thirty seconds later she reappeared and beckoned them forward.* ◆◇◇◇◇ VERB; V

reappearance /riːəpɪərəns/ **reappearances.** The **reappearance** of someone or something is their return after they have been away or out of sight for some time. *His sudden reappearance must have been a shock. ...the reappearance of Cossack culture in Russia.* N-COUNT: usu with poss

reappraisal /riːəpreɪzəl/ **reappraisals.** If there is a **reappraisal** of something such as an idea or plan, people think about the idea carefully and decide whether they want to change it; a formal word. *Britain's worst jail riot will force a fundamental reappraisal of prison policy... It is a time for quiet analysis and reappraisal.* N-VAR =review, reassessment

reappraise /riːəpreɪz/ **reappraises, reappraising, reappraised.** If you **reappraise** something such as an idea or a plan, you think carefully about it and decide whether it needs to be changed; a formal word. *It did not persuade them to abandon the war but it did force them to reappraise their strategy.* VERB =rethink; V n

rear /rɪəʳ/ **rears, rearing, reared** ◆◆◆◇◇

1 The **rear** of something such as a building or vehicle is the back part of it. *He settled back in the rear of the taxi. ...a stairway in the rear of the building.* ► Also an adjective. *Manufacturers have been obliged to fit rear seat belts in all new cars.* N-SING: the N, usu N of n =back ≠front; ADJ: ADJ n

2 If you are at the **rear** of a queue or of a moving line of people, you are the last person in it; a formal use. *Musicians played at the front and rear of the procession... The Lord Mayor follows at the rear in his gilded coach.* N-SING: the N, usu N of n =back ≠front

3 Your can refer to someone's buttocks as their **rear**; an informal use. *I turned away from the phone to see Lewis pat a waitress on her rear.* N-COUNT: usu poss N =behind, buttocks

4 If you **rear** children, you bring them up until they are old enough to look after themselves. If you say that someone **was reared** in a particular way or in a particular place, you are describing how or where they were brought up. The more usual American word is **raise**. *She reared sixteen children, six her own and ten her husband's... I was reared in east Texas.* VERB =bring up; V n; be V-ed prep

5 If you **rear** a young animal, you keep and look after it until it is old enough to be used for work or food, or until it can look after itself. *She spends a lot of time rearing animals.* VERB; V n

6 When a horse **rears**, it moves the front part of its body upwards, so that its front legs are high in the air and it is standing on its back legs. *The horse reared and threw off its rider.* ► **Rear up** means the same as **rear**. *...an army pony that didn't rear up at the sound of gunfire.* VERB; V; PHRASAL VERB; V P

7 If you say that something such as a building or mountain **rears** above you, you mean that is very tall and close to you. *The exhibition hall reared above me behind a high fence... The mountains reared up on each side, steep and white.* VERB =loom; V prep/adv

8 If a person or vehicle is **bringing up the rear**, they are the last person or vehicle in a moving line of them. *...police motorcyclists bringing up the rear of the procession.* PHRASES; V inflects

9 If something unpleasant **rears its head** or **rears its ugly head**, it begins to become apparent. *The threat of strikes reared its head again this summer... The extreme right reared its ugly head in the 1980s.* V and N inflect

rear up. See **rear** 6 PHRASAL VERB

Rear Admiral, Rear Admirals. Rear Admiral is a rank in the navy. It is the rank below **Vice Admiral**. *...Rear Admiral Douglas Cap, commander of the USS America.* N-TITLE; N-COUNT

rear-end, rear-ends, rear-ending, rear-ended. If a driver or vehicle **rear-ends** the vehicle in front, they crash into the back of it; an informal word. *A few days earlier somebody had rear-ended him.* VERB; V n

rearguard /rɪəʳgɑːʳd/

1 The rearguard is a group of soldiers who protect the back part of an army in a battle, especially when the army is retreating. N-SING: the N

2 If someone is **fighting a rearguard action** or **mounting a rearguard action**, they are trying very hard to prevent something from happening, even though it is probably too late for them to succeed. *Mr Urban looks increasingly like someone fighting a rearguard action to keep their job.* PHRASE: V inflects

rearm /riː ɑːʳm/ **rearms, rearming, rearmed;** also spelled **re-arm**. If a country **rearms** or **is rearmed** it starts to build up a new stock of military weapons. *They neglected to rearm in time and left Britain exposed to disaster. ...NATO's decision to rearm West Germany.* V-ERG; V; V n

rearmament /riː ɑːʳməmənt/. **Rearmament** is the process of building up a new stock of military weapons. N-UNCOUNT

rearrange /riːəreɪndʒ/ **rearranges, rearranging, rearranged** ◆◇◇◇◇

1 If you **rearrange** things, you change the way in which they are organized or ordered. *When she returned, she found Malcolm had rearranged all her furniture... A waiter was rapidly rearranging tables for the big group.* VERB; V n

2 If you **rearrange** a meeting or an appointment, you arrange for it to take place at a different time to that originally intended. *You may cancel or rearrange the appointment... The meeting on 31 October is rearranged for 30 January.* VERB =reschedule; V n

rearrangement /riːəreɪndʒmənt/ **rearrangements.** A **rearrangement** is a change in the way that something is arranged or organized. *...a rearrangement of the job structure.* N-VAR

rear-view mirror, rear-view mirrors. Inside a car, the **rear-view mirror** is the mirror that enables you to see the traffic behind when you are driving. N-COUNT

rearward /rɪəʳwəʳd/. If something moves or faces **rearward**, it moves or faces backwards. *...a rearward facing infant carrier... The centre of pressure moves rearward and the aeroplane becomes unbalanced.* ► Also an adjective. *...the rearward window.* ADV: ADV with v =backward ≠forward; ADJ: ADJ n

reason /riːzən/ **reasons, reasoning, reasoned** ◆◆◆◆◆

1 The **reason** for something is a fact or situation which explains why it happens or what causes it to happen. *There is a reason for every important thing that happens... Who would have a reason to want to kill her? ...the reason why Italian tomatoes have so much flavour... The only reason I went was because I was told to... My parents came to Germany for business reasons... The exact locations are being kept secret for reasons of security.* N-COUNT: usu with supp, oft N for n, N to-inf

2 If you say that you have **reason** to believe something or to have a particular emotion, you mean that you have evidence for your belief or there is a definite cause of your feeling. *They had reason to believe there could be trouble... He had every reason to be upset... He doesn't trust me. With good reason.* N-UNCOUNT: usu N to-inf =cause

3 The ability that people have to think and to make sensible judgements can be referred to as **reason**. *...a conflict between emotion and reason... Mike is my voice of reason. He thinks logically and points out where I'm going wrong.* N-UNCOUNT =common sense

4 If you **reason** that something is true, you decide that it is true after thinking carefully about all the facts. *I reasoned that changing my diet would lower my cholesterol level... 'Listen,' I reasoned, 'it doesn't* VERB; V that; V with quote *take a genius to figure out what Adam's up to.'* • See also **reasoned, reasoning.**

5 If you do not know why someone did something, you can say that they did it **for reasons best known to** themselves. You usually use this expression when you do not agree with what they did. *For reasons best known to himself, Algie changed his name.* PHRASES PHR with cl PRAGMATICS

6 If one thing happens **by reason of** another, it happens because of it; a formal expression. *The boss retains enormous influence by reason of his position... He pleaded innocent by reason of insanity.* PHR n

7 If you try to make someone **listen to reason**, you try to persuade them to listen to sensible arguments and be influenced by them. *The company's top executives had refused to listen to reason.* V inflects

8 If you say that something happened or was done **for no reason, for no good reason**, or **for no reason at all**, you mean that there was no obvious reason why it happened or was done. *The guards, he said, would punch them for no reason... For no reason at all the two men started to laugh.* PHR with cl

9 If you say that someone or something is someone's **reason for living** or their **reason for being**, you mean that it is the most important thing in their life. *Chloe is my reason for living.* usu poss PHR

10 If you say that something happened or is true **for some reason**, you mean that you know it happened or is true, but you do not know why. *For some reason, the curtains were shut... For some inexplicable reason she was attracted to Patrick.* PHR with cl

11 If you say that you will do anything **within reason**, you mean that you will do anything that is fair or reasonable and not too extreme. *I will take any job that comes along, within reason... It means working, within reason, for whatever time is necessary.* PHR with cl, n PHR

12 • **rhyme or reason**: see **rhyme.** • **to see reason**: see **see.** • **it stands to reason**: see **stand.**

reason with. If you try to **reason with** someone, you try to persuade them to do something or to accept something by using sensible arguments. *I have watched parents trying to reason with their children and have never seen it work.* PHRASAL VERB V P n

reasonable /riːzənəbᵊl/ ◆◆◆◇◇

1 If you think that someone is fair and sensible you can say they are **reasonable**. *He's a reasonable sort of chap... Oh, come on, be reasonable.* ♦ **reasonably** /riːzənəbli/ *'I'm sorry, Andrew,' she said reasonably.* ♦ **reasonableness** *'I can understand how you feel,' Desmond said with great reasonableness.* ADJ-GRADED ≠unreasonable ADV N-UNCOUNT

2 If you say a decision or action is **reasonable**, you mean that it is fair and understandable. *...a perfectly reasonable decision... At the time, what he'd done had seemed reasonable.* ADJ-GRADED =fair

3 If you say that an expectation or explanation is **reasonable**, you mean that there are good reasons why it may be correct. *It seems reasonable to expect rapid urban growth.* ♦ **reasonably** *You can reasonably expect your goods to arrive within six to eight weeks.* ADJ-GRADED: oft *it* v-link ADJ to-inf ADV: ADV with v

4 If you say that something's price is **reasonable**, you mean that it is fair and not too high. *You get an interesting meal for a reasonable price... His fees were quite reasonable.* ♦ **reasonably** *...reasonably priced accommodation.* ADJ-GRADED ≠overpriced ADV-GRADED: ADV with v

5 You can use the word **reasonable** to describe something that is fairly good, but not very good. *The boy answered him in reasonable French... He had never been able to make a reasonable living from his writing.* ♦ **reasonably** *I can dance reasonably well.* ADJ-GRADED ADV-GRADED: ADV adj/adv

6 A **reasonable** amount of something is a fairly large amount of it. *They will need a reasonable amount of desk area and good light.* ♦ **reasonably** *From now on events moved reasonably quickly.* ADJ-GRADED ADV: ADV adj/adv

reasoned /riːzᵊnd/. A **reasoned** discussion or argument is based on sensible reasons, rather than on an appeal to people's emotions; used showing approval. *Abortion is an issue which produces a lot of sound and fury, but little reasoned argument.* ◆◇◇◇◇ ADJ-GRADED: usu ADJ n PRAGMATICS =rational ≠irrational

reasoning /riːzənɪŋ/ **reasonings. Reasoning** is the process by which you reach a conclusion after thinking about all the facts. *...the reasoning behind the decision... She was not really convinced by this line of reasoning.* ◆◇◇◇◇ N-VAR

reassemble /riːəsembᵊl/ **reassembles, reassembling, reassembled**

1 If you **reassemble** something, you put it back together after it has been taken apart. *We will now try to reassemble pieces of the wreckage... The table had to be taken apart and hoisted through the window before it was reassembled.* VERB V n

2 If a group of people **reassembles** or if you **reassemble** them, they gather together again in a group. *We shall reassemble in the car park in thirty minutes... Mr Lukanov reassembled his team in September.* V-ERG V V n

reassert /riːəsɜːʳt/ **reasserts, reasserting, reasserted** ◆◇◇◇◇

1 If you **reassert** your control or authority, you make it clear that you are still in a position of power, or you strengthen the power that you had. *...the government's continuing effort to reassert its control in the region... The adults had reasserted their old authority.* VERB V n

2 If something such as an idea or habit **reasserts** itself, it becomes noticeable again. *His sense of humour was beginning to reassert itself.* VERB V pron-refl

reassess /riːəses/ **reassesses, reassessing, reassessed.** If you **reassess** something, you think about it and decide whether you need to change your opinion about it. *I will reassess the situation when I get home... Security in the area will have to be reassessed.* ◆◇◇◇◇ VERB =reappraise V n

reassessment /riːəsesmənt/ **reassessments.** If you make a **reassessment** of something, you think about it and decide whether you need to change your opinion about it. *Forty, more than any other birthday seems to mark the moment when we make a reassessment of ourselves.* N-VAR =reappraisal

reassurance /riːəʃʊərəns/ **reassurances** ◆◇◇◇◇

1 If someone needs **reassurance**, they are very worried about something and need someone to help them stop worrying by saying kind or helpful things. *She needed reassurance that she belonged somewhere... 'You really won't tell?' she asked, begging for reassurance.* N-UNCOUNT

2 Reassurances are things that you say to help people stop worrying about something. *...reassurances that pesticides are not harmful.* N-COUNT

reassure /riːəʃʊəʳ/ **reassures, reassuring, reassured.** If you **reassure** someone, you say or do things to make them stop worrying about something. *I tried to reassure her, 'Don't worry about it. We won't let it happen again.'... She just reassured me that everything was fine.* ◆◆◇◇◇ VERB V n V n that Also V n *about* n

reassured /riːəʃʊəʳd/. If you feel **reassured**, you feel less worried about something, especially as a result of something someone has said or done. *I feel much more reassured when I've been for a health check.* ◆◇◇◇◇ ADJ-GRADED: usu v-link ADJ

reassuring /riːəʃʊərɪŋ/. If you find someone's words or actions **reassuring**, they make you feel less worried about something. *It was reassuring to hear John's familiar voice... She gave me some reassuring news.* ♦ **reassuringly** *'It's okay now,' he said reassuringly.* ◆◇◇◇◇ ADJ-GRADED: oft *it* v-link ADJ to-inf/that =comforting ADV-GRADED: usu ADV with v, also ADV adj

reawaken /riːəweɪkən/ **reawakens, reawakening, reawakened.** If something **reawakens** an issue, or an interest or feeling that you used to have, it makes you think about it or feel it again. *The King's stand is bound to reawaken the painful debate about abortion... The food reawakens memories of dishes that their mothers once cooked.* ► Also a noun. *These sales heralded a reawakening of interest in stained glass.* VERB =rekindle V n N-UNCOUNT

rebate /riːbeɪt/ **rebates.** A **rebate** is an amount of money which is paid to you when you have paid more tax, rent, or rates than you needed to. *...a tax rebate... Customers are to benefit from a* ◆◇◇◇◇ N-COUNT: usu with supp, oft n N, adj N, N *on* n *rebate on their electricity bills... There's no rebate on VAT.*

rebel, rebels, rebelling, rebelled. The noun is pronounced /rebəl/. The verb is pronounced /rɪbel/. ◆◆◆◆◇

1 **Rebels** are people who are fighting against their own country's army in order to change the political system there. *...fighting between rebels and government forces. ...rebel forces in Liberia.* N-COUNT: usu pl

2 Politicians who oppose some of their own party's policies can be referred to as **rebels**. *The rebels want another 1% cut in interest rates. ...rebel MPs.* N-COUNT

3 If politicians **rebel** against one of their own party's policies, they show that they oppose it. *More than forty Conservative MPs rebelled against the government and voted against the bill. ...MPs planning to rebel over the Maastricht vote.* VERB V *against* n V

4 You can say that someone is a **rebel** if you think that they behave differently from other people and have rejected the values of society or of their parents. *She had been a rebel at school.* N-COUNT

5 When someone **rebels**, they start to behave differently from other people and reject the values of society or of their parents. *The child who rebels is unlikely to be overlooked... I was very young and rebelling against everything.* VERB V V *against* n

rebellion /rɪbeliən/ **rebellions** ◆◆◇◇◇

1 A **rebellion** is a violent organized action by a large group of people who are trying to change their country's political system. *The British soon put down the rebellion. ...the ruthless and brutal suppression of rebellion.* N-VAR =revolt, insurrection

2 A situation in which politicians show their opposition to their own party's policies can be referred to as a **rebellion**. *...the Tory rebellion against pit closures.* N-VAR =revolt

rebellious /rɪbeliəs/ ◆◇◇◇◇

1 If you think someone behaves in an unacceptable way and does not do what they are told, you can say they are **rebellious**. *...a rebellious teenager... He grew older and more rebellious.* ADJ-GRADED ♦ **rebelliousness** *...the normal rebelliousness of youth.* N-UNCOUNT

2 A **rebellious** group of people is a group involved in taking violent action against the rulers of their own country, usually in order to change the system of government there. *The rebellious officers, having seized the radio station, broadcast the news of the overthrow of the monarchy.* ADJ: ADJ n

rebirth /riːbɜːʳθ/. You can refer to a change that leads to a new period of growth and improvement in something as its **rebirth**. *...the rebirth of democracy in Latin America... The hotel is awaiting its rebirth.* ◆◇◇◇◇ N-UNCOUNT: oft N *of* n =revival

reborn /riːbɔːʳn/. If you say that someone or something **has been reborn**, you mean that they have become active again after a period of inactivity. *Shilling has been reborn as an artist... Russia was being reborn as a great power.* ◆◇◇◇◇ V-PASSIVE be V-ed *as* n

rebound, rebounds, rebounding, rebounded. The verb is pronounced /rɪbaʊnd/. The noun is pronounced /riːbaʊnd/. ◆◇◇◇◇

1 If something **rebounds** from a solid surface, it bounces or springs back from it. *His shot in the 21st minute of the game rebounded from a post... The hot liquid splashed down on the concrete and rebounded.* VERB V prep V

2 If an action or situation **rebounds** on you, it has an unpleasant effect on you, especially when this effect was intended for someone else. *Mia realised her trick had rebounded on her... The CIA was extremely wary of interfering with the foreign Press; in the past, such interference had rebounded.* VERB V *on/upon* n V

3 If you say that someone is **on the rebound**, you mean that they have just ended a relationship with a girlfriend or boyfriend. This often makes them do things they would not normally do. *He took heroin for the first time when he was on the rebound from a broken relationship.* PHRASE: usu v-link PHR

rebuff /rɪbʌf/ **rebuffs, rebuffing, rebuffed.** If you **rebuff** someone or **rebuff** a suggestion that they make, you refuse to do what they suggest. *He wanted sex with Julie but she rebuffed him... His proposals have already been rebuffed by the Prime Minister.* ◆◇◇◇◇ VERB =reject V n Also be V-ed *in* n ► Also a noun. *The results of the poll dealt a humiliating rebuff to Mr Jones.* N-VAR: usu with supp

rebuild /riːbɪld/ **rebuilds, rebuilding, rebuilt** ◆◆◇◇◇

1 When people **rebuild** something such as a building or a city, they build it again after it has been damaged or destroyed. *They say they will stay to rebuild their homes rather than retreat to refugee camps... The castle was rebuilt by his great grandson in 1859.* VERB =restore V n

2 When people **rebuild** something such as an institution, a system, or an aspect of their lives, they take action to restore it to its previous condition. *The East Europeans want aid to help rebuild their economies... Jane began to rebuild her social life which had been non-existent since her marriage... The agency has been rebuilding under new management.* VERB V n V

3 If doctors **rebuild** part of someone's body that has been damaged, they operate on that person to make them well again. *Two weeks later, surgeons carried out the operation to rebuild his face.* VERB V n

rebuke /rɪbjuːk/ **rebukes, rebuking, rebuked.** If you **rebuke** someone, you speak severely to them because they have said or done something that you do not approve of; a formal use. *The president rebuked the House and Senate for not passing those bills within 100 days.* ◆◇◇◇◇ VERB =reprimand V n ► Also a noun. *The Prime Minister delivered a tough rebuke to Tory Euro-rebels... 'Silly little boy' was his favourite expression of rebuke to his pupils.* N-VAR: usu with supp =reprimand

rebut /rɪbʌt/ **rebuts, rebutting, rebutted.** If you **rebut** a charge or criticism that is made against you, you give reasons why it is untrue or unjustified. *He spent most of his speech rebutting criticisms of his foreign policy.* VERB =refute V n

rebuttal /rɪbʌtəl/ **rebuttals.** If you make a **rebuttal** of a charge or accusation that has been made against you, you make a statement which gives reasons why the accusation is untrue. *He is conducting a point-by-point rebuttal of charges from former colleagues... Pakistan has still not issued an official rebuttal to the latest Indian statements.* N-COUNT: oft N *of/to* n

recalcitrant /rɪkælsɪtrənt/. If you describe someone or something as **recalcitrant**, you mean that they are stubborn, unco-operative, or unwilling to obey orders; a formal word. *King William moved rapidly to establish Norman power over a recalcitrant Saxon majority... He had a knack for coaxing even the most recalcitrant engine to life.* ADJ-GRADED: usu ADJ n =disobedient ♦ **recalcitrance** /rɪkælsɪtrəns/. *It is losing patience with their recalcitrance over introducing even the smallest political reform.* N-UNCOUNT =stubbornness

recall, recalls, recalling, recalled. The verb is pronounced /rɪkɔːl/. The noun is pronounced /riːkɔːl/. ◆◆◆◆◇

1 When you **recall** something, you remember it and tell others about it. *Henderson recalled that he first met Pollard during a business trip to Washington... Her teacher recalled: 'She was always on about modelling.'... Colleagues today recall with humor how meetings would crawl into the early morning hours... I recalled the way they had been dancing together... I have no idea what she said, something about airline travel, I seem to recall.* VERB =remember V that V with quote V wh V n V Also V -ing

2 You can say **as I recall, you might recall**, or **you will recall** to someone that you are talking to when you want to mention something that you are both already aware of which is relevant to the discussion. *As I recall, you're not on the board, Joe; you're only a minor shareholder... You will recall that I sent you a warning of troubled times. Well now, almost everything I forecast has come about.* VERB PRAGMATICS V V that

3 **Recall** is the ability to remember something that has happened in the past or the act of remembering it. *He had a good memory, and total recall of her spoken words.* N-UNCOUNT

4 If you are **recalled** to your home, country, or the place where you work, you are ordered to return there. *Spain has recalled its Ambassador after a row* VERB V n

over refugees seeking asylum at the embassy... Parliament was recalled from its summer recess. ▸ Also a noun. N-SING: the N of n *The recall of ambassador Alan Green is a public signal of America's concern.*

5 In sport, if a player is **recalled** to a team, they are asked to rejoin that team after being left out. VERB V n to n be V-ed *Dean Richards has been recalled to the England squad for Saturday's match with Wales... I had done enough after being recalled against Pakistan to have got on the tour to India.* ▸ Also a noun. N-SING *It would be great to get a recall to the England squad for Sweden.*

6 If a company **recalls** a product, they ask the shops or the people who have bought that item to return it because there is something wrong with it. VERB V n *The company said it was recalling one of its drugs and had stopped selling two others... More than 3,000 cars were recalled yesterday because of a brake problem.*

7 If something is **beyond recall**, it is no longer possible to recreate it. PHRASE *The ground has been polluted beyond recall... Buthelezi appeals desperately for a Zulu unity which now looks lost beyond recall.*

recant /rɪkænt/ **recants, recanting, recanted.** VERB If you **recant**, you say publicly that you no longer hold a set of beliefs that you had in the past; a formal word. V V n *Alarmed by the furor the letter created, White House officials ordered Williams to recant. ...a man who had refused after torture to recant his heresy.*

recap /riːkæp/ **recaps, recapping, recapped.** VERB PRAGMATICS =sum up, recapitulate You can say that you are going to **recap** when you want to draw people's attention to the fact that you are going to repeat the main points of an explanation, argument, or description, as a summary of it. V V n *To recap briefly, an agreement negotiated to cut the budget deficit in the coming year was rejected 10 days ago by a large majority... Can you recap the points included in the regional conference proposal?* ▸ Also a noun. N-SING *Many of us would also like to hear a recap of Labour's defence policies.*

recapitalize /riːkæpɪtəlaɪz/ **recapitalizes, recapitalizing, recapitalized.** VERB In American English, if a company **recapitalizes**, they alter the way the company manages its financial affairs, for example by borrowing money or reissuing shares. V V n *Mr Warnock resigned as the company abandoned a plan to recapitalize... He plans to recapitalize the insurance fund.* ♦ **recapitalization** /riːkæpɪtəlaɪzeɪʃən/ **recapitalizations** N-COUNT *A substantial thrust of the effort of management is to explore a recapitalization of the company.*

recapitulate /riːkəpɪtʃʊleɪt/ **recapitulates, recapitulating, recapitulated.** VERB PRAGMATICS =recap, sum up You can say that you are going to **recapitulate** the main points of an explanation, argument, or description when you want to draw attention to the fact that you are going to repeat the most important points as a summary. V n V *Let's just recapitulate the essential points... It will shortly be put up for sale under the terms already communicated to you, which, to recapitulate, call for a very minimum of publicity.* ♦ **recapitulation** /riːkəpɪtʃʊleɪʃən/ N-SING *Chapter 9 provides a valuable recapitulation of the material already presented.*

recapture /riːkæptʃəʳ/ **recaptures, recapturing, recaptured** ♦◇◇◇◇

1 When soldiers **recapture** an area of land or a place, they win control of it again from an opposing army who had taken it from them. VERB =retake V n *They said the bodies were found when rebels recaptured the area.* ▸ Also a noun. N-SING: usu N of n *...an offensive to be launched for the recapture of the city.*

2 When people **recapture** something that they have lost to a competitor, they win it back again. VERB =win back V n *One poll shows that Labour is recapturing the voters who helped the Tories to victory.*

3 To **recapture** a person or animal which has escaped from somewhere means to catch them again. VERB V n *Police have recaptured Alan Lord, who escaped from a police cell in Bolton.* ▸ Also a noun. N-SING: usu N of n *...the swift recapture of a renegade police chief in Panama.*

4 When you **recapture** something such as an experience, emotion, or a quality you had in the past, you experience it again. VERB When something **recaptures** an experience for you, it makes you remember it. V n *He couldn't recapture the form he'd shown in getting to the semi-final... These cookies seem to recapture all the textures and flavors we remember from childhood.*

recast /riːkɑːst, -kæst/ **recasts, recasting.** The form **recast** is used in the present tense and is also the past tense and past participle.

1 If you **recast** something, you change it by organizing it in a different way. VERB V n *The shake-up aims to recast IBM as a federation of flexible and competing subsidiaries.* ♦ **recasting** N-SING: N of n *...the recasting of the political map of Europe.*

2 If the producers of a play or a film **recast** an actor's role, they give the role to another actor. VERB V n *Stoppard had to recast four of the principal roles.*

recce /reki/ **recces, recceing, recced.** VERB =check out In British English, if you **recce** an area, you visit that place in order to become familiar with it. People usually recce an area when they are going to return at a later time to do something there. V n *The first duty of a director is to recce his location before asking a cameraman to shoot a single foot of film.* ▸ Also a noun. N-COUNT *Uncle Jim took the air rifle and went on a recce to the far end of the quarry.*

recd. In written English, **recd.** can be used as an abbreviation for 'received'.

recede /rɪsiːd/ **recedes, receding, receded** ♦◇◇◇◇

1 If something **recedes** from you, it moves away. VERB V prep V V-ing *Luke's footsteps receded into the night... As she receded he waved goodbye. ...the receding lights of the car.*

2 When something such as a quality, problem, or illness **recedes**, it becomes weaker, smaller, or less intense. VERB V V-ing Also V prep *Just as I started to think that I was never going to get well, the illness began to recede... Dealers grew concerned over the sliding dollar and receding prospects for economic recovery.*

3 If a man's hair starts to **recede**, it no longer grows on the front of his head. VERB V V-ing Also V *at/from* n *...a youngish man with dark hair just beginning to recede... The bartender had a florid face and a receding hairline.*

4 If your gums start to **recede**, they begin to cover less of your teeth, usually as the result of an infection. VERB V V-ing *If untreated, the gums recede, become swollen and bleed... Receding gums can be the result of disease or simply incorrect brushing.*

receipt /rɪsiːt/ **receipts** ♦♦◇◇◇

1 A **receipt** is a piece of paper that you get from someone as confirmation that they have received money or goods from you. N-COUNT *I wrote her a receipt for the money.*

2 Receipts are the amount of money received during a particular period, for example by a shop or theatre. N-PLURAL: usu with supp =takings *The film opened to healthy box office receipts before rapidly falling off... He was tallying the day's receipts.*

3 The **receipt** of something is the act of receiving it; a formal use. N-UNCOUNT *Goods should be supplied within 28 days after the receipt of your order.*

4 If you are **in receipt of** something, you have received it or you receive it regularly; a formal expression. PHRASE *We are taking action, having been in receipt of a letter from him... I am in receipt of a state pension.*

receive /rɪsiːv/ **receives, receiving, received** ♦♦♦♦♦

1 When you **receive** something, you get it after someone gives it to you or sends it to you. VERB =get V n *They will receive their awards at a ceremony in Stockholm... I received your letter of November 7.*

2 You can use **receive** to say that certain kinds of thing happen to someone. For example if they are injured, you can say that they **received** an injury. VERB V n *He received more of the blame than anyone when the plan failed to work... She was suffering from whiplash injuries received in a car crash.*

3 When you **receive** a visitor or a guest, you greet VERB them. *The following evening the duchess was again receiving guests... The shop assistant received me indifferently while leaning on a counter.* V n

4 If you say that something **is received** in a particular way, you mean that people react to it in that way. *The resolution had been received with great disappointment within the PLO... The proposals have been well received by many deputies.* VB: usu passive be V-ed prep/adv be V-ed with adv

5 When a radio or television **receives** signals that are being transmitted, it picks them up and converts them into sound or pictures. *The reception was a little faint but clear enough for him to receive the signal.* VERB V n Also V

6 If someone **receives** stolen goods, they buy or are given things that have been stolen; a legal term, used mainly in British English. *He went to prison for receiving stolen scrap iron... He received the shoes when stolen, and then passed them on to the men who would sell them.* VERB =fence V n

7 If you **are on the receiving end** or **at the receiving end** of something unpleasant, you are the person that it happens to. *You saw hate in their eyes and you were on the receiving end of that hate... Bullying can indeed be distressing and frightening for those at the receiving end.* PHRASE

received /rɪsiːvd/. The **received** opinion about something or the **received** way of doing something is generally accepted by people as being correct; a formal word. *He was among the first to question the received wisdom of the time... The judgments expressed are largely what is called received opinion.* ADJ: ADJ n

Received Pronunciation. **Received Pronunciation** is a way of pronouncing British English that is often used as a standard in the Teaching of English as a Foreign Language. The abbreviation **RP** is also used. The accent represented by the pronunciations in this dictionary is Received Pronunciation. N-UNCOUNT

receiver /rɪsiːvəʳ/ **receivers** ◆◆◇◇◇

1 A telephone's **receiver** is the part that you hold near to your ear and speak into. N-COUNT

2 A **receiver** is the part of a radio or television that picks up incoming signals and converts them into sound or pictures. *Auto-tuning VHF receivers are now common in cars.* N-COUNT

3 The **receiver** is someone who is appointed by a court of law to manage the affairs of a business, usually when it has gone into bankruptcy. *Between July and September, a total of 1,059 firms called in the receiver.* N-COUNT: usu *the* N

receivership /rɪsiːvəʃɪp/ **receiverships.** If a company goes into **receivership**, it becomes bankrupt and the administration of its business is handled by the receiver. *The company has now gone into receivership with debts of several million... Accountants Touche Ross say that there were 45 receiverships among hotels and caterers.* ◆◇◇◇◇ N-VAR: oft *in/into* N

recent /riːsᵊnt/. A **recent** event or period of time happened only a short while ago. *In the most recent attack one man was shot dead and two others were wounded... Sales have fallen by more than 75 percent in recent years.* ◆◆◆◆◆ ADJ-GRADED: usu ADJ n

recently /riːsᵊntli/. If you have done something **recently** or if something happened **recently**, it happened only a short time ago. *The bank recently opened a branch in Germany... It is only fairly recently that historians have begun to investigate the question... He was until very recently the most powerful banker in the city.* ◆◆◆◆◇ ADV-GRADED: ADV with v, *until* ADV

receptacle /rɪseptɪkəl/ **receptacles.** A **receptacle** is an object which you use to put or keep things in; a formal word. N-COUNT =container

reception /rɪsepʃᵊn/ **receptions** ◆◆◇◇◇

1 The **reception** in a hotel, office, or hospital is the part of the building where people are received and their reservations, appointments, or enquiries are dealt with; used mainly in British English. *Have him bring a car round to the reception... Wait at reception for me. ...the hotel's reception desk.* N-SING: *the* N, oft N n, also *at* N

2 A **reception** is a formal party which is given to welcome someone or to celebrate a special event. *At the reception they served smoke salmon. ...a glittering wedding reception.* N-COUNT

3 If someone or something has a particular kind of **reception**, that is the way people react to them. *Mr Mandela has been given a tumultuous reception in Washington... He received a cool reception to his speech.* N-COUNT: usu sing, usu supp N

4 The **reception** of guests is the act of formally welcoming them; a formal use. *The preparations for the reception of his Royal Highness proceeded.* N-SING: *the* N *of* n

5 If you get good **reception** from your radio or television, the sound or picture is clear because the signal is strong. If the **reception** is poor, the sound or picture is unclear because the signal is weak. *Adjust the aerial's position and direction for the best reception.* N-UNCOUNT

reception centre, reception centres; spelled **reception center** in American English. A **reception centre** is a place which provides temporary accommodation for people who are homeless or who are being looked after by the government authorities; used mainly in British English. N-COUNT

reception class, reception classes. In Britain, a **reception class** is a class that children go into when they first start infant school. N-COUNT

receptionist /rɪsepʃənɪst/ **receptionists.** In a hotel, office, or hospital, the **receptionist** is the person whose job is to answer the telephone, arrange reservations or appointments, and deal with people when they first arrive. ◆◇◇◇◇ N-COUNT

reception room, reception rooms. A **reception room** is a room in a house, for example a living room or a dining room, where people can sit; used mainly in British English. This expression is often used by estate-agents to describe houses that are for sale. N-COUNT

receptive /rɪseptɪv/ ◆◇◇◇◇

1 Someone who is **receptive** to new ideas or suggestions is prepared to consider them or accept them. *The voters had seemed receptive to his ideas... Do you think that there is any receptive audience for his remarks.* ♦ **receptiveness** *There was less receptiveness to liberalism in some areas.* ♦ **receptivity** /riːseptɪvɪti/ *There was a lack of receptivity to the advances in science.* ADJ-GRADED: oft ADJ *to* n; N-UNCOUNT; N-UNCOUNT

2 If someone who is ill is **receptive** to treatment, they start to get better when they are given treatment. *For those patients who are not receptive to treatment, the chance for improvement is small.* ADJ-GRADED: v-link ADJ *to* n

receptor /rɪseptəʳ/ **receptors.** **Receptors** are nerve endings in your body which react to changes and stimuli and make your body respond in a particular way; a technical term in biology. *Our sense of smell is just as crucial to the information receptors in our brain as our other senses.* ◆◇◇◇◇ N-COUNT

recess /rɪses, riːses/ **recesses, recessing, recessed** ◆◇◇◇◇

1 A **recess** is a break between the sessions of work of an official body such as a committee, a court of law, or a government. *The conference broke for a recess, but the 10-minute break stretched to two hours... Some in Congress are concerned the war option could be adopted in November when Congress is in recess... Parliament returns to work today after its summer recess.* N-COUNT: also *in/from* N

2 When formal proceedings **recess**, they stop temporarily. *The hearings have now recessed for dinner... Before the trial recessed today, the lawyer read her opening statement.* VERB V *for* n V

3 In a room, a **recess** is part of a wall which is built further back than the rest of the wall. Recesses are often used as a place to put furniture such as bookshelves. *...a discreet recess next to a fireplace.* N-COUNT =alcove

4 The **recesses** of something or somewhere are the parts of it which are hard to see because light does not reach them or they are hidden from view. *He emerged from the dark recesses of the garage... From the recesses of his coat Richard produced a bottle of champagne.* N-COUNT: usu pl, usu with supp

5 If you refer to the **recesses** of the someone's mind or soul, you are referring to thoughts or feelings N-COUNT: usu pl, usu with supp they have which are hidden or difficult to describe. *...the inner recesses of the soul... There was something in the darker recesses of his unconscious that was troubling him.*

recessed /riːsest/. If something such as a door or window is **recessed**, it is set into the wall that surrounds it. *...a wide passage, lit from one side by recessed windows. ...thick glass recessed into the ceiling.* ADJ

recession /rɪseʃᵊn/ **recessions.** A **recession** is a period when the economy of a country is doing badly, for example because industry is producing less and more people are becoming unemployed. *The recession caused sales to drop off... We should concentrate on sharply reducing interest rates to pull the economy out of recession... The oil price increases sent Europe into deep recession.* ◆◆◆◆◇ N-VAR =slump

recessional /rɪseʃənᵊl/

1 The **recessional** is a hymn which is sung at the end of a church service. N-SING

2 **Recessional** means related to an economic recession. *Despite stirrings in the property market, many home sellers remain stuck in a recessional rut.* ADJ: ADJ n

recessionary /rɪseʃᵊnri/. **Recessionary** means relating to an economic recession or having the effect of creating a recession. *Reduced interest rates would help ease recessionary pressures in the economy.* ◆◇◇◇◇ ADJ-GRADED: ADJ n

recessive /rɪsesɪv/. A **recessive** gene produces a particular characteristic only if a person has two of these genes, one from each parent; a technical term in biology. Compare **dominant**. *It's possible for two brown-eyed parents to have a child with blue eyes if both parents have inherited a recessive gene for blue eyes.* ADJ: usu ADJ n

recharge /riːtʃɑːʳdʒ/ **recharges, recharging, recharged** ◆◇◇◇◇

1 If you **recharge** a battery, you put an electrical charge back into the battery by connecting it to a machine that draws power from another source of electricity such as the mains. *He is using your mains electricity to recharge his car battery.* VERB V n

2 If you **recharge** your **batteries**, you take a break from activities which are tiring or stressful in order to relax and be refreshed when you return to work. *He wanted to recharge his batteries and come back feeling fresh and positive.* PHRASE: V inflects

rechargeable /riːtʃɑːʳdʒəbᵊl/ **rechargeables.** **Rechargeable** batteries can be recharged and used again. Some electrical products are described as **rechargeable** when they contain rechargeable batteries. *...a portable phone which will run for a month on a rechargeable battery. ...a rechargeable drill.* ► Also a noun. *It is more expensive to run a personal stereo on disposable batteries than on rechargeables.* ADJ: usu ADJ n; N-COUNT

recherché /rəʃeəʳʃeɪ/. If you describe something as **recherché**, you mean that it is very sophisticated or is associated with people who like things which are unusual and of a very high quality; a formal word. *Only extra-virgin, cold-pressed olive oil will do on the most recherché dinner tables.* ADJ-GRADED

recidivist /rɪsɪdɪvɪst/. **recidivists.** A **recidivist** is someone who has committed crimes in the past and has begun to commit crimes again, for example after a period of being in prison. *Six prisoners are still at large along with four dangerous recidivists.* ♦ **recidivism** /rɪsɪdɪvɪzəm/ *Their basic criticism was that prisons do not reduce the crime rate, they cause recidivism.* N-COUNT; N-UNCOUNT

recipe /resɪpi/ **recipes** ◆◆◇◇◇

1 A **recipe** is a list of ingredients and a set of instructions that tell you how to cook something. *...a traditional recipe for oatmeal biscuits. ...a recipe book.* N-COUNT

2 If you say that something is **a recipe for** a particular situation, you mean that it is likely to result in that situation. *Large-scale inflation is a recipe for disaster.* N-SING: a N for n

recipient /rɪsɪpiənt/ **recipients.** The **recipient** of something is the person who receives it; a formal word. *...the largest recipient of American foreign aid... A suppressed immune system puts a transplant recipient at risk of other infections.* ◆◆◇◇◇ N-COUNT: oft N of n

reciprocal /rɪsɪprəkᵊl/. A **reciprocal** action or agreement involves two people or groups who do the same thing to each other or agree to help each another in a similar way; a formal word. *They expected a reciprocal gesture before more hostages could be freed... The department said many countries had reciprocal agreements for health care with Britain.* ♦ **reciprocally** *Both sides had reciprocally observed restraints.* ◆◇◇◇◇ ADJ: usu ADJ n; ADV

reciprocate /rɪsɪprəkeɪt/ **reciprocates, reciprocating, reciprocated.** If your feelings or actions towards someone are **reciprocated**, the other person feels or behaves in the same way towards you as you have felt or behaved towards them. *Mr Tian is reciprocating the visit to Peking earlier this year by Mr Maude... Their attraction to each other as friends is reciprocated... He needs these people to fulfill his ambitions and reciprocates by bringing out the best in each of them.* ♦ **reciprocation** /rɪsɪprəkeɪʃᵊn/ *There was no reciprocation of esteem, let alone affection.* ◆◇◇◇◇ VERB V n; V by -ing; N-UNCOUNT

reciprocity /resɪprɒsɪti/. **Reciprocity** is the exchange of something between people or groups of people when each person or group gives or allows something to the other; a formal word. *The protest went ahead despite government assurances that they would press for reciprocity with Greece in the issuing of visas.* N-UNCOUNT

recital /rɪsaɪtᵊl/ **recitals** ◆◇◇◇◇

1 A **recital** is a performance of music or poetry, usually given by one person. *...a solo recital by the harpsichordist Maggie Cole.* N-COUNT: oft with supp

2 If someone speaks for a long time, or says something that is boring or that has been heard many times before, you can describe it as a **recital**; used in written English. *Before long we all grew bored with his frequent recital of the foods he couldn't eat... I had their total attention during the thirty-five minutes that my recital took.* N-COUNT: usu with supp

recitation /resɪteɪʃᵊn/ **recitations**

1 When someone does a **recitation**, they say aloud a piece of poetry or other writing that they have learned. *The transmission began with a recitation from the Koran.* N-VAR

2 A **recitation** of something is a statement of it; used in written English. *The letter was short – a simple recitation of their problem.* N-COUNT: oft N of n

recite /rɪsaɪt/ **recites, reciting, recited** ◆◇◇◇◇

1 When someone **recites** a poem or other piece of writing, they say it aloud after they have learned it. *They recited poetry to one another.* VERB V n Also V

2 If you **recite** something such as a list, you say it aloud. *All he could do was recite a list of Government failings... She suddenly realized that Wim was reciting Kirk's telephone number.* VERB V n

reckless /rekləs/. If you say that someone is **reckless**, you mean that they act in a way which shows that they do not care about danger or the effect their behaviour will have on other people. *She loved to ride; on horseback, she was reckless and utterly without fear... He is charged with causing death by reckless driving.* ♦ **recklessly** *He was leaning recklessly out of the unshuttered window... A congressional report charges that federal safety laws were recklessly violated.* ♦ **recklessness** *He felt a surge of recklessness... The headstrong recklessness of youth may be fine in some areas, but not behind the wheel of a car.* ◆◇◇◇◇ ADJ-GRADED; ADV-GRADED: ADV with v, ADV adj; N-UNCOUNT

reckon /rekən/ **reckons, reckoning, reckoned** ◆◆◆◇◇

1 If you **reckon** that something is true, you think that it is true; an informal use. *Toni reckoned that it must be about three o'clock... He reckoned he was still fond of her.* VERB =think V that

2 If you say that something **is reckoned** to be true, you mean that people think that it is true; an informal use. *The sale has been held up because the price is reckoned to be too high.* VB: usu passive =thought be V-ed to-inf

3 If you say that someone **reckons** to do something, you mean that they expect to do it; an informal use. *The merged banks reckon to raise 4 billion dollars of new equity next year... Police officers on the case are reckoning to charge someone very shortly.* VERB =expect V to-inf

4 If something **is reckoned** to be a particular figure, it is calculated to be roughly that amount. *The market's revised threshold is now reckoned to be 22,000-22,500 on the Nikkei index... The amount being poured into East Germany was reckoned at 140 billion marks.* VB: usu passive =calculate be V-ed to-inf be V-ed at n

reckon on. If you **reckon on** something, you feel certain that it will happen and therefore make your plans based on it happening. *They are typical of couples who plan a family without reckoning on the small fortune it will cost... He reckons on being world heavyweight champion.* PHRASAL VERB V P n/-ing (not pron)

reckon with PHRASAL VERB

1 If you say that you had not **reckoned with** something, you mean that you had not expected it and so were not prepared for it. *Giles had not reckoned with the strength of Sally's feelings for him.* with brd-neg V P n

2 If you say that there is someone or something **to be reckoned with**, you mean that they must be dealt with and it will be difficult. *This act was a signal to his victim's friends that he was someone to be reckoned with... He will have to demonstrate that his Movement for Democracy is really a force to be reckoned with in Algerian politics.* n PHR

reckon without. If you say that you had **reckoned without** something, you mean that you had not expected it and so were not prepared for it. *I thought that it would take only a day of hard driving to reach Chengdu. But I had reckoned without the landslides.* PHRASAL VERB V P n

reckoning /rekənɪŋ/ **reckonings** ◆◇◇◇◇

1 Someone's **reckoning** is a calculation they make about something, especially a calculation that is not very exact. *By my reckoning we were seven or eight kilometres from Borj Mechaab.* N-VAR: usu poss N

2 If you say that you will have a **reckoning** with someone, you mean that you will confront them at some time in the future and punish them for something they have done. *She knew their truce would not last. There would be a reckoning. There would be another fight.* ● see also **day of reckoning**. N-COUNT: usu sing

reclaim /rɪkleɪm/ **reclaims, reclaiming, reclaimed** ◆◇◇◇◇

1 If you **reclaim** something that you have lost or that has been taken away from you, you succeed in getting it back. *In 1986, they got the right to reclaim South African citizenship... She was given 15 minutes to scurry into the building and reclaim what she could of her life's possessions.* VERB V n

2 If you **reclaim** an amount of money, for example tax that you have paid, you claim it back. *There are an estimated eight million people currently thought to be eligible to reclaim income tax.* VERB V n

3 When people **reclaim** land, they make it suitable for a purpose such as farming or building, for example by draining it or by building a barrier against the sea. *The Netherlands has been reclaiming farmland from water. ...a scheme to build a residential development on 1,100 acres of reclaimed land in Tokyo Bay.* VERB V n V-ed

4 If a piece of land that was used for farming or building **is reclaimed** by a desert, or forest, or by the sea, it turns back into desert, forest, or sea. *The diamond towns are gradually being reclaimed by the desert... This method of spraying would allow the land to be reclaimed by the rain forests.* VB: usu passive be V-ed by n

5 If you **reclaim** a person who has been involved in bad or criminal behaviour, you cause them to stop acting in that way. *He set out to fight the drug infestation of Omaha by reclaiming a youth from the local gangs.* VERB V n

reclamation /rekləmeɪʃən/. **Reclamation** is the process of changing land that is unsuitable for farming or building into land that is usable. *...centuries of sea-wall construction and the reclamation of dry land from the marshes... The area is needed for a land reclamation project.* N-UNCOUNT

recline /rɪklaɪn/ **reclines, reclining, reclined** ◆◇◇◇◇

1 If you **recline** on something, you sit or lie on it with the upper part of your body supported at an angle. *She proceeded to recline on a chaise longue... Move to a reclining position on the mattress and rest for 15 minutes.* VERB =lie V prep V-ing Also V n

2 When a seat **reclines** or when you **recline** it, you lower the back so that it is more comfortable to sit in. *Air France first-class seats recline almost like beds... Ramesh had reclined his seat and was lying back smoking... He was comfortably seated in a soft reclining chair.* V-ERG V V n V-ing

recluse /rɪkluːs, AM rekluːs/ **recluses.** A **recluse** is a person who lives alone and deliberately avoids other people. *His widow became a virtual recluse for the remainder of her life.* N-COUNT: usu sing

reclusive /rɪkluːsɪv/. A **reclusive** person or animal lives alone and deliberately avoids the company of others. *A reclusive millionaire left his luxury home to the housekeeper he had hardly spoken to for 21 years... She had become increasingly ill and reclusive.* ADJ-GRADED

recognise /rekəgnaɪz/. See **recognize**.

recognition /rekəgnɪʃən/ ◆◆◆◇◇

1 Recognition is the act of recognizing someone or identifying something when you see it. *George said, 'Ida, how are you?' She frowned for a moment and then recognition dawned. 'George Black. Well, I never.'... He searched for a sign of recognition on her face, but there was none.* N-UNCOUNT

2 Recognition of something is an understanding and acceptance of it. *The CBI welcomed the Chancellor's recognition of the recession and hoped for a reduction in interest rates.* N-UNCOUNT: with supp =acceptance

3 When a government gives diplomatic **recognition** to another country, they officially accept that its status is valid. *Mr Mulroney said Canada was extending diplomatic recognition to the Baltic republics... His government did not receive full recognition by Britain until July.* N-UNCOUNT: with supp

4 When a person receives **recognition** for the things that they have done, people acknowledge the value or skill of their work. *At last, her father's work has received popular recognition... He is an outstanding goalscorer who doesn't get the recognition he deserves.* N-UNCOUNT: with supp

5 If you say that someone or something has changed **beyond recognition** or **out of all recognition**, you mean that person or thing has changed so much that you can no longer recognize them. *The bodies were mutilated beyond recognition... The facilities have improved beyond all recognition... The situation in Eastern Europe has changed out of all recognition.* PHRASES PHR after v

6 If something is done **in recognition of** someone's achievements, it is done as a way of showing official appreciation of them. *Brazil is about to normalise its diplomatic relations with South Africa in recognition of the steps taken to end apartheid... He had just received a doctorate in recognition of his contributions to seismology.* PREP

recognizable /rekəgnaɪzəbəl/; also spelled **recognisable** in British English. If something can be easily recognized or identified, you can say it is easily **recognizable**. *The vault was opened and the body found to be well preserved, his features easily recognizable... This tree is always recognizable by its extremely beautiful silvery bark. ...the world's most recognizable athlete.* ◆◇◇◇◇ ADJ-GRADED: oft adv ADJ, ADJ *as/by/to* n

♦ **recognizably** /rekəgnaɪzəbli/; *The request, naturally, is politely phrased but is still recognizably a command... At seven weeks, an embryo is about three-fourths of an inch long and recognizably human.* ADV-GRADED: usu ADV n, ADV adj

recognizance /rɪkɒgnɪzəns, -kɒn-/; also spelled **recognisance.** If someone who has been charged with a crime is released on their own **recognizance**, they are allowed to leave the courtroom after promising to return on a specified date. **Recognizance** also refers to an amount of money N-UNCOUNT: oft poss N that is pledged as a guarantee of someone's return after they are released; a legal term used mainly in American English. *His attorneys are requesting that he be released on his own recognizance while he awaits trial. ...a $100,000 personal recognizance bond.*

recognize /rekəgnaɪz/ **recognizes, recognizing, recognized;** also spelled **recognise** in British English. ◆◆◆◆◇
1 If you **recognize** someone or something, you know who that person is or what that thing is. To **recognize** someone or something you must have seen or heard them before, or someone must have described them to you. *The receptionist recognized him at once... He did not think she could recognize his car in the snow... A man I easily recognized as Luke's father sat with a newspaper on his lap.* VB: no cont; V n; V n as n
2 If someone says that they **recognize** something, they acknowledge that it exists or that it is true. *I recognize my own shortcomings... Well, of course I recognize that evil exists.* VB: no cont =accept; V n; V that
3 If people or organizations **recognize** something as valid, they officially accept it or approve of it. *Most doctors appear to recognize homeopathy as a legitimate form of medicine... France is on the point of recognizing the independence of the Baltic States. ...a nationally recognized expert on psychology.* VERB =accept; V n as n; V n; V-ed; Also V that
4 When people **recognize** the work someone has done, they show their appreciation of it, often by giving that person an award of some kind. *The RAF recognized him as an outstandingly able engineer... He had the insight to recognize their talents... Nichols was recognized by the Hall of Fame in 1949.* VERB; V n as n; V n

recoil, recoils, recoiling, recoiled. The verb is pronounced /rɪkɔɪl/. The noun is pronounced /riːkɔɪl/. ◆◇◇◇◇
1 If something makes you **recoil**, you move your body quickly away from it because it frightens, offends, or hurts you. *For a moment I thought he was going to kiss me. I recoiled in horror... We are attracted by nice smells and recoil from nasty ones.* VERB; V; V from n ► Also a noun. *His reaction was as much of a rebuff as a physical recoil. ...his small body jerking in recoil from the volume of his shouting.* N-UNCOUNT
2 If you say that someone **recoils** from doing something or **recoils** at the idea of something, you mean that they are reluctant to do it because they dislike it so much. *People used to recoil from the idea of getting into debt... She recoiled at the number of young girls who had to live by selling their bodies.* VERB; V from n; V at n
3 The **recoil** of a gun is the quick backward movement that it makes when it is fired. *The policeman fires again, tensed against the recoil, unleashing round after round at his assailant... I assembled the weapon, checked the firing and recoil mechanism and loaded it.* N-SING: also no det

recollect /rekəlekt/ **recollects, recollecting, recollected.** If you **recollect** something, you remember it. *Ramona spoke with warmth when she recollected the doctor who used to be at the county hospital... His efforts, the Duke recollected many years later, were distinctly half-hearted.* VERB =remember; V n; V that; Also V

recollection /rekəlekʃən/ **recollections.** If you have a **recollection** of something, you remember it. *Pat has vivid recollections of the trip, and remembers some of the frightening aspects I had forgotten... He had no recollection of the crash... Suddenly his mind filled with the recollection of a song she used to sing... She had a sudden burst of recollection and had to share it with me.* ◆◇◇◇◇ N-VAR =memory

recommence /riːkəmens/ **recommences, recommencing, recommenced.** If you **recommence** something or if it **recommences**, it begins again after having stopped; used in written English. *He recommenced work on his novel... His course at Sheffield University will not recommence until next year.* V-ERG; V n; V

recommend /rekəmend/ **recommends, recommending, recommended** ◆◆◆◆◇
1 If someone **recommends** something or someone to you, they suggest that you would find them good or useful. *I have just spent a holiday there and would recommend it to anyone... 'You're a good worker, boy,' he told him. 'I'll recommend you for a promotion.'... Ask your doctor to recommend a suitable therapist.* VERB; V n to/for/as n; V n ► Also an adjective. *Though ten years old, this book is highly recommended... There are a number of recommended restaurants.* ADJ-GRADED
2 If you **recommend** that something is done, you advise that it should be done. *The judge recommended that he serve 20 years in prison... We strongly recommend reporting the incident to the police... It is recommended that you should consult your doctor... The recommended daily dose is 12 to 24 grams.* VERB; V that; V n/-ing; it be V-ed that; V-ed; Also V n to-inf
3 If something or someone has a particular quality to **recommend** it, that quality makes it attractive or gives it an advantage over similar things. *La Noblesse restaurant has much to recommend it... He had little but his enthusiasm to recommend him... These qualities recommended him to Olivier.* VERB; V n; V n to n

recommendation /rekəmendeɪʃən/ **recommendations** ◆◆◆◇◇
1 The **recommendations** of a person or a committee are their suggestions or advice on what is the best thing to do. *The committee's recommendations are unlikely to be made public... Lord Justice Woolf will make recommendations for reform in his report... The decision was made on the recommendation of the Interior Minister.* N-VAR: oft with poss
2 A **recommendation** of something is the suggestion that someone should have or use it because it is good. *On O'Leary's recommendation, they started with tortellini... The best way of finding a solicitor is though personal recommendation.* N-VAR

recompense /rekəmpens/ **recompenses, recompensing, recompensed**
1 If you are given something, usually money, in **recompense**, you are given it as a reward or because you have suffered; a formal use. *He demands no financial recompense for his troubles... Substantial damages were paid in recompense.* N-UNCOUNT: oft N for n, in N =compensation
2 If you **recompense** someone for their efforts or their loss, you give them something, usually money, as a payment or reward; a formal use. *The fees offered by the NHS do not recompense dental surgeons for their professional time... If they succeed in court, they will be fully recompensed for their loss.* VERB =compensate; V n for n

reconcile /rekənsaɪl/ **reconciles, reconciling, reconciled** ◆◆◇◇◇
1 If you **reconcile** two beliefs, facts, or demands that seem to be opposed or completely different, you find a way in which they can both be true or both be fulfilled. *It's difficult to reconcile the demands of my job and the desire to be a good father... We suggest that it is possible to reconcile these apparently opposing perspectives... Negotiators must now work out how to reconcile these demands with American demands for access.* VERB; V pl-n; V n with n
2 If you **are reconciled** with someone, you become friendly with them again after a quarrel or disagreement. *He never believed he and Susan would be reconciled... Devlin was reconciled with the Catholic Church in his last few days.* V-RECIP-PASSIVE; pl-n be V-ed; be V-ed with n
3 If you **reconcile** two people, you make them become friends again after a quarrel or disagreement. *...my attempt to reconcile him with Toby.* VERB; V n with n
4 If you **reconcile** yourself to an unpleasant situation, you accept it, although it does not make you happy to do so. *She had reconciled herself to never seeing him again.* VERB; V pron-refl to n/-ing ♦ **reconciled** *She felt, if not grateful for her own lot, at least a little more reconciled to it.* ADJ-GRADED: v-link ADJ to n/-ing

reconciliation /rekənsɪlieɪʃən/ **reconciliations** ◆◆◇◇◇
1 **Reconciliation** between two people or countries who have quarrelled is the process of their becoming friends again. A **reconciliation** is an instance of this. *...an appeal for reconciliation between Catholics and Protestants... The couple have separated but he wants a reconciliation... Their handshake appeared to be a gesture of reconciliation.* N-VAR: oft N between/with/of n
2 The **reconciliation** of two beliefs, facts, or demands that seem to be opposed or completely different is the act or process of bringing them N-SING: N between/of/with n

together so that they can both be true or both be fulfilled. *...the ideal of democracy based upon a reconciliation of the values of equality and liberty.*

recondite /rɪkɒndaɪt, rekən-/. **Recondite** areas of knowledge or learning are difficult to understand, and not many people know about them; a formal word. *...such recondite areas as deconstruction, hermeneutics and the analysis of discourse.*
ADJ-GRADED: usu ADJ n =esoteric

recondition /riːkəndɪʃən/ **reconditions, reconditioning, reconditioned.** To **recondition** a machine or piece of equipment means to repair or replace all the parts that are damaged or broken. *He made contact with someone with an idea for reconditioning laser copiers... They sell used and reconditioned motorcycle parts.*
VERB
Vn
V-ed

reconfirm /riːkənfɜːʳm/ **reconfirms, reconfirming, reconfirmed. Reconfirm** means the same as **confirm.**
VERB

reconnaissance /rɪkɒnɪsəns/. **Reconnaissance** is the activity of obtaining military information about a place by sending soldiers or planes there, or by the use of satellites. *The helicopter was returning from a reconnaissance mission... The aircraft will be used for reconnaissance rather than combat.*
◆◇◇◇◇
N-UNCOUNT: oft N n

reconnect /riːkənekt/ **reconnects, reconnecting, reconnected.** If a company **reconnects** your electricity, water, gas, or telephone after it has been stopped, they provide you with it once again. *They charge a £66.10 fee for reconnecting cut-off customers... Local electricity companies say some homes won't be reconnected until the end of the week.* ♦ **reconnection** /riːkənekʃən/ *The cost of reconnection after supplies are cut off is high.*
VERB
Vn
N-UNCOUNT

reconnoitre /rekənɔɪtəʳ/ **reconnoitres, reconnoitring, reconnoitred;** spelled **reconnoiter** in American English. To **reconnoitre** an area means to obtain information about its geographical features or about the size and position of an army there. *He was sent to Eritrea to reconnoitre the enemy position... I left a sergeant in command and rode forward to reconnoitre.*
VERB
Vn
V

reconquer /riːkɒŋkəʳ/ **reconquers, reconquering, reconquered.** If an army **reconquers** a country or territory after having lost it, they win control over it again. *A crusade left Europe in an attempt to reconquer the Holy City.*
VERB
Vn

reconsider /riːkənsɪdəʳ/ **reconsiders, reconsidering, reconsidered.** If you **reconsider** a decision or opinion, you think about it and try to decide whether it should be changed. *We want you to reconsider your decision to resign from the board... This has forced the United States to seriously reconsider its position... If at the end of two years you still feel the same, we will reconsider.* ♦ **reconsideration** /riːkənsɪdəreɪʃən/ *The report urges reconsideration of the decision.*
◆◇◇◇◇
VERB
Vn
V
N-UNCOUNT: oft N of n

reconstitute /riːkɒnstɪtjuːt, AM -tuːt/ **reconstitutes, reconstituting, reconstituted**
◆◇◇◇◇

1 If an organization or state **is reconstituted,** it is formed again in a different way. *The five regions in East Germany will have to be reconstituted. ...the reconstituted Communist Party, now called the Party of Democratic Socialism.* ♦ **reconstitution** /riːkɒnstɪtjuːʃən, AM -tuːʃ-/ *They oppose any sort of reconstitution of the Soviet Union.*
VB: usu passive
be V-ed
V-ed
N-UNCOUNT: oft N of n

2 To **reconstitute** dried food means to add water to it so that it can be eaten. *To reconstitute dried tomatoes, simmer in plain water until they are tender... Try eating reconstituted dried prunes, figs or apricots.*
VERB
Vn
V-ed

reconstruct /riːkənstrʌkt/ **reconstructs, reconstructing, reconstructed**
◆◇◇◇◇

1 If you **reconstruct** something that has been destroyed or badly damaged, you build it and make it work again. *The government must reconstruct the shattered economy... He had plastic surgery to help reconstruct his badly damaged face... Although this part of Normandy was badly bombed during the war it has been completely reconstructed.*
VERB =rebuild
Vn

2 To **reconstruct** a system or policy means to change it so that it works in a different way. *She actually wanted to reconstruct the state and transform society... It is important to think about how these institutions might be reconstructed in our own societies.*
VERB
Vn

3 If you **reconstruct** an event that happened in the past, you try to get a complete understanding of it by combining a lot of small pieces of information. *He began to reconstruct the events of 21 December 1988, when flight 103 disappeared... Elaborate efforts were made to reconstruct what had happened.*
VERB
Vn
V wh

reconstruction /riːkənstrʌkʃən/ **reconstructions**
◆◆◇◇◇

1 **Reconstruction** is the process of making a country normal again after a war, for example by making the economy stronger and by replacing buildings that have been damaged. *...America's part in the post-war reconstruction of Germany.*
N-UNCOUNT

2 The **reconstruction** of a building, structure, or road is the activity of building it again, because it has been damaged. *Work began on the reconstruction of the road.*
N-UNCOUNT

3 The **reconstruction** of a crime or event is when people try to understand or show exactly what happened, often by acting it out. *Mrs Kerr was too upset to take part in a reconstruction of her ordeal.*
N-COUNT: usu with supp

reconstructive /riːkənstrʌktɪv/. **Reconstructive** surgery or treatment involves rebuilding a part of someone's body because it has been badly damaged, or because the person wants to change its shape. *I needed reconstructive surgery to give me a new nose.*
ADJ: ADJ n

reconvene /riːkənviːn/ **reconvenes, reconvening, reconvened.** If a parliament, court, or conference **reconvenes** or if someone **reconvenes** it, it meets again after a break. *The Commons reconvenes in mid-October... It was certainly serious enough for him to reconvene Parliament... An international conference on the future of Cambodia should be reconvened.*
◆◇◇◇◇
V-ERG
V
Vn

record, records, recording, recorded. The noun is pronounced /rekɔːʳd, AM -kərd/. The verb is pronounced /rɪkɔːʳd/.
◆◆◆◆◆

1 If you keep a **record** of something, you keep a written account or photographs of it so that it can be referred to later. *Keep a record of all the payments... There's no record of any marriage or children... The result will go on your medical records.*
N-COUNT

2 If you **record** a piece of information or an event, you write it down, photograph it, or put it into a computer so that in the future people can refer to it. *Her letters record the domestic and social details of diplomatic life in China. ...a place which has rarely suffered a famine in its recorded history.*
VERB
Vn
V-ed

3 If you **record** something such as a speech or performance, you put it on tape or film so that it can be heard or seen again later. *There is nothing to stop viewers recording the films on videotape... The call was answered by a recorded message saying the company had closed early.*
VERB
Vn
V-ed

4 If a musician or performer **records** a piece of music or a television or radio show, they perform the music or show so that it can be put onto record, tape, or film. *It took the musicians two and a half days to record their soundtrack for the film... She has recently recorded a programme for television.*
VERB
Vn

5 A **record** is a round, flat piece of black plastic on which sound, especially music, is stored, and which can be played on a record player. You can also refer to the music stored on this piece of plastic as a **record**. *This is one of my favourite records. ...the biggest and best-known record company in England.*
N-COUNT

6 If a dial, gauge, or other measuring device **records** a certain measurement or value, it shows that measurement or value. *An EEG records the electrical activity of the brain... The index of the performance of leading shares recorded a 16 per cent fall.*
VERB
Vn

7 A **record** is the best result that has ever been achieved in a particular sport or activity, for example the fastest time, the furthest distance, or the greatest number of victories. *Roger Kingdom set*
N-COUNT

the world record of 12.92 seconds... The painting was sold for £665,000 – a record for the artist. ...the 800 metres, where she is the world record holder.

8 You use **record** to say that something is higher, lower, better, or worse than has ever been achieved before. *Profits were at record levels... She won the race in record time.* ADJ: ADJ n

9 Someone's **record** is the facts that are known about their achievements or character. *His record reveals a tough streak... He had a distinguished record as a chaplain... His country is making a big effort to improve its human rights record.* N-COUNT: with supp

10 If someone has a criminal **record**, it is officially known that they have committed crimes in the past. *...a heroin addict with a criminal record going back 15 years... Where the accused has a record of violence, they should always be kept in custody.* N-COUNT

11 See also **recording**, **track record**.

12 If you say that what you are going to say next is **for the record**, you mean that you are saying it publicly and officially and you want it to be written down and remembered. *We're willing to state for the record that it has enormous value.* PHRASES

13 If you give some information **for the record**, you give it in case people might find it useful at a later time, although it is not a very important part of what you are talking about. *For the record, most Moscow girls leave school at about 18... Perhaps you'd like to tell me what you were doing Monday. Just for the record.*

14 If something that you say is **off the record**, you do not intend it to be taken as official, or published with your name attached to it. *May I speak off the record?... At the end of the lunch, I said I had some off-the-record comments.* usu PHR after v, PHR n

15 If you are **on record** as saying something, you have said it publicly and officially and it has been written down. *The Chancellor is on record as saying that the increase in unemployment is 'a price worth paying' to keep inflation down.*

16 If you keep information **on record**, you write it down or store it in a computer so that it can be referred to later. *The practice is to keep on record any analysis of samples.*

17 If something is the best, worst, or biggest **on record**, it is the best, worst, or biggest thing of its kind that has been noticed and written down. *It's the shortest election campaign on record... The 1980s were the hottest decade on record.*

18 If you **set the record straight** or **put the record straight**, you show that something which has been regarded as true is in fact not true. *Let me set the record straight on the misconceptions contained in your article.*

record-breaker, record-breakers; also spelled **record breaker**. A **record-breaker** is someone or something who beats the previous best result in a sport or other activity. *The movie became a box-office record breaker.* N-COUNT

record-breaking. A **record-breaking** success, result, or performance is one that beats the previous best success, result, or performance. *Australia's rugby union side enjoyed a record-breaking win over France.* ◆◇◇◇◇ ADJ: ADJ n

recorded delivery. In Britain, if you send a letter or parcel **recorded delivery**, you send it using a Post Office service which gives you an official record of the fact that it has been posted and delivered. The usual American word is **registered mail**. *Use recorded delivery for large cheques or money orders.* N-UNCOUNT

recorder /rɪkɔːʳdəʳ/ **recorders** ◆◆◇◇◇

1 You can refer to a cassette recorder, a tape recorder, or a video recorder as a **recorder.** *Rodney put the recorder on the desk top and pushed the play button.* • See also **cassette recorder**, **tape recorder**, **video recorder**. N-COUNT

2 A **recorder** is a musical instrument in the shape of a wooden or plastic pipe. You play the recorder by blowing into the mouthpiece and covering and uncovering the holes with your fingers. N-VAR: oft *the* N

3 In the legal system of England and Wales, a **recorder** is a barrister or solicitor who is appointed as a part-time judge in the Crown Court. N-COUNT; N-TITLE

4 A **recorder** is a machine or instrument that keeps a record of something, for example in an experiment or on a vehicle. *Data recorders also pin-point mechanical faults rapidly, reducing repair times.* • See also **flight recorder.** N-COUNT

recording /rɪkɔːʳdɪŋ/ **recordings** ◆◆◆◇◇

1 A **recording** of something is a record, CD, tape, or video of it. *...a video recording of a police interview.* N-COUNT

2 **Recording** is the process of making records, tapes, or videos. *...the recording industry.* N-UNCOUNT: usu N n

record player, record players; also spelled **record-player**. A **record player** is a machine on which you can play a record in order to listen to the music or other sounds on it. N-COUNT

recount, recounts, recounting, recounted. ◆◇◇◇◇ The verb is pronounced /rɪkaʊnt/. The noun is pronounced /riːkaʊnt/.

1 If you **recount** a story or event, you tell or describe it to people; a formal use. *He then recounted the story of the interview for his first job... He recounted how heavily armed soldiers forced him from the presidential palace.* VERB V n V wh Also V that

2 A **recount** is a second count of votes in an election when the result is very close. *She wanted a recount. She couldn't believe that I had got more votes than her.* N-COUNT

recoup /rɪkuːp/ **recoups, recouping, recouped.** If you **recoup** a sum of money that you have spent or lost, you get it back. *Insurance companies are trying to recoup their losses by increasing premiums.* ◆◇◇◇◇ VERB =recover V n

recourse /rɪkɔːʳs/. If you say that you can achieve something without **recourse** to a particular course of action, you mean that you can succeed in what you are trying to do without carrying out that action. If you have to have **recourse** to something you would rather not do, you believe you have to do it in order to succeed in something else. *It enabled its members to settle their differences without recourse to war... The public believes its only recourse is to take to the streets.* ◆◇◇◇◇ N-UNCOUNT: usu N *to* n

recover /rɪkʌvəʳ/ **recovers, recovering, recovered** ◆◆◆◇◇

1 When you **recover** from an illness or an injury, you become well again. *He is recovering from a knee injury... A policeman was recovering in hospital last night after being stabbed... He is fully recovered from the virus.* VERB V *from* n/-ing V V-ed

2 If you **recover** from an unhappy or unpleasant experience, you stop being upset by it. *...a tragedy from which he never fully recovered... Her plane broke down and it was 18 hours before she got there. It took her three days to recover.* VERB V *from* n V

3 If something **recovers** from a period of weakness or difficulty, it improves or gets stronger again. *He recovered from a 4-2 deficit to reach the quarter-finals... The stockmarket index fell by 80% before it began to recover.* VERB V *from* n V

4 If you **recover** something that has been lost or stolen, you find it or get it back. *Police raided five houses in south-east London and recovered stolen goods... Rescue teams recovered more bodies from the rubble.* VERB =retrieve V n

5 If you **recover** a mental or physical state, it comes back again. For example, if you **recover** consciousness, you become conscious again. *For a minute he looked uncertain, and then recovered his composure... She had a severe attack of asthma and it took an hour to recover her breath... She never recovered consciousness.* VERB =regain V n

6 If you **recover** money that you have spent, invested, or lent to someone, you get the same amount back. *Legal action is being taken to try to recover the money... The British market alone was not large enough to recover their costs of production.* VERB =recoup V n

recoverable /rɪkʌvərəbᵊl/. If something is **recoverable**, it is possible for you to get it back. *If you decide not to buy, the money you have spent on the survey is not recoverable.* ADJ

recovery /rɪkʌvəri/ **recoveries** ◆◆◆◇◇
1 If a sick person makes a **recovery**, he or she becomes well again. *He made a remarkable recovery from a shin injury... He had been given less than a one in 500 chance of recovery by his doctors.* N-VAR
2 When there is a **recovery** in a country's economy, it improves. *Interest-rate cuts have failed to bring about economic recovery... In many sectors of the economy the recovery has started.* N-VAR
3 You talk about the **recovery** of something when you get it back after it has been lost or stolen. *A substantial reward is being offered for the recovery of a painting by Turner... She has a reasonable prospect of recovery from the insurer.* N-UNCOUNT: usu N *of* n
4 You talk about the **recovery** of someone's physical or mental state when they return to this state. *...the abrupt loss and recovery of consciousness.* N-UNCOUNT: N *of* n
5 If someone is **in recovery**, they are being given a course of treatment to help them recover from something such as drug addiction or mental illness. *...Carole, a compulsive pot smoker and alcoholic in recovery.* PHRASE

recreate /riːkrieɪt/ **recreates, recreating, recreated.** ◆◇◇◇◇ If you **recreate** something, you succeed in making it exist or seem to exist in a different time or place to its original time or place. *The rooms are furnished and recreate the atmosphere of the castle's medieval heyday... I am trying to recreate family life far from home.* VERB V n

recreation, recreations. ◆◆◇◇◇ Pronounced /rekrieɪʃᵊn/ for meaning 1, and /riːkrieɪʃᵊn/ for meaning 2.
1 **Recreation** consists of things that you do in your spare time to relax. *Saturday afternoon is for recreation and outings... All the family members need to have their own interests and recreations.* N-VAR
2 A **recreation** of something is an act or process of making it exist or seem to exist again in a different time or place to its original time or place. *They are seeking to build a faithful recreation of the original Elizabethan theatre.* N-COUNT

recreational /rekrieɪʃənᵊl/. ◆◇◇◇◇ **Recreational** means relating to things people do in their spare time to relax. *...parks and other recreational facilities. ...recreational use of alcohol.* ADJ: usu ADJ n

recrimination /rɪkrɪmɪneɪʃᵊn/ **recriminations.** ◆◇◇◇◇ **Recriminations** are accusations that two people or groups make about each other. *The bitter rows and recriminations have finally ended the relationship... The war sweeps up everyone in hatred and recrimination.* N-UNCOUNT: also N in pl

recruit /rɪkruːt/ **recruits, recruiting, recruited** ◆◆◆◇◇
1 If you **recruit** people for an organization, you select them and persuade them to join it or work for it. *The police are trying to recruit more black and Asian officers... She set up her stand to recruit students to the Anarchist Association... He helped to recruit volunteers to go to Pakistan to fight.* VERB V n V n *to/for* n V n to-inf
♦ **recruiter, recruiters** *...a Marine recruiter.* N-COUNT
♦ **recruiting** *A bomb exploded at an army recruiting office.* N-UNCOUNT: oft N n
2 A **recruit** is a person who has recently joined an organization or an army. N-COUNT

recruitment /rɪkruːtmənt/. ◆◇◇◇◇ The **recruitment** of workers, soldiers, or members is the act or process of selecting them for an organization or army and persuading them to join. *...the examination system for the recruitment of civil servants. ...a crisis in teacher recruitment.* N-UNCOUNT

rectal /rektəl/. **Rectal** means relating to the rectum; a medical term. *...rectal cancer.* ADJ: ADJ n

rectangle /rektæŋgᵊl/ **rectangles.** ◆◇◇◇◇ A **rectangle** is a four-sided shape whose corners are all ninety degree angles. Each side of a rectangle is the same length as the one opposite to it. N-COUNT

rectangular /rektæŋgjʊləʳ/. ◆◇◇◇◇ Something that is **rectangular** is shaped like a rectangle. *...a rectangular table.* ADJ

rectification /rektɪfɪkeɪʃᵊn/. The **rectification** of something that is wrong is the act of changing it to make it correct or satisfactory. *...the rectification of an injustice.* N-UNCOUNT

rectify /rektɪfaɪ/ **rectifies, rectifying, rectified.** ◆◇◇◇◇ If you **rectify** something that is wrong, you change it so that it becomes correct or satisfactory. *Only an act of Congress could rectify the situation... That mistake could have been rectified within 28 days.* VERB =correct V n

rectitude /rektɪtjuːd, AM -tuːd/. **Rectitude** is a quality or attitude that makes people behave honestly and virtuously according to accepted standards; a formal word. *...people of the utmost moral rectitude.* N-UNCOUNT

rector /rektəʳ/ **rectors** ◆◇◇◇◇
1 A **rector** is an Anglican priest who is in charge of a parish. *He was rector of All Hallows Church in Wellingborough.* N-COUNT
2 A **rector** is a high-ranking official in some universities. *...the Rector of Imperial College, London.* N-COUNT

rectory /rektəri/ **rectories.** A **rectory** is a house in which a rector and his family live. N-COUNT

rectum /rektəm/ **rectums.** Someone's **rectum** is the bottom end of the tube down which waste food passes out of their body; a medical term. N-COUNT

recumbent /rɪkʌmbənt/. A **recumbent** figure or person is lying down; a formal word. *He looked down at the recumbent figure.* ADJ: usu ADJ n

recuperate /rɪkuːpəreɪt/ **recuperates, recuperating, recuperated.** ◆◇◇◇◇ When you **recuperate**, you recover your health or strength after you have been ill or injured. *I went away to the country to recuperate... He is recuperating from a serious back injury.* VERB =recover V V *from* n
♦ **recuperation** /rɪkuːpəreɪʃᵊn/ *Leonard was very pleased with his powers of recuperation.* N-UNCOUNT =recovery

recuperative /rɪkuːpərətɪv/. Something that is **recuperative** helps you to recover your health and strength after an illness or injury. *Human beings have great recuperative powers.* ADJ: usu ADJ n

recur /rɪkɜːʳ/ **recurs, recurring, recurred.** ◆◇◇◇◇ If something **recurs**, it happens more than once. *...a theme that was to recur frequently in his work. ...a recurring nightmare she has had since childhood.* VERB V V-ing

recurrence /rɪkʌrəns, AM -kɜːr-/ **recurrences.** ◆◇◇◇◇ If there is a **recurrence** of something, it happens again. *Police are out in force to prevent a recurrence of the violence.* N-VAR: oft N *of* n

recurrent /rɪkʌrənt, AM -kɜːr-/. ◆◇◇◇◇ A **recurrent** event or feeling happens or is experienced more than once. *Race is a recurrent theme in the work. ...buildings in which staff suffer recurrent illness.* ADJ: usu ADJ n =recurring

recyclable /riːsaɪkələbᵊl/. **Recyclable** waste or materials can be processed and used again. *...a separate bin for recyclable waste products.* ADJ-GRADED

recycle /riːsaɪkᵊl/ **recycles, recycling, recycled.** ◆◆◇◇◇ If you **recycle** things that have already been used, such as bottles or sheets of paper, you process them so that they can be used again. *The objective would be to recycle 98 per cent of domestic waste... All glass bottles which can't be refilled can be recycled... It is printed on recycled paper.* VERB V n V-ed
♦ **recycling** *...a recycling scheme.* N-UNCOUNT

red /red/ **reds; redder, reddest** ◆◆◆◆◆
1 Something that is **red** is the colour of blood or of a ripe tomato. *...a bunch of red roses... She had small hands with nails painted bright red.* COLOUR
2 If you say that someone's face is **red**, you mean that it is redder than its normal colour, because they are embarrassed, angry, or out of breath. *With a bright red face I was forced to admit that I had no real idea... She was red with shame.* ADJ-GRADED
3 You describe someone's hair as **red** when it is between red and brown in colour. *...a girl with red hair... He is still vain enough to dye his hair red.* ADJ
4 Your **red** blood cells or **red** corpuscles are the cells in your blood which carry oxygen around your body. ADJ: ADJ n
5 You can refer to red wine as **red**. *The spicy flavours in these dishes call for reds rather than whites.* N-MASS
6 If you refer to someone as a **red** or a **Red**, you disapprove of the fact that they are a communist, a N-COUNT PRAGMATICS

socialist or have left-wing ideas in general; an informal use. *They're all so terrified of Reds.*

7 If a person or company is **in the red** or if their bank account is **in the red**, they have spent more money than they have in their account and therefore they owe money to the bank. *The theatre is £500,000 in the red... If you do go into the red you get charged 30p for each transaction.* PHRASES v-link PHR =in debt

8 If you **see red**, you suddenly become very angry. *I didn't mean to break his nose. I just saw red.* V inflects

9 • **like a red rag to a bull**: see **rag**.

red alert, red alerts. If a hospital, a police force, or a military force is on **red alert**, they have been warned that there may be an emergency, so they can be ready to deal with it. *All the Plymouth hospitals are on red alert... Sirens sounded an end to the red alert.* N-VAR

red-blooded. If a man is described as **red-blooded**, he is considered to be strong and healthy and have a strong interest in sex; an informal expression. *Hers is a body which every red-blooded male cannot fail to have noticed.* ADJ: ADJ n =virile

redbrick /redbrɪk/. In Britain, a **redbrick** university is one of the universities that were established in large cities outside London in the late 19th and early 20th centuries, as opposed to much older universities such as Oxford and Cambridge. ADJ: ADJ n

red cabbage, red cabbages. A **red cabbage** is a round vegetable with dark red leaves. It is often sold pickled in vinegar. N-VAR

red carpet, red carpets. The **red carpet** is special treatment given to an important or honoured guest, for example the laying of a strip of red carpet for them to walk on. *We'll give her some VIP treatment and roll out the red carpet... He is embarrassed by the red carpet treatment.* N-COUNT: usu sing

Red Crescent. **The Red Crescent** is an organization in Muslim countries that helps people who are suffering because of war, famine, or natural disaster. N-PROPER: the N

Red Cross. **The Red Cross** is an international organization that helps people who are suffering because of war, famine, or natural disaster. ◆◆◇◇◇ N-PROPER: the N

redcurrant /redkʌrənt, AM -kɜːr-/ **redcurrants.** **Redcurrants** are very small, bright red berries that grow in bunches on a bush and can be eaten as a fruit or cooked to make a sauce for meat. The bush on which they grow can also be called a **redcurrant**. *...roast lamb and redcurrant jelly.* N-COUNT

redden /redᵊn/ **reddens, reddening, reddened.** If someone **reddens** or their face **reddens**, their face turns pink or red, often because they are embarrassed or angry; used in written English. *He was working himself up to a fury, his face reddening... She reddened instantly... Pearson massaged his reddened cheek.* VERB V V-ed

reddish /redɪʃ/. **Reddish** means slightly red in colour. *He had reddish brown hair... A pale reddish glow lit the sky.* ◆◇◇◇◇ ADJ: usu ADJ n

redecorate /riːdekəreɪt/ **redecorates, redecorating, redecorated.** If you **redecorate** a room or a building, you put new paint or wallpaper on it. *Americans redecorate their houses and offices every few years... Our children have left home, and we now want to redecorate.* ♦ **redecoration** /riːdekəreɪʃᵊn/ *The house is in desperate need of redecoration.* ◆◇◇◇◇ VERB V n V N-UNCOUNT

redeem /rɪdiːm/ **redeems, redeeming, redeemed** ◆◇◇◇◇

1 If you **redeem** yourself or your reputation, you do something that makes people have a good opinion of you again after you have behaved or performed badly. *He had realized the mistake he had made and wanted to redeem himself... The sole redeeming feature of your behaviour is that you're not denying it.* VERB V n V-ing

2 When something **redeems** an unpleasant thing or situation, it prevents it from being completely bad. *Work is the way that people seek to redeem their lives from futility. ...a long face with too prominent features that were redeemed by a fine pair of brown eyes... It was not a year to linger in the memory even if it did have some redeeming features.* VERB V n V-ing

3 If you **redeem** a debt or an obligation, you pay money that you owe or that you promised to pay. *The amount required to redeem the mortgage was £358,587... Take the voucher to your local branch of Woolworths and it will be redeemed for one toy.* VERB V n

4 If you **redeem** an object you possess, you get it back from someone by repaying them money that you have borrowed from them, using the object as a guarantee. *Make sure you know exactly what you will be paying back at the date upon which you plan to redeem the item.* VERB V n

5 In religions such as Christianity, to **redeem** someone means to save them by freeing them from sin and evil. *...a new female spiritual force to redeem the world.* VERB =save V n

redeemable /rɪdiːməbᵊl/. If something is **redeemable**, it can be exchanged for a particular sum of money or for goods worth a particular sum. *Their full catalogue costs $5, redeemable against a first order.* ADJ: oft ADJ *against/for* n

Redeemer /rɪdiːməʳ/. In the Christian religion, **the Redeemer** is Jesus Christ. N-PROPER: the N

redefine /riːdɪfaɪn/ **redefines, redefining, redefined.** If you **redefine** something, you cause people to consider it in a new way. *...a new treaty to redefine the relationship between the central Soviet authorities and the republics... Feminists have redefined the role of women.* ◆◇◇◇◇ VERB V n

redefinition /riːdefɪnɪʃᵊn/. The **redefinition** of something is the act or process of causing people to consider it in a new way. *...the redefinition of the role of the intellectual.* N-UNCOUNT

redemption /rɪdempʃᵊn/ **redemptions** ◆◇◇◇◇

1 **Redemption** is the act of redeeming something or of being redeemed by something. *He craves redemption for his sins. ...redemption of the loan. ...regional differences in the frequency of cash redemptions and quota payment.* N-VAR

2 If you say that someone or something is **beyond redemption**, you mean that they are so bad it is unlikely that anything can be done to improve them. *No man is beyond redemption... I have no doubt that we are polluting the environment beyond redemption.* PHRASE: v-link PHR, PHR after v

redemptive /rɪdemptɪv/. In Christianity, a **redemptive** act or quality is something which leads to freedom from the consequences of sin and evil. *...the redemptive power of Christ.* ADJ: usu ADJ n

redeploy /riːdɪplɔɪ/ **redeploys, redeploying, redeployed**

1 If forces or troops **are redeployed** or if they **redeploy**, they go to new positions so that they are ready for action. *We were forced urgently to redeploy our forces... US troops are redeploying to positions held earlier.* V-ERG V n V

2 If resources or workers **are redeployed**, they are used for a different purpose or task. *Some of the workers there will be redeployed to other sites... It would give us an opportunity to redeploy our resources.* VERB be V-ed V n

redeployment /riːdɪplɔɪmənt/ **redeployments.** The **redeployment** of forces, troops, workers, or resources involves putting them in a different place from where they were before, or using them for a different task or purpose. *...a redeployment of troops in the border areas... Moira had accepted their offer of redeployment to the school in Tarbert.* N-VAR

redesign /riːdɪzaɪn/ **redesigns, redesigning, redesigned.** If a building, vehicle, or system **is redesigned**, it is rebuilt according to a new design in order to improve it. *The hotel has recently been redesigned and redecorated... The second step is to redesign the school system so that it produces a well-educated population. ...the completely redesigned car.* ◆◇◇◇◇ VERB be V-ed V n V-ed

redevelop /riːdɪveləp/ **redevelops, redeveloping, redeveloped.** When an area **is redeveloped**, existing buildings and roads are removed VERB and new ones are built in their place. *Birmingham is now going to be redeveloped again.* be V-ed

redevelopment /riːdɪveləpmənt/. When **redevelopment** takes place, the buildings in one area of a town are knocked down and new ones are built in their place. ◆◇◇◇◇ N-UNCOUNT

red-eye, red-eyes; also spelled **redeye** in meaning 2.
1 A **red-eye** or a **red-eye flight** is an overnight plane journey; an informal use in American English. *She was running to catch a red-eye to New York... He decided not to take the red-eye flight home but to wait and take a nine o'clock flight the following morning.* N-COUNT
2 In photography, **redeye** is the unwanted effect that you sometimes get in photographs of people or animals where their eyes appear red because of the reflection of a camera flash or other light. *Quite surprisingly for a budget-priced camera, it incorporates a redeye reduction facility.* N-UNCOUNT: usu N n

red-faced. A **red-faced** person has a face that looks red, often because they are embarrassed or angry. *A red-faced Mr Jones was led away by police... Whenever he felt ill from any cause he became red-faced.* ADJ-GRADED

red flag, red flags
1 A **red flag** is a flag that is red in colour and is used as a symbol to represent communism and socialism or to indicate danger or as a symbol to stop. *They waved red flags and shouted, 'Lenin, yes'... Then the rain came and the red flag went up to signal a halt.* N-COUNT
2 If you refer to something as a **red flag**, you mean that it acts as a danger signal. *The abnormal bleeding is your body's own red flag of danger.* N-COUNT

red-handed. If someone **is caught red-handed**, they are caught while they are in the act of doing something wrong. *My boyfriend and I robbed a store and were caught red-handed.* PHRASE: V inflects

redhead /redhed/ **redheads.** A **redhead** is person, especially a woman, whose hair is a colour that is between red and brown. N-COUNT

redheaded /redhedɪd/. A **redheaded** person is a person whose hair is between red and brown in colour. ADJ: usu ADJ n

red herring, red herrings. If you say that something is a **red herring**, you mean that it is irrelevant and takes your attention away from the main subject or problem you are considering. *As Dr Smith left he said that the inquiry was something of a red herring.* N-COUNT

red-hot ◆◇◇◇◇
1 **Red-hot** metal or rock has been heated to such a high temperature that it has turned red. *...red-hot iron.* ADJ: usu ADJ n
2 A **red-hot** object is too hot to be touched safely or comfortably. *In the main rooms red-hot radiators were left exposed.* ADJ
3 **Red-hot** is used to describe something or someone who is very popular, especially something new or someone who is very good at what they do; an informal word used in journalism. *Some traders are already stacking the red-hot book on their shelves. ...red-hot guitarist David Grissom.* ADJ: usu ADJ n
4 If someone or something is described as **red-hot**, they show a lot of passion, enthusiasm, or excitement; an informal use. *...a red-hot sex-life. ...a red-hot fury she had never realized she possessed.* ADJ: usu ADJ n
5 The **red-hot** favourite in a race or contest is the person who is most definitely expected to win; an informal use. *His team are red-hot favourites.* ADJ: ADJ n

Red Indian, Red Indians. The Native Americans who were living in North America when the Europeans arrived there used to be called **Red Indians**; an old-fashioned word which is now considered offensive. N-COUNT

redirect /riːdɪrekt, -daɪ-/ **redirects, redirecting, redirected** ◆◇◇◇◇
1 If you **redirect** your energy, resources, or ability, you begin doing something different or trying to achieve something different. *Controls were used to redistribute or redirect resources.* ♦ **redirection** /riːdɪrekʃən, -daɪ-/ *A redirection of resources would be required.* VERB V n N-UNCOUNT: also a N, usu N of n
2 If you **redirect** someone or something, you change their course or destination. *She redirected them to the men's department.* ♦ **redirection** *...the Royal Mail redirection service.* VERB V n N-UNCOUNT

rediscover /riːdɪskʌvər/ **rediscovers, rediscovering, rediscovered.** If you **rediscover** something good or valuable that you had forgotten or lost, you become aware of it again or find it again. *Since Alan was disabled she has rediscovered the comfort of the Catholic faith in which she was brought up... Some of Naomi's earlier writings have been rediscovered in the 1980s and 1990s... Despite the newly rediscovered friendship, there's no doubt that more difficulties lie ahead.* ◆◇◇◇◇ VERB V n V-ed

rediscovery /riːdɪskʌvəri/ **rediscoveries.** The **rediscovery** of something good or valuable that you had forgotten or lost is the fact or the process of becoming aware of it again or finding it again. *The best part of his expedition had been the rediscovery of his natural passion for making things.* N-VAR: N of n

redistribute /riːdɪstrɪbjuːt/ **redistributes, redistributing, redistributed.** If something such as money or property **is redistributed**, it is shared among people or organizations in a different way from the way that it was previously shared. *Wealth was redistributed more equitably among society... Taxes could be used to redistribute income.* ♦ **redistribution** /riːdɪstrɪbjuːʃən/ *Labour will still be committed to a redistribution of wealth.* ◆◇◇◇◇ VERB be V-ed V n N-UNCOUNT: oft N of n

red-letter day, red-letter days. A **red-letter day** is a day that you will always remember because something good happens to you then. N-COUNT

red light, red lights ◆◇◇◇◇
1 A **red light** is a traffic signal which shines red to indicate that drivers must stop. N-COUNT
2 The **red-light** district of a city is the area where prostitutes work. ADJ: ADJ n

red meat, red meats. Red meat is meat such as beef or lamb, which is dark brown in colour after it has been cooked. N-MASS

redneck /rednek/ **rednecks.** If someone describes a white man, especially a lower class, rural American, as a **redneck**, they disapprove of him because they think he is ignorant and has strong, unreasonable opinions; a use that is often considered offensive. *A large Texan redneck was shouting obscenities at Ali.* N-COUNT PRAGMATICS

redness /rednəs/. **Redness** is the quality of being red. *Slowly the redness left Sophie's face.* N-UNCOUNT

redo /riːduː/ **redoes, redoing, redid, redone.** If you **redo** a piece of work, you do it again in order to improve it or change it. *They had redone their sums.* VERB V n

redolent /redələnt/
1 If something is **redolent** of something else, it has features that make you think of that other thing; a literary use. *...percussion instruments, redolent of Far Eastern cultures. ...a sad tale, redolent with regret.* ADJ-GRADED: v-link ADJ, usu ADJ of n
2 If something is **redolent** of something else, it smells strongly of that other thing; a literary use. *...the air redolent of cinnamon and apple. ...redolent with the scent of rosemary.* ADJ-GRADED: v-link ADJ, usu ADJ of n

redouble /riːdʌbəl/ **redoubles, redoubling, redoubled.** If you **redouble** your efforts, you try much harder to achieve something. If something **redoubles**, it increases in volume or intensity. *The president also called on nations to redouble their efforts to negotiate an international trade agreement... The applause redoubled.* V-ERG V n V

redoubt /rɪdaʊt/ **redoubts.** A **redoubt** is a place or situation in which someone feels safe because they know that nobody can attack them or spoil their peace; a literary use. *...the last redoubt of hippy culture.* N-COUNT =haven

redoubtable /rɪdaʊtəbəl/. If you describe someone as **redoubtable**, you respect them because they have a very strong character, even though ADJ: usu ADJ n =formidable you are slightly afraid of them. *...the redoubtable Mr Brooks... He is a redoubtable fighter.*

redound /rɪdaʊnd/ **redounds, redounding, redounded.** If an action or situation **redounds** to your benefit or advantage, it gives people a good impression of you or brings you something that can improve your situation. *The success in the Middle East redounds to his benefit... My skill in such matters might redound to my advantage.* VERB V to n

red pepper, red peppers ◆◇◇◇◇
1 **Red peppers** are ripe peppers which are sweet-tasting and can be used in cooking or eaten raw in salads. *...2 large green or red peppers. ...cheese, lettuce and chopped red pepper.* N-VAR =capsicum
2 **Red pepper** is a hot-tasting spicy powder made from the flesh and seeds of small, dried, red peppers. It is used for flavouring food. *...oil flavored with hot red peppers.* N-MASS =cayenne pepper

redraft /riːdrɑːft, -dræft/ **redrafts, redrafting, redrafted.** If you **redraft** something you have written, you write it again in order to improve it or change it. *Parliament plans to redraft the law on privatisation... The speech had already been redrafted 22 times.* VERB V n

redraw /riːdrɔː/ **redraws, redrawing, redrew, redrawn** ◆◇◇◇◇
1 If people in a position of authority **redraw** the boundaries or borders of a country or region, they change the borders so that the country or region covers a slightly different area than before. *They have redrawn the country's boundaries along ethnic lines... The map of post-war Europe was redrawn.* VERB V n
2 If people **redraw** something, for example an arrangement or plan, they change it because circumstances have changed. *With both countries experiencing economic revolutions, it might be time to redraw the traditional relationship... The Treaty of Union should be redrawn.* VERB =revise V n

redress /rɪdres/ **redresses, redressing, redressed.** The noun is also pronounced /riːdres/ in American English. ◆◇◇◇◇
1 If you **redress** something such as a wrong or a grievance, you do something to correct it or to improve things for the person who has been badly treated; a formal use. *More and more victims turn to litigation to redress wrongs done to them.* VERB V n
2 If you **redress** the balance or the imbalance between two things that have become unequal, you make them equal again because the fact that they were unequal was considered unfair or undesirable; a formal use. *So we're trying to redress the balance and to give teachers a sense that both spoken and written language are equally important. ...to redress the economic imbalance between the developed countries and the developing countries.* VERB V n
3 **Redress** is compensation for something wrong that has been done; a formal use. *They are continuing their legal battle to seek some redress from the government.* N-UNCOUNT =compensation

red tape. You refer to official rules and procedures as **red tape** when they seem unnecessary and cause delay. *The little money that was available was tied up in bureaucratic red tape.* ◆◇◇◇◇ N-UNCOUNT

reduce /rɪdjuːs, AM -duːs/ **reduces, reducing, reduced** ◆◆◆◆◇
1 If you **reduce** something, you make it smaller in size or amount, or less in degree. *It reduces the risks of heart disease... Consumption is being reduced by 25 per cent... The reduced consumer demand is also affecting company profits.* VERB ≠increase V n V-ed
2 If someone **is reduced** to a weaker or inferior state, they become weaker or inferior as a result of something that happens to them. *They were reduced to extreme poverty... They wanted the army reduced to a police force.* VB: usu passive be V-ed to n V-ed
3 If you say that someone **is reduced** to doing something, you mean that they have to do it, although it is unpleasant or humiliating. *He was reduced to begging for a living.* VB: usu passive be V-ed to n/-ing
4 If something is changed to a different or less complicated form, you can say that it **is reduced** to that form. *All the buildings in the town have been reduced to rubble... Politics has been reduced to class struggle.* VB: usu passive be V-ed to n
5 If you **reduce** liquid when you are cooking, or if it **reduces**, it is boiled in order to make it less in quantity and thicker. *Boil the liquid in a small saucepan to reduce it by half... Simmer until mixture reduces.* V-ERG V n V
6 If you say that someone is living in **reduced circumstances**, you mean that they do not have as much money as they used to have; a formal expression. *They are the descendants of emperors and kings and are now living in reduced circumstances.* PHRASES usu in PHR
7 If someone or something **reduces** you **to silence**, they make you feel so helpless that you cannot speak. *Her challenge reduced them to silence.* V inflects
8 If someone or something **reduces** you **to tears**, they make you feel so sad that you cry. *The attentions of the media reduced her to tears.* V inflects

reducible /rɪdjuːsɪbᵊl, AM -duːs-/. If you say that an idea, problem, or situation is not **reducible** to something simple, you mean that it is complicated and cannot be described in a simple way; a formal word. *The structure of the universe may not be reducible to a problem in physics.* ADJ: v-link ADJ to n, usu with brd-neg

reduction /rɪdʌkʃᵊn/ **reductions** ◆◆◆◇◇
1 When there is a **reduction** in something, it is made smaller. *...a future reduction in UK interest rates... Many companies have announced dramatic reductions in staff.* N-COUNT: usu with supp ≠increase
2 **Reduction** is the act of making something smaller in size or amount, or less in degree. *...a new strategic arms reduction agreement.* N-UNCOUNT: usu with supp

reductionist /rɪdʌkʃənɪst/. **Reductionist** describes a way of analysing problems and things by dividing them into simpler parts. *...reductionist science... This encourages reductionist explanations of fascist ideology.* ADJ: usu ADJ n

reductive /rɪdʌktɪv/. If you describe something such as a theory or a work of art as **reductive**, you disapprove of it because it reduces complex things to simple elements; a formal word. *Jill Mann persuasively resists such a cynical reductive interpretation.* ADJ-GRADED: usu ADJ n PRAGMATICS

redundancy /rɪdʌndənsi/ **redundancies** ◆◆◇◇◇
1 When there are **redundancies**, an organization dismisses some of its employees because their jobs are no longer necessary or because the organization can no longer afford to pay them; used in British English. The usual American word is **layoff**. *The ministry has said it hopes to avoid compulsory redundancies.* N-COUNT: usu pl
2 **Redundancy** means being made redundant. *Thousands of bank employees are facing redundancy as their employers cut costs... The company has had to make redundancy payments of £472 million.* N-UNCOUNT

redundant /rɪdʌndənt/ ◆◆◇◇◇
1 If you are made **redundant**, you are dismissed by your employer because your job is no longer necessary or because your employer cannot afford to keep paying you; used in British English. The usual American expression is **be laid off**. *My husband was made redundant late last year. ...a redundant miner.* ADJ: usu v-link ADJ
2 Something that is **redundant** is no longer needed because its job is being done by something else or because its job is no longer necessary or useful. *Changes in technology may mean that once-valued skills are now redundant. ...the conversion of redundant buildings to residential use.* ADJ: usu v-link ADJ =unwanted

redwood /redwʊd/ **redwoods.** A **redwood** is an extremely tall tree which grows in California. ► **Redwood** is the wood from this tree. N-COUNT N-UNCOUNT

reed /riːd/ **reeds** ◆◇◇◇◇
1 **Reeds** are tall plants that grow in large groups in shallow water or marshy ground. They have strong, hollow stems that can be used for making things such as mats or baskets. N-COUNT: usu pl
2 A **reed** is a small piece of cane or metal inserted into the mouthpiece of a woodwind instrument. The reed vibrates when you blow through it and makes a sound. N-COUNT

re-educate, re-educates, re-educating, re-educated. If an organization such as a government tries to **re-educate** a group of people, they try to make them adopt new attitudes, beliefs, or types of behaviour. *We are having to re-educate the public very quickly about something they have always taken for granted.* ♦ **re-education** *...a programme of punishment and re-education of political dissidents.* VERB; V n; N-UNCOUNT

reedy /riːdi/. If you say that someone has a **reedy** voice, you think their voice is unpleasant because it is high and unclear. *The big man had a high-pitched reedy voice.* ADJ: usu ADJ n

reef /riːf/ **reefs.** A **reef** is a long line of rocks or sand, the top of which is just above or just below the surface of the sea. *An unspoilt coral reef encloses the bay.* ◆◇◇◇◇ N-COUNT

reefer /riːfəʳ/ **reefers**

1 A **reefer** or **reefer coat** is a short thick coat which is often worn by sailors; used mainly in British English. N-COUNT

2 A **reefer** is a cigarette containing marijuana and tobacco; an old-fashioned, informal use. N-COUNT =joint

reek /riːk/ **reeks, reeking, reeked** ◆◇◇◇◇

1 If something **reeks** of something else, usually something unpleasant, it smells very strongly of it. *Your breath reeks of stale cigar smoke... The entire house reeked for a long time.* ► Also a noun. *He smelt the reek of whisky.* VERB =stink; V of n; V; N-SING: usu N of n

2 If you say that something **reeks** of unpleasant ideas, feelings, or practices, you disapprove of it because it gives a firm impression that it involves those ideas, feelings, or practices. *The whole thing reeks of hypocrisy.* VERB PRAGMATICS; V of n

reel /riːl/ **reels, reeling, reeled** ◆◆◆◇◇

1 A **reel** is a cylindrical object around which you wrap something such as cinema film, magnetic tape, fishing line, or cotton thread. American English usually uses the term **spool** to refer to thicker reels. *...a 30m reel of cable.* N-COUNT: oft N of n

2 You can talk about a **reel** as a way of referring to all the scenes in a film which fit onto one reel of film. *I shall not reveal the movie's final reel.* N-COUNT: usu with supp

3 If someone **reels**, they move about unsteadily as if they were going to fall. *He was reeling a little. He must be very drunk... He lost his balance and reeled back... I stood up and almost fell, reeling against the deck rail.* VERB; V; V adv/prep

4 If you are **reeling** from a shock, you are feeling extremely surprised or upset because of it. *I'm still reeling from the shock of hearing of it... It left us reeling with disbelief.* VB: usu cont; V from n; V prep

5 If you say that your brain or your mind **is reeling**, you mean that you are very confused because you have too many things to think about. *His mind reeled at the question.* VERB; V

6 A **reel** is a type of fast Scottish dance. N-COUNT

reel in. If you **reel in** something such as a fish, you pull it towards you by winding around a reel the wire or line that it is attached to. *Gleacher reeled in the first fish... The crew of the US space shuttle Atlantis were preparing to reel in the craft.* PHRASAL VERB; V P n (not pron); Also V n P

reel off. If you **reel off** information, you repeat it from memory quickly and easily. *She reeled off the titles of a dozen or so of the novels.* PHRASAL VERB; V P n (not pron); Also V n P

re-elect, re-elects, re-electing, re-elected. When someone such as a politician or a trade union official **is re-elected**, they win a new election and are therefore able to continue in their position as, for example, president or member of parliament, or union official. *The president will pursue lower taxes if he is re-elected... Mr Bush has the necessary experience to be re-elected president... He was overwhelmingly re-elected as party leader.* ♦ **re-election** /riːɪlekʃən/ *I would like to see him stand for re-election... His re-election campaign is floundering.* ◆◆◇◇◇ VERB; be V-ed; be V-ed n; be V-ed as n; N-UNCOUNT

re-enact, re-enacts, re-enacting, re-enacted. If you **re-enact** a scene or incident, you repeat the actions that occurred in the scene or incident. *He re-enacted scenes from his TV series.* VERB; V n

re-enactment, re-enactments. When a **re-enactment** of a scene or incident takes place, people re-enact it. N-COUNT: usu N of n

re-enter, re-enters, re-entering, re-entered. If you **re-enter** a place, organization, or area of activity that you have left, you return to it. *Ten minutes later he re-entered the hotel.* ◆◇◇◇◇ VERB; V n

re-entry

1 **Re-entry** is the act of returning to a place, organization, or area of activity that you have left. *The house has been barred and bolted to prevent re-entry... The military men are contemplating a re-entry into politics.* N-UNCOUNT: also a N

2 **Re-entry** is used to refer to the moment when a spacecraft comes back into the earth's atmosphere after being in space. *The station would burn up on re-entry into the earth's atmosphere.* N-UNCOUNT: also a N

re-examine, re-examines, re-examining, re-examined. If a person or group of people **re-examines** their ideas, beliefs, or attitudes, they think about them carefully because they are no longer sure if they are correct. *The European Community is to re-examine its policy towards South Africa... Her husband and children will also have to re-examine their expectations.* ♦ **re-examination, re-examinations** *It was time for a re-examination of the situation... Energy policy is badly in need of radical re-examination.* ◆◇◇◇◇ VERB =reassess; V n; N-VAR: usu N of n =reassessment

ref /ref/ **refs** ◆◇◇◇◇

1 **Ref.** is an abbreviation for 'reference'. It is written in front of a code at the top of business letters and documents. The code refers to a file where all the letters and documents about the same matter are kept. *Our Ref: JAH/JW.*

2 The **ref** in a sports match, such as football or boxing, is the same as the **referee**. *The ref gave a penalty and Platini scored.* N-COUNT: usu the N

refectory /rɪfektəri/ **refectories.** A **refectory** is a large dining hall in a monastery, university, or other institution. N-COUNT =canteen

refer /rɪfɜːʳ/ **refers, referring, referred** ◆◆◆◆◇

1 If you **refer** to a particular subject or person, you talk about them or mention them. *In his speech, he referred to a recent trip to Canada.* VERB; V to n

2 If you **refer** to someone or something as a particular thing, you use a particular word, expression, or name to mention or describe them. *Marcia had referred to him as a dear friend... He simply referred to him as Ronnie... Our economy is referred to as a free market.* VERB; V to n as n

3 If a word **refers** to a particular thing, situation, or idea, it describes it in some way. *The term electronics refers to electrically-induced action.* VERB; V to n

4 If a person who is ill **is referred** to a hospital or a specialist, they are sent there by a doctor in order to be treated. *Patients are mostly referred to hospital by their general practitioners... The patient should be referred for tests immediately.* VB: usu passive; be V-ed to n; be V-ed

5 If you **refer** a task or a problem to a person or an organization, you formally tell them about it, so that they can deal with it. *He could refer the matter to the high court.* VERB; V n to n

6 If you **refer** someone to a person or organization, you send them there for the help they need. *Now and then I referred a client to him.* VERB; V n to n

7 If you **refer** to a book or other source of information, you look at it in order to find something out. *He referred briefly to his notebook.* VERB; V to n

8 If you **refer** someone to a source of information, you tell them the place where they will find the information which they need or which you think will interest them. *Mr Bryan also referred me to a book by the American journalist Anthony Scaduto.* VERB; V n to n

referee /refəriː/ **referees, refereeing, refereed** ◆◆◇◇◇

1 The **referee** is the official who controls a sports match such as a football match or boxing match. N-COUNT

2 When someone **referees** a sports match or contest, they act as referee. *The match will be refereed by Derek Bevan from Wales... Vautrot has refereed in two World Cups.* VERB; be V-ed; V

3 A **referee** is a person who gives you a reference, for example when you are applying for a job. N-COUNT

reference /refərəns/ **references, referencing, referenced** ◆◆◆◇◇

1 Reference to someone or something is the act of talking about them or mentioning them. A **reference** to someone or something is an instance of this. *He made no reference to any agreement... The crowd chanted 'No Poll Tax', a reference to the government's new local taxation system... He summed up his philosophy, with reference to Calvin.* N-VAR

2 Reference means consulting someone or something for information or advice. *This might be done without reference to Parliament... Please keep this sheet in a safe place for reference.* N-UNCOUNT

3 Reference books are ones you look at when you need specific information or facts about a subject. *There are several reference books which have been compiled to help you make your choice. ...a useful reference work for teachers.* ADJ: ADJ n

4 A **reference** is a word, phrase, or idea which comes from something such as a book, poem, or play and which you use when making a point about something. *...a reference from the Quran. ...historical references.* N-COUNT

5 A **reference** is something such as a number or a name that tells you where you can obtain the information you want. *...a map reference... Make a note of the reference number shown on the form.* N-COUNT

6 A **reference** is a letter written by someone who knows you which describes your character and abilities. When you apply for a job, an employer might ask for **references**. *The firm offered to give her a reference.* N-COUNT

7 If you **reference** a particular book or writer, you make a precise reference to them in what you are saying or writing. *It specifically referenced Hermann Noordung's classic 1928 book on this subject.* VERB =refer to; V n

8 See also **cross-reference, frame of reference, point of reference, terms of reference.**

9 If you keep information **for future reference**, you keep it because it might be useful in the future. *Read these notes carefully and keep them for future reference.* PHRASES; PHR after v

10 You use **with reference to** or **in reference to** in order to indicate what something relates to. *I am writing with reference to your article on salaries for scientists... I'm calling in reference to your series on prejudice.* PREP

reference library, reference libraries. A **reference library** is a library that contains books which you can look at in the library itself but which you cannot borrow. N-COUNT

referendum /refərendəm/ **referendums** or **referenda** /refərendə/. If a country holds a **referendum** on a particular policy, they ask the people to vote on the policy and show whether or not they agree with it. *Estonia said today it too plans to hold a referendum on independence.* ◆◆◆◇◇ N-COUNT: oft N *on* n

referral /rɪfɜːrəl/ **referrals. Referral** is the act of officially sending someone to a person or authority that is authorized or better qualified to deal with them. A **referral** is an instance of this. *Legal Aid can often provide referral to other types of agencies... Ask your doctor for a referral to a clinical psychologist.* ◆◇◇◇◇ N-VAR: oft N *to* n

refill, refills, refilling, refilled. The verb is pronounced /riːfɪl/. The noun is pronounced /riːfɪl/. ◆◇◇◇◇

1 If you **refill** something, you fill it again after it has been emptied. *I refilled our wine glasses.* ▶ Also a noun. *Max held out his cup for a refill.* VERB; V n; N-COUNT

2 A **refill** of a particular product, such as detergent, is a quantity of that product sold in a cheaper container than the container it is usually sold in. You use a refill to replace the contents of an empty container. *Refill packs are cheaper and lighter.* N-COUNT

refinance /riːfaɪnæns/ **refinances, refinancing, refinanced.** If a person or a company **refinances** a debt or if they **refinance**, they borrow some money in order to pay the debt. *A loan was arranged to refinance existing debt... It can be costly to refinance.* ◆◇◇◇◇ VERB; V n; V

refine /rɪfaɪn/ **refines, refining, refined** ◆◇◇◇◇

1 When a substance **is refined**, it is made pure by having all other substances removed from it. *Oil is refined to remove naturally occurring impurities.* ♦ **refining** *...oil refining.* VB: usu passive; be V-ed; N-UNCOUNT

2 If something such as a process, a theory, or a machine **is refined**, it is improved by having small alterations made to it. *Surgical techniques are constantly being refined.* VB: usu passive =improve; be V-ed

refined /rɪfaɪnd/ ◆◇◇◇◇

1 A **refined** substance has been made pure by having other substances removed from it. *...refined sugar.* ADJ-GRADED: usu ADJ n

2 If you say that someone is **refined**, you mean that they are very polite and well-mannered and have good taste. *...refined and well-dressed ladies... His speech and manner are refined.* ADJ-GRADED =genteel

3 If you describe a machine or a process as **refined**, you mean that it has been carefully developed and is therefore very efficient or elegant. *...a more refined engine... This technique is becoming more refined and more acceptable all the time.* ADJ-GRADED

refinement /rɪfaɪnmənt/ **refinements** ◆◇◇◇◇

1 Refinements are small alterations or additions that you make to something in order to improve it. **Refinement** is the process of making refinements. *Older cars inevitably lack the latest safety refinements. ...development and refinement of the game.* N-VAR

2 Refinement is politeness and good manners, combined with a way of behaving which shows that you dislike anything vulgar. *...a girl who possessed both dignity and refinement.* N-UNCOUNT

refiner /rɪfaɪnəʳ/ **refiners. Refiners** are people or organizations that refine substances such as oil or sugar in order to sell them. N-COUNT

refinery /rɪfaɪnəri/ **refineries.** A **refinery** is a factory where a substance such as oil or sugar is refined. ◆◇◇◇◇ N-COUNT

refit, refits, refitting, refitted. The verb is pronounced /riːfɪt/. The noun is pronounced /riːfɪt/. When a ship **is refitted**, it is repaired or is given new parts, equipment, or furniture. *During the war, Navy ships were refitted here.* ▶ Also a noun. *The ship finished an extensive refit last year.* ◆◇◇◇◇ VB: usu passive; be V-ed; N-COUNT

reflate /riːfleɪt/ **reflates, reflating, reflated.** In British English, if a government tries to **reflate** its country's economy, it increases the amount of money that is available for use in order to encourage more economic activity; a technical term in economics. *The administration may try to reflate the economy next year.* ♦ **reflation** /riːfleɪʃᵊn/ *Ministers are again talking about reflation and price controls.* VERB; V n; N-UNCOUNT

reflect /rɪflekt/ **reflects, reflecting, reflected** ◆◆◆◆◇

1 If something **reflects** an attitude or situation, it shows that the attitude or situation exists or it shows what the nature of the attitude or situation is. *The Los Angeles riots reflected the bitterness between the black and Korean communities in the city... Concern at the economic situation was reflected in the government's budget.* VERB =show; V n

2 When light, heat or other rays **reflect** off a surface or when a surface **reflects** them, they are sent back from the surface and do not pass through it. *The sun reflected off the snow-covered mountains... The glass appears to reflect light naturally.* V-ERG; V prep; V n

3 When something **is reflected** in a mirror or in water, you can see its image in the mirror or in the water. *His image seemed to be reflected many times in the mirror.* VB: usu passive; be V-ed

4 When you **reflect**, you think deeply about something. *We should all give ourselves time to reflect... I reflected on the child's future.* VERB; V; V *on/upon* n

5 You can use **reflect** to indicate that a particular thought occurs to someone. *Things were very much changed since before the war, he reflected.* VERB; V that

6 If an action or situation **reflects** in a particular way on someone or something, it gives people a good or bad impression of them. *The affair hardly reflected well on the British... Your own personal* VERB; V adv *on* n; V *on* n *behavior as a teacher, outside of school hours, reflects on the school itself.*

reflection /rɪflekʃən/ **reflections** ◆◆◇◇◇

1 A **reflection** is an image that you can see in a mirror or in glass or water. *Meg stared at her reflection in the bedroom mirror.* N-COUNT

2 Reflection is the process by which light and heat are sent back from a surface and do not pass through it. *...the reflection of a beam of light off a mirror.* N-UNCOUNT

3 If you say that something is a **reflection** of a person's attitude or a situation, you mean that it is caused by that attitude or situation and therefore reveals something about it. *Inhibition in adulthood seems to be very clearly a reflection of a person's experiences as a child.* N-COUNT: usu N *of* n

4 If you say that something is a **reflection** on someone or a **sad reflection** on someone, you mean that it gives a bad impression of them. *Infection with head lice is no reflection on personal hygiene... The library is unique and its break-up would be a sad reflection on the value we place on our heritage.* N-SING: usu N *on* n

5 Reflection is careful thought about a particular topic. Your **reflections** are your thoughts about a particular topic. *After days of reflection she decided to write back... He paused, absorbed by his reflections.* N-UNCOUNT: also N in pl • If someone admits or accepts something **on reflection**, they admit or accept it after having thought carefully about it. *On reflection, he says, he very much regrets the comments.* PHRASE

6 Reflections on something are comments or writings that express someone's ideas about it. *In his latest collection of poems readers are confronted with a series of reflections on death.* N-COUNT: usu pl

reflective /rɪflektɪv/ ◆◇◇◇◇

1 If you are **reflective**, you are thinking deeply about something; used in written English. *I walked on in a reflective mood to the car, thinking about the poor honeymooners... Mike is a quiet, reflective man.* ADJ-GRADED =thoughtful ♦ **reflectively** *'The first part of her life hasn't been all that good,' he said reflectively... He gazed reflectively at his companion.* ADV-GRADED: ADV with v

2 If something is **reflective** of a particular situation or attitude, it is typical of that situation or attitude, or is a consequence of it. *The German government's support of the US is not entirely reflective of German public opinion... The pupil's answers may not have been reflective of what the class as a whole had understood.* ADJ-GRADED: v-link ADJ *of* n

3 A **reflective** surface or material sends back light or heat; a formal use. *...a garden of flowing streams, water basins, waterfalls, and a reflective pool... Avoid pans with a shiny, reflective base as the heat will be reflected back.* ADJ-GRADED

reflector /rɪflektəʳ/ **reflectors**

1 A **reflector** is a small piece of specially patterned glass or plastic which is fitted to the back of a bicycle or car or to a post beside the road, and which glows when light shines on it. N-COUNT

2 A **reflector** is a type of telescope which has a spherical mirror. N-COUNT

reflex /riːfleks/ **reflexes** ◆◇◇◇◇

1 A **reflex** or a **reflex action** is something that you do automatically and without thinking, as a habit or as a reaction to something. *Walsh fumbled in his pocket, a reflex from his smoking days... I turned to look inside the house in a reflex action.* N-COUNT

2 A **reflex** or a **reflex action** is a normal, uncontrollable reaction of your body to something that you feel, see, or experience. *...tests for reflexes, like tapping the knee or the heel with a rubber hammer. ...the stress hormone adrenaline, released by reflex action from the adrenal glands.* N-COUNT

3 Your **reflexes** are your ability to react quickly with your body when something unexpected happens, for example when you are involved in sport or when you are driving a car. *It takes great skill, cool nerves and the reflexes of an athlete.* N-PLURAL =reactions

reflexive /rɪfleksɪv/. A **reflexive** reaction or movement occurs immediately in response to something that happens; a formal word. *...that reflexive urge for concealment.* ADJ: usu ADJ n ♦ **reflexively** *He felt his head jerk reflexively.* ADV: usu ADV with v

reflexive pronoun, reflexive pronouns. A **reflexive pronoun** is a pronoun such as 'myself' which refers back to the subject of a sentence or clause. For example, in the sentence 'He made himself a cup of tea', the reflexive pronoun 'himself' refers back to 'he'. N-COUNT

reflexive verb, reflexive verbs. A **reflexive verb** is a transitive verb whose subject and object always refer to the same person or thing, so the object is always a reflexive pronoun. An example is 'to enjoy yourself', as in 'Did you enjoy yourself?'. N-COUNT

reflexology /riːfleksɒlədʒi/. **Reflexology** is the practice of massaging particular areas of the body, especially the feet, in the belief that it can heal particular organs. ◆◇◇◇◇ N-UNCOUNT ♦ **reflexologist, reflexologists** *A reflexologist can often tell what is wrong with his client by the condition of certain parts of the feet.* N-COUNT

reforest /riːfɒrɪst/ **reforests, reforesting, reforested.** To **reforest** an area where there used to be a forest means to plant trees over it. *He decided to do something about reforesting man-made wastes of western Australia.* VERB V n

reforestation /riːfɒrɪsteɪʃən/. **Reforestation** of an area where there used to be a forest is planting trees over it. *...the reforestation of the Apennine Mountains. ...a reforestation project.* N-UNCOUNT

reform /rɪfɔːʳm/ **reforms, reforming, reformed** ◆◆◆◆◇

1 Reform consists of changes and improvements to a law, social system, or institution. A **reform** is an instance of such a change or improvement. *The party embarked on a programme of economic reform... He has urged reform of the welfare system... The Socialists introduced fairly radical reforms.* N-VAR

2 If someone **reforms** something such as a law, social system, or institution, they change or improve it. *...his plans to reform the country's economy... The reformed Communist Party is still a force to be reckoned with.* VERB V n V-ed

3 When someone **reforms** or when something **reforms** them, they stop doing something that society does not approve of, such as breaking the law or drinking too much alcohol. *When his court case was coming up, James promised to reform... We will try to reform him within the community.* V-ERG V V n ♦ **reformed** *...a reformed alcoholic.* ADJ: usu ADJ n

4 See also **re-form.**

re-form, re-forms, re-forming, re-formed; also spelled **reform**. When an organization, group, or shape **re-forms**, or when someone **re-forms** it, it is created again after a period during which it did not exist or existed in a different form. *The appearance of Colonel Washington's cavalry had given the militia opportunity to re-form... The 40-year-old singer reformed his band.* V-ERG V V n

reformation /refəʳmeɪʃən/ ◆◇◇◇◇

1 The **reformation** of something is the act or process of changing and improving it. *He devoted his energies to the reformation of science.* N-UNCOUNT

2 The Reformation is the movement to reform the Catholic Church in the sixteenth century, which led to the Protestant church being set up. *...a famous statue of the Virgin which was destroyed during the Reformation.* N-PROPER: *the* N

reformer /rɪfɔːʳməʳ/ **reformers.** A **reformer** is someone who tries to change and improve something such as a law or a social system. ◆◆◇◇◇ N-COUNT

reformism /rɪfɔːʳmɪzəm/. **Reformism** is the belief that a system or law should be reformed. N-UNCOUNT

reformist /rɪfɔːʳmɪst/ **reformists. Reformist** groups or policies are trying to reform a system or law. *...a strong supporter of reformist policies.* ◆◇◇◇◇ ADJ-GRADED ► A **reformist** is someone with reformist views. N-COUNT

refract /rɪfrækt/ **refracts, refracting, refracted.** When a ray of light or a sound wave **refracts** or **is refracted**, the path it follows bends at a particular point, for example when it enters water or glass. *As we age the lenses of the eyes thicken, and* V-ERG V n *thus refract light differently.* ♦ **refraction** /rɪfrækʃən/ *...the refraction of the light on the dancing waves.* N-UNCOUNT

refractory /rɪfræktəri/. **Refractory** people are stubborn and difficult to control; a formal word. *...refractory priests who refused to side with the king.* ADJ-GRADED: usu ADJ n =recalcitrant

refrain /rɪfreɪn/ **refrains, refraining, refrained** ◆◇◇◇◇
1 If you **refrain** from doing something, you deliberately do not do it. *Mrs Hardie refrained from making any comment... He appealed to all factions to refrain from violence.* VERB V from -ing/n
2 A **refrain** is a short, simple part of a song, which is repeated many times. *...a refrain from an old song.* N-COUNT
3 A **refrain** is a comment or saying that people often repeat. *Rosa's constant refrain is that she doesn't have a life.* N-COUNT

refresh /rɪfreʃ/ **refreshes, refreshing, refreshed** ◆◇◇◇◇
1 If something **refreshes** you when you have become hot, tired, or thirsty, it makes you feel cooler or more energetic. *The lotion cools and refreshes the skin... They had stopped by a spring to refresh themselves.* ♦ **refreshed** *He awoke feeling completely refreshed.* VERB V n ADJ-GRADED: usu v-link ADJ
2 If you **refresh** something old or faded, you make it as strong or fresh as it was when it was new. *Many view these meetings as an occasion to share ideas and refresh friendship... Lettie appeared, her make-up refreshed.* VERB V n V-ed
3 If someone **refreshes** your memory, they tell you something that you had forgotten. *Allow me to refresh your memory... He walked on the opposite side of the street to refresh his memory of the building.* VERB =remind V n

refresher course, refresher courses. A **refresher course** is a training course in which people improve their knowledge or skills and learn about new developments that are related to the job that they do. N-COUNT

refreshing /rɪfreʃɪŋ/ ◆◆◇◇◇
1 You say that something is **refreshing** when it is pleasantly different from what you are used to. *It's refreshing to hear somebody speaking common sense... It made a refreshing change to see a good old-fashioned movie.* ♦ **refreshingly** *He was refreshingly honest.* ADJ-GRADED ADV-GRADED
2 A **refreshing** bath or drink makes you feel energetic or cool again after you have been uncomfortably tired or hot. *Herbs have been used for centuries to make refreshing drinks.* ADJ-GRADED

refreshment /rɪfreʃmənt/ **refreshments** ◆◇◇◇◇
1 **Refreshments** are drinks and small amounts of food that are provided, for example, during a meeting or a journey. N-PLURAL
2 You can refer to food and drink as **refreshment**; a formal use. *May I offer you some refreshment?* N-UNCOUNT

refrigerate /rɪfrɪdʒəreɪt/ **refrigerates, refrigerating, refrigerated.** If you **refrigerate** food, you make it cold, for example by putting it in a fridge, usually in order to preserve it. *Refrigerate the dough overnight. ...a lorry with refrigerated cargo.* ♦ **refrigeration** /rɪfrɪdʒəreɪʃən/ *Refrigeration will make olive oil cloudy.* ◆◇◇◇◇ VERB V n V-ed N-UNCOUNT

refrigerator /rɪfrɪdʒəreɪtəʳ/ **refrigerators.** A **refrigerator** is a large container which is kept cool inside, usually by electricity, so that the food and drink in it stays fresh. ◆◇◇◇◇ N-COUNT =fridge

refuel /riːfjuːəl/ **refuels, refuelling, refuelled;** spelled **refueling, refueled** in American English. When an aircraft or other vehicle **refuels** or when someone **refuels** it, it is filled with more fuel so that it can continue its journey. *His plane stopped in France to refuel... The airline's crew refuelled the plane.* ♦ **refuelling** *Tankers will accompany the Tornados for in-flight refuelling.* ◆◇◇◇◇ V-ERG V V n N-UNCOUNT

refuge /refjuːdʒ/ **refuges** ◆◆◇◇◇
1 If you take **refuge** somewhere, you try to protect yourself from physical harm by going there. *They took refuge in a bomb shelter... His home became a place of refuge for the believers.* N-UNCOUNT
2 A **refuge** is a place where you go for safety and protection, for example from violence or from bad weather. *Eventually Suzanne fled to a refuge for battered women... We climbed up a winding track towards a mountain refuge.* N-COUNT
3 If you take **refuge** in a particular way of behaving or thinking, you try to protect yourself from unhappiness or unpleasantness by behaving or thinking in that way. *All too often, they get bored, and seek refuge in drink and drugs... Father Rowan took refuge in silence.* N-UNCOUNT

refugee /refjuːdʒiː/ **refugees. Refugees** are people who have been forced to leave their homes or their country, either because there is a war there or because of their political or religious beliefs. ◆◆◆◆◇ N-COUNT

refund, refunds, refunding, refunded. The noun is pronounced /riːfʌnd/. The verb is pronounced /rɪfʌnd/. ◆◆◇◇◇
1 A **refund** is a sum of money which is returned to you, for example because you have paid too much or because you have returned goods to a shop. N-COUNT
2 If someone **refunds** your money, they return it to you, for example because you have paid too much or because you have returned goods to a shop. *We guarantee to refund your money if you're not delighted with your purchase... Take the goods back to your retailer who will refund you the purchase price.* VERB V n V n n

refundable /rɪfʌndəbəl/. A **refundable** deposit or charge will be paid back in certain circumstances. *A refundable deposit of 700 francs per apartment is payable on arrival... Tickets are not refundable.* ADJ

refurbish /riːfɜːʳbɪʃ/ **refurbishes, refurbishing, refurbished.** To **refurbish** a building or room means to clean it and decorate it and make it more attractive or better equipped. *We have spent money on refurbishing the offices... This hotel has recently been completely refurbished.* ◆◇◇◇◇ VERB V n

refurbishment /riːfɜːʳbɪʃmənt/ **refurbishments.** The **refurbishment** of something is the act or process of cleaning it, decorating it, and providing it with new equipment or facilities. ◆◇◇◇◇ N-UNCOUNT: also N in pl

refusal /rɪfjuːzəl/ **refusals** ◆◆◇◇◇
1 Someone's **refusal** to do something or **refusal** of something is the fact of them showing or saying that they will not do it, allow it, grant it, or accept it. *Her country suffered through her refusal to accept change... His letter in response to her request had contained a firm refusal. ...the Council's refusal of planning permission for a major shopping centre... We would appreciate confirmation of your refusal of our invitation to take part.* N-VAR
2 If someone has **first refusal** on something, they have the right to decide whether or not to buy it or take it before it is offered to anyone else. *If you have a good rapport with a dealer, they will always let you have first refusal on anything interesting... A tenant may have a right of first refusal if a property is offered for sale.* PHRASE: PHR after v

refuse, refuses, refusing, refused. The verb is pronounced /rɪfjuːz/. The noun is pronounced /refjuːs/. ◆◆◆◆◇
1 If you **refuse** to do something, you deliberately do not do it, or you say firmly that you will not do it. *He refused to comment after the trial... He expects me to stay on here and I can hardly refuse.* VERB V to-inf V
2 If someone **refuses** you something, they do not give it to you or do not allow you to have it. *The United States has refused him a visa... She was refused access to her children... The town council had refused permission for the march.* VERB V n n V n
3 If you **refuse** something that is offered to you, you do not accept it. *He offered me a second drink which I refused... The patient has the right to refuse treatment.* VERB =turn down V n
4 **Refuse** consists of the rubbish and all the things that are not wanted in a house, shop, or factory, and that are regularly thrown away; used mainly in official language. *The District Council made a weekly collection of refuse.* N-UNCOUNT =waste, rubbish

refutation /refjuːteɪʃən/ **refutations.** A **refutation** of an allegation, argument, or theory is N-VAR something that proves it is wrong or untrue; a formal word. *He concentrated on preparing a complete refutation of the Republicans' most serious charges.*

refute /rɪfjuːt/ **refutes, refuting, refuted** ◆◇◇◇◇
1 If you **refute** an allegation, an argument, or a theory, you prove that it is wrong or untrue; a formal use. *It was the kind of rumour that it is impossible to refute.* VERB =disprove V n
2 If you **refute** an allegation or accusation, you deny that it is true; a formal use. *Isabelle is quick to refute any suggestion of intellectual snobbery.* VERB =deny V n

regain /rɪgeɪn/ **regains, regaining, regained** ◆◆◇◇◇
1 If you **regain** something that you have lost, you get it back again. *Troops have regained control of the city... It took him a while to regain his composure.* VERB V n
2 If you **regain** a place that you have left, you succeed in getting back there; a formal use. *Davis went to regain his carriage.* VERB V n

regal /riːgᵊl/. If you describe something as **regal**, you mean that it is suitable for a king or queen, because it is very splendid or dignified. *He sat with such regal dignity... Never has she looked more regal.* ♦ **regally** *He inclined his head regally.* ◆◇◇◇◇ ADJ-GRADED ADV-GRADED

regale /rɪgeɪl/ **regales, regaling, regaled.** If someone **regales** you with stories or jokes, they tell you a lot of them, whether you want to hear them or not. *He was constantly regaled with tales of woe.* VERB V n with n

regalia /rɪgeɪliə/. **Regalia** consists of all the traditional clothes and items which someone such as a king or a judge wears and carries on official occasions. *...a military band in full regalia.* N-UNCOUNT

regard /rɪgɑːʳd/ **regards, regarding, regarded** ◆◆◆◆◇
1 If you **regard** someone or something as being a particular thing or as having a particular quality, you believe that they are that thing or have that quality. *He was regarded as the most successful Chancellor of modern times... Many Conservatives disapprove of the tax, regarding it as unfair.* VERB be V-ed as n V n as n
2 If you **regard** something or someone with a feeling such as dislike or respect, you have that feeling about them. *He regarded drug dealers with loathing... Displays of emotion are regarded with suspicion... He was a highly regarded scholar.* VERB V n with n adv V-ed
3 If you **regard** someone in a certain way, you look at them in that way; a literary use. *She regarded him curiously for a moment... The clerk regarded him with benevolent amusement.* VERB =look at V n V n with n
4 If you have **regard** for someone or something, you respect them and care about them. If you hold someone in high **regard**, you have a lot of respect for them. *I have a very high regard for him and what he has achieved... There were armed people about, people with little regard for human life... The Party ruled the country without regard for the people's views.* N-UNCOUNT
5 **Regards** are greetings. You use **regards** in expressions like **best regards** and **with kind regards** as a way of expressing friendly feelings towards someone, especially in a letter. *Give my regards to your family... My best regards to Mary.* N-PLURAL: oft N *to* n PRAGMATICS
6 You can use **as regards** to indicate the subject that is being talked or written about. *As regards the war, Haig believed in victory at any price.* PHRASES PREP PRAGMATICS =regarding
7 You can use **with regard to** or **in regard to** to indicate the subject that is being talked or written about. *The department is reviewing its policy with regard to immunisation.* PREP PRAGMATICS =regarding
8 You can use **in this regard** or **in that regard** to refer back to something you have just said. *In this regard nothing has changed... I may have made a mistake in that regard.* PHR with cl PRAGMATICS

regarding /rɪgɑːʳdɪŋ/. You can use **regarding** to indicate the subject that is being talked or written about. *He refused to divulge any information regarding the man's whereabouts.* ◆◆◇◇◇ PREP PRAGMATICS =concerning, about

regardless /rɪgɑːʳdləs/ ◆◆◇◇◇
1 If something happens **regardless of** something else, it is not affected or influenced at all by that other thing. *It takes in anybody regardless of religion, colour, or creed... Regardless of whether he is right or wrong, we have to abide by his decisions.* PHR-PREP
2 If you say that someone did something **regardless**, you mean that they did it even though there were problems or factors that could have stopped them, or perhaps should have stopped them. *Despite her recent surgery she has been carrying on regardless.* ADV: ADV after v =anyway

regatta /rɪgætə/ **regattas.** A **regatta** is a sports event consisting of races between yachts or rowing boats. ◆◇◇◇◇ N-COUNT: oft in names

regency /riːdʒᵊnsi/ **regencies;** usually spelled **Regency** for meaning 1.
1 **Regency** is used to refer to the period in Britain at the beginning of the nineteenth century, and to the style of architecture, literature, and furniture that was popular at the time. *...a huge, six-bedroomed Regency house. ...the Regency period.* ADJ: usu ADJ n
2 A **regency** is a period of time when a country is governed by a regent, because the king or queen is unable to rule. N-COUNT

regenerate /rɪdʒenəreɪt/ **regenerates, regenerating, regenerated** ◆◇◇◇◇
1 To **regenerate** something means to develop and improve it to make it more active, successful, or important, especially after a period when it has been declining. *The government will continue to try to regenerate inner city areas.* ♦ **regeneration** /rɪdʒenəreɪʃᵊn/ *...the physical and economic regeneration of the area.* VERB V n N-UNCOUNT
2 If organs or tissues **regenerate** or if something **regenerates** them, they heal and grow again after they have been damaged. *Nerve cells have limited ability to regenerate if destroyed... Newts can regenerate their limbs.* ♦ **regeneration** *Vitamin B assists in red-blood-cell regeneration.* V-ERG V V n N-UNCOUNT

regenerative /rɪdʒenərətɪv/. **Regenerative** powers or processes cause something to heal or become active again after it has declined or been damaged. *...the regenerative power of nature.* ADJ: usu ADJ n

regent /riːdʒᵊnt/ **regents.** A **regent** is a person who rules a country when the king or queen is unable to rule, for example because they are too young or too ill. N-COUNT

reggae /regeɪ/. **Reggae** is a kind of West Indian popular music with a very strong beat. *Many people will remember Bob Marley for providing them with their first taste of Reggae music.* ◆◆◇◇◇ N-UNCOUNT: oft N n

regicide /redʒɪsaɪd/ **regicides**
1 **Regicide** is the act of killing a king. *He had become czar through regicide.* N-UNCOUNT
2 A **regicide** is a person who kills a king. *Some of the regicides were sentenced to death.* N-COUNT

regime /reɪʒiːm/ **regimes** ◆◆◆◇◇
1 If you refer to a government or system of running a country as a **regime**, you are critical of it because you think it is not democratic and uses unacceptable methods. *...the collapse of Communist regimes in Eastern Europe... Pujol was imprisoned and tortured under the Franco regime.* N-COUNT: oft supp N PRAGMATICS
2 A **regime** is the way that something such as an institution, company, or economy is run, especially when it involves tough or restrictive action. *The authorities moved him to the less rigid regime of an open prison. ...a drastic regime of economic reform and financial discipline.* N-COUNT
3 A **regime** is a set of rules about food, exercise, or beauty that some people follow in order to stay healthy or attractive. *He has a new fitness regime to strengthen his back.* N-COUNT: oft supp N =regimen

regimen /redʒɪmen/ **regimens.** A **regimen** is a set of rules about food and exercise that some people follow in order to stay healthy. *Whatever regimen has been prescribed should be rigorously followed.* N-COUNT =regime

regiment /redʒɪmənt/ **regiments** ◆◆◇◇◇
1 A **regiment** is a large group of soldiers that is commanded by a colonel. N-COUNT
2 A **regiment of** people is a large number of them. *...robust food, good enough to satisfy a regiment of hungry customers.* N-COUNT: N *of* n =army

regimental /rẹdʒɪmẹntᵊl/. **Regimental** means belonging to a particular regiment. *Mills was regimental colonel.* ◆◇◇◇◇ ADJ: ADJ n

regimentation /rẹdʒɪmenteɪʃᵊn/. **Regimentation** is very strict control over the way a group of people behave or the way something is done. *Democracy is incompatible with excessive, bureaucratic regimentation of social life.* N-UNCOUNT

regimented /rẹdʒɪmentɪd/. Something that is **regimented** is very strictly controlled. *...the regimented atmosphere of the orphanage.* ADJ-GRADED

region /riːdʒᵊn/ **regions** ◆◆◆◆◇

1 A **region** is a large area of land that is different from other areas of land, for example because it is one of the different parts of a country with its own customs and characteristics, or because it has a particular geographical feature. *...Barcelona, capital of the autonomous region of Catalonia. ...a remote mountain region.* N-COUNT

2 In British English, **the regions** are the parts of a country that are not the capital city and its surrounding area. *...London and the regions... Tax incentives would be used to attract firms to the regions, away from the South-East.* N-PLURAL: the N

3 You can refer to a part of your body as a **region**. *...the pelvic region. ...the frontal region of the brain.* N-COUNT: with supp =area

4 You say **in the region of** to indicate that an amount that you are stating is approximate. *The scheme will cost in the region of six million pounds.* PHRASE =around

regional /riːdʒənᵊl/. **Regional** is used to describe things which relate to a particular area of a country or of the world. *...the autonomous regional government of Andalucia. ...concern about regional security... Many people in Minnesota and Tennessee have noticeable regional accents.* ◆◆◆◆◇ ADJ: usu ADJ n
♦ **regionally** *The impact of these trends has varied regionally.* ADV

regionalism /riːdʒənəlɪzəm/. **Regionalism** is a strong feeling of pride or loyalty that people in a region have for that region, often including a desire to govern themselves. *A grass-roots regionalism appears to be emerging.* N-UNCOUNT

register /rẹdʒɪstəʳ/ **registers, registering, registered** ◆◆◆◇◇

1 A **register** is an official list or record of things. *...registers of births, deaths and marriages... He signed the register at the hotel... She calls the register for her class of thirty 12 year olds.* N-COUNT

2 If you **register** to do something, you put your name on an official list, in order to be able to do that thing or to receive a service. *Have you come to register at the school?... Thousands lined up to register to vote... There were massive queues in Hong Kong trying to register for British citizenship... About 26 million people are not registered with a dentist. ...registered voters.* VERB V V to-inf V for n V-ed

3 If you **register** something, such as the name of someone who has just died, or the details of ownership of something, you have these facts recorded on an official list. *In order to register a car in Japan, the owner must have somewhere to park it... We registered his birth... The house is registered in her name, not her husband's. ...a registered charity.* VERB V n V-ed

4 When something **registers** on a scale or measuring instrument or when a scale or measuring instrument **registers** it, it shows on the scale or instrument. *It will only register on sophisticated X-ray equipment... The earthquake registered 5.3 points on the Richter scale... The scales registered a gain of 1.3 kilograms.* V-ERG V V n

5 If you **register** your feelings or opinions about something, you do something that makes them clear to other people. *Voters wish to register their dissatisfaction with the ruling party... Workers stopped work to register their protest.* VERB V n

6 If a feeling **registers** on someone's face, their expression shows clearly that they have that feeling. *Surprise again registered on Rodney's face.* VERB =show V

7 If a piece of information does not **register** or if you do not **register** it, you do not really pay attention to it, and so you do not remember it or react to it. *It wasn't that she couldn't hear me, it was just that what I said sometimes didn't register in her brain... The sound was so familiar that she didn't register it.* V-ERG V V n Also V that

8 If you sing or play something in a high or low **register**, you sing, or play it using high or low notes. If you say something in a high or low **register**, you say it in a high or low voice. N-COUNT

9 In linguistics, the **register** of a piece of speech or writing is its level and style of language, which is usually appropriate to the situation or circumstances in which it is used. N-VAR

10 See also **cash register, electoral register.**

registered /rẹdʒɪstəʳd/. A **registered** letter or parcel is sent by a special postal service, for which you pay extra money to insure it in case it is lost. *He asked his mother to send it by registered mail. ...an urgent registered letter.* ◆◇◇◇◇ ADJ: usu ADJ n

register office, register offices. In British English, a **register office** is a place where births, marriages, and deaths are officially recorded, and where people can get married without a religious ceremony. N-COUNT =registry office

registrar /rẹdʒɪstrɑːʳ, AM -strɑːr/ **registrars** ◆◇◇◇◇

1 In Britain, a **registrar** is a person whose job is to keep official records, especially of births, marriages, and deaths. N-COUNT

2 A **registrar** is a senior administrative official in a British college or university. N-COUNT

registration /rẹdʒɪstreɪʃᵊn/ **registrations.** The **registration** of something such as a person's name or the details of an event is the recording of it in an official list. *They have campaigned strongly for compulsory registration of dogs... With the high voter registration, many will be voting for the first time.* ◆◆◇◇◇ N-UNCOUNT: usu with supp

registration number, registration numbers. In British English, the **registration number** or the **registration** of a car or other road vehicle is the series of letters and numbers that are shown at the front and back of it. The American expression is **license plate number**. *Another driver managed to get the registration number of the car.* N-COUNT

registry /rẹdʒɪstri/ **registries.** A **registry** is a collection of all the official records relating to something, or the place where they are kept. *It agreed to set up a central registry of arms sales.* ◆◇◇◇◇ N-COUNT

registry office, registry offices. A **registry office** is the same as a **register office**; used mainly in British English. N-COUNT

regress /rɪgrẹs/ **regresses, regressing, regressed.** When people or things **regress**, they return to an earlier and less advanced stage of development; a formal word. *If your child regresses to babyish behaviour, all you know for certain is that the child is under stress... Such countries are not 'developing' at all, but regressing.* ◆◇◇◇◇ VERB V to/into n V
♦ **regression** /rɪgrẹʃᵊn/ **regressions** *Calderdale accepts that this can cause regression in a pupil's learning process.* N-VAR

regressive /rɪgrẹsɪv/. **Regressive** behaviour, activities, or processes involve a return to an earlier and less advanced stage of development; a formal word. *This regressive behaviour is more common in boys.* ADJ-GRADED

regret /rɪgrẹt/ **regrets, regretting, regretted** ◆◆◆◇◇

1 If you **regret** something that you have done, you wish that you had not done it. *I simply gave in to him, and I've regretted it ever since... Ellis seemed to be regretting that he had asked the question... Five years later she regrets having given up her home.* VERB V n V that V -ing

2 **Regret** is a feeling of sadness or disappointment, which is caused by something that has happened or something that you have done or not done. *My great regret in life is that I didn't bring home the America's Cup... Lillee said he had no regrets about retiring.* N-VAR

3 You can say that you **regret** something as a polite way of saying that you are sorry about it. You use expressions such as **I regret to say** or **I regret to inform you** to show that you are sorry about something; a formal use. *'I very much regret the injuries* VERB PRAGMATICS V n

he sustained,' he said... I regret that the United States has added its voice to such protests... Her lack of co-operation is nothing new, I regret to say... I regret to inform you he died as a consequence of his injuries. V that V to-inf

4 If someone expresses **regret** about something, they say that they are sorry about it; a formal use. *He expressed great regret and said that surgeons would attempt to reverse the operation... President Aquino says she has accepted his resignation with regret.* N-UNCOUNT

regretful /rɪgretfʊl/. If you are **regretful**, you show that you regret something. *Mr Griffin gave a regretful smile... Surprisingly, she didn't feel nervous, or regretful about her actions.* ADJ-GRADED: oft ADJ *about* n, ADJ that ♦ **regretfully** *He shook his head egretfully.* ADV-GRADED

regrettable /rɪgretəbᵊl/. ◆◇◇◇◇ You describe something as **regrettable** when you think that it is bad and that it should not happen or have happened. *The army said it had started an investigation into what it described as a regrettable incident... It is regrettable that strike leaders seem intent on spoiling holidays.* ADJ-GRADED PRAGMATICS =unfortunate ♦ **regrettably** *Regrettably we could find no sign of the man and the search was terminated... The incidents are regrettably true.* ADV-GRADED: ADV with cl, ADV adj =unfortunately

regroup /riːgruːp/ **regroups, regrouping, regrouped.** ◆◇◇◇◇ When people, especially soldiers, **regroup**, or when someone **regroups** them, they form an organized group again, in order to continue fighting. *Now the rebel army has regrouped and reorganised... The armed forces have refused to observe the truce, saying that the rebels may simply be using it to regroup their forces.* V-ERG V V n

regular /regjʊləʳ/ **regulars** ◆◆◆◆◇

1 **Regular** events have equal amounts of time between them, so that they happen, for example, at the same time each day or each week. *Take regular exercise... Now it's time for our regular look at the world of international sport... We're going to be meeting there on a regular basis... The cartridge must be replaced at regular intervals.* ADJ-GRADED: usu ADJ n ≠irregular ♦ **regularly** *Exercise regularly... He also writes regularly for 'International Management' magazine.* ADV-GRADED: ADV with v ♦ **regularity** /regjʊlærɪti/ *The overdraft arrangements had been generous because of the regularity of the half-yearly payments.* N-UNCOUNT

2 **Regular** events happen often. *...after a morning punctuated by regular volleys of gunfire... Although it may look unpleasant, this condition is harmless, and usually clears up with regular shampooing.* ADJ-GRADED: usu ADJ n =frequent ≠infrequent ♦ **regularly** *Fox, badger, weasel and stoat are regularly seen here... Potentially dangerous bacteria are regularly sent from one laboratory to another.* ADV-GRADED: ADV with v =frequently ♦ **regularity** *Closures and job losses are again being announced with monotonous regularity.* N-UNCOUNT

3 If you are, for example, a **regular** customer at a shop or a **regular** visitor to a place, you go there often. *'Tell me, Mr Mentakis, was Mrs Savalas one of your regular customers?'... She has become a regular visitor to Houghton Hall. ...people who are not regular churchgoers.* ADJ-GRADED: ADJ n

4 The **regulars** at a place or in a team are the people who often go to the place or are often in the team. *Regulars at his local pub have set up a fund to help out... I wasn't one of their regulars.* N-COUNT

5 You use **regular** when referring to the thing, person, time, or place that is usually used by someone or involved in something. For example, someone's **regular** place is the place where they usually sit. *The man shook his hand and then sat at his regular table near the windows. ...samples from one of their regular suppliers.* ADJ: det ADJ n =usual

6 A **regular** rhythm consists of a series of sounds or movements with equal periods of time between them. *...a very regular beat... He stood in the doorway, listening to her quiet, regular breathing.* ADJ-GRADED ≠irregular ♦ **regularly** *Remember to breathe regularly.* ADV-GRADED: ADV with v ♦ **regularity** *Experimenters have succeeded in controlling the rate and regularity of the heartbeat.* N-UNCOUNT

7 **Regular** is used, mainly in American English, to mean 'normal'. *The product looks and burns like a regular cigarette... He describes himself as just a regular guy from suburban Chicago.* ADJ: ADJ n =ordinary

8 In some restaurants, a **regular** drink or portion of food is of medium size; used mainly in American English. *...a cheeseburger and regular fries.* ADJ: ADJ n

9 A **regular** pattern or arrangement consists of a series of things with equal spaces between them. *...strange small rounded sandy hillocks, that look as if they've been scattered in a regular pattern on the ground. ...regular rows of wooden huts.* ADJ-GRADED ≠irregular

10 If something has a **regular** shape, both halves are the same and it has straight edges or a smooth outline. *...some regular geometrical shape.* ADJ-GRADED ≠irregular ♦ **regularity** *...the chessboard regularity of their fields.* N-UNCOUNT

11 **Regular** troops are professional soldiers who are a permanent part of an official national army. *Most schemes attempt to reduce the cost of defence through a smaller regular army... Only about a third of the reinforcements will be regular troops.* ADJ: ADJ n ≠irregular ▶ **Regulars** are regular troops. *...the presence of a garrison of British regulars.* N-COUNT: usu pl ≠irregular

12 In grammar, a **regular** verb, noun, or adjective inflects in the same way as most verbs, nouns, or adjectives in the language. ADJ ≠irregular

regularity /regjʊlærɪti/ **regularities** ◆◇◇◇◇

1 A **regularity** is the fact that the same thing always happens in the same circumstances; a formal word. *Children seek out regularities and rules in acquiring language.* N-COUNT

2 See also **regular**.

regularize /regjʊləraɪz/ **regularizes, regularizing, regularized;** also spelled **regularise** in British English. If someone **regularizes** a situation or system, they make it officially acceptable or put it under a system of rules; a formal word. *Cohabiting couples would regularise their unions, they said... The whole system of financing is being regularized.* VERB V n

regulate /regjʊleɪt/ **regulates, regulating, regulated.** ◆◆◇◇◇ To **regulate** an activity or process means to control it, especially by means of rules. *The powers of the European Commission to regulate competition in the Community are increasing... As we get older the temperature-regulating mechanisms in the body tend to become a little less efficient.* VERB V n V-ing ♦ **regulated** *...a planned, state-regulated economy... It's a treatment that can carry risks, and in Britain it's strictly regulated.* ADJ-GRADED

regulation /regjʊleɪʃᵊn/ **regulations** ◆◆◆◇◇

1 **Regulations** are rules made by a government or other authority in order to control the way something is done or the way people behave. *The European Community has proposed new regulations to control the hours worked by its employees... Under pressure from the American government, Fiat and other manufacturers obeyed the new safety regulations.* N-COUNT: usu pl =rule ▶ Also an adjective. *...a noisy cheerful group of people in regulation black parade tunics.* ADJ: ADJ n

2 **Regulation** is the controlling of an activity or process, usually by means of rules. *Social services also have responsibility for the regulation of nurseries... Some in the market now want government regulation in order to reduce costs.* N-UNCOUNT: oft N *of* n

regulator /regjʊleɪtəʳ/ **regulators** ◆◆◆◇◇

1 A **regulator** is a person or organization appointed by a government to regulate an area of activity such as banking or industry. *Congress is being asked to investigate why took so long for government regulators to shut the plant down... An independent regulator will be appointed to ensure fair competition.* N-COUNT ♦ **regulatory** /regjʊleɪtəri, AM -lətɔːri/ *...the UK's financial regulatory system.* ADJ: ADJ n

2 A **regulator** is a device or mechanism that automatically controls something, such as the temperature in a room or the growth of a body. *An automatic voltage regulator ensured a constant output from the generator.* N-COUNT

regurgitate /rɪgɜːʳdʒɪteɪt/ **regurgitates, regurgitating, regurgitated**

1 If you say that someone is **regurgitating** ideas or facts, you mean that they are repeating them VERB PRAGMATICS =repeat

without understanding them properly; used showing disapproval. *You can get sick to death of a friend regurgitating her partner's opinions.* Vn

2 If a person or animal **regurgitates** food, they bring it back up from the stomach before they digest it; a formal use. *Sometimes he regurgitates the food we give him because he cannot swallow.* VERB =bring up Vn

rehab /riːhæb/. **Rehab** is the process of helping someone to lead a normal life again after they have been ill, or when they are addicted to drugs or alcohol; an informal word. **Rehab** is short for rehabilitation. *She went through the drug rehab programme twice because she was such an extreme case.* N-UNCOUNT: oft N n

rehabilitate /riːhəbɪlɪteɪt/ **rehabilitates, rehabilitating, rehabilitated** ◆◆◇◇◇

1 To **rehabilitate** someone who has been ill or in prison means to help them to live a normal life again. To **rehabilitate** someone who is addicted to drugs or alcohol means to help them stop using drugs and alcohol and to live without them. *Considerable efforts have been made to rehabilitate patients who have suffered in this way.* VERB Vn ♦ **rehabilitation** /riːhəbɪlɪteɪʃᵊn/ *A number of other techniques are now being used by psychologists in the rehabilitation of young offenders. ...an alcohol and drug rehabilitation centre.* N-UNCOUNT

2 If someone **is rehabilitated**, they begin to be considered acceptable again after a period during which they have been rejected or severely criticized. *Ten years later, Dreyfus was rehabilitated... His candidacy has divided the Republican Party; while most have scorned him, others have sought to rehabilitate him.* VERB be V-ed Vn ♦ **rehabilitation** *The European Community has taken an important step towards Peking's rehabilitation in the West.* N-UNCOUNT

3 To **rehabilitate** a building or an area means to improve its condition so that it can be used again. *...a program for rehabilitating low-income housing.* VERB Vn ♦ **rehabilitation** *We have to support the rehabilitation and reconstruction of Cambodia.* N-UNCOUNT

rehash, rehashes, rehashing, rehashed. The noun is pronounced /riːhæʃ/. The verb is pronounced /riːhæʃ/.

1 If you describe something as a **rehash**, you are criticizing it because it repeats old ideas, facts, or themes while rearranging them so that they appear new. *The Observer found the play 'a feeble rehash of familiar Miller themes'... Most of the 'new' models promised by American car makers look set to be little more than rehashes of existing products.* N-COUNT: usu sing, N of n PRAGMATICS

2 If you say that someone **rehashes** old ideas, facts, or accusations, you disapprove of the fact that they present them in a slightly different way so that they seem new or original. *They've taken some of the best bits out of the best things and rehashed them... They are just bringing up all their old rehashed claims with no prospect or vision for the future.* VERB PRAGMATICS Vn V-ed ♦ **rehashing** *...the embarrassing rehashing of an old scandal.* N-SING: usu N of n

rehearsal /rɪhɜːʳsᵊl/ **rehearsals** ◆◆◇◇◇

1 A **rehearsal** of a play, dance, or piece of music is a practice of it in preparation for a performance. *The band was scheduled to begin rehearsals for a concert tour... When 'Can-Can' was in rehearsal, Porter felt that the title song needed a musical introduction.* • See also **dress rehearsal**. N-VAR: oft N for/of n

2 You can describe an event or object which is a preparation for a more important event or object as a **rehearsal for** it. *The sketch should be a kind of rehearsal for the eventual painting... Daydreams may seem to be rehearsals for real-life situations, but we know they are not.* N-COUNT: N for n

rehearse /rɪhɜːʳs/ **rehearses, rehearsing, rehearsed** ◆◇◇◇◇

1 When people **rehearse** a play, dance, or piece of music, they practise it in order to prepare for a performance. *In his version, a group of actors are rehearsing a play about Joan of Arc... Tens of thousands of people have been rehearsing for the opening ceremony in the workers' stadium... The cast and crew, who'd never worked together, were only given three and a half weeks to rehearse.* VERB Vn V for n V

2 If you **rehearse** something that you are going to say or do, you silently practise it by imagining that you are saying or doing it. *Anticipate any tough questions and rehearse your answers... We encouraged them to rehearse what they were going to say.* VERB Vn V wh

3 If you **rehearse** something, you repeat it in detail; a formal use. *Yesterday's speech to the Scottish party conference rehearsed the arguments again.* VERB Vn

rehouse /riːhaʊz/ **rehouses, rehousing, rehoused.** If someone **is rehoused**, their council or another authority provides them with a different house to live in. *Many of the 100,000 or so families who lost their homes in the earthquake have still not been rehoused... The council has agreed to rehouse the family.* VERB be V-ed Vn

reign /reɪn/ **reigns, reigning, reigned** ◆◆◇◇◇

1 If you say, for example, that silence **reigns** in a place or confusion **reigns** in a situation, you mean that the place is silent or the situation is confused. *Last night confusion reigned about how the debate, which continues today, would end... A relative calm reigned over the city.* VERB V V over n

2 When a king or queen **reigns**, he or she rules a country. *...Henry II, who reigned from 1154 to 1189. ...George III, Britain's longest reigning monarch.* ► Also a noun. *...Queen Victoria's reign.* VERB V V-ing N-COUNT: with poss

3 If you say that a person **reigns** in a situation or area, you mean that they are very powerful or successful. *Connors reigned as the world No. 1 for 159 consecutive weeks... Coco Chanel reigned over fashion for half a century.* ► Also a noun. *...a new book celebrating 21 years of Giles Havergal's reign as artistic director of the Citizens' Theatre.* VERB V V over n N-COUNT: with poss

4 Someone or something that **reigns supreme** is the most important or powerful element in a situation or period of time. *The bicycle reigned supreme as Britain's most popular mode of transport... Senator Sam Nunn reigns supreme over the Senate Armed Services Committee.* PHRASES V inflects

5 A **reign of terror** is a period during which there is a lot of violence and killing, especially by people who are in a position of power. *The commanders accused him of carrying out a reign of terror.*

reigning /reɪnɪŋ/. The **reigning** champion is the most recent winner of a contest or competition at the time you are talking about. *The result means that the reigning world champion has extended his lead in this season's championship.* ◆◇◇◇◇ ADJ: ADJ n

reimburse /riːɪmbɜːʳs/ **reimburses, reimbursing, reimbursed.** If you **reimburse** someone for something, you pay them back the money that they have spent or lost because of it; a formal word. *I'll be happy to reimburse you for any expenses you might have incurred... The funds are supposed to reimburse policyholders in the event of insurer failure.* ◆◇◇◇◇ VERB Vn for n Vn

reimbursement /riːɪmbɜːʳsmənt/ **reimbursements. Reimbursement** is the repayment to someone of money that they have spent or lost, for example while doing something for another person; a formal word. *She is demanding reimbursement for medical and other expenses... It can take up to six months before reimbursements are paid.* ◆◇◇◇◇ N-VAR

rein /reɪn/ **reins, reining, reined** ◆◆◇◇◇

1 **Reins** are the thin leather straps attached to a horse's bridle which are used to control the horse. N-PLURAL

2 Journalists sometimes use the expression **the reins** or **the reins of power** to refer to the control of a country or organization. *Mr Castro, who is sixty-five today, shows no sign of handing over the reins of power.* N-PLURAL: oft the N of n

3 If you **give a free rein to** someone, you give them a lot of freedom to do what they want. *The government continued to believe it should give free rein to the private sector in transport.* PHRASES V inflects =carte blanche

4 If you **keep a tight rein on** someone, you control them firmly. *Her parents had kept her on a tight rein with their narrow and inflexible views.* V inflects

rein back. To **rein back** something such as PHRASAL VERB spending means to control it strictly. *He promised that between now and the end of the year the government would try to rein back inflation.* =check V P n (not pron) Also V n P

rein in PHRASAL VERB
1 To **rein in** something means to control it. *His administration's economic policy would focus on reining in inflation and reducing the budget deficit... Mary spoiled both her children, then tried too late to rein them in.* =control V P n (not pron) V n P
2 If you **rein in** a horse, you stop it or cause it to go more slowly by pulling its reins. *The horsemen reined in and shouted at the men behind to turn back... Mrs Glick reined in the horse and stopped at the crossroads.* V P V P n (not pron) Also V n P

reincarnate /riːɪŋkɑːʳneɪt/ **reincarnates, reincarnating, reincarnated.** If people believe that they will **be reincarnated** when they die, they believe that their spirit will be born again and will live in the body of another person or animal. *...their belief that human souls were reincarnated in the bodies of turtles. ...a reincarnated soul.* VB: usu passive be V-ed V-ed Also V

reincarnation /riːɪŋkɑːʳneɪʃᵊn/ **reincarnations** ◆◇◇◇◇
1 If you believe in **reincarnation**, you believe that you will be reincarnated after you die. *Many African tribes believe in reincarnation.* N-UNCOUNT
2 A **reincarnation** is a person or animal whose body is believed to contain the spirit of a dead person. N-COUNT

reindeer /reɪndɪəʳ/. **Reindeer** is both the singular and the plural form. A **reindeer** is a deer with large antlers that lives in northern areas of Europe, Asia, and America. N-COUNT

reinforce /riːɪnfɔːʳs/ **reinforces, reinforcing, reinforced** ◆◆◇◇◇
1 If something **reinforces** a feeling, situation, or process, it makes it stronger or more intense. *A stronger European Parliament would, they fear, only reinforce the power of the larger countries... This sense of privilege tends to be reinforced by the outside world.* VERB =consolidate V n
2 If something **reinforces** an idea or point of view, it provides more evidence or support for it. *The delegation hopes to reinforce the idea that human rights are not purely internal matters.* VERB =strengthen V n
3 To **reinforce** an object means to make it stronger or harder. *Eventually, they had to reinforce the walls with exterior beams.* VERB V n with n ♦ **reinforced** *Its windows were of reinforced glass.* ADJ
4 To **reinforce** an army or a group of police means to make it stronger by increasing its size or providing it with more weapons. To **reinforce** a position or place means to make it stronger by sending more soldiers or weapons. *Both sides have been reinforcing their positions after yesterday's fierce fighting... Troops and police have been reinforced in the southern Pakistan city of Hyderabad.* VERB V n

reinforced concrete. **Reinforced concrete** is concrete that is made with pieces of metal inside it to make it stronger. *The prison was the safest building in the whole area because it was made of reinforced concrete.* N-UNCOUNT

reinforcement /riːɪnfɔːʳsmənt/ **reinforcements** ◆◇◇◇◇
1 **Reinforcements** are soldiers or policemen who are sent to join an army or group of police in order to make it stronger. *Mr Vlok promised new measures to protect residents, including the despatch of police and troop reinforcements.* N-PLURAL
2 The **reinforcement** of something is the process of making it stronger. *I am sure that this meeting will contribute to the reinforcement of peace and security all over the world... What the teacher now has to do is remove the reinforcement for this bad behaviour... There are reinforcement bars on all doors.* N-VAR: oft N of n

reinstate /riːɪnsteɪt/ **reinstates, reinstating, reinstated** ◆◇◇◇◇
1 If you **reinstate** someone, you give them back a job or position which had been taken away from them. *The governor is said to have agreed to reinstate five senior workers who were dismissed... Thailand's prime minister announced his resignation today, but he is widely expected to be reinstated within a few days.* VERB V n
2 To **reinstate** a law, facility, or practice means to start having it again. *She says the public response was a factor in the decision to reinstate the grant... There have now been 139 executions since the death penalty was reinstated in 1976.* VERB =restore V n

reinstatement /riːɪnsteɪtmənt/ ◆◇◇◇◇
1 **Reinstatement** is the act of giving someone back a job or position which has been taken away from them. *Parents campaigned in vain for her reinstatement.* N-UNCOUNT: usu with poss
2 The **reinstatement** of a law, facility, or practice is the act of causing it to exist again. *He welcomed the reinstatement of the 10 per cent bank base rate.* N-UNCOUNT: usu with poss =restoration

reissue /riː ɪʃuː/ **reissues, reissuing, reissued** ◆◇◇◇◇
1 A **reissue** is a book, record, or film that has not been available for some time but is now is published or produced again. *...this welcome reissue of a 1955 Ingmar Bergman classic.* N-COUNT
2 If something such as a book, record, or film **is reissued** after it has not been available for some time, it is published or produced again. *Evelyn Waugh's novels have just been reissued by Penguin with eye-catching new covers.* VB: usu passive be V-ed

reiterate /riːɪtəreɪt/ **reiterates, reiterating, reiterated.** If you **reiterate** something, you say it again or emphasize it; a formal word used especially in broadcast news. *He reiterated his opposition to the creation of a central bank... I want to reiterate that our conventional weapons are superior.* ◆◇◇◇◇ VERB =repeat V n V that Also V quote ♦ **reiteration** /riːɪtəreɪʃᵊn/ **reiterations** *It was really a reiteration of the same old entrenched positions.* N-VAR: oft N of n =repetition

reject, rejects, rejecting, rejected. The verb is pronounced /rɪdʒekt/. The noun is pronounced /riːdʒekt/. ◆◆◆◆◇
1 If you **reject** something such as a proposal or request, you do not accept it or you do not agree to it. *The British government is expected to reject the idea of state subsidy for a new high speed railway.* VERB V n ♦ **rejection** /rɪdʒekʃᵊn/ **rejections** *The rejection of such initiatives by no means indicates that voters are unconcerned about the environment.* N-VAR: oft N of n
2 If you **reject** a belief or a political system, you refuse to believe in it or to live by its rules. *...the children of Eastern European immigrants who had rejected their parents' political and religious beliefs.* VERB V n ♦ **rejection** *His rejection of our values is far more complete than that of D. H. Lawrence.* N-VAR
3 If someone **is rejected** for a job or course of study, it is not offered to them. *One of my most able students was rejected by another university.* VERB be V-ed Also V n ♦ **rejection** *Be prepared for lots of rejections before you land a job.* N-COUNT
4 If someone **rejects** another person who expects affection from them, they are cold and unfriendly towards them. *You make friends with people and then make unreasonable demands so that they reject you. ...people who had been rejected by their lovers.* VERB V n ♦ **rejection** *These feelings of rejection and hurt remain.* N-VAR
5 If a person's body **rejects** something such as a new heart that has been transplanted into it, it tries to attack and destroy it. *It was feared his body was rejecting a kidney he received in a transplant four years ago.* VERB V n ♦ **rejection** *...a special drug which stops rejection of transplanted organs.* N-VAR
6 If a machine **rejects** a coin that you put in it, the coin comes out and the machine does not work. VERB
7 A **reject** is a product that has not been accepted for use or sale, because there is something wrong with it. N-COUNT

rejig /riːdʒɪg/ **rejigs, rejigging, rejigged.** If someone **rejigs** an organization or a piece of work, they completely rearrange it. *The adjustments needed to rejig the industry are undeniably complex.* VERB V n

rejoice /rɪdʒɔɪs/ **rejoices, rejoicing, rejoiced** ◆◇◇◇◇
1 If you **rejoice**, you are very pleased about something and you show it in your behaviour. *Garbo plays the Queen, rejoicing in the love she has found* VERB V in/at n V that Also V

with Antonio... A Foreign Ministry statement said that the French government rejoiced at the happy outcome to events... Party activists in New Hampshire rejoiced that the presidential campaign had finally started. ♦ **rejoicing** *There was general rejoicing at the news.* N-UNCOUNT

2 If you say that someone or something **rejoices in the name of** something, you mean that they are called that and you find it amusing. *...their tortoise, who rejoiced in the name of Carruthers.* PHRASE: V inflects PRAGMATICS

rejoin, rejoins, rejoining, rejoined. Pronounced /riːdʒɔɪn/ for meanings 1, 2, and 3, and /rɪdʒɔɪn/ for meaning 4. ◆◇◇◇◇

1 If you **rejoin** a group, club, or organization, you become a member of it again after not being a member for a period of time. *The Prime Minister of Fiji has said Fiji is in no hurry to rejoin the Commonwealth... He rejoined Sadler's Wells Royal Ballet as Assistant Administrator in 1988.* VERB Vn Also V

2 If you **rejoin** someone, you go back to them after a short time away from them. *Mimi and her family went off to Tunisia to rejoin her father.* VERB Vn

3 If you **rejoin** a route, you go back to it after travelling along a different route for a time. *At Dorset Wharf go left to rejoin the river... In the morning I rejoined Highway 127 south.* VERB Vn

4 To **rejoin** means to answer quickly what someone has said, usually in a witty or critical manner; a formal use found mainly in written English. *'I dare say they do,' rejoined his wife drily. 'And who's to say who's right?'* VB: no cont =retort V with quote Also V that

rejoinder /rɪdʒɔɪndəʳ/ **rejoinders.** A **rejoinder** is a reply, especially a quick, witty, or critical one, to a question or remark; a formal word. N-COUNT =retort

rejuvenate /rɪdʒuːvəneɪt/ **rejuvenates, rejuvenating, rejuvenated** ◆◇◇◇◇

1 If something **rejuvenates** you, it makes you feel or look young again. *Shelley was advised that the Italian climate would rejuvenate him... When it was time to leave and return to civilization we both felt rejuvenated... This rejuvenated economy will turn its face to the people.* ♦ **rejuvenating** *The hotel's new Spa offers every kind of rejuvenating treatment and therapy.* VERB Vn V-ed ADJ

2 If you **rejuvenate** an organization or system, you make it more lively and more efficient, for example by introducing new ideas. *The government pushed through schemes to rejuvenate the inner cities... They should concentrate on rejuvenating the existing vegetation, like grass and shrubs.* ♦ **rejuvenation** /rɪdʒuːvəneɪʃən/ *The way Britain organises its politics needs rejuvenation.* VERB Vn N-UNCOUNT

rekindle /riːkɪndəl/ **rekindles, rekindling, rekindled** ◆◇◇◇◇

1 If something **rekindles** an interest, feeling, or thought that you used to have, it makes you think about it or feel it again. *Ben Brantley's article on Sir Ian McKellen rekindled many memories... Her interest was rekindled when she saw herbs in everyday medicinal use there.* VERB =reawaken Vn

2 If something **rekindles** an unpleasant situation, it makes the unpleasant situation happen again. *The continuing disintegration of the Soviet empire is rekindling old national and ethnic tensions.* VERB Vn

relapse /rɪlæps/ **relapses, relapsing, relapsed.** The noun can be pronounced /rɪlæps/ or /riːlæps/. ◆◇◇◇◇

1 If you say that someone **relapses into** a way of behaving that is undesirable, you mean that they start to behave in that way again. *'I wish I did,' said Phil Jordan, relapsing into his usual gloom... It is by no means clear that the financial markets will not relapse into panic.* ► Also a noun. *...a relapse into the nationalism of the nineteenth century.* VERB V into n N-COUNT: oft N into n

2 If a sick person **relapses**, their health suddenly gets worse after it had been improving. *In 90 per cent of cases the patient will relapse within six months.* ► Also a noun. *The treatment is usually given to women with a high risk of relapse after surgery... The sufferer can experience frequent relapses.* VERB V N-VAR

relate /rɪleɪt/ **relates, relating, related** ◆◆◆◇◇

1 If something **relates to** a particular subject, it concerns that subject. *Other recommendations relate to the details of how such data is stored... It does not matter whether the problem you have relates to food, drink, smoking or just living... I had papers relating to the children which my wife and I had to sign.* VERB V to n

2 The way that two things **relate**, or the way that one thing **relates** to another, is the sort of connection that exists between them. *More studies will be required before we know what the functions of these genes are and whether they relate to each other... Cornell University offers a course that investigates how language relates to particular cultural codes... Many Christians today feel the need to relate their experience to that of the Hindu, the Buddhist and the Muslim. ...a paper called 'Language and freedom' in which Chomsky tries to relate his linguistic and political views.* V-RECIP-ERG pl-n V V to n V n to n V pl-n

3 If you can **relate** to someone, you can understand how they feel or behave so that you are able to communicate with them or deal with them easily. *He is unable to relate to other people... I think it is important for children to have brothers and sisters they can relate to... When people are cut off from contact with others for any length of time, they lose all ability to relate.* V-RECIP V to n pl-n V

4 If you **relate** a story, you tell it; a formal use. *In Kathmandu there were Tibetan-speaking officials to whom he could relate the whole story... The poet sought support for a point he was making by relating the tale of an Irish peasant.* VERB =tell V n to n V n

related /rɪleɪtɪd/ ◆◆◆◇◇

1 If two or more things are **related**, there is a connection between them. *The philosophical problems of chance and of free will are closely related. ...equipment and accessories for diving and related activities.* ADJ =connected

2 People who are **related** belong to the same family. *...people in countries like Bangladesh who have been able to show they are related to a spouse or parent living in Britain.* ADJ: v-link ADJ, oft ADJ to n

3 If you say that different types of animal or different languages are **related**, you mean that they have developed from the same type of animal or language. *He recognized that Sanskrit, the language of India, was related very closely to Latin, Greek, and the Germanic and Celtic languages. ...closely related species.* ADJ: oft ADJ to n

-related /-rɪleɪtɪd/. **-related** combines with nouns to form adjectives with the meaning 'connected with the thing referred to by the noun'. *More than 50 arrests were made, mostly for drug-related offences... Twelve people die every hour from smoking-related diseases.* COMB in ADJ: usu ADJ n

relation /rɪleɪʃən/ **relations** ◆◆◆◆◇

1 **Relations** between people, groups, or countries are contacts between them and the way in which they behave towards each other. *Greece has established full diplomatic relations with Israel... Apparently relations between husband and wife had not improved... The company has a track record of good employee relations.* • See also **industrial relations, public relations, race relations.** N-COUNT: usu pl

2 If you talk about the **relation** of one thing to another, you are talking about the ways in which they are connected. *It is a question of the relation of ethics to economics. ...a relation between youthful unemployment and drug-related offences... This theory bears no relation to reality.* N-COUNT: usu sing, usu N of/to/between n =relationship

3 Your **relations** are the members of your family. *...visits to friends and relations. ...Frederick Bush, a former aide to President Bush (no relation).* • See also **poor relation.** N-COUNT =relatives

4 You can talk about something **in relation to** something else when you want to compare the size, condition, or position of the two things. *The money he'd been ordered to pay was minimal in relation to his salary. ...women's position in relation to men in the context of the family... You are given a map so that you can see where your villa is in relation to the swimming pool.* PHRASES PREP

5 If something is said or done **in relation to** a PREP

subject, it is said or done in connection with that subject. *...a question which has been asked many times in relation to Irish affairs... He is the sixth person to be arrested in relation to the coup plot.* =in connection with

relational /rɪleɪʃənəl/. **Relational** means concerning relationships and connections; a formal word. *...in the middle of a relational crisis... Language, for example, is a relational whole.* ADJ: ADJ n

relationship /rɪleɪʃənʃɪp/ **relationships** ◆◆◆◆◇

1 The **relationship** between two people or groups is the way in which they feel and behave towards each other. *The Chinese President has said that China will maintain its traditional friendly relationship with Bangladesh... Money problems place great stress on close family relationships.* N-COUNT: with supp

2 A **relationship** is a close friendship between two people, especially one involving romantic or sexual feelings. *We had been together for two years, but both of us felt the relationship wasn't really going anywhere.* N-COUNT

3 The **relationship** between two things is the way in which they are connected. *A number of small-scale studies have already indicated that there is a relationship between diet and cancer. ...an analysis of market mechanisms and their relationship to state capitalism and political freedom.* N-COUNT: N between/to/of n

relative /relətɪv/ **relatives** ◆◆◆◇◇

1 Your **relatives** are the members of your family. *Do relatives of yours still live in Siberia?... Get a relative to look after the children.* N-COUNT =relations

2 You use **relative** to say that something is true to a certain degree, especially when compared with other things of the same kind. *The fighting resumed after a period of relative calm... It is a cancer that can be cured with relative ease... Pedestrian zones mean that children can play in relative safety.* ADJ: ADJ n =comparative

3 You use **relative** when you are comparing the quality or size of two things. *They chatted about the relative merits of London and Paris as places to live... I reflected on the relative importance of education in 50 countries. ...the relative strength of the central and state governments.* ADJ: ADJ n

4 **Relative to** something means with reference to it or in comparison with it. *Japanese interest rates rose relative to America's... House prices now look cheap relative to earnings... The satellite remains in one spot relative to the earth's surface.* PHR-PREP =in relation to

5 If you say that something is **relative**, you mean that it needs to be considered and judged in relation to other things. *Fitness is relative; one must always ask 'Fit for what?'... Truth is relative.* ADJ-GRADED: usu v-link ADJ ≠absolute

6 If one animal, plant, language, or invention is a **relative** of another, they have both evolved or developed from the same type of animal, plant, language, or invention. *The pheasant is a close relative of the Guinea hen.* N-COUNT: usu N of n

relative clause, relative clauses. A **relative clause** is a subordinate clause which specifies or gives information about a person or thing. Relative clauses come after a noun or pronoun and, in English, often begin with a relative pronoun such as 'who', 'which', or 'that'. N-COUNT

relatively /relətɪvli/. **Relatively** means to a certain degree, especially when compared with other things of the same kind. *The sums needed are relatively small... I like to think I'm relatively easy to get along with.* ◆◆◆◇◇ ADV: ADV adj/adv PRAGMATICS =comparatively

relative pronoun, relative pronouns. A **relative pronoun** is a word such as 'who', 'that', or 'which' that is used to introduce a relative clause. 'Whose', 'when', 'where', and 'why' are generally called **relative pronouns**, though they are actually adverbs. N-COUNT

relativism /relətɪvɪzəm/. **Relativism** is the belief that the truth is not always the same but varies according to circumstances. *Traditionalists may howl, but in today's world, cultural relativism rules... Bennett launched a crusade for 'moral values' against decadent 'liberal relativism.'* N-UNCOUNT ≠absolutism

relativist /relətɪvɪst/ **relativists.** A **relativist** position or argument is one according to which the truth is not always the same, but varies according to circumstances. *Bonger advocated a relativist position. In his view, what is considered immoral depends on the social structure.* ▶ A **relativist** is someone with relativist views. ADJ ≠absolutist; N-COUNT

relativity /relətɪvɪti/. The theory of **relativity** is Einstein's theory concerning space, time, and motion; a technical term in physics. ◆◇◇◇◇ N-UNCOUNT

relax /rɪlæks/ **relaxes, relaxing, relaxed** ◆◆◆◇◇

1 If you **relax** or if something **relaxes** you, you feel more calm and less worried or tense. *I ought to relax and stop worrying about it... For the first time since his arrival he relaxed slightly... Do something that you know relaxes you.* V-ERG V V n

2 When a part of your body **relaxes**, or when you relax it, it becomes less stiff or firm. *Massage is used to relax muscles, relieve stress and improve the circulation... His face relaxes into a contented smile.* V-ERG V n V

3 If you **relax** your grip or hold on something, you hold it less tightly than before. *He gradually relaxed his grip on the arms of the chair.* VERB ≠tighten V n

4 If you **relax** a rule or your control over something, or if it **relaxes**, it becomes less firm or strong. *Rules governing student conduct relaxed somewhat in recent years... How much can the President relax his grip over the nation without emboldening it to rise in open revolt?... Some analysts believe China soon will begin relaxing economic controls.* V-ERG ≠tighten V V n

relaxation /riːlækseɪʃən/ ◆◆◇◇◇

1 **Relaxation** is ways of spending time that are pleasant and restful. *You should be able to find the odd moment for relaxation... Relaxation techniques are taught in hospitals in order to help all sorts of conditions.* N-UNCOUNT: oft N n

2 If there is **relaxation** of a rule or control, it is made less firm or strong. *The relaxation of travel restrictions means they are free to travel and work.* N-UNCOUNT: oft N of/in n

relaxed /rɪlækst/ ◆◆◇◇◇

1 If you are **relaxed**, you are calm and not worried or tense. *As soon as I had made the final decision, I felt a lot more relaxed... Try to adopt a more relaxed manner.* ADJ-GRADED

2 If a place or situation is **relaxed**, it is calm and peaceful. *The atmosphere at lunch was relaxed.* ADJ-GRADED

relaxing /rɪlæksɪŋ/. Something that is **relaxing** is pleasant and helps you to relax. *I find cooking very relaxing... We come here once a year expecting a quiet, relaxing holiday.* ◆◇◇◇◇ ADJ-GRADED =restful

relay, relays, relaying, relayed. The noun is pronounced /riːleɪ/. The verb is pronounced /rɪleɪ/. ◆◆◇◇◇

1 A **relay** or a **relay race** is a race between two or more teams, for example teams of runners or swimmers. Each member of the team runs or swims one section of the race. *Britain's prospects of beating the United States in the relay looked poor.* N-COUNT

2 To **relay** television or radio signals means to send them on or broadcast them. *The satellite will be used mainly to relay television programmes... This system continuously monitors levels of radiation and relays the information to a central computer... The event will be relayed to a giant TV screen a mile away.* ▶ Also a noun. *More than a thousand people outside listened to a relay of the proceedings.* VERB V n V n to/from n; N-COUNT

3 A **relay** is a piece of equipment that receives television or radio signals from one place and sends them on to another place. *...a security system with satellite relays. ...a television relay station.* N-COUNT

4 If you **relay** something that has been said to you, you repeat it to another person; a formal use. *She relayed the message, then frowned... The decision will be relayed to Iraq's ambassador at the UN.* VERB V n be V-ed to/from n

release /rɪliːs/ **releases, releasing, released** ◆◆◆◆◆

1 If a person or animal **is released** from somewhere where they have been imprisoned or looked after, they are set free or allowed to go. *He was released from custody the next day... He is expected to be released from hospital today... Fifty-five foxes were released from a fur farm by animal rights activists... He was released on bail.* VB: usu passive be V-ed from n be V-ed

2 When someone is released, you refer to their **release**. *He called for the immediate release of all political prisoners. ...the secret negotiations necessary* N-COUNT: with supp

to secure hostage releases... Serious complications have delayed his release from hospital.

3 If someone or something **releases** you from an obligation, task, or feeling, they free you from it; a formal use. *Divorce releases both the husband and wife from all marital obligations to each other... This releases the teacher to work with individuals who are having extreme difficulty.* ► Also a noun. *Our therapeutic style offers release from stored tensions, traumas and grief... They look on life at college as a blessed release from the obligation to work.* — VERB; V n *from* n; V n; N-UNCOUNT: also *a* N, oft N *from* N

4 To **release** feelings or abilities means to allow them to be expressed. *Becoming your own person releases your creativity... I personally don't want to release my anger on anyone else... Humour is wonderful for releasing tension.* ► Also a noun. *She felt the sudden sweet release of her own tears.* — VERB; V n; N-UNCOUNT

5 If someone in authority **releases** something such as a document or information, they make it available. *They're not releasing any more details yet... Figures released yesterday show retail sales were down in March.* ► Also a noun. *Action had been taken to speed up the release of cheques.* — VERB; V n; V-ed; N-COUNT: with supp

6 If you **release** someone or something, you stop holding them; a formal use. *He stopped and faced her, releasing her wrist. ...the twisting action before a bowler releases the ball.* — VERB =let go; V n

7 If you **release** a device, you move it so that it stops holding something. *Wade released the hand brake and pulled away from the curb.* — VERB

8 If something **releases** gas, heat, or a substance, it causes it to leave its container or the substance that it was part of and enter the surrounding atmosphere or area. *...a weapon which releases toxic nerve gas... The contraction of muscles uses energy and releases heat... The drug is surgically implanted into a woman's arm where it gradually releases the hormones into the body.* ► Also a noun. *Under the agreement, releases of cancer-causing chemicals will be cut by about 80 per cent.* — VERB; V n; N-COUNT: with supp

9 When an entertainer or company **releases** a new record, video, or film, it becomes available so that people can buy it or see it. *He is releasing an album of love songs.* — VERB; V n

10 A new **release** is a new record, video, or film that has just become available for people to buy or see. *Of the new releases that are out there now, which do you think are really good?* — N-COUNT

11 If a film or video is **on release** or **on general release**, it is available for showing in public cinemas or for people to buy. *The video has sold three million copies in its first three weeks on release.* — N-UNCOUNT: *on* N

12 See also **day release**, **news release**, **press release**.

relegate /relɪgeɪt/ **relegates, relegating, relegated** ◆◆◇◇◇

1 If you **relegate** someone or something to a less important or less prominent position, you give them this position. *Might it not be better to relegate the King to a purely ceremonial function?... Other newspapers relegated the item to the middle pages.* — VERB; V n to-inf

2 If a team that competes in a league **is relegated**, it has to compete in a lower division in the next competition, because it was one of the least successful teams in the higher division; used mainly in British English. *If Leigh lose, they'll be relegated. ...a team about to be relegated to the second division.* — VB: usu passive =demote ≠promote; *be* V-ed; *be* V-ed *to* n

♦ **relegation** /relɪgeɪʃən/ *Relegation to the Third Division would prove catastrophic.* — N-UNCOUNT ≠promotion

relent /rɪlent/ **relents, relenting, relented** ◆◇◇◇◇

1 If you **relent**, you allow someone to do something that you had previously refused to allow them to do. *Finally his mother relented and gave permission for her youngest son to marry.* — VERB; V

2 If bad weather **relents**, it improves. *If the weather relents, the game will be finished today.* — VERB; V

relentless /rɪlentləs/ ◆◆◇◇◇

1 Something bad that is **relentless** never stops or never becomes less intense. *The pressure now was relentless.* ♦ **relentlessly** *The sun is beating down relentlessly.* — ADJ-GRADED =remorseless; ADV-GRADED

2 Someone who is **relentless** is determined to do something and refuses to give up, even if what they are doing is unpleasant or cruel. *Relentless in his pursuit of quality, his technical ability was remarkable... He was the most relentless enemy I have ever known.* ♦ **relentlessly** *She always questioned me relentlessly.* — ADJ-GRADED; ADV-GRADED

relevance /reləvəns/. Something's **relevance** to a situation or person is its importance or significance in that situation or to that person. *Politicians' private lives have no relevance to their public roles... There are additional publications of special relevance to new graduates.* — ◆◇◇◇◇ N-UNCOUNT: with supp, oft N *to* n

relevant /reləvənt/ ◆◆◇◇◇

1 Something that is **relevant** to a situation or person is important or significant in that situation or to that person. *Is socialism still relevant to people's lives?... We have passed all relevant information on to the police.* — ADJ-GRADED =pertinent ≠irrelevant

2 **The relevant** thing of a particular kind is the one that is appropriate. *Make sure you enclose all the relevant certificates.* — ADJ: *the* ADJ n

reliable /rɪlaɪəbəl/ ◆◆◆◇◇

1 People or things that are **reliable** can be trusted to work well or to behave in the way that you want them to. *She was efficient and reliable... Japanese cars are so reliable.* ♦ **reliably** /rɪlaɪəbli/ *It's been working reliably for years.* ♦ **reliability** /rɪlaɪəbɪlɪti/ *He's not at all worried about his car's reliability.* — ADJ-GRADED =dependable; ADV-GRADED; N-UNCOUNT

2 Information that is **reliable** or that is from a **reliable** source is very likely to be correct. *There is no reliable information about civilian casualties... It's very difficult to give a reliable estimate... We have reliable sources.* ♦ **reliably** *Sonia, we are reliably informed, loves her family very much.* ♦ **reliability** *Both questioned the reliability of recent opinion polls.* — ADJ-GRADED; ADV-GRADED; N-UNCOUNT

reliance /rɪlaɪəns/. A person's or thing's **reliance** on something is the fact that they need it and often cannot live or work without it. *...the country's increasing reliance on foreign aid.* — ◆◇◇◇◇ N-UNCOUNT: usu poss N *on/upon* n =dependence

reliant /rɪlaɪənt/. A person or thing that is **reliant** on something needs it and often cannot live or work without it. *These people are not wholly reliant on Western charity... Lithuania is heavily reliant on Moscow for almost all its oil.* • See also **self-reliant**. — ◆◇◇◇◇ ADJ-GRADED: v-link ADJ *on/upon* n =dependent

relic /relɪk/ **relics** ◆◇◇◇◇

1 If you refer to something or someone as a **relic** of an earlier period, you mean that they belonged to that period but have survived into the present. *The tower is a relic of grim days when big houses had to be fortified against invaders... Germany's asylum law is a relic of an era in European history which has passed... He found himself thinking of the man as a relic from the past.* — N-COUNT: usu N *of/from* n

2 A **relic** is something which was made or used a long time ago and which is kept for its historical significance. *...a museum of war relics. ...ancient Egyptian relics.* — N-COUNT: usu with supp

3 A **relic** is the body of a saint or something else associated with a saint, which some people regard as holy. — N-COUNT

relief /rɪliːf/ **reliefs** ◆◆◆◆◇

1 If you feel a sense of **relief**, you feel glad because something unpleasant has not happened or is no longer happening. *I breathed a sigh of relief... The news will come as a great relief to the French authorities... To his relief a loud knock on the door spared him from giving an explanation... It's a relief to get out of the office once in a while.* — N-UNCOUNT: also *a* N

2 If something provides **relief** from pain or distress, it stops the pain or distress. *This brought considerable relief from the pain. ...a self-help programme which can give lasting relief from the torment of hay fever.* — N-UNCOUNT: oft N *from* n =respite

3 **Relief** is money, food, or clothing that is provided for people who are very poor or hungry, or who have been affected by war or a natural disaster. *Relief agencies are stepping up efforts to provide food, shelter and agricultural equipment. ...famine relief.* — N-UNCOUNT: oft N n, n N

4 A **relief** worker is someone who does your work — N-COUNT:

when you go home, or who is specially employed to do it instead of you when you are sick. *No relief drivers were available.* usu N n

5 A **relief** is a sculpture that is carved out of a flat vertical surface; a technical term in art. N-COUNT

6 See also **bas-relief, tax relief.**

relieve /rɪliːv/ **relieves, relieving, relieved** ◆◆◇◇◇

1 If something **relieves** an unpleasant feeling or situation, it makes it less unpleasant or causes it to disappear completely. *Drugs can relieve much of the pain... This should save her from boredom and will also relieve the pressure on you to keep her entertained.* VERB V n

2 If someone or something **relieves** you of an unpleasant feeling or difficult task, they take it from you. *A part-time bookkeeper will relieve you of the burden of chasing unpaid invoices and paying bills.* VERB V n of n

3 If someone **relieves** you of something, they take it away from you; a formal use. *A porter relieved her of the three large cases.* VERB V n of n

4 If you **relieve** someone, you take their place and continue to do the job or duty that they have been doing. *At seven o'clock the night nurse came in to relieve her.* VERB V n

5 If someone **is relieved** of their duties or **is relieved** of their post, they are told that they are no longer required to continue in their job; a formal use. *The officer involved was relieved of his duties because he had violated strict guidelines... The party leader has been relieved of his post.* VB: usu passive be V-ed of n

6 If an army **relieves** a town or another place which has been surrounded by enemy forces, it frees it. *The offensive began several days ago as an attempt to relieve the town.* VERB V n

7 If people or animals **relieve** themselves, they urinate or defecate; an old-fashioned use. *It is not difficult to train your dog to relieve itself on command.* VERB V pron-refl

relieved /rɪliːvd/. If you are **relieved**, you feel glad because something unpleasant has not happened or is no longer happening. *We are all relieved to be back home... I am very relieved that it is over... He was relieved at the result.* ◆◆◇◇◇ ADJ-GRADED: usu v-link ADJ, oft ADJ to-inf/that

religion /rɪlɪdʒ³n/ **religions** ◆◆◆◇◇

1 **Religion** is belief in a god or gods and the activities that are connected with this belief, such as prayer or worship in a church or temple. *...his understanding of Indian philosophy and religion... Do avoid potentially contentious subjects such as religion, sex or politics.* N-UNCOUNT

2 A **religion** is a particular system of belief in a god or gods and the activities that are connected with this system. *...the Christian religion.* N-COUNT

3 If you say that someone **has got religion**, you are referring in a mocking way to the fact that they have suddenly decided to follow a particular religion; an informal expression. *This guy got religion about a year back.* PHRASE: V inflects PRAGMATICS

religiosity /rɪlɪdʒiɒsɪti/. If you refer to a person's **religiosity**, you are referring to the fact that they are religious in a way which seems exaggerated and insincere; a formal word. *...their skin-deep religiosity which denounced only the most open scandal.* N-UNCOUNT: usu with supp

religious /rɪlɪdʒəs/ ◆◆◆◆◇

1 You use **religious** to describe things that are connected with religion or with one particular religion. *Religious groups are now able to meet quite openly. ...different religious beliefs.* ADJ: ADJ n ♦ **religiously** *India has always been one of the most religiously diverse countries.* ADV: usu ADV adj/adv, ADV -ed

2 Someone who is **religious** has a strong belief in a god or gods. *They are both very religious and felt it was a gift from God.* ADJ-GRADED

3 See also **religiously.**

religiously /rɪlɪdʒəsli/

1 If you do something **religiously**, you do it very regularly because you feel you have to. *She didn't stick religiously to the program... Do these exercises religiously every day.* ADV-GRADED: ADV with v

2 See also **religious.**

relinquish /rɪlɪŋkwɪʃ/ **relinquishes, relinquishing, relinquished.** If you **relinquish** something such as power or control, you give it up; a formal word. *He does not intend to relinquish power.* ◆◇◇◇◇ VERB =give up V n

reliquary /relɪkwəri, AM -kweri/ **reliquaries.** A **reliquary** is a container in which the relic of a saint is kept. N-COUNT

relish /relɪʃ/ **relishes, relishing, relished** ◆◆◇◇◇

1 If you **relish** something, you get a lot of enjoyment from it. *I relish the challenge of doing jobs that others turn down... He ate quietly, relishing his meal.* ► Also a noun. *The three men ate with relish.* VERB =enjoy V n; N-UNCOUNT

2 If you **relish** the idea, thought, or prospect of something, you are looking forward to it very much. *Jacqueline is not relishing the prospect of another spell in prison... He relished the idea of getting some cash.* VERB =look forward to V n

3 **Relish** is a sauce or a pickle that you eat with other food in order to give it more flavour. N-MASS

relive /riːlɪv/ **relives, reliving, relived.** If you **relive** something that has happened to you in the past, you remember it and imagine that you are experiencing it again. *There is no point in reliving the past... Last night he relived his terrifying ordeal.* ◆◇◇◇◇ VERB V n

reload /riːloʊd/ **reloads, reloading, reloaded.** If someone **reloads** a gun, they load it again by putting in more bullets or explosive. If you **reload** a container, you fill it again. *She reloaded the gun as quickly as she could... He reloaded and nodded to the gamekeeper.* VERB V n V

relocate /riːloʊkeɪt, AM -loʊkeɪt/ **relocates, relocating, relocated.** If people or businesses **relocate** or if someone **relocates** them, they move to a different place. *If the company was to relocate, most employees would move... Ray Bonner first relocated to Africa several years ago... There will be the problem of where to relocate the returning troops... Its headquarters will soon be relocated from Westminster to the Greenwich site.* ◆◇◇◇◇ V-ERG V V n ♦ **relocation** /riːloʊkeɪʃ³n/ **relocations** *The company says the cost of relocation will be negligible. ...the forcible relocation of large numbers of civilians from urban to rural areas.* N-UNCOUNT: also N in pl

reluctant /rɪlʌktənt/. If you are **reluctant** to do something, you are unwilling to do it and hesitate before doing it, or do it slowly and without enthusiasm. *Mr Spero was reluctant to ask for help... The police are very reluctant to get involved in this sort of thing.* ◆◆◆◇◇ ADJ-GRADED: usu v-link ADJ to-inf ≠eager, keen, willing ♦ **reluctantly** *We have reluctantly agreed to let him go.* ADV-GRADED: ADV with v ♦ **reluctance** *Ministers have shown extreme reluctance to explain their position to the media.* N-UNCOUNT: oft N to-inf

rely /rɪlaɪ/ **relies, relying, relied** ◆◆◆◇◇

1 If you **rely** on someone or something, you need them and depend on them in order to live or work properly. *They relied heavily on the advice of their professional advisers... The Association relies on member subscriptions for most of its income.* VERB V on/upon n V on/upon n for n

2 If you can **rely** on someone to work well or to behave as you want them to, you can trust them to do this. *I know I can rely on you to sort it out... The Red Cross are relying on us.* VERB V on/upon n to-inf V on/upon n

REM /ɑːr iː em/. **REM** sleep is a period of sleep that is very deep, during which your eyes and muscles make many small movements. It is the period during which most of your dreams occur. REM is an abbreviation for 'rapid eye movement'. ADJ: ADJ n

remain /rɪmeɪn/ **remains, remaining, remained** ◆◆◆◆◆

1 If someone or something **remains** in a particular state or condition, they stay in that state or condition and do not change. *The three men remained silent... The situation remains tense... The government remained in control... He remained a formidable opponent... It remains possible that bad weather could tear more holes in the tanker's hull.* V-LINK V adj V prep V n it V adj that/to-inf/wh Also it V n that

2 If you **remain** in a place, you stay there and do not move away. *Souness will have to remain in hos-* VERB ≠leave V prep

pital for at least 10 days... From time to time, James remained at home with his family. Also V

3 You can say that something **remains** when it still exists. *Many of the differences in everyday life remain... The wider problem remains... There remains deep mistrust of his government.* VERB V there V n

4 If something **remains** to be done, it has not yet been done and still needs to be done. *Major questions remain to be answered about his work... Huge amounts of weapons remain to be collected.* V-LINK V to-inf-passive

5 The **remains** of something are the parts of it that are left after most of it has been taken away or destroyed. *They were tidying up the remains of their picnic. ...the charred remains of a tank. ...the remains of an ancient mosque.* N-PLURAL: usu *the* N *of* n

6 The **remains** of a person or animal are the parts of their body that are left after they have died, sometimes after they have been dead for a long time. *The unrecognizable remains of a man had been found... More human remains have been unearthed in the north of the country.* N-PLURAL: usu with supp

7 Historical **remains** are things that have been found from an earlier period of history, usually buried in the ground, for example parts of buildings and pieces of pottery. *There are Roman remains all around us.* N-PLURAL: usu supp N

8 You can use **remain** in expressions such as **the fact remains that** or **the question remains whether** to introduce and emphasize something that you want to talk about. *The fact remains that inflation is unacceptably high... The question remains whether he was fully aware of the claims.* V-LINK PRAGMATICS V that V wh

9 See also **remaining**.

10 If you say that it **remains to be seen** whether something will happen, you mean that nobody knows whether it will happen. *It remains to be seen whether her parliamentary colleagues will agree.* PHRASE: usu *it* PHR whether PRAGMATICS

remainder /rɪmeɪndəʳ/ **remainders, remaindering, remaindered** ◆◆◇◇◇

1 **The remainder** of a group are the things or people that still remain after the other things or people have gone or have been dealt with. *He gulped down the remainder of his coffee... I spent the remainder of the day feeling terrible.* ► Also a pronoun. *Only 5.9 per cent of the area is now covered in trees. Most of the remainder is farmland... Of the 59 committee members, 40 were against legalisation, 13 were in favour and the remainder were undecided.* QUANT: QUANT *of* def-n =rest PRON

2 In arithmetic, **the remainder** is the amount that remains when one amount cannot be exactly divided by another. For example, if you divide 22 by 7, the answer is 3 and the remainder is 1. N-SING: *the* N

3 If a book **is remaindered**, it is sold at a reduced price because it has not been selling very well and the publishers have decided not to produce any more copies of it. *It failed to sell and was soon remaindered.* VB: usu passive *be* V-ed

4 A **remainder** is a book that has been remaindered. N-COUNT

remaining /rɪmeɪnɪŋ/ ◆◆◆◇◇

1 The **remaining** things or people out of a group are the things or people that still exist, are still present, or have not yet been dealt with. *The three parties will meet next month to work out remaining differences... The United States has withdrawn the remaining staff from its embassy... Stir in the remaining ingredients.* ADJ: ADJ n

2 See also **remain**.

remake, remakes, remaking, remade. The noun is pronounced /riːmeɪk/. The verb is pronounced /riːmeɪk/. ◆◇◇◇◇

1 A **remake** is a film that has the same story, and often the same title, as a film that was made earlier. *...a 1952 remake of the thirties musical 'Roberta'.* N-COUNT

2 If a film **is remade**, a new film is made that has the same story, and often the same title, as a film that was made earlier. *'A Face In The Crowd' is tipped to be remade with Richard Gere.* VB: usu passive *be* V-ed

3 If you have something **remade**, you ask someone to make it again, especially in a way that is better than before. *He had paid hundreds of pounds to have all the window frames in the room remade so that they would fit perfectly.* VERB *have* n V-ed Also V n

remand /rɪmɑːnd, -mænd/ **remands, remanding, remanded** ◆◇◇◇◇

1 If a person who is accused of a crime **is remanded** in custody or on bail, they are told to return to the court at a later date, when their trial will take place. *Carter was remanded in custody for seven days... Both were remanded on bail by Wrexham magistrates until March 24.* VB: usu passive *be* V-ed prep

2 **Remand** is used to refer to the process of remanding someone in custody or on bail, or to the period of time until their trial begins. *The remand hearing is often over in three minutes... This will mean more remand prisoners being held in police cells... She has already served a year on remand.* N-UNCOUNT: also N in pl, oft N n, *on* N

remand centre, remand centres. In Britain, a **remand centre** is an institution where people who are accused of a crime are sent until their trial begins or until a decision about their punishment has been made. N-COUNT

remark /rɪmɑːʳk/ **remarks, remarking, remarked** ◆◆◆◇◇

1 If you **remark** that something is the case, you say that it is the case. *I remarked that I would go shopping that afternoon... 'Some people have more money than sense,' Winston had remarked... On several occasions she had remarked on the boy's improvement... Everyone has remarked on what a lovely lady she is.* VERB V that V with quote V *on/upon* n/wh

2 If you make a **remark** about something, you say something about it. *Mr Samaras made his remarks about human rights during the summit... Geoff Cooke's recent remark that no one is indispensable will certainly not have escaped him.* N-COUNT: with supp =comment

remarkable /rɪmɑːʳkəbᵊl/. Someone or something that is **remarkable** is unusual or exceptional in some way that causes people to notice them and be surprised or impressed. *He was a remarkable man... It was a remarkable achievement... It is quite remarkable that doctors have been so wrong about this.* ♦ **remarkably** /rɪmɑːʳkəbli/ *It's been a remarkably successful year for Labour... Remarkably, the system continued until as recently as 1817.* ◆◆◆◇◇ ADJ-GRADED ADV-GRADED: usu ADV adj/adv, also ADV with cl

remarriage /riːmærɪdʒ/ **remarriages. Remarriage** is the act of remarrying. *The question of divorce and remarriage in church remains highly contentious.* N-VAR

remarry /riːmæri/ **remarries, remarrying, remarried.** If someone **remarries**, they marry again after they have obtained a divorce from their previous husband or wife, or after their previous husband or wife has died. *Her mother had never remarried.* ◆◇◇◇◇ VERB V Also V n

remaster /riːmɑːstəʳ, -mæstəʳ/ **remasters, remastering, remastered.** If a film or musical recording **is remastered**, a new recording is made of the old version, using modern technology to improve the quality. *A special remastered version of Casablanca is being released on video.* VERB V-ed Also V n

rematch /riːmætʃ/ **rematches.** In sport, a **rematch** is a second match that is played between two people or teams, either because their first match was a draw or because there was a dispute about some aspect of it. *Duff said he would be demanding a rematch.* N-COUNT

remedial /rɪmiːdiəl/ ◆◇◇◇◇

1 **Remedial** education is intended to improve a person's ability to read, write, or do maths. *...children who required special remedial education... His remedial teacher sees signs of progress in his reading and writing.* ADJ: usu ADJ n

2 **Remedial** activities are intended to improve a person's health when they are ill; a formal use. *He is already walking normally and doing remedial exercises.* ADJ: usu ADJ n

3 **Remedial** action is intended to correct something that has been done wrong or that has not been successful; a formal use. *Some authorities are now having to take remedial action.* ADJ: usu ADJ n

remedy /remədi/ **remedies, remedying, remedied** ◆◆◇◇◇

1 A **remedy** is a successful way of dealing with a problem. *The remedy lies in the hands of the government. ...a remedy for economic ills.* N-COUNT

2 A **remedy** is something that is intended to cure you when you are ill or in pain. *There are many different kinds of natural remedies to help overcome winter infections.* N-COUNT

3 If you **remedy** something that is wrong or harmful, you correct it or improve it. *A great deal has been done internally to remedy the situation.* VERB V n

remember /rɪmembəʳ/ **remembers, remembering, remembered** ◆◆◆◆◆

1 If you **remember** people or events from the past, your still have an idea of them in your mind and you are able to think about them. *You wouldn't remember me. I was in another group... I certainly don't remember talking to you at all... I remember her being a dominant figure... I remembered that we had drunk the last of the coffee the week before... I can remember where and when I bought each one... I used to do that when you were a little girl, remember?* VERB V n/-ing V n -ing V that V wh V

2 If you **remember** that something is the case, you become aware of it again after a time when you did not think about it. *She remembered that she was going to the social club that evening... Then I remembered the cheque, which cheered me up.* VERB V that V n

3 If you cannot **remember** something, you are not able to bring it back into your mind when you make an effort to do so. *If you can't remember your number, write it in code in a diary... I couldn't remember ever having felt so safe and secure... I don't remember you asking me about that... I can't remember what I said... Don't tell me you can't remember.* VB: usu with brd-neg V n/-ing V n -ing V wh V

4 If you **remember** to do something, you do it when you intend to. *I did remember to take the present... Please remember to enclose a stamped addressed envelope when writing.* VERB ≠forget V to-inf

5 You tell someone to **remember** that something is the case when you want to emphasize its importance. It may be something that they already know about or a new piece of information. *It is important to remember that each person reacts differently... It is worth remembering that children tend to copy their parents in this respect... It should be remembered that this loss of control can never be regained.* VERB PRAGMATICS V that *it* modal *be* V-ed that

6 If you say that someone will **be remembered** for something that they have done, you mean that people will think of this whenever they think about the person. *At his grammar school he is remembered for being bad at games... He will always be remembered as one of the great Chancellors of the Exchequer.* VB: usu passive *be* V-ed *for* n/-ing *be* V-ed *as* n

7 If you ask someone to **remember** you to a person who you have not seen for a long time, you are asking them to pass your greetings on to that person. *'Remember me to Lyle, won't you?' I said... She asked to be remembered to you.* VB: no cont, usu imper V n *to* n

8 If you make a celebration an occasion to **remember**, you make it very enjoyable for all the people involved. *We'll give everyone a night to remember... I'll make it a birthday to remember.* VB: only to-inf V

remembrance /rɪmembrəns/ **remembrances** ◆◇◇◇◇

1 If you do something in **remembrance** of a dead person, you do it as a way of showing that you want to remember them and that you respect them; a formal use. *They wore black in remembrance of those who had died.* N-UNCOUNT

2 A **remembrance** is a memory that you have of someone or something; a formal use. *He had clung to the remembrance of things past. ...happier remembrances of family holidays.* N-VAR

Remembrance Day. In Britain, **Remembrance Day** or **Remembrance Sunday** is the Sunday nearest to the 11th of November, when people honour the memory of those who died in the two world wars. *During their stay, they will attend a Remembrance Day service at a cemetery for British prisoners of war.* N-UNCOUNT: oft N n

remind /rɪmaɪnd/ **reminds, reminding, reminded** ◆◆◆◇◇

1 If someone **reminds** you of a fact or event that you already know about, they say something which makes you think about it. *He reminded Mrs Thatcher of an interview she had given five years ago... I had to remind myself that being confident is not the same as being perfect!* VERB V n *of* n V n that

2 In spoken English, you use **remind** in expressions such as **Let me remind you that** and **May I remind you that** to introduce a piece of information that you want to emphasize. It may be something that the hearer already knows about or a new piece of information. Sometimes these expressions can sound unfriendly. *'Let me remind you,' said Marianne, 'that Manchester is also my home town.'... May I remind you that the care of your health is a religious duty... Need I remind you who the enemy is?* VERB PRAGMATICS V n that V n wh

3 If someone **reminds** you to do something, they say something which makes you remember to do it. *Can you remind me to buy a bottle of Martini?... The note was to remind him about something he had to explain to one of his students.* VERB V n to-inf V n *about* n

4 If you say that someone or something **reminds** you **of** another person or thing, you mean that they are similar to the other person or thing and that they make you think about them. *She reminds me of the wife of the pilot who used to work for you... This reminds me of Christmas parties.* VERB V n *of* n

reminder /rɪmaɪndəʳ/ **reminders** ◆◆◇◇◇

1 Something that serves as a **reminder** of another thing makes you think about the other thing; used in written English. *The British are about to be given a sharp reminder of what fighting abroad really means... Violence has broken out in the capital, a stark reminder that the religious tensions are refusing to go away.* N-COUNT: usu sing, oft N *of* n/wh, N that

2 A **reminder** is a letter or note that is sent to tell you that you have not done something such as pay a bill or return library books; used mainly in British English. *...the final reminder for the gas bill.* N-COUNT

reminisce /remɪnɪs/ **reminisces, reminiscing, reminisced.** If you **reminisce** about something from your past, you write or talk about it, often with pleasure; a formal word. *Ray and I ate our meal and reminisced about the trip... I don't like reminiscing because it makes me feel old.* ◆◇◇◇◇ VERB V *about* V Also V with quote

reminiscence /remɪnɪsəns/ **reminiscences.** Someone's **reminiscences** are things that they remember from the past, and which they talk or write about. **Reminiscence** is the process of remembering these things and talking or writing about them. This is a formal word. *Here I am boring you with my reminiscences. ...reminiscences of her Jewish childhood... A faint smile of reminiscence appeared on her face..* ◆◇◇◇◇ N-VAR: oft poss N, N *of* n =memory

reminiscent /remɪnɪsənt/ ◆◆◇◇◇

1 If you say that one thing is **reminiscent of** another, you mean that it reminds you of it; a formal use. *The decor was reminiscent of a municipal arts-and-leisure centre... She bowed her head in a gesture somehow reminiscent of royalty.* ADJ-GRADED: v-link ADJ *of* n

2 A **reminiscent** look or smile is a look or smile which shows that you are remembering something from the past, usually with pleasure; a formal use. *A slow, reminiscent smile spread over her face.* ADJ-GRADED: usu ADJ n

♦ **reminiscently** *Both of them smiled at the picture reminiscently.* ADV-GRADED: ADV after v

remiss /rɪmɪs/. If someone is **remiss**, they are careless about doing things which ought to be done; a formal word. *I would be remiss if I did not do something about it.* ADJ-GRADED: v-link ADJ, oft ADJ *in* n/-ing =negligent

remission /rɪmɪʃən/ **remissions** ◆◇◇◇◇

1 If someone who has had a serious disease such as cancer is in **remission** or if the disease is in **remission**, the disease has been controlled so that they are not as ill as they were. *Brain scans have confirmed that the disease is in remission... After six years of remission, cancer reappeared.* N-VAR

2 If someone in prison gets **remission**, their prison sentence is reduced, usually because they have N-UNCOUNT

behaved well; used in British English. *With remission for good behaviour, she could be freed in a year.*

remit, remits, remitting, remitted. The noun is pronounced /riːmɪt/. The verb is pronounced /rɪmɪt/. ◆◇◇◇◇

1 Someone's **remit** is the area of activity which they are expected to deal with, or which they have authority to deal with; used in British English. *That issue is not within the remit of the working group... The centre has a remit to advise Asian businesses and entrepreneurs.* N-COUNT: usu sing, oft poss N, N *of* n =brief

2 If you **remit** money to someone, you send it to them; a formal use. *Many immigrants regularly remit money to their families.* VERB =send V n *to* n

3 In an appeal court, if a case **is remitted** to the court where it was originally dealt with, it is sent back to be dealt with there; a legal use. *The matter was remitted to the justices for a rehearing.* VB: usu passive *be* V-ed

remittance /rɪmɪtəns/ **remittances.** A **remittance** is a sum of money that you send to someone; a formal word. *Please enclose your remittance, making cheques payable to Thames Valley Technology.* ◆◇◇◇◇ N-VAR =payment

remix, remixes, remixing, remixed. The noun is pronounced /riːmɪks/. The veb is pronounced /riːmɪks/. ◆◇◇◇◇

1 A **remix** is a new version of a piece of music which has been created by putting together the individual instrumental and vocal parts in a different way. *Their new album features remixes of some of their previous hits.* N-COUNT

2 If a record producer **remixes** a piece of music, he or she makes a new version of it by putting together the individual instrumental and vocal parts in a different way. *The band are remixing some tracks... Both tracks are remixed versions of tracks from her forthcoming album.* VERB V n V-ed

remnant /remnənt/ **remnants** ◆◇◇◇◇

1 The **remnants** of something are small parts of it that are left over when the main part has disappeared or been destroyed. *After twenty-four hours of fighting, the remnants of the force were fleeing... Beneath the present church were remnants of Roman flooring... Obedience by women towards men is a remnant of religious teaching.* N-COUNT: usu N *of* n

2 A **remnant** is a small piece of cloth that is left over when most of the cloth has been sold. Shops usually sell remnants cheaply. N-COUNT

remodel /riːmɒdᵊl/ **remodels, remodelling, remodelled;** spelled **remodeling, remodeled** in American English. To **remodel** something such as a building or a room is to give it a different form or shape. *Workmen were hired to remodel and enlarge the farm buildings... The house was remodelled by its present owner.* ♦ **remodelling** *...the remodelling of Barcelona's airport.* VERB V n N-UNCOUNT

remonstrate /remənstreɪt, AM rɪmɒnstreɪt/ **remonstrates, remonstrating, remonstrated.** If you **remonstrate** with someone, you protest to them about something you do not approve of or agree with, and you try to get it changed or stopped; a formal word. *He remonstrated with the referee... I jumped in the car and went to remonstrate.* ♦ **remonstration** /remənstreɪʃᵊn/ **remonstrations** *There had been remonstrations from the Town Clerk.* VERB V *with* n V Also V prep N-VAR

remorse /rɪmɔːʳs/. **Remorse** is a strong feeling of guilt and regret about something wrong that you have done. *He was full of remorse and asked Beatrice what he could do to make amends... He has shown no remorse for his actions.* ◆◇◇◇◇ N-UNCOUNT =regret

remorseful /rɪmɔːʳsfʊl/. If you are **remorseful**, you feel very guilty and sorry about something wrong that you have done. *He was genuinely remorseful.* ♦ **remorsefully** *'My poor wife!' he said, remorsefully.* ADJ-GRADED ADV-GRADED: ADV with v

remorseless /rɪmɔːʳsləs/

1 If you describe something, especially something unpleasant, as **remorseless**, you mean that it continues in a persistent way and cannot be stopped. *...the remorseless pressure of recession and financial constraint. ...General Sherman's remorseless progress through Georgia.* ♦ **remorselessly** *There have been record bankruptcies and remorselessly rising unemployment.* ADJ-GRADED =relentless ADV-GRADED: usu ADV with v

2 Someone who is **remorseless** is prepared to be cruel to other people and feels no pity for them. *...the capacity for quick, remorseless violence. ...remorseless thieves.* ♦ **remorselessly** *They remorselessly beat up anyone they suspected of supporting the opposition.* ADJ-GRADED =merciless ADV-GRADED: ADV with v

remote /rɪmoʊt/ **remoter, remotest** ◆◆◆◇◇

1 **Remote** areas are far away from cities and places where most people live, and are therefore difficult to get to. *Landslides have cut off many villages in remote areas. ...a remote farm in the Yorkshire dales.* ♦ **remoteness** *...the remoteness of the island.* ADJ-GRADED: usu ADJ n N-UNCOUNT

2 The **remote** past or **remote** future is a time that is many years distant from the present. *Slabs of rock had slipped sideways in the remote past, and formed this hole.* ADJ-GRADED: usu ADJ n =distant

3 If something is **remote** from a particular subject or area of experience, it is not relevant to it because it is very different. *This government depends on the wishes of a few who are remote from the people... Teenagers are forced to study subjects that seem remote from their daily lives.* ♦ **remoteness** *...the remoteness of the officers from their men.* ADJ-GRADED: usu v-link ADJ *from* n N-UNCOUNT

4 If you say that there is a **remote** possibility or chance that something will happen, you are emphasizing that there is only a very small chance that it will happen. *I use a sunscreen whenever there is even a remote possibility that I will be in the sun... The chances of his surviving are pretty remote.* ADJ-GRADED PRAGMATICS

5 If you describe someone as **remote**, you mean that they behave as if they do not want to be friendly or closely involved with other people. *She looked so beautiful, and at the same time so remote.* ♦ **remoteness** *His remoteness was resented.* ADJ-GRADED N-UNCOUNT

remote control, remote controls ◆◇◇◇◇

1 **Remote control** is a system of controlling a machine or a vehicle from a distance by using radio or electronic signals. *The bomb was detonated by remote control.* N-UNCOUNT

2 The **remote control** for a television or video recorder is the device that you use to control the machine from a distance, by pressing the buttons on it. N-COUNT

remote-controlled. A **remote-controlled** machine or device is controlled from a distance by the use of radio or electronic signals. *Three soldiers were killed by a remote-controlled bomb.* ADJ: usu ADJ n

remotely /rɪmoʊtli/ ◆◇◇◇◇

1 You use **remotely** with a negative statement to emphasize the statement. *We had never seen anything remotely like it before... Nobody was remotely interested. ...a reluctance to say or do anything that might remotely provoke or offend.* ADV: with brd-neg, usu ADV group, also ADV before v PRAGMATICS

2 If someone or something is **remotely** placed or situated, they are a long way from other people or places. *...the remotely situated, five bedroom house.* ADV-GRADED: ADV -ed

remote sensing. **Remote sensing** is the gathering of information about something by observing it from space or from the air. *It can translate data from maps or remote sensing instruments into images.* N-UNCOUNT: oft N n

remould, remoulds, remoulding, remoulded; spelled **remold** in American English. The noun is pronounced /riːmoʊld/. The verb is pronounced /riːmoʊld/.

1 In British English, a **remould** is an old tyre which has been given a new surface and can be used again. The usual American term is **retread.** N-COUNT =retread

2 To **remould** something such as an idea or an economy is to change it so it has a new structure or is based on new principles. *...the crusade by Chairman Mao to remould the world view of the people.* VERB V n

remount /riːmaʊnt/ **remounts, remounting, remounted.** When you **remount** a bicycle or horse, you get back on it after you have got off it or fallen off it. *He was told to remount his horse and to accompany the officers back to Lexington...* VERB V n V

The pony scrabbled up and waited for the rider, who remounted and carried on.

removable /rɪmuːvəbəl/. A **removable** part of something is a part that can easily be moved from its place or position. *...a cake tin with a removable base.* ADJ: usu ADJ n

removal /rɪmuːvəl/ **removals** ◆◆◇◇◇

1 The **removal** of something is the act of removing it. *What they expected to be the removal of a small lump turned out to be major surgery... Parliament had decided that his removal from power was illegal. ...popular methods of hair removal.* N-UNCOUNT: usu with supp

2 **Removal** is the process of transporting furniture from one building to another; used mainly in British English. *Home removals are best done in cool weather... They were both in the furniture removal business. ...a removal van.* N-COUNT: usu with supp, oft N n

remove /rɪmuːv/ **removes, removing, removed** ◆◆◆◆◇

1 If you **remove** something from a place, you take it away; used mainly in written English. *As soon as the cake is done, remove it from the oven... At least three bullets were removed from his wounds... Often, the simplest answer is just to remove yourself from the situation... He went to the refrigerator and removed a bottle of wine.* VERB V n *from* n V n

2 If you **remove** clothing, you take it off; used mainly in written English. *He removed his jacket.* VERB V n

3 If you **remove** a stain from something, you make the stain disappear by treating it with a chemical or by washing it. *This treatment removes the most stubborn stains... Try using lemon juice to remove tobacco stains from your fingers.* VERB V n V n *from* n

4 If people **remove** someone from power or from something such as a committee, they stop them being in power or being a member of the committee. *The student senate voted to remove Fuller from office... The president could only be removed from power once free elections were organised... All senior officers involved in the coup will have to be removed.* VERB V n *from* n be V-ed

5 If you **remove** an obstacle, a restriction, or a problem, you get rid of it. *The agreement removes the last serious obstacle to the signing of the arms treaty... Most of her fears had been removed.* VERB V n

6 If you do or experience something **at** one **remove**, you do not do it or experience it yourself, but someone else does it or experiences it for you. *She enjoyed his company and the excitement of feeling herself linked at one remove to London society... She can know the world only at several removes.* PHRASE: N inflects, usu PHR after v

removed /rɪmuːvd/ ◆◇◇◇◇

1 If you say that an idea or situation is far **removed from** something, you mean that it is very different from it. *He found it hard to concentrate on conversation so far removed from his present preoccupations... The country had witnessed scenes of tumult not far removed from civil war... His style could scarcely be further removed from that of his famous predecessor.* ADJ: v-link adv ADJ *from* n

2 If someone is your cousin once **removed**, they are your cousin's child or your parent's cousin. ADJ: n ADJ

remover /rɪmuːvəʳ/ **removers**. **Remover** is a substance that you use for removing an unwanted stain, mark, or coating from a surface. *We got some paint remover and scrubbed it off.* N-MASS: usu supp N

remunerate /rɪmjuːnəreɪt/ **remunerates, remunerating, remunerated.** If you **are remunerated** for work that you do, you are paid for it; a formal word. *You will be remunerated and so will your staff. ...an adequately remunerated job.* VB: usu passive =pay be V-ed V-ed

remuneration /rɪmjuːnəreɪʃən/ **remunerations.** Someone's **remuneration** is the amount of money that they are paid for the work that they do; a formal word. *...the continuing marked increase in the remuneration of the company's directors... $31,000 is a generous remuneration.* N-VAR

remunerative /rɪmjuːnərətɪv/. **Remunerative** work is work that you are paid for; a formal word. *A doctor advised her to seek remunerative employment.* ADJ-GRADED: usu ADJ n =paid

renaissance /rɪneɪsɒns, AM renɪsɑːns/ ◆◆◇◇◇

1 **The Renaissance** was the period in Europe, especially Italy, in the 14th, 15th, and 16th centuries, when there was a great revival of interest in art, literature, science, and learning. *...the Renaissance masterpieces in London's galleries... Science took a new and different turn in the Renaissance.* N-PROPER: *the* N, oft N n

2 If something experiences a **renaissance**, it becomes popular or successful again after a time when people were not interested in it. *Popular art is experiencing a renaissance... They gathered to protest against the renaissance of the extreme right.* N-SING =revival

renal /riːnəl/. **Renal** describes things that concern or are related to the kidneys; a medical term. *He collapsed from acute renal failure... Blood enters the kidneys via the renal artery.* ADJ: ADJ n

rename /riːneɪm/ **renames, renaming, renamed.** If you **rename** something, you change its name to a new name. *The Prime Minister is being pressed to rename child benefit 'child allowance'... The party leader said the street should be renamed Freedom Avenue... The former Communist party, now renamed Socialists, have won nearly half the vote.* ◆◇◇◇◇ VERB V n n V-ed

rend /rend/ **rends, rending, rent**

1 If something or someone **rends** something, they tear it; a literary use. *...pain that rends the heart. ...a twisted urge to rend and tear.* VERB V n V

2 If a loud sound **rends** the air, it is heard suddenly and violently; a literary use. *He bellows, rends the air with anguish.* VERB V n

3 See also **heart-rending**.

render /rendəʳ/ **renders, rendering, rendered** ◆◆◇◇◇

1 You can use **render** with an adjective that describes a particular state to say that someone or something is changed into that state. For example, if someone or something makes a thing harmless, you can say that they **render** it harmless. *It contained so many errors as to render it worthless. ...barrel-makers whose trade was rendered obsolete by the introduction of stainless steel wine vats.* VERB =make V n adj

2 If you **render** someone help or assistance, you help them; a formal use. *He had a chance to render some service to his country... Any assistance you can render him will be appreciated... The money was in fact payment by the CIA for services rendered.* VERB =give V n *to* n V n n V-ed

3 When a jury or authority **renders** a verdict, decision, or response, they announce it; a formal use. *The Board had been slow to render its verdict.* VERB =announce V n

4 To **render** something in a particular language or in a particular way means to translate it into that language or in that way; a formal use. *...'Zensho shimasu,' which the translator rendered literally as, 'I will do my best.'... All the signs and announcements were rendered in English and Spanish.* VERB =translate V n *as/in/into* n

5 To **render** a wall means to cover it with a layer of plaster or cement, in order to protect it; used mainly in British English. VERB

rendering /rendərɪŋ/ **renderings** ◆◇◇◇◇

1 A **rendering** of a play, poem, or piece of music is a performance of it. *...a rendering of Verdi's Requiem by the BBC Symphony Orchestra.* N-COUNT: usu N *of* n =performance

2 A **rendering** of an expression or piece of writing or speech is a translation of it. *This phrase may well have been a rendering of a popular Arabic expression.* N-COUNT: usu N *of* n =translation

3 The **rendering** on a wall is a layer of plaster or cement which covers and protects it; used mainly in British English. The usual American word is **stucco**. N-COUNT

rendezvous /rɒndeɪvuː/ **rendezvousing, rendezvoused.** The form **rendezvous** is pronounced /rɒndeɪvuːz/ when it is the plural of the noun or the third person singular of the verb. ◆◇◇◇◇

1 A **rendezvous** is a meeting, often a secret one, that you have arranged with someone for a particular time and place. *I had almost decided to keep my rendezvous with Tony.* N-COUNT

2 A **rendezvous** is the place where you have arranged to meet someone, often secretly. *Their rendezvous would be the Penta Hotel at Heathrow Airport.* N-COUNT

3 If you **rendezvous** with someone or if the two of you **rendezvous**, you meet them at a time and place that you have arranged. *The plan was to rendezvous with him on Sunday afternoon... She wondered where they were going to rendezvous afterwards.* V-RECIP =meet V with n pl-n V

rendition /rendɪʃən/ **renditions.** A **rendition** of a play, poem, or piece of music is a performance of it. *The musicians burst into a rousing rendition of 'Paddy Casey's Reel'.* ◆◇◇◇◇ N-COUNT: usu N of n =performance

renegade /renɪgeɪd/ **renegades** ◆◇◇◇◇

1 A **renegade** is a person who abandons the religious, political, or philosophical beliefs that he or she used to have, and accepts opposing or different beliefs. N-COUNT

2 **Renegade** is used to describe a member of a group or profession who does or believes things which are completely against the normal behaviour or beliefs of that group or profession. *Three men were shot dead by a renegade policeman.* ADJ: ADJ n

renege /rɪniːg, AM -nɪg/ **reneges, reneging, reneged.** If someone **reneges** on a promise or an agreement, they do not do what they have promised or agreed to do. *He reneged on a promise to leave his wife.* ◆◇◇◇◇ VERB V on n Also V

renew /rɪnjuː, AM -nuː/ **renews, renewing, renewed** ◆◆◆◇◇

1 If you **renew** an activity, you begin it again. *He renewed his attack on government policy towards Europe... He believes the peace talks will be renewed soon... Reports from Lebanon say there was renewed fighting yesterday.* VERB =resume V n V-ed

2 If you **renew** a relationship with someone, you start it again after you have not seen them or have not been friendly with them for some time. *When the two men met again after the war they renewed their friendship... In December 1989 Syria renewed diplomatic relations with Egypt.* V-RECIP =resume pl-n V n V n with n

3 When you **renew** something such as a licence or a contract, you extend the period of time for which it is valid. *Larry's landlord threatened not to renew his lease... The job was for a fixed term and the contract is not being renewed.* VERB V n

4 You can say that something **is renewed** when it grows again or is replaced after it has been destroyed or lost. *Nature's repair process is slow and steady, with cells being constantly renewed. ...a renewed interest in public transport systems.* VB: usu passive be V-ed V-ed

renewable /rɪnjuːəbəl, AM -nuː-/ ◆◇◇◇◇

1 **Renewable** resources are ones such as wind, water, and sunlight, which are constantly replacing themselves and therefore do not become used up. *renewable energy sources.* ADJ-GRADED: usu ADJ n

2 If a contract or agreement is **renewable**, it can be extended when it reaches the end of a fixed period of time. *A formal contract is signed which is renewable annually.* ADJ

renewal /rɪnjuːəl, -nuː-/ **renewals** ◆◆◇◇◇

1 If there is a **renewal** of an activity or a situation, it starts again. *They will discuss the possible renewal of diplomatic relations... Is he really considering a renewal of hostilities at this stage?* N-UNCOUNT: usu N of n

2 The **renewal** of a document such as a licence or a contract is an official extension of the time for which it remains valid. *His contract came up for renewal... The premium should be received in this office within fourteen days of the renewal date.* N-VAR

3 **Renewal** of something lost, dead, or destroyed is the process of it growing again or being replaced. *...a political lobbyist concentrating on urban renewal and regeneration... Now it is spring, a time of renewal.* N-UNCOUNT: oft supp N

renounce /rɪnaʊns/ **renounces, renouncing, renounced** ◆◇◇◇◇

1 If you **renounce** a belief or a way of behaving, you decide and declare publicly that you no longer have that belief or will no longer behave in that way. *After a period of imprisonment she renounced terrorism... Britain's small Communist Party has voted to renounce Marxism-Leninism.* VERB V n

2 If you **renounce** an official post, rank, or title, you formally give it up. *He renounced his claim to the French throne.* VERB =give up V n

renovate /renəveɪt/ **renovates, renovating, renovated.** If someone **renovates** an old building, they repair and improve it and get it back into good condition. *The couple spent thousands renovating the house... She lives in a large, renovated farmhouse.* ♦ **renovation** /renəveɪʃən/ **renovations** *...a property which will need extensive renovation.* ◆◇◇◇◇ VERB V n V-ed N-VAR

renown /rɪnaʊn/. A person of **renown** is well known, usually because they do or have done something good. *She used to be a singer of some renown... Mailly's work achieved little renown.* N-UNCOUNT: oft n of N

renowned /rɪnaʊnd/. A person or place that is **renowned** for something, usually something good, is well known because of it. *The area is renowned for its Romanesque churches... James was renowned as a forward thinker. ...Sir William Crookes, the renowned chemist.* ◆◆◇◇◇ ADJ-GRADED: oft ADJ for/as n

rent /rent/ **rents, renting, rented** ◆◆◆◇◇

1 If you **rent** something, you regularly pay its owner a sum of money in order to be able to have it and use it yourself. *She rents a house with three other girls... He left his hotel in a rented car.* VERB V n V-ed

2 If you **rent** something to someone, you let them have it and use it in exchange for a sum of money which they pay you regularly. *She rented rooms to university students.* ► **Rent out** means the same as **rent**. *Last summer Brian Williams rented out his house and went camping... He repaired the boat, and rented it out for $150.* VERB V n to n PHRASAL VERB V P n (not pron) V n P

3 **Rent** is the amount of money that you pay regularly to use a house, flat, or piece of land. *She worked to pay the rent while I went to college... Traders in Marble Arch are facing huge rent increases.* N-VAR

4 **Rent** is the past tense and past participle of **rend**.

• See also **ground rent, peppercorn rent.**

rent out. See **rent** 2. PHRASAL VERB

rental /rentəl/ **rentals** ◆◆◇◇◇

1 The **rental** of something such as a car or television is the fact of paying an amount of money in order to have and use it. *We can organise car rental from Chicago O'Hare Airport. ...Scotland's largest video rental company.* N-UNCOUNT: also N in pl, with supp

2 The **rental** is the amount of money that you have to pay to use something such as a television, telephone, car, or property; used mainly in British English. *It has been let at an annual rental of £393,000.* N-COUNT

3 You use **rental** to describe things that are connected with the renting out of goods, properties, and services. *A friend drove her to Oxford, where she picked up a rental car... Repairs and improvements can lead to higher rental rates.* ADJ: ADJ n

rent boy, rent boys. A **rent boy** is a boy or young man who has sex with men for money. N-COUNT

rent-free. If you have a **rent-free** house or office, you do not have to pay anything to use it. *He was given a new rent-free apartment.* ► Also an adverb. *They told James he could no longer live rent-free.* ADJ: usu ADJ n ADV: ADV after v

renunciation /rɪnʌnsieɪʃən/ **renunciations**

1 The **renunciation** of a belief or a way of behaving is the public declaration that you reject it and have decided to stop having that belief or behaving in that way. *The talks were dependent on a renunciation of terrorism.* N-UNCOUNT: also N in pl

2 The **renunciation** of a claim, title, or privilege is the act of officially giving it up. *...the renunciation of territory in the Mediterranean.* N-UNCOUNT

3 **Renunciation** is the act of denying yourself certain pleasures for moral or religious reasons. *Gandhi exemplified the virtues of renunciation, asceticism and restraint.* N-UNCOUNT =self-denial

reopen /riəʊpən/ **reopens, reopening, reopened** 

1 If you **reopen** a public building such as a factory, airport, or school, or if it **reopens**, it opens and starts working again after it has been closed for some time. *Iran reopened its embassy in London...* V-ERG V n

It plans to reopen the shipyard tomorrow... The Theatre Royal, Norwich, will reopen in November. V

2 If police or the courts **reopen** a legal case, they investigate it again because it has never been solved or because there was something wrong in the way it was investigated before. *There was a call today to reopen the investigation into the bombing.* VERB Vn

3 If people or countries **reopen** talks or negotiations or if talks or negotiations **reopen**, the talks or negotiations begin again after they have stopped for some time. *US and Soviet negotiators reopened talks in Geneva. ...the possibility of reopening negotiations with the government... Middle East peace talks reopen in Washington on Wednesday.* V-RECIP-ERG =resume pl-n V n, V n *with* n, V

4 If people or countries **reopen** ties or relations, they start being friendly again after a time when they did not have any friendly links. *He reopened ties with Moscow earlier this year... Britain and Argentina reopened diplomatic relations.* V-RECIP V n *with* n, pl-n V n

5 If something **reopens** a question or debate, it makes the question or debate relevant again and causes people to start discussing it again. *His results are likely to reopen the debate on race and education.* VERB Vn

6 If a country **reopens** a border or route or if the border or route **reopens**, it becomes possible to cross or travel along it again. *Jordan plans to reopen its border with Iraq... The important Peking Shanghai route has reopened.* V-ERG Vn, V

reorganize /riɔːʳgənaɪz/ **reorganizes, reorganizing, reorganized;** also spelled **reorganise** in British English. To **reorganize** something means to change the way in which it is organized, arranged, or done. *It is the mother who is expected to reorganize her busy schedule... Four thousand troops have been reorganized into a fighting force... They'll have to reorganise and that might cause them problems. ...the newly reorganized local health service.* ◆◆◇◇◇ V-ERG Vn, V n *into* n, V, V-ed ♦ **reorganization** /riɔːʳgənaɪzeɪʃən/ **reorganizations** *...the reorganization of the legal system... David was worried about major reorganisations at work.* N-VAR

rep /rep/ **reps** ◆◇◇◇◇

1 A **rep** is a person whose job is to sell a company's products or services, especially by travelling round and visiting other companies. **Rep** is short for representative. *I'd been working as a sales rep for a photographic company.* N-COUNT: oft supp N

2 A **rep** is a person who acts as a representative for a group of people, usually a group of colleagues. *Contact the health and safety rep at your union.* N-COUNT: usu supp N

3 In the theatre, **rep** is the same as **repertory**. *A play is tested in rep before ever hitting a West End stage.* N-UNCOUNT

Rep. In the United States, **Rep.** is a written abbreviation for **Representative**. *...Rep. Barbara Boxer.* ◆◆◇◇◇

repaid /rɪpeɪd/. **Repaid** is the past tense and past participle of **repay**.

repair /rɪpeəʳ/ **repairs, repairing, repaired** ◆◆◆◇◇

1 If you **repair** something that has been damaged or is not working properly, you mend it. *Goldsmith has repaired the roof to ensure the house is windproof... The cost of repairing earthquake damage could be more than seven-thousand-million dollars... A woman drove her car to the garage to have it repaired.* VERB Vn, *have* n V-ed ♦ **repairer, repairers** *...services provided by builders, plumbers and TV repairers.* N-COUNT: usu n N =repairman

2 If you **repair** a relationship or someone's reputation after it has been damaged, you do something to improve it. *The government continued to try to repair the damage caused by the minister's interview... The first and most important thing was to repair my relationship with my father.* VERB Vn

3 A **repair** is something that you do to mend a machine, building, piece of clothing, or other thing that has been damaged or is not working properly. *Many women know how to carry out repairs on their cars... Many of the buildings are in need of repair... There is no doubt now that her marriage is beyond repair.* N-VAR

4 If someone **repairs to** a particular place, they go there; a formal use. *We then repaired to the pavilion for lunch.* VERB =go V *to* n

5 If something such as a building is **in good repair**, it is in good condition. If it is **in bad repair**, it is in bad condition. *The monks of Ettal keep the abbey in good repair... The road was in bad repair in parts.* PHRASE

repairman /rɪpeəʳmæn/ **repairmen.** A **repairman** is a man who mends broken machines such as televisions and telephones. *...a cheerful telephone repairman.* N-COUNT: usu supp N

reparation /repəreɪʃən/ **reparations** ◆◇◇◇◇

1 Reparations are sums of money that are paid after a war by the defeated country for the damage and injuries it caused in other countries. *Israel accepted billions of dollars in war reparations.* N-UNCOUNT: also N in pl

2 If you make **reparation** for something wrong that you have done to someone, you give them something or do something to help them because you have made them suffer. *There is a clear demand amongst victims for some sort of reparation from offenders.* N-UNCOUNT

repartee /repɑːʳtiː, AM -pərteɪ/. **Repartee** is conversation that consists of quick, witty comments and replies. *She was good at repartee.* N-UNCOUNT

repast /rɪpɑːst, -pæst/ **repasts.** A **repast** is a meal; a literary word. N-COUNT

repatriate /riːpætrieɪt, AM -peɪt-/ **repatriates, repatriating, repatriated** ◆◆◇◇◇

1 If a country **repatriates** someone, it sends them back to their home country. *It was not the policy of the government to repatriate genuine refugees... About 300 French hostages are to be repatriated.* VERB Vn ♦ **repatriation** /riːpætrieɪʃən, AM -peɪt-/ **repatriations** *Today they begin the forced repatriation of Vietnamese boat people.* N-VAR

2 If a company **repatriates** profits that it has made in another country, it brings them back into its home country. *Foreign investors are to be allowed to repatriate profits over one billion rupees.* VERB Vn ♦ **repatriation** *...penalties on the repatriation of profits.* N-VAR

repay /rɪpeɪ/ **repays, repaying, repaid** ◆◆◇◇◇

1 If you **repay** a loan or a debt, you pay back the money that you owe to the person who you borrowed or took it from. *It will take 30 years to repay the loan... He advanced funds of his own to his company, which was unable to repay him.* VERB Vn

2 If you **repay** a favour that someone did for you, you do something or give them something in return. *It was very kind. I don't know how I can ever repay you... I owe them a debt that cannot easily be repaid.* VERB Vn

repayable /rɪpeɪəbəl/. A loan that is **repayable** within a certain period of time must be paid back within that time; used mainly in British English. The usual American word is **payable**. *The loan is repayable over twenty years.* ADJ: usu v-link ADJ

repayment /rɪpeɪmənt/ **repayments** ◆◆◇◇◇

1 Repayments are amounts of money which you pay at regular intervals to a person or organization in order to repay a debt. *They were unable to meet their mortgage repayments... You can pay it off or make a minimum repayment.* N-COUNT

2 The **repayment** of money is the act or process of paying it back to the person you owe it to. *He failed to meet last Friday's deadline for repayment of a £114m loan... Brazil is putting forward a new debt repayment plan.* N-UNCOUNT

repeal /rɪpiːl/ **repeals, repealing, repealed.** If the government **repeals** a law, it officially ends it, so that it is no longer valid. *The government has just repealed the law segregating public facilities.* ◆◇◇◇◇ VERB Vn ► Also a noun. *Next year will be the 60th anniversary of the repeal of Prohibition.* N-UNCOUNT: N *of* n

repeat /rɪpiːt/ **repeats, repeating, repeated** ◆◆◆◆◇

1 If you **repeat** something, you say or write it again. You can say **I repeat** to show that you feel strongly about what you are repeating. *He repeated that he had been mis-quoted... I repeat that medicine is on the brink of a revolution... The Libyan leader Colonel Gadaffi has repeated his call for the release of hostages... 'You fool,' she kept repeating.* VERB =reiterate V that, V n, V with quote

2 If you **repeat** something that someone else has said or written, you say or write the same thing, or tell it to someone else. *She had an irritating habit of repeating everything I said to her... I trust you not to repeat that to anyone else... Now, brother, repeat after me, 'All praise to Allah, Lord of All the Worlds'.* VERB V n V n to n V after n with quote

3 If you **repeat** yourself, you say something which you have said before, usually by mistake. *He spoke well to begin with, but then started rambling and repeating himself.* VERB V pron-refl

4 People sometimes say **repeat** before saying again a word they have just said, in order to emphasize it or to make sure that people hear it; a formal use. *We are not, I repeat, not actually in the negotiating process... Find and destroy, repeat destroy, these units.* CONVENTION PRAGMATICS

5 If you **repeat** an action, you do it again. *The next day I repeated the procedure... He said Japan would never repeat its mistakes... Hold this position for 30 seconds, release and repeat on the other side.* VERB V n V

6 If an event or series of events **repeats** itself, it happens again. *The UN will have to work hard to stop history repeating itself... The cycle then repeats itself.* VERB V pron-refl Also V

7 If there is a **repeat** of an event, usually an undesirable event, it happens again. *There were fears that there might be a repeat of last year's campaign of strikes. ...in order to prevent a repeat tragedy.* N-COUNT: usu sing, oft N of n =repetition

8 If a company gets **repeat** business or **repeat** customers, people who have bought their goods or services before buy them again. *Nearly 60% of our bookings come from repeat business and personal recommendation.* ADJ: ADJ n

9 A **repeat** is a television or radio programme that has been broadcast before; used mainly in British English. The usual American word is **re-run**. *There's nothing except sport and repeats on TV.* N-COUNT

10 If there is **a repeat performance** of something, usually an undesirable event, it happens again. *This year can only see a repeat performance of the decline.* PHRASE =repeat

repeated /rɪpi̲ːtɪd/. **Repeated** actions or events are ones which happen many times. *Mr Lawssi apparently did not return the money, despite repeated reminders... During that time there have been repeated attempts to re-introduce capital punishment.* ◆◆◇◇◇ ADJ: ADJ n =frequent

repeatedly /rɪpi̲ːtɪdli/. If you do something **repeatedly**, you do it many times. *Both men have repeatedly denied the allegations... The rebel soldiers tried repeatedly to storm the building.* ◆◆◇◇◇ ADV: ADV with v

repel /rɪpe̲l/ **repels, repelling, repelled** ◆◇◇◇◇

1 When an army **repels** an attack or an invasion, they successfully fight and drive back soldiers from another army; a formal use. *They have fifty-thousand troops along the border ready to repel any attack.* VERB =repulse V n

2 When a magnetic pole **repels** another magnetic pole, it exerts a force that pushes the opposite pole away. You can also say that two magnetic poles **repel** each other or that they **repel**; a technical term in physics. *Like poles repel, unlike poles attract... As these electrons are negatively charged they will attempt to repel each other.* V-RECIP pl-n V V n

3 If something **repels** you, you find it horrible and disgusting. *...a violent excitement that frightened and repelled her.* ♦ **repelled** *She was very striking but in some way I felt repelled.* VB: no cont =revolt V n ADJ-GRADED

repellant /rɪpe̲lənt/. See **repellent**.

repellent /rɪpe̲lənt/ **repellents;** also spelled **repellant** for meaning 2. ◆◇◇◇◇

1 If you think that something is horrible and disgusting you can say it is **repellent**; a formal use. *...a very large, very repellent toad... She still found the place repellent.* ADJ-GRADED =repugnant, repulsive

2 Insect **repellent** is a product containing chemicals that you spray into the air or on your body in order to keep insects away. *...mosquito repellent.* N-MASS: usu n N

repent /rɪpe̲nt/ **repents, repenting, repented.** If you **repent**, you show or say that you are sorry for something wrong you have done. *Those who refuse to repent, he said, will be punished... Did he repent of anything in his life?* VERB V V of/for n Also V n

repentance /rɪpe̲ntəns/. If you show **repentance** for something wrong that you have done, you make it clear that you are sorry for doing it. *They showed no repentance during their trial.* N-UNCOUNT =remorse

repentant /rɪpe̲ntənt/. Someone who is **repentant** shows or says that they are sorry for something wrong they have done. *He was feeling guilty and depressed, repentant and scared. ...a repentant criminal.* ADJ-GRADED =penitent ≠unrepentant

repercussion /ri̲ːpəʳkʌ̲ʃᵊn/ **repercussions.** If an action or event has **repercussions**, it causes unpleasant things to happen some time after the original action or event; a formal word. *It was an effort which was to have painful repercussions... Members of congress were warned of possible repercussions if their vote went through.* ◆◇◇◇◇ N-COUNT: usu pl =consequence

repertoire /re̲pəʳtwɑːʳ/ **repertoires** ◆◇◇◇◇

1 A performer's **repertoire** is all the pieces of music or parts in plays that he or she has learned and can perform. *Meredith D'Ambrosio has thousands of songs in her repertoire.* N-COUNT: usu sing, with supp =repertory

2 The **repertoire** of a person or thing is all the things of a particular kind that the person or thing is capable of doing. *What I do remember is Mike's impressive repertoire of funny stories from childhood to present day... This has been one of the most successful desserts in my repertoire.* N-SING: with supp

3 You can refer to all the plays or music of a particular kind as, for example, the classical **repertoire** or the cello's **repertoire**. *It is no coincidence that the works in the 'standard repertoire' tend to have names.* N-SING: with supp

repertory /re̲pəʳtri, AM -tɔːri/ ◆◇◇◇◇

1 A **repertory** company is a group of actors and actresses who perform a small number of plays for just a few weeks at a time. They work in a **repertory** theatre. *...a well-known repertory company in Boston... He was in repertory in Dundee.* N-UNCOUNT: usu N n =rep

2 A performer's **repertory** is all the plays or pieces of music that he or she has learnt and is able to perform. *Her repertory was vast and to her it seemed that each song told some part of her life.* N-SING: usu poss N =repertoire

repetition /re̲pɪtɪ̲ʃᵊn/ **repetitions** ◆◇◇◇◇

1 If there is a **repetition** of an event, usually an undesirable event, it happens again. *Today the city government has taken measures to prevent a repetition of last year's confrontation... Collins wants to avoid repetition of the confusion that followed the discovery in 1989 of the cystic fibrosis gene.* N-VAR: usu N of n

2 **Repetition** means using the same words again. *He could also have cut out much of the repetition and thus saved many pages.* N-VAR

repetitious /re̲pɪtɪ̲ʃəs/. Something that is **repetitious** involves actions or elements that are repeated many times and is therefore boring. *The manifesto is long-winded, repetitious and often ambiguous or poorly drafted.* ADJ-GRADED PRAGMATICS =repetitive

repetitive /rɪpe̲tɪtɪv/ ◆◇◇◇◇

1 Something that is **repetitive** involves actions or elements that are repeated many times and is therefore boring. *...factory workers who do repetitive jobs... Suddenly music that seemed dull and repetitive comes alive.* ADJ-GRADED PRAGMATICS

2 **Repetitive** movements or sounds are repeated many times. *This technique is particularly successful where problems occur as the result of repetitive movements.* ADJ: usu ADJ n

repe̲titive strai̲n injury. People who suffer from **repetitive strain injury** have pain in their hands and arms as a result of performing many similar movements over a long period of time, usually as part of their job. The abbreviation **RSI** is also used. *One problem known to be associated with the increasing use of word processors is repetitive strain injury.* N-UNCOUNT

rephrase /ri̲ːfre̲ɪz/ **rephrases, rephrasing, rephrased.** If you **rephrase** a question or statement, you ask it or say it again in a different way. *Holidays can be horrendous. All right, I'll rephrase* VERB V n *that. The first few days are invariably hell... Again, the executive rephrased the question.*

replace /rɪpleɪs/ **replaces, replacing, replaced** ◆◆◆◆◇

1 If one thing or person **replaces** another, the first is used or acts instead of the second. *The council tax replaces the poll tax next April. ...the city lawyer who replaced Bob as chairman of the company... The smile disappeared to be replaced by a doleful frown.* VERB V n V n as n be V-ed with/by n

2 If you **replace** one thing or person with another, you put something or someone else in their place to do their job. *I clean out all the grease and replace it with oil so it works better in very low temperatures... The BBC decided it could not replace her.* VERB V n with/by n V n

3 If you **replace** something that is broken, damaged, or lost, you get a new one to use instead. *The shower that we put in a few years back has broken and we cannot afford to replace it.* VERB V n

4 If you **replace** something, you put it back where it was before. *The line went dead. Whitlock replaced the receiver... Replace the caps on the bottles.* VERB V n V n prep

replaceable /rɪpleɪsəbᵊl/

1 If something is **replaceable**, you can throw it away when it is finished and put a new one in its place. *...replaceable butane gas cartridges.* ADJ =disposable

2 If you say that someone is **replaceable**, you mean that they are not so important that someone else could not take their place. *Things would be better now. He would see I was not so easily replaceable.* ADJ-GRADED: usu v-link ADJ ≠irreplaceable

replacement /rɪpleɪsmənt/ **replacements** ◆◆◆◇◇

1 If you refer to the **replacement** of one thing by another, you mean that the second thing takes the place of the first. *...the replacement of damaged or lost books.* • See also **hormone replacement**. N-UNCOUNT: with supp =substitution

2 Someone who takes someone else's place in an organization, government, or team can be referred to as their **replacement**. *Taylor has nominated Adams as his replacement... The 18-year-old made his debut last week as a replacement for the injured Gordon Durie.* N-COUNT

replay, replays, replaying, replayed. ◆◆◇◇◇ The verb is pronounced /riːpleɪ/. The noun is pronounced /riːpleɪ/.

1 If a match between two sports teams **is replayed**, the two teams play it again, because neither team won the first time; used mainly in British English. *Drawn matches were replayed three or four days later.* ► You can refer to a match that is replayed as a **replay**. *If there has to be a replay we are confident of victory.* VB: usu passive be V-ed N-COUNT

2 If you **replay** something that you have recorded on film or tape, you play it again in order to watch it or listen to it. *He stopped the machine and replayed the message.* ► Also a noun. *I watched a slow-motion videotape replay of his fall.* VERB V n N-COUNT

3 If you **replay** an event in your mind, you think about it again and again. *She spends her nights lying in bed, replaying the fire in her mind.* VERB V n

4 See also **action replay**.

replenish /rɪplenɪʃ/ **replenishes, replenishing, replenished.** ◆◇◇◇◇ VERB If you **replenish** something, you make it full or complete again; a formal word. *Three hundred thousand tons of cereals are needed to replenish stocks... The insurance fund will need to be replenished.* V n

replenishment /rɪplenɪʃmənt/. **Replenishment** is the process by which something is made full or complete again; a formal word. *There is a concern about replenishment of the population. ...cell replenishment.* N-UNCOUNT: usu with supp

replete /rɪpliːt/

1 To be **replete with** something means to be full of it; a formal use. *The Harbor was replete with boats... History is replete with examples of populations out of control.* ADJ-GRADED: v-link ADJ with n =full of

2 If you are **replete**, you are pleasantly full of food and drink; a formal use. *Replete, guests can then retire to the modern conservatory for coffee.* ADJ: usu v-link ADJ PRAGMATICS =full up

replica /replɪkə/ **replicas** ◆◇◇◇◇

1 A **replica** of something such as a statue, building, or weapon is an accurate copy of it. *...a human-sized replica of the Statue of Liberty... Royce Hall was an exact replica of the basilica of Sant Ambrogio in Milan... It was a replica gun, for display only.* N-COUNT: usu N of n =model

2 If you say that one person is a **replica** of another, you mean that the first person looks very like the second. *Tina as a child was a replica of her mother.* N-COUNT: usu sing, usu N of n

replicate /replɪkeɪt/ **replicates, replicating, replicated** ◆◇◇◇◇

1 If you **replicate** someone's experiment, work, or research, you do it yourself in exactly the same way; a formal use. *He invited her to his laboratory to see if she could replicate the experiment.* VERB =duplicate, repeat V n

2 If a molecule **replicates**, it divides into smaller molecules which are exact copies of itself; a technical term in biology. *Cells can reproduce but only molecules can replicate.* ♦ **replication** /replɪkeɪʃᵊn/ *The process of replication is very quick and efficient.* VERB V Also V pron-refl N-UNCOUNT

reply /rɪplaɪ/ **replies, replying, replied** ◆◆◆◆◇

1 When you **reply** to something that someone has said or written to you, you say or write something as an answer. *'That's a nice dress,' said Michael. 'Thanks,' she replied solemnly... He replied that this was absolutely impossible... Grace was too terrified to reply... I've not replied to Lee's letter yet... To their surprise, hundreds replied to the advertisement.* VERB =answer V with quote V that V V to n

2 A **reply** is something that you say or write when you answer someone or answer a letter or advertisement. *I called out a challenge, but there was no reply... David has had 12 replies to his ad... They went ahead without waiting for a reply from the Germans... He said in reply that the question was unfair.* N-COUNT: oft N to/from n, also in N =answer, response

3 In sport, if you **reply** to a goal or a number of runs scored by your opponents, you then score a goal or a number of runs; used in journalism. *Graeme Hick scored an unbeaten 58 as Worcestershire replied to Middlesex's 202 with 132-3... Deryck Fox gave Featherstone the lead early in the first half with a penalty, but Saints were quick to reply.* VERB V to n V

4 If you **reply** to something such as an attack with violence or with another action, you do something in response. *During a number of violent incidents farmers threw eggs and empty bottles at police, who replied with tear gas... The National Salvation Front has already replied to this series of opposition moves with its own demonstrations.* VERB V with n V to n with n

report /rɪpɔːʳt/ **reports, reporting, reported** ◆◆◆◆◆

1 If you **report** something that has happened, you tell people about it. *They had been called in to clear drains after local people reported a foul smell... I reported the theft to the police... The officials also reported that two more ships were apparently heading for Malta... 'He seems to be all right now,' reported a relieved Taylor... The foreign secretary is reported as saying that force will have to be used if diplomacy fails... She reported him missing the next day... Between forty and fifty people are reported to have died in the fighting.* VERB V n V n to n V that V with quote be V-ed as -ing/-ed V n adj be V-ed to-inf Also it be V-ed that, V

2 If you **report** on an event or subject, you tell people about it, because it is your job or duty to do so. *Many journalists based outside of Sudan have been refused visas to enter the country to report on political affairs... I'll now call at the vicarage and report to you in due course.* VERB V on n V to n

3 A **report** is a news article or broadcast which gives information about something that has just happened. *According to a report in London's Independent newspaper, he still has control over the remaining shares... With a report on these developments, here's Jim Fish in Belgrade... Press reports said that 65mm of water fell in twenty four hours.* N-COUNT: usu with supp

4 A **report** is an official document which a group of people issue after investigating a situation or event. *The education committee will today publish its report on the supply of teachers for the 1990's... A report by the Association of University Teachers finds that only 22 per cent of lecturers in our universities are women.* N-COUNT: oft N on n, N by n

5 If you give someone a **report** on something, you tell them what has been happening. *She came back* N-COUNT *to give us a progress report on how the project is going... It seemed obvious from his report of that meeting that you were trying to focus suspicion on Mr Hirsch.*

6 If you say that there are **reports** that something has happened, you mean that some people say it has happened but you have no direct evidence of it. *There are unconfirmed reports that two people have been shot in the neighbouring town of Lalitpur... There were no reports of casualties.* N-COUNT: usu pl, N of/n, N that PRAGMATICS

7 If someone **reports** you to a person in authority, they tell that person about something wrong that you have done. *His ex-wife reported him to police a few days later... The Princess was reported for speeding twice on the same road within a week.* VERB; V n to n; be V-ed for -ing/n

8 If you **report** to a person or place, you go to that person or place and say that you are ready to start work or say that you are present. *According to protocol, he first reported to the Director of the hospital... Mr Ashwell has to surrender his passport and report to the police every five days... None of the men had reported for duty.* VERB; V to n; V for n

9 If you say that one employee **reports** to another, you mean that the first employee is told what to do by the second one and is responsible to them; a formal use. *He reported to a section chief, who reported to a division chief, and so on up the line.* VB: no cont; V to n

10 In British English, a school **report** is an official written account of how well or how badly a pupil has done during the term or year that has just finished. The American term is **report card**. *And now she was getting bad school reports.* N-COUNT

11 A **report** is a sudden loud noise made, for example, by a gun being fired or an explosion; a formal use. *Soon afterwards there was a loud report as the fuel tanks exploded.* N-COUNT

12 See also **reporting**.

report back PHRASAL VERB

1 If you **report back** to someone, you tell them about something that they asked you to find out about. *The teams are due to report back to the Prime Minister early next year... I'll report back the moment I have located him... He would, of course, report back on all deliberations... The repairman reported back that the computer had a virus.* V P to n; V P; V P on n; V P that; Also V n P, V P n (not pron)

2 If you **report back** to a place, you go back there and say that you are ready to start work or say that you are present. *The authorities have ordered all soldiers who have returned from the front line to report back to barracks... They were sent home and told to report back in the afternoon.* V P to n; V P; Also V P for n

3 If you **report back** a comment or remark, often a critical one, you repeat it to the person it was about. *We reported this back to Krajicek... They're scared that their sentiments might be reported back to the government.* V n P to n

reportage /rɪpɔːʳtɪdʒ, repɔːʳtɑːʒ/. **Reportage** is news reporting or documentary; a formal word. *...the magazine's acclaimed mix of reportage, fashion/beauty, and human interest stories.* N-UNCOUNT

report card, report cards

1 In American English, a **report card** is an official written account of how well or how badly a pupil has done during the term or year that has just finished. The British word is **report**. *The only time I got their attention was when I brought home straight A's on my report card.* N-COUNT

2 In American English, a **report card** is a report on how well a person, organization, or country has been doing recently; used in journalism. *The President today issued his final report card on the state of the economy.* N-COUNT

reported clause, reported clauses. A **reported clause** is a subordinate clause which indicates what someone said. For example, in 'She said that she was hungry', 'she was hungry' is a reported clause. N-COUNT

reportedly /rɪpɔːʳtɪdli/. If you say that something is **reportedly** true, you mean that someone has said that it is true, but you have no direct evidence of it; a formal word. *More than two hundred people have reportedly been killed in the past week's fighting... Now Moscow has reportedly agreed that the sale can go ahead... General Breymann had been shot dead, reportedly by one of his own men.* ◆◆◇◇◇ ADV: ADV with cl/group, ADV before v PRAGMATICS =apparently, allegedly

reported question, reported questions. A **reported question** is a question which is reported using a clause beginning with a word such as 'why' or 'whether', as in 'I asked her why she'd done it'. N-COUNT =indirect question

reported speech. **Reported speech** is speech which is reported using a report structure rather than the actual words used by the speaker, as in 'They said you didn't like it' and 'I asked him what his plans were'. N-UNCOUNT =indirect speech

reporter /rɪpɔːʳtəʳ/ **reporters.** A **reporter** is someone who writes news articles or who broadcasts news reports. *...a TV reporter. ...a trainee sports reporter... Our reporter Chris Loosemore sums up the findings.* ◆◆◆◆◇ N-COUNT =correspondent

reporting /rɪpɔːʳtɪŋ/. **Reporting** is the presenting of news in newspapers, on radio, and on television. *This newspaper has achieved a reputation for honest and impartial political reporting.* ◆◆◆◆◇ N-UNCOUNT

reporting clause, reporting clauses. A **reporting clause** is a clause which indicates that you are talking about what someone said or thought. For example, in 'She said that she was hungry', 'She said' is a reporting clause. N-COUNT

report structure, report structures. A **report structure** is a structure containing a reporting clause and a reported clause or a quote. N-COUNT

repose /rɪpoʊz/ **reposes, reposing, reposed**

1 **Repose** is a state in which you are resting and feeling calm; a literary use. *He had a still, almost blank face in repose... Its atmosphere is one of repose rather than excitement.* N-UNCOUNT

2 If something **reposes** somewhere, it is there; a formal use. *Exquisite china soup dishes reposed on silver plates.* VERB =lie; V prep/adv

repository /rɪpɒzɪtri, AM -tɔːri/ **repositories** ◆◇◇◇◇

1 A **repository** is a place where something is kept safely; a formal use. *A church in Moscow became a repository for police files.* N-COUNT: usu N for n =store

2 A **repository** of information is a person or group of people who know a lot of information about a particular place or subject. *The repository of all important knowledge in a small town was the chief barman of the local pub.* N-COUNT: usu N of n

repossess /riːpəzes/ **repossesses, repossessing, repossessed.** If your car or house **is repossessed**, the people who supplied it take it back because they are still owed money for it. *His car was repossessed by the company... The firm's sales of repossessed properties is up by 40 per cent.* ◆◇◇◇◇ VB: usu passive; be V-ed; V-ed

repossession /riːpəzeʃᵊn/ **repossessions** ◆◇◇◇◇

1 The **repossession** of someone's house is the act of repossessing it. *...the problem of home repossessions. ...families facing repossession of their homes.* N-VAR

2 You can refer to a house or car that has been repossessed as a **repossession**. *Many of the cars you will see at auction are repossessions.* N-COUNT

repossession order, repossession orders. In Britain, if a bank or building society enforces a **repossession order**, they officially tell someone that they are going to repossess their home. N-COUNT

repot /riːpɒt/ **repots, repotting, repotted.** If you **repot** a plant, you take it out of its pot and put it in a larger one. *As your plants flourish, you'll need to repot them in bigger pots.* VERB; V n

reprehensible /reprɪhensɪbᵊl/. If you think that a type of behaviour or an idea is very bad and morally wrong, you can say that it is **reprehensible**; a formal word. *Mr Cramer said the violence by anti-government protestors was reprehensible. ...behaving in the most reprehensible manner.* ADJ-GRADED: usu v-link ADJ

represent /reprɪzent/ **represents, representing, represented** ◆◆◆◆◇

1 If someone such as a lawyer or a politician **represents** a person or group of people, they act on behalf of that person or group. *...the politicians we elect to represent us... The offer has yet to be accepted by the lawyers representing the victims.* VERB; V n

2 If you **represent** a person or group at an official event, you go there on their behalf. *The general secretary may represent the president at some official ceremonies.* VERB V n

3 If you **represent** your country or town in a competition or sports event, you take part in it on behalf of the country or town where you live. *My only aim is to represent Britain at the Olympics next year.* VERB V n

4 If a group of people or things **is** well **represented** in a particular activity or in a particular place, a lot of them can be found there. *Women are already well represented in the area of TV drama... In New Mexico all kinds of cuisines are represented.* V-PASSIVE be adv V-ed be V-ed

5 If you say that something **represents** a change, achievement, or victory, you mean that it is a change, achievement, or victory. *The USSR represents a truly unique example in the history of human civilization... These developments represented a major change in the established order.* V-LINK =amount to, constitute V n

6 If a sign or symbol **represents** something, it is accepted as meaning that thing. *...a black dot in the middle of the circle is supposed to represent the source of the radiation.* VB: no cont =stand for, symbolize V n

7 If you say that something or someone **represents** an idea or quality, you mean that they are a symbol or an expression of that idea or quality. *We believe you represent everything British racing needs.* VB: no cont, no passive =embody V n

8 If you **represent** a person or thing as a particular thing, you describe them as being that thing. *The popular press tends to represent him as an environmental guru.* VERB =depict, portray V n *as* n

representation /re̲prɪzenteɪ̲ʃᵊn/ **representations** ◆◆◇◇◇

1 If a group or person has **representation** in a parliament or on a committee, someone in parliament or on the committee will vote or make decisions on their behalf. *Puerto Ricans are U.S. citizens but they have no representation in Congress.* ● See also **proportional representation.** N-UNCOUNT: oft N prep

2 You can describe a picture, model, or statue of a person or thing as a **representation** of them; a formal use. *...a lifelike representation of Christ... Historians looked to artists' representations of the lion to piece together a picture of how the lion once looked.* N-COUNT: usu N *of* n

3 If you make **representations** to a government or other official group, you make formal complaints or requests to them. *We have made representations to ministers but they just don't seem to be listening to us.* N-PLURAL: oft N *to/from* n

representational /re̲prɪzenteɪ̲ʃənᵊl/. In a **representational** painting, the artist attempts to show things as they really are; a formal word. *His painting went through both representational and abstract periods.* ADJ-GRADED

representative /re̲prɪze̲ntətɪv/ **representatives** ◆◆◆◆◇

1 A **representative** is a person who has been chosen to act or make decisions on behalf of another person or a group of people. *...trade union representatives... Employees from each department elect a representative.* N-COUNT =delegate

2 A **representative** is someone whose job is to sell a company's products or services, usually by travelling round other companies and organizations; used mainly in British English. *She had a stressful job as a sales representative.* N-COUNT: usu with supp =rep

3 A **representative** group consists of a small number of people who have been chosen to make decisions on behalf of a larger group. *The new head of state should be chosen by an 87 member representative council. ...the institutions of a representative government.* ADJ: ADJ n

4 Someone who is typical of the group to which they belong can be described as **representative**. *He was in no way representative of dog-trainers in general. ...fairly representative groups of adults.* ADJ-GRADED: oft ADJ *of* n
♦ **representativeness** *...a process designed to ensure the representativeness of the sample interviewed.* N-UNCOUNT

5 See also **House of Representatives.**

repress /rɪpre̲s/ **represses, repressing, repressed** ◆◇◇◇◇

1 If you **repress** a feeling, you make a deliberate effort not to show it or to have this feeling; used showing disapproval. *People who repress their emotions risk having nightmares... It is anger that is repressed that leads to violence and loss of control. ...repressed aggression.* VERB PRAGMATICS =suppress V n V-ed

2 If you **repress** a smile, sigh, or moan, you try hard not to smile, sigh, or moan. *He repressed a smile... I couldn't repress a sigh of admiration.* VERB V n

3 If a section of society **is repressed**, their freedom is restricted by the people who have authority over them; used showing disapproval. *The Cossacks were brutally repressed under Communist rule. ...a UN resolution banning him from repressing his people.* VERB PRAGMATICS =subjugate be V-ed V n

repressed /rɪpre̲st/. A **repressed** person is someone who does not allow themselves to have natural feelings and desires, especially sexual ones; used showing disapproval. *Some have charged that the Puritans were sexually repressed and inhibited.* ADJ-GRADED PRAGMATICS =frustrated

repression /rɪpre̲ʃᵊn/ **repressions** ◆◆◇◇◇

1 **Repression** is the use of force to restrict and control a society or other group of people. *...a society conditioned by violence and repression.* N-UNCOUNT: also N in pl =oppression

2 **Repression** of feelings, especially sexual ones, is the way in which some people do not allow themselves to have natural feelings and desires; used showing disapproval. *Much of the anger he's felt during his life has stemmed from the repression of his feelings about men.* N-UNCOUNT PRAGMATICS

repressive /rɪpre̲sɪv/. A **repressive** government is one that restricts people's freedom and controls them by using force; used showing disapproval. *The military regime in power was unpopular and repressive.* ◆◇◇◇◇ ADJ-GRADED PRAGMATICS
♦ **repressively** *The country, which had been repressively ruled for ten years, became increasingly engulfed in a civil war.* ADV-GRADED: ADV with v

reprieve /rɪpri̲ːv/ **reprieves, reprieved** ◆◇◇◇◇

1 If someone who has been sentenced in a court **is reprieved**, their punishment is officially postponed or cancelled. *Fourteen people, waiting to be hanged for the murder of a former prime minister, have been reprieved.* VB: usu passive, no cont be V-ed

2 A **reprieve** is a delay before a very unpleasant or difficult situation which may or may not take place. *Ministers agreed to postpone the abolition of duty-free sales in Europe. The reprieve may only be temporary, however.* N-COUNT: usu sing =respite

reprimand /re̲prɪmɑːnd, -mæ̲nd/ **reprimands, reprimanding, reprimanded.** If someone **is reprimanded**, they are spoken to angrily or seriously for doing something wrong, usually by someone in authority; a formal word. *He was reprimanded by a teacher for talking in the corridor... Her attempts to reprimand him were quickly shouted down.* ► Also a noun. *He has been fined five thousand pounds and given a severe reprimand.* ◆◇◇◇◇ VERB =admonish be V-ed *for* -ing/n V n N-VAR

reprint, reprints, reprinting, reprinted. The verb is pronounced /riːprɪ̲nt/. The noun is pronounced /ri̲ːprɪnt/. ◆◇◇◇◇

1 If a book **is reprinted**, further copies of it are printed when all the other ones have been sold. *It remained an exceptionally rare book until it was reprinted in 1918.* VB: usu passive be V-ed

2 A **reprint** is a process in which new copies of a book or article are printed because all the other ones have been sold. *Demand picked up and a reprint was required last November.* N-COUNT

3 A **reprint** is a new copy of a book or article, printed because all the other ones have been sold or because minor changes have been made to the original. *...a reprint of a 1962 novel.* N-COUNT

reprisal /rɪpra̲ɪzᵊl/ **reprisals.** If you do something to someone in **reprisal**, you do something violent or unpleasant to them because they have done something violent or unpleasant to you. *There were fears that some of the Western hostages might be killed in reprisal.* ◆◇◇◇◇ N-VAR =retaliation

reprise /rɪpriːz/ **reprises, reprising, reprised** ◆◇◇◇◇
1 In music, if there is a **reprise**, an earlier section of music is repeated. N-COUNT
2 If someone **reprises** a role or a song, they play or sing it again; used in written English. *He then proceeded to play for more than two hours, reprising every one of his hits.* VERB; V n

reproach /rɪproʊtʃ/ **reproaches, reproaching, reproached** ◆◇◇◇◇
1 If you **reproach** someone, you say or show that you are disappointed, upset, or angry because they have done something wrong. *She is quick to reproach anyone who doesn't live up to her own high standards... She had not even reproached him for breaking his promise.* VERB; V n; V n *for*-ing/n
2 If you look at or speak to someone with **reproach**, you show or say that you are disappointed, upset, or angry because they have done something wrong. *He looked at her with reproach... Women in public life must be beyond reproach.* N-VAR
3 If you **reproach** yourself, you think with regret about something you have done wrong. *You've no reason to reproach yourself, no reason to feel shame... We begin to reproach ourselves for not having been more careful.* VERB =blame; V pron-refl; V pron-refl *for* -ing/n
4 If you consider someone's actions or behaviour to be a **reproach** to a group of people, you consider them to be harmful or insulting to that group. *The shootings and bombings were 'a scandal and reproach to all of us in Europe'.* N-SING: usu N *to* n

reproachful /rɪproʊtʃfʊl/. **Reproachful** expressions or remarks show that you are disappointed, upset, or angry because someone has done something wrong. *She gave Isabelle a reproachful look... He turned to Alex and his tone was reproachful.* ♦ **reproachfully** *Luke's mother stopped smiling and looked reproachfully at him.* ADJ-GRADED; ADV-GRADED: ADV after v

reprobate /reprəbeɪt/ **reprobates.** If you think someone behaves in a foolish and immature way you can say they are a **reprobate**; an old-fashioned word. *Far from being the drunken reprobate of popular legend, they found him punctual and hard-working.* N-COUNT

reproduce /riːprədjuːs, AM -duːs/ **reproduces, reproducing, reproduced** ◆◆◇◇◇
1 If you try to **reproduce** something, you try to copy it. *I shall not try to reproduce the policemen's English... The effect has proved hard to reproduce.* VERB =copy; V n
2 If you **reproduce** a picture, speech, or a piece of writing, you make a photograph or printed copy of it. *We are grateful to you for permission to reproduce this article.* VERB; V n
3 If you **reproduce** an action or an achievement, you repeat it. *If we can reproduce the form we have shown in the last couple of months we will be successful.* VERB =repeat; V n
4 When people, animals, or plants **reproduce**, they produce young. *...a society where women are defined by their ability to reproduce... We are reproducing ourselves at such a rate that our numbers threaten the ecology of the planet.* ♦ **reproduction** /riːprədʌkʃən/ *Genes are those tiny bits of biological information swapped in sexual reproduction. ...the acids which are vital for normal cell reproduction.* VERB =procreate; V; V pron-refl; N-UNCOUNT

reproduction /riːprədʌkʃən/ **reproductions** ◆◇◇◇◇
1 A **reproduction** is a copy of something such as an antique or a painting. *...a reproduction of a popular religious painting. ...high-quality reproduction furniture.* N-COUNT: oft N n
2 Sound **reproduction** is the recording of sound onto cassettes, records, or films so that it can be heard by a large number of people. *...the increasingly high technology of music reproduction.* N-UNCOUNT

reproductive /riːprədʌktɪv/. **Reproductive** processes and organs are concerned with the reproduction of living things. *...the female reproductive system.* ◆◇◇◇◇ ADJ: usu ADJ n

reproof /rɪpruːf/ **reproofs.** If you say or do something in **reproof**, you say or do it to show that you disapprove of what someone has done or said; a formal word. *She raised her eyebrows in reproof... They spoke in tones of gentle reproof. ...a reproof that she responded to right away.* N-VAR

reprove /rɪpruːv/ **reproves, reproving, reproved.** If you **reprove** someone, you speak angrily or seriously to them because they have behaved wrongly or foolishly; a formal word. *'There's no call for talk like that,' Mrs Evans reproved him... Women were reproved if they did not wear hats in court.* VERB =reprimand, admonish; V with quote; V n

reproving /rɪpruːvɪŋ/. If you give someone a **reproving** look, or speak in a **reproving** voice, you show or say that you think they have behaved wrongly or foolishly; a formal word. *'Flatterer,' she said giving him a mock reproving look.* ♦ **reprovingly** *'I'm trying to sleep,' he lied, speaking reprovingly.* ADJ-GRADED: usu ADJ n; ADV-GRADED: ADV after v

reptile /reptaɪl, AM -tɪl/ **reptiles. Reptiles** are a group of animals which have scaly skins and lay eggs. Snakes, lizards, and crocodiles are reptiles. ◆◇◇◇◇ N-COUNT

reptilian /reptɪliən/
1 A **reptilian** creature is a reptile. *...a prehistoric jungle occupied by reptilian creatures.* ADJ: usu ADJ n
2 You can also use the word **reptilian** to describe something that is characteristic of a reptile or that is like a reptile. *The chick hatches after 43-45 days. Dark, ugly and almost reptilian in its appearance.* ADJ

republic /rɪpʌblɪk/ **republics.** A **republic** is a country which has a president or whose system of government is based on the idea that every citizen has equal status. *In 1918, Austria became a republic. ...the Baltic republics. ...the Republic of Ireland.* • See also **banana republic**. ◆◆◆◆◇ N-COUNT: oft in names

republican /rɪpʌblɪkən/ **republicans** ◆◆◆◆◇
1 A **republican** government has a president or is based on the idea that every citizen has equal status. *...the nations that had adopted the republican form of government.* ADJ
2 In the United States, if someone is **Republican**, they belong to or support the Republican Party. *Lower taxes made Republican voters happier with their party... Some families have been republican for generations.* ► A **Republican** is someone who has Republican views. *What made you decide to become a Republican, as opposed to a Democrat?* ADJ; N-COUNT
3 In Northern Ireland, if someone is **Republican**, they believe that Northern Ireland should not be ruled by Britain but should become part of the Republic of Ireland. *...a Republican paramilitary group.* ► A **Republican** is someone who has Republican views. *...a Northern Ireland republican.* ADJ; N-COUNT

republicanism /rɪpʌblɪkənɪzəm/
1 **Republicanism** is the belief that the best system of government is a republic. N-UNCOUNT
2 **Republicanism** is support for or membership of the Republican Party in the United States. N-UNCOUNT

Republican Party. The **Republican Party** is one of the two main political parties in the United States. Its members are considered to have conservative views and it is the party usually associated with business. There are also Republican Parties in some other countries. ◆◇◇◇◇ N-PROPER

repudiate /rɪpjuːdieɪt/ **repudiates, repudiating, repudiated.** If you **repudiate** something or someone, you show that you strongly disagree with them and do not want to be connected with them in any way. *Leaders urged people to turn out in large numbers to repudiate the violence... The Prime Minister has repudiated racist remarks made by a member of the Conservative Party.* ♦ **repudiation** /rɪpjuːdieɪʃən/ **repudiations** *He believes his public repudiation of the conference decision will enhance his standing as a leader.* ◆◇◇◇◇ VERB =reject, denounce; V n; N-VAR =rejection, denunciation

repugnant /rɪpʌgnənt/. If you think that something is horrible and disgusting, you can say that it is **repugnant**; a formal word. *The odour of vitamin in skin is repugnant to insects... The Committee said his actions were improper and repugnant.* ♦ **repugnance** *She felt a deep sense of shame and repugnance.* ADJ-GRADED: oft ADJ *to* n =repellent; N-UNCOUNT =disgust

repulse /rɪpʌls/ **repulses, repulsing, repulsed**
1 If you **are repulsed** by something, you think that it is horrible and disgusting and you want to avoid VB: usu passive =repel ≠attract

it. *Evil has charisma. Though people are repulsed by it, they also are drawn to its power.* — beV-ed

2 If an army or other group **repulses** a group of people, they drive it back using force. *The armed forces were prepared to repulse any attacks.* — VERB; V n

repulsion /rɪpʌlʃən/

1 **Repulsion** is an extremely strong feeling of disgust. *She gave a dramatic shudder of repulsion.* — N-UNCOUNT =revulsion

2 **Repulsion** is a force that pushes two things apart, such as the force that there is in magnets. *...the electric repulsion between charged electrons.* — N-UNCOUNT ≠attraction

repulsive /rɪpʌlsɪv/

1 If you find something or someone **repulsive**, you find them horrible and disgusting and you want to avoid them. *...repulsive fat white slugs. ...the most repulsive mass murderer America has known.* — ADJ-GRADED =revolting, disgusting
♦ **repulsively** *He once fired at a repulsively large rat as it dragged itself across the lane.* — ADV-GRADED: ADV adj

2 A **repulsive** force is a force which pushes away what is around it; a technical use in physics. *The repulsive force within the nucleus is enormous.* — ADJ: usu ADJ n

reputable /repjʊtəbəl/. A **reputable** company or person is reliable and trustworthy. *You are well advised to buy your car through a reputable dealer.* — ◆◇◇◇◇ ADJ-GRADED: usu ADJ n =reliable

reputation /repjʊteɪʃən/ **reputations** — ◆◆◆◇◇

1 To have a **reputation** for something means to be known or remembered for it. *Alice Munro has a reputation for being a very depressing writer. ...Barcelona's reputation as a design-conscious, artistic city.* — N-COUNT: usu with supp

2 Something's or someone's **reputation** is the opinion that people have about how good they are. If they have a good reputation, people think they are good. *This college has a good academic reputation... The stories ruined his reputation.* — N-COUNT: usu with supp

3 If you know someone **by reputation**, you have never met them but you have heard of their reputation. *She was by reputation a good organiser.* — PHRASE

repute /rɪpjuːt/

1 A person or thing **of repute** or **of** high **repute** is respected and known to be good; a formal use. *He was a writer of repute... Chicago has 6 graduate and professional schools of high repute.* — PHRASE: n PHR

2 A person's or organization's **repute** is their reputation, especially when this is good; a formal use. *Under his stewardship, the UN's repute has risen immeasurably.* — N-UNCOUNT: usu with supp =reputation

3 If you know someone **by repute**, you have never met them but you have heard or read about them; a formal use. *I only knew him by repute.* — PHRASE =by reputation

reputed /rɪpjuːtɪd/. If you say that something **is reputed** to be true, you mean that people say it is true, but you do not know if it is definitely true; a formal word. *Maradona is reputed to earn ten million pounds a year.* — ◆◇◇◇◇ V-PASSIVE PRAGMATICS; beV-ed to-inf
♦ **reputedly** /rɪpjuːtɪdli/ *He reputedly earns two million pounds a year... Both women have dramatic dark looks and, reputedly, fiery temperaments.* — ADV: ADV with cl/group, ADV before v

request /rɪkwest/ **requests, requesting, requested** — ◆◆◆◆◇

1 If you **request** something, you ask for it politely or formally; a formal use. *Mr Dennis said he had requested access to a telephone... She had requested that the door to her room be left open.* — VERB; V n; V that

2 If you **request** someone to do something, you politely or formally ask them to do it; a formal use. *They requested him to leave... Students are requested to park at the rear of the Department.* — VERB; V n to-inf; Also V with quote

3 If you make a **request**, you politely ask for something or ask someone to do something. *France had agreed to his request for political asylum... Vietnam made an official request that the conference be postponed.* — N-COUNT: oft N for n, N that/to-inf

4 A **request** is a song or piece of music which someone has asked a performer or disc jockey to play. *If you have any requests, I'd be happy to play them for you.* — N-COUNT

5 If you do something **at** someone's **request**, you do it because they have asked you to. *The evacuation is being organised at the request of the United Nations Secretary General.* — PHRASES

6 If something is given or done **on request**, it is given or done whenever you ask for it. *Leaflets giving details are available on request... Chambermaids will bring an iron or hair dryer on request.*

requiem /rekwiem/ **requiems** — ◆◇◇◇◇

1 A **requiem** or a **requiem mass** is a Catholic church service in memory of someone who has recently died. — N-COUNT

2 A **requiem** is a piece of music for singers and musicians that can be performed either as part of a requiem mass or as part of a concert. *...a performance of Verdi's Requiem.* — N-COUNT: oft in names

require /rɪkwaɪəʳ/ **requires, requiring, required** — ◆◆◆◆◇

1 If you **require** something or if something **is required**, you need it or it is necessary; a formal use. *If you require further information, you should consult the registrar... This isn't the kind of crisis that requires us to drop everything else... Some of the materials required for this technique may be difficult to obtain.* — VERB =need; V n; V n to-inf; V-ed

2 If a law or rule **requires** you to do something, you have to do it; a formal use. *The rules also require employers to provide safety training... At least 35 manufacturers have flouted a law requiring prompt reporting of such malfunctions... The law now requires that parents serve on the committees that plan and evaluate school programs... Then he'll know exactly what's required of him.* — VERB; V n to-inf; V n; V that; beV-ed of n

3 If you say that something is **required reading** for a particular group of people, you mean that you think it is essential for them to read it because it will give them information which they should have. *...an important research study that should be required reading for every member of the cabinet.* — PHRASE: v-link PHR, oft PHR for n

requirement /rɪkwaɪəʳmənt/ **requirements** — ◆◆◆◇◇

1 A **requirement** is a quality or qualification that you must have in order to be allowed to do something or to be suitable for something. *Its products met all legal requirements... Graduate status is the minimum requirement for entry to the teaching profession... I knew that concentration was the first requirement for learning.* — N-COUNT: usu with supp

2 Your **requirements** are the things that you need; a formal use. *Variations of this programme can be arranged to suit your requirements. ...a packaged food which provides 100 percent of your daily requirement of one vitamin.* — N-COUNT: usu pl, usu with supp

requisite /rekwɪzɪt/ **requisites** — ◆◇◇◇◇

1 You can use the word **requisite** to indicate that something is necessary for a particular purpose; a formal use. *She filled in the requisite paperwork.* — ADJ: usu *the* ADJ n =required

2 A **requisite** is something which is necessary for a particular purpose; a formal use. *An understanding of accounting techniques is a major requisite for the work of the analysts. ...his little bag of hunting requisites.* — N-COUNT: usu with supp

requisition /rekwɪzɪʃən/ **requisitions, requisitioning, requisitioned**

1 If people in authority **requisition** a vehicle, building, or food, they formally demand it and take it for official use; a formal use. *Authorities requisitioned hotel rooms to lodge more than 3,000 stranded Christmas vacationers.* — VERB =commandeer; V n

2 A **requisition** is a written document which allows a person or organization to obtain goods. *...a requisition for a replacement typewriter.* — N-COUNT

re-route, re-routes, re-routing, re-routed; also spelled **reroute**. If vehicles or planes **are re-routed**, they are directed along a different route because the usual route cannot be used. *The heavy traffic was re-routed past my front door... They rerouted the planes at La Guardia airport.* — VERB =redirect; beV-ed; V n

re-run, re-runs, re-running, re-ran. The form **re-run** is used in the present tense and is also the past participle of the verb. The noun is pronounced /riː rʌn/, and the verb is pronounced /riː rʌn/ — ◆◇◇◇◇

1 If you say that something is a **re-run of** a particular event or experience, you mean that what happens now is very similar to what happened in the past. *It was the world's second worst air disaster, a* — N-SING: N of n =repeat

horrific re-run of the runway collision in 1977... It seems likely that this year will see a re-run of last year's fight over the elementary-school budget.
2 If someone **re-runs** a process or event, they do it or organize it again. *Edit the input text and re-run the software... He re-ran in his mind his conversation with Smith.* ► Also a noun. *In the re-run he failed to make the final at all, finishing sixth.* VERB Vn N-COUNT
3 If an election **is re-run**, it is organized again, for example because the correct procedures were not followed or because no candidate got an overall majority. *The ballot was re-run on Mr Todd's insistence after accusations of malpractice.* ► Also a noun. *The opposition has demanded a re-run of parliamentary elections held yesterday.* VB: usu passive =repeat be V-ed N-COUNT: oft N of n
4 If a theatre company or cinema **re-runs** a play or a film, it puts it on or shows it again. *In honour of Jane Fonda's visit they re-ran one of her films at the cinema.* VERB Vn
5 A **re-run** is a film, play, or television programme, that is broadcast or put on again. *Viewers will have to make do with tired re-runs and second-rate movies... Thames television announced a re-run of the Benny Hill Show.* N-COUNT: usu with supp, oft N of n =repeat

resat /riːsæt/. **Resat** is the past tense and past participle of **resit**.

reschedule /riːʃedjuːl, AM -skedʒuːl/ **reschedules, rescheduling, rescheduled** ◆◇◇◇◇
1 If someone **reschedules** an event, they change the time at which it is due to happen. *Since I'll be away, I'd like to reschedule the meeting... They've rescheduled the vigil for February 14th... The programme was rescheduled to 9.30pm by Alan Yentob,controller of BBC1.* ♦ **rescheduling, reschedulings** *All this could lead up to a rescheduling of the trip to Asia.* VERB Vn V n for/to n N-VAR: usu N of n
2 To **reschedule** a debt means to arrange for the person, organization, or country that owes money to pay it back over a longer period because they are in financial difficulty. *...companies that have gone bust or had to reschedule their debts... The Commonwealth Development Corporation has agreed to reschedule Tanzania's debt.* ♦ **rescheduling** *The President is also expected to request a rescheduling of loan repayments.* VERB Vn N-VAR: usu N of n

rescind /rɪsɪnd/ **rescinds, rescinding, rescinded.** If a government or a group of people in power **rescind** a law or agreement, they officially withdraw it and state that it is no longer valid; a formal word. *Trade Union leaders have demanded the government rescind the price rise.* ◆◇◇◇◇ VERB Vn

rescue /reskjuː/ **rescues, rescuing, rescued** ◆◆◆◇◇
1 If you **rescue** someone, you get them out of a dangerous or unpleasant situation. *Helicopters rescued nearly 20 people from the roof of the burning building... He had rescued her from a horrible life.* ♦ **rescuer, rescuers** *It took rescuers 90 minutes to reach the trapped men.* VERB Vn N-COUNT
2 **Rescue** is help which gets someone out of a dangerous or unpleasant situation. *Lights clipped onto life jackets improve the chances of rescue... A big rescue operation has been launched for a trawler missing in the English Channel.* N-UNCOUNT: oft N n
3 A **rescue** is an attempt to save someone from a dangerous or unpleasant situation. *A major air-sea rescue is under way... Five children were pulled from the smoke-filled house in heroic rescues by fire crews.* N-COUNT
4 If you **go to** someone's **rescue** or **come to** their **rescue**, you help them when they are in danger or difficulty. *The 23-year-old's screams alerted a passerby who went to her rescue... The crisis puts strong political pressure on the state government to come to the rescue.* PHRASE: V inflects

research /rɪsɜːʳtʃ/ **researches, researching, researched** ◆◆◆◆◆
1 **Research** is work that involves studying something and trying to discover facts about it. *65 percent of the 1987 budget went for nuclear weapons research and production. ...cancer research. ...his researches into which kinds of flowers bees get their best honey from.* N-UNCOUNT: also N in pl
2 If you **research** something, you try to discover facts about it. *She spent two years in South Florida researching and filming her documentary... So far we haven't been able to find anything, but we're still researching.* ♦ **researcher, researchers** *He chose to join the company as a market researcher.* VERB Vn V N-COUNT

resell /riːsel/ **resells, reselling, resold.** If you **resell** something that you have bought, you sell it again. *Shopkeepers buy them in bulk and resell them for £150 each... It makes sense to buy at dealer prices so you can maximize your profits if you resell.* VERB Vn V

resemblance /rɪzembləns/ **resemblances.** If there is a **resemblance** between two people or things, they are similar to each other. *There was a remarkable resemblance between him and Pete... Our tour prices bore little resemblance to those in the holiday brochures.* ◆◇◇◇◇ N-VAR: oft adj N, N between/to n =likeness, similarity

resemble /rɪzembəl/ **resembles, resembling, resembled.** If one thing or person **resembles** another, they are similar to each other. *Some of the commercially produced venison resembles beef in flavour... She so resembles her mother.* ◆◆◇◇◇ VB: no cont Vn

resent /rɪzent/ **resents, resenting, resented.** If you **resent** someone or something, you feel bitter and angry about them. *She resents her mother for being so tough on her... I resent being dependent on her.* ◆◆◇◇◇ VERB V n/-ing

resentful /rɪzentfʊl/. If you are **resentful**, you feel resentment. *At first I felt very resentful and angry about losing my job... He turned away in sullen, resentful silence.* ♦ **resentfully** *For a moment she continued to look at him resentfully.* ◆◇◇◇◇ ADJ-GRADED =aggrieved, angry ADV-GRADED: usu ADV with v

resentment /rɪzentmənt/ **resentments.** **Resentment** is bitterness and anger that someone feels about something. *She expressed resentment at being interviewed by a social worker... But the problems of inflation and unemployment still cause a lot of resentment.* ◆◆◇◇◇ N-UNCOUNT: also N in pl =anger, bitterness

reservation /rezəʳveɪʃən/ **reservations** ◆◆◇◇◇
1 If you have **reservations** about something, you are not sure that it is entirely good or right. *I told him my main reservation about his film was the ending... After three days, the strikers' demands were met almost without reservation.* N-VAR: oft N about n
2 If you make a **reservation**, you arrange for something such as a table in a restaurant or a room in a hotel to be kept for you. *He went to the desk to enquire and make a reservation... Accommodation is restricted so a reservation is essential.* N-COUNT =booking
3 A **reservation** is an area of land that is kept separate for a particular group of people to live in. *Seventeen thousand native Indians live in Arizona on a reservation.* N-COUNT
4 See also **central reservation**.

reserve /rɪzɜːʳv/ **reserves, reserving, reserved** ◆◆◆◆◇
1 If something **is reserved** for a particular person or purpose, it is kept specially for that person or purpose. *A double room with a balcony overlooking the sea had been reserved for him... In the United States lanes are reserved for cars with more than one occupant.* VB: usu passive =set aside be V-ed for n
2 If you **reserve** something such as a table, ticket, or magazine, you arrange for it to be kept specially for you, rather than sold or given to someone else. *I'll reserve a table for five... Demand will be huge, so ask your newsagent to reserve your copy today.* VERB Vn
3 A **reserve** is a supply of something that is available for use when it is needed. *The Gulf has 65 per cent of the world's oil reserves... A friend can be a reserve of help in times of trouble.* N-COUNT: usu with supp
4 In sport, a **reserve** is someone who is available to play as part of a team if one of the members is ill or cannot play; used mainly in British English. *He ended up as a reserve, but still qualified for a team gold medal.* N-COUNT =substitute
5 A nature **reserve** is an area of land where the animals, birds, and plants are officially protected. *Marine biologists are now calling for Cardigan Bay to be created a marine nature reserve to protect the dolphins.* N-COUNT: usu supp N

6 If someone shows **reserve**, they keep their feelings hidden. *The subject is one which must be discussed with reserve... I do hope that you'll overcome your reserve and let me know.* N-UNCOUNT

7 If you have something **in reserve**, you have it available for use when it is needed. *He poked around the top of his cupboard for the small bottle of whisky that he kept in reserve... There were patrol cars on the streets and riot police standing by in reserve.* PHRASE: PHR after v

8 • to **reserve judgement**: see **judgement**. • to **reserve the right**: see **right**.

reserved /rɪzɜːʳvd/ ◆◆◇◇◇

1 Someone who is **reserved** keeps their feelings hidden. *He was unemotional, quite quiet, and reserved... Even though I'm quite a reserved person, I like meeting people.* ADJ-GRADED =aloof

2 A table in a restaurant or a seat in a theatre that is **reserved** is being kept for someone rather than given or sold to anyone else. *Seats, or sometimes entire tables, were reserved.* ADJ

reserve price, reserve prices. A **reserve price** is the lowest price which is acceptable to the owner of property being auctioned or sold; used in British English. N-COUNT

reservist /rɪzɜːʳvɪst/ **reservists. Reservists** are soldiers who are not serving in the regular army of a country, but who can be called to serve whenever they are needed. ◆◇◇◇◇ N-COUNT

reservoir /rezəʳvwɑːʳ/ **reservoirs** ◆◆◇◇◇

1 A **reservoir** is a lake that is used for storing water before it is supplied to people. N-COUNT

2 A **reservoir** of something is a large quantity of it that is available for use when needed. *...the huge oil reservoir beneath the Kuwaiti desert. ...the body's short-term reservoir of energy.* N-COUNT: with supp, oft N of n, adj N

reset /riːset/ **resets, resetting.** The form **reset** is used in the present tense and is also the past tense and past participle. ◆◇◇◇◇

1 If you **reset** a machine or device, you adjust or set it, so that it is ready to work again or ready to perform a particular function. *As soon as you arrive at your destination, step out of the aircraft and reset your wrist-watch.* VERB V n

2 If a doctor **resets** a broken bone, they put it back into its correct position. *He is recovering from an operation to reset his arm.* VERB V n

resettle /riːsetᵊl/ **resettles, resettling, resettled.** If people **are resettled** by a government or organization, or if people **resettle**, they move to a different place to live because they are no longer able or allowed to stay in the area where they used to live. *The refugees were put in camps in Italy before being resettled... In 1990, 200,000 Soviet Jews resettled on Israeli territory.* ◆◇◇◇◇ V-ERG be V-ed V

resettlement /riːsetᵊlmənt/. **Resettlement** is the process of moving people to a different place to live, because they are no longer allowed to stay in the area where they used to live. *Only refugees are eligible for resettlement abroad. ...the forcible resettlement of villagers from the countryside into towns. ...resettlement agencies.* ◆◇◇◇◇ N-UNCOUNT: oft N of n

reshape /riːʃeɪp/ **reshapes, reshaping, reshaped.** To **reshape** something means to change its structure or organization. *If they succeed on Europe, then they will have reshaped the political and economic map of the world... Recession has simply accelerated changes that have been reshaping the industry anyway.* ◆◇◇◇◇ VERB V n ♦ **reshaping** *This thesis led to a radical reshaping of many Labour policies.* N-SING: also no det, usu N of n

reshuffle, reshuffles, reshuffling, reshuffled. The noun is pronounced /riːʃʌfᵊl/. The verb is pronounced /riːʃʌfᵊl/. When a political leader **reshuffles** the ministers in a government, he or she changes their jobs so that some of the ministers change their responsibilities. *The prime minister told reporters this morning that he plans to reshuffle his entire cabinet.* ◆◇◇◇◇ VERB =reorganize V n ► Also a noun. *The Prime Minister is expected to announce details of a government reshuffle later today... He has carried out a partial cabinet reshuffle.* N-COUNT: usu sing, with supp

reside /rɪzaɪd/ **resides, residing, resided** ◆◇◇◇◇

1 If someone **resides** somewhere, they live there or are staying there; a formal use. *Margaret resides with her invalid mother in a London suburb... All single full-time students must reside in university residence halls.* VERB =live V prep/adv

2 If a quality **resides** in something, it is in that thing; a formal use. *Happiness does not reside in strength or money... The military is based on the principle that the ultimate authority resides in the armed forces.* VB: no cont V in n

residence /rezɪdəns/ **residences** ◆◆◇◇◇

1 A **residence** is a house where people live; a formal use. *The two leaders met over lunch at Mr Kohl's private residence... She travels constantly, moving among her several residences around the world.* N-COUNT =home, house

2 Your place of **residence** is the place where you live; a formal use. *The were significant differences among women based on age, place of residence and educational levels.* N-UNCOUNT

3 Someone's **residence** in a particular place is the fact that they live there or that they are officially allowed to live there. *They had entered the country and had applied for permanent residence... She moved out of 28 Barbary Lane to take up residence in a house in Pacific Heights.* N-UNCOUNT

4 See also **hall of residence**.

5 If someone is **in residence** in a particular place, they are living there. *Windsor is open to visitors when the Royal Family is not in residence.* PHRASES v-link PHR

6 An artist or writer **in residence** is one who teaches in an institution such as a university or theatre company. *Wakoski is writer in residence at Michigan State University. ...former Chicago Symphony composer in residence, John Corliano.* n PHR

residency /rezɪdənsi/. Someone's **residency** in a particular place, especially in a country, is the fact that they live there or that they are officially allowed to live there. *He applied for British residency... Foreigners found without residency cards can be fined or imprisoned.* ◆◇◇◇◇ N-UNCOUNT

resident /rezɪdənt/ **residents** ◆◆◆◆◇

1 The **residents** of a house or area are the people who live there. *The Archbishop called upon the government to build more low cost homes for local residents... More than 10 percent of Munich residents live below the poverty line.* N-COUNT: usu pl, with supp

2 Someone who is **resident** in a country or a town lives there. *He moved to Belgium in 1990 to live with his son, who had been resident in Brussels since 1967.* ADJ: v-link ADJ, usu ADJ in n

3 A **resident** doctor or tutor lives in the place where he or she works. *The morning after your arrival, you meet with the resident physician for a private consultation.* ADJ: usu ADJ n =live-in

4 If an institution has a **resident** specialist, that specialist works for the institution. *Having begun her career at Gray's Pottery, she stayed there as resident designer for seven years.* ADJ: ADJ n

residential /rezɪdenʃᵊl/ ◆◆◇◇◇

1 A **residential** area contains houses rather than offices or factories. *He was born in Kensington, West London, then a smart residential area of large terrace houses... Fontbonne is a liberal arts college, located in a residential suburb of St. Louis.* ADJ: usu ADJ n

2 A **residential** institution is one where people live while they are studying there or being cared for there. *Training involves a two-year residential course... She works as an officer in charge of a residential home for children with disabilities.* ADJ: usu ADJ n

residents' association, residents' associations. A **residents' association** is an organization of people who live in a particular area. Residents' associations have meetings and take action to make the area more pleasant to live in. N-COUNT

residual /rɪzɪdʒuəl/. **Residual** is used to describe what remains of something when most of it has gone. *...residual radiation from nuclear weapons testing... Turn the hotplate off and allow the residual heat to keep the mixture gently simmering.*  ADJ: usu ADJ n

residue /rezɪdjuː, AM -duː/ **residues.** A **residue** of something is a small amount that remains after most of it has gone. *Always using the same shampoo means that a residue can build up on the hair.* ◆◇◇◇◇ N-COUNT: usu with supp

resign /rɪzaɪn/ **resigns, resigning, resigned** ◆◆◆◇◇
1 If you **resign** from a job or position, you formally announce that you are leaving it. *A hospital administrator has resigned over claims he lied to get the job... Mr Robb resigned his position last month.* VERB =quit V V n
2 If you **resign** yourself to an unpleasant situation or fact, you accept it because you realize that you cannot change it. *Pat and I resigned ourselves to yet another summer without a boat... He had resigned himself to watching the European Championships on television.* VERB =reconcile V pron-refl to n/-ing
3 See also **resigned.**

resignation /rezɪgneɪʃᵊn/ **resignations** ◆◆◆◇◇
1 Your **resignation** is a formal statement of your intention to leave a job or position. *Mr Morgan has offered his resignation and it has been accepted... The minister has agreed to withdraw his letter of resignation.* N-VAR: usu with poss
2 **Resignation** is the acceptance of an unpleasant situation or fact because you realize that you cannot change it. *There was no grief in his expression, only deep resignation... He sighed with profound resignation.* N-UNCOUNT

resigned /rɪzaɪnd/. If you are **resigned** to an unpleasant situation or fact, you accept it without complaining because you realize that you cannot change it. *He is resigned to the noise, the mess, the constant upheaval... Pauline was already resigned to losing her home.* ◆◆◇◇◇ ADJ: usu v-link ADJ, usu ADJ to n/-ing =reconciled ♦ **resignedly** /rɪzaɪnɪdli/ *'I know you don't believe me,' I said resignedly.* ADV: ADV with v

resilient /rɪzɪliənt/ ◆◇◇◇◇
1 Something that is **resilient** is strong and not easily damaged by being hit, stretched, or squeezed. *Cotton is more resistant to being squashed and polyester is more resilient. ...an armchair of some resilient plastic material.* ADJ-GRADED: usu v-link ADJ ♦ **resilience** *Do you feel that your muscles do not have the strength and resilience that they should have?* N-UNCOUNT: also a N
2 People and things that are **resilient** are able to recover easily and quickly from unpleasant or damaging events. *George Fraser was clearly a good solider, calm and resilient... When the U.S. stock market collapsed in October 1987, the Japanese stock market was the most resilient.* ADJ-GRADED: usu v-link ADJ ♦ **resilience** *...the resilience of human beings to fight after they've been attacked.* N-UNCOUNT: also a N

resin /rezɪn/ **resins** ◆◇◇◇◇
1 **Resin** is a sticky substance that is produced by some trees. *...a tropical tree which is bled regularly for its resin.* N-MASS
2 **Resin** is a substance that is produced chemically and used to make plastics. *Two of the lorries, carrying industrial resin and paint thinner, burst into flames.* N-MASS

resinous /rezɪnəs/. Something that is **resinous** is like resin or contains resin. *Propolis is a hard resinous substance made by bees from the juices of plants. ...great resinous logs burning in the wide hearth.* ADJ-GRADED

resist /rɪzɪst/ **resists, resisting, resisted** ◆◆◆◇◇
1 If you **resist** something such as a change, you refuse to accept it and try to prevent it. *The Prime Minister says she will resist a single European currency being imposed... They resisted our attempts to modernize the distribution of books.* VERB =oppose V n -ing V n
2 If you **resist** someone or **resist** an attack by them, you fight back against them. *The man was shot outside his house as he tried to resist arrest... When she had attempted to cut his nails he resisted.* VERB V n V
3 If you **resist** doing something, or **resist** the temptation to do something, you stop yourself from doing it although you would like to do it. *Students should resist the temptation to focus on exams alone... She cannot resist giving him advice.* VB: oft with neg V n/-ing
4 If someone or something **resists** damage of some kind, they remain unharmed or undamaged by it. *...bodies trained and toughened to resist the cold... Chemicals form a protective layer that resists both oil and water-based stains.* VERB =withstand V n

resistance /rɪzɪstəns/ **resistances** ◆◆◆◇◇
1 **Resistance** to something such as a change or a new idea is a refusal to accept it. *The US wants big cuts in European agricultural export subsidies, but this is meeting resistance.* N-UNCOUNT: oft N to n
2 **Resistance** to an attack consists of fighting back against the people who have attacked you. *A BBC correspondent in Colombo says the troops are encountering stiff resistance... Police in riot gear cleared the noisy demonstrators, who offered no resistance.* N-UNCOUNT
3 The **resistance** of your body to germs or diseases is its power to remain unharmed or unaffected by them. *This disease is surprisingly difficult to catch as most people have a natural resistance to it.* N-UNCOUNT: oft N to n
4 Wind or air **resistance** is a force which slows down a moving object or vehicle. *The design of the bicycle has managed to reduce the effects of wind resistance and drag.* N-UNCOUNT: usu supp N
5 In electrical engineering or physics, **resistance** is the ability of a substance or an electrical circuit to stop the flow of an electrical current through it. *Superconductors, materials that lose all their electrical resistance, conduct electricity faster than ordinary materials.* N-VAR
6 In a country which is occupied by the army of another country, or which has a dictatorship, **the resistance** is an organized group of people who are involved in illegal activities against the people in power. *They managed to escape after being arrested by the resistance.* N-SING: the N
7 If you take or follow the **line of least resistance** in a situation, you take the easiest course of action, even though you think that it may not be the right thing to do; used in British English. The usual American expression is **path of least resistance.** *They would rather take the line of least resistance than become involved in arguments.* PHRASE: PHR after v

resistant /rɪzɪstənt/ ◆◆◇◇◇
1 Someone who is **resistant** to something is opposed to it and wants to prevent it. *Some people are very resistant to the idea of exercise.* ADJ-GRADED: oft ADJ to n
2 If something is **resistant** to a particular thing, it is not harmed by it. *...how to improve plants to make them more resistant to disease... The body may be less resistant if it is cold.* ADJ-GRADED: oft ADJ to n

-resistant /-rɪzɪstənt/. **-resistant** is added to nouns to form adjectives that describe something as not being harmed or affected by the thing mentioned. *Children's suncare products are normally water-resistant. ...heat-resistant glass dishes. ...bullet-resistant glass.* COMB in ADJ-GRADED =-proof

resistor /rɪzɪstəʳ/ **resistors.** A **resistor** is a device which is designed to increase the ability of an electric circuit to stop the flow of an electric current through it; a technical term. N-COUNT

resit, resits, resitting, resat. The verb is pronounced /riːsɪt/. The noun is pronounced /riːsɪt/. If someone **resits** a test or examination, they take it again, usually because they failed the first time; used in British English. The usual American word is **retake.** *This year, Jim is resitting the exams he failed... If they fail, they can often resit the next year.* VERB =retake V n V ► Also a noun. *He failed his First Year exams and didn't bother about the resits.* N-COUNT =retake

resold /riːsoʊld/. **Resold** is the past tense and past participle of **resell.**

resolute /rezəluːt/. If you describe someone as **resolute**, you approve of them because they are absolutely determined not to change their mind or not to give up a course of action; a formal word. *Voters perceive him as a decisive and resolute international leader... He described the situation as very dangerous and called for resolute action.* ◆◇◇◇◇ ADJ-GRADED PRAGMATICS =firm, determined ≠irresolute ♦ **resolutely** *He resolutely refused to speak English unless forced to... The United States remains resolutely opposed to this.* ADV-GRADED: ADV with v, ADV adj

resolution /rezəluːʃᵊn/ **resolutions** ◆◆◆◆◇
1 A **resolution** is a formal decision taken at a N-COUNT:

meeting by means of a vote. *He replied that the UN had passed two major resolutions calling for a complete withdrawal. ...a draft resolution on the occupied territories.* usu N supp, oft N num

2 If you make a **resolution**, you decide to try very hard to do something. *They made a resolution to lose all the weight gained during the Christmas period.* • See also **New Year's resolution**. N-COUNT

3 **Resolution** is determination to do something or not do something. *'I think I'll try a hypnotist,' I said with sudden resolution.* N-UNCOUNT

4 The **resolution** of a problem or difficulty is the final solving of it; a formal use. *...the successful resolution of a dispute involving UN inspectors in Baghdad. ...in order to find a peaceful resolution to the crisis.* N-SING: oft N *to/of* n

5 The **resolution** of an image is how clear the image is; a technical use in science. *Now this machine gives us such high resolution that we can see very small specks of calcium.* N-UNCOUNT: usu with supp

resolve /rɪzɒlv/ **resolves, resolving, resolved** ◆◆◆◇◇

1 To **resolve** a problem, argument, or difficulty means to find a solution to it; a formal use. *We must find a way to resolve these problems before it's too late... They hoped the crisis could be resolved peacefully.* VERB =sort out, solve V n

2 If you **resolve** to do something, you make a firm decision to do it; a formal use. *She resolved to report the matter to the hospital's nursing manager... She resolved that, if Mimi forgot this promise, she would remind her.* VERB V to-inf V that

3 **Resolve** is absolute determination to do what you have decided to do; a formal use. *So you're saying this will strengthen the American public's resolve to go to war if necessary?* N-VAR: oft N to-inf =determination

4 If you **resolve** something into a clearer form, or if it **resolves** into a clearer form, its shape or the different parts it contains become clear; a formal use. *...like a musician resolving a confused mass of sound into melodic or harmonic order... Each of the spirals of light resolved into points.* V-ERG V n *into* n V *into* n

resolved /rɪzɒlvd/. If you are **resolved** to do something, you are determined to do it; a formal use. *Most folk with property to lose were resolved to defend it.* ◆◇◇◇◇ ADJ-GRADED: v-link ADJ to-inf =determined

resonance /rezənəns/ **resonances** ◆◇◇◇◇

1 If something has a **resonance** for someone, it has a special meaning or is particularly important to them, for example because they agree with it or because it is similar in some way to something else. *The ideas of order, security, family, religion and country had the same resonance for them as for Michael.* N-VAR

2 If a sound has **resonance**, it is deep, clear, and echoing. *His voice had lost its resonance; it was tense and strained.* N-UNCOUNT

3 A **resonance** is the sound which is produced by an object when it vibrates at the same rate as the sound waves from another object; a technical use in physics. *The ear has a set of filaments to vibrate in resonance with incoming sound-waves.* N-VAR

resonant /rezənənt/ ◆◇◇◇◇

1 A sound that is **resonant** is deep and strong. *His voice sounded oddly resonant in the empty room... He responded with a resonant laugh.* ADJ-GRADED

2 Something that is **resonant** has a special meaning or is particularly important to people, for example because they agree with it or because it reminds them of something else; a literary word. *It is a country resonant with cinematic potential, from its architecture to its landscape.* ♦ **resonantly** *The third resonantly poetic language of Scotland this century is Gaelic.* ADJ ADV-GRADED

resonate /rezəneɪt/ **resonates, resonating, resonated** ◆◇◇◇◇

1 If something **resonates**, it vibrates and produces a deep, strong sound. *The bass guitar began to thump so loudly that it resonated in my head.* VERB V

2 You say that something **resonates** when it has a special meaning or when it is particularly important to someone, for example because they agree with it or because it reminds them of something else. *London is confident and alive, resonating with all the qualities of a civilised city.* VERB V *with* n

resort /rɪzɔːʳt/ **resorts, resorting, resorted** ◆◆◆◇◇

1 If you **resort** to a course of action that you do not really approve of, you adopt it because you cannot see any other way of achieving what you want to achieve. *His punishing work schedule had made him resort to drugs... Some schools have resorted to recruiting teachers from overseas.* VERB =turn V *to* n/-ing

2 If you say that you can achieve something without **resort** to a particular course of action, you mean that you can succeed in what you are trying to do without carrying out that action. If you have to have **resort** to something you would rather not do, you believe you have to do it in order to succeed in something else. *Congress has a responsibility to ensure that all peaceful options are exhausted before resort to war.* N-UNCOUNT: N *to* n =recourse

3 If you do something **as a last resort**, you do it because you can find no other way of getting out of a difficult situation or of solving a problem. *Nuclear weapons should be used only as a last resort... As a last resort you may have to accept their point of view.* PHRASE: PHR with cl

4 You use **in the last resort** when stating the most basic or important fact that will still be true in a situation whatever else happens. *...telling the Americans that the British would in the last resort support them whatever they did.* PHRASE: PHR with cl =ultimately

5 A **resort** is a place where a lot of people spend their holidays. *The ski resorts are expanding to meet the growing number of skiers that come here.* N-COUNT: usu supp N

resound /rɪzaʊnd/ **resounds, resounding, resounded**

1 When a noise **resounds**, it is heard very loudly and clearly; a literary use. *A roar of approval resounded through the Ukranian parliament... The soldiers' boots resounded in the street.* VERB =resonate V prep

2 If a place **resounds** with particular noises, it is filled with them; a literary use. *The whole place resounded with music... Tonight the Maysfield Leisure Centre resound to the strains of the Richie Valens song 'La Bamba'.* VERB V *with* n V *to* n

resounding /rɪzaʊndɪŋ/ ◆◇◇◇◇

1 A **resounding** sound is loud and echoing. *There was a resounding slap as Andrew struck him violently across the face... She got a resounding round of applause... The answer, Segal says, was a resounding yes!* ♦ **resoundingly** *Leatherdale was hit resoundingly on the side of the head.* ADJ: usu ADJ n ADV

2 You can refer to a very great success as a **resounding** success. *The good weather helped to make the occasion a resounding success.* ♦ **resoundingly** *They resoundingly support government programs for the poor... International trading remains resoundingly successful.* ADJ: usu ADJ n ADV-GRADED: ADV with v, ADV adj

resource /rɪzɔːʳs, AM riːsɔːrs/ **resources** ◆◆◆◆◇

1 The **resources** of an organization or person are the materials, money, and other things that they have and can use in order to function properly. *Some families don't have the resources to feed themselves properly... There's a great shortage of resource materials in many schools.* N-COUNT: usu pl

2 A country's **resources** are the things that it has and can use to increase its wealth, such as coal, oil, or land. *...resources like coal, tungsten, oil and copper... Today we are overpopulated, straining the earth's resources.* N-COUNT: usu pl

resourced /rɪzɔːʳst, AM riːsɔːrst/. If an organization is **resourced**, it has all the things, such as money and materials, that it needs to function properly; used in British English. *We are not yet fully resourced in Northern Ireland... The school is very well resourced – we have a language laboratory and use computers and videos.* ADJ: usu adv ADJ

resourceful /rɪzɔːʳsfʊl/. Someone who is **resourceful** is good at finding ways of dealing with problems. *He was amazingly inventive and resourceful, and played a major role in my career... Her mother was a resourceful and energetic woman.* ♦ **resourcefulness** *Because of his* ◆◇◇◇◇ ADJ-GRADED N-UNCOUNT *adventures, he is a person of far greater experience and resourcefulness.*

respect /rɪspe̲kt/ **respects, respecting, respected** ◆◆◆◆◇

1 If you **respect** someone, you have a good opinion of their character or ideas. *I want him to respect me as a career woman... He needs the advice of people he respects, and he respects you.* VERB V n

2 If you have **respect** for someone, you have a good opinion of them. See also **self-respect**. *I have tremendous respect for Dean... His voice was warm with friendship and respect.* N-UNCOUNT: usu N *for* n

3 You can say **with respect** when you are politely disagreeing with someone or criticizing them. *With respect, Minister, you still haven't answered my question... With respect, I hardly think that's the point.* PHRASE: PHR with cl PRAGMATICS

4 If you **respect** someone's wishes, rights, or customs, you avoid doing things that they would dislike or regard as wrong. *Finally, trying to respect her wishes, I said I'd leave.* VERB V n

5 If you show **respect** for someone's wishes, rights, or customs, you avoid doing anything they would dislike or regard as wrong. *They will campaign for the return of traditional lands and respect for aboriginal rights and customs.* N-UNCOUNT: usu N *for* n

6 If you **respect** a law or moral principle, you agree not to break it. *It is about time tour operators respected the law and their own code of conduct.* VERB V n ▶ Also a noun. *...respect for the law and the rejection of the use of violence.* N-UNCOUNT: usu N *for* n

7 If you **pay** your **respects** to someone, you go to see them or speak to them. You usually do this to be polite, and not necessarily because you want to do it; a formal use. *Carl had asked him to visit the hospital and to pay his respects to Francis.* PHRASES V inflects

8 If you **pay** your **last respects** to someone who has just died, you show your respect or affection for them by coming to see their body or their grave. *The son had nothing to do with arranging the funeral, but came along to pay his last respects.* V inflects

9 You use expressions like **in this respect** and **in many respects** to indicate that what you are saying applies to the feature you have just mentioned or to many features of something. *The children are not unintelligent – in fact, they seem quite normal in this respect... In many respects Asian women see themselves as equal to their men.* PHR with cl PRAGMATICS

10 You use **with respect to**, or in British English **in respect of**, to say what something relates to; a formal use. *Parents often have little choice with respect to the way their child is medically treated... Where Dr Shapland feels the system is not working most effectively is in respect of professional training and development.* PHR with cl

respectable /rɪspe̲ktəbᵊl/ ◆◆◇◇◇

1 Someone or something that is **respectable** is approved of by society and considered to be morally correct. *He came from a perfectly respectable middle-class family... It was a highly respectable and what was called an 'old-fashioned' hotel situated not far from Piccadilly.* ♦ **respectably** /rɪspe̲ktəbli/ *She's respectably dressed in jeans and sweatshirt.* ♦ **respectability** /rɪspe̲ktəbɪ̲lɪti/ *If she divorced Tony, she would lose the respectability she had as Mrs Tony Tatterton.* ADJ-GRADED =reputable; ADV-GRADED; N-UNCOUNT

2 You can say that something is **respectable** when you mean that it is adequate or acceptable. *...investments that offer respectable and highly attractive rates of return... At last I have something respectable to wear!* ADJ-GRADED =decent

respected /rɪspe̲ktɪd/. Someone or something that is **respected** is admired and considered important by many people. *He is highly respected for his novels and plays as well as his translations of American novels... She is a well respected member of the international community.* ◆◆◇◇◇ ADJ-GRADED: oft adv ADJ =admired

respecter /rɪspe̲ktəʳ/ **respecters**

1 If you say that someone is a **respecter** of something such as a belief or idea, you mean that they behave in a way which shows that they have a high opinion of it. *Ford was a respecter of proprieties and liked to see things done properly.* N-COUNT: usu N *of* n

2 If you say that someone or something is **no respecter of** a rule or tradition, you mean that the rule or tradition is not important to them. *The British Sports Council is no respecter of privacy or careers as it tries to stamp out the cheats... Accidents and sudden illnesses are no respecters of age.* PHRASE: v-link PHR

respectful /rɪspe̲ktfʊl/. If you are **respectful**, you show respect for someone. *He was always so polite and respectful... The children in our family are always respectful to their elders... The patient has the right to considerate and respectful care.* ♦ **respectfully** *'You are a true artist,' she said respectfully.* ◆◇◇◇◇ ADJ-GRADED: oft ADJ *of/towards/to* n; ADV-GRADED: usu ADV with v

respective /rɪspe̲ktɪv/. **Respective** means relating or belonging separately to the individual people you have just mentioned. *Steve and I were at very different stages in our respective careers... They went into their respective bedrooms to pack.* ◆◇◇◇◇ ADJ: ADJ n, usu poss ADJ pl-n

respectively /rɪspe̲ktɪvli/. **Respectively** means in the same order as the items that you have just mentioned. *Their sons, Ben and Jonathan, were three and six respectively... They finished first and second respectively.* ◆◆◇◇◇ ADV: ADV with cl/group

respiration /re̲spɪreɪ̲ʃᵊn/. Your **respiration** is your breathing; a medical term. *His respiration grew fainter throughout the day.* • See also **artificial respiration**. N-UNCOUNT =breathing

respirator /re̲spɪreɪtəʳ/ **respirators**

1 A **respirator** is a device that allows people to breathe when they cannot breathe naturally, for example because they are ill or have been injured. *She was so ill that she was put on a respirator.* N-COUNT

2 A **respirator** is a device you wear over your mouth and nose in order to breathe when you are surrounded by smoke or poisonous gas. N-COUNT

respiratory /re̲spərətri, AM -tɔːri/. **Respiratory** means relating to breathing; a medical term. *...people with severe respiratory problems... If you smoke then the whole respiratory system is constantly under attack.* ◆◇◇◇◇ ADJ: ADJ n

respite /re̲spaɪt, -pɪt/ ◆◇◇◇◇

1 A **respite** is a short period of rest from something unpleasant; a formal use. *It was some weeks now since they had had any respite from shellfire.* N-SING: also no det, oft N *from* n

2 A **respite** is a short delay before a very unpleasant or difficult situation which may or may not take place; a formal use. *Devaluation would only give the economy a brief respite.* N-SING: also no det =reprieve

resplendent /rɪsple̲ndənt/. If you describe someone or something as **resplendent**, you mean that their appearance is very impressive and expensive-looking; a formal word. *Bessie, resplendent in royal blue velvet, was hovering beside the table. ...the resplendent hotel banqueting-room.* ADJ-GRADED: oft ADJ *in* n =dazzling

respond /rɪspɒ̲nd/ **responds, responding, responded** ◆◆◆◆◇

1 When you **respond** to something that is done or said, you react to it by doing or saying something yourself. *They are likely to respond positively to the President's request for aid... The army responded with gunfire and tear gas... 'Are you well enough to carry on?'—'Of course,' she responded scornfully... Baker responded that the administration would look at the suggestion.* VERB V *to* n V V with quote V that

2 When you **respond** to a need, crisis, or challenge, you take the necessary or appropriate action. *This modest group size allows our teachers to respond to the needs of each student.* VERB =react V *to* n

3 If a patient or their injury or illness **is responding** to treatment, the treatment is working and they are getting better. *I'm pleased to say that he is now doing well and responding to treatment.* VERB V *to* n

respondent /rɪspɒ̲ndənt/ **respondents** ◆◇◇◇◇

1 The **respondents** to a survey or questionnaire are the people who answer the questions in it. *60 per cent of the respondents said they disapproved of the president's performance.* N-COUNT: usu pl

2 A **respondent** is someone against whom a petition or appeal is brought; a legal use. *In addition,* N-COUNT ≠complainant, appellant *the respondent disclosed professional confidences to one of the patients.*

response /rɪspɒns/ **responses.** Your **response** to an event or to something that is said is your reply or reaction to it. *There has been no response to his remarks from the government... Your positive response will reinforce her actions... The meeting was called in response to a request from Venezuela.* ◆◆◆◆◇ N-COUNT: oft N *to/from* n, also *in* N

responsibility /rɪspɒnsɪbɪlɪti/ **responsibilities** ◆◆◆◆◇

1 If you have **responsibility** for something or someone, or if they are your **responsibility**, it is your job or duty to deal with them and to take decisions relating to them. *Each manager had responsibility for just under 600 properties... We need to take responsibility for looking after our own health... 'She's not your responsibility,' he said gently.* N-UNCOUNT: oft N *for* n/-ing

2 If you accept **responsibility** for something that has happened, you agree that you were to blame for it or you caused it. *British Rail has admitted responsibility for the accident... Someone had to give orders and take responsibility for mistakes.* N-UNCOUNT: oft N *for* n

3 Your **responsibilities** are the duties that you have because of your job or position. *I am told that he handled his responsibilities as a counselor in a highly intelligent and caring fashion. ...programmes to help employees balance work and family responsibilities.* N-PLURAL: usu with supp

4 If someone is given **responsibility**, they are given the right or opportunity to make important decisions or to take action without having to get permission from anyone else. *She would have loved to have a better-paying job with more responsibility... Carrington held a position of responsibility within the government.* N-UNCOUNT

5 If you think that you have a **responsibility** to do something, you feel that you ought to do it because it is morally right to do it. *The court feels it has a responsibility to ensure that customers are not misled... As parents we have a responsibility to give our children a sense of belonging.* N-SING: usu N to-inf =duty

6 If you think that you have a **responsibility to** someone, you feel that it is your duty to take action that will protect their interests. *She had decided that as a doctor she had a responsibility to her fellow creatures.* N-SING: N *to/towards* n

responsible /rɪspɒnsɪbᵊl/ ◆◆◆◆◇

1 If someone or something is **responsible** for a particular event or situation, they are the cause of it or they can be blamed for it. *He still felt responsible for her death... I want you to do everything you can to find out who's responsible.* ADJ: v-link ADJ, usu ADJ *for* n/-ing

2 If you are **responsible** for something, it is your job or duty to deal with it and make decisions relating to it. *...the minister responsible for the environment... The man responsible for finding the volunteers is Dr. Charles Weber.* ADJ: v-link ADJ, usu ADJ *for* n/-ing

3 If you are **responsible to** a person or group, they have authority over you and you have to report to them about what you do. *I'm responsible to my board of directors... The government will be responsible to the President alone.* ADJ: v-link ADJ *to* n

4 **Responsible** people behave properly and sensibly, without needing to be supervised. *He's a very responsible sort of person... He feels that the media should be more responsible in what they report.* ADJ-GRADED ♦ **responsibly** *He urged everyone to act responsibly.* ADV-GRADED: ADV with v

5 **Responsible** jobs involve making important decisions or carrying out important tasks. *I work in a government office. It's a responsible position, I suppose, but not very exciting... They have been demoted to less responsible jobs.* ADJ-GRADED: ADJ n

responsive /rɪspɒnsɪv/ ◆◇◇◇◇

1 A **responsive** person is quick to react to people or events and to show emotions such as pleasure and affection. *Harriet was an easy, responsive little girl... This is a responsive class with plenty of ideas... Three months before birth babies are already responsive to sound.* ADJ-GRADED ♦ **responsiveness** *This condition decreases sexual desire and responsiveness.* N-UNCOUNT

2 If someone or something is **responsive**, they react quickly and favourably. *With an election coming soon, your MP should be very responsive to your request.* ADJ-GRADED: usu ADJ *to* n ♦ **responsiveness** *Such responsiveness to public pressure is extraordinary.* N-UNCOUNT

3 A **responsive** action is made as a reaction to something that has just been said or done. *At hearing his name spoken, the dog gave a responsive wag of his tail.* ADJ: ADJ n

rest 1 quantifier uses

rest /rest/ ◆◆◆◆◇

1 **The rest** is used to refer to all the parts of something or all the things in a group that remain or that you have not already mentioned. *It was an experience I will treasure for the rest of my life... I'm going to throw a party, then invest the rest of the money... He was unable to travel to Barcelona with the rest of the team.* QUANT: QUANT *of* def-n ► Also a pronoun. *Only 55 per cent of the raw material is canned. The rest is thrown away, or fed to cows.* PRON

2 You can add **and the rest** or **all the rest of it** to the end of a statement or list when you want to refer vaguely to other things like or associated with the ones you have already mentioned; an informal expression, used in spoken English. *...a man with nice clothes, a Range Rover and the rest... And what about racism and all the rest of it?* PHRASE PRAGMATICS =and so on, et cetera

rest 2 verb and noun uses

rest /rest/ **rests, resting, rested** ◆◆◆◆◇

1 If you **rest** or if you **rest** your body, you do not do anything active for a time. *He's tired and exhausted, and has been advised to rest for two weeks... Try to rest the injured limb as much as possible.* VERB V V n

2 If you get some **rest** or have a **rest**, you do not do anything active for a time. *'You're worn out, Laura,' he said. 'Go home and get some rest.'... After I've had a good rest, I'll tell you everything.* N-VAR

3 If something such as a theory or someone's success **rests** on a particular thing, it depends on that thing; a formal use. *Such a view rests on a number of incorrect assumptions... The long-term future of the country rests on how we teach our children.* VERB =hang, depend V *on/upon* n/wh

4 If authority, a responsibility, or a decision **rests** with you, you have that authority or responsibility, or you are the one who will make that decision; a formal use. *The judge said that 'whether Miss Bergman wishes to admit it or not, the responsibility rests with her.'... The final decision rested with the President.* VERB V *with* n

5 If you **rest** something somewhere, you put it there so that its weight is supported. *He rested his arms on the back of the chair... He rested one of his crutches against the rail.* VERB =lean V n prep

6 If something **is resting** somewhere, or if you **are resting** it there, it is in a position where its weight is supported. *His head was resting on her shoulder... He had been resting his head in his hands, deep in thought.* V-ERG V prep/adv V n prep/adv

7 If you **rest** on or against someone or something, you lean on them so that they support the weight of your body. *He rested on his pickaxe for a while.* VERB =lean V prep

8 A **rest** is an object that is used to support something, especially your head, arms, or feet. *When you are sitting, keep your elbow on the arm rest.* N-COUNT: usu n N =support

9 If your eyes **rest** on a particular person or object, you look directly at them, rather than somewhere else; used in written English. *As she spoke, her eyes rested on her husband's face.* VERB =settle V *on/upon* n

10 See also **rested.**

11 When an object that has been moving **comes to rest**, it finally stops; a formal expression. *The plane had plowed a path through a patch of forest before coming to rest in a field.* PHRASES V inflects =stop

12 If you say that someone can **rest easy**, you mean that they don't need to worry about a particular situation. *In that case, we can rest easy. Gagnier is the most helpful superintendent they have.*

13 If someone tells you to **give** something **a rest**, they want you to stop doing it because it annoys them or because they think it is harming you; an V inflects PRAGMATICS

informal expression. *Give it a rest, will you? We're trying to get some sleep... I think you ought to give football a rest for a time.*

14 If you say that someone who has died is **laid to rest**, you mean that they are buried. *His dying wish was to be laid to rest at the church near his Somerset home.* V inflects

15 If you **lay** something such as fears or rumours **to rest** or you **put** them **to rest**, you succeed in proving that they are not true. *His speech should lay those fears to rest... I am determined to put to rest these rumours that we are in financial trouble.* V inflects =allay

16 If someone refuses to **let** a subject **rest**, they refuse to stop talking about it, especially after they have been talking about it for a long time. *I am not prepared to let this matter rest... Let it rest, Rachel. Leave her in peace.* V inflects =drop

17 If someone or something **puts** your **mind at rest** or **sets** your **mind at rest**, they tell you something that stops you worrying. *She was quick to put his mind at rest. 'Mrs Barrett will be delighted to have your brothers back,' she said... A brain scan last Friday finally set his mind at rest.* V and N inflect =reassure

18 • **rest assured**: see **assured**. • to **rest on your laurels**: see **laurel**. • to **rest in peace**: see **peace**.

restart /riːstɑːʳt/ **restarts, restarting, restarted.** If you **restart** something that has been interrupted or stopped, or if it **restarts**, it starts to happen or function again. *The commissioners agreed to restart talks as soon as possible... The race was restarted after a break of around 20 minutes... The trial will restart today with a new jury.* ► Also a noun. *After a goalless first half, Australia took the lead within a minute of the restart.* ◆◇◇◇◇ V-ERG; V n; V; N-COUNT

restate /riːsteɪt/ **restates, restating, restated.** If you **restate** something, you say it again in words or writing, usually in a slightly different way; a formal word. *He continued throughout to restate his opposition to violence... The letter merely restated the law of the land.* ◆◇◇◇◇ VERB =reiterate; V n

restatement /riːsteɪtmənt/ **restatements.** A **restatement** of something that has been said or written is a repetition of it, usually in a slightly different form; a formal word. *I hope this book is not yet another restatement of the prevailing wisdom... Mr Smith concentrated on offering a classic restatement of Labour values.* N-COUNT: usu N *of* n =reiteration

restaurant /restərɒnt, AM -rɑnt/ **restaurants.** A **restaurant** is a place where you can pay for and eat a meal. In restaurants your food is usually served to you at your table by a waiter or waitress. *They ate in an Italian restaurant in Forth Street... We had dinner in the hotel's restaurant.* ◆◆◆◆◇ N-COUNT

restaurant car, restaurant cars. In British English, a **restaurant car** is the same as a **dining car**. N-COUNT

restaurateur /restərətɜːʳ/ **restaurateurs.** A **restaurateur** is a person who owns and manages a restaurant; a formal word. ◆◇◇◇◇ N-COUNT

rested /restɪd/. If you feel **rested**, you feel more energetic because you have just had a rest. *He looked tanned and well rested after his vacation.* ADJ-GRADED: v-link ADJ

restful /restfʊl/. Something that is **restful** helps you to feel calm and relaxed. *Adjust the lighting so it is soft and restful... After a joyous and restful three days, I left this beautiful city.* ADJ-GRADED =soothing, peaceful

rest home, rest homes. A **rest home** is the same as an **old people's home**. N-COUNT

resting place, resting places

1 A **resting place** is a place where you can stay and rest, usually for a short period of time. *The area was an important resting place for many types of migrant birds.* N-COUNT

2 You can refer to the place where a dead person is buried as their **resting place** or their final **resting place**. *The hill is supposed to be the resting place of the legendary King Lud.* N-COUNT: usu with poss

restitution /restɪtjuːʃᵊn, AM -tuː-/. **Restitution** is the act of giving back to a person something that was lost or stolen, or of paying them money for the loss; a formal word. *The victims are demanding full restitution... We have asked that they rehire the people that were fired and that they make restitution to them.* N-UNCOUNT

restive /restɪv/. If you are **restive**, you are impatient, bored, or dissatisfied; a formal word. *The audience grew restive. ...restive national minorities.* ♦ **restiveness** *There were signs of restiveness among the younger members.* ADJ-GRADED; N-UNCOUNT

restless /restləs/ ◆◆◇◇◇

1 If you are **restless**, you are bored, impatient, or dissatisfied, and you want to do something else. *By 1982, she was restless and needed a new impetus for her talent. ...a major new initiative to placate the country's restless intellectuals.* ♦ **restlessness** *From the audience came increasing sounds of restlessness.* ADJ-GRADED; N-UNCOUNT

2 If someone is **restless**, they keep moving around because they find it difficult to keep still. *My father seemed very restless and excited.* ♦ **restlessness** *Karen complained of hyperactivity and restlessness.* ♦ **restlessly** *He paced up and down restlessly, trying to put his thoughts in order.* ADJ-GRADED =fidgety; N-UNCOUNT; ADV: usu ADV with v

3 If you have a **restless** sleep, you do not sleep properly and when you wake up you feel tired and uncomfortable. *The shocking revelations of the 700-page report had caused him several restless nights... Hurt had spent a restless few hours on the plane from Paris.* ADJ-GRADED: ADJ n ≠restful

restock /riːstɒk/ **restocks, restocking, restocked**

1 If you **restock** something such as a shelf, fridge, or shop, you fill it with food or other goods to replace the food or goods that you have used or sold. *I have to restock the freezer... Back on Flatbush Avenue, Pong is busy restocking his shelves with cucumbers and coconuts.* VERB; V n; V n *with* n; Also V

2 To **restock** a lake means to put more fish in it because there are very few left. *McNicholl will use her stock of Orkney oysters to restock lochs and estuaries throughout Scotland and England.* VERB; V n; Also V n *with* n, V

Restoration /restəreɪʃᵊn/ ◆◆◇◇◇

1 The Restoration was the event in 1660 when Charles the Second became King of England, Scotland, and Ireland after a period when there had been no King or Queen. N-PROPER: *the* N

2 Restoration is used to refer to the style of drama and architecture that were popular during and just after the reign of Charles the Second in England. *...a Restoration comedy.* ADJ: ADJ n

restorative /rɪstɔːrətɪv/ **restoratives**

1 Something that is **restorative** makes you feel healthier, stronger, or more cheerful after you have been feeling tired, weak, or miserable. *She opened the door to her bedroom, thinking how restorative a hot bath would feel tonight.* ADJ-GRADED

2 If you describe something as a **restorative**, you mean that it makes you feel healthier, stronger, or more cheerful after you have been feeling tired, weak, or miserable. *Seven days off could be a wonderful restorative.* N-COUNT

restore /rɪstɔːʳ/ **restores, restoring, restored** ◆◆◆◇◇

1 To **restore** a situation or practice means to cause it to exist again. *The army has recently been brought in to restore order... As they smiled at each other, harmony was restored again... The death penalty was never restored.* ♦ **restoration** /restəreɪʃᵊn/ *His visit is expected to lead to the restoration of diplomatic relations... They were committed to the eventual restoration of a traditional monarchy.* VERB; V n; N-UNCOUNT: usu N *of* n

2 To **restore** someone or something to a previous condition means to cause them to be in that condition once again. *We will restore her to health but it may take time... He said the ousted president must be restored to power... His country desperately needs Western aid to restore its ailing economy.* ♦ **restoration** *I owe the restoration of my hearing to this remarkable new technique.* VERB; V n *to* n; V n; N-UNCOUNT: usu N *of* n

3 When someone **restores** something such as an old building, painting, or piece of furniture, they repair and clean it, so that it looks like it did when it was new. *...experts who specialise in examining and restoring ancient parchments. ...the beautifully* VERB; V n; V-ed *restored old town square.* ♦ **restoration, restorations** *I specialized in the restoration of old houses... The bones were 'mislaid' during the seventeenth-century restorations.* N-VAR

4 If something that was lost or stolen **is restored** to its owner, it is returned to them; a formal use. *The following day their horses and goods were restored to them... The looted property was restored and the charge d'affaires was told that the soldiers responsible had been arrested.* VB: usu passive =return *be* V-ed *to* n *be* V-ed

restorer /rɪstɔːrəʳ/ **restorers.** A **restorer** is someone whose job it is to repair old buildings, paintings, and furniture so that they look like they did when they were new. *...an antiques restorer from Bermondsey.* N-COUNT: oft n N

restrain /rɪstreɪn/ **restrains, restraining, restrained** ◆◆◇◇◇

1 If you **restrain** someone, you stop them from doing what they intended or wanted to do, usually by using your physical strength. *Wally gripped my arm, partly to restrain me and partly to reassure me... One onlooker had to be restrained by police.* VERB V n

2 If you **restrain** an emotion or you **restrain** yourself from doing something, you prevent yourself from showing that emotion or doing what you wanted or intended to do. *She was unable to restrain her desperate anger... Unable to restrain herself, she rose and went to the phone... Gladys wanted to ask, 'Aren't you angry with him?' But she restrained herself from doing so.* VERB V n V n *from* -ing/n

3 To **restrain** something that is growing or increasing means to prevent it from getting too large. *The radical 500-day plan was very clear on how it intended to try to restrain inflation... In the 1970s, the government tried to restrain corruption.* VERB =curb, check V n

restrained /rɪstreɪnd/ ◆◇◇◇◇

1 Someone who is **restrained** is very calm and unemotional. *In the circumstances he felt he'd been very restrained... Livy thought Caroline's greeting seemed a little restrained.* ADJ-GRADED

2 If you describe someone's clothes or the decorations in a house as **restrained**, you mean that you like them because they are subtle and tasteful. *She chose restrained earrings and a large brooch.* ADJ-GRADED PRAGMATICS =tasteful

restraint /rɪstreɪnt/ **restraints** ◆◆◇◇◇

1 **Restraints** are rules or conditions that limit or restrict someone or something. *The Prime Minister is calling for new restraints on trade unions... With open frontiers and lax visa controls, criminals could cross into the country without restraint.* N-VAR: usu with supp, oft N *on* n

2 **Restraint** is calm, controlled, and unemotional behaviour. *They behaved with more restraint than I'd expected... I'll speak to the staff and ask them to exercise restraint and common sense.* N-UNCOUNT

3 **Restraint** of something is the act of preventing it from increasing too much or from being done freely; a formal use. *For a year and a half, wage restraint on a voluntary basis worked... He sued them for restraint of trade and won.* N-UNCOUNT: with supp

restrict /rɪstrɪkt/ **restricts, restricting, restricted** ◆◆◇◇◇

1 If you **restrict** something, you put a limit on it in order to reduce it or prevent it becoming too great. *There is talk of raising the admission requirements to restrict the number of students on campus... The French, I believe, restrict Japanese imports to a maximum of 3 per cent of their market.* VERB =limit V n V n *to* amount

♦ **restriction** /rɪstrɪkʃᵊn/ *Since the costs of science were rising faster than inflation, some restriction on funding was necessary.* N-UNCOUNT =limit

2 To **restrict** the movement or actions of someone or something means to prevent them from moving or acting freely. *Villagers say the fence would restrict public access to the hills... The government imprisoned dissidents, forbade travel, and restricted the press... These dams have restricted the flow of the river downstream.* ♦ **restriction** *...the justification for this restriction of individual liberty.* VERB V n Also V n *from* -ing N-UNCOUNT

3 If you **restrict** someone or their activities to one thing, they can only do, have, or deal with that thing. If you **restrict** them to one place, they cannot go anywhere else. *He was, however, allowed to stay on at the temple as long as he restricted himself to his studies... The patient isn't restricted to a meagre diet... For the first two weeks patients are restricted to the grounds.* VERB =confine V n *to* n

4 If you **restrict** something to a particular group, only that group can do it or have it. If you **restrict** something to a particular place, it is allowed only in that place. *The International Shooting Union is to restrict the competition to men from 1996... Camping is restricted to five designated campgrounds.* VERB =confine V n *to* n

restricted /rɪstrɪktɪd/ ◆◆◇◇◇

1 Something that is **restricted** is quite small or limited. *...the monotony of a heavily restricted diet... Plants, like animals, often have restricted habitats.* ADJ-GRADED

2 If something is **restricted to** a particular group, only members of that group have it. If it is **restricted** to a particular place, it exists only in that place. *Discipline problems are by no means restricted to children in families dependent on benefits... The problem is not restricted to the southeast.* ADJ: v-link ADJ *to* n

3 A **restricted** area is one that only people with special permission can enter. *...a highly restricted area close to the old Khodinka airfield.* ADJ-GRADED

4 A **restricted** document is one that only people with special permission can read; used in British English. The usual American word is **classified**. *The charge was that, in February 1975, he had leaked a restricted document to a journalist.* ADJ

restriction /rɪstrɪkʃᵊn/ **restrictions** ◆◆◆◇◇

1 A **restriction** is an official rule that limits what you can do or that limits the amount or size of something. *...the lifting of restrictions on political parties and the news media... The relaxation of travel restrictions means they are free to travel and work.* N-COUNT: oft N *on* n

2 You can refer to anything that limits what you can do as a **restriction**. *His parents are trying to make up to him for the restrictions of urban living... The second restriction upon the president's power is the limited time at his disposal.* N-COUNT =limitation

3 See also **restrict**.

restrictive /rɪstrɪktɪv/. Something that is **restrictive** prevents people from doing what they want to do, or from moving freely. *Britain is to adopt a more restrictive policy on arms sales. ...increasingly restrictive immigration laws... Do not wear restrictive clothing.* ◆◇◇◇◇ ADJ-GRADED

restrictive practice, restrictive practices. In British English, **restrictive practices** are ways in which people involved in an industry, trade, or profession protect their own interests, rather than having a system which is fair to the public, employers, and other workers. *The Act was introduced to end restrictive practices in the docks.* N-COUNT: usu pl

rest room, rest rooms; also spelled **restroom.** In American English, a **rest room** is a toilet in a public place such as a restaurant or theatre. The usual British word is **ladies** or **gents**. N-COUNT

restructure /riːstrʌktʃəʳ/ **restructures, restructuring, restructured.** To **restructure** an organization or system means to change the way it is organized, usually in order to make it work more effectively. *The President called on educators and politicians to help him restructure American education... How can I begin to restructure my life so that I'm happier with it?* ◆◆◇◇◇ VERB V n Also V

♦ **restructuring, restructurings** *Pirelli, the Italian tyre company, is to lay off 1,520 workers as part of a restructuring.* N-VAR

result /rɪzʌlt/ **results, resulting, resulted** ◆◆◆◆◆

1 A **result** is something that happens or exists because of something else that has happened. *Compensation is available for people who have developed asthma as a direct result of their work... A real pizza oven gives better results than an ordinary home oven.* N-COUNT: oft *as a* N

2 If something **results** in a particular situation or event, it causes that situation or event to happen. *Fifty per cent of road accidents result in head injuries... Regular trips back to her adopted motherland have resulted in her first book, Tiger Balm.* VERB V *in* n

3 If something **results** from a particular event or action, it is caused by that event or action. *Many hair problems result from what you eat... Ignore the early warnings and illness could result.* VERB V from n V

4 A **result** is the situation that exists at the end of a contest. *'What was the result?'—'One-nil to Leeds.'... The final election results will be announced on Friday. ...the football results.* N-COUNT

5 A **result** is the number that you get when you do a calculation. *They found their computers producing different results from exactly the same calculation.* N-COUNT =answer

6 Your **results** are the marks or grades that you get for examinations you have taken; used mainly in British English. The usual American term is **scores**. *Kate's exam results were excellent.* N-COUNT: usu pl

resultant /rɪzʌltənt/. **Resultant** means caused by the event just mentioned; a formal word. *At least a quarter of a million people have died in the fighting and the resultant famines.* ◆◇◇◇◇ ADJ: ADJ n =consequent, ensuing

resume /rɪzjuːm, AM -zuːm/ **resumes, resuming, resumed** ◆◆◆◇◇

1 If you **resume** an activity or if it **resumes**, it begins again; a formal or written use. *After the war he resumed his duties at Emmanuel College... The search is expected to resume early today.* ♦ **resumption** /rɪzʌmpʃən/ *It is premature to speculate about the resumption of negotiations.* V-ERG =recommence V n V; N-UNCOUNT: usu N of n

2 If you **resume** your seat or position, you return to the seat or position you were in before you moved; a formal or written use. *'I changed my mind,' Blanche said, resuming her seat.* VERB =return to V n

3 If someone **resumes**, they begin speaking again after they have stopped for a short time; a written use. *'Hey, Judith,' he resumed, 'tell me all about yourself.'* VERB V with quote

résumé /rezjʊmeɪ, AM -zʊm-/ **résumés;** also spelled **resumé**. ◆◇◇◇◇

1 A **résumé** is a short account, either spoken or written, of something that has happened or that someone has said or written. *I will leave with you a resumé of his most recent speech... We used to begin each so-called planning meeting with a résumé of how we were doing as a division.* N-COUNT: oft N of n/wh =summary

2 In American English, your **résumé** is a brief account of your personal details, your education, and the jobs you have had. You are often asked to send a résumé when you are applying for a job. The usual British term is **curriculum vitae**. N-COUNT

resurface /riːsɜːʳfɪs/ **resurfaces, resurfacing, resurfaced** ◆◇◇◇◇

1 If something such as an idea or problem **resurfaces**, it becomes important or noticeable again. *These ideas resurfaced again in the American civil rights movement... The disease was said to have resurfaced in three countries.* VERB V

2 If someone who has not been seen for a long time **resurfaces**, they suddenly reappear; an informal use. *It is likely that they would go into hiding for a few weeks, and resurface when the publicity has died down.* VERB =reappear V

3 If someone or something that has been under water **resurfaces**, they come back to the surface of the water again. *George struggled wildly, going under and resurfacing at regular intervals.* VERB V

4 To **resurface** something such as a road means to put a new surface on it. *Meanwhile the race is on to resurface the road before next Wednesday.* VERB V n

resurgence /rɪsɜːʳdʒəns/. If there is a **resurgence** of an attitude or activity, it reappears and grows; a formal word. *Police say drugs traffickers are behind the resurgence of violence. ...a period of economic resurgence.* ◆◇◇◇◇ N-SING: also no det, oft N of n

resurgent /rɪsɜːʳdʒənt/. You use **resurgent** to say that something is becoming stronger and more popular after a period when it has been weak and unimportant. *...the threat from the resurgent nationalist movement.* ADJ-GRADED: usu ADJ n

resurrect /rezərekt/ **resurrects, resurrecting, resurrected.** If you **resurrect** something, you cause it to exist again after it had disappeared or ended. *Attempts to resurrect the ceasefire have already failed once... Sam Torrance is the man I have to thank for resurrecting my career.* ♦ **resurrection** /rezərekʃən/ *This is a resurrection of an old story from the mid-70s.* ◆◇◇◇◇ VERB V n; N-UNCOUNT

Resurrection /rezərekʃən/. In Christian belief, **the Resurrection** is the event in which Jesus Christ came back to life after he had been killed. ◆◇◇◇◇ N-PROPER: the N

resuscitate /rɪsʌsɪteɪt/ **resuscitates, resuscitating, resuscitated** ◆◇◇◇◇

1 If you **resuscitate** someone who has stopped breathing, you cause them to start breathing again. *A policeman and then a paramedic tried to resuscitate her.* ♦ **resuscitation** /rɪsʌsɪteɪʃən/ *Despite attempts at resuscitation, Mr Lynch died a week later in hospital.* VERB V n; N-UNCOUNT

2 If you **resuscitate** something, you cause it to become active or successful again. *He has submitted a bid to resuscitate the weekly magazine, which closed in April with losses of £1million a year.* ♦ **resuscitation** *The economy needs vigorous resuscitation.* VERB =revive V n; N-UNCOUNT

retail, retails, retailing, retailed. The pronunciation is /riːteɪl/ for meanings 1 to 3, and /riːteɪl/ for meaning 4. ◆◆◆◇◇

1 **Retail** is the activity of selling goods direct to the public, usually in small quantities. Compare **wholesale**. *Retail stores usually count on the Christmas season to make up to half of their annual profits... Retail sales grew just 3.8 percent last year.* N-UNCOUNT: usu N n

2 If something is sold **retail**, it is sold in ordinary shops direct to the public. ADV: ADV after v

3 If an item in a shop **retails** at or for a particular price, it is on sale at that price. *It originally retailed at £23.50.* VERB =sell V at/for n

4 If someone **retails** a story or event, they tell it to someone else, often in detail and in an exciting way; a literary use. *Mr Hastings gleefully retailed the story to Mr Anderson over lunch.* VERB =recount V n

retailer /riːteɪləʳ/ **retailers.** A **retailer** is a person or business that sells goods to the public. *Furniture and carpet retailers are among those reporting the sharpest annual decline in sales.* ◆◆◇◇◇ N-COUNT

retailing /riːteɪlɪŋ/. **Retailing** is the activity of selling goods direct to the public, usually in small quantities. Compare **wholesaling**. *She spent fourteen years in retailing. ...the car retailing industry.* ◆◇◇◇◇ N-UNCOUNT: oft N n

retail price index. In Britain, **the retail price index** is a list of prices of typical goods which shows how much the cost of living changes from one month to the next. *The retail price index for September, to be released on Friday, is expected to show inflation edging up to about 10.8 per cent.* N-PROPER: the N

retain /rɪteɪn/ **retains, retaining, retained** ◆◆◆◇◇

1 To **retain** something means to continue to have that thing; a formal use. *The interior of the shop still retains a nineteenth-century atmosphere... He retains a deep respect for the profession... Other countries retained their traditional and habitual ways of doing things... If left covered in a warm place, this rice will retain its heat for a good hour.* VERB =keep V n

2 If you **retain** a lawyer, you pay him or her a fee to make sure that he or she will represent you when your case comes before the court; a legal use. *He decided to retain him for the trial.* VERB V n

retainer /rɪteɪnəʳ/ **retainers** ◆◇◇◇◇

1 A **retainer** is a fee that you pay to someone in order to make sure that they will be available to do work for you if you need them to. *I'll need a five-hundred-dollar retainer... Liz was being paid a regular monthly retainer.* N-COUNT

2 A servant who has been with one family for a long time can be referred to as a **retainer**; an old-fashioned use. *I found the gardener, a family retainer, morosely surveying the scene.* N-COUNT =servant

retaining wall, retaining walls. A **retaining wall** is a wall that is built to prevent the earth behind it from moving. N-COUNT

retake, retakes, retaking, retook, retaken. The verb is pronounced /riːteɪk/. The noun is pronounced /riːteɪk/. ◆◇◇◇◇

1 If a military force **retakes** a place or building which it has lost in a war or battle, it captures it VERB =recapture again. *Residents were moved 30 miles away as the rebels retook the town.* V n

2 If during the making of a film there is a **retake** of a particular scene, that scene is filmed again because it needs to be changed or improved. *The director, Ron Howard, was dissatisfied with Nicole's response even after several retakes.* N-COUNT

3 If you **retake** an exam, you take it again because you failed it the first time. *I had one year in the sixth form to retake my O levels.* ► Also a noun. *Limits will be placed on the number of exam retakes students can sit.* VERB V n N-COUNT =resit

retaliate /rɪtæ̱lieɪt/ **retaliates, retaliating, retaliated.** If you **retaliate** when someone harms or annoys you, you do something which harms or annoys them in return. *I was sorely tempted to retaliate... Christie retaliated by sending his friend a long letter detailing Carl's utter incompetence... The militia responded by saying it would retaliate against any attacks... They may retaliate with sanctions on other products if the bans are disregarded.* ♦ **retaliation** /rɪtæ̱lieɪʃᵊn/ *Police said they believed the attack was in retaliation for the death of the drug trafficker.* ◆◆◇◇◇ VERB V V by -ing V against/for n V with n N-UNCOUNT

retaliatory /rɪtæ̱liətəri, AM -tɔːri/. If you take **retaliatory** action, you try to harm or annoy someone who has harmed or annoyed you; a formal word. *There's been talk of a retaliatory blockade to prevent supplies getting through.* ADJ: usu ADJ n

retard, retards, retarding, retarded. The verb is pronounced /rɪtɑ̱ːʳd/. The noun is pronounced /ri̱ːtɑːʳd/.

1 If something **retards** a process, or the development of something, it makes it happen more slowly; a formal use. *Continuing violence will retard negotiations over the country's future.* VERB =slow down V n

2 If you describe someone as a **retard**, you mean that they have not developed normally, either mentally or socially; an offensive use. *What the hell do I want with an emotional retard?* N-COUNT PRAGMATICS

retardation /ri̱ːtɑːʳde̱ɪʃᵊn/. **Retardation** is the process of making something happen or develop more slowly, or the fact of having developed more slowly; a formal use. *Meeting other parents whose children had mental retardation helped us accept some of Ted's limitations.* N-UNCOUNT: usu supp N

retarded /rɪtɑ̱ːʳdɪd/. Someone who is **retarded** is much less advanced mentally than most people of their age; an old-fashioned use. *...a special school for mentally retarded children.* ◆◇◇◇◇ ADJ-GRADED

retch /re̱tʃ/ **retches, retching, retched.** If you **retch**, your stomach moves as if you are vomiting. *The smell made me retch.* VERB =heave V

retd. **retd** is a written abbreviation for **retired**. It is used after someone's name to indicate that they have retired from the army, navy, or air force. *...Commander J. R. Simpson, RN (retd).* =retired

retell /ri̱ːte̱l/ **retells, retelling, retold.** If you **retell** a story, you write it, tell it, or present it again, often in a different way from its original form. *Lucilla often asks her sisters to retell the story... It is a tale which has often been retold within West Indian literature.* ♦ **retelling, retellings** *...this briskly attractive retelling of the Biblical creation story.* VERB V n N-COUNT

retention /rɪte̱nʃᵊn/. The **retention** of something is the keeping of it; a formal word. *The Citizens' Forum supported special powers for Quebec but also argued for the retention of a strong central government.* ◆◇◇◇◇ N-UNCOUNT: oft N of n, n N

retentive /rɪte̱ntɪv/. If you have a **retentive** memory, you are able to remember things very well. *Luke was very quick and had an amazingly retentive memory.* ADJ-GRADED: usu ADJ n

rethink /ri̱ːθɪ̱ŋk/ **rethinks, rethinking, rethought** ◆◇◇◇◇

1 If you **rethink** something such as a problem, a plan, or a policy, you think about it again and change it. *Both major political parties are having to rethink their policies... I think all of us need to rethink our attitudes toward health and sickness.* ♦ **rethinking** *...some fundamental rethinking of the way in which pilots are trained.* VERB =reconsider V n Also V N-UNCOUNT =reconsideration

2 If you have a **rethink** of a problem, a plan, or a policy, you think about it again and change it; used especially by journalists. *There must be a rethink of government policy towards this vulnerable group.* N-SING: oft N of/on n

rethought /ri̱ːθɔ̱ːt/. **Rethought** is the past tense and past participle of **rethink**.

reticent /re̱tɪsənt/. Someone who is **reticent** does not tell people about things. *She is so reticent about her achievements... Mrs. Smith, normally a reticent woman, took it upon herself to write to the President.* ♦ **reticence** *Pearl didn't mind his reticence; in fact she liked it.* ◆◇◇◇◇ ADJ-GRADED: oft ADJ about/on n =reserved N-UNCOUNT =reserve

retina /re̱tɪnə/ **retinas.** Your **retina** is the part of your eye at the back of your eyeball. It receives the image that you see and then sends the image to your brain. ◆◇◇◇◇ N-COUNT

retinal /re̱tɪnᵊl/. **Retinal** means relating to a person's retina; a technical term in biology. *Successful medical research means nine out of ten children with retinal cancer will survive.* ADJ: ADJ n

retinue /re̱tɪnjuː, AM -nuː/ **retinues.** An important person's **retinue** is the group of servants, friends, or assistants who go with them and look after their needs. *Mind trainers are now as much a part of a tennis star's retinue as the body trainers.* N-COUNT: usu with supp, oft N of n =entourage

retire /rɪta̱ɪəʳ/ **retires, retiring, retired** ◆◆◆◇◇

1 When older people **retire**, they leave their job and usually stop working altogether. *At the age when most people retire, he is ready to face a new career... Although their careers are important many said they plan to retire at 50... In 1974 he retired from the museum.* VERB V V from n

2 When a sports player **retires** from their sport, they stop playing competitively. When they **retire** from a race or a match, they stop competing in it. *I have decided to retire from Formula One racing at the end of the season... One of the most serious injuries was to Simon Littlejohn, who was forced to retire from the race with a leg injury.* VERB V from n Also V

3 If you **retire** to another room or place, you go there; a formal use. *Eisenhower left the White House and retired to his farm in Gettysburg.* VERB V to n

4 When a jury **retires**, the members of it leave the courtroom in order to decide their verdict. *The jury will retire to consider its verdict today.* VERB V

5 When you **retire**, you go to bed; a formal use. *She retires early most nights, exhausted... Some time after midnight, he retired to bed.* VERB V V to n

6 See also **retired, retiring.**

retired /rɪta̱ɪəʳd/ ◆◆◇◇◇

1 A **retired** person is an older person who has left his or her job and has usually stopped working altogether. *...a seventy-three-year-old retired teacher from Florida.* ADJ: usu ADJ n

2 See also **retire.**

retiree /rɪta̱ɪəri̱ː/ **retirees.** A **retiree** is a retired person; used mainly in American English. *We have newer generations of retirees who have completely different expectations of what later life might bring to them.* ◆◇◇◇◇ N-COUNT

retirement /rɪta̱ɪəʳmənt/ **retirements** ◆◆◆◇◇

1 **Retirement** is the time when a worker retires. *The proportion of the population who are over retirement age has grown tremendously in the past few years... The Governor of the prison and another official are to take early retirement.* N-VAR: oft N n

2 A person's **retirement** is the period in their life after they have retired. *'Growing Older' considered the needs of the elderly for financial support during retirement.* N-UNCOUNT

retiring /rɪta̱ɪərɪŋ/

1 Someone who is **retiring** is shy and avoids meeting other people. *I'm still that shy, retiring little girl who was afraid to ask for sweets in the shop.* ADJ-GRADED =reserved, shy

2 See also **retire.**

retold /ri̱ːto̱ʊld/. **Retold** is the past tense and past participle of **retell**.

retook /ri̱ːtʊ̱k/. **Retook** is the past tense of **retake**.

retool /riːtuːl/ **retools, retooling, retooled.** If the machines in a factory or the items of equipment used by a firm **are retooled**, they are replaced or changed so that they can do new tasks. *Each time the product changes, the machines have to be retooled and the workers retrained.*
VERB — *be* V-ed; Also V n, V

♦ **retooling** *Most East European companies have to go through a massive retooling in order to become compatible with the rest of the world.*
N-UNCOUNT

retort /rɪtɔːᶦt/ **retorts, retorting, retorted.** To **retort** means to reply angrily to someone; used in written English. *Was he afraid, he was asked. 'Afraid of what?' he retorted... Others retort that strong central power is a dangerous thing in Russia.* ► Also a noun. *His sharp retort clearly made an impact.*
◆◆◇◇◇ VERB — V with quote; V that; Also V — N-COUNT =rejoinder

retouch /riːtʌtʃ/ **retouches, retouching, retouched.** If something such as a painting or a photograph **is retouched**, it is restored, changed, or improved by painting over parts of it. *He said the photographs had been retouched... She put on fresh clothes and retouched her make-up.*
VERB — *be* V-ed; V n

retrace /rɪtreɪs/ **retraces, retracing, retraced.** If you **retrace** your steps or **retrace** your way, you return to the place you started from by going back along the same route. *He retraced his steps to the spot where he'd left the case.*
◆◇◇◇◇ VERB — V n

retract /rɪtrækt/ **retracts, retracting, retracted**
◆◇◇◇◇

1 If you **retract** something that you have said or written, you say that you did not mean it; a formal use. *Mr Smith hurriedly sought to retract the statement, but it had just been broadcast on national radio... He's hoping that if he makes me feel guilty, I'll retract.* ♦ **retraction** /rɪtrækʃᵊn/ **retractions** *Miss Pearce said she expected an unqualified retraction of his comments within twenty four hours.*
VERB — V n; V — N-COUNT: usu sing =withdrawal

2 When a part of a machine, or a part of a person's or animal's body **retracts** or **is retracted**, it moves inwards or back; a formal use. *Torn muscles retract, and lose strength, structure, and tightness. ...when the aircraft's wheels were retracted.*
V-ERG — V; *be* V-ed; Also V n

retractable /rɪtræktəbᵊl/. A **retractable** part of a machine or a building can be moved inwards or backwards. *A 20,000-seat arena with a retractable roof is planned.*
ADJ: usu ADJ n

retrain /riːtreɪn/ **retrains, retraining, retrained.** If you **retrain**, or if someone **retrains** you, you learn new skills, especially in order to get a new job. *Look at what you can do to retrain for a job which will make you happier... Union leaders have called upon the government to help retrain workers.* ♦ **retraining** *...measures such as the retraining of the workforce at their place of work... What is the good of retraining programmes if there are not any jobs to go to?*
◆◇◇◇◇ V-ERG — V; V n — N-UNCOUNT: oft N n

retread /riːtred/ **retreads**

1 If you describe something such as a book, film, or song as a **retread**, you mean that it contains ideas or elements that have been used before, and that it is not very interesting or original; used showing disapproval. *His last book, 'Needful Things', was a retread of tired material.*
N-COUNT: usu sing, oft N *of* n — PRAGMATICS

2 A **retread** is an old tyre which has been given a new outer surface.
N-COUNT =remould

retreat /rɪtriːt/ **retreats, retreating, retreated**
◆◆◆◇◇

1 If you **retreat**, you move away from something or someone. *'I've already got a job,' I said quickly, and retreated from the room... The young nurse pulled a face at the Matron's retreating figure.*
VERB — V prep; V-ing; Also V

2 When an army **retreats**, it moves away from enemy forces in order to avoid fighting them. *The French, suddenly outnumbered, were forced to retreat... Retreating soldiers were dousing homes and shops with petrol and setting them on fire.* ► Also a noun. *In June 1942, the British 8th Army was in full retreat.*
VERB — V; V-ing — N-VAR

3 If you **retreat** from something such as a plan or a way of life, you give it up, usually in order to do something safer or less extreme. *I believe people should live in houses that allow them to retreat from the harsh realities of life... From bouncing confidence she had retreated into self-pity.* ► Also a noun. *The President's remarks appear to signal that there will be no retreat from his position... It's a retreat into the adolescence they never really had.*
VERB — V *from/into* n — N-VAR: usu N *from/into* n

4 A **retreat** is a quiet, secluded place that you go to in order to rest or to do things in private. *He spent yesterday hidden away in his country retreat.*
N-COUNT: oft supp N

5 If you **beat a retreat**, you leave a place quickly in order to avoid an embarrassing or dangerous situation. *Cockburn decided it was time to beat a hasty retreat.*
PHRASE: V inflects

retrench /rɪtrentʃ/ **retrenches, retrenching, retrenched.** If a person or organization **retrenches**, they spend less money; a formal word. *Shortly afterwards, cuts in defence spending forced the aerospace industry to retrench.*
VERB =cut back, economize — V

retrenchment /rɪtrentʃmənt/ **retrenchments.** **Retrenchment** means spending less money; a formal word. *Defense planners predict an extended period of retrenchment. ...a need for industrial retrenchment and restructuring.*
N-VAR

retrial /riːtraɪəl/ **retrials.** A **retrial** is a second trial of someone for the same offence. *An Old Bailey judge yesterday ordered the retrial of a policeman accused of planting soft drugs on a black car mechanic.*
N-COUNT: usu sing

retribution /retrɪbjuːʃᵊn/. **Retribution** is punishment for a crime, especially punishment which is carried out by someone other than the official authorities; a formal word. *He didn't want any further involvement for fear of retribution.*
◆◇◇◇◇ N-UNCOUNT =punishment

retrieval /rɪtriːvᵊl/
◆◇◇◇◇

1 The **retrieval** of information from a computer is the process of getting it back. *...electronic storage and retrieval systems.*
N-UNCOUNT

2 The **retrieval** of something is the process of getting it back from a particular place, especially from a place where it should not be. *Its real purpose is the launching and retrieval of small aeroplanes in flight.*
N-UNCOUNT =recovery

retrieve /rɪtriːv/ **retrieves, retrieving, retrieved**
◆◆◇◇◇

1 If you **retrieve** something, you get it back from the place where you left it. *He reached over and retrieved his jacket from the back seat... The men were trying to retrieve weapons left when the army abandoned the island.*
VERB =recover, get back — V n

2 If you manage to **retrieve** a situation, you succeed in bringing it back into a more acceptable state. *He, the one man who could retrieve that situation, might receive the call.*
VERB =save — V n

3 To **retrieve** information from a computer or from your memory means to get it back. *Computers can instantly retrieve millions of information bits... As the child gets older, so his or her strategies for storing and retrieving information improve.*
VERB — V n

retriever /rɪtriːvəᶦ/ **retrievers.** A **retriever** is a kind of dog. Retrievers are traditionally used by hunters to bring back birds and animals which they have shot.
N-COUNT

retro /retrou/. **Retro** clothes, music, and objects are based on the styles of the past; used by journalists. *...clothes shops where original versions of many of today's retro looks can be found for a fraction of the price.*
◆◇◇◇◇ ADJ

retro- /retrou-/. **Retro-** is used to form adjectives and nouns which indicate that something goes back or goes backwards. *...exotic effects and retro-style photography.*
PREFIX

retroactive /retrouæktɪv/. If a decision or action is **retroactive**, it is intended to take effect from a date in the past; a formal word. *There are few precedents for the sort of retroactive legislation the banks want.* ♦ **retroactively** *It isn't yet clear whether the new law can actually be applied retroactively.*
ADJ =retrospective — ADV: ADV with v =retrospectively

retrofit /retroufɪt/ **retrofits, retrofitting, retrofitted.** To **retrofit** a machine or a building means to put a new part or new equipment in it after it has been in use for some time, especially to improve its safety or efficiency. *Much of this business involves retrofitting existing planes...*
VERB — V n

Damaged houses have been repaired, roads repaved and buildings retrofitted.

retrograde /re̱trəgreɪd/. A **retrograde** action is one that you think makes a situation worse rather than better; a formal word. *The Prime Minister described transferring education to central government funding as 'a retrograde step'.* ADJ-GRADED: usu ADJ n

retrogression /re̱trəgre̱ʃᵊn/. **Retrogression** means moving back to an earlier and less efficient stage of development; a formal word. *There has been a retrogression in the field of human rights since 1975.* N-UNCOUNT: also a N =regression

retrogressive /re̱trəgre̱sɪv/. If you describe an action or idea as **retrogressive**, you disapprove of it because it returns to old ideas or beliefs and does not take advantage of recent progress; a formal word. *The Prime Minister is still hoping that the voters will choose his forward-looking policies over the often retrogressive policies of the National parties.* ADJ PRAGMATICS =regressive

retrospect /re̱trəspekt/. When you consider something **in retrospect**, you think about it afterwards, and often have a different opinion about it from the one that you had at the time. *In retrospect, I wish that I had thought about alternative courses of action... It was a very strange feeling in retrospect – I was frightened, but excited at the same time.* ◆◇◇◇◇ PHRASE: PHR with cl

retrospective /re̱trəspe̱ktɪv/ **retrospectives** ◆◇◇◇◇

1 A **retrospective** is an exhibition or showing of work done by an artist over many years, rather than his or her most recent work. *...a retrospective of the films of Judy Garland... They honoured him with a retrospective exhibition in 1987.* N-COUNT

2 **Retrospective** feelings or opinions concern things that happened in the past. *Afterwards, retrospective fear of the responsibility would make her feel almost faint.* ♦ **retrospectively** *Retrospectively, it seems as if they probably were negligent... To ascribe opinions retrospectively is of course very dangerous.* ADJ: usu ADJ n; ADV: ADV with cl, ADV with v =in retrospect

3 **Retrospective** laws or legal actions take effect from a date before the date when they are officially approved. *Bankers are quick to condemn retrospective tax legislation.* ♦ **retrospectively** *...a decree which retrospectively changes the electoral law under which last year's national elections were held.* ADJ: usu ADJ n =retroactive; ADV: ADV with v =retroactively

return /rɪtɜ̱ːʳn/ **returns, returning, returned** ◆◆◆◆◆

1 When you **return** to a place, you go back there after you have been away. *There are unconfirmed reports that Aziz will return to Moscow within hours... Our correspondent Stephen Sackur has just returned from the camps on the border... So far more than 350,000 people have returned home.* VERB V to/from n V adv Also V

2 Your **return** is your arrival back at a place where you had been before. *Ryle explained the reason for his sudden return to London.* N-SING: with poss

3 If you **return** something that you have borrowed or taken, you give it back or put it back. *I enjoyed the book and said so when I returned it... The car was not returned on time, then was reported stolen.* ► Also a noun. *The main demand of the Indians is for the return of one-and-a-half-million acres of forest to their communities.* VERB V n; N-SING: usu N of n

4 If you **return** something somewhere, you put it back where it was. *He returned the notebook to his jacket.* VERB V n to n

5 If you **return** someone's action, you do the same thing to them as they have just done to you. If you **return** someone's feeling, you feel the same way towards them as they feel towards you. *Back at the station the Chief Inspector returned the call... She will be disappointed if her feelings are not returned.* VERB V n

6 If a feeling or situation **returns**, it comes back or happens again after a period of absence. *Official reports in Algeria suggest that calm is returning to the country... The pain returned in waves.* ► Also a noun. *It was like the return of his youth.* VERB V; N-SING: with supp

7 If you **return** to a state that you were in before, you start being in that state again. *Life has improved and returned to normal.* ► Also a noun. *He made an uneventful return to normal health... The opposition now fears a return to martial rule.* VERB V to n; N-SING: N to n

8 If you **return** to a subject that you have mentioned before, you begin talking about it again. *The power of the Church is one theme all these writers return to.* VERB V to n

9 If you **return** to an activity that you were doing before, you start doing it again. *At that stage he will be 52, young enough to return to politics if he wishes to do so.* ► Also a noun. *He has not ruled out the shock possibility of a return to football.* VERB V to n; N-SING: N to n

10 When a judge or jury **returns** a verdict, they announce whether they think the person on trial is guilty or not. *They returned a verdict of not guilty.* VERB V n

11 In British English, a **return** ticket is a ticket for a journey from one place to another and then back again. The American term is **round trip**. *He bought a return ticket and boarded the next train for home.* ► Also a noun. *BA and Air France charge more than £400 for a return to Nice.* ● See also **day return**. ADJ: usu ADJ n ≠single, one way; N-COUNT

12 In British English, the **return** trip or journey is the part of a journey that takes you back to where you started from. *Buy an extra ticket for the return trip.* ADJ: ADJ n ≠outward

13 The **return** on an investment is the profit that you get from it. *Profits have picked up this year but the return on capital remains tiny... Higher returns and higher risk usually go hand in hand.* ● See also **tax return**. N-COUNT =yield

14 **Returns** are the results of votes in various places as part of an election or ballot. *Early returns show Bulgaria's opposition party may have won.* N-PLURAL

15 When it is someone's birthday, people sometimes say **'Many happy returns'** to them as a way of congratulating them. PHRASES CONVENTION

16 If you do something **in return** for what someone else has done for you, you do it because they did that thing for you. *You pay regular premiums and in return the insurance company will pay out a lump sum.*

17 If you say that you have reached **the point of no return**, you mean that you now have to continue with what you are doing and it is too late to stop. *The release of Mr Nelson Mandela marked the point of no return in South Africa's movement away from apartheid.*

18 ● to **return fire**: see **fire**.

returnable /rɪtɜ̱ːʳnəbᵊl/

1 **Returnable** containers are intended to be taken back to the place they came from so that they can be used again. *Under the new rules, all beverages, except dairy products and cider, must be sold in returnable containers.* ADJ: usu ADJ n ≠non-returnable

2 If something such as a sum of money or a document is **returnable**, it will eventually be given back to the person who provided it. *Landlords can charge a returnable deposit, usually the equivalent of one month's rent.* ADJ: usu ADJ n

returnee /rɪtɜ̱ːʳni̱ː/ **returnees.** A **returnee** is a person who returns to the country where they were born, usually after they have been away for a long time. *The spokeswoman said the number of returnees could go as high as half a million.* N-COUNT: usu pl

returner /rɪtɜ̱ːʳnəʳ/ **returners.** A **returner** is someone who returns to work after a period when they did not work, especially a woman who returns after having children; used mainly in British English. *Many 'returners' are far more skilled at working with people than they were when they were younger.* N-COUNT

retu̱rning officer, returning officers. In Britain, the **returning officer** for a particular town or district is an official who is responsible for arranging an election and who formally announces the result. N-COUNT

retu̱rn match, return matches. A **return match** is the second of two matches that are played by two sports teams or two players; used mainly in British English. N-COUNT: usu sing

retu̱rn vi̱sit, return visits. If you make a **return visit**, you visit someone who has already visited you, or you go back to a place where you have N-COUNT already been once. *Towards the end of his career he made a nostalgic return visit to Germany.*

reunification /riːjuːnɪfɪkeɪʃᵊn/. The **reunification** of a country or city that has been divided into two or more parts for some time is the joining of it together again. *...the reunification of East and West Beirut in 1991.* ◆◇◇◇◇ N-UNCOUNT: with supp

reunion /riːjuːniən/ **reunions** ◆◇◇◇◇
1 A **reunion** is a party attended by members of the same family, school, or other group who have not seen each other for a long time. *The Association holds an annual reunion... The whole family was there for this big family reunion.* N-COUNT: usu with supp
2 A **reunion** is a meeting between people who have been separated for some time. *The children weren't allowed to see her for nearly a week. It was a very emotional reunion.* N-VAR: usu with supp

reunite /riːjuːnaɪt/ **reunites, reuniting, reunited** ◆◇◇◇◇
1 If people **are reunited**, or if they **reunite**, they meet each other again after they have been separated for some time. *She and her youngest son were finally allowed to be reunited with their family... She spent the post-war years of her marriage trying to reunite father and son.* V-ERG; be V-ed; V n; Also V
2 If a divided organization or country **is reunited**, or if it **reunites**, it becomes one united organization or country again. *Both expressed the hope that Korea could be reunited by the end of the 1990's... His first job will be to reunite the army... The end of family rule may now give Congress a chance to reunite.* V-ERG; be V-ed; V n; V

reusable /riːjuːzəbᵊl/; also spelled **re-usable.** Things that are **reusable** can be used more than once. *The average family in Europe throws as much as £20 worth of reusable materials into its dustbin each year. ...re-usable plastic containers.* ADJ =disposable

reuse, reuses, reusing, reused. The verb is pronounced /riːjuːz/. The noun is pronounced /riːjuːs/. When you **reuse** something, you use it again instead of throwing it away. *In several countries public pressure for recycling plastics is greater than the pressure to reuse paper.* ▶ Also a noun. *Copper, brass and aluminium are separated and remelted for reuse.* VERB; V n; N-UNCOUNT

rev /rev/ **revs, revving, revved** ◆◇◇◇◇
1 When the engine of a vehicle **revs**, or when you **rev** it, the engine speed is increased as the accelerator is pressed. *The engine started, revved and the car jerked away down the hill... The old bus was revving its engine, ready to start the journey back towards Madrid.* ▶ **Rev up** means the same as **rev.** *...drivers revving up their engines... Then there would be the sound of a car revving up, accompanied by the smell of petrol.* V-ERG; V; V n; PHRASAL VERB ERG; V P n (not pron); V P
2 If you talk about the **revs** of an engine, you are referring to its speed, which is measured in revolutions per minute. *The engine is impressive at all speeds, delivering instant acceleration whatever the revs.* N-PLURAL

rev up PHRASAL VERB
1 See **rev** 1.
2 If you **rev** something **up**, or if it **revs up**, it becomes more intense or more active; an informal use. *The temptation to rev up the arms race with high-tech weapons is especially dangerous... Now he plans to rev up publicity with a regional media campaign.* ERG; V P n (not pron); Also V n P

Rev. **Rev** is a written abbreviation for **Reverend.** *...the Rev John Roberts.* ◆◆◇◇◇ =Revd

revalue /riːvæljuː/ **revalues, revaluing, revalued** ◆◇◇◇◇
1 When a country **revalues** its currency, it increases the currency's value so that it can buy more foreign currency than before. *The Germans began talking openly about revaluing the mark.* ♦ **revaluation** /riːvæljuːeɪʃᵊn/ **revaluations** *There was a general revaluation of other currencies but not the pound.* VERB; V n; N-VAR: oft N of n
2 To **revalue** something means to increase the amount that you calculate it is worth so that its value stays roughly the same in comparison with other things, even if there is inflation. *It is now usual to revalue property assets on a more regular basis.* ♦ **revaluation** *Some British banks have used doubtful property revaluations to improve their capital ratios.* VERB; V n; N-VAR: oft N of n

revamp /riːvæmp/ **revamps, revamping, revamped.** If someone **revamps** something, they make changes to it in order to try and improve it. *All Italy's political parties have accepted that it is time to revamp the system... Ricardo Bofill, the Catalan architect, has designed the revamped airport.* ▶ Also a noun. *The revamp includes replacing the old navy uniform with a crisp blue and white cotton outfit.* ♦ **revamping** *Expected changes include a revamping of the courts and an adding of safeguards to curb corruption.* ◆◇◇◇◇ VERB; V n; V-ed; N-SING; N-SING: with supp

rev counter. In British English, a **rev counter** is an instrument in a car or an aeroplane which shows the speed of the engine. N-SING =tachometer

Revd. **Revd** is a written abbreviation for **Reverend.** *...the Revd Alfred Gatty.* =Rev

reveal /rɪviːl/ **reveals, revealing, revealed** ◆◆◆◆◇
1 To **reveal** something means to make people aware of it. *She has refused to reveal the whereabouts of her daughter... A survey of the British diet has revealed that a growing number of people are overweight... After the fire, it was revealed that North Carolina officials had never inspected the factory... No test will reveal how much of the drug was taken.* VERB; V n; V that; it be V-ed that; V wh; Also be V-ed as n
2 If you **reveal** something that has been out of sight, you uncover it so that people can see it. *In the principal room, a grey carpet was removed to reveal the original pine floor.* VERB =show; V n

revealing /rɪviːlɪŋ/ ◆◆◇◇◇
1 A **revealing** statement, account, or action tells you something that you did not know, especially about the person doing it or making it. *...a revealing interview. ...Sophie Tucker's revealing autobiography.* ♦ **revealingly** *Even more revealingly, he says: 'There's no such thing as failure.'* ADJ-GRADED; ADV-GRADED
2 **Revealing** clothes allow more of the wearer's body to be seen than is usual. *She was wearing a tight and revealing gold dress.* ADJ-GRADED

reveille /rɪvæli, AM revəli/. **Reveille** is the time when soldiers have to get up in the morning. *It must be nearly six; soon would be reveille and the end of the night's rest.* N-UNCOUNT

revel /revᵊl/ **revels, revelling, revelled;** spelled **reveling, reveled** in American English. ◆◇◇◇◇
1 If you **revel** in a situation or experience, you enjoy it very much. *Revelling in her freedom, she took a hotel room and stayed for several days even though she was expected home... Cats positively revel in heat, whether natural or man-made.* VERB; V in n
2 **Revels** are noisy celebrations; a literary use. *The revels often last until dawn.* N-COUNT: usu pl

revelation /revəleɪʃᵊn/ **revelations** ◆◆◇◇◇
1 A **revelation** is a surprising or interesting fact that is made known to people. *...the seemingly everlasting revelations about his private life. ...the revelation that William had survived the initial attack.* N-COUNT: oft N about n, N that
2 The **revelation** of something is the act of making it known. *...following the revelation of his affair with a former secretary... Further revelations are expected.* N-VAR: oft N of n
3 If you say that something you experienced was a **revelation**, you are emphasizing that it was very surprising or very good. *The noise, the buildings, the people, came as a revelation... Degas's work had been a revelation to her.* N-SING: a N, oft N to n PRAGMATICS
4 A divine **revelation** is a sign or explanation from God about his nature or purpose. *The whole system was based on divine revelation in the Scriptures.* N-VAR

revelatory /revələtəri, AM -tɔːri/. A **revelatory** account or statement tells you a lot that you did not know. *...Barbara Stoney's revelatory account of the author's life.* ADJ-GRADED

reveller /revələʳ/ **revellers;** spelled **reveler** in American English. **Revellers** are people who are enjoying themselves in a noisy and often drunk- N-COUNT: usu pl en way; a literary word. *Many of the revellers are tourists and British day-trippers.*

revelry /revəlri/ **revelries. Revelry** is people enjoying themselves in a noisy and often drunken way; a literary word. *As we got close to Broadway, we heard the sounds of revelry getting louder and louder. ...New Year revelries.* [N-UNCOUNT: also N in pl]

revenge /rɪvendʒ/ **revenges, revenging, revenged** [◆◆◇◇◇]

1 Revenge involves hurting or punishing someone who has hurt or harmed you. *The attackers were said to be taking revenge on the 14-year-old, claiming he was a school bully... The killings were said to have been in revenge for the murder of her lover.* [N-UNCOUNT: oft N *on/for/against* n]

2 If you **revenge** yourself on someone who has hurt you, you hurt them in return; used in written English. *Birmingham's Sunday Mercury accused her of trying to revenge herself on her former lover... She would be killed by the relatives of murdered villagers wanting to revenge the dead.* [VERB =avenge; V pron-refl *on* n; V n]

revenue /revənjuː/ **revenues. Revenue** is money that a company, organization, or government receives from people. *...a boom year at the cinema, with record advertising revenue and the highest ticket sales since 1980... One study said the government would gain about $12 billion in tax revenues over five years.* • See also **Inland Revenue**. [◆◆◆◇◇ N-UNCOUNT: also N in pl, usu with supp]

reverb /riːvɜːʳb, rɪvɜːʳb/. **Reverb** is a shaking or echoing effect added to a sound by an electronic device. *All the sounds are what I actually do with my voice, except for a little reverb.* [N-UNCOUNT]

reverberate /rɪvɜːʳbəreɪt/ **reverberates, reverberating, reverberated** [◆◇◇◇◇]

1 When a loud sound **reverberates** through a place, it echoes through it. *Day in and day out, the flat crack of the tank guns reverberates through the little Bavarian town... A woman's shrill laughter reverberated in the courtyard.* [VERB =echo; V prep; V]

2 You can say that an event or idea **reverberates** when it has a powerful effect which lasts a long time. *The controversy surrounding the take-over yesterday continued to reverberate around the television industry... The news sent shock waves through the community that have continued to reverberate to this day.* [VERB; V prep; V]

reverberation /rɪvɜːʳbəreɪʃən/ **reverberations**

1 Reverberations are serious effects that follow a sudden, dramatic event. *The move by the two London colleges is sending reverberations through higher education.* [N-COUNT: usu pl =repercussion]

2 A **reverberation** is the shaking and echoing effect that you hear after a loud sound has been made. *Jason heard the reverberation of the slammed door and felt rooted where he stood.* [N-VAR =echo]

revere /rɪvɪəʳ/ **reveres, revering, revered.** If you **revere** someone or something, you respect and admire them greatly; a formal word. *The Chinese revered corn as a gift from heaven... Today he's still revered as the father of the nation.* [◆◇◇◇◇ VERB; V n] ♦ **revered** *...some of the country's most revered institutions.* [ADJ-GRADED: usu ADJ n]

reverence /revərəns/. **Reverence** for someone or something is a feeling of great respect for them; a formal word. *We stand together now in mutual support and in reverence for the dead.* [◆◇◇◇◇ N-UNCOUNT]

Reverend /revərənd/. **Reverend** is a title used before the name or rank of an officially appointed religious leader. The abbreviation 'Rev' or 'Revd' is also used. *The service was led by the Reverend Jim Simons. ...the Bishop of Norwich, the Right Reverend Peter Knott.* [◆◆◇◇◇ N-TITLE: oft *the* N n]

reverent /revərənt/. If you describe someone's behaviour as **reverent**, you mean that it shows great respect for someone or something. *...the reverent hush of a rapt audience... Ellen looks almost reverent.* [ADJ ≠irreverent] ♦ **reverently** *He got up and took the book out almost reverently.* [ADV: usu ADV after v]

reverential /revərenʃəl/. Something that is **reverential** has the qualities of respect, admiration, and awe; a formal word. *'That's the old foresters' garden,' she whispered in reverential tones.* [ADJ-GRADED] ♦ **reverentially** *He reverentially returned the novel to a glass-fronted bookcase.* [ADV-GRADED: ADV with v]

reverie /revəri/ **reveries.** A **reverie** is a kind of short pleasant daydream; a formal word. *The announcer's voice brought Holden out of his reverie.* [N-COUNT =daydream]

reversal /rɪvɜːʳsəl/ **reversals** [◆◇◇◇◇]

1 A **reversal** of a process, policy, or trend is a complete change in it. *The Financial Times says the move represents a complete reversal of previous US policy... This marked a 7% increase on the previous year and the reversal of a steady five-year downward trend.* [N-COUNT: oft N *of* n]

2 When there is a role **reversal** or a **reversal of** roles, two people or groups exchange their positions or functions. *When children end up taking care of their parents, it is a strange role reversal indeed.* [N-COUNT: n N, N *of* n]

3 A **reversal** is a failure, usually involving the loss of money; a formal use. *They teach managers to accept reversals as a fact of business life.* [N-COUNT: usu pl =setback]

reverse /rɪvɜːʳs/ **reverses, reversing, reversed** [◆◆◆◇◇]

1 When someone or something **reverses** a decision, policy, or trend, they change it to the opposite decision, policy, or trend. *They have made it clear they will not reverse the decision to increase prices... The rise, the first in 10 months, reversed the downward trend in Belgium's jobless rate.* [VERB; V n]

2 If you **reverse** the order of a set of things, you arrange them in the opposite order, so that the first thing comes last. *In the squares place a penny, nickel, dime and quarter in that order. The object is to reverse the order of these coins... Because the normal word order is reversed in passive sentences, they are sometimes hard to follow.* [VERB; V n]

3 If you **reverse** the positions or functions of two things, you change them so that each thing has the position or function that the other one had. *He reversed the position of the two stamps.* [VERB; V n]

4 When a car **reverses** or when you **reverse** a car, the car is driven backwards; used mainly in British English. The usual American expression is **back up**. *Another car reversed out of the drive... He reversed and drove away... He reversed his car straight at the umpire.* [V-ERG; V; V n]

5 If your car is in **reverse**, you have changed gear so that you can drive it backwards. *He lurched the car in reverse along the ruts to the access road.* [N-UNCOUNT: usu *in/into* N]

6 Reverse means opposite to what you expect or to what has just been described. *The wrong attitude will have exactly the reverse effect.* [ADJ: usu ADJ n =opposite]

7 If you say that one thing is **the reverse** of another, you are emphasizing that the first thing is the exact opposite of the second thing. *There is absolutely no evidence at all that spectators want longer cricket matches. Quite the reverse... This would lead one to expect a fat, dense and detailed autobiography. The reverse is true. The book is short and spare.* [N-SING: *the* N PRAGMATICS]

8 A **reverse** is a serious failure or setback; a formal word. *It's clear that the party of the former Prime Minister has suffered a major reverse.* [N-COUNT =reversal, setback]

9 The **reverse** or the **reverse** side of a flat object which has two sides is the less important or the other side. *Cheques should be made payable to Country Living, and your address written on the reverse.* [N-SING: *the* N =back ≠front]

10 If something happens **in reverse** or goes **into reverse**, things happen in the opposite way to what usually happens or to what has been happening. *Amis tells the story in reverse, from the moment the man dies... The downward trend went into reverse and the scores started to creep up again.* [PHRASES v PHR]

11 In British English, if you **reverse the charges** when you make a telephone call, the person who you are phoning pays the cost of the call and not you. The usual American term is to **call collect**. [V inflects]

reverse charge call, reverse charge calls. In British English, a **reverse charge call** is a telephone call which is paid for by the person who receives the call. Reverse charge calls are made through the operator. The usual American term is **collect call**. [N-COUNT]

reverse discrimination. **Reverse discrimination** is the same as **positive discrimination.** *The Scheme wants a policy of reverse discrimination in favour of children from working-class and ethnic backgrounds.* N-UNCOUNT

reverse gear, reverse gears. The **reverse gear** of a vehicle is the gear which you use in order to make the vehicle go backwards. N-VAR

reversible /rɪvɜːʳsɪbᵊl/

1 If a process or an action is **reversible**, its effects can be reversed so that the original situation is restored. *Heart disease is reversible in some cases, according to a study published last summer.* ADJ ≠irreversible

2 **Reversible** clothes, bedclothes, or materials have been made so that either side can be worn or shown. *He wore the powder-blue side of a reversible waistcoat.* ADJ

reversing light, reversing lights. **Reversing lights** are the white lights on the back of a motor vehicle which shine when the vehicle is in reverse gear; used mainly in British English. N-COUNT: usu pl

reversion /rɪvɜːʳʃᵊn/ **reversions**

1 A **reversion** to a previous state, system, or kind of behaviour is a change back to it. *This is a reversion to the system under which the Royals were paid for nearly 200 years. ...a reversion to the emotions of her baby years.* N-SING: also no det, N to n =return

2 In law, the **reversion** of land or property to a person, family, or country is the return to them of the ownership or control of the land or property. *...the reversion of Hong Kong to Chinese sovereignty in 1997.* N-VAR: oft the N of n to n

revert /rɪvɜːʳt/ **reverts, reverting, reverted** ◆◇◇◇◇

1 When people or things **revert** to a previous state, system, or type of behaviour, they go back to it. *Jackson said her boss became increasingly depressed and reverted to smoking heavily.* VERB V to n

2 When someone **reverts** to a previous topic, they start talking or thinking about it again; used in written English. *In the car she reverted to the subject uppermost in her mind. 'You know, I really believe what Gran told you.'* VERB V to n

3 If you **revert** to your usual language, you start using that language again; a literary use. *After all these years she had reverted to her Veneto dialect and nobody could understand what she was saying.* VERB V to n

4 In law, if property, rights, or money **reverts** to someone, it becomes theirs again after someone else has had it for a period of time. *When the lease ends, the property reverts to the freeholder.* VERB V to n

5 If you say that someone has **reverted to type**, you mean that they are now behaving as you would expect them to, after having behaved in an unexpected and better way; usually used showing disapproval. *He was adamant that this setback does not mean he has reverted to type.* PHRASE: V inflects PRAGMATICS

review /rɪvjuː/ **reviews, reviewing, reviewed** ◆◆◆◆◇

1 A **review** of a situation or system is its formal examination by people in authority. This is usually done in order to see whether it can be improved or corrected. *The president ordered a review of US economic aid to Jordan... The White House quickly announced that the policy is under review.* N-COUNT: oft N of n, also prep N =evaluation

2 If you **review** a situation or system, you consider it carefully to see what is wrong with it or how it could be improved. *The Prime Minister reviewed the situation with his Cabinet yesterday... The next day we reviewed the previous day's work.* VERB =evaluate V n

3 A **review** is a report in a newspaper or magazine, or on television or radio, in which someone gives their opinion of a new book, film, television programme, record, play, or concert. *Disney's 'Beauty And The Beast' has won rave reviews... We've never had a good review in the music press.* N-COUNT

4 If someone **reviews** something such as a new book or play, they write a report or give a talk on television or radio in which they express their opinion of it. *Richard Coles reviews all of the latest video releases... His book about Afghanistan is reviewed here by Anthony Hyman.* VERB V n

5 When a military or political leader **reviews** troops, they inspect the troops or watch them in a military parade. *When he reviewed the troops they cheered him as he smiled and raised his hat.* VERB V n

reviewer /rɪvjuːəʳ/ **reviewers.** A **reviewer** is a person who reviews new books, films, television programmes, records, plays, or concerts. *...the reviewer for the Times Literary Supplement.* ◆◇◇◇◇ N-COUNT

reviewing stand, reviewing stands. A **reviewing stand** is a special raised platform from which military and political leaders watch military parades. N-COUNT

revile /rɪvaɪl/ **reviles, reviling, reviled.** If someone or something **is reviled**, people hate them intensely or show their hatred of them; a formal word. *He was just as feared and reviled as his tyrannical parents... Those who earlier hailed Mr Singh as an incorruptible man of principle now revile him for opportunism.* ♦ **reviled** *He is probably the most reviled man in contemporary theatre.* VERB =hate, despise be V-ed V n ADJ-GRADED

revise /rɪvaɪz/ **revises, revising, revised** ◆◆◇◇◇

1 If you **revise** the way you think about something, you adjust your thoughts, usually in order to make them better or more suited to how things are. *With time he fairly soon came to revise his opinion of the profession.* VERB =adjust, change V n

2 If you **revise** a price, amount, or estimate, you change it to make it more realistic, competitive, or accurate. *They realised that some of their prices were higher than their competitors' and revised prices accordingly... The United Nations has been forced to revise its estimates of population growth upwards.* VERB =adjust, change V n

3 When you **revise** an essay, a book, a law, or a piece of music, you change it in some way to improve it, update it, or adapt it for a particular purpose. *Three editors handled the work of revising the articles for publication... The staff should work together to improve or revise the syllabus or school curriculum.* VERB =change, improve V n for n V n

4 When you **revise** for an examination, you read things again and make notes in order to be prepared for the examination; used mainly in British English. *I have to revise for maths... After Friday, 17th May girls may stay at home to revise.* VERB =study V for n V

revision /rɪvɪʒᵊn/ **revisions** ◆◇◇◇◇

1 A **revision** of something that is written or something that has been decided is an alteration of it. The revision may be made to improve it, to update it, or to adapt it for a particular purpose. *The phase of writing that is actually most important is revision... The government will also make a number of revisions to reflect better data since the original figures were released.* N-VAR: oft N of n

2 When people who are studying do their **revision**, they read things again and make notes in preparation for an examination; used mainly in British English. *Some girls prefer to do their revision at home.* N-UNCOUNT: oft poss N =studying

revisionism /rɪvɪʒənɪzəm/. **Revisionism** is a theory of socialism that is more moderate than orthodox Marxist theory, and is therefore considered to be wrong and dangerous by orthodox Marxists; a technical term, used showing disapproval. *The Guardian says the reforms come after decades of hostility to revisionism in any shape or size.* N-UNCOUNT PRAGMATICS

revisionist /rɪvɪʒənɪst/ **revisionists**

1 If you describe a person or their views as **revisionist**, you mean that they reject traditionally held beliefs about historical events; a formal use which often shows disapproval. *Revisionist history must be challenged by historical research. ...the revisionist interpretation of the French Revolution.* ADJ PRAGMATICS

► A **revisionist** is a person who has revisionist views. *The reputation of the navigator is under assault from historical revisionists.* N-COUNT

2 If a socialist describes another socialist's actions or opinions as **revisionist**, they mean that they are wrong because they are more moderate than orthodox Marxist theory allows. *This revisionist thesis departs even further from Marxist assertions.* ADJ PRAGMATICS

► A **revisionist** is a person who has revisionist N-COUNT

views. *...ferocious infighting between Stalinist hardliners and revisionists.*

revisit /riːvɪzɪt/ **revisits, revisiting, revisited.** ◆◇◇◇◇
VERB If you **revisit** a place, you return there for a visit after you have been away for a long time, often after the place has changed a lot. V n *I myself was in Cambodia in the early 1970s, and then I revisited the country two years ago.*

revitalize /riːvaɪtəlaɪz/ **revitalizes, revitalizing, revitalized;** also spelled **revitalise** in British English. ◆◇◇◇◇
VERB =revive, revivify To **revitalize** something that has lost its activity or its health means to make it active or healthy again. V n *This hair conditioner is excellent for revitalizing dry, lifeless hair.* V-ed *...the revitalized Democratic Party.* V-ing *...a revitalizing mid-afternoon treat.*

revival /rɪvaɪvəl/ **revivals** ◆◆◇◇◇
1 N-COUNT: oft N of n When there is a **revival** of something, it becomes active or popular again. *This return to realism has produced a revival of interest in a number of artists... There is little chance of a revival in new car sales until at least August next year.*
2 N-COUNT A **revival** is a new and exciting production of a play, an opera, or a ballet. *...John Clement's revival of Chekhov's 'The Seagull'.*

revivalism /rɪvaɪvəlɪzəm/. N-UNCOUNT: usu adj N **Revivalism** is a movement whose aim is to make a religion more popular and more influential. *...a time of intense religious revivalism. ...Hindu revivalism.*

revivalist /rɪvaɪvəlɪst/ **revivalists.** ADJ: ADJ n **Revivalist** people or activities are involved in trying to make a particular religion more popular and more influential. *...the Hindu revivalist party... They attended a revivalist meeting and became born-again Christians.* ▶ N-COUNT Also a noun. *Booth was a revivalist intent on his Christian vocation.*

revive /rɪvaɪv/ **revives, reviving, revived** ◆◆◇◇◇
1 V-ERG When something such as the economy, a business, a trend, or a feeling **is revived** or when it **revives**, it becomes active, popular, or successful again. V n *...an attempt to revive the British economy...* V *His trial revived memories of French suffering during the war... There is no doubt that grades have improved and interest in education has revived.* ▶ ADJ Also an adjective. *Habib grimaced at the revived memories.*
2 VERB When someone **revives** a play, opera, or ballet, they present a new production of it. V n *The Gaiety is reviving John B. Kean's comedy 'The Man from Clare'.*
3 V-ERG If you manage to **revive** someone who has fainted or if they **revive**, they become conscious again. V n *She and a neighbour tried in vain to revive him...* V *With a glazed stare she revived for one last instant.*

revivify /riːvɪvɪfaɪ/ **revivifies, revivifying, revivified.** VERB =revitalize To **revivify** a situation, event, or activity means to make it more active, lively, or efficient; a formal word. V n *They've revivified rhythm and blues singing by giving it dance beats which are applicable to today.*

revoke /rɪvoʊk/ **revokes, revoking, revoked.** ◆◇◇◇◇
VERB =rescind When people in authority **revoke** something such as a licence, a law, or an agreement, they cancel it; a formal word. V n *The government revoked her husband's license to operate migrant labor crews.* ♦ **revocation** /revəkeɪʃən/ N-UNCOUNT *Now the Montserrat government has announced its revocation of 311 banking licences.*

revolt /rɪvoʊlt/ **revolts, revolting, revolted** ◆◆◇◇◇
1 N-VAR =insurrection, rebellion A **revolt** is an illegal and often violent attempt by a group of people to change their country's political system. *It was undeniably a revolt by ordinary people against their leaders... In July, 20,000 Tibetans had risen in revolt, many of them being killed.*
2 VERB When people **revolt**, they make an illegal and often violent attempt to change their country's political system. V *In 1375 the townspeople revolted...* V against n *Zanzibar's fortunes declined after the islanders revolted against the sultanate in 1964.*
3 N-VAR =rebellion A **revolt** by a person or group against someone or something is a rejection of the authority of that person or thing. *The prime minister is facing a revolt by Conservative party activists over his refusal to hold a referendum... Soon the entire armed forces were in open revolt.*
4 VERB =rebel When people **revolt** against someone or something, they reject the authority of that person or reject that thing. V *The prime minister only reacted when three of his senior cabinet colleagues revolted* V against n *and resigned in protest on Friday night... Caroline revolted against her ballet training at sixteen.*

revolting /rɪvoʊltɪŋ/. ◆◇◇◇◇ ADJ-GRADED =disgusting If you say that something or someone is **revolting**, you mean you think they are horrible and disgusting. *The smell in the cell was revolting... It was the most revolting thing I have ever tasted.*

revolution /revəluːʃən/ **revolutions** ◆◆◆◇◇
1 N-COUNT A **revolution** is a successful attempt by a large group of people to change the political system of their country by force. *The period since the revolution has been one of political turmoil. ...after the French Revolution. ...before the 1917 Revolution.*
2 N-COUNT: with supp A **revolution** in a particular area of human activity is an important change in that area. *The nineteenth century witnessed a revolution in ship design and propulsion. ...the industrial revolution.*

revolutionary /revəluːʃənri, AM -neri/ **revolutionaries** ◆◆◆◇◇
1 ADJ **Revolutionary** activities, organizations, or people have the aim of causing a political revolution. *Do you know anything about the revolutionary movement? ...the Cuban revolutionary leader, Jose Marti.*
2 N-COUNT A **revolutionary** is a person who tries to cause a revolution or who takes an active part in one. *The revolutionaries laid down their arms and its leaders went into voluntary exile.*
3 ADJ-GRADED **Revolutionary** ideas and developments involve great changes in the way that something is done or made. *Invented in 1951, the rotary engine is a revolutionary concept in internal combustion... His playing as a trumpet player was quite revolutionary.*

revolutionize /revəluːʃənaɪz/ **revolutionizes, revolutionizing, revolutionized;** also spelled **revolutionise** in British English. ◆◇◇◇◇
VERB When something **revolutionizes** an activity, it causes great changes in the way that it is done. V n *Over the past forty years plastics have revolutionised the way we live... Automation revolutionized the olive industry in the early 1970s.*

revolve /rɪvɒlv/ **revolves, revolving, revolved** ◆◇◇◇◇
1 VERB If you say that one thing **revolves** around another thing, you mean that the second thing is the main feature or focus of the first thing. V around n *Since childhood, her life has revolved around tennis... This plot revolves around a youngster who is shown various stages of his life.*
2 VERB If a discussion or conversation **revolves** around a particular topic, it is mainly about that topic. V around n *The debate revolves around specific accounting techniques... The conversation revolved around the terrible condition of the road.*
3 VERB If one object **revolves** around another object, the first object turns in a circle around the second object. V around n *The satellite revolves around the Earth once every hundred minutes.*
4 V-ERG When something **revolves** or when you **revolve** it, it moves or turns in a circle around a central point or line. V *Overhead, the fan revolved slowly...* V n *Monica picked up her Biro and revolved it between her teeth.*

revolver /rɪvɒlvər/ **revolvers.** ◆◇◇◇◇ N-COUNT =gun A **revolver** is a kind of hand gun. Its bullets are kept in a revolving cylinder in the gun.

revolving door, revolving doors
1 N-COUNT: usu pl Some large buildings have **revolving doors** instead of an ordinary door. They consist of four glass doors which turn together in a circle around a vertical post. *As he went through the revolving doors he felt his courage deserting him. ...the doorman by the revolving door.*
2 N-COUNT: usu sing PRAGMATICS In business, when you talk about a **revolving door**, you mean a situation in which the em-

ployees or owners of an organization keep changing; used showing disapproval. *They have accepted an offer from another firm with a busy revolving door.*

revue /rɪvjuː/ **revues.** A **revue** is a light theatrical entertainment consisting of songs, dances, and jokes about recent events. ◆◇◇◇◇ N-COUNT

revulsion /rɪvʌlʃᵊn/. Someone's **revulsion** at something is the strong feeling of disgust or disapproval they have towards it. *...their revulsion at the act of desecration... His voice was filled with horror and revulsion.* ◆◇◇◇◇ N-UNCOUNT: also a N =disgust

revved up. If someone is **revved up**, they are prepared for an important or exciting activity; an informal word. *Every single day my people would come to work and I would get them all revved up, and I would say, 'Give me an action plan on this'.* ADJ-GRADED: v-link ADJ =psyched-up, hyped-up

reward /rɪwɔːʳd/ **rewards, rewarding, rewarded** ◆◆◆◇◇

1 A **reward** is something that you are given, for example because you have behaved well, worked hard, or provided a service to the community. *A bonus of up to 5 per cent can be added to a pupil's final exam marks as a reward for good spelling, punctuation and grammar... He was given the job as a reward for running a successful leadership bid.* N-COUNT: oft N *for* n

2 A **reward** is a sum of money offered to anyone who can give information about lost or stolen property or about someone who is wanted by the police. *The firm last night offered a £10,000 reward for information leading to the conviction of the killer.* N-COUNT

3 If you do something and **are rewarded** with a particular benefit, you receive that benefit as a result of doing that thing. *Make the extra effort to impress the buyer and you will be rewarded with a quicker sale at a better price.* VERB *be* V-ed Also V n

4 The **rewards** of something are the benefits that you receive as a result of doing or having that thing. *The company is only just starting to reap the rewards of long-term investments... Potentially high financial rewards are attached to senior hospital posts.* N-COUNT: usu pl =benefit

5 If you say that something **rewards** your attention or effort, you mean that it is worth spending some time or effort on it; a fairly formal use. *The compression and density make this a difficult book to read, but it richly rewards the effort.* VERB V n

rewarding /rɪwɔːʳdɪŋ/. An experience or action that is **rewarding** gives you satisfaction or brings you benefits. *...a career which she found stimulating and rewarding... Life for the successful doctor can be emotionally and financially rewarding.* ◆◇◇◇◇ ADJ-GRADED =satisfying, worthwhile

rewind, rewinds, rewinding, rewound. The verb is pronounced /riːwaɪnd/. The noun is pronounced /riːwaɪnd/.

1 When the tape in a video or tape recorder **rewinds** or when you **rewind** it, the tape goes backwards so that you can play it again. Compare **fast forward**. *Waddington rewound the tape and played the message again... He switched the control to the answer-play mode and waited for the tape to rewind.* V-ERG V n V

2 If you put a video or cassette tape on **rewind**, you make the tape go backwards. Compare **fast forward**. *Press the rewind button... Press rewind or fast-forward.* N-UNCOUNT: usu N n

rewire /riːwaɪəʳ/ **rewires, rewiring, rewired.** If someone **rewires** a building or an electrical appliance, a new system of electrical wiring is put into it. *Their first job was to rewire the whole house and install central heating... I have had to spend a lot of money having my house replumbed and rewired.* ♦ **rewiring** *The replumbing and rewiring of the flat ran very smoothly.* VERB V n *have* n V-ed N-UNCOUNT

reword /riːwɜːʳd/ **rewords, rewording, reworded.** When you **reword** something that is spoken or written, you try to express it in a way that is more accurate, more acceptable, or more easily understood. *All right, I'll reword my question... The rules were reworded in 1986.* VERB =rephrase V n

rework /riːwɜːʳk/ **reworks, reworking, reworked.** If you **rework** something such as an idea or a piece of writing, you reorganize it and make changes to it in order to improve it or bring it up to date. *She reworked a lot of her compositions to make them more danceable... See if you can rework your schedule and come up with practical ways to reduce the number of hours you're on call.* ♦ **reworking, reworkings** *Her latest novel seems at first sight to be a reworking of similar themes.* ◆◇◇◇◇ VERB =revise V n N-COUNT: usu N *of* n

rewound /riːwaʊnd/. **Rewound** is the past tense and past participle of **rewind**.

rewrite, rewrites, rewriting, rewrote, rewritten. The verb is pronounced /riːraɪt/. The noun is pronounced /riːraɪt/. ◆◇◇◇◇

1 If someone **rewrites** a piece of writing such as a book, a script, or a law, they write it in a different way in order to improve it. *Following this critique, students rewrite their papers and submit them for final evaluation... The script was rewritten constantly during filming.* VERB =revise, rework V n

2 If governments **rewrite** history, they select and present historical events in a way that suits their own purposes; used showing disapproval. *We have always been an independent people, no matter how they rewrite history... As Orwell pointed out, history can be and often is rewritten to suit the needs of the present.* VERB PRAGMATICS V n

3 When journalists say that a sports player **has rewritten** the record books or the history books, they mean that he or she has broken a record or several records. *...the extraordinary West Country team that have rewritten all the record books in those three years... Kournikova is poised to rewrite the tennis history books.* VERB V n

4 In the film industry, a **rewrite** is the writing of parts of a script again to improve it. *Only after countless rewrites and the most intense effort did John consider the script ready.* N-COUNT =revision

rhapsodic /ræpsɒdɪk/. Language and feelings that are **rhapsodic** are very powerful and full of delight in something; a formal word. *One letter from Vivian is rhapsodic about the birth of her first baby.* ADJ-GRADED

rhapsodize /ræpsədaɪz/ **rhapsodizes, rhapsodizing, rhapsodized;** also spelled **rhapsodise** in British English. If you **rhapsodize** about someone or something, you express great delight or enthusiasm about them; a formal word. *The critics rhapsodized over her performance in 'Autumn Sonata'... 'Orchards would take the place of the jungle,' he rhapsodized.* VERB V *over/about* n V with quote

rhapsody /ræpsədi/ **rhapsodies.** A **rhapsody** is a piece of music which has an irregular form and is full of feeling. *...George Gershwin's Rhapsody In Blue.* N-COUNT: oft in names

rhesus factor /riːsəs fæktəʳ/. The **rhesus factor** is something that is in the blood of most people. If someone's blood contains this factor, they are rhesus positive. If it does not, they are rhesus negative. N-SING =Rh factor

rhetoric /retərɪk/ ◆◆◇◇◇

1 If you refer to fine-sounding speech or writing as **rhetoric**, you disapprove of it because it is meant to convince and impress people but may lack sincerity or honesty. *The change is largely cosmetic, a matter of acceptable political rhetoric rather than social reality... The harsh rhetoric had so soured officials that the two sides were barely speaking.* N-UNCOUNT PRAGMATICS

2 **Rhetoric** is the skill or art of using language effectively; a formal use. *...the noble institutions of political life, such as political rhetoric, public office and public service.* N-UNCOUNT

rhetorical /rɪtɒrɪkᵊl, AM -tɔːr-/ ◆◇◇◇◇

1 A **rhetorical** question is one which is asked in order to make a statement rather than to get an answer. *He grimaced slightly, obviously expecting no answer to his rhetorical question... He made no answer to the Commandante's question, which had been rhetorical in any case.* ♦ **rhetorically** ADJ: usu ADJ n ADV:

/rɪtɒrɪkli, AM -tɔːr-/ *'Do these kids know how lucky they are?' Jackson asked rhetorically.* ADV with v

2 **Rhetorical** language is intended to be grand and impressive; a formal use. *These arguments may have been used as a rhetorical device to argue for a perpetuation of a United Nations role.* ADJ-GRADED: usu ADJ n
♦ **rhetorically** *Suddenly, the narrator speaks in his most rhetorically elevated mode.* ADV

rhetorician /retərɪʃən/ **rhetoricians.** A **rhetorician** is a person who is good at public speaking or who is trained in the art of rhetoric. *...an able and fiercely contentious rhetorician.* N-COUNT

rheumatic /ruːmætɪk/

1 **Rheumatic** is used to describe conditions and pains that are related to rheumatism. **Rheumatic** joints are swollen and painful because they are affected by rheumatism. *...new treatments for a range of rheumatic diseases... It gives rapid relief from rheumatic aches and pains.* ADJ: ADJ n

2 Someone who is **rheumatic** suffers from rheumatism. ADJ-GRADED

rheumatic fever. **Rheumatic fever** is a disease which causes fever, and swelling and pain in your joints. N-UNCOUNT

rheumatism /ruːmətɪzəm/. **Rheumatism** is an illness that makes your joints or muscles stiff and painful. Older people, especially, suffer from rheumatism. N-UNCOUNT

rheumatoid arthritis /ruːmətɔɪd ɑːʳθraɪtɪs/. **Rheumatoid arthritis** is a long-lasting disease that causes your joints, for example your hands or knees, to swell up and become painful. ◆◇◇◇◇ N-UNCOUNT

rheumatology /ruːmətɒlədʒi/. **Rheumatology** is the area of medicine that is concerned with rheumatism, arthritis, and related diseases. N-UNCOUNT
♦ **rheumatologist, rheumatologists** *He was consultant rheumatologist at the Royal Hampshire Hospital.* N-COUNT

rheumy /ruːmi/. If someone has **rheumy** eyes, their eyes are moist and watery, usually because they are very ill or old; a literary word. ADJ: usu ADJ n

Rh factor /ɑːr eɪtʃ fæktəʳ/. The **Rh factor** is the same as the **rhesus factor**. N-UNCOUNT

rhinestone /raɪnstoʊn/ **rhinestones.** **Rhinestones** are shiny, glass jewels that are used in cheap jewellery and to decorate clothes. N-COUNT: oft N n

rhinitis /raɪnaɪtɪs/. If you suffer from **rhinitis** or allergic **rhinitis**, you have a constantly sore and runny nose; a medical term. N-UNCOUNT

rhino /raɪnoʊ/ **rhinos.** A **rhino** is the same as a **rhinoceros**; an informal word. ◆◇◇◇◇ N-COUNT

rhinoceros /raɪnɒsərəs/ **rhinoceroses.** A **rhinoceros** is a large Asian or African animal with thick grey skin and a horn, or two horns, on its nose. N-COUNT

rhizome /raɪzoʊm/ **rhizomes.** **Rhizomes** are the horizontal stems from which some plants, such as irises, grow. Rhizomes are found on or just under the surface of the earth. N-COUNT

rhododendron /roʊdədendrən/ **rhododendrons.** A **rhododendron** is a large bush with large flowers which are usually pink, red, or purple. ◆◇◇◇◇ N-VAR

rhombus /rɒmbəs/ **rhombuses.** A **rhombus** is a geometrical shape which has four equal sides but is not a square; a technical term in geometry. N-COUNT

rhubarb /ruːbɑːʳb/. **Rhubarb** is a plant with large leaves and long red stems. You can cook the stems with sugar to make jam or puddings. N-UNCOUNT

rhyme /raɪm/ **rhymes, rhyming, rhymed** ◆◇◇◇◇

1 If one word **rhymes** with another or if two words **rhyme**, they have a very similar sound. Words that rhyme with each other are often used in poems. *June always rhymes with moon in old love songs. ...the sort of people who give their children names that rhyme: Donnie, Ronnie, Connie. ...a singer rhyming 'eyes' with 'realise'. ...rhymed couplets.* V-RECIP-ERG; V *with* n; pl-n V; V n *with* n; V-ed; Also V n (non-recip)

2 If a poem or song **rhymes**, the lines end with words that have very similar sounds. *In his efforts to make it rhyme he seems to have chosen the first word that comes into his head. ...rhyming couplets.* VERB; V; V-ing

3 A **rhyme** is a word which rhymes with another word, or a set of lines which rhyme. *The one rhyme for passion is fashion... The lyrics are banal and the rhymes clumsy.* N-COUNT

4 A **rhyme** is a short poem which has rhyming words at the ends of its lines. *He was teaching Helen a little rhyme.* ● See also **nursery rhyme**. N-COUNT =poem, verse

5 **Rhyme** is the use of rhyming words as a technique in poetry. If something is written **in rhyme**, it is written as a poem in which the lines rhyme. *Porter stayed within the rules of rhyme... The plays are in rhyme.* N-UNCOUNT

6 If something happens or is done **without rhyme or reason**, there seems to be no logical reason for it to happen or be done. *He picked people on a whim, without rhyme or reason.* PHRASE: PHR after v

rhyming slang. **Rhyming slang** is a colloquial form of language in which you do not use the normal word for something, but say a word or phrase that rhymes with it instead. In Cockney rhyming slang, for example, people say 'apples and pears' to mean 'stairs'. N-UNCOUNT

rhythm /rɪðəm/ **rhythms** ◆◆◆◇◇

1 A **rhythm** is a regular series of sounds or movements. *His music of that period fused the rhythms of Jazz with classical forms... He had no sense of rhythm whatsoever... She could hear the constant rhythm of his breathing.* N-VAR

2 A **rhythm** is a regular pattern of changes, for example changes in your body, in the seasons, or in the tides. *Begin to listen to your own body rhythms. ...the seasonal rhythm of the agricultural year.* N-COUNT

rhythm and blues. **Rhythm and blues** is a style of popular music developed in the 1940's from blues music, but using electrically amplified instruments. The abbreviation 'R & B' is also used. N-UNCOUNT

rhythmic /rɪðmɪk/ or **rhythmical** /rɪðmɪkəl/. A **rhythmic** movement or sound is repeated at regular intervals, forming a regular pattern or beat. *Good breathing is slow, rhythmic and deep. ...the rhythmical beat of the drum.* ◆◇◇◇◇ ADJ-GRADED
♦ **rhythmically** /rɪðmɪkli/ *She stood, swaying her hips, moving rhythmically.* ADV-GRADED: ADV after v

rhythm method. The **rhythm method** is a form of contraception in which a couple try to prevent pregnancy by having sex only at times when the woman is not likely to become pregnant. N-SING: usu *the* N

rhythm section. The **rhythm section** of a band is the musicians whose main job is to supply the rhythm. It usually consists of bass and drums, and sometimes keyboard instruments. N-SING

rib /rɪb/ **ribs, ribbing, ribbed** ◆◆◇◇◇

1 Your **ribs** are the curved bones that go from your backbone around your chest. *Her heart was thumping against her ribs... My face was covered with bruises and I had a broken rib.* N-COUNT

2 A **rib** of beef, pork, or veal is a piece of meat that has been cut to include one of the animal's ribs. *...a rib of beef. ...pork ribs in sweet sauce.* N-COUNT: usu N *of* n, n N

3 **Rib** is a method of knitting that makes a raised pattern of parallel lines. You use rib, for example, around the cuffs and the bottom of sweaters so that the material can stretch without losing its shape. N-UNCOUNT

4 If you **rib** someone about something, you tease them about it in a friendly way; an informal use. *The guys in my local pub used to rib me about drinking 'girly' drinks.* VERB =tease; V n

5 See also **ribbed, ribbing.**

ribald /rɪbəld/. A **ribald** remark or sense of humour is rather rude and refers to sex in a humorous way. *...her ribald comments about a fellow guest's body language.* ADJ-GRADED: usu ADJ n

ribbed /rɪbd/. A **ribbed** surface, material, or garment has a raised pattern of parallel lines on it. *...ribbed cashmere sweaters. ...special ribbed tyres.* ADJ: usu ADJ n

ribbing /rɪbɪŋ/

1 **Ribbing** is friendly teasing; an informal use. *I got quite a lot of ribbing from my team-mates.* N-UNCOUNT =teasing

2 **Ribbing** is a method of knitting that makes a N-UNCOUNT

raised pattern of parallel lines. You use ribbing, for example, round the cuffs and the bottom of sweaters so that the material can stretch without losing its shape. =rib

ribbon /rɪbən/ **ribbons** ◆◆◇◇◇

1 A **ribbon** is a long, narrow piece of cloth that you use for tying things together or as a decoration. *She had tied back her hair with a peach satin ribbon. ...a piece of ribbon.* N-VAR

2 A typewriter or printer **ribbon** is a long, narrow piece of cloth containing a special ink that you put into a typewriter or printer. When you type or print something, a device presses against the ribbon and pushes the ink onto the paper. N-COUNT

rib cage, rib cages; also spelled **ribcage**. Your **rib cage** is the structure of ribs in your chest. It protects your lungs and other organs. N-COUNT

riboflavin /raɪboʊfleɪvɪn/. **Riboflavin** is a vitamin that occurs in green vegetables, milk, fish, eggs, liver, and kidney. N-UNCOUNT

rice /raɪs/ **rices. Rice** consists of white or brown grains taken from a cereal plant. You cook rice and usually eat it with meat or vegetables. *...a meal consisting of chicken, rice and vegetables... Thailand exports its fine rices around the world.* ◆◆◆◇◇ N-MASS
• See also **brown rice.**

rice paper. Rice paper is very thin paper made from rice plants. It is used in cooking. N-UNCOUNT

rich /rɪtʃ/ **richer, richest; riches** ◆◆◆◆◇

1 A **rich** person has a lot of money or valuable possessions. *You're going to be a very rich man... Their one aim in life is to get rich... With nothing but his own talent, he made himself rich and famous.* ADJ-GRADED ≠poor
► **The rich** are rich people. *This is a system in which the rich are cared for and the poor are left to suffer... Only the very rich have really benefited. ...a gossip page featuring the rich and famous.* N-PLURAL: the N

2 **Riches** are valuable possessions or large amounts of money. *An Olympic gold medal can lead to untold riches for an athlete... Some people want fame or riches – I just wanted a baby.* N-PLURAL

3 A **rich** country has a strong economy and produces a lot of wealth, so many people who live there have a high standard of living. *There is hunger in many parts of the world, even in some rich countries.* ADJ-GRADED ≠poor

4 If you talk about the earth's **riches**, you are referring to things that exist naturally in large quantities and that are useful and valuable, for example minerals, wood, and oil. *...Russia's vast natural riches. ...the oil riches of the Middle East.* N-PLURAL: usu supp N

5 If something is **rich in** a useful or valuable substance or is a **rich source** of it, it contains a lot of it. *Liver and kidney are particularly rich in vitamin A... Fish is a rich source of protein.* ADJ-GRADED: v-link ADJ in n, ADJ n

6 **Rich** food contains a lot of fat or oil. *...the hearty, rich foods of Gascony... Additional cream would make it too rich.* ADJ-GRADED
♦ **richness** *The coffee flavour complemented the richness of the pudding.* N-UNCOUNT

7 **Rich** soil contains large amounts of substances that make it good for growing crops or flowers in. *Farmers grow rice in the rich soil.* ADJ-GRADED ≠poor

8 A **rich** deposit of a mineral or other substance consists of a large amount of it. *...the country's rich deposits of the metal, lithium.* ADJ-GRADED
♦ **richness** *...the richness of Tibet's mineral deposits.* N-UNCOUNT

9 If you say that something is a **rich** vein or source of something such as humour, ideas, or information, you mean it can provide a lot of that thing. *The director discovered a rich vein of sentimentality... My collection of Victorian literature turned out to be a rich and often hilarious source of information.* ADJ-GRADED: ADJ n

10 **Rich** smells are strong and very pleasant. **Rich** colours and sounds are deep and very pleasant. *...a rich and luxuriously perfumed bath essence. ...an attractive, glossy rich red colour.* ADJ-GRADED
♦ **richness** *...the richness of colour in Gauguin's paintings.* N-UNCOUNT

11 A **rich** life or history is one that is interesting because it is full of different events and activities. *A rich and varied cultural life is essential for this couple. ...the rich history of the island... Manchester has a rich cultural, economic and sporting heritage.* ADJ-GRADED
♦ **richness** *It all adds to the richness of human life.* N-UNCOUNT

12 A **rich** collection or mixture contains a wide and interesting variety of different things. *Visitors can view a rich and colorful array of aquatic plants and animals... Australia has a rich cultural mix. ...a rich vocabulary.* ADJ-GRADED
♦ **richness** *...Birmingham, with its richness of cultural diversity.* N-UNCOUNT

13 If you say that something someone says or does is **rich**, you are making fun of it because you think it is a surprising and inappropriate thing for them to say or do; an informal use. *Gil says that women can't keep secrets. That's rich, coming from him, the professional sneak.* ADJ-GRADED: v-link ADJ PRAGMATICS =ironic

14 If you say that someone is **filthy rich** or **stinking rich**, you dislike them or are jealous of them because they have a lot of money; an informal expression. *He's stinking rich, and with no more talent than he ever had before. ...a handful of filthy rich young men who work eight months a year.* PHRASE: v-link PHR, PHR n PRAGMATICS =loaded

-rich /-rɪtʃ/. **-rich** combines with the names of useful or valuable substances to form adjectives that describe something as containing a lot of a particular substance. *...Angola's northern oil-rich coastline... It would be wise to include plenty of mineral rich foods in your diet.* COMB in ADJ-GRADED: usu ADJ n

richly /rɪtʃli/ ◆◇◇◇◇

1 If something is **richly** coloured, flavoured, or scented, it has a pleasantly strong colour, flavour, or scent. *...an opulent display of richly coloured fabrics. ...the richly flavoured, hearty foods of the region.* ADV-GRADED: usu ADV -ed/adj

2 If something is **richly** decorated, patterned, or furnished, it has a lot of elaborate and beautiful decoration, patterns, or furniture. *Coffee steamed in the richly decorated silver pot. ...a richly illustrated introduction to the art of the Islamic world.* ADV-GRADED: usu ADV -ed/adj =lavishly

3 If you say that someone **richly** deserves an award, success, or victory, you approve of what they have done and feel very strongly that they deserve it. *He achieved the success he so richly deserved. ...a deeply affecting performance that won him a richly deserved Oscar.* ADV-GRADED: ADV before v, ADV -ed PRAGMATICS

4 If a person or place is **richly** endowed or supplied with something, they have a lot of it. *...a boy richly endowed with courage... The hands are richly supplied with nerve endings.* ADV-GRADED: ADV -ed

5 If someone is **richly** rewarded for doing something, they get something very valuable or pleasurable in return for doing it. *It is a difficult book to read, but it richly rewards the effort... Their caution has been richly rewarded.* ADV-GRADED: ADV before v, ADV -ed

Richter scale /rɪktəʳ skeɪl/. **The Richter scale** is a scale which is used for measuring how severe an earthquake is. *An earthquake measuring 6.1 on the Richter Scale struck California yesterday.* ◆◇◇◇◇ N-SING: the N

rick /rɪk/ **ricks, ricking, ricked**

1 If you **rick** your neck, you hurt it by pulling or twisting it in an unusual way. *Kernaghan missed the United game after he ricked his neck... He recovered from a ricked neck.* VERB V n V-ed

2 A **rick** is a large pile of hay or straw that is built in a regular shape with a thatched top. N-COUNT

rickets /rɪkɪts/. **Rickets** is a disease that children can get when their food does not contain enough Vitamin D. It makes their bones soft and causes their liver and spleen to become too large. N-UNCOUNT

rickety /rɪkɪti/. A **rickety** structure or piece of furniture is not very strong or well made, and seems likely to collapse or break. *Mona climbed the rickety wooden stairway.* ADJ-GRADED: usu ADJ n =ramshackle

rickshaw /rɪkʃɔː/ **rickshaws.** A **rickshaw** is a simple vehicle that is used in Asia for carrying passengers. Some rickshaws are pulled by a man who walks or runs in front. N-COUNT

ricochet /rɪkəʃeɪ, AM -ʃeɪ/ **ricochets, ricocheting, ricocheted.** When a bullet **ricochets**, it hits a surface and bounces away from it. *The bullets ricocheted off the bonnet and windscreen.* VERB V prep/adv Also V
► Also a noun. *He was wounded in the shoulder by a ricochet.* N-COUNT

rid /rɪd/ **rids, ridding.** The form **rid** is used in the present tense and is the past tense and past participle of the verb. ◆◆◆◇◇

1 When you **get rid of** something that you do not want or do not like, you take action so that you no longer have it or suffer from it. *The owner needs to get rid of the car for financial reasons... There's corruption, and we're going to get rid of it... She will have to get rid of the excess weight on her hips.*
PHRASE: V inflects, PHR n

2 If you **get rid of** someone who is causing problems for you or who you do not like, you do something to prevent them affecting you any more, for example by making them leave. *He believed that his manager wanted to get rid of him for personal reasons... You seem in rather a hurry to get rid of me.*
PHRASE: V inflects, PHR n

3 If you **rid** a place or person **of** something undesirable or unwanted, you succeed in removing it completely from that place or person. *The proposals are an attempt to rid the country of political corruption... The new vaccine may rid the world of one of its most terrifying diseases.*
VERB =free
V n *of* n

4 If you **rid** yourself **of** something you do not want, you take action so that you no longer have it or are no longer affected by it. *Why couldn't he ever rid himself of those thoughts, those worries? ...the country's efforts to rid itself of poverty and hunger.*
VERB =free
V pron-refl *of* n

5 If you **are rid of** someone or something that you did not want or that caused problems for you, they are no longer with you or causing problems for you. *The family had sought a way to be rid of her and the problems she had caused them.*
ADJ: v-link ADJ *of* n

6 If you say that someone **is well rid of** someone, you think it is good that the person has gone because you did not like them or you think they caused a lot of problems. *It seems to me your wife was a shallow woman and you're well rid of her.*
PHRASE: V inflects

riddance /rɪdəns/. You say **'good riddance'** to indicate that you are glad that someone has left or that something has gone. *He's gone back to London in a huff and good riddance... I left Texas and said good riddance to all that.*
PHRASE: oft PHR *to* n
PRAGMATICS

ridden /rɪdən/. **Ridden** is the past participle of **ride**.

-ridden /-rɪdən/. **-ridden** combines with nouns to form adjectives that describe something as having a lot of a particular undesirable thing or quality, or suffering very much because of it. *...the debt-ridden economies of Latin America... Too many women are like me, guilt ridden about the kids.*
COMB in ADJ-GRADED

riddle /rɪdəl/ **riddles, riddling, riddled** ◆◇◇◇◇

1 A **riddle** is a puzzle or joke in which you ask a question that seems to be nonsense but which has a clever or amusing answer.
N-COUNT

2 You can describe something as a **riddle** if people have been trying to understand or explain it but have not been able to. *Scientists claimed yesterday to have solved the riddle of the birth of the Universe.*
N-COUNT =mystery, puzzle

3 If someone **riddles** something **with** bullets or bullet holes, they fire a lot of bullets into it. *Unknown attackers riddled two homes with gunfire... The darkness saved me from being riddled with bullets.*
VERB
V n *with* n

riddled /rɪdəld/ ◆◇◇◇◇

1 If something **is riddled with** bullets or bullet holes, it is full of bullet holes. *The bodies of four people were found riddled with bullets.*
ADJ-GRADED: usu v-link ADJ *with* n

2 If something **is riddled with** undesirable qualities or features, it is full of them. *They were the principal shareholders in a bank riddled with corruption... The report was riddled with errors.*
ADJ-GRADED: v-link ADJ *with* n

-riddled /-rɪdəld/. **-riddled** combines with nouns to form adjectives that describe something as being full of a particular undesirable thing or quality. *She pushed the bullet-riddled door open... It is a dangerous, crime-riddled, filthy city.*
COMB in ADJ: usu ADJ n

ride /raɪd/ **rides, riding, rode, ridden** ◆◆◆◆◇

1 When you **ride** a horse, you sit on it and control its movements. *I saw a girl riding a horse... Can you ride?... He was riding on his horse looking for the castle... They still ride around on horses.*
VERB
V n
V
V *on* n
V adv/prep

2 When you **ride** a bicycle or a motorcycle, you sit on it, control it, and travel along on it. *Riding a bike is great exercise... Two men riding on motorcycles opened fire on him... He rode to work on a bicycle.*
VERB
V n
V *on* n
V prep/adv

3 When you **ride** in a vehicle such as a car, you travel in it. *He prefers travelling on the Tube to riding in a limousine... I was riding on the back of a friend's bicycle... I remember the village full of American servicemen riding around in jeeps... I rode to Lily's in a cab.*
VERB
V *in/on* n
V adv/prep

4 A **ride** is a journey on a horse or bicycle, or in a vehicle. *She took some friends for a ride in the family car... Would you like to go for a ride?... She lives just a short bus ride from school.*
N-COUNT

5 If you say that one thing **is riding on** another, you mean that it the first thing is dependent on the other. *Billions of pounds are riding on the outcome of the election... Everything rides on the judgment of these few men.*
VB: oft cont =depend
V *on* n

6 See also **riding**.

7 If you say that someone or something **is riding high**, you mean that they are popular or successful at the present time. *He was riding high in the public opinion polls... His team is riding high.*
PHRASES
V inflects, usu cont

8 If you say that someone faces **a rough ride**, you think that things are going to be difficult for them because people will criticize or bully them; an informal expression. *The Chancellor could face a rough ride unless the plan works... The woman who is brave enough to pursue her own path must prepare herself for a rough ride.*
usu PHR after v =tough time

9 If you say that someone has **been taken for a ride**, you mean that they have been deceived or cheated; an informal expression. *You've been taken for a ride. Why did you give him five thousand francs?*
V inflects

10 • to **ride roughshod over** something: see **roughshod**.

ride out. If someone **rides out** a storm or a crisis, they manage to survive a difficult period without suffering serious harm. *The ruling party think they can ride out the political storm... He has to just ride this out and hope that it turns in his favor.*
PHRASAL VERB =survive
V P n (not pron)
V n P

ride up. If a garment **rides up**, it moves upwards, out of its proper position. *My underskirt had ridden up into a thick band around my hips.*
PHRASAL VERB
V P

rider /raɪdəʳ/ **riders.** A **rider** is someone who rides a horse, a bicycle, or a motorcycle as a hobby or job. You can also refer to someone who is riding a horse, a bicycle, or a motorcycle as a rider. *She is a very good and experienced rider... As we came out of the stables, a rider came towards us.*
◆◆◆◇◇
N-COUNT

ridge /rɪdʒ/ **ridges** ◆◆◇◇◇

1 A **ridge** is a long, narrow piece of raised land.
N-COUNT

2 A **ridge** is a raised line on a flat surface. *...the bony ridge of the eye socket.*
N-COUNT: with supp

ridged /rɪdʒd/. A **ridged** surface has raised lines on it. *...boots with thick, ridged soles for walking.*
ADJ-GRADED: usu ADJ n

ridicule /rɪdɪkjuːl/ **ridicules, ridiculing, ridiculed** ◆◇◇◇◇

1 If you **ridicule** someone or **ridicule** their ideas or beliefs, you make fun of them in an unkind way. *I admired her all the more for allowing them to ridicule her and never striking back... I don't think his faith should be ridiculed.*
VERB =mock
V n

2 If someone or something is an object of **ridicule** or is held up to **ridicule**, someone makes fun of them in an unkind way. *As a heavy child, she became the object of ridicule from classmates... The process of judicial selection was held up to ridicule... Davis was subjected to public ridicule.*
N-UNCOUNT

ridiculous /rɪdɪkjʊləs/. If you say that something or someone is **ridiculous**, you mean that they are very foolish. *It is ridiculous to suggest we are having a romance... It was an absolutely ridiculous decision.*
◆◆◇◇◇
ADJ-GRADED: oft *it* v-link ADJ that/to-inf =absurd

ridiculously /rɪdɪkjʊləsli/. You use **ridiculously** to emphasize the fact that you think something is unreasonable or very surprising. *Dena bought rolls of silk that seemed ridiculously*
◆◇◇◇◇
ADV-GRADED: usu ADV adj/adv
PRAGMATICS

cheap... She looked ridiculously young to be a mother.

riding /raɪdɪŋ/. **Riding** is the activity or sport of riding horses. *The next morning we went riding again... She runs a riding school in Devon.* ◆◆◇◇◇ N-UNCOUNT

rife /raɪf/. If you say that something, usually something bad, is **rife** in a place or that the place is **rife** with it, you mean that it is very common. *Speculation is rife that he will be sacked... Bribery and corruption were rife in the industry... Hollywood soon became rife with rumors.* ◆◇◇◇◇ ADJ-GRADED: v-link ADJ, oft ADJ *with* n

riff /rɪf/ **riffs.** In jazz and rock music, a **riff** is a short repeated tune. ◆◇◇◇◇ N-COUNT

riffle /rɪfᵊl/ **riffles, riffling, riffled.** If you **riffle** through the pages of a book or **riffle** them, you turn them over quickly, without reading everything that is on them. *I riffled through the pages until I reached the index.* VERB =flick V *through* n Also V n

riff-raff /rɪf ræf/; also spelled **riffraff**. If you refer to a group of people as **riff-raff**, you disapprove of them because you think that they are not respectable. N-UNCOUNT PRAGMATICS

rifle /raɪfᵊl/ **rifles, rifling, rifled** ◆◆◇◇◇

1 A **rifle** is a gun with a long barrel. *They shot him at point blank range with an automatic rifle... Neighbours heard the sound of rifle fire and alerted the police.* N-COUNT

2 If you **rifle** through things or **rifle** them, you make a quick search among them in order to find something or steal something. *I discovered my husband rifling through the filing cabinet... The men rifled through his clothing and snatched the wallet... There were lockers by each seat and I quickly rifled the contents.* VERB V *through* n V n

rifleman /raɪfᵊlmæn/ **riflemen.** A **rifleman** is a person, especially a soldier, who is skilled in the use of a rifle. N-COUNT

rifle range, rifle ranges. A **rifle range** is a place where you can practise shooting with a rifle. N-COUNT

rift /rɪft/ **rifts** ◆◇◇◇◇

1 A **rift** between people or countries is a serious quarrel that stops them having a co-operative relationship. *The interview reflected a growing rift between the President and the government... He has warned that the serious rifts within the country could lead to civil war... They hope to heal the rift with their father.* N-COUNT: usu with supp, oft adj N, N prep

2 A **rift** is a split that appears in something solid, especially in the ground. N-COUNT

rig /rɪg/ **rigs, rigging, rigged** ◆◆◇◇◇

1 If someone **rigs** an election, a job appointment, or a game, they dishonestly arrange it to get the result they want or to give someone an unfair advantage. *She accused her opponents of rigging the vote... They rig their domestic markets in favour of local businesses. ...the blatantly rigged elections which allowed him to retain power.* VERB V n V-ed

2 A **rig** is a large structure that is used for looking for oil or gas and for taking it out of the ground or the sea bed. *...a supply vessel for gas rigs in the North Sea.* N-COUNT: oft n N

3 See also **rigging**.

rig out. If you **rig** yourself **out** or **are rigged out** in a particular way, you are wearing a particular kind of clothes; an informal expression. *I rigged myself out in thick jeans and heavy belt... I was rigged out in my usual green suit.* PHRASAL VERB V pron-refl P

rig up. If you **rig up** a device or structure, you make it or fix it in place using any materials that are available. *When it rained I rigged up a partial shelter with a tarpaulin... Election officials have rigged up speakers to provide voters with music.* PHRASAL VERB V P n (not pron) Also V n P

rigging /rɪgɪŋ/ ◆◇◇◇◇

1 Vote or ballot **rigging** is the act of dishonestly organizing an election to get a particular result. *She was accused of corruption, and of vote rigging on a massive scale.* N-UNCOUNT: usu supp N

2 On a ship, the **rigging** is the ropes which support the ship's masts and sails. N-UNCOUNT

right 1 correct, appropriate, or acceptable

right /raɪt/ **rights, righting, righted** ◆◆◆◆◆

1 If something is **right**, it is correct and agrees with the facts. *That's absolutely right... Clocks never told the right time... You chip away at the problem until somebody comes up with the right answer... The barman tells me you saw Ann on Tuesday morning. Is that right?* ► Also an adverb. *He guessed right about some things.* ♦ **rightly** *She attended one meeting only, if I remember rightly.* ADJ =correct ≠wrong ADV: ADV after v ADV: ADV after v

2 If you do something in the **right** way or in the **right** place, you do it as or where it should be done or was planned to be done. *Walking, done in the right way, is a form of aerobic exercise... They have computerized systems to ensure delivery of the right pizza to the right place... The chocolate is then melted down to exactly the right temperature.* ► Also an adverb. *To make sure I did everything right, I bought a fat instruction book.* ADJ: usu ADJ n =correct ≠wrong ADV: ADV after v

3 If you say that someone is seen in all the **right** places or knows all the **right** people, you mean that they go to places which are socially acceptable or know people who are socially acceptable. *He was always to be seen in the right places... Through his father, he had met all the right people.* ADJ: usu ADJ n ≠wrong

4 If someone is **right** about something, they are correct in what they say or think about it. *Ron has been right about the result of every General Election but one... Is that true? Was she right?... Am I right in thinking you're the only person in the club who's actually played at Wembley?* ♦ **rightly** *He rightly assumed that the boy was hiding.* ADJ =correct ≠wrong ADV

5 If something such as a choice, action, or decision is the **right** one, it is the best or most suitable one. *She'd made the right choice in leaving New York... The right decision was made, but probably for the wrong reasons... They decided the time was right for their escape.* ♦ **rightly** *She hoped she'd decided rightly.* ADJ =correct ≠wrong ADV: ADV with v

6 If something is not **right**, there is something unsatisfactory about the situation or thing that you are talking about. *Ratatouille doesn't taste right with any other oil... The name Sue Anne never seemed quite right to Molly... He went into hospital and came out after a week. But he still wasn't right.* ADJ: v-link ADJ, with brd-neg ≠wrong

7 If you think that someone was **right** to do something, you think that there were good moral reasons why they did it. *You were right to do what you did, under the circumstances... The president was absolutely right in ordering the bombing raid.* ♦ **rightly** *The crowd screamed for a penalty but the referee rightly ignored them... Education, quite rightly, is currently at the forefront of the political agenda.* ADJ: v-link ADJ, usu ADJ to-inf ≠wrong ADV: ADV before v, ADV with cl

8 **Right** is used to refer to activities or actions that are considered to be morally good and acceptable. *It's not right, leaving her like this... Fox hunting is popular among some people in this country. It doesn't make it right though... The BBC thought it was right and proper not to show the film.* ► Also a noun. *At least he knew right from wrong.* ♦ **rightness** *Many people have very strong opinions about the rightness or wrongness of abortion.* ADJ: v-link ADJ, oft with brd-neg ≠wrong N-UNCOUNT N-UNCOUNT: usu N *of* n

9 If you **right** something or if it **rights** itself, it returns to its normal or correct state, after being in an undesirable state. *They recognise the urgency of righting the economy... Your eyesight rights itself very quickly.* VERB V n V pron-refl

10 If you **right** a wrong, you do something to make up for a mistake or something bad you did in the past. *We've made progress in righting the wrongs of the past... Having spent 25 years righting his own mistakes, he is anxious that children should not waste opportunities.* VERB =rectify V n

11 If you **right** something that has fallen or rolled over or if it **rights** itself, it returns to its normal upright position. *He righted the yacht and continued the race... The helicopter turned at an awful angle before righting itself.* VERB V n V pron-refl

12 The **right** side of a material is the side that is intended to be seen and that faces outwards when it is made into something. ADJ: ADJ n ≠wrong

13 If you say that things **are going right**, you mean that your life or a situation is developing as you intended or expected and you are pleased with it. *I* PHRASES V inflects ≠go wrong

can't think of anything in my life that's going right... I was pleased with my performance on Saturday – everything went right.

14 If someone has behaved in a way which is morally or legally right, you can say that they are **in the right**. You usually use this expression when the person is involved in an argument or dispute. *She wasn't entirely in the right... Legally, the local tax office is in the right.* usu v-link PHR ≠in the wrong

15 If you **put** something **right**, you correct something that was wrong or that was causing problems. *We've discovered what's gone wrong and are going to put it right.* V inflects

16 • **heart in the right place**: see **heart**. • **it serves** you **right**: see **serve**. • **on the right side of** someone: see **side**.

right 2 direction and political groupings

right /raɪt/; also written **Right** for meanings 3 and 4. ◆◆◆◆◇

1 The **right** is one of two opposite directions, sides, or positions. If you are facing north and you turn to the right, you will be facing east. In the word 'to', the 'o' is to the right of the 't'. *Ahead of you on the right will be a lovely garden... He looks to his left, up at the screen, then to his right.* ► Also an adverb. *Turn right into the street.* N-SING: usu *the*N ≠left; ADV: ADV after v

2 Your **right** arm, leg, or ear, for example, is the one which is on the right side of your body. Your **right** shoe or glove is the one which is intended to be worn on your right foot or hand. *He broke his right leg playing football.* ADJ: ADJ n ≠left

3 You can refer to people who support the political ideals of capitalism and conservatism as **the right**. They are often contrasted with **the left**, who support the political ideals of socialism. *The Tory Right still despise him... The right attacks me for being irreligious.* N-SING-COLL: *the*N ≠left

4 If you say that someone has moved to **the right**, you mean that their political beliefs have become more right-wing. *They see the shift to the Right as a worldwide phenomenon.* N-SING: *the*N ≠left

5 If someone is **at** a person's **right hand**, they work closely with that person so they can help and advise them. *I think he ought to be at the right hand of the president.* PHRASE: usu v-link PHR

right 3 entitlement

right /raɪt/ **rights** ◆◆◆◆◆

1 Your **rights** are what you are morally or legally entitled to do or to have. *They don't know their rights... You must stand up for your rights. ...voting rights.* N-PLURAL: usu poss N

2 If you have a **right** to do or to have something, you are morally or legally entitled to do it or to have it. *...a woman's right to choose... People have the right to read any kind of material they wish.* N-SING: usu N to-inf

3 If someone has **the rights** to a story or book, they are legally allowed to publish it or reproduce it in another form, and nobody else can do so without their permission. *An agent bought the rights to his life... He'd tried to buy the film rights of all George Bernard Shaw's plays.* N-PLURAL: *the*N, usu with supp

4 If something is not the case but you think that it should be, you can say that **by rights**, it should be the case. *She did work which by rights should be done by someone else.* PHRASES PHR with cl

5 If someone is a successful or respected person **in** their **own right**, they are successful or respected because of their own efforts and talents rather than those of the people they are closely connected with. *Although now a celebrity in her own right, actress Lynn Redgrave knows the difficulties of living in the shadow of her famous older sister... Their baby is a person in his own right.* usu n adj PHR

6 If you say that you **reserve the right** to do something, you mean that you will do it if you feel that it is necessary. *He reserved the right to change his mind... The ministry said it reserved the right to take whatever action necessary.* V inflects, PHR to-inf

7 If you say that someone is **within** their **rights** to do something, you mean they are morally or legally entitled to do it. *You were quite within your rights to refuse to co-operate with him.* usu v-link PHR =justified

right 4 discourse uses

right /raɪt/ ◆◆◆◆◇

1 You use **right** in order to attract someone's attention or to indicate that you have dealt with one thing so you can go on to another; used in spoken English. *Right, I'll be back in a minute... Wonderful. Right, let's go to our next caller.* ADV: ADV cl PRAGMATICS

2 You can use **right** to check whether what you have just said is right; used in spoken English. *They have a small plane, right?... So if it's not there now, the killer has it. Right?* CONVENTION PRAGMATICS

3 You can say **'right'** to show that you are listening to what someone is saying and that you accept it or understand it; used in spoken English. *'Your children may well come away speaking with a bit of a broad country accent'—'Right.'—'because they're mixing with country children.'* ADV: ADV as reply PRAGMATICS =yes

4 See also **all right**.

5 In informal spoken English, you say **'right on'** to express your support, encouragement, or approval. *He suggested that many of the ideas just would not work. But the tenor of his input was 'Right on! Please show us how to make them work'.* PHRASES CONVENTION PRAGMATICS

6 If someone says **'right you are'**, they are agreeing to do something in a very willing and happy way; used in informal spoken English. *'I want a word with you when you stop.'—'Right you are.'* PRAGMATICS =OK

right 5 used for emphasis

right /raɪt/ ◆◆◆◆◇

1 You can use the word **right** to emphasize the precise place, position, or time of something. *The back of a car appeared right in front of him. ...a charming resort right on the Italian frontier... I had to decide right then.* ADV: ADV adv/prep PRAGMATICS

2 You can use the word **right** to emphasize how far something moves or extends or how long it continues. *...the highway that runs through the Indian zone right to the army positions... She was kept very busy right up to the moment of her departure... It was taken right there on a conveyor belt.* ADV: ADV prep/adv PRAGMATICS =all the way

3 You can use the word **right** to emphasize the completeness of an action or of a state. *The candle had burned right down... If somebody fell in that water we could throw them a rope and pull them right out!* ADV: ADV adv/prep PRAGMATICS

4 In informal British English, you can use the word **right** to emphasize a noun, usually a noun referring to something bad. *He gave them a right telling off... England's European Championship plans are in a right mess.* ADJ: ADJ n PRAGMATICS =real

5 If you say that something happened **right** after a particular time or event or **right** before it, you mean that it happened immediately after or before it. *All of a sudden, right after the summer, Mother gets married... She then decided right before the opening to make a dramatic announcement.* ADV: ADV prep/adv PRAGMATICS =just

6 If you say **I'll be right there** or **I'll be right back**, you mean that you will get to a place or get back to it in a very short time. *I'm going to get some water. I'll be right back.* ADV: ADV adv PRAGMATICS

7 If you do something **right away** or **right off**, you do it immediately; an informal expression. *He wants to see you right away... I knew right away she was dead... Right off I want to confess that I was wrong.* PHRASES PHR after v, PHR with cl PRAGMATICS =straight away

8 You can use the expression **right now** to emphasize that you are referring to the present moment in time; an informal expression. *Right now I'm feeling very excited... I'm warning you; stop it right now!* PHR with cl PRAGMATICS

right 6 used in titles

Right /raɪt/. The word **Right** is used in some British titles. It indicates high rank or status. *...The Right Reverend John Baker.* ◆◆◇◇◇ ADV: ADV adj

right angle, right angles; also spelled **right-angle**. ◆◇◇◇◇

1 A **right angle** is an angle of ninety degrees. A square has four right angles. N-COUNT

2 If two things are **at right angles**, they are situated so that they form an angle of 90° where they touch each other. You can also say that one thing is **at right angles** to another. *...two lasers at right angles.* PHRASE: oft PHR *to* n

right-angled
1 A **right-angled** triangle has one angle that is a right angle; used in British English. The usual American term is **right triangle**. ADJ: ADJ n
2 A **right-angled** bend is a sharp bend that turns through approximately ninety degrees. ADJ: ADJ n

righteous /raɪtʃəs/. If you think that someone behaves or lives in a way that is morally good you can say that they are **righteous**. People sometimes use **righteous** to express their disapproval when they think someone is only behaving in this way so that others will admire or support them; a formal word. *Aren't you afraid of being seen as a righteous crusader?... He was full of righteous indignation. ...petty dictators and righteous politicians.* ♦ **righteousness** *Both sides in the dispute have been adopting a tone of moral righteousness.* ♦ **righteously** *They righteously maintain that they do not practise rationing.* ◆◇◇◇◇ ADJ-GRADED PRAGMATICS N-UNCOUNT ADV-GRADED

rightful /raɪtfʊl/. If you say that someone or something has returned to its **rightful** place or position, they have returned to the place or position that you think they should have. *The Baltics' own democratic traditions would help them to regain their rightful place in Europe... He had been denied what he believed to be his rightful position at the center of things... The car must be returned to its rightful owner.* ♦ **rightfully** *Jealousy is the feeling that someone else has something that rightfully belongs to you... She's inherited the money which is rightfully hers... Killing a police officer is something that's taken very seriously and rightfully so.* ◆◇◇◇◇ ADJ: ADJ n PRAGMATICS ADV: ADV group

right-hand. If something is on the **right-hand** side of something, it is positioned on the right of it. *...a church on the right-hand side of the road. ...the upper right-hand corner of the picture.* ◆◆◇◇◇ ADJ: ADJ n ≠left-hand

right-hand drive. A **right-hand drive** vehicle has its steering wheel on the right side. It is designed to be driven in countries such as Britain, Japan, and Australia where people drive on the left side of the road. ADJ: usu ADJ n ≠left-hand drive

right-handed. Someone who is **right-handed** uses their right hand rather than their left hand for activities such as writing and painting and for picking things up. ► Also an adverb. *I batted left-handed and bowled right-handed.* ◆◇◇◇◇ ADJ ≠left-handed ADV: ADV after v

right-hander, right-handers. You can describe someone as a **right-hander** if they use their right hand rather than their left hand for activities such as writing and painting and for picking things up. N-COUNT ≠left-hander

right-hand man, right-hand men. Someone's **right-hand man** is the person who acts as their chief assistant and helps and supports them a lot in their work. *He is Rupert Murdoch's right-hand man at News International.* N-COUNT: usu poss N

rightist /raɪtɪst/ **rightists**
1 If someone is described as a **rightist**, they are politically conservative and traditional. Rightists support the ideals of capitalism. N-COUNT ≠leftist
2 If someone has **rightist** views or takes part in **rightist** activities, they are politically conservative and traditional and support the ideas of capitalism. ADJ-GRADED: usu ADJ n ≠leftist

right-minded. If you think that someone's opinions or beliefs are sensible and you agree with them, you can describe them as a **right-minded** person. *He is an able, right-minded, and religious man.* ADJ: usu ADJ n PRAGMATICS =right-thinking

righto /raɪtoʊ/; also spelled **right oh**. In British English, some people say **righto** to show that they have heard what someone has said and are willing to do what they want or to do something to please them; an informal word. *Righto, Harry. I'll put Russ Clements in charge.* EXCLAM PRAGMATICS =OK

right-of-centre. You can describe a person or political party as **right-of-centre** if they have political views which are closer to capitalism and conservatism than to socialism but which are not very extreme. *...the new right-of-centre civilian government.* ADJ: usu ADJ n ≠left-of-centre

right of way, rights of way
1 A **right of way** is a public path across private land. N-COUNT
2 When someone has **right of way** or the **right of way**, they have the right to continue along a particular route, and other people must stop for them. N-UNCOUNT

right-on. You can describe someone as **right-on** if they have modern, liberal, or left-wing ideas, especially if you disagree with them or want to make fun of them. *The people that come to watch the play are all those right-on left-wing sort of people. ...the young, right-on student crowd.* • **right on**: see **right**. ◆◆◇◇◇ ADJ-GRADED: usu ADJ n PRAGMATICS =politically correct

right-thinking. If you think that someone's opinions or beliefs are sensible and you agree with them, you can describe them as a **right-thinking** person. *Every right-thinking American would be proud of them.* ADJ: usu ADJ n PRAGMATICS =right-minded

right triangle, right triangles. A **right triangle** has one angle that is a right angle; used in American English. The usual British term is **right-angled triangle**. N-COUNT

rightward /raɪtwəʳd/; the form **rightwards** is also used. If there is a **rightward** trend in the politics of a person or party, their views become more right-wing. *The result reflects a modest rightward shift in opinion.* ► Also an adverb. *The last-minute switching was strongly rightwards, from Labour to Liberal Democrat.* ADJ: ADJ n ADV: ADV after v

right-wing; also spelled **right wing** for meaning 2. ◆◆◆◇◇
1 A **right-wing** person or group has conservative or capitalist views. *...a right-wing government... Liberals say the paper is too right-wing.* ADJ-GRADED: usu ADJ n
2 **The right wing** of a political party consists of the members who have the most conservative or the most capitalist views. *...the right wing of the Conservative Party... Why did the right wing have so much power within the Kremlin?* N-SING: the N

right-winger, right-wingers. If you think someone has views which are more right-wing than most other members of their party, you can say they are a **right-winger**. ◆◇◇◇◇ N-COUNT ≠left-winger

rigid /rɪdʒɪd/ ◆◆◇◇◇
1 Laws, rules, or systems that are **rigid** cannot be changed or varied, and are therefore considered to be rather severe; used showing disapproval. *Several colleges in our study have rigid rules about student conduct... Hospital routines for nurses are very rigid.* ♦ **rigidity** /rɪdʒɪdɪti/ *...the rigidity of government policy.* ♦ **rigidly** *The caste system was so rigidly enforced that non-Hindus were not even allowed inside a Hindu house.* ADJ-GRADED PRAGMATICS ≠flexible N-UNCOUNT ADV-GRADED: ADV with v
2 If you disapprove of someone because you think they are not willing to change their way of thinking or behaving, you can describe them as **rigid**. *She was a fairly rigid person who had strong religious views... My father is very rigid in his thinking.* ADJ-GRADED PRAGMATICS
3 A **rigid** substance or object is stiff and does not bend, stretch, or twist easily. *...rigid plastic containers... These plates are fairly rigid.* ♦ **rigidity** *...the strength and rigidity of glass.* ADJ-GRADED N-UNCOUNT
4 If someone goes **rigid**, their body becomes very straight and stiff, usually as a result of shock or fear. *I went rigid with shock... Andrew went rigid when he saw a dog, any dog, anywhere.* ♦ **rigidly** *She stood rigidly and stared into the room.* ADJ-GRADED: usu v-link ADJ, oft ADJ *with* n ADV-GRADED: ADV after v

rigmarole /rɪgməroʊl/ **rigmaroles.** You can describe a long and complicated process as a **rigmarole**;used showing disapproval. *Then the whole rigmarole starts over again... I couldn't be bothered to go through the rigmarole of changing clothes.* N-COUNT: usu sing PRAGMATICS

rigor /rɪgəʳ/. See **rigour**.

rigor mortis /rɪgəʳ mɔːʳtɪs/. In a dead body, when **rigor mortis** sets in, the joints and muscles become very stiff. N-UNCOUNT

rigorous /rɪgərəs/ ◆◆◇◇◇
1 A test, system, or procedure that is **rigorous** is very thorough and strict. *The selection process is based on rigorous tests of competence and experience. ...a rigorous system of blood analysis. ...rigor-* ADJ-GRADED: usu ADJ n

ous military training. ♦ **rigorously** *...rigorously conducted research.* ADV-GRADED

2 If someone is **rigorous** in the way that they do something, they are very careful and thorough in the way that they do it. *He is rigorous in his control of expenditure.* ADJ-GRADED: usu v-link ADJ, oft ADJ *in* -ing/n

rigour /rɪgəʳ/ **rigours;** spelled **rigor** in American English. ◆◇◇◇◇

1 If you refer to the **rigours** of an activity or job, you mean the difficult, demanding, or unpleasant things that are associated with it. *He found the rigours of the tour too demanding. ...the rigours of childbirth.* N-PLURAL: usu *the* N *of* n

2 If something is done with **rigour**, it is done in a strict, thorough way. *The new current affairs series promises to address challenging issues with freshness and rigour.* N-UNCOUNT

rile /raɪl/ **riles, riling, riled.** If something **riles** you, it makes you angry. *Cancellations and late departures rarely rile him.* ♦ **riled** *He saw I was riled.* VERB V n ADJ-GRADED

rim /rɪm/ **rims** ◆◇◇◇◇

1 The **rim** of a container such as a cup or glass is the edge that goes all the way round the top. *She looked at him over the rim of her glass.* N-COUNT: usu with supp

2 The **rim** of a circular object is its outside edge. *...a round mirror with white metal rim.* N-COUNT: usu with supp

3 If there is a **rim** of dirt around a surface there is a dirty mark around it. *There was already a rim of dark hairs and soap round the basin.* N-COUNT: usu N *of* n

4 See also **rimmed, -rimmed.**

rimless /rɪmləs/. **Rimless** glasses are glasses which have no frame around the lenses or which have a frame only along the top of the lenses. ADJ: usu ADJ n

rimmed /rɪmd/ ◆◇◇◇◇

1 If something is **rimmed** with a substance or colour, it has that substance or colour around its border. *The plates and glassware were rimmed with gold.* ADJ: usu v-link ADJ *with* n

2 See also **rim, -rimmed.**

-rimmed /-rɪmd/

1 **-rimmed** combines with nouns to form adjectives that describe something as having a border or frame made of a particular substance. *...horn-rimmed spectacles.* COMB in ADJ

2 See also **rim, rimmed.**

rind /raɪnd/ **rinds** ◆◇◇◇◇

1 The **rind** of a fruit such as a lemon or orange is its thick outer skin. *...grated lemon rind.* N-VAR: usu with supp

2 The **rind** of cheese or bacon is the hard outer edge which you do not usually eat. *Discard the bacon rind and cut each rasher in half.* N-VAR: usu with supp

ring 1 telephoning or making a sound

ring /rɪŋ/ **rings, ringing, rang, rung** ◆◆◆◆◇

1 In British English, when you **ring** someone, you phone them. In American English you **call** someone. *He rang me at my mother's... If you'd like more information, ring the Hotline on 414 3929... I would ring when I got back to the hotel... She has rung home just once... Could someone ring for a taxi?* VERB =phone V n V V adv V *for* n

► **Ring up** means the same as **ring.** *You can ring us up anytime... John rang up and invited himself over for dinner... A few months ago I rang up about some housing problems... Nobody rings up a doctor in the middle of the night for no reason.* PHRASAL VERB V n P V P V P *about* n V P n (not pron)

2 When a telephone **rings**, the bell inside it makes a sound, to let you know that someone is phoning you. *As soon as he got home, the phone rang... The phone never stopped ringing.* ► Also a noun. *After at least eight rings, an ancient-sounding maid answered the phone.* ♦ **ringing** *She was jolted out of her sleep by the ringing of the telephone.* VERB V N-COUNT N-UNCOUNT

3 When you **ring** a bell or when a bell **rings**, it makes a metallic sound. *He heard the school bell ring... The door was opened before she could ring the bell.* ► Also a noun. *There was a ring at the bell.* ♦ **ringing** *...the ringing of church bells.* V-ERG V V n N-COUNT N-UNCOUNT

4 If you **ring** for something, you ring a bell to call someone to bring it to you. If you **ring** for someone, you ring a bell so that they come to you. *Shall I ring for a fresh pot of tea?... He rang for the guard to let him out.* VERB V *for* n

5 If you say that a place **is ringing** with sound, usually pleasant sound, you mean that it is completely filled with it; a literary use. *The whole place was ringing with music.* VERB V *with* n Also V

6 You can use the word **ring** to describe a quality that something such as a statement, discussion, or argument seems to have. For example, if an argument **has a plausible ring**, it seems quite plausible. *The announcement had a familiar ring to it.* N-SING: usu *a* adj N

7 If you say that someone **rings the changes**, you mean that they make alterations or improvements to the way something is organized or done. *Ring the changes by adding spices, dried fruit or olives.* PHRASES V inflects

8 If you say that someone's words **ring in** your **ears** or **ring in** your **head**, you mean that you remember them vividly, usually when you would rather forget them; a literary expression. *She shivered as the sound of that man's abuse rang in her ears.* V and N inflect

9 In British English, if you **give** someone **a ring**, you phone them; an informal expression. *We'll give him a ring as soon as we get back.* V inflects

10 If a statement **rings true**, it seems to be true or genuine. If it **rings hollow**, it does not seem to be true or genuine. *Joanna's denial rang true... The rumpus has made all the optimistic statements about unity and harmony ring a little hollow.* V inflects

11 ● to **ring a bell**: see **bell**.

ring around. See **ring round.** PHRASAL VERB

ring back. In British English, if you **ring** someone **back**, you phone them either because they phoned you earlier and you were not there or because you did not finish an earlier telephone conversation; an informal expression. *Tell her I'll ring back in a few minutes... If there's any problem I'll ring you back.* PHRASAL VERB no passive V P V n P

ring in. In British English, if you **ring in**, you phone a place, such as the place where you work, in order to tell them something. *Cecil wasn't there, having rung in to say he was taking the day off.* PHRASAL VERB V P

ring off. In British English, when you **ring off**, you put down the receiver at the end of a telephone call. *She had rung off before he could press her for an answer.* PHRASAL VERB V P

ring out. If a sound **rings out**, it can be heard loudly and clearly. *A single shot rang out.* PHRASAL VERB V P

ring round. In British English, if you **ring round** or **ring around**, you phone several people, usually when you are trying to organize something or to find out some information. *She'd ring around and get back to me... She immediately started ringing round her friends and relatives.* PHRASAL VERB V P V P n (not pron)

ring up PHRASAL VERB

1 See **ring** 1.

2 If a shop assistant **rings up** a sale on a cash register, he or she presses the keys in order to record the amount that is being put into it. *She was ringing up her sale on an ancient cash register.* V P n (not pron) Also V n P

3 If a company **rings up** an amount of money, usually a large amount of money, it makes that amount of money in sales or profits. *The advertising agency rang up 1.4 billion dollars in yearly sales.* V P n (not pron)

ring 2 shapes and groups

ring /rɪŋ/ **rings, ringing, ringed** ◆◆◆◇◇

1 A **ring** is a small circle of metal that you wear on your finger. You wear it as an ornament or to show that you are engaged or married. *She wore several diamond rings. ...a gold wedding ring.* N-COUNT

2 An object or substance that is in the shape of a circle can be described as a **ring.** *Frank took a large ring of keys from his pocket. ...a ring of blue smoke.* N-COUNT: usu with supp

3 A group of people or things arranged in a circle can be described as a **ring.** *They then formed a ring around the square. ...grilled fish surrounded by a ring of thinly cut carrots.* N-COUNT: usu with supp =circle

4 A gas or electric **ring** is a small plate, usually on a cooker, that heats up. You heat up saucepans of food or water on it. N-COUNT: usu supp N

5 At a boxing match or circus, the **ring** is the place where the contest or performance takes place. It is an enclosed space with seats round it. *He will never again be allowed inside a British boxing ring.* N-COUNT: usu with supp

6 You can refer to an organized group of people N-COUNT:

who are involved in an illegal activity as a **ring**. *Police are investigating the suspected drug ring at the school. ...an international spy ring.* usu n N

7 If a building or place **is ringed** with something, it is surrounded by it. *The areas are sealed off and ringed by troops.* VB: usu passive =surrounded be V-ed

8 If you **ring** a bird, you put a small metal ring around its leg so that you can identify it easily and study its movements and habits; used mainly in British English. The usual American word is **tag**. *He demonstrated his techniques for ringing birds.* VERB V n

9 If you say that someone **runs rings round** you or **runs rings around** you, you mean that they are a lot better or a lot more successful than you at a particular activity; an informal expression. *Mentally, he can still run rings round men half his age!* PHRASE: V inflects

ring binder, ring binders. A **ring binder** is a file with hard covers, which you can insert pages into. The pages are held in by metal rings on a bar attached to the inside of the file. N-COUNT

ringer /rɪŋəʳ/ **ringers**

1 If you say that one person is **a dead ringer** for another, you mean that they look exactly like each other; an informal expression. PHRASE: usu v-link PHR for n

2 A bell **ringer** is someone who rings church bells or hand bells as a hobby. N-COUNT

ring-fence, ring-fences, ring-fencing, ring-fenced. To **ring-fence** a grant or fund means to put restrictions on it, so that it can only be used for a particular purpose. *The Treasury has now agreed to ring-fence the money to ensure that it goes directly towards helping elderly people... There should be ring-fenced funding for local crime prevention initiatives.* VERB V n V-ed

ring finger, ring fingers. Your **ring finger** is the third finger of your left or right hand. In some countries, people wear a wedding ring or engagement ring on this finger. N-COUNT

ringing /rɪŋɪŋ/ ◆◇◇◇◇

1 A **ringing** sound is loud and can be heard very clearly. *He hit the metal steps with a ringing crash.* ADJ: ADJ n =resounding

2 A **ringing** statement or declaration is one that is made forcefully and is intended to make a powerful impression. *So far we have had ringing declarations, but only limited action. ...a ringing endorsement of the Clinton economic plan.* ADJ: ADJ n

ringleader /rɪŋliːdəʳ/ **ringleaders.** The **ringleaders** in a quarrel, disturbance, or illegal activity are the people who started it and who cause the most trouble; used showing disapproval. *The soldiers were well informed about the ringleaders of the protest.* N-COUNT PRAGMATICS

ringlet /rɪŋlət/ **ringlets.** **Ringlets** are long curls of hair that hang down. N-COUNT: usu pl

ringmaster /rɪŋmɑːstəʳ, -mæst-/ **ringmasters.** A circus **ringmaster** is the person who introduces the performers and the animals. N-COUNT

ring-pull, ring-pulls. In British English, a **ring-pull** is a metal strip that you pull off the top of a can of drink in order to open it. The American term is **tab**. N-COUNT

ring road, ring roads. A **ring road** is a road that goes all the way round the edge of a town so that traffic does not have to go through the town centre; used mainly in British English. N-COUNT

ringside /rɪŋsaɪd/

1 The **ringside** is the area immediately around the edge of a circus ring, boxing ring, or show jumping ring. *Most of the top British trainers were at the ringside.* N-SING

2 If you have a **ringside** seat or a **ringside** view, you have a clear and uninterrupted view of an event. ADJ: ADJ n

ringworm /rɪŋwɜːʳm/. **Ringworm** is a skin disease caused by a fungus. It produces itchy red patches on a person's or animal's skin, especially on their scalp, their groin, or between their toes. N-UNCOUNT

rink /rɪŋk/ **rinks.** A **rink** is a large area where people go to ice-skate or roller-skate. *The other skaters were ordered off the rink. ...outings to a skating rink.* ◆◇◇◇◇ N-COUNT: oft supp N

rinse /rɪns/ **rinses, rinsing, rinsed** ◆◇◇◇◇

1 When you **rinse** something, you wash it in clean water in order to remove dirt or soap from it. *After shampooing, always rinse the hair several times in clear water... It's important to rinse the rice to remove the starch.* ▶ Also a noun. *Clean skin means plenty of lather followed by a rinse with water.* VERB V n N-COUNT

2 If you **rinse** your mouth, you wash it with a mouthful of water or an antiseptic mouthwash. *Use a toothbrush on your tongue as well, and rinse your mouth frequently.* ▶ **Rinse out** means the same as **rinse**. *After her meal she invariably rinsed out her mouth... You should rinse your mouth out after eating.* ▶ Also a noun. *...mouth rinses with fluoride solutions.* VERB V n PHRASAL VERB V P n (not pron) V n P N-MASS

3 A hair **rinse** is a dye which gradually fades after you have washed your hair a number of times rather than being permanent. N-COUNT

riot /raɪət/ **riots, rioting, rioted** ◆◆◆◇◇

1 When there is a **riot**, a crowd of people behave violently in a public place, for example they fight, throw stones, or damage buildings and vehicles. *Twelve inmates have been killed during a riot at the prison.* N-COUNT

2 If people **riot**, they behave violently in a public place. *Last year 600 inmates rioted, starting fires and building barricades... They rioted in protest against the government.* ♦ **rioter, rioters** *The militia dispersed the rioters.* ♦ **rioting** *At least fifteen people are now known to have died in three days of rioting.* VERB V N-COUNT N-UNCOUNT

3 If you say that there is **a riot of** something pleasant such as colour, you mean that there is a large amount of various types of it. *All the cacti were in flower, so that the desert was a riot of colour... With Indian cuisine, you expect a riot of tastes and spices.* N-SING: a N of n PRAGMATICS

4 If someone in authority **reads** you **the riot act**, they tell you that you will be punished unless you start behaving as they would like you to. *I'm glad you read the riot act to Billy. He's still a kid and still needs to be told what to do.* PHRASES V inflects

5 If people **run riot**, they behave in a wild and uncontrolled manner. *Rampaging prisoners ran riot through Strangeways jail.* V inflects

6 If something such as imagination or speculation **runs riot**, it expresses itself or spreads in an uncontrolled way. *She dressed strictly for comfort and economy, but let her imagination run riot with costume jewelry... We have no proof and when there is no proof, rumour runs riot.* V inflects

riotous /raɪətəs/

1 If you say that someone has a **riotous** lifestyle, you mean that they frequently behave in a excessive and uncontrolled way, for example by eating or drinking too much; a formal use. *...aristocrats who wasted their inheritances in riotous living.* ADJ-GRADED: usu ADJ n =wild

2 You can describe someone's behaviour or an event as **riotous** when it is noisy and lively in a rather wild way. *The dinner was often a riotous affair enlivened by superbly witty speeches. ...a riotous exhibition of boogie-woogie piano playing.* ♦ **riotously** *...a slapstick affair which I found riotously amusing.* ADJ-GRADED: usu ADJ n ADV: ADV adj/-ed

3 You can describe things as **riotous** when they are very colourful or decorative rather than plain or functional. *...a riotous collection of gaudy and glamorous dresses.* ADJ: ADJ n

riot police. The **riot police** are the section of the police force that is trained to deal with rioters. *After about 10 minutes the riot police arrived.* ◆◇◇◇◇ N-SING-COLL

riot shield, riot shields. **Riot shields** are see-through shields used by police officers to control crowds and protect themselves from attack. N-COUNT: usu pl

rip /rɪp/ **rips, ripping, ripped** ◆◆◇◇◇

1 When something **rips** or when you **rip** it, you tear it forcefully with your hands or with a tool such as a knife. *I felt the banner rip as we were pushed in opposite directions... I tried not to rip the paper as I unwrapped it.* V-ERG =tear V V n

2 A **rip** is a long cut or split in something made of cloth or paper. *Looking at the rip in her new dress, she flew into a rage.* N-COUNT =tear

3 If you **rip** something away, you remove it quickly and forcefully. *He ripped away a wire that led to the* VERB =tear V with adv *alarm button... She ripped off her dress and let it fall to the floor... He had the microphone ripped from his hand as he prepared to speak.* V prep

4 If something **rips** into someone or something or **rips** through them, it enters that person or thing so quickly and forcefully that it often goes completely through them before heading in another direction. *A volley of bullets ripped into the facing wall... Their minibus was ripped apart by a bomb... The fire ripped through the living room... A violent streak of pain ripped through her whole body.* VERB =tear V prep/adv

5 If you **let rip**, you do something forcefully and without restraint; an informal expression. *Turn the guitars up full and let rip... 'Yaaaaaaa,' Carla let rip with the cry of the Valkyries.* PHRASES *let* inflects

6 If you **let** something **rip**, you do it as quickly or as forcefully as possible. You can say **'let it rip'** or **'let her rip'** to someone when you want them to make a vehicle go as fast as it possibly can. *The ecological disaster is partly a product of letting everything rip in order to increase production.* *let* inflects

rip apart PHRASAL VERB

1 If something **rips** people **apart**, it causes them to quarrel or fight very bitterly, so that they can no longer be friends. *He said that communal carnage was ripping the country apart... To have fought Paul on this would have risked ripping the family apart.* =tear apart V n P (not pron) Also V P n

2 If you **rip** someone **apart** or **rip** their opinion **apart**, you say publicly that they are wrong, often by ridiculing what they have said or done. *The presenters and audience ripped her apart, enjoying a laugh at her expense... Baker himself would be ripped apart in the American press for negotiating a deal.* =tear apart V n P Also V P n (not pron)

rip into. If someone **rips into** you, they verbally attack you for the things you have said or done; an informal use. *If they disputed his allegation, Paul would rip into them with every foul word you could imagine.* PHRASAL VERB =lay into V P n

rip off. If someone **rips** you **off**, they cheat you by charging you too much money for something or by selling you something that is faulty; an informal expression. *The Consumer Federation claims banks are ripping you off by not passing along savings on interest rates... Ticket touts ripped off soccer fans to the tune of £138,000 in the FA Cup Final.* PHRASAL VERB V n P V P n (not pron)
● See also **rip-off**.

rip up. If you **rip** something **up**, you tear it into small pieces. *If we wrote I think he would rip up the letter... She took every photograph of me that was in our house and ripped it up.* PHRASAL VERB =tear up V P n (not pron) V n P

R.I.P /ɑːr aɪ piː/. **R.I.P.** is written on gravestones and expresses the hope that the person buried there may rest in peace. It is an abbreviation for the Latin expression 'requiescat in pace' or 'requiescant in pace'. CONVENTION

ripcord /rɪpkɔːʳd/ **ripcords;** also spelled **rip cord**. A **ripcord** is the cord that you pull to open a parachute. N-COUNT

ripe /raɪp/ **riper, ripest** ◆◆◇◇◇

1 **Ripe** fruit or grain is fully grown and ready to eat. *Always choose firm, but ripe fruit. ...fields of ripe wheat.* ♦ **ripeness** *Test the figs for ripeness.* ADJ-GRADED N-UNCOUNT

2 If a situation **is ripe for** a particular development or event, you mean that development or event is likely to happen soon. *A hospital consultant said conditions were ripe for an outbreak of cholera and typhoid... This society is ripe for change.* ADJ-GRADED: v-link ADJ *for* n/-ing

3 If someone lives to a **ripe old age**, they live until they are very old. *He lived to the ripe old age of 95.* PHRASES prep PHR

4 If something is **ripe for picking** or **ripe for plucking**, it will be very easy to obtain. *Haig's message was that victory was ripe for picking.* usu v-link PHR

5 If you say **the time is ripe**, you mean that a suitable time has arrived for something to be done. *He told reporters that he thought the time was ripe for a normalisation of relations... The British Foreign Office has decided the time is ripe to send its first female ambassador to the region.* V inflects, oft PHR *for* n, PHR to-inf

ripen /raɪpən/ **ripens, ripening, ripened.** When crops **ripen** or when the sun **ripens** them, they become ripe. *I'm waiting for the apples to ripen... You can ripen the tomatoes on a sunny windowsill for a day or two. ...an abundance of sun ripened fruit.* ◆◇◇◇◇ V-ERG V V n V-ed

rip-off, rip-offs ◆◇◇◇◇

1 If you say that something that you bought was a **rip-off**, you mean that you were cheated by the person who sold it to you, either because you were charged too much money or because the item you bought was faulty; an informal expression. *If he thinks £3.40 a day for parking at Luton Airport is a rip-off, he should try Heathrow.* N-COUNT

2 If you say that something is a **rip-off** of something else, you mean that it is a copy of that thing and has no original features of its own; an informal use. *In a rip-off of the hit movie Green Card, Billy marries one of his students so he can stay in the country.* N-COUNT: oft N *of* n

riposte /rɪpɒst, AM -poʊst/ **ripostes, riposting, riposted**

1 A **riposte** is a quick, clever reply to something that someone has said; used in written English. *Laura glanced at Grace, expecting a cheeky riposte.* N-COUNT =retort

2 If you **riposte**, you make a quick, clever response to something someone has said; used in written English. *'It's tough at the top,' he said. 'It's tougher at the bottom,' riposted the billionaire.* VERB =retort V with quote

3 You can refer to an action as a **riposte** to something when it is a reaction to that thing; used by journalists. *The operation is being seen as a swift riposte to the killing of a senior army commander.* N-COUNT: oft N *to* n

ripple /rɪpᵊl/ **ripples, rippling, rippled** ◆◇◇◇◇

1 **Ripples** are little waves on the surface of water caused by the wind or by something moving in or on the water. N-COUNT

2 When the surface of an area of water **ripples** or when something **ripples** it, a number of little waves appear on it. *You throw a pebble in a pool and it ripples... I could see the dawn breeze rippling the shining water. ...the rippling deep blue water of the lake.* V-ERG V V n V-ing

3 When the wind **ripples** plants or trees or when they **ripple**, they move in a wave-like motion; a literary use. *A slight wind rippled the crops in the valley... The tops of the trees rippled in the breeze.* V-ERG V n V

4 If something such as a feeling **ripples** over someone's body, it moves across it or through it; a literary use. *A chill shiver rippled over his skin.* VERB V prep

5 If an event causes **ripples**, its effects gradually spread, causing several other events to happen one after the other. *The ripples of Europe's currency crisis continue to be felt in most of the ERM's member states... The problems of the auto industry have created economic ripples through the rest of the economy as well... Delayed flights have a ripple effect. Just one late flight could be carrying passengers for a dozen connecting services.* N-COUNT: usu pl, with supp

ripple effect, ripple effects. If an event or action has a **ripple effect**, it causes several other events to happen one after the other. *Delayed flights have a ripple effect. Just one late flight could be carrying passengers for a dozen connecting services.* N-COUNT =knock-on effect

rip-roaring. If you describe something as **rip-roaring**, you mean that it is very exciting and full of energy; an informal word. *...a rip-roaring movie with a great array of special effects.* ADJ: ADJ n

riptide /rɪptaɪd/ **riptides;** also spelled **rip-tide**. A **riptide** is an area of sea where two different currents meet or where the water is extremely deep. Riptides make the water very rough and dangerous. N-COUNT

rise /raɪz/ **rises, rising, rose, risen** ◆◆◆◆◆

1 If something **rises**, it moves upwards. *Wilson's ice-cold eyes watched the smoke rise from his cigarette... The powdery dust rose in a cloud around him.* ► **Rise up** means the same as **rise**. *Spray rose up from the surface of the water... Black dense smoke rose up.* VERB V *from/to* n V PHRASAL VERB V P *from/to* n V P

2 When you **rise**, you stand up; a formal use. *Luther rose slowly from the chair... He looked at Livy and Mark, who had risen to greet him.* ► **Rise up** means VERB V *from* n V PHRASAL VERB

the same as **rise**. *The only thing I wanted was to rise up from the table and leave this house.* V P *from* n Also V P

3 When you **rise**, you get out of bed; a formal use. *Tony had risen early and gone to the cottage to work.* VERB V

4 When the sun or moon **rises**, it appears from below the horizon. *He wanted to be over the line of the ridge before the sun had risen.* VERB ≠set V

5 You can say that something **rises** when it appears as a large tall shape; a literary use. *The building rose before him, tall and stately... The towers rise out of a concrete podium.* ▶ **Rise up** means the same as **rise**. *The White Mountains rose up before me.* VERB V prep/adv PHRASAL VERB V P prep/adv

6 If the level of something such as the water in a river **rises**, it becomes higher. *The waters continue to rise as more than 1,000 people are evacuated. ...the tides rise and fall.* VERB ≠fall V

7 If land **rises**, it slopes upwards. *He looked up the slope of land that rose from the house... The ground begins to rise some 20 yards away... The great house stood on rising ground.* VERB ≠fall V prep/adv V V-ing

8 A **rise** is an area of ground that slopes upwards. *The pub itself was on a rise, commanding views across the countryside... I climbed to the top of a rise overlooking the ramparts.* N-COUNT: usu sing =slope

9 If an amount **rises**, it increases. *Pre-tax profits rose from £842,000 to £1.82m... Tourist trips of all kinds in Britain rose by 10.5% between 1977 and 1987... Exports in June rose 1.5% to a record $30.91 billion... Investment levels have fallen, while the number of business failures has risen... The increase is needed to meet rising costs.* VERB ≠fall V *from/to* amount V *by* amount V amount V V-ing

10 A **rise in** the amount of something is an increase in it. *...the prospect of another rise in interest rates... Foreign nationals have begun leaving because of a sharp rise in violence.* N-COUNT: N *in* n =leap

11 In British English, a **rise** is an increase in your wages or your salary. The American word is **raise**. *He will get a pay rise of nearly £4,000.* N-COUNT =increase

12 **The rise of** a movement or activity is an increase in its popularity or influence. *The rise of racism in America is a serious concern. ...the rise of home ownership.* N-SING: *the* N *of* n =growth

13 If the wind **rises**, it becomes stronger. *The wind was still rising, approaching a force nine gale.* ▶ **Rise up** means the same as **rise**. *Foxworth shivered as the wind rose up and roared through the beech trees.* VERB V PHRASAL VERB V P

14 If a sound **rises** or if someone's voice **rises**, it becomes louder or higher. *'Bernard?' Her voice rose hysterically... His voice rose almost to a scream.* VERB V V *to* n

15 If a sound **rises** from a group of people, it comes from them. *There were low, muffled voices rising from the hallway.* ▶ **Rise up** means the same as **rise**. *From the people, a cheer rose up.* VERB V *from* n PHRASAL VERB V P

16 If an emotion **rises** in someone, they suddenly feel it very intensely so that it affects their behaviour. *A tide of emotion rose and clouded his judgement... The thought made anger rise in him and he went into a bar and had a double whisky.* VERB V V *in* n

17 If your colour **rises** or if a blush **rises** in your cheeks, you turn red because you feel angry, embarrassed, or excited. *Amy felt the colour rising in her cheeks at the thought.* VERB V *in* n Also V

18 When the people in a country **rise**, they rebel against the people in authority and start fighting them. *The National Convention has promised armed support to any people who wish to rise against armed oppression.* ▶ **Rise up** means the same as **rise**. *He warned that if the government moved against him the people would rise up... A woman called on the population to rise up against the government.* ♦ **rising, risings** *...popular risings against tyrannical rulers.* VERB =rebel V *against* n Also V PHRASAL VERB V P V P *against* n N-COUNT

19 If someone **rises** to a higher position or status, they become more important, successful, or powerful. *She is a strong woman who has risen to the top of a deeply sexist organisation... From an unlikely background he has risen rapidly through the ranks of government.* ▶ **Rise up** means the same as **rise**. *I started with Hoover 26 years ago in sales and rose up through the ranks.* VERB V prep PHRASAL VERB V P prep

20 The **rise** of someone is the process by which they become more important, successful, or powerful. *Haig's rise was fuelled by an all-consuming sense of patriotic duty... The group celebrated the regime's rise to power in 1979.* N-SING: with poss ≠fall

21 If something **gives rise to** an event or situation, it causes that event or situation to happen. *Low levels of choline in the body can give rise to high blood-pressure... The picture gave rise to speculation that the three were still alive and being held captive.* PHRASE: V inflects, PHR n =provoke

22 • to **rise to the bait**: see **bait**. • to **rise to the challenge**: see **challenge**. • to **rise to the occasion**: see **occasion**.

rise above. If you **rise above** a difficulty or problem, you manage not to let it affect you. *It tells the story of an aspiring young man's attempt to rise above the squalor of the street.* PHRASAL VERB V P n

rise up See **rise** 1, 2, 5, 13, 15, 18, 19. PHRASAL VERB

risen /rɪzᵊn/. **Risen** is the past participle of **rise**.

riser /raɪzəʳ/ **risers**

1 An early **riser** is someone who likes to get up early in the morning. A late **riser** is someone who likes to get up late. *He was an early riser and he would be at the breakfast table at half past seven.* N-COUNT: supp N

2 A **riser** is the flat vertical part of a step or a staircase; a technical term. N-COUNT

risible /rɪzɪbᵊl/. If you describe something as **risible**, you mean that it is ridiculous and does not deserve to be taken seriously; a formal word. ADJ-GRADED PRAGMATICS =ludicrous

rising damp. If a building has **rising damp**, moisture that has entered the brickwork has moved upwards from the floor, causing damage to the walls. N-UNCOUNT

risk /rɪsk/ **risks, risking, risked** ◆◆◆◆◇

1 If there is a **risk** of something unpleasant, there is a possibility that it will happen. *There is a small risk of brain damage from the procedure... In all the confusion, there's a serious risk that the main issues will be forgotten. ...mentally disordered women who pose a serious risk to the public... I suppose people do it because there is that element of danger and risk... Obesity is still a major risk factor in many diseases.* N-VAR: oft N *of* n, N that =danger

2 If something that you do is a **risk**, it might have unpleasant or undesirable results. *You're taking a big risk showing this to Kravis... This was one risk that paid off.* N-COUNT

3 If you say that something or someone is a **risk**, you mean they are likely to cause harm. *It's being overfat that constitutes a health risk... The restaurant has been refurbished – it was found to be a fire risk... He was not seen as a risk to national security.* N-COUNT: usu with supp

4 If you are considered a good **risk**, a bank or shop thinks that it is safe to lend you money or let you have goods without paying for them at the time. *Before providing the cash, they will have to decide whether you are a good or bad risk... If you are already considered a credit risk by a bank, a secured loan might be your only alternative.* N-COUNT: supp N

5 If you **risk** something unpleasant, you do something which might result in that thing happening or affecting you. *Those who fail to register risk severe penalties... Pregnant women who are heavy drinkers risk damaging the unborn foetus.* VERB V n/-ing

6 If you **risk** doing something, you do it, even though you know that it might have undesirable consequences. *The skipper was not willing to risk taking his ship through the straits until he could see where he was going... At the top, I risked a glance back... Don't risk it. It isn't worth it.* VERB V -ing/n

7 If you **risk** someone's life or something that is worth having, you do something which might result in it being lost or harmed. *She risked her own life to help a disabled woman... Why should anyone have risked all that to become an agent of a foreign power?* VERB V n

8 If someone or something is **at risk**, they are in a situation where something unpleasant might happen to them. *Up to 25,000 jobs are still at risk... An estimated seven million people are at risk of starva-* PHRASES v-link PHR, oft PHR *of* n

tion... If they have the virus they are putting patients at risk.

9 If you do something **at the risk of** something unpleasant happening, you do it even though you know that the unpleasant thing might happen as a result. *At the risk of being repetitive, I will say again that statistics are only a guide... Americans wanted to aid Britain even at the risk of war.* PHR n/-ing

10 If you tell someone that they are doing something **at** their **own risk**, you are warning them that, if they are harmed, it will be their own responsibility. *Those who wish to come here will do so at their own risk.* PHR after v PRAGMATICS

11 If you **run** the **risk** of doing or experiencing something undesirable, you do something knowing that the undesirable thing might happen as a result. *The officers had run the risk of being dismissed... I knew I was running a great many risks.* V and N inflect

12 ● to **risk your neck**: see **neck**.

risk-taking. **Risk-taking** means taking actions which might have unpleasant or undesirable results. *...a more entrepreneurial climate, with positive encouragement of risk-taking and innovation.* N-UNCOUNT

risky /rɪski/ **riskier, riskiest.** If an activity or action is **risky**, it is dangerous or likely to fail. *Investing in airlines is a very risky business... It's risky to assume that we know what voters will be thinking in a year's time.* ◆◆◇◇◇ ADJ-GRADED: oft *it* v-link ADJ to-inf

risotto /rɪzɒtoʊ/ **risottos.** **Risotto** is an Italian dish consisting of rice cooked with ingredients such as tomatoes, meat, or fish. N-VAR

risqué /rɪskeɪ, AM rɪskeɪ/. If you describe something as **risqué**, you mean that it is slightly rude because it refers to sex. *Madonna's show will be lively, full of risqué dance routines.* ADJ-GRADED =racy

rissole /rɪsoʊl, AM rɪsoʊl/ **rissoles.** In British English, **rissoles** are small balls of chopped meat or vegetables which are cooked in hot oil. N-COUNT: usu pl

rite /raɪt/ **rites.** A **rite** is a traditional ceremony that is carried out by a particular group or within a particular society. *Most traditional societies have transition rites at puberty. ...a fertility rite.* ● See also **last rites.** ◆◆◇◇◇ N-COUNT

ritual /rɪtʃuəl/ **rituals** ◆◆◇◇◇

1 A **ritual** is a religious service or other ceremony which involves a series of actions performed in a fixed order. *This is the most ancient, and holiest of the Shinto rituals... These ceremonies were already part of pre-Christian ritual in Mexico.* N-VAR

2 **Ritual** activities happen as part of a ritual or tradition. *...fastings and ritual dancing. ...an act of ritual suicide.* ♦ **ritually** *The statue was ritually bathed and purified.* ADJ: ADJ n; ADV: ADV with v

3 A **ritual** is a way of behaving or a series of actions which people regularly carry out in a particular situation, because it is their custom to do so. *The whole Italian culture revolves around the ritual of eating... Cocktails at the Plaza was a nightly ritual of their sophisticated world.* N-VAR

4 You can describe something as a **ritual** action when it is done in exactly the same way whenever a particular situation arises; used showing disapproval. *I realized that here the conventions required me to make the ritual noises.* ADJ: ADJ n PRAGMATICS

ritualistic /rɪtʃuəlɪstɪk/

1 **Ritualistic** actions or behaviour follow a similar pattern every time they are used. *Each evening she bursts into her apartment with a ritualistic shout of 'Honey I'm home!'* ADJ: usu ADJ n

2 **Ritualistic** acts are the fixed symbolic parts of a religious service or ceremony. *...the meditative and ritualistic practices of Buddhism.* ADJ-GRADED: usu ADJ n

ritualized /rɪtʃuəlaɪzd/; also spelled **ritualised** in British English. **Ritualized** acts are carried out in a fixed, structured way rather than being spontaneous. *...ritualized family gatherings intended to promote the myth of the happy family. ...highly ritualised courtship displays.* ADJ-GRADED: usu ADJ n ≠spontaneous

ritzy /rɪtsi/ **ritzier, ritziest.** If you describe something as **ritzy**, you mean that it is fashionable, glamorous, or expensive; an informal word. *Palm Springs has a lot of ritzy restaurants and a lot of glitzy nightlife.* ADJ-GRADED =fancy

rival /raɪvəl/ **rivals, rivalling, rivalled;** spelled **rivaling, rivaled** in American English. ◆◆◆◆◇

1 Your **rival** is a person, business, or organization who you are competing or fighting against in the same area or for the same things. *The world champion finished more than two seconds ahead of his nearest rival... He eliminated his rivals in a brutal struggle for power... The police believe the fight was due to a dispute between rival teenage gangs.* N-COUNT

2 If you say that someone or something has no **rivals** or is without **rival**, you mean that it is best of its type. *The area is famous for its wonderfully fragrant wine which has no rivals in the Rhone... He is a pastry chef without rival.* N-COUNT: with brd-neg

3 If you say that one thing **rivals** another, you mean that they are both of the same standard or quality. *Cassette recorders cannot rival the sound quality of CDs... An epidemic to rival that which killed 26,000 in 1989 may hit the UK.* VERB V n

rivalry /raɪvəlri/ **rivalries.** **Rivalry** is competition or fighting between people, businesses, or organizations who are in the same area or want the same things. *The rivalry between the Inkatha and the ANC has resulted in violence in the black townships... He had a lot of rivalry with his brothers and sisters. ...a city torn by deep ethnic rivalries.* ◆◆◇◇◇ N-VAR

riven /rɪvən/. If a country or organization is **riven** by conflict, its unity is torn apart by a violent disagreement between its people. *The four provinces are riven by deep family and tribal conflicts... The Communist movement has been riven with factional fighting.* ADJ: usu v-link ADJ *by/with* n =torn apart

river /rɪvəʳ/ **rivers.** A **river** is a large amount of fresh water flowing continuously in a long line across the land. *...a chemical works on the banks of the river. ...boating on the River Danube.* ◆◆◆◆◇ N-COUNT: oft in names before n

river bank, river banks; also spelled **riverbank.** A **river bank** is the land along the edge of a river. N-COUNT

river basin, river basins. A **river basin** is the area of land which is drained of water by a river and its tributaries. N-COUNT

river bed, river beds; also spelled **riverbed.** A **river bed** is the ground which a river flows over. N-COUNT

riverboat /rɪvəʳboʊt/ **riverboats.** A **riverboat** is a large boat that carries passengers along a river. N-COUNT: also *by* N

riverfront /rɪvəʳfrʌnt/. The **riverfront** is an area of land next to a river with buildings such as houses, shops, or restaurants on it. N-SING: *the* N, N n

riverside /rɪvəʳsaɪd/. The **riverside** is the area of land by the banks of a river. *They walked back along the riverside.* ◆◇◇◇◇ N-SING: *the* N, N n

rivet /rɪvɪt/ **rivets, riveting, riveted** ◆◇◇◇◇

1 If you **are riveted** by something, it fascinates you and holds your interest completely. *As a child I remember being riveted by my grandfather's appearance... He was riveted to the John Wayne movie... The scar on her face had immediately riveted their attention.* VERB *be* V-ed; *be* V-ed *to* n; V n

2 A **rivet** is a short metal pin with a flat head which is used to fasten flat pieces of metal together. N-COUNT

riveting /rɪvɪtɪŋ/. If you describe something as **riveting**, you mean that it is extremely interesting and exciting, and that it holds your attention completely. *I find snooker riveting though I don't play myself.* ADJ-GRADED

rivulet /rɪvjʊlɪt/ **rivulets.** A **rivulet** is a small stream; a formal word. N-COUNT

RM /ɑːr em/. **RM** is written after someone's name to show that they are an officer of the Royal Marines, one of the units which make up the United Kingdom's armed forces. *...Captain Alastair Rogers, RM.*

RN /ɑːr en/. In British English, **RN** is a written abbreviation for 'Royal Navy', the navy of the United Kingdom. It is written after someone's name to show that they are an officer of the Royal Navy. *...RN Museum, Portsmouth. ...Commander Richard Aylard RN.*

RNA /ɑːr en eɪ/. **RNA** is an acid in the chromosomes of the cells of living things, and plays a vital part in passing information about a cell's protein structure between different cells. **RNA** is an abbreviation for 'ribonucleic acid'; a technical term. ◆◇◇◇◇ N-UNCOUNT

RNAS. **RNAS** is a written abbreviation for 'Royal Naval Air Services', one of the units which make up the United Kingdom's armed forces.

roach /roʊtʃ/ **roaches.** The form **roach** can be used as the plural for meaning 2. ◆◆◆◇◇

1 A **roach** is the same as a **cockroach**; used especially in American English. *He found his brother in a seedy, roach-infested apartment.* N-COUNT

2 A **roach** is a fish that lives in European rivers and lakes. N-COUNT

road /roʊd/ **roads** ◆◆◆◆◆

1 A **road** is a long piece of hard ground which is built between two places so that people can drive or ride easily from one place to the other. *There was very little traffic on the roads... We just go straight up the Bristol Road... He was coming down the road the same time as the girl was turning into the lane... Buses carry 30 per cent of those travelling by road... You mustn't lay all the blame for road accidents on young people.* N-COUNT: oft in names, also *by* N

2 The **road** to a particular result is the means of achieving it or the process of achieving it. *We are bound to see some ups and downs along the road to recovery.* N-COUNT: usu sing, N *to* n

3 If you **hit the road**, you set out on a journey; an informal expression. *I was relieved to get back in the car and hit the road again.* PHRASES V inflects

4 If you are **on the road**, you are going on a long journey or a series of journeys by road. *He still hoped someday to get a new truck and go back on the road.* usu v-link PHR

5 If you say that someone is **on the road** to something, you mean that they are likely to achieve it. *The government took another step on the road to political reform. ...the stunning fashion pictures which launched unknown teenager Jane March on the road to stardom.* usu PHR after v, PHR *to* n =on the way

6 • **the end of the road**: see **end**.

roadblock /roʊdblɒk/ **roadblocks;** also spelled **road block**. When the police or the army put a **roadblock** across a road, they stop all the traffic going through, for example because they are looking for a criminal. *In other parts of the city police set up roadblocks to check passing vehicles.* ◆◇◇◇◇ N-COUNT

roadhog /roʊdhɒg/ **roadhogs;** also spelled **road hog**. If you describe someone as a **roadhog**, you mean that they drive in an inconsiderate way which is dangerous to other people; an informal word used showing disapproval. N-COUNT PRAGMATICS

roadhouse /roʊdhaʊs/ **roadhouses.** In American English, a **roadhouse** is a bar or restaurant on a road outside a city. N-COUNT

roadie /roʊdi/ **roadies.** A **roadie** is a person who transports and sets up equipment for a pop band. N-COUNT

road pricing. In British English, **road pricing** is a system of making motorists pay money for driving on certain roads by electronically recording the movement of vehicles on those roads. N-UNCOUNT

roadshow /roʊdʃoʊ/ **roadshows.** A **roadshow** is a travelling show organized by a radio station, magazine, or company. *The BBC Radio 2 Roadshow will broadcast live from the exhibition.* ◆◇◇◇◇ N-COUNT: usu supp N

roadside /roʊdsaɪd/ **roadsides.** The **roadside** is the area at the edge of a road. *Bob was forced to leave the car at the roadside and run for help... Roadside cafes are now a big part of the catering industry.* ◆◇◇◇◇ N-COUNT: usu sing, *the* N, N n

roadster /roʊdstəʳ/ **roadsters.** A **roadster** is a car with no roof and only two seats; an old fashioned word. N-COUNT =sports car

road tax. In Britain, **road tax** is a tax paid every year by the owners of every motor vehicle which is being used on the roads. N-UNCOUNT

roadway /roʊdweɪ/ **roadways.** The **roadway** is the part of a road that is used by traffic. *Marks in the roadway seem to indicate that he skidded taking a sharp turn.* N-COUNT: oft *the* N in sing =road

roadworks /roʊdwɜːʳks/. **Roadworks** are repairs or other work being done on a road. N-PLURAL

roam /roʊm/ **roams, roaming, roamed.** If you **roam** an area or **roam around** it, you wander or travel around it without having a particular purpose. *Barefoot children roamed the streets... They're roaming around the country shooting at anything that moves... Farmers were encouraged to keep their livestock in pens rather than letting them roam freely.* ◆◇◇◇◇ VERB =wander V n V prep/adv V

roan /roʊn/ **roans.** A **roan** is a horse that is brown or black with some white hairs. N-COUNT

roar /rɔːʳ/ **roars, roaring, roared** ◆◆◇◇◇

1 If something, usually a vehicle, **roars** somewhere, it goes there very fast, making a loud noise; used in written English. *A police car roared past... The plane roared down the runway for takeoff... Flames roared hundreds of feet into the air.* VERB V adv/prep

2 If something **roars**, it makes a very loud noise; used in written English. *The engine roared, and the vehicle leapt forward... Her heart was pounding and the blood roared in her ears. ...the roaring waters of Niagara Falls.* ► Also a noun. *...the roar of traffic... Local residents saw it plunge towards Earth with a deafening roar.* VERB V V-ing N-COUNT: usu sing

3 If someone **roars** with laughter, they laugh in a very noisy way. *Max threw back his head and roared with laughter.* ► Also a noun. *There were roars of laughter as he stood up.* VERB V *with* n Also V N-COUNT: N *of* n

4 If someone **roars**, they shout something in a very loud voice; used in written English. *'I'll kill you for that,' he roared... During the playing of the national anthem the crowd roared and whistled... The audience roared its approval.* ► Also a noun. *There was a roar of approval.* VERB V with quote V V n Also V *for* n N-COUNT

5 When a lion **roars**, it makes the loud sound that lions typically make. *The lion roared once, and sprang.* ► Also a noun. *...the roar of lions in the distance.* VERB V N-COUNT

roaring /rɔːrɪŋ/ ◆◇◇◇◇

1 A **roaring** fire has large flames and is sending out a lot of heat. ADJ: ADJ n

2 If something is a **roaring** success, it is very successful indeed. *The government's first effort to privatize a company has been a roaring success.* ADJ: ADJ n =resounding

3 See also **roar**.

4 If someone **does a roaring trade** in a type of goods, they sell a lot of them. *Salesmen of unofficial souvenirs have also been doing a roaring trade.* PHRASE: V inflects

roast /roʊst/ **roasts, roasting, roasted** ◆◆◇◇◇

1 When you **roast** meat or other food you cook it by dry heat in an oven or over a fire. *I personally would rather roast a chicken whole.* VERB V n

2 **Roast** meat has been cooked by roasting. *They serve the most delicious roast beef.* ADJ: ADJ n

3 A **roast** is a piece of meat that is cooked by roasting. *Come into the kitchen. I've got to put the roast in.* N-COUNT

roasting /roʊstɪŋ/. If someone gives you a **roasting**, they criticize you severely about something in a way that shows that they are very annoyed with you; used in informal British English. *A roasting from his old boss helped rescue his footballing career.* N-SING: usu *a* N

rob /rɒb/ **robs, robbing, robbed** ◆◆◇◇◇

1 If someone **is robbed**, they have money or property stolen from them. *Mrs Yacoub was robbed of her £3,000 designer watch at her West London home... Police said Stefanovski had robbed a man just hours earlier.* VERB be V-ed *of* n V n Also V

2 If someone **is robbed** of something that they deserve, have, or need, it is taken away from them. *When Miles Davis died last September, jazz was robbed of its most distinctive voice... I can't forgive Lewis for robbing me of an Olympic gold.* VERB be V-ed *of* n V n *of* n

robber /rɒbəʳ/ **robbers.** A **robber** is someone who steals money or property from a bank, a shop, or a vehicle, often by using force or threats. *Armed robbers broke into a jeweller's through a hole in the wall.* ◆◇◇◇◇ N-COUNT: oft supp N

robber baron, robber barons. If you refer to someone as a **robber baron**, you mean that they have made a very large amount of money and have been prepared to act immorally or illegally in order to do so. *...the vast wealth accumulated by America's robber barons from industry and transport.* N-COUNT

robbery /rɒbəri/ **robberies. Robbery** is the crime of stealing money or property from a bank, shop, or vehicle, often by using force or threats. *The gang members committed dozens of armed robberies over the past year... The man was serving a sentence for robbery with violence.* ◆◆◇◇◇ N-VAR: oft supp N

robe /roʊb/ **robes** ◆◇◇◇◇

1 A **robe** is a loose piece of clothing which covers all of your body and reaches the ground. You can describe someone as wearing a **robe** or as wearing **robes**; a formal use. *Pope John Paul II knelt in his white robes before the simple altar. ...a fur-lined robe of green silk.* N-COUNT

2 A **robe** is a piece of clothing, usually made of towelling, which people wear in the house, especially when they have just got up or had a bath. *Ryle put on a robe and went down to the kitchen.* N-COUNT =bathrobe

-robed /-roʊbd/. **-robed** combines with the names of colours to indicate that someone is wearing robes of a particular colour. *...a brown-robed monk.* COMB in ADJ: ADJ n

robin /rɒbɪn/ **robins.**

1 A **robin** is a small brown bird found in Europe. The male has an orangey-red neck and breast. N-COUNT

2 A **robin** is a brown bird found in North America. The male has a reddish-brown breast. North American robins are larger than European ones, and are a completely different species of bird. N-COUNT

3 See also **round-robin**.

robot /roʊbɒt, AM -bət/ **robots.** A **robot** is a machine which is programmed to move and perform certain tasks automatically. *...very lightweight robots that we could send to the moon for planetary exploration.* ◆◇◇◇◇ N-COUNT

robotic /roʊbɒtɪk/

1 **Robotic** equipment can perform certain tasks automatically. *Astronaut Pierre Thuot tried to latch the 15-foot robotic arm onto the satellite.* ADJ: ADJ n

2 If you describe someone as **robotic**, you mean that they speak or move in a stiff and mechanical way like a robot; used showing disapproval. *There is something a little robotic about him.* ADJ-GRADED PRAGMATICS

robotics /roʊbɒtɪks/. **Robotics** is the science of designing and building robots. N-UNCOUNT

robust /roʊbʌst, roʊbʌst/ ◆◆◇◇◇

1 Someone or something that is **robust** is very strong or healthy. *More women than men go to the doctor. Perhaps men are more robust or worry less?... We've always specialised in making very robust, simply designed machinery.* ♦ **robustly** *He became robustly healthy.* ♦ **robustness** *The robustness of diesel engines is another attractive quality.* ADJ-GRADED =sturdy; ADV-GRADED; N-UNCOUNT =strength

2 **Robust** views or opinions are strongly held and forcefully expressed. *A British Foreign Office minister has made a robust defence of the agreement... He has the keen eye and robust approach needed.* ♦ **robustly** *In the decisions we have to make about Europe, we have to defend our position very robustly indeed.* ♦ **robustness** *...a prominent industrialist renowned for the robustness of his right-wing views.* ADJ-GRADED: usu ADJ n; ADV-GRADED; N-UNCOUNT: oft *the* N *of* n

rock /rɒk/ **rocks, rocking, rocked** ◆◆◆◆◇

1 **Rock** is the hard substance which the Earth is made of. *The hills above the valley are bare rock... A little way below the ridge was an outcrop of rock that made a rough shelter.* N-UNCOUNT

2 A **rock** is a large piece of rock that sticks up out of the ground or the sea, or that has broken away from a mountain or a cliff. *She sat cross-legged on the rock. ...the sound of the sea crashing against the rocks... He and two friends were climbing a rock face when they heard cries for help.* N-COUNT

3 A **rock** is a piece of rock that is small enough for you to pick up. *She bent down, picked up a rock and threw it into the trees.* N-COUNT =stone

4 When something **rocks** or when you **rock** it, it moves slowly and regularly backwards and forwards or from side to side. *His body rocked from side to side with the train... He stood a few moments, rocking back and forwards on his heels... She sat on the porch and rocked the baby.* V-ERG; V prep/adv; V n; Also V

5 If an explosion or an earthquake **rocks** a building or an area, or makes it rock, it causes the building or area to shake; used by journalists. *Three people were injured yesterday when an explosion rocked one of Britain's best known film studios. ...a country that's rocked by dozens of earthquakes every year... As the buildings rocked under heavy shell-fire, he took refuge in the cellars.* V-ERG =shake; V n; V

6 If an event or a piece of news **rocks** a group or society, it shocks them or makes their position less secure; used by journalists. *His death rocked the fashion business. ...the latest scandal to rock the monarchy... Wall Street was rocked by the news and shares fell 4.3 per cent by the end of trading.* VERB =shake; V n

7 **Rock** is loud music with a strong beat that is usually played and sung by a small group of people using a variety of instruments including electric guitars and drums. *He once told an interviewer that he didn't even like rock music. ...a rock concert. ...famous rock stars.* N-UNCOUNT: oft N n

8 **Rock** is a sweet made in long, hard sticks which are often sold in seaside towns in Britain. *...a stick of rock.* N-UNCOUNT

9 If you are caught **between a rock and a hard place**, you are in a difficult situation where you have to choose between two equally unpleasant courses of action. PHRASES; PHR after v

10 If you have an alcoholic drink such as whisky **on the rocks**, you have it with ice cubes in it. *I could do with a Scotch on the rocks.* usu n PHR =with ice

11 If something such as a marriage or a business is **on the rocks**, it is experiencing very severe difficulties and looks likely to end very soon. *She confided to her mother six months ago that her marriage was on the rocks... Our film industry is on the rocks.* v-link PHR

12 • to **rock the boat**: see **boat**.

rockabilly /rɒkəbɪli/. **Rockabilly** is a kind of fast rock music which developed in the southern United States in the 1950s. N-UNCOUNT

rock and roll; also spelled **rock'n'roll. Rock and roll** is a kind of popular music developed in the 1950s which has a strong beat and is played on electrical instruments. *...Elvis Presley – the King of Rock and Roll. ...the greatest rock 'n' roll band in the world.* ◆◇◇◇◇ N-UNCOUNT: oft N n

rock bottom; also spelled **rock-bottom.** ◆◇◇◇◇

1 If something has reached **rock bottom**, it is at such a low level that it cannot go any lower. *Morale in the armed forces was at rock bottom... Prices have hit rock bottom.* N-UNCOUNT

2 If someone has reached **rock bottom**, they are in such a bad state or are so completely depressed that their situation could not get any worse. *She was at rock bottom. Her long-term love affair was breaking up and so was she.* N-UNCOUNT

3 A **rock-bottom** price or level is a very low one; used showing approval, mainly in advertisements. *What they do offer is a good product at a rock-bottom price.* ADJ: usu ADJ n

rock climber, rock climbers. A **rock climber** is a person whose hobby or sport is climbing cliffs or large rocks. N-COUNT

rock climbing; also spelled **rock-climbing. Rock climbing** is the activity of climbing cliffs or large rocks, as a hobby or sport. N-UNCOUNT

rocker /rɒkəʳ/ **rockers** ◆◇◇◇◇

1 In American English, a **rocker** is a chair that is built on two curved pieces of wood so that you can rock yourself backwards and forwards while you are sitting in it. The British term is **rocking chair**. *Claire spent the morning in a wicker rocker on the screened porch with a book.* N-COUNT =rocking chair

2 A **rocker** is someone who performs rock music. *...American rockers Guns 'N' Roses.* N-COUNT

rockery /rɒkəri/ **rockeries.** A **rockery** is a raised part of a garden which is built of stones and soil, with small plants growing between the rocks. N-COUNT

rocket /rɒkɪt/ **rockets, rocketing, rocketed** ◆◆◆◇◇

1 A **rocket** is a space vehicle that is shaped like a long tube. N-COUNT =spacecraft

2 A **rocket** is a missile containing explosive that is powered by gas. *There has been a renewed rocket attack on the capital.* N-COUNT: oft N n

3 A **rocket** is a firework that quickly goes high into the air and then explodes. N-COUNT

4 If things such as prices or social problems **rocket**, they increase very quickly and suddenly; used by journalists. *Fresh food is so scarce that prices have rocketed... The nation has experienced four years of recession, rocketing crime and escalating social injustice.* VERB =soar V V-ing

rocket launcher, rocket launchers. A **rocket launcher** is a cylindrical device that can be carried and used by soldiers for firing rockets. N-COUNT

rock garden, rock gardens. A **rock garden** is a garden which consists of an arrangement of rocks with small plants growing among them. ◆◇◇◇◇ N-COUNT

rock-hard; also spelled **rock hard**. Something that is **rock-hard** is very hard indeed. *During the dry season the land is rock hard.* ADJ ≠soft

rocking chair, rocking chairs. A **rocking chair** is a chair that is built on two curved pieces of wood so that you can rock yourself backwards and forwards when you are sitting in it. N-COUNT

rocking horse, rocking horses. A **rocking-horse** is a toy horse which a child can sit on and which can be made to rock backwards and forwards. N-COUNT

rock-like. Something that is **rock-like** is very strong or firm, and is unlikely to change. *He affected fellow writers with his rock-like integrity.* ADJ: usu ADJ n

rock music. **Rock music** is loud music with a strong beat that is usually played and sung by a small group of people using a variety of instruments including electric guitars and drums. ◆◇◇◇◇ N-UNCOUNT =rock

rock'n'roll /rɒkənroʊl/. See **rock and roll.** ◆◇◇◇◇

rock pool, rock pools. A **rock pool** is a small pool between rocks on the seashore. N-COUNT

rock salt. **Rock salt** is salt that is formed in the ground. It is obtained by mining. N-UNCOUNT

rock-solid; also spelled **rock solid**.

1 Something that is **rock-solid** is extremely hard. *Freeze it only until firm but not rock solid.* ADJ

2 If you describe someone or something as **rock-solid**, you approve of them because they are extremely reliable or unlikely to change. *Mayhew is a man of rock-solid integrity... I'll need rock solid proof... The firm is rock-solid financially... The pound was rock solid at 2.88 Deutschmarks.* ADJ PRAGMATICS

rock steady; also spelled **rock-steady**. Something that is **rock steady** is very firm and does not shake or move about. *He reached for a cigarette and lit it, fingers rock steady.* ADJ

rocky /rɒki/ ◆◇◇◇◇

1 A **rocky** place is covered with rocks or consists of large areas of bare rock. *The paths are often very rocky so strong boots are advisable. ...a rocky headland.* ADJ-GRADED

2 A **rocky** situation or relationship is unstable and full of difficulties. *They had gone through some rocky times together when Ann was first married... Their relationship had gotten off to a rocky start.* ADJ-GRADED

rococo /rəkoʊkoʊ, AM roʊkəkoʊ/. **Rococo** is a decorative style that was popular in Europe in the eighteenth century. **Rococo** buildings, furniture, and works of art have complicated curly decoration. N-UNCOUNT: oft N n

rod /rɒd/ **rods.** A **rod** is a long, thin metal or wooden bar. *...a 15-foot thick roof that was reinforced with steel rods.* • See also **fishing rod, lightning rod.** ◆◆◇◇◇ N-COUNT

rode /roʊd/. **Rode** is the past tense of **ride**.

rodent /roʊdənt/ **rodents.** **Rodents** are small mammals which have sharp front teeth. Rats, mice, rabbits, and squirrels are rodents. ◆◇◇◇◇ N-COUNT

rodeo /roʊdioʊ, roʊdeɪoʊ/ **rodeos.** In the United States, a **rodeo** is a public entertainment in which cowboys show different skills, including riding wild horses and catching calves with ropes. ◆◇◇◇◇ N-COUNT: usu sing

roe /roʊ/ **roes.** Roe is the eggs or sperm of a fish, which is eaten as food. *...smoked cod's roe.* N-VAR: oft supp N

roe deer; **roe deer** is both the singular and the plural form. A **roe deer** is a small deer which lives in woods in Europe and Asia. N-COUNT

roger /rɒdʒəʳ/ **rogers, rogering, rogered.** If a man **rogers** a woman, he has sex with her; used in informal British English. ◆◇◇◇◇ VERB: V n

rogue /roʊg/ **rogues** ◆◇◇◇◇

1 A **rogue** is a man who behaves in a dishonest or criminal way. *Mr Ward wasn't a rogue at all.* N-COUNT

2 If a man behaves in a way that you do not approve of but you like him anyway, you can refer to him as a **rogue**. *...Falstaff, the loveable rogue.* N-COUNT: oft adj N PRAGMATICS

3 A **rogue** element is someone or something that behaves differently from others of its kind, often causing damage. *Computer systems throughout the country are being affected by a series of mysterious rogue programmes, known as viruses... The rogue male is not a twentieth-century phenomenon.* ADJ: ADJ n

rogues' gallery

1 A **rogues' gallery** is a collection of photographs of criminals kept by the police for identification purposes; an informal use. *...a Rogues' Gallery of juvenile crime gangs.* N-SING: oft N of n

2 You can refer to a group of people or things that you consider undesirable as a **rogues' gallery**. *He and others in the rogues gallery of international terrorists may be running out of time.* N-SING: oft N of n PRAGMATICS

roguish /roʊgɪʃ/. If someone has a **roguish** expression or manner, they look as though they are about to do or say something mischievous. *She was a mature lady with dyed ginger hair and a roguish grin.* ADJ-GRADED

roil /rɔɪl/ **roils, roiling, roiled**

1 If water **roils**, it is rough and cloudy; used especially in American English. *The water roiled to his left as he climbed carefully at the edge of the waterfall.* VERB =churn V

2 Something that **roils** a state or situation makes it disturbed and confused. *Times of national turmoil generally roil a country's financial markets.* VERB V n

role /roʊl/ **roles** ◆◆◆◆◆

1 If you have a **role** in a situation or in society, you have a particular position and function in it. *Until now scientists had very little clear evidence about the drug's role in preventing more serious effects of infection... Under Communist rule, the role of the monarchy was absolutely discredited... Both sides have roles to play.* N-COUNT: with supp, oft N in/of/as n

2 A **role** is one of the characters that an actor or singer can play in a film, play, or opera. *The lead role of Princess Ida has been given to soprano Lesley Garrett... Shakespearean women's roles were originally written to be played by men.* N-COUNT: usu with supp

role model, role models. A **role model** is someone you admire and try to imitate. *Five out of the ten top role models for British teenagers are black.* ◆◇◇◇◇ N-COUNT

role play, role plays, role playing, role played; also spelled **role-play**. ◆◇◇◇◇

1 **Role play** is the act of imitating the character and behaviour of someone who is different from yourself, for example as a training exercise. *Group members have to communicate with each other, or with members of other groups, through role-play.* N-VAR

2 If people **role play**, they do a role play. *Rehearse and role-play the interview with a friend beforehand.* ♦ **role playing** *We did a lot of role playing.* VERB V n Also V N-UNCOUNT

roll /roʊl/ **rolls, rolling, rolled** ◆◆◆◆◇

1 When something **rolls** or when you **roll** it, it moves along a surface, turning over many times. *The ball rolled into the net... Their car went off the road and rolled over... I rolled a ball across the carpet... Roll the meat in coarsely ground black pepper to season it.* V-ERG V prep/adv V n prep

2 If you **roll** somewhere, you move on a surface VERB

while lying down, turning your body over and over, so that you are sometimes on your back, sometimes on your side, and sometimes on your front. V prep/adv *When I was a little kid I rolled down a hill and broke my leg... They just rolled about on the floor punching each other like schoolboys... She rolled over and propped herself up on her elbows.*

3 When vehicles **roll** along, they move along slowly. VERB *More than 100 tanks rolled into eastern Croatia...* V prep/adv *The lorry quietly rolled forward and demolished all the old wooden fencing.*

4 If a machine **rolls**, it is operating. VERB *He slipped and fell on an airplane gangway as the cameras rolled...* V *The newspaper presses are rolling in Pittsburgh again today.*

5 If drops of liquid **roll down** a surface, they move quickly down it. VERB *She looked at Ginny and tears* V *down* n *rolled down her cheeks.*

6 If you **roll** something flexible into a cylinder or a ball, you form it into a cylinder or a ball by wrapping it several times around itself or by shaping it between your hands. VERB *He took off his sweater, rolled it into a pillow and lay down on the grass...* V n *into* n *He rolled and lit another cigarette.* V n ▶ **Roll up** means the same as **roll**. PHRASAL VERB *Stein rolled up the paper bag with the money inside.* V P n (not pron) Also V n P

7 A **roll** of paper, plastic, cloth, or wire is a long piece of it that has been wrapped many times around itself or around a tube. N-COUNT: usu N *of* n *The photographers had already shot a dozen rolls of film. ...a roll of blue insulated wire.* ● See also **toilet roll**.

8 If you **roll** something such as a car window or a blind up, you cause it to move upwards by turning a handle. If you **roll** it down, you cause it to move downwards by turning a handle. VERB *In mid-afternoon, shopkeepers began to roll down their shutters...* V n with adv *She rolled up the window and drove on... He rolled his window down and gave the man the money without saying a word.*

9 If you **roll** your eyes or if your eyes **roll**, they turn up or turn from one side to another. People sometimes roll their eyes when they are very frightened or upset, or because they disapprove of something; used in written English. V-ERG *People may roll their eyes and talk about overprotective, interfering grandmothers...* V n *His eyes rolled and he sobbed.* V

10 A **roll** is a very small loaf of bread that is eaten by one person. Rolls can be round or long, and are eaten plain, with butter, or with some kind of filling. N-COUNT *He sipped at his coffee and spread butter and marmalade on a roll.*

11 A **roll** of drums is a long, rumbling sound made by drums. N-COUNT *He made a roll on the drums.* ● See also **drum roll**.

12 A **roll** is an official list of people's names. N-COUNT: with supp =register *Pro-democracy activists say a new electoral roll should be drawn up.*

13 See also **rolling**; **rock and roll**, **sausage roll**.

14 If someone is **on a roll**, they are having great success which seems likely to continue; an informal expression. PHRASES usu v-link PHR *I made a name for myself and I was on a roll, I couldn't see anything going wrong.*

15 In informal British English, if you say **roll on** something, you mean that you would like it to come soon, because you are looking forward to it. PHR n PRAGMATICS *Roll on the day someone develops an effective vaccine against malaria.*

16 If something is several things **rolled into one**, it combines the main features or qualities of those things. pl-n PHR, v-link PHR *Experts claimed that teachers had to be Einstein, Marie Curie and Linford Christie rolled into one to help children grasp the new national curriculum... This is our kitchen, sitting and dining room all rolled into one.*

17 ● to **start the ball rolling**: see **ball**. ● **heads will roll**: see **head**.

roll back. PHRASAL VERB To **roll back** a change or the power of something means to gradually reduce it or bring it to an end. *Last week he was performing strongly, winning applause with promises 'to roll back the state'...* V P n (not pron) Also V n P *Most major political reforms of the past five years would be rolled back.* ● See also **rollback**.

roll in or **roll into** PHRASAL VERB

1 If something such as money **is rolling in**, it is being received in large quantities; an informal expression. usu cont *Don't forget, I have always kept the money rolling in.* V P Also V P n

2 If someone **rolls into** a place or **rolls in**, they arrive in a casual way, often late. *'I've made you late.'—'No that's all right. I can roll in when I feel like it.'...* V P *The brothers usually roll into their studio around midday.* V P n

roll up PHRASAL VERB

1 If you **roll up** your sleeves or trouser legs, you fold the ends back several times, making them shorter. V P n (not pron) *The jacket was too big for him so he rolled up the cuffs...* V n P *Walking in the surf, she had to roll her pants up to her knees.* ● See also **rolled-up**.

2 If people **roll up** somewhere, they arrive there, especially in large numbers, to see something interesting. *Roll up, roll up, come and join The Greatest Show on Earth...* V P *The first reporters rolled up to the laboratory within minutes.* V P prep/adv

3 See also **roll** 6, **rolled-up**.

rollback /roʊlbæk/ **rollbacks.** A **rollback** of taxes, wages, or prices is a reduction in them. A **rollback** of a change is a reversal of it; used especially in American English. N-COUNT: usu with supp *Silber says the tax rollback would decimate basic services for the needy... The rollback of reform is already putting off private western investors.*

roll call, roll calls; also spelled **roll-call.**

1 If you take a **roll call**, you check which of the members of a group are present by reading their names out. N-VAR *In the late winter we were compelled to stand in the snow every morning for roll call.*

2 A **roll call of** a particular type of people or things is a list of them; used by journalists. N-SING: N *of* n *Her list of pupils read like a roll-call of the great and good.*

rolled-up ◆◇◇◇◇

1 Rolled-up objects have been folded or wrapped into a cylindrical shape. ADJ: ADJ n *...a rolled-up newspaper.*

2 Rolled-up sleeves or trouser legs have been made shorter by being folded over at the lower edge. ADJ: ADJ n *He was wearing cotton pants and an open-necked shirt, with rolled-up sleeves.*

roller /roʊlər/ **rollers** ◆◆◇◇◇

1 A **roller** is a cylinder that turns round in a machine or device. N-COUNT

2 Rollers are hollow tubes that women roll their hair round in order to make it curly. N-COUNT =curler

roller-coaster, roller-coasters; also spelled **roller coaster** or **rollercoaster**. ◆◇◇◇◇

1 At a fairground, a **roller-coaster** is a small railway that goes up and down steep slopes fast and that people ride on for pleasure. N-COUNT =big dipper *It's great to go on the roller coaster five times and not be sick.*

2 If you say that someone or something is on a **roller coaster**, you mean that they go through many dramatic changes in a short time; used mainly by journalists. N-COUNT: usu sing *I've been on an emotional roller coaster since I've been here... Over the last few years Japan's socialists have seen their electoral popularity take a roller-coaster ride.*

roller-skate, roller-skates, roller-skating, roller-skated

1 Roller-skates are shoes with four small wheels on the bottom. N-COUNT: usu pl

2 If you **roller-skate**, you move over a flat surface wearing roller-skates. VERB *On the day of the accident, my son Gary was roller-skating outside our house.* V ♦ **roller-skating** N-UNCOUNT *The craze for roller skating spread throughout the U.S.*

rollicking /rɒlɪkɪŋ/

1 A **rollicking** occasion is lighthearted, jolly, and usually noisy. A **rollicking** book or film is entertaining and enjoyable, and not very serious. ADJ: ADJ n *The fourth volume of Tony Benn's diaries is a rollicking read, like the others.* ▶ Also an adverb. ADV: ADV adj *I'm having a rollicking good time.*

2 If you give someone a **rollicking**, you tell them off in a very angry way; used in informal British English. N-SING: usu *a* N *'The boss gave us a rollicking,' said McGoldrick.*

rolling /rəʊlɪŋ/ ◆◇◇◇◇

1 **Rolling** hills are small hills with gentle slopes that extend a long way into the distance. *...the rolling countryside of south western France.* ADJ: ADJ n

2 If someone has a **rolling** walk, they have a slow and swaying way of walking. *Burns is a big lad with a rolling gait.* ADJ: ADJ n

3 If you say that someone **is rolling in it** or **is rolling in money**, you mean that they are very rich; an informal expression. PHRASE: V inflects =loaded

rolling mill, rolling mills. A **rolling mill** is a machine or factory which uses rollers to flatten metal into sheets or bars. N-COUNT

rolling pin, rolling pins. A **rolling pin** is a cylinder that you roll backwards and forwards over uncooked pastry in order to make the pastry flat. N-COUNT

rolling stock. **Rolling stock** is the engines, carriages, and wagons that are used on a railway. *Many stations needed repairs or rebuilding and there was a shortage of rolling stock.* N-UNCOUNT

roll of honour. In British English, a **roll of honour** is a list of the names of people who are admired or respected for something they have done, such as doing very well in a sport or exam. The American term is **honor roll**. N-SING

roll-on, roll-ons. A **roll-on** is a deodorant or cosmetic that you apply to your body by means of a ball which rotates in the neck of the container. *I use unperfumed roll-on deodorant.* N-COUNT: oft N n

roll-on roll-off. In British English, a **roll-on roll-off** ship is designed so that cars and lorries can drive on at one end before the ship sails, and then drive off at the other end after the voyage. *...roll-on roll-off ferries.* ADJ: ADJ n

roll-top desk, roll-top desks; also spelled **rolltop desk**. A **roll-top desk** is a desk which has a wooden cover which can be pulled down over the writing surface when the desk is not being used. N-COUNT

roly-poly /rəʊli pəʊli/. **Roly-poly** people are pleasantly fat and round; an informal word. *...a short, roly-poly man with laughing eyes.* ADJ: ADJ n

ROM /rɒm/. **ROM** is the permanent part of a computer's memory. The information stored there can be read but not changed. **ROM** is an abbreviation for 'read-only memory'. • See also **CD-ROM**. ◆◇◇◇◇ N-UNCOUNT

Roman /rəʊmən/ **Romans** ◆◆◆◇◇

1 **Roman** means related to or connected with ancient Rome and its empire. *...the fall of the Roman Empire. ...the third-century Roman historian Dio Cassius. ...the remains of a Roman fort.* ► A **Roman** was a citizen of ancient Rome or its empire. *When they conquered Britain, the Romans brought this custom with them.* ADJ: usu ADJ n; N-COUNT

2 **Roman** means related to or connected with modern Rome. *...a Roman hotel room.* ► A **Roman** is someone who lives in or comes from Rome. *...soccer-mad Romans.* ADJ: usu ADJ n; N-COUNT

3 **Roman** is the most common style of printing in books and magazines. It consists of upright letters. The definitions in this dictionary are printed in roman. N-UNCOUNT

Roman alphabet. The **Roman alphabet** is the alphabet that was used by the Romans in ancient times and that is used for writing most western European languages, including English. N-SING: the N

Roman Catholic, Roman Catholics ◆◆◇◇◇

1 The **Roman Catholic** Church is the same as the **Catholic** Church. *He had been ordained as a deacon in the Roman Catholic Church. ...a Roman Catholic priest.* ADJ: usu ADJ n =Catholic

2 A **Roman Catholic** is the same as a **Catholic**. *Like her, Maria was a Roman Catholic.* N-COUNT =Catholic

Roman Catholicism. **Roman Catholicism** is the same as **Catholicism**. N-UNCOUNT

romance /rəmæns, rəʊmæns/ **romances, romancing, romanced** ◆◆◇◇◇

1 A **romance** is a relationship between two people who are in love with each other but who are not married to each other. *After a whirlwind romance the couple announced their engagement in July. ...a holiday romance.* N-COUNT

2 **Romance** refers to the actions and feelings of people who are in love, especially behaviour which is very caring, impulsive, or extravagant. *He still finds time for romance by cooking candlelit dinners for his girlfriend... He takes a rather sceptical view of love and romance.* N-UNCOUNT

3 You can refer to the pleasure and excitement of doing something new or exciting as **romance**. *We want to recreate the romance and excitement that used to be part of rail journeys.* N-UNCOUNT

4 A **romance** is a novel or film about a love affair. *Her taste in fiction was for chunky historical romances.* N-COUNT

5 **Romance** is used to refer to novels about love affairs. *Since taking up writing romance in 1967 she has brought out over fifty books.* N-UNCOUNT

6 A medieval **romance** is a story about someone's adventures, for example the battles they fought. *...Arthurian Romances.* N-VAR

7 When a man **romances** a woman, he has a love affair with her; used in journalism. *He has romanced some of the world's most eligible women.* VERB: V n

8 **Romance** languages are languages such as French, Spanish, and Italian, which are derived from Latin; a technical term in linguistics. ADJ: ADJ n

Romanesque /rəʊmənesk/. **Romanesque** architecture is in the style that was common in western Europe from the ninth to the twelfth centuries. It is characterized by rounded arches and thick pillars. ADJ: usu ADJ n

Romanian /ru:meɪniən/ **Romanians;** also spelled **Rumanian**. ◆◆◆◆◇

1 **Romanian** means belonging or relating to Romania, or to its people, language, or culture. *...a visit to the Romanian capital, Bucharest. ...the Romanian people.* ADJ: usu ADJ n

2 A **Romanian** is a Romanian citizen, or a person of Romanian origin. N-COUNT

3 **Romanian** is the language spoken in Romania. N-UNCOUNT

Roman numeral, Roman numerals. **Roman numerals** are the letters used by the ancient Romans to represent numbers, for example I, IV, VIII, and XL, which represent 1, 4, 8, and 40. Roman numerals are still sometimes used today. N-COUNT: usu pl

romantic /rəʊmæntɪk/ **romantics** ◆◆◆◇◇

1 Someone who is **romantic** or does **romantic** things says and does things that make their wife, husband, girlfriend, or boyfriend feel special and loved. *When we're together, all he talks about is business. I wish he were more romantic... They enjoyed a romantic dinner for two at one of their favourite restaurants.* ♦ **romantically** /rəʊmæntɪkli/ *He lived with his pretty wife Helga – his barge was romantically called after her.* ADJ-GRADED; ADV-GRADED

2 **Romantic** means connected with sexual love. *...his early romantic experiences... He was not interested in a romantic relationship with Ingrid.* ♦ **romantically** *We are not romantically involved.* ADJ: ADJ n; ADV

3 A **romantic** play, film, or story describes or represents a love affair. *It is a lovely romantic comedy, well worth seeing. ...romantic novels.* ADJ: ADJ n

4 If you say that someone has a **romantic** view or idea of something, you are critical of them because their view of it is unrealistic and they think that thing is better or more exciting than it really is. *He has a romantic view of rural society... I don't have any romantic notions about having a baby. It's a really tough job.* ► A **romantic** is a person who has romantic views. *You're a hopeless romantic.* ♦ **romantically** *They suffered from tuberculosis, then still romantically called consumption.* ADJ-GRADED: usu ADJ n PRAGMATICS =unrealistic; N-COUNT ≠realist; ADV-GRADED

5 Something that is **romantic** is beautiful in a way that strongly affects your feelings. *Seacliff House is one of the most romantic ruins in Scotland. ...romantic images from travel brochures.* ♦ **romantically** *...the romantically named, but very muddy, Cave of the Wild Horses.* ADJ-GRADED; ADV-GRADED

6 **Romantic** means connected with the artistic movement of the eighteenth and nineteenth centuries which was concerned with the expression of ADJ: ADJ n

the individual's feelings and emotions. *...the poems and prose of the English romantic poets.*

romanticism /roʊmæntɪsɪzəm/ ◆◇◇◇◇

1 **Romanticism** is thoughts and feelings which are idealistic and romantic, rather than realistic. *Her determined romanticism was worrying me... His poetry tended towards a dreamy romanticism.* N-UNCOUNT ≠realism

2 **Romanticism** is the artistic movement of the eighteenth and nineteenth centuries which was concerned with the expression of the individual's feelings and emotions. N-UNCOUNT

romanticize /roʊmæntɪsaɪz/ **romanticizes, romanticizing, romanticized;** also spelled **romanticise** in British English. If you **romanticize** someone or something, you think or talk about them in a way which is not at all realistic and which makes them seem better than they really are. *He was forced to romanticize the past as he became increasingly disillusioned with his present.* ♦ **romanticized** *Mr. Lane's film takes a highly romanticized view of life on the streets.* VERB =idealize; V n; ADJ-GRADED

Romany /rɒʊməni/ **Romanies**

1 A **Romany** is the same as a **gypsy**. Many travelling people call themselves Romanies rather than gypsies. N-COUNT

2 **Romany** means related or connected to the Romany people. *...the Romany community.* ADJ: usu ADJ n

Romeo /roʊmioʊ/ **Romeos.** You can describe a man as a **Romeo** if you want to indicate in a humorous way that he is very much in love with a woman, or that he frequently has sexual relationships with women; an informal word. *Asked if any other children were planned, the 54-year-old Romeo said: 'Maybe, I dunno.' ...one of Hollywood's most notorious Romeos.* N-COUNT PRAGMATICS

romp /rɒmp/ **romps, romping, romped** ◆◇◇◇◇

1 Journalists use **romp** in expressions like **romp home**, **romp in**, or **romp to victory**, to say that a person or horse has won a race or competition very easily. *Mr Foster romped home with 141 votes.* VERB; V adv/prep

2 When children or animals **romp**, they play noisily and happily. *Dogs and little children romped happily in the garden.* VERB; V

3 If two people have a **romp**, they have sex in a light-hearted and very casual way. N-COUNT

4 Journalists describe a book, film, or play as a **romp** when it is funny, light-hearted, and full of action. *...a riveting, readable romp.* N-COUNT

romp through. If you **romp through** something, you do it or deal with it quickly and easily. *He had romped through the maze of questions with unexpected ease.* PHRASAL VERB; VP n

romper suit, romper suits. A **romper suit** is a piece of clothing worn by babies or young children. It consists of loose trousers and a top that are joined together. N-COUNT

roof /ruːf/ **roofs.** The plural can be pronounced /ruːfs/ or /ruːvz/. ◆◆◆◇◇

1 The **roof** of a building is the covering on top of it that protects the people and things inside from the weather. *...a small stone cottage with a red slate roof... A pail stood in one corner of the room to catch the drips where the roof leaked.* N-COUNT

2 The **roof** of a car or other vehicle is the top part of it, which protects passengers or goods from the weather. *The car rolled onto its roof, trapping him.* N-COUNT

3 **The roof** of your mouth is the highest part of the inside of your mouth. *She clicked her tongue against the roof of her mouth.* N-COUNT: the N of n =palate

4 The **roof** of an underground space such as a cave or mine is the highest part of it. *The cave roof collapsed.* N-COUNT

5 If the level of something such as the price of a product or the rate of inflation **goes through the roof**, it suddenly increases very rapidly indeed; an informal expression. *Prices for Korean art have gone through the roof.* PHRASES; V inflects

6 If you **hit the roof** or **go through the roof**, you become very angry indeed, and usually show your anger by shouting at someone; an informal expression. *Sergeant Long will hit the roof when I tell him you've gone off.* V inflects =go mad

7 If you have a **roof over** your **head**, you have somewhere to live. *I am just thankful that we have a roof over our heads.* head inflects

8 If a group of people **raise the roof**, or in British English **lift the roof**, they make a very loud noise inside a building, for example by cheering, singing, or shouting. *Thatcher loyalists are expected to raise the roof when she steps onto the stage.* V inflects

9 If a number of things or people are **under one roof** or **under the same roof**, they are in the same building. *The firms intend to open either together under one roof or alongside each other in shopping malls... While his relations with his mother were reasonably satisfactory, having her living under the same roof was a totally different matter!* PHR after v, v-link PHR

10 If something happens **under** your **roof**, it happens in your home. *Lionel has forbidden her ever to mention that name again under his roof.* PHR after v, v-link PHR

roofed /ruːft, ruːvd/. A **roofed** building or area is covered by a roof. *...a roofed corridor... Nowadays, only the two big houses remain roofed. ...a peasant hut roofed with branches.* ADJ

-roofed /-ruːft, -ruːvd/. **-roofed** combines with adjectives and nouns to form adjectives that describe what kind of roof a building has. *...a huge flat-roofed concrete and glass building. ...tile-roofed farmhouses.* COMB in ADJ: usu ADJ n

roofer /ruːfəʳ/ **roofers.** A **roofer** is a person whose job is to put roofs on buildings and to repair damaged roofs. N-COUNT

roof garden, roof gardens. A **roof garden** is a garden on the flat roof of a building. N-COUNT

roofing /ruːfɪŋ/

1 **Roofing** is material used for making or covering roofs. *A gust of wind pried loose a section of sheet-metal roofing... Stone began to be used as a roofing material.* N-UNCOUNT: oft N n

2 **Roofing** is the work of putting new roofs on houses. *...a roofing company.* N-UNCOUNT: oft N n

roofless /ruːfləs/. A **roofless** building has no roof, usually because the building has been damaged or has not been used for a long time. ADJ

roof rack, roof racks; also spelled **roof-rack**. A **roof rack** is a metal frame that is fixed on top of a car and used for carrying large objects. N-COUNT

rooftop /ruːftɒp/ **rooftops;** also spelled **roof-top.** ◆◇◇◇◇

1 A **rooftop** is the outside part of the roof of a building. *Below us you could glimpse the rooftops of a few small villages.* N-COUNT

2 If you shout something **from the rooftops**, you say it or announce it in a very public way. *When we have something definite to say, we shall be shouting it from the rooftops.* PHRASE: PHR after v

rook /rʊk/ **rooks**

1 A **rook** is a large black bird. Rooks are members of the crow family. N-COUNT

2 In chess, a **rook** is one of the chess pieces which stand in the corners of the board at the beginning of a game. Rooks can move forwards, backwards, or sideways, but not diagonally. N-COUNT =castle

rookie /rʊki/ **rookies** ◆◇◇◇◇

1 In American English, a **rookie** is a new recruit without much experience, especially a recruit in the army or police force; an informal use. *I don't want to have another rookie to train. ...a rookie police officer.* N-COUNT: oft N n

2 In American English, a **rookie** is a person who has been competing in a professional sport for less than a year. N-COUNT: oft N n

room /ruːm, rʊm/ **rooms, rooming, roomed** ◆◆◆◆◆

1 A **room** is one of the separate sections in a building. Rooms have their own walls, ceiling, floor, and door, and are usually used for a particular kind of activity. You can refer to all the people who are in a room as **the room**. *A minute later he excused himself and left the room... Downstairs are two small rooms: a kitchen and a sitting room... The largest conference room could seat 5,000 people... The whole room roared with laughter.* N-COUNT

2 If you talk about your **room**, you are referring to the room that you alone use, especially your bed- N-COUNT: poss N

room at home or your office at work. *If you're running upstairs, go to my room and bring down my sweater, please.*
3 A **room** is a bedroom in a hotel. *Toni booked a room in an hotel not far from Arzfeld.* N-COUNT
4 In American English, if you **room** with someone, you share a rented room, apartment, or house with them, for example when you are a student. *I had roomed with him in New Haven when we were both at Yale Law School.* VERB V *with* n Also V *together*
5 If there is **room** somewhere, there is enough empty space there for people or things to be fitted in, or for people to move freely or do what they want to. *There is usually room to accommodate up to 80 visitors... There wasn't enough room in the baggage compartment for all the gear... The old artist's studio is a brilliant place for a party with a high ceiling and plenty of room.* • See also **leg room**, **standing room**. N-UNCOUNT
6 If there is **room** for a particular kind of behaviour or action, people are able to behave in that way or to take that action. *The intensity of the work left little room for personal grief or anxiety... Once the plaster was dry there was no room for correction... There's lots of room to express yourself creatively.* N-UNCOUNT: usu N *for* n
7 If you have **room for manoeuvre**, you have the opportunity to change your plans if it becomes necessary or desirable. *With an election looming, he has little room for manoeuvre.* PHRASE: PHR after v, poss PHR, *with* PHR
8 See also **changing room**, **common room**, **consulting room**, **dining room**, **drawing room**, **dressing room**, **elbow room**, **ladies' room**, **leg room**, **living room**, **locker room**, **men's room**, **morning room**, **powder room**, **reading room**, **reception room**, **rest room**, **spare room**, **standing room**.
• to **give something house room**: see **houseroom**.

-roomed /-ru:md/. **-roomed** combines with numbers to form adjectives which tell you how many rooms a house or flat contains. *They found a little two-roomed flat to rent.* COMB in ADJ: usu ADJ n

roomful /ru:mfʊl/ **roomfuls.** A **roomful** of things or people is a room that is full of them. You can also refer to the amount or number of things or people that a room can contain as a **roomful**. *It was like a teacher disciplining a roomful of second-year pupils... I accumulated a roomful of documents and tape recordings.* N-COUNT: usu N *of* n

rooming house, rooming houses. In American English, a **rooming house** is a building that is divided into small flats or single rooms which people rent to live in. N-COUNT

roommate /ru:mmeɪt, rʊm-/ **roommates;** also spelled **room-mate**.
1 In American English, your **roommate** is the person you share a rented room, apartment, or house with, for example when you are at university. N-COUNT
2 In British English, your **roommate** is the person you share a rented room with, for example when you are at university. N-COUNT

room service. Room service is a service in a hotel by which meals or drinks are provided for guests in their rooms. *The hotel did not normally provide room service... Let's call room service, I need a bottle of wine.* N-UNCOUNT

roomy /ru:mi/ **roomier, roomiest**
1 If you describe a place as **roomy**, you mean that you like it because it is large inside and you can move around freely and comfortably. *The car is roomy and a good choice for anyone who needs to carry equipment.* ADJ-GRADED PRAGMATICS =spacious ≠cramped
2 If you describe a piece of clothing as **roomy**, you mean that you like it because it is large and fits loosely. *...roomy jackets.* ADJ-GRADED PRAGMATICS ≠tight

roost /ru:st/ **roosts, roosting, roosted** ◆◇◇◇◇
1 A **roost** is a place where birds or bats rest or sleep. N-COUNT
2 When birds or bats **roost** somewhere, they rest or sleep there. *The peacocks roost in nearby shrubs.* VERB V prep/adv
3 If bad or wrong things that someone has done in the past **have come home to roost**, or if their **chickens have come home to roost**, that they are now experiencing the unpleasant effects of these actions. *Appeasement has come home to roost... Politicians can fool some people some of the time, but in the end, the chickens will come home to roost.* PHRASES *come* inflects
4 If you say that someone **rules the roost** in a particular place, you mean that they have control and authority over the people there; an informal expression. *Today the country's nationalists rule the roost and hand out the jobs.* V inflects

rooster /ru:stəʳ/ **roosters.** A **rooster** is an adult male chicken; used mainly in American English. N-COUNT

root /ru:t/ **roots, rooting, rooted** ◆◆◆◇◇
1 The **roots** of a plant are the parts of it that grow under the ground. *...the twisted roots of an apple tree.* N-COUNT: usu pl
2 If you **root** a plant or cutting or if it **roots**, roots form on the bottom of its stem and it starts to grow. *Most plants will root in about six to eight weeks... Root the cuttings in a heated propagator.* V-ERG V V n
3 **Root** vegetables or **root** crops are grown for their roots which are large and can be eaten. *...root crops such as carrots and potatoes.* ADJ: ADJ n
4 The **root** of a hair or tooth is the part of it beneath the skin. *...decay around the roots of teeth. ...wax strips which remove hairs cleanly from the root.* N-COUNT
5 You can refer to the place or culture that a person or their family comes from as their **roots**. *I am proud of my Brazilian roots... It's 21 years since she first moved to Britain from the Lebanon, but she hasn't forgotten her roots.* N-PLURAL: usu poss N =origins
6 **Roots** is used to refer to types of pop music, especially types of reggae, that are strongly influenced by the traditional music of their culture of origin. *...superb roots reggae by the likes of Little Roy and Wailing Souls.* N-UNCOUNT: oft N n
7 You can refer to the cause of a problem or of an unpleasant situation as the **root** of it or the **roots** of it. *We got to the root of the problem... This lack of recognition was at the root of the dispute... His sense of guilt had its roots in his childhood loss of his younger sister... They were treating symptoms and not the root cause.* N-COUNT: usu *the* N *of* n
8 The **root** of a word is the part that contains its meaning and that does not change; a technical term in linguistics. *The word 'secretary' comes from the same Latin root as the word 'secret'.* N-COUNT
9 If you **root** through something or **root** in something, you look for something in it, moving things around as you search. *She rooted through the bag, found what she wanted, and headed toward the door... Dogs root in the debris at the roadside.* VERB =rummage V prep
10 See also **rooted**; **cube root**, **grass roots**, **square root**.
11 If something has been completely changed or destroyed, you can say that it has been changed or destroyed **root and branch**; used in written English. *The forces of National Socialism were transforming Germany root and branch... Some prison practices are in need of root and branch reform.* PHRASES PHR after v, PHR n
12 If someone **puts down roots**, they make a place their home, for example by taking part in activities there or by making a lot of friends there. *When they got to Montana, they put down roots and built a life.* V inflects =settle down
13 If an idea, belief, or custom **takes root**, it becomes established among a group of people. *Time would be needed for democracy to take root... Without a sensible sex education all kinds of strange and fantastic ideas will take root.* V inflects

root around; the form **root about** is also used in British English. If you **root around** or **root about** in something, you look for something there, moving things around as you search. *'It's in here somewhere,' he said, rooting about in his desk.* PHRASAL VERB =rummage V P prep Also V P

root for. If you **are rooting for** someone, you are giving them your support while they are doing something difficult or trying to defeat someone else; an informal expression. *Good luck, we'll be rooting for you... It's one of those movies in which you're forced to root for the villain.* PHRASAL VERB V P n

root out PHRASAL VERB
1 If you **root out** a person, you find them and force them from the place they are in, usually in order to punish them. *The generals have to root out traitors... It shouldn't take too long to root him out.* =flush out V P n (not pron) V n P

2 If you **root out** a problem or an unpleasant situation, you find out who or what is the cause of it and put an end to it. *There would be a major drive to root out corruption... Any sort of wrong-doing had to be rooted out.* V P n (not pron) Also V pron P

root beer, root beers. Root beer is a fizzy non-alcoholic drink flavoured with the roots of various plants and herbs. It is popular in the United States. N-UNCOUNT ▶ A glass, can, or bottle of root beer can be referred to as a **root beer**. *Kevin buys a root beer.* N-COUNT

rooted /ruːtɪd/ ◆◇◇◇◇

1 If you say that one thing is **rooted in** another, you mean that it is strongly influenced by it or has developed from it. *The crisis is rooted in deep rivalries between the two groups. ...powerful songs rooted in traditional African music.* ADJ: v-link ADJ *in* n

2 If someone has deeply **rooted** opinions or feelings, they believe or feel something extremely strongly and are unlikely to change. *Racism is a deeply rooted prejudice which has existed for thousands of years.* ● See also **deep-rooted**. ADJ-GRADED: usu ADJ n, usu adv ADJ

3 If you are **rooted to the spot**, you are unable to move because you are very frightened or shocked. *We just stopped there, rooted to the spot.* PHRASE

rootless /ruːtləs/. If someone has no permanent home or job and is not settled in any community, you can describe them as **rootless**. *These rootless young people have nowhere else to go. ...people who refused to integrate within society and instead lived rootless, jobless lives.* ADJ-GRADED: usu ADJ n

♦ **rootlessness** *...a social mobility that threatens to become rootlessness.* N-UNCOUNT

rope /roʊp/ **ropes, roping, roped** ◆◆◇◇◇

1 A **rope** is a very thick cord or wire that is made by twisting together several thinner cords or wires. Ropes are used for jobs such as towing cars, mooring boats, or tying large things together. *He tied the rope around his waist. ...a climbing rope. ...a piece of rope.* N-VAR

2 If you **rope** one thing to another, you tie the two things together with a rope. *I roped myself to the chimney.* VERB V n *to* n Also V n *together*

3 **The ropes** refers to the fence made of ropes that surrounds a boxing ring or a wrestling ring. *He was knocked through the ropes by Tafer.* N-PLURAL: *the* N

4 If you **give** someone **enough rope to hang** themselves, you give them the freedom to do a job in their own way because you hope that their attempts will fail and that they will look foolish. *The King has merely given the politicians enough rope to hang themselves... If we give her enough rope, she will hang herself.* PHRASES *give* inflects

5 If you **are learning the ropes**, you are learning how a particular task or job is done; an informal expression. V inflects

6 If you **know the ropes**, you know how a particular job or task should be done; an informal expression. *The moment she got to know the ropes, there was no stopping her.* V inflects

7 If you describe a payment as **money for old rope**, you are emphasizing that it is earned very easily, for very little effort; used in informal British English. *This is money for old rope.* usu v-link PHR PRAGMATICS =easy money

8 If you say that someone is **on the ropes**, you mean that they are very near to giving up or being defeated. *The army claims the rebels are on the ropes.* v-link PHR

9 If you **show** someone **the ropes**, you show them how to do a particular job or task; an informal expression. V inflects

rope in. If you say that you **were roped in** to do a particular task, you mean that someone persuaded you to help them do that task; an informal expression, used mainly in British English. *Visitors were roped in for potato picking and harvesting... I got roped in to help with the timekeeping.* PHRASAL VERB usu passive *be* V-ed P *for* n *be* V-ed P to-inf Also *be* V-ed P

rope off. If you **rope off** an area, you tie ropes between posts all around its edges so that people cannot enter it without permission. *You should rope off a big field and sell tickets. ...a large roped-off area.* PHRASAL VERB V P n (not pron) V-ed P Also V n P

rope ladder, rope ladders; also spelled **rope-ladder**. A **rope ladder** is a ladder made of two long ropes connected by short pieces of rope, wood, or metal. N-COUNT

ropey /roʊpi/ **ropier, ropiest.** In informal British English, if you say that something is **ropey**, you mean that its quality is poor or unsatisfactory. *Your spelling's a bit ropey... Their health-care system suffers from queues, shortages and ropey equipment.* ADJ-GRADED =poor

rosary /roʊzəri/ **rosaries.** A **rosary** is a string of beads that members of certain religions, especially Catholics, use for counting prayers. A series of prayers counted in this way is also called a **rosary**. *Estrada took a rosary from his tunic and ran the beads through the fingers of one hand... He's saying three rosaries a day.* N-COUNT

rose /roʊz/ **roses** ◆◆◆◇◇

1 **Rose** is the past tense of **rise**.

2 A **rose** is a flower, often with a pleasant smell, which grows on a bush with thorny stems. *She bent to pick a red rose. ...a bunch of yellow roses.* N-COUNT

3 Something that is **rose** is reddish-pink in colour. *...the rose and violet hues of a twilight sky.* COLOUR

4 A **rose** is a device with very small holes in it that fits onto the end of a hose or the spout of a watering can. The water comes out of the rose in a fine spray so that you can water plants. N-COUNT

5 If you say that a situation is not a **bed of roses**, you mean that it is not all pleasant, and that there are some unpleasant aspects to it as well. *We all knew that life was unlikely to be a bed of roses back in England.* PHRASES v-link PHR, usu with brd-neg

6 If you say that everything **is coming up roses** for someone, you mean that they are experiencing a lot of success in what they are doing and that everything is going well for them. *Earlier this year, everything was coming up roses for them. Their 'Going Black Again' album was selling well, and their British tour was a virtual sell-out.* V inflects

rosé /roʊzeɪ, AM roʊzeɪ/ **rosés. Rosé** is wine which is pink in colour. *The vast majority of wines produced in this area are reds or rosés.* ◆◇◇◇◇ N-MASS

rosebud /roʊzbʌd/ **rosebuds.** A **rosebud** is a young rose whose petals have not yet opened out fully. N-COUNT

rose-coloured; spelled **rose-colored** in American English. If you say that someone is looking at a person or situation through **rose-coloured spectacles** or **rose-coloured glasses**, you mean that they are only noticing the pleasant things about that person or situation and that therefore their view of them is unrealistic. You can also say that someone is looking through **rose-tinted spectacles** or **rose-tinted glasses**. *Its influence can make you view life through rose-coloured glasses... People are looking at the past with rose-tinted spectacles.* PHRASE: usu PHR after v PRAGMATICS

rosehip /roʊzhɪp/ **rosehips.** A **rosehip** is a bright red or orange fruit that grows on some kinds of rose bushes. N-COUNT

rosemary /roʊzməri, AM -meri/. **Rosemary** is a herb used in cooking. It comes from an evergreen plant with small spiky leaves. The plant is also called **rosemary**. ◆◇◇◇◇ N-UNCOUNT

rose-tinted. To look through **rose-tinted spectacles** means the same as to look through **rose-coloured spectacles**: see **rose-coloured**. PHRASE: usu PHR after v =rose-coloured

rosette /roʊzet/ **rosettes** ◆◇◇◇◇

1 A **rosette** is a large circular badge made from coloured ribbons which is worn to show support for a political party or sports team, or is given as a prize in a competition. *I saw her father with his rosette on, canvassing for the Conservatives... They have won over 100 rosettes together in dressage competitions up and down Britain.* N-COUNT

2 A **rosette** is a decoration or design that looks rather like a rose. *...intricately carved wood rosettes... Garnish the plate with whipped cream rosettes and fresh fruits.* N-COUNT

rosewater /rouzwɔtəʳ/. **Rosewater** is a liquid which is made from roses and which has a pleasant smell. It is used as a perfume and in cooking. N-UNCOUNT

rose window, rose windows. A **rose window** is a large round stained glass window in a church. N-COUNT

rosewood /rouzwud/. **Rosewood** is a hard dark-coloured wood that is used for making furniture. Rosewood comes from a species of tropical tree. *...a heavy rosewood desk.* N-UNCOUNT

roster /rɒstəʳ/ **rosters** ◆◇◇◇◇

1 A **roster** is a list which gives details of the order in which different people have to do a particular job. *The next day he put himself first on the new roster for domestic chores... He was in his office, preparing his duty roster for the coming month.* N-COUNT =rota

2 A **roster** is a list, especially a list of the people employed by a particular organization, or available to do a particular job. You can also refer to the people or things mentioned in a list as a **roster** of people or things. *The Amateur Softball Association's roster of umpires has declined to 57,000... From the studio's roster of leading men, Robert Walker was an obvious choice to play the part.* N-COUNT: usu with supp, oft N of n =register

rostrum /rɒstrəm/ **rostrums** or **rostra** /rɒstrə/. A **rostrum** is a raised platform on which someone stands when they are speaking to an audience, receiving a prize, or conducting an orchestra. *As he stood on the winner's rostrum, he sang the words of the national anthem.* N-COUNT

rosy /rouzi/ **rosier, rosiest** ◆◇◇◇◇

1 If you say that someone has a **rosy** face, you mean that they have pink cheeks and look very healthy. *Bethan's round, rosy face seemed hardly to have aged at all... She had bright, rosy cheeks.* ADJ

2 Something that is **rosy** is reddish-pink in colour. *...the rosy brick buildings.* ADJ

3 If you say that a situation looks **rosy** or that the picture looks **rosy**, you mean that the situation seems likely to be good or successful. *Little over a year ago, things looked very rosy for the Social Democrats... The job prospects for those graduating in engineering are far less rosy now than they used to be... Is the picture really so rosy?* ADJ-GRADED =good

rot /rɒt/ **rots, rotting, rotted** ◆◆◇◇◇

1 When food, wood, or other substances **rot**, or when something **rots** them, they decay and fall apart. *If we don't unload it soon, the grain will start rotting in the silos... Sugary canned drinks rot your teeth. ...the smell of rotting fish.* V-ERG V Vn V-ing

2 If there is **rot** in something, especially something that is made of wood, parts of it have decayed and fallen apart. *Investigations had revealed extensive rot in the beams under the ground floor... Neither the timber frame nor metal chassis were protected against rot.* N-UNCOUNT

3 You can use **the rot** to refer to a gradual worsening of something. For example, if you are talking about the time when **the rot** set in, you are talking about the time when a situation began to get steadily worse and worse. *In many schools, the rot is beginning to set in. Standards are falling all the time... The country's leaders are unwilling to take unpopular measures to stop the rot.* N-SING: the N

4 If you say that someone is being left to **rot** in a particular place, especially in a prison, you mean that they are being left there and their physical and mental condition is being allowed to get worse and worse. *Most governments simply leave the long-term jobless to rot on the dole.* VERB Also V

5 If you say that what someone is saying is **rot**, you mean that they are saying very silly things; an old-fashioned, informal British use. *What a load of pompous, pseudo-intellectual rot... You do talk rot!* N-UNCOUNT =nonsense, rubbish

6 See also **dry rot**.

rot away. When something **rots away**, it decays until it falls to pieces or none of it remains. *The pillars rotted away and were replaced.* PHRASAL VERB =decay VP

rota /routə/ **rotas.** In British English, a **rota** is a list which gives details of the order in which different people have to do a particular job. *I suggest that you work out a careful rota which will make it clear who tidies the room on which day. ...the washing-up rota... The tea is prepared on a rota basis by the lady members.* N-COUNT =roster

rotary /routəri/ ◆◇◇◇◇

1 **Rotary** means turning or able to turn round a fixed point. *...turning linear into rotary motion. ...heavy-duty rotary blades.* ADJ: ADJ n

2 **Rotary** is used in the names of some machines that have parts that turn round a fixed point. *...a rotary engine.* ADJ: ADJ n

rotate /routeɪt, AM routeɪt/ **rotates, rotating, rotated** ◆◆◇◇◇

1 When something **rotates** or when you **rotate** it, it turns with a circular movement. *The Earth rotates round the sun... Take each foot in both your hands and rotate it to loosen and relax the ankle.* V-ERG V Vn

2 If people or things **rotate**, or if someone **rotates** them, they take it in turns to do a particular job or serve a particular purpose. *The members of the club can rotate and one person can do all the preparation for the evening... They will swap posts in a year's time, according to new party rules which rotate the leadership.* ♦ **rotating** *Luxembourg will take the rotating presidency of the EC on January 1st.* V-ERG V Vn ADJ: ADJ n

rotation /routeɪʃən/ **rotations** ◆◇◇◇◇

1 **Rotation** is circular movement. A **rotation** is the movement of something through one complete circle. *...the daily rotation of the earth upon its axis.* N-VAR

2 The **rotation** of a group of things or people is the fact of them taking turns to do a particular job or serve a particular purpose. If people do something **in rotation**, they take turns to do it. *He grew a different crop on the same field five years in a row, what researchers call crop rotation... Once a month we met for the whole day, and in rotation each one led the group.* N-UNCOUNT: oft in N

rote /rout/. **Rote** learning is learning things by repeating them without thinking about them or trying to understand them. If you learn something **by rote**, you learn it by repeating it without thinking about it or trying to understand it; used showing disapproval. *He is very sceptical about the value of rote learning... You are merely reciting facts that you have learned by rote.* N-UNCOUNT: N n, by N PRAGMATICS

rotor /routəʳ/ **rotors.** The **rotors** or **rotor blades** of a helicopter are the four long, flat, thin pieces of metal on top of it which go round and lift it off the ground. ◆◇◇◇◇ N-COUNT

rotten /rɒtən/ ◆◆◇◇◇

1 If food, wood, or another substance is **rotten**, it has decayed and can no longer be used. *The smell outside this building is overwhelming – like rotten eggs... The front bay window is rotten.* ADJ

2 If you describe something as **rotten**, you think it is very unpleasant or of very poor quality; an informal use. *I personally think it's a rotten idea... I had a pretty rotten day yesterday... What rotten luck!* ADJ-GRADED: usu ADJ n =terrible ≠good

3 If you describe someone as **rotten**, you are insulting them or criticizing them because you think that they are very unpleasant or unkind; an informal use. *You rotten swine! How dare you?... That's a rotten thing to say!* ADJ-GRADED: usu ADJ n =horrible ≠nice

4 If you feel **rotten**, you feel bad, either because you are ill or because you are sorry about something; an informal use. *I had glandular fever and spent that year feeling rotten... Suddenly, Sarah felt rotten about the whole thing.* ADJ-GRADED: usu v-link ADJ =awful

5 You use **rotten** to emphasize your dislike for something or your anger or frustration about it; an informal use. *She was a rotten coward... Keep your rotten mouth shut.* ADJ: ADJ n PRAGMATICS

rotter /rɒtəʳ/ **rotters.** If you call someone a **rotter**, you are criticizing them because you think that they have behaved in a very unkind or selfish way; an old-fashioned informal word, used mainly in British English. N-COUNT PRAGMATICS

rottweiler /rɒtvaɪləʳ/ **rottweilers.** A **rottweiler** is a breed of dog which is large, black and very muscular and is often used as a guard dog. N-COUNT

rotund /rəʊtʌnd/. If someone is **rotund**, they are round and fat; a formal word. *A rotund, smiling, red-faced gentleman appeared.* ADJ-GRADED =fat ≠slim

rotunda /rəʊtʌndə/ **rotundas.** A **rotunda** is a round building or room, especially one with a dome. *...the rotunda of the Hotel des Invalides in Paris.* N-COUNT

rouble /ruːbəl/ **roubles.** The **rouble** is the unit of money of Russia and some of the other republics that form the Commonwealth of Independent States. ◆◆◇◇◇ N-COUNT: usu num N

rouge /ruːʒ/ **rouges, rouging, rouged** ◆◆◆◇◇

1 Rouge is a red powder or cream which women and actors can put on their cheeks in order to give them more colour; an old-fashioned word. N-UNCOUNT =blusher

2 If a woman or an actor **rouges** their cheeks or lips, they put red powder or cream on them to give them more colour. *Florentine women rouged their earlobes... She had curly black hair and rouged cheeks.* VERB V n V-ed

rough /rʌf/ **rougher, roughest; roughs, roughing, roughed** ◆◆◆◇◇

1 If a surface is **rough**, it is uneven and not smooth. *His hands were rough and calloused, from years of karate practice... Grace made her way slowly across the rough ground.* ♦ **roughness** *She rested her cheek against the roughness of his jacket.* ADJ-GRADED ≠smooth N-UNCOUNT

2 You say that people or their actions are **rough** when they use too much force and not enough care or gentleness. *Rugby's a rough game at the best of times... They have complained of discrimination and occasional rough treatment.* ♦ **roughly** *A hand roughly pushed him aside.* ♦ **roughness** *He regretted his roughness.* ADJ-GRADED ≠gentle ADV-GRADED N-UNCOUNT

3 A **rough** area, city, school, or other place is unpleasant and dangerous because there is a lot of violence or crime there. *It was quite a rough part of our town.* ADJ-GRADED

4 If you say that someone has had a **rough** time, you mean that they have had some difficult or unpleasant experiences. *All women have a rough time in our society... Tomorrow, he knew, would be a rough day.* ADJ-GRADED: usu ADJ n =tough

5 If you feel **rough**, you feel ill; used in informal British English. *The virus won't go away and the lad is still feeling a bit rough.* ADJ-GRADED: v-link ADJ =ill

6 A **rough** calculation or guess is approximately correct, but not exact. *We were only able to make a rough estimate of how much fuel would be required... As a rough guide, a horse needs 2.5 per cent of his body weight in food every day.* ♦ **roughly** *Gambling and tourism pay roughly half the entire state budget... The Ukraine is roughly equal to France in size and population. ...a period of very roughly 30 million years.* ADJ-GRADED: usu ADJ n =approximate ADV-GRADED: ADV with cl/group =approximately

7 If you give someone a **rough** idea, description, or drawing of something, you indicate only the most important features, without much detail. *I've got a rough idea of what he looks like... It often helps to make a rough sketch showing where the vehicles were.* ♦ **roughly** *He knew roughly what was about to be said... Roughly speaking, a scientific humanist is somebody who believes in science and in humanity but not in God.* ADJ-GRADED ADV-GRADED: ADV with cl/group, ADV after v

8 You can say that something is **rough** when it is not neat and well made. *The bench had a rough wooden table in front of it. ...chairs set in a rough circle in the middle of the room.* ♦ **roughly** *Roughly chop the tomatoes and add them to the casserole. ...houses, roughly painted white or blue.* ADJ-GRADED ADV-GRADED: ADV with v

9 If the sea or the weather at sea is **rough**, the weather is windy or stormy and there are very big waves. *A fishing vessel and a cargo ship collided in rough seas.* ADJ-GRADED =choppy ≠calm

10 When people sleep or live **rough**, they sleep in unusual places, often out of doors, usually because they have no home. *It makes me so sad when I see young people begging or sleeping rough on the streets.* ADV: ADV after v

11 If you have to **rough** it, you have to live without the possessions and comforts that you normally have. *You won't be roughing it; each room comes equipped with a telephone and a 3-channel radio.* VERB V it

12 ● **rough justice**: see **justice**.

rough out. If you **rough out** a drawing or an idea, you draw or write the main features of it before you do it in detail. *Wood roughed out a possible framework for their story.* PHRASAL VERB =sketch V P n (not pron) Also V n P

rough up. If someone **roughs** you **up**, they attack you and hit or beat you; an informal expression. *They threw him in a cell and roughed him up a bit... He was fired from his job after roughing up a colleague.* PHRASAL VERB =beat up V n P V P n (not pron)

roughage /rʌfɪdʒ/. **Roughage** consists of substances in food such as bran or fibre that make digestion easier and help your bowels to work properly. N-UNCOUNT =fibre

rough and ready; also spelled **rough-and-ready.**

1 A **rough and ready** solution or method is one that is rather simple and not very exact because it has been thought of or done in a hurry. *Here is a rough and ready measurement.* ADJ-GRADED

2 A **rough and ready** person is not very polite or gentle. *Soldiers are soldiers everywhere – a bit rough and ready!* ADJ-GRADED

rough and tumble; also spelled **rough-and-tumble.**

1 You can use **rough and tumble** to refer to a situation in which the people involved try hard to get what they want, and do not worry about upsetting or harming others, and you think this is acceptable and normal. *Many would maintain that all this is part of the rough-and-tumble of political combat.* N-UNCOUNT: oft *the* N *of* n

2 Rough and tumble is physical playing that involves noisy and slightly violent behaviour. *He enjoys rough and tumble play.* N-UNCOUNT

roughen /rʌfən/ **roughens, roughening, roughened.** If something has **been roughened**, its surface has become less smooth. *...complexions that have been roughened by long periods in the hot sun... She lifted her big, roughened hands.* VB: usu passive *be* V-ed V-ed

rough-hewn. **Rough-hewn** wood or stone has been cut into a shape but has not yet been smoothed or finished off. *It is a rough-hewn carving of a cat's head.* ADJ-GRADED: usu ADJ n

roughneck /rʌfnek/ **roughnecks**

1 A **roughneck** is a man who works on an oil rig or oil well; an informal use, used especially in American English. N-COUNT

2 If you describe a man as a **roughneck**, you disapprove of him because you think he is not gentle or polite, and can be violent; an informal use. N-COUNT PRAGMATICS

roughshod /rʌfʃɒd/. If you say that someone **is riding roughshod over** a person or their views, you disapprove of them because they are using their power or authority to do what they want, completely ignoring that person's wishes. *These laws allow the security forces to continue to ride roughshod over the human rights of the people.* PHRASE: V inflects PRAGMATICS

roulette /ruːlet/. **Roulette** is a gambling game in which a ball is dropped onto a revolving wheel with numbered holes in it. The players bet on which hole the ball will be in when the wheel stops spinning. ● See also **Russian roulette**. N-UNCOUNT

round 1 preposition and adverb uses

round /raʊnd/ ◆◆◆◆◇

Round is an adverb and preposition that has the same meanings as 'around'. **Round** is often used with verbs of movement, such as 'walk' and 'drive', and also in phrasal verbs such as 'get round' and 'hand round'. **Round** is commoner in British English than American English, and it is slightly more informal.

1 To be positioned **round** a place or object means to surround it or be on all sides of it. To move **round** a place means to go along its edge, back to your starting-point. *They were sitting round the kitchen table... The nightdress has handmade lace round the armholes and neckline... All round us was desert... I shivered and pulled my scarf more tightly round my neck... He tramped hurriedly round the lake towards the garden. ...cycling round* PREP *and round the park.* ► Also an adverb. *Visibility was good all round... The goldfish swam round and round in their tiny bowls.* ADV: ADV after v

2 If you move **round** a corner or obstacle, you move to the other side of it. If you look **round** a corner or obstacle, you look to see what is on the other side. *Suddenly a car came round a corner on the opposite side... Stay on the left-hand pavement to follow a road downhill round a curve... One of his men tapped and looked round the door.* PREP

3 You use **round** to say that something happens in or relates to different parts of a place or area, or is near a place or area. *He happens to own half the land round here... I think he has earned the respect of leaders all round the world... She's been on at me for weeks to show her round the stables... They need some way of getting round the country.* PREP ► Also an adverb. *Shirley found someone to show them round... So you're going to have a look round?* ADV: ADV after v, n ADV

4 If a wheel or object spins **round**, it turns on its axis. *Holes can be worn remarkably quickly by a wheel going round at 60mph... Stars appeared everywhere, spinning round and round, faster and faster.* ADV: ADV after v

5 If you turn **round**, you turn so that you are facing or going in the opposite direction. *She paused, but did not turn round... The end result was that the ship had to turn round, and go back to Djibouti... The wind veered round to the east... Tricia looked round in surprise.* ADV: ADV after v

6 If you move things **round**, you move them so they are in different places. *He will be glad to refurnish where possible, change things round and redecorate... I've already moved things round a bit to make it easier for him.* ADV: ADV after v

7 If you hand or pass something **round**, it is passed from person to person in a group. *John handed round the plate of sandwiches. ...as the whiskey bottle is passed round.* ADV: ADV after v ► Also a preposition. *They started handing the microphone out round the girls at the front... The word is passed round the industry if you think there's a troublesome driver.* PREP

8 If you go **round** to someone's house, you visit them. *I think we should go round and tell Kevin to turn his music down... He came round with a bottle of champagne.* ADV: ADV after v ► Also a preposition in non-standard English. *I went round my wife's house.* PREP

9 You use **round** in informal expressions such as **sit round** or **hang round** when you are saying that someone is spending time in a place and not doing anything very important. *As we sat round chatting, I began to think I'd made a mistake... I was running round all hyped up.* ADV: ADV after v ► Also a preposition. *She would spend the day hanging round street corners... Leonard pottered round the greenhouse, tying up canes for the tomatoes.* PREP

10 If something is built or based **round** a particular idea, that idea is the basis for it. *That was for a design built round an existing American engine... The core of the Festival's programme centres round performances of new and 20th century work.* PREP

11 If you get **round** a problem or difficulty, you find a way of dealing with it. *Don't just immediately give up but think about ways round a problem... There are ways of getting round most things!* PREP

12 If you win someone **round**, or if they come **round**, they change their mind about something and start agreeing with you. *He did his best to talk me round, but I wouldn't speak to him... The Chandler twins were coming round to the same opinion.* ADV: ADV after v

13 You use **round** in expressions such as **this time round** or **to come round** when you are describing something that has happened before or things that happen regularly. *In the past, the elections have been marked by hundreds of murders, but this time round the violence has been much more limited... Of course, it isn't the same first time round... We were very keen when the 1954 Rally came round.* ADV: n ADV, ADV after v

14 When you are giving measurements, you can use **round** to mention the diameter of something. *I'm about two inches larger round the waist. ...forty-eight inches round the hip.* PREP ► Also an adverb. *It's six feet high and five feet round.* ADV

15 You use **round** in front of times or amounts to indicate that they are approximate. *I go to bed round 11:00 at night.* ADV: ADV amount

16 In spoken English, **round about** means approximately; used mainly in British English. *Round about one and a half million people died. ...a system that was abolished round about 1902.* PHRASES PREP

17 You say **all round** to emphasize that something affects all parts of a situation or all members of a group; used mainly in British English. *It ought to make life much easier all round... Nerves are frayed all round.* cl PHR PRAGMATICS

18 If you say that something **is going round and round** in your head, you mean that you can't stop thinking about it. *It all keeps going round and round in my head till I don't know where I am.* V inflects

19 If something happens **all year round**, it happens throughout the year. *Many of these plants are evergreen, so you can enjoy them all year round... It's a treat to be enjoyed all the year round.* PHR after v

20 • **round the corner**: see **corner**. • **the other way round**: see **way**.

round 2 noun uses

round /raund/ **rounds** ◆◆◆◆◇

1 A **round** of events is a series of related events, especially one which comes after or before a similar series of events. *It was agreed that another round of preliminary talks would be held in Peking... This is the latest round of job cuts aimed at making the company more competitive... There will be more frequent rounds of inspection by our security personnel.* N-COUNT: with supp, oft N *of*n

2 In sport, a **round** is a series of games in a competition. The winners of these games go on to play in the next round, and so on, until only one player or team is left. *...in the third round of the Pilkington Cup... After round three, two Americans share the lead.* N-COUNT: usu adj N, N num =heat

3 In a boxing or wrestling match, a **round** is one of the periods during which the boxers or wrestlers fight. *He was declared the victor in the 11th round... Gibson's left eye is completely closed before the end of round one.* N-COUNT: usu adj N, N num

4 A **round** of golf is one game, usually including 18 holes. *...two rounds of golf... Ronan Rafferty shot six birdies in a round of 67.* N-COUNT: usu N *of*n, N *of*num

5 A **round** is a circular shape. *...small fresh rounds of goats' cheese... A cucumber was sliced into rounds.* N-COUNT: oft N *of*n

6 A **round** of bread is a slice of bread. A **round** of sandwiches is a sandwich made from two slices of bread; used mainly in British English. *...four rounds of toast.* N-COUNT: usu with supp, oft N *of*n

7 If you do your **rounds** or your **round**, you make a series of visits to different places or people, for example as part of your job. *The consultants still did their morning rounds... He got out of the car, and carried on with his paper round.* N-COUNT: usu supp N

8 If you buy a **round** of drinks, you buy a drink for each member of the group of people that you are with. *They sat on the clubhouse terrace, downing a round of drinks... I think it's my round.* N-COUNT: usu with supp

9 A **round** of ammunition is the bullet or bullets that are released when a gun is fired. *...firing 1650 rounds of ammunition during a period of ten minutes. ...the use of live rounds of ammunition.* N-COUNT: usu num N, N *of*n

10 If there is a **round** of applause, everyone claps. *Sue got a sympathetic round of applause.* N-COUNT: N *of*n

11 In music, a **round** is a simple song sung by several people in which each person sings a different part of the song at the same time. N-COUNT

12 If a story, idea, or joke **is going the rounds** or **doing the rounds**, a lot of people have heard it and are passing it on. *This story was going the rounds 20 years ago.* PHRASES V inflects

13 If you **make the rounds** or **do the rounds**, you visit a series of different places. *After school, I had picked up Nick and Ted and made the rounds of the dry cleaner and the grocery store... We could do the rounds of the galleries.* V inflects, usu PHR *of*n

round 3 adjective uses

round /raʊnd/ **rounder, roundest** ◆◆◇◇◇

1 Something that is **round** is shaped like a circle or ball. *She had small feet and hands and a flat, round face. ...the round church known as The New Temple. ...large round loaves dusted with flour.* ADJ-GRADED

2 If someone has **round** eyes, their eyes are open wide, for example because they are surprised, excited, or afraid. *The boy sucked his thumb and stared at Hebburn with huge, round eyes.* ADJ-GRADED

3 A **round** number is a whole number, especially a multiple of 10, 100, 1000, and so on. Round numbers are used instead of precise ones to give the general idea of a quantity or proportion. *I asked how much silver could be bought for a million pounds, which seemed a suitably round number... The money goes into the team pool, which this summer, in round figures, has now reached £78,000.* ADJ: ADJ n

round 4 verb uses

round /raʊnd/ **rounds, rounding, rounded** ◆◆◇◇◇

1 If you **round** a place or obstacle, you move in a curve past the edge or corner of it. *The house disappeared from sight as we rounded a corner... After rounding Cape Finisterre the boats ride the north-easterly trades.* VERB =go round V n

2 If you **round** an amount up or down, or if you **round** it off, you change it to the nearest whole number or nearest multiple of a number. *We needed to do decimals to round up and round down numbers... The fraction was then multiplied by 100 and rounded to the nearest half or whole number... I'll round it off to about £30.* VERB V n with adv; be V-ed *to* amount; V n adv *to* amount

3 See also **rounded**.

round off. If you **round off** an activity with something, you end the activity by doing something that provides a clear or satisfactory conclusion to it. *The Italian way is to round off a meal or evening with an ice-cream. ...a dazzling firework display which rounded off a lovely day... This rounded the afternoon off perfectly... He rounds off by proposing a toast to the attendants.* PHRASAL VERB =conclude V P n (not pron); V n P; V P *by*-ing

round on. In informal English, if someone **rounds on** you, they criticize you fiercely and attack you with aggressive words. *The Conservative Party rounded angrily on him for damaging the Government... He says that he will stand by his men and he has rounded on his critics.* PHRASAL VERB =attack V P n

round up PHRASAL VERB

1 If the police or army **round up** a number of people, they arrest or capture them. *The police rounded up a number of suspects... She says the patrolmen rounded them up at the village school and beat them with rifle butts.* V P n (not pron); V n P

2 If you **round up** animals or things, you gather them together. *He had sought work as a cowboy, rounding up cattle... We've rounded up a selection of products.* V P n (not pron)

3 See also **roundup**.

roundabout /raʊndəbaʊt/ **roundabouts** ◆◇◇◇◇

1 A **roundabout** is a circular structure in the road at a place where several roads meet. You drive round it until you come to the road that you want; used mainly in British English. N-COUNT =island

2 In British English, a **roundabout** at a funfair is a large, circular mechanical device with seats, often in the shape of animals or cars, on which children sit and go round and round. The American word is **carousel**. N-COUNT

3 In British English, a **roundabout** in a playground is a circular platform that children sit or stand on. People push the platform to make it spin round. N-COUNT

4 If you go somewhere by a **roundabout** route, you do not go there by the shortest and quickest route. *He left today on a roundabout route for Jordan and is also due soon in Egypt.* ADJ-GRADED: usu ADJ n =circuitous

5 If you do or say something in a **roundabout** way, you do not do or say it in a simple, clear, and direct way. *We made a bit of a fuss in a roundabout way. ...using indirect or roundabout language in place of a precise noun.* ADJ-GRADED: usu ADJ n =indirect ≠direct

6 • **round about**: see **round**. • **swings and roundabouts**: see **swing**.

rounded /raʊndɪd/ ◆◇◇◇◇

1 Something that is **rounded** is curved in shape, without any points or sharp edges. *...a low rounded hill... The barge had a rounded bow and stern.* ADJ-GRADED =curved ≠pointed

2 You describe something or someone as **rounded** or **well-rounded** when you are expressing approval of them because they are balanced, with no single aspect or characteristic dominating the others. *...his carefully organised narrative, full of rounded, believable and interesting characters. ...a well-rounded, well-educated and highly intelligent man... This cheese is matured for at least 10 months producing a nutty, well rounded flavour.* ADJ-GRADED PRAGMATICS =balanced

roundel /raʊndəl/ **roundels.** A **roundel** is a circular design, for example one painted on an aircraft to identify it. N-COUNT

rounders /raʊndəʳz/. In Britain, **rounders** is a game played by two teams of schoolchildren, in which a player scores points by hitting a ball thrown by a member of the other team and then running round all four sides of a square. N-UNCOUNT

roundly /raʊndli/. If you are **roundly** condemned or criticized, you are condemned or criticized forcefully or by many people. If you are **roundly** defeated, you are defeated completely. *Political leaders have roundly condemned the shooting... The Labour Party was roundly defeated in last year's general election.* ADV-GRADED: usu ADV before v

round-robin, round-robins; also spelled **round robin**. A **round-robin** is a sports competition in which each player or team plays against every other player or team. *They beat England 4-1 in their last round-robin match at Nagoya in Japan.* N-COUNT: usu N n ≠knock-out

round-shouldered. If someone is **round-shouldered**, they bend forward when they sit or stand, and their shoulders are curved rather than straight; used showing disapproval. *Cissie was round-shouldered and dumpy.* ADJ-GRADED PRAGMATICS

round table, round tables; also spelled **round-table** or **roundtable**. A **round table** discussion is a meeting where experts gather together in order to discuss a particular topic. *...a round-table conference of the leading heart specialists of America.* ◆◇◇◇◇ N-COUNT: usu N n

round-the-clock. See **clock**.

round trip, round trips; also spelled **round-trip**. ◆◇◇◇◇

1 If you make a **round trip**, you travel to a place and then back again. *The train operates the 2,400-mile round trip once a week.* N-COUNT

2 In American English, a **round-trip** ticket is a ticket for a train, bus, or plane that allows you to travel to a particular place and then back again. The usual British term is **return ticket**. *Mexicana Airlines has announced cheaper round-trip tickets between Los Angeles and cities it serves in Mexico. ...the lowest round-trip fare available between Washington and Dallas.* ADJ: ADJ n ≠single, one way

roundup /raʊndʌp/ **roundups;** also spelled **round-up**. ◆◇◇◇◇

1 In journalism, especially television or radio, a **roundup** of news is a summary of the main events that have happened. *First, we have this roundup of the day's news... We'll also have an election roundup from the streets of New York to the Via Veneto.* N-COUNT: usu with supp, oft N *of* n, adj N =summary

2 When there is a **roundup** of people, they are arrested or captured by the police or army and brought to one place. *There are reports that round ups of westerners are still taking place.* N-COUNT

3 In American English, a **roundup** is an occasion when cattle, horses, or other animals are collected together so that they can be counted or sold. *What is it that keeps a cowboy looking strong, young and ready for another roundup?* N-COUNT

roundworm /raʊndwɜːʳm/ **roundworms.** A **roundworm** is a very small worm that lives in the intestines of people, pigs, and other animals. N-VAR

rouse /raʊz/ **rouses, rousing, roused** ◆◇◇◇◇

1 If someone **rouses** you when you are sleeping or if you **rouse**, you wake up; a literary use. *Hilton roused him at eight-thirty by rapping on the door...* V-ERG =wake, arouse V n

When I put my hand on his, he stirs but doesn't quite rouse. V

2 If you **rouse** yourself, you stop being inactive and start doing something. *She seemed to be unable to rouse herself to do anything... Hong Kong's voters did not rouse themselves from their traditional political apathy.* VERB =stir V pron-refl to-inf V pron-refl *from* n

3 If something or someone **rouses** you, they make you very emotional or excited. *He did more to rouse the crowd there than anybody else... Ben says his father was good-natured, a man not quickly roused to anger or harsh opinions.* VERB =stir V n *be* V-ed *to* n ♦ **rousing** *...a rousing speech to the convention in support of the president.* ADJ-GRADED: usu ADJ n

4 If something **rouses** a feeling in you, it causes you to have that feeling. *It roused a feeling of rebellion in him... This roused my interest in politics and I went to work for the Democrats.* VERB =awaken, excite V n

roust /raʊst/ **rousts, rousting, rousted.** In American English, if you **roust** someone, you disturb, upset, or hit them, or make them move from their place. *Relax, kid, we're not about to roust you. We just want some information... Bruce had gone to bed, but they rousted him out.* VERB V n V n *out* Also V n *from* n

roustabout /raʊstəbaʊt/ **roustabouts.** In American English, a **roustabout** is a unskilled labourer, especially one who works in the docks or on an oil rig. N-COUNT

rout /raʊt/ **routs, routing, routed.** If an army, sports team, or other group **routs** its opponents, it defeats them completely and easily. *...the Battle of Hastings at which the Norman army routed the English opposition.* ◆◇◇◇◇ VERB =defeat V n ► used as a noun. *One after another the Italian bases in the desert fell as the retreat turned into a rout.* N-COUNT

route /ruːt/ **routes, routing, routed.** Also pronounced /raʊt/ in American English. ◆◆◆◆◇

1 A **route** is a way from one place to another. *...the most direct route to the town centre... All escape routes were blocked by armed police... Tens of thousands lined the route from Dublin airport.* N-COUNT

2 A bus, air, or shipping **route** is the way between two places along which buses, planes, or ships travel regularly. *...the main shipping routes to Japan.* N-COUNT: oft supp N

3 In the United States, **Route** is used in front of a number in the names of main roads between major cities. *From San Francisco take the freeway to the Broadway-Webster exit on Route 580.* N-IN-NAMES: N num

4 You can refer to a way of achieving something as a **route**. *Researchers are trying to get at the same information through an indirect route... Buying the best is as sure a route to success in investment as in any other field.* N-COUNT: usu with supp =way

5 If vehicles, goods, or passengers **are routed** in a particular direction, they are made to travel in that direction. *Double-stack trains are taking a lot of freight that used to be routed via trucks... Approaching cars will be routed into two lanes.* VB: usu passive *be* V-ed prep/adv

6 If telephone calls or other electronic signals **are routed** in a particular way, the signals are sent through a particular series of connections; a technical use in electronics. *...plans to route every emergency call in Britain through just three telephone exchanges.* VERB V n prep/adv

7 En route to a place means on the way to that place. **En route** is sometimes spelled **on route** in non-standard English. *They have arrived in London en route to the United States... One of the bags was lost en route.* PHRASES oft PHR *to/from/for* n =on the way

8 Journalists sometimes use **en route** when they are mentioning an event that happened as part of a longer process or before another event. *The German set three tournament records and equalled two others en route to grabbing golf's richest prize.* oft PHR *to* n/-ing

routine /ruːtiːn/ **routines** ◆◆◆◇◇

1 A **routine** is the usual series of things that you do at a particular time. A **routine** is also the practice of regularly doing things in a fixed order. *The players had to change their daily routine and lifestyle... They include the floor exercises as a regular part of their fitness routine... He checked up on you as a matter of routine.* N-VAR: usu with supp, oft N n, adj N

2 You use **routine** to describe activities that are done as a normal part of a job or process. *...a series of routine medical tests including X-rays and blood tests... The operator has to be able to carry out routine maintenance of the machine.* ADJ: usu ADJ n

3 A **routine** situation, action, or event is one which seems completely ordinary, rather than interesting, exciting, or different; used showing disapproval. *So many days are routine and uninteresting, especially in winter. ...this routine thriller about a CIA man and a KGB operative.* ADJ-GRADED PRAGMATICS =humdrum, dull

4 You use **routine** to refer to a way of life that is uninteresting and ordinary, or hardly ever changes; used showing disapproval. *...the mundane routine of her life... Family holidays are meant to be a break from routine.* N-VAR PRAGMATICS

5 A **routine** is a short sequence of jokes, remarks, actions, or movements that forms part of a longer performance. *... like a Marx Brothers routine. ...an athletic dance routine.* N-COUNT: usu n N

routinely /ruːtiːnli/ ◆◇◇◇◇

1 If something is **routinely** done, it is done as a normal part of a job or process. *Vitamin K is routinely given in the first week of life to prevent bleeding.* ADV: usu ADV with v, also ADV adj =regularly

2 If something happens **routinely**, it happens repeatedly and is not surprising, unnatural, or new. *Any outside criticism is routinely dismissed as interference... He is routinely described as the greatest scientist since Einstein.* ADV: ADV with v

rove /rouv/ **roves, roving, roved**

1 If someone **roves** about an area or **roves** an area, they wander around there. *...roving about the town in the dead of night and seeing something peculiar. ...organised anti-foreign bands called the Boxers who roved the countryside and the provinces.* VERB =roam, wander V prep/adv V n

2 If you say that someone's eyes **rove** round a place, you mean that they are looking around to see what is interesting. *Houston's eyes roved restlessly about the room... His eyes roved to see how many of the group appreciated his heavy humour.* VERB =wander V prep V

3 See also **roving**.

roving /rouvɪŋ/ ◆◇◇◇◇

1 You use **roving** to describe a person who travels around, rather than staying in a fixed place. *He is to join the BBC to cover the Olympic Games in Barcelona next month as a roving reporter... Left to raise themselves on the streets, these children form roving bands of delinquents.* ADJ: ADJ n

2 If you say that a man has **a roving eye**, you are criticizing him for continually paying attention to different women. PHRASE: N inflects PRAGMATICS

row 1 arrangement or sequence

row /rou/ **rows** ◆◆◆◇◇

1 A **row** of things or people is a number of them arranged in a line. *...a row of pretty little cottages... Several men are pushing school desks and chairs into neat rows.* N-COUNT: oft N *of* n =line

2 In a theatre or cinema, each line of seats is called a **row**. *She was sitting in the front row.* N-COUNT

3 Row is sometimes used in the names of streets. *...the house at 236 Larch Row.* N-IN-NAMES: n N

4 See also **death row, skid row**.

5 If something happens several times **in a row**, it happens that number of times without a break. If something happens several days **in a row**, it happens on each of those days. *They have won five championships in a row... If I'm inside for three days in a row, I go crazy... It is the sixth month in a row in which imports have fallen.* • **a hard row to hoe**: see **hoe**. PHRASE: PHR after v

row 2 making a boat move

row /rou/ **rows, rowing, rowed.** When you **row**, you sit in a boat and make it move through the water by using oars. If you **row** someone somewhere, you take them there in a boat, using oars. *He rowed as quickly as he could to the shore... We could all row a boat and swim almost before we could walk... The boatman refused to row him back.* ◆◆◇◇◇ VERB V prep V n V n adv/prep ► used as a noun. *I took Daniel for a row on the lake.* N-COUNT

• See also **rowing**.

row 3 disagreement or noise

row /raʊ/ **rows, rowing, rowed** ◆◆◆◇◇

1 A **row** is a serious disagreement between people or organizations; used mainly in informal British English. *This is likely to provoke a further row about the bank's role in the affair... The ministers must have realized that they risked what could be a major diplomatic row with France.* N-COUNT: oft adj N, N prep =dispute

2 If two people have a **row**, they have a noisy argument; used mainly in informal British English. *We never seem to stay together for very long before we have a dreadful row... A man had been stabbed to death in a family row.* N-COUNT =quarrel, argument

3 If two people **row** or if one person **rows** with another, they have a noisy argument; used mainly in informal British English. *They rowed all the time and thought it couldn't be good for the baby... He had earlier rowed with his girlfriend.* V-RECIP =quarrel, argue pl-n V V with n

4 If you say that someone is making a **row**, you mean that they are making a loud, unpleasant noise; used mainly in informal British English. *'Whatever is that row?' she demanded. 'Pop festival,' he answered.* N-SING =din, racket

rowan /roʊən/ **rowans.** A **rowan** or a **rowan** tree is a tree with a silvery bark that has red berries in autumn. ▶ **Rowan** is the wood of this tree. N-VAR =mountain ash N-UNCOUNT

rowboat /roʊboʊt/ **rowboats.** In American English, a **rowboat** is a small boat that you move through the water by using oars. The usual British term is **rowing boat**. N-COUNT

rowdy /raʊdi/ **rowdier, rowdiest; rowdies** ◆◇◇◇◇

1 When people are **rowdy**, they are noisy, rough, and likely to cause trouble. *He has complained to the police about rowdy neighbours... There were rowdy scenes inside parliament during the debate.* ADJ-GRADED =noisy

♦ **rowdiness** *...adolescent behaviour like vandalism and rowdiness.* N-UNCOUNT

2 In informal English, if you describe people as **rowdies**, you mean that they are noisy, rough, and likely to cause trouble. *...a bar in New York where the owner kept a baseball bat to deal with rowdies.* N-PLURAL

rower /roʊəʳ/ **rowers.** A **rower** is a person who rows a boat, especially as a sport. N-COUNT

row house /roʊ haʊs/ **row houses;** also spelled **rowhouse**. In American English, a **row house** is one of a row of similar houses joined together by their side walls. The usual British term is **terraced house**. N-COUNT

rowing /roʊɪŋ/. **Rowing** is a sport in which people or teams race against each other in boats with oars. *...competitions in rowing, swimming and water skiing.* ◆◇◇◇◇ N-UNCOUNT

rowing boat, rowing boats; also spelled **rowing-boat**. In British English, a **rowing boat** is a small boat that you move through the water by using oars. The usual American word is **rowboat**. N-COUNT

rowing machine, rowing machines. A **rowing machine** is an exercise machine with moving parts which you move as if you were rowing a rowing boat. N-COUNT

rowlock /rɒlək, roʊlɒk/ **rowlocks.** In British English, the **rowlocks** on a rowing-boat are the U-shaped pieces of metal that keep the oars in position while you move them backwards and forwards. N-COUNT: usu pl

royal /rɔɪəl/ **royals** ◆◆◆◆◇

1 **Royal** is used to indicate that something is connected with a king, queen, or emperor, or their family. A **royal** person is a king, queen, or emperor, or a member of their family. *...an invitation to a royal garden party. ...the Japanese royal couple, Emperor Akihito and Empress Michiko.* ADJ: usu ADJ n

2 **Royal** is used in the names of institutions or organizations that are officially appointed or supported by a member of a royal family. *...the Royal Academy of Music. ...several pilots of the Royal Navy's 846 Squadron.* ADJ: ADJ n

3 In informal English, members of the royal family are sometimes referred to as the **royals**. *The royals have always been patrons of charities pulling in large donations.* N-COUNT: usu pl

royal blue. Something that is **royal blue** is deep blue in colour. COLOUR

royal family, royal families. The **royal family** of a country is the king, queen, or emperor, and all the members of their family. ◆◆◇◇◇ N-COUNT

Royal Highness, Royal Highnesses. Expressions such as **Your Royal Highness** and **Their Royal Highnesses** are used to address or refer to members of royal families who are not kings or queens. ◆◇◇◇◇ N-VOC: poss N; PRON: poss PRON

royalist /rɔɪəlɪst/ **royalists.** A **royalist** is someone who supports their country's royal family or who believes that their country should have a king or queen. *He was hated by the royalists and mistrusted by the communists.* ◆◇◇◇◇ N-COUNT: oft N n =monarchist ≠republican

royal jelly. **Royal jelly** is a substance that bees make in order to feed young bees and queen bees. N-UNCOUNT

royally /rɔɪəli/. If you say that something is done **royally**, you are emphasizing that it is done impressively or grandly, or that it is very great in degree. *They were royally received in every aspect... They then get royally drunk in his memory.* ADV: usu ADV with v, also ADV adj PRAGMATICS

royalty /rɔɪəlti/ **royalties** ◆◆◇◇◇

1 The members of royal families are sometimes referred to as **royalty**. *Royalty and government leaders from all around the world are gathering in Japan. ...a ceremony attended by royalty.* N-UNCOUNT

2 **Royalties** are payments made to authors and musicians when their work is sold or performed. They usually receive a fixed percentage of the profits from these sales or performances. *I lived on about £3,000 a year from the royalties on my book.* N-PLURAL

3 Payments made to someone whose invention, idea, or property is used by a commercial company can be referred to as **royalties**. *The royalties enabled the inventor to re-establish himself in the business.* N-COUNT: usu pl

RP /ɑːʳ piː/. **RP** is an abbreviation for 'received pronunciation'. It is a way of pronouncing British English that is often considered to be the standard accent. Pronunciations in this dictionary are given in RP.

rpm /ɑːʳ piː em/. **rpm** is an abbreviation for 'revolutions per minute'. It is used to indicate the speed of something by saying how many times per minute it will go round in a circle. *Both engines were running at 2500 rpm.* ◆◇◇◇◇

RSI /ɑːr es aɪ/. **RSI** is an abbreviation for **repetitive strain injury**. *The women developed painful RSI because of poor working conditions.* N-UNCOUNT

RSVP /ɑːr es viː piː/. **RSVP** is an abbreviation for 'répondez s'il vous plaît', which means 'please reply'. It is written on the bottom of invitations.

Rt Hon. /raɪt ɒn/. **Rt Hon.** is an abbreviation for 'Right Honourable'. It is used in Britain as part of the formal title of some members of the Privy Council and some judges. *...the Rt Hon. Margaret Thatcher.* ADJ: the ADJ n

rub /rʌb/ **rubs, rubbing, rubbed** ◆◆◇◇◇

1 If you **rub** a part of your body, you move your hand or fingers backwards and forwards over it while pressing firmly. *He rubbed his arms and stiff legs... 'I fell in a ditch', he said, rubbing at a scrape on his hand.* VERB V n V prep/adv

2 If you **rub** against a surface or **rub** a part of your body against a surface, you move it backwards and forwards while pressing it against the surface. *A cat was rubbing against my leg... He kept rubbing his leg against mine.* VERB V prep V n prep

3 If you **rub** an object or a surface, you move a cloth backward and forward over it in order to clean or dry it. *She took off her glasses and rubbed them hard... He rubbed and rubbed but couldn't seem to get clean.* VERB V n V

4 If you **rub** a substance into a surface or **rub** something such as dirt from a surface, you spread it over the surface or remove it from the surface using your hand or something such as a cloth. *He rubbed oil into my back... I pretended to rub a fleck of grit from one eye.* VERB V n prep

5 If you **rub** two things together or if they **rub** to- V-ERG

gether, they move backwards and forwards, pressing against each other. *He rubbed his hands together a few times. ...the 650-mile rift that separates the Pacific and North American geological plates as they rub together.* V n together V together

6 If something you are wearing or holding **rubs**, it makes you sore because it keeps moving backwards and forwards against your skin. *Smear cream on to your baby's skin at the edges of the plaster to prevent it from rubbing.* VERB =chafe V Also V n

7 **Rub** is used in expressions such as **there's the rub** and **the rub is** when you are mentioning a difficulty that makes something hard or impossible to achieve; a formal use. *'What do you want to write about?'. And there was the rub, because I didn't yet know.* N-SING: the N =obstacle, snag

8 A massage can be referred to as a **rub**. *She sometimes asks if I want a back rub.* N-COUNT: usu sing

9 A **rub** is a substance that you massage into your skin. *...a fresh cucumber rub for your whole face.* N-COUNT: usu with supp

10 See also **rubbing**.

11 In British English, if you **rub** someone **up the wrong way**, you offend or annoy them without intending to; an informal expression. The usual American expression is **rub** someone **the wrong way**. *What are you going to get out of him if you rub him up the wrong way?* PHRASE: V inflects =annoy

12 • to **rub** someone's **nose in** it: see **nose**. • to **rub salt into the wound**: see **salt**. • to **rub shoulders**: see **shoulder**.

rub along. If two people **rub along** or if one person **rubs along** with another, they are able to live or work together in a fairly friendly way, usually when you would not expect them to; used in informal British English. *North and South had officials at the meeting and they rubbed along tolerably... Mr Nicholson respects soldiers, and he rubs along with them.* PHRASAL VERB RECIP pl-n V P V P with n

rub down PHRASAL VERB

1 If you **rub down** a rough surface, you make it smooth by rubbing it with something such as sandpaper. *They were settling to their work, rubbing down the woodwork with sandpaper.* V P n (not pron) Also V n P

2 If you **rub** someone **down**, you dry them or massage them with something such as a towel or cloth. *He set him on the bed and rubbed him down with a coarse towel... After a bath or shower rub down the whole body with a loofah.* V n P V P n (not pron)

rub in PHRASAL VERB

1 If you **rub** a substance **in**, you press it into something by continuously moving it over its surface. *When hair is dry, rub in a little oil to make it smooth and glossy.* V P n (not pron) Also V n P

2 If someone keeps reminding you of something you would rather forget you can say that they **are rubbing** it **in**. *Officials couldn't resist rubbing it in... It was by way of rubbing in his brother's inadequacy that Noel took the lead part for himself.* V n P V P n (not pron)

rub off. If someone's qualities or habits **rub off** on you, you develop some of their qualities or habits after spending time with them. *He was a tremendously enthusiastic teacher and that rubbed off on all the children... I was hoping some of his genius might rub off.* PHRASAL VERB V P on n V P

rub out PHRASAL VERB

1 If you **rub out** something that you have written on paper or a blackboard, you remove it by rubbing it with a rubber or cloth. *She began rubbing out the pencilled marks in the margin.* =erase V P n (not pron) Also V n P

2 If one person **rubs out** another, they kill them; an informal expression. *Nobody else believed that they had tried to rub out the pope.* =kill V P n (not pron) Also V n P

rubber /rʌbəʳ/ **rubbers** ◆◆◇◇◇

1 **Rubber** is a strong, waterproof, elastic substance made from the sap of a tropical tree or produced chemically. It is used for making tyres, boots, and other products. *...the smell of burning rubber.* N-UNCOUNT

2 **Rubber** things are made of rubber. *...rubber gloves. ...a rubber ball.* ADJ: usu ADJ n

3 In British English, a **rubber** is a small piece of rubber or other material used to rub out mistakes that you have made while writing, drawing, or typing. The American word is **eraser**. N-COUNT

4 In American English, a **rubber** is a condom; an informal use. N-COUNT

5 In some card games, for example bridge or whist, a **rubber** is a match of three games. *Let's have a few rubbers of bridge.* N-COUNT

rubber band, rubber bands. A **rubber band** is a thin circle of very elastic rubber. You put it around things such as papers in order to keep them together. N-COUNT =elastic band

rubber boot, rubber boots. In American English, **rubber boots** are long boots made of rubber that you wear to keep your feet dry. The British word is **wellington**. N-COUNT: usu pl

rubber bullet, rubber bullets. A **rubber bullet** is a bullet made of a metal ball coated with rubber. It is intended to injure people rather than kill them, and is used by police or soldiers to control crowds during a riot. *Teargas and rubber bullets were used to break up a demonstration by students.* N-COUNT

rubber plant, rubber plants. A **rubber plant** is a type of plant with shiny leaves. It grows naturally in Asia but is also grown as a house plant in other parts of the world. N-COUNT

rubber stamp, rubber stamps, rubber stamping, rubber stamped; also spelled **rubber-stamp**. ◆◇◇◇◇

1 A **rubber stamp** is a small device with a name, date, or symbol on it. You press it on to an ink pad and then on to a document in order to show that the document has been officially dealt with. *In Post Offices, virtually every document that's passed across the counter is stamped with a rubber stamp.* N-COUNT

2 When someone in authority **rubber-stamps** a decision, plan, or law, they agree to it. *Parliament's job is to rubber-stamp his decisions... Nearly 60 banks have rubber-stamped a refinancing deal.* VERB =approve V n

rubbery /rʌbəri/

1 Something that is **rubbery** looks or feels soft or elastic like rubber. *She had the most rubbery face... The mask is left on for about 15 minutes while it sets to a rubbery texture.* ADJ-GRADED

2 Food such as meat that is **rubbery** is difficult to chew. ADJ-GRADED =tough

rubbing /rʌbɪŋ/ **rubbings**

1 A **rubbing** is a picture that you make by putting a piece of paper over a carved surface and rubbing crayon, charcoal, or chalk over it. *We want to go in and do a brass rubbing.* N-COUNT: oft n N

2 See also **rub**.

rubbish /rʌbɪʃ/ **rubbishes, rubbishing, rubbished** ◆◆◇◇◇

1 **Rubbish** consists of unwanted things or waste material such as used paper, empty tins, and bottles, and waste food; used mainly in British English. The usual American word is **garbage** or **trash**. *...unwanted household rubbish... They had piled most of their rubbish into yellow skips.* N-UNCOUNT =refuse, waste

2 If you think that something is of very poor quality you can say that it is **rubbish**; an informal use, used mainly in British English. *He described her book as absolute rubbish.* N-UNCOUNT

3 If you think that an idea or a statement is foolish or wrong you can say that it is **rubbish**; ; an informal use, used mainly in British English. *He's talking rubbish... These reports are total and utter rubbish.* N-UNCOUNT =nonsense

4 In British English, if you think that someone is not very good at something, you can say that they are **rubbish** at it; an informal use. *He was rubbish at his job... I tried playing golf, but I was rubbish.* ADJ: v-link ADJ, usu ADJ at n ≠good

5 In British English, if you **rubbish** a person, their ideas or their work, you say they are of little value. *Five whole pages of script were devoted to rubbishing her political opponents... Officials have simply rubbished all positive ideas.* VERB V n

rubbishy /rʌbɪʃi/. In British English, if you describe something as **rubbishy**, you think it is of very poor quality; an informal word. *...some old rubbishy cop movie.* ADJ: usu ADJ n

rubble /rʌbəl/ ◆◇◇◇◇
1 When a building is destroyed, the pieces of brick, stone, or other materials that remain are referred to as **rubble**. *Thousands of bodies are still buried under the rubble... Entire suburbs have been reduced to rubble.* N-UNCOUNT
2 The word **rubble** is used to refer to the small pieces of stone that are used to build the foundations of roads, paths, and houses. *Brick rubble is useful as the base for paths and patios.* N-UNCOUNT

rubella /ruːbelə/. **Rubella** is a disease. The symptoms are a cough, a sore throat, and red spots on your skin; a medical term. N-UNCOUNT =German measles

Rubicon /ruːbɪkɒn/. If you say that someone **has crossed the Rubicon**, you mean that they have reached a point where they cannot change a decision or course of action; used in journalism. *He's crossed the Rubicon with regard to the use of military force as an option.* PHRASE: V inflects

rubicund /ruːbɪkənd/. If someone has a **rubicund** face, they have a red face; an old-fashioned, literary word. *She watched the colour drain from Colin's rubicund face.* ADJ =ruddy

ruble /ruːbəl/. See **rouble**.

rubric /ruːbrɪk/ **rubrics**
1 A **rubric** is a set of rules or instructions, for example the rules at the beginning of an examination paper; a formal use. *There was a firm rubric in the book about what had to be observed when interrogating anyone under seventeen.* N-COUNT
2 A **rubric** is a title or heading under which something operates or is studied; a formal use. *The aid comes under the rubric of technical co-operation between governments.* N-COUNT =title, heading

ruby /ruːbi/ **rubies** ◆◇◇◇◇
1 A **ruby** is a dark red jewel. *...a ruby and diamond ring.* N-COUNT
2 Something that is **ruby** is dark red in colour. *...a glass of ruby-red Cabernet Sauvignon.* COLOUR

ruched /ruːʃt/. **Ruched** curtains or garments are gathered so that they hang in soft folds. ADJ

ruck /rʌk/ **rucks, rucking, rucked** ◆◇◇◇◇
1 A **ruck** is a situation where a group of people are fighting or struggling; used in British English. *There'll be a huge ruck with the cops as they try to take photographs... Ministers will find their budgets being decided in a political ruck with their colleagues.* N-COUNT =scrap, fight
2 In the sport of rugby, a **ruck** is a situation where a group of players struggle for possession of the ball. N-COUNT
3 A **ruck** is a fold or crease in cloth or clothing. *...a small ruck in the carpet.* N-COUNT

ruck up. If cloth or someone's clothing **rucks up** or if someone or something **rucks it up**, it forms folds and covers a smaller area than it did before. *His designer suits ruck up round his middle... His shoe had rucked up one corner of the pale rug.* PHRASAL VERB ERG V P; V P n (not pron); Also V n P

rucksack /rʌksæk/ **rucksacks.** A **rucksack** is a bag with straps that go over your shoulders, so that you can carry things on your back, for example when you are walking or climbing; used mainly in British English. The usual American word is **pack** or **backpack**. ◆◇◇◇◇ N-COUNT =backpack

ruckus /rʌkəs/. In informal American English, if someone or something causes a **ruckus**, they cause a great deal of noise, argument, or confusion. *This caused such a ruckus all over Japan that they had to change their mind.* N-SING

ruction /rʌkʃən/ **ructions.** If someone or something causes **ructions**, they cause strong protests, quarrels, or other trouble; an informal word. *Both activities have caused some ructions.* N-COUNT: usu pl

rudder /rʌdər/ **rudders** ◆◇◇◇◇
1 A **rudder** is a device for steering a boat. It consists of a vertical piece of wood or metal at the back of the boat. N-COUNT
2 An aeroplane's **rudder** is a vertical piece of metal at the back which is used to make the plane turn to the right or to the left. N-COUNT

rudderless /rʌdərləs/. A country or a person that is **rudderless** does not have a good leader to follow or a clear aim to pursue. *The country was politically rudderless for almost three months. ...a feeling in the country that the Government was drifting rudderless.* ADJ

ruddy /rʌdi/ **ruddier, ruddiest** ◆◇◇◇◇
1 If you describe someone's face as **ruddy**, you mean that their face is a reddish colour, usually because they are healthy or have been working hard, or because they are angry or embarrassed. *He had a naturally ruddy complexion, even more flushed now from dancing... His face is still ruddy and handsome.* ADJ-GRADED
2 Something that is **ruddy** is reddish in colour; a literary use. *...barges, with their sails ruddy brown from regular dressing of ochre.* ADJ-GRADED
3 **Ruddy** is used as a mild swear word to add emphasis or to express anger; used mainly in old-fashioned British English. *He took the paraffin stove on a picnic and the ruddy thing wouldn't work.* ADJ: ADJ n

rude /ruːd/ **ruder, rudest** ◆◆◇◇◇
1 When people are **rude**, they act in an impolite way towards other people or say impolite things about them. *He's rude to her friends and obsessively jealous... People were quite often rude about him, often the people he had helped... Unfair bosses and rude customers make us unhappy on the job.* ADJ-GRADED: oft ADJ *to/about* n =impolite ≠polite
♦ **rudely** *I could not understand why she felt compelled to behave so rudely to a friend.* ADV-GRADED: usu ADV with v ♦ **rudeness** *Mother is cross at Caleb's rudeness, but I can forgive it.* N-UNCOUNT: oft with poss
2 **Rude** is used to describe words and behaviour that are likely to embarrass or offend people, because they relate to sex or to bodily functions. *Fred keeps cracking rude jokes with the guests... Luke made a rude gesture with his finger.* ADJ-GRADED: usu ADJ n =obscene
3 If someone receives a **rude** shock, something unpleasant happens unexpectedly. *It will come as a rude shock when their salary or income-tax refund cannot be cashed.* ADJ-GRADED: ADJ n ♦ **rudely** *People were awakened rudely by a siren just outside their window.* ADV-GRADED: ADV with v
4 Objects can be described as **rude** when they are very simply and roughly made; a literary use. *Roden had already constructed a rude cabin for himself and his family in case of necessity.* ADJ: ADJ n
5 If someone has a **rude awakening**, something shocking or unpleasant happens to them unexpectedly. *Asian investors have had a rude awakening with the BCCI scandal... This country has lived beyond its means and faces a rude awakening to the facts of economic life.* PHRASES N inflects, v PHR
6 If someone is in **rude health**, they are strong and healthy. *He is in rude health and can cycle 40 or 50 miles non-stop.*

rudimentary /ruːdɪmentri/ ◆◇◇◇◇
1 **Rudimentary** things are very basic or undeveloped and therefore unsatisfactory; a formal use. *The earth surface of the courtyard extended into a kind of rudimentary kitchen... They are deprived of the ability to exercise the most rudimentary workers' rights.* ADJ-GRADED =basic
2 **Rudimentary** knowledge includes only the simplest and most basic facts; a formal use. *He had only a rudimentary knowledge of French. ...a rudimentary grasp of economics.* ADJ-GRADED =basic

rudiments /ruːdɪmənts/. When you learn the **rudiments** of something, you learn the simplest or most essential things about it. *She helped to build a house, learning the rudiments of bricklaying as she went along.* N-PLURAL: usu *the* N *of* n =basics

rue /ruː/ **rues, ruing, rued** ◆◆◇◇◇
1 If you **rue** something that you have done, you are sorry that you did it, because it has had unpleasant results; a literary word. *Tavare was probably ruing his decision.* VERB =regret V n
2 If you **rue the day** that you did something, you are sorry that you did it, because it has had unpleasant results; a literary expression. *You'll live to rue the day you said that to me, my girl.* PHRASE: V inflects

rueful /ruːfʊl/. If someone is **rueful**, they feel or express regret or sorrow in a quiet and gentle way; a literary word. *He shook his head and gave me a rueful smile... 'Our marriage was a mistake,'* ◆◇◇◇◇ ADJ-GRADED *she said, looking rueful.* ♦ **ruefully** *He grinned at her ruefully.* ADV-GRADED: usu ADV with v

ruff /rʌf/ **ruffs**
1 A **ruff** is a stiff strip of cloth or other material with many small folds in it, which some people wore round their neck in former times. *...an Elizabethan ruff.* N-COUNT
2 A **ruff** is a thick band of feathers or fur round the neck of a bird or animal. N-COUNT

ruffian /rʌfiən/ **ruffians.** A **ruffian** is a man who behaves violently and is involved in crime; an old-fashioned word. *...gangs of ruffians who lurk about intent on troublemaking.* N-COUNT

ruffle /rʌfᵊl/ **ruffles, ruffling, ruffled** ◆◇◇◇◇
1 If you **ruffle** someone's hair, you move your hand backwards and forwards through it as a way of showing your affection towards them. *'Don't let that get you down,' he said ruffling Ben's dark curls.* VERB =rumple V n
2 When the wind **ruffles** something such as the surface of the sea, it causes it to move gently in a wave-like motion; a literary use. *The evening breeze ruffled the pond... A gust of breeze moved down the hillside, ruffling the grass.* VERB V n
3 If something **ruffles** someone, it causes them to panic and lose their confidence or to become angry or upset. *The catcalls didn't ruffle the Princess as she wandered around the temple... Nothing could ruffle the perfect composure with which she casually greets members of staff.* VERB V n
4 If a bird **ruffles** its feathers or if its feathers **ruffle**, they stand out on its body, for example when it is cleaning itself or when it is frightened. *Tame birds, when approached, will stretch out their necks and ruffle their neck feathering... Its body plumage suddenly began to ruffle and swell so that he seemed almost twice his size. ...a ruffling of wings.* V-ERG V n V V-ing
5 **Ruffles** are folds of cloth formed at the neck or cuffs of a piece of clothing or sewn on as a decoration. *...a white blouse with ruffles at the neck and cuffs.* N-COUNT: usu pl
6 If someone or something **ruffles** some **feathers** or **ruffles** someone's **feathers**, they cause people to become very angry, nervous, or upset. *His direct, often abrasive approach will doubtless ruffle a few feathers... Politicians are usually careful not to ruffle the feathers of their constituents.* PHRASE: V inflects

ruffled /rʌfᵊld/
1 Something that is **ruffled** is no longer smooth or neat. *Her short hair was oddly ruffled and then flattened around her head.* ADJ-GRADED =rumpled, dishevelled
2 **Ruffled** clothes are decorated with small folds of material. *She was wearing a white ruffled blouse and a blue velvet skirt.* • See also **ruffle**. ADJ: ADJ n

rug /rʌg/ **rugs** ◆◆◇◇◇
1 A **rug** is a piece of thick material that you put on a floor. It is like a carpet but covers a smaller area. *A Persian rug covered the hardwood floors.* N-COUNT
2 A **rug** is a small blanket which you use to cover your shoulders or your knees to keep them warm; used mainly in British English. *The old lady was seated in her chair at the window, a rug over her knees. ...a travel rug.* N-COUNT
3 If someone **pulls the rug from under** someone or something or **pulls the rug from under** someone's **feet**, they withdraw their help or support. *If the banks opt to pull the rug from under the ill-fated project, it will go into liquidation.* • **sweep something under the rug**: see **sweep**. PHRASE: V inflects

rugby /rʌgbi/. **Rugby** or **rugby football** is a game played by two teams using an oval ball. Players try to score points by carrying the ball to their opponents' end of the pitch, or by kicking it over a bar fixed between two goalposts. ◆◆◆◇◇ N-UNCOUNT =rugger

rugged /rʌgɪd/ ◆◇◇◇◇
1 A **rugged** area of land is rocky and uneven, with few trees or plants; a literary use. *We left the rough track and bumped our way over a rugged mountainous terrain.* ♦ **ruggedly** *...a ruggedly beautiful wilderness.* ♦ **ruggedness** *The island's ruggedness symbolises our history and the character of the people.* ADJ-GRADED: usu ADJ n; ADV: ADV adj; N-UNCOUNT
2 If you describe a man as **rugged**, you mean that he has strong, masculine features; used showing approval. *A look of pure disbelief crossed Shankly's rugged face.* ♦ **ruggedly** *He was six feet tall and ruggedly handsome.* ADJ-GRADED: usu ADJ n PRAGMATICS; ADV: ADV adj, ADV -ed
3 If you describe someone's character as **rugged**, you mean that they are strong and determined, and have the ability to cope with difficult situations; used showing approval. *Rugged individualism forged America's frontier society.* ADJ-GRADED: usu ADJ n PRAGMATICS
4 A **rugged** piece of equipment is made of strong material and is designed to last a long time, even if it is treated roughly. *The camera combines rugged reliability with unequalled optical performance and speed.* ♦ **ruggedness** *The body is 90% titanium for ruggedness.* ADJ-GRADED; N-UNCOUNT

rugger /rʌgəʳ/. In informal British English, **rugger** is the same as **rugby**. *We played rugger together at College. ...a rugger match.* N-UNCOUNT =rugby

ruin /ruːɪn/ **ruins, ruining, ruined** ◆◆◆◇◇
1 To **ruin** something means to severely harm, damage, or spoil it. *My wife was ruining her health through worry... Entire villages have been washed away. Roads and bridges have been destroyed and crops ruined.* VERB =destroy V n
2 To **ruin** someone means to cause them to no longer have any money. *She accused him of ruining her financially with his taste for the high life.* VERB V n
3 **Ruin** is the state of no longer having any money. *The farmers say recent inflation has driven them to the brink of ruin.* N-UNCOUNT
4 **Ruin** is the state of being severely damaged or spoiled, or the process of reaching this state. *The vineyards were falling into ruin... She wasn't going to let her plans go to ruin.* N-UNCOUNT
5 **The ruins of** something are the parts of it that remain after it has been severely damaged or weakened. *The new Turkish republic he helped to build emerged from the ruins of a great empire... He stood very still, staring in at the ruins of his work.* N-PLURAL: *the* N *of* n
6 The **ruins** of a building are the parts of it that remain after the rest has fallen down or been destroyed. *One dead child was found in the ruins almost two hours after the explosion... There's only the mountain in this direction, and higher up an old ruin, an abandoned castle.* N-COUNT: usu pl
7 See also **ruined**.
8 If something is **in ruins**, it is completely spoiled. *Its heavily-subsidized economy is in ruins... This country was once proud of its education system. Now it seems to be in ruins.* PHRASES oft v-link PHR
9 If a building or place is **in ruins**, most of it has been destroyed and only parts of it remain. *The abbey was in ruins... Within Germany, the city of Berlin lay in ruins.* usu v-link PHR

ruination /ruːɪneɪʃᵊn/. The **ruination** of someone or something is the act of ruining them or the process of being ruined. *Money was the ruination of him... The clerics have brought ruination on our people.* N-UNCOUNT: oft *the* N *of* n

ruined /ruːɪnd/. A **ruined** building or place has been very badly damaged or has gradually fallen down because of neglect. *...a ruined church.* ◆◇◇◇◇ ADJ: ADJ n

ruinous /ruːɪnəs/
1 If you describe the cost of something as **ruinous**, you mean that it costs far more money than you can afford or than is reasonable. *Many Britons will still fear the potentially ruinous costs of their legal system.* ♦ **ruinously** *...a ruinously expensive court case.* ADJ: usu ADJ n; ADV: ADV adj
2 A **ruinous** process or course of action is one that is likely to lead to ruin. *The economy of the state is experiencing the ruinous effects of the conflict.* ♦ **ruinously** *...cities ruinously choked by uncontrolled traffic.* ADJ-GRADED: usu ADJ n; ADV: usu ADV -ed

rule /ruːl/ **rules, ruling, ruled** ◆◆◆◆◆
1 **Rules** are instructions that tell you what you are allowed to do and what you are not allowed to do. *...a thirty-two-page pamphlet explaining the rules of basketball... Sikhs were expected to adhere strictly to the religious rules concerning appearance... Strictly speaking, this was against the rules. ...the amendment to Rule 22.* N-COUNT: oft N *of* n, N num

2 A **rule** is a statement telling people what they should do in order to achieve success or a benefit of some kind. *An important rule is to drink plenty of water during any flight... By and large, the rules for healthy eating are the same during pregnancy as at any other time.* N-COUNT: oft N *for/of* n

3 The **rules** of something such as a language or a science are statements that describe the way that things usually happen in a particular situation. *It is a rule of English that adjectives generally precede the noun they modify. ...according to the rules of quantum theory.* N-COUNT: oft N *of* n

4 If something is **the rule**, it is the normal state of affairs. *However, for many Americans today, weekend work has unfortunately become the rule rather than the exception.* N-SING: *the* N

5 The person or group that **rules** a country controls its affairs. *For four centuries, he says, foreigners have ruled Angola... He ruled for eight months. ...the long line of feudal lords who had ruled over this land.* ► Also a noun. *...demands for an end to one-party rule.* VERB V n V V *over* n N-UNCOUNT: usu supp N

6 If something **rules** your life, it influences or restricts your actions in a way that is not good for you. *Scientists have always been aware of how fear can rule our lives and make us ill.* VERB V n

7 When someone in authority **rules** that something is true or should happen, they state that they have officially decided that it is true or should happen; a formal use. *The court ruled that laws passed by the assembly remained valid... The Israeli court has not yet ruled on the case... A provincial magistrates' court last week ruled it unconstitutional... Kenneth Clarke, the home secretary, ruled against her being allowed to stay in Britain.* VERB =pronounce V that V *on* n V n adj/n V *against* n Also V *in favour of* n

8 If you **rule** a straight line, you draw it using something that has a straight edge. *...a ruled grid of horizontal and vertical lines.* VERB V-ed Also V n

9 See also **golden rule**, **ground rule**, **ruling**, **slide rule**.

10 If you say that something happens **as a rule**, you mean that it usually happens. *As a rule, however, such attacks have been aimed at causing damage rather than taking life.* PHRASES PHR with cl =generally, usually

11 If someone in authority **bends the rules** or **stretches the rules**, they do something or allow something to happen, even though it is against the rules. *There happens to be a particular urgency in this case, and it would help if you could bend the rules.* V inflects

12 A **rule of thumb** is a rule or principal that you follow which is not based on exact calculations but rather on experience. *A good rule of thumb is that a broker must generate sales of ten times his salary if his employer is to make a profit... As a rule of thumb, a cup of filter coffee contains about 80mg of caffeine.* *rule* inflects

13 If workers **work to rule**, or if they go on a **work to rule**, they protest by working strictly according to the rules of their job but doing no extra work and taking no new decisions, with the result that they work more slowly and achieve less. *Nurses are continuing to work to rule.* V inflects

rule out PHRASAL VERB

1 If you **rule out** a course of action, an idea, or a solution, you decide that it is impossible or unsuitable. *The Prime Minister is believed to have ruled out cuts in child benefit or pensions... Local detectives have ruled out foul play.* V P n (not pron) Also V n P

2 If something **rules out** a situation, it prevents it from happening or from being possible. *A serious car accident in 1986 ruled out a permanent future for him in farming.* V P n (not pron)

rule out of. If someone **rules** you **out of** a contest or activity, they say that you cannot or will not be involved in it. If something **rules** you **out of** a contest or activity, it prevents you from being involved in it. *He has ruled himself out of the world championships next year in Stuttgart... A damaged hamstring has ruled him out of contention for Wednesday's international against Spain.* PHRASAL VERB V n P P n

rule book, rule books

1 A **rule book** is a book containing the official rules for a particular game, job, or organization. *...one of the most serious offences mentioned in the Party rule book.* N-COUNT

2 If you say that someone is doing something by **the rule book**, you mean that they are doing it in the normal, accepted way. *This was not the time to take risks; he knew he should play it by the rule book.* N-COUNT: *the* N

rule of law. The **rule of law** refers to a situation in which the people in a society obey its laws and enable it to function properly; a formal expression. *I am confident that we can restore peace, stability and respect for the rule of law.* ◆◇◇◇◇ N-SING: usu *the* N

ruler /ruːlə^r/ **rulers** ◆◆◇◇◇

1 The **ruler** of a country is the person who rules the country. *The former military ruler of Lesotho has been placed under house arrest... He was a weak-willed and indecisive ruler.* N-COUNT: oft with poss

2 A **ruler** is a long flat piece of wood, metal, or plastic with straight edges marked in centimetres or inches. Rulers are used to measure things and to draw straight lines. N-COUNT

ruling /ruːlɪŋ/ **rulings** ◆◆◆◇◇

1 The **ruling** group of people in a country or organization is the group that controls its affairs. *...the Mexican voters' growing dissatisfaction with the ruling party. ...the domination of the ruling class. ...the sport's ruling body, the International Cricket Council.* ADJ: ADJ n

2 A **ruling** is an official decision made by a judge or court. *Goodwin tried to have the court ruling overturned... She appealed against a High Court ruling that she should be forcibly fed to save her life.* N-COUNT: oft N that

3 Someone's **ruling** passion or emotion is the feeling they have most strongly, which influences their actions. *Even my love of literary fame, my ruling passion, never soured my temper.* ADJ: ADJ n

rum /rʌm/ **rums** ◆◇◇◇◇

1 **Rum** is an alcoholic drink made from sugar cane juice. *...a bottle of rum. ...a rum punch.* N-MASS

2 In British English, if you describe people or things as **rum**, you mean that they are rather strange; an old-fashioned use. *It was a joke, of course, but surely a rum sort of joke?* ADJ-GRADED: ADJ n

Rumanian /ruːmeɪniən/. See **Romanian**.

rumba /rʌmbə/ **rumbas.** The **rumba** is a type of ballroom dance that comes from Cuba, or the music that the dance is performed to. N-COUNT: oft *the* N

rumble /rʌmbᵊl/ **rumbles, rumbling, rumbled** ◆◇◇◇◇

1 A **rumble** is a low, continuous, throbbing sound. *The silence of the night was punctuated by the distant rumble of traffic... The rain was teeming down and she thought she heard a rumble of thunder.* N-COUNT: oft N *of* n

2 If a vehicle **rumbles** somewhere, it moves slowly forward while making a loud, continuous, throbbing noise. *A bus rumbled along the road at the top of the path... A line of tractors rumbled onto the motorway through a cordon of police... The air reeked of kerosene and huge aircraft rumbled overhead.* VERB V adv/prep

3 If you refer to the **rumble** of someone's voice, you mean their voice sounds very low, making it hard to hear exactly what they are saying. *Rose's voice dropped and was interrupted by the rumble of Dagmar's.* N-COUNT: oft N *of* n

4 If something **rumbles**, it makes a low, throbbing noise. *The sky, swollen like a black bladder, rumbled and crackled... Speeches rumbled within the walls of the churches.* VERB V

5 If your stomach **rumbles**, it makes a vibrating noise, usually because you are hungry. *Her stomach rumbled. She hadn't eaten any breakfast.* VERB V

6 In informal British English, if someone **is rumbled**, the truth about them or something they were trying to conceal is discovered. *When his fraud was rumbled he had just £20.17 in the bank.* VB: usu passive *be* V-ed

rumble on. In British English, if you say that something such as an argument **rumbles on**, you mean that it continues long after it should have been settled; used by journalists. *And still the row* PHRASAL VERB =drag on V P *rumbles on over who is to blame for the steadily surging crime statistics... The scandal surrounding the collapse of the bank looked set to rumble on for a third year.*

rumbling /rʌmblɪŋ/ **rumblings** ◆◇◇◇◇

1 A **rumbling** is a low, continuous, throbbing noise. *...the rumbling of an empty stomach... Our peace was soon shattered by loud rumblings and explosions like cannon fire.* N-COUNT: usu with supp

2 **Rumblings** are signs that a bad situation is developing or that people are becoming dissatisfied. *Even Bayldon had become aware that there were rumblings of discontent within the ranks.* N-COUNT: usu pl, oft N prep

rumbustious /rʌmbʌstʃuəs/. In British English, a **rumbustious** person is energetic in a cheerful, noisy way. The usual American word is **rambunctious**. *...the flamboyant and somewhat rumbustious prime minister.* ADJ-GRADED: usu ADJ n =boisterous

ruminate /ruːmɪneɪt/ **ruminates, ruminating, ruminated**

1 If you **ruminate** on something, you think about it very carefully; a formal use. *He ruminated on the terrible wastage that typified American life... Obsessional personalities commonly ruminate excessively about death.* VERB =ponder V *on/about/over* n Also V

2 When animals **ruminate**, they bring food back from their stomach into their mouth and chew it again; a technical use. *He wanted to have a look at the two oxen, both ruminating without raising their eyes.* VERB V

rumination /ruːmɪneɪʃən/ **ruminations.** Your **ruminations** are your careful thoughts about something; a formal word. *Many of Vasari's ruminations on the subject are not always to be believed. ...profound ruminations about life.* N-COUNT: oft with poss =thoughts

ruminative /ruːmɪnətɪv, AM -neɪt-/. If you are **ruminative**, you are thinking very deeply and carefully about something; a formal word. *He was uncharacteristically depressed and ruminative.* ♦ **ruminatively** *He smiles and swirls the ice ruminatively around his almost empty glass.* ADJ =thoughtful ADV: ADV with v

rummage /rʌmɪdʒ/ **rummages, rummaging, rummaged** ◆◇◇◇◇

1 If you **rummage** through something, you search for something you want by moving things around in a careless or hurried way. *They rummage through piles of second-hand clothes for something that fits... Marianne went to rummage in the refrigerator.* ► Also a noun. *A brief rummage will provide several pairs of gloves. ...a rummage through his wardrobe for some tennis whites.* ► **Rummage about** and **rummage around** mean the same as **rummage**. *I opened the fridge and rummaged about... He rummaged around the post room and found the document.* VERB =root V prep Also V N-SING: a N PHRASAL VERB V P V P n (not pron)

2 In American English, **rummage** is old or unwanted things that people give away to charities. The British word is **jumble**. *...loads of pitiful rummage... I was taking a bunch of things to the church rummage sale.* N-UNCOUNT

rummy /rʌmi/. **Rummy** is a card game in which players try to collect cards of the same value or cards in a sequence in the same suit. N-UNCOUNT

rumor /ruːmər/. See **rumour**.

rumour /ruːməʳ/ **rumours;** spelled **rumor** in American English. A **rumour** is a story or piece of information that may or may not be true, but that people are talking about. *Simon denied rumours that he was planning to visit Bulgaria later this month... There have been persistent rumours of quarrels within the movement... There's a strange rumour going around at the moment about Peter.* ◆◆◆◇◇ N-VAR: oft N that, N *of/about* n

rumoured /ruːməʳd/; spelled **rumored** in American English. If something **is rumoured** to be the case, people are suggesting that it is the case, but they do not know for certain. *Her parents are rumoured to be on the verge of splitting up... It was rumoured that he had been interned in an asylum for a while. ...his rumoured relationship with a young singer.* ◆◇◇◇◇ V-PASSIVE =be said *be* V-ed to-inf *it be* V-ed that V-ed Also *there be* V-ed to-inf, *be* V-ed

rump /rʌmp/ **rumps** ◆◇◇◇◇

1 The **rump** of a group, organization, or country consists of the members who remain in it after the rest have left; used mainly in British English. *The rump of the party does in fact still have considerable assets... He finds himself heading a rump party largely out of tune with his own views.* N-SING: with supp

2 An animal's **rump** is its rear end. *The cows' rumps were marked with their owner's initials and a number.* N-COUNT: usu poss N

3 **Rump** or **rump** steak is meat cut from the rear end of a cow. N-UNCOUNT

4 A person's **rump** is his or her buttocks; an informal use. *...jeans stretching across her rump.* N-COUNT: usu sing

rumple /rʌmpəl/ **rumples, rumpling, rumpled.** If you **rumple** someone's hair, you move your hand backwards and forwards through it as your way of showing affection to them. *I leaned forward to rumple his hair, but he jerked out of the way.* VERB =ruffle V n

rumpled /rʌmpəld/. **Rumpled** means creased, untidy, or disordered. *I hurried to the tent and grabbed a few clean, if rumpled, clothes. ...a sprawl of white, rumpled sheets... He arrived, somewhat rumpled and unshaven.* ADJ-GRADED =crumpled

rump steak, rump steaks. Rump steak is meat from the top back part of a cow's leg. N-VAR

rumpus /rʌmpəs/ **rumpuses.** If someone or something causes a **rumpus**, they cause a lot of noise or argument. *He had actually left the company a year before the rumpus started.* N-COUNT

run /rʌn/ **runs, running, ran.** The form **run** is used in the present tense and is also the past participle of the verb. ◆◆◆◆◆

1 When you **run**, you move quickly, leaving the ground during each stride, because you are in a hurry to get somewhere or to get away, or for exercise. *I excused myself and ran back to the telephone... Police believe the gunmen ran off into the woods... Neighbouring shopkeepers ran after the man and caught him... He ran the last block to the White House with two cases of gear... Antonia ran to meet them.* ► Also a noun. *After a six-mile run, Jackie returns home for a substantial breakfast.* VERB V adv/prep V n/amount V N-COUNT: usu sing

2 When someone **runs** in a race, they run in competition with other people. *...when I was running in the New York Marathon... Phyllis Smith ran a controlled race to qualify in 51.32 sec.* VERB V V n

3 When a horse **runs** in a race or when its owner **runs** it, it competes in a race. *He was overruled by the owner, Peter Bolton, who insisted on Cool Ground running in the Gold Cup... If we have a wet spell, Cecil could also run Armiger in the Derby.* V-ERG V V n

4 If you say that something long, such as a road, **runs** in a particular direction, you are describing its course or position. You can also say that something **runs** the length or width of something else. *...the sun-dappled trail which ran through the beech woods. ...a gas-filled glass tube with a thin wire running down the centre... The hallway ran the length of the villa.* VERB V prep/adv V n

5 If you **run** a wire or tube somewhere, you install it or arrange it so that it is in a particular position. *Our host ran a long extension cord out from the house and set up a screen and a projector.* VERB V n prep/adv

6 If you **run** your hand or an object over something or through something, you move your hand or the object over it or through it. *It hurt to breathe, and he winced as he ran his hand over his ribs... He laughed and ran his fingers through his hair... I ran the brush through my hair and dashed out... Fumbling, he ran her card through the machine.* VERB V n prep

7 If you **run** something through a machine, process, or series of tests, you make it undergo a process. *They have gathered the best statistics they can find and run them through their own computers.* VERB V n *through* n

8 If someone **runs** for office in an election, they take part as a candidate; used mainly in American English. *It was only last February that he announced he would run for president... It is no easy job to run against John Glenn, Ohio's Democratic* VERB =stand V *for* n V *against* n V

senator... Women are running in nearly all the contested seats in Los Angeles.

9 In American English, a **run for** office is an attempt to be elected to office. The usual British word is **bid**. *He was already preparing his run for the presidency.* N-SING: N *for* n

10 If you **run** something such as a business or an activity, you are in charge of it or you organize it. *His stepfather ran a prosperous paint business... Is this any way to run a country?... Each teacher will run a different workshop that covers a specific area of the language. ...a well-run, profitable organisation.* VERB V n V-ed

11 If you talk about how a system, an organization, or someone's life **is running**, you are saying how well it is operating or progressing. *Officials in charge of the camps say the system is now running extremely smoothly. ...the staff who have kept the bank running.* VB: usu cont V adv V

12 If you **run** an experiment, computer program, or other process, or start it **running**, you start it and let it continue. *He ran a lot of tests and it turned out I had an infection called mycoplasma... You can check your program one command at a time while it's running.* V-ERG V n V

13 When you **run** a recording tape or video tape or when it **runs**, it moves through the machine as the machine operates. *Leaphorn pushed the play button again, ran the tape, pushed stop, pushed rewind... When I checked my answering machine, I found the tape had run to the end but recorded nothing.* V-ERG =play V n V

14 When a machine **is running** or when you **are running** it, it is switched on and operating. *He had failed to realise that the tape recorder was still running... We told him to wait out front with the engine running. ...with everybody running their appliances all at the same time.* V-ERG: usu cont V V n

15 A machine that **runs** on or off a particular source of energy functions using that source of energy. *Black cabs run on diesel... The Biotrace Hygiene Monitor is totally portable and runs off both mains and batteries.* VERB V *on/off* n

16 If you **run** a car or a piece of equipment, you have it and use it; used mainly in British English. *I ran a 1960 Rover 100 from 1977 until 1983. ...information about how much various electrical appliances cost to run.* VERB V n

17 When you say that vehicles such as trains and buses **run** from one place to another, you mean they regularly travel along that route. *A shuttle bus runs frequently between the Inn and the Country Club. ...a government which can't make the trains run on time.* VERB V prep V

18 If you **run** someone somewhere in a car, you drive them there; an informal use. *Could you run me up to Baltimore?* VERB =drive V n prep/adv

19 If you **run** over or down to a place that is quite near, you drive there; an informal use. *I'll run over to Short Mountain and check on Mrs Adams.* VERB =drive V adv

20 A **run** is a journey somewhere. *A run to Southampton showed the car was capable of a reasonable journey. ...doing the morning school run. ...after their bombing runs against ground troops.* N-COUNT

21 If a liquid **runs** in a particular direction, it flows in that direction. *Tears were running down her cheeks... There were cisterns to catch rainwater as it ran off the castle walls... Wash the rice in cold water until the water runs clear.* VERB =flow V prep/adv V adj

22 If you **run** water, or if you **run** a tap or a bath, you cause water to flow from a tap. *She went to the sink and ran water into her empty glass... They heard him running the kitchen tap... I threw off my clothing quickly and ran a warm bath.* VERB V n

23 If a tap or a bath **is running**, water is coming out of a tap. *You must have left a tap running in the bathroom... He came fully awake to hear the bath running.* VB: only cont V

24 If your nose **is running**, mucus is flowing out of it, usually because you have a cold. *Timothy was crying, mostly from exhaustion, and his nose was running.* VB: usu cont =drip V

25 If a surface **is running** with a liquid, that liquid is flowing down it. *After an hour he realised he was completely running with sweat... The window panes were running with condensation.* VB: usu cont V *with* n

26 If the dye in some cloth or the ink on some paper **runs**, it comes off or spreads when the cloth or paper gets wet. *The ink had run on the wet paper.* VERB V

27 If a feeling **runs** through your body or a thought **runs** through your mind, you experience it or think it quickly. *She felt a surge of excitement run through her... All sorts of thoughts were running through my head.* VERB =go V *through* n

28 If a feeling or noise **runs** through a group of people, it spreads among them. *A buzz of excitement ran through the crowd.* VERB =go V *through* n

29 If a theme or feature **runs** through something such as someone's actions or writing, it is present in all of it. *Another thread running through this series is the role of doctors in the treatment of the mentally ill. ...the theme running through the book... There was something of this mood running throughout the Congress's deliberations.* VERB V *through* n V *throughout* n

30 When newspapers or magazines **run** a particular item or story, or if it **runs**, it is published or printed. *The New Orleans Times-Picayune ran a series of four scathing editorials entitled 'The Choice of Our Lives.' ...an editorial that ran this weekend entitled 'Mr. Cuomo Backs Out.'* V-ERG =carry, print V n V

31 You can use **run** to indicate that you are quoting someone else's words or ideas. *'Whoa, I'm goin' to Barbay-dos!' ran the jaunty lyrics of a 1970s hit song.* VERB =go V with quote

32 If an amount **is running** at a particular level, it is at that level. *Today's RPI figure shows inflation running at 10.9 per cent... The deficit is now running at about 300 million dollars a year.* VERB =stand V *at* n

33 If a play, event, or legal contract **runs** for a particular period of time, it lasts for that period of time. *It pleased critics but ran for only three years in the West End... The contract was to run from 1992 to 2020... I predict it will run and run.* VERB V *for* amount V prep V

34 If someone or something **is running** late, they have taken more time than had been planned. If they **are running** to time or ahead of time, they have taken the time planned or less than the time planned. *Tell her I'll call her back later, I'm running late again... The steward will be able to tell you whether the event is running to time or is ahead of schedule.* VB: usu cont V adv/prep

35 If you **are running** a temperature or a fever, you have a high temperature because you are ill. *The little girl is running a fever and she needs help.* VERB V n

36 A **run** of a play or television programme is the period of time during which performances are given or programmes are shown. *The show will transfer to the West End on October 9, after a month's run in Birmingham... Meanwhile, Dusty Springfield's new TV series began a run on BBC 1.* N-COUNT: with supp

37 A **run** of successes or failures is a series of successes or failures. *The England skipper is haunted by a run of low scores... The Scottish Tories' run of luck is holding.* N-SING: usu N *of* n

38 A **run** of a product is the amount that a company or factory decides to produce at one time. *Wayne plans to increase the print run to a heady 1,000... Their defense markets are too small to sustain economically viable production runs.* N-COUNT: usu supp N

39 In cricket or baseball, a **run** is a score of one, which is made by players running between marked places on the pitch after hitting the ball. *At 20 he became the youngest player to score 2,000 runs in a season.* N-COUNT

40 If someone gives you **the run of** a place, they give you permission to go where you like in it and use it as you wish. *He had the run of the house and the pool.* N-SING: *the* N *of* n

41 If you say that someone or something is different from the average **run** or common **run** of people or things, you mean that they are different from ordinary people or things. *...a man who was outside the common run of professional athletes at the* N-SING: with supp *time. ...trying to accomplish the usual run of maintenance jobs and write a column too.*

42 If there is a **run on** something, a lot of people want to buy it or get it at the same time; a technical use in economics. *A run on sterling has killed off hopes of a rate cut... Loss of confidence could trigger a run on Citibank that would threaten the entire financial system.* N-SING: N *on* n

43 A ski **run** or bobsleigh **run** is a course or route that has been designed for skiing or competing in a bobsleigh. N-COUNT: usu n N =course

44 See also **running**, **dummy run**, **test run**, **trial run**.

45 If something happens **against the run of** play or **against the run of** events, it is different from what is generally happening in a game or situation. *The decisive goal arrived against the run of play... Against the run of the polls, the Socialist Workers' Party won Sunday's general election by an unexpectedly large margin.* PHRASES

46 If you **run someone close**, **run them a close second**, or **run a close second**, you almost beat them in a race or competition. *The Under-21 team has defeated Wales and Scotland this season, and ran England very close... The party won at least one county, and ran a close second in several others.* V inflects

47 If a river or well **runs dry**, it ceases to have any water in it. If an oil well **runs dry**, it no longer produces any oil. *Streams had run dry for the first time in memory.* V inflects =dry up

48 If a source of information or money **runs dry**, no more information or money can be obtained from it. *Three days into production, the kitty had run dry.* V inflects =dry up

49 If a characteristic **runs in** someone's **family**, it often occurs in members of that family, in different generations. *The insanity which ran in his family haunted him.* V inflects

50 If you **make a run for it** or if you **run for it**, you run away in order to escape from someone or something. *A helicopter hovered overhead as one of the gang made a run for it... Cody, get out, run for it.* V inflects

51 If people's feelings **are running high**, they are very angry, concerned, or excited. *Feelings there have been running high in the wake of last week's killing.* V inflects

52 If you talk about what will happen **in the long run**, you are saying what you think will happen over a long period of time in the future. If you talk about what will happen **in the short run**, you are saying what you think will happen in the near future. *Sometimes expensive drugs or other treatments can be economical in the long run... In fact, things could get worse in the short run.* PHR with cl, PHR with v

53 If you say that someone would **run a mile** if faced with something, you mean that they are very frightened of it and would try to avoid it. *Yasmin admits she would run a mile if Mark asked her out.* V inflects

54 If you say that someone could **give** someone else **a run for** their **money**, you mean you think they are almost as good as the other person. *...a youngster who even now could give Meryl Streep a run for her money.* V inflects

55 If someone is **on the run**, they are trying to escape or hide from someone such as the police or an enemy. *Fifteen-year-old Danny is on the run from a local authority home.* v-link PHR, PHR after v

56 If someone is **on the run**, they are being severely defeated in a contest or competition. *His opponents believe he is definitely on the run... I knew I had him on the run.* usu v-link PHR

57 If you say that a person or group **is running scared**, you mean that they are frightened of what someone might do to them or what might happen. *The administration is running scared.* V inflects

58 If you **are running short** of something or **running low** on something, you do not have much of it left. If a supply of something **is running short** or **running low**, there is not much of it left. *Government forces are running short of ammunition and fuel... We are running low on drinking water... Time is running short.* V inflects

59 • to **run amok**: see **amok**. • to **make your blood run cold**: see **blood**. • to **run counter to** something: see **counter**. • to **run** its **course**: see **course**. • to **cut and run**: see **cut**. • to **run deep**: see **deep**. • to **run** someone **to earth**: see **earth**. • to **run an errand**: see **errand**. • to **run the gamut of** something: see **gamut**. • to **run the gauntlet**: see **gauntlet**. • to **run rings round** someone: see **ring**. • to **run riot**: see **riot**. • to **run a risk**: see **risk**. • to **run to seed**: see **seed**. • to **run wild**: see **wild**.

run across. If you **run across** someone or something, you meet them or find them unexpectedly. *We ran across some old friends in the village.* PHRASAL VERB =come across V P n

run after. If you **are running after** someone, you are trying to start a relationship with them, usually a sexual relationship; used showing disapproval. *By the time she was fifteen Maria was already running after men twice her age.* PHRASAL VERB PRAGMATICS V P n

run along. If you tell a child to **run along**, you mean that you want them to go away; an informal expression. *Run along now and play for a bit.* PHRASAL VERB usu imper

run around. If you **run around**, you go to a lot of places and do a lot of things, often in a rushed or disorganized way. *No one noticed we had been running around emptying bins and cleaning up... I spend all day running around after the family... Jackie was running around with all these brilliant people... I will not have you running around the countryside without my authority.* PHRASAL VERB V P; V P *after/with* n; V P n (not pron)

run away PHRASAL VERB

1 If you **run away** from a place, you leave it because you are unhappy there. *I ran away from home when I was sixteen... After his beating Colin ran away and hasn't been heard of since... Three years ago I ran away to Mexico to live with a circus.* V P *from* n; V P; V P *to* n

2 If you **run away** with someone, you secretly go away with them in order to live with them or marry them. *She ran away with a man called McTavish last year... He and I were always planning to run away together.* RECIP =run off; V P *with* n; pl-n V P *together*

3 If you **run away** from something unpleasant or new, you try to avoid dealing with it or thinking about it. *They run away from the problem, hoping it will disappear of its own accord... You can't run away for ever.* V P *from* n; V P

4 See also **runaway**.

run away with PHRASAL VERB

1 If you let your imagination or your emotions **run away with** you, you fail to control them and cannot think sensibly. *You're letting your imagination run away with you... Radford sometimes allows his enthusiasm to run away with him.* V P P pron

2 If someone **runs away with** a competition, race, or prize, they win it easily. *Theresa Zabell ran away with the women's gold medal.* V P P n

3 If you **run away with** a particular idea, you accept it without thinking about it carefully, even though it is wrong. *It's very easy for us to run away with the idea that we can control everything.* V P P n

run by. If you **run** something **by** someone, you tell them about it or mention it, to see if they think it is a good idea, or can understand or recognize it; used mainly in American English and journalism. *I'm definitely interested, but I'll have to run it by Larry Estes... Run that by me again.* PHRASAL VERB =run past; V n P n

run down PHRASAL VERB

1 If you **run** people or things **down**, you criticize them strongly. *He last night denounced the British 'genius for running ourselves down'. ...that chap who was running down state schools.* =criticize; V n P; V P n (not pron)

2 If people **run down** an industry or an organization, they deliberately reduce its size or activity; used mainly in British English. *The government is cynically running down Sweden's welfare system... The property business could be sold or run down.* V P n (not pron)

3 If someone **runs down** an amount of something, they reduce it or allow it to decrease; used mainly in British English. *But the survey also revealed firms were running down stocks instead of making new products... Its $25m reserve fund had been run down to around $8m.* =reduce; V P n (not pron)

4 If a vehicle or its driver **runs** someone **down**, the =knock down,

vehicle hits them and injures them. *Lozano claimed that motorcycle driver Clement Lloyd was trying to run him down.* run over V n P
5 If a machine or device **runs down**, it gradually loses power or works more slowly. *The batteries are running down.* V P
6 See also **run-down**.

run into PHRASAL VERB
1 If you **run into** problems or difficulties, you unexpectedly begin to experience them. *Wang agreed to sell IBM systems last year after it ran into financial problems... But the government's plans have run into strong opposition from civil rights campaigners.* =encounter V P n (not pron)
2 If you **run into** someone, you meet them unexpectedly. *He ran into Krettner in the corridor a few minutes later.* =meet, bump into V P n
3 If a vehicle **runs into** something, it accidentally hits it. *The driver failed to negotiate a bend and ran into a tree.* =crash into, hit V P n
4 You use **run into** when indicating that the cost or amount of something is very great. *He said companies should face punitive civil penalties running into millions of pounds.* =amount to V P amount

run off PHRASAL VERB
1 If you **run off** with someone, you secretly go away with them in order to live with them or marry them. *The last thing I'm going to do is run off with somebody's husband... We could run off together, but neither of us wants to live the rest of our lives abroad.* RECIP =run away V P *with* n pl-n V P *together*
2 If you **run off** copies of a piece of writing, you produce them using a machine. *If you want to run off a copy sometime today, you're welcome to.* V P n (not pron) Also V n P

run out PHRASAL VERB
1 If you **run out** of something, you have no more of it left. *They have run out of ideas... We're running out of time... By now the plane was running out of fuel... We had lots before but now we've run out.* V P *of* n V P
• to **run out of steam**: see **steam**.
2 If something **runs out**, it becomes used up so that there is no more left. *Conditions are getting worse and supplies are running out... Time is running out.* V P
3 When a legal document **runs out**, it becomes no longer valid. *When the lease ran out the family moved to Campigny. ...the day my visa ran out.* =expire V P

run out on. If someone **runs out on** you, they go away and abandon you, leaving you with problems. *You can't run out on my wife and me like that.* PHRASAL VERB =abandon V P P n

run over. If a vehicle or its driver **runs** a person or animal **over**, it knocks them down or rolls over them. *You can always run him over and make it look like an accident... He ran over a six-year-old child as he was driving back from a party. ...if I were ever run over by a bus.* PHRASAL VERB =knock down, run down V n P V P n

run past. To **run** something **past** someone means the same as to **run** it **by** them. *Before agreeing, he ran the idea past Johnson.* PHRASAL VERB V n P n

run through PHRASAL VERB
1 If you **run through** a list of items, you read or mention all the items quickly. *I ran through the options with him.* =go through V P n
2 If you **run through** a performance or a series of actions, you rehearse it or practise it. *Doug stood still while I ran through the handover procedure.* =go through V P n
3 See also **run-through**.

run to PHRASAL VERB
1 If you **run to** someone, you go to them for help or to tell them something. *What would I do? Whom would I run to? Momma was still away... If you were at a party and somebody was getting high, you didn't go running to a cop.* V P n
2 If something **runs to** a particular amount or size, it is that amount or size. *The finished manuscript ran to the best part of fifty double-sided pages.* =amount to V P n (not pron)
3 If you cannot **run to** a particular item, you cannot afford to buy it or pay for it. *The entire set retails at just over £100. If you can't run to that, consider the recording of Wolf's complete Spanish Songbook.* with brd-neg =afford V P n
4 If your tastes or interests **run to** a particular type of thing, that is the type of thing you like. *My own tastes run to a comfortable apartment, somewhere high in a modern building.* V P n (not pron)

run up PHRASAL VERB
1 If someone **runs up** bills or debts, they acquire them by buying a lot of things or borrowing money. *He ran up a £1,400 bill at the Britannia Adelphi Hotel, saying the club would pay... Many ran up huge debts as they spent millions to buy foreign players..* V P n (not pron)
2 See also **run-up**.

run up against. If you **run up against** problems, you suddenly begin to experience them. *I ran up against the problem of getting taken seriously long before I became a writer... He ran up against a solid wall of opposition when it came to the sensitive issue of party privileges.* PHRASAL VERB =encounter V P P n

runabout /rʌnəbaʊt/ **runabouts.** A **runabout** is a small car used mainly for short journeys; an informal word, used mainly in British English. *...a small 1-litre runabout.* N-COUNT

runaround /rʌnəraʊnd/; also spelled **run-around**. If someone **gives** you **the runaround**, they deliberately do not give you all the information or help that you want, and send you to another person or place to get it; an informal expression. PHRASE: V inflects

runaway /rʌnəweɪ/ **runaways** ◆◇◇◇◇
1 You use **runaway** to describe a situation in which something increases or develops very quickly and cannot be controlled. *Our Grand Sale in June was a runaway success. ...a runaway best-seller. ...in an era of runaway inflation.* ADJ: ADJ n
2 A **runaway** is someone, especially a child, who leaves home without telling anyone or without permission. *...a teenage runaway. ...a runaway slave.* N-COUNT: oft N n
3 A **runaway** vehicle or animal is moving forward quickly, and its driver or rider has lost control of it. *The runaway car careered into a bench, hitting an elderly couple... The narrative pulls you along like a runaway train. ...a runaway horse.* ADJ: ADJ n

run-down; also spelled **rundown**. The adjective is pronounced /rʌn daʊn/. The noun is pronounced /rʌn daʊn/. ◆◇◇◇◇
1 If someone is **run-down**, they are tired or slightly ill; an informal use. *When 23-year-old Marilyn Brown started to feel run-down last December, it never occurred to her that she could have tuberculosis.* ADJ-GRADED: usu v-link ADJ =under the weather
2 A **run-down** building or area is in very poor condition. *They have put substantial funds into rebuilding one of the most run-down areas in Scotland. ...a run-down block of flats.* ADJ-GRADED: usu ADJ n
3 A **run-down** place of business is not as active as it used to be or does not have many customers. *...a run-down slate quarry... He bought a run-down television station.* ADJ-GRADED: usu ADJ n
4 When the **run-down of** an industry or organization takes place, it is reduced in size or activity; used mainly in British English. *...the impetus behind the rundown of the coal industry.* N-SING: N *of* n
5 If you give someone a **run-down** of a group of things or a **run-down** on something, you give them details about it; an informal use. *Here's a rundown of the options... This full-colour supplement includes full race details, plus a comprehensive rundown on all the British hopefuls.* N-SING: usu N *of/on* n

rune /ruːn/ **runes. Runes** are letters from an ancient alphabet that were carved in wood or stone by people in Northern Europe in former times. They were believed to have magical properties. ◆◇◇◇◇ N-COUNT

rung /rʌŋ/ **rungs** ◆◇◇◇◇
1 Rung is the past participle of **ring**.
2 The **rungs** on a ladder are the wooden or metal bars that form the steps. *I swung myself onto the ladder and felt for the next rung.* N-COUNT
3 If you reach a particular **rung** in your career, in an organization, or in a process, you reach that level in it. *I first worked with him in 1971 when we were both on the lowest rung of our careers... There has never been a better time to get on the first rung of the property ladder.* N-COUNT: with supp

run-in, run-ins ◆◆◇◇◇

1 A **run-in** is an argument or quarrel with someone; an informal use. *I had a monumental run-in with him a couple of years ago.* N-COUNT: oft N *with* n =row

2 The **run-in** to a sporting event is the period of time or series of matches leading up to it. *If Bob is at his best, we'll be able to win the most difficult game of our run-in.* N-SING

runner /rʌnəʳ/ **runners** ◆◆◆◇◇

1 A **runner** is a person who runs, especially for sport or pleasure. *...a marathon runner... I am a very keen runner and am out training most days.* N-COUNT

2 The **runners** in a horse race are the horses taking part. *There are 18 runners in the top race of the day.* N-COUNT

3 A drug **runner** or gun **runner** is someone who illegally takes drugs or guns into a country. N-COUNT: n N

4 Someone who is a **runner** for a particular person or company is employed to take messages, collect money, or do other small errands for them. *...a bookie's runner.* N-COUNT

5 **Runners** are thin strips of wood or metal underneath something which help it to move smoothly. *...the runners of his sled.* N-COUNT: usu pl

6 On a plant, **runners** are long shoots that grow from the main stem and put down roots to form a new plant. *...strawberry runners.* N-COUNT: usu pl

7 A **runner** is a long narrow mat that is put on a piece of furniture or on the floor. N-COUNT

8 If someone **does a runner**, they leave a place hurriedly, for example in order to escape arrest or to avoid paying for something; an informal expression. *At this point, the accountant did a runner – with all my bank statements, expenses and receipts.* PHRASE: V inflects =do a bunk

runner bean, runner beans. Runner beans are long green beans that are eaten as a vegetable. They grow on a tall climbing plant and are the cases that contain the seeds of the plant. *I've just picked some runner beans.* N-COUNT: usu pl =string bean

runner-up, runners-up. A **runner-up** is someone who has finished in second place in a race or competition. *The ten runners-up will receive a case of wine. ...Paul Azinger, the American who was runner-up to Faldo at Muirfield in 1987.* ◆◆◇◇◇ N-COUNT: oft N *to* n

running /rʌnɪŋ/ ◆◆◆◆◇

1 **Running** is the activity of moving as fast as you can, with your feet leaving the ground with every stride, especially as a sport. *We chose to do cross-country running. ...running shoes.* N-UNCOUNT

2 **The running of** something such as a business is the managing or organizing of it. *...the committee in charge of the day-to-day running of the party.* N-SING: *the* N *of* n

3 You use **running** to describe things that continue or keep occurring over a period of time. *He also began a running feud with Dean Acheson... The song turned into a running joke between him and the press.* ADJ: ADJ n =ongoing

4 A **running** total or tally is a total to which numbers keep being added as something progresses. *He kept a running tally of who had called him, who had visited, who had sent flowers... So far, his running total in transfers fees is £12million.* ADJ: ADJ n

5 You can use **running** when indicating that something keeps happening. For example, if something has happened every day for three days, you can say that it has happened for the third day **running** or for three days **running**. *He said drought had led to severe crop failure for the second year running... She changes her look so often that she never seems the same woman two days running.* ADJ: n ADJ =in a row, on the trot

6 **Running** water is water that is flowing rather than standing still. *The forest was filled with the sound of running water... Wash the lentils under cold running water.* ADJ: ADJ n

7 If a house has **running** water, water is supplied to the house through pipes and taps. *...a house without electricity or running water in a tiny African village.* ADJ: ADJ n

8 If someone is **in the running** for something, they have a good chance of winning or obtaining it. If they are **out of the running**, they have no chance of winning or obtaining it. *...the effort to persuade the American people that Bush was still in the running... Until this week he appeared to have ruled himself out of the running because of his age.* PHRASES usu v-link PHR

9 If someone **is making the running** in a situation, they are more active than the other people involved; used mainly in British English. *Republicans are furious that the Democrats currently seem to be making all the running.* V inflects

10 If something such as a system or place is **up and running**, it is operating normally. *We're trying to get the medical facilities up and running again.* v-link PHR, PHR after v

-running /-rʌnɪŋ/. **-running** combines with nouns to form nouns which refer to the illegal importing of drugs or guns. *...a serviceman suspected of drug-running.* COMB in N-UNCOUNT

running battle, running battles. When two groups of people fight a **running battle**, they keep attacking each other in various parts of a place. *They fought running battles in the narrow streets with police.* N-COUNT ≠pitched battle

running commentary, running commentaries. If someone provides a **running commentary** on an event, they give a continuous description of it whilst it is taking place. *John gave the police control room a running commentary on the driver's antics as he followed him at 90mph.* N-COUNT

running costs

1 The **running costs** of a business are the amount of money that is regularly spent on things such as salaries, heating, lighting, and rent. *The aim is to cut running costs by £90 million per year.* N-PLURAL =overheads

2 The **running costs** of an appliance such as a heater or a refrigerator are the amount of money that you spend on the gas, electricity, or other source of power which it uses. *Always buy a heater with thermostat control to save on running costs.* N-PLURAL

running mate, running mates. In an election campaign, a candidate's **running mate** is the person that they have chosen to have the next-ranking political office if they win. *...Clinton's selection of Al Gore as his running mate.* ◆◇◇◇◇ N-COUNT: oft poss N

running order. The **running order** of the items in a broadcast, concert, or show is the order in which the items will come. *John had seemed a little surprised that we had reversed the running order.* N-SING: usu *the* N

runny /rʌni/ **runnier, runniest** ◆◇◇◇◇

1 Something that is **runny** is more liquid than usual or than was intended. *Warm the honey until it becomes runny. ...a runny soft cheese.* ADJ-GRADED

2 If someone has a **runny** nose or **runny** eyes, liquid is flowing from their nose or eyes. *Symptoms are streaming eyes, a runny nose, headache and a cough.* ADJ-GRADED: usu ADJ n

run-off, run-offs; also spelled **runoff.**

1 A **run-off** is an extra vote or contest which is held in order to decide the winner of an election or competition, because no-one has yet clearly won. *There will be a run-off between these two candidates on December 9th... He claimed the title after beating the American Sean Moran in a run-off at Bradford. ...next month's presidential runoff election.* N-COUNT: usu sing, oft N *between* pl-n

2 **Run-off** is rainwater that forms a stream rather than being absorbed by the ground. *The sewers collected sewage and storm runoff and discharged it, untreated, into the harbour. ...runoff water flashing down a gully.* N-UNCOUNT

run-of-the-mill; also spelled **run of the mill.** A **run-of-the-mill** person or thing is very ordinary, with no special or interesting features; used showing disapproval. *I was just a very average run-of-the-mill kind of student... For many they clearly represent an alternative to run-of-the-mill estate cars.* ADJ-GRADED: usu ADJ n PRAGMATICS =ordinary

runt /rʌnt/ **runts**

1 The **runt** of a group of animals born to the same mother at the same time is the smallest and weakest of them. *Animals reject the runt of the litter.* N-COUNT: oft N *of* n

2 In informal British English, if you call a small person a **runt**, you are expressing your dislike for them. *You little runt!... My research owes nothing to anybody, least of all to a little runt like you.* N-COUNT PRAGMATICS

run-through, run-throughs. A **run-through** for a show or event is a rehearsal or practice for it. *Charles and Eddie are getting ready for their final run-through before the evening's recording.* N-COUNT =rehearsal

run-up, run-ups ◆◆◇◇◇

1 The **run-up** to an event is the period of time just before it. *The issue of the monarchy is complicating politics in the run-up to the elections... The company believes the products will sell well in the run-up to Christmas.* N-SING: usu *the* N *to* n

2 In sport, a **run-up** is a running approach made by a player or athlete, for example before throwing a ball or a javelin. *When I began to compete again, I was struggling with my run-up.* N-COUNT

runway /rʌnweɪ/ **runways.** At an airport, the **runway** is the long strip of ground with a hard surface which an aeroplane takes off from or lands on. *The plane started taxiing down the runway.* ◆◇◇◇◇ N-COUNT: usu *the* N

rupee /ruːpiː/ **rupees.** A **rupee** is a unit of money that is used in India, Pakistan, and some other countries. *He earns 20 rupees a day.* ◆◇◇◇◇ N-COUNT

rupture /rʌptʃər/ **ruptures, rupturing, ruptured** ◆◇◇◇◇

1 A **rupture** is a severe injury in which an internal part of your body tears or bursts open, especially the part between the bowels and the abdomen. N-COUNT

2 If a person or animal **ruptures** a part of their body or if it **ruptures**, it tears or bursts open. *His stomach might rupture from all the acid... Whilst playing badminton, I ruptured my Achilles tendon. ...a ruptured appendix.* V-ERG V V n V-ed

3 If you **rupture** yourself, you rupture a part of your body, usually because you have lifted something heavy. *He ruptured himself playing football.* VERB V pron-refl

4 If an object **ruptures** or if something **ruptures** it, it bursts open. *Certain truck gasoline tanks can rupture and burn in a collision... Sloshing liquids can rupture the walls of their containers.* V-ERG =burst V V n

5 A **rupture** between people is the severe worsening or ending of relations between them. *The incidents have not yet caused a major rupture in the political ties between countries. ...a rupture of the family unit.* N-COUNT: usu with supp

6 If someone or something **ruptures** relations between people, they damage them, causing them to become worse or to end. *Brutal clashes in Berlin between squatters and police yesterday ruptured the city's governing coalition between Social Democrats and Greens.* VERB =damage V n

rural /rʊərəl/ ◆◆◆◇◇

1 **Rural** places are far away from large towns or cities. *These plants have a tendency to grow in the more rural areas. ...the closure of rural schools.* ADJ-GRADED: usu ADJ n ≠urban

2 **Rural** means having features which are typical of areas that are far away from large towns or cities. *...the old rural way of life... He spoke with a heavy rural accent.* ADJ-GRADED: ADJ n

ruse /ruːz, AM ruːs/ **ruses.** A **ruse** is an action or plan which is intended to deceive someone; a formal word. *It is now clear that this was a ruse to divide them.* ◆◇◇◇◇ N-COUNT

rush /rʌʃ/ **rushes, rushing, rushed** ◆◆◆◇◇

1 If you **rush** somewhere, you go there quickly. *A schoolgirl rushed into a burning flat to save a man's life... Someone inside the building rushed out... I've got to rush. Got a meeting in a few minutes... Shop staff rushed to get help.* VERB =dash, hurry V prep/adv V V to-inf

2 If people **rush** to do something, they do it as soon as they can, because they are very eager to do it. *Russian banks rushed to buy as many dollars as they could... Before you rush to book a table, bear in mind that lunch for two would cost £100.* VERB =hurry V to-inf

3 A **rush** is a situation in which you need to go somewhere or do something very quickly. *The men left in a rush... It was all rather a rush... Then there was the mad rush not to be late for school.* N-SING

4 If there is a **rush** for something, many people suddenly try to get it or do it. *Record stores are expecting a huge rush for the single. ...the rush for contracts.* N-SING: usu N *for* n

5 The **rush** is a period of time when many people go somewhere or do something. *The shop's opening coincided with the Christmas rush... Apply before the rush starts. ...the annual rush to the beaches.* N-SING: *the* N, oft supp N

6 If you **rush** something, you do it in a hurry, often too quickly and without much care. *You can't rush a search... Chew your food well and do not rush meals... Instead of rushing at life, I wanted something more meaningful.* ♦ **rushed** *The report had all the hallmarks of a rushed job.* VERB V n V *at* n ADJ-GRADED

7 If you **rush** someone or something to a place, you take them there quickly. *We got an ambulance and rushed her to hospital... Federal agents rushed him into a car... We'll rush it round today if possible.* VERB V n prep V n with adv

8 If you **rush** into something or **are rushed** into it, you do it without thinking about it for long enough. *He will not rush into any decisions... They had rushed in without adequate appreciation of the task... Ministers won't be rushed into a response... Don't rush him or he'll become confused.* ♦ **rushed** *At no time did I feel rushed or under pressure.* V-ERG V *into* n V *in* *be* V-ed *into* n V n ADJ-GRADED: usu v-link ADJ

9 If you **rush** something or someone, you move quickly and forcefully at them, often in order to attack them. *They rushed the entrance and forced their way in... Tom came rushing at him from another direction.* VERB V n V *at* n

10 If air or liquid **rushes** somewhere, it flows there suddenly and quickly. *Water rushes out of huge tunnels... The air was rushing past us all the time. ...the sound of rushing water.* ► Also a noun. *A rush of air on my face woke me. ...the perpetual rush of the mill stream.* VERB V prep/adv V-ing N-COUNT: usu sing, with supp

11 If you experience a **rush** of a feeling, you suddenly experience it very strongly. *A rush of pure affection swept over him... He felt a sudden rush of panic at the thought.* N-COUNT: usu sing, with supp

12 **Rushes** are plants with long thin stems that grow near water. N-PLURAL

13 The **rushes** of a film are the parts of it that have been filmed but have not yet been edited; a technical term in film-making. N-PLURAL

14 If you are **rushed off your feet**, you are extremely busy; an informal expression. *We used to be rushed off our feet at lunchtimes.* PHRASE: usu v-link PHR

rush out. If a document or product **is rushed out**, it is produced very quickly. *A statement was rushed out... Studios are rushing out monster movies to take advantage of our new-found enthusiasm for dinosaurs.* PHRASAL VERB *be* V-ed P V P n (not pron) Also V n P

rush through. If you **rush** something **through**, you deal with it quickly so that it is ready in a shorter time than usual. *The government rushed through legislation aimed at Mafia leaders... They rushed the burial through so no evidence would show up.* PHRASAL VERB V P n (not pron) V n P

rush hour, rush hours; also spelled **rush-hour.** The **rush hour** is one of the periods of the day when most people are travelling to or from work. *During the evening rush hour it was often solid with vehicles... Try to avoid rush-hour traffic... I had to drive eight miles at rush hour.* ◆◇◇◇◇ N-COUNT: also *at/during* N

rusk /rʌsk/ **rusks. Rusks** are hard, dry biscuits that are given to babies and young children; used mainly in British English. N-VAR

russet /rʌsɪt/ **russets. Russet** is used to describe things that are reddish-brown in colour. *...a russet apple... The maple trees were in their autumn glory of russets, reds and browns.* COLOUR

Russian /rʌʃən/ **Russians** ◆◆◆◆◇

1 **Russian** means belonging or relating to Russia, or to its people, language, or culture. *...the Russian parliament. ...Russian dolls.* ADJ

2 A **Russian** is a Russian citizen, or a person of Russian origin. *Three-quarters of Russians live in cities.* N-COUNT

Russian roulette

1 If you say that someone is playing **Russian roulette**, or that what they are doing is like playing **Russian roulette**, you mean that what they are doing is very dangerous because it involves unpredictable risks. *You are playing Russian roulette every time you have unprotected sex.* N-UNCOUNT

2 If someone plays **Russian roulette**, they fire a N-UNCOUNT

gun with only one bullet at their head without knowing whether it will release the bullet.

rust /rʌst/ **rusts, rusting, rusted** ◆◇◇◇◇

1 **Rust** is a brown substance that forms on iron or steel when it comes into contact with water. *...a decaying tractor, red with rust... Manufacturers are looking into building cars out of plastic to avoid the problem of rust.* N-UNCOUNT

2 When a metal object **rusts**, it becomes covered in rust and often loses its strength. *Copper nails are better than iron nails because the iron rusts... There was an old rusting bolt on the door.* VERB V V-ing

3 **Rust** is sometimes used to describe things that are reddish-brown in colour. *...turquoise woodwork with accent colours of rust and ochre. ...a rust-coloured blouse.* COLOUR

4 **Rust** is a disease which affects plants. It is caused by a fungus. N-UNCOUNT

rust away. When a metal object **rusts away**, it is gradually weakened and destroyed by rust. *...an old car which had been rusting away for years.* PHRASAL VERB V P

Rust Belt. In the United States and some other countries, **the Rust Belt** is a region which used to have a lot of manufacturing industry, but which is now in economic decline. *...in the rust belt of the mid-west.* N-SING: the N

rustic /rʌstɪk/ **rustics** ◆◇◇◇◇

1 You can use **rustic** to describe things or people that you approve of because they are simple or unsophisticated in a way that is typical of the countryside. *...the rustic charm of a country life-style. ...a half dozen or so wonderfully rustic old log cabins.* ADJ-GRADED: usu ADJ n PRAGMATICS

2 You can refer to someone who comes from the countryside as a **rustic** if you find their behaviour amusing or very different from that of people who live in towns and cities. *...lots of opera-loving Italian rustics in from the country.* N-COUNT

rusticity /rʌstɪsɪti/. You can refer approvingly to the simple, peaceful character of life in the countryside as **rusticity**; used in written English. *It pleases me to think of young Tyndale growing up here in deep rusticity.* N-UNCOUNT PRAGMATICS

rustle /rʌsᵊl/ **rustles, rustling, rustled** ◆◇◇◇◇

1 When something thin and dry **rustles** or when you **rustle** it, it makes soft sounds as it moves. *The leaves rustled in the wind... She rustled her papers impatiently... A snake rustled through the dry grass.* V-ERG V V n V prep

► Also a noun. *She sat perfectly still, without even a rustle of her frilled petticoats.* ♦ **rustling, rustlings** *We were all terrified by a rustling sound coming from beneath one of the seats. ...the rustlings of women's dresses.* N-COUNT N-VAR: oft N of n

2 See also **rustling**.

rustle up PHRASAL VERB

1 If you **rustle up** something to eat or drink, you make or prepare it quickly, with very little planning. *Let's see if somebody can rustle up a cup of coffee... Many tasty and nutritious meals can be rustled up in next to no time.* V P n (not pron)

2 If you **rustle** something **up**, you provide or obtain it quickly, with very little planning; an informal use. *He managed to rustle up a couple of blankets... He has had no trouble rustling up 35 friends and colleagues to invite to his wedding.*

rustler /rʌsləʳ/ **rustlers.** **Rustlers** are thieves who steal farm animals, especially cattle; used especially in American English. *...the old Wyoming Trail once used by cattle rustlers and outlaws.* N-COUNT: usu pl, oft n N

rustling /rʌsəlɪŋ/

1 **Rustling** is the activity of stealing farm animals, especially cattle; used especially in American English. *Her thievery was confined mostly to cattle rustling and horse stealing.* N-UNCOUNT: usu n N

2 See also **rustle**.

rusty /rʌsti/ **rustier, rustiest** ◆◇◇◇◇

1 A **rusty** metal object such as a car or a machine has a lot of rust on it. *We spent years travelling around in a rusty old van. ...a rusty iron gate.* ADJ-GRADED: usu ADJ n

2 If a skill that you have or your knowledge of something is **rusty**, it is not as good as it used to be, because you have not used it for a long time. *...skills which have gone rusty since the previous winter... You may be a little rusty, but past experience and teaching skills won't have been lost.* ADJ-GRADED

3 **Rusty** is sometimes used to describe things that are reddish-brown in colour. *Her hair was rusty brown.* ADJ

rut /rʌt/ **ruts** ◆◇◇◇◇

1 If you say that someone is in a **rut**, you disapprove of the fact that they have become fixed in their way of thinking and doing things, and find it difficult to change. You can also say that someone's life or career is in a **rut**. *I don't like being in a rut - I like to keep moving on... Many over 30s feel stuck in a financial rut.* N-COUNT: usu sing, usu in a N PRAGMATICS

2 A **rut** is a deep, narrow mark made in the ground by the wheels of a vehicle. *Our driver slowed up as we approached the ruts in the road. ...the deep ruts left by the trucks' heavy wheels.* N-COUNT: oft N in n

3 The **rut** is the period of the year when some animals such as deer are sexually active, and males fight each other before mating with the females. *...two elks sparring during the autumn rut. ...a stag in rut.* N-SING: usu the N, also in N

4 See also **rutted, rutting**.

rutabaga /ruːtəbeɪgə/ **rutabagas.** In American English, a **rutabaga** is a round yellow root vegetable with a brown or purple skin. The usual British word is **swede**. N-VAR

ruthless /ruːθləs/ ◆◆◇◇◇

1 If you say that someone is **ruthless**, you mean that you disapprove of them because they are very harsh or cruel, and will do anything that is necessary to achieve what they want. *The President was ruthless in dealing with any hint of internal political dissent. ...an invasion by a ruthless totalitarian power... The late newspaper tycoon is condemned for his ruthless treatment of employees.* ADJ-GRADED: oft ADJ in n PRAGMATICS =merciless, callous

♦ **ruthlessly** *The Party has ruthlessly crushed any sign of organised opposition.* ♦ **ruthlessness** *...a powerful political figure with a reputation for ruthlessness.* ADV-GRADED: ADV with v N-UNCOUNT

2 A **ruthless** action or activity is done forcefully and thoroughly, without much concern for its effects on other people. *Her lawyers have been ruthless in thrashing out a divorce settlement... Successfully merging two banks requires a fast and ruthless attack on costs.* ♦ **ruthlessly** *Ghislaine showed signs of turning into the ruthlessly efficient woman her father wanted her to be.* ♦ **ruthlessness** *...a woman with a brain and business acumen and a certain healthy ruthlessness.* ADJ-GRADED: oft ADJ in n ADV-GRADED N-UNCOUNT

rutted /rʌtɪd/

1 A **rutted** road or track is very uneven because it has a lot of ruts in it. *...an agonisingly slow and uncomfortable ride along the deeply rutted roads.* ADJ-GRADED: oft adv ADJ

2 See also **rut**.

rutting /rʌtɪŋ/

1 **Rutting** male animals such as deer are in a period of sexual excitement and activity. *...jokes about bitches in heat and rutting stags.* ► Also a noun. *During the rutting season the big boars have the most terrible mating battles.* ADJ N-UNCOUNT: oft N n

2 See also **rut**.

RV /ɑːʳ viː/ **RVs.** In American English, an **RV** is a van which is equipped with such things as beds and cooking equipment, so that people can live in it, usually while they are on holiday. RV is an abbreviation for 'recreational vehicle'. The usual British term is **camper**. *...a group of RVs pulled over on the side of the highway.* N-COUNT

rye /raɪ/ ◆◇◇◇◇

1 **Rye** is a cereal grown in cold countries. Its grains can be used to make flour, bread, or other foods. *One of the first crops that I grew when we came here was rye. ...100g wholemeal or rye flour.* N-UNCOUNT: oft N n

2 You can refer to rye bread as **rye**, especially when you are buying or ordering a sandwich; used especially in American English. *I was eating ham and Swiss cheese on rye.* N-UNCOUNT: usu on N

rye bread. **Rye bread** is brown bread made with rye flour. *...two slices of rye bread.* N-UNCOUNT

S s

S, s /es/ **S's, s's**

1 S is the nineteenth letter of the English alphabet. N-VAR

2 S or s is an abbreviation for words beginning with s, such as 'south', 'seconds', and 'son'.

3 **s.** was a written abbreviation for **shilling** or **shillings** in Britain before decimal currency was introduced in 1971.

-s; also spelled **-es**. The suffix **-s** is pronounced /-s/ after the consonant sounds /p, t, k, f/ or /θ/. After other sounds **-s** is pronounced /-z/. The suffix **-es** is pronounced /-z/ after vowel sounds, and /-ɪz/ after consonant sounds.

1 **-s** or **-es** is added to a noun to form a plural. *...her two beloved cats. ...a few problems. ...new houses and flats... Most bosses are traditional.* SUFFIX

2 **-s** or **-es** is added to a verb to form the third person singular, present tense. *He never thinks about it... She likes her job... No-one wishes to see that.* SUFFIX

-'s. Pronounced /-s/ after the consonant sounds /p, t, k, f/ or /θ/, and /-ɪz/ after the consonant sounds /s, z, ʃ, ʒ, tʃ/ or /dʒ/. After other sounds **-'s** is pronounced /-z/. A final **-s'** is pronounced in the same way as a final **-s.**

1 **-'s** is added to nouns to form possessives. However, with plural nouns ending in '-s', and sometimes with names ending in '-s', you form the possessive by adding -'. *...the chairman's son. ...Britain's coal mines. ...women's rights. ...a boys' boarding-school. ...Sir Charles' car.*

2 **-'s** is the shortened form of 'is' in spoken or informal English. For example, 'he is' can be shortened to 'he's'. *She's a counselor... It's a disaster... That's right... There's plenty of time.*

3 **-'s** is the shortened form of 'has' in spoken or informal English, especially where 'has' is an auxiliary verb. For example, 'It has gone' can be shortened to 'It's gone'. *It's been a great experience... He's got a four year contract... There's been a lot of rewriting.*

4 **-'s** is sometimes added to numbers, letters, and abbreviations to form plurals, although many people think you should just add '-s'. *...new strategies for the 1990's. ...p's and q's.*

sab /sæb/ **sabs.** Some people refer to the people who try to stop blood sports such as fox hunting as a **sab**; an informal word. **Sab** is short for saboteur. *One sab was threatened with arrest for shouting too loud.* N-COUNT =saboteur

Sabbath /sæbəθ/. The **Sabbath** is the day of the week when members of some religious groups do not work. The Jewish Sabbath is on Saturday and the Christian Sabbath is on Sunday. *...a deeply religious man who will not discuss politics on the Sabbath... Remember the Sabbath day, to keep it holy.* N-PROPER: *the*N, oftN n

sabbatical /səbætɪkəl/ **sabbaticals.** A **sabbatical** is a period of time during which someone such as a teacher or university lecturer can leave their ordinary work and travel or study. *He took a year's sabbatical from the Foreign Office... He's been on sabbatical writing a novel.* N-COUNT: also *on*N

saber /seɪbəʳ/. See **sabre.**

sable /seɪbəl/. **sables** A **sable** is a small furry animal with valued fur. ► **Sable** is the fur of a sable. *...her full-length sable coat with matching hat.* N-COUNT; N-UNCOUNT: oftN n

sabotage /sæbətɑːʒ/ **sabotages, sabotaging, sabotaged** ◆◇◇◇◇

1 If a machine, railway line, or bridge **is sabotaged,** it is deliberately damaged or destroyed, for example in a war or as a protest. *The main pipeline supplying water was sabotaged by rebels.* ► Also a noun. *The bombing was a spectacular act of sabotage.* VB: usu passive beV-ed; N-UNCOUNT

2 If someone **sabotages** a plan or a meeting, they deliberately prevent it from being successful. *He accused the opposition of doing everything they could to sabotage the election... My ex-wife deliberately sabotages my access to the children.* VERB V n

saboteur /sæbətɜːʳ/ **saboteurs.** A **saboteur** is a person who deliberately damages or destroys things such as machines, railway lines, and bridges in order to weaken the enemy or to make a protest. People who try to stop blood sports such as fox hunting are also referred to as **saboteurs.** *The saboteurs had planned to bomb buses and offices. ...a confrontation between huntsmen and saboteurs.* ◆◇◇◇◇ N-COUNT

sabre /seɪbəʳ/ **sabres;** spelled **saber** in American English. A **sabre** is a heavy sword with a curved blade that was formerly used by soldiers on horseback. ◆◇◇◇◇ N-COUNT

sabre-rattling. If you describe a threat, especially a threat of military action, as **sabre-rattling,** you do not believe that the threat will actually be carried out. *It is too early to say whether the threats are mere sabre-rattling. ...sabre-rattling by the military.* N-UNCOUNT PRAGMATICS

sac /sæk/ **sacs.** A **sac** is a small part of an animal's body, shaped like a little bag. It contains air, liquid, or some other substance. *The lungs consist of millions of tiny air sacs.* ◆◇◇◇◇ N-COUNT

saccharin /sækərɪn/; also spelled **saccharine. Saccharin** is a very sweet chemical substance that some people use instead of sugar, especially when they are trying to lose weight. N-UNCOUNT

saccharine /sækərɪn, -riːn/. You describe something as **saccharine** when you find it unpleasantly sweet and sentimental. *...a saccharine-sweet, nostalgic sequel to the Peter Pan story... She smiled with saccharine sweetness.* ADJ-GRADED: usu ADJ n =sickly

sachet /sæʃeɪ, AM sæʃeɪ/ **sachets.** A **sachet** is a small closed plastic or paper packet, containing a very small quantity of something. *...individual sachets of instant coffee.* N-COUNT: oftN *of*n =packet

sack /sæk/ **sacks, sacking, sacked** ◆◆◆◇◇

1 A **sack** is a large bag made of rough woven material. Sacks are used to carry or store things such as vegetables or coal. *...a sack of potatoes.* N-COUNT: oftN *of*n

2 If your employers **sack** you, they tell you that you can no longer work for them because you have done something that they did not like or because your work was not good enough. *Earlier today the Prime Minister sacked 18 government officials for corruption... Science teacher James Wood was sacked for slapping a schoolboy.* ► Also a noun. *People who make mistakes can be given the sack the same day.* VERB =fire, dismiss V n; N-SING: *the*N

3 When an army **sacks** a town or city, they destroy it, taking away all valuable things. *In 1527 Imperial troops sacked the French ambassador's residence in Rome.* ► Also a noun. *The Odyssey tells what happened to the Greek heroes after the sack of Troy.* VERB =destroy V n; N-SING: *the*N *of*n =destruction

4 Some people refer to bed as **the sack**; used mainly in informal American English. N-SING: *the*N

sackcloth /sækklɒθ/

1 **Sackcloth** is rough woven material that is used to make sacks. *He kept the club wrapped in sackcloth.* N-UNCOUNT =hessian

2 If you talk about **sackcloth** or **sackcloth and ashes** you are referring to an exaggerated attempt by someone to apologize or compensate for doing something wrong. *I swore I would forgo silk nighties, and would wear sackcloth and ashes.* N-UNCOUNT

sackful /sækfʊl/ **sackfuls.** A **sackful** is the amount of something held by a sack. *...a sackful of presents... Letters and cards of support have been pouring in by the sackful.* N-COUNT: oft N *of* n =sack

sacking /sækɪŋ/ **sackings** ◆◇◇◇◇

1 **Sacking** is rough woven material that is used to make sacks. N-UNCOUNT =hessian

2 A **sacking** is the dismissal of a person from their job. *...the sacking of twenty-three-thousand miners.* N-COUNT =dismissal

sacrament /sækrəmənt/ **sacraments**

1 A **sacrament** is a Christian religious ceremony such as communion, baptism, or marriage. *...the holy sacrament of baptism.* N-COUNT

2 In the Roman Catholic church, **the Sacrament** is the holy bread eaten at the Eucharist. In the Anglican church, **the Sacrament** is the holy bread and wine taken at Holy Communion. N-SING: *the* N

sacramental /sækrəmentᵊl/

1 Something that is **sacramental** is connected with the sacraments. *...the sacramental wine.* ADJ

2 **Sacramental** is also used to describe something that is considered holy or religious. *The genuine sacramental pilgrimage.* ADJ =religious

sacred /seɪkrɪd/ ◆◆◇◇◇

1 Something that is **sacred** is believed to be holy and to have a special connection with God. *The owl is sacred for many Californian Indian people. ...shrines and sacred places.* ADJ-GRADED ≠profane, secular ♦ **sacredness** *...the sacredness of the site.* N-UNCOUNT: oft *the* N *of* n

2 Something connected with religion or used in religious ceremonies is described as **sacred**. *...sacred art. ...sacred songs or music.* ADJ: ADJ n

3 You can describe something as **sacred** when it is regarded as too important to be changed or interfered with. *My memories are sacred... He said the unity of the country was sacred.* ADJ-GRADED =sacrosanct ♦ **sacredness** *...the sacredness of his given word.* N-UNCOUNT

sacred cow, sacred cows. If you describe a belief, custom, or institution as a **sacred cow**, you disapprove of people treating it with too much respect and being afraid to criticize or question it. *...the sacred cow of monetarism.* N-COUNT

sacrifice /sækrɪfaɪs/ **sacrifices, sacrificing, sacrificed** ◆◆◆◇◇

1 To **sacrifice** an animal or person means to kill them in a special religious ceremony as an offering to a god. *The priest sacrificed a chicken... Two white bulls were sacrificed and a feast was held.* ► Also a noun. *...animal sacrifices to the gods.* VERB; V n; Also V n *to* n; N-COUNT

2 If you **sacrifice** something that is valuable or important, you give it up, usually to obtain something else for yourself or for other people. *She sacrificed family life to her career... Her husband's pride was a small thing to sacrifice for their children's security... Kitty Aldridge has sacrificed all for her first film... He sacrificed himself and so saved his country.* ► Also a noun. *She made many sacrifices to get Anita a good education... He was willing to make any sacrifice for peace.* ● See also **self-sacrifice.** VERB =give up; V n *to/for* n; V *to/for* n; V n; V pron-refl; N-VAR

sacrificial /sækrɪfɪʃᵊl/. **Sacrificial** means connected with or used in a sacrifice. *...the sacrificial altar. ...a sacrificial victim.* ADJ: ADJ n

sacrificial lamb, sacrificial lambs. If you refer to someone as a **sacrificial lamb**, you mean that they have been blamed unfairly for something they did not do or for which they are only partly responsible, usually in order to protect another more powerful person or people. *He was a sacrificial lamb to a system that destroyed him.* N-COUNT PRAGMATICS =scapegoat

sacrilege /sækrɪlɪdʒ/

1 **Sacrilege** is behaviour that shows great disrespect for a holy place or object. *For centuries, stealing from a place of worship was regarded as sacrilege.* N-UNCOUNT: also *a* N

2 You can use **sacrilege** to refer to disrespect that is shown for someone who is widely admired or for a belief that is widely accepted. *It is a sacrilege to offend democracy.* N-UNCOUNT: also *a* N

sacrilegious /sækrɪlɪdʒəs/. If someone's behaviour or actions are **sacrilegious**, they show great disrespect towards something holy or towards something that people think should be respected. *A number of churches were sacked and sacrilegious acts committed.* ADJ-GRADED

sacristy /sækrɪsti/ **sacristies.** A **sacristy** is the room in a church where the priest or minister changes into official clothes and where sacred objects are kept. N-COUNT

sacrosanct /sækroʊsæŋkt/. If you describe something as **sacrosanct**, you consider it to be special and are unwilling to see it criticized or changed. *Freedom of the press is sacrosanct and should remain so. ...weekend rest days were considered sacrosanct.* ADJ-GRADED: usu v-link ADJ =sacred

sad /sæd/ **sadder, saddest** ◆◆◆◆◇

1 If you are **sad**, you feel unhappy, usually because something has happened that you do not like. *The relationship had been important to me and its loss left me feeling sad and empty... I'm sad that Julie's marriage is on the verge of splitting up... I'd grown fond of our little house and felt sad to leave it... I'm sad about my toys getting burned in the fire.* ADJ-GRADED: oft ADJ that/to-inf, ADJ *about* n =unhappy ≠happy ♦ **sadly** *...a gallant man who will be sadly missed by all his comrades... He could not help adding sadly: 'I'm desperately upset not to be playing for Queensland.'* ADV-GRADED: usu ADV with v ≠happily ♦ **sadness** *It is with a mixture of sadness and joy that I say farewell.* N-UNCOUNT ≠happiness

2 **Sad** stories and **sad** news make you feel sad. *...a desperately humorous, impossibly sad novel... Yesterday, I received the sad news that one of them had been killed in a motor-cycle accident.* ADJ-GRADED: usu ADJ n

3 A **sad** event or situation is unfortunate or undesirable. *It's a sad truth that children are the biggest victims of passive smoking.* ADJ-GRADED ♦ **sadly** *Sadly, bamboo plants die after flowering... The vast majority of special care babies grow up to be perfectly healthy but, sadly, a few don't survive.* ADV: usu ADV adj, ADV with cl

4 If you describe someone as **sad**, you do not have any respect for them and think their behaviour or ideas are ridiculous; an informal use. *...sad old bikers and youngsters who think that Jim Morrison is God.* ADJ-GRADED: usu ADJ n =pathetic

5 You can use the expression **sad to say** when you are describing an situation which you find unfortunate. *How does a suffering alcoholic get into one of these hospitals? Sad to say, there are not very many of them around... He died five or six years ago I'm sad to say.* PHRASE: PHR with cl PRAGMATICS

sadden /sædᵊn/ **saddens, saddened.** If something **saddens** you, it makes you feel sad. *The cruelty in the world saddens me incredibly.* ◆◇◇◇◇ VB: no cont; V n ♦ **saddened** *He was disappointed and saddened that legal argument had stopped the trial.* ADJ-GRADED: v-link ADJ ♦ **saddening** *I find public squalor very saddening. ...a saddening experience.* ADJ-GRADED

saddle /sædᵊl/ **saddles, saddling, saddled** ◆◆◇◇◇

1 A **saddle** is a leather seat that you put on the back of an animal so that you can ride the animal. ● See also **side-saddle.** N-COUNT

2 If you **saddle** a horse or pony, you put a saddle on it so that you can ride it. *Why don't we saddle a couple of horses and go for a ride?* ► **Saddle up** means the same as **saddle.** *I want to be gone from here as soon as we can saddle up... She saddled up a horse.* VERB; V n; PHRASAL VERB; V P; V P n (not pron)

3 A **saddle** is a seat on a bicycle or motorcycle. N-COUNT

4 A **saddle** of lamb, hare, or venison is a large joint of meat taken from the middle of the animal's back. N-COUNT: usu N *of* n

5 If you **saddle** someone with a problem or with a responsibility, you put them in a position where they have to deal with it. *The war devastated the economy and saddled the country with a huge foreign debt.* VERB =lumber with; V n *with* n

6 If you are **in the saddle**, you are riding a horse. *When I watch horse racing on television, I wish I was back in the saddle.* PHRASES

7 If you are **in the saddle**, you are in power or in =in control

control of a situation. *The armed forces and the hardliners are now going to be in the saddle.*

saddle up. See **saddle** 2. PHRASAL VERB

saddlebag /sædəlbæg/ **saddlebags;** also spelled **saddle-bag.** A **saddlebag** is a bag fastened to the saddle of bicycle or motorcycle. N-COUNT =pannier

saddler /sædləʳ/ **saddlers.** A **saddler** is a person who makes, repairs, and sells saddles and other equipment for riding horses. N-COUNT

saddlery /sædləri/. Saddles and other leather goods made by a saddler can be referred to as **saddlery.** N-UNCOUNT

sadism /seɪdɪzəm/. **Sadism** is a type of behaviour in which a person obtains pleasure from hurting other people and making them suffer physically or mentally. *Psychoanalysts tend to regard both sadism and masochism as arising from childhood deprivation.* N-UNCOUNT ♦ **sadist** /seɪdɪst/ **sadists** *The man was a sadist who tortured animals and people.* N-COUNT

sadistic /sədɪstɪk/. A **sadistic** person obtains pleasure from hurting other people and making them suffer physically or mentally. *The prisoners rioted against mistreatment by sadistic guards and a starvation diet... There was a sadistic streak in him.* ◆◇◇◇◇ ADJ-GRADED ♦ **sadistically** /sədɪstɪkli/ *Many were killed, often most sadistically.* ADV-GRADED

sado-masochism /seɪdoʊ mæsəkɪzəm/; also spelled **sadomasochism. Sado-masochism** is the enjoyment by a person of both sadism and masochism. *...the sado-masochism of the Marquis de Sade.* N-UNCOUNT ♦ **sado-masochist** N-COUNT

sado-masochistic /seɪdoʊ mæsəkɪstɪk/; also spelled **sadomasochistic.** Something that is described as **sado-masochistic** is connected with the practice of sado-masochism. *...a sado-masochistic relationship.* ADJ-GRADED: usu ADJ n

s.a.e. /es eɪ iː/ **s.a.e.s.** An **s.a.e.** is an envelope on which you have stuck a stamp and written your own name and address. You send it to a person or organization so that they can send you something such as information in it. s.a.e. is an abbreviation for 'stamped addressed envelope' or 'self addressed envelope'. *Send an s.a.e. for a free information pack.* N-COUNT

safari /səfɑːri/ **safaris.** A **safari** is an expedition for observing or hunting wild animals, especially in East Africa. *He'd like to go on safari to photograph snakes and tigers.* ◆◆◇◇◇ N-COUNT: also *on* N

safari park, safari parks. In Britain, a **safari park** is a large enclosed area of land where wild animals, such as lions and elephants, live freely. People can pay to drive through the park and look at the animals. N-COUNT

safari suit, safari suits. A **safari suit** is a casual suit made from a light-coloured material such as linen or cotton. Safari suits are usually worn in hot weather. N-COUNT

safe /seɪf/ **safer, safest; safes** ◆◆◆◆◇

1 Something that is **safe** does not cause physical harm or danger. *Officials arrived to assess whether it is safe to bring emergency food supplies into the city... Most foods that we eat are safe for birds. ...a safe and reliable birth control option. ...a programme to make Russian nuclear reactors safer.* ADJ-GRADED: oft *it* v-link ADJ to-inf ≠dangerous

2 If someone or something is **safe** from something, they cannot be harmed or damaged by it. *In the future people can go to a football match knowing that they are safe from hooliganism... On beaches, keep your camera safe from sand by enveloping it inside a plastic bag... Crime Prevention Officers can visit your home and suggest ways to make it safer.* ADJ-GRADED: v-link ADJ, usu ADJ *from* n ≠at risk

3 If you are **safe**, you have not been harmed, or you are not in danger of being harmed. *Where is Sophy? Is she safe?... A baby boy is safe after rescue workers pulled him from a 12-foot-deep construction hole... He kissed me twice and I realized suddenly that I felt warm and safe.* ADJ-GRADED: v-link ADJ ♦ **safely** *All 140 guests were brought out of the building safely by firemen.* ADV: ADV with v

4 A **safe** place is one where it is unlikely that any harm, damage, or unpleasant things will happen to the people or things that are there. *The continuing tension has prompted more than half the inhabitants of the refugee camp to flee to safer areas... The elimination of all nuclear weapons would make the world a safer place... We shall take the treasure away to a safe place.* ADJ-GRADED ♦ **safely** *The banker keeps the money tucked safely under his bed.* ADV-GRADED: ADV after v

5 If people or things have a **safe** journey, they reach their destination without harm, damage, or unpleasant things happening to them. *'I'm heading back to Ireland again for another weekend.'—'Have a safe journey.' ...the UN plan to deploy 500 troops to ensure the safe delivery of food and other supplies.* ADJ: ADJ n ♦ **safely** *The space shuttle returned safely today from a 10-day mission... Once Mrs Armsby was safely home, she called the police again.* ADV: ADV with v, ADV adv

6 If you are at a **safe** distance from something or someone, you are far enough away from them to avoid any danger, harm, or unpleasant effects. *I shall conceal myself at a safe distance from the battlefield... He thinks he can find a way to vaccinate the elephants from a safe distance.* ADJ: ADJ n

7 If something you have or expect to obtain is **safe,** you cannot lose it or be prevented from having it. *We as consumers need to feel confident that our jobs are safe before we will spend spare cash... Is the National Health Service safe with the Conservative party?... Rovers made the game safe with a spectacular second goal in the 84th minute.* ADJ-GRADED: usu v-link ADJ =secure

8 A **safe** course of action is one in which there is very little risk of loss or failure. *Electricity shares are still a safe investment... It might not be safe politically for the President to leave the country.* ADJ-GRADED: usu ADJ n, also *it* v-link ADJ to-inf ♦ **safely** *We reveal only as much information as we can safely risk at a given time.* ADV: usu ADV before v

9 If you disapprove of something that someone chooses to do because you think it is not very adventurous, interesting, or original, you can describe it as **safe.** *...frustrated artists who became lawyers at an early age because it seemed a safe option... Rock'n'roll has become so commercialised and safe since punk.* ADJ-GRADED PRAGMATICS

10 If it is **safe** to say or assume something, you can say it with very little risk of being wrong. *I think it is safe to say that very few students expend the effort to do quality work in school... It is a safe assumption that modern terrorists are not suicidal, and will not be on board a bombed plane.* ADJ-GRADED: oft *it* v-link ADJ to-inf PRAGMATICS ♦ **safely** *If I go to a grocer I know and trust, I can safely assume the eggs will be fresh... I think you can safely say she will not be appearing in another of my films.* ADV-GRADED: ADV before v PRAGMATICS

11 If you say to someone that their secret is **safe** with you, you are promising not to tell it to anyone. *Don't worry, Mr Palin, your secret is safe with me.* ADJ-GRADED: usu v-link ADJ, usu ADJ *with* n

12 A **safe** is a strong metal cupboard with special locks, in which you keep money, jewellery, or other valuable things. *The files are now in a safe to which only he has the key.* N-COUNT

13 See also **safely, safe seat.**

14 If you say that someone or something is **in safe hands,** or is **safe in** someone's **hands,** you mean that they are being looked after by a reliable person and will not be harmed or damaged. *I had a huge responsibility to ensure these packets remained in safe hands... Don't worry, Uncle Tim, your future is safe in our hands.* PHRASES usu v-link PHR

15 If you say that something or someone is **as safe as houses,** you mean that they are completely safe. *The Government insisted that Britain's nuclear power stations are as safe as houses.* usu v-link PHR

16 If you refer to someone's attempts to **make** a place **safe for** a particular activity, you mean that they intend to make the place suitable for the activity to be successful, but that their efforts may have some very undesirable effects. *Why did these men fight and die? Supposedly it was to make the world safe for democracy.* V inflects, PHR n

17 If you **play safe** or **play it safe,** you do not take any risks. *If you want to play safe, cut down on the amount of salt you eat... The pilot decided that Christchurch was too far away, and played it safe and landed at Wellington.* V inflects

18 If you say you are doing something **to be on the** PHR with cl

safe side, you mean that you are doing it as a precaution, in case something unexpected or unpleasant happens. *You might still want to go for an X-ray, however, just to be on the safe side.*
19 If you say **'it's better to be safe than sorry'**, you are advising someone to take precautions in order to avoid possible unpleasant consequences later, even if these precautions might seem a waste of time. *Don't be afraid to have this checked by a doctor – better safe than sorry!*
20 You say that someone is **safe and sound** when they are still alive or unharmed after being in danger. *All I'm hoping for is that wherever Trevor is he will come home safe and sound.* PHR after v, v-link PHR
21 • **a safe pair of hands**: see **hands**. • **safe in the knowledge**: see **knowledge**.

safe area, safe areas. If part of a country that is involved in a war is declared or designated a **safe area**, neutral forces will try to keep peace there so that it is safe for people. *The UN declared it a safe area.* ◆◇◇◇◇ N-COUNT

safe conduct; also spelled **safe-conduct**. If you are given **safe conduct**, the authorities officially allow you to travel somewhere, guaranteeing that you will not be arrested or harmed while doing so. *Her family was given safe conduct to Britain when civil war broke out. ...a guarantee of safe conduct signed personally by General Williams.* N-UNCOUNT: also a N

safe deposit box, safe deposit boxes; also spelled **safe-deposit box**. A **safe deposit box** is a small box, usually kept in a special room in a bank, in which you can store valuable objects. N-COUNT

safeguard /seɪfgɑːʳd/ **safeguards, safeguarding, safeguarded** ◆◆◇◇◇
1 To **safeguard** something or someone means to protect them from being harmed, lost, or badly treated; a formal use. *They will press for international action to safeguard the ozone layer... The interests of minorities will have to be safeguarded under a new constitution... They are taking precautionary measures to safeguard their forces from the effects of chemical weapons.* VERB =protect V n V n *from* n
2 A **safeguard** is a law, rule, or measure intended to prevent someone or something from being harmed. *As an additional safeguard against weeds you can always use an underlay of heavy duty polythene... A system like ours lacks adequate safeguards for civil liberties.* N-COUNT: oft N *against* n

safe haven, safe havens ◆◇◇◇◇
1 If part of a country is declared a **safe haven**, people who need to escape from a dangerous situation such as a war can go there and be protected. *Countries overwhelmed by the human tide of refugees want safe havens set up at once.* N-COUNT
2 In American English, if a country provides **safe haven** for refugees or other people in difficulties, it allows them to stay there under its official protection. *Some Democrats support granting the Haitians temporary safe haven in the US.* N-UNCOUNT
3 A **safe haven** is a place, a situation, or an activity which provides people with an opportunity to escape from things that they find unpleasant or worrying. *...the idea of the family as a safe haven from the brutal outside world.* N-COUNT: usu sing, oft N *from* n

safe house, safe houses; also spelled **safe-house**. You can refer to a building as a **safe house** when it is used as a place where someone can stay and be protected. Safe houses are often used by spies, criminals, or the police. *...a farm which operates as a safe house for criminals on the run.* N-COUNT

safekeeping /seɪfkiːpɪŋ/. If something is given to you for **safekeeping**, it is given to you so that you will make sure that it is not harmed or stolen. *Hampton had been given the bills for safekeeping by a business partner.* N-UNCOUNT: usu *for* N

safely /seɪfli/ ◆◆◇◇◇
1 If something is done **safely**, it is done in a way that makes it unlikely that anyone will be harmed. *The waste is safely locked away until it is no longer radioactive... 'Drive safely,' he said and waved goodbye... More people will be doing the work with proper supervision and thus, more safely.* ADV-GRADED: usu ADV with v
2 You also use **safely** to say that there is no risk of a situation being changed. *Once events are safely in the past, this idea seems to become less alarming... The number two seed is safely through to the second round of the tournament.* ADV: usu ADV with v
3 See also **safe**.

safe passage. If someone is given **safe passage**, they are allowed to go somewhere safely, without being attacked or arrested. *They were unwilling, or unable, to guarantee safe passage from the city to the aircraft... We try to negotiate a safe passage for relief convoys which will travel that stretch of road.* N-UNCOUNT: also a N, oft N *for/to* n

safe seat, safe seats. In politics a **safe seat** is a constituency in which the candidate from one particular party nearly always wins with a large majority of votes. *...the safe seat Sir Geoffrey Howe has held since 1974... The constituency I live in is a safe Labour seat.* N-COUNT

safe sex or **safer sex. Safe sex** is sexual activity in which people protect themselves against the risk of AIDS and other such diseases, usually by using condoms. *People who have multiple sexual partners are now more apt to practise safe sex.* ◆◇◇◇◇ N-UNCOUNT

safety /seɪfti/ ◆◆◆◆◇
1 Safety is the state of being safe from harm or danger. *The report goes on to make a number of recommendations to improve safety on aircraft.* N-UNCOUNT
2 If you reach **safety**, you reach a place where you are safe from danger. *He stumbled through smoke and fumes given off from her burning sofa to pull her to safety... Guests ran for safety as the device went off in a ground-floor men's toilet... The refugees were groping their way through the dark, trying to reach safety. ...the safety of one's own home.* N-UNCOUNT: oft prep N
3 If you are concerned about the **safety** of something, you are concerned that it might be harmful or dangerous. *Three reactors at Chernobyl have continued to operate even though there is concern about the safety of their design... The safety of tacrine has not yet been proven, and there is concern that it causes damage to the liver.* N-SING: with poss
4 If you are concerned for someone's **safety**, you are concerned that they might be in danger. *There is grave concern for the safety of witnesses... The two youths today declined to testify because they said they feared for their safety.* N-SING: with poss
5 Safety features or measures are intended to make something less dangerous. *The built-in safety device compensates for a fall in water pressure. ...safety glasses.* ADJ: ADJ n
6 If you say that there is **safety in numbers**, you mean that you are safer doing something if there are a lot of people doing it rather than doing it alone. *Many people still feel there is safety in numbers when belonging to a union.* PHRASE: usu v-link PHR

safety belt, safety belts; also spelled **safety-belt**. A **safety belt** is a strap attached to a seat in a car or aeroplane. You fasten it round your body and it stops you being thrown forward if there is an accident. N-COUNT =seat belt

safety catch, safety catches. The **safety catch** on a gun is a device that stops you firing the gun accidentally. *Eddie slipped the safety catch on his automatic back into place.* N-COUNT

safety glass. Safety glass is very strong glass that does not splinter if it breaks. N-UNCOUNT

safety net, safety nets ◆◇◇◇◇
1 A **safety net** is something that you can rely on to help you if you get into a difficult situation. *Welfare is the only real safety net for low-income workers.* N-COUNT
2 In a circus, a **safety net** is a large net that is placed below performers on a high wire or trapeze in order to catch them and prevent them being injured if they fall off. N-COUNT

safety pin, safety pins. A **safety pin** is a bent metal pin used for fastening things together. The point of the pin has a cover so that when the pin is closed it cannot hurt anyone. *...trousers which were held together with safety pins.* N-COUNT

safety valve, safety valves
1 A **safety valve** is a device which allows liquids or gases to escape from a machine when the pressure inside it becomes too great. *Residents heard an enormous bang as a safety valve on the boiler failed.* N-COUNT
2 A **safety valve** is something that allows you to release strong feelings without hurting yourself or others. *...crying is a natural safety valve.* N-COUNT

saffron /sæfrɒn/ ◆◇◇◇◇
1 **Saffron** is a yellowish-orange powder obtained from a flower and used to give flavour and colouring to some foods. *...saffron rice.* N-UNCOUNT
2 **Saffron** is a yellowish-orange colour. *...a Buddhist in saffron robes.* COLOUR

sag /sæg/ **sags, sagging, sagged** ◆◇◇◇◇
1 When something **sags**, it hangs down loosely or sinks downwards in the middle. *The shirt's cuffs won't sag and lose their shape after washing... The roof sagged at one corner, where the ceiling beams had snapped with rot... He sat down in the sagging armchair.* VERB V V-ing
2 When someone's body begins to **sag**, it starts to lose its firmness, because of old age. *He is heavily built, but beginning to sag. ...flabby thighs and sagging bottoms.* VERB =droop V V-ing
3 To **sag** means to become weaker. *The pound continued to sag despite four interventions by the Bank of England... Some of the tension Altman builds up starts to sag... They failed to revive her sagging spirits.* VERB =flag V V-ing

saga /sɑːgə/ **sagas** ◆◇◇◇◇
1 A **saga** is a long story, account, or sequence of events. *...a 600 page saga about 18th century slavery... The continuing saga of unexpected failures by leading companies.* N-COUNT
2 A **saga** is a long story composed in medieval times in Norway or Iceland. *...a Nordic saga of giants and trolls.* N-COUNT

sagacious /səgeɪʃəs/. A **sagacious** person is intelligent and has the ability to make good decisions; a formal word. *...a wise and sagacious leader.* ADJ-GRADED =discerning, wise

sagacity /səgæsɪti/. **Sagacity** is the quality of being sagacious; a formal word. *...a man of great sagacity and immense experience.* N-UNCOUNT =wisdom

sage /seɪdʒ/ **sages** ◆◇◇◇◇
1 A **sage** is a person who is regarded as being very wise. *...ancient Chinese sages.* N-COUNT
2 **Sage** means wise and knowledgeable, especially as the result of a lot of experience; a literary use. *He was famous for his intellectual integrity and sage advice to younger painters.* ♦ **sagely** *Susan nodded sagely as if what I had said was profoundly significant... The family sagely married into American money many years ago.* ADJ-GRADED =wise ADV: ADV with v =wisely
3 **Sage** is a herb used in cooking. N-UNCOUNT
4 A **sage** is a plant with grey-green leaves and purple, blue, or white flowers. N-COUNT

saggy /sægi/ **saggier, saggiest.** If you describe something as **saggy**, you mean that it has lost its firmness over a period of time and become unattractive. *Is the mattress lumpy and saggy?... Exercise for just 20 minutes a day to firm up even the saggiest bottom.* ADJ-GRADED =droopy

Sagittarius /sædʒɪteəriəs/ ◆◆◇◇◇
1 **Sagittarius** is one of the twelve signs of the zodiac. Its symbol is a creature that is half-horse, half-man and that is shooting an arrow. People who are born approximately between the 22nd of November and the 21st of December come under this sign. N-UNCOUNT
2 **A Sagittarius** is a person whose sign of the zodiac is Sagittarius. N-SING: aN

sago /seɪgoʊ/. **Sago** is a white starchy substance obtained from the trunk of some palm trees. Sago is used for making sweet puddings. N-UNCOUNT

sahib /sɑːb, sɑːhɪb/ **sahibs. Sahib** is a term used by some people in India to address or to refer to a man in a position of authority. Sahib was used especially of white government officials in the period of British rule. *'It is most urgent, sahib,' he said. ...British Sahibs and Memsahibs.* N-TITLE; N-COUNT PRAGMATICS

said /sed/. **Said** is the past tense and past participle of **say**.

sail /seɪl/ **sails, sailing, sailed** ◆◆◆◇◇
1 **Sails** are large pieces of material attached to the mast of a ship. The wind blows against the sails and pushes the ship along. *The white sails billow with the breezes they catch.* N-COUNT
2 You say a ship **sails** when it moves over the sea. *The trawler had sailed from the port of Zeebrugge... The Kruzenshtern is expected to sail for Boston this week.* VERB V prep/adv
3 If you **sail** a boat or if a boat **sails**, it moves across water using its sails. *I shall get myself a little boat and sail her around the world... For nearly two hundred miles she sailed on, her sails hard with ice... She sails beautifully in winds over 60 knots.* V-ERG V n prep V adv/prep V
4 If someone or something **sails** somewhere, they move there steadily and fairly quickly. *We got into the lift and sailed to the top floor... He launched the folded envelope and it sailed across the room.* VERB V prep/adv
5 See also **sailing**.
6 When a ship **sets sail**, it leaves a port. *He loaded his vessel with another cargo and set sail... Christopher Columbus set sail for the New World in the Santa Maria.* PHRASES V inflects, oft PHR prep
7 If you cross the sea **under sail**, you cross it in a ship that has sails rather than an engine. *...the challenge and fun of going to sea under sail. ...a big ship under sail.*
8 • to **sail close to the wind**: see **wind**. • to **take the wind out of** someone's **sails**: see **wind**.

sail through. If someone or something **sails through** a difficult situation or experience, they deal with it easily and successfully. *While she sailed through her maths exams, he struggled... The agreement sailed through the French national assembly by 495 votes to 61.* PHRASAL VERB V P n Also V P

sailboat /seɪlbout/ **sailboats.** A **sailboat** is the same as a **sailing boat**; used especially in American English. N-COUNT

sailcloth /seɪlklɒθ, AM -klɔːθ/
1 **Sailcloth** a strong heavy cloth that is used for making things such as sails or tents. *The mainsails are hand-cut and sewn from real sailcloth.* N-UNCOUNT
2 **Sailcloth** is a light canvas material that is used for making clothes. *...red sailcloth trousers.* N-UNCOUNT

sailing /seɪlɪŋ/ **sailings** ◆◆◇◇◇
1 **Sailings** are voyages made by a ship carrying passengers. *Ferry companies are providing extra sailings from Calais... We'll get the next sailing.* N-COUNT: usu pl, oft supp N
2 **Sailing** is the activity or sport of sailing boats. *There was swimming and sailing down on the lake.* N-UNCOUNT
3 If you say that a task was not all **plain sailing**, you mean that it was not very easy. *Pregnancy wasn't all plain sailing and once again there were problems... We know it won't be plain sailing at Wembley because there are no easy games at this level.* PHRASE: usu v-link PHR

sailing boat, sailing boats; also spelled **sailing-boat**. A **sailing boat** is a boat with sails. N-COUNT

sailing ship, sailing ships. A **sailing ship** is a large ship with sails, especially of the kind that were used to carry passengers or cargo. *American clippers were the ultimate sailing ships.* N-COUNT

sailor /seɪləʳ/ **sailors.** A **sailor** is a man who works on a ship as a member of its crew. ◆◆◇◇◇ N-COUNT

sailplane /seɪlpleɪn/ **sailplanes.** A **sailplane** is a plane that glides through the air on air currents rather than using an engine. N-COUNT =glider

saint /seɪnt/ **saints;** the title is usually pronounced /sənt/. ◆◆◆◇◇
1 A **saint** is someone who has died and been officially recognized and honoured by the Christian church because his or her life was a perfect example of the way Christians should live. *Every parish was named after a saint. ...Saint John.* N-COUNT; N-TITLE
2 If you refer to a living person as a **saint**, you mean that they are extremely kind, patient, and unselfish. *My girlfriend Geraldine must be a bit of a saint to put up with me.* N-COUNT

sainthood /seɪnthʊd/. **Sainthood** is the state of being a saint. *His elevation to sainthood is entirely justified. ...a candidate for sainthood.* N-UNCOUNT: usu supp N

saintly /seɪntli/. A **saintly** person behaves in a very good or very holy way. *...his saintly mother... She has been saintly in her self-restraint.* ♦ **saintliness** /seɪntlɪnəs/ *They were praised for their courage and saintliness.* ADJ-GRADED N-UNCOUNT

sake /seɪk/ **sakes** ♦♦♦◇◇
1 If you do something **for the sake of** something, you do it for that purpose or in order to achieve that result. You can also say that you do it **for** something's **sake**. *Let's assume for the sake of argument that we manage to build a satisfactory database... For the sake of historical accuracy, please permit us to state the true facts... For safety's sake, never stand directly behind a horse.* PHRASES PHR n
2 Something that is done or obtained **for its own sake** is done or obtained because someone wants to do it or have it, and not for any other reason. You can also talk about, for example, **art for art's sake** or **sport for sport's sake**. *Economic change for its own sake did not appeal to him... I just like car trips for their own sake. ...a love of truth and learning for its own sake.* usu n PHR
3 When you do something **for** someone's **sake**, you do it in order to help them or make them happy. *I trust you to do a good job for Stan's sake... Linda knew that for both their sakes she must take drastic action.* N inflects, PHR with cl
4 In informal speech, some people use expressions such as **for God's sake**, **for heaven's sake**, **for goodness sake**, or **for Pete's sake** in order to express annoyance or impatience, or to add force to a question or request. Some people find 'for God's sake' and 'for Christ's sake' offensive. *For goodness sake, why didn't you ring me?... You've got a computer system, for heaven's sakes.* N inflects, PHR with cl PRAGMATICS

saké /sɑːki, -keɪ/; also spelled **sake**. **Saké** is a Japanese alcoholic drink that is made from rice. N-UNCOUNT

salaam /səlɑːm/ **salaams, salaaming, salaamed**
1 When someone **salaams** they bow with their right hand on their forehead. This is used as a formal and respectful way of greeting someone in India and Muslim countries. *He looked from one to the other of them, then salaamed and left.* VERB V n
2 Some Muslims greet people by saying **'Salaam'**. CONVENTION

salacious /səleɪʃəs/. If you describe something such as a book or joke as **salacious**, you think that it deals with sexual matters in an unnecessarily detailed way. *The newspapers once again filled their columns with salacious details. ...a wildly salacious novel.* ♦ **salaciousness** *The book is written without a hint of salaciousness.* ADJ-GRADED: usu ADJ n =prurient N-UNCOUNT =prurience

salad /sæləd/ **salads** ♦♦◇◇◇
1 A **salad** is a mixture of uncooked vegetables. It is usually eaten with other food as part of a meal. *...a salad of tomato, onion and cucumber. ...potato salad.* ● See also **fruit salad**. N-VAR
2 If you refer to your **salad days**, you are referring to a period of your life when you were young and inexperienced. *The Grand Hotel did not seem to have changed since her salad days.* PHRASE

salad bowl, salad bowls. A **salad bowl** is a large bowl from which salad is served at a meal. N-COUNT

salad cream salad creams. Salad cream is a yellow creamy sauce that you eat with salad. N-MASS

salad-dressing, salad-dressings. Salad-dressing is a mixture of oil, vinegar, herbs, and other flavourings, which you pour over a salad. *...low-calorie salad dressings.* N-MASS

salamander /sæləmændəʳ/ **salamanders.** A **salamander** is an animal that looks rather like a lizard, and that can live both on land and in water. N-COUNT

salami /səlɑːmi/ **salamis. Salami** is a type of strong-flavoured sausage made from chopped meat and spices. It is usually thinly sliced and eaten cold. N-VAR

salaried /sælərid/. **Salaried** people receive a salary from their job. *...salaried employees... James accepted the generously salaried job at the bank.* ♦◇◇◇◇ ADJ: usu ADJ n

salary /sæləri/ **salaries.** A **salary** is the money that someone is paid each month by their employer, especially when they are in a profession such as teaching, law, or medicine. *...the lawyer was paid a huge salary... The government has decided to increase salaries for all civil servants.* ♦♦♦◇◇ N-VAR =wage

sale /seɪl/ **sales** ♦♦♦♦♦
1 The **sale** of goods is the act of selling of them for money. *Efforts were made to limit the sale of alcohol. ...a proposed arms sale to Saudi Arabia... He had never intended living there after his wife's death and immediately set about trying to make a sale.* N-SING: usu with supp
2 The **sales** of a product are the quantity of it that is sold. *The newspaper has sales of 1.72 million. ...the huge Christmas sales of computer games. ...retail sales figures.* N-PLURAL
3 The part of a company that deals with **sales** deals with selling the company's products. *Until 1983 he worked in sales and marketing... She was their Dusseldorf sales manager.* N-PLURAL
4 A **sale** is an occasion when a shop sells things at less than their normal price. *...a pair of jeans bought half-price in a sale... Many stores have started their January sales a month early.* N-COUNT
5 A **sale** is an event when goods are sold to the person who offers the highest price. *The Old Master was bought by London dealers at the Christie's sale.* N-COUNT =auction
6 See also **car boot sale, jumble sale.**
7 If something is **for sale**, it is being offered to people to buy. *His former home is for sale at £495,000... There was a Leica camera for sale in the window... The company is not for sale.* PHRASES
8 Products that are **on sale** can be bought in shops; used mainly in British English. *English textbooks and dictionaries are on sale everywhere... All tickets go on sale this Friday.* =for sale
9 In American English, if products in a shop are **on sale**, they can be bought for less than their normal price. *He bought a sports jacket on sale at Gowings Men's Store.*
10 If a property or company is **up for sale**, its owner is trying to sell it. *The castle has been put up for sale.* =on the market

saleable /seɪləbᵊl/; also spelled **salable**. Something that is **saleable** is easy to sell to people. *The Oxfam shops depend on regular supplies of saleable items.* ADJ-GRADED

saleroom /seɪlruːm/ **salerooms.** A **saleroom** is a place where things are sold by auction; used in British English. N-COUNT =auction room

sales clerk, sales clerks. In American English, a **sales clerk** is a person who works in a shop selling things to customers and helping them to find what they want. The British expression is **shop assistant**. N-COUNT

sales force, sales forces; also spelled **salesforce**. A company's **sales force** is all the people that work for that company selling its products. N-COUNT

salesgirl /seɪlzgɜːʳl/ **salesgirls.** A **salesgirl** is a young woman who sells things, especially in a shop. Many women prefer to be called a **saleswoman** or a **salesperson** rather than a salesgirl. N-COUNT

salesman /seɪlzmən/ **salesmen.** A **salesman** is a man whose job is to sell things, especially directly to shops or other businesses on behalf of a company. *...an insurance salesman.* ♦♦◇◇◇ N-COUNT: usu supp N

salesmanship /seɪlzmənʃɪp/. **Salesmanship** is the skill of persuading people to buy things. *I was captured by his brilliant salesmanship.* N-UNCOUNT

salesperson /seɪlzpɜːʳsᵊn/ **salespeople** or **salespersons.** A **salesperson** is a person who sells things, either in a shop or directly to customers on behalf of a company. ♦◇◇◇◇ N-COUNT

sales pitch, sales pitches. Someone's **sales pitch** is what they say in order to persuade someone to buy something. *His sales pitch was smooth and convincing.* N-COUNT

sales slip, sales slips. In American English, a **sales slip** is a piece of paper given to someone N-COUNT confirming that they have bought something and showing the amount money they have paid for it. The British word is **receipt**.

sales tax, sales taxes. A **sales tax** is an amount of money which people pay to the government when they buy something. ◆◇◇◇◇ N-VAR

saleswoman /seɪlzwʊmən/ **saleswomen.** A **saleswoman** is a woman who sells things, either in a shop or directly to customers on behalf of a company. N-COUNT

salient /seɪliənt/ **salients** ◆◇◇◇◇

1 The **salient** points or facts of a situation are the most important ones. *He read the salient facts quickly... Chronic fatigue is also one of the salient features of depression.* ♦ **salience** *...the salience of social reforms.* ADJ-GRADED: usu ADJ n; N-UNCOUNT

2 A **salient** is a narrow area where an army has pushed its front line forward into enemy territory. *The soldiers had to remain in a deathtrap salient for most of the rest of the war.* N-COUNT: usu sing

saline /seɪlaɪn, AM -liːn/. A **saline** substance or liquid contains salt. *...a saline solution. ...warm, saline water.* ♦ **salinity** /səlɪnɪti/ *The Atlantic Ocean had undergone changes in temperature and salinity. ...a problem of soil salinity.* ADJ: usu ADJ n; N-UNCOUNT

saliva /səlaɪvə/. **Saliva** is the watery liquid that forms in your mouth and helps you to chew and digest food. ◆◇◇◇◇ N-UNCOUNT

salivary gland /səlaɪvəri glænd, AM sælɪveri -/ **salivary glands.** Your **salivary glands** are the glands that produce saliva in your mouth. N-COUNT: usu pl

salivate /sælɪveɪt/ **salivates, salivating, salivated.**

1 When people or animals **salivate**, they produce a lot of saliva in their mouth, often as a result of seeing or smelling food. *Any dog will salivate when presented with food.* ♦ **salivation** /sælɪveɪʃən/ VERB =drool; V; N-UNCOUNT

2 If you say that someone is **salivating** over something such as the chance to make a lot of money, you are emphasizing that you disapprove of the impulse motivating their desire for it. *Johnson was salivating over the millions he stood to make... These companies are salivating at the juicy contracts for rebuilding Kuwait.* VERB PRAGMATICS; V over/at n

sallow /sæloʊ/. If a person has **sallow** skin, their skin, especially on their face, is a pale yellowish colour and looks unhealthy. *Her sallow skin was drawn tightly across the bones of her face... His face was sallow and shiny with sweat.* ADJ-GRADED

sally /sæli/ **sallies, sallying, sallied** ◆◆◇◇◇

1 **Sallies** are clever and amusing remarks; a literary use. *He had thus far succeeded in fending off my conversational sallies.* N-COUNT

2 If someone **sallies** forth or **sallies** somewhere, they go there quickly or energetically, without any fear or hesitation; a literary use. *...worrying about her when she sallies forth on her first date... Tamara would sally out on a bitterly cold night to keep her appointments.* ▶ Also a noun. *...their first sallies outside the student world.* VERB; V forth; V prep/adv; N-COUNT

salmon /sæmən/; **salmon** is both the singular and the plural form. A **salmon** is a large silver-coloured fish. ▶ **Salmon** is the pink flesh of this fish which is eaten as food. It is often smoked and eaten raw. *He gave them a splendid lunch of smoked salmon.* ◆◆◇◇◇ N-COUNT; N-UNCOUNT

salmonella /sælmənelə/. **Salmonella** is a disease caused by bacteria in food. You can also refer to the bacteria itself as **salmonella**. *He thought he was suffering from salmonella poisoning because he'd been sick.* N-UNCOUNT

salmon pink. Something that is **salmon pink** or **salmon** is the orange-pink colour of a salmon's flesh. COLOUR

salon /sælɒn, AM səlɑːn/ **salons** ◆◆◇◇◇

1 A **salon** is a place where hairdressers or beauticians work. *...a new hair salon. ...a beauty salon.* N-COUNT: usu n N

2 A **salon** is a shop where smart, expensive clothes are sold. N-COUNT

3 A **salon** is an informal meeting of fashionable writers or artists, which is held at the house of someone who is well-known. Salons were more common in former times. *His apartment was the most famous literary salon in Russia.* N-COUNT

4 A **salon** is a sitting room in a large, grand house. N-COUNT

saloon /səluːn/ **saloons** ◆◇◇◇◇

1 In British English, a **saloon** or a **saloon car** is a car with seats for four or more people, a fixed roof, and a boot that is separated from the rear seats. The American word is **sedan**. N-COUNT

2 In American English, a **saloon** is a place where alcoholic drinks are sold and drunk. N-COUNT =bar

3 In Britain, the **saloon** or **saloon bar** in a pub or hotel is a comfortable bar where the drinks are more expensive than in the other bars; an old-fashioned expression. N-COUNT =lounge

salsa /sælsə, AM sɑːlsə/ **salsas** ◆◇◇◇◇

1 **Salsa** is a hot, spicy sauce made from onions and tomatoes, usually eaten with Mexican or Spanish food. N-MASS

2 **Salsa** is a type of dance music especially popular in Latin America. *A band played salsa, and spectators danced wildly.* N-UNCOUNT

salt /sɔːlt/ **salts, salting, salted** ◆◆◆◇◇

1 **Salt** is a strong-tasting substance, in the form of white powder or crystals, which is used to improve the flavour of food or to preserve it. Salt occurs naturally in sea water. *Season lightly with salt and pepper. ...a pinch of salt.* N-UNCOUNT

2 When you **salt** food, you add salt to it. *Salt the stock to your taste and leave it simmering very gently.* ♦ **salted** *Put a pan of salted water on to boil. ...lightly salted butter.* VERB; V n; ADJ-GRADED: usu ADJ n

3 **Salts** are substances like salt that are formed when an acid reacts with an alkaline. *The rock is rich in mineral salts... The rain leaches the salts from the soil.* N-COUNT: usu pl

4 See also **epsom salts, smelling salts.**

5 If you describe someone as the **salt of the earth**, you have a lot of respect for them as the type of person who deals with difficult or demanding situations without making any unnecessary fuss. *Most of the people there are salt-of-the-earth, good, working-class people.* PHRASES; oft v-link PHR

6 If you **take** something **with a pinch of salt**, you do not believe that it is completely accurate or true. *You have to take these findings with a pinch of salt because respondents tend to give the answers they feel they should.* V inflects

7 If you say, for example, that any doctor **worth** his or her **salt** would do something, you mean that any doctor who was good at his or her job or who deserved respect would do it. *No golf teacher worth his salt would ever recommend that you grip the club tightly.* n PHR

8 If someone or something **rubs salt into** the **wound**, they make the unpleasant situation that you are in even worse, often by reminding you of your failures or faults. *At least Mr Major had the dignity not to rub salt into his opponent's wounds.* V and *wound* inflect

salt away. If someone **salts away** sums of money, they save the money for the future, often illegally. *Yesterday its president was accused of salting away tens of millions of dollars in foreign accounts.* PHRASAL VERB; V P n (not pron); Also V n P

salt cellar, salt cellars. A **salt cellar** is a small container for salt with holes in the top for shaking salt onto food; used mainly in British English. N-COUNT

salt marsh, salt marshes. A **salt marsh** is an area of flat ground where a lot of salt water lies, making the ground very muddy and wet. N-VAR

salt water; also spelled **saltwater**. **Salt water** is water from the sea, which has salt in it. N-UNCOUNT ≠fresh water

salty /sɔːlti/ **saltier, saltiest.** Something that is **salty** contains salt or tastes of salt. *...salty foods such as ham and bacon. ...a cool salty sea breeze.* ♦ **saltiness** *The saltiness of the cheese is balanced by the sweetness of the red peppers.* ◆◇◇◇◇ ADJ-GRADED; N-UNCOUNT

salubrious /səluːbriəs/

1 A place that is **salubrious** is pleasant and healthy; a formal use. *...your salubrious lochside hotel.* ADJ-GRADED

2 Something that is described as **salubrious** is respectable or socially desirable; a formal use. *...London's less salubrious quarters.* ADJ-GRADED

salutary /sæljʊtəri, AM -teri/. A **salutary** experience is good for you, even though it may seem difficult or unpleasant at first. *It was a new and salutary experience to be in the minority... The letter had a very salutary effect.* ADJ-GRADED: usu ADJ n

salutation /sæljʊteɪʃən/ **salutations**

1 **Salutation** or a **salutation** is a greeting to someone. *Jackson turned his head and nodded a salutation... The old man moved away, raising his hand in salutation.* N-COUNT: also in/of N

2 The **salutation** of a letter is the phrase that is used at the beginning of it, such as 'Dear Sir' or 'Dear Mr Rodd'; a formal use. N-COUNT

salute /səluːt/ **salutes, saluting, saluted** ◆◆◇◇◇

1 If you **salute** someone, you greet them or show your respect with a formal sign. Soldiers usually salute officers by raising their right hand so that their fingers touch their forehead. *One of the company stepped out and saluted the General... I stood to attention and saluted.* ▶ Also a noun. *The soldier gave the clenched-fist salute... He raised his hand in salute.* VERB; V n; V; N-COUNT: also in N

2 To **salute** a person or their achievements means to publicly show or state your admiration for them. *I salute Governor Castle for the leadership role that he is taking... The statement salutes the changes of the past year.* ▶ Also a noun. *...a special salute to Anne Scargill for her plucky underground protest.* VERB =praise; V n; N-COUNT

salvage /sælvɪdʒ/ **salvages, salvaging, salvaged** ◆◆◇◇◇

1 If something **is salvaged**, someone manages to save it, for example from a ship that has sunk, or from a building that has been destroyed. *The team's first task was to decide what equipment could be salvaged... The investigators studied flight recorders salvaged from the wreckage.* VB: usu passive; be V-ed; V-ed

2 **Salvage** is the act of salvaging things from somewhere such as a wrecked ship or destroyed building. *The salvage operation went on. ...the cost of salvage.* N-UNCOUNT: oft N n

3 The **salvage** from somewhere such as a wrecked ship or destroyed building is the things that are saved from it. *They climbed up on the rock with their salvage.* N-UNCOUNT

4 If you manage to **salvage** a difficult situation, you manage to get something useful from it so that it is not a complete failure. *Officials tried to salvage the situation... Diplomats are still hoping to salvage something from the meeting.* VERB; V n; V n from n

5 If you **salvage** something such as your pride or your reputation, you manage not to lose it even though it seems likely that you will, or you regain it after losing it. *We definitely wanted to salvage some pride for British tennis... Chantal was lucky to be able to salvage her career.* VERB; V n

salvation /sælveɪʃən/ ◆◆◇◇◇

1 In Christianity, **salvation** is the fact that Christ has saved a person from evil. *The church's message of salvation has changed the lives of many.* N-UNCOUNT

2 The **salvation** of someone or something is the act of saving them from harm, destruction, or an unpleasant situation. *...a poor, lost, lonely woman clinging for salvation to a son whom she knew was as lost as she was. ...those whose marriages are beyond salvation.* N-UNCOUNT

3 If someone or something is your **salvation**, they are responsible for saving you from harm, destruction, or an unpleasant situation. *The country's salvation lies in forcing through democratic reforms... I consider books my salvation.* N-SING: with poss

Salvation Army. The **Salvation Army** is a Christian organization that aims to preach Christianity and care for the poor. Its members wear military-style uniforms. *...a Salvation Army hostel.* ◆◇◇◇◇ N-PROPER: the N, N n

salve /sælv, AM sæv/ **salves, salving, salved**

1 If you do something to **salve** your conscience, you do it in order to feel less guilty or worried. *I give myself treats and justify them to salve my conscience.* VERB =ease; V n

2 **Salve** is an oily substance that is put on sore skin or a wound to help it heal. *...a soothing salve for sore, dry lips.* N-MASS =balm

salver /sælvəʳ/ **salvers.** A **salver** is a tray or large plate, usually made of silver. *...silver salvers laden with flutes of champagne.* N-COUNT

salvo /sælvoʊ/ **salvoes** ◆◇◇◇◇

1 A **salvo** is the firing of several guns or missiles at the same time in a battle or ceremony. *They were to fire a salvo of blanks, after the national anthem.* N-COUNT

2 A **salvo** of activity such as laughing or shouting is a sudden outburst of it. *His testimony, however, was only one in a salvo of new attacks.* N-COUNT: with supp

Samaritan /səmærɪtən/ **Samaritans.** You refer to someone as a **Samaritan** if they help you when you are in difficulty. *A good Samaritan offered us a room in his house.* N-COUNT

samba /sæmbə/ **sambas.** A **samba** is a lively Brazilian dance. N-COUNT

same /seɪm/ ◆◆◆◆◆

1 If two or more things, actions, or qualities are the **same**, or if one is the **same** as another, the two are very similar or exactly like each other in some way. *The houses were all the same – square, close to the street, needing paint... In essence, all computers are the same... People with the same experience in the job should be paid the same... Driving a boat is not the same as driving a car... I want my son to wear the same clothes as everyone else at the school... Bihar had a population roughly the same as that of England.* ADJ: the ADJ, oft ADJ as n/-ing

2 If something is happening **the same as** something else, the two things are happening in a similar or identical way to each other. *I mean, it's a relationship, the same as a marriage is a relationship... I want to go home having won a game of football the same as you leave the ground and you want to go away with your team having won... He just wanted the war to end, the same as Wally did.* PHR-CONJ-SUBORD

3 You use **same** to indicate that you are referring to only one place, time, or thing, and not to different ones. *Bernard works at the same institution as Arlette... It's impossible to get everybody together at the same time... Members of his staff learn to work the same 13-hour days that he imposes on himself... John just told me that your birthday is on the same day as mine. ...business people who spoke the same language as himself... Gary plays football with the other children of the same age.* ADJ: the ADJ, oft ADJ n as n, ADJ n that

4 Something that is still **the same** has not changed in any way. *Taking ingredients from the same source means the beers stay the same... Only 17% said the economy would improve, but 25% believed it would stay the same.* ADJ: the ADJ

5 You use **the same** to refer to something that has previously been mentioned or suggested. *We made the decision which was right for us. Other parents must do the same... In the United States small specialised bookshops survive quite well. The same applies to small publishers... We like him very much and he says the same about us.* ▶ Also an adjective. *Dwight Eisenhower possessed much the same ability to appear likeable.* PRON: the PRON; ADJ: the ADJ

6 You use **same** in formal written English to refer to the exact thing that has already been mentioned in a document such as a business letter, bill, or receipt. *Wrist watches: £5. Inscription of same: £25.* PRON: of PRON

7 You say **'same here'** in order to suggest that you feel the same way about something as the person who has just spoken to you, or that you have done the same thing; an informal expression. *'Nice to meet you,' said Michael. 'Same here,' said Mary Ann... 'I hate going into stores.'—'Same here,' said William.* CONVENTION PRAGMATICS =likewise

8 You say **'same to you'** in response to someone who wishes you well with something. *'Have a nice Easter.'—'And the same to you Bridie.'... 'Goodbye, then, and thanks. Good luck.'—'The same to you.'* CONVENTION PRAGMATICS

9 In informal English, you say **'same again'** when you want to order another drink of the same kind as the one you have just had. *Give Roger another pint, Imogen, and I'll have the same again.* PHRASES PRAGMATICS

10 You can say **all the same** or **just the same** to PHR with cl

introduce a statement which indicates that a situation or your opinion has not changed, in spite of what has happened or what has just been said. *I arranged to pay him the dollars when he got there, a purely private arrangement. All the same, it was illegal... He was unable to pay attention to the papers on his desk. Just the same, he pulled over the stack of papers and started to examine them... Matt is weak and dependent, but you love him all the same. ...jokes that she did not understand but laughed at just the same.* PRAGMATICS

11 If you say **'It's all the same to me'**, you mean that you do not care which of several things happens or is chosen. *Whether I've got a moustache or not it's all the same to me... What's the difference between a white lie and a lie? I mean, it's all the same to me.*

12 When two or more people or things are thought to be distinct or separate and you say that they are **one and the same**, you mean that they are in fact one single person or thing. *Luckily, Nancy's father and her attorney were one and the same person... I'm willing to work for the party because its interests and my interests are one and the same.* v-link PHR

13 You say **'the same'** or **'the very same'** in reply to someone's question when you are saying that they have identified a person or thing correctly; a fairly formal expression. *'This Sawtry guy, he is John Sawtry?'—'Yes, sir. The very same.'*

14 ● **at the same time**: see **time**.

sameness /seɪmnəs/. The **sameness** of something is its lack of variety. *He grew bored by the sameness of the speeches.* N-UNCOUNT: usu with supp

samizdat /sæmɪzdæt, AM sɑːm-/. **Samizdat** referred to a system in the former USSR and Eastern Europe by which books and magazines banned by the state were illegally printed by dissident groups. *...a publisher specialising in samizdat literature.* N-UNCOUNT: usu N n

samovar /sæməvɑːʳ/ **samovars.** A **samovar** is a large decorated container for heating water, traditionally used in Russia for making tea. N-COUNT

sample /sɑːmpᵊl, sæm-/ **samples, sampling, sampled** ◆◆◆◇◇

1 A **sample** of a substance or product is a small quantity of it that shows you what it is like. *You'll receive samples of paint, curtains and upholstery... We're giving away 2000 free samples... They asked me to do some sample drawings.* N-COUNT

2 A **sample** of a substance is a small amount of it that is examined and analysed scientifically. *They took samples of my blood. ...urine samples.* N-COUNT =specimen

3 A **sample** of people or things is a number of them chosen out of a larger group and then used in tests or used to provide information about the whole group. *We based our analysis on a random sample of more than 200 males.* N-COUNT

4 If you **sample** food or drink, you taste a small amount of it in order to find out if you like it. *We sampled a selection of different bottled waters.* VERB =taste V n

5 If you **sample** a place or situation, you experience it for a short time in order to find out about it. *...the chance to sample a different way of life.* VERB =try V n

6 When musicians or pieces of their music **are sampled**, parts of their music are used by other musicians in their own work. *I don't actually mind being sampled as long as people give credit where it's due.* VB: usu passive be V-ed

sampler /sɑːmpləʳ, sæm-/ **samplers** ◆◇◇◇◇

1 A **sampler** is a piece of cloth embroidered with various patterns, which is intended to show the skill of the person who made it. N-COUNT

2 A **sampler** is a piece of equipment that is used for copying and remixing a piece of music into a new piece of music. N-COUNT

samurai /sæmjʊraɪ, AM -mʊr-/; **samurai** is both the singular and the plural form. In former times a **samurai**, was a member of a powerful class of warriors in Japan. N-COUNT

sanatorium /sænətɔːriəm/ **sanatoriums** or **sanatoria** /sænətɔːriə/; also spelled **sanitarium.** A **sanatorium** is an institution that provides medical treatment and rest, often in a healthy climate, for people who have been ill for a long time. *I had tuberculosis and was told I'd be in the sanatorium for two years.* N-COUNT =clinic

sanctify /sæŋktɪfaɪ/ **sanctifies, sanctifying, sanctified**

1 If someone or something **is sanctified** by a priest or other holy person, the priest or holy person officially blesses them and declares that they should be considered holy. *She is trying to make amends for her marriage not being sanctified.* VB: usu passive be V-ed

2 If an organization such as the Church **sanctifies** an activity, they approve of it, support it, and want it to remain exactly as it is. *The Church sanctified these sordid property rights. ...just another ideology as twisted as the one that sanctified the placing of the bombs.* VERB V n

sanctimonious /sæŋktɪmoʊniəs/. If you disapprove of someone because you think that they trying to appear virtuous and morally better than other people, you can say that they are **sanctimonious**. *He writes smug, sanctimonious rubbish... You sanctimonious little hypocrite!* ADJ-GRADED PRAGMATICS =self-righteous
♦ **sanctimoniousness** *She displays none of the sanctimoniousness often associated with spirituality.* N-UNCOUNT

sanction /sæŋkʃᵊn/ **sanctions, sanctioning, sanctioned** ◆◆◆◆◇

1 If someone in authority **sanctions** an action or practice, they officially approve of it and allow it to be done. *He may now be ready to sanction the use of force... He seemed to be preparing to sanction an increase in public borrowing.* VERB =approve V n ▸ Also a noun. *The king could not enact laws without the sanction of Parliament.* N-UNCOUNT: with supp =approval

2 **Sanctions** are measures taken by countries to restrict trade and official contact with a country that has broken international law. *...Margaret Thatcher's refusal to impose sanctions against South Africa... He expressed his opposition to the lifting of sanctions.* N-PLURAL: oft N *against*/*on* n

3 A **sanction** is a severe course of action which is intended to make people obey instructions, customs, or laws. *As an ultimate sanction, they can sell their shares if they disagree with the company's investment policy.* N-COUNT

4 If a country or an authority **sanctions** another country or a person for doing something, it declares that the country or person is guilty of doing it and imposes sanctions on them. *...their failure to sanction Japan for butchering whales in violation of international conservation treaties.* VERB V n

sanctity /sæŋktɪti/. If you talk about the **sanctity** of something, you mean that it is very important and must be treated with respect. *...the sanctity of human life.* N-UNCOUNT: oft *the* N *of* n

sanctuary /sæŋktʃuəri, AM -tʃueri/ **sanctuaries** ◆◆◇◇◇

1 A **sanctuary** is a place of safety and refuge for people, especially people who are being persecuted. *His church became a sanctuary for thousands of people who fled the civil war.* N-COUNT =haven

2 **Sanctuary** is the safety provided in a sanctuary. *Some of them have sought sanctuary in the church.* N-UNCOUNT

3 A **sanctuary** is a place where birds or animals are protected and allowed to live freely. *...a bird sanctuary. ...a wildlife sanctuary.* N-COUNT: oft n N

sanctum /sæŋtəm/ **sanctums**

1 A **sanctum** is a holy place inside a temple or mosque. N-COUNT

2 If you refer to someone's inner **sanctum**, you mean a place which is private and sometimes secret, in which they can be quiet and alone. *...His bedroom's his inner sanctum.* N-COUNT: usu sing

sand /sænd/ **sands, sanding, sanded** ◆◆◆◇◇

1 **Sand** is a powdery substance that consists of extremely small pieces of stone. Some deserts and many beaches are made up of sand. *They all walked barefoot across the damp sand to the water's edge. ...grains of sand.* N-UNCOUNT

2 **Sands** are a large area of sand, for example a beach. *...miles of golden sands.* N-PLURAL

3 If you **sand** a wood or metal surface, you rub VERB

sandpaper over it in order to make it smooth or clean. *Sand the surface softly and carefully.* ► **Sand down** means the same as **sand**. *I was going to sand down the chairs and repaint them... Simply sand them down with a fine grade of sandpaper.* Vn PHRASAL VERB V P n (not pron) V n P

4 If you refer to the **shifting sands** of a situation, you mean that it changes so often that it is difficult to deal with. *He had been a rock in the shifting sands of her existence. ...his shrewd tactical skills in the shifting sands of Arab politics.* PHRASE: oft PHR of n

sand down. See **sand** 3. PHRASAL VERB

sandal /sændəl/ **sandals. Sandals** are light shoes that you wear in warm weather, which have straps instead of a solid part over the top of your foot. ◆◇◇◇◇ N-COUNT

sandalwood /sændəlwʊd/

1 Sandalwood is the sweet-smelling wood of a tree that is found in South Asia and Australia. It is also the name of the tree itself. N-UNCOUNT

2 Sandalwood is the oil extracted from the wood of the tree. It is used to make perfume. N-UNCOUNT

sandbag /sændbæg/ **sandbags, sandbagging, sandbagged**

1 A **sandbag** is a sack filled with sand. Sandbags are usually used to build a wall for protection against floods or explosions. N-COUNT

2 To **sandbag** something means to protect or strengthen it using sandbags. *Residents sandbagged their homes to keep out flood waters.* VERB V n

sandbank /sændbæŋk/ **sandbanks.** A **sandbank** is a bank of sand below the surface of the sea or a river. *The ship hit a sandbank and capsized.* N-COUNT

sandbar /sændbɑːʳ/ **sandbars;** also spelled **sand bar**. A **sandbar** is a sandbank formed by moving currents, which is found especially at the mouth of a river or harbour. N-COUNT

sandbox /sændbɒks/ **sandboxes.** In American English, a **sandbox** is a shallow hole or box in the garden with sand in it where small children can play. The usual British word is **sandpit**. N-COUNT

sand castle, sand castles. A **sand castle** is a heap of sand, usually shaped roughly like a castle, which children make when they are playing on the beach. N-COUNT

sand dune, sand dunes. A **sand dune** is a hill of sand near the sea or in a sand desert. N-COUNT: usu pl =dune

sander /sændəʳ/ **sanders.** A **sander** is a machine for making wood or metal surfaces smoother. N-COUNT

sandpaper /sændpeɪpəʳ/. **Sandpaper** is strong paper that has a coating of sand on it. It is used for rubbing wood or metal surfaces to make them smoother. N-UNCOUNT

sandpit /sændpɪt/ **sandpits;** also spelled **sand-pit**. In British English, a **sandpit** is a shallow hole or box in the ground with sand in it where small children can play. The usual American word is **sandbox**. N-COUNT

sandstone /sændstoʊn/ **sandstones. Sandstone** is a type of rock which contains a lot of sand. It is often used for building houses and walls. *...the reddish sandstone walls. ...sandstone cliffs.* ◆◇◇◇◇ N-MASS

sandstorm /sændstɔːʳm/ **sandstorms.** A **sandstorm** is a strong wind in a desert area, which creates a mass of swirling sand. N-COUNT

sandwich /sænwɪdʒ, -wɪtʃ/ **sandwiches, sandwiching, sandwiched** ◆◆◇◇◇

1 A **sandwich** consists of two slices of bread with a layer of food such as cheese or meat between them. *...a ham sandwich.* N-COUNT

2 If you **sandwich** two things together with something else, you put that other thing between them. If you **sandwich** one thing between two other things, you put it between them. *Carefully split the sponge ring, then sandwich the two halves together with whipped cream... When you write, avoid sandwiching the bad news between an irrelevant, indirect, or overly cushioned beginning and end.* VERB V pl-n *together* V n *between* pl-n

3 See also **sandwiched**.

sandwich course, sandwich courses. In British English, a **sandwich course** is an educational course in which you alternate periods of study between periods of being at work. N-COUNT

sandwiched /sænwɪdʒd, -wɪtʃt/. If something is **sandwiched between** two other things, it is in a narrow space between them. *The original kitchen was sandwiched between the breakfast room and the toilet.* • See also **sandwich**. ADJ: v-link ADJ *between* pl-n

sandy /sændi/ ◆◆◇◇◇

1 A **sandy** area is covered with sand. *...long, sandy beaches. ...a sandy path.* ADJ-GRADED

2 Sandy hair is light orange-brown in colour. ADJ-GRADED

sane /seɪn/ **saner, sanest** ◆◇◇◇◇

1 Someone who is **sane** is able to think and behave normally and reasonably, and is not mentally ill. *He seemed perfectly sane... It wasn't the act of a sane person.* ADJ-GRADED ≠insane

2 If you refer to a **sane** person, action, or system, you mean one that you think is reasonable and sensible. *No sane person wishes to see conflict or casualties. ...a sane and safe energy policy.* ADJ-GRADED: usu ADJ n ≠insane

sang /sæŋ/. **Sang** is the past tense of **sing**.

sang-froid /sɒŋ frwɑː/; also spelled **sangfroid**. A person's **sang-froid** is their ability to remain calm in a dangerous or difficult situation; a formal word. *He behaves throughout with a certain sang-froid.* N-UNCOUNT

sangria /sæŋgriːə/. **Sangria** is a Spanish drink made of red wine, orange or lemon juice, soda, and brandy. N-UNCOUNT

sanguine /sæŋgwɪn/. If you are **sanguine** about something, you are cheerful and confident that things will happen in the way you want them to. *He's remarkably sanguine about the problems involved... They have begun to take a more sanguine view.* ◆◇◇◇◇ ADJ-GRADED: usu v-link ADJ, oft ADJ *about* n

sanitarium /sænɪteəriəm/ **sanitariums.** See **sanatorium**.

sanitary /sænɪtri, AM -teri/ ◆◇◇◇◇

1 Sanitary means concerned with keeping things clean and hygienic, especially by providing a sewage system and a clean water supply. *Sanitary conditions are appalling... The vast majority live in tin shacks without electricity, clean water or sanitary facilities.* ADJ: ADJ n

2 If you say that a place is not **sanitary**, you mean that it is not very clean. *It's not the most sanitary place one could swim.* ADJ-GRADED: usu with brd-neg =hygienic

sanitary napkin, sanitary napkins. In American English, a **sanitary napkin** is the same as a **sanitary towel**. N-COUNT

sanitary protection. Sanitary protection is sanitary towels or tampons. N-UNCOUNT

sanitary towel, sanitary towels. In British English, a **sanitary towel** is a pad of thick soft material which women wear to absorb the blood during their periods. The usual American expression is **sanitary napkin**. N-COUNT

sanitation /sænɪteɪʃən/. **Sanitation** is the process of keeping places clean and hygienic, especially by providing a sewage system and a clean water supply. *...the hazards of contaminated water and poor sanitation.* ◆◇◇◇◇ N-UNCOUNT

sanitize /sænɪtaɪz/ **sanitizes, sanitizing, sanitized;** also spelled **sanitise** in British English. If someone or something **sanitizes** an activity or a situation that is unpleasant or unacceptable, they describe it in a way that makes it seem more pleasant or acceptable. *...the cosy English school of crime writers who sanitise violence and make it respectable... He's worried that he's only going to get a sanitized version of what actually happened.* VERB V n V-ed

sanity /sænɪti/ ◆◇◇◇◇

1 A person's **sanity** is their ability to think and behave normally and reasonably. *He and his wife finally had to move from their apartment just to preserve their sanity.* N-UNCOUNT

2 If there is **sanity** in a situation or activity, there is a purpose and a regular pattern, rather than confusion and worry. *Rafsanjani has been considering various ways of introducing some sanity into the currency market.* N-UNCOUNT

sank /sæŋk/. **Sank** is the past tense of **sink**.

Sanskrit /sænskrɪt/. **Sanskrit** is an ancient language which used to be spoken in India and is now used only in religious writings and ceremonies. N-UNCOUNT

Santa Claus /sæntə klɔːz, AM - klɔːz/. **Santa Claus** or **Santa** is an imaginary old man with a long white beard and a red coat. Traditionally, young children in many countries are told that he brings their Christmas presents. ◆◇◇◇◇ N-PROPER =Father Christmas

sap /sæp/ **saps, sapping, sapped** ◆◇◇◇◇
1 If something **saps** your strength or confidence, it gradually weakens or destroys it. *I was afraid the sickness had sapped my strength... Analysts say the recession in Japan has sapped investor confidence.* VERB =diminish V n
2 **Sap** is the watery liquid in plants and trees. *The leaves, bark and sap are also common ingredients of local herbal remedies.* N-UNCOUNT
3 In American English, if you describe someone as a **sap**, you mean that you think they are foolish. *...her poor sap of a husband.* N-COUNT PRAGMATICS

sapiens /sæpienz/. See **homo sapiens**.

sapling /sæplɪŋ/ **saplings.** A **sapling** is a young tree. *...newly planted saplings swaying gently in the spring breeze.* N-COUNT

sapper /sæpəʳ/ **sappers.** A **sapper** is a soldier whose job is to carry out building, digging, and other engineering work. *They requested sappers to mend bridges or remove mines.* N-COUNT

sapphire /sæfaɪəʳ/ **sapphires** ◆◇◇◇◇
1 A **sapphire** is a precious stone which is blue in colour. *...a sapphire engagement ring.* N-VAR: oft N n
2 Something that is **sapphire** is bright blue in colour; a literary use. *...white snow and sapphire skies.* COLOUR

sappy /sæpi/
1 A **sappy** plant contains a lot of sap. *Do not overfeed them, as this will encourage soft sappy growth.* ADJ-GRADED
2 In American English, if you describe someone or something as **sappy**, you mean that you think they are foolish. *I wrote this sappy love song.* ADJ-GRADED PRAGMATICS

sarcasm /sɑːʳkæzəm/. **Sarcasm** is speech or writing which actually means the opposite of what it seems to say. Sarcasm is usually intended to mock or insult someone. *'I hope I didn't get you out of your shower,' Philpott said with thinly veiled sarcasm... His voice was heavy with sarcasm... Fred ignored the sarcasm.* ◆◇◇◇◇ N-UNCOUNT

sarcastic /sɑːʳkæstɪk/. Someone who is **sarcastic** says or does the opposite of what they really mean in order to mock or insult someone. *She poked fun at people's shortcomings with sarcastic remarks.* ♦ **sarcastically** /sɑːʳkæstɪkli/ *'What a surprise!' Caroline murmured sarcastically.* ◆◇◇◇◇ ADJ-GRADED; ADV-GRADED: ADV with v

sarcoma /sɑːʳkoʊmə/ **sarcomas**
1 **Sarcoma** is one of two general forms of cancer. It affects tissues such as muscle and bone. Compare **carcinoma**. N-UNCOUNT
2 **Sarcomas** are malignant tumours. N-COUNT

sarcophagus /sɑːʳkɒfəgəs/ **sarcophagi** or **sarcophaguses.** A **sarcophagus** is a large decorative coffin that was used in ancient times. *...an Egyptian sarcophagus.* N-COUNT =casket

sardine /sɑːʳdiːn/ **sardines** ◆◇◇◇◇
1 **Sardines** are a kind of small sea fish, often eaten as food. *They opened a tin of sardines.* N-COUNT
2 If you say that a crowd of people are **packed like sardines**, you are emphasizing that they are sitting or standing so close together that they cannot move easily. *The refugees were packed like sardines.* PHRASE: usu v-link PHR PRAGMATICS

sardonic /sɑːʳdɒnɪk/. If you describe someone as **sardonic**, you think their behaviour is mocking or scornful, often because they think that they are better than other people. *He was a big, sardonic man, who intimidated even the most self-confident students. ...a sardonic sense of humour.* ♦ **sardonically** /sɑːʳdɒnɪkli/ *He grinned sardonically and bowed towards her.* ◆◇◇◇◇ ADJ-GRADED: usu ADJ n; ADV-GRADED: ADV with v

sarge /sɑːʳdʒ/. A sergeant is sometimes addressed as **sarge** or referred to as **the sarge**; an informal word. *'Good luck, sarge,' he said... The sarge isn't here guv.* N-VOC; N-SING: the N

sari /sɑːri/ **saris.** A **sari** is a piece of clothing worn especially by Indian women. It consists of a long piece of thin material that is wrapped around the body. ◆◇◇◇◇ N-COUNT

sarnie /sɑːʳni/ **sarnies.** In informal British English, a **sarnie** is a sandwich. *...two crates of beer and a plate of sarnies.* N-COUNT =butty

sarong /sərɒŋ, AM -rɔːŋ/ **sarongs.** A **sarong** is a piece of clothing that is worn especially by Malaysian men and women. It consists of a long piece of cloth attached around the waist or under the armpit. N-COUNT

sartorial /sɑːʳtɔːriəl/. **Sartorial** means relating to clothes and to the way they are made or worn; a formal word. *...Sebastian's sartorial elegance... James gave him some sartorial advice.* ♦ **sartorially** *He was sartorially impeccable.* ADJ: ADJ n; ADV

SAS /es eɪ es/. **The SAS** is a group of highly trained British soldiers who work on secret or very difficult military operations. **SAS** is an abbreviation for 'Special Air Service'. N-PROPER: the N

sash /sæʃ/ **sashes**
1 A **sash** is a long piece of cloth which people wear round their waist or over one shoulder, especially with formal or official clothes. *She wore a white dress with a thin blue sash... She arrived to receive the sash of office from the outgoing president.* N-COUNT
2 A **sash** is one of the sliding frames in a sash window. N-COUNT

sashay /sæʃeɪ, AM sæʃeɪ/ **sashays, sashaying, sashayed.** If someone **sashays**, they walk in a graceful but rather noticeable way. *The models sashayed down the catwalk.* VERB V prep/adv

sash window, sash windows. A **sash window** is a window which consists of two frames placed one above the other. The window can be opened by sliding one frame over the other. N-COUNT

sassy /sæsi/
1 In American English, if an older person describes a younger person as **sassy**, they mean that they are cheeky and disrespectful; an informal word. *Are you that sassy with your parents, young lady?.* ADJ-GRADED =cheeky
2 In American English, **sassy** is used to describe people or things that are smart, trendy, and streetwise; an informal word. *...his sharp sassy style. ...colourful and sassy fashion accessories.* ADJ-GRADED

sat /sæt/. **Sat** is the past tense and past participle of **sit**.

Sat. **Sat.** is a written abbreviation for **Saturday**. ◆◆◇◇◇

SAT /sæt/ **SATs;** also spelled **sat.**
1 In the United States, the **SAT** is an examination which is often taken by students who wish to enter a college or university as undergraduates. **SAT** is an abbreviation for 'Scholastic Aptitude Test'. N-PROPER
2 In Britain, **SATs** are a set of tasks given to seven-year old school children in order to test their ability. **SAT** is an abbreviation for 'Standard Assessment Task'. N-COUNT

Satan /seɪtᵊn/. **Satan** is the Devil, considered to be the embodiment of evil and the chief opponent of God. ◆◇◇◇◇ N-PROPER

satanic /sətænɪk/ ◆◇◇◇◇
1 Something that is **satanic** is considered to be caused by or influenced by Satan. *...satanic cults. ...satanic ritual.* ADJ: usu ADJ n
2 A person or thing that is **satanic** is extremely wicked and evil. *...satanic mass murderers.* ADJ-GRADED: usu ADJ n

Satanism /seɪtənɪzəm/; also spelled **satanism**. **Satanism** is worship of the devil. *...black magic and satanism.* ♦ **Satanist** /seɪtənɪst/ **Satanists** *Police arrested a young Satanist accused of fire attacks on churches.* N-UNCOUNT; N-COUNT

satay /sæteɪ, AM sɑːteɪ/. **Satay** is pieces of meat cooked on skewers and served with a peanut sauce. *...chicken satay.* N-UNCOUNT

satchel /sætʃəl/ **satchels.** A **satchel** is a bag with a long strap that schoolchildren use for carrying books. N-COUNT

sated /seɪtɪd/. If you are **sated** with something, you have had more of it than you can enjoy at one time. *...children happily sated with ice cream.* ADJ-GRADED: v-link ADJ

satellite /sætəlaɪt/ **satellites** ◆◆◆◇◇
1 A **satellite** is an object which has been sent into space in order to collect information or to be part of a communications system. Satellites move continually round the earth or around another planet. *The rocket launched two communications satellites... The signals are sent by satellite link... President Bush spoke by satellite last night to 34 campaign rallies across the country.* N-COUNT: also *by* N
2 **Satellite** television is broadcast using a satellite. *They have four satellite channels.* ADJ: ADJ n
3 A **satellite** is a natural object in space that moves round a planet or star. *...the satellites of Jupiter.* N-COUNT
4 You can refer to a country, area, or organization as a **satellite** when you mean that it has no real power of its own, but is dependent on a larger and more powerful country, area, or organization. *...China's satellite territories. ...Russia and its former satellites.* N-COUNT: oft N n

satellite dish, satellite dishes. A **satellite dish** is a piece of equipment which people need to have on their house in order to receive satellite television. N-COUNT

satiate /seɪʃieɪt/ **satiates, satiating, satiated.** If something such as food or pleasure **satiates** you, you have all that you need or all that you want of it, often so much that you become tired of it; a formal word. *There is usually enough fruit on one apple tree to satiate several children... The Edinburgh International Festival offers enough choice to satiate most appetites.* ♦ **satiated** *She finished the meal and sat back with a satiated sigh.* VERB V n ADJ

satin /sætɪn, AM -tᵊn/ **satins** ◆◇◇◇◇
1 **Satin** is a smooth, shiny kind of cloth, usually made from silk. *...a peach satin ribbon. ...stylish dresses in silks and satins.* N-MASS
2 If something such as a paint, wax, or cosmetic gives something a **satin** finish, it reflects light to some extent but is not very shiny. *The final stage of waxing left it with a satin sheen.* ADJ: ADJ n

satinwood /sætɪnwʊd/. **Satinwood** is a smooth hard wood which comes from an East Indian tree and is used to make furniture. N-UNCOUNT

satire /sætaɪəʳ/ **satires** ◆◇◇◇◇
1 **Satire** is the use of humour, irony, or exaggeration in order to show how foolish or wicked some people's behaviour or ideas are. *The commercial side of the Christmas season is an easy target for satire.* N-UNCOUNT
2 A **satire** is a play, film, or novel that uses satire to criticize something. *...a sharp satire on the American political process.* N-COUNT: oft N *on* n

satiric /sətɪrɪk/. **Satiric** means the same as **satirical**. *...Ibsen's satiric attack on bourgeois convention.* ADJ-GRADED

satirical /sətɪrɪkᵊl/. A **satirical** drawing, piece of writing, or comedy show uses satire to criticize something. *...a satirical novel about London life in the late 80s.* ◆◇◇◇◇ ADJ-GRADED

satirist /sætɪrɪst/ **satirists.** A **satirist** is someone who writes or uses satire. *He built a reputation in the 1970s as a social satirist.* N-COUNT

satirize /sætɪraɪz/ **satirizes, satirizing, satirized;** also spelled **satirise** in British English. If you **satirize** a person or group of people, you use satire to criticize them or make fun of them in something such as a novel or a film. *His last movie satirized the class struggle between economic winners and losers during the Thatcher years.* VERB V n

satisfaction /sætɪsfækʃᵊn/ ◆◆◇◇◇
1 **Satisfaction** is the pleasure that you feel when you do something or get something that you wanted or needed to do or get. *She felt a small glow of satisfaction... Both sides expressed satisfaction with the progress so far... I doubt I'll ever get rich, but I get job satisfaction.* N-UNCOUNT
2 If you get **satisfaction** from someone, you get money or an apology from them because of some harm or injustice which has been done to you; a formal use. *If you can't get any satisfaction, complain to the park owner.* N-UNCOUNT
3 If you do something **to** someone's **satisfaction**, they are happy with the way that you have done it. *She never could seem to do anything right or to his satisfaction... It is hard to see how the issue can be resolved to everyone's satisfaction.* PHRASE: PHR after v

satisfactory /sætɪsfæktəri/. Something that is **satisfactory** is acceptable to you or fulfils a particular need or purpose. *I never got a satisfactory answer... It seemed a very satisfactory arrangement... Neither solution seemed satisfactory.* ♦ **satisfactorily** /sætɪsfæktərɪli/ *Their motives have never been satisfactorily explained.* ◆◆◇◇◇ ADJ-GRADED =acceptable ADV-GRADED: ADV with v

satisfied /sætɪsfaɪd/ ◆◆◆◇◇
1 If you are **satisfied** with something, you are happy because you have got what you wanted or needed. *We are not satisfied with these results. ...satisfied customers.* ADJ-GRADED: usu v-link ADJ, oft ADJ *with* n
2 If you are **satisfied** that something is true or has been done properly, you are convinced about this after checking it. *People must be satisfied that the treatment is safe.* ADJ-GRADED: v-link ADJ, oft ADJ that

satisfy /sætɪsfaɪ/ **satisfies, satisfying, satisfied** ◆◆◇◇◇
1 If someone or something **satisfies** you, they give you enough of what you want or need to make you pleased or contented. *The pace of change has not been quick enough to satisfy everyone... We just can't find enough good second-hand cars to satisfy demand... The scandal stories satisfy people's curiosity for a few hours.* VERB V n
2 If someone or something **satisfies** you that something is true or has been done properly, they convince you by giving you more information or by showing you what has been done. *He has to satisfy the environmental lobby that real progress will be made to cut emissions... He wanted to satisfy himself that he had given his best performance.* VERB =convince V n that
3 If you **satisfy** the requirements for something, you are good enough or have the right qualities to fulfil these requirements. *The Executive Committee recommends that the procedures should satisfy certain basic requirements.* VERB V n

satisfying /sætɪsfaɪɪŋ/. Something that is **satisfying** gives you a feeling of pleasure and fulfilment. *I found wood carving satisfying... Success has made it a satisfying and enriching task.* ♦ **satisfyingly** *...a series of satisfyingly detailed and painstakingly constructed documentaries.* ◆◆◇◇◇ ADJ-GRADED ADV-GRADED: usu ADV adj

satsuma /sætsuːmə/ **satsumas.** A **satsuma** is a fruit that looks like a small orange. N-COUNT

saturate /sætʃʊreɪt/ **saturates, saturating, saturated** ◆◇◇◇◇
1 If people or things **saturate** a place or object, they fill it completely so that no more can be added. *In the last days before the vote, both sides are saturating the airwaves... As the market was saturated with goods and the economy became more balanced, inflation went down.* ♦ **saturated** *As the domestic market becomes saturated, firms begin to export the product.* VERB =flood V n *be* V-ed *with* n ADJ
2 If someone or something **is saturated**, they become extremely wet. *If the filter has been saturated with motor oil, it should be discarded and replaced.* ♦ **saturated** *His work clothes, having become saturated with oil, had to be cleaned.* VERB =soaked *be* V-ed Also V n ADJ

saturated /sætʃʊreɪtɪd/. **Saturated** fats are types of fat that are found in some foods, especially dairy products, eggs, and meat. They are believed to contribute to heart disease and some other illnesses if eaten too often. *...foods rich in cholesterol and saturated fats.* ◆◇◇◇◇ ADJ-GRADED: usu ADJ n

saturation /sætʃʊreɪʃᵊn/ 
1 **Saturation** is the process or state that occurs when a place or thing is filled completely with people or things, so that no more can be added. *Japanese car makers have been equally blind to the saturation of their markets at home and abroad... Road traffic has reached saturation point.* N-UNCOUNT
2 **Saturation** is used to describe a campaign or other activity that is carried out very thoroughly, so ADJ: ADJ n

that nothing is missed. *The concept of saturation marketing makes perfect sense... Newspapers, television and radio are all providing saturation coverage. ...saturation bombing.*

Saturday /sætəʳdeɪ, -di/ **Saturdays. Saturday** is the day after Friday and before Sunday. *She had a call from him on Saturday morning at the studio... Every Saturday dad made a beautiful pea and ham soup... The overnight train runs every night of the week except Saturdays.* ◆◆◆◆◇ N-VAR

saturnine /sætəʳnaɪn/. Someone who is **saturnine** is gloomy and unfriendly. *He had a rather forbidding, saturnine manner.* ADJ: usu ADJ n =morose

satyr /sætəʳ/ **satyrs.** In classical mythology a **satyr** is a creature that is half man and half goat. N-COUNT

sauce /sɔːs/ **sauces.** A **sauce** is a thick liquid which is served with other food. *...pasta cooked in a sauce of garlic, tomatoes, and cheese. ...vanilla ice cream with chocolate sauce.* ◆◆◆◇◇ N-MASS

saucepan /sɔːspən, AM -pæn/ **saucepans.** A **saucepan** is a deep metal cooking pot, usually with a long handle and a lid. *Place the potatoes and turnips in a large saucepan, cover with cold water and bring to the boil.* ◆◇◇◇◇ N-COUNT =pan

saucer /sɔːsəʳ/ **saucers.** A **saucer** is a small curved plate on which you stand a cup. • See also **flying saucer**. ◆◇◇◇◇ N-COUNT

saucy /sɔːsi/ **saucier, sauciest.** Someone or something that is **saucy** refers to sex in a light-hearted, amusing way. *...a saucy joke.* ADJ-GRADED =cheeky

Saudi /saʊdi/ **Saudis** ◆◆◆◆◇

1 Saudi or **Saudi Arabian** means belonging or relating to Saudi Arabia or to its people, language, or culture. *Saudi officials have dismissed such reports as rumours. ...the Saudi Arabian delegation.* ADJ: usu ADJ n

2 The **Saudis** or **Saudi Arabians** are the people who come from Saudi Arabia. N-COUNT

sauerkraut /saʊəʳkraʊt/. **Sauerkraut** is cabbage which has been cut into very small pieces and pickled. It is eaten mainly in Germany. N-UNCOUNT

sauna /sɔːnə/ **saunas** ◆◇◇◇◇

1 If you have a **sauna**, you sit or lie in a room heated to a high temperature by the steam from burning charcoal. N-COUNT

2 A **sauna** is a room or building where you can have a sauna. N-COUNT

saunter /sɔːntəʳ/ **saunters, sauntering, sauntered.** If you **saunter** somewhere, you walk there in a slow, casual way. *We watched our fellow students saunter into the building... He sauntered along the river to the mill.* ► Also a noun. *She began a slow saunter toward the bonfires.* ◆◇◇◇◇ VERB V prep/adv N-SING

sausage /sɒsɪdʒ, AM sɔːs-/ **sausages** ◆◆◇◇◇

1 Sausage is finely minced meat which is mixed with other ingredients and put into a thin casing like a tube. N-UNCOUNT

2 A **sausage** is a tube-shaped piece of sausage meat. *...sausages and chips.* N-COUNT

sausage roll, sausage rolls. A **sausage roll** is a small amount of sausage meat which is covered with pastry and cooked; used mainly in British English. N-COUNT

sauté /soʊteɪ, AM sɔːteɪ/ **sautés, sautéing, sautéed.** When you **sauté** food, you fry it quickly in hot oil or butter. *Sauté the chicken until golden brown. ...sautéed mushrooms.* ◆◇◇◇◇ VERB V n V-ed

savage /sævɪdʒ/ **savages, savaging, savaged** ◆◆◇◇◇

1 Someone or something that is **savage** is extremely cruel, violent, and uncontrolled. *This was a savage attack on a defenceless young girl. ...the savage wave of violence that swept the country in November 1987. ...a savage dog lunging at the end of a chain.* ♦ **savagely** *He was savagely beaten.* ADJ-GRADED =vicious ADV-GRADED

2 If you refer to people as **savages**, you dislike them because you think that they are cruel, violent, or uncivilized. *...their conviction that the area was a frozen desert peopled with uncouth savages.* N-COUNT: usu pl PRAGMATICS

3 If someone **is savaged** by a dog or other animal, the animal attacks them violently. *The animal then turned on him and he was savaged to death.* VB: usu passive be V-ed

4 If someone or something that they have done **is savaged** by another person, that person criticizes them severely. *The show had already been savaged by critics... Speakers called for clearer direction and savaged the Chancellor.* VERB be V-ed V n

savagery /sævɪdʒri/. **Savagery** is extremely cruel and violent behaviour. *...the sheer savagery of war.* N-UNCOUNT

savannah /səvænə/ **savannahs;** also spelled **savanna.** A **savannah** is an open, flat stretch of grassland, usually in Africa. ◆◇◇◇◇ N-VAR

savant /sævᵊnt, AM sævɑːnt/ **savants**

1 A **savant** is a person of great learning or natural ability; a formal word. *The opinion of the savants on the composition of the lunar surface is not as united as you appear to believe.* N-COUNT

2 You can refer to someone as an idiot **savant** who seems to be less intelligent than normal people but who has other qualities or abilities which makes them an exceptional person. *...an idiot savant, an autistic with a gift for numbers.* N-COUNT

save /seɪv/ **saves, saving, saved** ◆◆◆◆◇

1 If you **save** someone or something, you help them to avoid harm or to escape from a dangerous or unpleasant situation. *...a final attempt to save 40,000 jobs in Britain's troubled aero industry... One man was still missing last night after the Belgian trawler Lucky capsized off the Dutch coast. Three other men were saved... A new machine no bigger than a 10p piece could help save babies from cot death... The national health system saved him from becoming a cripple.* ♦ **-saving** *His boxing career was ended after two sight-saving operations.* VERB V n V n *from* n/-ing COMB in ADJ

2 If you **save**, you gradually collect money by spending less than you get, usually in order to buy something that you want. *The majority of people intend to save, but find that by the end of the month there is nothing left... Tim and Barbara are now saving for a house in the suburbs... They could not find any way to save money.* ► **Save up** means the same as **save**. *Julie wanted to put some of her money aside for holidays or save up for something special... People often put money aside in order to save up enough to make one major expenditure.* VERB V V *for* n V n PHRASAL VERB V P *for* n V P n (not pron) Also V n P

3 If you **save** something such as time or money, you prevent the loss or waste of it. *It saves time in the kitchen to have things you use a lot within reach... More cash will be saved by shutting studios and selling outside-broadcast vehicles... I'll try to save him the expense of a flight from Perth... I got the fishmonger to skin the fish which helped save on the preparation time.* ♦ **-saving** *America was among the first to invent and use labor-saving devices in industry and mining.* VERB ≠waste V n V n n V *on* n Also V n *on* n COMB in ADJ

4 If you **save** something, you keep it because it will be needed later. *Drain the beans thoroughly and save the stock for soup... Scraps of material were saved, cut up and pieced together for quilts.* VERB V n Also V n n

5 If someone or something **saves** you from doing something or **saves** you from an unpleasant experience, they do it for you or change the situation so that you do not have to do it or experience it. *The scanner will reduce the need for exploratory operations which will save risk and pain for patients... She was hoping that something might save her from having to make a decision... He arranges to collect the payment from the customer, thus saving the client the paperwork.* VERB V n V n *from* n/-ing V n n

6 If a goalkeeper **saves** or **saves** a shot, they succeed in preventing the ball from going into the goal. *He saved one shot when the ball hit him on the head... Eck's shot was saved by Feuer, who leapt across his goal to turn the ball on the post.* ► Also a noun. *Spurs could have had several goals but for some brilliant saves from John Hallworth.* VERB V n N-COUNT

7 You can use **save** to introduce the only things, people, or ideas that your main statement does not apply to; a formal use. *There is almost no water at all in Mochudi save that brought up from bore holes.* • **Save for** means the same as **save**. *The parking lot was virtually empty save for a few cars clustered to one side.* PREP =apart from PHR-PREP =apart from

8 • to **save** someone's **bacon**: see **bacon**. • **to save the day**: see **day**. • to **save face**: see **face**.

save up. see **save** 2. PHRASAL VERB

saver /seɪvəʳ/ **savers.** A **saver** is a person who regularly saves money by paying it into a bank account or a building society. *Low interest rates are bad news for savers, who have seen their income halved over the last year.* ◆◇◇◇◇ N-COUNT

-saver /-seɪvəʳ/ **-savers. -saver** combines with words such as 'time' and 'energy' to indicate that something prevents the thing mentioned from being wasted. *These potatoes are sold ready sorted and washed, and can prove a great time-saver for the busy cook... These zip-top bags are great space-savers if storage is limited.* COMB in N-COUNT ≠-waster

saving /seɪvɪŋ/ **savings** ◆◆◆◇◇

1 A **saving** is a reduction in the amount of time or money that is used or needed. *Fill in the form below and you will be making a saving of £6.60 on a one-year subscription. ...a program of household savings on energy use.* N-COUNT: usu with supp

2 Your **savings** are the money that you have saved, especially in a bank or a building society. *Her savings were in the Post Office Savings Bank. ...a savings account.* N-PLURAL

saving grace, saving graces. A **saving grace** is a good quality or feature in a person or thing that prevents them from being completely bad or worthless. *That is ageing's single saving grace; you worry less about what people think about you.* N-COUNT: with supp

saviour /seɪvjəʳ/ **saviours;** spelled **savior** in American English. ◆◇◇◇◇

1 A **saviour** is a person who saves someone or something from danger, ruin, or defeat. *...the saviour of his country. ...the saviour of English football... She regarded him as her saviour.* N-COUNT: oft N *of* n

2 In the Christian religion, **the Saviour** is Jesus Christ. N-PROPER: *the* N

savoir-faire /sævwɑːʳ feəʳ/. **Savoir-faire** is the confidence and ability to do the appropriate thing in a social situation; a formal expression. *...a certain savoir-faire that comes from living with the best.* N-UNCOUNT

savour /seɪvəʳ/ **savours, savouring, savoured;** spelled **savor** in American English. ◆◇◇◇◇

1 If you **savour** an experience, you enjoy it as much as you can. *President Clinton savored his first major legislative victory today... We won't pretend we savour the prospect of a month in prison... There's something about the Loire Valley that makes you want to savour every moment.* VERB V n

2 If you **savour** food or drink, you eat or drink it slowly in order to taste its full flavour and to enjoy it properly. *Savour the flavour of each mouthful, and chew your food well.* VERB V n

savoury /seɪvəri/ **savouries;** spelled **savory** in American English. ◆◇◇◇◇

1 **Savoury** food has a salty or spicy flavour rather than a sweet one. *Italian cooking is best known for savoury dishes.* ADJ: usu ADJ n

2 **Savouries** are small portions of savoury food that are usually eaten as a snack. N-COUNT: usu pl

savvy /sævi/

1 In informal American English, if you describe someone as having **savvy**, you think that they have a good understanding and practical knowledge of something. *He is known for his political savvy and strong management skills.* N-UNCOUNT: oft supp N

2 In informal American English, if you describe someone as **savvy**, you think that they show a lot of practical knowledge. *She was a pretty savvy woman.* ADJ-GRADED

saw /sɔː/ **saws, sawing, sawed, sawn** ◆◇◇◇◇

1 **Saw** is the past tense of **see**.

2 A **saw** is a tool for cutting wood, which has a blade with sharp teeth along one edge. Some saws are pushed backwards and forwards by hand, and others are powered by electricity. • See also **chain saw.** N-COUNT

3 If you **saw** something, you cut it with a saw. *He escaped by sawing through the bars of his cell... Your father is sawing wood.* VERB V prep/adv V n

sawdust /sɔːdʌst/. **Sawdust** is dust and very small pieces of wood which are produced when you saw wood. *...a layer of sawdust.* N-UNCOUNT

sawed-off shotgun, sawed-off shotguns. A **sawed-off shotgun** is the same as a **sawn-off shotgun**; used in American English. N-COUNT =sawn-off shotgun

sawmill /sɔːmɪl/ **sawmills.** A **sawmill** is a factory in which wood is sawn up into planks using a power-driven saw. N-COUNT

sawn /sɔːn/. **Sawn** is the past participle of **saw.**

sawn-off shotgun or **sawed-off shotgun sawn-off shotguns.** A **sawn-off shotgun** is a shotgun on which the barrel has been cut short. They are often used by criminals because they can be easily hidden. *The men burst in wearing balaclavas and brandishing sawn-off shotguns.* N-COUNT

sax /sæks/ **saxes.** A **sax** is the same as a **saxophone**; an informal word. N-COUNT: oft *the* N

Saxon /sæksᵊn/ **Saxons** ◆◇◇◇◇

1 In former times, **Saxons** were members of a West Germanic tribe. Some members of this tribe settled in Britain and were known as **Anglo-Saxons.** N-COUNT

2 Something that is **Saxon** is related to or characteristic of, the ancient Saxons, the Anglo-Saxons or their descendents. *...a seventh-century Saxon church.* ADJ

3 **Saxons** are people who come from Saxony. N-COUNT

saxophone /sæksəfoʊn/ **saxophones.** A **saxophone** is a musical instrument in the shape of a curved metal tube with keys and a curved mouthpiece. You play the saxophone by blowing into the mouthpiece and pressing the keys with your fingers. ◆◇◇◇◇ N-VAR: oft *the* N

saxophonist /sæksɒfənɪst, AM sæksəfoʊn-/ **saxophonists.** A **saxophonist** is someone who plays the saxophone. ◆◇◇◇◇ N-COUNT

say /seɪ/ **says** /sez/ **saying, said** /sed/ ◆◆◆◆◆

1 When you **say** something, you speak words. *'I'm sorry,' he said... She said they were very impressed... Forty-one people are said to have been seriously hurt... I packed and said goodbye to Charlie... I hope you didn't say anything about Gretchen... You didn't say much when you telephoned... Did he say where he was going?... It doesn't sound exactly orthodox, if I may say so.* VERB V with quote V that *be* V-ed to-inf V n *to* n V n V wh V *so* Also V to-inf

2 You use **say** in expressions such as **I would just like to say** to introduce what you are actually saying, or to indicate that you are expressing an opinion or admitting a fact. If you state that you **can't say** something or you **wouldn't say** something, you are indicating in a polite or indirect way that it is not the case. *I would just like to say that this is the most hypocritical thing I have ever heard in my life... I have to say I didn't even know Fox Lane Police Station existed till about four or five years ago... I must say that rather shocked me, too... Dead? Well, I can't say I'm sorry.* VERB PRAGMATICS V that

3 You can mention the contents of a piece of writing by mentioning what it **says** or what someone **says** in it. *The report says there is widespread and routine torture of political prisoners in the country... Auntie Winnie wrote back saying Mam wasn't well enough to write... You can't have one without the other, as the song says... 'Highly inflammable,' it says on the spare canister... Jung believed that God speaks to us in dreams. The Bible says so too.* VERB V that V with quote *it* V with quote V *so*

4 If you **say** something to yourself, you think it. *Perhaps I'm still dreaming, I said to myself... 'Keep your temper,' he said to himself.* VERB V *to* pron-refl with quote

5 If you have a **say** in something, you have the right to give your opinion and influence decisions relating to it. *You can get married at sixteen, and yet you haven't got a say in the running of the country... The students wanted more say in the government of the university.* N-SING: usu *a* N, also *more/some* N

6 You indicate the information given by something such as a clock, dial, or map by mentioning what it **says.** *The clock said four minutes past eleven... The map says there's six of them.* VERB V n V that

7 If something **says** something about a person, situation, or thing, it reveals something about them. *I think that says a lot about how well Seles is* VERB V amount *about*

playing... The appearance of the place and the building says something about the importance of the project.
n
V pron *about* n

8 If something **says** a lot for a person or thing, it shows that this person or thing is very good or has a lot of good qualities. *That the Escort is still the nation's bestselling car in 1992 says a lot for the power of Ford's marketing people... It says much for Brookner's skill that while the book is suffused with sadness, it is never depressing.*
VERB PRAGMATICS
V amount *for* n
it V amount *for* n that

9 You use **say** in expressions such as **I'll say that for them** and **you can say this for them** after or before you mention a good quality that someone has, usually when you think they do not have many good qualities. *He's usually smartly-dressed, I'll say that for him... At the very least, he is devastatingly sure of himself, you can say that.*
VERB PRAGMATICS
V pron *for* n
V pron

10 You can use **say** when you want to discuss something that might possibly happen or be true. *Say you lived in Boston, Massachusetts, and dug straight down through the center of the Earth, what country would you come out nearest to?*
VB: only imper PRAGMATICS
=suppose
V that

11 You can use **say** or **let's say** when you mention something as an example. *To see the problem here more clearly, let's look at a different biological system, say, an acorn... Someone with, say, between 300 and 500 acres could be losing thousands of pounds a year.*
PRAGMATICS

12 In informal American English, **say** is used to attract someone's attention or to express surprise, pleasure, or admiration. *Say, Leo, how would you like to have dinner one night, just you and me?*
EXCLAM PRAGMATICS

13 If you say that something **says it all**, you mean that it shows you very clearly the truth about a situation or someone's feelings. *This is my third visit in a week, which says it all.*
PHRASES
V inflects PRAGMATICS

14 You can use **'You don't say'** to express surprise at what someone has told you. People often use this expression sarcastically. *'Apparently, people who had given to Tory party funds were more likely to receive honours than those who hadn't.'—'You don't say.'*
CONVENTION PRAGMATICS

15 If you say there is a lot **to be said for** something, you mean you think it has a lot of good qualities or aspects. *There's a lot to be said for being based in the country.*
amount PHR PRAGMATICS

16 If you say that someone **doesn't have much to say for** himself or herself, you mean that they are not speaking very much during a conversation; an informal expression. *He's never got much to say for himself.*

17 If someone asks **what** you **have to say for** yourself, they are asking what excuse you have for what you have done. *'Well,' she said eventually, 'what have you to say for yourself?'*
PRAGMATICS

18 If something **goes without saying**, it is obvious or is bound to be true. *It goes without saying that if someone has lung problems they should not smoke.*
oft *it* PHR that

19 When one of the people or groups involved in a discussion **has** their **say**, they give their opinion. *The Football Association have had their say and so have the Football League.*
V inflects

20 You use **'Say what you like about** someone or something' when you are about to mention one good thing about a person or thing that many people do not like. *Say what you like about Mrs Thatcher, at least she knew where she was going.*
PHR cl PRAGMATICS

21 You use **'I wouldn't say no'** to indicate that you would like something, especially something that has just been offered to you; an informal expression. *I wouldn't say no to a drink.*
CONVENTION PRAGMATICS

22 You can use **not to say** when adding a stronger or more extreme description than the one you have just used. *To those who've never received million dollar royalty cheques, this sounded a little odd, not to say offensive.*
usu PHR adj PRAGMATICS

23 You use **to say nothing of** when you mention an additional thing which gives even more strength to the point you are making. *Unemployment leads to a sense of uselessness, to say nothing of financial problems.*
PHR n PRAGMATICS

24 You use **shall I say** and **shall we say** in order to warn someone that what you are about to say may cause offence or be surprising. *We're all watching George Bush's problems, shall I say, with immense interest... My involvement has not been altogether, shall we say, ethical.*
PHR with cl/group PRAGMATICS

25 You use **that is to say** or **that's to say** to indicate that you are about to express the same idea more clearly or precisely; a formal expression. *We're basically talking about an independent state in the territories that were occupied in 1967, that is to say, in the West Bank and Gaza.*
PHR with cl/group PRAGMATICS
=that is

26 You can use **'You can say that again'** to express strong agreement with what someone has just said; an informal expression. *'Must have been a fiddly job.'—'You can say that again.'*
CONVENTION PRAGMATICS

27 • **to say the least**: see **least**. • **needless to say**: see **needless**.

saying /seɪɪŋ/ **sayings** ◆◇◇◇◇

1 A **saying** is a memorable sentence that people often say and that gives advice or information about human life and experience. *We also realize the truth of that old saying: Charity begins at home... One of Margaret Thatcher's favourite sayings is that 'the unexpected always happens'.*
N-COUNT

2 The **sayings** of a person, especially a religious or political leader, are important things that they said or pieces of advice that they gave. *The sayings of Confucius offer guidance on this matter.*
N-COUNT: usu pl

say-so. If you do something on someone's **say-so**, they tell you to do it or they give you permission to do it; an informal word. *Directors call the shots and nothing happens on set without their say-so.* ◆◇◇◇◇
N-SING: oft with poss

scab /skæb/ **scabs**

1 A **scab** is a hard, dry covering that forms over the surface of a wound. *The area can be very painful until scabs form after about ten days.*
N-COUNT

2 People who continue to work during a strike are called **scabs** by the people who are on strike. *Groups of pickets circled the plant, yelling obscenities at the men they called scabs.* ► Also an adjective. *The mill was started up with scab labor.*
N-COUNT PRAGMATICS
ADJ: ADJ n

3 **Scab** is a fungal disease that can affect apple trees, pear trees, and potato plants.
N-UNCOUNT

scabbard /skæbə^r^d/ **scabbards.** A **scabbard** is a holder for a sword, especially one that hangs from a belt.
N-COUNT

scabby /skæbi/. If a person, an animal, or a part of their body is **scabby**, it has scabs on it. *He had short trousers and scabby knees.*
ADJ-GRADED

scabies /skeɪbiːz/. **Scabies** is a very infectious skin disease caused by a parasite, which makes you want to scratch a lot.
N-UNCOUNT

scabrous /skeɪbrəs, skæb-/. If you describe something as **scabrous**, you mean that it deals with sex or describes sex in a shocking way; a literary word, often used showing disapproval. *...the scabrous lower reaches of the film business.*
ADJ-GRADED PRAGMATICS

scaffold /skæfoʊld/ **scaffolds**

1 A **scaffold** is a temporary raised platform which is used by house decorators.
N-COUNT

2 A **scaffold** is a raised platform on which criminals used to be hanged or beheaded. *Ascending the shaky ladder to the scaffold, More addressed the executioner.*
N-COUNT

scaffolding /skæfəldɪŋ/. **Scaffolding** is a temporary framework of poles and boards that is used by workers to stand on while they are building, repairing, or painting the outside walls of a building. ◆◇◇◇◇
N-UNCOUNT

scald /skɔːld/ **scalds, scalding, scalded**

1 If you **scald** yourself, you burn yourself with very hot liquid or steam. *A patient jumped into a bath being prepared by a member of staff and scalded herself. ...a child with a scalded hand.*
VERB
V n
V-ed

2 A **scald** is a burn caused by very hot liquid or steam.
N-COUNT

scalding /skɔːldɪŋ/. **Scalding** or **scalding hot** liquids are extremely hot. *I tried to sip the tea but it was scalding. ...scalding hot water.*
ADJ

scale /skeɪl/ **scales, scaling, scaled** ◆◆◆◆◇

1 If you refer to the **scale** of something, you are re-
N-SING:

ferring to its size or extent, especially when it is very big. *However, he underestimates the scale of the problem... You may feel dwarfed by the sheer scale of the place... The break-down of law and order could result in killing on a massive scale... The British aid programme is small in scale.* ● See also **full-scale, large-scale, small-scale.** also no det, with supp

2 A **scale** is a set of levels or numbers which are used in a particular system of measuring things or are used when comparing things. *...an earthquake measuring five-point-five on the Richter scale... The patient rates the therapies on a scale of zero to ten... The higher up the social scale they are, the more the men have to lose.* ● See also **sliding scale, time scale.** N-COUNT: usu with supp

3 A pay **scale** or **scale** of fees is a list of amounts of money which indicates how much someone should be paid, depending, for example, on their age or what work they do. *...those on the high end of the pay scale... A Registered Osteopath will be pleased to tell you his scale of fees before you decide on a consultation.* N-COUNT: usu with supp

4 The **scale** of a map, plan, or model is the relationship between the size of something in the map, plan, or model and its size in the real world. *The map, on a scale of 1:10,000, shows over 5,000 individual paths.* ● See also **full-scale, large-scale.** N-COUNT: usu with supp

5 A **scale** model or **scale** replica of a building or object is a model of it which is smaller but has all the same parts and features. *Franklin made his mother an intricately detailed scale model of the house.* ADJ: ADJ n

6 In music, a **scale** is a fixed sequence of musical notes, each one higher than the next, which begins at a particular note. *...the scale of C major.* N-COUNT

7 The **scales** of a fish or reptile are the small, flat pieces of hard skin that cover its body. N-COUNT: usu pl

8 **Scales** are a piece of equipment used for weighing things, for example for weighing amounts of food that you need in order to make a particular meal. *...a pair of kitchen scales. ...bathroom scales... I step on the scales practically every morning.* N-PLURAL: also *a pair of* N

9 If you **scale** something such as a mountain or a wall, you climb up it or over it. *...Rebecca Stephens, the first British woman to scale Everest... The men scaled a wall and climbed down scaffolding on the other side.* VERB =climb V n

10 If something is **out of scale** with the things near it, it is too big or too small in relation to them. *...the tower surmounted by its enormous golden statue of the Virgin, utterly out of scale with the building.* PHRASES usu v-link PHR, oft PHR *with* n

11 If the different parts of a map, drawing, or model are **to scale**, they are the right size in relation to each other. *...a miniature garden, with little pagodas and bridges all to scale.* v-link PHR, PHR after v

scale back. To **scale back** means the same as to **scale down**; used mainly in American English. *Despite current price advantage, UK manufacturers are still having to scale back production.* PHRASAL VERB =decrease V P n (not pron) Also V n P

scale down. If you **scale down** something, you make it smaller in size, amount, or extent than it used to be. *One Peking factory has had to scale down its workforce from six hundred to only six... The air rescue operation has now been scaled down... The Romanian government yesterday unveiled a new, scaled-down security force.* PHRASAL VERB =decrease V P n (not pron) V-ed P Also V n P

scale up. If you **scale up** something, you make it greater in size, amount, or extent than it used to be. *Simply scaling up a size 10 garment often leads to disaster... Since then, Wellcome has been scaling up production to prepare for clinical trials.* PHRASAL VERB =increase V P n (not pron) Also V n P

scallion /skæljən/ **scallions.** In American English, a **scallion** is a small onion with long green leaves. The British expression is **spring onion.** N-COUNT

scallop /skɒləp, skæl-/ **scallops** ◆◇◇◇◇

1 **Scallops** are large shellfish with two flat fan-shaped shells. Scallops can be eaten. N-COUNT: usu pl

2 **Scallops** are a series of small curves that form an ornamental border on things such as clothes, tablecloths, or handkerchiefs. N-COUNT: usu pl

scalloped /skɒləpt, skæl-/. **Scalloped** objects are decorated with a series of small curves along the edges. *The quilt has pretty, scalloped edges and intricate quilting.* ADJ: usu ADJ n

scallywag /skæliwæg/ **scallywags.** If you call a boy or a man a **scallywag**, you mean that he behaves badly but you like him, so you find it difficult to be really angry with him; an old fashioned, informal word. *It's his idea of a joke, I suppose, the scallywag.* N-COUNT PRAGMATICS =scamp, rascal

scalp /skælp/ **scalps, scalping, scalped** ◆◇◇◇◇

1 Your **scalp** is the skin under the hair on your head. *He smoothed his hair back over his scalp... Massage the shampoo into the scalp.* N-COUNT: usu sing

2 To **scalp** someone means to remove the skin and hair from the top of their head. *He pretended to scalp me with his sword.* VERB V n

3 A **scalp** is the piece of skin and hair that is removed when someone is scalped. N-COUNT

4 If you say that you want someone's **scalp**, you mean that you want to defeat or punish them; an informal use. *Stock speculators wanted his scalp... He told friends I was after his scalp.* N-COUNT: with poss

5 In American English, if someone **scalps** tickets, they sell them outside a sports ground or theatre, usually for more than their original value. The British word is **tout**. *He was trying to pick up some cash scalping tickets.* VERB V n

scalpel /skælpəl/ **scalpels.** A **scalpel** is a knife with a short, thin, sharp blade. Scalpels are used by surgeons during operations. N-COUNT

scalper /skælpər/ **scalpers.** In American English, a **scalper** is someone who sells tickets outside a sports ground or theatre, usually for more than their original value. The British word is **tout**. *Another scalper said he'd charge a $1000 for a $125 ticket.* N-COUNT

scaly /skeɪli/. **Scaly** skin is covered in small dry patches of hard or flaking skin. *The brown rat has prominent ears and a long scaly tail.* ADJ-GRADED: usu ADJ n

scam /skæm/ **scams.** A **scam** is a large-scale illegal trick, usually with the purpose of getting money from people or avoiding paying tax; an informal word. *They believed they were participating in an insurance scam, not a murder... The duo set up a scam to settle their respective debts.* ◆◇◇◇◇ N-COUNT =swindle, racket

scamp /skæmp/ **scamps.** If you call a boy a **scamp**, you mean that he is naughty or cheeky but you like him, so you find it difficult to be angry with him; an informal word. *Have some respect for me, you scamp! ...cheeky young scamps.* N-COUNT PRAGMATICS =rascal

scamper /skæmpər/ **scampers, scampering, scampered.** When people or small animals **scamper** somewhere, they move there quickly with small, light steps. *Children scampered off the yellow school bus and into the playground... The flash sent the foxes scampering away.* VERB V prep/adv

scampi /skæmpi/. **Scampi** is a dish of large prawns that have been fried in batter. N-UNCOUNT

scan /skæn/ **scans, scanning, scanned** ◆◆◇◇◇

1 When you **scan** written material, you look through it quickly in order to find important or interesting information. *She scanned the advertisement pages of the newspapers... I haven't read much into it as yet. I've only just scanned through it.* VERB V n V *through* n

► Also a noun. *I just had a quick scan through your book again.* N-SING

2 When you **scan** a place or group of people, you look at it carefully, usually because you are looking for something or someone. *The officer scanned the room... She was nervous and kept scanning the crowd for Paul... He raised the binoculars to his eye again, scanning across the scene.* VB: no passive V n V n *for* n V prep

3 If a machine **scans** luggage or other items, it examines it, for example by moving X-rays over it. *Their approach is to scan every checked-in bag with a bomb detector.* ♦ **scanning** *...routine scanning of luggage.* VERB V n Also V, V *for* n N-UNCOUNT

4 If a picture or document **is scanned** into a computer, a machine passes a beam of light over it to make a copy of it in the computer. *The entire paper contents of all libraries will eventually be scanned into computers... Designs can also be scanned in from paper.* VB: usu passive be V-ed *into/onto* n be V-ed *in/on*

5 If a radar or sonar machine **scans** an area, it examines or searches it by sending radar or sonar beams over it. *The ship's radar scanned the sea ahead.* VERB V n

6 A **scan** is a medical test in which a machine sends a beam of X-rays over a part of your body in order to check that your organs are healthy and working normally. *He was rushed to hospital for a brain scan. ...a breast scan to check for cancer.* N-COUNT: usu with supp

7 If a pregnant woman has a **scan**, a machine using sound waves produces an image of her womb on a screen so that a doctor can see if her baby is developing normally. *I've had two scans during this pregnancy.* N-COUNT

8 In a poem, if a line does not **scan**, it does not fit into the poem's regular rhythmic pattern. *He had written a few poems. Sid told him they didn't scan.* VB: usu with brd-neg V

scandal /skændᵊl/ **scandals** ◆◆◆◇◇

1 A **scandal** is a situation or event that a lot of people think is very shocking and immoral and that everybody knows about. *...a financial scandal.* N-COUNT: usu with supp

2 **Scandal** is talk about the shocking and immoral aspects of someone's behaviour or something that has happened. *He loved gossip and scandal... These mothers often abandoned their children because of fear of scandal.* N-UNCOUNT

3 If you say that something is a **scandal**, you are angry about it and think that the people responsible for it should be ashamed. *It is a scandal that a person can be stopped for no reason by the police.* N-SING: oft N that PRAGMATICS =disgrace

scandalize /skændəlaɪz/ **scandalizes, scandalizing, scandalized;** also spelled **scandalise** in British English. If something **scandalizes** people, they are shocked or offended by it. *As a young woman, she scandalised her family by falling in love with a married man.* VERB V n

scandalous /skændələs/ ◆◇◇◇◇

1 **Scandalous** behaviour or activity is considered immoral and shocking. *They would be sacked for criminal or scandalous behaviour... He spoke of scandalous corruption and incompetence.* ADJ-GRADED: usu ADJ n =shocking

♦ **scandalously** *He asked only that Ingrid stop behaving so scandalously.* ADV-GRADED: ADV with v

2 **Scandalous** stories or remarks are concerned with the immoral and shocking aspects of someone's behaviour or something that has happened. *Newspaper columns were full of scandalous tales... A jealous colleague could spread scandalous gossip about you.* ADJ-GRADED: usu ADJ n

3 You can describe something as **scandalous** if it makes you very angry and you think the people responsible for it should be ashamed. *It is absolutely scandalous that a fantastic building like this is just left to rot away. ...a scandalous waste of money.* ADJ PRAGMATICS =disgraceful

♦ **scandalously** *...scandalously over-priced Beaujolais Nouveau.* ADV: usu ADV adj

Scandinavian /skændɪneɪviən/ **Scandinavians** ◆◇◇◇◇

1 **Scandinavian** means belonging or relating to Scandinavia or to its people, language, or culture. *The three Baltic republics have called on the Scandinavian countries for help in starting negotiations with Moscow. ...a festival of Scandinavian culture in London.* ADJ

2 **Scandinavians** are people from Scandinavian countries. N-COUNT

scanner /skænəʳ/ **scanners.** A **scanner** is a machine which is used to examine, identify, or record things, for example by moving a beam of light, sound, or X-rays over them. Scanners are used in places such as hospitals, airports, and supermarkets. *...brain scanners. ...an optical scanner.* ◆◇◇◇◇ N-COUNT

scant /skænt/ ◆◇◇◇◇

1 You use **scant** to indicate that there is very little of something or not as much of something as there should be. *She began to berate the police for paying scant attention to the theft from her car. ...forces that have shown scant respect for Red Cross markings or UN flags... There is scant evidence of strong economic growth to come.* ADJ-GRADED: usu ADJ n

2 If you describe an amount as **scant**, you are emphasizing that it is small. *In the no-confidence vote, Mr Singh is expected to muster a scant 128 votes from his dwindling supporters... In fact, Richard Savage had known Edward Bellamy a scant five hours.* ADJ: a ADJ amount PRAGMATICS =mere

scanty /skænti/ **scantier, scantiest**

1 You describe something as **scanty** when there is less of it than you think there should be. *So far, what scanty evidence we have points to two suspects.* ADJ-GRADED

2 If someone is wearing **scanty** clothing, he or she is wearing clothes which are sexually revealing. *...a model in scanty clothing.* ADJ-GRADED =flimsy

♦ **scantily** *...a troupe of scantily-clad dancers. ...pictures of scantily dressed women on every page.* ADV-GRADED: ADV -ed/adj

scapegoat /skeɪpgoʊt/ **scapegoats, scapegoating, scapegoated** ◆◇◇◇◇

1 If you say that someone is made a **scapegoat** for something bad that has happened, you mean that people blame them and may punish them for it although it may not be their fault. *I don't think I deserve to be messed about and made the scapegoat for a couple of bad results.* N-COUNT: oft N for n

2 To **scapegoat** someone means to blame them publicly for something bad that has happened, even though it was not their fault. *...a climate where ethnic minorities are continually scapegoated for the lack of jobs and housing problems.* VERB V n

♦ **scapegoating** *The teachers are fair and avoid favouritism and scapegoating.* N-UNCOUNT

scapula /skæpjʊlə/ **scapulae.** Your **scapula** is your shoulder blade; a medical term. N-COUNT

scar /skɑːʳ/ **scars, scarring, scarred** ◆◆◇◇◇

1 A **scar** is a mark on the skin which is left after a wound has healed. *He had a scar on his forehead. ...facial injuries which have left permanent scars.* N-COUNT

2 If your skin **is scarred**, it is badly marked as a result of a wound. *He was scarred for life during a pub fight... His scarred face crumpled with pleasure.* VB: usu passive be V-ed V-ed

3 If a surface **is scarred**, it is damaged and there are ugly marks on it. *The arena was scarred by deep muddy ruts. ...scarred wooden table tops.* VB: usu passive be V-ed V-ed

4 If an unpleasant physical or emotional experience leaves a **scar** on someone, it has a permanent effect on their mind. *The early years of fear and the hostility left a deep scar on the young boy. ...emotional scars that come from having been abused.* N-COUNT

5 If an unpleasant physical or emotional experience **scars** you, it has a permanent effect on your mind. *This is something that's going to scar him forever.* VERB V n

scarce /skeəʳs/ **scarcer, scarcest** ◆◆◇◇◇

1 If something is **scarce**, there is not enough of it. *Food was scarce and expensive... Jobs are becoming increasingly scarce. ...the allocation of scarce resources.* ADJ-GRADED: usu v-link ADJ

2 If you **make** yourself **scarce**, you quickly leave the place you are in, usually in order to avoid a difficult or embarrassing situation; an informal expression. *It probably would be a good idea if you made yourself scarce.* PHRASE: V inflects

scarcely /skeəʳsli/ ◆◆◇◇◇

1 You use **scarcely** to emphasize that something is only just true or only just the case. *He could scarcely breathe... I scarcely knew him... She seemed scarcely aware of him... He was scarcely more than a boy... Scarcely a week goes by without the news providing fresh examples of police racism... She was scarcely 18 when she made her debut.* ADV-BRD-NEG: ADV before v, ADV group, oft ADV amount PRAGMATICS

2 You can use **scarcely** in a humorous way to say that something is certainly not true or is certainly not the case. *It can scarcely be coincidence... Yesterday, however, his views seemed scarcely relevant... It was scarcely in their interest to let too many people know.* ADV-BRD-NEG: ADV before v, ADV group PRAGMATICS =hardly

3 If you say **scarcely** had one thing happened when something else happened, you mean that the first event was followed immediately by the second. *Scarcely had they left the university campus before soldiers armed with bayonets and rifles charged into the students... Bruce had scarcely shaken our hands when the phone rang.* ADV-BRD-NEG: ADV before v PRAGMATICS

scarcity /skeəʳsɪti/ **scarcities.** If there is a **scarcity** of something, there is not enough of it for the people who need it or want it; a rather formal word. *...an ever increasing scarcity of water.* ◆◇◇◇◇ N-VAR =shortage

scare /skeəʳ/ **scares, scaring, scared** ◆◆◇◇◇

1 If something **scares** you, it frightens or worries you. *You're scaring me... What scares me most is that I'm going to end up not being married... The prospect of failure scares me rigid... It scared him to realise how close he had come to losing everything.* VERB =frighten V n V n adj *it* V n to-inf
• If you want to emphasize that something scares you a lot, you can say that it **scares the hell out of** you or **scares the life out of** you; an informal expression. PHRASE: V inflects PRAGMATICS

2 If a sudden unpleasant experience gives you a **scare**, it frightens you. *Don't you realize what a scare you've given us all?... We got a bit of a scare.* N-SING

3 A **scare** is a situation in which many people are afraid or worried because they think something dangerous is happening which will affect them all. *...the doctor at the centre of an Aids scare... Despite the scare there are no plans to withdraw the drug.* N-COUNT: oft n N

4 A bomb **scare** or a security **scare** is a situation in which there is believed to be a bomb in a place. *Despite many recent bomb scares, no one has yet been hurt. ...a security scare over a suspect package.* N-COUNT: usu n N =alert

5 See also **scared**.

scare away. See **scare off** 1. PHRASAL VERB

scare off PHRASAL VERB

1 If you **scare off** or **scare away** a person or animal, you frighten them so that they go away. *...an alarm to scare off an attacker. ...the problem of scaring birds away from airport runways.* =frighten off V P n (not pron) V n P

2 If you **scare** someone **off**, you accidentally discourage them from becoming involved with you. *I don't think that revealing your past to your boyfriend scared him off... The new Democratic Party is not likely to scare off voters.* =put off, frighten off V n P V P n (not pron)

scarecrow /skeəʳkroʊ/ **scarecrows.** A **scarecrow** is an object in the shape of a person, which is put in a field where crops are growing in order to frighten birds away. N-COUNT

scared /skeəʳd/ ◆◆◇◇◇

1 If you are **scared** of someone or something, you are frightened of them. *I'm certainly not scared of him... I was too scared to move... Why are you so scared?* ADJ-GRADED: usu v-link ADJ, oft ADJ *of* n, ADJ to-inf =frightened

2 If you are **scared** that something unpleasant might happen, you are nervous and worried because you think that it might happen. *I was scared that I might be sick... He was scared of letting us down.* ADJ-GRADED: usu v-link ADJ, oft ADJ that, ADJ *of*-ing =frightened

3 If you are **scared to death** or **scared stiff**, you are extremely scared. *In high school I was scared to death of you... He's scared stiff of the relationship breaking down.* PHRASE =terrified

scaremongering /skeəʳmʌŋgərɪŋ/. If one person or group accuses another person or group of **scaremongering**, they accuse them of deliberately spreading worrying stories to try and frighten people. *The Government has repeatedly accused Labour of scaremongering.* N-UNCOUNT

scare story, scare stories. A **scare story** is something that is said or written to make people feel frightened and think that a situation is much more unpleasant or dangerous than it really is. *He described talk of sackings as scare stories.* N-COUNT

scarf /skɑːʳf/ **scarfs** or **scarves.** A **scarf** is a piece of cloth that you wear round your neck or head, usually to keep yourself warm. *He reached up to loosen the scarf around his neck.* ◆◇◇◇◇ N-COUNT

scarlet /skɑːʳlət/ **scarlets** ◆◇◇◇◇

1 Something that is **scarlet** is bright red. *...her scarlet lipstick.* COLOUR

2 If someone with pale skin turns or goes **scarlet**, their face becomes redder than usual because they are very embarrassed or angry. *She turned scarlet from embarrassment, once she realized what she had done... Her face went bright scarlet.* COLOUR: usu v-link COLOUR

scarlet fever. **Scarlet fever** is an infectious disease which causes a painful throat, a high temperature, and a red rash. N-UNCOUNT

scarper /skɑːʳpəʳ/ **scarpers, scarpering, scarpered.** If someone **scarpers**, they leave a place quickly; used in informal British English. *He owed Vince money for drugs, which is perhaps the reason he scarpered.* VERB V

-scarred /-skɑːʳd/

1 **-scarred** is used after nouns such as 'bullet' and 'fire' to form adjectives which indicate that something has been damaged or marked by the thing mentioned. *Crying orphans were loaded back into a bullet-scarred bus. ...a lightning-scarred tree.* COMB in ADJ: ADJ n

2 **-scarred** is used after nouns such as 'battle' or 'drug' to form adjectives which indicate that the thing mentioned has had a permanent effect on someone's mind. *...battle-scarred soldiers. ...a war-scarred orphan.* COMB in ADJ-GRADED: usu ADJ n

3 See also **scar**.

scarves /skɑːʳvz/. **Scarves** is a plural of **scarf**.

scary /skeəri/ **scarier, scariest.** Something that is **scary** is rather frightening; an informal word. *I think prison is going to be a scary thing for Harry... There's something very scary about him... We watched scary movies.* ◆◇◇◇◇ ADJ-GRADED ♦ **scarily** /skeərɪli/ *...the scarily unstable new world order.* ADV-GRADED: usu ADV adj

scat /skæt/. **Scat** is a type of jazz singing in which the singer sings sounds rather than complete words. N-UNCOUNT

scathing /skeɪðɪŋ/. If you say that someone is being **scathing** about something, you mean that they are being very critical and scornful of it. *The society has been particularly scathing about the planning record of West Somerset District Council... He then launched a scathing attack on previous leaders.* ◆◇◇◇◇ ADJ-GRADED ♦ **scathingly** *'Oh, they want to be excused,' the other girl said scathingly.* ADV-GRADED: usu ADV with v

scatological /skætəlɒdʒɪkəl/. If you describe something as **scatological**, you mean that it deliberately refers to or represents faeces in some way; a formal word. *...scatological anecdotes.* ADJ-GRADED: usu ADJ n

scatter /skætəʳ/ **scatters, scattering, scattered** ◆◆◇◇◇

1 If you **scatter** things over an area, you throw or drop them so that they spread all over the area. *She tore the rose apart and scattered the petals over the grave... They've been scattering toys everywhere... He began by scattering seed and putting in plants.* VERB V n prep/adv V n

2 If a group of people **scatter** or if you **scatter** them, they suddenly separate and move in different directions. *After dinner, everyone scattered... The cavalry scattered them and chased them off the field.* V-ERG V V n

3 A **scatter** of things is a number of them spread over an area in an irregular way; a literary use. *On the table was a pile of books and a scatter of papers.* N-SING: usu N *of* n

4 See also **scattered**, **scattering**.

scatterbrained /skætəʳbreɪnd/; also spelled **scatter-brained**. If you describe someone as **scatterbrained**, you mean that they often forget things and are unable to organize their thoughts properly. ADJ-GRADED =forgetful

scattered /skætəʳd/ ◆◆◇◇◇

1 **Scattered** things are spread over an area in an untidy or irregular way. *He picked up the scattered toys... Tomorrow there will be a few scattered showers... The fridge door was open and food was scattered across the floor.* ADJ: ADJ n, v-link ADJ prep/adv

2 If something is **scattered with** a lot of small things, they are spread all over it. *Every surface is scattered with photographs.* ADJ: v-link ADJ *with* n

scattering /skætərɪŋ/ **scatterings.** A **scattering** of things or people is a small number of them spread over an area. *...the scattering of houses east of the village... Mr. James had had a scattering of very wealthy friends.* ◆◇◇◇◇ N-COUNT: usu N *of* n

scattershot. A **scattershot** approach or method does not seem to follow any organized plan or pattern. *The report condemns America's scattershot approach to training workers.* ADJ-GRADED: usu ADJ n

scatty /skæti/. If you describe someone as **scatty**, you mean that they are dreamy and often ADJ-GRADED =scatterbrained, forgetful

forget things or behave in a silly way; used in informal British English. *Her mother is scatty and absent-minded.*

scavenge /skævɪndʒ/ **scavenges, scavenging, scavenged.** If people or animals **scavenge** for things, they collect them by searching among waste or unwanted objects. *Many are orphans, their parents killed as they scavenged for food... Children scavenge through garbage... The foxes come and scavenge the bones... Cruz had to scavenge information from newspapers and journals.* ◆◇◇◇◇ VERB V *for* n V prep/adv V n Also V

♦ **scavenger, scavengers** *...scavengers such as rats.* N-COUNT

scenario /sɪnɑːrioʊ, AM -ner-/ **scenarios** ◆◆◇◇◇

1 If you talk about a likely or possible **scenario**, you are talking about the way in which a situation may develop. *...the nightmare scenario of a divided and irrelevant Royal Family... In the worst-case scenario, you could become a homeless person... Try to imagine all the possible scenarios and what action you would take.* N-COUNT

2 The **scenario** of a film is a piece of writing that gives an outline of the story. N-COUNT =outline

scene /siːn/ **scenes** ◆◆◆◆◇

1 A **scene** in a play, film, or book is part of it in which a series of events happen in the same place. *I found the scene in which Percy proposed to Olive tremendously poignant. ...the opening scene of 'A Christmas Carol'. ...love scenes. ...Act I, scene 1.* N-COUNT

2 You refer to a place as a **scene** when you are describing its appearance and indicating what impression it makes on you. *It's a scene of complete devastation... Thick black smoke billowed over the scene... You can just picture the scene, can't you?* N-COUNT: usu sing

3 You can describe an event that you see, or that is broadcast or shown in a picture, as a **scene** of a particular kind. *There were emotional scenes as the refugees enjoyed their first breath of freedom... Television broadcasters were warned to exercise caution over depicting scenes of violence... It was a bizarre scene.* N-COUNT: with supp

4 The **scene** of an event is the place where it happened. *The area has been the scene of fierce fighting for three months. ...traces left at the scene of a crime... Fire and police crews rushed to the scene, but the couple were already dead... Riot vans were on the scene in minutes.* N-COUNT: usu sing, oft N *of* n

5 You can refer to an area of activity as a particular type of **scene**. *Sandman's experimentation has made him something of a cult figure on the local music scene. ...when he first burst onto the national political scene at age 28. ...a youth guide to London's club scene.* N-SING: supp N, usu *the* supp N

6 Paintings and drawings of places are sometimes called **scenes**. *...James Lynch's country scenes.* N-COUNT: usu with supp

7 If you make a **scene**, you embarrass people by publicly showing your anger about something. *I'm sorry I made such a scene.* N-COUNT: usu sing

8 If something is done **behind the scenes**, it is done secretly rather than publicly. *But behind the scenes Mr Cain will be working quietly to try to get a deal done. ...behind-the-scenes discussions.* PHRASES PHR with cl, PHR n

9 If you refer to what happens **behind the scenes**, you are referring to what happens during the making of a film, play, or radio or television programme. *It's an exciting opportunity to learn what goes on behind the scenes.* PHR after v, PHR n

10 If you have **a change of scene**, you go somewhere different after being in a particular place for a long time. *What you need is a change of scene. Why not go on a cruise?* usu v PHR =a change of scenery

11 If you **set the scene** for someone, you tell them what they need to know in order to understand what is going to happen or be said next. *But first to set the scene: I was having a drink with my ex-boyfriend.* V inflects

12 Something that **sets the scene for** a particular event creates the conditions in which the event is likely to happen. *Mr Yeltsin's declaration set the scene for a further confrontation with Mr Gorbachev.* V inflects

13 When someone or something appears **on the scene**, they come into being or become involved in something. When they disappear **from the scene**, they are no longer there or are no longer involved. *He could react rather jealously when and if another child comes on the scene... Harris disappeared from the scene as suddenly as he had appeared.* usu v PHR

14 If you say that an activity or place **is not** your **scene**, you mean that you do not like it or enjoy it; an informal expression. *Lying on the beach all week isn't my scene.* V inflects

scenery /siːnəri/ ◆◇◇◇◇

1 The **scenery** in a country area is the land, water, or plants that you can see around you. *...the island's spectacular scenery... Sometimes they just drive slowly down the lane enjoying the scenery.* N-UNCOUNT

2 In a theatre, the **scenery** consists of the structures and painted backcloths that give an indication of where the action in the play takes place. N-UNCOUNT

3 If you have **a change of scenery**, you go somewhere different after being in a particular place for a long time. *A change of scenery might do you the power of good.* PHRASE =a change of scene

scenic /siːnɪk/ ◆◇◇◇◇

1 A **scenic** place has attractive scenery. *This is an extremely scenic part of America. ...a 2-hour drive through scenic country.* ADJ-GRADED: usu ADJ n =beautiful, picturesque

2 A **scenic** route goes through attractive scenery and has nice views. *It was even marked on the map as a scenic route... I went some miles out of my way to take the scenic road into Macon.* ADJ-GRADED: usu ADJ n

3 If a place has **scenic** beauty, its scenery is attractive. *...a land of unparalleled scenic beauty.* ADJ: ADJ n

♦ **scenically** /siːnɪkli/ *The Azores are scenically stunning.* ADV: usu ADV adj

scent /sent/ **scents, scenting, scented** ◆◆◇◇◇

1 Something's **scent** is the pleasant smell that it has. *Flowers are chosen for their scent as well as their look.* N-COUNT: usu with supp =fragrance

2 If something **scents** a place or thing, it makes it smell pleasant. *Jasmine flowers scent the air... Scent your drawers and wardrobe with your favourite aromas.* VERB V n V n *with* n

3 **Scent** is a pleasant-smelling liquid which women put on their necks and wrists to make themselves smell nice; used mainly in British English. *She dabbed herself with scent.* N-MASS =perfume

4 The **scent** of a person or animal is the smell that they leave and that other people sometimes follow when looking for them. *A police dog picked up the murderer's scent... Many kinds of insect find their mates by scent.* N-VAR: usu with supp

5 When an animal **scents** something, it becomes aware of it by smelling it. *...dogs which scent the hidden birds.* VB: no cont =smell V n

6 If you **scent** a situation, you feel that it is going to happen. *Republicans from Pennsylvania and New York are scenting victory.* VERB =sense V n

scented /sentɪd/. **Scented** things have a pleasant smell, either naturally or because perfume has been added to them. *The white flowers are pleasantly scented. ...scented body lotion.* ◆◇◇◇◇ ADJ =perfumed

scepter /septəʳ/ **scepters.** See **sceptre**.

sceptic /skeptɪk/ **sceptics;** spelled **skeptic** in American English. A **sceptic** is a person who has doubts about things that other people believe. *He was a born sceptic... But he now has to convince sceptics that he has a serious plan.* ◆◇◇◇◇ N-COUNT

sceptical /skeptɪkᵊl/; spelled **skeptical** in American English. If you are **sceptical** about something, you have doubts about it. *Other archaeologists are sceptical about his findings. ...scientists who are sceptical of global warming and its alleged consequences... The party has always had a cautious and sceptical attitude to Europe.* ◆◆◇◇◇ ADJ-GRADED: oft v-link ADJ *about/of* n =dubious

♦ **sceptically** /skeptɪkli/ *I looked at him skeptically, sure he was exaggerating... 'What's your point?' demanded the old man sceptically.* ADV-GRADED: ADV after v =dubiously

scepticism /skeptɪsɪzəm/; spelled **skepticism** in American English. **Scepticism** is great doubt about whether something is true or useful. *There was considerable scepticism about President* ◆◇◇◇◇ N-UNCOUNT =doubt

Gorbachev's plans for economic reforms... The report has inevitably been greeted with scepticism.

sceptre /septər/ **sceptres;** spelled **scepter** in American English. A **sceptre** is an ornamental rod that a king or queen carries on ceremonial occasions as a symbol of his or her power. N-COUNT

schedule /ʃedju:l, AM skedʒu:l/ **schedules, scheduling, scheduled** ◆◆◆◆◇

1 A **schedule** is a plan that gives a list of events or tasks and the times at which each one should happen or be done. *He has been forced to adjust his schedule... We both have such hectic schedules.* N-COUNT =timetable

2 You can use the word **schedule** to refer to the time or way something is planned to be done. For example, if something is completed **on schedule**, it is completed at the time planned. *The jet arrived in Johannesburg two minutes ahead of schedule... Everything went according to schedule... It will be completed several weeks behind schedule.* N-UNCOUNT: prep N

3 If something **is scheduled** to happen at a particular time, arrangements are made for it to happen at that time. *The space shuttle had been scheduled to blast off at 04:38... A presidential election was scheduled for last December... No new talks are scheduled.* VB: usu passive be V-ed to-inf be V-ed for n V-ed

4 A **schedule** is a written list of things, for example a list of prices, details, or conditions. N-COUNT =list

5 A **schedule** is a list of all the times when trains, boats, buses, or aircraft are supposed to arrive or depart from a particular place. *...a bus schedule.* N-COUNT =timetable

schema /ski:mə/ **schemas** or **schemata** /ski:mətə/. A **schema** is an outline of a plan or theory; a formal word. *...a definite position in the schema of the economic process.* N-COUNT

schematic /ski:mætɪk/. A **schematic** diagram or picture shows in a simplified way how something works. *This is represented in the schematic diagram below. ...a schematic picture of the solar system.* ♦ **schematically** /ski:mætɪkli/ *Let me schematically show what happens.* ADJ-GRADED: usu ADJ n; ADV-GRADED: ADV with v

scheme /ski:m/ **schemes, scheming, schemed** ◆◆◆◆◇

1 A **scheme** is a large-scale plan or arrangement produced by a government or other organization. *...schemes to help combat unemployment. ...a private pension scheme... The company was pouring around $30 million into the scheme.* N-COUNT: oft N to-inf, n N =plan

2 A **scheme** is someone's plan for achieving something. *...a quick money-making scheme to get us through the summer... They would first have to work out some scheme for getting the treasure out.* N-COUNT: oft N to-inf, N *for*-ing =plan

3 If you say that people **are scheming**, you mean that they are making secret plans in order to gain something for themselves; used showing disapproval. *Everyone's always scheming and plotting... The bride's family were scheming to prevent a wedding... They claimed that their opponents were scheming against them... You're a scheming little devil, aren't you?* ♦ **scheming** *...their favourite pastimes of scheming and gossiping.* VB: oft cont PRAGMATICS =plot V V to-inf V *against* n V-ing; N-UNCOUNT

4 See also **colour scheme**.

5 Someone's **scheme of things** is the way in which they think that things in their life should be organized. *He did not quite know how to place women in his scheme of things.* PHRASES poss PHR

6 When people talk about **the scheme of things** or **the grand scheme of things** , they are referring to the way that everything in the world seems to be organized. *We realize that we are infinitely small within the scheme of things.*

schemer /ski:mər/ **schemers.** If you refer to someone as a **schemer**, you mean that they make secret plans in order to get some benefit for themselves; used showing disapproval. *This is not to say we all want to turn into office schemers, thinking of nothing but our own advancement.* N-COUNT PRAGMATICS =plotter

scherzo /skeərtsoʊ/ **scherzos.** A **scherzo** is a short, lively piece of classical music which is usually part of a longer piece of music such as a symphony or a sonata. N-COUNT

schism /skɪzəm, sɪz-/ **schisms.** When there is a **schism**, a group or organization divides into two groups as a result of differences in thinking and beliefs; a formal word. *...the great schism which divided the Christian world in the 11th century... The church seems to be on the brink of schism.* N-VAR =split

schizoid /skɪtsɔɪd/

1 If you describe someone as **schizoid**, you mean that they seem to have very different opinions and purposes at different times; an informal use. *...a rather schizoid fellow.* ADJ-GRADED

2 Someone who is **schizoid** suffers from schizophrenia. *...a schizoid personality.* ADJ

schizophrenia /skɪtsəfri:niə/. **Schizophrenia** is a serious mental illness. People who suffer from it are unable to relate their thoughts and feelings to what is happening around them and often withdraw from society. ◆◇◇◇◇ N-UNCOUNT

schizophrenic /skɪtsəfrenɪk/ **schizophrenics** ◆◇◇◇◇

1 A **schizophrenic** is a person who is suffering from schizophrenia. *He was diagnosed as a paranoid schizophrenic.* ► Also an adjective. *...a schizophrenic patient. ...schizophrenic tendencies.* N-COUNT; ADJ

2 Someone's attitude or behaviour can be described as **schizophrenic** when they seem to have very different opinions or purposes at different times; an informal use. *...the schizophrenic mood of the American public.* ADJ-GRADED

schlep /ʃlep/ **schleps, schlepping, schlepped;** also spelled **schlepp.**

1 If you **schlep** something somewhere, you take it there awkwardly or with difficulty; used in informal American English. *You didn't just schlep your guitar around from folk club to folk club.* VERB =lug V n adv/prep

2 If you **schlep** somewhere, you go there; used in informal American English. *It's too cold to schlepp around looking at property.* VERB =trudge V adv/prep

schlock /ʃlɒk/. If you refer to films, pop songs, or books as **schlock**, you mean that they have no artistic or social value; an informal word. *...a showman with a good eye for marketable schlock.* N-UNCOUNT

schmaltz /ʃmælts, AM ʃmɑ:lts/. If you describe a play, film, or book as **schmaltz**, you do not like it because it is so sentimental. N-UNCOUNT PRAGMATICS =slush

schmaltzy /ʃmæltsi, AM ʃmɑ:ltsi/. If you describe songs, films, or books as **schmaltzy**, you do not like them because they are so sentimental. ADJ-GRADED PRAGMATICS =slushy

schmooze /ʃmu:z/ **schmoozes, schmoozing, schmoozed.** If you **schmooze**, you talk casually and socially with someone; used mainly in informal American English. *...those coffee houses where you can schmooze for hours.* VERB =chat V

schnapps /ʃnæps/. **Schnapps** is a strong alcoholic drink made from potatoes. ► A **schnapps** is a glass of schnapps. N-UNCOUNT; N-SING

scholar /skɒlər/ **scholars** ◆◆◇◇◇

1 A **scholar** is a person who studies an academic subject and knows a lot about it; a formal use. *The library attracts thousands of scholars and researchers. ...an influential Islamic scholar.* N-COUNT

2 You can use the word **scholar** to refer to someone who learns things at school in a particular way. For example, if someone is a good **scholar**, they are good at learning things. An old-fashioned use. *She could be a good scholar if she didn't let her mind wander so much.* N-COUNT: usu adj N =student

3 A **scholar** is a student who has obtained a scholarship. *He came to Oxford as a Rhodes scholar and studied law.* N-COUNT: usu n N

scholarly /skɒlərli/ ◆◇◇◇◇

1 A **scholarly** person spends a lot of time studying and knows a lot about academic subjects. *He was an intellectual, scholarly man.* ADJ-GRADED

2 A **scholarly** book or article contains a lot of academic information and is intended for academic readers. *...the more scholarly academic journals.* ADJ-GRADED

3 **Scholarly** matters and activities relate to scholars or their work. *This has been the subject of intense scholarly debate... Faculty members devote most of their time to scholarly research.* ADJ: usu ADJ n

scholarship /skɒlərʃɪp/ **scholarships** ◆◆◇◇◇

1 If you get a **scholarship** to a school or university, your studies are paid for by the school or university N-COUNT

or by some other organization. *He got a scholarship to the Pratt Institute of Art. ...scholarships for women over 30.*

2 **Scholarship** is serious academic study and the knowledge that is obtained from it. *I want to take advantage of your lifetime of scholarship.* N-UNCOUNT

scholastic /skəlæstɪk/. Your **scholastic** achievement or ability is your academic achievement or ability while you are at school; a formal word. *...the values which encouraged her scholastic achievement.* ADJ: ADJ n =academic

school /skuːl/ **schools, schooling, schooled** ◆◆◆◆◆

1 A **school** is a place where children are educated. You usually refer to this place as **school** when you are talking about the time that children spend there and the activities that they do there. *...a boy who was in my class at school... Even the good students say homework is what they most dislike about school... I took the kids for a picnic in the park after school. ...a school built in the Sixties... He favors extending the school day and school year. ...two boys wearing school uniform.* N-VAR: usu prep N

2 A **school** is the pupils or staff at a school. *Deirdre, the whole school's going to hate you. ...a children's writing competition open to schools or individuals.* N-COUNT-COLL

3 A privately-run place where a particular skill or subject is taught can be referred to as a **school**. *...a riding school and equestrian centre near Chepstow. ...the Kingsley School of English.* N-COUNT: with supp, oft in names

4 A university, college, or university department specializing in a particular type of subject can be referred to as a **school**. *...a lecturer in the school of veterinary medicine at the University of Pennsylvania... Stella, 21, is at art school training to be a fashion designer.* N-VAR: with supp, oft in names

5 In informal American English, **school** is used to refer to university or college. *Bill Clinton's an Oxford man – he went to school in England.* N-UNCOUNT

6 A particular **school** of writers, artists, or thinkers is a group of them whose work, opinions, or theories are similar. *...the Chicago school of economists... O'Keeffe was influenced by various painters and photographers, but she was never a member of any school.* N-COUNT-COLL: usu with supp

7 A **school of** fish or dolphins is a large group of them moving through water together. N-COUNT-COLL: N *of* n

8 If you **school** someone in something, you train or educate them to have a certain skill, type of behaviour, or way of thinking; used in written English. *Many mothers schooled their daughters in the myth of female inferiority... He is schooled to spot trouble.* VERB =train V n *in* n *be* V-ed to-inf Also V n to-inf

9 In American English and in formal British English, to **school** a child means to educate him or her. *She's been schooling her kids herself.* ♦ **schooled** *...a cross-cultural study with Indian children, both schooled and unschooled, and American children.* VERB =educate V n ADJ-GRADED ≠unschooled

10 If you **school** a horse, you train it so that it can be ridden in races or competitions. *She bought him as a £1,000 colt of six months and schooled him.* VERB =train V n

11 See also **schooled**, **schooling**; **after-school**, **approved school**, **boarding school**, **church school**, **convent school**, **driving school**, **finishing school**, **grade school**, **graduate school**, **grammar school**, **high school**, **infant school**, **junior school**, **middle school**, **night school**, **nursery school**, **pre-school**, **prep school**, **primary school**, **private school**, **public school**, **special school**, **state school**, **summer school**, **Sunday school**.

12 If you approve of someone because they have good qualities that used to be more common in the past, you can describe them as one **of the old school**. *He is one of the old school who still believes in honour in public life. ...an elderly gentleman of the old school.* • **school of thought**: see **thought**. PHRASE: usu n PHR PRAGMATICS

school age. When a child reaches **school age**, he or she is old enough to go to school. *Most of them have young children below school age.* ► Also an adjective. *...families with school-age children.* N-UNCOUNT: oft prep N ADJ: usu ADJ n

schoolbag /skuːlbæg/ **schoolbags;** also spelled **school bag**. A **schoolbag** is a bag such as a satchel or a holdall that children use to carry books and other things to and from school. N-COUNT

school board, school boards. In the United States, a **school board** is a committee in charge of education in a particular city or area, or in a particular school. *Colonel Richard Nelson served on the school board until this year.* ◆◇◇◇◇ N-COUNT-COLL

school book, school books; also spelled **schoolbook**. **School books** are textbooks that children use at school. N-COUNT: usu pl

schoolboy /skuːlbɔɪ/ **schoolboys** ◆◇◇◇◇

1 A **schoolboy** is a boy who goes to school. *...a group of ten-year-old schoolboys.* N-COUNT

2 If you think a man's sense of humour is silly or immature, you can describe it as **schoolboy** humour. *...tiresome schoolboy jokes.* ADJ: ADJ n PRAGMATICS

school bus, school buses. A **school bus** is a special bus which takes children to and from school. N-COUNT

schoolchild /skuːltʃaɪld/ **schoolchildren.** **Schoolchildren** are children who go to school. *Last year I had an audience of schoolchildren and they laughed at everything.* ◆◇◇◇◇ N-COUNT: usu pl

schooldays /skuːldeɪz/; also spelled **school days**. Your **schooldays** are the period of your life when you were at school. *He was happily married to a girl he had known since his schooldays.* N-PLURAL: usu poss N

school dinner, school dinners. In British English, **school dinners** are midday meals provided for children at a school. *Overcooked greens are my most vivid recollection of school dinners.* N-VAR

schooled /skuːld/. If you are **schooled** in something, you have learned about it as the result of training or experience; used in written English. *They were both well schooled in the ways of the Army... She is a professional economist and therefore schooled in the arguments against that sort of state intervention.* • See also **school**. ADJ-GRADED: v-link ADJ *in* n, oft adv ADJ =trained

school friend, school friends; also spelled **schoolfriend**. A **school friend** is a friend of yours who is at the same school as you, or who used to be at the same school when you were children. *His school friends and his teachers visited him and he got loads of presents and cards... I spent the evening with an old schoolfriend.* N-COUNT: oft with poss =schoolmate

schoolgirl /skuːlgɜːʳl/ **schoolgirls.** A **schoolgirl** is a girl who goes to school. *...half a dozen giggling schoolgirls.* ◆◇◇◇◇ N-COUNT

schoolhouse /skuːlhaʊs/ **schoolhouses.** In American English, a **schoolhouse** is a small building used as a school. *McCreary lives in a converted schoolhouse outside Charlottesville.* N-COUNT

schooling /skuːlɪŋ/. **Schooling** is education that children receive at school. *His formal schooling continued erratically until he reached the age of eleven. ...a voucher scheme to help poorer families pay for private schooling.* ◆◇◇◇◇ N-UNCOUNT: oft with poss =education

school kid, school kids; also spelled **schoolkid**. **School kids** are **schoolchildren**; used in spoken English. *...young school kids in short pants.* N-COUNT: usu pl

school leaver, school leavers; also spelled **school-leaver**. In British English, **school leavers** are young people who have just left school, because they have completed their time there. *...the lack of job opportunities, particularly for school-leavers.* ◆◇◇◇◇ N-COUNT: usu pl

schoolmaster /skuːlmɑːstəʳ, -mæst-/ **schoolmasters.** A **schoolmaster** is a man who teaches children in a school; an old-fashioned word. ◆◇◇◇◇ N-COUNT

schoolmate /skuːlmeɪt/ **schoolmates.** A **schoolmate** is a child who goes to the same school as you, especially one who is your friend. *He started the magazine with an unemployed former schoolmate... He was a favorite with his schoolmasters but not his schoolmates.* N-COUNT: oft with poss =schoolfriend

schoolmistress /skuːlmɪstrəs/ **schoolmistresses.** A **schoolmistress** is a woman who teaches children in a school; an old-fashioned word. N-COUNT

schoolroom /skuːlruːm/ **schoolrooms.** A **schoolroom** is a classroom, especially the only classroom in a small school. N-COUNT =classroom

schoolteacher /skuːltiːtʃəʳ/ **schoolteachers.** A **schoolteacher** is a teacher in a school. ◆◇◇◇◇ N-COUNT

school teaching. **School teaching** is the work that schoolteachers do; a formal word. *He returned to school teaching.* N-UNCOUNT =teaching

schoolwork /skuːlwɜːʳk/. **Schoolwork** is the work that a child does at school or as homework. *My mother would help me with my schoolwork.* N-UNCOUNT

schoolyard /skuːljɑːʳd/ **schoolyards;** also spelled **school yard**. The **schoolyard** is the large open area with a hard surface just outside a school building, where the schoolchildren can play and do other activities. *...the sound of the kids in the schoolyard.* N-COUNT: usu *the* N in sing =playground

schooner /skuːnəʳ/ **schooners**

1 A **schooner** is a medium-sized sailing ship. N-COUNT

2 In British English, a **schooner** is a large glass which you use for sherry. N-COUNT

schwa /ʃwɑː/ **schwas.** In the study of language, **schwa** is the name of the neutral vowel sound represented by the symbol /ə/ in this dictionary. N-VAR

sciatica /saɪætɪkə/. **Sciatica** is a severe pain in the nerve in your legs or the lower part of your back; a medical term. N-UNCOUNT

science /saɪəns/ **sciences** ◆◆◆◆◇

1 **Science** is the study of the nature and behaviour of natural things and the knowledge that we obtain about them. *The best discoveries in science are very simple. ...science and technology.* N-UNCOUNT

2 A **science** is a particular branch of science such as physics, chemistry, or biology. *Physics is the best example of a science which has developed strong, abstract theories. ...the science of microbiology.* N-COUNT: usu with supp

3 A **science** is the study of some aspect of human behaviour, for example sociology or anthropology. *...the modern science of psychology.* N-COUNT: usu with supp

4 See also **domestic science**, **exact science**, **Master of Science**, **political science**, **social science**.

science fiction. **Science fiction** consists of stories in books, comics, and films about events that take place in the future or in other parts of the universe. ◆◇◇◇◇ N-UNCOUNT =sci-fi

science park, science parks. A **science park** is an area, usually linked to a university, where there are a lot of private companies, especially ones concerned with high technology. N-COUNT

scientific /saɪəntɪfɪk/ ◆◆◆◇◇

1 **Scientific** is used to describe things that relate to science or to a particular science. *Scientific research is widely claimed to be the source of the high standard of living in the US. ...the use of animals in scientific experiments. ...scientific instruments.* ADJ: usu ADJ n
♦ **scientifically** /saɪəntɪfɪkli/ *...scientifically advanced countries.* ADV

2 If you do something in a **scientific** way, you do it carefully and thoroughly, using experiments or tests. *It's not a scientific way to test their opinions. ...the scientific study of capitalist development.* ADJ-GRADED: usu ADJ n =methodical
♦ **scientifically** *Efforts are being made to research it scientifically.* ADV-GRADED =methodically

scientist /saɪəntɪst/ **scientists.** A **scientist** is someone who has studied science and whose job is to teach or do research in science. *Scientists say they've already collected more data than had been expected.* • See also **social scientist**. ◆◆◆◆◇ N-COUNT

sci-fi /saɪ faɪ/. **Sci-fi** is **science fiction**; an informal word. *...a two-and-a-half hour sci-fi film.* ◆◇◇◇◇ N-UNCOUNT

scimitar /sɪmɪtəʳ/ **scimitars.** A **scimitar** is a sword with a curved blade that was used in former times in some Eastern countries. N-COUNT

scintilla /sɪntɪlə/. If you say that there is **not** a **scintilla of** evidence, hope, or doubt about something, you are emphasizing that there is none at all; a literary word. *He says there is 'not a scintilla of evidence' to link him to any controversy.* QUANT: with brd-neg, QUANT *of* n-uncount PRAGMATICS =shred

scintillating /sɪntɪleɪtɪŋ/. A **scintillating** conversation or performance is very lively and interesting. *You can hardly expect scintillating conversation from a kid that age.* ADJ-GRADED: usu ADJ n =sparkling

scion /saɪən/ **scions.** A **scion** of a rich or famous family is one of its younger or more recent members; a literary word. *Nabokov was the scion of an aristocratic family that lost its fortune in the Revolution.* N-COUNT: usu N *of* n

scissors /sɪzəʳz/; the form **scissor** is used as a modifier. **Scissors** are a small cutting tool with two sharp blades that are screwed together. You use scissors for cutting things such as paper and cloth. *He told me to get some scissors... She picked up a pair of scissors from the windowsill.* ◆◇◇◇◇ N-PLURAL: also *a pair of* N

sclerosis /sklərəʊsɪs/. **Sclerosis** is a medical condition in which the tissue in a part of your body becomes abnormally hard; a medical term. • See also **multiple sclerosis**. ◆◇◇◇◇ N-UNCOUNT

scoff /skɒf/ **scoffs, scoffing, scoffed** ◆◇◇◇◇

1 If you **scoff** at something, you speak in a scornful, mocking way about it because you think it is ridiculous or inadequate. *At first I scoffed at the notion... You may scoff but I honestly feel I'm being cruel only to be kind... 'You'll have to do better than that,' Joanna scoffed.* VERB =mock V *at* n V V with quote

2 If you **scoff** food, you eat it quickly and greedily; used in informal British English. *The pancakes were so good that I scoffed the lot.* VERB =wolf, gobble V n

scold /skəʊld/ **scolds, scolding, scolded.** If you **scold** someone, you speak angrily to them because they have done something wrong; a formal word. *If he finds out, he'll scold me... Later she scolded her daughter for having talked to her father like that... 'You should be at school,' he scolded.* ◆◇◇◇◇ VERB =reprimand, tell off V n V n *for* n V with quote Also V

sconce /skɒns/ **sconces.** A **sconce** is a decorated bracket that holds candles or an electric light, and that is attached to the wall of a room. N-COUNT

scone /skɒn, skəʊn/ **scones.** A **scone** is a small cake made from flour and fat, usually eaten with butter; used mainly in British English. *We chatted over tea and scones.* ◆◇◇◇◇ N-COUNT

scoop /skuːp/ **scoops, scooping, scooped** ◆◆◇◇◇

1 If you **scoop** someone or something somewhere, you put your hands or arms under or round them and quickly move them there. *Michael knelt next to her and scooped her into his arms.* VERB V n prep/adv Also V n

2 If you **scoop** something from a container, you remove it with something such as a spoon. *...the sound of a spoon scooping dog food out of a can.* VERB V n prep/adv

3 A **scoop** is an object like a spoon which is used for picking up a quantity of a food such as ice cream or an ingredient such as flour. *...a small ice-cream scoop.* ► A **scoop** of food is the amount that a scoop will hold. *She gave him an extra scoop of clotted cream.* N-COUNT N-COUNT: usu N *of* n

4 You can use the word **scoop** to refer to an exciting news story which is reported in one newspaper or on one television programme before it appears anywhere else. *...one of the biggest scoops in the history of newspapers.* N-COUNT =exclusive

5 If you **scoop** a prize or award, you win it; used in journalism. *...films which scooped awards around the world.* VERB =win V n

scoop out. If you **scoop out** part of something, you remove it using a spoon or other tool. *Cut a marrow in half and scoop out the seeds.* PHRASAL VERB V P n (not pron) Also V n P

scoop up. If you **scoop** something **up**, you put your hands or arms under it and lift it in a quick movement. *Use both hands to scoop up the leaves... He began to scoop his things up frantically.* PHRASAL VERB V P n (not pron) V n P

scoot /skuːt/ **scoots, scooting, scooted.** If you **scoot** somewhere, you go there very quickly; an informal word. *Sam said, 'I'm going to hide,' and scooted up the stairs.* VERB =rush V prep/adv Also V

scooter /skuːtəʳ/ **scooters**

1 A **scooter** is a small light motorcycle which has a low seat. N-COUNT

2 A **scooter** is a type of child's bicycle which has two wheels joined by a wooden board and a handle on a long pole attached to the front wheel. The child stands on the board with one foot, and uses the other foot to move forwards. N-COUNT

scope /skoup/ ◆◆◇◇◇

1 If there is **scope** for a particular kind of behaviour or activity, people have the opportunity to behave in this way or do that activity. *He believed in giving his staff scope for initiative... Banks had increased scope to develop new financial products.* N-UNCOUNT: oft N for n, N to-inf

2 The **scope** of an activity, topic, or piece of work is the whole area which it deals with or includes. *Mr Chavis promised to widen the organisation's scope of activity. ...the scope of a novel.* N-SING: usu N of n =range

scorch /skɔːʳtʃ/ **scorches, scorching, scorched** ◆◇◇◇◇

1 To **scorch** something means to burn it slightly. *The bomb scorched the side of the building.* VERB V n ♦ **scorched** *...scorched black earth.* ADJ-GRADED

2 If something **scorches** or **is scorched**, it becomes marked or discoloured by too much heat or by a chemical. *The leaves are inclined to scorch in hot sunshine... If any of the spray goes onto the lawn it will scorch the grass.* ♦ **scorched** *...the lamp with its scorched plastic shade.* V-ERG V V n ADJ-GRADED

3 If you **scorch** round a place, you move round it very quickly, either in a car or on foot; used in informal British English. *Many people dream of scorching round a racetrack.* VERB =tear V prep/adv

scorched earth. A **scorched earth** policy is the deliberate burning, destruction, and removal by an army of everything that would be useful to an enemy that might invade the area. *He employed a stringent scorched-earth policy, destroying villages, burning crops and cutting down trees. ...an army scorched earth campaign.* N-UNCOUNT: usu N n

scorching /skɔːʳtʃɪŋ/. **Scorching** or **scorching hot** weather or temperatures are very hot indeed; an informal word. *That race was run in scorching weather... It was a scorching hot day.* ◆◇◇◇◇ ADJ: usu ADJ n PRAGMATICS

score /skɔːʳ/ **scores, scoring, scored;** in meaning 10, the plural form is **score**. ◆◆◆◆◇

1 In a sport or game, if a player **scores** a goal or a point, they gain a goal or point. *Against which country did Ian Wright score his first international goal?... England scored 282 in their first innings... Gascoigne almost scored in the opening minute.* VERB V n V

2 If you **score** a particular number or amount, for example as a mark in a test, you achieve that number or amount. *Kelly had scored an average of 147 on three separate IQ tests... Congress as an institution scores low in public opinion polls.* VERB V n V adv

3 Someone's **score** in a game or test is a number, for example, a number of points or runs, which shows what they have achieved or what level they have reached. *The U.S. Open golf tournament was won by Ben Hogan, with a score of 287... Robin Smith made 167, the highest score by an England batsman in this form of cricket... There was also a strong link between children's low maths scores and parents' numeracy problems.* N-COUNT

4 The **score** in a game is the result of it or the current situation, as indicated by the number of goals, runs, or points obtained by the two teams or players. *4-1 was the final score... They beat the Giants by a score of 7 to 3... Even in Zurich he kept up with the County cricket scores.* N-COUNT

5 If you **score** a success, a victory, or a hit, you are successful in what you are doing; used in written English. *His abiding passion was ocean racing, at which he scored many successes... In recent months, the rebels have scored some significant victories... Soldiers using a multiple rocket launcher scored a direct hit on the steeple of a church.* VERB V n

6 The **score** of a film, play, or similar production is the music which is written or used for it. *The dance is accompanied by an original score by Henry Torgue. ...the composer of classic film scores such as West Side Story.* N-COUNT

7 The **score** of a piece of music is the written version of it. *He recognizes enough notation to be able to follow a score.* N-COUNT

8 If you **score** a piece of music, you write it or arrange it for specific instruments or voices. *Strauss spent much of 1941 scoring his last opera, Capriccio... He has mastered enough of the complexities of arrangement to write and score a piece for a chamber music ensemble.* VERB V n V n for n

9 If you refer to **scores of** things or people, you are emphasizing that there are very many of them; used in written English. *Campaigners lit scores of bonfires in ceremonies to mark the anniversary.* ▶ Also a pronoun. *Two people were killed and scores were injured.* QUANT: QUANT of pl-n PRAGMATICS PRON

10 A **score** is twenty or approximately twenty; used in written English. *It's thought a score of countries may be either producing or planning to obtain chemical weapons... The company already has around four score titles commissioned and planned for publication... The Bible states that the life of man is three score and ten.* NUM: usu a/num NUM

11 If you **score** a surface with something sharp, you cut or scratch a line in it. *Lightly score the surface of the steaks with a sharp cook's knife.* VERB V n

12 If someone **scores** drugs, they buy them illegally; an informal use. *Me and my mate went to score a kilo of amphetamine down in London.* VERB V n Also V

13 If things happen or exist **by the score**, they happen or exist in large numbers. *The companies brought out new products by the score.* PHRASES usu PHR after v

14 If you **keep score** of the number of things that are happening in a certain situation, you count them and record them. *You can keep score of your baby's movements before birth by recording them on a kick chart.* V inflects, oft PHR of n

15 If you **know the score**, you know what the real facts of a situation are and how they affect you, even though you may not like them; used in spoken English. *I don't feel sorry for Carl. He knew the score, he knew what he had to do and couldn't do it.* V inflects

16 You can use **on that score** or **on this score** to refer to something that has just been mentioned, especially an area of difficulty or concern. *I became pregnant easily. At least I've had no problems on that score... If someone you know has cancer, don't let worry on this score stop you from visiting them.* PRAGMATICS =in that respect, in this respect

17 If you **score a point over** someone, or **score points off** them, you gain an advantage over them, usually by saying something clever or making a better argument. *The Prime Minister was trying to score a political point over his rivals... The politicians might be forced to touch on the real issues rather than scoring points off each other.* V and N inflect, PHR n

18 If you **settle a score** or **settle an old score** with someone, you take revenge on them for something they have done in the past. *The groups had historic scores to settle with each other.* V and N inflect

scoreboard /skɔːʳbɔːʳd/ **scoreboards.** A **scoreboard** is a large board, for example at a sports ground, which shows how many goals, runs, or points have been scored in a match or competition. *The figures flash up on the scoreboard.* N-COUNT

scorecard /skɔːʳkɑːʳd/ **scorecards**

1 A **scorecard** is a printed card which tells you who is playing in a match or race, and on which spectators, players, or officials can record the scores of the players. N-COUNT

2 In American English, a **scorecard** is a system or procedure that is used for checking or testing something. *This commission would keep environmental scorecards on UN member nations. ...a set of recognized standards, a sort of scorecard of security features that can be used to test any given computer system.* N-COUNT: with supp

scoreless /skɔːʳləs/. In football, baseball, and some other sports, a **scoreless** game is one in which neither team has scored any goals, runs, or points; used in journalism. *Norway had held Holland to a scoreless draw in Rotterdam... The next six innings were scoreless.* ADJ

scoreline /skɔːʳlaɪn/ **scorelines.** In British journalism, the **scoreline** of a football, rugby, or tennis match is the score or the final result of it. *Victory was not as easy as the scoreline suggests. ...the excitingly close scoreline of 2-1.* N-COUNT: usu sing, usu the N =result

scorer /skɔːrəʳ/ **scorers** ◆◆◇◇◇

1 In football, cricket, and many other sports and games, a **scorer** is a player who scores a goal, runs, N-COUNT: usu with supp

or points. *...David Hirst, the scorer of 11 goals this season.*
2 A **scorer** is an official who writes down the score of a match or competition as it is being played. N-COUNT
3 You can refer to someone as a **scorer** when you are talking about what mark they achieved in a test. *...the top 2 per cent of scorers in IQ tests.* N-COUNT: usu with supp

scoresheet /skɔːʳʃiːt/; also spelled **score sheet.** In football, rugby, and some other sports, if a player **gets on the scoresheet**, he scores one or more goals, tries, or points; used in journalism. *Although Stewart did not get on the scoresheet, he was directly involved in both goals.* PHRASE: V inflects

scorn /skɔːʳn/ **scorns, scorning, scorned** ◆◇◇◇◇
1 If you treat someone or something with **scorn**, you show contempt for them. *Researchers greeted the proposal with scorn... Franklin shared the family's scorn for his wife's new friends... He became the object of ridicule and scorn.* N-UNCOUNT: oft *with* N, N *for* n =contempt, disrespect
2 If you **scorn** someone or something, you feel or show contempt for them. *Several leading officers have quite openly scorned the peace talks... People scorn me as a single parent.* VERB V n V n as n
3 If you **scorn** something, you refuse to have it or accept it because you think it is not good enough or suitable for you. *...people who scorned traditional methods.* VERB =reject V n
4 If you **pour scorn on** someone or something or **heap scorn on** them, you say that you think they are stupid and worthless. *It is fashionable these days to pour scorn on those in public life... He used to heap scorn on Dr Vazquez's socialist ideas.* PHRASE: V inflects =deride

scornful /skɔːʳnfəl/. If you are **scornful** of someone or something, you show contempt for them. *He is deeply scornful of politicians. ...a scornful simile.* ♦ **scornfully** *'I didn't think so,' the judge said scornfully.* ◆◇◇◇◇ ADJ-GRADED: oft ADJ *of* n =contemptuous ADV-GRADED: usu ADV with v =contemptuously

Scorpio /skɔːʳpioʊ/ **Scorpios** ◆◆◇◇◇
1 **Scorpio** is one of the twelve signs of the zodiac. Its symbol is a scorpion. People who are born approximately between the 23rd of October and the 21st of November come under this sign. N-UNCOUNT
2 A **Scorpio** is a person whose sign of the zodiac is Scorpio. N-COUNT

scorpion /skɔːʳpiən/ **scorpions.** A **scorpion** is a small creature which looks like a large insect. Scorpions have a long curved tail, and some of them are poisonous. N-COUNT

Scot /skɒt/ **Scots** ◆◆◇◇◇
1 A **Scot** is a person of Scottish origin. N-COUNT
2 **Scots** is a dialect of the English language that is spoken in Scotland. *There are things you can express in Scots that you can't say in English.* N-UNCOUNT
3 **Scots** means the same as **Scottish**. *...his guttural Scots accent. ...the Scots Tories.* ADJ: usu ADJ n

scotch /skɒtʃ/ **scotches, scotching, scotched.** If you **scotch** a rumour, plan, or idea, you put an end to it before it can develop any further. *They have scotched rumours that they are planning a special London show... Mr Major is taking every opportunity to scotch any notion that he sympathises with the rebels.* ◆◇◇◇◇ VERB V n

Scotch /skɒtʃ/ **Scotches** ◆◇◇◇◇
1 **Scotch** or **Scotch whisky** is whisky made in Scotland. *...a bottle of Scotch.* ► A **Scotch** is a glass of Scotch. *He poured himself a Scotch.* N-MASS =whisky N-COUNT
2 **Scotch** means the same as **Scottish**. This use is considered incorrect by many people. ADJ: usu ADJ n

Scotch egg, Scotch eggs. A **Scotch egg** is a hard boiled egg that is covered with sausage meat and breadcrumbs, then fried; used mainly in British English. N-COUNT

Scotch tape. In American English, **Scotch tape** is a clear sticky tape that is sold in rolls and that you use to stick paper or card together or onto a wall. The British word is **Sellotape**. **Scotch tape** and **Sellotape** are trademarks. N-UNCOUNT

scot-free. If you say that someone got away **scot-free**, you are emphasizing that they escaped punishment for something that you believe they should have been punished for. *Others who were guilty were being allowed to get off scot-free.* ADV: ADV after v PRAGMATICS

Scotsman /skɒtsmən/ **Scotsmen.** A **Scotsman** is a man of Scottish origin. ◆◇◇◇◇ N-COUNT

Scotswoman /skɒtswʊmən/ **Scotswomen.** A **Scotswoman** is a woman of Scottish origin. ◆◇◇◇◇ N-COUNT

Scottish /skɒtɪʃ/. Something that is **Scottish** belongs or relates to Scotland, its people, or its language. *...Scottish football. ...the Scottish Highlands.* ◆◆◆◆◇ ADJ

scoundrel /skaʊndrəl/ **scoundrels.** If you refer to a man as a **scoundrel**, they mean that he behaves very badly towards other people, especially by cheating them or deceiving them; an old-fashioned word. *He is a lying scoundrel!* N-COUNT

scour /skaʊəʳ/ **scours, scouring, scoured** ◆◇◇◇◇
1 If you **scour** something such as a place or book, you make a thorough search of it for someone or something. *Rescue crews had scoured an area of 30 square miles... We scoured the telephone directory for clues.* VERB =search V n V n *for* n
2 If you **scour** something such as a sink, floor, or pan, you clean its surface by rubbing it hard with something rough. *He decided to scour the sink.* VERB =scrub V n

scourge /skɜːʳdʒ/ **scourges, scourging, scourged** ◆◇◇◇◇
1 A **scourge** is something that causes a lot of trouble or suffering to a group of people. *...the best chance in 20 years to end the scourge of terrorism... Drugs are a scourge that is devastating our society.* N-COUNT: oft N *of* n
2 If something **scourges** a place or group of people, it causes great pain and suffering to people. *Economic anarchy scourged the post-war world.* VERB V n

scout /skaʊt/ **scouts, scouting, scouted.** ◆◇◇◇◇
1 A **scout** is someone who is sent to an area of countryside to find out the position of an enemy army. *They set off, two men out in front as scouts, two behind in case of any attack from the rear.* N-COUNT
2 A **scout** is the same as a **talent scout**. N-COUNT
3 If you **scout** somewhere for something, you go through that area searching for it. *I wouldn't have time to scout the area for junk... A team of four was sent to scout for a nuclear test site... I have people scouting the hills already.* VERB =search V n *for* n V *for* n V n

scout around or **scout round.** If you **scout around** or **scout round** for something, you go to different places looking for it. *They scouted around for more fuel... I scouted round in the bushes.* PHRASAL VERB =look around V P *for* n V P

scout out. If you **scout** something **out**, you succeed in finding it after you have been through an area searching for it. *Their mission is simply to scout out places where helicopters can land.* PHRASAL VERB =locate V P n (not pron) Also V n P

Scout, Scouts ◆◇◇◇◇
1 **The Scouts** is an organization for children and young people which teaches them to become disciplined, practical, and self-sufficient. *The Scouts are having difficulty in recruiting in the inner cities.* N-PROPER-COLL: *the* N
2 A **Scout** is a member of the Scouts. *...a party of seven Scouts and three leaders on a camping trip. ...a Scout troop.* N-COUNT

scoutmaster /skaʊtmɑːstəʳ, -mæs-/ **scoutmasters.** A **scoutmaster** is a man who is in charge of a troop of Scouts. N-COUNT

scowl /skaʊl/ **scowls, scowling, scowled.** When someone **scowls**, they frown to show that they are angry or displeased. *He scowled, and slammed the door behind him... She scowled at the two men as they entered the room.* ► Also a noun. *Chris met the remark with a scowl.* ◆◇◇◇◇ VERB =frown, glower V V *at* n N-COUNT

scrabble /skræbəl/ **scrabbles, scrabbling, scrabbled**
1 If you **scrabble** for something, especially something that you cannot see, you move your hands or your feet about quickly and wildly in order to find it. *He grabbed his jacket and scrabbled in his desk drawer for some loose change... I hung there, scrabbling with my feet to find a foothold.* ► **Scrabble around** or **scrabble about** means the same as **scrabble**. *Alberg scrabbled around for pen and paper... Gleb scrabbled about in the hay, pulled out a book and opened it.* VERB V *for* n V to-inf PHRASAL VERB V P *for* n V P
2 If you say that someone **is scrabbling** to do something, you mean that they are having difficulty because they are in too much of a hurry, or be- VERB

cause the task is almost impossible. *The banks are now desperately scrabbling to recover their costs... The opportunity had gone. His mind scrabbled for alternatives.* V to-inf V *for*n ▶ **Scrabble around** means the same as **scrabble**. *You get a six-month contract, and then you have to scrabble around for the next job, which could be anywhere in Britain.* PHRASAL VERB V P *for*n Also V P to-inf

scraggy /skrægi/ **scraggier, scraggiest.** If you describe a person or animal as **scraggy**, you mean that they look unattractive because they are so thin and bony; used mainly in British English. *...his scraggy neck. ...a flock of scraggy sheep.* ADJ-GRADED PRAGMATICS =scrawny, skinny

scramble /skræmbᵊl/ **scrambles, scrambling, scrambled** ◆◆◇◇◇

1 If you **scramble** over rocks or up a hill, you move quickly over them or up it using your hands to help you. *Tourists were scrambling over the rocks looking for the perfect camera angle... He scrambled up a steep bank.* VERB =clamber V prep/adv

2 If you **scramble** to a different place or position, you move there in a hurried, undignified way. *Ann threw back the covers and scrambled out of bed... He scrambled to his feet.* VERB V prep/adv

3 If a number of people **scramble** for something, they compete with each other for it, in a rough and undignified way. *More than three million fans are expected to scramble for tickets... Business is booming and foreigners are scrambling to invest.* VERB V *for*n V to-inf ▶ Also a noun. *...the scramble for jobs. ...a scramble to get a seat on the early morning flight.* N-COUNT: usu sing, oft N *for*n, N to-inf

4 If you **scramble** eggs, you mix the whites and yolks of the eggs, then cook the mixture by stirring and heating it in a pan. *Make the toast and scramble the eggs.* VERB V n ♦ **scrambled** *...scrambled eggs and bacon.* ADJ: usu ADJ n

5 If a device **scrambles** a radio or telephone message, it interferes with the sound so that the message can only be understood by someone with special equipment. *The latest machines scramble the messages so that the conversation cannot easily be intercepted.* VERB V n

scrambler /skræmbləʳ/ **scramblers.** A **scrambler** is an electronic device which alters the sound of a radio or telephone message so that it can only be understood by someone who has special equipment. N-COUNT

scrap /skræp/ **scraps, scrapping, scrapped** ◆◆◇◇◇

1 A **scrap** of something is a very small piece or amount of it. *A crumpled scrap of paper was found in her handbag. ...a fire fueled by scraps of wood... They need every scrap of information they can get.* N-COUNT: usu N *of*n

2 **Scraps** are pieces of unwanted food which are thrown away or given to animals. *...the scraps from the Sunday dinner table.* N-PLURAL =leftovers

3 If you **scrap** something, you get rid of it or cancel it. *President Hussein called on all countries in the Middle East to scrap nuclear or chemical weapons... It had been thought that passport controls would be scrapped.* VERB V n

4 **Scrap** metal or paper is no longer wanted for its original purpose, but may have some other use. *There's always tons of scrap paper in Dad's office.* ADJ: ADJ n

5 **Scrap** is metal from old or damaged machinery or cars. *Thousands of tanks, artillery pieces and armored vehicles will be cut up for scrap.* N-UNCOUNT

6 You can refer to a fight or a quarrel as a **scrap**, especially if it is not very serious; an informal use. *Billy Bonds has never been one to avoid a scrap.* N-COUNT =fight

scrapbook /skræpbʊk/ **scrapbooks.** A **scrapbook** is a book with blank pages. People stick things such as pictures or newspaper articles into scrapbooks in order to make a collection. N-COUNT

scrape /skreɪp/ **scrapes, scraping, scraped** ◆◆◇◇◇

1 If you **scrape** something from a surface, you remove it, especially by pulling a sharp object over the surface. *She went round the car scraping the frost off the windows... Young children were trying to scrape up some of the rice that spilled from the sacks.* VERB V n with adv

2 If something **scrapes** against something else or if you **scrape** it against something else, it rubs against it, making a noise or causing slight damage. *The only sound is that of knives and forks scraping against china... The cab driver struggled with her luggage, scraping a bag against the door as they came in... The car hurtled past us, scraping the wall and screeching to a halt... There was a scraping sound as she dragged the heels of her shoes along the pavement.* V-ERG V prep V n prep V n V-ing ▶ Also a noun. *From the other side of the door came the scrape of a guard's boot.* N-SING: usu N *of*n ♦ **scraping** *The house was silent but for the scraping of a branch on the slates.* N-SING: N *of*n

3 If you **scrape** a part of your body, you accidentally rub it against something hard and rough, and damage it slightly. *She stumbled and fell, scraping her palms and knees.* VERB =graze V n

4 If you are in a **scrape**, you are in a difficult situation which you have caused yourself; an old-fashioned use. *We got into terrible scrapes.* N-COUNT: usu *in/into* N =fix

5 ● to **scrape the barrel**: see **barrel**. ● to **scrape a living**: see **living**.

scrape by. If someone **scrapes by**, they earn just enough money to live on with difficulty. *We're barely scraping by on my salary.* PHRASAL VERB V P

scrape through. If you **scrape through** an examination, you just succeed in passing it. If you **scrape through** a competition or a vote, you just succeed in winning it. *Both my brothers have university degrees. I just scraped through a couple of A-levels... If we can get an early goal and then try and defend for the rest of the game, we might scrape through.* PHRASAL VERB V P n V P

scrape together. If you **scrape together** an amount of money or a number of things, you succeed in obtaining it with difficulty. *They only just managed to scrape the money together... It's possible the Congress Party will scrape together a majority with the support of smaller parties.* PHRASAL VERB V n P V P n (not pron)

scraper /skreɪpəʳ/ **scrapers.** A **scraper** is a tool with a small handle and a metal or plastic blade which can be used for scraping a particular surface clean. For example, you use a scraper to scrape old paint off a wall when you are decorating or to scrape ice off a car. N-COUNT

scrapheap /skræphiːp/; also spelled **scrap heap**.

1 If you say that someone has been thrown on the **scrapheap**, you strongly disapprove of the way that their employers have dismissed them from their jobs without any concern for their future welfare. *Thousands of miners have been thrown on the scrapheap with no jobs and no prospects.* N-SING: usu prep *the* N PRAGMATICS

2 If things such as machines or weapons are thrown on the **scrapheap**, they are thrown away because they are no longer needed. *Thousands of Europe's tanks and guns are going to the scrap heap.* N-SING: usu prep *the* N

scrapings /skreɪpɪŋz/. **Scrapings** are small amounts or pieces of something that have been scraped or scratched off a surface. *There might be scrapings under his fingernails.* N-PLURAL

scrappy /skræpi/. If you describe something as **scrappy**, you disapprove of it because it seems to be badly planned or untidy. *...a scrappy affair... The final chapter is no more than a scrappy addition.* ADJ-GRADED: usu ADJ n PRAGMATICS

scrapyard /skræpjɑːʳd/ **scrapyards;** also spelled **scrap yard**. In British English, a **scrapyard** is a place where old machines such as cars or ships are destroyed and where useful parts are saved. The usual American word is **junkyard**. N-COUNT

scratch /skrætʃ/ **scratches, scratching, scratched** ◆◆◇◇◇

1 If you **scratch** yourself, you rub your fingernails against your skin because it is itching. *He scratched himself under his arm... The old man lifted his cardigan to scratch his side... I had to wear long sleeves to stop myself scratching.* VERB V pron-refl V n V

2 If a sharp object **scratches** someone or something, it makes small shallow cuts on their skin or surface. *The branches tore at my jacket and scratched my hands and face... Knives will scratch the worktop.* VERB V n

3 **Scratches** on someone or something are small N-COUNT

shallow cuts. *The seven-year-old was found crying with scratches on his face and neck... I pointed to a number of scratches in the tile floor.*

4 If you do something **from scratch**, you do it without making use of anything that has been done before. *Building a home from scratch can be both exciting and challenging... Hong Kong's manufacturing industry did not start from scratch in the post-war period.* PHRASES PHR after v

5 If you say that someone is **scratching** their **head**, you mean that they are thinking hard and trying to solve a problem or puzzle. *The Institute spends a lot of time scratching its head about how to boost American productivity.* V inflects

6 If you only **scratch the surface** of a subject or problem, you deal with it in a superficial way, but not enough to understand or solve it fully. *Officials say they've only scratched the surface of the drug problem... We had only two weeks to tour Malaysia, which was hardly enough time to scratch the surface.* V inflects, oft PHR *of* n

7 If you say that someone or something is not **up to scratch**, you mean that they are not good enough. *My mother always made me feel I wasn't coming up to scratch.* PHR after v, v-link PHR, usu with brd-neg

scratchy /skrætʃi/

1 **Scratchy** sounds are thin and harsh. *Listening to the scratchy recording, I recognized Walt Whitman immediately.* ADJ-GRADED

2 **Scratchy** clothes or fabrics are rough and make you itch. *Wool is so scratchy that it irritates the skin.* ADJ-GRADED

scrawl /skrɔːl/ **scrawls, scrawling, scrawled** ◆◇◇◇◇

1 If you **scrawl** something, you write it in a careless and untidy way. *He scrawled a hasty note to his wife... Someone had scrawled 'Scum' on his car. ...racist graffiti scrawled on school walls.* VERB V n prep V with quote V-ed Also V n

2 You can refer to writing that looks careless and untidy as a **scrawl**. *The letter was handwritten, in a hasty, barely decipherable scrawl.* N-VAR =scribble

scrawny /skrɔːni/ **scrawnier, scrawniest.** If you describe a person or animal as **scrawny**, you mean that they look unattractive because they are so thin and bony. *...a scrawny woman with dyed black hair... The vulture extended his scrawny neck.* ADJ-GRADED PRAGMATICS =scraggy, skinny

scream /skriːm/ **screams, screaming, screamed** ◆◆◆◇◇

1 When someone **screams**, they make a very loud, high-pitched cry, for example because they are in pain or are very frightened. *Women were screaming; some of the houses nearest the bridge were on fire... If I hear one more joke about my hair, I shall scream... He staggered around the playground, screaming in agony... To play in front of 40,000 screaming fans was a great experience.* ▶ Also a noun. *Hilda let out a scream. ...screams of terror.* VERB =shriek V V *in* n V-ing N-COUNT

2 If you **scream** something, you shout it in a loud, high-pitched voice. *'Brigid!' she screamed. 'Get up!'... I was screaming at them to get out of my house... They started screaming abuse at us.* VERB =yell V with quote V *at* n to-inf V n

3 When something makes a loud, high-pitched noise, you can say that it **screams**; used in written English. *She slammed the car into gear, the tyres screaming as her foot jammed against the accelerator... As he talked, an airforce jet screamed over the town.* ▶ Also a noun. *There was a scream of brakes from the carriageway outside.* VERB =screech V V prep/adv N-COUNT =screech

4 If you say that someone is **a scream**, you think they are very funny; an informal use. N-SING: *a* N

screamingly /skriːmɪŋli/. If you say that something is, for example, **screamingly** funny or **screamingly** boring, you mean that it is extremely funny or extremely boring. *...a screamingly funny joke.* ADV: ADV adj

scree /skriː/ **screes. Scree** is a mass of loose stones on the side of a mountain. *Occasionally scree fell in a shower of dust and noise... He scrambled sideways down the scree slope.* N-VAR

screech /skriːtʃ/ **screeches, screeching, screeched** ◆◇◇◇◇

1 If a vehicle **screeches** somewhere or if its tyres **screech**, its tyres make an unpleasant high-pitched noise on the road. *A black Mercedes screeched to a halt beside the helicopter... The car wheels screeched as they curved and bounced over the rough broken ground.* VERB V prep/adv V

2 When you **screech** something, you shout it in a loud, unpleasant, high-pitched voice. *'Get me some water, Jeremy!' I screeched... Sometimes for no apparent reason she'd run out onto the highway, waving her hands and screeching at the traffic.* ▶ Also a noun. *The figure gave a screech.* VERB V with quote V *at* n Also V, V n N-COUNT

3 When a bird, animal, or thing **screeches**, it makes a loud, unpleasant, high-pitched noise. *A macaw screeched at him from its perch. ...tropical birds screeching in an aviary... The air-conditioning screeched all the time... Bronka is somewhat infamous for his screeching electric guitar work.* ▶ Also a noun. *He heard the screech of brakes.* VERB V *at* n V V-ing N-COUNT

screen /skriːn/ **screens, screening, screened** ◆◆◆◆◇

1 A **screen** is a flat vertical surface on which pictures or words are shown. Television sets and computer terminals have screens, and films are shown on a screen in cinemas. ● See also **big screen, small screen.** N-COUNT

2 You can refer to film or television as the **screen.** *Many viewers have strong opinions about violence on the screen... She was the ideal American teenager, both on and off screen.* N-SING: *the* N, also *on/off* N

3 When a film or a television programme **is screened**, it is shown in the cinema or broadcast on television. *The series is likely to be screened in January... TV firms were later banned from screening any pictures of the demo.* ♦ **screening, screenings** *The film-makers will be present at the screenings to introduce their works.* VERB =broadcast *be* V-ed V n N-COUNT

4 A **screen** is a vertical panel which can be moved around. It is used to keep cold air away from part of a room, or to create a smaller area within a room. *They put a screen in front of me so I couldn't see what was going on.* N-COUNT

5 If something **is screened** by another thing, it is behind it and hidden by it. *Most of the road behind the hotel was screened by a block of flats.* VB: usu passive *be* V-ed *by* n

6 To **screen** for a disease means to examine people to make sure that they do not have it. *...a quick saliva test that would screen for people at risk of tooth decay.* ♦ **screening** *Britain has an enviable record on breast screening for cancer.* VERB V *for* n Also V n N-VAR: usu N *for* n

7 When an organization **screens** people, it investigates them to make sure that they are not likely to be dangerous or disloyal. *They will screen all their candidates. ...screening procedures for the regiment.* VERB V n V-ing

8 To **screen** people or luggage means to check them using special equipment to make sure they are not carrying a weapon or a bomb. *The airline had not been searching unaccompanied baggage by hand, but only screening it on X-ray machines.* VERB V n

screen off. If part of a room or area **is screened off**, it is made into a separate area, using a screen. *Her bed was screened off from the other patients.* PHRASAL VERB usu passive *be* V-ed P

screen out. If an organization or country **screens out** certain people, it keeps them out because it thinks they may cause problems. *The company screened out applicants motivated only by money.* PHRASAL VERB V P n (not pron)

screenplay /skriːnpleɪ/ **screenplays.** A **screenplay** is a script for a film including instructions for the cameras. ◆◇◇◇◇ N-COUNT =script

screen test, screen tests. When a film studio gives an actor a **screen test**, they film a short scene in order to test how good he or she would be in films. N-COUNT

screenwriter /skriːnraɪtəʳ/ **screenwriters.** A **screenwriter** is a person who writes screenplays. ◆◇◇◇◇ N-COUNT

screenwriting /skriːnraɪtɪŋ/. **Screenwriting** is the process of writing screenplays. N-UNCOUNT

screw /skruː/ **screws, screwing, screwed** ◆◆◇◇◇

1 A **screw** is a metal object similar to a nail, with a spiral ridge around it. You turn a screw using a screwdriver so that it goes through two things, for example two pieces of wood or metal, and fastens N-COUNT

them together. *Each bracket is fixed to the wall with just three screws.*

2 If you **screw** something somewhere or if it **screws** somewhere, you fix it in place by means of a screw or screws. *I had screwed the shelf on the wall myself... Screw down any loose floorboards... I particularly like the type of shelving that screws to the wall.* V-ERG Vn prep Vn with adv V prep/adv

3 A **screw** lid or fitting is one that has a spiral ridge on the inside or outside of it, so that it can be fixed in place by twisting. *...an ordinary jam jar with a screw lid.* ADJ: ADJ n

4 If you **screw** something somewhere or if it **screws** somewhere, you fix it in place by twisting it round and round. *'Yes, I know that,' Kelly said, screwing the silencer onto the pistol... Screw down the lid fairly tightly... This device screws into the shutter release button. ...several aluminium poles that screw together to give a maximum length of 10 yards.* V-ERG Vn prep Vn with adv V prep/adv

5 If you **screw** something such as a piece of paper **into** a ball, you squeeze it or twist it tightly so that it is in the shape of a ball. *He screwed the paper into a ball and tossed it into the fire.* VERB Vn *into* n

6 If you **screw** your face or your eyes **into** a particular expression, you tighten the muscles of your face to form that expression, for example because you are in pain or because the light is too bright. *He screwed his face into an expression of mock pain.* VERB Vn *into* n

7 If someone **screws** someone else or if two people **screw**, they have sex together; a rude and offensive use which you should avoid using. V-RECIP

8 Some people use **screw** in expressions such as **screw you** or **screw that** to show that they are not concerned about someone or something or that they feel contempt for them; a rude and offensive use that you should avoid using. VB: only imper PRAGMATICS

9 If someone says that they **have been screwed**, they mean that someone else has cheated them, especially by getting money from them dishonestly; an informal use which some people find offensive. *They haven't given us accurate information. We've been screwed... The consumer is getting screwed by cover charges as well.* VB: usu passive *be* V-ed *get* V-ed

10 If someone **screws** something, especially money, **out of** you, they get it from you by means of strong persuasion or by putting strong pressure on you; used mainly in informal British English. *After decades of rich nations screwing money out of poor nations, it's about time some went the other way.* VERB Vn *out of* n

11 Prisoners often refer to prison officers as **screws**; an informal use. N-COUNT

12 A **screw** is a propeller on a ship or an aircraft; a technical use in engineering. N-COUNT

13 If you **turn** or **tighten the screw** on someone, you increase the pressure which is already on them, for example by using threats, in order to force them to do a particular thing. *Parisian taxi drivers are threatening to mount a blockade to turn the screw on the government.* PHRASES V and N inflect, oft PHR *on* n

14 You can refer to each of a series of threats or actions which are intended to force someone to do a particular thing as another **turn of the screw**. *Every rebel raid is another turn of the screw, increasing the pressure on the President.*

screw up. PHRASAL VERB

1 If you **screw up** your eyes or your face or if your face **screws up**, you tighten the muscles of your face to form wrinkles, for example because you are in pain or because the light is too bright. *She had screwed up her eyes, as if she found the sunshine too bright... Close your eyes and screw them up tight... His face screwed up in agony.* ERG =mess up VPn (not pron) VnP VP

2 If you **screw up** a piece of paper, you squeeze it tightly so that becomes very creased and no longer flat, usually when you are throwing it away. *He would start writing to his family and would screw the letter up in frustration... He screwed up his first three efforts after only a line or two.* VnP VPn (not pron)

3 If someone **screws** something **up**, or if they **screw up**, they cause something to fail or be spoiled; an informal expression. *You can't open the window because it screws up the air conditioning... Get out. Haven't you screwed things up enough already!... Somebody had screwed up; they weren't there.* VPn (not pron) VnP VP

screwball /skruːbɔːl/. **Screwball** comedy is silly and eccentric in an amusing and harmless way; an informal word. *...a remake of a '50s classic screwball comedy.* ADJ: ADJ n

screwdriver /skruːdraɪvəʳ/ **screwdrivers.** A **screwdriver** is a tool that is used for turning screws. It consists of a metal rod with a flat or cross-shaped end that fits into the top of the screw. N-COUNT

screwed up. If you say that someone is **screwed up**, you mean that they are very confused or worried, or that they have psychological problems; an informal expression. *He was really screwed up with his emotional problems... How many screwed-up adults are there now whose parents stayed together for the children's sake?* ◆◇◇◇◇ ADJ-GRADED

screw-top. A **screw-top** bottle or jar has a lid that is secured by being twisted on. ADJ: ADJ n

scribble /skrɪbəl/ **scribbles, scribbling, scribbled** ◆◇◇◇◇

1 If you **scribble** something, you write it quickly and roughly. *She scribbled a note to tell Mum she'd gone out... As I scribbled in my diary the light went out.* VERB Vn V prep/adv

2 To **scribble** means to make meaningless marks or rough drawings using a pencil or pen. *When Caroline was five she scribbled on a wall.* VERB V prep/adv Also V

3 **Scribble** is something that has been written or drawn quickly and roughly. *I'm sorry what I wrote was such a scribble.* N-VAR =scrawl

scribble down. If you **scribble down** something, you write it quickly or roughly. *I attempted to scribble down the names... He took my name and address, scribbling it down in his notebook.* PHRASAL VERB VPn (not pron) VnP

scribbler /skrɪbələʳ/ **scribblers.** People sometimes refer to writers as **scribblers** when they think they are not very good writers. *The world is full of scribblers. I don't intend to join their ranks.* N-COUNT: usu pl PRAGMATICS

scribe /skraɪb/ **scribes.** In the days before printing was common, a **scribe** was a person who wrote copies of things such as letters or documents. N-COUNT

scrimp /skrɪmp/ **scrimps, scrimping, scrimped.** If you **scrimp** on things, you live cheaply and spend as little money as possible. *Scrimping on safety measures can be a false economy... He has had to give up luxuries as he scrimps and saves while looking for a job.* VERB =skimp V *on* n V

script /skrɪpt/ **scripts, scripting, scripted** ◆◆◆◇◇

1 The **script** of a play, film, or television programme is the written version of it. *Jenny's writing a film script.* N-COUNT

2 The person who **scripts** a film or a radio or television play writes it. *...James Cameron, who scripted and directed both films.* VERB Vn

3 You can refer to a particular system of writing as a particular **script**. *...a text in the Malay language but written in Arabic script.* N-VAR: usu adj N

scripted /skrɪptɪd/. A **scripted** speech has been written in advance, although the speaker may pretend that it is spoken without preparation. *It's much easier to prepare scripted answers when a panel of journalists is asking the questions.* ADJ: usu ADJ n

scriptural /skrɪptʃərəl/. **Scriptural** is used to describe things that are written in or based on the Christian Bible. *...scriptural accounts of the process of salvation.* ADJ: ADJ n

scripture /skrɪptʃəʳ/ **scriptures. Scripture** or **the scriptures** refers to writings that are regarded as sacred in a particular religion, for example the Bible in Christianity. *...a quote from scripture. ...the Holy Scriptures.* ◆◇◇◇◇ N-VAR: oft *the* N

scriptwriter /skrɪptraɪtəʳ/ **scriptwriters.** A **scriptwriter** is a person who writes scripts for films or for radio or television programmes. N-COUNT

scroll /skroul/ **scrolls, scrolling, scrolled** ◆◇◇◇◇

1 A **scroll** is a long roll of paper, parchment, or other material with writing on it. *Ancient scrolls were found in caves by the Dead Sea.* N-COUNT

2 A **scroll** is a painted or carved decoration made to N-COUNT

look like a scroll. *...a handsome suite of chairs incised with Grecian scrolls.*
3 If you **scroll** through text on a computer screen, you move the text up or down to find the information that you need. *I scrolled down to find 'United States of America'.* VERB V prep/adv

Scrooge /skruːdʒ/ **Scrooges.** If you call someone a **Scrooge**, you disapprove of them because they are very mean and hate spending money. *What a bunch of Scrooges.* N-VAR PRAGMATICS

scrotum /skrəʊtəm/ **scrotums.** A man's **scrotum** is the bag of skin that contains his testicles. N-COUNT

scrounge /skraʊndʒ/ **scrounges, scrounging, scrounged.** If you say that someone **scrounges** something such as food or money, you mean they get it by asking someone for it, rather than by buying it or earning it, and that you think this is wrong; an informal word. *There were tales of Williams having to scrounge enough money to get his car out of the long-term park... The Indians accused the government of not giving them money once they had arrived, forcing them to scrounge for food.* ♦ **scrounger, scroungers** *They are just scroungers.* VERB PRAGMATICS V n V for n N-COUNT: usu pl

scrub /skrʌb/ **scrubs, scrubbing, scrubbed** ◆◆◇◇◇
1 If you **scrub** something, you rub it hard in order to clean it, using a stiff brush and water. *Surgeons began to scrub their hands and arms with soap and water before operating... The corridors are scrubbed clean.* ▶ Also a noun. *That floor needs a jolly good scrub.* VERB V n be V-ed adj N-SING: a N
2 If you **scrub** dirt or stains off something, you remove them by rubbing hard. *I started to scrub off the dirt... Matthew scrubbed the coal dust from his face.* VERB V n with off/away V n prep
3 **Scrub** consists of low trees and bushes, especially in an area that has very little rain. *There is an area of scrub and woodland beside the railway.* N-UNCOUNT

scrubber /skrʌbəʳ/ **scrubbers.** In British English, if someone refers to a woman as a **scrubber**, they are saying in a very rude and offensive way that she has had sex with a lot of men. N-COUNT PRAGMATICS

scrubby /skrʌbi/. **Scrubby** land is rough and dry and covered with scrub. *The hot, scrubby hills of western Eritrea.* ADJ: usu ADJ n

scrubland /skrʌblænd/ **scrublands. Scrubland** is an area of land which is covered with low trees and bushes. *Thousands of acres of forests and scrubland have been burnt.* N-VAR

scruff /skrʌf/. If someone grabs you **by the scruff of the neck**, they take hold of the back of your neck or collar suddenly and roughly. *He picked the dog up by the scruff of the neck and hurled her down the stairs.* PHRASE: V n PHR

scruffy /skrʌfi/ **scruffier, scruffiest.** Someone or something that is **scruffy** is dirty and untidy. *...a young man, pale, scruffy and unshaven. ...a scruffy basement flat in London.* ◆◇◇◇◇ ADJ-GRADED =tatty, shabby

scrum /skrʌm/ **scrums** ◆◇◇◇◇
1 In rugby, a **scrum** is a formation in which players from each side form a tight group and push against each other with their heads down in an attempt to get the ball. N-COUNT =scrummage
2 A **scrum** is a confused, disorderly group of people. *She pushed through the scrum of photographers. ...the scrum of shoppers.* N-COUNT: usu sing, oft N of n

scrummage /skrʌmɪdʒ/ **scrummages.** In rugby, a **scrummage** is the same as a **scrum**. N-COUNT

scrumptious /skrʌmpʃəs/. If you describe food as **scrumptious**, you mean that it tastes extremely good; an informal word. *...a scrumptious apple pie.* ADJ-GRADED =delicious

scrumpy /skrʌmpi/. **Scrumpy** is a strong kind of cider; used in informal British English. *...a pint of scrumpy.* N-UNCOUNT =cider

scrunch /skrʌntʃ/ **scrunches, scrunching, scrunched**
1 If something **scrunches**, it makes a loud sound as it is pressed or crushed or as it presses or crushes something else. *The sand on the floor scrunched under our feet... Her feet scrunch on the gravel.* VERB =crunch V prep Also V
2 If you **scrunch** something, you squeeze it or bend it so that it is no longer in its natural shape and is often crushed. *Her father scrunched his nose... Her mother was sitting bolt upright, scrunching her white cotton gloves into a ball.* ▶ **Scrunch up** means the same as **scrunch**. *She scrunched up three pages of notes and threw them in the bin... Stand straight or walk about a bit – don't scrunch yourself up.* VERB V n V n into n PHRASAL VERB V P n (not pron) V n P

scruple /skruːpəl/ **scruples. Scruples** are moral principles or beliefs that make you reluctant to do something that seems wrong. *...a man with no moral scruples.* N-VAR: usu pl

scrupulous /skruːpjʊləs/ ◆◇◇◇◇
1 Someone who is **scrupulous** takes great care to do what is fair, honest, or morally right. *You're being very scrupulous, but to what end?... I have been scrupulous about telling them the dangers... The Board is scrupulous in its consideration of all applications for licences.* ♦ **scrupulously** *He is scrupulously fair, and popular with his staff... Namibia has scrupulously upheld political pluralism.* ADJ-GRADED: usu v-link ADJ ADV-GRADED
2 **Scrupulous** means thorough, exact, and careful about details. *Both readers commend Knutson for his scrupulous attention to detail.* ♦ **scrupulously** *The streets and parks were scrupulously clean... Hillsden scrupulously avoided any topic likely to arouse suspicion as to his motives.* ADJ-GRADED: usu ADJ n =meticulous ADV-GRADED

scrutineer /skruːtɪnɪəʳ/ **scrutineers.** A **scrutineer** is a person who checks that an election or a race is carried out according to the rules; used in British English. N-COUNT

scrutinize /skruːtɪnaɪz/ **scrutinizes, scrutinizing, scrutinized;** also spelled **scrutinise** in British English. If you **scrutinize** something, you examine it very carefully, often to find out some information from it or about it. *Her purpose was to scrutinize his features to see if he was an honest man... Lloyds' results were carefully scrutinised as a guide to what to expect from the other banks.* ◆◇◇◇◇ VERB =examine V n

scrutiny /skruːtɪni/. If a person or thing is under **scrutiny**, they are being studied or observed very carefully. *His private life came under media scrutiny... The President promised a government open to public scrutiny.* ◆◆◇◇◇ N-UNCOUNT: oft prep N

scuba diving /skuːbə daɪvɪŋ/. **Scuba diving** is the activity of swimming under water using a special type of breathing equipment. The equipment consists of cylinders of compressed air which you carry on your back connected to your mouth by rubber tubes. N-UNCOUNT

scud /skʌd/ **scuds, scudding, scudded.** If clouds **scud** along, they move quickly and smoothly through the sky; a literary use. *...heavy, rain-laden clouds scudding across from the south-west.* VERB =sail V adv/prep

scuff /skʌf/ **scuffs, scuffing, scuffed**
1 If you **scuff** something or if it **scuffs**, you mark the surface by scraping it against other things or by scraping other things against it. *Constant wheelchair use will scuff almost any floor surface... Moulded plastic is almost indestructible, but scuffs easily.* ♦ **scuffed** *...scuffed brown shoes.* V-ERG V n V adv ADJ-GRADED
2 If you **scuff** your feet, you drag them along the ground as you walk. *Polly, bewildered and embarrassed, dropped her head and scuffed her feet.* VERB =drag V n

scuffle /skʌfəl/ **scuffles, scuffling, scuffled** ◆◇◇◇◇
1 A **scuffle** is a short, disorganized fight or struggle. *Violent scuffles broke out between rival groups demonstrating for and against independence.* N-COUNT =fight
2 If people **scuffle**, they fight for a short time in a disorganized way. *Police scuffled with some of the protesters... He and Hannah had been scuffling in the yard outside his house.* V-RECIP V with n pl-n V

scuffling /skʌflɪŋ/. A **scuffling** noise is a noise made by someone or something moving about, usually someone or something that you cannot see. *There was a scuffling noise in the background.* ADJ: ADJ n

scuff mark, scuff marks. Scuff marks are marks made on a smooth surface when something is rubbed against it. *Wooden floors can look* N-COUNT: usu pl *quite smart, but scuff marks from shoes are difficult to remove.*

scull /skʌl/ **sculls, sculling, sculled**
1 **Sculls** are small oars which are held by one person and used to move a boat through water. N-COUNT: usu pl
2 A **scull** is a small light racing boat which is rowed with two sculls. N-COUNT
3 To **scull** a boat means to row it using sculls. *An old woman sculling a coracle came alongside.* VERB V n Also V

scullery /skʌləri/ **sculleries.** In old-fashioned British English, a **scullery** is a small room next to a kitchen where washing and other domestic work is done. N-COUNT

sculpt /skʌlpt/ **sculpts, sculpting, sculpted** ◆◇◇◇◇
1 When an artist **sculpts** something, they carve or shape it out of a hard material such as stone or clay. *An artist sculpted a full-size replica of her head... When I sculpt, my style is expressionistic.* VERB V n V
2 If something **is sculpted**, it is made into a particular shape. *More familiar landscapes have been sculpted by surface erosion... Michael smoothed and sculpted Jane's hair into shape.* VERB be V-ed V n into n

sculptor /skʌlptəʳ/ **sculptors.** A **sculptor** is someone who creates sculptures. ◆◇◇◇◇ N-COUNT

sculptural /skʌlptʃərəl/. **Sculptural** means relating to sculpture. *He enjoyed working with clay as a sculptural form... The sculptural style of the classical and Hellenistic periods.* ADJ: usu ADJ n

sculpture /skʌlptʃəʳ/ **sculptures** ◆◆◇◇◇
1 A **sculpture** is a work of art that is produced by carving or shaping stone, wood, clay, or other materials. *...stone sculptures of figures and animals. ...a collection of 20th-century art and sculpture.* N-VAR
2 **Sculpture** is the art of creating sculptures. *Both studied sculpture.* N-UNCOUNT

sculptured /skʌlptʃəʳd/. **Sculptured** objects have been carved or shaped from something. *...a beautifully sculptured bronze horse.* ADJ

scum /skʌm/ ◆◇◇◇◇
1 If you refer to people as **scum**, you are expressing your feelings of dislike and disgust for them; an offensive use. N-PLURAL PRAGMATICS
2 **Scum** is a layer of a dirty or unpleasant-looking substance on the surface of a liquid. *...scum marks around the bath.* N-UNCOUNT

scumbag /skʌmbæg/ **scumbags.** If you refer to someone as a **scumbag**, you are expressing your feelings of dislike and disgust for them; an offensive word. N-COUNT PRAGMATICS

scupper /skʌpəʳ/ **scuppers, scuppering, scuppered.** To **scupper** a plan or attempt means to spoil it completely; used mainly in British journalism. *Any increase in the female retirement age would scupper the plans of women like Gwen Davis... If the Commission has its way, the entire deal will be scuppered.* ◆◇◇◇◇ VERB =scuttle, foil V n

scurrilous /skʌrɪləs, AM skɜːr-/. **Scurrilous** accusations or stories are untrue and unfair, and are likely to damage the reputation of the person that they relate to. *Scurrilous and untrue stories were being invented. ...scurrilous rumours.* ADJ-GRADED: usu ADJ n =defamatory

scurry /skʌri, AM skɜːri/ **scurries, scurrying, scurried** ◆◇◇◇◇
1 When people or small animals **scurry** somewhere, they move quickly and hurriedly, especially because they are frightened; used mainly in written English. *The attack began, sending residents scurrying for cover... The rats scurry around, searching for scraps of food in the rubbish.* VERB =scuttle V prep/adv
2 If people **scurry** to do something, they do it as soon as they can; used mainly in written English. *Pictures of starving children have sent many people scurrying to donate money.* VERB =rush, hurry V to-inf

scurvy /skɜːʳvi/. **Scurvy** is a disease that is caused by a lack of vitamin C. N-UNCOUNT

scuttle /skʌtᵊl/ **scuttles, scuttling, scuttled** ◆◇◇◇◇
1 When people or small animals **scuttle** somewhere, they run there with short quick steps. *Two very small children scuttled away in front of them... Crabs scuttle along the muddy bank.* VERB =scurry V adv/prep
2 To **scuttle** a plan or a proposal means to make it fail or cause it to stop. *Such threats could scuttle the peace conference.* VERB =scupper, foil V n
3 To **scuttle** a ship means to sink it deliberately by making holes in the bottom. *He personally had received orders from Commander Lehmann to scuttle the ship.* VERB V n Also V
4 A **scuttle** is the same as a **coal scuttle**; used mainly in British English. N-COUNT

scythe /saɪð/ **scythes, scything, scythed**
1 A **scythe** is a tool with a long curved blade at right angles to a long handle. It is used to cut long grass or grain. N-COUNT
2 If you **scythe** grass or grain, you cut it with a scythe. *Two men were attempting to scythe the grass that grew waist deep in the yard.* VERB V n

SE. **SE** is a written abbreviation for **south-east.**

sea /siː/ **seas** ◆◆◆◆◇
1 The **sea** is the salty water that covers about three-quarters of the earth's surface. *Most of the kids have never seen the sea... All transport operations, whether by sea, rail or road, are closely monitored at all times.* N-SING: the N, also by N
2 You use **seas** when you are describing the sea at a particular time or in a particular area; a literary use. *He drowned after 30 minutes in the rough seas... The seas are warm further south.* N-PLURAL
3 A **sea** is a large area of salty water that is part of an ocean or is surrounded by land. *...the North Sea. ...the huge inland sea of Turkana.* N-COUNT: oft in names
4 A **sea of** people or things is a very large number of them together. *Down below them was the sea of upturned faces... His eyes ran over the sea of bottles and glasses on the table.* N-SING: N of n
5 You can say that someone is **all at sea** when they are in a state of confusion or uncertainty; used mainly in journalism. *If you had never seen a telly ad, you would be all at sea with popular culture.* PHRASES usu v-link PHR
6 **At sea** means on or under the sea, far away from land. *The boats remain at sea for an average of ten days at a time... His body was found at sea in waters off the Canary Islands.* v-link PHR, PHR after v
7 If you go or look out **to sea**, you go or look across the sea. *...fishermen who go to sea for two weeks at a time... He pointed out to sea.* PHR after v

sea air. The **sea air** is the air at the seaside, which is regarded as being good for people's health. *I took a deep breath of the fresh sea air.* N-UNCOUNT

seabed /siːbed/; also spelled **sea bed**. The **seabed** is the ground under the sea. N-SING

seabird /siːbɜːʳd/ **seabirds;** also spelled **sea-bird**. **Seabirds** are birds that live near the sea and get their food from it. *The island is covered with seabirds.* N-COUNT

seaboard /siːbɔːʳd/ **seaboards.** The **seaboard** is the part of a country that is next to the sea; used especially of the coasts of North America. *...the Eastern seaboard of the USA.* N-COUNT: usu the N in sing =coast

seaborne /siːbɔːʳn/; also spelled **sea-borne. Seaborne** actions or events take place on the sea in ships. *He postponed the seaborne invasion until the spring. ...seaborne trade.* ADJ: ADJ n

sea breeze, sea breezes. A **sea breeze** is a light wind blowing from the sea towards the land. N-COUNT

sea captain, sea captains. A **sea captain** is a person in command of a ship, usually a ship that carries goods for trade. N-COUNT

sea change, sea changes; also spelled **sea-change**. A **sea change** in someone's attitudes or behaviour is a complete change. *A sea change has taken place in young people's attitudes to their parents.* N-COUNT

sea dog, sea dogs; also spelled **seadog**. A **sea dog** is a sailor is who has spent many years at sea; an old-fashioned word. N-COUNT

seafarer /siːfeərəʳ/ **seafarers. Seafarers** are people who work on ships or people who travel regularly on the sea; used mainly in written English. *The Estonians have always been seafarers.* N-COUNT: usu pl

seafaring /siːfeərɪŋ/. **Seafaring** means working as a sailor or travelling regularly on the sea. *The* ADJ: ADJ n

Lebanese were a seafaring people. ...a seafaring vessel.

seafloor /siːflɔːʳ/. The **seafloor** is the ground under the sea. N-SING =seabed

seafood /siːfuːd/ **seafoods. Seafood** is shellfish such as lobsters, mussels, and crabs, and sometimes other sea creatures that you can eat. *...a seafood restaurant.* ◆◇◇◇◇ N-UNCOUNT: also N in pl

seafront /siːfrʌnt/ **seafronts.** The **seafront** is the part of a seaside town that is next to the sea. It usually consists of a road with buildings facing the sea. *They decided to meet on the seafront.* N-COUNT: usu *the* N in sing

seagoing /siːgoʊɪŋ/; also spelled **sea-going. Seagoing** boats and ships are designed for travelling on the sea, rather than on lakes, rivers, or canals. ADJ: ADJ n

sea-green; also spelled **sea green**. Something that is **sea-green** is a bluish-green colour like the colour of the sea. *...her sea-green eyes.* COLOUR

seagull /siːgʌl/ **seagulls.** A **seagull** is a common kind of seabird with white or grey feathers. ◆◇◇◇◇ N-COUNT

seahorse /siːhɔːʳs/ **seahorses;** also spelled **sea horse**. A **seahorse** is a type of small fish which appears to swim in a vertical position and whose head looks a little like the head of a horse. N-COUNT

seal 1 closing

seal /siːl/ **seals, sealing, sealed** ◆◆◆◇◇

1 When you **seal** an envelope, you close it by sticking down the flap, so that it cannot be opened without being torn. If you **seal** something **in** an envelope, you put it inside and then seal the envelope. *He sealed the envelope and put on a stamp... Write your letter and seal it in a blank envelope... A courier was despatched with two sealed envelopes.* VERB V n V n *in* n V-ed

2 If you **seal** a container or an opening, you cover it with something in order to prevent air, liquid, or other material getting in or out. If you **seal** something **in** a container, you put it inside and then seal the container. *She merely filled the containers, sealed them with a cork, and pasted on labels... A woman picks them up and seals them in plastic bags. ...a lid to seal in heat and keep food moist. ...a hermetically sealed, leak-proof packet.* VERB V n V n with *in* V-ed

3 The **seal** on a container or opening is the part where it has been sealed. *When assembling the pie, wet the edges where the two crusts join, to form a seal.* N-COUNT

4 A **seal** is a device or a piece of material, for example in a machine or a system of pipes, which closes an opening tightly so that air, liquid or other substances cannot get in or out. *Checks seals on fridges and freezers regularly.* N-COUNT: oft N *on* n

5 A **seal** is something such as a piece of sticky paper or wax that is fixed to a container or door and must be broken before the container or door can be opened. *The seal on the box broke when it fell from its hiding-place... Protestors banged on the sides of the lorry and broke customs seals on the doors.* N-COUNT: oft N *on* n

6 A **seal** is a special mark or design, for example on a document, representing someone or something. It may be used to show that something is genuine or officially approved. *...a supply of note paper bearing the Presidential seal... The best wines are entitled to a numbered seal of quality.* N-COUNT: usu with supp

7 If someone in authority **seals** an area, they stop people entering or passing through it, for example by placing barriers in the way. *The soldiers were deployed to help paramilitary police seal the border... A wide area round the two-storey building is sealed to all traffic except the emergency services.* ▸ **Seal off** means the same as **seal**. *Police and troops sealed off the area after the attack... Soldiers there are going to seal the airport off.* VERB V n V-ed PHRASAL VERB V P n (not pron) V n P

8 If something or someone **seals** something, they make it definite or confirm how it is going to be; used in written English. *British Aerospace is close to sealing a deal with Taiwan Aerospace... A General Election will be held which will seal his destiny one way or the other... His artistic character was sealed by his experiences of the First World War.* VERB V n

9 If something **sets** or **puts the seal on** something, it makes it definite or confirms how it is going to be; used in written English. *Such a visit may set the seal on a new relationship between the two governments... They see this election as a chance to put the final seal on the defeat of communism.* PHRASES V inflects

10 If a document is **under seal**, it is in a sealed envelope or package and cannot be looked at, for example because it is confidential; a formal expression. *Because the transcript is still under seal, I am precluded by law from discussing the evidence.* v-link PHR, n PHR

11 ● **seal of approval**: see **approval**. ● to **seal** someone's **fate**: see **fate.** ● my **lips are sealed**: see **lip.** ● **signed and sealed**: see **sign.**

seal in. If something **seals in** a smell or liquid, it prevents it from getting out of a food. *The coffee is freeze-dried to seal in all the flavour.* PHRASAL VERB V P n (not pron) Also V n P

seal off PHRASAL VERB

1 If one object or area **is sealed off** from another, there is a physical barrier between them, so that nothing can pass between them. *Windows are usually sealed off. ...the anti-personnel door that sealed off the chamber.* *be* V-ed P V P n (not pron) Also V n P

2 See **seal** 7.

seal up. If you **seal** something **up**, you close it completely so that nothing can get in or out. *The paper was used for sealing up holes in walls and roofs.* PHRASAL VERB V P n (not pron) Also V n P

seal 2 animal

seal /siːl/ **seals.** A **seal** is a large animal with flippers, which eats fish and lives partly on land and partly in the sea, usually in cold parts of the world. ◆◇◇◇◇ N-COUNT

sea lane, sea lanes. Sea lanes are particular routes which ships regularly use in order to cross a sea or ocean. N-COUNT: usu pl

sealant /siːlənt/ **sealants.** A **sealant** is a substance that is used to seal holes, cracks, or gaps. N-MASS =sealer

sealer /siːləʳ/ **sealers.** A **sealer** is the same as a **sealant.** N-MASS

sea level; also spelled **sea-level. Sea level** is the average level of the sea with respect to the land. The height of mountains or other areas is calculated in relation to **sea level**. *The stadium was 2275 metres above sea level... The whole place is at sea level... The melting ice caused a rise in sea level.* ◆◇◇◇◇ N-UNCOUNT

sealing wax. Sealing wax is a hard, usually red, substance that melts quickly and is used for putting seals on documents or letters. N-UNCOUNT

sea lion, sea lions; also spelled **sea-lion**. A **sea lion** is a type of large seal. N-COUNT

sealskin /siːlskɪn/. **Sealskin** is the fur of a seal, used to make coats and other clothing. *...waterproof sealskin boots.* N-UNCOUNT: oft N n

seam /siːm/ **seams** ◆◇◇◇◇

1 A **seam** is a line of stitches which joins two pieces of cloth together. N-COUNT

2 A **seam** of coal is a long, narrow layer of it beneath the ground. *The average UK coal seam is one metre thick.* N-COUNT: usu with supp

3 If something **is coming apart at the seams** or **is falling apart at the seams**, it is no longer working properly and may soon stop working completely. *Britain's university system is in danger of falling apart at the seams.* PHRASES V inflects

4 If a place is very full, you can say that it is **bursting at the seams.** *The hotels of Warsaw, Prague and Budapest were bursting at the seams.* V inflects

seaman /siːmən/ **seamen.** A **seaman** is a sailor, especially one who is not an officer. *The men emigrate to work as seamen.* ◆◇◇◇◇ N-COUNT =sailor

seamanship /siːmənʃɪp/. **Seamanship** is skill in managing a boat and controlling its movement through the sea. *...the art of seamanship and navigation.* N-UNCOUNT

seamless /siːmləs/. You use **seamless** to describe something that has no breaks or gaps in it or which continues without stopping. *It was a seamless procession of wonderful electronic music. ...the seamless blue sky.* ♦ **seamlessly** *It's a class move, allowing new and old to blend seamlessly.* ◆◇◇◇◇ ADJ ADV-GRADED: ADV with v

seamstress /siːmstrəs, sem-/ **seamstresses.** A **seamstress** is a woman who sews and makes clothes as her job. N-COUNT

seamy /siːmi/ **seamier, seamiest.** If you describe something as **seamy**, you mean that it involves unpleasant aspects of life such as crime, sex, or violence. *Hamburg's seamy St Pauli's district. ...the seamier side of life.* ADJ-GRADED: usu ADJ n =sordid

seance /seɪɑːns/ **seances.** A **seance** is a meeting in which people try to make contact with people who have died. N-COUNT

seaplane /siːpleɪn/ **seaplanes.** A **seaplane** is a type of aeroplane that can take off from or land on water. N-COUNT

seaport /siːpɔːʳt/ **seaports.** A **seaport** is a town with a large harbour that is used by ships. *The Baltic seaport of Rostock.* N-COUNT

sea power, sea powers
1 Sea power is the size and strength of a country's navy. *The transformation of American sea power began in 1940.* N-UNCOUNT
2 A **sea power** is a country that has a large navy. N-COUNT

sear /sɪəʳ/ **sears, searing, seared**
1 To **sear** something means to burn its surface with a sudden intense heat. *Grass fires have seared the land near the farming village of Basekhai.* VERB V n
2 If something **sears** a part of your body, it causes a painful burning feeling there; a literary use. *I distinctly felt the heat start to sear my throat.* VERB V n
3 See also **searing.**

search /sɜːʳtʃ/ **searches, searching, searched** ◆◆◆◆◇
1 If you **search** for something or someone, you look carefully for them. *The Turkish security forces have started searching for the missing men... They searched for a spot where they could sit on the floor... Mr Li will no doubt be searching for ways of raising China's profile in the region.* VERB V for n, Also V
2 If you **search** a place, you look carefully for something or someone there. *Armed troops searched the hospital yesterday... She searched her desk for the necessary information... Relief workers are still searching through collapsed buildings looking for victims.* VERB V n, V n for n, V prep
3 A **search** is an attempt to find something or someone by looking for them carefully. *There was no chance of him being found alive and the search was abandoned... Egypt has said there is no time to lose in the search for a Middle East settlement.* N-COUNT: oft N for n
4 If a police officer or someone else in authority **searches** you, they look carefully to see whether you have something hidden on you. *The man took her suitcase from her and then searched her... His first task was to search them for weapons.* VERB V n, V n for n
5 See also **searching, strip-search.**
6 If you go **in search of** something or someone, you try to find them. *Miserable, and unexpectedly lonely, she went in search of Jean-Paul... The law already denies entry to people in search of better economic opportunities.* PHRASES PHR after v, PHR n
7 You say **'search me'** when someone asks you a question and you want to emphasize that you do not know the answer; an informal expression. *'So why did he get interested all of a sudden?'—'Search me.'* CONVENTION PRAGMATICS =no idea

search out. If you **search** something **out**, you keep looking for it until you find it. *Traditional Spanish food is delicious and its specialities are worth searching out... Many people want jobs. They try to search them out every day.* PHRASAL VERB =seek out, V P n (not pron), V n P

searcher /sɜːʳtʃəʳ/ **searchers**
1 Searchers are people who are looking for someone or something that is missing. *In Oregon, searchers have found three mountain climbers missing since Saturday on Mount Hood.* N-COUNT: usu pl
2 A **searcher** is someone who is trying to find something such as the truth or the answer to a problem. *He's not a real searcher after truth.* N-COUNT: oft N after/for n =seeker

searching /sɜːʳtʃɪŋ/. A **searching** question or look is intended to discover the truth about something. *They asked her some searching questions on moral philosophy and logic.* ● See also **soul-searching.** ADJ-GRADED: usu ADJ n

searchlight /sɜːʳtʃlaɪt/ **searchlights.** A **searchlight** is a large powerful light that can be turned to shine a long way in any direction. N-COUNT

search party, search parties. A **search party** is an organized group of people who are searching for someone who is missing. N-COUNT

search warrant, search warrants. A **search warrant** is a special document that gives the police permission to search a house or other building. *Officers armed with a search warrant entered the flat.* N-COUNT

searing /sɪərɪŋ/ ◆◇◇◇◇
1 Searing is used to indicate that something such as pain or heat is very intense. *She woke to feel a searing pain in her feet. ...the searing heat of the Saudi Arabian desert.* ADJ: ADJ n
2 A **searing** speech or piece of writing is very critical. *The British civil service has long been subject to searing criticism.* ADJ-GRADED: ADJ n

seascape /siːskeɪp/ **seascapes.** A **seascape** is a painting or photograph of a scene at sea. N-COUNT

seashell /siːʃel/ **seashells;** also spelled **sea shell. Seashells** are the empty shells of small sea creatures. N-COUNT: usu pl =shell

seashore /siːʃɔːʳ/ **seashores.** The **seashore** is the part of a coast where the land slopes down into the sea. *She takes her inspiration from shells and stones she finds on the seashore.* N-COUNT: usu *the* N in sing =beach

seasick /siːsɪk/. If someone is **seasick** when they are travelling in a boat, they vomit or feel sick because of the way the boat is moving. *It was quite rough at times, and she was seasick.* ADJ-GRADED: usu v-link ADJ
♦ **seasickness** *He was very prone to seasickness and already felt queasy.* N-UNCOUNT

seaside /siːsaɪd/. You can refer to an area that is close to the sea, especially one where people go for their holidays, as **the seaside**; used mainly in British English. *I went to spend a few days at the seaside... The town was Redcar, a seaside resort on the Cleveland coast.* ◆◇◇◇◇ N-SING: *the* N

season /siːzᵊn/ **seasons, seasoning, seasoned** ◆◆◆◆◆
1 The **seasons** are the main periods into which a year can be divided and which each have their own typical weather conditions. *Autumn's my favourite season. ...the only region of Brazil where all four seasons are clearly defined. ...the rainy season.* N-COUNT: usu with supp =experienced
2 You can use **season** to refer to the period during each year when a particular activity or event takes place. For example, the planting **season** is the period when a particular plant or crop is planted. *...birds arriving for the breeding season... For law students, autumn brings the recruiting season.* N-COUNT: usu sing, usu *the*-ing N
3 You can use **season** to refer to the period when a particular fruit, vegetable, or other food is ready for eating and is widely available. *The plum season is about to begin... Now British asparagus is in season.* N-COUNT: n N, also *in/out of* N
4 You can use **season** to refer to a fixed period during each year when a particular sport is played. *...the baseball season... It is his first race this season.* N-COUNT: usu sing, with supp
5 A **season** is a period in which a play or show, or a series of plays or shows, is performed in one place. *...a season of three new plays. ...the Royal Ballet's summer season.* N-COUNT: with supp
6 A **season** of films is several of them shown as a series because they are connected in some way. *...a brief season of films in which Artaud appeared.* N-COUNT: usu sing, usu with supp
7 The holiday **season** is the time when most people have their holiday. *...the peak holiday season... There are discos and clubs but these are often closed out of season.* N-COUNT: usu sing, usu supp N, also *in/out of* N
8 If you **season** food with salt, pepper, or spices, you add them to it in order to improve its flavour. *Season the meat with salt and pepper... I believe in seasoning food before putting it on the table.* VERB V n *with* n, V n
9 If wood **is seasoned**, it is made suitable for making into furniture or for burning, usually by being allowed to dry out gradually. *Ensure that new wood has been seasoned.* VB: usu passive *be* V-ed
10 See also **seasoned, seasoning.**

11 If a female animal is **in season**, she is in a state where she is ready for mating. PHRASE: usu v-link PHR

seasonal /siːzənəl/. A **seasonal** factor, event, or change occurs during one particular time of the year. *The EC's jobless rate is adjusted for seasonal factors... Seasonal variations need to be taken into account.* ♦ **seasonally** *The seasonally adjusted unemployment figures show a rise of twelve-hundred.* ◆◆◇◇◇ ADJ: ADJ n; ADV: usu ADV -ed

seasonal affective disorder. **Seasonal affective disorder** is a feeling of tiredness and depression that some people have during the autumn and winter when there is very little sunshine. N-UNCOUNT

seasoned /siːzənd/. You can use the word **seasoned** to describe someone who has a lot of experience of something. For example, a **seasoned** traveller is someone who has travelled a lot. *The author is a seasoned academic... He began acting with the confidence of a seasoned performer.* ◆◇◇◇◇ ADJ-GRADED: usu ADJ n

seasoning /siːzənɪŋ/ **seasonings.** **Seasoning** is salt, pepper, or other spices that are added to food to improve its flavour. *Mix the meat with the onion, carrot, and some seasoning. ...seasonings such as coriander, chives and ginger.* ◆◇◇◇◇ N-MASS

season ticket, **season tickets.** A **season ticket** is a ticket that you can use repeatedly during a certain period, without having to pay each time. You can buy **season tickets** for things such as buses, trains, regular sporting events, or theatre performances. *We went to renew our monthly season ticket.* ◆◇◇◇◇ N-COUNT =pass

seat /siːt/ **seats, seating, seated** ◆◆◆◆◇

1 A **seat** is an object that you can sit on, for example a chair. *Stephen returned to his seat... Ann could remember sitting in the back seat of their car.* N-COUNT

2 The **seat** of a chair is the part that you sit on. *The stool had a torn, red plastic seat.* N-COUNT

3 If you **seat** yourself somewhere, you sit down; used in written English. *He waved towards a chair, and seated himself at the desk. ...a portrait of one of his favourite models seated on an elegant sofa.* VERB V pron-refl prep/adv V-ed Also V pron-refl

4 A building or vehicle that **seats** a particular number of people has enough seats for that number. *The Theatre seats 570.* VERB V amount

5 The **seat** of a piece of clothing is the part that covers your bottom. *Then he got up, brushed off the seat of his jeans, and headed slowly down the slope.* N-SING: usu *the* N *of* n

6 In British English, when someone is elected to parliament, you can say that they, or their party, have won a **seat**. *Independent candidates won the majority of seats on the local council.* N-COUNT

7 If someone has a **seat** on the board of a company or on a committee, they are a member of it. *He has been unsuccessful in his attempt to win a seat on the board of the company.* N-COUNT

8 The **seat** of an organization, a wealthy family, or an activity is its base. *Gunfire broke out early this morning around the seat of government in Lagos. ...Weston Park, family seat of the Earl of Bradford.* N-COUNT: with supp

9 See also **deep-seated, hot seat.**

10 If you **take a back seat**, you allow other people to have all the power and to make all the decisions. *You need to take a back seat and think about both past and future... This is a country where women usually take a back seat.* PHRASES V inflects

11 If you **take a seat**, you sit down; a formal expression. *'Take a seat,' he said in a bored tone... Rachel smiled at him as they took their seats on opposite sides of the table.* V and N inflect =sit down

12 • **bums on seats**: see **bum.** • **in the driving seat**: see **driving.** • **by the seat of** your **pants**: see **pants.**

seat belt, **seat belts;** also spelled **seatbelt.** A **seat belt** is a strap attached to a seat in a car or an aircraft. You fasten it across your body in order to prevent yourself being thrown out of the seat if there is a sudden movement. *The fact I was wearing a seat belt saved my life.* ◆◇◇◇◇ N-COUNT =safety belt

-seater /-siːtər/ **-seaters.** **-seater** combines with numbers to form adjectives and nouns which indicate how many people something such as a car has seats for. *...a two-seater sports car. ...a three-seater sofa... The plane is an eight-seater with twin propellers.* • See also **all-seater.** COMB in ADJ and N-COUNT

seating /siːtɪŋ/ ◆◇◇◇◇

1 You can refer to the seats in a place as the **seating**. *The stadium has been fitted with seating for over eighty thousand spectators.* N-UNCOUNT

2 The **seating** at a public place or a formal occasion is the arrangement of where people will sit. *She made a mental note to check the seating arrangements before the guests filed into the dining-room.* N-UNCOUNT: oft N n

seat of learning, **seats of learning.** People sometimes refer to a university or a similar institution as a **seat of learning**. *...one department of that great seat of learning.* N-COUNT

sea turtle, **sea turtles.** In American English, a **sea turtle** is a large reptile which has a thick shell covering its body and which lives in the sea most of the time. The usual British word is **turtle.** N-COUNT

sea urchin, **sea urchins.** A **sea urchin** is a small round sea creature that has a hard shell covered with sharp points. N-COUNT

sea wall, **sea walls.** A **sea wall** is a wall built along the edge of the sea to stop the sea flowing over the land or eroding it. *Cherbourg had a splendid harbour enclosed by a long sea wall.* N-COUNT

seaward /siːwərd/; the form **seawards** can be used for meaning 1.

1 Something that moves or faces **seaward** or **seawards** moves or faces in the direction of the sea or further out to sea. *A barge was about a hundred yards away, waiting to return seaward... It faced seawards to the north.* ADV: ADV after v ≠inland

2 The **seaward** side of something faces in the direction of the sea or further out to sea. *The houses on the seaward side of the road were all in ruins.* ADJ: usu ADJ n

sea water; also spelled **seawater.** **Sea water** is salt water from the sea. ◆◇◇◇◇ N-UNCOUNT

seaweed /siːwiːd/ **seaweeds.** **Seaweed** is a plant that grows in the sea. There are many kinds of seaweed. *...seaweed washed up on a beach.* ◆◇◇◇◇ N-MASS

seaworthy /siːwɜːrði/. A ship or boat which is **seaworthy** is fit to travel at sea. *The ship was completely seaworthy. ...a seaworthy boat.* ♦ **seaworthiness** *It didn't reach required standards of safety and seaworthiness.* ADJ-GRADED; N-UNCOUNT

sebum /siːbəm/. **Sebum** is an oily substance produced by glands in your skin. N-UNCOUNT

sec /sek/ **secs.** If you ask someone to wait a **sec**, you are asking them to wait for a very short time; an informal word. *Can you just hang on a sec?... Be with you in a sec.* N-COUNT: usu *a* N in sing =tick, mo

sec. /sek/ **secs**

1 **Sec.** is a written abbreviation for **second** or **seconds**. *The first woman to finish was Grete Waitz of Norway, with a time of 2 hrs, 29 min., 30 sec.* =second

2 **Sec.** is a written abbreviation for **Secretary**, especially when it is used as part of a person's title. *Details are available from the Hon. Sec. A.R. Bushby.* =Secretary

secateurs /sekətɜːrz/. In British English, **secateurs** are a gardening tool that look like a pair of strong, heavy scissors. Secateurs are used for cutting the stems of plants. The American term is **pruning shears.** N-PLURAL: also *a pair of* N

secede /sɪsiːd/ **secedes, seceding, seceded.** If a region or group **secedes** from the country or larger group to which it belongs, it formally becomes a separate country or stops being a member of the larger group. *Singapore seceded from the Federation of Malaysia and became an independent sovereign state... On 20 August 1960 Senegal seceded.* ◆◇◇◇◇ VERB V *from* n V

secession /sɪseʃən/. The **secession** of a region or group from the country or larger group to which it belongs is its formal separation from it. *...the Ukraine's secession from the Soviet Union.* ◆◇◇◇◇ N-UNCOUNT

secessionist /sɪseʃənɪst/ **secessionists.** **Secessionists** are people who want their region or group to become separate from the country or larger group to which it belongs. *...Lithuanian secessionists... The government is trying to crush a secessionist movement.* ◆◇◇◇◇ N-COUNT: usu pl, N n

secluded /sɪklu:dɪd/. A **secluded** place is quiet, private, and undisturbed. *We were tucked away in a secluded corner of the room... We found a secluded beach a few miles further on.* ◆◇◇◇◇ ADJ-GRADED: usu ADJ n

seclusion /sɪklu:ʒᵊn/. If you are living in **seclusion**, you are in a quiet place away from other people. *She lived in seclusion with her husband on their farm in Panama... They love the seclusion of their garden.* N-UNCOUNT

second 1 part of a minute

second /sekənd/ **seconds.** A **second** is one of the sixty parts that a minute is divided into. People often say **'a second'** or **'seconds'** when they simply mean a very short length of time. *For a few seconds nobody said anything... It only takes forty seconds... Her orbital speed must be a few hundred meters per second... Within seconds the other soldiers began firing too... Seconds later, firemen reached his door.* ◆◆◆◆◆ N-COUNT

second 2 coming after something else

second /sekənd/ **seconds, seconding, seconded** ◆◆◆◆◆

1 The **second** item in a series is the one that you count as number two. *...the second day of his visit to Delhi. ...their second child... My son just got married for the second time. ...the Second World War... She was the second of nine children. ...King Charles the Second... Britain came second in the Prix St Georges Derby.* ORD

2 **Second** is used before superlative adjectives to indicate that there is only one thing better or larger than the thing you are referring to. *The party is still the second strongest in Italy. ...the second-largest city in the United States.* ORD: ORD adj-superl

3 You say **second** when you want to make a second point or give a second reason for something. *First, the weapons should be intended for use only in retaliation after a nuclear attack. Second, the possession of the weapons must be seen as a temporary expedient.* ADV: ADV cl PRAGMATICS

4 In Britain, an upper **second** is a good honours degree and a lower **second** is an average honours degree. *I then went up to Lancaster University and got an upper second.* N-COUNT

5 If you have **seconds**, you have a second helping of food; an informal use. *There's seconds if you want them.* N-PLURAL

6 **Seconds** are goods that are sold cheaply in shops because they are slightly faulty. *It's a new shop selling discounted lines and seconds.* N-COUNT: usu pl

7 The **seconds** of someone who is taking part in a boxing match or chess tournament are the people who assist and encourage them. *He shouted to his seconds, 'I did it! I did it!'* N-COUNT: usu pl

8 If you **second** a proposal in a meeting or debate, you formally express your agreement with it so that it can then be discussed or voted on. *...Bryan Sutton, who seconded the motion against fox hunting... Your application must be proposed and seconded by current members.* ♦ **seconder, seconders** *The names of Mr Heseltine's proposer and seconder will be revealed this morning.* VERB V n N-COUNT

9 If you **second** what someone has said, you say that you agree with them or say the same thing yourself. *The Prime Minister seconded the call for discipline and austerity in a speech to the assembly last week.* VERB V n

10 If you experience something **at second hand**, you are told about it by other people rather than experiencing it yourself. *Most of them, after all, had not been at the battle and had only heard of the massacre at second hand.* ● See also **second-hand**. PHRASES PHR after v

11 If you say that something is **second to none**, you are emphasizing that it is very good indeed or the best that there is. *Our scientific research is second to none.* v-link PHR PRAGMATICS

12 If you say that something is **second only to** something else, you mean that it is exceeded or excelled only by that thing. *As a major health risk hepatitis is second only to tobacco.* usu v-link PHR

13 ● **second nature**: see **nature**. ● **in the second place**: see **place**.

second 3 sending someone to do a job

second /sɪkɒnd/ **seconds, seconding, seconded.** If you **are seconded** somewhere, you are sent there temporarily by your employer in order to do special duties; used mainly in British English. *In 1937 he was seconded to the Royal Canadian Air Force in Ottawa as air armament adviser... Several hundred soldiers have been seconded to help farmers.* VB: usu passive be V-ed prep/adv be V-ed to-inf

secondary /sekəndri, AM -deri/ ◆◆◇◇◇

1 If you describe something as **secondary**, you mean that it is less important than something else. *The street erupted in a huge explosion, with secondary explosions in the adjoining buildings... They argue that human rights considerations are now of only secondary importance... The actual damage to the brain cells is secondary to the damage caused to the blood supply.* ADJ: usu ADJ n, also v-link ADJ to n

2 **Secondary** diseases or infections happen as a result of another disease or infection that has already happened. *These patients had been operated for the primary cancer but there was evidence of secondary tumours.* ADJ: usu ADJ n

3 **Secondary** education is given to pupils between the ages of 11 or 12 and 18. *Examinations for the GCSE are taken after about five years of secondary education.* ADJ

secondary modern, secondary moderns. Secondary moderns were schools which existed until recently in Britain for children aged between about eleven and sixteen, where more attention was paid to practical skills and less to academic study than in a grammar school. N-COUNT

secondary school, secondary schools. A **secondary school** is a school for pupils between the ages of 11 or 12 and 18. *She taught history at a secondary school... One in four pupils leaving secondary school can't read or write properly.* ◆◇◇◇◇ N-VAR

second best; also spelled **second-best.** ◆◇◇◇◇

1 **Second best** is used to describe something that is not as good as the best thing of its kind but is better than all the other things of that kind. *We polished and wore our second-best boots.* ADJ: usu ADJ n

2 You can use **second best** to describe something that you have to accept even though you would have preferred something else. *...a messy, second-best solution... He refused to settle for anything that was second best.* ► Also a noun. *Oatmeal is a good second best.* ADJ N-SING

second chamber. The **second chamber** is one of the two bodies that a parliament is divided into. In Britain, the second chamber is the House of Lords. N-SING

second childhood. If you say that an old person is in their **second childhood**, you mean that their mind is becoming weaker and that their behaviour is similar to that of a young child. *...his rapid descent into a second childhood.* N-SING

second-class; also spelled **second class.** ◆◇◇◇◇

1 If someone treats you as a **second-class** citizen, they treat you as if you are less valuable and less important than other people. *Too many airlines treat our children as second-class citizens... Mr Karimov said he was not prepared to see Uzbekistan become a second class republic.* ADJ: ADJ n

2 If you describe something as **second-class**, you mean that it is of poor quality. *I am not prepared to see children in some parts of this country having to settle for a second-class education.* ADJ: usu ADJ n =second-rate, mediocre

3 In the past, the **second-class** accommodation on a train or ship was the ordinary accommodation, which was cheaper and less luxurious than the first-class accommodation. Nowadays, this type of accommodation is usually called 'standard class'. *He sat in the corner of a second-class carriage... Seven second-class passengers prepared to disembark. ...a second-class ticket.* ► Also an adverb. *I recently travelled second class from Pisa to Ventimiglia.* ► **Second-class** was the second-class accommodation on a train or ship. *In second class the fare is £85 one-way.* ADJ: ADJ n ADV: ADV after v N-UNCOUNT

4 In Britain, **second-class** postage is the slower and ADJ:

cheaper type of postage. In the United States, **second-class** postage is the type of postage that is used for sending newspapers and magazines. *...a second-class stamp. ...second class letters.* ▶ Also an adverb. *They're going to send it second class.* ADJ n; ADV: ADV after v

5 In Britain, a **second-class** degree is a good university degree, but not as good as a first-class degree. *A second-class honours degree is the minimum requirement.* ADJ: ADJ n

second coming. When Christians refer to **the second coming**, they mean the expected return to earth of Jesus Christ. N-SING: the N

second cousin, second cousins. Your **second cousins** are the children of your parents' first cousins. N-COUNT

second-degree

1 In the United States, **second-degree** is used to describe crimes that are considered to be less serious than first-degree crimes. *The judge reduced the charge to second-degree murder.* ADJ: ADJ n

2 A **second-degree** burn is more severe than a first-degree burn but less severe than a third-degree burn. *James Bell suffered second-degree burns in an explosion.* ADJ: ADJ n

second-guess, second-guesses, second-guessing, second-guessed. If you try to **second-guess** something, you try to guess in advance what someone will do or what will happen. *Editors and contributors are trying to second-guess the future.* VERB; V n; Also V

second-hand ◆◇◇◇◇

1 **Second-hand** things are not new and have been owned by someone else. *Buying a second-hand car can be a risky business. ...a stack of second-hand books.* ▶ Also an adverb. *Far more boats are bought second-hand than are bought brand new.* ADJ: usu ADJ n ≠brand-new; ADV: ADV after v

2 A **second-hand** shop sells second-hand goods. ADJ

3 **Second-hand** stories, information, or opinions are those you learn about from other people rather than directly or from your own experience. *He conceded that second-hand accounts are leading to rumour and counter-rumour... The denunciation was made on the basis of second-hand information.* ADJ: usu ADJ n

● **at second hand**: see **second**.

second-in-command; also spelled **second in command.** A **second-in-command** is someone who is next in rank to the leader of a group, and who has authority to give orders when the leader is not there. *He was posted to Hong Kong as second-in-command of C Squadron... The President was replaced by his second-in-command.* N-SING

second language, second languages. Someone's **second language** is a language which is not their native language but which they use at work or at school. *Lucy teaches English as a second language... French remained her second language for the rest of her life.* N-COUNT

second lieutenant, second lieutenants. A **second lieutenant** is an officer in the army who ranks directly below a lieutenant. N-COUNT

secondly /sekəndli/. You say **secondly** when you want to make a second point or give a second reason for something. *The problems were numerous. Firstly, I didn't know exactly when I was going to America; secondly, who was going to look after Doran and Lili?* ◆◆◇◇◇ ADV: ADV with cl (not last in cl) PRAGMATICS

secondment /sɪkɒndmənt/ **secondments.** In British English, someone who is on **secondment** from their normal employer has been sent somewhere else temporarily in order to do special duties. *We have two full-time secretaries, one of whom is on secondment from the Royal Navy.* N-VAR: oft *on* N, N *from/to* n

second opinion, second opinions. If you seek a **second opinion**, you ask another qualified person for their opinion about something such as your health. *I would like to see a specialist for a second opinion on my doctor's diagnosis.* N-COUNT

second person. A statement in **the second person** is a statement about the person or people you are talking to. The subject of a statement like this is 'you'. N-SING: the N

second-rate. If you describe something as **second-rate**, you mean that it is of poor quality. *...second-rate restaurants. ...another second-rate politician.* ◆◇◇◇◇ ADJ-GRADED =second-class, mediocre

second sight. If you say that someone has **second sight**, you mean that they seem to have the ability to know or see things that are going to happen in the future, or are happening in a different place. N-UNCOUNT

second string; also spelled **second-string.** If you describe a person or thing as someone's **second string**, you mean that they are a substitute and only used if someone or something else is not available. *...a second string team. ...her second-string horse.* N-SING: oft N n

second thought, second thoughts ◆◇◇◇◇

1 If you do something without **a second thought**, you do it without thinking about it carefully, usually because you do not have enough time or you do not care very much. *This murderous lunatic could kill them both without a second thought... Roberto didn't give a second thought to borrowing $2,000 from him.* N-SING: with brd-neg, a N

2 If you have **second thoughts** about a decision that you have made, you begin to doubt whether it was the best thing to do. *I had never had second thoughts about my decision to leave the company.* N-PLURAL: oft N *about* n

3 You can say **on second thoughts** or **on second thought** when you suddenly change your mind about something that you are saying or something that you have decided to do. *'Wait there!' Kathryn rose. 'No, on second thought, follow me.'* PHRASE: PHR with cl

second wind. When you get your **second wind**, you become able to continue doing a difficult or strenuous task after you have been tired or out of breath. *Finding a second wind, he rode away from his pursuers.* N-SING

Second World War. **The Second World War** is the major war that was fought between 1939 and 1945. ◆◆◇◇◇ N-PROPER: the N

secrecy /siːkrəsi/. **Secrecy** is the act of keeping something secret, or the state of being kept secret. *The British government has thrown a blanket of secrecy over the details... He shrouds his business dealings in secrecy.* ◆◆◇◇◇ N-UNCOUNT: oft prep N

secret /siːkrɪt/ **secrets** ◆◆◆◆◇

1 If something is **secret**, it is known about by only a small number of people, and is not told or shown to anyone else. *Soldiers have been training at a secret location... The police have been trying to keep the documents secret.* ● See also **top secret**. ADJ-GRADED: ADJ n, v n ADJ, v-link ADJ

♦ **secretly** *He wore a hidden microphone to secretly tape-record conversations. ...secretly organised events.* ADV-GRADED: ADV with v, ADV adj/n

2 A **secret** is a fact that is known by only a small number of people, and is not told to anyone else. *I think he enjoyed keeping our love a secret... I didn't want anyone to know about it, it was my secret.* N-COUNT

3 If you say that a particular way of doing things is **the secret** of achieving something, you mean that it is the best or only way to achieve it. *The secret of success is honesty and fair dealing... I learned something about writing. The secret is to say less than you need.* N-SING: the N, oft the N of n

4 Something's **secrets** are the things about it which have never been fully explained. *We have an opportunity now to really unlock the secrets of the universe... The past is riddled with deep dark secrets.* N-COUNT: usu pl, oft with poss

5 If you do something **in secret**, you do it without anyone else knowing. *Dan found out that I had been meeting my ex-boyfriend in secret.* PHRASES PHR after v

6 If you say that someone can **keep a secret**, you mean that they can be trusted not to tell other people a secret that you have told them. *Tom was utterly indiscreet, and could never keep a secret.* V inflects

7 If you **make no secret** of something, you tell others about it openly and plainly. *His wife made no secret of her hatred for the formal occasions... Ministers are making no secret about their wish to buy American weapons.* V inflects, PHR of n

secret agent, secret agents. A **secret agent** is a person who is employed by a government to find out the secrets of other governments. N-COUNT =spy

secretarial /sekrəteəriəl/. **Secretarial** work or training involves the work of a secretary. *I was doing temporary secretarial work.* ◆◇◇◇◇ ADJ: ADJ n

secretariat /sekrəteəriæt/ **secretariats.** A **secretariat** is a department that is responsible for the administration of an international political organization. *...the UN secretariat.* ◆◇◇◇◇ N-COUNT

secretary /sekrətri, AM -teri/ **secretaries** ◆◆◆◆◆

1 A **secretary** is a person who is employed to do office work, such as typing letters, answering phone calls, and arranging meetings. N-COUNT

2 The **secretary** of an organization such as a trade union, a political party, or a club is its official manager. *My grandfather was secretary of the Scottish Miners' Union.* N-COUNT

3 The **secretary** of a company is the person who has the legal duty of keeping the company's records. N-COUNT

4 **Secretary** is used in the titles of ministers and officials who are in charge of main government departments. *...the British Foreign Secretary. ...Defense Secretary Caspar Weinberger.* N-COUNT: usu *the* N in sing; N-TITLE

secretary-general, secretaries-general; also spelled **Secretary General**. The **secretary-general** of an international political organization is the person in charge of its administration. *...the United Nations Secretary-General.* ◆◆◆◇◇ N-COUNT: usu *the* N in sing

Secretary of State, Secretaries of State ◆◆◆◇◇

1 In the United States, **the Secretary of State** is the head of the government department which deals with foreign affairs. N-COUNT: usu *the* N in sing

2 In Britain, **the Secretary of State** for a particular government department is the head of that department. *...the Secretary of State for Education.* N-COUNT: usu *the* N in sing

secrete /sɪkriːt/ **secretes, secreting, secreted** ◆◇◇◇◇

1 If part of a plant, animal, or human **secretes** a liquid, it produces it. *The sweat glands secrete water.* VERB V n

2 If you **secrete** something somewhere, you hide it there so that nobody will find it; a literary use. *She secreted the gun in the kitchen cabinet.* VERB =hide V n prep/adv

secretion /sɪkriːʃən/ **secretions** ◆◇◇◇◇

1 **Secretion** is the process by which certain liquid substances are secreted by parts of plants or bodies. *...the secretion of adrenaline. ...insulin secretion.* N-UNCOUNT

2 **Secretions** are liquid substances that parts of plants or bodies secrete. *...gastric secretions.* N-PLURAL

secretive /siːkrətɪv, sɪkriːt-/. If you are **secretive**, you like to have secrets and to keep your knowledge, feelings, or intentions hidden. *Billionaires are usually fairly secretive about the exact amount that they're worth. ...the secretive world of spying.* ♦ **secretively** *...a banknote handed over secretively in the entrance to a building.* ♦ **secretiveness** *He was evasive, to the point of secretiveness.* ◆◇◇◇◇ ADJ-GRADED: oft ADJ *about* n; ADV-GRADED: ADV after v; N-UNCOUNT

secret police. The **secret police** is a police force, especially in a non-democratic country, that works secretly and is concerned with political crimes. ◆◇◇◇◇ N-UNCOUNT: also *the* N

secret service, secret services. A country's **secret service** is a secret government department whose job is to find out enemy secrets and to prevent its own government's secrets from being discovered. ◆◇◇◇◇ N-COUNT

sect /sekt/ **sects.** A **sect** is a group of people that has separated from a larger group and has a particular set of religious or political beliefs. ◆◇◇◇◇ N-COUNT

sectarian /sekteəriən/. **Sectarian** means resulting from the differences between different religions. *He was the fifth person to be killed in sectarian violence last week... The police said the murder was sectarian. ...both sides of the sectarian divide.* ◆◇◇◇◇ ADJ: usu ADJ n

sectarianism /sekteəriənɪzəm/. **Sectarianism** is strong support for a particular sect and its beliefs. *There is a great deal of political rivalry and sectarianism within out movement.* N-UNCOUNT

section /sekʃən/ **sections, sectioning, sectioned** ◆◆◆◆◇

1 A **section** of something is one of the parts into which it is divided or from which it is formed. *He said it was wrong to single out any section of society for Aids testing... They moulded a complete new bow section for the boat. ...a large orchestra, with a vast percussion section. ...the Georgetown section of Washington, D.C. ...a geological section of a rock.* ● See also **cross-section**. N-COUNT: usu with supp

2 If something **is sectioned**, it is divided into sections. *It holds vegetables in place while they are being peeled or sectioned.* VB: usu passive *be* V-ed

3 A **section** of an official document such as a report or a law is one of the parts into which it is divided. *...section 14 of the Trade Descriptions Act 1968. ...the all-important section on the powers of the federal government.* N-COUNT: usu N num

4 A **section** is a diagram of something such as a building or a part of the body. It shows how the object would appear to you if it were cut from top to bottom and looked at from the side. *For some buildings a vertical section is more informative than a plan.* N-COUNT

5 ● **Caesarean section**: see **Caesarean**.

section off. If an area **is sectioned off**, it is separated by a wall, fence, or other barrier from the surrounding area. *The kitchen is galley shaped, sectioned off from the rest of the room by a half wall.* PHRASAL VERB usu passive *be* V-ed P

sectional /sekʃənəl/. **Sectional** interests are those of a particular group within a community or country. *He urged his countrymen to greater efforts and criticized the selfish attitude of certain sectional interests.* ADJ: ADJ n

sector /sektəʳ/ **sectors** ◆◆◆◆◇

1 A particular **sector** of a country's economy is the part connected with that specified type of industry. *...the nation's manufacturing sector. ...the service sector of the Hong Kong economy.* ● See also **public sector**, **private sector**. N-COUNT: supp N

2 A **sector** of a large group is a smaller group which is part of it. *Workers who went to the Gulf came from the poorest sectors of Pakistani society.* N-COUNT: usu with supp

3 A **sector** is an area of a city or country which is controlled by a military force. *Officers were going to retake sectors of the city.* N-COUNT: usu with supp

4 A **sector** is a part of a circle which is formed when you draw two straight lines from the centre of the circle to the edge; a technical term in mathematics. N-COUNT

sectoral. **Sectoral** means relating to the various economic sectors of a society or to a particular economic sector; a technical term in economics. *...sectoral differences within social classes.* ADJ: ADJ n

secular /sekjʊləʳ/. You use **secular** to describe things that have no connection with religion. *He spoke about preserving the country as a secular state. ...secular and religious education.* ◆◇◇◇◇ ADJ-GRADED: usu ADJ n ≠religious

secularism /sekjʊlərɪzəm/. **Secularism** is a system of social organization and education where religion is not allowed to play a part in civil affairs. ♦ **secularist, secularists** *The country is being torn to pieces by conflict between fundamentalists and secularists.* N-UNCOUNT; N-COUNT

secularized /sekjʊləraɪzd/; also spelled **secularised**. **Secularized** societies are no longer under the control or influence of religion. *The Pope had no great sympathy for the secularized West.* ADJ-GRADED

secure /sɪkjʊəʳ/ **secures, securing, secured** ◆◆◆◆◇

1 If you **secure** something that you want or need, you obtain it after a lot of effort; a formal use. *Federal leaders continued their efforts to secure a ceasefire... Graham's achievements helped secure him the job.* VERB V n V n n Also V n *for* n

2 If you **secure** a place, you make it safe from harm or attack; a formal use. *Staff withdrew from the main part of the prison but secured the perimeter... The shed was secured by a hasp and staple fastener.* VERB V n

3 A **secure** place is tightly locked or well protected, so that people cannot enter it or leave it. *...the secure unit at Cane Hill hospital... We shall make sure our home is as secure as possible from now on.* ADJ-GRADED

♦ **securely** *He locked the heavy door securely and* ADV:

kept the key in his pocket. ...territory once securely under the control of the rebels. usu ADV with v

4 If you **secure** an object, you fasten it firmly to another object. *He helped her close the cases up, and then he secured the canvas straps as tight as they would go... The frames are secured by horizontal rails to the back wall.* VERB V n

5 If an object is **secure**, it is fixed firmly in position. *Check joints are secure and the wood is sound... Shelves are only as secure as their fixings.* ADJ-GRADED: usu v-link ADJ ♦ **securely** *Ensure that the frame is securely fixed to the ground with bolts... Builders must fasten down roofs of newly-built homes more securely.* ADV-GRADED: ADV with v

6 If you describe something such as a job as **secure**, it is safe and certain not to be lost. *...trade union demands for secure wages and employment. ...the failure of financial institutions once thought to be secure.* ADJ-GRADED

7 A **secure** base or foundation is strong and reliable. *He was determined to give his family a secure and solid base... For many young blacks, the only jobs that offer a secure future are in the armed forces.* ADJ-GRADED: usu ADJ n

8 If you feel **secure**, you feel safe and happy and are not worried about life. *She felt secure and protected when she was with him... The government must feel secure before it will be willing to make the concessions needed for peace.* ADJ-GRADED: usu v-link ADJ

9 If a loan **is secured**, it is guaranteed by assets such as a house which becomes the property of the lender if the borrower fails to repay the loan. *The loan is secured against your home... His main task is to raise enough finance to repay secured loans.* VB: usu passive be V-ed adv/prep V-ed

security /sɪkjʊərɪti/ **securities** ◆◆◆◆◆

1 **Security** refers to all the measures that are taken to protect a place, or to ensure that only authorized people enter it or leave it. *They are now under a great deal of pressure to tighten their airport security... Strict security measures are in force in the capital. ...a top security jail.* N-UNCOUNT: with supp, oft N n

2 A feeling of **security** is a feeling of being safe and free from worry. *He loves the security of a happy home life... If an alarm gives you that feeling of security, then it's worth carrying.* N-UNCOUNT: usu with supp, oft N of n ● If something gives you **a false sense of security**, it makes you believe that you are safe when you are not. *Wearing helmets gave cyclists a false sense of security and encouraged them to take risks.* PHRASE: PHR after v

3 If you pledge something as **security** for a loan, you promise to give it to the person who lends you money, if you fail to pay the money back. *The central bank will provide special loans, and the banks will pledge the land as security.* N-UNCOUNT =collateral

4 **Securities** are stocks, shares, bonds, or other certificates that you buy in order to earn regular interest from them or to sell them later for a profit; a technical use. *National banks can package their own mortgages and underwrite them as securities. ...US government securities and bonds.* N-PLURAL

5 See also **social security**.

security blanket, security blankets

1 If you refer to something as a **security blanket**, you mean that it provides someone with a feeling of safety and comfort when they are in a situation that worries them or makes them feel nervous. *Alan sings with shy intensity, hiding behind the security blanket of his guitar.* N-COUNT

2 A baby's **security blanket** is a piece of cloth or clothing which the baby holds and chews in order to feel comforted. N-COUNT

Security Council. ◆◆◆◇◇ **The Security Council** is the committee which governs the United Nations. It has permanent representatives from the United States, Russia, China, France, and the United Kingdom, and temporary representatives from some other countries. N-PROPER: *the* N

security guard, security guards. ◆◇◇◇◇ A **security guard** is someone whose job is to protect a building or to collect and deliver large amounts of money. N-COUNT

security risk, security risks. If you describe someone as a **security risk**, you mean that they may be a threat to the safety of a country or organization. N-COUNT

sedan /sɪdæn/ **sedans.** ◆◇◇◇◇ In American English, a **sedan** is a car with seats for four or more people, a fixed roof, and a boot that is separate from the part of the car that you sit in. The British word is **saloon.** N-COUNT

sedan chair, sedan chairs. A **sedan chair** is an enclosed chair for one person carried on two poles by two men, one in front and one behind. **Sedan chairs** were used in the 17th and 18th centuries. N-COUNT

sedate /sɪdeɪt/ **sedates, sedating, sedated** ◆◇◇◇◇

1 If you describe someone as **sedate**, you mean that they are quiet and rather dignified, though perhaps dull. *She took them to visit her sedate, elderly cousins... Her London life was sedate, almost mundane.* ADJ-GRADED: usu ADJ n ♦ **sedately** *He saw her come out of the lift alone and walk sedately across the carpeting. ...sedately dressed in business suit with waistcoat.* ADV-GRADED: ADV with v

2 **Sedate** places are peaceful and rather dignified, though unexciting. *I live in a sedate little village in the Midlands... The normally sedate suburb of Coon Rapids faced the problem of mischievous teenagers. ...sedate hotel grounds.* ADJ-GRADED: usu ADJ n ♦ **sedately** *The rooms were neat and sedately furnished.* ADV-GRADED: ADV -ed

3 If you describe something such as a car or an event as **sedate**, you mean that it is slow and unexciting. *...a heavy car with solid but sedate performance... The party turned out to be a sedate affair.* ADJ-GRADED: usu ADJ n ♦ **sedately** *He pulled sedately out of the short driveway... He did not gallop like his opponent, but trotted sedately.* ADV-GRADED: ADV after v

4 If someone **is sedated**, they are given a drug to calm them or to make them sleep. *The patient is sedated with intravenous use of sedative drugs... Doctors have been told not to sedate children with an anaesthetic that may be linked to five deaths. ...a sedating massage oil.* VERB be V-ed V n V-ing ♦ **sedated** *Grace was asleep, lightly sedated.* ADJ-GRADED: v-link ADJ

sedation /sɪdeɪʃᵊn/. If someone is under **sedation**, they have been given medicine or drugs in order to calm them or make them sleep. *His mother was under sedation after the boy's body was brought back from Germany.* N-UNCOUNT: oft *under* N

sedative /sedətɪv/ **sedatives** ◆◇◇◇◇

1 A **sedative** is a medicine or drug that calms you or makes you sleep. *They use opium as a sedative, rather than as a narcotic.* N-COUNT

2 Something that has a **sedative** effect calms you or makes you sleep. *Amber bath oil has a sedative effect.* ADJ: ADJ n

sedentary /sedəntəri, AM -teri/. Someone who has a **sedentary** lifestyle or job, sits down a lot of the time and does not take much exercise. *Obesity and a sedentary lifestyle has been linked with an increased risk of heart disease.* ADJ-GRADED: usu ADJ n

sedge /sedʒ/ **sedges.** ◆◇◇◇◇ **Sedge** is a grass-like plant that grows in wet, marshy ground. N-MASS

sediment /sedɪmənt/ **sediments.** ◆◇◇◇◇ **Sediment** is solid material that settles at the bottom of a liquid, especially earth and pieces of rock that have been carried along and then left somewhere by water, ice, or wind. *Many organisms that die in the sea are soon buried by sediment. ...ocean sediments.* N-VAR

sedimentary /sedɪmentəri, AM -teri/. **Sedimentary** rocks are formed from sediment left by water, ice, or wind. ADJ: ADJ n

sedition /sɪdɪʃᵊn/. **Sedition** is speech, writing, or behaviour intended to encourage rebellion or resistance against the government. *Government officials charged him with sedition.* N-UNCOUNT

seditious /sɪdɪʃəs/. A **seditious** act, utterance, or piece of writing encourages rebellion or resistance against the government. *He fell under suspicion for distributing seditious pamphlets.* ADJ-GRADED: usu ADJ n

seduce /sɪdjuːs, AM -duːs/ **seduces, seducing, seduced** ◆◆◇◇◇

1 If something **seduces** you, it is so attractive that it tempts you into doing something that you would not otherwise do. *The view of lake and plunging* VERB =tempt V n

cliffs seduces visitors... He argues that the clever advertising employed by U.S. cigarette companies would seduce more people into smoking. — V n *into*-ing/n
♦ **seduction** /sɪdʌkʃən/ **seductions** *...the seduction of words... The country had resisted the seductions of mass tourism.* — N-VAR

2 If someone **seduces** another person, they use their charm to persuade that person to have sex with them. *She has set out to seduce Stephen.* — VERB; V n
♦ **seduction** *Her methods of seduction are subtle. ...a slow seduction.* — N-VAR

seducer /sɪdjuːsər, AM -duːs-/ **seducers.** A **seducer** is a man who seduces someone. *He is proud of his reputation as a seducer of young women.* — N-COUNT

seductive /sɪdʌktɪv/ ◆◇◇◇◇
1 Something that is **seductive** is very attractive or tempting. *It's a seductive argument.* — ADJ-GRADED
♦ **seductively** *...his seductively simple assertion... The film opens seductively.* — ADV-GRADED: usu ADV adj, also ADV with v
2 A person who is **seductive** is very attractive sexually. *...a seductive woman... I love dressing up to look seductive.* — ADJ-GRADED
♦ **seductively** *...looking seductively over her shoulder... Her mouth is seductively large and full.* — ADV-GRADED: usu ADV with v, also ADV adj

seductress /sɪdʌktrəs/ **seductresses.** A **seductress** is a woman who seduces someone. *Few males can resist a self-confident seductress.* — N-COUNT

see /siː/ **sees, seeing, saw, seen** ◆◆◆◆◆
1 When you **see** something, you notice it using your eyes. *You can't see colours at night... I saw a man making his way towards me... She can see, hear, touch, smell, and taste... As he neared the farm, he saw that a police car was parked outside it... Did you see what happened?* — VB: no cont; V n; V n -ing; V; V that; V wh
2 If you **see** someone, you visit them or meet them. *I saw him yesterday... Mick wants to see you in his office right away... You need to see a doctor.* — VERB; V n
3 If you **see** an entertainment such as a play, film, concert, or sports game, you watch it. *He had been to see a Semi-Final of the FA Cup... It was one of the most amazing films I've ever seen.* — VB: no cont; =watch; V n
4 If you **see** that something is true or exists, you realize by observing it that it is true or exists. *I could see she was lonely... We saw what happened to Labour in the 1980s... You see young people going to school inadequately dressed for the weather... My taste has changed a bit over the years as you can see... You've just been cleaning it, I see... The army must be seen to be taking firm action.* — VB: no cont; V that; V wh; V n -ing; V; *be* V-ed to-inf
5 If you **see** what someone means or **see** why something happened, you understand what they mean or understand why it happened. *Oh, I see what you're saying... I don't see why you're complaining... I really don't see any reason for changing it... Now I see that I was wrong.* — VB: no cont, no passive; =understand; V wh; V n; V that
6 If you **see** someone or something as a certain thing, you have the opinion that they are that thing. *She saw him as a visionary, but her father saw him as a man who couldn't make a living... They have a normal body weight but see themselves as being fat... Others saw it as a betrayal... I don't see it as my duty to take sides... As I see it, Llewelyn has three choices open to him... Women are sometimes seen to be less effective as managers.* — VERB; =perceive; V n *as* n/-ing; V *it as* n; V *it as* n to-inf; V *it*; *be* V-ed to-inf
7 If you **see** a particular quality in someone, you believe they have that quality. If you ask what someone **sees** in a particular person or thing, you want to know what they find attractive about that person or thing. *Frankly, I don't know what Paul sees in her... Young and old saw in him an implacable opponent of apartheid.* — VB: no cont, no passive; V n *in* n; V *in* n n
8 If you **see** something happening in the future, you imagine it, or predict that it will happen. *A good idea, but can you see Taylor trying it?... We can see a day where all people live side by side.* — VB: no cont; =imagine, picture; V n -ing; V n
9 If you say that a period of time or a person **sees** a particular change or event, you mean that the change or event takes place during that period of time or while that person is alive. *Yesterday saw the resignation of the acting Interior Minister... He had worked with the General for three years and was sorry to see him go... Mr Frank has seen the economy of his town slashed by the uprising.* — VB: no passive; =witness; V n; V n inf; V n -ed
10 You can use **see** in expressions to do with finding out information. For example, if you say **'I'll see what's happening'**, you mean that you intend to find out what is happening. *Let me just see what the next song is... Every time we asked our mother, she said, 'Well, see what your father says.'... Shake him gently to see if he responds.* — VERB; =find out; V wh
11 You can use **see** to promise to try and help someone. For example, if you say **'I'll see if I can do it'**, you mean that you will try to do the thing concerned. *I'll see if I can call her for you... We'll see what we can do, miss.* — VERB; PRAGMATICS; V if; V what
12 If you **see** that something is done or if you **see** to it that it is done, you make sure that it is done. *See that you take care of him... Catherine saw to it that the information went directly to Walter.* — VERB; V that; V *to it* that
13 If you **see** someone to a particular place, you accompany them to make sure that they get there safely, or to show politeness. *He didn't offer to see her to her car... 'Goodnight.'—'I'll see you out.'* — VERB; =accompany; V n prep/adv
14 If you **see** a lot **of** someone, you often meet each other or visit each other. *We used to see quite a lot of his wife, Carolyn... We didn't see much of each other after that because he was touring.* — VERB; V amount *of* n
15 If you **are seeing** someone, you spend time with them socially, and are having a romantic or sexual relationship. *My husband was still seeing her and he was having an affair with her.* — VERB; V n
16 Some writers use **see** in expressions such as **we saw** and **as we have seen** to refer to something that has already been explained or described. *We saw in Chapter 16 how annual cash budgets are produced... Using the figures given above, it can be seen that machine A pays back the initial investment in two years... As we have seen in previous chapters, visualization methods are varied.* — VERB; PRAGMATICS; V wh; V that
17 See is used in books to indicate to readers that they should look at another part of the book, or at another book, because more information is given there. *Surveys consistently find that men report feeling safe on the street after dark. See, for example, Hindelang and Garofalo (1978)... See Chapter 7 below for further comments on the textile industry.* — VB: only imper; PRAGMATICS; V n
18 You can use **seeing that** or **seeing as** to introduce a reason for what you are saying or a reason why you think something is the case. *He is in the marriage bureau business, which is mildly ironic seeing that his dearest wish is to get married himself... Seeing as Mr Moreton is a doctor, I would assume he has a modicum of intelligence.* — PHRASES; CONJ-SUBORD; PRAGMATICS; =since
19 You can say **'I see'** to indicate that you understand what someone is telling you; used in spoken English. *'He came home in my car.'—'I see.'* — CONVENTION; PRAGMATICS
20 People say **'I'll see'** or **'We'll see'** to indicate that they do not intend to make a decision immediately, and will decide later. *We'll see. It's a possibility.* — CONVENTION; PRAGMATICS
21 People say **'let me see'** or **'let's see'** when they are trying to remember something, or are trying to find something. *Let's see, they're six – no, make that five hours ahead of us... Now let me see, who's the man we want?* — CONVENTION; PRAGMATICS
22 If you try to make someone **see sense** or **see reason**, you try to make them realize that they are wrong because you think they are behaving stupidly. *He was hopeful that by sitting together they could both see sense and live as good neighbours... He tried again to get her to see reason.* — V inflects
23 You can say **'you see'** when you are explaining something to someone, to encourage them to listen and understand; used in spoken English. *Well, you see, you shouldn't really feel that way about it... She was a prime target for blackmail, don't you see?* — CONVENTION; PRAGMATICS
24 'See you', **'be seeing you'**, and **'see you later'** are informal ways of saying goodbye to someone when you expect to meet them again soon; they are used in spoken English. *'Talk to you later.'—'All right. See you love.'... 'No time for chattering now.'—'Be seeing you, then.'* — CONVENTION; PRAGMATICS; =bye
25 You can say **'You'll see'** to someone if they do not agree with you about what you think will hap- — CONVENTION; PRAGMATICS

pen in the future, and you believe that you will be proved right. *The thrill wears off after a few years of marriage. You'll see.*

26 • to **see the back of** someone: see **back.** • to **have seen better days**: see **day.** • to **see the light of day**: see **day.** • to **be seen dead**: see **dead.** • **as far as the eye can see**: see **eye.** • to **see eye to eye**: see **eye.** • **as far as I can see**: see **far.** • to **see fit**: see **fit.** • to **see the light**: see **light.** • to **see red**: see **red.** • **it remains to be seen**: see **remain.** • **wait and see**: see **wait.**

see about. When you **see about** something, you arrange for it to be done or provided. *Tony announced it was time to see about lunch... I must see about selling the house.* PHRASAL VERB V P n/-ing

see off PHRASAL VERB

1 If you **see off** an opponent, you defeat them. *There is no reason why they cannot see off the Socialist challenge.* V P n (not pron) Also V n P

2 When you **see** someone **off**, you go with them to the station, airport, or port that they are leaving from, and say goodbye to them there. *Ben had planned a steak dinner for himself after seeing Jackie off on her plane.* V n P Also V P n (not pron)

see through. If you **see through** someone or their behaviour, you realize what their intentions are, even though they are trying to hide them. *I saw through your little ruse from the start.* • See also **see-through.** PHRASAL VERB V P n

see to. If you **see to** something that needs attention, you deal with it. *While Franklin saw to the luggage, Sara took Eleanor home.* PHRASAL VERB V P n

seed /siːd/ **seeds, seeding, seeded** ◆◆◆◆◇

1 A **seed** is the small, hard part of a plant from which a new plant grows. *...a packet of cabbage seed... I sow the seed in pots of soil-based compost. ...sunflower seeds.* N-VAR

2 If you **seed** a piece of land, you plant seeds in it. *Men mowed the wide lawns and seeded them... The primroses should begin to seed themselves down the steep hillside. ...his newly seeded lawns.* VERB =sow V n V pron-refl V-ed

3 You can refer to the **seeds of** something when you want to talk about the beginning of a feeling or process that gradually develops and becomes stronger or more important; a literary use. *He raised questions meant to plant seeds of doubts in the minds of jurors... He considered that there were, in these developments, the seeds of a new moral order.* N-PLURAL: N of n

4 In sports such as tennis or badminton, a **seed** is a player who has been ranked according to his or her ability; a technical use. *...Pete Sampras, Wimbledon's top seed and the world No.1... In the final Capriati, the third seed, defeated Katerina Maleeva.* N-COUNT: usu supp N, oft ord/num N

5 In competitive sporting events, when a player or a team **is seeded**, they are ranked according to their ability; a technical use. *In the UEFA Cup the top 16 sides are seeded for the first round... He now meets Richey Reneberg, seeded eight... The top four seeded nations are through to the semi-finals.* VB: usu passive =ranked be V-ed adv/prep V-ed

6 If vegetable plants **go to seed** or **run to seed**, they produce flowers and seeds as well as leaves. *If unused, winter radishes run to seed in spring.* PHRASES V inflects

7 If you say that someone or something has **gone to seed** or **run to seed**, you mean that their health, strength, or efficiency has started to diminish or decay. *He says the economy has gone to seed... He was a big man in his forties; once he had a lot of muscle but now he was running to seed.* V inflects PRAGMATICS

seedbed /siːdbed/ **seedbeds;** also spelled **seed-bed.**

1 A **seedbed** is an area of ground, usually with specially prepared earth, where young plants are grown from seed. N-COUNT

2 You can refer to a place or a situation as a **seedbed** when it seems likely that rebellion or conflict will develop there easily. *Crises and conflicts are a seedbed for international terrorism... My region is a seedbed of crime.* N-COUNT: oft N for/of n

seed corn. **Seed corn** is money that businesses spend at the beginning of a project in the hope that it will eventually produce profits. *The scheme offers seed corn finance with loans of up to £5,000 at only 4% interest.* N-UNCOUNT

seedless /siːdləs/. A **seedless** fruit has no seeds in it. *...seedless grapes.* ADJ

seedling /siːdlɪŋ/ **seedlings.** A **seedling** is a young plant that has been grown from a seed. ◆◇◇◇◇ N-COUNT

seedy /siːdi/ **seedier, seediest.** If you describe a person or place as **seedy**, you disapprove of them because they look dirty and untidy, or they have a bad reputation. *Frank ran dodgy errands for a seedy local villain... We were staying in a seedy hotel close to the red light district... They suck you in to their seedy world.* ♦ **seediness** *...the atmosphere of seediness and decay about the city.* ◆◇◇◇◇ ADJ-GRADED: usu ADJ n PRAGMATICS N-UNCOUNT

seek /siːk/ **seeks, seeking, sought** ◆◆◆◆◆

1 If you **seek** something such as a job or a place to live, you try to find one; a formal use. *They have had to seek work as labourers... Four people who sought refuge in the Italian embassy have left voluntarily... Candidates are urgently sought for the post of Conservative party chairman.* VERB V n be V-ed for n

2 When someone **seeks** something, they try to obtain it; a formal use. *The prosecutors have warned they will seek the death penalty... Haemophiliacs are seeking compensation for being given contaminated blood.* VERB V n

3 If you **seek** someone's help or advice, you contact them in order to ask for it; a formal use. *Always seek professional legal advice before entering into any agreement... On important issues, they seek a second opinion... The couple have sought help from marriage guidance counsellors.* VERB V n V n from n

4 If you **seek** to do something, you try to do it; a formal use. *He also denied that he would seek to annex the country... Moscow is seeking to slow the growth of Russian inflation.* VERB V to-inf

seek out. If you **seek out** someone or something or **seek** them **out**, you keep looking for them until you find them. *Now is the time for local companies to seek out business opportunities in Europe... Ellen spent the day in the hills and sought me out when she returned.* PHRASAL VERB V P n (not pron) V n P

seeker /siːkəʳ/ **seekers.** A **seeker** is someone who is looking for or trying to get something. *I am a seeker after truth... The beaches draw sun-seekers from all over Europe.* • See also **asylum seeker, job seeker.** ◆◆◇◇◇ N-COUNT: usu pl, usu n N

seem /siːm/ **seems, seeming, seemed** ◆◆◆◆◆

1 You use **seem** to say that someone or something gives the impression of having a particular quality, or that something gives the impression of happening in the way you describe. *We heard a series of explosions. They seemed quite close by... Everyone seems busy except us... To everyone who knew them, they seemed an ideal couple... £20 seems a lot to pay... The calming effect seemed to last for about ten minutes... The government seems not to be troubled by its inconsistent policies on minority rights... It was a record that seemed beyond reach... The proposal seems designed to break opposition to the government's economic programme... It seems that the attack this morning was very carefully planned to cause few casualties... It seems clear that he has no reasonable alternative... It seemed as if she'd been gone forever... There seems to be a lot of support in Congress for this move... There seems no possibility that such action can be averted... This phenomenon is not as outrageous as it seems.* V-LINK: no cont V adj V n V to-inf V prep V-ed it V that it V adj that it V as if there V to-inf there V n V

2 You use **seem** when you are describing your own feelings or thoughts, or describing something that has happened to you, in order to make your statement less forceful. *I seem to have lost all my self-confidence... I seem to remember giving you very precise instructions... I seemed to have contracted the stomach problem... Excuse me I seem to be a little bit lost.* V-LINK: no cont V to-inf

3 If you say that you **cannot seem** or **could not seem** to do something, you mean that you have tried to do it and were unable to. *No matter how* PHRASE: PHR to-inf

hard I try I cannot seem to catch up on all the bills... Kim's mother couldn't seem to stop crying.

4 See also **seeming**.

seeming /siːmɪŋ/. **Seeming** means appearing to be the case, but not necessarily the case. For example, if you talk about someone's **seeming** ability to do something, you mean that they appear to be able to do it, but you are not certain; a formal word. *Wall Street analysts have been highly critical of the company's seeming inability to control costs... Whatever troubles arise, we'll have peace of mind amidst seeming chaos.* ADJ: ADJ n PRAGMATICS =apparent

seemingly /siːmɪŋli/ ◆◆◇◇◇

1 If something is **seemingly** the case, you mean that it appears to be the case, even though it may not really be so. *A seemingly endless line of trucks waits in vain to load up. ...bread made from a seemingly limitless variety of ingredients.* ADV: ADV adj/adv =apparently

2 You use **seemingly** when you want to say that something seems to be true. *He has moved to Spain, seemingly to enjoy a slower style of life... He is a man with seemingly not an ounce of malice in him.* ADV: ADV with cl/group, ADV before v PRAGMATICS

seemly /siːmli/. **Seemly** behaviour or dress is appropriate in the particular circumstances; an old-fashioned word. *It wasn't seemly for a boy still in school to be courting a young woman who worked.* ADJ-GRADED

seen /siːn/. **Seen** is the past participle of **see**.

seep /siːp/ **seeps, seeping, seeped** ◆◇◇◇◇

1 If something such as liquid or gas **seeps** somewhere, it leaks slowly and in small amounts into a place where it should not go. *Radioactive water had seeped into underground reservoirs... The gas is seeping out of the rocks... Engineers said that plutonium could begin seeping from the corroded sub.* VERB =leak V prep/adv

► Also a noun. *...an oil seep.* N-COUNT

2 If something such as secret information or an unpleasant emotion **seeps** somewhere, it comes out gradually. *...the tide of racism which is sweeping Europe seeps into Britain. ...letting information seep out of the Treasury.* VERB V prep/adv

seepage /siːpɪdʒ/. **Seepage** is the slow flow of a liquid through something. *The industry's chemical seepage and waste have caused untold damage.* N-UNCOUNT

seer /siːəʳ/ **seers.** A **seer** is a person who tells people what will happen in the future; a literary word. *...the writings of the 16th century French seer, Nostradamus. ...the economic seers who regularly provide The Economist with forecasts.* N-COUNT

seesaw /siːsɔː/ **seesaws, seesawing, seesawed;** also spelled **see-saw**.

1 A **seesaw** is a long board which is balanced on a fixed part in the middle. Children play on seesaws by making the board tilt up and down when one child sits on each end. *There was a sandpit, a seesaw and a swing in the playground.* N-COUNT

2 In a **seesaw** situation, something continually changes from one state to another and back again. *...a seesaw price situation. ...the seesaw way of politics.* ADJ: ADJ n

► Also a noun. *Marriage, however, is an emotional seesaw.* N-COUNT: usu sing

3 If someone's emotions **see-saw**, or a particular situation **see-saws**, they continually change from one state to another and back again. *The Tokyo stock market see-sawed up and down.* VERB V

seethe /siːð/ **seethes, seething, seethed** ◆◇◇◇◇

1 When you **are seething**, you are very angry about something but do not express your feelings about it. *She took it calmly at first but under the surface was seething... She put a hand on her hip, grinning derisively, while I seethed with rage... He is seething at all the bad press he is getting. ...a seething anger fueled by decades of political oppression.* VERB =fume V V prep V-ing

2 If you say that a place **is seething** with people or things, you are emphasizing that it is very full of them and that they are all moving about. *The forest below him seethed and teemed with life... Madrigueras station was a seething mass of soldiers.* VERB PRAGMATICS =swarm, throb V with n V-ing Also V

see-through. **See-through** clothes are made of thin cloth, so that you can see a person's body or underclothes through them. ◆◇◇◇◇ ADJ-GRADED: usu ADJ n =transparent

segment /segmənt/ **segments** ◆◆◆◇◇

1 A **segment of** something is one part of it, considered separately from the rest. *...the poorer segments of society. ...the third segment of his journey.* N-COUNT: N of n =section

2 A **segment** of fruit such as an orange or grapefruit is one of the sections into which it is easily divided. N-COUNT

3 A **segment** of a circle is one of the two parts into which it is divided when you draw a straight line through it. N-COUNT: usu N of n

segmentation /segmenteɪʃən/. **Segmentation** is the dividing of something into loosely-connected parts; a technical word. N-UNCOUNT

segmented /segmentɪd/. **Segmented** means divided into parts that are loosely connected to each other. *...segmented oranges.* ADJ: ADJ n

segregate /segrɪgeɪt/ **segregates, segregating, segregated.** To **segregate** two groups of people or things means to keep them physically apart from each other. *A large detachment of police was used to segregate the two rival camps of protesters... They segregate you from the rest of the community.* VERB V n V n prep

segregated /segrɪgeɪtɪd/. **Segregated** buildings or areas are kept for the use of one group of people who are the same race, sex, or religion, and no other group is allowed to use them. *...racially segregated schools... John grew up in Baltimore when that city was segregated.* ◆◇◇◇◇ ADJ

segregation /segrɪgeɪʃən/. **Segregation** is the official practice of keeping people apart, usually people of different sexes, races, or religions. *The Supreme Court unanimously ruled that racial segregation in schools was unconstitutional... Connecticut agreed to end its segregation of prison inmates suffering from AIDS.* ◆◇◇◇◇ N-UNCOUNT: usu with supp

segregationist /segrɪgeɪʃənɪst/ **segregationists.** A **segregationist** is someone who thinks people of different races should be segregated. *I'm a segregationist, but I'm not a White supremacist... Alabama may have been legally forced by the courts to kill off its segregationist policies.* N-COUNT: oft N n

segue /segweɪ/ **segues, segueing, segued** If something such as a piece of music or conversation **segues into** another piece of music or conversation, it changes into it or is followed by it without a break. *The piece segues into his solo with the strings. ...his film's attempt, in its latter sections, to segue into comedy.* VERB V into n Also V from n, V

► Also a noun. *...a neat segue into an arrangement of 'Eleanor Rigby'.* N-COUNT: usu sing

seismic /saɪzmɪk/. **Seismic** means caused by or relating to an earthquake; a technical term. *Earthquakes produce two types of seismic waves... The latest seismic activity was also felt in northern Kenya.* ◆◇◇◇◇ ADJ: ADJ n

seismograph /saɪzməgrɑːf, -græf/ **seismographs.** A **seismograph** is an instrument for recording and measuring the strength of earthquakes. N-COUNT

seismology /saɪzmɒlədʒi/. **Seismology** is the scientific study of earthquakes. N-UNCOUNT

♦ **seismological** *...the Seismological Society of America.* ADJ: usu ADJ n

♦ **seismologist, seismologists** *Peter Ward is a seismologist with the US Geological Survey.* N-COUNT

seize /siːz/ **seizes, seizing, seized** ◆◆◆◇◇

1 If you **seize** something, you take hold of it quickly, firmly, and forcefully. *'Leigh,' he said seizing my arm to hold me back. ...an otter seizing a fish.* VERB V n

2 When a group of people **seize** a place or **seize** control of it, they take control of it quickly and suddenly, using force. *Troops have seized the airport and railroad terminals... Army officers plotted a failed attempt yesterday to seize power.* VERB =take V n

3 If a government or other authority **seize** someone's property, they take it from them, often by force. *Police were reported to have seized all copies of this mornings edition of the newspaper...* VERB V n

Bailiffs need a certificate from the county court to seize goods for rent arrears.

4 When someone **is seized**, they are arrested or captured. *UN officials say two military observers were seized by the Khmer Rouge yesterday... Men carrying sub-machine guns seized the five soldiers and drove them away.* VERB be V-ed V n

5 When you **seize** an opportunity, you take advantage of it and do something that you want to do. *During the riots hundreds of people seized the opportunity to steal property... The government now hopes to seize the initiative on education.* VERB V n

seize on. If you **seize on** something or **seize upon** it, you show great interest in it, often because it is useful to you. *His opponents had seized enthusiastically on the issue as a weapon against Mr Yeltsin... The main fear was that both sides may seize upon a ceasefire and free food aid to rearm.* PHRASAL VERB V P n

seize up
PHRASAL VERB

1 If a part of your body **seizes up**, it suddenly stops working, because you have strained it or because you are getting old. *After two days' exertions, it's the arms and hands that seize up, not the legs... We are all born flexible but as we grow older, we tend to seize up a little.* V P

2 If something such as an engine **seizes up**, it stops working, because it has not been properly cared for. *She put diesel fuel, instead of petrol, into the tank causing the motor to seize up.* V P

seizure /siːʒəʳ/ **seizures** ◆◇◇◇◇

1 If someone has a **seizure**, they have a sudden violent attack of an illness, especially a heart attack or an epileptic fit. *...a mild cardiac seizure... I was prescribed drugs to control seizures.* N-COUNT

2 If there is a **seizure** of power or a **seizure** of an area of land, a group of people suddenly take control of the place, using force. *...the seizure of territory through force.* N-COUNT: oft N *of* n

3 When an organization such as the police or customs service makes a **seizure** of illegal goods, they confiscate them. *Police have made one of the biggest seizures of heroin there's ever been in Britain. ...arms seizures.* N-COUNT: oft N *of* n

4 If a financial institution or a government makes a **seizure** of someone's assets, they take their money or property from them because they have not paid money that they owe. *A Greek court has ordered the seizure of two ships in compensation for non-payment of a debt.* N-COUNT: oft N *of* n

seldom /seldəm/. If something **seldom** happens, it happens only occasionally. *They seldom speak... I've seldom felt so happy... We were seldom at home.* ◆◆◇◇◇ ADV-BRD-NEG, ADV before v, ADV with cl/group

select /sɪlekt/ **selects, selecting, selected** ◆◆◆◇◇

1 If you **select** something, you choose it from a number of things of the same kind. *Voters are selecting candidates for both US Senate seats and for 52 congressional seats... With a difficult tee shot, select a club which will keep you short of the trouble... The movie is being shown in selected cities.* VERB =choose V n V-ed Also V n *for/from* n

2 A **select** group is a small group of some of the best people or things of their kind. *He was one of the small select group assembled by Penney, at the High Explosive Research centre. ...a select group of French cheeses... As Faldo's final putt rattled in, he qualified to join a select band of illustrious sportsmen.* ADJ-GRADED: ADJ n

3 If you describe something as **select**, you mean it has many desirable features, but is available only to people who have a lot of money or who belong to a high social class. *Christian Lacroix is throwing a very lavish and very select party. ...a meeting of a very select club.* ADJ-GRADED: usu ADJ n =elite, exclusive

select committee, select committees. A **select committee** is a committee which is composed of members of a parliament, senate, or other elected assembly, and which is set up to investigate and report back on a particular matter. ◆◇◇◇◇ N-COUNT

selection /sɪlekʃᵊn/ **selections** ◆◆◆◇◇

1 **Selection** is the act of selecting of one or more people or things from a group. *...Darwin's principles of natural selection... Dr. Sullivan's selection to head the Department of Health was greeted with satisfaction... The children have to sit a tough selection test.* N-UNCOUNT: with supp

2 A **selection** of people or things is a set of them that have been selected from a larger group. *...this selection of popular songs. ...a dramatic rendition of selections from Dickens' A Christmas Carol.* N-COUNT: oft N *of* n

3 The **selection** of goods in a shop is the particular range of goods that it has available and from which you can choose what you want. *It offers the widest selection of antiques of every description in a one day market.* N-COUNT: usu sing, usu N *of* n =range

selective /sɪlektɪv/ ◆◆◇◇◇

1 A **selective** process applies only to a few things or people. *Selective breeding may result in a greyhound running faster and seeing better than a wolf. ...selective education.* ♦ **selectively** *Within the project, trees are selectively cut on a 25-year rotation.* ♦ **selectivity** /sɪlektɪvɪti/ *The soldiers specialized in going out in small groups, to kill with a very high degree of selectivity.* ADJ-GRADED: ADJ n; ADV: usu ADV with v; N-UNCOUNT: usu with supp

2 When someone is **selective**, they choose things carefully, for example the things that they buy or do. *Sales still happen, but buyers are more selective... If public figures seek publicity to further their careers, they can't be selective about it.* ♦ **selectively** *...people on small incomes who wanted to shop selectively.* ADJ-GRADED: usu v-link ADJ; ADV-GRADED: ADV with v

3 If you say that someone has a **selective** memory, you disapprove of the fact that they remember certain facts about something and deliberately forget others, often because it is convenient for them to do so. *We seem to have a selective memory for the best bits of the past... Mr Robins, suffering from selective amnesia about his role in the affair, was contradicted in nearly every instance by other witnesses.* ♦ **selectively** *...a tendency to remember only the pleasurable effects of the drug and selectively forget all the adverse effects.* ADJ-GRADED: usu ADJ n PRAGMATICS; ADV-GRADED: ADV with v

self /self/ **selves** ◆◆◆◇◇

1 Your **self** is your basic personality or nature, especially considered in terms of what you are really like as a person. *You're looking more like your usual self... She was back to her old self again.* N-COUNT: usu adj N

2 A person's **self** is the essential part of their nature which makes them different from everyone and everything else. *I want to explore and get in touch with my inner self... The face is the true self visible to others. ...our subconscious selves.* N-COUNT: usu adj N

self- /self-/

1 **Self-** is used to form words which indicate that you do something to yourself or by yourself. *He is a self-proclaimed racist. ...self-destructive behaviour... She was a woman utterly without self-knowledge.* COMB in ADJ and N

2 **Self-** is used to form words which describe something such as a device that does something automatically by itself. *...a self-loading pistol.* COMB in ADJ and N

self-absorbed. Someone who is **self-absorbed** thinks so much about things concerning themselves that they do not notice other people or the things around them. ADJ-GRADED

self-access. In a school or college, a **self-access** centre is a place where students can choose and use books, tapes, or other materials. *...a self-access study centre.* ADJ

self-addressed. A **self-addressed** envelope is an envelope which you have written your address on and which you send to someone in another envelope so that they can send something back to you. *A stamped self-addressed envelope must be enclosed if you require the return of your entry.* ADJ: usu ADJ n

self-adhesive. Something that is **self-adhesive** is covered on one side with a sticky substance like glue, so that it will stick to surfaces. *...self-adhesive labels. ...self-adhesive tiles.* ADJ: usu ADJ n

self-aggrandizement /self əgrændɪzmənt/; also spelled **self-aggrandisement**. If you say that someone is guilty of **self-aggrandizement**, you mean that they do certain things in order to make themselves more powerful, wealthy, or im- N-UNCOUNT PRAGMATICS portant; used showing disapproval. *Above all, he wanted to serve rather than use his position for self-aggrandisement.*

self-appointed. A **self-appointed** leader or ruler has taken the position of leader or ruler without anyone else asking them or choosing them to have it. *...the new self-appointed leaders of the movement.* ADJ: usu ADJ n

self-assembly. **Self-assembly** is used to refer to furniture and other goods that you buy in parts and that you have to put together yourself. *...a range of self-assembly bedroom furniture.* ADJ: usu ADJ n

self-assertion. **Self-assertion** is confidence that you have in speaking firmly about your opinions and demanding the rights that you believe you should have. *...her silence and lack of self-assertion... They are driven on partly by a wish for democracy, but also by a desire for national self-assertion.* N-UNCOUNT

self-assertive. Someone who is **self-assertive** acts in a confident way, speaking firmly about their opinions and demanding the rights that they believe they should have. *If you want good relationships, you must have the confidence to be self-assertive when required.* ADJ-GRADED

self-assurance. Someone who has **self-assurance** shows confidence in the things that they say and do because they are sure of their abilities. N-UNCOUNT =self-confidence

self-assured. Someone who is **self-assured** shows confidence in what they say and do because they are sure of their own abilities. *He's a self-assured, confident negotiator.* ADJ-GRADED =self-confident

self-catering. If you go on a **self-catering** holiday or you stay in **self-catering** accommodation, you stay in a place where you have to provide your own meals. *...a week's self-catering in Majorca for £139... The self-catering flats are usually reserved for postgraduate students.* N-UNCOUNT: usu N n

self-centred; spelled **self-centered** in American English. Someone who is **self-centred** is only concerned with their own wants and needs and never thinks about other people. *He was selfish, he was self-centred, he was stingy, but he wasn't cruel.* ADJ-GRADED

self-confessed. If you describe someone as a **self-confessed** murderer or a **self-confessed** perfectionist, for example, you mean that they admit openly that they are a murderer or a perfectionist. *The self-confessed drug addict was arrested 13 months ago... She is a self-confessed workaholic.* ADJ: ADJ n

self-confidence. If you have **self-confidence** you behave confidently because you feel sure of your abilities or value. *With the end of my love affair, I lost all the self-confidence I once had... Richard's self confidence is growing steadily.* ◆◇◇◇◇ N-UNCOUNT =self-assurance

self-confident. Someone who is **self-confident** behaves confidently because they feel sure of their abilities or value. *She'd blossomed into a self-confident young woman.* ADJ-GRADED =self-assured

self-congratulation. If someone keeps emphasizing how well they have done or how good they are, you can refer to their behaviour as **self-congratulation**. *This is not a matter for self-congratulation.* N-UNCOUNT

self-congratulatory. If you describe someone or their behaviour as **self-congratulatory**, you mean that they keep emphasizing how well they have done or how good they are; used showing disapproval. *Officials were self-congratulatory about how well the day had gone. ...self-congratulatory chatter.* ADJ-GRADED PRAGMATICS

self-conscious ◆◇◇◇◇

1 Someone who is **self-conscious** is easily embarrassed and nervous because they feel that everyone is looking at them and judging them. *I felt a bit self-conscious in my swimming costume... Bess was self-conscious about being shorter than her two friends.* ADJ-GRADED: usu v-link ADJ, oft ADJ about n ♦ **self-consciously** *I glanced down at my dress jacket a little self-consciously... She was fiddling self-consciously with her wedding ring.* ADV-GRADED: ADV with v ♦ **self-consciousness** *...her painful self-consciousness.* N-UNCOUNT

2 If you describe someone or something as **self-conscious**, you mean that they are strongly aware of who or what they are; a formal use. *They were forged by them, moreover, into a self-conscious nation as early as the 10th century... Putting the work together is a very self-conscious process.* ADJ-GRADED ♦ **self-consciously** *The world which the book inhabits seems too self-consciously literary, too introverted... The place is as self-consciously trendy as they come.* ADV-GRADED: ADV adj

self-contained ◆◇◇◇◇

1 You can describe someone or something as **self-contained** when they are complete and separate and do not need help or resources from outside. *He seems completely self-contained and he doesn't miss you when you're not there... The world trade system seems set to divide into large self-contained economic blocs.* ADJ-GRADED

2 **Self-contained** accommodation such as a flat has all its own facilities, so that a person living there does not have to share rooms such as a kitchen or bathroom with other people. ADJ-GRADED: usu ADJ n

self-contradictory. If you say or write something that is **self-contradictory**, you make two statements which cannot both be true. *He is notorious for making unexpected, often self-contradictory, comments.* ADJ-GRADED

self-control. Your **self-control** is your ability to control your feelings so that you do not show the emotions that you feel or do the things you instinctively want to do. *His self-control, reserve and aloofness were almost inhuman... I began to wish I'd shown more self-control.* ◆◇◇◇◇ N-UNCOUNT

self-controlled. Someone who is **self-controlled** is able to control their feelings so that they do not show the emotions that they feel or do the things they instinctively want to do. *My father, who had always been very self-controlled, became bad-tempered and unpredictable.* ADJ-GRADED

self-defeating. A plan or action that is **self-defeating** is likely to cause problems or difficulties instead of producing useful results. *Dishonesty is ultimately self-defeating. ...self-defeating patterns of thought and behavior.* ADJ-GRADED

self-defence; spelled **self-defense** in American English. ◆◇◇◇◇

1 **Self-defence** is the use of force to protect yourself against someone who is attacking you. *Richards claimed he acted in self-defence after Pagett opened fire on him during a siege. ...courses in karate or some other means of self-defence.* N-UNCOUNT: usu with supp, oft *in/of* N

2 **Self-defence** is the use of non-violent action to protect yourself from someone or something that you feel is threatening you. *Jokes were a natural self-defence mechanism against the tedium of communism.* N-UNCOUNT

self-delusion. **Self-delusion** is the state of having a false idea about yourself or the situation you are in. *...the grandiose self-delusion of the addict.* N-UNCOUNT

self-denial. **Self-denial** is the habit of refusing to do or have things that you would like, either because you cannot afford them, or because you believe it is morally good for you not to do them or have them. *Should motherhood necessarily mean sacrifice and self-denial? ...an unprecedented act of self-denial.* N-UNCOUNT

self-denying. Someone who is **self-denying** refuses to do or have things that they would like, either because they cannot afford them, or because they believe it is morally good for them not to do them or have them. *They believed that good parents should be self-sacrificing and self-denying... They belong to an older, more self-denying generation.* ADJ-GRADED

self-deprecating. If you describe someone's behaviour as **self-deprecating**, you mean that they criticize themselves or represent themselves as foolish in a light-hearted way. *Sharon tells the story of that night with self-deprecating humour.* ADJ-GRADED: usu ADJ n

self-destruct, self-destructs, self-destructing, self-destructed. If someone **self-destructs**, they do something that seriously damages their chances of success. *They're going to be famous, but unless something happens, they're going to self-destruct... He won the election because the Democrats self-destructed in their primary.* VERB V

self-determination. **Self-determination** is the right of a country to be independent, instead of being controlled by a foreign country, and to choose its own form of government. ◆◇◇◇◇ N-UNCOUNT =independence

self-discipline. **Self-discipline** is the ability to control yourself and to make yourself work hard or behave in a particular way without needing anyone else to tell you what to do. *Exercising at home alone requires a tremendous amount of self-discipline.* N-UNCOUNT

self-disciplined. Someone who is **self-disciplined** has the ability to control themselves and to make themselves work hard or behave in a particular way without needing anyone else to tell them what to do. *Most religions teach you to be truthful, self-disciplined, kind to others.* ADJ-GRADED

self-doubt. **Self-doubt** is a lack of confidence in yourself and your abilities. N-UNCOUNT ≠confidence

self-drive

1 In British English, a **self-drive** car is one which you hire and drive yourself. The usual American expression is **rental** car. *Any holiday in the USA and Canada is enhanced by renting a self-drive car.* ADJ: ADJ n

2 A **self-drive** holiday is one where you drive yourself to the place where you are staying, rather than being taken there by plane or coach. *...the growth in popularity of self-drive camping holidays.* ADJ: ADJ n

self-educated. People who are **self-educated** have acquired knowledge or a skill by themselves, rather than being taught it by someone else such as a teacher at school. *...a self-educated man from a working class background.* ADJ

self-effacement. Someone's **self-effacement** is their modesty and reluctance to talk about themselves or draw attention to themselves. *Modest to the point of self-effacement, he would be easy to forget immediately after a short meeting.* N-UNCOUNT =modesty

self-effacing. Someone who is **self-effacing** is modest and does not like talking about themselves or drawing attention to themselves. *As women we tend to be self-effacing and make light of what we have achieved. ...the slightly self-effacing manner adopted by many diplomats.* ADJ-GRADED =modest

self-employed. If you are **self-employed**, you organize your own work and taxes and are paid by people for a service you provide, rather than being paid a regular salary by a person or a firm. *There are no paid holidays or sick leave if you are self-employed. ...a self-employed builder.* ◆◇◇◇◇ ADJ ► Also a noun. *We want more support for the self-employed.* N-PLURAL: the N

self-esteem. Your **self-esteem** is how you feel about yourself. For example, if you have low **self-esteem**, you do not like yourself, you do not think that you are a valuable person, and therefore you do not behave confidently. *Poor self-esteem is at the centre of many of the difficulties we experience in our relationships.* ◆◆◇◇◇ N-UNCOUNT

self-evident. A fact or situation that is **self-evident** is so obvious that there is no need for proof or explanation. *It is self-evident that we will never have enough resources to meet the demand... The implications for this country are self-evident.* ◆◇◇◇◇ ADJ-GRADED: usu v-link ADJ =obvious ♦ **self-evidently** *The task was self-evidently impossible... Self-evidently a handful of companies will benefit.* ADV-GRADED: ADV adj, ADV with cl/group

self-examination

1 **Self-examination** is thought that you give to your own character and actions, for example in order to judge whether you have been behaving in a way that is acceptable to your own set of values. *The events in Los Angeles have sparked a new national self-examination... Once you've picked a company that seems right for you, you have to make sure you're right for it. This is a time for some more self-examination.* N-UNCOUNT: also a N

2 **Self-examination** is the act of examining your own body to check whether or not you have any signs of a particular disease or illness. *Breast self-examination is invaluable for detecting cancer in its very early stages.* N-UNCOUNT

self-explanatory. Something that is **self-explanatory** is clear and easy to understand without needing any extra information or explanation. *I hope the graphs on the following pages are self-explanatory.* ADJ-GRADED: usu v-link ADJ

self-expression. A person's **self-expression** is the expression of their own personality, feelings, or opinions, for example through a creative activity such as drawing or dancing. *The conflict between the urge for self-expression and the pressure to conform is a central one for her... Clothes are a fundamental form of self-expression.* N-UNCOUNT

self-fulfilling. If you describe a statement or belief about the future as **self-fulfilling**, you mean that what is said or believed comes true because people expect it to come true. *It's a case of the self-fulfilling prophecy. If you think a group is hostile, then you behave towards them as if they were hostile and they in return act with hostility.* ADJ

self-governing. A **self-governing** region or organization is governed or run by its own people rather than by the people of another region or organization. *...a self-governing province... The local hospital was one of the first to apply to become self-governing.* ◆◇◇◇◇ ADJ =self-rule

self-government. **Self-government** is government of a country or region by its own people rather than by others. ◆◇◇◇◇ N-UNCOUNT

self-help ◆◇◇◇◇

1 **Self-help** consists of people providing support and help for each other in an informal way, rather than relying on the authorities or other official organizations. *She helped her Mum set up a self-help group for parents with over-weight children.* N-UNCOUNT: oft N n

2 **Self-help** consists of doing things yourself to try and solve your own problems without depending on other people. *...a society that encourages competitiveness and self-help among the very young. ...a self-help book.* N-UNCOUNT

self-image, self-images. Your **self-image** is your opinion of yourself. *You must strive constantly to improve your self-image... A person with a poor self-image will feel inadequate.* ◆◇◇◇◇ N-COUNT: usu supp N

self-important. If you say that someone is **self-important**, you disapprove of them because they behave as if they are more important than they really are. *He was self-important, vain and ignorant. ...self-important officials.* ADJ-GRADED PRAGMATICS =pompous, arrogant ♦ **self-importance** *Many visitors complained of his bad manners and self-importance.* N-UNCOUNT

self-imposed. A **self-imposed** restriction, task, or situation is one that you have deliberately created or accepted for yourself. *He returned home in the summer of 1974 after eleven years of self-imposed exile... Sometimes a well-defined job becomes cluttered with self-imposed tasks.* ◆◇◇◇◇ ADJ: usu ADJ n

self-indulgence, self-indulgences. **Self-indulgence** is the act of allowing yourself to have or do the things that you enjoy very much. *He prayed to be saved from self-indulgence... Going to the movies in the afternoon is one of my big self-indulgences.* N-VAR

self-indulgent. If you say that someone is **self-indulgent**, you mean that they allow themselves to have or do the things that they enjoy very much. *Why give publicity to this self-indulgent, adolescent oaf?... To buy flowers for myself seems wildly self-indulgent.* ADJ-GRADED

self-inflicted. A **self-inflicted** wound or injury is one that you do to yourself deliberately. *He is being treated for a self-inflicted gunshot wound.* ADJ

self-interest. If you accuse someone of **self-interest**, you disapprove of them because they always want to do what is best for themselves ra- ◆◇◇◇◇ N-UNCOUNT PRAGMATICS ther than for anyone else. *Their current protests are motivated purely by self-interest.*

self-interested. If you describe someone as **self-interested**, you disapprove of them because they always want to do what is best for themselves rather than for other people. *Narrowly self-interested behaviour is ultimately self-defeating.* ADJ-GRADED PRAGMATICS

selfish /selfɪʃ/. If you say that someone is **selfish**, you mean that he or she cares only about himself or herself, and not about other people. *I think I've been very selfish. I've been mainly concerned with myself. ...the selfish interests of a few people.* ◆◆◇◇◇ ADJ-GRADED ♦ **selfishly** *The government's image has been tarnished because Cabinet Ministers are selfishly pursuing their own vested interests.* ADV: usu ADV with v ♦ **selfishness** *The arrogance and selfishness of different interest groups never ceases to amaze me.* N-UNCOUNT: usu with supp

self-knowledge. **Self-knowledge** is knowledge that you have about your own character and nature. *The more self-knowledge we have, the more control we can exert over our feelings and behaviour.* N-UNCOUNT

selfless /selfləs/. If you say that someone is **selfless**, you approve of them because they care about other people more than themselves. *She was a wonderful companion and her generosity to me was entirely selfless... Perhaps the only all-enduring and selfless love was that of a mother for her child.* ◆◇◇◇◇ ADJ-GRADED ♦ **selflessly** *I've never known anyone who cared so selflessly about children.* ADV-GRADED ♦ **selflessness** *I have enormous regard for his selflessness on behalf of his fellow man.* N-UNCOUNT

self-loathing. If someone feels **self-loathing**, they feel great dislike and disgust for themselves. N-UNCOUNT

self-made. **Self-made** is used to describe people who have become successful and rich through their own efforts, especially if they started life without money, education, or high social status. *He is a self-made man. ...a self-made millionaire.* ADJ: usu ADJ n

self-pity. **Self-pity** is a feeling of unhappiness and depression that you have about yourself and your problems, especially when this is unnecessary or greatly exaggerated. *I was unable to shake off my self-pity... Throughout, he showed no trace of self-pity.* ◆◇◇◇◇ N-UNCOUNT

self-pitying. Someone who is **self-pitying** is full of self-pity. *At the risk of sounding self-pitying, I'd say it has been harder on me than it has on Joanne.* ADJ-GRADED

self-portrait, self-portraits. A **self-portrait** is a drawing, painting, or written description that you do of yourself. N-COUNT

self-possessed. Someone who is **self-possessed** is calm and confident and in control of their emotions. *She is clearly the most articulate and self-possessed member of her family.* ADJ-GRADED =self-assured

self-possession. **Self-possession** is the quality of being self-possessed. *She found her customary self-possession had deserted her.* N-UNCOUNT =self-assurance

self-preservation. **Self-preservation** is the instinctive behaviour that makes you keep yourself safe from injury or death in a dangerous situation. *The police have the same human urge for self-preservation as the rest of us.* N-UNCOUNT

self-raising flour. In British English, **self-raising flour** is flour that makes cakes rise when they are cooked because it has chemicals added to it. The American term is **self-rising flour**. N-UNCOUNT

self-reliance. **Self-reliance** is the ability to do things and make decisions by yourself, without needing other people to help you. *People learned self-reliance because they had to... The Prime Minister called for more economic self-reliance.* N-UNCOUNT =independence

self-reliant. If you are **self-reliant**, you are able to do things and make decisions by yourself, without needing other people to help you; used showing approval. *She is intelligent and self-reliant, speaking her mind and not suffering fools gladly.* ADJ-GRADED PRAGMATICS =independent

self-respect. **Self-respect** is a feeling of confidence and pride in your own ability and worth. *They have lost not only their jobs, but their homes, their self-respect and even their reason for living.* ◆◇◇◇◇ N-UNCOUNT

self-respecting. If you say what any **self-respecting** person of a particular type would do, you are saying what is a typical, normal, or necessary thing for that type of person to do. *He died as any self-respecting gangster should – in a hail of bullets... No self-respecting gourmet would travel in France without the Michelin red guide.* ADJ: ADJ n

self-righteous. If you describe someone as **self-righteous**, you disapprove of them because they are convinced that they are right in their beliefs, attitudes, and behaviour and that other people are wrong. *He is critical of the monks, whom he considers narrow-minded and self-righteous. ...self-righteous reformers.* ADJ-GRADED PRAGMATICS ♦ **self-righteousness** *Her aggressiveness and self-righteousness caused prickles of anger at the back of his neck.* N-UNCOUNT

self-rising flour. In American English, **self-rising flour** is flour that makes cakes rise when they are cooked because it has chemicals added to it. The British term is **self-raising flour**. N-UNCOUNT

self-rule. **Self-rule** is the same as **self-government**. *The agreement gives the territory limited self-rule.* N-UNCOUNT

self-sacrifice. **Self-sacrifice** is the giving up of what you want so that other people can have what they need or want. *I thanked my parents for all their self-sacrifice on my behalf.* N-UNCOUNT

self-sacrificing. Someone who is **self-sacrificing** gives up what they want so that other people can have what they need or want. *He was a generous self-sacrificing man.* ADJ-GRADED

self-same; also spelled **selfsame**. You use **self-same** when you want to emphasize that the person or thing mentioned is exactly the same as the one mentioned previously. *In the USA and England the governing political parties are calling for a return to traditional methods, while in France the government wants to move away from these self-same traditions.* ADJ: ADJ n PRAGMATICS

self-satisfaction. **Self-satisfaction** is the feeling you have when you are self-satisfied. *He tried hard not to smile in smug self-satisfaction.* N-UNCOUNT =smugness

self-satisfied. If you describe someone as **self-satisfied**, you mean that they are so pleased and proud about their achievements or their situation that they do not feel they need to do anything more; used showing disapproval. *You're so bloody self-satisfied... She handed the cigar back to Jason with a self-satisfied smile.* ADJ-GRADED PRAGMATICS =smug

self-seeking. If you describe someone as **self-seeking**, you disapprove of them because they are interested only in doing things which give them an advantage over other people. *He said that democracy would open the way for self-seeking politicians to abuse the situation.* ADJ-GRADED PRAGMATICS

self-service. A **self-service** shop, restaurant, or garage is one where you serve yourself rather than being served by another person. ADJ

self-serving. If you describe someone or their motives as **self-serving**, you are critical of them because they are only interested in their own advantage or profit. *They suggest that my motives for proposing reform are self-serving and mercenary. ...corrupt, self-serving politicians.* ADJ-GRADED PRAGMATICS

self-styled. If you describe someone as a **self-styled** leader or expert, you disapprove of them because they claim to be a leader or expert but they do not actually have the right to call themselves this. *Two of those arrested are said to be self-styled area commanders... He fiercely criticised self-styled educational experts for ignoring Shakespeare.* ◆◇◇◇◇ ADJ: ADJ n PRAGMATICS

self-sufficiency. **Self-sufficiency** is the state of being self-sufficient. ◆◇◇◇◇ N-UNCOUNT

self-sufficient ◆◇◇◇◇

1 If a country or group is **self-sufficient**, it is able to ADJ-GRADED:

produce or make everything that it needs. *This enabled the country to become self-sufficient in sugar... Using traditional methods poor farmers can be virtually self-sufficient.* usu v-link ADJ

2 Someone who is **self-sufficient** is able to live happily without anyone else. *Although she had various boyfriends, Madeleine was, and remains, fiercely self-sufficient... He'd created a tiny, self-sufficient world for himself.* ADJ-GRADED =independent

self-supporting. **Self-supporting** is used to describe organizations, schemes, and people who earn enough money to not need financial help from anyone else. *The income from visitors makes the museum self-supporting... The parents were determined that the two girls should be fully self-supporting.* ADJ

self-sustaining. A **self-sustaining** process or system is able to continue without any intervention from outside. *Asia's emerging economies will be on a self-sustaining cycle of growth... Biologists say the area might be large enough to support a self-sustaining population.* ADJ

self-taught. If you are **self-taught**, you have learnt a skill by yourself rather than being taught it by someone else such as a teacher at school. *Paul is self-taught and became interested in photography just four years ago. ...a self-taught musician.* ADJ

self-will. Someone's **self-will** is their determination to do what they want without caring what other people think. *She had a little core of self-will that gave her a sparkle lacking in Isabel.* N-UNCOUNT

self-willed. Someone who is **self-willed** is determined to do the things that they want to do and will not take advice from other people. *He was very independent and self-willed.* ADJ-GRADED

sell /sel/ **sells, selling, sold** ◆◆◆◆◆

1 If you **sell** something that you own, you let someone have it in return for money. *I sold everything I owned except for my car and my books... His heir sold the painting to the London art dealer Agnews... The directors sold the business for £14.8 million... It's not a very good time to sell at the moment.* VERB V n, V n to n, V n for n, V, Also V n n, V to n

2 If a shop **sells** a particular thing, it is available for people to buy there. *It sells everything from hair ribbons to oriental rugs... Bean sprouts are also sold in cans.* VERB V n, Also V n n

3 If something **sells** for a particular price, that price is paid for it. *Unmodernised property can sell for up to 40 per cent of its modernised market value. ...a brand-new Yamaha moped, which sells at £1,374.* VERB V for/at n

4 If something **sells**, it is bought by the public, usually in fairly large quantities. *Even if this album doesn't sell and the critics don't like it, we wouldn't ever change... The company believes the products will sell well in the run-up to Christmas.* VERB V, V adv

5 Something that **sells** a product makes people want to buy the product. *It is only the sensational that sells news magazines. ...car manufacturers' long-held maxim that safety doesn't sell.* VERB V n, V

6 If you **sell** someone an idea or proposal, or **sell** someone **on** an idea, you convince them that it is a good one. *She tried to sell me the idea of buying my own paper shredder... She is hoping she can sell the idea to clients... An employee sold him on the notion that cable was the medium of the future... You know, I wasn't sold on this trip in the beginning.* VERB V n n, V n to n, V n on n, V-ed

7 If someone **sells** their **body**, they have sex for money. *85 per cent said they would rather not sell their bodies for a living.* PHRASES V and N inflect

8 If someone **sells** you **down the river**, they betray you for some personal profit or advantage. *He has been sold down the river by the people who were supposed to protect him.* V inflects

9 If you **sell** someone **short**, you do not point out their good qualities as much as you should or do as much for them as you should. *They need to improve their image – they are selling themselves short... Selling their fans short in such a shabby way is not acceptable.* V inflects

10 If you talk about someone **selling** their **soul** in order to get something, you are criticizing them for abandoning their principles. *...a man who would sell his soul for political viability.* V and N inflect PRAGMATICS

11 • to **sell like hot cakes**: see **cake**.

sell off. If you **sell** something **off**, you sell it because you need the money. *The company is selling off some sites and concentrating on cutting debts... We had to sell things off to pay the brewery bill.* • See also **sell-off**. PHRASAL VERB V P n (not pron), V n P

sell on. If you buy something and then **sell** it **on**, you sell it to someone else soon after buying it, usually in order to make a profit. *Mr Farrier bought cars at auctions and sold them on... The arms had been sold to a businessman; he sold them on to paramilitary groups.* PHRASAL VERB V n P, V n P to n

sell out PHRASAL VERB

1 If a shop **sells out** of something, it sells all its stocks of it, so that there is no longer any left for people to buy. *Hardware stores have sold out of water pumps and tarpaulins... The next day the bookshops sold out.* V P of n, V P

2 If a performance, sports event, or other entertainment **sells out**, all the tickets for it are sold. *Football games often sell out well in advance.* V P

3 When things **sell out**, all of them that are available are sold. *Sleeping bags sold out almost immediately... Tickets for the show sold out in 70 minutes.* V P

4 If you accuse someone of **selling out**, you disapprove of the fact that they do something which used to be against their principles, or give in to an opposing group. *The young in particular see him as a man who will not sell out or be debased by the compromises of politics... The Communists denounced the Socialists as Right-wingers who had sold out to the big business lobby.* PRAGMATICS V P, V P to n

5 In American English, **sell out** also means the same as **sell up**. *I hear she's going to sell out and move to the city.* V P

6 See also **sell-out, sold out.**

sell up. If you **sell up**, you sell everything you have, such as your house or your business, because you need the money; used mainly in British English. The usual American expression is **sell out**. *...all these farmers going out of business and having to sell up... He advised Evans to sell up his flat and move away to the country.* PHRASAL VERB V P, V P n (not pron)

sell-by date, sell-by dates

1 The **sell-by date** on a food container is the date by which the food should be sold or eaten, before it starts to deteriorate. *...a piece of cheese four weeks past its sell-by date.* N-COUNT

2 If you say that someone or something is **past** their **sell-by date**, you mean they are no longer effective, interesting, or useful. *They are tired of clapped-out formulas being regurgitated by people long past their sell-by date.* PHRASE: N inflects, v-link PHR

seller /seləʳ/ **sellers** ◆◆◇◇◇

1 A **seller** of a type of thing is a person or company that sells that type of thing. *...a flower seller. ...Kraft, the largest seller of cheese in the United States.* N-COUNT: n N, N of n =vendor

2 In a business deal, the **seller** is the person who is selling something to someone else. *In theory, the buyer could ask the seller to have a test carried out... Housing became a seller's market, and prices zoomed up.* N-COUNT: usu the N =vendor ≠buyer, purchaser

3 If you describe a product as, for example, a big **seller**, you mean that large numbers of it are being sold. *The gift shop's biggest seller is a photo of Nixon meeting Presley.* • See also **best seller.** N-COUNT: adj N

selling point, selling points. A **selling point** is a desirable quality or feature that something has which makes it likely that people will want to buy it. N-COUNT

selling price, selling prices. The **selling price** of something is the price for which it is sold. N-COUNT: usu sing

sell-off, sell-offs; also spelled **selloff**. The **sell-off** of something, for example a state-owned industry, assets, or shares, is the selling of it. *Labour yesterday set out its alternative to the rail sell-off... There is no question of any 'sell-off' of Russian land or assets.* ◆◇◇◇◇ N-COUNT: usu with supp

Sellotape /seləteɪp/ **Sellotapes, Sellotaping, Sellotaped**

1 In British English, **Sellotape** is a clear sticky tape that you use to stick paper or card together or onto a wall. The American term is **Scotch tape**. **Sellotape** and **Scotch tape** are trademarks. N-UNCOUNT

2 In British English, if you **Sellotape** one thing to another, you stick them together using Sellotape. *I sellotaped the note to his door.* VERB V n adv/prep

sell-out, sell-outs; also spelled **sellout**. ◆◇◇◇◇

1 If a play, sports event, or other entertainment is a **sell-out**, all the tickets for it are sold. *Their concert there was a sell-out. ...sell-out shows.* N-COUNT: usu sing, oft N n

2 If you describe someone's behaviour as a **sell-out**, you disapprove of the fact that they have done something which used to be against their principles, or given in to an opposing group. *For some, his decision to become a Socialist candidate at Sunday's election was simply a sell-out.* N-COUNT: usu sing, oft N *to* n PRAGMATICS

selves /selvz/. **Selves** is the plural of **self**.

semantic /sɪmæntɪk/. **Semantic** is used to describe something which concerns the meaning of words and sentences. *He did not want to enter into a semantic debate.* ADJ: usu ADJ n

semantics /sɪmæntɪks/. The form **semantic** is used as a modifier. **Semantics** is the branch of linguistics that deals with the meaning of words or sentences in isolation. Compare **pragmatics**. N-UNCOUNT

semaphore /seməfɔːʳ/. **Semaphore** is a system of sending messages by using two flags. You hold a flag in each hand and move your arms to various positions representing different letters of the alphabet. N-UNCOUNT

semblance /sembləns/. If there is a **semblance of** a particular condition or quality, it appears to exist, even though this may be a false impression. *At least a semblance of normality has been restored to parts of the country... They had nursed Peter back to some semblance of health.* ◆◇◇◇◇ N-UNCOUNT: N *of* n

semen /siːmen/. **Semen** is the liquid containing sperm that is produced by the sex organs of men and male animals. ◆◇◇◇◇ N-UNCOUNT

semester /sɪmestəʳ/ **semesters.** In colleges and universities in the United States and some other countries, a **semester** is one of the two periods into which the year is divided. N-COUNT

semi /semi/ **semis** ◆◇◇◇◇

1 In British English, a **semi** is a semi-detached house; an informal word. N-COUNT =semi-detached

2 In a sporting competition, the **semis** are the semi-finals; an informal use. *He reached the semis after beating Lendl in the quarterfinal.* N-COUNT: usu pl, usu *the* N

semi- /semi-/ **Semi-** combines with adjectives and nouns to form other adjectives and nouns that describe someone or something as being partly, but not completely, in a particular state. *He found Isabel's room in semi-darkness. ...semi-skilled workers.* PREFIX

semi-circle, semi-circles; also **semicircle**. A **semi-circle** is one half of a circle, or something having the shape of half a circle. *They stood in a semi-circle round the teacher's chair and answered questions.* N-COUNT

semi-circular; also spelled **semicircular**. Something that is **semi-circular** has the shape of a semi-circle. *...a semi-circular amphitheatre.* ADJ

semi-colon, semi-colons. A **semi-colon** is the punctuation mark (;) which is used in writing to separate different parts of a sentence or list or to indicate a pause. N-COUNT

semiconductor /semikəndʌktəʳ/ **semiconductors**; also spelled **semi-conductor**. A **semiconductor** is a substance used in electronics whose ability to conduct electricity increases with greater heat. ◆◇◇◇◇ N-COUNT

semi-detached. In British English, a **semi-detached** house is a house that is joined to another house on one side by a shared wall. *...a semi-detached house in Highgate.* ADJ =semi ▶ A **semi-detached** is the same as a semi-detached house. *It was an ordinary, post-war semi-detached.* N-SING

semi-final, semi-finals. A **semi-final** is one of the two matches or races in a competition that are held to decide who will compete in the final. *Steve Lewis won the first semi-final.* ◆◆◇◇◇ N-COUNT ▶ The **semi-finals** is the round of a competition in which these two matches or races are held. *He was beaten in the semi-finals by Chris Dittmar.* N-PLURAL: usu *the* N

semi-finalist, semi-finalists. A **semi-finalist** is a player, athlete, or team that is competing in a semi-final. N-COUNT

seminal /semɪnəl/. **Seminal** is used to describe things such as books, works, events, and experiences that have a great influence in a particular field; a formal word. *...author of the seminal book 'Animal Liberation'... The reforms have been a seminal event in the history of the NHS.* ◆◇◇◇◇ ADJ: usu ADJ n

seminar /semɪnɑːʳ/ **seminars** ◆◆◇◇◇

1 A **seminar** is a meeting where a group of people discuss a problem or topic. *...a series of half-day seminars to help businessmen get the best value from investing in information technology.* N-COUNT

2 A **seminar** is a class at a college or university in which the teacher and a small group of students discuss a topic. *Students are asked to prepare material in advance of each weekly seminar.* N-COUNT

seminarian /semɪneəriən/ **seminarians.** A **seminarian** is a student at a seminary. N-COUNT

seminary /semɪnəri, AM -neri/ **seminaries.** A **seminary** is a college where priests or rabbis are trained. N-COUNT

semiotics /semiɒtɪks/. **Semiotics** is the academic study of the relationship of language and other signs to their meanings. N-UNCOUNT

semi-precious. **Semi-precious** stones are stones such as turquoises and agates that are used in jewellery but that are less valuable than precious stones such as diamonds and rubies. ADJ: usu ADJ n

semi-professional. **Semi-professional** sports players, musicians, and singers receive some money for playing their sport or for performing but they also have an ordinary job as well. *...a semi-professional country musician... I played semi-professional soccer for Walsall.* ADJ

semi-skilled; also spelled **semiskilled**. A **semi-skilled** worker has some training and skills, but not enough to do specialized work. ADJ: usu ADJ n

Semitic /sɪmɪtɪk/ ◆◇◇◇◇

1 **Semitic** languages are a group of languages that include Arabic and Hebrew. ADJ: usu ADJ n

2 **Semitic** people belong to one of the groups of people who speak a Semitic language. *...the Semitic races.* ADJ: usu ADJ n

3 **Semitic** is sometimes used to mean Jewish. ● See also **anti-Semitic**. ADJ: usu ADJ n

semitone /semitoʊn/ **semitones.** In Western music, a **semitone** is the smallest interval between two musical notes. Two semitones are equal to one tone. N-COUNT

semi-tropical

1 **Semi-tropical** places have a climate that is warm and humid. *...a semi-tropical island.* ADJ: usu ADJ n

2 **Semi-tropical** plants and trees are plants and trees that grow in places that are warm and humid. *The inn has a garden of semi-tropical vegetation.* ADJ: usu ADJ n

semolina /seməliːnə/. **Semolina** consists of small hard grains of wheat that are used for making foods such as spaghetti and macaroni and for making sweet puddings with milk. N-UNCOUNT

Senate /senɪt/ **Senates** ◆◆◆◆◇

1 **The Senate** is the smaller and more important of the two councils in the government of some countries, for example in the United States and Australia. *The Senate is expected to pass the bill shortly. ...a Senate committee.* N-PROPER-COLL: usu *the* N

2 **Senate** or **the Senate** is the governing council at some universities. *By the time I was Vice Chancellor, Senate had become a much larger and a much more democratic body... The new bill would remove student representation from the university Senate.* N-PROPER-COLL

senator /senɪtəʳ/ **senators.** A **senator** is a member of a law-making Senate, for example in the United States or Australia. ◆◆◆◇◇ N-COUNT; N-TITLE

senatorial /senɪtɔːriəl/. **Senatorial** means belonging to or relating to a Senate; a formal word. *He has senatorial experience in defence and foreign policy.* ADJ: ADJ n

send /send/ **sends, sending, sent** ◆◆◆◆◆

1 When you **send** someone something, you arrange for it to be taken and delivered to them, for example by post. *Myra Cunningham sent me a note thanking me for dinner... I sent a copy to the minister for transport... He sent a basket of exotic fruit and a card... Sir Denis took one look and sent it back... More than half a million sheep are sent from Britain to Europe for slaughter every year.* VERB V n n, V n to n, V n, V n with adv, be V-ed from n

2 If you **send** someone somewhere, you tell them to go there. *Inspector Banbury came up to see her, but she sent him away... He had been sent here to keep an eye on Benedict. ...the government's decision to send troops to the region... I suggested that he rest, and sent him for an X-ray... Reinforcements were being sent from the neighbouring region..* VERB V n with adv, V n to n, V n for n, be V-ed from n

3 If you **send** someone to an institution such as a school or a prison, you arrange for them to stay there for a period of time. *He even sent his children to comprehensive schools... You're saying they are sending too many people to prison?* VERB V n to n

4 To **send** a signal means to cause it to go to a place by means of radio waves or electricity. *The transmitters will send a signal automatically to a local base station... In 1959, the Soviet moon probe Luna II sent back the first pictures of the dark side of the moon.* VERB V n to n, V n with adv, Also V n, V n n

5 If something **sends** things or people in a particular direction, it causes them to move in that direction. *The explosion sent shrapnel flying through the sides of cars on the crowded highway... He let David go with a thrust of his wrist that sent the lad reeling... The slight back and forth motion sent a pounding surge of pain into his skull.* VERB V n -ing, V n prep

6 If something **sends** someone or something into a particular state, it causes them to be in that state. *My attempt to fix it sent Lawrence into fits of laughter. ...before civil war and famine sent the country plunging into anarchy... An obsessive search for our inner selves, far from saving the world, could send us all mad.* VERB V n into n, V n -ing, V n adj

7 • to **send** someone **packing**: see **pack**. • to **send** someone **to Coventry**: see **Coventry**.

send away for. To **send away for** something means the same as to **send for** something. *She sent away for a collection of china birds and a clock.* PHRASAL VERB V P P n

send down PHRASAL VERB

1 In British English, if a student **is sent down** from their university or college, they are made to leave because they have behaved very badly. *She wondered if he had been sent down for gambling.* usu passive, be V-ed P

2 If someone who is on trial **is sent down**, they are convicted and sent to prison. *The two rapists were sent down for life in 1983.* usu passive, be V-ed P

send for PHRASAL VERB

1 If you **send for** someone, you send them a message asking them to come and see you. *I've sent for the doctor.* V P n

2 If you **send for** something, you write and ask for it to be sent to you. *Send for your free catalogue today.* V P n

send in PHRASAL VERB

1 If you **send in** something such as an application or a competition entry, you post it to the organization concerned. *Applicants are asked to send in a CV and a covering letter... We're hoping that readers will send in their ideas for saving money.* V P n (not pron), Also V n P

2 When a government **sends in** troops or police officers, it orders them to deal with a crisis or problem somewhere. *He has asked the government to send in troops to end the fighting.* V P n (not pron), Also V n P

send off PHRASAL VERB

1 When you **send off** a letter or parcel, you send it somewhere by post. *He sent off copies to various people for them to read and make comments.* V P n (not pron), Also V n P

2 If a footballer **is sent off**, the referee makes them leave the field during a game, as a punishment for seriously breaking the rules. *The 30-year-old Scottish international was sent off for arguing with a linesman.* • See also **sending-off**. usu passive, be V-ed P

send off for. To **send off for** something means the same as to **send for** something. *I sent off for the Hoseasons catalogue.* PHRASAL VERB V P P n

send on. If you **send on** something you have received, especially a document, you send it to another place or person. *We coordinate the reports from the overseas divisions, and send them on to headquarters in Athens.* PHRASAL VERB V n P

send out PHRASAL VERB

1 If you **send out** things such as letters, leaflets, or bills, you send them to a large number of people at the same time. *She had sent out well over four hundred invitations that afternoon.* V P n (not pron), Also V n P

2 To **send out** a signal, sound, light, or heat means to produce it. *The crew did not send out any distress signals... Like bats, they send out sound waves and make sense of their environment from the echoes they receive back.* V P n (not pron)

3 When a plant **sends out** roots or shoots, they grow. *If you cut your rubber plant back, it should send out new side shoots.* =produce, V P n (not pron)

send out for. If you **send out for** food, for example pizzas or sandwiches, you phone and ask for it to be delivered to you. *Let's send out for a pizza and watch The Late Show.* PHRASAL VERB V P P n

send up. If you **send** someone or something **up**, you imitate them amusingly in a way that makes them appear foolish; an informal expression, used mainly in British English. *You sense he's sending himself up as well as everything else. ...a spoof that sends up the macho world of fighter pilots.* • See also **send-up**. PHRASAL VERB =mock, V n P, V P n (not pron)

sender /sendəʳ/ **senders. The sender** of a letter, parcel, or radio message is the person who sent it. *The sender of the best letter every week will win a cheque for £10.* ◆◇◇◇◇ N-COUNT: the N, oft N of n

sending-off, sendings-off. If there is a **sending-off** during a football match, a player is told to leave the field by the referee, as a punishment for seriously breaking the rules. *He is about to begin a three-match ban after his third sending-off of the season.* N-COUNT: oft poss N

send-off, send-offs. If a group of people give someone who is going away a **send-off**, they come together to say goodbye to them; an informal expression. *All the people in the buildings came to give me a rousing send-off.* N-COUNT: usu adj N

send-up, send-ups. A **send-up** is a piece of writing or acting in which someone or something is amusingly imitated in a way that makes them appear foolish; an informal expression, used mainly in British English. *...his classic send-up of sixties rock, 'Get Crazy'.* N-COUNT: usu sing, oft N of n =parody

Senegalese /senɪgəliːz/. **Senegalese** is both the singular and plural form. ◆◆◆◆◇

1 Senegalese means belonging or relating to Senegal, or to its people or culture. *...the Senegalese navy.* ADJ

2 A **Senegalese** is a Senegalese citizen, or a person of Senegalese origin. N-COUNT

senile /siːnaɪl/. If old people become **senile**, they become confused, can no longer remember things, and are unable to look after themselves. ◆◇◇◇◇ ADJ-GRADED
♦ **senility** /sɪnɪlɪti/ *The old man was forced to resign after showing unmistakable signs of senility.* N-UNCOUNT

senile dementia. Senile dementia is a mental illness that effects some old people and that causes them to become confused and to forget things. *She is suffering from senile dementia.* N-UNCOUNT

senior /siːnjəʳ/ **seniors** ◆◆◆◆◇

1 The **senior** people in an organization or profession have the highest and most important jobs. *...senior officials in the Israeli government. ...the company's senior management... Television and radio needed many more women in senior jobs.* ADJ-GRADED: ADJ n ≠junior

2 If someone is **senior** to you in an organization or profession, they have a higher and more important job than you or they are considered to be superior to you because they have worked there for longer and have more experience. *The position had to be* ADJ: usu v-link ADJ to n ≠junior *filled by an officer senior to Haig... Williams felt himself to be senior to all of them.* ► Your **seniors** are the people who are senior to you. *He was described by his seniors as a model officer.* N-PLURAL: poss N ≠junior

3 Senior is used when indicating how much older one person is than another. For example, if someone is ten years your **senior**, they are ten years older than you. *She became involved with a married man many years her senior.* N-SING: poss N ≠junior

4 In American English, **seniors** are students in a school or college who are the oldest and who have reached an advanced level in their studies. N-COUNT

5 If you take part in a sport at **senior** level, you take part in competitions with adults and people who have reached a high degree of achievement in that sport. *This will be his fifth international championship and his third at senior level.* ADJ: ADJ n ≠junior

senior citizen, senior citizens. A **senior citizen** is a person who is old enough to receive an old-age pension. ◆◇◇◇◇ N-COUNT =pensioner

seniority /siːniɒrɪti, AM -ɔːrɪti/. A person's **seniority** in an organization is the degree of importance and power that they have. *He has said he will fire editorial employees without regard to seniority.* N-UNCOUNT

sensation /senseɪʃən/ **sensations** ◆◆◇◇◇

1 A **sensation** is a physical feeling. *Floating can be a very pleasant sensation... A sensation of burning or tingling may be experienced in the hands.* N-COUNT: with supp =feeling

2 **Sensation** is your ability to feel things physically, especially through your sense of touch. *The pain was so bad that she lost all sensation. ...nerve damage which can lead to loss of sensation in the limbs.* N-UNCOUNT: supp N =feeling

3 You can use **sensation** to refer to the general feeling or impression caused by a particular experience. *It's a funny sensation to know someone's talking about you in a language you don't understand.* N-COUNT: usu adj N =feeling

4 If a person, event, or situation is a **sensation**, it causes great excitement or interest. *...the film that turned her into an overnight sensation.* N-COUNT

5 If a person, event, or situation causes **a sensation**, they cause great interest or excitement. *She was just 14 when she caused a sensation at the Montreal Olympics.* N-SING: a N

sensational /senseɪʃənəl/ ◆◇◇◇◇

1 A **sensational** result, event, or situation is so remarkable that it causes great excitement and interest. *The world champions suffered a sensational defeat.* ♦ **sensationally** *The rape trial was sensationally halted yesterday.* ADJ-GRADED =dramatic; ADV-GRADED: usu ADV with v

2 You can describe stories or reports as **sensational** if you disapprove of them because they present facts in a way that is intended to cause feelings of shock, anger, or excitement. *...sensational tabloid newspaper reports.* ADJ-GRADED: usu ADJ n PRAGMATICS

3 You can describe something as **sensational** when you think that it is extremely good; an informal use. *Her voice is sensational... Experts agreed that this was a truly sensational performance.* ♦ **sensationally** *...sensationally good food.* ADJ =terrific, fantastic; ADV

sensationalism /senseɪʃənəlɪzəm/. **Sensationalism** is the presentation of facts or stories in a way that is intended to produce strong feelings of shock, anger, or excitement; used showing disapproval. *The report criticises the newspaper for errors and sensationalism and for being 'irresponsible in the extreme'.* N-UNCOUNT PRAGMATICS

sensationalist /senseɪʃənəlɪst/. **Sensationalist** news reports and television and radio programmes present the facts in a way that makes them seem worse or more shocking than they really are; used showing disapproval. *...sensationalist headlines... The pictures were sensationalist and could seriously disturb younger readers.* ADJ-GRADED PRAGMATICS

sensationalize /senseɪʃənəlaɪz/ **sensationalizes, sensationalizing, sensationalized;** also spelled **sensationalise** in British English. If someone **sensationalizes** a situation or event, they make it seem worse or more shocking than it really is; used showing disapproval. *Local news organizations are being criticized for sensationalizing the story.* VERB PRAGMATICS; V n

sense /sens/ **senses, sensing, sensed** ◆◆◆◆◆

1 Your **senses** are the physical abilities of sight, smell, hearing, touch, and taste. *She stared at him again, unable to believe the evidence of her senses. ...a keen sense of smell.* ● See also **sixth sense.** N-COUNT

2 If you **sense** something, you become aware of it or you realize it, although it is not very obvious. *She probably sensed that I wasn't telling her the whole story... He looks about him, sensing danger... Prost had sensed what might happen.* VERB V that V n V wh

3 If you have a **sense** that something is the case, you think that it is the case, although you may not have firm, clear evidence for this belief. *Suddenly you got this sense that people were drawing themselves away from each other... There is no sense of urgency on either side.* ● See also **sense of occasion.** N-SING: N that, N of n

4 If you have a **sense of** guilt or shame, for example, you feel guilty or ashamed. *When your child is struggling for life, you feel this overwhelming sense of guilt... Lulled into a false sense of security, we eagerly awaited their return.* N-SING: N of n =feeling

5 If you have a **sense of** something such as duty or justice, you are aware of it and believe it is important. *My sense of justice was offended... We must keep a sense of proportion about all this... She needs to regain a sense of her own worth.* N-SING: N of n

6 Someone who has a **sense** of timing or style has a natural ability with regard to timing or style. You can also say that someone has a bad **sense** of timing or style. *He has an impeccable sense of timing... Her dress sense is appalling. ...his astute business sense.* ● See also **sense of humour.** N-SING: N of n, also n N

7 Sense is the ability to make good judgements and to behave sensibly. *...when he was younger and had a bit more sense... When that doesn't work they sometimes have the sense to seek help... And I'll buzz over to talk some sense into old Ocker.* ● See also **common sense.** N-UNCOUNT

8 If you say that there is no **sense** or little **sense** in doing something, you mean that it is not a sensible thing to do because nothing useful would be gained by doing it. *There's no sense in pretending this doesn't happen... There's little sense in trying to outspend a competitor with a much larger service factory.* N-SING: with neg, N *in* -ing, N -ing =point

9 A **sense** of a word or expression is one of its possible meanings. *...a noun which has two senses... Then she remembered that they had no mind in any real sense of that word.* N-COUNT =meaning

10 The sense of something that is written or spoken is its general meaning. *In a letter to the Literary Gazette in 1937 Pasternak clarified the sense of the passage.* N-SING: the N of n

11 Sense is used in several expressions to indicate how true your statement is. For example, if you say that something is true **in a sense**, you mean that it is partly true, or that it is true in one way. If you say that something is true **in a** technical **sense**, you mean that it is technically true. *In a sense, both were right... In one sense, the fact that few new commercial buildings can be financed does not matter... He's not the leader in a political sense... Though his background was modest, it was in no sense deprived.* PHRASES PHR with cl PRAGMATICS

12 If something **makes sense**, you can understand it. *He was sitting there saying, 'Yes, the figures make sense.'... It all makes sense now.* V inflects

13 When you **make sense of** something, you succeed in understanding it. *Provided you didn't try to make sense of it, it sounded beautiful... This is to help her to come to terms with her early upbringing and make sense of past experiences.* V inflects =understand

14 If a course of action **makes sense**, it seems sensible. *It makes sense to look after yourself... The project should be re-appraised to see whether it made sound economic sense... They all said 'This is crazy, this makes no sense'.* V inflects, oft *it* PHR to-inf

15 If you say that someone **has come to** their **senses** or **has been brought to** their **senses**, you mean that they have stopped being foolish and are being sensible again. *Eventually the world will* V inflects

come to its senses and get rid of them... May her death bring these people to their senses.

16 If you say that someone seems to **have taken leave of** their **senses**, you mean that they have done or said something very foolish; an old-fashioned expression. *They looked at me as if I had taken leave of my senses.* V inflects

17 If you say that someone **talks sense**, you mean that what they say is sensible. V inflects

18 ● to **see sense**: see **see**.

senseless /sensləs/ ◆◇◇◇◇

1 If you describe an action as **senseless**, you think it is wrong because it has no purpose and produces no benefit. *...people whose lives have been destroyed by acts of senseless violence... If your child is thirsty for learning, then it is senseless to hold her back.* ADJ-GRADED =pointless

2 If someone is **senseless**, they are unconscious. *They were knocked to the ground, beaten senseless and robbed of their wallets... Then I saw my boy lying senseless on the floor.* ADJ: ADJ after v, v-link ADJ

sense of direction

1 Your **sense of direction** is your ability to know roughly where you are, or which way to go, even when you are in an unfamiliar place. *He had a poor sense of direction, and when he passed the barn for the second time, he was forced to admit that he was lost.* N-SING

2 If you say that someone has a **sense of direction**, you mean that they seem to have clear ideas about what they want to do or achieve; used showing approval. *The country now had a sense of direction, he said, after a twenty month period in which its democracy and its integrity were threatened.* N-SING PRAGMATICS

sense of humour; spelled **sense of humor** in American English. Someone who has a **sense of humour** often finds things amusing, rather than being serious all the time. *He had enormous charm and a great sense of humour. ...someone with a very warped sense of humour.* ◆◆◇◇◇ N-SING

sense of occasion. If there is a **sense of occasion** when a planned event takes place, people feel that something special and important is happening. *There is a great sense of occasion and a terrific standard of musicianship.* N-SING

sense organ, sense organs. Your **sense organs** are the parts of your body, for example your eyes and your ears, with which you perceive things around you; a formal expression. N-COUNT: usu pl

sensibility /sensɪbɪlɪti/ **sensibilities** ◆◇◇◇◇

1 **Sensibility** is the ability to experience deep feelings. *Everything he writes demonstrates the depth of his sensibility. ...a man of sensibility.* N-UNCOUNT: usu supp N

2 Someone's **sensibility** is their tendency to be influenced or offended by things. *He was unable to control his sensibility... The challenge offended their sensibilities.* N-VAR: usu poss N

sensible /sensɪbəl/ ◆◆◆◇◇

1 **Sensible** actions or decisions are good because they are based on reasons rather than emotions. *It might be sensible to get a solicitor... The sensible thing is to leave them alone. ...sensible advice.* ADJ-GRADED: oft it v-link ADJ to-inf
♦ **sensibly** /sensɪbli/ *He sensibly decided to lie low for a while... They have very sensibly adjusted their diet.* ADV-GRADED

2 **Sensible** people behave in a sensible way. *She was a sensible girl and did not panic... Oh come on, let's be sensible about this... I'm trying to persuade you to be more sensible.* ADJ-GRADED: oft ADJ about n/-ing

3 **Sensible** shoes or clothes are practical and strong rather than fashionable and attractive. *Wear loose clothing and sensible footwear.* ADJ-GRADED: usu ADJ n ♦ **sensibly** *They were not sensibly dressed.* ADV-GRADED: ADV after v, ADV -ed

sensitive /sensɪtɪv/ ◆◆◆◇◇

1 If you are **sensitive** to other people's needs, problems, or feelings, you show understanding and awareness of them. *The classroom teacher must be sensitive to a child's needs... He was always so sensitive and caring.* ADJ-GRADED: oft ADJ to n ♦ **sensitively** *The abuse of women needs to be treated seriously and sensitively.* ADV-GRADED: usu ADV with v
♦ **sensitivity** /sensɪtɪvɪti/ *A good relationship involves concern and sensitivity for each other's feelings.* N-UNCOUNT: oft N for n

2 If you are **sensitive** about something, you are easily worried and offended when people talk about it. *Young people are very sensitive about their appearance... Take it easy. Don't be so sensitive.* ADJ-GRADED: oft ADJ about n
♦ **sensitivity, sensitivities** *...people who suffer extreme sensitivity about what others think... They are aware of American political sensitivities about their country's role.* N-VAR: oft N about n

3 A **sensitive** subject or issue needs to be dealt with carefully because it is likely to cause disagreement or make people angry or upset. *Employment is a very sensitive issue. ...politically sensitive matters.* ADJ-GRADED
♦ **sensitivity** *Due to the obvious sensitivity of the issue he would not divulge any details.* N-UNCOUNT: oft N of n

4 **Sensitive** documents or reports contain information that needs to be kept secret and dealt with carefully. *He instructed staff to shred sensitive documents. ...sensitive information which, in the wrong hands, could jeopardise the safety of British troops.* ADJ-GRADED: usu ADJ n

5 Something that is **sensitive** to a physical force, substance, or treatment is easily affected by it and often harmed by it. *...a chemical which is sensitive to light. ...gentle cosmetics for sensitive skin.* ADJ-GRADED: oft ADJ to n
♦ **sensitivity** *...the sensitivity of cells to damage by chemotherapy.* N-UNCOUNT: oft N of n

6 A **sensitive** piece of scientific equipment is capable of measuring or recording very small changes. *...an extremely sensitive microscope.* ADJ-GRADED: usu ADJ n
♦ **sensitivity** *...the sensitivity of the detector.* N-UNCOUNT

sensitize /sensɪtaɪz/ **sensitizes, sensitizing, sensitized;** also spelled **sensitise** in British English.

1 If you **sensitize** people to a particular problem or situation, you make them aware of it; a formal use. *It seems important to sensitize people to the fact that depression is more than the blues... How many judges in our male-dominated courts are sensitized to women's issues?* VERB V n to n V-ed Also V n

2 If a substance **is sensitized** to something such as light or touch, it is made sensitive to it. *Skin is easily irritated, chapped, chafed, and sensitized. ...sensitised nerve endings.* VB: usu passive be V-ed V-ed

sensor /sensəʳ/ **sensors.** A **sensor** is an instrument which reacts to certain physical conditions or impressions such as heat or light, and which is used to provide information. *The latest Japanese vacuum cleaners contain sensors that detect the amount of dust and type of floor. ...a light sensor.* ◆◇◇◇◇ N-COUNT

sensory /sensəri/. **Sensory** means relating to the physical senses; a formal word. *Almost all sensory information from the trunk and limbs passes through the spinal cord. ...our body's sensory system.* ◆◇◇◇◇ ADJ: ADJ n

sensual /senʃuəl/ ◆◇◇◇◇

1 Someone or something that is **sensual** shows or suggests a great liking for physical pleasures, especially sexual pleasures. *He was a very sensual person... Clothing doesn't need to be overt to be sensual. ...a wide, sensual mouth.* ADJ-GRADED ♦ **sensuality** /senʃuælɪti/ *The wave and curl of her blonde hair gave her sensuality and youth.* N-UNCOUNT

2 Something that is **sensual** gives pleasure to your physical senses rather than to your mind. *It was an opera, very glamorous and very sensual. ...sensual dance rhythms.* ADJ-GRADED ♦ **sensuality** *These perfumes have warmth and sensuality.* N-UNCOUNT

sensuous /senʃuəs/ ◆◇◇◇◇

1 Something that is **sensuous** gives pleasure to the mind or body through the senses. *The film is ravishing to look at and boasts a sensuous musical score... It is a sensuous but demanding car to drive.* ADJ-GRADED
♦ **sensuously** *She lay in the deep bath for a long time, enjoying its sensuously perfumed water.* ADV-GRADED: ADV adj, ADV with v

2 Someone or something that is **sensuous** shows or suggests a great liking for sexual pleasure. *...his sensuous young mistress, Marie-Therese. ...wide sensuous lips... His voice was deep but gentle, almost sensuous.* ADJ-GRADED =sensual ♦ **sensuously** *The nose was straight, the mouth sensuously wide and full.* ADV-GRADED: ADV adj, ADV with v

sent /sent/. **Sent** is the past tense and past participle of **send**.

sentence /sentəns/ **sentences, sentencing, sentenced** ◆◆◆◆◇

1 A **sentence** is a group of words which, when they are written down, begin with a capital letter and end with a full stop, question mark, or exclamation mark. Most sentences contain a subject and a verb. N-COUNT

2 In a law court, a **sentence** is the punishment that a person receives after they have been found guilty of a crime. *They are already serving prison sentences for their part in the assassination... He was given a four-year sentence... The offences carry a maximum sentence of 10 years. ...demands for tougher sentences... The court is expected to pass sentence later today.* ● See also **death sentence, life sentence, suspended sentence.** N-VAR

3 When a judge **sentences** someone, he or she states in court what their punishment will be. *A military court sentenced him to death in his absence... She was sentenced to nine years in prison... He has admitted the charge and will be sentenced later.* VERB V n to n, be V-ed, Also V n to-inf

sentence adverb, sentence adverbs. Adverbs such as 'fortunately' and 'perhaps' which apply to the whole clause, rather than to part of it, are sometimes called **sentence adverbs**. N-COUNT

sentient /sentiənt, -ʃᵊnt/. A **sentient** being is capable of experiencing things through its senses; a formal word. *...sentient creatures human and nonhuman alike.* ADJ: usu ADJ n

sentiment /sentɪmənt/ **sentiments** ◆◆◇◇◇

1 A **sentiment** that people have is an attitude which is based on their thoughts and feelings. *Public sentiment rapidly turned anti-American... He's found growing sentiment for military action. ...nationalist sentiments that threaten to split the country.* N-VAR: supp N =feeling

2 A **sentiment** is an idea or feeling that someone expresses in words. *I must agree with the sentiments expressed by John Prescott... The Foreign Secretary echoed this sentiment.* N-COUNT: usu with supp

3 **Sentiment** is an emotion such as tenderness, romance, or sadness, which influences a person's behaviour, sometimes to an extent that is considered exaggerated and foolish. *Laura kept that letter out of sentiment... The coronation was an occasion for extravagant myth and sentiment.* N-UNCOUNT

sentimental /sentɪmentᵊl/ ◆◆◇◇◇

1 Someone or something that is **sentimental** feels or arouses emotions such as tenderness, romance, or sadness, sometimes to an extent that is considered exaggerated and foolish. *I'm trying not to be sentimental about the past... It's a very sentimental play.* ♦ **sentimentally** *Childhood had less freedom and joy than we sentimentally attribute to it.* ♦ **sentimentality** /sentɪmentælɪti/ *In this book there is no sentimentality.* ADJ-GRADED; ADV-GRADED: usu ADV with v; N-UNCOUNT

2 You use **sentimental** to describe things relating to or affecting a person's emotions. *Our paintings and photographs are of sentimental value only... Perhaps he has returned for sentimental reasons.* ADJ: usu ADJ n

sentimentalist /sentɪmentəlɪst/ **sentimentalists.** If you describe someone as a **sentimentalist**, you believe that they are sentimental about things. N-COUNT ≠realist

sentimentalize /sentɪmentəlaɪz/ **sentimentalizes, sentimentalizing, sentimentalized;** also spelled **sentimentalise** in British English. If you **sentimentalize** something, you make it seem sentimental or think about it in a sentimental way. *He seems either to fear women or to sentimentalize them... He's the kind of filmmaker who doesn't hesitate to over sentimentalize. ...Rupert Brooke's sentimentalised glorification of war.* VERB V n, V, V-ed

sentinel /sentɪnᵊl/ **sentinels.** A **sentinel** is a sentry; an old-fashioned or literary word. N-COUNT

sentry /sentri/ **sentries.** A **sentry** is a soldier who guards a camp or a building. *The sentry would not let her enter... Aren't you supposed to be on sentry duty?* ◆◇◇◇◇ N-COUNT

sentry box, sentry boxes; also spelled **sentry-box**. A **sentry box** is a narrow shelter with an open front in which a sentry can stand while on duty. N-COUNT

Sep. **Sep.** is a written abbreviation for **September**. The more usual abbreviation is **Sept.** *...Friday Sep 21, 1990.* ◆◆◇◇◇

separable /sepərəbᵊl/. If things are **separable**, they can be separated from each other. *Character is not separable from physical form but is governed by it.* ADJ: usu v-link ADJ, oft ADJ *from* n

separate, separates, separating, separated. ◆◆◆◆◇ The adjective and noun are pronounced /sepərət/. The verb is pronounced /sepəreɪt/.

1 If one thing is **separate** from another, there is a partition, space, or division between them, so that they are clearly two things. *Each villa has a separate sitting-room... They are now making plans to form their own separate party... Business bank accounts were kept separate from personal ones.* ♦ **separateness** *...establishing Australia's cultural separateness from Britain.* ADJ: oft ADJ *from* n; N-UNCOUNT

2 If you refer to **separate** things, you mean several different things, rather than just one thing. *Use separate chopping boards for raw meats, cooked meats, vegetables and salads... Men and women have separate exercise rooms... The authorities say six civilians have been killed in two separate attacks.* ADJ: usu ADJ n =different

3 If you **separate** people or things that are together, or if they **separate**, they move apart. *Police moved in to separate the two groups... The pans were held in both hands and swirled around to separate gold particles from the dirt... The front end of the car separated from the rest of the vehicle... They separated. Stephen returned to the square... They're separated from the adult inmates.* V-RECIP-ERG V pl-n, V n *from* n, V *from* n, pl-n V, V-ed

4 If you **separate** people or things that have been connected, or if one **separates** from another, the connection between them is ended. *They want to separate teaching from research... It's very possible that we may see a movement to separate the two parts of the country... He announced a new ministry to deal with Quebec's threat to separate from Canada.* V-RECIP-ERG V n *from* n, V pl-n, V *from* n, Also pl-n V

5 If a couple who are married or living together **separate**, they decide to live apart. *Her parents separated when she was very young... Since I separated from my husband I have gone a long way.* V-RECIP pl-n V, V *from* n

6 An object, obstacle, distance, or period of time which **separates** two people, groups, or things exists between them. *...the white-railed fence that separated the yard from the paddock. ...although they had undoubtedly made progress in the six years that separated the two periods... Rural communities are widely separated and often small... But a group of six women and 23 children got separated from the others.* VERB V n *from* n, V pl-n, *get* V-ed

7 If you **separate** one idea or fact from another, you consider them individually and see or show the distinction between them. *It is difficult to separate legend from truth. ...learning how to separate real problems from imaginary illnesses... It is difficult to separate the two aims.* ► **Separate out** means the same as **separate**. *How can one ever separate out the act from the attitudes that surround it?* VERB =distinguish V n *from* n, V pl-n; PHRASAL VERB V P n *from* n

8 A quality or factor that **separates** one thing from another is the reason why the two things are different from each other. *The single most important factor that separates ordinary photographs from good photographs is the lighting... What separates terrorism from other acts of violence?* VERB =distinguish V n *from* n

9 If a particular number of points **separate** two teams or competitors, one of them is winning or has won by that number of points. *In the end only three points separated the two teams.* VERB V pl-n

10 If you **separate** a group of people or things into smaller groups or elements, or if a group **separates**, the group is divided into smaller groups or elements. *The police wanted to separate them into smaller groups... Wallerstein's work can be separated into three main component themes... Let's* V-ERG =split V n *into* n, V *into* n, V

separate into smaller groups... So all the colours that make up white light are sent in different directions and they separate. ▸ **Separate out** means the same as **separate**. *If prepared many hours ahead, the mixture may separate out.* PHRASAL VERB V P

11 Separates are clothes such as skirts, trousers, and shirts which cover just the top half or the bottom half of your body. N-PLURAL

12 See also **separated**.

13 When two or more people who have been together for some time **go** their **separate ways**, they go to different places or end their relationship or partnership. *Sue was 27 when she and her husband decided to go their separate ways.* PHRASE: V inflects

14 • to **separate the wheat from the chaff**: see **chaff**.

separate out. If you **separate out** something from the other things it is with, you take it out. *The ability to separate out reusable elements from other waste is crucial.* • See also **separate** 7, 10. PHRASAL VERB V P n *from* n Also V P n (not pron)

separated /sepəreɪtɪd/ ◆◆◇◇◇

1 Someone who is **separated** from their wife or husband lives apart from them, but is not divorced. *Most single parents are either divorced or separated... Tristan had been separated from his wife for two years.* ADJ: v-link ADJ, oft ADJ *from* n

2 If you are **separated** from someone, for example your family, you are not able to be with them. *The idea of being separated from him, even for a few hours, was torture... They're trying their best to bring together those separated families.* ADJ: oft ADJ *from* n

separately /sepərətli/. If people or things are dealt with **separately** or do something **separately**, they are dealt with or do something at different times or in different places, rather than together. *Cook each vegetable separately until just tender... Chris had insisted that we went separately to the club.* ◆◆◇◇◇ ADV: ADV with v, oft ADV *from* n ≠together

separation /sepəreɪʃən/ **separations** ◆◆◇◇◇

1 The **separation** of two or more things or groups is the fact that they are separate or become separate, and are not linked. *He believes in the separation of the races. ...a 'Christian republic' in which there was a clear separation between church and state.* N-VAR: oft N *of/from/between* n

2 During a **separation**, people who usually live together are not together. *She wondered if Harry had been unfaithful to her during this long separation... All children will tend to suffer from separation from their parents and siblings.* N-VAR

3 If a couple who are married or living together have a **separation**, they decide to live apart. *They agreed to a trial separation. ...loss of a loved one through death, separation or divorce.* N-VAR

separatism /sepərətɪzəm/. **Separatism** is the beliefs and activities of separatists. N-UNCOUNT

separatist /sepərətɪst/ **separatists** ◆◆◇◇◇

1 **Separatist** organizations and activities involve members of an ethnic or cultural group of people within a country who want to establish their own separate government or are trying to do so. *Spanish police say they have arrested ten people suspected of being members of the Basque separatist movement... Nearly 2,500 have died in separatist violence this year.* ADJ: ADJ n

2 **Separatists** are people who want their own separate government or are involved in separatist activities. *The army has come under attack by separatists.* N-COUNT

sepia /siːpiə/. Something that is **sepia** is deep brown in colour, like the colour of very old photographs. *The walls are hung with sepia photographs of old school heroes.* COLOUR

Sept. **Sept.** is a written abbreviation for **September**. *I've booked it for Thurs. 8th Sept.* ◆◆◇◇◇ =Sep.

September /septembəʳ/ **Septembers. September** is the ninth month of the year in the Western calendar. *Her son, Jerome, was born in September... They returned to Moscow on 22 September 1930... They spent a couple of nights here last September.* ◆◆◆◆◇ N-VAR

septic /septɪk/. If a wound or a part of your body becomes **septic**, it becomes infected. *A flake of plaster from the ceiling fell into his eye, which became septic. ...a septic toe.* ADJ

septicaemia /septɪsiːmiə/. **Septicaemia** is blood poisoning; a medical term. N-UNCOUNT

septic tank, septic tanks. A **septic tank** is an underground tank where faeces, urine, and other waste matter is made harmless using bacteria. N-COUNT

septuagenarian /septʃuədʒɪneəriən/ **septuagenarians.** A **septuagenarian** is a person between 70 and 79 years old; a formal word. *...septuagenarian author Mary Wesley.* N-COUNT: oft N n

sepulchral /sɪpʌlkrəl/. Something that is **sepulchral** is gloomy and solemn; a literary word. *'He's gone,' Rory whispered in sepulchral tones.* ADJ-GRADED

sepulchre /sepəlkəʳ/ **sepulchres;** spelled **sepulcher** in American English. A **sepulchre** is a large tomb in which a dead person is buried; a literary word. N-COUNT

sequel /siːkwəl/ **sequels** ◆◇◇◇◇

1 A book or film which is a **sequel** to an earlier one continues the story of the earlier one. *She is currently writing a sequel to Daphne du Maurier's 'Rebecca'... Richard Chamberlain has agreed to make a sequel to 'The Thorn Birds'.* N-COUNT: oft N *to* n

2 The **sequel** to something that has happened is an event or situation that happens after it or as a result of it. *The police said the clash was a sequel to yesterday's nationwide strike... The arrests were a 'direct sequel' to investigations.* N-COUNT: usu sing

sequence /siːkwəns/ **sequences** ◆◆◇◇◇

1 A **sequence** of events or things is a number of events or things that come one after another in a particular order. *...the sequence of events which led to the murder. ...a dazzling sequence of novels by John Updike.* N-COUNT: oft N *of* n =series

2 A particular **sequence** is a particular order in which things happen or are arranged. *...the colour sequence yellow, orange, purple, blue, green and white... The chronological sequence gives the book an element of structure.* N-COUNT

3 A film **sequence** is a part of a film that shows a single set of actions. *The best sequence in the film occurs when Roth stops at a house he used to live in.* N-COUNT

sequencer /siːkwənsəʳ/ **sequencers.** A **sequencer** is an electronic instrument that can be used for recording and storing sounds so that they can be replayed as part of a new piece of music. N-COUNT

sequential /sɪkwenʃəl/. Something that is **sequential** follows a fixed order and thus forms a pattern; a formal word. *...the sequential story of the universe... In this way the children are introduced to sequential learning.* ♦ **sequentially** *The pages are numbered sequentially.* ADJ: usu ADJ n; ADV: ADV after v

sequester /sɪkwestəʳ/ **sequesters, sequestering, sequestered**

1 **Sequester** means the same as **sequestrate**. *Everything he owned was sequestered.* VERB *be* V-ed Also V n

2 If someone **is sequestered** somewhere, they are isolated from other people. *This jury is expected to be sequestered for at least two months.* VERB *be* V-ed

sequestered /sɪkwestəʳd/. A **sequestered** place is quiet, undisturbed, and far away from other people and places; a literary word. ADJ-GRADED =secluded

sequestrate /siːkwestreɪt/ **sequestrates, sequestrating, sequestrated.** When property **is sequestrated**, it is taken officially from someone who has debts, usually after a decision in a court of law. If the debts are paid off, the property is returned to its owner. *He promised to do all that he could to prevent union money from being sequestrated by the courts.* ♦ **sequestration** /siːkwestreɪʃən/ *...the sequestration of large areas of land.* VB: usu passive =sequester; *be* V-ed; N-UNCOUNT

sequin /siːkwɪn/ **sequins. Sequins** are small, shiny discs that are sewn on clothes to decorate them. *The frocks were covered in sequins, thousands of them.* N-COUNT: usu pl

sequinned /siːkwɪnd/; spelled **sequined** in American English. Something that is **sequinned** is decorated or covered with sequins. *...a strapless sequinned evening gown.* ADJ

seraph /serəf/ **seraphim** /serəfɪm/ or **seraphs.** In the Bible, a **seraph** is one of the angels that guard God's throne. N-COUNT

Serbo-Croat /sɜːʳbou krouæt/. **Serbo-Croat** is one of the languages spoken in the former Yugoslavia. N-UNCOUNT

serenade /serɪneɪd/ **serenades, serenading, serenaded** ◆◇◇◇◇

1 If one person **serenades** another, they sing or play a piece of music for them. Traditionally men did this outside the window of the woman they loved. *In the interval a blond boy dressed in white serenaded the company on the flute... It happened to be my birthday, and after breakfast I was serenaded by the crew.* ► Also a noun. *Placido Domingo sang his serenade of love.* VERB Vn N-COUNT

2 In classical music, a **serenade** is a piece in several parts written for a small orchestra. *...Vaughan Williams's Serenade to Music.* N-COUNT: oft in names

serendipitous /serendɪpɪtəs/. A **serendipitous** event is unplanned but has a beneficial result; a literary word. *...her serendipitous choice of careers as an antique dealer.* ADJ-GRADED

serendipity /serendɪpɪti/. **Serendipity** is the luck some people have in finding or creating interesting or valuable things by chance; a literary word. *Some of the best effects in my garden have been the result of serendipity.* N-UNCOUNT

serene /sɪriːn/. Someone or something that is **serene** is calm and quiet. *She looked as calm and serene as she always did... He didn't speak much, he just smiled with that serene smile of his. ...the beautiful, serene park.* ♦ **serenely** *We sailed serenely down the river... She carried on serenely sipping her gin and tonic. ...serenely beautiful.* ♦ **serenity** /sɪrenɪti/ *I had a wonderful feeling of peace and serenity when I saw my husband.* ◆◇◇◇◇ ADJ-GRADED ADV-GRADED: ADV with v, ADV adj N-UNCOUNT =tranquility

serf /sɜːʳf/ **serfs.** In former times, **serfs** were a class of people who had to work on their master's land and could not leave without his permission. N-COUNT

serfdom /sɜːʳfdəm/

1 The system of **serfdom** was the social and economic system by which the land was cultivated by serfs. N-UNCOUNT

2 If someone was in a state of **serfdom**, they were a serf. N-UNCOUNT

serge /sɜːʳdʒ/. **Serge** is a type of strong woollen cloth used to make clothes such as skirts, coats, and trousers. *He wore a blue serge suit.* ◆◇◇◇◇ N-UNCOUNT

sergeant /sɑːʳdʒᵊnt/ **sergeants** ◆◆◇◇◇

1 A **sergeant** is a non-commissioned officer of middle rank in the army or airforce. *A sergeant with a detail of four men came into view. ...Sergeant Black.* N-COUNT; N-TITLE; N-VOC

2 In the British police force, a **sergeant** is an officer with the next to lowest rank. In American police forces, a **sergeant** is an officer with the rank immediately below a captain. *The unit was staffed by 11 officers from Greater Manchester Police headed by Sergeant Bell.* N-COUNT; N-TITLE; N-VOC

sergeant major, sergeant majors; also spelled **sergeant-major.** A **sergeant major** is a non-commissioned army officer of the highest rank. N-COUNT; N-TITLE; N-VOC

serial /sɪəriəl/ **serials** ◆◆◇◇◇

1 A **serial** is a story which is broadcast on television or radio or published in a magazine in a number of parts over a period of time. *...one of BBC television's most popular serials, Eastenders... Maupin's novels have all appeared originally as serials.* N-COUNT

2 **Serial** killings or attacks are a series of killings or attacks committed by the same person. This person is known as a **serial** killer or attacker. *...serial murders... The serial killer claimed to have killed 400 people.* ADJ: ADJ n

serialization /sɪəriəlaɪzeɪʃᵊn/ **serializations;** also spelled **serialisation** in British English.

1 **Serialization** is the act of serializing a book. N-UNCOUNT

2 A **serialization** is a story, originally written as a book, which is being published or broadcast in a number of parts. *...in the serialisation of Jane Austen's Pride and Prejudice.* N-COUNT

serialize /sɪəriəlaɪz/ **serializes, serializing, serialized;** also spelled **serialise** in British English. If a book **is serialized**, it is broadcast on the radio or television or published in a magazine in a number of parts. *A few years ago Tom Brown's Schooldays was serialised on television.* VB: usu passive be V-ed

serial number, serial numbers. The **serial number** of an object is a number on that object which identifies it. *...the gun's serial number. ...your bike's serial number... All the bills had the same serial number. The cash was counterfeit.* N-COUNT: oft with poss

series /sɪəriz/; **series** is both the singular and plural form. ◆◆◆◆◇

1 A **series** of things or events is a number of them that come one after the other. *...a series of meetings with students and political leaders. ...a series of explosions.* N-COUNT: usu sing: oft N of n =succession

2 A radio or television **series** is a set of programmes of a particular kind which have the same title. *...the TV series 'The Trials of Life' presented by David Attenborough. ...the world's longest-running radio series, Britain's 'The Archers'.* N-COUNT: usu sing

serious /sɪəriəs/ ◆◆◆◆◆

1 **Serious** problems or situations are very bad and cause people to be worried or afraid. *Crime is an increasingly serious problem in Russian society... The government still face very serious difficulties... Doctors said his condition was serious but stable.* ♦ **seriously** *If this ban was to come in it would seriously damage my business... They are not thought to be seriously hurt.* ♦ **seriousness** *...the seriousness of the crisis.* ADJ-GRADED =grave ADV-GRADED: ADV adj/adv, ADV with v N-UNCOUNT: oft N of n

2 **Serious** matters are important and deserve careful and thoughtful consideration. *I regard this as a serious matter... Don't laugh boy. This is serious. ...the serious business of running the country.* ADJ-GRADED

3 When important matters are dealt with in a **serious** way, they are given careful and thoughtful consideration. *My parents never really faced up to my drug use in any serious way... It was a question which deserved serious consideration. ...serious discussions.* ♦ **seriously** *The management will have to think seriously about their positions.* ADJ-GRADED: usu ADJ n ADV-GRADED: ADV with v

4 **Serious** music or literature requires concentration to understand or appreciate it. *...serious classical music. ...a serious newspaper.* ADJ: ADJ n

5 If someone is **serious** about something, they are sincere about what they are saying, doing, or intending to do. *You really are serious about this, aren't you?... I hope you're not serious.* ♦ **seriously** *Are you seriously jealous of Erica?* ♦ **seriousness** *In all seriousness, there is nothing else I can do... They had shown a commitment and seriousness of purpose.* ADJ-GRADED: oft ADJ *about* n ADV: ADV adj/adv, ADV with v N-UNCOUNT: oft N of n

6 **Serious** people are thoughtful and quiet, and do not laugh very often. *He's quite a serious person... She looked at me with big, serious eyes.* ♦ **seriously** *They spoke to me very seriously but politely.* ADJ-GRADED ADV-GRADED: ADV with v

7 **Serious** money is a very large amount of money; an informal use. *He started earning serious money only in the sixties.* ♦ **seriously** *What's it like to be seriously rich at 15?* ADJ: ADJ n ADV: ADV adj

seriously /sɪəriəsli/ ◆◆◆◇◇

1 You use **seriously** to indicate that you are not joking and that you really mean what you say. *Seriously, I only smoke in the evenings.* ADV: ADV with cl

2 You say **'seriously'** when you are surprised by what someone has said, as a way of asking them if they really mean it; used in spoken English. *'I tried to chat him up at the general store.' He laughed. 'Seriously?'* CONVENTION

3 See also **serious.**

4 If you **take** someone or something **seriously**, you believe that they are important and deserve attention. *It's hard to take them seriously in their pretty grey uniforms... The phrase was not meant to be taken seriously.* PHRASE: V inflects

sermon /sɜːʳmən/ **sermons.** A **sermon** is a talk on a religious or moral subject that is given by a member of the clergy as part of a church service. ◆◇◇◇◇ N-COUNT

serpent /sɜːʳpənt/ **serpents.** A **serpent** is a snake; a literary word. *...the serpent in the Garden of Eden.* ◆◇◇◇◇ N-COUNT

serpentine /sɜːʳpəntaɪn/. Something that is **serpentine** is curving and winding in shape, like a snake when it moves; a literary word. *...serpentine woodland pathways.* ADJ-GRADED =winding

serrated /sereɪtɪd/. A **serrated** object such as a knife or blade has a row of V-shaped points along the edge. *Bread knives should have a serrated edge.* ADJ: usu ADJ n

serried /serid/. **Serried** things or people are closely crowded together in rows; a literary word. *...serried rows of law books and law reports. ...the serried ranks of fans.* ADJ: ADJ n =dense

serum /sɪərəm/ **serums** ◆◇◇◇◇
1 A **serum** is a liquid that is injected into someone's blood to protect them against a poison or disease. N-VAR =antitoxin
2 **Serum** is the watery, pale yellow part of blood. N-UNCOUNT

servant /sɜːʳvᵊnt/ **servants** ◆◆◆◇◇
1 A **servant** is someone who is employed to work in another person's house, for example as a cleaner or a gardener. N-COUNT =domestic
2 You can also use the word **servant** to refer to someone or something that provides a service for people or can be used by them. *Like any other public servants, police must respond to public demand... The question is whether technology is going to be our servant or our master.* • See also **civil servant**. N-COUNT

serve /sɜːʳv/ **serves, serving, served** ◆◆◆◆◇
1 If you **serve** your country, an organization, or a person, you do useful work for them. *It is unfair to soldiers who have served their country well for many years... I have always said that I would serve the Party in any way it felt appropriate.* VERB V n
2 If you **serve** in a particular place or as a particular official, you perform official duties, especially in the armed forces, as a civil servant, or as a politician. *During the second world war he served with RAF Coastal Command... He also served on the National Front's national executive committee... For seven years until 1991 he served as a district councillor in Solihull.* VERB V prep/adv
3 If something **serves** as a particular thing or **serves** a particular purpose, it performs a particular function, which is often not its intended function. *She ushered me into the front room, which served as her office... I really do not think that an inquiry would serve any useful purpose... Their brief visit has served to underline the deep differences between the two countries... The old drawing room serves her as both sitting room and study.* VERB V *as/for* n, V n, V to-inf, V n *as/for* n
4 If something **serves** people or an area, it provides them with something that they need. *This could mean the closure of thousands of small businesses which serve the community. ...improvements in the public water-supply system serving the Nairobi area... Cuba is well served by motorways. ...a desire to make education serve the needs of politicians and business.* VERB V n
5 Something that **serves** someone's interests benefits them. *The economy should be organized to serve the interests of all the people... They may well decide that their interests would be best served by joining in.* VERB V n
6 When you **serve** food and drink, you give people food and drink. *Serve it with French bread... Serve the cakes warm... Prepare the garnishes shortly before you are ready to serve the soup. ...the pleasure of having someone serve you champagne and caviar in bed... They are expected to baby-sit, run errands, and help serve at cocktail parties.* ▶ **Serve up** means the same as **serve.** *After all, it is no use serving up TV dinners if the kids won't eat them... He served it up on delicate white plates.* VERB V n prep, V n adj, V n, V n n, V, Also V n *to* n; PHRASAL VERB V P n (not pron), V n P
7 **Serve** is used to indicate how much food a recipe produces. For example, a recipe that **serves** six provides enough food for six people. *Garnish with fresh herbs. Serves 4.* VB: no cont V n
8 Someone who **serves** customers in a shop or a bar helps them and provides them with what they want to buy. *They wouldn't serve me in any pubs 'cos I looked too young... Auntie and Uncle suggested she serve in the shop.* VERB V n, V
9 When the police or other officials **serve** someone with a legal order or **serve** an order on them, they give or send the legal order to them; a legal term. *...as immigration officers accompanied by the police tried to serve her with a deportation order... Police said they had been unable to serve a summons on 25-year-old Lee Jones.* VERB V n *with* n, V n *on* n, Also V n
10 If you **serve** something such as a prison sentence or an apprenticeship, you spend a period of time doing it. *...Leo, who is currently serving a life sentence for murder... He was able to serve his apprenticeship as a trainer with Eddie Futch.* VERB V n
11 When you **serve** in games such as tennis and badminton, you throw up the ball or shuttlecock and hit it to start play. *He served 17 double faults... If you serve like this nobody can beat you.* ▶ Also a noun. *His second serve clipped the net.* VERB V n, V; N-COUNT
12 When you describe someone's **serve**, you are indicating how well or how fast they serve a ball or shuttlecock. *His powerful serve was too much for the defending champion.* N-COUNT
13 See also **serving**.
14 If you say **it serves** someone **right** when something unpleasant happens to them, you mean that it is their own fault and you have no sympathy for them. *Serves her right for being so stubborn.* PHRASE: V inflects, oft PHR *for* -ing PRAGMATICS

serve out. If someone **serves out** their term of office, contract, or prison sentence, they do not leave before the end of the agreed period of time. *The governor has declared his innocence and says he plans to fight and serve out his term... I was resigned to serving out the sentence.* PHRASAL VERB V P n (not pron)

serve up. See **serve** 6. PHRASAL VERB

server /sɜːʳvəʳ/ **servers** ◆◇◇◇◇
1 In tennis and badminton, the **server** is the player whose turn it is to hit the ball or shuttlecock to start play. *...a brilliant server and volleyer.* N-COUNT: oft adj N
2 A **server** is something such as a fork or spoon that is used for serving food. *...salad servers.* N-COUNT: oft n N
3 In computing, a **server** is part of a computer network which does a particular task, for example storing or processing information, for all or part of the network. N-COUNT

service /sɜːʳvɪs/ **services, servicing, serviced** ◆◆◆◆◆
1 A **service** is something that the public needs, such as transport, communications facilities, hospitals, or energy supplies, which is provided in a planned and organized way by the government or an official body. *Britain still boasts the cheapest postal service... We have started a campaign for better nursery and school services... The authorities have said they will attempt to maintain essential services.* N-COUNT: usu with supp
2 You can sometimes refer to an organization or private company as a particular **service** when it provides something for the public or acts on behalf of the government. *...Mr John Tusa, managing director of the BBC World Service. ...Careers Advisory Services.* N-COUNT: oft in names
3 If an organization or company provides a particular **service**, they can do a particular job or a type of work for you. *The kitchen maintains a twenty-four hour service and can be contacted via Reception... The larger firm was capable of providing a better range of services.* N-COUNT
4 **Services** are activities such as tourism, banking, and selling which contribute to a country's economy, but which are not directly concerned with producing or manufacturing goods. *Mining rose by 9.1%, manufacturing by 9.4% and services by 4.3%. ...the doctrine that a highly developed service sector was the sign of a modern economy.* N-PLURAL
5 The level or standard of **service** provided by an organization or company is the amount or quality of the work it can do for you. *Taking risks is the only way employees can provide effective and efficient customer service... The current level of service will* N-UNCOUNT

be maintained except that the evening 'Network Express' trains will be withdrawn.

6 A bus or train **service** is a route or regular journey that is part of a transport system. *A bus service operates between Bolton and Salford.* N-COUNT: usu n N

7 Your **services** are the things that you do or the skills that you use in your job, which other people find useful and are usually willing to pay you for. *I have obtained the services of a top photographer to take our pictures... The performers have all offered their services free of charge.* N-PLURAL: with poss

8 If you refer to someone's **service** or **services** to a particular organization or activity, you mean that they have done a lot of work for it or devoted a lot of their time to it. *You've given a lifetime of service to athletics... More than half his long service in parliament has been as a cabinet minister. ...the two policemen, who have a total of 31 years' service between them... He was awarded the OBE in 1990 for services to fashion.* N-UNCOUNT: also N in pl, oft N *to* n

9 The **Services** are the army, the navy, and the air force. *In June 1945, Britain still had forty-five per cent of its workforce in the Services and munitions industries.* N-COUNT: usu pl

10 **Service** is the work done by people or equipment in the army, navy, or air force, for example during a war. *The regiment was recruited from the Highlands specifically for service in India. ...an aircraft carrier that saw service in World War II.* N-UNCOUNT

11 When you receive **service** in a restaurant, hotel, or shop, an employee asks you what you want or gives you what you have ordered. *A five-course meal including coffee, service and VAT is £25. ...clean stores with respectful service and fair prices.* N-UNCOUNT

12 A **service** is a religious ceremony that takes place in a church with a congregation present. *After the hour-long service, his body was taken to a cemetery in the south of the city. ...the church in which the President was attending morning service.* N-COUNT: also no det

13 A dinner **service** or a tea **service** is a complete set of plates, cups, saucers, and other pieces of china. *...a 60-piece dinner service.* N-COUNT: usu n N

14 A **services** is a place where you can stop on a motorway and where there is a petrol station, a restaurant, a shop, and toilets. The plural **services** can be used to refer either to one or to more than one of these places. *They had to pull up, possibly go to a motorway services or somewhere like that... We have repeatedly told planners that services are vital on a motorway like the M40.* N-COUNT =service station

15 In tennis, badminton, and some other sports, when it is your **service**, it is your turn to serve. *She conceded just three points on her service during the first set.* N-COUNT: oft with poss

16 **Service** is used to describe parts of a building or structure that are used by people such as technical and maintenance staff, and not usually by the public. *He wheeled the trolley down the corridor and disappeared with it into the service lift. ...the bigger tunnels, which run either side of the service tunnel.* ADJ: ADJ n

17 If someone is in **service**, they are working as a servant. *If a young woman did not have a dowry, she went into domestic service.* N-UNCOUNT: oft *in/into* N

18 If you have a vehicle or machine **serviced**, you arrange for someone to examine, adjust, and clean it so that it will keep working efficiently and safely. *...if you had had your car serviced at the local garage... Make sure that all gas fires and central heating boilers are serviced annually.* ▸ Also a noun. *The car needs a service... The company sends a service engineer to fix the disk drive before it fails.* VERB *have* n V-ed, *be* V-ed, Also V n; N-COUNT: usu sing, oft N n

19 If a country or organization **services** its debts, it pays the interest on them. *Almost a quarter of the country's export earnings go to service a foreign debt of $29 billion.* VERB V n

20 If someone or something **services** something such as an organization, a project or a group of people, they provide it with things that it needs in order to function properly or effectively. *There are now 400 staff at headquarters, servicing our regional and overseas work... Fossil fuels such as coal, oil and gas will service our needs for some considerable time to come.* VERB V n

21 See also **active service, Civil Service, community service, emergency services, in-service, National Health Service, national service, public service, room service.**

22 If someone or something is **at the service of** a person or organization, they are fully available to help or to be used by that person or organization. *The intellectual and moral potential of the world's culture must be put at the service of politics.* PHRASES PHR n, usu PHR after v

23 You can use **'at your service'** after your name as a formal way of introducing yourself to someone and saying that you are willing to help them in any way you can. *She bowed dramatically. 'Anastasia Krupnik, at your service,' she said.* CONVENTION PRAGMATICS

24 If you **do** someone **a service**, you do something that helps or benefits them. *You are doing me a great service, and I'm very grateful to you... 'You don't feel that you've betrayed your country?'—'Not at all, I think I've done a service to my country.'* V inflects

25 If a piece of equipment or type of vehicle is **in service**, it is being used or is able to be used. If it is **out of service**, it is not being used, usually because it is not working properly. *Cuts in funding have meant that equipment has been kept in service long after it should have been replaced... In 1882, London's first electric tram cars went into service... Some two hundred obsolete warships and submarines have been taken out of service during the past five years.* usu PHR after v, v-link PHR

26 If someone or something is **of service** to you, they help you or are useful to you. *That is, after all, the primary reason we live – to be of service to others.* v-link PHR, oft PHR *to* n

27 • **be pressed into service**: see **press**.

serviceable /sɜːʳvɪsəbᵊl/. If you describe something as **serviceable**, you mean that it is good enough to be used and to perform its function adequately. *His Arabic was not as good as his English, but serviceable enough... A customer took a perfectly serviceable washing machine in for repair, only to be told it needed replacing.* ADJ-GRADED

service area, service areas. A **service area** is an area beside a motorway where you can stop and buy petrol and something to eat. N-COUNT =service station

service charge, service charges. A **service charge** is an amount that is added to your bill in a restaurant to pay for the work of the waiter or waitress who serves you. *Most restaurants add a 10 per cent service charge to the bill.* N-COUNT

service industry, service industries. A **service industry** is an industry such as banking or insurance that provides a service but does not produce anything. ◆◇◇◇◇ N-COUNT

serviceman /sɜːʳvɪsmən/ **servicemen.** A **serviceman** is a man who is in the army, navy, or air force. ◆◆◇◇◇ N-COUNT

service station, service stations

1 A **service station** is a garage that sells things such as petrol, oil, and spare parts. Service stations often sell food, drink, and other goods. N-COUNT

2 A motorway **service station** is an area beside a motorway where you can stop, and buy petrol and something to eat. N-COUNT =service area

serviette /sɜːʳviet/ **serviettes.** In British English, a **serviette** is a square of cloth or paper that you use to protect your clothes or to wipe your mouth when you are eating. The usual American term is **table napkin.** N-COUNT =napkin

servile /sɜːʳvaɪl, AM -vᵊl/. If you say that someone is **servile**, you disapprove of them because they are too eager to obey someone or do things for them. *He was subservient and servile... They said she had a servile attitude to her employer.* ADJ-GRADED PRAGMATICS =obsequious

♦ **servility** /sɜːʳvɪlɪti/ *She's a curious mixture of stubbornness and servility.* N-UNCOUNT

serving /sɜːʳvɪŋ/ **servings** ◆◇◇◇◇

1 A **serving** is an amount of food that is given to one person at a meal. *Quantities will vary according to how many servings of soup you want to prepare... Each serving contains 240 calories.* N-COUNT: oft N *of* n

2 A **serving** spoon or dish is used for giving out food at a meal. *Pile the potatoes into a warm serving dish.* ADJ: ADJ n

servitude /sɜːʳvɪtjuːd, AM -tuːd/. **Servitude** is the condition of being a slave or of being completely under the control of someone else. *...a life of servitude.* • See also **penal servitude**. N-UNCOUNT

sesame /sesəmi/. **Sesame** is a plant grown for its seeds and oil which are used in cooking. *...sesame seeds... I've put some sesame crackers in the oven to bake.* ◆◇◇◇◇ N-UNCOUNT: usu N n

session /seʃᵊn/ **sessions** ◆◆◆◆◇

1 A **session** is a meeting of a court, parliament, or other official group. *...an emergency session of parliament... After two late night sessions, the Security Council has failed to reach agreement... The court was in session.* N-COUNT: also *in* N

2 A **session** is a period during which the meetings of a court, parliament, or other official group are regularly held. *The parliamentary session ends on October 4th... From September until December, Congress remained in session.* N-COUNT: also *in* N

3 A **session** of a particular activity is a period of that activity. *The two leaders emerged for a photo session. ...group therapy sessions.* N-COUNT: usu with supp =period

4 **Session** musicians are employed to play backing music in recording studios. *He established himself as a session musician. ...a session drummer.* ADJ: ADJ n

set 1 noun uses

set /set/ **sets** ◆◆◆◆◆

1 A **set** of things is a number of things that belong together or that are thought of as a group. *There must be one set of laws for the whole of the country... I might need a spare set of clothes... The computer repeats a set of calculations... Only she and Mr Cohen had complete sets of keys to the shop... The mattress and base are normally bought as a set. ...a chess set.* N-COUNT: oft N *of* n

2 In tennis, a **set** is one of the groups of six or more games that form part of a match. *Graf was leading 5-1 in the first set.* N-COUNT: oft supp N

3 In mathematics, a **set** is a group of mathematical quantities that have some characteristic in common. N-COUNT

4 A band's or musician's **set** is the group of songs or tunes that they perform at a concert. *The band continued with their set after a short break... He plays a solo acoustic set.* N-COUNT

5 You can refer to a group of people as a **set** if they meet together socially or have the same interests and lifestyle. *...what the press called 'The Chelsea Set' – upper-class rakes forced by lack of cash to fraternise with criminals.* • See also **jet set**. N-SING: supp N

6 The **set** for a play, film, or television show is the furniture and scenery that is on the stage when the play is being performed or in the studio where filming takes place. *From the first moment he got on the set, he wanted to be a director too... He achieved fame for his stage sets for the Folies Bergeres. ...a movie set. ...stars who behave badly on set.* N-COUNT: also *on/off* N

7 The **set** of someone's face or part of their body is the way that it is fixed in a particular expression or position, especially one that shows determination. *Matt looked at Hugh and saw the stubbornness in the set of his shoulders... Artist Richard Stone has captured in her eyes and the set of her face her steely determination.* N-SING: usu *the* N *of* n

8 A **set** is an appliance. For example, a television set is a television. *Children spend so much time in front of the television set... We got our first set—black and white—in 1963.* N-COUNT: oft supp N

set 2 verb and adjective uses

set /set/ **sets, setting.** The form **set** is used in the present tense and is the past tense and past participle of the verb. ◆◆◆◆◆

1 If you **set** something somewhere, you put it there, especially in a careful or deliberate way. *He took the case out of her hand and set it on the floor... When he set his glass down he spilled a little drink.* VERB =put V n prep V n with adv

2 If something is **set** in a particular place or position, it is in that place or position. *The castle is set in 25 acres of beautiful grounds... Quiberon is set on an eight-mile peninsula.* ADJ: v-link ADJ prep/adv =situated

3 If something is **set** into a surface, it is fixed there and does not stick out. *The man unlocked a gate set in a high wall and let me through... Set into an alcove under the side deck is a tiny wash basin.* ADJ: v-link ADJ prep/adv

4 You can use **set** to say that a person or thing causes something to be in a particular condition or situation. For example, if something **sets** someone free, it causes them to be free, and if someone **sets** something doing something, they cause it to do that thing. *Set the kitchen timer going... A phrase from the conference floor set my mind wandering... Dozens of people have been injured and many vehicles set on fire... Churchill immediately set into motion a daring plan.* VERB V n -ing *be* V-ed adj/adv V n with prep

5 When you **set** a clock or control, you adjust it to a particular point or level. *Set the volume as high as possible... I forgot to set my alarm and I overslept.* VERB V n adv/prep V n

6 If you **set** a date, price, goal, or level, you decide what it will be. *The conference chairman has set a deadline of noon tomorrow... A date will be set for a future meeting... The German government has set a tight budget for next year... The pass mark is set at 50 per cent.* VERB =fix V n *be* V-ed *at* n

7 If you **set** a certain value on something, you think it has that value. *She sets a high value on autonomy... If you set no value on being a woman yourself, how can you expect others to?* VERB V n *on* n/-ing

8 If you **set** something such as a record, an example, or a precedent, you create it for people to copy or to try to achieve. *Mr Hashimoto said Japan would not comply because it might set a dangerous international precedent... A new world marathon record of 2 hrs, 8 min, 5 sec, was set by Stephen Jones of Great Britain... They set the pace in cutting ozone-damaging emissions... If you are smoking in front of the children then you are setting them a bad example.* VERB =establish V n V n n

9 If someone **sets** you a task or aim or if you **set** yourself a task or aim, you have to do that task or achieve that aim. *I have to plan my academic work very rigidly and set myself clear objectives... We will train you first before we set you a task... The secret to happiness is to keep setting yourself new challenges.* VERB V n n

10 To **set** an examination or a question paper means to decide what questions will be asked in it. *He broke with the tradition of setting examinations in Latin.* VERB V n

11 You use **set** to describe something which is fixed and cannot be changed. *Investors can apply for a package of shares at a set price... A set period of fasting is supposed to bring us closer to godliness... There is a set menu from £24.00 for two courses with coffee.* ADJ: usu ADJ n =fixed

12 A **set** book must be studied by students taking a particular course. *One of the set books is Jane Austen's Emma.* ADJ: ADJ n

13 If a play, film, or story is **set** in a particular place or period of time, the events in it take place in that place or period. *The play is set in a small Midwestern town. ...a 1964 science fiction novel by Philip K Dick, set in 1994 in a colony of humans on Mars... The Hungarian director has completed her powerful Diary trilogy, set against the background of events in her country.* ADJ: v-link ADJ prep/adv

14 If you are **set** to do something, you are ready to do it or are likely to do it. If something is **set** to happen, it is about to happen or likely to happen. *Roberto Baggio is set to become one of the greatest players of all-time... The talks are set to continue through the week.* ADJ: v-link ADJ to-inf

15 If you are **set on** something, you are strongly determined to do or have it. If you are **set against** something, you are strongly determined not to do or have it. *She was set on going to an all-girls school... Margaret was always mischievous and set on her own individual course... France is also set against devaluation.* ADJ: v-link ADJ *on/against* n/-ing

16 If you **set** your face or jaw, you put on a fixed expression of determination. *Mr Bush bangs his fist* VERB V n

on the table and sets his jaw... He came insolently towards Mr. Won, his features set in a scowl.

17 When something such as jelly, melted plastic, or cement **sets**, it becomes firm or hard. *You can add ingredients to these desserts as they begin to set... Lower the heat and allow the omelet to set on the bottom... The material requires higher temperatures and pressures to set hard.* VERB V V adj

18 When the sun **sets**, it goes below the horizon. *They watched the sun set behind the distant dales... The scene was touched by the red glow of the setting sun.* VERB V V-ing

19 When someone **sets** a trap, they prepare it to catch someone or something. *He seemed to think I was setting some sort of trap for him... They dug trenches in their path and set booby traps.* VERB V n for n V n

20 When someone **sets** the table, they prepare it for a meal by putting plates and cutlery on it. *They are setting the table while Margarita prepares the boy's eggs, beans and tortillas.* VERB =lay V n

21 If someone **sets** a poem or a piece of writing **to** music, they write music for the words to be sung to. *He has attracted much interest by setting ancient religious texts to music.* VERB V n *to* n

22 See also **setting, set-to.**

23 If someone **sets the scene** or **sets the stage** for an event to take place, they make preparations so that it can take place. *The Democrat convention has set the scene for a ferocious election campaign this autumn... The company has been setting the stage recently for progress in the US.* PHRASES V inflects

24 If you say that someone **is set in** their **ways**, you are being critical of the fact that they have fixed habits and ideas which they will not easily change, even though they may be old-fashioned. V inflects PRAGMATICS

25 • to **set eyes on** something: see **eyes.** • to **set fire to** something: see **fire.** • to **set foot** somewhere: see **foot.** • to **set** your **heart on** something: see **heart.** • to **set sail**: see **sail.** • to **set great store by** or **on** something: see **store.** • to **set to work**: see **work.**

set against PHRASAL VERB

1 If one argument or fact **is set against** another, it is considered in relation to it. *These are relatively small points when set against her expertise on so many other issues... £1,000 was a considerable sum in those days and particularly when set against the maximum wage.* PRAGMATICS =compare with *be* V-ed P n Also V n P n

2 To **set** one person **against** another means to cause them to become enemies or rivals. *The case has set neighbour against neighbour in the village.* V n P n

set apart. If a characteristic **sets** you **apart** from other people, it makes you different from the others in a noticeable way. *What sets it apart from hundreds of similar small French towns is the huge factory... Li blends right into the crowd of teenagers. Only his accent sets him apart.* PHRASAL VERB V n P *from* n V n P

set aside PHRASAL VERB

1 If you **set** something **aside** for a special use or purpose, you keep it available for that use or purpose. *Some doctors advise setting aside a certain hour each day for worry... £130 million would be set aside for repairs to schools.* V P n (not pron) Also V n P

2 If you **set aside** a belief, principle, or feeling, you decide that you will not be influenced by it. *He urged the participants to set aside minor differences for the sake of achieving peace.* V P n (not pron) Also V n P

set back PHRASAL VERB

1 If something **sets** you **back** or **sets back** a project or scheme, it causes a delay. *It has set us back in so many respects that I'm not sure how long it will take for us to catch up... There will be a risk of public protest that could set back reforms.* V n P V P n (not pron)

2 If something **sets** you **back** a certain amount of money, it costs you that much money. *In 1981 dinner for two in New York would set you back £5.* =cost V n P amount

3 See also **setback.**

set down PHRASAL VERB

1 If a committee or organization **sets down** rules or guidelines for doing something, they decide what they should be and officially record them. *The Dublin Convention of June 1990 sets down rules for deciding which EC country should deal with an asylum request.* =lay down V P n (not pron) Also V n P

2 If you **set down** your thoughts or experiences, you write them all down. *Old Walter is setting down his memories of village life.* =write down V P n (not pron) Also V n P

set forth PHRASAL VERB

1 If you **set forth** a number of facts, beliefs, or arguments, you explain them in writing or speech in a clear, organized way; a formal expression. *Dr. Mesibov set forth the basis of his approach to teaching students.* =set out V P n (not pron)

2 If you **set forth**, you start a journey; a literary expression. *It was during the reign of Queen Isabella that Christopher Columbus set forth on his epic voyage of discovery.* =set out V P

set in. If something unpleasant **sets in**, it begins and seems likely to continue or develop. *Then disappointment sets in as they see the magic is no longer there... Winter is setting in and the population is facing food and fuel shortages.* PHRASAL VERB V P

set off PHRASAL VERB

1 When you **set off**, you start a journey. *Nichols set off for his remote farmhouse in Connecticut... The President's envoy set off on another diplomatic trip... I set off, full of optimism.* =set out V P prep/adv V P

2 If something **sets off** something such as an alarm or a bomb, it activates it so that the alarm rings or the bomb explodes. *Any escape, once it's detected, sets off the alarm... Someone set off a fire extinguisher... It could take months before evidence emerges on how the bomb was made, and who set it off.* =trigger V P n (not pron) V n P

3 If something **sets off** an event or a series of events, it causes it to start happening. *The arrival of the charity van set off a minor riot as villagers scrambled for a share of the aid... If he attended a party without the Princess, it set off a storm of speculation.* =trigger V P n (not pron) Also V n P

4 If something **sets** someone **off**, they start talking a lot because it makes them angry, or makes them remember something. *The smallest thing sets him off, and he can't stop talking about his childhood.* V n P Also V P n (not pron)

5 If one colour, flavour, or object **sets off** another, it makes it look more attractive, often by providing a contrast. *Blue suits you, sets off the colour of your hair. ...perfectly proportioned galleries that set off the contents to their best advantage.* V P n (not pron) Also V n P

set on. To **set** animals **on** someone means to cause the animals to attack them. *They brought the young men in and set the dogs on them.* PHRASAL VERB V n P n

set out PHRASAL VERB

1 When you **set out**, you start a journey. *When setting out on a long walk, always wear suitable boots.* =set off V P prep/adv Also V P

2 If you **set out** to do something, you start trying to do it. *He has achieved what he set out to do three years ago... We set out to find the truth behind the mystery.* V P to-inf

3 If you **set** things **out**, you arrange or display them somewhere. *Set out the cakes attractively, using lacy doilies.* =arrange V P n (not pron) Also V n P

4 If you **set out** a number of facts, beliefs, or arguments, you explain them in writing or speech in a clear, organized way. *He has written a letter to The Times setting out his views... You will be given a Back To Work plan which sets out how you can best help yourself.* =set forth V P n (not pron) V P wh Also V n P

set up PHRASAL VERB

1 If you **set** something **up**, you make the preparations that are necessary for it to start. *The two sides agreed to set up a commission to investigate claims. ...an organization which sets up meetings about issues of interest to women... Tell us when and why you started your business and how you went about setting it up.* V P n (not pron) V n P ♦ **setting up** *The British government announced the setting up of a special fund.* N-UNCOUNT: usu N *of* n

2 If you **set up** a temporary structure, you place it or build it somewhere. *They took to the streets, setting up roadblocks of burning tyres... 200 peace activists are planning to set up a peace camp at the border.* =erect V P n (not pron)

3 If you **set up** a device or piece of machinery, you make the preparations and adjustments that are necessary for it to start working. *Setting up the camera can be tricky... I set up the hardware so that they could work from home.* V P n (not pron) Also V n P

4 If you **set up** somewhere or **set** yourself **up** somewhere, you establish yourself in a new business or new area. *The Hong Kong-based Bank of East Asia is thinking of setting up in Canada... He worked as a dance instructor in London before setting himself up in Bucharest... Grandfather set them up in a liquor business.* V P prep/adv V pron-refl P prep/adv V n P prep/adv

5 If you **set up** home or **set up** shop, you buy a house or business of your own and start living or working there. *They married, and set up home in Ramsgate. ...20 businessmen hoping to set up shop in Japan.* V P n

6 If something **sets up** a phenomenon or process, it creates it or causes it to begin. *The secondary current sets up a magnetic field inside the tube... This can help you satisfy the craving without setting up problems later on.* V P n (not pron) Also V n P

7 If something **sets** you **up** for something, it puts you in a good condition or position to deal with it, for example by making you feel healthy and energetic. *I have my cornflakes and smell the fresh air and the grass and it sets me up for the day... The win sets us up perfectly for the match in Belgium.* V n P

8 If you **are set up** by someone, they make it seem that you have done something wrong when you have not; an informal use. *He claimed yesterday that he had been set up after drugs were discovered at his home... Maybe Angelo tried to set us up.* =frame be V-ed P V n P Also V P n (not pron)

9 See also **set-up**.

set upon. If you **are set upon** by people, they make a sudden and unexpected physical attack on you. *We were set upon by about twelve youths and I was kicked unconscious.* PHRASAL VERB usu passive be V-ed P

set-aside. In the European Union, **set-aside** is a scheme in which an area of land is taken out of production in order to reduce surpluses or maintain the price of a specific crop. *...set-aside land... A Brockhampton farm is paid £87 per acre for the 1,700 acres it has in set-aside.* N-UNCOUNT: oft N n

setback /setbæk/ **setbacks;** also spelled **set-back**. A **setback** is an event that delays your progress or reverses some of the progress that you have made. *The move represents a setback for the Middle East peace process... He has suffered a serious setback in his political career.* ◆◆◇◇◇ N-COUNT: oft N *for/in/to* n

set piece, set pieces; also spelled **set-piece**. ◆◇◇◇◇

1 A **set piece** is an occasion such as a battle or a move in a football match that is planned and carried out in an ordered way. *Guerrillas avoid fighting set-piece battles... The first three Oldham goals came from set-pieces.* N-COUNT: oft N n

2 A **set piece** is a part of a film, novel, or piece of music which has a strong dramatic effect and which is often not an essential part of the main story. *...the film's martial arts set pieces.* N-COUNT

sett /set/ **setts.** A **sett** is the place where a badger lives. N-COUNT

settee /setiː/ **settees.** A **settee** is a long comfortable seat with a back and arms, which two or more people can sit on. ◆◇◇◇◇ N-COUNT =couch, sofa

setter /setəʳ/ **setters.** A **setter** is a long-haired dog that can be trained to show hunters where birds and animals are. ◆◇◇◇◇ N-COUNT

setting /setɪŋ/ **settings** ◆◆◇◇◇

1 A particular **setting** is a particular place or type of surroundings where something is or takes place. *Rome is the perfect setting for romance... Perth was the setting for the SNP's conference this year... The house is in a lovely setting in the Malvern hills.* N-COUNT. usu with supp, oft N *for* n

2 A **setting** is one of the positions to which the controls of a device such as a cooker or heater can be adjusted. *You can boil the fish fillets on a high setting.* N-COUNT

3 A table **setting** is the complete set of equipment that one person needs to eat a meal, including knives, forks, spoons, and glasses. N-COUNT

settle /setəl/ **settles, settling, settled** ◆◆◆◆◇

1 If two people **settle** an argument or problem, or if someone or something **settles** it, they solve it by making a decision about who is right or about what to do. *They agreed to try to settle their dispute by negotiation... Both sides are looking for ways to settle their differences... Tomorrow's vote is unlikely to settle the question of who will replace their leader..* VERB V n

2 If people **settle** a legal dispute or if they **settle**, they agree to end the dispute without going to a court of law, for example by paying some money or by apologizing. *In an attempt to settle the case, Molken has agreed to pay restitution... She got much less than she would have done if she had settled out of court... His company settled with the American authorities by paying a $200 million fine.* VERB V n V V *with* n

3 If you **settle** a bill or debt, you pay the amount that you owe. *I settled the bill for my coffee and his two glasses of wine... They settled with Colin at the end of the evening.* VERB V n V *with* n

4 If something **is settled**, it has all been decided and arranged. *As far as we're concerned, the matter is settled... That's settled then. We'll exchange addresses tonight.* VB: usu passive be V-ed

5 To **settle** money **on** someone means to formally give it to them, for example in a will. *She offered to settle a legacy on Katharine.* VERB V n *on* n

6 When people **settle** a place or in a place, or when a government **settles** them there, they start living there permanently. *Refugees settling in Britain suffer from a number of problems... He visited Paris and eventually settled there... This was one of the first areas to be settled by Europeans... Thirty-thousand-million dollars is needed to settle the immigrants.* V-ERG V prep/adv V n Also V n prep/adv, V

7 If you **settle** yourself somewhere or **settle** somewhere, you sit down or make yourself comfortable. *Albert settled himself on the sofa... Jessica settled into her chair with a small sigh of relief.* VERB V pron-refl prep/adv V prep/adv

8 If something **settles** or if you **settle** it, it sinks slowly down and becomes still. *A black dust settled on the walls... Once its impurities had settled, the oil could be graded... Tap each one firmly on your work surface to settle the mixture.* V-ERG V prep/adv V V n

9 If your eyes **settle** on something, you stop looking around and look at that thing for some time. *The man let his eyes settle upon Cross's face.* VERB =rest V *on/upon* n

10 When birds or insects **settle on** something, they land on it from above. *Moths flew in front of it, eventually settling on the rough painted metal.* VERB =light V *on* n

11 See also **settled**.

12 • **when the dust settles**: see **dust**. • **to settle a score**: see **score**.

settle down PHRASAL VERB

1 When someone **settles down**, they start living a quiet life in one place, especially when they get married or buy a house. *One day I'll want to settle down and have a family... Before she settled down in Portugal, she had run her own antiques shop in London.* V P V P prep/adv

2 If a situation or a person that has been going through a lot of problems or changes **settles down**, they become calm. *It'd be fun, after the situation in Europe settles down, to take a trip over to France... We saw the therapist four times, and the children have now settled down.* V P

3 If you **settle down** to do something or to something, you prepare to do it and concentrate on it. *He got his coffee, came back and settled down to listen... They settled down to some serious work.* V P to-inf V P *to* n

4 If you **settle down** for the night, you get ready to lie down and sleep. *They put up their tents and settled down for the night.* V P

settle for. If you **settle for** something, you choose or accept it, especially when it is not what you really want but there is nothing else available. *Virginia was a perfectionist. She was just not prepared to settle for anything mediocre... England will have to settle for third or fourth place.* PHRASAL VERB V P n

settle in. If you **settle in**, you become used to living in a new place, doing a new job, or going to a new school. *I enjoyed King Edward's School enormously once I'd settled in.* PHRASAL VERB V P

settle on. If you **settle on** a particular thing, you choose it after considering other possible choices. PHRASAL VERB =decide on V P n

I finally settled on a Mercedes estate. It's the ideal car for me.
settle up. When you **settle up**, you pay a bill or a debt. *When we approached the till to settle up, he reduced our bill by 50 per cent.* PHRASAL VERB V P

settled /setᵊld/ ◆◆◇◇◇
1 If you have a **settled** way of life, you stay in one place, in one job, or with one person, rather than moving around or changing. *He decided to lead a more settled life with his partner... His house was the only settled home I had as a child.* ADJ-GRADED: usu ADJ n =steady
2 A **settled** situation or system stays the same all the time. *Cats are creatures of habit – they seem to appreciate a settled routine... There has been a period of settled weather.* ADJ-GRADED: usu ADJ n
3 If you feel **settled**, you have been living or working in a place long enough to feel comfortable there. *After a few years of being a diplomat, she still didn't feel settled.* ADJ-GRADED: v-link ADJ

settlement /setᵊlmənt/ **settlements** ◆◆◆◆◇
1 A **settlement** is an official agreement between two sides who were involved in a conflict or argument. *Our objective must be to secure a peace settlement... They are not optimistic about a settlement of the eleven year conflict.* N-COUNT: usu with supp =agreement
2 A **settlement** is an agreement to end a disagreement or dispute without going to a court of law, for example by offering someone money. *She accepted an out-of-court settlement of £4,000. ...a libel settlement.* N-COUNT: usu with supp
3 The **settlement** of a debt is the act of paying back money that you owe. *...ways to delay the settlement of debts.* N-UNCOUNT: usu N of n
4 A **settlement** is a place where people have come to live and have built homes. *The village is a settlement of just fifty houses. ...a Muslim settlement.* N-COUNT: usu with supp
5 The **settlement of** a group of people is the process in which they settle in a place where people from their country or ethnic group have never lived before. *...the settlement of immigrants in the occupied territories.* N-UNCOUNT: N of n

settler /setələʳ/ **settlers. Settlers** are people who go to live in a new country. *The first German village in south-western Siberia was founded a century ago by settlers from the Volga region.* ◆◆◇◇◇ N-COUNT

set-to, set-tos. A **set-to** is a dispute or fight; an informal word. *This was the subject of a bit of a set-to between Smith and his record company.* ◆◆◆◇◇ N-COUNT

set-up, set-ups; also spelled **setup.** ◆◆◆◆◇
1 A particular **set-up** is a particular system or way of organizing something; an informal use. *It appears to be an idyllic domestic set-up... I gradually got rather disillusioned with the whole setup of the university.* N-COUNT
2 If you describe a situation as a **set-up**, you mean that people have planned it in order to deceive you or to make it look as if you have done something wrong; an informal use. *He was asked to pick somebody up and bring them to a party, not realizing it was a setup.* N-COUNT

seven /sevᵊn/ **sevens. Seven** is the number 7. *Sarah and Ella have been friends for seven years.* ◆◆◆◆◆ NUM

seventeen /sevᵊntiːn/ **seventeens. Seventeen** is the number 17. *Jenny is seventeen years old.* ◆◆◆◆◆ NUM

seventeenth /sevᵊntiːnθ/ **seventeenths.** ◆◆◆◆◇
1 The **seventeenth** item in a series is the one that you count as number seventeen. *She gave birth to Annabel just after her seventeenth birthday.* ORD
2 A **seventeenth** is one of seventeen equal parts of something. FRACTION

seventh /sevᵊnθ/ **sevenths** ◆◆◆◆◇
1 The **seventh** item in a series is the one that you count as number seven. *I was the seventh child in the family. There were 11 of us altogether.* ORD
2 A **seventh** is one of seven equal parts of something. *A million people died, a seventh of the population.* FRACTION

Seventh Day Adventist /sevᵊnθ deɪ ædventɪst/ **Seventh Day Adventists**
1 **Seventh Day Adventist** churches are churches that believe that Jesus Christ will return very soon, and that celebrate the Sabbath on Saturday. ADJ: ADJ n
2 A **Seventh Day Adventist** is a member of the Seventh Day Adventist church. N-COUNT

seventh heaven. If you say that you are **in seventh heaven**, you mean that you are in a state of complete happiness; an informal expression. *After I was given my first camera I was in seventh heaven.* N-UNCOUNT: in N

seventieth /sevᵊntiəθ/ **seventieths.** ◆◆◆◆◇
1 The **seventieth** item in a series is the one that you count as number seventy. *...the seventieth anniversary of the discovery of Tutankhamun's tomb.* ORD
2 A **seventieth** is one of seventy equal parts of something. FRACTION

seventy /sevᵊnti/ **seventies.** ◆◆◆◆◆
1 **Seventy** is the number 70. *Seventy people were killed.* NUM
2 When you talk about the **seventies**, you are referring to numbers between 70 and 79. For example, if you are **in your seventies**, you are aged between 70 and 79. If the temperature is **in the seventies**, the temperature is between 70 and 79. *I thought it was a long way to go for two people in their seventies, but Sylvia loved the idea.* N-PLURAL
3 **The seventies** is the decade between 1970 and 1979. *In the late Seventies, things had to be new, modern, revolutionary.* N-PLURAL: the N

sever /sevəʳ/ **severs, severing, severed** ◆◇◇◇◇
1 To **sever** something means to cut completely through it or to cut it completely off. *Richardson severed his right foot in a motorbike accident. ...oil still gushing from a severed fuel line.* VERB V n V-ed
2 If you **sever** a relationship or connection that you have with someone, you end it suddenly and completely. *She severed her ties with England... He was able to sever all emotional bonds to his family.* VERB V n

several /sevrəl/. **Several** is used to refer to an imprecise number of people or things that is not large but is greater than two. *I had lived two doors away from this family for several years... Several blue plastic boxes under the window were filled with record albums... Several hundred students gathered on campus to sing protest songs and hear speeches.* ► Also a quantifier. *Supporters are urging him to take action against the demonstrators, several of whom are members of the parliament... According to several of their friends, their 25-year marriage has suffered some difficulties.* ► Also a pronoun. *No one drug will suit or work for everyone and sometimes several may have to be tried... Ben's case is not unique but one of several I have come up against during the past few years.* ◆◆◆◆◆ DET: DET pl-n QUANT: QUANT of pl-n PRON

severance /sevərəns/
1 **Severance** from a person or group, or the severance of a connection, involves the ending of a relationship or connection; a formal word. *...his bitter sense of severance from his family. ...the complete severance of diplomatic relations.* N-UNCOUNT
2 **Severance** pay is money that a firm pays its employees as compensation when it has to stop employing them. *We were offered 13 weeks' severance pay.* ADJ: ADJ n

severe /sɪvɪəʳ/ **severer, severest** ◆◆◆◆◇
1 You use **severe** to indicate that something bad or undesirable is great or intense. *...a business with severe cash flow problems... I suffered from severe bouts of depression... Steve passed out on the floor and woke up blinded and in severe pain... Shortages of professional staff are very severe in some places.* ADJ-GRADED
♦ **severely** *The UN wants to send food aid to 10 countries in Africa severely affected by the drought... An aircraft overshot the runway and was severely damaged. ...the severely depressed construction industry.* ADV-GRADED: usu ADV with v, also ADV adj ♦ **severity** /sɪverɪti/ *Several drugs are used to lessen the severity of the symptoms.* N-UNCOUNT: usu with supp
2 **Severe** punishments or actions are harsh and show an unforgiving attitude. *This was a dreadful crime and a severe sentence is necessary... Before she could reply, my mother launched into a severe reprimand.* ADJ-GRADED =harsh ♦ **severely** *...a campaign to try to change the law to punish dangerous drivers more severely.* ADV-GRADED: ADV with v
♦ **severity** *The Bishop said he was sickened by the* N-UNCOUNT:

severity of the sentence... Believers were treated with the same severity as the Christians had been a few years earlier. usu with supp

3 If you describe the appearance of someone or something as **severe**, you do not like its plain appearance and lack of decoration. *...wearing her felt hats and severe grey suits... The cushions add a touch of colour in a room that might otherwise look severe.* ♦ **severity** *When women started working in offices, they opted for severity in dress in order to imply sobriety.* ADJ-GRADED PRAGMATICS =austere; N-UNCOUNT: usu with supp =austerity

sew /soʊ/ **sews, sewing, sewed, sewn** ◆◇◇◇◇

1 When you **sew** something such as clothes, you make them or repair them by joining pieces of cloth together by passing thread through them with a needle. *She sewed the dresses on the sewing machine... Anyone can sew on a button, including you... Mrs Roberts was a dressmaker, and she taught her daughter to sew.* VERB; V n; V n with *on*; V; Also V n prep

2 When something such as a hand or finger **is sewn** back by a doctor, it is joined with the patient's body using a needle and thread. *The hand was preserved in ice by neighbours and sewn back on in hospital... Surgeons at Odstock Hospital, Wilts, sewed the thumb on.* ● See also **sewing.** VERB; *be* V-ed adv; V n with adv

sew up PHRASAL VERB

1 If you **sew up** pieces of cloth or tears in cloth or skin, you join them together using a needle and thread. *Next day, Miss Stone decided to sew up the rip... This material was then put into cotton bags which were weighed and then sewn up.* V P n (not pron); Also V n P

2 If someone **sews up** something such as a business deal, an election, or a game, they make sure that they will get the result they want; an informal use. *If they didn't move fast, Johnson could sew this deal up within days... The Italians think they've got it all sewn up.* V n P; Also V P n (not pron)

sewage /suːɪdʒ/. **Sewage** is waste matter such as faeces or dirty water from homes and factories, which flows away through sewers. *...the MPs' call for more treatment of raw sewage.* ◆◇◇◇◇ N-UNCOUNT

sewer /suːəʳ/ **sewers.** A **sewer** is a large underground channel that carries waste matter and rain water away, usually to a place where it is treated and made harmless. *...the city's sewer system. ...open sewers.* ◆◇◇◇◇ N-COUNT

sewerage /suːərɪdʒ/. **Sewerage** is the system by which waste matter is carried away in sewers and made harmless. *The town has already put in a proper sewerage system. ...without access to any services such as water or sewerage.* N-UNCOUNT: usu N n

sewing /soʊɪŋ/ ◆◇◇◇◇

1 Sewing is the activity of making or mending clothes or other things using a needle and thread. *Her mother had always done all the sewing.* N-UNCOUNT

2 Sewing is clothes or other things that are being sewn. *We all got out our own sewing and sat in front of the log fire.* N-UNCOUNT

sewing machine, sewing machines. A **sewing machine** is a machine that you use for sewing. ◆◇◇◇◇ N-COUNT

sewn /soʊn/. **Sewn** is the past participle of **sew.**

sex /seks/ **sexes, sexing, sexed** ◆◆◆◆◇

1 The two **sexes** are the two groups, male and female, into which people and animals are divided according to the function they have in producing young. *She found it hard to form relationships with the opposite sex. ...an entertainment star who appeals to all ages and both sexes. ...differences between the sexes.* ● See also **fair sex.** N-COUNT: usu with supp

2 The **sex** of a person or animal is their characteristic of being either male or female. *She continually failed to gain promotion because of her sex... The new technique has been used to identify the sex of foetuses. ...sex discrimination.* N-COUNT: oft with poss =gender

3 Sex is the physical activity by which people can produce young. *He was very open in his attitudes about sex... The entire film revolves around drugs, sex and violence... We have a very active sex life.* N-UNCOUNT

4 If an animal **is sexed**, someone finds out whether it is male or female. *The birds must be weighed, sexed and tagged.* VB: usu passive; *be* V-ed

5 If two people **have sex**, they perform the act of sex. *Have you ever thought about having sex with someone other than your husband?* PHR-RECIP: V inflects, pl-n PHR, PHR *with* n

sex appeal. Someone's **sex appeal** is their sexual attractiveness. *She still has the energy and sex appeal of a woman less than half her age.* ◆◇◇◇◇ N-UNCOUNT

-sexed /-sekst/. **-sexed** is used after adverbs such as 'over' and 'under' to form adjectives which indicate that someone wants to have sex too often or not often enough. *My husband has always been a bit over-sexed. ...a highly sexed woman who takes complete control in the bedroom.* COMB in ADJ-GRADED

sex education. **Sex education** is education in schools on the subject of sexual activity and sexual relationships. ◆◇◇◇◇ N-UNCOUNT

sex goddess, sex goddesses. If you refer to a woman, especially a film star, as a **sex goddess**, you mean that many people consider her to be sexually attractive; used mainly in journalism. *Raquel Welch was at the height of her popularity as a sex goddess.* N-COUNT

sexism /seksɪzəm/. **Sexism** is the belief that the members of one sex, usually women, are less intelligent or less capable than those of the other sex and need not be treated equally. It is also the behaviour which is the result of this belief. *Groups like ours are committed to eradicating homophobia, racism and sexism.* ◆◇◇◇◇ N-UNCOUNT

sexist /seksɪst/ **sexists.** If you describe people, things, or behaviour as **sexist**, you mean that they are influenced by the belief that the members of one sex, usually women, are less intelligent or less capable than those of the other sex and need not be treated equally; used showing disapproval. *Old-fashioned sexist attitudes are still common... I think the whole thing is very unfair and if I may say so I think it's very sexist... I am not being sexist.* ► A **sexist** is someone with sexist views or behaviour. ◆◇◇◇◇ ADJ-GRADED PRAGMATICS; N-COUNT

sexless /sekslәs/. If you describe a person as **sexless**, you mean that they have no sexual feelings or that they are not sexually active. A **sexless** relationship does not involve sex. *Malcolm is a brilliant but frustrated surgeon who is married to a neurotic and sexless woman.* ADJ-GRADED

sex object, sex objects. If someone is described as a **sex object**, he or she is considered only in terms of their physical attractiveness and not their character or abilities. *Now she had a boyfriend who cared for her as a whole person rather than just a sex object.* N-COUNT

sexologist /seksɒlәdʒɪst/ **sexologists.** A **sexologist** is a person who studies sexual relationships and gives advice or makes reports. *...Alfred Kinsey, the pioneering sexologist.* N-COUNT

sex shop, sex shops. A **sex shop** is a shop that sells products that are associated with sexual pleasure, for example magazines, videos, and special clothing or equipment. N-COUNT

sex symbol, sex symbols. A **sex symbol** is a famous person, especially an actor or a singer, who is considered by many people to be sexually attractive. *...Hollywood sex symbols of the Forties.* N-COUNT

sextant /sekstәnt/ **sextants.** A **sextant** is an instrument used for measuring angles, for example between the sun and the horizon, so that the position of a ship or aeroplane can be calculated. N-COUNT

sextet /sekstet/ **sextets**

1 A **sextet** is a group of six musicians or singers who play or sing together. *...the Paul Rogers Sextet.* N-COUNT

2 A **sextet** is a piece of music written for six performers. N-COUNT

sexual /sekʃuәl/ ◆◆◆◆◇

1 Sexual feelings or activities are connected with the act of sex or with people's desire for sex. *This was the first sexual relationship I had had... Men's sexual fantasies often have little to do with their sexual desire. ...the horror of sexual abuse.* ♦ **sexually** *...sexually transmitted diseases... How many kids in this school are sexually active?* ADJ: usu ADJ n; ADV: ADV with v, ADV adj

2 Sexual means relating to the differences between ADJ:

male and female people. *Womens groups denounced sexual discrimination. ...sexual and racial equal opportunities.* ♦ **sexually** *If you're sexually harassed, you ought to do something about it.* usu ADJ n / ADV: ADV with v

3 **Sexual** means relating to the differences between heterosexuals and homosexuals. *...discrimination based on sexual orientation. ...couples of all sexual persuasions.* ADJ: usu ADJ n

4 **Sexual** means relating to the biological process by which people and animals produce young. *Girls generally reach sexual maturity two years earlier than boys. ...sexual reproduction.* ♦ **sexually** *The first organisms that reproduced sexually were free-floating plankton.* ADJ: usu ADJ n / ADV: ADV with v, ADV adj

sexual harassment. **Sexual harassment** is repeated unwelcome sexual comments, looks, or physical contact, usually by men against women. This usually occurs in the workplace or in public places. *Sexual harassment of women workers by their bosses is believed to be widespread.* ◆◇◇◇◇ N-UNCOUNT

sexual intercourse. **Sexual intercourse** is the physical act of sex between two people; a formal expression. ◆◇◇◇◇ N-UNCOUNT

sexuality /sekʃuælɪti/ ◆◆◇◇◇

1 A person's **sexuality** is their sexual feelings. *In Britain, the growing discussion of women's sexuality raised its own disquiet.* N-UNCOUNT: oft poss N

2 You can refer to a person's **sexuality** when you are talking about whether they are heterosexual, homosexual, or bisexual. *He believes he has been discriminated against because of his sexuality.* N-UNCOUNT

sexy /seksi/ **sexier, sexiest.** You can describe people and things as **sexy** if you think they are sexually exciting or sexually attractive. *She was one of the sexiest women I had seen... It was a wonderful voice which women found incredibly sexy. ...sexy underwear.* ♦ **sexily** *He says I don't dress sexily enough.* ♦ **sexiness** *Our image of sexiness is changing.* ◆◆◇◇◇ ADJ-GRADED =raunchy / ADV-GRADED: ADV with v, ADV adj / N-UNCOUNT

SF /es ef/. **SF** is the same as **science fiction**. *Arthur C Clarke likes to quote his friend and fellow SF writer Ray Bradbury.* N-UNCOUNT: usu N n

Sgt. **Sgt** is the written abbreviation for 'Sergeant' when it is used as a title. *...Sgt Johnston.* N-TITLE

sh /ʃ/; also spelled **shh**. You can say **'Sh!'** to tell someone to be quiet; an informal word. *Sh! You want to listen or don't you?* ◆◇◇◇◇ CONVENTION PRAGMATICS =shush

shabby /ʃæbi/ **shabbier, shabbiest** ◆◇◇◇◇

1 **Shabby** things or places look old and in bad condition. *His clothes were old and shabby... He walked past her into a tiny, shabby room. ...one of the shabbiest and poorest areas of London.* ♦ **shabbily** /ʃæbɪli/ *...a shabbily dressed young man.* ♦ **shabbiness** *...the shabbiness of the building.* ADJ-GRADED =scruffy / ADV-GRADED: usu ADV with v / N-UNCOUNT

2 A person who is **shabby** is wearing old, worn clothes. *...a shabby, tall man with dark eyes.* ADJ-GRADED =scruffy

3 If you describe someone's behaviour as **shabby**, you think they behave in an unfair or unacceptable way. *It was hard to say why the man deserved such shabby treatment... I knew it was shabby of me, but I couldn't help feeling slightly disappointed.* ♦ **shabbily** *I feel I behaved shabbily.* ADJ-GRADED PRAGMATICS / ADV-GRADED

shack /ʃæk/ **shacks, shacking, shacked.** A **shack** is an old or flimsy hut built from tin, wood, or other materials. ◆◇◇◇◇ N-COUNT

shack up. If you say that someone **has shacked up** with someone else or that two people **have shacked up** together, you disapprove of the fact that they have started living together as lovers; an informal expression. *...the deserters who had shacked up with local women... The Government was keen for people to get married rather than shack up... It turned out she was shacked up with a lawyer in New York.* PHRASAL VERB RECIP PRAGMATICS / V P *with* n / pl-n V P / *be* V-ed P

shackle /ʃækᵊl/ **shackles, shackling, shackled** ◆◇◇◇◇

1 If you **are shackled** by something, it prevents you from doing what you want to do; a formal use. *The trade unions are shackled by the law. ...people who find themselves shackled to a high-stress job.* VB: usu passive =hamper *be* V-ed *by/to* n

2 If you throw off the **shackles** of something, you reject it or free yourself from it because it was preventing you from doing what you wanted to do; a literary use. *He had not yet thrown off the intellectual shackles of Marxism.* N-PLURAL: with supp

3 **Shackles** are two metal rings joined by a chain which are fastened around someone's wrists or ankles in order to prevent them from moving or escaping. *He unbolted the shackles on Billy's hands.* N-PLURAL

4 To **shackle** someone means to put shackles on them. *...the chains that were shackling his legs... She was shackled to a wall.* VERB V n / V-ed *to* n

shade /ʃeɪd/ **shades, shading, shaded** ◆◆◆◇◇

1 A **shade** of a particular colour is any of its different forms. For example, emerald green and olive green are shades of green. You often use **shade** when you are referring to the colour of a decorating product or cosmetic. *In the mornings the sky appeared a heavy shade of mottled gray... The walls were painted in two shades of green. ...new eyeshadows in a choice of 80 shades.* N-COUNT: oft N *of* n, *in* N

2 **Shade** is an area of darkness under or next to an object such as a tree, where sunlight does not reach. *Temperatures in the shade can reach forty-eight degrees celsius at this time of year... Alexis walked up the coast, and resumed his reading in the shade of an overhanging cliff. ...exotic trees provide welcome shade.* N-UNCOUNT: oft *in the* N

3 If you say that a place or person **is shaded** by objects such as trees, you mean that the place or person cannot be reached, harmed, or bothered by strong sunlight because those objects are in the way. *...a health resort whose beaches are shaded by palm trees... Most plants prefer to be lightly shaded from direct, hot sunlight... Umbrellas shade outdoor cafes along winding cobblestone streets.* ♦ **shaded** *These plants will grow happily in a sunny or partially shaded spot.* VERB *be* V-ed / *be* V-ed *from* n / V n / ADJ-GRADED: oft adv ADJ

4 If you **shade** your eyes, you put your hand or an object partly in front of your face in order to prevent a bright light from shining into your eyes. *You can't look directly into it; you've got to shade your eyes or close them altogether... I had to stop at the traffic lights and put down the sun visor to shade my eyes from the light.* VERB =shield / V n / V n *from* n

5 **Shade** is darkness or shadows as they are shown in a picture. *...Rembrandt's skilful use of light and shade to create the atmosphere of movement.* N-UNCOUNT ≠light

6 The **shades** of something abstract are its many, slightly different forms. *...the capacity to convey subtle shades of meaning. ...literally dozens of newspapers of every shade of opinion.* N-COUNT: usu pl, N *of* n

7 If something **shades** into something else, there is no clear division between the two things, so that you cannot tell where or when the first thing ends and the second thing begins. *As the dusk shaded into night, we drove slowly through narrow alleys... The tail feathers are dark blue at their bases, shading to pale blue at their tips.* VERB / V *into* n / V *to* n

8 **Shades** are sunglasses; an informal use. N-PLURAL

9 A **shade** is the same as a **lampshade**. N-COUNT

10 In American English, a **shade** is a piece of stiff cloth or heavy paper that you can pull down over a window in order to prevent sunlight from coming into a room. The usual British word is **blind**. *Nancy left the shades down and the lights off.* N-COUNT =blind

11 The **shade** of a dead person is their spirit, which is thought to be still alive in some way and in contact with the real world; a literary use. *His writing benefits from the shade of Lincoln hovering over his shoulder.* N-COUNT: usu N *of* n

12 See also **shaded, shading**.

13 If you say that something is, for example, **a shade** unusual or **a shade** disappointing, you mean that it is slightly unusual or disappointing. *The first two goals were a shade fortunate... He found her charming, but perhaps just a shade too ingenuous for him... The South is now only a shade behind the rest of the affluent United States.* PHRASES PHR adj/adv/prep =a little

14 If you say that there is **light and shade** in something such as a performance, you mean you like it because it has a lot of variation or contrast; used in written English. *...a faltering, artless voice that is* PRAGMATICS

pleasant enough, if rather lacking in light and shade.

15 If someone or something **puts** someone or something else **in the shade**, they are so impressive that they make the other person or thing seem unimportant by comparison. *...a run that put every other hurdler's performance in the shade.* V inflects

shaded /ʃeɪdɪd/. A **shaded** area on something such as a map is one that is coloured darker than the surrounding areas, so that it can be distinguished from them. ◆◇◇◇◇ ADJ

-shaded /-ʃeɪdɪd/. **-shaded** combines with nouns to form adjectives which indicate that sunlight is prevented from reaching a certain place by the thing mentioned. *She turned the car into the winding, tree-shaded driveway of the mansion.* COMB: COMB in ADJ

shading /ʃeɪdɪŋ/ **shadings**

1 **Shading** is material such as nets or dark paint that provide shade, especially for plants. *The conservatory will get very hot in summer unless shading is used.* N-UNCOUNT

2 Dark areas or patches in a picture or on an object can be referred to as **shading**. *Trees are depicted with blocks of flat colour or shading.* N-UNCOUNT

3 You can refer to very small changes or differences between things as **shading** or **shadings**. *Their language is particularly difficult to learn because of its subtle shading of tone and emphasis. ...the nuances and intricate shadings of diplomatic messages.* N-UNCOUNT: also N in pl, with supp

4 See also **shade**.

shadow /ʃædoʊ/ **shadows, shadowing, shadowed** ◆◆◆◇◇

1 A **shadow** is a dark shape on a surface that is made when something stands between a light and the surface. *An oak tree cast its shadow over a tiny round pool... Nothing would grow in the shadow of the grey wall... All he could see was his shadow.* N-COUNT

2 **Shadow** is darkness in a place caused by something preventing light from reaching it. *Most of the lake was in shadow. ...a combination of light and shadow.* N-UNCOUNT: oft *in* N =shade

3 If something **shadows** a thing or place, it covers it with a shadow. *The hood shadowed her face.* VERB V n

4 If someone **shadows** you, they follow you very closely wherever you go. *Soviet spies had been shadowing him for some time.* VERB =follow V n

5 A British Member of Parliament who is a member of the **shadow** cabinet or who is a **shadow** cabinet minister belongs to the main opposition party and takes a special interest in matters which are the responsibility of a particular government minister. *...the shadow chancellor.* ► Also a noun. *Clarke swung at his shadow the accusation that he was 'a tabloid politician'.* ADJ: ADJ n; N-COUNT: poss N

6 If you say that something is true without **a shadow of a doubt** or without **a shadow of doubt**, you are emphasizing that there is no doubt at all that it is true. *It was without a shadow of a doubt the best we've played.* PHRASES usu with brd-neg PRAGMATICS

7 If you live **in the shadow of** someone or **in** their **shadow**, their achievements and abilities are so great that you are not noticed or valued. *He has always lived in the shadow of his brother.* N inflects

8 If you say that someone is **a shadow of** their **former self**, you mean that they are much less strong or capable than they used to be. *Johnson returned to the track after his ban but was a shadow of his former self.* Ns inflect

shadowy /ʃædoʊi/ ◆◇◇◇◇

1 A **shadowy** place is dark or full of shadows. *I watched him from a shadowy corner. ...a broad, shadowy room.* ADJ-GRADED: usu ADJ n

2 A **shadowy** figure or shape is someone or something that you can hardly see because they are in a dark or misty place. *...a tall, shadowy figure silhouetted against the pale wall. ...the shadowy shape of a big barge loaded with logs.* ADJ-GRADED: ADJ n

3 You describe activities and people as **shadowy** when very little is known about them. *...the shadowy world of spies. ...a shadowy group calling itself the People's Army.* ADJ =mysterious

shady /ʃeɪdi/ **shadier, shadiest** ◆◇◇◇◇

1 You can describe a place as **shady** when you like the fact that it is sheltered from bright sunlight, for example by trees or buildings. *After flowering, place the pot in a shady spot in the garden... The rooms are admirably cool and shady after the hot brown monotony of the countryside.* ADJ-GRADED

2 **Shady** trees provide a lot of shade. *Clara had been reading in a lounge chair under a shady tree.* ADJ: usu ADJ n

3 You can describe activities as **shady** when you think that they might be dishonest or illegal. You can also use **shady** to describe people who are involved in such activities. *In the 1980s, the company was notorious for shady deals... Joseph watched a shady-looking bunch playing cards aboard a Mississippi steamer.* ADJ-GRADED: usu ADJ n

shaft /ʃɑːft, ʃæft/ **shafts** ◆◆◇◇◇

1 A **shaft** is a long vertical passage, for example for a lift. *He was found dead at the bottom of a lift shaft. ...old mine shafts.* N-COUNT: oft n N

2 In a machine, a **shaft** is a rod that turns round continually in order to transfer movement in the machine. *...a drive shaft. ...the propeller shaft.* N-COUNT: usu n N

3 A **shaft** is a long thin piece of wood or metal that forms part of a spear, axe, golf club, or other object. *...golf clubs with steel shafts.* N-COUNT

4 A **shaft** of light is a beam of light, for example sunlight shining through an opening. *A brilliant shaft of sunlight burst through the doorway.* N-COUNT: usu N *of* n

shag /ʃæg/ **shags, shagging, shagged** ◆◇◇◇◇

1 A **shag** is a black seabird with a yellow beak, found mainly in Europe and North Africa. N-COUNT =cormorant

2 In informal British English, if someone **shags** another person, or if two people **shag**, they have sex together; a use which some people find offensive. ► Also a noun. *...a spy movie with car chases, a murder, a shag and a happy ending.* VERB: V n, V; N-COUNT: usu sing

shaggy /ʃægi/ **shaggier, shaggiest. Shaggy** hair or fur is long and untidy. *Tim, who still has longish, shaggy hair, used to turn up at official dinners in jeans and T-shirt.* ◆◇◇◇◇ ADJ-GRADED

Shah /ʃɑː/ **Shahs.** In former times, **the Shah** of Iran was its ruler. ◆◇◇◇◇ N-PROPER: *the* N

shaikh /ʃeɪk/ **shaikhs.** See **sheikh**.

shake /ʃeɪk/ **shakes, shaking, shook, shaken;** the form **shook** can be used as the past participle for meaning 2 of the phrasal verb **shake up**. ◆◆◆◆◇

1 If you **shake** something, you hold it and move it quickly backwards and forwards or up and down. You can also **shake** a person, for example, because you are angry with them or because you want them to wake up. *The nurse took the thermometer, shook it, and put it under my armpit... Shake the rugs well and hang them for a few hours before replacing on the floor... I've even seen her shake Zara when she's been naughty.* ► Also a noun. *She picked up the Cellophane bag of salad and gave it an angry shake.* VERB V n; N-COUNT: usu sing

2 If you **shake** yourself or your body, you make a lot of quick, small, repeated movements without moving from the place where you are. *As soon as he got inside, the dog shook himself... Shake your right hand downwards until you feel your fingers getting hot with blood.* ► Also a noun. *Take some slow, deep breaths and give your body a bit of a shake.* VERB V pron-refl V n; N-COUNT

3 If you **shake** your head, you turn it from side to side in order to say 'no' or to show disbelief or sadness. *'Anything else?' Colum asked. Kathryn shook her head wearily... We were amazed, shocked, dumbfounded, shaking our heads in disbelief.* ► Also a noun. *'The elm trees are all dying,' said Palmer, with a sad shake of his head.* VERB V n; N-COUNT

4 If you **are shaking**, or a part of your body **is shaking**, you are making quick, small movements that you cannot control, for example because you are cold or afraid. *He roared with laughter, shaking in his chair... My hand shook so much that I could hardly hold the microphone... I stood there, crying and shaking with fear.* VERB V V *with* n

5 If you have **the shakes**, your body is shaking uncontrollably because you are afraid or ill, or because you have drunk too much alcohol; an N-PLURAL: *the* N

informal use. *Another man constantly chain-smoked and seemed to have the shakes.*

6 If you **shake** your fist or an object such as a stick at someone, you wave it in the air in front of them because you are angry with them. *The colonel rushed up to Earle, and shaking his gun at him exclaimed in a voice quivering with passion: 'Curse you!'... The protesters burst through police lines into the cathedral square, shaking clenched fists.*
VERB — V n at n; V n

7 If a force **shakes** something, or if something **shakes**, it moves from side to side or up and down with quick, small, but sometimes violent movements. *...an explosion that shook buildings several kilometers away... The hiccups may shake your baby's body from head to foot... The breeze grew in strength, the flags shook, plastic bunting creaked.*
V-ERG — V n; V

8 To **shake** something into a certain place or state means to bring it into that place or state by moving it quickly up and down or from side to side. *Small insects can be collected from nettle beds by shaking them into an upturned umbrella and tipping the contents into a jam jar... She frees her mass of hair from a rubber band and shakes it off her shoulders... Shake off any excess flour before putting livers in the pan... The prop shaft vibrated like mad and shook the exhaust mounting loose.*
VERB — V n prep; V n with adv; V n adj

9 If your voice **is shaking**, you cannot control it properly and it sounds very unsteady, for example because you are nervous or angry. *His voice shaking with rage, he asked how the committee could keep such a report from the public.*
VERB — V *with* n; Also V

10 If an event or a piece of news **shakes** you, or **shakes** your confidence, it makes you feel shocked or upset, and unable to think calmly or clearly. *There was no doubt that the news of Tandy's escape had shaken them all... She was close to both of her parents and was undeniably shaken by their divorce... Your optimism has been badly shaken over the past months.* ♦ **shaken** *Unhurt, but a bit shaken, she was trying not to cry.*
VERB — V n; ADJ-GRADED: usu v-link ADJ

11 If an event **shakes** a group of people or their beliefs, it causes great uncertainty and makes them question their beliefs. *It won't shake the football world if we beat Torquay... When events happen that shake these beliefs, our fear takes control... The reforms announced by the health minister aim to win back confidence in a system shaken by a major scandal.*
VERB — V n; V-ed

12 If you **shake** someone **out of** an attitude or belief that you dislike or disapprove of, you cause them to change their attitude or belief to one that is more responsible or sensible. *No amount of reasoning could shake him out of his conviction... Many businessmen still find it hard to shake themselves out of the old state-dependent habit.*
VERB — V n *out of* n

13 A **shake** is the same as a **milkshake**. *He sent his driver to fetch him a strawberry shake.*
N-COUNT

14 A **shake** of a liquid or a powder is a small amount of it that comes out of something such as a bottle when you shake it. *Season with salt and pepper and a good shake of vinegar.*
N-COUNT: usu sing, N *of* n

15 If you do not get **a fair shake**, you are not given a reasonable opportunity to succeed or to achieve something; used mainly in American English. *A lot of people think that they're not going to get a fair shake from the courts.*
PHRASES — PHR after v =a fair chance

16 If you say that someone or something is **no great shakes**, you mean that they are not very skilful or effective; an informal expression. *I'm no great shakes as a detective... Democracies, in general, are no great shakes at confronting terrorism.*
v-link PHR

17 If you **shake** someone's **hand** or **shake** someone **by the hand**, you shake hands with them. *I said congratulations and walked over to him and shook his hand... The Secretary emerged, a big fat man who quickly shook us all by the hand.*
V inflects

18 If you **shake hands** with someone, you hold their right hand in your own for a few moments, often moving it up and down slightly, when you are meeting them, saying goodbye to them, or congratulating them. You can also say that two people **shake hands**. *He nodded greetings to Mary Ann and Michael and shook hands with Burke... We shook hands and parted on good terms.*
RECIP: V inflects, PHR *with* n, pl-n PHR

19 • to **shake the foundations of** something: see **foundation**. • to **shake like a leaf**: see **leaf**. • **more things than** you **can shake a stick at**: see **stick**. • **shaken but not stirred**: see **stir**.

shake down. In American English, if someone **shakes** you **down**, they use threats or search you physically in order to obtain something from you. *He ordered the dismantling of police checkpoints on highways, which were being used to shake down motorists for bribes... Residents complain about being harassed on the street, roughed up, sometimes even shaken down for their money.*
PHRASAL VERB — V P n (not pron); Also V n P

shake off
PHRASAL VERB

1 If you **shake off** something that you do not want such as an illness or a bad habit, you manage to recover from it or get rid of it. *Businessmen are frantically trying to shake off the bad habits learned under six decades of a protected economy... Get your body moving to boost energy, stay supple and shake off winter lethargy... He had difficulty in breathing and was generally feeling bad. He just couldn't shake it off.*
V P n (not pron); V n P

2 If you **shake off** someone who is following you, you manage to get away from them, for example by running faster than them. *I caught him a lap later, and although I could pass him I could not shake him off... It seems that he was unaware that they had shaken off their pursuers.*
V n P; V P n (not pron)

3 If you **shake off** someone who is touching you, you move your arm or body sharply so that they are no longer touching you. *He grabbed my arm. I shook him off... She shook off his restraining hand.*
V n P; V P n (not pron)

shake out. If you **shake out** a cloth or a piece of clothing, you hold it by one of its edges and move it up and down one or more times, in order to open it out, make it flat, or remove dust. *While the water was heating she decided to shake out the carpet... I took off my poncho, shook it out, and hung it on a peg by the door.* • See also **shake-out**.
PHRASAL VERB — V P n (not pron); V n P

shake up
PHRASAL VERB

1 If someone **shakes up** something such as an organization, an institution, or a profession, they make major changes to it. *The government wanted to accelerate the reform of the institutions, to find new ways of shaking up the country... Directors and shareholders are preparing to shake things up in the corporate boardrooms of America.* • See also **shake-up**.
V P n (not pron); V n P

2 If you **are shaken up** or **shook up** by an unpleasant experience, it makes you feel shocked and upset, and unable to think calmly or clearly. *The jockey was shaken up when he was thrown twice from his horse yesterday... He was in the car when those people died. That really shook him up... He said that the accident had left her a bit shook up, but she was going to be just fine.*
be V-ed P; V n P; V-ed P; Also V P n (not pron)

shaken /ʃeɪkən/. **Shaken** is the past participle of **shake**.

shake-out, shake-outs; spelled **shakeout** in American English. A **shake-out** is a major set of changes in a system or an organization which results in a large number of companies closing or a large number of people losing their jobs; used in journalism. *This should be the year of a big shake-out in Italian banking... The party needs a shake-out, if it is to be the driving-force of the new politics.*
N-COUNT: usu sing

shake-up, shake-ups; spelled **shakeup** in American English. A **shake-up** is a major set of changes in an organization or a system; used in journalism. *The report proposed an unexpectedly radical shake-up of the secondary education system... Doctors yesterday delivered an overwhelming vote of no confidence in controversial health service shake-ups.*
◆◇◇◇◇ N-COUNT: usu with supp, oft N *of*/*in* n

shaky /ʃeɪki/ **shakier, shakiest**
◆◇◇◇◇

1 If you describe a situation as **shaky**, you mean that it is weak or unstable, and seems unlikely to last long or be successful. *A shaky ceasefire is holding after three days of fighting between rival*
ADJ-GRADED

groups... I'm afraid that this school year is off to a shaky start... The Prime Minister's political position is becoming increasingly shaky.

2 If your body or your voice is **shaky**, you cannot control it properly and it trembles, for example because you are ill or nervous. You can also describe someone's movements as **shaky**. *We have all had a shaky hand and a dry mouth before speaking in public... Even small operations can leave you feeling a bit shaky... His speech was difficult to understand, his signature shaky and unrecognizable.* ADJ-GRADED

♦ **shakily** /ʃeɪkɪli/ *He made his way down the aircraft steps unaided but moved shakily as he did so... 'I'm okay,' she said shakily.* ADV-GRADED: ADV with v

shale /ʃeɪl/ **shales. Shale** is smooth soft rock that breaks easily into thin layers. ◆◇◇◇◇ N-MASS

shall /ʃəl STRONG ʃæl/ ◆◆◆◆◇

Shall is a modal verb. It is used with the base form of a verb.

1 You use **shall** with 'I' and 'we' in questions in order to make offers or suggestions, or to ask for advice. *Shall I get the keys?... I bought some lovely raisin buns at the bakery. Shall I bring you one with some tea?... Shall I telephone her and ask her to come here?... Well, shall we go?... Let's have a nice little stroll, shall we?... What shall I do?.* MODAL PRAGMATICS

2 You use **shall**, usually with 'I' and 'we', when you are referring to something that you intend to do, or when you are referring to something that you are sure will happen to you in the future. *We shall be landing in Paris in sixteen minutes, exactly on time... I shall sail out on the twenty-second... I shall know more next month, I hope... I shall miss him terribly.* MODAL

3 You use **shall** with 'I' or 'we' during a speech or piece of writing to say what you are going to discuss or explain later. *In Chapter 3, I shall describe some of the documentation that I gathered... We shall refer here to three significant trends that arose in the previous decade... The building, as we shall see, is very different in its internal planning, with a great complex of halls and rooms.* MODAL

4 You use **shall** to indicate that something must happen, usually because of a rule or law. You use **shall not** to indicate that something must not happen. *The president shall hold office for five years... The Security Council shall decide what measures shall be taken to restore peace and security... The bank shall be entitled to debit the amount of such liability and all costs incurred in connection with it to your Account... You shall not make this speech... If you want to pry into other people's business you shall not do it here, young man.* MODAL PRAGMATICS

5 You use **shall**, usually with 'you', when you are assuring someone that they will be able to do something or that something will happen. *Very well, if you want to go, go you shall... 'I want to hear all the gossip, all the scandal.'—'You shall, dearie, you shall!'... 'What I would like, is a membership list and some information on how the Society is run.'—'Then that is what you shall have.'* MODAL PRAGMATICS

6 In formal English, you use **shall** with verbs such as 'look forward to' and 'hope' to say politely that you are looking forward to something or hoping to do something. *Well, we shall look forward to seeing him tomorrow... I shall hope to see you in my office, young lady, and we'll review your portfolio.* MODAL PRAGMATICS

7 You use **shall** when you are referring to the likely result or consequence of a particular action or situation. *When the big City law firms finally decide to put the lid on their entertainments, we shall know that times really are hard... This is our last chance and we shall need to take it if we are to compete and survive.* MODAL

8 • **shall I say**: see **say**.

shallot /ʃəlɒt/ **shallots. Shallots** are small round vegetables that are the roots of a crop and are similar to onions. They have a strong taste and are used for flavouring other food. ◆◇◇◇◇ N-VAR: usu pl

shallow /ʃæloʊ/ **shallower, shallowest** ◆◆◇◇◇

1 A **shallow** container, hole, or area of water measures only a short distance from the top to the bottom. *Put the milk in a shallow dish... The water is quite shallow for some distance. ...the remains of a young woman found in a shallow grave.* ADJ-GRADED ≠deep

2 If you describe a person, piece of work, or idea as **shallow**, you disapprove of them because they do not show or involve any serious or careful thought. *I think he is shallow, vain and untrustworthy... The evening news is often criticized for being shallow.* ADJ-GRADED PRAGMATICS

♦ **shallowness** *...intellectual shallowness.* N-UNCOUNT

3 If your breathing is **shallow**, you take only a very small amount of air into your lungs at each breath. *She began to hear her own taut, shallow breathing.* ADJ-GRADED ≠deep

♦ **shallowly** *He was breathing, quickly and shallowly.* ADV-GRADED: ADV with v

shallows /ʃæloʊ/. **The shallows** are the shallow part of an area of water. *At dusk more fish come into the shallows.* ◆◇◇◇◇ N-PLURAL: the N

shalt /ʃəlt, STRONG ʃælt/. **Shalt** is an old-fashioned form of **shall**. *Thou shalt not kill.* MODAL

sham /ʃæm/ **shams.** Something that is a **sham** is not real or is not really what it seems to be; used showing disapproval. *The government's promises were exposed as a hollow sham... Many of the world's leaders have already denounced this election as a sham. ...sham marriages.* ◆◇◇◇◇ N-COUNT: usu sing PRAGMATICS

shaman /ʃeɪmən/ **shamans** ◆◇◇◇◇

1 A **shaman** is a priest or priestess in shamanism. N-COUNT

2 In some North American tribes, a **shaman** is a person who is believed to have powers to heal sick people or to rid them of evil spirits. N-COUNT

shamanism /ʃeɪmənɪzəm/. **Shamanism** is a religion which is based on the belief that the world is controlled by good and evil spirits, and that these spirits can be directed by people with special powers. Shamanism is a belief which is traditionally found in some Asian countries. N-UNCOUNT

shamble /ʃæmbəl/ **shambles, shambling, shambled** ◆◇◇◇◇

1 If a place, event, or situation is a **shambles** or is **in a shambles**, everything is in disorder. *The ship's interior was an utter shambles... The economy is in a shambles.* N-SING =mess

2 If you **shamble** somewhere, you walk clumsily, dragging your feet. *The conductor shambled to the next carriage. ...his tall, shambling figure.* VERB V prep/adv V-ing

shambolic /ʃæmbɒlɪk/. If you describe a situation, person, or place as **shambolic**, you mean that they are very disorganized. *...a shambolic public relations disaster... John lived in a stylishly shambolic artist's studio.* ADJ-GRADED

shame /ʃeɪm/ **shames, shaming, shamed** ◆◆◆◇◇

1 **Shame** is an uncomfortable feeling that you get when you have done something wrong or embarrassing, or when someone close to you has. *She felt a deep sense of shame... They feel shame and guilt as though it is their fault... Her father and her brothers would die of shame... I was, to my shame, a coward.* N-UNCOUNT

2 If someone brings **shame** on you, they make other people lose their respect for you. *I don't want to bring shame on the family name... He committed suicide rather than face the shame of being linked to the scandal.* N-UNCOUNT =disgrace

3 If something **shames** you, it causes you to feel shame. *Her son's affair had humiliated and shamed her.* VERB V n

4 If you **shame** someone close to you, you make people lose their respect for that person, by behaving in an unacceptable way. *I wouldn't shame my father by trying that.* VERB V n

5 If you **shame** someone into doing something, you force them to do it by making them feel ashamed not to. *He would not let neighbours shame him into silence... Museums have now been shamed out of selling the treasures from their collections.* VERB V n into/out of n/-ing

6 If you say that something is a **shame**, you are expressing your regret about it and indicating that you wish it had happened differently. *It's a crying shame that police have to put up with these mindless attacks... They did not have enough money to adopt a child. It was such a shame.* N-SING: a N, oft it v-link N that PRAGMATICS

7 You can use **shame** in expressions such as **shame** CONVENTION

on you and **shame on him** to indicate that someone ought to feel shame for something they have said or done. *He tried to deny it. Shame on him!* PRAGMATICS

8 If someone **puts** you **to shame**, they make you feel ashamed because they do something much better than you do. *His playing really put me to shame.* PHRASE: V inflects

shamefaced /ʃeɪmfeɪst, AM -feɪst/. If you are **shamefaced**, you feel embarrassed because you have done something that you know you should not have done; a formal word. *There was a long silence, and my father looked shamefaced.* ADJ-GRADED

shameful /ʃeɪmfʊl/. If you describe a person's action or attitude as **shameful**, you think that it is so bad that the person ought to be ashamed. *...the most shameful episode in US naval history.* ◆◇◇◇◇ ADJ-GRADED PRAGMATICS
♦ **shamefully** *At times they have been shamefully neglected.* ADV-GRADED: ADV with v, ADV adj

shameless /ʃeɪmləs/. If you describe someone as **shameless**, you mean that they should be ashamed of their behaviour, which is unacceptable to other people. *...a shameless attempt to stifle democratic debate. ...a shameless hustler and dealer in stolen goods.* ♦ **shamelessly** *...a shamelessly lazy week-long trip.* ◆◇◇◇◇ ADJ-GRADED PRAGMATICS ADV-GRADED: ADV with v, ADV adj

shampoo /ʃæmpuː/ **shampoos, shampooing, shampooed** ◆◇◇◇◇
1 **Shampoo** is a soapy liquid that you use for washing your hair. *...a bottle of shampoo. ...bubble baths, soaps and shampoos.* N-MASS
2 When you **shampoo** your hair, you wash it using shampoo. *Shampoo your hair and dry it.* VERB V n

shamrock /ʃæmrɒk/ **shamrocks.** A **shamrock** is a small plant with three round leaves on each stem. The shamrock is the national emblem of Ireland. N-COUNT

shandy /ʃændi/ **shandies. Shandy** is a drink which is made by mixing beer and lemonade; used in British English. ► A glass of shandy can be referred to as a **shandy**. N-UNCOUNT N-COUNT

shank /ʃæŋk/ **shanks** ◆◇◇◇◇
1 The **shank** of an object is the long, thin, straight part of the object. *These hooks are sharp with long shanks. ...the shank of the club.* N-COUNT
2 **Shanks** are the lower parts of the legs; used especially with reference to meat. *Turn the shanks and baste them once or twice as they cook.* N-COUNT: usu pl

shan't /ʃɑːnt, ʃænt/. In informal English, 'shall not' is usually said or written as **shan't**.

shanty /ʃænti/ **shanties** ◆◇◇◇◇
1 A **shanty** is a small rough hut which poor people live in, built from tin, cardboard, or other materials that are not very strong. N-COUNT
2 A **shanty** is a song which sailors used to sing while they were doing work on a ship. *...one of my father's favourite sea-shanties.* N-COUNT

shanty town, shanty towns; also spelled **shantytown**. A **shanty town** is a collection of rough huts which poor people live in, usually in or near a large city. N-COUNT

shape /ʃeɪp/ **shapes, shaping, shaped** ◆◆◆◆◇
1 The **shape** of an object, a person, or an area is the appearance of their outside edges or surfaces, for example whether they are round, square, curved, or fat. *Each mirror is made to order and can be designed to almost any shape or size. ...little pens in the shape of baseball bats... The glass bottle is the shape of a woman's torso. ...sofas and chairs of contrasting shapes and colours... The buds are conical or pyramidal in shape... These bras should be handwashed to help them keep their shape... Walking is extremely beneficial to your body shape.* N-COUNT: oft N of n, also in N
2 You can refer to something that you can see as a **shape** if you cannot see it clearly, or if its outline is the clearest or most striking aspect of it. *The great grey shape of a tank rolled out of the village... Lying in bed we often see dark shapes of herons silhouetted against the moon.* N-COUNT
3 A **shape** is a space enclosed by an outline, for example a circle, a square, or a triangle. *...if you imagine a sort of a kidney shape... He suggested that the shapes represented a map of Britain and Ireland.* N-COUNT
4 The **shape** of something that is planned or organized is its structure and character. *European Community leaders are meeting in Dublin to plan the future shape of Western Europe... Ultimately, we can change the shape of people's lives.* N-SING: usu N of n
5 Someone or something that **shapes** a situation or an activity has a very great influence on the way it develops. *Christian Democratic leaders are meeting to discuss their role in shaping the future of Europe... Like it or not, our families shape our lives and make us what we are.* VERB V n
6 If you **shape** an object, you give it a particular shape, using your hands or a tool. *Cut the dough in half and shape each half into a loaf. ...machinery for shaping the plutonium core of nuclear weapons.* VERB V n into n V n
7 See also **shaped.**
8 If you say that something is **the shape of things to come**, you mean that it is the start of a new trend or development, and in future things will be like this. *British Rail says its new Liverpool Street station is the shape of things to come.* PHRASES v-link PHR
9 If you say, for example, that you will not accept something **in any shape or form**, or **in any way, shape or form**, you are emphasizing that you will not accept it for any reason or in any circumstances. *I don't condone violence in any shape or form... There is absolutely no reason for consumers to be panicking in any way, shape or form.* PHR after v PRAGMATICS
10 If someone or something is **in shape**, or **in good shape**, they are in a good state of health or in a good condition. If they are **in bad shape**, they are in a bad state of health or in a bad condition. *...the Fatburner Diet Book, a comprehensive guide to getting in shape... He was still in better shape than many young men... The trees were in bad shape from dry rot.* PHR after v, v-link PHR
11 You can use **in the shape of** to state exactly who or what you are referring to, immediately after referring to them in a general way. *The Prime Minister found a surprise ally today in the shape of Jacques Delors, the Commission President... What industry needed now was a little hope in the shape of an interest-rate cut.* PHR n
12 If you **lick, knock,** or **whip** someone or something **into shape**, you use whatever methods are necessary to change or improve them so that they are in the condition that you want them to be in. *You'll have four months in which to lick the recruits into shape... Few people doubt his ability to whip the economy into shape.* V inflects
13 If something is **out of shape**, it is no longer in its proper or original shape, for example because it has been damaged or wrongly handled. *Once most wires are bent out of shape, they don't return to the original position.* PHR after v
14 If you are **out of shape**, you are unhealthy and unable to do a lot of physical activity without getting tired. v-link PHR =unfit ≠fit
15 If you say that things or people of a certain type **come in all shapes and sizes**, you mean that there are a large number of them, and that they are often very different from each other. *Colleges and universities come in all shapes and sizes.* V inflects
16 When something **takes shape**, it develops or starts to appear in such a way that it becomes fairly clear what its final form will be. *In 1912 women's events were added, and the modern Olympic programme began to take shape.* V inflects

shape up PHRASAL VERB
1 If something **is shaping up**, it is starting to develop or seems likely to happen; used mainly in American English. *There are also indications that a major tank battle may be shaping up for tonight... The accident is already shaping up as a significant environmental disaster... It's shaping up to be a terrible winter.* V P V P as n V P to-inf Also V P into n
2 If you ask how someone or something **is shaping up**, you want to know how well they are doing in a particular situation or activity. *I did have a few worries about how Hugh and I would shape up as parents... Girls are being recruited now. I heard they are shaping up very well.* V P as n V P adv

3 If you tell someone to **shape up**, you are telling them to start behaving in a sensible and responsible way. *It is of no value simply to tell one's adolescent children to shape up and do something useful.* VP

shaped /ʃeɪpt/. Something that is **shaped** like a particular object or in a particular way has the shape of that object or a shape of that type. *A new perfume from Russia came in a bottle shaped like a tank. ...oddly shaped little packages.* ◆◆◆◇◇ ADJ: v-link ADJ *like* n, adv ADJ

-shaped /-ʃeɪpt/. **-shaped** combines with nouns to describe the shape of an object. *...large, heart-shaped leaves. ...an L-shaped settee.* COMB in ADJ

shapeless /ʃeɪpləs/. Something that is **shapeless** does not have a distinct or attractive shape. *Aunt Mary never wore anything but shapeless black dresses.* ADJ-GRADED: usu ADJ n

shapely /ʃeɪpli/. If you describe a woman as **shapely**, you mean that she has an attractive shape. *...her shapely legs.* ADJ-GRADED: usu ADJ n

shard /ʃɑːʳd/ **shards. Shards** are pieces of broken glass, pottery, or metal. *Eyewitnesses spoke of rocks and shards of glass flying in the air.* N-COUNT: oft N of n

share /ʃeəʳ/ **shares, sharing, shared** ◆◆◆◆◆

1 A company's **shares** are the many equal parts into which its ownership is divided. Shares can be bought by people as an investment. *This is why Sir Colin Marshall, British Airways' chairman, has been so keen to buy shares in US-AIR... They faced a period of some months when the share price would remain fairly static.* N-COUNT: oft N *in* n

2 If you **share** something with another person, you both have it, use it, or occupy it. You can also say that two people **share** something. *...the small income he had shared with his brother from his father's estate... Two Americans will share this year's Nobel Prize for Medicine... Scarce water resources are shared between states who cannot trust each other... Most hostel tenants would prefer single to shared rooms.* V-RECIP V n *with* n, pl-n V n, *be* V-ed *between* pl-n, V-ed

3 If you **share** a task, duty, or responsibility with someone, you each carry out or accept part of it. You can also say that two people **share** something. *You can find out whether they are prepared to share the cost of the flowers with you... The republics have worked out a plan for sharing control of nuclear weapons.* V-RECIP V n *with* n, pl-n V n

4 If you **share** an experience with someone, you have the same experience, often because you are with them at the time. You can also say that two people **share** something. *Yes, I want to share my life with you... I felt we both shared the same sense of loss, felt the same pain.* V-RECIP V n *with* n, pl-n V n

5 If you **share** someone's opinion, you agree with them. *The forum's members share his view that business can be a positive force for change in developing countries... Prosperity and economic success remain popular and broadly shared goals.* VB: no cont V n, V-ed

6 If one person or thing **shares** a quality or characteristic with another, they have the same quality or characteristic. You can also say that two people or things **share** something. *La Repubblica and El Pais are politically independent newspapers which share similar characteristics with certain British newspapers. ...two groups who share a common language.* V-RECIP: no cont V n *with* n, pl-n V n

7 If you **share** something that you have with someone, you give some of it to them or let them use it. *The village tribe is friendly and they share their water supply with you... Scientists now have to compete for funding, and do not share information among themselves... Toddlers are notoriously antisocial when it comes to sharing toys.* VERB V n *with* n, V n *among* pl-n, V n, Also V

8 If you **share** something personal such as a thought or a piece of news with someone, you tell them about it. *It can be beneficial to share your feelings with someone you trust... Film critic Bob Mondello shares his thoughts on the movie 'City of Hope'.* VERB V n *with* n, V n

9 If something is divided or distributed among a number of different people or things, each of them has, or is responsible for, a **share** of it. *Sara also pays a share of the gas, electricity and phone bills... He is counting on winning seats and perhaps a share in the new government of Macedonia.* N-COUNT: usu sing, oft N *of/in* n

10 If you have or do your **share** of something, you have or do the amount that it is reasonable or fair for you to expect, or for other people to expect of you. *Women must receive their fair share of training for good-paying jobs... I have had more than my full share of adventures.* N-COUNT: usu sing with poss, N *of* n

11 See also **lion's share, market share, power-sharing.**

share in. If you **share in** something such as a success or a responsibility, you are one of a number of people who achieve or accept it. *The company is offering you the chance to share in its success... Everybody shares in the cooking chores.* PHRASAL VERB V P n

share out. If you **share out** an amount of something, you give each person in a group an equal or fair part of it. *If you start taking the prize money off the people from the top then you could share it out a bit more equally... Warsaw Pact members have failed to agree on how to share out proposed cuts in tank numbers. ...a formula for sharing out power among the various clans.* • See also **share-out.** PHRASAL VERB V n P, V P n (not pron), V P n *among/between* pl-n

sharecropper /ʃeəʳkrɒpəʳ/ **sharecroppers.** A **sharecropper** is a farmer who pays the rent for his land with some of the crops they produce. N-COUNT

shareholder /ʃeəʳhoʊldəʳ/ **shareholders.** A **shareholder** is a person who owns shares in a company. *...a shareholders' meeting.* ◆◆◆◇◇ N-COUNT

share index, share indices or **share indexes.** A **share index** is an indicator of the state of a stock market. It is based on the combined share prices of a set of companies. *The FT 30 share index was up 16.4 points to 1,599.6.* ◆◇◇◇◇ N-COUNT

share-out, share-outs. If there is a **share-out** of something, several people are given equal or fair parts of it. *...a referendum on independence and the share-out of seats in the transitional government.* N-COUNT: usu sing

shareware /ʃeəʳweəʳ/; also spelled **Shareware. Shareware** is computer software that you can try before you buy the legal right to use it; a technical term. *...a shareware program.* N-UNCOUNT: oft N n

shark /ʃɑːʳk/ **sharks** The form **shark** can also be used as the plural form for meaning 1. ◆◇◇◇◇

1 A **shark** is a very large fish. Some sharks have very sharp teeth and may attack people. N-VAR

2 If you refer to a person as a **shark**, you disapprove of them because they trick people out of their money by giving bad advice about buying, selling, or investments; an informal use. *Beware the sharks when you are making up your mind how to invest.* • See also **loan shark.** N-COUNT PRAGMATICS

sharp /ʃɑːʳp/ **sharper, sharpest** ◆◆◆◆◇

1 A **sharp** point or edge is very small or thin and can cut through things very easily. A **sharp** knife, tool, or other object has a point or edge of this kind. *The other end of the twig is sharpened into a sharp point to use as a toothpick... Using a sharp knife, cut away the pith and peel from both fruits... The ground was strewn with sharp-edged pebbles.* ADJ-GRADED ≠blunt

2 You can describe a shape or an object as **sharp** if part of it or one end of it comes to a point or forms an angle. *His nose was thin and sharp. ...black sharp-toed cowboy boots.* ADJ-GRADED

3 A **sharp** bend or turn is one that changes direction suddenly. *I was approaching a fairly sharp bend that swept downhill to the left.* ► Also an adverb. *Do not cross the bridge but turn sharp left to go down on to the towpath.* ♦ **sharply** *Room number nine was at the far end of the corridor where it turned sharply to the right.* ADJ-GRADED =tight; ADV: ADV adv; ADV-GRADED: ADV after v

4 If you describe someone as **sharp**, you are praising them because they are quick to notice, hear, understand, or react to things. *He is very sharp, a quick thinker and swift with repartee... Gates is known to be a superb analyst with a sharp eye and an excellent memory.* ♦ **sharpness** *I much preferred working for Americans: I liked their enthusiasm and sharpness of mind.* ADJ-GRADED PRAGMATICS; N-UNCOUNT: oft N *of* n

5 If someone says something in a **sharp** way, they say it suddenly and rather firmly or angrily, for ex- ADJ-GRADED

ample because they are warning or criticizing you. *'Don't contradict your mother,' was Charles's sharp reprimand... That ruling had drawn sharp criticism from civil rights groups.* ♦ **sharply** *'You've known,' she said sharply, 'and you didn't tell me?'... Environmentalists were sharply critical of the policy for its failure to encourage conservation.* ADV-GRADED: ADV with v, ADV adj
♦ **sharpness** *'Let them find their own way out,' said his father with unaccustomed sharpness.* N-UNCOUNT

6 A **sharp** change, movement, or feeling occurs suddenly, and is great in amount, force, or degree. *There's been a sharp rise in the rate of inflation... Tennis requires a lot of short sharp movements... He felt a sharp pain in the abductor muscle in his right thigh.* ADJ-GRADED ♦ **sharply** *Unemployment among the over forties has risen sharply in recent years... I turned my body sharply in the chair... The latest survey shows buying plans for homes are sharply lower than in June.* ADV-GRADED: ADV with v, ADV adj

7 A **sharp** difference, image, or sound is very easy to see, hear, or distinguish. *Many people make a sharp distinction between humans and other animals... Her reticence was in sharp contrast to the glamour and star status of her predecessors... All the footmarks are quite sharp and clear... We heard a voice sing out in a clear, sharp tone.* ADJ-GRADED: usu ADJ n ♦ **sharply** *Opinions on this are sharply divided... The woman's figure is sharply brought out by the intense Provençal light... The things she saw and heard every day made her ever more sharply aware of the separation between herself and her family.* ADV-GRADED: usu ADV with v, also ADV adj ♦ **sharpness** *The telescope will show us our Universe as we've never seen it before, with wonderful sharpness and clarity.* N-UNCOUNT

8 A **sharp** taste or smell is rather strong or bitter, but is often also clear and fresh. *...a colourless, almost odourless liquid with a sharp, sweetish taste... In the hot sun the rain-washed herbs smelled sharp and spicy and sweet all at once.* ADJ-GRADED ♦ **sharpness** *The pesto vinaigrette added a stimulating sharpness.* N-UNCOUNT

9 A **sharp** wind, or **sharp** cold, is so strong or intense that it almost hurts you when you are exposed to it. *The wind was not as sharp and cruel as it had been.* ADJ-GRADED =biting

10 **Sharp** clothes are neat, elegant, and fashionable. *Now politics is all about the right haircut and a sharp suit.* ADJ-GRADED

11 **Sharp** is used after stating a particular time to show that something happens at exactly the time stated. *She planned to unlock the store at 8.00 sharp this morning.* ADV: n ADV =precisely

12 **Sharp** is used after a letter representing a musical note to show that the note should be played or sung half a tone higher than the note which otherwise corresponds to that letter. **Sharp** is often represented by the symbol ♯. *A solitary viola plucks a lonely, soft F sharp.* ADJ: n ADJ ≠flat

13 See also **razor-sharp**.

14 If you say that someone is **at the sharp end** of a particular activity or type of work, you mean that they are involved in the most difficult or dangerous aspects of it. *Vincent French is a real estate broker at the sharp end of a tough and exacting business... Working at the sharp end, many of us have noted an increase in the number of patients attending surgeries.* ● **short, sharp shock**: see **shock**. PHRASE: usu v-link PHR, oft PHR of n

sharpen /ʃɑːʳpən/ **sharpens, sharpening, sharpened** ◆◇◇◇◇

1 If your senses, understanding, or skills **sharpen** or **are sharpened**, you become better at noticing things, thinking, or doing something. *Her gaze sharpened, as if she had seen something unusual... You can sharpen your skills with rehearsal.* V-ERG; V; V n

2 If you **sharpen** an object, you make its edge very thin or you make its end pointed. *He started to sharpen his knife. ...sharpened pencils.* VERB; V n; V-ed

3 If disagreements or differences between people **sharpen**, or if they **are sharpened**, they become bigger or more important. *The difference has sharpened during this recession, as men have lost jobs faster than women... The case of Harris has sharpened the debate over capital punishment.* V-ERG; V; V n

sharpen up. If you **sharpen** something **up**, or if it **sharpens up**, it becomes smarter or better than it was; an informal expression. *The fashion designers have sharpened up their act in the last few years... If he really wants to sell his product, he'll have to get his marketing boys to sharpen up.* PHRASAL VERB ERG; V n; V

sharpener /ʃɑːʳpnəʳ/ **sharpeners.** A **sharpener** is a tool or machine used for sharpening pencils or knives. *...a pencil sharpener.* N-COUNT: usu n N

sharp-eyed. A **sharp-eyed** person is good at noticing and observing things. *A sharp-eyed shop assistant spotted the fake and police were called.* ADJ-GRADED: usu ADJ n

sharpish /ʃɑːʳpɪʃ/. In British English, if you do something **sharpish**, you do it quickly, without any delay. *She was asked to leave, sharpish.* ADV-GRADED: ADV after v

sharp practice. You can use **sharp practice** to refer to an action or a way of behaving, especially in business or professional matters, that you think is clever but dishonest. *He accused some solicitors of sharp practice in quoting low fees which were later increased.* N-UNCOUNT

sharpshooter /ʃɑːʳpʃuːtəʳ/ **sharpshooters.** A **sharpshooter** is a person who can fire a gun very accurately; used mainly in American English. N-COUNT =marksman

sharp tongue, sharp tongues. If you say that someone has a **sharp tongue**, you are critical of the fact that they say things which are unkind though often clever. *Despite her moods and sharp tongue, she inspires fierce loyalty from her friends.* N-COUNT PRAGMATICS

sharp-tongued. If you describe someone as **sharp-tongued**, you being critical of them for speaking in a way which is unkind though often clever. *Julia was a very tough, sharp-tongued woman.* ADJ-GRADED: usu ADJ n PRAGMATICS

shatter /ʃætəʳ/ **shatters, shattering, shattered** ◆◇◇◇◇

1 If something **shatters** or if something or someone **shatters** it, it breaks into a lot of small pieces. *...safety glass that won't shatter if it's broken... The car shattered into a thousand burning pieces in a 200mph crash... One bullet shattered his skull.* V-ERG; V; V into n; V n; Also V n into n ♦ **shattering** *...the shattering of glass.* N-UNCOUNT

2 If something **shatters** your dreams, hopes, or beliefs, it completely destroys them. *A failure would shatter the hopes of many people... Something like that really shatters your confidence. ...broken hearts and shattered dreams.* VERB =destroy; V n; V-ed

3 If someone **is shattered** by an event, it shocks and upsets them very much. *He had been shattered by his son's death. ...the tragedy which had shattered his life.* VERB; be V-ed; V n

4 See also **shattered**, **shattering**.

shattered /ʃætəʳd/ ◆◆◇◇◇

1 If you are **shattered** by something, you are extremely shocked and upset about it. *It is desperately sad news and I am absolutely shattered to hear it.* ADJ-GRADED: usu v-link ADJ =devastated

2 If you say you are **shattered**, you mean you are extremely tired and have no energy left. *He was shattered and too tired to concentrate on schoolwork.* ADJ-GRADED: usu v-link ADJ =exhausted

shattering /ʃætərɪŋ/ ◆◇◇◇◇

1 Something that is **shattering** shocks and upsets you very much. *The experience of their daughter's death had been absolutely shattering... Yesterday's decision was another shattering blow.* ADJ-GRADED =devastating

2 See also **shatter**, **earth-shattering**.

shave /ʃeɪv/ **shaves, shaving, shaved** ◆◆◇◇◇

1 When a man **shaves**, he cuts the hair from his face using a razor or shaver. *He took a bath and shaved before dinner... He had shaved his face until it was smooth... It's a pity you shaved your moustache off.* VERB; V; V n; V n with off ► Also a noun. *He never seemed to need a shave.* N-COUNT ♦ **shaving** *...a range of shaving products.* N-UNCOUNT

2 If someone **shaves** a part of their body, they cut hair from it using a razor or shaver. *Many women shave their legs... If you have long curly hair, don't shave it off.* VERB; V n; V n with off

3 If you **shave** someone, you cut the hair from their face or other part of their body with a razor or shaver. *The doctors shaved his head... She had to call a barber to shave him.* VERB; V n

4 If you **shave off** part of a piece of wood or other VERB material, you cut very thin pieces from it. *I set the log on the ground and shaved off the bark... She was shaving thin slices off a courgette.* — V n with off; V n off n

5 If you **shave** a small amount off something such as a record, cost, or price, you reduce it by that amount. *She's already shaved four seconds off the national record for the mile... Supermarket chains have shaved prices.* — VERB; V n off/from n; V n

6 See also **shaving**.

7 If you describe a situation as a **close shave**, you mean that there was nearly an accident or a disaster but it was avoided. *I can't quite believe the close shaves I've had just recently.* — PHRASE: N inflects

shaven /ʃeɪvᵊn/. If a part of someone's body is **shaven**, it has been shaved. *...a small boy with a shaven head.* • See also **clean-shaven**. — ◆◇◇◇◇ ADJ

shaver /ʃeɪvəʳ/ **shavers.** A **shaver** is an electric device, used for shaving hair from the face and body. *...men's electric shavers.* — ◆◇◇◇◇ N-COUNT: oft adj N

shaving /ʃeɪvɪŋ/ **shavings. Shavings** are small very thin pieces of wood or other material which have been cut from a larger piece. *The floor was covered with shavings from his wood carvings. ...metal shavings.* • See also **shave**. — ◆◇◇◇◇ N-COUNT: usu pl

shaving cream, shaving creams. Shaving cream is soap or foam which men put on their face before they shave. *...a tube of shaving cream.* — N-MASS

shawl /ʃɔːl/ **shawls.** A **shawl** is a large piece of woollen cloth which a woman wears over her shoulders or head, or which is wrapped around a baby to keep it warm. — ◆◇◇◇◇ N-COUNT

she /ʃi, STRONG ʃiː/ — ◆◆◆◆◆

She is a third person singular pronoun. **She** is used as the subject of a verb.

1 You use **she** to refer to a woman, girl, or female animal who has already been mentioned or whose identity is clear. *When Ann arrived home that night, she found Brian in the house watching T.V... She was seventeen and she had no education or employment... She was a little fluffy baby duck which we reared until she was fully grown.* — PRON-SING

2 In written English, some writers may use **she** to refer to a person who is not identified as either male or female. They do this because they wish to avoid using the pronoun 'he' all the time. Some people dislike this use and prefer to use 'he or she' or 'they'. *The student may show signs of feeling the strain of responsibility and she may give up... Very early in life when the baby feels the pangs of hunger, she learns to scream.* — PRON-SING

3 She is sometimes used to refer to a country or nation. *Now Britain needs new leadership if she is to play a significant role shaping Europe's future development.* — PRON-SING

4 Some people use **she** to refer to a car or a machine. People who sail often use **she** to refer to a ship or boat. *Hundreds of small boats clustered round the yacht as she sailed into Southampton docks.* — PRON-SING

s/he. Some writers use **s/he** instead of either 'he' or 'she' when they are referring to someone who might exist but who has not been identified. By using 's/he', the writer does not need to say whether the person is male or female. *Talk to your doctor and see if s/he knows of any local groups.* — PRON-SING =he or she

sheaf /ʃiːf/ **sheaves**

1 A **sheaf** of papers is a bundle of papers. *He took out a sheaf of papers and leafed through them.* — N-COUNT: usu N of n

2 A **sheaf** is a bundle of ripe corn plants tied together. — N-COUNT

shear /ʃɪəʳ/ **shears, shearing, sheared, shorn** — ◆◇◇◇◇

1 To **shear** a sheep means to cut its wool off. *In the Hebrides they shear their sheep later than anywhere else.* ♦ **shearing** *...a display of sheep shearing.* — VERB; V n; N-UNCOUNT

2 A pair of **shears** is a tool like a very large pair of scissors. Shears are used especially for cutting garden hedges. *Trim the shrubs with shears.* — N-PLURAL: also a pair of N

shear off. If something such as a piece of metal **shears off**, or if it **is sheared off**, it breaks. *It was not yet clear how the rudder had sheared off... The aircraft's wings were sheared off in the crash.* — PHRASAL VERB; ERG; V P; be V-ed P

sheath /ʃiːθ/ **sheaths** — ◆◇◇◇◇

1 A **sheath** is a covering for the blade of a knife. — N-COUNT

2 A **sheath** is a rubber covering for a man's penis that is used as a contraceptive. — N-COUNT =condom

sheathe /ʃiːð/ **sheathes, sheathing, sheathed**

1 If something is **sheathed** in a material or other covering, it is closely covered with it; a literary use. *The television was sheathed in a snug coverlet. ...her long legs, sheathed in sheer black tights.* — VB: usu passive; be V-ed in n; V-ed

2 When someone **sheathes** a knife, they put it in its sheath; a literary use. *He sheathed the knife and strapped it to his shin.* — VERB; V n

sheaves /ʃiːvz/. **Sheaves** is the plural of **sheaf.**

shebang /ʃɪbæŋ/. **The whole shebang** is the whole situation or business that you are describing; an informal expression. — PHRASE

shed /ʃed/ **sheds, shedding.** The form **shed** is used in the present tense and is the past tense and past participle of the verb. — ◆◆◆◇◇

1 A **shed** is a small building that is used for storing things such as garden tools. *...a garden shed.* — N-COUNT

2 A **shed** is a large shelter or building, for example at a railway station, port, or factory. *...disused railway sheds.* — N-COUNT: usu n N

3 When a tree **sheds** its leaves, its leaves fall off in the autumn. When an animal **sheds** hair or skin, some of its hair or skin drops off. *Some of the trees were already beginning to shed their leaves. ...a snake who has shed its skin.* — VERB; V n

4 To **shed** something means to get rid of it; a formal use. *The firm is to shed 700 jobs... He had maintained a rigid diet, shedding some twenty pounds. ...a city trying to shed its rough image.* — VERB; V n

5 If a lorry **sheds** its load, the goods that it is carrying accidentally fall onto the road. *A lorry piled with scrap metal had shed its load.* — VERB; V n

6 If you **shed** tears, you cry. *They will shed a few tears at their daughter's wedding.* — VERB; V n

7 To **shed** blood means to kill people in a violent way. If someone **sheds** their blood, they are killed in a violent way, usually when they are fighting in a war. *Gunmen in Ulster shed the first blood of the new year... Others promised to 'shed our blood and sacrifice our lives to oppose the Communists'.* ♦ **shedding** *The Pope called for a halt to the shedding of innocent blood.* — VERB; V n; N-UNCOUNT: N of n

8 • to **shed light on** something: see **light**.

she'd /ʃiːd, ʃɪd/

1 She'd is the usual spoken form of 'she had', especially when 'had' is an auxiliary verb. *She'd rung up to discuss the divorce... She would go for a swim when she'd unpacked.*

2 She'd is a spoken form of 'she would'. *She'd do anything for a bit of money... I got the impression she'd like a word with you, sir.*

sheen /ʃiːn/. If something has a **sheen**, it has a smooth and gentle brightness on its surface. *The carpet had a silvery sheen to it.* — ◆◇◇◇◇ N-SING: oft adj N

sheep /ʃiːp/; **sheep** is both the singular and plural form. — ◆◆◇◇◇

1 A **sheep** is a farm animal with a thick woolly coat. Sheep are kept for their wool or for their meat. *...grassland on which a flock of sheep were grazing.* — N-COUNT

2 If you say that a group of people are like **sheep**, you disapprove of them because if one person does something, all the others copy that person. — N-PLURAL: usu like N; PRAGMATICS

3 • See also **black sheep**. — PHRASES

sheepdog /ʃiːpdɒg/ **sheepdogs.** A **sheepdog** is a breed of dog. Some sheepdogs are used for controlling sheep. — N-COUNT

sheepish /ʃiːpɪʃ/. If you look **sheepish**, you look slightly embarrassed because you feel foolish or you have done something silly. *I asked him why. He looked a little sheepish when he answered.* ♦ **sheepishly** *He grinned sheepishly.* — ◆◇◇◇◇ ADJ-GRADED; ADV-GRADED

sheepskin /ʃiːpskɪn/ **sheepskins. Sheepskin** is the skin of a sheep with the wool still attached to it, used especially for making coats and rugs. *...a sheepskin coat.* — N-VAR: oft N n

sheer /ʃɪəʳ/ **sheerer, sheerest** — ◆◆◇◇◇

1 You can use **sheer** to emphasize that a state or situation is complete and does not involve or is not — ADJ: ADJ n; PRAGMATICS mixed with anything else. *His music is sheer delight... Sheer chance quite often plays an important part in sparking off an idea. ...acts of sheer desperation.* =pure

2 A **sheer** cliff or drop is extremely steep or completely vertical. *There was a sheer drop just outside my window... A young man plunged from a sheer rock face to his death.* ADJ-GRADED: usu ADJ n

3 **Sheer** material is very thin, light, and delicate. *...sheer black tights.* ADJ-GRADED

sheet /ʃiːt/ **sheets** ◆◆◆◇◇

1 A **sheet** is a large rectangular piece of cotton or other cloth that you sleep on or cover yourself with in a bed. *Once a week, a maid changes the sheets. ...the luxury of silk sheets.* N-COUNT

2 A **sheet** of paper is a rectangular piece of paper. *...a sheet of newspaper... I was able to fit it all on one sheet.* N-COUNT

3 You can use the word **sheet** to refer to a piece of paper which gives information about something. *...information sheets on each country in the world.* N-COUNT: usu n N

4 A **sheet** of glass, metal, or wood is a large, flat, thin piece of it. *...a cracked sheet of glass... Overhead cranes were lifting giant sheets of steel... Vinyl can be laid in sheet or tile form.* N-COUNT: usu N of n

5 A **sheet** of something is a thin wide layer of it over the surface of something else. *...a sheet of ice. ...a blue-grey sheet of dust.* N-COUNT: usu N of n

6 A **sheet** of fire or water is a fast-moving mass of it that is difficult to see through. *The streets were now in one fierce sheet of flame... Sheets of rain slanted across the road.* N-COUNT: usu N of n

7 In sailing, a **sheet** is a line or rope used for controlling the position of a sail on a boat. N-COUNT: oft n N

8 See also **balance sheet**, **broadsheet**, **charge sheet**, **dust sheet**, **fact sheet**, **groundsheet**, **newssheet**, **scoresheet**, **spreadsheet**, **worksheet**. ● **as white as a sheet**: see **white**.

sheeting /ʃiːtɪŋ/

1 **Sheeting** is metal, plastic, or other material that is made in the form of sheets. *They put plastic sheeting on the insides of our windows.* N-UNCOUNT: oft n N

2 **Sheeting** is cloth that is used for making sheets. *...six yards of white sheeting.* N-UNCOUNT

sheet metal. **Sheet metal** is metal which is made into thin sheets rather than being made into solid bars or cast in moulds. N-UNCOUNT

sheet music. **Sheet music** is music that is printed on sheets of paper without a hard cover. *...a copy of the sheet music to 'Happy Days'.* N-UNCOUNT

sheikh /ʃeɪk, AM ʃiːk/ **sheikhs;** also spelled **sheik** or **shaikh**. A **sheikh** is a male Arab chief or ruler. *...Sheikh Khalifa. ...the sheik's role in global oil affairs.* ◆◆◇◇◇ N-TITLE; N-COUNT

sheikhdom /ʃeɪkdəm, AM ʃiːk-/ **sheikhdoms;** also spelled **sheikdom**. A **sheikhdom** is a country or region that is ruled by a sheikh. N-COUNT

shelf /ʃelf/ **shelves** ◆◆◇◇◇

1 A **shelf** is a flat piece of wood, metal, or glass which is attached to a wall or to the sides of a cupboard. Shelves are used for keeping things on. *He took a book from the shelf. ...the middle shelf of the oven.* N-COUNT

2 A **shelf** is a section of rock on a cliff or mountain or underwater that sticks out like a shelf. *The house stands on a shelf of rock among pines.* ● See also **continental shelf**. N-COUNT

3 If you buy something **off the shelf**, you buy something that is not specially made for you. *Any car you can buy off the shelf in a pastel pink has got to be saying something. ...off-the-shelf software.* PHRASES PHR after v, PHR n ≠tailor-made

4 If you say that someone or something is **on the shelf**, you mean that no one wants them; an informal expression. *I was afraid of getting left on the shelf. ...first-rate plans which sit on the shelf.* v-link PHR, PHR after v

shelf life, shelf lives. The **shelf life** of a product, especially food, is the length of time that it can be kept in a shop or at home before it becomes too old to sell or use. *Mature flour produces better baking results and has a longer shelf life.* N-COUNT: usu sing

shell /ʃel/ **shells, shelling, shelled** ◆◆◆◇◇

1 The **shell** of a nut or egg is the hard covering which surrounds it. *They cracked the nuts and removed their shells... Once the eggs have hatched the shells are left behind.* ► **Shell** is the substance that a shell is made of. *...beads made from ostrich egg shell.* N-COUNT N-UNCOUNT

2 The **shell** of a tortoise, snail, or crab is the hard protective covering that it has on its back. N-COUNT

3 **Shells** are hard objects found on beaches. They are usually pink, white, or brown and are the covering which surrounds, or used to surround, small sea creatures. *I collect shells and interesting seaside items. ...sea shells.* N-COUNT

4 If you **shell** nuts, peas, prawns, or other food, you remove their natural outer covering. *She shelled and ate a few nuts. ...shelled prawns.* VERB V n V-ed

5 If someone comes out of their **shell**, they become more friendly and interested in other people and less quiet, shy, and reserved. *Her normally shy son had come out of his shell. ...a lonely boy struggling to emerge from his shell.* N-COUNT: usu poss N

6 The **shell** of a building, boat, car, or other structure is the outside frame of it. *...the shells of burned buildings... The solid feel of the car's shell is impressive.* N-COUNT: usu with supp

7 A **shell** is a weapon consisting of a metal container filled with explosives that can be fired from a large gun over long distances. N-COUNT

8 To **shell** a place means to fire explosive shells at it. *The rebels shelled the densely-populated suburbs near the port.* ♦ **shelling, shellings** *Out on the streets, the shelling continued.* VERB V n N-VAR

shell out. If you **shell out** for something, you spend a lot of money on it. *You won't have to shell out a fortune for it... If I'm shelling out a few hundred pounds, I don't want someone telling me what I can or can't do. ...an insurance premium which saves you from having to shell out for repairs... The very fact that you shelled out money to come and see us is a good sign.* PHRASAL VERB =fork out V P n for/on n V P n V P for/on n V P n to-inf Also V P to-inf

she'll /ʃiːl, ʃɪl/. **She'll** is the usual spoken form of 'she will'. *Sharon was a wonderful lady and I know she'll be greatly missed.*

shellac /ʃəlæk/. **Shellac** is a kind of natural varnish which you paint on to wood to give it a shiny surface. N-UNCOUNT

shellfire /ʃelfaɪəʳ/. **Shellfire** is the firing of large military guns. *The radio said other parts of the capital also came under shellfire.* N-UNCOUNT

shellfish /ʃelfɪʃ/; **shellfish** is both the singular and plural form. **Shellfish** are small creatures that live in the sea and have a shell. *Fish and shellfish are the specialities.* ◆◇◇◇◇ N-VAR: usu pl

shell shock; also spelled **shell-shock**. **Shell shock** is the confused or nervous mental condition of people who have been under fire in a war. *The men were suffering from shell shock.* N-UNCOUNT

shell-shocked; also spelled **shell shocked**.

1 If you say that someone is **shell-shocked**, you mean that they are very shocked, usually because something bad has happened; an informal use. *We were shell-shocked when Chelsea took the lead. ...shell-shocked investors.* ADJ-GRADED =stunned

2 If someone is **shell-shocked**, they have a confused or nervous mental condition as a result of a shocking experience such as being in a war or an accident. *...a shell-shocked war veteran.* ADJ-GRADED

shell suit, shell suits; also spelled **shell-suit**. A **shell suit** is a casual suit which is made of thin nylon. *...someone in a shell suit from Stirchley.* N-COUNT

shelter /ʃeltəʳ/ **shelters, sheltering, sheltered** ◆◆◆◇◇

1 A **shelter** is a small building or covered place which is made to protect people from bad weather or danger. *The city's bomb shelters were being prepared for possible air raids. ...a bus shelter.* N-COUNT

2 If a place provides **shelter**, it provides you with a place to stay or live, especially when you need protection from bad weather or danger. *The number of families seeking shelter rose by 17 percent... Although horses do not generally mind the cold,* N-UNCOUNT

shelter from rain and wind is important. ...the hut where they were given food and shelter.

3 A **shelter** is a building where homeless people can sleep and get food. *...a shelter for homeless women.* N-COUNT =refuge

4 If you **shelter** in a place, you stay there and are protected from bad weather or danger. *...a man sheltering in a doorway... Twelve Cubans left the embassy after sheltering there for several days.* VERB V prep/adv

5 If a place or thing **is sheltered** by something, it is protected by that thing from wind and rain. *...a wooden house, sheltered by a low pointed roof.* VB: usu passive V-ed

6 If you **shelter** someone, usually someone who is being hunted by police or other people, you provide them with a place to stay or live. *A neighbor sheltered the boy for seven days. ...people sheltering illegal immigrants.* VERB V n

7 See also **sheltered**.

sheltered /ʃeltəʳd/ ◆◇◇◇◇

1 A **sheltered** place is protected from wind and rain. *...a shallow-sloping beach next to a sheltered bay.* ADJ-GRADED

2 If you say that someone has led a **sheltered** life, you mean that they have not experienced things that most people of their age have experienced, for example because their parents have protected them too much, and that as a result they are rather naive. *Perhaps I've just led a really sheltered life... My mother, who had a sheltered upbringing, has fantastic memories of childhood.* ADJ-GRADED: usu ADJ n

3 **Sheltered** accommodation or work is designed for old or disabled. It allows them to be independent but also gives them supervision when they need it. *For the last few years I have been living in sheltered accommodation. ...sheltered employment for people with severe disabilities.* ADJ: ADJ n

4 See also **shelter**.

shelve /ʃelv/ **shelves, shelving, shelved** ◆◇◇◇◇

1 If someone **shelves** a plan or project, they decide not to continue with it, either for a while or permanently. *Atlanta has shelved plans to include golf in the 1996 Games... Sadly, the project has now been shelved.* VERB V n

2 If a stretch of land **shelves**, it slopes or drops downwards, especially on a seashore. *The shoreline shelves away steeply. ...A gentle shelving beach.* VERB V adv/prep V-ing

3 **Shelves** is the plural of **shelf**.

shelving /ʃelvɪŋ/. **Shelving** is a set of shelves, or material which is used for making shelves. *...the shelving on the long, windowless wall. ...a pyramid-shaped shelving unit.* N-UNCOUNT

shenanigans /ʃɪnænɪgənz/. You can use **shenanigans** to refer to rather dishonest or immoral behaviour, especially when you think it is amusing or interesting; an informal word. *Media people knew about the private shenanigans of public figures.* N-PLURAL

shepherd /ʃepəʳd/ **shepherds, shepherding, shepherded** ◆◆◇◇◇

1 A **shepherd** is a person, especially a man, whose job is to look after sheep. N-COUNT

2 If you **are shepherded** somewhere, someone takes you there to make sure that you arrive at the right place safely. *She was shepherded by her guards up the rear ramp of the aircraft.* VB: usu passive *be* V-ed prep/adv

shepherdess /ʃepəʳdes/ **shepherdesses.** A **shepherdess** is a woman whose job is to look after sheep. N-COUNT

shepherd's pie, shepherd's pies. In Britain, **shepherd's pie** is a dish consisting of minced meat, usually lamb, covered with a layer of mashed potato. N-VAR

sherbet /ʃɜːʳbət/ **sherbets**

1 **Sherbet** is a type of ice cream made with fruit juices, sugar, and water; used mainly in American English. *...lemon sherbet.* N-VAR

2 In British English, **sherbet** is a sweet dry powder that tastes fizzy and is eaten as a sweet. *...sherbet dips.* N-UNCOUNT: oft N n

sheriff /ʃerɪf/ **sheriffs** ◆◇◇◇◇

1 In the United States, a **sheriff** is a person who is elected to make sure that the law is obeyed in a particular county. *...the local sheriff. ...Sheriff Bob Cahill.* N-COUNT; N-TITLE

2 In Scotland, a **sheriff** is a legal officer whose chief duty is to act as judge in a Sheriff Court. These courts deal with all but the most serious crimes and with most civil actions. *...the presiding judge, Sheriff John Mowatt.* N-COUNT; N-TITLE

3 In England and Wales, the **Sheriff** of a city or county is a person who is elected or appointed to carry out mainly ceremonial duties. *...the Sheriff of Oxford.* N-COUNT: usu N *of* n

sherry /ʃeri/ **sherries. Sherry** is a type of strong wine that is made in south-western Spain. It is usually drunk before a meal. *I poured us a glass of sherry. ...some of the world's finest sherries.* ► A glass of sherry can be referred to as a **sherry**. *I'll have a sherry please.* ◆◆◇◇◇ N-MASS N-COUNT

she's /ʃiːz, ʃɪz/

1 **She's** is the usual spoken form of 'she is'. *She's an exceptionally good cook... Have they told you, she's having a baby in October?*

2 **She's** is a spoken form of 'she has', especially when 'has' is an auxiliary verb. *She's been married for seven years and has two daughters.*

shh /ʃ/. See **sh**.

shibboleth /ʃɪbəleθ/ **shibboleths.** If you describe a popular idea or belief as a **shibboleth**, you mean that it may be meaningless or wrong although many people believe it; a formal word. *It is time to go beyond the shibboleth that conventional forces, unlike nuclear ones, cannot deter.* N-COUNT

shield /ʃiːld/ **shields, shielding, shielded** ◆◆◇◇◇

1 Something or someone which is a **shield** against a particular danger or risk provides protection from it. *He used his left hand as a shield against the reflecting sunlight. ...asbestos heat shields.* N-COUNT: usu sing

2 If something or someone **shields** you **from** a danger or risk, they protect you from it. *He shielded his head from the sun with an old sack... The company does not bet its own money on equities, and so is shielded from market risk.* VERB =protect V n *from* n

3 If you **shield** your eyes, you put your hand above your eyes to protect them from direct sunlight. *He squinted and shielded his eyes.* VERB =shade V n

4 A **shield** is a large piece of metal or leather which soldiers used to carry to protect their bodies while they were fighting. N-COUNT

5 A **shield** is a sports trophy or a badge that is shaped like a shield. N-COUNT

shift /ʃɪft/ **shifts, shifting, shifted** ◆◆◆◇◇

1 If you **shift** something or if it **shifts**, it moves slightly. *He stopped, shifting his cane to his left hand... He shifted from foot to foot... The entire pile shifted and slid, thumping onto the floor. ...the squeak of his boots in the snow as he shifted his weight.* V-ERG V n prep/adv V prep/adv V V n

2 If someone's opinion, a situation, or a policy **shifts** or **is shifted**, it changes slightly. *Attitudes to mental illness have shifted in recent years... The emphasis should be shifted more towards Parliament.* ► Also a noun. *...a shift in government policy. ...the shift in opinion away from the Prime Minister.* V-ERG V *be* V-ed prep/adv Also V adv N-COUNT: usu N prep

3 If someone **shifts** the responsibility or blame for something onto you, they unfairly make you responsible or make people blame you for it, instead of them; used showing disapproval. *It was a vain attempt to shift the responsibility for the murder to somebody else... Their husbands try to shift the blame by accusing them of having 'suspicious minds'.* VERB PRAGMATICS V n prep V n

4 If a shop or company **shifts** goods, they sell goods that are difficult to sell. *Some suppliers were selling at a loss to shift stock.* VERB

5 In American English, if you **shift** gears in a car or if you **shift** up or **shift** down, you put the car into a different gear. In British English, you **change** gears, or **change up** or **change down**. VERB

6 If a group of factory workers, nurses, or other people work **shifts**, they work for a set period before being replaced by another group, so that there is always a group working. Each of these set periods is called a **shift**. You can also use **shift** to refer N-COUNT: oft n N

to a group of workers who work together on a particular shift. *His father worked shifts in a steel mill. ...workers coming home from the afternoon shift... The night shift should have been safely down the mine long ago.*
7 See also **shifting**.

shifting /ʃɪftɪŋ/. **Shifting** is used to describe something which is made up of parts that are continuously moving and changing position in relation to other parts. *...the shifting sand beneath their feet... The Croatian town of Ilok is a classic case of shifting populations.* • See also **shift**. ◆◆◇◇◇ ADJ: ADJ n

shiftless /ʃɪftləs/. If you describe someone as **shiftless**, you mean that they are lazy and have no desire to achieve anything. *...a shiftless husband.* ADJ

shifty /ʃɪfti/. Someone who looks **shifty** gives the impression of being dishonest; an informal word. *He had a shifty face and previous convictions.* ADJ-GRADED

shilling /ʃɪlɪŋ/ **shillings.** A **shilling** was a unit of money used in Britain until 1971 which was the equivalent of 5p. There were twenty shillings in a pound. ◆◇◇◇◇ N-COUNT

shilly-shally /ʃɪli ʃæli/ **shilly-shallies, shilly-shallying, shilly-shallied.** In British English, if you say that someone **is shilly-shallying**, you disapprove of the fact that they are hesitating when they should make a decision; an informal word. *It's time for Brooke to stop shilly-shallying.* VB: usu cont PRAGMATICS =dither V

shimmer /ʃɪməʳ/ **shimmers, shimmering, shimmered.** If something **shimmers**, it shines with a faint, unsteady light or has an unclear, unsteady appearance. *The lights shimmered on the water... The trees shimmered in the afternoon heat.* ► Also a noun. *...a shimmer of starlight.* ◆◇◇◇◇ VERB V N-SING

shimmy /ʃɪmi/ **shimmies, shimmying, shimmied.** If you **shimmy**, you dance or move in a way that involves shaking your hips and shoulders from side to side. *Dancers embraced and shimmied in the streets of New Orleans' French Quarter... Tina Turner shimmied across the stage in an incredibly sexy dress.* VERB V V prep/adv

shin /ʃɪn/ **shins, shinning, shinned** ◆◇◇◇◇
1 Your **shins** are the front parts of your legs between your knees and your ankles. *She punched him on the nose and kicked him in the shins.* N-COUNT
2 In British English, **shin** of beef or veal is the meat from the lower fore-leg of a cow. N-UNCOUNT

shin up. If you **shin up** a tree or a pole, you climb it quickly and easily, using your hands and legs to grip it. *Nancy shinned up the tree.* PHRASAL VERB V P n

shindig /ʃɪndɪg/ **shindigs.** A **shindig** is a large, noisy, enjoyable party; an informal word. N-COUNT =knees-up

shine /ʃaɪn/ **shines, shining, shined, shone.** The past tense and past participle of the verb is **shone**, except for meaning 5 when it is **shined**. ◆◆◇◇◇
1 When the sun or a light **shines**, it gives out bright light. *It is a mild morning and the sun is shining... A few scattered lights shone on the horizon.* VERB V
2 If you **shine** a torch or other light somewhere, you point it there, so that you can see something when it is dark. *One of the men shone a torch in his face... The container is invisible until you shine an ultraviolet light on it... The man walked slowly towards her, shining the flashlight.* VERB V n prep V n
3 Something that **shines** is very bright and clear because it is reflecting light. *Her blue eyes shone and caught the light. ...a pair of patent shoes that shone like mirrors. ...shining aluminum machines.* VERB =gleam V V-ing
4 Something that has a **shine** is bright and clear because it is reflecting light. *This gel gives a beautiful shine to the hair... The wood had been recently polished to bring back the shine.* N-SING =sheen
5 If you **shine** a wooden, leather, or metal object, you make it bright by rubbing or polishing it. *Let him dust and shine the furniture... His high black boots had been shined to a gleaming finish.* VERB =polish V n
6 Someone who **shines** at a skill or activity does it extremely well. *Did you shine at school?... He failed to shine academically.* VERB =excel V
7 See also **shining**.
8 If you say that someone has **taken a shine to** another person, you mean that he or she liked them very much at their first meeting; an informal expression. *Seems to me you've taken quite a shine to Miss Richmond.* • **rain or shine**: see **rain**. PHRASE: V inflects

shingle /ʃɪŋgəl/ **shingles** ◆◇◇◇◇
1 **Shingle** is a mass of small rough pieces of stone on the shore of a sea or a river. *...a beach of sand and shingle.* N-UNCOUNT
2 **Shingles** are thin, rectangular tiles, especially ones made of wood, which are laid in overlapping rows to cover a roof or wall. *The roofs had shingles missing.* N-COUNT: usu pl
3 **Shingles** is a disease which causes a rash of painful red spots which spread in bands over a person's body, especially around their waist. N-UNCOUNT

shining /ʃaɪnɪŋ/. A **shining** achievement or quality is a very good one which should be greatly admired. *She is a shining example to us all... The Ariane space-rocket project has had a shining success.* • See also **shine**. ◆◆◇◇◇ ADJ

Shinto /ʃɪntoʊ/. **Shinto** is the traditional religion of Japan. N-UNCOUNT

shiny /ʃaɪni/ **shinier, shiniest. Shiny** things are bright and reflect light. *Her blonde hair was shiny and clean. ...a shiny new sports car.* ◆◆◇◇◇ ADJ-GRADED

ship /ʃɪp/ **ships, shipping, shipped** ◆◆◆◆◇
1 A **ship** is a large boat which carries passengers or cargo. *Within ninety minutes the ship was ready for departure... We went by ship over to America. ...merchant ships.* N-COUNT: also by N
2 If people or things **are shipped** somewhere, they are sent there on a ship or by some other means of transport. *Food is being shipped to drought-stricken Southern Africa.* VB: usu passive be V-ed prep/adv
3 See also **shipping**.

shipboard /ʃɪpbɔːʳd/. **Shipboard** means taking place on a ship. *...a shipboard romance.* ADJ: ADJ n

shipbuilder /ʃɪpbɪldəʳ/ **shipbuilders.** A **shipbuilder** is a company or a person that builds ships. N-COUNT

shipbuilding /ʃɪpbɪldɪŋ/. **Shipbuilding** is the industry of building ships. ◆◇◇◇◇ N-UNCOUNT

shipload /ʃɪploʊd/ **shiploads.** A **shipload** of people or goods is as many people or goods as a ship can carry. *...a shipload of refugees... A shipload of supplies arrived in Havana, Cuba, last night.* N-COUNT: usu N of n

shipmate /ʃɪpmeɪt/ **shipmates.** Sailors who work together on the same ship are **shipmates**. *His shipmates stayed at their stations during the attack.* N-COUNT: oft poss N

shipment /ʃɪpmənt/ **shipments** ◆◆◇◇◇
1 A **shipment** is an amount of a particular kind of cargo that is sent to another country on a ship, train, aeroplane, or other vehicle. *Mr de Michelis said the money was for food shipments. ...a shipment of weapons.* N-COUNT: usu N n, N of n
2 The **shipment** of a cargo somewhere is the sending of it there by ship, train, aeroplane, or some other vehicle. *Bananas are packed before being transported to the docks for shipment overseas.* N-UNCOUNT

shipowner /ʃɪpoʊnəʳ/ **shipowners.** A **shipowner** is someone who owns a ship or ships or who has shares in a shipping company. N-COUNT

shipper /ʃɪpəʳ/ **shippers. Shippers** are people or companies who ship cargo as a business. N-COUNT: usu pl

shipping /ʃɪpɪŋ/ ◆◆◇◇◇
1 **Shipping** is the transport of cargo as a business, especially on ships. *...the international shipping industry... The Greeks are still powerful players in world shipping.* N-UNCOUNT: usu with supp
2 You can refer to the amount of money that you pay to a company to transport cargo as **shipping**. *It is $39.95 plus $3 shipping.* N-UNCOUNT
3 You can refer to ships as **shipping** when considering them as a group. *They sent naval forces to protect merchant shipping.* N-UNCOUNT

shipshape /ʃɪpʃeɪp/. If something is **shipshape**, it looks tidy, neat, and in good condition. *The* ADJ-GRADED: usu v-link ADJ *house only needs an occasional coat of paint to keep it shipshape.*

shipwreck /ʃɪprek/ **shipwrecks; shipwrecked**

1 If there is a **shipwreck**, a ship is destroyed in an accident at sea. *He was drowned in a shipwreck off the coast of Spain. ...the perils of storm and shipwreck.* N-VAR

2 A **shipwreck** is a ship which has been destroyed in an accident at sea. N-COUNT =wreck

3 If someone **is shipwrecked**, their ship is destroyed in an accident at sea but they survive and manage to reach land. *He was shipwrecked after visiting the island... The shipwrecked couple were rescued by two fishermen.* V-PASSIVE be V-ed V-ed

shipwright /ʃɪpraɪt/ **shipwrights.** A **shipwright** is a person who builds or repairs ships as a job. N-COUNT

shipyard /ʃɪpjɑːʳd/ **shipyards.** A **shipyard** is a place where ships are built and repaired. ◆◇◇◇◇ N-COUNT

shire /ʃaɪəʳ/ **shires** ◆◇◇◇◇

1 **The Shires** or **the shire counties** are the mainly rural counties of England. *Smart country people are fleeing back to the shires.* N-COUNT: usu *the* N in pl

2 A **shire** or **shire horse** is a large heavy horse used for pulling loads; used mainly in British English. N-COUNT

shirk /ʃɜːʳk/ **shirks, shirking, shirked.** If someone does not **shirk** their responsibility or duty, they do what they have a responsibility to do. *We in the Congress have our role to play, and we can't shirk our responsibility... The Government will not shirk from considering the need for further action.* ♦ **shirker, shirkers** *They know I'm not a shirker.* VB: usu with neg V n V *from* -ing/n Also V N-COUNT

shirt /ʃɜːʳt/ **shirts** ◆◆◆◇◇

1 A **shirt** is a piece of clothing that you wear on the upper part of your body. Shirts have a collar, sleeves, and buttons down the front. N-COUNT

2 See also **dress shirt**, **stuffed shirt**, **sweatshirt**, **T-shirt**.

-shirted /-ʃɜːʳtɪd/. **-shirted** is used to form adjectives which indicate what colour or type of shirt someone is wearing. *...white-shirted men.* COMB in ADJ

shirtsleeve /ʃɜːʳtsliːv/ **shirtsleeves.** **Shirtsleeves** are the sleeves of a shirt. If a man is **in shirtsleeves** or **in his shirtsleeves**, he is wearing a shirt but not a jacket. *He rolled up his shirtsleeves... Franklin went to work in his shirtsleeves.* N-COUNT: usu pl

shirt-tail, shirt-tails; also spelled **shirttail**. **Shirt-tails** are the long parts of a shirt below the waist. *He wore sandals and old jeans and his shirt-tails weren't tucked in.* N-COUNT

shirty /ʃɜːʳti/. In British English, if someone gets **shirty**, they behave in a bad-tempered and rude way because they are annoyed about something; an informal word. *He got quite shirty with me.* ADJ-GRADED: usu v-link ADJ =stroppy

shit /ʃɪt/ **shits, shitting, shat** ◆◆◇◇◇

1 Some people use the word **shit** to refer to waste matter from the body of a human being or animal; an informal use that some people find offensive. N-UNCOUNT

2 To **shit** means to get rid of faeces from the body; an informal use that some people find offensive. VERB: V

3 To have a **shit** means to get rid of faeces from the body; an informal use which some people find offensive. N-SING

4 If someone says that they have **the shits**, they mean that they have got diarrhoea; an informal use that some people find offensive. N-PLURAL: *the* N

5 People sometimes refer to things that they do not like as **shit**; an informal use that some people find offensive. *This is a load of shit.* N-UNCOUNT

6 People sometimes insult someone they do not like by referring to them as a **shit**; an informal use that some people find offensive. N-COUNT PRAGMATICS

7 **Shit** is used to express anger, impatience, or disgust; an informal use that some people find offensive. EXCLAM

8 If someone says they **are shitting** themselves, they mean that they are very frightened; an informal use that some people find offensive. VERB: V pron-refl

9 To **beat** or **kick the shit out of** someone means to beat or kick them so violently that they are badly injured; an informal use that some people find offensive. PHRASES V inflects

10 If someone says that **the shit hit the fan**, they mean that there was suddenly a lot of trouble or angry arguments; an informal expression that some people find offensive. V inflects

11 If someone says that they do not **give a shit** about something, they mean that they do not care about it at all; an informal expression that some people find offensive. V inflects, usu with brd-neg PRAGMATICS

12 If someone is **in the shit** or **in deep shit**, they are in a lot of trouble; an informal expression that some people find offensive. usu v-link PHR

13 **Tough shit** can be used as a way of telling someone that they will have to accept a situation they do not like because they have no choice; an informal expression that some people find offensive. CONVENTION =hard luck

shite /ʃaɪt/. In British English, if someone describes something as **shite**, they do not like it or think that it is very poor quality; an informal word that some people find offensive. ADJ-GRADED

shitless /ʃɪtləs/. If someone says that they are scared **shitless** or bored **shitless**, they are emphasizing that they are extremely scared or bored; an informal word that some people find offensive. ADV: adj ADV PRAGMATICS

shitty /ʃɪti/. If someone describes something as **shitty**, they do not like it or think that it is of poor quality; an informal word that some people find offensive. ADJ-GRADED

shiver /ʃɪvəʳ/ **shivers, shivering, shivered.** When you **shiver**, your body shakes slightly because you are cold or frightened. *He shivered in the cold... I was sitting on the floor shivering with fear.* ► Also a noun. *The emptiness here sent shivers down my spine... Alice gave a shiver of delight.* ◆◆◇◇◇ VERB =shake V N-COUNT

shivery /ʃɪvəri/. If you are **shivery**, you cannot stop shivering because you feel cold, frightened, or ill. *She felt shivery and a little sick.* ADJ-GRADED

shoal /ʃoʊl/ **shoals.** A **shoal** of fish is a large group of them swimming together. *Among them swam shoals of fish. ...tuna shoals.* ◆◇◇◇◇ N-COUNT: oft N *of* n

shock /ʃɒk/ **shocks, shocking, shocked** ◆◆◆◆◇

1 If you have a **shock**, something suddenly happens which is unpleasant, upsetting, or very surprising. *The extent of the violence came as a shock... He has never recovered from the shock of your brother's death... It was quite a shock to see my face on that screen!* N-COUNT

2 **Shock** is a person's emotional and physical condition when something very frightening or upsetting has happened to them. *The little boy was speechless with shock... She's still in a state of shock.* N-UNCOUNT

3 If someone is in **shock**, they are suffering from a serious physical condition in which their blood cannot circulate properly, for example because they have had a bad injury. *He was found beaten and in shock... They escaped the blaze but were rushed to hospital suffering from shock.* N-UNCOUNT: oft *in* N

4 If something **shocks** you, it makes you feel very upset, because it involves death or suffering and because you had not expected it. *After forty years in the police force nothing much shocks me... Relief workers were shocked by what they saw.* ♦ **shocked** *This was a nasty attack and the woman is still very shocked.* VERB V n ADJ-GRADED

5 If someone or something **shocks** you, it upsets or offends you because you think it is rude or morally wrong. *You can't shock me... They were easily shocked in those days... We were always trying to be creative and to shock.* ♦ **shocked** *Don't look so shocked.* VERB V n V-ed V ADJ-GRADED

6 A **shock** announcement or event is one which shocks people because it is unexpected. *...the shock announcement that she is to resign. ...a shock defeat.* ADJ: ADJ n

7 A **shock** is something sudden and unexpected that threatens the economy, traditions, or way of life of a group of people. *This is the latest in a series of shocks to the Scandinavian banking system. ...the economic pain of two oil shocks.* N-COUNT: usu with supp

8 A **shock** is a slight movement in something when it is hit or jerked by something else. *Steel barriers can bend and absorb the shock.* N-VAR

9 A **shock** is the same as an **electric shock**. N-COUNT

10 A **shock of** hair is a very thick mass of hair on a person's head. *...a very old priest with a shock of white hair.* N-COUNT: N *of* n

11 See also **shocking**; **culture shock**, **electric shock**, **shell shock**.

12 A **short, sharp shock** is a punishment that is fairly harsh and severe but only lasts for a short time. PHRASE: N inflects

shock absorber, shock absorbers; also spelled **shock-absorber**. A **shock absorber** is a device fitted near the wheels of a car or other vehicle to reduce the effects of travelling over bumpy surfaces. *...a pair of simple rear shock absorbers.* N-COUNT

shocker /ʃɒkəʳ/ **shockers.** A **shocker** is something such as a story, a piece of news, or a film that shocks people or that is intended to shock them; an informal word. *Marsha Hunt's second novel, 'Free', is a shocker.* N-COUNT

shock horror

1 A **shock horror** story is presented in a way that is intended to cause great shock or anger; an informal use. *The media is full of shock-horror headlines about under-age crime.* ADJ: ADJ n =sensational

2 You can say **shock horror!** in reaction to something that other people may find shocking or surprising, to indicate in a humorous way that you do not find it shocking or surprising at all; an informal use. *I have felt intellectually superior to most of them despite – shock, horror – my total lack of educational qualifications.* EXCLAM PRAGMATICS

shocking /ʃɒkɪŋ/ ◆◆◇◇◇

1 You can say that something is **shocking** if you think that it is very bad; an informal use. *The media coverage was shocking... I must have been in a shocking state last night.* ♦ **shockingly** *His memory was becoming shockingly bad.* ADJ-GRADED =appalling; ADV: ADV adj/adv

2 You can say that something is **shocking** if you think that it is morally wrong. *It is shocking that nothing was said... This was a shocking invasion of privacy.* ♦ **shockingly** *Shockingly, this useless and dangerous surgery did not end until the 1930s.* ADJ-GRADED: oft *it* v-link ADJ that/to-inf; ADV

3 See also **shock**.

shocking pink. Something that is **shocking pink** is very bright pink. *...a shocking-pink T-shirt.* COLOUR

shock tactic, shock tactics. Shock tactics are a way of trying to influence people's attitudes to a particular matter by shocking them. *We must use shock tactics if we are to stop Aids becoming another accepted 20th-century disease.* N-COUNT: usu pl

shock therapy

1 You can refer to the use of extreme policies or actions to solve a particular problem quickly as **shock therapy**. *...Prague's policy of economic shock therapy.* N-UNCOUNT =shock treatment

2 **Shock therapy** is a way of treating mentally ill patients by passing an electric current through their brain. *...the electrodes used for shock therapy.* N-UNCOUNT =shock treatment

shock treatment, shock treatments. Shock treatment is the same as shock therapy. N-UNCOUNT: also N in pl

shock troops. Shock troops are soldiers who are specially trained to carry out a quick attack. N-PLURAL

shock wave, shock waves; also spelled **shockwave**. ◆◇◇◇◇

1 A **shock wave** is an area of very high pressure moving through the air, earth, or water. It is caused by an explosion or an earthquake, or by an object travelling faster than sound. *The shock waves yesterday were felt from Las Vegas to San Diego.* N-COUNT

2 A **shock wave** is the effect of something surprising, such as a piece of unpleasant news, that causes strong reactions when it spreads through a place. *The crime sent shock waves throughout the country.* N-COUNT

shod /ʃɒd/

1 You can use **shod** when you are describing the kind of shoes that a person is wearing; a formal use. *He has demonstrated a strong preference for being shod in running shoes. ...her stoutly shod feet.* ADJ: v-link ADJ *in/with* n, adv ADJ

2 **Shod** is the past participle of **shoe**.

shoddy /ʃɒdi/ **shoddier, shoddiest. Shoddy** work or a **shoddy** product has been done or made carelessly or badly. *I'm normally quick to complain about shoddy service... American customers no longer tolerate shoddy goods.* ♦ **shoddily** *These products are shoddily produced. ...shoddily-built cars.* ◆◇◇◇◇ ADJ-GRADED: usu ADJ n; ADV-GRADED: usu ADV with v

shoe /ʃuː/ **shoes, shoeing, shoed, shod** ◆◆◆◇◇

1 **Shoes** are objects which you wear on your feet. They cover most of your foot and you wear them over socks or stockings. *...a pair of shoes... Low-heeled comfortable shoes are best... You don't mind if I take my shoes off, do you?* • See also **snowshoe**, **training shoe**. N-COUNT

2 A **shoe** is the same as a **horseshoe**. N-COUNT

3 When a blacksmith **shoes** a horse, he or she fixes horseshoes onto its hooves. *Blacksmiths spent most of their time repairing tools and shoeing horses... He helped his father by holding the horses steady while they were being shod.* VERB V n

4 See also **shod**.

5 If you **fill** someone's **shoes** or **step into** their **shoes**, you take their place by doing the job they were doing. *No one has been able to fill his shoes... Now that Chris is gone she wants me to step into his shoes.* PHRASES V inflects

6 If you talk about being **in** someone's **shoes**, you talk about what you would do or how you would feel if you were in their situation. *I wouldn't want to be in his shoes.* usu v-link PHR

shoehorn /ʃuːhɔːʳn/ **shoehorns, shoehorning, shoehorned**

1 A **shoehorn** is a piece of metal or plastic with a slight curve that you put in the back of your shoe so that your heel will go into the shoe easily. N-COUNT

2 If you **shoehorn** something into a tight place, you manage to get it in there even though it is difficult. *Their cars are shoehorned into tiny spaces... I was shoehorning myself into my skin-tight ball gown.* VERB *be* V-ed *into* n; V n *into* n

shoelace /ʃuːleɪs/ **shoelaces. Shoelaces** are long, narrow pieces of material like pieces of string that you use to fasten your shoes. *He began to tie his shoelaces.* N-COUNT: usu pl

shoemaker /ʃuːmeɪkəʳ/ **shoemakers.** A **shoemaker** is a person whose job is making shoes and boots. N-COUNT

shoestring /ʃuːstrɪŋ/ **shoestrings**

1 In American English, **shoestrings** are long, narrow pieces of material like pieces of string that you use to fasten your shoes; the British word is **shoelace**. N-COUNT: usu pl

2 A **shoestring** budget is one where you have very little money to spend. *The British-produced film was made on a shoestring budget.* ADJ: ADJ n =tight

3 If you do something or make something **on a shoestring**, you do it using very little money. *The theatre will be run on a shoestring.* PHRASE: PHR after v

shone /ʃɒn, AM ʃoʊn/. **Shone** is the past tense and past participle of **shine**.

shoo /ʃuː/ **shoos, shooing, shooed**

1 If you **shoo** an animal or a person away, you make them go away by waving your hands or arms at them. *You'd better shoo him away... I shooed him out of the room.* VERB V n with adv; V n prep

2 You say **'shoo!'** to an animal when you want it to go away. *Shoo, bird, shoo.* EXCLAM

shoo-in, shoo-ins. In American English, a **shoo-in** is a person or thing that seems sure to succeed; an informal word. *George Bush looked like a shoo-in for a second term in the White House.* N-COUNT

shook /ʃʊk/. **Shook** is the past tense of **shake**.

shoot /ʃuːt/ **shoots, shooting, shot** ◆◆◆◆◇

1 If someone **shoots** a person or an animal, they kill them or injure them by firing a bullet or arrow at them. *The police had orders to shoot anyone who attacked them... Namibian law permits ranchers to shoot cheetahs to protect their livestock... Gunmen shot dead the brother of the minister... The man was shot dead by the police during a raid on his house... Her father shot himself in the head with a shotgun.* VERB V n; V n with adj; V n *in* n

2 To **shoot** means to fire a bullet from a weapon VERB

such as a gun. *He taunted armed officers by pointing to his head, as if inviting them to shoot... The police came around the corner and they started shooting at us... She had never been able to shoot straight... Troops began shooting in all directions.* V V atn V adv/prep

3 If someone or something **shoots** in a particular direction, they move in that direction quickly and suddenly. *They had almost reached the boat when a figure shot past them... Another car shot out of a junction and smashed into the back of them.* VERB V adv/prep

4 If you **shoot** something somewhere or if it **shoots** somewhere, it moves there quickly and suddenly. *Masters shot a hand across the table and gripped his wrist... As soon as she got close, the old woman's hand shot out... You'd turn on the water, and it would shoot straight up in the air.* V-ERG V n prep/adv V adv/prep

5 If you **shoot** a glance at someone, you look at them quickly and briefly, often in a way that expresses your feelings. *Mary Ann shot him a rueful look... The man in the black overcoat shot a penetrating look at the other man.* VERB V n n V n *at* n

6 If someone **shoots** to fame, they become famous or successful very quickly. *Alina Reyes shot to fame a few years ago with her extraordinary first novel... She shot to stardom on Broadway in a Noel Coward play.* VERB V *to* n

7 When people **shoot** a film or **shoot** photographs, they make a film or take photographs using a camera. *He'd love to shoot his film in Cuba... Three CBS cameramen were on site to shoot and edit taped reports.* ► Also a noun. *...a barn presently being used for a video shoot.* VERB V n N-COUNT

8 **Shoots** are plants that are beginning to grow, or new parts growing from a plant or tree. N-COUNT: usu pl

9 In sports such as football or basketball, when someone **shoots**, they try to score by kicking, throwing, or hitting the ball towards the goal. *Spencer scuttled away from Young to shoot wide when he should have scored... A time limit was set for a team to shoot at the basket.* VERB V adv/prep Also V, V n

10 In American English, when someone **shoots** pool or **shoots** craps, they play a game of pool or the dice game called craps. *People are still hanging out drinking beer, maybe shooting some pool.* VERB V n

11 See also **shooting**, **shot**.

12 If you **shoot the breeze** or **shoot the bull** with someone, you talk to them about things which are not very serious or important; an informal expression used especially in American English. *They expected me to sit up and shoot the breeze with them till one or two in the morning... I also met with Pollack again to kind of shoot the bull.* PHRASES RECIP: V inflects, PHR *with* n, pl-n V

13 If you **shoot** yourself **in the foot**, something you say or do causes you harm. *If I was to insult the contestants I would be shooting myself in the foot.* V inflects

14 • to **shoot from the hip**: see **hip**.

shoot down PHRASAL VERB

1 If someone **shoots down** an aeroplane, a helicopter, or a missile, they make it fall to the ground by hitting it with a bullet or missile. *They claimed to have shot down one incoming missile... His plane was shot down over North Vietnam in 1967.* V P n (not pron) Also V n P

2 If one person **shoots down** another, they shoot them with a gun. *He was prepared to suppress rebellion by shooting down protesters... They shot him down in cold blood.* V P n (not pron) V n P

3 If you **shoot** someone **down** or **shoot down** their ideas, you ridicule that person or their ideas. *She was able to shoot the rumour down in flames with ample documentary evidence.* V n P Also V P n (not pron)

shoot up PHRASAL VERB

1 If something **shoots up**, it grows or increases very quickly. *Sales shot up by 9% last month... The fair market value of the property shot up.* V P *by/to* n V P

2 If a drug addict **shoots up**, they inject a quantity of drugs into their body. *Drug addicts shoot up in the back alleys... We shot up heroin in the playground.* V P V P n (not pron)

shooter /ʃuːtəʳ/ **shooters** ◆◇◇◇◇

1 A **shooter** is a person who shoots a gun. *An eyewitness identified him as the shooter... I have been a shooter for 16 years and enjoy my sport.* N-COUNT

2 A **shooter** is a gun; an informal use. N-COUNT

shooting /ʃuːtɪŋ/ **shootings** ◆◆◇◇◇

1 A **shooting** is an occasion when someone is killed or injured by being shot with a gun. *Two more bodies were found nearby after the shooting... A drug-related gang war led to a series of shootings in the city.* N-COUNT

2 In British English, **shooting** is hunting animals with a gun as a form of sport or recreation. The usual American word is **hunting**. *Grouse shooting begins in August.* N-UNCOUNT

3 The **shooting** of a film is the act of filming it. *Ingrid was busy learning her lines for the next day's shooting... The shooting of The Maltese Falcon proceeded without a hitch.* N-UNCOUNT: usu with supp

shooting gallery, shooting galleries. A **shooting gallery** is a place where people use rifles to shoot at targets, especially in order to win prizes. N-COUNT

shooting star, shooting stars. A **shooting star** is a piece of rock or metal that burns very brightly when it enters the earth's atmosphere from space, and is seen from earth as a bright star travelling very fast across the sky. N-COUNT

shooting war, shooting wars. When two countries in conflict engage in a **shooting war**, they fight each other with weapons rather than opposing each other by diplomatic or other means; used in journalism. N-COUNT

shoot-out, shoot-outs ◆◇◇◇◇

1 A **shoot-out** is a fight in which people shoot at each other with guns. *Three IRA men were killed in the shoot-out. ...a bloody shoot-out between rival gangs that killed 18 people.* N-COUNT

2 In games such as football, if the result of a match where the scores are equal is decided by a **shoot-out** or a penalty **shoot-out**, each side takes a series of penalties after the game has ended in a draw in order to determine the winner. *The Danes won that UEFA tie in a shoot-out.* N-COUNT

shop /ʃɒp/ **shops, shopping, shopped** ◆◆◆◆◇

1 In British English, a **shop** is a building or part of a building where things are sold. The more usual American word is **store**. *...health food shops. ...a record shop... It's not available in the shops.* N-COUNT =store

2 When you **shop**, you go to shops and buy things. *He always shopped at the Co-op. ...some advice that's worth bearing in mind when shopping for a new carpet. ...customers who shop once a week.* VERB V prep/adv V

♦ **shopper, shoppers** *...crowds of Christmas shoppers.* N-COUNT

3 You can refer to a place where a particular service is offered as a particular type of **shop**. *...the barber shop where Rodney sometimes had his hair cut. ...betting shops. ...your local video shop.* N-COUNT: n N

4 You can refer to a place where things are made or done as a particular kind of **shop**. *...the blacksmith's shop. ...a repair shop.* N-COUNT: n N

5 In informal British English, if you **shop** someone, you report them to the police for doing something illegal. *His father was so disgusted to discover his son was dealing drugs he shopped him to police... Fraudsters are often shopped by honest friends and neighbours.* VERB V n *to* n *be* V-ed

6 See also **shopping**; **bucket shop, chip shop, coffee shop, corner shop, paper shop, pawn shop, print shop, sex shop, tea shop, talking shop, thrift shop.**

7 In informal British English, if something is happening **all over the shop**, it is happening in many different places or throughout a wide area. *This gave them the freedom to make trouble all over the shop without fear of retribution.* PHRASES PHR after v =everywhere

8 If you **set up shop**, you start a business. *He set up shop as an independent PR consultant... He has just set up shop in Cherbourg.* V inflects

9 In British English, when a shop, office, or firm **shuts up shop**, it stops doing business and closes, either at the end of the day or permanently. *If they had been faced with the bill they'd have shut up shop and fled the country.* V inflects

10 If you say that people **are talking shop**, you V inflects

mean that they are talking about their work, and this is boring for other people who do not do the same work. *Although I get on well with my colleagues, if you hang around together all the time you just end up talking shop.* PRAGMATICS

11 • **a bull in a china shop**: see **bull**.

shop around. If you **shop around**, you go to different shops or companies in order to compare the prices and quality of goods or services before you decide to buy them. *Prices may vary so it's well worth shopping around before you buy... He shopped around for a firm that would be flexible.* PHRASAL VERB VP VP for n

shopaholic /ʃɒpəhɒlɪk/ **shopaholics.** A **shopaholic** is a person who spends money compulsively; an informal word. N-COUNT

shop assistant, shop assistants. In British English, a **shop assistant** is a person who works in a shop selling things to customers. The usual American word is **sales clerk**. ◆◇◇◇◇ N-COUNT

shop floor; also spelled **shop-floor** or **shopfloor**. The **shop floor** is used to refer to all the workers in a factory or the area where they work, especially in contrast to the management or the area where the management work. *Cost must be controlled, not just on the shop floor but in the boardroom too. ...shop floor workers.* N-SING: oft N n

shop front, shop fronts; also spelled **shopfront.** A **shop front** is the outside part of a shop which faces the street, including the door and windows; used mainly in British English. The usual American term is **storefront**. N-COUNT

shopkeeper /ʃɒpkiːpəʳ/ **shopkeepers.** A **shopkeeper** is a person who owns or manages a small shop; used mainly in British English. The usual American term is **storekeeper**. ◆◇◇◇◇ N-COUNT

shoplift /ʃɒplɪft/ **shoplifts, shoplifting, shoplifted.** If someone **shoplifts**, they steal goods from a shop by hiding them in a bag or in their clothes. *He openly shoplifted from a supermarket... They had shoplifted thousands of dollars' worth of merchandise.* ♦ **shoplifter, shoplifters** *A persistent shoplifter has been banned from every Marks & Spencer store in Britain.* VERB V V n N-COUNT

shoplifting /ʃɒplɪftɪŋ/. **Shoplifting** is stealing from a shop by hiding things in a bag or in your clothes. *The grocer accused her of shoplifting and demanded to look in her bag... He admitted five shoplifting offences.* N-UNCOUNT

shopping /ʃɒpɪŋ/ ◆◆◆◇◇

1 When you do the **shopping**, you go to shops and buy things. *I'll do the shopping this afternoon.* • See also **window shopping**. N-UNCOUNT

2 Your **shopping** is the things that you have bought from shops, especially food and groceries. *We put the shopping away.* N-UNCOUNT

shopping cart, shopping carts. A **shopping cart** is the same as a **shopping trolley**; used in American English. N-COUNT

shopping centre, shopping centres; also spelled **shopping center**. ◆◇◇◇◇

1 In British English, a **shopping centre** is a covered area where many shops have been built and where cars are not allowed. The American term is **shopping mall**. *The new shopping centre was constructed at a cost of 1.1 million.* N-COUNT

2 In British English, a **shopping centre** is an area in a town where a lot of shops have been built close together. N-COUNT

shopping list, shopping lists. A **shopping list** is a list of the things that you want to buy when you go shopping, which you write on a piece of paper. ◆◇◇◇◇ N-COUNT

shopping mall, shopping malls. A **shopping mall** is a covered area where many shops have been built and where cars are not allowed. ◆◇◇◇◇ N-COUNT

shopping trolley, shopping trolleys. In British English, a **shopping trolley** is a large metal basket on wheels which is provided by shops such as supermarkets for customers to use while they are in the shop. The American word is **shopping cart**. N-COUNT

shop steward, shop stewards. A **shop steward** is a trade union member who is elected by the other members in a factory or office to speak for them at official meetings; used mainly in British English. N-COUNT

shore /ʃɔːʳ/ **shores, shoring, shored** ◆◆◆◇◇

1 The **shores** or the **shore** of a sea, lake, or wide river is the land along the edge of it. Someone who is **on shore** is on the land rather than on a ship. *They walked down to the shore. ...elephants living on the shores of Lake Kariba... I have spent less time on shore than most men... As soon as they were safely back to shore, Dirk raced for the nearest phone.* N-COUNT: also prep N

2 When someone or something reaches the **shores** of a country or continent, they arrive in that country or continent; a literary use. *It is feared that a similar epidemic will soon reach the shores of Europe... This youngster is another destined to leave these shores.* N-PLURAL: with supp

shore up. If you **shore up** something that is weak or about to fail, you do something in order to strengthen it or support it. *The democracies of the West may find it hard to shore up their defences.* PHRASAL VERB V P n (not pron) Also V n P

shoreline /ʃɔːʳlaɪn/ **shorelines.** A **shoreline** is the edge of a sea, lake, or wide river. ◆◇◇◇◇ N-COUNT

shorn /ʃɔːʳn/

1 If grass or hair is **shorn**, it has been cut very short; a literary use. *...his shorn hair.* ADJ

2 If someone or something is **shorn** of something that was an important part of them, it has been removed from them; a literary use. *She looks terrible, shorn of all her beauty and dignity. ...an age increasingly shorn of religious and political faith.* ADJ: v-link ADJ of n

3 **Shorn** is the past participle of **shear**.

short 1 adjective and adverb uses

short /ʃɔːʳt/ **shorter, shortest** ◆◆◆◆◆

1 If something is **short** or lasts for a **short** time, it does not last very long. *The announcement was made a short time ago... How could you do it in such a short period of time?... Mr Mandela took a short break before resuming his schedule... Kemp gave a short laugh... We had a short meeting.* ADJ-GRADED ≠long

2 If you talk about a **short** hour, day, or year, you mean that it seems to have passed very quickly or will seem to pass very quickly. *For a few short weeks there was peace... Only five short years later, your money will have grown by $94,000.* ADJ-GRADED: usu ADJ n ≠long

3 A **short** speech, letter, or book does not have many words or pages in it. *They were performing a short extract from Shakespeare's Two Gentlemen of Verona... This is a short note to say thank you.* ADJ-GRADED: usu ADJ n ≠long

4 Someone who is **short** is not as tall as most people are. *I'm tall and thin and he's short and fat. ...a short, elderly woman with grey hair... He's the shortest of four brothers.* ADJ-GRADED ≠tall

5 Something that is **short** measures only a small amount from one end to the other. *The city centre and shops are only a short distance away... A short flight of steps led to a grand doorway... His black hair was very short.* ADJ-GRADED ≠long

6 If you are **short of** something or if it is **short**, you do not have enough of it. If you are running **short of** something or if it is running **short**, you do not have much of it left. *Her father's illness left the family short of money... Government forces are running short of ammunition and fuel... Supplies of everything are unreliable, food is short... Time is running short.* ADJ-GRADED: v-link ADJ, usu ADJ of n

7 If someone or something is or stops **short of** a place, they have not quite reached it. If they are or fall **short of** an amount, they have not quite achieved it. *He stopped a hundred yards short of the building... Opinion polls have suggested Mr Vargas may fall short of an absolute majority... Inflation is just short of 11 per cent... They were still 91 short of their target.* ADJ: v-link ADJ of n

8 **Short of** a particular thing means except for that thing or without actually doing that thing. *Short of climbing railings four metres high, there was no way into the garden from this road... They have no means, short of civil war, to enforce their will upon the minorities.* PHR-PREP: PREP n/-ing =except for

9 If something is cut **short** or stops **short**, it is stopped before people expect it to or before it has finished. *His glittering career was cut short by a heart attack... Jackson cut short his trip to Africa... His voice stopped short as he saw the blade emerge from Desmond's pocket.* ADV: ADV after v

10 If a name or abbreviation is **short for** another name, it is the short version of that name. *Her friend Kes (short for Kesewa) was in tears... 'O.O.B.E.' is short for 'Out Of Body Experience'.* ADJ: v-link ADJ *for* n

11 If you have a **short** temper, you get angry very easily. *...an awkward, self-conscious woman with a short temper.* • See also **short-tempered.** ADJ-GRADED

12 If you are **short with** someone, you speak briefly and rather rudely to them, because you are impatient or angry. *She seemed nervous or tense, and she was definitely short with me.* ADJ-GRADED: v-link ADJ, usu ADJ *with* n =terse

13 If you **are caught short** or **are taken short**, you feel a sudden strong need to urinate, especially when you can not easily find a toilet; an informal expression. PHRASES V inflects

14 If a person or thing is called something **for short**, that is the short version of their name. *Opposite me was a woman called Jasminder (Jazzy for short)... This condition is called seasonal affective disorder, or SAD for short.* usu n PHR

15 If you **go short** of something, especially food, you do not have as much of it as you want or need. *Some people may manage their finances badly and therefore have to go short of essentials.* V inflects, oft PHR *of* n

16 You use the expression **in short** when you have been giving a lot of details and you want to give a conclusion or summary. *Try tennis, badminton or windsurfing. In short, anything challenging... She was surrounded by doctors, lawyers, housewives – people, in short, like herself.* PHR with cl

17 You use **nothing short of** or **little short of** to emphasize how great or extreme something is. For example, if you say that something is **nothing short of** a miracle or **nothing short of** catastrophic, you are emphasizing that it is a miracle or it is catastrophic. *The results are nothing short of magnificent... His last visit to Washington was little short of a fiasco.* v-link PHR adj/n PRAGMATICS

18 If you say that someone is, for example, **several cards short of a full deck** or **one sandwich short of a picnic**, you think they are stupid, foolish, or crazy; used in informal English. v-link PHR

19 If someone or something **is short on** a particular good quality, they do not have as much of it as you think they should have; used showing disapproval. *He was very short on enthusiasm... The proposals were short on detail.* V inflects PRAGMATICS

20 If someone **stops short of** doing something, they come close to doing it but do not actually do it. *He stopped short of explicitly criticizing the government... The resolution stopped short of an outright declaration of independence.* V inflects, PHR -ing/n

21 If workers are put on **short time**, they are asked to work less hours than the normal working week, because their employer can not afford to pay them a full time wage. *Workers across the country have been put on short time because of the slump in demand... Most manufacturers have had to introduce short-time working.* *on* PHR, PHR n

22 If something **pulls** you **up short** or **brings** you **up short**, it makes you suddenly stop what you are doing. *The name on the gate pulled me up short.* V inflects

23 If you **make short work of** someone or something, you deal with them or defeat them very quickly; an informal expression. *Stefan Edberg made short work of his opponent.* V inflects, PHR n

24 • **short of breath**: see **breath.** • **at short notice**: see **notice.** • to **sell** someone **short**: see **sell.** • to **get short shrift**: see **shrift.** • to **cut a long story short**: see **story.** • to **draw the short straw**: see **straw.** • **in short supply**: see **supply.** • **in the short term**: see **term.**

short 2 noun uses

short /ʃɔːʳt/ **shorts** ◆◆◇◇◇

1 **Shorts** are trousers with very short legs, that people wear in hot weather or for taking part in sport. *...two women in bright cotton shorts and tee shirts.* N-PLURAL: also *a pair of* N

2 **Shorts** are men's underpants that usually reach to mid-thigh; used especially in American English. N-PLURAL: also *a pair of* N

3 A **short** is a small, strong alcoholic drink of a spirit such as whisky, gin, or vodka, rather than a weaker alcoholic drink like beer or wine that you can drink in larger quantities; used mainly in British English. N-COUNT

4 A **short** is a short film, especially one that is shown before the main film at the cinema. N-COUNT

shortage /ʃɔːʳtɪdʒ/ **shortages.** If there is a **shortage** of something, there is not enough of it. *A shortage of funds is preventing the UN from monitoring relief... Vietnam is suffering from food shortage... There's no shortage of ideas when it comes to improving the education of children.* ◆◆◆◇◇ N-VAR: usu with supp, N *of* n, n N

short back and sides; also spelled **short-back-and-sides.** A **short back and sides** is a haircut in which the hair is cut very short at the back and sides with slightly thicker, longer hair on the top of the head. N-SING

shortbread /ʃɔːʳtbred/ **shortbreads. Shortbread** is a kind of biscuit made from flour, sugar, and butter. N-VAR

shortcake /ʃɔːʳtkeɪk/.

1 **Shortcake** is the same as **shortbread**; used in British English. N-UNCOUNT

2 **Shortcake** is a cake or dessert which consists of a crisp cake with layers of fruit and cream; used mainly in American English. *...desserts like strawberry shortcake and pumpkin pie.* N-UNCOUNT

short-change, short-changes, short-changing, short-changed

1 If someone **short-changes** you, they do not give you enough change after you have bought something from them. *The cashier made a mistake and short-changed him.* VERB V n

2 If you **are short-changed**, you are treated unfairly or dishonestly, often because you are given less of something than you deserve. *Women are in fact still being short-changed in the press.* ♦ **short-changed** *Some theatre-goers may feel short-changed when they arrive expecting to see an international superstar perform.* VB: usu passive be V-ed; ADJ-GRADED: v-link ADJ

short-circuit, short-circuits, short-circuiting, short-circuited

1 If an electrical system or device **short-circuits** or **is short-circuited**, a wrong connection or damaged wire causes electricity to travel along the wrong route and damage the system or device. *Carbon dust and oil build up in large motors and cause them to short-circuit... Once inside they short-circuited the electronic security.* ▶ Also a noun. *Ensure that any electrical gadgets are fitted expertly to eliminate the risk of a short-circuit.* V-ERG V, V n; N-COUNT

2 If someone or something **short-circuits** a process or system, they avoid long or difficult parts of it and use a quicker, more direct method to achieve their aim. *Mr Abrahams said the approach was intended to short-circuit normal complaints procedures.* VERB V n

shortcoming /ʃɔːʳtkʌmɪŋ/ **shortcomings.** Someone's or something's **shortcomings** are the faults or weaknesses which they have. *Marriages usually break down as a result of the shortcomings of both partners... His book has its shortcomings.* ◆◇◇◇◇ N-COUNT: usu pl, oft with poss =failing

shortcrust /ʃɔːʳtkrʌst/. **Shortcrust** pastry is a kind of pastry that is easy to make and that crumbles easily. ADJ: ADJ n

short cut, short cuts; also spelled **short-cut** or **shortcut.** ◆◇◇◇◇

1 A **short cut** is a quicker way of getting somewhere than the usual route. *I tried to take a short cut and got lost.* N-COUNT

2 A **short cut** is a method of achieving something more quickly or more easily than if you use the usual methods. *Fame can be a shortcut to love and money... There is no short cut from dictatorship to democracy.* N-COUNT: oft N *to* n

shorten /ʃɔːʳtᵊn/ **shortens, shortening, shortened** ◆◇◇◇◇

1 If you **shorten** an event or the length of time that something lasts, or if it **shortens**, it does not last as long as it would otherwise do or as it used to do. *Smoking can shorten your life... The trading day is shortened in observance of the Labor Day holiday... When the days shorten in winter some people suffer depression.* V-ERG ≠lengthen V n V

2 If you **shorten** an object or if it **shortens**, it becomes smaller in length. *Her father paid £1,000 for an operation to shorten her nose.* V-ERG ≠lengthen V n Also V

3 If you **shorten** a name or other word, you change it by removing some of the letters. *Originally called Lili, she eventually shortened her name to Lee.* VERB V n

4 ● **to shorten the odds**: see **odds**.

shortening /ʃɔːʳtnɪŋ/ **shortenings. Shortening** is cooking fat that you use with flour in order to make pastry or dough; used especially in American English. N-MASS

shortfall /ʃɔːʳtfɔːl/ **shortfalls.** If there is a **shortfall** in something, there is less of it than you need. *The government has refused to make up a £30,000 shortfall in funding.* ◆◇◇◇◇ N-COUNT: usu with supp =deficit

shorthand /ʃɔːʳthænd/ ◆◇◇◇◇

1 **Shorthand** is a way of writing which uses signs to represent words or syllables. Shorthand is used by secretaries to quickly write down what someone is saying. *Ben took notes in shorthand.* N-UNCOUNT ≠longhand

2 You can also use **shorthand** to mean a quick or simple way of referring to something. *Laslett uses the shorthand of 'second age' for the group of younger people who are creating families... The fiction that 'he' is a neutral shorthand for 'he or she' is no longer acceptable to many.* N-UNCOUNT: also a N

short-handed; also spelled **shorthanded.** If a company or organization is **short-handed**, it does not have enough people to work on a particular job. *We're actually a bit short-handed at the moment.* ADJ-GRADED: usu v-link ADJ =short-staffed

shorthand typist, shorthand typists. A **shorthand typist** is a person who types and does shorthand, usually in an office. N-COUNT

short-haul. Short-haul is used to describe things that involve transporting passengers or goods over short distances. *Short-haul flights operate from Heathrow and Gatwick.* ADJ: ADJ n ≠long-haul

shortish /ʃɔːʳtɪʃ/. **Shortish** means fairly short. *...a shortish man, with graying hair.* ADJ: usu ADJ n

shortlist /ʃɔːʳtlɪst/ **shortlists, shortlisting, shortlisted.** The noun is also spelled **short list**, especially in American English. ◆◇◇◇◇

1 If someone is on a **shortlist**, for example for a job or a prize, they are one of a small group of people who have been chosen from a larger group. The successful person is then chosen from the small group. *If you've been asked for an interview you are probably on a short list of no more than six.* N-COUNT

2 If someone or something **is shortlisted** for a job or a prize, they are put on a shortlist; used mainly in British English. *He was shortlisted for the Nobel Prize for literature several times... Mr Afzal has been shortlisted as a parliamentary candidate.* VB: usu passive be V-ed for/as n

short-lived. Something that is **short-lived** does not last very long. *Any hope that the speech would end the war was short-lived... Chantal told Martine about her short-lived marriage.* ◆◇◇◇◇ ADJ-GRADED

shortly /ʃɔːʳtli/ ◆◆◆◇◇

1 If something happens **shortly** after or before something else, it happens not long after or before it. If something is going to happen **shortly**, it is going to happen soon. *Their trial will shortly begin... The work will be completed very shortly... Shortly after moving into her apartment, she found a job... She kept a diary until shortly before her death... Christine didn't answer, and shortly afterwards she left.* ADV-GRADED: ADV with v, ADV *after/before* n, ADV adv

2 If you speak to someone **shortly**, you speak to them in a cross or impatient way. *'I don't know you,' he said shortly, 'and I'm in a hurry.'* ADV-GRADED: ADV after v =tersely

short-range. Short-range weapons or missiles are designed to be fired across short distances. ◆◇◇◇◇ ADJ-GRADED: ADJ n

short-sighted; also spelled **shortsighted.** ◆◇◇◇◇

1 If you are **short-sighted**, you cannot see things properly when they are far away, because there is something wrong with your eyes. *Testing showed her to be very short-sighted.* ♦ **short-sightedness** *Radical eye surgery promises to cure short-sightedness.* ADJ-GRADED N-UNCOUNT

2 If someone is **short-sighted** about something, or if their ideas are **short-sighted**, they do not make proper or careful judgements about the future. *Environmentalists fear that this is a short-sighted approach to the problem of global warming... I think we're being very short-sighted.* ♦ **short-sightedness** *The government now recognises the short-sightedness of this approach.* ADJ-GRADED N-UNCOUNT

short-staffed. A company or place that is **short-staffed** does not have enough people working there. *The hospital is desperately short-staffed.* ADJ-GRADED =short-handed

short story, short stories. A **short story** is a piece of prose fiction that is only a few pages long. *He published a collection of short stories.* ◆◇◇◇◇ N-COUNT

short-tempered. Someone who is **short-tempered** gets angry very quickly. *I'm a bit short-tempered sometimes.* ADJ-GRADED

short-term. Short-term is used to describe things that will last for a short time, or things that will have an effect soon rather than in the distant future. *Investors weren't concerned about short-term profits over the next few years... This is a cynical manipulation of the situation for short-term political gain... The company has 90 staff, almost all on short-term contracts... The short-term outlook for employment remains gloomy... There is no easy short-term solution to Britain's economic malaise.* ◆◆◆◇◇ ADJ-GRADED: usu ADJ n ≠long-term

short-time. See **short.**

short-wave; also spelled **short wave** or **shortwave. Short-wave** is a range of short radio wavelengths used for broadcasting. *I use the short-wave radio to get the latest war news... Until now, the BBC has only been available in South Africa on short wave.* N-UNCOUNT: oft N n

shot /ʃɒt/ **shots** ◆◆◆◆◇

1 **Shot** is the past tense and past participle of **shoot.**

2 A **shot** is an act of firing a gun. *He had murdered Perceval at point blank range with a single shot... A man fired a volley of shots at them.* N-COUNT

3 Someone who is a good **shot** can shoot well. Someone who is a bad **shot** cannot shoot well. *He was not a particularly good shot because of his eyesight.* N-COUNT: adj N

4 In sports such as football, golf, or tennis, a **shot** is an act of kicking, hitting, or throwing the ball, especially in an attempt to score a point. *He had only one shot at goal.* N-COUNT

5 A **shot** is a photograph or a particular sequence of pictures in a film. *I decided to try for a more natural shot of a fox peering from the bushes... He received praise for the atmospheric monochrome shots in David Lynch's The Elephant Man.* N-COUNT

6 If you have a **shot at** something, you attempt to do it; an informal use. *The heavyweight champion will be given a shot at Holyfield's world title.* N-COUNT: usu sing, usu N *at* n

7 A **shot** of a drug is an injection of it. *He administered a shot of Nembutal.* N-COUNT: usu N *of* n

8 A **shot** of a strong alcoholic drink is a small glass of it; used especially in American English. *...a shot of vodka. ...spirits and liqueurs, served in a shot glass.* N-COUNT

9 If you **give** something your **best shot**, you do it as well as you possibly can; an informal expression. *I don't expect to win. But I am going to give it my best shot.* PHRASES V inflects

10 If you describe someone's actions as **a shot across the bow** of another person, you mean that it is a warning to that person to stop or change what they are doing. *As a warning shot across the bows of rivals, it is already setting aggressive prices.* Ns inflect, usu v-link PHR

11 The person who **calls the shots** is in a position V inflects

to tell others what to do. *The directors call the shots and nothing happens without their say-so.*

12 If you do something **like a shot**, you do it without any delay or hesitation; an informal expression. *I heard the key turn in the front door and I was out of bed like a shot... If he thought it his duty to arrest me, he'd do it like a shot.* PHR after v

13 If you describe something as a **long shot**, you mean that it is unlikely to succeed, but is worth trying. *The deal was a long shot, but Bagley had little to lose... I thought about meeting a handsome stranger but it seemed a bit of a long shot.* v-link PHR

14 People sometimes use the expression **by a long shot** to emphasize the opinion they are giving. *The missile-reduction treaty makes sweeping cuts, but the arms race isn't over by a long shot.* PRAGMATICS

15 If something **is shot through with** an element or feature, it contains a lot of that element or feature. *His work was deeply refreshing, and all of it shot through with humour... This is an argument shot through with inconsistency.* V inflects, PHR n

16 ● **a shot in the dark**: see **dark**.

shotgun /ʃɒtgʌn/ **shotguns.** A **shotgun** is a gun used for shooting birds and animals which fires a lot of small metal balls at one time. ◆◇◇◇◇ N-COUNT

shot put. In athletics, the **shot put** is a competition in which the contestants throw a heavy metal ball as far as possible. N-SING: usu *the* N ♦ **shot putter, shot putters** ...*Canadian shot-putter Georgette Reed.* N-COUNT

should /ʃəd, STRONG ʃʊd/ ◆◆◆◆◆

Should is a modal verb. It is used with the base form of a verb.

1 You use **should** or **should not** when you are giving advice or recommendations. You also use **should** when you are mentioning things that are not the case but that you think ought to be. *I should exercise more... The diet should be maintained unchanged for about a year... He's never going to be able to forget it. And I don't think he should... Sometimes I am not as brave as I should be... Should our children be taught to swim at school?* MODAL PRAGMATICS

2 You use **should** or **should not** to tell someone what to do or to report a rule or law which tells someone what to do. *A High Court judge has ruled that the two men should stand trial... The European Commission ruled that British Aerospace should pay back tens of millions of pounds.* MODAL PRAGMATICS

3 If you say that something **should have** happened, you mean that it did not happen, but that you wish it had happened or that you expected it to happen. If you say that something **should not have** happened, you mean that it did happen, but that you wish it had not. *I should have gone this morning but I was feeling a bit ill... I should have been in the shade like all the other tourists, then I wouldn't have got burned... You should have done that yesterday you idiot!... You should have written to the area manager again... I shouldn't have said what I did.* MODAL

4 You use **should** when you are saying that something is probably the case or will probably happen in the way you are describing. If you say that something **should have** happened by a particular time, you mean that it will probably have happened by that time. *You should have no problem with reading this language... The voters should by now be in no doubt what the parties stand for... The doctor said it will take six weeks and I should be fine by then... We should have finished by a quarter past two and the bus doesn't leave till half past.* MODAL

5 You use **should** in questions when you are asking someone for advice, permission, or information. *Should I or shouldn't I go to university?... What should I do?... Please could you advise me what I should do?... Should I go back to the motel and wait for you to telephone?... Should I fetch your slippers?... Should we tell her about it?* MODAL PRAGMATICS

6 You say **'I should'**, usually with the expression 'if I were you', when you are giving someone advice by telling them what you would do if you were in their position; a formal use. *I should look out if I were you!... James, I should refuse that consultancy with Shapiro, if I were you... I should go if I were you.* MODAL PRAGMATICS

7 You use **should** in conditional clauses when you are talking about things that might happen; a formal use. *If you should be fired, your health and pension benefits will not be automatically cut off... Should you buy a home from Lovell, the company promises to buy it back at the same price after three years... Should Havelock become the first Englishman to retain his world title, he will be the last to do so under the present system.* MODAL

8 You use **should** in 'that' clauses after certain verbs, nouns, and adjectives when you are talking about a future event or situation. In formal English the subjunctive is used instead of this structure. *He raised his glass and indicated that I should do the same... I insisted that we should have a look at every car... My father was very keen that I should fulfill my potential... George was sincerely anxious that his son should find happiness and security... It seems such a pity that a distinguished and honored name should be commercialized in such a manner... There is a wish among competitors that the Federation should change the test every four years.* MODAL

9 You use **should** in expressions such as **I should think** and **I should imagine** to indicate that you think something is true but you are not sure. *I should think it's going to rain soon... 'I suppose that was the right thing to do.'—'I should imagine so.'... 'Can we be talking about the same thing?'—'I should hope so.'* MODAL PRAGMATICS

10 You use **should** in expressions such as **I should like** and **I should be happy** to show politeness when you are saying what you want to do, or when you are requesting, offering, or accepting something. *I should be happy if you would bring them this evening... 'I should like to know anything you can tell me,' said Kendal... I should like a word with the carpenter... I should like to ask you to come with us for a quiet supper... That is very kind of you both. I should like to come... 'You can go and see her tomorrow afternoon if you feel like it.'—'I should be delighted to do so.'... She thought, 'I should like her for a friend.'.* MODAL PRAGMATICS

11 You use **should have** with 'you' when reporting an event, to emphasize how funny, shocking, or impressive it was; used in spoken English. *You should have heard him last night!... You should have seen him when he first came out – it was so sad... He started crying and I cried too. You should have seen us... You should have seen his roses! As good a show as in the Botanic Garden... You should have seen Boris's face when Hugh tapped him on the shoulder. Talk about surprise!* MODAL PRAGMATICS

12 You use **should** in interrogative structures with words like 'who' and 'what' when you are reporting an event to emphasize how surprising or shocking it was; used in spoken English. *I'm making these plans and who should I meet but this blonde guy and John.* MODAL PRAGMATICS

shoulder /ʃoʊldəʳ/ **shoulders, shouldering, shouldered** ◆◆◆◆◇

1 Your **shoulders** are between your neck and the tops of your arms. *She led him to an armchair, with her arm round his shoulder... He glanced over his shoulder and saw me watching him.* N-COUNT: oft poss N

2 The **shoulders** of a piece of clothing are the parts that cover your shoulders. ...*extravagant fashions with padded shoulders.* N-COUNT

3 When you talk about someone's problems or responsibilities, you can say that they carry them on their **shoulders**. *No one suspected the anguish he carried on his shoulders... I fervently hope he recognizes and understands the burden that's on his shoulders.* N-PLURAL: poss N

4 If you **shoulder** the responsibility or the blame for something, you accept it. *He has had to shoulder the responsibility of his father's mistakes... Some of the blame for the disastrous night must be shouldered by the promoters.* VERB =accept V n

5 If you **shoulder** something heavy, you put it across one of your shoulders so that you can carry VERB it more easily. *The rest of the group shouldered their bags, gritted their teeth and set off... He shouldered his bike and walked across the finish line.* V n

6 If you **shoulder** someone aside or if you **shoulder** your way somewhere, you push past people roughly using your shoulder. *The policemen rushed past him, shouldering him aside... She could do nothing to stop him as he shouldered his way into the house... He shouldered past Harlech and opened the door.* VERB; V n with *aside*; V *way* prep/adv; V *past/through* n

7 A **shoulder** is a joint of meat from the upper part of the front leg of an animal. *...shoulder of lamb.* N-VAR

8 See also **cold-shoulder, hard shoulder.**

9 If someone offers you **a shoulder to cry on** or is **a shoulder to cry on**, they listen sympathetically to all your troubles. *Mrs Barrantes longs to be at her daughter's side to offer her a shoulder to cry on... Roland sometimes saw me as a shoulder to cry on.* PHRASES; usu PHR after v

10 If you say that someone or something stands **head and shoulders** above other people or things, you mean that they are a lot better than them. *The two candidates stood head and shoulders above the rest... I am very impressed by your magazine. It is head and shoulders above any other.* PHR *above* n

11 If you say that someone is **looking over** their **shoulders**, you mean that they feel anxious or insecure about someone or something that threatens them. *When a company keeps making people redundant, those who are left behind might start looking over their shoulder.* V and N inflect

12 If you **rub shoulders with** famous or notorious people, you meet them and talk to them. *He regularly rubs shoulders with the likes of Elizabeth Taylor and Kylie Minogue.* V inflects, PHR n

13 If two or more people stand **shoulder to shoulder**, they are standing next to each other, with their shoulders touching. *They fell into step, walking shoulder to shoulder with their heads bent against the rain... We went on board and saw these people packed shoulder to shoulder on the decks.* PHR after v, v-link PHR

14 If people work **shoulder to shoulder**, they work cooperatively together in order to achieve a common aim. *They could fight shoulder-to-shoulder against a common enemy... We will need you and the chairman standing shoulder to shoulder on basic positions.* usu v PHR =side by side

15 • **a chip on** one's **shoulder**: see **chip**.

shoulder-bag, shoulder-bags. A **shoulder-bag** is a bag that has a long strap so that it can be carried on a person's shoulder. N-COUNT

shoulder blade, shoulder blades. Your **shoulder blades** are the two large, flat, triangular bones that you have in the upper part of your back, below your shoulders. N-COUNT

shoulder-high. A **shoulder-high** object is as high as your shoulders. *...a shoulder-high hedge.* ADJ: usu ADJ n
► Also an adverb. *They picked up Oliver and carried him shoulder high into the garage.* ADV: ADV after v

shoulder-length. **Shoulder-length** hair is long enough to reach your shoulders. ADJ: usu ADJ n

shoulder pad, shoulder pads. **Shoulder pads** are small pads that are put inside the shoulders of a jacket, coat, or other article of clothing in order to raise them. N-COUNT

shoulder-strap, shoulder-straps

1 The **shoulder-straps** on a piece of clothing such as a dress are two narrow straps that go over the shoulders. N-COUNT

2 A **shoulder-strap** on a bag is a long strap that you put over your shoulder to carry the bag. N-COUNT

shouldn't /ʃʊdᵊnt/. In informal English, 'should not' is usually said or written as **shouldn't**.

should've /ʃʊdəv/. **Should've** is the usual spoken form of 'should have', especially when 'have' is an auxiliary verb.

shout /ʃaʊt/ **shouts, shouting, shouted** ◆◆◆◇◇

1 If you **shout**, you say something very loudly, usually because you want people a long distance away to hear you or because you are angry. *He had to shout to make himself heard above the near gale-force wind... 'She's alive!' he shouted triumphantly... Andrew rushed out of the house, shouting for help... You don't have to shout at me... I shouted at mother to get the police... The driver managed to escape from the vehicle and shout a warning.* VERB; V; V with quote; V *for* n; V *at* n; V *at* n to-inf; V n; Also V that
► Also a noun. *The decision was greeted with shouts of protest from opposition MPs... I heard a distant shout.* N-COUNT ♦ **shouting** *One of my grandchildren heard the shouting first.* N-UNCOUNT

2 If you are in a pub and someone you are with says **'It's your shout'** or **'It's my shout'**, they mean that it is your turn or their turn to buy a round of drinks; an informal expression, used mainly in British English. CONVENTION PRAGMATICS

shout down. If people **shout down** someone who is trying to speak, they prevent that person from being heard by shouting at them. *They shouted him down when he tried to explain why Zaire needed an interim government... There were scuffles when UDF hecklers began to shout down the speakers.* PHRASAL VERB; V n P; V P n (not pron)

shout out. If you **shout** something **out**, you say it very loudly so that people can hear you clearly. *They shouted out the names of those detained... I shouted out 'I'm OK'... I wanted to shout it out, let her know what I had overheard.* PHRASAL VERB; V P n (not pron); V P with quote; V n P; Also V P

shouting match, shouting matches. A **shouting match** is an angry quarrel in which people shout at each other. *We had a real shouting match with each other.* N-COUNT: oft N *with/between* n

shove /ʃʌv/ **shoves, shoving, shoved** ◆◆◇◇◇

1 If you **shove** someone or something, you push them with a quick, violent movement. *He shoved her out of the way... He was then shoved face down on the pavement... He's the one who shoved me... She shoved as hard as she could.* VERB; V n prep/adv; V n; V
► Also a noun. *She gave Gracie a shove towards the house.* N-COUNT

2 If you **shove** something somewhere, you push it there quickly and carelessly. *We shoved a copy of the newsletter beneath their door... He shoved a cloth in my hand.* VERB; V n prep/adv

3 If you talk about what you think will happen if **push comes to shove**, you are talking about what you think will happen if a situation becomes very bad or difficult; an informal expression. *If push comes to shove, if you should lose your case in the court, what will you do?... When push comes to shove, you are on your own.* PHRASE: V inflects

shovel /ʃʌvᵊl/ **shovels, shovelling, shovelled;** spelled **shoveling, shoveled** in American English. ◆◇◇◇◇

1 A **shovel** is a tool like a spade, used for lifting and moving earth, coal, or snow. *...a coal shovel... She dug the foundation with a pick and shovel.* N-COUNT

2 If you **shovel** earth, coal, or snow, you lift and move it with a shovel. *He has to get out and shovel snow... Pendergood had shovelled the sand out of the caravan.* VERB; V n; V n prep/adv

3 If you **shovel** something somewhere, you push a lot of it quickly into that place. *There was silence, except for Randall, who was obliviously shoveling food into his mouth.* VERB; V n prep/adv

show /ʃoʊ/ **shows, showing, showed, shown.** ◆◆◆◆◆

1 If something **shows** that a state of affairs exists, it gives information that proves it or makes it clear to people. *Research shows that a high-fibre diet may protect you from bowel cancer... Opinion polls show as much as 86 percent of the American public supports Mr. Bush... These figures show an increase of over one million in unemployment... It was only later that the drug was shown to be addictive... You'll be given regular blood tests to show whether you have been infected.* VERB; V that; V n; *be* V-ed to-inf; V wh

2 If a picture, chart, film, or piece of writing **shows** something, it represents it or gives information about it. *Figure 4.1 shows the respiratory system. ...a coin showing Cleopatra... The cushions, shown left, measure 20 x 12 inches and cost $39.95... Much of the film shows the painter simply going about his task... Our photograph shows how the plants will turn out.* VERB; V n; V-ed; V n -ing; V wh

3 If you **show** someone something, you give it to them, take them to it, or point to it, so that they can see it or know what you are referring to. *Cut out this article and show it to your bank manager... He* VERB; V n *to* n; V n n; V n wh *showed me the flat he shares with Esther... I showed them where the gun was... Show me which one you like and I'll buy it for you.*

4 If you **show** someone to a room or seat, you lead them there. *It was very good of you to come. Let me show you to my study... Milton was shown into the office... John will show you upstairs, Mr Penry... Your office is ready for you. I'll show you the way.* VERB V n prep/adv V n

5 If you **show** someone how to do something, you do it yourself so that they can watch you and learn how to do it. *Claire showed us how to make a chocolate roulade... There are seasoned professionals who can teach you and show you what to do... Mother asked me to show you how the phones work... Dr. Reichert has shown us a new way to look at those behavior problems.* VERB V n wh V n n

6 If something **shows** or if you **show** it, it is visible or noticeable. *He showed his teeth in a humourless grin... His beard was just beginning to show signs of grey... Faint glimmers of daylight were showing through the treetops... I'd driven both ways down this road but my tracks didn't show.* V-ERG V n V

7 If you **show** a particular attitude, quality, or feeling, or if it **shows**, you behave in a way that makes this attitude, quality, or feeling clear to other people. *Elsie has had enough time to show her gratitude... She showed no interest in her children... Ferguson was unhappy and it showed... You show me respect... Mr Clarke has shown himself to be resolutely opposed to compromise... The baby was tugging at his coat to show that he wanted to be picked up.* V-ERG V n V V n n V n to-inf V that

8 If something **shows** a quality or characteristic or if that quality or characteristic **shows** itself, the quality or characteristic can be noticed or observed. *The story shows a strong narrative gift and a vivid eye for detail... Middle East peace talks in Washington showed signs of progress yesterday... Her popularity clearly shows no sign of waning... How else did his hostility to women show itself?* VERB V n

9 A **show** of a feeling or quality is an attempt by someone to make it clear that they have that feeling or quality. *Miners gathered in the centre of Bucharest in a show of support for the government... A crowd of more than 10,000 has gathered in a show of strength... She said goodbye to Hilda with a convincing show of affection... Mr Morris was determined to put on a show of family unity.* N-COUNT: usu *a* N *of* n

10 If you say that something is for **show**, you mean that it has no real purpose and is done just to give a good impression. *The change in government is more for show than for real... 'It's all show,' said Linus. 'The girls don't take it seriously.'* N-UNCOUNT

11 If a company **shows** a profit or a loss, its accounts indicate that it has made a profit or a loss. *It is the only one of the three companies expected to show a profit for the quarter... Lonrho's mining and minerals businesses showed some improvement.* VERB V n

12 If a person you are expecting to meet does not **show**, they do not arrive at the place where you expect to meet them; used mainly in American English. *There was always a chance he wouldn't show.* VERB =turn up V
▸ **Show up** means the same as **show**. *We waited until five o'clock, but he did not show up... He always shows up in a fancy car... If I don't show up for class this morning, I'll be kicked out.* PHRASAL VERB V P V P *for*/*to* n

13 A television or radio **show** is a programme on television or radio. *I had my own TV show... This is the show in which Loyd Grossman visits the houses of the famous. ...a popular talk show on a Cuban radio station... A daily one-hour news show can cost $250,000 to produce.* N-COUNT: oft supp N =programme

14 A **show** in a theatre is an entertainment or concert, especially one that includes different items such as music, dancing, and comedy. *How about going shopping and seeing a show in London?... He has earned a reputation as the man who can close a show with a bad review... The band are playing a handful of shows at smaller venues.* N-COUNT

15 If someone **shows** a film or television programme, it is broadcast or appears on television or in the cinema. *The BBC World Service Television news showed the same film clip... The drama will be shown on American TV next year... American films are showing at Moscow's cinemas.* VERB V n V ♦ **showing, showings** *I gave him a private showing of the film.* N-COUNT

16 A **show** is a public exhibition of things, such as works of art, fashionable clothes, or things that have been entered in a competition. *The venue for the show is Birmingham's National Exhibition Centre Hall... Gucci will be holding fashion shows to present their autumn collection... Two complementary exhibitions are on show at the Africa Centre... Today his picture goes on show at the National Portrait Gallery.* N-COUNT: also *on* N

17 To **show** things such as works of art means to put them in an exhibition where they can be seen by the public. *50 dealers will show oils, watercolours, drawings and prints from 1900 to 1992. ...one of East Village's better-known galleries, where he showed and sold his work.* VERB V n

18 A **show** home, house, or flat is one of a group of newly-built homes. It is decorated and furnished by the building company, and people who want to buy one of the homes come and look round it. ADJ: ADJ n

19 If a question is decided by a **show of hands**, people vote on it by raising their hands to indicate whether they vote yes or no. *Parliamentary leaders agreed to take all such decisions by a show of hands... Russell then asked for a show of hands concerning each of the targets.* PHRASES

20 If you **have** something **to show for** your efforts, you have achieved something as a result of what you have done. *I'm nearly 31 and it's about time I had something to show for my time in my job... It always amazed her how little she had to show for the amount she spent.* *have* inflects, PHR n

21 You can say **'I'll show you'** to threaten or warn someone that you are going to make them admit that they are wrong. *She shook her fist. 'I'll show you,' she said... I'll show him, leave it to me.* PRAGMATICS

22 If you say **it just goes to show** or **it just shows** that something is the case, you mean that what you have just said or experienced demonstrates that it is the case. *I forgot all about the ring. Which just goes to show that getting good grades in school doesn't mean you're clever... It's crazy and just shows the inconsistency of refereeing.* PHR that, PHR n

23 If you say that someone **is running the show**, you mean that they are in control or in charge of a situation. *They made it clear who is now running the show... There's some serious problems with the way the state's leadership has been running the show.* V inflects

24 If you say that someone **steals the show**, you mean that they get a lot of attention or praise because they perform better than anyone else in a show or other event. *It was Chinese women who stole the show on the first day of competition... Brad Pitt steals the show as the young man doomed by his zest for life.* V inflects

25 • to **show** someone **the door**: see **door**. • to **show** your **face**: see **face**.

show around or **show round.** If you **show** someone **around** or **show** them **round**, you go with them to show them all the interesting, useful, or important features of a place when they first visit it. *Would you show me around?... She showed me round and introduced me to everybody... Spear showed him around the flat.* PHRASAL VERB V n P V n P n

show off PHRASAL VERB

1 If you say that someone is **showing off**, you are criticizing them for trying to impress people by showing in a very obvious way what they can do or what they own. *All right, there's no need to show off... He had been showing off for her at the poker table.* PRAGMATICS V P

2 If you **show off** something that you own or an attribute that you have, you show it to a lot of people or make it obvious, because you are proud of it. *Naomi was showing off her engagement ring... Body builders shave their chests to show off their muscles... He actually enjoys his new hair-style and has decided to start showing it off.* V P n (not pron) V n P

3 If something **shows** something **off**, it emphasizes its good features so that it looks especially attractive. *She had made Helen a dress which showed off her tiny waist.* VPn (not pron) Also VnP

4 See also **show-off**.

show round. See **show around.** PHRASAL VERB

show up PHRASAL VERB

1 If an object or phenomenon **shows up** or if something **shows** it **up**, it can be clearly seen or noticed. *You may have some strange disease that may not show up for 10 or 15 years... The orange tip shows up well against most backgrounds. ...a telescope so powerful that it can show up galaxies billions of light years away... There have been four hundred escapes this year showing up the lack of security.* ERG VP VPn (not pron)

2 If someone or something **shows** you **up**, they make you feel embarrassed or ashamed of them. *He wanted to teach her a lesson for showing him up in front of Leonov... She kept saying I ought to try some, but I wasn't going to show myself up... We expected every drawing exercise to show us up as hopeless artists.* VnP VnP as n

3 See **show** 12.

showbiz /ʃoʊbɪz/. **Showbiz** is the same as **show business**; an informal word. ◆◇◇◇◇ N-UNCOUNT

show business. **Show business** is the entertainment industry of film, theatre, and television. *He started his career in show business by playing the saxophone and singing. ...show business personalities.* ◆◇◇◇◇ N-UNCOUNT

showcase /ʃoʊkeɪs/ **showcases, showcasing, showcased** ◆◇◇◇◇

1 A **showcase** is a glass container with valuable objects inside it, for example at an exhibition or in a museum. N-COUNT

2 You use **showcase** to refer to a situation or setting in which something is displayed or presented to its best advantage. *The festival remains a valuable showcase for new talent.* N-COUNT: with supp

3 If something **is showcased**, it is displayed or presented to its best advantage; used in journalism. *Restored films are being showcased this month at a festival in Paris.* VB: usu passive be V-ed

showdown /ʃoʊdaʊn/ **showdowns;** also spelled **show-down**. A **showdown** is a big argument or conflict which is intended to settle a dispute that has lasted for a long time. *They may be pushing the Prime Minister towards a final showdown with his party.* ◆◇◇◇◇ N-COUNT: usu sing

shower /ʃaʊəʳ/ **showers, showering, showered** ◆◆◇◇◇

1 A **shower** is a device used for washing yourself. It consists of a pipe or hose which ends in a flat piece with a lot of holes in it so that water comes out in a spray. *She heard him turn on the shower.* N-COUNT

2 A **shower** is a cubicle that contains a shower. N-COUNT

3 The **showers** or the **shower** in somewhere such as a sports centre is the area containing showers. *The showers are a mess... We all stood in the women's shower.* N-COUNT

4 If you have a **shower**, you wash yourself by standing under a spray of water from a shower. *I think I'll have a shower before dinner... She took two showers a day.* N-COUNT

5 If you **shower**, you wash yourself by standing under a spray of water from a shower. *There wasn't time to shower or change clothes.* VERB V

6 A **shower** is a short period of rain, especially light rain. *There'll be bright or sunny spells and scattered showers this afternoon.* N-COUNT

7 You can refer to a lot of things that are falling as a **shower** of them. *Showers of sparks flew in all directions. ...a shower of meteorites.* N-COUNT: usu N of n

8 If you **are showered with** a lot of small objects or pieces, they are scattered over you. *They were showered with rice in the traditional manner... Mr Reagan was showered with glass.* VB: usu passive be V-ed with n

9 If you **shower** a person **with** presents or kisses, you give them a lot of presents or kisses in a very generous and extravagant way. *He showered her with emeralds and furs... Her parents showered her with kisses.* VERB Vn with n

showery /ʃaʊəri/. If the weather is **showery**, there are showers of rain but it does not rain all the time. ADJ-GRADED

showgirl /ʃoʊgɜːʳl/ **showgirls.** A **showgirl** is a young woman who sings and dances as part of the chorus in a musical show. N-COUNT

showground /ʃoʊgraʊnd/ **showgrounds.** A **showground** is a large, open-air area where events such as agricultural shows or competitions are held. N-COUNT

show jumper, show jumpers. A **show jumper** is a person who takes part in the sport of show jumping. *I loved horses as a child and was a junior show jumper.* ◆◇◇◇◇ N-COUNT

show jumping; also spelled **showjumping**. **Show jumping** is a sport in which horses are ridden in competitions to demonstrate their skill in jumping over fences and walls. ◆◇◇◇◇ N-UNCOUNT

showman /ʃoʊmæn/ **showmen.** A **showman** is a person who is very entertaining and dramatic in the way that they perform, or the way that they present things. N-COUNT

showmanship /ʃoʊmənʃɪp/. **Showmanship** is a person's skill at performing or presenting things in an entertaining and dramatic way. N-UNCOUNT

shown /ʃoʊn/. **Shown** is the past participle of **show**.

show-off, show-offs. If you say that someone is a **show-off**, you are criticizing them for trying to impress people by showing in a very obvious way what they can do or what they own; an informal expression. ◆◇◇◇◇ N-COUNT PRAGMATICS

showpiece /ʃoʊpiːs/ **showpieces;** also spelled **show-piece**. A **showpiece** is something that is admired as a fine example of its type, especially something which is intended to show its owner or creator in a favourable light. *The factory was to be a showpiece of Western investment in the East... Wembley is the showpiece stadium in this country.* ◆◇◇◇◇ N-COUNT: with supp

showroom /ʃoʊruːm/ **showrooms.** A **showroom** is a shop in which goods are displayed for sale, especially goods such as cars or electrical or gas appliances. *...a car showroom... Further information is available from your local electricity showroom.* ◆◇◇◇◇ N-COUNT: usu n N

show-stopper, show-stoppers; also spelled **showstopper**. If something is a **show-stopper**, it is very impressive; an informal word. *Her natural creativity and artistic talent make her home a real show stopper.* N-COUNT

show-stopping; also spelled **showstopping**. A **show-stopping** performance or product is very impressive; an informal word. ADJ: ADJ n

showtime /ʃoʊtaɪm/. **Showtime** is the time when a particular stage or television show is due to begin. *It's close to showtime now, so you retire into the dressing room.* N-UNCOUNT

show trial, show trials. People describe a trial as a **show trial** if they believe that the trial is unfair and is held for political reasons rather than in order to find out the truth; used showing disapproval. *Amnesty International has denounced the show trials of political dissidents.* N-COUNT PRAGMATICS

showy /ʃoʊi/ **showier, showiest.** Something that is **showy** is very noticeable because it is large, colourful, or bright. *Since he was color blind, he favored large, showy flowers... They were smart but not showy.* ADJ-GRADED =gaudy

shrank /ʃræŋk/. **Shrank** is the past tense of **shrink**.

shrapnel /ʃræpnᵊl/. **Shrapnel** consists of small pieces of metal which are scattered from exploding bombs and shells. *He was hit by shrapnel from a grenade.* ◆◇◇◇◇ N-UNCOUNT

shred /ʃred/ **shreds, shredding, shredded** ◆◆◇◇◇

1 If you **shred** something such as food or paper, you cut it or tear it into very small, narrow pieces. *They may be shredding documents... Finely shred the carrots, cabbage and cored apples.* VERB Vn

2 If you cut or tear food or paper into **shreds**, you N-COUNT:

cut or tear it into small, narrow pieces. *Cut the cabbage into fine long shreds.* usu pl

3 If there is not a **shred** of something, there is not even a small amount of it. *He said there was not a shred of evidence to support such remarks... There is not a shred of truth in the story... He was left without a shred of self-esteem.* N-COUNT: N *of*n, usu with brd-neg =scrap

4 If you **tear** someone **to shreds** or **rip** them **to shreds**, you criticize them very thoroughly and severely. PHRASE: V inflects

shredder /ʃredəʳ/ **shredders.** A **shredder** is a machine for shredding things such as documents or twigs. *...a document shredder. ...a garden shredder.* N-COUNT

shrew /ʃruː/ **shrews.** A **shrew** is a small brown animal like a mouse with a long pointed nose. N-COUNT

shrewd /ʃruːd/ **shrewder, shrewdest.** A **shrewd** person is able to understand and judge a situation quickly and to use this understanding to their own advantage. *She's a shrewd businesswoman... His grey eyes were shrewd but kindly... It should prove a shrewd investment.* ♦ **shrewdly** *She looked at him shrewdly. ...a shrewdly worded statement.* ♦ **shrewdness** *His natural shrewdness tells him what is needed to succeed.* ◆◇◇◇◇ ADJ-GRADED; ADV-GRADED: usu ADV with v; N-UNCOUNT

shriek /ʃriːk/ **shrieks, shrieking, shrieked** ◆◇◇◇◇

1 When someone **shrieks**, they make a short, very loud cry, for example because they are startled or in pain, or are laughing. *She shrieked and leapt from the bed... Miranda shrieked with laughter.* ► Also a noun. *Sue let out a terrific shriek and leapt out of the way. ...the groans of the wounded, or the shrieks of the dying. ...a shriek of joy.* VERB; V; N-COUNT

2 If you **shriek** something, you shout it in a loud, high-pitched voice. *'Stop it! Stop it!' shrieked Jane... He was shrieking obscenities and weeping.* VERB =scream; V with quote; V n

shrift /ʃrɪft/. If someone or something gets **short shrift**, they are paid very little attention. *The idea has been given short shrift by philosophers.* PHRASE: PHR after v

shrill /ʃrɪl/ **shriller, shrillest; shrills, shrilling, shrilled** ◆◇◇◇◇

1 A **shrill** sound is high-pitched, piercing, and unpleasant to listen to. *Shrill cries and startled oaths flew up around us as pandemonium broke out. ...the shrill whistle of the engine... Mary Ann's voice grew shrill.* ♦ **shrilly** *'What are you doing?' she demanded shrilly.* ♦ **shrillness** *...that ugly shrillness in her voice.* ADJ-GRADED =piercing; ADV-GRADED: usu ADV with v; N-UNCOUNT

2 If you describe a demand, protest, or statement as **shrill**, you disapprove of it and do not like the strong, forceful way it is said. *I disregard these shrill protests from groups closely associated with the terrorists.* ADJ-GRADED: usu ADJ n PRAGMATICS

3 If a bell or whistle **shrills**, it makes a loud, high-pitched sound. *The phone shrilled, making her jump.* VERB; V

4 If someone with a high-pitched voice **shrills** something, they say it loudly; used in written English. *'No, no, no,' she shrilled.* VERB; V with quote

shrimp /ʃrɪmp/ **shrimps; shrimp** can also be used as the plural form. **Shrimps** are small shellfish with long tails and many legs. *Add the shrimp and cook for 30 seconds... I'm going to have shrimps for my tea.* ◆◇◇◇◇ N-COUNT

shrine /ʃraɪn/ **shrines** ◆◇◇◇◇

1 A **shrine** is a holy place of worship which is associated with a sacred person or object. *...the holy shrine of Mecca.* N-COUNT

2 A **shrine** is a place that people visit and treat with respect because it is connected with a dead person or with dead people that they want to remember. *Yazukuni is Japan's shrine to all of its dead soldiers.* N-COUNT

shrink /ʃrɪŋk/ **shrinks, shrinking, shrank, shrunk** ◆◆◇◇◇

1 If cloth or clothing **shrinks**, it becomes smaller in size, usually as a result of being washed. *All my jumpers have shrunk.* VERB; V

2 If something **shrinks** or something else **shrinks** it, it becomes smaller. *The vast forests of West Africa have shrunk... Hungary may have to lower its hopes of shrinking its state sector.* V-ERG ≠grow; V; V n

3 If you **shrink** away from someone or something, you move away from them because you are frightened or horrified by them. *One child shrinks away from me when I try to talk to him... Siegfried cringed and shrank against the wall... She shrank back with an involuntary gasp.* VERB; V prep/adv

4 If you do not **shrink** from a task or duty, you do it even though it is unpleasant or dangerous. *We must not shrink from the legitimate use of force if we are to remain credible... They didn't shrink from danger.* VB: usu with neg; V *from* n

5 A **shrink** is a psychiatrist; an informal use. *I've seen a shrink already.* N-COUNT

6 • **no shrinking violet**: see **violet**.

shrinkage /ʃrɪŋkɪdʒ/. **Shrinkage** is a decrease in the size or amount of something. *Allow for some shrinkage in both length and width. ...a shrinkage in industrial output.* N-UNCOUNT

shrink-wrapped. A **shrink-wrapped** product is sold in a tight-fitting polythene cover. *...a shrink-wrapped cassette.* ADJ: usu ADJ n

shrivel /ʃrɪvᵊl/ **shrivels, shrivelling, shrivelled;** spelled **shriveling, shriveled** in American English. When something **shrivels** or when something else **shrivels** it, it becomes dry and wrinkled, usually because it loses moisture in the heat. *The plant shrivels and dies. ...dry weather that shrivelled this summer's crops.* ► **Shrivel up** means the same as **shrivel**. *The leaves started to shrivel up.* ♦ **shrivelled** *...a shriveled chestnut... It looked old and shrivelled.* ◆◇◇◇◇ V-ERG; V; V n; PHRASAL VERB V P; ADJ-GRADED

shroud /ʃraʊd/ **shrouds, shrouding, shrouded** ◆◇◇◇◇

1 A **shroud** is a cloth which is used for wrapping a dead body. N-COUNT

2 You can refer to something that surrounds an object or situation as a **shroud of** something. *...a parked car huddled under a shroud of grey snow... Ministers are as keen as ever to wrap their activities in a shroud of secrecy.* N-COUNT: N *of*n

3 If something **has been shrouded** in mystery or secrecy, very little information about it has been made available. *For years the teaching of acting has been shrouded in mystery. ...the secrecy which has shrouded the whole affair.* ♦ **shrouded** *His demise is as shrouded in mystery as ever.* VERB; *be* V-ed *in* n; V n; ADJ-GRADED: v-link ADJ *in* n

4 If darkness, fog, or smoke **shrouds** an area, it covers it so that it is difficult to see. *Mist shrouded the outline of Buckingham Palace.* ♦ **shrouded** *The area is shrouded in smoke.* VERB; V n; ADJ-GRADED: v-link ADJ *in* n

Shrove Tuesday /ʃroʊv tjuːzdeɪ, AM tuːz-/. **Shrove Tuesday** is the Tuesday before Ash Wednesday. People traditionally eat pancakes on Shrove Tuesday. N-UNCOUNT =Pancake Day

shrub /ʃrʌb/ **shrubs. Shrubs** are low plants like small trees with several woody stems instead of a trunk. *...flowering shrubs.* ◆◆◇◇◇ N-COUNT

shrubbery /ʃrʌbəri/ **shrubberies**

1 A **shrubbery** is a part of a garden where a lot of shrubs are growing. N-COUNT

2 You can refer to a lot of shrubs or to shrubs in general as **shrubbery**. N-UNCOUNT

shrubby /ʃrʌbi/. A **shrubby** plant is like a shrub. *...a shrubby tree.* ADJ: usu ADJ n

shrug /ʃrʌg/ **shrugs, shrugging, shrugged.** If you **shrug**, you raise your shoulders to show that you are not interested in something or that you do not know or care about something. *I shrugged, as if to say, 'Why not?'... The man shrugged his shoulders.* ► Also a noun. *'I suppose so,' said Anna with a shrug.* ◆◆◇◇◇ VERB; V; V n; N-COUNT

shrug off. If you **shrug** something **off**, you ignore it or treat it as if it is not really important or serious. *He shrugged off the criticism... He just laughed and shrugged it off.* PHRASAL VERB; V P n (not pron); V n P

shrunk /ʃrʌŋk/. **Shrunk** is the past participle of **shrink**.

shrunken /ʃrʌŋkən/. Someone or something that is **shrunken** has become smaller than they used to be. *She now looked small, shrunken and pathetic... His shrunken thighs were barely strong enough to support the weight of his body.* ADJ-GRADED

shuck /ʃʌk/ **shucks, shucking, shucked**

1 In American English, the **shuck** of something is N-COUNT

its outer covering, for example the husk of an ear of maize, or the shell of an oyster or clam. *...corn shucks.*

2 In American English, if you **shuck** something such as maize or shellfish, you remove it from its outer covering. *On a good day, each employee will shuck 3,500 oysters.* VERB Vn

3 In informal American English, if you **shuck** something that you are wearing, you take it off. *He shucked his coat and set to work.* VERB Vn

4 **Shucks** is an exclamation that is used to express embarrassment, disappointment, or annoyance; an informal word, used mainly in American English. *Terry actually says 'Oh, shucks!' when complimented on her singing.* EXCLAM PRAGMATICS

shudder /ʃʌdəʳ/ **shudders, shuddering, shuddered** ◆◇◇◇◇

1 If you **shudder**, you tremble with fear, horror, or disgust, or with cold. *Lloyd had urged her to eat caviar. She had shuddered at the thought... Elaine shuddered with cold.* ▶ Also a noun. *She gave a violent shudder... She recoiled with a shudder.* VERB V prep/adv Also V N-COUNT: usu sing

2 If something such as a machine or vehicle **shudders**, it shakes suddenly and violently. *The train began to pull out of the station – then suddenly shuddered to a halt... The whole ship shuddered and trembled at the sudden strain.* VERB V prep/adv V

3 If something sends **a shudder** or **shudders** through a group of people, it causes them worry or alarm. *The next crisis sent a shudder of fear through the UN community... The word still causes a shudder among some of my students.* N-COUNT

4 If you say that you **shudder to think** what would happen in a particular situation, you mean that you expect it to be so awful or disastrous that you do not really want to think about it. *I shudder to think what would have happened if he hadn't acted as quickly as he did.* PHRASE: V inflects, usu PHR wh

shuffle /ʃʌfᵊl/ **shuffles, shuffling, shuffled** ◆◆◇◇◇

1 If you **shuffle** somewhere, you walk there without lifting your feet properly off the ground. *Moira shuffled across the kitchen... They shuffled along somewhat reluctantly.* ▶ Also a noun. *She noticed her own proud walk had become a shuffle.* VERB V prep/adv N-SING

2 If you **shuffle** around, you move your feet about while standing or you move your bottom about while sitting, often because you feel uncomfortable or embarrassed. *He shuffles around in his chair... He grinned and shuffled his feet.* VERB V prep/adv Vn

3 If you **shuffle** a pack of cards, you mix them up before you begin a game. *There are various ways of shuffling and dealing the cards.* VERB Vn Also V

4 If you **shuffle** things such as pieces of paper, you move them around so that they are in a different order. *The silence lengthened as Thorne unnecessarily shuffled some papers.* VERB Vn

shun /ʃʌn/ **shuns, shunning, shunned.** If you **shun** someone or something, you deliberately avoid them or keep away from them. *From that time forward everybody shunned him... He has always shunned publicity... This extremist organization has shunned conventional politics.* ◆◇◇◇◇ VERB =avoid Vn

shunt /ʃʌnt/ **shunts, shunting, shunted** ◆◇◇◇◇

1 If someone or something **is shunted** somewhere, they are moved or sent there, usually because someone finds them inconvenient; used showing disapproval. *He has spent most of his life being shunted between his mother, father and various foster families... Independent thinkers are shunted into minor jobs or refused promotion.* VB: usu passive be V-ed prep/adv

2 When railway engines **shunt** wagons or carriages, they push or pull them from one railway line to another. *The GM diesel engine shunted the coaches to Platform 4.* VERB V n prep/adv

shush /ʃʊʃ, ʃʌʃ/ **shushes, shushing, shushed**

1 You say **shush** when you are telling someone to be quiet. *Shush! Here he comes. I'll talk to you later.* CONVENTION PRAGMATICS

2 If you **shush** someone, you tell them to be quiet by saying 'shush' or 'sh', or by indicating in some other way that you want them to be quiet. *Frannie shushed her with a forefinger to the lips.* VERB Vn Also V

shut /ʃʌt/ **shuts, shutting.** The form **shut** is used in the present tense and is the past tense and past participle. ◆◆◆◇◇

1 If you **shut** something such as a door or if it **shuts**, it moves so that it fills a hole or a space. *Just make sure you shut the gate after you... The screen door shut gently.* ▶ Also an adjective. *They have warned residents to stay inside and keep their doors and windows shut... The exit doors were locked shut.* V-ERG =close Vn V ADJ: ADJ after v, v-link ADJ

2 If you **shut** your eyes, you lower your eyelids so that you cannot see anything. *Lucy shut her eyes so she wouldn't see it happen.* ▶ Also an adjective. *His eyes were shut and he seemed to have fallen asleep.* VERB =close Vn ADJ: v-link ADJ

3 If your mouth **shuts** or if you **shut** your mouth, you place your lips firmly together. *Daniel's mouth opened, and then shut again... He opened and shut his mouth, unspeaking.* ▶ Also an adjective. *She was silent for a moment, lips tight shut, eyes distant.* V-ERG V Vn ADJ: v-link ADJ

4 When a shop or pub **shuts** or when someone **shuts** it, it is closed and you cannot go into it until the next time that it is open. *There is a tendency to shut museums or shops at a moment's notice... Shops usually shut from noon-3pm, and stay open late... What time do the pubs shut?* ▶ Also an adjective. *Make sure you have food to tide you over when the local shop may be shut.* V-ERG =close Vn V ADJ: v-link ADJ =closed

5 If you say that someone **shuts their eyes to** something, you mean that they deliberately ignore something which they should face; used showing disapproval. *We shut our eyes to the plainest facts, refusing to admit the truth... She was shutting her eyes to reality, just as she had done after Matthew died.* PHRASES V inflects, PHR n PRAGMATICS

6 If someone tells you to **keep** your **mouth shut** about something, they are telling you not to let anyone else know about it. *I don't have to tell you how important it is for you to keep your mouth shut about all this... He paid my brother to kill Norton and keep his mouth shut.* V inflects

7 If you **keep** your **mouth shut**, you do not express your opinions about something, even though you would like to. *If she had kept her mouth shut she would still have her job now.* V inflects

8 If someone tells you to **shut** your **mouth** or **shut** your **face**, they are telling you very rudely to stop talking; an informal expression. *'Oi, shut your mouth and have respect for elders,' Langda said to the boy.* N inflects PRAGMATICS

9 ● **shut up shop**: see **shop**.

shut away. If you **shut** yourself **away**, you avoid going out and seeing other people, usually because you are feeling depressed. *Depressed and ill, he had again shut himself away in his darkened studio.* PHRASAL VERB V pron-refl P

shut down. If a factory or business **shuts down** or if someone **shuts** it **down**, work there stops or it no longer trades as a business. *Smaller contractors had been forced to shut down... It is required by law to shut down banks which it regards as chronically short of capital... Mr Buzetta sold the newspaper's assets to its competitor and shut it down.* ● See also **shutdown**. PHRASAL VERB ERG V P V P n (not pron) V n P

shut in PHRASAL VERB

1 If you **shut** someone or something **in** a room, you close the door so that they cannot leave it. *The door enables us to shut the birds in the shelter in bad weather.* V n P n

2 If you **shut** yourself **in** a room, you stay in there and make sure nobody else can get in. *After one particular bad result, he shut himself in the shower room for an hour... He shut himself in his office, telling his secretary to hold all calls.* V pron-refl P n

shut off PHRASAL VERB

1 If you **shut off** something such as an engine or an electrical item, you turn it off to stop it working. *They pulled over and shut off the engine... Will somebody for God's sake shut that alarm off.* =switch off V P n (not pron) V n P

2 If you **shut** yourself **off**, you avoid seeing other people, usually because you are feeling depressed. *Billy tends to keep things to himself more and shut himself off... She shut herself off from all the social aspects of life.* V pron-refl P V pron-refl P from n

3 If an official organization **shuts off** the supply of something, they no longer send it to the people they supplied in the past. *In Britain the DTI is shutting off national aid to small companies... The State Water Project has shut off all supplies to farmers.* V P n (not pron)

shut out PHRASAL VERB

1 If you **shut** something or someone **out**, you prevent them from getting into a place, for example by closing the doors. *'I shut him out of the bedroom,' says Maureen... I was set to shut out anyone else who came knocking.* V n P *of* n; V P n (not pron); Also V n P

2 If you **shut out** a thought or a feeling, you prevent yourself from thinking or feeling it. *I shut out the memory which was too painful to dwell on... The figures represent such overwhelming human misery that the mind wants to shut it out.* =block out; V P n (not pron); V n P

3 If you **shut** someone **out** of something, you prevent them from having anything to do with it. *She is very reclusive, to the point of shutting me out of her life... They refused to allow Republicans to offer amendments, effectively shutting them out of the process... She had effectively shut him out by refusing to listen.* V n P *of* n; V n P

shut up. If someone **shuts up** or if someone or something **shuts** them **up**, they stop talking. You can say **'shut up'** to someone to tell them to stop talking. *Just shut up, will you?... I don't feel like shutting up; I think statements about injustice should be made... A sharp verbal put-down was the only way he knew of shutting her up.* PHRASAL VERB ERG; V P; V n P

shutdown /ʃʌtdaʊn/ **shutdowns.** A **shutdown** is the closing of a factory, shop, or other business, either for a short time or for ever. *The shutdown is the latest in a series of painful budget measures... All seven plants have had temporary shutdowns this year.* ◆◇◇◇◇ N-COUNT

shut-eye; also spelled **shuteye**. **Shut-eye** is sleep; an informal word. *Go home and get some shut-eye, Craig.* N-UNCOUNT =sleep

shutter /ʃʌtəʳ/ **shutters** ◆◇◇◇◇

1 The **shutter** in a camera is the part which opens to allow light through the lens when a photograph is taken. *There are a few things you should check before pressing the shutter release. ...a slow shutter speed.* N-COUNT

2 **Shutters** are wooden or metal covers fitted on the outside of a window. They can be opened to let in the light, or closed to keep out the sun or the cold or to protect the windows from damage. *She opened the shutters and gazed out over village roofs.* N-COUNT: usu pl

shuttered /ʃʌtəʳd/

1 A **shuttered** window, room, or building has its shutters closed. *I opened a shuttered window... Schools and government offices have been closed, and many shops remain shuttered.* ADJ

2 A **shuttered** window, room, or building has shutters fitted to it. *The stone-built property is in good condition, with a new tiled roof, shuttered windows and electric heating. ...green-shuttered colonial villas.* ADJ: ADJ n

shuttle /ʃʌtəl/ **shuttles, shuttling, shuttled** ◆◆◇◇◇

1 A **shuttle** is the same as a **space shuttle**. N-COUNT

2 A **shuttle** is a plane, bus, or train which makes frequent journeys between two places. *...the BA shuttle to Glasgow. ...shuttle flights between London and Manchester.* N-COUNT: oft N n

3 If someone or something **shuttles** or **is shuttled** from one place to another place, they frequently go from one place to the other. *He and colleagues have shuttled back and forth between the three capitals... Machine parts were also being shuttled across the border without authorisation.* V-ERG; V prep/adv; *be* V-ed prep/adv; Also V n prep/adv

4 A **shuttle** is a piece of equipment used in weaving. It takes a thread backwards and forwards over the other threads in order to make a piece of cloth. N-COUNT

shuttlecock /ʃʌtəlkɒk/ **shuttlecocks.** A **shuttlecock** is the small object that you hit over the net in a game of badminton. It is rounded at one end and has real or artificial feathers fixed in the other end. N-COUNT

shuttle diplomacy. **Shuttle diplomacy** is the movement of diplomats between countries whose leaders refuse to talk directly to each other, in order to try to settle the argument between them. *UN mediators are conducting shuttle diplomacy between the two sides.* N-UNCOUNT

shy /ʃaɪ/ **shyer, shyest; shies, shying, shied** ◆◆◇◇◇

1 A **shy** person is nervous and uncomfortable in the company of other people. *She was a shy, quiet-spoken girl... She was a shy and retiring person off-stage... He is painfully shy of women.* ♦ **shyly** *The children smiled shyly.* ♦ **shyness** *Eventually he overcame his shyness.* ADJ-GRADED; ADV-GRADED: usu ADV with v; N-UNCOUNT

2 If you are **shy** of doing something, you are unwilling to do it because you are afraid of what might happen. *You should not be shy of having your say in the running of the school.* ADJ-GRADED: oft ADJ *of* -ing

3 When a horse **shies**, it moves away suddenly, because something has frightened it. *Llewelyn's stallion shied as the wind sent sparks flying.* VERB; V

4 You say **'once bitten, twice shy'** when you want to indicate that someone will not do something a second time because they had a bad experience the first time they did it. PHRASES

5 If you **fight shy** of something, you try very hard to avoid it. *It is no use fighting shy of publicity and then complaining when sponsors pass us by... Until now television had fought shy of covering by-elections.* V inflects

6 A number or amount that is just **shy of** another number or amount is just under it. *...a high-school dropout rate just shy of 53%... He died two days shy of his 95th birthday.* PREP =short of

shy away from. If you **shy away from** doing something, you avoid doing it, often because you are afraid or not confident enough. *We frequently shy away from making decisions... Alan doesn't shy away from controversy.* PHRASAL VERB; V P P -ing/n

-shy /-ʃaɪ/. **-shy** is added to nouns to form adjectives which indicate that someone does not like a particular thing, and tries to avoid it. For example, someone who is camera-shy is nervous and uncomfortable about being filmed or about having their photograph taken. *Normally coy and camera-shy, Diana made it known she wanted him to photograph her... The publicity-shy singer spoke frankly in his first interview in three years.* COMB in ADJ

shyster /ʃaɪstəʳ/ **shysters.** If you refer to someone, especially a lawyer or politician, as a **shyster**, you mean that they are dishonest and immoral; an informal word, used mainly in American English. N-COUNT

Siamese cat /saɪəmiːz kæt/ **Siamese cats.** A **Siamese cat** is a type of cat with short cream and brown fur, blue eyes, dark ears, and a dark tail. N-COUNT

Siamese twin /saɪəmiːz twɪn/ **Siamese twins.** **Siamese twins** are twins who are born joined to each other by a part of their bodies. N-COUNT

sibilant /sɪbɪlənt/. **Sibilant** sounds are soft, hissing sounds, like the sounds a snake makes; a formal word. *A sibilant murmuring briefly pervaded the room... She heard Eve's voice, cold and sibilant. 'What are you doing here?'* ADJ: usu ADJ n

sibling /sɪblɪŋ/ **siblings.** Your **siblings** are your brothers and sisters. *His siblings are mostly in their early twenties... Sibling rivalry often causes parents anxieties.* ◆◇◇◇◇ N-COUNT

sic. You write **sic** in brackets after a word or expression when you want to indicate to the reader that although the word or expression looks odd or wrong, you intended to write it in that way or the original writer wrote it like that. *The latest school jobs page advertises a 'wide rnage (sic) of 6th form courses.'* ◆◆◇◇◇

Sicilian /sɪsɪliən/ **Sicilians** ◆◇◇◇◇

1 **Sicilian** means belonging or relating to Sicily, or to its people or culture. *...the Sicilian village of Corleone.* ADJ

2 A **Sicilian** is a Sicilian citizen, or a person of Sicilian origin. N-COUNT

sick /sɪk/ **sicker, sickest** ◆◆◆◇◇

1 If you are **sick**, you are ill. **Sick** usually means ADJ-GRADED physically ill, but it can sometimes be used to mean mentally ill. *He's very sick. He needs medication... She found herself with two small children, a sick husband, and no money... He was not evil, but he was sick.* ► **The sick** are people who are sick. *There were no doctors to treat the sick.* =ill N-PLURAL: the N

2 If you are **sick**, the food that you have eaten comes up from your stomach and out of your mouth. If you feel **sick**, you feel as if you are going to be sick. *She got up and was sick in the handbasin... The very thought of food made him feel sick... Orange juice makes him sick so don't give it to him.* ADJ-GRADED: v-link ADJ

3 In British English, **sick** is vomit; an informal use. N-UNCOUNT

4 If you say that you are **sick of** something or **sick and tired of** it, you are emphasizing that you are very annoyed by it and want it to stop; an informal use. *I am sick and tired of hearing all these people moaning... Most people here are sick of violence.* ADJ-GRADED: v-link ADJ of n/-ing PRAGMATICS =fed up

5 If you describe something such as a joke or story as **sick**, you mean that it deals with death or suffering in an unpleasantly frivolous way; used showing disapproval. *...a sick joke about a cat... That's really sick.* ADJ-GRADED PRAGMATICS

6 If you say that something or someone **makes** you **sick**, you mean that they make you feel angry or disgusted; an informal use. *It makes me sick that young people commit offences time after time and never seem to get punished... The British press makes me sick.* PHRASES V inflects, oft it PHR that

7 If you are **off sick**, you are not at work because you are ill. *When we are off sick, we only receive half pay.* usu v-link PHR

8 If you say that you are **worried sick**, you are emphasizing that you are extremely worried; an informal expression. *He was worried sick about what our mothers would say.* v-link PHR PRAGMATICS

sick bay, sick bays; also spelled **sick-bay**. A **sick bay** is an area, especially on a ship or in a school or university, where medical treatment is given and where beds are provided for people who are ill. *...a free 16-bed sick bay for students needing continuous care... You'd better go to Sick Bay.* N-COUNT: also prep N

sickbed /sɪkbed/ **sickbeds;** also spelled **sickbed**. Your **sickbed** is the bed that you are lying in while you are ill. *Michael left his sickbed to entertain his house guests.* N-COUNT: usu poss N

sick building syndrome. **Sick building syndrome** is a group of symptoms, including headaches, eye irritation, and tiredness, which people who work in air-conditioned offices may experience. *Built-up static contributes to sick building syndrome.* N-UNCOUNT

sicken /sɪkən/ **sickens, sickening, sickened** ◆◇◇◇◇

1 If something **sickens** you, it makes you feel disgusted. *The notion that art should be controlled by intellectuals sickened him... What he saw there sickened him, despite all his years of police work.* VERB =disgust V n

2 If you **sicken**, you become ill; an old-fashioned use. *Many of them sickened and died.* VERB V

sickening /sɪkənɪŋ/. You describe something as **sickening** when it gives you feelings of horror or disgust, or makes you feel sick in your stomach. *This was a sickening attack on a pregnant and defenceless woman... He described the Foreign Office's decision as sickening and cynical.* ◆◇◇◇◇ ADJ-GRADED

♦ **sickeningly** *The interview was offensive and sickeningly irresponsible.* ADV-GRADED: usu ADV adj/adv

sickle /sɪkəl/ **sickles.** A **sickle** is a tool that is used for cutting grass and grain crops. It has a short handle and a long curved blade. ◆◇◇◇◇ N-COUNT

sick leave. **Sick leave** is the time that a person spends away from work because of illness or injury. *I have been on sick leave for seven months with depression.* N-UNCOUNT: oft on N

sickle-cell anaemia; spelled **sickle-cell anemia** in American English. **Sickle-cell anaemia** is a hereditary disease in which the red blood cells become sickle-shaped, causing jaundice, ulcers, and a high temperature. N-UNCOUNT

sickly /sɪkli/ **sicklier, sickliest** ◆◇◇◇◇

1 A **sickly** person or animal is weak, unhealthy, and often ill. *He had been a sickly child.* ADJ-GRADED

2 A **sickly** smell or taste is unpleasant and makes you feel slightly sick, often because it is extremely sweet. *...the sickly smell of rum.* ADJ-GRADED

3 A **sickly** colour or light is unpleasantly pale or weak. *Wallpapers designed specifically for children are too often available only in sickly pastel shades.* ADJ-GRADED: usu ADJ n

sickness /sɪknəs/ **sicknesses** ◆◆◇◇◇

1 **Sickness** is the state of being ill or unhealthy. *In fifty-two years of working he had one week of sickness... There appears to be another outbreak of sickness among seals in the North Sea.* N-UNCOUNT

2 **Sickness** is the uncomfortable feeling that you are going to vomit. *He felt a great rush of sickness... After a while, the sickness gradually passed and she struggled to the mirror.* ● See also **morning sickness, travel sickness.** N-UNCOUNT =nausea

3 A **sickness** is a particular illness. *More than 930 local people are registered as suffering from radiation sickness.* N-VAR

sickness benefit. In British English, **sickness benefit** is money that you receive regularly from the government when you are unable to work because of illness. N-UNCOUNT

sick pay. When you are ill and unable to work, **sick pay** is the money that you get from your employer instead of your normal wages. *...if they are not eligible for sick pay.* N-UNCOUNT

sickroom /sɪkruːm/ **sickrooms;** also spelled **sick room**. A **sickroom** is a room in which a sick person is lying in bed. *Close friends were allowed into the sickroom now, provided they didn't stay too long.* N-COUNT

side /saɪd/ **sides, siding, sided** ◆◆◆◆◆

1 The **side** of something is a position to the left or right of it, rather than in front of it, behind it, or on it. *On one side of the main entrance there's a red plaque. ...a photograph with me in the centre and Joe and Ken on each side of me. ...the nations on either side of the Pacific... There's nothing but woods on the other side of the highway... There has been a build-up of troops on both sides of the border... To the side of the large star is a smaller star... PC Dacre knocked on Webb's door and, opening it, stood to one side.* N-COUNT: usu prep N of n

2 The **side** of an object, building, or vehicle is any of its flat surfaces which is not considered to be its front, its back, its top, or its bottom. *We put a notice on the side of the box. ...a van bearing on its side the name of a company... There was a stone staircase against the side of the house... A carton of milk lay on its side. ...a huge vacation house on the side of a mountain.* N-COUNT: usu with poss

3 The **sides** of a hollow or a container are its inside vertical surfaces. *The rough rock walls were like the sides of a deep canal... Line the base of the dish with greaseproof paper and lightly grease the sides. ...narrow valleys with steep sides.* N-COUNT

4 The **sides** of an area or surface are its edges. *Park on the side of the road. ...a small beach on the north side of the peninsula... Coyne slid his legs over the side of the bed.* N-COUNT: usu prep N of n =edge

5 The two **sides** of an area, surface, or object are its two halves. *She turned over on her stomach on the other side of the bed... The major centre for language is in the left side of the brain. ...the right side of your face.* N-COUNT: usu prep N of n =half

6 The two **sides** of a road are its two halves on which traffic travels in opposite directions. *It had gone on to the wrong side of the road and hit a car coming in the other direction.* N-COUNT

7 If you talk about the other **side** of a town or of the world, you mean a part of the town or of the world that is very far from where you are. *He lives the other side of London... He saw the ship that was to transport them to the other side of the world... Are you working on this side of the city?* N-COUNT: with supp

8 Your **sides** are the parts of your body under your arms from your armpits down to your hips. *His* N-COUNT: usu poss N

arms were limp at his sides... They had laid him on his side.

9 If someone is **by your side** or **at your side**, they stay near you and give you comfort or support. *He was constantly at his wife's side... He calls me 20 times a day and needs me by his side in the evening. He was too sick to travel to his son's side.* N-COUNT: usu sing, by/at poss N

10 The two **sides** of something flat, for example a piece of paper, are its two flat surfaces. You can also refer to one side of a piece of paper filled with writing as one **side** of writing. *The new copiers only copy onto one side of the paper... Fry the chops until brown on both sides... Your cv should be short – two sides of a sheet of A4 paper should normally be enough.* N-COUNT

11 One **side** of a tape or record is what you can hear or record if you play the tape or record from beginning to end without turning it over. *We want to hear side A... In those days symphonies were recorded on both sides of four twelve-inch records.* N-COUNT

12 A **side of** beef, bacon, or other meat consists of the meat from half the animal cut along its backbone. N-COUNT: N of n

13 **Side** is used to describe things that are not the main or most important ones of their kind. *She slipped in and out of the theatre by a side door. ...a little fish restaurant on a side street. ...a prawn curry with a lentil side dish.* ADJ: ADJ n ≠main

14 The different **sides** in a war, argument, or negotiation are the different groups of people who are fighting, arguing, or negotiating with each other. *Both sides appealed for a new ceasefire... Any solution must be acceptable to all sides. ...the elections which his side lost... The other side denied that any money was owed to me.* N-COUNT: usu with supp

15 The different **sides** of an argument or deal are the different points of view or positions involved in it. *His words drew sharp reactions from people on both sides of the issue. ...those with the ability to see all sides of a question... We shall be able to tell whether you've kept your side of the bargain.* N-COUNT: usu N of n

16 If one person or country **sides** with another, they support them in an argument or a war. If people or countries **side** against another person or country, they support each other in arguing or fighting against that person or country. *There has been much speculation that America might be siding with the rebels... You need to confront those who have sided against you.* VERB V with/against n

17 In sport, a **side** is a team. *Italy were definitely a better side than West Germany... The captain made the decision to include four men in their 40s in his side.* N-COUNT: usu with supp =team

18 A particular **side** of something such as a situation or someone's character is one aspect of it. *He is in charge of the civilian side of the UN mission... It shows that your child can now see the funny side of things... There's a puritanical side to me... Anxiety has a mental and a physical side.* N-COUNT: usu supp N

19 The **mother's side** and the **father's side** of your family are your mother's relatives and your father's relatives. *So was your father's side more well off? ...a relative on the maternal side of his family.* N-COUNT: usu supp N

20 See also **-sided, siding.**

21 If two people or things are **side by side**, they are next to each other. *We sat side by side on two wicker seats... Put the eggplants side by side in a serving dish.* PHRASES usu PHR after v

22 If people work or live **side by side**, they work or live closely and peacefully together. *...areas where different nationalities have lived side by side for centuries... We're usually working side by side with the men.* usu PHR after v =shoulder to shoulder

23 If you say that someone **has let the side down,** you mean that they have embarrassed their family or friends by behaving badly or not doing very well at something. *Brown was constantly letting the side down.* V inflects

24 If something moves **from side to side**, it moves repeatedly to the left and to the right. *She was shaking her head from side to side.* PHR after v

25 If you are **on** someone's **side**, you are supporting them in an argument or a war. *He has the Democrats on his side... Get that employee on your side and then work together towards a solution... Some of the younger people seem to be on the side of reform.* PHR after v

26 If something is **on** your **side** or if you have it **on** your **side**, it helps you when you are trying to achieve something. *The weather is rather on our side... The law is not on their side.* PHR after v, v-link PHR

27 If you get **on the wrong side of** someone, you do something to annoy them and make them dislike you. If you stay **on the right side of** someone, you try to please them and avoid annoying them. *I wouldn't like to get on the wrong side of him... You'll need to get on the right side of Carmela.* usu PHR after v

28 If you say that something is **on the** small **side**, you are saying politely that you think it is slightly too small. If you say that someone is **on the** young **side**, you are saying politely that you think they are slightly too young. *He's quiet and a bit on the shy side.* usu v-link PHR PRAGMATICS

29 If someone does something **on the side**, they do it in addition to their main work. *...ways of making a little bit of money on the side.* usu PHR after v

30 If you **put** something **to one side** or **put** it **on one side**, you temporarily ignore it in order to concentrate on something else. *In order to maintain profit margins health and safety regulations are often put to one side.* V inflects

31 If you **take** someone **to one side** or **draw** them **to one side**, you speak to them privately, usually in order to give them advice or a warning. *He took Sabrina to one side and told her about the safe.* V inflects

32 If you **take sides** or **take** someone**'s side** in an argument or war, you support one of the sides against the other. *We cannot take sides in a civil war... See? You're taking his side again.* V inflects

33 If you say that something will not happen **this side of** a date or event, you mean that it will not happen before that date or event. *A race between the two is now unlikely to take place this side of the world championships.* PREP: PREP n =before

34 • **on the side of the angels**: see **angel.** • **look on the bright side**: see **bright.** • **the other side of the coin**: see **coin.** • **two sides of the same coin**: see **coin.** • to **err on the side of** something: see **err.** • to **be on the safe side**: see **safe.** • someone's **side of the story**: see **story.**

sidearm /saɪdɑːʳm/ **sidearms. Sidearms** are weapons, usually small guns, that you carry at your side in a holster or belt. *Two guards with sidearms patrolled the wall.* N-COUNT: usu pl

sideboard /saɪdbɔːʳd/ **sideboards**

1 A **sideboard** is a long cupboard which is about the same height as a table. Sideboards are usually kept in dining rooms to put plates and glasses in. N-COUNT

2 In British English, **sideboards** are the same as **sideburns.** N-PLURAL

sideburns /saɪdbɜːʳnz/. If a man has **sideburns**, he has a strip of hair growing down the side of each cheek. *...a young man with long sideburns.* N-PLURAL

sidecar /saɪdkɑːʳ/ **sidecars.** A **sidecar** is a kind of box with wheels which you can attach to the side of a motorcycle so that you can carry a passenger in it. N-COUNT

-sided /-saɪdɪd/. **-sided** combines with numbers or adjectives to describe how many sides something has, or what kind of sides something has. *...a three-sided pyramid... We drove up a steep-sided valley.* • See also **one-sided.** COMB in ADJ: usu ADJ n

side dish, side dishes. A **side dish** is a portion of food that is served at the same time as and in addition to the main dish. *These mushrooms would make a delicious side dish to serve with grilled chicken.* N-COUNT

side-effect, side-effects; also spelled **side effect.** ◆◆◇◇◇

1 The **side-effects** of a drug are the effects, usually bad ones, that the drug has on you in addition to its function of curing illness or pain. *The treatment has a whole host of extremely unpleasant side-* N-COUNT: usu pl *effects including weight gain, acne, skin rashes and headaches... Most patients suffer no side-effects.*

2 A **side-effect** of a situation is something that is unplanned, and usually unpleasant, that happens in addition to the main results or effects of that situation. *One side effect of modern life is stress... In Eastern Europe, one of the side effects of freedom appears to be crime.* N-COUNT: usu N *of* n/-ing

side issue, side issues. A **side issue** is an issue or subject that is not considered to be as important as the main one. *I must forget these side issues and remember my mission.* N-COUNT

sidekick /saɪdkɪk/ **sidekicks.** Someone's **sidekick** is a companion or colleague who helps them with routine tasks, and who you consider to be inferior, less intelligent, or less important than the other person; an informal word. *His sons, brother and nephews were his armed sidekicks. ...a dim-witted sidekick.* N-COUNT: oft poss N

sidelight /saɪdlaɪt/ **sidelights**

1 In British English, the **sidelights** on a vehicle are the small lights at the front that help other drivers to notice the vehicle and to judge its width. The usual American term is **parking lights**. N-COUNT

2 A **sidelight** on a particular situation is a piece of information about that situation which is interesting but which is not particularly important. *The book's interspersed with interesting and often amusing sidelights on his family background.* N-COUNT: oft N *on* n

sideline /saɪdlaɪn/ **sidelines, sidelining, sidelined** ◆◇◇◇◇

1 A **sideline** is something that you do in addition to your main job in order to earn extra money. *It was quite a lucrative sideline... Mr. Means sold computer disks as a sideline.* N-COUNT

2 The **sidelines** are the lines marking the long sides of the playing area, for example on a football pitch or tennis court. N-PLURAL

3 If you are on **the sidelines** in a situation, you do not influence events at all, either because you have chosen not to be involved, or because other people have not involved you. *France no longer wants to be left on the sidelines when critical decisions are taken... He has watched from the sidelines the great developments unrolling in Eastern Europe... The government has just stood on the sidelines up to now and let the situation get worse.* N-PLURAL: *the* N, usu *on/from* N

4 If someone or something **is sidelined,** they are made to seem unimportant and not included in what people are doing. *For months he had been under pressure to resign and was about to be sidelined anyway... What they fear is that environment policy will be sidelined until it is too late.* VB: usu passive *be* V-ed

5 In sport, if a player **is sidelined**, he or she is prevented from playing for a period of time, for example because of an injury. *Mercer will have his jaw wired up tomorrow and will be sidelined for six to eight weeks.* VB: usu passive

sidelong /saɪdlɒŋ, AM -lɔːŋ/. If you give someone a **sidelong** look, you look at them out of the corner of your eyes. *She gave him a quick sidelong glance, then steadied her eyes on the road.* ADJ: ADJ n

side-on. A **side-on** collision or view is a collision or view from the side of an object. *The German car also features steel beams built into the doors for added protection against a side-on crash.* ◆◇◇◇◇ ADJ

side-saddle. When you ride a horse **side-saddle**, you sit on a special saddle with both your legs on one side rather than one leg on each side of the horse. *Instead of riding a bicycle, Naomi was given a pony and taught to ride side-saddle.* ► Also an adjective. *Katie Moore took the ladies' side-saddle award.* ADV: ADV after v; ADJ: ADJ n

sideshow /saɪdʃoʊ/ **sideshows;** also spelled **side-show.**

1 A **sideshow** is a less important or less significant event or situation related to a larger, more important one that is happening at the same time. *In the end, the meeting was a sideshow to a political storm that broke Thursday... Radio work for him was very much a sideshow.* N-COUNT: oft N *to* n

2 At a circus or fair, a **sideshow** is a performance that you watch or a game of skill that you play, that is provided in addition to the main entertainment. *Sideshows at the championship include highland dancing and a play by The Wanlockhead Players.* N-COUNT

side-splitting. Something that is **side-splitting** is very funny and makes you laugh so much that you ache all over; an informal word. *...a side-splitting joke.* ADJ

sidestep /saɪdstep/ **sidesteps, sidestepping, sidestepped;** also spelled **side-step.** ◆◇◇◇◇

1 If you **sidestep** a problem, you avoid discussing it or dealing with it. *Rarely, if ever, does he sidestep a question... He was trying to sidestep responsibility.* VERB =evade V n Also V

2 If you **sidestep**, you step sideways in order to avoid something or someone that is coming towards you or going to hit you. *As I sidestepped, the bottle hit me on the left hip... He made a grab for her but she sidestepped him and kicked him.* VERB V V n

sideswipe /saɪdswaɪp/ **sideswipes;** also spelled **side-swipe.** If you take a **sideswipe** at someone or something, you make an unexpected critical remark about them while you are talking about something else. *Despite the increasingly hostile sideswipes at him, the Chancellor is secure in his post.* N-COUNT: usu N *at* n

sidetrack /saɪdtræk/ **sidetracks, sidetracking, sidetracked;** also spelled **side-track.** If you **are sidetracked** by something, it makes you forget what you intended to do or say, and start instead doing or talking about a different thing. *He was relieved that he'd managed to avoid being sidetracked by Schneider or Matthew Armstrong's problems... The leadership moved to sidetrack the proposal... They have a tendency to try to sidetrack you from your task.* VERB *be* V-ed V n V n *from* n Also *be* V-ed *into* n/-ing

sidewalk /saɪdwɔːk/ **sidewalks.** In American English, a **sidewalk** is a path with a hard surface by the side of a road. The British word is **pavement**. *Two men and a woman were walking briskly down the sidewalk toward him.* ◆◇◇◇◇ N-COUNT

sideways /saɪdweɪz/ ◆◇◇◇◇

1 **Sideways** means from or towards the side of something or someone. *Piercey glanced sideways at her... The ladder blew sideways... He was facing sideways.* ► Also an adjective. *Alfred shot him a sideways glance.* ADV: ADV after v; ADJ-GRADED: ADJ n

2 If you are moved **sideways** at work, you move to another job at the same level as your old job. *He would be moved sideways, rather than demoted.* ► Also an adjective. *...her recent sideways move.* ADV: ADV after v; ADJ: ADJ n

3 If you **are knocked sideways** by something, it makes you feel amazed, confused, or very upset; an informal expression. *He was knocked sideways by the result... A week ago I met my ex-boyfriend and it knocked us both sideways.* PHRASE: V inflects

siding /saɪdɪŋ/ **sidings.** A **siding** is a short railway track beside the main tracks, where engines and carriages are left when they are not being used. N-COUNT

sidle /saɪdᵊl/ **sidles, sidling, sidled.** If you **sidle** somewhere, you walk there uncertainly or cautiously, as if you do not want anyone to notice you. *A young man sidled up to me and said, 'May I help you?'... He was sidling into the bar, obviously trying to be inconspicuous.* VERB V prep/adv

siècle. See **fin de siècle**.

siege /siːdʒ/ **sieges** ◆◆◇◇◇

1 A **siege** is a military or police operation in which soldiers or police surround a place in order to force the people there to surrender or to come out. *We must do everything possible to lift the siege... They are hopeful of bringing the siege to a peaceful conclusion... The journalists found a city virtually under siege.* • See also **state of siege.** N-COUNT: also *under* N

2 If police, soldiers, or journalists **lay siege** to the place where someone is, they surround it in order to force the people there to surrender or to come out. *The rebels laid siege to the governor's residence... The press laid siege to the club.* PHRASES V inflects, usu PHR *to* n

3 If someone or something is **under siege**, they are being severely criticized or put under a great deal v-link PHR

of pressure. *The guy'll think he's under siege... Radio One is under siege from all sides.*

siege mentality. If someone has a **siege mentality**, they refuse to co-operate with other people, because they think that other people are constantly trying to harm or defeat them. *The commission said police officers had a siege mentality that isolated them from the people they served.* N-SING: also no det

siesta /siestə/ **siestas.** A **siesta** is a short sleep or rest which you have in the early afternoon, especially in hot countries. *Many cultures have a siesta during the hottest part of the day.* N-COUNT

sieve /sɪv/ **sieves, sieving, sieved** ◆◇◇◇◇
1 A **sieve** is a tool used for separating solids from liquids or larger pieces of something from smaller pieces. It consists of a metal or plastic ring with a wire or plastic net underneath, which the liquid or smaller pieces pass through. *Press the raspberries through a fine sieve to form a puree.* N-COUNT
2 When you **sieve** a liquid or powdery substance, you put it through a sieve. *Cream the margarine in a small bowl, then sieve the icing sugar into it.* VERB =sift V n

sift /sɪft/ **sifts, sifting, sifted** ◆◇◇◇◇
1 If you **sift** a loose or powdery substance such as flour or sand, you put it through a sieve in order to remove large pieces or lumps. *Sift the flour and baking powder into a medium-sized mixing bowl.* VERB =sieve V n
2 If you **sift** through something such as evidence, you examine it thoroughly. *Police officers have continued to sift through the wreckage following yesterday's bomb attack... Brook has sifted the evidence and summarises it clearly.* VERB V *through* n V n

sigh /saɪ/ **sighs, sighing, sighed** ◆◆◆◇◇
1 When you **sigh**, you let out a deep breath, as a way of expressing feelings such as disappointment, tiredness, or pleasure. *Michael sighed wearily... Roberta sighed with relief... Dad sighed and stood up.* ► Also a noun. *She kicked off her shoes with a sigh... Prue heaved a weary sigh.* VERB V prep/adv V N-COUNT
2 If you **sigh** something, you say it with a sigh. *'Oh, sorry. I forgot.'—'Everyone forgets,' the girl sighed.* VERB V with quote
3 If the wind **sighs** through a place, it moves through the place with a sound like a sigh; a literary use. *The wind sighed through the valley.* VERB V prep
4 If people breathe or heave a **sigh of relief**, they feel very glad because something unpleasant has not happened or is no longer happening. *With monetary mayhem now retreating into memory, European countries can breathe a collective sigh of relief... There was an audible sigh of relief in Washington when the foreign ministers decided to postpone the meeting.* PHRASE: *sigh* inflects, PHR after v

sight /saɪt/ **sights, sighting, sighted** ◆◆◆◆◇
1 Someone's **sight** is their ability to see. *My sight is failing, and I can't see to read any more... I use the sense of sound much more than the sense of sight.* N-UNCOUNT: oft poss N =vision
2 **The sight of** something is the act of seeing it or an occasion on which you see it. *I faint at the sight of blood... The sight of him entering a room could flood her with desire.* N-SING: *the* N *of* n
3 A **sight** is something that you see. *The practice of hanging clothes across the street is a common sight in many parts of the city... We encountered the pathetic sight of a family packing up its home... Among the most spectacular sights are the great sea-bird colonies.* N-COUNT: usu with supp, oft adj N
4 If you **sight** someone or something, you suddenly see them, often briefly. *The security forces sighted a group of young men that had crossed the border... A fleet of French ships was sighted in the North Sea.* VERB =spot V n
5 The **sights** of a weapon such as a rifle are the part which helps you aim it more accurately. N-COUNT: usu pl
6 The **sights** are the places that are interesting to see and that are often visited by tourists. *We'd toured the sights of Paris... I am going to show you the sights of our wonderful city... Once at Elgin day-trippers visit a number of local sights.* N-PLURAL: usu *the* N, oft N *of* n
7 You can use **a sight** to mean a lot. For example, if you say that something is **a sight** worse than it was before, you are emphasizing that it is much worse than it was; an informal use. *She's been no more difficult than most daughters and a sight better than some I could mention... We weren't doing anything different to what we've always done. We're just doing it a damn sight quicker.* ADV: ADV adj/adv PRAGMATICS
8 See also **sighted, sighting.**
9 If you **catch sight of** someone, you suddenly see them, often briefly. *Then he caught sight of her small black velvet hat in the crowd... Every time I catch sight of myself in the mirror, I feel so disappointed.* PHRASES V inflects, PHR n =see
10 If you say that something seems to have certain characteristics **at first sight**, you mean that it appears to have the features you describe when you first see it but later it is found to be different. *It promised to be a more difficult undertaking than might appear at first sight... At first sight it resembles a traditional village of two-storeyed, balconied houses, set among well-tended gardens.* PHR with cl
11 If something is **in sight** or **within sight**, you can see it. If it is **out of sight**, you cannot see it. *The sandy beach was in sight... The Atlantic coast is within sight of the hotel... My companion suggested that we park out of sight of passing traffic to avoid attracting attention.* usu v-link PHR
12 If a result or a decision is **in sight** or **within sight**, it is likely to happen within a short time. *An agreement on many aspects of trade policy was in sight... There is no end in sight to the struggle for power... She was within sight of Navratilova's record of seventy-four consecutive wins.* v-link PHR
13 If you **lose sight of** an important aspect of something, you no longer pay attention to it because you are worrying about less important things. *In some cases, US industry has lost sight of customer needs in designing products... We shouldn't lose sight of the fact that education is important for its own sake.* V inflects, PHR n =forget
14 If you **know** someone **by sight**, you can recognize them when you see them, although you have never met them and talked to them. *I knew him by sight but had never spoken with him.* V inflects
15 If you say **'out of sight, out of mind'**, you mean that people quickly forget someone if he or she goes away. *The problems of the poor are largely invisible – out of sight, out of mind.*
16 If someone is ordered to do something **on sight**, they have to do it without delay, as soon as a person or thing is seen. *Troops shot anyone suspicious on sight... Magee was set free but British authorities were asked to arrest him on sight.*
17 If you say that someone or something is **not a pretty sight**, you mean that it is not pleasant to look at; an informal expression. *The bathroom is not a pretty sight. The wallpaper's peeling, the tiles are crumbling.* v-link PHR
18 If you **set** your **sights on** something, you decide that you want it and try hard to get it. *They have set their sights on the world record... Although she came from a family of bankers, Franklin set her sights on a career in scientific research.* V inflects, PHR n
19 If you agree to buy something **sight unseen**, you agree to buy it, even though you have not seen it and do not know what condition it is in. *Although people sometimes buy property sight unseen, it's a remarkably bad idea.* PHR after v
20 ● **love at first sight**: see **love.**

sighted /saɪtɪd/. **Sighted** people have the ability to see. This word is usually used to contrast people who can see with people who are blind. *Blind children tend to be more passive in this area of motor development than sighted children.* ● See also **clear-sighted, far-sighted, long-sighted, near-sighted, short-sighted.** ◆◇◇◇◇ ADJ: ADJ n ≠blind

sighting /saɪtɪŋ/ **sightings.** A **sighting** of something, especially something unusual or unexpected is an occasion on which it is seen. *...the sighting of a rare sea bird at Lundy island... The National Weather Service has reported several tornado sightings in Illinois.* ◆◇◇◇◇ N-COUNT: oft N *of* n

sightless /saɪtləs/. Someone who is **sightless** is blind; a literary word. *He wiped a tear from his sightless eyes.* ADJ

sight-read, sight-reads, sight-reading. The form **sight-read** is used in the present tense, where it is pronounced /saɪt riːd/, and is the past tense and past participle, pronounced /saɪt red/. Someone who can **sight-read** can play or sing music from a printed sheet the first time they see it, without practising it beforehand. *Symphony musicians cannot necessarily sight-read.* VERB V Also V n

sightseeing /saɪtsiːɪŋ/; also spelled **sight-seeing**. If you go **sightseeing** or do some **sight-seeing**, you travel around visiting the interesting places that tourists usually visit. *...a day's sight-seeing in Venice. ...a sightseeing tour.* ◆◇◇◇◇ N-UNCOUNT

sightseer /saɪtsiːəʳ/ **sightseers.** A **sightseer** is someone who is travelling around visiting the interesting places that tourists usually visit. *...coachloads of sightseers.* N-COUNT =tourist

sign /saɪn/ **signs, signing, signed** ◆◆◆◆◆

1 A **sign** is a mark or shape that always has a particular meaning, for example in mathematics or music. *Equations are generally written with a two-bar equals sign.* N-COUNT =symbol

2 A **sign** is a movement of your arms, hands, or head which is intended to have a particular meaning. *They gave Lavalle the thumbs-up sign... The priest made the sign of the cross over him.* N-COUNT

3 If you **sign**, you communicate with someone using sign language. If a programme or performance **is signed**, someone uses sign language so that deaf people can understand it. *All programmes will be either 'signed' or subtitled.* VERB be V-ed Also V, V n

4 A **sign** is a piece of wood, metal, or plastic with words or pictures on it. Signs give you information about something, or give you a warning or an instruction. *...a sign saying that the highway was closed because of snow. ...a cardboard sign, which stated 'No to Poll Tax'... As soon as the seat belt sign had been switched off, we rushed out.* N-COUNT

5 If there is a **sign** of something, there is something which shows that it exists or is happening. *They are prepared to hand back a hundred prisoners of war a day as a sign of good will... His face and movements rarely betrayed a sign of nerves... Your blood would have been checked for any sign of kidney failure.* N-VAR: usu with supp, oft N *of* n

6 When you **sign** a document, you write your name on it, usually at the end or in a special space. You do this to indicate that you have written the document, that you agree with what is written, or that you were present as a witness. *World leaders are expected to sign a treaty pledging to increase environmental protection... Before an operation the patient will be asked to sign a consent form.* VERB V n

7 If an organization **signs** someone or if someone **signs** for an organization, they sign a contract agreeing to work for that organization for a specified period of time. *It cost the Minnesota Vikings 12 players to sign Herschel Walker from the Dallas Cowboys... The band then signed to Slash Records.* V-ERG V n V *to/for* n Also V

8 In astrology, a **sign** of the zodiac is one of the twelve areas into which the heavens are divided. *The New Moon takes place in your opposite sign of Libra on the 15th.* N-COUNT

9 See also **signing**; **call sign**.

10 If you say that there is **no sign of** someone, you mean that they have not yet arrived, although you are expecting them to come. *The London train was on time, but there was no sign of my Finnish friend.* PHRASES v-link PHR n

11 If you say that an agreement is **signed and sealed**, or **signed, sealed and delivered**, you mean that it is absolutely definite because everybody involved has signed all the legal documents. *President Bush would like to have this treaty signed and sealed before he leaves office... A government spokesman said the bill must be signed, sealed and delivered by tomorrow.* usu v-link PHR

12 • to **sign** one's **own death warrant**: see **death warrant**.

sign away. If you **sign** something **away**, you sign official documents that mean that you no longer own it or have a right to it. *The Duke signed away his inheritance ... They signed the rights away when they sold their idea to DC Comics.* PHRASAL VERB V P n (not pron) V n P

sign for. If you **sign for** something, you officially state that you have received it, by signing a form or book. *When the postal clerk delivers your order, check the carton before signing for it.* PHRASAL VERB V P n

sign in. If you **sign in**, you officially indicate that you have arrived at a hotel or club by signing a book or form. *I signed in and crunched across the gravel to my room.* PHRASAL VERB V P

sign off PHRASAL VERB

1 If someone **signs off**, they write a final message at the end of a letter or they say a final message at the end of telephone conversation. You can say that people such as entertainers **sign off** when they finish a broadcast. *O.K. I'll sign off. We'll talk at the beginning of the week... He would sign off each week with the catch-phrase, 'I'll see thee!'.* V P

2 In British English, when someone who has been unemployed **signs off**, they officially inform the authorities that they have found a job, so that they no longer receive money from the government. *If he sold his art he would be breaking the law, but if he signed off the dole he wouldn't.* V P n (not pron) Also V P

sign on. In British English, when an unemployed person **signs on**, they officially inform the authorities that they are unemployed, so that they can receive money from the government in order to live. *He has signed on at the Labour Exchange... I had to sign on the dole on Monday.* PHRASAL VERB V P prep V P n (not pron)

sign on for. If you **sign on for** something, you officially agree to work for an organization or do a course of study by signing a contract or form. *Andrew joined up in 1989 and was planning to sign on for nine more years... He had signed on for a driving course.* PHRASAL VERB V P P n

sign over. If you **sign** something **over**, you sign documents that give someone else property, possessions, or rights that were previously yours. *Two years ago, he signed over his art collection to the New York Metropolitan Museum of Art... Last June, he closed his business voluntarily and signed his assets over to someone else.* PHRASAL VERB V P n (not pron) V n P

sign up. If you **sign up** for an organization or if an organization **signs** you **up**, you sign a contract officially agreeing to do a job or course of study. *He signed up as a steward with P&O Lines... He saw the song's potential, and persuaded the company to sign her up.* PHRASAL VERB ERG V P *as/for* n V n P

signal /sɪgnəl/ **signals, signalling, signalled;** spelled **signaling, signaled** in American English. ◆◆◆◇◇

1 A **signal** is a gesture, sound, or action which is intended to give a particular message to the person who sees or hears it. *They fired three distress signals... As soon as it was dark, Mrs Evans gave the signal... You mustn't fire without my signal.* N-COUNT

2 If you **signal** to someone, you make a gesture or sound in order to send them a particular message. *The United manager was to be seen frantically signalling to McClair... He stood up, signalling to the officer that he had finished with his client... She signalled a passing taxi and ordered him to take her to the rue Marengo.* VERB V prep/adv V that V n Also V

3 If an event or action is a **signal** of something, it suggests that this thing exists or is going to happen. *Kurdish leaders saw the visit as an important signal of support... The first warning signals came in March... The Red Cross said it is withdrawing its staff until they receive clear signals from all sides that their presence is welcomed.* N-COUNT: with supp =sign

4 If someone or something **signals** an event, they suggest that the event is happening or likely to happen. *She will be signalling massive changes in energy policy... Britain was signalling its readiness to have the embargo lifted... The outcome of that meeting could signal whether there truly exists a political will to begin negotiating.* VERB =indicate V n V wh

5 A **signal** is a piece of equipment beside a railway, which indicates to train drivers whether they should stop the train or not. N-COUNT

6 A **signal** is a series of radio waves, light waves, or electrical impulses, which carry information. *...high-frequency radio signals.* N-COUNT

7 You use **signal** to describe a triumph, success, or ADJ:

failure when you are emphasizing the fact that it has occurred and indicating that the consequences are significant. *His final round was a signal triumph in a career marked by many sweet moments. ...John Major's signal failure to grab America's attention.* ♦ **signally** *...a demoralised party which its leader signally failed to reassure.* ADJ n PRAGMATICS ADV: usu ADV before v

signal box, signal boxes. A **signal box** is a small building near a railway, which contains the switches used to control the signals. N-COUNT

signalman /sɪgnəlmæn/ **signalmen.** A **signalman** is a person whose job is to control the signals on a particular section of a railway. N-COUNT

signatory /sɪgnətri, AM -tɔːri/ **signatories.** The **signatories** of an official document are the people, organizations, or countries that have signed it; a formal word. *Both countries are signatories to the Nuclear Non-Proliferation Treaty.* ♦◇◇◇◇ N-COUNT: oft N *of/to* n

signature /sɪgnətʃəʳ/ **signatures** ♦♦◇◇◇

1 Your **signature** is your name, written in your own characteristic way, often at the end of a document to indicate that you wrote the document or that you agree with what it says. *I was writing my signature at the bottom of the page. ...a petition containing 170 signatures.* N-COUNT

2 If you **put** your **signature to** a document, you sign it as a way of officially showing that you agree with what is written. *The two sides met to put their signatures to a formal agreement.* PHRASE: V and N inflect, PHR n =sign

signature tune, signature tunes. A **signature tune** is the tune which is always played at the beginning or end of a particular television or radio programme, or which people always associate with a particular performer; used mainly in British English. *Doesn't that sound like the signature tune from The Late Late Show? ...BB King's signature tune 'Worried Life Blues'.* N-COUNT

signboard /saɪnbɔːʳd/ **signboards.** A **signboard** is a piece of wood which has been painted with pictures or words and which gives some information about a particular place, product, or event. *The signboard at the entrance to the factory read 'baby milk plant' in English and in Arabic.* N-COUNT

signer /saɪnəʳ/ **signers.** A **signer** is someone who communicates to deaf people using sign language. *I'm keen on providing signers for deaf people and readers for the blind.* N-COUNT

signet ring /sɪgnət rɪŋ/ **signet rings.** A **signet ring** is a ring which has a flat oval or circular section at the front with a pattern or letters carved into it. N-COUNT

significance /sɪgnɪfɪkəns/. The **significance** of something is the importance that it has, usually because it will have an effect on a situation or shows something about a situation. *Ideas about the social significance of religion have changed over time... A sacred site might be a mountain that is of some significance to a tribe.* ♦♦◇◇◇ N-UNCOUNT: usu with supp, oft N prep =importance

significant /sɪgnɪfɪkənt/ ♦♦♦♦◇

1 A **significant** amount of something is large enough to be important or make a difference. *Most 11-year-olds are not encouraged to develop reading skills; a small but significant number are illiterate. ...foods that offer a significant amount of protein.* ADJ-GRADED: usu ADJ n ≠insignificant
♦ **significantly** *The number of MPs now supporting him had increased significantly... America's airlines have significantly higher productivity than European ones... None is prepared to admit that their prices overall are significantly above those of their principal rivals.* ADV-GRADED: ADV with v, ADV adj/adv/prep

2 If one thing has a **significant** effect on another, it has an important and fundamental effect on it. *Her upbringing had a significant effect on her adult life and relationships... All their customs and cultures have made a very significant contribution to the way we live... It is significant that the time when we cut welfare is almost always during recessions.* ADJ-GRADED: usu ADJ n =important
♦ **significantly** *The 1990 Clean Air Act will significantly improve the environment. ...the virtues of positive liberty and more significantly humanitarian equality.* ADV-GRADED: ADV with v, ADV with cl/group

3 A **significant** action or gesture is intended to have a special meaning. *Mrs Bycraft gave Rose a significant glance.* ♦ **significantly** *She looked up at me significantly, raising an eyebrow.* ADJ-GRADED: usu ADJ n =meaningful ADV-GRADED: ADV after v

significant other, significant others. If you refer to your **significant other**, you are referring to your wife, husband, or the person you are having a relationship with. N-COUNT

signify /sɪgnɪfaɪ/ **signifies, signifying, signified** ♦◇◇◇◇

1 If an event, a sign, or a symbol **signifies** something, it is a sign of that thing or represents that thing. *He said Mr Singh's visit signified a step forward in relations between their two countries... A 'Les Routiers' symbol proudly displayed outside a restaurant signifies there's excellent cuisine to be enjoyed inside.* VERB V n V that

2 If you **signify** something, you make a sign or gesture in order to convey a particular meaning. *Two jurors signified their dissent... The UN flag was raised at the airport yesterday to signify that control had passed into its hands.* VERB =indicate, signal V n V that

signing /saɪnɪŋ/ **signings** ♦♦◇◇◇

1 The **signing of** a document is the act of writing your name to indicate that you agree with what it says or to say that you have been present to witness other people writing their signature. *Spain's top priority is the signing of an EMU treaty.* N-UNCOUNT: N *of* n

2 A **signing** is someone who has recently signed a contract agreeing to play for a football club or work for a record company. *...Steve McMahon, Manchester City's recent £900,000 signing from Liverpool.* N-COUNT: usu with supp

3 The **signing of** a player by a football club or a group by a record company is the act of drawing up a legal document setting out the length and terms of the association between them. *...Aston Villa's signing of the Australian goalkeeper Mark Bosnich.* N-UNCOUNT: N *of* n

4 **Signing** is the use of sign language to communicate to someone who is deaf or between deaf people. *The two deaf actors converse solely in signing.* N-UNCOUNT

sign language, sign languages. Sign language is a method of communicating by using movements of your hands and arms. There are several formal systems of sign language, used for example by deaf people, as well as informal methods that you might invent when you talk to someone who does not speak the same language as you. *Her son used sign language to tell her what happened.* N-VAR

signpost /saɪnpoʊst/ **signposts**

1 A **signpost** is a sign by a road junction, telling you which direction to go to reach a particular place. *The lights of the car lit up a signpost... Turn off at the signpost for Attlebridge.* N-COUNT =sign

2 A **signpost** is something that helps you to know how a situation or a course of action will develop. *The outcome of tomorrow's elections will be studied carefully as a signpost of voter intentions on the really big day this year... These events were all signposts pointing toward change.* N-COUNT: usu with supp, oft N *to/of* n

signposted /saɪnpoʊstɪd/. A place or route that is **signposted** has signposts beside the road to show the way. *The entrance is well signposted and is in Marbury Road.* ADJ

Sikh /siːk/ **Sikhs** A **Sikh** is a person who follows the Indian religion of Sikhism. *The rise of racism concerns Sikhs because they are such a visible minority. ...a Sikh temple. ...Sikh festivals.* ♦♦◇◇◇ N-COUNT: oft N n

Sikhism /siːkɪzəm/. **Sikhism** is an Indian religion which separated from Hinduism in the sixteenth century and which teaches that there is only one God. N-UNCOUNT

silage /saɪlɪdʒ/. **Silage** is food for cattle that is made by harvesting a crop such as grass or corn when it is green and then partly fermenting it. N-UNCOUNT

silence /saɪləns/ **silences, silencing, silenced** ♦♦♦◇◇

1 If there is **silence**, nobody is speaking. *They stood in silence... He never lets those long silences develop during dinner... Then he bellowed 'Silence!'* N-VAR: oft *in/of* N

2 The **silence** of a place is the extreme quietness there. *...the silence of that rainless, all-concealing fog... She breathed deeply, savouring the silence.* N-UNCOUNT: oft *the* N *of* n

3 Someone's **silence** about something is their failure or refusal to speak to other people about it. *He broke his silence for the first time yesterday about his lovechild... The district court ruled that Popper's silence in court today should be entered as a plea of not guilty.* N-UNCOUNT: oft poss N

4 To **silence** someone or something means to stop them speaking or making a noise. *A ringing phone silenced her... The shock silenced him completely.* VERB V n

5 If someone **silences** you, they stop you expressing opinions that they do not agree with. *Like other tyrants, he tried to silence anyone who spoke out against him. ...an unsuccessful attempt by the government to silence the debate.* VERB V n

6 To **silence** someone means to kill them in order to stop them revealing something secret. *A hit man had been sent to silence her over the affair.* VERB V n

silencer /saɪlənsəʳ/ **silencers**

1 A **silencer** is a device that is fitted onto a gun to make it very quiet when it is fired. *...a pistol that was equipped with a silencer.* N-COUNT

2 In British English, a **silencer** is a device on a car exhaust that makes it quieter. The American word is **muffler**. N-COUNT

silent /saɪlənt/ ◆◆◆◇◇

1 Someone who is **silent** is not speaking. *Trish was silent because she was reluctant to put her thoughts into words... He spoke no English and was completely silent during the visit... They both fell silent.* ADJ-GRADED: v-link ADJ =quiet ♦ **silently** *She and Ned sat silently for a moment, absorbing the peace of the lake... Most of those attending the funeral stood silently showing little emotion.* ADV: ADV with v =quietly

2 If you describe someone as a **silent** person, you mean that they do not talk to people very much, and sometimes give the impression of being unfriendly. *He was a serious, silent man.* ADJ-GRADED: ADJ n =quiet

3 A place that is **silent** is completely quiet, with no sound at all. Something that is **silent** makes no sound at all. *The room was silent except for the slight crunching coming from John's mouth as he ground his teeth together... The heavy guns have again fallen silent.* ADJ-GRADED: usu v-link ADJ =quiet ♦ **silently** *Strange shadows moved silently in the almost permanent darkness.* ADV-GRADED: ADV with v

4 If someone is **silent about** something, they do not tell people anything about it, because they think it is a private matter or because they want to keep the information secret. *Douglas was noticeably silent about his feelings for his father... The administration has recently become silent about abuses in Haiti.* ADJ-GRADED: v-link ADJ about n

5 A **silent** emotion or action is not expressed in speech. *The attacker still stood there, watching her with silent contempt... She offered a silent prayer of thanks.* ADJ: ADJ n ♦ **silently** *Whitlock silently cursed Graham for heaping more suspicion on him.* ADV: ADV with v

6 A **silent** film has pictures usually accompanied by music but does not have the actors' voices or any other sounds. *...one of the famous silent films of Charlie Chaplin. ...comedy stars of the silent era.* ADJ: ADJ n

7 A **silent** letter in a word is written but not pronounced. For example, the 'k' in the word 'know' is silent. ADJ

silent majority. If you believe that, in society or in a particular group, the opinions of most people are very different from the opinions that are most often heard in public, you can refer to these people as the **silent majority**. *...arguing that a silent majority should never again allow extremists to take control of the country... It may now be time for the silent majority of supportive parents and teachers to make their views known to MPs.* N-SING-COLL

silent partner, silent partners. In American English, a **silent partner** is a person who provides some of the capital for a business but who does not take an active part in managing the business. The British term is **sleeping partner**. N-COUNT

silhouette /sɪluet/ **silhouettes** ◆◇◇◇◇

1 A **silhouette** is the solid dark shape that you see when someone or something has a bright light or pale background behind them. *The dark silhouette of the castle ruins stood out boldly against the fading light.* N-COUNT

2 The **silhouette** of something is the outline that it has, which often helps you to recognize it. *He put on a hat that came down over his squarish skull and changed the distinctive silhouette of his ears... The shirt's ideal worn loose over leggings or tuck it in for a streamlined silhouette.* N-COUNT

3 If you see something **in silhouette**, you see it as a dark shape with no detail except for the outline. *Even from behind in silhouette, Billy recognized the figure.* PHRASE

silhouetted /sɪluetɪd/. If someone or something is **silhouetted** against a background, you can see their silhouette. *Silhouetted against the sun stood the figure of a man.* ADJ: usu v-link ADJ against n

silica /sɪlɪkə/. **Silica** is silicon dioxide, a compound of silicon which is found in sand, quartz, and flint, and which is used to make glass. N-UNCOUNT

silicate /sɪlɪkət/ **silicates.** A **silicate** is a compound of silica which does not dissolve. There are many different kinds of silicate. *...large amounts of aluminum silicate.* N-MASS

silicon /sɪlɪkən/. **Silicon** is a non-metallic element that is found combined with oxygen in sand and in minerals such as quartz and granite. Silicon is used to make parts of computers and other electronic equipment. *...a thin layer of silicon oxide... Each new chip will contain over three million transistors on a piece of silicon about the size of a standard postage stamp.* ◆◇◇◇◇ N-UNCOUNT

silicon chip, silicon chips. A **silicon chip** is a very small piece of silicon inside a computer. It has electronic circuits on it and can hold large quantities of information or perform mathematical or logical operations. N-COUNT =microchip

silicone /sɪlɪkoun/. **Silicone** is a tough artificial substance made from silicon, which is used to make things such as lubricants and polishes, and which is also used in cosmetic surgery and plastic surgery. *...silicone lubricants. ...women who suffered health problems from silicone breast implants that leak.* ◆◇◇◇◇ N-UNCOUNT: usu N n

silk /sɪlk/ **silks** ◆◆◇◇◇

1 **Silk** is a substance produced by silkworms which is made into smooth fine cloth and sewing thread. You can also refer to this cloth or thread as silk. *They continued to get their silks from China... Pauline wore a silk dress with a strand of pearls. ...softer-looking shades in silk.* N-MASS

2 You can refer to the substance produced by some creatures such as spiders as **silk**. *...the silk threads of a spider's web.* N-UNCOUNT: oft N n

silken /sɪlkən/

1 **Silken** is used to describe things that are very pleasantly smooth and soft; a literary use. *Christabel ran her fingers slowly through her long silken hair. ...her long, silken legs.* ADJ: usu ADJ n =silky

2 A **silken** garment, fabric, or rope is made of silk or a material that looks like silk; a literary use. *...a silken nightshirt. ...silken cushions.* ADJ: ADJ n

silk-screen; also spelled **silkscreen**. **Silk-screen** printing is a method of printing patterns onto cloth by forcing paint or dyes through silk or similar material. *...silk-screen prints. ...an Andy Warhol silk-screen portrait of Marilyn Monroe.* ADJ: ADJ n

silkworm /sɪlkwɜːʳm/ **silkworms.** A **silkworm** is a type of caterpillar that produces silk. N-COUNT

silky /sɪlki/ **silkier, silkiest** ◆◇◇◇◇

1 If something has a **silky** texture, it is smooth, soft, and shiny, like silk. *...dresses in seductively silky fabrics... Claire smoothed Katy's silky hair. ...skin that's silky and unblemished.* ADJ-GRADED: usu ADJ n

2 If you describe someone's voice as **silky**, you mean that it sounds confident but gentle and you find it attractive. *...a well-spoken man with a silky voice.* ADJ-GRADED: usu ADJ n

3 If you describe the way someone or something moves as **silky**, you mean that they move effortlessly and gracefully. *Some people moved in silky, liquid movements, others were jerky, probably drunk... I had the car for two years and much*

enjoyed its excellent handling, quietness and silky gearchange.

sill /sɪl/ **sills.** A **sill** is a ledge at the bottom of a window, either inside or outside a building. *Whitlock was perched on the sill of the room's only window.* ◆◇◇◇◇ N-COUNT

silly /sɪli/ **sillier, silliest** ◆◆◇◇◇

1 If you say that someone or something is **silly**, you mean that they are foolish, childish, or ridiculous. *My best friend tells me that I am silly to be upset about this... You silly boy; why did you tramp about so long in the cold?... I thought it would be silly to be too rude at that stage... That's a silly question. ...a silly hat.* ADJ-GRADED =stupid ♦ **silliness** *She looked round to make sure there was no giggling or silliness.* N-UNCOUNT

2 If you do something such as laugh or drink yourself **silly**, you do it so much that you are unable to think or behave sensibly; an informal use. *Right now the poor old devil's drinking himself silly... Poor Donald's been worrying himself silly.* ADJ: v n ADJ =stupid

silly season. **The silly season** is the time of the year, usually around August, when the newspapers are full of trivial or silly news stories because parliament is in recess and there is often very little real news to report; used mainly in British English. N-PROPER: *the* N

silo /saɪloʊ/ **silos**

1 A **silo** is a tall round metal tower on a farm, in which silage, grain, or some other substance is stored. *Before silos were invented, cows gave less milk during winter because they had no green grass to eat. ...a grain silo.* N-COUNT

2 A **silo** is a specially built place underground where a nuclear missile is kept. *...underground nuclear missile silos.* N-COUNT

silt /sɪlt/ **silts, silting, silted.** **Silt** is fine sand, soil, or mud which is carried along by a river. *The lake was almost solid with silt and vegetation.* ◆◇◇◇◇ N-UNCOUNT

silt up. If a river or lake **silts up** or something **silts** it **up**, it becomes blocked with silt. *Without huge investment the reservoirs will silt up... The soil washed from the hills is silting up the hydroelectric dams.* PHRASAL VERB ERG V P V P n

silver /sɪlvər/ **silvers** ◆◆◆◇◇

1 Silver is a valuable greyish-white metal that is used for making jewellery and ornaments. *...a hand-crafted brooch made from silver. ...amber earrings set in silver. ...silver teaspoons.* N-UNCOUNT: oft N n

2 Silver consists of coins that are made from silver or that look like silver. *...the basement where £150,000 in silver was buried.* N-UNCOUNT

3 You can use **silver** to refer to all the things in a house that are made of silver, especially the cutlery and dishes. *He beat the rugs and polished the silver.* N-UNCOUNT: also *the* N =silverware

4 Silver is used to describe things that are shiny greyish-white in colour or look as if they are made from silver. *He had thick silver hair which needed cutting. ...a silver sports car... Using silver tape, they taped all the doors and windows shut.* COLOUR

5 A **silver** is the same as a **silver medal**. *Britain went on to take bronze and then followed it up by winning silver in the World Cup.* N-VAR

6 • **born with a silver spoon in** your **mouth**: see **spoon.**

silver birch, silver birches; silver birch can also be used as the plural form. A **silver birch** is a tree with a greyish-white trunk and branches. N-COUNT

silvered /sɪlvərd/. You can describe something as **silvered** when it has become silver in colour; a literary word. *He had a magnificent head of silvered hair.* ADJ: usu ADJ n

silver jubilee, silver jubilees. A **silver jubilee** is the 25th anniversary of an important event, such as a king or queen coming to the throne, or the founding of a particular organization. *She arrived in St Ives to celebrate the Queen's Silver Jubilee. ...the group's silver jubilee concert.* N-COUNT

silver lining

1 If you say that **every cloud has a silver lining**, you mean that every sad or unpleasant situation has a positive side to it. *As they say, every cloud has a silver lining. We have drawn lessons from the decisions taken.* PHRASE

2 If you talk about a **silver lining**, you are talking about something positive that comes out of a sad or unpleasant situation. *The fall in inflation is the silver lining of the prolonged recession.* N-SING

silver medal, silver medals. If you win a **silver medal**, you come second in a competition, especially a sports contest, and are given a medal made of silver as a prize. *Gillingham won the silver medal in the 200 metres at Seoul.* ◆◇◇◇◇ N-COUNT =silver

silver plate

1 Silver plate is metal that has been coated with a thin layer of silver. *They are available in polished brass, antique brass or silver-plate. ...silver-plate cutlery.* N-UNCOUNT: oft N n

2 Silver plate is dishes, bowls, and cups that are made of silver. *...gold and silver plate, jewellery, and roomfuls of antique furniture.* N-UNCOUNT

silver-plated. Something that is **silver-plated** is covered with a very thin layer of silver. *...silver-plated cutlery.* ADJ

silver screen. People sometimes refer to the films that are shown in cinemas as **the silver screen**. *Marlon Brando, Steve McQueen, and James Dean are now legends of the silver screen... We don't see much of dear old Peter O'Toole on the silver screen these days.* N-SING: *the* N

silversmith /sɪlvərsmɪθ/ **silversmiths.** A **silversmith** is a person who makes things out of silver. N-COUNT

silver-tongued. A **silver-tongued** person is very skilful at persuading people to believe what they say or to do what they want them to do. *...a silver-tongued lawyer. ...the luckless lady who fell for his silver-tongued charm.* ADJ-GRADED: usu ADJ n

silverware /sɪlvərweər/. You can use **silverware** to refer to all the things in a house that are made of silver, especially the cutlery and dishes. *There was a serving spoon missing when Nina put the silverware back in its box.* N-UNCOUNT =silver

silver wedding, silver weddings. A married couple's **silver wedding** or **silver wedding anniversary** is the 25th anniversary of their wedding. *He and Helen celebrated their silver wedding last year.* N-COUNT: usu poss N

silvery /sɪlvəri/. **Silvery** things look like silver or are the colour of silver. *...a small, intense man with silvery hair... There was a full moon and its silvery light seeped through the curtains.* ◆◇◇◇◇ ADJ: usu ADJ n

simian /sɪmiən/

1 If someone has **simian** features or mannerisms, their features or mannerisms are like those of a monkey or ape; a formal use. *Ada Buck was small and ancient, with a wrinkled, simian face. ...his simian jaw.* ADJ: usu ADJ n

2 Simian is used to describe things relating to monkeys or apes; a technical use in biology. *...a simian virus that affects several types of monkeys.* ADJ: usu ADJ n

similar /sɪmɪlər/. If one thing is **similar to** another, or if two things are **similar**, they have features that are the same. *...a savoury cake with a texture similar to that of carrot cake. ...the accident was similar to one that happened in 1973. ...a group of similar pictures.* ◆◆◆◆◇ ADJ-GRADED: oft ADJ *to* n ≠different

similarity /sɪmɪlærɪti/ **similarities** ◆◆◇◇◇

1 If there is a **similarity** between two or more things, they are similar to each other. *The astonishing similarity between my brother and my first-born son... There was a very basic similarity in our philosophy... She is also 25 and a native of Birmingham, but the similarity ends there.* N-UNCOUNT: oft N *between/in/with* n

2 Similarities are features that things have which make them similar to each other. *There were significant similarities between mother and son... The similarities between Mars and Earth were enough to keep alive hopes of some form of Martian life.* N-COUNT: usu pl, oft N *between/in/with* n ≠difference

similarly /sɪmɪlərli/ ◆◆◇◇◇

1 You use **similarly** to say that something is similar to something else. *Most of the men who now gathered round him again were similarly dressed.* ADV-GRADED: ADV adj/adv, ADV with v ≠differently

2 You use **similarly** to say that there is a correspondence or similarity between the way two ADV: ADV with cl =likewise things happen or are done. *A mother somehow memorises the feel of her child's skin from the very first touches and can recognise it even when blindfolded. Similarly a baby's cry is instantly identified by the mother.*

simile /sɪmɪli/ **similes.** A **simile** is an expression which describes a person or thing as being similar to someone or something else. For example, the sentences 'She runs like a deer' and 'He's as white as a sheet' contain similes. N-COUNT

simmer /sɪməʳ/ **simmers, simmering, simmered** ◆◆◇◇◇

1 When you **simmer** food or when it **simmers**, you cook it by keeping it at boiling point or just below boiling point. *Make an infusion by boiling and simmering the rhubarb and camomile together... Turn the heat down so the sauce simmers gently.* ▶ Also a noun. *Combine the stock, whole onion and peppercorns in a pan and bring to a simmer.* V-ERG; V n; V; N-SING

2 If a conflict or a quarrel **simmers**, it does not actually happen for a period of time, but eventually builds up to the point where it does. *...bitter divisions that have simmered for more than half a century... The gardener exploded with the rage that had simmered all morning... The province was attacked a month ago after weeks of simmering tension.* VERB; V; V-ing

simmer down. If someone's feelings **simmer down**, they become less intense; an informal expression. *There's a great deal of suspicion and fear, and it's hard to say when all of this will simmer down... Ginny's initial rage at his treatment of Chris had simmered down to resentment.* PHRASAL VERB =subside; V P; V P to n

simper /sɪmpəʳ/ **simpers, simpering, simpered.** When someone **simpers**, they smile in a rather silly way. *The maid lowered her chin and simpered.* ▶ Also a noun. *'Thank you doctor,' said the nurse with a simper.* VERB; V; N-COUNT

simple /sɪmpəl/ **simpler, simplest** ◆◆◆◆◇

1 If you describe something as **simple**, you mean that it is not complicated, and is therefore easy to understand. *...simple pictures and diagrams. ...pages of simple advice on filling in your tax form... Buddhist ethics are simple but its practices are very complex to a western mind.* ♦ **simply** *When applying for a visa extension state simply and clearly the reasons why you need an extension.* ADJ-GRADED =uncomplicated, straightforward ≠complicated; ADV-GRADED: ADV with v

2 If you describe people or things as **simple**, you mean that they have all the basic or necessary things they require, but nothing extra. *The Holy Family Church was closed and the parish now celebrates mass in this simple side chapel... He ate a simple dinner of rice and beans. ...the simple pleasures of childhood... He lives a very simple life for a man who has become incredibly rich... Nothing is simpler than a cool white shirt.* ♦ **simply** *The living room is furnished simply with white wicker furniture and blue-and-white fabrics... He dressed simply and led a quiet family life.* ADJ-GRADED =basic; ADV-GRADED: ADV after v

3 If a problem is **simple** or if its solution is **simple**, the problem can be solved easily. *Some puzzles look difficult but once the solution is known are actually quite simple... The answer is simple... I cut my purchases dramatically by the simple expedient of destroying my credit cards.* ADJ-GRADED

4 A **simple** task is easy to do. *The job itself had been simple enough... The simplest way to install a shower is to fit one over the bath.* ♦ **simply** *Simply dial the number and tell us your area.* ADJ-GRADED: oft ADJ to-inf =easy; ADV-GRADED: ADV with v

5 If you say that someone is **simple**, you mean that they are not very intelligent or that they are mentally retarded. *He was simple as a child.* ADJ-GRADED

6 You use **simple** to emphasize that the thing you are referring to is the only important or relevant reason for something. *His refusal to talk was simple stubbornness.* ADJ: ADJ n PRAGMATICS =plain

7 In English grammar, **simple** tenses are ones which are not formed using an auxiliary verb 'be', as in 'I dressed and went for a walk' and 'These wines taste awful'. Simple verb groups are used especially to refer to completed actions, habitual actions, and situations. Compare **continuous**. ADJ

8 In English grammar, a **simple** sentence consists of one main clause. Compare **compound, complex**. ADJ

9 See also **simply**.

simple interest. **Simple interest** is interest that is calculated on an original sum of money and not also on interest which has previously been added to the sum. N-UNCOUNT

simple-minded. If you describe someone as **simple-minded**, you believe that they interpret things in a way that is too simple and do not understand how complicated things are; used showing disapproval. *Sylvie was a simple-minded romantic... His politics were also simple minded. ...those simple-minded solutions.* ♦ **simple-mindedness** *...the simple-mindedness of the theme in this film.* ADJ-GRADED PRAGMATICS; N-UNCOUNT

simpleton /sɪmpəltən/ **simpletons.** If you call someone a **simpleton**, you believe they are easily fooled or not very intelligent. *'But Ian's such a simpleton', she laughed... He was a lightweight, a political simpleton.* N-COUNT

simplicity /sɪmplɪsɪti/ ◆◇◇◇◇

1 The **simplicity** of something is the fact that it is uncomplicated and can be understood or done easily. *The apparent simplicity of his plot is deceptive... Because of its simplicity, this test could be carried out easily by a family doctor.* N-UNCOUNT: usu with supp

2 When you talk about something's **simplicity**, you approve of it because it is natural and simple rather than elaborate or ornate. *...fussy details that ruin the simplicity of the design... A pair of jewelled earrings will liven up this dress without detracting from its simplicity.* N-UNCOUNT: usu with supp PRAGMATICS

3 If you say that the way something looks is **simplicity itself**, you mean that it is attractive because it is simple and functional rather than elaborate or ornate. *The kitchen is simplicity itself, relying on a combination of good design, craftsmanship and quality materials for its effect.* PHRASES v-link PHR

4 If you say that doing something is **simplicity itself**, you mean that it is very easy to do. *Using a credit card to pay for an order is simplicity itself.* v-link PHR

simplification /sɪmplɪfɪkeɪʃən/ **simplifications**

1 You can use **simplification** to refer to the thing that is produced when you make something simpler or when you reduce it to its basic elements. *Like any such diagram, it is a simplification.* N-COUNT

2 **Simplification** is the act or process of making something simpler. *Everyone favours the simplification of court procedures.* N-UNCOUNT ≠complication

simplify /sɪmplɪfaɪ/ **simplifies, simplifying, simplified.** If you **simplify** something, you make it easier to understand or you remove the things which make it complex. *The aim of the scheme is to simplify the complex social security system... He reduced his needs to the minimum by simplifying his life.* ♦ **simplified** *Last night, the president presented a shorter, simplified version of his speech.* ◆◇◇◇◇ VERB ≠complicate; V n; ADJ-GRADED

simplistic /sɪmplɪstɪk/. A **simplistic** view or interpretation of something makes it seem much simpler than it really is. *He has a simplistic view of the treatment of eczema... The whole process is flawed because the logic behind the questions is too simplistic.* ♦ **simplistically** /sɪmplɪstɪkli/ *The impact of religion on voting has been analysed far too simplistically.* ◆◇◇◇◇ ADJ-GRADED; ADV-GRADED: usu ADV after v, also ADV adj

simply /sɪmpli/ ◆◆◆◆◇

1 You use **simply** to emphasize that something consists of only one thing, happens for only one reason, or is done in only one way. *The table is simply a chipboard circle on a base... Most of the damage that's occurred was simply because of fallen trees... Many people switch on the television simply to stave off boredom over the Christmas break... A sitting room can be transformed into a guest bedroom simply by adding a sofabed.* ADV: ADV before v, ADV with cl/group =just

2 You use **simply** to emphasize what you are saying. *This sort of increase simply cannot be justified... So many of these questions simply don't have answers... In a poll of those leaving the theatre nine out of ten thought it was simply marvellous.* ADV: ADV before v, ADV adj PRAGMATICS =just

3 See also **simple**.

simulate /sɪmjʊleɪt/ **simulates, simulating, simulated** ♦◇◇◇◇

1 If you **simulate** an action or a feeling, you pretend that you are doing it or feeling it. *They rolled about on the Gilligan Road, simulating a bloodthirsty fight... He performed a simulated striptease.* VERB V n V-ed

2 If you **simulate** an object, a substance, or a noise, you produce something that looks or sounds like it. *The wood had been painted to simulate stone... Smoke was used to simulate steam coming from a smashed radiator... Cadets are having to use football rattles to simulate gunfire because blank ammunition is too costly.* VERB V n

3 If you **simulate** a set of conditions, you reproduce them in some form, for example in order to conduct an experiment. *The scientist developed one model to simulate a full year of the globe's climate... Cars are tested to see how much damage they suffer in simulated crashes.* VERB V n V-ed

simulation /sɪmjʊleɪʃən/ **simulations** **Simulation** is the process of simulating something or the result of simulating it. *Training includes realistic simulation of casualty procedures. ...a simulation of the greenhouse effect.* ♦◇◇◇◇ N-VAR

simulator /sɪmjʊleɪtəʳ/ **simulators.** A **simulator** is a device which is designed to reproduce actual conditions. Simulators are used in training people such as pilots or astronauts. *...pilots practising a difficult landing in a flight simulator.* N-COUNT

simultaneous /sɪməlteɪniəs, AM saɪm-/. Things which are **simultaneous** happen or exist at the same time. *...the simultaneous release of the book and the album... The theatre will provide simultaneous translation in both English and Chinese.* ♦♦◇◇◇ ADJ
♦ **simultaneously** *...the two guns fired almost simultaneously... The stage version of 'The Butcher Boy' was written simultaneously with the novel.* ADV: ADV with v, ADV with cl/group

sin /sɪn/ **sins, sinning, sinned** ♦♦◇◇◇

1 **Sin** or a **sin** is an action or type of behaviour which is believed to break the laws of God. *The Vatican's teaching on abortion is clear: it is a sin... Was it the sin of pride to have believed too much in themselves?.* • See also **cardinal sin, mortal sin**. N-VAR

2 If you **sin**, you do something that is believed to break the laws of God. *The Spanish Inquisition charged him with sinning against God and man... You have sinned and unless you repent your ways you will surely roast in hell.* ♦ **sinner** /sɪnəʳ/ **sinners** *I was shown that I am a sinner, that I needed to repent of my sins.* VERB V *against* n V; N-COUNT

3 A **sin** is any action or behaviour that people disapprove of or consider morally wrong. *...the sin of arrogant hard-heartedness... The ultimate sin was not infidelity, but public mention which led to scandal.* N-COUNT

4 If you say that a man and a woman **are living in sin**, you mean that they are living together as a couple although they are not married; an old-fashioned use. *She was living in sin with her boyfriend.* • **a multitude of sins**: see **multitude**. PHRASE: V inflects

sin-bin; also spelled **sin bin**. In the sports of ice-hockey or rugby league, if a player is sent to the **sin-bin**, they are ordered to leave the playing area for a short period of time because they have done something wrong such as making an illegal tackle or fighting. N-SING

since /sɪns/ ♦♦♦♦♦

1 You use **since** when you are mentioning a time or event in the past and indicating that a situation has continued from then until now. *Jacques Arnold has been a member of parliament since 1987... She had a sort of breakdown some years ago, and since then she has been very shy... I've been here since the end of June.* ► Also an adverb. *When we first met, we had a row, and we have rowed frequently ever since... They went to Dartmouth College together in the 1960s and have frequently done business together since... I returned home to Sussex and have since worked as a solicitor.* ► Also a conjunction. *I've earned my own living since I was seven, doing all kinds of jobs. ...the problems the movie company had had ever since it set up camp on Sketon Island.* PREP; ADV: ADV with v; CONJ-SUBORD

2 You use **since** to mention a time or event in the past when you are describing an event or situation that has happened after that time. *The percentage increase in reported crime in England and Wales this year is the highest since the war... He turned out to have more battles with the Congress than any president since Andrew Johnson.* ► Also a conjunction. *So much has changed in the sport since I was a teenager... Since I have become a mother, the sound of children's voices has lost its charm. ...a slight accent she had acquired since he last saw her.* PREP; CONJ-SUBORD

3 When you are talking about an event or situation in the past, you use **since** to indicate that another event happened at some point later in time. *About six thousand people were arrested, several hundred of whom have since been released... His style of leadership has attracted increasing criticism among his supporters, many of whom have since left Central Office.* ADV: ADV with v

4 If you say that something has **long since** happened, you mean that it happened a long time ago. *Even though her parents have long since died, she still talks about them in the present tense.* PHRASE: PHR with v

5 You use **since** to introduce reasons or explanations. *I'm forever on a diet, since I put on weight easily... Since she did not make enough money to live in her own house, she went back to live with her mother.* CONJ-SUBORD =as

sincere /sɪnsɪəʳ/. If you say that someone is **sincere**, you approve of them because they really mean the things they say. You can also describe someone's behaviour and beliefs as **sincere**. *He's sincere in his views... He accepted her apologies as sincere... There was such a sincere expression of friendliness on both their faces that it was a joy to see.* ♦ **sincerity** /sɪnserɪti/ *I was impressed with his deep sincerity... The film is made with sincerity.* ♦♦◇◇◇ ADJ-GRADED PRAGMATICS =genuine ≠insincere; N-UNCOUNT

sincerely /sɪnsɪəʳli/ ♦◇◇◇◇

1 If you say or feel something **sincerely**, you really mean or feel it, and are not pretending. *'Congratulations,' he said sincerely. ...sincerely held religious beliefs... 'I sincerely hope we shall meet again', he said... He sincerely believed he was acting in both women's best interests.* ADV-GRADED: usu ADV with v, also ADV adj =genuinely

2 In Britain, people write **Yours sincerely** before their signature at the end of a formal letter when they have addressed it to someone by name. In the United States, people often write **Sincerely yours** before their signature at the end of a formal letter. *Yours sincerely, James Brown.* CONVENTION

sinecure /sɪnɪkjʊəʳ, saɪn-/ **sinecures.** A **sinecure** is a job for which you receive payment but which does not involve much work or responsibility. *She found him an exalted sinecure as a Fellow of the Library of Congress. ...a lucrative sinecure with a big law firm.* N-COUNT

sine qua non /sɪni kwɑː noʊn, AM - nɑːn/. A **sine qua non** is something that is essential if you want to achieve a particular thing; a formal expression. *Successful agricultural reform is also a sine qua non of Mexico's modernisation.* N-SING: aN

sinew /sɪnjuː/ **sinews.** A **sinew** is a cord in your body that connects a muscle to a bone. *...the sinews of the neck.* N-COUNT

sinewy /sɪnjuːi/. Someone who is **sinewy** has a lean body with strong muscles. *A short, sinewy young man... When muscles are exercised often and properly, they keep the arms firm and sinewy. ...his long sinewy hands.* ADJ-GRADED

sinful /sɪnfʊl/. If you describe someone or something as **sinful**, you mean that they are wicked or immoral. *'I am a sinful man, Magda,' he said quietly. ...this is a sinful world... He reminded us that smoking was sinful.* ♦ **sinfulness** *...the sinfulness of apartheid.* ADJ-GRADED =wicked; N-UNCOUNT

sing /sɪŋ/ **sings, singing, sang, sung** ♦♦♦♦◇

1 When you **sing**, you make musical sounds with your voice, usually producing words that fit a tune. *I can't sing... I sing about love most of the time...* VERB V V *about* n V n

They were all singing the same song... Go on, then, sing us a song!... 'You're getting to be a habit with me,' sang Eddie. ...an operatic aria sung by Luciano Pavarotti. V n n / V with quote / V-ed

2 When birds or insects **sing**, they make pleasant high-pitched sounds. *Birds were already singing in the garden.* VERB / V

3 • to **sing** someone's **praises**: see **praise**. See also **singing**.

sing along. If you **sing along** with a piece of music, you sing it while you are listening to someone else perform it. *We listen to children's shows on the radio, and Janey can sing along with all the tunes... Would-be Elvis Presleys can sing along to 'Jailhouse Rock', 'Love me Tender' and 'Blue Suede Shoes'. ...fifteen hundred people all singing along and dancing.* • See also **singalong**. PHRASAL VERB / V P *with* n / V P *to* n / V P

sing out. If someone **sings out** something, they say it in a loud, cheerful voice. *'See you,' Geoff sang out.* PHRASAL VERB / no cont / V P with quote / Also V P n

sing. Sing. is a written abbreviation for **singular**.

singalong /sɪŋəlɒŋ, AM -lɔːŋ/ **singalongs;** also spelled **sing-along**. A **singalong** is an occasion when a group of people sing songs together for pleasure. *How about a nice sing-along around the piano?* N-COUNT

Singaporean /sɪŋgəpɔːriən/ **Singaporeans.** ◆◆◆◆◇

1 Singaporean means belonging or relating to Singapore, or to its people or culture. *...the Singaporean economy.* ADJ

2 A **Singaporean** is a citizen of Singapore or a person of Singaporean origin. *All Singaporeans have to pass exams in the official language of their ethnic group as well as English.* N-COUNT

singe /sɪndʒ/ **singes, singeing, singed.** If you **singe** something or if it **singes**, it burns very slightly and changes colour but does not catch fire. *The electric fire had begun to singe the bottoms of his trousers... Her hair was singed and her anorak was burnt.* V-ERG / V n / V-ed / Also V

singer /sɪŋəʳ/ **singers.** A **singer** is a person who sings, especially as a job. *My mother was a singer in a dance band. ...Dame Joan Sutherland, one of the great opera singers of the century.* ◆◆◆◇◇ N-COUNT

singer-songwriter, singer-songwriters. A **singer-songwriter** is someone who writes and performs their own songs, especially popular songs. *Twenty years ago singer-songwriter John Prine released his first album.* ◆◇◇◇◇ N-COUNT

singing /sɪŋɪŋ/. **Singing** is the activity of making musical sounds with your voice. *...a people's carnival, with singing and dancing in the streets. ...the singing of a traditional hymn. She's having singing lessons.* ◆◆◇◇◇ N-UNCOUNT

single /sɪŋgəl/ **singles, singling, singled** ◆◆◆◆◆

1 You use **single** to emphasize that you are referring to one thing, and no more than one thing. *A single shot rang out... Over six hundred people were wounded in a single day... She hadn't uttered a single word.* ADJ: ADJ n / PRAGMATICS

2 You use **single** to indicate that you are considering something on its own and separately from other things like it. *Every single house in town had been damaged... The Middle East is the world's single most important source of oil.* ADJ: det ADJ / PRAGMATICS

3 Someone who is **single** is not married. You can also use **single** to describe someone who does not have a girlfriend or boyfriend. *Is it difficult being a single mother?... I now have to face the rest of my life as a single person... Gay men are now eligible to become foster parents whether they are single or have partners.* ADJ

4 A **single** room is a room intended for one person to stay or live in. *A single room at the Astir Hotel costs £56 a night. ...a modern single bedsitter.* ► Also a noun. *It's £65 for a single, £98 for a double and £120 for an entire suite.* ADJ: usu ADJ n / N-COUNT

5 A **single** bed is wide enough for one person to sleep in. **Single** bedclothes are designed to fit single beds. ADJ: ADJ n

6 In British English, a **single** ticket is a ticket for a journey from one place to another but not back again. The usual American term is **one-way** ticket. *The price of a single ticket is thirty-nine pounds.* ► Also a noun. *...a Club Class single to Los Angeles.* ADJ: usu ADJ n / ≠return / N-COUNT

7 A **single** is a small record which has one short song on each side. You can also refer to the main song on a small record as a **single**. *Kids today don't buy singles... The collection includes all the band's British and American hit singles.* N-COUNT

8 Singles is a game of tennis or badminton in which one player plays another. The plural **singles** can be used to refer to one or more of these matches. *Boris Becker of West Germany won the men's singles... She is equally at home on the singles or doubles court.* N-UNCOUNT / ≠doubles

9 In cricket, a **single** is a hit from which one run is scored. In baseball, a **single** is a hit by which a batter reaches first base. N-COUNT

10 See also **single-**. • **in single file**: see **file**.

single out. If you **single** someone **out** from a group, you choose them and give them special attention or treatment. *The gunman had singled Debilly out and waited for him... His immediate superior has singled him out for a special mention... We wanted to single out the main threat to civilisation.* PHRASAL VERB / V n P / V n P *for/as* n / V P n (not pron) / Also V P n (not pron) *for/as* n

single- /sɪŋgəl-/. **single-** is used to form words which describe something that has one part or feature, rather than having two or more of them. *The single-engine plane landed in western Arizona. ...a single-sex school. ...a single-track road.* COMB in ADJ

single-breasted. A **single-breasted** coat, jacket, or suit fastens in the centre of the chest and has only one row of buttons. ADJ

single cream. In British English, **single cream** is thin cream that does not have a lot of fat in it. N-UNCOUNT

single-decker, single-deckers. In British English, a **single-decker** or a **single-decker bus** is a bus with only one deck. N-COUNT

single-handed. If you do something **single-handed**, you do it on your own, without help from anyone else. *I brought up my seven children single-handed... She changed the face of British politics almost single-handed.* ► Also an adjective. *...a single-handed yachtsman. ...a single-handed struggle.* ♦ **single-handedly** *Olga Korbut single-handedly turned gymnastics into a major event.* ◆◇◇◇◇ ADV: ADV after v / ADJ / ADV: ADV with v

single-minded. Someone who is **single-minded** has only one aim or purpose and is determined to achieve it. *They were effective politicians, ruthless and single-minded in their pursuit of political power. ...a single-minded determination to win.* ♦ **single-mindedly** *He was single-mindedly devoted to the hastening of freedom for the oppressed.* ♦ **single-mindedness** *...the single-mindedness of the athletes as they train.* ◆◇◇◇◇ ADJ-GRADED / ADV-GRADED: ADV with v, ADV adj / N-UNCOUNT

single parent, single parents. A **single parent** is someone who is bringing up a child on their own, because the other parent is not living with them. *I was bringing up my three children as a single parent. ...single-parent families. ...a single-parent household.* ◆◇◇◇◇ N-COUNT: oft N n

singles bar, singles bars. In North America, a **singles bar** is a bar where single people can go on order to drink and meet other single people. N-COUNT

singlet /sɪŋglət/ **singlets**

1 A **singlet** is a sleeveless sports shirt worn by athletes and boxers; used mainly in British English. *...a grubby running singlet.* N-COUNT / =vest

2 A **singlet** is a plain sleeveless piece of underwear like a vest which is worn on the upper half of the body; used mainly in British English. *He was wearing a blue silk singlet and boxer shorts.* N-COUNT / =vest

singly /sɪŋgli/. If people do something **singly**, they each do it on their own, or do it one by one. *They marched out singly or in pairs... Patients went singly into the consulting room.* ADV: ADV with v / =one by one

sing-song, sing-songs; also spelled **singsong**.

1 A **sing-song** voice repeatedly rises and falls in pitch. *He started to speak in a nasal sing-song voice.* ADJ: ADJ n

2 A **sing-song** is an occasion on which a group of N-COUNT people sing songs together for pleasure; used mainly in British English. =singalong

singular /sɪŋgjʊləʳ/ ◆◇◇◇◇

1 The **singular** form of a word is the form that is used when referring to one person or thing. *...the fifteen case endings of the singular form of the Finnish noun... The word 'you' can be singular or plural.* ADJ ≠plural

2 **The singular** of a noun is the form of it that is used to refer to one person or thing. *The inhabitants of the Arctic are known as the Inuit. The singular is Inuk.* N-SING: the N ≠plural

3 **Singular** means very great and remarkable; a formal use. *...a smile of singular sweetness... Barre was quickly drawn into the electoral arena, although with singular lack of success.* ♦ **singularly** *At the time, however, it seemed a singularly ill-judged enterprise for Truman to undertake. ...a former sales executive singularly unsuited for the job.* ADJ: ADJ n =remarkable; ADV: ADV adj/adv =extremely, remarkably

4 If you describe someone or something as **singular**, you mean that they are strange or unusual; an old-fashioned use. *Cardinal Meschia was without doubt a singular character... Where he got that singular notion I just can't think.* ♦ **singularity** /sɪŋgjʊlærɪti/ *...his abrupt, turbulent style and the singularity of his appearance.* ADJ-GRADED: usu ADJ n =peculiar; N-UNCOUNT =peculiarity

singular noun, singular nouns. A **singular noun** is a noun such as 'standstill' or 'vicinity' that does not have a plural form and always has a determiner such as 'a' or 'the' in front of it. N-COUNT

sinister /sɪnɪstəʳ/. Something that is **sinister** seems evil or harmful. *There was something sinister about him that she found disturbing. ...a sinister and frightening place. ...a sinister conspiracy by well-trained terrorists or gangs.* ◆◆◇◇◇ ADJ-GRADED

sink /sɪŋk/ **sinks, sinking, sank, sunk** ◆◆◆◇◇

1 A **sink** is a large basin in a kitchen with taps that supply water. It is used for washing dishes. *The sink was full of dirty dishes. ...the kitchen sink.* N-COUNT

2 A **sink** is the same as a **washbasin**. *The bathroom is furnished with 2 toilets, 2 showers, and 2 sinks.* N-COUNT

3 If a boat **sinks** or someone or something **sinks** it, it disappears below the surface of a mass of water. *In a naval battle your aim is to sink the enemy's ship... The boat was beginning to sink fast... The lifeboat crashed against the side of the sinking ship.* ♦ **sinking, sinkings** *...the sinking of the Titanic.* V-ERG V n V V-ing; N-COUNT

4 If something **sinks**, it disappears below the surface of a mass of water. *A fresh egg will sink and an old egg will float.* VERB ≠float

5 If something **sinks**, it moves slowly downwards. *Far off to the west the sun was sinking... When they came to build the southern spire the foundations began to sink.* VERB V

6 If you **sink**, you move into a lower position, for example by sitting down in a chair or kneeling; used mainly in written English. *Kate laughed, and sank down again to her seat... She sank into an armchair and crossed her legs... 'Don't you understand?' I moaned, sinking dramatically to my knees.* VERB V adv/prep

7 If something **sinks** to a lower level or standard, it falls to that level or standard. *Share prices would have sunk - hurting small and big investors... Pay increases have sunk to around seven per cent... The pound has sunk 10 per cent against the schilling.* VERB =drop V V to/from/by amount/n V amount

8 If your voice **sinks**, it becomes quieter; used in written English. *Her voice sank, and he moved closer to catch what she was saying... Her voice had sunk to a whisper.* VERB =fall V V to/into n

9 To **sink** into an unpleasant or undesirable mood, situation, or state means to pass gradually into it; used in written English. *She'd sometimes sink into depression... That night he sank into a deep coma... Bulgaria's economy has sunk into chaos.* VERB V into n

10 If your heart or your spirits **sink**, you become depressed or lose hope. *My heart sank because I thought he was going to dump me for another girl... Her spirits sank lower and lower.* VERB V

11 If something sharp **sinks** or **is sunk** into something solid, it goes deeply into it. *He sinks the needle into my arm... I sank my teeth into a peppermint cream... The spade sank into a clump of overgrown bushes.* V-ERG V n into n V into n

12 If someone **sinks** a well, mine, or other large hole, they make a deep hole in the ground, usually by digging or drilling. *...the site where Stephenson sank his first mineshaft... If they carry on sinking boreholes then the land is likely to subside. ...a one-thousand foot deep hole sunk into the rock.* VERB V n V-ed

13 If you **sink** money into a business or project, you spend money on it in the hope of making more money. *He has already sunk $25million into the project.* VERB =plough V amount into n

14 In British English, if someone **sinks** a number of alcoholic drinks, they drink them quickly; an informal use. *She sank two glasses of white wine.* VERB =down V n

15 In golf, snooker, and some other games, if you **sink** a ball or a putt, you successfully hit the ball into a hole. *He sank two crucial putts in the last three holes.* VERB V n

16 See also **sinking, sunk**.

17 If you say that someone will have to **sink or swim**, you mean that they will have to succeed through their own efforts, or fail. *The government doesn't want to force inefficient firms to sink or swim too quickly... It was very much sink or swim.* PHRASE

● to **sink without trace**: see **trace**.

sink in. When a statement or fact **sinks in**, you finally understand or realize it fully. *The implication took a while to sink in.* PHRASAL VERB V P

sinker /sɪŋkəʳ/. You can use **hook, line, and sinker** to emphasize that someone is tricked or forced into a situation completely. *We fell for it hook, line, and sinker... I was caught hook, line and sinker.* PHRASE: PHR after v PRAGMATICS

sinking /sɪŋkɪŋ/. If you have a **sinking** feeling, you suddenly become depressed or lose hope. *I began to have a sinking feeling that I was not going to get rid of her.* ● See also **sink**. ADJ: ADJ n

sinking fund, sinking funds. A **sinking fund** is money that a company or government has invested in order to pay off a long-term debt. N-COUNT

Sino- /saɪnoʊ-/. **Sino-** is added to adjectives indicating nationality to form adjectives which describe relations between China and another country. *...Sino-Vietnamese friendship. ...Sino-Japanese trade and investment.* COMB in ADJ: ADJ n

sinuous /sɪnjʊəs/

1 Something that is **sinuous** moves with smooth twists and turns; a literary word. *...the silent, sinuous approach of a snake through the long grass... He has a distinctively sinuous way of walking.* ADJ-GRADED: usu ADJ n

2 Something that is **sinuous** has many smooth turns and curves; a literary word. *I drove along sinuous mountain roads.* ADJ-GRADED: usu ADJ n

sinus /saɪnəs/ **sinuses.** Your **sinuses** are the spaces in the bones of your skull just behind your nose. *I still suffer from catarrh and sinus problems.* ◆◇◇◇◇ N-COUNT: usu pl

sinusitis /saɪnəsaɪtɪs/. If you have **sinusitis**, the membranes lining your sinuses become swollen and painful, which can cause headaches and a blocked-up nose. *I have had antibiotics for my sinusitis but it doesn't seem to be clearing up.* N-UNCOUNT

sip /sɪp/ **sips, sipping, sipped** ◆◆◇◇◇

1 If you **sip** a drink or **sip at** it, you drink by taking just a small amount at a time. *Jessica sipped her drink thoughtfully... He sipped at the glass and then put it down... She sipped from her coffee mug, watching him over the rim... He lifted the water-bottle to his lips and sipped.* VERB V n V at/from n V

2 A **sip** is a small amount of drink that you take into your mouth. *Harry took a sip of bourbon... Katherine took another sip from her glass to calm herself.* N-COUNT: oft N of n

siphon /saɪfᵊn/ **siphons, siphoning, siphoned;** also spelled **syphon**. ◆◇◇◇◇

1 If you **siphon** liquid from a container, you draw it out of the container through a tube by using atmospheric pressure. *She puts a piece of plastic tubing in her mouth and starts siphoning gas from a huge metal drum... Tell Mac to siphon petrol out of his wagon.* ► **Siphon off** means the same as **siphon**. *Surgeons siphoned off fluid from his left lung... The water had to be siphoned off.* VERB V n prep Also V n; PHRASAL VERB V P n (not pron) Also V n P

2 A **siphon** is a tube that you use for siphoning liquid. N-COUNT

3 If you **siphon** money or resources from something, you cause them to be used for a purpose for which they were not intended. *He had siphoned thousands of pounds a week from the failing business... They siphon foreign aid money into their personal bank accounts.* ► **Siphon off** means the same as **siphon**. *He had siphoned off a small fortune in aid money from the United Nations.* VERB V n prep PHRASAL VERB V P n (not pron) Also V n P

sir /sɜːʳ/ **sirs** ◆◆◆◆◆

1 People sometimes say **sir** as a very formal and polite way of addressing a man whose name they do not know or a man of superior rank. For example, a shop assistant might address a male customer as **sir**. *Excuse me sir, but would you mind telling me what sort of car that is?... Good afternoon to you, sir.* N-VOC PRAGMATICS

2 **Sir** is the title used in front of the name of a knight or baronet. *...the former deputy Prime Minister, Sir Geoffrey Howe... She introduced me to Sir Tobias and Lady Clarke.* N-TITLE

3 You use the expression **Dear sir** at the beginning of a formal letter or a business letter when you are writing to a man. You use **Dear sirs** when you are writing to an organization. *Dear Sir, Your letter of the 9th October addressed to the editor of The Independent has been referred to us for reply.* CONVENTION

sire /saɪəʳ/ **sires, siring, sired** ◆◇◇◇◇

1 When a male animal, especially a horse, **sires** offspring, he makes a female pregnant and she gives birth to a young animal; a technical use. *Comet also sired the champion foal out of Spinway Harvest.* VERB V n

2 If a man **sires** a child, he makes a woman pregnant and she gives birth to a child; an old-fashioned use. *Hunt married three women and sired 15 children.* VERB =father V n

3 Your **sire** is your father; an old-fashioned use. N-COUNT

siren /saɪərən/ **sirens** ◆◇◇◇◇

1 A **siren** is a warning device which makes a long, loud, wailing noise. Most fire engines, ambulances, and police cars have sirens. *It sounds like an air raid siren.* N-COUNT: oft supp N

2 Some people refer to a woman as a **siren** when they think that she is attractive to men but dangerous in some way; a literary use. *He maligns the innocent princess as a siren who has drawn him to his ruin. ...the voluptuous siren with a husky voice.* N-COUNT =femme fatale

3 A **siren call** or **siren song** is the appeal that something has although it is harmful or dangerous. *Unable to resist the siren call of the cards, he withdrew their savings and headed for Las Vegas... They are finding themselves seduced by Mr Kravchuk's siren song.* PHRASE: N inflects

sirloin /sɜːʳlɔɪn/ **sirloins.** A **sirloin** is a piece of beef which is cut from the bottom and side parts of a cow's back. *...fresh beef sirloin steaks.* N-VAR

sisal /saɪzəl/. **Sisal** is the fibre from the leaves of a plant that is grown in the West Indies, South America, and Africa. **Sisal** is used to make rope, cord, and mats. N-UNCOUNT

sissy /sɪsi/ **sissies;** also spelled **cissy.**

1 Some people, especially men, describe a boy as a **sissy** when they disapprove of them because they think he is not manly enough, for example that he does not like sport or is afraid to do things that are slightly dangerous; an informal use. *They were rough kids, and thought we were sissies... 'Last one in the sea is a sissy,' proclaimed Idris.* N-COUNT PRAGMATICS

2 If you describe an action or activity as **sissy**, you disapprove of it because you think it is unmanly; an informal use. *Far from being sissy, it takes a real man to accept that he is not perfect. ...men who feel that writing is essentially a sissy occupation.* ADJ PRAGMATICS

sister /sɪstəʳ/ **sisters** ◆◆◆◆◆

1 Your **sister** is a girl or woman who has the same parents as you. *His sister Sarah helped him. ...Vanessa Bell, the sister of Virginia Woolf... I didn't know you had a sister.* • See also **half-sister, stepsister.** N-COUNT: oft poss N

2 **Sister** is a title given to a woman who belongs to a religious community such as a convent. *Sister Francesca entered the chapel. ...the Hospice of the Sisters of Charity at Lourdes.* N-COUNT; N-TITLE; N-VOC

3 In Britain, a **sister** is a senior female nurse who supervises a hospital ward. *Ask to speak to the sister on the ward... Sister Middleton followed the coffee trolley.* N-COUNT; N-TITLE, also N-VOC

4 You might use **sister** to describe a woman who belongs to the same race, religion, country, profession, or trade union as you, or who has ideas that are similar to yours. *Modern woman has been freed from many of the duties that befell her sisters in times past. ...our Jewish brothers and sisters.* N-COUNT: usu poss N

5 You can use **sister** to describe something that is of the same type or is connected in some way to another thing you have mentioned. For example, if a company has a **sister** company, they are connected, perhaps because they are both part of a larger organization. *...the International Monetary Fund and its sister organisation, the World Bank. ...Voyager 2 and its sister ship, Voyager 1.* ADJ: ADJ n

sisterhood /sɪstəʳhʊd/. **Sisterhood** is the affection and loyalty that women feel for other women who they have something in common with. *There was a degree of solidarity and sisterhood among the women.* N-UNCOUNT

sister-in-law, sisters-in-law. Someone's **sister-in-law** is the sister of their husband or wife, or the woman who is married to their brother. ◆◇◇◇◇ N-COUNT: oft poss N

sisterly /sɪstəʳli/. A woman's **sisterly** feelings are the feelings of love and loyalty which you expect a sister to show. *We just had a sisterly relationship... Bernadette gave him a shy, sisterly kiss.* ADJ-GRADED: usu ADJ n

sit /sɪt/ **sits, sitting, sat.** ◆◆◆◆◆

1 If you **are sitting** somewhere, for example in a chair, your weight is supported by your buttocks rather than your feet and the upper part of your body is upright. *Mother was sitting in her chair in the kitchen... They sat there in shock and disbelief... They had been sitting watching television... He was unable to sit still for longer than a few minutes.* VERB V prep/adv Also V

2 When you **sit** somewhere, you lower your body until you are sitting on something. *He set the cases against a wall and sat on them... Eva pulled over a chair and sat beside her husband... When you stand, they stand; when you sit, they sit.* ► To **sit down** means the same as to **sit**. *I sat down, stunned... Hughes beckoned him to sit down on the sofa.* VERB V prep/adv V PHRASAL VERB V P V P prep/adv

3 If you **sit** someone somewhere, you tell them to sit there or put them in a sitting position. *He used to sit me on his lap... He'll sit you in front of his computer and give you a glimpse of the problem.* ► To **sit** someone **down** somewhere means to **sit** them there. *She helped him out of the water and sat him down on the rock... They sat me down and had a serious discussion about sex.* VERB V n prep/adv PHRASAL VERB V n P prep/adv V n P Also V P n (not pron)

4 If you **sit** for an artist or photographer, you place yourself in a sitting position so you can be painted or photographed. *A person may well have been sitting for the artist for eight hours at a stretch.* VERB V for n

5 In British English, if you **sit** an examination, you do it. In American English, you **take** an examination. *June and July are the traditional months for sitting exams.* VERB =take V n

6 If you **sit** on a committee or other official group, you are a member of it. *He was asked to sit on numerous committees... I know of no professional person who has ever sat on a jury... The party's three MPs will continue to sit in parliament.* VB: no cont V on/in n

7 When a parliament, court, or other official body **sits**, it officially carries out its work; a formal use. *Parliament sits for only 28 weeks out of 52... The court would sit all night.* VERB V

8 If a building or object **sits** in a particular place, it is in that place; used in written English. *Our new house sat next to a stream... On the table sat a box decorated with little pearl triangles.* VERB =stand V prep/adv

9 See also **sitting.**

10 If you **sit tight**, you remain in the same place or situation and do not take any action, usually be- PHRASE: V inflects

cause you are waiting for something to happen. *Sit tight. I'll be right back... Life would continue to be hard but if they sat tight and trusted him things would get better.* • **sit on the fence**: see **fence**.

sit around; the form **sit about** is also used in British English. If you **sit around** or **sit about**, you spend time doing nothing useful or interesting; an informal expression. *Eve isn't the type to sit around doing nothing... We sat about in the gloomy airport lounge.* PHRASAL VERB; V P

sit back. If you **sit back** while something is happening, you relax and do not become involved in it; an informal expression. *They didn't have to do anything except sit back and enjoy life... American firms handed over technologies to their partners and then sat back to enjoy the cash flow.* PHRASAL VERB; V P; V P to-inf

sit by. If you **sit by** while something wrong or illegal is happening, you allow it to happen and do not do anything about it. *We can't just sit by and watch you throw your life away... The use of ozone-depleting chemicals grew dramatically and the government sat idly by.* PHRASAL VERB =stand by; V P

sit down PHRASAL VERB

1 See **sit** 2, 3.

2 If you **sit down** and do something, you spend time and effort doing it in order to try to achieve something. *Have you both sat down and worked out a budget together?... 150 countries sat down to discuss the impact of human activities on the atmosphere.* V P

3 See also **sit-down**.

sit in on. If you **sit in on** a lesson, meeting, or discussion, you are present while it is taking place but do not take part in it. *Will they permit you to sit in on a few classes?... People can sit in on meetings, even if it's not really in their subject area.* PHRASAL VERB; V P P n

sit on. If you say that someone **is sitting on** something, you mean that they are delaying dealing with it; an informal expression. *He had been sitting on the document for at least two months.* PHRASAL VERB; V P n

sit out. If you **sit** something **out**, you wait patiently for it to finish, without taking any action. *The only thing I can do is keep quiet and sit this one out... He can afford to sit out the property slump.* PHRASAL VERB; V n P; V P n (not pron)

sit through. If you **sit through** something such as a film, lecture, or meeting, you stay until it is finished although you are not enjoying it. *...movies so bad you can hardly bear to sit through them.* PHRASAL VERB; V P n

sit up PHRASAL VERB

1 If you **sit up**, you move into a sitting position when you have been leaning back or lying down. *Her head spins dizzily as soon as she sits up.* V P

2 If you **sit** someone **up**, you move them into a sitting position when they have been leaning back or lying down. *She sat him up and made him comfortable.* V n P; Also V P n (not pron)

3 If you **sit up**, you do not go to bed although it is very late. *We sat up drinking and talking... I didn't feel like sitting up all night.* =stay up; V P

4 If something makes you **sit up**, it makes you suddenly pay attention to what is happening. *A defeat like that makes you sit up and think.* V P

5 See also **sit-up**.

sitar /sɪtɑːʳ/ **sitars.** A **sitar** is an Indian musical instrument with two layers of strings, a long neck, and a round body. N-VAR: oft *the* N

sitcom /sɪtkɒm/ **sitcoms.** A **sitcom** is a television comedy series which shows the same set of characters in each episode, in amusing situations that are similar to everyday life. **Sitcom** is an abbreviation for **situation comedy**. *...the classic '70s TV sitcom 'Rising Damp'.* ◆◇◇◇◇ N-COUNT

sit-down ◆◆◇◇◇

1 If you have **a sit-down**, you sit down and rest for a short time; an informal use. *All he wanted was a cup of tea and a sit-down.* N-SING: *a* N

2 A **sit-down** meal is served to people sitting at tables. *A sit-down dinner was followed by a disco.* ADJ: ADJ n

3 In a **sit-down** protest, people refuse to leave a place until they get what they want. *A number of university teachers staged a sit-down protest in front of the president's office.* ADJ: ADJ n

site /saɪt/ **sites, siting, sited** ◆◆◆◆◇

1 A **site** is a piece of ground that is used for a particular purpose or where a particular thing happens. *He became a hod carrier on a building site. ...a bat sanctuary with special nesting sites... Apprentice carpenters are trained on site by expert craftsmen.* N-COUNT: oft n N, also *on* N

2 The **site** of an important event is the place where it happened. *Scientists have described the Aral sea as the site of the worst ecological disaster on earth... Plymouth Hoe is renowned as the site where Drake played bowls before tackling the Spanish Armada.* N-COUNT: usu *the* N *of* n

3 A **site** is a piece of ground where something such as a statue or monument stands or used to stand. *...the site of Moses' tomb. ...the Church of the Holy Sepulchre in Jerusalem, which is regarded by some as Christianity's holiest site.* N-COUNT

4 If something **is sited** in a particular place or position, it is put there or built there. *He said chemical weapons had never been sited in Germany. ...a damp, old castle, romantically sited on a river estuary.* ♦ **siting** *...controls on the siting of gas storage vessels.* VB: usu passive; *be* V-ed prep/adv; V-ed; N-SING: usu *the* N *of* n

sit-in, sit-ins. A **sit-in** is a protest in which people go to a public place and stay there for a long time. *The campaigners held a sit-in outside the Supreme Court.* ◆◆◇◇◇ N-COUNT

sitter /sɪtəʳ/ **sitters.** A **sitter** is the same as a **babysitter**: see **babysit**. ◆◇◇◇◇ N-COUNT

sitting /sɪtɪŋ/ **sittings**

1 A **sitting** is one of the periods when a meal is served when there is not enough space for everyone to eat at the same time. *Dinner was in two sittings.* N-COUNT

2 A **sitting** of a parliament, court, or other official body is one of the occasions when it meets in order to carry out its work. *...the recent emergency sittings of the UN Security Council.* N-COUNT: usu N *of* n =session

3 A **sitting** president or member of parliament is a present one, not a future or past one. *...the greatest clash in our history between a sitting president and an ex-president.* ADJ: ADJ n =incumbent

4 See also **sit**.

5 If you are **sitting pretty**, you are in a very favourable situation; an informal expression. *If we'd let them buy it for a quarter of a million, we'd be sitting pretty by now.* PHRASE: usu v-link PHR

sitting duck, sitting ducks. If you say that someone is a **sitting duck**, you mean that they are an obvious target and that it would be easy to attack or cheat them; an informal expression. *Nancy knew she'd be a sitting duck when she raised the trap door.* N-COUNT

sitting-room, sitting-rooms. A **sitting-room** is a room in a house where people sit and relax; used mainly in British English. ◆◇◇◇◇ N-COUNT =living room

sitting tenant, sitting tenants. In Britain, a **sitting tenant** is a person who rents a house or flat as their home and has a legal right to live there. *1.4 million council homes have been sold, mostly to sitting tenants.* N-COUNT

situate /sɪtʃueɪt/ **situates, situating, situated.** If you **situate** something such as an idea or fact in a particular context, you relate it to that context, especially in order to understand it better; a formal word. *How do we situate Christianity in the context of modern physics and psychology.* VERB; V n adv/prep

situated /sɪtʃueɪtɪd/. If something is **situated** in a particular place or position, it is in that place or position. *His hotel is situated in one of the loveliest places on the Loire... The pain was situated above and around the eyes... The new store is better situated to attract customers.* ◆◆◇◇◇ ADJ: v-link ADJ prep, adv ADJ =located

situation /sɪtʃueɪʃᵊn/ **situations** ◆◆◆◆◆

1 You use the word **situation** to refer generally to what is happening in a particular place at a particular time, or to refer to what is happening to you. *Army officers said the situation was under control... And now for a look at the travel situation in the rest of the country... She's in a hopeless situation... If you want to improve your situation you must adopt a positive mental attitude.* N-COUNT: usu with supp, oft poss N

2 The **situation** of a building or town is the kind of surroundings that it has; a formal use. *The garden is in a beautiful situation on top of a fold in the rolling Hampshire landscape.* [N-COUNT: usu supp N =location]

3 **Situations Vacant** is the title of a column or page in a newspaper where jobs vacancies are advertised. [PHRASE: oft PHR n]

situation comedy, situation comedies. A **situation comedy** is television comedy series which shows the same set of characters in each episode, in amusing situations that are similar to everyday life. The abbreviation **sitcom** is also used. *...a situation comedy that was set in an acupuncture clinic.* [N-VAR =sitcom]

sit-up, sit-ups. Sit-ups are exercises that you do to strengthen your stomach muscles. They involve sitting up from a lying position while keeping your legs straight on the floor. ◆◇◇◇◇ [N-COUNT: usu pl]

six /sɪks/ **sixes** ◆◆◆◆◆

1 **Six** is the number 6. *...a glorious career spanning more than six decades.* [NUM]

2 In cricket, if a player hits a **six**, they score six runs by hitting the ball so that it crosses the boundary at the edge of the playing area before it touches the ground. [N-COUNT: usu sing]

3 If someone or something **is hit for six** or **knocked for six**, they are surprised or overwhelmed by something that has happened to them; an informal British expression. *The loss of my wife hit me for six; it took me months to recover... Many areas in the North were knocked for six by that first recession.* [PHRASES V inflects]

4 If you say that someone or something is **at sixes and sevens**, you mean that they are confused or disorganized; an informal expression. *The government is at sixes and sevens over the issue of domestic security.* [usu v-link PHR]

six footer, six footers. Someone who is six foot tall can be called a **six footer**; an informal expression. *...a strapping six-footer. ...the brunette six-footer.* [N-COUNT]

six-pack, six-packs. A **six-pack** is a pack containing six bottles or cans sold together. *He picked up a six-pack of beer.* [N-COUNT: oft N of n]

sixpence /sɪkspəns/ **sixpences.** A **sixpence** is a small silver coin which was used in Britain before the decimal money system was introduced in 1971. It was the equivalent of 2.5 pence. [N-COUNT]

six-shooter, six-shooters. A **six-shooter** is a revolver that holds six bullets. [N-COUNT]

sixteen /sɪkstiːn/ **sixteens. Sixteen** is the number 16. *...exams taken at the age of sixteen... He worked sixteen hours a day... The number of under-sixteens in low-paid jobs is increasing.* ◆◆◇◇◇ [NUM]

sixteenth /sɪkstiːnθ/ **sixteenths** ◆◇◇◇◇

1 The **sixteenth** item in a series is the one that you count as number sixteen. *...the sixteenth century AD.* [ORD]

2 A **sixteenth** is one of sixteen equal parts of something. *...a sixteenth of a second. ...fifteen sixteenths of an inch.* [FRACTION]

sixth /sɪksθ/ **sixths** ◆◆◆◆◇

1 The **sixth** item in a series is the one that you count as number six. *...the sixth round of the World Cup. ...the sixth of December.* [ORD]

2 A **sixth** is one of six equal parts of something. *The company yesterday shed a sixth of its workforce. ...five-sixths of a mile.* [FRACTION]

sixth form, sixth forms; also spelled **sixth-form**. The **sixth form** in a British school consists of the classes that pupils go into at the age of about sixteen, usually in order to study for A levels. *She was offered her first modelling job while she was still in the sixth-form... The couple met at a sixth form college in Solihull.* ◆◇◇◇◇ [N-COUNT: usu sing]

sixth former, sixth formers; also spelled **sixth-former**. A **sixth former** is a pupil who is in the sixth form at school. [N-COUNT]

sixth sense. If you say that someone has a **sixth sense**, you mean that they seem to know things instinctively or intuitively, without any direct evidence of them. *The interesting thing about O'Reilly is his sixth sense for finding people who have good ideas.* [N-SING]

sixtieth /sɪkstiəθ/ **sixtieths.** ◆◆◆◆◇

1 The **sixtieth** item in a series is the one that you count as number sixty. *He is to retire on his sixtieth birthday.* [ORD]

2 A **sixtieth** is one of sixty equal parts of something. [FRACTION]

sixty /sɪksti/ **sixties** ◆◆◆◆◆

1 **Sixty** is the number 60. *...the sunniest April in Britain for more than sixty years.* [NUM]

2 When you talk about the **sixties**, you are referring to numbers between 60 and 69. For example, if you are **in your sixties**, you are aged between 60 and 69. If the temperature is **in the sixties**, the temperature is between 60 and 69 degrees. *...a lively widow in her sixties.* [N-PLURAL]

3 **The sixties** is the decade between 1960 and 1969. *The most recent attempt was made by the Labour government in the late sixties.* [N-PLURAL: the N]

sizable /saɪzəbᵊl/. See **sizeable**.

size /saɪz/ **sizes, sizing, sized** ◆◆◆◆◇

1 The **size** of something is how big or small it is. Something's size is determined by comparing it to other things, counting it, or measuring it. *Scientists have found the bones of a hoofed grazing animal about the size of a small horse... In 1970 the average size of a French farm was 19 hectares... Iraq itself has oil reserves second in size only to Saudi Arabia's. ...shelves containing books of various sizes.* [N-VAR: usu *the* N *of* n]

2 The **size** of something is the fact that it is very large. *He knows the size of the task... Jack walked around the hotel and was mesmerized by its sheer size.* [N-UNCOUNT: usu *the* N *of* n]

3 A **size** is one of a series of graded measurements, especially for things such as clothes or shoes. *My sister is the same height but only a size 12... I tried them on and they were the right size.* [N-COUNT]

4 If someone is **cut down to size**, something happens to make them realize that they are not as important as they think they are; an informal expression. *The once-powerful post unions have been cut down to size.* [PHRASES V inflects]

5 If an object **is cut to size**, its size is altered to make it suitable for a particular purpose. *Every piece of timber was planed, cut to size and stained with cedar preservative.* [V inflects]

6 If you try something **for size**, you try it to see if it is suitable for you. *She was trying on an £8,000 jacket for size... He suggests that Nietzsche was trying each style on for size.* [PHR after v]

7 ● **comes in all shapes and sizes**: see **shape**.

size up. If you **size up** a person or situation, you carefully look at the person or think about the situation, so that you can decide how to act; an informal expression. *Some US manufacturers have been sizing up the UK as a possible market for their clothes... He spent the evening sizing me up intellectually.* [PHRASAL VERB =weigh up] [V P n (not pron)] [V n P]

-size /-saɪz/ or **-sized**

1 You can use **-size** or **-sized** in combination with nouns to form adjectives which indicate that something is the same size as something else. *...golfball-sized lumps of coarse black rock.* [COMB in ADJ]

2 You can use **-size** or **-sized** in combination with adjectives to form adjectives which describe the size of something. *...full-size gymnasiums. ...a medium-sized college.* [COMB in ADJ]

3 You can use **-size** or **-sized** in combination with nouns to form adjectives which indicate that something is big enough or small enough to be suitable for a particular job or purpose. *...a small passport-size photograph. ...a child-sized knife.* [COMB in ADJ]

sizeable /saɪzəbᵊl/; also spelled **sizable**. **Sizeable** means fairly large. *Harry has inherited the house and a sizeable chunk of land that surrounds it... These polls give a very sizeable vote to the candidate of the M19 Movement.* ◆◇◇◇◇ [ADJ-GRADED: usu ADJ n =substantial]

-sized /-saɪzd/. See **-size**.

sizzle /sɪzᵊl/ **sizzles, sizzling, sizzled.** If something **sizzles**, it makes a hissing sound like the sound made by frying food. *The sausages and*  [VERB] [V]

burgers sizzled on the barbecue. ...a frying pan of sizzling oil. V-ing

skate /skeɪt/ **skates, skating, skated** ◆◆◇◇◇
1 **Skates** are **ice-skates**. N-COUNT
2 **Skates** are **roller-skates**. N-COUNT
3 If you **skate**, you move about wearing ice-skates or roller-skates. *I actually skated, and despite some teetering I did not fall on the ice... Dan skated up to him.* ♦ **skating** *They all went skating together in the winter.* ♦ **skater, skaters** *West Lake, an outdoor ice-skating rink, attracts skaters during the day and night.* VERB V V adv/prep Also V n N-UNCOUNT N-COUNT
4 In British English, a **skate** is a kind of flat sea fish. The plural of **skate** is **skate**. *Boats had plenty of mackerel and a few skate.* ► **Skate** is this fish eaten as food. N-COUNT =ray N-UNCOUNT
5 If you **skate** over or round a difficult subject, you avoid discussing it. *Scientists have tended to skate over the difficulties of explaining dreams... When pressed, he skates around the subject of those women who he met as a 19-year-old.* VERB V over n V round/around n

skateboard /skeɪtbɔːʳd/ **skateboards.** A **skateboard** is a narrow board with wheels at each end, which people stand on and ride for pleasure. N-COUNT

skateboarder /skeɪtbɔːʳdəʳ/ **skateboarders.** A **skateboarder** is someone who goes skateboarding. N-COUNT

skateboarding /skeɪtbɔːʳdɪŋ/. **Skateboarding** is the activity of riding on a skateboard. N-UNCOUNT

skating rink, skating rinks. A **skating rink** is the same as a **rink**. N-COUNT

skein /skeɪn/ **skeins.** A **skein** is a loosely coiled length of thread, especially wool or silk. *...a skein of wool.* N-COUNT =hank

skeletal /skelɪtəl/ ◆◇◇◇◇
1 **Skeletal** means relating to skeletons. *...the skeletal remains of seven adults. ...the skeletal system.* ADJ: ADJ n
2 A **skeletal** person is so thin that you can see their bones through their skin. *...a hospital filled with skeletal children.* ADJ-GRADED
3 Something that is **skeletal** has been reduced to its basic structure. *Passenger services can best be described as skeletal.* ADJ-GRADED

skeleton /skelɪtən/ **skeletons** ◆◆◇◇◇
1 Your **skeleton** is the framework of bones in your body. *...a human skeleton.* N-COUNT
2 A **skeleton** staff is the smallest number of staff necessary in order to run an organization or service. *Only a skeleton staff remains to show anyone interested around the site.* ADJ: ADJ n
3 The **skeleton** of something such as a building or a plan is its basic framework. *The town of Rudbar had ceased to exist, with only skeletons of buildings remaining. ...a skeleton of policy guidelines.* N-COUNT: usu N of n
4 If you say that someone has **a skeleton in the closet**, or in British English **a skeleton in the cupboard**, you mean that they are keeping secret something that is scandalous or embarrassing. *Mr Worthing is this election's Mr Nice Guy, without any skeletons in his cupboard.* PHRASE: Ns inflect

skeleton key, skeleton keys. A **skeleton key** is a key which has been specially made so that it will open many different locks. N-COUNT

skeptic /skeptɪk/. See **sceptic**.
skeptical /skeptɪkəl/. See **sceptical**.
skepticism /skeptɪsɪzəm/. See **scepticism**.

sketch /sketʃ/ **sketches, sketching, sketched** ◆◆◇◇◇
1 A **sketch** is a drawing that is done quickly without a lot of details. Artists often use sketches as a preparation for a more detailed painting or drawing. *...a sketch of a soldier by Orpen.* N-COUNT
2 If you **sketch** something, you make a quick, rough drawing of it. *Clare and David Astor are sketching a view of far Spanish hills... I always sketch with pen and paper. ...balconies and gates sketched on holidays in Spain and Italy... Her hobbies were playing the guitar and sketching.* VERB V n V V-ed V-ing
3 A **sketch** of a situation, person, or incident is a brief description of it without many details. *...thumbnail sketches of heads of state and political figures... I had a basic sketch of a plan.* N-COUNT: usu N of n
4 If you **sketch** a situation or incident, you give a short description of it, including only the most important facts. *Cross sketched the story briefly, telling the facts just as they had happened.* ► **Sketch out** means the same as **sketch**. *Luxembourg sketched out an acceptable compromise between Britain, France and Germany.* VERB =outline V n PHRASAL VERB V P n (not pron)
5 A **sketch** is a short humorous piece of acting, usually forming part of a comedy show. *...a five-minute sketch about a folk singer.* N-COUNT

sketch in. If you **sketch in** details about something, you tell them to people. *We sat in Lily's sunroom while I sketched in the situation.* PHRASAL VERB V P n (not pron)

sketch out. See **sketch** 4. PHRASAL VERB

sketchbook /sketʃbʊk/ **sketchbooks;** also spelled **sketch-book**. A **sketchbook** is a book of blank pages for drawing on. N-COUNT =sketchpad

sketchpad /sketʃpæd/ **sketchpads;** also spelled **sketch-pad**. A **sketchpad** is a pad of blank pages for drawing on. N-COUNT

sketchy /sketʃi/ **sketchier, sketchiest.** ◆◇◇◇◇ **Sketchy** knowledge or accounts of something do not have many details and are therefore incomplete or inadequate. *Details of what actually happened are still sketchy... Only sketchy information exists on the stock of natural resources such as fish.* ♦ **sketchily** /sketʃɪli/ *The ideas seem sketchily developed, the textures thin, the images vague.* ADJ-GRADED =vague ADV-GRADED: usu ADV with v

skew /skjuː/ **skews, skewing, skewed.** ◆◇◇◇◇ If information or a situation **is skewed**, it is altered or distorted by external factors, so that people do not get an accurate view of it. *The arithmetic of nuclear running costs has been skewed by the fall in the cost of other fuels... Today's election will skew the results in favor of the northern end of the county.* ♦ **skewed** *Policies are definitely more skewed towards economic growth than before. ...a handful of schools which constitute a skewed and highly selective sample.* VERB be V-ed V n ADJ-GRADED

skewer /skjuːəʳ/ **skewers, skewering, skewered** ◆◇◇◇◇
1 A **skewer** is a long metal pin which is used to hold pieces of food together during cooking. N-COUNT
2 If you **skewer** something, you push a long, thin, pointed object through it. *He skewered his victim through the neck. ...skewered beef with vegetables.* VERB V n prep V-ed

ski /skiː/ **skis, skiing, skied** ◆◆◆◇◇
1 **Skis** are long, flat, narrow pieces of wood, metal, or plastic that are fastened to boots so that you can move easily on snow. *...a pair of skis.* N-COUNT
2 When people **ski**, they move over snow on skis. *They surf, ski and ride... The whole party then skied off.* ♦ **skier** /skiːəʳ/ **skiers** *He is an enthusiastic skier.* ♦ **skiing** *My hobbies were skiing and scuba diving. ...a skiing holiday.* VERB V V adv/prep N-COUNT N-UNCOUNT: oft N n
3 You use **ski** to refer to things that are concerned with skiing. *...the Swiss ski resort of Klosters. ...a private ski instructor. ...artificial ski slopes.* ADJ: ADJ n
4 See also **water-ski**.

skid /skɪd/ **skids, skidding, skidded** ◆◇◇◇◇
1 If a vehicle **skids**, it slides sideways or forwards while moving, for example when you are trying to stop it suddenly on a wet road. *The car pulled up too fast and skidded on the dusty shoulder of the road... The plane skidded off the runway while taking off in a snow storm.* ► Also a noun. *I slammed the brakes on and went into a skid.* VERB V V prep N-COUNT
2 If you say that something is **on the skids** you believe that it is out of control and certain to fail. *His career is on the skids. ...my marriage was on the skids.* PHRASE: v-link PHR

skid row /skɪd roʊ/; also spelled **Skid Row**. You can refer to the poorest part of town where drunks and vagrants live as **skid row**; used mainly in American English. *He was suspended from his job and actually became a skid row type of drunkard.* N-UNCOUNT: oft N n

skiff /skɪf/ **skiffs.** A **skiff** is a small light rowing-boat or sailing-boat, which usually has room for only one person. N-COUNT

ski jump, ski jumps. A **ski jump** is a specially-built steep slope covered in snow with one end curving upwards. People ski down it and jump into the air at the end. N-COUNT

skilful /skɪlfʊl/; spelled **skillful** in American English. Someone who is **skilful** at something does it very well. *He is widely regarded as Hungary's most skilful politician. ...Rembrandt's skilful use of light and shade.* ♦◇◇◇◇ ADJ-GRADED ♦ **skilfully** *He had a clear idea of his company's strengths and skilfully exploited them.* ADV-GRADED: ADV with v

ski lift, ski lifts; also spelled **ski-lift.** A **ski lift** is a machine for taking people to the top of a slope so that they can ski down it. It consists of a series of seats hanging down from a moving wire. N-COUNT

skill /skɪl/ **skills** ♦♦♦♦◇

1 A **skill** is a type of work or activity which requires special training and knowledge. *Most of us will know someone who is always learning new skills, or studying new fields.* N-COUNT

2 **Skill** is the knowledge and ability that enables you to do something well. *The cut of a diamond depends on the skill of its craftsman.* N-UNCOUNT

skilled /skɪld/ ♦♦◇◇◇

1 Someone who is **skilled** has the knowledge and ability to do something well. *Few doctors are actually trained, and not all are skilled, in helping their patients make choices. ...a network of amateur but highly skilled observers of wildlife.* ADJ-GRADED: oft ADJ *in/at* n/-ing

2 **Skilled** work can only be done by people who have had some training. *New industries demanded skilled labour not available locally. ...skilled workers, such as plumbers and electricians.* ADJ: usu ADJ n ≠unskilled

skillet /skɪlɪt/ **skillets.** A **skillet** is a shallow cast-iron pan which is used for frying. N-COUNT

skillful /skɪlfʊl/. See **skilful.**

skim /skɪm/ **skims, skimming, skimmed** ♦◇◇◇◇

1 If you **skim** something from the surface of a liquid, you remove it. *Rough seas today prevented specially equipped ships from skimming oil off the water's surface... Skim off the fat.* VERB V n *off/from* n V n with *off*

2 If something **skims** a surface, it moves quickly along just above it. *...seagulls skimming the waves... The little boat was skimming across the sunlit surface of the bay.* VERB V n V *over/across* n

3 If you **skim** a piece of writing, you read through it quickly. *He skimmed the pages quickly, then read them again more carefully... I only had time to skim through the script before I flew over here.* VERB V n V *through* n

skim off. If someone **skims off** the best part of something, or money which belongs to other people, they take it for themselves. *He has been accused of skimming the cream off the economy... Rich Italian clubs such as AC Milan cannot simply skim off all of Europe's stars... If I read this right, he skimmed off about thirty million.* PHRASAL VERB V n P n V P n (not pron)

skimmed milk. In British English, **skimmed milk** is milk from which the cream has been removed. The American term is **skim milk.** N-UNCOUNT

skimp /skɪmp/ **skimps, skimping, skimped.** If you **skimp on** something, you use less time, money, or material for it than you really need, so that the result is not good enough. *Many families must skimp on their food and other necessities just to meet the monthly rent.* VERB =scrimp V *on* n

skimpy /skɪmpi/ **skimpier, skimpiest.** Something that is **skimpy** is too small in size or quantity. *...skimpy underwear... They suffered long hours, unsafe working conditions and skimpy pay.* ADJ-GRADED

skin /skɪn/ **skins, skinning, skinned** ♦♦♦♦◇

1 Your **skin** is the natural covering of your body. *His skin is clear and smooth... There are three major types of skin cancer... The only difference between us is the colour of our skins.* N-VAR

2 An animal **skin** is skin which has been removed from a dead animal. Skins are used to make things such as coats and rugs. *That was real crocodile skin. ...a leopard skin coat.* N-VAR: usu supp N =pelt

3 The **skin** of a fruit or vegetable is its outer layer or covering. *The outer skin of the orange is called the 'zest'. ...banana skins.* N-VAR

4 If a **skin** forms on the surface of a liquid, a thin, fairly solid layer forms on it. *Stir the custard occasionally to prevent a skin forming.* N-SING

5 If you **skin** a dead animal, you remove its skin. *...with the expertise of a chef skinning a rabbit.* VERB V n

6 See also **-skinned; banana skin.**

7 If something makes you **jump out of** your **skin**, it surprises or shocks you very much. *He nearly jumped out of his skin when he saw two rats.* PHRASES V and N inflect

8 If you try to **save** your **own skin** or **save** your **skin**, you try to save yourself from something dangerous or unpleasant; used showing disapproval. *He'd have done anything to anybody to save his own skin.* V and N inflect PRAGMATICS

9 If you do something **by the skin of** your **teeth**, you just manage to do it. *He won, but only by the skin of his teeth.* PHR with cl

10 If you say that someone has **a thick skin**, you mean that they are able to listen to criticism about themselves without becoming offended. *You need a thick skin to be a headmaster.* N inflects, usu v PHR

11 ● to **make** your **skin crawl**: see **crawl.**

skin deep; also spelled **skin-deep.** Something that is only **skin deep** is not a major or important feature of something, although initially you may think that it is. *Beauty is only skin deep... He denies that racism is just skin-deep.* ADJ: usu v-link ADJ

skinflint /skɪnflɪnt/ **skinflints.** If you describe someone as a **skinflint**, you are saying that they are a mean person who hates spending money. N-COUNT =miser

skinhead /skɪnhed/ **skinheads.** In British English, a **skinhead** is a young person whose hair is shaved or cut very short. Skinheads are usually regarded as violent, aggressive, and racist. ♦◇◇◇◇ N-COUNT

skinless /skɪnləs/. **Skinless** meat has had its skin removed. *...skinless chicken breast fillets.* ADJ: usu ADJ n

-skinned /-skɪnd/. **-skinned** is used after adjectives such as 'dark' and 'clear' to form adjectives that indicate what kind of skin someone has. *Dark-skinned people rarely develop skin cancer... She was smooth-skinned and pretty.* COMB in ADJ-GRADED

skinny /skɪni/ **skinnier, skinniest.** A **skinny** person is extremely thin, in a way that you find unattractive; an informal word. *He was quite a skinny little boy... She had stringy hair and skinny legs.* ♦◇◇◇◇ ADJ-GRADED PRAGMATICS =scrawny

skint /skɪnt/. In informal British English, if you say that you are **skint**, you mean that you have no money. *I'm skint! Lend us a tenner.* ADJ-GRADED =broke

skin-tight; also spelled **skintight. Skin-tight** clothes fit very tightly so that they show the shape of your body. *...the youth with the slicked down hair and skin-tight trousers.* ADJ: usu ADJ n

skip /skɪp/ **skips, skipping, skipped** ♦♦◇◇◇

1 If you **skip** along, you move almost as if you are dancing, with a series of little jumps from one foot to the other. *They saw the man with a little girl skipping along behind him... We went skipping down the street arm in arm... She was skipping to keep up with him.* ► Also a noun. *The boxer gave a little skip as he came out of his corner.* VERB V adv/prep V N-COUNT

2 When someone **skips**, they jump up and down over a rope which they or two other people are holding at each end and turning round and round. *Outside a dozen children were skipping and singing a complicated rhyme.* ♦ **skipping** *Skipping is one of the most enjoyable aerobic activities.* VERB V N-UNCOUNT

3 If you **skip** something that you usually do or something that most people do, you decide not to do it. *It is important not to skip meals... Her daughter started skipping school.* VERB =miss V n

4 If you **skip** or **skip over** a part of something you are reading or a story you are telling, you miss it out or pass over it quickly and move on to something else. *You might want to skip the exercises in this chapter... She reinvented her own life story, skipping over the war years when she had a German lover.* VERB V n V *over/to* n

5 If you **skip** from one subject or activity to another, you move quickly from one to the other although there is no obvious connection between VERB =jump

them. *She kept up a continuous chatter, skipping from one subject to the next.* V from n to n
6 In British English, a **skip** is a large, open, metal container which is used to hold and take away large unwanted items and rubbish. N-COUNT

skipper /skɪpəʳ/ **skippers, skippering, skippered** ◆◆◇◇◇
1 You can use **skipper** to refer to the captain of a ship or boat. *...the skipper of an English fishing boat... Gunfire, skipper!* N-COUNT; N-VOC =captain
2 You can use **skipper** to refer to the captain of a sports team. *The England skipper is confident.* N-COUNT =captain
3 To **skipper** a team or a boat means to be the captain of it. *He skippered the second Rugby XV... The yacht was skippered by Pierre Mas.* VERB =captain V n

skipping rope, skipping ropes. A **skipping rope** is a piece of rope, usually with handles at each end. You exercise with it by turning it round and round and jumping over it; used mainly in British English. N-COUNT

skirmish /skɜːʳmɪʃ/ **skirmishes, skirmishing, skirmished** ◆◇◇◇◇
1 A **skirmish** is a minor battle. *Border skirmishes between India and Pakistan were common.* N-COUNT: oft N with/between n
2 If people **skirmish**, they fight. *They were skirmishing close to the minefield now... Police skirmished with youths on the estate last Friday evening.* ♦ **skirmishing** *On land there was minor skirmishing.* V-RECIP pl-n V V with n N-UNCOUNT
3 A **skirmish** is a short, sharp argument. *This difference in approach has resulted in several political skirmishes.* N-COUNT

skirt /skɜːʳt/ **skirts, skirting, skirted** ◆◆◇◇◇
1 A **skirt** is a piece of clothing worn by women and girls. It fastens at the waist and hangs down around the legs. N-COUNT
2 Something that **skirts** an area is situated around the edge of it. *We raced across a large field that skirted the slope of a hill.* VERB V n
3 If you **skirt** something, you go around the edge of it. *We shall be skirting the island on our way... She skirted round the edge of the room to the door.* VERB V n V round/around n
4 If you **skirt** a problem or question, you avoid dealing with it. *He skirted the hardest issues, concentrating on areas of possible agreement... He skirted round his main differences with her.* VERB V n V round/around n

skirting board, skirting boards. In British English, **skirting board** or **skirting** is a narrow length of wood which goes along the bottom of a wall in a room and makes a border between the walls and the floor. N-VAR

ski slope, ski slopes. A **ski slope** is a sloping surface down which you can ski, either on a snow-covered mountain or on a specially made structure. N-COUNT

skit /skɪt/ **skits.** A **skit** is a short performance in which the actors make fun of people, events, and types of literature by imitating them. *...clever skits on popular songs.* N-COUNT

skitter /skɪtəʳ/ **skitters, skittering, skittered.** If something **skitters**, it moves about very lightly and quickly. *The rats skittered around them in the drains and under the floorboards... Pieces of paper were skittering along the sidewalk.* VERB V adv/prep

skittish /skɪtɪʃ/
1 If you describe a person or animal as **skittish**, you mean they are very excitable and easily frightened. *The declining dollar gave heart to skittish investors.* ADJ-GRADED =nervous
2 Someone who is **skittish** does not concentrate on anything or take life very seriously. *His work shows a fertile talent at war with a relentlessly skittish sense of humour.* ADJ-GRADED

skittle /skɪtᵊl/ **skittles**
1 A **skittle** is a wooden object used as a target in the game of skittles; used especially in British English. N-COUNT =ninepins
2 **Skittles** is a game in which players try to knock over as many skittles as they can out of a group of nine by throwing a ball at them. N-UNCOUNT

skive /skaɪv/ **skives, skiving, skived.** In British English, if you **skive**, you avoid working, especially by staying away from the place where you should be working; an informal word. *The company treated me as though I were skiving.* ▶ **Skive off** means the same as **skive**. *'I absolutely hated school,' Rachel says. 'I skived off all the time.'... Almost everybody's kids skive off school.* ♦ **skiver, skivers** *He was a skiver, and a thief.* VERB V PHRASAL VERB VP VP n N-COUNT

skulduggery /skʌldʌgəri/. **Skulduggery** is behaviour in which someone acts in a dishonest way in order to achieve their aim; an old-fashioned word. *...accusations of intimidation and political skulduggery.* N-UNCOUNT

skulk /skʌlk/ **skulks, skulking, skulked.** If you **skulk** somewhere, you hide or move around quietly because you do not want to be seen. *You, meanwhile, will be skulking in the safety of the car... Harry skulked off.* VERB V prep/adv

skull /skʌl/ **skulls.** Your **skull** is the bony part of your head which encloses your brain. *Her husband was later treated for a fractured skull.* ◆◆◇◇◇ N-COUNT

skull and crossbones. A **skull and crossbones** is a picture of a human skull above a pair of crossed bones which warns of death or danger. It used to appear on the flags flown by pirate ships and is now sometimes found on containers holding poisonous or toxic substances. *Skull and crossbones stickers on the drums aroused the suspicion of the customs officers.* N-SING

skull cap, skull caps; also spelled **skullcap**. A **skull cap** is a small close-fitting cap. N-COUNT

skunk /skʌŋk/ **skunks.** A **skunk** is a small black and white animal which releases an unpleasant smelling liquid if it is frightened or attacked. Skunks live in America. N-COUNT

sky /skaɪ/ **skies** ◆◆◆◇◇
1 The **sky** is the space around the earth which you can see when you stand outside and look upwards. *The sun is already high in the sky. ...warm sunshine and clear blue skies... The night sky was lit up by flashes of light.* N-VAR
2 • **pie in the sky**: see **pie**.

sky-blue. Something that is **sky-blue** is a very pale blue in colour. *Her silk shirtdress was sky-blue, the colour of her eyes.* COLOUR

skydiver /skaɪdaɪvəʳ/ **skydivers;** also spelled **sky diver**. A **skydiver** is someone who goes skydiving. N-COUNT

skydiving /skaɪdaɪvɪŋ/. **Skydiving** is the sport of jumping out of an aeroplane and falling freely through the air before opening your parachute. N-UNCOUNT

sky-high. If you say that prices or confidence are **sky-high**, you are emphasizing that they are at a very high level. *Christie said: 'My confidence is sky high.' ...the effect of falling house prices and sky-high interest rates.* ▶ Also an adverb. *Their prestige went sky high.* ADJ PRAGMATICS ADV: ADV after v

skylark /skaɪlɑːʳk/ **skylarks.** A **skylark** is a small brown bird that sings while hovering high above the ground. N-COUNT

skylight /skaɪlaɪt/ **skylights.** A **skylight** is a window in a roof. N-COUNT

skyline /skaɪlaɪn/ **skylines.** The **skyline** is the line or shape that is formed where the sky meets buildings or the land. *The village church dominates the skyline.* ◆◇◇◇◇ N-COUNT: usu the N

skyrocket /skaɪrɒkɪt/ **skyrockets, skyrocketing, skyrocketed.** If prices or amounts **skyrocket**, they go up suddenly and steeply. *Production has dropped while prices and unemployment have skyrocketed. ...the skyrocketing costs of health care.* VERB V V-ing

skyscraper /skaɪskreɪpəʳ/ **skyscrapers.** A **skyscraper** is a very tall building in a city. ◆◇◇◇◇ N-COUNT

skyward /skaɪwəʳd/; also spelled **skywards**. If you look **skyward** or **skywards**, you look up towards the sky; a literary word. *He pointed skywards. ...people who look skywards at the first sound of an aircraft.* ADV: ADV after v

slab /slæb/ **slabs.** A **slab** of something is a thick, flat piece of it. *...slabs of stone. ...huge concrete paving slabs.* ◆◇◇◇◇ N-COUNT: with supp

slack /slæk/ **slacker, slackest; slacks, slacking, slacked** ◆◇◇◇◇
1 Something that is **slack** is loose and not firmly ADJ-GRADED

stretched or tightly in position. *The boy's jaw went slack.*

2 A **slack** period is one in which there is not much work or activity. *The workload can be evened out, instead of the shop having busy times and slack periods.* ADJ-GRADED =quiet

3 Someone who is **slack** in their work does not do it properly. *Many publishers have simply become far too slack.* ♦ **slackness** *He accused the government of slackness and complacency.* ADJ-GRADED N-UNCOUNT

4 If someone **is slacking**, they are not working as hard as they should. *He had never let a foreman see him slacking.* ► **Slack off** means the same as **slack**. *If someone slacks off, Bill comes down hard.* VB: only cont V PHRASAL VERB VP

5 To **take up the slack** or **pick up the slack** in an organization or system means to reduce its spare capacity so that it works more efficiently. *Exports could take up some of the slack but orders aren't coming in as strongly as earlier this year.* PHRASE: V inflects

slack off PHRASAL VERB

1 **Slack off** means the same as **slacken off**.

2 See **slack** 4.

slacken /slækən/ **slackens, slackening, slackened** ♦◇◇◇◇

1 If something **slackens** or if you **slacken** it, it becomes slower, less active, or less intense. *Inflationary pressures continued to slacken last month... The Conservative government will not slacken the pace of radical reform.* ♦ **slackening** *There was a slackening of western output during the 1930s.* V-ERG V Vn N-SING: oft N *of* n

2 If your grip or a part of your body **slackens** it becomes looser or more relaxed. *Her grip slackened on Arnold's arm... Muscles stretch, slacken and relax during child-birth.* V-ERG V Also V n

slacken off. If something **slackens off**, it becomes slower, less active, or less intense; used mainly in British English. *At about five o'clock, business slackened off.* PHRASAL VERB no passive =slack off VP

slacker /slækəʳ/ **slackers.** If you describe someone as a **slacker**, you mean that they are lazy and do less work than they should. *He's not a slacker, he's the best worker they've got.* N-COUNT

slack-jawed. If you say that someone is **slack-jawed**, you mean that their mouth is hanging open, often because they are surprised. *He just gazed at me slack-jawed without saying a word.* ADJ

slacks /slæks/. **Slacks** are casual trousers; an old-fashioned word. *She was wearing black slacks and a white sweater.* ♦◇◇◇◇ N-PLURAL: also *a pair of* N =trousers

slag /slæg/ **slags, slagging, slagged.** In informal British English, **slag** is an offensive word which some people use to refer to a woman who they disapprove of because they think she is sexually immoral. ♦◇◇◇◇ N-COUNT PRAGMATICS

slag off. To **slag** someone **off** means to criticize them in an unpleasant way; an informal expression, used mainly in British English. *All bands slag off their record companies. It's just the way it is... People have been slagging me off.* PHRASAL VERB V P n (not pron) V n P

slag heap, slag heaps; also spelled **slagheap**. A **slag heap** is a hill made from waste material, such as rock and mud, left over from mining. N-COUNT

slain /sleɪn/. **Slain** is the past participle of **slay**.

slake /sleɪk/ **slakes, slaking, slaked.** If you **slake** your thirst you drink something that stops you being thirsty; a literary word. *I slaked my thirst with three cans of Coke.* VERB V n

slalom /slɑːləm/ **slaloms.** A **slalom** is a race on skis or in canoes in which the competitors have to avoid a series of obstacles in a very twisting and difficult course. ♦◇◇◇◇ N-COUNT

slam /slæm/ **slams, slamming, slammed** ♦♦◇◇◇

1 If you **slam** a door or window or if it **slams**, it shuts noisily and with great force. *She slammed the door and locked it behind her... I was relieved to hear the front door slam... He slammed the gate shut behind him.* V-ERG V n V V n adj

2 If you **slam** something down, you put it there quickly and with great force. *She listened in a mixture of shock and anger before slamming the phone down.* VERB V n with adv

3 To **slam** someone or something means to criticize them very severely; used in journalism. *The famed film-maker slammed the claims as 'an outrageous lie.'... Britain has been slammed by the United Nations for having one of the worst race relations records in the world.* VERB V n

4 If one thing **slams** into or against another, it crashes into it with great force. *The plane slammed into the building after losing an engine shortly after take-off... He slammed me against the ground.* VERB V *into/against* n V n *into/against* n

5 See also **Grand Slam**.

slammer /slæməʳ/. **The slammer** is prison; an informal word. N-SING: *the* N

slander /slɑːndəʳ, slæn-/ **slanders, slandering, slandered** ♦◇◇◇◇

1 **Slander** is an untrue spoken statement about someone which is intended to damage their reputation. *Dr. Bach is now suing the company for slander... Korea has been a target of threats and slanders from the major western powers.* N-VAR =defamation

2 To **slander** someone means to say untrue things about them in order to damage their reputation. *He has been questioned on suspicion of slandering the Prime Minister.* VERB V n

slanderous /slɑːndərəs, slæn-/. A spoken statement that is **slanderous** is untrue and intended to damage the reputation of the person that it refers to. *Herr Kohler wanted an explanation for what he described as 'slanderous' remarks.* ADJ-GRADED

slang /slæŋ/. **Slang** consists of words, expressions, and meanings that are informal and are used by people who know each other very well or who have the same interests. *Archie liked to think he kept up with current slang. ...a slang term.* ♦◇◇◇◇ N-UNCOUNT

slanging match /slæŋɪŋ mætʃ/ **slanging matches.** In British English, **a slanging match** is an angry quarrel in which people insult each other. *They conducted a public slanging match on television.* N-COUNT =row

slangy /slæŋi/. **Slangy** speech or writing has a lot of slang in it. *The play was full of slangy dialogue.* ADJ: usu ADJ n

slant /slɑːnt, slænt/ **slants, slanting, slanted** ♦◇◇◇◇

1 Something that **slants** is sloping, rather than horizontal or vertical. *The morning sun slanted through the glass roof... Battered pine floors slanted down to a Georgian window. ...slanting green eyes.* VERB V adv/prep V-ing

2 If something is on a **slant**, it is in a slanting position. *You're slightly above the garden because the house is on a slant. ...long pockets cut on the slant.* N-SING

3 If information or a system **is slanted**, it is made to show favour towards a particular group or opinion. *The programme was deliberately slanted to make the home team look good.* ♦ **slanted** *The electoral system, which is heavily slanted towards the ruling party, needs to be changed. ...slanted news coverage.* VB: usu passive *be* V-ed Also *be* V-ed prep ADJ-GRADED

4 A particular **slant** on a subject is a particular way of thinking about it, especially one that is unfair, biased, or prejudiced. *The political slant at Focus can be described as centre-right... They give a slant to every single news item that's put on the air.* N-SING: usu with supp =bias

slap /slæp/ **slaps, slapping, slapped** ♦♦◇◇◇

1 If you **slap** someone, you hit them with the palm of your hand. *He would push or slap her once in a while... I slapped him hard across the face... He was slapping a woman around and I objected.* ► Also a noun. *He reached forward and gave her a slap.* VERB V n V n adv/prep N-COUNT: usu sing

2 If you **slap** someone **on** the back, you hit them in a friendly manner on their back. *A large middle-aged lady slapped me on the back and said 'Nice to see you again.'* VERB V n *on* n

3 If you **slap** something onto a surface, you put it there quickly, roughly, or carelessly. *'Coffee!' bellowed the barman, slapping the cup on to the waiting saucer.* VERB V n *on/onto* n

4 If journalists say that the authorities **slap** something such as a tax or a ban **on** something, they think that it is unreasonable or too hasty; an informal use. *The government slapped a ban on the export of unprocessed logs... Thankfully the Government still hasn't discovered a way of slapping a tax on love, sunshine or air.* VERB PRAGMATICS =stick V n *on* n

5 If you describe something that someone does as **a slap in the face**, you mean that it shocks or upsets you because it shows that they do not support you or respect you. *'The Sun' calls it a massive slap in the face for the United States government... Britons persist in treating any pay rise of less than 5% as a slap in the face.* PHRASES oft PHR for n

6 A **slap on the wrist** is a warning or a punishment that is not very severe. *The fine they gave her is just more or less a slap on the wrist.*

slap bang; also spelled **slap-bang**. In informal British English, **slap bang** is used in expressions such as **slap bang in the middle** of somewhere to mean exactly in that place. *Of course, slap-bang in the middle of town the rents are high.* ADV: ADV prep

slapdash /slæpdæʃ/; also spelled **slap-dash.** If you describe someone as **slapdash**, you mean that they do things carelessly without much thinking or planning. *...a slapdash student... Malcolm's work methods appear amazingly slapdash.* ADJ-GRADED

slap-happy. If you describe someone as **slap-happy**, you believe they are irresponsible and careless. *...a slap-happy kind of cook. ...a slap-happy ignorance of the danger.* ADJ-GRADED

slapstick /slæpstɪk/. **Slapstick** is a simple type of comedy in which the actors behave in a rough and foolish way. *...slapstick comedy. ...Laurel and Hardy's inspired bursts of slapstick.* N-UNCOUNT: oft N n

slap-up. A **slap-up** meal is a large enjoyable meal; an informal word used in British English. *We usually had one slap-up meal a day.* ADJ: ADJ n

slash /slæʃ/ **slashes, slashing, slashed** ◆◆◇◇◇

1 If you **slash** something, you make a long, deep cut in it. *He came within two minutes of bleeding to death after slashing his wrists.* ► Also a noun. *Make deep slashes in the meat and push in the spice paste.* VERB V n N-COUNT

2 If you **slash at** someone or something, you quickly hit at them with something. *He slashed at her, aiming carefully.* VERB V at n

3 To **slash** something such as costs or jobs means to reduce them by a large amount; used by journalists. *Car makers could be forced to slash prices after being accused of overcharging yesterday... Everyone agrees that subsidies have to be slashed.* VERB =cut V n

4 You say **slash** to refer to a diagonal line that separates letters, words, or numbers. For example, if you are giving the number 340/21/K, you say 'Three four zero, slash two one, slash K.'

slash and burn; also spelled **slash-and-burn**. **Slash and burn** is a method of farming that involves clearing land by destroying and burning all the trees and plants on it, farming there for a short time, and then moving on to clear a new piece of land. *Traditional slash and burn farming methods have exhausted the soil.* N-UNCOUNT: usu N n

slat /slæt/ **slats. Slats** are the narrow pieces of wood, metal, or plastic in things such as Venetian blinds or cupboard doors. N-COUNT: usu pl

slate /sleɪt/ **slates, slating, slated** ◆◆◇◇◇

1 **Slate** is a dark grey rock that can be easily split into thin layers. Slate is often used for covering roofs. ... *a stone-built cottage, with a traditional slate roof.* N-UNCOUNT: oft N n

2 A **slate** is one of the small flat pieces of slate that are used for covering roofs. N-COUNT

3 A **slate** is a list of candidates for an election, usually from the same party. *The leadership want to present a single slate of candidates to be approved in an open vote.* N-COUNT: usu with supp =list

4 If something **is slated** to happen, it is planned to happen at a particular time; used especially in American English. *Bromfield was slated to become U.S. Secretary of Agriculture... A controversial measure designed to set the nation's future energy course is slated for Senate debate within days.* V-PASSIVE =be scheduled be V-ed to-inf be V-ed for n

5 In British English, if something **is slated**, it is criticized very severely; used mainly by journalists. *Arnold Schwarzenegger's new restaurant has been slated by a top food critic... Slated by critics at the time, the film has since become a cult classic.* VB: usu passive be V-ed V-ed

6 If you start with **a clean slate**, you do not take account of previous mistakes or failures and make a fresh start. *The proposal is to pay everything you owe, so that you can start with a clean slate.* PHRASES

7 If you **wipe the slate clean**, you decide to forget previous mistakes, failures, or debts and to start again. *Why not wipe the slate clean and start all over again from scratch?* V inflects

slather /slæðəʳ/ **slathers, slathering, slathered.** If you **slather** something with a substance, or **slather** the substance onto something, you cover it thickly. *If your skin is dry, you have to slather on moisturiser to soften it. ...pieces of toast slathered with butter and marmalade.* VERB V n with adv be V-ed prep Also V n prep

slatted /slætɪd/. Something that is **slatted** is made with slats. *...yellow slatted wooden seats. ...slatted window blinds.* ADJ

slattern /slætəʳn/ **slatterns.** A **slattern** is a dirty untidy woman; an old-fashioned word. N-COUNT

slaughter /slɔːtəʳ/ **slaughters, slaughtering, slaughtered** ◆◆◇◇◇

1 If large numbers of people or animals **are slaughtered**, they are killed in a way that is cruel, unjust, or unnecessary. *Thirty four people were slaughtered while queuing up to cast their votes... Whales and dolphins are still being slaughtered for commercial gain.* ► Also a noun. *The West Europeans failed to halt the slaughter that accompanied the break-up of Yugoslavia... The annual slaughter of wildlife in Italy is horrific.* VB: usu passive =butcher be V-ed N-UNCOUNT

2 To **slaughter** animals such as cows and sheep means to kill them for their meat. *Lack of chicken feed means that chicken farms are having to slaughter their stock.* ► Also a noun. *More than 491,000 sheep were exported to the Continent for slaughter last year.* VERB V n N-UNCOUNT

3 • **like lambs to the slaughter**: see **lamb**.

slaughterhouse /slɔːtəʳhaʊs/ **slaughterhouses.** A **slaughterhouse** is a place where animals are killed for their meat. N-COUNT =abattoir

Slav /slɑːv/ **Slavs.** A **Slav** is a member of any of the peoples of Eastern Europe who speak a Slavonic language. ◆◇◇◇◇ N-COUNT

slave /sleɪv/ **slaves, slaving, slaved** ◆◆◇◇◇

1 A **slave** is someone who is the property of another person and has to work for that person. *The state of Liberia was formed a century and a half ago by freed slaves from the United States.* N-COUNT

2 You can describe someone as a **slave** when they are completely under the control of another person or of a powerful influence. *She may no longer be a slave to the studio system, but she still has a duty to her fans.* N-COUNT: with supp

3 If you say that someone **is slaving** over something or **is slaving** for someone, you mean that they work very hard. *When you're busy all day the last thing you want to do is spend hours slaving over a hot stove.* ► To **slave away** means the same as to **slave**. *He stares at the hundreds of workers slaving away in the intense sun.* VERB V over n Also V, V prep PHRASAL VERB V P

slave away. See **slave** 3. PHRASAL VERB

slave labour; spelled **slave labor** in American English.

1 **Slave labour** refers to slaves or to work done by slaves. *The children were used as slave labour in gold mines in the jungle... The report alleges that thousands of people have been forced into slave labour by the army.* N-UNCOUNT

2 If people work very hard for long hours for very little money, you can refer to it as **slave labour**; used showing disapproval. *He's been forced into slave labour at burger bars to earn a bit of cash.* N-UNCOUNT PRAGMATICS

slaver /slævəʳ/ **slavers, slavering, slavered**

1 If an animal **slavers**, saliva drips from its mouth. *Mad guard dogs slavered at the end of their chains. ...the wolf's slavering jaws.* VERB =slobber V V-ing

2 If you say that someone **is slavering**, you mean that they are so excited by something that they cannot control themselves, and that you find this disgusting. *I found myself skipping these passages, though no doubt many readers will slaver over them.* VERB PRAGMATICS V over n Also V

slavery /sleɪvəri/. **Slavery** is the system by which people are owned by other people as slaves. *My people have survived 400 years of slavery.* ◆◇◇◇◇ N-UNCOUNT

slave trade. **The slave trade** is the buying and selling of slaves, especially the sale into slavery of Black Africans from the 16th to the 19th centuries. *More than a century and a half since the transatlantic slave trade was abolished, slavery is far from dead.* N-SING: the N

Slavic /slævɪk, slɑːv-/. Something that is **Slavic** comes from or refers to the Slavs. *...Americans of Slavic descent. ...Slavic culture. ...his high Slavic cheekbones.* ADJ

slavish /sleɪvɪʃ/

1 You use **slavish** to describe things that copy or imitate something exactly, without any attempt to be original; used showing disapproval. *She herself insists she is no slavish follower of fashion.* ADJ-GRADED PRAGMATICS

♦ **slavishly** *Most have slavishly copied the design of IBM's big mainframe machines... When a political columnist describes a cabinet minister in slavishly adoring terms, shouldn't we be told whether the two are pals?* ADV-GRADED: ADV with v, ADV adj

2 If you describe someone as **slavish**, you are critical of the fact that they behave like a slave, for example by being completely obedient to another person. *Total devotion it certainly was, slavish devotion some would say.* ADJ-GRADED PRAGMATICS

Slavonic /sləvɒnɪk/; also spelled **Slavonic**. Something that is **Slavonic** relates to the language and study of the Slavs. *The Ukrainians speak a slavonic language similar to Russian. ...the department of Slavonic studies.* ADJ

slay /sleɪ/ **slays, slaying, slew, slayed, slain.** ◆◇◇◇◇

1 If someone **slays** an animal, they kill it in a violent way; a formal use. *...the hill where St George slew the dragon.* ♦ **slaying** *The festival commemorates the slaying of the demon buffalo.* ♦ **slayer, slayers** *...the story of the Monster Slayer.* VERB V n; N-UNCOUNT: usu N of n; N-COUNT =killer

2 In American English, journalists say that someone **has been slain** when they have been murdered. *Two Australian tourists were slain.* V-PASSIVE =murder be V-ed

slaying /sleɪɪŋ/ **slayings.** Journalists sometimes use the word **slaying** to refer to a murder; used mainly in American English. *...a trail of motiveless slayings.* N-COUNT: usu with supp =murder

sleaze /sliːz/. You use **sleaze** to describe activities that you consider immoral, dishonest, or not respectable, especially in politics, business, journalism, or entertainment; an informal word. *She claimed that an atmosphere of sleaze and corruption now surrounded the Government... The President denounced the press for engaging in 'sleaze' and called the story a lie. ...porn movies and sleaze.* N-UNCOUNT PRAGMATICS

sleazy /sliːzi/ **sleazier, sleaziest** ◆◇◇◇◇

1 If you describe a place as **sleazy**, you dislike it because it looks dirty and badly cared for, and not respectable; an informal word. *...sleazy bars. ...sleazy cinemas in London's Soho... Downstairs in the windowless basement, where the real work is done, it is sleazy and sweaty.* ADJ-GRADED PRAGMATICS

2 If you describe something or someone as **sleazy**, you disapprove of them because you think they are not respectable and are rather sordid; an informal word. *...sex shops and sleazy magazines. ...a sleazy fellow... The accusations are making the government's conduct appear increasingly sleazy.* ADJ-GRADED PRAGMATICS

sled /sled/ **sleds, sledding, sledded**

1 In American English, a **sled** is the same as a **sledge**. N-COUNT

2 In American English, if you go **sledding**, you ride on a sled. *We got home and went sledding on the small hill in our back yard.* VERB V-ing; Also V

sledge /sledʒ/ **sledges, sledging, sledged** ◆◇◇◇◇

1 In British English, a **sledge** is an object used for travelling over snow. It consists of a framework which slides on two strips of wood or metal. *She travelled 14,000 miles by sledge across Siberia to Kamchatka.* N-COUNT: also by N =sled

2 In British English, if you **sledge** or go **sledging**, you ride on a sledge. *Our hill is marvellous for sledging and we always have snow in January.* VERB V; Also V prep

sledgehammer /sledʒhæmər/ **sledgehammers;** also spelled **sledge-hammer.**

1 A **sledgehammer** is a large, heavy hammer with a long handle, used for smashing rocks and concrete. N-COUNT

2 If you say that someone is using **a sledgehammer to crack a nut**, you mean that they are using stronger measures than are really necessary to solve a problem. PHRASE: Ns inflect

sleek /sliːk/ **sleeker, sleekest** ◆◇◇◇◇

1 **Sleek** hair or fur is smooth and shiny and looks healthy. *...sleek black hair... The horse's sleek body gleamed.* ADJ-GRADED =glossy

2 If you describe someone as **sleek**, you mean that they look rich and stylish. *Lord White is as sleek and elegant as any other multi millionaire businessman.* ADJ-GRADED

3 **Sleek** vehicles, furniture, or other objects look smooth, shiny, and expensive. *... a sleek white BMW. ...sleek modern furniture.* ADJ-GRADED

sleep /sliːp/ **sleeps, sleeping, slept** ◆◆◆◆◇

1 **Sleep** is the natural state of rest in which your eyes are closed, your body is inactive, and your mind does not think. *They were exhausted from lack of sleep... Try and get some sleep... Be quiet and go to sleep... Often he would have bad dreams and cry out in his sleep.* N-UNCOUNT

2 When you **sleep**, you rest with your eyes closed and your mind and body inactive. *During the car journey, the baby slept... I've not been able to sleep for the last few nights. ...a pool surrounded by sleeping sunbathers.* VERB V; V-ing

3 A **sleep** is a period of sleeping. *I think he may be ready for a sleep soon.* N-COUNT: usu sing

4 If a building or room **sleeps** a particular number of people, it has beds for that number of people. *The villa sleeps 10 and costs £530 per person for two weeks.* VB: no cont, no passive; V amount

5 See also **sleeping.**

6 If you cannot **get to sleep**, you are unable to sleep. *I can't get to sleep with all that singing.* PHRASES V inflects

7 If you say that you didn't **lose** any **sleep** over something, you mean that you did not worry about it at all. *I didn't lose too much sleep over that investigation.* V inflects, usu PHR *over* n

8 If you are trying to make a decision and you say that you will **sleep on it**, you mean that you will delay making a decision on it until the following day, so you have time to think about it. V inflects

9 If a sick or injured animal **is put to sleep**, it is painlessly killed by a vet. *I'm going take the dog down to the vet's and have her put to sleep.* V inflects =put down

10 ● **sleep rough**: see **rough.**

sleep around. If you say that someone **sleeps around**, you disapprove of them because they have sex with a lot of different people; an informal expression. *I don't sleep around. ...a drunken husband who slept around with other women.* PHRASAL VERB PRAGMATICS V P; V P with n

sleep off. If you **sleep off** the effects of too much travelling, drink, or food, you recover from it by sleeping. *It's a good idea to spend the first night of your holiday sleeping off the jet lag... They had been up all night and were sleeping it off.* PHRASAL VERB V P n (not pron); V n P

sleep through. If you **sleep through** something, it does not wake you up. *Some children can sleep through any kind of noise.* PHRASAL VERB V P n

sleep together. If two people **are sleeping together**, they are having a sexual relationship, but are not usually married to each other. *I'm pretty sure they slept together before they were married.* PHRASAL VERB V P

sleep with. If you **sleep with** someone, you have sex with them. *He was old enough to sleep with a girl and make her pregnant.* PHRASAL VERB V P n

sleeper /sliːpər/ **sleepers** ◆◇◇◇◇

1 You can use the word **sleeper** to indicate how well someone sleeps. For example, if someone is a light **sleeper**, they are easily woken up. *I'm a very light sleeper and I can hardly get any sleep at all... Poor sleepers take longer to fall asleep than good sleepers.* N-COUNT: adj N

2 On a train, a **sleeper** is a bed or a carriage containing several beds; used mainly in British English. N-COUNT

3 A **sleeper** is a train with beds for passengers on overnight journeys; used mainly in British English. N-COUNT

4 Railway **sleepers** are large heavy beams that support the rails of a railway track; used in British English. N-COUNT: oft n N

5 If you describe something as a **sleeper**, you mean that it unexpectedly becomes successful, after a long period of inactivity or obscurity; an informal use. *...Menno Meyjes, a young Dutch writer, who had had his first success with the sleeper 'The Children's Crusade'.* N-COUNT

sleeping /sli:pɪŋ/. You use **sleeping** to describe places where people sleep or things concerned with where people sleep. *On the top floor we have sleeping quarters for women and children. ...investigations of people's finances, sleeping arrangements and housekeeping habits.* • See also **sleep.** ADJ: ADJ n

sleeping bag, sleeping bags. A **sleeping bag** is a large deep bag with a warm lining, used for sleeping in, especially when you are camping. ◆◇◇◇◇ N-COUNT

sleeping car, sleeping cars. A **sleeping car** is a railway carriage that provides beds for passengers to sleep in. N-COUNT

sleeping partner, sleeping partners. In British English, a **sleeping partner** is a person who provides some of the capital for a business but who does not take an active part in managing the business. The American expression is **silent partner.** N-COUNT

sleeping pill, sleeping pills. A **sleeping pill** is a pill that you can take to help you sleep. ◆◇◇◇◇ N-COUNT

sleeping sickness. **Sleeping sickness** is a serious tropical disease which causes great tiredness and often leads to death. N-UNCOUNT

sleeping tablet, sleeping tablets. A **sleeping tablet** is the same as a **sleeping pill.** N-COUNT

sleepless /sli:pləs/ ◆◇◇◇◇

1 A **sleepless** night is one during which you do not sleep. *I have sleepless nights worrying about her.* ADJ-GRADED: usu ADJ n

2 Someone who is **sleepless** is unable to sleep. *A sleepless baby can seem to bring little reward.* ADJ =restless

♦ **sleeplessness** *Sleeplessness is sometimes the side effect of certain medications.* N-UNCOUNT

sleepwalk /sli:pwɔ:k/ **sleepwalks, sleepwalking, sleepwalked.** If someone **is sleepwalking**, they are walking around while they are asleep. *He once sleepwalked to the middle of the road outside his home at 1 a.m.* ♦ **sleepwalker** *We don't know what makes a sleepwalker.* VERB V N-COUNT

sleepy /sli:pi/ **sleepier, sleepiest** ◆◇◇◇◇

1 If you are **sleepy**, you are very tired and are almost asleep. *I was beginning to feel amazingly sleepy... She was still tired and sleepy when he woke her.* ♦ **sleepily** *Joanna sat up, blinking sleepily.* ♦ **sleepiness** *He tried to fight the sleepiness that overwhelmed him.* ADJ-GRADED: usu v-link ADJ =drowsy ADV-GRADED: ADV with v N-UNCOUNT

2 A **sleepy** place is quiet and does not have much activity or excitement. *Valence is a sleepy little town just south of Lyon.* ADJ-GRADED: usu ADJ n ≠bustling

sleet /sli:t/. **Sleet** is rain that is partly frozen. *...blinding snow, driving sleet and wind.* N-UNCOUNT

sleeve /sli:v/ **sleeves** ◆◆◇◇◇

1 The **sleeves** of a coat, shirt, or other item of clothing are the parts that cover your arms. *His sleeves were rolled up to his elbows... He wore a black band on the left sleeve of his jacket.* N-COUNT

2 A record **sleeve** is the stiff envelope in which a record is kept. *There are to be no pictures of him on the sleeve of the new record. ...an album sleeve.* N-COUNT: usu N of n, n N

3 If someone **wears** their **heart on** their **sleeve**, they behave in a way that makes their feelings very obvious, for example when they are in love with someone. PHRASES V and Ns inflect

4 If you have something **up** your **sleeve**, you have an idea or plan which you have not told anyone about. You can also say that someone has **an ace, card,** or **trick up** their **sleeve.** *He wondered what Shearson had up his sleeve... I'd been doing some quiet investigating in the meantime and had an ace up my sleeve.* N inflects

-sleeved /-sli:vd/. **-sleeved** is added to adjectives such as 'long' and 'short' to form adjectives which indicate that an item of clothing has long or short sleeves. *...a short-sleeved blue shirt.* COMB in ADJ: usu ADJ n

sleeveless /sli:vləs/. A **sleeveless** T-shirt, dress, or other item of clothing has no sleeves. *She wore a sleeveless silk dress.* ADJ: usu ADJ n

sleeve note, sleeve notes. In British English, on record sleeves, the **sleeve notes** are short pieces of writing that tell you something about the record or the musicians playing on the record. The American term is **liner note.** N-COUNT: usu pl

sleigh /sleɪ/ **sleighs.** A **sleigh** is a vehicle which can slide over snow. Sleighs are usually pulled by horses. N-COUNT =sledge

sleight of hand /slaɪt əv hænd/ **sleights of hand. Sleight of hand** is a skilful piece of deception. *He accused Mr MacGregor of 'sleight of hand'. ...a financial sleight of hand.* N-VAR

slender /slendəʳ/ ◆◇◇◇◇

1 A **slender** person is attractively thin and graceful; used in written English. *She was slender, with delicate wrists and ankles. ...a tall, slender figure in a straw hat... He gazed at her slender neck.* ADJ-GRADED PRAGMATICS

2 You can use **slender** to describe a situation which exists but only to a very small degree; used in written English. *The United States held a slender lead... He has won a vote of confidence but only by a slender majority. ...the first slender hope of peace.* ADJ-GRADED: usu ADJ n =slim

slept /slept/. **Slept** is the past tense and past participle of **sleep.**

sleuth /slu:θ/ **sleuths.** A **sleuth** is a detective; an old-fashioned word. N-COUNT

sleuthing /slu:θɪŋ/. **Sleuthing** is the investigation of a crime or mystery by someone who is not a detective in the police force; a literary word. *I want to do a little sleuthing round the property to see if I can find any footprints.* N-UNCOUNT

slew /slu:/ **slews, slewing, slewed**

1 **Slew** is the past tense of **slay.**

2 If a vehicle **slews** or **is slewed** across a road, it slides or skids across it. *The bus slewed sideways... A seven-ton lorry slewed across their path... He slewed the car against the side of the building.* V-ERG =veer V adv/prep V n prep/adv

3 A **slew** of things is a large number of them; used mainly in American English. *There have been a whole slew of shooting incidents... They dealt with a slew of other issues.* N-COUNT: usu sing, usu N of n

slice /slaɪs/ **slices, slicing, sliced** ◆◆◆◇◇

1 A **slice** of bread, meat, fruit, or other food is a thin piece that has been cut from a larger piece. *Try to eat at least four slices of bread a day. ...water flavored with a slice of lemon.* N-COUNT: usu with supp, oft N of n

2 If you **slice** bread, meat, fruit, or other food, you cut it into thin pieces. *Helen sliced the cake... Slice the steak into long thin slices.* ► **Slice up** something means the same as **slice.** *I sliced up an onion... He began slicing the pie up.* VERB V n V n into n PHRASAL VERB V P n (not pron) V n P

3 You can use **slice** to refer to a part of a situation or activity. *Fiction takes up a large slice of the publishing market. ...a car that represents a slice of motoring history.* N-COUNT: usu N of n =proportion

4 In tennis, golf, and other sports, if you **slice** a ball, you hit its edge rather than its centre, so that it travels at an angle. *The captain swung his left foot, but sliced the ball wide.* ► Also a noun. *...a ball that would reduce hooks and slices.* VERB V n adv/adj Also V n N-COUNT

5 If something **slices** through a substance, it moves through it quickly, like a knife; a literary use. *The ship sliced through the water.* VERB =carve V through n Also V n

6 See also **sliced; fish slice.**

7 • **slice of the action**: see **action.**

slice up. See **slice** 2. PHRASAL VERB

sliced /slaɪst/. **Sliced** bread has been cut into slices before being wrapped and sold. *...a sliced white loaf.* ADJ: usu ADJ n

slick /slɪk/ **slicker, slickest; slicks, slicking, slicked** ◆◆◇◇◇

1 A **slick** performance, production, or advertisement is attractively and professionally presented. ADJ-GRADED

There's a big difference between an amateur video and a slick Hollywood production... His style is slick and visually exciting. ♦ **slickly** *The products had been slickly marketed.* ♦ **slickness** *These actors and directors brought a new sophistication and slickness to modern theatre.*
ADV-GRADED: ADV with v
N-UNCOUNT

2 A **slick** action is done quickly and smoothly, and without any obvious effort. *They were outplayed by the Colombians' slick passing and decisive finishing. ...a slick gear change.*
ADJ-GRADED: usu ADJ n

3 A **slick** person speaks easily and persuasively but is not sincere; used showing disapproval. *Don't be fooled by slick politicians. ...a slick, suit-wearing detective.* ♦ **slickness** *He had the slickness but not the sharpness.*
ADJ-GRADED PRAGMATICS
N-UNCOUNT

4 A **slick** is the same as an **oil slick**. *Experts are trying to devise ways to clean up the huge slick.*
N-COUNT

5 If someone **slicks** their hair back, they make it flat, smooth, and shiny by putting oil or water on it. *She had slicked her hair back... He slicked down his few remaining wisps of gray hair... His hair was slicked carefully into waves.*
VERB
V with *back/down*
be V-ed prep

slicker /slɪkə^{r}/ **slickers**

1 In American English, a **slicker** is a long loose waterproof coat. The British term is **oilskin**.
N-COUNT

2 See also **slick**.

slide /slaɪd/ **slides, sliding, slid** ◆◆◆◇◇

1 When something **slides** somewhere or when you **slide** it there, it moves there smoothly over or against something. *She slid the door open... I slid the wallet into his pocket... Tears were sliding down his cheeks.*
V-ERG
V n with adj
V n prep/adv
V prep/adv
Also V

2 If you **slide** somewhere, you move there smoothly and quietly. *He slid into the driver's seat... 'Nice meeting you, Zoe,' I said and slid off.*
VERB
V prep/adv

3 To **slide into** a particular mood, attitude, or situation means to gradually start to have that mood, attitude, or situation often without intending to. *She had slid into a depression... He needs them to stop the country sliding into chaos.*
VERB =slip
V *into* n

4 If currencies or prices **slide**, they gradually become worse or lower in value; used in journalism. *The US dollar continued to slide... The upset sent share prices sliding to their lowest level for almost 18 months... Shares slid 11p to 293p after brokers downgraded their profit estimates... Its share slid from 24.24 per cent to 22.17 per cent.* ► Also a noun. *...the dangerous slide in oil prices.*
VERB
V
V prep/adv
V amount
V *from/to/by* amount
N-COUNT

5 A **slide** is a small piece of photographic film which you project onto a screen so that you can see the picture. *...a slide show.*
N-COUNT

6 A **slide** is a piece of glass on which you put something that you want to examine through a microscope.
N-COUNT

7 A **slide** in a playground is a structure that has a steep slope for children to slide down.
N-COUNT

8 If you **let** something **slide**, you allow it to get into a worse state or condition by not attending to it. *The company had let environmental standards slide.*
PHRASE: *let* inflects

slide rule, slide rules. A **slide rule** is an instrument that you use for calculating numbers. It looks like a ruler and has a middle part that slides backwards and forwards.
N-COUNT

sliding door, sliding doors. Sliding doors are doors which slide together on runners rather than swinging on hinges.
N-COUNT

sliding scale, sliding scales. Payments such as wages or taxes that are calculated on a **sliding scale** are higher or lower depending on various different factors. *Many practitioners have a sliding scale of fees for those who need but can't afford treatment.*
N-COUNT: usu sing, oft N *of* n, *on a* N

slight /slaɪt/ **slighter, slightest; slights, slighting, slighted** ◆◆◆◇◇

1 Something that is **slight** is very small in degree or quantity. *Doctors say he has made a slight improvement... We have a slight problem... A slight smile flickered over his face... He's not the slightest bit worried.*
ADJ-GRADED: usu ADJ n =small

2 A **slight** person has a slim and delicate body. *She is smaller and slighter than Christie... He is a slight, bespectacled, intellectual figure.* ♦ **slightly** *...a slightly built man.*
ADJ-GRADED
ADV-GRADED: ADV -ed

3 If you **are slighted**, someone does or says something that insults you by treating you as if your views or feelings are not important. *They felt slighted by not being adequately consulted.* ► Also a noun. *It's difficult to persuade my husband that it isn't a slight on him that I enjoy my evening class.* ♦ **slighting** *...slighting references to her age.*
VB: usu passive
feel V-ed
N-COUNT: usu with supp
ADJ-GRADED

4 You use **in the slightest** to emphasize a negative statement. *That doesn't interest me in the slightest... 'Do you worry about ageing?' 'Not in the slightest.'*
PHRASE: with brd-neg PRAGMATICS

slightly /slaɪtli/. **Slightly** means to some degree but not to a very large degree. *His family then moved to a slightly larger house... They will be slightly more expensive but they last a lot longer... Each person learns in a slightly different way... You can adjust it slightly... The best activities for stamina are fairly energetic; they need to get you slightly out of breath.* ◆◆◆◆◇
ADV: ADV adj, ADV with v, ADV prep

slim /slɪm/ **slimmer, slimmest; slims, slimming, slimmed** ◆◆◆◇◇

1 A **slim** person has an attractively thin and well-shaped body. *The young woman was tall and slim... Jean is pretty, of slim build, with blue eyes.*
ADJ-GRADED PRAGMATICS =slender

2 If you **are slimming**, you are trying to make yourself thinner and lighter by eating less food. *Some people will gain weight, no matter how hard they try to slim... It makes sense to eat a reasonably balanced diet when slimming.* ► **Slim down** means the same as **slim**. *Doctors have told Benny to slim down. ...salon treatments that claim to slim down thighs.* ♦ **slimmer, slimmers** *...meals for slimmers.* ♦ **slimming** *We live in a society which is obsessed with slimming.*
VERB
V
Also V n
PHRASAL VERB
V P
V P n
N-COUNT
N-UNCOUNT

3 A **slim** book, wallet, or other object is thinner than usual. *The slim booklets describe a range of services and facilities... He published only three slim volumes of verse in his short life.*
ADJ-GRADED: usu ADJ n

4 A **slim** chance or possibility is a very small one. *There's still a slim chance that he may become Prime Minister.*
ADJ-GRADED =faint

5 If an organization **slims** its products, profits, or workforce, it reduces them. *The company recently slimmed its product line.*
VERB
V n

slim down
PHRASAL VERB

1 If a company or other organization **slims down** or is **slimmed down**, it employs less people, in order to save money or become more efficient. *Many firms have had little choice but to slim down. ...the plan to slim down the coal industry.*
ERG
V P
V P n (not pron)
Also V n P

2 See **slim** 2.

slime /slaɪm/. **Slime** is a thick, slippery substance which covers a surface or comes from the bodies of animals such as snails. *He swam down and retrieved his glasses from the muck and slime at the bottom of the pond.*
N-UNCOUNT

slimline /slɪmlaɪn/. **Slimline** objects are thinner or narrower than normal ones. *The slimline diary fits easily into a handbag.*
ADJ: usu ADJ n

slimy /slaɪmi/ **slimier, slimiest**

1 **Slimy** substances are thick, slippery, and unpleasant. **Slimy** objects have slippery unpleasant surfaces. *His feet slipped in the slimy mud... Her hand touched something cold and slimy.*
ADJ-GRADED

2 In informal British English, if you describe someone as **slimy**, you dislike them because they are friendly and pleasant in an insincere way. *I've worked hard for what I have and I don't want it taken away by some slimy business partner.*
ADJ-GRADED PRAGMATICS =oily

sling /slɪŋ/ **slings, slinging, slung** ◆◇◇◇◇

1 If you **sling** something somewhere, you throw it there carelessly. *Marla was recently seen slinging her shoes at Trump... I saw him take off his anorak and sling it into the back seat.*
VERB
V n prep/adv

2 If you **sling** something over your shoulder or over something such as a chair, you hang it there loosely. *She slung her coat over her desk chair... He had a small green rucksack slung over one shoulder. ...a police informer with a rifle slung across his back.*
VERB =chuck
V n prep

3 If a rope, blanket, or other object **is slung** be-
VB: usu passive

tween two points, someone has hung it loosely between them. *...two long poles with a blanket slung between them... We slept in hammocks slung beneath the roof.* beV-ed prep

4 A **sling** is an object made of ropes, straps, or cloth that is used for carrying things. *They used slings of rope to lower us from one set of arms to another.* N-COUNT

5 A **sling** is a piece of cloth which supports someone's broken or injured arm and is tied round their neck. *She was back at work with her arm in a sling.* N-COUNT

6 A baby **sling** is a device in which you carry a baby, either on your back or across your front. N-COUNT

7 See also **mud-slinging**.

8 **Slings and arrows** are unpleasant things that happen to you and that are not your fault; used in written English. *She had suffered her own share of slings and arrows in the quest for publicity.* PHRASE =tribulations

slingshot /slɪŋʃɒt/ **slingshots.** In American English, a **slingshot** is a **catapult**. N-COUNT

slink /slɪŋk/ **slinks, slinking, slunk.** If you **slink** somewhere, you move there in a slow and secretive way because you do not want to be seen. *He decided that he couldn't just slink away, so he went and sat next to his wife.* VERB =sneak V adv/prep

slinky /slɪŋki/ **slinkier, slinkiest. Slinky** clothes fit very closely to a woman's body in a way that makes her look sexually attractive. *She's wearing a slinky black mini-skirt.* ADJ-GRADED: usu ADJ n

slip /slɪp/ **slips, slipping, slipped** ◆◆◆◆◇

1 If you **slip**, you accidentally slide and lose your balance. *He had slipped on an icy pavement... Be careful not to slip.* VERB =slide V

2 If something **slips**, it slides out of place or out of your hand. *His glasses had slipped... The hammer slipped out of her grasp.* VERB V V prep/adv

3 If you **slip** somewhere, you go there quickly and quietly. *Amy slipped downstairs and out of the house... She slipped into the driving seat and closed the door.* VERB =slide V adv/prep

4 If you **slip** something somewhere, you put it there quickly in a way that does not attract attention. *I slipped a note under Louise's door... He found a coin in his pocket and slipped it into her collecting tin... Just slip in a piece of paper.* VERB =slide V n prep V n with adv

5 If you **slip** something to someone, you give it to them secretly. *Robert had slipped her a note in school... She looked round before pulling out a package and slipping it to the man.* VERB V n n V n *to* n

6 To **slip into** a particular state or situation means to pass gradually into it, in a way that is hardly noticed. *It amazed him how easily one could slip into a routine... There was 50-50 chance that the economy could slip back into recession.* VERB =slide V *into* n

7 If something **slips** to a lower level or standard, it falls to that level or standard. *Shares slipped to 117p... The club had slipped to the bottom of Division Four... In June, producer prices slipped 0.1% from May... Overall business activity is slipping.* ► Also a noun. *...a slip in consumer confidence.* VERB V *to/from/by* amount/n V amount V N-SING: oft N *in* n

8 If you **slip** into or out of clothes or shoes, you put them on or take them off quickly and easily. *She slipped out of the jacket and tossed it on the couch... I slipped off my woollen gloves.* VERB V *into/out of* n V n with *on/off*

9 A **slip** is a small or unimportant mistake. *We must be well prepared, there must be no slips.* N-COUNT =slip-up

10 A **slip** of paper is a small piece of paper. *...little slips of paper he had torn from a notebook... I put her name on the slip. ...credit card slips.* N-COUNT: oft N *of* n

11 A **slip** is a thin piece of clothing that a woman wears under her dress or skirt. N-COUNT =petticoat

12 If you refer to someone as a **slip of a** girl or a **slip of a** boy, you mean they are small, thin, and young; an informal use. *He's a mere slip of a lad compared to his brother... She was just a slip of a thing.* N-COUNT: usu sing, N *of* a n

13 See also **Freudian slip**.

14 If you **give** someone **the slip**, you escape from them when they are following you or watching you; an informal expression. *He gave reporters the slip by leaving at midnight.* PHRASES V inflects

15 If you **let slip** information, you accidentally tell it to someone, when you wanted to keep it secret. *I bet he let slip that I'd gone to America.* *let* inflects

16 If something **slips** your **mind**, you forget about it. *The reason for my visit had obviously slipped his mind.* V and N inflect

17 ● **slip through** your **fingers**: see **finger**. ● **slip of the tongue**: see **tongue**.

slip in. If you **slip in** a question or comment, you ask or make it without interrupting the flow of the conversation. *Slip in a few questions about other things... Skillfully Bush slipped in a reference to his own military service.* PHRASAL VERB V P n (not pron) Also V n P

slip through. If something **slips through** a set of checks or rules, it is accepted when in fact it should not be. *...hardened trouble-makers who have slipped through the security checks... The slightest little bit of inattention can let something slip through.* PHRASAL VERB V P n V P

slip up. If you **slip up**, you make a small or unimportant mistake. *There were occasions when we slipped up... You will see exactly where you are slipping up.* ● See also **slip-up**. PHRASAL VERB V P

slip-on, slip-ons. Slip-on shoes have no laces or buckles. *...slip-on boat shoes.* ► Also a noun. *He removed his brown slip-ons.* ADJ: ADJ n N-COUNT

slippage /slɪpɪdʒ/ **slippages. Slippage** is a failure to maintain a steady position or rate of progress, so that a particular target or standard is not achieved. *...a substantial slippage in the value of sterling... We want to stop the slippage of the quality of public services.* N-VAR

slipped disc, slipped discs. If you have a **slipped disc**, you have a bad back because one of the discs in your spine has moved out of its proper position. N-COUNT

slipper /slɪpəʳ/ **slippers. Slippers** are loose, soft shoes that you wear in the house. ◆◇◇◇◇ N-COUNT

slippery /slɪpəri/ ◆◇◇◇◇

1 Something that is **slippery** is smooth, wet, or greasy and is therefore difficult to walk on or to hold. *The tiled floor was wet and slippery... Motorists were warned to beware of slippery conditions.* ADJ-GRADED

2 You can describe someone as **slippery** if you think that they are dishonest in a clever way and cannot be trusted. *He is a slippery customer, and should be carefully watched.* ADJ-GRADED PRAGMATICS

3 If someone is on a **slippery slope**, they are involved in a course of action that is difficult to stop and that will eventually lead to failure or trouble. *The company started down the slippery slope of believing that they knew better than the customer.* PHRASE: N inflects, usu *down/on* PHR, oft PHR *to* n

slip road, slip roads. In British English, a **slip road** is a road which cars use to drive on and off a motorway. The usual American expressions are **entrance ramp** and **exit ramp**. N-COUNT

slipshod /slɪpʃɒd/. If something is **slipshod** it has been done without care or thoroughness. *The hotel had always been run in a slipshod way.* ADJ-GRADED: usu ADJ n =careless

slipstream /slɪpstriːm/ **slipstreams**

1 The **slipstream** of a fast-moving object such as a car, plane, or boat is the flow of air directly behind it. *Snow and ice will not collect during flight because of the slipstream of air around the hull.* N-COUNT: usu *the* N

2 If you are in the **slipstream** of someone, you are following their example. *...in the slipstream of various literary greats.* N-COUNT: with poss

slip-up, slip-ups. A **slip-up** is a small or unimportant mistake; an informal word. *There's been a slip-up somewhere... The girls had made three crucial slip-ups.* N-COUNT =slip

slipway /slɪpweɪ/ **slipways.** A **slipway** is a large platform that slopes down into the sea, from which boats are launched. N-COUNT

slit /slɪt/ **slits, slitting.** The form **slit** is used in the present tense and is the past tense and past participle. ◆◇◇◇◇

1 If you **slit** something, you make a long narrow cut in it. *They say somebody slit her throat... He began to slit open each envelope... She was wearing a white dress slit to the thigh.* VERB V n V n with *open* be V-ed *to/from* n

2 A **slit** is a long narrow cut. *Make a slit in the stem about half an inch long.* N-COUNT: oft N *in* n

3 A **slit** is a long narrow opening in something. *She watched them through a slit in the curtains.* N-COUNT: oft N in n

slither /slɪðəʳ/ **slithers, slithering, slithered** ◆◇◇◇◇
1 If you **slither** somewhere, you slide along in an uneven way. *Robert lost his footing and slithered down the bank.* VERB V prep/adv
2 If an animal such as a snake **slithers**, it moves along in a twisting way. *The snake slithered into the water.* VERB V prep/adv Also V

slithery /slɪðəri/. Something that is **slithery** is slippery and moves in a twisting way. *...slithery rice noodles. ...dresses in slithery fabrics.* ADJ-GRADED =slippery

sliver /slɪvəʳ/ **slivers.** A **sliver** of something is a small thin piece or amount of it. *Not a sliver of glass remains where the windows were... There was only one sliver of light in the darkness.* ◆◇◇◇◇ N-COUNT: usu N of n

Sloane /sloʊn/ **Sloanes.** Rich young people from upper middle class backgrounds in London are sometimes called **Sloanes** in British English; used showing disapproval. N-COUNT

slob /slɒb/ **slobs.** If you call someone a **slob**, you think they very lazy and untidy. *My boyfriend used to call me a fat slob.* N-COUNT

slobber /slɒbəʳ/ **slobbers, slobbering, slobbered.** If a person or an animal **slobbers**, they let liquid fall from their mouth. *...slobbering on his eternal cigarette end.* VERB =drool V prep Also V

sloe /sloʊ/ **sloes.** A **sloe** is a small, sour fruit that has a dark purple skin. It is often used to flavour gin. N-VAR

slog /slɒg/ **slogs, slogging, slogged** ◆◇◇◇◇
1 If you **slog** through something, you work hard and steadily through it; an informal use. *They secure their degrees by slogging through an intensive 11-month course... She has slogged her way through ballet classes since the age of six... While slogging at work, have you neglected your marriage?* ► **Slog away** means the same as **slog**. *Edward slogged away, always learning.* VERB V prep V way through n V PHRASAL VERB V P
2 If you describe a task as a **slog**, you mean that it is tiring and requires a lot of effort; an informal use. *I eventually got financial backing, but it was a slog... There is little to show for the two years of hard slog.* N-SING: also no det
3 If you **slog** somewhere, you make a long and tiring journey there; an informal use. *The men had to slog up a steep muddy incline... Why should Melissa have to slog around the supermarket on her own?.* VERB V prep/adv
4 A **slog** is a long tiring journey; an informal use. *...a slog through heather and bracken to the top of a hill.* N-SING
5 If two or more people **slog it out**, they work very hard to try to be the one who is successful or has their ideas and wishes accepted. *The leading contenders are still slogging it out.* PHRASE: V inflects =slug it out

slog away. See **slog** 1. PHRASAL VERB

slogan /sloʊgən/ **slogans.** A **slogan** is a short, easily-remembered phrase. Slogans are used in advertisements and by political parties and other organizations who want people to remember what they are saying or selling. *They could campaign on the slogan 'We'll take less of your money'. ...a group of angry demonstrators shouting slogans.* ◆◆◇◇◇ N-COUNT

sloganeering /sloʊgənɪərɪŋ/. **Sloganeering** is the use of slogans by people such as politicians or advertising agencies so that people will remember what they are saying or selling. *...the simple yet powerful sloganeering of her company's marketing department.* N-UNCOUNT

sloop /sluːp/ **sloops.** A **sloop** is a small sailing boat with one mast. N-COUNT

slop /slɒp/ **slops, slopping, slopped** ◆◇◇◇◇
1 If liquid **slops** or if you **slop** it, it spills over the edge of a container in a messy way. *A little cognac slopped over the edge of the glass... She slopped some tea into the saucer.* V-ERG V adv/prep V n adv/prep Also V, V n
2 You can use **slop** or **slops** to refer to liquid waste containing the remains of food. *Breakfast plates were collected and the slops emptied.* N-UNCOUNT: also N in pl

slope /sloʊp/ **slopes, sloping, sloped** ◆◆◇◇◇
1 A **slope** is the side of a mountain, hill, or valley. *Saint-Christo is perched on a mountain slope. ...the lower slopes of the Himalayas.* N-COUNT: usu with supp
2 A **slope** is a surface that is at an angle, so that one end is higher than the other. *The street must have been on a slope.* N-COUNT: usu sing =incline
3 If a surface **slopes**, it is at an angle, so that one end is higher than the other. *The bank sloped down sharply to the river... The garden sloped quite steeply.* ♦ **sloping** *...a brick building, with a sloping roof. ...the gently sloping beach.* VERB V adv/prep V ADJ-GRADED
4 If something **slopes**, it leans to the right or to the left rather than being upright. *The writing sloped backwards... He wonders why the digits on his calculator slope to the right.* VERB =slant V adv/prep
5 The **slope** of something is the angle at which it slopes. *The slope increases as you go up the curve. ...a slope of ten degrees.* N-COUNT: usu sing, oft N of n
6 If someone **slopes** into or out of a place, they enter or leave it quickly and quietly, especially because they are trying to avoid or escape something; an informal use. *She sloped off quietly on Saturday afternoon... They sloped into their hotel at 6am.* VERB =slink V adv/prep
7 See also **ski slope.**
8 ● **slippery slope**: see **slippery.**

slopping out; also spelled **slopping-out.** In prisons where prisoners have to use buckets as toilets, **slopping out** is the practice in which they empty the buckets. N-UNCOUNT

sloppy /slɒpi/ **sloppier, sloppiest** ◆◇◇◇◇
1 If you describe someone's work or activities as **sloppy**, you mean they have been done in a careless and lazy way. *He has little patience for sloppy work from colleagues... His language is disjointed and sloppy.* ♦ **sloppily** /slɒpɪli/ *They lost because they played sloppily.* ♦ **sloppiness** *Miss Furniss could not abide sloppiness.* ADJ-GRADED =slack ADV-GRADED: ADV with v N-UNCOUNT
2 If you describe someone or something as **sloppy**, you are laughing at them because you think they are sentimental and romantic. *It's ideal for people who like a sloppy movie. ...some sloppy love-story.* ADJ-GRADED PRAGMATICS =slushy

slosh /slɒʃ/ **sloshes, sloshing, sloshed**
1 If a liquid **sloshes** around or if you **slosh** it around, it splashes or moves around in a messy way. *The water sloshed around the bridge... He took a mouthful of the cheap wine and sloshed it around his mouth... The champagne sloshed and spilt.* V-ERG V adv/prep V n adv/prep V Also V n
2 If you **slosh** through mud or water, you walk through it, making a splashing sound. *The two girls joined arms and sloshed through the mud together.* VERB V adv/prep

sloshed /slɒʃt/. In British English, if someone is **sloshed**, they are drunk; an informal word. *Everyone else around them was getting sloshed.* ADJ-GRADED: v-link ADJ =plastered

slot /slɒt/ **slots, slotting, slotted** ◆◆◇◇◇
1 A **slot** is a narrow opening in a machine or container, for example a hole that you put coins in to make a machine work. *He dropped a coin into the slot and dialed.* N-COUNT
2 If you **slot** something into something else, or if it **slots** into it, you put it into a space where it fits. *He was slotting a CD into a CD player... The car seat belt slotted into place easily... She slotted in a fresh filter.* V-ERG V n into/in/onto n V into/in/onto n V n with adv
3 A **slot** in a schedule or scheme is a place in it where an activity can take place. *Visitors can book a time slot a week or more in advance... The first episode occupies a peak evening viewing slot.* N-COUNT: oft n N

sloth /sloʊθ/. **sloths**
1 **Sloth** is laziness, especially with regard to work; a formal word. *Employers claimed that the workers were lazy, bringing the sloth of the countryside to the mines.* N-UNCOUNT =idleness
2 A **sloth** is an animal from Central and South America. Sloths live in trees and move very slowly. N-COUNT

slothful /sloʊθfʊl/. Someone who is **slothful** is lazy and unwilling to make an effort to work; a formal word. *He was not slothful: he had been busy all night.* ADJ-GRADED =idle

slot machine, slot machines. A **slot machine** is a machine from which you can get food or cigarettes or on which you can gamble. You make it work by putting coins into a slot. N-COUNT

slotted spoon, slotted spoons. A **slotted spoon** is a large plastic or metal spoon with holes or slits in it. It is used to drain liquid from food.
N-COUNT

slouch /slaʊtʃ/ **slouches, slouching, slouched** ◆◇◇◇◇

1 If someone **slouches**, they sit or stand with their shoulders and head drooping so they look lazy and unattractive. *Try not to slouch when you are sitting down... She has recently begun to slouch over her typewriter.* ► Also a noun. *He straightened himself from a slouch.* ♦ **slouched** *The men were slouched on sofas and chairs... She had been slouched against the counter.*
VERB; V; V prep/adv; N-SING; ADJ: v-link ADJ, usu ADJ prep

2 If someone **slouches** somewhere, they walk around slowly with their shoulders and heads drooping looking lazy or bored. *Most of the time, they slouch around in the fields... Scowling, the lad slouched over.*
VERB; V adv/prep

3 If you say that someone is **no slouch** at a particular activity, you mean that they are skilful at it or are willing to work hard at it. *The Welsh are no slouches at cooking.*
PHRASE: N inflects, usu v-link PHR

slough /slʌf/ **sloughs, sloughing, sloughed.** ◆◇◇◇◇ When a plant **sloughs** its leaves, or an animal such as a snake **sloughs** its skin, the leaves or skin come off naturally. *All reptiles have to slough their skin to grow... The lemon geranium sloughs dry brown leaves at the base of its branches.* ► **Slough off** means the same as **slough**. *Our bodies slough off dead cells.*
VERB =shed; V n; Also V; PHRASAL VERB =shed; V P n (not pron); Also V n P

slough off
PHRASAL VERB

1 See **slough** 1.

2 If you **slough off** something that you no longer want or need, you get rid of it; used in written English. *She tried hard to slough off her old personality... The nation states of Eastern Europe finally sloughed off their totalitarian regimes.*
=get rid of; V P n (not pron); Also V n P

slovenly /slʌvᵊnli/. **Slovenly** people are careless, untidy, or inefficient. *Lisa was irritated by the slovenly attitude of her boyfriend Sean.*
ADJ-GRADED: usu ADJ n =sloppy

slow /sloʊ/ **slower, slowest; slows, slowing, slowed** ◆◆◆◆◇

1 Something that is **slow** moves, happens, or is done without much speed. *The traffic is heavy and slow... Electric whisks should be used on a slow speed. ...slow, regular breathing.* ♦ **slowly** *He spoke slowly and deliberately... Christian backed slowly away.* ♦ **slowness** *She lowered the glass with calculated slowness.*
ADJ-GRADED ≠fast; ADV-GRADED: ADV with v; N-UNCOUNT

2 In informal English, **slower** is used to mean 'at a slower speed' and **slowest** is used to mean 'at the slowest speed'. In non-standard English, **slow** is used to mean 'with little speed'. *I began to walk slower and slower... We got there by driving slow all the way.*
ADV-GRADED: ADV after v

3 Something that is **slow** takes a long time. *The distribution of passports has been a slow process.* ♦ **slowly** *My resentment of her slowly began to fade.* ♦ **slowness** *...the slowness of political and economic progress.*
ADJ-GRADED; ADV-GRADED: ADV with v; N-UNCOUNT

4 If someone is **slow** to do something, they do it after a delay. *The world community has been slow to respond to the crisis... I've been a bit slow in making up my mind.*
ADJ-GRADED: v-link ADJ, usu ADJ to-inf, ADJ *in*-ing

5 If something **slows** or if you **slow** it, it starts to move or happen more slowly. *The rate of bombing has slowed considerably... She slowed the car and began driving up a narrow road... Reactions were slowed by fatigue.*
V-ERG; V; V n

6 Someone who is **slow** is not very clever and takes a long time to understand things. *He got hit on the head and he's been a bit slow since.*
ADJ-GRADED ≠bright

7 If you describe a situation, place, or activity as **slow**, you mean that it is not very exciting. *Don't be faint-hearted when things seem a bit slow or boring... The island is too slow for her liking.*
ADJ-GRADED =quiet ≠lively

8 If a clock or watch is **slow**, it shows a time that is earlier than the correct time.
ADJ-GRADED: usu v-link ADJ ≠fast

9 See also **slow-**.

10 • **slow off the mark**: see **mark**. • **slowly but surely**: see **surely**. • **slow on the uptake**: see **uptake**.

slow down
PHRASAL VERB

1 If something **slows down** or is if something **slows** it **down**, it starts to move or happen more slowly. *The car slowed down as they passed Customs... There is no cure for the disease, although drugs can slow down its rate of development... Damage to the turbine slowed the work down.*
ERG =slow up ≠speed up; V P; V P n (not pron); V n P

2 If someone **slows down** or if something **slows** them **down**, they become less active. *You will need to slow down for a while... He was still taking some medication which slowed him down.*
ERG; V P; V n P

3 See also **slowdown.**

slow up. Slow up means the same as **slow down** 1. *Sales are slowing up... The introduction of a new code of criminal procedure has also slowed up the system.*
PHRASAL VERB ERG; V P; V P n (not pron); Also V n P

slow- /sloʊ-/ **slow-** is used to form words which describe something that happens slowly. *He was stuck in a line of slow-moving traffic. ...a slow-burning fuse.*
COMB in ADJ-GRADED

slowdown /sloʊdaʊn/ **slowdowns** ◆◇◇◇◇

1 A **slowdown** is a reduction in speed or activity. *There has been a sharp slowdown in economic growth.*
N-COUNT

2 In American English, a **slowdown** is a protest in which workers deliberately work slowly and cause problems for their employers. The British term is a **go-slow**. *It's impossible to assess how many officers are participating in the slowdown.*
N-COUNT

slow lane, slow lanes

1 On a motorway, the **slow lane** is the lane for vehicles which are moving more slowly than the other vehicles.
N-COUNT: usu sing

2 If you say that a country or company is in the **slow lane**, you mean that they are not progressing as fast as other countries or companies in a particular area of activity. *Germany was not trying to push Britain into the slow lane... If they are wrong, both of them will end up in the corporate slow lane.*
N-SING

slow motion; also spelled **slow-motion**. When film or television pictures are shown in **slow motion**, they are shown much more slowly than normal. *It seemed almost as if he were falling in slow motion... This can be seen easily with the benefit of slow motion video playback.*
◆◇◇◇◇ N-UNCOUNT: usu *in* N

slow-witted. Someone who is **slow-witted** is slow to understand things.
ADJ-GRADED

sludge /slʌdʒ/ **sludges. Sludge** is thick mud, sewage, or industrial waste. *All dumping of sludge will be banned by 1998.*
◆◇◇◇◇ N-VAR

slug /slʌg/ **slugs, slugging, slugged** ◆◇◇◇◇

1 A **slug** is a small slow-moving creature with a long slimy body, like a snail without a shell.
N-COUNT

2 If you take a **slug** of an alcoholic drink, you take a large mouthful of it; an informal use. *Edgar took a slug of his drink.*
N-COUNT: usu N *of* n =shot

3 If you **slug** someone, you hit them hard; an informal use. *She slugged her right in the face... He felt as if he had been slugged by a piece of lead pipe.*
VERB =sock; V n

4 A **slug** is a bullet; used mainly in informal American English.
N-COUNT

5 If two or more people **slug it out**, they work very hard to try to be the one who is successful or has their ideas and wishes accepted. *Four candidates are slugging it out in a dirty campaign.*
PHRASE: V inflects =slog it out

slugger /slʌgəʳ/ **sluggers.** In baseball, a **slugger** is a player who hits the ball very hard.
N-COUNT

sluggish /slʌgɪʃ/. You can describe something as **sluggish** if it moves, works, or reacts much slower than you would like or is normal. *The economy remains sluggish... Circulation is much more sluggish in the feet than in the hands. ...the sluggish pace of reforms.* ♦ **sluggishly** *The company has responded sluggishly to these changes in technology.* ♦ **sluggishness** *...the sluggishness of Britain's economic recovery.*
◆◇◇◇◇ ADJ-GRADED; ADV-GRADED: ADV after v, also ADV adj; N-UNCOUNT

sluice /sluːs/ **sluices, sluicing, sluiced**

1 A **sluice** is a passage that carries a current of water and has an opening, called a sluice-gate, which can be opened and closed to control the flow of water.
N-COUNT

2 If you **sluice** something or **sluice** if down or out,
VERB

you wash it with a stream of water. *After he had sluiced the bath and while waiting for it to fill he shaved himself... Ten minutes later we were sluicing off dust at the fountain in the town centre.* V n / V n with adv

slum /slʌm/ **slums, slumming, slummed** ◆◇◇◇◇
1 A **slum** is an area of a city where living conditions are very bad and where the houses are in bad condition. *...a slum area of St Louis. ...inner-city slums in the old cities of the north and east.* N-COUNT: oft N n =ghetto
2 If someone **is slumming it** or **is slumming**, they are spending time in a place or in conditions that are at a much lower social level than they are used to. *...rich kids slumming it. ...aristocratic types who enjoyed slumming around in musty old Scottish castles.* VB: usu cont / V it / V

slumber /slʌmbəʳ/ **slumbers, slumbering, slumbered.** **Slumber** is sleep; a literary word. *He had fallen into exhausted slumber... He roused Charles from his slumbers.* ► Also a verb. *The older three girls are still slumbering peacefully.* N-VAR / VERB / V

slump /slʌmp/ **slumps, slumping, slumped** ◆◆◇◇◇
1 If something such as the value of something **slumps**, it falls suddenly and by a large amount. *Net profits slumped by 41%... Government popularity in Scotland has slumped to its lowest level since the 1970s.* ► Also a noun. *The council's land is now worth much less than originally hoped because of a slump in property prices.* VERB / V prep / Also V / N-COUNT: oft N *in* n
2 A **slump** is a time when there is a lot of unemployment and poverty in a country. *...the slump of the early 1980s.* N-COUNT =recession
3 If you **slump** somewhere, you fall or sit down there heavily, for example because you are very tired or you feel ill. *She slumped into a chair... He saw the driver slumped over the wheel.* VERB / V prep/adv / V-ed

slung /slʌŋ/. **Slung** is the past tense and past participle of **sling**.

slunk /slʌŋk/. **Slunk** is the past tense and past participle of **slink**.

slur /slɜːʳ/ **slurs, slurring, slurred** ◆◇◇◇◇
1 A **slur** is an insulting remark which could damage someone's reputation. *This is yet another slur on the integrity of the Metropolitan Police. ...racial slurs.* N-COUNT: oft N *on* n =smear
2 If someone **slurs** their speech or if their speech **slurs**, they do not pronounce each word clearly and distinctly, because they are drunk, ill, or sleepy. *He repeated himself and slurred his words more than usual... The newscaster's speech began to slur... 'Hey, you're gorgeous,' he slurred.* ♦ **slurred** *Her speech was so slurred as to be almost incomprehensible.* V-ERG / V n / V / V with quote / ADJ-GRADED

slurp /slɜːʳp/ **slurps, slurping, slurped**
1 If you **slurp** a liquid, you drink it noisily. *He blew on his soup before slurping it off the spoon... He slurped down a cup of sweet, black coffee.* VERB / V n *from/off* n / V adv n / Also V n, V
2 A **slurp** is a noise that you make with your mouth when you drink noisily. It is also the mouthful of liquid that you are drinking noisily. *He takes a slurp from a cup of black coffee.* N-COUNT

slurry /slʌri, AM slɜːri/ **slurries.** **Slurry** is a watery mixture of something such as mud, animal waste, or dust. *...farm slurry and industrial waste.* N-VAR =sludge

slush /slʌʃ/
1 **Slush** is snow that has begun to melt and is therefore very wet and dirty. *Becker's eyes were as cold and grey as the slush on the pavements outside.* N-UNCOUNT
2 If you describe a love story as **slush**, you mean that you dislike it because it is too sentimental and cannot be taken seriously. N-UNCOUNT PRAGMATICS

slush fund, slush funds. A **slush fund** is a sum of money collected to pay for an illegal activity, especially in politics or business. *He's accused of misusing $17.5 million from a secret government slush fund.* N-COUNT

slushy /slʌʃi/ **slushier, slushiest**
1 **Slushy** ground is covered in dirty, wet snow. *Here and there a drift across the road was wet and slushy.* ADJ-GRADED
2 If you describe a story or idea as **slushy**, you mean you dislike it because it is extremely romantic and sentimental. ADJ-GRADED PRAGMATICS

slut /slʌt/ **sluts.** People sometimes refer to a woman as a **slut** when they consider her to be very immoral in her sexual behaviour; a rude and offensive word. N-COUNT PRAGMATICS

sly /slaɪ/ ◆◇◇◇◇
1 A **sly** look, expression, or remark shows that you know something that other people do not know or that was meant to be a secret. *His lips were spread in a sly smile... He gave me a sly, meaningful look.* ♦ **slyly** *Anna grinned slyly.* ADJ-GRADED: usu ADJ n / ADV-GRADED
2 If you describe someone as **sly**, you disapprove of them because they are secretive and clever at deceiving people. *She is devious and sly and manipulative... He's a sly old beggar if ever there was one.* ADJ-GRADED PRAGMATICS =cunning
3 If someone does something **on the sly**, they do it in a secretive way, often because it is something that they should not be doing; an informal expression. *Was she meeting some guy on the sly?* PHRASE: PHR after v =on the quiet

smack /smæk/ **smacks, smacking, smacked** ◆◆◇◇◇
1 If you **smack** someone, you hit them with your hand. *She smacked me on the side of the head.* ► Also a noun. *Sometimes he just doesn't listen and I end up shouting at him or giving him a smack.* VERB / V n / N-COUNT
2 If you **smack** something somewhere, you put it or throw it there so that it makes a loud, sharp noise. *He smacked his hands down on his knees... Ray Houghton smacked the ball against a post.* VERB / V n adv/prep
3 If one thing **smacks of** another thing that you consider bad, it reminds you of it or is like it. *The engineers' union was unhappy with the motion, saying it smacked of racism.* VERB / V *of* n
4 Something that is **smack** in a particular place is exactly in that place; an informal use. *In part that's because industry is smack in the middle of the city.* ADV: ADV prep =slap bang
5 In informal English, **smack** is **heroin**. N-UNCOUNT
6 If you **smack** your **lips**, you open and close your mouth noisily, especially before or after eating, to show that you are keen to eat or enjoyed eating. *'I really want some dessert,' Keaton says, smacking his lips.* PHRASE: V inflects

small /smɔːl/ **smaller, smallest** ◆◆◆◆◆
1 A **small** person, thing, or amount of something is not large in physical size. *She is small for her age... The window was far too small for him to get through... Next door to the garage is a small orchard area... Stick them on using a small amount of glue.* ♦ **smallness** *Amy had not mentioned the smallness and bareness of Luis's home.* ADJ-GRADED ≠big / N-UNCOUNT ≠largeness
2 A **small** group or quantity consists of only a few people or things. *A small group of students meets regularly to learn Japanese... Guns continued to be produced in small numbers.* ADJ-GRADED ≠large
3 A **small** child is a very young child. *I have a wife and two small children... What were you like when you were small?* ADJ-GRADED =young
4 You use **small** to describe something that is not significant or great in degree. *It's quite easy to make quite small changes to the way that you work... No detail was too small to escape her attention... He believes this to be a relatively small problem.* ADJ-GRADED =minor ≠major
5 **Small** businesses or companies employ a small number of people and do business with a small number of clients. *...shops, restaurants and other small businesses... Tool companies here are generally small.* ADJ-GRADED
6 If someone speaks in a **small** voice, they speak very quietly and softly, because they are frightened or ashamed. *'I'm scared,' she said in a very small voice.* ADJ-GRADED: ADJ n ≠loud
7 If someone makes you look or feel **small**, they make you look or feel stupid, so that you are ashamed or humiliated. *This may just be another of her schemes to make me look small... When your children misbehave tell them without making them feel small.* ADJ-GRADED: v-link ADJ =stupid
8 **The small of** your back is the bottom part of your back that curves inwards slightly. *Place your hands on the small of your back and breathe in.* N-SING: *the* N *of* n
9 See also **smalls.** • **the small hours**: see **hour**. • **small wonder**: see **wonder**.

small ad, small ads. The **small ads** in a newspaper are short advertisements in which you can N-COUNT: usu *the* N in pl advertise something such as an object for sale or a room to let. *Prospective buyers should study the small ads in the daily newspaper.*

small arms. **Small arms** are guns that are light and easy to carry. *The two sides exchanged small arms fire for about three hours.* N-PLURAL =handgun

small beer. In British English, if you say that something is **small beer**, you mean it is unimportant in comparison with something else. *The arrangement and furnishing of public spaces is small beer compared with saving the rainforests.* N-UNCOUNT =peanuts

small change. **Small change** is coins of low value. *She was counting out 30p, mostly in small change, into my hand.* N-UNCOUNT

small fry; **small fry** is both the singular and the plural form. **Small fry** is used to refer to someone or something that is considered to be unimportant. *They owed £92,897 to the Inland Revenue. But that is small fry compared to the overall £1.2 million debt... It's the small fry who are usually the last to get paid.* N-UNCOUNT: also N in pl

smallholder /smɔːlhoʊldəʳ/ **smallholders.** A **smallholder** is someone who has a smallholding. N-COUNT

smallholding /smɔːlhoʊldɪŋ/ **smallholdings.** A **smallholding** is a piece of land used for farming that is smaller than a normal farm. *A smallholding in the hills could not support a large family.* N-COUNT

small hours. If something happens in the **small hours**, it happens shortly after midnight, in the very early morning. *They were arrested in the small hours of Saturday morning.* N-PLURAL: usu *in the* N, oft N *of* n

smallish /smɔːlɪʃ/. Something that is **smallish** is fairly small. *Some smallish firms may close... The pool is smallish and more crowded than most.* ADJ ≠largish

small-minded. If you say that someone is **small-minded**, you are critical of them because they have fixed opinions and are unwilling to change them or to think about more general subjects. *...their small-minded preoccupation with making money.* ♦ **small-mindedness** *Helen's small-mindedness bored and disgusted her.* ADJ-GRADED PRAGMATICS ≠open-minded; N-UNCOUNT

smallpox /smɔːlpɒks/. **Smallpox** is a serious infectious disease that causes a rash and leaves deep scars on the skin. N-UNCOUNT

small print. The **small print** of a contract or agreement is the part of it that is written in very small print. You refer to this part as the **small print** especially when you think that it might include unfavourable conditions which someone might not notice or understand. *Read the small print in your contract to find out exactly what you are insured for.* ◆◇◇◇◇ N-UNCOUNT: usu *the* N =fine print

smalls /smɔːlz/. In informal British English, your **smalls** are your underwear. N-PLURAL

small-scale. A **small-scale** activity or organization is small in size and limited in extent. *...the small-scale production of farmhouse cheeses in Devon.* ◆◇◇◇◇ ADJ-GRADED: usu ADJ n ≠large-scale

small screen. When people talk about **the small screen**, they are referring to television, in contrast to films that are made for the cinema. *Now he is also to become a star of the small screen... Live concerts are never quite the same on the small screen.* N-SING: usu *the* N ≠big screen

small talk. **Small talk** is polite conversation about unimportant things that people make at social occasions. *Smiling for the cameras, the two men strained to make small talk.* N-UNCOUNT

small-time. If you refer to workers or businesses as **small-time**, you think they are not very important because they work only on a small-scale. *During my youth I knew all the small time drug dealers and criminals. ...a small-time actress and model.* ADJ-GRADED ≠big-time

smalltown /smɔːltaʊn/. In American English, **smalltown** is used to refer to people or places that have characteristics such as friendliness, honesty, and politeness. A smalltown person can also be considered narrow-minded. *She seemed to be living the dream teenage life in smalltown America... The guy in charge was the typical smalltown tyrant.* ADJ: usu ADJ n

smarmy /smɑːʳmi/ **smarmier, smarmiest.** In British English, if you describe someone as **smarmy**, you dislike them because they are unpleasantly polite and flattering, usually because they want you to like them or to do something for them. *Rick is slightly smarmy and eager to impress.* ADJ-GRADED =ingratiating

smart /smɑːʳt/ **smarter, smartest; smarts, smarting, smarted** ◆◆◆◇◇

1 **Smart** people and things are pleasantly neat and clean in appearance; used mainly in British English. *He was smart and well groomed but not good looking... I was dressed in a smart navy blue suit. ...smart new offices.* ♦ **smartly** *He dressed very smartly which was important in those days. ...a smartly-painted door.* ♦ **smartness** *The jumper strikes the perfect balance between comfort and smartness.* ADJ-GRADED =neat; ADV-GRADED: ADV with v; N-UNCOUNT

2 You can describe someone who is clever as **smart**. *He thinks he's smarter than Sarah is... Buying expensive furniture is not necessarily the smartest move to make.* ● See also **smartly**; **street smart**. ADJ-GRADED =clever

3 A **smart** place or event is connected with wealthy and fashionable people. *...smart London dinner parties. ...a smart residential district.* ADJ-GRADED: usu ADJ n

4 **Smart** bombs and weapons are guided by computers and lasers so that they hit their targets accurately. ADJ: ADJ n

5 If a part of your body or a wound **smarts**, you feel a sharp stinging pain in it. *My eyes smarted from the smoke.* VERB =sting V

6 If you **are smarting** from something such as criticism or failure, you feel upset about it; used mainly in journalism. *The Americans were still smarting from their defeat in the Vietnam War... He is still smarting over criticism of his victorious but clumsy performance.* VB: usu cont; V *from* n; V prep

7 **The smart set** is a group of fashionable and wealthy people; used mainly in journalism. *...Spago, favourite eating place of the Los Angeles smart set.* ● **the smart money**: see **money**. PHRASE

smart alec, smart alecs; also spelled **smart aleck**. If you describe someone as a **smart alec**, you dislike the fact that they think they are very clever and always have an answer for everything; an informal word. *...a fortyish smart-alec TV reporter... You'll end up no more than a smart alec and you're well down that road already.* N-COUNT: oft N n PRAGMATICS

smartarse /smɑːʳtɑːʳs/ **smartarses;** also spelled **smartass**. If you describe someone as a **smartarse**, you dislike the fact that they think they are very clever and like to show everyone this; an informal word which some people find offensive. *...smartass comments.* N-COUNT: oft N n PRAGMATICS

smart card, smart cards. A **smart card** is a plastic card which looks like a credit card and can store and process computer data. N-COUNT

smart drug, smart drugs. **Smart drugs** are drugs which some people think can improve your memory and intelligence. N-COUNT: usu pl

smarten /smɑːʳtᵊn/ **smartens, smartening, smartened**

smarten up. If you **smarten** yourself or a place **up**, you make yourself or the place look neater and tidier. *...a 10-year programme to smarten up the London Underground... She had wisely smartened herself up. ...a medical student who refused to smarten up.* PHRASAL VERB =tidy up; V P n (not pron); V n P; V P

smartly /smɑːʳtli/. If someone moves or does something **smartly**, they do it quickly and neatly; used in written English. *The housekeeper moved smartly to the Vicar's desk to answer the call... Stacey saluted smartly.* ● See also **smart**. ◆◇◇◇◇ ADV-GRADED: ADV with v

smash /smæʃ/ **smashes, smashing, smashed** ◆◆◆◇◇

1 If you **smash** something or if it **smashes**, it breaks into many pieces, for example when it is hit or dropped. *Someone smashed a bottle... A crowd of youths started smashing windows... Two or three glasses fell off and smashed into pieces.* V-ERG =break; V n; V *into* n

2 If you **smash** through a wall, gate, or door, you VERB get through it by hitting and breaking it. *The demonstrators used trucks to smash through embassy gates... Soldiers smashed their way into his office.* V through n; V way prep/adv

3 If something **smashes** or **is smashed** against something solid, it moves very fast and with great force against it. *The bottle smashed against a wall... He smashed his fist into Anthony's face.* V-ERG; V prep/adv; V n prep

4 To **smash** a political group or system means to deliberately destroy it; an informal use. *The President said he would smash the communists.* VERB; V n

5 A **smash** is the same as a **smash hit**. *It is the public who decide if a film is a smash or a flop.* N-COUNT

6 You can refer to a car crash as a **smash**; an informal use. *He was near to death after a car smash.* N-COUNT

7 See also **smashed, smashing**.

smash down. If you **smash down** a door, building, or other large heavy object, you hit it hard and break it until it falls on the ground. *The crowd tried to smash down the door of the police station.* PHRASAL VERB =break down; V P n (not pron); Also V n P

smash up PHRASAL VERB

1 If you **smash** something **up**, you completely destroy it by hitting it and breaking it into many pieces. *She took revenge on her ex-boyfriend by smashing up his home... You could smash the drawer up with a hammer... Office material worth hundreds of thousands of pounds was smashed up.* V P n (not pron); V n P

2 If you **smash up** your car, you damage it by crashing it into something. *All you told me was that he'd smashed up yet another car.* =wreck; V P n (not pron); Also V n P

smash-and-grab, smash-and-grabs; also spelled **smash and grab**. A **smash-and-grab** is a robbery in which a person smashes a shop window, seizes the things that are on display there, and rushes away with them. *...a smash and grab raid.* N-COUNT: oft N n

smashed /smæʃt/. Someone who is **smashed** is extremely drunk; an informal word. ADJ: usu v-link ADJ

smash hit, smash hits. A **smash hit** or **smash** is a very popular show, play, or song. *The show was a smash hit.* N-COUNT

smashing /smæʃɪŋ/. In British English, if you describe something or someone as **smashing**, you mean that you like them very much; an old-fashioned, informal word. *It was smashing. I really enjoyed it... She's a smashing girl.* ◆◇◇◇◇ ADJ

smattering /smætərɪŋ/. A **smattering** of something is a very small amount of it. *I had acquired a pretty competent knowledge of Latin and a smattering of Greek grammar.* N-SING: usu a N of n =modicum

smear /smɪəʳ/ **smears, smearing, smeared** ◆◇◇◇◇

1 If you **smear** a surface with a greasy or sticky substance or **smear** the substance onto the surface, you spread a layer of the substance over the surface. *My sister smeared herself with suntan oil and slept by the swimming pool... Smear a little olive oil over the inside of the salad bowl.* VERB; V n with n; V n prep

2 A **smear** is a dirty or greasy mark. *There was a smear of gravy on his chin.* N-COUNT: oft N of n

3 To **smear** someone means to spread unpleasant and untrue rumours or accusations about them in order to damage their reputation; used mainly in journalism. *The BBC last night launched an inquiry into an apparently crude attempt to smear its director-general.* VERB =sully; V n

4 A **smear** is an unpleasant and untrue rumour or accusation that is intended to damage someone's reputation; used mainly in journalism. *He puts all the accusations down to a smear campaign by his political opponents.* N-COUNT: oft N n =slur

5 A **smear** or a **smear test** is a medical test in which a few cells are taken from a woman's cervix and analysed to see if any cancer cells are present. N-COUNT

smeared /smɪəʳd/. If something is **smeared**, it has dirty or greasy marks on it. *The other child's face was smeared with dirt. ...long, smeared windows.* ◆◇◇◇◇ ADJ-GRADED

smell /smel/ **smells, smelling, smelled, smelt** ◆◆◆◇◇

1 The **smell** of something is a quality it has which you become aware of when you breathe in through your nose. *...the smell of freshly baked bread. ...horrible smells... What is your favourite smell?* N-COUNT: oft N of n

2 Your sense of **smell** is the ability that your nose has to detect things. *...people who lose their sense of smell.* N-UNCOUNT

3 If something **smells** in a particular way, it has a quality which you become aware of through your nose. *The room smelled of lemons... It smells delicious. ...a crumbly black substance that smells like fresh soil.* V-LINK; V of n; V adj; V like n; Also V as if

4 If you say that something **smells**, you mean that it smells unpleasant. *Ma threw that out. She said it smelled... Do my feet smell?* VERB; V

5 If you **smell** something, you become aware of it when you breathe in through your nose. *As soon as we opened the front door we could smell the gas.* VERB; V n

6 If you **smell** something, you put your nose near it and breathe in, so that you can discover its smell. *I took a fresh rose out of the vase on our table, and smelled it.* VERB =sniff; V n

7 If you **smell** something, you feel instinctively that it is likely to happen or be true. *He knew virtually nothing about music but he could smell a hit.* VERB; V n

8 ● to **smell a rat**: see **rat**.

-smelling /-smelɪŋ/. **-smelling** combines with adjectives to form adjectives which indicate how something smells. *...sweet-smelling dried flowers... The city is covered by a foul-smelling cloud of smoke.* COMB in ADJ-GRADED

smelling salts. A bottle of **smelling salts** contains a chemical with a strong smell which is used to help someone recover after they have fainted. N-PLURAL

smelly /smeli/ **smellier, smelliest.** Something that is **smelly** has an unpleasant smell. *He had extremely smelly feet... Pubs are dirty, smelly and unfriendly, according to the Good Pub Guide.* ◆◇◇◇◇ ADJ-GRADED

smelt /smelt/ **smelts, smelting, smelted**

1 Smelt is a past tense and past participle of **smell**.

2 To **smelt** a substance containing metal means to process it by heating it until it melts, so that the metal is extracted and changed chemically. *Darby was looking for a way to improve iron when he hit upon the idea of smelting it with coke instead of charcoal.* VERB; V n

smelter /smeltəʳ/ **smelters.** A **smelter** is a furnace for smelting metal. N-COUNT

smidgen /smɪdʒɪn/ **smidgens;** also spelled **smidgeon** or **smidgin**. A **smidgen** is a small amount of something; an informal word. *...a smidgen of tobacco. ...a smidgeon of luck... She arrives a smidgen ahead of time.* N-COUNT: oft N of n

smile /smaɪl/ **smiles, smiling, smiled** ◆◆◆◆◇

1 When you **smile**, the corners of your mouth curve upwards and you sometimes show your teeth. People smile when they are pleased or amused, or when they are being friendly. *When he saw me, he smiled and waved... He rubbed the back of his neck and smiled ruefully at me... His smiling face appears on T-shirts, billboards, and posters.* VERB; V; V at n; V-ing

2 A **smile** is the expression that you have on your face when you smile. *She gave a wry smile... 'There are some sandwiches if you're hungry,' she said with a smile... She had a big smile on her face.* N-COUNT

3 If you **smile** something, you say it with a smile or express it by a smile. *'Aren't we daft?' she smiled... She smiled her thanks and arranged the guitar under her arm.* VERB; V with quote; V n

4 If you say that something such as fortune **smiles** on someone, you mean that they are lucky or successful; a literary use. *When fortune smiled on him, he made the most of it... God is not smiling on our cause.* VERB; V on/upon n

5 If you say that someone is **all smiles**, you mean that they look very happy, often when they have previously been worried or upset about something. PHRASE: v-link PHR

smiley /smaɪli/. A **smiley** person smiles a lot or is smiling; an informal word. *Two smiley babies are waiting for their lunch.* ADJ-GRADED: usu ADJ n

smilingly /smaɪlɪŋli/. If someone does something **smilingly**, they smile as they do it; used in written English. *He opened the gate and smilingly welcomed the travellers home.* ADV: ADV with v

smirk /smɜːʳk/ **smirks, smirking, smirked.** If you **smirk**, you smile in an unpleasant way, often because you believe that you have gained an advantage over someone else or know something that they do not know. *Two men standing nearby looked at me, nudged each other and smirked... A dozen people were watching her, smirking at her discomfort.* ▶ Also a noun. *Her mouth was drawn back into a smirk of triumph.* ◆◇◇◇◇ VERB V V at n N-COUNT

smite /smaɪt/ **smites, smiting, smote, smitten.** To **smite** something meants to hit it hard; a literary word. *Agassi would smite the ball so hard that Becker was left groping at thin air.* ● See also **smitten.** VERB =smack V n

smithereens /smɪðəriːnz/. If something is smashed or blown to **smithereens**, it breaks into very small pieces. *She dropped the vase and smashed it to smithereens... They walked right into a booby-trap and got blown to smithereens.* N-PLURAL: usu *to* N =pieces

smithy /smɪði/ **smithies.** A **smithy** is a place where a blacksmith works. N-COUNT =forge

smitten /smɪtᵊn/

1 If you are **smitten**, you find someone so attractive that you are or seem to be in love with them. *They were totally smitten with each other.* ADJ-GRADED: usu v-link ADJ, oft ADJ *with/by* n

2 If you are **smitten** by something, you are very impressed by it and enthusiastic about it. *Simon Fraser was smitten by the landscapes he found in the wild southwest of the United States.* ADJ-GRADED: usu v-link ADJ, oft ADJ *with/by* n

3 **Smitten** is the past participle of **smite**.

smock /smɒk/ **smocks**

1 A **smock** is a loose garment, rather like a long blouse, usually worn by women. *She was wearing wool slacks and a paisley smock.* N-COUNT

2 A **smock** is a loose garment worn by people such as artists to protect their clothing. N-COUNT

smocked /smɒkt/. A **smocked** dress or top is decorated with smocking. *She was pretty and young, in a loose smocked sundress.* ADJ

smocking /smɒkɪŋ/. **Smocking** is a decoration on tops and dresses which is made by gathering the material into folds using small stitches. N-UNCOUNT

smog /smɒg/ **smogs. Smog** is a mixture of fog and smoke which occurs in some busy industrial cities. *Cars cause pollution, both smog and acid rain.* ◆◇◇◇◇ N-VAR

smoggy /smɒgi/ **smoggier, smoggiest.** A **smoggy** city or town is badly affected by smog. *The smoggy sprawl of Los Angeles is America's largest manufacturing and trading centre.* ADJ-GRADED

smoke /smoʊk/ **smokes, smoking, smoked** ◆◆◆◆◇

1 **Smoke** consists of gas and small bits of solid material that are sent into the air when something burns. *A cloud of black smoke blew over the city... The air was thick with cigarette smoke.* N-UNCOUNT

2 If something **is smoking**, smoke is coming from it. *The chimney was smoking fiercely. ...a pile of smoking rubble.* VERB V V-ing

3 When someone **smokes** a cigarette, cigar, or pipe, they suck the smoke from it into their mouth and blow it out again. If you **smoke**, you regularly smoke cigarettes, cigars, or a pipe. *He was sitting alone, smoking a big cigar... It's not easy to quit smoking cigarettes... Do you smoke?* ▶ Also a noun. *Someone came out for a smoke.* ♦ **smoker, smokers** *He was not a heavy smoker.* VERB V n V N-SING: *a* N N-COUNT

4 If fish or meat **is smoked**, it is hung over burning wood so that the smoke preserves it and gives it a special flavour. *...the grid where the fish were being smoked. ...smoked bacon.* VB: usu passive *be* V-ed V-ed

5 See also **smoked, smoking.**

6 If someone says **there's no smoke without fire** or **where there's smoke there's fire**, they mean that there are rumours or signs that something is true so it must be at least partly true. PHRASES

7 If something **goes up in smoke**, it is destroyed by fire. *More than 900 years of British history went up in smoke in the Great Fire of Windsor.* V inflects

8 If something that is very important to you **goes up in smoke**, it fails or ends without anything being achieved. *The dreams of hundreds of holidaymakers went up in smoke after the collapse of their travel agency.* V inflects

smoke out. If you **smoke out** someone who is hiding, you discover them and make them publicly known. *The committee have tried dozens of different ways to smoke him out. ...technology to smoke out tax evaders.* PHRASAL VERB V n P V P n (not pron)

smoke bomb, smoke bombs. A **smoke bomb** is a bomb that produces clouds of smoke when it explodes. N-COUNT

smoked /smoʊkt/. **Smoked** glass has been made darker by being treated with smoke. *...a white van with smoked glass windows.* ● See also **smoke.** ADJ

smoked salmon. Smoked salmon is the flesh of a salmon which is smoked and eaten raw. ◆◇◇◇◇ N-UNCOUNT

smoke-filled room, smoke-filled rooms. If you talk about a decision being made in a **smoke-filled room**, you mean that it is made by a small group of people in a private meeting, rather than in a more democratic or open way; used showing disapproval. *The danger is that the professionals in smoke-filled rooms will impose an over-centralised European Union.* N-COUNT PRAGMATICS

smokeless /smoʊkləs/. **Smokeless** fuel burns without producing smoke. ADJ

smokescreen /smoʊkskriːn/ **smokescreens;** also spelled **smoke screen.** If something that you do or say is a **smokescreen**, it is intended to hide the truth about your activities or intentions. *He was accused of putting up a smokescreen to hide poor standards in city schools.* N-COUNT

smoke signal, smoke signals. If someone such as a politician or businessman sends out **smoke signals**, they give an indication of their views and intentions. This indication is often not clear and needs to be worked out. *The vote could be influenced at this late stage by smoke signals from the Labour Party leader's office.* N-COUNT: usu pl

smokestack /smoʊkstæk/ **smokestacks.** A **smokestack** is a very tall chimney that carries smoke away from a factory. N-COUNT =chimney

smoking /smoʊkɪŋ/ ◆◆◆◇◇

1 **Smoking** is the act or habit of smoking cigarettes, cigars, or a pipe. *Smoking is now banned in many places of work. ...a no-smoking area.* N-UNCOUNT

2 A **smoking** area or compartment is intended for people who want to smoke. *...the decision to scrap smoking compartments on Kent trains.* ADJ: ADJ n

3 See also **smoke; passive smoking.**

smoking gun, smoking guns. A **smoking gun** is a piece of evidence that proves that someone is responsible for something or that something is true; used mainly in American journalism. *The search for other kinds of evidence tying him to trafficking has not produced a smoking gun.* N-COUNT: usu sing

smoky /smoʊki/ **smokier, smokiest;** also spelled **smokey.** ◆◇◇◇◇

1 A place that is **smoky** has a lot of smoke in the air. *His main problem was the extremely smoky atmosphere at work.* ADJ-GRADED

2 You can use **smoky** to describe something that looks like smoke, for example because it is slightly blue or grey or because it appears cloudy. *At the center of the dial is a piece of smoky glass... He had smoky grey-blue eyes.* ADJ: ADJ n, ADJ colour

3 Something that has a **smoky** flavour tastes as if it has been smoked. *Cooking with the lid on gives the food that distinctive smoky flavour.* ADJ-GRADED

smolder /smoʊldəʳ/. See **smoulder.**

smooch /smuːtʃ/ **smooches, smooching, smooched.** If two people **smooch**, they kiss and hold each other closely. People sometimes smooch while they are dancing. *I smooched with him on the dance floor... The customers smooch and chat.* ▶ Also a noun. *...a good smooch.* V-RECIP V *with* n pl-n V N-SING

smooth /smuːð/ **smoother, smoothest; smooths, smoothing, smoothed** ◆◆◆◇◇

1 A **smooth** surface has no roughness, lumps, or holes. *...a rich cream that keeps skin soft and smooth. ...a smooth surface such as glass... The flagstones beneath their feet were worn smooth by* ADJ-GRADED ≠rough

centuries of use. ♦ **smoothness** *...the smoothness of her skin.* N-UNCOUNT: with supp

2 A **smooth** liquid or mixture has been mixed well so that it has no lumps. *Continue whisking until the mixture looks smooth and creamy... Blend the cornflour to a smooth paste with a little cold water.* ADJ-GRADED ≠lumpy

3 If you describe a drink such as wine, whisky, or coffee as **smooth**, you mean that it is not bitter and is pleasant to drink. *This makes the whiskeys much smoother.* ADJ-GRADED ≠bitter

4 Something that is **smooth** happens or continues evenly and steadily with no sudden changes or breaks. *This exercise is done in one smooth motion. ...the smooth curve of the trunk.* ♦ **smoothly** *Make sure that you execute all movements smoothly and without jerking... 'I've no idea,' he said smoothly.* ♦ **smoothness** *Sayer was delighted with the smoothness of the engine.* ADJ-GRADED =even; ADV-GRADED: ADV with v =evenly; N-UNCOUNT: with supp

5 A **smooth** ride, flight, or sea crossing is very comfortable because there are no bumps or jolts. *The active suspension system gives the car a very smooth ride.* ♦ **smoothness** *The smoothness of the flight was memorable.* ADJ-GRADED ≠bumpy; N-UNCOUNT: with supp

6 You use **smooth** to describe something that is going well and is free of problems or trouble. *Political hopes for a swift and smooth transition to democracy have been dashed... A number of problems marred the smooth running of this event.* ♦ **smoothly** *So far, talks at GM have gone smoothly... The operation was moving along smoothly.* ♦ **smoothness** *The Albanians deserve a bit of credit, frankly, for the smoothness of the election.* ADJ-GRADED =easy; ADV-GRADED: ADV with v; N-UNCOUNT: with supp

7 If you describe a man as **smooth**, you mean that he is extremely smart, confident, and polite, often in a way that you find rather unpleasant. *Twelve extremely good-looking, smooth young men have been picked as finalists... He was the smoothest and probably the most powerful chief of staff in political memory.* ADJ-GRADED

8 If you **smooth** something, you move your hands over its surface to make it smooth and flat. *She stood up and smoothed down her frock... Bardo smoothed his moustache.* VERB V n with adv; V n

9 If you **smooth** something somewhere, you use your hands to spread it there. *She smoothed the lotion across his shoulder blades... His fingers smoothed the hair back from her face.* VERB V n prep; V n with adv

10 If you **smooth the path** or **smooth the way** towards something, you make it easier or more likely to happen. *Their talks were aimed at smoothing the path towards a treaty to limit long-range weapons.* PHRASES V inflects

11 If you say that someone has to **take the rough with the smooth**, you mean that they have to accept the unpleasant or difficult things that happen as well as the pleasant things. V inflects

smooth out. If you **smooth out** a problem or difficulty, you solve it, especially by talking to the people concerned. *Baker was smoothing out differences with European allies... It's O.K. I smoothed things out.* PHRASAL VERB =sort out; V P n (not pron); V n P

smooth over. If you **smooth over** a problem or difficulty, you make it less serious and easier to deal with, especially by talking to the people concerned. *...an attempt to smooth over the violent splits that have occurred... The Chancellor is trying to smooth things over.* PHRASAL VERB V P n (not pron); V n P

smoothie /smu̲ːði/ **smoothies.** If you describe a man as a **smoothie**, you mean that he is extremely smart, confident, and polite, often in a way that you find rather unpleasant. N-COUNT =charmer

smo̲oth-ta̲lking. A **smooth-talking** man talks very confidently and persuasively, but may not be sincere or honest. *...the smooth-talking conman who has wrecked their lives.* ADJ =silver-tongued

smorgasbord /smɔ̲ːʳgəsbɔːʳd/

1 **Smorgasbord** is a meal with a variety of hot and cold savoury dishes served as a buffet. N-SING: also no det

2 A **smorgasbord** of things is a number of different things that are combined together as a whole; used in journalism. *...a smorgasbord of paintings and sculpture. ...Further Education colleges with a smorgasbord of academic and vocational courses.* N-SING: usu N *of* n

smote /smo̲ʊt/. **Smote** is the past tense of **smite**.

smother /smʌ̲ðəʳ/ **smothers, smothering, smothered** ♦◇◇◇◇

1 If you **smother** a fire, you cover it with something in order to put it out. *The girl's parents were also burned as they tried to smother the flames.* VERB V n

2 To **smother** someone means to kill them by covering their face with something so that they cannot breathe. *A father was secretly filmed as he tried to smother his six-week-old son in hospital.* VERB =suffocate; V n

3 Things that **smother** something cover it completely. *Once the shrubs begin to smother the little plants, we have to move them.* ♦ **smothered** *...a hundred-year-old red-bricked house almost smothered in ivy... Make sure that your meal won't be smothered with white sauce.* VERB V n; ADJ: v-link ADJ, usu ADJ *in/with* n

4 If you **smother** someone, you show your love for them too much and protect them too much. *She loved her own children, almost smothering them with love. ...a smothering, overprotective mother.* VERB V n; V-ing

5 If you **smother** an emotion or a reaction, you control it so that people do not notice it. *She summoned up all her pity for him, to smother her self-pity. ...smothered giggles.* VERB =stifle; V n; V-ed

6 If an activity or process **is smothered**, it is prevented from continuing or developing. *Intellectual life in France was smothered by the occupation... The debts of both Poland and Hungary are beginning to smother the reform process.* VERB =stifle; be V-ed; V n

smoulder /smo̲ʊldəʳ/ **smoulders, smouldering, smouldered**; spelled **smolder** in American English. ♦◇◇◇◇

1 If something **smoulders**, it burns slowly, producing smoke but not flames. *A number of buildings around the Parliament were still smouldering today... Whole blocks had been turned into smouldering rubble.* VERB V; V-ing

2 If a feeling such as anger or hatred **smoulders** inside you, you continue to feel it but rarely show it. *Baxter smouldered as he drove home for lunch... That's a lot of people smouldering with resentment... There is a smouldering anger in the black community.* VERB V; V-ing

3 If you say that someone **smoulders**, you mean that they are sexually attractive, usually in a mysterious or very intense way. *Melanie Griffith seems to smoulder with sexuality... His darkly smouldering eyes never left her face.* VERB V prep; V-ing

smudge /smʌ̲dʒ/ **smudges, smudging, smudged** ♦◇◇◇◇

1 A **smudge** is a dirty mark. *There was a dark smudge on his forehead. ...smudges of blood.* N-COUNT

2 If you **smudge** something, you make it dirty or messy by touching it. *Smudge the outline using a cotton-wool bud... She stood there in the old coat and woollen cap, her face smudged with dirt... Her lipstick was smudged.* VERB V n; V-ed; Also V

smudgy /smʌ̲dʒi/ **smudgier, smudgiest.** Something that is **smudgy** is blurred and its outline is unclear. *The hand-writing is smudgy. ...smudgy photos.* ADJ-GRADED =blurred

smug /smʌ̲g/. If you say that someone is **smug**, you are criticizing the fact they seem very pleased with how good, clever, or fortunate they are. *Thomas and his wife looked at each other in smug satisfaction. ...a smug woman of about 45.* ♦ **smugly** *The Major smiled smugly and sat down.* ♦ **smugness** *He had the smugness that many lawyers show. ...a trace of smugness in his voice.* ♦◇◇◇◇ ADJ-GRADED PRAGMATICS; ADV-GRADED: usu ADV with v; N-UNCOUNT

smuggle /smʌ̲gəl/ **smuggles, smuggling, smuggled.** If someone **smuggles** things or people into a place or out of it, they take them there illegally or secretly. *My message is 'If you try to smuggle drugs you are stupid'... Police have foiled an attempt to smuggle a bomb into Belfast airport... Had it really been impossible to find someone who could smuggle out a letter?... Everything along the border has its price: drugs, teak, smuggled goods.* ♦ **smuggling** *An air hostess was arrested and charged with drug smuggling. ...the smuggling of arms.* ♦♦◇◇◇ VERB V n; V n prep; V n with adv; V-ed; N-UNCOUNT

smuggler /smʌɡələʳ/ **smugglers.** **Smugglers** are people who take goods into or out of a country illegally. *...drug smugglers.* ◆◇◇◇◇ N-COUNT

smut /smʌt/ **smuts**
1 If you refer to words or pictures that are related to nudity or sex as **smut**, you disapprove of them because you think that have been said or published just to shock or excite people, rather than for serious reasons. *I find the media's growing obsession with smut and sensation deplorable. ...schoolboy smut.* N-UNCOUNT PRAGMATICS
2 **Smut** or **smuts** refer to dirt such as soot which makes a dirty mark on something. N-UNCOUNT: also N in pl

smutty /smʌti/ **smuttier, smuttiest.** If you describe something such as a joke, book, or film as **smutty**, you disapprove of it because it refers to sex or features nudity in a way that you think is intended just to shock or excite people. *...smutty jokes... I detest smutty books.* ADJ-GRADED: usu ADJ n PRAGMATICS =dirty

snack /snæk/ **snacks, snacking, snacked** ◆◆◇◇◇
1 A **snack** is a simple meal that is quick to cook and to eat. *Lunch was a snack in the fields.* N-COUNT
2 A **snack** is something such as a chocolate bar that you eat between meals. *Do you eat sweets, cakes or sugary snacks?.* N-COUNT
3 If you **snack**, you eat snacks between meals. *Instead of snacking on crisps and chocolate, nibble on celery or carrot... She would improve her diet if she ate less fried food and snacked less.* VERB V on n V

snack bar, snack bars. A **snack bar** is a place where you can buy and eat simple meals such as sandwiches, and also drinks. N-COUNT

snaffle /snæfᵊl/ **snaffles, snaffling, snaffled**
1 A **snaffle** is a mouthpiece, or bit, made out of two short joined bars, which is placed in a horse's mouth. It is used to give the rider more control over the horse. N-COUNT
2 In British English, if you **snaffle** something, you quickly take it for yourself; an informal use. *Michael Stich then proceeded to snaffle the $2 million first prize.* VERB =snatch V n

snag /snæɡ/ **snags, snagging, snagged** ◆◇◇◇◇
1 A **snag** is a small problem or disadvantage. *A police clampdown on car thieves hit a snag when villains stole one of their cars... The school deals exclusively with children of high academic ability. There is a snag though, it costs £6,600 a year.* N-COUNT =hitch
2 If you **snag** part of your clothing on a sharp or rough object or if it **snags**, it gets caught on the object and tears. *She snagged a heel on a root and tumbled to the ground... Brambles snagged his suit... Local fishermen complained that their nets kept snagging on some underwater objects.* V-ERG =catch V n on n V n V on n

snail /sneɪl/ **snails** ◆◇◇◇◇
1 A **snail** is a small animal with a long, soft, slimy body and a spiral-shaped shell. Snails move very slowly. N-COUNT
2 If you say that someone does something **at a snail's pace**, you are emphasizing that they are doing it very slowly, usually when you think it would be better if they did it much more quickly. *The train was moving now at a snail's pace... The economy grew at a snail's pace in the first three months of this year.* PHRASE: PHR after v PRAGMATICS

snail mail. Some computer users refer to the postal system as **snail mail**, because it is very slow in comparison with the system of sending messages electronically from one computer to another by email. N-UNCOUNT

snake /sneɪk/ **snakes, snaking, snaked** ◆◆◇◇◇
1 A **snake** is a long, thin reptile without legs. N-COUNT
2 Something that **snakes** in a particular direction goes in that direction in a line with a lot of bends; a literary use. *The road snaked through forested mountains... The three-mile procession snaked its way through the richest streets of the capital.* VERB =wind V prep/adv V *way* prep/adv

snakebite /sneɪkbaɪt/ **snakebites;** also spelled **snake bite.** A **snakebite** is the bite of a snake, especially a poisonous one. N-VAR

snake charmer, snake charmers; also spelled **snake-charmers.** A **snake charmer** is a person who entertains people by controlling the behaviour of a snake, for example by playing music and causing the snake to rise out of a basket and drop back in again. N-COUNT

snakes and ladders. **Snakes and ladders** is a British children's game played with a board and dice. When you go up a ladder, you progress quickly. When you go down a snake, you go backwards. N-UNCOUNT

snakeskin /sneɪkskɪn/. **Snakeskin** is the skin of snakes used to make shoes and clothes. N-UNCOUNT: oft N n

snap /snæp/ **snaps, snapping, snapped** ◆◆◆◇◇
1 If something **snaps** or if you **snap** it, it breaks suddenly, usually with a sharp cracking noise. *He shifted his weight and a twig snapped... The brake pedal had just snapped off... She gripped the pipe with both hands, trying to snap it in half.* ► Also a noun. *Every minute or so I could hear a snap, a crack and a crash as another tree went down.* V-ERG V V adv/prep V n adv/prep Also V n N-SING
2 If you **snap** something into a particular position, or if it **snaps** into that position, it moves quickly into that position, with a sharp sound. *He snapped the notebook shut... He snapped the cap on his ballpoint... The bag snapped open.* ► Also a noun. *He shut the book with a snap and stood up.* V-ERG V n adv/prep V adv N-SING
3 If you **snap** your fingers, you make a sharp sound by moving your middle finger quickly across your thumb, for example in order to accompany music or to order someone to do something. *She had millions of listeners snapping their fingers to her first single... He snapped his fingers, and Wilson produced a sheet of paper... She snapped her fingers at a passing waiter.* ► Also a noun. *I could obtain with the snap of my fingers anything I chose.* VERB =click V n N-SING: N of n
4 If someone **snaps** at you, they speak to you in a sharp, unfriendly way. *'Of course I don't know her,' Roger snapped... I'm sorry, Casey, I didn't mean to snap at you like that.* VERB V with quote V at n
5 If someone **snaps**, if their patience **snaps**, or if something **snaps** inside them, they suddenly stop being calm and become very angry because the situation has become too tense or too difficult for them. *He finally snapped when she prevented their children from visiting him one weekend... For the first and only time Grant's self-control snapped... Then something seemed to snap in me. I couldn't endure any more.* VERB V
6 If an animal such as a dog **snaps** at you, it opens and shuts its jaws quickly near you, as if it were going to bite you. *His teeth clicked as he snapped at my ankle... The poodle yapped and snapped.* VERB V at n V
7 A **snap** decision or action is one that is taken suddenly, often without careful thought. *I think this is too important for a snap decision... It's important not to make snap judgments... The opposition is worried that a snap election will be held before they can get organised.* ADJ: ADJ n
8 A **snap** is a photograph; an informal use. *...a snap my mother took last year.* N-COUNT =photograph
9 If you **snap** someone or something, you take a photograph of them; an informal use. *He was the first ever non-British photographer to be invited to snap a royal.* VERB =photograph V n
10 **Snap** is a simple British card game in which the players take turns to put cards down on a pile, and try to be the first to shout 'snap' when two cards with the same number or picture are put down. N-UNCOUNT
11 In informal British English, you can say **'Snap!'** as an expression of surprise when you realize that two things are the same or very similar, for example if you meet a friend wearing the same shirt as you. EXCLAM
12 In American English, a **snap** is the same as a **snap fastener**. N-COUNT
13 See also **cold snap**.

snap out of. If someone who is depressed **snaps out of it** or **snaps out of** their depression, they suddenly become more cheerful, especially by making an effort. *Come on, snap out of it!... Often a patient cannot snap out of their negativity that easily.* PHRASAL VERB V P P it V P P n

snap up. If you **snap** something **up**, you buy it quickly because it is a bargain or because it is just what you want. *Every time we get a new delivery of* PHRASAL VERB V n P

Donna's clothes, there is a queue of people waiting to snap them up... One eagle-eyed collector snapped up a pair of Schiaparelli earrings for just £6. V P n (not pron)

snapdragon /snæpdrægən/ **snapdragons.** A **snapdragon** is a common garden plant with small colourful flowers that can open and shut like a mouth. N-COUNT

snap fastener, snap fasteners. In American English, a **snap fastener** is a small metal fastener for clothes, made up of two parts which can be pressed together. The British term is **press stud** or **popper**. N-COUNT

snapper /snæpəʳ/ **snappers; snapper** can also be used as the plural form. A **snapper** is a fish that has sharp teeth and lives in warm seas. N-COUNT
► **Snapper** is a piece of this fish eaten as food. N-UNCOUNT

snappish /snæpɪʃ/. If someone is **snappish**, they speak to people in a sharp, unfriendly manner. *'That is beautiful, Tony,' Momma said, no longer sounding at all snappish.* ADJ-GRADED: usu v-link ADJ =snappy ♦ **snappishly** *She frowned and her voice rose snappishly. 'I'm not pregnant, Brian.'* ADV-GRADED: ADV with v

snappy /snæpi/ **snappier, snappiest** ◆◇◇◇◇

1 If someone has a **snappy** style of speaking, they speak in a quick, clever, concise, and often funny way. *Each film gets a snappy two-line summary. ...snappy American film dialogue.* ADJ-GRADED: usu ADJ n

2 If someone is a **snappy** dresser or if they wear **snappy** clothes, they wear smart, stylish clothes. *She has already made a name for herself as a snappy dresser. ...snappy sports jackets.* ADJ-GRADED: ADJ n ♦ **snappily** *...his usual band of snappily dressed friends.* ADV-GRADED: ADV -ed, ADV after v

3 If someone is **snappy**, they speak to people in a sharp, unfriendly manner. *He wasn't irritable or snappy or anything, just slightly perplexed.* ADJ-GRADED: usu v-link ADJ =snappish

4 If you tell someone to **make it snappy**, you tell them to do something quickly; an informal use. *Look at the pamphlets, and make it snappy.* PHRASE

snapshot /snæpʃɒt/ **snapshots** ◆◇◇◇◇

1 A **snapshot** is a photograph that is taken quickly and casually. N-COUNT =photograph

2 If something provides you with a **snapshot** of a place or situation, it gives you a brief idea of what that place or situation is like. *The interviews present a remarkable snapshot of Britain in these dark days of recession.* N-COUNT: usu sing, usu N of n

snare /sneəʳ/ **snares, snaring, snared** ◆◇◇◇◇

1 A **snare** is a trap for catching birds or small animals. It consists of a loop of wire or rope which pulls tight around the animal. N-COUNT =trap

2 If you describe a situation as a **snare**, you mean that it is a trap from which it is difficult to escape; a formal use. *Given data which are free from bias there are further snares to avoid in statistical work... Worldly success could prove a snare unless used for the good of others.* N-COUNT =trap

3 If someone **snares** an animal, they catch it using a snare. *He'd snared a rabbit earlier in the day.* VERB V n

4 If someone **is snared**, they are caught in a trap. *A motor-cyclist was seriously injured when she was snared by a rope stretched across the road... The classic 'debt trap' has now snared Italy.* VB: usu passive be V-ed V n

5 If someone **snares** something, they get it by using cleverness and cunning. *Most of all I want to snare a husband... Possessed of such qualities, how do you bring them to the fore and snare the job?* VERB V n

snare drum, snare drums. A **snare drum** is a small cylindrical drum used in orchestras and bands. It has metal or gut springs stretched across the lower of its two surfaces which allow it to make a continuous sound. Snare drums are usually played with wooden sticks. N-COUNT =side drum

snarl /snɑːʳl/ **snarls, snarling, snarled** ◆◇◇◇◇

1 When an animal **snarls**, it makes a fierce, rough sound in its throat while showing its teeth. *He raced ahead up into the bush, barking and snarling... The dogs snarled at the intruders.* VERB V V at n ► Also a noun. *With a snarl, the second dog made a dive for his heel.* N-COUNT

2 If you **snarl** something, you say it in a fierce, angry way. *'Let go of me,' he snarled... I vaguely remember snarling at someone who stepped on my foot... 'Aubrey.' Hyde seemed almost to snarl the name.* VERB V with quote V at n V n ► Also a noun. *His eyes flashed, and his lips were drawn back in a furious snarl.* N-COUNT

3 A **snarl** is a tangled or disorganized mass of things. *...the snarl of logs and branches where she had gotten entangled... A radio-link automatically advises it of traffic snarls and plots a detour.* N-COUNT: usu with supp

snarl up. To **snarl** something **up** means to cause problems which prevent it continuing or making progress. *The ensuing row snarled up the work of the joint peace commission.* PHRASAL VERB V P n (not pron) Also V n P

snarl-up, snarl-ups. A **snarl-up** is a disorganized situation such as a traffic jam, in which things are unable to move or work normally; used in informal British English. N-COUNT

snatch /snætʃ/ **snatches, snatching, snatched** ◆◆◇◇◇

1 If you **snatch** something or **snatch** at something, you take it or pull it away quickly. *Mick snatched the cards from Archie's hand... He snatched up the telephone... The thin wind snatched at her skirt.* VERB V n prep V n with adv V at n

2 If something **is snatched** from you, it is stolen, usually using force. If a person **is snatched**, they are taken away by force. *If your bag is snatched, let it go... Mr Hillman was snatched by kidnappers last Thursday.* VB: usu passive be V-ed ♦ **snatcher, snatchers** *Wealthy tourists are tempting targets for bag snatchers.* N-COUNT: n N

3 If you **snatch** an opportunity, you take it quickly. If you **snatch** something to eat or a rest, you have it quickly in between doing other things. *I snatched a glance at the mirror... You can even snatch a few hours off... He was going out for a run, then snatching a piece of toast and a cup of coffee.* VERB V n

4 If you **snatch** victory in a competition, you defeat your opponent by a small amount or just before the end of the contest. *The American came from behind to snatch victory by a mere eight seconds... Chesterfield snatched a third goal.* VERB V n

5 A **snatch** of a conversation or a song is a very small piece of it. *I heard snatches of the conversation.* N-COUNT: usu N of n

6 If someone **snatches victory from the jaws of defeat**, they win when it seems that they are certain to lose. If someone **snatches defeat from the jaws of victory**, they lose when it seems that they are certain to win. Used in journalism. PHRASE: V inflects

snazzy /snæzi/ **snazzier, snazziest.** Something that is **snazzy** is stylish and attractive, often in a rather bright or noticeable way; an informal word. *...snazzy swimsuits. ...a snazzy new Porsche. ...the snazziest part of town.* ADJ-GRADED: usu ADJ n

sneak /sniːk/ **sneaks, sneaking, sneaked;** ◆◆◇◇◇ American English sometimes uses the form **snuck** for the past tense and past participle.

1 If you **sneak** somewhere, you go there very quietly on foot, trying to avoid being seen or heard. *Sometimes he would sneak out of his house late at night to be with me... Don't sneak away and hide.* VERB =slip V adv/prep

2 If you **sneak** something somewhere, you take it there secretly. *He smuggled papers out each day, photocopied them, and snuck them back... You even snuck me a cigarette.* VERB V n prep/adv V n n

3 If you **sneak** a look at someone or something, you secretly have a quick look at them. *You sneak a look at your watch to see how long you've got to wait.* VERB =steal V n prep

4 See also **sneaking**.

sneak up on PHRASAL VERB

1 If someone **sneaks up on** you, they try and approach you without being seen or heard, perhaps to surprise you or do you harm. *I managed to sneak up on him when you knocked on the door.* =creep up V P P n

2 If something **sneaks up on** you, it happens or occurs when you are not expecting it. *Sometimes our expectations sneak up on us unawares.* V P P n

sneaker /sniːkəʳ/ **sneakers. Sneakers** are casual shoes with rubber soles; used mainly in American English. The usual British word is **trainers**. ◆◇◇◇◇ N-COUNT: usu pl

sneaking /sniːkɪŋ/. A **sneaking** feeling is a slight or vague feeling, especially one that you are unwilling to accept. *I have a sneaking suspicion that* ADJ: ADJ n *they are going to succeed... I've always had this sneaking admiration for him.*

sneak preview, sneak previews. A **sneak preview** of something is an unofficial opportunity to have a look at it before it is officially published or shown to the public. N-COUNT: oft N *of* n

sneaky /sniːki/ **sneakier, sneakiest.** If you describe someone as **sneaky**, you disapprove of them because they do things secretly rather than openly; an informal word. *It is a sneaky and underhand way of doing business... One kid can generally tell when another kid is sneaky.* ADJ-GRADED PRAGMATICS =sly

sneer /snɪəʳ/ **sneers, sneering, sneered.** If you **sneer** at someone or something, you express your contempt for them by the expression on your face or by what you say. *There is too great a readiness to sneer at anything the Opposition does... If you go to a club and you don't look right, you're sneered at... 'Hypocrite,' he sneered... Although some may sneer, working as a secretary is for many the fastest route to career success.* ► Also a noun. *Canete's mouth twisted in a contemptuous sneer... There were always those who dismissed him with a sneer, saying he wasn't British by birth.* ◆◇◇◇◇ VERB V *at* n V with quote V Also V that N-COUNT

sneeringly /snɪərɪŋli/. If someone refers **sneeringly** to someone or something, they refer to them in a contemptuous way; used in written English. *...those in what the Tories sneeringly call the 'chattering classes'... They were sneeringly dismissive.* ADV-GRADED =scornfully

sneeze /sniːz/ **sneezes, sneezing, sneezed** ◆◇◇◇◇

1 When you **sneeze**, you suddenly and involuntarily take in your breath and then blow it down your nose noisily. People sneeze when they have a cold, or if something irritates their nose. *What exactly happens when we sneeze?... See your doctor now to beat summer sneezing.* ► Also a noun. *Coughs and sneezes spread infections.* VERB V V-ing N-COUNT

2 If you say that something is **not to be sneezed at**, you mean that it is worth having; an informal expression. *The money's not to be sneezed at.* PHRASE =not to be sniffed at

snicker /snɪkəʳ/ **snickers, snickering, snickered.** If you **snicker**, you laugh quietly and disrespectfully, for example at something rude or at someone's misfortune. *We all snickered at Mrs. Swenson.* ► Also a noun. *...a chorus of jeers and snickers.* VERB =snigger V *at* n Also V N-COUNT

snide /snaɪd/. A **snide** comment or remark is one which criticizes someone nastily, often in an indirect, sarcastic way. *He made a snide comment about her weight... They kept making snide remarks about each other... She couldn't tell if he was being snide, so she took the question straight.* ♦ **snidely** *'What are you doing here?' he asked snidely.* ADJ-GRADED: usu ADJ n =sarcastic ADV: ADV with v

sniff /snɪf/ **sniffs, sniffing, sniffed** ◆◆◇◇◇

1 When you **sniff**, you breathe in air through your nose hard enough to make a sound, for example when you are trying not to cry, or in order to show disapproval or scorn. *She wiped her face and sniffed loudly... Moira looked around and sniffed. 'This place badly needs a decorator.'... Then he sniffed. There was a smell of burning... He sniffed back the tears.* ► Also a noun. *At last the sobs ceased, to be replaced by sniffs.* VERB V V n with adv N-COUNT

2 If you **sniff** something or **sniff at** it, you smell it by sniffing. *Suddenly, he stopped and sniffed the air... She sniffed at it suspiciously.* VERB V n V *at* n

3 You can use **sniff** to indicate that someone says something disapproving or scornful. *'Tourists!' she sniffed.* VERB V with quote

4 If you say that something is not to be **sniffed at**, you mean you think it is very good or worth having. If someone **sniffs at** something, they do not think it is adequate, or they express their scorn of it. *The salary was not to be sniffed at either... Only last weekend, Foreign Office sources sniffed at reports that up to 4,000 British troops might be sent.* VB: usu passive, usu with brd-neg =scoff *be* V-ed *at* V *at* n

5 If someone **sniffs** a substance such as glue, they deliberately breathe in the substance or its fumes as a drug. *He felt light-headed, as if he'd sniffed glue.* ♦ **sniffer, sniffers** *...teenage glue sniffers.* VERB V n N-COUNT

6 If you get a **sniff** of something, you learn or guess that it might be happening or might be near; an informal use. *You know what they'll be like if they get a sniff of a murder investigation... Have the Press got a sniff yet?... Then, at the first sniff of danger, he was back at his post.* N-SING: usu N *of* n =whiff, hint

7 If you say that someone has not had a **sniff** of something, you mean that they have not had even a small chance of getting it; an informal use. *Winterton has never had a sniff of a government job in his entire twenty-one years in parliament.* N-SING: usu *a* N *of*, usu with brd-neg,

sniff around or **sniff round** PHRASAL VERB

1 If someone **is sniffing around** or **sniffing round,** they are trying to find out information about someone or something, especially information that someone else does not want known; an informal use. *But really, what harm could it possibly do to pop down there and just sniff around?... They might have sent a couple of plain-clothes men to sniff round his apartment while the doctors patched him up.* =nose around V P V P n

2 If a person or organization **is sniffing around** someone or **sniffing round** them, they are trying to get them, for example as a lover, employee, or client; an informal use. *When I had to go away to university, I was convinced that other men would be sniffing round her... Rioch knows the big clubs have been sniffing around Andy Walker.* no passive V P n

sniff out PHRASAL VERB

1 If you **sniff out** something, you discover it after some searching; an informal use. *...journalists who are trained to sniff out sensation or scandal. ...those who like sniffing out bargains.* V P n (not pron) Also V n P

2 When a dog used by a group such as the police **sniffs out** hidden explosives or drugs, it finds them using its sense of smell. *A police dog, trained to sniff out explosives, found evidence of a bomb in the apartment.* V P n (not pron) Also V n P

sniff round. See **sniff around.** PHRASAL VERB

sniffer dog, sniffer dogs. A **sniffer dog** is a dog used by the police or army to find explosives or drugs by their smell. N-COUNT

sniffle /snɪfᵊl/ **sniffles, sniffling, sniffled**

1 If you **sniffle**, you keep sniffing, usually because you are crying or have a cold. *'Please don't yell at me.' She began to sniffle.* VERB =snuffle V

2 A **sniffle** is a slight cold. You can also say that someone has **the sniffles**. Used in informal English. N-COUNT: also *the* N in pl

sniffy /snɪfi/ **sniffier, sniffiest.** Someone who is **sniffy** has a scornful and contemptuous attitude towards something; an informal word. *Some people are a bit sniffy about television. ...sniffy art critics.* ♦ **sniffily** /snɪfɪli/ *The broadcast media sniffily affects to distance itself from the press.* ADJ-GRADED: oft ADJ *about* n =snobby ADV-GRADED: usu ADV with v

snifter /snɪftəʳ/ **snifters**

1 In informal British English, a **snifter** is a small amount of an alcoholic drink. N-COUNT: oft N *of* n

2 In American English, a **snifter** is a bowl-shaped glass used for drinking brandy. N-COUNT

snigger /snɪgəʳ/ **sniggers, sniggering, sniggered.** If someone **sniggers**, they laugh quietly and disrespectfully, for example at something rude. *Suddenly, three schoolkids sitting near me started sniggering... How can I forget, with people sniggering behind my back?... The tourists snigger at the locals' outdated ways and dress... 'We know what that means,' Robert sniggered.* ► Also a noun. *...trying to suppress a snigger.* ◆◇◇◇◇ VERB =snicker V V *at* n V with quote Also V *about* n N-COUNT

snip /snɪp/ **snips, snipping, snipped** ◆◇◇◇◇

1 If you **snip** something, or if you **snip at** or **through** something, you cut it using scissors or shears in a single quick action. *He has now begun to snip away at the piece of paper... He snipped a length of new bandage and placed it around Peter's chest.* VERB V adv/prep V n

2 In informal British English, if you say that something is **a snip** you mean that it is very good value. *The beautifully made briefcase is a snip at £74.25.* N-SING: *a* N =bargain

snipe /snaɪp/ **snipes, sniping, sniped; snipe** is both the singular and the plural form of the noun. ◆◇◇◇◇
1 If someone **snipes** at you, they criticize you. *The Spanish media were still sniping at the British press yesterday... This leaves him vulnerable to sniping from within his own party.* VERB V at n V-ing Also V
2 To **snipe** at someone means to shoot at them from a hidden position. *Gunmen have repeatedly sniped at US Army positions... A member of the security forces was killed and two others were wounded in sniping incidents.* VERB V at n V-ing
3 A **snipe** is a type of bird with a very long beak which normally lives in marshy areas. N-COUNT

sniper /snaɪpəʳ/ **snipers.** A **sniper** is someone who shoots at people from a hidden position. ◆◇◇◇◇ N-COUNT

snippet /snɪpɪt/ **snippets.** A **snippet** of something is a small piece of it. *...snippets of popular classical music... I read a snippet she had cut from a magazine.* ◆◇◇◇◇ N-COUNT: oft N of n

snitch /snɪtʃ/ **snitches, snitching, snitched**
1 If you **snitch** on someone, you tell someone in authority that another person has done something naughty or wrong; an informal use. *She felt like a fifth-grader who had snitched on a classmate.* VERB =grass V on n Also V
2 A **snitch** is a person who snitches on other people, an informal use. N-COUNT =grass
3 If you **snitch** something, you steal it quickly and quietly; an informal use. *Before I'd finished reading it, she snitched my copy of To Kill a Mockingbird.* VERB =pinch, nick V n

snivel /snɪvəl/ **snivels, snivelling, snivelled;** spelled **sniveling, sniveled** in American English. If someone **is snivelling**, they are crying, sniffing, and whining in a way that irritates you. *Billy started to snivel. His mother smacked his hand. ...a journalist snivelling with the flu.* ► Also a noun. *Carol managed a few proper snivels for the sake of appearance.* VERB V N-COUNT

snob /snɒb/ **snobs** ◆◇◇◇◇
1 If you call someone a **snob**, you disapprove of them because they admire upper-class people and despise lower-class people. *Going to a private school and spending weekends with other pupils whose parents had massive houses made her a snob... Kenneth is an arrogant, rude, social snob.* N-COUNT PRAGMATICS
2 If you call someone a **snob**, you mean you disapprove of them because they behave as if they are superior to other people because of their intelligence or taste. *She was an intellectual snob. ...a first class food snob.* N-COUNT: usu supp N PRAGMATICS

snobbery /snɒbəri/. **Snobbery** is the attitude of a snob. ◆◇◇◇◇ N-UNCOUNT

snobbish /snɒbɪʃ/. If you describe someone as **snobbish**, you disapprove of them because they are excessively proud of their social status, intelligence, or taste. *They had a snobbish dislike for their intellectual and social inferiors... I'd expected her to be snobbish but she was warm and friendly.* ♦ **snobbishness** *...his snobbishness and loathing of democracy.* ADJ-GRADED PRAGMATICS =snooty N-UNCOUNT

snobby /snɒbi/ **snobbier, snobbiest. Snobby** means the same as snobbish. ADJ-GRADED

snog /snɒg/ **snogs, snogging, snogged.** In informal British English, if one person **snogs** another, they kiss and cuddle that person for a period of time. You can also say that two people **are snogging**. *She snogged the rotund and balding Barry... A couple were snogging under a bridge... We went in for secret snogging sessions in the toilets at the restaurant.* ► Also a noun. *They went for a quick snog behind the bike sheds.* V-RECIP V n pl-n V V-ing N-COUNT: usu a N

snook /snuːk/. If you **cock a snook** at someone in authority or at an organization, you do something that they cannot punish you for, but which insults them or expresses your contempt; used mainly in British English, especially in journalism. *A majority of Tories in the House of Lords cocked a snook at their prime minister over a piece of legislation.* PHRASE: V inflects

snooker /snuːkəʳ, AM snʊk-/ **snookers, snookering, snookered** ◆◇◇◇◇
1 **Snooker** is a game involving balls on a large table. The players use a long stick to hit a white ball, and score points by knocking coloured balls into the pockets at the sides of the table. *...a game of snooker... They were playing snooker.* N-UNCOUNT
2 In British English, if you **are snookered** by something, it is difficult or impossible for you to take action or do what you want to do; an informal use. *The President has been snookered on this issue.* VB: usu passive be V-ed

snoop /snuːp/ **snoops, snooping, snooped**
1 If someone **snoops** around a place, they secretly look around it in order to find out things. *Ricardo was the one she'd seen snooping around Kim's hotel room.* ► Also a noun. *The second house that Grossman had a snoop around contained 'strong simple furniture'.* ♦ **snooper, snoopers** *St Barth's strange lack of street names is meant to dissuade journalistic snoopers.* VERB V adv/prep Also V N-COUNT N-COUNT
2 If someone **snoops on** a person, they watch them secretly in order to find out things about their life. *...the vast intelligence bureaucracy that America built up to snoop on the Soviets.* ♦ **snooper** *You bloody snooper! All the time you've been talking to me you've been prying into my family.* VERB =spy on V on n N-COUNT
3 A **snoop** is the same as a **snooper**. *Each neighborhood had its own organization of snoops who reported strangers to the authorities.* N-COUNT

snooty /snuːti/ **snootier, snootiest.** If you say that someone is **snooty**, you disapprove of them because they behave as if they are superior to other people. *...snooty intellectuals... Everyone thought Annabel was being snooty.* ADJ-GRADED PRAGMATICS =snobbish

snooze /snuːz/ **snoozes, snoozing, snoozed.**
1 A **snooze** is a short, light sleep, especially during the day; an informal word. N-COUNT =nap
2 If you **snooze**, you sleep lightly for a short period of time; an informal word. *Mark snoozed in front of the television... Patients are given an extra 15 minutes to snooze before being woken gently.* VERB V

snore /snɔːʳ/ **snores, snoring, snored.** When someone who is asleep **snores**, they make a loud noise each time they breathe. *His mouth was open, and he was snoring.* ► Also a noun. *Uncle Arthur, after a loud snore, woke suddenly.* ◆◇◇◇◇ VERB V N-COUNT

snorkel /snɔːʳkəl/ **snorkels, snorkelling, snorkelled;** spelled **snorkeling, snorkeled** in American English.
1 A **snorkel** is a tube through which a person swimming just under the surface of the sea can breathe. N-COUNT
2 When someone **snorkels** they swim under water using a snorkel. *After a rest on the boat, we would go snorkelling, and then return for lunch.* VERB V

snort /snɔːʳt/ **snorts, snorting, snorted** ◆◇◇◇◇
1 When people or animals **snort**, they breathe air noisily out through their noses. People sometimes snort in order to express disapproval or amusement. *Harrell snorted with laughter... He snorted loudly and shook his head.* ► Also a noun. *...snorts of laughter... He turned away with a snort.* VERB V with n V N-COUNT: oft N of n
2 If someone **snorts** something, they say it in a way that shows contempt. *'Reports,' he snorted. 'Anyone can write reports.'* VERB V with quote
3 To **snort** a drug such as cocaine means to breathe it in quickly through one nostril. *He died of cardiac arrest after snorting cocaine at a party.* VERB V n

snot /snɒt/. **Snot** is the slimy substance that is produced inside your nose; an informal word which some people find offensive. N-UNCOUNT

snotty /snɒti/
1 Something that is **snotty** is covered in snot; an informal use which some people find offensive. *He suffered from a snotty nose, runny eyes and a slight cough.* ADJ: ADJ n
2 If you describe someone as **snotty**, you disapprove of them because they have a very proud and superior attitude to other people; an informal use. *...snotty college kids... She smiled a snotty smile.* ADJ-GRADED PRAGMATICS

snout /snaʊt/ **snouts**
1 The **snout** of an animal such as a pig is its long nose. *Two alligators rest their snouts on the water's surface.* N-COUNT
2 Writers sometimes refer to the front of a car or the barrel of a gun as its **snout**. *The snout of the* N-COUNT: oft N of n

Mercedes poked through the gates... The tank stopped with the long snout of its gun turned to the ridge.

snow /snoʊ/ **snows, snowing, snowed** ◆◆◆◇◇

1 Snow consists of a lot of soft white bits of frozen water that fall from the sky in cold weather. *In Mid-Wales six inches of snow blocked roads... They put tramped through the falling snow.* N-UNCOUNT

2 You can refer to a great deal of snow in an area as the **snows**. *...the first snows of winter... As the snows melt, the flood waters rise.* N-PLURAL

3 When **it snows**, snow falls from the sky. *It had been snowing all night.* VERB *it* V

4 See also **snowed in, snowed under.**

snowball /snoʊbɔːl/ **snowballs, snowballing, snowballed** ◆◇◇◇◇

1 A **snowball** is a ball of snow. Children often throw snowballs at each other. N-COUNT

2 If something such as a project or campaign **snowballs**, it rapidly increases and grows. *From those early days the business has snowballed... The investigation snowballed from there and has since led to several arrests.* VERB V

snowbound /snoʊbaʊnd/. If people or vehicles are **snowbound**, they cannot go anywhere because of heavy snow. *The village became snowbound.* ADJ =snowed in

snow-capped. A **snow-capped** mountain is covered with snow at the top; a literary word. *...the snow-capped Himalayan peaks.* ADJ: ADJ n

snow-covered. Snow-covered places and things are covered over with snow. *...a Swiss chalet set in the snow-covered hills.* ADJ: usu ADJ n

snowdrift /snoʊdrɪft/ **snowdrifts.** A **snowdrift** is a deep pile of snow formed by the wind. N-COUNT

snowdrop /snoʊdrɒp/ **snowdrops.** A **snowdrop** is a small white flower which appears in the early spring. N-COUNT

snowed in. If you are **snowed in**, you cannot go anywhere because of heavy snow. *We may all be snowed in here together for days.* ADJ =snowbound

snowed under. If you say that you are **snowed under**, you are emphasizing that you have a lot of work or other things to deal with; an informal expression. *Ed was snowed under with fan mail when he was doing his television show.* ADJ-GRADED: v-link ADJ, usu ADJ *with* n

snowfall /snoʊfɔːl/ **snowfalls**

1 The **snowfall** in an area or country is the amount of snow that falls there during a particular period. *The total rain and snowfall amounted to 50mm.* N-UNCOUNT

2 A **snowfall** is a fall of snow. N-COUNT

snowfield /snoʊfiːld/ **snowfields.** A **snowfield** is a large area which is always covered in snow. N-COUNT

snowflake /snoʊfleɪk/ **snowflakes.** A **snowflake** is one of the soft, white bits of frozen water that fall as snow. N-COUNT

snowman /snoʊmæn/ **snowmen.** A **snowman** is a large shape which is made out of snow, especially by children, and is supposed to look like a person. N-COUNT

snowmobile /snoʊməbiːl/ **snowmobiles.** A **snowmobile** is a small vehicle built to move across snow and ice. N-COUNT

snowplough /snoʊplaʊ/ **snowploughs;** spelled **snowplow** in American English. A **snowplough** is a vehicle which is used to push snow off roads or railway lines. N-COUNT

snowshoe /snoʊʃuː/ **snowshoes. Snowshoes** are oval frames which have a strong net stretched across them and which you fasten to your feet so that you can walk on deep snow. N-COUNT: usu pl

snowstorm /snoʊstɔːʳm/ **snowstorms.** A **snowstorm** is a very heavy fall of snow, usually when there is also a strong wind blowing at the same time. N-COUNT

snow-white. Something that is **snow-white** is of a brilliant white colour. *His hair was snow white like an old man's.* ◆◇◇◇◇ ADJ

snowy /snoʊi/ **snowier, snowiest.** A **snowy** place is covered in snow. A **snowy** day is a day when a lot of snow has fallen. *...the snowy peaks of the Bighorn Mountains. ...a cold, snowy day in mid-February.* ◆◇◇◇◇ ADJ-GRADED: usu ADJ n

Snr. **Snr** is the written abbreviation for 'Senior'. It is used after someone's name to distinguish them from a younger member of their family who has the same name. Used especially in American English. *...Robert Trent Jones, Snr.*

snub /snʌb/ **snubs, snubbing, snubbed** ◆◇◇◇◇

1 If you **snub** someone, you deliberately insult them by ignoring them or by behaving or speaking rudely towards them. *He snubbed her in public and made her feel an idiot... They snubbed his invitation to a meeting of foreign ministers at the UN.* VERB V n

2 If you snub someone, your behaviour or your remarks can be referred to as a **snub**. *Ryan took it as a snub... The German move was widely seen as a deliberate snub to Mr Alphandery.* N-COUNT

3 Someone who has a **snub** nose has a short nose which points slightly upwards. ADJ: ADJ n

snuck /snʌk/. **Snuck** is a past tense and past participle of **sneak** used in American English.

snuff /snʌf/ **snuffs, snuffing, snuffed** ◆◇◇◇◇

1 Snuff is powdered tobacco which some people take by sniffing it up their nose. N-UNCOUNT

2 If someone **snuffs it**, they die; an informal British expression. *Perhaps he thought he was about to snuff it.* VERB V *it*

snuff out PHRASAL VERB

1 If someone or something **snuffs out** something such as a rebellion or disagreement, they stop it, usually in a forceful or sudden way. *Every time a new flicker of resistance appeared, the government snuffed it out... The recent rebound in mortgage rates could snuff out the housing recovery.* V n P, V P n (not pron)

2 If you **snuff out** a small flame, you stop it burning, usually by using your fingers or by covering it with something for a few seconds. *Tenzin snuffed out the candle.* V P n (not pron) Also V n P

snuffle /snʌfᵊl/ **snuffles, snuffling, snuffled.** If people or animals **snuffle**, they make sniffing noises, for example because they have a cold or are trying not to cry. *She snuffled and wiped her nose on the back of her hand.* VERB =sniffle V

snug /snʌg/ **snugs; snugger, snuggest** ◆◇◇◇◇

1 If you feel **snug** or are in a **snug** place, you are very warm and comfortable, especially because you are protected from cold weather. *They lay snug and warm amid the blankets and watched their sister hard at work. ...a snug log cabin.* ♦ **snugly** *Wrap your baby snugly in a shawl or blanket.* ADJ-GRADED =cosy; ADV: ADV with v

2 Something such as a piece of clothing that is **snug** fits very closely or tightly. *...a snug black T-shirt and skin-tight black jeans... Every dress is lined, ensuring a snug, firm fit.* ♦ **snugly** *His jeans fit snugly.* ADJ-GRADED; ADV-GRADED: ADV with v

3 In British English, a **snug** is a small room in a pub. N-COUNT

snuggle /snʌgᵊl/ **snuggles, snuggling, snuggled.** If you **snuggle** somewhere, you settle yourself into a warm, comfortable position, especially by moving closer to another person. *Jane snuggled up against his shoulder... I snuggled down in the big, comfortable seat.* VERB =nestle V adv/prep

so /soʊ/; usually pronounced /soʊ/ for meanings 1, 6, 7, 8, 9, 16 and 17. ◆◆◆◆◆

1 You use **so** to refer back to something that has just been mentioned. *'Do you think that made much of a difference to the family?'—'I think so.'... If you can't play straight, then say so... 'Is he the kind of man who can be as flexible as he needs to be?'—'Well, I hope so.'... Almost all young women who turn to prostitution do so as a means of survival.* ADV: ADV after v

2 You use **so** when you are saying that something which has just been said about one person or thing is also true of another one. *I enjoy Ann's company and so does Martin... They had a wonderful time and so did I... The police arrived, and so did reporters and a photographer from the 'Journal'.* ADV: ADV cl

3 You use the structures **as...so** and **just as...so** when you want to indicate that two events or situations are alike in some way. *As computer systems become even more sophisticated, so too do the methods of those who exploit the technology... Just* CONJ-COORD *as John has changed, so has his wife... Just as the teacher plays the role of leader in the classroom, so does the headteacher play a leadership role in the school.*

4 If you say that a state of affairs **is so**, you mean that it is the way it has been described. *The press reception for the Democratic ticket was favourable but chiefly where one would expect it to be so... In those days English dances as well as songs were taught at school, but that seems no longer to be so... It is strange to think that he held strong views on many things, but it must have been so.* ADV: v-link ADV

5 You can also use **so** with actions and gestures to show someone how to do something, or to indicate the size, height, or length of something. *Clasp the chain like so. ...holding the champagne glass with long red nails positioned just so.* ADV: ADV after v

6 You use **so** and **so that** to introduce the result of the situation you have just mentioned. *I am not an emotional type and so cannot bring myself to tell him I love him... People are living longer than ever before, so even people who are 65 or 70 have a surprising amount of time left... I was an only child, and so had no experience of large families... There was snow everywhere, so that the shape of things was difficult to identify.* CONJ-SUBORD

7 You use **so**, **so that**, and **so as** to introduce the reason for doing the thing that you have just mentioned. *Come to my suite so I can tell you all about this wonderful play I saw in Boston... He took her arm and hurried her upstairs so that they wouldn't be overheard... I was beginning to feel alarm, but kept it to myself so as not to worry our two friends.* CONJ-SUBORD

8 You can use **so** in stories and accounts to introduce the next event in a series of events or to suggest a connection between two events. *The woman asked if he could perhaps mend her fences, and so he stayed... She was free for five whole days, from Christmas Eve. And so she would be going to Charles, to join her family... I thought, 'Here's someone who'll understand me.' So I wrote to her... He said he'd like to meet Sharon. So I said all right... And so Christmas passed.* ADV: ADV cl

9 You can use **so** in conversations to introduce a new topic, or to introduce a question or comment about something that has been said. *So how was your day?... So you're a runner, huh?... So as for your question, Miles, the answer still has to be no... So, as I said to you, natural medicine is also known as holistic medicine... And so, to answer your question, that's why your mother is disappointed... 'I didn't find him funny at all.'—'So you won't watch the show again then?'... 'They're slow, heavy and cost a fortune,'—'So how have these motorbikes become a fashion statement?'* ADV: ADV cl

10 You can use **so** in conversations to show that you are accepting what someone has just said. *'It makes me feel, well, important.'—'And so you are.'... 'You can't possibly use this word.'—'So I won't.'... 'You know who Diana was, Grandfather.'—'So I do!'... 'Why, this is nothing but common vegetable soup!'—'So it is, madam.'... 'The car, Annie,' said Max rather grimly.—'So okay, the car. What about it?'* ADV: ADV cl

11 You say **'So?'** and **'So what?'** to indicate that you think that something that someone has said is unimportant; an informal use. *'My name's Bruno.'—'So?'... 'You take a chance on the weather if you holiday in the UK.'—'So what?'... I enjoy someone telling me I'm wonderful, but part of me thinks, 'So what? You won't say that tomorrow.'* CONVENTION

12 You can also use **so** in front of adjectives and adverbs to emphasize the quality that they are describing. *'I am so afraid,' Francis thought... He was surprised they had married – they had seemed so different... What is so compromising about being an employee of the state?* ADV: ADV adj/adv

13 You can use **so...that** and **so...as** to emphasize the degree of something by mentioning the result of consequence of it. *The tears were streaming so fast she could not see... The deal seems so attractive it would be ridiculous to say no... Frescoes are so familiar a feature of Italian churches that it is easy to take them for granted... He's not so daft as to listen to rumours.* ADV: ADV adj that, ADV adj *as* to-inf

14 You use **and so on** or **and so forth** at the end of a list to indicate that there are other items that you could also mention. *...the Government's policies on such important issues as health, education, tax and so on... The patient can have apples, apple juice, apple sauce, and so forth.* PHRASES cl/group PHR =etcetera

15 You use **so much** and **so many** when you are saying that there is a definite limit to something but you are not saying what this limit is. *There is only so much time in the day for answering letters... There is only so much fuel in the tank and if you burn it up too quickly you are in trouble... Even the greatest city can support only so many lawyers.* PHR n

16 You use the structures **not...so much** and **not so much...as** to say that something is one kind of thing rather than another kind. *I did not really object to Will's behaviour so much as his personality... A good birth depends not so much on who you are but where you are and how much you know.*

17 You use **or so** when you are giving an approximate amount. *Though rates are heading down, they still offer real returns of 8% or so... They'll be here within the next fortnight or so... The driver usually spends four hours or so helping to load and prepare his lorry.* amount PHR

18 • **so much the better**: see **better**. • **ever so**: see **ever**. • **so far so good**: see **far**. • **insofar as**: see **insofar**. • **so long**: see **long**. • **so much for**: see **much**. • **so much so**: see **much**. • **every so often**: see **often**. • **so there**: see **there**.

soak /soʊk/ **soaks, soaking, soaked** ◆◆◇◇◇

1 If you **soak** something or leave it to **soak**, you put it into a liquid and leave it there. *Soak the beans for 2 hours... He turned off the water and left the dishes to soak.* VERB V n V

2 If a liquid **soaks** something or when if **soak** something with a liquid, the liquid makes the thing very wet. *The water had soaked his jacket and shirt... Soak the soil around each bush with at least 4 gallons of water.* VERB V n V n with n

3 If a liquid **soaks** through something, it passes through it. *There was so much blood it had soaked through my boxer shorts... Rain had soaked into the sand.* VERB V prep/adv

4 If someone **soaks**, they spend a long time in a hot bath, because they enjoy it. *What I need is to soak in a hot tub.* ► Also a noun. *I was having a long soak in the bath.* VERB V N-COUNT

5 See also **soaked, soaking.**

soak up PHRASAL VERB

1 If a soft or dry material **soaks up** a liquid, the liquid goes into the substance. *The cells will promptly start to soak up moisture.* V P n (not pron) Also V n P

2 If you **soak up** the sun, you sit or lie in the sun, because you enjoy it; an informal use. *I was lying on my stomach soaking up the sun.* V P n (not pron)

3 If you **soak up** the atmosphere in a place that you are visiting, you observe or get involved in the way of life there, because you enjoy it or are interested in it; an informal use. *Keaton comes here once or twice a year to soak up the atmosphere.* =absorb V P n (not pron) Also V n P

4 If something **soaks up** something such as money or other resources, it uses a great deal of money or other resources. *Defence soaks up forty per cent of the budget... External broadcasting soaks up more resources in Britain than elsewhere.* V P n (not pron) Also V n P

soaked /soʊkt/. If someone or something gets **soaked** or **soaked through**, water or some other liquid makes them extremely wet or extremely damp. *I have to check my tent – it got soaked last night in the storm... My goodness, you're soaked through. Where's your car?... We got soaked to the skin... His torn clothes were soaked in blood.* ◆◇◇◇◇ ADJ: usu v-link ADJ =drenched

-soaked /-soʊkt/

1 **-soaked** combines with nouns such as 'rain' and 'blood' to form adjectives which describe someone or something that is extremely wet or extremely damp because of the thing mentioned. *...the* COMB in ADJ: usu ADJ n *possibility of a rain-soaked pitch causing a game to be cancelled. ...blood-soaked clothes.*

2 **-soaked** combines with nouns such as 'sun' to form adjectives which describe places, times, or events that have a lot of the thing mentioned. *...a sun-soaked Caribbean island. ...the cash-soaked Eighties... The champagne-soaked event took over the city's main thoroughfare.* [COMB in ADJ: usu ADJ n]

soaking /soʊkɪŋ/. If something is **soaking** or **soaking wet**, it is very wet. *My face and raincoat were soaking wet.* [◆◇◇◇◇ ADJ =sopping]

so-and-so, so-and-sos [◆◇◇◇◇]

1 You use **so-and-so** instead of a word, expression, or name when you are talking generally rather than giving a specific example of a particular thing. *It would be a case of 'just do so-and-so and here's your cash'... If Mrs So-and-so was ill then Mrs So-and-so down the street would go and clean for her.* [PRON-SING]

2 People sometimes refer to another person as a **so-and-so** when they are annoyed with them or think that they are foolish. People often use **so-and-so** in order to avoid using a swear word. Used in informal English. *All her fault, the wicked little so-and-so.* [N-COUNT PRAGMATICS]

soap /soʊp/ **soaps, soaping, soaped** [◆◆◇◇◇]

1 **Soap** is a substance that you use with water for washing yourself or sometimes for washing clothes. *...a bar of lavender soap. ...a large packet of soap powder. ...a soap bubble.* [N-MASS]

2 If you **soap** yourself, you rub soap on your body in order to wash yourself. *She soaped herself all over.* [VERB; V pron-refl; Also V n]

3 A **soap** is the same as a **soap opera**; an informal use. [N-COUNT]

soapbox /soʊpbɒks/ **soapboxes.**

1 A **soapbox** is a small temporary platform on which a person stands when he or she is making a speech outdoors to passers-by. *He stood on his soapbox, his head clearly visible above often hostile crowds. ...soapbox speeches.* [N-COUNT]

2 If you say that someone is on their **soapbox**, you mean that they are speaking or writing about something they feel passionate about. *We were interested in pushing forward certain issues and getting up on our soapbox about them... I wanted to talk about the pension age. It's rather a soapbox of mine.* [N-COUNT]

soap opera, soap operas. A **soap opera** is a popular television drama serial about the daily lives and problems of a group of people. [◆◇◇◇◇ N-COUNT]

soapy /soʊpi/ **soapier, soapiest.** Something that is **soapy** is full of soap or covered with soap. *Wash your hands thoroughly with hot soapy water before handling any food. ...the soapy plates.* [ADJ-GRADED: usu ADJ n]

soar /sɔːʳ/ **soars, soaring, soared** [◆◆◇◇◇]

1 If the amount, value, level, or volume of something **soars**, it quickly increases by a great deal; used in journalism. *Insurance claims are expected to soar... Shares soared on the stock exchange... Economists believe the jobless total will soar to 3.5 million by the spring... The temperature in the south will soar into the hundreds. ...soaring unemployment.* [VERB =rocket; V; V prep/adv; V-ing]

2 If something such as a bird **soars** into the air, it goes quickly up into the air; a literary use. *If you're lucky, a splendid golden eagle may soar into view... Buzzards soar overhead at a great height... The two sheets of flame clashed, soaring hundreds of feet high.* [VERB; V prep/adv; V n]

3 Trees or buildings that **soar** upwards are very tall; a literary use. *The steeple soars skyward. ...the soaring spires of churches like St Peter's.* [VERB; V prep/adv; V-ing]

4 If music **soars**, it rises greatly in volume or pitch; a literary use. *The music soared to the rafters, carrying its listeners' hearts... His soaring voice cuts straight to the heart.* [VERB; V prep; V-ing; Also V]

5 If your spirits **soar**, you suddenly start to feel very happy; a literary use. *For the first time in months, my spirits soared.* [VERB; V]

soaraway /sɔːrəweɪ/. If you describe something as a **soaraway** success, you mean that its success has suddenly increased; an informal word, used in journalism. *Her soaraway career took off after she was divorced from her first husband. ...soaraway sales.* [ADJ: ADJ n]

sob /sɒb/ **sobs, sobbing, sobbed** [◆◇◇◇◇]

1 When someone **sobs**, they cry in a noisy way, breathing in short breaths. *She began to sob again, burying her face in the pillow... Her sister broke down, sobbing into her handkerchief.* ♦ **sobbing** *The room was silent except for her sobbing.* [VERB =weep; V] [N-UNCOUNT =weeping]

2 If you **sob** something, you say it whilst you are crying. *'Everything's my fault,' she sobbed.* [VERB; V with quote]

3 A **sob** is one of the noises that you make when you are crying. [N-COUNT]

sober /soʊbəʳ/ **sobers, sobering, sobered** [◆◆◇◇◇]

1 When you are **sober**, you are not drunk. *He'd been drunk when I arrived. Now he was sober.* [ADJ-GRADED: usu v-link ADJ ≠drunk]

2 A **sober** person is serious and thoughtful. *We are now far more sober and realistic... It was a room filled with sad, sober faces... The euphoria is giving way to a more sober assessment of the situation.* ♦ **soberly** *'There's a new development,' he said soberly.* [ADJ-GRADED] [ADV-GRADED: usu ADV with v]

3 **Sober** colours and clothes are plain and rather dull. *He dresses in sober grey suits. ...sober-suited middle-aged men.* ♦ **soberly** *She saw Ellis, soberly dressed in a well-cut dark suit.* [ADJ-GRADED =sombre, staid] [ADV-GRADED: ADV with v]

4 See also **sobering.**

5 ● **stone-cold sober**: see **stone-cold.**

sober up. When someone **sobers up**, they become sober after being drunk. If someone or something **sobers** a person **up**, they make the person sober after he or she has been drunk. *He was left to sober up in a police cell. ...the idea that a cup of strong black coffee sobers you up.* [PHRASAL VERB ERG; V P; V n P]

sobering /soʊbərɪŋ/. You say that something is a **sobering** thought or has a **sobering** effect when a situation seems serious and makes you become serious and thoughtful. *It is a sobering thought that in the 17th century she could have been burnt as a witch... The events of October 1987 had a sobering effect on managers of large funds.* [◆◇◇◇◇ ADJ-GRADED: usu ADJ n]

sobriety /səbraɪɪti/

1 **Sobriety** is the state of being sober rather than drunk; a formal use. [N-UNCOUNT]

2 **Sobriety** is serious and thoughtful behaviour; a formal use. *...the values society depends upon, such as honesty, sobriety and trust.* [N-UNCOUNT]

sobriquet /soʊbrɪkeɪ/ **sobriquets;** also spelled **soubriquet**. A **sobriquet** is a humorous nickname or description that is applied to someone or something; used in written English. *In 1970, Lawton Chiles walked the length of Florida to win election to the US Senate, earning the sobriquet 'Walkin' Lawton'.* [N-COUNT: usu sing]

sob story, sob stories. You describe what someone tells you about their own or someone else's difficulties as a **sob story** when you think that they have told you about it in order to get your sympathy. *Any sob story moved Jarvis to generosity.* [N-COUNT PRAGMATICS]

Soc. /sɒk/. **Soc.** is the written abbreviation for **Society**.

so-called; also spelled **so called**. [◆◆◆◇◇]

1 You use **so-called** to indicate that you think the following word or expression is incorrect or misleading. *These are the facts that explode their so-called economic miracle... More and more companies have gone 'green' and started producing so-called environmentally-friendly products.* [ADJ: ADJ n PRAGMATICS]

2 You use **so-called** to indicate that something is generally referred to by the name that you are about to use. *...a summit of the world's seven leading market economies, the so-called G-7... She was one of the so-called Gang of Four.* [ADJ: ADJ n]

soccer /sɒkəʳ/. **Soccer** is a game played by two teams of eleven players using a round ball. Players kick the ball to each other and try to score goals by kicking the ball into a large net. In Europe and South America, this game is also referred to as **football**.  [N-UNCOUNT]

sociable /soʊʃəbəl/. **Sociable** people are friendly and enjoy talking to other people. *She was,* [◆◇◇◇◇ ADJ-GRADED =friendly]

and remained, extremely sociable, enjoying dancing, golf, tennis, skating and bicycling... Some children have more sociable personalities than others. ♦ **sociability** /soʊʃəbɪlɪti/ *Enthusiasm, adaptability, sociability, and good health are essential.*
≠anti-social
N-UNCOUNT

social /soʊʃəl/ **socials** ◆◆◆◆◆

1 Social means relating to society or to the way society is organized. *...the worst effects of unemployment, low pay and other social problems. ...long-term social change. ...the acceptance that social conditions influenced crime. ...changing social attitudes. ...the tightly woven social fabric of small towns. ...research into housing and social policy.* ♦ **socially** *Let's face it – drinking is a socially acceptable habit. ...one of the most socially deprived estates in the city.*
ADJ: ADJ n
ADV: ADV adj/-ed

2 Social means relating to the status or rank that someone has in society. *Higher education is unequally distributed across social classes... The guests came from all social backgrounds... Morisot and Degas moved in the same social circles. ...a prosperous upper-middle-class couple with social aspirations.* ♦ **socially** *For socially ambitious couples this is a problem. ...socially disadvantaged children... I felt there was a lot of pressure on me to achieve, both academically and socially.*
ADJ: ADJ n
ADV: usu ADV adj/-ed, also ADV with cl

3 Social means relating to leisure activities that involve meeting other people. *We ought to organize more social events... Social activities might include barbecues on the beach and walking tours of the Old Town.* ♦ **socially** *We have known each other socially for a long time... The two groups rarely meet socially... Socially I found him delightful.*
ADJ: ADJ n
ADV: usu ADV with v, also ADV with cl

4 A **social** is a party, dance, or informal gathering that is organized for the members of a club or institution; an old-fashioned use. *...church socials.*
N-COUNT

5 Social animals live in groups and do things together. *These endangered gentle giants are highly social animals. ...social insects like bees and ants.*
ADJ-GRADED: ADJ n

social climber, social climbers. You describe someone as a **social climber** when you disapprove of them because they try to have friends and acquaintances who belong to a higher social class, in order to be regarded as belonging to that class themselves. *That Rous was a snob and a social climber could scarcely be denied.*
N-COUNT PRAGMATICS

social climbing; also spelled **social-climbing**. You describe someone's behaviour as **social climbing** when you disapprove of it because they try to have friends and acquaintances who belong to a higher social class, in order to be regarded as belonging to that class themselves. *All that vulgar social-climbing!* ▶ Also an adjective. *...Leroy's ambitious social-climbing wife.*
N-UNCOUNT PRAGMATICS
ADJ: ADJ n

social club, social clubs. A **social club** is a club where members go in order to meet each other socially.
N-COUNT

social democracy, social democracies

1 Social democracy is a political system according to which social justice and equality can be achieved within the framework of a market economy. *...western-style social democracy.*
N-UNCOUNT

2 A **social democracy** is a country where there is social democracy.
N-COUNT

social democratic. A **social democratic** party is a political party whose principles are based on social democracy. *...a western-style social democratic party. ...relations with the social democratic governments in Europe.*
◆◇◇◇◇ ADJ: ADJ n

social housing. In Britain, **social housing** is housing which is provided for rent or sale at a fairly low cost by organizations such as housing associations and local councils.
N-UNCOUNT

socialisation /soʊʃəlaɪzeɪʃən/. See **socialization**.

socialise /soʊʃəlaɪz/. See **socialize**.

socialism /soʊʃəlɪzəm/. **Socialism** is a set of left-wing political principles whose general aim is to create a system in which everyone has an equal opportunity to benefit from a country's wealth. Under socialism, the country's main industries are usually owned by the state.
◆◆◇◇◇ N-UNCOUNT

socialist /soʊʃəlɪst/ **socialists** ◆◆◆◇◇

1 Socialist means based on socialism or relating to socialism. *...members of the ruling Socialist party. ...low-inflation policies practised by the socialist government... Capitalist reform is gradually dismantling the socialist state.*
ADJ: usu ADJ n

2 A **socialist** is a person who believes in socialism or who is a member of a socialist party. *The ruling Socialists are deeply unpopular.*
N-COUNT

socialistic /soʊʃəlɪstɪk/. If you describe a policy or organization as **socialistic**, you mean that it has some of the features of socialism; often used showing disapproval. *The Conservatives denounce it as socialistic... Most of these specific Socialistic policies have been abandoned.*
ADJ

socialite /soʊʃəlaɪt/ **socialites.** A **socialite** is a person who attends many fashionable upper-class social events and who is well known because of this; used mainly in journalism.
N-COUNT

socialization /soʊʃəlaɪzeɪʃən/; also spelled **socialisation**.

1 Socialization is the process by which people, especially children, are made to behave in a way which is acceptable in their culture or society; a technical use in sociology. *Female socialization emphasizes getting along with others, while male socialization stresses becoming independent.*
N-UNCOUNT

2 Socialization is the process by which something is made to operate on socialist principles; a technical use in politics.
N-UNCOUNT

socialize /soʊʃəlaɪz/ **socializes, socializing, socialized;** also spelled **socialise** in British English. ◆◆◇◇◇

1 If you **socialize**, you meet other people socially, for example at parties. *...an open meeting, where members socialized and welcomed any new members... It distressed her that she and Charles no longer socialized with old friends.* ♦ **socializing** *The hours were terrible, so socialising was difficult.*
VERB V V *with* n
N-UNCOUNT

2 When people, especially children, **are socialized**, they are made to behave in a way which is acceptable in their culture or society; a technical use in sociology. *You may have been socialized to do as you are told... From the time you are born you have to be socialised into being a good father.*
VB: usu passive
be V-ed

3 When something **is socialized**, it is made to operate on socialist principles; a technical use in politics. *...a socialist system in which the ownership of the means of production will be socialized. ...the debate over how a fully socialized economy might work.*
VB: usu passive
be V-ed V-ed

social life, social lives. Your **social life** consists of the activities in which you meet your friends and acquaintances, for example at parties or in pubs or bars.
◆◇◇◇◇ N-COUNT: with supp, oft with poss

social order, social orders. The **social order** in a place is the way that society is organized there. *...the threat to social order posed by right-wing extremists.*
◆◇◇◇◇ N-VAR

social science, social sciences ◆◇◇◇◇

1 Social science is the scientific study of society.
N-UNCOUNT

2 The **social sciences** are the various branches of social science, for example sociology and politics.
N-COUNT: usu pl

social scientist, social scientists. A **social scientist** is a person who studies or teaches social science.
N-COUNT

social security. **Social security** is a system under which a government pays money regularly to certain groups of people, for example the sick, the unemployed, or those with no other income. *...women who did not have jobs and were on social security... Families on social security benefits will be harshly affected.*
◆◆◇◇◇ N-UNCOUNT

social services. The **social services** in a district are the services provided by the local authority to help people who have serious family problems or financial problems. *I have asked the social services for help, but they have not done anything.*
◆◆◇◇◇ N-PLURAL

social studies. **Social studies** is a subject that is taught in British schools and colleges. It includes sociology, politics, and economics. N-UNCOUNT

social work. **Social work** is work which involves giving help and advice to people with serious family problems or financial problems. ◆◇◇◇◇ N-UNCOUNT

social worker, social workers. A **social worker** is a person whose job is to do social work. ◆◆◇◇◇ N-COUNT

societal /səsaɪɪtəl/. **Societal** means relating to society or to the way society is organized; a formal word. *...the societal changes that have taken place over the last two decades. ...societal norms.* ADJ: ADJ n =social

society /səsaɪɪti/ **societies** ◆◆◆◆◆

1 **Society** is people in general, thought of as a large organized group. *This reflects attitudes and values prevailing in society... He maintains Islam must adapt to modern society.* N-UNCOUNT

2 A **society** is the people who live in a country or region, their organizations, and their way of life. *We live in a capitalist society. ...those responsible for destroying our African heritage and the fabric of our society. ...the complexities of South African society.* N-VAR: with supp

3 A **society** is an organization for people who have the same interest or aim. *...the North of England Horticultural Society. ...the historical society.* N-COUNT =association

4 **Society** is the rich, fashionable people in a particular place who meet on social occasions. *The couple quickly became a fixture of society pages. ...the high season for society weddings.* N-UNCOUNT: oft N n

5 See also **building society**.

socio- /soʊsioʊ-/. **Socio-** is used to form adjectives and nouns which describe or refer to things relating to or involving social factors. *Sociobiology is the study of how animal behaviour evolves to fit function.* PREFIX

socio-economic; also spelled **socioeconomic**. **Socio-economic** circumstances or developments involve a combination of social and economic factors; a technical term in social science. *The age, education, and socio-economic status of these young mothers led to less satisfactory child care. ...the western European historical model of socio-economic development.* ◆◇◇◇◇ ADJ: ADJ n

sociology /soʊsiɒlədʒi/. **Sociology** is the study of society or of the way society is organized. ◆◆◇◇◇ N-UNCOUNT ♦ **sociological** /soʊsiəlɒdʒɪkəl/ *Psychological and sociological studies were emphasizing the importance of the family.* ADJ: usu ADJ n ♦ **sociologist, sociologists** *By the 1950s some sociologists were confident that they had identified the key characteristics of capitalist society.* N-COUNT

sociopath /soʊsiəpæθ/ **sociopaths.** A **sociopath** is the same as a **psychopath**. N-COUNT

socio-political; also spelled **sociopolitical**. **Socio-political** systems and problems involve a combination of social and political factors; a technical term in social science. *...contemporary sociopolitical issues such as ecology, human rights, and nuclear arms.* ADJ: ADJ n

sock /sɒk/ **socks, socking, socked** ◆◆◇◇◇

1 **Socks** are pieces of clothing which cover your foot and ankle and are worn inside shoes. *...a pair of knee-length socks.* N-COUNT

2 If someone **socks it to** another person, they do or say something that makes a big impact on them; an informal expression, used especially in journalism. *Come on, lads. Sock it to 'em.* PHRASES V inflects, PHR n

3 If you tell someone to **pull** their **socks up**, you mean that they should start working or studying harder, because they have been lazy or careless recently; an informal expression, used mainly in British English. *He needs to pull his socks up if he is to make a success of his career.* V inflects PRAGMATICS

socket /sɒkɪt/ **sockets** ◆◇◇◇◇

1 A **socket** is a device on a piece of electrical equipment into which you can put a bulb or plug. N-COUNT

2 In British English, a **socket** is a device or point in a wall where you can connect electrical equipment to the power supply. The usual American term is **outlet**. N-COUNT =power point

3 You can refer to any hollow part or opening in a structure which another part fits into as a **socket**. *Rotate the shoulders in their sockets five times... Her eyes were sunk deep into their sockets.* N-COUNT

sod /sɒd/ **sods** ◆◇◇◇◇

1 If someone calls another person or something such as a job a **sod**, they are expressing anger or annoyance towards that person or thing; an informal British use which many people find offensive. N-COUNT PRAGMATICS

2 If someone uses an expression such as '**Sod it**', '**Sod you**', or '**Sod that**', they are expressing anger or the fact that they do not care about someone or something. These expressions are used in informal British English and many people find them offensive. PRAGMATICS

3 The **sod** is the surface of the earth, with the grass and roots that are growing in it; a literary use. N-SING

4 **Sod all** means 'nothing at all'; an informal British expression which many people find offensive. PHRASES PRAGMATICS

5 **Sod's Law** is the idea that if something can go wrong, it will go wrong; an informal British expression which many people find offensive. *This was sod's law: when the spare tyre is in use, you will have a puncture.*

sod off. In informal British English, if someone tells someone else to **sod off**, they are telling them in a very offensive way to go away or leave them alone. PHRASAL VERB only imper PRAGMATICS

soda /soʊdə/ **sodas** ◆◇◇◇◇

1 **Soda** is the same as **soda water**. N-UNCOUNT

2 In American English, **soda** is a sweet fizzy drink. *...a glass of diet soda.* ► A **soda** is a bottle of soda. *They had liquor for the adults and sodas for the children.* N-MASS =soda pop N-COUNT =soda pop

3 See also **bicarbonate of soda, caustic soda, ice-cream soda**.

soda pop, soda pops. In American English, **soda pop** is a sweet fizzy drink. ► A **soda pop** is a bottle or a glass of soda pop. N-UNCOUNT =soda N-COUNT

soda siphon, soda siphons; also spelled **soda syphon**. A **soda siphon** is a special bottle from which you can squirt soda water into a drink. N-COUNT

soda water; also spelled **soda-water**. **Soda water** is fizzy water used for mixing with alcoholic drinks and fruit juice. N-UNCOUNT =soda

sodden /sɒdən/. Something that is **sodden** is extremely wet. *We stripped off our sodden clothes... His grey jersey and trousers were sodden with the rain.* ◆◇◇◇◇ ADJ =soaked

-sodden /-sɒdən/

1 **-sodden** combines with 'drink' and with the names of alcoholic drinks to form adjectives which describe someone who has drunk too much alcohol and is in a bad state as a result. *He portrays a whisky-sodden Catholic priest.* COMB in ADJ: usu ADJ n

2 **-sodden** combines with words such as 'rain' to form adjectives which describe someone or something that has become extremely wet as a result of the thing that is mentioned. *The porter put our scruffy rain-sodden luggage on a trolley.* COMB in ADJ: usu ADJ n

sodding /sɒdɪŋ/. In British English, **sodding** is a swear word that some people use to express their anger or annoyance; an informal use which many people find offensive. ADJ: ADJ n

sodium /soʊdiəm/ ◆◆◇◇◇

1 **Sodium** is a silvery-white chemical element which combines with other chemicals. Salt is a sodium compound. *The fish or seafood is heavily salted with pure sodium chloride. ...one level teaspoon of sodium bicarbonate powder.* N-UNCOUNT

2 **Sodium** lighting gives out a strong orange light. *...the orange glow of the sodium streetlamps.* ADJ: ADJ n

sodomy /sɒdəmi/. **Sodomy** is anal sexual intercourse, especially between men. N-UNCOUNT

sofa /soʊfə/ **sofas.** A **sofa** is a long, comfortable seat with a back and usually with arms, which two or three people can sit on; used mainly in British English. ◆◆◇◇◇ N-COUNT =settee

sofa-bed, sofa-beds. A **sofa-bed** is a sofa which is made with a special seat that folds out so that it can also be used as a bed. N-COUNT

soft /sɒft, AM sɔːft/ **softer, softest** ◆◆◆◆◇

1 Something that is **soft** is pleasant to touch, and ADJ-GRADED

not rough or hard. *Regular use of a body lotion will keep the skin soft and supple... When it's dry, brush the hair using a soft, nylon baby brush. ...warm, soft, white towels.* ≠rough ♦ **softness** *The sea air robbed her hair of its softness.* N-UNCOUNT

2 Something that is **soft** changes shape or bends easily when you press it. *She lay down on the soft, comfortable bed... Add enough milk to form a soft dough. ...soft cheese.* ADJ-GRADED ≠hard, firm

3 Something that has a **soft** appearance has smooth curves rather than sharp or distinct edges. *This is a smart, yet soft and feminine look. ...the soft curves of her body.* ADJ-GRADED =gentle ≠hard ♦ **softly** *She wore a softly tailored suit. ...a fresh, modern hairstyle which has long layers falling softly on the neck.* ADV-GRADED: ADV with v

4 Something that is **soft** is very gentle and has no force. For example, a **soft** sound or voice is quiet and not harsh. A **soft** light or colour is pleasant to look at because it is not bright. *There was a soft tapping on my door... When he woke again he could hear soft music. ...a soft Irish accent. ...soft muted colours... A soft spring rain had fallen all day.* ADJ-GRADED =gentle ≠harsh ♦ **softly** *'I'm sorry,' he said softly... She crossed the softly lit room... She bent forward and kissed him softly.* ADV-GRADED: ADV with v

5 If you are **soft** on someone, you do not treat them as strictly or severely as you should do; used showing disapproval. *The president says the measure is soft and weak on criminals... He had initially thought Byrnes too soft with the Russians.* ADJ-GRADED: usu v-link ADJ, oft ADJ *on* n PRAGMATICS ≠hard

6 If you say that someone has a **soft** heart, you mean that they are sensitive and sympathetic towards other people. *Her rather tough and worldly exterior hides a very soft and sensitive heart.* ADJ-GRADED =tender ≠hard

7 You use **soft** to describe a way of life that is easy and involves very little work. *The regime at Latchmere could be seen as a soft option... There is no way that 20 years of soft living could be lost in the first 30 minutes' exercise.* ADJ-GRADED =easy ≠hard

8 Soft drugs are drugs, such as marijuana, which are illegal but which many people do not consider to be strong, harmful, or addictive. ADJ: ADJ n

9 A **soft** target is a place or person that can easily be attacked. *It sums these terrorists up when they go after such soft targets.* ADJ-GRADED =easy

10 Soft water does not contain much calcium and so makes bubbles easily when you use soap to wash things. ADJ-GRADED ≠hard

11 If you have **a soft spot for** someone or something, you feel a great deal of affection for them or like them a lot. *Terry had a soft spot for me... I have a soft spot for London Zoo.* PHRASE: PHR after v, PHR n ● **a soft touch**: see **touch**.

softback /sɒftbæk/. A **softback** is a book with a thin cardboard, paper, or plastic cover. Compare **hardback** and **paperback**. *...published by Boxtree, at £5.99 for the softback and £15.99 for the hardback... This title was a best seller and is now available in softback.* N-SING: also *in* N

softball /sɒftbɔːl, AM sɔːft-/ **softballs**

1 Softball is a game similar to baseball, but played with a larger, softer ball. N-UNCOUNT

2 A **softball** is the ball used in the game of softball. N-COUNT

soft-boiled. A **soft-boiled** egg is one that has been boiled for only a few minutes, so that the yolk is still soft. ADJ ≠hard-boiled

soft-core; also spelled **softcore**. **Soft-core** pornography shows or mentions sexual acts or naked bodies, but not in a very explicit or violent way. Compare **hard-core**. ADJ: ADJ n

soft drink, soft drinks. A **soft drink** is a cold, non-alcoholic drink such as lemonade or fruit juice. ◆◇◇◇◇ N-COUNT

soften /sɒfᵊn, AM sɔːf-/ **softens, softening, softened** ◆◆◇◇◇

1 If you **soften** something or if it **softens**, it becomes less hard, stiff, or firm. *Soften the butter mixture in a small saucepan... Fry for about 4 minutes, until the onion has softened.* V-ERG V n V

2 If one thing **softens** the impact or the damaging effect of another thing, it makes the impact or effect seem less severe. *There were also pledges to soften the impact of the subsidy cuts on the poorer regions... In order to soften the blow of steep price rises, Yeltsin has announced a near doubling of many public-sector salaries.* VERB V n

3 If you **soften** your position, if your position **softens**, or if you **soften**, you become more sympathetic and less hostile or critical. *The letter shows no sign that the Americans have softened their position... His party's policy has softened a lot in recent years... Livy felt herself soften towards Caroline.* V-ERG ≠harden V n V

4 If your voice or expression **softens** or if you **soften** it, it becomes much more gentle and friendly. *All at once, Mick's serious expression softened into a grin... She did not smile or soften her voice.* V-ERG V V n

5 If you **soften** something such as light, a colour, or a sound, you make it less bright or harsh. *We wanted to soften the light without destroying the overall effect of space... Stark concrete walls have been softened by a show of fresh flowers.* VERB V n

6 Something that **softens** your skin makes it very smooth and pleasant to touch. *...products designed to moisturize and soften the skin.* VERB V n

soften up. If you **soften** someone **up**, you put them into a good mood before asking them to do something; an informal expression. *If they'd treated you well it was just to soften you up.* PHRASAL VERB =butter up V n P Also V P n (not pron)

softener /sɒfənəʳ, AM sɔːf-/ **softeners**

1 A water **softener** is a device or substance which removes certain minerals, for example calcium, from water, so that it makes bubbles easily when you use soap to wash things. N-COUNT

2 A fabric **softener** is a chemical substance that you add to water when you wash clothes in order to make the clothes feel softer. N-MASS

soft focus. If something in a photograph or film is in **soft focus**, it has been made to look slightly blurred to give it a more romantic effect. *In the background, in soft focus, we see his smiling wife.* N-UNCOUNT

soft fruit, soft fruits. In British English, **soft fruits** are small fruits with soft skins, such as strawberries and currants. N-VAR

soft furnishings. In British English, **soft furnishings** are cushions, curtains, lampshades, and furniture covers. N-PLURAL

soft-hearted. Someone who is **soft-hearted** has a very sympathetic and kind nature. ADJ-GRADED

softie /sɒfti/ **softies;** also spelled **softy**. If you describe someone as a **softie**, you mean that they are very emotional or that they can easily be made to feel sympathy towards other people; an informal use. *He's just a big softie... Oh, so you're one of those softies who believe you should reason with criminals!* N-COUNT

soft loan, soft loans. A **soft loan** is a loan with a very low interest rate. Soft loans are usually made to developing countries or to businesses in developing countries. N-COUNT

softly-softly; also spelled **softly, softly**. In British English, a **softly-softly** approach to something is cautious and patient and avoids direct action or force. *There is now a growing debate as to whether the government's softly, softly approach to the prison protest was the right one.* ADJ: ADJ n

soft-pedal, soft-pedals, soft-pedalling, soft-pedalled; spelled **soft-pedaling, soft-pedaled** in American English. If you **soft-pedal** something, you deliberately reduce the amount of activity or pressure that you have been using to get something done; used mainly in American English. *He refused to soft-pedal an investigation into the scandal.* VERB V n Also V *on* n

soft porn. **Soft porn** is pornography that shows or mentions sexual acts, but not in a very explicit or violent way. N-UNCOUNT

soft sell; also spelled **soft-sell**. A **soft sell** is a method of selling or advertising that involves gentle persuasion rather than putting a lot of pressure on people. *I think more customers probably prefer a soft sell.* N-SING ≠hard sell

soft-soap, soft-soaps, soft-soaping, soft-soaped. If you **soft-soap** someone, you flatter VERB them or tell them what you think they want to hear in order to try and persuade them to do something. *The government is not soft-soaping the voters here.* V n

soft-spoken. Someone who is **soft-spoken** has a quiet, gentle voice. *He was a gentle, soft-spoken intelligent man.* ADJ-GRADED

soft toy, soft toys. Soft toys are toys that look like animals. They are made of soft material and stuffed. N-COUNT

software /sɒftweəʳ, AM sɔːf-/. Computer programs are referred to as **software.** *...the people who write the software for big computer projects.* ◆◆◆◇◇ N-UNCOUNT

softwood /sɒftwʊd, AM sɔːft-/ **softwoods. Softwood** is the wood from trees such as pines, that grow quickly and can be sawn easily. N-MASS ≠hardwood

softy /sɒfti, AM sɔːfti/. See **softie**.

soggy /sɒgi/ **soggier, soggiest.** Something that is **soggy** is unpleasantly wet. *...soggy cheese sandwiches. ...a gray and soggy afternoon.* ◆◇◇◇◇ ADJ-GRADED

soignée /swɑːnjeɪ, AM -jeɪ/; also spelled **soigné** when referring to a man. If you describe a person as **soignée**, you mean that they are very elegant; a formal term. *...looking very soignée in black.* ADJ-GRADED =elegant

soil /sɔɪl/ **soils, soiling, soiled** ◆◆◆◇◇

1 **Soil** is the substance on the surface of the earth in which plants grow. *We have the most fertile soil in Europe. ...regions with sandy soils.* N-MASS

2 You can use **soil** in expressions like **'British soil'** to refer to a country's territory. *The issue of foreign troops on Turkish soil is a sensitive one.* N-UNCOUNT: with supp =land, territory

3 If you **soil** something, you make it dirty; a formal use. *Young people don't want to do things that soil their hands... He raised his eyes slightly as though her words might somehow soil him.* ♦ **soiled** *...a soiled white apron.* VERB =dirty V n; ADJ-GRADED =dirty

soiree /swɑːreɪ, AM swɑːreɪ/ **soirees;** also spelled **soirée.** A **soiree** is a social gathering held in the evening; a formal word. N-COUNT

sojourn /sɒdʒɜːʳn, AM soʊdʒ-/ **sojourns.** A **sojourn** is a short stay in a place that is not your home; a literary word. N-COUNT =stay

solace /sɒlɪs/ ◆◇◇◇◇

1 **Solace** is a feeling of comfort that makes you feel less sad; a formal use. *I found solace in writing when my father died three years ago... Henry was inclined to seek solace in drink.* N-UNCOUNT =comfort

2 If something is a **solace** to you, it makes you feel less sad; a formal use. *She found the companionship of Marcia a solace.* N-SING =comfort

solar /soʊləʳ/ ◆◆◇◇◇

1 **Solar** is used to describe things relating to the sun. *A total solar eclipse is due to take place some time tomorrow.* ADJ: usu ADJ n

2 **Solar** power is obtained from the sun's light and heat. ADJ: usu ADJ n

solar cell, solar cells. A **solar cell** is a device that produces electricity from the sun's rays. N-COUNT

solarium /soʊleəriəm/ **solariums.** A **solarium** is a place equipped with sun-lamps, where you can go to get an artificial suntan. N-COUNT

solar plexus /soʊləʳ pleksəs/. Your **solar plexus** is the part of your stomach, below your ribs, where it is painful if you are hit hard. N-SING: *the* N, N with poss

solar system, solar systems. The **solar system** is the sun and all the planets and comets that go round it. *Saturn is the second biggest planet in the solar system.* ◆◇◇◇◇ N-COUNT: usu sing, oft *the* N, poss N

sold /soʊld/. **Sold** is the past tense and past participle of **sell**.

solder /soʊldəʳ, AM sɑːdəʳ/ **solders, soldering, soldered**

1 If you **solder** two pieces of metal together, you join them by melting a small piece of soft metal and putting it between them so that it holds them together after it has cooled. *Fewer workers are needed to solder circuit boards... He then soldered the wire to the telephone terminal... He cuts the pieces and solders them together.* VERB V n V n *to/onto* n V n adv Also V

2 **Solder** is the soft metal used for soldering. N-UNCOUNT

soldering iron, soldering irons. A **soldering iron** is a tool used to solder things together. N-COUNT

soldier /soʊldʒəʳ/ **soldiers, soldiering, soldiered.** A **soldier** is a person who works in an army, especially a person who is not an officer. ◆◆◆◆◇ N-COUNT

soldier on. If you **soldier on** at something, you continue to do it although it is difficult or unpleasant. *The government has soldiered on as if nothing were wrong.* PHRASAL VERB V P

soldierly /soʊldʒəʳli/. If you act in a **soldierly** way, you behave like a good or brave soldier; a formal word. *There was a great deal of soldierly good fellowship.* ADJ: usu ADJ n

soldiery /soʊldʒəri/. **Soldiery** is a group or body of soldiers; a literary word. *...the distant shouts and songs of the drunken soldiery.* N-UNCOUNT

sold out ◆◇◇◇◇

1 If a performance, sports event, or other entertainment is **sold out**, all the tickets for it have been sold. *The premiere on Monday is sold out.* ADJ: v-link ADJ

2 If a shop is **sold out** of something, it has sold all of it that it had. *The stores are sometimes sold out of certain groceries.* ADJ: v-link ADJ, oft ADJ *of* n

sole /soʊl/ **soles** ◆◆◇◇◇

1 The **sole** thing or person of a particular type is the only one of that type. *Their sole aim is to destabilize the Indian government.* ADJ: ADJ n =only

2 If you have **sole** charge or ownership of something, you are the only person in charge of it or who owns it. *Many women are left as the sole providers in families after their husband has died... After 1997 China expects to be in sole political control.* ADJ: ADJ n

3 The **sole** of your foot or of a shoe or sock is the underneath surface of it. *...shoes with rubber soles... They were beaten on the soles of their feet.* N-COUNT: usu with supp

4 A **sole** is a kind of flat fish that you can eat. ● See also **lemon sole.** ▶ **Sole** is this fish eaten as food. N-COUNT N-UNCOUNT

-soled /-soʊld/. **-soled** combines with adjectives and nouns to form adjectives which describe shoes with a particular kind of sole. *The lad was wearing rubber-soled shoes.* COMB in ADJ: usu ADJ n

solely /soʊlli/. If something involves **solely** one thing, it involves only this thing and no others. *Too often we make decisions based solely upon what we see in the magazines... This program is a production of NPR, which is solely responsible for its content.* ◆◆◇◇◇ ADV: ADV with v, ADV with group/cl =exclusively

solemn /sɒləm/ ◆◆◇◇◇

1 Someone or something that is **solemn** is very serious rather than cheerful or humorous. *His solemn little face broke into smiles... He looked solemn.* ♦ **solemnly** *Her listeners nodded solemnly.* ♦ **solemnity** /səlemnɪti/ *The setting for this morning's signing ceremony matched the solemnity of the occasion.* ADJ-GRADED =serious, sombre; ADV-GRADED: ADV with v; N-UNCOUNT

2 A **solemn** promise or agreement is one that you make in a very formal, sincere way. *She made a solemn promise to him when they became engaged that she would give up cigarettes for good.* ♦ **solemnly** *Chancellor Kohl has solemnly pledged that Germany has no territorial claims against Poland.* ADJ-GRADED; ADV-GRADED: ADV with v

solicit /səlɪsɪt/ **solicits, soliciting, solicited** ◆◇◇◇◇

1 If you **solicit** money, help, support, or an opinion from someone, you ask them for it; a formal use. *He's already solicited their support on health care reform... No tuition was charged by the school, which solicited contributions from the society's members.* VERB V n V n *from* n

2 When prostitutes **solicit**, they offer to have sex with people in return for money. *Prostitutes were forbidden to solicit on public roads and in public places.* ♦ **soliciting** *Girls could get very heavy sentences for soliciting – nine months or more.* VERB V; N-UNCOUNT

solicitation /səlɪsɪteɪʃᵊn/ **solicitations. Solicitation** is the act of soliciting money, help, support, or an opinion from someone; used mainly in American English. *Republican leaders are making open solicitation of the Italian-American vote... The new measures are aimed at cutting back on intrusive telephone solicitations.* N-VAR

solicitor /səlɪsɪtəʳ/ **solicitors.** In Britain, a **solicitor** is a lawyer who gives legal advice, prepares legal documents and cases, and represents ◆◆◆◇◇ N-COUNT clients in the lower courts of law. Compare **barrister.**

Solicitor General; also spelled **solicitor-general.** In Britain, the **Solicitor General** is the second most important legal officer, next in rank below the Attorney General. N-SING: usu *the* N; N-TITLE

solicitous /səlɪsɪtəs/. A person who is **solicitous** shows anxious concern for someone or something. *He was so solicitous of his guests.* ADJ-GRADED: oft ADJ *of* n
♦ **solicitously** *He took her hand in greeting and asked solicitously how everything was.* ADV-GRADED: usu ADV with v

solicitude /səlɪsɪtjuːd, AM -tuːd/. **Solicitude** is anxious concern for someone; a formal word. *He is full of tender solicitude towards my sister.* N-UNCOUNT

solid /sɒlɪd/ **solids**

1 A **solid** substance or object stays the same shape whether it is in a container or not. *...the potential of greatly reducing our solid waste problem... He did not eat solid food for several weeks.* ADJ: usu ADJ n ≠liquid

2 A **solid** is a substance that stays the same shape whether it is in a container or not. *Solids turn to liquids at certain temperatures... No baby should be given any solids before four months old.* N-COUNT ≠liquid

3 A substance that is **solid** is very hard or firm. *The snow had melted, but the lake was still frozen solid... The concrete will stay as solid as a rock.* ADJ-GRADED

4 A **solid** object or mass does not have a space inside it, or holes or gaps in it. *...a tunnel carved through 50ft of solid rock. ...a solid wall of multi-coloured trees. ...a solid mass of colour... The car park was absolutely packed solid with people.* ADJ: usu ADJ n

5 If an object is made of **solid** gold or **solid** wood, for example, it is made of gold or wood all the way through, rather than just on the outside. *The taps appeared to be made of solid gold. ...solid wood doors. ...solid pine furniture.* ADJ: ADJ n

6 A structure that is **solid** is strong and is not likely to collapse or fall over. *Banks are built to look solid to reassure their customers... The car feels very solid.* ADJ-GRADED
♦ **solidly** *Their house, which was solidly built, resisted the main shock.* ADV-GRADED: ADV with v ♦ **solidity** /səlɪdɪti/ *...the solidity of walls and floors.* N-UNCOUNT

7 If you describe someone as **solid**, you mean that they are very reliable and respectable. *You want a husband who is solid and stable, someone who will devote himself to you... All the band come from good, solid, working-class backgrounds... Mr Zuma has a solid reputation as a grass roots organiser.* ADJ-GRADED =reliable, dependable
♦ **solidly** *Graham is so solidly consistent.* ADV-GRADED ♦ **solidity** *He had the proverbial solidity of the English.* N-UNCOUNT

8 Solid evidence or information is reliable because it is based on facts. *We don't have good solid information on where the people are... Some solid evidence was what was required... He has a solid alibi.* ADJ-GRADED =reliable

9 You use **solid** to describe something such as advice or a piece of work which is useful and reliable. *The CIU provides churches with solid advice on a wide range of subjects... All I am looking for is a good solid performance... I've always felt that solid experience would stand me in good stead.* ADJ-GRADED =sound ♦ **solidly** *She's played solidly throughout the spring.* ADV-GRADED: ADV with v

10 You use **solid** to describe something such as the basis for a policy or support for an organization when it is strong, because it has been developed carefully and slowly. *I am determined to build on this solid foundation. ...a Democratic nominee with solid support within the party and broad appeal beyond. ...Washington's attempt to build a solid international coalition.* ADJ-GRADED =firm, strong ♦ **solidly** *The Los Alamos district is solidly Republican... So far, majority public opinion in Egypt seems solidly behind the government's policy. ...a society based solidly on trust and understanding.* ADV-GRADED: ADV adj/prep, ADV with v ♦ **solidity** *...doubts over the solidity of Chinese backing for the American approach.* N-UNCOUNT

11 If you do something for a **solid** period of time, you do it without any pause or interruption throughout that time. *We had worked together for two solid years.* ADJ: ADJ n, -ed ADJ ♦ **solidly** *People who had worked solidly since Christmas enjoyed the chance of a Friday off.* ADV-GRADED: ADV with v

12 See also **rock-solid.**

13 ● **on solid ground**: see **ground.**

solidarity /sɒlɪdærɪti/. If a group of people show **solidarity**, they show complete unity and support for each other, especially in political or international affairs. *Supporters want to march tomorrow to show solidarity with their leaders.*   N-UNCOUNT: oft N *with* n

solid fuel, solid fuels. Solid fuel is fuel such as coal or wood, that is solid rather than liquid or gas. N-MASS

solidify /səlɪdɪfaɪ/ **solidifies, solidifying, solidified**

1 When a liquid **solidifies** or **is solidified**, it changes into a solid. *The thicker lava would have taken two weeks to solidify... The Energy Department plans to solidify the deadly waste in a high-tech billion-dollar factory. ...a frying-pan full of solidified fat.* V-ERG V V n V-ed

2 If something such as a position or opinion **solidifies**, or of something **solidifies** it, it becomes firmer and more definite and unlikely to change. *Her attitudes solidified through privilege and habit. ...his attempt to solidify his position as chairman... Her behavior this week has solidified her support within the Department of Justice.* V-ERG V V n

solid-state. Solid-state electronic equipment is made using transistors, silicon chips, or other semi-conductors, instead of valves or other mechanical parts; a technical term in physics. ADJ: ADJ n

soliloquy /səlɪləkwi/ **soliloquies.** A **soliloquy** is a speech in a play in which an actor or actress speaks to himself or herself and to the audience, rather than to another actor. N-COUNT

solitaire /sɒlɪteəʳ/ **solitaires**

1 Solitaire is a game for one person in which you move pegs to different positions on a board, with the aim of having one peg left at the end of the game. N-UNCOUNT

2 In American English, **solitaire** is a card game for only one player. The British word is **patience.** N-UNCOUNT

3 A **solitaire** is a diamond or other jewel that is set on its own in a ring or other piece of jewellery. N-COUNT

solitary /sɒlɪtri, AM -teri/

1 A person or animal that is **solitary** spends a lot of time alone. *Paul was a shy, pleasant, solitary man... They often have a lonely and solitary life to lead.* ADJ-GRADED: usu ADJ n

2 A **solitary** activity is one that you do alone. *His evenings were spent in solitary drinking.* ADJ: ADJ n

3 A **solitary** person or object is alone, with no others nearby. *...the occasional solitary figure making a study of wildflowers or grasses.* ADJ: ADJ n =lone

4 Solitary is the same as **solitary confinement**; an informal use. *Tom was in solitary across the way from me.* N-UNCOUNT: usu *in* N

solitary confinement. A prisoner who is in **solitary confinement** is being kept alone away from all other prisoners, usually as a punishment. *Last night he was being held in solitary confinement in Douglas jail.* N-UNCOUNT: usu *in* N

solitude /sɒlɪtjuːd, AM -tuːd/. **Solitude** is the state of being alone, especially when this is peaceful and pleasant. *He enjoyed his moments of solitude before the pressures of the day began... Imagine long golden beaches where you can wander in solitude.*  N-UNCOUNT

solo /soʊloʊ/ **solos.** A **solo** is a performance, especially of a piece of music, done by one person. *The original version featured a guitar solo.* ► Also an adjective. *He had just completed his final solo album.* ► Also an adverb. *Charles Lindbergh became the very first person to fly solo across the Atlantic.*  N-COUNT ADJ: usu ADJ n ADV: ADV after v

soloist /soʊloʊɪst/ **soloists.** A **soloist** is a person who performs a solo, usually a piece of music. N-COUNT

solstice /sɒlstɪs/ **solstices.** The **summer solstice** and the **winter solstice** are the two times of the year when the sun is farthest away from the equator. In the northern hemisphere, the summer solstice is on June 21 or 22, and the winter solstice is on December 21 or 22. In the southern hemisphere the summer solstice is in December and the winter solstice is in June.  N-COUNT

soluble /sɒljʊbᵊl/ ◆◇◇◇◇
1 A substance that is **soluble** will dissolve in a liquid. *Uranium is soluble in sea water.* ADJ-GRADED ≠insoluble
2 If something is **water-soluble** or **fat-soluble**, it will dissolve in water or in fat. *The red dye on the leather is water-soluble. ...fat-soluble vitamins.* COMB in ADJ

solution /səluːʃᵊn/ **solutions** ◆◆◆◆◇
1 A **solution** to a problem or difficult situation is a way of dealing with it so that the difficulty is removed. *Although he has sought to find a peaceful solution, he is facing pressure to use greater military force. ...the ability to sort out simple, effective solutions to practical problems.* N-COUNT: oft N *to* n =answer
2 The **solution** to a riddle or a puzzle is the answer to it. *...the solution to crossword No. 19721.* N-COUNT
3 A **solution** is a liquid in which a solid substance has been dissolved. *...a warm solution of liquid detergent... Vitamins in solution are more affected than those in solid foods.* N-COUNT: also *in* N

solve /sɒlv/ **solves, solving, solved.** If you **solve** a problem or a question, you find a solution or an answer to it. *Their domestic reforms did nothing to solve the problem of unemployment... We may now be able to get a much better idea of the true age of the universe, and solve one of the deepest questions of our origins.* ◆◆◆◇◇ VERB =resolve V n

solvency /sɒlvᵊnsi/. A person or organization's **solvency** is their ability to pay their debts. N-UNCOUNT: usu with supp

solvent /sɒlvᵊnt/ **solvents** ◆◇◇◇◇
1 If a person or a company is **solvent**, they have enough money to pay all their debts. *They're going to have to show that the company is now solvent.* ADJ: usu v-link ADJ ≠insolvent
2 A **solvent** is a liquid that can dissolve other substances. *...a small amount of cleaning solvent. ...industrial solvents.* N-MASS

solvent abuse. **Solvent abuse** is the dangerous practice of breathing in the vapour from solvents such as glue in order to feel as if you are drunk; a formal expression. N-UNCOUNT =glue sniffing

sombre /sɒmbəʳ/; spelled **somber** in American English. ◆◇◇◇◇
1 If someone is **sombre**, they are serious, sad, or pessimistic. *The pair were in sombre mood... His expression became increasingly sombre... Unfortunately, this happy story finishes on a more sombre note.* ♦ **sombrely** *'All the same, I wish he'd come back,' Martha said sombrely... She felt more sympathy for Neil's sombrely stolid manner than she ever had before.* ADJ-GRADED =serious, solemn ADV-GRADED: ADV after v, ADV adj
2 **Sombre** colours and places are dark and dull. *...a worried official in sombre black... It was a beautiful house, but it was dark and sombre and dead.* ADJ-GRADED

sombrero /sɒmbreəroʊ/ **sombreros.** A **sombrero** is a hat with a very wide brim which is worn especially in Mexico. N-COUNT

some /səm, STRONG sʌm/ ◆◆◆◆◆
1 You use **some** to refer to a quantity of something or to a number of people or things, when you are not stating the quantity or number precisely. *Robin opened some champagne... Heat a couple of tablespoons of olive oil, a chopped clove of garlic and some black pepper in a heavy saucepan... He went to fetch some books... Some children refuse to eat on time and others overeat.* ► Also a pronoun. *This year all the apples are all red. My niece and nephew are going out this morning with step-ladders to pick some.* DET: DET n-uncount/pl-n PRON
2 You use **some** to emphasize that a quantity or number is fairly large. For example, if an activity takes **some** time, it takes quite a lot of time. *The question of local government finance has been the subject of debate for some years... I have discussed this topic in some detail... He remained silent for some time... It took some effort to conceal her relief.* DET: DET n-uncount/pl-n
3 You use **some** to emphasize that a quantity or number is fairly small. For example, if something happens to **some** extent, it happens a little. *'Isn't there some chance that William might lead a normal life?' asked Jill... All mothers share to some extent in the tension of a wedding... Some fishing is still allowed, but limits have been imposed on the size of the catch.* DET: DET n-uncount/sing-n
4 If you refer to **some of** the people or things in a group, you mean a few of them but not all of them. If you refer to **some of** a particular thing, you mean a part of it but not all of it. *Some of the people already in work will lose their jobs... Remove the cover and spoon some of the sauce into a bowl... Boats crammed with hot and angry holidaymakers, some of whom had waited for up to two days to cross... Some of us are sensitive to smells, others find colours easier to remember.* ► Also a pronoun. *Shivering tourists had congregated in the only open bar in town. Some, desperate for the sun, headed down to Lisbon, while the rest of us decided to sample the sea air of Biarritz... When the chicken is cooked I'll freeze some.* QUANT: QUANT *of* n-uncount/pl-n ≠all PRON
5 If you refer to **some** person or thing, you are referring to that person or thing vaguely, without stating precisely which one you mean. *If you are worried about some aspect of your child's health, call us... Jim Partridge chucked himself off some bridge or other... Three years ago there was an incident at the local school when some bloke started shooting the place up.* DET: DET sing-n
6 You can also use **some** in front of a number to indicate that it is approximate. *I have kept birds for some 30 years... He waited some 80 to 100 yards from the big pink villa... The headquarters is some 30 miles due west.* ADV: ADV num =about
7 In American English, **some** is used to mean to a small extent or degree. *If Susanne is off somewhere, I'll kill time by looking around some... 'I party some,' said Jed... He decided we should spend Christmas in Acapulco. There we could ski some and relax.* ADV: ADV after v
8 You can use **some** in front of a noun in order to express your approval or disapproval of the person or thing you are mentioning; an informal use. *She lived to be ninety-nine years old and only weighed eighty pounds but she'd raised eight kids. That was some tough woman!... 'Some party!'—'Yep. One hell of a party.'* DET

somebody /sʌmbədi, AM -bɑːdi/. **Somebody** means the same as **someone**. ◆◆◆◆◇ PRON-INDEF

some day; also spelled **someday**. **Some day** means at a date in the future that is unknown or that has not yet been decided. *Some day I'll be a pilot... He took her left hand, hoping that it would someday bear a gold ring on the third finger.* ◆◇◇◇◇ ADV: ADV with v, ADV with cl

somehow /sʌmhaʊ/ ◆◆◆◇◇
1 You use **somehow** to say that you do not know or cannot say how something was done or will be done. *We'll manage somehow, you and me. I know we will... Channel 4 arrived and somehow created a different role for television... Somehow Karin managed to cope with the demands of her career... Somehow I knew he would tell me the truth... He's been very quiet and withdrawn, sort of different, somehow... This city is somehow different.* ADV: ADV with v, ADV adj
2 ● **somehow or other**: see **other**.

someone /sʌmwʌn/. The form **somebody** is also used. ◆◆◆◆◇
1 You use **someone** or **somebody** to refer to a person without saying exactly who you mean. *Her father was shot by someone trying to rob his small retail store... I need someone to help me... She fell in love with someone and ran off with him... If somebody asks me how my diet is going, I say, 'Fine'... He noticed a huge crowd gathered outside – someone really famous must be staying there... She was tired of him and wanted to leave him, perhaps to marry somebody else.* PRON-INDEF
2 If you say that a person is **someone** or **somebody** in a particular kind of work or in a particular place, you mean that they are considered to be important in that kind of work or in that place. *He was somebody in the law division... 'Before she came around,' she says, 'I was somebody in this town'.* PRON-INDEF: usu PRON *in* n

someplace /sʌmpleɪs/. In American English **someplace** means the same as **somewhere**. *Maybe if we could go someplace together, just you and I... They lived over around Coyote Canyon someplace.* ◆◇◇◇◇ ADV: ADV after v =somewhere

somersault /sʌməʳsɔːlt/ **somersaults, somersaulting, somersaulted**

1 If someone or something does a **somersault** they turn over completely in the air. N-COUNT

2 If you say that someone does a **somersault**, you mean that they change suddenly from having a particular opinion or policy about something to having a completely different opinion or policy. *What worries some of us is that the Prime Minister may feel simply unable to do a somersault... In the last 30 years, both sexes have performed a somersault in terms of expectations, roles and relationships.* N-COUNT

3 If someone or something **somersaults**, they perform one or more somersaults. *His boat hit a wave and somersaulted at speed... I hit him back and he somersaulted down the stairs.* VERB V, V prep

something /sʌmθɪŋ/ ◆◆◆◆◆

1 You use **something** to refer to a thing, situation, event, or idea, without saying exactly what it is. *He realized right away that there was something wrong... There was something vaguely familiar about him... The garden was something special... 'You said there was something you wanted to ask me,' he said politely... There was something in her attitude that bothered him... People are always out in their cars, watching television or busy doing something else.* PRON-INDEF: oft PRON adj, PRON adj *about* n

2 You can use **something** to say that the description or amount that you are giving is not exact. *He described the smell as something between a circus and a sea-port... Clive made a noise, something like a grunt... There was something around a thousand dollars in the office strong box... Their membership seems to have risen to something over 10,000.* PRON-INDEF: PRON prep

3 If you say that a person or thing is **something** or is really **something**, you mean that you are very impressed by them. *You're really something... The doors here are really something, all made of good wood like mahogany... This is really something. Someone actually thinks my records are all right!* PRON-INDEF

4 You can use **something** in expressions like **'that's something'** when you think that a situation is not very good but is better that it might have been. *Well, at least he was in town. That was something... Well, you're staying. That's something I suppose.* PRON-INDEF

5 If you say that a thing is **something of** a disappointment, you mean that it is quite disappointing. If you say that a person is **something of** an artist, you mean that they are quite good at art. *The city proved to be something of a disappointment... She received something of a surprise when Robert said that he was coming to New York... He is something of a fighter, and will certainly want to win.* PRON-INDEF: PRON *of* n

6 If you say that there is **something in** an idea or suggestion, you mean that it is quite good and should be considered seriously. *Christianity has stood the test of time, so there must be something in it... There had been something in Des's first statement... Could there be something in what he said?* PRON-INDEF: PRON *in* n

7 You use **something** in expressions such as **'or something'** and **'or something like that'** to indicate that you are referring to something similar to what you have just mentioned when you are not being exact. *This guy, his name was Briarly or Beardly or something... The air fare was about a hundred and ninety-nine pounds or something like that.* PRON-INDEF PRAGMATICS

8 ● **something like**: see **like**. ● **something or other**: see **other**.

-something /-sʌmθɪŋ/ **-somethings**

1 **-something** is combined with numbers such as twenty and thirty to form adjectives which indicate an approximate amount, especially someone's age. For example, if you say that someone is **thirty-something**, you mean they are between thirty and forty years old. COMB in ADJ

2 People of a similar age range are sometimes referred to as, for example, **twenty-somethings** or **thirty-somethings**; used in journalism. *Most American twenty-somethings do not read about politics.* COMB in N-COUNT

sometime /sʌmtaɪm/ ◆◆◇◇◇

1 You use **sometime** to refer to a time in the future or the past that is unknown or that has not yet been decided. *The sales figures won't be released until sometime next month... Why don't you come and see me sometime... I'm aiming to get to work by nine sometime... I really want to go to Spain sometime.* ADV: ADV with v, ADV with cl/group

2 You also use **sometime** to describe a job or role that a person used to have. *Cecile was in her early thirties, a sometime actress, dancer and singer. ...sometime boxer Frank Bruno.* ADJ: ADJ n =former, erstwhile

sometimes /sʌmtaɪmz/. You use **sometimes** to say that something happens on some occasions rather than all the time. *During the summer, my skin sometimes gets greasy... Sometimes I think he dislikes me... You must have noticed how tired he sometimes looks... Other people's jobs were exactly the same – sometimes good, sometimes bad.* ◆◆◆◆◇ ADV: ADV with cl/group, ADV with v

somewhat /sʌmʰwɒt/. You use **somewhat** to indicate that something is the case to a limited extent or degree. *He concluded that Oswald was somewhat abnormal... He explained somewhat unconvincingly that the company was paying for everything... Mr Kuwa said conditions in the village had improved somewhat since January... 'I believe you know him'—'Somewhat.'* ◆◆◆◇◇ ADV: ADV with cl/group

somewhere /sʌmʰweəʳ/ ◆◆◆◇◇

1 You use **somewhere** to refer to a place without saying exactly where you mean. *I've got a feeling I've seen him before somewhere... I'm not going home yet. I have to go somewhere else first... 'Perhaps we can talk somewhere privately,' said Kesler... Somewhere in Ian's room were some of the letters that she had sent him... Don't I know you from somewhere?... I needed somewhere to live in London.* ADV-INDEF: ADV after v, ADV with *be*, oft ADV cl/group, *from* ADV

2 You use **somewhere** when giving an approximate amount, number, or time. *The Queen is believed to earn somewhere between seven million and one hundred million pounds... Caray is somewhere between 73 and 80 years of age... The W.H.O. safety standard for ozone levels is somewhere about a hundred... He's American-bred, with a sort of Irish background somewhere along the line.* ADV-INDEF: ADV prep

3 If you say that you **are getting somewhere**, you mean that you are making progress towards achieving something. *At last they were agreeing, at last they were getting somewhere... This time it looks as if we're really going to get somewhere.* PHRASE: V inflects ≠be getting nowhere

● **somewhere or other**: see **other**.

somnolent /sɒmnələnt/

1 If you are **somnolent** you feel sleepy; a formal use. *The sedative makes people very somnolent.* ADJ: usu ADJ n

2 If a place is **somnolent** it is very peaceful and quiet; a literary use. *...the somnolent villages of Sicily.* ADJ: usu ADJ n

son /sʌn/ **sons** ◆◆◆◆◆

1 Someone's **son** is their male child. *He shared a pizza with his son Laurence... Sam is the seven-year-old son of Eric Davies... They have a son.* N-COUNT: oft with poss

2 A man, especially a famous man, can be described as a **son** of the place he comes from; used by journalists. *...New Orleans's most famous son, Louis Armstrong. ...sons of Africa.* N-COUNT: with poss

3 Some people use **son** as a form of address when they are showing kindness or affection to a boy or a man who is younger than them; an informal use. *Don't be frightened by failure, son.* N-VOC PRAGMATICS

sonar /soʊnɑːʳ/ **sonars. Sonar** is equipment on a ship which can calculate the depth of the sea or the position of an underwater object using sound waves. N-VAR

sonata /sənɑːtə/ **sonatas.** A **sonata** is a piece of classical music written either for a single instrument, or for one instrument and a piano. ◆◇◇◇◇ N-COUNT: oft in names

son et lumière /sɒn eɪ luːmieəʳ/. **Son et lumière** is an entertainment which is held at night in an old building such as a castle. A person describes the history of the place, and at the same time different parts of the building are brightly lit and music is played. N-SING

song /sɒŋ, AM sɔːŋ/ **songs** ◆◆◆◆◇

1 A **song** is words and music sung together. *...a voice singing a Spanish song. ...a love song.* N-COUNT

2 **Song** is the art of singing. *...dance, music, mime and song. ...the history of American popular song.* N-UNCOUNT

3 A bird's **song** is the pleasant, musical sounds that it makes. *It's been a long time since I heard a blackbird's song in the evening.* N-COUNT

4 See also **birdsong**, **song and dance**, **songbird**, **swan song**.

5 If someone **bursts into song** or **breaks into song**, they start singing. *I feel as if I should break into song.* PHRASES V inflects

6 If you buy something **for a song**, you buy it for much less than its real value; an informal expression. *We found two second-hand chairs that were going for a song.* after v

7 In British English, journalists sometimes describe sportsmen or sportswomen as being **on song** when they are playing really well. *Ward is not the most consistent of players, but when he is on song he looks a world-beater.* usu v-link PHR =on form

song and dance

1 A **song and dance** act is a theatrical performance in which a person or group of people both sing and dance. N-UNCOUNT: usu N n

2 In informal British English, if you say that someone is making a **song and dance** about something, you mean they are making an unnecessary fuss about it; used showing disapproval. *He used his money to help others – but he never made a song and dance about it.* PHRASE PRAGMATICS =fuss

songbird /sɒŋbɜːʳd, AM sɔːŋ-/ **songbirds;** also spelled **song bird**. A **songbird** is a bird that produces musical sounds which are like singing. There are many different kinds of songbird. N-COUNT

songster /sɒŋstəʳ, AM sɔːŋ-/ **songsters.** Journalists sometimes refer to a male popular singer as a **songster**. N-COUNT =singer

songstress /sɒŋstrəs, AM sɔːŋ-/ **songstresses.** Journalists sometimes refer to a female popular singer as a **songstress**. N-COUNT =singer

songwriter /sɒŋraɪtəʳ, AM sɔːŋ-/ **songwriters.** A **songwriter** is someone who writes the words or the music, or both, for popular songs. *...one of rock'n'roll's greatest songwriters.* ● See also **singer-songwriter**. ◆◇◇◇◇ N-COUNT

sonic /sɒnɪk/. **Sonic** is used to describe things related to sound; a technical word. *...the sonic boom of enemy fighter-bombers.* ◆◇◇◇◇ ADJ: ADJ n

son-in-law, sons-in-law. Someone's **son-in-law** is the husband of their daughter. ◆◇◇◇◇ N-COUNT: usu poss N

sonnet /sɒnɪt/ **sonnets.** A **sonnet** is a poem that has 14 lines. Each line has 14 syllables, and the poem has a fixed pattern of rhymes. ◆◇◇◇◇ N-COUNT

sonny /sʌni/. Some people address a boy or young man as **sonny**; an informal word. *Well, sonny, I'll give you a bit of advice.* N-VOC PRAGMATICS

son of a bitch, sons of bitches; also spelled **son-of-a-bitch**. If someone is very angry with another person, or if they want to insult them, they sometimes call them a **son of a bitch**; a rude and offensive word which you should avoid using. N-COUNT PRAGMATICS

sonority /sənɒrɪti, AM -nɔːr-/ **sonorities.** The **sonority** of a sound is its deep resonance; a formal word. *The lower strings contribute a splendid richness of sonority.* N-UNCOUNT: also N in pl

sonorous /sɒnərəs, AM sənɔːrəs/. A **sonorous** sound is deep and rich. *'Doctor McKee?' the man called in an even, sonorous voice.* ♦ **sonorously** *The church clock chimed sonorously.* ADJ-GRADED =resonant; ADV-GRADED

soon /suːn/ **sooner, soonest** ◆◆◆◆◆

1 If something is going to happen **soon**, it will happen after a short time. If something happened **soon** after a particular time or event, it happened a short time after it. *You'll be hearing from us very soon... This chance has come sooner than I expected... You'll find out soon enough... The plane was returning to the airport soon after takeoff when it burst into flames... Soon afterwards he separated from his wife.* ADV-GRADED: ADV with v, ADV after n/cl, ADV afterwards

2 If you say that something happens **as soon as** something else happens, you mean that it happens immediately after the other thing. *As soon as relations improve they will be allowed to go... You'll never guess what happened as soon as I left my room.* PHRASES CONJ-SUBORD

3 If you say that you **would just as soon** do something or you**'d just as soon** do it, you mean that you would prefer to do it. *These people could afford to retire to Florida but they'd just as soon stay put... I'd just as soon not have to make this public... I'd just as soon you put that thing away... She'd just as soon throw your plate in your face as serve you.* MODAL =would rather; MODAL inf; MODAL *not* inf; MODAL that; MODAL inf *as* inf

sooner /suːnəʳ/ ◆◆◇◇◇

1 **Sooner** is the comparative of **soon**.

2 You say **the sooner the better** when you think something should be done as soon as possible. *Detective Holt said: 'The kidnapper is a man we must catch and the sooner the better'.* PHRASES

3 If you say that something will happen **sooner or later**, you mean that it will happen at some time in the future, even though it might take a long time. *Sooner or later she would be caught by the police.* PHR with cl =eventually

4 If you say that **no sooner** has one thing happened **than** another thing happens, you mean that the second thing happens immediately after the first thing. *No sooner had he arrived in Rome than he was kidnapped.* CONJ-SUBORD =scarcely

5 If you say that you **would sooner** do something or you**'d sooner** do it, you mean that you would prefer to do it. *Unless they speak French already, they would sooner learn English... I'd sooner not talk about it... I'd sooner he didn't know till I've talked to Pete... I would sooner give up sleep than miss my evening class... I'd sooner not, if you don't mind.* MODAL =would rather; MODAL inf; MODAL *not* inf; MODAL that; MODAL inf *than* inf; MODAL *not*

soot /sʊt/. **Soot** is black powder which rises in the smoke from a fire and collects on the inside of chimneys. *... a wall blackened by soot.* ◆◇◇◇◇ N-UNCOUNT

soothe /suːð/ **soothes, soothing, soothed** ◆◆◇◇◇

1 If you **soothe** someone who is angry or upset, you make them feel calmer. *He would take her in his arms and soothe her... It did not take long for the central bank to soothe investors' fears.* ♦ **soothing** *Put on some nice soothing music... His casual, relaxed manner was very soothing.* ♦ **soothingly** *'Now don't you worry,' she said soothingly.* VERB V n; ADJ-GRADED; ADV: usu ADV after v

2 Something that **soothes** a part of your body where there is pain or discomfort makes the pain or discomfort less severe. *...body lotion to soothe dry skin.* ♦ **soothing** *Cold tea is very soothing for burns.* VERB; ADJ-GRADED

soothsayer /suːθseɪəʳ/ **soothsayers.** In former times, **soothsayers** were people who believed they could see into the future and say what was going to happen. N-COUNT =prophet

sooty /sʊti/. Something that is **sooty** is covered with soot. *Their uniforms are torn and sooty.* ADJ-GRADED

sop /sɒp/ **sops.** You describe something as a **sop** to someone when they are offered something small or unimportant in order to prevent them from getting angry or causing trouble; used showing disapproval. *This is an obvious sop to the large Irish-American audience... The government parties may be tempted to throw a few sops to the right-wingers.* N-COUNT: oft N *to* n PRAGMATICS =bribe

sophisticate /səfɪstɪkeɪt/ **sophisticates.** A **sophisticate** is someone who knows about culture, fashion, and other matters that are considered socially important. N-COUNT

sophisticated /səfɪstɪkeɪtɪd/ ◆◆◆◇◇

1 A **sophisticated** machine, device, or method is more advanced or complex than others. *Honeybees use one of the most sophisticated communication systems of any insect. ...a large and sophisticated new British telescope.* ADJ-GRADED =advanced ≠unsophisticated

2 Someone who is **sophisticated** is at ease in social situations and knows about culture, fashion, and other matters that are considered socially important. *Claude was a charming, sophisticated companion... Recently her tastes have become more sophisticated.* ADJ-GRADED =refined ≠unsophisticate

3 A **sophisticated** person is intelligent and well-informed, and shows an ability to understand ADJ-GRADED complicated matters. *These people are very sophisticated observers of the foreign policy scene.*

sophistication /sɒfɪstɪkeɪʃən/. The **sophistication** of people, places, machines, or methods is their quality of being sophisticated. *It would take many decades to build up the level of education and sophistication required. ...the sophistication of one of the world's richest cities... Given the sophistication of modern machines, there is little that cannot be successfully washed at home.* ◆◇◇◇◇ N-UNCOUNT: usu with supp

sophistries /sɒfɪstriz/. **Sophistries** are clever arguments that sound convincing but are in fact false; a formal word. *They refuted the 'sophistries of the economists'.* N-PLURAL

sophistry /sɒfɪstri/. **Sophistry** is the practice of using clever arguments that sound convincing but are in fact false; a formal word. *Political selection is more dependent on sophistry and less on economic literacy.* N-UNCOUNT

sophomore /sɒfəmɔːʳ/ **sophomores.** In the United States, a **sophomore** is a student in the second year of college or high school. N-COUNT

soporific /sɒpərɪfɪk/. Something that is **soporific** makes you feel sleepy. *The warmth of the room and the monotony of the speaker's voice grew soporific. ...the soporific effect of the alcohol.* ADJ-GRADED

sopping /sɒpɪŋ/. Something that is **sopping** or **sopping wet** is extremely wet; an informal word. *I pulled off my sopping mittens... They came back sopping wet.* ADJ

soppy /sɒpi/ **soppier, soppiest.** If you describe someone or something as **soppy**, you mean that they are foolishly sentimental; an informal word, used mainly in British English. *He's constantly on the phone to his girlfriend being soppy... She loves soppy love stories, old films, that sort of thing.* ADJ-GRADED =slushy

soprano /səprɑːnoʊ, -præn-/ **sopranos** ◆◇◇◇◇

1 A **soprano** is a woman, girl, or boy with a high singing voice. *She was the main soprano at the Bolshoi theatre. ...a pretty girl with a sweet soprano voice.* N-COUNT

2 A **soprano** saxophone or other musical instrument has a range of notes of high pitch. ADJ: ADJ n

sorbet /sɔːʳbeɪ, AM -bɪt/ **sorbets. Sorbet** is water ice that is usually made from fruit. *...a light lemon sorbet.* N-MASS

sorcerer /sɔːʳsərəʳ/ **sorcerers.** In stories and fairy tales, a **sorcerer** is a person who performs magic by using the power of evil spirits. N-COUNT =wizard, warlock

sorceress /sɔːʳsərɪs/ **sorceresses.** In stories and fairy tales, a **sorceress** is a woman who performs magic by using the power of evil spirits. N-COUNT =witch

sorcery /sɔːʳsəri/. **Sorcery** is the practice of performing magic by using the power of evil spirits. N-UNCOUNT =witchcraft

sordid /sɔːʳdɪd/ ◆◇◇◇◇

1 If you describe someone's behaviour as **sordid**, you mean that it is immoral or dishonest. *He sat with his head buried in his hands as his sordid double life was revealed... I don't want to hear the sordid details of your relationship with Sandra... She listened to Kate's explanation of the sordid affair.* ADJ-GRADED

2 If you describe a place as **sordid**, you mean that it is dirty, unpleasant, or depressing. *...the attic windows of their sordid little rooms.* ADJ-GRADED =seedy

sore /sɔːʳ/ **sorer, sorest; sores** ◆◆◇◇◇

1 If part of your body is **sore**, it causes you pain and discomfort. *It's years since I've had a sore throat like I did last night... My chest is still sore from the surgery.* ♦ **soreness** *The soreness lasted for about six weeks.* ADJ-GRADED =painful; N-UNCOUNT

2 If you are **sore** about something, you are angry and upset about it; an informal use, used mainly in American English. *The result is that they are now all feeling very sore at you... They are sore about losing to England in the quarter-finals.* ADJ-GRADED: v-link ADJ, oft ADJ *at/about* n/-ing =annoyed

3 A **sore** is a painful place on the body where the skin is infected. ● See also **cold sore**. N-COUNT

4 If something is **a sore point** with someone, it is likely to make them angry or embarrassed if you try to discuss it. *The continuing presence of American troops on Korean soil remains a very sore point with these students.* ● to **stick out like a sore thumb**: see **thumb**. PHRASE: oft PHR *with/for/between* n

sorely /sɔːʳli/. **Sorely** is used to emphasize that a feeling such as disappointment or need is very strong. *I for one was sorely disappointed. ...the potential to earn sorely needed money for Britain from overseas orders... National institutes in the east are sorely in need of renovation and modern equipment... He will be sorely missed.* ◆◇◇◇◇ ADV-GRADED: ADV adj/prep, ADV before v PRAGMATICS

sorghum /sɔːʳgəm/. **Sorghum** is a type of corn that is grown in warm countries. Its grain can be made into flour or syrup. N-UNCOUNT

sorority /sərɔːrɪti/ **sororities.** In the United States, a **sorority** is a society of women students that is formed for social purposes. *Eleanor had belonged to the same sorority as Betty Jean and they were still great friends.* N-COUNT

sorrel /sɒrəl, AM sɔːr-/. **Sorrel** is a plant with arrow-shaped leaves that have a bitter taste and are sometimes used in salads and sauces. N-UNCOUNT =dock

sorrow /sɒroʊ/. **Sorrow** is a feeling of deep sadness or regret. *It was a time of great sorrow... Words cannot express my sorrow.* ◆◇◇◇◇ N-UNCOUNT =anguish

sorrowful /sɒroʊfʊl/. **Sorrowful** means very sad; a literary word. *His father's face looked suddenly soft and sorrowful... Roy told his sorrowful tale with simple words anybody could understand.* ♦ **sorrowfully** *The postmaster shook his head sorrowfully.* ADJ-GRADED =mournful; ADV: ADV with v

sorrows /sɒroʊz/. **Sorrows** are events or situations that cause deep sadness. *...the joys and sorrows of everyday living.* ● to **drown** one's **sorrows**: see **drown**. N-PLURAL

sorry /sɒri/ **sorrier, sorriest** ◆◆◆◆◇

1 You say **'Sorry'** or **'I'm sorry'** as a way of apologizing to someone for something that you have done which has upset them or caused them difficulties. *'We're all talking at the same time.'—'Yeah. Sorry.'... Sorry I took so long... Sorry for barging in like this... I'm really sorry if I said anything wrong... I'm sorry to call so late, but I need a favour... The next morning she came into my room and said she was sorry.* CONVENTION PRAGMATICS

2 If you are **sorry** about a situation, you feel regret, sadness, or disappointment about it. *She was very sorry about all the trouble she'd caused... I'm sorry about what's happened... I'm sorry he's gone... He was sorry to see them go... Tell me I won't be sorry, she said.* ADJ-GRADED: v-link ADJ, usu ADJ *about* n, ADJ that/to-inf

3 You use **I'm sorry** or **sorry** as an introduction when you are telling someone something that you do not think they will want to hear, for example when you are disagreeing with them, refusing to do something, or giving them bad news. *No, I'm sorry, I can't agree with you... 'I'm sorry,' he told the real estate agent, 'but we really must go now.'... I'm sorry, but Miss Lee is resting and can't be disturbed... Sorry – no baths after ten o'clock... I'm sorry to have to tell you that Janet West is dead.* CONVENTION PRAGMATICS

4 If someone says **'You'll be sorry'**, they are threatening you or warning you and suggesting that something unpleasant will happen to you because of your actions. *I'll tell Daddy, and then you'll be sorry because he'll give you another black eye... Get back in there, or you'll be sorry.* PHRASE PRAGMATICS

5 You use the expression **I'm sorry to say** to express regret together with disappointment or disapproval. *I've only done half of it, I'm sorry to say... This, I am sorry to say, is almost entirely wishful thinking.* PHRASE: PHR with cl, PHR that PRAGMATICS

6 You say **'I'm sorry'** to express your regret and sadness when you hear sad or unpleasant news. *I've heard about Mollie – I'm so sorry... 'I'm afraid he's away ill.'—'I'm sorry to hear that.'* CONVENTION PRAGMATICS

7 If you feel **sorry for** someone who is unhappy or in an unpleasant situation, you feel sympathy and sadness for them. *I felt sorry for him and his colleagues – it must have been so frustrating for them... I am very sorry for the family.* ADJ-GRADED: v-link ADJ *for* n

8 You say that someone is feeling **sorry for** himself or herself when you disapprove of the fact that he or she is miserable and full of self-pity, rather than ADJ-GRADED: v-link ADJ *for* pron-refl PRAGMATICS

trying to be cheerful and positive. *What he must not do is to sit around at home feeling sorry for himself.*

9 You say **'Sorry?'** when you have not heard something that someone has said and you want them to repeat it.
CONVENTION PRAGMATICS =pardon, excuse me

10 You use **sorry** when you correct yourself and use different words to say what you have just said, especially when what you say the second time does not use the words you would normally choose to use. *Barcelona will be hoping to bring the trophy back to Spain (sorry, Catalonia) for the first time. ...refugees (sorry, economic migrants) who refuse to return to Vietnam.*
CONVENTION PRAGMATICS

11 If someone or something is in a **sorry** state, they are in a bad state, mentally or physically. *The fire has left Kuwait's oil industry in a sorry state... She is a sorry sight... They were a sorry lot.*
ADJ-GRADED: ADJ n

12 • **better safe than sorry**: see **safe**.

sort /sɔːʳt/ **sorts, sorting, sorted** ◆◆◆◆◆

1 If you talk about a particular **sort** of something, you are talking about a class of things that have particular features in common and that belong to a larger group of related things. *What sort of school did you go to?... There are so many different sorts of mushrooms available these days... A dozen trees of various sorts were planted... He had a nice, serious sort of smile... That's just the sort of abuse that he will be investigating... Eddie was playing a game of some sort... It is the last time I will take on this sort of work... Let's have some more articles of this sort.*
N-COUNT: with supp, usu N *of* n =type, kind

2 You describe someone as a particular **sort** when you are describing their character. *He seemed to be just the right sort for the job... She was a very vigorous sort of person... What sort of men were they?*
N-SING: with supp =type, kind

3 If you **sort** things, you separate them into different classes, groups, or places, for example so that you can do different things with them. *He sorted the materials into their folders... The students are sorted into three ability groups... He unlatched the box and sorted through the papers... I sorted the laundry.*
VERB V n *into* n V *through* n V n

4 If you get a problem or the details of something **sorted**, you do what is necessary to solve the problem or organize the details; an informal use. *I'm trying to get my script sorted... These problems have now been sorted.*
VB: usu passive =work out *get* n V-ed *be* V-ed

5 **All sorts** of things or people means a large number of different things or people. *There are all sorts of animals, including bears, pigs, kangaroos, and penguins... It was used by all sorts of people... Self-help groups of all sorts have been running for more than 20 years.*
PHRASES =all kinds

6 If you describe something as a thing **of sorts** or as a thing **of a sort**, you are suggesting that the thing is of a rather poor quality or standard. *He made a living of sorts selling pancakes from a van... She even managed a grimacing smile of sorts... They have had an education of a sort.*
n PHR =of a kind

7 You use **sort of** when you want to say that your description of something is not very accurate. *You could even order windows from a catalogue – a sort of mail order stained glass service... In the end, she sort of pushed it... I suppose it sort of made it more exciting.*
PRAGMATICS =kind of

8 If you are **out of sorts**, you feel slightly unwell, discontented, or annoyed.
v-link PHR

9 • to **sort the wheat from the chaff**: see **chaff**.
• **nothing of the sort**: see **nothing**.

sort out PHRASAL VERB

1 If you **sort out** a group of things, you separate them into different classes, groups, or places, for example so that you can do different things with them. *Sort out all your bills, receipts, invoices and expenses as quickly as possible and keep detailed accounts... Davina was sorting out scraps of material... How do we sort out fact from fiction?*
V P n (not pron) V P n (not pron) *from* n Also V n P

2 If you **sort out** a problem or the details of something, you do what is necessary to solve the problem or organize the details. *India and Nepal have sorted out their trade and security dispute... Have you sorted something out for tomorrow night?*
V P n (not pron) V n P

3 If you **sort** someone **out**, you make them realize that they have behaved wrongly, for example by talking to them or by punishing them; used mainly in British English. *It was the older women and young mothers who sorted all the troublemakers out... The crucial skill you need to develop is sorting out the parents.*
V n P V P n (not pron)

4 If you **sort** yourself **out**, you organize yourself or calm yourself so that you can act effectively and reasonably. *We're in a state of complete chaos here and I need a little time to sort myself out.*
=get yourself together V pron-refl P

sortie /sɔːʳti/ **sorties** ◆◇◇◇◇

1 A **sortie** is a brief trip away from your home base, especially a trip to an unfamiliar place; a formal use. *From here we plan several sorties into the countryside on foot. ...little sorties into antique shops.*
N-COUNT =foray

2 If a military force makes a **sortie**, it makes an attack or raid by leaving its own position and going briefly into enemy territory; a formal use. *His men made a sortie to Guazatan and took a prisoner... They flew 2,700 sorties in a day and didn't lose a single plane.*
N-COUNT =raid

sorting office, sorting offices. A **sorting office** is a place where letters and parcels are taken after posting and are sorted according to their delivery addresses.
N-COUNT

SOS /es oʊ es/. An **SOS** is a signal which indicates to other people that you are in danger and need help quickly. *The ferry did not even have time to send out an SOS.*
N-SING =mayday

so-so. If you say that something is **so-so**, you mean that it is average in quality, rather than being very good or very bad; an informal word. *Their lunch was only so-so... Sommers performed a flute solo a few weeks ago that got so-so reviews.*
◆◇◇◇◇ ADJ =middling, average

► Also an adverb. *'How's it going?'—'So-so.'*
ADV: ADV as reply

sotto voce /sɒtoʊ voʊtʃeɪ/. If you say something **sotto voce**, you say it in a soft voice; a literary expression.
ADV: usu ADV after v

soubriquet /soʊbrɪkeɪ/ **soubriquets.** See **sobriquet.**

soufflé /suːfleɪ, AM suːfleɪ/ **soufflés;** also spelled **souffle**. A **soufflé** is a light food made from a mixture of beaten egg whites and other ingredients that is baked in the oven. It can be either sweet or savoury. *...a superb cheese soufflé.*
◆◇◇◇◇ N-VAR

sought /sɔːt/. **Sought** is the past tense and past participle of **seek**.

sought-after. Something that is **sought-after** is in great demand, usually because it is rare or of very good quality. *An Olympic gold medal is the most sought-after prize in world sport.*
◆◇◇◇◇ ADJ-GRADED

souk /suːk/ **souks;** also spelled **suq**. A **souk** is an open-air marketplace in Muslim countries, especially in North Africa and the Middle East.
N-COUNT

soul /soʊl/ **souls** ◆◆◆◇◇

1 Your **soul** is the part of you that consists of your mind, character, thoughts, and feelings. Many people believe that your soul continues existing after your body is dead. *She went to pray for the soul of her late husband... 'I will put my heart and soul into the job,' he promises.*
N-COUNT: usu with supp =spirit ≠body

2 The **soul** of a nation or a political movement is its basic nature and beliefs. *...a struggle for the soul of the Republican Party.*
N-SING: with poss

3 You can refer to someone as a particular kind of **soul** when you are describing their character or condition. *He's a jolly soul... Her mother, poor soul, came to an even worse end.*
N-COUNT: adj N

4 You use **soul** in negative statements like **not a soul** to mean nobody at all. *I've never harmed a soul in my life... There was not a soul there.*
N-SING: with brd-neg

5 **Soul** or **soul music** is a type of pop music performed mainly by black American musicians. It developed from gospel and blues music and often expresses deep emotions. *...American soul singer Anita Baker.*
N-UNCOUNT

6 You can refer to the number of people who live in a particular place as **souls**; a literary use. *...a tiny village of only 100 souls.*
N-PLURAL: num N

7 If you say that someone **sells** their **soul**, you
PHRASE:

mean that they give up something very important such as their honesty in exchange for wealth or success. ...*politicians who would sell their soul for the sake of office.* V inflects, oft PHR *for/to* n

8 • to **bare** one's **soul**: see **bare**. • **body and soul**: see **body**. • to **keep body and soul together**: see **body**. • **the life and soul of the party**: see **life**.

soul-destroying. Activities or situations that are **soul-destroying** make you depressed, because they are boring or because there is no hope of improvement. *Believing yourself to be in the wrong job can be soul-destroying. ...an utterly soul-destroying experience.* ADJ-GRADED ≠inspiring

soulful /soulfʊl/. Something that is **soulful** expresses deep feelings, especially sadness or love. *...his great, soulful, brown eyes. ...soulful music.* ◆◇◇◇◇ ADJ-GRADED ≠soulless
♦ **soulfully** *She gazed at him soulfully.* ADV-GRADED

soulless /soulləs/. If you describe a thing or person as **soulless**, you mean that they lack human qualities and the ability to feel or produce deep feelings. *...a clean and soulless hotel. ...a grey and soulless existence... He was big and brawny with soulless eyes.* ADJ-GRADED ≠soulful

soul mate, soul mates; also spelled **soulmate**. A **soul mate** is someone with whom you share a close friendship and deep personal understanding. *Steve and I became soul mates, near-constant companions.* N-COUNT

soul music. **Soul music** or **soul** is a type of pop music performed mainly by black American musicians. It developed from gospel and blues music and often expresses deep emotions. N-UNCOUNT

soul-searching. **Soul-searching** is a long and careful examination of your thoughts and feelings, especially when you are trying to make a difficult moral decision or thinking about something that has gone wrong. *My year was really spent doing a lot of soul-searching and trying to find out what had gone wrong in my life.* N-UNCOUNT

sound 1 noun and verb uses

sound /saund/ **sounds, sounding, sounded** ◆◆◆◆◆

1 A **sound** is something that you hear. *Peter heard the sound of gunfire... Liza was so frightened she couldn't make a sound... There was a splintering sound as the railing gave way. ...the sounds of children playing.* N-COUNT

2 **Sound** is what you hear as a result of vibrations travelling through air or water. *...the waves of energy that we can hear as sound... The aeroplane will travel at twice the speed of sound.* N-UNCOUNT

3 **The sound** on a television, radio, or record player is what you hear coming from the machine. Its loudness can be controlled. *She went and turned the sound down... Compact discs have brought about a vast improvement in recorded sound quality.* N-SING: *the* N

4 A singer's or band's **sound** is the distinctive quality of their music. *They have started showing a strong soul element in their sound... He's got a unique sound and a unique style.* N-COUNT: with supp

5 If something such as a horn or a bell **sounds** or if you **sound** it, it makes a noise. *The buzzer sounded in Daniel's office... A young man sounds the bell to start the Sunday service.* V-ERG V V n

6 If you **sound** a warning, you publicly give it. If you **sound** a note of caution, scepticism, or optimism, you say publicly that you feel cautious, sceptical, or optimistic. *The Archbishop of Canterbury has sounded a warning to Europe's leaders on third world debt... Others consider the move premature and have sounded a note of caution... King Hussein sounded a deeply pessimistic note in an interview.* VERB V n

7 When you are describing a noise, you can talk about the way it **sounds**. *They heard what sounded like a huge explosion... The creaking of the hinges sounded very loud in that silence... It sounded as if he were trying to say something.* V-LINK V *like* n V adj V as if

8 When you talk about the way someone **sounds**, you are describing the impression you have of them when they speak. *She sounded a bit worried... Murphy sounds like a child... She sounded as if she really cared... I am dealing by telephone with Perry who sounds a real self-important Cockney.* V-LINK V adj V *like* n V as if V n

9 When you are describing your impression or opinion of something you have heard about or read about, you can talk about the way it **sounds**. *It sounds like a wonderful idea to me, does it really work?... It sounds as if they might have made a dreadful mistake... She decided that her doctor's advice sounded pretty good... The book is not as morbid as it sounds... I know this sounds a crazy thing for me to ask you.* V-LINK V *like* n V as if V adj V n

10 You can describe your impression **of** something you have heard about or read about by talking about **the sound of** it. *Here's a new idea we liked the sound of... I don't like the sound of Toby Osborne... From the sound of things, he might well be the same man... He was being paid danger money from the sound of it.* N-SING: *the* N *of* n

11 See also **-sounding, sounding**.

12 • to **sound the alarm**: see **alarm**. • to **sound the death knell**: see **death knell**. • **safe and sound**: see **safe**.

sound off. If someone **sounds off**, they express their opinions strongly and rather rudely to everyone without being asked; an informal expression. *It is surprising how many people start sounding off about something without really deciding what they think about it.* PHRASAL VERB V P *about/on* n Also V P

sound out. If you **sound** someone **out**, you question them in order to find out what their opinion is about something. *He is sounding out Middle Eastern governments on ways to resolve the conflict... Sound him out gradually. Make sure it is what he really wants.* PHRASAL VERB V P n (not pron) V n P

sound 2 adjective uses

sound /saund/ **sounder, soundest** ◆◆◇◇◇

1 If a structure, part of someone's body, or someone's mind is **sound**, it is in good condition or healthy. *When we bought the house, it was structurally sound... Although the car is basically sound, I was worried about certain areas... His body was still sound.* ♦ **soundness** *We had taken great pains to check the structural soundness of the coachwork.* ADJ-GRADED: usu v-link ADJ, oft adv ADJ ≠unsound N-UNCOUNT: usu with poss

2 **Sound** advice, reasoning, or evidence is reliable and sensible. *They are trained nutritionists who can give sound advice on diets... Buy a policy only from an insurance company that is financially sound... His reasoning is perfectly sound, but he misses the point... There is sound scientific evidence of what certain gases do to the atmosphere.* ♦ **soundness** *I can appreciate his humanitarian zeal; it is the soundness of his thought that I question... They have a strong record of financial soundness.* ADJ-GRADED =reliable ≠unsound N-UNCOUNT

3 If you describe someone's ideas as **sound**, you mean that you approve of them and think they are correct. *I am not sure that this is sound democratic practice... I think the idea of secularism is a very sound one... Can anyone suggest a method of deterring spiders which is ecologically sound?* ADJ-GRADED PRAGMATICS ≠unsound

4 If someone is in a **sound** sleep, they are sleeping very deeply. *She had woken me out of a sound sleep.* ▶ Also an adverb. *He was lying in bed, sound asleep.* ADJ: ADJ n ADV: ADV adj

5 See also **soundly**.

sound barrier. If an aircraft breaks the **sound barrier**, it reaches a speed that is faster than the speed of sound. N-SING: usu *the* N

soundbite /saundbaɪt/ **soundbites;** also spelled **sound-bite**. A **soundbite** is a short sentence or phrase, usually from a politician's speech, which is broadcast during a news bulletin. *...a 30-second sound bite on national television.* N-COUNT

sound effect, sound effects. **Sound effects** are the sounds that are created artificially to make a play more realistic, especially a radio play. N-COUNT: usu pl

sound engineer, sound engineers. A **sound engineer** is a person who works in a recording studio or for a radio or television company, whose job is to alter and balance the levels of different sounds as they are recorded. N-COUNT

sounding /saʊndɪŋ/ **soundings**

1 **The sounding of** a bell or a horn is the act of causing it to make a sound. *There were 15 minutes between the first air raid alert and the sounding of the all-clear signal.* N-SING: *the* N *of* n

2 If you take **soundings**, you try to find out people's opinions on a subject. *She will take soundings of the people's wishes before deciding on a course of action.* N-COUNT: usu pl

-sounding /-saʊndɪŋ/. **-sounding** combines with adjectives to indicate a quality that a word, phrase, or name seems to have. *Many literary academics simply parrot a set of impressive-sounding phrases. ...faraway places with strange-sounding names.* ● See also **high-sounding**. COMB in ADJ-GRADED

sounding board, sounding boards. If you use someone as a **sounding board**, you discuss your ideas with them in order to get another opinion. *It was one of those occasions when he needed a sounding board rather than thinking alone.* N-COUNT

soundless /saʊndləs/. Something that is **soundless** does not make a sound; a literary word. *My bare feet were soundless over the carpet.* ADJ =silent
♦ **soundlessly** *Joe's lips moved soundlessly.* ADV

soundly /saʊndli/ ◆◇◇◇◇

1 If someone is **soundly** defeated or beaten, they are defeated or beaten thoroughly. *In 1945, Churchill and the Conservatives were soundly beaten in the election.* ADV-GRADED: ADV -ed

2 If a decision, opinion, or statement is **soundly** based, there are sensible or reliable reasons behind it. *Are today's hopes more soundly based than the false ones of 1990?... Changes must be soundly based in economic reality.* ADV-GRADED: ADV -ed

3 If you sleep **soundly**, you sleep deeply and do not wake during your sleep. *How can he sleep soundly at night? He's the one responsible for all those crimes... She was too soundly asleep to hear Stefano's return.* ADV-GRADED: ADV after v, ADV adj =deeply

soundproof /saʊndpruːf/ **soundproofs, soundproofing, soundproofed;** also spelled **sound-proof.**

1 A **soundproof** room, door, or window is designed to prevent all sound from getting in or out. *The studio isn't soundproof.* ADJ

2 If you **soundproof** a room, you line it with special materials to stop all sound from getting in or out. *We've soundproofed our home studio... The dog was placed in a soundproofed room.* VERB V n V-ed
♦ **soundproofing** *We did make a mistake in not having enough soundproofing upstairs.* N-UNCOUNT

sound stage, sound stages; also spelled **sound-stage, soundstage**. A **sound stage** is a stage or set which is suitable for recording sound, especially for a film. N-COUNT

sound system, sound systems. A **sound system** is a set of equipment for playing and amplifying recorded music, or for amplifying live music. ◆◇◇◇◇ N-COUNT

soundtrack /saʊndtræk/ **soundtracks;** also spelled **sound track**. The **soundtrack** of a film is its sound, speech, and music. It is used especially to refer to the music. ◆◆◇◇◇ N-COUNT

sound wave, sound waves; also spelled **soundwave**. **Sound waves** are the waves of energy that we hear as sound. *Speech is made up of sound waves that vary in frequency and intensity.* N-COUNT

soup /suːp/ **soups, souping, souped** ◆◆◇◇◇

1 **Soup** is liquid food made by boiling meat, fish, or vegetables in water. *...home-made chicken soup.* N-MASS: usu supp N

2 If you say that someone is **in the soup**, you mean they are in trouble; an informal expression, used mainly in journalism. *She has a knack of landing herself right in the soup.* PHRASE: PHR after v, v-link PHR

soup up. To **soup up** something such as a car engine means to make it more powerful. To **soup up** something such as a piece of music or writing means to make it more interesting and exciting. *He had his first car at sixteen, a Mini, which he souped up and crashed.* PHRASAL VERB V P n (not pron)
♦ **souped-up** *...a souped-up Peugeot 205. ...a souped-up version of the theme from 'The Generation Game'.* ADJ: ADJ n

soup kitchen, soup kitchens; also spelled **soup-kitchen**. A **soup kitchen** is a place where homeless people or very poor people are provided with free food. *...a soup kitchen in Warsaw that's run by the Church.* N-COUNT

soup plate, soup plates. A **soup plate** is a deep plate with a wide rim in which soup is served. N-COUNT

soup spoon, soup spoons. A **soup spoon** is a spoon used for eating soup. The bowl-like part at the end of it is rounder than on other types of spoons. N-COUNT

soupy /suːpi/. **Soupy** things are like soup or look like soup. *...swirling soupy water... The rice is accompanied by a soup or a soupy stew.* ADJ

sour /saʊəʳ/ **sours, souring, soured** ◆◆◇◇◇

1 Something that is **sour** has a sharp taste like the taste of a lemon or an unripe apple. *The stewed apple was sour even with honey.* ● See also **sweet and sour**. ADJ-GRADED =bitter

2 **Sour** milk is milk that has an unpleasant taste because it is no longer fresh. ADJ ≠fresh

3 Someone who is **sour** is bad-tempered and unfriendly. *She made a sour face in his direction... Police, weary and increasingly sour in mood, wonder aloud why the situation has been allowed to deteriorate.* ADJ-GRADED =surly, churlish
♦ **sourly** *'Leave my mother out of it,' he said sourly.* ADV: ADV with v

4 If a situation or relationship turns **sour** or goes **sour**, it stops being enjoyable or satisfactory. *Everything turned sour for me there... Even the European dream is beginning to turn sour... Their songs are filled with tales of love gone sour.* ADJ

5 If a friendship, situation, or attitude **sours** or if something **sours** it, it becomes less friendly, enjoyable, or hopeful. *If anything sours the relationship, it is likely to be real differences in their world-views... Her mood soured a little.* V-ERG V n V

6 If you refer to someone's attitude as **sour grapes**, you mean that they say that something is worthless or undesirable because they want it themselves but cannot have it; used showing disapproval. *Page's response to the suggestion that this might be sour grapes because his company lost the bid is: 'Life's too short for that.'* PHRASE PRAGMATICS

source /sɔːʳs/ **sources, sourcing, sourced** ◆◆◆◆◇

1 The **source** of something is the person, place, or thing which you get it from. *For Iraqis, Baghdad Radio is the main official source of information... Renewable sources of energy must be used where practical... Tourism, which is a major source of income for the city, may be seriously affected.* N-COUNT: usu N *of* n

2 In business, if a person or firm **sources** a product or a raw material, they find someone who will supply it. *Together they travel the world, sourcing clothes for the small, privately owned company... About 60 per cent of an average car is sourced from outside of the manufacturer. ...furniture sourced from all over the world.* VERB V n V-ed Also V *from* n
♦ **sourcing** *The union is particularly concerned at the sourcing of products abroad.* N-UNCOUNT: oft N *of* n

3 A **source** is a person or book that provides information for a news story or for a piece of research. *Military sources say the boat was heading south at high speed... She quotes secondary and primary sources without distinction.* N-COUNT: usu with supp

4 The **source of** a difficulty is its cause. *This gave me a clue as to the source of the problem.* N-COUNT: N *of* n =cause

5 The **source** of a river or stream is the place where it begins. *...the source of the Tiber.* N-COUNT: usu sing

sour cream; also spelled **soured cream**. **Sour cream** is cream that has been artificially made sour by being mixed with bacteria. It is used in cooking. N-UNCOUNT

south /saʊθ/; also spelled **South**. ◆◆◆◆◆

1 The **south** is the direction which is on your right when you are looking towards the direction where the sun rises. *The town lies ten miles to the south of here... All around him, from east to west, north to south, the stars glittered in the heavens.* N-UNCOUNT: also *the* N

2 The **south** of a place, country, or region is the part which is in the south. *...holidays in the south of France.* N-SING: usu *the* N, oft N *of* n

3 If you go **south**, you travel towards the south. *We did an extremely fast U-turn and shot south up the Boulevard St. Michel... He went south to climb Taishan, a mountain sacred to the Chinese.* ADV: ADV after v

4 Something that is **south of** a place is positioned to the south of it. *They now own and operate a farm 50 miles south of Rochester... I was living in a house just south of Market Street.* ADV: ADV of n

5 The **south** edge, corner, or part of a place or country is the part which is towards the south. *...the south coast of Alderney.* ADJ: ADJ n

6 **'South'** is used in the names of some countries, states, and regions in the south of a larger area. *Next week the President will visit five South American countries in six days.* ADJ

7 A **south** wind is a wind that blows from the south. ADJ

southbound /saʊθbaʊnd/. **Southbound** roads, cars, and trains lead or are travelling towards the south. *...the southbound train from the Scottish Highlands. ...the southbound carriageway of the M61.* ADJ: usu ADJ n

south-east; also spelled **South-East**. ◆◆◆◆◇

1 The **south-east** is the direction which is halfway between south and east. *The city of Ch'eng Tu lies some seven hundred miles to the South-East.* N-UNCOUNT: also the N

2 The **south-east** of a place, country, or region is the part which is in the south-east. *...the regional electricity company serving the South-east of England... The heaviest snowfalls today are expected in the south east.* N-SING: usu the N, oft N of n

3 If you go **south-east**, you travel towards the south-east. *We turned south-east, making for Portoferraio.* ADV: ADV after v

4 Something that is **south-east of** a place is positioned to the south-east of it. *...the potteries of Iznik, some 120km south-east of Istanbul.* ADV: ADV of n

5 The **south-east** part of a place, country, or region is the part which is towards the south-east. *...South-East Asia. ...the south-east quarter of Lincolnshire. ...an island just off Shetland's south-east coast.* ADJ: ADJ n

6 A **south-east** wind is a wind that blows from the south-east. ADJ: ADJ n

south-easterly; also spelled **south easterly**.

1 A **south-easterly** point, area, or direction is to the south-east or towards the south-east. ADJ: usu ADJ n

2 A **south-easterly** wind is a wind that blows from the south-east. ADJ

south-eastern; also spelled **south eastern**. **South-eastern** means in or from the south-east of a region or country. *...this city on the south-eastern edge of the United States.* ◆◇◇◇◇ ADJ: usu ADJ n

southerly /sʌðəʳli/

1 A **southerly** point, area, or direction is to the south or towards the south. *We set off in a southerly direction. ...the most southerly areas of Zimbabwe and Mozambique.* ADJ-GRADED: usu ADJ n

2 A **southerly** wind is a wind that blows from the south. ADJ: usu ADJ n

southern /sʌðəʳn/. **Southern** means in or from the south of a region or country. *The Everglades National Park stretches across the southern tip of Florida. ...a place where you can sample southern cuisine.* ◆◆◆◆◇ ADJ: ADJ n

southerner /sʌðəʳnəʳ/ **southerners.** A **southerner** is a person who was born in or lives in the south of a country. *Bob Wilson is a Southerner, from Texas... Southerners smoke less and drink less than those in other parts of the country.* ◆◇◇◇◇ N-COUNT

southernmost /sʌðəʳnmoust/. The **southernmost** part of an area or the **southernmost** place is the one that is further towards the south than any other. *The ancient province of Satsuma lies in the southernmost part of the Japanese island of Kyushu. ...Aswan, Egypt's southernmost city.* ADJ-SUPERL: usu ADJ n

South Pole. **The South Pole** is the place on the surface of the earth which is farthest towards the south. N-PROPER: the N

southward /saʊθwəʳd/; the form **southwards** is also used. **Southward** or **southwards** means towards the south. *They drove southward... It was a visit that took him to Mogadishu and southwards to Kismayo.* ▶ Also an adjective. *Instead of her normal southward course towards Alexandria and home, she headed west.* ADV: ADV after v; ADJ

south-west; also spelled **South-West**. ◆◆◆◆◇

1 The **south-west** is the direction which is halfway between south and west. *...the village of Popplewell, some six miles to the south-west.* N-UNCOUNT: also the N

2 The **south-west** of a place, country, or region is the part which is towards the south-west. *...the mountains in the south west of the USA.* N-SING: usu the N, oft N of n

3 If you go **south-west**, you travel towards the south-west. *We took a plane south-west across the Anatolian plateau to Cappadocia.* ADV: ADV after v

4 Something that is **south-west of** a place is positioned to the south-west of it. *...a gold mine at Orkney, south-west of Johannesburg.* ADV: ADV of n

5 The **south-west** part of a place, country, or region is the part which is towards the south-west. *...a light aircraft crash near Stranraer in South-West Scotland. ...in the south-west corner of my garden.* ADJ: ADJ n

6 A **south-west** wind is a wind that blows from the south-west. ADJ: ADJ n

south-westerly; also spelled **south westerly**.

1 A **south-westerly** point, area, or direction is to the south-west or towards the south-west. *...the most south-westerly tip of Scotland.* ADJ: usu ADJ n

2 A **south-westerly** wind is a wind that blows from the south-east. ADJ

south-western; also spelled **south western**. **South-western** means in or from the south-west of a region or country. *...towns and villages in south-western Azerbaijan.* ◆◇◇◇◇ ADJ: usu ADJ n

souvenir /suːvənɪəʳ, AM -nɪr/ **souvenirs.** A **souvenir** is something which you buy or keep to remind you of a holiday, place, or event. *...a souvenir of the summer of 1992.* ◆◇◇◇◇ N-COUNT: oft N of n =memento

sou'wester /saʊwestəʳ/ **sou'westers.** A **sou'wester** is a waterproof hat that is worn especially by sailors in stormy weather. It has a wide brim at the back to keep your neck dry. N-COUNT

sovereign /sɒvrɪn/ **sovereigns** ◆◆◇◇◇

1 A **sovereign** state or country is independent and not under the authority of any other country. *For the first time the parties had accepted the existence of Bosnia as a sovereign state... The Russian Federation declared itself to be a sovereign republic.* ADJ: usu ADJ n =autonomous

2 **Sovereign** is used to describe the person or institution that has the highest power in a country. *Sovereign power will continue to lie with the Supreme People's Assembly.* ADJ

3 A **sovereign** is a king, queen, or other royal ruler of a country. *In March 1889, she became the first British sovereign to set foot on Spanish soil.* N-COUNT =monarch

sovereignty /sɒvrɪnti/. **Sovereignty** is the power that a country has to govern itself or another country or state. *Britain's concern to protect national sovereignty is far from new.* ◆◆◇◇◇ N-UNCOUNT: also N in pl =autonomy

Soviet /soʊviət, sɒv-/ **Soviets** ◆◆◆◆◇

1 **Soviet** is used to describe something that belonged or related to the former Soviet Union. *...Soviet athletes. ...the former Soviet empire.* ADJ: usu ADJ n

2 The **Soviets** were the people of the former Soviet Union. *In 1957, the Soviets launched Sputnik 1 into outer space.* N-PLURAL

3 A **soviet** was an elected local, regional, or national council in the former Soviet Union. *...the supreme soviet.* N-COUNT

Sovietologist /soʊviətɒlədʒɪst, sɒv-/ **Sovietologists.** A **Sovietologist** is a person who is an expert on the former Soviet Union. N-COUNT

sow 1 verb uses

sow /soʊ/ **sows, sowing, sowed, sown** ◆◇◇◇◇

1 If you **sow** seeds or **sow** an area of land with seeds, you plant the seeds in the ground. *Sow the seed in a warm place in February/March... Yesterday the field opposite was sown with maize.* VERB =plant V n be V-ed with n

2 If someone **sows** an undesirable feeling or situation, they cause it to begin and develop. *He cleverly sowed doubts into the minds of his rivals... Instead, the session has sowed confusion.* VERB V n

3 If one thing **sows the seeds of** another, it starts the process which leads eventually to the other PHRASE: V inflects, PHR n

thing. *By pushing for an agreement which lacks the approval of Mr Dostam, he may have sown the seeds of renewed conflict.*

sow 2 noun use

sow /saʊ/ **sows.** A **sow** is an adult female pig. N-COUNT

sown /soʊn/. **Sown** is the past participle of **sow**.

soya /sɔɪə/. **Soya** flour, butter, or other food is made from soya beans. ◆◇◇◇◇ N-UNCOUNT: usu N n

soya bean, soya beans; spelled **soybean** /sɔɪbiːn/ in American English. **Soya beans** are beans that can be eaten or used to make flour, oil, or soy sauce. N-COUNT

soy sauce /sɔɪ sɔːs/; also spelled **soya sauce**. **Soy sauce** is a dark brown liquid made from soya beans and used as a flavouring, especially in Chinese cooking. N-UNCOUNT

spa /spɑː/ **spas** ◆◇◇◇◇

1 A **spa** is a place where water with minerals in it bubbles out of the ground. People drink the water or bathe in it in order to improve their health. *...Fiuggi, a spa town famous for its water.* N-COUNT

2 A health **spa** is a place where people go to use facilities such as a pool, a gymnasium, and a sauna in order to improve their health. N-COUNT

space /speɪs/ **spaces, spacing, spaced** ◆◆◆◆◇

1 You use **space** to refer to an area that is empty or available. The area can be any size. For example, you can refer to a large area outside as a large open **space** or to a small area between two objects as a small **space** between the objects. *Under the plan, bits of open space – fields, golf-course borders and small parks – will be preserved. ...cutting down yet more trees to make space for houses... I had plenty of space to write and sew... The space underneath could be used as a storage area... He looked cautiously through a half-inch space between the curtains and saw an empty bedroom... The bird was enclosed in such a small space that it could not turn without bending its tail... List in the spaces below the specific changes you have made.* N-VAR

2 A particular kind of **space** is the area that is available for a particular activity or for putting a particular kind of thing in. *...the high cost of office space... You don't want your living space to look like a bedroom... Finding a parking space in the summer months is still a virtual impossibility... The Women's Gym is a women-only space dedicated to women of all ages, shapes and sizes.* N-VAR: usu supp N

3 If a place gives a feeling of **space**, it gives an impression of being large and open. *Large paintings can enhance the feeling of space in small rooms... The sense of space and emptiness is overwhelming.* N-UNCOUNT: oft n *of* N =spaciousness

4 If you give someone **space** to think about something or to develop as a person, you allow them the time and freedom to do this. *You need space to think everything over... We will give each other space to develop.* N-UNCOUNT =room

5 The amount of **space** for a topic to be discussed in a document is the number of words, paragraphs, or pages available to discuss the topic. *We can't promise to publish a reply as space is limited. ...some work which we couldn't include because of lack of space in this issue.* N-UNCOUNT

6 A **space of** time is a period of time. *They've come a long way in a short space of time... I have known dramatic changes occur in the space of a few minutes with this method.* N-SING: N *of* n

7 **Space** is the vast area that lies beyond the Earth's atmosphere and surrounds the stars and planets. *The six astronauts on board will spend ten days in space. ...launching satellites into space. ...developments in space technology. ...outer space.* N-UNCOUNT

8 **Space** is the whole area within which everything exists. *She felt herself transcending time and space... The physical universe is finite in space and time.* N-UNCOUNT

9 If you **space** a series of things, you arrange them so that they are not all together but have gaps or intervals of time between them. *Women once again are having fewer children and spacing them further apart... His voice was angry and he spaced the words for emphasis.* ► **Space out** means the same as **space**. *He talks quite slowly and spaces his words out... I was spacing out the seedlings into divided trays... They will have time to draw breath between matches, with their last four fixtures spaced out over three weeks.* ♦ **spaced** *Its houses are large, well-spaced and surrounded by gardens... The RAC is calling for rest areas spaced at regular intervals on major roads.* ♦ **spacing** *Generous spacing gives healthier trees and better crops.* VERB V n adv/prep V n PHRASAL VERB V n P V P n (not pron) V-ed P ADJ: adv ADJ, v-link ADJ adv/prep N-UNCOUNT

10 See also **spacing**; **airspace**, **breathing space**, **outer space**, **personal space**.

11 If you are staring **into space**, you are looking straight in front of you, without actually looking at anything in particular, for example because you are thinking or because you are feeling shocked. *He just sat in the dressing-room staring into space... Molly turned away and gazed off into space, a far-away look in her eyes.* PHRASES PHR after v

12 If you describe someone or something as a **waste of space**, you are indicating that you have a very low opinion of them; an informal expression. *Even Sarah treated him as if he were a waste of space... Are we expected to believe those scribblings are art? This piece of trash was a waste of space.* usu v-link PHR

13 Journalists write **'Watch this space'** in order to indicate in an informal way that they will be giving more information about something in the future. *Watch this space for details of our next event.*

space age; also spelled **space-age**.

1 **The space age** is the present period in the history of the world, when travel in space has become possible. N-SING: *the* N

2 You use **space-age** to describe something that is very modern and makes you think of the technology of the space age. *...a space-age tower of steel and glass.* ADJ: usu ADJ n =futuristic

spacecraft /speɪskrɑːft, -kræft/; **spacecraft** is both the singular and the plural form. A **spacecraft** is a rocket or other vehicle that can travel in space. ◆◇◇◇◇ N-COUNT

spaced-out; also spelled **spaced out**. Someone who is **spaced-out** feels as if nothing around them is real, usually because they have taken drugs or because they are very tired; an informal expression. *He's got this spaced-out look.* ADJ-GRADED

space flight, space flights. A **space flight** is a trip into space. *She made her first and only space flight last September... The future for manned space flight is looking increasingly uncertain.* N-VAR

spaceman /speɪsmæn/ **spacemen.** A **spaceman** is a male astronaut; used mainly by children. N-COUNT =astronaut

space probe, space probes. A **space probe** is a small unmanned spacecraft that is sent into space in order to transmit information about what space is like. N-COUNT =satellite

spaceship /speɪsʃɪp/ **spaceships.** A **spaceship** is a spacecraft that carries people through space. N-COUNT

space shuttle, space shuttles. A **space shuttle** or a **shuttle** is a spacecraft that is designed to travel into space and back to earth several times.  N-COUNT =shuttle

space station, space stations. A **space station** is an object which is sent into space and then goes around the earth, and which is used as a base by astronauts. ◆◇◇◇◇ N-COUNT

space suit, space suits; also spelled **spacesuit**. A **space suit** is a special protective suit that is worn by astronauts in space. N-COUNT

space walk, space walks. When an astronaut goes on a **space walk**, he or she leaves the spacecraft and works outside it while floating in space. N-COUNT

spacing /speɪsɪŋ/. **Spacing** refers to the way that typing or printing is arranged on a page, especially in relation to the amount of space that is left between words or lines. *Please type or write clearly in double spacing on one side of A4 paper only.* ● See also **space**. N-UNCOUNT

spacious /speɪʃəs/. A **spacious** room or other place is large in size or area, so that you can move around freely in it. *The house has a spacious kitchen and dining area.* ♦ **spaciousness** *A high ceiling creates a feeling of spaciousness.* ◆◇◇◇◇ ADJ-GRADED: usu ADJ n =roomy N-UNCOUNT

spade /speɪd/ **spades** ◆◇◇◇◇
1 A **spade** is a tool used for digging, with a flat metal blade and a long handle. ... *a garden spade... The girls happily played in the sand with buckets and spades.* N-COUNT
2 **Spades** is one of the four suits in a pack of playing cards. Each card in the suit is marked with one or more black symbols: ♠. ...*the ace of spades.* ► A **spade** is a playing card of this suit. N-UNCOUNT-COLL N-COUNT
3 If you say that someone **calls a spade a spade**, you mean that they speak frankly and directly, often about embarrassing or unpleasant subjects; an informal expression, used showing approval. *I'm not at all secretive, and I'm pretty good at calling a spade a spade.* PHRASE: V inflects PRAGMATICS

spadework /speɪdwɜːʳk/. The **spadework** is the uninteresting work that has to be done as preparation before you can start a project or activity. *It is now that the spadework has to be done to lay firm foundations for later success.* N-SING: usu *the* N

spaghetti /spəgeti/. **Spaghetti** is a type of pasta. It looks like long pieces of string and is usually served with a sauce. ◆◇◇◇◇ N-UNCOUNT

spaghetti western, spaghetti westerns. A **spaghetti western** is a film made in Europe by an Italian director about life in the American Wild West. N-COUNT

spake /speɪk/. **Spake** is the very old-fashioned form of the past tense of **speak**. It is usually only used humorously nowadays. *Thus spake George Bush at the peace conference in Madrid.* V

span /spæn/ **spans, spanning, spanned** ◆◆◇◇◇
1 A **span** is the period of time between two dates or events during which something exists, functions, or happens. *The batteries had a life span of six hours... Gradually the time span between sessions will increase.* N-COUNT: usu supp N
2 Your concentration **span** or your attention **span** is the length of time you are able to concentrate on something or be interested in it. *His ability to absorb information was astonishing, but his concentration span was short... Young children have a limited attention span and can't concentrate on one activity for very long.* N-COUNT: usu supp N
3 If something **spans** a long period of time, it lasts throughout that period of time or relates to that whole period of time. *His professional career spanned 16 years... The film, spanning almost a quarter-century, tells the story of Henry Hill... Lining a corridor is a wall of photographs spanning his rugby days.* VB: no passive V n
4 If something **spans** a range of things, all those things are included in it. *Bernstein's compositions spanned all aspects of music, from symphonies to musicals. ...a remarkable man whose interests spanned almost every aspect of nature.* VB: no passive V n
5 The **span** of something that extends or is spread out sideways is the total width of it from one end to the other. *It is a very pretty butterfly, with a 2 inch wing span... It may be that you are unaware of where your hip joint is; it is not at the waist but a good hand span below it.* N-COUNT: usu with supp
6 A bridge or other structure that **spans** something such as a river or a valley stretches right across it. *Travellers get from one side to the other by walking across a footbridge that spans a little stream. ...the humped iron bridge spanning the railway... Architects tell their clients that floors can span 100 metres without any visible means of support.* VERB V n
7 See also **spick and span**.

spangle /spæŋgᵊl/ **spangles. Spangles** are small pieces of metal or plastic which sparkle brightly and are used to decorate clothing or hair. ...*robes that glittered with spangles.* N-COUNT: usu pl

spangled /spæŋgᵊld/. Something that is **spangled** is covered with small shiny objects. ...*spangled, backless dresses. ...a dark night sky spangled with stars.* ADJ

spangly /spæŋgli/. Something that is **spangly** is covered with spangles. *He certainly liked spangly jackets.* ADJ

Spaniard /spænjəʳd/ **Spaniards.** A **Spaniard** is a Spanish citizen, or a person of Spanish origin. ◆◇◇◇◇ N-COUNT

spaniel /spænjəl/ **spaniels.** A **spaniel** is a type of dog with long ears that hang down. N-COUNT

Spanish /spænɪʃ/ ◆◆◆◆◇
1 **Spanish** means belonging or relating to Spain, or to its people, language, or culture. ...*a Spanish sherry. ...the Spanish Ambassador.* ADJ: usu ADJ n
2 **Spanish** is the main language spoken in Spain, and in many countries in South and Central America. N-UNCOUNT
3 The **Spanish** are the people who come from Spain. N-PLURAL: usu *the* N

spank /spæŋk/ **spanks, spanking, spanked.** If someone **spanks** a child, they punish them by hitting them on the bottom several times. *When I used to do that when I was a kid, my mom would spank me.* VERB =smack

spanking /spæŋkɪŋ/ **spankings**
1 If someone gives a child a **spanking**, they give the child a series of slaps with their hand, usually on the child's bottom, as a way of punishing the child. *Andrea gave her son a sound spanking.* N-COUNT
2 If you describe something as **spanking** new, **spanking** clean, or **spanking** white, you mean that it is very new, very clean, or very white; an informal use. ...*a spanking new Mercedes... The upstairs bedrooms were spanking clean.* ADV: ADV adj
3 If something moves at a **spanking** pace, it moves quickly. *The film moves along at a spanking pace... We rode at a spanking trot.* ADJ: ADJ n

spanner /spænəʳ/ **spanners** ◆◇◇◇◇
1 A **spanner** is a metal tool with a specially shaped end that fits round a nut so that you can loosen or tighten the nut; used mainly in British English. The usual American word is **wrench** or **monkey wrench**. N-COUNT =wrench
2 In British English, if someone **throws a spanner in the works**, they prevent something happening smoothly in the way that it was planned, by causing a problem or difficulty. The American expression is to **throw a wrench** or **throw a monkey wrench** into something. *A bad result is sure to throw a spanner in the works.* PHRASE: V inflects

spar /spɑːʳ/ **spars, sparring, sparred** ◆◇◇◇◇
1 If you **spar** with someone, you box using fairly gentle blows instead of hitting your opponent hard, either when you are training or when you want to test how quickly your opponent reacts. *He entered the ring to spar a few one-minute rounds with an old friend... They sparred for a moment, on the brink of a full fist-fight.* V-RECIP V *with* n pl-n V
2 If you **spar** with someone, you argue with them but not in an aggressive or serious way. *Over the years he sparred with his friend Jesse Jackson over political tactics... Morisot and Manet had always gotten along, even when they sparred.* V-RECIP V *with* n pl-n V
3 A **spar** is a strong pole, especially one that a sail is attached to on a sailing ship. *The mast, which was a solid spruce spar, bent like a bow, and for a moment I thought we were going to lose it.* N-COUNT

spare /speəʳ/ **spares, sparing, spared** ◆◆◆◇◇
1 You use **spare** to describe something that is the same as things that you are already using, but that you do not need yet and are keeping ready in case another one is needed. *If possible keep a spare pair of glasses accessible in case your main pair is broken or lost... Don't forget to take a few spare batteries... He could have taken a spare key... The wagons carried spare ammunition.* ► Also a noun. *Give me the trunk key and I'll get the spare.* ADJ: usu ADJ n N-COUNT
2 You use **spare** to describe something that is not being used by anyone, and is therefore available for someone to use. *They don't have a lot of spare cash... The spare bedroom is on the second floor... There was hardly a spare inch of space to be found.* ADJ: usu ADJ n
3 If you have something such as time, money, or space to **spare**, you have some extra time, money, or space that you have not used or which you do not need. *You got here with ninety seconds to spare... It's not as if he has money to spare... The car suddenly darted ahead, squeezing past him with* VB: only to-inf V

only inches to spare... Miranda has drive and energy to spare and has now taken on an even bigger challenge.

4 If you **spare** time or another resource for a particular purpose, you make it available for that purpose. *She said that she could only spare 35 minutes for our meeting... He's a very busy man, and it's good of him to spare the time to visit... He suggested that his country could not spare the troops for such an operation.*
VERB
V n

5 If a person or a place **is spared**, they are not harmed, although someone or something threatened them or harmed other people or places; a literary use. *We have lost everything, but thank God, our lives have been spared... Not a man was spared... Northern Somalia was largely spared from the famine.*
VB: usu passive
be V-ed
be V-ed *from* n

6 If you **spare** someone an unpleasant experience, you prevent them from suffering it. *I wanted to spare Frances the embarrassment of discussing this subject... Prisoners are spared the indignity of wearing uniforms... Spare me the gory details... She's just trying to spare Shawna's feelings... The policy has not spared the farming community from severe financial pressure.*
VERB
V n n
V n
V n *from* n

7 Someone who is described as **spare** is tall and not at all fat; a literary use. *She was thin and spare, with a sharply intelligent face.*
ADJ-GRADED
=lean

8 Something such as a room that is **spare** is very plain with no unnecessary features; a literary use. *Inside, the two small rooms were spare and neat, stripped bare of ornaments.*
ADJ-GRADED
=stark

9 See also **sparing**.

10 If you **spare no effort** in doing something, you do it as well as possible, without worrying about the amount of work involved. If you **spare no expense** in doing it, you do it as well as possible, without trying to save money. *The government is determined to spare no effort in investigating this case thoroughly... Officials say they'll spare no expense to prevent another riot.*
PHRASES
V inflects

11 If you **spare a thought for** an unfortunate person, you make an effort to think sympathetically about them and their bad luck. *Spare a thought for the nation's shopkeepers – consumer sales slid again in May... I do not think any of us spared a thought for the ordeal of her crew.*
V inflects, PHR n

12 • to **spare** someone's **blushes**: see **blush**.

spare part, spare parts. Spare parts are parts that you can buy separately to replace old or broken parts in a piece of equipment. They are usually parts that are designed to be easily removed or fitted. *In the future the machines will need spare parts and maintenance.*
◆◇◇◇◇
N-COUNT: usu pl

spare room, spare rooms. A **spare room** is a bedroom which is kept especially for visitors to sleep in.
N-COUNT

spare time. Your **spare time** is the time during which you do not have to work and you can do whatever you like. *In her spare time she read books on cooking... I spend a lot of my spare time watching videos.*
◆◇◇◇◇
N-UNCOUNT: usu poss N
=free time

spare tyre, spare tyres; spelled **spare tire** in American English.

1 A **spare tyre** is the same as a spare wheel.
N-COUNT

2 In British English, if you describe someone as having a **spare tyre**, you mean that they are fat around their waist.
N-COUNT

spare wheel, spare wheels. A **spare wheel** is a complete wheel with a tyre already on it that you keep in your car in case you have a puncture and need to replace one of your wheels.
N-COUNT
=spare

sparing /speərɪŋ/. Someone who is **sparing** with something uses it or gives it only in very small quantities. *I've not been sparing with the garlic... Her sparing use of make-up only seemed to enhance her classically beautiful features... Only a sparing amount is needed.* ♦ **sparingly** *Medication is used sparingly... Normally she ate sparingly.*
◆◇◇◇◇
ADJ-GRADED
≠unsparing
ADV-GRADED: ADV after v

spark /spɑːʳk/ **sparks, sparking, sparked**
◆◆◆◇◇

1 A **spark** is a tiny bright piece of burning material that flies up from something that is burning. *The fire gradually got bigger and bigger. Sparks flew off in all directions.*
N-COUNT

2 A **spark** is a flash of light caused by electricity. It often makes a crackling sound. *He passed an electric spark through a mixture of gases.*
N-COUNT

3 If something **sparks**, sparks of fire or light come from it. *The wires were sparking above me... I stared into the flames of the fire as it sparked to life.*
VERB
V
V prep

4 If a burning object or electricity **sparks** a fire, it causes a fire. *A dropped cigarette may have sparked the fire.*
VERB
=start
V n

5 A **spark of** a quality or feeling, especially a desirable one, is a small but noticeable amount of it. *His music lacked that vital spark of imagination... Even Oliver felt a tiny spark of excitement.*
N-COUNT: N *of* n

6 If one thing **sparks** another, the first thing causes the second thing to start happening. *What was it that sparked your interest in motoring?... The proposals are expected to spark heated debate. ...a row sparked by a comment about his sister.* ► **Spark off** means the same as **spark**. *That incident sparked it off... His book, Animal Liberation, sparked off a revolution in the way we think about animals. ...a political crisis sparked off by religious violence.*
VERB
=cause
V n
V-ed
PHRASAL VERB
V n P
V P n (not pron)
V-ed

7 See also **bright spark**.

8 If **sparks fly** between people, they discuss something in an excited or angry way. *They are not afraid to tackle the issues or let the sparks fly when necessary.*
PHRASE: V inflects

spark off. See **spark** 6.
PHRASAL VERB

sparkle /spɑːʳkəl/ **sparkles, sparkling, sparkled**
◆◆◇◇◇

1 If something **sparkles**, it is clear and bright and shines with a lot of very small points of light. *The jewels on her fingers sparkled... His bright eyes sparkled. ...the sparkling blue waters of the ocean.* ► Also a noun. *...the sparkle of coloured glass.*
VERB
=glitter
V
V-ing
N-UNCOUNT

2 **Sparkles** are small points of light caused by light reflecting off a clear bright surface. *...sparkles of light... There was a sparkle in her eye that could not be hidden.*
N-COUNT

3 Someone who **sparkles** is lively, intelligent, and witty. *She sparkles, and has as much zest as a person half her age... They'd been a dejected lot when he'd arrived at the shipyard, but now they sparkled with enthusiasm.* ► Also a noun. *There was little sparkle in their performance.* ♦ **sparkling** *He is sparkling and versatile in front of the camera.*
VERB
=shine
V
V *with* n
N-UNCOUNT
ADJ-GRADED
=scintillating

4 See also **sparkling**.

sparkler /spɑːʳkləʳ/ **sparklers.** A **sparkler** is a small firework that you can hold alight in your hand. It looks like a piece of thick wire and burns with a lot of small bright sparks.
N-COUNT

sparkling /spɑːʳklɪŋ/. **Sparkling** drinks are slightly fizzy. *...a glass of sparkling wine. ...a new lightly sparkling drink.* • See also **sparkle**.
◆◇◇◇◇
ADJ: usu ADJ n

sparkling wine, sparkling wines. Sparkling wine is wine that is slightly fizzy.
N-MASS

sparkly /spɑːʳkli/. **Sparkly** things sparkle; an informal word. *...a sparkly toy necklace... Her eyes were sparkly.*
ADJ-GRADED

spark plug, spark plugs. A **spark plug** is a device in the engine of a motor vehicle, which produces electric sparks to make the petrol burn.
N-COUNT

sparky /spɑːʳki/ **sparkier, sparkiest. Sparky** people or events are lively and entertaining; an informal word. *She's a terrific, sparky girl... London Fashion Week will be a sparky affair.*
ADJ-GRADED
=lively

sparring partner, sparring partners

1 A boxer's **sparring partner** is another boxer who he or she fights regularly in training.
N-COUNT

2 Your **sparring partner** is a person with whom you regularly have good-humoured arguments.
N-COUNT

sparrow /spærou/ **sparrows.** A **sparrow** is a small brown bird that is very common in Britain.
◆◇◇◇◇
N-COUNT

sparse /spɑːʳs/ **sparser, sparsest.** Something that is **sparse** is small in number or amount and spread out over an area. *Many slopes are rock fields with sparse vegetation... He was a tubby little man in his fifties, with sparse hair... Traffic was sparse on the highway.* ♦ **sparsely** *...the*
◆◇◇◇◇
ADJ-GRADED
ADV-GRADED:

sparsely populated interior region, where there are few roads. usu ADV -ed

spartan /spɑːʳtᵊn/. A **spartan** lifestyle or existence is very simple or strict, with no luxuries. *Their spartan lifestyle prohibits a fridge or a phone... Felicity's bedroom was spartan but functional.* ◆◇◇◇◇ ADJ-GRADED =simple, austere ≠luxurious

spasm /spæzəm/ **spasms** ◆◇◇◇◇
1 A **spasm** is a sudden tightening of your muscles, which you cannot control. *A muscular spasm in the coronary artery can cause a heart attack... A lack of magnesium causes muscles to go into spasm.* N-VAR: oft *into* N =convulsion
2 A **spasm** is a sudden strong pain or unpleasant emotion which lasts for a short period of time; used in written English. *A spasm of pain brought his thoughts back to the present... Kemp felt a spasm of fear.* N-COUNT: usu N *of* n =fit

spasmodic /spæzmɒdɪk/. Something that is **spasmodic** happens suddenly, for short periods of time, and at irregular intervals. *He managed to stifle the spasmodic sobs of panic rising in his throat... My husband's work was so spasmodic.* ADJ-GRADED =intermittent
♦ **spasmodically** /spæzmɒdɪkli/ *The tremor occurred in Bucharest, where buildings trembled spasmodically for forty-five seconds or so.* ADV-GRADED

spastic /spæstɪk/ **spastics.** Someone who is **spastic** is born with a disability which makes it difficult for them to control their muscles, especially in their arms and legs. Most people now refer to someone with this disability as having **cerebral palsy.** ► A **spastic** is someone who is spastic. ADJ; N-COUNT

spat /spæt/ **spats**
1 **Spat** is the past tense and past participle of **spit**.
2 A **spat** between people, countries, or organizations is a disagreement between them. *...a spat between America and Germany over interest rates and currencies.* N-COUNT =quarrel
3 **Spats** are specially shaped pieces of cloth or leather which button down one side and which were worn in former times by men over their ankles and part of their shoes. N-PLURAL

spate /speɪt/ **spates** ◆◇◇◇◇
1 A **spate** of things, especially unpleasant things, is a large number of them that happen or appear within a short period of time. *...the recent spate of attacks on horses. ...the current spate of scandals.* N-COUNT: usu sing, usu N *of* n =series
2 When a river is **in spate** it contains a lot more water than usual and is flowing very fast; used mainly in British English. *The Thames was in spate, with flocks of Canada geese speeding downriver.* PHRASE: v-link PHR

spatial /speɪʃᵊl/ ◆◇◇◇◇
1 **Spatial** is used to describe things relating to size, area, position, or distribution. *...the spatial distribution of black employment and population in South Africa. ...spatial constraints. ...the claustrophobic spatial dividers found in business offices.* ADJ: ADJ n =physical
♦ **spatially** *The growth of home ownership has been both socially and spatially uneven. ...jobs that are more spatially dispersed throughout the country.* ADV
2 Your **spatial** ability is your ability to see and understand the relationships between shapes, spaces, and areas. *His manual dexterity and fine spatial skills were wasted on routine tasks. ...spatial awareness.* ADJ: ADJ n

spatter /spætəʳ/ **spatters, spattering, spattered.** If a liquid **spatters** a surface or you **spatter** a liquid over a surface, drops of the liquid fall on an area of the surface. *He stared at the rain spattering on the glass... Gently turn the fish, being careful not to spatter any hot butter on yourself... Blood spattered the dark concrete... I always spatter my blouse with gravy when I eat... Her dress was spattered with mud.* V-ERG =splatter; V prep; V n prep; V n; V n *with* n; V-ed

-spattered /-spætəʳd/. **-spattered** is added to nouns to form adjectives which indicate that a liquid has spattered onto something. *...the blood-spattered body.* COMB in ADJ =-splattered

spatula /spætʃʊlə/ **spatulas.** A **spatula** is an object like a knife with a wide, flat blade. Spatulas are used in cooking. *Spoon the batter into the prepared pan, smoothing over the top with a spatula.* N-COUNT

spawn /spɔːn/ **spawns, spawning, spawned** ◆◇◇◇◇
1 **Spawn** is a soft, jelly-like substance containing the eggs of fish, or of frogs or other amphibians. *...her passion for collecting frog spawn.* N-UNCOUNT: usu n N
2 When fish, or frogs or other amphibians **spawn**, they lay their eggs. *...fish species like salmon and trout which go upstream, spawn and then die... The toads have settled in and accepted the pond as a good spawning ground.* VERB; V; V-ing
3 If something **spawns** something else, it causes it to happen or to be created; a literary use. *Tyndall's inspired work spawned a whole new branch of science... He wrote 54 crime novels, which spawned both movies and television shows.* VERB; V n

spay /speɪ/ **spays, spaying, spayed.** When a female animal **is spayed**, it has its ovaries removed so that it cannot become pregnant. *All bitches should be spayed unless being used for breeding.* VB: usu passive =neuter, sterilize; be V-ed

speak /spiːk/ **speaks, speaking, spoke, spoken** ◆◆◆◆◆
1 When you **speak**, you use your voice in order to say something. *He tried to speak, but for once, his voice had left him... He speaks with a lisp... I rang the hotel and spoke to Louie... She says she must speak with you at once... She cried when she spoke of Oliver. ...as I spoke these idiotic words.* ♦ **spoken** *...a marked decline in the standards of written and spoken English in Britain.* VERB; V; V *to/with* n; V *of/about* n; V n; ADJ: ADJ n
2 When someone **speaks** to a group of people, they make a speech. *Speaking to the House of Commons, Mr Jones accused some councils of using the new tax as an excuse for large increases in spending... He's determined to speak at the Democratic Convention... The President spoke of the need for territorial compromise.* VERB; V *to* n; V; V *of* n
3 If you **speak for** a group of people, you make their views and demands known, or represent them. *He said it was the job of the Church to speak for the underprivileged... I speak for all 7,000 members of our organization... Obviously I can't speak for other people, but certainly no one I know would entertain the idea.* VERB; V *for* n
4 If you **speak** a foreign language, you know the language and are able to have a conversation in it. *He doesn't speak English... Many of them can speak two or three or more languages.* VERB; V n
5 People sometimes mention something that has been written by saying what the author **speaks of.** *Throughout the book Liu speaks of the abuse of Party power... St Paul speaks of the body as the 'temple of the Holy Spirit'.* VERB; V *of* n; V *of* n *as* n
6 If two people **are** not **speaking**, they no longer talk to each other because they have quarrelled. *He is not speaking to his mother because of her friendship with his ex-wife... The co-stars are still not speaking.* V-RECIP: with neg; V *to* n; pl-n V
7 If you say that something **speaks** to you of a quality, experience, or feeling, you mean that it is evidence of it or conveys it. *His behaviour spoke of an early maturity... The length of the car and the high polish of its fittings both spoke of money... Their music speaks to us with an innate grandeur we can all understand.* VB: no cont; V *of* n; V *to* n
8 If you say that something **speaks for** itself, you mean that its meaning or quality is so obvious that it does not need explaining or pointing out. *The figures speak for themselves: six million people will have died of AIDS in Africa by the end of the century... The results speak for themselves.* VB: no cont; V *for* pron-refl
9 See also **speaking**.
10 If you say **'Speak for yourself'** when someone has said something, you mean that what they have said is only their opinion or applies only to them; an informal expression. *'We're not blaming you,' Kate said. 'Speak for yourself,' Boris muttered.* PHRASES; CONVENTION; PRAGMATICS
11 If something or someone **is spoken for** or **has been spoken for**, someone has claimed them or asked for them, so no-one else can have them. *She'd probably drop some comment about her 'fiancé' into the conversation so that he'd think she* V inflects

was already spoken for... By December last year most of the resources had been spoken for.

12 If you say that **actions speak louder than words**, you are saying that people's actions show their real attitudes, rather than what they say. This expression is sometimes used to advise someone to do something rather than just saying or writing something. PRAGMATICS

13 Nothing **to speak of** means 'hardly anything' or 'only unimportant things'. *They have no weaponry to speak of... 'Any fresh developments?'—'Nothing to speak of.'* n PHR, with brd-neg

14 You can use **not to speak of** when adding something which your previous statement also applies to, or applies to even more than other things. *This move caused consternation among universities and the government, not to speak of the students affected.* cl PHR n PRAGMATICS =not to mention

15 If you **speak well of** someone or **speak highly of** someone, you say good things about them. If you **speak ill of** someone, you criticize them. *Both spoke highly of the Russian president... It seemed she found it difficult to speak ill of anyone.* V inflects, PHR n

16 You use **so to speak** to draw attention to the fact that you are describing or referring to something in a metaphorical, colourful, or unusual way. *I ought not to tell you but I will, since you're in the family, so to speak... The five countries have now all passed, so to speak, their entry test.* PHR with cl PRAGMATICS =as it were

17 If you are **on speaking terms** with someone, you are quite friendly with them and often talk to them. *For a long time her mother and her grandmother had hardly been on speaking terms.* usu v-link PHR, oft PHR *with* n

18 • to **speak** your **mind**: see **mind**. • to **speak volumes**: see **volume**.

speak out. If you **speak out** against something or in favour of something, you say publicly that you think it is bad or good. *As tempers rose, he spoke out strongly against some of the radical ideas for selling off state-owned property... Viktor Shklovsky spoke out in defence of the book... Even then, she continued to speak out at rallies around the country.* PHRASAL VERB V P prep V P

speak up PHRASAL VERB

1 If you **speak up**, you say something, especially to defend someone or protest about something, rather than just saying nothing. *Uncle Herbert never argued, never spoke up for himself... Don't be afraid of speaking up... I am not suggesting that individuals never speak up about wrong-doing.* V P *for* n V P V P prep

2 If you ask someone to **speak up**, you are asking them to speak more loudly. *I'm quite deaf – you'll have to speak up.* no cont V P

-speak /-spiːk/. **-speak** is used to form nouns which refer to the kind of language used by a particular person or by people involved in a particular activity. You use **-speak** when you disapprove of this kind of language because it is difficult for other people to understand. *Solicitor-speak is believed to be a reason why two out of three people die without making a will... Unfortunately, the simplicity of this message is almost lost within his constant management-speak.* COMB in N-UNCOUNT PRAGMATICS

speakeasy /spiːkiːzi/ **speakeasies.** A **speakeasy** was a place where people could buy alcoholic drinks illegally in the U.S. between 1920 and 1933, when alcohol was banned. N-COUNT

speaker /spiːkəʳ/ **speakers** ◆◆◆◇◇

1 A **speaker** at a meeting, conference, or other gathering is a person who is making a speech or giving a talk. *Among the speakers at the gathering was Treasury Secretary Nicholas Brady... Bruce Wyatt will be the guest speaker at next month's meeting... He was not a good speaker.* N-COUNT

2 A **speaker** of a particular language is a person who speaks it, especially one who speaks it as their first language. *...in the Ukraine, where a fifth of the population are Russian speakers... The Department has a growing section which teaches English to speakers of other languages.* • See also **native speaker**. N-COUNT: n N, N *of* n

3 In the parliament of many countries, the **Speaker** is the person who is in charge of the meetings of the parliament. *For twenty minutes, the Speaker tried to keep order. ...the Speaker of the Polish Parliament... Mr. Speaker, our message to the president is simple.* N-PROPER; N-VOC: *Mr/Madam* N

4 A **speaker** is a person who is speaking. *From a simple gesture or the speaker's tone of voice, the Japanese listener gleans the whole meaning.* N-COUNT: usu *the* N

5 A **speaker** is a piece of equipment, for example part of a radio or hi-fi system, through which sound comes out. *For a good stereo effect, the speakers should not be too wide apart.* N-COUNT

speaking /spiːkɪŋ/ ◆◆◇◇◇

1 **Speaking** is the activity of giving speeches and talks. *It would also train women union members in public speaking and decision-making... His work schedule still includes speaking engagements and other public appearances.* N-UNCOUNT: oft supp N

2 You can say '**speaking as** a parent' or '**speaking as** a teacher', for example, to indicate that the opinion you are giving is based on your experience as a parent or as a teacher. *Well, speaking as a journalist I'm dismayed by the amount of pressure there is for pictures of combat.* PHRASES PREP PRAGMATICS

3 You can say **speaking of** something that has just been mentioned as a way of introducing a new topic which has some connection with that thing. *There's plenty of time to drop hints for Christmas presents! And speaking of presents, we have 100 exclusive fragrance collections to give away.* PREP PRAGMATICS =talking of

4 You use **speaking** in expressions such as **generally speaking** and **technically speaking** to indicate the range or relevance of the statement you are making. *Generally speaking there was no resistance to the idea... Politically speaking, do you think that these moves have been effective?* PHR with cl PRAGMATICS

-speaking /-spiːkɪŋ/. **-speaking** combines with nouns referring to languages to form adjectives which indicate what language someone speaks, or what language is spoken in a particular region. *Lessons with English-speaking instructors can be booked and paid for in the resort. ...in the mainly French-speaking province of Quebec.* COMB in ADJ: ADJ n

spear /spɪəʳ/ **spears, spearing, speared** ◆◇◇◇◇

1 A **spear** is a weapon consisting of a long pole with a sharp metal point attached to the end. N-COUNT

2 If you **spear** something, you push or throw a pointed object into it. *Spear a piece of fish with a carving fork and dip it in the batter... A police officer was speared to death.* VERB V n *be* V-ed *to* n

3 Asparagus or broccoli **spears** are individual stalks of asparagus or broccoli. N-COUNT: with supp

spearhead /spɪəʳhed/ **spearheads, spearheading, spearheaded** ◆◇◇◇◇

1 If someone **spearheads** a campaign or an attack, they lead it; used in journalism. *...Esther Rantzen, who is spearheading a national campaign against bullying... Helicopters can to some extent take the place of tanks by spearheading the airborne attack.* VERB V n

2 The **spearhead** of a campaign is the person or group that leads it; used in journalism. *The marines went ashore as a spearhead this morning to capture key targets.* N-COUNT: usu sing, usu with supp

spearmint /spɪəʳmɪnt/. **Spearmint** is a plant whose leaves have a strong smell and taste. It is often used for flavouring foods, especially sweets. N-UNCOUNT

spec /spek/ **specs** ◆◇◇◇◇

1 Someone's **specs** are their glasses; an informal use. *...a young businessman in his specs and suit.* N-PLURAL: also *a pair of* N

2 The **spec** for something, especially a machine or vehicle, is its design and the features included in it; an informal use. *The standard spec includes stainless steel holding tanks.* N-COUNT =specification

3 If you do something **on spec**, you do it hoping to get something that you want as a result, but without any certainty that you will get it; an informal expression. *When searching for a job Adrian favours networking and writing letters on spec.* PHRASE: PHR after v

special /speʃəl/ **specials** ◆◆◆◆◆

1 Someone or something that is **special** is better or more important than other people or things. *You're very special to me, darling... There are strong arguments for holidays at Easter and Christmas be-* ADJ-GRADED ≠ordinary

cause these are special occasions... Just to see him was something special... My special guest will be comedian Ben Elton.

2 Special means different from normal. *In special cases, a husband can deduct the travel expenses of his wife who accompanies him on a business trip... So you didn't notice anything special about him?... There is nothing worse than trying to relax and eat a special meal only to find clouds of cigarette smoke drifting over you. ...'Little Scarlet' strawberry jam, made from a special variety of strawberry.* ADJ: ADJ n ≠normal

3 You use **special** to describe someone who is officially appointed or who has a particular position specially created for them. *Due to his wife's illness, he returned to the State Department as special adviser to the President... Frank Deford is a special correspondent for Newsweek magazine.* ADJ: ADJ n

4 Special schools or institutions are for people who have particular problems such as physical or mental handicaps. *The 5-year-old has no speech and limited movement, and attends special school... Police are still searching for a convicted rapist, who escaped from Broadmoor special hospital yesterday.* ADJ: ADJ n

5 You use **special** to describe something that relates to one particular person, group, or place. *Every anxious person will have his or her own special problems or fears... Remember, Yugoslavia had a special brand of communism.* ADJ: ADJ n =unique

6 A **special** is a product, programme, or meal which is not normally available, or which is made for a particular purpose. *...complaints about the BBC's Hallowe'en special, 'Ghostwatch'... Grocery stores have to offer enough specials to bring people into the store. ...talk shows and news specials.* N-COUNT

Special Branch. **The Special Branch** is the department of the British police that is concerned with political security and deals with problems such as terrorism, visits by foreign leaders, and political refugees. ◆◇◇◇◇ N-PROPER: *the* N

special effect, **special effects.** In film, **special effects** are unusual pictures or sounds that are created by using special techniques. *...a Hollywood horror film with special effects that are not for the nervous.* ◆◇◇◇◇ N-COUNT: usu pl

specialise /speʃəlaɪz/. See **specialize.**

specialism /speʃəlɪzəm/ **specialisms**

1 Someone's **specialism** is a particular subject or skill which they study and know a lot about. *...a teacher with a specialism in mathematics.* N-COUNT =speciality

2 Specialism is the act of specializing in a particular subject. *The needs of children may not be best met by an over-emphasis on subject specialism.* N-UNCOUNT =specialization

specialist /speʃəlɪst/ **specialists.** A **specialist** is a person who has a particular skill or knows a lot about a particular subject. *If you are housebound, you can arrange for a home visit from a specialist adviser... Peckham, himself a cancer specialist, is well aware of the wide variations in medical practice. ...a specialist in diseases of the nervous system.* ◆◆◆◇◇ N-COUNT: usu N n, n N, N *in/on* n =expert

speciality /speʃiælɪti/ **specialities**

1 Someone's **speciality** is a particular type of work that they do most or do best, or a subject that they know a lot about. *My father was a historian of repute. His speciality was the history of Germany... Handpainted tiled murals for kitchens and bathrooms are Julie Eurich's speciality.* ◆◇◇◇◇ N-COUNT =field

2 A **speciality** of a particular place is a special food or product that is always very good there. *Rhineland dishes are a speciality of the restaurant... I started with the Viennese speciality frittatensuppe, or pancake soup.* N-COUNT: with supp

specialize /speʃəlaɪz/ **specializes, specializing, specialized;** also spelled **specialise** in British English. If you **specialize in** a thing, you know a lot about it and concentrate a great deal of your time and energy on it, especially in your work or when you are studying or training. *...a University professor who specializes in the history of the Russian empire. ...a Portuguese restaurant which specializes in seafood.* ◆◆◆◇◇ VERB V *in* n ♦ **specialization** /speʃəlaɪzeɪʃən/ **specializations** *This degree offers a major specialisation in Social Policy alongside a course in Sociology. ...an economist who has avoided narrow specialization.* N-VAR

specialized /speʃəlaɪzd/; also spelled **specialised.** Someone or something that is **specialized** is trained or developed for a particular purpose or area of knowledge. *Cocaine addicts get specialized support from knowledgeable staff. ...a specialized knowledge of American History.* ◆◆◇◇◇ ADJ-GRADED

specially /speʃəli/ ◆◆◇◇◇

1 If something has been done **specially** for a particular person or purpose, it has been done only for that person or purpose. *...a soap specially designed for those with sensitive skins... Patrick needs to use specially adapted computer equipment... The school is specially for children whose schooling has been disrupted by illness.* ADV: ADV with v, oft ADV *for* n

2 Specially is used to mean more than usually or more than other things; an informal use. *Stay in bed extra late or get up specially early... What was specially enjoyable about that job? ...something which you specially want... It can become extremely hot and dry, specially in a small glasshouse... Dryness at the roots can occur very easily specially when plants are grown in containers.* ADV: ADV with v, ADV with cl/group =particularly

special needs ◆◇◇◇◇

1 People with **special needs** are people who have particular problems, for example they are physically or mentally handicapped. *...a school for children with special needs. ...a teacher who's worked with special needs students for nearly two decades.* N-PLURAL: oft N n

2 You use **special needs** to refer to schemes, methods, and organizations which are intended for people with special needs. *The local authority has said the area could be redeveloped for special needs housing.* ADJ: ADJ n

special offer, **special offers.** A **special offer** is a product, service, or programme that is offered at reduced prices or rates. *The SHE directory is packed with money-saving special offers on the latest products.* ◆◇◇◇◇ N-COUNT

special pleading. If you say that someone is using **special pleading**, you mean that they are trying to persuade you to do something by only telling you the facts that support their case. *The Secretary of State has already given in to special pleading by interested parties.* N-UNCOUNT

special school, **special schools.** A **special school** is a school for children who have some kind of physical or mental handicap. N-COUNT

specialty /speʃəlti/ **specialties.** In American English, a **specialty** is the same as a **speciality.** *His specialty is international law... Both doctors and nurses have increasingly made a specialty of the care of the aged.* ◆◇◇◇◇ N-COUNT

species /spiːʃiz/; **species** is both the singular and the plural form. A **species** is a class of plants or animals whose members have the same main characteristics and are able to breed with each other. *Pandas are an endangered species... There are several thousand species of trees here.* ◆◆◆◇◇ N-COUNT

specific /spɪsɪfɪk/ ◆◆◆◆◇

1 You use **specific** to refer to a particular fixed area, problem, or subject. *Massage may help to increase blood flow to specific areas of the body... There are several specific problems to be dealt with... Specific groups may be formed to address specific issues. ...the specific needs of the individual.* ADJ-GRADED: ADJ n =particular

2 If someone is **specific**, they give a description that is precise and exact. You can also use **specific** to describe their description. *I asked him to be more specific... These nerve centres generate rhythmic movements; or to be more specific, rhythmic stomach movements... This report offered the most specific and accurate description of the problems.* ADJ-GRADED =exact, precise ≠vague, unspecific

♦ **specificity** /spesɪfɪsɪti/ *...the kind of extreme specificity normally associated only with computer programmes.* N-UNCOUNT

3 Something that is **specific** to a particular thing is connected with that thing only. *Send your resume with a cover letter that is specific to that particular* ADJ: usu v-link ADJ *to* n =peculiar *job.* ▶ Also after nouns. *Most studies of trade have been country-specific. ...a job-specific course.* COMB in ADJ-GRADED

specifically /spɪsɪfɪkli/ ◆◆◆◇◇

1 You use **specifically** to emphasize that something is given special attention and considered separately from other things of the same kind. *...the first nursing home designed specifically for people with AIDS... We haven't specifically targeted school children. ...the only book specifically about that event.* ADV: ADV with v PRAGMATICS =especially

2 You use **specifically** to add something more precise or exact to what you have already said. *Death frightens me, specifically my own death. ...the Christian, and specifically Protestant, religion. ...brain cells, or more specifically, neurons.* ADV: ADV with group PRAGMATICS

3 You use **specifically** to indicate that something has a restricted nature, as opposed to being more general in nature. *...a specifically female audience... Russia and Japan did not have specifically economic motives for their penetration of China.* ADV: ADV adj

4 If you state or describe something **specifically**, you state or describe it precisely and clearly. *I asked her to repeat specifically the words that Patti had used... I specifically asked for this steak rare.* ADV: ADV with v =distinctly, clearly

specification /spesɪfɪkeɪʃən/ **specifications.** ◆◇◇◇◇ N-COUNT A **specification** is a requirement which is clearly stated, for example about the necessary features in the design of something. *I'd like to buy some land and have a house built to my specification... Legislation will require UK petrol companies to meet an EEC specification for petrol. ...officials constrained by rigid job specifications.*

specifics /spɪsɪfɪks/. The **specifics** of a subject are the details of it that need to be considered. *Things improved when we got down to the specifics... Union officials won't discuss specifics of the negotiations.* ◆◇◇◇◇ N-PLURAL =particulars

specify /spesɪfaɪ/ **specifies, specifying, specified** ◆◆◇◇◇

1 If you **specify** something, you give information about what is required or should happen in a certain situation. *They specified a spacious entrance hall... He has not specified what action he would like them to take.* VERB V n V wh

2 If you **specify** that something should be done, you tell someone precisely what you want doing or how something should be done. *Each recipe specifies the size of egg to be used... One rule specifies that learner drivers must be supervised by adults... Patients eat together at a specified time.* VERB V n V that V-ed

specimen /spesɪmɪn/ **specimens** ◆◆◇◇◇

1 A **specimen** is a single plant or animal which is an example of a particular species or type and is examined by scientists. *200,000 specimens of fungus are kept at the Komarov Botanical Institute. ...North American fossil specimens... Collectors will pay $50,000 to $1 million for a rare specimen.* N-COUNT: usu with supp

2 A **specimen** of something is an example of it which gives an idea of what the whole of it is like. *Job applicants have to submit a specimen of handwriting. ...a specimen bank note.* N-COUNT: usu with supp

3 A **specimen** is a small quantity of someone's urine, blood, or other body fluid which is examined in a medical laboratory, in order to find out if they are ill or if they have been drinking alcohol or taking drugs. *He refused to provide a specimen... If your urine specimen shows the presence of bacteria, you'll be prescribed antibiotics.* N-COUNT =sample

4 You can use **specimen** to refer to someone who has a quality of a particular kind; used in written English. *What a poor specimen that child is!... He is a fine specimen of his class.* N-COUNT: with supp

specious /spiːʃəs/. Something that is **specious** seems to exist or be true, but is in fact false or an illusion. *It is unlikely that the Duke was convinced by such specious arguments.* ADJ-GRADED =false

speck /spek/ **specks** ◆◇◇◇◇

1 A **speck** is a very small stain, mark, or shape. *He has even cut himself shaving. There is a speck of blood by his ear.* N-COUNT: oft N of n

2 A **speck** is a very small piece of a powdery substance. *Billy leaned forward and brushed a speck of dust off his shoes.* N-COUNT: oft N of n

speckled /spekəld/. A **speckled** surface is covered with small marks, spots, or shapes. *...a large brown speckled egg... The sky was speckled with stars.* ADJ: usu ADJ n

specs /speks/. See **spec**.

spectacle /spektəkəl/ **spectacles** ◆◆◇◇◇

1 Glasses are sometimes referred to as **spectacles**; a formal use. *He looked at me over the tops of his spectacles. ...thick spectacle frames.* N-PLURAL: also a pair of N

2 A **spectacle** is a strange or interesting sight. *It was a spectacle not to be missed. ...the bizarre spectacle of three people desperately demanding an encore.* N-COUNT =sight

3 A **spectacle** is a grand and impressive event or performance. *94,000 people turned up for the spectacle. ...a director passionate about music and spectacle.* N-VAR =extravaganza

4 ● **rose-coloured spectacles**: see **rose-coloured**.

spectacular /spektækjʊləʳ/ **spectaculars** ◆◆◆◇◇

1 Something that is **spectacular** is very impressive or dramatic. *...spectacular views of the Sugar Loaf Mountain... They have revamped the business with spectacular success... The results have been spectacular.* ♦ **spectacularly** *My turnover increased spectacularly... Many of her movies had been spectacularly successful.* ADJ-GRADED ≠unspectacular; ADV-GRADED: ADV with v, ADV adj/adv

2 A **spectacular** is a show or performance which is very grand and impressive. *...a television spectacular. ...one of the world's great sporting spectaculars.* N-COUNT: usu n N =extravaganza

spectator /spekteɪtəʳ, AM spekteɪtər/ **spectators.** A **spectator** is someone who watches something, especially a sporting event. *Thirty thousand spectators watched the final game.* ◆◆◇◇◇ N-COUNT

spectator sport, spectator sports. A **spectator sport** is a sport that is interesting and entertaining to watch. *The most popular spectator sport is football.* N-COUNT

spectra /spektrə/. **Spectra** is a plural form of **spectrum**.

spectral /spektrəl/. If you describe someone or something as **spectral** you mean that they look like a ghost; a literary word. *She is compelling, spectral, fascinating, an unforgettably unique performer. ...the spectral quality of the light.* ADJ =ghostly

spectre /spektəʳ/ **spectres;** spelled **specter** in American English. ◆◇◇◇◇

1 If you refer to the **spectre** of something unpleasant, you are referring to something that you are frightened might occur. *Failure to arrive at a consensus over the issue raised the spectre of legal action... Like many others, Handford was relieved to see the spectre of 15% interest rates evaporate by the end of the day.* N-COUNT: usu *the* N *of* n

2 A **spectre** is a ghost; a literary use. N-COUNT

spectrum /spektrəm/ **spectra** or **spectrums** ◆◆◇◇◇

1 **The spectrum** is the range of different colours which is produced when light passes through a prism or through a drop of water. A rainbow shows the colours in the spectrum. N-SING: *the* N

2 A **spectrum** is a range of a particular type of thing. *She'd seen his moods range across the emotional spectrum... Politicians across the political spectrum have denounced the act... The term 'special needs' covers a wide spectrum of problems.* N-COUNT: usu sing, with supp

3 A **spectrum** is a range of light waves or radio waves within particular frequencies. *Vast amounts of energy, from X-rays right through the spectrum down to radio waves, are escaping into space... The individual colours within the light spectrum are believed to have an effect on health. ...the ultraviolet spectra of hot stars.* N-COUNT

speculate /spekjʊleɪt/ **speculates, speculating, speculated** ◆◆◆◇◇

1 If you **speculate** about something, you make guesses about its nature or identity, or about what might happen. *Mr Perez de Cuellar refused to speculate about the contents of the letter... It would be unfair to Debby's family to speculate on the reasons for her suicide... The doctors speculate that he died of a cerebral haemorrhage caused by a blow on the head... The reader can speculate what will hap-* VERB V prep V that V wh Also V, V with quote

pen next. ♦ **speculation** /spe̲kjʊleɪʃən/ **speculations** *The President has gone out of his way to dismiss speculation over the future of the economy minister... I had published my speculations about the future of the universe in the Review of Modern Physics.* N-VAR

2 If someone **speculates** financially, they buy property, stocks, or shares, in the hope of being able to sell them again at a higher price and make a profit. *Big farmers are moving in, not in order to farm, but in order to speculate with rising land prices... The banks made too many risky loans which now can't be repaid, and they speculated in property whose value has now dropped.* VERB V prep/adv Also V

speculative /spe̲kjʊlətɪv, AM -leɪt-/ ◆◇◇◇◇

1 A piece of information that is **speculative** is based on speculation rather than knowledge. *The papers ran speculative stories about the mysterious disappearance of Eddie Donagan... He has written a speculative biography of Christopher Marlowe.* ADJ-GRADED

2 Someone who has a **speculative** expression seems to be trying to guess something about someone or something. *His mother regarded him with a speculative eye.* ♦ **speculatively** *I caught her eyes on me speculatively. I imagined she was wondering about my relationship with Max.* ADJ-GRADED ADV-GRADED: ADV with v

3 **Speculative** is used to describe activities which involve buying goods or shares, or buildings and properties in the hope of being able to sell them again at a higher price and make a profit. *Thousands of pensioners were persuaded to mortgage their homes to invest in speculative bonds... The King's Reach hotel was built as a speculative venture but never completed.* ADJ

speculator /spe̲kjʊleɪtər/ **speculators.** A **speculator** is a person who speculates financially. ◆◇◇◇◇ N-COUNT

sped /spe̲d/. **Sped** is a past tense and past participle of **speed**.

speech /spi̲ːtʃ/ **speeches** ◆◆◆◆◇

1 **Speech** is the ability to speak or the act of speaking. *...the development of speech in children... Intoxication interferes with speech and coordination. ...a speech therapist specialising in stammering.* N-UNCOUNT

2 Your **speech** is the way in which you speak. *His speech became increasingly thick and nasal... I'd make fun of her dress and imitate her speech.* N-SING: usu poss N

3 **Speech** is spoken language. *He could imitate in speech or writing most of those he admired. ...the way common letter clusters are usually pronounced in speech.* N-UNCOUNT

4 A **speech** is a formal talk which someone gives to an audience. *She is due to make a speech on the economy next week... He delivered his speech in French. ...a dramatic resignation speech.* N-COUNT

5 A **speech** is a group of lines spoken by a character in a play. *...the hilarious speech from Alan Bennett's 'Forty Years On'.* N-COUNT

6 See also **direct speech**, **figure of speech**, **indirect speech**, **maiden speech**, **part of speech**, **reported speech**.

spe̲e̲ch day, speech days. In some British schools, **speech day** is a day, usually at the end of the school year, when prizes are presented to pupils and speeches are made by guest speakers and the head teacher. N-VAR

speechifying /spi̲ːtʃɪfaɪɪŋ/. **Speechifying** is the making of speeches, especially in a rather proud and self-important way; used showing disapproval. *...five tedious days of speechifying and punditing.* N-UNCOUNT PRAGMATICS

speechless /spi̲ːtʃləs/. If you are **speechless**, you are temporarily unable to speak, usually because something has shocked you. *Alex was almost speechless with rage and despair.* ADJ: usu v-link ADJ, oft ADJ *with* n =dumb

spe̲e̲ch the̲rapist, speech therapists. A **speech therapist** is a person whose job is to help people to overcome speech and language problems. N-COUNT

spe̲e̲ch the̲rapy. **Speech therapy** is the treatment of people who have speech and language problems. *The earlier a stammering child begins speech therapy, the better his or her chances of becoming fluent.* N-UNCOUNT

speechwriter /spi̲ːtʃraɪtər/ **speechwriters.** A **speechwriter** is a person who writes speeches for important people such as politicians. N-COUNT

speed /spi̲ːd/ **speeds, speeding, sped, speeded.** The form of the past tense and past participle is **sped** in meaning 5 but **speeded** for the phrasal verb. ◆◆◆◆◇

1 The **speed** of something is the rate at which it moves or travels. *He drove off at high speed... With this type of camera, the shutter speed is fixed... An electrical pulse in a wire travels close to the speed of light... Wind speeds reached force five.* N-VAR: with supp

2 The **speed** of something is the rate at which it happens or is done. *In the late 1850s the speed of technological change quickened... Each learner can proceed at his own speed.* N-COUNT: with supp =pace

3 **Speed** is very fast movement or travel. *Speed is the essential ingredient of all athletics... He put on a burst of speed... The car is quite noisy at speed.* N-UNCOUNT

4 **Speed** is a very fast rate at which something happens or is done. *I was amazed at his speed of working. ...the sheer speed of the unification process.* N-UNCOUNT: usu N *of* n/-ing =pace

5 If you **speed** somewhere, you move or travel there quickly, usually in a vehicle. *Trains will speed through the Channel Tunnel at 186mph... The engine noise rises only slightly as I speed along.* VERB =race V prep/adv

6 Someone who **is speeding** is driving a vehicle faster than the legal speed limit. *This man was not qualified to drive and was speeding.* ♦ **speeding** *He was fined for speeding last year.* VB: usu cont V N-UNCOUNT

7 **Speed** is an illegal drug which some people take to increase their energy and excitement and give them unusual sensations in their minds; an informal use. N-UNCOUNT

8 See also **-speed**.

9 ● **pick up speed**: see **pick**.

speed up PHRASAL VERB

1 When something **speeds up** or when you **speed** it **up**, it moves or travels faster. *You notice that your breathing has speeded up a bit... He pushed a lever that speeded up the car.* ERG V P V P n (not pron) Also V n P

2 When a process or activity **speeds up** or when something **speeds it up**, it happens at a faster rate. *Job losses are speeding up... I had already taken steps to speed up a solution to the problem... I kept praying that the DJ would speed the music up.* ERG V P V P n (not pron) V n P

-speed /-spiːd/. **-speed** is used after numbers to form adjectives that indicate that a bicycle or car has a particular number of gears. *...a 10-speed bicycle.* COMB in ADJ

speedboat /spi̲ːdbout/ **speedboats.** A **speedboat** is a boat that can go very fast because it has a powerful engine. N-COUNT

spe̲e̲d limit, speed limits. The **speed limit** on a road is the maximum speed at which you are legally allowed to drive. ◆◇◇◇◇ N-COUNT: usu *the* N

speedometer /spiːdɒ̲mɪtər/ **speedometers.** A **speedometer** is the instrument in a vehicle which shows how fast the vehicle is moving. N-COUNT

speedway /spi̲ːdweɪ/. **Speedway** is the sport of racing lightweight motorcycles on special tracks. N-UNCOUNT

speedy /spi̲ːdi/ **speedier, speediest.** A **speedy** process, event, or action happens or is done very quickly. *We wish Bill a speedy recovery... This would be a very speedy trial... I'll sell at a discount in return for a speedy sale.* ♦ **speedily** *This review is being conducted as speedily as possible.* ◆◇◇◇◇ ADJ-GRADED: usu ADJ n =quick, rapid ≠slow ADV-GRADED: ADV with v

spell /spe̲l/ **spells, spelling, spelled, spelt.** The form **spelled** is both the past tense and past participle. British English also uses the form **spelt**. ◆◆◆◇◇

1 When you **spell** a word, you write or speak each letter in the word in the correct order. *He gave his name and then helpfully spelt it... How do you spell 'potato'?... 'Tang' is 'Gnat' spelt backwards.* ► **Spell out** means the same as **spell**. *If I don't know a word, I ask them to spell it out for me... I never have to spell out my first name.* VERB V n V-ed PHRASAL VERB V n P V P n (not pron)

2 Someone who can **spell** knows the correct order of letters in words. *It's shocking how students can't* VB: no cont V

spell these days... You accused me of inaccuracy yet you can't spell 'Middlesex'. V n

3 If something **spells** a particular result, often an unpleasant one, it suggests that this will be the result. *If the irrigation plan goes ahead, it could spell disaster for the birds... A report has just arrived on government desks which spells more trouble.* VB: no cont =signal V n

4 A **spell** of a particular type of weather or a particular activity is a short period of time during which this type of weather or activity occurs. *There has been a long spell of dry weather... You join a barrister for two six-month spells of practical experience. ...sunny spells.* N-COUNT: usu N *of* n =period

5 A **spell** is a situation in which events are controlled by a magical power. *They say she died after a witch cast a spell on her. ...the kiss that will break the spell.* N-COUNT

6 See also **spelling**.

7 If something or someone **casts their spell** on you or **casts a spell** on you, you are fascinated or charmed by them. *For many years sundials have cast their spell over scientists and mathematicians... People said he was able to cast a spell on the public.* PHRASES V inflects, usu PHR *on/over* n

8 If you are **under** someone**'s spell**, you are so fascinated by them that you cannot think about anything else. *Even sensible Frank had fallen under her spell.* N inflects, PHR after v, v-link PHR

spell out PHRASAL VERB

1 If you **spell** something **out**, you explain it in detail or in a very clear way. *Be assertive and spell out exactly how you feel... How many times do I have to spell it out?* V P n (not pron) V n P

2 See **spell** 1.

spellbinding /spelbaɪndɪŋ/. A **spellbinding** image or sound is one that is so fascinating that you can think about nothing else. *Gray describes in dramatic and spellbinding detail the lives of these five ladies.* ADJ-GRADED: usu ADJ n =gripping

spellbound /spelbaʊnd/. If you are **spellbound** by something or someone, you are so fascinated that you cannot think about anything else. *His audience had listened like children, spellbound by his words... He was in awe of her; she held him spellbound.* ADJ: usu v-link ADJ, oft ADJ *by* n

speller /speləʳ/ **spellers.** If you describe someone as a good or bad **speller**, you mean that they find it easy or difficult to spell words correctly. *I am an absolutely appalling speller.* N-COUNT: adj N

spelling /spelɪŋ/ **spellings** ◆◇◇◇◇

1 A **spelling** is the correct order of the letters in a word. *In most languages adjectives have slightly different spellings for masculine and feminine... If we got a spelling wrong we were forced to get a dictionary out.* N-COUNT

2 Spelling is the ability to spell words in the correct way. It is also an attempt to spell a word in the correct way. *His spelling is very bad. ...basic skills in reading, writing, grammar and spelling... Spelling mistakes are often just the result of haste.* N-UNCOUNT

3 See also **spell**.

spelt /spelt/. In British English, **spelt** is a past tense and past participle form of **spell**.

spend /spend/ **spends, spending, spent** ◆◆◆◆◆

1 When you **spend** money, you pay money for things that you want. *By the end of the holiday I had spent all my lire... Businessmen spend enormous amounts advertising their products... Juventus have spent £23m on new players... The survey may cost at least £80 but is money well spent.* VERB V n V n -ing V amount/n *on* n V-ed
♦ **spending** *Has your spending on food increased?... Government spending is expected to fall.* N-UNCOUNT =expenditure

2 If you **spend** time or energy doing something, you use your time or energy doing it. *Engineers spend much time and effort developing brilliant solutions... This energy could be much better spent taking some positive action.* VERB V n -ing

3 If you **spend** a period of time in a place, you stay there for a period of time. *We spent the night in a hotel.* VERB V n adv/prep

4 ● **spend a penny**: see **penny**.

spender /spendəʳ/ **spenders.** If a person or organization is a big **spender** or a compulsive **spender**, for example, they spend a lot of money or are unable to stop themselves spending money. *The Swiss are Europe's biggest spenders on food... Once the compulsive spender stops at the mall, she will be unable to control her spending.* ◆◇◇◇◇ N-COUNT: usu adj N

spending money. **Spending money** is money that you have or are given to spend on personal things for pleasure, especially when you are on holiday. *Jo will use her winnings as spending money on her holiday to the Costa Brava.* ◆◇◇◇◇ N-UNCOUNT

spendthrift /spendθrɪft/ **spendthrifts.** If you call someone a **spendthrift**, you mean that they spend money in a wasteful or extravagant way; used showing disapproval. ► Also an adjective. *...his father's spendthrift ways.* N-COUNT PRAGMATICS ADJ-GRADED: usu ADJ n

spent /spent/

1 Spent is the past tense and past participle of **spend**.

2 Spent substances or containers have been used and cannot be used again. *Radioactive waste is simply spent fuel... Several spent cartridges have already been found. ...spent uranium.* ADJ: usu ADJ n

spent force. If you refer to someone who used to be powerful as **a spent force**, you mean that they no longer have any power or influence. *He had begun to look a spent force, a politician led by events rather than controlling them.* N-SING: *a* N

sperm /spɜːʳm/ **sperms; sperm** can also be used as the plural form. ◆◆◇◇◇

1 A **sperm** is a cell which is produced in the sex organs of a male animal and can enter a female animal's egg and fertilize it. *Conception occurs when a single sperm fuses with an egg... We had given up any hope of having a baby. My husband had a very low sperm count.* N-COUNT

2 Sperm is used to refer to the liquid that contains sperm when it is produced. *...a sperm donor.* N-UNCOUNT

spermatozoon /spɜːʳmətəzoʊɒn/ **spermatozoa** /spɜːʳmətəzoʊə/. A **spermatozoon** is a sperm; a technical term in biology. N-COUNT

spermicidal /spɜːʳmɪsaɪdəl/. A **spermicidal** cream or jelly contains spermicide. ADJ: ADJ n

spermicide /spɜːʳmɪsaɪd/ **spermicides.** **Spermicide** is a substance that kills sperm. *Although most condoms contain spermicide, there are some manufactured without.* N-MASS

sperm whale, sperm whales. A **sperm whale** is a large whale that has a cavity in its head that contains a large amount of oil. N-COUNT

spew /spjuː/ **spews, spewing, spewed** ◆◇◇◇◇

1 When something **spews** out a substance or when a substance **spews** from something, the substance flows out quickly in large quantities. *The volcano spewed out more scorching volcanic ashes, gases and rocks... Leaking oil spewed from the tanker... An oil tanker spewed its cargo into the sea.* V-ERG V n with adv V prep V n prep

2 If someone **spews** or **spews** up, they vomit; a very informal use. *He's pissed. Let's get out of his way before he starts spewing.* VERB V

sphere /sfɪəʳ/ **spheres** ◆◆◇◇◇

1 A **sphere** is an object that is perfectly round in shape like a ball. N-COUNT

2 A **sphere** of activity or interest is a particular area of activity or interest. *...the sphere of international politics. ...nurses, working in all spheres of the health service.* N-COUNT: usu N *of* n =field

3 A **sphere** of people is a group of them who are similar in social status or who have the same interests. *...the realities of life outside the government and academic spheres of society.* N-COUNT: usu N *of* n =circle

4 A country's **sphere of influence** is an area of the world where it is the dominant power and where it can affect events and developments. *...Germany's efforts to create a sphere of influence in northern Yugoslavia. ...countries traditionally within the British or American spheres of influence.* PHRASE: *sphere* inflects

spherical /sferɪkəl, AM sfɪr-/. Something that is **spherical** is round like a ball; a formal word. *...purple and gold spherical earrings.* ADJ

sphincter /sfɪŋktəʳ/ **sphincters.** A **sphincter** is a ring of muscle that surrounds an opening to the body and that can tighten to close this opening; a technical term in biology. *...the anal sphincter.* N-COUNT

sphinx /sfɪŋks/ **sphinxes.** The **Sphinx** is a huge statue of a monster with a human head and a lion's body that stands near the pyramids in Egypt and which was built by the ancient Egyptians. The sphinxes in mythology were supposed to set riddles, and so a person who seems mysterious or puzzling is sometimes referred to as a **sphinx**. *It suited him to play the sphinx.* N-COUNT: usu *the* N in sing

spice /spaɪs/ **spices, spicing, spiced** ◆◆◇◇◇

1 A **spice** is a part of a plant, or a powder made from that part, which you put in food to give it flavour. Cinnamon, ginger, and paprika are spices. *...herbs and spices. ...a row of spice jars.* N-MASS

2 If you **spice** something that you say or do, you add excitement or interest to it. *They spiced their conversations and discussions with intrigue. ...a boring film spiced with the occasional funny moment.* ► **Spice up** means the same as **spice**. *Her publisher wants her to spice up her stories with sex. ...a discovery which spiced the conversation up quite a bit.* VERB V n *with* n V-ed; PHRASAL VERB V P n (not pron) V n P

3 **Spice** is something which makes life more exciting. *Variety is the spice of life!... To add spice to the debate, they disagreed about method and ideology.* N-UNCOUNT

spice up. See **spice** 2. PHRASAL VERB

spiced /spaɪst/. Food that is **spiced** has had spices or other strong-tasting foods added to it. *Every dish was served heavily spiced. ...delicately spiced sauces. ...pork spiced with black pepper.* ◆◇◇◇◇ ADJ-GRADED: usu adv ADJ, oft ADJ *with* n

spick and span /spɪk ənd spæn/; also spelled **spick-and-span**. A place that is **spick and span** is very clean and tidy. *The apartment was spick and span.* ADJ: usu v-link ADJ

spicy /spaɪsi/ **spicier, spiciest. Spicy** food is strongly flavoured with spices. *Thai food is hot and spicy. ...a spicy tomato and coriander sauce.* ◆◇◇◇◇ ADJ-GRADED

spider /spaɪdəʳ/ **spiders.** A **spider** is a small creature with eight legs. Most types of spider make webs in which they catch insects for food. ◆◆◇◇◇ N-COUNT

spidery /spaɪdəri/. If you describe something such as handwriting as **spidery**, you mean that it consists of thin, dark, pointed lines. *He saw her spidery writing on the envelope.* ADJ: usu ADJ n

spiel /ʃpiːl, AM spiːl/ **spiels.** Someone's **spiel** is a well-prepared speech that they make, and that they have usually made many times before, in order to persuade you to do something or to buy something; an informal word, used showing disapproval. N-COUNT PRAGMATICS =patter

spiffing /spɪfɪŋ/. In British English, if someone describes something such as news or an event as **spiffing**, they mean that it is very good; an old-fashioned, informal word. *I came to give your mother a piece of perfectly spiffing news. ...a jolly spiffing film.* ADJ-GRADED

spigot /spɪgət/ **spigots.**

1 In British English, a **spigot** is a type of valve that controls the flow of a liquid from one source to another. N-COUNT

2 In American English, a **spigot** is a faucet or tap. N-COUNT

spike /spaɪk/ **spikes, spiking, spiked** ◆◆◇◇◇

1 A **spike** is a long piece of metal with a sharp point. *...a 15-foot wall topped with iron spikes... Yellowing receipts had been impaled on a metal spike.* N-COUNT

2 Any long pointed object can be referred to as a **spike**. *Her hair stood out in spikes. ...a long spike of white flowers.* N-COUNT: usu with supp

3 **Spikes** are a pair of sports shoes with pointed pieces of metal attached to the soles. They help runners' feet to grip the ground when they are running. N-PLURAL: also *a pair of* n

4 If your drink **is spiked**, someone has added alcohol or drugs to it without telling you; an informal use. *They wondered whether their drinks had been spiked. ...drinks spiked with tranquillisers.* VB: usu passive =lace *be* V-ed V-ed

5 See also **spiked**.

spiked /spaɪkt/ ◆◇◇◇◇

1 Something that is **spiked** has one or more spikes on it. *...spiked railings. ...spiked golf shoes.* ADJ: usu ADJ n

2 If someone has **spiked** hair, their hair is short and sticks up all over their head. ADJ: usu ADJ n

3 See also **spike**.

spike heels. In American English, **spike heels** are womens' shoes with very high narrow heels. The British term is **stilettos**. N-PLURAL: also *a pair of* n

spiky /spaɪki/. Something that is **spiky** has one or more sharp points. *Her short spiky hair is damp with sweat. ...tall, spiky evergreen trees.* ◆◇◇◇◇ ADJ-GRADED

spill /spɪl/ **spills, spilling, spilled, spilt.** The form **spilled** is both the past tense and past participle. British English also uses the form **spilt**. ◆◆◇◇◇

1 If a liquid **spills** or if you **spill** it, it accidentally flows over the edge of a container. *70,000 tonnes of oil spilled from the tanker. ...water behind a dam, getting ready to spill over... He always spilled the drinks... Don't spill water on your suit.* V-ERG V adv/prep V n V n adv/prep Also V

2 A **spill** is an amount of liquid that has spilled from a container. *She wiped a spill of milkshake off the counter... An oil spill could be devastating for wildlife.* N-COUNT: usu with supp

3 If the contents of a bag, box, or other container **spill** or **are spilled**, they come out of the container onto a surface. *A number of bags had split and were spilling their contents... He carefully balanced the satchel so that its contents would not spill out onto the floor.* V-ERG V n V adv/prep

4 If people or things **spill** out of a place, they come out of it in large numbers. *Tears began to spill out of the boy's eyes... When the bell rings, more than 1,000 children spill from classrooms.* VERB V adv/prep

5 If light **spills** or **is spilled** into a place, it shines brightly into it, usually through a gap. *She noticed the light spilling under Brian's door... The door swung open again, spilling light into the cell.* V-ERG V adv/prep V n adv/prep

6 If you **spill** someone's **blood**, you kill them or wound them; used in written English. *He is prepared to spill the blood of a million people... If blood is spilled the countries will be at war.* PHRASE: V inflects

7 • to **spill the beans**: see **bean.** • **thrills and spills**: see **thrill**.

spill out. If you **spill out** information or if it **spills out**, you tell someone about it in a hurried way, because you cannot or do not want to keep it secret. *The words spilled out in a rush... He was tempted to spill out his problems to Philip.* PHRASAL VERB ERG V P V P n (not pron) Also V n P

spillage /spɪlɪdʒ/ **spillages.** If there is a **spillage**, a substance such as crude oil escapes from its container. **Spillage** is also used to refer to the substance that escapes. *...an oil spillage off the coast of Texas. ...an accident in the workplace involving blood spillage.* N-VAR

spillover /spɪloʊvəʳ/ **spillovers.** A **spillover** is a situation or feeling that starts in one place but then begins to happen or have an effect somewhere else. *The army is taking precautions against any possible spillover as neighbouring troops move north towards the border... Spillover damage from the building's demolition was confined to some broken glass.* N-COUNT: usu with supp

spilt /spɪlt/. In British English, **spilt** is a past tense and past participle form of **spill**.

spin /spɪn/ **spins, spinning, spun** 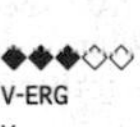

1 If something **spins** or if you **spin** it, it turns quickly around a central point. *The latest discs, used for small portable computers, spin 3600 times a minute... The Earth spins on its own axis... He spun the wheel sharply and made a U turn in the middle of the road... He spun his car round and went after them.* ► Also a noun. *This driving mode allows you to move off in third gear to reduce wheel-spin in icy conditions.* V-ERG V V n V n *round/around*; N-VAR

2 When you **spin** washing, it is turned round and round quickly in a spin drier or a washing machine to get the water out. *Just spin the washing and it's nearly dry.* ► Also a noun. *Set on a cool wash and finish with a short spin.* VERB V n; N-SING

3 If your head **is spinning**, you feel dizzy because you are excited, ill, or confused. *My head was spin-* VERB V *ning from the wine... All those figures make my poor head spin.*

4 If someone puts a certain **spin** on an event or situation, they interpret it and try to present it in a particular way; an informal use, used especially in American English. *He interpreted the vote as support for the constitution and that is the spin his supporters are putting on the results today. ...the wholly improper political spin given to the report, particularly by The New York Times.* • See also **spin doctor.** N-SING: with supp

5 If you go for **a spin** or take a car for **a spin**, you make a short journey in a car just to enjoy yourself. N-SING: a N

6 If someone **spins** a story or **spins** a tale, they give you an account of something that is untrue or only partly true. *He was surprised, and annoyed that she had spun a story which was too good to be condemned as a simple lie.* VERB V n Also V n n

7 When people **spin**, they make thread by twisting together pieces of a fibre such as wool or cotton using a device or machine. *Michelle will also spin a customer's wool fleece to specification at a cost of $2.25 an ounce.* ♦ **spinning** *They do their own cooking, spinning, and woodworking.* VERB V n Also V N-UNCOUNT

8 If a plane goes into **a spin**, it falls very rapidly towards the ground in a spiral movement. N-SING: a N

9 In a game such as tennis or cricket, if you put **spin** on a ball, you deliberately make it spin rapidly when you hit it or throw it. N-UNCOUNT

10 In informal British English, if you say that someone is **in a spin** or **in a flat spin**, you mean that they are confused and unable to act sensibly because of something that has happened. *Poor Jane was in rather a spin about the party.* PHRASE: v-link PHR =in a flap

spin out. If you **spin** something **out**, you make it last longer than it normally would. *My wife's solicitor was anxious to spin things out for as long as possible... The Government will try to spin out the conference into next autumn.* PHRASAL VERB =prolong, extend V n P V P n (not pron)

spina bifida /spaɪnə bɪfɪdə/. **Spina bifida** is a condition of the spine that some people are born with. It often causes paralysis. N-UNCOUNT

spinach /spɪnɪdʒ, -ɪtʃ/. **Spinach** is a vegetable with large dark green leaves that you chop up and boil in water before eating. ◆◇◇◇◇ N-UNCOUNT

spinal /spaɪnᵊl/. **Spinal** means relating to your spine. *...spinal fluid. ...spinal injuries.* ◆◇◇◇◇ ADJ: ADJ n

spinal column, spinal columns. Your **spinal column** is your spine; a formal or technical expression. N-COUNT =backbone

spinal cord, spinal cords. Your **spinal cord** is a thick cord of nerves inside your spine which connects your brain to nerves in all parts of your body. N-COUNT

spindle /spɪndᵊl/ **spindles** ◆◇◇◇◇

1 A **spindle** is a rod in a machine, around which another part of the machine turns. N-COUNT

2 A **spindle** is a pointed rod which you use when you are spinning wool by hand. You twist the wool with the spindle to make it into a thread. N-COUNT

spindly /spɪndli/ **spindlier, spindliest.** Something that is **spindly** is long and thin and looks very weak. *I did have rather spindly legs.* ADJ-GRADED

spin doctor, spin doctors. In politics, a **spin doctor** is someone who is skilled in public relations and who advises political parties on how to present their policies favourably; an informal expression. N-COUNT

spine /spaɪn/ **spines** ◆◆◇◇◇

1 Your **spine** is the row of bones down your back. N-COUNT

2 The **spine** of a book is the narrow stiff part which the pages and covers are attached to. N-COUNT

3 Spines are also long, sharp points on an animal's body or on a plant. N-COUNT

spine-chilling. A **spine-chilling** film or story makes you feel very frightened. ADJ-GRADED: usu ADJ n

spineless /spaɪnləs/. If you say that someone is **spineless**, you mean that they are weak and cowardly. *Clive's spineless son Marcus. ...bureaucrats and spineless politicians.* ADJ-GRADED

spinet /spɪnet, AM spɪnɪt/ **spinets.** A **spinet** is a small harpsichord. N-COUNT: oft *the* N

spine-tingling. A **spine-tingling** film or piece of music is enjoyable because it causes you to feel a strong emotion such as excitement or fear. *...Martin Scorsese's spine-tingling and stylish thriller. ...a spine-tingling rendition of 'Why Do Fools Fall In Love'.* ADJ-GRADED

spinnaker /spɪnəkəʳ/ **spinnakers.** A **spinnaker** is a large, light, triangular sail that is attached to the front mast on a racing yacht. N-COUNT

spinner /spɪnəʳ/ **spinners** ◆◇◇◇◇

1 A **spinner** is a cricketer who makes the ball spin when he or she bowls it so that it changes direction when it hits the ground or the bat. N-COUNT: usu supp N

2 A **spinner** is a person who makes thread by spinning. N-COUNT

spinney /spɪni/ **spinneys.** A **spinney** is a small area covered with trees; used mainly in British English. N-COUNT =copse

spinning wheel, spinning wheels; also spelled **spinning-wheel.** A **spinning wheel** is a wooden spinning machine used in people's homes, mainly in former times. It has a wheel which makes the spindle turn round. N-COUNT

spin-off, spin-offs ◆◇◇◇◇

1 A **spin-off** is an unexpected but useful or valuable result of an activity that was designed to achieve something else. *The company put out a report on commercial spin-offs from its research.* N-COUNT: usu with supp, oft N *from/of* n

2 A **spin-off** is a book, film, or television series that is derived from a similar book, film, or television series which has been very successful. N-COUNT

spinster /spɪnstəʳ/ **spinsters.** A **spinster** is a woman who has never been married, especially an old or middle-aged woman; an old-fashioned word. N-COUNT

spiny /spaɪni/. A **spiny** plant or animal is covered with long sharp points. *...a spiny lobster. ...a spiny cactus.* ADJ

spiral /spaɪərəl/ **spirals, spiralling, spiralled;** spelled **spiraling, spiraled** in American English. ◆◆◇◇◇

1 A **spiral** is a shape which winds round and round, with each curve above or outside the previous one. ► Also an adjective. *...a spiral staircase.* N-COUNT ADJ-GRADED: ADJ n

2 If something **spirals** or **is spiralled** somewhere, it grows or moves in a spiral curve. *Vines spiraled upward toward the roof. ...a bullet spiralling out of a gun barrel... A joss stick spiralled smoke.* ► Also a noun. *Larks were rising in spirals from the ridge.* V-ERG V adv/prep V n Also V N-COUNT

3 If an amount or level **spirals**, it rises quickly and at an increasing rate. *Production costs began to spiral. ...a spiralling trend of violence... The divorce rate is spiralling upwards.* ► Also a noun. *...an inflationary spiral.* VERB V V adv/prep N-SING: with supp

4 If an amount or level **spirals** downwards, it falls quickly and at an increasing rate. *House prices will continue to spiral downwards.* ► Also a noun. *...a spiral of debt.* VERB V adv/prep N-SING: usu N *of* n

spire /spaɪəʳ/ **spires.** The **spire** of a building such as a church is the tall cone-shaped structure on the top. ◆◇◇◇◇ N-COUNT =steeple

spirit /spɪrɪt/ **spirits, spiriting, spirited** ◆◆◆◆◇

1 Your **spirit** is the part of you that is not physical and that motivates you. It is connected with your character, behaviour, and feelings. *The human spirit is virtually indestructible... Marian retains a restless, youthful spirit, in search of new horizons.* • see also **kindred spirit.** N-SING =soul

2 A person's **spirit** is the non-physical part of them that is believed to remain alive after their death. *His spirit has left him and all that remains is the shell of his body.* N-COUNT: usu poss N =soul

3 A **spirit** is a ghost or supernatural being. *In the Middle Ages branches were hung outside country houses as a protection against evil spirits.* • See also **Holy Spirit.** N-COUNT =ghost

4 Spirit is the courage and determination that helps people to survive in difficult times and to keep their way of life and their beliefs. *She was a very brave girl and everyone who knew her admired her spirit.* N-UNCOUNT

5 Spirit is the liveliness and energy that someone shows in what they do. *They played with spirit.* N-UNCOUNT

6 The **spirit** in which you do something is the attitude you have when you are doing it. *Their problem can only be solved in a spirit of compromise... They approached the talks in a conciliatory spirit.* N-SING

7 A particular kind of **spirit** is the feeling of loyalty to a group that is shared by the people who belong to the group. *There is a great sense of team spirit among the British Olympic squad... The president has appealed to the Brazilian people for patriotism and community spirit.* N-UNCOUNT: usu with supp, oft n N

8 A particular kind of **spirit** is the set of ideas, beliefs, and aims that are held by a group of people. *...the real spirit of the Labour movement.* N-SING

9 **The spirit of** something such as a law or an agreement is the way that it was intended to be interpreted or applied. *The requirement for work permits violates the spirit of the 1950 treaty.* N-SING: *the* N *of*n

10 You can refer to a person as a particular kind of **spirit** if they show a certain characteristic or if they show a lot of enthusiasm in what they are doing. *I like to think of myself as a free spirit... He was the founder and guiding spirit of New York's Shakespeare Festival.* N-COUNT: usu adj N

11 Your **spirits** are your feelings at a particular time, especially feelings of happiness or unhappiness. *At supper, everyone was in high spirits... A bit of exercise will help lift his spirits.* N-PLURAL

12 If someone or something **is spirited** away, or if they **are spirited** out of somewhere, they are taken from a place quickly and secretly without anyone noticing. *He was spirited away and probably murdered... His parents had spirited him away to the country... It is possible that he has been spirited out of the country.* VERB *be* V-ed *away* V n *away* *be* V-ed prep/adv

13 **Spirits** are strong alcoholic drinks such as whisky and gin. N-MASS

14 **Spirit** or **spirits** is an alcoholic liquid that is used as a fuel, for cleaning things, or for other purposes. There are many kinds of spirit. • See also **surgical spirit, methylated spirits.** N-UNCOUNT

15 If you **enter into the spirit** of something, you take part in it in an enthusiastic way. PHRASES V inflects

16 If you say you are somewhere **in spirit** or with someone **in spirit**, you mean that although you are not with them, you feel as though you are with them because you are thinking about them a lot. *In spirit I was with you here.* PHR with cl

17 You use **in spirit** when you are talking about someone's true nature. *They seemed close in spirit to those first independent-minded Turkish women who took professions... It is independent in spirit.* adj PHR

18 **The spirit of the age** or **the spirit of the times** is the set of ideas, beliefs, and aims that is typical of people in a particular period in history.

spirited /spɪ̲rɪtɪd/ ◆◇◇◇◇

1 A **spirited** action shows great energy and courage. *President Gorbachev made a spirited defence of his reforms.* ♦ **spiritedly** *She had talked spiritedly about her adventures.* ADJ-GRADED: usu ADJ n; ADV-GRADED: ADV with v

2 A **spirited** person is very active, lively, and confident. *He was by nature a spirited little boy.* ADJ-GRADED: usu ADJ n

-spirited /-spɪ̲rɪtɪd/. **-spirited** combines with adjectives to describe the nature of a person's character, attitude, or behaviour. For example, a **mean-spirited** person behaves in a way that is unkind to other people; a **free-spirited** person behaves as they please and not as most people who follow normal rules and conventions do. *That's a mean-spirited thing for a mother to say... Murray was an affable, free-spirited man... Ten-year-olds are more knowledgeable and generous-spirited.* • See also **high-spirited**; **public-spirited.** COMB in ADJ-GRADED

spiritless /spɪ̲rɪtləs/. If someone is **spiritless**, they lack energy and motivation. *We pushed our way through the crowds who were too spiritless even to resist.* ADJ-GRADED =apathetic

spi̲rit level, spirit levels; also spelled **spirit-level**. A **spirit level** is a device for testing to see if a surface is level. It consists of a plastic, wood, or metal frame containing a glass tube of liquid with an air bubble in it. N-COUNT

spiritual /spɪ̲rɪtʃuəl/ **spirituals** ◆◆◆◇◇

1 **Spiritual** means relating to people's thoughts and beliefs, rather than to their bodies and physical surroundings. *She lived entirely by spiritual values, in a world of poetry and imagination.* ♦ **spiritually** *Our whole programme is spiritually oriented but not religious.* ♦ **spirituality** /spɪ̲rɪtʃuæ̲lɪti/ *...the peaceful spirituality of Japanese culture.* ADJ ≠temporal; ADV; N-UNCOUNT

2 **Spiritual** means relating to people's religious beliefs. *The Dalai Lama is a national leader of Tibetans as well as their spiritual leader... A man in priestly clothes offered spiritual guidance.* ADJ =religious ≠secular

3 A **spiritual** is a religious song of the type originally sung by Negro slaves in America. N-COUNT

4 Your **spiritual home** is the place where you feel that you belong, usually because your ideas or attitudes are the same as those of the people who live there. PHRASE: N inflects

spiritualism /spɪ̲rɪtʃuəlɪzəm/. **Spiritualism** is the belief that the spirits of people who are dead can communicate with people who are still alive. ♦ **spiritualist, spiritualists** *He was a poet and an ardent spiritualist.* N-UNCOUNT; N-COUNT

spit /spɪ̲t/ **spits, spitting, spat.** In American English, the form **spit** is used as the past tense and past participle. ◆◆◇◇◇

1 **Spit** is the watery liquid produced in your mouth. You usually use **spit** to refer to an amount of it that has been forced out of someone's mouth. N-UNCOUNT =saliva

2 If someone **spits**, they force an amount of liquid out of their mouth, often to show hatred or scorn. *The gang thought of hitting him too, but decided just to spit... They spat at me and taunted me... She spat into the little tray of mascara and brushed it on her lashes.* VERB V; V prep

3 If you **spit** liquid or food somewhere, you force a small amount of it out of your mouth. *Spit out that gum and pay attention... He felt as if a serpent had spat venom into his eyes... I started spitting blood and my mother panicked.* VERB V n with *out*; V n prep; V n

4 If something such as a machine or food that is cooking **spits**, it makes a series of short, sharp, hissing noises. *The engine spat and banged. ...the fire where pork chops were sizzling and spitting.* VERB =splutter V

5 If someone **spits** an insult or comment, they say it in an angry or hostile way; used in written English. *'Wait a damn minute,' Mindy spat. 'Nobody said anything about staying overnight.'... Cramer spat an obscenity.* ► **Spit out** means the same as **spit**. *He spat out. 'I don't like the way he looks at me.'... She spat the name out like an insult... He appeared to be angry, spitting out disconnected words.* VERB V with quote; V n; PHRASAL VERB V P with quote; V n P; V P n (not pron)

6 In British English, if **it is spitting**, it is raining very lightly. The American term is **sprinkle**. *It will stop in a minute - it's only spitting.* VB: usu cont *it* V

7 A **spit** is a long rod which is pushed through a piece of meat and hung over an open fire to cook the meat. *She roasted the meat on a spit.* N-COUNT

8 A **spit of** land is a long, flat, narrow piece of land that sticks out into the sea. N-COUNT: N *of*n

9 If one place is **within spitting distance** of another, they are very close to each other; an informal expression. *...a restaurant within spitting distance of the Tower of London.* PHRASES usu PHR *of*n

10 If you say that one person is **the spitting image of** another, you mean that they look very similar. *Nina looks the spitting image of Audrey Hepburn.* usu v-link PHR

spit out. See **spit** 5. PHRASAL VERB

spite /spa̲ɪt/ ◆◆◆◇◇

1 You use **in spite of** to introduce a fact which makes the rest of the statement you are making seem surprising. *Josef Krips at the State Opera hired her in spite of the fact that she had never sung on stage... Their love of life comes in spite of, almost in defiance of, considerable hardship.* PHR-PREP =despite

2 If you do something **in spite of** yourself, you do it although you did not really intend to or expect to. *The blunt comment made Richard laugh in spite of himself... She was deeply moved and in spite of herself could not help showing it.* PHR-PREP: PREP pron-refl

3 If you do something nasty out of **spite**, you do it N-UNCOUNT

because you want to hurt or upset someone. *I refused her a divorce, out of spite I suppose... Never had she met such spite and pettiness.*

4 If you do something nasty to **spite** someone, you do it in order to hurt or upset them. *Pantelaras was giving his art collection away for nothing, to spite Marie and her husband.* VB: only to-inf V n

5 • to **cut off** your **nose to spite** your **face**: see **nose**.

spiteful /spaɪtfʊl/. Someone who is **spiteful** does nasty things to people they dislike. *He could be spiteful. ...a stream of spiteful telephone calls.* ADJ-GRADED =malicious

♦ **spitefully** *We crept into our little sister's bedroom and spitefully defaced her pop posters.* ADV-GRADED: ADV with v

spittle /spɪtᵊl/. **Spittle** is the watery liquid which is produced in your mouth; an old-fashioned word. *A tiny roll of spittle oozed down his jaw.* N-UNCOUNT =spit

spiv /spɪv/ **spivs.** In informal British English, a **spiv** is a man who does not have a regular job and who makes money by business deals which are usually illegal. N-COUNT =wide boy

splash /splæʃ/ **splashes, splashing, splashed** ♦♦◇◇◇

1 If you **splash** about or **splash** around in water, you hit or disturb the water in a noisy way, causing some of it to fly up into the air. *A lot of people were in the water, swimming or simply splashing about... She could hear the voices of her friends as they splashed in a nearby rock pool... The gliders and their pilots splashed into the lake and had to be fished out.* VERB V about/around V V into n

2 If you **splash** a liquid somewhere or if it **splashes**, it hits someone or something and scatters in a lot of small drops. *He closed his eyes tight, and splashed the water on his face... A little wave, the first of many, splashed in my face... Beer splashed the carpet... Lorries rumbled past them, splashing them with filthy water from the potholes in the road... He heard the sounds of splashing water and glanced at the door to the bathroom.* V-ERG V n prep V prep/adv V n V n with n V-ing

3 A **splash** is the sound made when something hits water or falls into it. *There was a splash and something fell clumsily into the water.* N-SING

4 A **splash** of a liquid is a small quantity of it that has been spilt on something or added to something. *Wallcoverings and floors should be able to withstand steam and splashes... Add a splash of lemon juice to flavor the butter.* N-COUNT

5 A **splash** of colour is an area of a bright colour which contrasts strongly with the colours around it. *Anne has left the walls white, but added splashes of colour with the tablecloth and the paintings.* N-COUNT: with supp, oft N of n

6 If a magazine or newspaper **splashes** a story, it prints it in such a way that it is very noticeable. *The newspapers splashed the story all over their front pages... A picture of his girlfriend Sheryl had been splashed in the previous weekend's tabloids.* VERB V n

7 If you **make a splash**, you become noticed or become popular because of something that you have done. *Now she's made a splash in the American television show 'Civil Wars'.* PHRASE: V inflects =make an impression

splash out. If you **splash out** on something, especially on a luxury, you buy it even though it costs a lot of money; used in British English. *If he wanted to splash out on a new car it would take him a couple of days to get his hands on the cash... Can you afford to splash out a little? Is your budget unlimited?* PHRASAL VERB no passive V P on n V P

splashdown /splæʃdaʊn/ **splashdowns.** A **splashdown** is the landing of a spacecraft in the sea after a flight. N-COUNT

splat /splæt/. **Splat** is used to describe the sound of something wet hitting a surface with a lot of force. *The egg landed on my cheek with a splat.* N-SING; SOUND

splatter /splætəʳ/ **splatters, splattering, splattered.** If a thick wet substance **splatters** on something or is **splattered** on it, it drops or is thrown over it. *The rain splattered against the french windows... 'Sorry Edward,' I said, splattering the cloth with jam. ...a mud-splattered white shirt.* ♦◇◇◇◇ V-ERG =spatter V adv/prep V n V-ed

splay /spleɪ/ **splays, splaying, splayed.** If things **splay** or **are splayed**, their ends are spread out away from each other. *He splayed his fingers across his face... His fingers splay out in a star shape... He was on his stomach, his legs splayed apart.* V-ERG V n V adv/prep V-ed

spleen /spliːn/ **spleens** ♦◇◇◇◇

1 Your **spleen** is an organ near your stomach that controls the quality of your blood. N-COUNT

2 **Spleen** is violent and spiteful anger; a formal word. *Paul Fussell's latest book vents his spleen against everything he hates about his country... There were other targets for Mr Lamont's spleen.* N-UNCOUNT: usu poss N =anger

splendid /splendɪd/ ♦♦◇◇◇

1 If you say that something is **splendid**, you mean that it is very good. *The book includes a wealth of splendid photographs... Our house has got a splendid view across towards the Cotswolds... I found him to be splendid company during the hour of our acquaintance.* ♦ **splendidly** *I have heard him tell people that we get along splendidly.* ADJ-GRADED: usu ADJ n =marvellous ADV-GRADED: ADV with v

2 If you describe a building or work of art as **splendid**, you mean that it is beautiful, impressive, and extremely well made. *...a splendid Victorian mansion.* ♦ **splendidly** *The young women are splendidly dressed, some in floor-length ball gowns... Its historic buildings are being slowly and splendidly renovated. ...this splendidly readable and robust autobiography.* ADJ-GRADED: usu ADJ n =magnificent ADV-GRADED: ADV adj, ADV with v =magnificently

3 You can say **'splendid'** in a conversation to indicate that you approve of a particular situation or something that someone has said. *'I was thinking I might do a lemon cream sauce and baked potatoes.' 'Splendid!' Midge applauded.* EXCLAM PRAGMATICS =super, great

splendour /splendəʳ/ **splendours;** spelled **splendor** in American English. ♦◇◇◇◇

1 The **splendour** of something is its beautiful and magnificent appearance. *The foreign ministers are meeting in the splendour of Oktyabrskaya Hotel in central Moscow.* N-UNCOUNT

2 The **splendours** of a place or way of life are its beautiful and impressive features. *Montagu was extremely impressed by the splendours of the French court.* N-PLURAL: oft N of n

splenetic /splɪnetɪk/. If you describe someone as **splenetic**, you mean that they are bad-tempered and irritable; a formal word. *...retired military men with splenetic opinions.* ADJ-GRADED =peevish

splice /splaɪs/ **splices, splicing, spliced**

1 If you **splice** two pieces of rope, film, or tape together, you join them neatly at the ends so that they make one continuous piece. *He taught me to edit and splice film... The film will be spliced with footage of Cypress Hill to be filmed in America.* VERB V n be V-ed

2 When two people **get spliced**, they get married; an old-fashioned, informal expression. *An old friend of mine, newly spliced, recently invited me to dinner in his new marital home.* V-PASSIVE V-ed

spliff /splɪf/ **spliffs.** In informal English, a **spliff** is a cigarette which contains cannabis. N-COUNT =joint

splint /splɪnt/ **splints.** A **splint** is a long piece of wood or metal that is fastened to a broken arm, leg, or back to keep it still. N-COUNT

splinter /splɪntəʳ/ **splinters, splintering, splintered** ♦◇◇◇◇

1 A **splinter** is a very thin, sharp piece of wood, glass, or other hard substance, which has broken off from a larger piece. *...splinters of glass. ...a splinter in the finger.* N-COUNT

2 If something **splinters** or **is splintered**, it breaks into thin, sharp pieces. *The ruler cracked and splintered into pieces... The stone rocketed into the glass, splintering it.* V-ERG V prep/adv V n

splinter group, splinter groups. A **splinter group** or organization is a group of people who break away from a larger group and form a separate organization, usually because they no longer agree with the views of the larger group. N-COUNT

split /splɪt/ **splits, splitting.** The form **split** is used in the present tense and is the past tense and past participle of the verb. ♦♦♦♦◇

1 If something **splits** or if you **split** it, it is divided into two or more parts. *In a severe gale the ship split in two... If the chicken is fairly small, you may simply split it in half... We split the boards down the* V-ERG V in/into n V n in/into n V n

middle to use them for the back of the shelves. ...uniting families split by the Korean war.

2 If an organization **splits** or **is split**, one group of members disagree strongly with the other members, and may form a group of their own. *The Communist Party in the Soviet Republic of Latvia has split over whether to break ties with Moscow... Women priests are accused of splitting the church... The Labour Party will be split and divided by subtle dealings.* ▶ Also an adjective. *The Kremlin is deeply split in its approach to foreign policy.* V-ERG V V n ADJ-GRADED: usu v-link ADJ

3 A **split** in an organization is a disagreement between its members. *They accused both radicals and conservatives of trying to provoke a split in the party.* N-COUNT

4 A **split** between two things is a division or difference between them. *...a split between what is thought and what is felt.* N-SING: oft N *between* pl-n

5 If something such as wood or a piece of clothing **splits** or **is split**, a long crack or tear appears in it. *The seat of his short grey trousers split... Twist the mixture into individual sausages without splitting the skins... He had a split lip and an eye that wouldn't open properly.* V-ERG V V n V-ed

6 A **split** is a long crack or tear. *The plastic-covered seat has a few small splits around the corners.* N-COUNT =tear

7 If two or more people **split** something, they share it between them. *I would rather pay for a meal than watch nine friends pick over and split a bill... Split the wages between you... All exhibits are for sale, the proceeds being split between Oxfam and the artist.* VERB V n V n *between* pl-n

• See also **splitting**.

split off. If people **split off** from a group, they stop being part of the group and become separated from it. *Somehow, Quentin split off from his comrades. ...the Youth Wing which split off the National Liberal party earlier this year... A key member of the San Diego Yacht Club team is splitting off to form his own team.* PHRASAL VERB V P *from* n V P n V P

split up PHRASAL VERB

1 If two people **split up**, or if someone or something **splits** them **up**, they end their relationship or marriage. *Research suggests that children whose parents split up are more likely to drop out of high school... I was beginning to think that nothing could ever split us up... I split up with my boyfriend last year.* RECIP-ERG V P V n P V P *with* n

2 If a group of people **split up** or **are split up**, they go away in different directions. *Did the two of you split up in the woods?... This situation has split up the family... Touring the 'Lovey' album temporarily split the band up.* ERG V P V P n (not pron) V n P

3 If you **split** something **up**, or if it **splits up**, you divide it so that it is in a number of smaller separate sections. *Any thought of splitting up the company was unthinkable they said... We'll sell the show for £100 million and split it up, and move on to our next projects... Her company has had to split up and work from two locations.* ERG V P n (not pron) V n P V P

split ends. If you have **split ends**, some of your hairs are split at the ends because they are dry or damaged. N-PLURAL

split infinitive, split infinitives. A **split infinitive** is a construction in which an adverb is put between 'to' and the infinitive of a verb, as in 'to really experience it'. Some people think it is incorrect to use split infinitives. N-COUNT

split-level. A **split-level** house or room has part of the ground floor at a different level from another part, usually because the house has been built on ground that slopes. ADJ: usu ADJ n

split personality, split personalities. If you say that someone has a **split personality**, you mean that their moods can change so much that they seem to have two separate personalities. N-COUNT

split-screen, split-screens

1 **Split-screen** is used to describe the technique in making films and television programmes in which two different pieces of film are shown at the same time. *...split-screen movies.* ADJ: usu ADJ n

2 On a computer terminal, a **split-screen** is a display of two different sets of output in separate windows on the screen. N-COUNT

split second; also spelled **split-second.** A **split second** is an extremely short period of time. *Her gaze met Michael's for a split second... Soldiers had to make split-second decisions before opening fire, he said.* ◆◇◇◇◇ N-SING

splitting /splɪtɪŋ/. A **splitting** headache is a very severe and painful one. ADJ: ADJ n

splodge /splɒdʒ/ **splodges.** A **splodge** is a large uneven mark or stain, especially one that has been caused by a liquid. N-COUNT =splotch

splotch /splɒtʃ/ **splotches.** A **splotch** is the same as a splodge. N-COUNT =splodge

splurge /splɜːʳdʒ/ **splurges, splurging, splurged.** If you **splurge on** something, you spend a lot of money extravagantly, usually on things that you do not need. *We splurged on Bohemian glass for gifts, and for ourselves.* ▶ Also a noun. *I'm confident that there's enough in the bank for a splurge on a great pair of shoes.* VERB =splash out V *on* n N-COUNT

splutter /splʌtəʳ/ **splutters, spluttering, spluttered** ◆◇◇◇◇

1 If someone **splutters**, they make spitting sounds and have difficulty speaking clearly, for example because they are embarrassed or angry. *'But it cannot be', he spluttered... Molly leapt to her feet, spluttering and howling with rage.* ▶ Also a noun. *He gave a brief splutter of laughter.* VERB =sputter V with quote V N-COUNT

2 If something **splutters**, it makes a series of short, sharp sounds. *Suddenly the engine coughed, spluttered and died.* VERB =sputter

spoil /spɔɪl/ **spoils, spoiling, spoiled, spoilt.** ◆◆◇◇◇ The form **spoiled** is both the past tense and past participle. British English also uses the form **spoilt**.

1 If you **spoil** something, you prevent it from being successful or satisfactory. *It's important not to let mistakes spoil your life... Peaceful summer evenings can be spoilt by mosquitoes.* VERB V n

2 If you **spoil** children, you give them everything they want or ask for. This is considered to have a bad effect on a child's character. *Grand-parents are often tempted to spoil their grandchildren whenever they come to visit.* ♦ **spoilt, spoiled** *A spoilt child is rarely popular with other children... Oh, that child. He's so spoiled.* VERB V n ADJ-GRADED

3 If you **spoil** yourself or **spoil** someone you love, you give yourself or them something nice as a treat or do something special for them. *Spoil yourself with a new perfume this summer... Perhaps I could employ someone to iron his shirts, but I wanted to spoil him. He was my man.* VERB =pamper V pron-refl V n

4 If food **spoils** or if it **is spoilt**, it is no longer fit to be eaten. *We all know that fats spoil by becoming rancid... Some organisms are responsible for spoiling food and cause food poisoning... Some of my apples were spoilt last year by grubs inside the fruit. ...the potential health problems from spoiled food.* V-ERG V V n V-ed

5 If someone **spoils** their vote, they deface their voting paper, usually as a protest about the election. This makes their vote invalid. *They had broadcast calls for voters to spoil their ballot papers... The results showed that 7.2% of the voters cast blank or spoiled ballots.* VERB =deface V n V-ed

6 The **spoils** of something are things that people get as a result of winning a battle or of doing something successfully. *True to military tradition, the victors are now treating themselves to the spoils of war... Competing warlords and foreign powers scrambled for political spoils.* N-PLURAL: usu with supp

7 If you say that someone is **spoilt for choice** or **spoiled for choice**, you are emphasizing that they have a great many things of the same type to choose from. *At lunchtime, MPs are spoilt for choice in 26 restaurants and bars, each providing subsidised food.* PHRASE: v-link PHR

spoil for. If you **are spoiling for** a fight, you are very eager for it to happen. *A mob armed with guns was at the border between the two republics, spoiling for a fight.* PHRASAL VERB only cont V P n

spoilage /spɔɪlɪdʒ/. When **spoilage** occurs, something, usually food, decays or is harmed, so that it is no longer fit to be used; a technical term. N-UNCOUNT

spoiler /spɔɪləʳ/ **spoilers**
1 If you describe someone or something as a **spoiler**, you mean that they try to spoil the performance of other people or things. *I was a talentless spoiler. If I couldn't be good, why should they?... We could use pressure to make sure that Syria doesn't play the role of spoiler in the region.* N-COUNT
2 A **spoiler** is an object which forms part of an aeroplane's wings or part of the body of a car. It redirects the flow of air around the vehicle, allowing an aircraft to change direction or making a car's forward movement more efficient. N-COUNT

spoilsport /spɔɪlspɔːʳt/ **spoilsports.** If you say that someone is a **spoilsport**, you mean that they are behaving in a way that ruins other people's pleasure or enjoyment; an informal word. N-COUNT =killjoy

spoilt /spɔɪlt/. **Spoilt** is a past participle and past tense of **spoil**.

spoke /spoʊk/ **spokes**
1 **Spoke** is the past tense of **speak**.
2 The **spokes** of a wheel are the bars that connect the outer ring to the centre. N-COUNT: usu pl

spoken /spoʊkən/. **Spoken** is the past participle of **speak**.

-spoken /-spoʊkən/. **-spoken** combines with adverbs and adjectives to form adjectives which indicate how someone speaks. *The woman was smartly dressed and well-spoken. ...a soft-spoken man in his early thirties.* COMB in ADJ-GRADED

spoken word. The **spoken word** is used to refer to language expressed in speech, for example in contrast to written texts or music. *There is a potential educational benefit in allowing pictures to tell the story, rather than the spoken word. ...a spoken word CD by acclaimed novelist Derek Raymond.* N-SING: usu *the* N

spokesman /spoʊksmən/ **spokesmen.** A **spokesman** is a male spokesperson. *A UN spokesman said that the mission will carry 20 tons of relief supplies.* ◆◆◆◆◇ N-COUNT

spokesperson /spoʊkspɜːʳsᵊn/ **spokespersons** or **spokespeople.** A **spokesperson** is a person who speaks as the representative of a group or organization. *A spokesperson for Amnesty, Norma Johnston, describes some cases.* ◆◇◇◇◇ N-COUNT

spokeswoman /spoʊkswʊmən/ **spokeswomen.** A **spokeswoman** is a female spokesperson. *Vera Wollenberger is spokeswoman for the Green Party in the East German parliament.* ◆◆◇◇◇ N-COUNT

sponge /spʌndʒ/ **sponges, sponging, sponged** ◆◇◇◇◇
1 **Sponge** is a very light absorbent substance with lots of little holes in it. Sponge can be either man-made or natural and is capable of absorbing a lot of water or of acting as an insulating material. *...a sponge mattress.* N-COUNT
2 A **sponge** is a sea animal with a soft round body made of natural sponge. N-COUNT
3 A **sponge** is a piece of sponge that you use for washing yourself or for cleaning things. *He wiped off the table with a sponge.* N-COUNT
4 If you **sponge** something, you clean it by wiping it with a wet sponge. *Fill a bowl with water and gently sponge your face and body.* ▶ **Sponge down** means the same as **sponge**. *If your child's temperature rises, sponge her down gently with tepid water.* VERB V n PHRASAL VERB V n P Also V P n (not pron)
5 A **sponge** is a light cake or pudding made from flour, eggs, sugar, and sometimes fat. *It makes a superb filling for cakes and sponges.* N-VAR
6 If you say that someone **sponges off** other people or **sponges on** them, you mean that they regularly get money from other people when they should be trying to support themselves; used in informal English showing disapproval. *He should just get an honest job and stop sponging off the rest of us!... He spent his life grumbling about missed opportunities and sponging on his father for money.* VERB PRAGMATICS =scrounge off V *off* n V *on* n

spongebag /spʌndʒbæg/ **spongebags;** also spelled **sponge bag**. In British English, a **spongebag** is a small bag in which you keep things such as soap, a flannel, and a toothbrush when you are travelling. N-COUNT =toilet bag

sponge cake, sponge cakes. A **sponge cake** is a very light cake made from flour, eggs, and sometimes fat. N-VAR

sponger /spʌndʒəʳ/ **spongers.** If you describe someone as a **sponger**, you mean that they sponge off other people or organizations; used in informal English showing disapproval. N-COUNT PRAGMATICS =scrounger

spongy /spʌndʒi/. Something that is **spongy** is soft and squashy, like a sponge. *We liked the bike's spongy handgrip for keeping our hands away from cold metal... The earth was spongy from rain.* ADJ-GRADED

sponsor /spɒnsəʳ/ **sponsors, sponsoring, sponsored** ◆◆◆◇◇
1 If an organization or an individual **sponsors** something such as an event or someone's training, they pay some or all of the expenses connected with it, often in order to get publicity for themselves. *Mercury, in association with The Independent, is sponsoring Britain's first major Pop Art exhibition for over 20 years... The competition was sponsored by Ruinart Champagne... Most DES students are sponsored by the National Department of Education.* VERB =finance V n
2 In Britain, if you **sponsor** someone who is doing something to raise money for charity, for example trying to walk a certain distance, you agree to give them a sum of money for the charity if they succeed in doing it. *Please could you sponsor me for my school's campaign for Help the Aged?* VERB V n
3 If you **sponsor** a proposal or suggestion, you officially put it forward and support it. *Eight senators sponsored legislation to stop the military funding.* VERB V n
4 When a country or an organization such as the United Nations **sponsors** negotiations between countries, it suggests holding the negotiations and organizes them. *Given the strength of pressure on both sides, the superpowers may well have difficulties sponsoring negotiations... The agreement was reached during peace talks sponsored by the European Community.* VERB V n V-ed
5 If one country accuses another of **sponsoring** terrorism, they mean that the other country does not do anything to prevent it, and may even encourage it. *We have to make the states that sponsor terrorism pay a price.* VERB =support V n
6 A **sponsor** is a person or organization that sponsors something or someone. *I understand Coca-Cola are to be named as the new sponsors of the League Cup later this week... The chief sponsor of the New York law, state Senator Emanuel Gold, says he's not giving up.* N-COUNT

sponsored /spɒnsəʳd/. In Britain, a **sponsored** event is an event in which participants try to do something such as walk a certain distance in order to raise money for charity. *The sponsored walk will raise money for AIDS care.* ◆◇◇◇◇ ADJ: ADJ n

sponsorship /spɒnsəʳʃɪp/ ◆◆◇◇◇
1 **Sponsorship** is financial support given by a sponsor. *Campbell is one of an ever-growing number of skiers in need of sponsorship... Private sponsorships only accounted for a third of all arts funding last year.* N-UNCOUNT: also N in pl
2 **Sponsorship** of something is the act of sponsoring it. *When it is done properly, arts sponsorship can be more effective than advertising.* N-UNCOUNT: usu with supp

spontaneity /spɒntəneɪɪti/. **Spontaneity** is spontaneous, natural behaviour. *He had the spontaneity of a child.* ◆◇◇◇◇ N-UNCOUNT

spontaneous /spɒnteɪniəs/ ◆◆◇◇◇
1 **Spontaneous** acts are not planned or arranged, but are done because someone suddenly wants to do them. *Diana's house was crowded with happy people whose spontaneous outbursts of song were accompanied by lively music... I joined in the spontaneous applause.* ♦ **spontaneously** *As soon as the tremor passed, many people spontaneously arose* ADJ-GRADED ADV-GRADED: usu ADV with v, also ADV adj

and cheered... He was never spontaneously warm or friendly towards us.

2 A **spontaneous** event happens because of processes within something rather than being caused by things outside it. *I had another spontaneous miscarriage at around the 16th to 18th week. ...a spontaneous explosion.* ♦ **spontaneously** *Usually a woman's breasts produce milk spontaneously after the birth... These images surface spontaneously in dreams.* ADJ / ADV: ADV after v

spoof /spu:f/ **spoofs.** A **spoof** is something such as an article or television programme that seems to be about a serious matter but is actually a joke. *...a spoof on Hollywood life. ...Tim Robbins's spoof documentary about a presidential campaign.* N-COUNT

spook /spu:k/ **spooks, spooking, spooked** ◆◇◇◇◇

1 A **spook** is a ghost. N-COUNT

2 In American English, a **spook** is a spy. *...as a US intelligence spook said yesterday.* N-COUNT

3 If people **are spooked**, something has scared them or made them nervous; used especially in American English. *But was it the wind that spooked her?... Investors were spooked by slowing economies.* ♦ **spooked** *He was so spooked that he, too, began to believe that he heard strange clicks and noises on their telephones.* VERB =scare V n / ADJ-GRADED: v-link ADJ

spooky /spu:ki/ **spookier, spookiest.** A place that is **spooky** has a frightening atmosphere, and makes you feel that there are ghosts around. *The whole place has a slightly spooky atmosphere.* ◆◇◇◇◇ ADJ-GRADED =creepy

spool /spu:l/ **spools.** A **spool** is a round object onto which thread, tape, or film can be wound, especially before it is put in a sewing machine, tape recorder, or projector. ◆◇◇◇◇ N-COUNT =reel

spoon /spu:n/ **spoons, spooning, spooned** ◆◆◇◇◇

1 A **spoon** is an implement used for eating, stirring, and serving food. One end of it is shaped like a shallow bowl and it has a long handle. *He stirred his coffee with a spoon.* N-COUNT

2 You can refer to an amount of food resting on a spoon as a **spoon** of food. *...tea with two spoons of sugar.* N-COUNT: usu N *of* n

3 If you **spoon** food into something, you put it there with a spoon. *He spooned instant coffee into two of the mugs... Spoon the sauce over the meat.* VERB V n prep

4 See also **greasy spoon**, **soup spoon**, **slotted spoon**, **wooden spoon**.

5 If you think that someone has a lot of advantages because they have a rich or influential family, you can say that they have been **born with a silver spoon in** their **mouth**. *She was born with a silver spoon in her mouth and everything has been done for her.* PHRASE: Ns inflect

spoonerism /spu:nərɪzəm/ **spoonerisms.** A **spoonerism** is a mistake made by a speaker in which the first sounds of two words are changed over, often with a humorous result, for example when someone says 'wrong load' instead of 'long road'. N-COUNT

spoon-feed, spoon-feeds, spoon-feeding, spoon-fed

1 If you think that someone is being given too much help with something and is not making enough effort themselves, you can say they are being **spoon-fed**; used showing disapproval. *Students are unwilling to really work. They want to be spoon-fed... They've been spoon-fed, provided with a house, servants, bank balance.* VB: usu passive PRAGMATICS *be* V-ed

2 If you say that someone is **spoon-fed** ideas or information, you mean that they are told about them and are expected to accept them without questioning them; used showing disapproval. *They were less willing to be spoon-fed doctrines from Japan... The children who were spoon-fed consumerism have discovered that the years of excess are over.* VB: usu passive PRAGMATICS *be* V-ed n

3 If you **spoon-feed** a small child or a sick person, you feed them using a spoon. *It took two years for me to get better, during which time he spoon-fed me and did absolutely everything around the house.* VERB V n

spoonful /spu:nfʊl/ **spoonfuls.** You can refer to an amount of food resting on a spoon as a **spoonful** of food. *He took a spoonful of the stew and ate it. ...three spoonfuls of sugar.* ◆◇◇◇◇ N-COUNT: usu N *of* n

spoor /spʊəʳ/. The **spoor** of an animal is the visible trail that it leaves as it moves along. N-SING

sporadic /spərædɪk/. **Sporadic** occurrences of something happen at irregular intervals. *...a year of sporadic fighting over northern France... The sound of sporadic shooting could still be heard.* ♦ **sporadically** *The distant thunder from the coast continued sporadically... He attends school sporadically.* ◆◇◇◇◇ ADJ-GRADED ≠continuous / ADV-GRADED: ADV with v ≠continuously

spore /spɔ:ʳ/ **spores.** **Spores** are cells produced by bacteria and fungi which can develop into new bacteria. ◆◇◇◇◇ N-COUNT

sporran /spɒrən, AM spɔ:rən/ **sporrans.** A **sporran** is a large purse, usually made out of leather or fur, which is worn on a belt around their waists by Scotsmen when they are wearing a kilt. N-COUNT

sport /spɔ:ʳt/ **sports, sporting, sported** ◆◆◆◆◇

1 **Sports** are games such as football and basketball and other competitive leisure activities which need physical effort and skill. *I'd say football is my favourite sport... She excels at sport... Mark was mainly interested in sport at school, playing rugby as well as soccer... Billy turned on a radio to get the sports news.* N-VAR

2 If you say that someone is a **sport** or a good **sport**, you mean that they cope with a difficult situation or teasing in a cheerful way; an old-fashioned use. *He was accused of having no sense of humor, of not being a good sport.* N-COUNT

3 If you say that someone **sports** something such as a distinctive item of clothing, you mean that they wear it stylishly or without any shyness; used in written English. *He sported a collarless jacket with pleated black panels... He was heavily-built and sported a red moustache... People sported swastikas and walls were covered with inflammatory slogans.* VERB =wear V n

sporting /spɔ:ʳtɪŋ/ ◆◆◇◇◇

1 **Sporting** means relating to sport or used for sport. *...major sporting events, such as Wimbledon and the World Cup finals. ...a huge sporting goods store.* ADJ: ADJ n

2 If you have **a sporting chance** of doing something, it is quite likely that you will do that thing. *There was a sporting chance they would meet, but not necessarily at the party.* PHRASE

sports car, sports cars. A **sports car** is a low, fast car, usually with room for only two people. ◆◇◇◇◇ N-COUNT

sports day, sports days. In British schools, **sports day** is a day or an afternoon when pupils compete in activities such as races, the high jump, and throwing the javelin. Parents are often invited to come and watch the events. N-VAR

sports jacket, sports jackets. A **sports jacket** is a man's jacket, usually made of tweed. It is worn on informal occasions with trousers of a different colour or material. N-COUNT

sportsman /spɔ:ʳtsmən/ **sportsmen.** A **sportsman** is a man who takes part in sports. ◆◇◇◇◇ N-COUNT

sportsmanship /spɔ:ʳtsmənʃɪp/. **Sportsmanship** is behaviour and attitudes that show respect for the rules of a game and for the other players. *The team also won praise for sportsmanship and fair play.* N-UNCOUNT

sportswear /spɔ:ʳtsweəʳ/. **Sportswear** is the special clothing worn for playing sports or for informal leisure activities. N-UNCOUNT

sportswoman /spɔ:ʳtswʊmən/ **sportswomen.** A **sportswoman** is a woman who takes part in sports. N-COUNT

sports writer, sports writers. A **sports writer** is a journalist who writes about sport. N-COUNT

sporty /spɔ:ʳti/ **sportier, sportiest** ◆◇◇◇◇

1 You can describe a car as **sporty** when it performs like a racing car but can be driven on normal roads. *The steering and braking are exactly what you want from a sporty car.* ADJ-GRADED

2 Someone who is **sporty** likes playing sports. ADJ-GRADED

spot /spɒt/ **spots, spotting, spotted** ◆◆◆◆◇

1 **Spots** are small, round, coloured areas on a sur- N-COUNT:

face. *The leaves have yellow areas on the top and underneath are powdery orange spots... The swimsuit comes in navy with white spots or blue with green spots.* usu pl

2 **Spots** on a person's skin are small lumps or marks. *Never squeeze blackheads, spots or pimples.* N-COUNT: usu pl

3 A **spot of** a liquid is a small amount of it; used mainly in British English. *Spots of rain had begun to fall... Secure with a few spots of glue.* N-COUNT: N *of* n

4 If you have a **spot of** something, you have a small amount of it; used mainly in informal British English. *Mr Brooke is undoubtedly in a spot of bother... A year or two ago I found myself indulging in a spot of yachting in Finnish waters... We've given all the club members tea, coffee and a spot of lunch.* QUANT: QUANT *of* n-uncount =bit

5 You can refer to a particular place as a **spot**. *They stayed at several of the island's top tourist spots... They all stood there staring, as if frozen to the spot.* N-COUNT: usu supp N

6 A **spot** in a television or radio show is a part of it that is regularly reserved for a particular performer or type of entertainment. *Unsuccessful at screen writing, he got a spot on a CNN film show.* N-COUNT: usu with supp =slot

7 If you **spot** something or someone, you notice them. *Vicenzo failed to spot the error... He left the party seconds before smoke was spotted coming up the stairs.* • See also **spotted**; **black spot**, **blind spot**. VERB V n

8 If you are **on the spot**, you are at the actual place where something is happening. *...areas where troops are on the spot and protecting civilians... Mr Connolly is their 'man on the spot' and the person you can call if you have a complaint.* PHRASES v-link PHR

9 If you do something **on the spot**, you do it immediately. *James was called to see the producer and got the job on the spot... The surveyor will use a lap-top computer to give on the spot advice.* PHR after v, PHR n

10 If you **put** someone **on the spot**, you cause them to have to answer a difficult question or make a difficult decision. *He put me on the spot a bit because he invited me right in front of his mum and I didn't particularly want to go... Even clever people are not terribly clever when put on the spot.* V inflects

11 If you are **in a tight spot**, you are in a difficult situation; an informal expression. *In a tight spot there is no one I would sooner see than Frank.* PHR after v, PHR cl

12 • **rooted to the spot**: see **rooted**. • **have a soft spot for someone**: see **soft**.

spot check, spot checks. If someone carries out a **spot check**, they examine a randomly chosen thing from a group in order to make sure that it is satisfactory. N-COUNT: oft N *on* n

spotless /spɒtləs/. Something that is **spotless** is perfectly clean. *Each morning cleaners make sure everything is spotless... Even in the most spotless homes, carpets need regular cleaning to keep them looking good.* ♦ **spotlessly** *The house had huge, spotlessly clean rooms.* ADJ-GRADED; ADV: ADV adj

spotlight /spɒtlaɪt/ **spotlights, spotlighting, spotlighted** ◆◆◇◇◇

1 A **spotlight** is a powerful light, for example in a theatre, which can be directed so that it lights up a small area. N-COUNT

2 If something **spotlights** a particular problem or situation, it makes people notice it and think about it. *The budget crisis also spotlighted a weakening American economy. ...a new book spotlighting female entrepreneurs.* VERB =highlight V n

3 Someone or something that is **in the spotlight** is getting a great deal of public attention. *Webb is back in the spotlight.* PHRASES v-link PHR

4 If someone or something comes **under the spotlight**, they are thoroughly examined, especially by journalists and the public. *The economy will come under the spotlight today at the conference of the Trades Union Congress.* PHR after v

spotlit /spɒtlɪt/. Something that is **spotlit** is brightly lit up by one or more spotlights. *She caught a clear view upwards of the spotlit temple.* ADJ

spot-on; also spelled **spot on**. In informal British English, **spot-on** means exactly correct or accurate. *Schools were told their exam information had to be spot-on and accurate.* ◆◇◇◇◇ ADJ: usu v-link ADJ

spotted /spɒtɪd/. ◆◇◇◇◇

1 Something that is **spotted** has a pattern of spots on it. *...hand-painted spotted cups and saucers in green and blue... His cheeks were spotted with blackheads.* ADJ: oft ADJ *with* n

2 See also **spot**.

spotter /spɒtəʳ/ **spotters.** A **spotter** of something such as trains or aeroplanes is someone whose hobby is looking out for them. *I was a devoted train spotter.* ◆◇◇◇◇ N-COUNT: n N

-spotting /-spɒtɪŋ/. **-spotting** combines with nouns to form nouns which describe the activity of looking out for things such as birds or trains as a hobby. *...train-spotting. ...bird-spotting.* COMB in N-UNCOUNT

spotty /spɒti/

1 Someone who is **spotty** has spots or pimples on their face. *She was rather fat, and her complexion was muddy and spotty.* ADJ-GRADED =pimply

2 In American English, something that is **spotty** does not stay the same but is sometimes good and sometimes bad. *He quit in 1981 – had a spotty political career... His attendance record was spotty.* ADJ-GRADED =patchy

spousal /spaʊzəl/. In American English, **spousal** rights and duties are ones which you gain if you are married; a formal word. ADJ: ADJ n

spouse /spaʊs/ **spouses.** Someone's **spouse** is the person they are married to. ◆◆◇◇◇ N-COUNT

spout /spaʊt/ **spouts, spouting, spouted** ◆◇◇◇◇

1 If something **spouts** liquid or fire or if liquid or fire **spout** out of something, it comes out very quickly with a lot of force. *He replaced the boiler when the last one began to spout flames... The main square has a fountain that spouts water 40 feet into the air... In a storm, water spouts out of the blowhole just like a whale.* V-ERG =spurt V n; V n prep; V adv/prep

2 A **spout** of liquid is a long stream of it which is coming out of something very forcefully. N-COUNT =jet

3 If you say that someone **spouts** something, you disapprove of them because they say something which you do not agree with or they say something which you think they do not honestly feel. *My mother would go red in the face and spout bitter recriminations... You're the kind of person who affiliates himself with the kind of crap they spout.* ▶ **Spout forth** and **spout off** mean the same as **spout**. *...an estate agent spouting forth about houses... All too often he is spouting off about matters which should not concern him.* VERB PRAGMATICS V n; PHRASAL VERB V P *about* n

4 A **spout** is a long, hollow part of a container through which liquids can be poured out easily. N-COUNT

5 If you say that something is **up the spout**, you mean that it is wrong or it is no longer working; an informal expression. *If you only take a sample then all the statistics are up the spout.* PHRASES v-link PHR PRAGMATICS

6 If you say that a woman is **up the spout**, you mean that she is pregnant; an informal expression that some people find offensive. usu v-link PHR

sprain /spreɪn/ **sprains, spraining, sprained**

1 If you **sprain** a joint such as your ankle or wrist, you accidentally damage it by twisting it or bending it violently. *He fell and sprained his ankle.* ▶ Also an adjective. *...a badly sprained ankle. ...his wrist was sprained.* VERB V n; ADJ: usu ADJ n

2 A **sprain** is the injury caused by spraining a joint. N-COUNT

sprang /spræŋ/. **Sprang** is the past tense of **spring**.

sprat /spræt/ **sprats. Sprats** are very small European sea fish which can be eaten. N-COUNT

sprawl /sprɔːl/ **sprawls, sprawling, sprawled** ◆◇◇◇◇

1 If you **sprawl** somewhere, you sit or lie down with your legs and arms spread out in a careless way. *She sprawled on the bed as if she had left her, not even moving to cover herself up... They sprawled in lawn chairs, snoozing... He locked his knee against the man's inner thigh and sent him sprawling to the ground.* • See also **sprawled**. ▶ **Sprawl out** means the same as **sprawl**. *He would take two aspirin and sprawl out on his bed.* VERB V prep/adv; V prep; PHRASAL VERB V P prep

2 If you say that a place **sprawls**, you mean that it covers a large area of land. *The State Recreation Area sprawls over 900 acres on the southern tip of Key Biscayne... If we continue to sprawl across the* VERB V prep; V-ing *land, we're in for a terrible future... The sprawling city contained some 4m people.*

3 You can use **sprawl** to refer to an area where a city has expanded into the countryside without proper planning or regulation. *The whole urban sprawl of Ankara contains over 2.6m people.*
N-UNCOUNT: usu with supp

4 If something **sprawls**, its structure is disorganized or it lacks direction. *Boylan plays with language, letting the prose sprawl about before tightening it suddenly to great effect... He keeps forgetting the words and the song is a sprawling mess.*
VERB =ramble V adv V-ing

sprawled /sprɔːld/. If you are **sprawled** somewhere, you are sitting or lying with your legs and arms spread out in a careless way. *People are sprawled on makeshift beds in the cafeteria... Rolando lay sprawled on his stomach, snoring.*
◆◇◇◇◇ ADJ: v-link ADJ, ADJ after v

spray /spreɪ/ **sprays, spraying, sprayed** ◆◆◆◇◇

1 Spray is a lot of small drops of water which are being splashed or forced into the air. *The moon was casting a rainbow through the spray from the waterfall... The rope whipped clear of the water, throwing up a spray of droplets.*
N-VAR: oft N *from/of* n

2 A **spray** is a liquid kept under pressure in a can or other container, which you can force out in very small drops. *...hair spray. ...a can of insect spray.*
N-MASS

3 If you **spray** a liquid somewhere or if it **sprays** somewhere, drops of the liquid cover a place or shower someone. *A sprayer hooked to a tractor can spray five gallons onto ten acres... Two inmates hurled slates at prison officers spraying them with a hose... Drops of blood sprayed across the room.*
V-ERG V n prep/adv V n *with* n V prep

4 If a lot of small things **spray** somewhere or if something **sprays** them, they are scattered somewhere with a lot of force. *A shower of mustard seeds sprayed into the air and fell into the grass... The intensity of the blaze shattered windows, spraying glass on the streets below... The bullet slammed into the ceiling, spraying them with bits of plaster.*
V-ERG V prep V n prep V n *with* n

5 If someone **sprays** bullets somewhere, they fire a lot of bullets at a group of people or things. *He ran to the top of the building spraying bullets into shoppers below... The army lorries were sprayed with machinegun fire from guerrillas in the woods.*
VERB V n prep/adv V n *with* n Also V n

6 If something **is sprayed**, it is painted using paint from a pressurized container. *The bare metal was sprayed with several coats of primer.*
VB: usu passive *be* V-ed *with* n Also V n colour

7 When someone **sprays** against insects, they cover plants or crops with a chemical which prevents insects feeding on it. *He doesn't spray against pests or diseases... Confine the use of insecticides to the evening and do not spray plants that are in flower... Because of the immunity of the immature insects, it's important to spray regularly.*
VERB V *against* n V n V Also V n prep

8 A **spray** is a piece of equipment for spraying water or another liquid, especially over growing plants.
N-COUNT =sprayer

9 A **spray of** flowers or leaves is a number of flowers or leaves on one stem or branch. *...a small spray of freesias.*
N-COUNT: N *of* n

spray can, spray cans; also spelled **spray-can.** A **spray can** is a small metal container containing liquid such as paint under pressure so that it can be sprayed.
N-COUNT =aerosol

sprayer /spreɪəʳ/ **sprayers.** A **sprayer** is a piece of equipment used for spraying liquid somewhere.
N COUNT =spray

spray gun, spray guns; also spelled **spray-gun**. A **spray gun** is a piece of equipment which you use to spray paint under pressure onto a surface.
N-COUNT

spread /spred/ **spreads, spreading, spread** ◆◆◆◆◇

1 If you **spread** something somewhere, you open it out or arrange it over a place or surface, so that all of it can be seen or used easily. *She spread a towel on the sand and lay on it... His coat was spread over the bed.* ► **Spread out** means the same as **spread**. *He extracted several glossy prints and spread them out on a low coffee table... In his room, Tom was spreading out a map of Scandinavia on the bed.*
VERB V n prep PHRASAL VERB V n P V P n (not pron)

2 If you **spread** your arms, hands, fingers, or legs, you stretch them out until they are far apart. *Sitting on the floor, spread your legs as far as they will go without overstretching... He stepped back and spread his hands wide. 'You are most welcome to our home.'* ► **Spread out** means the same as **spread**. *David made a gesture, spreading out his hands as if he were showing that he had no explanation to make... You need a bed that's large enough to let you spread yourself out.*
VERB V n adv V n adj Also V n PHRASAL VERB V P n (not pron) V n P

3 If you **spread** a substance on a surface or **spread** the surface with the substance, you put a thin layer of the substance over the surface. *Spread the mixture in the cake tin and bake for 30 minutes... A thick layer of wax was spread over the surface... Spread the bread with the cheese.*
VERB V n prep V n *with* n

4 Spread is a soft food which is put on bread. *...a wholemeal salad roll with low fat spread.*
N-MASS: usu supp N

5 If something **spreads** or **is spread** by people, it gradually reaches or affects a larger and larger area or more and more people. *The industrial revolution which started a couple of hundred years ago in Europe is now spreading across the world. ...the sense of fear spreading in residential neighborhoods... He was fed-up with the lies being spread about him.* ► Also a noun. *The greatest hope for reform is the gradual spread of information... Thanks to the spread of modern technology, trained workers are now more vital than ever.*
V-ERG V prep/adv V V n N-SING: usu *the* N *of* n

6 If something such as a liquid, gas, or smoke **spreads** or **is spread**, it moves outwards in all directions so that it covers a larger area. *Fire spread rapidly after a chemical truck exploded... A dark red stain was spreading across his shirt... In Northern California, a wildfire has spread a haze of smoke over 200 miles.* ► Also a noun. *The situation was complicated by the spread of a serious forest fire.*
V-ERG V V prep V n prep N-SING

7 If you **spread** something **over** a period of time, it takes place regularly or continuously over that period, rather than happening at one time. *There seems to be little difference whether you eat all your calorie allowance in one go, or spread it over the day... The course is spread over a five week period.*
VERB V n *over* n

8 If you **spread** something such as wealth or work, you distribute it evenly or equally. *...policies that spread the state's wealth more evenly... The loss of jobs has been far more evenly spread across the regions than it was during the early 1980s.* ► Also a noun. *There are easier ways to encourage the even spread of wealth.*
VERB V n V n prep N-SING: usu N *of* n

9 A **spread** of ideas, interests, or other things is a wide variety of them. *A topic-based approach can be both hard to assess in primary schools with a typical spread of ability... We have an enormous spread of industries, mainly in the Home Counties and East Anglia.*
N-SING: usu N *of* n =range

10 A **spread** is a large meal, especially one that has been prepared for a special occasion.
N-COUNT

11 A **spread** is two pages of a book, magazine, or newspaper that are opposite each other when you open it at a particular place. *There was a double-page spread of a dinner for 46 people.*
N-COUNT

12 • **spread** your **wings**: see **wing**.

spread out PHRASAL VERB

1 If people, animals, or vehicles **spread out** they move apart from each other. *Felix watched his men move like soldiers, spreading out into two teams.*
V P

2 If something such as a city or forest **spreads out**, it gets larger and gradually begins to covers a larger area. *Cities such as Tokyo are spreading out... A crude oil slick quickly spreads out over water.*
V P

3 See **spread** 1.

4 See **spread** 2.

spreadeagled /spredi:gəld/; also spelled **spread-eagled**. Someone who is **spreadeagled** is lying with their arms and legs spread out. *They lay spreadeagled on the floor. ...the spreadeagled body.*
ADJ: usu v-link ADJ

spread out. If people or things are **spread out**, they are a long way apart. *The Kurds are spread out across five nations.*
◆◇◇◇◇ ADJ-GRADED: usu v-link ADJ

spreadsheet /spredʃi:t/ **spreadsheets.** A **spreadsheet** is a computer program that is used for entering and arranging numerical data. **Spreadsheets** are used mainly for financial planning and budgeting.
N-COUNT

spree /spriː/ **sprees.** If you spend a period of time doing something in an excessive way, you can say that you are going on a particular kind of **spree**. *Some Americans went on a spending spree in December to beat the new tax.* ◆◇◇◇◇ N-COUNT: usu n N

sprig /sprɪg/ **sprigs.** A **sprig** is a small twig or stem with leaves on it which has been picked from a bush or plant, especially so that it can be used in cooking or as a decoration. ◆◇◇◇◇ N-COUNT: usu N *of* n

sprigged /sprɪgd/. **Sprigged** material or paper has a pattern of sprigs on it. *...a sprigged cotton dress... She came out with two packages wrapped in holly-sprigged paper.* ADJ: usu ADJ n

sprightly /spraɪtli/ **sprightlier, sprightliest.** A **sprightly** person, especially an old person, is lively and active. *...the sprightly 85-year-old President.* ADJ-GRADED: usu ADJ n =spry

spring /sprɪŋ/ **springs, springing, sprang, sprung** ◆◆◆◆◇

1 **Spring** is the season between winter and summer when the weather becomes warmer and plants start to grow again. *The Labor government of Western Australia has an election due next spring... We met again in the spring of 1977.* N-VAR

2 A **spring** is a coil of wire which returns to its original shape after it is pressed or pulled. *Unfortunately, as a standard mattress wears, the springs soften and so do not support your spine... Both springs in the fuel pump were broken.* N-COUNT

3 A **spring** is a place where water comes up through the ground. It is also the water that comes from that place. *To the north are the hot springs of Banyas de Sant Loan.* N-COUNT: usu pl

4 When a person or animal **springs**, they jump upwards or forwards suddenly or quickly. *He sprang to his feet, grabbing his keys off the coffee table... Outside each door a guard sprang to attention as they approached... The lion roared once and sprang... Throwing back the sheet, he sprang from the bed.* VERB V prep

5 If something **springs** in a particular direction, it moves suddenly and quickly. *Sadly when the lid of the boot sprang open, it was empty.* VERB V V adj

6 If things or people **spring into action** or **spring to life**, they suddenly start being active or suddenly come into existence. *When she contacted me at the beginning of August to enlist support, Sharon and I sprang into action. ...new industries which had sprung into life during the 1920s.* VERB V prep

7 If one thing **springs from** another thing, it is the result of it. *Ethiopia's art springs from her early Christian as well as her Muslim heritage... His anger sprang from his suffering at the loss of the most important love he had ever known in his life.* VERB =stem V *from* n

8 If a boat or container **springs a leak**, water or some other liquid starts coming in or out through a hole or crack. *The yacht has sprung a leak in the hull.* VERB V n

9 If you **spring** some news or a surprise on someone, you tell them something that they did not expect to hear, without warning them. *The two superpower leaders sprang a surprise at a ceremony in the White House yesterday by signing a trade deal... Mclaren sprang a new idea on him.* VERB V n V n *on* n

10 • **spring to mind**: see **mind**.

spring up. If something **springs up**, it suddenly appears or comes into existence. *New theatres and arts centres sprang up all over the country.* PHRASAL VERB V P

springboard /sprɪŋbɔːʳd/ **springboards**

1 If something is a **springboard** for an action or enterprise, it makes it possible for the action or enterprise to begin. *The 1981 budget was the springboard for an economic miracle... It could provide a springboard to success.* N-COUNT: N *for/to* n

2 A **springboard** is a flexible board which you jump on before performing a dive or a gymnastic movement. N-COUNT

spring chicken, spring chickens. If you say that someone is **no spring chicken**, you are saying in a humorous way that they are not young. *At 85, he is no spring chicken, but Henry Cook is busier than ever.* PHRASE: usu v-link PHR

spring-clean, spring-cleans, spring-cleaning, spring-cleaned. When you **spring-clean** a house, you thoroughly clean everything in it. *It's almost as easy these days to give your rooms a new coat of paint as it is to spring-clean them.* ► Also a noun. *It needs a thorough spring clean.* ♦ **spring-cleaning** *The rooms inside were undergoing a spring-cleaning.* VERB V n N-SING N-SING

spring greens. In British English, young cabbages are sometimes referred to as **spring greens**. N-PLURAL

spring onion, spring onions. In British English, **spring onions** are small onions with long green leaves. They are often eaten raw in salads. The usual American term is **scallion**. ◆◇◇◇◇ N-VAR: usu pl

spring roll, spring rolls. A **spring roll** is an item of Chinese food consisting of a small roll of thin pastry filled with vegetables and sometimes meat, and then fried. N-COUNT

spring tide, spring tides. A **spring tide** is an unusually high tide that happens at the time of a new moon or a full moon. N-COUNT

springtime /sprɪŋtaɪm/. **Springtime** is the period of time during which spring lasts. N-UNCOUNT

springy /sprɪŋi/. If something is **springy**, it returns quickly to its original shape after you press it. *Steam for about 12 mins until the cake is risen and springy to touch in the centre.* ADJ-GRADED

sprinkle /sprɪŋkəl/ **sprinkles, sprinkling, sprinkled** ◆◆◇◇◇

1 If you **sprinkle** a thing with something such as a liquid or powder, you scatter the liquid or powder over it. *Sprinkle the meat with salt and place in the pan... At the festival, candles are blessed and sprinkled with holy water... Cheese can be sprinkled on egg or vegetable dishes.* VERB V n *with* n be V-ed *on* n

2 If something **is sprinkled** with particular things, it has them a few of them throughout it and they are far apart from each other. *Unfortunately, the text is sprinkled with errors... Men in green army uniforms are sprinkled throughout the huge auditorium.* VERB be V-ed *with* n be V-ed prep

3 In American English, if it **is sprinkling**, it is raining very lightly. The British word is **spit**. VERB

sprinkler /sprɪŋkləʳ/ **sprinklers.** A **sprinkler** is a device used to spray water. Sprinklers are used to water plants or lawns or to put out a fire in a building. N-COUNT

sprinkling /sprɪŋklɪŋ/. A **sprinkling** of something is a small quantity or amount of it, especially if it is spread over a large area. *...a light sprinkling of snow... Norway has a fair sprinkling of women ministers.* N-SING: usu N *of* n

sprint /sprɪnt/ **sprints, sprinting, sprinted** ◆◆◇◇◇

1 **The sprint** is a short, fast running race. *Rob Harmeling won the sprint in Bordeaux. ...the women's 100-metres sprint.* N-SING: *the* N

2 A **sprint** is a short race in which the competitors run, drive, ride, or swim very fast. *Lewis will compete in both sprints in Stuttgart... I knew there were other riders who could beat me in a sprint.* N-COUNT

3 **A sprint** is a fast run that someone does, either at the end of a race or because they are in a hurry. *Gilles Delion, of France, won the Tour of Lombardy in a sprint finish at Monza yesterday... The police retreated at a sprint... I broke into a sprint.* N-SING: *a* N

4 If you **sprint**, you run or ride as fast as you can over a short distance. *Sergeant Horne sprinted to the car.* VERB V adv/prep

sprinter /sprɪntəʳ/ **sprinters.** A **sprinter** is a person who takes part in short, fast races. ◆◇◇◇◇ N-COUNT

sprite /spraɪt/ **sprites.** In fairy stories and legends, a **sprite** is a small, magic creature which lives near water. N-COUNT

spritzer /sprɪtsəʳ/ **spritzers.** A **spritzer** is a drink consisting of white wine and soda water. N-COUNT

sprocket /sprɒkɪt/ **sprockets.** A **sprocket** is a wheel with teeth around the outer edge that fit into the holes in a chain or a reel of film or tape in order to turn it. N-COUNT

sprout /spraʊt/ **sprouts, sprouting, sprouted** ◆◇◇◇◇

1 When plants, vegetables, or seeds **sprout**, they VERB

produce new shoots or leaves. *It only takes a few days for beans to sprout.* V

2 When leaves, shoots, or plants **sprout** somewhere, they grow there. *Leaf-shoots were beginning to sprout on the hawthorn... Birch trees sprouted from the rubble and grew into a dense young wood.* VERB V prep

3 If a garden or other area of land **sprouts** plants, they start to grow there. *...the garden, which had had time to sprout a shocking collection of weeds.* VB: no passive V n

4 If you **sprout** beans or seeds, you make them grow small shoots before eating them. You usually do this by soaking them in water. *When you sprout seeds their nutritional content increases... Sprouted beans only need to be cooked for 1-2 minutes.* VERB V n V-ed

5 If something such as hair **sprouts** from a person or animal, or if they **sprout** it, it grows on them. *She is very old now, with little, round, wire-rimmed glasses and whiskers sprouting from her chin... As well as sprouting a few grey hairs, Kevin seems to be suffering the occasional memory loss.* V-ERG: no passive V prep V n

6 If a large number of things have appeared or developed somewhere, you can say that they **have sprouted** there or that the place has **sprouted** them. *More than a million satellite dishes have sprouted on homes across the country... Since its first shop was opened in 1976, it has sprouted outlets in 39 countries.* V-ERG V adv/prep V n Also V

7 Sprouts are vegetables that look like tiny cabbages. They are also called **brussels sprouts**. N-COUNT: usu pl

8 Sprouts are new shoots on plants. *After eleven days of growth the number of sprouts was counted.* N-COUNT: usu pl

spruce /spruːs/ **spruces, sprucing, spruced;** ◆◇◇◇◇ **spruce** is both the singular and the plural of the noun.

1 A **spruce** is a kind of evergreen tree. *Trees such as spruce, pine and oak have been planted. ...a young blue spruce. ...80-year-old spruces.* N-VAR ► **Spruce** is the wood from this tree. *Early settlers built frames of spruce, maple and pine.* N-UNCOUNT

2 Someone who is **spruce** is very neat and smart in appearance. *Chris was looking spruce in his stiff-collared black shirt and new short hair cut.* ADJ-GRADED =dapper

spruce up. If something **is spruced up**, its appearance is improved. *Many buildings have been spruced up... In the evening we spruced ourselves up a bit and went out for dinner.* PHRASAL VERB be V-ed P V n P

sprung /sprʌŋ/. **Sprung** is the past participle of **spring**.

spry /spraɪ/. Someone, especially an old person, who is **spry**, is lively and active. *The old gentleman was as spry as ever. ...a spry old lady.* ADJ-GRADED: usu v-link ADJ =sprightly

spud /spʌd/ **spuds. Spuds** are potatoes; an informal word. N-COUNT: usu pl

spun /spʌn/. **Spun** is the past tense and past participle of **spin**.

spunk /spʌŋk/. **Spunk** is courage; an informal word. *I admired her independence and her spunk.* N-UNCOUNT =guts

spunky /spʌŋki/ **spunkier, spunkiest.** A **spunky** person shows courage; an informal word. *...a spunky girl... She's so spunky and spirited.* ADJ-GRADED =gutsy

spur /spɜːʳ/ **spurs, spurring, spurred** ◆◆◆◇◇

1 If one thing **spurs** you to do another, it encourages you to do it. *It's the money that spurs these fishermen to risk a long ocean journey in their flimsy boats... His friend's plight had spurred him into taking part.* VERB =urge V n to-inf V n to/into n/-ing ► **Spur on** means the same as **spur**. *Their attitude, rather than reining him back, only seemed to spur Philip on... Criticism can be of great use; we may not like it at the time, but it can spur us on to greater things.* PHRASAL VERB V n P V n P to n Also V P n (not pron), V n P to-inf

2 If something **spurs** a change or event, it makes it happen faster or sooner; used in journalism. *The administration may put more emphasis on spurring economic growth... The trade pacts will spur an exodus of US businesses to Mexico.* VERB V n

3 Something that acts as a **spur** to something else encourages a person or organization to do that thing or makes it happen more quickly. *...a belief in competition as a spur to efficiency... Redundancy is the spur for many to embark on new careers.* N-COUNT: usu sing, oft N to n

4 Spurs are small metal wheels with sharp points attached to the heels of a rider's boots. The rider uses them to urge a horse to go faster. N-COUNT: usu pl

5 The **spur** of a hill or mountain is a piece of ground which sticks out from its side. N-COUNT

6 If you do something **on the spur of the moment**, you do it suddenly, without planning it beforehand. *They admitted they had taken a vehicle on the spur of the moment... It wasn't a spur-of-the-moment decision. We discussed it in detail beforehand.* PHRASES PHR after v, PHR n =on impulse

7 If you **win** your **spurs** or **earn** your **spurs**, you achieve a particular status by proving that you can do something skilfully. *Young conductors earn their spurs in a small orchestra or opera house.* V inflects

spurious /spjʊəriəs/ ◆◇◇◇◇

1 Something that is **spurious** seems to be genuine, but is false; used showing disapproval. *He was arrested in 1979 on spurious corruption charges... Quite a lot of allegations of misjustice are spurious.* ADJ-GRADED: usu ADJ n PRAGMATICS =bogus, false

2 A **spurious** argument or analysis is based on faulty reasoning and is therefore probably incorrect; used showing disapproval. *...a spurious framework for analysis... The justification of this chart is entirely spurious.* ADJ-GRADED: usu ADJ n PRAGMATICS =bogus ♦ **spuriously** *These figures were often spuriously computed by selecting particularly favorable sample groups. ...a spuriously scientific book.* ADV-GRADED: ADV adj, ADV with v

spurn /spɜːʳn/ **spurns, spurning, spurned.** If you **spurn** someone or something, you reject them. *He spurned the advice of management consultants... These gestures have been spurned. ...a spurned lover.* ◆◇◇◇◇ VERB =reject V n V-ed

spur-of-the-moment. See **spur**.

spurt /spɜːʳt/ **spurts, spurting, spurted** ◆◇◇◇◇

1 When something **spurts** liquid or fire or when liquid or fire **spurts** from somewhere or something, it comes out quickly in a thin, powerful stream. *They spurted blood all over me. I nearly passed out... He hit her on the head, causing her too to spurt blood. ...a fountain that spurts water nine stories high... I saw flames spurt from the roof.* V-ERG =gush, spray V n V prep Also V ► **Spurt out** means the same as **spurt**. *When the washing machine spurts out water at least we can mop it up... Wear eye protection when opening the container, since it's so easy for contents to spurt out.* PHRASAL VERB ERG V P n (not pron) V P

2 A **spurt** of liquid is a stream of it which comes out of something very forcefully. *A spurt of diesel came from one valve and none from the other.* N-COUNT: oft N of n =jet

3 A **spurt** of activity, effort, or emotion is a sudden, brief period of intense activity, effort, or emotion. *The average boy of 14 years old is only beginning his adolescent growth spurt... I flushed bright red as a spurt of anger flashed through me... The recent spurt in violence has demoralised the public.* N-COUNT: usu with supp =surge

4 If someone or something **spurts** somewhere, they suddenly increase their speed for a short while in order to get there. *The back wheels spun and the van spurted up the last few feet.* VERB V prep/adv ► Also a noun. *These muscles work in a steady state for most of the race except at the end when the athlete puts on a spurt.* N-COUNT

5 If something happens **in spurts**, there are periods of activity followed by periods of inactivity. *The deals came in spurts: three in 1977, none in 1978, three more in 1979.* PHRASE: PHR after v

sputter /spʌtəʳ/ **sputters, sputtering, sputtered**

1 If something such as an engine or a flame **sputters**, it works or burns in an uneven way and makes a series of soft popping sounds. *The truck sputtered and stopped... Engines sputtered to life again... The flame sputters out. ...the sputtering engine.* VERB =splutter V V prep/adv V-ing ► Also a noun. *All I could hear was the sputter of the fire.* N-COUNT: usu N of n

2 If a process, action, or state of affairs **sputters**, it progresses unevenly and with very little force. *The economy is already sputtering, with low or no growth... The battle sputtered to a halt in mid-October... The whole thing sputtered out.* VERB V V prep/adv

3 If you **sputter**, you speak or breathe with difficulty and make soft, spitting sounds, especially if you are agitated or angry. *Stunned, I sputtered, 'What do you mean?'... Our father's face had reddened* VERB =splutter V with quote V V n *with rage and he began to sputter... He began to sputter his reply.*

sputum /spjuːtəm/. **Sputum** is mucus which is coughed up from someone's chest or lungs; a medical term. N-UNCOUNT

spy /spaɪ/ **spies, spying, spied** ◆◆◇◇◇

1 A **spy** is a person whose job is to find out secret information about another country or organization. *He was jailed for five years as an alleged British spy... The spy ring passed secrets to the enemy.* N-COUNT

2 A **spy** satellite or **spy** plane obtains secret information about another country by taking aerial photographs of particular areas. ADJ: ADJ n

3 Someone who **spies** for a country or organization tries to find out secret information about another country or organization. *The agent had spied for East Germany for more than twenty years... Russian intelligence is still spying on Western countries... I never agreed to spy against the United States.* VERB V for n V on n V against n
♦ **spying** *...a ten-year sentence for spying.* N-UNCOUNT

4 If you **spy on** someone, you watch them secretly. *That day he spied on her while pretending to work on the shrubs... He had his wife spied on for evidence in a divorce case.* VERB V on n

5 If you **spy** someone or something, you notice them; a literary use. *He was walking down the street when he spied an old friend.* VERB =spot V n

spymaster /spaɪmɑːstəʳ, -mæs-/ **spymasters.** A **spymaster** is a spy who is in charge of a group of spies. N-COUNT

sq

1 **sq** is used as a written abbreviation for 'square' when you are giving the measurement of an area. *The building provides about 25,500 sq ft of air-conditioned offices.* =square

2 **Sq** is used as a written abbreviation for 'Square' in addresses and on maps and signs. *...Mortons Club, 28 Berkeley Sq, W1.* =square

squabble /skwɒbᵊl/ **squabbles, squabbling, squabbled.** When people **squabble**, they quarrel about something that is not really important. *Mother is devoted to Dad although they squabble all the time... The children were squabbling over the remote-control gadget for the television... My four-year-old squabbles with his friends... In recent months its government has been paralysed by political squabbling.* ► Also a noun. *There have been minor squabbles about phone bills.* ◆◇◇◇◇ V-RECIP =quarrel, bicker pl-n V pl-n V over/about n V with n V-ing N-COUNT

squad /skwɒd/ **squads** ◆◆◆◇◇

1 A **squad** is a section of a police force that is responsible for dealing with a particular type of crime. *The building was evacuated and the bomb squad called... The club is under investigation by the fraud squad.* N-COUNT: usu sing, usu supp N

2 A **squad** is a group of players from which a sports team will be chosen. *Sean O'Leary has been named in the England squad to tour Argentina.* N-COUNT

3 A **squad** of soldiers is a small group of them. *...a squad of commandos.* ● See also **death squad**, **firing squad**, **Flying Squad**, **vice squad**. N-COUNT: oft N of n

squad car, squad cars. A **squad car** is a car used by the police; used mainly in American English. The usual British term is **patrol car**. N-COUNT =patrol car

squaddie /skwɒdi/ **squaddies.** In British English, a **squaddie** is a soldier of the lowest rank in the army; an informal word. N-COUNT

squadron /skwɒdrən/ **squadrons.** A **squadron** is a section of one of the armed forces, especially the air force. *The government said it was preparing a squadron of eighteen Mirage fighter planes.* ◆◇◇◇◇ N-COUNT-COLL

squadron leader, squadron leaders. A **squadron leader** is an officer in the British air force who has a rank above that of flight lieutenant. N-COUNT; N-TITLE

squalid /skwɒlɪd/ ◆◇◇◇◇

1 A **squalid** place is dirty, untidy, and in bad condition. *He followed her up a rickety staircase to a squalid bedsit... The migrants have been living in squalid conditions.* ADJ-GRADED

2 **Squalid** activities are unpleasant and often dishonest. *The Labour Party called the bill 'the most squalid measure ever put before the Commons'. ...the squalid pursuit of profit.* ADJ-GRADED

squall /skwɔːl/ **squalls, squalling, squalled**

1 A **squall** is a sudden strong wind which often causes a brief, violent rain storm or snow storm. *The boat was hit by a squall north of the island.* N-COUNT =storm

2 If a person or animal **squalls**, they make a loud unpleasant noise like the noise made by a crying baby. *There was an infant squalling in the back of the church. ...squalling guitars.* VERB =wail V V-ing

squally /skwɔːli/. In **squally** weather, there are sudden strong winds which often cause brief, violent storms. *The competitors had to contend with squally weather conditions.* ADJ: usu ADJ n =stormy

squalor /skwɒləʳ/. You can refer to squalid conditions or surroundings as **squalor**. *He was out of work and living in squalor.* ◆◇◇◇◇ N-UNCOUNT

squander /skwɒndəʳ/ **squanders, squandering, squandered.** If you **squander** money, resources, or opportunities, you use them in a foolish and wasteful way. *Hooker didn't squander his money on flashy cars or other vices... He had squandered his chances to win.* ◆◇◇◇◇ VERB =waste V n

square /skweəʳ/ **squares, squaring, squared** ◆◆◆◆◇

1 A **square** is a shape with four sides that are all the same length and four corners that are all right angles. *Serve the cake warm or at room temperature, cut in squares... There was a calendar on the wall, with large squares around the dates... Most of the rugs are simple cotton squares.* N-COUNT

2 In a town or city, a **square** is a flat open place, often in the shape of a square. *The house is located in one of Pimlico's prettiest garden squares... The town centre is thick with churches and cafe-lined squares. ...St Mark's Square.* N-COUNT: oft in names after n

3 Something that is **square** has a shape the same as a square or similar to a square. *Round tables seat more people in the same space as a square table... His finger nails were square and cut neatly across.* ADJ-GRADED: usu ADJ n

4 **Square** is used before units of length when mentioning the area of something. For example, if a rectangle is three metres long and two metres wide, its area is six square metres. *Canary Wharf was set to provide 10 million square feet of office space... The Philippines has just 6,000 square kilometres of forest left.* ADJ: ADJ n

5 **Square** is used after units of length when you are giving the length of each side of something that is square in shape. *...a linen cushion cover, 45 cm square. ...two pieces of wood 4 inches square.* ADJ: amount ADJ

6 To **square** a number means to multiply it by itself. For example, **3 squared** is 3 x 3, or 9. **3 squared** is usually written as 3^2. *Take the time in seconds, square it, and multiply by 5.12... A squared plus B squared equals C squared.* VERB V n V-ed

7 The **square** of a number is the number produced when you multiply that number by itself. For example, the square of 3 is 9. *...the square of the speed of light, an exceedingly large number.* N-COUNT: usu with poss

8 If you **square** two different situations or ideas **with** each other or when they **square with** each other, they can be accepted together or they seem compatible. *That explanation squares with the facts, doesn't it... He set out to square his dreams with reality.* V-ERG V with n V n with n

9 If you **square** something **with** someone, you go to them to ask their permission or to check with them that what you are doing is acceptable to them. *I squared it with Dan, who said it was all right so long as I was back next Monday morning... She should have squared things with Jay before she went into this business with Walker.* VERB V n with n

10 See also **squared**; **squarely**.

11 If you say that someone **squares the circle**, you mean that they bring together two things which are normally thought to be so different that they cannot exist together. *He has squared the circle of keeping the City happy and doing something to improve business cash flow... 'Nirvana' squared the circle by making a record that was both superb pop and rock music at the same time.* PHRASES V inflects

12 If you are **back to square one**, you have to start v-link PHR,

dealing with something from the beginning again because the way you were dealing with it has failed. *If your complaint in not upheld, you may feel you are back to square one... We got a phone call from the lawyers and it was back to square one.* PHR after v

13 If you describe someone as a **square peg in a round hole**, you mean that they are completely unsuitable for the job they are doing or the situation they are in. *Taylor is clearly the wrong man for the job – a square peg in a round hole.*

14 ● **fair and square**: see **fair**.

square away. In American English, if you **square away** a problem or a task, you deal with it so that you are free to do something else. *Negotiators have already squared away a lot of the agreements that will be signed at the Earth Summit.* PHRASAL VERB V P n (not pron) Also V n P

square off. If you **square** something **off**, you alter it so that it has the shape of a square. *Peel a thick-skinned orange and square off the ends with a sharp knife. ...white modern buildings that look like squared-off wedding cakes.* PHRASAL VERB V P n (not pron) V-ed P Also V P n

square up. If you **square up** to a problem, person, or situation, you accept that you have to deal with it and take action to do so. *The world's most prestigious insurance company was last night squaring up to take on Tory MPs who have accused it of being riddled with corruption. ...a woman facing serious responsibility, squaring up to the deepest crisis she has yet had to face.* PHRASAL VERB V P V P *to*n

squared /skweəʳd/.

1 Something that is **squared** has the shape of a square, or has a pattern of squares on it. *Draw up a scale floor plan on squared paper, marking in the door opening and windows.* ADJ

2 See also **square**.

square dance, square dances

1 A **square dance** is a traditional American dance in which sets of four couples dance together, beginning the dance in a square formation. N-COUNT

2 A **square dance** is a social event where people dance square dances. N-COUNT

squarely /skweəʳli/ ◆◇◇◇◇

1 **Squarely** means directly and in the middle, rather than indirectly or at an angle. *I kept the gun aimed squarely at his eyes.* ADV: ADV with v =directly

2 If you face something **squarely**, you face it directly, without trying to avoid it. *The management committee have faced the situation squarely... They faced each other squarely as if ready for a fist fight.* ADV: ADV with v

square meal, square meals. A **square meal** is a meal which is big enough to satisfy you. *They haven't had a square meal for four or five days.* N-COUNT

square-rigged. A **square-rigged** sailing ship has large square sails. ADJ: ADJ n

square root, square roots. The **square root** of a number is another number which produces the first number when it is multiplied by itself. For example, the square root of 16 is 4. N-COUNT: usu N *of*num

squash /skwɒʃ/ **squashes, squashing, squashed** ◆◆◇◇◇

1 If someone or something **is squashed**, they are pressed or crushed with such force that they become injured or lose their shape. *Robert was lucky to escape with just a broken foot after being squashed against a fence by a car... Whole neighbourhoods have been squashed flat by shelling... She made clay models and squashed them flat again.* VERB *be*V-ed prep *be*V-ed adj V n adj Also V n

2 If people or things are **squashed into** a place, they are put or pushed into a place where there is not enough room for them to be. *There were 2000 people squashed into her recent show... The stage is squashed into a small corner of the field.* ADJ: v-link ADJ *into* n =cram

3 If you say that getting a number of people into a small space is **a squash**, you mean that it is only just possible for them all to get into it; an informal use. *It all looked a bit of a squash as they squeezed inside the small hatchback.* N-SING: *a*N =squeeze

4 If you **squash** something that is causing you trouble, you put a stop to it, often by force. *The troops would stay in position to squash the first murmur of trouble.* VERB V n

5 **Squash** is a game in which two players hit a small rubber ball against the walls of a court using rackets. N-UNCOUNT

6 In British English, **squash** is a drink made from fruit juice, sugar, and water. Squash is sold in bottles in a concentrated form to which you add water. *...a glass of orange squash.* N-MASS =cordial

7 A **squash** is any vegetable belonging to the marrow family. N-COUNT

squashy /skwɒʃi/. **Squashy** things are soft and able to be squashed easily. *...deep, squashy sofas.* ADJ-GRADED: usu ADJ n

squat /skwɒt/ **squats, squatting, squatted** ◆◇◇◇◇

1 If you **squat**, you lower yourself towards the ground, balancing on your feet with your legs bent. *He squatted, grunting at the pain in his knees... We squatted beside the pool and watched the diver sink slowly down... He came over and squatted on his heels, looking up at the boys.* ► **Squat down** means the same as **squat**. *Albert squatted down and examined it... She had squatted down on her heels.* ► Also a noun. *He bent to a squat and gathered the puppies on his lap.* VERB =crouch V V *on*n Also V PHRASAL VERB V P prep N-SING: *a*N

2 If you describe someone or something as **squat**, you mean they are short and thick, usually in an unattractive way. *Eddie was a short squat fellow in his forties with thinning hair. ...squat stone houses.* ADJ-GRADED: usu ADJ n

3 People who **squat** occupy an unused building or uncultivated land without having a legal right to do so. *You can't simply wander around squatting on other people's property... They earn their living by squatting the land and sharecropping.* VERB V V n

4 A **squat** is an empty building that people are living in illegally, without paying any rent or any property tax. *After returning from Paris, David moved to a squat in Brixton... Thomas now faces eviction from his squat.* N-COUNT

squatter /skwɒtəʳ/ **squatters** ◆◇◇◇◇

1 A **squatter** is someone who lives in an unused building without having a legal right to do so and without paying any rent or any property tax. N-COUNT

2 A **squatter** is someone who occupies unused land, either to farm it or to build a house on it, without having a legal right to do so. *When they returned to Tuol Sakor, they found all the best land taken by squatters.* N-COUNT

squaw /skwɔː/ **squaws.** In the past, people sometimes referred to a North American Indian woman as a **squaw**. Many people now find this word offensive. N-COUNT

squawk /skwɔːk/ **squawks, squawking, squawked**

1 When a bird **squawks**, it makes a loud harsh noise. *I threw pebbles at the hens, and that made them jump and squawk.* ► Also a noun. *A mallard suddenly took wing, rising steeply into the air with an angry squawk.* VERB V N-COUNT

2 If a person **squawks**, they complain loudly, often in a high-pitched, harsh tone; an informal use. *Mr Arbor squawked that the deal was a double-cross... 'Wait for me!' Melanie squawked. 'I'm not staying here alone.'* ► Also a noun. *She gave a loud squawk when the water was poured on her.* VERB V that V with quote Also V N-COUNT

squeak /skwiːk/ **squeaks, squeaking, squeaked** ◆◇◇◇◇

1 If something or someone **squeaks**, they make a short, high-pitched sound. *My boots squeaked a little as I walked... The door squeaked open... She squeaked with delight.* ► Also a noun. *He gave an outraged squeak.* VERB V V adj V *with*n N-COUNT

2 If someone or something **squeaks** through or **squeaks** by, they only just manage to get accepted, to get included in something, or to win something. *Mr Clinton's economic package squeaked through the House of Representatives by 219 votes to 213... In spite of a dismal record at school, she narrowly squeaked into design school.* VERB V prep/adv

3 See also **bubble and squeak**.

squeaky /skwiːki/. Something that is **squeaky** makes squeaking noises. *...squeaky floorboards... He had a squeaky voice.* ADJ-GRADED

squeaky clean; also spelled **squeaky-clean**. If you say that someone is **squeaky clean**, you ADJ-GRADED mean that they live a very moral life and that they do not appear to have any vices; an informal expression. *Maybe this guy isn't so squeaky clean after all. ...his desire to foster a squeaky-clean image.*

squeal /skwiːl/ **squeals, squealing, squealed.** ◆◇◇◇◇ If someone or something **squeals**, they make a long, high-pitched sound. *Jennifer squealed with delight and hugged me... The car's tires squealed again as it sped around the corner.* ► Also a noun. *At that moment there was a squeal of brakes and the angry blowing of a car horn.* VERB =screech, squawk V with n V N-COUNT

squeamish /skwiːmɪʃ/. If you are **squeamish**, you are easily upset by unpleasant sights or situations. *I'm terribly squeamish. I can't bear gory films... I am not squeamish about blood.* ADJ-GRADED: usu v-link ADJ
♦ **squeamishness** *When you've got over your squeamishness, there will be no stopping you.* N-UNCOUNT

squeeze /skwiːz/ **squeezes, squeezing, squeezed** ◆◆◆◇◇
1 If you **squeeze** something, you press it firmly, usually with your hands. *He squeezed her arm reassuringly... Dip the bread briefly in water, then squeeze it dry.* ► Also a noun. *I liked her way of reassuring you with a squeeze of the hand.* VERB V n V n adj N-COUNT: usu sing
2 If you **squeeze** a liquid or a soft substance out of an object, you get the liquid or substance out by pressing the object. *Joe put the plug in the sink and squeezed some detergent over the dishes. ...freshly squeezed lemon juice.* VERB V n V-ed
3 If you **squeeze** your eyes shut or if your eyes **squeeze** shut, you close them tightly, usually because you are frightened or to protect your eyes from something such as strong sunlight. *With a giant whoosh! the raft dropped over the edge. Nancy squeezed her eyes shut and prayed... If you keep your eyes squeezed shut, you'll miss the show... The priest's eyes were squeezed shut against the light.* V-ERG V n adj V adj V-ed
4 If you **squeeze** someone or something somewhere or if they **squeeze** there, they manage to get through or into a small space. *They lowered him gradually into the cockpit. Somehow they squeezed him in the tight space, and strapped him in... Many break-ins are carried out by youngsters who can squeeze through tiny windows.* V-ERG V n prep/adv V prep/adv
5 If you say that getting a number of people into a small space is **a squeeze**, you mean that it is only just possible for them all to get into it; an informal use. *It was a squeeze in the car with five of them... The lift holds six people at a squeeze.* N-SING: a N =squash
6 If you **squeeze** something out of someone, you persuade them to give it to you, although they may be uncooperative or unwilling to do this. *The investigators complained about the difficulties of squeezing information out of residents... The company intends to squeeze further savings from its suppliers.* VERB V n prep
7 If a government **squeezes** the economy, they put strict controls on people's ability to borrow money or on their own departments' freedom to spend money, in order to control the country's rate of inflation. *If a voluntary agreement is not reached the government will squeeze the economy into a severe recession to force inflation down... Defense experts say joint projects are increasingly squeezed by budget pressures.* ► Also a noun. *The CBI also says the squeeze is slowing down inflation.* VERB V n N-SING

squeeze in. If you **squeeze** something **in**, you manage to find time to do it. *The executives squeezed in a few meetings at the hotel before boarding the buses again.* PHRASAL VERB V P n (not pron) Also V n P

squeeze out. If someone or something **is squeezed out**, they are no longer included in something they were formerly involved in. *Other directors appear happy that Lord Hollick has been squeezed out... Latin and Greek will be squeezed out of school timetables.* PHRASAL VERB usu passive be V-ed P be V-ed P of n

squelch /skweltʃ/ **squelches, squelching, squelched**
1 To **squelch** means to make a wet, sucking sound, like the sound you make when you are walking on wet, muddy ground. *He squelched across the turf... His sodden trousers were clinging to his shins and his shoes squelched.* VERB V prep/adv V
2 If you **squelch** something that is causing you trouble, for example rumours or opposition, you firmly put a stop to it; an informal use. *The President wants to squelch any perception that the meeting is an attempt to negotiate.* VERB =squash V n

squib /skwɪb/ **squibs.** You can describe something such as an event or a performance as a **damp squib** when it is expected to be interesting, exciting, or impressive, but fails to be any of these things. *The all-party meeting was a damp squib.* PHRASE: N inflects, usu v-link PHR

squid /skwɪd/ **squids; squid** can also be used as the plural form. A **squid** is a sea creature with a long soft body and many tentacles. ► **Squid** is pieces of this creature eaten as food. *Add the prawns and squid and cook for 2 minutes on a medium heat.* ◆◇◇◇◇ N-COUNT N-UNCOUNT

squidgy /skwɪdʒi/. In British English, something that is **squidgy** is soft and can be squashed easily; an informal word. *...the squidgy end of a melon. ...a squidgy sofa.* ADJ-GRADED: usu ADJ n =squashy

squiggle /skwɪgᵊl/ **squiggles.** A **squiggle** is a line that bends and curls in an irregular way. N-COUNT

squiggly /skwɪgəli/. **Squiggly** lines are lines that bend and curl in an irregular way. *He drew three squiggly lines.* ADJ-GRADED

squint /skwɪnt/ **squints, squinting, squinted** ◆◇◇◇◇
1 If you **squint** at something, you look at it with your eyes partly closed. *The girl squinted at the photograph... The man squinted up at him... The bright sunlight made me squint... He squinted his eyes and looked at the floor.* VERB V prep/adv V V n
2 If someone has a **squint**, their eyes look in different directions from each other. N-COUNT

squire /skwaɪəʳ/ **squires**
1 In former times, the **squire** of an English village was the man who owned most of the land in it. N-COUNT; N-TITLE
2 In British English, some men use **squire** to address a man they do not know in a friendly but respectful way; an informal use. *Hard luck, squire.* N-VOC

squirm /skwɜːʳm/ **squirms, squirming, squirmed** ◆◇◇◇◇
1 If you **squirm**, you move your body from side to side, usually because you are nervous or uncomfortable. *He had squirmed and wriggled and screeched when his father had washed his face... He gave a feeble shrug and tried to squirm free... He squirmed out of the straps of his backpack before collapsing into a chair.* VERB =wriggle V V adj V adv/prep
2 If you **squirm**, you are very embarrassed or ashamed. *Mentioning religion is a sure way to make him squirm. ...the type of awful occasion that makes politicians squirm with embarrassment.* VERB V V with n

squirrel /skwɪrəl, AM skwɜːrəl/ **squirrels, squirrelling, squirrelled;** spelled **squirreling, squirreled** in American English. A **squirrel** is a small furry animal with a long bushy tail. Squirrels live mainly in trees. ◆◇◇◇◇ N-COUNT

squirrel away. If you **squirrel** things **away**, you hide or store them so that you can use them in the future. *She says the kid's been squirrelling money away like there's no tomorrow... Arlott squirrelled away books, pictures and porcelain plates.* PHRASAL VERB V n P V P n (not pron)

squirt /skwɜːʳt/ **squirts, squirting, squirted** ◆◇◇◇◇
1 If you **squirt** a liquid somewhere or if it **squirts** somewhere, the liquid comes out of a narrow opening in a thin fast stream. *Norman cut open his pie and squirted tomato sauce into it... The water squirted from its throat... The liquid is squirted out in powerful jets.* ► Also a noun. *It just needs a little squirt of oil.* V-ERG V n prep/adv V prep/adv be V-ed adv/prep N-COUNT: usu N of n
2 If you **squirt** something **with** a liquid, you squirt the liquid at it. *They squirted the politicians with manure... Its linings were simply squirted with oil.* VERB V n with n

Sr. **Sr** is a written abbreviation for 'Senior', and is written after a man's name. It is used in order to distinguish a man from his son when they both have the same name. *...Donald Cunningham, Sr.*

St; the form **SS** is used as the plural for meaning 2.
1 **St** is a written abbreviation for 'Street'. ...*116 Princess St.*
2 **St** is a written abbreviation for 'Saint'. ...*St Thomas. ...the Church of SS Cornelius and Cyprian.*

st. **st** is used as a written abbreviation for 'stone' when you are mentioning someone's weight. *He weighs 11st 8lb.*

-st. SUFFIX You add **-st** to numbers written in figures and ending in 1 (but not 11) in order to form ordinal numbers. ...*Sunday 1st August 1993. ...the 101st Airborne Division.*

stab /stæb/ **stabs, stabbing, stabbed** ◆◆◇◇◇
1 VERB If someone **stabs** you, they push a knife or sharp object into your body. *Somebody stabbed him in the stomach... Stephen was stabbed to death in an unprovoked attack nearly five months ago.* [V n; V to n]
2 VERB If you **stab** something or **stab at** it, you push at it with your finger or with something pointed that you are holding. *Bess stabbed a slice of cucumber... Goldstone flipped through the pages and stabbed his thumb at the paragraph he was looking for... He stabbed at the omelette with his fork.* [V n; V n at n; V at n]
3 N-SING: a N at n/-ing If you have **a stab at** something, you try to do it; an informal use. *Several tennis stars have had a stab at acting.*
4 N-SING: a N of n You can refer to a sudden, usually unpleasant feeling as **a stab of** that feeling; a literary use. *She felt a stab of pity for him.*
5 PHRASE: V inflects If you say that someone has **stabbed** you **in the back**, you mean that they have done something very harmful to you when you thought that you could trust them. You can refer to an action of this kind as **a stab in the back**. *She felt betrayed, as though her daughter had stabbed her in the back... He denounced the defection as a stab in the back.*
● **a stab in the dark**: see **dark**.

stabbing /stæbɪŋ/ **stabbings** ◆◇◇◇◇
1 N-COUNT A **stabbing** is an incident in which someone stabs someone else with a knife.
2 ADJ: ADJ n A **stabbing** pain is a sudden sharp pain. *He was struck by a stabbing pain in his midriff.*

stability /stəbɪlɪti/. See **stable**.

stabilize /steɪbɪlaɪz/ **stabilizes, stabilizing, stabilized;** also spelled **stabilise** in British English. ◆◆◇◇◇ V-ERG If something **stabilizes**, or if someone or something **stabilizes** it, it becomes stable. *Although her illness is serious, her condition is beginning to stabilize... Officials hope the move will stabilize exchange rates... I believe he would have had a stabilising effect on the team.* [V; V n; V-ing]
♦ **stabilization** /steɪbɪlaɪzeɪʃᵊn/ N-UNCOUNT ...*the stabilisation of property prices.*

stabilizer /steɪbɪlaɪzəʳ/ **stabilizers;** also spelled **stabiliser**. N-COUNT A **stabilizer** is a device, mechanism, or chemical that stabilizes something.

stable /steɪbᵊl/ **stabler, stablest; stables, stabling, stabled** ◆◆◆◆◇
1 ADJ-GRADED If something is **stable**, it is not likely to change or come to an end suddenly. *The price of oil should remain stable for the rest of 1992. ...a stable marriage.*
♦ **stability** /stəbɪlɪti/ N-UNCOUNT *It was a time of political stability and progress.*
2 ADJ-GRADED ≠unstable If someone has a **stable** personality, they are calm and reasonable and they do not have frequent changes of mood. *Their characters are fully formed and they are both very stable children.*
3 ADJ-GRADED You can describe someone who is seriously ill as **stable** when their condition has stopped getting worse. *The injured man was in a stable condition.*
4 ADJ-GRADED Chemical substances are described as **stable** when they tend to remain in the same chemical or atomic state; a technical use. *The less stable compounds were converted into a compound called Delta-A THC.*
5 ADJ-GRADED =secure ≠unstable If an object is **stable**, it is firmly fixed in position and is not likely to move or fall. *This structure must be stable.*
6 N-COUNT A **stable** or **stables** is a building in which horses are kept.
7 N-COUNT A **stable** or **stables** is an organization that breeds and trains racehorses. *Miss Curling won on two horses from Mick Trickey's stable.*
8 VB: usu passive When horses **are stabled**, they are put into a stable. *The animals had been fed and stabled... You should allow your stabled horse a couple of hours' freedom per day.* [be V-ed; V-ed]
9 N-COUNT: with supp, usu N of n You can say that someone has a **stable** of people when they manage and promote the careers of that group of people. *As chief executive, he assembled a polished stable of celebrities.*
10 PHRASE: V inflects If you say that someone has **closed** or **shut the stable door after the horse has bolted**, you mean that they have taken a precaution against something happening but they have done so too late to prevent damage being done.

stable boy, stable boys. N-COUNT A **stable boy** is the same as a **stable lad**.

stable lad, stable lads; also spelled **stable-lad**. N-COUNT A **stable lad** is a young man who works in a stable looking after the horses.

stablemate /steɪbᵊlmeɪt/ **stablemates**
1 N-COUNT: usu poss N **Stablemates** are race horses that come from the same stables and often compete against each other. *The head groom is responsible for seeing that Milton and his stablemates have safe journeys.*
2 N-COUNT: poss N A person's **stablemate** is someone who is managed by the same organization. A product's **stablemate** is something which is produced by the same company. *Tomorrow he will play his Cuemasters stablemate.*

stab wound, stab wounds. N-COUNT A **stab wound** is a wound that someone has when they have been stabbed with a knife.

staccato /stəkɑːtoʊ/
1 ADJ-GRADED: usu ADJ n A **staccato** noise consists of a series of short, sharp, separate sounds. *He spoke in Arabic, a short staccato burst. ...the staccato chattering of several machine-guns.*
2 ADV-GRADED: ADV after v The instruction **staccato** on a piece of music means that the notes should be played or sung very briefly with gaps between them. ► ADJ-GRADED Also an adjective. ...*a rapid staccato passage.*

stack /stæk/ **stacks, stacking, stacked** ◆◆◇◇◇
1 N-COUNT: usu N of n A **stack** of things is a pile of them. *There were stacks of books on the bedside table and floor.*
2 VERB If you **stack** a number of things, you arrange them in neat piles. *Mme Cathiard was stacking the clean bottles in crates... They are stacked neatly in piles of three.* [V n; V-ed] ► PHRASAL VERB **Stack up** means the same as **stack**. *He ordered them to stack up pillows behind his back. ...plates of delicious food stacked up on the counters.* [V P n (not pron); V-ed P; Also V n P]
3 N-PLURAL: N of n =loads If you say that someone has **stacks of** something, you mean that they have a lot of it; an informal use. *If the job's that good, you'll have stacks of money.*
4 VERB =pack If someone in authority **stacks** an organization or body, they fill it with their own supporters so that the decisions it makes will be the ones they want it to make; used mainly in American English. *They said they were going to stack the court with anti-abortion judges... The committee is stacked with members from energy-producing states.* [V n with n; Also V n]
5 See also **stacked**; **chimney stack**.
6 PHRASE: V inflects, PHR n If you say that **the odds are stacked against** someone, or that particular factors **are stacked against** them, you mean that they are unlikely to succeed in what they want to do because the conditions are not favourable. *The odds are stacked against civilians getting a fair trial... Everything seems to be stacked against us.*

stack up PHRASAL VERB
1 no passive =compare If you ask how one person or thing **stacks up** against other people or things, you are asking how the one compares with the others; used mainly in informal American English. *The British will be out to see how they stack up to the competition... How does this drug stack up when used on children?.* [V P against/to n; V P]
2 See **stack** 2.

stacked /stækt/. ADJ: usu v-link ADJ, ADJ with n If a place or surface is **stacked with** objects, it is filled with piles of them. *Shops in Ho Chi Minh City are stacked with goods. ...his house has 20 rooms stacked with paintings.*

stadium /steɪdiəm/ **stadiums** or **stadia** /steɪdiə/. A **stadium** is a large sports ground with rows of seats all round it. *...a baseball stadium... A concert in his honour will take place at Wembley Stadium.* ◆◆◆◇◇ N-COUNT: oft in names after n

staff /stɑːf, stæf/ **staffs, staffing, staffed** ◆◆◆◆◆
1 The **staff** of an organization are the people who work for it. *The staff were very good... The outpatient program has a staff of six people... He thanked his staff. ...members of staff... Many employers seek diversity in their staffs.* ● See also **Chief of Staff**. N-COUNT-COLL
2 People who are part of a particular staff are often referred to as **staff**. *10 staff were allocated to the task... He had the complete support of hospital staff.* N-PLURAL =employees
3 If an organization **is staffed** by particular people, they are the people who work for it. *They are staffed by volunteers... The center is staffed with highly trained physicians... The centre is staffed at all times... Some have regular clinics staffed by nursing officers.* ♦ **staffed** *The house allocated to them was pleasant and spacious, and well-staffed. ...poorly staffed hotels.* ● see also **short-staffed**. VB: usu passive be V-ed by/with n be V-ed V-ed; ADJ: adv ADJ
4 A **staff** is a strong stick or pole. N-COUNT

staffer /stɑːfəʳ, stæf-/ **staffers.** A **staffer** is a member of staff, especially in political organizations or in journalism; used mainly in American English. *The Sky News TV station is largely run by ex-BBC news staffers.* ◆◇◇◇◇ N-COUNT: usu n N

staffing /stɑːfɪŋ, stæf-/. **Staffing** refers to the number of workers employed to work in a particular organization or building. *Staffing levels in prisons are too low.* ◆◇◇◇◇ N-UNCOUNT

staff nurse, staff nurses. A **staff nurse** is a hospital nurse whose rank is just below that of a sister or charge nurse. N-COUNT

staff officer, staff officers. In the army and air-force, a **staff officer** is an officer who works for a commander or in the headquarters. N-COUNT

staff sergeant, staff sergeants; also spelled **Staff Sergeant**. In the British and US armies, a **staff sergeant** is a soldier who ranks just above sergeant. *His father is a staff sergeant in the army. ...Staff Sergeant Robert Daily.* N-COUNT; N-TITLE

stag /stæg/ **stags.** A **stag** is an adult male deer belonging to one of the larger species of deer. Stags usually have large branch-like horns called antlers. ◆◇◇◇◇ N-COUNT

stage /steɪdʒ/ **stages, staging, staged** ◆◆◆◆◆
1 A **stage** of an activity, process, or period is one part of it. *The way children talk about or express their feelings depends on their age and stage of development... Mr Douglas Hurd has arrived in Greece on the final stage of a tour which also included Egypt and Israel.* N-COUNT: usu with supp =phase
2 In a theatre, the **stage** is an area where actors or other entertainers perform. *The road crew needed more than 24 hours to move and rebuild the stage after a concert... I went on stage and did my show.* N-COUNT: also on N
3 You can refer to acting and the production of plays in a theatre as **the stage**. *Madge did not want to put her daughter on the stage... He was the first comedian I ever saw on the stage.* N-SING: the N
4 If someone **stages** a play or other show, they organize and present a performance of it. *Maya Angelou first staged the play 'And I Still Rise' in the late 1970s.* VERB =put on V n
5 If you **stage** an event or ceremony, you organize it and usually take part in it. *Russian workers have staged a number of strikes in protest at the republic's declaration of independence... At the middle of this year the government staged a huge military parade.* VERB =hold V n
6 You can refer to a particular area of activity as a particular **stage**, especially when you are talking about politics. *He hoped Mr Shevardnadze would not leave the political stage... Mr Li is now a more confident man and China a less isolated country on the international stage.* N-SING: usu supp N =arena
7 ● to **set the stage**: see **set**.

stagecoach /steɪdʒkoutʃ/ **stagecoaches;** also spelled **stage-coach**. **Stagecoaches** were large carriages pulled by horses which carried passengers and mail. N-COUNT: also by N

stagecraft /steɪdʒkrɑːft, -kræft/. **Stagecraft** is skill in writing or producing or directing plays in the theatre. N-UNCOUNT

stage direction, stage directions. Stage directions are the notes in the text of a play which say what the actors should do. N-COUNT

stage door, stage doors. The **stage door** of a theatre is the entrance used by actors and actresses and by employees of the theatre. N-COUNT: usu the N in sing

stage fright; also spelled **stage-fright**. **Stage fright** is a feeling of fear or nervousness that some people have just before they appear in front of an audience. N-UNCOUNT

stagehand /steɪdʒhænd/ **stagehands;** also spelled **stage hand**. A **stagehand** is a person whose job is to move the scenery and equipment on the stage in a theatre. N-COUNT

stage left. **Stage left** is the left-hand side of the stage for an actor standing facing the audience. *He entered stage left.* ADV: usu ADV after v, also prep ADV

stage-manage, stage-manages, stage-managing, stage-managed. If someone **stage-manages** an event, they carefully organize and control it, rather than let it happen spontaneously; used showing disapproval. *Some radicals may oppose him in protest at the attempt of his supporters to stage manage the congress... Today's council sessions have been carefully stage-managed to avoid embarrassing disclosures or signs of internal dissent. ...a stage-managed demonstration.* VERB PRAGMATICS V n V-ed

stage manager, stage managers; also spelled **stage-manager**. At a theatre, a **stage manager** is the person who is responsible for the scenery and lights and for the way that actors or other performers move about and use the stage during a performance. N-COUNT

stage name, stage names. A **stage name** is a name that an actor or entertainer uses professionally instead of his or her real name. *Under the stage name of Beverly Brooks, Patricia had small parts in several British films.* N-COUNT

stage right. **Stage right** is the right-hand side of the stage for an actor standing facing the audience. *Two armies are situated stage right and stage left with an open area separating them.* ADV: usu ADV after v, also prep ADV

stage-struck; also spelled **stagestruck**. Someone who is **stage-struck** is fascinated by the theatre and wants to become an actor or actress. ADJ-GRADED

stage whisper, stage whispers; also spelled **stage-whisper**. A **stage whisper** is a loud whisper that is meant to be heard by several people. N-COUNT

stagflation /stægfleɪʃᵊn/. If an economy is suffering from **stagflation**, inflation is high but there is no corresponding increase in demand for goods or in employment. N-UNCOUNT

stagger /stægəʳ/ **staggers, staggering, staggered** ◆◇◇◇◇
1 If you **stagger**, you walk very unsteadily, for example because you are ill or drunk. *He lost his balance, staggered back against the rail and toppled over... He was staggering and had to lean on the bar.* VERB V adv/prep V
2 If you say that someone or something **staggers** on, you mean that it is only just succeeds in continuing. *Truman allowed him to stagger on for nearly another two years. ...a government that staggered from crisis to crisis.* VERB V adv/prep
3 If something **staggers** you, it surprises you very much. *The whole thing staggers me.* ♦ **staggered** *I was simply staggered by the heat of the Argentinian high-summer.* VERB V n; ADJ-GRADED: v-link ADJ =astounded
4 To **stagger** things such as people's holidays or hours of work means to arrange them so that they do not all happen at the same time. *During the past few years the government has staggered the summer vacation periods for students.* VERB V n
5 See also **staggering**.

staggering /stægərɪŋ/. Something that is **staggering** is very surprising. *...a three-year contract reputed to be worth a staggering £25,000-a-* ◆◆◇◇◇ ADJ-GRADED =astounding *week... The results have been quite staggering.* ♦ **staggeringly** *The South Pole expedition proved to be staggeringly successful.* ADV-GRADED: ADV adj =astoundingly

staging post, staging posts; also spelled **staging-post.**
1 A place that is a **staging post** on a long journey is where people who are making that journey usually stop, for example to rest or to get new supplies. *The island is a staging-post for many visiting yachts on their way south.* N-COUNT
2 If you describe an action or achievement as a **staging post**, you mean that it helps you reach a particular goal that you have. *Privatisation is a necessary staging post to an open market.* N-COUNT

stagnant /stægnənt/ ◆◇◇◇◇
1 If something such as a business or society is **stagnant**, there is little activity or change; used showing disapproval. *He is seeking advice on how to revive the stagnant economy... Mass movements are often a factor in the awakening and renovation of stagnant societies.* ADJ-GRADED PRAGMATICS
2 **Stagnant** water is not flowing, and is therefore often dirty, smelly, and unhealthy. ADJ

stagnate /stægneɪt, AM stægneɪt/ **stagnates, stagnating, stagnated.** If something such as a business or society **stagnates**, it becomes inactive or unchanging; used showing disapproval. *Industrial production is stagnating... His career had stagnated.* ♦ **stagnation** /stægneɪʃᵊn/ *...the stagnation of the steel industry.* ◆◇◇◇◇ VERB PRAGMATICS V N-UNCOUNT

stag night, stag nights. A **stag night** is a party for a man who is getting married very soon, to which only men are invited. N-COUNT

stag party, stag parties. A **stag party** is the same as a **stag night**. N-COUNT

staid /steɪd/. If you say that someone or something is **staid**, you mean that they are serious, dull, and rather old-fashioned. *...a staid seaside resort.* ADJ-GRADED

stain /steɪn/ **stains, staining, stained** ◆◆◇◇◇
1 A **stain** is a mark on something that is difficult to remove. *Remove stains by soaking in a mild solution of bleach. ...a black stain.* N-COUNT: oft supp N
2 If a liquid **stains** something, the thing becomes coloured or marked by the liquid. *Some foods can stain the teeth, as of course can smoking.* ♦ **stained** *His clothing was stained with mud.* ♦ **-stained** *...ink-stained fingers.* VERB V n ADJ-GRADED: usu v-link ADJ COMB in ADJ

stained glass; also spelled **stained-glass.** **Stained glass** consists of pieces of glass of different colours which are fixed together to make decorative windows or other objects. ◆◇◇◇◇ N-UNCOUNT

stainless steel /steɪnləs stiːl/. **Stainless steel** is a metal made from steel and chromium which does not rust. *...a stainless steel sink.* ◆◇◇◇◇ N-UNCOUNT

stair /steəʳ/ **stairs** ◆◆◇◇◇
1 **Stairs** are a set of steps inside a building which go from one floor to another. *Nancy began to climb the stairs... We walked up a flight of stairs... He learned to walk safely up and down stairs... He stopped at the top of the stairs. ...a stair carpet.* N-PLURAL
2 A **stair** is a flight of stairs; a literary use. *I followed her down the stair.* N-SING =staircase
3 A **stair** is one of the steps in a flight of stairs. *Terry was sitting on the bottom stair.* N-COUNT

staircase /steəʳkeɪs/ **staircases.** A **staircase** is a set of stairs inside a building. *They walked down the staircase together.* ◆◇◇◇◇ N-COUNT

stairway /steəʳweɪ/ **stairways.** A **stairway** is a staircase or a flight of steps, inside or outside a building. ◆◇◇◇◇ N-COUNT

stairwell /steəʳwel/ **stairwells.** The **stairwell** is the part of a building that contains the staircase. N-COUNT

stake /steɪk/ **stakes, staking, staked** ◆◆◆◆◇
1 If something is **at stake**, it is being risked and might be lost or damaged if you are not successful. *The tension was naturally high for a game with so much at stake... At stake is the success or failure of world trade talks... At stake are more than 20,000 jobs in Britain's aerospace sector.* PHRASE =at risk
2 The **stakes** involved in a contest or a risky action are the things that can be gained or lost. *The game was usually played for high stakes between two large groups... By arresting the organisation's two top leaders the government and the army have now raised the stakes... For Mr Gorbachev the political stakes could hardly have been higher.* N-PLURAL: oft supp N
3 If you **stake** something such as your money or your reputation on the result of something, you risk your money or reputation on it. *He has staked his political future on an election victory... He has staked his reputation on the outcome.* VERB =risk V n on n
4 If you have a **stake in** something such as a business, it matters to you, for example because you own part of it or because its success or failure will affect you. *Mr Maude said China had a growing economic stake in Hong Kong's continued success... Detectives now believe the Mafia also had a stake in the plot and killed him when it went wrong.* N-COUNT: N in n =investment
5 You can use **stakes** to refer to something that is like a contest. For example, you can refer to the choosing of a leader as **the** leadership **stakes**. *Britain lags behind in the European childcare stakes.* N-PLURAL: the supp N
6 A **stake** is a pointed wooden post which is pushed into the ground, for example in order to support a young tree. N-COUNT =post
7 If you **stake a claim**, you say that something is yours or that you have a right to it. *Jane is determined to stake her claim as an actress... Baguet's success staked his claim for a place in Belgium's world championship team.* PHRASE: V inflects

stake out. If you **stake out** a position that you are stating or a claim that you are making, you are defending the boundaries or limits of the position or claim. *Those who want to take child abuse seriously today must stake out a humane child protection practice... The time has come for Hindus to stake out their claim to their own homeland.* PHRASAL VERB V P n (not pron)

stakeholder /steɪkhouldəʳ/ **stakeholders.** **Stakeholders** are people who have an interest in a company's or organization's affairs. N-COUNT

stake out, stake outs. If police officers are on a **stake out**, they are secretly watching a building for evidence of criminal activity. N-COUNT

stalactite /stæləktaɪt, AM stəlæk-/ **stalactites.** A **stalactite** is a long piece of rock which hangs down from the roof of a cave. Stalactites are formed by the dripping of water containing lime. N-COUNT

stalagmite /stæləgmaɪt, AM stəlæg-/ **stalagmites.** A **stalagmite** is a long piece of rock which sticks up from the floor of a cave. Stalagmites are formed by the dripping of water containing lime. N-COUNT

stale /steɪl/ **staler, stalest** ◆◇◇◇◇
1 **Stale** food is no longer fresh or good to eat. *Their daily diet consisted of a lump of stale bread, a bowl of rice and stale water.* ADJ-GRADED ≠fresh
2 **Stale** air or smells are unpleasant because they are no longer fresh. *A layer of smoke hung low in the stale air. ...the smell of stale sweat.* ADJ-GRADED
3 If you feel **stale**, you are bored because you have no new ideas or enthusiasm for what you are doing. *I believe in progression, in taking risks, in never getting stale.* ADJ-GRADED: v-link ADJ =jaded
4 If you say that a place, an activity, or an idea is **stale**, you mean that is has become boring because it is always the same. *Her relationship with Mark has become stale... Labour, said Mr Baker, were sticking to stale ideas.* ADJ-GRADED

stalemate /steɪlmeɪt/ **stalemates** ◆◇◇◇◇
1 **Stalemate** is a situation in which neither side in an argument or contest can win or in which no progress is possible. *There have been hopes that Mr Brooke's initiative could break the political stalemate in Northern Ireland... He said the war had reached a stalemate and that a political accord was the only solution.* N-VAR =impasse, deadlock
2 In chess, **stalemate** is a position in which a player cannot make any move which is permitted by the rules, so that the game ends and no one wins. N-VAR

stalk /stɔːk/ **stalks, stalking, stalked** ◆◆◇◇◇
1 The **stalk** of a flower, leaf, or fruit is the thin part that joins it to the plant or tree. *A single pale blue flower grows up from each joint on a long stalk. ...corn stalks.* N-COUNT: usu with supp =stem

2 If you **stalk** a person or a wild animal, you follow them quietly in order to kill them, catch them, or observe them carefully. *He stalks his victims like a hunter after a deer.* VERB =trail, track V n

3 If you **stalk** somewhere, you walk there in a stiff, proud, or angry way. *If his patience is tried at meetings he has been known to stalk out.* VERB V adv/prep

4 If something bad or dangerous **stalks** a place, it moves menacingly through it, causing death or disaster; a literary use. *The spectre of neo fascism, as he put it, was stalking the streets of Sofia and other big cities.* VERB V n

stalker /stɔːkəʳ/ **stalkers.** A **stalker** is someone who has become obsessed with a person, often a famous person whom they do not know or someone they used to have a relationship with, and has begun to pester and harass that person in a frightening way, for example by constantly telephoning them or by following them everywhere they go. N-COUNT

stalking horse, stalking horses

1 If you describe someone or something as a **stalking horse**, you mean that it is being used to obtain a temporary advantage so that someone can get what they really want; used showing disapproval. *The successful applicants will almost certainly use victory as a stalking horse for an altogether more lucrative prize.* N-COUNT PRAGMATICS

2 In politics, a **stalking horse** is someone who stands against a leader in order to see how strong the opposition is. The stalking horse then withdraws in favour of a stronger challenger. *The possibility of another stalking horse challenge this autumn cannot be ruled out.* N-COUNT: oft N n

stall /stɔːl/ **stalls, stalling, stalled** ◆◆◇◇◇

1 If a process **stalls**, or if someone or something **stalls** it, the process stops but may continue at a later time. *The Social Democratic Party has vowed to try to stall the bill until the current session ends. ...but the peace process stalled... Negotiations remained stalled yesterday in New York.* V-ERG V n V V-ed

2 If you **stall**, you try to avoid doing something until later. *Some parties have accused the governor of stalling... Thomas had spent all week stalling over his decision.* VERB V V *over/on* n

3 If you **stall** someone, you prevent them from doing something until a later time. *Shop manager Brian Steel stalled the man until the police arrived.* VERB V n

4 If a vehicle **stalls** or if you accidentally **stall** it, the engine stops suddenly. *The engine stalled... Your foot falls off the pedal and you stall the car.* V-ERG V V n

5 A **stall** is a large table on which you put goods that you want to sell, or information that you want to give people. *...market stalls selling local fruits.* N-COUNT =stand

6 **The stalls** in a theatre or concert hall are the seats on the ground floor directly in front of the stage; used mainly in British English. N-PLURAL: *the* N

7 A **stall** is a small enclosed area in a room which is used for a particular purpose, for example a shower; used in American English. N-COUNT =cubicle

stallholder /stɔːlhouldəʳ/ **stallholders.** A **stallholder** is a person who sells goods at a stall in a market. N-COUNT

stallion /stæliən/ **stallions.** A **stallion** is a male horse, especially one kept for breeding. ◆◇◇◇◇ N-COUNT

stalwart /stɔːlwəʳt/ **stalwarts** ◆◇◇◇◇

1 A **stalwart** is a loyal and hard-working worker or supporter of an organization, especially of a political party. *His free-trade policies aroused suspicion among Tory stalwarts... Moving to Germany, he became a stalwart of the revered Kurt Edelhagen Orchestra.* N-COUNT: usu with supp

2 A **stalwart** supporter or worker is loyal, steady, and completely reliable. *...a stalwart supporter of the colonial government... The stalwart volunteers marched in this morning ready to go to work.* ADJ-GRADED: usu ADJ n

3 A **stalwart** man is strong and sturdy; an old-fashioned or formal use. *I knew I was never in any danger with my stalwart bodyguard around me.* ADJ: ADJ n

stamen /steɪmen/ **stamens.** The **stamens** of a flower are the small, delicate stalks which grow at the flower's centre and produce pollen. N-COUNT

stamina /stæmɪnə/. **Stamina** is the physical or mental energy needed to do a tiring activity for a long time. *You have to have a lot of stamina to be a top-class dancer.* ◆◇◇◇◇ N-UNCOUNT =resilience

stammer /stæməʳ/ **stammers, stammering, stammered** ◆◇◇◇◇

1 If you **stammer**, you speak with difficulty, hesitating and repeating words or sounds. *Five per cent of children stammer at some point... 'Forgive me,' I stammered... People cursed and stammered apologies.* ♦ **stammering** *Of all speech impediments stammering is probably the most embarrassing.* VERB V V with quote V n N-UNCOUNT

2 Someone who has a **stammer** tends to stammer when they speak. *A speech-therapist cured his stammer.* N-SING

stamp /stæmp/ **stamps, stamping, stamped** ◆◆◆◇◇

1 A **stamp** or a **postage stamp** is a small piece of gummed paper which you stick on an envelope or parcel before you post it to pay for the cost of the postage. *...a book of stamps... It's FREEPOST, so there's no need for a stamp. ...two first class stamps.* ● see also **food stamp**. N-COUNT

2 A **stamp** is a small block of wood or metal which has a pattern or a group of letters on one side. You press it onto an pad of ink and then onto a piece of paper in order to produce a mark on the paper. The mark that you produce is also called a **stamp**. *...a date stamp and an ink pad... You may live only where the stamp in your passport says you may.* N-COUNT

3 If you **stamp** a mark or word on an object, you press the mark or word onto the object using a stamp or other device. *Car manufacturers stamp a vehicle identification number at several places on new cars to help track down stolen vehicles... In a department store when a gift voucher is exchanged it's stamped with the details of the store to cancel it... 'Eat before JULY 14' was stamped on the label.* VERB V n prep

4 If you **stamp** or **stamp** your foot, you lift your foot and put it down very hard on the ground, for example because you are angry or because your feet are cold. *Often he teased me till my temper went and I stamped and screamed, feeling furiously helpless... His foot stamped down on the accelerator... She stamped her feet on the pavement to keep out the cold.* ► Also a noun. *...hearing the creak of a door and the stamp of cold feet.* VERB V V adv/prep V n prep/adv Also V n N-COUNT: usu sing

5 If you **stamp** somewhere, you walk there putting your feet down very hard on the ground because you are angry. *'I'm going before things get any worse!' he shouted as he stamped out of the bedroom... Overweight and sweating in the humid weather, she stamped from room to room.* VERB =stomp V prep/adv

6 If you **stamp on** something, you put your foot down on it very hard. *He received the original ban last week after stamping on the referee's foot during the supercup final.* VERB =trample V *on* n

7 If something bears the **stamp** of a particular quality or person, it clearly has that quality or was done by that person. *...lawns and flowerbeds that bore the stamp of years of confident care... Most of us want to make our home a familiar place and put the stamp of our personality on its walls.* N-SING: usu *the* N *of* n =hallmark, mark

8 A quality, feature, or action that **stamps** someone or something **as** a particular thing shows clearly that they are this thing. *I talked to social workers and the police – that had stamped me as a bad woman... Chris Boardman stamped himself as the 4,000m favourite by setting the world's fastest outdoor time in Barcelona last night.* VERB =brand, mark V n *as* n V pron-refl *as* n

9 See also **rubber stamp**. ● **stamp of approval**: see **approval**.

stamp out. If you **stamp** something **out**, you put an end to it. *Dr Muffett stressed that he was opposed to bullying in schools and that action would be taken to stamp it out. ...on-the-spot fines to stamp the problems out.* PHRASAL VERB V n P Also V P n (not pron)

stamp on. If someone **stamps on** a dishonest or undesirable activity, they act immediately tc stop it happening or spreading. *The tone of her voice was designed to stamp on this topic of conversation once and for all... Mrs Amaury's story had to be stamped on before it got any further... The govern-* PHRASAL VERB V P n *ment's first duty is to defend the currency by stamping on inflation.*

stamp collecting. **Stamp collecting** is the hobby of building up a collection of stamps. N-UNCOUNT =philately

stamp duty. In Britain, **stamp duty** is a tax that you pay to the government when you buy a house. ◆◇◇◇◇ N-UNCOUNT

stamped /stæmpt/. A **stamped** envelope or parcel has a stamp stuck on it. ADJ: usu ADJ n

stamped addressed envelope, stamped addressed envelopes. A **stamped addressed envelope** is an envelope on which you have stuck a stamp and written your own name and address. You send it to an organization or a person so that they can use it to send you something without having to pay the cost of posting it to you. The abbreviation **s.a.e.** is also used. ◆◇◇◇◇ N-COUNT

stampede /stæmpiːd/ **stampedes, stampeding, stampeded** ◆◇◇◇◇

1 If there is a **stampede**, a group of people or animals run in a wild, uncontrolled way. *There was a stampede for the exit.* N-COUNT: usu sing

2 If a group of animals or people **stampede** or if something **stampedes** them, they run in a wild, uncontrolled way. *The crowd stampeded and many were crushed or trampled underfoot... Countryside robbers are learning the ways of the wild west by stampeding cattle to distract farmers before raiding their homes. ...a herd of stampeding cattle.* V-ERG V V n V-ing

3 If a lot of people all do the same thing at the same time, you can describe it as a **stampede**. *Generous redundancy terms had triggered a stampede of staff wanting to leave. ...a stampede by South African farmers to buy up cheap land in Mozambique.* N-COUNT: usu sing =rush

4 If people **are stampeded** into doing something, they are forced into doing it by pressure from other people, even though they do not think it is the right thing to do. *Do we really want to be stampeded in such a way?... It was widely believed that Powell had stampeded the Government into taking action.* VERB =railroad be V-ed V n *into* n

stamping ground, stamping grounds. Someone's **stamping ground** is a place where they like to go often. N-COUNT: usu with poss =haunt

stance /stæns/ **stances** ◆◆◇◇◇

1 Your **stance** on a particular matter is your attitude to it. *The Congress had agreed to reconsider its stance on the armed struggle... They have maintained a consistently neutral stance... His stance towards the story is quite similar to ours.* N-COUNT: usu sing, with supp =position

2 Your **stance** is the way that you are standing; a formal use. *Take a comfortably wide stance and flex your knees a little... The woman detective shifted her stance from one foot to another.* N-COUNT: usu sing, supp N =position

stanchion /stæntʃᵊn/ **stanchions.** A **stanchion** is a pole or bar that stands upright and is used as a support; a formal word. N-COUNT

stand /stænd/ **stands, standing, stood** ◆◆◆◆◆

1 When you **are standing**, your body is upright, your legs are straight, and your weight is supported by your feet. *She was standing beside my bed staring down at me... They told me to stand still and not to turn round... Overcrowding is so bad that prisoners have to sleep in shifts, while others have to stand.* ► **Stand up** means the same as **stand**. *We waited, standing up, for an hour. ...Mrs Fletcher, a shop assistant who has to stand up all day.* VERB V prep V adj V PHRASAL VERB V P

2 When someone who is sitting **stands**, they change their position so that they are upright and on their feet. *Becker stood and shook hands with Ben.* ► **Stand up** means the same as **stand**. *When I walked in, they all stood up and started clapping.* VERB V PHRASAL VERB V P

3 If you **stand** aside or **stand** back, you move a short distance sideways or backwards, so that you are standing in a different place. *I stood aside to let her pass me... The policemen stood back. Could it be a bomb?* VERB V adv/prep

4 If something such as a building or a piece of furniture **stands** somewhere, it is in that position, and is upright; used in written English. *The house stands alone on top of a small hill... I reached for the lamp, which stood in the middle of the table.* VERB V prep/adv

5 You can say that a building **is standing** when it remains after other buildings around it have fallen down or been destroyed. *The palace, which was damaged by bombs in World War II, still stood... There are very few buildings left standing.* VERB V

6 If you **stand** something somewhere, you put it there in an upright position. *Stand the plant in the open in a sunny, sheltered place.* VERB =place V n prep/adv

7 If you leave food or a mixture of something to **stand**, you leave it without disturbing it for some time. *The salad improves if made in advance and left to stand.* VERB V

8 If you take or make a **stand**, you do something or say something in order to make it clear what your attitude to a particular thing is. *He felt the need to make a stand against racism in South Africa... They must take a stand and cast their votes... His tough stand won some grudging admiration.* N-COUNT: usu sing, oft N *against/on* n

9 If you ask someone where or how they **stand** on a particular issue, you are asking them what their attitude or view is. *The amendment will force senators to show where they stand on the issue of sexual harassment... So far, the bishop hasn't said where he stands.* VERB *where* V *on* n *where* V

10 If you do not know where you **stand** with someone, you do not know exactly what their attitude to you is. *No-one knows where they stand with him; he is utterly unpredictable... All children need discipline, to know where they stand.* VERB *where* V *with* n *where* V

11 You can use **stand** instead of 'is' when you are describing the present state or condition of something or someone. *The alliance stands ready to do what is necessary... He stands accused of destroying the party in pursuit of his presidential ambitions... The peace plan as it stands violates basic human rights.* V-LINK V adj V

12 If a decision, law, or offer **stands**, it still exists and has not been changed or cancelled. *Although exceptions could be made, the rule still stands... The Supreme Court says that the convictions can stand.* VERB V

13 If something that can be measured **stands at** a particular level, it is at that level. *The inflation rate now stands at 3.6 per cent... Support for the two sides is standing at between 42 and 44 per cent.* VERB V *at* amount

14 You can describe how tall or high someone or something is by saying that they **stand** a particular height. *She stood five feet five inches tall and weighed 120 pounds... The dam will stand 600 feet high... She stood tall and aloof.* VERB V amount adj V adj

15 If something can **stand** a situation or a test, it is good enough or strong enough to experience it without being damaged, harmed, or shown to be inadequate. *These are the first machines that can stand the wear and tear of continuously crushing glass... I think these books can stand comparison quite happily with works by Dickens... Ancient wisdom has stood the test of time.* VERB V n

16 If you cannot **stand** something, you cannot bear it or tolerate it. *I can't stand any more. I'm going to run away... Stoddart can stand any amount of personal criticism... How does he stand the pain?* VERB =bear V n/-ing

17 If you cannot **stand** someone or something, you dislike them very strongly; an informal use. *I can't stand that man and his arrogance... He can't stand me smoking.* VERB =bear V n/-ing

18 If you **stand to gain** something, you are likely to gain it. If you **stand to lose** something, you are likely to lose it. *The management group would stand to gain millions of dollars if the company were sold... As many as 30,000 workers at 22 nuclear weapons sites stand to lose their jobs.* VERB V to-inf

19 In British English, if you **stand** in an election, you are a candidate in it. The usual American word is **run**. *He has not yet announced whether he will stand in the election... Some ardent supporters were urging him to stand... She is to stand as a Member of the European Parliament... Mr Walesa himself is likely to stand for president.* VERB V *in* n V V *as/for/against* n

20 If you **stand** someone a meal or a drink, you buy it for them; an informal use. *You can stand me a pint.* VERB V n n

21 A **stand** is a small shop or stall, outdoors or in a large public building. *He ran a newspaper stand* N-COUNT: oft n N =stall

outside the American Express office... She bought a hot dog from a stand on a street corner. • See also **newsstand**.

22 A **stand** at a sports ground is a large structure where spectators sit or stand to watch what is happening. • See also **grandstand**. N-COUNT

23 A **stand** is an object or piece of furniture that is designed for supporting or holding a particular kind of thing. *The teapot came with a stand to catch the drips.* N-COUNT

24 In a law court, **the stand** is the place where a witness stands to answer questions. *When the father took the stand today, he contradicted his son's testimony... The government has called nearly 50 witnesses to the stand.* N-SING: *the*N

25 See also **standing**.

26 If an idea, claim, or attempt **stands or falls** on something, its truth or success depends on that thing. *Airlines should stand or fall on their ability to attract passengers.* PHRASES V inflects, PHR *on/by*n

27 You can describe someone's final attempt to defend themselves before they are defeated as their **last stand**. *There they made their tragic and heroic last stand against the Roman legions.*

28 If you say it **stands to reason** that something is true or likely to happen, you mean that it is obvious; an informal expression. *It stands to reason that if you are considerate and friendly to people you will get a lot more back... Smith isn't his real name, that stands to reason.* V inflects, usu *it*PHR that

29 If you **stand in the way of** something or **stand in** someone's **way**, you prevent that thing from happening or prevent that person from doing something. *The British government would not stand in the way of such a proposal... It is his decision to go to America and who am I to stand in his way?* V inflects

30 • to **stand a chance**: see **chance**. • to **stand up and be counted**: see **count**. • to **stand firm**: see **firm**. • to **stand on** your **own two feet**: see **foot**. • to **stand** your **ground**: see **ground**. • to **stand** someone **in good stead**: see **stead**. • to **stand trial**: see **trial**.

stand aside PHRASAL VERB

1 If you **stand aside** from something, you allow it to happen without interfering in it or doing anything to prevent it. *Ireland stood aside from this conflict... The key question was whether they would stand aside or would disrupt the elections.* V P *from*n V P

2 See also **stand down**.

stand back. If you **stand back** and think about a situation, you think about it as if you were not involved in it. *Stand back and look objectively at the problem.* PHRASAL VERB =step back V P

stand by PHRASAL VERB

1 If you **are standing by**, you are ready and waiting to provide help or to take action. *British and American warships are standing by to evacuate their citizens if necessary... We will be holding the auditions from nine o'clock tomorrow night so stand by for details.* • See also **standby**. V P to-inf V P *for*n Also V P

2 If you **stand by** and let something bad happen, you do not do anything to stop it; used showing disapproval. *The Secretary of Defence has said that he would not stand by and let democracy be undermined... The police just stood by and watched as the missiles rained down on us.* PRAGMATICS V P

3 If you **stand by** someone, you continue to give them support, especially when they are in trouble; used showing approval. *I wouldn't break the law for a friend, but I would stand by her if she did.* PRAGMATICS =stick by V P n

4 If you **stand by** an earlier decision, promise, or statement, you continue to support it or keep it. *The decision has been made and I have got to stand by it... He continues to insist that all he wrote in the book is nothing but the truth, and that he will stand by his word.* =stick by V P n

stand down. If someone **stands down** or **stands aside**, they resign from an important job or position, often in order to let someone else take their place. *The President said he was willing to stand aside if that would stop the killing... Profits plunged and he stood down as chairman last January.* PHRASAL VERB =step down, resign V P V P *as*n

stand for PHRASAL VERB

1 If you say that a letter **stands for** a particular word, you mean that it is an abbreviation for that word. *AIDS stands for Acquired Immune Deficiency Syndrome... What does EEC stand for?* V P n

2 The ideas or attitudes that someone or something **stands for** are the ones that they support or represent. *The party is trying to give the impression that it alone stands for democracy... He hates us and everything we stand for.* =represent V P n

3 If you will **not stand for** something, you will not allow it to happen or continue. *It's outrageous, and we won't stand for it any more.* with neg V P n

stand in. If you **stand in** for someone, you take their place or do their job, because they are ill or away. *I had to stand in for her on Tuesday when she didn't show up. ...the acting president, who's standing in while Franco's out of the country.* • See also **stand-in**. PHRASAL VERB =deputize V P *for*n V P

stand out PHRASAL VERB

1 If something **stands out**, it is very noticeable. *Every tree, wall and fence stood out against dazzling white fields... Grammatical errors are always obvious to me, spelling mistakes stand out.* V P

2 If something **stands out**, it is much better or much more important than other things of the same kind. *He played the violin, and he stood out from all the other musicians... Many people were involved in this conspiracy, but three stand out.* V P *from*n V P

3 If something **stands out** from a surface, it rises up from it. *His tendons stood out like rope beneath his skin... Her hair stood out in spikes.* =stick out V P

stand up PHRASAL VERB

1 See **stand** 1, 2.

2 If something such as a claim or a piece of evidence **stands up**, it is accepted as true or satisfactory after being carefully examined. *He made wild accusations that did not stand up... How well does this thesis stand up to close examination?* V P V P *to*n

3 If a boyfriend or girlfriend **stands** you **up**, they fail to keep an arrangement to meet you; an informal expression. *We were to have had dinner together yesterday evening, but he stood me up... He was in a foul mood because he had been stood up.* V n P Also V P n (not pron)

stand up for. If you **stand up for** someone or something, you defend them and make your feelings or opinions very clear; used showing approval. *They stood up for what they believed to be right... Don't be afraid to stand up for yourself.* PHRASAL VERB PRAGMATICS =stick up for, defend V P P n

stand up to PHRASAL VERB

1 If something **stands up to** rough treatment, it remains almost undamaged or unharmed. *Is this building going to stand up to the strongest gales?* V P P n/-ing

2 If you **stand up to** someone, especially someone more powerful than you are, you defend yourself against their attacks or demands. *He hit me, so I hit him back – the first time in my life I'd stood up to him... Women are now aware of their rights and are prepared to stand up to their employers.* V P P n

standard /stændə^{r}d/ **standards** ◆◆◆◆◇

1 A **standard** is a level of quality or achievement, especially a level that is thought to be acceptable. *The standard of professional cricket has never been lower... There will be new national standards for hospital cleanliness.* N-COUNT: with supp

2 A **standard** is something that you use in order to judge the quality of something else. *...systems that were by later standards absurdly primitive.* N-COUNT: with supp

3 **Standards** are moral principles which affect people's attitudes and behaviour. *My father has always had high moral standards.* • See also **double standard**. N-PLURAL: usu with supp =principles

4 You use **standard** to describe things which are usual and normal. *It was standard practice for untrained clerks to advise in serious cases such as murder... No other executive car can offer you the same level of standard equipment at this price.* ADJ-GRADED: usu ADJ n

5 A **standard** work or text on a particular subject is one that is widely read and often recommended. ADJ: ADJ n

standard bearer, standard bearers; also spelled **standard-bearer**. If you describe someone as the **standard bearer** of a group, you mean N-COUNT: usu with supp that they act as the leader or public representative of a group of people who have the same aims or interests. *He is now certain to become the standard-bearer for about 60 Labour MPs who oppose the treaty.*

standardize /stændəʳdaɪz/ **standardizes, standardizing, standardized;** also spelled **standardise** in British English. ◆◇◇◇◇ VERB To **standardize** things means to change them so that they all have the same features. V n *There is a drive both to standardise components and to reduce the number of models on offer...* V-ed *He feels standardized education does not benefit those children who are either below or above average intelligence.*
♦ **standardization** /stændəʳdaɪzeɪʃᵊn, AM -dɪz-/ N-UNCOUNT *...the standardisation of working hours in Community countries.*

standard lamp, standard lamps. N-COUNT In British English, a **standard lamp** is a tall electric light which stands on the floor in a living-room. It consists of a bulb and shade fixed to the top of a wooden or metal pole on a base. The usual American expression is **floor lamp**.

standard of living, standards of living. ◆◇◇◇◇ N-COUNT Your **standard of living** is the level of comfort and wealth which you have. *We'll continue to fight for a decent standard of living for our members.*

standard time. N-UNCOUNT: usu supp N **Standard time** is the official local time of a region or country. *French standard time is GMT plus 1 hr.*

standby /stændbaɪ/ **standbys;** also spelled **stand-by**. ◆◇◇◇◇

1 N-COUNT: oft N n A **standby** is something or someone that is always ready to be used if they are needed. *Canned varieties of beans and pulses are a good standby... He sat through the trial as a standby juror.*

2 PHRASE: usu v-link PHR, PHR after v If someone or something is **on standby**, they are ready to be used if they are needed. *Five ambulances are on standby at the port... Security forces have been put on standby in case of violence.*

3 ADJ: ADJ n A **standby** ticket for something such as the theatre or a plane journey is a cheap ticket that you buy just before the performance starts or the plane takes off, if there are still some seats left. *Access International books standby flights from New York to Europe.* ► Also an adverb. ADV: ADV after v *Magda was going to fly standby.*

stand-in, stand-ins. N-COUNT A **stand-in** is a person who takes someone else's place or does someone else's job for a while, for example because the other person is ill or away. *He was a stand-in for my regular doctor.*

standing /stændɪŋ/ **standings** ◆◇◇◇◇

1 N-UNCOUNT: with supp, oft adj N, with poss =status Someone's **standing** is their reputation or status. *...an artist of international standing... He has improved his country's standing abroad... She had the wealth and social standing to command respect.*

2 N-COUNT: usu sing, with poss A party's or person's **standing** is their popularity, usually according to opinion polls. *There is one thing that Mr Clinton can do to improve his standing with the electorate... Mrs Thatcher's standing is clearly much higher in the US than at home.*

3 ADJ: ADJ n =permanent You use **standing** to describe something which is permanently in existence. *Israel has a relatively small standing army and its strength is based on its reserves... Elizabeth had a standing invitation to stay with her. ...the finance standing committee.*

4 N-PLURAL In a contest or competition, the list of competitors which shows their places during the event is called the **standings**; used in journalism. *Britain is 11th in the team standings.*

5 See also **free-standing, long-standing**.

6 PHRASE: n PHR You can use the expression **of many years' standing** to say that something has had a particular function or someone has had a particular role for many years. For example, if a place is your home **of ten years' standing**, it has been your home for ten years. Used in written English. *...a Congressman of 24 years' standing... My girlfriend of long standing left me.*

standing order, standing orders. N-COUNT: also by N A **standing order** is an instruction to your bank to pay a fixed amount of money to someone at regular times.

standing ovation, standing ovations. ◆◇◇◇◇ N-COUNT If a speaker or performer gets a **standing ovation** when they have finished speaking or performing, the audience stands up to applaud them in order to show great admiration or support for them.

standing room. N-UNCOUNT **Standing room** is space in a room or bus, where people can stand when all the seats have been occupied. *The place quickly fills up so it's soon standing room only.*

stand-off, stand-offs; also spelled **standoff**. ◆◇◇◇◇ N-COUNT A **stand-off** is a situation in which neither of two opposing groups or forces will make a move until the other one does something, so nothing can happen until one of them gives way. *There is no sign of an end to the stand-off between Mohawk Indians and the Quebec provincial police... The State Department was warning that this could lead to another diplomatic stand-off.*

stand-offish; also spelled **standoffish**. ADJ-GRADED =aloof, cold If you say that someone is **stand-offish**, you mean that they behave in a formal and rather unfriendly way. *He can be quite stand-offish and rude, even to his friends.*

standpipe /stændpaɪp/ **standpipes.** N-COUNT A **standpipe** is a vertical pipe that is connected to a water supply and stands in a street or other public place.

standpoint /stændpɔɪnt/ **standpoints.** ◆◇◇◇◇ N-COUNT: with supp, usu *from* N =point of view, perspective From a particular **standpoint** means looking at an event, situation, or idea in a particular way. *He believes that from a military standpoint, the situation is under control... From my standpoint, you know, this thing is just ridiculous.*

standstill /stændstɪl/. ◆◇◇◇◇ N-SING: a N, usu *to/at* N =halt If movement or activity comes to or is brought to **a standstill**, it stops completely. *Abruptly the group ahead of us came to a standstill... Production is more or less at a standstill.*

stand-up; also spelled **standup**. ◆◆◇◇◇

1 ADJ: ADJ n A **stand-up** comic or comedian stands alone in front of an audience and tells jokes. *He does all kinds of accents, he can do jokes – he could be a stand-up comic... Women do not normally break into the big time by doing stand-up comedy.*

2 ADJ: ADJ n If people have a **stand-up** fight or argument, they stand up and hit or shout at each other in an unrestrained way.

stank /stæŋk/. **Stank** is the past tense of **stink**.

Stanley knife /stænli naɪf/ **Stanley knives.** N-COUNT A **Stanley knife** is a very sharp knife used in crafts such as woodwork. It consists of a small triangular blade on the end of a short plastic handle. **Stanley knife** is a trademark.

stanza /stænzə/ **stanzas.** ◆◇◇◇◇ N-COUNT A **stanza** is a verse of a poem; a technical term in poetry.

staple /steɪpᵊl/ **staples, stapling, stapled** ◆◆◇◇◇

1 ADJ: ADJ n A **staple** food, product, or activity is one that is basic and important in people's everyday lives. *Rice is the staple food of more than half the world's population... The Chinese also eat a type of pasta as part of their staple diet... Staple goods are disappearing from the shops.* ► Also a noun. N-COUNT *Fish is a staple in the diet of many Africans. ...boutiques selling staples such as jeans and T-shirts.*

2 N-COUNT: usu N *of* n A **staple** is something that forms an important part of something else. *Political reporting has become a staple of American journalism.*

3 N-COUNT **Staples** are small pieces of wire that are used for holding sheets of paper together firmly. You push the staples through the paper using a special device called a stapler.

4 VERB If you **staple** something, you fasten it to something else or fix it in place using staples. V n with adv *Staple some sheets of paper together into a book.* V-ed *...polythene bags stapled to an illustrated card.* Also V n prep

staple gun, staple guns. N-COUNT A **staple gun** is a small machine used for forcing staples into wood or brick.

stapler /steɪpləʳ/ **staplers.** A **stapler** is a special device used for putting staples into sheets of paper. N-COUNT

star /stɑːʳ/ **stars, starring, starred** ◆◆◆◆◆

1 A **star** is a large ball of burning gas in space. Stars appear to us as small points of light in the sky on clear nights. *The nights were pure with cold air and lit with stars.* ● see **morning star, shooting star.** N-COUNT

2 You can refer to a shape or an object as a **star** when it has four, five, or more points sticking out of it in a regular pattern. *Children at school receive coloured stars for work well done.* N-COUNT

3 **Stars** are star-shaped marks that are printed against the name of something to indicate its quality. The more stars something has, the better it is. *...five star hotels.* N-COUNT

4 Famous actors, musicians, and sports players are often referred to as **stars.** *...Gemma, 41, star of the TV series Pennies From Heaven... By now Murphy is Hollywood's top male comedy star. ...former football stars Jackie and Bobby Charlton.* N-COUNT: oft supp N

5 If an actor or actress **stars in** a play or film, he or she has one of the most important parts in it. *The previous year Adolphson had starred in a play in which Ingrid had been an extra... He's starred in dozens of films.* VERB V *in* n

6 If a play or film **stars** a famous actor or actress, he or she has one of the most important parts in it. *...The BBC's new satirical show, That Was The Week That Was, which starred David Frost. ...a Hollywood film, The Secret of Santa Vittoria, directed by Stanley Kramer and starring Anthony Quinn.* VERB =feature V n

7 The horoscope in a newspaper or magazine is sometimes referred to as the **stars.** *There was nothing in my stars to say I'd have travel problems!* N-PLURAL =horoscope

8 If you say that someone should **thank** their **lucky stars** that something is the case, you mean that they should be very grateful that it is the case, because otherwise their situation would be a lot worse. *Thank your lucky stars you're out of London.. You ought to thank your lucky stars, Sefton, that I don't tell your mother.* PHRASE: V inflects, usu PHR that

starboard /stɑːʳbəʳd/. The **starboard** side of a ship is the right side when you are on it and facing towards the front; a technical term. *He detected a ship moving down the starboard side of the submarine.* ▶ Also a noun. *I could see the fishing boat to starboard.* ◆◇◇◇◇ ADJ ≠port; N-UNCOUNT: usu *to* N

starburst /stɑːʳbɜːʳst/ **starbursts.** A **starburst** is a bright light with rays coming from it, or a patch of bright colour with points extending from it; a literary word. *They shot past at treetop height and broke into a starburst of multi-coloured smoke.* N-COUNT

starch /stɑːʳtʃ/ **starches, starching, starched** ◆◇◇◇◇

1 **Starch** is a carbohydrate found in foods such as bread, potatoes, pasta, and rice. *She reorganised her eating so that she was taking more fruit and vegetables and less starch, salt, and fat.* N-MASS

2 **Starch** is a substance that is used for stiffening cloth, especially cotton and linen. N-UNCOUNT

3 If you **starch** cloth, you stiffen it using starch. *I took down the curtains, washed, and starched them.* VERB V n

starched /stɑːʳtʃt/. A **starched** garment or piece of cloth has been stiffened using starch. *...a starched white shirt. ...starched napkins.* ADJ: usu ADJ n

starchy /stɑːʳtʃi/ **starchier, starchiest. Starchy** foods contain a lot of starch. *...starchy and sticky glutinous rices.* ADJ-GRADED

star-crossed. If someone is **star-crossed,** they keep having bad luck. *...star-crossed lovers parted by war and conflict.* ADJ: usu ADJ n

stardom /stɑːʳdəm/. **Stardom** is the state of being very famous, usually as an actor, musician, or sportsplayer. *In 1929 she shot to stardom on Broadway in a Noel Coward play.* ◆◇◇◇◇ N-UNCOUNT =fame

stare /steəʳ/ **stares, staring, stared** ◆◆◆◇◇

1 If you **stare** at someone or something, you look at them for a long time. *Tamara stared at him in disbelief, shaking her head... Ben continued to stare out the window... Mahoney tried not to stare.* ▶ Also a noun. *Hlasek gave him a long, cold stare.* VERB V prep/adv V; N-COUNT

2 If a situation or the answer to a problem **is staring** you **in the face,** it is very obvious, although you may not be immediately aware of it; an informal expression. *Then the answer hit me. It had been staring me in the face ever since Lullington.* PHRASE: V inflects

stare out. If you **stare** someone **out,** you look steadily into their eyes for such a long time that they feel that they have to turn their eyes away from you. *He glared at Nikitin but the General Secretary stared him out with hard, pebble-like eyes.* PHRASAL VERB V n P

starfish /stɑːʳfɪʃ/; **starfish** is both the singular and plural form. A **starfish** is a flat, star-shaped creature with five arms that lives in the sea. N-COUNT

star-gazer, star-gazers; also spelled **stargazer.** A **star-gazer** is someone who studies the stars as an astronomer or astrologer; an informal word. N-COUNT

star-gazing; also spelled **stargazing. Star-gazing** is the activity of studying the stars as an astronomer or astrologer; an informal word. N-UNCOUNT

stark /stɑːʳk/ **starker, starkest** ◆◆◇◇◇

1 **Stark** choices or statements are harsh and unpleasant. *UK companies face a stark choice if they want to stay competitive... In his celebration speech, he issued a stark warning to Washington and other Western capitals.* ♦ **starkly** *That issue is presented starkly and brutally by Bob Graham and David Cairns... The point is a starkly simple one.* ADJ-GRADED =harsh; ADV-GRADED: ADV with v, ADV adj

2 If two things are in **stark** contrast to one another, they are very different from each other in a way that is very obvious. *...secret cooperation between London and Washington that was in stark contrast to official policy.* ♦ **starkly** *Angus's child-like paintings contrast starkly with his adult subject matter in these portraits... The outlook now is starkly different.* ADJ-GRADED; ADV-GRADED: ADV with v, ADV adj

3 Something that is **stark** is very bare and plain in appearance. *...the stark white, characterless fireplace in the drawing room.* ♦ **starkly** *The desert was luminous, starkly beautiful... The room was starkly furnished.* ADJ-GRADED; ADV-GRADED: ADV adj, ADV with v

stark naked. Someone who is **stark naked** is completely naked. *All contestants competed stark naked.* ADJ: ADJ after v, v-link ADJ

starlet /stɑːʳlɪt/ **starlets.** A **starlet** is a young actress who is expected to become a film star in the future; used in newspapers. N-COUNT

starlight /stɑːʳlaɪt/. **Starlight** is the light that comes from the stars at night. N-UNCOUNT

starling /stɑːʳlɪŋ/ **starlings.** A **starling** is a very common European bird with greenish-black feathers. Starlings often fly around together in large flocks. N-COUNT

starlit /stɑːʳlɪt/. **Starlit** means made lighter or brighter by the stars. *...a clear starlit sky. ...this cold, starlit night.* ADJ: ADJ n

starry /stɑːri/. A **starry** night or sky is one in which a lot of stars are visible. *She stared up at the starry sky.* ADJ: ADJ n

starry-eyed. If you say that someone is **starry-eyed,** you mean that they are so full of dreams, hopes, or idealistic thoughts that they do not see how things really are. *I'm not starry-eyed about Europe. ...a starry-eyed young couple.* ADJ-GRADED

Stars and Stripes. The Stars and Stripes is the name of the national flag of the United States of America. N-PROPER: *the* N

star sign, star signs. Your **star sign** is the sign of the zodiac under which you were born. *'What star sign are you?'—'Gemini.'* N-COUNT =birth sign

star-studded. A **star-studded** show, event, or cast is one that includes a large number of famous performers; used in journalism. *...a star-studded production of Hamlet... The film opened with a star-studded premiere last night.* ADJ: ADJ n

start /stɑːʳt/ **starts, starting, started** ◆◆◆◆◆

1 If you **start** to do something, you do something that you were not doing before and you continue doing it. *John then unlocked the front door and I started to follow him up the stairs... It was 1956 when Susanna started the work on the garden... She started cleaning the kitchen.* ▶ Also a noun. *After several starts, she read the report properly.* VERB =begin V to-inf V n/-ing Also V; N-COUNT

2 When something **starts**, or if someone **starts** it, it takes place from a particular time. *...the Crimson Drawing Room, where the fire is now known to have started... The Great War started in August of that year... Trains start at 11.00 and an hourly service will operate until 16.00... All of the passengers started the day with a swim.* ▶ Also a noun. *...1918, four years after the start of the Great War... She demanded to know why she had not been told from the start.* — V-ERG =begin; V; V prep; V n; N-SING: the N =beginning

3 If you **start by** doing something, or if you **start with** something, you do that thing first in a series of actions. *I started by asking how many day-care centers were located in the United States... He started with a good holiday in Key West, Florida.* — VERB =begin; V by -ing; V with n

4 You use **start** to say what someone's first job was. For example, if their first job was that of a porter, you can say that they **started as** a porter. *Betty started as a shipping clerk at the clothes factory... Grace Robertson started as a photographer with Picture Post in 1947.* ▶ **Start off** means the same as **start**. *Mr. Dambar had started off as an assistant to Mrs. Spear's husband.* — VERB =begin; V as n; PHRASAL VERB V P as n

5 When someone **starts** something such as a new business, they create it or cause it to begin. *George Granger has started a health centre and I know he's looking for qualified staff... Now is probably as good a time as any to start a business.* ▶ **Start up** means the same as **start**. *The cost of starting up a day care center for children ranges from $150,000 to $300,000... He said what a good idea it would be to start a community magazine up.* • See also **start-up**. — VERB; V n; PHRASAL VERB =set up; V P n (not pron); V n P

6 If you **start** an engine, car, or machine, or if it **starts**, it begins to work. *He started the car, which hummed smoothly... We were just passing one of the parking bays when a car's engine started.* ▶ **Start up** means the same as **start**. *He waited until they went inside the building before starting up the car and driving off... Put the key in the ignition and turn it to start the car up... The engine of the seaplane started up.* — V-ERG; V n; V; PHRASAL VERB ERG; V P n (not pron); V n P; V P

7 If you **start**, your body jerks as a result of surprise or fear. *She put the bottle on the coffee table beside him, banging it down hard. He started at the sound, his concentration broken... Rachel started forward on the sofa.—'You mean you've arrested Pete?'* ▶ Also a noun. *Sylvia woke with a start... He gave a start of surprise and astonishment.* — VERB; V; V adv; N-COUNT: usu sing

8 See also **head start**, **false start**.

9 You use **for a start** or **to start with** to introduce the first of a number of things or reasons that you want to mention or could mention. *You must get her name and address, and that can be a problem for a start... It comes as a surprise to be reminded that he is 70. For a start, he doesn't look it... To start with, where and when did it happen?* — PHRASES; PHR with cl/group; PRAGMATICS

10 If you **get off to a good start**, you are successful in the early stages of doing something. If you **get off to a bad start**, you are not successful in the early stages of doing something. *The new Prime Minister has got off to a good start, but he still has to demonstrate what manner of leader he is going to be... Mrs Thatcher's war on inflation got off to a bad start. The cost of living rose to 21.9% in May 1980.* — V inflects

11 **'To start with'** means at the very first stage of an event or process. *To start with, the pressure on her was very heavy, but it's eased off a bit now... Success was assured and, at least to start with, the system operated smoothly.* — PHR with cl =in the beginning

12 • **in fits and starts**: see **fits**. • **get off to a flying start**: see **flying**.

start off — PHRASAL VERB

1 If you **start off** by doing something, you do it as the first part of an activity. *She started off by accusing him of blackmail but he more or less ignored her... Joe Loss started off playing piano background music for silent films in the 1920's.* — V P by -ing; V P -ing

2 To **start** someone **off** means to cause them to begin doing something. *Her mother started her off acting in children's theatre.* — V n P

3 To **start** something **off** means to cause it to begin. *He became more aware of the things that started that tension off... Best results are obtained by starting the plants off in a warm greenhouse.* — V n P

4 See **start** 4.

start on. If you **start on** something that needs to be done, you start dealing with it. *No need for you to start on the washing-up yet... He has not finished his drama, in fact, he has not started on it.* — PHRASAL VERB; V P n

start out — PHRASAL VERB

1 If someone or something **starts out as** a particular thing, they are that thing at the beginning although they change later. *Daly was a fast-talking Irish-American who had started out as a salesman... What started out as fun quickly became hard work.* — V P as n; Also V P n as n

2 If you **start out by** doing something, you do it at the beginning of an activity. *We start out by advising people to sit down and identify seven experiences from any time of their life... The child'll start out by making relatively few distinctions in the language.* — V P by -ing

start over. If you **start over** or **start** something **over**, you begin something again from the beginning; used especially in American English. *...moving the kids to some other schools, closing them down and starting over with a new staff... It's just not enough money to start life over.* — PHRASAL VERB; V P; V n P

start up — PHRASAL VERB

1 See **start** 5.

2 See **start** 6.

starter /stɑːʳtəʳ/ **starters** ◆◆◇◇◇

1 A **starter** is a small quantity of food that is served as the first course of a meal; used mainly in British English. — N-COUNT =hors d'oeuvre

2 The **starter** of a car is the device that starts the engine. *A car's starter is basically an electric motor.* — N-COUNT

3 The **starters** in a race are the people or animals who take part at the beginning even if they do not finish. *Of the 10 starters, four were eliminated or retired.* — N-COUNT: usu pl

4 You use **for starters** when you mention something to indicate that it is the first item or point in a series. *These prizes are just for starters. Other exciting offers are flooding in... Her manager said, 'It will cost her 1.5 million pounds for starters if she loses.'* — PHRASE: PHR with cl/group

starting block, starting blocks. **Starting blocks** are blocks which sprinters put their feet against to help them move quickly forward at the start of a race. — N-COUNT: usu pl

starting point, starting points; also spelled **starting-point**. ◆◇◇◇◇

1 Something that is a **starting point** for a discussion or process can be used to begin it or act as a basis for it. *These proposals represent a realistic starting point for negotiation... A pair of pretty, faded pink antique curtains was the starting point for the room's colour scheme.* — N-COUNT: oft N for n =basis

2 When you make a journey, your **starting point** is the place from which you start. *The newly built airport acts as a starting point for safaris into the game parks and reserves of northern Tanzania... They had already walked a couple of miles or more from their starting point.* — N-COUNT: usu with supp

startle /stɑːʳtᵊl/ **startles, startling, startled.** ◆◆◇◇◇ If something sudden and unexpected **startles** you, it surprises and frightens you slightly. *The telephone startled him... Sorry, I didn't mean to startle you... The news will startle the City.* ♦ **startled** *Martha gave her a startled look.* — VERB =alarm; V n; ADJ-GRADED

startling /stɑːʳtəlɪŋ/. ◆◆◇◇◇ Something that is **startling** is so different, unexpected, or remarkable that people react to it with surprise. *Sometimes the results may be rather startling. ...startling new evidence... His hair was dyed a startling black.* ♦ **startlingly** *He was startlingly handsome... Then, startlingly, the back door was jerked open by Binton.* — ADJ-GRADED; ADV-GRADED: usu ADV adj, also ADV after v, ADV with cl

start-up

1 The **start-up** costs of something such as a new business or new product are the costs of starting to run or produce it. *That is enough to pay the start-up costs for fourteen research projects... The minimum* — ADJ: ADJ n

start-up capital for a Pizza franchise is estimated at $250,000 to $315,000.

2 A **start-up** company is a small business that has recently been started by someone. *Thousands and thousands of start-up firms have poured into the computer market.* ADJ: ADJ n

star turn, star turns. The **star turn** of a performance or show is the main item, or the one that is considered to be the most interesting or impressive. N-COUNT: usu *the*N in sing

starvation /stɑːˈveɪʃᵊn/. **Starvation** is extreme suffering or death, caused by lack of food. *Over three hundred people have died of starvation since the beginning of the year.* ◆◆◇◇◇ N-UNCOUNT: usu *of/from* N

starve /stɑːʳv/ **starves, starving, starved** ◆◆◇◇◇

1 If people **starve**, they suffer greatly from lack of food which sometimes leads to their death. *A number of the prisoners we saw are starving... In the 1930s, millions of Ukrainians starved to death or were deported... Getting food to starving people does nothing to stop the war.* VERB V V *to* n V-ing

2 To **starve** someone means not to give them any food. *Mr Le Pen said that to starve the Iraqi people was unworthy of civilised nations ... Judy decided I was starving myself.* VERB V n V pron-refl

3 If someone or something **is starved** of something that they need, they are suffering because they are not getting enough of it. *The electricity industry is not the only one to have been starved of investment... The most damaging thing the West could do is to starve Russia of new foreign capital. ...an audience hungry for American films and long starved of choice.* VERB *be* V-ed *of* n V n *of* n V-ed

starving /stɑːʳvɪŋ/. If you say that you are **starving**, you mean that you are very hungry; an informal use. *Apart from anything else I was starving.* ADJ: v-link ADJ =ravenous

stash /stæʃ/ **stashes, stashing, stashed** ◆◇◇◇◇

1 If you **stash** something valuable in a secret place, you store it there to keep it safe; an informal use. *We went for the bottle of whiskey that we had stashed behind the bookcase... Andrews had stashed money away in secret offshore bank accounts.* VERB V n prep V n with adv Also V n

2 A **stash** of something valuable is a secret store of it; an informal use. *A large stash of drugs had been found aboard the yacht.* N-COUNT: with supp, usu N *of* n =hoard

stasis /stæsɪs, AM steɪ-/. **Stasis** is a state in which something remains the same, and does not change or develop; a formal word. *All great art explores this tension between order and chaos, between growth and stasis.* N-UNCOUNT ≠dynamism

state /steɪt/ **states, stating, stated** ◆◆◆◆◆

1 You can refer to countries as **states**, particularly when you are discussing politics. *...Albania, Europe's only remaining communist state. ...students who have participated in exchanges with other member states of the European Community.* N-COUNT

2 Some large countries such as the USA are divided into smaller areas called **states**. *Leaders of the Southern states are meeting in Louisville.* N-COUNT

3 The USA is sometimes referred to as **the States**; an informal use. N-PROPER: *the*N

4 You can refer to the government of a country as **the state**. *The state does not collect enough revenue to cover its expenditure... Eastern Europe shows that worker-owned factories can be as inefficient as state-owned ones.* N-SING: *the*N

5 **State** industries or organizations are financed and organized by the government rather than private companies. *...reform of the state social-security system.* • See **state school**. ADJ: ADJ n

6 A **state** occasion is a formal one involving the head of a country. *Mr John Major and Mr Boris Yeltsin were on a state visit to India.* ADJ: ADJ n

7 When you talk about the **state** of someone or something, you are referring to the condition they are in or what they are like at a particular time. *For the first few months after Daniel died, I was in a state of clinical depression... When we moved here the walls and ceiling were in an awful state... Look at the state of my car!* N-COUNT: usu sing, with supp

8 If you **state** something, you say or write it in a formal or definite way. *Clearly state your address and telephone number... The police report stated that he was arrested for allegedly assaulting his wife... 'Our relationship is totally platonic,' she stated... Buyers who do not apply within the stated period can lose their deposits.* VERB =declare V n V that V with quote V-ed

9 See also **head of state, nation state, police state, welfare state.**

10 If you say that someone **is not in a fit state** to do something, you mean that they are too upset or ill to do it. *When you left our place, you weren't in a fit state to drive.* PHRASES V inflects, PHR to-inf

11 If you are **in a state** or if you get **into a state**, you are very upset or nervous about something. *I was in a terrible state because nobody could understand why I had this illness... People will work themselves up into a state about anything.* v-link PHR

12 If the dead body of an important person **lies in state**, it is publicly displayed for a few days before it is buried. V inflects

State Department. In the United States, **the State Department** is the government department that is concerned with foreign affairs. *Officials at the State Department say the issue is urgent. ...a senior State Department official.* ◆◆◆◇◇ N-PROPER: *the*N

statehood /steɪthʊd/. **Statehood** is the condition of being an independent state or nation. ◆◇◇◇◇ N-UNCOUNT

statehouse /steɪthaʊs/ **statehouses.** In the United States, a **statehouse** is where the governor of a state has his offices. N-COUNT

stateless /steɪtləs/. A person who is **stateless** is not a citizen of any country and therefore has no nationality. *If I went back I'd be a stateless person... The ethnic minorities will be effectively stateless.* ADJ

statelet /steɪtlət/ **statelets.** A **statelet** is a small, independent state which is usually formed by the break-up of a larger state; used in journalism. N-COUNT

stately /steɪtli/. Something or someone that is **stately** is impressive because they look very graceful and dignified. *Instead of moving at his usual stately pace, he was almost running. ...a stately mansion.* ◆◇◇◇◇ ADJ-GRADED

stately home, stately homes. A **stately home** is a large old house which has belonged to an aristocratic family for a long time, especially one that people can pay to visit; used mainly in British English. ◆◇◇◇◇ N-COUNT

statement /steɪtmənt/ **statements** ◆◆◆◆◇

1 A **statement** is something that you say or write which gives information in a formal or definite way. *'Things are moving ahead.' – I found that statement vague and unclear... Andrew now disowns that statement, saying he was depressed when he made it.* N-COUNT

2 A **statement** is an official or formal announcement that is issued on a particular occasion. *The statement by the military denied any involvement in last night's attack.* N-COUNT

3 You can refer to the official account of events which a suspect or a witness gives to the police as a **statement**. *The 350-page report was based on statements from witnesses to the events.* N-COUNT

4 If you describe an action or thing as a **statement**, you mean that it clearly expresses a particular opinion or idea that you have. *The following recipe is a statement of another kind – food is fun!* N-COUNT

5 A printed document showing how much money has been paid into and taken out of a bank or building society account is called a **statement**. N-COUNT

state of affairs. If you refer to a particular **state of affairs**, you mean the general situation and circumstances connected with someone or something. *This state of affairs cannot continue for too long, if parliament is to recover... The nation had a chance to move towards a more democratic, and modern, state of affairs.* ◆◇◇◇◇ N-SING: usu with supp

state of mind, states of mind. Your **state of mind** is your mood or mental state at a particular time. *I want you to get into a whole new state of mind... He's in hospital, and in a confused state of mind.* ◆◇◇◇◇ N-COUNT: usu sing, usu with supp =mood

state of siege. A **state of siege** is a situation in which a government or other authority puts restrictions on the movement of people into or out of a country, town, or building. *Under the state of siege, the police could arrest suspects without charges or warrants.* N-SING

state-of-the-art. If you describe something as **state-of-the-art**, you mean that it is the best available because it has been made using the most modern techniques and technology. *...the production of state-of-the-art military equipment. ...state-of-the-art technology.* ◆◇◇◇◇ ADJ: usu ADJ n

stateroom /steɪtruːm/ **staterooms**
1 On a passenger ship, a **stateroom** is a private room, especially one that is large and comfortable; an old-fashioned use. N-COUNT
2 In a palace or other impressive building, a **stateroom** is a large room for use on formal occasions; used mainly in British English. N-COUNT

state school, state schools. In British English, a **state school** is a school that is controlled and funded by the government or a local authority, and which children can attend without having to pay. The usual American term is **public school.** ◆◇◇◇◇ N-COUNT ≠private school

stateside /steɪtsaɪd/; also spelled **Stateside. Stateside** means in, from, or to the United States; an informal word, used mainly in American English and British journalism. *The band are currently planning a series of Stateside gigs. ...a well-known Stateside cop show.* ► Also an adverb. *His debut album was hugely successful Stateside.* ADJ =American; ADV: ADV after v

statesman /steɪtsmən/ **statesmen.** A **statesman** is an important and experienced politician, especially one who is widely known and respected. *Hamilton is a great statesman and political thinker.* • See also **elder statesman.** ◆◆◇◇◇ N-COUNT

statesmanlike /steɪtsmənlaɪk/. If you describe someone, especially a political leader, as **statesmanlike**, you approve of them because they give the impression of being very able and experienced. *They believe that among the three, Mr. Bush will come across as the most confident and statesmanlike... He is trying to project a more dignified, statesmanlike image in this election year.* ADJ-GRADED PRAGMATICS

statesmanship /steɪtsmənʃɪp/. **Statesmanship** is the skill and activities of a statesman. *He praised the two leaders warmly for their statesmanship.* N-UNCOUNT

statewide /steɪtwaɪd/. **Statewide** means across or throughout the whole of one of the states of the United States. *Each year they compete in a prominent statewide bicycle race... These voters often determine the outcome of statewide elections.* ► Also an adverb. *In the weeks since flooding began, 16 people have died statewide.* ◆◇◇◇◇ ADJ: usu ADJ n; ADV: ADV after v

static /stætɪk/ ◆◇◇◇◇
1 Something that is **static** does not move or change. *The numbers of young people obtaining qualifications has remained static or decreased... Both your pictures are of static subjects.* ADJ-GRADED
2 **Static** or **static electricity** is electricity which is caused by friction and which collects in things such as your body or metal objects. N-UNCOUNT
3 If there is **static** on the radio or television, you hear a series of loud crackling noises. N-UNCOUNT

station /steɪʃᵊn/ **stations, stationing, stationed** ◆◆◆◆◇
1 A **station** is a building by a railway line where trains stop so that people can get on or off. *Ingrid went with him to the railway station to see him off... Businessmen stream into one of Tokyo's main train stations.* N-COUNT: oft n N
2 A **bus station** or **coach station** is a building where buses or coaches start their journey. N-COUNT: n N
3 If you talk about a particular radio or television **station**, you are referring to the programmes broadcast by a particular radio or television company. *...an independent local radio station... It claims to be the most popular television station in the UK.* N-COUNT: oft n N
4 If soldiers or officials **are stationed** in a place, they are sent there to do a job or to work for a period of time. *Reports from the capital, Lome, say troops are stationed on the streets... I was stationed there just after the war. ...United States military personnel stationed in the Philippines.* V-PASSIVE be V-ed prep/adv V-ed
5 If you **station** yourself somewhere, you go there and wait, usually for a particular purpose; a formal use. *The musicians stationed themselves quickly on either side of the stairs... He stationed himself at the door.* VERB =position V pron-refl prep/adv
6 See also **fire station, gas station, petrol station, police station, power station, service station, space station, way station.**

stationary /steɪʃənri, AM -neri/. Something that is **stationary** is not moving. *Stationary cars in traffic jams cause a great deal of pollution... The train was stationary for 90 minutes.* ◆◇◇◇◇ ADJ: usu ADJ n

stationer /steɪʃənəʳ/ **stationers.** A **stationer** is a person who sells paper, envelopes, pens, and other equipment used for writing. N-COUNT

stationery /steɪʃənri, AM -neri/. **Stationery** is paper, envelopes, and other materials or equipment used for writing. ◆◇◇◇◇ N-UNCOUNT

stationmaster /steɪʃᵊnmɑːstəʳ, -mæstəʳ/ **stationmasters;** also spelled **station master.** A **stationmaster** is the official who is in charge of a railway station. N-COUNT

station wagon, station wagons. In American English, a **station wagon** is car with a long body, a door at the rear, and space behind the back seats. The British term is **estate car.** N-COUNT

statist /steɪtɪst/. When a country has **statist** policies, the state has a lot of control over the economy. *The Poles are demanding radical change, not a continuation of statist economic controls.* ADJ-GRADED: usu ADJ n

statistic /stətɪstɪk/ **statistics** ◆◆◆◇◇
1 **Statistics** are facts which are obtained from analysing information expressed in numbers, for example information about the number of times that something happens. *Official statistics show real wages declining by 24%... There are no reliable statistics for the number of deaths in the battle.* • See also **vital statistics.** N-COUNT: usu pl =figure
2 **Statistics** is a branch of mathematics concerned with the study of information that is expressed in numbers. *...a professor of Mathematical Statistics.* N-UNCOUNT

statistical /stətɪstɪkᵊl/. **Statistical** means relating to the use of statistics. *The report contains a great deal of statistical information... We need to back that suspicion up with statistical proof.* ◆◆◇◇◇ ADJ: usu ADJ n
♦ **statistically** /stətɪstɪkli/. *The results are not statistically significant... Statistically, ninety-eight percent of all acute sunstroke cases are fatal.* ADV: ADV with cl/group, ADV with v

statistician /stætɪstɪʃᵊn/ **statisticians.** A **statistician** is a person who studies statistics or who works using statistics. ◆◇◇◇◇ N-COUNT

stats /stæts/
1 **Stats** are facts which are obtained from analysing information expressed in numbers. **Stats** is an abbreviation for **statistics**; an informal word. *...a fall in April's retail sales stats.* N-PLURAL
2 **Stats** is a branch of mathematics concerned with the study of information that is expressed in numbers; an informal use. N-UNCOUNT

statuary /stætʃuəri, AM -ueri/. If you talk about the **statuary** in a place, you are referring to all the statues and sculpture there; a formal word. N-UNCOUNT

statue /stætʃuː/ **statues.** A **statue** is a large sculpture of a person or an animal, made of stone, marble, bronze, or some other hard material. ◆◆◇◇◇ N-COUNT

statuesque /stætʃuesk/. A woman who is **statuesque** is big and tall and has good posture; used in written English. *She was a statuesque brunette of thirty-eight.* ADJ-GRADED: usu ADJ n

statuette /stætʃuet/ **statuettes.** A **statuette** is a very small sculpture of a person or an animal which is often displayed on a shelf or stand. N-COUNT

stature /stætʃəʳ/. ◆◇◇◇◇
1 Someone's **stature** is their height. *It's more than his physical stature that makes him remarkable...* N-UNCOUNT: usu with poss, of supp N,

Mother was of very small stature, barely five feet tall... She was a little short in stature. in N

2 The **stature** of a person is the importance and reputation that they have. *Who can deny his stature as the world's greatest cellist?... This club has grown in stature over the last 20 years.* N-UNCOUNT: usu with poss, *of* supp N, *in* N

status /steɪtəs/ ◆◆◆◆◇

1 Your **status** is your social or professional position. *The status of children in society has long been underestimated. ...women and men of wealth and status. ...promoted to the status of foreman. ...his wife's former status as his secretary.* N-UNCOUNT: usu with supp

2 Status is the prestige and importance that someone has in the eyes of other people. *Nurses are undervalued, and they never enjoy the same status as doctors... He has risen to gain the status of a national hero.* N-UNCOUNT

3 The **status** of something is the importance that people give it. *Those things that can be assessed by external tests are being given unduly high status... The fact that the most senior judge of the High Court's Family Division had taken control of the case was proof of its urgency and status.* N-UNCOUNT =importance

4 Status is an official classification that a person, organization, or country receives, which gives them particular rights or advantages. *The Soviet president had insisted Lithuania return to its status of a Soviet republic. ...his status as a British citizen... The WHO recommendation has no legal status... The personal allowance depends on your age and marital status.* N-UNCOUNT: with supp

5 The **status** of something is its state of affairs at a particular time. *Mr. Bush immediately met with his senior advisers for a status report and to discuss how to respond to the Soviet proposal... What is your current financial status?... Please keep us informed of the status of this project.* N-UNCOUNT: with supp

status quo /steɪtəs kwoʊ/. The **status quo** is the state of affairs that exists at a particular time, especially in contrast to a different possible state of affairs. *By 492 votes to 391, the federation voted to maintain the status quo... They have no wish for any change in the status quo... We must not return to the status quo.* ◆◇◇◇◇ N-SING: usu *the* N

status symbol, status symbols. A **status symbol** is something that a person has or owns that shows they have prestige and importance in society. N-COUNT

statute /stætʃuːt/ **statutes.** A **statute** is a rule or law which has been made by a government or other organization and formally written down. *The new statute covers the care for, bringing up and protection of children... The independence of the judiciary in France is guaranteed by statute.* ◆◇◇◇◇ N-VAR

statute book, statute books. The **statute book** is a record of all the laws made by the government; used mainly in British English. *The Bill could reach the statute book by the summer if it attracts the support of Home Office ministers... Germany still has no insider-dealing offence in its statute books.* N-COUNT: *the* poss N

statutory /stætʃʊtəri, AM -tɔːri/. **Statutory** means relating to rules or laws which have been formally written down; a formal word. *We had a statutory duty to report to Parliament.* ♦ **statutorily** /stætʃʊtərɪli, AM -tɔːrɪli/. *Such tenants are statutorily protected... Broadcasting has had to be regulated statutorily.* ◆◆◇◇◇ ADJ: usu ADJ n; ADV: ADV with v

staunch /stɔːntʃ/ **stauncher, staunchest; staunches, staunching, staunched.** ◆◇◇◇◇

1 A **staunch** supporter or believer is very loyal to a person, organization, or a set of beliefs, and supports them strongly. *He's a staunch supporter of controls on government spending.* ♦ **staunchly** *He was staunchly opposed to a public confession.* ADJ-GRADED: usu ADJ n =steadfast; ADV-GRADED

2 To **staunch** the flow of something means to stop it; a formal use. *The government claims this is the only way to staunch the annual flow to Germany of hundreds of thousands of refugees... Efforts to staunch the spill of crude oil from a tanker off the north coast of Scotland are being held up by gale force winds.* VERB =stop V n

3 To **staunch** a wound, or to **staunch** the blood from a wound, means to stop the wound from bleeding; a formal use. *Tom tried to staunch the blood with his handkerchief.* VERB =stop V n

stave /steɪv/ **staves, staving, staved** ◆◇◇◇◇

1 A **stave** is a strong stick, especially one that is used as a weapon. *Many of the men had armed themselves with staves and pieces of iron.* N-COUNT =staff

2 A **stave** is the five lines that music is written on; used mainly in British English. N-COUNT

stave off. If you **stave off** something bad, or if you **stave** it **off**, you succeed in stopping it happening for a while. *Labour chose a new Prime Minister in a last-minute bid to stave off defeat... But the reality of discovery was a different matter, and he did all he could to stave it off.* PHRASAL VERB =fend off V P n (not pron) V n P

stay /steɪ/ **stays, staying, stayed** ◆◆◆◆◆

1 If you **stay** where you are, you continue to be there and do not leave. *'Stay here,' Trish said. 'I'll bring the car down the drive to take you back.'... In the old days the woman stayed at home and the man earned the money.* VERB V adv/prep

2 If you **stay** in a town, or hotel, or at someone's house, you live there for a short time. *Gordon stayed at The Park Hotel, Milan... He tried to stay a few months every year in Scotland.* ► Also a noun. *An experienced Indian guide is provided during your stay.* VERB V prep/adv V n; N-COUNT: usu supp N

3 If someone or something **stays** in a particular state or situation, they continue to be in it. *The Republican candidate said he would 'work like crazy to stay ahead'. ...community care networks that offer classes on how to stay healthy... Nothing stays the same for long.* V-LINK =remain V adv/prep V adj Also V n

4 If you **stay** away from a place, you do not go there. *Government employers and officers also stayed away from work during the strike... Every single employee turned up at the meeting, even people who usually stayed away.* VERB =keep V *away from* n V *away*

5 If you **stay out of** something, you do not get involved in it. *In the past, the UN has stayed out of the internal affairs of countries unless invited in... After months of staying well out of the problem, Washington has expressed a willingness to help find a solution.* VERB V *out of* n

6 If you say that something is **here to stay**, you mean that people have accepted it and it has become a part of everyday life. *Satellite TV is here to stay... Nuclear weapons are here to stay because they have changed the way countries approach the idea of war.* PHRASES v-link PHR

7 If you **stay put**, you remain somewhere. *He was forced by his condition to stay put and remain out of politics... Nigel says for the moment he is very happy to stay put in Lyon.* V inflects

8 If you **stay the night** in a place, you sleep there for one night. *They had invited me to come to supper and stay the night.* V inflects

stay in. If you **stay in** during the evening, you remain at home and do not go out. *If I stay in my boyfriend cooks a wonderful lasagne or chicken or steak... Before we had our child the idea of staying in every night would have been horrific.* PHRASAL VERB ≠go out V P

stay on. If you **stay on** somewhere, you remain there after other people have left or after the time when you were going to leave. *He had managed to arrange to stay on in Adelaide... So few teenage Britons stay on at school, compared with the rest of Europe... The board reversed its decision and asked Mr. Evans to stay on.* PHRASAL VERB ≠leave V P

stay out PHRASAL VERB

1 If you **stay out** at night, you remain away from home, especially when you are expected to be there. *That was the first time Elliot stayed out all night... I met some friends and stayed out until eleven or twelve.* =stop out ≠stay in V P

2 If workers who are striking **stay out**, they remain on strike. *The electricians at the power stations went on strike and stayed out nearly five days.* V P

stay up. If you **stay up**, you remain out of bed at a time when most people have gone to bed or at a PHRASAL VERB time when you are normally in bed yourself. *I used to stay up late with my mom and watch movies.* V P adv/prep

stay-at-home, stay-at-homes. If you describe someone as a **stay-at-home**, you mean that they stay at home rather than going out to work or travelling. *I was a stay-at-home mum until 1980 when my husband lost his job.* ◆◇◇◇◇ N-COUNT: usu N n

staying power; also spelled **staying-power.**

1 If you have **staying power**, you have the strength and stamina to keep going until you reach the end of what you are doing. *Goldie is an actress with phenomenal staying power.* N-UNCOUNT =stamina

2 If something such as an idea or a product has **staying power**, it remains popular or successful for a long time. *'A cashmere sweater still thrills me,' she admits. 'It has wonderful staying power; it looks chic and modern.'* N-UNCOUNT

stay of execution, stays of execution. If you are given a **stay of execution**, you are legally permitted to delay obeying an order of a court of law; a legal expression. N-COUNT

STD /es tiː diː/ **STDs. STD** is an abbreviation for 'sexually transmitted disease'; a medical term. *...an STD clinic.* N-COUNT: usu N n

stead /sted/ ◆◇◇◇◇

1 If you do something **in** someone's **stead**, you replace them and do it instead of them; a formal expression. *We hope you will consent to act in his stead... My grandmother and aunt will be there in my parents' stead.* PHRASES PHR after v

2 If you say that something will **stand** someone **in good stead**, you mean that it will be very useful to them in the future. *These two games here will stand them in good stead for the future... My years of teaching stood me in good stead.* V inflects

steadfast /stedfɑːst, -fæst/. If someone is **steadfast** in something that they are doing, they are convinced that what they are doing is right and they refuse to change it or to give up; used showing approval. *He remained steadfast in his belief that he had done the right thing.* ◆◇◇◇◇ ADJ-GRADED: oft ADJ *in* n PRAGMATICS =firm
♦ **steadfastly** *She steadfastly refused to look his way.* ADV-GRADED ♦ **steadfastness** *By now the government was well aware of the steadfastness and strength of his resistance.* N-UNCOUNT

steady /stedi/ **steadier, steadiest; steadies, steadying, steadied** ◆◆◆◇◇

1 A **steady** situation continues or develops gradually without any interruptions and is not likely to change quickly. *Despite the steady progress of building work, the campaign against it is still going strong... The improvement in standards has been steady and persistent, but has attracted little comment from educationalists... Despite the steady rain, the mood was friendly and festive... A student doesn't have a steady income.* ADJ-GRADED =constant ♦ **steadily** /stedɪli/ *Relax as much as possible and keep breathing steadily... The company has steadily been losing market share to Boeing and Airbus.* ADV-GRADED: ADV with v

2 If an object is **steady**, it is firm and does not shake or move about. *Get as close to the subject as you can and hold the camera steady... It takes a very steady hand and plenty of practice to paint a perfect line.* ADJ-GRADED ≠unsteady

3 If you look at someone or speak to them in a **steady** way, you look or speak in a calm, controlled way. *'Well, go on,' said Camilla, her voice fairly steady... Gail was silent for a moment, regarding Harry with his steady gaze.* ADJ GRADED =calm ♦ **steadily** *He moved back a little and stared steadily at Elaine.* ADV-GRADED: ADV after v

4 If you describe a person as **steady**, you mean that they are sensible and reliable. *He was firm and steady unlike other men she knew. ...a politician who's steady almost to the point of being boring.* ADJ-GRADED: usu v-link ADJ =dependable, reliable ≠unreliable

5 If you **steady** something or if it **steadies**, it stops shaking or moving about. *Two men were on the bridge-deck, steadying a ladder... Lovelock eased back the throttles and the ship steadied.* V-ERG =stabilize V n V

6 If you **steady** yourself, you control your voice or expression, so that people will think that you are calm and not nervous. *Somehow she steadied herself and murmured, 'Have you got a cigarette?'... She breathed in to steady her voice.* VERB =compose V pron-refl V n

7 You say **'steady on'** to someone to tell them to calm down or to be careful about what they are saying. *'What if there's another murder?'—'Steady on!'... 'One can't live with a man like that!'—'Steady on,' said Chris.* EXCLAM

steak /steɪk/ **steaks** ◆◆◇◇◇

1 A **steak** is a large flat piece of beef without much fat on it. You cook it by grilling or frying it. ● See also **rump steak, T-bone steak.** N-VAR

2 **Steak** is beef that is used for making stews and casseroles. It is often sold in the form of cubes of meat. *...steak and kidney pie.* ● See also **stewing steak.** N-UNCOUNT

3 A fish **steak** is a large piece of fish that contains few bones. *...fresh salmon steaks.* N-COUNT: usu n N

steak house, steak houses; also spelled **steakhouse.** A **steak house** is a restaurant where the main food served is steak. N-COUNT

steal /stiːl/ **steals, stealing, stole, stolen** ◆◆◆◇◇

1 If you **steal** something from someone, you take it away from them without their permission and without intending to return it. *He was accused of stealing a small boy's bicycle... Bridge stole the money from clients' accounts... People who are drug addicts come in and steal... She has since been jailed for six months for stealing from the tills.* VERB V n V n *from* n V V-ing ♦ **stolen** *We have now found the stolen car.* ADJ

2 If you **steal** someone else's ideas, you pretend that they are your own. *A writer is suing director Steven Spielberg for allegedly stealing his film idea... His team solved the engineering problem by stealing an idea from nature.* VERB V n

3 If someone **steals** somewhere, they move there quietly and cautiously. *They can steal away at night and join us... Leroy stole up the hall to the parlor.* VERB V adv/prep

4 If you describe something as **a steal**, you mean that it is very good value; an informal use. *At only £13.50, this champagne is a steal.* N-SING: a N =bargain, snip

5 ● to **steal a glance**: see **glance.** ● to **steal a march** on someone: see **march.** ● to **steal the show**: see **show.** ● to **steal** someone's **thunder**: see **thunder.**

stealth /stelθ/. If you use **stealth** when you do something, you do it in such a slow, quiet, and secretive way that other people do not notice what you are doing. *Wild animals demand secrecy and a certain amount of stealth from the photographer... Both sides advanced by stealth.* ◆◇◇◇◇ N-UNCOUNT: oft *by* N ≠openness

stealthy /stelθi/ **stealthier, stealthiest. Stealthy** actions or movements are performed quietly and secretively, so that no one will notice what you are doing. *I would creep in and with stealthy footsteps explore the second-floor... It was a stealthy sound made by someone anxious not to be heard.* ADJ-GRADED =furtive ≠overt ♦ **stealthily** /stelθɪli/ *Slowly and stealthily, someone was creeping up the stairs.* ADV-GRADED: ADV with v

steam /stiːm/ **steams, steaming, steamed** ◆◆◆◇◇

1 **Steam** is the hot mist that forms when water boils. **Steam** vehicles and machines are operated using steam as a means of power. *In an electric power plant the heat converts water into high-pressure steam... The invention of the steam engine changed ships, just as it had changed land transport.* N-UNCOUNT

2 If something **steams**, it gives off steam. *...restaurants where coffee pots steamed on their burners. ...a basket of steaming bread rolls.* VERB V V-ing

3 If you **steam** food or if it **steams**, you cook it in steam rather than in water. *Steam the carrots until they are just beginning to be tender... Leave the vegetables to steam over the rice for the 20 minutes cooking time. ...steamed clams and broiled chicken.* V-ERG V n V V-ed

4 If something such as a plan or a project goes **full steam ahead**, it proceeds quickly and efficiently so that a lot of progress is made. *The Government was determined to go full steam ahead with its privatisation programme... Plans are rolling full steam ahead for the Jamaica Festival.* PHRASES v PHR

5 If you **let off steam**, you get rid of your energy, anger, or strong emotions with physical activity or by behaving in a noisy or violent way; an informal expression. *Regular exercise helps to combat un-* V inflects

wanted stress and is a good way of relaxing or letting off steam.

6 If a belief, a plan, or a project **picks up steam**, it starts to develop and become more important. *Just as the presidential campaign was picking up steam, riots exploded in Los Angeles.* — V inflects =get going

7 If you **run out of steam**, you stop doing something because you have no more energy or enthusiasm left; an informal expression. *I decided to paint the bathroom ceiling but ran out of steam halfway through.* — V inflects

8 If you do something **under** your **own steam**, you do it without any help from anyone else. *Patients who are well enough to turn up under their own steam are well enough to wait to be seen by a doctor.* — PHR after v

steam up — PHRASAL VERB

1 If someone **gets steamed up** about something, they are very annoyed about it. *The general manager may have got steamed up about nothing... I remember going to the lecture in my first week and getting very steamed up.* — PASSIVE; get V-ed P about n; get V-ed P

2 When a window, mirror, or pair of spectacles **steams up**, it becomes covered with steam or mist. *...the irritation of living with lenses that steam up when you come in from the cold.* — V P ♦ **steamed-up** *The glass is all steamed up still.* — ADJ

steamboat /stiːmbout/ **steamboats.** A **steamboat** is a boat or ship that has an engine powered by steam. — N-COUNT =steamer

steamer /stiːməʳ/ **steamers** ◆◇◇◇◇

1 A **steamer** is a ship that has an engine powered by steam. — N-COUNT

2 A **steamer** is a special saucepan used for steaming food such as vegetables and fish. — N-COUNT

steam iron, steam irons. A **steam iron** is an electric iron that produces steam from water that you put into it. The steam makes it easier to get the creases out of your clothes. — N-COUNT

steamroller /stiːmroulə ʳ/ **steamrollers, steamrollering, steamrollered**

1 A **steamroller** is a large, heavy vehicle with wide solid wheels or rollers, which is used to flatten the surface of a road. In the past steamrollers were powered by steam. — N-COUNT

2 If you **steamroller** someone who disagrees with you or opposes you, you defeat them or you force them to do what you want by using your power or by putting a lot of pressure on them. *They could simply steamroller all opposition. ...the Prime Minister's attempt to steamroller the general into a job he did not want.* — VERB; V n; V n *into*

steamship /stiːmʃɪp/ **steamships.** A **steamship** is a ship that has an engine powered by steam. — N-COUNT =steamer

steamy /stiːmi/ ◆◇◇◇◇

1 **Steamy** means erotic or passionate; an informal use. *...a steamy thriller set in France... He'd had a steamy affair with an office colleague.* — ADJ-GRADED: usu ADJ n

2 A **steamy** place is very hot and humid because it is full of steam. *...a steamy cafe... The air was hot and steamy from the heat of a hundred bodies.* — ADJ-GRADED: usu ADJ n

steed /stiːd/ **steeds.** A **steed** is a large strong horse used for riding; a literary word. — N-COUNT

steel /stiːl/ **steels, steeling, steeled** ◆◆◆◇◇

1 **Steel** is a very strong metal which is made mainly from iron. Steel is used for making many things, for example bridges, buildings, vehicles, and cutlery. *...steel pipes. ...the iron and steel industry. ...a fall in demand for cement, bricks, steel and glass. ...a woman with steel-grey eyes and silvery-blonde hair.* — N-MASS: oft N n

• See also **stainless steel**.

2 **Steel** is used to refer to the industry that produces steel and items made of steel. *...a three-month study of European steel... The company has interests in steel and other products.* — N-UNCOUNT: oft N n

3 If you **steel** yourself, you prepare to deal with something unpleasant. *Those involved are steeling themselves for the coming battle... I was steeling myself to call round when Simon arrived.* — VERB; V pron-refl for/against n; V pron-refl to-inf

steel band, steel bands. A **steel band** is a band of people who play music on special metal drums. Steel bands originated in the West Indies. — N-COUNT

steelmaker /stiːlmeɪkəʳ/ **steelmakers.** A **steelmaker** is a company that makes steel. — N-COUNT

steel wool. **Steel wool** is a mass of fine steel threads twisted together into a small ball and used for cleaning hard surfaces or removing paint. — N-UNCOUNT

steelworker /stiːlwɜːʳkəʳ/ **steelworkers;** also spelled **steel worker**. A **steelworker** is a person who works in a steelworks. — N-COUNT

steelworks /stiːlwɜːʳks/; **steelworks** is both the singular and plural form. A **steelworks** is a factory where steel is made. — N-COUNT

steely /stiːli/ ◆◇◇◇◇

1 **Steely** is used to emphasize that a person is hard, strong, and determined. *Their indecision has been replaced by confidence and steely determination... Captain Grenville stared at him steely-eyed.* — ADJ-GRADED: usu ADJ n

2 You use **steely** to describe something that has a hard, greyish colour like steel. *...steely grey hair.* — ADJ: usu ADJ n

steep /stiːp/ **steeper, steepest; steeps, steeping, steeped** ◆◆◇◇◇

1 A **steep** slope rises at a very sharp angle and is difficult to go up. *San Francisco is built on 40 hills and some are very steep. ...a narrow, steep-sided valley.* — ADJ-GRADED ♦ **steeply** *The road climbs steeply, with good views of Orvieto through the trees. ...steeply terraced valleys. ...houses with steeply sloping roofs.* — ADV-GRADED: ADV with v

2 A **steep** increase or decrease in something is a very big increase or decrease. *Consumers are rebelling at steep price increases.* — ADJ-GRADED =sharp ♦ **steeply** *Unemployment is rising steeply.* — ADV-GRADED: ADV with v

3 If you say that the price of something is **steep**, you mean that it is expensive; an informal use. *The annual premium can be a little steep, but will be well worth it if your dog is injured.* — ADJ-GRADED: usu v-link ADJ

4 To **steep** food in a particular liquid means to immerse it in it, so that it becomes soft and absorbs the flavour of the liquid. *It's a drink made by steeping pineapple rind in water. ...green beans steeped in olive oil.* — VERB =marinate; V n; V-ed

steeped /stiːpt/. If a place or person is **steeped in** a quality or characteristic, they are surrounded by it or deeply influenced by it. *The castle is steeped in history and legend... He said they were unrealistic and steeped in the past.* — ◆◇◇◇◇ ADJ-GRADED: v-link ADJ *in* n

steeple /stiːpəl/ **steeples.** A **steeple** is a tall pointed structure on top of the tower of a church. — ◆◇◇◇◇ N-COUNT =spire

steeplechase /stiːpəltʃeɪs/ **steeplechases** ◆◇◇◇◇

1 A **steeplechase** is a long horse race in which the horses have to jump over obstacles such as hedges and water jumps. — N-COUNT

2 A **steeplechase** is a race over 3000 metres in which people jump over hurdles and water jumps round an athletics track. — N-COUNT

steer /stɪəʳ/ **steers, steering, steered** ◆◆◇◇◇

1 When you **steer** a car, boat, or plane, you control it so that it goes in the direction that you want. *What is it like to steer a ship this size?... When I was a kid, about six or seven, she would often let me steer the car along our driveway.* — VERB; V n; V n prep; Also V

2 If you **steer** people towards a particular course of action or attitude, you try to lead them gently in that direction. *The new government is seen as one that will steer the country in the right direction... I think you are perfectly correct in trying to steer your mother towards increased independence.* — VERB; V n prep

3 If you **steer** someone in a particular direction, you guide them there. *Nick steered them into the nearest seats.* — VERB =guide; V n prep

4 If you **steer** a particular **course**, you take a particular line of action. *Prime Minister Hun Sen has sought to steer a course between the two groups... In nearly all these issues the British steered a middle course.* — VERB; V n prep; V n

5 A **steer** is a bull that has been castrated. — N-COUNT

6 See also **steering**.

7 If you **steer clear** of someone or something, you deliberately avoid them. *I think a lot of people, women in particular, steer clear of these sensitive issues.* — PHRASE: V inflects

steering /stɪərɪŋ/ ◆◇◇◇◇

1 The **steering** in a car or other vehicle is the mechanical parts of it which make it possible to steer. N-UNCOUNT

2 A **steering** committee or a **steering** group is a group of people that manage the early stages of a project, in particular the order and priority of business, and oversee its progress. *There will be an economic steering committee with representatives of each of the republics.* ADJ: ADJ n

steering column, steering columns. In a car or other vehicle, the **steering column** is the rod on which the steering wheel is mounted. N-COUNT

steering wheel, steering wheels. The **steering wheel** in a car or lorry or other vehicle is the wheel which the driver holds when he or she is steering the vehicle. ◆◇◇◇◇ N-COUNT

stellar /stelər/

1 **Stellar** is used to describe anything connected with stars. *A stellar wind streams outward from the star.* ADJ: ADJ n

2 A **stellar** person or thing is considered to be excellent. *...a stellar education at Eton and Oxford... The French companies are registering stellar profits.* ADJ-GRADED: usu ADJ n =superlative, excellent

stem /stem/ **stems, stemming, stemmed** ◆◆◆◇◇

1 If a condition or problem **stems from** something, it was caused originally by that thing. *All my problems stem from drink... Much of the instability stems from the economic effects of the war.* VERB V *from* n

2 If you **stem** something, you stop it spreading, increasing, or continuing; a formal use. *Austria has sent three army battalions to its border with Hungary to stem the flow of illegal immigrants... The authorities seem powerless to stem the rising tide of violence... He was still conscious, trying to stem the bleeding with his right hand.* VERB =stop, halt V n

3 The **stem** of a plant is the thin, upright part on which the flowers and leaves grow. *He stooped down, cut the stem for her with his knife and handed her the flower.* N-COUNT =stalk

4 The **stem** of a glass or vase is the long thin part which connects the bowl to the base. N-COUNT

5 The **stem** of a pipe is the long thin part through which smoke is sucked. *He chewed the stem of his pipe and eyed her sceptically.* N-COUNT

6 In grammar, the **stem** of a word is the main part of it, which remains unchanged when the ending changes. N-COUNT

7 If something happens **from stem to stern** on a boat, it involves the whole of the boat. *A South African television report said the ship was ablaze from stem to stern.* PHRASE: usu PHR after v

-stemmed /-stemd/. **-stemmed** is added to adjectives to form adjectives which indicate what the stem of something is like. *...an enormous bouquet of long-stemmed roses.* COMB in ADJ: usu ADJ n

stench /stentʃ/ **stenches.** A **stench** is a strong and very unpleasant smell. *The stench of burning rubber was overpowering.* ◆◇◇◇◇ N-COUNT: oft N *of* n =stink

stencil /stensəl/ **stencils, stencilling, stencilled;** spelled **stenciling**, **stenciled** in American English. ◆◇◇◇◇

1 A **stencil** is a piece of paper, plastic, or metal which has a design cut out of it. You place the stencil on a surface and use it to create a design, by allowing ink or paint to go through the holes in the stencil onto the surface below. N-COUNT

2 If you **stencil** a design or if you **stencil** a surface with a design, you print a design on a surface using a stencil. *He then stencilled the ceiling with a moon and stars motif. ...a stencilled design.* VERB V n *with* n V-ed Also V n

stenographer /stənɒgrəfər/ **stenographers.** In American English, a **stenographer** is an office worker who can write shorthand and type. N-COUNT

stentorian /stentɔːriən/. A **stentorian** voice is very loud and strong; a formal word. *He bellowed in a stentorian voice.* ADJ-GRADED: usu ADJ n =strident

step /step/ **steps, stepping, stepped** ◆◆◆◆◆

1 If you take a **step**, you lift your foot and put it down in a different place, for example when you are walking. *I took a step towards him... She walked on a few steps... I followed her, five steps behind... He heard steps in the corridor.* N-COUNT

2 If you **step** on something or **step** in a particular direction, you put your foot on the thing or move your foot in that direction. *This was the moment when Neil Armstrong became the first man to step on the Moon... She accidentally stepped on his foot on a crowded commuter train... I tried to step back, but he held my upper arms too tightly.* VERB V prep/adv

3 **Steps** are a series of surfaces at increasing or decreasing heights, on which you put your feet in order to walk up or down to a different level. *This little room was along a passage and down some steps... A flight of stone steps leads to the terrace.* N-COUNT =stairs

4 A **step** is a raised flat surface in front of a door. *A little girl was sitting on the step of the end house... Leave empty milk bottles on the step.* ● See also **doorstep**. N-COUNT

5 A **step** is one of a series of actions that you take in order to achieve something. *He greeted the agreement as the first step towards peace... She is not content with her present lot and wishes to take steps to improve it... The elections were a step in the right direction, but there is a lot more to be done.* N-COUNT: oft N prep/adv

6 A **step** in a process is one of a series of stages. *The next step is to put the theory into practice... Aristotle took the scientific approach a step further.* N-COUNT =stage

7 The **steps** of a dance are the sequences of foot movements which make it up. N-COUNT =movement

8 Someone's **step** is the way they walk. *He quickened his step... There was a real spring in her step.* N-SING: poss N

9 **Steps** are the same as a **stepladder**; used mainly in British English. N-PLURAL

10 If you stay **one step ahead of** someone or something, you manage to achieve more than they do or avoid competition or danger from them. *Successful travel is partly a matter of keeping one step ahead of the crowd... Businessmen cluster together to get ideas, tips, personal contacts anything to get a step ahead of the computer. ...nations only a few steps ahead of famine.* PHRASES PHR after v, v-link PHR

11 If people who are walking or dancing are **in step**, they are moving their feet forward at exactly the same time as each other. If they are **out of step**, their feet are moving forward at different times. *They were almost the same height and they moved perfectly in step... They jogged in silence a while, faces lowered, out of step... She slipped her hand into his and fell into step beside him.* PHR after v

12 If people are **in step** with each other, their ideas or opinions are the same. If they are **out of step** with each other, their ideas or opinions are different. *Moscow is anxious to stay in step with Washington... The British Government is once more out of step with world opinion.* usu PHR *with* n

13 If you tell someone to **step on it**, you are telling them to go faster or hurry up. *We've only got thirty-five minutes so step on it.* PRAGMATICS =hurry up

14 If you do something **step by step**, you do it by progressing gradually from one stage to the next. *I am not rushing things and I'm taking it step by step... Follow our simple step-by-step instructions.* PHR with v, PHR n

15 If someone tells you to **watch** your **step**, they are warning you to be careful about how you behave or what you say so that you don't get into trouble. PRAGMATICS =be careful

step aside. See **step down**. PHRASAL VERB

step back. If you **step back** and think about a situation, you think about it as if you were not involved in it. *I stepped back and analysed the situation... It was necessary to step back from the project and look at it as a whole.* PHRASAL VERB =stand back V P V P *from* n

step down or **step aside.** If someone **steps down** or **steps aside**, they resign from an important job or position, often in order to let someone else take their place. *Mr Orlando was forced to step down as mayor despite his popularity with the voters... Many would prefer to see him step aside in favour of a younger man.* PHRASAL VERB =stand down V P *as* n V P

step in. If you **step in**, you get involved in a difficult situation because you think you can or should help with it. *If no agreement was reached, the army would step in... There are circumstances in which the State must step in to protect children.* PHRASAL VERB =intervene V P

step up. If you **step up** something, you increase it PHRASAL VERB or increase its intensity. *He urged donors to step up their efforts to send aid to Somalia... Security is being stepped up to deal with the increase in violence... There are reports of stepped-up fighting in El Salvador.* =increase V P n (not pron) V-ed P Also V n P

stepbrother /stepbrʌðəʳ/ **stepbrothers;** also spelled **step-brother**. Someone's **stepbrother** is the son of their stepfather or stepmother. N-COUNT: oft poss N

step-by-step. See **step**.

stepchild /steptʃaɪld/ **stepchildren;** also spelled **step-child**. Someone's **stepchild** is a child that was born to their husband or wife during a previous relationship. N-COUNT: oft poss N

stepdaughter /stepdɔːtəʳ/ **stepdaughters;** also spelled **step-daughter**. Someone's **stepdaughter** is a daughter that was born to their husband or wife during a previous relationship. N-COUNT: oft poss N

stepfather /stepfɑːðəʳ/ **stepfathers;** also spelled **step-father**. Someone's **stepfather** is the man who has married their mother after the death or divorce of their father. ◆◇◇◇◇ N-COUNT: oft poss N

stepladder /steplædəʳ/ **stepladders.** A **stepladder** is a portable ladder that is made of two sloping parts that are hinged together at the top so that it will stand up on its own. N-COUNT =steps

stepmother /stepmʌðəʳ/ **stepmothers;** also spelled **step-mother**. Someone's **stepmother** is the woman who has married their father after the death or divorce of their mother. ◆◇◇◇◇ N-COUNT: oft poss N

stepparent /steppeərənt/ **stepparents;** also spelled **step-parent**. Someone's **stepparent** is their stepmother or stepfather. N-COUNT: oft poss N

steppe /step/ **steppes. Steppes** are large areas of grassland where there are no trees. It is often used to refer to the area that stretches from Eastern Europe across the south of the former Soviet Union to Siberia. N-UNCOUNT: also N in pl

stepping stone, stepping stones; also spelled **stepping-stone**. ◆◇◇◇◇

1 You can describe a job or event as a **stepping stone** when it helps you to make progress, especially in your career. *Many students now see university as a stepping stone to a good job.* N-COUNT: oft N *to* n

2 **Stepping stones** are a line of large stones which you can walk on in order to cross a shallow stream or river. N-COUNT: usu pl

stepsister /stepsɪstəʳ/ **stepsisters;** also spelled **step-sister**. Someone's **stepsister** is the daughter of their stepfather or stepmother. N-COUNT: oft poss N

stepson /stepsʌn/ **stepsons;** also spelled **step-son**. Someone's **stepson** is a son born to their husband or wife during a previous relationship. N-COUNT: oft poss N

stereo /steriou/ **stereos** ◆◆◇◇◇

1 **Stereo** is used to describe a sound system or record in which the sound is played through two speakers. *...loudspeakers that give all-around stereo sound.* ADJ

2 A **stereo** is a record player with two speakers. N-COUNT

stereotype /steriətaɪp/ **stereotypes, stereotyping, stereotyped** ◆◆◇◇◇

1 A **stereotype** is a fixed general image or set of characteristics that a lot of people believe represent a particular type of person or thing. *There's always been a stereotype about successful businessmen... Accents can reinforce a negative stereotype.* N-COUNT

2 If someone **is stereotyped** as something, people form a fixed general idea or image of them, so that it is assumed that they will behave in a particular way. *He was stereotyped by some as a renegade... I get very worked up about the way women are stereotyped in a lot of mainstream films... You are likely to find many people who have stereotyped ideas about women.* VB: usu passive =typecast *be* V-ed *as* n *be* V-ed V-ed

stereotypical /sterioutɪpɪkᵊl/. A **stereotypical** idea of a type of person or thing is a fixed general idea that a lot of people have about it, that may be false in many cases. *These are men whose masculinity does not conform to stereotypical images of the unfeeling male.* ADJ-GRADED

sterile /steraɪl, AM -rəl/ ◆◇◇◇◇

1 Something that is **sterile** is completely clean and free from germs. *He always made sure that any cuts were protected by sterile dressings... Urine is sterile.* ADJ: usu ADJ n ♦ **sterility** /stərɪlɪti/ *...the antiseptic sterility of the hospital.* N-UNCOUNT

2 A person or animal that is **sterile** is unable to have or produce babies. *George was sterile. ...a sterile male.* ADJ ♦ **sterility** *This disease causes sterility in both males and females.* N-UNCOUNT

3 A **sterile** situation is lacking in energy and new ideas. *Too much time has been wasted in sterile debate.* ADJ-GRADED: usu ADJ n ♦ **sterility** *...the sterility of Dorothea's life in industry.* N-UNCOUNT

sterilize /sterɪlaɪz/ **sterilizes, sterilizing, sterilized;** also spelled **sterilise** in British English. ◆◇◇◇◇

1 If you **sterilize** a thing or a place, you make it completely clean and free from germs. *Sulphur is also used to sterilize equipment... The milk was sterilized and sealed in bottles.* VERB V n ♦ **sterilization** /sterɪlaɪzeɪʃᵊn, AM -lɪz-/ *...the pasteurization and sterilization of milk.* N-UNCOUNT

2 If a person or an animal **is sterilized**, they have a medical operation that makes it impossible for them to have or produce babies. *My wife was sterilized after the birth of her fourth child.* VB: usu passive *be* V-ed ♦ **sterilization, sterilizations** *In some cases, a sterilization is performed through the vaginal wall.* N-VAR

sterling /stɜːʳlɪŋ/ ◆◆◆◆◇

1 **Sterling** is the money system of Great Britain. *The stamps had to be paid for in sterling.* N-UNCOUNT

2 **Sterling** means excellent in quality; a formal word used to describe someone's work or character. *Those are sterling qualities to be admired in anyone. ...his years of sterling service.* ADJ: usu ADJ n =excellent

stern /stɜːʳn/ **sterner, sternest; sterns** ◆◆◇◇◇

1 **Stern** words or actions are very severe. *Mr de Klerk issued a stern warning to those who persist in violence... He said stern measures would be taken against the killers... Michael gave the dog a stern look.* ADJ-GRADED ♦ **sternly** *'We will take the necessary steps,' she said sternly.* ADV-GRADED: ADV with v, ADV adj

2 Someone who is **stern** is very serious and strict. *Her father was stern and hard to please.* ADJ-GRADED =strict

3 The **stern** of a boat is the back part of it. ● **From stem to stern**: see **stern**. N-COUNT ≠prow

4 If you say that someone is **made of sterner stuff**, you mean that they have a strong personality and are capable of overcoming difficulties and problems. *Whoever this woman is, she's made of sterner stuff than I am.* PHRASE

sternum /stɜːʳnəm/ **sternums.** Your **sternum** is the long flat bone which goes from your throat to the bottom of your ribs and to which your ribs are attached; a medical term. N-COUNT =breastbone

steroid /sterɔɪd, AM stɪr-/ **steroids.** A **steroid** is a type of chemical substance found in your body. Steroids can be artificially introduced into the bodies of athletes to improve their strength. ◆◇◇◇◇ N-COUNT

stethoscope /steθəskoup/ **stethoscopes.** A **stethoscope** is an instrument that a doctor uses to listen to your heart and breathing. It consists of a small disc that the doctor places on your body and a hollow tube that connects the disc to earpieces. N-COUNT

stetson /stetsᵊn/ **stetsons.** A **stetson** is a type of hat with a wide brim that is traditionally worn by cowboys. N-COUNT

stew /stjuː, AM stuː/ **stews, stewing, stewed** ◆◇◇◇◇

1 A **stew** is a meal which you make by cooking meat and vegetables in liquid at a low temperature. *She served him a bowl of beef stew... They made a stew.* N-VAR

2 When you **stew** meat, vegetables, or fruit, you cook them slowly in liquid in a closed dish. *Stew the apple and blackberries to make a thick pulp. ...stewed prunes.* VERB V n V-ed

3 If you are **in a stew**, you feel very worried. *He's been in a stew since early this morning... Highly charged emotions have you in a stew.* PHRASES PHR after v, v-link PHR

4 If you **let** someone **stew** or if you **leave** them **to stew**, you deliberately leave them to worry about something for a while, rather than telling them something which would make them feel better. *I'd* V inflects

rather let him stew... Leave them to stew in their own juice.

steward /stjuːəʳd, AM stuː-/ **stewards** ◆◆◇◇◇

1 A **steward** is a man who works on a ship, plane, or train, looking after passengers and serving meals to them. N-COUNT

2 A **steward** is someone who has the responsibility for looking after property. *The Earl didn't have the money or good judgement to employ a steward to manage the place for him.* N-COUNT =custodian

3 A **steward** is a man or woman who helps to organize a race, march, or other public event. *The steward at the march stood his ground while the rest of the marchers decided to run.* ● See also **shop steward**. N-COUNT

stewardess /stjuːəʳdes, stuː-/ **stewardesses.** A **stewardess** is a woman who works on a ship, plane, or train, looking after passengers and serving meals to them. N-COUNT =air hostess

stewardship /stjuːəʳdʃɪp, AM stuː-/. **Stewardship** is the responsibility of looking after property; a formal word. N-UNCOUNT: usu N *of* n

stewing steak. Stewing steak is beef which is suitable for cooking slowly in a stew. N-UNCOUNT

stick 1 noun uses

stick /stɪk/ **sticks** ◆◆◆◇◇

1 A **stick** is a thin branch which has fallen off a tree. *...people carrying bundles of dried sticks to sell for firewood.* N-COUNT =twig

2 A **stick** is a long thin piece of wood which is used for supporting someone's weight or for hitting people or animals. *He looks old, has diabetes and walks with a stick... Crowds armed with sticks and stones took to the streets.* ● See also **carrot and stick**. N-COUNT

3 A **stick** is a long thin piece of wood which is used for a particular purpose. *...kebab sticks. ...lolly sticks. ...drum sticks.* N-COUNT: usu n N

4 Some long thin objects used when taking part in sports are called **sticks**. *...lacrosse sticks. ...hockey sticks. ...ski-sticks.* N-COUNT: usu n N

5 A **stick** of something is a long thin piece of it. *...a stick of celery. ...cinnamon sticks.* N-COUNT: usu N *of* n, n N

6 If you give someone some **stick**, you criticize them or tease them roughly; used mainly in informal British English. *It's not motorists who give you the most stick, it's the general public... I get some stick from the lads because of my faith but I don't mind.* N-UNCOUNT

7 If you say that someone lives in **the sticks**, you mean that they live a long way from any large cities; an informal expression, used showing disapproval. *He lived out in the sticks somewhere.* N-PLURAL: *the* N

8 If you say that something is **a stick to beat** someone **with**, you mean that it is used, or could be used, as a basis for criticism; used mainly in journalism. *Unfortunately historic American fiction is constantly being used as a stick to beat contemporary British writers with.* PHRASES

9 If someone **gets the wrong end of the stick** or **gets hold of the wrong end of the stick**, they completely misunderstand something; an informal expression. V inflects

10 If you say that there are **more** things **than you could** or **can shake a stick at**, you are emphasizing in a light-hearted way that there are a lot of them; an old-fashioned, informal expression. *...a man with more medals than you can shake a stick at.* PRAGMATICS

stick 2 verb uses

stick /stɪk/ **sticks, sticking, stuck** ◆◆◆◆◇

1 If you **stick** something somewhere, you put it there in a rather casual way; an informal use. *He folded the papers and stuck them in his desk drawer... Jack opened his door and stuck his head out.* VERB V n prep/adv

2 If you **stick** a pointed object in something, or if it **sticks** in something, it pierces it. *They sent in loads of male nurses and stuck a needle in my back... Some punk stuck a knife in her last night... The soldiers went at once to the mound and began to stick their bayonets through it... The knife stuck in the ground at his feet.* V-ERG V n *in/into/through* n V *in* n

3 If something is **sticking out** from somewhere or **sticking into** something else, it extends away from something or through something. *They lay where they had fallen from the crane, sticking out of the water... Something was sticking from the pocket of the little man's grimy shorts... His hair sticks up in half a dozen directions. ...when we see her with lots of tubes and needles sticking into her little body.* VERB V adv/prep

4 If you **stick** one thing to another, you attach it using glue, sticky tape, or another sticky substance. *Don't forget to clip the token and stick it on your card... We just stuck it to the window... He has nowhere to stick up his posters... Stick down any loose bits of flooring.* VERB V n prep V n with adv

5 If one thing **sticks** to another, it becomes attached to it and is difficult to remove. *The soil sticks to the blade and blocks the plough... Peel away the waxed paper if it has stuck to the bottom of the cake... If left to stand, cooked pasta sticks together.* VERB =adhere V *to* n V *together*

6 If something **sticks in** your mind, you remember it for a long time. *The incident stuck in my mind because it was the first example I had seen of racism in that country... That song has stuck in my head for years.* VERB V *in* n

7 If you give someone or something a name and the name **sticks**, it becomes the name which most people use to refer to that person or thing. *A friend dubbed it 'The Sanctuary' and the name stuck.* VERB V

8 If someone manages to make a charge or accusation **stick**, they show that the person accused is guilty of the crime or wrong-doing they are accused of. *I don't see how they'll make the charges stick... But legal experts are not sure if such a charge can stick.* VB: no cont, with brd-neg V

9 If something which can usually be moved **sticks**, it becomes fixed in one position. *The needle on the dial went right round to fifty feet, which was as far as it could go, and there it stuck... The dagger stuck tightly in the silver scabbard.* VERB V

10 If you are in an unpleasant or difficult situation and can hardly **stick** it, you cannot bear to remain there long; an informal use. *Got a job bottle-washing at the brewery. I lasted a fortnight. I couldn't stick it... How long did you stick it for?* VERB =stand V n

11 See also **stuck**.

12 If you say that someone **can stick** something, especially a job, or tell them where **to stick** it, you are rudely refusing it or emphasizing that you do not want it or like it; an informal expression which some people find offensive. *It's a rotten play, so they can stick it... She then stormed out in a temper telling him to 'stick his job'.* PHRASE PRAGMATICS

stick around. If you **stick around**, you stay where you are, often because you are waiting for something; an informal expression. *Stick around a while and see what develops... I didn't stick around long enough to find out.* PHRASAL VERB V P Also V P n

stick at. If you **stick at** a task or activity, you continue doing it, even if it is difficult. *You will find it hard at first, but stick at it... He became more and more irritated by her inability to stick at anything.* PHRASAL VERB V P n

stick by PHRASAL VERB

1 If you **stick by** someone, you continue to give them help or support. *...friends who stuck by me during the difficult times as Council Leader... She'd stuck by Bob through thick and thin.* V P n

2 If you **stick by** a promise, agreement, decision, or principle, you do what you said you would do, or do not change your mind. *But I made my decision then and stuck by it.* =stick to V P n

stick out PHRASAL VERB

1 If you **stick out** part of your body, you extend it away from your body. *She made a face and stuck out her tongue at him... He stuck his hand out and he said, 'Good evening.'* ● to **stick your neck out**: see **neck**. V P n (not pron) V n P

2 If something **sticks out**, it is very noticeable because it is unusual. *The things that stuck out were his cockiness and his four-letter words... What had Cutter done to make him stick out from the crowd?* ● to **stick out a mile**: see **mile**. ● to **stick out like a sore thumb**: see **thumb**. =stand out V P V P *from* n

3 If someone in an unpleasant or difficult situation V inflects

sticks it out, they do not leave or give up. *I really didn't like New York, but I wanted to stick it out a little bit longer.* • to **stick in** your **throat**: see **throat**.

stick out for. If you **stick out for** something, you keep demanding it and do not accept anything different or less. *I stuck out for a handsome redundancy package.* PHRASAL VERB VPPn

stick to PHRASAL VERB

1 If you **stick to** something or someone when you are travelling, you stay close to them. *There are interesting hikes inland, but most ramblers stick to the clifftops... Stick to well-lit roads.* VPn

2 If you **stick to** something, you continue doing, using, saying, or talking about it, rather than changing to something else. *Perhaps he should have stuck to writing... Lionel, you just tell the cops what you saw; stick to your story.* VPn

3 If you **stick to** a promise, agreement, decision, or principle, you do what you said you would do, or do not change your mind. *Immigrant support groups are waiting to see if he sticks to his word. ...if Labour sticks to its plan to lift the upper earnings limit... But one problem is that few people can stick to a diet for long.* • to **stick to your guns**: see **gun**. =stick by VPn

4 If you **stick to** rules, you do what they say you must do. *Obviously we are disappointed but the committee could do nothing less than stick to the rules... Police must stick to the highest standards if they are to win back public confidence.* VPn

stick together. If people **stick together**, they stay with each other and support each other. *If we all stick together, we ought to be okay.* PHRASAL VERB VP

stick up for. If you **stick up for** a person or a principle, you support or defend them forcefully. *Dad spoils me. He loves me. He sticks up for me... I can stick up for myself... He has shown a great deal of courage in sticking up for democracy and civil liberties.* PHRASAL VERB =stand up for, defend VPPn

stick with PHRASAL VERB

1 If you **stick with** something, you do not change to something else. *If you're in a job that keeps you busy, stick with it... They prefer, in the end, to stick with what they know.* VPn

2 If you **stick with** someone, you stay close to them. *Tugging the woman's arm, she pulled her to her side saying: 'You just stick with me, dear.'* VPn

sticker /stɪkəʳ/ **stickers.** A **sticker** is a small piece of paper or plastic, with writing or a picture on one side, which you can stick onto a surface. • See also **bumper sticker**. ◆◇◇◇◇ N-COUNT

sticking plaster, sticking plasters. Sticking plaster is material that you can stick over a cut or blister in order to protect it. A **sticking plaster** is a piece of this. N-VAR

sticking point, sticking points; also spelled **sticking-point**. A **sticking point** in a discussion or series of negotiations is a point on which the people involved cannot agree and which may delay or stop the talks. A **sticking point** is also one aspect of a problem which you have trouble dealing with. *The main sticking point was the question of taxes.* ◆◇◇◇◇ N-COUNT: usu sing

stick insect, stick insects; also spelled **stick-insect**. A **stick insect** is an insect with a long thin body and legs. It looks like a small stick. N-COUNT

stick-in-the-mud, stick-in-the-muds. In British English, if you describe someone as a **stick-in-the-mud**, you mean that you disapprove of them because they do not like doing anything that is new or fun; an informal word. N-COUNT PRAGMATICS =fuddy-duddy

stickleback /stɪkəlbæk/ **sticklebacks.** A **stickleback** is a small fish which has spikes along its back. N-COUNT

stickler /stɪkləʳ/ **sticklers.** If you are a **stickler** for something, you always insist on it. *I'm a bit of a stickler for accuracy ... Lucy was a stickler for perfection, and everything had to be exactly right.* N-COUNT: usu N *for* n

stick-on. Stick-on labels, shapes, and objects have an adhesive material on one side so that they will stick to surfaces. ADJ: ADJ n =adhesive

sticky /stɪki/ **stickier, stickiest** ◆◆◇◇◇

1 A **sticky** substance is soft, or thick and liquid, and can stick to other things. **Sticky** things are covered with a sticky substance. *...sticky toffee... If the dough is sticky, add more flour... Peel away the sticky paper.* ♦ **stickiness** *...the stickiness of her hands.* ADJ-GRADED N-UNCOUNT

2 A **sticky** situation involves problems or is embarrassing; an informal use, used mainly in British English. *Inevitably the transition will yield some sticky moments... Her research was going through a sticky patch.* ADJ-GRADED: usu ADJ n =tricky

3 **Sticky** weather is unpleasantly hot and damp. *...four desperately hot, sticky days in the middle of August.* ADJ-GRADED =muggy

4 If someone **comes to a sticky end** or **meets a sticky end**, they suffer very badly or die in an unpleasant way; an informal expression. *Arminius also came to a sticky end, murdered by his own troops.* PHRASE: V inflects

sticky tape. Sticky tape is clear sticky tape that is sold in rolls and that you use to stick paper or card together or onto a wall. N-UNCOUNT

stiff /stɪf/ **stiffer, stiffest** ◆◆◇◇◇

1 Something that is **stiff** is firm or does not bend easily. *The furniture was stiff, uncomfortable, too delicate, and too neat... His gaberdine trousers were brand new and stiff... Her fingers were stiff with cold inside her leather gloves... Clean the mussels with a stiff brush under cold running water.* ♦ **stiffly** *Moira sat stiffly upright in her straight-backed chair.* ADJ-GRADED =rigid ≠flexible ADV-GRADED: ADV adj, ADV with v

2 Something such as a door or drawer that is **stiff** does not move as easily as it should. *Train doors have handles on the inside. They are stiff so that they cannot be opened accidentally.* ADJ-GRADED

3 If you are **stiff**, your muscles or joints ache when you move, because of illness or because of too much exercise. *The Mud Bath is particularly recommended for relieving tension and stiff muscles... I'm stiff all over right now – I hope I can recover for tomorrow's race.* ♦ **stiffly** *He climbed stiffly from the Volkswagen.* ♦ **stiffness** *Stiffness and discomfort can usually be eased with heat or a warm bath.* ADJ-GRADED ADV-GRADED N-UNCOUNT

4 **Stiff** behaviour is rather formal and not very friendly or relaxed. *She looked at him with a stiff smile... They always seemed a little awkward with each other, a bit stiff and formal.* ♦ **stiffly** *'Why don't you borrow your sister's car?' said Cassandra stiffly... He was sending a stiffly worded letter of complaint to the club.* ♦ **stiffness** *There had been stiffness and long silences and tension in the air.* ADJ-GRADED =reserved ≠relaxed ADV-GRADED: ADV with v, ADV adj N-UNCOUNT

5 **Stiff** can be used to mean difficult or severe. *The film faces stiff competition for the Best Film nomination... Under Greece's stiff anti-drugs laws they could face twenty years in jail.* ADJ-GRADED: usu ADJ n

6 A **stiff** drink is a large amount of a strong alcoholic drink. *...a stiff whisky.* ADJ-GRADED: ADJ n =large

7 A **stiff** breeze is blowing quite strongly. *Next morning dawned clear and sunny, with a stiff breeze rustling the trees.* ADJ-GRADED: usu ADJ n =strong

8 If you are bored **stiff**, worried **stiff**, or scared **stiff**, you are extremely bored, worried, or scared; an informal use. *Anna tried to look interested. Actually, she was bored stiff... I was scared stiff when I realized what I'd done.* ► Also an adjective. *Even if he bores you stiff, it is good manners not to let him know it.* ADV: adj ADV ADJ: ADJ after v

9 • **stiff upper lip**: see **lip**.

stiffen /stɪfᵊn/ **stiffens, stiffening, stiffened** ◆◇◇◇◇

1 If you **stiffen**, you stop moving and stand or sit with muscles that are suddenly tense, for example because you feel afraid or angry. *Ada stiffened at the sound of his voice... The father's face stiffened with dismay.* VERB V

2 If your muscles or joints **stiffen**, or if something **stiffens** them, they become difficult to bend or move. *The blood supply to the skin is reduced when muscles stiffen.* ► **Stiffen up** means the same as **stiffen**. *These clothes restrict your freedom of movement and stiffen up the whole body... 'I just stiffened* V-ERG V Also V n PHRASAL VERB ERG V P n (not pron) Also V n P,

up, and the more they told me to 'be natural', the more I felt not at all relaxed. V P

3 If attitudes or behaviour **stiffen**, or if something **stiffens** them, they become stronger or more severe, and less likely to be changed. *Russian resistance suddenly stiffened because there was no room for retreat... Canada has recently stiffened its immigration rules.* V-ERG =strengthen V V n

4 If something such as cloth **is stiffened**, it is made firm so that it does not bend easily. *This special paper was actually thin, soft Sugiwara paper that had been stiffened with a kind of paste... They peeled cold stiffened gloves from their hands.* VB: usu passive be V-ed V-ed

stiffen up. See **stiffen** 2. PHRASAL VERB

stiff-necked; also spelled **stiffnecked**. If you say that someone is **stiff-necked**, you mean that they are proud and stubborn; used showing disapproval. ADJ-GRADED PRAGMATICS =stubborn, proud

stifle /staɪfᵊl/ **stifles, stifling, stifled** ◆◇◇◇◇

1 If someone **stifles** something you consider to be a good thing, they prevent it from continuing. *Regulations on children stifled creativity... Critics have accused the US of trying to stifle debate.* VERB =repress V n

2 If you **stifle** a yawn or laugh, you prevent yourself from yawning or laughing. *She makes no attempt to stifle a yawn... His hand shot to his mouth to stifle a giggle.* VERB =suppress, smother V n

3 If you **stifle** your natural feelings or behaviour, you prevent yourself from having those feelings or behaving in that way. *It is best to stifle curiosity and leave birds' nests alone... He stifled his temptation to take hold of Ivy and shake her.* VERB =suppress V n

stifling /staɪfəlɪŋ/ ◆◇◇◇◇

1 **Stifling** heat is so intense that it makes you feel uncomfortable. You can also use **stifling** to describe a place that is extremely hot. *The stifling heat of the little room was beginning to make me nauseous.* ADJ-GRADED =suffocating

2 If a situation is **stifling**, it makes you feel uncomfortable because you cannot do what you want. *Life at home with her parents and two sisters was stifling. ...a stifling bureaucracy.* ADJ-GRADED =suffocating

3 See also **stifle**.

stigma /stɪgmə/ **stigmas** ◆◇◇◇◇

1 If something has a **stigma** attached to it, people consider it to be unacceptable or a disgrace. *There is still a stigma attached to cancer... There is very little stigma attached to crime and criminals.* N-VAR

2 The **stigma** of a flower is the top of the centre part which takes in pollen. N-COUNT

stigmata /stɪgmɑːtə/. If marks appear on a person's body in the same places where Christ was wounded when He was crucified, they are called **stigmata**. Some Christians believe that this is a sign of holiness. N-PLURAL

stigmatize /stɪgmətaɪz/ **stigmatizes, stigmatizing, stigmatized;** also spelled **stigmatise** in British English. If someone or something **is stigmatized**, they are unfairly regarded by many people as unacceptable or disgraceful. *Children in single-parent families must not be stigmatised... The AIDS epidemic has further stigmatised gays... They are often stigmatized by the rest of society as lazy and dirty.* ♦ **stigmatized** *It is a stigmatized illness.* VERB be V-ed V n be V-ed prep ADJ

stile /staɪl/ **stiles.** A **stile** is an entrance to a field or path that consists of a step on either side of a fence or wall. This allows you to get onto the field or path without opening the gate, which means that no animals can get out of the field. N-COUNT

stiletto /stɪletoʊ/ **stilettos. Stilettos** are women's shoes that have high, very narrow heels; used mainly in British English. The usual American expression is **spike heels**. N-COUNT: usu pl

still 1 adverb uses

still /stɪl/ ◆◆◆◆◆

1 If a situation that used to exist **still** exists, it has continued and exists now. *I still dream of home... Brian's toe is still badly swollen and he cannot put on his shoe... If you don't like the job, why are you still there?... There are still doubts about the final signing of the two treaties.* ADV: ADV before v, ADV group

2 If something that has not yet happened could **still** happen, it is possible that it will happen. If something that has not yet happened is **still** to happen, it will happen at a later time. *Big money could still be made if the crisis keeps oil prices high... We could still make it, but we won't get there till three... The details have still to be to be worked out... Still to come, the financial news and the weather at a quarter to two.* ADV: ADV before v

3 If you say that there **is still** an amount of something left, you are emphasizing that there is that amount left. *Bardi coloured the milk with the slightest touch of coffee, of which there was still plenty... There are still some outstanding problems... There's still time to catch up with them.* ADV: be ADV n

4 You use **still** to emphasize that something remains the case or is true in spite of what you have just said. *Even if politicians are Labour, they still can have minds of their own... Despite the ruling, Boreham was still found guilty.* ADV: ADV before v =nonetheless

5 You use **still** when you are dismissing a problem or difficulty as not really worth worrying about. *Their luck had simply run out. Still, never fear... 'Any idea who is going to be here this weekend?'—No. Still, who cares?'* ADV: ADV with cl

6 You use **still** in expressions such as **still further**, **still another**, and **still more** to show that you find the number or quantity of things you are referring to surprising or excessive. *We look forward to strengthening still further our already close cooperation with the police service... Why did the bank not conduct its own audit before lending still more?* ADV: ADV n/adv =even, yet

7 You use **still** with comparatives to indicate that something has even more of a quality than something else. *Formula One motor car racing is supposed to be dangerous. 'Indycar' racing is supposed to be more dangerous still.* ADV: ADV with compar

still 2 not moving or making a noise

still /stɪl/ **stiller, stillest; stills, stilling, stilled** ◆◆◆◆◆

1 If you stay **still**, you stay in the same position and do not move. *David had been dancing about like a child, but suddenly he stood still and looked at Brad... He played the tape through once, then sat very still for several minutes... He recalled her still face and the hurt in her eyes when he had refused her help... Gladys was still, then she shook her head slowly.* ADJ-GRADED: ADJ after v, v-link ADJ, ADJ n

2 If air or water is **still**, it is not moving. *The night air was very still... He watched the still water over the side of the boat.* ADJ-GRADED

3 If a place is **still**, it is quiet and shows no sign of activity. *In the room it was very still.* ♦ **stillness** *Four deafening explosions shattered the stillness of the night air.* ADJ-GRADED =quiet, tranquil N-UNCOUNT =tranquillity

4 If a sound **stills** or **is stilled**, it becomes quiet. *Her crying slowly stilled... The roar of the crowd stilled to an expectant murmur... The people's voice has been stilled.* V-ERG V be V-ed

5 A **still** is a photograph taken from a cinema film which is used for publicity purposes. N-COUNT: oft N n

still 3 apparatus

still /stɪl/ **stills.** A **still** is an apparatus used for distilling alcoholic drinks. N-COUNT

stillbirth /stɪlbɜːʳθ/ **stillbirths.** A **stillbirth** is the birth of a dead baby. N-VAR

stillborn /stɪlbɔːʳn/

1 A **stillborn** baby is dead when it is born. *It was a miracle that she survived the birth of her stillborn baby... Their first child was stillborn.* ADJ

2 An idea, action, or attempt which is **stillborn**, is completely ineffective or unsuccessful. *The current EC plan will be stillborn. ...stillborn agreements.* ADJ

still life, still lifes. A **still life** is a painting or drawing of an arrangement of objects such as flowers or fruit. It also refers to this type of painting or drawing. ◆◇◇◇◇ N-VAR

stilt /stɪlt/ **stilts**

1 **Stilts** are long upright pieces of wood or metal which are used to support some buildings, especially when the ground is wet or very soft. *They inhabit reed huts built on stilts above the water.* N-COUNT: usu pl, oft on N

2 Stilts are also two long pieces of wood with ledges high up on the sides that people such as circus clowns or children stand on in order to walk high up above the ground. N-COUNT

stilted /stɪltɪd/. If someone's behaviour or conversation is **stilted**, they behave or speak in a formal, self-conscious, or unnatural way. *We made polite, stilted conversation... His delivery was stilted and occasionally stumbling.* ADJ-GRADED =laboured ≠relaxed

stimulant /stɪmjʊlənt/ **stimulants.** A **stimulant** is a drug that makes your body work faster, often increasing your heart rate and making you less likely to sleep. ◆◇◇◇◇ N-COUNT

stimulate /stɪmjʊleɪt/ **stimulates, stimulating, stimulated** ◆◆◆◇◇

1 To **stimulate** something means to encourage it to begin or develop further. *America's priority is rightly to stimulate its economy... The Russian health service has stimulated public interest in home cures.* ♦ **stimulation** /stɪmjʊleɪʃᵊn/ *...an economy in need of stimulation.* VERB V n N-UNCOUNT

2 If you are **stimulated** by something, it makes you feel full of ideas and enthusiasm. *Bill was stimulated by the challenge... I was stimulated to examine my deepest thoughts.* ♦ **stimulating** *It is complex yet stimulating book... The atmosphere was always stimulating.* ♦ **stimulation** *Many enjoy the mental stimulation of a challenging job.* VB: usu passive be V-ed be V-ed to-inf ADJ-GRADED: usu ADJ n N-UNCOUNT: usu with supp

3 If something **stimulates** a part of a person's body, it causes it to move or function, usually automatically by a natural reflex. *Exercise stimulates the digestive and excretory systems... The production of melanin in the skin is stimulated by exposure to the sun... The body is stimulated to build up resistance.* ♦ **stimulating** *...the stimulating effect of adrenaline.* ♦ **stimulation** *...physical stimulation. ...the chemical stimulation of drugs.* VERB V n be V-ed to-inf ADJ-GRADED N-UNCOUNT: usu with supp

stimulative /stɪmjʊlətɪv/. If a government policy has a **stimulative** effect on the economy, it encourages the economy to grow. *It is possible that a tax cut might have some stimulative effect.* ADJ-GRADED: usu ADJ n

stimulus /stɪmjʊləs/ **stimuli** /stɪmjʊlaɪ/. A **stimulus** is something that encourages activity in people or things. *Interest rates could fall soon and be a stimulus to the US economy... It is through our nervous system that we adapt ourselves to our environment and to all external stimuli.* ◆◆◇◇◇ N-VAR

sting /stɪŋ/ **stings, stinging, stung** ◆◆◇◇◇

1 If a plant, animal, or insect **stings** you, it pricks your skin, usually with poison, so that you feel a sharp pain. *The nettles stung their legs... I jumped as if I had been stung by a scorpion... This type of bee rarely stings.* VERB V n V

2 The **sting** of an insect or animal is the part that stings you. *Remove the bee sting with tweezers.* N-COUNT

3 If you feel a **sting**, you feel a sharp pain in your skin or other part of your body. *This won't hurt - you will just feel a little sting.* N-COUNT: usu sing

4 If a part of your body **stings**, or if a substance **stings** it, you feel a sharp pain there. *His cheeks were stinging from the icy wind... Never put any essential oils near the eyes. They are very strong and could sting... Sprays can sting sensitive skin.* V-ERG V V n

5 If someone's remarks **sting** you, they make you feel hurt and annoyed. *He's a sensitive lad and some of the criticism has stung him... She burst into tears, stung by the harshness of his words.* ♦ **stinging** *...a stinging attack on the government's economic policy.* VB: no cont =hurt V n V-ed ADJ-GRADED: usu ADJ n

6 In American English, a **sting** is a clever secret plan by undercover police to catch criminals. *The police ran a sting operation to crack down on illegal guns. ...a sting set by the FBI.* N-COUNT: oft N n

7 If an announcement or decision has **a sting in the tail** or **a sting in its tail**, it contains a critical and unpleasant part, normally at the end. PHRASES usu PHR after v

8 If something **takes the sting out** of a situation, it makes it less hurtful or unpleasant. V inflects

stingray /stɪŋreɪ/ **stingrays.** A **stingray** is a type of large flat fish with a long tail which it can use as a weapon. N-COUNT

stingy /stɪndʒi/ **stingier, stingiest.** Someone who is **stingy** is very mean. *The West is stingy with aid... Winston was not a stingy man.* ADJ-GRADED =mean ≠generous

stink /stɪŋk/ **stinks, stinking, stank, stunk** ◆◇◇◇◇

1 If something **stinks**, it smells extremely unpleasant. *We all stank and nobody minded... The place stinks of fried onions... The pond stank like a sewer.* ► Also a noun. *He was aware of the stink of stale beer on his breath... The stink was overpowering.* ♦ **stinking** *They were locked up in a stinking cell.* VERB V V of n V like n N-SING =stench ADJ-GRADED

2 If you say that something **stinks**, you mean that you disapprove of it because it involves ideas, feelings, or practices that you do not like; an informal use. *I think their methods stink... The whole thing stinks of political corruption.* VERB PRAGMATICS V V of n

3 If someone makes **a stink** about something they are angry about, they show their anger in order to make people take notice; an informal use. *The family's making a hell of a stink... The tabloid press kicked up a stink about his seven-day visit.* N-SING: a N =fuss

stinker /stɪŋkəʳ/ **stinkers.** If you describe someone or something as a **stinker**, you mean that you think they are very unpleasant or bad; an informal word. *I think he's an absolute stinker to do that to her... I thought it was a right stinker.* N-COUNT

stinking /stɪŋkɪŋ/

1 You use **stinking** to describe something that is unpleasant or bad; an informal word. *I had a stinking cold.* ADJ: ADJ n

2 See also **stink**.

stinky /stɪŋki/ **stinkier, stinkiest. Stinky** means the same as **stinking**. ADJ-GRADED: usu ADJ n ≠smelly

stint /stɪnt/ **stints.** A **stint** is a period of time which you spend doing a particular job or activity or working in a particular place. *He is returning to this country after a five-year stint in Hong Kong.* ◆◇◇◇◇ N-COUNT: with supp, oft adj N, N prep

stipend /staɪpend/ **stipends.** A **stipend** is a sum of money that is paid regularly to a person, especially a magistrate or clergyman, as a salary or as living expenses. N-COUNT =allowance

stipendiary /staɪpendiəri, AM -dieri/. A **stipendiary** magistrate or clergyman receives a stipend. ADJ: ADJ n

stippled /stɪpᵊld/. A surface that is **stippled** is covered with tiny dots. *The room remains simple with bare, stippled green walls.* ADJ

stipulate /stɪpjʊleɪt/ **stipulates, stipulating, stipulated.** If you **stipulate** a condition or that something must be done, you say clearly that it must be done. *She could have stipulated that she would pay when she collected the computer... International rules stipulate the number of foreign entrants.* ♦ **stipulation** /stɪpjʊleɪʃᵊn/ **stipulations** *Clifford's only stipulation is that his clients obey his advice.* ◆◇◇◇◇ VERB =specify V that/wh V n N-COUNT =condition

stir /stɜːʳ/ **stirs, stirring, stirred** ◆◆◆◇◇

1 If you **stir** a liquid or other substance, you move it around or mix it in a container using something such as a spoon. *Stir the soup for a few seconds... There was Mrs Bellingham, stirring sugar into her tea... You don't add the peanut butter until after you've stirred in the honey.* VERB V n V n into n V n with in

2 If you **stir**, you move slightly, for example because you are uncomfortable or beginning to wake up ; used in written English. *Eileen shook him, and he started to stir... The two women lay on their backs, not stirring.* VERB =move V

3 If you do not **stir** from a place, you do not move from it; used in written English. *She had not stirred from the house that evening... There's something you could study without stirring from this room.* VB: usu with brd-neg =move V from n

4 If something **stirs** or if the wind **stirs** it, it moves gently in the wind; used in written English. *Palm trees stir in the soft Pacific breeze... Not a breath of fresh air stirred the long white curtains.* V-ERG =move V V n

5 If you **stir** yourself, or if something **stirs** you into action, you move in order to start doing something. *Stir yourself! We've got a visitor... You can't even stir yourself to have a drink with them... The sight of them stirred him into action.* VERB =shift V pron-refl V pron-refl to-inf V n prep

6 If something **stirs** you, it makes you react with a strong emotion; used in written English. *The voice,* VERB =move, affect

less coarse now, stirred her as it had then... I was intrigued by him, stirred by his intellect. Vn

7 If a particular memory, feeling, or mood **stirs** or **is stirred** in you, you begin to think about it or feel it; used in written English. *Then a memory stirs in you and you start feeling anxious... Amy remembered the anger he had stirred in her... Beneath my antipathy a powerful curiosity was stirring.* V-ERG =awaken V in n V n in n V

8 If an event causes a **stir**, it causes great excitement, shock, or anger among people. *His film has caused a stir in America.* N-SING =commotion

9 See also **stirring**.

10 If you say that someone has been **shaken but not stirred** by an experience, you mean that they have been slightly disturbed or emotionally affected by it, but not deeply enough to change their behaviour or way of thinking; an informal expression, used mainly in journalism. *A clash with America over farm subsidies had left the Europeans and their common agricultural policy shaken but not stirred.* PHRASE: usu v-link PHR

stir up PHRASAL VERB

1 If something **stirs up** dust or **stirs up** mud in water, it causes it to rise up and move around. *They saw first a cloud of dust and then the car that was stirring it up.* =disturb V n P Also V P n (not pron)

2 If you **stir up** a particular mood or situation, usually a bad one, you cause it. *As usual, Harriet is trying to stir up trouble... He said senior government officials were trying to stir up ethnic tension... I thought at first that Jay had been stirring things up.* =encourage V P n (not pron) V n P

stir-fry, stir-fries, stir-frying, stir-fried ◆◇◇◇◇

1 If you **stir-fry** vegetables, meat, or fish, you cook small pieces of them quickly by stirring them in a small quantity of very hot oil. This method is often used in Chinese cookery. *Stir-fry the vegetables until crisp. ...stir-fried vegetables.* VERB V n V-ed

2 A **stir-fry** is a Chinese dish consisting of small pieces of vegetables, meat, or fish which have been stir-fried. *Serve the stir-fry with 'instant' noodles.* N-COUNT

3 **Stir-fry** vegetables, meat, or fish or **stir-fry** dishes are cooked by the stir-fry method. ADJ: ADJ n

stirrer /stɜːrəʳ/ **stirrers.** If you refer to someone as a **stirrer**, you disapprove of them because they often try to cause trouble; an informal word. N-COUNT PRAGMATICS

stirring /stɜːrɪŋ/ **stirrings** ◆◇◇◇◇

1 A **stirring** event, performance, or account of something makes people very excited or enthusiastic. *The Prime Minister made a stirring speech... Stowe gives a stirring performance as a strong spirited female. ...a stirring account of the final months of the old regime.* ADJ-GRADED: usu ADJ n =rousing

2 A **stirring** of a feeling or thought is the beginning of one. *I feel a stirring of curiosity. ...the first stirrings of a sense of guilt.* N-COUNT: usu N of n

stirrup /stɪrəp, AM stɜːr-/ **stirrups. Stirrups** are the two metal loops which are attached to a horse's saddle by long pieces of leather, and which you place your feet in when riding a horse. N-COUNT

stitch /stɪtʃ/ **stitches, stitching, stitched** ◆◆◇◇◇

1 If you **stitch** cloth, you use a needle and thread to join two pieces together or to make a decoration. *Fold the fabric and stitch the two layers together... We stitched incessantly. ...those patient ladies who stitched the magnificent medieval tapestries.* VERB =sew V n adv/prep V V n

2 **Stitches** are the short pieces of thread that have been sewn in a piece of cloth. *...a row of straight stitches... You can use embroidery stitches for further decoration.* N-COUNT

3 In knitting and crochet, a **stitch** is a loop made by one turn of wool around a knitting needle or crochet hook. *Her mother counted the stitches on her knitting needles... She kept dropping stitches.* N-COUNT

4 If you sew or knit something in a particular **stitch**, you sew or knit in a way that produces a particular pattern. *The design can be worked in cross stitch. ...a woolly vest knitted in garter stitch.* N-UNCOUNT: usu n N

5 When doctors **stitch** a wound, they use a special needle and thread to sew the skin together. *Jill washed and stitched the wound.* ► **Stitch up** means the same as **stitch**. *Dr Armonson stitched up her wrist wounds... They've taken him off to hospital to stitch him up.* VERB =suture V n PHRASAL VERB V P n (not pron) V n P

6 A **stitch** is a piece of thread that has been used to sew the skin of a wound together. *He had six stitches in a head wound.* N-COUNT =suture

7 A **stitch** is a sharp pain in your side, usually caused by running or laughing a lot. N-SING

8 If you are **in stitches**, you cannot stop laughing; an informal expression. *Here's a book that will have you in stitches.* PHRASE: PHR after v, v-link PHR

stitch up PHRASAL VERB

1 To **stitch** someone **up** means to trick them so that they are put in a situation where they are at a disadvantage, or where they are blamed for something they have not done; an informal expression. *He claimed that a police officer had threatened to stitch him up and send him to prison.* =frame V n P Also V P n (not pron)

2 To **stitch up** an agreement, especially a complicated agreement between several people, means to arrange it; an informal use. *Shiraz has stitched up major deals all over the world to boost sales.* =secure V P n

3 See **stitch** 5.

stitching /stɪtʃɪŋ/. **Stitching** is a row of stitches that have been sewn in a piece of cloth. *The stitching had begun to fray at the edges... A star was done in red stitching.* N-UNCOUNT

stitch-up, stitch-ups; also spelled **stitch up**. If you describe a situation as a **stitch-up**, you mean that it has been altered in a way that makes it unfair; an informal word. *My view is that this is a stitch up, and has been from the very beginning.* N-COUNT: usu sing

stoat /stoʊt/ **stoats.** A **stoat** is a small wild animal that has brown fur and is similar to a weasel. Some stoats that live in northern Europe have fur that turns white in winter. N-COUNT

stock /stɒk/ **stocks, stocking, stocked** ◆◆◆◆◆

1 **Stocks** are shares in the ownership of a company, or investments on which a fixed amount of interest will be paid. *...the buying and selling of stocks and shares... As stock prices have dropped, so too has bank capital.* N-COUNT: usu pl

2 A company's **stock** is the amount of money which the company has through selling shares. *Two years later, when Compaq went public, their stock was valued at $38 million... The Fisher family holds 40% of the stock.* N-UNCOUNT: usu poss N

3 If a shop **stocks** particular goods, it keeps a supply of them to sell. *The shop stocks everything from cigarettes to recycled loo paper.* VB: no cont V n

4 A shop's **stock** is the total amount of goods which it has available to sell. *We took the decision to withdraw a quantity of stock from sale.* N-UNCOUNT

5 If you **stock** something such a cupboard, shelf, or room, you fill it with food or other things. *I worked stocking shelves in a grocery store... Some families stocked their cellars with food and water... The kitchen cupboard was stocked with tins of soup.* ► **Stock up** means the same as **stock**. *I had to stock the boat up with food... Customers travel from hundreds of miles away to stock up their deep freezes... Start planning for Christmas now by stocking up the freezer with some festive dishes.* VERB V n V n with n V-ed PHRASAL VERB V n P with n V P n (not pron) V P n (not pron) with n Also V n P

6 If you have a **stock** of things, you have a supply of them stored in a place ready to be used. *I keep a stock of cassette tapes describing various relaxation techniques... Stocks of ammunition were running low.* N-COUNT: with supp, usu N of n

7 The **stock** of something is the total amount of it that is available in a particular area. *...the stock of accommodation available to be rented.* N-SING: with supp

8 If you are from a particular **stock**, you are descended from a particular group of people; a formal use. *We are both from working class stock. ...blacks, Asians and people of Mediterranean stock.* N-UNCOUNT: usu supp N =descent

9 **Stock** are cattle, sheep, pigs, or other animals which are kept by a farmer, usually ones which have been specially bred. *I am carefully selecting the breeding stock... His herd of 170 dairy cattle and 200 young stock are kept on the land.* N-PLURAL =livestock

10 A **stock** answer, expression, or way of doing something is one that is very commonly used, especially because people cannot be bothered to ADJ: ADJ n PRAGMATICS =standard

think of something new; used showing disapproval. *My boss had a stock response – 'If it ain't broke, don't fix it!'... National security is the stock excuse for keeping things confidential.*

11 Stock is a liquid, usually made by boiling meat, bones, or vegetables in water. Stock is used to give flavour to soups and sauces. N-MASS

12 In former times, the **stocks** were an instrument of punishment. The criminal's hands and legs were locked into holes in a wooden frame while people threw things at them. N-PLURAL

13 See also **stocking**; **laughing stock**, **rolling stock**.

14 If goods are **in stock** a shop has them available to sell. If they are **out of stock**, it does not. *Check that your size is in stock... Lemon and lime juice were both temporarily out of stock.* PHRASES usu v-link PHR

15 If you **take stock**, you pause to think about all the aspects of a situation or event, before deciding what to do next. *It was time to take stock of the situation... I was forty, the age when people take stock and change their lives.* V inflects, usu PHR *of*n

16 • **lock, stock, and barrel**: see **barrel**.

stock up PHRASAL VERB

1 See **stock** 5.

2 If you **stock up** on something, you buy a lot of it, in case you cannot get it later. *The authorities have urged people to stock up on fuel... New Yorkers have been stocking up with bottled water.* V P *on/with*n

stockade /stɒkeɪd/ **stockades.** A **stockade** is a wall of large wooden posts built around an area to keep out enemies or wild animals. *Entry into this inner stockade was by a single, permanently-manned gateway.* N-COUNT

stockbroker /stɒkbroʊkəʳ/ **stockbrokers.** A **stockbroker** is a person whose job is to buy and sell stocks and shares for people who want to invest money. ◆◇◇◇◇ N-COUNT

stockbroker belt, stockbroker belts. The **stockbroker belt** is an area outside a city, especially London, where rich commuters live. *He grew up in the comfort of the Surrey stockbroker belt.* N-COUNT: usu *the*N

stockbroking /stɒkbroʊkɪŋ/. **Stockbroking** is the professional activity of buying and selling stocks and shares for clients. *His stockbroking firm was hit by the 1987 crash.* N-UNCOUNT: usu N n

stock car, stock cars. A **stock car** is an old car which has had changes made to it to make it suitable for races on a small dirt track, in which the cars often collide. *He acted as grand marshal of a stock car race.* N-COUNT

stock control. **Stock control** is the management of goods for sale so that a company has exactly the right amount of them at any one time. N-UNCOUNT

stock cube, stock cubes. A **stock cube** is a solid cube made from dried meat or vegetable juices and other flavourings. Stock cubes are used to add flavour to dishes such as stews and soups. N-COUNT

stock exchange, stock exchanges. A **stock exchange** is a place where people buy and sell stocks and shares. The **stock exchange** is also the trading activity that goes on there and the trading organization itself. *The shortage of good stock has kept some investors away from the stock exchange. ...the New York Stock Exchange.* ◆◆◆◇◇ N-COUNT: usu *the*N in sing =stock market

stockholder /stɒkhoʊldəʳ/ **stockholders.** In American English, a **stockholder** is a person who owns shares in a company. The usual British word is **shareholder**. ◆◇◇◇◇ N-COUNT

stockholding /stɒkhoʊldɪŋ/ **stockholdings.** **Stockholding** is the storage of raw materials or finished products before they are used or sold. N-VAR

stocking /stɒkɪŋ/ **stockings** ◆◇◇◇◇

1 Stockings are items of women's clothing which fit closely over their feet and legs. Stockings are usually made of nylon or silk and are held in place by suspenders. *...a pair of nylon stockings.* N-COUNT

2 A **stocking** is the same as a **Christmas stocking**. N-COUNT

3 See also **stock**; **body stocking**.

stockinged /stɒkɪŋd/. If someone is in their **stockinged** feet, they are wearing socks, tights, or stockings, but no shoes. *He tip-toed to the door in his stockinged feet.* ADJ: ADJ n

stocking filler, stocking fillers; also spelled **stocking-filler**. A **stocking filler** is a small present that is suitable for putting in a Christmas stocking. *Packed in a clear plastic display carton, it will make a lovely stocking filler at only 59p.* N-COUNT

stock-in-trade; also spelled **stock in trade**. If you say that something is someone's **stock-in-trade**, you mean that it is a usual part of their behaviour or work. *Patriotism is every politician's stock-in-trade... Delicious potted shrimps and prawns were once the stock-in-trade of the harbourside cafe.* N-SING: with poss =staple

stockist /stɒkɪst/ **stockists.** In British English, a **stockist** of a particular brand or type of goods is someone who sells this brand or type in their shop. *Take it to your nearest Kodak Photo CD stockist.* ◆◇◇◇◇ N-COUNT =retailer

stock market, stock markets. The **stock market** consists of the general activity of buying stocks and shares, and the people and institutions that organize it. *He's been studying and playing the stock market since he was 14... The company's shares promptly fell by 300 lire on the stock market.* ◆◆◆◇◇ N-COUNT: *the*N

stockpile /stɒkpaɪl/ **stockpiles, stockpiling, stockpiled** ◆◇◇◇◇

1 If people **stockpile** things such as food or weapons, they store large quantities of them for future use. *People are stockpiling food for the coming winter.* VERB =hoard V n

2 A **stockpile** of things is a large quantity of them that have been stored for future use. *The two leaders also approved treaties to cut stockpiles of chemical weapons.* N-COUNT: oft N *of*n =stock, store

stockroom /stɒkruːm/ **stockrooms;** also spelled **stock-room**. A **stockroom** is a room, especially in a shop or a factory, where a stock of goods is kept. N-COUNT

stock-still. If someone stands or sits **stock-still**, they do not move at all. *The lieutenant stopped and stood stock-still.* ADJ: ADJ after v

stocktaking /stɒkteɪkɪŋ/. **Stocktaking** is the activity of counting and checking all the goods that a shop or business has. N-UNCOUNT

stocky /stɒki/ **stockier, stockiest.** A **stocky** person has a body that is broad, solid, and often short. ◆◇◇◇◇ ADJ-GRADED: usu ADJ n

stodgy /stɒdʒi/ **stodgier, stodgiest**

1 Stodgy food is very solid and heavy. It makes you feel very full, and is difficult to digest. *He was disgusted with the stodgy pizzas on sale in London.* ADJ-GRADED: usu ADJ n

2 If you describe someone or something as **stodgy**, you dislike them or are bored by them because they are very old-fashioned or serious. *They're not cultured or interesting, they are boring stodgy old things.* ADJ-GRADED: usu ADJ n PRAGMATICS =stuffy

stoic /stoʊɪk/ **stoics**

1 Stoic means the same as **stoical**; a formal use. *...this noble image of the tall, stoic land-loving peasant withstanding hardship with humour and heroism.* ADJ-GRADED: usu ADJ n

2 If you say that someone is a **stoic**, you approve of them because they suffer hardship without showing their emotions; a formal use. N-COUNT

stoical /stoʊɪkəl/. If you say that someone behaves in a **stoical** way, you approve of them because they accept difficulties and suffering without complaining or getting upset; a formal word. *She never ceased to admire the stoical courage of those in Northern Ireland... He had been stoical at their parting.* ♦ **stoically** *She put up with it all stoically.* ADJ-GRADED PRAGMATICS; ADV-GRADED: usu ADV with v

stoicism /stoʊɪsɪzəm/. **Stoicism** is stoical behaviour; a formal word. *They bore their plight with stoicism and fortitude.* N-UNCOUNT

stoke /stoʊk/ **stokes, stoking, stoked** ◆◇◇◇◇

1 If you **stoke** a fire, you add coal or wood to it to keep it burning. *She was stoking the stove with* VERB V n *sticks of maple.* ▸ **Stoke up** means the same as **stoke.** *He stoked up the fire in the hearth.* PHRASAL VERB V P n (not pron)

2 If you **stoke** something such as a feeling, you cause it to be felt more strongly. *These demands are helping to stoke fears of civil war.* ▸ **Stoke up** means the same as **stoke.** *He has sent his proposals in the hope of stoking up interest for the idea.* VERB V n PHRASAL VERB V P n (not pron)

stoker /st**ou**kəʳ/ **stokers.** In former times a **stoker** was a person whose job was to stoke fires, especially on a ship or a steam train. N-COUNT

stole /st**ou**l/ **stoles**

1 Stole is the past tense of **steal.**

2 A **stole** is a long, wide scarf for women which is worn round the shoulders. *...fur stoles.* N-COUNT

stolen /st**ou**lᵊn/. **Stolen** is the past participle of **steal.**

stolid /st**ɒ**lɪd/. If you describe someone as **stolid,** you mean that they are rather solemn and conventional in their behaviour, and do not show much emotion. *He glanced furtively at the stolid faces of the two detectives. ...the conflict that emerges when stolid countryfolk find themselves confronted by flighty townsfolk.* ADJ-GRADED: usu ADJ n

stomach /st**ʌ**mək/ **stomachs, stomaching, stomached** ◆◆◆◇◇

1 Your **stomach** is the organ inside your body where food is digested before it moves into the intestines. *He had an upset stomach... My stomach is completely full.* N-COUNT =tummy

2 You can refer to the front part of your body below your waist as your **stomach.** *The children lay down on their stomachs. ...stomach muscles.* N-COUNT: oft poss N =abdomen

3 If the front part of your body below your waist feels uncomfortable because you are feeling worried or frightened, you can refer to it as your **stomach.** *His stomach was in knots.* N-COUNT: oft poss N

4 If you say that someone has a strong **stomach,** you mean that they are not disgusted by things that disgust most other people. *Surgery often demands actual physical strength, as well as the possession of a strong stomach.* N-COUNT

5 If you cannot **stomach** something, you cannot accept it because you dislike it or disapprove of it. *I could never stomach the cruelty involved in the wounding of animals.* VB: with brd-neg V n/-ing

6 If you do something **on an empty stomach,** you do it without having eaten. *Avoid drinking on an empty stomach.* PHRASES PHR after v

7 If you **have no stomach** for something, you do not have the courage to do it. *America has no stomach for a fight... The surgeon didn't have the stomach to look at Kelly's face.* with neg, V inflects, PHR *for* n, PHR to-inf

8 If you say that you feel **sick to** your **stomach** about something, you mean that you feel very angry or upset about it. *She felt sick to her stomach just thinking about it.* v-link PHR

9 If you say that something **turns** your **stomach** or makes your **stomach turn,** you mean that it is so unpleasant or offensive that it makes you feel sick. *The true facts will turn your stomach... I saw the shots of what happened on television and my stomach just turned over.* ERG: V inflects

10 ● **butterflies in** your **stomach**: see **butterfly.**

st<u>o</u>mach ache, stomach aches; also spelled **stomachache.** If you have a **stomach-ache,** you have a pain in your stomach. N-VAR

st<u>o</u>mach-churning. If you describe something as **stomach-churning,** you mean that it is so unpleasant that it makes you feel physically sick. *The stench from rotting food is stomach-churning. ...that rush of stomach-churning fear at the sound of a mortar exploding nearby.* ADJ-GRADED

stomp /st**ɒ**mp/ **stomps, stomping, stomped.** If you **stomp** somewhere, you walk there with very heavy steps, often because you are angry. *He turned his back on them and stomped off up the hill... He stomped out of the room.* ◆◇◇◇◇ VERB V prep/adv

stone /st**ou**n/ **stones, stoning, stoned.** The plural is usually **stone** in meaning 10. ◆◆◆◆◇

1 Stone is a hard solid substance found in the ground and often used for building houses. *He could not tell whether the floor was wood or stone... People often don't appreciate that marble is a natural stone. ...stone walls.* N-MASS

2 A **stone** is a small piece of rock that is found on the ground. *He removed a stone from his shoe... The crowd began throwing stones.* N-COUNT

3 A **stone** is a large piece of stone put somewhere in memory of a person or event, or as a religious symbol. *The monument consists of a circle of gigantic stones.* N-COUNT

4 Stone is used in expressions such as **set in stone** and **tablets of stone** to suggest that an idea or rule is firm and fixed, and cannot be changed. *He is merely throwing the idea forward for discussion, it is not cast in stone... Scientific opinions are not carved on tablets of stone; they change over the years.* N-UNCOUNT: oft with brd-neg

5 You can refer to a jewel as a **stone.** *...a diamond ring with three stones.* N-COUNT

6 A **stone** is a small hard ball of minerals and other substances which sometimes forms in a person's kidneys or gall bladder. *He had kidney stones.* N-COUNT: usu n N

7 In British English, the **stone** in a plum, cherry, or other fruit is the large hard seed in the middle of it. The American term is **pit.** N-COUNT

8 If you **stone** a fruit, you remove its stone. *Then stone the fruit and process the plums to a puree.* VERB V n

9 If people **stone** someone or something, they throw stones at them. *Youths burned cars and stoned police... The head of the local Communist Party was stoned by protesters when he tried to address a meeting.* VERB V n

10 In British English, a **stone** is a measurement of a person's weight, equal to 14 pounds or 6.35 kilograms. *I weighed around 16 stone.* N-COUNT: usu num N

11 See also **stoned; foundation stone, paving stone, precious stone, stepping stone.**

12 If you say that one place is **a stone's throw** from another, you mean that the places are close to each other. *...a two-bedroom apartment just a stone's throw from the beach... Just a stone's throw away is the City Art Gallery.* PHRASES PHR prep/adv

13 If you say that you will **leave no stone unturned,** you are emphasizing that you will try every way you can think of in order to achieve what you want. *He said he would leave no stone unturned in the search for peace.* V inflects PRAGMATICS

14 ● **kill two birds with one stone**: see **bird.**

St<u>o</u>ne Age. **The Stone Age** is a very early period of human history, when people used tools and weapons made of stone, not metal. N-PROPER: *the* N

st<u>o</u>ne-c<u>o</u>ld

1 If something that should be warm is **stone-cold,** it is very cold indeed. *Hillsden took a sip of tea, but it was stone cold.* ADJ

2 If someone is **stone-cold sober,** they are completely sober; an informal expression. PHRASE: v-link PHR

stoned /st**ou**nd/. If someone is **stoned,** their mind is greatly affected by a drug such as cannabis; an informal word. ● See also **stone.** ADJ-GRADED: usu v-link ADJ

st<u>o</u>ne-d<u>e</u>ad. If you **kill** something such as an idea or emotion **stone-dead,** you completely destroy it. *The prospect of having to pay a graduate tax until retirement would kill the students' enthusiasm stone dead.* PHRASE: V inflects

st<u>o</u>ne d<u>ea</u>f; also spelled **stone-deaf.** Someone who is **stone deaf** is completely deaf. ADJ: usu v-link ADJ

st<u>o</u>ne-ground; also spelled **stoneground. Stone-ground** flour or bread is made from grain that has been crushed between two large, heavy pieces of stone. ADJ: usu ADJ n

stonemason /st**ou**nmeɪsᵊn/ **stonemasons.** A **stonemason** is a person who is skilled at cutting and preparing stone so that it can be used for building walls and buildings. N-COUNT

stonewall /st**ou**nw**ɔ**ːl, AM -wɔːl/ **stonewalls, stonewalling, stonewalled.** If you say that someone **stonewalls,** you disapprove of them because they delay giving a clear answer or making a clear decision, often because there is something that they want to hide or avoid doing. *The administration is just stonewalling in an attempt to hide their political embarrassment... He did his* VERB PRAGMATICS V V n Also V *on* n

best this week to stonewall questions and to block even the most modest proposals. ♦ **stonewalling** *After 18 days of stonewalling, he at last came out and faced the issue.*
N-UNCOUNT

stoneware /stoʊnweəʳ/. **Stoneware** is very hard earthenware pottery which is baked at a high temperature. *...a selection of hand-painted blue-and-white stoneware. ...a large stoneware bowl.*
N-UNCOUNT: oft N n

stone-washed; also spelled **stonewashed.** **Stone-washed** jeans are jeans which have been specially washed with small pieces of stone so that when you buy them they look faded and worn.
ADJ

stonework /stoʊnwɜːʳk/. **Stonework** consists of objects or parts of a building that are made of stone. *...the crumbling stonework of the derelict church.*
N-UNCOUNT =masonry

stony /stoʊni/ **stonier, stoniest** ♦◇◇◇◇
1 Stony ground is rough and contains a lot of stones. *The steep, stony ground is well drained. ...a stony track.*
ADJ-GRADED =pebbly

2 A **stony** expression or attitude does not show any sympathy or friendliness. *She gave me the stoniest look I ever got... He drove us home in stony silence.*
ADJ-GRADED =icy

stood /stʊd/. **Stood** is the past tense and past participle of **stand.**

stooge /stuːdʒ/ **stooges.** If you refer to someone as a **stooge**, you are criticizing them because they are used by someone else to do unpleasant or dishonest tasks. *He has vehemently rejected claims that he is a government stooge... The latter had for decades acted largely as a stooge for the communists.*
N-COUNT: usu with supp PRAGMATICS =puppet

stool /stuːl/ **stools** ♦◇◇◇◇
1 A **stool** is a seat with legs but no support for your arms or back. *O'Brien sat on a bar stool and leaned his elbows on the counter.*
N-COUNT

2 If someone **has fallen between two stools**, they were unable to decide which of two courses of action to take and as a result they have not done either of them successfully; used mainly in British English.
PHRASE: V inflects

3 Stools are the pieces of solid waste matter that are passed out of a person's body through their bowels; a formal or medical use.
N-COUNT: usu pl =faeces

stoop /stuːp/ **stoops, stooping, stooped** ♦◇◇◇◇
1 If you **stoop**, you stand or walk with your shoulders bent forwards. *She was taller than he was and stooped slightly.* ► Also a noun. *He was a tall, thin fellow with a slight stoop.* ♦ **stooping** *...a slender slightly stooping American.*
VERB =hunch; V; N-SING; ADJ-GRADED: usu ADJ n

2 If you **stoop**, you bend your body forwards and downwards. *He stooped to pick up the carrier bag of groceries... Two men in shirt sleeves stooped over the car... Stooping down, he picked up a big stone and hurled it.*
VERB; V; V over n; V down/over

3 If you say that someone **stoops** to doing something, you are criticizing them because they do something wrong or immoral that they would not normally do. *He had not, until recently, stooped to personal abuse... They've stooped to using any and every weapon at their disposal... How could anyone stoop so low?*
VERB PRAGMATICS; V to n/-ing; V adj

4 In American English, a **stoop** is a small wooden platform at the door of a building, with steps leading it up to it. *They stood together on the stoop and rang the bell.*
N-COUNT

stop /stɒp/ **stops, stopping, stopped** ♦♦♦♦♦
1 If you have been doing something and then you **stop** doing it, you no longer do it. *Stop throwing those stones!... He can't stop thinking about it... I've been told to lose weight and stop smoking... I stopped working last year to have a baby... Does either of the parties want to stop the fighting?... She stopped in mid-sentence.*
VERB; V -ing; V n; V

2 If you **stop** something happening, you prevent it from happening or prevent it from continuing. *He proposed a new diplomatic initiative to try to stop the war... If the fire isn't stopped, it could spread to 25,000 acres... I think she really would have liked to stop us seeing each other... He put the radio on loud to stop himself thinking about it... Motherhood won't stop me from pursuing my acting career... There's nothing to stop you from doing a bit of exploring further afield.*
VERB; V n; V n -ing; V n from -ing

3 If an activity or process **stops**, it is no longer happening. *The rain had stopped and a star or two was visible over the mountains... The system overheated and filming had to stop... The music stopped and the lights were turned up... They're treating it like a game, a novelty. That's got to stop.*
VERB; V

4 If something such as machine **stops**, or someone or something **stops** it, it is no longer moving or working. *The clock had stopped at 2.12 a.m... His heart stopped three times... Arnold stopped the engine and got out of the car... He stopped the machine and replayed the message.*
V-ERG; V; V n

5 When a moving person or vehicle **stops** or **is stopped**, they no longer move and they remain in the same place. *The car failed to stop at an army checkpoint... He stopped and let her catch up with him... The event literally stopped the traffic... The van was stopped at customs in Harwich.*
V-ERG =halt; V; V n

6 If something that is moving comes **to a stop** or is brought **to a stop**, it slows down and no longer moves. *People often wrongly open doors before the train has come to a stop... He slowed the car almost to a stop.*
N-SING: *to a* N =halt

7 If someone does not **stop** to think or to explain, they continue with what they are doing without taking any time to think about or explain it. *She doesn't stop to think about what she's saying... There is something rather strange about all this if one stops to consider it... People who lead busy lives have no time to stop and reflect.*
VERB =pause; V to-inf; V

8 If you say that a quality or state **stops** somewhere, you mean that it exists or is true up to that point, but no further. *The cafe owner has put up the required 'no smoking' signs, but thinks his responsibility stops there... The good news did not stop there... Once you cross over the thin line to acts of lawlessness, who knows where it stops?*
VERB =end; V adv

9 A **stop** is a place where buses or trains regularly stop so that people can get on and off. *There was an Underground map above one of the windows and I counted the stops to West Hampstead... They waited at a bus stop.*
N-COUNT: oft supp N

10 If you **stop** somewhere on a journey, you stay there for a short while. *He insisted we stop at a small restaurant just outside of Atlanta... It would be a crime to travel all the way to Australia and not stop in Sydney.*
VERB; V prep/adv

11 A **stop** is a time or place at which you stop during a journey. *The last stop in Mr Baker's lengthy tour was Paris... Mack was driving down from Vermont, with a stop in Boston to pick Sarah up.*
N-COUNT: usu with supp

12 In music, organ **stops** are the knobs at the side of the organ, which you pull or push in order to control the type of sound that comes out of the pipes.
N-COUNT: usu pl

13 If you say that someone will **stop at nothing** to get or achieve something, you are emphasizing that they are very determined about it, and are willing to do things that are extreme, wrong, or dangerous in order to get or achieve it. *Their motive is money, and they will stop at nothing to get it.*
PHRASES V inflects PRAGMATICS

14 If you **pull out all the stops**, you do everything you can to make something happen or succeed. *New Zealand police vowed yesterday to pull out all the stops to find the killer.*
V inflects

15 If you **put a stop to** something you do not like or approve of, you prevent it from happening or continuing. *His daughter should have stood up and put a stop to all these rumours.*
V inflects

16 If you say that someone doesn't **know when to stop**, you mean that they do not control their own behaviour very well and so they often annoy or upset other people. *Like many politicians before him, Mr Bentley did not know when to stop... You should know when to stop asking questions.*
know inflects

17 ● to **stop dead**: see **dead.** ● to **stop short of**: see **short.** ● to **stop** someone **in** their **tracks**: see **track.**

stop by. If you **stop by** somewhere, you make a short visit to a person or place; an informal expres-
PHRASAL VERB

sion. *Perhaps I'll stop by the hospital... I'll stop by to see Leigh before going home.* V P n / V P

stop off. If you **stop off** somewhere or **stop off,** you stop for a short time in the middle of a journey. *The president stopped off in Poland on his way to Munich for the economic summit.* PHRASAL VERB / V P

stop up. If you **stop** something **up**, you cover or fill a hole or gap in it. *They stopped up leaks with chewing gum.* PHRASAL VERB / V P n (not pron) / Also V n P

stopcock /stɒpkɒk/ **stopcocks.** A **stopcock** is a tap on a pipe, which you turn in order to allow something to pass through the pipe or to stop it from passing through. N-COUNT

stopgap /stɒpgæp/ **stopgaps.** A **stopgap** is something that serves a purpose for a short time, but is replaced as soon as possible. *Gone are the days when work was just a stopgap between leaving school and getting married... Even if the bill were approved, it would be no more than a stopgap measure.* N-COUNT: oft N n

stop-go. **Stop-go** is used to describe processes in which inactivity and activity alternate. *...stop-go economic cycles.* ADJ: usu ADJ n

stoplight /stɒplaɪt/ **stoplights;** also spelled **stop light**. In American English, a **stoplight** is a set of coloured lights which controls the flow of traffic on a road. The British term is **traffic light**. N-COUNT

stopover /stɒpoʊvəʳ/ **stopovers.** A **stopover** is a short stay in a place in between parts of a journey. *During a brief stopover in Minsk, Mr Shevardnadze addressed a conference... The Sunday flights will make a stopover in Paris.* N-COUNT

stoppage /stɒpɪdʒ/ **stoppages** ◆◇◇◇◇
1 When there is a **stoppage**, people stop working because of a disagreement with their employers. *Mineworkers in the Ukraine have voted for a one-day stoppage next month.* N-COUNT: oft supp N =strike
2 In football and some other sports, when there is a **stoppage**, the game stops for a short time, for example because a player is injured, and the referee may add some extra time at the end to compensate for it. N-COUNT

stopper /stɒpəʳ/ **stoppers.** A **stopper** is a piece of glass, plastic, or cork that fits into the top of a bottle or jar to close it. *...a bottle of colourless liquid sealed with a cork stopper.* • See also **show-stopper**. N-COUNT

stop press. **Stop press** is sometimes printed next to an article in a newspaper to indicate that this is very recent news that was inserted after the rest of the newspaper had been printed. *STOP PRESS: The fourth National Photography Conference is being held in Bristol from September 24-26.*

stopwatch /stɒpwɒtʃ/ **stopwatches;** also spelled **stop-watch**. A **stopwatch** is a watch with buttons which you press at the beginning and end of an event, so that you can measure exactly how long it takes. N-COUNT

storage /stɔːrɪdʒ/ ◆◆◇◇◇
1 If you refer to the **storage** of something, you mean that it is kept in a special place until it is needed. *...the storage of toxic waste... Some of the space will at first be used for storage... The collection has been in storage for decades.* N-UNCOUNT
2 **Storage** is the process of storing data in a computer. *His task is to ensure the fair use and storage of personal information held on computer. ...data-storage devices.* N-UNCOUNT
3 See also **cold storage**.

store /stɔːʳ/ **stores, storing, stored** ◆◆◆◆◇
1 A **store** is a shop. In British English, **store** is used mainly to refer to a large shop selling a variety of goods, but in American English, a **store** can be any size shop. *Bombs were planted in stores in Manchester and Blackpool. ...grocery stores. ...a record store.* N-COUNT
2 When you **store** things, you put them in a container or other place and leave them there until they are needed. *Store the cookies in an airtight tin... Some types of garden furniture must be stored inside in the winter.* ▸ **Store away** means the same as **store**. *He simply stored the tapes away... He's stored away nearly one ton of potatoes.* VERB =keep / V n prep/adv / Also V n / PHRASAL VERB / V n P / V P n (not pron)
3 When you **store** information, you keep it in your memory, in a file, or in a computer. *Where in the brain do we store information about colours? ...chips for storing data in electronic equipment.* VERB / V n
4 A **store** of things is a supply of them that you keep somewhere until you need them. *I handed over my secret store of chocolate biscuits... Dolly's store of drinking glasses had run out.* N-COUNT: usu N *of* n =supply, stock
5 A **store** is a place where things are kept while they are not being used. *...a decision taken in 1982 to build a store for spent fuel from submarines. ...a grain store.* N-COUNT: usu with supp
6 If you have a **store** of knowledge, jokes, or stories, you have a large amount of them ready to be used. *He possessed a vast store of knowledge... Jessica dipped into her store of theatrical anecdotes.* N-COUNT: usu N *of* n
7 See also **chain store**, **cold store**, **department store**.
8 If something is **in store** for you, it is going to happen at some time in the future. *Surprises were also in store for me.* PHRASES / PHR after v, v-link PHR, usu PHR *for* n
9 If you **set great store by** something, you think that it is extremely important or necessary; a formal expression. *...a retail group which sets great store by traditional values.* V inflects, PHR n

store away. See **store** 2. PHRASAL VERB

store up. If you **store** something **up**, you keep it until you think that the time is right to use it. *Investors were storing up a lot of cash in anticipation of disaster... I got all the emotion out of me which had been stored up.* PHRASAL VERB / V P n (not pron) / Also V n P

storecard /stɔːʳkɑːʳd/ **storecards;** also spelled **store card**. A **storecard** is a plastic card that you use to buy goods on credit from a particular store or group of stores; used mainly in British English. The more usual American term is **charge card**. N-COUNT

storefront /stɔːʳfrʌnt/ **storefronts**
1 In American English, a **storefront** is the outside part of a shop which faces the street, including the door and windows. The British term is **shop front**. N-COUNT
2 In American English, a **storefront** is a small shop or office that opens onto the street and is part of a row of shops or offices. *Main Street in Great Barrington is lined with small storefronts and restaurants. ...a tiny storefront office on the main street.* N-COUNT: oft N n

storehouse /stɔːʳhaʊs/ **storehouses** ◆◇◇◇◇
1 A **storehouse** is a building in which things, usually food, are stored. *Some of the cottages were still lived in by old folk; others had been turned into barns and storehouses.* N-COUNT
2 When a lot of things can be found together in one place, you can refer to this place as a **storehouse** of a particular kind. *This book is a veritable storehouse of information... It is comforting to have a storehouse of treasured memories.* N-COUNT: usu N *of* n =wealth

storekeeper /stɔːʳkiːpəʳ/ **storekeepers.** A **storekeeper** is a shopkeeper; used mainly in American English. N-COUNT

storeroom /stɔːruːm/ **storerooms.** A **storeroom** is a room in which you keep things until they are needed. *...a storeroom filled with massive old furniture covered with dust.* N-COUNT

storey /stɔːri/ **storeys;** spelled **story** in American English. A **storey** of a building is one of its different levels, which is situated above or below other levels. *Houses must not be more than two storeys high. ...the upper storeys of the Empire State Building.* ◆◇◇◇◇ N-COUNT: usu supp N =floor

-storey /-stɔːri/; spelled **-story** in American English. **-storey** is used after numbers to form adjectives that indicate that a building has a particular number of floors or levels. *...a modern three-storey building.* • See also **multi-storey**. COMB in ADJ

-storeyed /-stɔːrid/. **-storeyed** means the same as **-storey**. *The narrow streets were lined with two-storeyed houses.* COMB in ADJ

stork /stɔːʳk/ **storks.** A **stork** is a large bird with a long beak and long legs, which lives near water. N-COUNT

storm /stɔ:ʳm/ **storms, storming, stormed** ◆◆◆◇◇

1 A **storm** is very bad weather, with heavy rain, strong winds, and often thunder and lightning. *...the violent storms which whipped America's East Coast.* N-COUNT

2 If something causes a **storm**, it causes an angry or excited reaction from a large number of people. *The photos caused a storm when they were first published... The announcement provoked an immediate storm of protest. ...the storm of publicity that Richard's book had generated.* N-COUNT: oft N *of*n =furore

3 A **storm** of applause or laughter is a sudden loud burst of applause or laughter from an audience or other group of people. *His speech was greeted with a storm of applause... Not since the 1968 Olympic Games has a medals ceremony caused such a storm of booing.* N-COUNT: usu sing, usu N *of*n =roar

4 If you **storm** into or out of a place, you enter or leave it quickly and noisily, because you are angry. *After a bit of an argument, he stormed out... He stormed into an office, demanding to know where the head of department was.* VERB =charge V adv/prep

5 If you **storm**, you say something in a very loud voice, because you are extremely angry; used in written English. *'It's a fiasco,' he stormed.* VERB =rage V with quote

6 If a place that is being defended **is stormed**, a group of people attack it, usually in order to get inside it. *Government buildings have been stormed and looted... The refugees decided to storm the embassy.* ♦ **storming** *...the storming of the Bastille.* VERB *be* V-ed V n N-UNCOUNT: N *of*n

7 See also **firestorm**.

8 If someone or something **takes** a place **by storm**, they are extremely successful. *Kenya's long distance runners have taken the athletics world by storm.* PHRASES V inflects =conquer

9 If someone **weathers the storm**, they succeed in reaching the end of a very difficult period without much harm or damage. *He insists he will not resign and will weather the storm.* V and N inflect

10 ● **the eye of the storm**: see **eye**. ● **a storm in a teacup**: see **teacup**.

storm cloud, storm clouds; also spelled **stormcloud**.

1 **Storm clouds** are the dark clouds which are seen before a storm. N-COUNT: usu pl

2 You can use **storm clouds** to refer to a sign that something very unpleasant is going to happen; a formal use. *Over the past three weeks, the storm clouds have gathered again over the government.* N-COUNT: usu pl

storm trooper, storm troopers; also spelled **stormtrooper**. **Storm troopers** were members of a force of soldiers in Nazi Germany, who were specially trained to be violent and ruthless. N-COUNT

stormy /stɔ:ʳmi/ **stormier, stormiest** ◆◇◇◇◇

1 If there is **stormy** weather, there are strong winds and heavy rain. *It had been a night of stormy weather, with torrential rain and high winds. ...the long stormy winter of 1942.* ADJ-GRADED: usu ADJ n ≠calm

2 **Stormy** seas have very large strong waves because there are strong winds. *They make the treacherous journey across stormy seas. ...the stormy waters that surround the British Isles.* ADJ-GRADED: usu ADJ n =turbulent ≠calm

3 If you describe a situation as **stormy**, you mean it involves a lot of angry argument or criticism. *The letter was read at a stormy meeting... Their working relationship was stormy at times.* ADJ-GRADED

story /stɔ:ri/ **stories** ◆◆◆◆◆

1 A **story** is a description of imaginary people and events, which is written or told in order to entertain. *The second story in the book is titled 'The Scholar'... I shall tell you a story about four little rabbits. ...a popular love story with a happy ending.* N-COUNT =tale

2 A **story** is a description of an event or something that happened to someone, especially a spoken description of it. *The parents all shared interesting stories about their children... Isak's story is typical of a child who has a specific learning disability.* N-COUNT =account

3 The **story** of something is a description of all the important things that have happened to it since it began. *...the story of the women's movement in Ireland.* N-COUNT: usu N *of*n

4 If someone invents a **story**, they give a false explanation or account of something. *He invented some story about a cousin.* N-COUNT =tale, yarn

5 A news **story** is a piece of news in a newspaper or in a news broadcast. *Those are some of the top stories in the news... They'll do anything for a story. ...front-page news stories.* N-COUNT

6 See **storey**.

7 See also **cock-and-bull story**, **short story**, **sob story**, **success story**, **tall story**.

8 You say **'but that's another story'** when you have mentioned a subject that you are not going to talk about or explain in detail; used in spoken English. *I'd met him at a dance I'd gone to on my own. But that's another story.* PHRASES V inflects PRAGMATICS

9 You use **to cut a long story short** to indicate that you are going to state the final result of an event and not give any more details; used in spoken English. *To cut a long story short, I ended up as managing director.* V inflects PRAGMATICS

10 You use **a different story** to refer to a situation, usually a bad one, which exists in one set of circumstances when you have mentioned that it does not exist in another set of circumstances. *Where Marcella lives, the rents are fairly cheap, but a little further north it's a different story.* usu v-link PHR PRAGMATICS

11 If you say it's **the same old story** or **the old story**, you mean that something unpleasant or undesirable seems to happen again and again. *It's the same old story. They want one person to do three people's jobs.* v-link PHR PRAGMATICS

12 If you say that something is **only part of the story** or is **not the whole story**, you mean that the explanation or information given is not enough for a situation to be fully understood. *This may be true but it is only part of the story... Jane goes to great lengths to explain that this is not the whole story.* usu v-link PHR PRAGMATICS =only part of the picture

13 If someone tells you **their side of the story**, they tell you why they behaved in a particular way and why they think they were right, when other people think that person behaved wrongly. *He had already made up his mind before even hearing her side of the story.* *side* inflects

storybook /stɔ:ribʊk/ **storybooks**

1 A **storybook** is a book of stories for children. *As a child she learned to draw by tracing pictures out of her mother's old storybooks. ...two of her favourite storybook characters.* N-COUNT

2 A **storybook** relationship, situation, or life is one that is perfect and ends happily, just as many fairy stories do. *In many ways it was a storybook life. Summers in Salzburg. Weekends hunting in Connecticut... It was a real storybook romance.* ADJ: ADJ n =fairy tale

storyline /stɔ:rilaɪn/ **storylines.** The **storyline** of a book, film, or play is its story and the way in which it develops. *The surprise twists in the storyline are the film's greatest strength.* ◆◇◇◇◇ N-COUNT =plot

storyteller /stɔ:ritelәʳ/ **storytellers;** also spelled **story-teller**. A **storyteller** is someone who tells or writes stories. *He was the one who first set down the stories of the Celtic storytellers.* ◆◇◇◇◇ N-COUNT

storytelling /stɔ:ritelɪŋ/; also spelled **story-telling**. **Storytelling** is the activity of telling or writing stories. *The programme is 90 minutes of dynamic Indian folk dance, live music and storytelling.* N-UNCOUNT

stout /staʊt/ **stouter, stoutest; stouts** ◆◇◇◇◇

1 A **stout** person is rather fat. *He was a tall, stout man with gray hair.* ADJ-GRADED =stocky

2 **Stout** shoes, branches, or other objects are thick and strong. *I hope you've both got stout shoes... The old man picked up a stout stick that lay by his feet. ...a stout oak door.* ADJ-GRADED =sturdy

3 If you use **stout** to describe someone's actions, attitudes, or beliefs, you approve of them because they are strong and determined. *He produced a stout defence of the car business... The invasion was held up by unexpectedly stout resistance.* ♦ **stoutly** *She stoutly defended her husband during the trial. ...stoutly anti-imperialist nations.* ADJ-GRADED PRAGMATICS =fierce ADV-GRADED: ADV with v, ADV adj

4 In British English, **stout** is a strong dark-coloured beer. *...Guinness and other Irish stouts.* N-MASS

stove /stoʊv/ **stoves.** A **stove** is an apparatus which provides heat, either for cooking or for heating a room. *She put the kettle on the gas stove... The cobwebs on the ceiling fluttered in the heat from the stove.* ◆◇◇◇◇ N-COUNT

stow /stoʊ/ **stows, stowing, stowed.** If you **stow** something somewhere, you carefully put it there until it is needed. *I helped her stow her bags in the boot of the car... Alistair had carefully folded up the paper and stowed it away under the sacks.* ◆◇◇◇◇ VERB V n prep/adv Also V n

stow away. If someone **stows away**, they hide in a ship, aeroplane, or other vehicle in order to make the journey secretly or without paying the fare. *He stowed away on a ferry and landed in North Shields.* PHRASAL VERB V P

stowage /stoʊɪdʒ/. **Stowage** is the space that is available for stowing things on a ship or aeroplane. *Stowage is provided in lined lockers beneath the berths.* N-UNCOUNT

stowaway /stoʊəweɪ/ **stowaways.** A **stowaway** is a person who hides in a ship, aeroplane, or other vehicle in order to make a journey secretly or without paying the fare. *The crew discovered the stowaway about two days into their voyage.* N-COUNT

straddle /strædᵊl/ **straddles, straddling, straddled** ◆◇◇◇◇

1 If you **straddle** something, you put or have one leg on either side of it. *He looked at her with a grin and sat down, straddling the chair.* VERB V n

2 If something **straddles** a river, road, border, or other place, it stretches across it or exists on both sides of it. *A small wooden bridge straddled the dike. ...this town that straddles the US-Mexico border.* VERB V n

3 Someone or something that **straddles** different periods, groups, or fields of activity exists in, belongs to, or takes elements from them all. *Our lives have straddled a period of greater change than perhaps any since the end of the Roman Empire... He straddles two cultures, having been brought up in Britain and later converted to Islam.* VERB V n

strafe /streɪf/ **strafes, strafing, strafed.** To **strafe** an enemy means to attack them by scattering bombs or bullets on them from a low-flying aircraft. *It seemed that the plane was going to swoop down and strafe the town, so we dived for cover.* VERB V n

straggle /strægᵊl/ **straggles, straggling, straggled**

1 If people **straggle** somewhere, they move there slowly, in small groups with large, irregular gaps between them. *They came straggling up the cliff road... The other boys straggled away, some to their work in the kitchen, some to the great hall.* VERB V prep/adv

2 When things **straggle** over an area, they cover it in an uneven or untidy way. *Her grey hair straggled in wisps about her face... They were beyond the last straggling suburbs now.* VERB V prep V-ing

straggler /strægələʳ/ **stragglers**

1 The **stragglers** are the people in a group who are moving more slowly or making less progress than the others. *There were two stragglers twenty yards back... Any straggler that fell behind or got lost in the darkness was easy prey for the enemy.* N-COUNT: usu pl =dawdler

2 The **stragglers** at an event such as a party are the people who are still there after most of the other people have left. *...round about two o'clock in the morning when there were only a few stragglers left.* N-COUNT: usu pl

straggly /strægəli/. Something that is **straggly** grows or spreads out untidily in different directions. *Her long fair hair was knotted and straggly... The yard held a few straggly bushes.* ADJ-GRADED

straight /streɪt/ **straighter, straightest; straights** ◆◆◆◆◇

1 A **straight** line or edge continues in the same direction and does not bend or curve. *Keep the boat in a straight line... Using the straight edge as a guide, trim the cloth to size... His teeth were perfectly straight... There wasn't a single straight wall in the building.* ► Also an adverb. *Stand straight and stretch the left hand to the right foot... Turn right and just basically walk straight, right over the river.* ADJ-GRADED ADV: ADV after v

2 **Straight** hair has no curls or waves in it. *Grace had long straight dark hair which she wore in a bun.* ADJ-GRADED: usu ADJ n ≠curly, wavy

3 You use **straight** to indicate that the way from one place to another is very direct, with no changes of direction. *...squirting the medicine straight to the back of the child's throat... He finished his conversation and stood up, looking straight at me... Straight ahead were the low cabins of the motel.* ADV: ADV prep/adv

4 If you go **straight** to a place, you go there immediately. *As always, we went straight to the experts for advice... We'll go to a meeting in Birmingham and come straight back.* ADV: ADV prep/adv =directly

5 If you give someone a **straight** answer, you speak honestly and frankly to them. *What a shifty arguer he is, refusing ever to give a straight answer to a straight question.* ► Also an adverb. *I lost my temper and told him straight that I hadn't been looking for any job.* ADJ-GRADED: ADJ n ADV-GRADED: ADV after v

6 **Straight** also means following one after the other. *They'd won 12 straight games before they lost.* ► Also an adverb. *He called from Weddington, having been there for 31 hours straight.* ADJ: ADJ n ADV: n ADV

7 A **straight** choice or a **straight** fight involves only two people or things. *It's a straight choice between low-paid jobs and no jobs... Each has several times beaten the other in a straight fight.* ADJ: ADJ n =clear

8 If you describe someone as **straight**, you mean that they are normal and conventional, for example in their opinions and in the way they live. *Dorothy was described as a very straight woman, a very strict Christian who was married to her job.* ADJ-GRADED =conventional

9 If you describe someone as **straight**, you mean that they are heterosexual rather than homosexual; an informal use. *His sexual orientation was a lot more gay than straight... Marty of New York describes herself as a straight female.* ► Also a noun. *...a standard of sexual conduct that applies equally to gays and straights.* ADJ: usu v-link ADJ ≠gay N-COUNT

10 On a racetrack, a **straight** is a section of the track that is straight, rather than curved; used mainly in British English. *Our cars were clearly too slow along the straights... I went to overtake him on the back straight on the last lap.* • See also **home straight**. N-COUNT

11 If you **get** something **straight**, you make sure that you understand it properly or that someone else does; used in spoken English. *You need to get your facts straight... Let's get things straight. I didn't lunch with her.* PHRASES V inflects

12 If a criminal **is going straight**, he or she is no longer involved in crime. V inflects

13 If something keeps people **on the straight and narrow**, it helps to keep them living an honest or healthy life. *All her efforts to keep him on the straight and narrow have been rewarded.* PHR after v

14 • **a straight face**: see **face**. • **set the record straight**: see **record**.

straight away; also spelled **straightaway**. If you do something **straight away**, you do it immediately and without delay. *I should go and see a doctor straight away... I wrote him a letter and posted it straightaway.* ◆◇◇◇◇ ADV: ADV with v =immediately

straighten /streɪtᵊn/ **straightens, straightening, straightened** ◆◇◇◇◇

1 If you **straighten** something, you make it tidy or put it in its proper position. *She sipped her coffee and straightened a picture on the wall. ...tidying, straightening cushions and organising magazines.* VERB V n

2 If you are standing in a relaxed or slightly bent position and then you **straighten**, you make your back or body straight and upright. *The three men straightened and stood waiting.* ► **Straighten up** means the same as **straighten**. *He straightened up and slipped his hands in his pockets.* VERB V PHRASAL VERB V P

3 If you **straighten** something, or it **straightens**, it becomes straight. *Straighten both legs until they are fully extended... The road straightened and we were on a plateau.* ► **Straighten out** means the same as **straighten**. *No one would dream of* V-ERG V n V PHRASAL VERB ERG V P n (not pron)

straightening out the knobbly spire at Empingham Church... The road twisted its way up the mountain then straightened out for the last two hundred yards. VP Also V n P

straighten out PHRASAL VERB
1 If you **straighten out** a confused situation, you succeed in getting it organized and tidied up. *He would make an appointment with him to straighten out a couple of things... My sister had come in with her calm common sense and straightened them out.* =sort out, clear up V P n (not pron) V n P
2 See **straighten** 3.

straighten up. See **straighten** 1. PHRASAL VERB

straight-faced. A **straight-faced** person appears not to be amused in a funny situation. *'Whatever gives you that idea?' she replied straight-faced... At that time it got around that he was a straight-faced, humourless character.* ADJ-GRADED: usu ADJ n, ADJ after v, also v-link ADJ

straightforward /streɪtfɔːʳwəʳd/ ◆◆◇◇◇
1 If you describe something as **straightforward**, you approve of it because it is easy to do or understand. *Disposable nappies are fairly straightforward to put on... The question seemed straightforward enough. ...simple straightforward language.* ♦ **straightforwardly** *Acid rain is not straightforwardly attributable to the burning of coal... Nor does scientific knowledge derive straightforwardly from experiments and observations.* ADJ-GRADED: oft ADJ to-inf PRAGMATICS; ADV: ADV adj, ADV with v
2 If you use **straightforward** to describe a person or their behaviour, you approve of them because they are honest and direct, and do not try to hide their feelings. *She is very blunt, very straightforward and very honest... I was impressed by his straightforward intelligent manner.* ♦ **straightforwardly** *His daughter says straightforwardly that he was not good enough.* ADJ-GRADED PRAGMATICS =frank; ADV-GRADED: ADV with v, ADV adj

strain /streɪn/ **strains, straining, strained** ◆◆◆◇◇
1 If **strain** is put on an organization or system, it has to do more than it is able to do. *The prison service is already under considerable strain... The vast expansion in secondary education is putting an enormous strain on the system. ...the credit crunch caused by strains on the banking system.* N-VAR: oft *under* N, N *on* n =pressure
2 To **strain** something means to make it do more than it is able to do. *The volume of scheduled flights is straining the air traffic control system... Resources will be further strained by new demands for housing.* VERB =stretch V n
3 **Strain** is a state of worry and tension caused by a difficult situation. *She was tired and under great strain. ...the stresses and strains of a busy and demanding career.* N-UNCOUNT: also N in pl =stress
4 If you say that a situation is **a strain**, you mean that it makes you worried and tense. *I sometimes find it a strain to be responsible for the mortgage.* N-SING: *a* N =worry
5 **Strain** is a force that pushes, pulls, or stretches something in a way that may damage it. *Place your hands under your buttocks to take some of the strain off your back... A build-up of strain on a section of the San Andreas Fault has been detected.* N-UNCOUNT
6 **Strain** is an injury to a muscle in your body, caused by using it too much or twisting it awkwardly. *Avoid muscle strain by warming up with slow jogging. ...a groin strain.* N-VAR: usu n N
7 If you **strain** a muscle, you injure it by using it too much or twisting it awkwardly. *He strained his back during a practice session.* VERB V n
8 If you **strain** to do something, you make a great effort to do it when it is difficult to do. *I had to strain to hear... Several thousand supporters strained to catch a glimpse of the new president... They strained their eyes, but saw nothing.* VERB V to-inf V n
9 When you **strain** food, you separate the liquid part of it from the solid parts. *Strain the stock and put it back into the pan.* VERB V n
10 You can use **strain** to refer to a particular quality in someone's character, remarks, or work. *There was a strain of bitterness in his voice. ...this cynical strain in the book.* N-SING: with supp =streak
11 A **strain** of a germ, plant, or other organism is a particular type of it. *Every year new strains of influenza develop. ...a particularly beautiful strain of Swiss pansies.* N-COUNT: usu N *of* n
12 If you hear the **strains** of music, you hear music being played; a literary use. *She could hear the tinny strains of a chamber orchestra.* N-PLURAL: usu N *of* n
13 See also **eye strain, repetitive strain injury**.

strained /streɪnd/ ◆◇◇◇◇
1 If someone's appearance, voice, or behaviour is **strained**, they seem worried and nervous. *She looked a little pale and strained... Gil sensed something wrong from her father's strained voice... His laughter seemed a little strained.* ADJ-GRADED =tense ≠relaxed
2 If relations between people are **strained**, those people do not like or trust each other. *...a period of strained relations between the prime minister and his deputy.* ADJ-GRADED

strainer /streɪnəʳ/ **strainers.** A **strainer** is a small sieve for separating liquids from solids. *Pour the broth through a strainer. ...a tea strainer.* N-COUNT

strait /streɪt/ **straits** ◆◇◇◇◇
1 You can refer to a narrow strip of sea which joins two large areas of sea as a **strait** or the **straits**. *An estimated 1600 vessels pass through the strait annually. ...the Straits of Gibraltar.* N-COUNT: oft in names
2 If someone is in dire or desperate **straits**, they are in a very difficult situation, usually because they do not have much money. *If we had a child, we'd be in really dire straits... The company's closure has left many small businessmen in desperate financial straits.* N-PLURAL: adj N

straitened /streɪtᵊnd/. If someone is living in **straitened** circumstances, they do not have as much money as they used to, and are finding it very hard to buy or pay for everything that they need; a formal word. *His father died when he was ten, leaving the family in straitened circumstances... There is much talk of cuts in the diplomatic service in these straitened times.* ADJ-GRADED: usu ADJ n =impoverished

straitjacket /streɪtdʒækɪt/ **straitjackets**
1 A **straitjacket** is a special jacket used to tie the arms of a violent person tightly around their body. *Occasionally his behavior became so uncontrollable that he had to be placed in a straitjacket.* N-COUNT
2 If you describe an idea or a situation as a **straitjacket**, you mean that it is very limited and restricting. *The national curriculum must be a guide, not a straitjacket. ...the ideological straitjacket of Marxism-Leninism.* N-COUNT

strait-laced; also spelled **straight-laced** or **straitlaced.** If you describe someone as **straitlaced**, you disapprove of them because they have a very strict and severe attitude towards questions of morality. *He was criticised for being boring, strait-laced and narrow-minded... Our unconventional behaviour did in fact shock some of our more straitlaced friends.* ADJ-GRADED PRAGMATICS =prudish

strand /strænd/ **strands, stranding, stranded** ◆◆◇◇◇
1 A **strand** of something such as hair, wire, or thread is a single thin piece of it. *She tried to blow a gray strand of hair from her eyes. ...high fences, topped by strands of barbed-wire... He began to feed in the spaghetti, carefully separating the strands.* N-COUNT: usu N *of* n
2 A **strand** of a plan or theory is a part of it. *There had been two strands to his tactics... He's trying to bring together various strands of radical philosophic thought.* N-COUNT =element
3 If you **are stranded**, you are prevented from leaving a place, for example because of bad weather. *The climbers had been stranded by a storm... The airport had to be closed, stranding tourists.* VERB *be* V-ed V n

strange /streɪndʒ/ **stranger, strangest** ◆◆◆◆◇
1 Something that is **strange** is unusual or unexpected, and makes you feel slightly uneasy or afraid. *Then a strange thing happened... There was something strange about the flickering blue light... It was so strange to see a policeman lying down, without his helmet... It's strange how things turn out.* ♦ **strangely** *She noticed he was acting strangely... America has no shortage of strangely named clubs... The hut suddenly seemed strangely silent.* ADJ-GRADED: oft *it* v-link ADJ that/to-inf/*how* =peculiar, odd; ADV-GRADED: ADV with v, ADV adj

♦ **strangeness** ...*the breathy strangeness of the music.* N-UNCOUNT =weirdness

2 A **strange** place is one that you have never been to before. A **strange** person is someone you have never met before. *I ended up alone in a strange city... She was faced with a new job, in unfamiliar surroundings with strange people.* ADJ: ADJ n =unknown ≠familiar

3 If you feel **strange**, you have an unpleasant or uncomfortable feeling, either physical or emotional. *I felt all dizzy and strange.* ADJ-GRADED: usu v-link ADJ

4 See also **stranger**.

strangely /streɪndʒli/. You use **strangely** to emphasize that what you are saying is surprising. *Strangely, the race didn't start until 8.15pm... No, strangely enough, this is not the case.* ◆◆◇◇◇ ADV: ADV with cl PRAGMATICS =surprisingly

stranger /streɪndʒəʳ/ **strangers** ◆◆◇◇◇

1 A **stranger** is someone you have never met before. *Telling a complete stranger about your life is difficult... Sometimes I feel like I'm living with a stranger.* N-COUNT

2 If two people are **strangers**, they do not know each other. *The women knew nothing of the dead girl. They were strangers.* N-PLURAL

3 If you are a **stranger** in a place, you do not know the place well. *'You don't know much about our town, do you?'—'No, I'm a stranger here.'* N-COUNT ≠local

4 If you are a **stranger** to something, you have had no experience of it or do not understand it. *He is no stranger to controversy... We were both strangers to diplomatic life.* N-COUNT: oft with brd-neg, N to n

5 See also **strange**.

strangle /stræŋgᵊl/ **strangles, strangling, strangled** ◆◇◇◇◇

1 To **strangle** someone means to kill them by squeezing their throat tightly so that they cannot breathe. *He tried to strangle a border policeman and steal his gun... He was almost strangled by his parachute harness straps.* ♦ **strangler** /strænglәʳ/ **stranglers** ...*a vigilante group looking for a strangler who's terrorising the town.* VERB =throttle V n N-COUNT

2 To **strangle** something means to prevent it from succeeding or developing. *The country's economic plight is strangling its scientific institutions... His creative drive has been strangled by his sense of political guilt.* VERB V n

strangled /stræŋgᵊld/. A **strangled** voice or cry sounds unclear and muffled. *In a strangled voice he said, 'This place is going to be unthinkable without you.'... Sue let out a strangled cry of shock.* ADJ: ADJ n

stranglehold /stræŋgᵊlhoʊld/. To have a **stranglehold** on something means to have control over it and prevent it from being free or from developing. *These companies are determined to keep a stranglehold on the banana industry... The troops are tightening their stranglehold on the city... To succeed, the new paper will need to break the stranglehold of the printing unions.* ◆◇◇◇◇ N-SING

strangulation /stræŋgjʊleɪʃᵊn/. **Strangulation** is the act of killing someone by squeezing their throat tightly so that they cannot breathe. *He is charged with the strangulation of two students.* N-UNCOUNT

strap /stræp/ **straps, strapping, strapped** ◆◆◇◇◇

1 A **strap** is a narrow piece of leather, cloth, or other material. Straps are used to carry things, fasten things together, or to hold a piece of clothing in place. *Nancy gripped the strap of her beach bag... Brian pulled the straps through the buckles of his suitcase... She pulled the strap of her nightgown onto her shoulder... I undid my watch strap.* N-COUNT

2 If you **strap** something somewhere, you fasten it there with a strap. *Strapping the skis on the roof, we boarded the hovercraft in Dover... She strapped the gun belt around her middle... Through the basement window I saw him strap on his pink cycling helmet... The carer will have to do all the work: placing the patient on the seat, strapping him in, taking him off again at the top.* VERB V n prep V n with *on/in/down*

strapless /stræpləs/. A **strapless** dress or bra does not have the usual narrow bands of material over the shoulders. ...*a black, strapless evening dress.* ADJ: usu ADJ n

strapped /stræpt/. If someone is **strapped** for money, they do not have enough money to buy or pay for the things they want or need. *My husband and I are really strapped for cash. ...the financially strapped state university.* ● See also **cash-strapped**. ◆◇◇◇◇ ADJ-GRADED: oft ADJ *for* n, adv ADJ

strapping /stræpɪŋ/. If you describe someone as **strapping**, you mean that they are tall, strong, and healthy-looking. *He was a bricklayer – a big, strapping fellow.* ADJ: usu ADJ n =brawny

strata /strɑːtə, AM streɪtə/. **Strata** is the plural of **stratum**.

stratagem /strætədʒəm/ **stratagems.** A **stratagem** is a plan that is intended to achieve a particular effect, often by deceiving people; a formal word. *Trade discounts may be used as a competitive stratagem to secure customer loyalty.* N-COUNT =ploy

strategic /strətiːdʒɪk/ ◆◆◆◇◇

1 **Strategic** means relating to the most important, general aspects of something such as a military operation or political policy, especially when these are decided in advance. ...*the new strategic thinking which NATO leaders produced at the recent London summit. ...a strategic plan for reducing the rate of infant mortality... Madagascar is also of strategic importance to France.* ♦ **strategically** /strətiːdʒɪkli/ ...*strategically important roads, bridges and buildings. ...integrating politics, economics and military affairs, thinking strategically, setting priorities and making choices.* ADJ: usu ADJ n ADV

2 **Strategic** weapons are very powerful, long-range weapons, and the decision to use them can be made only by a political leader, rather than by a military commander in battle. ...*strategic nuclear weapons.* ADJ: usu ADJ n ≠tactical

3 If you put something in a **strategic** position, you place it cleverly in a position where it will be most useful or have the most effect. ...*the marble benches Eve had placed at strategic points throughout the gardens, where the views were spectacular.* ♦ **strategically** *We had kept its presence hidden with a strategically placed chair.* ADJ: usu ADJ n ADV: usu ADV -ed

strategist /strætədʒɪst/ **strategists.** A **strategist** is someone who is skilled in planning the best way to gain an advantage or to achieve success, especially in war. *Military strategists had devised a plan that guaranteed a series of stunning victories. ...a clever political strategist.* ◆◇◇◇◇ N-COUNT =tactician

strategy /strætədʒi/ **strategies** ◆◆◆◆◇

1 A **strategy** is a general plan or set of plans intended to achieve something, especially over a long period. *The Labour Party launched its new strategy for industry... What should our marketing strategy have achieved?... Community involvement is now integral to company strategy.* N-VAR =policy

2 **Strategy** is the art of planning the best way to gain an advantage or achieve success, especially in war. *I've just been explaining the basic principles of strategy to my generals.* N-UNCOUNT

stratification /strætɪfɪkeɪʃᵊn/. **Stratification** is the division of something, especially society, into different classes or layers. *She was concerned about the stratification of American society.* N-UNCOUNT

stratified /strætɪfaɪd/. A **stratified** society is one that is divided into different classes or social layers; a formal word. ...*a highly stratified, unequal and class-divided society.* ADJ-GRADED

stratosphere /strætəsfɪəʳ/ ◆◇◇◇◇

1 **The stratosphere** is the layer of the earth's atmosphere which lies between 10 and 50 kilometres above the earth. N-SING: *the* N

2 If you say that someone or something climbs or is sent into **the stratosphere**, you mean that they reach a very high level; used in journalism. *This was enough to launch their careers into the stratosphere... If oil supplies were ever disrupted, it would send U.S. oil-import bills into the stratosphere.* N-SING: *the* N, usu *the* N

stratospheric /strætəsferɪk, AM -fɪrɪk/. **Stratospheric** means found in or related to the stratosphere. ...*stratospheric ozone.* ADJ: ADJ n

stratum /strɑːtəm, AM streɪtəm/ **strata** ◆◇◇◇◇

1 A **stratum** of society is a group of people in it who N-COUNT:

are similar in their education, income, or social status; a formal use. *It was an enormous task that affected every stratum of society... The rebels came overwhelmingly from the poorest strata of rural society.* usu with supp =class

2 The **strata** in the earth's crust are the different layers of rock; a technical use. *Contained within the rock strata is evidence that the region was intensely dry 15,000 years ago.* N-COUNT: usu pl

straw /strɔː/ **straws** ◆◆◇◇◇

1 **Straw** consists of the dried, yellowish stalks from crops such as wheat or barley. *The barn was full of bales of straw... I stumbled through mud to a yard strewn with straw. ...a wide-brimmed straw hat.* N-UNCOUNT

2 A **straw** is a thin tube of paper or plastic, which you use to suck a drink into your mouth. *...a bottle of lemonade with a straw in it.* N-COUNT

3 If you **are clutching at straws**, you are trying unusual or extreme ideas or methods because other ideas or methods have failed. *...a badly thought-out scheme from a Government clutching at straws.* PHRASES V inflects

4 If an event is **the last straw** or **the straw that broke the camel's back**, it is the latest in a series of unpleasant or undesirable events, and makes you feel that you cannot tolerate a situation any longer. *For him the Church's decision to allow the ordination of women had been the last straw... Then came the recession. Revenues dropped, but the straw to break the camel's back was the war.* usu v-link PHR

5 If you draw **the short straw**, you are chosen from a number of people to perform a job or duty that you will not enjoy. *...if a few of your guests have drawn the short straw and agreed to drive others home after your summer barbecue.* usu v PHR

6 If you say that an incident or piece of news is a **straw in the wind**, you mean that it gives an indication of what might happen in the future. *The latest straw in the wind is a pick-up in sales among the nation's retail giants.* *straw* inflects =hint

strawberry /strɔːbri, AM -beri/ **strawberries.** A **strawberry** is a small red fruit which is soft and juicy and has tiny yellow seeds on its skin. *...strawberries and cream. ...homemade strawberry jam.* ◆◆◇◇◇ N-COUNT

strawberry blonde, strawberry blondes; also spelled **strawberry blond.**

1 **Strawberry blonde** hair is reddish blonde. ADJ

2 A **strawberry blonde** is a person, especially a woman, who has strawberry blonde hair. N-COUNT

straw-coloured; spelled **straw-colored** in American English. If you describe something, especially hair, as **straw-coloured**, you mean that it is pale yellow. ADJ: usu ADJ n

straw poll, straw polls. A **straw poll** is the unofficial questioning of a group of people to find out their opinion about something. *A straw poll conducted at the end of the meeting found most people agreed with Mr Fortuna... Many parents wouldn't dream of buying the stuff for their daughters anyway, as a straw poll among my friends and acquaintances demonstrated.* N-COUNT

stray /streɪ/ **strays, straying, strayed** ◆◆◇◇◇

1 If someone **strays** somewhere, they wander away from where they are supposed to be. *Tourists often get lost and stray into dangerous areas... Crews stray outside to film the view from the pavement... A railway line crosses the park so children must not be allowed to stray.* VERB V prep/adv V

2 A **stray** dog or cat has wandered away from its owner's home. *A stray dog came up to him. ...a refuge for stray cats.* ▸ Also a noun. *The dog was a stray which had been adopted.* ADJ: ADJ n N-COUNT

3 If your mind or your eyes **stray**, you do not concentrate on or look at one particular subject, but start thinking about or looking at other things. *Even with the simplest cases I find my mind straying... She could not keep her eyes from straying towards him.* VERB =wander V

4 You use **stray** to describe something that exists separated from other similar things. *An 8-year-old boy was killed by a stray bullet... She shrugged a stray lock of hair out of her eyes.* ADJ: ADJ n

streak /striːk/ **streaks, streaking, streaked** ◆◆◇◇◇

1 A **streak** is a long stripe or mark on a surface which contrasts with the surface because it is a different colour. *There are these dark streaks on the surface of the moon... The flames begin as a few streaks of red against the pale brown of the walls.* N-COUNT

2 If something **streaks** a surface, it makes long stripes or marks on the surface. *Rain had begun to streak the window-panes... Fine shades of grey streaked his dark hair... His face was pale and streaked with dirt.* ♦ **-streaked** *Her bare feet were dirt-streaked and cracked with cold. ...soot-streaked silver trains.* VERB V n *be* V-ed *with* n COMB in ADJ

3 If someone has a **streak** of a particular type of behaviour, they sometimes behave in that way. *We're both alike - there is a streak of madness in us both... He's still got a mean streak.* N-COUNT: usu sing, with supp

4 If something or someone **streaks** somewhere, they move there very quickly. *A meteorite streaked across the sky... He got a near perfect start, streaking away from the pack.* VERB =dart V prep/adv

5 A winning **streak** or a lucky **streak** is a continuous series of successes, for example in gambling or sport. A losing **streak** or an unlucky **streak** is a series of failures or losses. *The casinos had better watch out since I'm obviously on a lucky streak! ...a losing streak that had extended back to June 1.* N-COUNT: adj N

streaker /striːkəʳ/ **streakers.** A **streaker** is someone who runs quickly through a public place wearing no clothes, as a joke. N-COUNT

streaky /striːki/ **streakier, streakiest.** Something that is **streaky** is marked with long stripes that are a different colour to the rest of it. *She has streaky fair hair and blue eyes. ...the empty house with its streaky windows.* ADJ-GRADED

streaky bacon. In British English, **streaky bacon** is bacon which has stripes of fat between stripes of meat. N-UNCOUNT

stream /striːm/ **streams, streaming, streamed** ◆◆◆◇◇

1 A **stream** is a small narrow river. *There was a small stream at the end of the garden. ...a mountain stream.* N-COUNT =brook

2 A **stream** of smoke, air, or liquid is a narrow moving mass of it. *He breathed out a stream of cigarette smoke... Add the oil in a slow, steady stream.* N-COUNT: with supp, usu N *of* n

3 A **stream** of vehicles or people is a long moving line of them. *There was a stream of traffic behind him.* N-COUNT: with supp, usu N *of* n

4 A **stream** of things is a large number of them occurring one after another. *The discovery triggered a stream of readers' letters. ...a never-ending stream of jokes... We had a constant stream of visitors.* N-COUNT: with supp, usu N *of* n =flood

5 If a liquid **streams** somewhere, it flows or comes out in large amounts. *Tears streamed down their faces... She came in, rain streaming from her clothes and hair.* VERB V prep/adv

6 If your eyes **are streaming**, liquid is coming from them, for example because you have a cold. You can also say that your nose **is streaming**. *Her eyes were streaming now from the wind... A cold usually starts with a streaming nose and dry throat.* VB: usu cont V V-ing

7 If people or vehicles **stream** somewhere, they move there quickly and in large numbers. *Refugees have been streaming into Travnik for months... The traffic streamed past him... The clock in the church struck twelve, and soon after people began to stream out.* VERB V prep/adv

8 When light **streams** into or out of a place, it shines strongly into or out of it. *Sunlight was streaming into the courtyard.* VERB V prep/adv

9 If something such as a flag or someone's hair **streams** in the wind, it is blown so that it is almost horizontal. *She was wearing a flimsy pink dress that streamed out behind her... He had been greeted by the sight of his mother, her red hair wildly streaming.* VERB V prep/adv V

10 In a school, a **stream** is a group of children of the same age and ability who are taught together; used mainly in British English. *Examinations may be used to choose which pupils are to move into the top streams.* N-COUNT: with supp

11 To **stream** pupils means to divide them into groups according to their ability; used mainly in British English. *He advocates streaming children, and educating them according to their needs.* ♦ **streaming** *There's no streaming at St Benedict's school.*
VERB; V n; Also V; N-UNCOUNT

12 See also **gulf stream, jet stream.**

streamer /striːməʳ/ **streamers. Streamers** are long rolls of coloured paper used for decorating rooms at parties.
N-COUNT

streamline /striːmlaɪn/ **streamlines, streamlining, streamlined.** To **streamline** an organization or process means to make it more efficient by removing unnecessary parts of it; used showing approval. *They're making efforts to streamline their normally cumbersome bureaucracy... They say things should be better now that they have streamlined application procedures.* ♦ **streamlined** *...streamlined companies using cheap freelance staff.*
◆◇◇◇◇ VERB; PRAGMATICS; V n; ADJ-GRADED: usu ADJ n

streamlined /striːmlaɪnd/. A **streamlined** vehicle, animal, or object has a shape that allows it to move quickly or efficiently through air or water. *...these beautifully streamlined and efficient cars. ...the sharks' sleek, streamlined bodies. ...streamlined helmets.*
◆◇◇◇◇ ADJ-GRADED: usu ADJ n; =aerodynamic

stream of consciousness, streams of consciousness; also spelled **stream-of-consciousness**. If you describe what someone writes or says as a **stream of consciousness**, you mean that it expresses their thoughts as they occur, rather than in a structured way; a formal expression. *The novel is an intensely lyrical stream-of-consciousness about an Indian woman who leaves her family home to be married... The stream-of-consciousness they expect of a friend over coffee is not really what they need of their president.*
N-VAR: oft N n

street /striːt/ **streets**
◆◆◆◆◆

1 A **street** is a road in a town or village, usually with houses along it. *He lived at 66 Bingfield Street... Boppard is a small, quaint town with narrow streets.*
N-COUNT: oft in names after n

2 You can use **street** or **streets** when talking about activities that happen out of doors in a town rather than inside a building. *Changing money on the street is illegal-always use a bank... Their aim is to raise a million pounds to get the homeless off the streets. ...a New York street gang.*
N-COUNT: *the* N, usu *on/off* N

3 See also **back street, civvy street, Downing Street, Fleet Street, high street, Wall Street.**

4 If someone is **streets ahead** of you, they are much better at something than you are. *He was streets ahead of the other contestants.*
PHRASES; usu v-link PHR, oft PHR *of* n

5 If you talk about **the man in the street** or **the man or woman in the street**, you mean ordinary people in general. *The average man or woman in the street doesn't know very much about immune disorders.*

6 If a job or activity is **up** your **street**, it is the kind of job or activity that you are very interested in. *She loved it, this was just up her street.*
usu v-link PHR

streetcar /striːtkɑːʳ/ **streetcars.** In American English, a **streetcar** is an electric vehicle for carrying people which travels on rails in the streets of a town. The British word is **tram.**
N-COUNT

street cred; also spelled **street-cred**. If someone says that you have **street cred**, they mean that ordinary young people would approve of you and consider you to be part of their culture, usually because you share their sense of fashion or their views; an informal expression. *At 16, she oozes street cred. She wears black, talks cool and looks 18... Having children was the quickest way to lose your street cred.*
N-UNCOUNT; PRAGMATICS; =cred

street credibility; also spelled **street-credibility**. **Street credibility** is the same as **street cred.**
N-UNCOUNT; =street cred, cred

streetlamp /striːtlæmp/ **streetlamps;** also spelled **street-lamp**. A **streetlamp** is the same as a **streetlight**. *He paused under a streetlamp and looked across at the cafe.*
N-COUNT; =streetlight

streetlight /striːtlaɪt/ **streetlights;** also spelled **street light**. A **streetlight** is a tall post with a light at the top, which stands by the side of a road to light it up, usually in a town. *As the day darkened the streetlights came on.*
N-COUNT; =streetlamp

street smart; also spelled **street-smart**. Someone who is **street smart** knows how to deal with intimidating people or dangerous situations, especially in big cities; used especially in informal American English. *He is street smart and is not afraid of this neighborhood.*
ADJ-GRADED; =streetwise

street value. The **street value** of a drug is the price that is paid for it when it is sold illegally to drug users; used in journalism. *Cocaine with a street value of two-and-a-half-million pounds was seized at Heathrow airport last night.*
N-SING: usu N *of* amount

streetwalker /striːtwɔːkəʳ/ **streetwalkers.** A **streetwalker** is a prostitute who stands or walks in the streets in order to get customers; an old-fashioned word.
N-COUNT

streetwise /striːtwaɪz/. Someone who is **streetwise** knows how to deal with difficult or dangerous situations, especially in big cities; an informal word. *He was not academic but he was streetwise. ...a cocky, streetwise kid who thought he knew it all.*
ADJ-GRADED

strength /streŋθ/ **strengths**
◆◆◆◆◇

1 Your **strength** is the physical energy that you have, which gives you the ability to perform various actions, such as lifting or moving things. *She has always been encouraged to swim to build up the strength of her muscles... He threw it forward with all his strength... You don't need strength to take part in this sport... He leant against the wall, fighting for strength to continue.*
N-UNCOUNT

2 Someone's **strength** in a difficult situation is their confidence or courage. *Something gave me the strength to overcome the difficulty... He copes incredibly well. His strength is an inspiration to me in my life... I think she showed great strength of character in turning down what must have been a very lucrative offer... You need strength of mind to stand up for yourself.*
N-UNCOUNT: also *a* N; ≠weakness

3 The **strength** of an object or material is its ability to be treated roughly, or to support or carry heavy weights, without being damaged or destroyed. *He checked the strength of the cables. ...the properties of a material, such as strength or electrical conductivity.*
N-UNCOUNT: also N in pl

4 The **strength** of a person, organization, or country is the power or influence that they have. *...information about the military, economic, and political strength of the Soviet Union... The Alliance in its first show of strength drew a hundred thousand-strong crowd to a rally... They have their own independence movement which is gathering strength.*
N-UNCOUNT: also N in pl

5 If you refer to the **strength** of a feeling, opinion, or belief, you are talking about how deeply it is felt or believed by people, or how much they are influenced by it. *He was surprised at the strength of his own feeling. ...the Civil War and the strength of feeling it had engendered among the Spanish people... What makes a mayor successful in Los Angeles is the strength of his public support.*
N-UNCOUNT; =intensity

6 Someone's **strengths** are the qualities and abilities that they have which are an advantage to them, or which make them successful. *Take into account your own strengths and weaknesses... Vision and ambition are his great strengths... Tact was never Mr Moore's strength... Organisation is the strength of any good army... The book's strength lay in its depiction of present-day Tokyo.*
N-VAR; =asset; ≠weakness

7 If you refer to the **strength** of a currency, economy, or industry, you mean that its value or productivity is steady or increasing. *...the long-term competitive strength of the American economy... The drop was caused partly by the pound's strength against the dollar.*
N-UNCOUNT; ≠weakness

8 The **strength** of a group of people is the total number of people in it. *...elite forces, comprising about one-tenth of the strength of the army.*
N-UNCOUNT: also N in pl

9 The **strength** of a wind, current, or other force is
N-UNCOUNT:

its power or speed. *Its oscillation depends on the strength of the gravitational field... A tropical storm is gaining strength in the eastern Atlantic.* also N in pl

10 The **strength** of a drink, chemical, or drug is the amount of the particular substance in it that gives it its particular effect. *It is very alcoholic, sometimes near the strength of port... Each capsule contains between 30 and 100 pellets of morphine sulphate according to the strength of dose required... What's the scale that's used to compare the strength of acids and alkalis?* N-UNCOUNT: also N in pl =concentration

11 You can talk about the **strength** of a flavour, smell, colour, sound, or light to describe how intense or easily noticed it is. *The wine has lots of strength of flavour.* N-UNCOUNT: also N in pl

12 If a person or organization **goes from strength to strength**, they become more and more successful or confident. *Since her heart and lung transplant operation she has gone from strength to strength... A decade later, the company has gone from strength to strength.* PHRASES V inflects

13 If a team or army is at **full strength**, all the members that it needs or usually has are present. *He needed more time to bring US forces there up to full strength... With a full-strength team, we will quickly make good progress.* PHR after v, v-link PHR, PHR n

14 If a group turns out **in strength**, they arrive in large numbers. *Miss Bhutto called on voters and party workers to turn out in strength... Security forces have been out in strength.* PHR after v

15 If one thing is done **on the strength of** another, it is done because of the influence of that other thing. *He was elected to power on the strength of his charisma... On the strength on those grades, he won a scholarship to Syracuse University.* PHR after v

16 If an army or team is **under strength** or **below strength**, it does not have all the members that it needs or usually has. *He was hampered by his regiments of regular troops being so much under strength... They had been beaten three days earlier by a below-strength Brazilian side.* PHR after v, v-link PHR, PHR n

strengthen /streŋθᵊn/ **strengthens, strengthening, strengthened** ◆◆◆◇◇

1 If something **strengthens** a person or group or if they **strengthen** their position, they become more powerful and secure, or more likely to succeed. *...the new constitution, which strengthens the government and enables it to balance and check the powers of parliament and president... To strengthen his position in Parliament, he held talks with leaders of the Peasant Party... He hoped to strengthen the position of the sciences in the leading universities.* VERB =fortify V n

2 If something **strengthens** a case or argument, it supports it by providing more reasons or evidence for it. *He does not seem to be familiar with research which might have strengthened his own arguments.* VERB =reinforce V n

3 If a currency, economy, or industry **strengthens**, or if something **strengthens** it, it increases in value or becomes more productive. *The dollar strengthened against most other currencies... If the Government wants to save the Pound it should start by strengthening the British economy.* V-ERG ≠weaken V V n

4 If a government **strengthens** laws or measures or if they **strengthen**, they are made more severe. *A London Labour MP is urging the Government to strengthen the laws against racial hatred... Community leaders want to strengthen controls at external frontiers... Because of the war, security procedures have strengthened.* V-ERG V n V

5 If something **strengthens** you or **strengthens** your resolve or character, it makes you more confident and determined. *Any experience can teach and strengthen you, but particularly the more difficult ones... This merely strengthens our resolve to win the league... She began to believe that Nick would survive, and every day that came and went strengthened her conviction.* VERB ≠weaken V n

6 If something **strengthens** a relationship or bond, or if it **strengthens**, it becomes closer and more likely to last for a long time. *It will draw you closer together, and it will strengthen the bond of your relationship... His visit is intended to strengthen ties between the two countries.* V-ERG V n Also V

7 If something **strengthens** an impression, feeling, or belief, or if it **strengthens**, it affects people more powerfully or affects more people. *His speech strengthens the impression he is the main power in the organization... Every day of sunshine strengthens the feelings of optimism... Amy's own Republican sympathies strengthened as the days passed.* V-ERG =intensify V n V

8 If something **strengthens** your body or a part of your body, it makes it healthier, often in such a way that you can move or carry heavier things. *Cycling is good exercise. It strengthens all the muscles of the body... Yoga can be used to strengthen the immune system.* VERB V n

9 If something **strengthens** an object or structure, it makes it able to be treated roughly or able to support heavy weights, without being damaged or destroyed. *The builders will have to strengthen the existing joists with additional timber.* VERB =reinforce V n

10 If the wind, current, or other force **strengthens**, it becomes faster or more powerful. *As it strengthened the wind was veering southerly... There was a short sharp shower followed by a strengthening breeze.* VERB V V-ing

strenuous /strenjuəs/. A **strenuous** activity or action involves a lot of energy or effort. *Avoid strenuous exercise in the evening... These trips were strenuous, and the couple did not enjoy them... Strenuous efforts had been made to improve conditions in the jail... Despite strenuous objections by the right wing, the grant was agreed.* ◆◇◇◇◇ ADJ-GRADED

♦ **strenuously** *Exercising too much or too strenuously is just as bad as not doing it at all... The company concerned has strenuously denied the accusations.* ADV-GRADED: ADV with v

stress /stres/ **stresses, stressing, stressed** ◆◆◆◆◇

1 If you **stress** a point in a discussion, you put extra emphasis on it because you think it is important. *The spokesman stressed that the measures did not amount to an overall ban... China's leaders have stressed the need for increased co-operation between Third World countries... 'We're not saying we're outside and above all this,' he stresses.* ► Also a noun. *Japanese car makers are laying ever more stress on European sales.* VERB =emphasize V that V n V with quote N-VAR: N *on* n =emphasis

2 If you feel under **stress**, you feel worried and tense because of difficulties in your life. *Katy could think clearly when not under stress... Of course, the British will suffer such daily stresses patiently. ...a wide range of stress-related problems.* N-VAR: oft *under* N

3 **Stresses** are strong physical pressures applied to an object. *Earthquakes happen when stresses in rock are suddenly released as the rocks fracture.* N-VAR

4 If you **stress** a word or part of a word when you say it, you put emphasis on it so that it sounds slightly louder. *She stresses the syllables as though teaching a child.* ► Also a noun. *...the misplaced stress on the first syllable of this last word.* VERB V n N-VAR

stressed /strest/ ◆◇◇◇◇

1 If you are **stressed**, you feel tension and anxiety because of difficulties in your life. *Work out what situations or people make you feel stressed and avoid them.* ADJ-GRADED: usu v-link ADJ ≠relaxed

2 A **stressed** object is affected by strong physical pressure which has been applied to it; a technical use in physics. *...stressed metal.* ADJ: ADJ n

3 If a word or part of a word is **stressed**, it is pronounced with emphasis. ADJ ≠unstressed

stressed out. If someone is **stressed out**, they are very tense and anxious because of difficulties in their lives; an informal expression. ADJ-GRADED

stressful /stresfʊl/. If a situation or experience is **stressful**, it causes the person involved to feel stress. *I think I've got one of the most stressful jobs there is.* ◆◇◇◇◇ ADJ-GRADED

stretch /stretʃ/ **stretches, stretching, stretched** ◆◆◆◇◇

1 Something that **stretches** over an area or distance covers or exists in the whole of that area or distance. *The procession stretched for several mi-* VB: no cont =extend V prep/adv *les... He had burns that stretched from his neck to his hips. ...an artificial reef stretching the length of the coast.* V n

2 A **stretch** of road, water, or land is a length or area of it. *It's a very dangerous stretch of road... This stretch of Lost River was broader and deeper. ...a long stretch of beach with fine white sand.* N-COUNT: usu N *of* n

3 When you **stretch**, you put your arms or legs out straight and tighten your muscles. *He yawned and stretched... Try stretching your legs and pulling your toes upwards... She arched her back and stretched herself.* ► Also a noun. *At the end of a workout spend time cooling down with some slow stretches.* VERB V V n N-COUNT
♦ **stretching** *Make sure no awkward stretching is required.* N-UNCOUNT

4 A **stretch** of time is a period of time. *He was fluent in French, having spent stretches of time in Southern France. ...after an 18-month stretch in the army... He would study for eight to ten hours at a stretch.* N-COUNT: oft N *of* n =spell

5 If an event or activity **stretches** or **is stretched** into a further period of time, it continues into that period, which is later than expected. *...as anti-abortion protests stretched into their second week... The talks could be stretched into the summer of 1993.* V-ERG =continue V *into/to* n *be* V-ed *into/to* n

6 If something **stretches** from one time to another, it begins at the first time and ends at the second, which is longer than expected. *...a working day that stretches from seven in the morning to eight at night.* VERB =last V *from* n *to/into* n

7 If a group of things **stretch** from one type of thing to another, the group includes a wide range of things. *...a trading empire, with interests that stretched from chemicals to sugar.* VERB =range V *from* n *to* n

8 When something soft or elastic **stretches** or **is stretched**, it is becomes longer or bigger as well as thinner, usually because it is pulled. *The cables are designed not to stretch... Ease the pastry into the corners of the tin, making sure you don't stretch it.* V-ERG V V n

9 **Stretch** fabric is soft and elastic and stretches easily. *...stretch fabrics such as Lycra. ...stretch cotton swimsuits.* ADJ: ADJ n

10 If you **stretch** an amount of something or if it **stretches**, you make it last longer than it usually would by being careful and not wasting any of it. *They're used to stretching their budgets... During his senior year his earnings stretched far enough to buy an old car.* V-ERG V n V

11 If your resources can **stretch to** something, you can just afford to do it. *If your pocket can stretch to it, do get some good advice.* VB: no cont V *to* n

12 If something **stretches** your money or resources, it uses them up so you have hardly enough for your needs. *The drought there is stretching American resources... Public expenditure was being stretched to the limit by having to support 3 million unemployed people.* ♦ **stretched** *The deal will also help the company's stretched finances.* VERB V n *be* V-ed prep/adv ADJ-GRADED

13 If you say that a job or task **stretches** you, you mean that you like it because it makes you work hard and use all your energy and skills so that you do not become bored or achieve less than you should. *I'm trying to move on and stretch myself with something different... They criticised the quality of teaching, claiming pupils were not stretched enough.* VERB PRAGMATICS =push V n

14 ● **home stretch**: see **home straight**.

15 If you are **at full stretch**, your arm is straight and extended as far as possible, usually because you are trying to reach something that is almost too far away. *He offered his lighter at full stretch.* PHRASES usu v PHR, v-link PHR

16 If you are **at full stretch**, you are using the maximum amount of effort or energy. *Everyone would be working at full stretch.* PHR after v

17 If you say that something is not true or possible **by any stretch of the imagination**, you are emphasizing that it is completely untrue or absolutely impossible. You can also say that **by no stretch of the imagination** can something be true or possible. *Her husband was not a womaniser by any stretch of the imagination... By no stretch of the imagination could his speech be described as impersonal.* PRAGMATICS

18 If you **stretch** your **legs**, you go for a short walk, usually after you have been sitting down for a long time. *I stopped at the square and got out to stretch my legs.* V inflects

19 If you **stretch a point**, you describe something in a way which is not accurate, although it may be partly true. *It is stretching a point to call this censorship.* V inflects, oft *it* PHR to-inf

stretch out PHRASAL VERB

1 If you **stretch out** or **stretch** yourself **out**, you lie with your legs and body in a straight line. *The jacuzzi was too small to stretch out in... Moira stretched herself out on the lower bench.* V P adv/prep V pron-refl P prep/adv Also V P

2 If you **stretch out** a part of your body, you hold it out straight. *He was about to stretch out his hand to grab me.* V P n (not pron) Also V n P

stretcher /stretʃəʳ/ **stretchers stretchered** ◆◇◇◇◇

1 A **stretcher** is a long piece of canvas with a pole along each side, which is used to carry an injured or sick person. *The two ambulance attendants quickly put Plover on a stretcher and got him into the ambulance.* N-COUNT

2 If someone **is stretchered** somewhere, they are carried there on a stretcher. *I was close by as Lester was stretchered into the ambulance... The goalkeeper was stretchered off just before half-time with a rib injury.* V-PASSIVE *be* V-ed prep/adv

stretch marks. **Stretch marks** are lines or marks on someone's skin caused by the skin stretching after the person's weight has changed rapidly. Women who have had children often have stretch marks. N-PLURAL

stretchy /stretʃi/ **stretchier, stretchiest.** **Stretchy** material is slightly elastic and stretches easily. ADJ-GRADED

strew /struː/ **strews, strewing, strewed, strewn.** To **strew** things somewhere, or to **strew** a place with things, means to scatter them there in an untidy way. *The racoons knock over the rubbish bins in search of food, and strew the contents all over the ground... An elderly woman was strewing the floor with French chalk so that the dancing shoes would not slip... By the end, bodies were strewn all round the headquarters building.* VERB V n prep/adv V n *with* n V-ed

strewn /struːn/ ◆◇◇◇◇

1 If a place is **strewn with** things, they are scattered there untidily. *The front room was strewn with books and clothes... The riverbed was strewn with big boulders.* ► Also a combining form. *...a litter-strewn street. ...a rock-strewn hillside.* ADJ: v-link ADJ *with* n COMB in ADJ

2 **Strewn** is the past participle of **strew**.

stricken /strɪkən/ ◆◇◇◇◇

1 **Stricken** is the past participle of some meanings of **strike**.

2 If a person or place is **stricken** by something such as an unpleasant feeling, an illness, or a natural disaster, they are severely affected by it. *...a family stricken by genetically inherited cancer... Foreign aid workers will not be allowed into the stricken areas.* ► Also a combining form. *He was panic-stricken at the thought he might never play again. ...a leukaemia-stricken child. ...drought-stricken areas.* ADJ-GRADED: oft ADJ *by/with* n COMB in ADJ-GRADED

strict /strɪkt/ **stricter, strictest** ◆◆◆◇◇

1 A **strict** rule or order is very clear and precise or severe and must be obeyed absolutely. *The officials had issued strict instructions that we were not to get out of the jeep... French privacy laws are very strict... All your replies will be treated in the strictest confidence... Even if you are on a fairly strict diet you can still go out for a good meal.* ♦ **strictly** *The acceptance of new members is strictly controlled... The law was strictly enforced.* ADJ-GRADED ADV-GRADED: ADV with v

2 Someone who is **strict** does not tolerate impolite or disobedient behaviour, especially from children. *My parents were very strict. ...a few schools selected for their high standards and their strict discipline.* ♦ **strictly** *My own mother was brought up very strictly and correctly.* ♦ **strictness** *The girl lied because she resented her parents' strictness.* ADJ-GRADED ADV-GRADED N-UNCOUNT

3 If you talk about the **strict** meaning of something, you mean the precise meaning of it. *It's not quite peace in the strictest sense of the word, rather the absence of war.* ♦ **strictly** *Actually, that is not strictly true... Strictly speaking, it is not one house at all, but three houses joined together.* ADJ-GRADED: ADJ n ADV: ADV adj

4 You use **strict** to describe someone who never does things that are against their beliefs. *Four million Britons are now strict vegetarians... He was a strict, old-school Freudian.* ADJ: ADJ n

strictly /strɪktli/. You use **strictly** to emphasize that something is of one particular type, or intended for one particular thing or person, rather than any other. *He seemed fond of her in a strictly professional way... This session was strictly for the boys.* ◆◆◇◇◇ ADV: ADV group PRAGMATICS =purely

stricture /strɪktʃəʳ/ **strictures**

1 You can use **strictures** to refer to severe criticism or disapproval of something; a formal use. *...Mencken's strictures on the 1920s, with its self-righteous prohibition on alcohol and unconventional ideas... This satirical address was a thinly disguised stricture against the doctrine of the rights of man.* N-COUNT: usu pl, oft N *on/against* n

2 You can refer to things that limit what you can do as **strictures** of a particular kind. Some people consider this use to be incorrect. A formal use. *Your goals are hindered by financial strictures. ...the power of the imagination to subdue the strictures of daily life.* N-COUNT: usu pl, usu with supp =restriction

stride /straɪd/ **strides, striding, strode** ◆◆◇◇◇

1 If you **stride** somewhere, you walk there with quick, long steps. *They were joined by a newcomer who came striding across a field... He turned abruptly and strode off down the corridor.* VERB V prep/adv

2 A **stride** is a long step which you take when you are walking or running. *With every stride, runners hit the ground with up to five times their bodyweight... He walked with long strides.* N-COUNT

3 Someone's **stride** is their way of walking with long steps. *He lengthened his stride to keep up with her.* N-SING: usu poss N

4 If you make **strides** in something that you are doing, you make rapid progress in it. *The country has made enormous strides politically but not economically.* N-COUNT: usu pl, usu adj N

5 If you **get into** your **stride** or **hit** your **stride**, you start to do something easily and confidently, after being slow and uncertain. *The campaign is just getting into its stride... He's still learning and when he hits his stride, he'll be unstoppable.* PHRASES V inflects

6 In British English, if you **take** a problem or difficulty **in** your **stride**, you deal with it calmly and easily. The usual American expression is to **take something in stride**. *Beth was struck by how Naomi took the mistake in her stride.* V inflects

stridency /straɪdᵊnsi/. **Stridency** is the quality of being strident. *Many voters were alarmed by the President's new stridency.* N-UNCOUNT

strident /straɪdᵊnt/ ◆◇◇◇◇

1 If you use **strident** to describe someone or the way they express themselves, you mean that they make their feelings or opinions known in a very noticeable or persistent manner, often in a way that disturbs other people. *She was increasingly seen as a strident feminist. ...the unnecessarily strident tone of the President's remarks... Demands for his resignation have become more and more strident.* ♦ **stridently** *He was arrested in 1984 on suspicion of being a spy – a charge he stridently denies... In the late 1920s the party began to adopt a more stridently nationalistic posture.* ADJ-GRADED ADV-GRADED: ADV with v, ADV adj

2 If a voice or sound is **strident**, it is loud, harsh, and unpleasant to listen to. *She tried to laugh, and the sound was harsh and strident... He could hear Hilton's strident voice rising in vehement argument with Houston.* ADJ-GRADED =raucous

strife /straɪf/. **Strife** is strong disagreement or fighting; a formal word. *Money is a major cause of strife in many marriages... The boardroom strife at the company is far from over... It remains a highly unstable and strife-torn country.* ◆◇◇◇◇ N-UNCOUNT =conflict

strike /straɪk/ **strikes, striking, struck, stricken.** The form **struck** is the past tense and past participle. The form **stricken** can also be used as the past participle for meanings 6, 17, and 19. ◆◆◆◆◇

1 When there is a **strike**, workers stop doing their work for a period of time, usually in order to try to get better pay or conditions for themselves. *French air traffic controllers have begun a three-day strike in a dispute over pay... Staff at the hospital went on strike in protest at the incidents. ...a call for strike action.* N-COUNT: also *on* N

2 When workers **strike**, they go on strike. *...their recognition of the workers' right to strike... They shouldn't be striking for more money... The government agreed not to sack any of the striking workers.* ♦ **striker, strikers** *The strikers want higher wages, which state governments say they can't afford.* VERB V V *for/against* n V-ing N-COUNT

3 If you **strike** someone or something, you deliberately hit them; a formal use. *She took two quick steps forward and struck him across the mouth... He struck the ball straight into the hospitality tents... I struck it away and got a bite on my forearm... It is impossible to say who struck the fatal blow.* VERB =hit V n prep/adv V n

4 If something that is falling or moving **strikes** something, it hits it; a formal use. *His head struck the bottom when he dived into the 6ft end of the pool... One 16-inch shell struck the control tower... He was killed when he was struck by a car as he walked to his hotel. ...the fire which began when the installation was struck by lightning.* VERB =hit V n

5 If you **strike** one thing against another, or if one thing **strikes** against another, the first thing hits the second thing; a formal use. *Wilde fell and struck his head on the stone floor... My right toe struck against a submerged rock.* V-ERG =bang V n *on/against* n V *against* n

6 If something such as an illness or disaster **strikes**, it suddenly happens. *Bank of England officials continued to insist that the pound would soon return to stability but disaster struck... Both of them were afflicted with a rare genetic disease, which struck in their thirties... A powerful earthquake struck the Italian island of Sicily early this morning... He was suddenly struck with such a sense of grief, of loss, that his eyes filled with tears. ...a young woman who had been stricken with polio.* VERB V V n

7 To **strike** means to attack someone or something quickly and violently. *Criminals and terrorists were able to strike in one country then flee to another... The killer says he will strike again... Then the scorpion struck.* VERB V

8 A military **strike** is a military attack, especially an air attack. *...a punitive air strike. ...a nuclear strike. ...strategic strikes against Italian air bases.* N-COUNT: with supp, oft N *against* n

9 If something **strikes at** the heart or foundation of something, it attacks or conflicts with the basic elements or principles of that thing; a literary use. *...a rejection of her core beliefs and values, which strikes at the very heart of her being... The issue strikes at the very foundation of our community.* VERB V *at* n

10 If an idea or thought **strikes** you, it suddenly comes into your mind. *A thought struck her. Was she jealous of her mother, then?... At this point, it suddenly struck me that I was wasting my time.* VB: no cont V n *it* V n that/*how*

11 If something **strikes** you as being a particular thing, it gives you the impression of being that thing. *He struck me as a very serious but friendly person... What struck me as interesting is how much we judge other people by the clothes they wear... You've always struck me as being an angry man.* VERB V n *as* n/adj V n *as* -ing

12 If you **are struck** by something, you think it is very impressive, noticeable, or interesting. *She was struck by his simple, spellbinding eloquence... Theresa was struck by her own lack of forethought... What struck me about the firm is how genuinely friendly and informal it is.* VERB be V-ed *by/with* n V n

13 If you **strike** a deal or a bargain with someone, you come to an agreement with them. *They struck a deal with their paper supplier, getting two years of newsprint on credit... The two struck a deal in which Rendell took half of what a manager would... He insists he has struck no bargains for their release.* V-RECIP V n *with* n pl-n V n V n (non-recip)

14 If you **strike** a balance, you do something that is VERB

halfway between two extremes. *At times like that you have to strike a balance between sleep and homework.* Vn

15 If you **strike** a pose or attitude, you put your body and limbs in a particular position, for example when someone is taking your photograph. *She struck a pose, one hand on her hip and the other waving an imaginary cigarette.* VERB =adopt Vn

16 If something **strikes** fear or terror into people, it makes them very frightened or anxious; a literary use. *If there is a single subject guaranteed to strike fear in the hearts of parents, it is drugs.* VERB Vn *into*n

17 If you **are struck** dumb or blind, you suddenly become unable to speak or to see; used in written English. *I was struck dumb by this and had to think it over for a moment... For this revelation he was struck blind by the goddess Hera.* VB: usu passive *be*V-ed adj

18 When a clock **strikes**, its bells make a sound to indicate what the time is. *The clock struck nine... Finally, the clock strikes.* VERB Vn V

19 If you **strike** words from a document or an official record, you delete them; a formal use. *Strike that from the minutes... Her achievements were struck from the record book.* ▸ **Strike out** means the same as **strike**. *The censor struck out the next two lines.* VERB Vn *from*n Also Vn PHRASAL VERB VPn (not pron) Also VnP

20 When you **strike** a match, you make it produce a flame by moving it quickly against something rough. *Robina struck a match and held it to the crumpled newspaper in the grate.* VERB Vn

21 If someone **strikes** oil or gold, they discover it in the ground as a result of mining or drilling. *Hamilton Oil recently announced that it had struck oil in the Liverpool Bay area of the Irish Sea.* VERB Vn

22 When a coin or medal **is struck**, it is made. *Another medal was specially struck for him.* VB: usu passive *be*V-ed

23 If someone or something has a **strike against** them, they have an undesirable characteristic or feature; an informal use, mainly in American English. *The Hotel has two strikes against it. One, it's an immense ugly concrete building. Second, it lies in a rather awkward position.* N-COUNT: N *against*n =black mark

24 See also **stricken, striking; hunger strike**.

25 If you are **within striking distance** of something, or if something is **within striking distance**, it is quite near, so it could be reached or achieved quite easily. *I believe we are within striking distance of an agreement... The airport was within striking distance: no more than sixty miles to the west.* PHRASES oft PHR *of*n =close

26 If you **strike gold**, you find, do, or produce something that brings you a lot of money or success; used in journalism. *The company has struck gold with its new holiday development, Center Parcs.* V inflects

27 If you **strike it rich**, you make a lot of money, especially in a short time; an informal expression. *He hoped to strike it rich by investing in ginseng.* V inflects

28 • to **strike a chord**: see **chord**. • to **strike home**: see **home**. • to **strike a happy medium**: see **medium**. • to **strike it lucky**: see **lucky**.

strike back. If you **strike back**, you harm or criticize someone who has harmed or criticized you. *Our instinctive reaction when someone causes us pain is to strike back... Sometimes, Kappy got angry and struck back at him in whatever way she could... The president struck back at critics who say he should be held accountable for conditions that contributed to the riots.* PHRASAL VERB =retaliate VP VP *at*n

strike down PHRASAL VERB

1 If someone **is struck down**, especially by an illness, they are killed or severely harmed; used in written English. *Frank had been struck down by a massive heart attack. ...a great sporting hero, struck down at 49.* usu passive *be*V-ed P V-ed P

2 In American English, if a judge or court **strikes down** a law or regulation, they abolish it. *The Supreme Court today struck down a law that prevents criminals from profiting from books or movies about their crimes.* VPn

strike off. If someone such as a doctor or lawyer **is struck off**, their name is removed from the official register and they are not allowed to do medical or legal work any more. *...a company lawyer who had been struck off for dishonest practices... He could be struck off the medical register.* PHRASAL VERB usu passive *be*V-ed P *be*V-ed P n

strike out PHRASAL VERB

1 If you **strike out**, you begin to do something different, often because you want to become more independent. *She wanted me to strike out on my own, buy a business. ...a desire to make changes and to strike out in new directions.* VP

2 If you **strike out** at someone, you hit, attack, or speak angrily to them. *He seemed always ready to strike out at anyone and for any cause... Frampton struck out blindly, hitting not Waddington, but an elderly man.* VP *at*n VP

3 If you **strike out** in a particular direction, you start travelling in that direction; a literary use. *They left the car and struck out along the muddy track... He was planning to dump her and strike out for New York alone.* =set out VP prep/adv

4 In baseball, if a pitcher **strikes out** a batter or if a batter **strikes out**, the batter fails to hit three balls thrown properly by the pitcher, and is out. *He struck out ten batters, and allowed only two runs... Canseco, nursing a back injury, struck out.* ERG VPn (not pron) VP

5 See also **strike** 19.

strike up PHRASAL VERB

1 When you **strike up** a conversation or friendship with someone, you begin one; used in written English. *I trailed her into Penney's and struck up a conversation... James struck up a friendship with a small boy who owned a pony on the island.* VPn (not pron)

2 When musicians **strike up** a piece of music, or when music **strikes up**, the music begins. *And then the orchestra struck up the National Anthem... Music struck up in one of the big old buildings along the seafront... The band struck up, and riders paraded round the ring.* ERG VPn (not pron) VP

strike-breaker, strike-breakers; also spelled **strikebreaker**.

striker /straɪkəʳ/ **strikers** ◆◆◇◇◇

1 In football and some other team sports, a **striker** is a player whose main function is to attack and score goals, rather than defend. *The England striker Alan Shearer scored twice.* N-COUNT

2 See also **strike**.

striking /straɪkɪŋ/ ◆◆◆◇◇

1 Something that is **striking** is very noticeable or unusual. *The most striking feature of those statistics is the high proportion of suicides... He bears a striking resemblance to Lenin. ...her striking good looks.* ♦ **strikingly** *In one respect, however, the men really were strikingly similar. ...a strikingly handsome man... Most strikingly, the amount consumers spent in the shops grew much more quickly than anyone expected.* ADJ-GRADED =marked ADV-GRADED: usu ADV adj

2 Someone who is **striking** is very attractive, in a noticeable way. *She was a striking woman with long blonde hair.* ADJ-GRADED =stunning

3 See also **strike**.

string /strɪŋ/ **strings, stringing, strung** ◆◆◆◇◇

1 **String** is thin rope made of twisted threads, used for tying things together or tying up parcels. *He held out a small bag tied with string. ...a shiny metallic coin on a string.* N-VAR

2 A **string** of things is a number of them on a piece of string, thread, or wire. *She wore a string of pearls around her neck. ...a string of fairy lights.* N-COUNT: usu N *of*n

3 A **string** of places or objects is a number of them that form a line. *The landscape is broken only by a string of villages... A string of five rowing boats set out from the opposite bank.* N-COUNT: usu sing, usu N *of*n

4 A **string** of similar events is a series of them that happen one after the other. *The incident was the latest in a string of attacks... Between 1940 and 1943 he had a string of 62 consecutive victories.* N-COUNT: usu sing, usu N *of*n

5 The **strings** on a musical instrument such as a violin or guitar are thin pieces of tightly-stretched wire or nylon. You make sounds by plucking the strings or by passing a bow across them. *He went off to change a guitar string. ...a twenty-one-string harp.* N-COUNT

6 The **strings** are the section of an orchestra which consists of stringed instruments played with a bow. *The strings provided a melodic background to the passages played by the soloist... There was a 20-member string section.* N-PLURAL: oft N n

7 If you **string** something somewhere, you hang it up between two or more objects. *He had strung a banner across the wall.* ► **String up** means the same as **string**. *People were stringing up decorations on the fronts of their homes.* VERB V n prep/adv PHRASAL VERB V P n (not pron) Also V n P

8 See also **highly-strung**, **purse strings**, **second string**, **strung out**.

9 If someone has more than one **string to** their **bow**, they have more than one ability or thing they can use if the first one they try is not successful. *I'm never out of work because I have so many strings to my bow.* PHRASES Ns inflect, PHR after v

10 If something is offered to you with **no strings attached** or with **no strings**, it is offered without any special conditions. *Aid should be given to developing countries with no strings attached. ...no-strings grants that last for five years.*

11 If you **pull strings**, you use your influence with other people in order to get something done, often unfairly. *Tony is sure he can pull a few strings and get you in.* V inflects

12 • **apron strings**: see **apron**.

string along. If you **string** someone **along**, you deceive them by letting them believe you have the same desires, beliefs, or hopes as them; an informal expression. *She took advantage of him, stringing him along even after they were divorced.* PHRASAL VERB V n P

string together. If you **string** things **together**, you form something from them by adding them to each other, one at a time. *As speech develops, the child starts to string more words together... The speaker strung together a series of jokes.* PHRASAL VERB =put together V n P V P n (not pron)

string up PHRASAL VERB

1 See **string** 7.

2 To **string** someone **up** means to kill them by hanging them; an informal expression. *Guards rushed into his cell and strung him up.* V n P Also V P n (not pron)

string bean, string beans

1 In American English, **string beans** are long, very narrow green vegetables consisting of the cases that contain the seeds of a climbing plant. The usual British expression is **French beans**. N-COUNT: usu pl

2 In British English, **string beans** are vegetables similar to French beans, but thicker and coarser. N-COUNT: usu pl =runner bean

stringed instrument, stringed instruments. A **stringed instrument** is a musical instrument that has strings, such as a violin or a guitar. N-COUNT

stringency /strɪndʒᵊnsi/. Financial **stringency** is a shortage of money, either for spending or for investing; a technical use in economics. *In times of financial stringency it is clear that public expenditure has to be closely scrutinized.* N-UNCOUNT: supp N

stringent /strɪndʒᵊnt/. **Stringent** laws, rules, or conditions are very severe or are strictly controlled; a formal word. *He announced that there would be more stringent controls on the possession of weapons... Its drug-testing procedures are the most stringent in the world.* ♦ **stringently** *He is determined to see the Act enforced more stringently.* ◆◇◇◇◇ ADJ-GRADED =rigorous ADV: ADV with v

stringer /strɪŋəʳ/ **stringers.** A **stringer** is a journalist who is employed part-time by a newspaper or news service in order to report on a particular area; a technical term in journalism. *He picked up extra money as a local stringer for the New York Herald.* ◆◇◇◇◇ N-COUNT

string quartet, string quartets

1 A **string quartet** is a group of four musicians who play stringed instruments together. The instruments are two violins, a viola, and a cello. *The guests were entertained by a string quartet. ...a recital by the Borodin String Quartet.* N-COUNT

2 A **string quartet** is a musical composition for two violins, a viola, and a cello. *...Dvorak's String Quartet Opus 34.* N-COUNT

string vest, string vests. In British English, a **string vest** is a sleeveless vest that is made from pieces of cotton string that have been woven loosely together so there are fairly large spaces between them. N-COUNT

stringy /strɪŋi/ **stringier, stringiest**

1 **Stringy** food is unpleasant to eat because it contains long, thin strands that are difficult to chew, or messy. *The meat was stringy... Thankfully, it wasn't smothered in stringy cheese like some pizzas.* ADJ-GRADED

2 **Stringy** hair is thin and unattractive. *...an enormously fat man with long, stringy gray hair.* ADJ-GRADED =straggly

strip /strɪp/ **strips, stripping, stripped** ◆◆◆◇◇

1 A **strip** of something such as paper, cloth, or food is a long, narrow piece of it. *...a new kind of manufactured wood made by pressing strips of wood together and baking them... The simplest rag-rugs are made with strips of fabric plaited together... Serve dish with strips of fresh raw vegetables.* N-COUNT: usu N *of* n

2 A **strip** of land or water is a long narrow area of it. *The coastal cities of Liguria sit on narrow strips of land lying under steep mountains. ...a short boat ride across a narrow strip of water.* N-COUNT: usu N *of* n =stretch, belt

3 In American English, a **strip** is a long road, usually just outside a town, where there are a lot of stores, restaurants, and hotels. *...Goff's Charcoal Hamburgers on Lover's Lane, a busy commercial strip in North Dallas.* N-COUNT

4 If you **strip**, you take off your clothes. *They stripped completely, and lay and turned in the damp grass... Women residents stripped naked in protest.* ► **Strip off** means the same as **strip**. *The children were brazenly stripping off and leaping into the sea.* VERB V V adj PHRASAL VERB V P

5 If someone **is stripped**, their clothes are taken off by another person, for example in order to search for hidden or illegal things. *One prisoner claimed he'd been dragged to a cell, stripped and beaten.* • See also **strip-search**. VB: usu passive *be* V-ed

6 To **strip** something means to remove everything that covers it. *After Mike left for work I stripped the beds and vacuumed the carpets... The floorboards in both this room and the dining room have been stripped, sanded and sealed.* VERB V n

7 If you **strip** an engine or a piece of equipment, you take it to pieces so that it can be cleaned or repaired. *Volvo's three-man team stripped the car and treated it to a restoration.* ► **Strip down** means the same as **strip**. *In five years I had to strip the water pump down four times... I stripped down the two SU carburettors, cleaned and polished the pieces and rebuilt the units.* VERB =dismantle V n PHRASAL VERB =dismantle V n P V P n (not pron)

8 To **strip** someone of their property, rights, or titles means to take those things away from them. *The soldiers have stripped the civilians of their passports, and every other type of document... A senior official had been stripped of his rank and all his privileges for publicly criticising his former employer.* VERB V n *of* n

9 In a newspaper or magazine, a **strip** is a series of drawings which tell a story. The words spoken by the characters are often written on the drawings. Used mainly in American English. *...the Doonesbury strip.* N-COUNT =comic strip

10 See also **landing strip**.

11 If you **tear a strip off** someone or if you **tear** them **off a strip**, you scold them angrily and severely; an informal expression. *He heard Nora tearing a strip off an orderly for not returning the food bins to the kitchen soon enough... When the police arrived to tear him off a strip he apologised for all the trouble he'd caused them.* PHRASE: V inflects

strip away PHRASAL VERB

1 To **strip away** something misleading or unnecessary means to remove it completely, so that people can see what is important or true. *Altman strips away the pretence and mythology to expose the film industry as a business like any other.* V P n (not pron)

2 To **strip away** a layer of something means to remove it completely. *Sensitive Cream will not strip away the skin's protective layer... She'd managed to strip the bloodied rags away from Nellie's body.* V P n (not pron) V n P *from* n

strip down. See **strip** 6. PHRASAL VERB

strip off. If you **strip off** your clothes, you take PHRASAL VERB them off. *He stripped off his wet clothes and stepped into the shower.* ● See also **strip** 4. V P n (not pron) Also V n P

strip cartoon, strip cartoons. In British English, a **strip cartoon** is the same as a **comic strip**. N-COUNT

strip club, strip clubs. A **strip club** is a club which people go to in order to see striptease. N-COUNT

stripe /straɪp/ **stripes** ◆◆◇◇◇

1 A **stripe** is a long line which is a different colour from the areas next to it. *She wore a bright green jogging suit with a white stripe down the sides... The walls in the front bedroom are painted with broad, pale blue and white stripes.* N-COUNT

2 In the armed forces or the police, **stripes** are V-shaped bands of material sewn onto a uniform to indicate the rank of corporal or sergeant. *...a soldier with a corporal's stripes on his arms... He'd lost his stripes for slovenliness and cheek.* N-COUNT: usu pl

striped /straɪpt/. Something that is **striped** has stripes on it. *...a bottle green and maroon striped tie. ...striped wallpaper.* ◆◇◇◇◇ ADJ: usu ADJ n

stripey /straɪpi/. See **stripy**.

strip joint, strip joints. A **strip joint** is the same as a **strip club**; an informal expression. N-COUNT

strip light, strip lights; also spelled **strip-light**. A **strip light** is an electric light in the form of a long tube which shines very brightly. N-COUNT

strip lighting; also spelled **strip-lighting**. **Strip lighting** is a method of lighting which uses long tubes rather than light bulbs. *Other causes of migraine are VDU screens and strip-lighting.* N-UNCOUNT

stripling /strɪplɪŋ/ **striplings.** People sometimes refer to a young man as a **stripling** when they want to indicate in a slightly humorous way that although he is no longer a boy, he is not yet really a man; an old-fashioned word. *...a stripling of 20.* N-COUNT

strip mine, strip mines. In American English, a **strip mine** is a mine in which the coal, metal, or mineral is near the surface, and so underground passages are not needed. The British term is **opencast mine**. N-COUNT

strip mining; also spelled **strip-mining**. In American English, **strip mining** is the method of mining that is used when the mineral is near the surface and underground passages are not needed. The British term is **opencast mining**. N-UNCOUNT

stripper /strɪpəʳ/ **strippers.** A **stripper** is a person who earns money by doing striptease. *She worked as a stripper and did some acting. ...a male stripper.* ◆◇◇◇◇ N-COUNT

strip-search, strip-searches, strip-searching, strip-searched; also spelled **strip search**. If a person **is strip-searched**, someone such as a police officer makes them take off all their clothes and searches them, usually to see if they are carrying drugs or weapons. *All 23 of them were strip-searched for drugs.* ► Also a noun. *They suspected that he might be carrying a weapon and ordered a strip search.* VB: usu passive; be V-ed for n; Also be V-ed; N-COUNT

striptease /strɪptiːz, AM -tiːz/; also spelled **strip-tease**. **Striptease** is a form of entertainment in which someone takes off their clothes slowly and in a sexy way to music. *Oscar, much the worse for vodka, did a striptease. ...a striptease artist.* N-UNCOUNT

stripy /straɪpi/; also spelled **stripey**. Something that is **stripy** has stripes on it; an informal word. *He was wearing a stripy shirt and baggy blue trousers.* ADJ: usu ADJ n =stripey

strive /straɪv/ **strives, striving.** The past tense is either **strove** or **strived**, and the past participle is either **striven** or **strived**. If you **strive** to do something or **strive** for something, you make a great effort to do it or get it. *He strives hard to keep himself very fit... She strove to read the name on the stone pillar... Mr Calderon said the region must now strive for economic development as well as peace.* ♦ **striving, strivings** *...a politician consumed by his own passionate striving for leadership.* ◆◆◇◇◇ VERB =labour, struggle; V to-inf; V for n; Also V; N-UNCOUNT: also N in pl

strobe /stroʊb/ **strobes.** A **strobe** or a **strobe light** is a very bright light which flashes on and off very quickly. *The band left their strobes on for 20 minutes. ...like strobe lighting at a disco.* N-COUNT: oft N n

strode /stroʊd/. **Strode** is the past tense and past participle of **stride**.

stroke /stroʊk/ **strokes, stroking, stroked** ◆◆◆◇◇

1 If you **stroke** someone or something, you move your hand slowly and gently over them. *Carla, curled up on the sofa, was smoking a cigarette and stroking her cat... She walked forward and embraced him and stroked his tousled white hair.* VERB =caress V n

2 If someone has a **stroke**, a blood vessel in their brain bursts or gets blocked, which may kill them or cause one side of their body to be paralysed. *He had a minor stroke in 1987, which left him partly paralysed.* N-COUNT: usu sing

3 The **strokes** of a pen or brush are the movements or marks you make with it when you are writing or painting. *Fill in gaps by using short, upward strokes of the pencil.* N-COUNT: usu pl

4 When you are swimming or rowing, your **strokes** are the repeated movements you make with your arms or the oars. *I turned and swam a few strokes further out to sea... The boatmen accompany the stroke of their oars with the sound of their voices.* N-COUNT: usu pl

5 A swimming **stroke** is a particular style or method of swimming. *She spent hours practicing the breast stroke.* N-COUNT: usu sing, supp N

6 The **strokes** of a clock are the sounds that indicate each hour. *On the stroke of 12, fireworks suddenly exploded into the night.* N-COUNT

7 In sports such as tennis, cricket, and golf, a **stroke** is the action of hitting the ball. *Compton was sending the ball here, there, and everywhere with each stroke.* N-COUNT

8 **A stroke of** luck or good fortune is something lucky that happens. *It didn't rain, which turned out to be a stroke of luck.* N-SING: a N of n

9 **A stroke of** genius or inspiration is a sudden idea or inspiration. *At the time, his appointment seemed a stroke of genius.* N-SING: a N of n

10 If something happens **at a stroke** or **in one stroke**, it happens suddenly and completely because of one single action. *Myxomatosis wiped out 40 million rabbits at a stroke... How can Britain reduce its prison population in one stroke?* PHRASES; PHR after v =at one go

11 If someone does not **do a stroke** of work, they are very lazy and do no work at all; an informal expression. *I never did a stroke of work at college.* with brd-neg, V inflects

stroll /stroʊl/ **strolls, strolling, strolled.** If you **stroll** somewhere, you walk there in a slow, relaxed way. *He collected some orange juice from the refrigerator and, glass in hand, strolled to the kitchen window... Afterwards, we strolled back, put the kettle on and settled down with the newspapers.* ► Also a noun. *After dinner, I took a stroll round the city.* ♦ **stroller** *The foggy streets were virtually empty, except for the occasional evening stroller.* ◆◆◇◇◇ VERB =wander V prep/adv; N-COUNT; N-COUNT

stroller /stroʊləʳ/ **strollers.** In American English, a **stroller** is a small chair on wheels, in which a baby or small child can sit and be wheeled around. The British word is **pushchair**. N-COUNT

strong /strɒŋ, AM strɔːŋ/ **stronger** /strɒŋgəʳ, AM strɔːŋgər/ **strongest** /strɒŋgɪst, AM strɔːŋgɪst/ ◆◆◆◆◆

1 Someone who is **strong** is healthy with good muscles and can move or carry heavy things, or do hard physical work. *I'm not strong enough to carry him... I feared I wouldn't be able to control such a strong horse.* ADJ-GRADED ≠weak

2 Someone who is **strong** is confident and determined, and is not easily influenced or worried by other people. *He is sharp and manipulative with a strong personality... It's up to managers to be strong and do what they believe is right... Eventually I felt strong enough to look at him.* ADJ-GRADED =forceful ≠weak

3 **Strong** objects or materials are not easily broken and can support a lot of weight or resist a lot of strain. *The vacuum flask has a strong casing, which won't crack or chip... Glue the mirror in with a strong adhesive... The fabric is strong enough to withstand harsh processing.* ♦ **strongly** *The fence was very strongly built, with very large posts.* ADJ-GRADED ≠weak; ADV-GRADED: ADV -ed

4 A **strong** wind, current, or other force has a lot of power or speed, and can cause heavy things to move. *Strong winds and torrential rain combined to make conditions terrible for golfers in the Scottish Open... A fairly strong current seemed to be moving the whole boat... A neutron star has a gravitational field strong enough to generate X-rays.* ♦ **strongly** *The metal is strongly attracted to the surface.*
ADJ-GRADED =powerful; ADV-GRADED: ADV with v

5 A **strong** impression or influence has a great effect on someone. *We're glad if our music makes a strong impression, even if it's a negative one... There will be a strong incentive to enter into a process of negotiation... Developments in the Gulf continue to exert a strong influence on the world economy... We had strong family traditions; we couldn't escape them.* ♦ **strongly** *He is strongly influenced by Spanish painters such as Goya and El Greco... They were so determined to learn and they were so strongly motivated.*
ADJ-GRADED; ADV-GRADED: ADV with v

6 If you have **strong** opinions on something or express them using **strong** words, you have extreme or very definite opinions which you are willing to express or defend. *She is known to hold strong views on Cuba... There has been strong criticism of the military regime... The paper is a strong supporter of President Mandela's reforms... It condemned in extremely strong language what it called Britain's iniquitous campaign... It's bad judgment, but it's not treason. I think treason is too strong a word.* ♦ **strongly** *Obviously you feel very strongly about this... We are strongly opposed to the presence of America in this region... The police have strongly criticised England's football authorities... The presidents issued a strongly-worded statement in support of the government.*
ADJ-GRADED: usu ADJ n; ADV-GRADED: usu ADV with v

7 If someone in authority takes **strong** action, they act firmly and severely. *The government has said it will take strong action against any further strikes... He has also said he will have to become a strong President to put things right.*
ADJ-GRADED: usu ADJ n =decisive

8 If there is a **strong** case or argument for something, it is supported by a lot of evidence. *The testimony presented offered a strong case for acquitting her on grounds of self-defense... The evidence that such investment promotes growth is strong... A strong link was found between parental mental illness and disturbance in their children.* ♦ **strongly** *He argues strongly for retention of NATO as a guarantee of peace... These are conditions said by doctors to be strongly indicative of heart failure.*
ADJ-GRADED =convincing; ADV-GRADED: ADV with v, ADV adj/adv

9 If there is a **strong** possibility or likelihood that something is true or will happen, it is very likely to be true or to happen. *There is a strong possibility that the cat contracted the condition by eating contaminated pet food.*
ADJ-GRADED

10 Your **strong** points are your best qualities or talents, or the things you are good at. *Discretion is not Jeremy's strong point... Exports may be the only strong point in the economy over the next six to 12 months... Foreign policy is supposed to be George Bush's strongest suit, his strongest issue... Cynics argue that the EC is far stronger on rhetoric than on concrete action.*
ADJ-GRADED: ADJ n, v-link ADJ *on* n

11 A **strong** competitor, candidate, or team is talented or likely to succeed. *She was a strong contender for Britain's Olympic team... The Green Party is said to be the strongest challenger to the Communists in the elections... They've got a strong squad and some great players... This show has several strengths – notably a strong cast.*
ADJ-GRADED: usu ADJ n

12 If a relationship or bond is **strong**, it is close and likely to last for a long time. *He felt he had a relationship strong enough to talk frankly to Sarah... This has tested our marriage, and we have come through it stronger than ever... Delhi first began to develop strong ties with Moscow in the 1950s.*
ADJ-GRADED

13 A **strong** currency, economy, or industry has a high value or is very productive. *The US dollar continued its strong performance in Tokyo today... The local economy is strong and the population is growing... The company was not financially strong enough to be floated on the Stock Exchange.*
ADJ-GRADED =robust ≠weak

14 If something is a **strong** element or part of something else, it is an important or large part of it. *We are especially encouraged by the strong representation, this year, of women in information technology disciplines... There is a strong element of truth to each of these explanations.*
ADJ-GRADED

15 You can use **strong** when you are saying how many people there are in a group. For example, if a group is twenty strong, there are twenty people in it. *Ukraine indicated that it would establish its own army, 400,000 strong. ...a 1,000-strong crowd.*
ADJ: num ADJ

16 A **strong** drink, chemical, or drug contains a lot of the particular substance which makes it effective. *Strong coffee or tea late at night may cause sleeplessness... In strong concentrations it can cause nausea and vomiting.*
ADJ-GRADED

17 A **strong** colour, flavour, smell, sound, or light is intense and easily noticed. *As she went past there was a gust of strong perfume... Strong colours would flatter her pale skin and dark hair... The wine goes with strong and mild cheese alike.* ♦ **strongly** *He leaned over her, smelling strongly of sweat... The effect only works well with strongly coloured subjects.*
ADJ-GRADED =intense; ADV-GRADED: ADV with v

18 If someone has a **strong** accent, they speak in a distinctive way that shows very clearly what country or region they come from. *'Good, Mr Ryle,' he said in English with a strong French accent.*
ADJ-GRADED =pronounced ≠faint

19 You can say someone has **strong** features or a **strong** face if they have large and distinctive facial features. *He had a strong Greek nose and olive-black eyes.*
ADJ-GRADED

20 If someone **comes on strong**, they make their intentions or feelings clear in an excessive or aggressive way; an informal expression. *'I come on strong sometimes. Don't know why.' She was beginning to feel like a bully.*
PHRASES V inflects

21 If someone or something is still **going strong**, they are still alive, in good condition, or popular after a long time; an informal expression. *The old machinery was still going strong.*
v-link PHR

strong-arm. If you refer to someone's behaviour as **strong-arm** tactics or methods, you disapprove of it because it consists of using threats or force in order to achieve something. *The money has been recovered without resorting to verbal abuse or strong-arm tactics... The paper is openly critical of the strong-arm president.*
ADJ: ADJ n PRAGMATICS

stronghold /strɒŋhould, AM strɔːŋ-/ **strongholds** ◆◇◇◇◇

1 If you say that a place or region is a **stronghold** of a particular attitude or belief, you mean that most people there share this attitude or belief. *The western-most part of north Wales is a stronghold of Welsh-speakers... The seat was a stronghold of the Labour party.*
N-COUNT: oft N *of* n =bastion

2 If you say that somewhere is a **stronghold** of a particular type of animal, you mean that a relatively large number of that type of animal lives there. *Shetland is the last stronghold of otters in the British Isles.*
N-COUNT: with poss

strongman /strɒŋmæn, AM strɔːŋ-/ **strongmen.** If you refer to a male political leader as a **strongman**, you mean that he has great power and control over people and events, although his methods may sometimes be brutal or morally wrong. *He was a military strongman who ruled the country after a coup.*
N-COUNT

strong-minded. If you describe someone, especially a woman, as **strong-minded**, you approve of them because they have their own firm attitudes and opinions, and are not easily influenced by other people. *She is a strong-minded, independent woman.*
ADJ-GRADED PRAGMATICS =determined

strong-willed. Someone who is **strong-willed** has a lot of determination and always tries to do what they want, even though other people may advise them not to. *He is a very determined and strong-willed person.*
ADJ-GRADED =headstrong ≠weak-willed

stroppy /strɒpi/ **stroppier, stroppiest.** In British English, someone who is **stroppy** is bad-tempered and obstinate; an informal word. *A*
ADJ-GRADED

mother I knew was going through a really unpleasant time with a stroppy teenage son... The gas people haven't called to repair the cooker so I shall have to get stroppy with them.

strove /strəʊv/. **Strove** is a past tense of **strive**.

struck /strʌk/. **Struck** is the past tense and past participle of **strike**.

structural /strʌktʃərəl/. ◆◆◇◇◇ **Structural** means relating to or affecting the structure of something. *The explosion caused little structural damage to the office towers themselves.* ADJ: usu ADJ n ♦ **structurally** *When we bought the house, it was structurally sound, but I decided to redecorate throughout.* ADV: ADV adj/-ed, ADV with cl

structuralism /strʌktʃərəlɪzəm/. **Structuralism** is a method of analysis applied to such things as language, literature, or systems of thought. According to structuralism, something such as a language or a literary work can be understood as a structure whose various parts or elements make sense only in relation to the whole; a technical term in language, literature, and social science. N-UNCOUNT

structuralist /strʌktʃərəlɪst/ **structuralists**

1 A **structuralist** is someone whose work is based on structuralism. N-COUNT

2 **Structuralist** is used to refer to people and things that are connected with structuralism. *There are two main structuralist techniques incorporated into critical social research.* ADJ: ADJ n

structure /strʌktʃəʳ/ **structures, structuring, structured** ◆◆◆◆◇

1 The **structure** of something is the way in which it is made, built, or organized. *The typical family structure of Freud's patients involved two parents and two children... The chemical structure of this particular molecule is very unusual.* N-VAR: usu with supp, oft N *of*n

2 A **structure** is something that consists of parts connected together in an ordered way. *The feet are highly specialised structures made up of 26 small delicate bones.* N-COUNT: usu with supp

3 A **structure** is something that has been built. *About half of those funds has gone to repair public roads, structures and bridges... The house was a handsome four-story brick structure.* N-COUNT =building

4 If you **structure** something, you arrange it in a careful, organized pattern or system. *By structuring the course this way, we're forced to produce something the companies think is valuable.* VERB V n ♦ **structured** *We have introduced a more structured training programme.* ADJ-GRADED

5 See also **report structure**.

struggle /strʌgəl/ **struggles, struggling, struggled** ◆◆◆◆◇

1 If you **struggle** to do something, you try hard to do it, even though other people or things may be making it difficult for you to succeed. *They had to struggle against all kinds of adversity... Those who have lost their jobs struggle to pay their supermarket bills.* VERB V prep V to-inf Also V

2 A **struggle** is an attempt to obtain something or to defeat someone who is denying you something, such as your freedom. *Life became a struggle for survival. ...a young lad's struggle to support his poverty-stricken family... He is currently locked in a power struggle with his Prime Minister.* N-VAR: oft N prep, N to-inf

3 If you **struggle** when you are being held, you twist, kick, and move violently in order to get free. *I struggled, but he was a tall man, well-built.* VERB V

4 If two people **struggle** with each other, they fight. *She screamed at him to 'stop it' as they struggled on the ground... We were struggling for the gun when it went off!... There were signs that she struggled with her attacker.* V-RECIP pl-n V pl-n V *for*n V *with*n ► Also a noun. *He died in a struggle with prison officers less than two months after coming to Britain.* N-COUNT

5 If you **struggle** to move yourself or to move a heavy object, you try to do it, but it is difficult. *I could see the young boy struggling to free himself... I struggled with my bags, desperately looking for a porter.* VERB V to-inf V prep

6 If you **struggle** to do something or go somewhere, you succeed in doing it or in going there but with great difficulty. *Catherine struggled to her feet... I struggled into a bathrobe and staggered down the stairs.* VERB V prep/adv

7 If a person or organization **is struggling**, they are likely to fail in what they are doing, even though they might be trying very hard. *The company is struggling to find buyers for its new product... One in five young adults was struggling with everyday mathematics... By the 1960s, many shipyards were struggling.* VB: only cont V to-inf V prep V

8 An action or activity that is **a struggle** is very difficult for you to do. *Losing weight was a terrible struggle.* N-SING: a N

struggle on. If you **struggle on**, you continue doing something although it is difficult, rather than stopping. *Why should I struggle on to please my parents?... The rest of the world struggles on with its perpetual problems, poverty and debt.* PHRASAL VERB V P V P *with*n

strum /strʌm/ **strums, strumming, strummed.** ◆◇◇◇◇ If you **strum** a stringed instrument such as a guitar, you play it by moving your fingers backwards and forwards across the strings. *In the corner, one youth sat alone, softly strumming a guitar... Vaska strummed away on his guitar.* VERB V n V prep/adv ► Also a noun. *A little while later, I heard the strum of my father's guitar as he began to sing.* N-SING: oft N *of*n

strung /strʌŋ/. **Strung** is the past tense and past participle of **string**.

strung out

1 If things are **strung out** somewhere, they are spread out in a line. *Colleges, temples and administrative buildings were strung out on the north side of the river.* ADJ: usu v-link ADJ, usu ADJ prep

2 If someone is **strung out** on drugs, they are heavily affected by drugs; an informal use. *Back in the Seventies, he was permanently strung out on heroin.* ADJ-GRADED: v-link ADJ, usu ADJ *on*n

strut /strʌt/ **struts, strutting, strutted** ◆◇◇◇◇

1 Someone who **struts** walks in a proud way, with their head held high and their chest out, as if they are very important; used showing disapproval. *He struts around town like he owns the place.* VERB PRAGMATICS V prep/adv ● If you **strut** your **stuff**, you act in a proud way and show off; an informal expression. *He got up to strut his stuff on the dance-floor.* PHRASE: V inflects

2 A **strut** is a piece of wood or metal which holds the weight of other pieces in a building. *...the struts of a suspension bridge.* N-COUNT

strychnine /strɪkniːn, AM -naɪn/. **Strychnine** is a very poisonous drug which is sometimes used in very small amounts as a medicine. N-UNCOUNT

stub /stʌb/ **stubs, stubbing, stubbed** ◆◇◇◇◇

1 The **stub** of a cigarette or a pencil is the last short piece of it which remains when the rest has been used. *He pulled the stub of a pencil from behind his ear. ...an ashtray of cigarette stubs.* N-COUNT: with supp

2 A ticket **stub** is the part that you keep when you go in to watch a performance. *Fans who still have their original ticket stubs should contact Sheffield Arena by July 3.* N-COUNT: usu n N

3 A cheque **stub** is the small part that you keep as a record of what you have paid. N-COUNT: usu n N

4 If you **stub** your toe, you hurt it by accidentally kicking something. *I stubbed my toes against a table leg.* VERB V n

stub out. When someone **stubs out** a cigarette, they put it out by pressing it against something hard. *Signs across the entrances warn all visitors to stub out their cigarettes.* PHRASAL VERB =put out V P n (not pron) Also V n P

stubble /stʌbəl/

1 The short stalks which are left standing in fields after corn or wheat has been harvested are referred to as **stubble**. *The stubble was burning in the fields.* N-UNCOUNT

2 The very short hairs on a man's face when he has not shaved recently are referred to as **stubble**. *His face was covered with the stubble of several nights.* N-UNCOUNT

stubbly /stʌbəli/. If a man has not shaved recently, he has a **stubbly** chin. *He had long unkempt hair and a stubbly chin.* ADJ-GRADED: usu ADJ n

stubborn /stʌbəʳn/ ◆◆◇◇◇

1 Someone who is **stubborn** or who behaves in a **stubborn** way is determined to do what they want ADJ-GRADED =obstinate

and is very unwilling to change their mind. *He is a stubborn character used to getting his own way... His face was set in an expression of stubborn determination.* ♦ **stubbornly** *He stubbornly refused to tell her how he had come to be in such a state.* ADV-GRADED ♦ **stubbornness** *I couldn't tell if his refusal to talk was simple stubbornness.* N-UNCOUNT

2 A **stubborn** stain or problem is difficult to remove or to deal with. *This treatment removes the most stubborn stains... The first and most stubborn problem was that of reductions in the number of aircraft.* ♦ **stubbornly** *Some interest rates have remained stubbornly high.* ADJ-GRADED: usu ADJ n =persistent; ADV-GRADED

stubby /stʌbi/. An object that is **stubby** is shorter and thicker than usual. *He pointed a stubby finger at a wooden chair opposite him.* ADJ-GRADED =stumpy

stucco /stʌkoʊ/. **Stucco** is a type of plaster used for covering walls and decorating ceilings. N-UNCOUNT: oft N n

stuck /stʌk/ ♦♦◇◇◇

1 **Stuck** is the past tense and past participle of **stick**.

2 If something is **stuck** in a particular position, it is fixed tightly in this position and is unable to move. *He said his car had got stuck in the snow... She had got something stuck between her teeth.* ADJ: v-link ADJ, oft ADJ prep/adv

3 If you are **stuck** in a place, you want to get away from it, but are unable to. *I was stuck at home with flu... Certainly, I wouldn't have wanted to be stuck on a desert island with her for any length of time.* ADJ: v-link ADJ prep/adv

4 If you are **stuck** in a boring or unpleasant situation, you are unable to change it or get away from it. *I don't want to get stuck in another job like that... I am stuck in a relationship which I don't enjoy.* ADJ: v-link ADJ prep/adv =trapped

5 If something is **stuck** at a particular level or stage, it is not progressing or changing. *The negotiations have got stuck on a number of key issues... US unemployment figures for March showed the jobless rate stuck at 7 per cent... The economy is still stuck in recession.* ADJ: v-link ADJ prep/adv

6 If you are **stuck with** something that you do not want, you cannot get rid of it. *Many people are now stuck with expensive fixed-rate mortgages... I know you think I'm stupid, but we're stuck with each other, aren't we?* ADJ: v-link ADJ *with* n =lumbered

7 If you get **stuck** when you are trying to do something, you are unable to continue doing it because it is too difficult. *They will be there to help if you get stuck... If he gets stuck on a word, he can make the computer prompt him.* ADJ: v-link ADJ, oft ADJ *on* n

8 If you **get stuck in**, you start what you are going to do with enthusiasm and determination; an informal expression. *We're bottom of the league and we have to get stuck in.* PHRASE: V inflects

stuck-up. If you say that someone is **stuck-up**, you mean that you dislike them because they think they are very important and are very proud and unfriendly; an informal word. *She was a famous actress, but she wasn't a bit stuck-up.* ADJ-GRADED PRAGMATICS =snooty

stud /stʌd/ **studs** ♦◇◇◇◇

1 **Studs** are small pieces of metal which are attached to a surface for decoration. *You see studs on lots of London front doors.* N-COUNT

2 **Studs** are earrings which consist of one small piece of jewellery attached to a bar which goes through your ear. *...plain gold studs.* N-COUNT

3 **Studs** are small round objects attached to the bottom of boots, especially sports boots, so that the wearer does not slip. N-COUNT

4 Horses or other animals that are kept for **stud** are kept to be used for breeding. *He was voted horse of the year and then was retired to stud.* N-UNCOUNT

5 If you refer to a man as a **stud**, you mean that he is thought to be very active sexually and good at satisfying women's sexual desires; an informal use. *You treat me halfway between a little boy and a stud.* N-COUNT

6 A **stud** is the same as a **stud farm**. N-COUNT

7 See also **press stud**.

stud book, stud books; also spelled **studbook**. A **stud book** is a written record of the breeding of a particular horse, especially a racehorse. N-COUNT

studded /stʌdɪd/ ♦◇◇◇◇

1 Something that is **studded** is decorated with studs or things that look like studs. *...studded leather jackets. ...a beautiful gold bracelet studded with diamonds.* ► Also after nouns. *...a gold and diamond-studded trophy.* ADJ: oft ADJ *with* n; COMB in ADJ

2 If you say that something is **studded with** another thing, you mean that there are a lot of the second thing in or on the first thing. *His collection was studded with Flemish masterpieces. ...a metal panel studded with small microphones.* ADJ: v-link ADJ, ADJ *with* n

3 See also **star-studded**.

student /stjuːdᵊnt, stuː-/ **students** ♦♦♦♦♦

1 A **student** is a person who is studying at a university or college. *She has known Mr Smith since they were students at Glasgow University. ...a 23-year-old medical student.* • See also **mature student**. N-COUNT

2 A **student** is a person who is studying at a secondary school; used mainly in American English. N-COUNT =pupil

3 Someone who is a **student of** a particular subject is interested in the subject and spends time learning about it. *...a passionate student of history and an expert on nineteenth century prime ministers.* N-COUNT: N *of* n

students' union, students' unions

1 In British English, the **students' union** or the **student union** is the students' organization in a university or college which organizes leisure activities, provides welfare services, and represents students' political interests. *...Jon Moore, president of the college's student union. ...Loughborough Students' Union.* N-COUNT: oft *the* N, oft in names

2 **The students' union** or the **student union** is the building where the students' union organization has its offices and which usually has a shop, a coffee bar, and a meeting place. N-SING: *the* N =guild

stud farm, stud farms. A **stud farm** is a place where horses are bred. N-COUNT

studied /stʌdid/. A **studied** action has been carefully thought about or planned and is not spontaneous or natural. *'We both have an interesting 10 days coming up,' said Alex Ferguson with studied understatement.* • See also **study**. ADJ: ADJ n ≠unstudied

studio /stjuːdioʊ, stuː-/ **studios** ♦♦♦♦◇

1 A **studio** is a room where a painter, photographer, or designer works. *She was in her studio again, painting onto a large canvas.* N-COUNT

2 A **studio** is a room where radio or television programmes are recorded, records are produced, or films are made. *She's much happier performing live than in a recording studio.* N-COUNT

3 You can also refer to film-making or recording companies as **studios**. *She wrote to Paramount Studios and asked if they would audition her.* N-COUNT: usu pl

4 A **studio**, a **studio flat**, or a **studio apartment** is a small flat with one room for living and sleeping in, a kitchen, and a bathroom. *I live on my own in a studio flat.* N-COUNT

studio audience, studio audiences. A **studio audience** is a group of people who are in a television or radio studio watching while a programme is being made, so that their clapping, laughter, or questions are recorded on the programme. N-COUNT-COLL

studious /stjuːdiəs, stuː-/. Someone who is **studious** spends a lot of time reading and studying books. *I was a very quiet, studious little girl.* ADJ-GRADED =bookish

studiously /stjuːdiəsli, stuː-/. If you do something **studiously**, you do it carefully and deliberately. *When I looked at Clive, he studiously avoided my eyes.* ADV-GRADED: usu ADV with v, also ADV adj

study /stʌdi/ **studies, studying, studied** ♦♦♦♦♦

1 If you **study**, you spend time learning about a particular subject or subjects. *...a relaxed and happy atmosphere that will allow you to study to your full potential... He went to Hull University, where he studied History and Economics... She came to Britain to study for her A levels.* VERB V; V n; V *for* n

2 **Study** is the activity of studying. *...the use of maps and visual evidence in the study of local history... She gave up her studies to have Alexander.* N-UNCOUNT: also N in pl

3 A **study** of a subject is a piece of research on it. *Recent studies suggest that as many as 5 in 1000* N-COUNT: usu with supp

new mothers are likely to have this problem. ...the first study of English children's attitudes.

4 You can refer to educational subjects or courses that contain several elements as **studies** of a particular kind. *Bulgaria's first institute for Islamic studies opened in Sofia yesterday... She is currently doing a business studies course at Leeds.*
N-PLURAL: supp N

5 If you **study** something, you look at it or watch it very carefully, in order to find something out. *Debbie studied her friend's face for a moment.*
VERB
V n

6 If you **study** something, you consider it or observe it carefully in order to be able to understand it fully. *I know that you've been studying chimpanzees for thirty years now... I invite every citizen to carefully study the document.*
VERB
V n

7 A **study** by an artist is a drawing which is done in preparation for a larger picture.
N-COUNT

8 A **study** is a room in a house which is used for reading, writing, and studying.
N-COUNT

9 See also **studied; case study**.

stuff /stʌf/ **stuffs, stuffing, stuffed** ◆◆◆◆◇

1 You can use **stuff** to refer to things such as a substance, a collection of things, events, or ideas, or the contents of something in a general way without mentioning the thing itself by name; an informal use. *I'd like some coffee, and I don't object to the powdered stuff if it's all you've got... I don't know anything about this antique stuff... 'What do you want to know?'—'About life and stuff.'... Don't tell me you still believe in all that stuff?... He pointed to a duffle bag. 'That's my stuff.'*
N-UNCOUNT: usu with supp

2 If you **stuff** something somewhere, you push it there quickly and roughly. *I stuffed my hands in my pockets... He stuffed the newspapers into a litter bin and headed down the street... His pants were stuffed inside the tops of his boots.*
VERB =shove
V n prep/adv

3 If you **stuff** a container or space with something, you fill it with something or with a quantity of things until it is full. *He grabbed my purse, opened it and stuffed it full, then gave it back to me... He still stood behind his cash register stuffing his mouth with popcorn. ...wallets stuffed with dollars.*
VERB =cram
V n adj
V n *with* n
V-ed

4 If you **stuff** yourself, you eat a lot of food; an informal use. *I could stuff myself with ten chocolate bars and half an hour later eat a big meal.* ♦ **stuffed** *But you're just so stuffed you won't be able to drink anything.*
VERB
V pron-refl prep
ADJ-GRADED: v-link ADJ

5 If you **stuff** a bird such as a chicken or a vegetable such as a pepper, you put a mixture of food inside it before cooking it. *Will you stuff the turkey and shove it in the oven for me? ...beef suet pudding, beer and stuffed tomatoes.*
VERB
V n
V-ed

6 If a dead animal **is stuffed**, it is filled with a substance so that it can be preserved and displayed. *A pike weighing 29 lb 8 oz taken in 1878 was stuffed and is on display at the estate office... He didn't much care for the stuffed animal heads that hung on the walls.*
VB: usu passive
be V-ed
V-ed

7 If you say that one thing is **the stuff of** another, you mean that the first thing is a very important feature or characteristic of the second thing, or that the second thing can be based or built on the first thing; a formal use. *The idea that we can be whatever we want has become the stuff of television commercials.*
N-SING: *the* N *of* n =essence

8 If you are angry with someone for something that they have said or done, you might say **'Get stuffed!'** to them; a rude expression, used mainly in British English.
EXCLAM PRAGMATICS

9 **Stuff** is used in front of nouns to emphasize that you do not care about something, or do not want to think about it; an informal use. *Ultimately my attitude was: stuff them... 'Stuff the poll tax'.*
VB: only imper PRAGMATICS
V n

10 If you **do** your **stuff**, you perform an activity in the way that people expect; an informal expression. *Once I get on the pitch I know I can do my stuff... All that was left was to plant the roses and wait for nature to do her stuff.*
PHRASES
V inflects

11 If you say that someone **knows** their **stuff**, you mean that they are good at doing something because they know a lot about it; an informal expression. *These chaps know their stuff after seven years of war.*
V inflects

12 • **strut one's stuff**: see **strut**.

stuffed shirt, stuffed shirts. If you describe someone, especially someone with an important position, as a **stuffed shirt**, you mean that they are extremely formal and old-fashioned; an informal expression. *He was so smart he charmed everybody from stuffed shirts all the way down to idiots.*
N-COUNT

stuffing /stʌfɪŋ/ **stuffings** ◆◇◇◇◇

1 **Stuffing** is a mixture of food that is put inside a bird such as a chicken, or a vegetable such as a pepper, before it is cooked. *Chestnuts can be used at Christmas time, as a stuffing for turkey, guinea fowl or chicken.*
N-MASS

2 **Stuffing** is material that is put inside pillows, cushions, or toys, in order to fill them and make them firm or solid.
N-UNCOUNT

3 If something **knocks the stuffing out of** you when you are feeling enthusiastic or confident about something, it causes you to lose your enthusiasm or confidence. *Men have had a hard time for the last fifteen years. The women's movement knocked the stuffing out of them.*
PHRASE: V inflects

stuffy /stʌfi/ **stuffier, stuffiest** ◆◇◇◇◇

1 **Stuffy** people or institutions are formal and old-fashioned. *Why were grown-ups always so stuffy and slow to recognize good ideas? ...a firm of lawyers in Lincoln's Inn, immensely stuffy and respectable. ...stuffy attitudes.*
ADJ-GRADED =staid

2 If it is **stuffy** in a place, it is unpleasantly warm and there is not enough fresh air. *It was hot and stuffy in the classroom even though two of the windows at the back had been opened.*
ADJ-GRADED =airless

3 If you have a **stuffy** nose, your nose is blocked with mucus, usually because of a cold. *Aromatic capsules are great for easing the discomfort of a stuffy nose.* ♦ **stuffiness** *Peppermint leaves are believed to relieve tiredness and nasal stuffiness.*
ADJ-GRADED: usu ADJ n =bunged up
N-UNCOUNT

stultify /stʌltɪfaɪ/ **stultifies, stultifying, stultified.** If something **stultifies** you, it makes you feel empty or dull in your mind, because it is so boring or repetitive. *You couldn't say that island life stultified the Eunson girls... Only a uniformed guard stultified with boredom might have overheard them.* ♦ **stultifying** *A rigid routine can be stultifying and boring.*
VERB
V n
V-ed
ADJ-GRADED

stumble /stʌmbəl/ **stumbles, stumbling, stumbled.** ◆◆◇◇◇

1 If you **stumble**, you put your foot down awkwardly while you are walking or running and nearly fall over. *He stumbled and almost fell... I stumbled into the telephone box and dialed 999.* ► Also a noun. *I make it into the darkness with only one stumble.*
VERB
V
V prep/adv
N-COUNT: usu sing

2 If you **stumble** while you are reading aloud or speaking, you make a mistake, and have to pause before saying the words properly. *Labour was delighted to see the Premier stumbling over answers to questions on Tory tax plans.*
VERB =falter
V *over* n
Also V

stumble across or **stumble on.** If you **stumble across** something or **stumble on** it, you find it or discover it unexpectedly. *I stumbled across an extremely simple but very exact method for understanding where my money went... History relates that they stumbled on a magnificent waterfall.*
PHRASAL VERB =come across
V P n

stumbling block, stumbling blocks. A **stumbling block** is a problem which stops you from achieving something. *Perhaps the major stumbling block to reunification is the military presence in South Korea.*
◆◇◇◇◇
N-COUNT: oft N *to/in* n

stump /stʌmp/ **stumps, stumping, stumped** ◆◆◇◇◇

1 A **stump** is a small part of something that remains when the rest of it has been removed or broken off. *If you have a tree stump, check it for fungus... The tramp produced a stump of candle from his deep pockets.*
N-COUNT: usu with supp

2 In cricket, the **stumps** are the three wooden sticks that are placed upright in the ground to form the wicket.
N-COUNT

3 If you **are stumped** by a question or problem,
VERB

you cannot think of any solution or answer to it. *John Diamond is stumped by an unexpected question... Well, maybe I stumped you on that one.* be V-ed; V n

4 If you **stump** somewhere, you walk there with heavy steps. *The Marshal stepped over the vacuum-cleaner and stumped out of the room.* VERB =stomp V prep/adv

5 If politicians **stump** the country or **stump** for a candidate, they travel around making campaign speeches before an election; used mainly in American English. *Mr Brazauskas has been stumping the country as though unsure of victory... He was in Georgia stumping for Senator Wyche Fowler, a Democrat.* VERB V n; V *for* n; Also V

6 If politicians are **on the stump**, they are campaigning for an election; used mainly in American English. *The presidential candidates are on the stump today.* PHRASE: usu v-link PHR

stump up. If you **stump up** a sum of money, you pay the money that is required for something, often reluctantly; an informal British expression. *Customers do not have to stump up any cash for at least four weeks.* PHRASAL VERB =cough up V P n (not pron) Also V P

stumpy /stʌmpi/. **Stumpy** things are short and thick. *Does this dress make my legs look too stumpy?* ADJ-GRADED =chunky

stun /stʌn/ **stuns, stunning, stunned** ◆◆◇◇◇

1 If you **are stunned** by something, you are very shocked or astonished by it and are therefore unable to speak or do anything. *Many cinema-goers were stunned by the film's violent and tragic end.* VB: usu passive =amaze, shock *be* V-ed ♦ **stunned** *When they told me she had gone missing I was totally stunned... His announcement did not produce any immediate cheers, only a stunned silence while the words sank in.* ADJ-GRADED

2 If something such as a blow on the head **stuns** you, it makes you unconscious or confused and unsteady. *Sam stood his ground and got a blow that stunned him.* VERB =daze V n

3 See also **stunning**.

stung /stʌŋ/. **Stung** is the past tense and past participle of **sting**.

stunk /stʌŋk/. **Stunk** is the past participle of **stink**.

stunner /stʌnəʳ/ **stunners**

1 A **stunner** is an extremely attractive woman; an informal use. *One of the girls was an absolute stunner.* N-COUNT =beauty

2 If you say that something is a **stunner**, you mean that it is very surprising or impressive; an informal use. *Their debut single is a stunner.* N-COUNT

stunning /stʌnɪŋ/ ◆◆◇◇◇

1 A **stunning** person or thing is extremely beautiful or impressive. *She was 55 and still a stunning woman... A stunning display of fireworks lit up the sky.* ADJ-GRADED: usu ADJ n =fabulous ♦ **stunningly** *The video is filmed in stunningly beautiful countryside.* ADV-GRADED: ADV adj

2 A **stunning** thing or event is so unusual or unexpected that people are astonished by it. *The minister resigned last night after a stunning defeat in Sunday's vote... The secret that the priest had confided to him was a stunning piece of news.* ADJ-GRADED: usu ADJ n =staggering ♦ **stunningly** *Sometimes people were quite stunningly rude to him.* ADV-GRADED

stunt /stʌnt/ **stunts, stunting, stunted** ◆◇◇◇◇

1 A **stunt** is something interesting that is done in order to attract attention and get publicity for the person or company responsible for it. *In a bold promotional stunt for the movie, he smashed his car into a passing truck.* N-COUNT

2 A **stunt** is a dangerous and exciting piece of action in a film. *Sean Connery insisted on living dangerously for his new film by performing his own stunts.* N-COUNT

3 If something **stunts** the growth or development of a person or thing, it prevents it from growing or developing as much as it should. *The heart condition had stunted his growth a bit... High interest rates have stunted economic growth.* VERB V n ♦ **stunted** *Damage may result in stunted growth and sometimes death of the plant. ...low stunted trees.* ADJ-GRADED

4 If someone **pulls a stunt**, they do something silly or risky. *The days when they needed to pull publicity stunts to get noticed are long gone.* PHRASE: V and N inflect

stunt man, stunt men; also spelled **stuntman.** A **stunt man** is a man whose job is to do dangerous things, either for publicity or in a film instead of the actor so that the actor does not risk being injured. *The British stunt man Eddie Kidd jumped over the Great Wall of China on a motorcycle.* N-COUNT

stupefy /stjuːpɪfaɪ, stuː-/ **stupefies, stupefying, stupefied.** If something **stupefies** you, it shocks or surprises you so much that you cannot think properly for a while. *...a violent slap on the side of the head, which stunned and stupefied him.* VERB V n ♦ **stupefied** *Primrose, stupefied by tiredness, began to wail that she was hungry.* ADJ ♦ **stupefying** *...a life of almost stupefying indolence.* ADJ-GRADED

stupendous /stjuːpendəs, AM stuː-/. Something that is **stupendous** is surprisingly impressive or large. *He was a man of stupendous stamina and energy... This stupendous novel keeps you gripped to the end. ...a stupendous amount of money.* ADJ-GRADED: usu ADJ n =staggering ♦ **stupendously** *He is a stupendously swift writer.* ADV

stupid /stjuːpɪd, AM stuː-/ **stupider, stupidest** ◆◆◆◇◇

1 If you say that someone or something is **stupid**, you mean that they show a lack of good judgement or intelligence and they are not at all sensible. *I'll never do anything so stupid again... I made a stupid mistake... Your father wouldn't have asked such a stupid question... If you give him half a chance he can make you look stupid.* ADJ-GRADED PRAGMATICS =foolish ≠wise, sensible ♦ **stupidly** *We had stupidly been looking at the wrong column of figures... He got rather drunk and behaved stupidly.* ADV-GRADED: usu ADV with v, also ADV adj ♦ **stupidity** /stjuːpɪdɪti, AM stuː-/ **stupidities** *I stared at him, astonished by his stupidity.* N-VAR: usu with poss

2 You say that something is **stupid** to indicate that you do not like it or that it annoys you. *I wouldn't call it art. It's just stupid and tasteless... Friendship is much more important to me than a stupid old ring!* ADJ-GRADED PRAGMATICS =silly

stupor /stjuːpəʳ, AM stuː-/ **stupors.** Someone who is in a **stupor** is almost unconscious and is unable to act or think normally, especially as a result of drink or drugs. *He fell back onto the sofa in a drunken stupor... He was drinking himself into a stupor every night.* N-COUNT: usu sing, oft *in/into* a N

sturdy /stɜːʳdi/ **sturdier, sturdiest.** Someone or something that is **sturdy** looks strong and is unlikely to be easily injured or damaged. *She was a short, sturdy woman in her early sixties... The camera was mounted on a sturdy tripod.* ◆◇◇◇◇ ADJ-GRADED =robust ♦ **sturdily** *It was a good table too, sturdily constructed of elm.* ADV-GRADED: usu ADV with v

sturgeon /stɜːʳdʒᵊn/; **sturgeon** is both the singular and the plural form. A **sturgeon** is a fish which lives in the northern hemisphere. Sturgeon are usually caught for their eggs, which are known as caviar. N-VAR

stutter /stʌtəʳ/ **stutters, stuttering, stuttered** ◆◇◇◇◇

1 If someone has a **stutter**, they find it difficult to say the first sound of a word, and so they often hesitate or repeat it two or three times. *He spoke with a pronounced stutter.* N-COUNT: usu sing =stammer

2 If someone **stutters**, they have difficulty speaking because they find it hard to say the first sound of a word. *I was trembling so hard, I thought I would stutter when I spoke.* VERB =stammer V ♦ **stuttering** *He had to stop talking because if he'd kept on, the stuttering would have started.* N-UNCOUNT

3 If something **stutters** along, it progresses slowly and unevenly. *The old truck stuttered along the winding road... The political debate stutters on.* VERB V prep/adv

sty /staɪ/ **sties.** A **sty** is the same as a **pigsty**. N-COUNT

stye /staɪ/ **styes.** A **stye** is an infection of the skin at the bottom of an eyelash, which makes the eyelid red and swollen. N-COUNT

style /staɪl/ **styles, styling, styled** ◆◆◆◆◇

1 The **style** of something is the general way in which it is done or presented, which often shows the attitudes of the people involved. *Our children's* N-COUNT: with supp, also *in* adj N

different needs and learning styles created many problems... Belmont Park is a broad sweeping track which will suit the European style of running... Sam celebrated in fine style.

2 If people or places have **style**, they are smart and elegant. *Bournemouth, you have to admit, has style... Both love doing things in style... She had not lost her grace and style.* N-UNCOUNT: oft *in* N

3 The **style** of a product is its design. *His 50 years of experience have given him strong convictions about style... Several styles of hat were available.* N-VAR

4 In the arts, a particular **style** is characteristic of a particular period or group of people. *...six scenes in the style of a classical Greek tragedy. ...a mixture of musical styles. ...the revival of the gothic style.* N-COUNT: usu with supp

5 If something such as a piece of clothing, a vehicle, or someone's hair **is styled** in a particular way, it is designed or shaped in that way. *His thick blond hair had just been styled before his trip. ...classically styled clothes.* VB: usu passive *be* V-ed V-ed

6 See also **old-style, self-styled, styling**.

7 If you say that something is **not** someone**'s style**, you mean that it is not the way in which they usually do things, or does not fit the way they usually see themselves. *Mr Baker was not off guard. That is not his style... To be honest, the house is not quite our style.* ● to **cramp** someone's **style**: see **cramp**. PHRASE: v-link PHR

-style /-staɪl/

1 **-style** combines with nouns and adjectives to form adjectives which describe the style or characteristics of something. *...the development of a Western-style political system. ...a hearty country-style dinner.* COMB in ADJ: usu ADJ n

2 **-style** combines with adjectives and nouns to form adverbs which describe how something is done. *Guests have been asked to dress 1920s-style.* COMB in ADV: ADV after v

styling /st<u>aɪ</u>lɪŋ/ ◆◇◇◇◇

1 The **styling** of an object is the design and appearance of it. *The car neatly blends classic styling into a smooth modern package.* N-UNCOUNT: oft supp N

2 The **styling** of someone's hair is the way in which it is cut and arranged. *...shampoos and styling products.* N-UNCOUNT: oft N n

3 See also **style**.

stylised /st<u>aɪ</u>laɪzd/. See **stylized**.

stylish /st<u>aɪ</u>lɪʃ/. Someone or something that is **stylish** is smart, elegant, and fashionable. *...a very attractive and very stylish woman of 27. ...a varied choice of stylish designs.* ♦ **stylishly** *...stylishly dressed middle-aged women.* ♦ **stylishness** *...a thoroughly modern Italian stylishness.* ◆◆◇◇◇ ADJ-GRADED =fashionable ADV-GRADED N-UNCOUNT

stylist /st<u>aɪ</u>lɪst/ **stylists** ◆◇◇◇◇

1 A **stylist** is a hairdresser. *Choose a stylist recommended by someone whose hair you like.* N-COUNT

2 A **stylist** is someone whose job is to create the style of something such as an advertisement or the image of people such as pop singers. *She is now a writer and fashion stylist.* N-COUNT

3 If you describe someone as a **stylist**, you mean that they pay a lot of attention to the way they write, say, or do something so that it is attractive and elegant. *He is the finest stylist in the English language of today.* N-COUNT

stylistic /staɪl<u>ɪ</u>stɪk/. **Stylistic** describes things relating to the methods and techniques used in creating a piece of writing, music, or art. *There are some stylistic elements in the statue that just don't make sense.* ♦ **stylistically** *While both share some similarities they are stylistically very different.* ◆◇◇◇◇ ADJ: usu ADJ n ADV: ADV adj, ADV with cl

stylized /st<u>aɪ</u>laɪzd/; also spelled **stylised**. Something that is **stylized** uses various artistic or literary conventions in order to create an effect, instead of being natural or true to life. *Some of it has to do with recent stage musicals, which have been very, very stylised. ...a stylized geometrical design.* ◆◇◇◇◇ ADJ-GRADED

stylus /st<u>aɪ</u>ləs/ **styluses.** The **stylus** on a record player is the small needle that picks up the sound signals on the records. N-COUNT =needle

stymie /st<u>aɪ</u>mi/ **stymies, stymieing, stymied.** If you **are stymied** by something, you find it very difficult to take action or to continue what you are doing; an informal word. *Companies have been stymied by the length of time it takes to reach an agreement... Relief efforts have been stymied in recent weeks by armed gunmen.* VB: usu passive =foil *be* V-ed

styrofoam /st<u>aɪə</u>rəfoʊm/. In American English, **styrofoam** is a very light, plastic substance, used especially to make containers or as an insulating material. The usual British word is **polystyrene**. N-UNCOUNT

suave /sw<u>ɑː</u>v/ **suaver, suavest.** Someone who is **suave** is charming, polite, and elegant, but may be insincere. *He is a suave, cool and cultured man.* ♦ **suavely** *...the skills needed to deal suavely with a company's senior managers.* ADJ-GRADED =debonair ADV-GRADED

sub /s<u>ʌ</u>b/ **subs** ◆◆◇◇◇

1 In team games such as football, a **sub** is a player who is brought into a match to replace another player; used mainly in British English. *We had a few injuries and had to use youth team kids as subs.* N-COUNT =substitute

2 A **sub** is a submarine; an informal use. N-COUNT

3 A fixed amount of money that you pay regularly in order to be a member of a club or society is called your **subs**; used in British English. *Subs will be raised as from next year.* N-PLURAL =subscription fees

sub- /sʌb-/

1 **Sub-** is used at the beginning of words that have 'under' as part of their meaning. *The waters were rising about the rock and would soon submerge it. ...a nuclear-powered submarine.* PREFIX

2 **Sub-** is added to the beginning of nouns in order to form other nouns that refer to things that are part of a larger thing. *...a subcommittee on family values and individual rights. ...the subdivision of farms into smallholdings.* PREFIX

3 **Sub-** is added to the beginning of adjectives in order to form other adjectives that describe someone or something as inferior, for example inferior to normal people or to normal things. *The cold has made already substandard living conditions even worse. ...educationally subnormal children.* PREFIX

subaltern /s<u>ʌ</u>bᵊltᵊn/ **subalterns.** A **subaltern** is any commissioned officer in the army below the rank of captain; used mainly in British English. N-COUNT

subatomic /s<u>ʌ</u>bət<u>ɒ</u>mɪk/. A **subatomic** particle is a particle which is part of an atom, for example an electron, a proton, or a neutron; a technical term in nuclear physics. ADJ: ADJ n

subcommittee /s<u>ʌ</u>bkəmɪti/ **subcommittees;** also spelled **sub-committee.** A **subcommittee** is a small committee made up of members of a larger committee. ◆◇◇◇◇ N-COUNT-COLL

subconscious /s<u>ʌ</u>bk<u>ɒ</u>nʃəs/ ◆◇◇◇◇

1 Your **subconscious** is the part of your mind that can influence you or affect your behaviour even though you are not aware of it. *...the hidden power of the subconscious... The memory of it all was locked deep in my subconscious.* N-SING: *the* N, N with poss

2 A **subconscious** feeling or action exists in or is influenced by your subconscious. *He caught her arm in a subconscious attempt to detain her. ...a subconscious cry for affection.* ♦ **subconsciously** *Subconsciously I had known that I would not be in personal danger.* ADJ: usu ADJ n =conscious ADV: usu ADV with v, also ADV adj

subcontinent /s<u>ʌ</u>bk<u>ɒ</u>ntɪnənt/ **subcontinents;** also spelled **sub-continent.** A **subcontinent** is part of a larger continent, made up of a number of countries that form a large mass of land. 'The subcontinent' is often used to refer to the area that contains India, Pakistan, and Bangladesh. N-COUNT: usu sing

subcontract, subcontracts, subcontracting, subcontracted. The verb is pronounced /s<u>ʌ</u>bkəntr<u>æ</u>kt/. The noun is pronounced /sʌbk<u>ɒ</u>ntrækt/.

1 If one firm **subcontracts** part of its work to another firm, it pays the other firm to do part of the work that it has been employed to do. *The company is subcontracting production of most of the parts... They are cutting costs by subcontracting work out to other local firms.* VERB =contract out V n V n *to* n

2 A **subcontract** is a contract between a firm which N-COUNT

is being employed to do a job and another firm which agrees to do part of that job.

subcontractor /sʌbkəntræktəʳ, AM -kɑːntræk-/ **subcontractors**; also spelled **sub-contractor**. A **subcontractor** is a person or firm that has a contract to do part of a job which another firm is responsible for. *The company was considered as a possible subcontractor to build the aeroplane.* N-COUNT

subculture /sʌbkʌltʃəʳ/ **subcultures**; also spelled **sub-culture**. A **subculture** is the ideas, art, and way of life of a group of people within a society, which are different from the ideas, art, and way of life of the rest of the society. *...the latest American subculture. ...the violent subculture of London youth gangs.* N-COUNT: usu with supp

subcutaneous /sʌbkjuteɪniəs/. **Subcutaneous** is used to indicate that something is situated, used, or put under your skin. *...subcutaneous fat.* ADJ: ADJ n

subdivide /sʌbdɪvaɪd/ **subdivides, subdividing, subdivided**; also spelled **sub-divide**. If something **is subdivided**, it is divided into several smaller areas, parts, or groups. *The verbs were subdivided into transitive and intransitive categories.* VB: usu passive; be V-ed into n

subdivision /sʌbdɪvɪʒən/ **subdivisions**; also spelled **sub-division**.

1 A **subdivision** is an area, part, or section of something which is itself a part of something larger. *Months are a conventional subdivision of the year.* N-COUNT

2 In American English, you can refer to a plot of land for building houses as a **subdivision**. *Rammick lives high on a ridge in a 400-home subdivision.* N-COUNT

subdue /səbdjuː, AM -duː/ **subdues, subduing, subdued** ◆◇◇◇◇

1 If soldiers or the police **subdue** a group of people, they defeat them or bring them under control by using force. *Senior government officials admit they have not been able to subdue the rebels.* VERB; V n

2 To **subdue** feelings means to make them less strong. *He forced himself to subdue and overcome his fears.* VERB; V n

subdued /səbdjuːd, AM -duːd/ ◆◇◇◇◇

1 Someone who is **subdued** is very quiet, often because they are sad or worried about something. *He faced the press, initially, in a somewhat subdued mood... The audience are strangely subdued, clapping politely after each song.* ADJ-GRADED

2 **Subdued** sounds are not very loud. *The conversation around them was resumed, but in subdued tones.* ADJ-GRADED

3 **Subdued** lights or colours are not very bright. *The lighting was subdued.* ADJ-GRADED

sub-editor, sub-editors; also spelled **subeditor**. A **sub-editor** is a person whose job is to check and correct articles in newspapers or magazines before they are printed; used in British English. *I was a sub-editor on the foreign desk of the News Chronicle.* N-COUNT

subgroup /sʌbgruːp/ **subgroups**; also spelled **sub-group**. A **subgroup** is a group that is part of a larger group. *The Action Group worked by dividing its tasks among a large number of subgroups.* N-COUNT

subheading /sʌbhedɪŋ/ **subheadings**; also spelled **sub-heading**. **Subheadings** are headings that divide a section of a piece of writing into shorter sections. *The three main sections take their headings from the title and are divided by subheadings.* N-COUNT

subhuman /sʌbhjuːmən/; also spelled **sub-human**. If you describe someone's behaviour or situation as **subhuman**, you mean that it is disgusting and not worthy of a civilized person. *...sub-human terrorist methods.* ADJ

subject, subjects, subjecting, subjected. ◆◆◆◆◇ The noun and adjective are pronounced /sʌbdʒɪkt/. The verb is pronounced /səbdʒekt/.

1 The **subject** of something such as a conversation, letter, or book is the thing that is being discussed or written about. *It was I who first raised the subject of plastic surgery. ...the president's own views on the subject. ...steering the conversation round to his favourite subject.* N-COUNT =topic

2 Someone or something that is the **subject of** criticism, study, or an investigation is being criticized, studied, or investigated. *Over the past few years, some of the positions Mr. Meredith has adopted have made him the subject of criticism... He's now the subject of an official inquiry.* N-COUNT: N of n

3 A **subject** is an area of knowledge or study, especially one that you study at school, college, or university. *Surprisingly, mathematics was voted their favourite subject. ...a tutor in maths and science subjects.* N-COUNT

4 In an experiment or piece of research, the **subject** is the person or animal that is being tested or studied; a formal use. *'White noise' was played into the subject's ears through headphones... Subjects in the study were asked to follow a modified diet.* N-COUNT

5 An artist's **subjects** are the people, animals, or objects that he or she paints, models, or photographs. *Her favourite subjects are shells spotted on beach walks.* N-COUNT: with supp

6 In grammar, the **subject** of a clause is the noun group that refers to the person or thing that is doing the action expressed by the verb. For example, in 'My cat keeps catching birds', 'my cat' is the subject. N-COUNT

7 If someone or something is **subject to** something, they are affected by it or are likely to be affected by it. *Prices may be subject to alteration... In addition, interest on Treasury issues isn't subject to state and local income taxes. ...a disorder in which the person's mood is subject to wild swings from mania to depression.* ADJ: v-link ADJ to n

8 If someone is **subject to** a particular set of rules or laws, they have to obey those rules or laws. *The tribunal is unique because Mr Jones is not subject to the normal police discipline code. ...arguing that as a sovereign state it could not be subject to another country's laws.* ADJ: v-link ADJ to n

9 If you **subject** someone to something unpleasant, you make them experience it. *...the man who had subjected her to four years of beatings and abuse... Innocent civilians are being arrested and subjected to inhumane treatment.* VERB; V n to n

10 The people who live in or belong to a particular country, usually one ruled by a monarch, are the **subjects** of that monarch or country; used mainly in British English. Compare **citizen**. *...his subjects regarded him as a great and wise monarch... Roughly half of them are British subjects.* N-COUNT: with supp

11 **Subject** peoples and countries are ruled or controlled by the government of another country; a formal use. *The subject peoples of her empire were anxious for their own independence. ...colonies and other subject territories.* ADJ: ADJ n

12 When someone involved in a conversation **changes the subject**, they start talking about something else, often because the previous subject was embarrassing. *He tried to change the subject, but she wasn't to be put off.* PHRASES; V inflects

13 If an event will take place **subject to** a condition, it will take place only if that thing happens. *They denied a report that Egypt had agreed to a summit, subject to certain conditions.* PREP

subjection /səbdʒekʃən/. **Subjection** to someone involves being controlled and oppressed by them. *...their complete subjection to their captors. ...to frighten the masses into law-abiding subjection. ...the worst forms of economic subjection and drudgery.* N-UNCOUNT: oft N to/of n

subjective /səbdʒektɪv/. Something that is **subjective** is based on personal opinions and feelings rather than on facts. *We know that taste in art is a subjective matter... The way they interpreted their past was highly subjective.* ◆◇◇◇◇ ADJ-GRADED ≠objective

♦ **subjectively** *Our preliminary results suggest that people do subjectively find the speech clearer.* ADV-GRADED ≠objectively

♦ **subjectivity** /sʌbdʒektɪvɪti/ *They accused her of flippancy and subjectivity in her reporting of events in their country.* N-UNCOUNT ≠objectivity

subject matter; also spelled **subject-matter**. The **subject matter** of something such as a book, lecture, film, or painting is the thing that is being written about, discussed, or shown. *Then, attitudes changed and artists were given greater freedom in their choice of subject matter... Her subject matter is herself.* ◆◇◇◇◇ N-UNCOUNT =subject

sub judice /sʌb dʒuːdɪsi/; also spelled **sub-judice**. When something is **sub judice**, people are not allowed to comment about it in the media because it is the subject of a trial in a court of law; a legal term. *He declined further comment on the grounds that the case was sub judice.* ADJ: usu v-link ADJ

subjugate /sʌbdʒʊgeɪt/ **subjugates, subjugating, subjugated**
1 If someone **subjugates** a group of people, they take complete control of them, especially by defeating them in a war. *Their costly and futile attempt to subjugate the Afghans lasted just 10 years.* VERB =conquer, overpower V n
♦ **subjugation** /sʌbdʒʊgeɪʃᵊn/ *...the brutal subjugation of native tribes.* N-UNCOUNT: usu N *of* n
2 If your wishes or desires **are subjugated** to something, they are treated as less important than that thing. *After having been subjugated to ambition, your maternal instincts are at last starting to assert themselves.* VB: usu passive *be* V-ed *to* n Also *be* V-ed

subjunctive /səbdʒʌŋktɪv/. In English, a clause expressing a wish or suggestion can be put in **the subjunctive**, or in the **subjunctive** mood, by using the base form of a verb or 'were'. Examples are 'He asked that they be removed' and 'I wish I were somewhere else'. These structures are formal. N-SING: *the* N

sublet /sʌblet/ **sublets, subletting.** The form **sublet** is used in the present tense and is the past tense and past participle of the verb. If you **sublet** a building or part of a building, you allow someone to use it and you take rent from them, although you are not the owner and pay rent for it yourself. *The company agreed to rent the whole building, occupy part itself and sublet the remainder.* VERB V n

sub-lieutenant, sub-lieutenants. A **sub-lieutenant** is a naval officer of the lowest rank. N-COUNT

sublimate /sʌblɪmeɪt/ **sublimates, sublimating, sublimated.** If you **sublimate** a strong desire or feeling, you express it in a way that is socially acceptable; a technical term in psychology. *He could try to sublimate the problem by writing, in detail, about it... The erotic impulse is sublimated into art.* ♦ **sublimation** /sʌblɪmeɪʃᵊn/ *In the play, talk is the sublimation of erotic attraction. ...sublimation of the sexual drive.* VERB V n *be* V-ed *into* n N-UNCOUNT

sublime /səblaɪm/ ◆◇◇◇◇
1 If you describe something as **sublime**, you mean that it has a wonderful quality that affects you deeply; a literary use. *Sublime music floats on a scented summer breeze to the spot where you lie. ...the sublime beauty of nature.* ► You can refer to sublime things as **the sublime**. *She elevated every rare small success to the sublime.* ● If you describe something as going **from the sublime to the ridiculous**, you mean that it changes from being of very high quality to being silly or trivial. *At times the show veered from the sublime to the ridiculous.* ADJ-GRADED: usu ADJ n =heavenly N-SING: *the* N PHRASE: PHR after v
2 If you describe someone's attitude or behaviour as **sublime**, you mean that they seem surprisingly ignorant or unaware of something; a formal use. *The administration's sublime incompetence is probably temporary... What sublime innocence and naivety!* ♦ **sublimely** *Mrs Trollope was sublimely uninterested in what she herself wore.* ADJ: usu ADJ n ADV: usu ADV adj

subliminal /sʌblɪmɪnᵊl/. **Subliminal** influences or messages affect your mind without you being aware of it. *Colour has a profound, though often subliminal influence on our senses and moods. ...subliminal advertising.* ♦ **subliminally** *I have read many books, perhaps they influenced me subliminally.* ADJ: usu ADJ n ADV

sub-machine gun, sub-machine guns; also spelled **sub-machine-gun, submachine gun**. A **sub-machine gun** is a light portable type of machine gun. N-COUNT

submarine /sʌbməriːn, AM -riːn/ **submarines** ◆◆◇◇◇
1 A **submarine** is a type of ship that can travel both above and below the surface of the sea. *...a nuclear submarine.* N-COUNT
2 **Submarine** means existing below the surface of the sea; a formal or technical use. *...submarine caves. ...submarine plants.* ADJ: ADJ n

submariner /sʌbmærɪnəʳ, AM also sʌbməriːnəʳ/ **submariners.** A **submariner** is a sailor who works on a submarine. N-COUNT

submerge /səbmɜːʳdʒ/ **submerges, submerging, submerged** ◆◇◇◇◇
1 If something **submerges** or if you **submerge** it, it goes below the surface of some water or another liquid. *Hippos are unable to submerge in the few remaining water holes... The river burst its banks, submerging an entire village.* V-ERG V V n
2 If you **submerge** yourself in an activity, you give all your attention to it and do not think about anything else. *He submerges himself in the world of his imagination.* VERB V pron-refl *in* n

submerged /səbmɜːʳdʒd/. If something is **submerged**, it is below the surface of some water. *My right toe struck against a submerged rock... Most of the mouth of the cave was submerged in the lake.* ADJ

submersible /səbmɜːʳsɪbᵊl/. If something is **submersible**, it can go or operate under water. *...a submersible pump.* ADJ

submission /səbmɪʃᵊn/ **submissions** ◆◇◇◇◇
1 **Submission** is a state in which people can no longer do what they want to do because they have been brought under the control of someone else. *The army intends to take the city or simply starve it into submission.* N-UNCOUNT: oft *into* N =capitulation
2 The **submission** of a proposal, application, or other document is the act of sending it to someone, so that they can decide whether to accept it or not; a formal use. *Diploma and certificate courses do not normally require the submission of a dissertation.* N-UNCOUNT: usu *the* N *of* n
3 A **submission** is a proposal, application, or other document that is sent or presented to someone, so that they can decide whether to accept it or not. *A written submission has to be prepared.* N-COUNT

submissive /səbmɪsɪv/. If you are **submissive**, you behave in a quiet, obedient way. *Most doctors want their patients to be submissive.* ♦ **submissively** *The troops submissively lay down their weapons.* ADJ-GRADED =passive ≠assertive ADV-GRADED

submit /səbmɪt/ **submits, submitting, submitted** ◆◆◇◇◇
1 If you **submit** to something, you accept it or undergo it reluctantly, for example because you are not powerful enough to resist it. *In desperation, Mrs. Jones submitted to an operation on her right knee to relieve the pain... If I submitted to their demands, they would not press the allegations.* VERB =give in, yield V *to* n Also V
2 If you **submit** a proposal or application to someone, you send it to them so that they can decide whether to accept it or not. *They submitted their reports to the Chancellor yesterday... Head teachers yesterday submitted a claim for a 9 per cent pay rise.* VERB =present V n *to* n V n

subnormal /sʌbnɔːʳmᵊl/; also spelled **sub-normal**. If someone is **subnormal**, they have less ability or intelligence than a normal person of their age. *...educationally subnormal children.* ► The **subnormal** are people who are subnormal. *She attended a school for the educationally subnormal.* ADJ N-PLURAL: *the* N

subordinate, subordinates, subordinating, subordinated. The noun and adjective are pronounced /səbɔːʳdɪnət/. The verb is pronounced /səbɔːʳdɪneɪt/. ◆◆◇◇◇
1 If someone is your **subordinate**, they have a less important position than you in the organization that you both work for. *Haig tended not to seek guidance from subordinates... Nearly all her subordinates adored her.* N-COUNT: oft poss N ≠superior
2 Someone who is **subordinate** to you has a less ADJ:

important position than you and has to obey you. *Sixty of his subordinate officers followed his example... Women were regarded as subordinate to free men.* oft ADJ *to* n ≠superior

3 Something that is **subordinate** to something else is less important than the other thing. *It was an art in which words were subordinate to images.* ADJ-GRADED: oft ADJ *to* n

4 If you **subordinate** something to another thing, you regard it or treat it as less important than the other thing. *He was both willing and able to subordinate all else to this aim.* ♦ **subordination** /səbɔːʳdɪneɪʃᵊn/ *...the social subordination of women. ...economic subordination to Europe.* VERB; V n *to* n; N-UNCOUNT: oft N *of/to* n

subordinate clause, subordinate clauses. A **subordinate clause** is a clause in a sentence which adds to or completes the information given in the main clause. It cannot usually stand alone as a sentence. Compare **main clause.** N-COUNT

subordinating conjunction, subordinating conjunctions. A **subordinating conjunction** is a word such as 'although', 'because', or 'when' which begins a subordinate clause. Compare **coordinating conjunction.** N-COUNT

sub-plot, sub-plots. The **sub-plot** in a play, film, or novel is a story that is separate from and less important than the main story. *...a fascinating sub-plot to the main drama.* N-COUNT

subpoena /səpiːnə/ **subpoenas, subpoenaing, subpoenaed** ◆◇◇◇◇

1 A **subpoena** is a legal document telling someone that they must attend a court of law and give evidence as a witness. *He has been served with a subpoena to answer the charges in court.* N-COUNT

2 If someone **subpoenas** someone, they serve them with a subpoena telling them to attend a court of law to give evidence. If someone **subpoenas** evidence, it must be produced in a court of law as evidence. *Select committees have the power to subpoena witnesses... The investigation will rely on existing powers to subpoena documents.* VERB; V n

subscribe /səbskraɪb/ **subscribes, subscribing, subscribed** ◆◇◇◇◇

1 If you **subscribe to** an opinion or belief, you are one of a number of people who have this opinion or belief. *I've personally never subscribed to the view that either sex is superior to the other.* VERB; V *to* n

2 If you **subscribe to** a magazine or a newspaper, you pay to receive copies of it regularly. *My main reason for subscribing to New Scientist is to keep abreast of advances in science.* VERB; V *to* n

3 If you **subscribe to** a charity or a campaign, you send money to it regularly. *I subscribe to a few favourite charities.* VERB =donate; V *to* n

4 If you **subscribe** for shares in a company, you apply to buy shares in that company. *Employees subscribed for far more shares than were available.* VERB; V *for* n; Also V n

subscriber /səbskraɪbəʳ/ **subscribers** ◆◇◇◇◇

1 A magazine's or a newspaper's **subscribers** are the people who pay to receive copies of it regularly. *I have been a subscriber to Railway Magazine for many years.* N-COUNT: usu pl, oft N *to* n

2 **Subscribers** to a service are the people who pay to receive the service. *China has almost 15 million subscribers to satellite and cable television.* N-COUNT: usu pl, oft N *to* n

3 The **subscribers** to a charity, campaign, or organization are the people who support it by sending money regularly to it. N-COUNT: usu pl, oft N *to* n

subscription /səbskrɪpʃᵊn/ **subscriptions.** A **subscription** is an amount of money that you pay regularly in order to belong to an organization, to help a charity or campaign, or to receive copies of a magazine or newspaper. *You can become a member by paying the yearly subscription.* ◆◆◇◇◇ N-COUNT

subsection /sʌbsekʃᵊn/ **subsections;** also spelled **sub-section.** A **subsection** of a text or a document such as a law is one of the smaller parts into which its main parts are divided. N-COUNT: also N num

subsequent /sʌbsɪkwənt/ ◆◆◆◇◇

1 You use **subsequent** to describe something that happened or existed after the time or event that has just been referred to; a formal word. *...the increase of population in subsequent years... Those concerns were overshadowed by subsequent events.* ♦ **subsequently** *She subsequently became the Faculty's President... Subsequently the arrangement was terminated.* ADJ: ADJ n ≠prior; ADV

2 If something happened **subsequent to** something else, it happened after that thing; a formal expression. *They won only one more game subsequent to their Cup semi-final win last year.* PHRASE: PHR n/-ing ≠prior to

subservient /səbsɜːʳviənt/ ◆◇◇◇◇

1 If you are **subservient**, you do whatever someone wants you to do. *Her willingness to be subservient to her children isolated her.* ♦ **subservience** /səbsɜːʳviəns/ *...an austere regime stressing obedience and subservience to authority.* ADJ-GRADED: oft ADJ *to* n; N-UNCOUNT

2 If you treat one thing as **subservient to** another, you treat it as less important than the other thing. *The woman's needs are seen as subservient to the group interest.* ADJ: v-link ADJ *to* n

subset /sʌbset/ **subsets.** A **subset** of a group of things is a smaller number of things that belong together within that group. *...subsets of the population such as men, women, ethnic groups, etc.* N-COUNT: oft N *of* n

subside /səbsaɪd/ **subsides, subsiding, subsided** ◆◇◇◇◇

1 If a feeling or a noise **subsides**, it becomes less strong or loud. *The pain had subsided during the night... Catherine's sobs finally subsided.* VERB; V

2 If fighting **subsides**, it becomes less intense or widespread. *Violence has subsided following two days of riots.* VERB; V

3 If the ground or a building **is subsiding**, it is sinking to a lower level. *Does that mean the whole house is subsiding?* VERB; V

4 If the level of water, especially flood water, **subsides**, it goes down. *Local officials say the flood waters have subsided.* VERB; V

subsidence /səbsaɪdᵊns, sʌbsɪdᵊns/. When there is **subsidence** in a place, the ground there sinks to a lower level. *A surveyor said that the problems were caused by subsidence and the house needed to be underpinned.* N-UNCOUNT

subsidiarity /səbsɪdiærɪti/. **Subsidiarity** is the principle of allowing the individual members of a large organization to make decisions on issues that affect them, rather than leaving those decisions to be made by the whole group. *The chancellor knows that the principle of subsidiarity must be guaranteed and shown to work.* ◆◇◇◇◇ N-UNCOUNT

subsidiary /səbsɪdiəri, AM -dieri/ **subsidiaries** ◆◆◇◇◇

1 A **subsidiary** or a **subsidiary** company is a company which is part of a larger and more important company. *...British Asia Airways, a subsidiary of British Airways.* N-COUNT: oft N *of* n, N n

2 If something is **subsidiary**, it is less important than something else with which it is connected. *The economics ministry has increasingly played a subsidiary role to the finance ministry.* ADJ =secondary

subsidize /sʌbsɪdaɪz/ **subsidizes, subsidizing, subsidized;** also spelled **subsidise** in British English. ◆◆◇◇◇

1 If a government or other authority **subsidizes** something, they pay part of the cost of it. *Around the world, governments have subsidized the housing of middle and upper-income groups... At the moment they are existing on pensions that are subsidised by the government.* ♦ **subsidized** *...heavily subsidized prices for housing, bread, and meat.* ♦ **subsidizing** *...the subsidising of London's transport.* ♦ **subsidization** /sʌbsɪdaɪzeɪʃᵊn/ *...the federal government's subsidisation of poorer parts of the country.* VERB; V n; ADJ-GRADED; N-UNCOUNT; N-UNCOUNT: usu N *of* n

2 If a government **subsidizes** an industry, they provide money in order to enable the industry to continue. *The government continues to subsidize the production of eggs and beef. ...a government decision to subsidise coal mining.* ♦ **subsidized** *...Scotland's subsidised theatre.* ♦ **subsidization** *...the subsidization of Japanese agriculture.* VERB; V n; ADJ-GRADED; N-UNCOUNT

subsidy /sʌbsɪdi/ **subsidies.** A **subsidy** is money that is paid by a government or other authority in order to help an industry or business, or to pay for a public service. *European farmers are*  N-COUNT

planning a massive demonstration against farm subsidy cuts... They've also slashed state subsidies to utilities and transportation.

subsist /səbsɪst/ **subsists, subsisting, subsisted.** If people **subsist**, they are just able to obtain the food or money that they need in order to stay alive. *The prisoners subsisted on one mug of the worst quality porridge three times a day... Almost every employee must moonlight in second jobs simply to subsist.* VERB =exist V on n V

subsistence /səbsɪstəns/ ◆◇◇◇◇

1 **Subsistence** is the condition of just having enough food or money to stay alive. *...below the subsistence level... The standard of living today is on the edge of subsistence.* N-UNCOUNT: oft N n

2 In **subsistence** farming or **subsistence** agriculture, farmers produce food to eat themselves rather than to sell. *Many black Namibians are subsistence farmers who live in the arid borderlands.* ADJ: ADJ n

subsoil /sʌbsɔɪl/. The **subsoil** is a layer of earth that is just below the surface soil but above hard rock. *...the chalk subsoil on the site.* N-UNCOUNT: also a N

subsonic /sʌbsɒnɪk/. **Subsonic** speeds or aeroplanes are very fast but slower than the speed of sound. *This is 20,000 feet higher than most subsonic airliners.* ADJ: ADJ n

sub-species; also spelled **subspecies**. **Sub-species** is both the singular and plural form. A **sub-species** of a plant or animal is a subdivision of a species; a technical term in biology. *Several other sub-species of gull are found in the region.* N-COUNT: oft N of n

substance /sʌbstəns/ **substances** ◆◆◆◇◇

1 A **substance** is a solid, powder, liquid, or gas with particular properties. *There's absolutely no regulation of cigarettes to make sure that they don't include poisonous substances... The substance that's causing the problem comes from the barley.* N-COUNT: usu with supp

2 **Substance** is the quality of being important or significant; a formal use. *It's questionable whether anything of substance has been achieved... Syria will attend only if the negotiations deal with issues of substance.* N-UNCOUNT: oft with brd-neg

3 **The substance of** what someone says or writes is the main thing that they are trying to say. *The substance of his discussions doesn't really matter.* N-SING: the N of n =gist

4 If you say that something has no **substance**, you mean that it is not true; a formal use. *There is no substance in any of these allegations.* N-UNCOUNT =truth

5 A person **of substance** has a lot of money, power, or influence; a formal expression. *...mature men of substance.* PHRASE

sub-standard; also spelled **substandard**. A **sub-standard** service or product is unacceptable because it is below a required standard. *Residents in general are poor and undereducated, and live in sub-standard housing.* ADJ-GRADED

substantial /səbstænʃᵊl/ ◆◆◆◇◇

1 **Substantial** means large in amount or degree; a formal use. *It's reported that Mr Heath has secured the release of a substantial number of people... That is a very substantial improvement in the present situation.* ADJ-GRADED: usu ADJ n =significant ≠insubstantial

2 A **substantial** building is large and strongly built; a formal use. *...those fortunate enough to have a fairly substantial property to sell.* ADJ-GRADED

substantially /səbstænʃəli/ ◆◆◇◇◇

1 If something increases or decreases **substantially**, it increases or decreases by a large amount. If something changes or improves **substantially**, it changes or improves to a great extent; a formal use. *The percentage of girls in engineering has increased substantially... Supplies of gas have been substantially reduced... The group does not expect market conditions to improve substantially in the second half of this year.* ADV-GRADED: ADV with v =significantly

2 If something is **substantially** different from something else, there is a large or basic difference between the two things; a formal use. *The skin of an eighty-year-old looks substantially different from that of a twenty-year-old... The price was substantially higher than had been expected... The warrants were sold to them at prices substantially below market value.* ADV-GRADED: ADV adj/prep =considerably

3 If you say that something is **substantially** correct or unchanged, you mean that it is generally correct or unchanged; a formal use. *He checked the details given and found them substantially correct... BBC Television remains otherwise substantially unchanged.* ADV: ADV adj =essentially

substantiate /səbstænʃieɪt/ **substantiates, substantiating, substantiated.** To **substantiate** a statement or a story means to supply evidence which proves that it is true; a formal word. *There is little scientific evidence to substantiate the claims.* ♦ **substantiation** /səbstænʃieɪʃᵊn/ *There may be alternative methods of substantiation other than written records.* ◆◇◇◇◇ VERB =validate V n N-UNCOUNT

substantive /səbstæntɪv/ ◆◇◇◇◇

1 **Substantive** negotiations or talks involve real issues and aim to arrive at a meaningful agreement; a formal word. *They plan to meet again in Rome very soon to begin substantive negotiations.* ADJ-GRADED: usu ADJ n =meaningful

2 **Substantive** issues or questions are real and important; a formal use. *All the delegates say they are prepared to discuss substantive issues tomorrow.* ADJ-GRADED: usu ADJ n

substation /sʌbsteɪʃᵊn/ **substations;** also spelled **sub-station**. A **substation** is a place where high voltage electricity from power plants is converted to lower voltage electricity for homes or factories. N-COUNT

substitute /sʌbstɪtjuːt, AM -tuːt/ **substitutes, substituting, substituted** ◆◆◆◇◇

1 If you **substitute** one thing for another, or if one thing **substitutes** for another, it takes the place or performs the function of the other thing. *They were substituting violence for dialogue... You could always substitute a low-fat soft cheese... Would phone conversations substitute for cosy chats over lunch or in the pub after work?... He was substituting for the injured William Wales.* ♦ **substitution** /sʌbstɪtjuːʃᵊn, AM -tuː-/ **substitutions** *In my experience a straight substitution of carob for chocolate doesn't work... Both Scotland and Northern Ireland had made last-minute substitutions.* V-ERG V n for n V n V for n Also V N-VAR: usu with supp, oft N of n

2 A **substitute** is something that you have or use instead of something else. *She is seeking a substitute for the very man whose departure made her cry. ...tests on humans to find a blood substitute made from animal blood.* N-COUNT: oft N for n

3 If you say that one thing is no **substitute** for another, you mean that it does not have certain desirable features that the other thing has, and is therefore unsatisfactory. If you say that there is no **substitute** for something, you mean that it is the only thing which is really satisfactory. *The printed word is no substitute for personal discussion with a great thinker... There is no substitute for practical experience.* N-COUNT: with neg, usu sing, N for n

4 In team games such as football and rugby, a **substitute** is a player who is brought into a match to replace another player. *Coming on as a substitute, he scored four crucial goals for Cameroon.* N-COUNT =sub

substratum /sʌbstrɑːtəm, AM -streɪt-/ **substrata.** A **substratum** of something is something that exists under the surface of something else, or is less obvious than something else; a formal word. *...its deep substratum of chalk... His re-creation of the city is credible, with a substratum of fact to bolster the fiction.* N-COUNT: with supp, usu N of n

subsume /səbsjuːm, AM -suːm/ **subsumes, subsuming, subsumed.** If something **is subsumed** within a larger group or class, it is included within it, rather than being considered as something separate; a formal word. *After that the two alliances might be subsumed into a new European security system... With unification, East Germany was subsumed by capitalist West Germany.* VERB be V-ed prep be V-ed Also V n, V n prep

subterfuge /sʌbtəʳfjuːdʒ/ **subterfuges. Subterfuge** is a trick or a dishonest way of getting what you want. *Most people can see right through that type of subterfuge... The party has predictably rejected the proposals as a subterfuge.* N-VAR

subterranean /sʌbtəreɪniən/. A **subterranean** river or tunnel is under the ground; a formal word. *London has 9 miles of such subterranean passages.* ◆◇◇◇◇ ADJ: usu ADJ n =underground

subtext /sʌbtekst/ **subtexts.** The **subtext** is the implied message or subject of something that is said or written. *Europe's divisions are the subtext of a new movie thriller called Zentropa.* N-VAR: usu with supp

subtitle /sʌbtaɪtᵊl/ **subtitles**
1 The **subtitle** of a piece of writing is a second title which is often longer and explains more than the main title. *'Kathleen' was, as its 1892 subtitle asserted, 'An Irish Drama'.* N-COUNT
2 **Subtitles** are the printed translation that you can read at the bottom of the screen when you are watching a foreign film. *The dialogue is in Spanish, with English subtitles.* N-PLURAL

subtitled /sʌbtaɪtᵊld/
1 If you say how a book or play **is subtitled**, you say what its subtitle is. *'Lorna Doone' is subtitled 'a Romance of Exmoor'.* V-PASSIVE be V-ed with quote
2 If a foreign film is **subtitled**, it has a printed translation of the spoken words of the film at the bottom of the screen. *Much of the film is subtitled. ...subtitled films.* ADJ

subtle /sʌtᵊl/ **subtler, subtlest** ◆◆◇◇◇
1 Something that is **subtle** is not immediately obvious or noticeable. *...the slow and subtle changes that take place in all living things... Intolerance can take subtler forms too.* ♦ **subtly** *The truth is subtly different... We change subtly all the time.* ADJ-GRADED ≠blatant, obvious; ADV-GRADED
2 A **subtle** person cleverly uses indirect methods to achieve something. *I even began to exploit him in subtle ways... He is a subtle character, you know.* ♦ **subtly** *What I've tried very subtly to do is to reclaim language.* ADJ-GRADED; ADV-GRADED: ADV with v
3 **Subtle** smells, tastes, sounds, or colours are pleasantly complex and delicate. *...subtle shades of brown. ...delightfully subtle scents. ...whole aubergines in a very subtle sauce.* ♦ **subtly** *...a white sofa teamed with subtly coloured rugs.* ADJ-GRADED ≠overpowering; ADV-GRADED

subtlety /sʌtᵊlti/ **subtleties** ◆◇◇◇◇
1 **Subtleties** are very small details or differences which are not obvious. *His fascination with the subtleties of human behaviour makes him a good storyteller... When a book goes into translation, all those linguistic subtleties get lost.* N-COUNT: usu pl, usu with supp, oft N of n
2 **Subtlety** is the quality of being not immediately obvious or noticeable, and therefore difficult to describe. *African dance is vigorous, but full of subtlety, requiring great strength and control... Many of the resulting wines lack the subtlety of the original model.* N-UNCOUNT
3 **Subtlety** is the ability to notice and recognize things which are not obvious, especially small differences between things. *She analyses herself with great subtlety.* N-UNCOUNT
4 **Subtlety** is the ability to use indirect methods to achieve something, rather than doing something that is obvious. *They had obviously been hoping to approach the topic with more subtlety.* N-UNCOUNT =sensitivity

subtotal /sʌbtoutᵊl/ **subtotals;** also spelled **sub-total**. A **subtotal** is a figure that is the result of adding some numbers together but is not the final total. N-COUNT

subtract /səbtrækt/ **subtracts, subtracting, subtracted.** If you **subtract** one number from another, you do a calculation in which you take it away from the other number. For example, if you subtract 3 from 5, you get 2. *Mandy subtracted the date of birth from the date of death... We have subtracted $25 per adult to arrive at a basic room rate.* ♦ **subtraction** /səbtrækʃᵊn/ **subtractions** *She's ready to learn simple addition and subtraction... I looked at what he'd given me and did a quick subtraction.* ◆◇◇◇◇ VERB ≠add; V n from n; V n; N-VAR ≠addition

sub-tropical; also spelled **subtropical**.
1 **Sub-tropical** places have a climate that is warm and humid, and are often near tropical regions. *...the sub-tropical region of the Chapare.* ADJ =semi-tropical
2 **Sub-tropical** plants and trees grow in places that are warm and humid. *...a remarkable garden of sub-tropical plants.* ADJ: usu ADJ n =semi-tropical

suburb /sʌbɜːʳb/ **suburbs** ◆◆◇◇◇
1 A **suburb** of a city or large town is a smaller area which is part of the city or large town but is outside its centre. *Anna was born in 1923 in Ardwick, a suburb of Manchester. ...the north London suburbs of Harrow, Barnet and Enfield.* N-COUNT: usu with supp, oft N of n
2 If you live in the **suburbs**, you live in the mainly residential area outside the centre of a large town or city. *His family lived in the suburbs. ...Bombay's suburbs.* N-PLURAL: oft *in the* N

suburban /səbɜːʳbən/ ◆◆◇◇◇
1 **Suburban** means relating to a suburb. *...a comfortable suburban home. ...a suburban shopping centre in Sydney.* ADJ: ADJ n
2 If you describe something as **suburban**, you mean that it is dull and conventional. *His clothes are conservative and suburban. ...ghastly good taste and suburban gentility.* ADJ-GRADED

suburbia /səbɜːʳbiə/. Journalists often use **suburbia** to refer to the suburbs of cities and large towns considered as a whole. *...images of bright summer mornings in leafy suburbia.* N-UNCOUNT

subversion /səbvɜːʳʃᵊn, AM -ʒᵊn/. **Subversion** is the attempt to weaken or destroy a political system or a government. *He was arrested in parliament on charges of subversion for organizing the demonstration.* ◆◇◇◇◇ N-UNCOUNT

subversive /səbvɜːʳsɪv/ **subversives** ◆◇◇◇◇
1 Something that is **subversive** is intended to weaken or destroy a political system or government. *The play was promptly banned as subversive and possibly treasonous.* ADJ-GRADED
2 **Subversives** are people who attempt to weaken or destroy a political system or government. *Agents regularly rounded up suspected subversives.* N-COUNT

subvert /səbvɜːʳt/ **subverts, subverting, subverted.** To **subvert** something means to destroy its power and influence; a formal word which is often used showing disapproval. *...an alleged plot to subvert the state. ...a last attempt to subvert culture from within.* ◆◇◇◇◇ VERB PRAGMATICS =undermine V n

subway /sʌbweɪ/ **subways** ◆◇◇◇◇
1 A **subway** is an underground railway; used mainly in American English. *...the Bay Area Rapid Transit subway system... I don't ride the subway late at night.* N-COUNT: oft N n, also *by* N
2 In British English, a **subway** is a passage for pedestrians that goes underneath a busy road or a railway track. *The majority of us feel worried if we walk through a subway.* N-COUNT =underpass

sub-zero; also spelled **subzero**. **Sub-zero** temperatures are below 0° centigrade. *...passengers stranded in sub-zero temperatures.* ADJ

succeed /səksiːd/ **succeeds, succeeding, succeeded** ◆◆◆◆◇
1 If you **succeed** in doing something, you manage to do it. *We have already succeeded in working out ground rules with the Department of Defense... Some people will succeed in their efforts to stop smoking... If they can succeed in America and Europe, then they can succeed here too.* VERB ≠fail V *in* -ing/n V
2 If something **succeeds**, it works in a satisfactory way or has the result that is intended. *If marriage is to succeed in the 1990's, then people have to recognise the new pressures it is facing. ...a move which would make any future talks even more unlikely to succeed.* VERB ≠fail V
3 Someone who **succeeds** gains a high position in what they do, for example in business or politics. *...the skills and qualities needed to succeed in small and medium-sized businesses.* VERB ≠fail V
4 If you **succeed** another person, you are the next person to have their job or position. *David Rowland is almost certain to succeed him as chairman on January 1... The present ruler, Prince Rainier III, succeeded to the throne on 9 May 1949.* VERB V n V *to* n
5 If one thing **is succeeded** by another thing, the other thing happens or comes after it. *A quick divorce can be succeeded by a much longer—and* VB: usu passive be V-ed

more agonising—period of haggling over the fate of the family.

success /səksesˌ/ **successes** ◆◆◆◆◇

1 **Success** is the achievement of something that you have been trying to do. *It's important for the long-term success of any diet that you vary your meals. ...the success of European business in building a stronger partnership between management and workers.* N-UNCOUNT ≠failure

2 **Success** is the achievement of a high position in a particular field, for example in business or politics. *Nearly all of the young people interviewed believed that work was the key to success.* N-UNCOUNT ≠failure

3 The **success** of something is the fact that it works in a satisfactory way or has the result that is intended. *Most of the cast was amazed by the play's success... Enthused by the success of the first exhibition, its organisers are hoping to repeat the experience.* N-UNCOUNT: usu with poss ≠failure

4 Someone or something that is a **success** achieves a high position, makes a lot of money, or is admired a great deal. *The jewellery was a great success... We hope it will be a commercial success.* N-COUNT ≠failure

successful /səksesfʊl/ ◆◆◆◆◇

1 Something that is **successful** achieves what it was intended to achieve. Someone who is **successful** achieves what they intended to achieve. *How successful will this new treatment be?... I am looking forward to a long and successful partnership with him... She has been comparatively successful in maintaining her privacy.* ♦ **successfully** *The doctors have successfully concluded preliminary tests.* ADJ-GRADED: oft ADJ *in* -ing ≠unsuccessful; ADV: ADV with v

2 Something that is **successful** is popular or makes a lot of money. *...the hugely successful movie that brought Robert Redford an Oscar for his directing... One of the keys to successful business is careful planning.* ADJ-GRADED

3 Someone who is **successful** achieves a high position in what they do, for example in business or politics. *Women do not necessarily have to imitate men to be successful in business... She is a successful lawyer.* ADJ-GRADED: oft ADJ *in* n ≠unsuccessful

succession /səkseʃᵊn/ **successions** ◆◆◇◇◇

1 A **succession** of things of the same kind is a number of them that exist or happen one after the other. *Adams took a succession of jobs which have stood him in good stead... Scoring three goals in quick succession, he made it 10-8... Fraser Clyne has won the Scottish Road Running Championship for the third year in succession.* N-SING: oft N *of* n, also *in* N =series

2 **Succession** is the act or right of being the next person to have an important job or position. *She is now seventh in line of succession to the throne.* N-UNCOUNT: also N in pl

successive /səksesɪv/. **Successive** means happening or existing one after another without a break. *Jackson was the winner for a second successive year... Britain was suffering from the failure of successive governments to co-ordinate a national transport policy.* ♦ **successively** *He successively won the British, European and World championships. ...the successively higher levels of unemployment we have endured during the past three recessions.* ◆◆◇◇◇ ADJ =consecutive; ADV: ADV with v, ADV adj-compar

successor /səksesəʳ/ **successors.** Someone's **successor** is the person who takes their job after they have left. *He set out several principles that he hopes will guide his successors... John Major got the leadership because he was seen as a natural successor to Mrs Thatcher.* ◆◆◇◇◇ N-COUNT: oft poss N, N *to* n

success story, success stories. Someone or something that is a **success story** is very successful, often unexpectedly or in spite of unfavourable conditions. *Her nationwide chain, Sock Shop, was one of the high-street success stories of the Eighties.* ◆◇◇◇◇ N-COUNT

succinct /səksɪŋkt/. Something that is **succinct** expresses facts or ideas clearly and in few words; used showing approval. *The book gives an admirably succinct account of the technology and its history... If you have something to say make sure that it is accurate, succinct and to the point.* ♦ **succinctly** *He succinctly summed up his manifesto as 'Work hard, train hard and play hard'.* ◆◇◇◇◇ ADJ-GRADED PRAGMATICS =concise; ADV-GRADED: ADV with v

succor /sʌkəʳ/. See **succour**.

succour /sʌkəʳ/ **succours, succouring, succoured;** spelled **succor** in American English.

1 **Succour** is help given to people who are suffering or in difficulties; a formal use. *...Italy's commitment to give succour to populations involved in an absurd conflict.* N-UNCOUNT =assistance, aid

2 If you **succour** someone who is suffering or in difficulties, you help them; a formal use. *Helicopters fly in appalling weather to succour shipwrecked mariners.* VERB =assist, aid V n

succulent /sʌkjʊlənt/ **succulents** ◆◇◇◇◇

1 **Succulent** food, especially meat or vegetables, is juicy and delicious. *Cook pieces of succulent chicken with ample garlic and a little sherry. ...succulent early vegetables.* ADJ-GRADED =juicy, mouth-watering

2 **Succulents** or **succulent** plants are types of plants which have thick, fleshy leaves. *His potted succulents were looking parched. ...hostas, delphiniums and other succulent plants.* N-COUNT

succumb /səkʌm/ **succumbs, succumbing, succumbed** ◆◇◇◇◇

1 If you **succumb to** persuasion or to a desire for something, you are unable to resist it although you feel it might be wrong; a formal use. *Don't succumb to the temptation to have just one cigarette... The Minister said his country would never succumb to pressure.* VERB =give in V *to* n

2 If you **succumb to** an illness, you become affected by it or die from it; a formal use. *A few years later, Katya succumbed to cancer in London... I was determined not to succumb to the virus.* VERB V *to* n

such /sʌtʃ/ ◆◆◆◆◆

When **such** is used as a predeterminer, it is followed by 'a' and a count noun in the singular. When it is used as a determiner, it is followed by a count noun in the plural or by an uncount noun.

1 You use **such** to refer back to the thing or person that you have just mentioned, or a thing or person like the one that you have just mentioned. You use **such as** and **such...as** to introduce a reference to the person or thing that has just been mentioned. *There have been previous attempts at coups. We regard such methods as entirely unacceptable... You say you feel that you're being made to choose, and so you are. Such choices as this are a by-product of freedom... There'd be no telling how John would react to such news as this.* ► Also a predeterminer. *If your request is for information about a child, please contact the Registrar to find out how to make such a request... She has told us that when she goes back to stay with her family, they make her pay rent. We could not believe such a thing... How can we make sense of such a story as this?* ► Also before **be**. *We are scared because we are being watched – such is the atmosphere in Pristina and other cities in Kosovo.* ► Also **as such**. *There should be a law ensuring products tested on animals have to be labelled as such.* ► Also **such as**. *Issues such as these were not really his concern... I wouldn't see another chance such as this in my lifetime.* DET: DET n, DET n *as* pron; PREDET: PREDET *a* n; *such be*; -ed *as such*; *such as* pron

2 You use **such...as** to link something or someone with a clause in which you give a description of the kind of thing or person that you mean. *Each member of the alliance agrees to take such action as it deems necessary, including the use of armed force... Britain is not enjoying such prosperity as it was in the mid-1980s.* ► Also **such as**. *Children do not use inflections such as are used in mature adult speech... His confessions to the two killings did reveal special knowledge such as could only have been known by the killer.* DET: DET n *as* cl PRAGMATICS; n *such as* cl

3 You also use **such...as** to introduce one or more examples of the kind of thing or person that you have just mentioned. *He was said to have written such books as The Day of Locusts and Miss Lovely Hearts. ...such careers as teaching, nursing, hairdressing and catering. ...delays caused by such things as bad weather or industrial disputes.* ► Also **such as**. *...serious offences, such as assault on a police officer... He definitely wants to perform further tests, such as a biopsy and some x-rays...* DET: DET n *as* n PRAGMATICS; *such as* n

When I get tired, such as when I'm working on my computer, I turn to biscuits.

4 You use **such** before noun groups to emphasize the extent of something or to emphasize that something is remarkable. *I think most of us don't want to read what's in the newspaper anyway in such detail... One will never be able to understand why these political issues can acquire such force... The economy was not in such bad shape, he says.* ▶ Also a predeterminer. *You know the health service is in such a state and it's getting desperate now... He had such a way with the ladies... It was such a pleasant surprise... He's such a sweet boy, isn't he.*
DET PRAGMATICS; PREDET: PREDET a n

5 You use **such...that** in order to emphasize the degree of something by mentioning the result or consequence of it. *The weather has brought such a demand for beer that one brewery will operate over the weekend... This is something where you can earn such a lot of money that there is not any risk that you will lose it... He was in such a hurry that he almost pushed me over on the stairs.* ▶ Also a determiner. *She looked at him in such distress that he had to look away.* ▶ Also after **be**. *Though Vivaldi had earned a great deal in his lifetime, his extravagance was such that he died in poverty... He kept thinking the pain was such that he would faint.*
PREDET: PREDET a n that PRAGMATICS; DET: DET n that; be such that

6 You use **such...that** or **such...as** in order to say what the result or consequence of something that you have just mentioned is. *The operation has uncovered such backstreet dealing in stolen property that police might now press for changes in the law.* ▶ Also a predeterminer. *He could put an idea in such a way that Alan would believe it was his own.* ▶ Also after **be**. *OFSTED's brief is such that it can conduct any inquiry or provide any advice which the Secretary of State requires.*
DET: DET n that PRAGMATICS; PREDET: PREDET a n that/as to; be such that

7 In spoken English, you use **such and such** to refer to a thing or person when you do not want to be exact or precise. *I said, 'Well what time'll I get to Leeds?' and he said such and such a time but I missed my connection... They're informed that we've got this money to spend and we will do such and such with it.*
PHRASES PHR a n, PHR after v

8 You use **such as it is** or **such as they are** to suggest that the thing you have just mentioned is not very good, important, or useful. *Well my toilet's all blocked up and I've got it all coming into my flat and it'll ruin my home, such as it is... The British Women's Movement, such as it is these days, came up with a programme of speeches at the House of Commons.*
n PHR PRAGMATICS

9 You use **as such** with a negative to indicate that a word or expression is not a very accurate description of the actual situation. *I am not a learner as such – I used to ride a bike years ago... Mark joined as an office boy at the age of fourteen with no academic qualifications as such at all... There is no rudder as such, so the craft can be steered only when under power.*
usu n PHR

10 You use **as such** after a noun to indicate that you are considering that thing on its own, separately from other things or factors. *House prices are easily upset by factors which have nothing to do with property as such. The fall in prices in the South-East results largely from the high rate of interest on mortgages... Mr Simon said he was not against taxes as such, 'but I do object when taxation is justified on spurious or dishonest grounds,' he says.*
n PHR

11 • **no such thing**: see **thing**.

suchlike /sʌtʃlaɪk/. You use **suchlike** to refer to things like the ones already mentioned. *...objets d'art, gold, silver, and ivory assortments, ceramics, and suchlike... I suppose you'd rather be in Chicago, eating waffles and hamburgers, or suchlike?* ▶ Also a determiner. *The prices of polymers and suchlike materials will decrease... Mother couldn't stand to be parted from me, miss my childhood and suchlike rubbish.*
PRON =the like; DET: DET pl-n/n-uncount =similar

suck /sʌk/ **sucks, sucking, sucked** ◆◆◇◇◇

1 If you **suck** something, you hold it in your mouth and pull at it with the muscles in your cheeks and tongue, for example in order to get liquid out of it. *They waited in silence and sucked their sweets... He sucked on his cigarette... Doran was clutching the bottle with both hands and sucking intently.*
VERB; V n; V on/at n; V

2 If something **sucks** a liquid, gas, or object in a particular direction, it draws it there with a powerful force. *The pollution-control team is at the scene and is due to start sucking up oil any time now... The air is sucked out by a high-powered fan... They sucked in deep lungfuls of air. ...the airline pilot who was almost sucked from the cockpit of his plane when a window shattered.*
VERB; V n with adv; be V-ed prep; Also V n prep

3 If you **are sucked** into a bad situation, you are unable to prevent yourself from becoming involved in it. *He warned that if the President tried to enforce control, the country would be sucked into a power vacuum. ...the extent to which they have been sucked into the cycle of violence.*
V-PASSIVE =be drawn; be V-ed into n

4 If someone says that something **sucks**, they are indicating that they think it is very bad; an informal use which many people find offensive. *The system sucks.*
VB: no cont; V

5 • to **suck** someone **dry**: see **dry**.

suck up. You say that someone **is sucking up** to a person in authority when you do not like the fact that they are trying to please the person because of his or her position; an informal expression. *She kept sucking up to the teachers, especially Mrs Clements.*
PHRASAL VERB PRAGMATICS; V P to n; Also V P

sucker /sʌkər/ **suckers, suckering, suckered** ◆◇◇◇◇

1 If you call someone a **sucker**, you mean that it is very easy to cheat them; an informal use showing disapproval. *But that is what the suckers want so you give it them... Keep giving us your money, sucker!*
N-COUNT; N-VOC PRAGMATICS

2 If you describe someone as a **sucker for** something, you mean that they find it very difficult to resist it; an informal use. *I'm such a sucker for romance.*
N-COUNT: N for n

3 If you **sucker** someone, or if you **sucker** them into doing something, you deceive them, usually so that they do something that is against their own interests; used mainly in American English. *If you tell those folks the truth, they won't vote for you. But if you sucker them, they'll vote for you twice over... It is becoming harder for the authorities to sucker healthy banks into taking over smaller ones.*
VERB; V n; V n into -ing

4 The **suckers** on some animals and insects are the parts on the outside of their body which they use in order to stick to a surface.
N-COUNT

5 A **sucker** is a small device used for attaching things to surfaces. It consists of a cup-shaped piece of rubber that sticks to a surface when it is pressed flat. *...sucker pads.*
N-COUNT

6 On a plant, a **sucker** is a new growth that is sent out from the base of the plant or from its root.
N-COUNT

suckle /sʌkəl/ **suckles, suckling, suckled**

1 When a mother **suckles** her baby, she feeds it by letting it suck milk from her breast; an old-fashioned use. *A young woman suckling a baby is one of life's most natural and delightful scenes.*
VERB =breastfeed; V n

2 When a baby **suckles**, it sucks milk from its mother's breast; a formal use. *As the baby suckles, a further supply of milk is generated.*
VERB =breastfeed; V

sucrose /su:krous/. **Sucrose** is a common type of sugar; a technical term in biochemistry. *...simple sugars like sucrose, glucose and fructose.*
N-UNCOUNT

suction /sʌkʃən/ **suctions, suctioning, suctioned**

1 **Suction** is the process by which liquids, gases, or other substances are drawn out of somewhere. *Dustbags act as a filter and suction will be reduced if they are too full... If the teat enters the cup, the suction of the milking machine ensures that it becomes attached.*
N-UNCOUNT

2 If a doctor or technician **suctions** a liquid, they remove it by using a machine which sucks it away. *Michael was showing the nurse how to suction his saliva... We found a cyst and I suctioned off the liquid within.*
VERB; V n; V n with adv

3 **Suction** is the process by which two surfaces stick together when the air between them is re-
N-UNCOUNT: oft N n

moved. *...their pneumatic robot which uses air to move and sticks to surfaces by suction.*

Sudanese /suːdəniːz/. **Sudanese** is both the singular and plural form. ◆◆◆◆◇

1 **Sudanese** means belonging or relating to the Sudan, or to its people or culture. *...the Sudanese government. ...the southern Sudanese town of Juba.* ADJ

2 The **Sudanese** are the people of Sudan. *...tens of thousands of Sudanese.* N-PLURAL

sudden /sʌdᵊn/ ◆◆◆◇◇

1 **Sudden** means happening quickly and unexpectedly. *He had been deeply affected by the sudden death of his father-in-law... 'I hope,' the stranger said, 'that the sudden change of venue did not inconvenience you.'... She started to thank him, but a sudden movement behind him caught her attention... It was all very sudden.* ADJ-GRADED: usu ADJ n ♦ **suddenness** *The enemy seemed stunned by the suddenness of the attack.* N-UNCOUNT: oft *the* N *of* n

2 If something happens **all of a sudden**, it happens quickly and unexpectedly. *All of a sudden she didn't look sleepy any more.* PHRASE: usu PHR with cl, PHR with v

sudden death. **Sudden death** is a way of quickly deciding the winner of something such as a football match or golf tournament when there are equal scores at the time when it would normally end. In a **sudden-death** situation, the team who next scores a goal or the golfer who next wins a hole is the winner. *Twenty games have gone to sudden death – a new cup record... He beat Bernhard Langer at the second hole of a sudden death play-off.* ◆◇◇◇◇ N-UNCOUNT: oft N n

suddenly /sʌdᵊnli/. If something happens **suddenly**, it happens quickly and unexpectedly. *Suddenly, she looked ten years older... Her expression suddenly altered... He sat down suddenly.* ◆◆◆◆◇ ADV-GRADED: usu ADV with cl, ADV with v, also ADV adj

suds /sʌdz/. **Suds** are the bubbles that are produced when soap or detergent is mixed with water. *He had soap suds in his ears. ...the greasy suds of a kitchen washing up bowl.* N-PLURAL

sue /suː/ **sues, suing, sued.** If you **sue** someone, you start a legal case against them, usually in order to claim money from them because they have harmed you in some way. *Mr Warren sued him for libel over the remarks... The company could be sued for damages... One former patient has already indicated his intention to sue.* ◆◆◇◇◇ VERB V n *for* n V Also V n

suede /sweɪd/. **Suede** is leather with a soft, slightly rough surface. *Albert wore a brown suede jacket and jeans.* ◆◇◇◇◇ N-UNCOUNT: oft N n

suet /suːɪt/. **Suet** is hard animal fat that is used in cooking. *You'd always have suet pudding for afters.* N-UNCOUNT: oft N n

suffer /sʌfəʳ/ **suffers, suffering, suffered** ◆◆◆◆◇

1 If you **suffer** pain, you feel it in your body or in your mind. *Within a few days she had become seriously ill, suffering great pain and discomfort... Can you assure me that my father is not suffering?* VERB V n V

2 If you **suffer from** an illness or from some other bad condition, you are badly affected by it. *He was eventually diagnosed as suffering from terminal cancer... I realized he was suffering from shock.* VERB V *from* n

3 If you **suffer** something bad, you are in a situation in which something painful, harmful, or very unpleasant happens to you. *The peace process has suffered a serious blow now... Romania suffered another setback in its efforts to obtain financial support for its reforms.* VERB V n

4 If you **suffer**, you are badly affected by an unfavourable event or situation. *There are few who have not suffered... It is obvious that Syria will suffer most from this change of heart.* VERB V V *from* n

5 If something **suffers**, it becomes worse in quality or condition because it has been neglected or because of an unfavourable situation. *Investment would suffer badly... I'm not surprised that your studies are suffering.* VERB V

6 See also **suffering**.

7 If you do not **suffer fools gladly**, you do not have much patience with people who are stupid. *She doesn't suffer fools gladly and, in her view, most people are fools.* PHRASE: V inflects, with brd-neg

sufferance /sʌfrəns/. If you are allowed to do something on **sufferance**, you can do it, although you know that the person who gave you permission would prefer that you did not do it. *His party held office on sufferance... The civilian authorities are only there on sufferance of the military.* N-UNCOUNT: usu *on* N

sufferer /sʌfərəʳ/ **sufferers.** A **sufferer** from an illness or some other bad condition is a person who is affected by the illness or condition. *Frequently sufferers of this kind of allergy are also sufferers of asthma. ...hay-fever sufferers.* ◆◆◇◇◇ N-COUNT: oft N *from/of* n, n N

suffering /sʌfərɪŋ/ **sufferings. Suffering** is serious pain which someone feels in their body or their mind. *They began to recover slowly from their nightmare of pain and suffering... It has caused terrible suffering to animals... His many novels have portrayed the sufferings of his race.* ● See also **long-suffering**. ◆◆◇◇◇ N-UNCOUNT: also N in pl =torment

suffice /səfaɪs/ **suffices, sufficing, sufficed** ◆◇◇◇◇

1 If you say that something will **suffice**, you mean it will be enough to achieve a purpose or to fulfil a need; a formal word. *A cover letter should never exceed one page; often a far shorter letter will suffice.* VB: no cont =do V Also V to-inf

2 **Suffice it to say** or **suffice to say** is used at the beginning of a statement to indicate that what you are saying is obvious, or that you will only give a short explanation. *Suffice it to say that afterwards we never met again... Suffice to say, it was more than a couple of years ago!* PHRASE: PHR that, PHR with cl

sufficiency /səfɪʃᵊnsi/. **Sufficiency** of something is enough of that thing to achieve a purpose or to fulfil a need; a formal word. *When foods from different plant sources are eaten together, deficiency in one is compensated for by sufficiency in another... There's a sufficiency of drama in these lives to sustain your interest.* ● See also **self-sufficiency**. ◆◇◇◇◇ N-UNCOUNT: also *a* N, oft N *of* n ≠insufficiency

sufficient /səfɪʃᵊnt/ ◆◆◆◇◇

1 If something is **sufficient** for a particular purpose, there is enough of it for the purpose. *One metre of fabric is sufficient to cover the exterior of an 18-in-diameter hatbox... Lighting levels should be sufficient for photography without flash... There was not sufficient evidence to secure a conviction.* ADJ: oft ADJ to-inf, ADJ n to-inf, ADJ *for* n ≠insufficient ♦ **sufficiently** *She recovered sufficiently to accompany Chou on his tour of Africa in 1964... The holes were sufficiently large to serve as nests.* ADV

2 If something is a **sufficient** cause or condition for something to happen, it can happen; a formal use. *Discipline is a necessary, but certainly not a sufficient condition for learning to take place.* ADJ: ADJ n, oft with brd-neg

suffix /sʌfɪks/ **suffixes**

1 A **suffix** is a letter or group of letters, for example '-ly' or '-ness', which is added to the end of a word in order to form a different word, often of a different word class. For example, the suffix '-ly' is added to 'quick' to form 'quickly'. Compare **affix** and **prefix**. N-COUNT

2 A **suffix** is one or more numbers or letters added to the end of a code number to indicate, for example, what area something belongs to. *These ships were all numbered with the suffix LBK.* N-COUNT

suffocate /sʌfəkeɪt/ **suffocates, suffocating, suffocated** ◆◇◇◇◇

1 If someone **suffocates** or **is suffocated**, they die because there is no air for them to breathe. *He either suffocated, or froze to death... They were suffocated as they slept.* V-ERG V *be* V-ed ♦ **suffocation** /sʌfəkeɪʃᵊn/ *Many of the victims died of suffocation.* N-UNCOUNT

2 If you say that you **are suffocating** or that something **is suffocating** you, you mean that you feel very uncomfortable because there is not enough fresh air and it is difficult to breathe. *That's better. I was suffocating in that cell of a room... The airlessness of the room suffocated her.* V-ERG V V n

3 You say that someone or something **is suffocating** or that something **is suffocating** them when the situation that they are in does not allow them to act freely or to develop. *After a few weeks with her parents, she felt she was suffocating... The governor's proposals would actually cost millions of jobs and suffocate the economy.* V-ERG V V n

suffrage /sʌfrɪdʒ/. **Suffrage** is the right of people to vote for a government or national leader; a formal word. *He was an advocate of universal suffrage as a basis for social equality. ...the women's suffrage movement.* N-UNCOUNT

suffragette /sʌfrədʒet/ **suffragettes.** In Britain, in the early twentieth century, a **suffragette** was a woman who was involved in the campaign for women to have the right to vote. *She was a suffragette and a birth control pioneer.* N-COUNT

suffuse /səfjuːz/ **suffuses, suffusing, suffused**
1 If something, especially a colour or feeling, **suffuses** someone or something, it gradually spreads over or through them; a literary word. *A dull red flush suffused Selby's face.* VERB V n
2 If something such as a book, film, or piece of music **is suffused** with a quality, it is full of that quality; a formal word. *This book is suffused with Shaw's characteristic wry Irish humour... Kingdon's broad experience, as writer and scholar, suffuses this important book.* VERB be V-ed with n, V n

Sufi /suːfi/ **Sufis.** A **Sufi** is someone who belongs to a mystical Muslim sect. *...the teachings of the Sufi mystics.* N-COUNT: oft N n

sugar /ʃʊgəʳ/ **sugars, sugaring, sugared** ◆◆◆◇◇
1 Sugar is a sweet substance that is used to sweeten food and drink. It is usually in the form of white or brown crystals. *...bags of sugar... Ice cream is high in fat and sugar.* • See also **caster sugar**, **confectioners' sugar**, **demerara sugar**, **granulated sugar**, **icing sugar**. N-UNCOUNT
2 If someone has one **sugar** in their tea or coffee, they have one small spoon of sugar or one sugar lump in it. *How many sugars do you take? ...a mug of tea with two sugars.* N-COUNT
3 If you **sugar** food or drink, you add sugar to it. *He sat down and sugared and stirred his coffee.* VERB V n
4 Sugars are substances that occur naturally in food. When you eat them, the body converts them into energy. *Plants produce sugars and starch to provide themselves with energy. ...the natural sugars found in grape juice.* N-COUNT: usu pl
5 If one person knows another person very well and likes them a lot, they sometimes call them **sugar**; an informal use. *I know how to make you feel better, sugar. I'll tell you a story.* N-VOC PRAGMATICS =honey
6 • to **sugar the pill**: see **pill**.

sugar beet, sugar beets. Sugar beet is a crop with a large round root. It is grown for the sugar which can be obtained from this root. N-VAR

sugar bowl, sugar bowls. A **sugar bowl** is a small bowl in which sugar is kept. N-COUNT

sugar cane; also spelled **sugarcane. Sugar cane** is a tall tropical plant. It is grown for the sugar that can be obtained from its thick stems. N-UNCOUNT

sugar-coated
1 Sugar-coated food is covered with a sweet substance made of sugar. *Some sugar-coated cereals are 50% sugar. ...sugar-coated popcorn.* ADJ: usu ADJ n
2 If you describe something such as a story as **sugar-coated**, you disapprove of it because it appears to be pleasant or attractive but in fact describes something very unpleasant. *The story presents a sugar-coated view of the young boy's introduction to sex.* ADJ: usu ADJ n PRAGMATICS

sugar daddy, sugar daddies; also spelled **sugar-daddy**. A woman's **sugar daddy** is a rich older man who gives her money and presents in return for her company, affection, and usually sexual intercourse; an informal expression. *Actor John Goodman plays Melanie Griffith's sugar daddy in his next screen role.* N-COUNT: usu poss N

sugared almond, sugared almonds. Sugared almonds are almonds which have been covered with a hard sweet coating. N-COUNT: usu pl

sugar lump, sugar lumps; also spelled **sugarlump. Sugar lumps** are small cubes of sugar. You put them in cups of tea and coffee. N-COUNT

sugary /ʃʊgəri/
1 Sugary food or drink contains a lot of sugar. *Sugary canned drinks rot your teeth. ...sugary tea.* ADJ-GRADED: usu ADJ n
2 If you describe a film or piece of music as **sugary**, you mean that it is sentimental and insincere; used showing disapproval. *The programme seemed false and sugary, and the characters smug.* ADJ-GRADED: usu ADJ n PRAGMATICS

suggest /sədʒest, AM səgdʒ-/ **suggests, suggesting, suggested** ◆◆◆◆◆
1 If you **suggest** something, you put forward a plan or idea for someone to think about. *He suggested a link between class size and test results of seven-year-olds... I suggest you ask him some specific questions about his past... I suggested to Mike that we go out for a meal with his colleagues... No one has suggested how this might occur... 'Could he be suffering from amnesia?' I suggested... So instead I suggested taking her out to dinner for a change.* VERB V n, V that, V to n that, V wh, V with quote, V -ing
2 If you **suggest** the name of a person or place, you recommend them to someone. *Could you suggest someone to advise me how to do this?... They can suggest where to buy one.* VERB V n, V wh to-inf
3 If you **suggest** that something is the case, you say something which you believe is the case. *I'm not suggesting that is what is happening... It is wrong to suggest that there are easy alternatives... Their success is conditional, I suggest, on this restriction.* VERB V that
4 If one thing **suggests** another, it implies it or makes you think that it might be the case. *Earlier reports suggested that a meeting would take place on Sunday... Its hairy body suggests a mammal.* VERB V that, V n
5 If one thing **suggests** another, it brings it to your mind through an association of ideas. *This onomatopoeic word suggests to me the sound a mousetrap makes when it snaps shut.* VERB V n

suggestible /sədʒestɪbəl, AM səgdʒ-/. Someone who is **suggestible** can be easily influenced by other people. *People tending to make false confessions are likely to be highly suggestible and compliant individuals.* ADJ-GRADED

suggestion /sədʒestʃən, AM səgdʒ-/ **suggestions** ◆◆◆◇◇
1 If you make a **suggestion**, you put forward an idea or plan for someone to think about. *The dietitian was helpful, making suggestions as to how I could improve my diet... Perhaps he'd followed her suggestion of a stroll to the river... I have lots of suggestions for the park's future.* N-COUNT: oft N of/for n/-ing
2 A **suggestion** is something that someone says which implies that something is the case. *We reject any suggestion that the law needs amending... There are suggestions that he might be supported by the Socialists.* N-COUNT: oft N that
3 If there is no **suggestion** that something is the case, there is no reason to think that it is the case. *There is no suggestion whatsoever that the two sides are any closer to agreeing... There is absolutely no suggestion of any mainstream political party involvement.* N-SING: usu with brd-neg, N that, N of n
4 If there is a **suggestion** of something, there is a slight indication or sign of it. *...that fashionably faint suggestion of a tan. ...a firm, well-sprung mattress with not one suggestion of a sag.* N-COUNT: usu sing, N of n =hint
5 Suggestion means giving people a particular idea by associating it with other ideas. *The power of suggestion is very strong.* N-UNCOUNT

suggestive /sədʒestɪv, AM səgdʒ-/ ◆◇◇◇◇
1 Something that is **suggestive of** something else gives a hint of it or reminds you of it. *The atmosphere is more suggestive of a relaxed lunchtime jazz session than an intense rock gig... The fingers were gnarled, lumpy, with long, curving nails suggestive of animal claws.* ADJ-GRADED: v-link ADJ of n =reminiscent
2 Suggestive remarks or looks cause people to think about sex, often in a way that makes them feel uncomfortable. *...another former employee who claims Thomas made suggestive remarks to her. ...advertisements containing words or pictures of a sexually suggestive nature.* ♦ **suggestively** *She winked suggestively.* ADJ-GRADED =provocative; ADV-GRADED

suicidal /suːɪsaɪdəl/ ◆◇◇◇◇
1 People who are **suicidal** want to kill themselves. *I was suicidal and just couldn't stop crying... Her suicidal tendencies continued for several more weeks.* ADJ
2 If you describe an action or behaviour as **suicidal**, you mean that it is very dangerous. *They real-* ADJ: oft it v-link ADJ to-inf

ized it would be suicidal to resist in the face of overwhelming military superiority. ...the suicidal bicycle rickshaws of New Delhi.

suicide /suːɪsaɪd/ **suicides** ◆◆◆◇◇

1 People who commit **suicide** deliberately kill themselves because they do not want to continue living. *She tried to commit suicide on several occasions. ...a case of attempted suicide. ...a growing number of suicides in the community.* N-VAR

2 You say that people commit **suicide** when they deliberately do something which ruins their career or position in society. *Quite a few have committed social suicide by writing their boring memoirs... They say it would be political suicide for the party to abstain.* N-UNCOUNT: supp N

3 The people involved in a **suicide** attack, mission, or bombing do not expect to survive. *According to the army, the teenager said he was on a 'suicide mission' for the movement. ...a suicide bomber.* ADJ: ADJ n

sui generis /suːi dʒenərɪs/. If you describe something or someone as **sui generis**, you mean that they are unique and cannot be judged by comparing them with something else; a formal word. *He is, in this country anyway, sui generis.* ADJ =unique

suit /suːt/ **suits, suiting, suited** ◆◆◆◆◇

1 A man's **suit** consists of a jacket, trousers, and sometimes a waistcoat, all made from the same fabric. *...a dark pin-striped business suit. ...a smart suit and tie.* N-COUNT

2 A woman's **suit** consists of a jacket and skirt, or sometimes trousers, made from the same fabric. *I was wearing my tweed suit.* N-COUNT

3 A particular type of **suit** is a piece of clothing that you wear for a particular activity. *The six survivors only lived through their North Sea ordeal because of the special rubber suits they were wearing.* N-COUNT: n N

4 If something **suits** you, it is convenient for you or is the best thing for you in the circumstances. *They will only release information if it suits them... They should be able to find you the best package to suit your needs.* VB: no cont V n

5 If something **suits** you, you like it. *I don't think a sedentary life would altogether suit me.* VB: no cont V n

6 If a piece of clothing or a particular style or colour **suits** you, it makes you look attractive. *Green suits you.* VB: no cont V n

7 If you **suit** yourself, you do something just because you want to do it, without bothering to consider other people. *The British have tended to suit themselves, not paying much heed to the reformers... He made a dismissive gesture. 'Suit yourself.'* VERB =please V pron-refl

8 In a court of law, a **suit** is a case in which a person tries to get justice for some wrong that has been done to them. *Up to 2,000 former employees have filed personal injury suits against the company... The judge dismissed the suit.* ▶ In American English, you can say that someone files or brings **suit** against another person. *One insurance company has already filed suit against the city of Chicago.* N-COUNT =lawsuit; N-UNCOUNT

9 A **suit** is one of the four types of card in a set of playing cards. These are hearts, diamonds, clubs, and spades. N-COUNT

10 See also **bathing suit**, **birthday suit**, **boiler suit**, **romper suit**, **trouser suit**.

11 If people **follow suit**, they do the same thing that someone else has just done. *Efforts to persuade the remainder to follow suit have continued.* PHRASES V inflects

12 If something **suits** you **down to the ground,** you like it a great deal or find it very convenient. *Their London house suits them down to the ground.* V inflects

suitable /suːtəbᵊl/. Someone or something that is **suitable** for a particular purpose or occasion is right or acceptable for it. *Employers usually decide within five minutes whether someone is suitable for the job... She had no other dress suitable for the occasion... The authority must make suitable accommodation available to the family.* ◆◆◆◇◇ ADJ-GRADED: oft ADJ for n/-ing

♦ **suitability** /suːtəbɪlɪti/ *...information on the suitability of a product for use in the home.* N-UNCOUNT: with supp

suitably /suːtəbli/ ◆◇◇◇◇

1 You use **suitably** to describe something that you think is right or appropriate for a particular purpose or occasion. *There are problems in recruiting suitably qualified scientific officers for NHS laboratories... Unfortunately I'm not suitably dressed for gardening.* ADV: ADV adj

2 If you say that someone or something is, for example, **suitably** impressed or **suitably** modest, you mean that they show as much of that quality as you would expect in the circumstances. *She flicked her eyes up to make certain I was suitably impressed... Her exit seemed suitably dramatic.* ADV: ADV adj

suitcase /suːtkeɪs/ **suitcases.** A **suitcase** is a box or bag with a handle and a hard frame in which you carry your clothes when you are travelling. *It did not take Andrew long to pack a suitcase.* ◆◆◇◇◇ N-COUNT

suite /swiːt/ **suites** ◆◆◇◇◇

1 A **suite** is a set of rooms in a hotel or other building. *They had a fabulous time during their week in a suite at the Paris Hilton. ...a new suite of offices.* N-COUNT
• See also **en suite**.

2 A **suite** is a set of matching armchairs and a sofa. *...a three-piece suite.* N-COUNT

3 A bathroom **suite** is a matching bath, basin, and toilet. N-COUNT

suited /suːtɪd/ ◆◇◇◇◇

1 If something is well **suited** to a particular purpose, it is right or appropriate for that purpose. If someone is well **suited** to a particular job, they are right or appropriate for that job. *The area is well suited to road cycling as well as off-road riding... Satellites are uniquely suited to provide this information.* ADJ-GRADED: v-link ADJ, usu adv ADJ *to* n/-ing, ADJ to-inf

2 If two people, especially a man and a woman, are **well suited**, they are likely to have a successful relationship because they have similar personalities or interests. *They were well suited to each other.* ADJ-GRADED: v-link ADJ, usu adv ADJ, oft ADJ *to* n

suiting /suːtɪŋ/ **suitings. Suiting** is cloth from which trousers, jackets, skirts, and men's suits are made. N-MASS

suitor /suːtəʳ/ **suitors** ◆◇◇◇◇

1 A woman's **suitor** is a man who wants to marry her; an old-fashioned use. *My mother had a suitor who adored her.* N-COUNT

2 A **suitor** is a company or organization that wants to buy another company. *The company was making little progress in trying to find a suitor... Whatever is offered by the bank is unlikely to be improved on by any rival suitor.* N-COUNT

sulfate /sʌlfeɪt/. See **sulphate**.

sulfide /sʌlfaɪd/. See **sulphide**.

sulfur /sʌlfəʳ/. See **sulphur**.

sulfuric acid /sʌlfjʊərɪk æsɪd/. See **sulphuric acid**.

sulk /sʌlk/ **sulks, sulking, sulked.** If you **sulk**, you are silent and bad-tempered for a while because you are annoyed about something; an informal word used showing disapproval. *He turned his back and sulked.* ▶ Also a noun. *He went off in a sulk... Now she must be tired of my sulks.* ◆◇◇◇◇ VERB PRAGMATICS V; N-COUNT: oft *in/into* a N =mood

sulky /sʌlki/. Someone who is **sulky** is sulking or is unwilling to enjoy themselves; an informal word used showing disapproval. *I was quite sulky, so I didn't take part in much. ...a sulky adolescent.* ADJ-GRADED PRAGMATICS

♦ **sulkily** *'You haven't got the right attitude,' he said sulkily.* ADV-GRADED: usu ADV with v

sullen /sʌlᵊn/. Someone who is **sullen** is bad-tempered and does not speak much. *The offenders lapsed into a sullen silence... Many of them remained sullen and resentful.* ◆◇◇◇◇ ADJ-GRADED

♦ **sullenly** *'I've never seen it before,' Harry said sullenly. ...a sullenly resentful crowd.* ADV-GRADED: usu ADV with v, also ADV adj

sully /sʌli/ **sullies, sullying, sullied**

1 If something **is sullied** by something else, it is damaged so that it is no longer pure or of such high value; a formal use. *The City's reputation has been sullied by scandals like those at Lloyd's... She claimed they were sullying the Conservative Party's good name.* VERB *be* V-ed V n

2 If someone **sullies** something, they make it dirty or imperfect; a formal use. *I felt loath to sully the gleaming brass knocker by handling it.* VERB V n

sulphate /sʌlfeɪt/ **sulphates;** spelled **sulfate** in American English. A **sulphate** is a salt of sulphuric acid. *...copper sulphate. ...sulphate of potash.* ◆◇◇◇◇ N-MASS: oft n N, N of n

sulphide /sʌlfaɪd/ **sulphides;** spelled **sulfide** in American English. A **sulphide** is a compound of sulphur with some other chemical elements. *...hydrogen sulphide.* N-MASS: oft n N

sulphur /sʌlfəʳ/; spelled **sulfur** in American English. **Sulphur** is a yellow chemical which has a strong smell. *The air reeks of sulphur. ...measures to reduce emissions of sulphur dioxide.* ◆◇◇◇◇ N-UNCOUNT

sulphuric acid /sʌlfjʊərɪk æsɪd/; spelled **sulfuric acid** in American English. **Sulphuric acid** is a colourless, oily, and very powerful acid. N-UNCOUNT

sulphurous /sʌlfərəs/; spelled **sulfurous** in American English. **Sulphurous** air or places contain sulphur or smell of sulphur. *...sulphurous volcanic gases. ...a sulphurous spring.* ADJ-GRADED: usu ADJ n

sultan /sʌltən/ **sultans.** A **sultan** is a ruler in some Muslim countries. *...during the reign of Sultan Abdul Hamid.* ◆◇◇◇◇ N-TITLE; N-COUNT

sultana /sʌltɑːnə, -tæn-/ **sultanas. Sultanas** are dried white grapes; used mainly in British English. N-COUNT: usu pl

sultry /sʌltri/

1 Sultry weather is hot and humid; used mainly in written English. *The climax came one sultry August evening.* ADJ-GRADED: usu ADJ n

2 Someone who is **sultry** is attractive in a way that suggests hidden passion; used mainly in written English. *...a dark-haired sultry woman.* ADJ-GRADED =sensual

sum /sʌm/ **sums, summing, summed** ◆◆◆◇◇

1 A **sum** of money is an amount of money. *Large sums of money were lost... Even the relatively modest sum of £50,000 now seems beyond his reach.* N-COUNT: oft N of n

2 A **sum** is a simple calculation in arithmetic. *I can't do my sums.* N-COUNT

3 In mathematics, **the sum of** two numbers is the number that is obtained when they are added together. *The sum of all the angles of a triangle is 180 degrees.* N-SING: the N of n

4 The sum of something is all of it. You often use 'sum' in this way to indicate that you are disappointed because the extent of something is rather small, or because it is not very good. *To date, the sum of my gardening experience had been futile efforts to rid the flower beds of grass... The sum of evidence points to the crime resting on them... Has it, in its 30 years, added much to the sum of human happiness?* N-SING: the N of n =sum total

5 See also **lump sum**.

6 You use **in sum** to introduce a statement that briefly describes a situation; a formal expression. *In sum, the two countries are now true economic partners... It is a situation, in sum, devoid of logic.* PHRASES PHR with cl PRAGMATICS

7 If you say that something is **more than the sum of** its **parts** or **greater than the sum of** its **parts**, you mean that it is better than you would expect from the individual parts, because the way they combine adds a different quality. *As individual members' solo careers have proved, each band was greater than the sum of its parts.* v-link PHR

sum up PHRASAL VERB

1 If you **sum** something **up**, you describe it as briefly as possible. *One voter in Brasilia summed up the mood – 'Politicians have lost credibility,' he complained... Obree summed his weekend up in one word: 'Disastrous.'* V P n (not pron) V n P

2 If something **sums** a person or situation **up**, it represents their most typical characteristics. *'I love my wife, my horse and my dog,' he said, and that summed him up... Sadly, the feud sums up the relationship between Lord Bath and the man who succeeds him.* =epitomize V n P V P n (not pron)

3 If you **sum up** after a speech or at the end of a piece of writing, you briefly state the main points again. When a judge **sums up** after a trial, he reminds the jury of the evidence and the main arguments of the case they have heard. *When the judge summed up, it was clear he wanted a guilty verdict... To sum up: We welcome the statement of the Government and appreciate its willingness and commitment to work cooperatively with us.* V P

4 See also **summing-up**.

summarize /sʌməraɪz/ **summarizes, summarizing, summarized;** also spelled **summarise** in British English. If you **summarize** something, you give a summary of it. *Table 3.1 summarizes the information given above... Basically, the article can be summarized in three sentences... To summarise, this is a clever approach to a common problem.* ◆◇◇◇◇ VERB V n be V-ed prep/adv V Also V with quote

summary /sʌməri/ **summaries** ◆◆◇◇◇

1 You use **in summary** to indicate that what you are about to say is a summary of what has just been said. *In summary, it is my opinion that this complete treatment process was very successful.* N-COUNT: oft N of n PRAGMATICS

2 Summary actions are done without delay, often when something else should have been done first or done instead; a formal use. *It says torture and summary execution are common... There is no doubt that some considered that a beating was no more than summary justice... The four men were killed after a summary trial.* ♦ **summarily** *Several detainees had been summarily executed.* ADJ: ADJ n ADV: ADV with v

summat /sʌmət/. **Summat** is used in writing to represent a regional spoken form of the word 'something'. *Are we going to write a story or summat?*

summation /sʌmeɪʃən/ **summations.** A **summation** is a summary of what someone has said or done; a formal word. *Her introduction is a model of fairness, a lively summation of Irish history.* N-COUNT: usu sing, oft N of n =summary

summer /sʌməʳ/ **summers. Summer** is the season between spring and autumn. In the summer the weather is usually warm or hot. *I escaped the heatwave in London earlier this summer and flew to Cork... It was a perfect summer's day. ...in the summer of 1987. ...the summer holidays... He used to spend childhood summers with his grandparents.* • See also **high summer**, **Indian summer**. ◆◆◆◆◇ N-VAR

summer house, summer houses; also spelled **summerhouse**.

1 A **summerhouse** is a small building in a garden. It contains seats, and people can sit there in the summer. N-COUNT

2 Someone's **summer house** is a house in the country or by the sea where they spend the summer. *He visited relatives at their summer house on the river.* N-COUNT

summer school, summer schools. A **summer school** is an educational course on a particular subject that is run during the summer. The students usually stay at the place where the summer school is being held. *...a summer school for young professional singers.* N-VAR

summer time; also spelled **summertime** for meaning 1. ◆◇◇◇◇

1 Summer time is the period of time during which the summer lasts. *It's a very beautiful place in the summertime.* N-UNCOUNT: also the N

2 In British English, **summer time** is a period in the spring and summer during which the clocks are put forward, so that people can have an extra hour of daylight in the evening. The American expression is **daylight saving time**. *When we put the clocks forward in March we go into British Summer Time.* N-UNCOUNT

summery /sʌməri/. Something that is **summery** is suitable for summer or characteristic of summer. *It's very flowery and summery. ...light summery fruit salads.* ADJ-GRADED

summing-up, summings-up; also spelled **summing up**. In a trial, the judge's **summing-up** is the speech he or she makes to the jury at the end of a trial to remind them of the evidence and the main arguments of the case they have heard. *There was pandemonium in court as the judge gave his summing-up.* ◆◇◇◇◇ N-COUNT

summit /sʌmɪt/ **summits** ◆◆◆◆◇

1 A **summit** is a meeting at which the leaders of two N-COUNT or more countries discuss important matters. *...next week's Washington summit. ...the NATO summit meeting in Rome.*

2 The **summit** of a mountain is the top of it. *...the first man to reach the summit of Mount Everest.* N-COUNT

summon /sʌmən/ **summons, summoning, summoned** ◆◆◇◇◇

1 If you **summon** someone, you order them to come to you; a formal use. *Howe summoned a doctor and hurried over... Suddenly we were summoned to the interview room... He has been summoned to appear in court on charges of incitement to law-breaking.* VERB V n be V-ed prep/adv be V-ed to-inf

2 If you **summon** a quality, you make a great effort to have it on a particular occasion. For example, if you **summon** the courage or strength to do something, you make a great effort to be brave or strong, so that you will be able to do it. *It took her a full month to summon the courage to tell her mother.* VERB V n

▶ **Summon up** means the same as **summon**. *Painfully shy, he finally summoned up courage to ask her to a game... We couldn't even summon up the energy to open the envelope.* PHRASAL VERB V P n (not pron)

summon up PHRASAL VERB

1 See **summon** 2.

2 If something **summons up** a memory or thought, it causes it to come to your mind; a literary use. *The oddest events will summon up memories.* V P n (not pron)

summons /sʌmənz/ **summonses, summonsing, summonsed** ◆◇◇◇◇

1 A **summons** is an order to come and see someone. *I received a summons to the Palace from Sir Robert Fellowes, the Queen's private secretary.* N-COUNT

2 A **summons** is an official order to appear in court. *She had received a summons to appear in court.* N-COUNT

3 If someone **is summonsed**, they are officially ordered to appear in court. *The men were summonsed and last week 30 appeared before Hove magistrates... She has been summonsed to appear at St Albans magistrates' court.* VB: usu passive be V-ed be V-ed to-inf

sumo /suːmoʊ/. **Sumo** is the Japanese style of wrestling. *...a sumo wrestler.* ◆◇◇◇◇ N-UNCOUNT: oft N n

sump /sʌmp/ **sumps**

1 The **sump** is the place under an engine which holds the engine oil. N-COUNT: oft N n

2 A **sump** is a deep cave which is often filled with water. *An attempt was then made to dive the sump.* N-COUNT

sumptuous /sʌmptʃuəs/. Something that is **sumptuous** is magnificent and obviously very expensive. *...a sumptuous feast. ...a variety of sumptuous fabrics. ...sumptuous silk brocades and damasks... Dinner that evening was even more sumptuous than lunch.* ◆◇◇◇◇ ADJ-GRADED ♦ **sumptuously** *...this sumptuously illustrated volume... A white cane sofa is sumptuously upholstered in gold taffeta and purple velvet.* ADV-GRADED: ADV adj, ADV with v

sum total. The **sum total** of a number of things is all the things added or considered together. You often use this expression to indicate that you are disappointed because the extent of something is rather small, or because it is not very good. *That small room contained the sum total of the family's possessions... We have already seen the sum total of his attributes.* N-SING: usu *the* N *of* n =sum

sun /sʌn/ **suns, sunning, sunned** ◆◆◆◆◇

1 The **sun** is the ball of fire in the sky that the Earth goes round, and that gives us heat and light. *The sun was now high in the southern sky... The sun came out, briefly. ...the sun's rays... The sun was shining.* N-SING: usu *the* N

2 You refer to the light and heat that reach us from the sun as the **sun**. *Dena took them into the courtyard to sit in the sun... They were trying to soak up some sun.* N-UNCOUNT: usu *the* N

3 If you **are sunning yourself**, you are sitting or lying in a place where the sun is shining on you. *She was last seen sunning herself in a riverside park.* VB: usu cont =sunbathing V pron-refl

4 A **sun** is any star which has planets revolving around it. N-COUNT

5 **Everything under the sun** means a very great number of things. **Anything under the sun** means anything at all. *We sat there for hours talking about everything under the sun... The fashion-conscious will go for anything under the sun!* ● **a place in the sun**: see **place**. PHRASE: PHR after v

Sun. **Sun.** is a written abbreviation for **Sunday**. *The Palace is open Mon-Sun.* ◆◆◇◇◇

sun-baked. **Sun-baked** land or earth has been made hard and dry by the sun shining on it. *...a dry, sun-baked lawn.* ADJ: ADJ n

sunbathe /sʌnbeɪθ/ **sunbathes, sunbathing, sunbathed.** When people **sunbathe**, they sit or lie in a place where the sun shines strongly on them, so that they get a suntan. *Franklin swam and sunbathed at the pool every morning.* ◆◇◇◇◇ VERB V ♦ **sunbather, sunbathers** *A week ago Bournemouth beach was thronged with sunbathers soaking up the 80 degrees heat.* N-COUNT ♦ **sunbathing** *Nearby there is a stretch of white sand beach perfect for sunbathing.* N-UNCOUNT

sunbeam /sʌnbiːm/ **sunbeams.** A **sunbeam** is a ray of sunlight. *A sunbeam slants through the west window.* N-COUNT

sunbed /sʌnbed/ **sunbeds.** A **sunbed** is a piece of equipment with ultraviolet lights, that you lie on to get a suntan. N-COUNT

sunblock /sʌnblɒk/ **sunblocks.** **Sunblock** is a cream which you put on your skin to protect it completely from the sun. N-MASS

sunburn /sʌnbɜːʳn/ **sunburns.** If someone has **sunburn**, their skin is bright pink and sore because they have spent too much time in hot sunshine. *The risk and severity of sunburn depend on the body's natural skin colour... I was concerned that I was not protected and would get a sunburn.* N-VAR

sunburnt /sʌnbɜːʳnt/; also spelled **sunburned.**

1 Someone who is **sunburnt** has sore bright pink skin because they have spent too much time in hot sunshine. *A badly sunburned face or back is extremely painful.* ADJ-GRADED =burnt

2 Someone who is **sunburnt** has very brown skin because they have spent a lot of time in the sunshine. *Mr Cooper looked fit and sunburnt.* ADJ-GRADED =bronzed, tanned

sunburst /sʌnbɜːʳst/ **sunbursts.** A **sunburst** is a pattern or design that resembles the sun with rays coming from it. *She designed a huge sunburst window. ...a bronze sunburst pendant.* N-COUNT

sundae /sʌndeɪ, -di/ **sundaes.** A **sundae** is a tall glass of ice cream with whipped cream and nuts or fruit on top. *...a chocolate sundae.* N-COUNT: usu n N

Sunday /sʌndeɪ, -di/ **Sundays.** **Sunday** is the day after Saturday and before Monday. *I thought we might go for a drive on Sunday... Naomi used to go to church in Granville every Sunday.* ◆◆◆◆◇ N-VAR

Sunday best. If you are in your **Sunday best**, you are wearing your best clothes, which you only wear for special occasions. *They looked as if they were dressed in their Sunday best, the girls in clean white dresses, the boys in dark trousers and plain white shirts.* N-SING: poss N

Sunday school, Sunday schools. **Sunday school** is a class organized by a church that some children go to on Sundays in order to learn about Christianity. *I went to the young people's service in the morning and to Sunday school in the afternoon. ...a Sunday School teacher.* ◆◇◇◇◇ N-VAR

sunder /sʌndəʳ/ **sunders, sundering, sundered.** If people or things **are sundered**, they are separated or split by something; a literary word. *The city is being sundered by racial tension... Police moved in to separate the two groups, already sundered by distrust.* VB: usu passive =split be V-ed V-ed

sundial /sʌndaɪəl/ **sundials.** A **sundial** is a device used for telling the time when the sun is shining. The shadow of a pointer falls onto a flat surface that is marked with the hours, and points to the correct hour. N-COUNT

sundown /sʌndaʊn/. In American English, **sundown** is the time when the sun sets. The usual British word is **sunset**. *The fighting broke out about two hours after sundown.* N-UNCOUNT

sun-drenched; also spelled **sundrenched.** **Sun-drenched** places have a lot of hot sunshine. ADJ-GRADED: ADJ n

He sat on the terrace of his sun-drenched villa in the South of France.

sundries /sʌndriz/. When someone is making a list of things, items that are not important enough to be listed individually are sometimes referred to together as **sundries**; a formal word. *The inn gift shop stocks quality Indian crafts and sundries.* N-PLURAL

sundry /sʌndri/ ◆◇◇◇◇

1 If someone refers to **sundry** people or things, they are referring to several people or things that are all different from each other and which they do not wish to describe individually; a formal use. *Scientists, business people, and sundry others gathered on Monday for the official opening... She could ring for food and drink, laundry and sundry services.* ADJ

2 **All and sundry** means everyone. *I made tea for all and sundry at the office... He was well known to all and sundry.* PHRASE: usu prep PHR

sunflower /sʌnflaʊəʳ/ **sunflowers.** A **sunflower** is a very tall plant with large yellow flowers. Oil from sunflower seeds is used in cooking and to make margarine. ◆◇◇◇◇ N-COUNT

sung /sʌŋ/. **Sung** is the past participle of **sing**.

sunglasses /sʌnglɑːsɪz, -glæs-/. **Sunglasses** are spectacles with dark lenses which you wear to protect your eyes from bright sunlight. *She slipped on a pair of sunglasses.* ◆◇◇◇◇ N-PLURAL: also *a pair of* N =dark glasses

sun hat, sun hats; also spelled **sunhat**. A **sun hat** is a wide-brimmed hat that protects your head from the sun. N-COUNT

sunk /sʌŋk/

1 **Sunk** is the past participle of **sink**.

2 If you say that someone is **sunk**, you mean that they have no hope of avoiding trouble or failure; an informal use. *Without him we'd be well and truly sunk.* ADJ: v-link ADJ

sunken /sʌŋkən/ ◆◇◇◇◇

1 **Sunken** ships have sunk to the bottom of a sea, ocean, or lake. *The sunken sailing-boat was a glimmer of white on the bottom... Try diving for sunken treasure.* ADJ: ADJ n

2 **Sunken** gardens, roads, or other features are below the level of their surrounding area. *Steps lead down to the sunken garden... The room was dominated by a sunken bath.* ADJ: ADJ n

3 **Sunken** eyes, cheeks, or other parts of the body curve inwards and make you look thin and unwell. *Her eyes were sunken and black-ringed. ...an elderly man with sunken cheeks.* ADJ

sun lamp, sun lamps; also spelled **sunlamp**. A **sun lamp** is a lamp that produces ultraviolet rays. People use sun lamps to get a suntan. N-COUNT

sunless /sʌnləs/

1 On **sunless** days, the sun does not shine. *The day dawned sunless and with a low cloud base.* ADJ ≠sunny

2 **Sunless** places are not lit by the sun. *Carmen stayed behind in the dark, sunless room.* ADJ: ADJ n

sunlight /sʌnlaɪt/. **Sunlight** is the light that comes from the sun during the day. *I saw her sitting at a window table, bathed in sunlight.* ◆◆◇◇◇ N-UNCOUNT

sunlit /sʌnlɪt/. **Sunlit** places are brightly lit by the sun. *Her house has two big sunlit rooms with floor-to-ceiling windows.* ADJ: ADJ n

sunny /sʌni/ **sunnier, sunniest** ◆◆◇◇◇

1 When it is **sunny**, the sun is shining brightly. *The weather was surprisingly warm and sunny... There is a chance of sunny spells in the West.* ADJ-GRADED =bright

2 **Sunny** places are brightly lit by the sun. *Most roses like a sunny position in a fairly fertile soil. ...a sunny terrace.* ADJ-GRADED =sunlit

3 Someone who has a **sunny** disposition is usually cheerful and happy. *He was a nice lad – bright and with a sunny disposition... The staff wear big sunny smiles.* ADJ-GRADED =cheery

sunrise /sʌnraɪz/ **sunrises** ◆◇◇◇◇

1 **Sunrise** is the time in the morning when the sun first appears in the sky. *The rain began before sunrise.* N-UNCOUNT =dawn

2 A **sunrise** is the colours and light that you see in the eastern part of the sky when the sun first appears. *There was a spectacular sunrise yesterday.* N-COUNT

sunroof /sʌnruːf/ **sunroofs.** A **sunroof** is a panel in the roof of a car that opens to let sunshine and air enter the car. N-COUNT

sunscreen /sʌnskriːn/ **sunscreens.** A **sunscreen** is a cream that protects your skin from the sun's rays, especially in hot weather. ◆◇◇◇◇ N-MASS

sunset /sʌnset/ **sunsets** ◆◆◇◇◇

1 **Sunset** is the time in the evening when the sun disappears out of sight from the sky. *The dance ends at sunset.* N-UNCOUNT =dusk, sundown

2 A **sunset** is the colours and light that you see in the western part of the sky when the sun disappears in the evening. *There was a red sunset over Paris.* N-COUNT

sunshine /sʌnʃaɪn/. **Sunshine** is the light and heat that comes from the sun. *In the marina yachts sparkle in the sunshine... She was sitting outside a cafe in bright sunshine... I awoke next morning to brilliant sunshine streaming into my room.* ◆◆◇◇◇ N-UNCOUNT

sunspot /sʌnspɒt/ **sunspots. Sunspots** are dark cool patches that appear on the surface of the sun and last for about a week. N-COUNT

sunstroke /sʌnstroʊk/. **Sunstroke** is an illness caused by spending too much time in hot sunshine. *I was suffering from acute sunstroke, starvation and exhaustion.* N-UNCOUNT

suntan /sʌntæn/ **suntans;** also spelled **sun-tan**.

1 If you have a **suntan**, the sun has turned your skin an attractive brown colour. N-COUNT =tan

2 **Suntan** lotion, oil, or cream protects your skin from the sun. *She playfully rubs suntan lotion on his neck.* ADJ: ADJ n

suntanned /sʌntænd/. Someone who is **suntanned** has an attractive brown colour from being in the sun. *He is always suntanned and incredibly fit.* ADJ-GRADED =tanned

sun-up; also spelled **sunup**. In American English, **sun-up** is the time of day when the sun rises. The usual British word is **sunrise**. *We worked from sunup to sunset.* N-UNCOUNT =dawn

sup /sʌp/ **sups, supping, supped**

1 If you **sup** something, you drink it, especially in fairly small sips; an old-fashioned or literary use. *We supped mulled wine.* VERB V n

2 If you **sup**, you eat dinner in the evening; an old-fashioned or literary use. *He had been invited to sup with a colleague and his wife.* VERB =dine V

super /suːpəʳ/ ◆◆◆◇◇

1 Some people use **super** to mean very nice or very good; an informal and slightly old-fashioned use, used mainly in British English. *We had a super time... That's a super idea... 'I think I could find you something.'—'That would be super.'* ADJ =great

2 **Super** is used before adjectives to indicate that something has a lot of a quality. *I'm going to Greece in the summer so I've got to be super slim. ...squads of super-fit athletes.* ADV: ADV adj ▸ Also a prefix. *...the development of superfast computers.* PREFIX

3 **Super** is used before nouns to indicate that something is larger, better, or more advanced than similar things. *...building Russia into a super state. ...a chance to test-drive a stunning Lotus super-car.* ADJ: ADJ n ▸ Also a prefix. *...planning and refining the next generation of superweapons.* PREFIX

super- /suːpəʳ-/. **Super-** is used to form adjectives which indicate that something is at a higher level than something else. *...his superhuman efforts to find work. ...a fragment of crystal with supernormal powers.* PREFIX

superannuated /suːpərænjueɪtɪd/. If you describe something as **superannuated**, you mean that it is old and no longer used for its original purpose; a formal word. *...the superannuated idealism of the Sixties.* ADJ: usu ADJ n =antiquated

superannuation /suːpərænjueɪʃən/. In British English, **superannuation** is money which people pay regularly into a special fund so that when they retire from their job they will receive money regularly as a pension. *The union pressed for a superannuation scheme.* N-UNCOUNT =pension

superb /suːpɜːʳb/ ◆◆◆◇◇

1 If something is **superb**, its quality is very good indeed. *There is a superb 18-hole golf course 6 miles away... The waters are crystal clear and offer a superb opportunity for swimming.* ♦ **superbly** *The orchestra played superbly.* ADJ-GRADED =excellent; ADV-GRADED: ADV with v, ADV adv/adj

2 If you say that someone has **superb** confidence, control, or skill, you mean that they have very great confidence, control, or skill. *With superb skill he managed to make a perfect landing.* ♦ **superbly** *...his superbly disciplined opponent... The sports complex is huge and superbly well-equipped.* ADJ-GRADED =great; ADV-GRADED: ADV with v, ADV adj/adv

supercharged /suːpəʳtʃɑːʳdʒd/. If a car engine is **supercharged**, it has more air than normal forced into it so that the petrol burns more quickly and the car has more power. ADJ

supercilious /suːpəʳsɪliəs/. If you say that someone is **supercilious**, you disapprove of them because they behave in a scornful way towards other people because they think they are superior to them. *His manner is supercilious and arrogant... Her eyebrows were arched in supercilious surprise.* ADJ-GRADED PRAGMATICS =disdainful

supercomputer /suːpəʳkəmpjuːtəʳ/ **supercomputers.** A **supercomputer** is a powerful computer that can process large amounts of data very quickly. ◆◇◇◇◇ N-COUNT

superconductivity /suːpəʳkɒndʌktɪvɪti/. **Superconductivity** is the ability of certain metals to allow electricity to pass through them without any resistance at very low temperatures; a technical term in electronics. N-UNCOUNT

superconductor /suːpəʳkəndʌktəʳ/ **superconductors.** A **superconductor** is a metal that allows electricity to pass through it without resistance at very low temperatures; a technical term in electronics. ◆◇◇◇◇ N-COUNT

super-ego, super-egos; also spelled **superego.** Your **super-ego** is the part of your mind which makes you aware of what is right and wrong, and which causes you to feel guilt when you have done something wrong; a technical term in psychology. N-COUNT =conscience

superficial /suːpəʳfɪʃəl/ ◆◆◇◇◇

1 If you describe someone as **superficial**, you disapprove of them because they do not think deeply, and have little understanding of anything serious or important. *This guy is a superficial yuppie with no intellect whatsoever... The tone of his book is consistently negative, occasionally arrogant, and often superficial.* ♦ **superficiality** /suːpəʳfɪʃiælɪti/ *He hated the superficiality, the neon glamour and the cheap prettiness of life in L.A.* ♦ **superficially** *Hill cannot write badly or superficially; his characters and plotting are, as usual, admirable.* ADJ-GRADED PRAGMATICS; N-UNCOUNT: oft N of n; ADV-GRADED: ADV after v

2 If you describe something such as an action, feeling, or relationship as **superficial**, you mean that it includes only the simplest and most obvious aspects of that thing, and not those aspects which require more effort to deal with or understand. *Their arguments do not withstand the most superficial scrutiny... His roommate had been pleasant on a superficial level... Father had no more than a superficial knowledge of music.* ♦ **superficiality** *His assessment only serves to demonstrate the superficiality of the judgements we make when we first meet people.* ♦ **superficially** *The film touches on these difficult questions, but only superficially.* ADJ-GRADED; N-UNCOUNT: oft N of n; ADV-GRADED: ADV with v

3 **Superficial** is used to describe the appearance of something or the impression that it gives, especially if its real nature is very different. *Despite these superficial resemblances, this is a darker work than her earlier novels... Spain may well look different but the changes are superficial.* ♦ **superficially** *Many of these killers are frequently glib and superficially charming... Superficially there have been many changes in Britain in recent years.* ADJ-GRADED; ADV-GRADED: ADV with cl/group, ADV with v

4 **Superficial** injuries are not very serious, and affect only the surface of the body. You can also describe damage to an object as **superficial.** *The 69-year-old clergyman escaped with superficial wounds... The explosion caused superficial damage to the fortified house.* ADJ-GRADED =slight

5 The **superficial** layers of the skin are the ones nearest the surface; a medical use. *...superficial blood vessels in the forearm.* ADJ: ADJ n

superfluity /suːpəʳfluːɪti/ **superfluities.** If there is a **superfluity of** something, there is more of it than is needed; a formal word. *The city has gone from a shortage to a superfluity of five-star hotels.* N-COUNT: usu N of n

superfluous /suːpɜːʳfluəs/. Something that is **superfluous** is unnecessary or is no longer needed. *My presence at the afternoon's proceedings was superfluous... I rid myself of many superfluous belongings and habits that bothered me.* ◆◇◇◇◇ ADJ-GRADED =redundant

supergrass /suːpəʳgrɑːs, -græs/ **supergrasses.** In informal British English, a **supergrass** is a person who gives the police information about a large group of criminals or terrorists. N-COUNT

supergroup /suːpəʳgruːp/ **supergroups.** A **supergroup** is a pop group that has become very popular and famous. *Supergroup U2 will be among a host of top bands appearing at Wembley Stadium on April 20.* N-COUNT

superheated /suːpəʳhiːtəd/. If a liquid is **superheated**, it has been heated to a temperature that is higher than its boiling point without being allowed to boil; a technical term in physics. ADJ

superhero /suːpəʳhɪərou/ **superheroes.** A **superhero** is a fictional character in a cartoon who has superhuman powers and fights against evil. *...superheroes like Batman and Superman.* N-COUNT

superhighway /suːpəʳhaɪweɪ/ **superhighways**

1 In American English, a **superhighway** is a large, fast motorway with several lanes. *He took off for the city on the eight-lane superhighway.* N-COUNT

2 The information **superhighway** is the network of computer links that enables computer users all over the world to communicate with each other. *...a superhighway using digital and fibre-optic technology to provide new telecommunications links.* N-COUNT

superhuman /suːpəʳhjuːmən/. If you describe a quality that someone has as **superhuman**, you mean that it seems to be much greater than that of ordinary people. *Officers were terrified of his superhuman strength... They saw their bills rising steadily, in spite of superhuman efforts to save water.* ADJ: usu ADJ n =herculean

superimpose /suːpərɪmpouz/ **superimposes, superimposing, superimposed** ◆◇◇◇◇

1 If one image **is superimposed** on another, it is put on top of it so that you can see the second image through it. *The image of a seemingly tiny dancer was superimposed on the image of the table... The features of different faces were superimposed over one another.* VB: usu passive; be V-ed on/over n

2 If features or characteristics from one situation **are superimposed** onto another, they are transferred onto or used in the second situation, though they may not fit. *Patterns of public administration and government are superimposed on traditional societies.* VB: usu passive; be V-ed on n

superintend /suːpərɪntend/ **superintends, superintending, superintended.** If you **superintend** something, you have responsibility for ensuring that it is carried out properly; a formal word. *During the interval, Linton superintended a prize draw.* VERB; V n

superintendent /suːpərɪntendənt/ **superintendents** ◆◆◇◇◇

1 In Britain, a **superintendent** is a senior police officer of the rank above an inspector. In the United States, a **superintendent** is the head of a police department. *He was stopped at the airport by an assistant superintendent of police. ...Detective Superintendent Kirby.* N-COUNT; N-TITLE

2 A **superintendent** is a person who is responsible for a particular thing or the work done in a particular department. *He became superintendent of the bank's East African branches... The Superintendent of Public Works gives orders for all watercourses to be inspected.* N-COUNT: N of n

superior /suːpɪəriəʳ/ **superiors** ◆◆◆◇◇
1 If one thing or person is **superior** to another, the first is better than the second. *We have a relationship infinitely superior to those of many of our friends. ...a woman greatly superior to her husband in education and sensitivity... Long-term stock market investments have produced superior returns compared with cash deposits.* ♦ **superiority** *The technical superiority of laser discs over tape is well established.* ADJ-GRADED: oft ADJ *to* n ≠inferior N-UNCOUNT: oft N *over/to* n
2 If you describe something as **superior**, you mean that it is good, and better than other things of the same kind. *A few years ago it was virtually impossible to find superior quality coffee in local shops... Lulu was said to be of very superior intelligence.* ADJ-GRADED
3 A **superior** person or thing has more authority or importance than another person or thing in the same organization or system. *...negotiations between the mutineers and their superior officers... Locally passed laws are of superior authority to those laws passed in Moscow.* ADJ: oft ADJ *to* n
4 Your **superior** in an organization that you work for is a person who has a higher rank than you. *Other army units are completely surrounded and cut-off from communication with their superiors... The company president, and my immediate superior, was the dynamic Harry Stokes.* N-COUNT: poss N ≠subordinate
5 If you describe someone as **superior**, you disapprove of them because they behave as if they are better, more important, or more intelligent than other people. *Finch gave a superior smile... You can stand there and feel superior as you point and laugh at them.* ♦ **superiority** *...a false sense of his superiority over mere journalists.* ADJ-GRADED PRAGMATICS N-UNCOUNT: oft N *over* n
6 If one group of people has **superior** numbers to another group, the first has more people than the second, and therefore has an advantage over it. *The demonstrators fled when they saw the authorities' superior numbers... His men were far superior numerically.* ADJ-GRADED
7 If you describe someone as your **superior** in a particular activity, you mean that they are better than you at that activity; used in written English. *Anthony sometimes felt that his mistress was his superior in will-power... Among his immediate rivals was Arnold Matters, probably his superior in comic roles.* N-COUNT: poss N, oft N *in* n ≠inferior

superiority /suːpɪəriɒrɪti, AM -ɔːrɪti/. If one side in a war or conflict has **superiority**, it has an advantage over its enemy, for example because it has more soldiers or better equipment. *The US will need a three-to-one superiority in forces to be sure of a successful attack... We have air superiority.* N-UNCOUNT: oft N *over/in* n

superlative /suːpɜːʳlətɪv/ **superlatives** ◆◇◇◇◇
1 If you describe something as **superlative**, you mean that it is extremely good. *Some superlative wines are made in this region... The Regent hotel has a superlative view of Hong Kong island.* ♦ **superlatively** *The Philharmonia played this staggeringly difficult music superlatively well.* ADJ ADV
2 If someone uses **superlatives** to describe something, they use adjectives and expressions which indicate that it is extremely good. *...a spectacle which has critics world-wide reaching for superlatives.* N-COUNT: usu pl
3 In grammar, the **superlative** form of an adjective or adverb is the form that indicates that something has more of a quality than anything else in a group. For example, 'biggest' is the superlative form of 'big'. Compare **comparative.** ► Also a noun. *...his tendency towards superlatives and exaggeration.* ADJ: ADJ n N-COUNT

superman /suːpəʳmæn/ **supermen.** A **superman** is a man who has extraordinarily great physical or mental powers or who is extremely good at something. *Collor nurtured the idea that he was a superman, who single-handedly could resolve Brazil's crisis.* N-COUNT

supermarket /suːpəʳmɑːʳkɪt/ **supermarkets.** A **supermarket** is a large shop which sells all kinds of food and some household goods. *Most of us do our food shopping in the supermarket... How do those prawns find their way from Norway to the supermarket shelf?* ◆◆◇◇◇ N-COUNT

supermodel /suːpəʳmɒdᵊl/ **supermodels.** A **supermodel** is a world-famous fashion model. ◆◇◇◇◇ N-COUNT

supernatural /suːpəʳnætʃrəl/. **Supernatural** creatures, forces, and events are believed by some people to exist or happen, although they are impossible according to scientific laws. *The Nakani were evil spirits who looked like humans and possessed supernatural powers. ...supernatural beings.* ► **The supernatural** are things that are supernatural. *He writes short stories with a touch of the supernatural.* ◆◇◇◇◇ ADJ-GRADED =preternatural N-SING: *the* N

supernova /suːpəʳnoʊvə/ **supernovas** or **supernovae** /suːpəʳnoʊviː/. A **supernova** is an exploding star. *At least one supernova occurs per decade in our galaxy.* ◆◇◇◇◇ N-COUNT

superpower /suːpəʳpaʊəʳ/ **superpowers.** A **superpower** is a very powerful and influential country, usually one that has nuclear weapons and is economically successful. *The United States could claim to be both a military and an economic superpower.* ◆◆◇◇◇ N-COUNT

supersede /suːpəʳsiːd/ **supersedes, superseding, superseded.** If something **is superseded** by something newer, it is replaced because it has become old-fashioned or unacceptable. *Hand tools are relics of the past that have now been superseded by the machine.* ◆◇◇◇◇ VB: usu passive =supplant *be* V-ed

supersonic /suːpəʳsɒnɪk/. **Supersonic** aircraft travel faster than the speed of sound. *There was a huge bang; it sounded like a supersonic jet.* ◆◇◇◇◇ ADJ: ADJ n

superstar /suːpəʳstɑːʳ/ **superstars.** A **superstar** is a very famous entertainer or sports player; an informal word. *He was more than a footballing superstar, he was a celebrity. ...a Hollywood superstar.* ◆◇◇◇◇ N-COUNT

superstate /suːpəʳsteɪt/ **superstates.** A **superstate** is a political alliance or union of several nations. *...a European superstate.* N-COUNT

superstition /suːpəʳstɪʃᵊn/ **superstitions.** **Superstition** is belief in things that are not real or possible, for example magic. *Fortune-telling is a very much debased art surrounded by superstition... The phantom of the merry-go-round is just a local superstition.* ◆◇◇◇◇ N-VAR

superstitious /suːpəʳstɪʃəs/ ◆◇◇◇◇
1 People who are **superstitious** believe in things that are not real or possible, for example magic. *Jean was extremely superstitious and believed the colour green brought bad luck.* ADJ-GRADED: usu v-link ADJ
2 **Superstitious** fears or beliefs are irrational and not based on fact. *A wave of superstitious fear spread among the townspeople... In the countryside as a young doctor she encountered ancient superstitious beliefs and prejudices.* ADJ-GRADED: ADJ n

superstore /suːpəʳstɔːʳ/ **superstores.** **Superstores** are very large supermarkets or shops selling household goods and equipment. Superstores are usually built outside city centres away from other shops. *...a Do-It-Yourself superstore.* ◆◇◇◇◇ N-COUNT

superstructure /suːpəʳstrʌktʃəʳ/ **superstructures.** The **superstructure** of a ship is the part of it that is above its main deck. *We might try to clear up some of the cabins in the superstructure.* N-COUNT: usu sing

supertanker /suːpəʳtæŋkəʳ/ **supertankers.** A **supertanker** is an extremely large ship that is used for transporting oil. *An oil slick caused by a spill from a supertanker has hit several beaches.* N-COUNT

supervise /suːpəʳvaɪz/ **supervises, supervising, supervised** ◆◆◇◇◇
1 If you **supervise** an activity or a person, you make sure that the activity is done correctly or that the person is doing a task or behaving correctly. *University teachers have refused to supervise students' examinations... He supervised and trained more than 400 volunteers.* VERB V n
2 If you **supervise** a place where work is done, you ensure that the work there is done properly. *He makes the wines and supervises the vineyards... One of his jobs was supervising the dining room.* VERB V n

supervision /suːpəʳvɪʒᵊn/. **Supervision** is the supervising of people, activities, or places. *A toddler requires close supervision and firm control at all times... The plan calls for a cease-fire and UN supervision of the country... First-time licence holders have to work under supervision.*
[◆◆◇◇◇ N-UNCOUNT: oft N *of* n, *under* N]

supervisor /suːpəʳvaɪzəʳ/ **supervisors.** A **supervisor** is a person who supervises activities or people, especially workers or students. *...a full-time job as a supervisor at a factory... Each student has a supervisor to advise on the writing of the dissertation.*
[◆◆◇◇◇ N-COUNT]

supervisory /suːpəʳvaɪzəri/. **Supervisory** means concerned with the supervision of people, activities, or places. *Most supervisory boards meet only twice a year. ...staff with a minor supervisory role.*
[◆◇◇◇◇ ADJ: ADJ n]

supine /suːpaɪn/
1 If you are **supine**, you are lying flat on your back; a formal word. *...bedridden persons confined to the supine position. ...a statue of a supine dog.* ► Also an adverb. *I lay supine on the poolside grass.*
[ADJ] [ADV: ADV after v]
2 If you describe someone as **supine**, you mean that they let events happen because they are too lazy or afraid to influence them; a formal use. *...a willing and supine executive.*
[ADJ-GRADED: usu ADJ n =submissive]

supper /sʌpəʳ/ **suppers**
[◆◆◇◇◇]
1 Some people refer to the main meal eaten in the early part of the evening as **supper**. *Some guests like to dress for supper.*
[N-VAR]
2 **Supper** is a simple meal eaten just before you go to bed at night. *She gives the children their supper, then puts them to bed.*
[N-VAR]
3 If someone has to **sing for** their **supper**, they have to do a job before they are allowed to do something they want to do. *They would have to 'sing for their supper' during the exhausting official round of duties.*
[PHRASE: V and N inflect]

suppertime /sʌpəʳtaɪm/. **Suppertime** is the period of the day when people have their supper. It can be in the early part of the evening or just before they go to bed at night. *They'll be back by suppertime... Sausages, eggs, chips and baked beans are available at suppertime in the dining room.*
[N-UNCOUNT]

supplant /səplɑːnt, -plænt/ **supplants, supplanting, supplanted.** If a person or thing **is supplanted**, another person or thing takes their place; a formal word. *He may be supplanted by a younger man... By the 1930s the wristwatch had almost completely supplanted the pocket watch.*
[◆◇◇◇◇ VERB =usurp] [be V-ed] [V n]

supple /sʌpᵊl/ **suppler, supplest**
[◆◇◇◇◇]
1 A **supple** object or material bends or changes shape easily without cracking or breaking; used showing approval. *The leather is supple and sturdy enough to last for years... Traditional cheesemaking skills give our brie its soft, supple, creamy texture.*
[ADJ-GRADED PRAGMATICS =pliant, flexible]
♦ **suppleness** *This luxurious talcum lotion restores softness and suppleness to dehydrated skin.*
[N-UNCOUNT]
2 A **supple** person can move and bend their body very easily. *Paul was incredibly supple and strong... Try these simple exercises to keep your feet supple.*
[ADJ-GRADED]
♦ **suppleness** *Exercise in pregnancy can build up your strength and suppleness.*
[N-UNCOUNT]
3 If you describe something such as a flavour or a sound as **supple**, you like it because it is smooth and rich; a literary use. *The wine has a medium-bodied, supple flavour. ...the haunting didgeridoo, the teasing keyboards and the supple bassline.*
[ADJ-GRADED PRAGMATICS]

supplement /sʌplɪmənt/ **supplements, supplementing, supplemented**
[◆◆◇◇◇]
1 If you **supplement** something, you add something to it in order to improve it. *...people doing extra jobs outside their regular jobs to supplement their incomes... I suggest supplementing your diet with vitamins E and A.* ► Also a noun. *Business sponsorship must be a supplement to, not a substitute for, public funding.*
[VERB] [V n] [V n *with* n] [N-COUNT: oft N *to* n]
2 A **supplement** is a pill that you take or a special kind of food that you eat in order to improve your health or diet. *...a multiple vitamin and mineral supplement... I took regular supplements and exercised every day.*
[N-COUNT]
3 A **supplement** is a separate part of a magazine or newspaper, often dealing with a particular topic. *...a special supplement to a monthly financial magazine.* ● See also **colour supplement**.
[N-COUNT]
4 A **supplement** to a book is an additional section, written some time after the main text and published either at the end of the book or separately. *...the supplement to the Encyclopedia Britannica.*
[N-COUNT: oft N *to* n]
5 A **supplement** is an extra amount of money that you pay in order to obtain special facilities or services, for example when you are travelling or staying at a hotel. *If you are travelling alone, the single room supplement is £11 a night.*
[N-COUNT]
6 A **supplement** is an extra amount of money that is paid to someone, in addition to their normal pension or income. *Some people may be entitled to a housing benefit supplement... It is hoped that all who need a supplement to their basic pension obtain it.*
[N-COUNT: usu N n, N *to* n]

supplemental /sʌplɪmentᵊl/. **Supplemental** means **supplementary**; a formal word used mainly in American English. *You'll probably be able to buy supplemental insurance at an extra cost... Large supplemental doses of vitamin E can slightly raise blood pressure.*
[ADJ: ADJ n =extra, additional]

supplementary /sʌplɪmentri, AM -teri/. **Supplementary** things are added to something in order to improve it. *...the question of whether or not we need to take supplementary vitamins... Provide them with additional background or with supplementary information.*
[◆◇◇◇◇ ADJ: usu ADJ n =additional, extra]

supplementary benefit, supplementary benefits. In Britain, **supplementary benefit** is the name that used to be given to money that the government gives regularly to people with no income or very low incomes. The new name for this amount of money is **income support**. *...the decline in the number of lone parent families on Supplementary Benefit. ...the supplementary benefits scheme.*
[N-UNCOUNT: also N in pl]

supplementation /sʌplɪmenteɪʃᵊn/. **Supplementation** is the use of drugs or special types of food in order to improve your health or diet; a medical term. *The product provided inadequate vitamin and mineral supplementation.*
[N-UNCOUNT]

supplicant /sʌplɪkənt/ **supplicants.** A **supplicant** is a person who humbly asks God or an important person to help them or to give them something that they want very much; a formal word. *He flung himself down in the flat submissive posture of a mere supplicant.*
[N-COUNT]

supplication /sʌplɪkeɪʃᵊn/ **supplications.** A **supplication** is a prayer or a humble request to God or someone in authority for help; a formal word. *He raised his arms in a gesture of supplication... The Tory government has to date resisted all supplications.*
[N-VAR]

supplied /səplaɪd/. If you say that a person or place is well **supplied with** particular things, you mean that they have a large number of them. *France is abundantly supplied with excellent family-run hotels.* ● See also **supply**.
[ADJ-GRADED: v-link ADJ *with* n]

supplier /səplaɪəʳ/ **suppliers.** A **supplier** is a person, company, or organization that sells or supplies something such as goods or equipment to customers. *...Hillsdown Holdings, one of the UK's biggest food suppliers... Japan is Asia's dominant supplier of imports and technology.*
[◆◆◇◇◇ N-COUNT: oft N n, N *of* n]

supply /səplaɪ/ **supplies, supplying, supplied**
[◆◆◆◆◇]
1 If you **supply** someone with something that they want or need, you give them a quantity of it. *...an agreement not to produce or supply chemical weapons. ...a pipeline which will supply the major Greek cities with Russian natural gas. ...the blood vessels supplying oxygen to the brain.*
[VERB] [V n] [V n *with* n] [V n *to* n]
2 You can use **supplies** to refer to food, equipment, and other essential things that people need, especially when these are provided in large quantities. *What happens when food and gasoline supplies run*
[N-PLURAL: oft n N]

low?... The country's only supplies are those it can import by lorry from Vietnam.

3 A **supply** of something is an amount of it which someone has or which is available for them to use. *The brain requires a constant supply of oxygen... Most urban water supplies in the United States now contain fluoride in varying amounts.*
N-VAR: N *of* n, n N

4 Supply is the quantity of goods and services that can made available for people to buy; a technical use in economics. *Prices change according to supply and demand.*
N-UNCOUNT ≠demand

5 If you **supply** a missing word or piece of information, for example in a puzzle, you say or write it because you know it. *Supply the missing word(s) and you could win a T-shirt.*
VERB =provide V n

6 If something is **in short supply**, there is very little of it available and it is difficult to find or obtain. *Food is in short supply all over the country... Nowadays that sort of innocence is in short supply.*
PHRASE: usu v-link PHR

supply line, supply lines. A **supply line** is a route along which goods and equipment are transported to an army during a war. *The bombing campaign appears aimed at cutting the supply lines between Germany and its army in occupied France.*
N-COUNT

supply teacher, supply teachers. In British English, a **supply teacher** is a teacher whose job is to take the place of other teachers at different schools when they are absent. The usual American term is **substitute teacher**.
N-COUNT

support /səpɔːʳt/ **supports, supporting, supported** ◆◆◆◆◆

1 If you **support** someone or their ideas or aims, you agree with them, and perhaps help them because you want them to succeed. *The vice president insisted that he supported the hard-working people of New York... The National Union of Mineworkers pressed the party to support a total ban on imported coal.* ► Also a noun. *The prime minister gave his full support to the government's reforms... They are prepared to resort to violence in support of their beliefs.*
VERB =back ≠oppose V n
N-UNCOUNT: usu with supp

2 If you give **support** to someone during a difficult or unhappy time, you are kind to them and help them. *It was hard to come to terms with her death after all the support she gave to me and the family... We hope to continue to have her close support and friendship.*
N-UNCOUNT

3 Financial **support** is money provided to enable an organization to continue. This money is usually provided by the government. *...the EC's proposal to cut agricultural support by only about 15%.*
N-UNCOUNT: oft supp N =funding, assistance

4 If you **support** someone, you provide them with money or the things that they need. *I have children to support, money to be earned, and a home to be maintained... She sold everything she'd ever bought in order to support herself through art school.*
VERB V n V pron-refl

5 If a fact **supports** a statement or a theory, it helps to show that it is true or correct. *The Freudian theory about daughters falling in love with their father has little evidence to support it.* ► Also a noun. *The two largest powers in any system must always be major rivals. History offers some support for this view.*
VERB =substantiate V n
N-UNCOUNT =evidence

6 If something **supports** an object, it is underneath the object and holding it up. *...the thick wooden posts that supported the ceiling... Let your baby sit on the floor propped up with plenty of cushions to support him.*
VERB =hold up V n

7 A **support** is a bar or other object that supports something.
N-COUNT

8 If you **support** yourself, you prevent yourself from falling by holding onto something or by leaning on something. *He supported himself by means of a nearby post.* ► Also a noun. *Alice, very pale, was leaning against him as if for support.*
VERB V pron-refl
N-UNCOUNT

9 If you **support** a sports team, especially a football team, you want them to win and perhaps go regularly to their games. *Tim, 17, supports Manchester United.*
VERB V n

10 See also **supporting**.

supporter /səpɔːʳtəʳ/ **supporters. Supporters** are people who support someone or something, for example a political leader or a sports team. *The fourth night of violence in the German city of Rostock was triggered by football supporters... Bradley was a major supporter of the 1986 tax reform plan.*
◆◆◆◆◇ N-COUNT: usu pl, with supp

supporting /səpɔːʳtɪŋ/.

1 In a film or play, a **supporting** actor or actress is one who has an important part, but not the most important part. *...the winner of the best supporting actress award. ...acting the supporting role in a Harrison Ford-type movie.*
ADJ: ADJ n

2 See also **support**.

supportive /səpɔːʳtɪv/. If you are **supportive**, you are kind and helpful to someone at a difficult or unhappy time in their life. *They were always supportive of each other... Her boss was very supportive and gave her time off work to see her mum.*
◆◆◇◇◇ ADJ-GRADED: oft ADJ *of* n ≠unsupportive

suppose /səpoʊz/ **supposes, supposing, supposed** ◆◆◆◆◇

1 You can use **suppose** or **supposing** to introduce a clause in which you state a possible situation or action. You usually then go on to consider the effects or results that this situation or action might have. *Suppose someone gave you an egg and asked you to describe exactly what was inside... Supposing he's right and I do die tomorrow? Maybe I should take out an extra insurance policy.*
VERB PRAGMATICS =say V that

2 If you **suppose** that something is true, you believe that it is probably true, because of other things that you know. *The policy is perfectly clear and I see no reason to suppose that it isn't working... I knew very well that the problem was more complex than he supposed... It had been supposed that by then Peter would be married.*
VERB PRAGMATICS V that *it be* V-ed that Also V n

3 You can say **'I suppose'** with a clause stating something that you believe to be true, or something that you think you should do, when you want to express slight uncertainty about it; used in spoken English. *I get a bit uptight these days. Hormones, I suppose... I suppose I'd better do some homework... Is that the right way up?—Yeah. I suppose so... There's nothing to keep us here, is there.—I suppose not.*
PHRASES oft PHR that, PHR *so/not* PRAGMATICS

4 You can say **'I suppose'** or **'I don't suppose'** to introduce a clause in which you report someone's thoughts or attitude, when you want to express impatience or slight anger at them; used in spoken English. *I suppose you think you're funny... I don't suppose it occurred to you to notify the police.*
PHR that PRAGMATICS

5 You can say **'I don't suppose'** as a way of introducing a polite request to someone when it might cause them some difficulty or inconvenience; used in spoken English. *I don't suppose you could tell me where James Street is could you?*
PHR that PRAGMATICS

6 You can use **'do you suppose'** to introduce a question when you want someone to give their opinion about something, although you know that they are unlikely to have any more knowledge or information about it than you; used in spoken English. *Do you suppose he was telling the truth?... What do you suppose they want with her?... You don't suppose they'd start the trip without us, do you?*
PHR that PRAGMATICS

7 You can use **'do you suppose'** as a polite way of suggesting or requesting that someone does something. *Do you suppose we could get together for a little chat sometime soon?.*
PHR that PRAGMATICS

supposed. Pronounced /səpoʊzd/ or /səpoʊst/ for meanings 1 to 4, and /səpoʊzɪd/ for meaning 5.

◆◆◆◆◇

1 If you say that something **is supposed to** happen, you mean that it is planned or expected. Sometimes this use suggests that the thing does not really happen in this way. *He produced a hand-written list of nine men he was supposed to kill... Public spending is supposed to fall, not rise, in the next few years.*
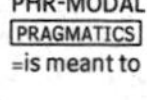
PHR-MODAL PRAGMATICS =is meant to

2 If something **was supposed to** happen, it was planned or intended to happen, but did not in fact
PHR-MODAL

happen. *He was supposed to go back to Bergen on the last bus, but of course the accident prevented him... The first debate was supposed to have been held on Tuesday.*

3 If you say that something **is supposed to** be true, you mean that people say it is true but you do not know for certain that it is true. *'The Whipping Block' has never been published, but it's supposed to be a really good poem... 'The President cannot be disturbed,' his son is supposed to have told an early morning caller.* PHR-MODAL PRAGMATICS =be meant to

4 You can use **'be supposed to'** to express annoyance at someone's ideas, or because something is not happening in the proper way. *You're supposed to be my friend!... Don't try to tell me what I'm supposed to be feeling... What am I supposed to have done wrong now?* PHR-MODAL

5 You can use **supposed** when you want to suggest that the following word or description is misleading, or when it is not definitely known to be true. *Not all indigenous regimes were willing to accept the supposed benefits of British trade. ...when the rule of law is broken by its supposed guardians.* ADJ: ADJ n PRAGMATICS =alleged

♦ **supposedly** /səpoʊzɪdli/ *He was more of a victim than any of the women he supposedly offended... Supposedly his last words to her were: 'You must not pity me.'* ADV: ADV with v, ADV with cl/group

supposition /sʌpəzɪʃᵊn/ **suppositions**

1 A **supposition** is an idea or statement which someone believes or assumes to be true, although they may have no evidence for it; a formal use. *There's a popular supposition that we're publicly funded but the bulk of our money comes from competitive contracts... But as with many such suppositions in natural history, no one had ever tested it.* N-COUNT: oft N that =assumption

2 You can describe someone's ideas or statements as **supposition** if you disapprove of the fact that they have no evidence to support them. *The report has been rejected by the authorities, who said much of it was based on supposition or inaccuracy.* N-UNCOUNT PRAGMATICS

suppository /səpɒzɪtri, AM -tɔːri/ **suppositories.** A **suppository** is a solid block of medicine that is put into the vagina or rectum where it gradually dissolves. N-COUNT

suppress /səpres/ **suppresses, suppressing, suppressed** ◆◆◇◇◇

1 If someone in authority **suppresses** an activity, they prevent it from continuing, by using force or making it illegal. *...drug traffickers, who continue to flourish despite international attempts to suppress them... The Orthodox religion, suppressed under communist rule, was encouraged to flourish again.* VERB =restrain, restrict V n V-ed

♦ **suppression** /səpreʃᵊn/ *...people who were imprisoned after the violent suppression of the pro-democracy movement protests.* N-UNCOUNT: usu N of n

2 If a natural function or reaction of your body **is suppressed**, it is stopped, for example by drugs or illness. *The reproduction and growth of the cancerous cells can be suppressed by bombarding them with radiation. ...the strongest evidence so far that ultraviolet light can suppress human immune responses.* VERB =check be V-ed V n

♦ **suppression** *Eye problems can indicate an unhealthy lifestyle with subsequent suppression of the immune system.* N-UNCOUNT: usu N of n

3 If you **suppress** your feelings or reactions, you do not express them, even though you might want to. *Liz thought of Barry and suppressed a smile... The Professor said that deep sleep allowed suppressed anxieties to surface.* VERB V n V-ed

♦ **suppression** *A mother's suppression of her own feelings can cause problems.* N-UNCOUNT: usu N of n

4 If someone **suppresses** a piece of information, they prevent other people from learning it. *At no time did they try to persuade me to suppress the information... The wrong criminal is in the dock either because a genuine mistake has been made or because evidence has been suppressed.* VERB V n

♦ **suppression** *The inspectors found no evidence which supported any allegation of suppression of official documents.* N-UNCOUNT: N of n

5 If someone or something **suppresses** a process or activity, they stop it continuing or developing. *'The Government is suppressing inflation by devastating the economy,' he said... Lawyers said today's ruling would lead to higher prices and would suppress innovation of new products.* VERB V n

suppressant /səpresənt/ **suppressants.** A **suppressant** is a drug which is used to stop one of the natural functions of the body; a medical term. *...the brief period in her life when she took Dexedrine as an appetite suppressant.* N-COUNT: n N

suppressor /səpresəʳ/. **Suppressor** cells or genes are ones that prevent a cancer from developing or spreading; a medical term. ADJ: ADJ n

supranational /suːprənæʃənəl/; also spelled **supra-national**. A **supranational** organization or authority involves or relates to more than one country. *...NATO and other Western supranational institutions.* ADJ: ADJ n

supremacist /suːpreməsɪst/ **supremacists** A **supremacist** is someone who believes that one group of people, usually white people, should be more powerful and have more influence than another group. *...a plot by White supremacists to blow up a Black church in Los Angeles. ...a white supremacist group.* N-COUNT: oft N n

supremacy /suːpreməsi/ ◆◇◇◇◇

1 If one group of people has **supremacy** over another group, they are more powerful politically or militarily than the other group. *The conservative old guard had re-established its political supremacy... The president has been able to assert his ultimate supremacy over the prime minister.* N-UNCOUNT: usu with poss, oft N over n =dominance

2 If someone or something has **supremacy** over another person or thing, they are better. *In the United States Open final, Graf has retained overall supremacy.* N-UNCOUNT: usu with poss, oft N over n =superiority

supreme /suːpriːm/ ◆◆◆◆◇

1 Supreme is used in the title of a person or an official group to indicate that they are at the highest level in a particular organization or system. *MacArthur was Supreme Commander for the allied powers in the Pacific. ...the Supreme Court. ...the Supreme Being.* ADJ: ADJ n

2 You use **supreme** to emphasize the greatness of a quality or thing. *Her approval was of supreme importance... The lady conspired to seize supreme power.* ADJ

♦ **supremely** *Mr Kohl is now in a supremely confident position... She gets on with her job and does it supremely well.* ADV: ADV adj/adv

supremo /suːpriːmoʊ/ **supremos.** In British English, a **supremo** is someone who is considered to have the most authority or skill in a particular organization, situation, or area of activity; an informal word. *Her new role as fashion supremo is something she can really get her teeth into. ...London's new arts supremo. ...an economics supremo.* ◆◇◇◇◇ N-COUNT: usu supp N

Supt. Supt is a written abbreviation for **superintendent** when it is part of the title of someone in the police force. *Det Supt Bassett, who is in charge of the murder enquiry, said he was confident of catching the killer.* =superintendent

surcharge /sɜːʳtʃɑːʳdʒ/ **surcharges.** A **surcharge** is an extra payment of money in addition to the usual payment for something. It is added for a specific reason, for example by a company because costs have risen or by a government as a tax. *The government introduced a 15% surcharge on imports... The prices of overseas holidays are subject to surcharges.* ◆◇◇◇◇ N-COUNT: oft N on/for n

sure /ʃʊəʳ/ **surer, surest** ◆◆◆◆◆

1 If you are **sure** that something is true, you are certain that it is true. If you are not **sure** about something, you do not know for certain what the true situation is. *He'd never been in a class before and he was not even sure that he should have been teaching... The president has never been sure which direction he wanted to go in on this issue... She was no longer sure how she felt about him... It is impossible to be sure about the value of land.* ADJ-GRADED: v-link ADJ, ADJ that, ADJ wh, ADJ about n =certain ≠doubtful

2 If someone is **sure of** getting something, they will certainly get it. *A lot of people think that it's better to pay for their education so that they can be sure of* ADJ: v-link ADJ of -ing/n *getting quality... It is the self-assurance of the new generation which makes them sure of their success.*

3 If you say that something **is sure to** happen, you are emphasizing your belief that it will happen. *With over 80 beaches to choose from, you are sure to find a place to lay your towel... Anyone who goes food shopping without a list is sure to forget the things they really need.* PHR-MODAL PRAGMATICS =be bound to

4 Sure is used to emphasize that something such as a sign or ability is reliable or accurate. *Sharpe's leg and shoulder began to ache, a sure sign of rain... She has a sure grasp of social issues such as literacy, poverty and child care.* ♦ **sureness** *New to the job, he was keen to demonstrate his sureness of mind.* ADJ-GRADED: ADJ n PRAGMATICS; N-UNCOUNT

5 If you tell someone to **be sure** to do something, you mean that they must not forget to do it. *Be sure to read about how mozzarella is made, on page 65... Be sure you get your daily quota of calcium and daily vitamins.* ADJ-GRADED: v-link ADJ, ADJ to-inf, ADJ that PRAGMATICS

6 Sure is an informal way of saying 'yes' or 'all right'. *'He rang you?'—'Sure. Last night.'... 'I'd like to be alone, O.K?'—'Sure. O.K.'... 'We'll phone and you can make an appointment'—'Sure. What time do you want to go?'* CONVENTION PRAGMATICS

7 You can use **sure** in order to emphasize what you are saying. *'Has the whole world just gone crazy?'—'Sure looks that way, doesn't it.'... It sure is hot, he thought.* ADV: ADV before v PRAGMATICS =certainly

8 You say **sure enough**, especially when telling a story, to confirm that something was really true or was actually happening. *We found the English treacle pudding too good to resist. Sure enough, it was delicious... I was in a shop when I saw a lady looking carefully at me. She'd recognised me, and sure enough, she came across.* PHRASES PHR with cl (not last in cl) PRAGMATICS

9 If you say that something is **for sure** or that you know it **for sure**, you mean that it is definitely true. *One thing's for sure, Astbury's vocal style hasn't changed much over the years... Even to this day we don't know what happened for sure.* PHR with cl (not first in cl) =for certain

10 If you **make sure** that something is done, you take action so that it is done. *Make sure that you follow the instructions carefully... He wants to make sure that schools are committed to providing alternative education.* V inflects, usu PHR that =check

11 If you **make sure** that something is the way that you want or expect it to be, you check that it is that way. *He looked in the bathroom to make sure that he was alone... Before you cut the cloth, make sure that the pattern matches up on both edges.* V inflects, usu PHR that =make certain, check

12 You use **to be sure** when you are admitting that something is true, although it seems to contradict a more general statement that you are making. *Parents make the rules. To be sure, many of the rules are no longer appropriate today.* PHR with cl PRAGMATICS =of course

13 If you are **sure of yourself**, you are very confident about your own abilities or opinions. *I'd never seen him like this, so sure of himself, so in command.* v-link PHR

sure-fire; also spelled **surefire**. A **sure-fire** thing is something that is certain to succeed or win; an informal word. *If something's a sure-fire hit then Radio One will play it. ...a surefire best seller.* ADJ: ADJ n =guaranteed

sure-footed; also spelled **surefooted**.

1 A person or animal that is **sure-footed** can move easily over steep or uneven ground without falling. *My horse is small but wiry and sure-footed.* ADJ-GRADED

2 If someone is **sure-footed**, they are confident in what they are doing. *The Labour Party is growing increasingly sure-footed.* ADJ-GRADED =confident

surely /ʃʊəʳli/ ◆◆◆◇◇

1 You use **surely** to emphasize that you think something should be true, and you would be surprised if it was not true. *You're an intelligent woman, surely you realize by now that I'm helping you... You surely haven't forgotten Dr Walters?... If I can accept this situation, surely you can.* ADV: ADV with cl/group PRAGMATICS

2 If something will **surely** happen or is **surely** the case, it will definitely happen or is certainly the case; a formal use. *He knew that under the surgeon's knife he would surely die... He is an artist, just as surely as Rembrandt or any other first-rate portrait painter is one.* ADV: ADV with cl, ADV before v =certainly

3 If you say that something is happening **slowly but surely**, you mean that it is happening gradually but it is definitely happening. *Slowly but surely she started to fall in love with him... He's recovering, slowly but surely.* PHRASE: PHR with cl

surety /ʃʊərɪti/ **sureties.** A **surety** is money or something valuable which you give to someone to show that you will do what you have promised. *The insurance company will take warehouse stocks or treasury bonds as surety... Bristol Crown Court granted conditional bail with a surety of £2,500.* N-VAR =guarantee

surf /sɜːʳf/ **surfs, surfing, surfed** ◆◇◇◇◇

1 Surf is the mass of white foam that is formed by waves as they fall upon the shore. *...surf rolling onto white sand beaches.* N-UNCOUNT

2 If you **surf**, you ride on big waves in the sea on a special board. *I'm going to buy a surfboard and learn to surf... I'm going to be surfing bigger waves when I get to Australia!* ♦ **surfer, surfers** *...this small fishing village, which continues to attract painters and surfers.* VERB V, V n; N-COUNT

surface /sɜːʳfɪs/ **surfaces, surfacing, surfaced** ◆◆◆◆◇

1 The **surface** of something is the flat top part of it or the outside of it. *Ozone forms a protective layer between 12 and 30 miles above the Earth's surface. ...tiny little waves on the surface of the water... The road surface has started breaking up... Its total surface area was seven thousand square feet.* N-COUNT: usu with supp

2 A work **surface** is a flat area, for example the top of a table, desk, or cupboard, on which you can work. *It can simply be left on the work surface... Place the fish on a flat surface and sprinkle the flesh with lemon juice and pepper.* N-COUNT: usu with supp

3 When you refer to the **surface** of a situation, you are talking about what can be seen easily rather than what is hidden or not immediately obvious. *Back in Britain, things appear, on the surface, simpler... Social unrest, never far below the surface in Brazil, has erupted over the last few days... It's brought to the surface a much wider controversy.* N-SING: usu *the* N

4 Surface is used to describe the parts of the armed forces which travel by ship or by land rather than underwater or in the air. *In contrast with its surface fleet, Britain's submarine force was relatively small. ...Soviet surface forces.* ADJ: ADJ n

5 If someone or something under water **surfaces**, they come up to the surface of the water. *He surfaced, gasping for air.* VERB V

6 When something such as a piece of news, a feeling, or a problem **surfaces**, it becomes known or becomes obvious. *The paper says the evidence, when it surfaces, is certain to cause uproar... The emotions will surface at some point in life... The same old problems would surface again.* VERB =emerge V

7 When someone **surfaces**, they appear after not being seen for some time, for example because they have been asleep; an informal use. *There's no chance that he'll surface because he's bound to have heard by now... What time do you surface?* VERB =emerge V

surface mail. Surface mail is the system of sending letters and parcels by road, rail, or sea, not by air. *Goods may be sent by surface mail or airmail.* N-UNCOUNT

surface-to-air. Surface-to-air missiles are fired from the land or sea at aircraft or at other missiles. ADJ: ADJ n

surfboard /sɜːʳfbɔːʳd/ **surfboards.** A **surfboard** is a long narrow board that is used for surfing. N-COUNT

surfeit /sɜːʳfɪt/. A **surfeit** of something is an amount which is too large; a formal word. *Rationing had put an end to a surfeit of biscuits long ago.* N-SING: usu N *of* n =surplus, excess

surfing /sɜːʳfɪŋ/. **Surfing** is the sport of riding on the top of a wave while standing or lying on a special board. ◆◇◇◇◇ N-UNCOUNT

surge /sɜːʳdʒ/ **surges, surging, surged** ◆◆◇◇◇

1 A **surge** is a sudden large increase in something that has previously been steady, or has only in- N-COUNT: usu sing, usu N *in/of* n creased or developed slowly. *Specialists see various reasons for the recent surge in inflation... The anniversary is bound to bring a new surge of interest in Dylan's work.*

2 If something **surges**, it increases suddenly and greatly, after being steady or developing only slowly. *The Freedom Party's electoral support surged from just under 10 per cent to nearly 17 per cent... Surging imports will add to the demand for hard currency.* — VERB =increase; V *from/to/by* amount; V-ing; Also V, V amount

3 If people **surge** forward, they move forward suddenly and powerfully, usually in a crowd. *The photographers and cameramen surged forward. ...the crowd surging out from the church.* — VERB; V adv/prep

4 A **surge** is a sudden powerful movement of a physical force such as wind or water. *The whole car shuddered with an almost frightening surge of power... In the year 1091, London Bridge was destroyed by a tidal surge during a storm.* — N-COUNT: usu sing with supp, oft N *of* n

5 If a physical force such as water or electricity **surges** through something, it moves through it suddenly and powerfully. *Thousands of volts surged through his car after he careered into a lamp post, ripping out live wires... Fish and seaweed rose, caught motionless in the surging water.* — VERB; V adv/prep; V-ing; Also V

6 If you feel a **surge** of a particular emotion or feeling, you experience it suddenly and powerfully. *'It must be very difficult,' said Hunter, feeling a surge of embarrassment for Diane's predicament... He was overcome by a sudden surge of jealousy.* — N-COUNT: usu sing, usu N *of* n

7 If an emotion or sensation **surges** in you or through you, you feel it suddenly and powerfully; a literary use. *Nausea surged in him and he retched violently... Panic surged through her.* — VERB; V *in/through* n ► **Surge up** means the same as **surge**. *A slow hatred for Hilton began to surge up in him... Memories surged up in Don's mind.* — PHRASAL VERB; V P *in* n

surgeon /sɜːʳdʒən/ **surgeons.** A **surgeon** is a doctor who is specially trained to perform surgery. *...a heart surgeon.* • See also **plastic surgeon.** — ◆◆◇◇◇ N-COUNT

surgery /sɜːʳdʒəri/ **surgeries** — ◆◆◆◇◇

1 Surgery is medical treatment in which someone's body is cut open so that a doctor can repair or remove a diseased or damaged part. *His father has just recovered from heart surgery... Mr Clark underwent five hours of emergency surgery.* — N-UNCOUNT
• See also **plastic surgery.**

2 In British English, a **surgery** is the room or house where a doctor or dentist works. *Bill was in the doctor's surgery demanding to know what was wrong with him.* — N-COUNT

3 In British English, a doctor's **surgery** is also the period of time each day when he or she sees patients at his or her surgery. *His surgery always ends at eleven.* — N-COUNT: oft with poss

surgical /sɜːʳdʒɪkəl/ — ◆◆◇◇◇

1 Surgical equipment and clothing is used in surgery. *...an array of surgical instruments. ...a pair of surgical gloves.* — ADJ: ADJ n

2 Surgical treatment involves surgery. *A biopsy is usually a minor surgical procedure. ...surgical removal of a tumor.* — ADJ: ADJ n ♦ **surgically** *In very severe cases, bunions may be surgically removed.* — ADV: ADV with v

3 Surgical military actions are designed to attack or destroy a particular target without harming other people or damaging other buildings nearby. *...a surgical strike aimed at a terrorist organization.* — ADJ: ADJ n

surgical spirit. **Surgical spirit** is a liquid which is used to clean and sterilize wounds or surgical instruments. It consists mainly of alcohol. — N-UNCOUNT

surly /sɜːʳli/ **surlier, surliest.** Someone who is **surly** behaves in a rude bad-tempered way; used in written English. *He became surly and rude towards me.* — ADJ-GRADED =churlish

surmise /səʳmaɪz/ **surmises, surmising, surmised**

1 If you **surmise** that something is true, you guess it from the available evidence, although you do not know for certain; a formal use. *There's so little to go on, we can only surmise what happened... He surmised that he had discovered one of the illegal streets.* — VERB =infer; V wh; V that; Also V, V n

2 If you say that a particular conclusion is **surmise**, you mean that it is a guess based on the available evidence and you do not know for certain that it is true; a formal use. *It is mere surmise that Bosch had Brant's poem in mind when doing this painting... His surmise proved correct.* — N-VAR =conjecture

surmount /səʳmaʊnt/ **surmounts, surmounting, surmounted** — ◆◇◇◇◇

1 If you **surmount** a problem or difficulty, you deal successfully with it. *I realized I had to surmount the language barrier.* — VERB =overcome; V n

2 If something **is surmounted** by a particular thing, that thing is on top of it; a formal use. *The island is surmounted by a huge black castle.* — VB: usu passive; *be* V-ed

surname /sɜːʳneɪm/ **surnames.** Your **surname** is the name that you share with other members of your family. In English speaking countries and many other countries it is your last name. *She'd never known his surname... The majority of British women adopt their husband's surname when they marry.* — ◆◇◇◇◇ N-COUNT

surpass /səʳpɑːs, -pæs/ **surpasses, surpassing, surpassed** — ◆◇◇◇◇

1 If one person or thing **surpasses** another, the first is better than, or has more of a particular quality than, the second. *He was determined to surpass the achievements of his older brothers... Warwick Arts Centre is the second largest Arts Centre in Britain, surpassed in size only by London's Barbican.* — VERB =exceed; V n; V-ed

2 If something **surpasses** expectations it is much better than it was expected to be. *Conrad Black gave an excellent party that surpassed expectations.* — VERB; V n

3 If something **surpasses** understanding, it is too difficult to understand. *...a clever and spectacularly successful system, the detailed complexity of which surpasses our full understanding.* — VERB; V n

surplice /sɜːʳplɪs/ **surplices.** A **surplice** is a loose white knee-length garment which is worn over a long robe by priests and members of the choir in some churches. *...the priest and choir in their lace surplices.* — N-COUNT

surplus /sɜːʳpləs/ **surpluses** — ◆◆◆◇◇

1 If there is a **surplus** of something, there is more than is needed. *Germany suffers from a surplus of teachers.* — N-VAR

2 Surplus is used to describe something that is extra or that is more than is needed. *Few people have large sums of surplus cash... Farmers can now sell all surplus beef to the European Community for storage... The houses are being sold because they are surplus to requirements.* — ADJ: usu ADJ n, also v-link ADJ *to* n =extra

3 If a country has a trade **surplus**, it exports more than it imports. *Japan's annual trade surplus is in the region of 100 billion dollars.* — N-COUNT: usu n N

4 If a government has a budget **surplus**, it has spent less than it received in revenue. *Norway's budget surplus has fallen from 5.9% in 1986 to an expected 0.1% this year.* — N-COUNT: usu n N

surprise /səʳpraɪz/ **surprises, surprising, surprised** — ◆◆◆◆◇

1 A **surprise** is an unexpected event, fact, or piece of news. *I have a surprise for you: We are moving to Switzerland!... It may come as a surprise to some that a normal, healthy child is born with many skills... It is perhaps no surprise to see another 60s singing star attempting a comeback.* — N-COUNT: oft N *to* n ► Also an adjective. *Baxter arrived here this afternoon, on a surprise visit... German intelligence expected Japan to launch a surprise attack on the US, and Pearl Harbor was the likely target.* — ADJ: ADJ n

2 Surprise is the feeling that you have when something unexpected happens. *The Foreign Office in London has expressed surprise at these allegations... 'You mean he's going to vote against her?' Scobie asked in surprise... I started working hard for the first time in my life. To my surprise, I found I liked it.* — N-UNCOUNT

3 If something **surprises** you, it gives you a feeling of surprise. *We'll solve the case ourselves and surprise everyone... It surprised me that a driver of* — VERB; V n; *it* V n that/if; V pron-refl

Alain's experience should make those mistakes... It wouldn't surprise me if there was such chaos after this election that another had to be held... They were served lamb and rosemary and she surprised herself by eating greedily.

4 If you **surprise** someone, you give them, tell them, or do something pleasant that they are not expecting. *Surprise a new neighbour with one of your favourite home-made dishes.* VERB V n *with* n Also V n

5 If you describe someone or something as a **surprise**, you mean that they are very good or pleasant although you were not expecting this. *...Senga MacFie, one of the surprises of the World Championships three months ago... My father decided to slip a little extra spending money into my purse as a surprise.* N-COUNT

6 If you **surprise** someone, you attack, capture, or find them when they are not expecting it. *Marlborough led his armies across the Rhine and surprised the French and Bavarian armies near the village of Blenheim.* VERB V n

7 See also **surprised, surprising**.

8 You can say **'surprise, surprise'** if you disapprove of something because it is not surprising or original, or could easily have been predicted. *There is a shortage of carrots. So everybody starts growing carrots. Next season, surprise, surprise, there is a glut of carrots.* PHRASES PHR with cl PRAGMATICS

9 You can say **'surprise, surprise'** if you meet someone you know or give them something when they are not expecting it; used in spoken English. *He came back in as I was heading up to the shower. 'Surprise, surprise,' he said.* PRAGMATICS

10 If something **takes** you **by surprise**, it happens when you are not expecting it or when you are not prepared for it. *His question took his two companions by surprise... Whenever it snows in Britain we are taken by surprise.* V inflects

surprised /səʳpraɪzd/. ◆◆◆◇◇

1 If you are **surprised** at something, you have a feeling of surprise, because it is unexpected or unusual. *This lady was genuinely surprised at what happened to her pet... Chang seemed surprised to find the big living-room empty... Reading the ideas of the so-called experts, I am not surprised the country is in such a state.* ADJ-GRADED: usu v-link ADJ, oft ADJ *at/by* n, ADJ to-inf, ADJ that/how

2 See also **surprise**.

surprising /səʳpraɪzɪŋ/. ◆◆◆◇◇

1 Something that is **surprising** is unexpected or unusual and makes you feel surprised. *It is not surprising that children learn to read at different rates... A surprising number of customers order the same sandwich every day.* ♦ **surprisingly** *...the Flemish Bloc, which did surprisingly well in the general election last year... Not surprisingly, he enjoyed telling tales about his time at the military academy.* ADJ-GRADED: oft *it* v-link ADJ that/to-inf ≠unsurprising ADV-GRADED: ADV with cl, ADV adj/adv

2 See also **surprise**.

surreal /səriːəl/. If you describe something as **surreal**, you mean that the elements in it are combined in a strange dreamlike way that you would not normally expect. *'Performance' is undoubtedly one of the most surreal movies ever made.* ◆◇◇◇◇ ADJ-GRADED

Surrealism /səriːəlɪzəm/. **Surrealism** is a style in art and literature in which ideas, images, and objects are combined in a strange dreamlike way. *His early work was influenced by the European surrealism of the 1930's.* N-UNCOUNT

surrealist /səriːəlɪst/ **surrealists** ◆◇◇◇◇

1 **Surrealist** means related to or in the style of surrealism. *Dali's shoe hat was undoubtedly the most surrealist idea he ever worked on with Schiaparelli.* ADJ-GRADED

2 A **Surrealist** is an artist or writer whose work is based on the ideas of surrealism. N-COUNT

surrealistic /səriːəlɪstɪk/

1 **Surrealistic** means the same as surreal. *What gives this movie a strange Sixties atmosphere is the surrealistic way it plays with time and character.* ADJ-GRADED

2 **Surrealistic** means related to or in the style of surrealism. *Man Ray's surrealistic study of a woman's face with glass teardrops.* ADJ: ADJ n

surrender /sərendəʳ/ **surrenders, surrendering, surrendered** ◆◆◆◇◇

1 If you **surrender**, you stop fighting or resisting someone and agree that you have been beaten. *General Martin Bonnet called on the rebels to surrender... We'll never surrender to the terrorists.* ► Also a noun. *...the government's apparent surrender to demands made by the religious militants.* VERB V V *to* n N-VAR: oft N *to* n

2 If you **surrender** something you would rather keep, you give it up or let someone else have it, for example after a struggle. *Nadja had to fill out forms surrendering all rights to her property... Gen. Morgan's troops yesterday surrendered their heavy weapons to Belgian and US troops.* ► Also a noun. *...the sixteen-day deadline for the surrender of weapons and ammunition.* VERB =relinquish V n V n *to* n N-UNCOUNT: usu N *of* n

3 If you **surrender** something such as a ticket or your passport, you give it to someone in authority when they ask you to; a formal use. *They have been ordered to surrender their passports.* VERB V n

4 You use **surrender** to refer to someone's attitude or behaviour when they lose the will to resist their feelings or the demands of other people; a literary use. *...the need for total personal surrender to and dependence on Jesus... Depression is a partial surrender to death... A look of disbelief came into his eyes, but was quickly replaced by one of dismal surrender.* N-UNCOUNT: also *a* N, oft N *to* n

surrender value, surrender values. The **surrender value** of a life insurance policy is the amount of money you receive if you decide you no longer wish to continue with the policy; a technical term in insurance. N-COUNT

surreptitious /sʌrəptɪʃəs, AM sɜːr-/. A **surreptitious** action is done secretly. *He made a surreptitious entrance to the club through the little door in the brick wall... They had several surreptitious conversations.* ♦ **surreptitiously** *Surreptitiously Mark looked at his watch.* ◆◇◇◇◇ ADJ-GRADED =furtive ADV-GRADED: ADV with v

surrogacy /sʌrəgəsi, AM sɜːr-/. **Surrogacy** is an arrangement by which a woman gives birth to a baby on behalf of a woman who cannot have babies herself because she is infertile. *In this country it is illegal to pay for surrogacy.* N-UNCOUNT

surrogate /sʌrəgeɪt, AM sɜːr-/ **surrogates.** You use **surrogate** to describe a person or thing that acts as a substitute for someone or something else. *Martin had become Howard Cosell's surrogate son... John Brown was the latest in a series of surrogate father figures in Victoria's life... Leningrad was the third alien city to offer him a surrogate home.* ► Also a noun. *Arms control should not be made into a surrogate for peace.* ◆◇◇◇◇ ADJ: ADJ n =substitute N-COUNT

surrogate mother, surrogate mothers. A **surrogate mother** is a woman who has agreed to give birth to a baby on behalf of another woman. N-COUNT

surround /səraʊnd/ **surrounds, surrounding, surrounded** ◆◆◆◆◇

1 If something or someone **is surrounded** by something, that thing is situated all around them. *The small churchyard was surrounded by a rusted wrought-iron fence... The shell surrounding the egg has many important functions. ...the snipers and artillerymen in the surrounding hills.* VERB *be* V-ed V n V-ing

2 If you **are surrounded** by soldiers or police, they spread out so that they are in positions all the way around you. *When the car stopped in the town square it was surrounded by soldiers and militiamen... He tried to run away but gave up when he found himself surrounded... Shooting broke out after the guards surrounded a villa in the city.* VERB =encircle *be* V-ed V-ed V n

3 The circumstances, feelings, or ideas which **surround** something are those that are closely associated with it. *The decision had been agreed in principle before today's meeting, but some controversy surrounded it... Once the euphoria surrounding this victory subsides, reality must return.* VERB V n

4 If you **surround** yourself **with** certain people or things, you make sure that you have a lot of them near you all the time. *He had made it his business to surround himself with a hand-picked group of* VERB V n *with/by* n

bright young officers... They love being surrounded by familiar possessions.

5 The **surround** of something such as a fireplace is the border, wall, or shelves around it. *...a small fireplace with a cast-iron surround.* N-COUNT

6 Your **surrounds** are your **surroundings**. *The entire team enjoyed hot showers in the spacious surrounds of a new, modern village hall.* N-PLURAL

surroundings /səra͟ʊndɪŋz/. When you are describing the place where you are at the moment, or the place where you live, you can refer to it as your **surroundings**. *Schumacher adapted effortlessly to his new surroundings. ...a peaceful holiday home in beautiful surroundings.* ◆◆◇◇◇ N-PLURAL: oft poss N, *in* N with supp

surtax /sɜ͟ːʳtæks/. **Surtax** is an additional tax on incomes higher than the level at which ordinary tax is paid. *...a 10% surtax for Americans earning more than $250,000 a year.* N-UNCOUNT

surveillance /səʳve͟ɪləns/. **Surveillance** is the careful watching of someone, especially by an organization such as the police or the army. *He was arrested after being kept under constant surveillance... Police swooped on the home after a two-week surveillance operation... Police keep track of the kidnapper using electronic surveillance equipment.* ◆◆◇◇◇ N-UNCOUNT

survey, surveys, surveying, surveyed. The noun is pronounced /sɜ͟ːʳveɪ/. The verb is pronounced /səʳve͟ɪ/, and can also be pronounced /sɜ͟ːʳveɪ/ in meanings 2 and 6. ◆◆◆◆◇

1 If you carry out a **survey**, you try to find out detailed information about a lot of different people or things, usually by asking people a series of questions. *The council conducted a survey of the uses to which farm buildings are put... According to the survey, overall world trade has also slackened.* N-COUNT

2 If you **survey** a number of people, companies, or organizations, you try to find out information about their opinions or behaviour, usually by asking them a series of questions. *Business Development Advisers surveyed 211 companies for the report... Only 18 percent of those surveyed opposed the idea.* VERB V n V-ed

3 If you **survey** something, you look at or consider the whole of it carefully. *He pushed himself to his feet and surveyed the room... He surveys American politics with a conservative world view.* VERB V n

4 If you give something a brief **survey** or a quick **survey**, you look at or consider all of it quickly, but not in detail. *...a brief survey of some important books on astrology... He sniffed the perfume she wore, then gave her a quick survey.* N-SING: with supp, oft N *of* n

5 If someone carries out a **survey** of an area of land, they examine it and measure it, usually in order to make a map of it. *...the organizer of the geological survey of India... The scientists conducted two aerial surveys followed by two ground surveys.* N-COUNT

6 If someone **surveys** an area of land, they examine it and measure it, usually in order to make a map of it. *Scarborough Council commissioned geological experts earlier this year to survey the cliffs.* VERB V n
♦ **surveying** *...data relating to astronomy, astrology, surveying and navigation. ...surveying equipment.* N-UNCOUNT

7 A **survey** is a careful examination of the condition and structure of a house, usually carried out in order to give advice to a person who wants to buy it; used mainly in British English. *...a structural survey undertaken by a qualified surveyor.* N-COUNT =inspection

8 If someone **surveys** a house, they examine it carefully and report on its structure, usually in order to give advice to a person who is thinking of buying it; used mainly in British English. *...the people who surveyed the house for the mortgage.* VERB =inspect V n
♦ **surveying** *In more than 30 years of surveying he has never yet known a building to collapse because of subsidence.* N-UNCOUNT

surveyor /səʳve͟ɪəʳ/ **surveyors** ◆◇◇◇◇

1 A **surveyor** is a person whose job is to survey land. *...the surveyor's maps of the Queen Alexandra Range.* N-COUNT

2 In British English, a **surveyor** is a person whose job is to survey buildings. *Our surveyor warned us that the house needed totally rebuilding.* N-COUNT

3 See also **quantity surveyor**.

survival /səʳva͟ɪvəl/ ◆◆◆◇◇

1 If you refer to the **survival** of something or someone, you mean that they manage to continue or exist in spite of difficult circumstances. *...companies which have been struggling for survival in the advancing recession... Ask for the free booklet 'Debt: a Survival Guide'.* N-UNCOUNT

2 If you refer to the **survival** of a person or living thing, you mean that they live through a dangerous situation in which it was possible that they might die. *If cancers are spotted early there's a high chance of survival... An animal's sense of smell is still crucial to its survival.* N-UNCOUNT

3 You can use **the survival of the fittest** to refer to a situation in which only the strongest people or things continue to live or be successful, while the others die or fail. PHRASE

survive /səʳva͟ɪv/ **survives, surviving, survived** ◆◆◆◆◇

1 If a person or living thing **survives** in a dangerous situation such as an accident or an illness, they do not die. *...the sequence of events that left the eight pupils battling to survive in icy seas for over four hours... Those organisms that are that are most suited to the environment will be those that will survive... Drugs that dissolve blood clots can help people survive heart attacks.* VERB V V n

2 If you **survive** in difficult circumstances, you manage to live or continue in spite of them and do not let them affect you very much. *On my first day here I thought, 'Ooh, how will I survive?' ...people who are struggling to survive without jobs... Jim Hogg survives on £65 pounds a fortnight after losing his job. ...a man who had survived his share of boardroom coups.* VERB V V *on* n V n

3 If something **survives**, it continues to exist although there is a risk of it being destroyed or abolished. *When the market economy is introduced, many factories will not survive... The chances of a planet surviving a supernova always looked terribly slim. ...surviving examples of 19th-century architecture in the Mid-West.* VERB V V n V-ing

4 If you **survive** someone, you continue to live after they have died. *Most women will survive their spouses... She is survived by two daughters from her first marriage. ...William Shakespeare's last surviving descendant.* VERB V n V-ing

survivor /səʳva͟ɪvəʳ/ **survivors** ◆◆◇◇◇

1 A **survivor** of a disaster, accident, or illness is someone who continues to live afterwards in spite of coming close to death. *Officials said there were no survivors of the plane crash.* N-COUNT: oft N *of* n

2 A **survivor** of a very unpleasant experience is a person who has had such an experience, and who is still affected by it. *This book is written with survivors of child sexual abuse in mind.* N-COUNT: oft N *of* n

3 If you describe someone as a **survivor**, you approve of the fact that they are able to carry on with their life even though they experience many difficulties. *Above all Susie is a great survivor, with a bright, indomitable spirit.* N-COUNT PRAGMATICS

4 If you describe someone or something as a **survivor** from an earlier period, you mean that they are still present or available, while other people or things from that period have disappeared or been lost. *Rafferty was the sole survivor from the successful Ireland team of 1988. ...a black 1950 Cyclops, which is the only known survivor of 30 test cars built by Rover.* N-COUNT: oft N *from* n

susceptibility /səse͟ptɪbɪ̱lɪti/ **susceptibilities** ◆◇◇◇◇

1 If you have a **susceptibility** to something unpleasant you are likely to be affected by it. *...his increased susceptibility to infections.* N-VAR =vulnerability

2 A person's **susceptibilities** are feelings which can be easily hurt. *I am well aware that in saying this I shall outrage a few susceptibilities.* N-PLURAL =sensibilities

susceptible /səse͟ptɪbəl/ ◆◇◇◇◇

1 If you are **susceptible to** something or someone, you are very likely to be influenced by them. *Young* ADJ-GRADED: v-link ADJ *to* n *people are the most susceptible to advertisements... James was extremely susceptible to flattery... He was, she believes, unusually susceptible to women.*

2 If you are **susceptible to** a disease or injury, you are very likely to be affected by it. *Walking with weights makes the shoulders very susceptible to injury... Diesel exhaust is particularly aggravating to many susceptible individuals.* — ADJ-GRADED: usu v-link ADJ *to* n =vulnerable

3 A **susceptible** person is very easily influenced emotionally. *Hers was a susceptible nature.* — ADJ-GRADED: ADJ n

sushi /suːʃi/. **Sushi** is a Japanese dish of rice with sweet vinegar, often served with raw fish. — N-UNCOUNT

suspect, suspects, suspecting, suspected. ◆◆◆◆◇ The verb is pronounced /səspekt/. The noun is pronounced /sʌspekt/.

1 You use **suspect** when you are stating something that you believe is probably true, in order to make it sound less strong or direct. *I suspect they were right... The above complaints are, I suspect, just the tip of the iceberg... Do women really share such stupid jokes? We suspect not.* — VERB [PRAGMATICS] V that, V *not/so*

2 If you **suspect** that something dishonest or unpleasant has been done, you believe that it has probably been done. If you **suspect** someone of doing an action of this kind, you believe that they probably did it. *He suspected that the woman staying in the flat above was using heroin... Interpol suspects there may be a terrorist attack in Rio de Janeiro next week... It was perfectly all right, he said, because the police had not suspected him of anything... You don't really think Webb suspects you?... Frears was rushed to hospital with a suspected heart attack.* — VERB: V that, V n *of* n, V n, V-ed, Also V wh

3 A **suspect** is a person who the police or authorities think may be guilty of a crime. *Police have arrested a suspect in a series of killings and sexual assaults in the city.* — N-COUNT

4 **Suspect** things or people cannot be trusted and must be dealt with cautiously, because there is some aspect of them that makes you think that they are not genuine or that they are less good than they appear. *Delegates evacuated the building when a suspect package was found... The firm has taken out adverts in national newspapers to urge customers to return suspect products... The whole affair has been highly suspect.* — ADJ-GRADED

suspend /səspend/ **suspends, suspending, suspended** ◆◆◆◇◇

1 If you **suspend** something, you delay it or stop it from happening for a while or until a decision is made about it. *The union suspended strike action this week... A UN official said aid programs will be suspended until there's adequate protection for relief convoys.* — VERB: V n

2 If someone **is suspended**, they are prevented from holding a particular job or position for a fixed length of time or until a decision is made about them. *Julie was suspended from her job shortly after the incident... Buchanan was suspended for a year from Georgetown University after brawling with police... The Lawn Tennis Association has also suspended Mr Castle from the British team.* — VERB: *be* V-ed, V n

3 If something **is suspended** from a high place, it is hanging from that place. *...a mobile of birds or nursery rhyme characters which could be suspended over the cot. ...chandeliers suspended on heavy chains from the ceiling.* — VB: usu passive *be* V-ed, V-ed

suspended animation

1 **Suspended animation** is a state in which the important body functions of an animal are slowed down for a period of time. This is done by freezing or because the animal hibernates. — N-UNCOUNT

2 If you describe someone as being in a state of **suspended animation**, you mean that they have become inactive and are doing nothing. *She lay in a state of suspended animation, waiting for dawnlight, when she would rise... The Hague conference is in suspended animation.* — N-UNCOUNT

suspended sentence, suspended sentences. If a criminal is given a **suspended sentence**, they are given a prison sentence which they have to serve if they commit another crime within a specified period of time. *John was given a four-month suspended sentence.* — N-COUNT

suspender /səspendəʳ/ **suspenders**

1 In British English, **suspenders** are the fastenings which hang down from a suspender belt and hold up a woman's stockings. The American word is **garter**. — N-COUNT: usu pl

2 In American English, **suspenders** are a pair of straps that go over someone's shoulders and are fastened to their trousers at the front and at the back to prevent the trousers from falling down. The British word is **braces**. — N-PLURAL: also *a pair of* N =braces

suspender belt, suspender belts. In British English, a **suspender belt** is a piece of underwear for women that is used for holding up stockings. The American expression is **garter belt**. — N-COUNT

suspense /səspens/ ◆◇◇◇◇

1 **Suspense** is a state of excitement or anxiety about something that is going to happen very soon, for example about some news that you are waiting to hear. *The suspense over the two remaining hostages ended last night when the police discovered the bullet ridden bodies. ...a writer who holds the suspense throughout her tale.* — N-UNCOUNT

2 If you **keep** or **leave** someone **in suspense**, you deliberately delay telling them something that they are very eager to know about. *Keppler kept all his men in suspense until that morning before announcing which two would be going... 'Go on, don't leave us in suspense,' Dennis said.* — PHRASE: V inflects, PHR after v

suspenseful /səspensfʊl/. A **suspenseful** story or situation has a lot of suspense in it. *...a suspenseful and sinister tale.* — ADJ-GRADED: usu ADJ n

suspension /səspenʃᵊn/ **suspensions** ◆◆◇◇◇

1 The **suspension** of something is the act of delaying or stopping it for a while or until a decision is made about it. *A strike by British Airways ground staff has led to the suspension of flights between London and Manchester... The terrorists say their so-called suspension of violence will end at midnight tonight.* — N-UNCOUNT

2 Someone's **suspension** is their removal from a job or position for a period of time or until a decision is made about them. *The minister warned that any civil servant not at his desk faced immediate suspension... The athlete received a two-year suspension following a positive drug test.* — N-VAR

3 A vehicle's **suspension** consists of the springs and shock absorbers attached to the wheels, which give a smooth ride in spite of bumps in the road. — N-VAR

suspension bridge, suspension bridges. A **suspension bridge** is a type of bridge that is supported from above by cables. — N-COUNT

suspicion /səspɪʃᵊn/ **suspicions** ◆◆◆◇◇

1 **Suspicion** or a **suspicion** is a belief or feeling that someone has committed a crime or done something wrong. *There was a suspicion that this runner attempted to avoid the procedures for dope testing... The police said their suspicions were aroused because Mr Owens had other marks on his body... Scotland Yard had assured him he was not under suspicion... An East German has been arrested in Switzerland on suspicion of spying.* — N-VAR: oft N that, N *of* n, *under* N, *on* N *of* n

2 If there is **suspicion** of someone or something, people do not trust them or consider them to be reliable. *This tendency in his thought is deepened by his suspicion of all Utopian political programmes... Our culture harbors deep suspicions of big-time industry... I was always regarded in the Army with a certain amount of suspicion because of my left-wing tendencies.* — N-VAR: oft N *of* n

3 A **suspicion** is a feeling that something is probably true or is likely to happen. *I have a sneaking suspicion that they are going to succeed... Astronomers will have to collect more spectra from these stars to confirm their suspicions.* — N-COUNT: oft N that

4 A **suspicion** of something is a very small amount or trace of it; used in written English. *...large blooms of white with a suspicion of pale pink.* — N-SING: usu N *of* n =hint

5 • to **point the finger of suspicion**: see **finger**.

suspicious /səspɪʃəs/ 

1 If you are **suspicious** of someone or something, — ADJ-GRADED:

you do not trust them, and deal with them cautiously. *He was rightly suspicious of meeting me until I reassured him I was not writing about him... He has his father's suspicious nature.* ♦ **suspiciously** *'What's the matter with you?' Jake asked suspiciously. 'What have you been up to?'* oft ADJ *of*n/-ing ADV-GRADED: ADV after v

2 If you are **suspicious** of someone or something, you believe that they are probably involved in a crime or some dishonest activity. *Two officers on patrol became suspicious of two men in a car... A woman kept prisoner in a basement was rescued after suspicious neighbours tipped off police.* ADJ-GRADED: oft ADJ *of*n

3 If you describe someone or something as **suspicious**, you mean that there is some aspect of them which makes you think that they are involved in a crime or a dishonest activity. *He reported that two suspicious-looking characters had approached Callendar... Nottingham police last night found what they described as a suspicious package.* ♦ **suspiciously** *They'll question them as to whether anyone was seen acting suspiciously in the area over the last few days... Police were told to arrest voters found with suspiciously large sums of money in their pockets.* ADJ-GRADED ADV-GRADED: ADV with v, ADV adj/adv

suspiciously /səspɪʃəsli/ ◆◇◇◇◇

1 If you say that something looks or sounds **suspiciously** like a particular thing, you mean that it probably is that thing, or something very similar to it, although it may give the impression of being something different. *The tan-coloured dog looks suspiciously like an American pit bull terrier... 'Yes,' he replied, though it sounded suspiciously like a question.* ADV: ADV prep

2 You can use **suspiciously** when you are describing something that you think is slightly strange or not as it should be. *He lives alone in a suspiciously tidy flat in Notting Hill Gate... The jellies were topped with suspiciously synthetic blobs of cream.* ADV: ADV adj/adv

3 See also **suspicious**.

suss /sʌs/ **susses, sussing, sussed.** In British English, if you **suss** a person or situation, you realize or work out what their real character or nature is; an informal word. *I think I've sussed the reason for it... The women began to suss that there was no reason why they should be impressed by him... We're getting the problem sussed.* ► **Suss out** means the same as **suss**. *They're sussing out the area to see how strong the police presence is... He susses his colleagues out and he knows who he can trust... I'd had the training to suss out what he was up to.* VERB =figure out V n V that get n V-ed Also V wh PHRASAL VERB V P n (not pron) V n P V P wh Also V that

sussed /sʌst/. In British English, if someone is **sussed**, they are clever and knowledgeable, often about a particular thing such as clothes, pop music, or politics; an informal word. ADJ-GRADED =smart

sustain /səsteɪn/ **sustains, sustaining, sustained** ◆◆◆◇◇

1 If you **sustain** something, you continue it or maintain it for a period of time. *Mandela has to be patient if he's to sustain his position as a great international figure... The parameters within which life can be sustained on Earth are extraordinarily narrow. ...a period of sustained economic growth throughout 1995.* VERB V n V-ed

2 If you **sustain** something such as a defeat, loss, or injury, it happens to you; a formal use. *Every aircraft in there has sustained some damage... A seventeen-year-old tourist died late last night of injuries sustained in yesterday's bomb blast.* VERB =suffer V n V-ed

3 If something **sustains** you, it supports you by giving you help, strength, or encouragement; a formal use. *The cash dividends they get from the cash crop would sustain them during the lean season... I am sustained by letters of support and what people say to me in ordinary daily life... Sustained by this wonderful breakfast, it was with restored morale that we re-boarded our plane.* VERB V n V-ed

sustainable /səsteɪnəbəl/ ◆◇◇◇◇

1 You use **sustainable** to describe the use of natural resources when this use is kept at a steady level that is not likely to damage the environment. *...the management, conservation and sustainable development of forests... Try to buy wood that you know has come from a sustainable source.* ♦ **sustainability** /səsteɪnəbɪlɪti/ *...the growing concern about environmental sustainability.* ♦ **sustainably** *It wants timber to come, where possible, from sustainably managed sources.* ADJ-GRADED N-UNCOUNT ADV: ADV with v

2 A **sustainable** plan, method, or system can be continued at the same pace or level of activity without harming its efficiency and the people affected by it. *The creation of an efficient and sustainable transport system is critical to the long-term future of London. ...a sustainable recovery in consumer spending.* ♦ **sustainability** *...doubts about the sustainability of the current economic expansion.* ADJ-GRADED ≠unsustainable N-UNCOUNT: oft *the* N *of*n

sustenance /sʌstɪnəns/. **Sustenance** is food or drink which a person, animal, or plant needs to remain alive and healthy; a formal word. *The state provided a basic quantity of food for daily sustenance, but little else.* N-UNCOUNT

suture /suːtʃəʳ/ **sutures.** A **suture** is a stitch made to join together the open parts of a wound, especially one made after a patient has been operated on; a medical term. N-COUNT

svelte /svelt, sfelt/. Someone who is **svelte** is attractively slim, elegant, and stylish. ADJ-GRADED =slender

SW. **SW** is a written abbreviation for **south-west**. *...King's Road, London SW 3.*

swab /swɒb/ **swabs, swabbing, swabbed**

1 A **swab** is a small piece of cotton wool used by a doctor or nurse for cleaning a wound or for applying ointment or disinfectant. N-COUNT

2 If you **swab** something, you clean it using a wet cloth or mop. *I noticed a lone man in the cafeteria swabbing the floor as I passed.* VERB V n

swaddle /swɒdəl/ **swaddles, swaddling, swaddled.** If you **swaddle** a baby, you wrap cloth or a shawl around it in order to keep it warm or to prevent it from moving; an old-fashioned word. *Swaddle your newborn baby so that she feels secure. ...a baby swaddled in silk brocade.* VERB V n V-ed

swag /swæg/ **swags**

1 **Swag** is stolen goods, or money obtained illegally; an old-fashioned, informal word. N-UNCOUNT

2 A **swag** is a piece of material that is hung above a window in such a way that it hangs down ornamentally. N-COUNT

swagger /swægəʳ/ **swaggers, swaggering, swaggered.** If you **swagger**, you walk in a proud, over-confident way, holding your body upright and swinging your hips. *A broad shouldered man wearing a dinner jacket swaggered confidently up to the bar... The burly brute swaggered forward, towering over me, and shouted... John Steed was an arrogant, swaggering young man.* ► Also a noun. *He walked with something of a swagger.* ◆◇◇◇◇ VERB =strut V prep/adv V-ing Also V N-SING

swain /sweɪn/ **swains.** A **swain** is a young man who is in love; an old-fashioned word. N-COUNT =beau

swallow /swɒloʊ/ **swallows, swallowing, swallowed** ◆◆◇◇◇

1 If you **swallow** something, you cause it to go from your mouth down into your stomach. *You are asked to swallow a capsule containing vitamin B... Polly took a bite of the apple, chewed and swallowed.* ► Also a noun. *Jan lifted her glass and took a quick swallow.* VERB V n V N-COUNT

2 If you **swallow**, you make a movement in your throat as if you are swallowing something, often because you are nervous or frightened. *Nancy swallowed hard and shook her head.* VERB V

3 If someone **swallows** a story or a statement, they believe it completely. *They cast doubt on his words when it suited their case, but swallowed them whole when it did not... I too found this story a little hard to swallow.* VERB V n

4 If you **swallow** your feelings, you do not express them, although you want to very much. *Gordon has swallowed the anger he felt... He flashed me a quick grin but rapidly swallowed it when he saw my expression.* VERB =stifle V n

5 A **swallow** is a kind of small bird with pointed wings and a forked tail. N-COUNT

6 • **a bitter pill to swallow**: see **pill**. • to **swallow** one's **pride**: see **pride**.

swallow up PHRASAL VERB

1 If one thing **is swallowed up** by another, it becomes part of the first thing and no longer has a separate identity of its own. *During the 1980s monster publishing houses started to swallow up smaller companies.* V P n (not pron) Also V n P

2 If something **swallows up** money or resources, it uses them entirely while giving very little in return. *A seven-day TV ad campaign could swallow up the best part of £50,000... Farmers could see a quarter of their income swallowed up by the interest rate rise.* V P n (not pron) V-ed P Also V n P

3 If someone or something **is swallowed up** by something, they disappear into it so that you cannot see them any more. *He headed back towards the flea market and was quickly swallowed up in the crowd... Weeds had swallowed up the garden.* be V-ed P V P n (not pron) Also V n P

swam /swæm/. **Swam** is the past tense of **swim**.

swamp /swɒmp/ **swamps, swamping, swamped** ◆◆◇◇◇

1 A **swamp** is an area of very wet land with wild plants growing in it. N-VAR

2 If something **swamps** a place or object, it fills it with water. *Their electronic navigation failed and a rogue wave swamped the boat... The Ventura river burst its banks, swamping a mobile home park.* VERB V n

3 If you **are swamped** by things or people, you have more of them than you can deal with. *He is swamped with work... The railway station was swamped with thousands of families trying to flee the city.* VB: usu passive be V-ed

swampland /swɒmplænd/ **swamplands.** N-VAR **Swampland** is an area that is permanently swampy.

swampy /swɒmpi/ **swampier, swampiest.** A **swampy** area of land consists mainly of swamps. ADJ-GRADED

swan /swɒn/ **swans, swanning, swanned** ◆◇◇◇◇

1 A **swan** is a large bird with a very long neck. Swans live on rivers and lakes and are usually white. N-COUNT

2 In informal British English, if you describe someone as **swanning around**, **swanning about**, or **swanning off**, you mean that they are wandering about or going somewhere in a leisurely and irresponsible manner. *She spends her time swanning around the world... Swanning about at a party he came face-to-face with his auntie... The mother was widowed and had swanned off.* VERB V prep/adv

swank /swæŋk/ **swanks, swanking, swanked**

1 If someone is **swanking**, they are speaking in a boastful way in order to impress other people; used showing disapproval; used mainly in informal British English. *I have always been against swanking about all the things I have been lucky enough to win.* ► Also a noun. *There was no swank in Martin.* VERB PRAGMATICS =brag V about n Also V N-UNCOUNT

2 **Swank** means the same as **swanky**; an informal word. *...a swank new shop on the outskirts of Beijing.* ADJ-GRADED: usu ADJ n

swanky /swæŋki/ **swankier, swankiest.** If you describe something as **swanky**, you mean that it is glamorous, fashionable, and expensive; an informal word. *...one of the swanky hotels that line the Pacific shore at Acapulco.* ADJ-GRADED: usu ADJ n =ritzy

swan song; also spelled **swan-song**. Someone's **swan song** is the last time that they do something for which they are famous, for example the last time that an actor gives a performance in the theatre. *I competed in the Commonwealth Games in Christchurch, which was my swan song.* N-SING

swap /swɒp/ **swaps, swapping, swapped;** also spelled **swop**. ◆◆◇◇◇

1 If you **swap** something with someone, you give it to them and receive something else in exchange. *Next week they will swap places and will repeat the switch weekly... I'd gladly swap places with mummy any day... I know a sculptor who swaps her pieces for drawings by a well-known artist... Some hostages were swapped for convicted prisoners.* ► Also a noun. *If she ever fancies a job swap, I could be interested.* V-RECIP =exchange V pl-n V pl-n with n V n for/with n N-COUNT: oft n N

2 If you **swap** one thing for another, you remove the first thing and replace it with the second, or you stop doing the first thing and start doing the second. *Despite the heat, he'd swapped his overalls for a suit and tie... He has swapped his hectic rock star's lifestyle for that of a country gentleman... Both sides swapped their goalies in the 30th minute.* VERB V n for n V n

3 If you **swap** stories or opinions with someone, you tell each other stories or give each other your opinions. *They all sat together at table, laughing and swapping stories.* VERB V pl-n

swarm /swɔːʳm/ **swarms, swarming, swarmed** ◆◇◇◇◇

1 A **swarm** of bees or other insects is a large group of them flying together. N-COUNT-COLL: oft N of n

2 When bees or other insects **swarm**, they move or fly in a large group. *A dark cloud of bees comes swarming out of the hive.* VERB V prep/adv Also V

3 When people **swarm** somewhere, they move there quickly in a large group. *People swarmed to the shops, buying up everything in sight.* VERB V prep/adv Also V n

4 A **swarm** of people is a large group of them moving about quickly. *A swarm of people encircled the hotel... Today at the crossing there were swarms of tourists taking photographs.* N-COUNT-COLL: oft N of n =horde

5 If a place **is swarming** with people, it is full of people moving about in a busy way. *Within minutes the area was swarming with officers who began searching a nearby wood.* VB: usu cont V with n

swarthy /swɔːʳði/. A **swarthy** person has a dark complexion. *He had a broad swarthy face.* ADJ-GRADED

swashbuckling /swɒʃbʌklɪŋ/. If you describe someone or something as **swashbuckling**, you mean that they remind you of the courageous and daring behaviour of pirates. *He has not been the same swashbuckling player since suffering a knee injury. ...a swashbuckling adventure story.* ADJ-GRADED

♦ **swashbuckler, swashbucklers** *He's a swashbuckler. He has such unbelievable charisma and energy.* N-COUNT

swastika /swɒstɪkə/ **swastikas.** A **swastika** is a symbol in the shape of a cross with each arm bent over at right angles. It is used in India as a good luck sign, but it was also used by the Nazis in Germany as their official symbol. ◆◇◇◇◇ N-COUNT

swat /swɒt/ **swats, swatting, swatted.** If you **swat** something such as an insect, you hit it with a quick, swinging movement, using your hand or a flat object. *Hundreds of flies buzz around us, and the workman keeps swatting them.* ► Also a noun. *Mother took a swat at Jack's arm.* VERB V n N-COUNT =swipe

swathe /sweɪð, AM swɑːð/ **swathes, swathing, swathed;** the noun is also spelled **swath**. ◆◇◇◇◇

1 A **swathe** of land is a long strip of land. *On May 1st the army took over another swathe of territory... Year by year great swathes of this small nation's countryside disappear.* N-COUNT: usu N of n

2 A **swathe** of cloth is a long strip of cloth, especially one that is wrapped round someone or something. *...swathes of white silk.* N-COUNT: usu N of n

3 To **swathe** someone or something **in** cloth means to wrap them in it completely. *She swathed her enormous body in thin black fabrics... His head was swathed in bandages made from a torn sheet.* VERB V n in n V-ed

4 If someone or something **cuts a swathe** through something, they pass through it causing great destruction or change. *The storm cut a swathe through southern England... Keegan's team have been cutting an irresistible swathe through the first division.* PHRASE: V inflects, PHR n

SWAT team /swɒt tiːm/ **SWAT teams.** A **SWAT team** is a group of policemen who have been specially trained to deal with incidents involving violence or terrorism. SWAT stands for Special Weapons and Tactics; used mainly in American English. N-COUNT

sway /sweɪ/ **sways, swaying, swayed** ◆◆◇◇◇

1 When people or things **sway**, they lean or swing slowly from one side to the other. *The people swayed back and forth with arms linked... The whole boat swayed and tipped. ...a coastal highway lined with tall, swaying palm trees.* VERB V adv/prep V V-ing

2 If you **are swayed** by someone or something, you are influenced by them. *Don't ever be swayed by fashion. ...last minute efforts by the main political parties to sway the voters in tomorrow's local elections.* VERB be V-ed V n

3 If someone or something **holds sway**, they have great power or influence over a particular place or activity. *South of the Usk, a completely different approach seems to hold sway... The 'families' are the basic units, each holding sway over a recognised territory.* PHRASES V inflects, oft PHR over n

4 If you are **under the sway** of someone or something, they have great influence over you. *How mothers keep daughters under their sway is the subject of the next five sections.* PHR after v, v-link PHR

swear /sweəʳ/ **swears, swearing, swore, sworn** ◆◆◇◇◇

1 If someone **swears**, they use language that is considered to be rude or offensive, usually because they are angry. *It's wrong to swear and shout... They swore at them and ran off.* VERB V V at n

2 If you **swear** to do something, you solemnly promise that you will do it. *Alan swore that he would do everything in his power to help us... We have sworn to fight cruelty wherever we find it... The police are the only civil servants who have to swear allegiance to the Crown... I have sworn an oath to defend her.* VERB V that V to-inf V n

3 If you say that you **swear** that something is true or that you can **swear** to it, you are saying very firmly that it is true. *I swear I've told you all I know... I swear on all I hold dear that I had nothing to do with this... Behind them was a confusion of noise, perhaps even a shot, but he couldn't swear to it.* VERB V that V on/by n that V to n

4 If someone **is sworn** to secrecy or **is sworn** to silence, they promise another person that they will not reveal a secret. *She was bursting to announce the news but was sworn to secrecy.* VB: usu passive be V-ed to n

5 See also **sworn**.

swear by. If you **swear by** something, you believe that it can be relied on to have a particular effect; an informal expression. *Many people swear by vitamin C's ability to ward off colds.* PHRASAL VERB V P n

swear in. When someone **is sworn in**, they solemnly promise to fulfil the duties of a new job or appointment. *Mary Robinson has been formally sworn in as Ireland's first woman president.* PHRASAL VERB usu passive be V-ed P

swearing-in. The **swearing-in** at the beginning of a trial or official appointment is the act of making solemn promises to fulfil the duties it involves. N-SING

swear word, swear words; also spelled **swearword**. A **swear word** is a word which is considered to be rude or offensive. Swear words are usually used when people are angry. N-COUNT

sweat /swet/ **sweats, sweating, sweated** ◆◆◇◇◇

1 **Sweat** is the salty colourless liquid which comes through your skin when you are hot, ill, or afraid. *Both horse and rider were dripping with sweat within five minutes... He wiped the sweat off his face and looked around... Her sweat-stained clothing clung to her body.* N-UNCOUNT

2 When you **sweat**, sweat comes through your skin. *Already they were sweating as the sun beat down upon them.* VERB V ♦ **sweating** *...symptoms such as sweating, irritability, anxiety and depression.* N-UNCOUNT

3 If someone is in a **sweat**, they are sweating a lot. *Every morning I would break out in a sweat... Cool down very gradually after working up a sweat... I really don't feel a bit sick, no night sweats, no fevers.* N-COUNT

4 In informal American English, **sweats** are the same as a **sweatsuit** or **sweatpants**. N-PLURAL

5 If someone is **in a cold sweat** or **in a sweat**, they feel frightened or embarrassed. *The very thought brought me out in a cold sweat.* PHRASES PHR after v, v-link ADJ

6 If someone **sweats it out**, they wait anxiously for a situation to improve or be resolved, because they cannot do anything about it. *The islanders can do little but sweat it out, wondering whether they will be forced to go and seek a new life elsewhere.* V inflects

7 If someone says **no sweat** when you ask them about something or to do something, they mean that it is not a problem or that it can be done without effort or difficulty; an informal expression. *'Many thanks.'—'No sweat. Anything else?'... No-one minds that she's a woman, that's no sweat at all.* CONVENTION =no problem

8 ● **blood, sweat, and tears**: see **blood**. ● to **sweat blood**: see **blood**.

sweater /swetəʳ/ **sweaters.** A **sweater** is a warm knitted piece of clothing which covers the upper part of your body and your arms. ◆◆◇◇◇ N-COUNT

sweatpants /swetpænts/. In American English, **sweatpants** are the part of a sweatsuit that covers your legs. The British term is **tracksuit trousers** or **tracksuit bottoms**. N-PLURAL

sweatshirt /swetʃɜːʳt/ **sweatshirts.** A **sweatshirt** is a loose warm piece of casual clothing, usually made of thick stretchy cotton, which covers the upper part of your body and your arms. ◆◇◇◇◇ N-COUNT

sweatshop /swetʃɒp/ **sweatshops;** also spelled **sweat shop**. If you describe a small factory or workshop as a **sweatshop**, you mean that many people work together there in poor conditions for low pay; used showing disapproval. *...the dingy, hidden world of garment sweatshops.* N-COUNT PRAGMATICS

sweatsuit /swetsuːt/ **sweatsuits.** In American English, a **sweatsuit** is a loose, warm, stretchy suit consisting of long pants and a top which people wear to relax and do exercise. The usual British word is **tracksuit**. N-COUNT =tracksuit

sweaty /sweti/ **sweatier, sweatiest** ◆◇◇◇◇

1 If parts of your body or your clothes are **sweaty**, they are soaked or covered with sweat. *...sweaty hands... She was hot and sweaty.* ADJ-GRADED

2 A **sweaty** place or activity makes you sweat because it is hot or tiring. *...a sweaty nightclub.* ADJ-GRADED

swede /swiːd/ **swedes.** In British English, a **swede** is a round yellow root vegetable with a brown or purple skin. The usual American word is **rutabaga**. N-VAR

Swede /swiːd/ **Swedes.** A **Swede** is a Swedish citizen, or a person of Swedish origin. ◆◇◇◇◇ N-COUNT

Swedish /swiːdɪʃ/ ◆◆◆◆◇

1 **Swedish** means belonging or relating to Sweden, or to its people, language, or culture. *...the Swedish ambassador to the European Community. ...the Swedish city of Gothenburg.* ADJ

2 **Swedish** is the language spoken in Sweden. *I had a chat with Lars in the morning and spoke Swedish.* N-UNCOUNT

sweep /swiːp/ **sweeps, sweeping, swept** ◆◆◆◇◇

1 If you **sweep** an area of floor or ground, you push dirt or rubbish off it with a long-handled brush. *The owner of the store was sweeping his floor when I walked in... She was in the kitchen sweeping crumbs into a dust pan... Norma picked up the broom and began sweeping.* VERB V n V n prep/adv V Also V n with adv

2 If you **sweep** things off something, you push them off with a quick smooth movement of your arm. *I swept rainwater off the flat top of a gravestone... With a gesture of frustration, she swept the cards from the table... 'Thanks friend,' he said, while sweeping the money into his pocket.* VERB V n prep/adv

3 If someone with long hair **sweeps** their hair into a particular style, they put it into that style. *...stylish ways of sweeping your hair off your face... Her long, fine hair was swept back in a ponytail.* VERB V n prep/adv V-ed

4 If your arm or hand **sweeps** in a particular direction, or if you **sweep** it there, it moves quickly and smoothly in that direction. *His arm swept around the room... Daniels swept his arm over his friend's shoulder. ...the long sweeping arm movements of a violinist.* ► Also a noun. *With one sweep of her hand she threw back the sheets.* V-ERG V prep/adv V n prep/adv V-ing N-COUNT

5 If wind, a stormy sea, or another strong force **sweeps** someone or something along, it moves them quickly along. *...landslides that buried homes and swept cars into the sea... Suddenly, she was swept along by the crowd.* VERB V n prep/adv

6 If you **are swept** somewhere, you are taken there very quickly. *The visitors were swept past various monuments... A limousine swept her along the busy freeway to the airport.* VERB be V-ed prep/adv V n prep/adv

7 If something **sweeps** from one place to another, it moves there extremely quickly; used in written English. *An icy wind swept through the streets... The car swept past the gate house.* VERB V prep/adv

8 If events, ideas, or beliefs **sweep** through a place, they spread quickly through it. *A flu epidemic is sweeping through Moscow. ...the wave of patriotism sweeping the country.* VERB V through/across n, V n

9 If someone **sweeps** into a place, they walk into it in a proud confident manner, often when they are angry; used in written English. *She swept into the conference room... Scarlet with rage, she swept past her employer and stormed up the stairs... The Chief turned and swept out.* VERB V prep/adv

10 If something or someone **sweeps** something away or aside, they remove it quickly and completely. *The commission's conclusions sweep away a decade of denials and cover-ups... In times of war, governments often sweep human rights aside... He swept the names from his mind.* VERB V n with adv, V n prep

11 If a light or someone's gaze **sweeps** an area, it moves across the area steadily from side to side. *Helicopters with searchlights swept the park which was sealed off... Her gaze sweeps rapidly around the room.* VERB V n, V prep/adv

12 If land or water **sweeps** somewhere, it stretches out in a long, wide, curved shape. *The land sweeps away from long areas of greenery. ...the arc of countries that sweeps down from South Korea to Indonesia.* VERB V prep/adv

13 A **sweep** of land or water forms a long, wide, curved shape. *The ground fell away in a broad sweep down to the river. ...the great sweep of the bay.* N-COUNT: with supp

14 If a person or group **sweeps** an election or **sweeps** to victory, they win the election easily. *Indira Gandhi swept the 1971 election... Mr Chretien swept to victory in an easy first ballot contest... Ms Bhutto is riding on a wave of acclaim that could well sweep her back to power. ...a sweeping victory.* VERB V n, V to n, V n to n, V-ing

15 If someone makes a **sweep** of a place, they search it, usually because they are looking for people who are hiding or for an illegal activity. *Two of the soldiers swiftly began making a sweep of the premises... There may be periodic police 'sweeps' of crime in the area.* N-COUNT: usu sing

16 If you refer to the **sweep** of something, you are indicating that it includes a large number of different events, qualities, or opinions. *...the whole sweep of German social and political history.* N-SING: with supp

17 See also **sweeping**; **chimney sweep**.

18 If someone **sweeps** something bad or wrong **under the carpet**, or if they **sweep** it **under the rug**, they try to prevent people from hearing about it. *For a long time this problem has been swept under the carpet.* PHRASES V inflects

19 If you make **a clean sweep** of something, such as a series of matches or tournaments, you win them all. *...the first club to make a clean sweep of all three trophies.* PHR n, usu v PHR

20 If someone **sweeps** you **off** your **feet**, you fall in love with them almost as soon as you see them because you find them very good-looking or exciting. *I was swept off my feet. I had always dreamed of being an officer's wife.* V inflects

21 • **sweep the board**: see **board**.

sweep up. If you **sweep up** rubbish or dirt, you push it together with a brush and then remove it. *Get a broom and sweep up that glass will you?... He started working for a gallery sweeping up and making the tea.* PHRASAL VERB V P n (not pron), V P, Also V n P

sweeper /swiːpəʳ/ **sweepers.** In football, a **sweeper** is a player who operates behind the main defenders but in front of the goalkeeper; used in British English. ◆◇◇◇◇ N-COUNT

sweeping /swiːpɪŋ/ ◆◇◇◇◇

1 A **sweeping** curve is a long wide curve. *...the long sweeping curve of Rio's Guanabara Bay.* ADJ: ADJ n

2 If someone makes a **sweeping** statement or generalization, they make a firm definite statement although they have not considered the relevant facts or details carefully; used showing disapproval. *It is far too early to make sweeping statements about gene therapy.* ADJ-GRADED: usu ADJ n PRAGMATICS

3 **Sweeping** changes or reforms are large in scale and have very important or significant results. *The new government has started to make sweeping changes in the economy... The armed forces would be given sweeping new powers. ...sweeping economic reforms.* ADJ-GRADED: usu ADJ n =far-reaching

4 See also **sweep**.

sweepstake /swiːpsteɪk/ **sweepstakes.** A **sweepstake** is a method of gambling in which each person pays a small amount of money and is given the name of a competitor before a race or contest. Then the person who has the name of the winner receives all the money. N-COUNT

sweet /swiːt/ **sweeter, sweetest; sweets** ◆◆◆◇◇

1 **Sweet** food and drink contains a lot of sugar. *...a mug of sweet tea... If the sauce seems too sweet, add a dash of red wine vinegar. ...the sweet taste of wild strawberries.* ♦ **sweetness** *Florida oranges have a natural sweetness.* ADJ-GRADED; N-UNCOUNT

2 In British English, **sweets** are sweet things such as toffees, chocolates, and mints. The American word is **candy**. N-COUNT

3 In British English, a **sweet** is something sweet, such as fruit or a pudding, that you eat at the end of a meal, especially in a restaurant. The American word is **dessert**. *The sweet was a mousse flavoured with whisky.* N-VAR =dessert

4 A **sweet** smell is pleasant and fragrant. *...the sweet smell of her shampoo... She'd baked some bread which made the air smell sweet.* ADJ-GRADED ≠foul

5 If you describe something such as air or water as **sweet**, you mean that it smells or tastes pleasantly fresh and clean. *I gulped a breath of sweet air. ...a stream of sweet water.* ADJ-GRADED ≠foul

6 A **sweet** sound is pleasant, smooth, and gentle. *Her voice was as soft and sweet as a young girl's. ...the sweet sounds of Mozart.* ♦ **sweetly** *He sang much more sweetly than he has before.* ADJ-GRADED; ADV-GRADED: usu ADV with v

7 If you describe something as **sweet**, you mean that it gives you great pleasure and satisfaction; used in written English. *There are few things quite as sweet as revenge. ...the sweet taste of illicit love... His success was all the sweeter for being at the expense of Europe's most admired team.* ADJ-GRADED ≠bitter

8 If you describe someone as **sweet**, you mean that they are pleasant, kind, and gentle towards other people. *He was a sweet man but when he drank he tended to quarrel... How sweet of you to think of me!* ♦ **sweetly** *I just smiled sweetly and said no.* ADJ-GRADED; ADV-GRADED

9 If you describe a small person or thing as **sweet**, you mean that they are attractive in an unsophisticated way; an informal use which can sound patronizing. *...a sweet little baby girl... The house was really sweet.* ADJ-GRADED =cute

10 You might address someone as **sweet** or **my sweet** if you are very fond of them; an old-fashioned use. *I am so proud of you, my sweet!* N-VOC =darling

11 See also **sweetly**.

12 If you **keep** someone **sweet**, you do something to please them in order to prevent them from becoming annoyed or dissatisfied; an informal expression. *Where's the money to keep us sweet?* PHRASES V inflects

13 • **a sweet tooth**: see **tooth**.

sweet and sour; also spelled **sweet-and-sour**. **Sweet and sour** is used to describe Chinese food that contains both a sweet flavour and something sharp or sour such as lemon or vinegar. ADJ: ADJ n

sweetbread /swiːtbred/ **sweetbreads. Sweetbreads** are meat obtained from the pancreas of a calf or a lamb. N-COUNT

sweetcorn /swiːtkɔʳn/; also spelled **sweet corn. Sweetcorn** is a long rounded vegetable covered in small yellow seeds. It is part of the maize plant. The seeds themselves can also be referred to as **sweetcorn**. ◆◇◇◇◇ N-UNCOUNT

sweeten /swiːtᵊn/ **sweetens, sweetening, sweetened** ◆◇◇◇◇

1 If you **sweeten** food or drink, you add sugar, honey, or another sweet substance to it. *He liberally* VERB V n

sweetened his coffee... The Australians fry their bananas and sweeten them with honey. V n with n

2 If you **sweeten** something such as an offer or a business deal, you try to make someone want it more by improving it or by increasing the amount you are willing to pay. *Kalon Group has sweetened its takeover offer for Manders... She had been careful to sweeten the deal with a rather generous cash payment.* VERB V n V n with n

sweetener /swiːtənəʳ/ **sweeteners** ◆◇◇◇◇

1 **Sweetener** is an artificial substance that can be used in drinks instead of sugar and is less fattening than sugar. N-MASS

2 A **sweetener** is something that you give or offer someone in order to persuade them to accept an offer or business deal. N-COUNT

sweetheart /swiːthɑːʳt/ **sweethearts** ◆◇◇◇◇

1 You call someone **sweetheart** if you are very fond of them. *Happy birthday, sweetheart.* N-VOC =darling

2 Your **sweetheart** is your boyfriend or your girlfriend; an old-fashioned or journalistic use. *I married Shurla, my childhood sweetheart, in Liverpool.* N-COUNT: usu supp N

sweetie /swiːti/ **sweeties**

1 You might call someone **sweetie** if you are fond of them, especially if they are younger than you; an informal use which can sound patronizing. N-VOC =dearie

2 If you say that someone is a **sweetie** you mean that they are kind, pleasant, and lovable; an informal use. N-COUNT

3 In British English, sweets are sometimes referred to as **sweeties** by children or adults speaking to children. N-COUNT PRAGMATICS

sweetish /swiːtɪʃ/. A **sweetish** smell or taste is fairly sweet. ADJ

sweetly /swiːtli/

1 If an engine or machine is running **sweetly**, it is working smoothly and efficiently. *He heard the car engine running sweetly beyond the open door.* ADV-GRADED: ADV with v

2 If you kick or hit a ball **sweetly**, you kick or hit it in the very middle of it so that it goes firmly and accurately to the place you are aiming for. *He could strike the ball as sweetly as when he was 28 years younger.* ADV-GRADED: ADV with v

3 See also **sweet**.

sweetmeat /swiːtmiːt/ **sweetmeats. Sweetmeats** are sweet items of food, especially delicacies that are considered to be rather special; an old-fashioned word. N-COUNT: usu pl

sweetness /swiːtnəs/.

1 If you say that a situation is not **all sweetness and light**, you mean that it is not proceeding entirely well although this may seem to be the case or someone may want people to think this is the case. *It has not all been sweetness and light between him and the Prime Minister.* PHRASE: with brd-neg, usu v-link PHR

2 See also **sweet**.

sweet nothings. If someone whispers **sweet nothings** in your ear, they quietly say nice, loving, and flattering things to you. N-PLURAL

sweet pea, sweet peas; also spelled **sweetpea**. A **sweet pea** is a climbing plant which has delicate, fragrant flowers. N-COUNT

sweet pepper, sweet peppers. A **sweet pepper** is a hollow green, red, or yellow vegetable. N-COUNT =capsicum

sweet potato, sweet potatoes. Sweet potatoes are vegetables that look like large ordinary potatoes but taste sweet. They have pinkish brown skins and yellow flesh. N-VAR

sweet shop, sweet shops; also spelled **sweetshop**. In British English, a **sweet shop** is a small shop that sells sweets and cigarettes, and sometimes newspapers and magazines. The usual American expression is **candy store**. N-COUNT: oft the N

sweet talk, sweet talks, sweet talking, sweet talked; also spelled **sweet-talk**. If you **sweet talk** someone, you talk to them very nicely so that they will do what you want. *She could always sweet-talk Pamela into letting her stay up late... He even tried to sweet-talk the policewoman who arrested him.* VERB V n into -ing/n V n

swell /swel/ **swells, swelling, swelled, swollen;** the forms **swelled** and **swollen** are both used as the past participle. ◆◆◇◇◇

1 If the amount or size of something **swells** or if something **swells** it, it becomes larger than it was before. *The human population swelled, at least temporarily, as migrants moved south... By the end of this month the size of the mission is expected to swell to 280 people... His bank balance has swelled by £222,000 in the last three weeks... Offers from other countries should swell the force to 35,000. ...the ever-swelling numbers of the homeless... Its population is swollen by 360,000 refugees.* V-ERG =increase V V to/by n V n to n V-ing V-ed Also V n

2 If something such as a part of your body **swells**, it becomes larger and rounder than normal. *Do your ankles swell at night?... The limbs swell to an enormous size.* ► **Swell up** means the same as **swell**. *When you develop a throat infection or catch a cold the glands in the neck swell up.* VERB V V to n PHRASAL VERB V P

3 If you **swell** with a feeling, you are suddenly full of that feeling; a literary use. *She could see her two sons swell with pride.* VERB V with n

4 If sounds **swell**, they get louder; a literary use. *Heavenly music swelled from nowhere.* VERB V

5 A **swell** is the regular movement of waves up and down in the open sea. *We bobbed gently up and down on the swell of the incoming tide.* N-COUNT

6 In informal American English, you can describe something as **swell** if you think it is really nice. *I've had a swell time.* ADJ-GRADED

7 See also **swelling, swollen; groundswell.**

swell up. See **swell** 2. PHRASAL VERB

swelling /swelɪŋ/ **swellings.** A **swelling** is a raised, curved shape on the surface of your body which appears as a result of an injury or an illness. *His eye was partly closed, and there was a swelling over his lid... There is some swelling and he is being detained for observation.* ◆◇◇◇◇ N-VAR

swelter /sweltəʳ/ **swelters, sweltering, sweltered.** If you **swelter**, you are very uncomfortable because the weather is extremely hot. *They sweltered in temperatures rising to a hundred degrees... Fred and Volodia sweltered at night in the stuffy, crowded cabins.* VERB V

sweltering /sweltərɪŋ/. If you describe the weather as **sweltering**, you mean that it is extremely hot and makes you feel uncomfortable. ADJ

swept /swept/. **Swept** is the past tense and past participle of **sweep**.

swerve /swɜːʳv/ **swerves, swerving, swerved.** If a vehicle or other moving thing **swerves**, or if you **swerve** it, it suddenly changes direction, often in order to avoid colliding with something else. *Drivers coming in the opposite direction swerved to avoid the bodies... Her car swerved off the road into a 6ft high brick wall... Suddenly Ned swerved the truck, narrowly missing a blond teenager on a skateboard.* ► Also a noun. *He swung the car to the left and that swerve saved Malone's life.* ◆◇◇◇◇ V-ERG V V prep/adv V n N-COUNT

swift /swɪft/ **swifter, swiftest; swifts** ◆◆◇◇◇

1 A **swift** event or process happens very quickly or without delay. *Our task is to challenge the UN to make a swift decision... The police were swift to act.* ♦ **swiftly** *The French have acted swiftly and decisively to protect their industries.* ♦ **swiftness** *The secrecy and swiftness of the invasion shocked and amazed army officers.* ADJ-GRADED =quick ADV-GRADED N-UNCOUNT: oft N of n

2 Something that is **swift** moves very quickly. *With a swift movement, Matthew Jerrold sat upright.* ♦ **swiftly** *Lenny moved swiftly and silently across the front lawn. ...a swiftly flowing stream.* ♦ **swiftness** *With incredible swiftness she ran down the passage.* ADJ-GRADED =quick ADV-GRADED: ADV with v N-UNCOUNT

3 A **swift** is a small bird with long curved wings. N-COUNT

swig /swɪg/ **swigs, swigging, swigged.** If you **swig** a drink, you drink it from a bottle or cup quickly and in large amounts. *I swigged down two white wines... He was still hanging around, swigging the Coke out of the can.* ► Also a noun. *Brian took a swig of his beer... McGuire took a long swig from his bottle of bitter lemon.* VERB V n with down/back V n N-COUNT

swill /swɪl/ **swills, swilling, swilled**

1 If you **swill** an alcoholic drink, you drink a lot of it. *A crowd of men were standing around swilling beer.*
VERB
V n

2 If a liquid **swills** around, or if you **swill** it around, it moves around the area that it is contained in. *Gallons of sea water had rushed into the cabin and were now swilling about in the bilges... She swilled the whisky around in her glass.*
V-ERG
V *around/about*
V n *around/about*

3 To **swill** out something means to clean it by pouring water over it; used mainly in British English. *Having finished his coffee, he swilled out the mug and left it on the draining board.*
VERB
V n with *out*

4 **Swill** is a liquid mixture containing waste food such as vegetable peelings that is given to pigs to eat.
N-UNCOUNT

swim /swɪm/ **swims, swimming, swam, swum** ◆◆◆◇◇

1 When you **swim**, you move through water by making movements with your arms and legs. *She learned to swim when she was really tiny... I went round to Jonathan's to see if he wanted to go swimming... He was rescued only when an exhausted friend swam ashore... I swim a mile a day.* ► Also a noun. *When can we go for a swim, Mam?*
VERB
V
V adv/prep
V amount/n
N-SING

2 If you **swim** a race, you take part in a swimming race. *She swam the 400 metres medley ten seconds slower than she did in 1980.*
VERB
V n
Also V

3 If you **swim** a stretch of water, you keep swimming until you have crossed it. *In 1875, Captain Matthew Webb became the first man to swim the English Channel.*
VERB
V n

4 When a fish **swims**, it moves through water by making movements with its tail and fins. *The barriers are lethal to fish trying to swim upstream.*
VERB
V adv/prep
Also V

5 If objects **swim**, they seem to be moving backwards and forwards, usually because you are ill. *Alexis suddenly could take no more: he felt too hot, he couldn't breathe, the room swam.*
VERB
V

6 If your head **is swimming**, you feel dizzy. *The musty aroma of incense made her head swim.*
VERB
=spin
V

7 If something **is swimming** in liquid or **is swimming** with liquid, it is surrounded by and covered with it. *He polished off a large steak, salad, broccoli swimming in thick sauce, and half a litre of wine.*
VB: only cont
V *in/with* n

8 ● **sink or swim**: see **sink**.

swimmer /swɪməʳ/ **swimmmers.** A **swimmer** is a person who swims, especially for sport or pleasure, or a person who is swimming. *You don't have to worry about me. I'm a good swimmer... She wants to become an Olympic swimmer... Apart from a few swimmers, the rest of us stretched out on the bank to sunbathe.*
◆◇◇◇◇
N-COUNT

swimming /swɪmɪŋ/. **Swimming** is the activity of swimming, especially as a sport or for pleasure. *Swimming is probably the best form of exercise you can get. ...swimming lessons.*
◆◆◇◇◇
N-UNCOUNT

swimming bath, swimming baths

1 In British English, a **swimming baths** or **swimming bath** is a building that contains an indoor public swimming pool. The plural **swimming baths** can be used to refer either to one or to more than one of these places. *It had been two years since I had been to the swimming baths.*
N-COUNT

2 In British English, a **swimming bath** is a public swimming pool, especially an indoor one.
N-COUNT

swimming cap, swimming caps. In British English, a **swimming cap** is a rubber cap which you wear to keep your hair dry when you are swimming. The usual American term is **bathing cap**.
N-COUNT

swimming costume, swimming costumes. In British English, a **swimming costume** is the same as a **swimsuit**.
N-COUNT
=swimsuit

swimmingly /swɪmɪŋli/. If you say that something **is going swimmingly**, you mean that everything is happening in a satisfactory way, without any problems; an informal expression. *The work has been going swimmingly.*
PHRASE:
V inflects

swimming pool, swimming pools. A **swimming pool** is a place that has been built for people to swim in. It consists of a large hole that has been tiled and filled with water.
◆◆◇◇◇
N-COUNT

swimming trunks. In British English, **swimming trunks** are the shorts that a man wears when he goes swimming. The usual American term is **bathing trunks**.
N-PLURAL:
also *a pair of* N

swimsuit /swɪmsuːt/ **swimsuits.** A **swimsuit** is a piece of clothing that is worn for swimming, especially by women and girls.
◆◇◇◇◇
N-COUNT
=bathing suit

swimwear /swɪmweəʳ/. **Swimwear** is the things people wear for swimming.
N-UNCOUNT

swindle /swɪndᵊl/ **swindles, swindling, swindled.** If someone **swindles** a person or an organization, they deceive them in order to get something valuable from them, especially money. *A City businessman swindled investors out of millions of pounds... An oil executive swindled £250,000 out of his firm.* ► Also a noun. *He fled to Switzerland rather than face trial for a tax swindle.* ♦ **swindler, swindlers** *Swindlers have cheated investors out of £12 million.*
◆◇◇◇◇
VERB
V n *out of* n
N-COUNT
N-COUNT

swine /swaɪn/ **swines.** The form **swines** is used as the plural for meaning 1; **swine** is used as both the singular and plural for meaning 2.

1 If you call someone a **swine**, you dislike them or think that they are a bad person, usually because they have behaved unpleasantly towards you; an informal word.
N-COUNT

2 A **swine** is a pig; an old-fashioned or technical use. *...imports of live swine from Canada. ...pigs with swine fever.* ● to **cast pearls before swine**: see **pearl**.
N-COUNT

swing /swɪŋ/ **swings, swinging, swung** ◆◆◆◇◇

1 If something **swings** or if you **swing** it, it moves repeatedly backwards and forwards or from side to side from a fixed point. *The sail of the little boat swung crazily from one side to the other... She was swinging a bottle of wine by its neck... Ian lit a cigarette and sat on the end of the table, one leg swinging.* ► Also a noun. *...a woman in a tight red dress, walking with a slight swing to her hips.*
V-ERG
V adv/prep
V n
V-ing
N-COUNT:
usu with supp

2 If something **swings** in a particular direction or if you **swing** it in that direction, it moves in that direction with a smooth, curving movement. *The torchlight swung across the little beach and out over the water, searching... The canoe found the current and swung around... Roy swung his legs carefully off the couch and sat up.* ► Also a noun. *When he's not on the tennis court, you'll find him practising his golf swing.*
V-ERG
V prep/adv
V n prep/adv
N-COUNT

3 If a vehicle **swings** in a particular direction, or if the driver **swings** it in a particular direction, they turn suddenly in that direction. *Joanna swung back on to the main approach and headed for the airport... The tyres dug into the grit as he swung the car off the road.*
V-ERG
V adv
V n prep/adv

4 If someone **swings** round, they turn around quickly, usually because they are surprised. *She swung around to him, spilling her tea without noticing it.*
VERB
V adv

5 If you **swing** at someone or something, you try to hit them with your arm or with something that you are holding. *Blanche swung at her but she moved her head back and Blanche missed... I picked up his baseball bat and swung at the man's head.* ► Also a noun. *I often want to take a swing at someone to relieve my feelings.*
VERB
V *at* n
Also V n *at* n
N-COUNT
=swipe

6 A **swing** is a seat hanging by two ropes or chains from a metal frame or from the branch of a tree. You can sit on the seat and move forwards and backwards through the air.
N-COUNT

7 **Swing** is a style of jazz dance music that was popular in the 1930's. It was played by big bands.
N-UNCOUNT

8 A **swing** in people's opinions, attitudes, or feelings is a significant change in them. *There was a massive twenty per cent swing away from the Conservatives to the Liberal Democrats... Educational practice is liable to sudden swings and changes... Dieters suffer from violent mood swings.*
N-COUNT:
usu with supp

9 If people's opinions, attitudes, or feelings **swing**, they change significantly. *In two years' time there is a presidential election, and the voters could swing again... The mood amongst Tory MPs seems to be swinging away from the Prime Minister.*
VERB
V
V adv/prep

10 If something is **in full swing**, it is operating fully and is no longer in its early stages. *When we returned, the party was in full swing and the dance floor was crowded... The international rugby season is in full swing.* PHRASES v-link PHR =well under way

11 If you **get into the swing of** something, you become very involved in it and enjoy what you are doing. *Everyone understood how hard it was to get back into the swing of things after such a long absence.* V inflects, PHR n

12 If you say that something **is going with a swing**, you mean that it is happening in a lively and exciting way. *Sara Lewis' impressive recipes are guaranteed to make the party go with a swing.* V inflects

13 If you say that a situation is **swings and roundabouts**, you mean that there are as many gains as there are losses.

14 • **no room to swing a cat**: see **cat**.

swing door, swing doors. Swing doors are doors that can open both towards you and away from you. N-COUNT: usu pl

swingeing /swɪndʒɪŋ/. In British English, a **swingeing** action, such as an attack or a cutback, causes serious harm or hardship; used in journalism. *The Party Conference has opened with a swingeing attack on Labour... There have been swingeing cuts on government subsidies, on housing, food and fuel.* ADJ: ADJ n =severe

swinger /swɪŋəʳ/ **swingers.** A **swinger** is a person who is lively and fashionable; an old-fashioned, informal word. N-COUNT

swinging /swɪŋɪŋ/. If you describe something or someone as **swinging**, you mean that they are lively and fashionable; an old-fashioned, informal word. *The stuffy '50s gave way to the swinging '60s. ...a young student in mid-1960s 'swinging London'.* ADJ-GRADED: usu ADJ n

swipe /swaɪp/ **swipes, swiping, swiped** ◆◇◇◇◇

1 If you **swipe** at a person or thing, you try to hit them with a stick or other object, making a swinging movement with your arm. *She swiped at Rusty as though he was a fly... He swiped me across the shoulder with the poker.* ► Also a noun. *He took a swipe at Andrew that deposited him on the floor.* VERB V at n V n N-COUNT

2 If you **swipe** something, you steal it quickly; an informal use. *Five soldiers were each fined £140 for swiping a wheelchair from a disabled tourist... Everywhere I went, people kept trying to swipe my copy of The New York Times.* VERB =whip, pinch V n

3 If you take a **swipe at** a person or an organization, you attack them, usually in an indirect way. *Mr Major also took a swipe at Tory right wingers... In a swipe at the president, he called for an end to 'begging for aid around the world'.* N-COUNT

swirl /swɜːʳl/ **swirls, swirling, swirled.** If you **swirl** something liquid or flowing, or if it **swirls**, it moves round and round quickly. *She smiled, swirling the wine in her glass... The black water swirled around his legs, reaching almost to his knees... She swirled the ice-cold liquid around her mouth. ...Carmen with her swirling gypsy skirts.* ► Also a noun. *...small swirls of chocolate cream... He breathes out a swirl of cigarette smoke.* ◆◇◇◇◇ V-ERG V n V prep/adv V n prep V-ing Also V n with adv, V N-COUNT

swish /swɪʃ/ **swishes, swishing, swished; swisher, swishest** ◆◇◇◇◇

1 If something **swishes** or if you **swish** it, it moves quickly through the air, making a soft sound. *A car swished by steady and fast heading for the coast... He swished his cape around his shoulders... He heard a swishing sound.* ► Also a noun. *She turned with a swish of her skirt.* V-ERG V adv/prep V n prep/adv V-ing N-COUNT

2 In British English, if you describe something as **swish**, you mean that it is smart and fashionable; an old-fashioned, informal use. *...a swish cocktail bar.* ADJ-GRADED

Swiss /swɪs/. **Swiss** is both the singular and plural form. ◆◆◆◆◇

1 **Swiss** means belonging or relating to Switzerland, or to its people or culture. *...Swiss cheese. ...an avalanche in the Swiss alps.* ADJ

2 The **Swiss** are the people of Switzerland. *The report shows the Swiss are among the world's top wage earners.* N-COUNT: usu pl, the N

swiss roll, swiss rolls; also spelled **swiss-roll.** In British English, a **swiss roll** is a cylindrical cake made from a thin flat sponge which is covered with jam or cream on one side, then rolled up. N-VAR

switch /swɪtʃ/ **switches, switching, switched** ◆◆◆◇◇

1 A **switch** is a small control for an electrical device which you use to turn the device on or off. *Leona put some detergent into the dishwasher, shut the door and pressed the switch. ...a light switch.* N-COUNT

2 If you **switch** to something different, for example to a different system, task, or subject of conversation, you change to it from what you were doing or saying before. *Estonia is switching to a market economy... The law would encourage companies to switch from coal to cleaner fuels... The encouragement of a friend spurred Chris into switching jobs.* ► Also a noun. *New technology made a switch to oil possible... The spokesman implicitly condemned the United States policy switch.* ► **Switch over** means the same as **switch**. *Everywhere communists are tending to switch over to social democracy.* VERB =change V to n V from n to n V pl-n Also V N-COUNT: usu with supp PHRASAL VERB V P to n Also V P

3 If you **switch** your attention from one thing to another or if your attention **switches**, you stop paying attention to the first thing and start paying attention to the second. *My mother's interest had switched to my health... As the era wore on, she switched her attention to films.* V-ERG V to n V n to n

4 If you **switch** two things, you replace one with the other. *In half an hour, they'd switched the tags on every cable... The ballot boxes have been switched.* VERB =swap V pl-n

switch off PHRASAL VERB

1 If you **switch off** a light or other electrical device, you stop it working by operating a switch. *She switched off the coffee-machine... Glass parked the car and switched the engine off.* =turn off V P n (not pron) V n P Also V P

2 If you **switch off**, you stop paying attention or stop thinking or worrying about something; an informal use. *Thankfully, I've learned to switch off and let it go over my head... You may find you've got so many things to think about that it's difficult to switch off.* V P

switch on. If you **switch on** a light or other electrical device, you make it start working by operating a switch. *She emptied both their mugs and switched on the electric kettle... He pointed the light at his feet and tried to switch it on.* PHRASAL VERB =turn on V P n (not pron) V n P Also V P

switch over. PHRASAL VERB

1 If you **switch over** when you are watching television, you change to another channel. *I just happened to switch over although I haven't been watching the Olympics... Let's switch over to Channel 4.* V P V P to n

2 See **switch** 2.

switchback /swɪtʃbæk/ **switchbacks.**

1 A **switchback** is a road which rises and falls sharply many times, or a sharp rise and fall in a road; used mainly in British English. *...a dizzy bus ride over a switchback road.* N-COUNT: oft N n

2 A **switchback** is a road which goes up a steep hill in a series of zigzags or sharp bends, or a sharp bend in a road; used mainly in American English. *Several hundred yards beyond the first switchback in the road, he came to the second bend.* N-COUNT

switchblade /swɪtʃbleɪd/ **switchblades.** A **switchblade** is a knife with a blade that is hidden in the handle and that springs out when a button is pressed; used mainly in American English. The usual British word is **flick-knife**. N-COUNT

switchboard /swɪtʃbɔːʳd/ **switchboards.** A **switchboard** is a place in a large office or business where all the telephone calls are connected. *He asked to be connected to the central switchboard at London University... The switchboard operator was the hotel owner's wife.* ◆◇◇◇◇ N-COUNT

swivel /swɪvəl/ **swivels, swivelling, swivelled;** spelled **swiveling, swiveled** in American English. ◆◇◇◇◇

1 If something **swivels** or if you **swivel** it, it turns around a central point so that it is facing in a different direction. *She swivelled her chair round and* V-ERG V n adv/prep

stared out across the back lawn... His chairs can swivel, but they can't move up or down. V Also V n

2 If you **swivel** in a particular direction, you turn suddenly in that direction. *He swivelled round to face Sarah.* VERB V adv/prep

3 If your head or your eyes **swivel** in a particular direction or if you **swivel** them in a particular direction, you quickly look in that direction. *Roger swivelled his head to look at her... His eyes swivelled from one girl to the other.* V-ERG V n V prep/adv Also V

swivel chair, swivel chairs. A **swivel chair** is a chair whose seat can be turned around a central point to face in a different direction without moving the legs. N-COUNT: usu sing

swollen /swoʊlən/ ◆◇◇◇◇

1 If a part of your body is **swollen**, it is larger and rounder than normal, usually as a result of injury or illness. *My eyes were so swollen I could hardly see.* ADJ-GRADED

2 A **swollen** river has more water in it and flows faster than normal, usually because of heavy rain. ADJ-GRADED

3 **Swollen** is the past participle of **swell**.

swoon /swuːn/ **swoons, swooning, swooned** VERB
If you **swoon**, you are strongly affected by your feelings for someone you love or admire very much. *Virtually every woman in the '20s swooned over Valentino... The ladies shriek and swoon at his every word.* V over n V Also V adv

swoop /swuːp/ **swoops, swooping, swooped** ◆◇◇◇◇

1 If police or soldiers **swoop** on a place, they go there suddenly and quickly, usually in order to arrest someone or to attack the place; used mainly in journalism. *The terror ended when armed police swooped on the car... The drugs squad swooped and discovered 240 kilograms of cannabis.* ▶ Also a noun. *Police held 10 suspected illegal immigrants after a swoop on a German lorry.* VERB V on n V N-COUNT

2 When a bird or aeroplane **swoops**, it suddenly moves downwards through the air in a smooth curving movement. *More than 20 helicopters began swooping in low over the ocean... The hawk swooped and soared away carrying something.* VERB V adv/prep V

3 If something is done **in one fell swoop** or **at one fell swoop**, it is done on a single occasion or by a single action. *In one fell swoop the bank wiped away the tentative benefits of this policy.* PHRASE: PHR with cl

swop /swɒp/. See **swap**.

sword /sɔːʳd/ **swords** ◆◆◇◇◇

1 A **sword** is a weapon with a handle and a long sharp blade. N-COUNT

2 If you **cross swords** with someone, you disagree with them and argue with them about something. *...a candidate who's crossed swords with Labor by supporting the free-trade pact... The fiercest of rivals, the last time they crossed swords was during the 1980s.* PHRASES RECIP: V inflects, PHR with n, pl-n PHR

3 If you say that something is a **double-edged sword** or a **two-edged sword**, you mean that its positive effects are balanced or outweighed by its negative effects. N inflects

4 ● **Sword of Damocles**: see **Damocles**.

swordfish /sɔːʳdfɪʃ/; **swordfish** is both the singular and plural form. A **swordfish** is a large sea fish with a very long upper jaw. ▶ **Swordfish** is this fish eaten as food. *...grilled swordfish with a yogurt dressing.* N-VAR N-UNCOUNT

swordsman /sɔːʳdzmən/ **swordsmen.** A **swordsman** is a man who is skilled at fighting with a sword. N-COUNT

swore /swɔːʳ/. **Swore** is the past tense of **swear**.

sworn /swɔːʳn/

1 **Sworn** is the past participle of **swear**.

2 If you make a **sworn** statement or declaration, you swear that everything that you have said in it is true. *The allegations against them were made in sworn evidence to the inquiry.* ADJ: ADJ n

3 If two people or two groups of people are **sworn** enemies, they dislike each other very much. *It somehow seems hardly surprising that Ms Player is now his sworn enemy.* ADJ: ADJ n

swot /swɒt/ **swots, swotting, swotted**

1 In British English, if you **swot**, you study very hard, especially when you are preparing for an examination; an informal word. *They swotted for their A levels.* ▶ **Swot up** means the same as **swot**. *...several hours spent swotting up on how to be a pop star... The orchestra's been swotting up their Holst and Stravinsky.* VERB V for n Also V PHRASAL VERB VP on n VP n (not pron)

2 In British English, if you call someone a **swot**, you disapprove of the fact that they study extremely hard and are not interested in other things; an informal word. N-COUNT PRAGMATICS

swot up. See **swot** 1. PHRASAL VERB

swum /swʌm/. **Swum** is the past participle of **swim**.

swung /swʌŋ/. **Swung** is the past tense and past participle of **swing**.

sybaritic /sɪbərɪtɪk/. A **sybaritic** person or way of life is lazy, luxurious, and devoted to pleasure. ADJ-GRADED: usu ADJ n

sycamore /sɪkəmɔːʳ/ **sycamores.** A **sycamore** or a **sycamore tree** is a tree that has yellow flowers and large leaves with five points. ▶ **Sycamore** is the wood of this tree. *The furniture is made of sycamore, beech and leather.* N-VAR N-UNCOUNT

sycophancy /sɪkəfænsi, AM -fənsi/. **Sycophancy** is the quality or action of being sycophantic; a formal word, used showing disapproval. N-UNCOUNT PRAGMATICS

sycophant /sɪkəfænt, AM -fənt/ **sycophants.** A **sycophant** is a person who behaves in a sycophantic way; a formal word, used showing disapproval. *...a dictator surrounded by sycophants, frightened to tell him what he may not like.* N-COUNT PRAGMATICS

sycophantic /sɪkəfæntɪk/. If you describe someone as **sycophantic**, you disapprove of them because they flatter people who are more important and powerful than they are in order to gain an advantage for themselves. *...his clique of sycophantic friends... We heard the sound of sycophantic laughter.* ADJ-GRADED

syllable /sɪləbəl/ **syllables.** A **syllable** is a part of a word that contains a single vowel sound and that is pronounced as a unit. So, for example, 'book' has one syllable, and 'reading' has two syllables. *We children called her Oma, accenting both syllables.* ◆◇◇◇◇ N-COUNT

syllabus /sɪləbəs/ **syllabuses.** You can refer to the subjects that are studied in a particular course as the **syllabus**; used mainly in British English. *...the GCSE history syllabus.* ◆◇◇◇◇ N-COUNT =curriculum

sylvan /sɪlvən/. **Sylvan** is used to describe things that have an association with woods and trees; a literary word. ADJ: usu ADJ n

symbiosis /sɪmbioʊsɪs, -baɪ-/

1 **Symbiosis** is a close relationship between two organisms of different kinds which benefits both organisms; a technical use. *...the link between bacteria, symbiosis, and the evolution of plants and animals.* N-UNCOUNT

2 **Symbiosis** is any relationship between different things, people, or groups that benefits all the things or people concerned. *...the cosy symbiosis of the traditional political parties. ...a symbiosis between monarch and church.* N-UNCOUNT

symbiotic /sɪmbiɒtɪk, -baɪ-/. A **symbiotic** relationship is one in which organisms, people, or things exist together in a way that benefits them all. *...fungi that have a symbiotic relationship with the trees of these northwestern forests... Racing has always had a symbiotic relationship with betting.* ADJ-GRADED: usu ADJ n

symbol /sɪmbəl/ **symbols** ◆◆◆◇◇

1 Something that is a **symbol** of a society or an aspect of life seems to represent it because it is very typical of it. *To them, the monarchy is the special symbol of nationhood... She was put under house arrest two years ago but remained a powerful symbol in last year's election.* N-COUNT: with supp

2 A **symbol** of something such as an idea is a shape or design that is used to represent it. *Later in this same passage Yeats resumes his argument for the Rose as an Irish symbol... I frequently use sunflowers as symbols of strength.* N-COUNT: with supp

3 A **symbol** for an item in a calculation or formula N-COUNT

is a number, letter, or shape that represents the item. *What's the chemical symbol for mercury?*
4 See also **sex symbol, status symbol**.

symbolic /sɪmbɒlɪk/ ◆◆◇◇◇
1 If you describe an event, action, or procedure as **symbolic**, you mean that it represents an important change, although it has little practical effect. *A lot of Latin-American officials are stressing the symbolic importance of the trip... The move today was largely symbolic.* ♦ **symbolically** /sɪmbɒlɪkli/ *It was a simple enough gesture, but symbolically important.* ADJ; ADV: ADV adj, ADV with cl
2 Something that is **symbolic of** someone or something else is regarded or used as a symbol of them. *Yellow clothes are worn as symbolic of spring... The change from long to short hair is symbolic of the woman's need for change in her whole life.* ♦ **symbolically** *Each circle symbolically represents the whole of humanity.* ADJ-GRADED: usu v-link ADJ of n; ADV: ADV with v
3 **Symbolic** is used to describe things involving or relating to symbols. *...symbolic representations of landscape.* ADJ: ADJ n

symbolise /sɪmbəlaɪz/. See **symbolize**.

symbolism /sɪmbəlɪzəm/ ◆◇◇◇◇
1 **Symbolism** is the use of symbols in order to represent something. *The scene is so rich in symbolism that any explanation risks spoiling the effect. ...a film much praised at the time for its visual symbolism.* N-UNCOUNT
2 You can refer to the **symbolism** of an event or action when it seems to show something important about a situation. *The symbolism of the two events will not be lost on most Albanians.* N-UNCOUNT: usu N of n

symbolize /sɪmbəlaɪz/ **symbolizes, symbolizing, symbolized;** also spelled **symbolise** in British English. If one thing **symbolizes** another, it is used or regarded as a symbol of it. *The fall of the Berlin Wall symbolised the end of the Cold War between East and West. ...the post-war world order symbolised by the United Nations.* ◆◇◇◇◇ VERB; V n; V-ed

symmetrical /sɪmetrɪkəl/. If something is **symmetrical**, it has two halves which are exactly the same, except that one half is the mirror image of the other. *...the neat rows of perfectly symmetrical windows.* ♦ **symmetrically** /sɪmetrɪkli/ *The south garden at Sissinghurst was composed symmetrically.* ◆◇◇◇◇ ADJ; ADV: ADV with v

symmetry /sɪmɪtri/ **symmetries** ◆◇◇◇◇
1 Something that has **symmetry** is symmetrical in shape, design, or structure. *...the incredible beauty and symmetry of a snowflake... I loved the house because it had perfect symmetry... Their own lives already seemed to possess the symmetries of narrative art.* N-VAR
2 **Symmetry** in a relationship or agreement is the fact of both sides giving and receiving an equal amount. *The superpowers pledged to maintain symmetry in their arms shipments.* N-UNCOUNT
3 You can refer to **symmetry** between countries, institutions, or situations if you think that there is a close similarity between them. *He said that Britain would not rejoin the ERM 'until there is much greater symmetry between our economy and other European economies.'* N-VAR

sympathetic /sɪmpəθetɪk/ ◆◆◇◇◇
1 If you are **sympathetic** to someone who has had a misfortune, you are kind to them and show that you understand their feelings. *She was very sympathetic to the problems of adult students... It may be that he sees you only as a sympathetic friend.* ♦ **sympathetically** /sɪmpəθetɪkli/ *She nodded sympathetically.* ADJ-GRADED: oft v-link ADJ to n; ADV-GRADED: ADV with v
2 If you are **sympathetic** to a proposal or action, you approve of it and are willing to support it. *Many of these early visitors were sympathetic to the Chinese socialist experiment... His speeches against corruption may find a sympathetic hearing among some Trinidadians.* ♦ **sympathetically** *After a year we will sympathetically consider an application for reinstatement.* ADJ-GRADED: oft v-link ADJ to n; ADV-GRADED: ADV with v
3 You describe someone as **sympathetic** when you like them and approve of the way that they behave. *She sounds a most sympathetic character.* ADJ-GRADED

sympathize /sɪmpəθaɪz/ **sympathizes, sympathizing, sympathized;** also spelled **sympathise** in British English. ◆◇◇◇◇
1 If you **sympathize** with someone who has had a misfortune, you show that you are sorry for them. *I must tell you how much I sympathize with you for your loss, Professor... He would sympathize but he wouldn't understand.* VERB; V with n; V
2 If you **sympathize** with someone's feelings, you understand them and are not critical of them. *Some Europeans sympathize with the Americans over the issue... He liked Max, and sympathized with his ambitions.* VERB; V with n; Also V
3 If you **sympathize** with a proposal or action, you approve of it and are willing to support it. *Most of the people living there sympathized with the guerrillas.* VERB; V with n

sympathizer /sɪmpəθaɪzəʳ/ **sympathizers;** also spelled **sympathiser**. The **sympathizers** of an organization or cause are the people who approve of it and support it. *Safta Hashmi was a well-known playwright and Communist sympathizer.* ◆◇◇◇◇ N-COUNT: usu pl, oft supp N

sympathy /sɪmpəθi/ **sympathies** ◆◆◆◇◇
1 If you have **sympathy** for someone who has had a misfortune, you are sorry for them, and show this in the way you behave towards them. *We expressed our sympathy for her loss... I have had very little help from doctors and no sympathy whatsoever... I wanted to express my sympathies on your resignation.* N-UNCOUNT: also N in pl
2 If you have **sympathy** with someone's ideas or opinions, you agree with them. *I have some sympathy with this point of view... Lithuania still commands considerable international sympathy for its cause... She has frequently expressed Republican sympathies.* N-UNCOUNT: also N in pl, oft N with/for n
3 If you take some action in **sympathy** with someone else, you do it in order to show that you support them. *Several hundred workers struck in sympathy with their colleagues at KBS... Milne resigned in sympathy because of the way Donald had been treated. ...calls for sympathy strikes.* N-UNCOUNT: oft N with n

symphonic /sɪmfɒnɪk/. **Symphonic** means relating to or like a symphony. ADJ: usu ADJ n

symphony /sɪmfəni/ **symphonies.** A **symphony** is a piece of music written to be played by an orchestra. Symphonies are usually made up of four separate sections called movements. ◆◆◇◇◇ N-COUNT: oft in names

symphony orchestra, symphony orchestras. A **symphony orchestra** is a large orchestra that plays classical music. ◆◇◇◇◇ N-COUNT: oft in names

symposium /sɪmpoʊziəm/ **symposia** /sɪmpoʊziə/ or **symposiums.** A **symposium** is a conference in which experts or scholars discuss a particular subject. *He had been taking part in an international symposium on population.* ◆◇◇◇◇ N-COUNT: oft N on n

symptom /sɪmptəm/ **symptoms** ◆◆◆◇◇
1 A **symptom** of an illness is something wrong with your body or mind that is a sign of the illness. *One of the most common symptoms of schizophrenia is hearing imaginary voices. ...patients with flu symptoms... If the symptoms persist, it is important to go to your doctor.* N-COUNT
2 A **symptom** of a bad situation is something that happens which is considered to be a sign of this situation. *Your problem with keeping boyfriends is just a symptom of a larger problem: making and keeping friends... The contradictory statements are symptoms of disarray in the administration.* N-COUNT: oft N of n

symptomatic /sɪmptəmætɪk/. If something is **symptomatic** of something else, especially something bad, it is a sign of it; a formal word. *The city's problems are symptomatic of the crisis that is spreading throughout the country.* ◆◇◇◇◇ ADJ: v-link ADJ, usu ADJ of n

synagogue /sɪnəgɒg/ **synagogues.** A **synagogue** is a building where Jewish people meet to worship or to study their religion. ◆◇◇◇◇ N-COUNT: oft in names after n

synapse /saɪnæps, AM sɪnæps/ **synapses.** A **synapse** is one of the points in the nervous system at N-COUNT which a nerve signal passes from one neuron to another; a technical term in biology.

sync /sɪŋk/; also spelled **synch**. If two things are **out of sync**, they are badly matched or do not work simultaneously as they should. If two things are **in sync**, they are well matched or work simultaneously as they should; an informal expression. *Normally, when demand and supply are out of sync, you either increase the supply, or you adjust the price mechanism... They swayed back and forth, more or less in sync with the music.* PHRASE: usu v-link PHR, oft PHR *with* n

synch /sɪŋk/. See **sync**.

synchronize /sɪŋkrənaɪz/ **synchronizes, synchronizing, synchronized;** also spelled **synchronise** in British English. If you **synchronize** two activities, processes, or movements, or **synchronize** one activity, process, or movement with another, you cause them to happen at the same time and speed as each other. *It was virtually impossible to synchronise our lives so as to take holidays and weekends together... Synchronise the score with the film action. ...a series of unexpected, synchronized attacks.* ◆◇◇◇◇ V-RECIP-ERG; V pl-n; V n *with* n; V-ed; Also V *with* n, pl-n V

♦ **synchronization** /sɪŋkrənaɪzeɪʃᵊn/ *With perfect synchronization, two other girls cartwheeled toward the ropes.* N-UNCOUNT

synchronized swimming; also spelled **synchronised swimming**. **Synchronized swimming** is a sport in which two or more swimmers perform complicated and carefully planned movements in water in time to music. N-UNCOUNT

syncopated /sɪŋkəpeɪtɪd/. In **syncopated** music, the weak beats in the bar are stressed instead of the strong beats. *Some spirituals are based on syncopated rhythms.* ADJ-GRADED

syncopation /sɪŋkəpeɪʃᵊn/ **syncopations.** **Syncopation** is the quality that music has when the weak beats in a bar are stressed instead of the strong ones. *There was some nice syncopation and it had a good swing to it... It was jazz music he loved, its syncopations.* N-VAR

syndicate /sɪndɪkət/ **syndicates, syndicating, syndicated** ◆◆◇◇◇

1 A **syndicate** is an association of people or organizations that is formed for business purposes or in order to carry out a project. *They formed a syndicate to buy the car in which they competed in the race. ...a syndicate of 152 banks. ...a major crime syndicate.* N-COUNT

2 When newspaper articles or television programmes **are syndicated**, they are sold to several different newspapers or television stations, who then publish the articles or broadcast the programmes. *Today his programme is syndicated to 500 stations... Myssi is well known in Finland for her quirky food column, which is syndicated across the country. ...a syndicated talk show.* VB: usu passive; *be* V-ed prep/adv; V-ed; Also *be* V-ed

♦ **syndication** /sɪndɪkeɪʃᵊn/ *The show was ready for syndication in early 1987... All together, Columbia has 23 sitcoms in syndication.* N-UNCOUNT

syndrome /sɪndroʊm/ **syndromes** ◆◆◇◇◇

1 A **syndrome** is a medical condition that is characterized by a particular group of signs and symptoms. *Irritable bowel syndrome seems to affect more women than men... The syndrome is more likely to strike those whose immune systems are already below par.* • See also **Down's syndrome, premenstrual syndrome.** N-COUNT: usu sing, oft in names after n

2 You can refer to an undesirable condition that is characterized by a particular type of activity or behaviour as a **syndrome**. *It's a bit like the exam syndrome where you write down everything you know regardless of what has been asked... Scientists call this the 'it won't affect me' syndrome.* N-COUNT: usu sing, usu supp N

synergy /sɪnərdʒi/ **synergies.** If you say that there is **synergy** between two or more organizations or groups, you mean that when they combine or work together, they are more successful than they are when they are on their own; used mainly by business people. *Of course, there's quite obviously a lot of synergy between the two companies... The synergies gained from the merger, Pirelli claimed, would create savings of about £130m over four years.* N-VAR

synod /sɪnɒd/ **synods.** A **synod** is a special council of members of a Church, which meets regularly to discuss religious issues. ◆◇◇◇◇ N-COUNT

synonym /sɪnənɪm/ **synonyms.** A **synonym** is a word or expression which means the same as another word or expression. *The term 'industrial democracy' is often used as a synonym for worker participation.* N-COUNT: oft N *for* n ≠antonym

synonymous /sɪnɒnɪməs/. If you say that one thing is **synonymous** with another, you mean that the two things are very closely associated with each other so that one suggests the other or one cannot exist without the other. *Paris has always been synonymous with elegance, luxury and style... Going grey is not necessarily synonymous with growing old... In politics, power and popularity are not synonymous.* ◆◇◇◇◇ ADJ: usu v-link ADJ, oft ADJ *with* n

synopsis /sɪnɒpsɪs/ **synopses** /sɪnɒpsiːz/. A **synopsis** is a summary of a longer piece of writing or work. *For each title there is a brief synopsis of the book.* N-COUNT =outline, summary

syntactic /sɪntæktɪk/. **Syntactic** means relating to syntax; a technical term. *...three common syntactic devices in English.* ADJ: ADJ n

syntax /sɪntæks/. **Syntax** is the ways that words can be put together, or are put together, in order to make sentences; a technical term. *His grammar and syntax, both in oral and written expression, were much better than the average.* N-UNCOUNT

synthesis /sɪnθɪsɪs/ **syntheses** ◆◇◇◇◇

1 A **synthesis** of different ideas or styles is a mixture or combination of these ideas or styles; a formal use. *His novels are a rich synthesis of Balkan history and mythology... Her synthesis of feminism and socialism ran counter to all other historical currents.* N-COUNT: usu sing, N *of* n =amalgamation

2 The **synthesis** of a substance is the production of it by means of chemical or biological reactions; a technical use. *...the genes that regulate the synthesis of these compounds... This kind of lighting encourages vitamin D synthesis in the skin.* N-VAR: usu with supp =production

synthesize /sɪnθɪsaɪz/ **synthesizes, synthesizing, synthesized;** also spelled **synthesise** in British English. ◆◇◇◇◇

1 To **synthesize** a substance means to produce it by means of chemical or biological reactions; a technical use. *After extensive research, Albert Hoffman first succeeded in synthesizing the acid in 1938... A vitamin is a chemical compound that cannot be synthesized by the human body.* VERB =manufacture; V n

2 If you **synthesize** different ideas, facts, or experiences, you combine them to form a single idea or impression; a formal use. *The movement synthesised elements of modern art that hadn't been brought together before, such as Cubism and Surrealism.* VERB =fuse; V n

synthesized /sɪnθɪsaɪzd/; also spelled **synthesised** in British English. **Synthesized** sounds are produced electronically using a synthesizer. *If the vehicle is going too fast, a synthesised voice tells the driver to slow down. ...synthesised dance music.* ADJ: ADJ n

synthesizer /sɪnθɪsaɪzəʳ/ **synthesizers;** also spelled **synthesiser** in British English. A **synthesizer** is an electronic machine that produces speech, music, or other sounds by using its computer to combine individual syllables or sounds that have been previously recorded and stored. *Now he can only communicate through a voice synthesiser. ...synthesizer music.* ◆◇◇◇◇ N-COUNT

synthetic /sɪnθetɪk/. **Synthetic** products are made from chemicals or artificial substances rather than from natural ones. *Boots made from synthetic materials can usually be washed in a machine. ...synthetic rubber.* ◆◇◇◇◇ ADJ: usu ADJ n =man-made

♦ **synthetically** *...the therapeutic use of natural and synthetically produced hormones.* ADV: ADV with v

synthetics /sɪnθetɪks/. You can refer to synthetic clothing, fabric, or materials as **synthetics**. N-PLURAL

Natural fabrics like silk and wool are better insulators than synthetics.

syphilis /sɪfɪlɪs/. **Syphilis** is a serious disease which is passed on through sexual intercourse. N-UNCOUNT

syphon /saɪfᵊn/ **syphons.** See **siphon.**

Syrian /sɪriən/ **Syrians** ◆◆◆◆◇

1 **Syrian** means belonging or relating to Syria, or to its people or culture. *...the Syrian capital of Damascus. ...a senior Syrian diplomat.* ADJ

2 A **Syrian** is a Syrian citizen, or a person of Syrian origin. *The crew-members were Syrians.* N-COUNT

syringe /sɪrɪndʒ/ **syringes.** A **syringe** is a small tube with a plunger and a fine hollow needle or pointed end. Syringes are used for putting liquids into things and for taking liquids out, for example for injecting drugs or for taking blood from someone's body. ◆◇◇◇◇ N-COUNT

syrup /sɪrəp/ **syrups** ◆◇◇◇◇

1 **Syrup** is a sweet liquid made by cooking sugar with water, and sometimes with fruit juice as well. *...canned fruit with sugary syrup.* N-MASS

2 **Syrup** is a very sweet thick liquid made from sugar. *...a heavy syrup pudding.* • See also **golden syrup, maple syrup.** N-UNCOUNT: oft supp N

3 **Syrup** is a medicine in the form of a thick, sweet liquid. *...cough syrup.* N-MASS: usu supp N

syrupy /sɪrəpi/

1 Liquid that is **syrupy** is sweet or thick like syrup. ADJ-GRADED

2 If you describe something as **syrupy**, you dislike it because it is too sentimental. *...this syrupy film version of Conroy's novel.* ADJ-GRADED PRAGMATICS

system /sɪstəm/ **systems** ◆◆◆◆◆

1 A **system** is a way of working, organizing, or doing something which follows a fixed plan or set of rules. You can use **system** to refer to an organization or institution that is organized in this way. *The present system of funding for higher education is unsatisfactory. ...a flexible and relatively efficient filing system. ...a multi-party system of government... The Court of Appeal has a pivotal role in the English legal system.* N-COUNT: usu with supp =method

2 A **system** is a device or set of devices powered by electricity, for example a hi-fi or a computer. *Viruses tend to be good at surviving when a computer system crashes.* N-COUNT: usu supp N

3 A **system** is a set of equipment or parts such as water pipes or electrical wiring, which is used to supply water, heat, or electricity. *...a central heating system.* N-COUNT: usu supp N

4 A **system** is a network of things that are linked together so that people or things can travel from one place to another or communicate. *...Australia's road and rail system. ...a news channel on a local cable system.* N-COUNT: usu supp N =network

5 Your **system** is your body's organs and other parts that together perform particular functions. *He had slept for over fourteen hours, and his system seemed to have recuperated admirably... These gases would seriously damage the patient's respiratory system. ...the reproductive system.* N-COUNT: usu supp N

6 A **system** is a particular set of rules, especially in mathematics or science, which is used to count or measure things. *...the decimal system of metric weights and measures. ...Trachtenberg's system of simplified mathematics.* N-COUNT: usu supp N

7 People sometimes refer to the government or administration of a country as **the system.** *These feelings are likely to make people attempt to overthrow the system... He wants to be the tough rebel who bucks the system.* N-SING: *the* N

8 See also **central nervous system, digestive system, ecosystem, immune system, metric system, nervous system, public address system, solar system, sound system.**

9 If you **get** something **out of** your **system**, you take some action so that you no longer want to do it or no longer have strong feelings about it. *I want to get boxing out of my system and settle down to enjoy family life.* PHRASE: V inflects

systematic /sɪstəmætɪk/. Something that is done in a **systematic** way is done according to a fixed plan, in a thorough and efficient way. *They went about their business in a systematic way... They had not found any evidence of a systematic attempt to rig the ballot.* ♦ **systematically** /sɪstəmætɪkli/ *The army has systematically violated human rights... She began applying systematically to colleges.* ◆◆◇◇◇ ADJ-GRADED: usu ADJ n =methodical; ADV: ADV with v =methodically

systematize /sɪstəmətaɪz/ **systematizes, systematizing, systematized;** also spelled **systematise** in British English. If you **systematize** things, you make them systematic or organize them into a system; a formal word. *The way to stay on top of changes is to systematize your approach to problem solving.* ♦ **systematization** /sɪstəmətaɪzeɪʃᵊn, AM -tɪz-/ *...a systematization of management practice.* VERB; V n; Also V; N-UNCOUNT: usu N *of* n

systemic /sɪstiːmɪk/ ◆◇◇◇◇

1 **Systemic** means affecting the whole of something. *The economy is locked in a systemic crisis.* ADJ: usu ADJ n

2 **Systemic** chemicals or drugs are absorbed into the whole of an organism such as a plant or person, rather than being applied to one area. ADJ

systems analyst, systems analysts. A **systems analyst** is someone whose job is to assess a company's computer needs and to provide the equipment and software needed to fulfil them. N-COUNT

Tt

T, t /tiː/ **T's, t's;** also spelled **tee** for meaning 3.

1 **T** is the twentieth letter of the English alphabet. N-VAR

2 **T** or **t** is a written abbreviation for words beginning with 't', such as 'ton' and 'time'.

3 In informal English, you can use **to a T** or **to a tee** to mean perfectly or exactly right. For example, if something suits you **to a T**, it suits you perfectly. If you have got an activity or a skill **down to a T**, you have succeeded in doing it exactly right. *The description fits us to a tee... Lucy was a stickler for perfection, and everything had to be exactly right, rehearsed down to a T.* PHRASE: PHR with cl

ta /tɑː/. In British English, **ta** means thankyou; an informal word. ◆◇◇◇◇ CONVENTION

tab /tæb/ **tabs** ◆◇◇◇◇

1 A **tab** is a small piece of cloth or paper that is attached to something, usually with information about that thing written on it. *A stupid medical clerk had slipped the wrong tab on his X-ray while reaching for a mug of tea. ...a small red tab sewn on to the left-hand side of the back right pocket.* N-COUNT =tag, label

2 In American English, a **tab** is a bill or check for goods or services that you have received. *At least one estimate puts the total tab at $7 million... 'I'll get my purse out of the bedroom.'—'No sweat, Mrs. Day. We can put it on your tab.'* N-COUNT =bill

3 In American English, a **tab** is a metal strip that you pull off the top of a can of drink in order to open it. The British term is **ring-pull.** N-COUNT

4 A **tab** is tablet of a drug that is sold illegally; an informal use. *One tab of Ecstasy costs at least £15.* N-COUNT

5 If someone **keeps tabs on** you, they make sure that they always know where you are and what you are doing, often in order to control you; an infor- PHRASES V inflects: PHR n

mal expression. *It was obvious Hill had come over to keep tabs on Johnson and make sure he didn't do anything drastic.*

6 If you **pick up the tab**, you pay a bill on behalf of a group of people or provide the money that is needed for something; an informal expression. *Pollard picked up the tab for dinner that night... Today any employee with back or shoulder pain can go straight to Mr Jay and the company will pick up the tab.* V inflects

Tabasco /tæbæskoʊ/. **Tabasco** is a hot spicy sauce made from peppers. **Tabasco** is a trademark. N-UNCOUNT

tabby /tæbi/ **tabbies.** A **tabby** or a **tabby cat** is a cat whose fur has dark stripes or wavy markings on a lighter background. N-COUNT

tabernacle /tæbəʳnækəl/ **tabernacles**

1 A **tabernacle** is a church used by certain Christian Protestant groups and by Mormons. *...the vision which led Earl Paulk to create his first tabernacle in Atlanta. ...the Brooklyn Tabernacle Choir.* N-COUNT: oft in names

2 **The Tabernacle** was a small tent which contained the most sacred writings of the ancient Jews and which they took with them when they were travelling. N-PROPER: *the* N

table /teɪbəl/ **tables, tabling, tabled** ◆◆◆◆◇

1 A **table** is a piece of furniture with a flat top that you put things on or sit at. *She was sitting at the kitchen table eating a currant bun... I placed his drink on the small table at his elbow.* N-COUNT

2 If you ask for a **table** in a restaurant, you want to have a meal there. *I'd like a table for two at about 8.30, please... I booked a table at the Savoy Grill... You will join us at our table, won't you?* N-COUNT

3 If someone **tables** a proposal, they say formally that they want it to be discussed at a meeting; used mainly in British English. *They've tabled a motion criticising the Government for doing nothing about the problem.* VERB =propose; V n

4 In American English, if someone **tables** a proposal or plan which has been put forward, they decide to discuss it or deal with it at a later date, rather than straight away. *We will table that for later.* VERB; V n

5 A **table** is a written set of facts and figures arranged in columns and rows. *Consult the table on page 104... Other research supports the figures in Table 3.3.* N-COUNT: also N num

6 A **table** is a list of the multiplications of numbers between one and twelve. Children often have to learn tables at school. *He didn't know his eleven-times table... I attempted to learn my tables.* N-COUNT =multiplication table

7 See also **coffee table, dressing table, negotiating table, round table, tea table.**

8 If you put something **on the table**, you present it at a meeting for it to be discussed. *This is one of the best packages we've put on the table in years... It means that all the options are at least on the table.* PHRASES; PHR after v, v-link PHR

9 If you **turn the tables** on someone, you change the situation completely, so that instead of them causing problems for you, you are causing problems for them. *The only question is whether the President can use his extraordinary political skills to turn the tables on his opponents.* V inflects, oft PHR *on* n

10 ● to **put** your **cards on the table**: see **card.**

tableau /tæbloʊ/ **tableaux** ◆◇◇◇◇

1 A **tableau** is a scene, for example from the Bible, history, or mythology, portrayed by people in costumes posing silently, sometimes on a float in a procession. *...a nativity tableau. ...tableaux depicting the foundation of Barcelona.* N-COUNT

2 A **tableau** is a piece of art such as a sculpture or painting that depicts a scene, especially one from the Bible, history, or mythology. *...Gaudi's luxuriant stone tableau of the Nativity on the cathedral's east face.* N-COUNT

tablecloth /teɪbəlklɒθ, AM -klɔːθ/ **tablecloths** A **tablecloth** is a cloth used to cover a table. ◆◇◇◇◇ N-COUNT

table lamp, table lamps. A **table lamp** is a small electric lamp which stands on a table or other piece of furniture. N-COUNT

table manners. You can use **table manners** to refer to the way you behave when you are eating a meal at a table. *He attacked the food as quickly as decent table manners allowed.* N-PLURAL: usu supp N

tablespoon /teɪbəlspuːn/ **tablespoons** ◆◆◇◇◇

1 A **tablespoon** is a fairly large spoon used for serving food and in cooking. N-COUNT

2 You can refer to an amount of food resting on a tablespoon as a **tablespoon** of food. *...a tablespoon of sugar.* N-COUNT: usu N *of* n

tablespoonful /teɪbəlspuːnfʊl/ **tablespoonsful** or **tablespoonfuls.** You can refer to an amount of food resting on a tablespoon as a **tablespoonful** of food. *Grate a tablespoonful of fresh ginger into a pan.* N-COUNT: usu N *of* n

tablet /tæblət/ **tablets** ◆◆◇◇◇

1 A **tablet** is a small solid round mass of medicine which you swallow. *It's time for your tablets, dear... It is never a good idea to take sleeping tablets regularly for this kind of wakefulness.* N-COUNT: oft n N =pill

2 Clay **tablets** or stone **tablets** are the flat pieces of clay or stone which people used to write on before paper was invented. *He also studied the ancient stone tablets from around the pyramids.* ● **not written on tablets of stone**: see **stone.** N-COUNT: oft n N

table tennis; also spelled **table-tennis. Table tennis** is a game played indoors by two or four people. The players stand at each end of a long table which has a low net across its middle and hit a small light ball to the other side of the table, using small bats. ◆◇◇◇◇ N-UNCOUNT

table top, table tops; also spelled **tabletop.** A **table top** is the flat surface on a table. N-COUNT

tableware /teɪbəlweəʳ/. **Tableware** consists of the objects used on the table at meals, for example plates, glasses, or cutlery; a formal word. N-UNCOUNT

table wine, table wines. Table wine is fairly cheap wine that is drunk with meals. N-MASS

tabloid /tæblɔɪd/ **tabloids.** A **tabloid** is a newspaper that has small pages, short articles, and lots of photographs. Tabloids are often considered to be less serious than other newspapers. *'The British tabloids called me "leggy" and "stunning"', she recalls.* ◆◆◇◇◇ N-COUNT ≠broadsheet

taboo /tæbuː/ **taboos.** If there is a **taboo** on a subject or activity, it is a social custom to avoid doing that activity or talking about that subject, because people find them embarrassing or offensive. *The topic of addiction remains something of a taboo... Religious dogmas often include strong sexual taboos and can create in children the impression that sex is sinful.* ► Also an adjective. *Cancer is a taboo subject and people are frightened or embarrassed to talk openly about it.* ◆◇◇◇◇ N-COUNT; ADJ-GRADED

tabulate /tæbjʊleɪt/ **tabulates, tabulating, tabulated.** To **tabulate** information means to arrange it in columns on a page so that it can be analyzed. *...methods of collecting, tabulating and analysing numerical data... Results for the test program haven't been tabulated.* ♦ **tabulation** /tæbjʊleɪʃən/ *...the tabulation of the election results.* VERB; V n; N-UNCOUNT: oft N *of* n

tachograph /tækəgrɑːf, -græf/ **tachographs.** In British English, a **tachograph** is a device that is put in vehicles such as lorries and coaches in order to record information such as how fast the vehicle goes, how far it travels, and the number of breaks the driver takes. N-COUNT

tacit /tæsɪt/. If you refer to someone's **tacit** agreement or approval, you mean they are agreeing to something or approving it without actually saying so, often because they are unwilling to admit to doing so. *The question was a tacit admission that a mistake had indeed been made... The rebels enjoyed the tacit support of elements in the army.* ♦ **tacitly** *He tacitly admitted that the government had breached regulations.* ◆◇◇◇◇ ADJ: usu ADJ n; ADV: ADV with v

taciturn /tæsɪtɜːʳn/. A **taciturn** person does not say very much and can seem unfriendly. *A taciturn man, he replied to my questions in monosyllables.* ADJ-GRADED

tack /tæk/ **tacks, tacking, tacked** 

1 A **tack** is a short nail with a broad, flat head, especially one that is used for fastening carpets to the N-COUNT

floor. • See also **thumbtack.** • **get down to brass tacks**: see **brass.**

2 If you **tack** something to a surface, you pin it there with tacks or drawing pins. *He had tacked this note to her door... She had recently taken a canvas from the theater and tacked it up on the wall.* VERB V n to n V n with adv

3 If you change **tack** or try a different **tack**, you try a different method for dealing with a situation. *In desperation I changed tack... This report takes a different tack from the 20 that have come before.* N-SING: also no det =approach

4 If a sailing boat **is tacking** or if the crew **tacks** it, it is sailing towards a particular point in a series of diagonal movements rather than in a straight line. *We were tacking fairly close inshore... Our last serious trip involved a coastal passage from Morocoy to Puerto la Cruz, tacking east against wind and current... The helmsman could tack the boat singlehanded... We had to tack the boat out of the way of an approaching ferry.* V-ERG V V adv/prep V n V n prep/adv

5 If you **tack** pieces of material together, you sew them together with big, loose stitches in order to hold them firmly or check that they fit, before sewing them properly. *Tack them together with a 1.5 cm seam... Tack the cord around the cushion with raw edges level.* VERB V pl-n with *together* V n prep/adv

tack on. If you say that something **is tacked on** to something else, you think that it is added in a hurry and in an unsatisfactory way. *The child-care bill is to be tacked on to the budget plan now being worked out in the Senate.* PHRASAL VERB *be* V-ed P *to* n Also V n P

tackle /tækəl/ **tackles, tackling, tackled** ◆◆◆◇◇

1 If you **tackle** a difficult problem or task, you deal with it in a very determined or efficient way. *He accused the cabinet of failing to tackle Somalia's severe economic and social problems... Firemen later tackled the blaze.* VERB V n

2 If you **tackle** someone in a game such as hockey or soccer, you try to take the ball away from them. If you **tackle** someone in rugby or American football, you knock them to the ground. *Foley tackled the quarterback.* ► Also a noun. *...a tackle by fullback Brian Burrows.* VERB V n N-COUNT

3 If you **tackle** someone about a matter, you speak to them frankly about it, usually in order to get something changed or done. *I tackled him about how anyone could live amidst so much poverty.* VERB =confront V n *about* wh/n

4 If you **tackle** someone, you attack them and fight them. *He claims Pasolini overtook and tackled him, pushing him into the dirt.* VERB V n

5 **Tackle** is the equipment that you need for a sport or activity, especially fishing. *...fishing tackle.* N-UNCOUNT

6 **Tackle** is the equipment, usually consisting of ropes and pulleys, needed for lifting or pulling something. *I finally hoisted him up with a block and tackle.* N-UNCOUNT

tacky /tæki/ **tackier, tackiest** ◆◇◇◇◇

1 If you describe something as **tacky**, you dislike it because it is cheap and badly made or vulgar; an informal use. *...a woman in a fake leopard-skin coat and tacky red sunglasses... The whole thing is dreadfully tacky.* ADJ-GRADED: usu ADJ n PRAGMATICS =tawdry

2 If something such as paint or glue is **tacky**, it is slightly sticky and not yet dry. *Test to see if the finish is tacky, and if it is, leave it to harden.* ADJ-GRADED =sticky

tact /tækt/. **Tact** is the ability to avoid upsetting or offending people by being careful not to say or do things that would hurt their feelings. *Her tact and intuition never failed. She was a discreet and sympathetic confidante. ...helping to smooth over problems with great tact and efficiency.* ◆◇◇◇◇ N-UNCOUNT =diplomacy

tactful /tæktfʊl/. If you use **tactful** to describe someone, or something they say or do, you approve of them because they are careful not to say or do something which would offend or upset another person. *He had been extremely tactful in dealing with the financial question... I decided it wouldn't be tactful to order another beer.* ◆◇◇◇◇ ADJ-GRADED: oft *it* v-link ADJ to-inf PRAGMATICS =diplomatic ≠tactless

♦ **tactfully** *Alex tactfully refrained from further comment.* ADV-GRADED: usu ADV with v

tactic /tæktɪk/ **tactics.** **Tactics** are the methods that you choose to use in order to achieve what you want in a particular situation. *The terrorists continue to express confidence that their guerrilla tactics can defeat a conventional force... He pressed on in the hope that a few others would join him. The tactic paid off.*  N-COUNT: usu pl

tactical /tæktɪkəl/ ◆◆◇◇◇

1 You use **tactical** to describe an action or plan which is intended to help someone achieve what they want in a particular situation. *It's not yet clear whether the Prime Minister's resignation offer is a serious one, or whether it's simply a tactical move... The security forces had made a tactical withdrawal from the area.* ADJ: usu ADJ n

♦ **tactically** /tæktɪkli/ *They cannot actually tell their supporters to vote tactically against the Conservatives... They were tactically superior too.* ADV: ADV after v, ADV adj, ADV with cl

2 **Tactical** weapons or forces are those which a military commander can decide to use in a battle, rather than waiting for a decision by a political leader. *They have removed all tactical nuclear missiles that could strike Europe. ...U.S. tactical air fighter squadrons.* ADJ: ADJ n

tactical voting. **Tactical voting** is the act of voting for a particular person or political party in order to prevent someone else from winning, rather than because you support that person or party; used mainly in British English. N-UNCOUNT

tactician /tæktɪʃən/ **tacticians.** If you say that someone is a good **tactician**, you mean that they are skilful at choosing the best methods in order to achieve what they want. *He is an extremely astute political tactician... She is a good enough tactician to wait and see what the election brings.* N-COUNT: usu supp N

tactile /tæktaɪl, AM -təl/

1 If you describe someone as **tactile**, you mean that they tend to touch other people a lot when talking to them. *I am a very tactile person. My father-in-law is always very surprised when I kiss him on both cheeks.* ADJ-GRADED

2 Something such as fabric which is **tactile** is pleasant or interesting to touch. *Tweed is timeless, tactile and tough.* ADJ-GRADED

3 **Tactile** experiences or sensations are received or felt by touch; a formal use. *Babies who sleep with their parents receive much more tactile stimulation than babies who sleep in a cot... Heat, cold, tactile and other sensations contribute to flavour.* ADJ: usu ADJ n

tactless /tæktləs/. If you describe someone as **tactless**, you think what they say or do is likely to offend other people. *Throughout his school life Darius was tactless and egocentric... He had alienated many people with his tactless remarks.* ADJ-GRADED ≠tactful

tad /tæd/. You can use **a tad** in expressions such as **a tad big** or **a tad small** when you mean that it is slightly too big or slightly too small; an informal word. *It was a tad confusing... The prices were a tad above average, but they're of the highest quality.* PHRASE: PHR adj/adv

tadpole /tædpoʊl/ **tadpoles.** **Tadpoles** are small water creatures which grow into frogs or toads. N-COUNT

taffeta /tæfɪtə/. **Taffeta** is shiny stiff material made of silk or nylon that is used mainly for making women's clothes. N-UNCOUNT

tag /tæg/ **tags, tagging, tagged** ◆◆◇◇◇

1 A **tag** is a small piece of card or cloth which is attached to an object or person and has information about that object or person on it. *Staff wore name tags and called inmates by their first names. ...baggage tags.* • See also **dog tag, price tag.** N-COUNT =label

2 An electronic **tag** is a device that is firmly attached to someone or something and sets off an alarm if that person or thing moves away or is removed. *A hospital is to fit new-born babies with electronic tags to foil kidnappers... Sometimes, they've snapped off the security tag and just taken the one shoe.* • See also **electronic tagging.** N-COUNT

3 If you **tag** something, you attach something to it or mark it so that it can be identified later. *Professor Orr has developed interesting ways of tagging chemical molecules using existing laboratory lasers... The most important trees were tagged to protect them from being damaged by construction machinery.* VERB V n

4 You can refer to a phrase that is used to describe or categorize someone or something as a **tag**; used in journalism. *In Britain, jazz is losing its elitist tag and gaining a much broader audience.* N-COUNT: usu with supp =label

5 If you **tag** someone with a particular label, you keep describing them using a particular phrase or thinking of them as a particular thing; used in journalism. *...the pundits were still tagging him with that age-old label, 'best of a bad bunch'... She has always lived in John's house and is still tagged 'Dad's girlfriend' by his children.* VERB =label V n *with* n, *be* V-ed n, Also V n *as* n, V n

6 A **tag** is a short quotation or saying. N-COUNT

7 **Tag** is a children's game in which one child chases the others and tries to touch them. N-UNCOUNT =tig

8 See also **question tag**.

tag along. If someone goes somewhere and you **tag along**, you go with them, especially when they have not asked you to. *I let him tag along because he had not been too well recently... She seems quite happy to tag along with them.* PHRASAL VERB V P, V P *with* n

tag on. If you **tag** something **on**, you add it; an informal expression. *It is also worth tagging on an extra day or two to see the capital... Johnson tagged on a happy ending and changed the title to 'Life Begins at 8:30'.* PHRASAL VERB =tack on V P n (not pron) Also V n P

tag line, tag lines; also spelled **tag-line**. The **tag line** of something such as a television commercial or a joke is the phrase that comes at the end and is meant to be memorable or amusing. N-COUNT

tail /teɪl/ **tails, tailing, tailed** ◆◆◆◇◇

1 The **tail** of an animal, bird, or fish is the part extending beyond the end of its body. *The cattle were swinging their tails to disperse the flies. ...a black dog with a long tail.* ♦ **-tailed** *...white-tailed deer.* N-COUNT; COMB in ADJ

2 You can use **tail** to refer to the end or back of something, especially something long and thin. *...the horizontal stabilizer bar on the plane's tail... Elsie tugged her husband's coat tail. ...a comet tail.* N-COUNT: usu with supp

3 If a man is wearing **tails**, he is wearing a formal jacket which has two long pieces hanging down at the back. N-PLURAL =tailcoat

4 To **tail** someone means to follow close behind them and watch where they go and what they do; an informal use. *Officers had tailed the gang from London during a major undercover inquiry... He trusted her so little that he had her tailed.* VERB =shadow V n, *have* n V-ed

5 A **tail** is someone who is paid to watch and to follow another person; an informal use. *He checked behind. No tail.* N-COUNT

6 If you toss a coin and it comes down **tails**, you can see the side of it that does not have a picture of a head on it. ADV: ADV after v ≠heads

7 If you say that **the tail is wagging the dog**, you mean that a small or unimportant part of something is becoming too important and is controlling the whole thing; used showing disapproval. *Past TV deals have seen the tail wagging the dog. Now football clubs feel they are equal partners with TV.* PHRASES V inflects PRAGMATICS

8 If you say that you have **your tail between your legs**, you are emphasizing that you feel defeated and humiliated. *His team retreated last night with tails tucked firmly between their legs.* PHR after v, *with* PHR PRAGMATICS

9 If you **turn tail**, you turn and run away. *I turned tail and fled in the direction of the main house.* V inflects

10 • **cannot make head or tail of** something: see **head**. • to **top and tail**: see **top**.

tail away or **tail off.** When a person's voice **tails away** or **tails off**, it gradually becomes quieter and then silent. *His voice tailed away in the bitter cold air... Benedict's voice tailed off, then resumed.* PHRASAL VERB V P

tail back. When traffic **tails back**, a long queue of it forms along a road, moving very slowly or not at all, for example because of road works or an accident; used in British English. *Southbound traffic tailed back for twenty miles on the M5 near Bristol.* • See also **tailback**. PHRASAL VERB V P

tail off. When something **tails off**, it gradually becomes less in amount or value, often before coming to an end completely. *Last year, economic growth tailed off to below four percent... The drug's effect does not tail off after it has been used repeatedly.* • See also **tail away**. PHRASAL VERB V P

tailback /teɪlbæk/ **tailbacks.** A **tailback** is a long queue of traffic stretching back along a road, moving very slowly or not at all, for example because of road works or an accident; used in British English. *The flooding led to six-mile tailbacks between west London and Heathrow Airport.* N-COUNT

tailcoat /teɪlkoʊt/ **tailcoats;** also spelled **tail-coat**. A **tailcoat** is a man's coat which is short at the front with long pieces at the back. Tailcoats were popular in the 19th century and are now worn only for very formal occasions, such as weddings. N-COUNT =tails

tail end; also spelled **tail-end**. The **tail end** of an event, situation, or period of time is the last part of it. *Barry had obviously come in on the tail-end of the conversation... This is the tail end of the season.* N-SING: usu N *of* n

tailgate /teɪlgeɪt/ **tailgates.** A **tailgate** is a door at the back of a truck or car, that is hinged at the bottom so that it opens downwards. *He let down the tailgate so the dog could jump out.* N-COUNT

tail-light, tail-lights; also spelled **taillight**. The **tail-lights** on a car or other vehicle are the two red lights at the back. *She stood watching the car's tail-lights disappear down the drive.* N-COUNT =rear light

tailor /teɪləʳ/ **tailors, tailoring, tailored** ◆◆◇◇◇

1 A **tailor** is a person whose job is to make men's clothes. N-COUNT

2 If you **tailor** something such as a plan or system to someone's needs, you make it suitable for a particular person or purpose by changing the details of it. *We can tailor the program to the patient's needs. ...how the local forces were trying to tailor their policing style to increase public confidence. ...scripts tailored to American comedy audiences.* VERB V n *to* n, V n to-inf, V-ed, Also V n

tailored /teɪləʳd/. **Tailored** clothes are designed to fit close to the body, rather than being loose and baggy. *...a white tailored shirt.* ADJ-GRADED: usu ADJ n =fitted

tailor-made ◆◇◇◇◇

1 If something is **tailor-made**, it has been specially designed for a particular person or purpose. *...tailor-made itineraries for tourists seeking something more individual than packaged holidays... Each client's portfolio is tailor-made.* ADJ =custom made

2 If you say that someone or something is **tailor-made** for a particular task, purpose, or need, you are emphasizing that they are perfectly suitable for it. *He was tailor-made, it was said, for the task ahead... These questions were tailor-made for Professor Posner.* ADJ: oft ADJ *for* n PRAGMATICS

3 **Tailor-made** clothes have been specially made by a tailor to fit a particular person. *He was wearing a tweed suit that looked tailor-made. ...his expensive tailor-made shirt.* ADJ =made-to-measure

tailor-make, tailor-makes, tailor-making, tailor-made. If someone **tailor-makes** something for you, they make or design it to suit your requirements. *The company can tailor-make your entire holiday... I tailor-make music according to the person.* • See also **tailor-made**. VERB V n

tailpipe /teɪlpaɪp/ **tailpipes.** In American English, a **tailpipe** is the same as an **exhaust** pipe. N-COUNT

tailwind /teɪlwɪnd/ **tailwinds;** also spelled **tail wind**. A **tailwind** is a wind that is blowing from behind an aeroplane, boat, or other vehicle, making it move faster. *A tailwind had cut the flying time by half an hour.* N-COUNT ≠headwind

taint /teɪnt/ **taints, tainting, tainted** ◆◇◇◇◇

1 If you say that something or someone **is tainted** by something undesirable or corrupt, you mean that their status or reputation is harmed because they are associated with it. *Opposition leaders said that the elections had been tainted by corruption. ...a series of political scandals that has tainted the political stars of a generation.* ♦ **tainted** *He came out only slightly tainted by telling millions of viewers he and his wife had marital problems. ...tainted evidence.* VERB *be* V-ed, V n; ADJ-GRADED

2 A **taint** is an undesirable quality which spoils the status or reputation of someone or something. *Her government never really shook off the taint of cor-* N-COUNT: usu sing, usu with supp

ruption... She could smell the taint of sin in the most innocent of passions.

3 If an unpleasant substance **taints** food or medicine, the food or medicine is spoiled or damaged by it. *Rancid oil will taint the flavour. ...blood tainted with the AIDS and hepatitis viruses.* VERB V n V-ed

take 1 used with nouns describing actions

take /teɪk/ **takes, taking, took, taken** ◆◆◆◆◆

Take is used in combination with a wide range of nouns, where the meaning of the combination is mostly given by the noun. Many of these combinations are common idiomatic expressions whose meanings can be found at the appropriate nouns. For example, the expression **take care** is explained at **care**.

1 You can use **take** followed by a noun to talk about an action or event, when it would also be possible to use a verb that is related to the noun or has the same form. For example, you can say **'she took a sip'** instead of 'she sipped'. *She was too tired to take a shower... Betty took a photograph of us... I've never taken a holiday since starting this job... There's not enough people willing to take the risk... Walk around the property and take a good look at it from the outside... We took a long walk through the pines.* VERB V n

2 In ordinary spoken or written English, people use **take** with a range of nouns when it is clear from the context what it means, often instead of a more specific verb. For example people often say **'he took control'** or **'she took a positive attitude'** instead of 'he assumed control' or 'she adopted a positive attitude'. *President Collor de Mello took power in March... I felt it was important for women to join and take a leading role... The constitution requires members of parliament to take an oath of allegiance... In Asia the crisis took a different form.* VERB V n

take 2 other uses

take /teɪk/ **takes, taking, took, taken** ◆◆◆◆◆

1 If you **take** something, you reach out for it and hold it. *Here, let me take your coat... Colette took her by the shoulders and shook her... She took her in her arms and tried to comfort her.* VERB V n V n *by* n V n prep

2 If you **take** something with you when you go somewhere, you carry it or have it with you. *Mark often took his books to Bess's house to study... I'll take these papers home and read them... You should take your passport with you when changing money... Don't forget to take your camera.* VERB V n prep/adv V n *with* n V n

3 If a person, vehicle, or path **takes** someone somewhere, they transport or lead them there. *She took me to a Mexican restaurant... The school bus takes them to school and brings them back... She was taken to hospital.* VERB V n prep/adv

4 If something such as a job or interest **takes** you to a place, it is the reason for you going there. *He was a poor student from Madras whose genius took him to Cambridge... My work takes me abroad a lot.* VERB V n prep/adv

5 If you **take** something such your problems or your custom to someone, you go to that person when you have problems you want to discuss or things you want to buy. *You need to take your problems to a trained counsellor... In a true market, the customer can take business elsewhere.* VERB V n prep/adv

6 If one thing **takes** another to a particular level, condition, or state, it causes it to reach that level or condition. *A combination of talent, hard work and good looks have taken her to the top... The managing director had given himself a pay rise of 20%, taking his salary to £220,000... Her latest research takes her point further.* VERB V n prep/adv

7 If you **take** something from a place, you remove it from there. *He took a handkerchief from his pocket and lightly wiped his mouth... Opening a drawer, she took out a letter.* VERB V n with prep/adv

8 If you **take** something from someone who owns it, you steal it or go away with it without their permission. *He has taken my money, and I have no chance of getting it back... The burglars took just about anything they could carry.* VERB V n

9 If an army or political party **takes** something or someone, they win or capture them from their enemy or opponent. *A Serb army unit took the town... Marines went in, taking 15 prisoners... Labour have made big gains in the local government elections, and took the key council of Bradford.* VERB V n

10 If you **take** one number or amount from another, you subtract it or deduct it. *Take off the price of the house, that's another five thousand.* VERB V n with adv/prep

11 If you cannot **take** something difficult, painful, or annoying, you can not endure or tolerate it without becoming upset, ill, or angry. *Don't ever ask me to look after those kids again. I just can't take it!... Harry's rudeness to everyone was becoming hard to take.* VB: no passive, usu with brd-neg =stand, bear V n

12 If you **take** something such as damage or loss, you suffer it, especially in war or in a battle. *They have taken heavy casualties.* VERB V n

13 If something **takes** a certain amount of time, that amount of time is needed in order to do it. *Since the roads are very bad, the journey took us a long time... Rebuilding Somalia will take years... The sauce takes 25 minutes to prepare and cook... The game took her less than an hour to finish... You must beware of those traps – you could take all day getting out of them... It takes 15 minutes to convert the plane into a car by removing the wings and the tail... It had taken Masters about twenty hours to reach the house... It took thirty-five seconds for the hour to strike.* VB: no passive V n n V n V n to-inf V n n to-inf V n -ing *it* V n to-inf *it* V n n to-inf *it* V n *for* n to-inf

14 If something **takes** a particular quality or thing, that quality or thing is needed in order to do it. *At one time, walking across the room took all her strength... We want to get married and start a family and all. But that takes money... It takes courage to say what you think... It takes the bark of three whole trees to make enough of the drug to treat a single patient... It takes a pretty bad level of performance before the teachers will criticize the students.* VB: no passive =require V n *it* V n to-inf *it* V n *before* cl

15 If you **take** something that is given or offered to you, you agree to accept it. *When I took the job I thought I could change the system, but it's hard... His sons took his advice.* VERB =accept V n

16 If you **take** a feeling such as pleasure, pride, or delight in a particular thing or activity, the thing or activity gives you that feeling. *They take great pride in their heritage... The government will take comfort from the latest opinion poll.* VERB =derive V n *in* n/-ing V n *from* n/-ing

17 If a shop, restaurant, theatre, or other business **takes** a certain amount of money, they get that amount from people buying goods or services; used mainly in British English. *The firm took £100,000 in bookings.* ► In American English, the usual expression is **take in**. *The average cabbie takes in about $600 a week in fares.* VERB V amount PHRASAL VERB V P amount

18 If you **take** a prize or medal, you win it. *'Poison' took first prize at the 1991 Sundance Film Festival... Christie took the gold medal in the 100 metres.* VERB V n

19 If you **take** the blame, responsibility, or credit for something, you agree to accept it. *His brother Raoul did it, but Leonel took the blame and kept his mouth shut... She's reluctant to take all the credit.* VERB =accept V n

20 If you **take** patients or clients, you accept them as your patients or clients. *Some universities would be forced to take more students than they wanted... They were told that Dr Albright wasn't taking any new patients.* VERB V n

21 If you **take** a telephone call, you speak to someone who is telephoning you. *Douglas telephoned Catherine at her office. She refused to take his calls.* VERB V n

22 If you **take** something in a particular way, you react in the way mentioned to a situation or to someone's beliefs or behaviour. *Unfortunately, no one took my messages seriously... Her husband had taken the news badly... I was determined to take the news in a calm and dignified manner.* VERB V n adv/prep

23 You use **take** when you are discussing or explaining a particular question, in order to introduce an example or to say how the question is being considered. *There's confusion and resentment, and it's almost never expressed out in the open. Take this office, for example... You can attack this problem from many angles, but let's take one thing* VB: usu imper PRAGMATICS =consider V n V n prep/adv V-ed at a time... Taken in isolation these statements can be dangerous fallacies.*

24 If you **take** someone's meaning or point, you understand and accept what they are saying. *They've turned sensible, if you take my meaning... 'I'm not saying it's right, I'm just saying that's what happens.'—'I take your point.'*
VERB =understand V n

25 If you **take** someone for something, you believe wrongly that they are that thing. *She had taken him for a journalist... Do you take me for an idiot?... I naturally took him to be the owner of the estate.*
VERB V n *for* n V n to-inf

26 If you **take** something from among a number of things, you choose to have or buy it. *'I'll take the grilled tuna,' Mary Ann told the waiter.*
VERB V n

27 If you **take** a road or route, you choose to travel along it. *From Wrexham centre take the Chester Road to the outskirts of town... He had to take a different route home... It forked in two directions. He had obviously taken the wrong fork.*
VERB V n prep/adv V n

28 If you **take** a house or flat, you rent it, usually for only a short time. *My wife and I have taken the cottage for a month.*
VERB V n

29 In British English, if you **take** something such as a newspaper, you buy it or have it delivered to your home on a regular basis. *Before the Chronicle I used to take the Guardian.*
VERB V n

30 If you **take** a car, train, bus, or plane, you use it to go from one place to another. *It's the other end of the High Street. We'll take the car, shall we?... She took the train to New York every weekend... We'll take a taxi home.*
VERB V n V n prep/adv

31 If you **take** a subject or course at school or university, you choose to study it. *Students are allowed to take European history and American history.*
VERB V n

32 If you **take** a test or examination, you do it in order to obtain a qualification. *She took her driving test in Greenford... She travelled to India after taking her A levels.*
VERB V n

33 If you **take** someone for a subject, you give them lessons in that subject; used mainly in British English. *The teacher that took us for economics was Miss Humphrey.*
VERB =teach V n *for* n

34 If someone **takes** drugs, pills, or other medicines, they take them into their body, for example by swallowing them. *She's been taking sleeping pills... I have never taken illegal drugs.*
VERB V n

35 If you **take** food or drink, you eat or drink it. *She made a habit of coming in to take tea with Nanny Crabtree... If you don't take milk, cheese or yoghurt, other sources of calcium are important.*
VERB V n

36 If you **take** something such as a note or a letter, you write down something you want to remember or something someone says. *She sat expressionless, carefully taking notes... Take a letter, Miss Singleton.*
VERB V n

37 If you **take** a measurement, you find out what it is by measuring. *By drilling, geologists can take measurements at various depths... If he feels hotter than normal, take his temperature.*
VERB V n

38 If a place or container **takes** a particular amount or number, there is enough space for that amount or number. *The place could just about take 2,000 people.*
VB: no passive V amount

39 If you **take** a particular size in shoes or clothes, that size fits you. *47 per cent of women in the UK take a size 16 or above.*
VERB V n

40 If something such as a drug or a dye **takes**, it has the effect or result that is intended. *If the cortisone doesn't take, I may have to have surgery.*
VERB V

41 A **take** is a short piece of action which is filmed in one continuous session for a cinema or television film. *She couldn't get it right – she never knew the lines and we had to do several takes.*
N-COUNT

42 Someone's **take** on a particular situation or fact is their attitude to it or their interpretation of it. *What's your take on the new government? Do you think it can work?... That sort of thing gives you a different take on who you are.*
N-SING: N *on* n, usu supp N =perspective

43 You can say **'I take it'** to check with someone that what you believe to be the case or what you understand them to mean is in fact the case, or is in fact what they mean. *I take it you're a friend of the Kellings, Mr Burr... I take it that neither of you reads 'The Times'... 'You've no objection, I take it?'—'Of course not.'*
PHRASES PHR with cl, oft PHR that PRAGMATICS =I presume

44 You can say **'take it from me'** to tell someone that you are absolutely sure that what you are saying is correct, and that they should believe you. *Take it from me – this is the greatest achievement by any Formula One driver ever.*
PHR with cl PRAGMATICS =believe me

45 If you say to someone **'take it or leave it'**, you are telling them that they can accept something or not accept it, but that you do are not prepared to discuss any other alternatives. *A 72-hour week, 12 hours a day, six days a week, take it or leave it.*
CONVENTION PRAGMATICS

46 If someone **takes** an insult or attack **lying down**, they accept it without protesting or retaliating. *The government is not taking such criticism lying down.*
take inflects

47 If something **takes a lot out of** you or **takes it out of** you, it requires a lot of energy or effort and makes you feel very tired and weak afterwards. *He looked tired, as if the argument had taken a lot out of him... Having loads of children takes it out of you.*
V inflects, PHR n

48 If something **takes you out of** yourself, it makes you feel better and so you forget all your worries and unhappiness. *Donating time and energy to others can take you out of yourself.*
V inflects, PHR pron-refl

49 • to be **taken aback**: see **aback**. • to **take up arms**: see **arm**. • to **take the biscuit**: see **biscuit**. • to **take the bull by the horns**: see **bull**. • to **take** your **hat off to** someone: see **hat**. • to **take the mickey**: see **mickey**. • to **take the piss**: see **piss**. • to **take** something **as read**: see **read**. • to **be taken for a ride**: see **ride**. • to **take** someone **by surprise**: see **surprise**. • **take my word for it**: see **word**.

take after. If you **take after** a member of your family, you resemble them in your appearance, your behaviour, or your character. *Ted's always been difficult, Mr Kemp – he takes after his dad.*
PHRASAL VERB no passive V P n

take against. If you **take against** someone or something, you develop a dislike for them, often for no good reason; used mainly in British English. *It is not an unsympathetic biography, but Sir Edward has taken against it.*
PHRASAL VERB no passive V P n

take apart
PHRASAL VERB

1 If you **take** something **apart**, you separate it into the different parts that it is made of. *When the clock stopped, he took it apart, found what was wrong, and put the whole thing together again.*
=dismantle V n P Also V P n (not pron)

2 If you **take apart** something such as an argument or an idea, you show what its weaknesses are, usually by analyzing it carefully. *They will take that problem apart and analyze it in great detail... He proceeds to take apart every preconception anyone might have ever had about him.*
V n P V P n

take away
PHRASAL VERB

1 If you **take** something **away** from someone, you remove it from them, so that they no longer possess it or have it with them. *They're going to take my citizenship away... 'Give me the knife,' he said softly, 'or I'll take it away from you.'... In prison they'd taken away his watch and everything he possessed.*
V n P V n P *from* n V P n (not pron)

2 If you **take** one number or amount **away** from another, you subtract one number from the other. *We take the time when he goes and we take the time when he comes back, take one away from the other and we know how long the horse has been out.*
=subtract ≠add V n P *from* n Also V P n

3 To **take** someone **away** means to bring them from their home to an institution such as a prison or hospital. You can also use this expression to say that someone has been forcefully removed from their home before being killed. *Two men claiming to be police officers called at the pastor's house and took him away... They were taken away in a police bus... Soldiers took away four people one of whom was later released.*
=take off V n P V P n (not pron)

4 See also **takeaway**.

take away from. If something **takes away from** an achievement, success, or quality, or **takes** something **away from it**, it makes it seem lower in value or worth than it should be. *'It's starting to rain again.'—'Not enough to take away from the charm of the scene.'... The victory looks rather*
PHRASAL VERB =detract V P P n V n P P n

hollow. That takes nothing away from the courage and skill of the fighting forces.

take back PHRASAL VERB

1 If you **take** something **back**, you return it to the place where you bought it or where you borrowed it from, because it is unsuitable or broken, or because you have finished with it. *If I buy something and he doesn't like it I'll take it back... I went to the library and took your books back... I once took back a pair of shoes that fell apart after a week.* V n P; V P n (not pron)

2 If you **take** something **back**, you admit that something that you said or thought is wrong. *I take it back, I think perhaps I am an extrovert... Take back what you said about Jeremy!* V n P; V P n (not pron)

3 If you **take** someone **back**, you allow them to come home again, after they have gone away because of a quarrel or other problem. *Why did she take him back?... The government has agreed to take back those people who are considered economic rather than political refugees.* V n P; V P n (not pron)

4 If you say that something **takes** you **back**, you mean that it reminds you of a period of your past life and makes you think about it again. *I enjoyed experimenting with colours – it took me back to being five years old... This takes me back.* V n P *to* n/-ing; V n P

take down PHRASAL VERB

1 If you **take** something **down**, you reach up and get it from a high place such as a shelf. *Alberg took the portrait down from the wall... Gil rose and went to his bookcase and took down a volume.* V n P; V P n (not pron)

2 If you **take down** a structure, you remove each piece of it. *The Canadian army took down the barricades erected by the Indians... They put up the bird table, but it got in everyone else's way so Les tried to take it down.* ≠put up; V P n (not pron); V n P

3 If you **take down** a piece of information or statement, you write it down. *We've been trying to get back to you, Tom, but we think we took your number down incorrectly... I took down his comments in shorthand.* =write down; V n P; V P n (not pron)

take in PHRASAL VERB

1 If you **take** someone **in**, you allow them to stay in your house or country, especially when they are homeless or in trouble. *He persuaded Jo to take him in... The monastery has taken in 26 refugees.* V n P; V P n (not pron)

2 If the police **take** someone **in**, they remove them from their home in order to question them. *The police have taken him in for questioning in connection with the murder of a girl.* V n P; Also V P n (not pron)

3 If you are **taken in** by someone or something, you are deceived by them, so that you get a false impression of them. *I married in my late teens and was taken in by his charm – which soon vanished... I know I was a naive fool to trust him but he is a real charmer who totally took me in.* be V-ed P; V n P; Also V P n (not pron)

4 If you **take** something **in**, you pay attention to it and understand it when you hear it or read it. *Lesley explains possible treatments but you can tell she's not taking it in... Gazing up into his eyes, she seemed to take in all he said.* V n P; V P n (not pron)

5 If you **take** something **in**, you see all of it at the same time or with just one glance. *The eyes behind the lenses were dark and quick-moving, taking in everything at a glance.* V P n (not pron); Also V n P

6 If you **take in** something such as a film or a museum, you go to see it. *I was wondering if you might want to take in a movie with me this evening.* no passive; V P n (not pron); Also V n P

7 If people, animals, or plants **take in** air, drink, or food, they allow it to enter their body, usually by breathing or swallowing. *They will certainly need to take in plenty of liquid.* V P n (not pron); Also V n P

8 If one thing **takes in** another, it is big enough to include the other thing within it. *Ethiopia's large territorial area takes in a population of more than 40 million people.* no passive; V P n (not pron); Also V n P

9 If you **take in** a dress, jacket, or other item of clothing, you make it smaller and tighter by altering its seams. *She had taken in the grey dress so that it hugged her thin body.* ≠let out; V P n (not pron); Also V n P

take off PHRASAL VERB

1 When an aeroplane **takes off**, it leaves the ground and starts flying. *We eventually took off at 11 o'clock and arrived in Venice at 1.30.* ≠land; V P

2 If something such as a product, an activity, or someone's career **takes off**, it suddenly becomes very successful. *They need to expand the number of farmers who are involved if the scheme's going to really take off... In 1944, he met Edith Piaf, and his career took off.* V P

3 If you **take off** or **take** yourself **off**, you go away, often suddenly and unexpectedly. *He took off at once and headed back to the motel... He took himself off to Mexico.* V P; V pron-refl P

4 If you **take** a garment **off**, you remove it. *He wouldn't take his hat off... She took off her spectacles.* ≠put on; V n P; V P n (not pron)

5 If you **take** time **off**, you obtain permission not to go to work for a short period of time. *Mitchel's schedule had not permitted him to take time off... She took two days off work.* V n (not pron) P; V n (not pron) P n

6 If you **take** someone **off**, you make them go with you to a particular place, especially when they do not want to go there. *The police stopped her and took her off to a police station... Martinez was taken off to jail.* =take away; V n P prep/adv

7 If you **take** someone **off**, you imitate them and the things that they do and say, in such a way that you make other people laugh; used mainly in British English. *Mike can take off his father to perfection.* =mimic; V P n (not pron); Also V n P

8 If something such as a service or entertainment **is taken off**, it is withdrawn so that people can no longer use it or watch it. *We would very much deplore it if a popular programme were taken off as a result of political pressure... The network took it off the air in 1971.* be V-ed P; V n P n; Also V n P, V P n (not pron)

9 See also **takeoff**.

take on PHRASAL VERB

1 If you **take on** a job or responsibility, especially a difficult one, you accept it. *No other organisation was able or willing to take on the job... Don't take on more responsibilities than you can handle.* V P n (not pron); Also V n P

2 If something **takes on** a new appearance or quality, it develops that appearance or quality. *Believing he had only a year to live, his writing took on a feverish intensity.* no passive; =assume; V P n (not pron); Also V n P

3 If a vehicle such as a bus or ship **takes on** passengers, goods, or fuel, it stops in order to allow them to get on or to be loaded on. *This is a brief stop to take on passengers and water.* V P n (not pron); Also V n P

4 If you **take** someone **on**, you employ them to do a job. *He's spoken to a publishing firm. They're going to take him on... The party has been taking on staff, including temporary organisers.* V n P; V P n (not pron)

5 If you **take** someone **on**, you fight them or compete against them, especially when they are bigger or more powerful than you are. *Democrats were reluctant to take on a president whose popularity ratings were historically high... I knew I couldn't take him on.* no passive; V P n (not pron); V n P

6 If you **take** something **on** or **upon** yourself, you decide to do it without asking anyone for permission or approval. *Knox had taken it on himself to choose the wine... He took upon himself the responsibility for protecting her... The President absolved his officers and took the blame upon himself.* no passive; V *it* P pron-refl to-inf; V P pron-refl n; V n P pron-refl

take out PHRASAL VERB

1 If you **take** something **out**, you remove it permanently from its place. *I got an abscess so he took the tooth out... When you edit the tape you can take out the giggles.* V n P; V P n (not pron)

2 If you **take out** something such as a loan, a licence, or an insurance policy, you obtain it by fulfilling the conditions and paying the money that is necessary. *They find a house, agree a price, and take out a mortgage through their building society.* V P n (not pron); Also V n P

3 If you **take** someone **out**, they go to something such as a restaurant or theatre with you after you have invited them, and usually you pay for them. *Jessica's grandparents took her out for the day... Reichel took me out to lunch. ...a father taking out his daughter for a celebratory dinner.* V n P; V n P *to* n; V P n

4 If you **take** someone **out**, you kill them, or injure them so badly that they can no longer fight or do anything to harm you; an informal expression. *In my neighbourhood, the local crack dealers would have taken him out a long time ago.* V n P Also V P n (not pron)

take out on. If you **take** something **out on** someone, you behave in an unpleasant way towards them because you feel angry or upset, even though this is not their fault. *Jane's always annoying her and she takes it out on me sometimes.* PHRASAL VERB V n P P n

take over PHRASAL VERB

1 If you **take over** a company, you get control of it, for example by buying its shares. *A British newspaper says British Airways plan to take over Trans World Airways.* V P n (not pron) Also V n P

2 If someone **takes over** a country or building, they get control of it by force, for example with the help of the army. *The Communists took over China in 1949... The parliament in Madrid was taken over by civil guards.* V P n (not pron) Also V n P

3 If you **take over** a job or role or you **take over**, you become responsible for the job after someone else has stopped doing it. *His widow has taken over the running of his empire, including six London theatres... In 1966, Pastor Albertz took over from him as governing mayor... She took over as chief executive of the Book Trust.* V P n (not pron) V P *from* n V P

4 If one thing **takes over** from something else, it becomes more important, successful, or powerful than the other thing, and eventually replaces it. *Cars gradually took over from horses... When the final vote came, rationality took over.* V P *from* n V P

5 See also **takeover**.

take to PHRASAL VERB ≠take against

1 If you **take to** someone or something, you like them, especially after knowing them or thinking about them for only a short time. *Did the children take to him?... The first series was really bad. But for some reason the public took to it.* V P n

2 If you **take to** doing something, you begin to do it as a regular habit. *They had taken to wandering through the streets arm-in-arm.* V P -ing

take up PHRASAL VERB

1 If you **take up** an activity or a subject, you become interested in it and spend time doing it, either as a hobby or as a career. *He did not particularly want to take up a competitive sport... He left a job in the City to take up farming... Angela used to be a model and has recently decided to take it up again.* V P n (not pron) V n P

2 If you **take up** a question, problem, or cause, you act on it or discuss how you are going to act on it. *Mr de Garis's MP, Max Madden, has taken up the case... Today the United Nations takes up the issue of Somalia... Dr Mahathir intends to take up the proposal with the prime minister... If the bank is unhelpful take it up with the Ombudsman.* V P n (not pron) V P n *with* n V n P *with* n Also V n P

3 If you **take up** a job, you begin to work at it. *He will take up his post as the head of the civil courts at the end of next month.* V P n Also V n P

4 If you **take up** an offer or a challenge, you accept it. *Increasingly, more wine-makers are taking up the challenge of growing Pinot Noir... 96 per cent of the eligible employees took up the offer.* V P n (not pron) Also V n P

5 If something **takes up** a particular amount of time, space, or effort, it uses that amount. *I know how busy you must be and naturally I wouldn't want to take up too much of your time... The entire memo took up all of two pages... A good deal of my time is taken up with reading critical essays and reviews... The aim was not to take up valuable time with the usual boring pictures.* V P n (not pron) *be* V-ed P *with* -ing/n V P n *with* n/-ing

6 If you **take up** a particular position, you get into a particular place in relation to something else. *He had taken up a position in the centre of the room... UN peacekeeping forces are expected to take up positions along the border.* no passive V P n (not pron) Also V n P

7 If you **take up** something such as a task or a story, you begin doing it after it has been interrupted or after someone else has begun it. *Gerry's wife Jo takes up the story... 'No, no, no,' says Damon, taking up where Dave left off.* V P n (not pron) V P where Also V n P

8 See also **take-up**.

take up on PHRASAL VERB

1 If you **take** someone **up on** their offer or invitation, you accept it. *Since she'd offered to babysit, I took her up on it.* V n P P n

2 If you **take** someone **up on** something, you ask them to explain or justify something that they have just said or done, because you think it is wrong or strange. *She was making herself unnaturally casual. But he did not take her up on it.* V n P P n

take upon. See **take on** 6. PHRASAL VERB

take up with PHRASAL VERB

1 You say that someone **has taken up with** someone unsuitable when they have begun a sexual or friendly relationship with them, and you disapprove of this. *Sandy took up with a widow 21 years his junior... He took up with smugglers.* no passive PRAGMATICS V P P n

2 If you **are taken up with** something, it keeps you busy or fully occupied. *His mind was wholly taken up with the question.* PASSIVE *be* V-ed P P n

takeaway /teɪkəweɪ/ **takeaways**

1 In British English, a **takeaway** is a shop or restaurant which sells hot cooked food that you eat somewhere else. The American word is **takeout**. N-COUNT

2 In British English, a **takeaway** is hot cooked food that you buy from a shop or restaurant and eat somewhere else. The American word is **takeout**. *...a Chinese takeaway.* N-COUNT

take-home pay. Your **take-home pay** is the amount of your wages or salary that is left after deductions such as income tax have been made. *He was earning £215 a week before tax: take-home pay, £170.* N-UNCOUNT =net pay ≠gross pay

taken /teɪkən/

1 **Taken** is the past participle of **take**.

2 If you are **taken** with something or someone, you are very interested in them or attracted to them; a rather informal use. *She seems very taken with the idea... I was quite taken with him when I was young.* ADJ-GRADED: v-link ADJ, usu ADJ *with* n

takeoff /teɪkɒf, AM -ɔːf/ **takeoffs;** also spelled **take-off**.

1 **Takeoff** is the beginning of a flight, when an aircraft leaves the ground. *The aircraft crashed after takeoff from Heathrow in a reservoir... The commuter plane was waiting for takeoff.* N-VAR

2 A **takeoff** of someone is a humorous imitation of the way in which they behave. *The programme was worth watching for an inspired take off of the Collins sisters.* N-COUNT: usu sing, usu N *of* n

3 **Takeoff** is the point in the development of something, such as an economy or a business, when it begins to be successful. *The 1950s were the decade of Hong Kong's industrial take-off.* N-UNCOUNT

takeout /teɪkaʊt/ **takeouts**

1 In American English, a **takeout** is a shop or restaurant which sells hot cooked food that you eat somewhere else. The British word is **takeaway**. N-COUNT

2 In American English, a **takeout** or **takeout** food is hot cooked food which you buy from a shop or restaurant and eat somewhere else. The British word is **takeaway**. N-COUNT: oft N n

takeover /teɪkoʊvəʳ/ **takeovers** ◆◆◆◇◇

1 A **takeover** is the act of gaining control of a company by buying enough of its shares to be the major shareholder. *...the proposed £3.4 billion takeover of Midland Bank by the Hong Kong and Shanghai. ...a hostile takeover bid for NCR, America's fifth-biggest computer-maker.* N-COUNT

2 A **takeover** is the act of taking control of a country, political party, or movement by force. *There's been a military takeover of some kind.* N-COUNT: usu with supp =coup

taker /teɪkəʳ/ **takers.** If there are no **takers** for something such as an investment or a challenge, nobody is willing to accept it. *Over 100 buyers or investors were approached, but there were no takers... He hasn't found any takers for that idea.* ◆◇◇◇◇ N-COUNT: usu with brd-neg, usu pl, oft N *for* n

-taker /-teɪkəʳ/ **-takers. -taker** combines with nouns to form other nouns which refer to people who take things, for example decisions or notes. *Of these, 40% told census-takers they were Muslims... They've got some terrific penalty-takers.* COMB in N-COUNT

take-up. **Take-up** is the rate at which people apply for or buy something which is offered, for example financial help from the government or shares in a company; used mainly in British English. *...a major campaign to increase the take-up of welfare benefits.* N-UNCOUNT: usu with supp, oft N *of* n

takings /teɪkɪŋz/. You can use **takings** to refer to the amount of money that a business such as a shop or a cinema gets from selling its goods or tickets during a certain period; used mainly in British English. *The pub said that their takings were fifteen to twenty thousand pounds a week.* N-PLURAL

talc /tælk/. **Talc** is the same as **talcum powder**; an informal word. N-UNCOUNT

talcum powder /tælkəm paʊdər/. **Talcum powder** is fine, perfumed powder which people put on their bodies after they have had a bath or a shower. N-UNCOUNT =talc

tale /teɪl/ **tales** ◆◆◆◇◇

1 A **tale** is a story, often involving adventure or magic. *...a collection of stories, poems and folk tales... Episodes 1 and 2 of Tales of the City will be shown together on Tuesday.* N-COUNT: oft in names

2 You can refer to an interesting, exciting, or dramatic account of a real event as a **tale**. *The media have been filled with tales of horror and loss resulting from Monday's earthquake. ...a property analyst, full of cheery tales about soaring share prices and new capital pouring into property companies.* N-COUNT: usu with supp, oft N *of* n =story

3 See also **fairy tale, old wives' tale, tall tale**.

4 If you survive a dangerous or frightening experience and so are able to tell people about it afterwards, you can say that you **lived to tell the tale**. *You lived to tell the tale this time but who knows how far you can push your luck.* PHRASES V inflects

5 If someone **tells tales** about you, they tell other people things about you which are untrue or which you wanted to be kept secret. *I hesitated, not wanting to tell tales about my colleague.* • See also **telltale**. V inflects

talent /tælənt/ **talents. Talent** is the natural ability to do something well. *She is proud that both her children have a talent for music... The player was given hardly any opportunities to show off his talents... He's got lots of talent.* • See also **talent show**. ◆◆◆◇◇ N-VAR: oft N *for* n

talented /tæləntɪd/. Someone who is **talented** has a natural ability to do something well. *Howard is a talented pianist... She has a huge army of young fans, and is extremely talented.* ◆◆◇◇◇ ADJ-GRADED =gifted

talent scout, talent scouts. A **talent scout** is someone whose job is to find people who have talent, for example as actors, footballers, or musicians, so that they can be offered work. N-COUNT

talent show, talent shows. A **talent show**, **talent competition**, or **talent contest** is a show where ordinary people perform an act on stage, usually in order to try to win a prize for the best performance. *He began his musical career in talent shows... At the age of 18, she won first prize in a talent contest.* N-COUNT

talisman /tælɪzmən/ **talismans.** A **talisman** is an object which you believe has magic powers to protect you or bring you luck. N-COUNT =amulet, charm

talk /tɔːk/ **talks, talking, talked** ◆◆◆◆◆

1 When you **talk**, you use spoken language to express your thoughts, ideas, or feelings. *He was too distressed to talk... A teacher reprimanded a girl for talking in class... The boys all began to talk at once... Though she can't talk yet, she understands what is going on.* ► Also a noun. *That's not the kind of talk one usually hears from accountants.* VERB V N-UNCOUNT

2 If you **talk** to someone, you have a conversation with them. You can also say that two people **talk**. *We talked and laughed a great deal... I talked to him yesterday... A neighbour saw her talking with Craven... When she came back, they were talking about American food... Can't you see I'm talking? Don't interrupt.* ► Also a noun. *We had a long talk about her father, Tony, who was a friend of mine.* V-RECIP pl-n V, V *to* n, V *with* n, pl-n V *about* n, V (non-recip), Also V *to* n *about* n; N-COUNT =conversation

3 If you **talk** to someone, you tell them about the things that are worrying you. You can also say that two people **talk**. *Your first step should be to talk to a teacher or school counselor... There's no one she can talk to, and she's on the verge of collapse... We need to talk alone... Do ring if you want to talk about it... I have to sort some things out. We really needed to talk.* ► Also a noun. *I think it's time we had a talk.* V-RECIP V *to* n, pl-n V, V *about* n (non-recip), V (non-recip); N-COUNT

4 If you **talk** on or about something, you make an informal speech telling people what you know or think about it. *She will talk on the issues she cares passionately about including education and nursery care... He intends to talk to young people about the dangers of AIDS.* ► Also a noun. *A guide gives a brief talk on the history of the site... He then set about campaigning, giving talks and fund-raising.* VERB =speak V *on/about* n, V *to* n; N-COUNT: oft N *on/about* n

5 **Talks** are formal discussions intended to produce an agreement, usually between different countries or between employers and employees. *...the next round of Middle East peace talks... Talks between striking railway workers and the Polish government have broken down... They are holding hostages to try to force the authorities into talks on possible amnesties for drugs offences.* N-PLURAL: oft N *with/between* n, N *on/about* n =negotiations

6 If one group of people **talks** to another, or if two groups **talk**, they have formal discussions in order to do a deal or produce an agreement. *We're talking to some people about opening an office in London... The company talked with many potential investors... It triggered broad speculation that GM and Jaguar might be talking.* V-RECIP V *to* n *about* n/-ing, V *with/to* n, pl-n V

7 When different countries or different sides in a dispute **talk**, or **talk** to each other, they discuss their differences in order to try and settle the dispute. *The Foreign Minister said he was ready to talk to any country that had no hostile intentions... They are collecting information in preparation for the day when the two sides sit down and talk... Croats and Serbs still aren't prepared to talk to each other... The speed with which the two sides came to the negotiating table shows that they are ready to talk.* V-RECIP =negotiate V *to* n, pl-n V, V *to/with* pron-recip, V (non-recip)

8 If people **are talking** about another person or **are talking**, they are discussing that person and gossiping about them. *Everyone is talking about him... People will talk, but you have to get on with your life.* ► Also a noun. *There has been a lot of talk about me getting married... There was even talk that charges of fraud would be brought.* VERB =gossip V *about/of* n, V; N-UNCOUNT: usu N *about/of* n/-ing, N that

9 If someone **talks** when they are being held by police or soldiers, they reveal important or secret information, usually unwillingly. *They'll talk, they'll implicate me.* VERB V

10 If you **talk** a particular language or **talk** with a particular accent, you use that language or have that accent when you speak. *You don't sound like a foreigner talking English... They were amazed that I was talking in an Irish accent.* VB: no passive V n, V prep/adv

11 If you **talk** something such as politics or sport, you discuss it. *The guests were mostly middle-aged men talking business.* VB: no passive V n

12 You can use **talk** to say what you think of the ideas that someone is expressing. For example, if you say that someone is **talking sense**, you mean that you think the opinions they are expressing are sensible. *You must admit George, you're talking absolute rubbish.* VERB V n

13 In informal conversations, you can say that you **are talking** a particular thing to draw attention to your topic or to point out a characteristic of what you are discussing. *We're not talking ax murder here; we're talking poker machines or gambling – things that are misdemeanors in most states... We're talking megabucks this time.* VB: no passive PRAGMATICS V n

14 If you say that something such as an idea or threat is just **talk**, you mean that it does not mean or matter much, because people are exaggerating about it or do not really intend to do anything about it. *Has much of this actually been tried here? Or is it just talk?... Conditions should be laid down. Otherwise it's all talk.* N-UNCOUNT

15 In informal English, you can say **talk about** before mentioning a particular expression or situation, when you mean that something is a very striking or clear example of that expression or situation. PHRASES PHR n/-ing PRAGMATICS

Took us quite a while to get here, didn't it? Talk about Fate moving in a mysterious way!... She threw the cake I'd made on the floor and stood on it. Talk about being humiliated!

16 You can use the expression **talking of** to introduce a new topic that you want to discuss, and to link it to something that has already been mentioned. *I'll give a prize to the best idea. Talking of good ideas, here's one to break the ice at a wedding party... As it says in the Bible, my cup is running over. Talking of which, I must get you a cup of tea.* PHR n/-ing PRAGMATICS =speaking of

17 ● to **talk shop**: see **shop**.

talk back. If you **talk back** to someone in authority such as a parent or teacher, you answer them in a rude way. *How dare you talk back to me!... I talked back and asked questions.* PHRASAL VERB =answer back; V P to n; V P

talk down PHRASAL VERB

1 To **talk down** someone who is flying an aircraft in an emergency means to give them instructions so that they can land safely. *The pilot began to talk him down by giving instructions over the radio.* V n P

2 If someone **talks down** a particular thing, they make it less interesting, valuable, or likely than it originally seemed. *They even blame the government for talking down the nation's fourth biggest industry... Businessmen are tired of politicians talking the economy down.* ≠talk up; V P n (not pron); V n P

3 To **talk** someone **down** in negotiations means to persuade them to accept less money than they originally asked for; used mainly in British English. *We talked them down and struck a deal... When he makes you an offer, you send me in and I'll talk him down another thousand... This leaves the Prime Minister, like his predecessors, earnestly trying to talk down wages.* V n P; V n P amount; V P n (not pron)

talk down to. If you say that someone **talks down to** you, you disapprove of the way they talk to you, treating you as if you are not very intelligent or not very important. *She was a gifted teacher who never talked down to her students.* PHRASAL VERB PRAGMATICS =patronize; V P P n

talk into PHRASAL VERB

1 If you **talk** someone **into** doing something they do not want to do, especially something wrong or stupid, you persuade them to do it. *He talked me into marrying him. He also talked me into having a baby... I was a fool to have let her talk me into it.* ≠talk out of; V n P -ing/n

2 If you **talk** yourself **into** a particular situation or state, you get yourself into it by talking. *He has talked himself into a position where he will have no option but to go.* V pron-refl P n

talk out. If you **talk out** something such as a problem, you discuss it thoroughly in order to settle it. *Talking things out with someone else can be helpful... Talk out your problems. Do not keep them bottled up.* PHRASAL VERB =talk through; V n P; V P n (not pron)

talk out of PHRASAL VERB

1 If you **talk** someone **out of** doing something they want or intend to do, you persuade them not to do it. *My mother tried to talk me out of getting a divorce... People tried to talk him out of it, but he insisted.* ≠talk into; V n P P -ing/n

2 If you **talk** yourself **out of** a particular situation or state, you get yourself out of it by talking. *I tried to talk myself out of a fight.* V pron-refl P n

talk over. If you **talk** something **over**, you discuss it thoroughly and honestly. *He always talked things over with his friends... We should go somewhere quiet, and talk it over... Talk over problems, don't bottle them up inside.* PHRASAL VERB; V n P with n; V n P; V P n (not pron)

talk round. If you **talk** someone **round**, you persuade them to change their mind so that they agree with you, or agree to do what you want them to do; used mainly in British English. *He went to the house to try to talk her round... It advises salesmen to talk round reluctant customers over a cup of tea.* PHRASAL VERB; V n P; V P n (not pron)

talk through PHRASAL VERB

1 If you **talk** something **through** with someone, you discuss it with them thoroughly. *He and I have talked through this whole tricky problem... Now her children are grown-up and she has talked through with them what happened... It had all seemed so simple when they'd talked it through, so logical... He had talked it through with Judith.* RECIP; pl-n V P n (not pron); V P with n n; pl-n V n P; V n P with n

2 If someone **talks** you **through** something that you do not know, they explain it to you carefully. *Now she must talk her sister through the process a step at a time.* V n P n

talk up PHRASAL VERB

1 If someone **talks up** a particular thing, they make it sound more interesting, valuable, or likely than it originally seemed. *Politicians accuse the media of talking up the possibility of a riot... He'll be talking up his plans for the economy.* ≠talk down; V P n (not pron); Also V n P

2 To **talk** someone or something **up** in negotiations means to persuade someone to pay more money than they originally offered or wanted to; used mainly in British English. *Allan Clarke kept talking the price up, while Wilkinson kept knocking it down.* ≠talk down; V n P; Also V P n (not pron)

talkative /tɔːkətɪv/. Someone who is **talkative** talks a lot. *He suddenly became very talkative, his face slightly flushed, his eyes much brighter.* ADJ-GRADED =chatty

talker /tɔːkəʳ/ **talkers.** You can use **talker** to refer to someone when you are considering how much they talk, or how good they are at talking to people. *...a fluent talker.* N-COUNT: usu supp N

talkie /tɔːki/ **talkies.** A **talkie** is a cinema film made with sound, as opposed to a silent film; an old-fashioned word. *Garbo made two dozen films, first silent pictures then talkies.* ◆◇◇◇◇ N-COUNT =talking picture

talking head, talking heads. In informal English, **talking heads** are people who appear in television discussion programmes and interviews to give their opinions about a topic. N-COUNT =pundit

talking point, talking points. A **talking point** is an interesting subject for discussion or argument. *It's bound to be the main talking point during discussions between the Prime Minister and the President.* N-COUNT

talking shop, talking shops. If you say that a conference or a committee is just a **talking shop**, you disapprove of it because nothing is achieved as a result of what is discussed; used mainly in British English. N-COUNT PRAGMATICS

talking-to. If you give someone **a talking-to**, you speak to them severely, usually about something unacceptable that they have done, in order to show them they were wrong; an informal word. *The team manager said: 'Tony has had a good talking-to and regrets his action'.* N-SING: a N

talk show, talk shows; also spelled **talk-show.** A **talk show** is a television or radio show in which an interviewer and his or her guests talk in an informal way about different topics. ◆◇◇◇◇ N-COUNT =chat show

tall /tɔːl/ **taller, tallest** ◆◆◆◇◇

1 Someone or something that is **tall** has a greater height than is normal or average. *Being tall can make you feel incredibly self-confident... She was a young woman, fairly tall and fairly slim... The windows overlooked a lawn of tall waving grass.* ADJ-GRADED

2 You use **tall** to ask or talk about the height of someone or something. *How tall are you?... I'm only 5ft tall, and I look younger than my age... I am already as tall as she is... Tony, my oldest, is already taller than me, and he's only eleven.* ADJ-GRADED: how ADJ, amount ADJ, as ADJ as, ADJ-compar than

3 If something is **a tall order**, it is very difficult. *Financing your studies may seem like a tall order, but there is plenty of help available.* PHRASES N inflects, v-link PHR

4 If you say that someone **walks tall**, you mean that they behave in a way that shows that they have pride in themselves and in what they are doing. V inflects

tallow /tæloʊ/. **Tallow** is hard animal fat used for making candles and soap. N-UNCOUNT

tall story, tall stories. A **tall story** is the same as a **tall tale**. N-COUNT

tall tale, tall tales. A **tall tale** is a long and complicated story that is very difficult to believe because most of the events it describes seem unlikely or impossible. *...the imaginative tall tales of sailors.* N-COUNT =tall story

tally /tæli/ **tallies, tallying, tallied** ◆◇◇◇◇

1 A **tally** is a record of amounts or numbers which you keep changing and adding to as the activity which affects it progresses. *They do not keep a tally* N-COUNT: usu sing, oft N of n *of visitors to the palace, but it is very popular... The final tally was 817 votes for her and 731 for Mr Lee.*

2 If one number or statement **tallies** with another, they agree with each other or are exactly the same. You can also say that two numbers or statements **tally**. *Its own estimate of three hundred tallies with that of another survey... This description didn't seem to tally with what we saw... The figures didn't seem to tally.* V-RECIP =correspond; V *with* n; pl-n V

3 If you **tally** numbers, items, or totals, you count them. *...as we tally the number of workers who have been laid off this year... When the final numbers are tallied, sales will almost certainly have fallen.* VERB; V n

► **Tally up** means the same as **tally**. *Bookkeepers haven't yet tallied up the total cost.* PHRASAL VERB; V P n (not pron); Also V n P

Talmud /tælmʊd/. **The Talmud** is the collection of ancient Jewish laws which governs the religious and non-religious life of Orthodox Jews. N-PROPER: *the* N

talon /tælən/ **talons.** The **talons** of a bird of prey, are its hooked claws. N-COUNT: usu pl

tamarind /tæmərɪnd/ **tamarinds.** A **tamarind** is a fruit which grows on a tropical evergreen tree which has pleasant-smelling flowers. You can also refer to the tree on which this fruit grows as a **tamarind**. N-VAR

tamarisk /tæmərɪsk/ **tamarisks.** A **tamarisk** is a bush or small tree which grows mainly around the Mediterranean and in Asia, and which has feathery pink or white flowers. N-COUNT

tambourine /tæmbəriːn/ **tambourines.** A **tambourine** is a musical instrument which you shake or hit with your hand. It consists of a drum skin on a circular frame with pairs of small round pieces of metal all around the edge. N-COUNT: oft *the* N

tame /teɪm/ **tamer, tamest; tames, taming, tamed** ◆◇◇◇◇

1 A **tame** animal or bird is one that is not afraid of humans. *They never became tame; they would run away if you approached them.* ADJ-GRADED

2 If you say that something or someone is **tame**, you are criticizing them for being weak and unadventurous, rather than forceful or shocking. *Some of today's political demonstrations look rather tame... The report was pretty tame stuff.* ADJ-GRADED PRAGMATICS ♦ **tamely** *There was no excuse though when Thomas shot tamely wide from eight yards.* ADV-GRADED: ADV with v

3 If someone **tames** a wild animal or bird, they train it not to be afraid of humans and to be obedient. *The Amazons were believed to have been the first to tame horses.* VERB; V n

4 If you **tame** someone or something that is dangerous, uncontrolled, or likely to cause trouble, you bring them under control. *Two regiments of cavalry were called out to tame the crowds.* VERB; V n

tamp /tæmp/ **tamps, tamping, tamped.** If you **tamp** something, you press it down by tapping it several times so that it becomes more solid and compact. *Then I tamp down the soil with the back of a rake... Philpott tamped a wad of tobacco into his pipe.* VERB; V n with adv; V n prep/adv; Also V n

tamper /tæmpəʳ/ **tampers, tampering, tampered.** If someone **tampers** with something, they interfere with it or try to change it when they have no right to do so. *I don't want to be accused of tampering with the evidence... He found his computer had been tampered with.* ◆◇◇◇◇ VERB; V *with* n ♦ **tampering** *...discovering a motive for a crime like product tampering.* N-UNCOUNT: usu n N

tampon /tæmpɒn/ **tampons.** A **tampon** is a piece of cotton wool that a woman puts inside her vagina in order to absorb the blood during menstruation. ◆◇◇◇◇ N-COUNT

tan /tæn/ **tans, tanning, tanned** ◆◆◇◇◇

1 If you have a **tan**, your skin has become darker than usual because you have been in the sun. *She is tall and blonde, with a permanent tan.* N-SING: usu *a* N =suntan

2 If a part of your body **tans** or if you **tan** it, your skin becomes darker than usual because you spend a lot of time in the sun. *I have very pale skin that never tans... I don't tan... Leigh rolled over on her stomach to tan her back.* V-ERG; V; V n ♦ **tanned** *Their skin was tanned and glowing from their weeks at the sea.* ADJ-GRADED

3 Something that is **tan** is a light brown colour. *...a tan leather jacket.* COLOUR

4 To **tan** animal skins means to make them into leather by treating them with tannin or other chemicals. *...the process of tanning animal hides.* VERB; V n

tandem /tændəm/ **tandems** ◆◇◇◇◇

1 A **tandem** is a bicycle designed for two riders, on which one rider sits behind the other. N-COUNT

2 If one thing happens or is done **in tandem** with another thing, the two things happen at the same time. *Malcolm's contract will run in tandem with his existing one.* PHRASES; usu PHR after v, oft PHR *with* n

3 If one person does something **in tandem** with another person, the two people do it by working together. *He is working in tandem with officials of the Serious Fraud Office.* usu PHR after v, oft PHR *with* n

tandoori /tændʊəri/. **Tandoori** dishes are Indian meat dishes which are cooked in a clay oven. ADJ: usu ADJ n

tang /tæŋ/. A **tang** is a strong, sharp smell or taste. *She could smell the salty tang of the sea.* N-SING

tangent /tændʒənt/ **tangents**

1 A **tangent** is a line that touches the edge of a curve or circle at one point, but does not cross it. N-COUNT

2 If someone **goes off at a tangent**, they start saying or doing something that is not directly connected with what they were saying or doing before. *The conversation went off at a tangent.* PHRASE: V and N inflect

tangential /tændʒenʃəl/

1 If you describe something as **tangential**, you mean that it has only a slight or indirect connection with the thing you are concerned with, and is therefore not worth considering seriously; a formal use. *Too much time was spent discussing tangential issues... They thought the whole thing was a sideshow, tangential to the real world of business.* ADJ-GRADED

2 If something is **tangential** to something else, it is at a tangent to it. *...point T, where the demand curve is tangential to the straight line L. ...the street tangential to the courthouse square.* ADJ: oft ADJ *to* n

tangerine /tændʒəriːn/ **tangerines.** A **tangerine** is a small sweet orange. N-COUNT

tangible /tændʒɪbəl/. If something is **tangible**, it is clear enough or definite enough to be easily seen, felt, or noticed. *There should be some tangible evidence that the economy is starting to recover... The relief was almost tangible.* ◆◇◇◇◇ ADJ-GRADED ♦ **tangibly** *This tangibly demonstrated that the world situation could be improved.* ADV-GRADED: usu ADV with v, also ADV adj

tangle /tæŋgəl/ **tangles, tangling, tangled** ◆◆◇◇◇

1 A **tangle** of something is a mass of it twisted together in an untidy way. *A tangle of wires is all that remains of the computer and phone systems... There he stood: hair in wild tangles, dark stubble shadowing his chin.* N-COUNT: usu N *of* n

2 If something **is tangled** or **tangles**, it becomes twisted together in an untidy way. *Animals get tangled in fishing nets and drown... She tried to kick the pajamas loose, but they were tangled in the satin sheet... Lee and I fell in a tangled heap... Her hair tends to tangle... He suggested that tangling fishing gear should be made a criminal offence.* V-ERG; *get/be* V-ed in n; V-ed; V; V n; Also *get/be* V-ed

3 You can refer to a confusing or complicated situation as a **tangle**. *I was thinking what a tangle we had got ourselves into. ...the tangle of domestic politics.* N-SING: oft N *of* n

4 If ideas or situations **are tangled**, they become confused and complicated. *The themes get tangled in Mr. Mahfouz's elliptical storytelling... You are currently in a quagmire where financial and emotional concerns are tangled together.* VB: usu passive; *get/be* V-ed; V-ed ♦ **tangled** *His personal life has become more tangled than ever.* ADJ-GRADED

5 ● **a tangled web**: see **web**.

tangle up PHRASAL VERB

1 If something or someone **is tangled up** in something such as a mass of wire or ropes, they are caught or trapped in it. *Sheep kept getting tangled up in it and eventually the wire was removed... The teeth are like razors. Once you get tangled up it will never let you go.* usu passive; *get/be* V-ed P in n; *get/be* V-ed P

2 If you **are tangled up** in a complicated or unpleasant situation, you are involved in it and cannot get free of it. *Politicians normally avoid getting* usu passive; *get/be* V-ed P *in/with* n

tangled up in anything to do with their electorate's savings. ♦ **tangled up** *For many days now Buddy and Joe had appeared to be more and more tangled up in secrets.* ADJ-GRADED: v-link ADJ

tangle with. If you **tangle with** another person, you get involved in a conflict with them. *In the past Clinton has tangled with the teachers' unions in Arkansas... All the newspapers wanted to do was to photograph the police officers tangling with the demonstrators.* PHRASAL VERB V P n

tango /tæŋgoʊ/ **tangos, tangoing, tangoed** ◆◇◇◇◇

1 The **tango** is a South American dance in which two people hold each other closely, walk quickly in one direction, then walk quickly back again. N-SING: usu *the* N

2 A **tango** is a piece of music intended for tango dancing. *A tango was playing on the jukebox... The sounds of tango filled the air.* N-VAR

3 If you **tango**, you dance the tango. *They can rock and roll, they can tango, but they can't bop.* VERB V

4 ● **it takes two to tango**: see **two**.

tangy /tæŋi/ **tangier, tangiest.** A **tangy** flavour or smell is one that is sharp, especially a flavour like that of lemon juice or a smell like that of sea air. ◆◇◇◇◇ ADJ-GRADED

tank /tæŋk/ **tanks** ◆◆◆◇◇

1 A **tank** is a large container for holding liquid or gas. *...an empty fuel tank... Two water tanks provide a total capacity of 400 litres. ...a tank full of goldfish.* ▶ A **tank** of a liquid or gas is an amount of it contained in a tank. *A lorry can drive up to 600 miles on a single tank of fuel.* N-COUNT: oft n N; N-COUNT: usu N *of* n

2 A **tank** is a military vehicle covered with armour and equipped with weapons which moves along on metal tracks fitted over the wheels. N-COUNT

3 See also **septic tank, think-tank.**

tankard /tæŋkəʳd/ **tankards.** A **tankard** is a large metal mug with a handle, which you can drink beer from. *...a large pewter tankard.* ▶ A **tankard** of beer is an amount of it contained in a tankard. *...a tankard of ale.* N-COUNT; N-COUNT: usu N *of* n

tanked up. In informal British English, if someone is **tanked up**, they are drunk. ADJ-GRADED: usu v-link ADJ

tanker /tæŋkəʳ/ **tankers** ◆◆◇◇◇

1 A **tanker** is a very large ship used for transporting large quantities of gas or liquid, especially oil. *A Greek oil tanker has run aground.* N-COUNT: oft supp N, also *by* N

2 A **tanker** is a large truck, railway vehicle, or aircraft used for transporting large quantities of a substance. *...an accident involving a petrol tanker on the M27, east of Southampton.* N-COUNT: usu supp N, also *by* N

tanner /tænəʳ/ **tanners.** A **tanner** is someone whose job is making leather from animal skins. N-COUNT

tannin /tænɪn/. **Tannin** is a yellow or brown chemical that is found in plants such as tea. It is used in the process of making leather and in dyeing. N-UNCOUNT

Tannoy /tænɔɪ/. In British English, a **Tannoy** is a system of loudspeakers used to make public announcements, for example at a fete or at a sports stadium. **Tannoy** is a trademark. N-SING: oft *over* N

tantalize /tæntəlaɪz/ **tantalizes, tantalizing, tantalized;** also spelled **tantalise** in British English. If someone or something **tantalizes** you, they make you feel hopeful and excited about getting something, usually before disappointing you by not letting you have what they appeared to offer. *The boy would come into the room and tantalize the dog with his feed. ...the dreams of democracy that have so tantalized them.* ♦ **tantalizing** *A tantalising aroma of roast beef fills the air.* ♦ **tantalizingly** *She went away disappointed after getting tantalisingly close to breaking the record... A political settlement remains tantalisingly out of reach.* ◆◇◇◇◇ VERB; V n *with* n; V n; Also V; ADJ-GRADED; ADV-GRADED: ADV adj, ADV with v, ADV with cl

tantamount /tæntəmaʊnt/. If you say that one thing is **tantamount to** a second, more serious thing, you are emphasizing how bad, unacceptable, or unfortunate the first thing is by comparing it to the second; a formal word. *What Bracey is saying is tantamount to heresy... He said the decision was tantamount to protecting terrorist organisations around the world.* ◆◇◇◇◇ ADJ: v-link ADJ *to* n/-ing PRAGMATICS =as good as

tantrum /tæntrəm/ **tantrums.** If a child has a **tantrum**, they suddenly lose their temper in a noisy and uncontrolled way. If you say that an adult is throwing a **tantrum**, you are criticizing them for losing their temper and acting childishly. *My son had a tantrum and banged his fist on the ground... He immediately threw a tantrum, screaming and stomping up and down like a child.* ◆◇◇◇◇ N-COUNT PRAGMATICS

Taoism /taʊɪzəm/. **Taoism** is a Chinese religious philosophy which believes that people should lead a simple honest life and not interfere with the course of natural events. N-UNCOUNT

tap /tæp/ **taps, tapping, tapped** ◆◆◆◇◇

1 A **tap** is a device that controls the flow of a liquid or gas from a pipe or container, for example on a sink; used mainly in British English. The usual American word is **faucet**. *...a cold-water tap... The honey runs out of a tap at the bottom of the drum.* N-COUNT

2 If you **tap** something, you hit it with a quick light blow or a series of quick light blows. *He tapped the table to still the shouts of protest... Tap the eggs gently with a teaspoon to crack the shells... Grace tapped on the bedroom door and went in... There was a comfortable-looking clerk on duty, tapping away on a manual typewriter... To hold the carpet in place, it's a good idea to tap in a few nails temporarily.* ▶ Also a noun. *A tap on the door interrupted him and Sally Pierce came in.* VERB V n; V adv/prep; N-COUNT: usu N *on/at* n

3 If you **tap** your fingers or feet, you make a rhythmic sound by hitting a surface lightly and repeatedly with them, especially while you are listening to music. *The song's so catchy it makes you bounce round the living room or tap your feet.* VERB V n

4 If you **tap** a resource or situation, you make use of it by getting from it something that you need or want. *He owes his election to having tapped deep public disillusion with professional politicians... The company is tapping shareholders for £15.8 million... The Campbell Soup Company says it will try to tap into Japan's rice market.* VERB V n; V n *for* n; V *into* n

5 If someone **taps** your telephone, they attach a special device to the line so that they can secretly listen to your conversations. *The government passed laws allowing the police to tap telephones... We suspected the telephone line was tapped.* ● See also **phone-tapping, wiretap.** ▶ Also a noun. *He assured MPs that ministers and MPs were not subjected to phone taps.* VERB =bug; V n; N-COUNT: oft n N

6 If drinks are **on tap**, they come from a tap rather than from a bottle. *Filtered water is always on tap, making it very convenient to use.* PHRASES usu v-link PHR

7 If something is **on tap**, you can have as much of it as you want whenever you want; an informal expression. *The advantage of group holidays is company on tap but time alone if you want it.* usu v-link PHR

tap out. If you **tap out** a rhythm, a code, or a number, you indicate it by hitting a surface or a machine such as a telephone. *Dermot joined her, his eyes on the dance floor, his fingers tapping out a rhythm on the table... Thirteen people tap out numbers on touch-tone phones in the nightly search for votes for President Bush.* PHRASAL VERB V P n (not pron)

tapas /tæpæs/. In Spain, **tapas** are small portions of food that are served with drinks or before a main meal. N-PLURAL

tap dancer, tap dancers. A **tap dancer** is a dancer who does tap dancing. N-COUNT

tap dancing; also spelled **tap-dancing**. **Tap dancing** is a style of dancing in which the dancers wear special shoes with pieces of metal on the heels and toes. The shoes make clicking noises as the dancers move their feet. N-UNCOUNT

tape /teɪp/ **tapes, taping, taped** ◆◆◆◆◇

1 **Tape** is a narrow plastic strip covered with a magnetic substance. It is used to record sounds, pictures, and computer information. *Tape is expensive and loses sound quality every time it is copied... Many students declined to be interviewed on tape.* N-UNCOUNT: oft *on* N

2 A **tape** is a cassette or spool with magnetic tape N-COUNT

wound round it. ...*a new cassette tape... She still listens to the tapes I made her.* =cassette

3 If you **tape** music, sounds, or television pictures, you record them using a tape recorder or a video recorder. *She has just taped an interview... He shouldn't be taping without the singer's permission. ...taped evidence from prisoners.* ♦ **taping** ...*an unauthorized taping.* VERB Vn V V-ed N-COUNT

4 A **tape** is a strip of cloth used to tie things together or to identify who a piece of clothing belongs to. *The books were all tied up with tape.* N-VAR

5 A **tape** is a ribbon that is stretched across the finishing line of a race. ...*the finishing tape.* N-COUNT: supp N

6 **Tape** is an adhesive strip of plastic used for sticking things together. ...*strong adhesive tape.* N-UNCOUNT

7 If you **tape** one thing to another, you attach it using sticky tape. *I taped the base of the feather onto the velvet... There are notes from years ago taped to the walls... The envelope has been tampered with and then taped shut again.* VERB V n *onto/to* n be V-ed adj

8 See also **magnetic tape**, **masking tape**, **red tape**, **sticky tape**, **videotape**.

tape up. If you **tape** something **up**, you fasten tape around it firmly, in order to protect it or hold it in a fixed position. *Put the bottles into boxes and tape them up... Shopkeepers were taping up their windows.* PHRASAL VERB V n P V P n (not pron)

tape deck, tape decks; also spelled **tape-deck**. A **tape deck** is the machine on which you can play or record tapes. N-COUNT

tape measure, tape measures. A **tape measure** is a strip of metal, plastic, or cloth which has markings on and which is used for measuring things. N-COUNT

taper /teɪpəʳ/ **tapers, tapering, tapered** ♦◇◇◇◇

1 If something **tapers**, or if you **taper** it, it becomes gradually thinner at one end. *Unlike other trees, it doesn't taper very much. It stays fat all the way up. ...beautiful hands with long, tapering fingers... Taper the shape of your eyebrows towards the outer corners.* ♦ **tapered** ...*the elegantly tapered legs of the dressing-table.* V-ERG V V-ing V n Also V prep ADJ-GRADED

2 If something **tapers** or **is tapered**, it gradually becomes reduced in amount, number, or size until it is greatly reduced. *There are signs that inflation is tapering... If you take these drugs continuously, withdrawal must be tapered.* ► **Taper off** means the same as **taper**. *Immigration is expected to taper off... I suggested that we start to taper off the counseling sessions.* V-ERG V be V-ed PHRASAL VERB V P V P n (not pron) Also V n P

3 A **taper** is a long, thin, fast-burning candle or a thin wooden strip that is used for lighting fires. N-COUNT

taper off. See **taper** 2. PHRASAL VERB

tape-record, tape-records, tape-recording, tape-recorded; also spelled **tape record**. If you **tape-record** speech, music, or another kind of sound, you record it on tape, using a tape recorder or a tape deck. ...*a factory worker who allegedly tape-recorded two officers verbally abusing him... The conversation was tape-recorded and played in court. ...a tape-recorded interview.* VERB =tape V n V-ed

tape recorder, tape recorders; also spelled **tape-recorder**. A **tape recorder** is a machine used for recording and playing music, speech, or other sounds. ♦◇◇◇◇ N-COUNT

tape recording, tape recordings. A **tape recording** is a recording of sounds that has been made on tape. ...*a tape recording of several dogs barking.* N-COUNT: oft N *of* n

tapestry /tæpɪstri/ **tapestries** ♦◇◇◇◇

1 A **tapestry** is a large piece of heavy cloth with a picture sewn on it using coloured threads. *The seats of the chairs had been recovered in tapestry... He sat on a tapestry cushion next to the hearth... On the opposite wall is a large tapestry.* N-VAR

2 You can refer to something as a **tapestry** when it is made up of many varied types of people or things; a literary use. *Hedgerows and meadows are thick with a tapestry of wild flowers. ...Chicago's political tapestry.* N-COUNT: with supp

tapeworm /teɪpwɜːʳm/ **tapeworms.** A **tapeworm** is a long, flat, parasitic creature which lives in the stomach and intestines of animals or people. N-COUNT

tapioca /tæpioʊkə/. **Tapioca** is a food consisting of white grains, rather like rice, which come from the cassava plant. N-UNCOUNT

tap water. **Tap water** is the water that comes out of a tap in a building such as a house or a hotel. *He never drinks tap water.* N-UNCOUNT

tar /tɑːʳ/ **tars, tarring, tarred** ♦◇◇◇◇

1 **Tar** is a thick black sticky substance that is used especially for making roads. *The oil has hardened to tar... They drove across the river to New Hampshire on a hot tar road.* N-UNCOUNT

2 **Tar** is one of the poisonous substances contained in tobacco. N-UNCOUNT

3 If some people in a group behave badly and if people falsely think that all of the group is equally bad, you can say that the whole group **is tarred with the same brush**. *I am a football supporter and I have to often explain that I'm not one of the hooligan sort because we'll all get tarred with the same brush when there's trouble.* PHRASE: V inflects

4 See also **tarred**.

taramasalata /tærəməsəlɑːtə/. **Taramasalata** is a pink creamy food made from the eggs of a fish such as cod or mullet. It is usually eaten at the beginning of a meal. N-UNCOUNT

tarantula /tərænt∫ʊlə/ **tarantulas.** A **tarantula** is a large hairy spider which has a poisonous bite. N-COUNT

tardy /tɑːʳdi/ **tardier, tardiest**

1 If you describe something or someone as **tardy**, you think that they are later than they should be or later than expected; a literary use. *He wept for the loss of his mother and his tardy recognition of her affection... I was as tardy as ever for the afternoon appointments.* ♦ **tardiness** *His legendary tardiness left audiences waiting for hours.* ADJ-GRADED N-UNCOUNT

2 If you describe someone or something as **tardy**, you are criticizing them because they are slow to act. ...*companies who are tardy in paying bills... The agency was heavily criticised for its tardy response to the hurricane.* ♦ **tardiness** ...*England's tardiness in giving talented young players greater international experience.* ADJ-GRADED: oft ADJ *in* -ing/n PRAGMATICS N-UNCOUNT: oft N *in* -ing/n

target /tɑːʳgɪt/ **targets, targeting, targeted;** also spelled **targetting, targetted**. ♦♦♦♦◇

1 A **target** is something at which someone is aiming a weapon or other object. *The village lies beside a main road, making it an easy target for bandits... The missiles missed their target... He missed the target only once yesterday... We threw knives at targets.* N-COUNT

2 A **target** is a result that you are trying to achieve. *He's won back his place too late to achieve his target of 20 goals this season. ...school leavers who failed to reach their target grades.* N-COUNT

3 If someone **targets** someone or something, they decide to attack or criticize them. *In 23 attacks, the terrorists targeted military bases... Mr Heseltine targeted rumours of a whispering campaign against the Shadow Chancellor.* ► Also a noun. *In the past they have been the target of racist abuse... The professor has been a frequent target for animal rights extremists.* VERB V n N-COUNT: oft N *of/for* n

4 If you **target** a particular group of people, you try to appeal to those people or affect them. *The campaign will target American insurance companies... The company has targeted adults as its primary customers.* ► Also a noun. *Yuppies are a prime target group for marketing strategies.* VERB V n N-COUNT

5 If someone or something is **on target**, they are making good progress and are likely to achieve the result that is wanted. *We were still right on target for our deadline.* PHRASE: v-link PHR

tariff /tærɪf/ **tariffs** ♦♦◇◇◇

1 A **tariff** is a tax that a government collects on goods coming into a country. *America wants to eliminate tariffs on items such as electronics.* N-COUNT: oft N *on* n

2 In formal British English, a **tariff** is the rate at which you are charged for public services such as gas and electricity, or for accommodation and services in a hotel. *The daily tariff includes accommo-* N-COUNT: usu supp N *dation and unlimited use of the pool and gymnasium. ...electricity tariffs and telephone charges.*

tarmac /tɑːʳmæk/ ◆◇◇◇◇

1 In British English, **tarmac** is a material used for making road surfaces, consisting of crushed stones mixed with tar. The usual American word is **blacktop**. **Tarmac** is a trademark. *...a strip of tarmac. ...tarmac paths.* N-UNCOUNT

2 **The tarmac** is an area that has a surface of tarmac, especially airport runways. *Standing on the tarmac were two American planes.* N-SING: *the*N

tarn /tɑːʳn/ **tarns.** A **tarn** is a small lake in an area of mountains. N-COUNT: oft in names

tarnish /tɑːʳnɪʃ/ **tarnishes, tarnishing, tarnished** ◆◇◇◇◇

1 If you say that something **tarnishes** someone's reputation or image, you mean that it causes people to have a worse opinion of them than they would otherwise have had. *The affair could tarnish the reputation of the prime minister... His image was tarnished by the savings and loan scandal.* VERB =blemish V n
♦ **tarnished** *He says he wants to improve the tarnished image of his country.* ADJ-GRADED

2 If a metal **tarnishes** or if something **tarnishes** it, it becomes stained and loses its brightness. *It never rusts or tarnishes.* ♦ **tarnished** *...its brown surfaces of tarnished brass.* V-ERG V Also V n ADJ-GRADED

3 **Tarnish** is a substance which forms of the surface of some metals and which stains them or causes them to lose their brightness. *The tarnish lay thick on the inside of the ring.* N-UNCOUNT

Tarot /tæroʊ/. The **Tarot** is a pack of cards with pictures on them that is used to predict what will happen to people in the future. **Tarot** is also used to refer to the system of predicting people's futures using these cards. *...the suits of the Tarot... Today there is a considerable revival of tarot. ...tarot cards.* ◆◇◇◇◇ N-UNCOUNT: also *the*N, oft N n

tarpaulin /tɑːʳpɔːlɪn/ **tarpaulins**

1 **Tarpaulin** is a fabric made of canvas or similar material coated with tar, wax, paint, or some other waterproof substance. *... a piece of tarpaulin. ...tarpaulin covers.* N-UNCOUNT: oft N n

2 A **tarpaulin** is a sheet of heavy waterproof material that is used as a protective cover. N-COUNT

tarragon /tærəgɒn/. **Tarragon** is a small European herb with narrow leaves which are used to add flavour to food. N-UNCOUNT

tarred /tɑːʳd/. A **tarred** road or roof has a surface of tar. *The side tracks off the tarred road were rutted and uneven... The road was narrow but tarred.* ADJ

tarry, tarries, tarrying, tarried. The verb is pronounced /tæri/. The adjective is pronounced /tɑːri/.

1 If you **tarry** somewhere, you stay there longer than you meant to and delay leaving; an old-fashioned use. *Two old boys tarried on the street corner discussing cattle.* VERB =linger V

2 If you describe something as **tarry**, you mean that it has a lot of tar in it or is like tar. *I smelled tarry melted asphalt. ...cups of tarry coffee.* ADJ

tart /tɑːʳt/ **tarts, tarting, tarted** ◆◇◇◇◇

1 A **tart** is a shallow pastry case with a filling of food, especially sweet food. *...jam tarts. ...a slice of home-made tart.* N-VAR

2 If something such as fruit is **tart**, it has a sharp taste. *The blackberries were a bit too tart on their own, so we stewed them gently with some apples. ...a slightly tart wine.* ADJ-GRADED =sharp

3 A **tart** remark or way of speaking is sharp and unpleasant, often in a way that is rather cruel. *The words were more tart than she had intended... He also made a tart reference to the Kuwaiti government.* ♦ **tartly** *'There are other patients on the ward, Lovell,' the staff nurse reminded her tartly.* ADJ-GRADED =acid ADV-GRADED: usu ADV with v

4 If someone refers to a woman or girl as a **tart**, they are criticizing her behaviour or her appearance because they think she is sexually immoral or dresses in a vulgar way in order to attract men's sexual interest; an offensive use, used mainly in British English. *He was nasty about my appearance. If I dressed up he'd say I looked like a tart.* N-COUNT PRAGMATICS

tart up. In British English, if someone **tarts up** a room or building, they try to improve its appearance, often with the result that it looks vulgar; an informal expression used showing disapproval. *'Have you ever wondered why British Rail would rather tart up their stations than improve services?' he asked. ...tarted-up pubs.* PHRASAL VERB V P n (not pron) V-ed P Also V n P

tartan /tɑːʳtᵊn/ **tartans.** **Tartan** is a design for cloth traditionally associated with Scotland, which has a number of distinctive types. **Tartan** is composed of a lines of different widths and colours crossing each other at right angles. **Tartan** is also used to refer to cloth which has this pattern. *The corridors are carpeted in tartan. ...traditional tartan kilts.* ◆◇◇◇◇ N-VAR: oft N n

tartar /tɑːʳtəʳ/ **tartars**

1 **Tartar** is a hard yellowish substance that forms on your teeth and causes them to decay if it is not removed. N-UNCOUNT

2 If you describe someone, especially a woman in a position of authority, as a **tartar**, you mean that they are fierce, bad-tempered, and demanding; an informal use. *She can be quite a tartar.* N-COUNT

3 See also **cream of tartar**.

tartare sauce; also spelled **tartar sauce**. **Tartare sauce** is a thick cold sauce, usually eaten with fish, consisting of chopped onions and capers mixed with mayonnaise. N-UNCOUNT

tarty /tɑːʳti/ **tartiest.** If you describe a woman or her clothes as **tarty**, you are critical of her because she tries to make herself look sexually attractive in a vulgar way; an offensive use. *That coat made her look so tarty.* ADJ-GRADED PRAGMATICS

task /tɑːsk, tæsk/ **tasks** ◆◆◆◆◇

1 A **task** is an activity or piece of work which you have to do, usually as part of a larger project. *Walker had the unenviable task of breaking the bad news to Hill... She used the day to catch up with administrative tasks.* N-COUNT: usu N *of*-ing, supp N

2 If you **take** someone **to task**, you criticize them or reprimand them in a severe or angry way because of something bad or wrong that they have done. *The country's intellectuals are also being taken to task for their failure to speak out against the regime.* PHRASE: V inflects, oft PHR *for*n/-ing =rebuke, scold

task-based. In language teaching, a **task-based** activity or syllabus is based on the successful completion of tasks by language learners. ADJ

task force, task forces; also spelled **taskforce.** ◆◆◇◇◇

1 A **task force** is a small section of an army, navy, or air force that is sent to a particular place to deal with a military crisis. *The United States is sending a naval task force to the area to evacuate American citizens.* N-COUNT

2 A **task force** is a group of people working together on a particular task. *We have set up a task force to look at the question of women returning to work.* N-COUNT

taskmaster /tɑːskmɑːstəʳ, tæskmæstəʳ/ **taskmasters.** If you refer to someone as a hard **taskmaster**, you mean that they expect the people they supervise to work very hard. *They're both tough taskmasters, but Stephen is much more supportive.* N-COUNT: usu adj N

tassel /tæsᵊl/ **tassels.** **Tassels** are bunches of short pieces of wool or other material tied together at one end and attached as decorations to something such as a piece of clothing or a lampshade. N-COUNT

tasselled /tæsᵊld/. **Tasselled** means decorated with tassels. *...tasselled cushions.* ADJ

taste /teɪst/ **tastes, tasting, tasted** ◆◆◆◆◇

1 **Taste** is one of the five senses that people have. When you have food or drink in your mouth, your sense of taste makes it possible for you to recognize what it is. *...a keen sense of taste.* N-UNCOUNT

2 The **taste** of something is the individual quality which it has when you put it in your mouth and which distinguishes it from other things. For example, something may have a sweet, bitter, sour, or salty taste. *I like the taste of wine and enjoy trying different kinds... The taste of blood in her throat* N-COUNT: usu with supp =flavour

made her want to vomit... Nettles are surprisingly good – much like spinach but with a sweetish taste.

3 If you have a **taste** of some food or drink, you try a small amount of it in order to see what the flavour is like. *He swirled the caramel liquor around in his cupped palm and savoured its bouquet before taking another small taste.* N-SING

4 If food or drink **tastes** of something, it has that particular flavour, which you notice when you eat or drink it. *I drank a cup of tea that tasted of diesel... It tastes like chocolate... The pizza tastes delicious without any cheese at all.* VB: no cont; V of/like n; V adj

5 If you **taste** some food or drink, you eat or drink a small amount of it in order to try its flavour, for example to see if you like it or not. *He finished his aperitif and tasted the wine the waiter had produced... Before proceeding any further, cut off a small bit of the meat and taste it.* VERB =sample, try; V n

6 If you can **taste** something that you are eating or drinking, you are aware of its flavour. *You can taste the chilli in the dish but it is a little sweet.* VB: no passive; V n

7 If you have a **taste of** a particular way of life or activity, you have a brief experience of it. *But having had a taste of the big time, he won't want to go back to playing in the reserves... This voyage was his first taste of freedom.* N-SING: N of n

8 If you **taste** something such as a way of life or a pleasure, you experience it for a short period of time. *Once you have tasted the outdoor life in southern California, it takes a peculiar kind of masochism to return to a Nottingham winter.* VB: no passive; V n

9 If you have a **taste for** something, you have a liking or preference for it. *She developed a taste for journeys to isolated hazardous regions in North America... That gave me a taste for reading.* N-SING: N for n/-ing =liking

10 A person's **taste** is their choice in the things that they like or buy, for example their clothes, possessions, or favourite music. If you say that someone has good **taste**, you mean that you approve of their choices. If you say that they have poor **taste**, you disapprove of their choices. *His taste in clothes is extremely good... Oxford's social circle was far too liberal for her taste. ...a large family with different tastes and preferences... How could so many people have such bad taste in music?* N-UNCOUNT: also N in pl

11 If you say that something that is said or done is **in bad taste** or **in poor taste**, you mean that it is offensive, often because it concerns death or sex and is inappropriate for the situation. If you say that something is **in good taste**, you mean that it is not offensive and that it is appropriate for the situation. *He rejects the idea that his film is in bad taste... I do not feel your actions were either appropriate or done in good taste.* PHRASES v-link PHR, PHR after v

12 When a recipe tells you to add a particular spice or other flavouring **to taste**, it means that you can add as much of that ingredient as you like. *Add tomato paste, salt and pepper to taste.* PHR after v

taste bud, taste buds; also spelled **tastebud**. Your **taste buds** are the little points on the surface of your tongue which enable you to recognize the flavour of a food or drink. N-COUNT: usu pl, oft poss N

tasteful /teɪstfʊl/. If you say that something is **tasteful**, you consider it to be attractive, elegant, and in good taste. *The decor is tasteful and restrained. ...tasteful jewelry.* ♦ **tastefully** *...a large and tastefully decorated home... The rectory has been sensitively restored and tastefully furnished.* ◆◇◇◇◇ ADJ-GRADED ≠tasteless; ADV-GRADED: usu ADV with v, also ADV adj

tasteless /teɪstləs/

1 If you describe something such as furniture, clothing, or the way that a house is decorated as **tasteless**, you consider it to be vulgar and unattractive. *...a flat crammed with spectacularly tasteless objets d'art.* ADJ-GRADED

2 If you describe something such as a remark or joke as **tasteless**, you mean that it is offensive. *I think that is the most vulgar and tasteless remark I ever heard in my life.* ADJ-GRADED =vulgar

3 If you describe food or drink as **tasteless**, you mean that it has very little or no flavour. *The fish was mushy and tasteless.* ADJ-GRADED =flavourless

taster /teɪstəʳ/ **tasters** ◆◇◇◇◇

1 A **taster** is someone whose job is to taste different wines, teas, or other foods or drinks, in order to test their quality. *...a wine taster.* N-COUNT

2 If you refer to something as a **taster** of something greater, or of something that will come later, you mean that the first thing gives you an idea what the second thing is like, and often makes you interested in it or want more of it; used mainly in British English. *...a taster of things to come... The book is essentially a taster for those unfamiliar with the subject.* N-COUNT: usu sing, oft N of n

tasting /teɪstɪŋ/ **tastings. Tasting** is used in expressions such as **wine tasting** to refer to a social event at which people try different kinds of the specified drink or food in small amounts. N-COUNT: usu supp N

tasty /teɪsti/ **tastier, tastiest** ◆◇◇◇◇

1 If you say that food, especially savoury food, is **tasty**, you mean that it has a fairly strong and pleasant flavour which makes it good to eat. *Try this tasty dish for supper with a crispy salad... I thought the food was very tasty.* ADJ-GRADED

2 In British English, if someone describes a person, especially a woman, as **tasty**, they think they are sexually desirable; an informal use which some people find offensive. ADJ-GRADED

tat /tæt/. You can use **tat** to refer to ornaments, second-hand goods, cheap clothes, or other items which you think are cheap and of bad quality; used mainly in informal British English. *...souvenir shops selling an astounding variety of tat.* N-UNCOUNT

ta-ta /tæ tɑː/; also spelled **ta ta**. In informal British English, **ta-ta** is used to say goodbye. *Okay John. See you again. Ta-ta... Ta-ta for now.* CONVENTION PRAGMATICS =bye

tattered /tætəʳd/ ◆◇◇◇◇

1 If something such as clothing or a book is **tattered**, it is damaged, torn, or crumpled, especially because it has been used a lot over a long period of time. *He fled wearing only a sarong and a tattered shirt. ...a very old, tattered, phone directory.* ADJ-GRADED =ragged

2 If you describe something as **tattered**, you mean that it has been badly damaged or has failed completely. *But, two-and-a-half years later, things haven't quite gone to plan and Stanley's dreams of fame and fortune lie tattered and torn. ...the last tattered remnants of a defeated army.* ADJ-GRADED

tatters /tætəʳz/

1 Clothes that are in **tatters** are badly torn in several places, so that pieces can easily come off. *His jersey was left in tatters.* N-PLURAL: usu in N =in rags

2 If you say that something such as a plan or a person's state of mind is in **tatters**, you are emphasizing that it is weak, has suffered a lot of damage, and is likely to fail completely. *The economy is in tatters.* N-PLURAL: usu in N PRAGMATICS

tattle /tætᵊl/. See **tittle-tattle**.

tattoo /tætuː/ **tattoos, tattooing, tattooed** ◆◇◇◇◇

1 A **tattoo** is a design on someone's skin, made by pricking little holes and filling them with coloured dye. N-COUNT

2 If someone **tattoos** you, they give you a tattoo. *In the old days, they would paint and tattoo their bodies for ceremonies... He had the words 'Angie loves Ian' tattooed on his left shin.* VERB; V n; V-ed

3 A military **tattoo** is a public display of exercises and music given by members of the armed forces; used mainly in British English. N-COUNT

4 If you beat a **tattoo**, you hit something quickly and repeatedly. N-COUNT: usu sing

tatty /tæti/. If you describe something as **tatty**, you think it is untidy, rather dirty, and looks as if it has not been cared for. *There were a lot of guest houses which were very tatty. ...a very tatty old bathrobe.* ADJ-GRADED =scruffy

taught /tɔːt/. **Taught** is the past tense and past participle of **teach**.

taunt /tɔːnt/ **taunts, taunting, taunted.** If someone **taunts** you, they say unkind or insulting things to you, especially about your weaknesses or failures. *A gang taunted a disabled man... Other youths taunted him about his* ◆◇◇◇◇ VERB; V n; V n about n *clothes.* ▶ Also a noun. *For years they suffered racist taunts.* N-COUNT

taupe /toʊp/. Something that is **taupe** is a pale brownish-pink colour. *...a pale wool jacket in taupe, apricot, and cream.* COLOUR

Taurus /tɔːrəs/ ◆◆◇◇◇

1 Taurus is one of the twelve signs of the zodiac. Its symbol is a bull. People who are born approximately between the 20th of April and the 20th of May come under this sign. N-UNCOUNT

2 A Taurus is a person whose sign of the zodiac is Taurus. N-SING: a N

taut /tɔːt/ **tauter, tautest** ◆◇◇◇◇

1 Something that is **taut** is stretched very tight. *When muscles are taut or cold there is more chance of injury or strain... The clothes line is pulled taut and secured.* ADJ-GRADED

2 If a person or their body is **taut**, they are very lean with firm muscles. *That summer she had shed the weight gained during pregnancy, her body was trim and taut.* ADJ-GRADED

3 If someone has a **taut** expression, they look very worried and tense. *Ben sat up quickly, his face taut and terrified... Little by little she lost the taut, strained air of perpetual anxiety.* ADJ-GRADED

4 If you describe a piece of writing or a film as **taut**, you mean that it is good because it is concentrated and has no unnecessary or irrelevant details. *...Eric Rochant's 'Aux yeux du monde', a taut thriller about the kidnapping of a school bus.* ADJ-GRADED =spare

tauten /tɔːtᵊn/ **tautens, tautening, tautened.** If a part of your body **tautens** or if you **tauten** it, it becomes stiff or firm. *Her whole body tautened violently... There are exercises that tauten facial muscles.* V-ERG V Vn

tautological /tɔːtəlɒdʒɪkᵊl/. A **tautological** statement involves tautology. ADJ-GRADED

tautology /tɔːtɒlədʒi/ **tautologies. Tautology** is the use of different words to say the same thing twice in the same statement. 'The money should be adequate enough' is an example of tautology. N-VAR

tavern /tævəʳn/ **taverns.** A **tavern** is a bar or pub; an old-fashioned word. ◆◇◇◇◇ N-COUNT: oft in names

tawdry /tɔːdri/ **tawdrier, tawdriest**

1 If you describe something such as clothes or decorations as **tawdry**, you mean that they are cheap and show a lack of taste. *...tawdry jewellery.* ADJ-GRADED =tacky

2 If you describe something such as a story or an event as **tawdry**, you mean that it is unpleasant or immoral. *...the yawning gulf between her fantasies and the tawdry reality. ...the tawdry business of day-to-day bartering and bargaining.* ADJ-GRADED: usu ADJ n

tawny /tɔːni/. **Tawny** hair, fur, or skin is a pale golden brown colour. *She had tawny hair. ...a large, tawny dog.* COLOUR

tax /tæks/ **taxes, taxing, taxed** ◆◆◆◆◆

1 Tax is an amount of money that you have to pay to the government so that it can pay for public services. *No-one enjoys paying tax... They are calling for large spending cuts and tax increases. ...a cut in tax on new cars. ...a pledge not to raise taxes on people below a certain income... His decision to return to a form of property tax is the right one.* N-VAR

2 When a person or company **is taxed**, they have to pay a part of their income or profits to the government. When goods **are taxed**, a percentage of their price has to be paid to the government. *Husband and wife are now taxed separately on their incomes. ...the government's commitment to simplifying the way companies are taxed... The Bonn government taxes profits of corporations at a rate that is among the highest in Europe.* VERB be V-ed Vn Also V

3 If something **taxes** your strength, your patience, or your resources, it uses nearly all of them, so that you have great difficulty in carrying out what you are trying to do. *Overcrowding has taxed the city's ability to deal with waste... These dilemmas would tax the best of statesmen.* VERB Vn

4 See also **taxing; council tax, income tax, poll tax, value added tax.**

taxable /tæksəbᵊl/. **Taxable** income is income on which you have to pay tax.  ADJ: usu ADJ n

taxation /tækseɪʃᵊn/ ◆◆◇◇◇

1 Taxation is the system by which a government takes money from people and spends it on things such as education, health, and defence. N-UNCOUNT

2 Taxation is the amount of money that people have to pay in taxes. *The result will be higher taxation.* N-UNCOUNT

tax avoidance. Tax avoidance is the use of legal methods to pay the smallest possible amount of tax. N-UNCOUNT

tax break, tax breaks. If the government gives a **tax break** to a particular group of people or type of organization, it reduces the amount of tax they have to pay or changes the tax system in a way that benefits them; used mainly in American English. *Today they'll consider tax breaks for businesses that create jobs in inner cities.* ◆◇◇◇◇ N-COUNT

tax-deductible. If an expense is **tax-deductible**, it can be paid out of your untaxed income, so that the amount of your income which you pay tax on is reduced. *The cost of private childcare should be made tax-deductible... Keep track of tax-deductible expenses, such as the supplies and equipment you buy.* ADJ

tax disc, tax discs. In Britain, a **tax disc** is a small round piece of paper displayed on cars and motorcycles which proves that the owner has paid road tax. N-COUNT

tax evasion. Tax evasion is the crime of not paying the full amount of tax that you should pay. ◆◇◇◇◇ N-UNCOUNT

tax-free; also spelled **tax free. Tax-free** is used to describe income on which you do not have to pay tax. *...a tax-free investment plan. ...a return of 16.5% tax free... Redundancy payments are tax-free up to £30,000.* ◆◇◇◇◇ ADJ: ADJ n, amount ADJ, v-link ADJ

tax haven, tax havens. A **tax haven** is a country or place which has a low rate of taxation, so that people choose to live there or register companies there in order to avoid paying higher tax in their own countries. N-COUNT

taxi /tæksi/ **taxis, taxiing, taxied** ◆◆◇◇◇

1 A **taxi** is a car driven by a person whose job is to take people where they want to go in return for money. *The taxi drew up in front of the Riviera Club... He set off by taxi.* N-COUNT: also by N =cab

2 When an aircraft **taxis** along the ground or when a pilot taxis a plane somewhere, it moves slowly along the ground. *She gave permission to the plane to taxi into position and hold for takeoff... The pilot taxied the plane to the end of the runway.* V-ERG V prep/adv V n prep/adv Also V, V n

taxicab /tæksikæb/ **taxicabs;** also spelled **taxi-cab.** A **taxicab** is the same as a **taxi**; used mainly in American English. N-COUNT

taxidermist /tæksidɜːʳmɪst/ **taxidermists.** A **taxidermist** is a person whose job is to stuff dead animals and birds so that they look lifelike and can be displayed. N-COUNT

taxidermy /tæksidɜːʳmi/. **Taxidermy** is the craft of stuffing dead animals and birds so that they look lifelike and can be displayed. N-UNCOUNT

taxing /tæksɪŋ/. A **taxing** task or problem is one that requires a lot of mental or physical effort. *How to manage relations with these East European states will be one of the most taxing issues for the EC... It's unlikely that you'll be asked to do anything too taxing.* ADJ-GRADED =demanding

taxi rank, taxi ranks. In British English, a **taxi rank** is a place where taxis wait for passengers, for example at an airport or outside a station. The usual American term is **taxi stand**. N-COUNT

taxi stand, taxi stands. In American English, a **taxi stand** is a place where taxis wait for passengers, for example at an airport or outside a station. The usual British expression is **taxi rank**. N-COUNT

taxonomy /tæksɒnəmi/ **taxonomies. Taxonomy** is the classification and naming of things such as animals and plants in groups within a larger system, according to their similarities and differences; a technical term. N-VAR

taxpayer /tækspeɪəʳ/ **taxpayers.** **Taxpayers** are people who pay a percentage of their income to the government as tax. ◆◆◇◇◇ N-COUNT

tax relief. **Tax relief** is a reduction in the amount of tax that a person or company has to pay, for example because of expenses associated with their business or property. *...mortgage interest tax relief.* ◆◇◇◇◇ N-UNCOUNT

tax return, tax returns. A **tax return** is an official form on which you declare your income and give details about your personal circumstances, so that the authorities can decide how much tax you should pay. *We analyzed a sample of 2,400 tax returns filed between 1980 and 1984.* ◆◇◇◇◇ N-COUNT

tax year, tax years. A **tax year** is a particular period of twelve months which is used by the government as a basis for calculating taxes and for organizing its own finances and accounts. In Britain, the tax year begins on April 6th and ends on April 5th. N-COUNT

TB /tiː biː/. **TB** is an extremely serious infectious disease that affects someone's lungs and other parts of their body. **TB** is an abbreviation for **tuberculosis**. ◆◇◇◇◇ N-UNCOUNT

tba. **tba** is sometimes written in announcements about events to indicate that a date, time, or event has not yet been arranged and will be announced at a later date. **tba** is an abbreviation for 'to be arranged' or 'to be announced'.

T-bone steak, T-bone steaks. A **T-bone steak** is a thick piece of beef that contains a T-shaped bone. N-VAR

tbs. In recipes, **tbs.** is a written abbreviation for **tablespoonful**.

tbsp., tbsps. In recipes, **tbsp.** is a written abbreviation for **tablespoonful**. N-COUNT

tea /tiː/ **teas** ◆◆◆◆◇

1 **Tea** is a drink made by adding hot water to tea leaves or tea bags. Many people add milk to the drink and some add sugar. *...a cup of tea... Would you like some tea?... Four or five men were drinking tea from flasks.* N-MASS ► A cup of tea can be referred to as a **tea**. *Would anybody like a tea or coffee?* N-COUNT

2 Drinks such as mint **tea** or chamomile **tea** are made by pouring hot water on the dried leaves of the particular plant or flower. N-MASS: usu n N

3 The chopped dried leaves of the plant tea is made from is referred to as **tea**. *...a packet of tea... America imports about 190 million pounds of tea a year... Earl Grey, Darjeeling and Jasmine are best-selling traditional teas.* N-MASS

4 In Britain, **tea** is a meal some people eat in the late afternoon. It consists of food such as sandwiches and cakes, with tea to drink. *I'm doing the sandwiches for tea... I took her to tea at the Ritz.* • See also **afternoon tea**, **high tea**. N-VAR

5 In British English, some people refer to the main meal that they eat in the early part of the evening as **tea**. *At five o'clock he comes back for his tea.* N-VAR

6 If you say that someone or something is not your **cup of tea**, you mean that they are not the kind of person or thing that you like. *Politics was not his cup of tea... I know I'm not everyone's cup of tea.* PHRASE: v-link PHR, usu with brd-neg

tea bag, tea bags; also spelled **teabag**. **Tea bags** are small paper bags with tea leaves in them. You put them into hot water to make tea. N-COUNT

tea break, tea breaks. If you have a **tea break**, you stop working and have a cup of tea or coffee; used mainly in British English. The usual American expression is **coffee break**. *He had a tea-break about twelve.* N-COUNT =coffee break

tea caddy, tea caddies. A **tea caddy** is a small tin in which you keep tea; used mainly in British English. N-COUNT

teacake /tiːkeɪk/ **teacakes.** In British English, **teacakes** are round flat bread cakes. They usually contain raisins and are often toasted and eaten with butter. N-COUNT

teach /tiːtʃ/ **teaches, teaching, taught** ◆◆◆◆◇

1 If you **teach** someone something, you give them instructions so that they know about it or how to do it. *The trainers have a programme to teach them vocational skills... George had taught him how to ride a horse... She taught Julie to read... The computer has simplified the difficult task of teaching reading to the deaf.* VERB V n n, V n wh, V n to-inf, V n to n

2 To **teach** someone something means to make them think, feel, or act in a new or different way. *Their daughter's death had taught him humility... He taught his followers that they could all be members of the kingdom of God... Teach them to voice their feelings.* VERB V n n, V n that, V n to-inf, Also V n wh, V n *about* n

3 If you **teach** or **teach** a subject, you help students to learn about it by explaining it or showing them how to do it, usually as a job at a school, college, or university. *Ingrid is currently teaching Mathematics at Shimla Public School... The topic is not taught in degree courses... She taught English to Japanese business people... She has taught for 34 years... She taught children French. ...this twelve month taught course.* VERB V n, V n to n, V, V n n, V-ed

4 See also **teaching**. • to **teach someone a lesson**: see **lesson**.

teacher /tiːtʃəʳ/ **teachers.** A **teacher** is a person who teaches, usually as a job at a school or similar institution. *I'm a teacher with 21 years' experience. ...her chemistry teacher.* • See also **supply teacher**. ◆◆◆◆◇ N-COUNT

tea chest, tea chests. In British English, a **tea chest** is a large wooden box in which tea is packed when it is exported. People also use tea chests for putting things in when they move from one house to another. N-COUNT

teach-in, teach-ins. A **teach-in** is a meeting, usually between students and teachers, with discussions on important or controversial topics. Teach-ins are not usually part of a formal academic course. N-COUNT

teaching /tiːtʃɪŋ/ **teachings** ◆◆◆◇◇

1 **Teaching** is the work that a teacher does in helping students to learn. *The Government funds university teaching. ...the teaching of English in schools.* N-UNCOUNT

2 The **teachings** of a particular person, school of thought, or religion are all the ideas and principles that they teach. *...the teachings of Jesus. ...their teachings on sexuality and marriage.* N-COUNT: usu pl, with poss

teaching hospital, teaching hospitals. A **teaching hospital** is a hospital that is linked with a medical school, where medical students and newly qualified doctors receive practical training. N-COUNT

teaching practice. **Teaching practice** is a period that a student teacher spends at a school doing practical teaching as part of his or her training; used mainly in British English. N-UNCOUNT

tea cloth, tea cloths; also spelled **tea-cloth**. In British English, a **tea cloth** is the same as a **tea towel**. N-COUNT =tea towel

tea cosy, tea cosies; also spelled **tea-cosy**. A **tea cosy** is a soft knitted or fabric cover which you put over a teapot in order to keep the tea hot. N-COUNT

teacup /tiːkʌp/ **teacups;** also spelled **tea-cup**.

1 A **teacup** is a cup that you use for drinking tea. N-COUNT

2 If you describe a situation as **a storm in a teacup**, you think that a lot of fuss is being made about something that is not important; used mainly in informal British English. *Both are trying to present the disagreement as a storm in a teacup.* PHRASE: PHR after v, v-link PHR

teak /tiːk/. **Teak** is the wood of a tall tree with very hard, light-coloured wood which grows in South-East Asia. *The door is beautifully made in solid teak.* ◆◇◇◇◇ N-UNCOUNT

teal /tiːl/ **teals.** The plural can be either **teal** or **teals**. A **teal** is a small duck found in Europe and Asia. N-COUNT

tea leaf, tea leaves; also spelled **tea-leaf**. **Tea leaves** are the small pieces of dried leaves that are left in a teapot or a cup after the tea has been drunk. N-COUNT: usu pl

team /tiːm/ **teams, teaming, teamed** ◆◆◆◆◆

1 A **team** is a group of people who play a particular sport or game together against other similar groups of people. *The team failed to qualify for the* N-COUNT-COLL

African Nations Cup finals... He had lost his place in the England team.

2 You can refer to any group of people who work together as a **team**. *Each specialist consultant has a team of doctors under him... The governors were joined by Mr Birt and his management team.* N-COUNT-COLL

team up. If you **team up** with someone, you join them in order to work together for a particular purpose. You can also say that two people or groups **team up**. *Elton teamed up with Eric Clapton to wow thousands at a Wembley rock concert... Recently a friend suggested that we team up for a working holiday in Europe in the summer.* PHRASAL VERB RECIP V P with n pl-n V

team-mate, team-mates. In a game or sport, your **team-mates** are the other members of your team. ◆◆◇◇◇ N-COUNT: oft poss N

team spirit. **Team spirit** is the feeling of pride and loyalty that exists among the members of a team and that makes them want their team to do well or to be the best. N-UNCOUNT

teamster /tiːmstəʳ/ **teamsters.** In American English, a **teamster** is a person who drives a truck. The British expression is **lorry driver**. N-COUNT

teamwork /tiːmwɜːʳk/. **Teamwork** is the ability a group of people have to work well together. *Today's complex buildings require close teamwork between the architect and the builders.* N-UNCOUNT

tea party, tea parties; also spelled **tea-party**. A **tea party** is a social gathering in the afternoon at which tea, cakes, and sandwiches are served; an old-fashioned expression. N-COUNT

teapot /tiːpɒt/ **teapots;** also spelled **tea pot**. A **teapot** is a container with a lid, a handle, and a spout, used for making and serving tea. ◆◇◇◇◇ N-COUNT

tear 1 crying

tear /tɪəʳ/ **tears** ◆◆◆◇◇

1 **Tears** are the drops of salty liquid that come out of your eyes when you are crying. *Her eyes filled with tears... I just broke down and wept with tears of joy... I didn't shed a single tear.* N-COUNT: usu pl

2 You can use **tears** in expressions such as **in tears**, **burst into tears**, and **close to tears** to indicate that someone is crying or is almost crying. *He was in floods of tears on the phone... She burst into tears and ran from the kitchen... She was conscious of being very near to tears.* N-PLURAL

3 See also **crocodile tears**. • **blood, sweat, and tears**: see **blood**.

tear 2 damaging or moving

tear /teəʳ/ **tears, tearing, tore, torn** ◆◆◆◆◇

1 If you **tear** paper, cloth, or another material, or if it **tears**, you pull it into two pieces or you pull it so that a hole appears in it. *She very nearly tore my overcoat... Mary Ann tore the edge off her napkin... He took a small notebook from his jacket pocket and tore out a page... Too fine a material may tear... Nancy quickly tore open the envelope... He noticed that fabric was tearing away from the plane's wing... He went ashore leaving me to start repairing the torn sail.* ▶ **Tear up** means the same as **tear**. *She tore the letter up... Don't you dare tear up her ticket. ...a torn up photograph.* V-ERG =rip V n V n prep V n with adv V V n with adj V prep/adv V-ed PHRASAL VERB V n P V P n (not pron) V-ed P

2 A **tear** in paper, cloth, or another material is a hole that has been made in it. *I peered through a tear in the van's curtains.* N-COUNT =rip

3 If something **tears** your flesh or skin, it scratches or cuts it violently. *Canine teeth are for piercing and killing prey, and tearing flesh... He had stumbled down and torn the skin from his knees.* VERB =rip V n V n prep

4 If you **tear** one of your muscles or ligaments, or if it **tears**, you injure it by accidentally moving it in the wrong way. *He tore a muscle in his right thigh... If the muscle is stretched again it could even tear. ...torn ligaments.* V-ERG V n V V-ed

5 To **tear** something from somewhere means to remove it roughly and violently. *She tore the windscreen wipers from his car... He tore down the girl's photograph, and crumpled it into a ball.* VERB =rip V n prep V n with adv

6 If a person or animal **tears at** something, they pull it violently and try to break it into pieces. *Female fans fought their way past bodyguards and tore at his clothes.* VERB =rip V at n

7 If you **tear** somewhere, you move there very quickly, often in an uncontrolled or dangerous way. *The door flew open and Miranda tore into the room... Without looking to left or to right, he tore off down the road.* VERB =rush V prep/adv

8 If you say that a place **is torn** by particular events, you mean that unpleasant events which cause suffering and division among people are happening there. *...a country that has been torn by civil war and foreign invasion since its independence.* ♦ **-torn** *...the riot-torn areas of Los Angeles.* V-PASSIVE =be riven be V-ed by n COMB in ADJ

9 See also **torn, wear and tear.** • to **tear a strip off**: see **strip.** • to **tear** someone **to pieces**: see **piece.** • to **tear** someone **to shreds**: see **shred.**

tear apart PHRASAL VERB

1 If something **tears** people **apart**, it causes them to quarrel or to leave each other. *The quarrel tore the party apart... War and revolution have torn families apart.* V n P

2 If something **tears** you **apart**, it makes you feel very upset, worried, and unhappy. *Don't think it hasn't torn me apart to be away from you.* V n P

tear away. If you **tear** someone **away** from a place or activity, you force them to leave the place or stop doing the activity, even though they want to remain there or carry on. *Fame hasn't torn her away from her beloved Liverpool... Japan's education ministry ordered the change to encourage students to tear themselves away from textbooks... I stared at the man, couldn't tear my eyes away.* PHRASAL VERB oft with brd-neg V n P from n V pron-refl P from n V n P Also V pron-refl P

tear down. If you **tear** something **down**, you destroy it or remove it completely. *Angry Russians may have torn down the statue of Felix Dzerzhinsky... I imagine they'll be tearing the building down sooner or later.* PHRASAL VERB V P n (not pron) V n P

tear into. If you **tear into** someone, you criticize them very angrily and strongly; an informal expression. *I had a real row with him. I tore into him.* PHRASAL VERB V P n

tear off. If you **tear off** your clothes, you take them off in a rough and violent way. *Totally exhausted, he tore his clothes off and fell into bed... Fuentes tore off his hat and flung it to the ground.* PHRASAL VERB V n P V P n (not pron)

tear up PHRASAL VERB

1 If something such as a road, railway, or area of land **is torn up**, it is completely removed or destroyed. *Dozens of miles of railway track have been torn up... The company came under furious attack from environmentalists for tearing up the forests.* be V-ed P V P n (not pron)

2 See **tear** 1.

tearaway /teərəweɪ/ **tearaways.** In British English, if you refer to a young person as a **tearaway**, you mean that they behave in a wild and uncontrolled way. *He blamed lack of parental control for the young tearaways' behaviour.* N-COUNT

teardrop /tɪəʳdrɒp/ **teardrops.** A **teardrop** is a large tear that comes from your eye when you are crying quietly. N-COUNT =tear

tearful /tɪəʳfʊl/. If someone is **tearful**, their face or voice shows signs that they have been crying or that they want to cry. *She became very tearful when pressed to talk about it. ...a tearful farewell.* ♦ **tearfully** *Gwendolen smiled tearfully.* ◆◇◇◇◇ ADJ-GRADED ADV-GRADED

tear gas /tɪəʳ gæs/; also spelled **tear-gas**. **Tear gas** is a gas that causes your eyes to sting and fill with tears so that you cannot see. It is sometimes used by the police or army to control crowds. *Police used tear gas to disperse the demonstrators.* N-UNCOUNT

tear-jerker /tɪəʳ dʒɜːʳkəʳ/ **tear-jerkers;** also spelled **tearjerker**. If you refer to a play, film, or book as a **tear-jerker**, you are indicating that it is very sad or sentimental; an informal expression. N-COUNT

tea room, tea rooms; also spelled **tearoom**. A **tea room** is the same as a **tea shop**. N-COUNT: oft in names

tease /tiːz/ **teases, teasing, teased** ◆◆◇◇◇

1 To **tease** someone means to laugh at them or make jokes about them in order to embarrass, annoy, or upset them. *He told her how the boys in East Poldown had set on him, teasing him... He teased me mercilessly about going Hollywood... 'You must be expecting a young man,' she teased.* ▶ Also a noun. *Calling her by her real name had always been* VERB V n V n about n/-ing V with quote N-COUNT

one of his teases. ♦ **teasing** *She tolerated the teasing, until the fourth grade.* N-UNCOUNT: also *the*N

2 If you refer to someone as a **tease**, you mean that they like laughing at people or making jokes about them. *My brother's such a tease... The best way to deal with a tease is to ignore him.* N-COUNT: usu sing

3 If you say that someone **is teasing**, you mean that they are pretending to offer you something that you want, especially sex, but then not giving it to you. *I thought she was teasing, playing the innocent, but looking back, I'm not so sure... When did you last flirt with him or tease him?* VERB V Vn

4 If you refer to someone as a **tease**, you mean that they pretend to offer someone something that they want, especially sex, but then do not give it to them; used showing disapproval. *Later she heard he had told one of her friends she was a tease.* N-COUNT: usu sing PRAGMATICS

5 See also **teasing**; **striptease**.

tease out. If you **tease out** information or a solution, you succeed in obtaining it even though this is difficult. *They try to tease out the answers without appearing to ask... There had to be an answer – he was sure he could tease it out if only he had time.* PHRASAL VERB V P n (not pron) V n P Also V n P *of*n

teasel /tiːzᵊl/ **teasels;** also spelled **teazel** or **teazle**. A **teasel** is a plant with dry prickly flower-heads and prickly leaves. N-COUNT

teaser /tiːzəʳ/ **teasers**

1 A **teaser** is a difficult question, especially one in a quiz or competition; an informal use. N-COUNT =poser

2 A **teaser** is someone who makes fun of people in a slightly cruel way. N-COUNT

tea service, tea services. A **tea service** is the same as a **tea set**. N-COUNT

tea set, tea sets. A **tea set** is a set of cups, saucers, and plates, with a milk jug, sugar bowl, and teapot. N-COUNT

tea shop, tea shops; also spelled **teashop**. In British English, a **tea shop** is a small restaurant or café where tea, coffee, cakes, sandwiches, and light meals are served. N-COUNT: oft in names =tea room

teasing /tiːzɪŋ/. A **teasing** expression or manner shows that the person is not completely serious about what they are saying or doing. *'But we're having such fun, aren't we?' he protested with a teasing smile... Smith was at his most teasing.* ADJ-GRADED

♦ **teasingly** *'My, what a lot of things you want to know, Sergeant', she said teasingly.* ADV-GRADED: usu ADV with v

teaspoon /tiːspuːn/ **teaspoons** ◆◆◇◇◇

1 A **teaspoon** is a small spoon that you use to put sugar into tea or coffee. *Drop the dough onto a baking sheet with a teaspoon.* N-COUNT

2 You can refer to an amount of food resting on a teaspoon as a **teaspoon** of food. *He wants three teaspoons of sugar in his coffee.* N-COUNT: usu N *of*n

teaspoonful /tiːspuːnfʊl/ **teaspoonfuls; teaspoonful** can also be used as the plural form. You can refer to an amount of food resting on a teaspoon as a **teaspoonful** of food. *...a heaped teaspoonful of salt.* N-COUNT: usu N *of*n

teat /tiːt/ **teats**

1 A **teat** is a pointed part on the body of a female animal which her offspring suck in order to get milk. N-COUNT

2 A **teat** is a piece of rubber or plastic that is shaped like a teat, especially one that is fitted to a bottle so that a baby can suck liquids from it. N-COUNT

tea table; also spelled **tea-table**. You refer to a table as **the tea table** when it is being used for a meal eaten in the late afternoon or early evening; used mainly in British English. *...cakes and sandwiches on the tea-table.* N-SING: *the*N

teatime /tiːtaɪm/ **teatimes. Teatime** is the period of the day when people have their tea. It can be eaten in the late afternoon or in the early part of the evening; used mainly in British English. *We left at teatime.* N-VAR

tea towel, tea towels. In British English, a **tea towel** is a cloth used to dry dishes after they have been washed. The usual American term is **dish towel**. N-COUNT =tea cloth

teazel /tiːzᵊl/. See **teasel**.

teazle /tiːzᵊl/. See **teasel**.

tech /tek/ **techs.** In informal British English, a **tech** is the same as a **technical college**. ◆◇◇◇◇ N-COUNT: also *at*N

techie /teki/ **techies.** Some people refer to someone who works in a technological industry, especially computing, as a **techie**; an informal word. N-COUNT

technical /teknɪkᵊl/ ◆◆◆◇◇

1 **Technical** means involving the sorts of machines, processes, and materials that are used in industry, transport, and communications. *In order to reach this limit a number of technical problems will have to be solved. ...jobs that require technical knowledge... Many technical experts at the time had doubts about the technology.* ADJ: usu ADJ n

♦ **technically** /teknɪkli/ *...the largest and most technically advanced furnace company in the world.* ADV: ADV adj

2 You use **technical** to describe the practical skills and methods used to do an activity such as an art, a craft, or a sport. *Their technical ability is exceptional... In the realm of sculpture too, the technical skill of foreign artists was long recognised.* ADJ: usu ADJ n

♦ **technically** *While Sade's voice isn't technically brilliant it has a quality which is unmistakable.* ADV: ADV adj

3 **Technical** language involves using special words to describe the details of a specialized activity. *The technical term for sunburn is erythema... He's just written a book: large format, nicely illustrated and not too technical.* ADJ-GRADED

4 See also **technically**.

technical college, technical colleges. In Britain, a **technical college** is a college where you can study arts and technical subjects, often as part of the qualifications and training required for a particular job. N-VAR: oft in names

technicality /teknɪkælɪti/ **technicalities** ◆◇◇◇◇

1 The **technicalities** of a process or activity are the detailed methods used to do it or to carry it out. *...the technicalities of classroom teaching.* N-PLURAL: usu N *of*n

2 A **technicality** is a point, especially a legal one, that is based on a strict interpretation of the law or of a set of rules. *The earlier verdict was overturned on a legal technicality.* N-COUNT

technically /teknɪkəli/. If something is **technically** the case, it is the case according to a strict interpretation of facts, laws, or rules, but may not be important or relevant in a particular situation. *Nude bathing is technically illegal but there are plenty of unspoilt beaches where no one would ever know... Technically, the two sides have been in a state of war ever since 1949.* ◆◇◇◇◇ ADV: ADV adj, ADV with cl

technician /teknɪʃᵊn/ **technicians** ◆◆◇◇◇

1 A **technician** is someone whose job involves skilled practical work with scientific equipment, for example in a laboratory. *...a laboratory technician.* N-COUNT

2 A **technician** is someone who is very good at the detailed technical aspects of an activity. *...a versatile, veteran player, a superb technician.* N-COUNT

Technicolor /teknɪkʌləʳ/; also spelled **technicolour** in British English for meaning 2.

1 **Technicolor** is a system of colour photography used in making cinema films. **Technicolor** is a trademark. *...films in Technicolor.* N-UNCOUNT

2 You can use **technicolour** to describe real or imagined scenes when you want to emphasize that they are very colourful, especially in an exaggerated way; an informal use. *I was seeing it all in glorious technicolour: mountains, valleys, lakes, summer sunshine. ...Technicolor dreams.* N-UNCOUNT

technique /tekniːk/ **techniques** ◆◆◆◆◇

1 A **technique** is a particular method of doing an activity, usually a method that involves practical skills. *...tests performed using a new technique.* N-COUNT: with supp

2 **Technique** is skill and ability in an artistic, sporting, or other practical activity that you develop through training and practice. *He went off to the Amsterdam Academy to improve his technique.* N-UNCOUNT

techno /teknoʊ/. **Techno** is a form of modern electronic music with a very fast beat. N-UNCOUNT

techno- /teknoʊ-/. **Techno-** is used at the beginning of words that refer to technology. *He* PREFIX *tried to implement a technocratic economic policy. ...a group of futurist technofreaks.*

technocracy /teknɒkrəsi/ **technocracies**
1 A **technocracy** is a group of scientists, engineers, and other experts who have political power as well as technical knowledge. *...the power of the Brussels technocracy.* N-COUNT-COLL
2 A **technocracy** is a country or society that is controlled by scientists, engineers, and other experts. *...a centralised technocracy.* N-COUNT

technocrat /teknəkræt/ **technocrats.** A **technocrat** is a scientist, engineer, or other expert who is one of a group of similar people who have political power as well as technical knowledge. ◆◇◇◇◇ N-COUNT

technocratic /teknəkrætɪk/. **Technocratic** means consisting of or influenced by technocrats. *...the current technocratic administration.* ADJ: usu ADJ n

technological /teknəlɒdʒɪkəl/. **Technological** means relating to or associated with technology. *...an era of very rapid technological change.* ◆◆◇◇◇ ADJ: ADJ n
♦ **technologically** /teknəlɒdʒɪkli/ *...technologically advanced aircraft.* ADV: usu ADV adj

technology /teknɒlədʒi/ **technologies.** **Technology** refers to methods, systems, and devices which are the result of scientific knowledge being used for practical purposes. *Technology is changing fast... They should be allowed to wait for cheaper technologies to be developed. ...modern nuclear weapons technology.* ◆◆◆◆◇ N-VAR
♦ **technologist** /teknɒlədʒɪst/ **technologists** *...the scientists and technologists that we will need for the future.* N-COUNT

tectonic /tektɒnɪk/. **Tectonic** means relating to the structure of the earth's surface or crust; a technical term in geology. *...the tectonic plates of the Pacific region which are separating from the East Pacific Ridge.* ADJ: ADJ n

tectonics /tektɒnɪks/. See **plate tectonics**.

Ted /ted/ **Teds.** A **Ted** is the same as a **Teddy boy**; an informal British word. N-COUNT

teddy /tedi/ **teddies.** A **teddy** is the same as a **teddy bear**. Children often call their teddies 'Teddy' when they are talking to them or about them. *This is Teddy. He was my mummy's teddy and now he's mine.* ◆◇◇◇◇ N-COUNT

teddy bear, teddy bears; also spelled **teddy-bear**. A **teddy bear** is a children's soft toy which looks like a friendly bear. ◆◇◇◇◇ N-COUNT

Teddy boy, Teddy boys. In British English, a **Teddy boy** is a man who dresses in a style that became popular in the 1950's. Teddy boys were associated with early rock and roll music, and often regarded as bad or violent. N-COUNT

tedious /tiːdiəs/. If you describe something such as a job, task, or situation as **tedious**, you mean it is boring and rather frustrating. *Such lists are long and tedious to read. ...the tedious business of line-by-line programming.* ◆◇◇◇◇ ADJ-GRADED =boring
♦ **tediously** *...the most tediously boring aspects of international relations.* ADV-GRADED: usu ADV adj

tedium /tiːdiəm/. If you talk about the **tedium** of a job, task, or situation, you think it is boring and rather frustrating. *She began to wonder whether she wouldn't go mad with the tedium of the job.* N-UNCOUNT: oft N *of* n =boredom

tee /tiː/ **tees, teeing, teed** ◆◇◇◇◇
1 In golf, a **tee** is a small piece of wood or plastic which is used to support the ball before it is hit at the start of each hole. N-COUNT
2 On a golf course, a **tee** is one of the small flat areas of ground from which people hit the ball at the start of each hole. N-COUNT
3 • **to a tee**: see **T**.

tee off. In golf, when you **tee off**, you hit the ball from a tee at the start of a hole. *In a few hours time most of the world's top golfers tee off in the US Masters.* PHRASAL VERB V P

tee up. In golf, when you **tee up** a ball, you place it on a tee so that it is ready for you to hit it. *I bent down to tee up my ball... I never dreamed that I'd tee up with Bob Hope.* PHRASAL VERB V P n (not pron) V P Also V n P

teem /tiːm/ **teems, teeming, teemed.** If you say that a place **is teeming** with people or animals, you mean that it is crowded and the people and animals are moving around a lot. *For most of the year, the area is teeming with tourists.* ◆◇◇◇◇ VB: usu cont =swarm V with n

teen /tiːn/ **teens** ◆◆◇◇◇
1 If you are in your **teens**, you are between thirteen and nineteen years old. *Most people who smoke began smoking in their teens... My late teens and early twenties were really rough years... I spent most of my teen years reading diet books.* N-PLURAL: with supp, usu poss N
2 **Teen** is used to describe things such as films, magazines, bands, or activities that are aimed at or are done by people who are in their teens; used mainly in American English. *...a teen movie starring George Carlin... Pop isn't pop without huge teen sensations. ...teen violence.* ADJ: ADJ n =teenage
3 In American English, a **teen** is someone aged between thirteen and nineteen years old. The usual British word is **teenager**. *It used to be that any teen who wanted a summer job could get one.* N-COUNT =teenager

teenage /tiːneɪdʒ/ ◆◆◇◇◇
1 **Teenage** children are aged between thirteen and nineteen years old. *Almost one in four teenage girls now smoke.* ADJ: ADJ n =teenaged
2 **Teenage** is used to describe things such as films, magazines, bands, or activities that are aimed at or are done by teenage children. *...'Smash Hits', a teenage magazine. ...teenage pregnancies.* ADJ: ADJ n

teenaged /tiːneɪdʒd/. **Teenaged** people are aged between thirteen and nineteen. *She is the mother of two teenaged daughters.* ADJ: ADJ n

teenager /tiːneɪdʒəʳ/ **teenagers.** A **teenager** is someone who is between thirteen and nineteen years old. *As a teenager he attended Tulse Hill Senior High School.* ◆◆◆◇◇ N-COUNT

teeny /tiːni/ **teenier, teeniest.** If you describe something as **teeny**, you are emphasizing that it is very small; an informal word, often used by young children. *...little teeny bugs... Sue never carried anything other than the teeniest purse.* ADJ-GRADED: ADJ n PRAGMATICS =wee

teenybopper /tiːnibɒpəʳ/ **teeny-boppers;** also spelled **teeny-bopper**. A **teenybopper** is a teenager, usually a girl, who is very interested in pop music; an old-fashioned, informal word. N-COUNT

teepee /tiːpiː/. See **tepee**.

tee-shirt. See **T-shirt**.

teeter /tiːtəʳ/ **teeters, teetering, teetered** ◆◇◇◇◇
1 **Teeter** is used in expressions such as **teeter on the brink** and **teeter on the edge** to emphasize that something seems to be in a very unstable situation or position. *Three of the hotels are in receivership, and others are teetering on the brink of bankruptcy... His voice teetered on the edge of hysteria. ...white towns teetering precariously on the edge of cliffs.* VERB PRAGMATICS V on n
2 If someone or something **teeters**, they shake in an unsteady way, and seem to be about to lose their balance and fall over. *Hyde shifted his weight and felt himself teeter forward, beginning to overbalance... He watched the cup teeter on the edge before it fell.* VERB V adv/prep Also V

teeth /tiːθ/. **Teeth** is the plural of **tooth**.

teething /tiːðɪŋ/. When babies **are teething**, their teeth are starting to appear through their gums, often causing them pain. *Emma broke off a bit of rusk and gave it to Jacinta, who was teething... Camomile has long been used as a remedy for teething babies.* ► Also a noun. *Teething can be painful and make your baby irritable.* VB: only cont V V-ing N-UNCOUNT

teething problems. If a project or new product has **teething problems**, it has problems in its early stages or when it first becomes available; used in British English. *There are bound to be teething problems with something so new.* N-PLURAL

teething troubles. **Teething troubles** are the same as **teething problems**; used in British English. *As the director of the project explains, there are still a few teething troubles to overcome.* N-PLURAL

teetotal /tiːtoʊtəl, AM tiːtoʊtəl/. Someone who is **teetotal** makes it a rule never to drink alcohol. *He will not be having a celebratory drink, as he is teetotal.* ADJ: usu v-link ADJ

teetotaller /tiːtoʊtələʳ/ **teetotallers.** A **teetotaller** is someone who makes it a rule never to drink alcohol. *He is a strict teetotaller.* N-COUNT

TEFL /tefᵊl/. **TEFL** is the teaching of English to people whose first language is not English, especially people from a country where English is not spoken. **TEFL** is an abbreviation for 'teaching English as a foreign language'. N-UNCOUNT

Teflon /teflɒn/. **Teflon** is a type of plastic which is often used to coat cooking pans. Teflon provides a very smooth, slippery surface which food does not stick to, so the pan can be cleaned easily. **Teflon** is a trademark. N-UNCOUNT

tel. **Tel.** is a written abbreviation for 'telephone number'. *Cobuild Ltd; tel: 0121 414 3925.*

telecast /telɪkɑːst, -kæst/ **telecasts.** In American English, a **telecast** is a programme that is broadcast on the television, especially a programme that is broadcast live. N-COUNT

telecommunications /telɪkəmjuːnɪkeɪʃᵊnz/; the form **telecommunication** is used as a modifier. **Telecommunications** is the technology of sending signals and messages over long distances using electronic equipment, for example by radio and telephone. *...the UK telecommunications industry. ...a Japanese telecommunication company.* ◆◆◇◇◇ N-UNCOUNT: usu N n

telecommuter /telɪkəmjuːtəʳ/ **telecommuters.** **Telecommuters** are the same as **teleworkers**; used mainly in British English. N-COUNT =teleworker

telecommuting /telɪkəmjuːtɪŋ/. **Telecommuting** is the same as **teleworking**; used mainly in British English. N-UNCOUNT =teleworking

telegenic /telɪdʒenɪk/. Someone who is **telegenic** looks good on the television. *The bright and telegenic Miss Foster is being paid around £90,000 a year for her exclusive deal.* ADJ-GRADED

telegram /telɪgræm/ **telegrams.** A **telegram** is a message that is sent by telegraph and then printed and delivered to someone's home or office. *Scores of congratulatory telegrams and letters greeted Franklin on his return... The President received a briefing by telegram.* ◆◇◇◇◇ N-COUNT: also *by* N

telegraph /telɪgrɑːf, -græf/ **telegraphs, telegraphing, telegraphed** ◆◇◇◇◇

1 **Telegraph** is a system of sending messages over long distances, either by means of electricity or by radio signals. Telegraph was more commonly used before the invention of telephones. N-UNCOUNT: also *the* N

2 To **telegraph** someone means to send them a message by telegraph. *Churchill telegraphed an urgent message to Wavell... 'Please,' he telegraphed, 'just leave it alone.'... He telegraphed to me asking me to do something.* VERB V n *to* n, V with quote, V *to* n, Also V n, V

3 If someone **telegraphs** something that they are planning or intending to do, they make it obvious, either deliberately or accidentally, that they are going to do it. *The commission telegraphed its decision earlier this month by telling an official to prepare the order.* VERB V n

telegraph pole, telegraph poles. A **telegraph pole** is a tall wooden pole with telephone wires attached to it, connecting several different buildings to the telephone system. N-COUNT

telemetry /təlemɪtri/. **Telemetry** is the science of using automatic equipment to make scientific measurements and transmit them by radio to a receiving station; a technical term. N-UNCOUNT

telepathic /telɪpæθɪk/. If you believe that someone is **telepathic**, you believe that they have mental powers which cannot be explained by science, such as being able to communicate with other people's minds without using speech, writing, or any other normal signals. *About half the subjects considered themselves to be telepathic... I could not know that. I'm not telepathic.* ADJ

♦ **telepathically** /telɪpæθɪkli/ *I used to communicate with her telepathically.* ADV: ADV with v

telepathy /tɪlepəθi/. If you refer to **telepathy**, you mean the direct communication of thoughts and feelings between people's minds, without the need to use speech, writing, or any other normal signals. *Many of us find it very difficult to state our needs. We expect people to know by telepathy what we are feeling.* N-UNCOUNT

telephone /telɪfoʊn/ **telephones, telephoning, telephoned** ◆◆◆◆◇

1 The **telephone** is an electrical system of communication that you use to talk directly to someone else in a different place. You use the telephone by dialling a number on a piece of equipment and speaking into it. *They usually exchanged messages by telephone... I dread to think what our telephone bill is going to be... She was wanted on the telephone.* N-UNCOUNT =phone

2 A **telephone** is the piece of equipment that you use when you talk to someone by telephone. *He got up and answered the telephone... The telephone in Rizzoli's room rang.* N-COUNT =phone

3 If you **telephone** someone, you dial their telephone number and speak to them by telephone. *I felt so badly I had to telephone Owen to say I was sorry... They usually telephone first to see if she is at home.* VERB =call, ring, phone V n, V

4 If you are **on the telephone**, you are speaking to someone by telephone. *Linda remained on the telephone to the police for three hours... We talked on the telephone for quite a while.* PHRASE: v-link PHR, PHR after v =on the phone

5 To be **on the telephone** means to have a telephone in your house or office which is connected to the rest of the telephone system. *She wasn't on the telephone... Are you on the telephone at home?* PHRASE: v-link PHR =on the phone

telephone book, telephone books. The **telephone book** is a book that contains an alphabetical list of the names, addresses, and telephone numbers of the people in a particular area. *Directory enquiries will give you the number if you cannot find it in the telephone book.* N-COUNT =telephone directory, phone book

telephone booth, telephone booths. A **telephone booth** is a place in a public building or in the street where there is a telephone that can be used by the public; a formal expression. N-COUNT

telephone box, telephone boxes. In British English, a **telephone box** is a small shelter in the street in which there is a public telephone. The American term is **phone booth**. N-COUNT =phone box, call box

telephone directory, telephone directories. The **telephone directory** is the same as the **telephone book**. N-COUNT

telephone exchange, telephone exchanges. A **telephone exchange** is a building where connections are made between telephone lines; used mainly in British English. N-COUNT

telephone number, telephone numbers. Your **telephone number** is the number that other people dial when they want to talk to you on the telephone. ◆◇◇◇◇ N-COUNT =phone number

telephonist /tɪlefənɪst/ **telephonists.** In British English, a **telephonist** is someone who works at a telephone exchange or whose job is to answer the telephone for a business or other organization. The usual American term is **telephone operator.** N-COUNT

telephony /tɪlefəni/. **Telephony** is a system of sending messages and signals over long distances using electronic equipment. *These optical fibres may be used for new sorts of telephony.* N-UNCOUNT

telephoto lens /telɪfoʊtoʊ lenz/ **telephoto lenses.** A **telephoto lens** is a powerful camera lens which allows you to take close-up pictures of something that is far away. N-COUNT

telescope /telɪskoʊp/ **telescopes.** A **telescope** is a long instrument shaped like a tube. It has lenses inside it that make distant things seem larger and nearer when you look through it. *It's hoped that the telescope will enable scientists to see deeper into the universe than ever before.* ◆◆◇◇◇ N-COUNT

telescopic /telɪskɒpɪk/

1 **Telescopic** lenses and instruments are used to make things seem larger and nearer, and are usually longer than others of the same type. *...a sporting rifle fitted with a telescopic sight.* ADJ: usu ADJ n

2 A **telescopic** object is made of cylindrical sections that fit or slide into each other, so that it can ADJ: usu ADJ n be made longer or shorter, for example to save space when it is not being used. *...this new lightweight telescopic ladder.*

televise /telɪvaɪz/ **televises, televising, televised.** ◆◆◇◇◇ If an event or programme **is televised**, it is broadcast so that it can be seen on television. *The Grand Prix will be televised by the BBC.* VB: usu passive; be V-ed

television /telɪvɪʒᵊn, -vɪʒ-/ **televisions** ◆◆◆◆◇

1 A **television** or **television set** is a piece of electrical equipment consisting of a box with a glass screen on it on which you can watch programmes with pictures and sounds. *She turned the television on and flicked around between news programmes.* N-COUNT =TV, telly

2 Television is the system of sending pictures and sounds by electrical signals over a distance so that people can receive them on a television in their home. *Toy manufacturers began promoting some of their products on television... Television is increasingly being transmitted by satellites.* N-UNCOUNT =TV

3 Television refers to all the programmes that you can watch. *I don't have much time to watch very much television.* N-UNCOUNT =TV

4 Television is the business or industry concerned with making programmes and broadcasting them on television. *British commercial television has been steadily losing its lead as the most advanced sector of the industry in Europe.* N-UNCOUNT

televisual /teləvɪʒuəl/. **Televisual** means broadcast on or related to television; used mainly in British English. *...a televisual masterpiece... He made televisual history when he used that word in 1965.* ADJ: ADJ n

teleworker /teliwɜːʳkəʳ/ **teleworkers. Teleworkers** are people who work from home using equipment such as telephones, fax machines, and modems to contact their colleagues and customers. N-COUNT =telecommuter

teleworking /teliwɜːʳkɪŋ/. **Teleworking** is working from home using equipment such as telephones, fax machines, and modems to contact colleagues and customers. N-UNCOUNT =telecommuting

telex /teleks/ **telexes, telexing, telexed** ◆◇◇◇◇

1 Telex is an international system of sending written messages. Messages are converted into signals which are transmitted, either by means of electricity or by radio signals, and then printed out by a machine in another place. N-UNCOUNT

2 A **telex** is a machine that transmits and receives telex messages. N-COUNT

3 A **telex** is a message that you send or that has been received and printed by telex. *He sent a telex to the British High Commission in Delhi.* N-COUNT

4 If you **telex** a message to someone, you send it to them by telex. *The embassy says it has telexed their demands to the foreign ministry... They telexed British Airways.* VERB; V n to n; V n

tell /tel/ **tells, telling, told** ◆◆◆◆◆

1 If you **tell** someone something, you give them information. *In the evening I returned to tell Phyllis our relationship was over... I called Andie to tell her how spectacular the stuff looked... Claire had made me promise to tell her the truth... I only told the truth to the press when the single was released as it seemed the perfect time to do it... Tell us about your moment on the summit... Her voice breaking with emotion, she told him: 'It doesn't seem fair'.* VERB; V n that; V n wh; V n n; V n to n; V n about n; V with quote; Also V of n

2 If you **tell** something such as a joke, a story, or your personal experiences, you communicate it to other people using speech. *His friends say he was always quick to tell a joke... He told his story to The Sunday Times and produced photographs... Will you tell me a story?* VERB; V n; V n to n; V n n

3 If you **tell** someone to do something, you order, instruct, or advise them to do it. *A passer-by told the driver to move his car so that it was not causing an obstruction... She told me on the telephone to come help clean the house.* VERB; V n to-inf

4 If you **tell** yourself something, you put it into words in your own mind because you need to encourage or persuade yourself about something. *'Come on', she told herself... I told myself I would be satisfied with whatever I could get.* VERB; V pron-refl with quote; V pron-refl that

5 If you can **tell** what is happening or what is true, you are able to judge correctly what is happening or what is true. *It was already impossible to tell where the bullet had entered... I couldn't tell if he had been in a fight or had just fallen down... You can tell he's joking.* VB: no cont, oft with brd-neg; V wh; V that

6 If you can **tell** one thing from another, you are able to recognize the difference between it and other similar things. *I can't really tell the difference between their policies and ours... How do you tell one from another?... I had to look twice to tell which was Martinez; they all looked alike.* VB: no cont, oft with brd-neg; V n between pl-n; V n from n; V wh

7 If you **tell**, you reveal or give away a secret; an informal use. *Many of the children know who they are but are not telling.* VERB; V

8 If facts or events **tell** you something, they reveal certain information to you through ways other than speech. *The facts tell us that this is not true... I don't think the unemployment rate ever tells us much about the future... The evidence of our eyes tells us a different story... While most of us feel fairly complacent about the nutrients we're getting from our diets, the facts tell a very different story.* VERB; V n that; V n amount; V n n; V n

9 If an unpleasant or tiring experience begins to **tell**, it begins to have a serious effect. *The pressure began to tell as rain closed in after 20 laps... The strains of office are beginning to tell on the prime minister.* VERB; V; V on n

10 See also **telling, kiss and tell.**

11 You use **as far as I can tell** or **so far as I could tell** to indicate that what you are saying is based on the information you have, but that there may be things you do not know. *As far as I can tell, Jason is basically a nice guy... So far as anyone can tell, there's evidence that there was a Robin Hood... As far as I could tell, neither of us was under observation.* PHRASES PRAGMATICS

12 You can say **'I tell you'**, **'I can tell you'**, or **'I can't tell you'** to add emphasis to what you are saying; an informal expression. *I tell you this, I will not rest until that day has come... This little letter gave us a few chuckles, I can tell you... I can't tell you how glad I was to leave that place.* CONVENTION PRAGMATICS

13 If you say **'You never can tell'**, you mean that the future is always uncertain and it is never possible to know exactly what will happen. *You never can tell what life is going to bring you.* CONVENTION

14 If someone disagrees with you or refuses to do what you suggest and you are eventually proved to be right, you can say **'I told you so'**; an informal expression which some people may find impolite. *Her parents did not approve of her decision and, if she failed, her mother would say, 'I told you so.'* CONVENTION

15 In spoken English, you use **I'll tell you what** or **I tell you what** to introduce a suggestion or a new topic of conversation. *I tell you what, I'll bring the water in a separate glass.* CONVENTION PRAGMATICS

16 • to **tell the time**: see **time.** • **time will tell**: see **time.**

tell against. If a feature or characteristic **tells against** someone, it spoils their chance of success when they are being considered for something, for example a job. *His record of misjudgments tells against him.* PHRASAL VERB; V P n

tell apart. If you can **tell** people or things **apart**, you are able to recognize the differences between them and can therefore identify them individually. *Perhaps it is the almost universal use of flavourings that makes it so hard to tell the products apart.* PHRASAL VERB; V n P

tell off. If you **tell** someone **off**, you speak to them angrily or seriously because they have done something wrong. *He never listened to us when we told him off... I'm always being told off for being so awkward... Dutch police told off two of the gang, aged 10 and 11.* PHRASAL VERB; V n P; V n P for n/-ing; V P n (not pron)

tell on. If you **tell on** someone, you give information about them to someone in authority, especially if they have done something wrong; an informal expression. *Never mind, I won't tell on you... I'll tell my mummy on you.* PHRASAL VERB; V P n; V n P n

teller /teləʳ/ **tellers.** A **teller** is a someone who works in a bank and who customers pay money to or get money from; used mainly in American ◆◇◇◇◇ N-COUNT =cashier

and Scottish English. *Every bank pays close attention to the speed and accuracy of its tellers.*

telling /telɪŋ/ **tellings** ◆◇◇◇◇

1 The **telling** of a story or of something that has happened is the repetition of it to other people. *Herbert sat quietly through the telling of this saga... These stories grow in the telling.* N-VAR

2 If something is **telling**, it shows the true nature of a person or situation. *It was her expression that was the most telling... How a man shaves may be a telling clue to his age.* ♦ **tellingly** *Most tellingly, Labour's vote was well down on its 1990 performance.* ADJ-GRADED =revealing; ADV-GRADED: ADV with cl, ADV with v

3 A **telling** argument or criticism is a very effective one. *He spoke reasonably, carefully, and with telling effect... The most telling condemnation of the system was that it failed to fulfil its function.* ADJ-GRADED: usu ADJ n

4 You use **there's no telling** to introduce a statement when you want to say that it is impossible to know what will happen in a situation. *There's no telling how long the talks could drag on... There's no telling what diseases a person can get.* PHRASE: usu PHR wh

telling-off, tellings-off; also spelled **telling off**. If you give someone a **telling-off**, you tell them that you are very angry with them about something they have done; an informal word. *I got a severe telling off for not phoning him.* N-COUNT: usu sing

tell-tale; also spelled **telltale**. Something that is described as **telltale** gives away information, often about something bad that would otherwise not be noticed. *Only occasionally did the telltale redness around his eyes betray the fatigue he was suffering.* ADJ: ADJ n

telly /teli/ **tellies.** In informal British English, a **telly** is a television. The usual American word is **TV**. *After a hard day's work most people want to relax in front of the telly.* ◆◇◇◇◇ N-VAR =box, TV

temerity /tɪmerɪti/. If you say that someone has the **temerity** to do something, you are annoyed about something they have done which you think showed a lack of respect. *He has even had the temerity to invoke the names of Martin Luther King Jr and Malcolm X in defence of his actions. ...'difficult' patients who have the temerity to challenge their doctors' decisions.* N-UNCOUNT: usu N to-inf PRAGMATICS =presumption

temp /temp/ **temps, temping**

1 A **temp** is a person, usually a secretary, who is employed by an agency that sends him or her to work in different offices for short periods of time, for example to replace someone who is ill or on holiday. N-COUNT

2 If someone **is temping**, they are working as a temp. *Like so many aspiring actresses, she ended up waiting tables and temping in office jobs... Mrs Reynolds has been temping since losing her job.* VB: only cont V

temper /tempəʳ/ **tempers, tempering, tempered** ◆◆◇◇◇

1 If you refer to someone's **temper** or say that they have a **temper**, you mean that they become angry very easily. *He had a temper and could be nasty... His short temper had become notorious... I hope he can control his temper.* N-VAR

2 Your **temper** is the way you are feeling at a particular time. If you are in a good **temper**, you feel cheerful. If you are in a bad **temper**, you feel angry and impatient. *I was in a bad temper last night... He was in a very good temper... In a fit of bad temper, Dougie threw the deep fat fryer overboard.* N-VAR: with supp, oft adj N, oft *in* N =mood

3 To **temper** something means to make it less extreme; a formal use. *For others, especially the young and foolish, the state will temper justice with mercy... He had to learn to temper his enthusiasm.* VERB V n *with* n V n

4 If someone is **in a temper** or gets **into a temper**, the way that they are behaving shows that they are feeling angry and impatient. *She was still in a temper when Colin arrived... When I try to explain how I feel he just flies into a temper.* PHRASES v-link PHR, PHR after v =in a rage

5 If you **lose** your **temper**, you become so angry that you shout at someone or show in some other way that you are no longer in control of yourself. *I've never seen him get cross or lose his temper... I lost my temper and banged my book down on the desk.* V inflects

temperament /temprəmənt/ **temperaments** ◆◇◇◇◇

1 Your **temperament** is your basic nature, especially as it is shown in the way that you react to situations or to other people. *His impulsive temperament regularly got him into difficulties... She was furtive and vicious by temperament.* N-VAR

2 **Temperament** is the tendency to behave in an uncontrolled, bad-tempered, or unreasonable way. *Mark does have a habit of allowing his temperament to get the better of him... Some of the models were given to fits of temperament.* N-UNCOUNT

temperamental /temprəmentəl/

1 If you say that someone is **temperamental**, you are criticizing them for not being calm or quiet by nature, but having moods that change often and suddenly. *He is very temperamental and critical. ...a man given to temperamental outbursts and paranoia.* ADJ-GRADED PRAGMATICS

2 If you describe something such as a machine or car as **temperamental**, you mean that it often does not work properly. *I first started cruising in yachts with temperamental petrol engines... Vickers machine-guns could be temperamental.* ADJ-GRADED

temperamentally /temprəmentəli/. **Temperamentally** means because of someone's basic nature or related to someone's basic nature. *He is a quitter who is temperamentally unsuited to remaining a champion.* ADV: ADV with cl/group, ADV after v

temperance /tempərəns/

1 If you believe in **temperance**, you disapprove of drinking alcohol. *...a reformed alcoholic extolling the joys of temperance.* N-UNCOUNT

2 A person who shows **temperance** is very self-controlled and does not eat too much, drink too much, or do anything to excess; a formal use. *The age of hedonism is being ushered out by a new era of temperance.* N-UNCOUNT =moderation

temperate /tempərɪt/ ◆◇◇◇◇

1 **Temperate** is used to describe a climate or a place which is never extremely hot or extremely cold. *The Nile Valley keeps a temperate climate throughout the year.* ADJ-GRADED: usu ADJ n =mild

2 If a person's behaviour is **temperate**, it is calm and self-controlled, so that they do not get angry or lose their temper easily; a formal use. *His final report to the President was far more temperate and balanced than the earlier memorandum.* ADJ-GRADED =moderate

temperature /temprətʃəʳ/ **temperatures** ◆◆◆◇◇

1 The **temperature** of something is a measure of how hot or cold it is. *Winter closes in and the temperature drops below freezing... The temperature of the water was about 40 degrees... Coping with severe drops in temperature can be very difficult.* N-VAR

2 Your **temperature** is the temperature of your body. A normal temperature is about 37° centigrade. *His temperature continued to rise and the cough worsened until Tania finally persuaded a doctor to come.* N-UNCOUNT: oft poss N

3 You can use **temperature** to talk about the feelings and emotions that people have in particular situations. *There's also been a noticeable rise in the political temperature.* N-COUNT: usu sing

4 If something is at **room temperature**, its temperature is neither hot nor cold. *Just before serving, stir the parsley into the potatoes. Serve at room temperature.* PHRASES usu PHR after v, v-link PHR

5 If you **are running a temperature** or if you **have a temperature**, your temperature is higher than it usually is. *He began to run an extremely high temperature. I begged him to let me call a doctor... Little Constance had a temperature that day.* V inflects

6 If you **take** someone's **temperature** you use a thermometer to measure the temperature of their body in order to see if they are ill. *He will probably take your child's temperature too.* V inflects

tempest /tempɪst/ **tempests**

1 A **tempest** is a very violent storm; a literary use. *Torrential rain and a howling tempest cut a swathe of destruction across the country.* N-COUNT =storm

2 You can refer to a situation in which people are very angry or excited as a **tempest**. *I hadn't foreseen* N-COUNT: usu with supp =furore,

the tempest my request would cause... The takeover provoked a tempest of criticism. storm

tempestuous /tempestʃuəs/. If you describe a relationship or a situation as **tempestuous**, you mean that very strong and passionate emotions, especially anger, are involved. *For years, the couple's tempestuous relationship made the headlines... Somehow the marriage lasted for eight tempestuous months.* ADJ-GRADED: usu ADJ n =stormy ≠peaceful

tempi /tempi/. **Tempi** is a plural of **tempo**.

template /templeɪt, AM -plɪt/ **templates**

1 A **template** is a thin piece of metal or plastic which is cut into a particular shape. It is used to help you cut wood, paper, metal, or other materials accurately, or to reproduce the same shape many times. *Trace around your template and transfer the design onto a sheet of card.* N-COUNT

2 If one thing is a **template** for something else, the second thing is based on the first thing. *The template for Adair's novel is not somebody else's fiction, but fact.* N-COUNT: usu sing

temple /tempəl/ **temples** ◆◆◆◇◇

1 A **temple** is a building used for the worship of a god or gods, especially in the Buddhist and Hindu religions, and in ancient Greek and Roman times. *...a small Hindu temple. ...the Temple of Diana at Ephesus.* N-COUNT: oft in names

2 Your **temples** are the flat parts on each side of the front part of your head, near your forehead. *Threads of silver ran through his beard and the hair at his temples.* N-COUNT: usu pl

tempo /tempoʊ/ **tempos; tempi** can also be used as the plural form. ◆◇◇◇◇

1 The **tempo** of an event is the speed at which it happens. *Pressure from inside Albania as well as outside is likely to speed up the tempo of change further... Both teams played with a lot of quality, pace and tempo.* N-SING =pace

2 The **tempo** of a piece of music is the speed at which it is played. *In a new recording, the Boston Philharmonic tried the original tempo... Elgar supplied his works with precise indications of tempo.* N-VAR

temporal /tempərəl/ ◆◇◇◇◇

1 **Temporal** powers or matters relate to ordinary institutions and activities rather than to religious or spiritual ones; a technical use in theology. *...the spiritual and temporal leader of the Tibetan people. ...firmly believing in the need for the clergy not to become pre-occupied with temporal matters.* ADJ: ADJ n =worldly ≠spiritual

2 The **temporal** parts of your brain are the parts near your temples, at the sides of your head; a medical use. *...a small but important area of the temporal lobe of the brain.* ADJ: ADJ n

3 **Temporal** means relating to time; a formal use. *One is also able to see how specific acts are related to a temporal and spatial context... The present world crisis should in principle be analysed from different temporal perspectives.* ♦ **temporally** /tempərəli/ *In the last stages of dementia, persons will be spatially and temporally disoriented.* ADJ: ADJ n / ADV

temporary /tempərəri, AM -reri/. Something that is **temporary** lasts for only a limited time. *His job here is only temporary... Most adolescent problems are temporary. ...a temporary loss of memory.* ♦ **temporarily** /tempəreərɪli/ *The peace agreement has at least temporarily halted the civil war... Checkpoints between the two zones were temporarily closed.* ◆◆◆◇◇ ADJ ≠permanent / ADV: ADV with v, ADV adj ≠permanently

temporize /tempəraɪz/ **temporizes, temporizing, temporized;** also spelled **temporise** in British English. If you say that someone **is temporizing**, you mean that they keep doing something unimportant, in order to delay something important such as making a decision or stating their real opinion; a formal word. *They are still temporizing in the face of what can only be described as a disaster... 'Not exactly, sir,' temporized Sloan.* VERB / V / V with quote

tempt /tempt/ **tempts, tempting, tempted** ◆◇◇◇◇

1 Something that **tempts** you attracts you and makes you want it, even though it may be wrong or harmful. *Reducing the income will further impoverish these families and could tempt an offender into further crime... It is the fresh fruit that tempts me at this time of year... Can I tempt you with a little puff pastry?... The fact that she had become wealthy did not tempt her to alter her frugal way of life.* VERB / V n into n/-ing / V n / V n with n / V n to-inf

2 If you **tempt** someone, you offer them something they want in order to encourage them to do something that you want them to do. *...a million dollar marketing campaign to tempt American tourists back to Britain... Having spent so long at a great club like Rangers, no other Scottish team could tempt him away... Don't let credit tempt you to buy something you can't afford... She will be offering a package worth about 40 million dollars, to tempt the rebels into agreeing to disarm.* VERB / V n prep/adv / V n to-inf / V n into -ing/n

3 See also **tempted**.

4 If someone says that something they say or do **is tempting fate** or **is tempting providence**, they mean they are worried that it may cause the good luck they have had so far to end. *As soon as you start to talk about never having played on a losing side, it is tempting fate.* PHRASE: V inflects

temptation /tempteɪʃən/ **temptations.** If you feel you want to do something or have something, even though you know you really should avoid it, you can refer to this feeling as **temptation**. You can refer to the thing you want to do or have as a **temptation**. *Will they be able to resist the temptation to buy? ...the many temptations to which you will be exposed.* ◆◆◇◇◇ N-VAR

tempted /temptɪd/. If you say that you are **tempted** to do something, you mean that you would like to do it. *I'm very tempted to sell my house... She'd never even felt tempted to return.* ◆◆◇◇◇ ADJ-GRADED: v-link ADJ, usu ADJ to-inf

tempting /temptɪŋ/. If something is **tempting**, it makes you want to do it or have it. *In the end, I turned down Raoul's tempting offer of the Palm Beach trip... If you're slimming, resisting tempting goodies becomes a measure of your 'success' as a woman... At first glance, it would be tempting to agree.* ♦ **temptingly** *The good news is that prices are still temptingly low.* ◆◇◇◇◇ ADJ-GRADED / ADV

temptress /temptrəs/ **temptresses.** If you describe a woman as a **temptress**, you mean that she uses her female charm and sexuality to encourage men to have sexual relations with her. *Supermodel Jane Bracknel plays a nubile temptress out to seduce him.* N-COUNT

ten /ten/ **tens. Ten** is the number 10. *Over the past ten years things have changed.* • See also **Number Ten.** • **ten a penny**: see **penny**. ◆◆◆◆◆ NUM

tenable /tenəbəl/. If you say that an argument, point of view, or situation is **tenable**, you believe that it is reasonable and could be successfully defended against criticism. *This argument is simply not tenable... The only way his role can be clarified and his position made tenable again is if there's a public inquiry.* ADJ-GRADED ≠untenable

tenacious /tɪneɪʃəs/ ◆◇◇◇◇

1 If you are **tenacious**, you are very determined and do not give up easily. *She is very tenacious and will work hard and long to achieve objectives... He is regarded at the BBC as a tenacious and persistent interviewer.* ♦ **tenaciously** *In spite of his illness, he clung tenaciously to his job.* ADJ-GRADED / ADV-GRADED: usu ADV after v

2 If you describe something such as an idea or belief as **tenacious**, you mean that it has a strong influence on people and is difficult to change or remove. *...a remarkably tenacious belief that was to dominate future theories of military strategy.* ADJ-GRADED =deep-seated

tenacity /tɪnæsɪti/. If you have **tenacity**, you are very determined and do not give up easily. *Talent, hard work and sheer tenacity are all crucial to career success.* ◆◇◇◇◇ N-UNCOUNT

tenancy /tenənsi/ **tenancies. Tenancy** is the use that you have of land or property belonging to someone else, for which you pay rent. *His father took over the tenancy of the farm 40 years ago... Tenants should check their tenancy agreements closely.* ◆◇◇◇◇ N-VAR

tenant /tenənt/ **tenants.** A **tenant** is someone who pays rent for the place they live in, or for land or buildings that they use. *Regulations* ◆◆◇◇◇ N-COUNT *placed clear obligations on the landlord for the benefit of the tenant... Landowners frequently left the management of their estates to tenant farmers.* • See also **sitting tenant**.

tench /tentʃ/; **tench** is both the singular and the plural form. **Tench** are dark green European fish that live in lakes and rivers. N-VAR

tend /tend/ **tends, tending, tended** ◆◆◆◆◇

1 If something **tends** to happen, it usually happens or it often happens. *A problem for manufacturers is that lighter cars tend to be noisy... In older age groups women predominate because men tend to die younger... They tend to buy cheap processed foods like canned chicken and macaroni.* VERB =be apt V to-inf

2 If you **tend** towards a particular characteristic, you often display that characteristic. *Artistic and intellectual people tend towards left-wing views.* VERB V *towards* n Also V *to* n

3 You can say that you **tend** to think something when you want to give your opinion, but do not want it to seem too forceful or definite. *I tend to think that members of parliament by and large do a good job.* VERB PRAGMATICS V to-inf

4 If you **tend** someone or something, you do what is necessary to keep them in a good condition or to improve their condition; a formal use. *For years he tended her in her painful illness... He tends the flower beds and evergreens that he has planted in the driveway.* VERB =look after V n

5 If you **tend to** someone or something, you pay attention to them and deal with their problems and needs. *In our culture, girls are brought up to tend to the needs of others... She hurried away to pour more coffee and tend to the grill.* VERB =attend V *to* n

tendency /tendənsi/ **tendencies** ◆◆◆◇◇

1 A **tendency** is a worrying or unpleasant habit or action that keeps occurring. *The army has become increasingly restless over the mounting separatist tendencies of the northern republics. ...the government's tendency towards secrecy in recent years.* N-COUNT: with supp

2 A **tendency** is a part of your character that makes you behave in an unpleasant or worrying way. *He is spoiled, arrogant and has a tendency towards snobbery... Helen had been struggling against suicidal tendencies.* N-COUNT: with supp

tendentious /tendenʃəs/. Something that is **tendentious** expresses a particular opinion or point of view very strongly, especially one that many people disagree with; a formal word. *His analysis was rooted in a somewhat tendentious reading of French history.* ADJ-GRADED =controversial

tender 1 adjective uses

tender /tendəʳ/ **tenderer, tenderest** ◆◆◇◇◇

1 Someone or something that is **tender** expresses gentle and caring feelings. *Her voice was tender, full of pity... Patients may not receive the tender, loving care once associated with a hospital stay.* ADJ-GRADED

♦ **tenderly** *Mr. White tenderly embraced his wife.* ADV-GRADED: ADV with v

♦ **tenderness** *She smiled, politely rather than with tenderness or gratitude.* N-UNCOUNT

2 If you say that someone does something at a **tender** age, you mean that they do it when they are still young and inexperienced. *He had become attracted to the game at the tender age of seven. ...the loss of her father at such a tender age.* ADJ-GRADED: ADJ n

3 Meat or other food that is **tender** is easy to cut or chew. *Cook for a minimum of 2 hours, or until the meat is tender. ...tender young dwarf beans.* ADJ-GRADED ≠tough

4 If part of your body is **tender**, it is sensitive and painful when it is touched. *My tummy felt very tender... Treat any tender points by massaging.* ADJ-GRADED =sore

♦ **tenderness** *There is still some tenderness in her tummy.* N-UNCOUNT

tender 2 noun and verb uses

tender /tendəʳ/ **tenders, tendering, tendered** ◆◆◇◇◇

1 A **tender** is a formal offer to supply goods or to do a particular job, and a statement of the price that you or your company will charge. If a contract is **put out to tender**, formal offers are invited. If a company **wins a tender**, their offer is accepted. *Builders will then be sent the specifications and asked to submit a tender for the work... Some services are now compulsorily put out to tender. ...the consortium that has won the tender to build the second Severn Bridge.* N-VAR

2 If a company **tenders for** something, it makes a formal offer to supply goods or do a job for a particular price. *The staff are forbidden to tender for private-sector work... He tendered for and was awarded the contract.* VERB V *for* n

♦ **tendering** *...compulsory competitive tendering for council leisure and recreation services.* N-UNCOUNT

3 If you **tender** something such as a suggestion, your resignation, or money, you formally offer or present it. *She quickly tendered her resignation... He took his wallet from his inside coat pocket and tendered the permit.* VERB V n

4 See also **legal tender**.

tender-hearted. If you are **tender-hearted**, you have a gentle and caring nature. ADJ-GRADED

tenderize /tendəraɪz/ **tenderizes, tenderizing, tenderized;** also spelled **tenderise** in British English. If you **tenderize** meat, you make it more tender by preparing it in a particular way. *Wine vinegar tenderises meat.* VERB V n

tendon /tendən/ **tendons.** A **tendon** is a strong cord in a person's or animal's body which joins a muscle to a bone. • See also **Achilles tendon**. ◆◇◇◇◇ N-COUNT

tendril /tendrɪl/ **tendrils**

1 A **tendril** is something thin and wispy, for example a piece of hair which hangs loose away from the main part. *Tendrils of hair strayed to the edge of her pillow.* N-COUNT

2 **Tendrils** are thin stems which grow on some plants so that they can attach themselves to supports such as walls or other plants. N-COUNT: usu pl

tenement /tenəmənt/ **tenements**

1 A **tenement** is a large, old terraced building which is divided into a number of individual flats. *...elegant 19th century tenement buildings.* N-COUNT

2 A **tenement** is one of the flats in a tenement. *...the cramped Edinburgh tenement in which Connery grew up.* N-COUNT

tenet /tenɪt/ **tenets.** The **tenets** of a theory or belief are the main principles on which it is based; a formal word. *Non-violence and patience are the central tenets of their faith... The judge's ruling was based on the simple commonsense tenet that no man is above the law.* ◆◇◇◇◇ N-COUNT: with supp, oft N *of* n =principle

tenner /tenəʳ/ **tenners.** In informal British English, a **tenner** is ten pounds or a ten-pound note. N-COUNT

tennis /tenɪs/. **Tennis** is a game played by two or four players on a rectangular court. The players use rackets to hit a ball over a net which is placed across the middle of the court. ◆◆◆◇◇ N-UNCOUNT

tenor /tenəʳ/ **tenors** ◆◇◇◇◇

1 A **tenor** is a male singer whose voice is fairly high. *...a free, open-air concert given by the Italian tenor, Luciano Pavarotti.* N-COUNT: oft N n

2 A **tenor** saxophone or other musical instrument has a range of notes that are of a fairly low pitch. *...one of the best tenor sax players ever.* ADJ

3 The **tenor** of something is the general meaning or mood that it expresses; a formal use. *The whole tenor of discussions has changed... Her dreams were troubled, reflecting the tenor of her waking hours.* N-SING: with poss

ten-pin bowling; also spelled **tenpin bowling**. **Ten-pin bowling** is a game like skittles in which you try to knock down ten bottle-shaped objects by rolling a heavy ball towards them. It is usually played in a bowling alley. This expression is mainly used in British English, and the usual American word is **bowling**. N-UNCOUNT

tense /tens/ **tenser, tensest; tenses, tensing, tensed** ◆◆◇◇◇

1 A **tense** situation or period of time is one that makes people anxious, because they do not know what is going to happen next. *This gesture of goodwill did little to improve the tense atmosphere at the talks... After three very tense weeks he phoned again... There was a tense silence.* ADJ-GRADED

2 If you are **tense**, you are anxious and nervous and cannot relax. *Dart, who had at first been very tense, at last relaxed.* ADJ-GRADED

♦ **tensely** *She waited tensely for the next bulletin... 'Tony, I can explain everything,' she* ADV-GRADED: usu ADV with v *said tensely.* ♦ **tenseness** *McKay walked slowly toward this screen, feeling a growing tenseness.* N-UNCOUNT

3 If your body is **tense**, your muscles are tight and not relaxed. *She lay, eyes shut, body tense... A bath can relax tense muscles.* ♦ **tenseness** *If you feel a tenseness around the eyes, relax your muscles.* ADJ-GRADED N-UNCOUNT

4 If your muscles **tense**, if you **tense**, or if you **tense** your muscles, your muscles become tight and stiff, often because you are anxious or frightened. *Newman's stomach muscles tensed... He tensed as the big West Indian gripped his shoulder... Jane tensed her muscles to stop them from shaking.* ► **Tense up** means the same as **tense**. *When we are under stress our bodies tend to tense up... I tried not to tense up, or become obviously wary... Tense up the muscles in both of your legs.* V-ERG V V n PHRASAL VERB ERG V P V P n (not pron) Also V n P

5 The **tense** of a verb group is its form, which usually shows whether you are referring to past, present, or future time. *It was as though Corinne was already dead: they were speaking of her in the past tense.* N-COUNT

tense up. See **tense** 4. PHRASAL VERB

tensile /te̲nsaɪl, AM -sɪl/. You use **tensile** when you are talking about the amount of stress that materials such as wire, rope, and concrete can take without breaking; a technical term in engineering. *Certain materials can be manufactured with a high tensile strength.* ADJ: ADJ n

tension /te̲nʃᵊn/ **tensions** ♦♦♦◊◊

1 **Tension** is the feeling that is produced in a situation when people are anxious and do not trust each other, and when there is a possibility of sudden violence or conflict. *The tension between the two countries is likely to remain... The years of his government are remembered for political tension and conflict. ...continued tension over the killing of demonstrators.* N-UNCOUNT: also N in pl

2 **Tension** is a feeling of worry and nervousness which makes it difficult for you to relax. *She has done her best to keep calm but finds herself trembling with tension and indecision... Smiling and laughing has actually been shown to relieve tension and stress.* N-UNCOUNT: also N in pl

3 If there is a **tension** between forces, arguments, or influences, there are differences between them that cause difficulties. *The film explored the tension between public duty and personal affections.* N-VAR: usu N *between* pl-n

4 The **tension** in something such as a rope or wire is the extent to which it is stretched tight. N-UNCOUNT

tent /te̲nt/ **tents.** A **tent** is a shelter made of canvas or nylon which is held up by poles and ropes, used mainly by people who are camping. ♦♦◊◊◊ N-COUNT

tentacle /te̲ntəkᵊl/ **tentacles** ♦◊◊◊◊

1 The **tentacles** of an animal such as an octopus are the long thin parts that are used for feeling and holding things, for getting food, and for moving. N-COUNT: usu pl

2 If you talk about the **tentacles** of a political, commercial, or social organization, you are referring to the power and influence that it has in the outside community; used showing disapproval. *Free speech is being gradually eroded year after year by new tentacles of government control.* N-COUNT: usu pl, with supp PRAGMATICS

tentative /te̲ntətɪv/ ♦♦◊◊◊

1 **Tentative** agreements, plans, or arrangements are not definite or certain, but have been made as a first step. *Political leaders have reached a tentative agreement to hold a preparatory conference next month... Such theories are still very tentative.* ♦ **tentatively** *The next round of talks is tentatively scheduled to begin October 21st in Washington.* ADJ-GRADED =provisional ≠firm ADV-GRADED: ADV with v

2 If someone is **tentative**, they are cautious and not very confident because they are uncertain or afraid. *My first attempts at complaining were rather tentative... She did not return his tentative smile.* ♦ **tentatively** *Perhaps, he suggested tentatively, they should send for Dr Band.* ADJ-GRADED ≠confident ADV-GRADED: ADV with v

tented /te̲ntɪd/

1 A **tented** field or a **tented** camp is an area where a number of people are living in tents. *He said the refugees would be moved to a tented camp.* ADJ: usu ADJ n

2 A **tented** room has long pieces of material hanging down from the centre of the ceiling to the walls, so that the room has the appearance of the inside of a large tent. *...a tented dining area... The tented ceiling hides a maze of water pipes.* ADJ: usu ADJ n

tenterhooks /te̲ntəʳhʊks/. If you are **on tenterhooks**, you are very nervous and excited because you are wondering what is going to happen in a particular situation. *He was still on tenterhooks waiting for his directors' decision about the job.* PHRASE: v-link PHR

tenth /te̲nθ/ **tenths** ♦♦♦♦◊

1 The **tenth** item in a series is the one that you count as number ten. ORD

2 A **tenth** is one of ten equal parts of something. *He finished three-tenths of a second behind Prost.* FRACTION

tenuous /te̲njuəs/. If you describe something such as a connection, a reason, or someone's position as **tenuous**, you mean that it is very uncertain or weak. *The cultural and historical links between the many provinces were seen to be very tenuous... This decision puts the President in a somewhat tenuous position.* ♦ **tenuously** *The sub-plots are only tenuously interconnected.* ♦◊◊◊◊ ADJ-GRADED ≠strong ADV-GRADED: ADV with v

tenure /te̲njəʳ/ ♦◊◊◊◊

1 **Tenure** is the legal right to live in a particular building or to use a particular piece of land during a fixed period of time. *Lack of security of tenure was a reason for many families becoming homeless.* N-UNCOUNT

2 **Tenure** is the period of time during which someone holds an important job. *...the three-year tenure of President Bush... During his tenure as foreign minister, Mr Shevardnadze presided over a revolution in Soviet foreign policy.* N-UNCOUNT: with supp

3 If you have **tenure** in your job, you have the right to keep it until you retire. *Junior staff have only a slim chance of getting tenure.* N-UNCOUNT

tepee /ti̲ːpiː/ **tepees;** also spelled **teepee**. A **tepee** is a cone-shaped tent. Tepees were first made by Native American peoples from animal skins or bark. N-COUNT =wigwam

tepid /te̲pɪd/ ♦◊◊◊◊

1 Water or another liquid that is **tepid** is slightly warm. *She bent her mouth to the tap and drank the tepid water.* ADJ =lukewarm

2 If you describe something such as a feeling or reaction as **tepid**, you mean that it lacks enthusiasm or liveliness. *His nomination, while strongly backed by the President, has received tepid support in the Senate.* ADJ-GRADED =lukewarm

tercentenary /tɜ̲ːʳsentiː̲nəri, AM -te̲n-/. A **tercentenary** is a day or a year which is exactly three hundred years after an important event such as the birth of a famous person. *...the tercentenary of Purcell's death.* N-SING: oft *the* N *of* n

term /tɜ̲ːʳm/ **terms, terming, termed** ♦♦♦♦♦

1 If you talk about something **in terms of** something or **in** particular **terms**, you are specifying which aspect of it you are discussing or from what point of view you are considering it. *Our goods compete in terms of product quality, reliability and above all variety... Paris has played a dominant role in France, not just in political terms but also in economic power.* PHRASE: PHR after v, PHR with cl

2 If you say or express something **in** particular **terms**, you say or express it using a particular type or level of language or using language which clearly shows your attitude. *The video explains in simple terms how the new tax works... The document is expressed in terms that are readily understood and agreed.* PHRASE: usu PHR after v, PHR with cl

3 A **term** is a word or expression with a specific meaning, especially one which is used in relation to a particular subject. *Myocardial infarction is the medical term for a heart attack.* N-COUNT: usu with supp

4 If you say that something **is termed** a particular thing, you mean that that is what people call it or that is their opinion of it. *He had been termed a temporary employee... He termed the war a humanitarian nightmare.* VERB *be* V-ed n V n n Also V n *as* n

5 A **term** is one of the periods of time that a school, college, or university divides the year into. *...the summer term. ...the last day of term.* N-VAR

6 A **term** is a period of time between two elections during which a particular party, prime minister, or N-COUNT: with supp

president is in power. *Felipe Gonzalez won a fourth term of office in Spain's election.*

7 A **term** is a period of time that someone spends doing a particular job or in a particular place. *...a 12 month term of service... Offenders will be liable to a seven-year prison term.* N-COUNT: with supp

8 A **term** is the period for which a legal contract or insurance policy is valid. *Premiums are guaranteed throughout the term of the policy.* N-COUNT: with supp

9 The **term** of a woman's pregnancy is the nine month period that it lasts. **Term** is also used to refer to the end of the nine month period. *That makes her the first TV presenter to work the full term of her pregnancy... Women over 40 seem to be just as capable of carrying a baby to term as younger women.* N-UNCOUNT

10 The **terms** of an agreement, treaty, or other arrangement are the conditions that must be accepted by the people involved in it. *...the terms of the Helsinki agreement... Mayor Rendell imposed the new contract terms.* N-PLURAL: usu with supp

11 If you **come to terms with** something difficult or unpleasant, you learn to accept and deal with it. *She had come to terms with the fact that her husband would always be crippled.* PHRASES V inflects, PHR n

12 If two people or groups compete **on equal terms** or **on the same terms**, neither of them has an advantage over the other. *I had at last found a sport where I could compete on equal terms with able-bodied people... The focus was on women gaining access to work on the same terms as men.* PHR after v

13 If two people are **on good terms** or **on friendly terms**, they are friendly with each other. *Madeleine is on good terms with Sarah... We shook hands and parted on good terms.* v-link PHR, PHR after v

14 You use the expressions **in the long term, in the short term**, and **in the medium term** to talk about what will happen over a long period of time, over a short period of time, and over a medium period of time. *The agreement should have very positive results in the long term... In the short term, chemical sprays are clearly an effective way to control pests... In the medium term the UK car industry has a brighter outlook.* • See also **long-term, medium-term, short-term.** PHR with cl

15 If you do something **on** your **terms**, you do it under conditions that you decide because you are in a position of power. *They will sign the union treaty only on their terms.* PHR after v

16 If you say that you **are thinking in terms of** doing a particular thing, you mean that you are considering it. *United should be thinking in terms of winning the European Cup... She was thinking in terms of a career.* V inflects, PHR -ing/n

17 • a **contradiction in terms**: see **contradiction.** • **in no uncertain terms**: see **uncertain.** • **in real terms**: see **real.** • **on speaking terms**: see **speak.**

terminal /tɜːʳmɪnəl/ **terminals** ◆◆◇◇◇

1 A **terminal** illness or disease causes death, often slowly, and cannot be cured. *...terminal cancer. ...his illness was terminal.* ♦ **terminally** *The patient is terminally ill.* ADJ: usu ADJ n ADV: ADV adj

2 A **terminal** patient is dying of a terminal illness or disease. *They have started a hospice for terminal patients.* ADJ: usu ADJ n

3 A **terminal** is a place where vehicles, passengers, or goods begin or end a journey. *Plans are underway for a fifth terminal at Heathrow airport.* N-COUNT: usu supp N

4 A computer **terminal** is a piece of equipment consisting of a keyboard and a screen that is used for putting information into a computer or getting information from it. *Carl sits at a computer terminal 40 hours a week.* N-COUNT

5 On a piece of electrical equipment, a **terminal** is one of the points where electricity enters or leaves it. *...the positive terminal of the battery.* N-COUNT

terminate /tɜːʳmɪneɪt/ **terminates, terminating, terminated** ◆◆◇◇◇

1 When you **terminate** something or when it **terminates**, it ends completely; a formal use. *Her next remark abruptly terminated the conversation... His contract terminates at the season's end.* V-ERG V n V

♦ **termination** /tɜːʳmɪneɪʃən/ *...a dispute which led to the abrupt termination of trade.* N-UNCOUNT

2 To **terminate** a pregnancy means to end it; a medical use. *After a lot of agonizing she decided to terminate the pregnancy... In the world as a whole, about ten per cent of all pregnancies are terminated.* ♦ **termination, terminations** *You should also have a medical check-up after the termination of a pregnancy.* VERB V n N-VAR

3 When a train or bus **terminates** somewhere, it ends its journey there; a formal use. *This train will terminate at Taunton.* VERB V prep/adv

termini /tɜːʳmɪnaɪ/. **Termini** is the plural of **terminus.**

terminology /tɜːʳmɪnɒlədʒi/ **terminologies.** ◆◇◇◇◇ The **terminology** of a subject is the set of special words and expressions used in connection with it. *...gastritis, which in medical terminology means an inflammation of the stomach.* N-VAR: usu with supp

terminus /tɜːʳmɪnəs/ **termini.** On a bus or train route, the **terminus** is the last stop or station, where the bus or train turns round or starts a journey in the opposite direction. *...the London terminus of the Channel Tunnel rail link.* N-COUNT

termite /tɜːʳmaɪt/ **termites. Termites** are small white insects which live in hot countries in nests made of earth. Termites do a lot of damage by eating wood. N-COUNT

terms of reference. Terms of reference are the instructions given to someone when they are asked to consider or investigate a particular subject, telling them what they must deal with and what they can ignore; a formal expression. *The government has announced the terms of reference for its proposed committee of inquiry.* N-PLURAL

tern /tɜːʳn/ **terns.** A **tern** is a small black and white seabird with long wings and a forked tail. N-COUNT

terrace /terɪs/ **terraces** ◆◆◇◇◇

1 In British English, a **terrace** is a row of similar houses joined together by their side walls. *...a terrace of stylish Victorian houses. ...3 Queensborough Terrace.* N-COUNT: oft in names after n

2 A **terrace** is a flat area of stone or grass next to a building where people can sit. *Some guests recline in lounge chairs on the sea-facing terrace.* N-COUNT

3 **Terraces** are a series of flat areas of ground built like steps on a hillside so that crops can be grown there. *...massive terraces of maize and millet carved into the mountainside like giant steps.* N-COUNT: usu pl

4 **The terraces** at a football ground are wide steps that people can stand on when they are watching a game; used in British English. N-PLURAL: the N

terraced /terɪst/. A **terraced** slope or hillside has flat areas of ground like steps cut into it, where crops or other plants can be grown. ◆◇◇◇◇ ADJ: usu ADJ n

terraced house, terraced houses. In British English, a **terraced house** or a **terrace house** is one of a row of similar houses joined together by their side walls. The usual American term is a **row house.** N-COUNT

terracing /terəsɪŋ/

1 **Terracing** is a sloping piece of land that has had flat areas of ground like steps built on it, for example so that people can grow crops there. *The traditional lawn has been replaced by low-cost terracing, with a raised pool and waterfall.* N-UNCOUNT

2 At a football stadium, **terracing** is an area of wide steps that people can stand on when they are watching the game; used in British English. N-UNCOUNT

terracotta /terəkɒtə/; also spelled **terra-cotta.** ◆◇◇◇◇

1 **Terracotta** is a brownish-red clay that has been baked but not glazed and that is used for making things such as flower pots, small statues, and tiles. *...plants in terracotta pots.* N-UNCOUNT: oft N n

2 **Terracotta** is used to describe things that are brownish-red in colour. *...the soft tones of blue, cream and terracotta.* COLOUR

terra firma /terə fɜːʳmə/. If you describe the ground as **terra firma**, you mean that it feels safe in contrast to being in the air or at sea. *...his relief on finding himself once more on terra firma.* N-UNCOUNT

terrain /tər**e**ɪn/ **terrains.** **Terrain** is used to refer to an area of land or a type of land when you are considering its physical features. *The terrain changed quickly from arable land to desert. ...a tortuous eight-hour coach ride around 1,200 bends of rough terrain.* ◆◇◇◇◇ N-VAR: usu with supp

terrapin /t**e**rəpɪn/ **terrapins.** A **terrapin** is a reptile which has a thick shell covering its body and which lives partly in water and partly on the land. N-COUNT

terrestrial /tɪr**e**striəl/ ◆◇◇◇◇
1 A **terrestrial** animal or plant lives on land or on the ground rather than in the sea, in trees, or in the air; a technical use in zoology and botany. *Terrestrial and aquatic fauna may sometimes be found resting together under a loose stone.* ADJ: usu ADJ n
2 **Terrestrial** means relating to the planet Earth rather than to some other part of the universe. *...terrestrial life forms.* ADJ: ADJ n
3 **Terrestrial** television channels are transmitted using equipment situated at ground level, and not by satellite; used mainly in British English. ADJ: usu ADJ n

terrible /t**e**rɪbᵊl/ ◆◆◆◆◇
1 A **terrible** experience or situation is very serious or very unpleasant. *Tens of thousands more suffered terrible injuries in the world's worst industrial disaster... I often have the most terrible nightmares... Prison life, he told me, was terrible.* ADJ-GRADED =dreadful ♦ **terribly** *My son has suffered terribly. He has lost his best friend.* ADV-GRADED: ADV after v
2 If you **feel terrible**, you feel extremely ill or unhappy. If you tell someone that they **look terrible**, you mean that they look as if they are extremely ill or unhappy. *He did feel terrible at the time but seems to be fine now... Are you all right? You look terrible. Are you sick?* ADJ-GRADED: *feel/look* ADJ =awful
3 If something is **terrible**, it is very bad or of very poor quality. *She admits her French is terrible.* ADJ-GRADED =dreadful
4 You use **terrible** to emphasize the great extent or degree of something. *I was a terrible fool, you know. I remember that now... Her death is a terrible waste.* ADJ: ADJ n ♦ **terribly** *I'm terribly sorry to bother you at this hour... I suffered terribly when she died.* ADV-GRADED: usu ADV adj

terrier /t**e**riəʳ/ **terriers.** A **terrier** is a small breed of dog. There are many different types of terrier. ● See also **bull terrier**, **pit bull terrier**. ◆◇◇◇◇ N-COUNT

terrific /tər**ɪ**fɪk/ ◆◆◇◇◇
1 If you describe something or someone as **terrific**, you are very pleased with them or very impressed by them; an informal use. *What a terrific idea!... Everybody there was having a terrific time... You look terrific, Ann. You really do.* ADJ-GRADED =great
2 **Terrific** means very great in amount, degree, or intensity. *He did a terrific amount of fundraising... All of a sudden there was a terrific bang and a flash of smoke.* ADJ-GRADED: ADJ n =tremendous ♦ **terrifically** /tər**ɪ**fɪkli/ *She really is terrifically pretty. ...the only child of terrifically repressed parents.* ADV: usu ADV adj/-ed

terrify /t**e**rɪfaɪ/ **terrifies, terrifying, terrified.** If something **terrifies** you, it makes you feel extremely frightened. *Flying terrifies him... The thought of dying slowly and painfully terrified me.* ◆◆◇◇◇ VERB =petrify V n ♦ **terrified** *He was terrified of heights... She was terrified that Ronnie would kidnap Sam... I'm terrified to think about the fact that my mother will die someday.* ADJ-GRADED: oft ADJ *of*n, ADJ that, ADJ to-inf

terrifying /t**e**rɪfaɪɪŋ/. If something is **terrifying**, it makes you very frightened. *I still find it terrifying to find myself surrounded by large numbers of horses... Rabies has been described as one of the most terrifying diseases known to man.* ◆◆◇◇◇ ADJ-GRADED: oft ADJ to-inf =horrifying ♦ **terrifyingly** *Below was a terrifyingly deep crevasse... Costs can escalate terrifyingly.* ADV-GRADED

territorial /t**e**rɪt**ɔː**riəl/ **territorials** ◆◆◇◇◇
1 **Territorial** means concerned with the ownership of a particular area of land or water. *It is the only republic which has no territorial disputes with the others... Both Chile and Argentina feel very strongly about their territorial claims to Antarctica.* ADJ: usu ADJ n
2 In Britain, the **Territorials** are the members of the **Territorial Army**. N-COUNT: usu *the*N in pl
3 If you describe an animal or its behaviour as **territorial**, you mean that it has an area which it regards as its own, and which it defends when other animals try to enter it. *Two cats or more in one house will also exhibit territorial behaviour.* ADJ-GRADED

Te**rritorial** A**rmy.** **The Territorial Army** is a British armed force whose members are not professional soldiers but train as soldiers in their spare time. N-PROPER: *the*N =Territorials

te**rritorial w**a**ters.** A country's **territorial waters** are the parts of the sea close to its coast which are recognized by international agreement to be under its control, especially with regard to fishing rights. *A number of governments banned the ship from their territorial waters.* N-PLURAL: usu poss/adj N

territory /t**e**rətri, AM -tɔːri/ **territories** ◆◆◆◆◇
1 **Territory** is land which is controlled by a particular country or ruler. *The government denies that any of its territory is under rebel control. ...Russian territory.* N-VAR
2 A **territory** is a country or region that is controlled by another country. *They just want to return to their families in the occupied territories... He toured some of the disputed territories now under UN control.* N-COUNT
3 You can use **territory** to refer to an area of knowledge or experience. *Even on their own familiar territory of trade, the EC's 12 member states have failed to reach agreement... Reading from a tedious technical brief for hours on end, he would stray into difficult territory.* ● **virgin territory**: see **virgin.** N-UNCOUNT: with supp =terrain
4 An animal's **territory** is an area which it regards as its own and which it defends when other animals try to enter it. *The territory of a cat only remains fixed for as long as the cat dominates the area.* N-VAR: usu with supp
5 **Territory** is land with a particular character. *...mountainous territory. ...a vast and uninhabited territory.* N-UNCOUNT: with supp, usu adj N
6 If you say that something **comes with the territory**, you mean that you accept it as a natural result of the situation you are in. *Doing human rights work is risky business. That comes with the territory... You can't expect not to have a debate; that's what comes with the territory in a democracy.* PHRASE: V inflects

terror /t**e**rəʳ/ **terrors** ◆◆◇◇◇
1 **Terror** is very great fear. *I shook with terror whenever I was about to fly in an aeroplane... The day of terror ended after police used teargas and stormed the house.* N-UNCOUNT
2 **Terror** is violence or the threat of violence, especially when it is used for political reasons. *The bomb attack on the capital could signal the start of a pre-election terror campaign.* N-UNCOUNT: oft N n
3 A **terror** is something that makes you very frightened. *As a boy, he had a real terror of facing people. ...the terrors of violence.* N-COUNT
4 If someone describes a child as a **terror**, they think that he or she is naughty and difficult to control; an informal use. *He was a terror. He had been a difficult child for as long as his parents could remember.* N-COUNT =horror
5 If something **holds no terrors for** you, you are not at all frightened or worried by it. *Childbirth now held fewer terrors for her than it once had.* PHRASE: V inflects
6 ● to **live in terror**: see **live.** ● **reign of terror**: see **reign.**

terrorise /t**e**rəraɪz/. See **terrorize.**

terrorism /t**e**rərɪzəm/. **Terrorism** is the use of violence, especially murder, kidnapping, and bombing, in order to achieve political aims or to force a government to do something; used showing disapproval. ◆◆◇◇◇ N-UNCOUNT PRAGMATICS

terrorist /t**e**rərɪst/ **terrorists.** A **terrorist** is a person who uses violence, especially murder, kidnapping, and bombing, in order to achieve political aims; used showing disapproval. *One American was killed and three were wounded in terrorist attacks.* ◆◆◆◇◇ N-COUNT: oft N n PRAGMATICS

terrorize /t**e**rəraɪz/ **terrorizes, terrorizing, terrorized;** also spelled **terrorise** in British English. If someone **terrorizes** you, they keep you in a state of fear by making it seem likely that they ◆◇◇◇◇ VERB will attack you. *Bands of gunmen have hijacked food shipments and terrorized relief workers. ...pensioners terrorised by anonymous telephone calls.* — V n; V-ed

terry /teri/. **Terry** or **terry cloth** is a type of fabric which has a lot of very small loops covering both sides. It is used especially for making things like towels and babies' nappies. *...a terry nappy.* — N-UNCOUNT: usu N n

terse /tɜːʳs/ **terser, tersest.** A **terse** statement or comment is brief and unfriendly. *He issued a terse statement, saying he is discussing his future with colleagues before announcing his decision on Monday... His tone was terse as he asked the question.* ♦ **tersely** *'It's too late,' he said tersely.* — ◆◇◇◇◇ ADJ-GRADED =abrupt, curt; ADV-GRADED: ADV with v

tertiary /tɜːʳʃəri, AM -ʃieri/
1 Tertiary means third in order, third in importance, or at a third stage of development; a formal use. *He must have come to know those philosophers through secondary or tertiary sources. ...the complementary tertiary colours, russet and olive green.* — ADJ
2 Tertiary education is education at university or college level. *...institutions of tertiary education. ...Selby Tertiary College.* — ADJ: ADJ n

TESL /tesᵊl/. **TESL** is the teaching of English to people who live in an English-speaking country, but whose first language is not English. **TESL** is an abbreviation for 'teaching English as a second language'. — N-UNCOUNT

TESOL /tiːsɒl/. **TESOL** is the teaching of English to people whose first language is not English. **TESOL** is an abbreviation for 'teaching English to speakers of other languages'. — N-PROPER

test /test/ **tests, testing, tested** ◆◆◆◆◆
1 When you **test** something, you try it, for example by touching it or using it for a short time, in order to find out what it is, what condition it is in, or how well it works. *Either measure the temperature with a bath thermometer or test the water with your wrist... Here the army has its ranges where Rapier missiles and other weaponry are tested... The drug must first be tested in clinical trials to see if it works on other cancers.* — VERB; V n
2 A **test** is a deliberate action or experiment to find out how well something works. *...the banning of nuclear tests.* — N-COUNT
3 If you **test** someone, you ask them questions or tell them to perform certain actions in order to find out how much they know about a subject or how well they are able to do something. *There was a time when each teacher spent an hour, one day a week, testing pupils in every subject... She decided to test herself with a training run in London.* — VERB; V n; V pron-refl
4 A **test** is a series of questions that you must answer or actions that you must perform in order to show how much you know about a subject or how well you are able to do something. *Out of a total of 2,602 pupils only 922 passed the test... She had sold her bike, taken a driving test and bought a car.* — N-COUNT
5 If you **test** someone, you deliberately make things difficult for them in order to see how they react. *From the first day, Rudolf was testing me, seeing if I would make him tea, bring him a Coke.* — VERB; V n
6 If an event or situation is a **test** of a person or thing, it reveals their qualities or effectiveness. *It is a commonplace fact that holidays are a major test of any relationship... The test of any civilised society is how it treats its minorities.* — N-COUNT: usu sing, oft N of n
7 If you **are tested** for a particular disease or medical condition, you are examined or undergo various procedures in order to find out whether you have that disease or condition. *My doctor wants me to be tested for diabetes... Girls in an affected family can also be tested to see if they carry the defective gene.* — VB: usu passive; be V-ed for n; be V-ed
8 A medical **test** is an examination of a part of your body in order to check that you are healthy or to find out what is wrong with you. *If necessary X-rays and blood tests will also be used to aid diagnosis... The family doctor ordered numerous, expensive medical tests, which revealed no physical problem.* — N-COUNT
9 In British English, a **test** or a **test match** is a sports match between two international sides, usually at cricket, rugby union, or rugby league. — N-COUNT
10 See also **testing, acid test, breath test, means test, litmus test.**
11 If you **put** something **to the test**, you find out how useful or effective it is by using it. *The Liverpool team are now putting their theory to the test... Arriving at the railway station, I put local knowledge to the test and ask a taxi driver.* — PHRASES; V inflects
12 If new circumstances or events **put** something **to the test**, they put strain on it and indicate how strong or stable it really is. *Sooner or later, life will put the relationship to the test – and it's those relationships with the strongest foundations that weather the course.* — V inflects
13 If you say that something **will stand the test of time**, you mean that it is strong or effective enough to last for a very long time. *It says a lot for her culinary skills that so many of her recipes have stood the test of time.* — V inflects
14 ● **to test the waters**: see **water.**

testament /testəmənt/ **testaments** ◆◇◇◇◇
1 If one thing is a **testament** to another, it shows that the other thing exists or is true; a formal use. *Braka's house, just off Sloane Square, is a testament to his Gothic tastes... The fact that these scandals are now public is testament to the relative openness of America's government.* — N-VAR: usu N to n =testimony
2 Someone's **last will and testament** is the most recent will that they have made, especially the last will that they make before they die; a legal expression. — PHRASE: Ns inflect, usu with poss
3 See also **New Testament, Old Testament.**

test case, test cases. A **test case** is a legal case which becomes an example for deciding other similar cases. — ◆◇◇◇◇ N-COUNT

tester /testəʳ/ **testers** ◆◇◇◇◇
1 A **tester** is a person who has been asked to test a particular thing. *Our tester found the conditioner added body but did not leave her hair completely smooth.* — N-COUNT
2 A **tester** is a machine or device that you use to test whether another machine or device is working properly. *I have a battery tester in my garage.* — N-COUNT: usu n N

testicle /testɪkᵊl/ **testicles.** A man's **testicles** are the two sex glands between his legs that produce sperm. — ◆◇◇◇◇ N-COUNT =testis

testify /testɪfaɪ/ **testifies, testifying, testified** ◆◆◇◇◇
1 When someone **testifies** in a court of law, they give a statement of what they saw someone do or what they know of a situation, after having promised to tell the truth. *Several eyewitnesses testified that they saw the officers hit Miller in the face... Eva testified to having seen Herndon with his gun on the stairs... He hopes to have his 12-year prison term reduced by testifying against his former colleagues.* — VERB; V that; V to -ing/n; V against/for/about n; Also V
2 If one thing **testifies** to another, it supports the belief that the second thing is true; a formal use. *Recent excavations testify to the presence of cultivated inhabitants on the hill during the Arthurian period.* — VERB; V to n

testimonial /testɪmoʊniəl/ **testimonials** ◆◇◇◇◇
1 A **testimonial** is a written statement about a person's character and abilities, often written by their employer. *She could hardly expect her employer to provide her with testimonials to her character and ability.* — N-COUNT =reference
2 A **testimonial** is a sports match which is specially arranged so that part of the profit from the tickets sold can be given to a particular player or to a particular player's family. — N-COUNT

testimony /testɪməni, AM -moʊni/ **testimonies** ◆◆◇◇◇
1 In a court of law, someone's **testimony** is a formal statement that they make about what they saw someone do or what they know of a situation, after having promised to tell the truth. *His testimony was an important element of the Prosecution case... Prosecutors may try to determine if Robb gave false testimony when he appeared before the grand jury.* — N-VAR: oft poss N
2 If you say that one thing is **testimony** to another, you mean that it shows clearly that the second thing has a particular quality. *The environmental* — N-UNCOUNT: also a N, usu N to n

movement is testimony to the widespread feelings of support for nature's inherent worth... Her living room is also her office, filled with desks, books, papers, a testimony to her dedication to her work.

testing /tₑstɪŋ/ ◆◆◆◇◇
1 A **testing** problem or situation is very difficult to deal with and shows a lot about the character of the person who is dealing with it. *The most testing time is undoubtedly in the early months of your return to work... The papers in maths and English are very testing.* ADJ-GRADED
2 **Testing** is the activity of testing something or someone in order to find out information. *...product testing and labelling... The National Collegiate Athletic Association introduced drug testing in the mid-1980s.* N-UNCOUNT

testis /tₑstɪs/ **testes** /tₑstiːz/. A man's **testes** are his **testicles**; a medical term. N-COUNT: usu pl

Test match, Test matches. In cricket and rugby, a **Test match** is a one of a series of matches played between teams representing two countries. ◆◇◇◇◇ N-COUNT =test

testosterone /testɒstəroʊn/. **Testosterone** is a hormone found in men and male animals, which can also be produced artificially. It is thought to be responsible for the male sexual instinct and male characteristics such as aggression. ◆◇◇◇◇ N-UNCOUNT

test pilot, test pilots. A **test pilot** is a pilot who flies aircraft of a new design in order to test their performance. ◆◇◇◇◇ N-COUNT

test run, test runs. If you give a machine or system a **test run**, you try it out to see if it will work properly when it is actually in use. *Japan's space ambitions have had a set-back after the failure of an engine in a test run... The vote was seen as a test run for elections to come.* N-COUNT =trial run

test tube, test tubes; also spelled **test-tube**. A **test tube** is a small tube-shaped container made from glass. Test tubes are used in laboratories. ◆◇◇◇◇ N-COUNT

test-tube baby, test-tube babies; also spelled **test tube baby**. A **test-tube baby** is a baby that develops from an egg which has been removed from the mother's body, fertilized, and then replaced in her womb in order that it can continue developing. N-COUNT

testy /tₑsti/. If you describe someone as **testy**, you mean that they easily become impatient or angry. *Ben's getting a little testy in his old age.* ADJ-GRADED: usu v-link ADJ =crotchety
♦ **testily** *He reacted testily to reports that he'd opposed military involvement.* ADV-GRADED: ADV with v

tetanus /tₑtənəs/. **Tetanus** is a serious painful disease caused by bacteria getting into wounds. It makes your muscles, especially your jaw muscles, go stiff. N-UNCOUNT

tetchy /tₑtʃi/ **tetchier, tetchiest.** In informal British English, if you say that someone is **tetchy**, you mean they are irritable and likely to get angry suddenly without an obvious reason. *You always get tetchy when you're hungry... He was in a particularly tetchy mood yesterday.* ADJ-GRADED =touchy

tether /tₑðəʳ/ **tethers, tethering, tethered** ◆◇◇◇◇
1 If you say that you are at **the end of** your **tether**, you mean that you are so worried, tired, and unhappy because of your problems that you feel you cannot cope. *She was jealous, humiliated, and emotionally at the end of her tether... I've reached the end of my tether.* PHRASE: *tether* inflects, usu *at* PHR, v PHR
2 A **tether** is a rope or chain which used to tie an animal to a post or fence so that it can only move around within a small area. N-COUNT
3 If you **tether** an animal or object to something, you attach it there with a rope or chain so that it cannot move very far. *The officer dismounted, tethering his horse to a tree.* VERB: V n *to* n, Also V n

Teutonic /tjuːtɒnɪk, AM tuː-/. **Teutonic** means typical of or relating to German people; a formal word. *There was sweat pouring over her Teutonic face... The coach was a masterpiece of Teutonic engineering.* ADJ: usu ADJ n

text /tₑkst/ **texts** ◆◆◆◇◇
1 **The text** of a book is the main part of it, rather than the introduction, pictures, notes, or index. *The text is precise and informative, while the many photographs and illustrations enhance its clarity.* N-SING: *the* N
2 **Text** is any written material. *The machine can recognise hand-written characters and turn them into printed text... A CD-ROM can store more than 250,000 pages of typed text.* N-UNCOUNT
3 The **text** of a speech, broadcast, or recording is the written version of it. *A spokesman said a text of Dr Runcie's speech had been circulated to all of the bishops.* N-COUNT: usu sing, usu N *of* n
4 A **text** is a book or other piece of writing, especially one connected with science or learning. *Her text is believed to be the oldest surviving manuscript by a female physician.* N-COUNT
5 A **text** is a written or spoken passage, especially one that is used in a school or university for discussion or in an examination. *Right, I'll read the text aloud first... His early plays used to be set texts in universities.* N-COUNT

textbook /tₑkstbʊk/ **textbooks;** also spelled **text book.** ◆◇◇◇◇
1 A **textbook** is a book containing facts about a particular subject that is used by people studying that subject. *She wrote a textbook on international law. ...a chemistry textbook.* N-COUNT
2 If you say that something is a **textbook** case or example, you are emphasizing that it provides a clear example of a type of situation or event. *The house is a textbook example of medieval domestic architecture... France Telecom is a textbook model of what can be achieved by a state-owned company.* ADJ: ADJ n

textile /tₑkstaɪl/ **textiles** ◆◆◇◇◇
1 **Textiles** are types of cloth or fabric, especially ones that have been woven. *...decorative textiles for the home. ...the Scottish textile industry.* N-COUNT: usu pl, usu with supp
2 **Textiles** are the industries concerned with the manufacture of cloth. *Another 75,000 jobs will be lost in textiles and clothing.* N-PLURAL: no det

textual /tₑkstʃuəl/. **Textual** means relating to written texts, especially literary texts. *...close textual analysis of Shakespeare.* ADJ: ADJ n

texture /tₑkstʃəʳ/ **textures** ◆◆◇◇◇
1 The **texture** of something is the way that it feels when you touch it, for example how smooth or rough it is. *It is used in moisturisers to give them a wonderfully silky texture... Her skin is pale, the texture of fine wax.* ♦ **-textured** *...a medium-textured toothbrush.* N-VAR
2 The **texture** of something, especially food or soil, is its structure, for example whether it is light with lots of holes, or very heavy and dense. *Matured over 18 months, this cheese has an open, crumbly texture with a strong flavour... Earthworms consume large amounts of soil, and produce a rich humus, perfect in texture.* N-VAR
3 The **texture** of a piece of music or a work of literature is the impression that it makes on you as a result of the way that its different elements are combined. *The very texture of his prose bears the influence of his familiarity with drugs.* N-VAR: usu with supp

textured /tₑkstʃəʳd/. A **textured** surface is not smooth, but has a particular texture, for example, it is rough or fluffy. *...a mixture of textured and lacy stitches... The shoe's sole had a slightly textured surface.* ◆◇◇◇◇ ADJ: usu ADJ n

-th /-θ/. You add **-th** to numbers written in figures and ending in 4, 5, 6, 7, 8, 9, 10, 11, 12, or 13 in order to form ordinal numbers. These numbers are pronounced as if they were written as words. For example, 7th is pronounced the same as 'seventh', and 5th is pronounced the same as 'fifth'. *The first meeting was held on Thursday, 10th May, 1990. ...between Broadway and 6th Avenue. ...the 25th amendment to the American constitution.* SUFFIX

Thai /taɪ/ **Thais** ◆◆◆◆◇
1 **Thai** means belonging or relating to Thailand, or to its people, language, or culture. *Thai food is terrific. ...Thai businessmen.* ADJ
2 A **Thai** is a citizen of Thailand, or a person of Thai origin. N-COUNT
3 **Thai** is the language spoken in Thailand. N-UNCOUNT

thalidomide /θəlɪdəmaɪd/

1 **Thalidomide** is a drug which used to be given to pregnant women as a tranquillizer, and which was withdrawn from use after it was discovered to cause abnormalities in developing foetuses. N-UNCOUNT

2 **Thalidomide** is used to describe someone whose body is deformed because their mother took thalidomide when she was pregnant with them. *...the special needs of thalidomide children.* ADJ: ADJ n

than /ðən, STRONG ðæn/ ◆◆◆◆◆

1 You use **than** after a comparative adjective or adverb in order to link two parts of a comparison. *The radio only weighs a few ounces and is smaller than a cigarette packet... Indian skins age far more slowly than American or Italian ones.* ► Also a conjunction. *He wished he could have helped her more than he did... Sometimes patients are more depressed six months later than when they first hear the bad news.* PREP: compar PREP group; CONJ-SUBORD: compar CONJ cl

2 You use **than** when you are stating a number, quantity, or value approximately by saying that it is above or below another number, quantity, or value. *They talked on the phone for more than an hour. ...the three-match Test series in England, starting in less than two months time... Head teachers yesterday demanded a nine per cent rise, more than twice the rate of inflation.* PREP: *more/less* PREP n

3 You use **than** in order to link two parts of a contrast, for example in order to state a preference. *The arrangement was more a formality than a genuine partnership of two nations... I would rather stare at a clear, star-filled sky than a TV set... I would sooner give up sleep than miss my evening class.* CONJ-COORD

4 • **easier said than done**: see **easy.** • **less than**: see **less.** • **more than**: see **more.** • **more often than not**: see **often.** • **other than**: see **other.** • **rather than**: see **rather.**

thank /θæŋk/ **thanks, thanking, thanked** ◆◆◆◆◆

1 You use **thank you** or, in more informal English, **thanks** to express your gratitude when someone does something for you or gives you something. *Thank you very much for your call... Thanks for the information... Oh thank you so much! They're so pretty!... Thanks a lot, Suzie. You've been great.* CONVENTION PRAGMATICS

2 You use **thank you** or, in more informal English, **thanks** to politely accept or refuse something that has just been offered to you. *'You'd like a cup as well, would you, Mr Secombe?'—'Thank you, Jane, I'd love one.'... 'Would you like a cigarette?'—'No thank you.'... 'A whisky?'—'I'd better not, thanks.'* CONVENTION PRAGMATICS

3 You use **thank you** or, in more informal English, **thanks**, to politely acknowledge what someone has said to you, especially when they have paid you a compliment or answered your question. *The policeman smiled at her. 'Pretty dog.' 'Oh well, thank you.'... 'His eyes were glassy?'—'And dilated. They were watery.'—'Thank you.'... 'It's great to see you.'—'Thanks. Same to you.'* CONVENTION PRAGMATICS

4 You use **thank you** or **thank you very much** in order to say firmly that you do not want someone's help or to tell them that you do not like the way that they are behaving towards you. *I can stir my own tea, thank you... We know where we can get it, thank you very much.* CONVENTION PRAGMATICS

5 When you **thank** someone for something, you express your gratitude to them for it. *I thanked them for their long and loyal service... When the decision was read out Mrs Gardner thanked the judges.* VERB V n *for* n, V n

6 When you express your **thanks** to someone, you express your gratitude to them for something. *They accepted their certificates with words of thanks.* N-PLURAL

7 See also **thankyou.**

8 When people **give thanks**, they thank God for something good that has happened. *We give thanks for this food.* PHRASES V inflects, oft PHR *for* n

9 You say **'Thank God', 'Thank Goodness'**, or **'Thank heavens'** when you are very relieved about something. *I was wrong, thank God... Thank heavens we have you here.* oft PHR with cl, PHR that PRAGMATICS

10 If you say that you **have** someone **to thank** for something, you mean that you are grateful to them because they caused it to happen. *I have her to thank for my life... For all this I have only you to thank.* V inflects, oft PHR *for* n

11 If you say that something happens **thanks to** someone or something, you mean that they are responsible for it happening or caused it to happen. *It is thanks to this committee that many new sponsors have come forward... Thanks to recent research, effective treatments are available.* PHR n, usu PHR with cl, v-link PHR, PHR after v

12 If you say that something happens **no thanks to** someone or something, you mean that they did not help it to happen, or that it happened in spite of them. *It is no thanks to the Government that net assets did rise.* PHR n, usu PHR with cl, v-link PHR

13 • to **thank** your **lucky stars**: see **star.**

thankful /θæŋkfʊl/. When you are **thankful**, you are very happy and relieved that something has happened. *Most of the time I'm just thankful that I've got a job... I was so thankful for his support... She's thankful to be alive.* ♦ **thankfully** *Simon thankfully slipped off his uniform and relaxed.* ◆◇◇◇◇ ADJ-GRADED: usu v-link ADJ, oft ADJ that, ADJ *for* n =grateful; ADV-GRADED: ADV with v

thankfully /θæŋkfʊli/. You use **thankfully** in order to express approval or relief about a statement that you are making. *Thankfully, she was not injured... The next day dawned, thankfully with a drop in wind and waves.* ADV: ADV with cl/group PRAGMATICS

thankless /θæŋkləs/. If you describe a job or task as **thankless**, you mean that it is hard work and brings very few rewards. *Soccer referees have a thankless task.* ADJ-GRADED: usu ADJ n

thanksgiving /θæŋksgɪvɪŋ/. **Thanksgiving** is the giving of thanks to God, especially in a religious ceremony. *The Prince's unexpected recovery was celebrated with a thanksgiving service in St Paul's. ...prayers of thanksgiving.* N-UNCOUNT

Thanksgiving, Thanksgivings. In the United States, **Thanksgiving** or **Thanksgiving Day** is a public holiday on the fourth Thursday in November. It was originally a day when people celebrated the end of the harvest and thanked God for it. *No matter where his business took him, he always managed to be home for Thanksgiving... It's going to be the most magnificent Thanksgiving dinner we ever had.* ◆◇◇◇◇ N-VAR

thankyou /θæŋkju:/ **thankyous;** also spelled **thank-you.** If you refer to something as a **thankyou** for something that someone has done for you, you mean that it is intended as a way of thanking them. *The surprise gift is a thankyou for our help. ...a thank-you note.* • See also **thank.** N-COUNT: oft N n

that 1 demonstrative uses

that /ðæt/ ◆◆◆◆◆

1 You use **that** to refer back to an idea or situation expressed in a previous sentence or sentences. *They said you particularly wanted to talk to me. Why was that?... 'Hey, is there anything the matter with my sisters?'—'Is that why you're phoning?'... Some members feared Germany might raise its interest rates on Thursday. That could have set the scene for a confrontation with the US.* ► Also a determiner. *The most important purpose of our Health Care is to support you when making a claim for medical treatment. For that reason the claims procedure is as simple and helpful as possible.* PRON PRAGMATICS; DET

2 You use **that** to refer to someone or something already mentioned. *The Commissioners get between £50,000 and £60,000 a year in various allowances. But that amount can soar to £90,000 a year... The biggest increase is on the cheapest model, the CRX-HF. That car will have a 1990 base price of $9,145.* DET

3 When you have been talking about a particular period of time, you use **that** to indicate that you are still referring to the same period. You use expressions such as **that morning** or **that afternoon** to indicate that you are referring to an earlier period of the same day. *The story was published in a Sunday newspaper later that week... That morning I had put on a pair of black slacks and a long-sleeved black blouse.* DET

4 You use **that** in expressions such as **that of** and PRON:

that which to introduce more information about something already mentioned, instead of repeating the noun which refers to it; a formal use. *A recession like that of 1973-74 could put one in ten American companies into bankruptcy... Indoor pollution falls into two categories, that which we can see or smell, and pollution which is invisible and produces no odour.*
PRON *of* n, PRON pron-rel

5 You use **that** in front of words or expressions which express agreement, responses, or reactions to what has just been said. *'She said she'd met you in England.'—'That's true.'... 'I've never been to Paris.'—'That's a pity. You should go one day.'*
PRON PRAGMATICS

6 You use **that** to introduce a person or thing which you are going to give details or information about; a formal use. *In my case I chose that course which I considered right... That person who violates the law and discriminates should suffer in his career.* ▶ **That which** is used to introduce a subject in very general terms. *Too much time is spent worrying over that which one can't change.*
DET PRAGMATICS; PRON: PRON pron-rel

7 You use **that** when you are referring to someone or something which is a distance away from you in position or time, especially when you indicate or point to them. When there are two or more things near you, **that** refers to the more distant one. *Look at that guy. He's got red socks... Where did you get that hat?... You see that man over there, that man who has just walked into the room?* ▶ Also a pronoun. *Leo, what's that you're writing?... That looks heavy. May I carry it for you?*
DET; PRON

8 You use **that** when you are identifying someone or asking about their identity. *That's my wife you were talking to... That's John Gibb, operations chief for New York Emergency Management... 'Who's that with you?'—'A friend of mine.'... I answered the phone and this voice went, 'Hello? Is that Alison?'*
PRON

9 You can use **that** when you expect your hearer to know what or who you are referring to, without needing to identify the particular person or thing fully; used in spoken English. *I really thought I was something when I wore that hat and my patent leather shoes... Did you get that cheque I sent?... That idiot porter again knocked on my door!* ▶ Also a pronoun. *That was a terrible case of blackmail in the paper today... That was a good year, wasn't it?*
DET; PRON

10 If something is not **that** bad, funny, or expensive for example, it is not as bad, funny, or expensive as it might be or as has been suggested. *Not even Gary, he said, was that stupid... It isn't that funny... He didn't look that bad... Kids don't change that fast.*
ADV: with brd-neg, ADV adj/adv

11 You can use **that** to emphasize the degree of a feeling or quality; an informal use. *I would have walked out, I was that angry... Do I look that stupid?... They actually moved down from upstairs because the rent's that expensive.*
ADV: ADV adj/adv PRAGMATICS =so

12 See also **those**.

13 You use **and all that** or **and that** to refer generally to everything else which is associated with what you have just mentioned; an informal expression. *I hate to be nasty and all that... I'm not a cook myself but I am interested in nutrition and that.*
PHRASES cl/group PHR

14 You use **at that** after a statement which modifies or emphasizes what you have just said. *Success never seems to come but through hard work, often physically demanding work at that... The café was popular with locals, and not with the more respectable locals at that.*
n/adj PHR PRAGMATICS =too

15 You use **that is** or **that is to say** to indicate that you are about to express the same idea more clearly or precisely. *I am a disappointing, though generally dutiful, student. That is, I do as I'm told... Education Ministers ought to have placed the interests of consumers – that is to say pupils – first.*
PHR with cl/group PRAGMATICS

16 You use **that's it** to indicate that nothing more needs to be done or that the end has been reached. *When he left the office, that was it, the workday was over.*
V inflects

17 You use **that's it** to express agreement, approval, or confirmation of what has just been said or done. *'You got married, right?'—'Yeah, that's it.'*
CONVENTION PRAGMATICS =exactly

18 You use **just like that** to emphasize that something happens or is done immediately or in a very simple way, often without much thought or discussion; an informal expression. *Just like that, I was in love... You mean he sent you back just like that?*
PHR with cl

19 You use **that's that** to say there is nothing more you can do or say about a particular matter; used in spoken English. *'Well, if that's the way you want it,' he replied, tears in his eyes, 'I guess that's that.'... 'I want you to go home.'—'I'm staying here, and that's that.'*
V inflects

20 • **like that**: see **like**. • **this and that**: see **this**. • **this, that and the other**: see **this**.

that 2 conjunction and relative pronoun uses

that /ðət, STRONG ðæt/ ◆◆◆◆◆

1 You can use **that** after many verbs, adjectives, nouns, and expressions to introduce a clause in which you report what someone has said, or what they think or feel. *He called her up one day and said that he and his wife were coming to New York... We were worried that she was going to die... I welcome the news that attacks on women on the railways are 19 per cent down.*
CONJ-SUBORD

2 You use **that** after 'it' and a link verb and an adjective to comment on a situation or fact. *It's interesting that you like him... I've made up my mind, but it's obvious that you need more time to think... It's extraordinary that he left without making a public statement about the situation.*
CONJ-SUBORD: it v-link adj CONJ cl

3 You use **that** to introduce a clause which gives more information to help identify the person or thing you are talking about. *...pills that will make the problem disappear. ...a car that won't start... You should have learned to walk away from things that don't concern you. ...the house that they have lived in throughout their married lives.*
PRON-REL

4 You use **that** after expressions with 'so' and 'such' in order to introduce the result or effect of something. *She became so nervous that she shook violently... She came towards me so quickly that she knocked a chair over... Unfortunately it made such a revolting brew that it was worse than drinking no tea at all... The effect on our blood chemistry is such that it produces physical changes in our entire body.*
CONJ-SUBORD: *so/such* group CONJ cl

thatch /θætʃ/ **thatches**

1 A **thatch** or a **thatch roof** is a roof made from straw or reeds. *They would live in a small house with a green door and a new thatch.*
N-COUNT

2 **Thatch** is straw or reeds used to make a roof. *Thatch is naturally warm in winter and cool in summer.*
N-UNCOUNT

3 You can refer to someone's hair as their **thatch** of hair, especially when it is very thick and untidy. *Teddy ran thick fingers through his unruly thatch of hair.*
N-SING: oft N *of* n

thatched /θætʃt/. A **thatched** house or a house with a **thatched** roof has a roof made of straw or reeds.
◆◇◇◇◇ ADJ: usu ADJ n

thatcher /θætʃəʳ/ **thatchers.** A **thatcher** is a person whose job is making roofs from straw or reeds.
N-COUNT

thatching /θætʃɪŋ/

1 **Thatching** is straw or reeds used to make a roof.
N-UNCOUNT

2 **Thatching** is the skill or activity of making roofs from straw or reeds.
N-UNCOUNT

that's /ðæts/. **That's** is a spoken form of **that is.**

thaw /θɔː/ **thaws, thawing, thawed** ◆◇◇◇◇

1 When ice, snow, or something else that is frozen **thaws**, it melts. *It's so cold the snow doesn't get a chance to thaw... The ground has thawed.*
VERB V

2 A **thaw** is a period of warmer weather when snow and ice melt, usually at the end of winter. *We slogged through the mud of an early spring thaw.*
N-COUNT

3 When you **thaw** frozen food or when it **thaws**, you leave it in a place where it can reach room temperature so that it is ready for use. *Always thaw pastry thoroughly... The food in the freezer had thawed during a power cut.* ▶ **Thaw out** means the same as **thaw**. *Thaw it out completely before reheating in a saucepan... I remember to thaw out the chicken before I leave home.*
V-ERG =defrost V n V; PHRASAL VERB ERG V n P V P n (not pron) Also V P

4 If something **thaws** relations between people or if relations **thaw**, they become friendly again after a period of tension. *At least this second meeting had helped to thaw the atmosphere... It took up to Christmas for political relations to thaw.* ▶ Also a noun. *His visit is one of the most striking results of the thaw in relations between East and West.* V-ERG Vn V N-SING

thaw out PHRASAL VERB
1 See **thaw** 3.
2 If someone who is very cold **thaws out**, or if another person or thing **thaws** them **out**, they begin to feel warmer. *Amy's feet were beginning to thaw out... Peter thawed us all out with coffee... Bob and Louise had prepared a sumptuous meal to thaw out our bodies.* ERG VP VnP VPn (not pron)

the. Usually pronounced /ðə/ before a consonant and /ði/ before a vowel, but pronounced /ði:/ when you are emphasizing it. ◆◆◆◆◆
The is the definite article. It is used at the beginning of noun groups.
1 You use **the** at the beginning of noun groups to refer to someone or something that you have already mentioned or identified. *A waiter came and hovered. John caught my look and we both got up and, ignoring the waiter, made our way to the buffet... Six of the 38 people were Soviet citizens.* DET
2 You use **the** at the beginning of a noun group when the first noun is followed by an 'of' phrase or a clause which identifies the person or thing. *There has been a slight increase in the consumption of meat... Of the 9,660 cases processed last year, only 10 per cent were totally rejected.* DET
3 You use **the** in front of some nouns that refer to something in our general experience of the world. *It's always hard to speculate about the future... Amy sat outside in the sun... He lay in the darkness, pretending to sleep.* DET
4 You use **the** in front of nouns that refer to people, things, services, or institutions that are associated with everyday life. *The doctor's on his way... Who was that on the phone?... You're old enough to travel on the train by yourself... They have a generator when the electricity fails... Four executive journalists were detained for questioning by the police today... He took a can of beer from the fridge.* DET
5 You use **the** instead of a possessive determiner, especially when you are talking about a part of someone's body or a member of their family. *'How's the family?'—'Just fine, thank you.'... I patted him on the head... She took Gill by the hand.* DET
6 You use **the** in front of a singular noun when you want to make a general statement about things or people of that type. *An area in which the computer has made considerable strides in recent years is in playing chess... After dogs, the horse has had the closest relationship with man.* DET: DET sing-n
7 You use **the** with the name of a musical instrument when you are talking about someone's ability to play the instrument. *Did you play the piano as a child?... She was trying to teach him to play the guitar.* DET
8 You use **the** with nationality adjectives and nouns to talk about the people who live in a country. *The Japanese, Americans, and even the French and Germans, judge economic policies by results.* DET: DET pl-n
9 You use **the** with words such as 'rich', 'poor', 'old', or 'unemployed' to refer to all people of a particular type. *Conditions for the poor in Los Angeles have not improved. ...care for the elderly, the mentally handicapped and the disabled.* DET: DET pl-n
10 If you want to refer to a whole family or to a married couple, you can make their surname into a plural and use **the** in front of it. *...a 400 acre farm owned by the Allens... The Taylors decided that they would employ an architect to do the work.* DET: DET pl-n-proper
11 You use **the** in front of an adjective when you are referring to a particular thing that is described by that adjective. *He knows he's wishing for the impossible... I thought you might like to read the enclosed.* DET: DET adj/-ed
12 You use **the** to indicate that you have enough of the thing mentioned for a particular purpose. *She may not have the money to maintain or restore her property... We must have the patience to continue to work until we will find a peaceful solution... Carl couldn't even raise the energy for a smile.* DET: DET n to-inf, DET n for n =sufficient
13 You use **the** with some titles, place-names, and other names. *...the SUN, the DAILY STAR and the DAILY EXPRESS. ...the Albert Hall... The King has already agreed that the President of the Nepal Congress should be the Prime Minister.* DET
14 You use **the** in front of ordinal numbers. *The meeting should take place on the fifth of May... Marco Polo is said to have sailed on the Pacific on his way to Java in the thirteenth century... One ferry operator 'Sealink' said it was now running a full service for the first time in five weeks.* DET: DET ord
15 You use **the** in front of numbers when they refer to decades. *It's sometimes hard to imagine how bad things were in the thirties.* DET: DET pl-num
16 You use **the** in front of superlative adjectives and adverbs. *Brisk daily walks are still the best exercise for young and old alike... The Mayor of West Berlin described the Germans as the happiest people in the world... This engine uses all the most modern technology... The third girl answered the most audibly.* DET: DET superl
17 You use **the** in front of each of two comparative adjectives or adverbs when you are describing how one amount or quality changes in relation to another. *The longer you have been in shape in the past, the quicker you will regain fitness in future... The more confidence you build up in yourself, the greater are your chances of success.* DET: DET compar DET compar
18 When you express rates, ratios, prices, and measurements, you can use **the** to say how many units apply to each of the items being measured. *New Japanese cars averaged 13 km to the litre in 1981... Some analysts predicted that the exchange rate would soon be $2 to the pound.* DET: DET sing-n =per
19 You use **the** to indicate that something or someone is the most famous, important, or best thing of its kind. In spoken English, you put more vocal stress on it. In written English, you often underline it or write it in capitals or in italics. *Camden Market is the place to be on a Saturday or Sunday... 'Olympia is in America, where K Records was founded.'—'No! Surely you don't mean THE K Records?'* DET

theatre /θi̲ːətəʳ/ **theatres;** spelled **theater** in American English. ◆◆◆◆◇
1 A **theatre** is a building with a stage in it, on which plays, shows, and other performances take place. *If we went to the theatre it was a very big event... I worked at the Grand Theatre.* N-COUNT: oft in names
2 You can refer to work in the theatre such as acting or writing plays as **the theatre**. *You can move up to work in films and the theatre... Very soon he took the first steps towards a career in the theatre.* N-SING: the N
3 **Theatre** is entertainment that involves the performance of plays. *Companies across the country are beginning to show a healthy interest in theatre for children.* N-UNCOUNT
4 In American English, a **theater** or a **movie theater** is a place where people go to watch films for entertainment. The British term is **cinema**. N-COUNT =cinema
5 In a hospital, a **theatre** is a special room where surgeons carry out medical operations. *She is back from theatre and her condition is comfortable.* N-COUNT: also prep N
6 A **theatre** of war or other conflict is the area or region in which the war or conflict is happening. *The Middle East has often been a theatre of war.* N-COUNT: usu sing, usu N of n

theatre-goer, theatre-goers; spelled **theatergoer** in American English. **Theatre-goers** are people who are at the theatre to see a play, or who regularly go to the theatre to see plays. *Other theatre-goers complained Joan was on stage for just half an hour... I'm a keen theatre-goer.* N-COUNT

theatrical /θiæ̲trɪkəl/ **theatricals** ◆◆◇◇◇
1 **Theatrical** means relating to the theatre. *These are the prizes given for the most outstanding British theatrical performances of the year. ...major theatrical productions.* ♦ **theatrically** /θiæ̲trɪkli/ *Shaffer's great gift lies in his ability to animate ideas theatrically.* ADJ: ADJ n ADV

2 **Theatrical** behaviour is exaggerated and unnatural, and intended to create an effect. *In a theatrical gesture Glass clamped his hand over his eyes.* ♦ **theatricality** /θiætrɪkælɪti/ *There was no theatricality in her long silence.* ♦ **theatrically** *He looked theatrically at his watch.* ADJ-GRADED N-UNCOUNT ADV

3 **Theatrical** can be used to describe something that is grand and dramatic, as if it is part of a performance in a theatre. *There was a theatrical air about the whole scene which had a great appeal for me... The clothes were very showy, very theatrical.* ♦ **theatricality** *I'd hate to miss out on the theatricality of a wedding. ...the architectural theatricality of Venice.* ♦ **theatrically** *...a white hotel theatrically set along a ridge.* ADJ-GRADED N-UNCOUNT: usu N *of* n ADV-GRADED

4 **Theatricals** are performances of plays and other entertainments, especially when they are done by amateur actors; an old-fashioned word. *I always was good at amateur theatricals.* N-PLURAL =dramatics

thee /ðiː/. **Thee** is an old-fashioned, poetic, or religious word for 'you' when you are talking to only one person. It is used as the object of a verb or preposition. *I miss thee, beloved father.* PRON-SING: v PRON, prep PRON

theft /θeft/ **thefts.** **Theft** is the crime of stealing. *Art theft is now part of organised crime. ...the theft of some classified documents from a car in London.* ◆◆◇◇◇ N-VAR: oft n N, N *of* n

their /ðeəʳ/ ◆◆◆◆◆

Their is the third person plural possessive determiner.

1 You use **their** to indicate that something belongs or relates to the group of people, animals, or things that you are talking about. *Janis and Kurt have announced their engagement... Horses were poking their heads over their stall doors. ...as the trees shed their leaves and the year begins to die.* DET-POSS

2 You use **their** instead of 'his or her' to indicate that something belongs or relates to a person without saying whether that person is a man or a woman. Some people think this use is incorrect. *It is up to the student to improve their own lot by regular and proper practice of yoga techniques... But anyone looking for income from their investments is in a much worse state.* DET-POSS

theirs /ðeəʳz/ ◆◆◇◇◇

Theirs is the third person plural possessive pronoun.

1 You use **theirs** to indicate that something belongs or relates to the group of people, animals, or things that you are talking about. *There was a big group of a dozen people at the table next to theirs... It would cost about £1000 to install a new heating system in a flat such as theirs... Theirs had been a happy and satisfactory marriage.* PRON-POSS

2 You use **theirs** instead of 'his or hers' to indicate that something belongs or relates to a person without saying whether that person is a man or a woman. Some people think this use is incorrect. *He would leave the trailer unlocked. If there was something inside someone wanted, it would be theirs for the taking... This child is nobody's child until someone makes her theirs officially.* PRON-POSS

them /ðəm, STRONG ðem/ ◆◆◆◆◆

Them is a third person plural pronoun. **Them** is used as the object of a verb or preposition.

1 You use **them** to refer to a group of people, animals, or things. *The Beatles – I never get tired of listening to them... Kids these days have no one to tell them what's right and wrong... She let the dogs into the house and fed them... His dark socks, I could see, had a stripe on them.* PRON-PLURAL: v PRON, prep PRON

2 You use **them** instead of 'him or her' to refer to a person without saying whether that person is a man or a woman. Some people think this use is incorrect. *It takes great courage to face your child and tell them the truth.* PRON-PLURAL: v PRON, prep PRON

3 In non-standard spoken English, **them** is sometimes used instead of 'those'. *'Our Billy doesn't eat them ones,' Helen said.* DET

thematic /θiːmætɪk/. **Thematic** means concerned with the subject or theme of something, or with themes and topics in general; a formal word. *...assembling this material into thematic groups. ...the whole thematic approach to learning.* ♦ **thematically** /θiːmætɪkli/ *...another thematically-linked threesome of songs.* ADJ-GRADED: usu ADJ n ADV

theme /θiːm/ **themes** ◆◆◆◇◇

1 A **theme** in a piece of writing, a talk, or a discussion is an important idea or subject that runs through it. *The theme of the conference is renaissance Europe... 'That's another element in choosing a style of writing, you see,' he says, returning to his main theme... The need to strengthen the family has been a recurrent theme for the Prime Minister.* N-COUNT: usu with supp

2 A **theme** in an artist's work or in a work of literature is an idea in it that the artist or writer develops or repeats. *The novel's central theme is the perennial conflict between men and women... This painting points to another recurring theme in Munch's work.* N-COUNT: usu with supp

3 A **theme** is a short simple tune on which a piece of music is based. *...variations on themes from Mozart's The Magic Flute.* N-COUNT

4 **Theme** music is a piece of music that is played at the beginning and end of a film or of a television or radio programme. *...the theme from Dr Zhivago... The BBC used Vangelis's Chariots of Fire as its Olympic theme tune in 1984.* N-COUNT: usu N n

themed /θiːmd/. A **themed** place or event has been built or created so that it reflects a particular historical time or way of life, or recreates a well-known story; used mainly in British English. *...themed restaurants, bars, and nightclubs. ...a huge space laid out as a series of small themed areas.* ADJ: usu ADJ n

theme park, **theme parks.** A **theme park** is a large outdoor area where people pay to go to enjoy themselves. All the different attractions in a theme park are usually based on the same idea or theme. ◆◇◇◇◇ N-COUNT

themself /ðəmself/. **Themself** is sometimes used instead of 'themselves' when it clearly refers to a singular subject. Some people consider this use to be incorrect. *No one perceived themself to be in a position to hire such a man. ...if the person themself wouldn't give me the permission to talk to their GP.* PRON-REFL: v PRON, prep PRON

themselves /ðəmselvz/ ◆◆◆◆◆

Themselves is the third person plural reflexive pronoun.

1 You use **themselves** to refer to people, animals, or things when the object of a verb or preposition refers to the same people or things as the subject of the verb. *They all seemed to be enjoying themselves... The men talked amongst themselves... All artists have part of themselves that they can never share with anyone else.* PRON-REFL: v PRON, prep PRON

2 You use **themselves** to emphasize the people or things that you are referring to. **Themselves** is also sometimes used instead of 'them' as the object of a verb or preposition. *Many mentally ill people are themselves unhappy about the idea of community care... Cities themselves are changing rapidly... Care-givers get a chance to socialize with men and women who are in the same position as themselves.* PRON-REFL-EMPH PRAGMATICS

3 You use **themselves** instead of 'himself or herself' to refer back to the person who is the subject of sentence without saying whether it is a man or a woman. Some people think this use is incorrect. *What can a patient with emphysema do to help themselves?... Nobody was prepared to commit themselves.* PRON-REFL: v PRON, prep PRON

4 You use **themselves** instead of 'himself or herself' to emphasize the person you are referring to without saying whether it is a man or a woman. **Themselves** is also sometimes used as the object of a verb or preposition. Some people think this use is incorrect. *Each student makes only one item themselves... After all, what more can anyone be than themselves?* PRON-REFL-EMPH PRAGMATICS

5 ● **by themselves**: see **by**.

then /ðen/ ◆◆◆◆◆

1 **Then** means at a particular time in the past or in the future. *He wanted to have a source of income af-* ADV: ADV with cl, oft prep ADV

ter his retirement; until then, he wouldn't require additional money... Groucho Marx died in 1977. Since then Woody Allen has described him as the best comedian the United States has ever produced... I spent years on the dole trying to get bands together and I never worried about money then. ≠now

2 Then is used when you refer to something which was true at a particular time in the past but is not true now. *...the Race Relations Act of 1976 (enacted by the then Labour Government)... He was known by many for his role in the then record-breaking robbery of the mail train from Glasgow to London in August 1963.* ► Also an adverb. *Richard Strauss, then 76 years old, suffered through the war years in silence... Roberts was then a newly married man.* ADJ: ADJ n; ADV: ADV group

3 You use **then** to say that one thing happens after another, or is after another on a list. *Add the oil and then the scallops to the pan, leaving a little space for the garlic... I felt myself blush. Then I sniffed back a tear... New mothers have been observed to touch the feet and hands first, then the body, and then the baby's face.* ADV: ADV cl/group, ADV before v

4 You use **then** in conversation to indicate that what you are about to say follows logically in some way from what has just been said or implied. *'I wasn't a very good scholar at school.'—'What did you like doing best then?'... You're not gonna tell me, are you? Do I have to guess, then?... 'I got a load of money out of them.'—'So you're okay, then.'* ADV: cl/group ADV

5 You use **then** at the end of a topic or at the end of a conversation. *'I can meet you after work. Six o'clock?'—'Fine.'—'Six o'clock, then?'... 'I'll talk to you on Friday anyway.'—'Yep. Okay then.'... He stood up. 'That's settled then.'* ADV: cl/group ADV

6 You use **then** with words like 'now', 'well', and 'okay', to introduce a new topic or a new point of view. *Now then, I think the Queen should be taxed... Well then, I'll put the kettle on and make us some tea... Okay then let me ask how you do that.* ADV: adv ADV PRAGMATICS

7 You use **then** to introduce a summary of what you have said or the conclusions that you are drawing from it; used mainly in written English. *This, then, was the music that appeared to dominate the world of serious concert music in the mid-1960s... By 1931, then, France alone in Europe was a country of massive immigration.* ADV: ADV with cl PRAGMATICS =therefore

8 You use **then** to introduce the second part of a sentence which begins with 'if'. The first part of the sentence describes a possible situation, and **then** introduces the result of the situation. *If the answer is 'yes', then we must decide on an appropriate course of action... If the people feel that way, then does this enhance Bill Clinton's image as a leader?* ADV: ADV cl

9 You use **then** at the beginning of a sentence or after 'and' or 'but' to introduce a comment or an extra piece of information to what you have already said. *The National Engineering Firm said they would get it out of the museum for us. And then we have two trucking firms that are willing to bring it back for us... He sounded sincere, but then, he always did.* ADV: ADV cl PRAGMATICS

10 • **now and then**: see **now**. • **there and then**: see **there**.

thence /ðens/

1 Thence means from a particular place, especially when you are giving directions about how to get somewhere; a formal use. *I ran straight up to Columbia County, then turned East, came down the Harlem Valley and thence home... The mosaics were sent to Munich, and thence to Geneva.* ADV: usu ADV adv/prep, also ADV before v

2 Thence is used to say that something changes from one state or condition to another; a formal use. *...the conversion of sunlight into heat and thence into electricity.* ADV: usu ADV prep, also ADV before v

thenceforth /ðensfɔːʳθ/. **Thenceforth** means from a particular time in the past that you have mentioned onwards; a formal word. *...my life was totally different thenceforth.* ADV: ADV with cl =thereafter

theocracy /θiɒkrəsi/ **theocracies.** A **theocracy** is a society which is ruled by priests who represent a god; a technical term in political science. *...a medieval theocracy run by Buddhist monks.* N-VAR

theocratic /θiːəkrætɪk/. A **theocratic** society is ruled by priests who represent a god; a technical term in political science. *It is a movement that threatens the choice of the people and threatens to install a theocratic state.* ADJ: usu ADJ n ≠secular

theologian /θiːəloʊdʒən/ **theologians.** A **theologian** is someone who studies the nature of God, religion, and religious beliefs. ◆◇◇◇◇ N-COUNT

theology /θiɒlədʒi/ **theologies** ◆◇◇◇◇

1 Theology is the study of the nature of God and of religion and religious beliefs. *...questions of theology.* ♦ **theological** /θiːəlɒdʒɪkəl/ *...theological books.* N-UNCOUNT; ADJ: usu ADJ n

2 A **theology** is a particular set of religious beliefs and ideas. *...cults, sects and bizarre theologies.* N-COUNT

theorem /θiːərəm/ **theorems.** A **theorem** is a statement in mathematics or logic that can be proved to be true by reasoning. N-COUNT

theoretical /θiːəretɪkəl/ ◆◆◇◇◇

1 A **theoretical** study or explanation is based on or uses the ideas and abstract principles that relate to a particular subject, rather than the practical aspects or uses of it. *...theoretical physics.* ADJ: usu ADJ n

2 If you describe a situation as a **theoretical** one, you mean that although it is supposed to be true or to exist in the way stated, it may not in fact be true or exist in that way. *This is certainly a theoretical risk but in practice there is seldom a problem... These fears are purely theoretical.* ADJ: usu ADJ n

theoretically /θiːəretɪkli/. You use **theoretically** to say that although something is supposed to be true or to happen in the way stated, it may not in fact be true or happen in that way. *Theoretically, the price is supposed to be marked on the shelf... Emigration was still theoretically a matter of choice.* ◆◇◇◇◇ ADV: ADV with cl/group

theoretician /θɪərətɪʃən/ **theoreticians.** A **theoretician** is the same as a **theorist**. *...socialist theoreticians.* N-COUNT =theorist, thinker

theorist /θiːərɪst/ **theorists.** A **theorist** is someone who develops an abstract idea or set of ideas about a particular subject in order to explain it. *...theorists unaligned with any particular doctrine.* ◆◇◇◇◇ N-COUNT =theoretician, thinker

theorize /θiːəraɪz/ **theorizes, theorizing, theorized;** also spelled **theorise** in British English. If you **theorize** that something is true or **theorize** about it, you develop an abstract idea or set of ideas about something in order to explain it. *Police are theorizing that the killers may be posing as hitchhikers... By studying the way people behave, we can theorize about what is going on in their mind.* ♦ **theorizing** *This was no time for theorizing.* ◆◇◇◇◇ VERB: V that, V about n, Also V; N-UNCOUNT

theory /θɪəri/ **theories** ◆◆◆◆◇

1 A **theory** is a formal idea or set of ideas that is intended to explain something. *Marx produced a new theory about historical change based upon conflict between competing groups... Einstein formulated the Theory of Relativity in 1905.* N-VAR: usu with supp

2 If you have a **theory** about something, you have your own opinion about it which you cannot prove but which you think is true. *There was a theory that he wanted to marry her... My theory about divorce is that it's not the split-up that damages children, it's how it is handled.* N-COUNT =hypothesis

3 The **theory** of a practical subject or skill is the set of rules and principles that form the basis of it. *He taught us music theory. ...graduates who are well-trained in both the theory and practice of statistics.* N-UNCOUNT: usu with supp, supp N, N of n

4 You use **in theory** to say that although something is supposed to be true or to happen in the way stated, it may not in fact be true or happen in that way. *A school dental service exists in theory, but in practice, there are few dentists to work in them.* PHRASE: PHR with cl =theoretically ≠in practice

therapeutic /θerəpjuːtɪk/ ◆◇◇◇◇

1 If something is **therapeutic**, it helps you to relax or to feel better about things, especially about a situation that made you unhappy. *It's so therapeutic, a bit like meditation.* ADJ-GRADED

2 Therapeutic treatment is designed to treat a disease or to improve a person's health, rather than to ADJ: usu ADJ n prevent a disease or ill-health; a medical use. *...therapeutic drugs.*

therapist /θerəpɪst/ **therapists.** A **therapist** is a person who is skilled in a particular type of therapy. *My therapist helped me feel my anger. ...family therapists.*
◆◆◇◇◇ N-COUNT: usu supp N

therapy /θerəpi/ **therapies** ◆◆◆◇◇

1 Therapy is the treatment of someone with mental or physical illness without the use of drugs or operations. *In therapy, she began to let go of her obsession with Mike... He is having therapy to conquer his phobia.*
N-UNCOUNT

2 A **therapy** is a particular treatment of someone with a particular illness; a medical use. *...hormonal therapies. ...conventional drug therapy.*
N-VAR: with supp

there. Pronounced /ðəʳ, STRONG ðeəʳ/ for meanings 1 and 2, and /ðeəʳ/ for meanings 3 to 19. ◆◆◆◆◆

1 There is used as the subject of the verb 'be' to say that something exists or does not exist, or to draw attention to it. *There's roadworks and temporary traffic lights between Camblesforth and Carlton... Are there some countries that have been able to tackle these problems successfully?... There were differences of opinion, he added, on very basic issues... There's nothing in this room; there's not a single chair, there's no bed, and not a single shelf... There's no way we can afford to buy a house at the moment... There's no question she is the best comedienne in this country.*
PRON: PRON *be* n

2 You use **there** in front of certain verbs when you are saying that something exists, develops, or can be seen. Whether the verb is singular or plural depends on the noun which follows the verb. *There remains considerable doubt over when the intended high-speed rail link will be complete... There appeared no imminent danger... There rose before us the great pyramid of Gaza... There developed a practice that came to a tragic and terrible end.*
PRON: PRON v n

3 There is used after 'hello' or 'hi' when you are greeting someone. *'Hello there,' said the woman, smiling at them.—'Hi!' they chorused... Oh, hi there. You must be Sidney.*
CONVENTION

4 If something is **there**, it exists or is available. *The group of old buildings on the corner by the main road is still there today... The book is there for people to read and make up their own mind... Nothing will be spent until he has made sure the money is there to pay for it.*
ADV: *be* ADV, oft ADV *for* n, ADV to-inf

5 You use **there** to refer to a place which has already been mentioned. *Mr Mandela travels to Lusaka tomorrow. While he's there, he's also expected to meet some of the leaders of the frontline states... 'Come on over, if you want.'—'How do I get there?'... The Bonn government is making plans to evacuate more than two-hundred of its citizens from Liberia if the fighting there increases... It's one hell of a train trip, about five days there and back... What if Spain reacts to the similar economic pressures which are appearing over there?*
ADV: *be* ADV, ADV with v, n ADV, oft prep ADV

6 You use **there** to indicate a place that you are pointing to or looking at, in order to draw someone's attention to it. *There it is, on the corner over there... There she is on the left up there... The toilets are over there, dear... You'll find the details there.*
ADV: ADV with *be*, ADV after v, oft prep ADV

7 You use **there** in expressions such as **'there he was'** or **'there we were'** to summarize part of a story or to slow a story down for dramatic effect; used in spoken English. *So there we were with Amy and she was driving us crazy... I looked, and there he was, riding a horse, with a double barreled shotgun on his shoulder.*
ADV: ADV cl PRAGMATICS

8 You use **there** when speaking on the telephone to ask if someone is available to speak to you. *Hello, is Gordon there please?*
ADV: ADV with *be*

9 You use **there** to refer to a point that someone has made in a conversation. *Death is terrible. I agree with you there... I think you're right there John... Can I just stop you there sir?... If you'll excuse me, ladies and gentlemen, we'd better leave it there.*
ADV: ADV after v

10 You use **there** to refer to a stage that has been reached in an activity or process. *We are making further investigations and will take the matter from there... And there we end this edition of Science in Action... And there we have a question that most women would find uncomfortable to answer. Do we really want the men to be at home?*
ADV: ADV with cl, oft prep ADV

11 You use **there** to indicate that something has reached a point or level which is completely successful. *We had hoped to fill the back page with extra news; we're not quite there yet... Life has not yet returned to normal but we are getting there.*
ADV: *be* ADV, ADV after v

12 You can use **there** in expressions such as **there you go** or **there we are** when accepting that an unsatisfactory situation cannot be changed; used in spoken English. *I'm the oldest and, according to all the books, should be the achiever, but there you go... It's the wages that count. Not over-generous, but there you are... 'They didn't seem to know anything about it.'—'Oh well there we are.'*
ADV: ADV cl

13 You can use **there** in expressions such as **there you go** and **there we are** when emphasizing that something proves that you were right; used in spoken English. *You see? There you go. That's why I didn't mention it earlier. I knew you'd take it the wrong way... 'There you are, you see!' she exclaimed. 'I knew you'd say that!'... Victoria Street, that's the name of the street. There we are, look.*
ADV: ADV cl PRAGMATICS

14 You use **there again** to introduce an extra piece of information which either contradicts what has been said or gives an alternative to it. *At 18 stone, I can't run around the way I used to. There again, some people say I never did... I mean small cars are the answer surely. Or there again a good system of public transport might do the same thing.*
PHRASES PHR cl

15 Phrases such as **there** you **go again**, are used to show annoyance at someone who is repeating something that has annoyed you in the past. *'There you go again, upsetting the child!' said Shirley... 'There you go again, Dad, with your silly words.'—'Sorry, son.'... Careful, there I go again, getting sentimental.*
V inflects

16 You can add **'so there'** to what you are saying to show that you will not change your mind about a decision you have made, even though the person you are talking to disagrees with you; an informal expression. *'Take That' are the best group in the whole world. So there... I think that's sweet, so there.*
cl PHR

17 If something happens **there and then** or **then and there**, it happens immediately. *Many felt that he should have resigned there and then... There and then he made his decision... A friend of Pip's invited them then and there to his college ball that night.*
PHR after v, PHR with cl

18 You say **'there there'** to someone who is very upset, especially a small child, in order to comfort or soothe them. *'There, there,' said Mum. 'You've been having a really bad dream.'*
CONVENTION PRAGMATICS

19 You say **'there you are'** or **'there you go'** when you are offering something to someone. *Nora picked up the boy, and gave him a biscuit. 'There you are, Lennie, you take the nice biscuit.'*
CONVENTION PRAGMATICS

thereabouts /ðeərəbaʊts/. You add **or thereabouts** after a number or date to indicate that it is approximate. *He told us that her age was forty-eight or thereabouts... By 1997 or thereabouts Athens will have a new airport, plus the best underground railway in Europe.*
PHRASE: n/num PHR

thereafter /ðeərɑːftəʳ, -æftəʳ/. **Thereafter** means after the event or date mentioned; a formal word. *Inflation will fall and thereafter so will interest rates... It was the only time she had ever discouraged him from dangerous activities and she regretted it thereafter.*
◆◆◇◇◇ ADV: ADV with cl =subsequently

thereby /ðeəʳbaɪ/. You use **thereby** to introduce an important result or consequence of the event or action you have just mentioned; a formal word. *Our bodies can sweat, thereby losing heat by evaporation... A firm might sometimes sell at a loss to drive a competitor out of business, and thereby increase its market power.*
◆◆◇◇◇ ADV: ADV with cl PRAGMATICS =thus

therefore /ðeəʳfɔːʳ/. You use **therefore** to introduce a logical result or conclusion. *Muscle cells need lots of fuel and therefore burn lots of calories... Nothing was to prevent him now from be-*
◆◆◆◆◇ ADV: ADV with cl/group PRAGMATICS =consequently

coming the richest, and therefore the happiest, man in the world.

therein /ðeə̲rɪn/ ◆◇◇◇◇

1 **Therein** means contained in the place that has been mentioned; a literary use. *By burning tree branches, pine needles, and pine cones, many not only warm their houses but improve the smell therein.* ADV: n ADV

2 **Therein** means relating to something that has just been mentioned; a formal use. *Afternoon groups relate to the specific addictions and problems therein.* ADV: n ADV

3 When you say **therein lies** a situation or problem, you mean that an existing situation has caused that situation or problem; a formal or old-fashioned expression. *Santa Maria di Castellabate is barely mentioned in guidebooks; therein lies its charm.* PHRASE: V inflects, PHR n

thereof /ðeərɒ̲v/. **Thereof** is used after a noun to relate that noun to a situation or thing that you have just mentioned; a formal word. *...his belief in God – or the lack thereof. ...a charge of £2 per hour or part thereof.* ADV: n ADV

thereon /ðeərɒ̲n/

1 **Thereon** means on the object or surface just mentioned; a formal use. *There was a card on each door with a guest's name inscribed thereon.* ADV: ADV after v

2 **Thereon** can be used to refer back to a thing that has previously been mentioned to show that the word just used relates to that thing; a formal use. *You will, in addition, pay to the Bank any losses, costs, expenses or legal fees (including VAT thereon).* ADV: n ADV, ADV after v

thereupon /ðeə̲rəpɒ̲n/. **Thereupon** means happening immediately after something else has happened and usually as a result of it; a formal word. *Some months ago angry demonstrators mounted a noisy demonstration beneath his window. His neighbours thereupon insisted upon more security.* ADV: ADV with cl

therm /θɜ̲ːʳm/ **therms.** A **therm** is a measurement of heat. N-COUNT: num N

thermal /θɜ̲ːʳməl/ **thermals** ◆◇◇◇◇

1 **Thermal** means relating to or caused by heat or by changes in temperature. *...thermal power stations. ...financial assistance with repair, thermal insulation and improvements to homes through Government grants.* ADJ: ADJ n

2 **Thermal** streams or baths contain water which is naturally hot or warm. *Volcanic activity has created thermal springs and boiling mud pools.* ADJ: ADJ n

3 **Thermal** clothes are specially designed to keep you warm in cold weather. *My feet were like blocks of ice despite the thermal socks... I put on my thermal leggings, long socks and the rest of my clothes.* ADJ: ADJ n

► **Thermals** are thermal clothes. *Have you got your thermals on?* N-PLURAL

4 A **thermal** is a movement of rising warm air. *Birds use thermals to lift them through the air.* N-COUNT

thermo /θɜ̲ːʳmoʊ/. **Thermo** means using or relating to heat. *The main thermo power station in the area has been damaged.* ► Also a combining form. *...the dangers of thermo-nuclear war.* ► Also combines to form nouns. *The body is made of mineral-reinforced thermo-plastic.* ADJ: ADJ n; COMB in ADJ; COMB in NOUNS

thermodynamics /θɜ̲ːʳmoʊdaɪnæ̲mɪks/; the form **thermodynamic** is used as a modifier. **Thermodynamics** is the branch of physics that is concerned with the relationship between heat and other forms of energy. N-UNCOUNT

thermometer /θəʳmɒ̲mɪtəʳ/ **thermometers.** A **thermometer** is an instrument for measuring temperature. It usually consists of a narrow glass tube containing a thin column of mercury which rises and falls as the temperature rises and falls. ◆◇◇◇◇ N-COUNT

thermonuclear /θɜ̲ːʳmoʊnju̲ːkliəʳ, AM -nu̲ːk-/; also spelled **thermo-nuclear**. A **thermonuclear** weapon or device is one which uses the high temperatures that are generated in nuclear fission to detonate it. ADJ: ADJ n

thermoplastic /θɜ̲ːʳmoʊplæstɪk/ **thermoplastics.** **Thermoplastic** materials are types of plastic which become soft when they are heated and hard when they cool down. N-COUNT: usu N n

Thermos /θɜ̲ːʳmɒs/ **Thermoses.** A **Thermos** or a **Thermos flask** is a container which is used to keep hot drinks hot or cold drinks cold. It has two thin silvery glass walls with a vacuum between them. **Thermos** is a trademark. N-COUNT =vacuum flask, flask

thermostat /θɜ̲ːʳməstæt/ **thermostats.** A **thermostat** is a device that switches a system or motor on or off according to the temperature. Thermostats are used, for example, in central heating systems and refrigerators. N-COUNT

thesaurus /θɪsɔ̲ːrəs/ **thesauruses.** A **thesaurus** is a reference book in which words with similar meanings are grouped together. N-COUNT

these. The determiner is pronounced /ðiːz/. The pronoun is pronounced /ði̲ːz/. ◆◆◆◆◆

1 You use **these** at the beginning of noun groups to refer to someone or something that you have already mentioned or identified. *Switch to an interest-paying current account and stay in credit. Most banks and larger building societies now offer these accounts... A steering committee has been formed. These people can make decisions in ten minutes which would usually take us months.* DET: DET pl-n PRAGMATICS

► Also a pronoun. *AIDS kills mostly the young population of a nation. These are the people who contribute most to a country's economic development.* PRON

2 You use **these** to introduce people or things that you are going to talk about. *Check out these advanced Canon features: Text Memory with easy editing of stored text on the LCD display and a search and replace facility... If you're converting your loft, these addresses will be useful.* ► Also a pronoun. *Look after yourself properly while you are pregnant. These are some of the things you can do for yourself.* DET: DET pl-n; PRON

3 In spoken English, people use **these** to introduce people or things into a story; an informal use. *I was on my own and these fellows came along towards me... She used to make all these chocolate puddle puddings, you know, with the sauce underneath and all this sort of thing.* DET: DET pl-n

4 You use **these** when you are identifying someone or asking about their identity. *These are my children.* PRON

5 You use **these** to refer to people or things that are near you, especially when you touch them or point to them. *What I try to do in putting these pictures up here is to show how varied children are in solving the problem... These scissors are awfully heavy.* DET: DET pl-n

► Also a pronoun. *These are the people who are doing our loft conversion for us... These are my favourite biscuits.* PRON

6 You use **these** when you refer to something which you expect the hearer to know about or when you are checking that you are both thinking of the same person or thing. *You know these last few months when we've been expecting it to warm up a little bit?... You know these funny cigarettes I smoke?* DET: DET pl-n

7 You use **these** in the expression **these days** to mean 'at the present time'. *Living in Bootham these days can be depressing... Trying to make it as a single parent raising your children would be the main concern to me these days.* DET: DET pl-n

thesis /θi̲ːsɪs/ **theses** /θi̲ːsiːz/ ◆◆◇◇◇

1 A **thesis** is an idea or theory that is expressed as a statement and is discussed in a logical way. *This thesis does not stand up to close inspection. ...proponents of the thesis that computers can be programmed to do anything which a human mind does.* N-COUNT =argument

2 A **thesis** is a long piece of writing based on your own ideas and research that you do as part of a university degree, especially a PhD. *He was awarded his PhD for a thesis on industrial robots.* N-COUNT

thespian /θe̲spiən/ **thespians**

1 A **thespian** is an actor or actress; an old-fashioned use. N-COUNT

2 Thespian means relating to drama and the theatre; an old-fashioned use. ADJ: ADJ n

they /ðeɪ/ ◆◆◆◆◆
They is a third person plural pronoun. **They** is used as the subject of a verb.
1 You use **they** to refer to a group of people, animals, or things. *The two men were far more alike than they would ever admit... People matter because of what they are, not what they have... The young horses broke in a pack, and over the first furlong, they remained in a pack.* PRON-PLURAL
2 You use **they** instead of 'he or she' to refer to a person without saying whether that person is a man or a woman. Some people think this use is incorrect. *The teacher is not responsible for the student's success or failure. They are only there to help the student learn... I never saw anyone go in to buy. Whether they ever did I don't know.* PRON-PLURAL
3 You also use **they** in expressions such as 'they say' or 'they call it' to refer vaguely to people in general when you are making general statements about what people say, think, or do. *They say there's plenty of opportunities out there, you just have to look carefully and you'll find them... They call us terrorists and say we must be destroyed.* PRON-PLURAL

they'd /ðeɪd/
1 They'd is a spoken form of 'they had', especially when 'had' is an auxiliary verb. *They'd both lived in this road all their lives.*
2 They'd is a spoken form of 'they would'. *He agreed that they'd visit her after they stopped at Jan's for coffee.*

they'll /ðeɪəl/. **They'll** is the usual spoken form of 'they will'. *They'll probably be here Monday and Tuesday.*

they're /ðeəʳ, ðeɪəʳ/. **They're** is the usual spoken form of 'they are'. *People eat when they're depressed.*

they've /ðeɪv/. **They've** is the usual spoken form of 'they have', especially when 'have' is an auxiliary verb. *The worst thing is when you call friends and they've gone out.*

thick /θɪk/ **thicker, thickest** ◆◆◆◇◇
1 Something that is **thick** has a large distance between its two opposite sides. *For breakfast I had a thick slice of bread and syrup... He wore glasses with thick rims... This material is very thick and this needle is not strong enough to go through it.* ♦ **thickly** *An old man sat in a great carved armchair of black wood, thickly padded with soft cushions... Slice the meat thickly.* ADJ-GRADED ≠thin; ADV-GRADED: ADV with v ≠thinly
2 You can use **thick** to talk or ask about how wide or deep something is. *The folder was two inches thick... How thick are these walls? ...a finger as thick as a sausage.* ► Also a combining form. *His life was saved by a quarter-inch-thick bullet-proof steel screen.* ♦ **thickness, thicknesses** *The size of the fish will determine the thickness of the steaks... The egg had a shell thickness of 0.14mm and the newly-hatched chick weighed nine grams. ...a relatively dense layer of gases about 200 miles in thickness.* ADJ: n ADJ, *how* ADJ, amount ADJ, *as* ADJ *as*; COMB in ADJ: ADJ n; N-VAR: oft N *of* n, N *of* amount, amount *in* N
3 If something that consists of several things is **thick**, it has a large number of them very close together. *She inherited our father's thick, wavy hair... They walked through thick forest.* ♦ **thickly** *I rounded a bend where the trees and brush grew thickly... The interior flatlands and valleys are thickly planted with coconuts.* ADJ-GRADED =dense; ADV-GRADED: ADV after v, ADV -ed
4 If something is **thick with** another thing, the first thing is full of or covered with the second. *The air is thick with acrid smoke from the fires... She ate scones thick with butter.* ADJ-GRADED: v-link ADJ *with* n
5 Thick clothes are made from heavy cloth, so that they will keep you warm in cold weather. *In the winter she wears thick socks, Wellington boots and gloves... She wore a thick tartan skirt and a red cashmere sweater.* ADJ-GRADED ≠thin
6 Thick smoke, fog, or cloud is difficult to see through. *The smoke was bluish-black and thick... It wasn't very thick fog.* ADJ-GRADED
7 Thick liquids are fairly stiff and solid and do not flow easily. *They had to battle through thick mud to reach construction workers... The sauce is thick and rich so don't bother trying to diet.* ADJ-GRADED
8 If someone's voice is **thick**, they are not speaking clearly, for example because they are ill, upset, or drunk. *When he spoke his voice was thick with bitterness.* ♦ **thickly** *'It's all my fault,' he mumbled thickly.* ADJ-GRADED: usu v-link ADJ; ADV-GRADED: ADV after v
9 A **thick** accent is very obvious and easy to identify. *He answered our questions in English but with a thick accent... 'What do you want?' a teenage girl demanded in a thick German accent.* ADJ-GRADED: usu ADJ n =strong, pronounced
10 If you describe someone as **thick**, you think they are stupid; used mainly in informal British English. *How could she have been so thick?* ADJ-GRADED: usu v-link ADJ [PRAGMATICS] =stupid
11 If things happen **thick and fast**, they happen very quickly and in large numbers. *The rumours have been coming thick and fast... Distress calls were pouring in thick and fast from all over the area.* PHRASES PHR after v
12 If you are **in the thick of** an activity or situation, you are very involved in it. *I enjoy being in the thick of things... Peterson suddenly found himself in the thick of desperate fighting.* PHR n, usu v-link PHR, PHR after v =in the middle of
13 If you do something **through thick and thin**, you do it although the conditions or circumstances are very bad. *She'd stuck by Bob through thick and thin... I will go on loving James through thick and thin no matter what happens.* PHR after v
14 ● to **lay it on thick**: see **lay**. ● **a thick skin**: see **skin**.

thicken /θɪkən/ **thickens, thickening, thickened** ◆◇◇◇◇
1 When you **thicken** a liquid or it **thickens**, it becomes stiffer and more solid. *Thicken the broth with the cornflour... Keep stirring until the sauce thickens.* V-ERG V n V
2 If something **thickens**, it becomes more closely grouped together or denser than it was before. *The crowds around him began to thicken... As the ice sheet grows and thickens it chills the nearby air.* VERB V
3 People sometimes say '**the plot thickens**' when a situation or series of events is getting more and more complicated and mysterious. *'Find anything?' he asked. 'Yeah. The plot thickens,' I said.* PHRASE: V inflects

thickener /θɪkənəʳ/ **thickeners.** A **thickener** is a substance that is added to a liquid in order to make it stiffer and more solid. *...cornstarch, used as a thickener... How much thickener is used?* N-MASS

thicket /θɪkɪt/ **thickets** ◆◇◇◇◇
1 A **thicket** is a small group of trees or bushes which are growing closely together. *...a bamboo thicket.* N-COUNT
2 If you refer to a **thicket** of ideas or events, you mean that there a lot of them together, and often that they are confusing or difficult to identify. *The novel is a thicket of literary references... To try to open a foreign-owned business is to enter a thicket of regulations from which few emerge.* N-COUNT: with supp, usu N *of* n

thickset /θɪkset/; also spelled **thick-set**. A man who is **thickset** is broad and heavy, with a solid-looking body. *He was of middle height, thick-set. ...his stout, thickset figure.* ADJ-GRADED =stocky

thick-skinned. If you say that someone is **thick-skinned**, you mean that they are not easily upset by criticism or unpleasantness. *He was thick-skinned enough to cope with it.* ADJ-GRADED: usu v-link ADJ

thief /θiːf/ **thieves** /θiːvz/. A **thief** is a person who steals something from another person. *The thieves snatched the camera. ...car thieves.* ◆◆◇◇◇ N-COUNT

thieving /θiːvɪŋ/
1 Thieving is the act of stealing things from people; an old-fashioned use. *An ex-con who says he's given up thieving.* N-UNCOUNT
2 Thieving means involved in stealing things or intending to steal something. *...a thieving grocer who put sand in the sugar. ...a string of convictions from a thieving career.* ADJ: ADJ n

thigh /θaɪ/ **thighs.** Your **thighs** are the top parts of your legs, between your knees and your hips. ◆◆◇◇◇ N-COUNT

thimble /θɪmbəl/ **thimbles.** A **thimble** is a small metal or plastic object which you use to protect your finger when you are sewing. N-COUNT

thin /θɪn/ **thinner, thinnest; thins, thinning, thinned** ◆◆◆◇◇

1 Something that is **thin** is much narrower than it is long. *A thin cable carries the signal to a computer... James's face was thin, finely boned, and sensitive.* ADJ-GRADED

2 A person or animal that is **thin** has no extra fat on their body . *He was a tall, thin man with grey hair that fell in a wild tangle to his shoulders... He is small and very thin and has pale-white skin.* ● **as thin as a rake**: see **rake**. ♦ **thinness** *There was something familiar about him, his fawn raincoat, his thinness, the way he moved.* ADJ-GRADED; N-UNCOUNT

3 Something such as paper or cloth that is **thin** is flat and has only a very small distance between its two opposite surfaces. *...a small, blue-bound book printed in fine type on thin paper... A thin layer of topsoil was swept away.* ♦ **thinly** *Peel and thinly slice the onion... Roll the pasta out as thinly as possible.* ADJ-GRADED ≠thick; ADV-GRADED: ADV with v

4 Liquids that are **thin** are weak and watery. *The soup was thin and clear, yet mysteriously rich... They are stirring huge pots of rice and thin vegetable soup over a fire made of charcoal.* ADJ-GRADED ≠thick

5 A crowd or audience that is **thin** does not have many people in it. *The crowd, which had been thin for the first half of the race, had now grown considerably.* ♦ **thinly** *The island is thinly populated. ...thinly attended meetings.* ADJ-GRADED; ADV-GRADED: ADV -ed

6 A **thin** smile is one that is not genuinely warm or humorous. *All she could manage was a thin, wan smile.* ♦ **thinly** *Wilson smiled thinly. 'We have decided to name the new Home after Councillor Minford.'* ADJ-GRADED: usu ADJ n; ADV-GRADED: ADV after v

7 Thin clothes are made from light cloth and are not warm to wear. *Her gown was thin, and she shivered, partly from cold.* ♦ **thinly** *Mrs Brown wrapped the thinly clad man in her own fur coat and very likely saved his life.* ADJ-GRADED; ADV-GRADED: ADV adj/-ed

8 If you describe an argument or explanation as **thin**, you mean that it is weak and unconvincing. *However, the evidence is thin and, to some extent, ambiguous... Even if the optimists' theory is true, it still seems a thin argument against reform.* ♦ **thinly** *Much of the speech was a thinly disguised attack on British Airways. ...a series of what correspondents describe as thinly veiled threats to use force.* ADJ-GRADED =weak ≠strong; ADV: usu ADV -ed, also ADV before v

9 A voice or sound that is **thin** is high-pitched and not very loud. *Her thin voice rose high in complaint.* ADJ-GRADED

10 If someone's hair is described as **thin**, they do not have a lot of hair. *She had pale thin yellow hair she pulled back into a bun.* ADJ-GRADED ≠thick

11 When you **thin** something or if it **thins**, it becomes less crowded because people or things have been removed from it. *It would have been better to have thinned the trees over several winters rather than all at one time... By midnight the crowd had thinned.* ► **Thin out** means the same as **thin**. *NATO will continue to thin out its forces... When the crowd began to thin out, I realized that most of the food was still there... Further up the river, the vineyards start to thin out and the orange groves and almond trees take over.* V-ERG; V n; V; PHRASAL VERB ERG; V P n (not pron); V P; Also V n P

12 To **thin** a sauce or liquid means to make it weaker and more watery by adding another liquid to it. *It may be necessary to thin the sauce slightly... Aspirin thins the blood, letting it flow more easily through narrowed blood vessels.* ► **Thin down** means the same as **thin**. *Thin down your mayonnaise with soured cream or natural yoghurt. ...an oil-based paint that was thinned down with white spirit.* VERB; V n; PHRASAL VERB; V P n (not pron)

13 If a man's hair **is thinning** he is beginning to go bald. *His hair is thinning and his skin has lost all hint of youth.* ● **thin on top**: see **top**. VERB; V

14 If someone's patience, for example, **is wearing thin**, they are beginning to become impatient or angry with someone. *Parliament has not yet begun to combat the deepening economic crisis, and public patience is wearing thin.* PHRASES

15 ● **on thin ice**: see **ice**. ● to **disappear into thin air**: see **air**.

thin down. See **thin** 12 PHRASAL VERB

thin out. See **thin** 11 PHRASAL VERB

thine /ðaɪn/. **Thine** is an old-fashioned, poetic, or religious word for 'yours' when you are talking to only one person. *I am Thine, O Lord, I have heard Thy voice.* PRON-POSS

thing /θɪŋ/ **things** ◆◆◆◆◆

1 You can use **thing** to refer to any object, feature, or event when you cannot, need not, or do not want to refer to it more precisely. *'What's that thing in the middle of the fountain?'—'Some kind of statue, I guess.'... She was in the middle of clearing the breakfast things... If you could change one thing about yourself, what would it be?... A strange thing happened... We get blamed for all kinds of things.* N-COUNT: usu with supp

2 Thing is used in lists and descriptions to give examples or to widen the range of what you are referring to. *These are genetic disorders that only affect males normally. They are things like muscular dystrophy and haemophilia... The Earth is made mainly of iron and silicon and things like that... Big things, such as hospitals and social security, are paid for by the Government... You can spot them fairly easily because of their short haircuts and things.* N-COUNT: usu pl, usu with supp PRAGMATICS

3 The word **thing** is often used after an adjective, where it would also be possible just to use the adjective. For example, you can say **it's a different thing** instead of **it's different**. *Of course, literacy isn't the same thing as intelligence... To be a parent is a terribly difficult thing... Perhaps it's a good thing that Dizzy retired.* N-COUNT: adj N

4 The word **thing** is often used instead of the pronouns 'anything,' or 'everything' in order to emphasize what you are saying. *It isn't going to solve a single thing... Don't you worry about a thing... 'It's all here,' she said. 'Every damn thing.'* N-SING: oft with brd-neg PRAGMATICS

5 The word **thing** is used in expressions such as **such a thing** or **things like that**, especially in negative statements, in order to emphasize the bad or difficult situation you are referring back to. *I don't believe he would tell Leo such a thing... 'Are you accusing me of being a thief?—'I have done no such thing, Tony.'... How do you actually go about discovering a thing like that?... I'm trying to cope. These things happen. You have to cope.* N-COUNT: usu with brd-neg, with supp PRAGMATICS

6 You can use **thing** to refer in a vague way to a situation, activity, or idea, especially when you want to suggest that it is not very important; an informal use. *I'm a bit unsettled tonight. This war thing's upsetting me... These folks clearly take this ballroom thing very seriously. ...the man who had spoken dismissively of the 'vision thing' when running for the presidency in 1988.* N-COUNT: supp N, usu n N PRAGMATICS

7 You can use **thing** when you referring to something that you are uncertain or vague about, after mentioning something that it resembles or could possibly be; an informal use. *She'd actually taken it home and she put it in this jar thing... The captain of the submarine has got this periscope thing.* N-COUNT: n N

8 You often use the word **thing** to indicate to the person you are addressing that you are about to mention something important, or something that you particularly want them to know. *One thing I am sure of was that she was scared... The first thing parents want to know is: will the baby survive?... The funny thing is that the rest of us have known that for years... The most important thing to remember about fish is to buy it really fresh.* N-COUNT: with supp, oft adj N PRAGMATICS

9 Thing is often used to refer back to something that has just been mentioned, either to emphasize it or to give more information about it. *Getting drunk is a thing all young men do... I never wanted to be normal. It was not a thing I ever thought desirable... The Captain stretched his left leg on one of the empty chairs. He knew it was not a polite thing to do.* N-COUNT =something

10 A **thing** is a physical object that is considered as having no life of its own. *It's not a thing, Beauchamp. It's a human being!* N-COUNT

11 Thing is used to refer to something, especially a physical object, when you want to express contempt or irritation towards it; used in spoken English. *This thing's virtually useless... Turn that thing off!... They're armed with sub-machine-guns or machine-pistols or whatever you call those things.* N-COUNT PRAGMATICS

12 You can call a person or an animal a particular **thing** when you want to mention a particular quality that they have and express your feelings towards them, usually affectionate feelings; an informal use. *You really are quite a clever little thing... Oh you lucky thing!* N-COUNT: adj N

13 Your **things** are your clothes or possessions. *Sara told him to take all his things and not to return... Is there anything you'd like to borrow, before your own things are unpacked?* N-PLURAL: poss N

14 Things can refer to the situation or life in general and the way it is changing or affecting you. *Everyone agrees things are getting better... A change of ownership might improve things... How are things going?* N-PLURAL

15 Things can refer to a particular aspect of life, such as the physical or spiritual aspect. *...a movement away from the things of this world to the things of the spirit... I think I'm more aware now of some spiritual things and I do believe in good and evil.* N-PLURAL: with supp, oft N of n, adj N

16 You can refer to a monster or something else that is too frightening, strange, or horrible to describe clearly as a **thing**. *...John W. Campbell, author of 'The Thing From Another World.'* N-COUNT

17 If you say that something is **the thing** you mean that it is fashionable or popular. *I feel under pressure to go out and get drunk because it's the thing to do... They were obviously of the opinion that his taste was not quite the thing.* N-SING: the N, oft N to-inf

18 In all things means in every situation and at all times; a literary expression. *Sara wished Franklin to follow family tradition, in this as in all things. ...the old rule of health, which prescribes moderation in all things.* PHRASES n/adj PHR, PHR after v

19 If you say that someone or something is trying to **be all things to all men** or **to all people**, you are criticizing them because they are trying to behave in a way that will please everybody, and this is impossible. *I realised I had a big problem. I wanted to be all things to all people... The film tries to be all things to all men – comedy, romance, fantasy, and satire.* V inflects PRAGMATICS

20 If, for example, you **do the** right **thing** or **do the** decent **thing** in a situation, you do something which is considered correct or socially acceptable in that situation. *People want to do the right thing and buy 'green'... Carrington did the honourable thing and resigned... I think I did the wrong thing.* V inflects

21 If you say that something is **the done thing**, you mean it is the socially acceptable way to behave. *It was not the done thing. In those days the man was supposed to be the provider.* oft with brd-neg, v-link PHR

22 If you do something **first thing**, you do it at the beginning of the day, before you do anything else. If you do it **last thing**, you do it at the end of the day, before you go to bed or go to sleep. *I'll go see her, first thing... Take the money to your office without fail, first thing in the morning... I always do it last thing on a Saturday... Last thing at night, he thought of her.* PHR after v, PHR with cl, oft PHR prep

23 If you **have a thing about** someone or something, you have very strong feelings about them; an informal expression. *I had always had a thing about red hair... He's got this thing about ties.* V inflects, PHR n/-ing

24 You say **it is a** good **thing to** do something to introduce a piece of advice or a comment on a situation or activity. *Can you tell me whether it is a good thing to prune an apple tree and does it apply to other fruit trees apart from apples?... In a new democracy, it is no bad thing to master the art of compromise... It is a terrible thing to doubt someone you have trusted all your life.* PHR inf

25 If you **make a thing of** something or **make a thing about** it, you talk about it or do it in an exaggerated way, so that it seems much more important than it really is; an informal expression. *Gossips made a big thing about him going on shopping trips with her... I took his hand to make a big thing of introducing him to my mother... I didn't have time to tell you, and anyway, I didn't want to make a big thing out of it.* V inflects, PHR n/-ing

26 You can say that the first of two ideas, actions, or situations **is one thing** when you want to contrast it with a second idea, action, or situation and emphasize that the second one is much more difficult, important, or extreme. *It was one thing to talk about leaving; it was another to physically walk out the door... Borrowing $100,000 is one thing. Owing $425,000 is another!* V inflects, oft *it* PHR to-inf PRAGMATICS

27 You can say **for one thing** when you are explaining a statement or answering a question, to suggest that your explanation or answer is only partial, and that there are other points that you could add to it. *She was a monster. For one thing, she really enjoyed cruelty... She was unable to sell it, because for one thing its size was awkward... 'How have the sanctions affected your life in Belgrade?'—'Well, for one thing, we already have shortages.'* PHR with cl PRAGMATICS

28 In spoken English, you can use the expression **'one thing and another'** to suggest that there are several reasons for something or several items on a list, but you are not going to explain or mention them all. *What with one thing and another, it was fairly late in the day when we returned to Shrewsbury... Everybody came in with their Christmas order for beer and spirits and port and one thing and another.* oft *with* PHR

29 If you say **it is just one of those things** you mean that you cannot explain something because it seems to happen by chance. *'I wonder why.' Mr. Dambar shrugged. 'It must be just one of those things, I guess.'... It was simply one of those things, pure coincidence.* V inflects

30 You say **one thing led to another** when you are explaining how something happened, but you do not really want to give the details or you think people will be able to imagine the details. *He came by on Saturday to see if she was lonely. One thing led to another and he stayed the night.* V inflects

31 If you **do** your **own thing**, you live, act, or behave in the way you want to, without paying attention to convention or depending on other people; an informal expression. *We accept the right of all men and women to do their own thing, however bizarre... She was allowed to do her own thing as long as she kept in touch by phone.* V inflects

32 If something is **a thing of the past**, it no longer exists or happens, or is being replaced by something new. *Painful typhoid injections are a thing of the past, thanks to the introduction of an oral vaccine... Cheap computers, faxes and phone calls will make commuting to work a thing of the past.* v-link PHR, PHR after v

33 If you say that someone **is seeing** or **hearing things**, you mean that they believe they are seeing or hearing something that is not really there. *Dr Payne led Lana back into the examination room and told her she was seeing things... I thought I was hearing things yesterday. I thought I heard a cuckoo.* V inflects, usu cont

34 You can say there is **no such thing** as something to emphasize that it does not exist or is not possible. *There really is no such thing as a totally risk-free industry... 'I found a mermaid.'—'Don't be daft. There's no such thing.'* usu v-link PHR, oft PHR *as* n

35 You say **'the thing is'** to introduce an explanation, comment, or opinion, that relates to something that has just been said. **'The thing is'** is often used to identify a problem relating to what has just been said. *'What does your market research consist of?'—'Well, the thing is, it depends on our target age group.'... I'm getting a grant for a speech therapy course. But the thing is, I don't know whether I want to do it any more.* PHR cl PRAGMATICS

36 If you say that something is **just the thing** or is **the very thing**, you are emphasizing that it is exactly what is wanted or needed *Kiwi fruit are just* usu v-link PHR, oft PHR *for* n, PHR to-inf PRAGMATICS *the thing for a healthy snack... I know the very thing to cheer you up.*

37 If you say that someone knows **a thing or two** about something or could teach someone **a thing or two** about it, you mean that they are very knowledgeable about it or good at it. *Patricia Hewitt knows a thing or two about how to be well-organised... They do agree Africa could teach America a thing or two about family values... The peace movement has learnt a thing or two from Vietnam.*
PHR after v, oft PHR *about* n

38 • **other things being equal**: see **equal**. • **first things first**: see **first**. • **the real thing**: see **real**. • **the shape of things to come**: see **shape**.

thingummy /θɪŋəmi/ **thingummies.** In informal spoken English, you refer to something or someone as **thingummy** or **thingummyjig** when you cannot remember or do not know the proper word or name for them, or when you cannot be bothered to use the proper word or name for them. *I once bought a thingummy out of one of those catalogues... I must say, I mean, it sounded like er thingummyjig all over again without the politics.*
N-COUNT

thingy /θɪŋi/ **thingies.** In informal spoken English, you refer to something or someone as **thingy** when you cannot remember or do not know the proper word or name for them, or when you cannot be bothered to use the proper word or name for them. *...the new phone thingy. ...what's his name, Sir Jack Thingy.*
N-COUNT

think /θɪŋk/ **thinks, thinking, thought** ◆◆◆◆◆

1 If you **think** that something is the case, you have the opinion that it is the case. *I certainly think there should be a ban on tobacco advertising... Do you think I ought to seal the boxes up?... A generation ago, it was thought that babies born this small could not survive... Tell me, what do you think of my theory?... Peter is useless, far worse than I thought... He manages a good deal better than I thought possible... 'It ought to be stopped.'—'Yes, I think so.'*
VB: no cont; V that; *it be* V-ed that; V *of/about* n; V; V adj; V *so/not*; Also V n to-inf

2 If you say that you **think** that something is true or will happen, you mean that you have the impression that it is true or will happen, although you are not certain of the facts. *Nora thought he was seventeen years old... Do you think she was embarrassed about it?... She's in Napa, I think... The storm is thought to be responsible for as many as four deaths... 'Did Mr Stevens ever mention her to you?'—'No, I don't think so.'.*
VB: no cont; V that; *be* V-ed to-inf; V *so/not*

3 If you **think** in a particular way, you have those general opinions or attitudes. *You wouldn't think like that if you were in Somalia or Bosnia... He can keep matters under control by silencing the demonstrators and others who think like them... If you think as I do, vote as I do... I don't blame you for thinking that way.*
VB: no cont, no passive; V *like* n; V *as/like* cl; V n

4 When you **think** about ideas or problems, you make a mental effort to consider them. *She closed her eyes for a moment, trying to think... I have often thought about this problem... Next time you have a problem, think about how you can improve the situation instead of dwelling on all the negative aspects... Let's think what we can do... We had to think what to do next.* ▶ Also a noun in British English. *I'll have a think about that.*
VERB; V; V *about* n/wh; V wh; V wh-to-inf; N-SING: a N

5 If you **think** in a particular way, you consider things, solve problems, or make decisions in this way, for example because of your job or your background. *To make the computer work at full capacity, the programmer has to think like the machine... I meet many businessmen, and I see they think in terms of the overall picture... The referee has to think the way the players do.*
VB: no passive =reason; V prep; V n

6 If you **think** of something, it comes into your mind or you remember it. *Nobody could think of anything to say... I can't think of any reason why he should do that... I just can't think of his name... I was trying to think what else we had to do.*
VB: no cont; V *of* n; V wh

7 If you **think of** an idea, you make a mental effort and use your imagination and intelligence to create it or develop it. *He thought of another way of getting out of the marriage... I don't know why I never thought of that.*
VERB; V *of* n

8 If you **are thinking** something at a particular moment, you have words or ideas in your mind without saying them out loud. *She must be ill, Tatiana thought... I remember thinking how lovely he looked... I'm trying to think positive thoughts.*
VB: no passive; V with quote; V wh/that; V n

9 If you **think of** someone or something as having a particular quality or purpose, you regard them as having this quality or purpose. *We all thought of him as a father... He thinks of it as his home... In China bats are thought of as being very lucky... Nobody had thought him capable of that kind of thing.*
VB: no cont; V *of* n *as* n/-ing; V n adj

10 If you **think** a lot **of** someone or something, you admire them very much or think they are very good. *To tell the truth, I don't think much of psychiatrists... The Director thought a good deal of him... People at the club think very highly of him... He seemed to be a good man, well thought of by all.*
VB: no cont; V amount *of* n; V adv *of* n

11 If you **think** of someone, you show consideration for them and pay attention to their needs. *I'm only thinking of you... You never think of anyone but yourself... We have the interest of 500,000 customers to think of... You don't have to think about me and Hugh.*
VERB; V *of* n; V *about* n

12 If you **are thinking of** taking a particular course of action, you are considering it as a possible course of action. *Martin was thinking of taking legal action against Zuckerman... Have you ever thought of marrying?... It would be unwise for the government to think of privatisation as a means of saving money.*
VERB; V *of*-ing/n

13 You can say that you **are thinking of** a particular aspect or subject, in order to introduce an example or explain more exactly what you are talking about. *I'm primarily thinking of the first year... There is a theme of tragedy that runs through it: I'm thinking in particular of the story of Tom Howard.*
VB: usu cont; PRAGMATICS; V *of* n

14 You use **think** in questions where you are expressing your anger or shock at someone's behaviour. *Who does she think she is? Trying to make a fool of me like that... You can't do this! What do you think you're doing?... What were you thinking of? You shouldn't steal.*
VB: only interrog; PRAGMATICS; V that; V *of* n/-ing

15 You use **think** when you are commenting on something which you did or experienced in the past and which now seems surprising, foolish, or shocking to you. *To think I left you alone in a place with a madman at large!... When I think of how you've behaved and the trouble you've got into!*
VB: no cont, no passive; PRAGMATICS; V that; V *of* n

16 You can use **think** in expressions such as **you would think** or **I would have thought** when you are criticizing someone because they ought to or could be expected to do something, but have not done it. *You'd think you'd remember to wash your ears... We would have thought he would have a more responsible attitude... 'Surely to God she should have been given some proper help.'—'Well I would have thought so.'*
VB: no cont; PRAGMATICS; V that; V *so*; Also V

17 You can use **think** in expressions such as **anyone would think** and **you would think** to express your surprise or disapproval at the way someone is behaving, and to suggest that their behaviour gives a particular wrong impression. *Anyone would think you were in love with the girl... You'd think you had never seen a door before!*
VB: no cont; V that

18 See also **thinking, thought.**

19 You use expressions such as **come to think of it**, **when you think about it**, or **thinking about it**, when you mention something that you have suddenly remembered or realized. *He was her distant relative, as was everyone else on the island, come to think of it... When you think about it, he's probably right.*
PHRASES; PHR with cl; PRAGMATICS

20 You use **'I think'** as a way of being polite when you are explaining or suggesting to someone what you want to do, or when you are accepting or refusing an offer. *I think I'll go home and have a shower... We need a job, and I thought we could go around and ask if people need odd jobs done... Time for a pint of beer, I think... 'Would you like to do that another time.'—'Yes I think so.'*
PHR that, PHR with cl, PHR *so/not*; PRAGMATICS

21 You use **'I think'** in conversations or speeches to make your statements and opinions sound less forceful, rude, or direct. *I think he means 'at' rather than 'to'... Thanks, but I think I can handle it... This is, I think, much, much more important... 'You've got it wrong.'—'I think not.'* PHR that, PHR with cl, PHR *so/not* PRAGMATICS

22 You say **just think** when you feel excited, fascinated, or shocked by something, and you want the person to whom you are talking to feel the same. *Just think; tomorrow we shall walk out of this place and leave it all behind us forever... Just think how snug and cosy we could be.* PHR with cl, PHR wh PRAGMATICS =imagine

23 If you **think again** about an action or decision, you consider it very carefully, often with the result that you change your mind and decide to do things differently. *It has forced politicians to think again about the wisdom of trying to evacuate refugees... He intends to ask the court to think again.* oft PHR *about* n/-ing =reconsider

24 If you **think nothing of** doing something that other people might consider difficult, strange, or wrong, you consider it to be easy or normal, and you do it often or would be quite willing to do it. *I thought nothing of betting £1,000 on a horse.* V inflects, PHR -ing

25 If something happens and you **think nothing of it**, you do not pay much attention to it or think of it as strange or important, although later you realize that it is. *When she went off to see her parents for the weekend I thought nothing of it... One of Tony's friends, David, kept coming to my house but I didn't think anything of it.* V inflects

26 • you **can't hear** yourself **think**: see **hear**. • to **shudder to think**: see **shudder**. • to **think better of it**: see **better**. • to **think big**: see **big**. • to **think twice**: see **twice**. • to **think the world of**: see **world**.

think back. If you **think back**, you make an effort to remember things that happened to you in the past. *I thought back to the time in 1975 when my son was desperately ill... When you think back on it, do you think that it was the right thing to do?... Thinking back, I don't know how I had the courage.* PHRASAL VERB =look back V P prep V P

think out. If you **think** something **out**, you consider all the aspects and details of it before doing anything or making a decision. *I need time alone to think things out... The book is detailed and well thought out... He chewed at the end of his pencil, thinking out the next problem.* PHRASAL VERB V n P V-ed P V P n (not pron)

think over. If you **think** something **over**, you consider it carefully before making a decision. *She said she needs time to think it over... I suggest you think over your position very carefully.* PHRASAL VERB V n P V P n (not pron)

think through. If you **think** a situation **through**, you consider it thoroughly, together with all its possible effects or consequences. *I didn't think through the consequences of promotion... The administration has not really thought through what it plans to do once the fighting stops... It was the first time she'd had a chance to think it through.* PHRASAL VERB V P n (not pron) V P wh V n P

think up. If you **think** something **up**, for example an idea or plan, you invent it using mental effort. *Julian has been thinking up new ways of raising money... 'Where do you get that idea about the piano?'—'Well, I just thought it up.'* PHRASAL VERB V P n (not pron) V n P

thinker /θɪŋkəʳ/ **thinkers.** A **thinker** is a person who spends a lot of time thinking deeply about important things, especially a philosopher who is famous for thinking of new ideas. *There were few influential Marxist thinkers.* ◆◇◇◇◇ N-COUNT

thinking /θɪŋkɪŋ/ ◆◆◆◆◇

1 The general ideas or opinions of a person or group can be referred to as their **thinking**. *There was undeniably a strong theoretical dimension to his thinking. ...the direction of the ANC's thinking on the country's political future... The thinking of economic bureaucrats tends to lag behind changes in world conditions.* N-UNCOUNT: with poss

2 **Thinking** is the activity of using your brain by considering a problem or possibility or creating an idea. *This is a time of decisive action and quick thinking... After the pain of defeat passes, England have some thinking to do.* N-UNCOUNT

3 If you describe someone as **thinking**, you mean that they are intelligent and take an interest in important events and issues, and you approve of this. *Thinking people on both sides will applaud this book... A newspaper had called him 'the thinking man's Tory'.* ADJ: ADJ n PRAGMATICS

4 See also **wishful thinking**. • **to** my **way of thinking**: see **way**.

think-tank, think-tanks. A **think-tank** is a group of experts who are gathered together by an organization, especially by a government, in order to consider various problems and try and work out ways to solve them. *...Moscow's leading foreign policy think-tank.* ◆◇◇◇◇ N-COUNT-COLL

thin-skinned. If you say that someone is **thin-skinned**, you mean that they are easily upset by criticism or unpleasantness; used showing disapproval. *Some fear he is too thin-skinned to survive the rough-and-tumble of a presidential campaign.* ADJ-GRADED: usu v-link ADJ PRAGMATICS =sensitive ≠thick-skinned

third /θɜːʳd/ **thirds** ◆◆◆◆◇

1 The **third** item in a series is the one that you count as number three. *I sleep on the third floor... It was the third time one of his cars had gone up in flames... He came third in the poll with 149 votes... The attack was the third so far this year.* ORD

2 A **third** is one of three equal parts of something. *A third of the cost went into technology and services... Only one third get financial help from their fathers... He divided their kingdom into thirds.* FRACTION

3 You say **third** when you want to make a third point or give a third reason for something. *First, interest rates may take longer to fall than is hoped. Second, in real terms, lending may fall. Third, bad loans could wipe out much of any improvement.* ADV: ADV with cl (not last in cl) PRAGMATICS =thirdly

4 A **third** is the lowest honours degree that can be obtained from a British university. N-COUNT: usu sing

third-class

1 A **third-class** degree is the lowest honours degree that can be obtained from a British university. ADJ: ADJ n

2 In the past, the **third-class** accommodation on a train or ship was the cheapest and least comfortable accommodation. *...third-class passengers.* ADJ: usu ADJ n

► Also an adverb. *...travelling third class.* ADV: ADV after v

third-degree

1 **Third-degree** burns are very severe, destroying tissue under the skin. *He suffered third-degree burns over 98 per cent of his body.* ADJ: ADJ n

2 If you say that someone has been given the **third degree**, you mean that they have been questioned or reprimanded extremely severely, sometimes with physical violence; an informal expression. *The next thing you know, she's phoned to complain and you're suddenly being given the third degree.* N-SING: usu *the* N

thirdly /θɜːʳdli/. You use **thirdly** when you want to make a third point or give a third reason for something. *First of all, there are not many of them, and secondly, they have little money and, thirdly, they have few big businesses.* ◆◇◇◇◇ ADV: ADV with cl (not last in cl) PRAGMATICS =third

third party, third parties. ◆◇◇◇◇

1 A **third party** is someone who is not one of the main people involved in a business agreement or legal case, but who is involved in it in a minor role. *You can instruct your bank to allow a third party to remove money from your account.* N-COUNT

2 **Third-party** insurance is a type of insurance you have that gives financial compensation to people who are hurt or whose property is damaged as a result of something you have done. *Premiums for third-party cover are set to rise by up to 25 per cent.* ADJ

third person. A statement in **the third person** is a statement about another person or thing, and not directly about yourself or about the person you are talking to. The subject of a statement like this is 'he', 'she', 'it', or a name or noun. N-SING: *the* N

third-rate. If you describe something as **third-rate**, you mean that it is of a very poor quality or standard. *...a third-rate movie.* ADJ-GRADED: usu ADJ n

Third World. The countries of Africa, Asia, and South America are sometimes referred to collectively as **the Third World**, especially those parts that are poor, do not have much power, and are ◆◆◆◇◇ N-PROPER: *the* N, N n considered to be underdeveloped. *...development in the Third World. ...Third World debt.*

thirst /θɜːʳst/ **thirsts, thirsting, thirsted** ◆◇◇◇◇

1 Thirst is the feeling that you need to drink something. *Coca is well-known for reducing hunger, thirst and fatigue... Instead of tea or coffee, drink water to quench your thirst... I had such a thirst.* N-VAR

2 Thirst is the condition of not having enough to drink. *They died of thirst on the voyage.* N-UNCOUNT

3 A **thirst** for something is a very strong desire for that thing. *Children show a real thirst for learning. ...their ever-growing thirst for cash.* N-SING: usu N *for* n =hunger

4 If you say that someone **thirsts** for something, you mean that they have a strong desire for it; a literary use. *We all thirst for the same things.* VERB =hunger V *for/after* n

thirsty /θɜːʳsti/ **thirstier, thirstiest** ◆◇◇◇◇

1 If you are **thirsty**, you feel a need to drink something. *If a baby is thirsty, it feeds more often... Drink whenever you feel thirsty during exercise.* ADJ-GRADED: usu v-link ADJ

♦ **thirstily** /θɜːʳstɪli/ *The child nodded, drinking her milk thirstily.* ADV: ADV after v

2 If you are **thirsty for** something, you have a strong desire for it; a literary use. *People should understand how thirsty for revenge they are.* ADJ-GRADED: v-link ADJ *for* n =hungry

thirteen /θɜːʳtiːn/ **thirteens. Thirteen** is the number 13. ◆◆◆◆◆ NUM

thirteenth /θɜːʳtiːnθ/. The **thirteenth** item in a series is the one that you count as number thirteen. ◆◆◆◆◇ ORD

thirtieth /θɜːʳtiəθ/. The **thirtieth** item in a series is the one that you count as number thirty. ◆◆◆◆◇ ORD

thirty /θɜːʳti/ **thirties.** ◆◆◆◆◆

1 Thirty is the number 30. NUM

2 When you talk about the **thirties**, you are referring to numbers between 30 and 39. For example, if you are **in your thirties**, you are aged between 30 and 39. If the temperature is **in the thirties**, the temperature is between 30 and 39 degrees. *Mozart clearly enjoyed good health throughout his twenties and early thirties.* N-PLURAL

3 The thirties is the decade between 1930 and 1939. *She became quite a notable director in the thirties and forties.* N-PLURAL: *the* N

this. The determiner is pronounced /ðɪs/. In other cases, **this** is pronounced /ðɪs/. ◆◆◆◆◆

1 You use **this** to refer back to a particular person or thing that has been mentioned or implied. *When food comes out of any oven, it should stand a while. During this delay the centre carries on cooking... On 1 October the US suspended a proposed $574 million aid package for 1991. Of this amount, $250 million is for military purchases.* ► Also a pronoun. *He's had these turns before but he has never had one like this.* DET: DET sing-n/ n-uncount PRAGMATICS; PRON

2 You use **this** to introduce someone or something that you are going to talk about. *This is what I will do. I will telephone Anna and explain.* ► Also a determiner. *This report from David Cook of our Science Unit: "One of the biggest questions surrounding animal evolution is why did the dinosaurs become extinct about 70 million years ago?".* PRON; DET: DET sing-n/ n-uncount

3 You use **this** to refer back to an idea or situation expressed in a previous sentence or sentences. *You feel that it's uneconomic to insist that people work together in groups. Why is this?... A job is pretty much nine-to-five. Is this what you feel would make you happy?* ► Also a determiner. *There have been continual demands for action by the political authorities to put an end to this situation.* PRON PRAGMATICS; DET: DET sing-n/ n-uncount

4 In spoken English, people use **this** to introduce a person or thing into a story; an informal use. *I came here by chance and was just watching what was going on, when this girl attacked me... So I just walked up the steps into this big, beautiful church.* DET: DET sing-n PRAGMATICS

5 You use **this** to refer to a person or thing that is near you, especially when you touch them or point to them. When there are two or more people or things near you, **this** refers to the nearest one. *'If you'd prefer something else I'll gladly have it changed for you.'—'No, this is great.'... 'Is this what you were looking for?' Bradley produced the handkerchief... This is my colleague, Mr Arnold Landon.* PRON ► Also a determiner. *David beckons me to an archway behind the lectern. 'This church was built by the Emperor Constantine Monomarchus in the eleventh century.'* DET: DET sing-n

6 You use **this** when you refer to a general situation, activity, or event which is happening or has just happened and which you feel involved in. *I thought, this is why I've travelled thousands of miles... Tim, this is awful. I know what you must think, but it's not so... Is this what you want to do with the rest of your life?* PRON: PRON with *be*

7 You use **this** when you refer to the place you are in now or to the present time. *We've stopped shipping weapons to this country by train... This place is run like a hotel ought to be run... I think coffee is probably the best thing at this point... Nothing seems certain in this crucial period in Pakistan's political life.* ► Also a pronoun. *This is the worst place I've come across... This could have been one of the coldest golf tournaments on record.* DET: DET sing-n/ n-uncount; PRON

8 You use **this** to refer to the next occurrence in the future of a particular day, month, season, or festival. *...this Sunday's 7.45 performance... We're getting married this June... Jordan's own-label collection of sweatshirts, T-shirts and caps will be available this Christmas.* DET: DET sing-n

9 You use **this** when you are indicating the size or shape of something with your hands. *They'd said the wound was only about this big you see and he showed me with his fingers.* ADV: ADV adj

10 You use **this** when you are going to specify how much you know or how much you can tell someone. *I am not going to reveal what my seven-year plan is, but I will tell you this much, if it works out, the next seven years will be very interesting.* ADV: ADV adv

11 If you say **this is it**, you are agreeing with what someone else has just said. *'You know, people conveniently forget the things they say.'—'Well this is it.'* CONVENTION PRAGMATICS =this is true

12 You use **this** in order to say who you are or what organization you are representing, when you are speaking on the telephone, radio, or television. *Hello, this is John Thompson... 'Hello, is this Raymond Brown?'—'Yeah, who's this?'... This is NPR, National Public Radio.* PRON

13 You use **this** to refer to the medium of communication that you are using at the time of speaking or writing. *What I'm going to do in this lecture is focus on something very specific... What a book can do, and what this one will try to accomplish, is to present examples of how life can be made more enjoyable... Later in this chapter, I recommend several specific steps we need to take.* DET: DET sing-n

14 See also **these**.

15 If you say that you are doing or talking about **this and that**, or **this, that, and the other** you mean that you are doing or talking about a variety of things that you do not want to specify. *'And what are you doing now?'—'Oh this and that.'... I want to make a point about all these charges going up, water rates and all this that and the other.* PHRASE

thistle /θɪsᵊl/ **thistles.** A **thistle** is a wild plant with prickly leaves and purple flowers. N-COUNT

thither /ðɪðəʳ/. **Thither** means to the place that has already been mentioned; an old-fashioned word. *They have dragged themselves thither for shelter.* ● **hither and thither**: see **hither**. ADV: ADV after v =there

tho'; also spelled **tho. Tho'** and **tho** are very informal written forms of **though**.

thong /θɒŋ, AM θɔːŋ/ **thongs**

1 A **thong** is a long thin strip of leather, plastic, or rubber. N-COUNT

2 A **thong** is a narrow band of cloth that is worn between a person's legs to cover up his or her sexual organs, and that is held up by a piece of string around the waist. N-COUNT

3 In American English, **thongs** are sandals which are held on your foot by a V-shaped strap that goes between your big toe and the toe next to it. The usual British word is **flip-flops**. N-COUNT: usu pl

thoracic /θɔːræsɪk/. **Thoracic** means relating to or affecting your thorax; a medical term. *...diseases of the thoracic area.* ADJ: ADJ n

thorax /θɔːræks/ **thoraxes** or **thoraces** /θɔːrəsiːz/

1 Your **thorax** is the part of your body between your neck and your waist; a medical use. N-COUNT: usu sing

2 An insect's **thorax** is the central part of its body to which the legs and wings are attached; a technical use in biology. N-COUNT: usu sing

thorn /θɔːʳn/ **thorns** ◆◇◇◇◇

1 **Thorns** are the sharp points on some plants and trees, for example on a rose bush. *Roses will always have thorns but with care they can be avoided.* N-COUNT =prickle

2 A **thorn** or a **thorn bush** or a **thorn tree** is a bush or tree such as a hawthorn which has a lot of thorns on it. *...the shade of a thorn bush. ...the thorn and bramble thickets.* N-VAR

3 If you describe someone or something as a **thorn in** your **side** or **a thorn in** your **flesh**, you mean that they are a constant problem or annoyance to you. *She's a real thorn in his side... The Party was a thorn in the flesh of his coalition.* PHRASE: v-link PHR

thorny /θɔːʳni/ **thornier, thorniest** ◆◇◇◇◇

1 A **thorny** plant or tree is covered with thorns. *...thorny hawthorn trees.* ADJ: usu ADJ n

2 If you describe a problem as **thorny**, you mean that it is very complicated and difficult to solve, and that people are often unwilling to discuss it. *...the thorny issue of immigration policy... It is essential that we tackle this thorny problem.* ADJ-GRADED: usu ADJ n =knotty

thorough /θʌrə, AM θɜːroʊ/ ◆◆◆◇◇

1 A **thorough** action or activity is one that is done very carefully and methodically so that nothing is forgotten. *We are making a thorough investigation... This very thorough survey goes back to 1784... How thorough is the assessment?* ADJ-GRADED: usu ADJ n =exhaustive ♦ **thoroughly** *Food that is being offered hot must be reheated thoroughly. ...a thoroughly researched and illuminating biography.* ADV-GRADED: ADV with v ♦ **thoroughness** *The thoroughness of the evaluation process we went through was impressive.* N-UNCOUNT

2 Someone who is **thorough** is always very careful and methodical in their work. *Martin would be a good judge, I thought. He was calm and thorough... The men were expert, thorough and careful.* ADJ-GRADED: usu v-link ADJ ♦ **thoroughness** *His thoroughness and attention to detail is legendary.* N-UNCOUNT

3 **Thorough** is used to emphasize the great degree or extent of something. *I was a thorough little academic snob... We regard the band as a thorough shambles.* ADJ: det ADJ PRAGMATICS =complete ♦ **thoroughly** *I thoroughly enjoy your programme... We returned home thoroughly contented.* ADV-GRADED: ADV before v, ADV adj

thoroughbred /θʌrəbred, AM θɜːroʊ-/ **thoroughbreds** ◆◇◇◇◇

1 A **thoroughbred** is a horse that has parents that are of the same high quality breed. N-COUNT

2 A **thoroughbred** is a particular breed of racing horse. *...a thoroughbred stallion.* N-COUNT: oft N n

thoroughfare /θʌrəfeəʳ, AM θɜːroʊ-/ **thoroughfares.** A **thoroughfare** is a main road in a town or city which usually has shops along it and a lot of traffic; a formal word. *...a busy thoroughfare.* N-COUNT: usu supp N

thoroughgoing /θʌrəgoʊɪŋ, AM θɜːroʊ-/; also spelled **thorough-going.**

1 You use **thoroughgoing** to emphasize that someone or something is fully or completely the type of person or thing specified. *...a thoroughgoing conservative. ...readers who are unhappy with such thoroughgoing materialism.* ADJ-GRADED: usu ADJ n PRAGMATICS

2 If you describe a piece of work as **thoroughgoing**, you approve of it because it has been carefully and thoroughly put together. *...a thoroughgoing review of prison conditions. ...this splendidly thoroughgoing biography.* ADJ-GRADED: usu ADJ n PRAGMATICS =thorough

those. The determiner is pronounced /ðoʊz/. The pronoun is pronounced /ðoʊz/. ◆◆◆◆◆

1 You use **those** to refer to people or things which have already been mentioned. *Theoretically he had control over more than $400 million in US accounts. But, in fact, it was the US Treasury and State Department who controlled those accounts... They have the aircraft capable of doing significant damage, because most of those aircraft are capable of launching anti-ship missiles.* DET: DET pl-n PRAGMATICS ► Also a pronoun. *I understand that there are a number of projects going on. Could you tell us a little bit about those?... Waterfalls never fail to attract and those at the Falls of Clyde are no exception.* PRON

2 You use **those** when you are referring to people or things that are a distance away from you in position or time, especially when you indicate or point to them. *What are those buildings?... Oh, those books! I meant to put them away before this afternoon.* DET: DET pl-n ► Also a pronoun. *Those are nice shoes. Where'd you get them?... Excuse me. What are those for?... I think those are my earrings.* PRON

3 You use **those** to refer to someone or something when you are going to give details or information about them; a formal use. *Those people who took up weapons to defend themselves are political prisoners... The point of home bread-making is to avoid those additives used in much commercial baking.* DET: DET pl-n

4 You use **those** to introduce more information about something already mentioned, instead of repeating the noun which refers to it; a formal use. *The interests he is most likely to enjoy will be those which enable him to show off himself or his talents... The cells of the body, especially those of the brain, can live only minutes without circulating blood.* PRON: PRON pron-rel, PRON *of* n

5 You use **those** to mean 'people'. *A little selfish behaviour is unlikely to cause real damage to those around us... A number of leading opposition figures were said to be among those arrested.* PRON: PRON prep/adj/-ed, PRON pron-rel

6 You use **those** when you refer to things that you expect the hearer to know about or when you are checking that you are both thinking of the same people or things. *He did buy me those daffodils a week or so ago... I have been putting pressure onto the Cleansing Services to replace those dustbin lids... I believe they've doubled their turnover since those advertisements appeared in the press. ...those embarrassing moments we all have.* DET: DET pl-n

thou /ðaʊ/. **Thou** is an old-fashioned, poetic, or religious word for 'you' when you are talking to only one person. It is used as the subject of a verb. ● See also **holier-than-thou.** ◆◇◇◇◇ PRON-SING

though. Pronounced /ðoʊ/ for meanings 1 and 2, and /ðoʊ/ for meanings 3 to 5. ◆◆◆◆◆

1 You use **though** to introduce a statement in a subordinate clause which contrasts with the statement in the main clause. You often use **though** to indicate that the statement in the main clause is surprising or unexpected, or to admit a fact which you regard as less important than the fact in the main clause. *Gaelic has been a dying language for many years, though children are nowadays taught it in school... After news of this new court case Ford broke down again, though he blamed the breakdown on his work... He's very attractive, though certainly not a ladykiller... Cleveland has always had a reputation for being a dirty, ugly, boring city, though now they say it is much better.* CONJ-SUBORD PRAGMATICS =although

2 You use **though** to introduce a subordinate clause which gives some information that is relevant to the main clause and weakens the force of what it is saying. *I look back on it as the bloodiest (though not literally) winter of the war... The problem was finally, though not conclusively, identified as a severely pinched nerve... His achievements, though hardly exciting, were widely admired.* CONJ-SUBORD PRAGMATICS =although

3 You use **though** to indicate that the information in a clause contrasts with or modifies information given in a previous sentence or sentences. *I like him. Though he makes me angry sometimes... I want to try my hand at politics, or go back to the law. I don't want to go to school for it, though... It might be worth your while to go to court. This is tricky, though, and you'll need expert advice.* ADV: ADV with cl PRAGMATICS =although

4 You say **though I say it myself** or **though I say so myself** after praising yourself or something you have done, in order to sound less boastful. *I'm a good cook, though I say it myself.* PHRASE: PHR with cl PRAGMATICS

5 ● **as though**: see **as.** ● **even though**: see **even.**

thought /θɔːt/ **thoughts** ◆◆◆◆◆
1 **Thought** is the past tense and past participle of **think**.
2 A **thought** is an idea that you have in your mind. *The thought of Nick made her throat tighten... I tormented myself with the thought that life was just too comfortable... He pushed the thought from his mind... I've just had a thought.* N-COUNT: oft N *of* n/-ing, N that
3 A person's **thoughts** are their mind, or all the ideas in their mind when they are concentrating on one particular thing. *I jumped to my feet so my thoughts wouldn't start to wander... Usually at this time our thoughts are on Christmas... If he wasn't there physically, he was always in her thoughts.* N-PLURAL: usu poss N
4 A person's **thoughts** are their opinions on a particular subject. *Many of you have written to us to express your thoughts on the conflict... Mr Goodman, do you have any thoughts on that?* N-PLURAL: oft poss N, N *on/about* n
5 **Thought** is the activity of thinking, especially deeply, logically, or with concentration. *Alice had been so deep in thought that she had walked past her car without even seeing it... He had given some thought to what she had told him... After much thought I decided to end my marriage. ...the differences between his thought processes and ours.* N-UNCOUNT
6 A **thought** is an intention, hope, or reason for doing something. *Sarah's first thought was to run back and get Max... They had no thought of surrender... Mansell has now banished all thoughts of retirement.* N-COUNT: oft N *of* n
7 A **thought** is an act of kindness or an offer of help; used especially when you are thanking someone, or expressing admiration of someone. *'Would you like to move into the ward?'—'A kind thought, but no, thank you.'... 'She has given them this seven hundred pounds.' 'What a lovely thought.'* N-SING: with supp, oft adj N PRAGMATICS
8 **Thought** is the group of ideas and beliefs or way of thinking which belongs, for example, to a particular religion, philosopher, political party, or scientist. *Aristotle's scientific theories dominated Western thought for fifteen hundred years... This school of thought argues that depression is best treated by drugs.* N-UNCOUNT
9 See also **second thought**.

thoughtful /θɔːtfʊl/ ◆◆◇◇◇
1 If you are **thoughtful**, you are quiet and serious because you are thinking about something. *Nancy, who had been thoughtful for some time, suddenly spoke... He was looking very thoughtful... She had a thoughtful expression on her face.* ♦ **thoughtfully** *Daniel nodded thoughtfully.* ADJ-GRADED =pensive; ADV-GRADED: ADV with v
2 If you describe someone as **thoughtful**, you approve of them because they remember what other people want, need, or feel, and try not to upset them. *...a thoughtful and caring man... Thank you. That's very thoughtful of you... It was a very kind and thoughtful gesture.* ♦ **thoughtfully** *...the bottle of wine he had thoughtfully purchased for the celebrations.* ♦ **thoughtfulness** *I can't tell you how much I appreciate your thoughtfulness.* ADJ-GRADED: oft ADJ *of* n PRAGMATICS =considerate ≠thoughtless; ADV-GRADED: ADV with v; N-UNCOUNT
3 If you describe something such as a book, film, or speech as **thoughtful**, you mean that it is serious and well thought out. *...a thoughtful and scholarly book.* ♦ **thoughtfully** *...these thoughtfully designed machines.* ADJ-GRADED; ADV-GRADED: ADV with v

thoughtless /θɔːtləs/. If you describe someone as **thoughtless**, you are critical of them because they forget or ignore other people's wants, needs, or feelings. *...a small minority of thoughtless and inconsiderate people... It was thoughtless of her to mention it... It was just a thoughtless remark.* ♦ **thoughtlessly** *They thoughtlessly planned a picnic without him... Nobody is perfect, and everyone acts thoughtlessly on occasion.* ♦ **thoughtlessness** *What women mistake as thoughtlessness is often just diffidence.* ADJ-GRADED PRAGMATICS ≠thoughtful; ADV-GRADED: ADV with v; N-UNCOUNT

thousand /θaʊzənd/ **thousands** The plural form is **thousand** after a number, or after a word or expression referring to a number, such as 'several' or 'a few'. ◆◆◆◆◆
1 A **thousand** or one **thousand** is the number 1,000. *...five thousand acres... Visitors can expect to pay about a thousand pounds a day.* NUM: usu *a*/num NUM
2 If you refer to **thousands of** things or people, you are emphasizing that there are very many of them. *Thousands of refugees are packed into overcrowded towns and villages... I must have driven past that place thousands of times.* ► Also a pronoun. *Hundreds have been killed in the fighting and thousands made homeless.* QUANT: QUANT *of* pl-n PRAGMATICS; PRON
3 ● **a thousand and one**: see **one**.

thousandth /θaʊzənθ/ **thousandths**
1 The **thousandth** item in a series is the one that you count as number one thousand. *The magazine has just published its six thousandth edition.* ► If you say that something has happened for the **thousandth** time, you are emphasizing that it has happened again and that it has already happened a great many times. *The phone rings for the thousandth time.* ORD; ORD PRAGMATICS
2 A **thousandth** is one of a thousand equal parts of something. *...a dust particle weighing only a thousandth of a gram.* FRACTION

thrall /θrɔːl/. If you say that someone is in **thrall** to a person or thing, you mean that they are completely in their power or are greatly influenced by them; a formal word. *He is not in thrall to the media... Tomorrow's children will be even more in the thrall of the silicon chip.* N-UNCOUNT: oft *in* N *to* n

thrash /θræʃ/ **thrashes, thrashing, thrashed** ◆◇◇◇◇
1 If one player or team **thrashes** another in a game or contest, they defeat them easily or by a large score; an informal use. *Second-placed Rangers thrashed St Johnstone 5-nil.* VERB =hammer; V n amount, Also V n
2 If you **thrash** someone, you hit them several times as a punishment. *'Liar!' Sarah screamed, as she thrashed the child. 'You stole it.'* VERB; V n
3 If someone **thrashes** about, or **thrashes** their arms or legs about, they move in a wild or violent way, often hitting against something. You can also say that someone's arms or legs **thrash** about. *Many of the crew died a terrible death as they thrashed about in shark-infested waters. ...dreams so vivid that I thrash inside my sleeping bag and cry out... Jimmy collapsed on the floor, thrashing his legs about like an injured racehorse.* V-ERG; V adv/prep, V n adv/prep
4 If something or someone **thrashes** something, or **thrashes** at something, they hit it continually in a violent or noisy way. *...a magnificent paddle-steamer on the mighty Mississippi, her huge wheel thrashing the muddy water... Three shaggy-haired men thrash tunelessly at their guitars.* ► Also a noun. *...the thrash of the horses' hooves.* VERB; V n, V *at* n; N-SING
5 **Thrash** or **thrash metal** is a type of pop music that consists of loud, fast, simple guitar tunes; used in pop music journalism. *...a dozen high energy throwaway thrash tunes.* N-UNCOUNT
6 A **thrash** is a party; an informal use. *Harry always invited Charlie when he threw a thrash in his office.* N-COUNT =bash
7 See also **thrashing**.

thrash out PHRASAL VERB
1 If people **thrash out** something such as a plan or an agreement, they decide on it after a great deal of discussion. *The foreign ministers have thrashed out a suitable compromise formula... How foreign fund-managers will be compensated has yet to be thrashed out.* =hammer out; V P n (not pron)/wh, Also V n P
2 If people **thrash out** a problem or a dispute, they discuss it thoroughly until they reach an agreement. *...a sincere effort by two people to thrash out differences about which they have strong feelings.* =settle, resolve; V P n (not pron), Also V n P

thrashing /θræʃɪŋ/ **thrashings** ◆◇◇◇◇
1 If one player or team gives another one a **thrashing**, they defeat them easily or by a large score; an informal use. *She dropped only eight points in the 43-minute thrashing of the former Wimbledon champion. ...a school renowned for handing out 10-goal thrashings in association football.* N-COUNT: usu with supp =hammering
2 If someone gives someone else a **thrashing**, they hit them several times as a punishment. *If Sarah caught her, she would get a thrashing.* N-COUNT =hiding, beating
3 See also **thrash**.

thread /θred/ **threads, threading, threaded** ◆◆◇◇◇

1 **Thread** or a **thread** is a long very thin piece of a material such as cotton, nylon, or silk, especially one that is used in sewing. *This time I'll do it properly with a needle and thread. ...a tiny Nepalese hat embroidered with golden threads.* N-VAR

2 The **thread** of an argument, a story, or a situation is an aspect of it that connects all the different parts together. *The thread running through many of these proposals was the theme of individual power and opportunity... All religions are united by the common threads of fighting evil and helping others... The possible consequences so filled his mind that he lost the thread of Wan Da's narrative.* N-COUNT: usu with supp

3 A **thread** of something such as liquid, light, or colour is a long thin line or piece of it. *A thin, glistening thread of moisture ran along the rough concrete sill. ...Venetian glass decorated with embedded threads of white. ...a corpulent man with threads of black hair plastered across his brow.* N-COUNT: usu N *of* n

4 In American English, you can refer to clothes as **threads**; an informal use. *...a cheap place to pick up natty threads.* N-PLURAL

5 The **thread** on a screw, or on something such as a lid or a pipe, is the raised spiral line of metal or plastic around it which allows it to be fixed in place by twisting. *The screw threads will be able to get a good grip.* N-COUNT

6 If you **thread** your way through a group of people or things, or **thread** through it, you move through it carefully or slowly, changing direction frequently as you move. *Slowly she threaded her way back through the moving mass of bodies. ...threading our way past little boats... We threaded through a network of back streets.* VERB V *way* prep/adv V prep

7 If you **thread** a long thin object through something, you pass it through one or more holes or narrow spaces. *...threading the laces through the eyelets of his shoes... Air ducts and electrical cables were threaded through the complex structure... Instruments developed at the hospital allow doctors to thread microscopic telescopes into the digestive tract.* VERB V n *through* n V n *into* n

8 If you **thread** small objects such as beads onto a string or thread, you join them together by pushing the string through them. *Wipe the mushrooms clean and thread them on a string.* VERB V n prep

9 When you **thread** a needle, you put a piece of thread through the hole in the top of the needle in order to sew with it. *I sit down, thread a needle, snip off an old button.* VERB V n

10 If you say that something **is hanging by a thread**, you mean that it is in a very uncertain state and is unlikely to survive or succeed. *The fragile peace was hanging by a thread as thousands of communist hardliners took to the streets.* PHRASES V inflects

11 If you **pick up the threads of** an activity, you start it again after an interruption. If you **pick up the threads of** your **life**, you become more active again after a period of failure or bad luck. *Many women have been able to pick up the threads of their former career.* V inflects

threadbare /θredbeəʳ/

1 **Threadbare** clothes, carpets, and other pieces of cloth look old, dull, and very thin, because they have been worn or used too much. *She sat cross-legged on a square of threadbare carpet.* ADJ-GRADED =worn

2 If you describe an activity, an idea, or an argument as **threadbare**, you mean that it is very weak, or inadequate, or old and no longer interesting. *...the government's threadbare domestic policies.* ADJ-GRADED

threat /θret/ **threats** ◆◆◆◆◇

1 A **threat** to someone or something is a danger that something unpleasant might happen to them. A **threat** is also the cause of this danger. *Some couples see single women as a threat to their relationships... The Hurricane Center warns people not to take the threat of tropical storms lightly... All countries in the region had the right to protect themselves against external threat.* N-VAR: with supp, oft N *to/from* n, N *of* n

2 A **threat** is a statement by someone that they will do something unpleasant, especially if you do not do what they want. *He may be forced to carry out his threat to resign... The priest remains in hiding after threats by former officials of the ousted dictatorship... The terrorist made a death threat.* N-COUNT: usu with supp, oft N to-inf

3 If someone or something is **under threat**, there is a danger that something unpleasant might be done to them, or that they might cease to exist. *His position as leader will be under threat at a party congress due next month... She lives daily under threat of violence... Even the most security-conscious computer user is under constant threat from computer viruses.* PHRASE: oft PHR *of/from* n

threaten /θretᵊn/ **threatens, threatening, threatened** ◆◆◆◆◇

1 If someone **threatens** to do something unpleasant to you, or if they **threaten** you, they say or imply that they will do something unpleasant to you, especially if you do not do what they want. *He said army officers had threatened to destroy the town... He tied her up and threatened her with a six-inch knife... If you threaten me or use any force, I shall inform the police.* VERB V to-inf V n *with* n V n Also V that

2 If something or someone **threatens** a person or thing, they are likely to harm that person or thing. *The newcomers directly threaten the livelihood of the established workers... The unity of our society is threatened by troublesome and restless minorities... 30 percent of reptiles, birds, and fish are currently threatened with extinction.* VERB V n be V-ed *with* n

3 If something unpleasant **threatens** to happen, it seems likely to happen. *The fighting is threatening to turn into full-scale war... Plants must be covered with a leaf-mould or similarly protected if frost threatens.* VERB V to-inf V

4 See also **threatened, threatening.**

threatened /θretᵊnd/. If you feel **threatened**, you feel as if someone is trying to harm you. *Anger is the natural reaction we experience when we feel threatened or frustrated... The survey found that 4 per cent of people felt threatened by the sight of beggars.* • See also **threaten.** ◆◇◇◇◇ ADJ-GRADED: v-link ADJ, oft ADJ *by* n

threatening /θretənɪŋ/. You can describe someone's behaviour as **threatening**, when you think that they are trying to harm you. *The police could have charged them with threatening behaviour... She said Denny had received a threatening letter and asked me if I sent it.* ♦ **threateningly** *'This ain't no affair of yours, boy!' McClosky said threateningly.* • See also **threaten; life-threatening.** ◆◆◆◇◇ ADJ-GRADED: usu ADJ n ADV-GRADED: usu ADV with v

three /θriː/ **threes.** **Three** is the number 3. *We waited three months before going back to see the specialist.* ◆◆◆◆◆ NUM

three-cornered. If you describe something such as a disagreement, competition, or game as **three-cornered**, you mean that it involves three people, groups, or teams; used mainly in British English. *...the three-cornered struggle between employers and male and female workers. ...a three-cornered contest.* ADJ: usu ADJ n

three-dimensional ◆◇◇◇◇

1 A **three-dimensional** object is solid rather than flat, because it can be measured in three dimensions, usually the height, depth, and width. The abbreviation '3-D' can also be used. *...a three-dimensional model. ...the three-dimensional structure of DNA.* ADJ

2 A **three-dimensional** picture, image, or film looks as though it is deep or solid rather than flat. The abbreviation '3-D' can also be used. *...new software, which generates both two-dimensional drawings and three-dimensional images. ...three dimensional pictures created by lasers.* ADJ

3 If you describe fictional characters as **three-dimensional** you mean that they seem real and lifelike; used showing approval. *She emerges as a full, three-dimensional character in a way that few horror genre heroines ever do.* ADJ-GRADED PRAGMATICS

4 **Three-dimensional** art or design is produced by carving or shaping stone, wood, clay, or other materials. The abbreviation '3-D' can also be used. *...a degree in three-dimensional art.* ADJ: ADJ n

three-fourths. In American English, **three-fourths of** a particular thing is an amount that is equal to three out of four equal parts of that thing. The commoner American word and the usual British word is **three-quarters.** *Three-fourths of the apartments in the ghetto had no heat... Government expenditures absorbed nearly three-fourths of the national income.* ► Also a pronoun. *He has just under 1,600 delegates, about three-fourths what he needs to win the Democratic presidential nomination.*
QUANT: QUANT of n
PRON

three-line whip, three-line whips. In some countries, when a political party issues a **three-line whip**, the MPs in that party are ordered to attend parliament and vote in a particular way on a particular issue; used in British English.
N-COUNT

three-point turn, three-point turns. When the driver of a vehicle does a **three-point turn**, he or she turns the vehicle by driving forwards in a curve, then backwards in a curve, and then forwards in a curve.
N-COUNT

three-quarter; also spelled **three quarter.** You can use **three-quarter** to describe something which is three fourths of the usual size or three fourths of a standard measurement. *Choose short or three-quarter sleeves for summer. ...a session which lasted one and three-quarter hours. ...three-quarter length coats... There was a three-quarter moon tonight.*
◆◇◇◇◇ ADJ: ADJ n

three-quarters; also spelled **three quarters. Three-quarters** is an amount that is three out of four equal parts of something. *Three-quarters of the country's workers took part in the strike... It took him about three-quarters of an hour.* ► Also a pronoun. *Road deaths have increased by three-quarters... I'm 29 and three-quarters.* ► Also an adverb. *We were left with an open bottle of champagne three-quarters full... Remove the vegetables from the steamer when they are three-quarters cooked.*
◆◆◇◇◇ QUANT: QUANT of n =three-fourths
PRON
ADV: ADV adj/-ed

three Rs. When talking about children's education, **the three Rs** are the basic skills of reading, writing, and arithmetic. *...ministers who want teachers to concentrate on the three Rs.*
N-PLURAL: the N

threesome /θriːsəm/ **threesomes.** A **threesome** is a group of three people.
N-COUNT

three-wheeler, three-wheelers. A **three-wheeler** is a bicycle or car with three wheels.
N-COUNT

thresh /θreʃ/ **threshes, threshing, threshed.** When a cereal such as corn, wheat, or rice **is threshed**, it is beaten in order to separate the grains from the rest of the plant. *The corn was still sown, cut and threshed as it was a hundred years ago.* ♦ **threshing** *Spring and summer are taken up by the reaping of hay and the threshing of corn. ...a threshing machine.*
VB: usu passive
be V-ed Also V
N-UNCOUNT: oft N n

threshold /θreʃhoʊld/ **thresholds**
◆◆◇◇◇

1 The **threshold** of a building or room is the floor in the doorway, or the doorway itself. *He stopped at the threshold of the bedroom... The bride was carried over the threshold.*
N-COUNT: usu sing

2 A **threshold** is an amount, level, or limit on a scale. When the **threshold** is reached, something else happens or changes. *She has a low threshold of boredom and needs the constant stimulation of physical activity... The consensus has clearly shifted in favour of raising the nuclear threshold... Fewer than forty per cent voted – the threshold for results to be valid.*
N-COUNT: usu with supp, oft N of n, n N

3 If you are **on the threshold of** something exciting or new, you are about to experience it. *We are on the threshold of a new era in astronomy. ...a lovely girl on the threshold of growing up.*
PHRASE: PHR n/-ing

threw /θruː/. **Threw** is the past tense of **throw.**

thrice /θraɪs/

1 Something that happens **thrice** happens three times; an old-fashioned use. *They should think not twice, but thrice, before ignoring such advice... She plays tennis thrice weekly.*
ADV: ADV with v, ADV adv, ADV n

2 You can use **thrice** to indicate that something is three times the size, value, or intensity of something else; an old-fashioned use. *The metal had been valued at twice or thrice its current price. ...moving at thrice the speed of sound.*
ADV: ADV n

thrift /θrɪft/ **thrifts**
◆◆◇◇◇

1 **Thrift** is the quality and practice of being careful with money and not wasting things; used showing approval. *They were rightly praised for their thrift and enterprise.*
N-UNCOUNT PRAGMATICS ≠extravagance

2 In America, a **thrift** or a **thrift institution** is a kind of savings bank.
N-COUNT

thrift shop, thrift shops. In American English, a **thrift shop** or a **thrift store** is a shop that sells second-hand goods cheaply and gives its profits to a charity. The British term is **charity shop.**
N-COUNT

thrifty /θrɪfti/ **thriftier, thriftiest.** If you say that someone is **thrifty**, you are praising them for saving money, not buying unnecessary things, and not wasting things. *My mother taught me to be thrifty. ...thrifty shoppers.*
ADJ-GRADED PRAGMATICS

thrill /θrɪl/ **thrills, thrilling, thrilled**
◆◆◇◇◇

1 If something gives you a **thrill**, it gives you a sudden feeling of great excitement, pleasure, or fear. *I can remember the thrill of not knowing what I would get on Christmas morning... It's a great thrill for a cricket-lover like me to play at the home of cricket. ...the realization that new adventures, new thrills, and new worlds lie ahead.*
N-COUNT: usu sing, oft N of n/-ing

2 If something **thrills** you, or if you **thrill** at it, it gives you a feeling of great pleasure and excitement. *The electric atmosphere both terrified and thrilled him... The children will thrill at all their favourite characters.*
V-ERG
V n
V at/to n

3 See also **thrilled, thrilling.**

4 If you refer to **thrills and spills**, you are referring to an experience which is exciting and full of surprises. *Its prime audience lies in the 17 to 24 age group, and they want instant thrills and spills.*
PHRASE

thrilled /θrɪld/.
◆◇◇◇◇

1 If someone is **thrilled**, they are extremely pleased about something. *I was so thrilled to get a good report from him... Sue and John were especially thrilled with this award... I'm really thrilled that the public have taken to the song.* ● If you say that someone is **thrilled to bits**, you are emphasizing the fact that they are extremely pleased about something. *I'm thrilled to bits to have won the cash... He's thrilled to bits at the news... He just thoroughly enjoyed reading it with me and was thrilled to bits that it was his very own story.*
ADJ-GRADED: v-link ADJ, oft ADJ to-inf, ADJ prep, ADJ that
PHRASE: v-link PHR, oft PHR to-inf, PHR at/with n/-ing PRAGMATICS

2 See also **thrill.**

thriller /θrɪləʳ/ **thrillers.** A **thriller** is a book, film, or play that tells an exciting fictional story about something such as criminal activities or spying. *...a tense psychological thriller.*
◆◆◇◇◇ N-COUNT

thrilling /θrɪlɪŋ/.
◆◇◇◇◇

1 Something that is **thrilling** is very exciting and enjoyable. *Our wildlife trips offer a thrilling encounter with wildlife in its natural state.* ♦ **thrillingly** *Watson has a wonderful voice, with thrillingly clear top notes... I have seen them play many times, but never as thrillingly and flawlessly as tonight.*
ADJ-GRADED =exciting
ADV-GRADED: ADV adj, ADV with v

2 See also **thrill.**

thrive /θraɪv/ **thrives, thriving, thrived**
◆◆◇◇◇

1 If someone or something **thrives**, they do well and are successful, healthy, or strong. *Today his company continues to thrive... Lavender thrives in poor soil. ...the river's thriving population of kingfishers.*
VERB
V
V-ing

2 If you say that someone **thrives on** a particular situation, you mean that they enjoy it or that they can deal with it very well, especially when other people find it unpleasant or difficult. *Many people thrive on a stressful lifestyle... Creative people are usually very determined and thrive on overcoming obstacles.*
VERB
V on n/-ing

thro'; also spelled **thro. Thro'** is sometimes used in informal written English as an abbreviation for **through.**

throat /θroʊt/ **throats**

1 Your **throat** is the back of your mouth and the top part of the tubes that go down into your stomach
N-COUNT: oft poss N

and your lungs. *She had a sore throat... As she stared at him she felt her throat go dry.*

2 Your **throat** is the front part of your neck. *His striped tie was loosened at his throat.* N-COUNT: oft poss N

3 If you **clear** your **throat**, you cough once in order to make it easier to speak or to attract people's attention. *Cross cleared his throat and spoke in low, polite tones.* PHRASES V inflects

4 If you **ram** something **down** someone's **throat** or **force** it **down** their **throat**, you keep mentioning something such as an idea in order to make them accept it or believe it. *I've always been close to my dad but he's never rammed his career down my throat... I can't understand why we're trying to ram Shakespeare down their throats.* V inflects

5 If two people or groups are **at each other's throats**, they are quarrelling or fighting violently with each other. *The idea that Billy and I are at each other's throats couldn't be further from the truth.* v-link PHR, PHR after v =at loggerheads

6 If something **sticks in** your **throat**, you find it unacceptable. *What sticks in my throat is that I wasn't able to win the trophy... She wanted to ask if he had news of Keith, but the words stuck in her throat.* V inflects

7 ● **a lump in** your **throat**: see **lump**.

throaty /θroʊti/. A **throaty** voice, whisper, or laugh is low and rather rough. ADJ-GRADED =hoarse

throb /θrɒb/ **throbs, throbbing, throbbed** ◆◇◇◇◇

1 If part of your body **throbs**, you feel a series of strong and usually painful beats there. *His head throbbed... Presently George's ankle began to throb with pain. ...the throbbing tooth whose pain had woken her.* ► Also a noun. *The bruise on his stomach ached with a steady throb.* VERB V V *with* n V-ing N-SING

2 If something **throbs**, it vibrates and makes a rhythmical noise; a literary use. *The engines throbbed... The music throbbed hypnotically... The gardens blazed with colour and throbbed with birdsong.* ► Also a noun. *Jake's head jerked up at the throb of the engine.* VERB V V *with* n N-SING

throes /θroʊz/ ◆◇◇◇◇

1 If someone is experiencing something very unpleasant or emotionally painful, you can say that they are in the **throes** of it, especially when it is in its final stages; a formal use. *...when the country was going through the final throes of civil war. ...the agonising throes of transition.* N-PLURAL: usu prep N, N *of* n

2 If you are **in the throes of** doing or experiencing something, especially something difficult, you are busy doing it or are deeply involved in it; a formal expression. *The country is in the throes of a general election... Despite being in the throes of school exams, Tamsin made the long trek from Liverpool.* PHR-PREP

3 See also **death throes**.

thrombosis /θrɒmboʊsɪs/ **thromboses** /θrɒmboʊsiːz/. **Thrombosis** is the formation of a blood clot in a person's heart or in one of their blood vessels, which can cause death; a medical term. *It is generally accepted that thinning of the blood reduces the chances of thrombosis. ...a lady with a thrombosis in her lung.* ● See also **coronary thrombosis**. N-VAR

throne /θroʊn/ **thrones** ◆◆◇◇◇

1 A **throne** is an ornate chair used by a king, queen, or emperor on important official occasions. N-COUNT

2 You can talk about **the throne** as a way of referring to the position of being king, queen, or emperor. *...the Queen's 40th anniversary on the throne. ...the heir to the throne.* N-SING: *the* N

throng /θrɒŋ/, AM /θrɔːŋ/ **throngs, thronging, thronged** ◆◇◇◇◇

1 A **throng** is a large crowd of people; a literary use. *An official pushed through the throng.* N-COUNT =crowd

2 When people **throng** somewhere, they go there in great numbers; a literary use. *The crowds thronged into the mall... The multitudes that throng around the Pope.* VERB =flock V *to/into/around* n

3 If people **throng** a place, they are present there in great numbers. *They throng the beaches between late June and early August.* ♦ **thronged** *The streets are thronged with people.* VERB =crowd V n ADJ: v-link ADJ *with* n

throttle /θrɒtəl/ **throttles, throttling, throttled** ◆◇◇◇◇

1 To **throttle** someone means to kill or injure them by squeezing their throat or tightening something around it and preventing them from breathing. *The attacker then tried to throttle her with wire... He throttled her and hid her body.* VERB =strangle V n

2 If you say that something or someone **is throttling** a process, institution, or group, you mean that they are restricting it severely or destroying it. *He said the over-valuation of sterling was throttling industry.* VERB V n

3 The **throttle** of a motor vehicle or aircraft is a device, lever, or pedal that controls the quantity of fuel entering the engine and is used to control the vehicle's speed. *He gently opened the throttle, and the ship began to ease forward... You have to push the throttle forward for more power.* N-COUNT

4 **Throttle** is the power that is obtained by using a throttle. *...motor bikes revving at full throttle. ...a little more throttle.* N-UNCOUNT

5 If you say that something is done **at full throttle**, you mean that it is done with great speed and eagerness. *He lived his life at full throttle.* PHRASE: PHR after v, v-link PHR

throttle back. If you **throttle back**, or you **throttle back** the engine, when driving a motor vehicle or flying an aircraft, you make it go slower by reducing the quantity of fuel entering the engine. *The pilot throttles back slightly to maintain level flight... He stepped swiftly to the controls to throttle back the engine.* PHRASAL VERB V P V P n (not pron)

through The preposition is pronounced /θruː/. In other cases, **through** is pronounced /θruː/ ◆◆◆◆◆

In addition to the uses shown below, **through** is used in phrasal verbs such as 'see through', 'think through', and 'win through'.

1 To move **through** something such as a hole, opening, or pipe means to move directly from one side or end of it to the other. *The theatre was evacuated when rain poured through the roof at the Liverpool Playhouse... Go straight through that door under the EXIT sign... Visitors enter through a side entrance... The main path continues through a tunnel of trees.* ► Also an adverb. *He went straight through to the kitchen and took a can of beer from the fridge... She opened the door and stood back to allow the man to pass through.* PREP ADV: ADV after v

2 To cut **through** something means to cut it in two pieces or to make a hole in it. *Use a proper fish knife and fork if possible as they are designed to cut through the flesh but not the bones... Rabbits still manage to find a way in. I am sure that some have even taken to gnawing through the metal.* ► Also an adverb. *Score lightly at first and then repeat, scoring deeper each time until the board is cut through.* PREP ADV: ADV after v

3 To go **through** a town, area, or country means to travel across it or in it. *Go up to Ramsgate, cross into France, go through Andorra and into Spain. ...travelling through pathless woods... The couple set off in August from Morocco, drove through the Sahara, visited Nigeria and were heading for Zimbabwe... President Bush leaves tomorrow for a trip through Asia.* ► Also an adverb. *Few know that the tribe was just passing through.* PREP ADV: ADV after v

4 If you move **through** a group of things or a mass of something, it is on either side of you or all around you. *We made our way through the crowd to the river... Sybil's fingers ran through the water... Nancy kept running, plunging through the sand... He hurried through the rain, to the patrol car.* ► Also an adverb. *He pushed his way through to the edge of the crowd where he waited.* PREP ADV: ADV after v

5 To get **through** a barrier or obstruction means to get from one side of it to the other. *Allow twenty-five minutes to get through Passport Control and Customs... He was one of the last of the crowd to pass through the barrier... Traders generally travel safely through the border.* ► Also an adverb. *...a maze of concrete and steel barriers, designed to prevent vehicles driving straight through.* PREP ADV: ADV after v

6 If something goes into an object and comes out of the other side, you can say that it passes **through** PREP the object. *The ends of the net pass through a wooden bar at each end... Zita was herself unconventional, keeping a safety-pin stuck through her ear lobe.* ► Also an adverb. *I bored a hole so that the fixing bolt would pass through.* ADV: ADV after v

7 To go **through** a system means to move around it or to pass from one end of it to the other. *...electric currents travelling through copper wires... What a lot of cards you've got through the post! ...a child's successful passage through the education system.* ► Also an adverb. *It is also expected to consider a resolution which would allow food to go through immediately with fewer restrictions.* PREP; ADV: ADV after v

8 If you see, hear, or feel something **through** a particular thing, that thing is between you and the thing you can see, hear, or feel. *Alice gazed pensively through the wet glass... They could hear music pulsing through the walls of the house... I am sure I can feel a vibration through the soles of my feet.* PREP

9 If something such as a feeling, attitude, or quality, happens or exists **through** an area, organization, or a person's body, it happens or exists everywhere in it or affects all of it. *An atmosphere of anticipation vibrated through the crowd... The melody that ran through his brain was composed of bad notes... What was going through his mind when he spoke those amazing words?... A mood of optimism swept through the company and its customers.* PREP

10 If something happens or exists **through** a period of time, it happens or exists from the beginning until the end. *We're playing in New Zealand, Australia and Japan through November... Saga features trips for older people at home and abroad all through the year... She kept quiet all through breakfast.* ► Also an adverb. *We've got a tough programme, hard work right through to the summer... He worked right through.* PREP; ADV: ADV after v

11 In American English, if something happens from a particular period of time **through** another, it starts at the first period and continues until the end of the second period. The usual British word is **to**. *...open Monday through Sunday from 7:00 am to 10:00 pm... During her busy season (March through June), she often completes as many as fifty paintings a week.* PREP

12 If you go **through** a particular experience or event, you experience it, and if you behave in a particular way **through** it, you behave in that way while it is happening. *Men go through a change of life emotionally just like women. ...a humorous woman who had lived through two world wars in Paris... Why was I putting myself through all this misery?... Through it all, Mark was outwardly calm.* PREP

13 If you are **through** with something or if it is **through**, you have finished doing it and will never do it again. If you are **through** with someone, you do not want to have anything to do with them again. *I'm through with the explaining... Training as a marriage counsellor would guarantee her some employment once her schooling was through... They were through. They wanted out. Forever... I'm through with women.* ADJ: v-link ADJ, oft ADJ *with* n

14 You use **through** in expressions such as **halfway through** and **all the way through** to indicate to what extent an action or task is completed. *A thirty-nine-year-old competitor collapsed half-way through the marathon and died shortly afterwards.* ► Also an adverb. *Stir the pork about until it turns white all the way through.* PREP: n PREP n; ADV: n ADV

15 If something happens because of something else, you can say that it happens **through** it. *They are understood to have retired through age or ill health... The thought of someone suffering through a mistake of mine makes me shiver.* PREP =because of

16 You use **through** when stating the means by which a particular thing is achieved. *Those who seek to grab power through violence deserve punishment... You simply can't get a ticket through official channels.* PREP

17 If you do something **through** someone else, they take the necessary action for you. *Do I need to go through my doctor or can I make an appointment direct?... Speaking through an interpreter, he called for some new thinking from the West.* PREP =via

18 If something such as a proposal or idea goes **through**, it is accepted by people in authority and is made legal or official. *It is possible that the present Governor General will be made interim President, if the proposals go through... The secretary of state during the Nixon-Ford transition did not wish to push the proposals through.* ► Also a preposition. *They want to get the plan through Congress as quickly as possible.* ADV: ADV after v; PREP

19 If someone gets **through** an examination or a round of a competition, they succeed or win. *She was bright, learned languages quickly, and sailed through her exams... All the seeded players got through the first round.* ► Also an adverb. *Nigeria also go through from that group.* PREP; ADV: ADV after v

20 When you get **through** while making a telephone call, the call is connected and you can speak to the person you are phoning. *He may find the line cut on the telephone so that he can't get through... Smith tried to get through to Frank at Warm Springs the next morning.* ADV: ADV after v

21 If you look or go **through** a lot of things, you look at them or deal with them one after the other. *Let's go through the numbers together and see if a workable deal is possible... When you have finished your list of personal preferences, go through it again... David ran through the agreement with Guy, point by point... He, too, had a lot of paperwork to get through.* PREP

22 If you read **through** something, you read it from beginning to end. *She read through pages and pages of the music I had brought her... I only had time to skim through the script before I flew over here.* ► Also an adverb. *The article had been authored by Raymond Kennedy. He read it straight through, looking for any scrap of information that might have passed him by.* PREP; ADV: ADV after v

23 A **through** train goes directly to a particular place, so that the people who want to go there do not have to change trains. *...Britain's longest through train journey, 685 miles.* ADJ: ADJ n

24 If you say that someone or something is wet **through**, you are emphasizing how wet they are. *I returned to the inn cold and wet, soaked through by the drizzling rain... She went on crying, and cried and cried until the pillow was wet through.* ADV: adj ADV PRAGMATICS

25 Through and through means completely and to the greatest extent possible. *I've gotten my feet thoroughly soaked in the cold and feel frozen through and through... People assume they know me through and through the moment we meet.* PHRASE: usu n/adj PHR, PHR after v

throughout /θruːaʊt/ ◆◆◆◆◇

1 If you say that something happens **throughout** a particular period of time, you mean that it happens during the whole of that period. *The national tragedy of rival groups killing each other continued throughout 1990... Movie music can be made memorable because its themes are repeated throughout the film. ...a single-minded devotion to racing which Gaye has shown throughout her career.* ► Also an adverb. *The first song, 'Blue Moon', didn't go too badly except that everyone talked throughout.* PREP; ADV: ADV with cl

2 If you say that something happens or exists **throughout** a place, you mean that it happens or exists in all parts of that place. *'Sight Savers', founded in 1950, now runs projects throughout Africa, the Caribbean and South East Asia... As we have tried to show throughout this book, companies that provide outstanding service don't do it by luck.* ► Also an adverb. *The route is well sign-posted throughout... Throughout, the walls are white.* PREP; ADV: ADV with cl

throughput /θruːpʊt/. The **throughput** of an organization or system is the amount of things it can do or deal with in a particular period of time. *...technologies which will allow us to get much higher throughput... There's still a reasonable throughput of business.* N-UNCOUNT

throw /θroʊ/ **throws, throwing, threw, thrown** ◆◆◆◆◇

1 When you **throw** an object that you are holding, VERB

you move your hand or arm quickly and let go of the object, so that it moves through the air. *He spent hours throwing a tennis ball against a wall... On one occasion, his father threw a radio at his mother... The crowd began throwing stones... Sophia jumps up and throws down her knitting... He threw Brian a rope.* ▸ Also a noun. *One of the judges thought it was a foul throw... A throw of the dice allows a player to move himself forward.* ♦ **throwing** *He didn't really know very much about javelin throwing.*
V n prep/adv
V n
V n with adv
V n n
N-COUNT: oft N *of* n
N-UNCOUNT: usu with supp

2 If you **throw** your body or part of your body into a particular position or place, you move it there suddenly and with a lot of force. *She threw her arms around his shoulders... She threatened to throw herself in front of a train... He set his skinny legs apart and threw back his shoulders.*
VERB =fling
V n prep
V pron-refl prep/adv
V n with adv

3 If you **throw** something into a particular place or position, you put it there in a quick and careless way. *He struggled out of his bulky jacket and threw it on to the back seat... Why not throw it all in the pot and see what happens?*
VERB
V n prep/adv

4 To **throw** someone into a particular place or position means to force them roughly into that place or position. *He threw me to the ground and started to kick... The device exploded, throwing Mr Taylor from his car.*
VERB
V n prep/adv

5 If you say that someone **is thrown** into prison, you mean that they are sent there by the authorities, often in a brutal way. *Those two should have been thrown in jail... Police should have the power to fine people who hamper rescue efforts. In fact I'd throw them into prison for a night.*
VERB
be V-ed *in/into* n
V n *in/into* n

6 If a horse **throws** its rider, it makes him or her fall off, by suddenly jumping or moving violently. *The horse reared, throwing its rider and knocking down a youth standing beside it.*
VERB
V n

7 If a person or thing **is thrown** into an unpleasant situation or state, something causes them to be in that situation or state. *Abidjan was thrown into turmoil because of a protest by taxi drivers... Economic recession had thrown millions out of work... The border dispute has threatened to throw next week's OPEC meeting in Geneva into confusion.*
VERB
be V-ed prep
V n prep

8 If something **throws** light or a shadow on a surface, it causes that surface to have light or a shadow on it. *The sunlight is white and blinding, throwing hard-edged shadows on the ground.*
VERB =cast
V n *on/onto* n

9 If something **throws** doubt or suspicion on a person or thing, it causes people to doubt or suspect them. *This new information does throw doubt on their choice... She did not attempt to throw any suspicion upon you.*
VERB =cast
V n *on/upon* n

10 If you **throw** a look or smile at someone or something, you look or smile at them quickly and suddenly. *Emily turned and threw her a suggestive grin.*
VB: no cont
V n n
Also V n *at* n

11 If you **throw** yourself, your energy, or your money into a particular job or activity, you become involved in it very actively or enthusiastically. *She threw herself into a modelling career... They threw all their military resources into the battle.*
VERB
V pron-refl *into* n
V n *into* n

12 If you **throw** a fit or a tantrum, you suddenly start to behave in an uncontrolled way. *I used to get very upset and scream and swear, throwing tantrums all over the place.*
VERB
V n

13 If something such as a remark or an experience **throws** you, it surprises you or confuses you because it is unexpected. *The professor rather threw me by asking if I went in for martial arts... Obviously the puncture threw me a little, but I'm reasonably happy.* ▸ **Throw off** means the same as **throw**. *I lost my first serve in the first set, it threw me off a bit.*
VERB
V n
PHRASAL VERB
V n P

14 If you **throw** a punch, you punch someone. *Everything was fine until someone threw a punch.*
VERB
V n

15 When someone **throws** a party, they organize one, usually in their own home; an informal use. *Why not throw a party for your friends?*
VERB
V n

16 When someone **throws** a switch, they turn it on or off. *Prince Edward threw the switch to light the illuminations.*
VERB
V n

17 In sport, if a player **throws** a game or contest, they lose it as a result of a deliberate action or intention. *...offering him a bribe to throw the game.*
VERB
V n

18 If things cost a particular amount of money **a throw**, they cost that amount each; an informal expression. *Most applications software for personal computers cost over $500 a throw.*
PHRASES
amount PHR

19 If someone **throws** themselves **at** you, they make it very obvious that they want to begin a relationship with you, by behaving in a bold and flirtatious way. *I'll say you started it, that you threw yourself at me.*
V inflects

20 • to **throw the baby out with the bath water**: see **baby**. • to **throw the book at** someone: see **book**. • to **throw** someone **in at the deep end**: see **end**. • to **throw down the gauntlet**: see **gauntlet**. • to **throw up** your **hands**: see **hand**. • to **throw light on** something: see **light**. • to **throw in** your **lot with** someone: see **lot**. • to **throw money at** something: see **money**. • to **throw good money after bad**: see **money**. • to **throw a spanner in the works**: see **spanner**. • **a stone's throw**: see **stone**. • to **throw in the towel**: see **towel**. • to **throw cold water on** something: see **water**. • to **throw** your **weight about**: see **weight**. • to **throw a wrench**: see **wrench**.

throw around. If you say that someone **throws around** a word or name, you disapprove of the fact that they mention it frequently, often in a silly or irrelevant way in order to impress someone; an informal expression. *Occasionally, he throws fancy words around... The name that I've heard thrown around a lot is Jim Morrison.*
PHRASAL VERB
PRAGMATICS
V n P
V-ed P
Also V P n (not pron)

throw aside. If you **throw aside** a way of life, a principle, or an idea, you abandon it or reject it. *Detectives threw aside professional training and caution, and looked for a different explanation... Exceptional patients have the ability to throw statistics aside to say, 'I can be a survivor'.*
PHRASAL VERB
V P n (not pron)
V n P

throw away or **throw out**
PHRASAL VERB

1 When you **throw away** or **throw out** something that you do not want, you get rid of it, for example by putting it in a dustbin. *I never throw anything away... I'm not advising you to throw away your makeup or forget about your appearance.*
V n P
V P n (not pron)

2 If you **throw away** an opportunity, advantage, or benefit, you waste it, rather than using it sensibly. *Failing to tackle the deficit would be throwing away an opportunity we haven't had for a generation... We should have won. We threw it away.* • See also **throwaway**.
V P n (not pron)
V n P

throw back
PHRASAL VERB

1 If you **throw** something **back** at someone, you remind them of something bad they did in the past, in order to hurt them. *I should never have told you that. I knew you'd throw it back at me.*
V n P *at* n
Also V P *at* n n

2 If someone **is thrown back** on their own powers or resources, they have to use them, because there is nothing else they can use. *We are constantly thrown back on our own resources.*
usu passive
be V-ed P *on* n

throw down. If you **throw down** a challenge to someone, you do something new or unexpected in a bold or forceful manner that will probably cause them to reply or react equally strongly. *The regional parliament threw down a new challenge to the central authorities by passing a law allowing private ownership of businesses... Government ministers have been responding to the challenge thrown down by their former colleague.*
PHRASAL VERB
V P n (not pron)
V-ed P

throw in
PHRASAL VERB

1 If you **throw in** a remark when having a conversation, you add it in a casual or unexpected way. *Occasionally Farling threw in a question.*
V P n (not pron)
Also V n P

2 If someone who is selling something **throws in** something extra, they give you the extra thing and only ask you to pay for the first thing. *Pay £2.80 for larger prints and they throw in a free photo album... They were offering me a weekend break in Paris—with free beer thrown in.*
=include
V P n (not pron)
V-ed P
Also V n P

throw off
PHRASAL VERB

1 If you **throw off** something that is restricting you or making you unhappy, you get rid of it. *He had not yet thrown off the intellectual shackles of Marx-*
=cast off
V P n (not pron)
V n P

ism... One day depression descended upon him, and wherever he went after that he could never throw it off.

2 If something **throws off** a substance, it produces it and releases it into the air. *The belt may make a squealing noise and throw off sooty black particles of rubber... The star grew 30% brighter and threw off huge amounts of radiation.* =give off; V P n (not pron)

3 If you **throw off** people who are chasing you or trying to find you, you do something unexpected that makes them unable to catch you or find you. *He is said to have thrown off pursuers by pedaling across the Wisconsin state line... He tried to throw police off the track of his lover.* V P n (not pron); V n P n; Also V n P

4 See also **throw** 13.

throw out PHRASAL VERB

1 See **throw away** 1.

2 If a judge **throws out** a case, he or she rejects it and the accused person does not have to stand trial. *The defense wants the district Judge to throw out the case.* V P n (not pron); Also V n P

3 If you **throw** someone **out**, you force them to leave a place or group. *He was thrown out of the Olympic team after testing positive for drugs... I wanted to kill him, but instead I just threw him out of the house... The party threw out the Trotskyist Militant Tendency.* be/get V-ed P of n; V n P of n; V P n (not pron); Also V n P

throw together PHRASAL VERB

1 If you **throw** something **together**, for example a meal or a costume, you make it quickly and not very carefully; an informal expression. *Too often, picnic preparation consists of throwing together some sandwiches and grabbing an apple.* V P n (not pron); Also V n P

2 If people **are thrown together** by a situation or event, or if one person or group **is thrown together** with another, the situation or event causes them to meet and get to know each other, even though they may not want to. *The cast and crew were thrown together for 12 hours a day, six days a week, until the filming was completed... If you have men and women thrown together in inhospitable surroundings, you are going to get some sexual tension... My husband is constantly thrown together with young people through his work.* RECIP; pl-n be V-ed P; V-ed P; be V-ed P with n; Also V pl-n P, V P pl-n (not pron), V n P with n

throw up PHRASAL VERB

1 When someone **throws up**, they vomit; an informal expression. *She said she had thrown up after reading reports of the trial.* V P

2 If something **throws up** dust, stones, or water, when it moves or hits the ground, it causes them to rise up into the air. *If it had hit the Earth, it would have made a crater 100 miles across and thrown up an immense cloud of dust.* V P n (not pron); Also V n P

3 If you say that a building or structure **is thrown up**, you mean that it is built or made very quickly, usually so that it is not of very good quality. *...living in the slums where wood and scrap metal dwellings are thrown up in any available space... Youths threw up barricades on the streets.* be V-ed P; V P n (not pron); Also V n P

4 To **throw up** a particular person or thing means to produce them or cause them to become noticeable; used mainly in British English. *The political struggle threw up a strong leader... These studies have already thrown up some interesting results.* V P n (not pron); Also V n P

throwaway /θroʊəweɪ/ **throwaways**

1 A **throwaway** product is intended to be used only for a short time, and then to be thrown away. *Now they are producing throwaway razors.* ▸ A **throwaway** is a throwaway product. *She's taken surplus goods and throwaways and given them useful new lives with the aid of paint and imagination.* ADJ: ADJ n; N-COUNT

2 If you say that someone makes a **throwaway** remark or gesture, you mean that they make it in a casual way, although it may be important, or have some serious or humorous effect. *...a throwaway remark she later regretted... The humour and throwaway lines ensure that the piece never loses its pace.* ADJ: ADJ n

throwback /θroʊbæk/ **throwbacks.** If you say that something is a **throwback** to a former time, you mean that it is like something that existed a long time ago. *The hall is a throwback to another era with its old prints and stained-glass.* N-COUNT: usu sing, oft N to n

throw-in, throw-ins. When there is a **throw-in** in a football or rugby match, the ball is thrown back onto the field after it has been kicked off it. ◆◇◇◇◇ N-COUNT

thrown /θroʊn/. **Thrown** is the past participle of **throw**.

thru. **Thru** is sometimes used in written English as an abbreviation for **through**; used mainly in American English.

thrum /θrʌm/ **thrums, thrumming, thrummed.** When something such as a machine or engine **thrums**, it makes a low beating sound. *The air-conditioner thrummed.* ▸ Also a noun. *...the thrum of refrigeration motors... My head was going thrum thrum thrum.* VERB; V; N-COUNT; SOUND

thrush /θrʌʃ/ **thrushes** ◆◇◇◇◇

1 A **thrush** is a fairly small bird with a brown back and a spotted breast. N-COUNT

2 **Thrush** is a medical condition cause by a fungus. It most often occurs in a baby's mouth or in a woman's vagina. N-UNCOUNT

thrust /θrʌst/ **thrusts, thrusting, thrust** ◆◆◇◇◇

1 If you **thrust** something or someone somewhere, you push or move them there quickly with a lot of force. *They thrust him into the back of a jeep... She grabs a stack of baby photos and thrusts them into my hands.* ▸ Also a noun. *Two of the knife thrusts were fatal.* VERB =shove; V n prep/adv; N-COUNT

2 If you **thrust** your way somewhere, you move there, pushing between people or things which are in your way. *She thrust her way into the crowd... He reached the garden gate and thrust his way through it.* VERB =push; V way prep/adv

3 If something **thrusts** up or out of something else, it sticks up or sticks out in a noticeable way; a literary use. *A small dish aerial thrust up from the grass verge... A ray of orange sunlight thrust out through the clouds.* VERB; V adv/prep

4 **Thrust** is the power or force that is required to make a vehicle move in a particular direction. *It provides the thrust that makes the craft move forward.* N-UNCOUNT

5 The **thrust** of an activity or of an idea is the main or essential things it expresses. *The real thrust of the film is its examination of New York's Hasidic community... The main thrust of the research will be the study of the early Universe and galaxy formation... The conductor brought home the full thrust of the work's emotional resolution.* N-SING: adj N, usu N of n

thrust upon. If something **is thrust upon** you, you are forced to have it, deal with it, or experience it. *Why has such sadness been thrust upon us?... She had not wanted to be Queen, but the role was thrust upon her... Some are born great, some achieve greatness, and some have greatness thrust upon them.* PHRASAL VERB usu passive; be V-ed P n; have n V-ed P n

Thu. See **Thurs.**

thud /θʌd/ **thuds, thudding, thudded** ◆◇◇◇◇

1 A **thud** is a dull sound, such as that which a heavy object makes when it hits something soft. *She tripped and fell with a sickening thud... Much of their study and revision was done to the thud of hammers and pneumatic drills... I heard the regular thud thud thud of running shoes behind me.* N-COUNT: usu sing, oft N of n; SOUND =thump

2 If something **thuds** somewhere, it makes a dull sound, usually when it falls onto something else or hits something else. *She ran up the stairs, her bare feet thudding on the wood... The windscreen wipers thudded back and forth... There was a heavy thudding noise against the bedroom door.* ♦ **thudding** *...the thudding of the bombs beyond the hotel.* VERB; V prep/adv; V-ing; Also V; N-UNCOUNT: oft N of n

3 When your heart **thuds**, it beats strongly and rather quickly, for example because you are very frightened or very happy. *My heart had started to thud, and my mouth was dry... Jessica's heart was thudding against her ribcage. ...exercises to help you slow your breathing and quiet your thudding heart.* VERB =pound; V; V prep/adv; V-ing

thug /θʌg/ **thugs.** You can refer to a violent person or criminal as a **thug**; used showing disapproval. *...the cowardly thugs who mug old people.* ◆◇◇◇◇ N-COUNT

thuggery /θʌgəri/. **Thuggery** is rough, violent behaviour. N-UNCOUNT

thumb /θʌm/ **thumbs, thumbing, thumbed** ◆◆◇◇◇
1 Your **thumb** is the short thick digit on the side of your hand next to your first finger. *She bit the tip of her left thumb, not looking at me.* N-COUNT
2 The **thumb** of a glove or mitten is the part which a person's thumb fits into. N-COUNT
3 If you **thumb** a lift or **thumb** a ride, you stand by the side of the road holding out your thumb until a driver stops and gives you a lift. *It may interest you to know that a boy answering Rory's description thumbed a ride to Howth... Thumbing a lift had once a carefree, easy-going image.* VERB =hitch V n to n V n
4 See also **well-thumbed**.
5 If you say that someone or something **sticks out like a sore thumb** or **stands out like a sore thumb**, you are emphasizing that they are very noticeable, usually because they are unusual or inappropriate. *Does the new housing stick out like a sore thumb or blend into its surroundings?... In Japan a European stands out like a sore thumb.* PHRASES V and N inflect PRAGMATICS
6 If you say that someone is **twiddling** their **thumbs**, you mean that they do not have anything to do and are waiting for something to happen. *The prospect of waiting around just twiddling his thumbs was appalling... The Government cannot expect graduates to twiddle their thumbs on the dole.* V inflects
7 If you are **under** someone's **thumb**, you are under their control, or very heavily influenced by them. *I cannot tell you what pain I feel when I see how much my mother is under my father's thumb... She has Rachel firmly under her thumb.* v-link PHR, PHR after v
8 • **green thumb**: see **green**. • **to thumb** your **nose at** someone: see **nose**. • **rule of thumb**: see **rule**.

thumb through. If you **thumb through** something such as a book or magazine, you turn the pages quickly and glance at the contents rather than reading each page carefully. *He thumbed through a couple of pages, feigning just a slight interest... In a second, he had the drawer open and was thumbing through the files.* PHRASAL VERB V P n

thumbnail /θʌmneɪl/ **thumbnails;** also spelled **thumb-nail**.
1 Your **thumbnail** is the nail on your thumb. N-COUNT
2 A **thumbnail** sketch or account is a very short description of an event, idea, or plan which gives only the main details. ADJ: ADJ n

thumbscrew /θʌmskru:/ **thumbscrews;** also spelled **thumb screw**.
1 A **thumbscrew** is an object that was used in the past to torture people by crushing their thumbs. N-COUNT
2 If someone puts the **thumbscrews** on you, they start to put you under extreme pressure in order to force you to do something. N-COUNT

thumbs-down; also spelled **thumbs down**. If you say that someone gives a plan, idea, or suggestion **the thumbs-down**, you are indicating that they do not approve of it and refuse to accept it; an informal expression. N-SING ≠thumbs-up

thumbs-up; also spelled **thumbs up**.
1 A **thumbs-up** or a **thumbs-up sign** is a sign that you make by raising your thumb to show that you agree with someone, that you are happy with an idea or situation, or that everything is all right. *She checked the hall, then gave the others a thumbs-up sign.* N-SING
2 If you give a plan, idea, or suggestion **the thumbs-up**, you indicate that you approve of it and are willing to accept it; an informal use. *The financial markets have given the thumbs up to the new policy... It more or less gets the thumbs up from everyone.* N-SING: the N ≠thumbs-down

thumbtack /θʌmtæk/ **thumbtacks.** In American English, a **thumbtack** is a short pin with a broad flat top which is used for fastening papers or pictures to a board, wall, or other surface. The usual British term is **drawing pin**. N-COUNT

thump /θʌmp/ **thumps, thumping, thumped** ◆◇◇◇◇
1 If you **thump** something, you hit it hard, usually with your fist. *He thumped my shoulder affectionately, nearly knocking me over... I heard you thumping on the door.* ► Also a noun. *He felt a thump on his shoulder.* VERB V n V on n N-COUNT
2 If you **thump** someone, you attack them and hit them with your fist; used mainly in informal British English. *Don't say it serves me right or I'll thump you.* VERB V n
3 If you **thump** something somewhere or if it **thumps** there, it makes a loud, dull sound by hitting something else. *She thumped her hand on the witness box... Waiters went scurrying down the aisles, thumping down tureens of soup. ...paving stones and bricks which have been thumping down on police shields and helmets... She dashed out through the door, her stockinged feet thumping softly as she ran up the stairs... Where's that thumping noise coming from?* ► Also a noun. *There was a loud thump as the horse crashed into the van.* V-ERG =bang V n prep V n with adv V prep/adv V V-ing N-COUNT
4 When your heart **thumps**, it beats strongly and quickly, usually because you are afraid or excited. *My heart was thumping wildly but I didn't let my face show any emotion.* VERB =pound V
5 See also **thumping**.

thumping /θʌmpɪŋ/. ◆◇◇◇◇
1 In British English, **thumping** is used to emphasize that something is very great or severe; an informal use. *The Right has a thumping majority... The gloom deepened after a thumping £145m loss at British Rail.* ► Also an adverb. *A thumping good time was had by all.* ADJ: ADJ n PRAGMATICS =whopping ADV: ADV adj
2 See also **thump**.

thunder /θʌndə^r/ **thunders, thundering, thundered** ◆◆◇◇◇
1 **Thunder** is the loud noise that you hear from the sky after a flash of lightning, especially during a storm. *There was frequent thunder and lightning, and torrential rain. ...a distant clap of thunder.* N-UNCOUNT
2 When it **thunders**, a loud noise comes from the sky after a flash of lightning. *The day was heavy and still. It would probably thunder later.* VERB it V
3 The **thunder of** something that is moving or making a sound is the loud deep noise it makes. *The thunder of the sea on the rocks seemed to blank out other thoughts... Khalil heard the thunder of an avalanche.* N-UNCOUNT: N of n =crashing, roar
4 If something or someone **thunders** somewhere, they move there quickly and with a lot of noise. *The horses thundered across the valley floor... Niccolini was thundering up the stairs, taking them two at a time... A lorry thundered by.* VERB V prep/adv
5 If something **thunders**, it makes a very loud noise, usually continuously. *She heard the sound of the guns thundering in the fog. ...thundering applause.* VERB =resound V V-ing
6 If you **thunder** something, you say it loudly and forcefully, especially because you are angry; used in written English. *'It's your money. Ask for it!' she thundered... The Prosecutor looked toward Napoleon, waiting for him to thunder an objection.* VERB =bellow V with quote V n
7 If you **steal** someone's **thunder**, you get the attention or praise that they thought they would get, usually by saying or doing what they had intended to say or do. *He had no intention of letting the Foreign Secretary steal any of his thunder.* PHRASE: V inflects

thunderbolt /θʌndə^rboult/ **thunderbolts.** A **thunderbolt** is a flash of lightning, accompanied by thunder, which strikes something such as a building or a tree. N-COUNT

thunderclap /θʌndə^rklæp/ **thunderclaps.** A **thunderclap** is a short loud bang that you hear in the sky just after you see a flash of lightning. N-COUNT

thundercloud /θʌndə^rklaud/ **thunderclouds.** A **thundercloud** is a large dark cloud that is likely to produce thunder and lightning. N-COUNT

thunderous /θʌndərəs/. If you describe a noise as **thunderous**, you mean that it is very loud and deep. *The audience responded with thunderous applause. ...the thunderous roar of an explosion.* ◆◇◇◇◇ ADJ-GRADED: usu ADJ n =deafening

thunderstorm /θʌndə^rstɔ:^rm/ **thunderstorms.** A **thunderstorm** is a storm in which there is thunder and lightning and a lot of heavy rain. ◆◇◇◇◇ N-COUNT

thunderstruck /θʌndəʳstrʌk/. If you say that someone is **thunderstruck**, you mean that they are extremely surprised or shocked; a formal word. ADJ: usu v-link ADJ =stunned

thundery /θʌndəri/. When the weather is **thundery**, there is a lot of thunder, or there are heavy clouds which make you think that there will be thunder soon. *Thundery weather is forecast... Heavy thundery rain fell throughout Thursday.* ADJ-GRADED

Thurs. Also spelled **Thur.** or **Thu.**. **Thurs.** is a written abbreviation for **Thursday**. *Its opening hours are Mon-Wed 10am-12.30am; Thurs-Fri 10am-1am.* ◆◆◇◇◇

Thursday /θɜːʳzdeɪ, -di/ **Thursdays. Thursday** is the day after Wednesday and before Friday. *On Thursday Barrett invited me for a drink... We go and do the weekly shopping every Thursday morning... I'm always terribly busy on Thursdays.* ◆◆◆◆◇ N-VAR

thus /ðʌs/ ◆◆◆◆◇

1 You use **thus** to show that what you are about to mention is the result or consequence of something else that you have just mentioned; a formal use. *Neither of them thought of turning on the lunchtime news. Thus Caroline didn't hear of John's death until Peter telephoned... Even in a highly skilled workforce some people will be more capable and thus better paid than others. ...women's access to the basic means of production and thus to political power.* ADV: ADV with cl/group PRAGMATICS =therefore, hence

2 If you say that something is **thus** or happens **thus** you mean that it is, or happens, as you have just described or as you are just about to describe; a formal use. *Joanna was pouring the drink. While she was thus engaged, Charles sat on one of the bar-stools... Martin helped his father dig the water gardens out by hand. Thus he discovered his interest in gardening.* ADV: ADV with v, ADV cl PRAGMATICS

3 ● **thus far**: see **far**.

thwack /θwæk/ **thwacks.** A **thwack** is a sound made when two solid objects hit each other hard. *I listened to the thwack of the metal balls... Then the woodcutter let his axe fly – Thwack! Everyone heard it.* N-COUNT; SOUND

thwart /θwɔːʳt/ **thwarts, thwarting, thwarted.** If you **thwart** someone or **thwart** their plans, you prevent them from doing or getting what they want. *The security forces were doing all they could to thwart terrorists... Her ambition to become an artist was thwarted by failing eyesight.* ◆◇◇◇◇ VERB V n

thy /ðaɪ/. **Thy** is an old-fashioned, poetic, or religious word for 'your' when you are talking to one person. *Honor thy father and thy mother.* ◆◇◇◇◇ DET-POSS

thyme /taɪm/. **Thyme** is a type of herb used in cooking. ◆◇◇◇◇ N-UNCOUNT

thyroid /θaɪrɔɪd/ **thyroids.** Your **thyroid** or your **thyroid gland** is a gland in your neck that produces chemicals which control the way your body grows and functions. ◆◇◇◇◇ N-COUNT

thyself /ðaɪself/. **Thyself** is an old-fashioned, poetic, or religious word for 'yourself' when you are talking to only one person. *Love thy neighbour as thyself.* PRON-REFL

tiara /tiɑːrə/ **tiaras.** A **tiara** is a semicircular metal band decorated with jewels which a woman of very high social rank wears on her head at formal social occasions. N-COUNT

Tibetan /tɪbetᵊn/ **Tibetans** ◆◆◆◆◇

1 **Tibetan** means belonging or relating to Tibet, or to its people, language, or culture. ADJ

2 A **Tibetan** is a Tibetan citizen or a person of Tibetan origin. N-COUNT

3 **Tibetan** is a language spoken by people who live Tibet. N-UNCOUNT

tibia /tɪbiə/ **tibias.** Your **tibia** is the inner bone of the two bones in the lower part of your leg; a medical term. N-COUNT

tic /tɪk/ **tics.** If someone has a **tic**, a part of their face or body keeps making an uncontrollable twitching movement, for example because they are tired or have a nervous illness. *...people with nervous tics... She developed a tic in her left eye.* N-COUNT

tick /tɪk/ **ticks, ticking, ticked** ◆◆◇◇◇

1 A **tick** is a written mark like a V with the right side extended. It is used to show that something is correct or has been selected or dealt with; used mainly in British English. *His exercise books were full of well deserved red ticks... Place a tick in the appropriate box.* N-COUNT

2 If you **tick** something that is written on a piece of paper, you put a tick next to it; used mainly in British English. *Please tick this box if you do not wish to receive such mailings... As each boy said yes, he ticked their name.* VERB V n

3 When a clock or watch **ticks**, it makes a regular series of short sounds as it works. *A wind-up clock ticked busily from the kitchen counter.* ► **Tick away** means the same as **tick**. *A grandfather clock ticked away in a corner.* ♦ **ticking** *...the endless ticking of clocks.* VERB V PHRASAL VERB V P N-UNCOUNT: oft N of n

4 The **tick** of a clock or watch is the series of short sounds it makes when it is working, or one of those sounds. *He sat listening to the tick of the grandfather clock.* N-COUNT

5 In British English, you can use **tick** to refer to a very short period of time; an informal use. *Just hang on a tick, we may be able to help... I'll be back in a tick... I shall be with you in two ticks.* N-COUNT =sec

6 If you talk about what makes someone **tick**, you are talking about the beliefs, wishes, and feelings that make them behave in the way that they do; an informal use. *He wanted to find out what made them tick... I'm interested in how people tick.* VERB V

7 A **tick** is a small creature like a flea which lives on the bodies of people or animals and uses their blood as food. *...chemicals that destroy ticks and mites... Tick bites can cause Lyme disease.* N-COUNT

tick away or **tick by** or **tick on.** If you say that the clock or time is **ticking away**, **ticking by**, or **ticking on**, you mean that time is passing, especially when there is something urgent that needs to be done or when someone is waiting for something to happen. *The clock ticks away, leaving little time for talks... The minutes towards departure ticked by, until finally the pilot arrived... The clock ticked on towards the president's visit.* ● See also **tick** 3. PHRASAL VERB V P

tick by. See **tick away**. PHRASAL VERB

tick off PHRASAL VERB

1 If you **tick off** items on a list, you write a tick or other mark next to them, in order to show that they have been dealt with; used mainly in British English. *He ticked off my name on a piece of paper... Tick it off in the box.* V P n (not pron) V n P

2 In British English, if you **tick** someone **off**, you speak angrily to them because they have done something wrong; an informal expression. *His mum ticked him off at home... Abdel felt free to tick him off for smoking too much... Traffic police ticked off a pensioner for jumping a red light.* ● See also **ticking off**. =tell off V n P V n P *for*-ing/n V P n (not pron) *for*-ing/n Also V P n (not pron)

3 In American English, if you say that something **ticks** you **off**, you mean that it annoys you; an informal expression. *I just think it's rude and it's ticking me off... She's still ticked off at him for brushing her off and going out with you instead.* V n P V-ed P

tick on. See **tick away**. PHRASAL VERB

tick over PHRASAL VERB

1 If an engine **is ticking over**, it is running at a low speed or rate, for example when it is switched on but you are not actually using it; used mainly in British English. *Very slowly he moved forward, the engine ticking over.* =idle V P

2 If a person, system, or business **is ticking over**, they are working steadily, but not producing very much or making much progress; used mainly in British English. *The market is at least ticking over... It keeps you ticking over, stops you being complacent.* V P

ticker /tɪkəʳ/ **tickers.** Your **ticker** is your heart; an old-fashioned, informal word, used mainly in British English. N-COUNT

ticker tape. **Ticker tape** consists of long narrow strips of paper on which information such as stock exchange prices is printed by a machine. In N-UNCOUNT: oft N n

American cities, people sometimes throw ticker tape from high windows as a way of celebrating and honouring someone in public. *A half million people watched the troops march in New York's ticker tape parade.*

ticket /tɪkɪt/ **tickets** ◆◆◆◆◇

1 A **ticket** is an official piece of paper or card which shows that you have paid to enter a place of entertainment such as a cinema or a sports ground, or shows that you have paid for a journey. *I queued for two hours to get a ticket to see the football game... I love opera and last year I got tickets for Covent Garden... Entrance is free, but by ticket only... Her brother Bernard became a ticket collector at Waterloo Station.* N-COUNT: also *by*N

2 A **ticket** is an official piece of paper which orders you to pay a fine or to appear in court because you have committed a driving or parking offence. *I want to know at what point I break the speed limit and get a ticket.* N-COUNT

3 A **ticket** for something such as a raffle or a lottery is a piece of paper with a number on it. If the number on your ticket matches the number chosen, you win a prize. *She bought a lottery ticket and won more than $33 million.* N-COUNT: usu n N

4 The particular **ticket** on which a person fights an election is the party they represent or the policies they support. *He first ran for president on a far-left ticket... She would want to fight the election on a ticket of parliamentary democracy... It's a ticket that was designed to appeal to suburban and small town voters.* N-SING: usu with supp

5 If you say that something is **just the ticket**, you mean that it is exactly what is needed; an informal expression. *Young kids need all the energy and protein they can get and whole milk is just the ticket.* PHRASE: usu v-link PHR

6 See also **ticketing**; **big-ticket**, **dream ticket**, **meal ticket**, **parking ticket**, **season ticket**.

ticketing /tɪkɪtɪŋ/.

1 **Ticketing** is the act or activity of selling tickets. *The two airlines will cooperate on ticketing and schedules. ...automatic ticketing machines.* N-UNCOUNT: oft N n

2 See also **ticket**.

ticking off, tickings off. If you give someone a **ticking off**, you speak angrily to them because they have done something wrong; an informal expression. *They got a ticking off from the police.* N-COUNT: usu sing =telling-off

tickle /tɪkəl/ **tickles, tickling, tickled** ◆◇◇◇◇

1 When you **tickle** someone, you move your fingers lightly over a sensitive part of their body, often in order to make them laugh. *I was tickling him, and he was laughing and giggling.* VERB; V n

2 If something **tickles** you or **tickles**, it causes an irritating feeling by lightly touching a part of your body. *...a yellow hat with a great feather that tickled her ear... A beard doesn't scratch, it just tickles.* VERB; V n; V

3 If a fact or a situation **tickles** you, it amuses you or gives you pleasure. *It tickles me to see him riled... The story was really funny – it tickled me.* ♦ **tickled** *They all sounded just as tickled.* VERB; it V n to-inf; V n; ADJ-GRADED: usu v-link ADJ

4 If you **are tickled pink**, you are extremely pleased about something. *'I'm tickled pink,' said Jimmy after his wife gave birth.* PHRASE: V inflects

ticklish /tɪkəlɪʃ/

1 A **ticklish** problem, situation, or task is difficult and needs to be dealt with carefully. *Policy-makers are considering the ticklish question of the future of the European Community.* ADJ-GRADED: usu ADJ n =delicate

2 Someone who is **ticklish** is sensitive to being tickled, and laughs as soon as you tickle them. *This massage method is not recommended for anyone who is very ticklish.* ADJ-GRADED

tidal /taɪdəl/. **Tidal** means relating to or produced by tides. *The tidal stream or current gradually decreases in the shallows... The 20-minute boat ride through a maze of tidal rivers and marshes is wonderful.* ◆◇◇◇◇ ADJ: usu ADJ n

tidal wave, tidal waves ◆◇◇◇◇

1 A **tidal wave** is a very large wave, often caused by an earthquake, that flows onto the land and destroys things. *A massive tidal wave swept the ship up and away.* N-COUNT

2 If you describe a very large number of emotions, things, or people as a **tidal wave**, you mean that they all occur at the same time. *The trade union movement was swept along by the same tidal wave of patriotism which affected the country as a whole... The recession is deepening and we are now seeing a tidal wave of job losses in all sections of the economy.* N-COUNT: usu sing, usu N *of*n =deluge

tidbit /tɪdbɪt/. See **titbit**.

tiddler /tɪdləʳ/ **tiddlers**

1 In informal British English, a **tiddler** is a very small fish of any kind. N-COUNT

2 In informal British English, if you refer to a person or thing as a **tiddler**, you mean that they are very insignificant or small, especially when compared to other people or things of the same type. *Conde Nast's British division is a relative tiddler compared with the giant IPC.* N-COUNT: usu with supp

tiddly /tɪdəli/

1 In informal British English, if someone is **tiddly**, they are slightly drunk; an informal use. ADJ-GRADED =tipsy

2 In informal British English, if you describe a thing as **tiddly**, you mean that it is very small. *It's a tiddly little thing.* ADJ-GRADED =tiny

tiddlywink /tɪdəliwɪŋk/ **tiddlywinks**

1 **Tiddlywinks** is a game in which the players try to make small round pieces of plastic jump into a container, by pressing their edges with a larger piece of plastic. N-UNCOUNT

2 **Tiddlywinks** are the small round piece of plastic used in the game of tiddlywinks. N-COUNT

tide /taɪd/ **tides, tiding, tided** ◆◆◆◇◇

1 The **tide** is the regular change in the level of the sea on the shore. *The tide was at its highest... The tide was going out, and the sand was smooth and glittering... State police say that high tides and severe flooding have damaged beaches.* N-COUNT

2 A **tide** is a current in the sea that is caused by the regular and continuous movement of large areas of water towards and away from the shore. *Roman vessels used to sail with the tide from Boulogne to Richborough.* N-COUNT

3 The **tide of** opinion, for example, is what the majority of people think at a particular time. *The tide of opinion seems overwhelmingly in his favour.* N-SING: N *of*n

4 People sometimes refer to events or forces that are difficult or impossible to control as **the tide of** history, for example. *They talked of reversing the tide of history... The tide of war swept back across their country.* N-SING: *the*N *of*n

5 You can talk about a **tide of** something, especially something which is unpleasant, when there is a large and increasing amount of it. *...an ever increasing tide of crime... The tide of nationalism is still running high in a number of republics.* N-SING: N *of*n

6 See also **high tide**, **low tide**.

tide over. If you do something for someone to **tide** them **over**, you help them through a period when they are having difficulties, especially by lending them money. *He wanted money to tide him over... The banks were prepared to put up 50 million guilders to tide over the company.* PHRASAL VERB; V n P; V P n (not pron)

tidings /taɪdɪŋz/. You can use **tidings** to refer to news that someone tells you; a formal, old-fashioned word. *He hated always to be the bearer of bad tidings... I dare to hope that your heart will be touched by the tidings of my survival.* N-PLURAL: usu adj N, oft N *of*n =news

tidy /taɪdi/ **tidier, tidiest; tidies, tidying, tidied** ◆◆◇◇◇

1 Something that is **tidy** is neat and arranged in an orderly way. *Having a tidy desk can seem impossible if you have a busy, demanding job... I'll do your garden, I'll keep that tidy for you.* ♦ **tidily** /taɪdɪli/ *...books and magazines stacked tidily on shelves. ...some tidily arranged papers.* ♦ **tidiness** *Employees are expected to maintain a high standard of tidiness in their dress and appearance.* ADJ-GRADED ≠untidy; ADV: ADV after v, ADV -ed; N-UNCOUNT

2 Someone who is **tidy** likes everything to be neat and arranged in an orderly way. *She's obsessively tidy, always hoovering and polishing.* ♦ **tidiness** *I'm very impressed by your tidiness and order.* ADJ-GRADED ≠untidy; N-UNCOUNT

3 When you **tidy** a place such as a room or cupboard, you make it neat by putting things in their VERB

proper places. *She made her bed, and tidied her room.* — V n

4 A **tidy** amount of money is a large amount; an informal use. *The opportunities are there to make a tidy profit.* — ADJ-GRADED: ADJ n =sizeable

tidy away. When you **tidy** something **away**, you put it in something else so that it is not in the way; used mainly in British English. *The large log basket can be used to tidy toys away... When they'd gone, McMinn tidied away the glasses and tea-cups.* — PHRASAL VERB; V n P; V P n (not pron)

tidy up. When you **tidy up** or **tidy** a place **up**, you put things back in their proper places so that everything is neat. *I really must start tidying the place up... He tried to tidy up, not wanting the maid to see the disarray... Anne made the beds and tidied up the nursery.* — PHRASAL VERB; V n P; V P; V P n (not pron)

tie /taɪ/ **ties, tying, tied** ◆◆◆◆◇

1 If you **tie** two things together or **tie** them, you fasten them together with a knot. *He tied the ends of the plastic bag together... They tied the ends of the bags securely... Mr Saunders tied her hands and feet.* — VERB; V n adv/prep; V n

2 If you **tie** something or someone in a particular place or position, you put them in that place or position and fasten them there using rope or string. *He had tied the dog to one of the trees near the canal... He tied her hands behind her back.* — VERB =attach; V n to n; V n prep/adv

3 If you **tie** a piece of string or cloth around something or **tie** something with a piece of string or cloth, you put a piece of string or cloth around it and fasten the ends together in a knot or bow. *She tied her scarf over her head... Roll the meat and tie it with string... Dad handed me a big box wrapped in gold foil and tied with a red ribbon.* — VERB; V n prep/adv; V n with n; V-ed

4 If you **tie** a knot or bow in something or **tie** something in a knot or bow, you fasten the ends together in a knot or bow. *He took a short length of rope and swiftly tied a slip knot... She tied a knot in a cherry stem... She grabbed her hair in both hands and swept it back, tying it in a loose knot... She wore a checked shirt tied in a knot above the navel.* — VERB; V n; V n in n; V-ed

5 When you **tie** something or when something **ties**, you close or fasten it using a bow or knot. *He pulled on his heavy suede shoes and tied the laces. ...a long white thing around his neck that tied in front in a floppy bow.* — V-ERG; V n; V

6 A **tie** is a long narrow piece of cloth that is worn round the neck under a shirt collar and tied in a knot at the front. Ties are worn mainly by men. *Jason had taken off his jacket and loosened his tie.* — N-COUNT

7 A **tie** is a long narrow piece of cloth, plastic, or wire that is used to attach one thing to another, or to close or fasten something. *...plastic bag ties.* — N-COUNT

8 If one thing **is tied** to another or two things **are tied**, the two things have a close connection or link. *Their cancers are not so clearly tied to radiation exposure... My social life and business life are closely tied.* — VB: usu passive =link, connect; be V-ed to n; pl-n be V-ed

9 If you **are tied** to a particular place or situation, you are forced to accept it and cannot change it. *They had children and were consequently tied to the school holidays... I wouldn't like to be tied to catching the last train home.* — VB: usu passive; be V-ed to n/-ing

10 Ties are the connections you have with people or a place. *Quebec has always had particularly close ties to France... I can't find any tie between her and the town... Louise herself had family ties in Nimes.* — N-COUNT: usu pl, oft N prep =connection, link

11 If two people **tie** in a competition or game or if they **tie** with each other, they have the same number of points or the same degree of success. *Both teams had tied on points and goal difference... Ronan Rafferty had tied with Frank Nobilo.* ► Also a noun. *The first game ended in a tie.* — V-RECIP =draw; pl-n V; V with n; N-COUNT

12 In sport, a **tie** is a match that is part of a competition. The losers are eliminated and the winners go on to the next round. *They'll meet the winners of the first round tie.* — N-COUNT

13 See also **tied**; **black tie**, **bow tie**, **old school tie**. • your **hands are tied**: see **hand**. • **to tie the knot**: see **knot**. • **to tie yourself in knots**: see **knot**.

tie down. A person or thing that **ties** you **down** restricts your freedom in some way. *We'd agreed from the beginning not to tie each other down... The reason he didn't have a family was that he didn't want to be tied down!* — PHRASAL VERB; V n P

tie in with or **tie up with.** If something such as an idea or fact **ties in with** or **ties up with** something else, or if it is **tied in with** or **tied up with** it, it is compatible with it or connected with it. *Our wedding had to tie in with David leaving the army... I've got a feeling that the death may be tied up with his visit in some way.* — PHRASAL VERB ERG; V P P n; Also V n P P n

tie up — PHRASAL VERB

1 When you **tie** something **up**, you fasten string or rope round it so that it is firm or secure. *He tied up the bag and took it outside.* — V P n (not pron); Also V n P

2 If someone **ties** another person **up**, they fasten ropes or chains around them so that they cannot move or escape. *Masked robbers broke in, tied him up, and made off with $8,000... At about 5 a.m. they struck again in Fetcham, tying up a couple and ransacking their house.* — V n P; V P n (not pron)

3 If you **tie** an animal **up**, you fasten it to a fixed object with a piece of rope so that it cannot run away. *Would you go and tie your horse up please... They dismounted, tied up their horses and gave them the grain they had brought.* — =tether; V n P; V P n (not pron)

4 If you **tie up** an issue or problem, you deal with it in a way that gives definite conclusions or answers. *Kingfisher confirmed that it hopes to tie up a deal within the next two weeks... We could have tied the whole case up without getting you and Smith shot at.* — V P n (not pron); V n P

5 See also **tied up**.

tie up with. See **tie in with**. — PHRASAL VERB

tie-break, tie-breaks. A **tie-break** is an extra game which is played in a tennis match when the score in a set is 6-6. The player who wins the tie-break wins the set. — N-COUNT

tie-breaker, tie-breakers. A **tie-breaker** is an extra question or round that decides the winner of a competition or game when two or more people have the same score at the end. — N-COUNT

tied /taɪd/.

1 A **tied** cottage or house belongs to a farmer or other employer and is rented to someone who works for him or her; used in British English. *He lives with his wife in a tied cottage in Hamsey.* — ADJ: usu ADJ n

2 See also **tie**.

tied up. If someone or something is **tied up**, they are busy or being used, with the result that they are not available for anything else; an informal word. *He's tied up with his new book. He's working hard, you know... More and more old people have capital tied up in a house.* — ◆◇◇◇◇ ADJ-GRADED: v-link ADJ, oft ADJ with/in n

tie-dye, tie-dyes, tie-dyeing, tie-dyed

1 If a piece of cloth or a garment is **tie-dyed**, it is tied in knots and then put into dye, so that some parts become more deeply coloured than others. *He wore a T-shirt that had been tie-dyed in bright colours... I bought a great tie-dyed silk scarf.* — VB: usu passive; be V-ed; V-ed

2 A **tie-dye** is a garment or piece of cloth that has been tie-dyed. *They wore tie-dyes and ponchos. ...a hideous tie-dye shirt.* — N-VAR: usu N n

tie-pin, tie-pins; also spelled **tiepin**. A **tie-pin** is a narrow brooch used to pin a person's tie to their shirt. — N-COUNT

tier /tɪə/ **tiers** ◆◇◇◇◇

1 A **tier** is a row or layer of something that has other layers above or below it. *...the auditorium with the tiers of seats around and above it.* ► Also a combining form. *...a three-tier wedding cake.* — N-COUNT: oft N of n; COMB in ADJ

2 A **tier** is a level in an organization or system. *Islanders have campaigned for the abolition of one of the three tiers of municipal power on the island.* ► Also a combining form. *...the possibility of a two-tier system of universities.* — N-COUNT: oft N of n; COMB in ADJ

tiff /tɪf/ **tiffs.** A **tiff** is a small unimportant quarrel, especially between two close friends or between a husband and wife. — N-COUNT

tiger /taɪgə/ **tigers.** A **tiger** is a large fierce animal belonging to the cat family. Tigers are orange with black stripes. • See also **paper tiger**. — ◆◇◇◇◇ N-COUNT

tight /taɪt/ **tighter, tightest** ◆◆◆◇◇

1 **Tight** clothes or shoes are rather small and fit closely to your body. *She walked off the plane in a miniskirt and tight top... His jeans were too tight.* ADJ-GRADED ≠loose
♦ **tightly** *He buttoned his collar tightly round his thick neck.* ADV-GRADED: ADV with v
2 If you hold someone or something **tight**, you hold them firmly and securely. *She just fell into my arms, clutching me tight for a moment... Just hold tight to my hand and follow along... Hold on tight!* ADV-GRADED: ADV after v
► Also an adjective. *As he and Henrietta passed through the gate he kept a tight hold of her arm.* ADJ-GRADED: usu ADJ n
♦ **tightly** *She climbed back into bed and wrapped her arms tightly round her body.* ADV-GRADED: ADV after v
3 **Tight** controls or rules are very strict. *The measures include tight control of media coverage... The Government were prepared to keep a tight hold on public sector pay rises... Security is tight this week at the polling sites.* ADJ-GRADED ♦ **tightly** *The internal media is tightly controlled by the Communist Party.* ADV-GRADED: ADV after v, ADV -ed
4 Something that is shut **tight** is shut very firmly. *The baby lay on his back with his eyes closed tight... I keep the flour and sugar in individual jars, sealed tight with their glass lids... Within minutes she was outside, closing her bedroom door tight behind her... She kept her eyes tight closed.* ADV-GRADED: ADV -ed, ADV after v ♦ **tightly** *Pemberton frowned and closed his eyes tightly... Despite the heat its windows remained tightly closed with wooden shutters.* ADV-GRADED: ADV after v, ADV -ed
5 Skin, cloth, or string that is **tight** is stretched or pulled so that it is smooth or straight. *My skin feels tight and lacking in moisture... Pull the elastic tight and knot the ends.* ADJ-GRADED ♦ **tightly** *Her sallow skin was drawn tightly across the bones of her face.* ADV-GRADED: ADV with v
6 **Tight** is used to describe a group of things or an amount of something that is closely packed together. *She curled up in a tight ball, with her knees tucked up at her chin... The men came in a tight group.* ADJ-GRADED: usu ADJ n ► Also an adverb. *The people sleep on sun lounges packed tight, end to end.* ADV ♦ **tightly** *Many animals travel in tightly packed lorries and are deprived of food, water and rest.* ADV-GRADED: ADV after v, ADV -ed
7 If a part of your body is **tight**, it feels rather uncomfortable and painful, for example because you are ill, anxious, or angry. *It is better to stretch the tight muscles first... Sarah came forward with a tight and angry face... 'There were no survivors, of course,' said Fred, his throat tight.* ADJ-GRADED =taut ♦ **tightness** *Heart disease often shows itself first as pain or tightness in the chest.* N-UNCOUNT
8 A **tight** group of people is one whose members are closely linked by beliefs, feelings, or interests. *He is one of a small, tight knot of people who have been with Madonna since the beginning.* ADJ-GRADED =close
9 A **tight** bend or corner is one that changes direction very quickly so that you cannot see very far round it. *They collided on a tight bend and both cars were extensively damaged.* ADJ-GRADED: usu ADJ n =sharp
10 A **tight** schedule or budget allows very little time or money for unexpected events or expenses. *It's difficult to cram everything into a tight schedule ... Emma is on a tight budget for clothes... Financially things are a bit tight.* ADJ-GRADED
11 A **tight** contest is one where none of the competitors has a clear advantage or looks likely to win, so that it is difficult to say who the winner will be. *It was a very tight match... The most recent polls predict a tight three-way race.* ADJ-GRADED
12 If you say that someone is **tight**, you disapprove of them because they are unwilling to spend their money; an informal use. *What about getting new ones – or are you so tight you won't even spend three roubles?* ADJ-GRADED PRAGMATICS =tight-fisted, mean, stingy
13 See also **airtight, skin-tight.**
14 If you are in **a tight corner** or in **a tight spot**, you are in a difficult situation; an informal expression. *That puts the president in a tight spot if the vote is not a resounding 'yes'... They teach you to use your head to get out of a tight corner.* PHRASES usu prep PHR
15 You can say **'sleep tight'** to someone when they are going to bed as an affectionate way of saying that you hope they will sleep well. *Good night, Davey. Sleep tight.* CONVENTION PRAGMATICS
16 ● to **keep a tight rein on**: see **rein.** ● to **sit tight**: see **sit.**

tighten /taɪtᵊn/ **tightens, tightening, tightened** ◆◆◇◇◇

1 If you **tighten** your grip on something, or if your grip **tightens**, you hold the thing more firmly or securely. *Luke answered by tightening his grip on her shoulder... Her arms tightened about his neck in gratitude... Stefano's grip tightened and his tone became colder.* V-ERG ≠loosen V n V prep V
2 If you **tighten** a rope or chain, or if it **tightens**, it is stretched or pulled hard until it is straight. *The anchorman flung his whole weight back, tightening the rope... The cables tightened and he was lifted gradually from the deck.* V-ERG =tauten ≠slacken V n V
3 If a government or organization **tightens** its grip on a group of people or an activity, or if its grip **tightens**, it begins to have more control over it. *He knows he has considerable support for his plans to tighten his grip on the machinery of central government... As the communist grip on the mainland tightened over the next few years, hundreds of thousands more people fled south.* V-ERG V n V
4 When you **tighten** a screw, nut, or other device, you turn it or move it so that it is more firmly in place or holds something more firmly. *I used my thumbnail to tighten the screw on my lamp... All the bolts were fully tightened.* VERB V n ► **Tighten up** means the same as **tighten**. *It's important to tighten up the wheels properly, otherwise they vibrate loose and fall off.* PHRASAL VERB V P n (not pron) Also V n P
5 If a part of your body **tightens**, the muscles in it become tense and stiff, for example because you are angry or afraid. *Sofia's throat had tightened and she couldn't speak... She saw his jaw tighten and his face lose its colour.* VERB ≠relax V ♦ **tightening** *...a headache caused by tension which results in tightening of the muscles in the neck. ...a slight tightening of the throat.* N-UNCOUNT: usu N *of* n
6 If someone in authority **tightens** a rule, a policy, or a system, they make it stricter or more efficient. *The United States plans to tighten the economic sanctions currently in place... They have tightened security along the border... Take-off and landing procedures have been tightened after two jets narrowly escaped disaster.* VERB ≠relax V n ► **Tighten up** means the same as **tighten**. *Until this week, every attempt to tighten up the law had failed... He accused ministers of breaking election pledges to tighten up on immigration.* PHRASAL VERB V P n (not pron) V P *on* n Also V n P ♦ **tightening** *...the tightening of state control over press and broadcasting.* N-UNCOUNT: oft N *of* n
7 ● to **tighten** your **belt**: see **belt.** ● to **tighten the screw**: see **screw.**

tighten up. If a group, team, or organization **tightens up**, they make an effort to control what they are doing more closely, in order to become more efficient and successful. *I want us to be a bit more sensible this time and tighten up.* PHRASAL VERB ≠loosen up V P ● See also **tighten** 4 and 6.

tight-fisted. If you describe someone as **tight-fisted**, you disapprove of them because they are unwilling to spend money. *He had the reputation of being one of the most tight-fisted and demanding of employers. ...the government's tight-fisted monetary policy.* ADJ-GRADED PRAGMATICS =mean, stingy ≠generous

tight-lipped

1 If you describe someone as **tight-lipped**, you mean that they are unwilling to give any information about something. *Military officials are still tight-lipped about when or whether their forces will launch a ground offensive.* ADJ-GRADED: oft ADJ *about* n/wh ≠forthcoming
2 Someone who is **tight-lipped** has their lips pressed tightly together, especially because they are angry or disapproving. *He was sitting at the other end of the table, tight-lipped and angry.* ADJ-GRADED

tightrope /taɪtroʊp/ **tightropes** ◆◇◇◇◇

1 A **tightrope** is a tightly stretched piece of rope on which an acrobat balances and performs tricks. N-COUNT
2 You can use **tightrope** in expressions such as **walk a tightrope** and **live on a tightrope** to indi- N-COUNT: usu sing

cate that someone is in a difficult situation and has to be very careful about what they say or do. *School administrators walk a tightrope between the demands of the community and the realities of how children really behave... For the past few days Corinne has been living on an emotional tightrope.*

tights /taɪts/. In British English, **tights** are a piece of clothing made of thin material such as nylon that covers your hips and each of your legs and feet separately. Tights are usually worn by women and girls. In American English, the usual word is **pantyhose** when referring to the kind of tights worn by women and girls. *...a new pair of tights.* ◆◇◇◇◇ N-PLURAL: also *a pair of* N

tigress /taɪgrɪs/ **tigresses.** A **tigress** is a female tiger. N-COUNT

tilde /tɪldə/ **tildes.** A **tilde** is a symbol that is written over the letter 'n' in Spanish (ñ) and the letters 'o' (õ) and 'a' (ã) in Portuguese to indicate the way in which they should be pronounced. N-COUNT

tile /taɪl/ **tiles, tiling, tiled** ◆◆◇◇◇

1 Tiles are flat, square pieces of baked clay, carpet, cork, or other substance, which are fixed as a covering onto a floor or wall. *Amy's shoes squeaked on the tiles as she walked down the corridor... The cabins had linoleum tile floors. ...a broken piece of tile.* N-VAR

2 Tiles are flat pieces of baked clay which are used for covering roofs. *...a fine building, with a neat little porch and ornamental tiles on the roof.* N-VAR

3 When someone **tiles** a surface such as a roof or floor, they cover it with tiles. *He wants to tile the bathroom... The terracotta tiled floor gives the place a wonderfully homely character.* ♦ **-tiled** *...a slate-tiled floor. ...a narrow white-tiled room.* VERB V n V-ed COMB in ADJ

4 See also **tiling.**

5 If someone has a night **on the tiles** or is out **on the tiles**, they go out in the evening, for example to a bar or a disco, and do not return home until very late; used in informal British English. *Charlotte was dressed for a night on the tiles... I used to be out on the tiles every night.* PHRASE: n PHR, prep PHR =on the town

tiling /taɪlɪŋ/.

1 You can refer to a surface that is covered by tiles as **tiling**. *The kitchen has smart black tiling, worksurfaces and cupboards.* N-UNCOUNT

2 See also **tile.**

till /tɪl/ **tills, tilling, tilled** ◆◆◆◇◇

1 In spoken English and informal written English, **till** is often used instead of **until.** *They had to wait till Monday to ring the bank manager... I've survived till now, and will go on doing so without help from you.* ► Also a conjunction. *I hadn't left home till I was nineteen... They slept till the alarm bleeper woke them at four.* PREP =until CONJ-SUBORD =until

2 In a shop or other place of business, a **till** is a counter or cash register where money is kept, and where customers pay for what they have bought. *...long queues at tills that make customers angry. ...money stolen from the till in a public house.* N-COUNT =cash register

3 When people **till** land, they prepare the earth and work on it in order to grow crops; a literary use. *Workers were singing as they tilled the rice paddy fields. ...freshly tilled fields.* VERB V n V-ed

tiller /tɪlər/ **tillers.** The **tiller** of a boat is a handle that is fixed to the rudder. It is used to turn the rudder, which then steers the boat. N-COUNT

tilt /tɪlt/ **tilts, tilting, tilted** ◆◆◇◇◇

1 If you **tilt** an object or if it **tilts**, it moves into a sloping position with one end or side higher than the other. *She tilted the mirror and began to comb her hair... Leonard tilted his chair back on two legs and stretched his long body... The boat instantly tilted, filled and sank.* V-ERG V n V n adv/prep V Also V adv/prep

2 If you **tilt** part of your body, usually your head, you move it slightly upwards or to one side. *Mari tilted her head back so that she could look at him... His wife tilted his head to the side and inspected the wound... She tilted her face to kiss me quickly on the chin.* ► Also a noun. *He opened the rear door for me with an apologetic tilt of his head.* VERB V n with adv V n prep V n N-COUNT: usu sing

3 The **tilt** of something is the fact that it tilts or slopes, or the angle at which it tilts or slopes. *...calculations based on our understanding of the tilt of the earth's axis. ...the abrupt tilt of the hill... The 3-metre-square slabs are on a tilt.* N-COUNT: usu sing, oft N *of* n

4 If something or someone **tilts** towards a particular opinion or if something **tilts** them towards it, they change slightly so that they become more in agreement with that opinion or position. *When the political climate tilted towards fundamentalism he was threatened... He continued to urge the Conservative Party to tilt rightwards... The paper has done much to tilt American public opinion in favour of military intervention.* V-ERG V prep/adv V n prep/adv

5 If there is a **tilt towards** a particular opinion or position, that opinion or position is favoured or begins to be favoured. *The chairman also criticised the plan for its tilt towards higher taxes rather than lower spending.* N-SING: N *towards* n

6 A **tilt at** something is an attempt to win or conquer it; used in journalism. *His first tilt at Parliament came in the same year but he failed to win the seat... He was determined to use his remaining year with Manchester United for one last tilt at the League title.* N-COUNT: N *at* n

7 If something is moving or happening **full tilt** or **at full tilt**, it is moving or happening with as much speed, energy, or force as possible. *As John approached at full tilt he saw one lane completely closed off and a queue of traffic blocking the other... Larry Layton's trial is going full tilt right now.* PHRASE: PHR after v

timber /tɪmbər/ **timbers** ◆◆◇◇◇

1 Timber is wood that is used for building houses and making furniture. You can also refer to trees that are grown for this purpose as **timber**. *These Severn Valley woods have been exploited for timber since Saxon times. ...a single-story timber building.* N-UNCOUNT

2 The **timbers** of a ship or house are the large pieces of wood that have been used to build it. *...a bird nestling in the timbers of the roof.* N-COUNT: usu pl

timbered /tɪmbərd/. A **timbered** building has a wooden frame or wooden beams showing on the outside. *Timbered cottages stood around a triangular green.* • See also **half-timbered.** ADJ: usu ADJ n

timber yard, timber yards. In British English, a **timber yard** is a place where timber is stored and sold. The usual American word is **lumberyard** . N-COUNT

timbre /tæmbər/ **timbres.** The **timbre** of someone's voice or of a musical instrument is the particular quality of sound that it has; a formal word. *His voice had a deep timbre... The timbre of the violin is far richer than that of the mouth organ.* N-COUNT: usu sing, oft N *of* n

time /taɪm/ **times, timing, timed** ◆◆◆◆◆

1 Time is what we measure in minutes, hours, days, and years. *...a two-week period of time... Time passed, and still Ma did not appear... As time went on the visits got more and more regular... The social significance of religion has changed over time.* N-UNCOUNT

2 You use **time** to ask or talk about a specific point in the day, which can be stated in hours and minutes and is shown on clocks. *'What time is it?'—'Eight o'clock.'... He asked me the time... What time did he leave?... I phoned my mother to ask what time she was coming home... The time is now 19 minutes past the hour.* N-SING: *what/the* N

3 The **time** when something happens is the point in the day when it happens or is supposed to happen. *Departure times are 0815 from St Quay, and 1815 from St Helier.* • See also **opening time.** N-COUNT

4 You use **time** to refer to the system of expressing time and counting hours that is used in a particular part of the world. *The tidal predictions are expressed in Greenwich Mean Time. Add one hour for British Summer Time... The incident happened just after ten o'clock local time.* N-UNCOUNT: supp N

5 You use **time** to refer to the period that someone spends doing something or when something has been happening. *Adam spent a lot of time in his grandfather's office... He wouldn't have the time or money to take care of me... Listen to me, I haven't got much time... It's obvious that you need more* N-UNCOUNT: also *a* N *time to think... The route was blocked for some time... For a long time I didn't tell anyone... A short time later they sat down to eat... Thank you very much for your time.*

6 If you say that something has been happening for **a time** you mean that it has been happening for a fairly long period of time. *He was also for a time the art critic of 'The Scotsman'... He stayed for quite a time... After a time they came to a pond.* N-SING: a N

7 You use **time** to refer to a period of time or a point in time, when you are describing what is happening then. For example, if something happened **at** a particular **time**, that is when it happened. If it happens **at all times**, it always happens. *We were in the same college, which was male-only at that time... By this time he was thirty... During the time I was married I tried to be the perfect wife... It was a time of terrible uncertainty... Homes are more affordable than at any time in the past five years... It seemed like a good time to tell her... There were times when he would ring his bell at all hours of the day or night.* N-COUNT: with supp, oft prep N

8 You use **time** or **times** to talk about a particular period in history or in your life. *They were hard times and his parents had been struggling to raise their family... We'll be alone together, quite like old times... We are in one of the most severe recessions in modern times... A 'Felucca' is the traditional Nile sailboat, unchanged since the time of the pharaohs.* N-COUNT: with supp, usu adj N, N of n

9 You can use **the times** to refer to the present time and to modern fashions, tastes, and developments. For example, if you say that someone **keeps up with the times**, you mean they are fashionable or aware of modern developments. If you say they are **behind the times**, you mean they are unfashionable or not aware of them. *He is unafraid to move with the times... This approach is now seriously out of step with the times... Johnny has changed his image to fit the times.* N-PLURAL: the N

10 When you describe the **time** that you had on a particular occasion or during a particular part of your life, you are describing the sort of experience that you had then. *Sarah and I had a great time while the kids were away... She's had a really tough time the last year and a half... You had an easy time of it at home... I try to remember all the good times I've had here.* N-COUNT: adj N

11 Your **time** is the amount of time that you have to live, or to do a particular thing. *Now Martin has begun to suffer the effects of AIDS, and he says his time is running out... Every administration has its time. And when your time is over, you leave... I doubt I would change anything if I had my time again.* N-SING: poss N

12 If you say it is **time** for something, **time** to do something, or **time** someone did something, you mean that this thing ought to happen or be done now. *I think it's time for a change so I'll be voting Labour... It was time for him to go to work... This was no time to make a speech... The time has come to put an end to the conflict... It's time you went to school.* N-UNCOUNT: oft N for n, N to-inf, N that

13 When you talk about a **time** when something happens, you are referring to a specific occasion when it happens. *Every time she travels on the bus it's delayed by at least three hours... The last time I saw her was about sixteen years ago... House prices are rising for the first time since November... Next time you go shopping, throw in a few extra fruit and vegetables... Remember that time she picked up my daughter when I was ill?.* N-COUNT: with supp

14 You use **time** after numbers to say how often something happens. *It was her job to make tea three times a day... How many times has your mother told you never to talk to strangers?... The Masters golf tournament was won a second time by the American Ben Hogan.* N-COUNT: usu num/ord N

15 You use **times** after numbers when comparing one thing to another and saying, for example, how much bigger, smaller, better, or worse it is. *Its profits are rising four times faster than the average company... Young people were several times more likely to be out of work than older members of the workforce... He polled four times as many votes as his rival. ...an area five times the size of Britain.* N-PLURAL: num N compar, num N as adj/adv, num N n

16 You use **times** in arithmetic to link numbers or amounts that are multiplied together to reach a total. *Four times six is 24.* CONJ-COORD

17 Someone's **time** in a race is the amount of time it takes them to finish the race. *He was over a second faster than his previous best time... She recorded a time of two minutes 8.74 seconds.* N-COUNT: with supp, oft poss N, N of n

18 The **time** of a piece of music is the number of beats that the piece has in each bar. *A reel is in four-four time, and a jig is in six-eight time.* N-UNCOUNT: usu supp N, oft in N

19 If you **time** something for a particular time, you plan or decide to do it or cause it to happen at this time. *He timed the election to coincide with new measures to boost the economy... We had timed our visit for March 7... He had timed his intervention well... Operation Amazon is timed to coincide with the start of the dry season.* VERB V n to-inf, V n for n, V n adv, V-ed, Also V n

20 If you **time** an action or activity, you measure how long someone takes to do it or how long it lasts. *He timed each performance with a stopwatch.* VERB V n

21 See also **timing**.

22 If you say it is **about time** that something was done, you are saying in an emphatic way that it should happen or be done now, and really should have happened or been done sooner. *It's about time a few movie makers with original ideas were given a chance... 'Here she is.'—'About time too.'* PHRASES it v-link PHR that, PHR as reply PRAGMATICS

23 If you do something **ahead of time**, you do it before a particular event or before you need to, in order to be well prepared. *Find out ahead of time what regulations apply to your situation.* PHR after v =in advance

24 If someone is **ahead of** their **time** or **before** their **time**, they have new ideas a long time before other people start to think in the same way. *He was indeed ahead of his time in employing women, ex-convicts, and the handicapped... His only fundamental mistake, he insists, is that he was 20 years before his time.* v-link PHR, oft PHR in -ing

25 If something happens or is done **all the time**, it happens or is done continually. *We can't be together all the time... I get the two of them mixed up all the time, they're so similar.* PHR after v =continually

26 You say **at a time** after an amount to say how many things or how much of something is involved in one action, place, or group. *Beat in the eggs, one at a time... She ran for the staircase and down the steps, taking them two at a time... Do you sometimes find that you are doing very little physical exercise for several weeks at a time?* amount PHR

27 If something could happen **at any time**, it is possible that it will happen very soon, though nobody can predict exactly when. *Conditions are still very tense and the fighting could escalate at any time.* PHR with cl =at any moment

28 You say **at the best of times** when you are making a negative or critical comment to emphasize that it is true even when the circumstances are as favourable as possible. *His voice is hardly resonant at the best of times. Today he is almost inaudible.* PHR with cl PRAGMATICS

29 If you say that something was the case **at one time**, you mean that it was the case during a particular period in the past. *At one time 400 men, women and children lived in the village. ...enormous glaciers, which at one time covered vast areas of the northern hemisphere.* PHR with cl

30 If two or more things exist, happen, or are true **at the same time**, they exist, happen, or are true together although they seem to contradict each other. *I was afraid of her, but at the same time I really liked her... She was somehow able to look sad and cheerful at the same time.* PHR with cl

31 **At the same time** is used to introduce a statement that slightly changes or contradicts the previous statement. *I don't think I set out to come up with a different sound for each album. At the same time, I do have a sense of what is right for the moment.* PHR with cl PRAGMATICS

32 You use **at times** to say that something happens or is true on some occasions or at some moments. PHR with cl/group =sometimes

The debate was highly emotional at times... At times she had an overwhelming desire to see him... He went on listening to her, at times impatient and at times fascinated.

33 If you say that something was **before** your **time**, you mean that it happened or existed before you were born or before you were able to know about it or remember it. *'You've never seen the Marilyn Monroe film?'—'No, I think it was a bit before my time.'* usu v-link PHR

34 If someone has reached a particular stage in life **before** their **time**, they have reached it at a younger age than is normal. *The small print has forced me, years before my time, to buy spectacles... There is nothing like a college town to make you feel old before your time.* PHR after v

35 In British English, if you say **not before time** after a statement has been made about something that has been done, you are saying in an emphatic way that you think it should have been done sooner. *The virus is getting more and more attention, and not before time... Not before time, that is about to change.* PHR with cl PRAGMATICS

36 Someone who **is doing time** is in prison; an informal expression. *He is serving 11 years for robbery, and did time for a similar offence before that.* V inflects

37 If you say that something will be the case **for all time**, you mean that it will be the case forever. *The desperate condition of the world is that madness has always been here, and that it will remain so for all time.* usu PHR with v, PHR with group

38 If something is the case or will happen **for the time being**, it is the case or will happen now, but only until something else becomes possible or happens. *For the time being, however, immunotherapy is still in its experimental stages... The situation is calm for the time being.* PHR with cl =for now

39 If you do something **from time to time**, you do it occasionally but not regularly. *Her daughters visited him from time to time when he was ill.* PHR with v, PHR with cl =now and again

40 If you say that something is the case **half the time** you mean that it often is the case; an informal expression. *Half the time, I don't have the slightest idea what he's talking about.* PHR with cl

41 In informal English, if you say that you **have no time for** someone or something, you mean you do not like them or approve of them, and if you say that you **have a lot of time for** someone or something, you mean you like them or approve of them very much. *When I think of what he's done to my mother and me, I've just got no time for him... I have got a lot of time for people who are prepared to put the welfare of their party above their own vanity.* V inflects, PHR n

42 If you say that **it is high time** that something happened or was done, you are saying in an emphatic way that it should happen or be done now, and really should have happened or been done sooner. *It is high time the Government displayed a more humanitarian approach towards victims of the recession... It is high time to consider the problem on a global scale.* V inflects, PHR that, PHR to-inf PRAGMATICS

43 If you are **in time** for a particular event, you are not too late for it. *I arrived just in time for my flight to London... She set the alarm so she'd wake up in time to give her two sons their medication.* PHR after v, oft PHR *for* n, PHR to-inf

44 If you say that something will happen **in time** or **given time**, you mean that it will happen eventually, when a lot of time has passed. *He would sort out his own problems, in time... Tina believed that, given time, her business would become profitable.* PHR with cl

45 If you are playing, singing, or dancing **in time** with a piece of music, you are following the rhythm and speed of the music correctly. If you are **out of time** with it, you are not following the rhythm and speed of the music correctly. *Her body swayed in time with the music... We were standing onstage playing completely out of time.* PHR after v, oft PHR *with* n

46 If you say that something will happen, for example, **in** a week**'s time** or **in** two years**' time**, you mean that it will happen a week from now or two years from now. *Presidential elections are due to be held in ten days' time... In a year's time we will all be laughing about it.* PHR with cl

47 If you arrive somewhere **in good time**, you arrive early so that there is time to spare before a particular event. *If we're out, we always make sure we're home in good time for the programme.* PHR after v, oft PHR *for* n

48 If you tell someone that something will happen **in good time** or **all in good time**, you are telling them to be patient because it will happen eventually. *There will be many advanced exercises that you won't be able to do at first. You will get to them in good time... 'I can't wait to be grown up.'—'All in good time.'* PHR after v, PHR as reply

49 If something happens **in no time** or **in next to no time**, it happens almost immediately or very quickly. *He's going to be just fine. At his age he'll heal in no time... He expects to be out of prison in next to no time.* PHR with cl

50 If you do something **in** your **own time**, you do it at the speed or pace that you choose, rather than allowing anyone to hurry you. *Now, in your own time, tell me what happened.* PHR with cl

51 In British English, if you do something such as work **in** your **own time**, you do it in your free time rather than, for example, at work or school. The usual American expression is **on** your **own time**. *If I choose to work on other projects in my own time, then I say that is my business.* PHR with cl

52 If you **keep time** to a beat when playing or singing music, you follow or play the beat, without going too fast or too slowly. *As he sang he kept time on a small drum.* V inflects

53 When you talk about how well a watch or clock **keeps time**, you are talking about how accurately it measures time. *Some pulsars keep time better than the earth's most accurate clocks.* V inflects

54 If you **make time** for a particular activity or person, you arrange to have some free time so that you can do the activity or spend time with the person. *Before leaving the city, be sure to make time for a shopping trip... She had made time for me in the midst of her busy schedule... I think you should always make time to see your friends.* V inflects, oft PHR *for* n, PHR to-inf

55 If you say that you **made good time** on a journey, you mean it did not take you very long compared to the length of time you expected it to take. *They had left early in the morning, on quiet roads, and made good time.* V inflects

56 If someone is **making up for lost time**, they are doing something intensively and with enthusiasm because they have not had the opportunity to do it before or when they were younger. *Five years older than the majority of officers of his same rank, he was determined to make up for lost time.* V inflects

57 If you **are marking time**, you are doing something that is not particularly useful or interesting while you wait for something more important or interesting to happen. *I think they're all simply marking time until they see what the Clinton administration has in store for them.* V inflects

58 If you say that something happens or is the case **nine times out of ten** or **ninety-nine times out of a hundred**, you mean that it happens on nearly every occasion or is almost always the case. *When they want something, nine times out of ten they get it... Ninety-nine times out of a hundred when parents say to their children 'I know how you feel', they are lying.* PHR with cl

59 If you say that someone or something is, for example, the best writer **of all time**, or the most successful film **of all time**, you mean that they are the best or most successful that there has ever been. *'Monopoly' is one of the best-selling games of all time... This is my favourite song of all time.* n PHR, usu PHR after adj-superl

60 If you are **on time**, you are not late. *Don't worry, she'll be on time... Their planes usually arrive on time.* v-link PHR, PHR after v

61 If you say that it is **only a matter of time** or **only a question of time** before something happens, you mean that it is unavoidable and will definitely happen at some future date. *It now seems only a matter of time before they resign... The doctors are confi-* v-link PHR, oft *it* v-link PHR *before* cl

dent he'll make a full recovery. It's just a question of time.

62 When you refer to **our time** or **our times** you are referring to the present period in the history of the world. *It would be wrong to say that the Church doesn't enter the great moral debates of our time.* — usu *of/in/for* PHR

63 If you do something to **pass the time** you do it because you have some time available and not because you really want to do it. *Without particular interest and just to pass the time, I read a story... During a lunch break, he and the buyer passed the time with some chitchat.* — V inflects

64 If you **pass the time of day** with someone, you have a short friendly conversation with them. *One or two people went up and passed the time of day with her... They can't even say 'good morning' or pass the time of day.* — V inflects, oft PHR *with* n

65 If you **play for time**, you try to make something happen more slowly, because you do not want it to happen or because you need time to think about what to do if it happens. *The president's decision is being seen as an attempt to play for time.* — V inflects

66 If you say that something will **take time**, you mean that it will take a long time. *Change will come, but it will take time... It takes time to build up intimacy.* — V inflects, oft *it* PHR to-inf

67 If you **take** your **time** doing something, you do it quite slowly and do not hurry. *'Take your time,' Cross told him. 'I'm in no hurry.'... He took his time answering, knowing that he must select his words with great care.* — V inflects, oft PHR -ing

68 If a child can **tell the time**, they are able to find out what the time is by looking at a clock or watch. *My four-year-old daughter cannot quite tell the time.* — V inflects

69 If something happens **time after time**, it happens in a similar way on many occasions. *Burns had escaped from jail time after time... Time after time, I hear these stories of missing children on the news.* — PHR with cl, PHR after v =repeatedly

70 If you say that **time flies**, you mean that it seems to pass very quickly. *Time flies when you're having fun.* — V inflects

71 If you have **the time of** your **life**, you enjoy yourself very much indeed. *We're taking our little grandchild away with us. We'll make sure he has the time of his life... For some it was awful, for others, particularly the young, it was the time of their lives.* — Ns inflect, PHR after v, v-link PHR

72 If you say there is **no time to lose** or **no time to be lost**, you mean you must hurry as fast as you can to do something. *He rushed home, realising there was no time to lose.* — v-link PHR, PHR after v

73 If you say that **time will tell** whether something is true or correct, you mean that it will not be known until some time in the future whether it is true or correct. *Only time will tell whether Broughton's optimism is justified... I can't see any problems, but time will tell.* — oft PHR whether/if

74 If you **waste no time** in doing something, you take the opportunity to do it immediately or quickly. *Tom wasted no time in telling me why he had come.* — V inflects, usu PHR *in* -ing

75 • **time and again**: see **again**. • **to the end of time**: see **end**. • **in the fullness of time**: see **fullness**. • **there's no time like the present**: see **present**. • **the time is ripe**: see **ripe**.

time and motion. A **time and motion** study is an analysis of industrial or work procedures in order to discover the most efficient methods of working. — N-UNCOUNT: usu N n

time bomb, time bombs; also spelled **time-bomb**.

1 A **time bomb** is a bomb with a mechanism that causes it to explode at a particular time. — N-COUNT

2 If you describe something as a **time bomb**, you mean that it is likely to have a serious effect on a person or situation at a later date, especially if you think it will cause a lot of damage. *This proposal is a political time bomb that could cost the government the next election... Unemployment is building up into a social time bomb across the industrialised world.* — N-COUNT: oft adj N

time-consuming; also spelled **time consuming**. If something is **time-consuming**, it takes a lot of time. *It's just very time consuming to get such a large quantity of data... Starting a new business, however small, is a time-consuming exercise.* — ◆◇◇◇◇ ADJ-GRADED: oft *it* v-link ADJ to-inf

time frame, time frames. The **time frame** of an event is the length of time during which it happens or develops; a formal expression. *The time frame within which all this occurred was from September 1985 to March 1986... Discussions at the UN could include a time frame for action.* — N-COUNT =time scale

time-honoured. A **time-honoured** tradition or way of doing something is one that has been used and respected for a very long time. *The beer is brewed in the time-honoured way at the Castle Eden Brewery.* — ADJ: ADJ n =age-old

timekeeper /taɪmkiːpəʳ/ **timekeepers;** also spelled **time-keeper**.

1 A **timekeeper** is a person or an instrument that records or checks the time. — N-COUNT

2 If you say that someone is a good **timekeeper**, you mean that they regularly arrive on time at work. If you say that they are a poor **timekeeper**, you mean that they are often late. — N-COUNT: supp N

timekeeping /taɪmkiːpɪŋ/

1 If you talk about someone's **timekeeping**, you are talking about how good they are at arriving in time for things. *I am trying to improve my timekeeping... He was penalized for bad timekeeping.* — N-UNCOUNT: poss N, adj N

2 **Timekeeping** is the process or activity of timing an event or series of events. *Who did the timekeeping? ...improvements in timekeeping technology.* — N-UNCOUNT

time lag, time lags; also spelled **time-lag**. A **time lag** is a fairly long interval of time between one event and another related event that happens after it. *...the time-lag between theoretical research and practical applications.* — N-COUNT: usu sing, oft N *between* pl-n

timeless /taɪmləs/. If you describe something as **timeless**, you mean that it is so good or beautiful that it cannot be affected by changes in society or fashion. *There is a timeless quality to his best work. ...the timeless appeal of her designs.* — ◆◇◇◇◇ ADJ-GRADED
♦ **timelessness** *Maybe it was the trees that gave this place its atmosphere of mystery and timelessness.* — N-UNCOUNT

time limit, time limits. A **time limit** is a date before which a particular task must be completed. *We have extended the time limit for claims until July 30.* — ◆◇◇◇◇ N-COUNT

timely /taɪmli/. If you describe an event as **timely**, you approve of it because it happens exactly at the moment when it is most useful, effective, or relevant. *The recent outbreaks of cholera are a timely reminder that this disease is still a serious health hazard... The exhibition is timely, since 'self-taught' art is catching on in a big way.* — ◆◇◇◇◇ ADJ-GRADED PRAGMATICS =opportune

time out, time outs; also spelled **time-out**. — ◆◇◇◇◇

1 In basketball, ice hockey, and some other sports, when a team calls a **time out**, they call a stop to the game for a few minutes in order to rest and discuss tactics. — N-VAR

2 If you take **time out** from a job or activity, you have a break from it and do something different instead. *He took time out from campaigning to accompany his mother to dinner. ...women returning to the labour market after time out to raise young families.* — N-UNCOUNT: oft N *from* n, N to-inf

timepiece /taɪmpiːs/ **timepieces;** also spelled **time piece**. A **timepiece** is a clock, watch, or other device that measures and shows time; an old-fashioned word. — N-COUNT

timer /taɪməʳ/ **timers.** A **timer** is a device that measures time, especially one that is part of a machine and causes it to start or stop working at specific times. *...electronic timers that automatically switch on the lights when it gets dark.* • See also **egg timer**. — ◆◇◇◇◇ N-COUNT

time scale, time scales; also spelled **timescale**. The **time scale** of an event is the length of time during which it happens or develops. *The likelihood is that these companies now will show excellent profits on a two-year time scale... He gave no time-scale for these steps.* N-COUNT: oft *on* N with supp =time frame

time-server, time-servers; also spelled **timeserver**. If you refer to someone as a **time-server**, you disapprove of them because they are making very little effort at work and are just waiting until they retire or leave for a new job. N-COUNT PRAGMATICS

time-share, time-shares; also spelled **time share**. If you have a **time-share**, you have the right to use a particular property as holiday accommodation for a specific amount of time each year. N-VAR

time signal, time signals. In Britain, the **time signal** is the series of high-pitched sounds that are broadcast at certain times on the radio, for example at exactly one o'clock or exactly six o'clock. N-COUNT: usu *the* N in sing =the pips

time signature, time signatures. The **time signature** of a piece of music consists of two numbers written at the beginning that show how many beats there are in each bar. N-COUNT

time switch, time switches. A **time switch** is a device that causes a machine to start or stop working at specific times. N-COUNT

timetable /taɪmteɪbəl/ **timetables, timetabling, timetabled** ◆◆◇◇◇

1 A **timetable** is a plan of the times when particular events are to take place. *The timetable was hopelessly optimistic... Don't you realize we're working to a timetable? We have to have results... The two countries are to try to agree a timetable for formal talks.* N-COUNT =schedule

2 In a school or college, a **timetable** is a chart that shows the times in the week at which particular subjects are taught. You can also refer to the range of subjects that a student learns or the classes that a teacher teaches as their **timetable**. *Options are offered subject to staff availability and the constraints of the timetable... Members of the union will continue to teach their full timetables.* N-COUNT

3 A **timetable** is a list of the times when trains, boats, buses, or aeroplanes are supposed to arrive at or depart from a particular place. *For a local bus timetable, contact Dyfed County Council.* N-COUNT

4 If something **is timetabled**, it is scheduled to happen or do something at a particular time; used mainly in British English. *On both days, three very different trains will be timetabled... Opie is timetabled to work a four-day week.* ♦ **timetabling** *Timetabling is a nightmare for all schools.* VB: usu passive *be* V-ed *be* V-ed to-inf N-UNCOUNT

time trial, time trials. In cycling and some other sports, a **time trial** is a contest in which competitors race along a course individually, in as fast a time as possible, instead of racing directly against each other. ◆◇◇◇◇ N-COUNT

time-worn; also spelled **timeworn**. Something that is **time-worn** is old or has been used a lot over a long period of time. *Even in the dim light the equipment looked old and time-worn... These time-worn techniques are often very effective approaches to the illnesses of the present day.* ADJ-GRADED

time zone, time zones; also spelled **timezone**. A **time zone** is one of the areas into which the world is divided where the time is calculated as being a particular number of hours behind or ahead of GMT. ◆◇◇◇◇ N-COUNT

timid /tɪmɪd/ ◆◇◇◇◇

1 **Timid** people are shy, nervous, and have no courage or self-confidence. *A timid child, Isabella had learned obedience at an early age.* ♦ **timidity** /tɪmɪdɪti/ *She doesn't ridicule my timidity.* ♦ **timidly** *The little boy stepped forward timidly and shook Leo's hand.* ADJ-GRADED ≠confident N-UNCOUNT ADV-GRADED: usu ADV with v

2 If you describe someone's attitudes or actions as **timid**, you are criticizing them for being too cautious or slow to act, because they are nervous about the possible consequences of their actions. *The President's critics say he has been too timid in responding to changing international developments... The newspaper called the plan timid and unimaginative.* ♦ **timidity** *He was soon disillusioned by the government's timidity on social reform.* ♦ **timidly** *A number of these states are moving timidly towards multi-party democracy.* ADJ-GRADED PRAGMATICS =half-hearted ≠assertive N-UNCOUNT ADV-GRADED: ADV with v

timing /taɪmɪŋ/ ◆◆◇◇◇

1 **Timing** is the skill or action of judging the right moment in a situation or activity at which to do something. *His photo is a wonderful happy moment caught with perfect timing... If your timing is right, you may be fortunate enough to stumble across a village fiesta.* N-UNCOUNT: usu supp N

2 **Timing** is used to refer to the time at which something happens or is planned to happen, or to the length of time that something takes. *The timing of the announcement from the Iraqi leader is seen as significant.* N-UNCOUNT: usu N *of* n

3 See also **time**.

timorous /tɪmərəs/

1 If you describe someone as **timorous**, you mean that they are frightened and nervous of other people and situations; a literary word. *He is a reclusive, timorous creature.* ADJ-GRADED =timid

2 If you describe someone's actions or decisions as **timorous**, you are criticizing them for being too cautious or weak, because the person is not very confident and is worried about the possible consequences of their actions. *Some delegates believe the final declaration is likely to be too timorous.* ADJ-GRADED PRAGMATICS =feeble

timpani /tɪmpəni/. **Timpani** are kettledrums that are played in an orchestra. N-PLURAL =kettledrum

tin /tɪn/ **tins** ◆◆◇◇◇

1 **Tin** is a soft silvery-white metal. *...a factory that turns scrap metal into tin cans. ...a tin-roofed hut.* N-UNCOUNT

2 In British English, a **tin** is a metal container which is filled with food and sealed in order to preserve the food for long periods of time. The usual American word is **can**. *She popped out to buy a tin of soup.* ► A **tin** of food is the amount of food contained in a tin. *He had survived by eating a small tin of fruit every day.* N-COUNT: oft N *of* n N-COUNT: oft N *of* n

3 A **tin** is a metal container with a lid in which things such as biscuits, cakes, or tobacco can be kept. *Store the cookies in an airtight tin... He reached for a tin of tobacco on the shelf behind him.* ► A **tin** of things is the amount of things contained in a tin. *They emptied out the remains of the tin of paint and smeared it on the inside of the van.* N-COUNT: oft supp N, N *of* n N-COUNT: oft N *of* n

4 In British English, a baking **tin** is a metal container used for baking things such as cakes and bread in an oven. The usual American word is **pan**. *Pour the mixture into the cake tin and bake for 45 minutes. ...a 2 lb loaf tin.* N-COUNT: usu supp N

tincture /tɪŋktʃəʳ/ **tinctures.** A **tincture** is a medicine consisting of alcohol and a small amount of a drug. *...a few drops of tincture of iodine.* N-VAR: oft N *of* n

tinder /tɪndəʳ/. **Tinder** consists of small pieces of something dry, especially wood or grass, that burns easily and can be used for lighting a fire. N-UNCOUNT =kindling

tinderbox /tɪndəʳbɒks/ **tinderboxes;** also spelled **tinder box**. If you say that a situation is a **tinderbox**, you mean that it is very tense and something dangerous or unpleasant is likely to happen very soon. N-COUNT: usu sing

tine /taɪn/ **tines.** The **tines** of something such as a fork, a rake, or a deer's antlers are the long pointed parts; a formal word. N-COUNT

tinfoil /tɪnfɔɪl/; also spelled **tin foil. Tinfoil** consists of shiny metal in the form of a thin sheet which is used for wrapping food. N-UNCOUNT =foil

tinge /tɪndʒ/ **tinges.** A **tinge** of a colour, feeling, or quality is a small amount of it. *His skin had an unhealthy greyish tinge... Could there have been a slight tinge of envy in Eva's voice?* ◆◇◇◇◇ N-COUNT: usu with supp =hint

tinged /tɪndʒd/

1 If something is **tinged** with a particular colour, it has a small amount of that colour in it. *His dark hair was just tinged with grey... The living room was tinged yellow by light filtered through the curtains.* ► Also a combining form. *...pink-tinged flowers.* ADJ-GRADED: usu v-link ADJ, oft ADJ *with* n, ADJ colour COMB in ADJ

2 If something is **tinged with** a particular feeling or quality, it has or shows a small amount of that feeling or quality. *Her homecoming was tinged with sadness.* ► Also a combining form. *...the jazz-tinged rock of the early Seventies.* ADJ-GRADED: usu v-link ADJ, oft ADJ *with* n; COMB in ADJ

tingle /tɪŋgᵊl/ **tingles, tingling, tingled** ◆◇◇◇◇

1 When a part of your body **tingles**, you feel a slight prickling or stinging sensation there. *The backs of his thighs tingled. ...a taste which is first sweet, then bitter, leaving a tingling sensation on the tongue.* VERB V V-ing
♦ **tingling** *Its effects on the nervous system include weakness, paralysis, and tingling in the hands and feet.* N-UNCOUNT

2 If you **tingle** with a feeling such as excitement or anticipation, you feel it very strongly. *She tingled with excitement... When I look over and see Terry I tingle all over.* ► Also a noun. *I felt a sudden tingle of excitement.* VERB V *with* n V N-COUNT: usu sing

tingly /tɪŋgli/

1 If something makes your body feel **tingly**, it gives you a prickling feeling. *These lotions tend to give the skin a tingly sensation.* ADJ-GRADED

2 If something pleasurable or exciting makes you feel **tingly**, it gives you a strange warm feeling. *He had a way of sounding so sincere. It made me warm and tingly... I go all tingly when I think of what might happen.* ADJ-GRADED

tinker /tɪŋkəʳ/ **tinkers, tinkering, tinkered** ◆◇◇◇◇

1 If you **tinker with** something, you make some small adjustments to it, in an attempt to improve it or repair it. *Instead of the Government admitting its error, it just tinkered with the problem... They tinkered with the engine... It is not enough to tinker at the edges; our objective must be to reconstruct the entire system.* ♦ **tinkering** *No amount of tinkering is going to improve matters.* VERB V *with* n V N-UNCOUNT

2 In former times, a **tinker** was a person who did not have a fixed home, but travelled from place to place mending metal pots and doing other small repair jobs. N-COUNT

3 In British English, some people refer to any traveller or gipsy, especially one who is Irish, as a **tinker**; an offensive use. N-COUNT

tinkle /tɪŋkᵊl/ **tinkles, tinkling, tinkled**

1 If something **tinkles**, it makes a clear, high-pitched, ringing noise, especially as small parts of it strike a surface. *A fresh cascade of splintered glass tinkled to the floor... We strolled past tinkling fountains and perfumed gardens.* ► Also a noun. *...a tinkle of broken glass.* VERB V prep/adv V-ing Also V N-COUNT: usu sing

2 If a bell **tinkles** or if you **tinkle** it, it makes a quiet ringing noise as you shake it. *An old-fashioned bell tinkled as he pushed open the door... Miss Peel tinkled her desk bell and they all sat down again.* ► Also a noun. *...the tinkle of goat bells.* V-ERG V V n N-COUNT: usu sing

tinned /tɪnd/. **Tinned** food is food that has been preserved by being sealed in a tin; used mainly in British English. The usual American word is **canned**. *...tinned tomatoes. ...tinned salmon.* ◆◇◇◇◇ ADJ: usu ADJ n

tinny /tɪni/

1 If you describe a sound as **tinny**, you mean that it has an irritating, high-pitched quality. *He could hear the tinny sound of a radio playing a pop song. ...a small tinny voice.* ADJ-GRADED

2 If you use **tinny** to describe something such as a cheap car, you mean that it is made of thin metal and is of poor quality. *It is one of the cheapest cars on the market, with tinny bodywork.* ADJ-GRADED

tin opener, tin openers; also spelled **tin-opener**. A **tin opener** is a tool that is used for opening tins of food; used mainly in British English. The usual American word is **can opener**. N-COUNT

tinpot /tɪnpɒt/; also spelled **tin-pot**. You can use **tinpot** to describe a leader, country, or government that you consider to be unimportant and inferior to most others; used mainly in British English. *The territories are ruled by a tinpot dictator, who only holds power because the president allows him to.* ADJ: ADJ n PRAGMATICS

tinsel /tɪnsᵊl/. **Tinsel** consists of small strips of shiny paper attached to long pieces of thread. People use tinsel as a decoration at Christmas. N-UNCOUNT

Tinseltown /tɪnsᵊltaʊn/. People sometimes refer to Hollywood as **Tinseltown**, especially when they want to show that they disapprove of it or when they are making fun of it. N-PROPER PRAGMATICS

tint /tɪnt/ **tints, tinting, tinted** ◆◇◇◇◇

1 A **tint** is a small amount of colour. *Its large leaves often show a delicate purple tint... Green has many different shades and tints.* N-COUNT

2 If you put a **tint** on your hair, you dye it a slightly different colour. *You've had a tint on your hair... Haircuts cost £6, tints £10.* N-COUNT

3 If something **is tinted**, it has a small amount of a particular colour or dye in it. *Eyebrows can be tinted with the same dye... Glass bottles are filled with water tinted with food colourings... Most of the dirt was on the outside of the tinted glass.* ♦ **-tinted** *He wore green-tinted glasses.* VB: usu passive *be* V-ed V-ed COMB in ADJ

tin whistle, tin whistles. A **tin whistle** is a simple musical instrument in the shape of a metal pipe with holes. Tin whistles make a high sound and are often used in folk music. N-COUNT =penny whistle

tiny /taɪni/ **tinier, tiniest.** Something or someone that is **tiny** is extremely small. *The living room is tiny... Though she was tiny, she had a very loud voice... The crop represents a tiny fraction of U.S. production.* ◆◆◆◇◇ ADJ-GRADED

-tion /-ʃᵊn/ **-tions.** See **-ation**.

tip /tɪp/ **tips, tipping, tipped** ◆◆◆◇◇

1 The **tip** of something long and narrow is the end of it. *The sleeves covered his hands to the tips of his fingers... She poked and shifted things with the tip of her walking stick... Hurricane Andrew has passed over the southern tip of Florida.* N-COUNT: oft N *of* n

2 If you **tip** an object or part of your body or if it **tips**, it moves into a sloping position with one end or side higher than the other. *He leaned away from her, and she had to tip her head back to see him... A young boy is standing on a stool, reaching for a cookie jar, and the stool is about to tip... The north pole is slightly tipped towards the sun.* V-ERG V n adv/prep V V-ed

3 If you **tip** something somewhere, you pour it there. *Tip the vegetables into a bowl... She took out the plate, stared blankly at the dried-up food on it, and tipped it into the bin... Tip away the salt and wipe the pan.* VERB V n prep V n with adv

4 In British English, to **tip** rubbish means to get rid of it by leaving it somewhere. *...the costs of tipping rubbish in landfills... How do you stop people tipping?... We live in a street off Soho Road and there's rubbish tipped everywhere.* VERB V n V V-ed

5 A **tip** is a place where rubbish is left; used mainly in British English. *Officers had found a large bread knife on the rubbish tip... I took a load of rubbish and grass cuttings to the tip.* N-COUNT

6 In British English, if you describe a place as a **tip**, you mean it is very untidy; an informal use. *The flat is an absolute tip.* N-COUNT =pigsty

7 If you **tip** someone such as a waiter, you give them some money in order to thank them for their services. *Do you really think it's customary to tip the waiters?... She tipped the barmen 10 dollars and bought drinks all round.* ♦ **tipping** *A 10 percent service charge is added in lieu of tipping.* VERB V n V n amount Also V N-UNCOUNT

8 If you give a **tip** to someone such as a waiter, you give them some money to thank them for their services. *I gave the barber a tip... The Head Porter was keeping all the tips.* N-COUNT

9 A **tip** is a useful piece of advice. *It shows how to prepare a CV, and gives tips on applying for jobs. ...tips for busy managers... A good tip is to buy the most expensive lens you can afford.* N-COUNT: oft N *on/for* -ing/n =hint

10 If a person **is tipped to** do something or **is tipped for** success at something, experts or journalists believe that they will do that thing or achieve that success; used mainly in British English. *He is tipped to be the country's next foreign minister... He was widely tipped for success.* VB: usu passive *be* V-ed to-inf *be* V-ed *for* n

11 Someone's **tip** for a race or competition is their advice on its likely result, especially to someone who wants to bet money on the result. *I've a tip for the races... United are still my tip for the Title.* N-COUNT: oft N *for* n

12 If you say that a problem is **the tip of the** PHRASES

iceberg, you mean that it is one small part of a much larger problem. *Unless we're all a lot more careful, the people who have died so far will be just the tip of the iceberg.* v-link PHR

13 If something **tips the scales** or **tips the balance**, it gives someone a slight advantage. *Today's slightly shorter race could well help to tip the scales in his favour... If the trial were evenly poised the newspapers might tip the balance against them.* V inflects, oft PHR prep

14 If a comment or question is **on the tip of** your **tongue**, you really want to say it or ask it, but you decide not to say it. *It was on the tip of Mahoney's tongue to say the boss was out... A sarcastic remark was on the tip of her tongue.* v-link PHR

tip off. If someone **tips** you **off**, they give you information about something that has happened or is going to happen. *Greg tipped police off on his car phone about a suspect drunk driver... He was arrested two days later after a friend tipped off the FBI.* PHRASAL VERB V n P; V P n (not pron)

tip over. If you **tip** something **over** or if it **tips over**, it falls over or turns over. *He tipped the table over in front of him... She tipped over the chair and collapsed into the corner with a splintering crash... We grabbed it just as it was about to tip over.* PHRASAL VERB ERG V n P; V P n (not pron); V P

tip up. If you **tip** something **up** or if it **tips up**, it moves into a sloping position with one end or side higher than the other. *We had to tip up the bed and the model was in grave danger of falling off it!... Tip the bottle up so it's in the same position as it would be when feeding the baby... The aircraft leveled out, and tipped up again for its climb to 20,000 feet.* PHRASAL VERB ERG V P n (not pron); V n P; V P

tip-off, tip-offs. A **tip-off** is a piece of information or a warning that you give to someone, often privately or secretly. *The man was arrested at his home after a tip-off to police from a member of the public.* ◆◇◇◇◇ N-COUNT

-tipped /-tɪpt/. **-tipped** combines with nouns to form adjectives that describe something as having a tip made of a particular substance or covered with a particular material. *In his hand, he carried a gold-tipped crook. ...poison-tipped arrows.* COMB in ADJ

tipple /tɪpᵊl/ **tipples.** In British English, a person's **tipple** is the alcoholic drink that they usually drink; an informal use. *My favourite tipple is a glass of port.* N-COUNT: usu supp N

tipster /tɪpstəʳ/ **tipsters.** A **tipster** is someone who tells you, usually in exchange for money, which horses they think will win particular races, so that you can bet money on the horses. N-COUNT

tipsy /tɪpsi/. If someone is **tipsy**, they are slightly drunk. *I'm feeling a bit tipsy.* ADJ-GRADED =tiddly

tiptoe /tɪptoʊ/ **tiptoes, tiptoeing, tiptoed** ◆◇◇◇◇

1 If you **tiptoe** somewhere, you walk there very quietly without putting your heels on the floor when you walk. *She slipped out of bed and tiptoed to the window.* VERB V prep/adv Also V

2 If you do something **on tiptoe** or **on tiptoes**, you do it standing or walking on the front part of your foot, without putting your heels on the ground. *She leaned her bike against the stone wall and stood on tiptoe to peer over it.* PHRASE: PHR after v, v-link PHR

tip-top; also spelled **tiptop**. You can use **tip-top** to indicate that something is extremely good; an old-fashioned, informal expression. *Her hair was thick, glossy and in tip-top condition.* ADJ: usu ADJ n

tirade /taɪreɪd/ **tirades.** A **tirade** is a long angry speech in which someone criticizes something or someone. *She launched into a tirade against the policies that ruined her business... He too has met a tirade of abuse.* N-COUNT =diatribe

tire /taɪəʳ/ **tires, tiring, tired** ◆◇◇◇◇

1 If something **tires** you or you **tire**, you feel that you have used a lot of energy and you want to rest or sleep. *If driving tires you, take the train... He tired easily, though he was unable to sleep well at night.* V-ERG V n; V

2 If you **tire of** something, you no longer wish to do it, because you have become bored of it or unhappy with it. *He felt he would never tire of international cricket... Sooner or later he may tire of constantly putting himself last.* VB: no passive =weary V of n/-ing

3 See **tyre**.

tire out. If something **tires** you **out**, it makes you exhausted. *The oppressive afternoon heat had quite tired him out... His objective was to tire out the climbers.* ♦ **tired out** *He was obviously tired out.* PHRASAL VERB V n P; V P n (not pron); ADJ

tired /taɪəʳd/ ◆◆◆◇◇

1 If you are **tired**, you feel that you want to rest or sleep. *Michael is tired and he has to rest after his long trip.* ♦ **tiredness** *He had to cancel some engagements because of tiredness.* ADJ-GRADED; N-UNCOUNT

2 You can describe a part of your body as **tired** if it looks or feels as if you need to rest it or to sleep. *Cucumber is good for soothing tired eyes... My arms are tired, and my back is tense.* ADJ-GRADED

3 If you are **tired of** something, you do not want it to continue because you are bored of it or unhappy with it. *I am tired of all the speculation... I was tired of being a bookkeeper.* ADJ-GRADED: v-link ADJ *of* n/-ing =sick

4 If you describe something as **tired**, you are critical of it because you have heard it or seen it many times. *I didn't want to hear another one of his tired excuses... What we see at Westminster is a tired old ritual.* ADJ-GRADED: usu ADJ n PRAGMATICS

tireless /taɪəʳləs/. If you describe someone or their efforts as **tireless**, you approve of the fact that they put a lot of hard work into something, and refuse to give up or take a rest. *He was a tireless worker for justice. ...Mother Teresa's tireless efforts to help the poor.* ♦ **tirelessly** *He worked tirelessly for the cause of health and safety.* ◆◇◇◇◇ ADJ-GRADED PRAGMATICS; ADV-GRADED: ADV with v

tiresome /taɪəʳsəm/. If you describe someone or something as **tiresome**, you mean that you find them irritating or boring. *...the tiresome old lady next door... It would be too tiresome to wait in the queue.* ◆◇◇◇◇ ADJ-GRADED

tiring /taɪərɪŋ/. If you describe something as **tiring**, you mean that it makes you tired so that you want to rest or sleep. *It had been a long and tiring day... Travelling is tiring.* ◆◇◇◇◇ ADJ-GRADED

tissue /tɪʃuː, tɪsjuː/ **tissues** ◆◆◆◇◇

1 In animals and plants, **tissue** consists of cells that are similar to each other in appearance and that have the same function. *As we age we lose muscle tissue... Athletes have hardly any fatty tissue... All the cells and tissues in the body benefit from the increased intake of oxygen.* N-UNCOUNT: also N in pl

2 **Tissue** or **tissue paper** is thin paper that is used for wrapping things that are easily damaged, such as objects made of glass or china. N-UNCOUNT

3 A **tissue** is a piece of thin soft paper that you use as a handkerchief. *...a box of tissues.* N-COUNT

tit /tɪt/ **tits** ◆◇◇◇◇

1 A **tit** is a small European bird that eats insects and seeds. There are several kinds of tit. • See also **blue tit**. N-COUNT

2 A woman's **tits** are her breasts; an informal use which some people find offensive. N-COUNT: usu pl

3 If you call someone a **tit**, you are insulting them and saying that they are stupid; an informal British use which some people find offensive. N-COUNT PRAGMATICS

titan /taɪtᵊn/ **titans.** If you describe someone as a **titan** of a particular field, you mean that they are very important and powerful or successful in that field. *...the country's two richest business titans. ...the titans of Renaissance literature: Spenser, Shakespeare, Donne and Milton.* N-COUNT: usu N n, N *of* n

titanic /taɪtænɪk/. If you describe something as **titanic**, you mean that it is very big or important, and usually that it involves very powerful forces. *The world had witnessed a titanic struggle between two visions of the future.* ADJ: usu ADJ n =monumental

titanium /taɪteɪniəm/. **Titanium** is a strong white metal used in making lightweight alloys. ◆◇◇◇◇ N-UNCOUNT

titbit /tɪtbɪt/ **titbits.** The form **tidbit** is used in American English.

1 You can refer to a small piece of information about someone's private affairs as a **titbit**, especially when it is interesting and shocking. *...titbits of gossip gleaned from the corridors of power... Who passed that titbit on to you?* N-COUNT

2 A **titbit** is a small delicious piece of food. *She offered Molly tidbits: a chicken drumstick, some cheese.* N-COUNT

tit-for-tat. A **tit-for-tat** action is one where someone takes revenge on another person for what they have done by doing something similar to them. *The two countries have each expelled another diplomat following a round of tit-for-tat expulsions.* ADJ: usu ADJ n

tithe /taɪð/ **tithes.** A **tithe** is a fixed amount of money or goods that is given regularly in order to support a church, a priest, or a charity. N-COUNT

titillate /tɪtɪleɪt/ **titillates, titillating, titillated.** ◆◇◇◇◇ VERB If something **titillates** someone, it pleases and excites them, especially in a sexual way. *The pictures were not meant to titillate audiences. ...food to titillate the most jaded of palates.* V n ♦ **titillating** ADJ-GRADED *...deliberately titillating lyrics.* ♦ **titillation** N-UNCOUNT /tɪtɪleɪʃᵊn/ *People buy sex manuals for titillation.*

title /taɪtᵊl/ **titles, titling, titled** ◆◆◆◆◇

1 The **title** of a book, play, film, or piece of music is its name. *'Patience and Sarah' was first published in 1969 under the title 'A Place for Us'.* N-COUNT

2 When a writer, composer, or artist **titles** a work, they give it a title. *Pirandello titled his play 'Six Characters in Search of an Author'... The single is titled 'White Love'... Their story is the subject of a new book titled 'The Golden Thirteen'.* VERB V n n be V-ed n V-ed ♦ **-titled** COMB in ADJ *This oddly-titled book is a beginner's guide to the bits that make up a PC. ...his aptly titled autobiography, Life is Meeting.*

3 Publishers and booksellers often refer to books or periodicals as **titles**. *It has become the biggest publisher of new poetry in Britain, with 50 new titles a year.* N-COUNT: usu pl

4 An aristocratic person's **title** is a word such as 'Sir', 'Lord', or 'Lady' that is used in front of their name, or a phrase that is used instead of their name, which indicates that they have a high rank in society. *Her husband has also been honoured with his title 'Sir Denis'... Princess Alexandra was to inherit the title of Duchess of Fife... He had no title and was not the heir to a great estate.* N-COUNT: oft poss N

5 Someone's **title** is a word such as 'Mr', 'Mrs', or 'Doctor', that is used before their own name in order to show their status or profession. *She has been awarded the title Professor.* N-COUNT: oft poss N

6 Someone's **title** is a name that describes their job or status in an organization. *He was given the title of deputy prime minister... 'Could you tell me your official job title?'—'It's Data Processing Manager.'* N-COUNT: oft poss N

7 In sports competitions, a **title** is the position of champion. Usually a person keeps a title until someone else defeats them. *He became Jamaica's first Olympic gold medallist when he won the 400m title in 1948... Gary Kasparov has retained his title as world chess champion.* N-COUNT: usu with supp, oft poss N

8 **Title** is the legal ownership of something, especially land or property. *He never had title to the property.* N-UNCOUNT

titled /taɪtᵊld/. Someone who is **titled** has a name such as 'Lord', 'Lady', 'Sir', or 'Princess' before their own name showing that they are a member of the aristocracy. *Her mother was a titled lady.* ◆◆◇◇◇ ADJ

title-holder, title-holders; also spelled **title holder**. The **title-holder** is the person who holds the position of champion in a sports competition that is held regularly. *Kasparov became the youngest world title-holder at 22.* N-COUNT

title role, title roles. The title role in a play or film is the role referred to in the name of the play or film. *My novel 'The Rector's Wife' is being adapted for TV, with Lindsay Duncan in the title role.* N-COUNT: the N

title track, title tracks. The **title track** on a CD, record, or tape is a song or piece of music that has the same title as the CD, record, or tape. *They come from Tuam, a place they refer to on the title track of their album, 'All the Way From Tuam'.* ◆◇◇◇◇ N-COUNT: usu sing

titter /tɪtəʳ/ **titters, tittering, tittered.** If someone **titters**, they give a short nervous laugh, especially when they are embarrassed about something. *Mention sex therapy and most people will titter in embarrassment.* VERB =giggle, snigger V ► Also a noun. *Mollie gave an uneasy little titter.* N-COUNT ♦ **tittering** *There was nervous tittering in the studio audience.* N-UNCOUNT

tittle-tattle /tɪtᵊl tætᵊl/. If you refer to something that a group of people talk about as **tittle-tattle**, you mean that you disapprove of it because it is trivial gossip, and there is no real evidence that it is true. *...tittle-tattle about the private lives of minor celebrities.* N-UNCOUNT PRAGMATICS =gossip

titular /tɪtʃʊləʳ/. A **titular** job or position has a name that makes it seem important, although the person who has it is not really important or powerful. *He is titular head, and merely signs laws occasionally.* ADJ: ADJ n =nominal

tizzy /tɪzi/. If you get **in a tizzy** or **into a tizzy**, you get excited, worried, or nervous about something, especially something that is not important; an informal expression. *He was in a right tizzy, muttering and swearing... Male journalists have been sent into a tizzy by the idea of female fighter pilots.* PHRASE: v-link PHR, PHR after v

T-junction, T-junctions. If you arrive at a **T-junction**, the road that you are on ends at right angles to another road, so that you have to turn either left or right to continue. N-COUNT

TM /tiː em/

1 **TM** is a kind of meditation derived from Hinduism, in which people mentally relax by silently repeating over and over again a special formula of words; an abbreviation for 'transcendental meditation'. N-UNCOUNT

2 **TM** is a written abbreviation for **trademark**.

TNT /tiː en tiː/. **TNT** is a powerful explosive substance; an abbreviation for 'trinitrotoluene'. N-UNCOUNT

to 1 preposition and adverb uses

to. Usually pronounced /tə/ before a consonant and /tu/ before a vowel, but pronounced /tuː/ when you are emphasizing it. ◆◆◆◆◆

In addition to the uses shown below, **to** is used after some verbs, nouns, and adjectives in order to introduce extra information, and in phrasal verbs such as 'see to' and 'come to'. It is also used with some verbs that have two objects in order to introduce the second object.

1 You use **to** when indicating the place that someone or something visits, moves towards, or points at. *Two friends and I drove to Florida during college spring break... Ramsay made a second visit to Italy. ...a five-day road and rail journey to Peking... She went to the window and looked out... He pointed to a chair, signalling for her to sit.* PREP

2 If you go **to** an event, you go where it is taking place. *We went to a party at the leisure centre... He came to dinner... I do hope you'll be able to come to the wedding... Eliza accepted Charles' invitation to a house party.* PREP

3 If something is attached **to** something larger or fixed **to** it, the two things are joined together. *There was a piece of cloth tied to the dog's collar... Many patients prefer hand-held shower heads rather than those fixed to the wall... Scrape off all the meat juices stuck to the bottom of the pan.* PREP

4 You use **to** when indicating the position of something. For example, if something is **to** your left, it is nearer your left side than your right side. *Hemingway's studio is to the right... You will see the chapel on the hill to your left... Atlanta was only an hour's drive to the north.* PREP

5 When you give something **to** someone, they receive it. *He picked up the knife and gave it to me... Firms should be allowed to offer jobs to the long-term unemployed at a lower wage.* PREP: v n PREP n

6 You use **to** to indicate who or what an action or a feeling is directed towards. *Marcus has been most unkind to me today. ...troops loyal to the government. ...the problem of cruelty to children... I have had to pay for repairs to the house.* PREP: adj/n PREP n

7 You use **to** with certain nouns and adjectives to show that a following noun is related to them. *He is a witty man, and an inspiration to all of us... Marriage is not the answer to everything... She was very sympathetic to the problems of adult students.* PREP: adj/n PREP n

8 If you say something **to** someone, you want that person to listen and understand what you are saying. *I'm going to have to explain to them that I can't pay them.* PREP

9 You use **to** when indicating someone's reaction to something or someone's feelings about a situation or event. For example, if you say that something happens **to** someone's relief, you mean that they are relieved when it happens. *To his surprise, the bedroom door was locked... He survived, to the amazement of surgeons.* PREP

10 You use **to** when indicating the person whose opinion you are stating. *It was clear to me that he respected his boss... Everyone seemed to her to be amazingly kind.* • **according to**: see **according**. PREP

11 You use **to** when indicating what something or someone is becoming, or the state or situation that they are progressing towards. *The shouts changed to screams of terror. ...an old ranch house that has been converted to a nature centre. ...a return to active politics... Charles has been promoted to general sales and marketing manager.* PREP

12 **To** can be used as a way of introducing the person or organization you are employed by, when you perform some service for them. *Rickman worked as a dresser to Nigel Hawthorne... He was an official interpreter to the government of Nepal.* PREP: n PREP n

13 You use **to** to indicate that something happens until the time or amount mentioned is reached. *Every vehicle was banned from coming into Mexico City one day a week from Monday to Friday... From 1977 to 1985 the United States gross national product grew 21 percent... The annual rate of inflation in Britain has risen to its highest level for eight years.* PREP

14 You use **to** when indicating the last thing in a range of things, usually when you are giving two extreme examples of something. *I read everything from fiction to history and science. ...mechanical toys and gadgets, from typewriters to toy cars. ...new orders for everything from computers to trucks.* PREP: *from* n PREP n

15 If someone goes from place **to** place or from job **to** job, they go to several places, or work in several jobs, and spend only a short time in each one. *Larry and Andy had drifted from place to place, worked at this and that.* PREP: *from* n PREP n

16 If someone moves **to and fro**, they move repeatedly from one place to another and back again, or from side to side. *She stood up and began to pace to and fro... The boat was rocking gently to and fro in the water.* • See also **to-ing and fro-ing**. PHRASE: PHR after v

17 You use **to** when you are stating a time which is less that thirty minutes before an hour. For example, if it is 'five **to** eight', it is five minutes before eight o'clock. *At twenty to six I was waiting by the entrance to the station... At exactly five minutes to nine, Ann left her car and entered the building.* PREP: num/n PREP num

18 You use **to** when giving ratios and rates. *...engines that can run at 60 miles to the gallon. ...a mixture of one part milk to two parts water.* PREP: amount PREP amount

19 You use **to** when indicating that two things happen at the same time. For example, if something is done **to** music, it is done at the same time as music is being played. *Romeo left the stage, to enthusiastic applause... Amy woke up to the sound of her doorbell ringing... 'I've got an idea,' said Edward to a chorus of groans.* PREP

20 If you say **'There's nothing to it'**, **'There's not much to it'**, or **'That's all there is to it'**, you are emphasizing how simple you think something is. *'There is nothing to it,' those I asked about it told me... She's going through a difficult time. That's all there is to it.* CONVENTION

21 If you push or shut a door **to**, you close it but may not shut it completely. *He slipped out, pulling the door to.* ADV: ADV after v

to 2 used before the base form of a verb

to Pronounced /tə/ before a consonant and /tu/ before a vowel. ◆◆◆◆◆

1 You use **to** before the base form of a verb to form the 'to-infinitive'. You use the to-infinitive after certain verbs, nouns, and adjectives, and after words such as 'how', 'which', and 'where'. *The management wanted to know what I was doing there... She told ministers of her decision to resign... Trish was the first to see him... Nuclear plants are expensive to build, though cheap to operate... Darling! It's lovely to see you... She did not take the judge's advice about how to do her job... The Foreign Minister is to visit China... The youngest child, John, was to die at the age of fourteen.* to inf

2 You use **to** before the base form of a verb to indicate the purpose or intention of an action. *...using the experience of big companies to help small businesses... He was doing this to make me more relaxed... He is leaving tomorrow to play his first match. ...programs set up to save animals... To help provide essential nourishment, we've put together these nutritious drinks.* • **in order to**: see **order**. to inf =in order to

3 You use **to** before the base form of a verb when you are commenting on a statement that you are making, for example when saying that you are being honest or brief, or that you are summing up or giving an example. *I'm disappointed, to be honest... Well, to sum up, what is the message that you are trying to get across?* to inf

4 You use **to** before the base form of a verb in exclamations when you are emphasizing a very strong emotion, such as a desire or wish, or a regret or disappointment. *Oh, to think of his poor wife, standing there helpless... But then to be let down like that, oh it's so unfair!* to inf

5 You use **to** before the base form of a verb when indicating what situation follows a particular action. *He made his way to the kitchen to find Francis cooking... From the garden you walk down to discover a large and beautiful lake... He awoke to find Charlie standing near the bed.* to inf

6 You use **to** with 'too' and 'enough' in expressions like **too much to** and **old enough to**; see **too** and **enough**.

toad /tоʊd/ **toads.** A **toad** is a creature which is similar to a frog but which has a drier skin and spends less time in water. ◆◇◇◇◇ N-COUNT

toadstool /toʊdstu:l/ **toadstools.** A **toadstool** is a fungus that you cannot eat because it is poisonous. N-COUNT

toady /toʊdi/ **toadies, toadying, toadied**

1 If you refer to someone as a **toady**, you disapprove of them because they flatter or are pleasant towards an important or powerful person in the hope of getting some advantage from them. N-COUNT PRAGMATICS

2 If you say that someone **is toadying** to an important or powerful person, you disapprove of them because they are flattering or being pleasant towards that person in the hope of getting some advantage from them. *They came backstage afterward, cooing and toadying to him.* VERB PRAGMATICS V *to* n Also V

toast /toʊst/ **toasts, toasting, toasted** ◆◆◇◇◇

1 **Toast** is bread which has been cut into slices and made brown and crisp by cooking at a high temperature. *...a piece of toast.* N-UNCOUNT

2 When you **toast** something such as bread, you cook it at a high temperature in a toaster or under a grill so that it becomes brown and crisp. *Toast the bread lightly on both sides. ...a toasted sandwich.* VERB V n V-ed

3 When you drink a **toast** to someone or something, you drink some wine or another alcoholic drink as a symbolic gesture, in order to show your appreciation of them or to wish them success. *Eleanor and I drank a toast to Miss Jacobs... At the end of the meal Burgoyne was asked to propose a toast.* N-COUNT

4 When you **toast** someone or something, you drink a toast to them. *Party officials and generals toasted his health... They toasted her in champagne.* VERB V n V n *in/with* n

5 If someone is **the toast of** a place, they are very popular and greatly admired there, because they have done something very successfully or well. *She was the toast of Paris.* N-SING: *the* N *of* n

toaster /toʊstəʳ/ **toasters.** A **toaster** is a piece of electric equipment used to toast bread. N-COUNT

toastmaster /toʊstmɑ:stəʳ, -mæs-/ **toastmasters.** At a reception or formal dinner, the N-COUNT

toastmaster is the person who proposes toasts and introduces the speakers.

toast rack, toast racks. A **toast rack** is an object that is designed to hold pieces of toast in an upright position and separate from each other, ready for people to eat. N-COUNT

tobacco /təbækoʊ/ **tobaccos** ◆◆◇◇◇

1 Tobacco is the dried leaves of a plant which people smoke in pipes, cigars, and cigarettes. You can also refer to pipes, cigars, and cigarettes collectively as **tobacco**. *Try to do without tobacco and alcohol... I believe it is time to ban tobacco advertising altogether.* N-MASS

2 Tobacco is the plant from which tobacco is obtained. N-UNCOUNT

tobacconist /təbækənɪst/ **tobacconists**

1 A **tobacconist** is a shopkeeper who sells things such as tobacco, cigarettes, and cigars. N-COUNT

2 A **tobacconist** or a **tobacconist's** is a shop that sells things such as tobacco, cigarettes, and cigars. N-COUNT: oft *the* N

toboggan /təbɒgən/ **toboggans.** A **toboggan** is an object that is designed to be used for travelling downhill on snow or ice. N-COUNT =sledge

toccata /təkɑːtə/ **toccatas.** A **toccata** is a fast piece of music for the piano, organ, or other keyboard instrument. N-COUNT: oft in names

today /tədeɪ/ ◆◆◆◆◆

1 You use **today** to refer to the day on which you are speaking or writing. *How are you feeling today?... I wanted him to come with us today, but he couldn't.* ► Also a noun. *Today is Friday, September 14th... The Prime Minister remains the main story in today's newspapers.* ADV: ADV with cl; N-UNCOUNT

2 You can refer to the present period of history as **today**. *The United States is in a serious recession today... He thinks pop music today is as exciting as it's ever been.* ► Also a noun. *In today's America, health care is one of the very biggest businesses. ...the Africa of today.* ADV: ADV with cl, n ADV; N-UNCOUNT

toddle /tɒdəl/ **toddles, toddling, toddled.** When a child **toddles**, it walks unsteadily with short quick steps. *...once your baby starts toddling... She fell while toddling around.* VERB: V; V adv/prep

toddler /tɒdləʳ/ **toddlers.** A **toddler** is a young child who has only just learnt to walk or who still walks unsteadily with small, quick steps. ◆◇◇◇◇ N-COUNT

toddy /tɒdi/ **toddies.** A **toddy** is a drink that is made by adding hot water and sugar to whisky, rum, or brandy. *...a hot toddy.* N-VAR: usu supp N

to-do /tə duː/. When there is a **to-do**, people are very excited, confused, or angry about something; an informal word. ◆◇◇◇◇ N-SING

toe /toʊ/ **toes, toeing, toed** ◆◆◇◇◇

1 Your **toes** are the five movable parts at the end of each foot. N-COUNT: usu pl

2 The **toe** of a shoe or sock is the part that covers the end of your foot. N-COUNT

3 If you **dip** your **toes into** something or **dip** your **toes into the waters of** something, you start doing that thing slowly and carefully, because you are not sure whether it will be successful or whether you will like it. *This may encourage gold traders to dip their toes back into the markets... Universities are dipping their toes in the waters of management education.* PHRASES: V inflects, usu PHR n

4 If you say that someone or something **keeps** you **on** your **toes**, you mean that they cause you to remain alert and ready for anything that might happen. *His fiery campaign rhetoric has kept opposition parties on their toes for months.* V inflects

5 If you **toe the line**, you behave in the way that people in authority expect you to. *...attempts to persuade the rebel members to toe the line... He's one of the politicians that wouldn't toe the party line.* V inflects

6 If you **tread on** someone's **toes**, you offend them by criticizing the way that they do something or by interfering in something that is their responsibility; an informal expression. *I must be careful not to tread on their toes. My job is to challenge, but not threaten them.* V inflects

toecap /toʊkæp/ **toecaps;** also spelled **toe-cap.** A **toecap** is a piece of leather or metal which is fitted over the end of a shoe or boot in order to protect or strengthen it. N-COUNT

TOEFL /toʊfəl/. **TOEFL** is an English language examination which is often used to evaluate the level of English of students who want to study at universities in English-speaking countries. TOEFL is an abbreviation of 'Test of English as a Foreign Language'. N-PROPER

toehold /toʊhoʊld/ **toeholds;** also spelled **toe-hold.** If you have a **toehold** in a situation, you have managed to gain an uncertain position or a small amount of power in it, which you hope will give you the opportunity to get a better or more powerful position. *Mitsubishi Motors were anxious to get a toehold in the European market.* N-COUNT: usu sing, usu N *in/on* n

toenail /toʊneɪl/ **toenails;** also spelled **toe nail.** Your **toenails** are the thin hard areas at the end of each of your toes. N-COUNT: usu pl

toff /tɒf/ **toffs.** In informal British English, if you refer to someone as a **toff**, you are saying in an unkind way that they come from the upper classes or are very rich. N-COUNT PRAGMATICS =nob

toffee /tɒfi, AM tɔːfi/ **toffees.** A **toffee** is a sticky chewy sweet that is made by boiling sugar and butter together with water. N-VAR

toffee-nosed. If you say that someone is **toffee-nosed**, you disapprove of them because they have a high opinion of themselves and a low opinion of other people; used in informal British English. ADJ-GRADED PRAGMATICS

tog /tɒg/ **togs**

1 A **tog** is an official measurement that shows how warm a blanket or quilt is; used in British English. *The range of tog values has been extended to 15 togs.* ► Also a combining form. *...a snug 13.5-tog winter duvet.* N-COUNT: usu N n, num N; COMB in ADJ

2 Togs are clothes, especially ones for a particular purpose; an informal use. *The photograph showed him wearing football togs.* N-PLURAL =gear

toga /toʊgə/ **togas.** A **toga** is a piece of clothing which was worn by the ancient Romans. N-COUNT

together /təgeðəʳ/ ◆◆◆◆◆

In addition to the uses shown below, **together** is used in phrasal verbs such as 'piece together', 'pull together', and 'sleep together'.

1 If people do something **together**, they do it with each other. *We went on long bicycle rides together... He and I worked together on a book... They all live together in a three-bedroom house... Together they swam to the ship.* ADV: usu ADV after v, also ADV cl ≠alone

2 If things are joined **together**, they are joined with each other so that they touch or form one whole. *Mix the ingredients together thoroughly... She clasped her hands together on her lap... If a window is broken, you can't stick it back together again.* ADV: ADV after v

3 If things or people are situated **together**, they are in the same place and very near to each other. *The trees grew close together... Ginette and I gathered our things together... People stood packed together tightly.* ADV: ADV after v

4 If a group of people are held or kept **together**, they are united with each other in some way. *He has done enough to pull the party together... I want us all to be a happy family together... His tough brand of communism was largely successful in holding the country together.* ► Also an adjective. *We are together in the way we're looking at this situation.* ADV: ADV after v; ADJ: v-link ADJ =united

5 If two people are **together**, they are married or having a sexual relationship with each other. *We were together for five years... Towards the end of our time together he was impossible... Passion kept us together.* ADJ: v-link ADJ, n ADJ, v n ADJ ≠apart

6 If two things happen or are done **together**, they happen or are done at the same time. *Three horses crossed the finish line together... 'Yes,' they said together.* ADV: ADV after v ≠separately

7 You use **together** when you are adding two or more amounts or things to each other in order to consider a total amount or effect. *The two main* ADV: ADV before v, n ADV, ADV cl *right-wing opposition parties together won 29.8 per cent... The companies have together spent £600 million... Together they account for less than five per cent of the population... The two together are particularly deadly.*

8 If you say that two things **go together**, or that one thing **goes together** with another, you mean that they are compatible with each other or cannot be separated from each other. *I can see that some colours go together and some don't... Winckelmann declared that art and freedom went together... Poverty and illiteracy go together with high birth rates.*
PHR-RECIP: pl-n PHR, PHR *with* n/-ing

9 If you describe someone as **together**, you admire them because they are very confident, organized, and know what they want; an informal use. *She was very headstrong, and very together... I know on the surface I appear to be quite a together person... I had to take a break for a cup of tea before I could really get myself together.*
ADJ-GRADED PRAGMATICS

10 You use **together with** to mention someone or something else that is also involved in an action or situation. *Every month we'll deliver the very best articles, together with the latest fashion and beauty news... A famine started which, together with the war, carried away millions of lives... Together with his wife, he helped to draft the ANC's 1955 'Freedom Charter'.*
PHR-PREP =along with

11 • to **get** your **act together**: see **act**. • to **put** your **heads together**: see **head**. • **put together**: see **put**.

togetherness /təgeðərnəs/. **Togetherness** is a happy feeling of affection and closeness to other people, especially your friends and family. *Nothing can ever take the place of real love and family togetherness.*
N-UNCOUNT

toggle /tɒgəl/ **toggles.** A **toggle** is a small rod of wood or plastic which is sewn to something such as a coat or bag, and which is pushed through a loop or hole as a fastener.
N-COUNT

toil /tɔɪl/ **toils, toiling, toiled** ◆◇◇◇◇

1 When people **toil**, they work very hard doing unpleasant or tiring tasks; a literary use. *People who toiled in dim, dank factories were too exhausted to enjoy their family life... Workers toiled long hours.*
VERB V V n Also V *at/on* n

▸ **Toil away** means the same as **toil**. *She has toiled away at the violin for years... Nora toils away serving burgers at the local cafe.*
PHRASAL VERB V P *at/on* n V P

2 If you **toil** somewhere, you move there slowly and with difficulty, usually because you are very tired; a literary use. *Arnold had his head down, gasping as he toiled up the hill.*
VERB V prep/adv

3 **Toil** is unpleasant work that is very tiring physically; a literary use.
N-UNCOUNT

toilet /tɔɪlət/ **toilets** ◆◆◇◇◇

1 A **toilet** is a large bowl with a seat, or a platform with a hole, which is connected to a water system and which you use when you want to get rid of urine or faeces from your body. *She made Tina flush the pills down the toilet.*
N-COUNT

2 A **toilet** is a room in a house or public building that contains a toilet. *Annette ran and locked herself in the toilet... Fred never uses public toilets.*
N-COUNT

3 You can say that someone **goes to the toilet** to mean that they urinate or defecate, especially when you want to avoid using words that you think may offend people. *He gave me a bucket to go to the toilet in.*
PHRASE: V inflects

toilet paper. **Toilet paper** is thin absorbent paper that people use to clean themselves after they have got rid of urine or faeces from their body.
N-UNCOUNT

toiletries /tɔɪlətriz/. **Toiletries** are things that you use when washing or taking care of your body, for example soap, deodorant, and toothpaste.
N-PLURAL

toilet roll, toilet rolls. A **toilet roll** is a long narrow strip of toilet paper that is wound around a small cardboard tube.
N-VAR

toilet water, toilet waters. **Toilet water** is fairly weak and inexpensive perfume.
N-MASS

to-ing and fro-ing. If you say that there is a lot of **to-ing and fro-ing**, you mean that the same actions or movements or the same arguments are being repeated many times. *After some to-ing and fro-ing, Elsie and the children moved back to London.*
N-UNCOUNT

token /toʊkən/ **tokens** ◆◆◇◇◇

1 You use **token** to describe things or actions which are small and insignificant but are meant to show particular intentions or feelings, which may or may not be sincere. *The announcement was welcomed as a step in the right direction, but was widely seen as a token gesture... Miners have staged a two-hour token stoppage to demand better pay and conditions... You described her as the token woman on the shortlist.*
ADJ: ADJ n

2 A **token** is a piece of paper or card that can be exchanged for goods, either in a particular shop or as part of a special promotional offer. *...£10 book tokens... Here is the fifth token towards our offer. You need six of these tokens.*
N-COUNT: oft n N

3 A **token** is a round flat piece of metal or plastic that is sometimes used instead of money. *Some of the older telephones still only accept tokens.*
N-COUNT

4 If you give something to someone or do something for them as a **token** of your feelings, you give it or do it as a way of expressing those feelings. *He kept sending gifts and assured her that they were merely small tokens of his appreciation... As a token of goodwill, I'm going to write another letter. ...the custom of exchanging love tokens to celebrate February 14.*
N-COUNT: usu with supp, oft N *of* n

5 You use **by the same token** to introduce a statement that you think is true for the same reasons that were given for a previous statement. *If you give up exercise, your muscles shrink and fat increases. By the same token, if you expend more energy you will lose fat.*
PHRASE: PHR with cl PRAGMATICS

tokenism /toʊkənɪzəm/. If you refer to an action as **tokenism**, you disapprove of it because you think it is just done for effect, in order to show a particular intention or to impress a particular type of person. *Is his promotion evidence of the minorities' advance, or mere tokenism?*
N-UNCOUNT PRAGMATICS

told /toʊld/

1 **Told** is the past tense and past participle of **tell**.

2 You can use **all told** to introduce or follow a summary, generalization, or total. *All told there were 104 people on the payroll... All told, it seems like an awful mess... The cost of the immunizations was about $600,000 all told.*
PHRASE: PHR with cl, amount PHR PRAGMATICS =altogether

tolerable /tɒlərəbəl/ ◆◇◇◇◇

1 If you describe something as **tolerable**, you mean that it is bearable, even though it is unpleasant or painful. *The levels of tolerable pain vary greatly from individual to individual... He described their living conditions as tolerable.* ♦ **tolerably** /tɒlərəbli/ *Their captors treated them tolerably well. ...tolerably hot water.*
ADJ-GRADED =bearable ≠intolerable
ADV: usu ADV adj/adv, also ADV after v

2 If you describe something as **tolerable**, you mean that it is fairly good and reasonably satisfactory, but not of the highest quality or standard; a formal use. *He fell asleep just past midnight with tolerable ease... Is there anywhere tolerable to eat in town?* ♦ **tolerably** *He can see tolerably well and he can read.*
ADJ-GRADED =reasonable
ADV-GRADED

tolerance /tɒlərəns/ **tolerances** ◆◆◇◇◇

1 **Tolerance** is the quality of allowing other people to say and do as they like, even if you do not agree or approve of it; used showing approval. *...his tolerance and understanding of diverse human nature. ...the acceptance and tolerance of other ways.*
N-UNCOUNT: oft N *of* n PRAGMATICS ≠intolerance

2 **Tolerance** is the ability to bear something painful or unpleasant. *There is lowered pain tolerance, lowered resistance to infection. ...a low tolerance of errors.*
N-UNCOUNT: usu with supp, n N, N *of* n

3 If someone or something has a **tolerance to** a substance, they are exposed to it so often that it does not have very much effect on them. *As with any drug taken in excess, your body can build up a tolerance to it.*
N-VAR: with supp, usu N *to* n

tolerant /tɒlərənt/ ◆◇◇◇◇

1 If you describe someone as **tolerant**, you approve of the fact that they allow other people to say and do as they like, even if they do not agree with or
ADJ-GRADED: oft v-link ADJ *of* n PRAGMATICS

like it. *They need to be tolerant of different points of view... Other changes include more tolerant attitudes to unmarried couples having children.* ≠intolerant
♦ **tolerantly** *She had listened tolerantly to his jumbled account.* ADV-GRADED: ADV with v

2 If a plant, animal, or machine is **tolerant of** particular conditions or types of treatment, it is able to endure them without being damaged or hurt. *...plants which are more tolerant of dry conditions... Today's floppy disc drives are tolerant of poor quality discs.* ADJ-GRADED: v-link ADJ *of* n

tolerate /tɒləreɪt/ **tolerates, tolerating, tolerated** ♦♦◇◇◇

1 If you **tolerate** a situation or person, you accept them although you do not particularly like them. *She can no longer tolerate the position that she's in... The cousins tolerated each other, but did not really get on well together.* VERB =put up with V n
♦ **toleration** /tɒləreɪʃᵊn/ *...his views on religious toleration, education, and politics.* N-UNCOUNT

2 If you can **tolerate** something unpleasant or painful, you are able to bear it. *The ability to tolerate pain varies from person to person.* VERB =bear V n

toll /toʊl/ **tolls, tolling, tolled** ♦♦◇◇◇

1 When a bell **tolls** or when someone **tolls** it, it rings slowly and repeatedly, often as a sign that someone has died. *Church bells tolled and black flags fluttered... The pilgrims tolled the bell.* V-ERG V V n

2 A **toll** is a small sum of money that you have to pay in order to use a particular bridge or road. N-COUNT

3 A **toll** is a total number of deaths, accidents, or disasters that occur in a particular period of time; used by journalists. *There are fears that the casualty toll may be higher. ...the second highest annual murder toll in that city's history.* ● See also **death toll**. N-COUNT: usu sing, supp N

4 If you say that something **takes** its **toll** or **takes a heavy toll**, you mean that it has a bad effect on something or someone, or causes a lot of suffering. *Winter takes its toll on your health... Higher fuel prices took their toll. ...a high exchange rate took a heavy toll on industry.* PHRASE: V inflects, oft PHR *on* n

toll-free. In American English, a **toll-free** telephone number is one which you can dial without having to pay for the call. The usual British word is **freefone**. ► Also an adverb. *Call our customer-service staff toll-free.* ADJ: usu ADJ n; ADV: ADV after v

toll road, toll roads. In British English, a **toll road** is a road which people have to pay to drive on. N-COUNT

tom /tɒm/ **toms.** A **tom** is a male cat. N-COUNT

tomahawk /tɒməhɔːk/ **tomahawks.** A **tomahawk** is a small light axe that is used by Native American peoples. N-COUNT

tomato /təmɑːtoʊ, AM -meɪ-/ **tomatoes. Tomatoes** are small, soft, red fruit that you can eat raw in salads or cooked as a vegetable. ♦♦◇◇◇ N-VAR

tomb /tuːm/ **tombs.** A **tomb** is a large grave that is above ground and that usually has a sculpture or other decoration on it. ♦◇◇◇◇ N-COUNT

tomboy /tɒmbɔɪ/ **tomboys.** If you say that a girl is a **tomboy**, you mean that she likes playing rough or noisy games, or doing things that were traditionally considered to be things that boys enjoy. N-COUNT

tombstone /tuːmstoʊn/ **tombstones.** A **tombstone** is a large stone with words carved into it, which is placed on a grave. ♦◇◇◇◇ N-COUNT =gravestone

tom cat, tomcats; also spelled **tomcat**. A **tom cat** is a male cat. N-COUNT =tom

tome /toʊm/ **tomes.** A **tome** is a very large, heavy book; a formal word. ♦◇◇◇◇ N-COUNT

tomfoolery /tɒmfuːləri/. **Tomfoolery** is playful behaviour, usually of a rather silly, noisy, or rough kind. *Were you serious, or was that a bit of tomfoolery?* N-UNCOUNT =horseplay

tomorrow /təmɒroʊ, AM -mɔːr-/ **tomorrows** ♦♦♦♦◇

1 You use **tomorrow** to refer to the day after today. *Bye, see you tomorrow... The first official results will be announced tomorrow.* ► Also a noun. *What's on your agenda for tomorrow?... Davies plays for the Barbarians in tomorrow's match against England... Tomorrow is Christmas Day.* ADV: ADV with cl; N-UNCOUNT

2 You can refer to the future, especially the near future, as **tomorrow**. *What is education going to look like tomorrow?* ► Also a noun. *...tomorrow's computer industry... Experiences in the past become a part of us, affecting our tomorrows.* ADV: ADV with cl; N-UNCOUNT: also N in pl

tom-tom, tom-toms. A **tom-tom** is a tall narrow drum that is usually played with the hands. N-COUNT

ton /tʌn/ **tons** ♦♦♦◇◇

1 A **ton** is a unit of weight that is equal to 2240 pounds in Britain and to 2000 pounds in the United States. *Hundreds of tons of oil spilled into the sea... Getting rid of rubbish can cost $100 a ton.* N-COUNT: num N, oft N *of* n

2 A **ton** is the same as a **tonne**. N-COUNT

3 If someone **comes down on** you **like a ton of bricks**, they are extremely angry with you and tell you off because of something wrong that you have done; an informal expression. *If you do something awful they all come down on you like a ton of bricks.* PHRASES V inflects

4 If you say that something **weighs a ton**, you mean that it is extremely heavy; an informal expression. V inflects

tonal /toʊnᵊl/. **Tonal** means relating to the qualities or pitch of a sound or to the tonality of a piece of music. *There is little tonal variety in his voice. ...tonal music.* ADJ: usu ADJ n

tonality /toʊnælɪti/ **tonalities. Tonality** is the presence of a musical key in a piece of music; a technical term. N-VAR

tone /toʊn/ **tones, toning, toned** ♦♦♦◇◇

1 The **tone** of a sound is its particular quality. *Cross could hear him speaking in low tones to Sarah. ...the clear tone of the bell.* N-COUNT: with supp, usu pl

2 Someone's **tone** is a quality in their voice which shows what they are feeling or thinking. *I still didn't like his tone of voice... Suddenly he laughed again, this time with a cold, sharp tone... Her tone implied that her patience was limited.* N-COUNT: usu with supp

3 The **tone** of a speech or piece of writing is its style and the opinions or ideas expressed in it. *The spokesman said the tone of the letter was very friendly... His comments to reporters were conciliatory in tone... The whole tone of President Suharto's speech was one of continuity and stability.* N-UNCOUNT =tenor

4 The **tone** of a place or an event is its general atmosphere. *The high tone of the occasion was assured by the presence of a dozen wealthy patrons... The service desk at the entrance, with its friendly, helpful and efficient staff, sets the tone for the rest of the store.* N-SING: *the* N, usu with supp

5 The **tone** of someone's body, especially their muscles, is its degree of firmness and strength. *...stretch exercises that aim to improve muscle tone... Keeping your muscles strong and in tone helps you to avoid back problems.* N-UNCOUNT

6 Something that **tones** your body makes it firm and strong. *This movement lengthens your spine and tones the spinal nerves... Try these toning exercises before you start the day. ...finely toned muscular bodies.* ► **Tone up** means the same as **tone**. *Exercise tones up your body... Although it's not strenuous exercise, you feel toned-up, supple and relaxed.* VERB V n V-ing V-ed; PHRASAL VERB V P n (not pron) V-ed P Also V n P

7 A **tone** is one of the lighter, darker, or brighter shades of the same colour. *Each brick also varies slightly in tone, texture and size... I'm a cheery sort of person, so I like cheerful tones. ...two-tone, striped wallpaper.* N-VAR

8 If one thing **tones** with another, the two things look nice together because their colours are similar in quality or brightness; used mainly in British English. *Princess Margaret toned with her in a turquoise print dress.* ► **Tone in** means the same as **tone**; used mainly in British English. *The bowls tone in cleverly with the mugs.* VERB V *with* n; PHRASAL VERB V P *with* n

9 A **tone** is one of the sounds that you hear when you are using a telephone, for example the sound that tells you that a number is engaged. *They phoned at the same time, and got the engaged tone.* N-SING: usu with supp

10 A **tone** is a difference in pitch between two musical notes equal to two semitones. N-COUNT

11 If you say that something **lowers the tone** of a place or event, you mean that it is not appropriate PHRASE: V inflects PRAGMATICS

and makes the place or event seem less respectable. *Councillors say plastic-framed windows lower the tone of the neighbourhood.*

tone down [PHRASAL VERB]
1 If you **tone down** something that you have written or said, you make it less forceful, severe, or offensive. *The fiery right-wing leader toned down his militant statements after the meeting... The forecasts have since had to be toned down, as the economy has exhibited unmistakable signs of slowing... We have had to ask the agency and their client to tone their ads down.* [V P n (not pron); V n P]
2 If you **tone down** a colour or a flavour, you make it less bright or strong. *When Ken Hom wrote his first book for the BBC he was asked to tone down the spices and garlic in his recipes.* [V P n (not pron); Also V n P]

tone in. See **tone** 8. [PHRASAL VERB]

tone up. See **tone** 6. [PHRASAL VERB]

-toned /-təʊnd/. **-toned** combines with adjectives to indicate that something has a particular kind of tone. *...a beautiful silver-toned voice ideal for Mozart. ...soft, pastel-toned drawings.* [COMB in ADJ]

tone-deaf. If you say that someone is **tone-deaf**, you mean that they cannot sing in tune or recognize different tunes. [ADJ; PRAGMATICS]

toneless /təʊnləs/. A **toneless** voice is dull and does not express any feeling; used in written English. *'What shall we do?' Milton said again in a toneless voice.* ♦ **tonelessly** *'That's most kind of him,' Eleanor said tonelessly.* [ADJ-GRADED; ADV-GRADED: ADV after v]

toner /təʊnəʳ/ **toners.** A **toner** is a substance which you can put on your skin, for example to clean it or make it less oily. ◆◇◇◇◇ [N-MASS]

tongs /tɒŋz, AM tɔːŋz/. **Tongs** are a tool that you use to grip and pick up objects that you do not want to touch. They consist of two long narrow pieces of metal joined together at one end. *The waiter lifted rolls from a basket with a pair of silver tongs.* ● **hammer and tongs**: see **hammer**. [N-PLURAL: also *a pair of* N]

tongue /tʌŋ/ **tongues** ◆◆◇◇◇
1 Your **tongue** is the soft movable part inside your mouth which you use for tasting, licking, and speaking. *I walked over to the mirror and stuck my tongue out... She ran her tongue around her lips.* [N-COUNT: usu poss N]
2 You can use **tongue** to refer to the kind of things that a person says. *...her sharp wit and quick tongue... She had a nasty tongue, but I liked her.* [N-COUNT: usu supp N]
3 A **tongue** is a language; a literary use. *The French feel passionately about their native tongue.* ● See also **mother tongue**. [N-COUNT =language]
4 **Tongue** is the cooked tongue of an ox or sheep. It is usually eaten cold. [N-VAR]
5 The **tongue** of a shoe or boot is the piece of leather which is underneath the laces. [N-COUNT]
6 A **tongue of** something such as fire or land is a long thin piece of it; a literary use. *A yellow tongue of flame shot upwards. ...a silver, frozen tongue of water.* [N-COUNT: N *of* n]
7 A **tongue-in-cheek** remark or attitude is ironic and not serious, although it may seem to be serious. *...a lighthearted, tongue-in-cheek approach... This is all slightly tongue-in-cheek, I'd like to make that clear... Were they written tongue-in-cheek, or with an underlying conviction?* [PHRASES; PHR n, v-link PHR, PHR after v]
8 If you **hold** your **tongue**, you do not say anything even though you might want to or be expected to, because it is the wrong time to say it. *Douglas held his tongue, preferring not to speak out on a politically sensitive issue.* [V inflects]
9 If you say that you can not **get** your **tongue round** a word or phrase, you mean that you find it very difficult to pronounce. [V inflects, PHR n, usu with brd-neg]
10 If you describe something you said as **a slip of the tongue**, you mean that you said it by mistake. *At one stage he referred to Anna as John's fiancée, but later said that was a slip of the tongue.* [*slip* inflects]
11 ● to **bite** your **tongue**: see **bite**.

tongue-in-cheek. See **tongue**.

tongue lashing, tongue lashings. If someone gives you a **tongue lashing**, they shout at you or criticize you in a very forceful way; an informal word. *After a cruel tongue lashing, he threw the girl out of the group.* [N-COUNT]

tongue-tied. If someone is **tongue-tied**, they are unable to say anything because they feel shy or nervous. *In their presence I became self-conscious and tongue-tied.* [ADJ-GRADED: usu v-link ADJ]

tongue-twister, tongue-twisters; also spelled **tongue twister.** A **tongue-twister** is a sentence or expression which is very difficult to say properly, especially when you try to say it quickly. An example of a tongue-twister is 'She sells seashells on the seashore'. [N-COUNT]

tonic /tɒnɪk/ **tonics** ◆◇◇◇◇
1 **Tonic** or **tonic water** is a colourless fizzy drink that has a slightly bitter flavour and is often mixed with alcoholic drinks, especially gin. *Keeler sipped at his gin and tonic. ...low-calorie tonics.* ► A glass of tonic can be referred to as a **tonic** or a **tonic water**. *I'll just have a tonic water.* [N-MASS; N-COUNT]
2 A **tonic** is a medicine that makes you feel stronger, healthier, and less tired. *Britons are spending twice as much on health tonics as they were five years ago... Ginseng is generally known for its tonic properties.* [N-MASS =pick-me-up]
3 A **tonic** is anything that makes you feel stronger, more cheerful, or more enthusiastic. *Seeing Marcus at that moment was a great tonic... His generous offer was a tremendous tonic for our morale.* [N-COUNT: oft adj N, N *for* n =boost]
4 Skin **tonic** or hair **tonic** is a liquid that you put on your skin or hair in order to improve it. [N-MASS]
5 The **tonic** of a musical scale is its first note; a technical term in music. [N-COUNT]

tonight /tənaɪt/. **Tonight** is used to refer to the evening of today or the night that follows today. *I'm at home tonight... Tonight, I think he proved to everybody what a great player he was... There they will stay until 11 o'clock tonight.* ► Also a noun. *Tonight is the opening night of the opera. ...tonight's flight to London.* ◆◆◆◆◇ [ADV: ADV with cl, n ADV; N-UNCOUNT]

tonnage /tʌnɪdʒ/ **tonnages**
1 The **tonnage** of a ship is its size or the amount of space that it has inside it for cargo; a technical term in shipping. [N-VAR]
2 **Tonnage** is the total number of tons that something weighs, or the total amount that there is of it. [N-VAR]

tonne /tʌn/ **tonnes.** A **tonne** is a metric unit of weight that is equal to 1000 kilograms. *...65.5 million tonnes of coal... Top quality Thai rice fetched $340 a tonne.* ◆◆◇◇◇ [N-COUNT: num N, oft N *of* n]

tonsillitis /tɒnsɪlaɪtɪs/. **Tonsillitis** is a painful swelling of your tonsils caused by an infection. [N-UNCOUNT]

tonsils /tɒnsɪlz/; the form **tonsil** is used as a modifier. Your **tonsils** are the two small soft lumps in your throat at the back of your mouth. [N-PLURAL]

too 1 adding something or responding

too /tuː/ ◆◆◆◆◆
1 You use **too** after mentioning another person, thing, or aspect that a previous statement applies to or includes. *'Nice to talk to you.'—'Nice to talk to you too.'... 'I've got a great feeling about it.'—'Me too.'... Depression may be expressed physically too... He doesn't want to meet me. I, too, have been afraid to talk to him... We talked to her agent. He's your agent, too, right?* [ADV: cl/group ADV; PRAGMATICS]
2 You use **too** after adding a piece of information or a comment to a statement, in order to emphasize that it is surprising or important. *We did learn to read, and quickly too... People usually think of it as a 'boys' book', which of course it is, and a very good one too.* [ADV: cl/group ADV; PRAGMATICS =as well]
3 You use **too** at the end of a sentence to emphasize an opinion that you have added after a statement made by you or by another person. *'That money's mine.'—'Of course it is, and quite right too.'... 'Oh excuse me.'—'I should think so too.'... The banks are being told to think about small businesses a little more. And about time too.* [ADV: cl ADV; PRAGMATICS]
4 You use **too** in order to emphasize in a humorous or childish way your contradiction of what someone else has said or your refusal to obey them; an informal use. *'I'm getting a bike for my birthday.'—'You are not.'—'I am too.'* [ADV: ADV after aux; PRAGMATICS]

too 2 indicating excess

too /tuː/ ◆◆◆◆◆

1 You also use **too** in order to indicate that there is a greater amount or degree of something than is desirable, necessary, or acceptable. *Leather jeans that are too big will make you look larger... Eggs shouldn't be kept in the fridge, it's too cold... The shaking inside may be due to low blood sugar, too much caffeine or too many cigarettes... She was drinking too much, eating too much, having too many late nights... 'I've come to see Miss Ridley.'—'Then I'm afraid you're too late, sir. She's gone.'... I know you need your freedom too much to stay with me.* ADV: ADV adj/adv, oft ADV adj/adv to-inf

2 You use **too** with a negative to make what you are saying sound less forceful or more polite or cautious. *Americans are never too keen to leave their beloved country... I wasn't too happy with what I'd written so far... He won't be too pleased to see you.* ADV: with brd-neg, ADV adj PRAGMATICS =very

3 You also use **too** when you want to emphasize in a fairly formal way your thanks to someone for something that they have done for you. *'I'll try and get you a cake.'—'Oh Ann you're too kind.'* ADV: ADV adj PRAGMATICS

4 You use **all too** or **only too** to emphasize that something happens to a greater extent or degree than is pleasant or desirable. *She remembered it all too well... She is all too aware that we should be grateful for good health... The letter spoke only too clearly of his anxiety for her.* PHRASES PHR adv/adj PRAGMATICS

5 If you describe a situation as **too little too late**, you are blaming someone for not doing enough to prevent a problem and for taking action only after the problem had become very bad. *They think this is too little too late... The government is now bringing in laws to reduce air pollution. But, is it a case of too little, too late?* v-link PHR, PHR after v

6 • **too bad**: see **bad**. • **too clever**: see **clever**. • **none too**: see **none**.

took /tʊk/. **Took** is the past tense of **take**.

tool /tuːl/ **tools** ◆◆◆◇◇

1 A **tool** is any instrument or simple piece of equipment that you hold in your hands and use to do a particular kind of work. For example, spades, hammers, and knives are all tools. *I find the best tool for the purpose is a pair of shears.* • See also **machine tool**. N-COUNT

2 You can refer to anything that you use for a particular purpose as a particular type of **tool**. *Writing is a good tool for discharging overwhelming feelings... The video has become an invaluable teaching tool... The threat of bankruptcy is a legitimate tool to extract money from them.* N-COUNT: usu with supp, oft N *for*-ing/n

3 If you describe someone as a **tool** of a particular person, group, or ideology, you mean that they are controlled and used by that person, group, or ideology, especially to do unpleasant or dishonest things; used showing disapproval. *He became the tool of the security services... Mr Torr said he would not serve in an army which was a tool of apartheid.* N-COUNT: usu N *of*n PRAGMATICS =puppet

4 In British English, if you say that workers **down tools**, you mean that they stop working suddenly in order to strike or to make a protest of some kind. PHRASES V inflects

5 **The tools of** your **trade** or **the tools of the trade** are the skills, instruments, and other equipment that you need in order to do your job properly. *They're here to learn the tools of their trade from their American colleagues... Black-leather jackets and tattoos are the standard tools of the trade for heavy-metal musicians.* PHR after v, oft v-link PHR

tool box, tool boxes. A **tool box** is a metal or plastic box which contains general tools that you need at home, for example to do repairs in your house or car. N-COUNT

tool kit, tool kits. A **tool kit** is a special set of tools that are kept together and that are often used for a particular purpose. N-COUNT

toot /tuːt/ **toots, tooting, tooted.** If someone **toots** their car horn or if a car horn **toots**, it produces a short sound or series of sounds. *People set off fireworks and tooted their car horns... Car horns toot as cyclists dart precariously through the traffic... A man behind her tooted angrily.* ◆◇◇◇◇ V-ERG =hoot V n V

► Also a noun. *The driver gave me a wave and a toot.* N-SING

tooth /tuːθ/ **teeth** ◆◆◆◇◇

1 Your **teeth** are the hard white objects in your mouth and which you use for biting and chewing. *She had very pretty straight teeth... If a tooth feels very loose, your dentist may recommend that it's taken out.* N-COUNT: oft poss N

2 The **teeth** of something such as a comb, saw, cog, or zip are the parts that stick out in a row on its edge. *The front cog has 44 teeth.* N-PLURAL

3 If you say that something such as an official group or a law has **teeth**, you mean that it has power and is able to be effective. *The opposition argues that the new council will be unconstitutional and without teeth... The law must have teeth, and it must be enforced.* N-PLURAL =power, authority

4 See also **wisdom tooth**.

5 Someone who is **armed to the teeth** is armed with a lot of weapons or with very effective weapons. *Both sides were armed to the teeth.* PHRASES usu v-link PHR

6 If you say that someone **cut their teeth** doing a particular thing, at a particular time, or in a particular place, you mean they began their career and learned some of their skills doing that thing, at that time, or in that place. *...director John Glen, who cut his teeth on Bond movies... He cut his teeth in the sixties as director of Edinburgh's Traverse Theatre.* V inflects, PHR prep, PHR -ing

7 If you say that something **sets** your **teeth on edge**, you mean that you find it extremely unpleasant or irritating. *Their voices set your teeth on edge.* V inflects

8 If you **fight tooth and nail** to do something, you do everything you can in order to achieve it. If you **fight** something **tooth and nail**, you do everything you can in order to prevent it. *He fought tooth and nail to keep his job... Furious Tory rebels last night vowed to fight the treaty tooth and nail.* V inflects, oft PHR to-inf

9 If you describe a task or activity as something you can **get your teeth into**, you mean that you like it because it is substantial or complex enough to hold all your interest. *This role gave her something to get her teeth into... They have to get involved and get their teeth into some police work.* V inflects, oft PHR n PRAGMATICS

10 If you do something **in the teeth of** a difficulty or danger, you do it in spite of the difficulty or danger. *I was battling my way along the promenade in the teeth of a force ten gale... In the teeth of the longest recession since the 1930s, the company continues to perform well.* PHR n =despite

11 If you say that someone **is lying through** their **teeth**, you are emphasizing that they are telling lies. V inflects PRAGMATICS

12 You can describe someone as **long in the tooth** if they are old or getting old; an informal expression. *Aren't I a bit long in the tooth to start being an undergraduate?* v-link PHR

13 If you have **a sweet tooth**, you like sweet food very much. *Add more honey if you have a sweet tooth.* usu PHR after v

14 • to **get the bit between** your **teeth**: see **bit**. • to **give** one's **eye teeth for** something: see **eye**. • to **gnash** one's **teeth**: see **gnash**. • to **grit** your **teeth**: see **grit**. • a **kick in the teeth**: see **kick**. • **by the skin of** your **teeth**: see **skin**.

toothache /tuːθeɪk/. **Toothache** is pain in one of your teeth. N-UNCOUNT

toothbrush /tuːθbrʌʃ/ **toothbrushes.** A **toothbrush** is a small brush that you use for cleaning your teeth. ◆◇◇◇◇ N-COUNT

toothless /tuːθləs/

1 You use **toothless** to describe a person or their smile when they have no teeth. ADJ: usu ADJ n

2 If you describe something such as an official group or a law as **toothless**, you mean it has no real power and is not effective. *In his view, the Commission remains a toothless and ineffectual body.* ADJ-GRADED

toothpaste /tuːθpeɪst/ **toothpastes.** **Toothpaste** is a thick substance which you put on your toothbrush and use to clean your teeth. ◆◇◇◇◇ N-MASS

toothpick /tu:θpɪk/ **toothpicks.** A **toothpick** is a small stick which you use to remove food from between your teeth. N-COUNT

toothy /tu:θi/. A **toothy** smile is one in which a person shows a lot of teeth. ADJ-GRADED: ADJ n

tootle /tu:tᵊl/ **tootles, tootling, tootled**

1 If you **tootle** somewhere, you travel or go there without rushing or without any particular aim; an informal use, used mainly in British English. *I'm sure Ted is tootling down the motorway at this very moment.* VERB V prep/adv

2 If you **tootle** a tune on an instrument, you play it quietly, without concentrating or taking it seriously; an informal use. *McCann tootled a tune on the piano.* VERB V n Also V

top /tɒp/ **tops, topping, topped** ♦♦♦♦♦

1 The **top** of something is its highest point or part. *I waited at the top of the stairs. ...the picture at the top of the page... Bake the biscuits for 20-25 minutes, until the tops are lightly browned.* ► Also an adjective. *The bullet had entered the top part of the brain. ...the top corner of his newspaper.* N-COUNT: usu *the* N in sing, oft N *of* n ≠bottom ADJ: ADJ n ≠bottom

2 The **top** thing or layer in a series of things or layers is the highest one. *I can't reach the top shelf... Our new flat was on the top floor... A plastic surgeon can remove the top layer of skin.* ADJ: ADJ n =bottom

3 The **top** of something such as a bottle, jar, or tube is a cap, lid, or other device that fits or screws onto one end of it. *...the plastic tops from aerosol containers. ...a bottle top.* N-COUNT

4 The **top** of a street, garden, bed, or table is the end of it that is farthest away from where you usually enter it or from where you are; used mainly in British English. *...a little shop at the top of the street... He moved to the empty chair at the top of the table.* ► Also an adjective. *...the hill near the top end of the garden. ...the top corridor of the main building.* N-SING: *the* N, oft N *of* n =end, head ADJ: ADJ n

5 A **top** is a piece of clothing that you wear on the upper half of your body, for example a blouse or T-shirt; an informal use. *Look at my new top.* N-COUNT

6 You can use **top** to indicate that something or someone is at the highest level of a scale or measurement. *The vehicles have a top speed of 80 kilometres per hour. ...a top-ranking Saudi officer.* ADJ: ADJ n ≠bottom

7 The **top** of an organization or career structure is the highest level in it. *We started from the bottom and we had to work our way up to the top. ...his dramatic rise to the top of the military hierarchy. ...the man at the top.* ► Also an adjective. *I need to have the top people in this company pull together.* N-SING: *the* N, oft N *of* n ≠bottom ADJ: ADJ n

8 You can use **top** to describe the most important or famous people or things in a particular area of work or activity. *So you want to be a top model... The President met this afternoon with his top military advisers... Those are some of the top stories in the news.* ADJ: ADJ n

9 If someone is **at the top** of a table or league or is **the top** of the table or league, their performance is better than that of all the other people involved. *The United States will be at the top of the medal table... Labour was top of the poll with forty-six per cent.* ► Also an adjective. *He was the top student in physics... I usually came top in English.* N-SING: *the* N ≠bottom ADJ

10 You can use **top** to indicate that something is the first thing you are going to do, because you consider it to be the most important. *Cleaning up the water supply is their top priority... On arrival, a six-course meal was top of the agenda.* ADJ: oft ADJ *of* n

11 You can use **top** to indicate that someone does a particular thing more times than anyone else or that something is chosen more times than anything else. *Schillaci was Italy's top scorer during the World Cup matches... Semtex is terrorists' top choice of explosive.* ADJ: ADJ n

12 If someone or something **tops** a list, poll, or chart, they are mentioned or chosen more times than anyone or anything else; used by journalists. *It was the first time a Japanese manufacturer had topped the list for imported vehicles... Yeltsin has topped the poll in the first round of voting.* VERB V n

13 If something **tops** a particular amount, it is larger than that amount; used by journalists. *Imports topped £10 billion last month... These five schools are in the state's top 5% in achievement scores, one school topping the score for the whole state.* VERB V n

14 If something **is topped** with something, it has that thing as its highest part. *The holiest of their chapels are topped with gilded roofs... To serve, top the fish with the cooked leeks.* ♦ **-topped** *...the glass-topped table.* VERB be V-ed *with/by* n V n *with* n Also V n COMB in ADJ

15 If you **top** a story, remark, or action, you follow it with a better or more impressive one. *How are you going to top that?* VERB V n

16 In informal English, you can use **tops** after mentioning a quantity, to say that it is the maximum possible. *The publisher expected the book to sell 1,500 copies, tops... Be here in half an hour, tops.* ► Also an adjective. *He reckons a hundred is tops.* ADV: num ADV =max ADJ: v-link ADJ

17 See also **topping**.

18 If you say that something **is tops** or **is the tops**, you mean that it is better or more successful than anything else; an informal expression. *Majorca and Ibiza are tops for holiday bargain-hunters in June... The United States was tops in finance and services... I thought it was the tops so I bought it.* PHRASES V inflects

19 If someone **blows** their **top**, they become very angry about something; an informal expression. *He blew his top after airport officials refused to let him on a plane.* V inflects

20 If a person, organization, or country **comes out on top**, they are more successful than the others that they have been competing with. *The only way to come out on top is to adopt a different approach.* V inflects

21 If you say that you clean, tidy, or examine something **from top to bottom**, you are emphasizing that you do it completely and thoroughly. *She would clean the house from top to bottom.* PHR after v PRAGMATICS

22 You can use **from top to toe** to emphasize that the whole of someone's body is covered or dressed in a particular thing or type of clothing. *They were sensibly dressed from top to toe in rain gear.* PHR after v PRAGMATICS

23 When something **gets on top of** you, it makes you feel depressed and helpless because it is very difficult or worrying, or because it involves more work than you can cope with. *Things have been getting on top of me lately.* V inflects, PHR n

24 If you say something **off the top of** your **head**, you say it without thinking about it much before you speak, especially because you do not have enough time. *It was the best I could think of off the top of my head.* PHR after v, PHR with cl

25 If one thing is **on top** of another, it is placed over it or on its highest part. *...the vacuum flask that was resting on top of the stove. ...the fairy on top of the Christmas tree... Place the sliced pork fillet on top and pour a little sauce over it.* v-link PHR, PHR after v, oft PHR *of* n

26 You can use **on top** or **on top of** to indicate that a particular problem exists in addition to a number of other problems. *A stepfamily faces all the problems that a normal family has, with a set of additional problems on top... An extra 700 jobs are being cut on top of the 2,000 that were lost last year.*

27 You say that someone is **on top** when they have reached the most important position in an organization or business. *How does he stay on top, 17 years after becoming foreign minister?* usu v-link PHR

28 If you **are on top of** or **get on top of** something that you are doing, you are dealing with it successfully. *...the government's inability to get on top of the situation.* V inflects, PHR n

29 If you say that you feel **on top of the world**, you are emphasizing that you feel extremely happy and healthy. *Mr Mandela said he was feeling on top of the world after his stay in hospital.* usu v-link PHR PRAGMATICS

30 If one thing is **over the top** of another, it is placed over it so that it is completely covering it. *I have overcome this problem by placing a sheet of polythene over the top of the container... Stir the sauce and pour it over the top.* PHR after v, v-link PHR, oft PHR *of* n

31 You describe something as **over the top** when you think that it is exaggerated, and therefore unacceptable; an informal expression, used mainly in usu v-link PHR =OTT

British English. *The special effects are a bit over the top but I enjoyed it.*
32 If you **top and tail** fruit such as gooseberries, you cut off the top and bottom of them when you are preparing them to be eaten; used in British English. Vs inflect
33 If you say that someone is at **the top of the tree**, you mean that they have reached the highest level in their career or profession; used in British English. *He sees himself going right to the top of the tree.* usu prep PHR
34 If you say something **at the top of** your **voice**, you say it very loudly. *'Stephen!' shouted Marcia at the top of her voice.* PHR after v
35 • **at the top of the heap**: see **heap**.
top off. If you **top off** an event or period with a particular thing, you end it in an especially satisfactory, dramatic, or annoying way by doing that thing. *He topped off his career with an Olympic gold medal... The evening was topped off by a special showing of the museum's new Degas exhibit... To top it all off one of the catering staff managed to slice their finger cutting cheese.* PHRASAL VERB V P n (not pron) V n P
top up. If you **top** something **up**, you make it full again when part of it has been used; used mainly in British English. *We topped up the water tanks... He topped her glass up after complaining she was a slow drinker.* • See also **top-up**. PHRASAL VERB V P n (not pron) V n P
topaz /tɒʊpæz/ **topazes.** A **topaz** is a precious stone which is usually yellowish-brown in colour. N-VAR
top-class also spelled **top class**. **Top-class** means amongst the finest of its kind. *He's a great prospect and we think he'll turn into a top-class player. ...a top-class hotel.* ◆◇◇◇◇ ADJ
topcoat /tɒpkoʊt/ **topcoats;** also spelled **top coat**.
1 A **topcoat** is a thick, warm coat. N-COUNT
2 A **topcoat** is the final layer of paint or varnish that is put on something. **Topcoat** is the type of paint or varnish that you use for the final layer. • See also **undercoat**. N-VAR
top-drawer. If you describe someone or something as **top-drawer**, you are saying, often in a humorous way, that they have a high social standing or are of very good quality. ADJ: usu ADJ n
top hat, top hats. A **top hat** is a man's tall hat with a narrow brim. Top hats are now worn only on special occasions, for example at some weddings. N-COUNT
top-heavy
1 Something that is **top-heavy** is larger or bulkier at the top than at the bottom, and is therefore not stable. *...top-heavy flowers such as sunflowers.* ADJ-GRADED
2 If you describe a business or other organization as **top-heavy**, you mean that it has too many senior managers in relation to the number of junior managers or workers; used showing disapproval. *...top-heavy bureaucratic structures.* ADJ-GRADED PRAGMATICS
topiary /toʊpiəri, AM -eri/. **Topiary** is the art of cutting hedges and bushes into different shapes, for example into the shapes of birds or animals. N-UNCOUNT
topic /tɒpɪk/ **topics.** A **topic** is a particular subject that you discuss or write about. *The weather is a constant topic of conversation in Britain... The main topic for discussion is political union... They offer tips on topics such as home safety.* ◆◆◇◇◇ N-COUNT =subject
topical /tɒpɪkᵊl/. **Topical** is used to describe something that concerns or relates to events that are happening at the present time. *The magazine's aim is to discuss topical issues within a Christian framework... The sinking of the tanker has made aspects of marine pollution particularly topical.* ♦ **topicality** /tɒpɪkælɪti/ *The book has all the lively topicality of first-rate journalism.* ◆◆◇◇◇ ADJ-GRADED N-UNCOUNT
topknot /tɒpnɒt/ **topknots;** also spelled **top-knot**. If someone, especially a woman, has her hair in a **topknot**, her hair is arranged in a small neat pile on top of her head. N-COUNT
topless /tɒpləs/ ◆◇◇◇◇
1 If a woman goes **topless**, she does not wear anything to cover her breasts. *I wouldn't sunbathe topless if I thought I might offend anyone.* ADJ: ADJ after v, ADJ n, v-link ADJ
2 A **topless** show or bar is one in which the female entertainers or staff do not wear anything to cover their breasts. ADJ: ADJ n
top-level. A **top-level** discussion or activity is one that involves the people with the greatest amount of power and authority in an organization or country. *...a top-level meeting of American generals at the Pentagon.* ◆◇◇◇◇ ADJ: ADJ n
topmost /tɒpmoʊst/. The **topmost** thing in a number of things is the one that is highest or nearest the top. *...the topmost branches of a gigantic oak tree.* ADJ: ADJ n =uppermost, highest
top-notch; also spelled **top notch**. If you describe someone or something as **top-notch**, you mean that they are of a very high standard or quality; an old-fashioned, informal word. ADJ =first-rate
topographical /tɒpəgræfɪkᵊl/. A **topographical** survey or map relates to or shows the physical features of an area of land, for example its hills, valleys, and rivers. ADJ: usu ADJ n
topography /təpɒgrəfi/ **topographies**
1 **Topography** is the study and description of the physical features of an area, for example its hills, valleys, or rivers, or the representation of these features on maps. N-UNCOUNT
2 The **topography** of a particular area is its physical shape, including its hills, valleys, and rivers. *The topography of the river's basin has changed significantly since the floods.* N-COUNT: usu sing, with poss
topping /tɒpɪŋ/ **toppings.** A **topping** is food, such as cream or cheese, that is poured or put on top of other food in order to decorate it or add to its flavour. • See also **top**. ◆◇◇◇◇ N-MASS
topple /tɒpᵊl/ **topples, toppling, toppled** ◆◆◇◇◇
1 If someone or something **topples** somewhere or if you **topple** them, they become unsteady or unstable and fall over. *He just released his hold and toppled slowly backwards... Winds and rain toppled trees and electricity lines.* ► **Topple over** means the same as **topple**. *The tree is so badly damaged they are worried it might topple over... We lost our balance and toppled over on to a table.* V-ERG V adv/prep V n Also V PHRASAL VERB V P
2 To **topple** a government or leader, especially one that is not democratically elected, means to cause them to lose power; used in journalism. *...the revolution which toppled the communist regime.* VERB =overthrow V n
top-ranked. A **top-ranked** sports player or team is the most successful player or team in a particular sport; used by journalists. ADJ: ADJ n
top-ranking. A **top-ranking** person is someone who has a very high rank or status in a particular organization or field of activity. *...400 of Germany's top-ranking military officials... Top-ranking sumo wrestlers attain superstar status.* ADJ: ADJ n
top-rated. A **top-rated** show or service is the most successful or highly regarded of its kind; used in journalism. *...the top-rated American television series. ...the company's top-rated hotel.* ADJ: ADJ n
top secret; also spelled **top-secret**. **Top secret** information or activity is intended to be kept completely secret, for example in order to prevent a country's enemies from finding out about it. *The top secret documents had to do with the most advanced military equipment... Four of the most powerful men in Russia set out on a top-secret mission.* ◆◇◇◇◇ ADJ: usu ADJ n
topside /tɒpsaɪd/ **topsides**
1 In British English, **topside** is a joint of beef that is cut from the upper part of the leg. It is usually cooked by roasting. N-UNCOUNT
2 On a ship, if you go **topside**, you go up onto the top deck; a technical use. *He left the control station and went topside.* ADV: ADV after v
3 The **topside** or **topsides** of a ship or boat are the top deck or the parts which you can see above the water; a technical use. N-COUNT: usu pl
topsoil /tɒpsɔɪl/. **Topsoil** is the layer of soil nearest the surface of the ground. N-UNCOUNT
topsy-turvy /tɒpsi tɜːʳvi/. Something that is **topsy-turvy** is in a confused or disorganized state; an informal word. *The world has turned topsy-turvy in my lifetime. ...the moss-covered, topsy-turvy gravestones.* ADJ

top-up, top-ups ◆◇◇◇◇
1 A **top-up** is another serving of a drink in the same glass that you have just used; used in British English. *Anyone ready for a top-up?* N-COUNT
2 In British English, a **top-up** loan or payment is added to an amount of money in order to bring it up to a required level. *Student grants will be frozen at existing levels and top-up loans made available.* ADJ: ADJ n

torch /tɔːʳtʃ/ **torches, torching, torched** ◆◆◇◇◇
1 A **torch** is a small electric light which is powered by batteries and which you can carry in your hand; used mainly in British English. The usual American word is **flashlight**. N-COUNT
2 A **torch** is a long stick with burning material at one end, used to provide light or to set things on fire. *They lit a torch and set fire to the chapel's thatch. ...a torch-lit march for peace.* N-COUNT
3 A **torch** is a device that uses a hot flame for a task such as welding or cutting metal. *The gang worked for up to ten hours with acetylene torches to open the vault.* • See also **blowtorch**. N-COUNT: supp N
4 If someone **torches** a building or vehicle, they set fire to it deliberately. *The rioters torched the local library... Cars and trucks have been torched, bottles and bricks thrown.* VERB V n
5 If you say that someone **is carrying a torch for** someone else, you mean that they secretly admire them or love them. *He has always carried a torch for Barbara.* PHRASES V inflects, PHR n
6 If you say that someone is **carrying the torch** of a particular belief or movement, you mean that they are working hard to ensure that it is not forgotten and continues to grow stronger. *This group aims to carry the torch for the millions who demonstrated and the thousands who died... Since his death in 1985 his widow has carried the torch of his Stalinist legacy.* V inflects, usu PHR *for/of* n

torchlight /tɔːʳtʃlaɪt/. If you do something by **torchlight**, you do it using the light that is produced by a torch or torches. *Surgeons are performing operations in tents by torchlight... The marchers held a torchlight procession.* N-UNCOUNT: oft *by* N, N n

tore /tɔːʳ/. **Tore** is the past tense of **tear**.

torment, torments, tormenting, tormented. ◆◇◇◇◇
The noun is pronounced /tɔːʳment/. The verb is pronounced /tɔːʳment/.
1 **Torment** is extreme suffering, usually mental suffering. *She is my first ever girlfriend, a source both of wonder and torment... He spent days in torment while the police searched for his stolen car.* N-UNCOUNT =anguish
2 A **torment** is something that causes extreme suffering, usually mental suffering. *Sooner or later most writers end up making books about the torments of being a writer... Outdoors, mosquitoes and midges were a perpetual torment.* N-COUNT
3 If something **torments** you, it causes you extreme mental suffering. *At times the memories returned to torment her... He had lain awake all night, tormented by jealousy.* VERB =torture V n V-ed
4 If you **torment** a person or animal, you annoy them in a playful, rather cruel way for your own amusement. *My older brother and sister used to torment me by singing it to me.* VERB V n

tormentor /tɔːʳmentəʳ/ **tormentors.** Someone's **tormentor** is a person who deliberately causes them physical or mental pain. *...cases where women subjected to years of brutality lose control and kill their tormentors.* N-COUNT: usu poss N

torn /tɔːʳn/ ◆◇◇◇◇
1 **Torn** is the past participle of **tear**.
2 If you are **torn** between two or more things, you cannot decide which to choose, and so you feel anxious or troubled. *Robb is torn between becoming a doctor and a career in athletics... I know the administration was very torn on this subject.* ADJ-GRADED: usu v-link ADJ, oft ADJ *between* pl-n =divided

tornado /tɔːʳneɪdoʊ/ **tornadoes** or **tornados.** A **tornado** is a violent wind storm whose centre is a cloud in the shape of a funnel. ◆◇◇◇◇ N-COUNT

torpedo /tɔːʳpiːdoʊ/ **torpedoes, torpedoing, torpedoed** ◆◇◇◇◇
1 A **torpedo** is bomb that is shaped like a tube and that travels under water. N-COUNT
2 If a ship **is torpedoed**, it is hit, and usually sunk, by a torpedo or torpedoes. *More than a thousand people died when the Lusitania was torpedoed.* VB: usu passive *be* V-ed
3 If someone **torpedoes** negotiations or plans, they deliberately prevent them from being completed or from being successful; an informal use. *These attacks are seen as an effort to torpedo the talks.* VERB =sabotage, wreck V n

torpid /tɔːʳpɪd/. If you are **torpid**, you are mentally or physically inactive, especially because you are feeling lazy or sleepy; a formal word. ADJ-GRADED =lethargic

torpor /tɔːʳpəʳ/. **Torpor** is the state of being completely inactive mentally or physically, for example because of illness or laziness. *He had slumped into a state of torpor from which nothing could rouse him... The sick person gradually falls into a torpor.* N-UNCOUNT: also *a* N

torque /tɔːʳk/. **Torque** is a force that causes something to spin around a central point such as an axle; a technical term in engineering. N-UNCOUNT

torrent /tɒrənt, AM tɔːr-/ **torrents** ◆◇◇◇◇
1 A **torrent** is a lot of water falling or flowing rapidly or violently. *Torrents of water gushed into the reservoir... The rain came down in torrents, and we could see nothing... The trip involved crossing a raging torrent.* N-COUNT: oft N *of* n =flood
2 A **torrent** of abuse or questions is a lot of abuse or questions directed continuously at someone. *He turned round and directed a torrent of abuse at me. ...a £45,000 offer which prompted a torrent of criticism in the media.* N-COUNT: usu N *of* n

torrential /tərenʃəl, AM tɔːr-/. **Torrential** rain pours down very rapidly and in great quantities. ◆◇◇◇◇ ADJ: usu ADJ n

torrid /tɒrɪd, AM tɔːrɪd/
1 **Torrid** weather is extremely hot and dry. *...the torrid heat of a Spanish summer.* ADJ-GRADED: usu ADJ n
2 A **torrid** relationship or incident involves very strong emotions connected with love and sex. *She began a torrid love affair with a theatrical designer. ...torrid bedroom scenes.* ADJ-GRADED: usu ADJ n =passionate
3 In British English, if someone or something has a **torrid** time, they experience a lot of difficulties; used mainly in journalism. *Seles, the victim of a death threat earlier this week, has had a torrid time during the Championships... The minister suffered yet another torrid day of criticism.* ADJ-GRADED: usu ADJ n

torsion /tɔːʳʃən/. **Torsion** is a twisting effect on something such as a piece of metal or an organ of the body; a technical term in engineering and medicine. N-UNCOUNT

torso /tɔːʳsoʊ/ **torsos.** Your **torso** is the main part of your body, excluding your arms, head, and legs; a formal word. ◆◇◇◇◇ N-COUNT: oft poss N =trunk

tort /tɔːʳt/ **torts.** A **tort** is something that you do or fail to do which harms someone else and for which you can be sued for damages; a legal term. N-VAR

tortilla /tɔːʳtiːjə/ **tortillas.** A **tortilla** is a Mexican pancake made from corn and eggs. N-VAR

tortoise /tɔːʳtəs/ **tortoises.** A **tortoise** is a slow-moving animal with a shell into which it can pull its head and legs for protection. ◆◇◇◇◇ N-COUNT

tortoiseshell /tɔːʳtəsʃel/ **tortoiseshells**
1 **Tortoiseshell** is the hard shell of a kind of sea turtle. It is brown and yellow in colour and is often polished and used to make jewellery and ornaments. N-UNCOUNT
2 **Tortoiseshell** means made of tortoiseshell or made of a material which resembles tortoiseshell. *He wears huge spectacles with thick tortoiseshell frames.* ADJ: usu ADJ n
3 A **tortoiseshell** is a butterfly with brown and orange wings. N-COUNT

tortuous /tɔːʳtʃuəs/ ◆◇◇◇◇
1 A **tortuous** road is full of bends and twists. *The only road access is a tortuous mountain route.* ADJ-GRADED: usu ADJ n
2 A **tortuous** process or piece of writing is very long and complicated. *...these long and tortuous negotiations aimed at ending the conflict... The parties must now go through the tortuous process of picking their candidates.* ADJ-GRADED: usu ADJ n =convoluted

torture /tɔːʳtʃəʳ/ **tortures, torturing, tortured** ◆◆◆◇◇
1 If someone **is tortured**, another person deliberately causes them great pain over a period of time, VERB

in order to punish them or to make them reveal information. *French police are convinced that she was tortured and killed... Three members of the group had been tortured to death... They never again tortured a prisoner in his presence.* ► Also a noun. *...alleged cases of torture and murder by the security forces... Many died under torture, others committed suicide... I had thought this was a medieval torture that had mercifully disappeared.* — be V-ed; V n; N-VAR

2 To **torture** someone means to cause them to suffer mental pain or anxiety. *He would not torture her further by trying to argue with her... She tortured herself with fantasies of Bob and his new girlfriend.* — VERB =torment; V n; V pron-refl

3 If you say that something is **torture** or a **torture**, you mean that it causes you great mental or physical suffering; an informal use. *Waiting for the result was torture... The friction of the sheets against his skin was torture... Learning – something she had always loved – became a torture.* — N-UNCOUNT: also a N

torturer /tɔːʳtʃərəʳ/ **torturers.** A **torturer** is someone who tortures people. — N-COUNT

torturous /tɔːʳtʃərəs/. Something that is **torturous** is extremely painful and causes great suffering. *His breathing was torturous... This is a torturous, agonizing way to kill someone.* — ADJ-GRADED

Tory /tɔːri/ **Tories.** In Britain, a **Tory** politician or voter is a member of or votes for the Conservative Party. *...the former Tory Party chairman, Lord Tebbit. ...the constituency with the largest Tory majority in the country.* ► Also a noun. *...the first budget since the Tories won the 1992 general election.* — ◆◆◆◆◇ ADJ =Conservative; N-COUNT

toss /tɒs, AM tɔːs/ **tosses, tossing, tossed** — ◆◆◇◇◇

1 If you **toss** something somewhere, you throw it there lightly, often in a rather careless way. *He screwed the paper into a ball and tossed it into the fire... He tossed his blanket aside and got up... He tossed Malone a can of beer, and took one himself.* — VERB; V n prep/adv; V n n

2 If you **toss** your head or **toss** your hair, you move your head backwards, quickly and suddenly, often as a way of expressing an emotion such as anger or contempt. *'I'm sure I don't know.' Cook tossed her head... Gasping, she tossed her hair out of her face.* ► Also a noun. *With a toss of his head and a few hard gulps, Bob finished the last of his beer.* — VERB; V n; V n prep/adv; N-COUNT

3 In sports and informal situations, if you decide something by **tossing** a coin, you spin a coin into the air and guess which side of the coin will face upwards when it lands. *We tossed a coin to decide who would go out and buy the buns.* ► Also a noun. *It would be better to decide it on the toss of a coin.* — VERB; V n; N-COUNT: usu sing

4 The toss is a way of deciding something, such as who is going to go first in a game, that consists of spinning a coin into the air and guessing which side of the coin will face upwards when it lands. *Bangladesh won the toss and decided to bat first.* — N-SING: the N

5 If something such as the wind or sea **tosses** an object, it causes it to move from side to side or up and down; a literary use. *The seas grew turbulent, tossing the small boat like a cork... As the plane was tossed up and down, the pilot tried to stabilise it.* — VERB; V n; be V-ed adv/prep

6 If you **toss** food while preparing it, you put pieces of it into a liquid and lightly shake them so that they become covered with the liquid. *Do not toss the salad until you're ready to serve... Add the grated orange rind and toss the apple slices in the mixture... Serve straight from the dish with a tossed green salad.* — VERB; V n; V n in n; V-ed

7 See also **toss-up**.

8 In British English, if you say that someone **argues the toss**, you are criticizing them for continuing to argue for longer than is necessary about something that is not very important. *They were still arguing the toss about the first goal... They spend so much time arguing the toss over inconsequential matters.* — PHRASES; V inflects, oft PHR prep; PRAGMATICS

9 In spoken British English, if you say that you do not **give a toss** about someone or something, you are emphasizing that you do not care about them at all; an informal expression. *Well, who gives a toss about sophistication anyway?... I don't give a toss what people think... The rest of us really couldn't give a toss; money's what we want.* — with brd-neg, V inflects, oft PHR about n, PHR wh; PRAGMATICS

10 If you **toss and turn**, you move restlessly in bed and cannot sleep properly, for example because you are ill or worried. *You feel as if you've been tossing and turning all night, and wake up feeling worn out.* — V inflect

toss-up, toss-ups. If you say that it is a **toss-up** whether one thing will happen or another thing will happen, you mean that either outcome seems equally likely. *It's a toss-up whether oil prices will go up or down over the days ahead.* — N-COUNT: usu a N in sing, oft N wh, N *between* pl-n

tot /tɒt/ **tots, totting, totted** — ◆◇◇◇◇

1 A **tot** is a very young child; an informal word used in journalism. — N-COUNT

2 A **tot** of a strong alcoholic drink such as whisky or brandy is a small amount of it in a glass; used mainly in British English. — N-COUNT: usu N of n

tot up. To **tot up** a total or a list of numbers means to add up several numbers in order to reach a total; used mainly in British English. *I finally sat down to tot up the full extent of my debt... Now tot up the points you've scored.* — PHRASAL VERB =add up; V P n (not pron); Also V n P

total /toʊtᵊl/ **totals, totalling, totalled** — ◆◆◆◆◆

1 A **total** is the number that you get when you add several numbers together or when you count how many things there are in a group. *The companies have a total of 1,776 employees... Mr Smith said the true jobless total was 4 million.* — N-COUNT

2 The **total** number or cost of something is the number or cost that you get when you add together or count all the parts in it. *They said that the total number of cows dying from BSE would be twenty thousand... The total cost of the project would be more than $240 million.* — ADJ: ADJ n

3 If there are a number of things **in total**, there are that number when you count or add them all together. *I was with my husband for eight years in total... In total, 45 per cent of adults in Britain are exposed to tobacco smoke at home.* — PHRASE: PHR after v, PHR with cl, amount PHR

4 If several numbers or things **total** a certain figure, that figure is the total of all the numbers or all the things. *The unit's exports will total $85 million this year... They will compete for prizes totalling nearly £300.* — VERB; V amount

5 When you **total** a set of numbers or objects, you add them all together. *They haven't totalled the exact figures.* — VERB; V n

6 You can use **total** to emphasize that something is as great in extent, degree, or amount as it possibly can be. *You were a total failure if you hadn't married by the time you were about twenty-three... There was an almost total lack of management control... Why should we trust a total stranger?... I have total confidence that things will change.* ♦ **totally** *Young people want something totally different from the old ways... The fire totally destroyed the top floor.* — ADJ: usu ADJ n; PRAGMATICS; =complete; ADV: ADV adj/adv, ADV with v =completely

totalitarian /toʊtælɪteəriən/ **totalitarians.** A **totalitarian** political system is one in which there is only one political party which controls everything and does not allow any opposition parties; used showing disapproval. ► **Totalitarians** are people who support totalitarian political ideas and systems. *They feared that totalitarians might yet conquer the entire world.* — ◆◇◇◇◇ ADJ; PRAGMATICS; N-COUNT

totalitarianism /toʊtælɪteəriənɪzəm/. **Totalitarianism** is the ideas, principles, and practices of totalitarian political systems. — N-UNCOUNT

totality /toʊtælɪti/. The **totality** of something is the whole of it; a formal word. *...a process of social, economic and political change which involves the totality of human experience... He did not want to reform the criminal justice system in its totality.* — N-UNCOUNT: oft N of n, in its/their N

tote /toʊt/ **totes, toting, toted** — ◆◇◇◇◇

1 In British English, **the Tote** is a system of betting money on horses at a racetrack. — N-SING: the N

2 To **tote** something, especially a gun, means to carry it with you in such a way that people can see it. *The demonstrators fled when soldiers toting machine guns advanced on the crowd.* ♦ **-toting** *They* — VERB; V n; COMB in ADJ *are too frightened to speak out against the gun-toting thugs... Durham has much to offer the camera-toting visitor.*

totem /tɒutəm/ **totems** ◆◇◇◇◇

1 In some societies, a family's **totem** is the particular animal, plant, or natural object which they regard as a special symbol and which they believe has spiritual significance. N-COUNT

2 Something that is a **totem** of another thing is a symbol of it; used in written English. *This opera is one of the cultural totems of Western civilisation.* N-COUNT: oft N of n

totem pole, totem poles. A **totem pole** is a long wooden pole with symbols and pictures carved and painted on it. Totem poles are made by some Native American peoples and placed outside their homes. N-COUNT

totter /tɒtəʳ/ **totters, tottering, tottered** ◆◇◇◇◇

1 If someone **totters** somewhere, they walk there in an unsteady way, for example because they are ill or drunk. *He tottered to the fridge, got a beer and slumped at the table... The baby began to crawl, then managed her first tottering steps.* VERB V prep/adv V-ing

2 If something such as a market or government **is tottering**, it is weak and likely to collapse or fail completely. *The property market is tottering. ...further criticism of the tottering government.* VERB V V-ing

toucan /tuːkən, AM -kæn/ **toucans.** A **toucan** is a South American bird with a large brightly-coloured beak. N-COUNT

touch /tʌtʃ/ **touches, touching, touched** ◆◆◆◆◇

1 If you **touch** something, you put your hand onto it in order to feel it or to make contact with it. *Her tiny hands gently touched my face... Don't touch that dial... She reached down, touching her toes with opposite hands... The virus is not passed on through touching or shaking hands.* ▶ Also a noun. *Sometimes even a light touch on the face is enough to trigger off this pain.* VERB V n V-ing N-COUNT: usu sing

2 If two things **are touching**, or if one thing **touches** another, or if you **touch** two things, their surfaces come into contact with each other. *Their knees were touching ... A cyclist crashed when he touched wheels with another rider... If my arm touches the wall, it has to be washed again... In some countries people stand close enough to touch elbows... He touched the cow's side with his switch.* V-RECIP-ERG pl-n V V pl-n *with* n V n V pl-n V n *with* n

3 Your sense of **touch** is your ability to tell what something is like when you feel it with your hands. *The evidence suggests that our sense of touch is programmed to diminish with age. ...boys and girls who are blind and who want to be able to read and write by touch.* N-UNCOUNT

4 To **touch** something means to strike it, usually quite gently. *He scored the first time he touched the ball... As the aeroplane went down the runway the wing touched a pile of rubble.* VERB V n

5 If something **has** not **been touched**, nobody has dealt with it or taken care of it. *When John began to restore the house in the 1960, nothing had been touched for 40 years.* VB: usu passive, with brd-neg *be* V-ed

6 If you say that you did not **touch** someone or something, you are emphasizing that you did not attack them or harm or destroy them, especially when someone has accused you of doing so. *Pearce remained adamant, saying 'I didn't touch him'... I was in the garden. I never touched the sandwiches.* VB: with brd-neg PRAGMATICS V n

7 You say that you never **touch** something or that you have not **touched** something for a long time to emphasize that you never use or consume it, or you have not used or consumed it for a long time. *He doesn't drink much and doesn't touch drugs... His diet is vegetarian, and he hasn't touched alcohol for six years... Jones hasn't touched a trumpet in 10 years.* VB: no passive, with brd-neg PRAGMATICS V n

8 If you **touch on** a particular subject or problem, you mention it or write briefly about it. *The film touches on these issues, but only superficially... She writes about women's idealisation of men, touching briefly on the topic of women's fantasy life.* VERB V *on/upon* n

9 If something **touches** you, it affects you in some way for a short time. *...a guilt that in some sense touches everyone... Nor had the benefits of the war years touched all sectors of the population.* VERB V n

10 If something that someone says or does **touches** you, it affects you emotionally, often because you see that they are suffering a lot or that they are being very kind. *It has touched me deeply to see how these people live... Her enthusiasm touched me.* ♦ **touched** *I was touched to find that he regards me as engaging... He was touched that we came.* VERB =move *it* V n to-inf V n ADJ-GRADED: v-link ADJ

11 If something **is touched with** a particular quality, it has a certain amount of that quality; used in written English. *His crinkly hair was touched with grey... Kasparov understood the boy was touched with genius.* VB: usu passive *be* V-ed *with* n

12 If you say about someone that nobody can **touch** him or her **for** a particular thing, you mean that he or she is much better at it than anyone else. *No one can touch these girls for professionalism.* VB: no cont, no passive V n *for* n Also V n

13 To **touch** a particular level, amount, or score, especially a high one, means to reach it; used mainly in British English. *By the third lap Kinkead had touched 289 m.p.h... The winds had touched storm-force the day before.* VB: no passive V n

14 If you **touch** someone **for** money, you ask them to give it to you; an informal use. *Now is the time to touch him for a loan.* VERB V n *for* n

15 A **touch** is a detail which is added to something to improve it. *They called the event 'a tribute to heroes', which was a nice touch... Small touches to a room such as flowers can be what gives a house its vitality.* N-COUNT: supp N

16 If someone has a particular kind of **touch**, they have a particular way of doing something. *The dishes he produces all have a personal touch... The striker was unable to find his scoring touch.* N-SING: with supp

17 **A touch of** something is a very small amount of it. *She thought she just had a touch of flu... At university he wrote a bit, did a touch of acting, and indulged in internal college politics.* QUANT: QUANT *of* n-uncount

18 You can use **a touch** to mean slightly or to a small extent, especially in order to make something you say seem less extreme. For example, if you say that something is **a touch** expensive, you might really think that it is very expensive. *We were all a touch uneasy, I think... I found it a touch distasteful.* PHRASE: PHR adj/adv/prep PRAGMATICS =a bit

19 See also **touching**.

20 You use **at the touch of** in expressions such as **at the touch of a button** and **at the touch of a key** to indicate that something is possible by simply touching a switch or one of the keys of a keyboard. *Staff will be able to trace calls at the touch of a button. ...seats that flip out at the touch of a lever.* PHRASES PHR n, usu PHR after v

21 If you say that someone has **the common touch**, you mean that they have the natural ability to have a good relationship with ordinary people and be popular with them. *Unlike many senior judges, he has consistently shown that he has the common touch.* usu PHR after v

22 If you get **in touch** with someone, you contact them by writing to them or telephoning them. If you are, keep, or stay **in touch** with them, you write, phone, or visit each other regularly. *I will get in touch with solicitors about this... The organisation would be in touch with him tomorrow... My parents were constantly in touch.* PHR after v, v-link PHR, usu PHR *with* n

23 If you are **in touch** with a subject or situation, or if someone keeps you **in touch** with it, you know the latest news or information about it. If you are **out of touch** with it, you do not know the latest news or information about it. *You'll also be kept in touch with local Oxfam events. ...keeping the unemployed in touch with the labour market... Mr Cavazos' problem was that he was out of touch.* PHR after v, v-link PHR, usu PHR *with* n

24 If you **lose touch** with someone, you gradually stop writing, telephoning, or visiting them. *In my job one tends to lose touch with friends... We lost touch after that.* V inflects, usu PHR *with* n

25 If you **lose touch** with something, you no longer have the latest news or information about it. *Their leaders have lost touch with what is happening in the country.* V inflects, usu PHR *with* n

26 If you say that something is **touch and go**, you mean that you are uncertain whether it will happen or succeed. *It was touch and go whether we'd go bankrupt.* v-link PHR, oft PHR whether

27 If you say that someone is **a soft touch** or **an easy touch**, you mean that they can easily be persuaded to lend you money or to do things for you; an informal expression. *Mr Wilson is no soft touch... Pamela was an easy touch when she needed some cash.* v-link PHR

28 • **would not touch** someone or something **with a bargepole**: see **barge**. • **the finishing touch**: see **finish**. • **touch wood**: see **wood**.

touch down. When an aircraft **touches down**, it lands. *Spacecraft Columbia touched down yesterday... The first large contingent of troops touches down on American soil today.* PHRASAL VERB =land V P

touch off. If something **touches off** a situation or series of events, it causes it to start happening. *Is the massacre likely to touch off a new round of violence?* PHRASAL VERB V P n (not pron) Also V n P

touchdown /tʌtʃdaʊn/ **touchdowns** ◆◇◇◇◇

1 **Touchdown** is the landing of an aircraft or spacecraft. *...a perfect touchdown... The astronauts are preparing for touchdown tomorrow morning.* N-VAR =landing

2 In rugby and American football, a **touchdown** is when a team scores points by taking the ball over the opposition's goal line. N-COUNT

touché /tuːʃeɪ/. You say **'touché'** when you want to admit that the other person in an argument has won a point, usually with a short and witty remark. CONVENTION

touching /tʌtʃɪŋ/. If something is **touching**, it causes feelings of sadness or sympathy. *Her story is the touching tale of a wife who stood by the husband she loved... It was a very, very touching moment.* ♦ **touchingly** *He was touchingly naive about sex.* • See also **touch**. ◆◇◇◇◇ ADJ-GRADED =moving; ADV-GRADED: usu ADV adj

touchline /tʌtʃlaɪn/. In sports such as rugby and football, the **touchline** is one of the two lines which mark the side of the playing area; used mainly in British English. ◆◇◇◇◇ N-SING: usu *the* N

touch paper; also spelled **touchpaper**. If someone **lights the touch paper** or **lights the blue touch paper**, they do something which causes anger or excitement; used in British journalism. *This kind of remark is guaranteed to light the blue touch paper with some Labour politicians.* PHRASE: V inflects

touchstone /tʌtʃstoʊn/ **touchstones.** If you use one thing as a **touchstone** of another, you use it as a test, standard, or criterion by which you judge and assess the second thing. *Job security has become the touchstone of a good job for many employees.* N-COUNT: usu N *of/for* n

touchy /tʌtʃi/ **touchier, touchiest**

1 If you describe someone as **touchy**, you mean that they are easily upset, offended, or irritated. *She is very touchy about her past... Don't be so touchy.* ADJ-GRADED: oft ADJ *about* n =sensitive

2 If you say that something is a **touchy** subject, you mean that it is a subject that needs to be dealt with carefully and tactfully, because it might upset or offend people. *...the touchy question of political reform.* ADJ-GRADED: usu ADJ n =delicate

touchy-feely /tʌtʃi fiːli/. If you describe something as **touchy-feely**, you mean that it involves people expressing emotions such as love and affection openly in a way which you find embarrassing and silly. *...a touchy-feely song about making your life worth living.* ADJ-GRADED PRAGMATICS

tough /tʌf/ **tougher, toughest; toughs, toughing, toughed** ◆◆◆◆◇

1 A **tough** person has a strong, determined character and can tolerate difficulty or hardship. *He built up a reputation as a tough businessman... She is tough and ambitious.* ♦ **toughness** *Mrs Potter has won a reputation for toughness and determination on her way to the top.* ADJ-GRADED; N-UNCOUNT

2 If you describe someone as **tough**, you mean that they are rough and violent. *He had shot three people dead earning himself a reputation as a tough guy.* ▶ A **tough** is a tough person. *Three burly toughs elbowed their way to the front.* ADJ-GRADED; N-COUNT

3 A **tough** place or area is considered to have a lot of crime and violence. *She doesn't seem cut out for this tough neighbourhood... Arthur grew up in a tough city.* ADJ-GRADED: usu ADJ n =rough

4 A **tough** way of life or period of time is difficult or full of hardship. *She had a pretty tough childhood... It's been a tough day... He was having a really tough time at work.* ADJ-GRADED: usu ADJ n =rough

5 A **tough** task or problem is difficult to do or solve. *It was a very tough decision but we feel we made the right one... Whoever wins the election is going to have a tough job getting the economy back on its feet... It may be tough to raise cash... Change is often tough to deal with.* ADJ-GRADED: oft *it* v-link ADJ to-inf, ADJ to-inf =hard

6 **Tough** policies or actions are strict and firm. *He is known for taking a tough line on security... He announced tough measures to limit the money supply.* ADJ-GRADED =strict

7 A **tough** substance is strong, and difficult to break, cut, or tear. *In industry, diamond can form a tough, non-corrosive coating for tools. ...dark brown beans with a rather tough outer skin.* ADJ-GRADED

8 **Tough** meat is difficult to cut and chew. *The steak was tough and the peas were like bullets.* ADJ-GRADED

9 • **a tough row to hoe**: see **hoe**. • **tough luck**: see **luck**. • **a tough nut**: see **nut**.

tough out. If you **tough out** a difficult situation, you do not give in or show any weakness in that situation. *I think it was very brave of him to tough it out... Cabinet ministers signalled their determination to tough out the controversy.* PHRASAL VERB V n P; V P n (not pron)

tough cookie, tough cookies. If you describe someone as a **tough cookie**, you mean that they are unemotional and are not easily hurt by what people say or do. *She really is a tough cookie.* N-COUNT

toughen /tʌfᵊn/ **toughens, toughening, toughened** ◆◇◇◇◇

1 If you **toughen** something or if it **toughens**, you make it stronger so that it will not break easily. *Do not add salt to beans when cooking as this tends to toughen the skins. ...toughened glass.* V-ERG V n; V-ed; Also V

2 If a person, institution, or law **toughens** its policies, regulations, or penalties, it makes them firmer or stricter. *Talks are under way to toughen trade restrictions... They have put considerable pressure on the Government to toughen its stance... British regulations are also being toughened.* ▶ **Toughen up** means the same as **toughen**. *The new law toughens up penalties for those that misuse guns.* VERB V n; PHRASAL VERB V P n (not pron) Also V n P

3 If an experience **toughens** you, it makes you stronger and more independent in character. *They believe that participating in fights toughens boys and shows them how to be men. ...people who have been toughened by their daily circumstances.* ▶ **Toughen up** means the same as **toughen**. *He thinks boxing is good for kids, that it toughens them up... My father tried to teach me to toughen up.* VERB V n; PHRASAL VERB V n P; V P; Also V P n (not pron)

toupee /tuːpeɪ, AM tuːpeɪ/ **toupees.** A **toupee** is a small wig worn by a man to cover a bald patch on his head. N-COUNT

tour /tʊəʳ/ **tours, touring, toured** ◆◆◆◆◇

1 A **tour** is an organized trip that people such as musicians, politicians, or theatre companies go on to several different places, stopping to meet people or perform. *The band are currently on a two-month tour of Europe... It will be the first official cricket tour of South Africa for 22 years. ...a presidential campaign tour in Illinois.* • When people are travelling on a tour, you can say that they are **on tour**. *The band will be going on tour... The Royal Opera is on tour... There were mixed fortunes for French rugby teams on tour.* N-COUNT: usu with supp; PHRASE: PHR after v, v-link PHR

2 When people such as musicians, politicians, or theatre companies **tour**, they go on a tour, for example in order to perform or to meet people. *A few years ago they toured the country in a roadshow... He toured for nearly two years and played 500 sell-out shows... Dean Jones is with the Australian touring team in Sri Lanka.* VERB V n; V; V-ing

3 A **tour** is a journey during which you visit several N-COUNT:

places that interest you. *It was week five of my tour of the major cities of Europe.* oft N *of* n

4 A **tour** is a short trip that you make round a place, for example round a historical building, so that you can look at it. *...a guided tour of a ruined Scottish castle.* N-COUNT: oft N *of* n

5 If you **tour** a place, you go on a journey or trip round it. *You can also tour the site on modern coaches equipped with videos... We toured the streets of Milan.* VERB V n

tour de force /tʊəʳ də fɔːʳs/ **tours de force;** also spelled **tour-de-force.** If you call something such as a performance or a creation a **tour de force**, you are emphasizing that it is extremely good or extremely well done or made. *Stevenson's deeply felt performance is a tour-de-force... His tour de force is an elephant sculpture.* N-COUNT: usu sing

tourism /tʊərɪzəm/. **Tourism** is the business of providing services for people on holiday, for example hotels, restaurants, and sightseeing trips. *Tourism is vital for the Spanish economy.* ◆◆◇◇◇ N-UNCOUNT

tourist /tʊərɪst/ **tourists.** A **tourist** is a person who is visiting a place for pleasure and interest, especially when they are on holiday. *...foreign tourists... Blackpool is the top tourist attraction in England. ...the tourist season.* ◆◆◆◇◇ N-COUNT: oft N n

touristy /tʊərɪsti/. If you describe a place as **touristy**, you do not like it because it is full of tourists or full of things for tourists to buy and do; an informal word. *Visit some of the less touristy islands.* ADJ-GRADED PRAGMATICS

tournament /tʊəʳnəmənt/ **tournaments.** A **tournament** is a sports competition in which players who win a match continue to play further matches in the competition until just one person or team is left. ◆◆◆◇◇ N-COUNT: oft supp N

tourniquet /tʊəʳnɪkeɪ/ **tourniquets.** A **tourniquet** is a strip of cloth that is tied tightly round an injured arm or leg in order to stop it bleeding. N-COUNT

tour operator, tour operators. A **tour operator** is a company that provides holidays in which your travel and accommodation are booked for you. ◆◇◇◇◇ N-COUNT

tousled /taʊzᵊld/. If you have **tousled** hair, your hair is untidy and looks as though it has not been combed. ADJ-GRADED =ruffled, dishevelled

tout /taʊt/ **touts, touting, touted** ◆◇◇◇◇

1 If someone **touts** something, they try to sell it or convince people that it is good; used showing disapproval. *It has the trappings of an election campaign in the United States, with slick television ads touting the candidates. ...a popular advertising industry practice of using performers to tout products... He was being touted as the most interesting thing in pop... The product is touted as being completely natural. ...a couple of highly touted novels.* VERB PRAGMATICS V n *be* V-ed *as* n/adj/-ing V-ed

2 If someone **touts for** business or custom, they try to obtain it; used mainly in British English. *He visited Hong Kong and Singapore to tout for investment... Minicabs are not allowed to tout for hire on the streets.* VERB V *for* n

3 In British English, if someone **touts** tickets, they sell them outside a sports ground or theatre, usually for more than their original value. The American word is **scalp**. *...a man who made his money touting tickets... The queue stretches several hundred yards and tickets are touted for a tenner.* VERB V n

4 In British English, a **tout** is someone who sells things such as tickets unofficially, usually at prices which are higher than the official ones. The American word is **scalper**. N-COUNT

tow /toʊ/ **tows, towing, towed** ◆◆◇◇◇

1 If one vehicle **tows** another, it pulls it along behind it. *There may be supplementary charges if you are towing a caravan or a trailer... They threatened to tow away my car... The British navy boarded the vessel and towed it to New York.* ► Also a noun. *I can give you a tow if you want.* VERB V n V n with adv V n prep N-SING: *a* N

2 If you have someone **in tow**, they are following you closely because you are looking after them or you are leading them somewhere; an informal expression. *There she was on my doorstep with child in tow... She had a reporter and a photographer in tow.* PHRASE: *with* n PHR, PHR after v

towards /təwɔːʳdz, AM tɔːrdz/. The form **toward** is also used, and is the more usual form in American English. ◆◆◆◆◆

In addition to the uses shown below, **towards** is used in phrasal verbs such as 'count towards' and 'lean towards'.

1 If you move, look, or point **towards** something or someone, you move, look, or point in their direction. *Caroline leant across the table towards him... Anne left Artie and walked down the corridor towards the foyer... When he looked towards me, I smiled and waved... Patterson pointed toward a plain cardboard box beneath a long wooden table.* PREP

2 If things develop **towards** a particular situation, that situation becomes nearer in time or more likely to happen. *The talks made little evident progress towards agreement... She also began moving toward a different life-style. ...the trend towards couples living together rather than marrying.* PREP: PREP n/-ing

3 If you have a particular attitude **towards** something or someone, you have that attitude when you think about them or deal with them. *It's the business of the individual to determine his own attitude towards religion... Not everyone in the world will be kind and caring towards you... My feelings towards Susan have changed over the years.* PREP

4 If something happens **towards** a particular time, it happens just before that time. *The Channel tunnel was due to open towards the end of 1993... There was a forecast of cooler weather toward the end of the week.* PREP

5 If something is **towards** part of a place or thing, it is near that part. *The home of the Morgan family was up Gloucester Road, towards the top of the hill... The most popular items are located toward the back of the store.* PREP

6 If you give money **towards** something, you give it to help pay for that thing. *He gave them £20,000 towards a house... 71 percent of the entire budget went towards the military... Families could use the money as a contribution towards the cost of sending their children to a public school.* PREP

towel /taʊəl/ **towels, towelling, towelled;** spelled **toweling, toweled** in American English. ◆◆◇◇◇

1 A **towel** is a piece of thick soft cloth that you use to dry yourself. *...a bath towel.* N-COUNT

2 If you **towel** something or **towel** it dry, you dry it with a towel. *James came out of his bedroom, towelling his wet hair... I towelled myself dry... He stepped out of the shower and began towelling himself down.* VERB V n V n adj V n *down/off*

3 If you **throw in the towel**, you stop trying to do something because you realize that you cannot succeed; an informal expression. *It seemed as if the police had thrown in the towel and were abandoning the investigation.* PHRASE: V inflects =give in

4 See also **sanitary towel, tea towel.**

towelling /taʊəlɪŋ/; spelled **toweling** in American English. **Towelling** is a kind of fairly thick soft cloth that is used especially for making towels. *...a towelling bathrobe.* N-UNCOUNT: oft N n

tower /taʊəʳ/ **towers, towering, towered** ◆◆◆◇◇

1 A **tower** is a tall, narrow building, that either stands alone or forms part of another building such as a church or castle. *...an eleventh century castle with 120-foot high towers. ...the Leaning Tower of Pisa.* N-COUNT: oft in names

2 Someone or something that **towers** over surrounding people or things is a lot taller than they are. *He stood up and towered over her... At school, a girl may tower over most boys her age... The icebergs towered above them.* VERB V *over/above* n

3 A **tower** is a tall structure that is used for sending radio or television signals. *Troops are still in control of the television and radio tower.* N-COUNT

4 A **tower** is the same as a **tower block**. *...his design for a new office tower in Frankfurt.* N-COUNT

5 See also **clock tower, control tower, ivory tower.**

6 If you refer to someone as a **tower of strength**, you appreciate them because they give you a lot of PHRASE: *tower* inflects, v-link PHR, help, support, and encouragement when you have problems or are in a difficult situation. *Pat was a tower of strength to our whole family.* oft PHR *to* n

tower block, tower blocks. In British English, a **tower block** is a tall building divided into flats or offices. *...a 23-storey tower block.* ◆◇◇◇◇ N-COUNT

towering /taʊərɪŋ/ ◆◇◇◇◇

1 If you describe something such as a mountain or cliff as **towering**, you mean that it is very tall and therefore impressive; a literary use. *...towering cliffs of black granite which rise straight out of the sea.* ADJ: ADJ n

2 If you describe someone or something as **towering**, you are emphasizing that they are impressive because of their importance, skill, or intensity; a literary use. *He remains a towering figure in modern British politics... I saw her in a towering rage only once.* ADJ: ADJ n

town /taʊn/ **towns** ◆◆◆◆◆

1 A **town** is a place with many streets and buildings where people live and work. Towns are larger than villages and smaller than cities. *...the small town of St Augustine, in north-east Florida... Parking can be tricky in the town centre.* N-COUNT ► You can use **the town** to refer to the people of a town. *The town takes immense pride in recent achievements.* N-COUNT: usu sing

2 You use **town** in order to refer to the town where you live. *He admits he doesn't even know when his brother is in town. ...attractive and fun loving Americans, new to town... She left town.* N-UNCOUNT

3 You use **town** in order to refer to the central area of a town where most of the shops and offices are. *I walked around town... I caught a bus into town.* N-UNCOUNT

4 If you refer to **the town**, you are referring to town and city areas in general, as opposed to country areas; used mainly in British English. *More people are going to want to escape from the town into the country... It had the advantages of town and country combined.* N-SING

5 See also **ghost town, hometown, new town.**

6 If you say that someone **goes to town** on something or someone, you mean that they deal with them with a lot of enthusiasm or intensity. *We really went to town on it, turning it into a full, three-day show... The papers got hold of it and went to town on it... With £150 spending money for each couple, you can really go to town!* PHRASES V inflects, oft PHR *on* n

7 If you describe someone as a **man about town** or a **woman about town**, you mean that they are sophisticated, like to go out and spend money, and have a busy social life. *He was known as a tall, handsome man about town... He is an old flame of Diana's, from her days as a single girl about town.*

8 If you go out **on the town** or go for a night **on the town**, you enjoy yourself by going to a town centre in the evening and spending a long time there visiting several places of entertainment. *My idea of luxury used to be going out on the town and coming back in the early hours of the morning... Last Saturday, I was out on the town with my mate... Tim was just arriving home from a long night on the town.* prep PHR, n PHR =on the tiles

town council, town councils. A **town council** is a group of people who have been elected to govern a town. *The town council has refused permission for the march.* N-COUNT-COLL: oft in names

town crier, town criers. In former times, a **town crier** was a man whose job was to walk through the streets of a town shouting out news and official announcements. N-COUNT

town hall, town halls; also spelled **Town Hall.** A **town hall** in a town is a large building owned and used by the town council, often as its headquarters. You can also use **town hall** to refer to the town council that uses this building. ◆◇◇◇◇ N-COUNT

town house, town houses

1 A **town house** is a tall narrow house in a town, usually in a row of similar houses. N-COUNT

2 The **town house** of a wealthy person is the house that they own in a town or city, rather than another house that they own in the country. N-COUNT: with poss

townie /taʊni/ **townies.** If someone who lives in the countryside refers to someone from a town or city as a **townie**, they disapprove of that person because they think they have no knowledge of the countryside or country life. N-COUNT PRAGMATICS

town planning. **Town planning** is the planning and design of all the new buildings, roads, and parks in a place in order to make them attractive and convenient for the people who live there. N-UNCOUNT: oft N n

townsfolk /taʊnzfoʊk/. The **townsfolk** of a town or city are the people who live there; an old-fashioned word. *...some of the prominent townsfolk of the 1860s.* N-PLURAL =townspeople

township /taʊnʃɪp/ **townships** ◆◆◇◇◇

1 In South Africa, a **township** was a town where only black people lived. *...the South African township of Soweto. ...a black township.* N-COUNT

2 In the United States and Canada, a **township** is an area of land, especially a part of a county which is organized as a unit of local government. N-COUNT

townspeople /taʊnzpiːpᵊl/. The **townspeople** of a town or city are the people who live there. *Food shortages forced many townspeople into the country to grow their own food.* N-PLURAL

towpath /toʊpɑːθ, -pæθ/ **towpaths.** A **towpath** is a path along the side of a canal or river, which horses used to walk on when they towed boats. N-COUNT

towrope /toʊroʊp/ **towropes;** also spelled **tow rope.** A **towrope** is a strong rope that is used for towing vehicles. N-COUNT

tow truck, tow trucks. A **tow truck** is a motor vehicle which is used to tow away broken or damaged vehicles. N-COUNT

toxic /tɒksɪk/. A **toxic** substance is poisonous. *...the cost of cleaning up toxic waste... These products are not toxic to humans.* ◆◆◇◇◇ ADJ-GRADED =poisonous ♦ **toxicity** /tɒksɪsɪti/ **toxicities** *...data on the toxicity of chemicals.* N-VAR

toxicology /tɒksɪkɒlədʒi/. **Toxicology** is the study of poisons; a technical term in science. N-UNCOUNT ♦ **toxicological** /tɒksɪkəlɒdʒɪkᵊl/ *There were no adverse toxicological effects.* ADJ: ADJ n ♦ **toxicologist, toxicologists** *Toxicologists attempt to identify and understand toxic hazards.* N-COUNT

toxin /tɒksɪn/ **toxins.** A **toxin** is any poisonous substance produced by bacteria, animals, or plants. *Experts have linked this condition to a build-up of toxins in the body... Tests showed increased levels of toxin in shellfish.* ◆◇◇◇◇ N-VAR

toy /tɔɪ/ **toys, toying, toyed** ◆◆◆◇◇

1 A **toy** is an object that children play with, for example a doll or a model car. *He was really too old for children's toys. ...a toy telephone.* ● See also **soft toy.** N-COUNT

2 You can refer to objects that adults use for fun rather than for a serious purpose as **toys**. *Computers have become household toys.* N-COUNT: oft supp N

toy with PHRASAL VERB

1 If you **toy with** an idea, you consider it casually without making any decisions about it. *He toyed with the idea of going to China... For a time he had toyed with the notion of becoming a doctor.* V P n

2 If you **toy with** an object, you keep moving it around with your fingers, especially while you are thinking about something else. *He picked up a pencil and toyed with it idly.* =play with V P n

3 If you **toy with** food or drink, you do not eat or drink it with any enthusiasm, but only take a bite or a sip from time to time. *She had no appetite, and merely toyed with the bread and cheese.* V P n

toyboy /tɔɪbɔɪ/ **toyboys.** In informal British English, people sometimes refer humorously to a woman's lover as her **toyboy** when he is much younger than she is. N-COUNT

toytown /tɔɪtaʊn/. You use **toytown** to show that you think something is silly, childish, or worthless; used mainly in British English. *He denounced what he called toytown revolutionaries advocating non-payment of taxes... Inflation has turned the rouble into a toytown currency.* ADJ: ADJ n PRAGMATICS

trace /treɪs/ **traces, tracing, traced** 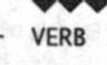

1 If you **trace** the origin or development of something, you find out or describe how it started or de- VERB veloped. *The exhibition traces the history of graphic design in America from the 19th century to the present... I first went there to trace my roots, visiting my mum's home island of Jamaica... The psychiatrist successfully traced some of her problems to severe childhood traumas.* ► **Trace back** means the same as **trace**. *Britain's Parliament can trace its history back to the English Parliament of the 13th century... She has never traced back her lineage, but believes her grandparents were from Aberdeenshire.* Vn / Vn to n / PHRASAL VERB / V n P to n / V P n (not pron)

2 If you **trace** someone or something, you find them after looking for them. *Police are anxious to trace two men seen leaving the house just before 8am... We are currently trying to trace the whereabouts of certain sums of money... They traced the van to a New Jersey car rental agency.* VERB / V n / V n to n

3 If you **trace** something such as a pattern or a shape, for example with your finger or toe, you mark its outline on a surface. *I traced the course of the river on the map spread out on my briefcase.* VERB / V n

4 If you **trace** a picture you copy it by covering it with a piece of transparent paper and drawing over the lines underneath. *She learned to draw by tracing pictures out of old storybooks.* VERB / V n

5 A **trace** of something is a very small amount of it. *Wash them in cold water to remove all traces of sand... He took great pains to write on his subject without a trace of sensationalism.* N-COUNT: usu N of n

6 A **trace** is a sign which shows you that someone or something has been in a place. *The local church has traces of fifteenth-century frescoes... There's been no trace of my aunt and uncle... Finally, and mysteriously, Hoffa disappeared without trace.* N-COUNT: usu N of n, also without N

7 If you say that someone or something **sinks without trace** or **sinks without a trace**, you mean that they stop existing or stop being successful very suddenly and completely. *The Social Democratic Party has sunk without trace at these elections... Pop groups are like Olympic swimmers – they hit gold once, then they sink without trace.* PHRASE: V inflects

trace back. See **trace** 1. PHRASAL VERB

traceable /treɪsəbᵊl/. If one thing is **traceable** to another, there is evidence to suggest that the first thing was caused by or is connected to the second thing. *The probable cause of his death is traceable to an incident in November 1724... Britain's inflation is probably traceable in part to the Chancellor's failure to get the exchange rate right.* ADJ: usu v-link ADJ, usu ADJ to n

trachea /trəkiːə, AM treɪkiə/ **tracheas** or **tracheae** /trəkiːiː, AM treɪkiiː/. Your **trachea** is your windpipe; a medical term. N-COUNT

tracing paper. **Tracing paper** is special transparent paper which you put over an illustration so that you can draw over the lines in order to produce a copy. N-UNCOUNT

track /træk/ **tracks, tracking, tracked** ◆◆◆◆◇

1 A **track** is a narrow road or path. *We set off once more, over a rough mountain track.* N-COUNT =path

2 A **track** is a piece of ground, often oval-shaped, that is used for races involving athletes, cyclists, cars, horses, or greyhounds. *The two men turned to watch the horses going round the track. ...the athletics track.* N-COUNT

3 Railway **tracks** are the rails that a train travels along. *A woman fell on to the tracks.* N-COUNT: usu pl

4 A **track** is one of the songs or pieces of music on a CD, record, or tape. *Graeme Naysmith has produced two of the ten tracks on this album.* N-COUNT

5 **Tracks** are footprints or other marks left in the ground by animals or people. *The only evidence of pandas was their tracks in the snow... McKee suddenly noticed tire tracks on the bank ahead.* N-PLURAL: oft supp N

6 If you **track** animals or people, you try to find them by following their footprints or other signs that they have left behind. *He thought he had better track this wolf and kill it... I followed him, tracking him in the snow until finally he got tired.* VERB / V n

7 To **track** someone or something means to follow their movements by means of a special device, such as a satellite or radar. *Our radar began tracking the jets... Forecasters are also tracking hurricane Josephine.* VERB / V n

8 If you **track** someone or something, you investigate them, because you are interested in finding out more about them. *If it's possible, track the rumour back to its origin... The player is being tracked by Juventus.* VERB / V n

9 See also **backtrack, fast track, racetrack, sidetrack, soundtrack, title track.**

10 If someone **covers** their **tracks**, they hide or destroy evidence of their identity or their actions, because they want to keep them secret. *He covered his tracks, burnt letters and diaries... The killer may have returned to the scene of the crime to cover his tracks.* PHRASES / V inflects

11 If you say that someone **has the inside track**, you mean that they have an advantage, for example special knowledge about something; used mainly in American journalism. *Denver has the inside track among 10 sites being considered... As an agent, you may have an inside track when good deals become available.* V inflects

12 If you **keep track of** a situation or a person, you have accurate and up-to-date information about them all the time. *With eleven thousand employees, it's very difficult to keep track of them all... It's hard to keep track of time in here.* V inflects, PHR n ≠lose track of

13 If you **lose track of** someone or something, you no longer know where they are or what is happening. *You become so deeply absorbed in an activity that you lose track of time... It's so easy to lose track of who's playing who and when.* V inflects, PHR n ≠keep track of

14 If you **make tracks**, you leave the place where you are, especially when you are in a hurry; an informal expression. *We'd better make tracks soon, hadn't we?* V inflects

15 If someone or something is **on track**, they are acting or progressing in a way that is likely to result in success. *It may take some time to get the British economy back on track... David put me back on track... He believes the talks are still on track.* PHR after v, v-link PHR

16 If you are **on the track of** someone or something, you are trying to find them, or find information about them. *He was on the track of an escaped criminal... The research institute is on the track of what causes the artery damage.* PHR n, usu v-link PHR =on the trail of

17 If you are **on the right track**, you are acting or progressing in a way that is likely to result in success. If you are **on the wrong track**, you are acting or progressing in a way that is likely to result in failure. *Guests are returning in increasing numbers – a sure sign that we are on the right track... We need a convincing win to put us back on the right track... We thought we were on the wrong track when we heard their description of you... The country was headed on the wrong track, economically.* v-link PHR, PHR after v

18 If someone or something **stops** you **in** your **tracks**, or if you **stop dead in** your **tracks**, you suddenly stop moving or doing something because you are very surprised, impressed, or frightened. *This magnificent church cannot fail to stop you in your tracks... They stopped in their tracks and stared at him in amazement... The thought almost stopped me dead in my tracks.* V inflects

19 If someone or something **stops** a process or activity **in its tracks**, or if it **stops dead in its tracks**, they prevent the process or activity from continuing or developing. *Francis felt he would like to stop this conversation in its tracks... U.S. manufacturers may find the export boom stopping dead in its tracks.* V inflects

20 ● **off the beaten track**: see **beaten**.

track down. If you **track down** someone or something, you find them, or find information about them, after a difficult or long search. *She had spent years trying to track down her parents... I don't know where that old story came from, I've never been able to track it down.* PHRASAL VERB / V P n (not pron) / V n P

track and field. **Track and field** refers to athletics as opposed to other sports; used mainly in American English. N-UNCOUNT =athletics

tracker /trækəʳ/ **trackers.** A **tracker** is a person or animal that finds other people or animals by following footprints and other signs that show where they have been. N-COUNT

track event, track events. A **track event** is an event in athletics which involves running or walking around a racetrack, in contrast to events that involve only jumping or throwing. N-COUNT

track record, track records. If you talk about the **track record** of a person, company, or product, you are referring to their past performance, achievements, or failures in it. *The job needs someone with a good track record in investment... His track record as a headmaster was excellent.* ◆◇◇◇◇ N-COUNT: usu with supp, oft N *in* n, N *of*-ing

tracksuit /træksuːt/ **tracksuits;** also spelled **track suit**. In British English, a **tracksuit** is a loose, warm suit consisting of trousers and a top which people wear to relax and do exercise. The usual American word is **sweatsuit**. ◆◇◇◇◇ N-COUNT

tract /trækt/ **tracts** ◆◇◇◇◇

1 A **tract** of land or **tracts** of land is a very large area of land. *A vast tract of land is ready for development... They cleared large tracts of forest for farming, logging and ranching.* N-COUNT: usu N *of* n

2 A **tract** is a short article expressing a strong opinion on a religious, moral, or political subject in order to try to influence people's attitudes. *She produced a feminist tract, 'Comments on Birth-Control', in 1930.* N-COUNT =pamphlet

3 A **tract** is a system of organs and tubes in an animal's or person's body that has a particular function, especially the function of processing a substance in the body; a medical term. *Foods are broken down in the digestive tract... A cold is an infection of the upper respiratory tract. ...urinary tract infections.* N-COUNT: usu supp N

tractable /træktəbəl/. If you say that a person, problem, or device is **tractable**, you mean that they can be easily controlled or dealt with; a formal word. *He could easily manage his tractable and worshipping younger brother. ...the country's least tractable social problems.* ADJ-GRADED ≠intractable

traction /trækʃən/ ◆◇◇◇◇

1 Traction is a form of medical treatment, in which weights and pulleys are used to gently pull or stretch an injured part of the body for a period of time. You say that a person who is having this treatment is **in traction**. *Is there an alternative to traction for a broken leg?... Isabelle's legs were in traction for about two and a half weeks.* N-UNCOUNT: oft *in* N

2 Traction is a particular form of power that makes a vehicle move. N-UNCOUNT: usu supp N

3 Traction is the grip that something has on the ground, especially the wheels of a vehicle. N-UNCOUNT

tractor /træktəʳ/ **tractors.** A **tractor** is a farm vehicle that is used to pull farm machinery and to provide the energy needed for the machinery to work. ◆◇◇◇◇ N-COUNT

trad /træd/. **Trad** or **trad jazz** is a kind of jazz based on the jazz that was played in the 1920s; used mainly in British English. N-UNCOUNT

trade /treɪd/ **trades, trading, traded** ◆◆◆◆◆

1 Trade is the activity of buying, selling, or exchanging goods or services between people, firms, or countries. *The ministry had direct control over every aspect of foreign trade. ...negotiations on a new international trade agreement... Texas has a long history of trade with Mexico.* N-UNCOUNT: usu with supp

2 When people, firms, or countries **trade**, they buy, sell, or exchange goods or services between themselves. *They may refuse to trade, even when offered attractive prices... They had years of experience of trading with the West... He has been trading in antique furniture for 25 years.* ♦ **trading** *Trading on the stock exchange may be suspended... Sunday trading laws will be reformed.* VERB; V; V *with* n; V *in* n; N-UNCOUNT: usu with supp

3 A **trade** is a particular area of business or industry. *They've completely ruined the tourist trade for the next few years. ...the arms trade.* N-COUNT: usu supp N

4 Someone's **trade** is the kind of work that they do, especially when they have been trained to do it over a period of time. *He learnt his trade as a diver in the North Sea... Allyn was a jeweller by trade... She is a patron of small businesses and trades.* N-COUNT: oft poss N, also *by* N

5 If someone **trades** one thing for another or if two people **trade** the things, they agree to exchange one thing for the other thing; used mainly in American English. *They traded land for goods and money... He still claims the arms weren't traded for hostages... Kids used to trade baseball cards... They suspected that Neville had traded secret information with Mr Foster.* ► Also a noun. *I am willing to make a trade with you... It wouldn't exactly have been a fair trade.* V-RECIP =exchange; V n *for* n (non-recip); pl-n V n; V n *with* n; N-COUNT

6 If you **trade** places with someone or the two of you **trade** places, you move into the other person's position or situation, and they move into yours; used mainly in American English. *Mike asked George to trade places with him so he could ride with Tod... Kennedy mischievously suggested that professors ought to trade jobs for a time with janitors... The receiver and the quarterback are going to trade positions.* V-RECIP =exchange; V n *with* n; pl-n V n

7 If two people or groups **trade** something such as blows, insults, or jokes, they hit each other, insult each other, or tell each other jokes; used mainly in American English. *Children would settle disputes by trading punches or insults in the schoolyard... They traded artillery fire with government forces inside the city.* V-RECIP =exchange; pl-n V n; V n *with* n

trade in. If you **trade in** an old car or appliance, you give it to a dealer when you buy a new one so that you get a reduction on the price. *He had a Rolls-Royce, and he traded it in for two matching silver Range Rovers... Richard refused to trade in his old Canon cameras.* ● See also **trade-in**. PHRASAL VERB; V n P; V P n (not pron)

trade off PHRASAL VERB

1 If you **trade off** one thing against another, you exchange all or part of one thing for another, as part of a negotiation or compromise. *They cynically tried to trade off a reduction in the slaughter of dolphins against a resumption of commercial whaling... There is a possibility of being able to trade off information for a reduced sentence.* ● See also **trade-off**. V P n *against* n; V P n *for* n

2 If someone **trades off** something, they make use of it for their own advantage, often in an unfair way. *They would be able to trade off their looks and manage on that alone.* V P n

trade on. If someone **trades on** something, they make use of it for their own advantage, often in an unfair way. *He was a man who traded on the achievements of others.* PHRASAL VERB; V P n

trade fair, trade fairs. A **trade fair** is an exhibition where manufacturers show their products to other people in industry and try to get business. N-COUNT

trade gap, trade gaps. If a country imports goods worth more than the value of the goods that it exports, this is referred to as a **trade gap**. N-COUNT: usu sing

trade-in, trade-ins. A **trade-in** is an arrangement in which someone buys something such as a new car or washing machine at a reduced price by giving their old one, as well as money, in payment. *...the trade-in value of the car.* ◆◆◇◇◇ N-COUNT: oft N n =part exchange

trademark /treɪdmɑːʳk/ **trademarks;** also spelled **trade mark**. ◆◇◇◇◇

1 A **trademark** is a name or symbol that a company uses on its products and that cannot legally be used by another company. N-COUNT

2 If you say that something is the **trademark** of a particular person or place, you mean that it is characteristic of them or typically associated with them. *...the spiky punk hairdo that became his trademark. ...the designer bars which have become the new trademark of the city.* N-COUNT: with poss

trade name, trade names. A **trade name** is the name which manufacturers give to a product or to a range of products. *It's marketed under the trade name 'Tattle'.* N-COUNT =brand name

trade-off, trade-offs; also spelled **tradeoff**. A **trade-off** is a situation where you make a compromise between two things, or where you exchange all or part of one thing for another; used by journalists. *The newspaper's headline indicates*  N-COUNT

that there was a trade-off at the summit. ...the trade-off between inflation and unemployment. ...the tradeoff of territory or land for peace.

trader /treɪdəʳ/ **traders.** A **trader** is a person whose job is to trade in goods or stocks. *Market traders display an exotic selection of the island's produce. ...a fur trader. ...traders at the Stock Exchange.* ◆◆◆◇◇ N-COUNT: oft n N

trade route, trade routes. A **trade route** is a route, often covering long distances, that used by traders. N-COUNT

trade secret, trade secrets

1 A **trade secret** is information that is known, used, and kept secret by a particular firm, for example about a method of production or a chemical formula. *The nature of the polymer is currently a trade secret.* N-COUNT

2 A **trade secret** is a piece of knowledge that you have, especially about how to do something, that you are not willing to tell other people. *I'd rather not talk about it too much because I don't like giving trade secrets away.* N-COUNT

tradesman /treɪdzmən/ **tradesmen.** A **tradesman** is a person, usually a man, who sells goods or services, especially one who owns and runs a shop. N-COUNT

tradespeople /treɪdzpiːpəl/. **Tradespeople** are people who sell goods or services as their job. N-PLURAL

trades union, trades unions. See **trade union.**

Trades Union Congress. **The Trades Union Congress** in Britain is the same as the **TUC**. N-PROPER: the N

trade union, trade unions; also spelled **trades union**. In British English, a **trade union** is an organization that has been formed by workers in order to represent their rights and interests to their employers, for example in order to improve working conditions or wages. The American term is **labor union.** ◆◆◇◇◇ N-COUNT: oft N n

trade unionism. **Trade unionism** is the system, practices, and ideology of trade unions. N-UNCOUNT

trade unionist, trade unionists; also spelled **trades unionist**. A **trade unionist** is an active member of a trade union. ◆◇◇◇◇ N-COUNT

trading estate, trading estates. A **trading estate** is the same as an **industrial estate**; used in British English. N-COUNT: oft in names

tradition /trədɪʃən/ **traditions** ◆◆◆◇◇

1 A **tradition** is a custom or belief that has existed for a long time. *...the rich traditions of Afro-Cuban music, and dance... Mary has carried on the family tradition of giving away plants... The story of King Arthur became part of oral tradition.* N-VAR

2 If you say that something or someone is **in the tradition of** a person or thing from the past, you mean that they have many features that remind you of that person or thing. *They're marvellous pictures in the tradition of Gainsborough. ...a Catholic novelist in the tradition of Graham Greene.* PHR-PREP

traditional /trədɪʃənəl/ ◆◆◆◆◇

1 **Traditional** customs, beliefs, or methods are ones that have existed for a long time without changing. *Traditional teaching methods sometimes only succeeded in putting students off learning. ...traditional Indian music.* ♦ **traditionally** *Married women have traditionally been treated as dependent on their husbands... Hell is traditionally associated with suffering... Traditionally, election campaigns start on Labor Day.* ADJ-GRADED: usu ADJ n; ADV-GRADED: ADV with cl/group

2 A **traditional** organization or person prefers older methods and ideas to modern ones. *We're still a traditional school in a lot of ways. ...traditional parents, who believed in laying down the law for their children.* ♦ **traditionally** *He is loathed by some of the more traditionally minded officers.* ADJ-GRADED: usu ADJ n ≠progressive; ADV-GRADED: ADV -ed/adj

traditionalism /trədɪʃənəlɪzəm/. **Traditionalism** is behaviour and ideas that support established customs and beliefs, rather than modern ones. N-UNCOUNT ≠progressivism

traditionalist /trədɪʃənəlɪst/ **traditionalists** ◆◇◇◇◇

1 A **traditionalist** is a person who supports the established customs and beliefs of his or her society or group, and does not want to change them. N-COUNT ≠progressive

2 A **traditionalist** idea, argument, or organization supports the established customs and beliefs of a society or group, rather than modern ones. ADJ ≠progressive

traduce /trədjuːs, AM -duːs/ **traduces, traducing, traduced.** If someone has **been traduced**, unpleasant and untrue things have deliberately been said about them; a formal word. *We have been traduced in the press as xenophobic bigots.* VB: usu passive; be V-ed

traffic /træfɪk/ **traffics, trafficking, trafficked** ◆◆◆◇◇

1 **Traffic** refers to all the vehicles that are moving along the roads in a particular area. *There was heavy traffic on the roads... Traffic was unusually light for that time of day. ...the problems of city life, such as traffic congestion.* • See also **traffic jam.** N-UNCOUNT: also the N

2 **Traffic** refers to the movement of ships, trains, or aircraft between one place and another. **Traffic** also refers to the people and goods that are being transported. *Air traffic had returned to normal... The railways will carry a far higher proportion of freight traffic... The ferries can cope with the traffic of both goods and passengers.* • See also **air traffic control.** N-UNCOUNT: with supp, usu n N

3 **Traffic** in something such as drugs or stolen goods is an illegal trade in them. *Traffic in illicit drugs was now worth some 500 thousand million dollars a year.* N-UNCOUNT: with supp, usu N in n

4 Someone who **traffics** in something such as drugs or stolen goods buys and sells them even though it is illegal to do so. *The president said illegal drugs are hurting the entire world and anyone who traffics in them should be brought to justice.* ♦ **trafficking** *He was sentenced to ten years in prison on charges of drug trafficking. ...the trafficking of illegal weapons.* VERB: V in n; N-UNCOUNT: usu n N

traffic calming; also spelled **traffic-calming**. **Traffic calming** consists of measures designed to make roads safer, for example making them narrower or placing obstacles in them, so that drivers are forced to slow down; used mainly in British English. *The government increased the budget for traffic calming schemes this year to £42 million.* N-UNCOUNT: usu N n

traffic cone, traffic cones. **Traffic cones** are plastic cone-shaped objects that are placed on a road to prevent people from driving or parking there. N-COUNT

traffic jam, traffic jams. A **traffic jam** is a long line of vehicles that cannot move forward because there is too much traffic, or because the road is blocked by something. ◆◇◇◇◇ N-COUNT

trafficker /træfɪkəʳ/ **traffickers.** A **trafficker** in particular goods, especially drugs, is a person who illegally buys or sells these goods. *They have been arrested as suspected drug traffickers.* ◆◇◇◇◇ N-COUNT: usu n N

traffic light, traffic lights. A **traffic light** or **traffic lights** are sets of red, green, and amber lights at a road junction that control the flow of traffic by signalling when vehicles have to stop and when they can go. ◆◇◇◇◇ N-COUNT: usu pl

traffic warden, traffic wardens. A **traffic warden** is a person whose job is to make sure that cars are not parked illegally; used mainly in British English. N-COUNT

tragedy /trædʒɪdi/ **tragedies** ◆◆◆◇◇

1 A **tragedy** is an extremely sad event or situation. *They have suffered an enormous personal tragedy... Maskell's life had not been without tragedy.* N-VAR

2 **Tragedy** is a type of literature, especially drama, that is serious and sad, and often ends with the death of the main character. *The story has elements of tragedy and farce. ...a classic Greek tragedy.* N-VAR ≠comedy

tragic /trædʒɪk/ ◆◆◇◇◇

1 A **tragic** event or situation is extremely sad, usually because it involves death or suffering. *It was just a tragic accident. ...the tragic loss of so many lives... The circumstances are tragic but we have to act within the law.* ♦ **tragically** /trædʒɪkli/ *Tragically, she never saw the completed building because she died before it was finished... My father died very suddenly and very tragically.* ADJ-GRADED; ADV-GRADED: ADV with cl, ADV with v, ADV adj/adv

2 **Tragic** is used to refer to tragedy as a type of lit- ADJ:

erature. *...Michael Henchard, the tragic hero of 'The Mayor of Casterbridge'.* ADJ n

tragi-comedy /trædʒi kɒmədi/ **tragi-comedies.** N-COUNT A **tragi-comedy** is a play or other written work that is both sad and amusing.

tragi-comic /trædʒi kɒmɪk/. Something that is **tragi-comic** is both sad and amusing at the same time. ADJ

trail /treɪl/ **trails, trailing, trailed** ◆◆◆◇◇

1 A **trail** is a rough path across open country or through forests. *He was following a broad trail through the trees.* N-COUNT =track

2 A **trail** is a route along a series of paths or roads, often one that has been planned and marked out for a particular purpose. *...a large area of woodland with hiking and walking trails.* N-COUNT

3 A **trail** is a series of marks or other signs of movement or other activities left by someone or something. *Everywhere in the house was a sticky trail of orange juice... He left a trail of clues at the scenes of his crimes... The typhoon has left a trail of death and destruction across much of central Japan.* N-COUNT: usu sing, oft N of n

4 If you **trail** someone or something, you follow them secretly, often by finding the marks or signs that they have left. *Two detectives were trailing him... I trailed her to a shop in Kensington.* VERB =follow V n V n prep/adv

5 You can refer to all the places that a politician visits in the period before an election as their campaign **trail**. *During a recent speech on the campaign trail, he was interrupted by hecklers. ...at the end of a hard day on the election trail.* N-COUNT: n N

6 If you **trail** something or it **trails**, it hangs down loosely behind you as you move along. *She came down the stairs slowly, trailing the coat behind her... He let his fingers trail in the water.* V-ERG =drag V n V prep

7 If someone **trails** somewhere, they move there slowly, without any energy or enthusiasm, often following someone else. *He trailed through the wet Manhattan streets... I spent a long afternoon trailing behind him.* VERB V adv/prep

8 If a person or team in a sports match or other contest **is trailing**, they have a lower score than their opponents. *He scored again, leaving Dartford trailing 2-0 at the break... The polls showed the Government trailing behind the Labour Party by 17 per cent.* VB: usu cont V amount V *behind* n

9 If you are **on the trail of** a person or thing, you are trying hard to find them or find out about them, often by following clues. *The police were hot on his trail... There was a newspaper on the trail of the story.* PHRASE: usu v-link PHR =on the track of

10 See also **nature trail, paper trail.** ● **to blaze a trail**: see **blaze.**

trail off or **trail away.** If a speaker's voice or a speaker **trails off** or **trails away**, their voice becomes quieter and they hesitate until they stop speaking completely. *'But he had no reason. He of all men...' Kate's voice trailed off.* PHRASAL VERB =tail away V P

trailblazer /treɪlbleɪzəʳ/ **trailblazers.** A **trailblazer** is a person who is the leader in a particular field, or who does a particular thing before anybody else does. *He has been the trailblazer and given British sprinters the belief that we are able to take on and beat the world's best.* N-COUNT

trail-blazing. A **trail-blazing** idea, event, or organization is new, exciting, and daring. *...a trail-blazing agreement that could lead to a global ban on nuclear weapons... The Festival aims to live up to its reputation as a trail-blazing event.* ADJ: ADJ n

trailer /treɪləʳ/ **trailers** ◆◆◇◇◇

1 A **trailer** is a vehicle which is pulled by a car or van and which is used for transporting large or heavy items. N-COUNT

2 A **trailer** is the long rear section of an articulated lorry, in which the goods are carried. N-COUNT

3 In American English, a **trailer** is a long vehicle which people use as a home or office and which can be pulled behind a car. The British word is **caravan.** N-COUNT

4 A **trailer** for a film or television programme is a set of short extracts which are shown to advertise it. *...a misleadingly violent trailer for the film.* N-COUNT: oft N *for* n

train 1 noun uses

train /treɪn/ **trains** ◆◆◆◆◇

1 A **train** is a number of carriages or trucks which are all connected together and which are pulled by an engine along a railway. Trains carry people and goods from one place to another. *The train pulled into a station... We can catch the early morning train... He arrived in Shenyang by train yesterday.* N-COUNT: also *by* N

2 A **train** of vehicles, people, or animals is a long line of them travelling slowly in the same direction. *In the old days this used to be done with a baggage train of camels. ...a long train of oil tankers.* N-COUNT: with supp, usu N *of* n

3 A **train** of thought or a **train** of events is a connected sequence, in which each thought or event seems to arise naturally or logically as a result of the previous one. *He lost his train of thought for a moment, then recovered it... Giles set in motion a train of events which would culminate in tragedy.* N-COUNT: usu sing, N *of* n

4 The **train** of a woman's formal gown or wedding dress is the long part at the back of it which flows along the floor behind her when she is wearing it. N-COUNT

5 If a process or event is **in train** or has been set **in train**, it is happening or starting to happen; used mainly in British English. *In a moment the ceremony was in train... He praised the economic reforms set in train by the government.* PHRASES v-link PHR, PHR after v =in motion

6 If something brings problems or difficulties **in** its **train**, the problems or difficulties occur as a natural or logical result of it. *The cars have brought in their train a host of other problems.* PHR after v

train 2 verb uses

train /treɪn/ **trains, training, trained** ◆◆◆◆◇

1 If someone **trains** you to do something, they teach you the skills that you need in order to do it. If you **train** to do something, you learn the skills that you need in order to do it. *The US was ready to train its troops to participate... Stavros was training to be a priest... Psychiatrists initially train as doctors... We don't train them only in bricklaying, but also in other building techniques... Companies tend to favour the lawyer who has trained with a good quality City firm... I'm a trained nurse... Our workforce is highly trained and competitive.* ♦ **-trained** *Mr. Koutab is an American-trained lawyer. ...French-trained Indian troops.* ♦ **trainer, trainers** *...a book for both teachers and teacher trainers.* V-ERG V n to-inf V to-inf V *as/in* n V n *as/in* n V V-ed Also V n COMB in ADJ N-COUNT

2 To **train** a natural quality or talent that someone has, for example their intellect or voice, means to help them to develop it. *I see my degree as something which will train my mind and improve my chances of getting a job... Some children come to school with more finely trained perceptual skills than others.* VERB V n V-ed

3 If you **train** for a physical activity such as a race or if someone **trains** you for it, you prepare for it by doing particular physical exercises. *Strachan is training for the new season... He has spent a year training crews for next month's round the world race.* ♦ **trainer** *She went to the gym with her trainer.* V-ERG V *for* n V n *for* n Also V, V n N-COUNT

4 If an animal or bird **is trained** to do particular things, it is taught to do them, for example in order to be able to work for someone or to be a good pet. *Sniffer dogs could be trained to track them down. ...a man who trained hundreds of dogs... She had brought her trained sheepdog to help in the rescue.* ♦ **trainer** *The horse made a winning start for his new trainer.* VERB *be* V-ed to-inf V n V-ed Also V n to-inf N-COUNT

5 If you **train** something such as a gun, a camera, or a light **on** someone or something, you aim it at them and keep it pointing steadily towards them. *She trained her binoculars on the horizon... Police cameras had been specifically trained on that area.* VERB V n *on* n

6 If you **train** a tree, bush, or plant in a particular direction, you tie it and cut it so that it grows in that direction. *Instead of training the shoots up the fence, lay them flat in both directions alongside it... You could even put a trellis on your walls and train plants to grow up it.* VERB V n prep V n to-inf

7 See also **training.**

train up. In British English, if someone **trains** you **up**, they teach you new skills or give you the necessary preparation so that you will reach the stand- PHRASAL VERB ard required for a particular job or activity; an informal expression. *The first companies to go in are taking a policy of employing East Germans and training them up... He usually preferred to train up a crew of enthusiastic young sailors from scratch.* V n P; V P n (not pron)

trainee /treɪni:/ **trainees.** A **trainee** is someone who is employed at a junior level in a particular job in order to learn the skills needed for that job. *He is a 24-year-old trainee reporter... My first job was as a graduate trainee with a bank.* ◆◇◇◇◇ N-COUNT: oft N n

trainer /treɪnə^r/ **trainers.** In British English, **trainers** are special shoes that people wear for running or jogging. The American word is **sneakers.** • See also **train.** ◆◇◇◇◇ N-COUNT: usu pl =training shoe

training /treɪnɪŋ/ ◆◇◇◇◇
1 **Training** is the process of learning the skills that you need for a particular job or activity. *He called for much higher spending on education and training... Kennedy had no formal training as a decorator. ...a one-day training course.* N-UNCOUNT
2 **Training** is physical exercise that you do regularly in order to keep fit or to prepare for an activity such as a race. *The emphasis is on developing fitness through exercises and training. ...her busy training schedule.* N-UNCOUNT • If you are **in training**, you are preparing yourself for a physical activity such as a race, by taking a lot of exercise and eating a special diet. *He will soon be back in training for next year's National... Redman broke a toe in training.* PHRASE: v-link PHR, PHR after v
3 See also **circuit training, potty training.**

training camp, training camps. A **training camp** for soldiers or sports players is an organized period of training at a particular place. ◆◇◇◇◇ N-COUNT

training shoe, training shoes. Training shoes are the same as **trainers.** N-COUNT: usu pl

traipse /treɪps/ **traipses, traipsing, traipsed**
1 If you **traipse** somewhere, you go there reluctantly, because you are tired or dissatisfied and do not wish to go there. *If traipsing around shops does not appeal to you, perhaps using a catalogue will... Joyce traipsed from one doctor to another, praying that someone would listen.* VERB =trudge; V prep/adv
2 If you talk about people **traipsing** somewhere, you mean that they are going there or moving about there in a way that annoys someone or gets in their way. *You will have to get used to a lot of people traipsing in and out of your home... She doesn't want security men traipsing round with her every minute of the day.* VERB PRAGMATICS; V prep/adv

trait /treɪt, treɪ/ **traits.** A **trait** is a particular characteristic, quality, or tendency that someone or something has. *The study found that some alcoholics had clear personality traits showing up early in childhood... Creativity is a human trait.* ◆◇◇◇◇ N-COUNT: with supp

traitor /treɪtə^r/ **traitors** ◆◇◇◇◇
1 If you call someone a **traitor**, you mean that they have betrayed beliefs that they used to hold, or that their friends hold, by their words or actions. *Some say he's a traitor to the working class.* N-COUNT: oft N *to* n
2 If someone is a **traitor**, they betray their country or a group of which they are a member by helping their enemies, especially during wartime. *...rumours that there were traitors among us who were sending messages to the enemy.* N-COUNT

traitorous /treɪtərəs/. A **traitorous** action will betray or bring danger to a country or to the group of people that someone belongs to. *...the monstrous betrayal of men by their most traitorous companions. ...the movement could be labeled as divisive, even traitorous.* ADJ-GRADED

trajectory /trədʒektəri/ **trajectories** ◆◇◇◇◇
1 The **trajectory** of a moving object is the path that it follows as it moves. *...the trajectory of an artillery shell.* N-COUNT: with supp
2 The **trajectory** of something such as a person's career is the course that it follows over time. *...a relentlessly upward career trajectory.* N-COUNT: with supp

tram /træm/ **trams.** A **tram** is a public transport vehicle, usually powered by electricity from overhead lines, which travels along rails laid in the surface of a street; used mainly in British English. The usual American word is **streetcar.** *You can get to the beach easily from the centre of town by tram.* ◆◇◇◇◇ N-COUNT: also *by* N

tramline /træmlaɪn/ **tramlines.** In British English, a **tramline** is one of the rails laid in the surface of a road that trams travel along. The American term is **streetcar line.** N-COUNT

tramp /træmp/ **tramps, tramping, tramped** ◆◇◇◇◇
1 A **tramp** is a person who has no home or job, and very little money. Tramps go from place to place, and get food or money by begging or by doing casual work. N-COUNT =down-and-out, hobo
2 If you **tramp** somewhere, you walk there slowly and with regular, heavy steps, for a long time. *They put on their coats and tramped through the falling snow... She spent all day yesterday tramping the streets, gathering evidence.* VERB =trudge, plod; V prep/adv; V n
3 The **tramp** of people is the sound of their heavy, regular walking. *He heard the slow, heavy tramp of feet on the stairs. ...the tramp of heavy boots.* N-UNCOUNT: usu N *of* n
4 If someone refers to a woman as a **tramp**, they are insulting her, because they think that she is immoral in her sexual behaviour; an offensive word used mainly in American English. N-COUNT PRAGMATICS =slut

trample /træmpəl/ **tramples, trampling, trampled** ◆◇◇◇◇
1 To **trample** on someone's rights or values or **trample** them means to deliberately ignore or disregard them. *They say loggers are destroying rain forests and trampling on the rights of natives... Diplomats denounced the leaders for trampling their citizens' civil rights... When a tribe encounters civilization, the first things to get trampled underfoot are the religious beliefs of the tribe.* VERB; V *on* n; V n
2 If someone **is trampled**, they are injured or killed by being trodden on by animals or by other people. *Many people were trampled in the panic that followed... Thousands of victims perished, trampled underfoot.* VB: usu passive; *be* V-ed; V-ed
3 If someone **tramples** something or **tramples** on it, they tread heavily and carelessly on it and damage it. *They don't want people trampling the grass, pitching tents or building fires. ...half-ripe apples that were being trampled underfoot by the fighting men... Please don't trample on the azaleas... There was a smell of trampled grass and earth.* VERB; V n; V *on* n; V-ed

trampoline /træmpəli:n/ **trampolines.** A **trampoline** is a piece of gymnastic apparatus on which you do acrobatic jumps. It consists of a large piece of strong cloth held by springs in a frame. N-COUNT

tramway /træmweɪ/ **tramways.** A **tramway** is a set of rails laid in the surface of a road for trams to travel along; used mainly in British English. N-COUNT

trance /trɑ:ns, træns/ **trances.** A **trance** is a state of mind in which someone seems to be asleep and to have no conscious control over their thoughts or actions, but in which they can see and hear things and respond to commands given by other people. *Like a man in a trance, Blake found his way back to his rooms... They went into a trance to communicate with the spirit world.* ◆◇◇◇◇ N-COUNT: oft prep N

tranche /trɑ:nʃ/ **tranches**
1 In economics, a **tranche** of shares in a company, or a **tranche** of a company, is a number of shares in that company. *On February 12th he put up for sale a second tranche of 32 state-owned companies.* N-COUNT: usu N *of* n
2 A **tranche** of something is a piece, section, or part of it. A **tranche** of things is a group of them; a formal use. *They risk losing the next tranche of funding... The next tranche of managers consists of assistant general managers and board directors.* N-COUNT: usu N *of* n

tranquil /træŋkwɪl/. Something that is **tranquil** is calm and peaceful. *The tranquil atmosphere of The Connaught allows guests to feel totally at home... The place was tranquil and appealing.* ◆◇◇◇◇ ADJ-GRADED =serene
♦ **tranquillity** /træŋkwɪlɪti/ or **tranquility** *The hotel is a haven of peace and tranquillity.* N-UNCOUNT

tranquillize /træŋkwɪlaɪz/ **tranquillizes, tranquillizing, tranquillized;** also spelled **tranquillise** in British English, and **tranquilize** in American English. To **tranquillize** a person or an ani- VERB =sedate mal means to make them become calm, sleepy, or unconscious by means of a drug. *This powerful drug is used to tranquilize patients undergoing surgery.* Vn

tranquillizer /træŋkwɪlaɪzəʳ/ **tranquillizers;** ◆◇◇◇◇ N-COUNT also spelled **tranquilliser** in British English, and **tranquilizer** in American English. A **tranquillizer** is a drug that makes people feel calmer or less anxious. Tranquillizers are sometimes used to make people or animals become sleepy or unconscious.

trans. **trans.** is a written abbreviation for 'translated by'.

trans- /trænz-/

1 trans- is used to form adjectives which indicate that something involves or enables travel from one side of an area to the other. For example, a trans-continental journey is a journey across a continent. *...trans-Pacific flights between Asia and America. ...the Trans-Siberian railway.* PREFIX

2 trans- is used to form words which indicate that someone or something moves from one group, thing, state, or place to another. *...trans-racial adoption.* PREFIX

transact /trænzækt/ **transacts, transacting, transacted.** If you **transact** business, you enter into a deal with someone, for example by buying or selling something; a formal word. *The ecu has yet to make an impact on the way in which companies transact their business... Mr. Harrison reckons half of his business could be transacted by computer.* VERB =carry out Vn

transaction /trænzækʃᵊn/ **transactions.** A **transaction** is a piece of business, for example an act of buying or selling something; a formal word. ◆◆◆◇◇ N-COUNT

transatlantic /trænzətlæntɪk/ ◆◇◇◇◇

1 Transatlantic flights or signals go across the Atlantic Ocean, usually between the United States and Britain. *Many transatlantic flights land there. ...the first transatlantic radio signal.* ADJ: ADJ n

2 In British English, **transatlantic** is used to refer to something that happens, exists, or originates in the United States. *...transatlantic fashions.* ADJ: ADJ n

transcend /trænsend/ **transcends, transcending, transcended.** Something that **transcends** normal limits or boundaries goes beyond them, because it is more significant than them. *...issues like European union that transcend party loyalty.* ◆◇◇◇◇ VERB Vn

transcendence /trænsendəns/. **Transcendence** is the quality of being able to go beyond normal limits or boundaries. *...the transcendence of class differences.* N-UNCOUNT

transcendent /trænsendənt/. Something that is **transcendent** goes beyond normal limits or boundaries, because it is more significant than them. *...the idea of a transcendent God who stood apart from mankind.* ◆◇◇◇◇ ADJ

transcendental /trænsendentᵊl/. **Transcendental** refers to things that lie beyond the practical experience of ordinary people, and cannot be discovered or understood by ordinary reasoning. *...the transcendental nature of God.* ADJ: usu ADJ n

transcendental meditation. **Transcendental meditation** is a kind of meditation derived from Hinduism, in which people mentally relax by silently repeating over and over again a special formula of words. The abbreviation 'TM' is also used. N-UNCOUNT

transcribe /trænskraɪb/ **transcribes, transcribing, transcribed** ◆◇◇◇◇

1 If you **transcribe** a speech or text, you write it out in a different form from the one in which it exists, for example by writing it out in full from notes or from a tape recording. *She is transcribing, from his dictation, the diaries of Simon Forman... Every telephone conversation will be recorded and transcribed.* VERB Vn

2 If you **transcribe** a piece of music for an instrument which is not the one for which it was originally written, you rewrite it so that it can be played on that instrument. *He gave up trying to write for the guitar and decided to transcribe the work for piano.* VERB Vn for n Also Vn

transcript /trænskrɪpt/ **transcripts.** A **transcript** of a conversation or speech is a written text of it, based on a recording or notes. *They wouldn't let me have a transcript of the interview.* ◆◆◇◇◇ N-COUNT: oft N of n

transcription /trænskrɪpʃᵊn/ **transcriptions**

1 Transcription of speech or text is the process of transcribing it. N-UNCOUNT

2 A **transcription** of a conversation or speech is a written text of it, based on a recording or notes. *The transcriptions of the text were available as early as 1960.* N-COUNT

transept /trænsept/ **transepts.** In a cathedral or church the **transepts** are the parts which project to the north or south of the main part of the building, at right-angles to it. N-COUNT

transfer, transfers, transferring, transferred. The verb is pronounced /trænsfɜːʳ/. The noun is pronounced /trænsfɜːʳ/. ◆◆◆◆◇

1 If you **transfer** something or someone from one place to another, or they **transfer** from one place to another, they go from the first place to the second. *Remove the wafers with a spoon and transfer them to a plate... He was transferred from Weston Hospital to Frenchay... He wants to transfer some money to the account of his daughter... The person can transfer from wheelchair to seat with relative ease.* ► Also a noun. *Arrange for the transfer of medical records to your new doctor... The bank reserves the right to reverse any transfers or payments.* V-ERG Vn from/to n V from/to n N-VAR: oft N of n

2 If something **is transferred**, or **transfers**, from one person or group of people to another, the second person or group gets it instead of the first. *I realized she'd transferred all her love from me to you... The chances of the disease being transferred to humans is extremely remote... On 1 December the presidency of the Security Council automatically transfers from the US to Yemen.* ► Also a noun. *...the transfer of power from the old to the new regimes.* V-ERG Vn from/to n V from/to n N-VAR: usu N of n

3 Technology **transfer** is the process or act by which a country or organization which has developed new technology enables another country or organization to use the technology. *The Philippines needs capital and technology transfer... There will be a transfer of technology from this country to Taiwan.* N-VAR: supp N, N of n

4 In professional sport, especially football, if a player **transfers** or **is transferred** from one club to another, they stop playing for the first club and start playing for the second club; used mainly in British English. The usual American word is **trade.** *A deal to allow Diego Maradona to transfer from Napoli to Seville was tentatively agreed last night... He was transferred from Crystal Palace to Arsenal for £2.5 million.* ► Also a noun. *...Gascoigne's transfer to the Italian club, Lazio.* V-ERG V from/to n be V-ed from/to n Also Vn from/to n N-COUNT

5 If you **are transferred**, or if you **transfer**, to a different job or place, you move to a different job or start working in a different place. *I was transferred to the book department... Many personnel departments began to take charge of deciding who should be transferred... Anton was able to transfer from Lavine's to an American company.* ► Also a noun. *They will be offered transfers to other locations.* V-ERG be V-ed from/to n be V-ed V from/to n Also Vn, Vn from/to n N-VAR: oft N to n

6 When information **is transferred** onto a different medium, it is copied from one medium to another. *Such information is easily transferred onto microfilm. ...systems to create film-quality computer effects and then transfer them to film.* ► Also a noun. *It can be connected to a PC for the transfer of information. ...data transfer.* VERB be V-ed onto/to n Vn onto/to n N-UNCOUNT: usu with supp, N of n, n N

7 When property or land **is transferred**, it stops being owned by one person or institution and becomes owned by another; a legal use. *He has already transferred ownership of most of the works to a British foundation... Certain kinds of property are transferred automatically at death.* ► Also a noun. *...an outright transfer of property.* VERB Vn from/to n be V-ed Also Vn N-VAR: oft N of n

8 If you **transfer** or **are transferred** when you are on a journey, you change from one vehicle to an- V-ERG other. *He likes to transfer from the bus to the Blue Line at 103rd Street in Watts... 1,654 passengers were transferred at sea to a Norwegian cruise ship.* [Grammar: V from/to n; be V-ed from/to n]

9 Transfers are pieces of paper with a design on one side. The design can be transferred by heat or pressure onto material, paper, or china for decoration. *...gold letter transfers.* [Grammar: N-COUNT]

transferable /trænsfɜːrəbᵊl/. If something is **transferable**, it can be passed or moved from one person or organization to another and used by them. *Use the transferable skills acquired from your previous working background... Your Railcard is not transferable to anyone else.* [Grammar: ADJ]

transference /trænsfərəns/. The **transference** of something such as power, information, or affection from one person or place to another is the action of transferring it. *It is a struggle for a transference of power... His transference of devotion from Nicola to Susan was complete.* [Grammar: N-UNCOUNT: oft N of n; =transfer]

transfigure /trænsfɪgəʳ, AM -fɪgjər/ **transfigures, transfiguring, transfigured.** If someone or something **is transfigured**, they are completely transformed into something great or beautiful; a literary word. *They are transfigured by the healing powers of art... He smiled back, which for an instant transfigured his unrevealing features.* [Grammar: VERB; be V-ed; V n]

transfix /trænsfɪks/ **transfixes, transfixing, transfixed.** If you **are transfixed** by something, it captures all of your interest or attention, so that you are unable to think of anything else or unable to act. *We were all transfixed by the images of the war.* ♦ **transfixed** *Her eyes were transfixed with terror... For hours he stood transfixed.* [Grammar: VERB; =mesmerize; be V-ed; ADJ-GRADED: v-link ADJ, ADJ after v]

transform /trænsfɔːʳm/ **transforms, transforming, transformed** ◆◆◆◇◇

1 To **transform** something into something else means to change or convert it into that thing. *Your metabolic rate is the speed at which your body transforms food into energy... Delegates also discussed transforming them from a guerrilla force into a regular army.* ♦ **transformation** /trænsfəʳmeɪʃᵊn/ **transformations** *Norah made plans for the transformation of an attic room into a study... Chemical transformations occur.* [Grammar: VERB; V n into n; V n from n into n; Also V n; N-VAR: usu with supp]

2 To **transform** something or someone means to change them completely and suddenly so that they are much better or more attractive. *The Minister said the Urban Development Corporation was now transforming the area... A cheap table can be transformed by an interesting cover... He said she had transformed him from a hard-drinking womaniser into a devoted husband and father.* [Grammar: VERB; V n; V n from n into n; Also V n into n]

♦ **transformation** *In the last five years he's undergone a personal transformation. ...one of the most astonishing economic transformations seen since the second world war.* [Grammar: N-VAR: usu with supp]

transformer /trænsfɔːʳməʳ/ **transformers.** A **transformer** is a piece of electrical equipment which changes the voltage of a current. [Grammar: N-COUNT]

transfusion /trænsfjuːʒᵊn/ **transfusions.** A **transfusion** is the same as a **blood transfusion**. ◆◇◇◇◇ [Grammar: N-VAR]

transgress /trænzgres/ **transgresses, transgressing, transgressed.** If someone **transgresses**, they break a moral law or a rule of behaviour. *If a politician transgresses, that is not the fault of the media. ...a monk who had transgressed against the law of celibacy... It seemed to me that he had transgressed the boundaries of good taste.* ♦ **transgression** /trænzgreʃᵊn/ **transgressions** *Tales of the candidate's alleged past transgressions have begun springing up.* [Grammar: VERB; V; V against n; V n; N-VAR]

transgressor /trænzgresəʳ/ **transgressors.** A **transgressor** is someone who has broken a particular rule or law or has done something that is generally considered unacceptable; a formal word. [Grammar: N-COUNT]

transience /trænziəns, AM -nʃəns/. If you talk about the **transience** of a situation, you mean that it lasts only a short time or is constantly changing; a formal word. *There is a sense of transience about her, a feeling that she has only stopped off here en route to another place. ...the superficiality and transience of the club scene.* [Grammar: N-UNCOUNT]

transient /trænziənt, AM -nʃənt/ **transients** ◆◇◇◇◇

1 Transient is used to describe a situation that lasts only a short time or is constantly changing; a formal use. *...the transient nature of high fashion... In most cases, pain is transient.* [Grammar: ADJ-GRADED; =transitory]

2 Transients are people who stay in a place for only a short time and then move somewhere else; a formal use. *...a hotel for transients.* [Grammar: N-COUNT: usu pl]

transistor /trænzɪstəʳ/ **transistors** ◆◇◇◇◇

1 A **transistor** is a small electronic component in something such as a television or radio, which is used for amplification and switching. [Grammar: N-COUNT]

2 A **transistor** or a **transistor radio** is a small portable radio; an old-fashioned use. [Grammar: N-COUNT]

transit /trænzɪt/ ◆◆◇◇◇

1 Transit is the carrying of goods or people by vehicle from one place to another. *They halted transit of EC livestock. ...a transit time of about 42 minutes.* [Grammar: N-UNCOUNT]

• If people or things are **in transit**, they are travelling or being taken from one place to another. *They were in transit to Bombay... We cannot be held responsible for goods lost in transit.* [Grammar: PHRASE: v-link PHR, PHR after v]

2 A **transit** area is an area where people wait or where goods are kept between different stages of a journey. *...refugees arriving at the two transit camps. ...a transit lounge at Moscow airport.* [Grammar: ADJ: ADJ n]

3 In American English, a **transit** system is a system for moving people or goods from one place to another, for example on buses or trains. *The president wants to improve the nation's highways and mass transit systems. ...the New York City Transit Authority.* [Grammar: N-UNCOUNT: oft N n; =transport]

transition /trænzɪʃᵊn/ **transitions. Transition** is the process in which something changes from one state to another. *The transition to a multi-party democracy is proving to be difficult. ...a period of transition.* ◆◆◆◇◇ [Grammar: N-VAR]

transitional /trænzɪʃənᵊl/ ◆◇◇◇◇

1 A **transitional** period is one in which things are changing from one state to another. *...a transitional period following more than a decade of civil war... We are still in the transitional stage between the old and new methods.* [Grammar: ADJ: ADJ n]

2 Transitional is used to describe something that happens or exists during a transitional period. *The main rebel groups have agreed to join in a meeting to set up a transitional government.* [Grammar: ADJ: ADJ n]

transitive /trænzɪtɪv/. A **transitive** verb has a direct object. [Grammar: ADJ; ≠intransitive]

transitivity /trænzɪtɪvɪti/. The **transitivity** of a verb is whether or not it is used with a direct object. [Grammar: N-UNCOUNT]

transitory /trænzɪtəri, AM -tɔːri/. If you say that something is **transitory**, you mean that it lasts only for a short time. *Most teenage romances are transitory. ...a sad reminder of the transitory nature of political success.* [Grammar: ADJ-GRADED; =transient]

translate /trænzleɪt/ **translates, translating, translated** ◆◆◇◇◇

1 If something that someone has said or written **is translated**, it is said or written again in a different language. *Only a small number of Kadare's books have been translated into English... Martin Luther translated the Bible into German... The Celtic word 'geis' is usually translated as 'taboo'... The girls waited for Mr Esch to translate. ...Mr Mani by Yehoshua, translated from Hebrew by Hillel Halkin.* ♦ **translation** *The papers have been sent to Saudi Arabia for translation.* [Grammar: VERB; be V-ed into/from n; V n into/from n; be V-ed as n; V; V-ed; Also V n, V n as n; N-UNCOUNT]

2 If a name, a word, or expression **translates** as something in a different language, that is what it means in that language. *His family's Cantonese nickname for him translates as Never Sits Still.* [Grammar: VERB; V as n]

3 If one thing **translates** or **is translated** into another, the second happens or is done as a result of the first. *Reforming Warsaw's stagnant economy requires harsh measures that would translate into job losses... Your decision must be translated into specific, concrete actions.* [Grammar: V-ERG; V into n; be V-ed into n]

4 If you say that a remark, a gesture, or an action [Grammar: V-ERG]

translates as something, or that you **translate** it as something, you decide that this is what its significance is. *'I love him' often translates as 'He's better than nothing'... I translated this as a mad desire to lock up every single person with HIV.* V as n / V n as n
5 See also **translation.**

translation /trænzleɪʃᵊn/ **translations** ◆◆◇◇◇
1 A **translation** is a piece of writing or speech that has been translated from a different language. *...Macneice's excellent English translation of 'Faust'... I've only read Solzhenitsyn in translation.* N-COUNT: also *in* N
2 If you say that a quality of something has **been lost in translation**, or that the thing **loses something in translation**, you mean that it is not very good as a result of being translated into another language or retold in another form. *Much of the wit is lost in translation... French filmmakers say American remakes are losing something in the translation.* PHRASE: V inflects

translator /trænzleɪtəʳ/ **translators.** A **translator** is a person whose job is translating writing or speech from one language to another. ◆◆◇◇◇ N-COUNT

translucent /trænzluːsᵊnt/ ◆◇◇◇◇
1 If a material is **translucent**, some light can pass through it. *The building is roofed entirely with translucent corrugated plastic.* ADJ-GRADED
2 You use **translucent** to describe something that has a glowing appearance, as if light is passing through it. *She had fair hair, blue eyes and translucent skin... The sky was changing from translucent blue to thicker grey.* ADJ-GRADED

transmission /trænzmɪʃᵊn/ **transmissions** ◆◆◇◇◇
1 The **transmission** of something is the passing or sending of it to a different person or place. *Heterosexual contact is responsible for the bulk of HIV transmission. ...the fax machine and other forms of electronic data transmission. ...the transmission of knowledge and skills.* N-UNCOUNT: usu with supp, n N, N *of* n
2 The **transmission** of television or radio programmes is the broadcasting of them. N-UNCOUNT
3 A **transmission** is a broadcast. N-COUNT
4 The **transmission** on a car or other vehicle is the system of gears and shafts by which the power from the engine reaches and turns the wheels. *The car was fitted with automatic transmission. ...a four-speed manual transmission.* N-VAR

transmit /trænzmɪt/ **transmits, transmitting, transmitted** ◆◆◇◇◇
1 When radio and television programmes, computer data, or other electronic messages **are transmitted**, they are sent from one place to another, using wires, radio waves, or satellites. *The game was transmitted live in Spain and Italy... The information is electronically transmitted to schools and colleges... This is currently the most efficient way to transmit certain types of data like electronic mail... The device is not designed to transmit to satellites.* VERB be V-ed / V n / V *to* n
2 If one person or animal **transmits** a disease to another, they have the disease and cause the other person or animal to have it; a formal use. *...mosquitoes that transmit disease to humans... There was no danger of transmitting the infection through operations. ...the spread of sexually transmitted diseases.* VERB V n *to* n / V n / V-ed
3 If you **transmit** an idea or feeling to someone else, you make them understand and share the idea or feeling; a literary use. *The message they are transmitting to their daughters is very different from that of previous generations... He transmitted his keen enjoyment of singing to the audience.* VERB =convey V n *to* n
4 If an object or substance **transmits** something such as sound or vibrations, the sound or vibrations are able to pass through it or along it. *These thin crystals transmit much of the power... There was no vibration transmitted to the handles and the machine wasn't noisy either.* VERB V n / V-ed

transmitter /trænzmɪtəʳ/ **transmitters.** A **transmitter** is a piece of apparatus that is used for broadcasting television or radio programmes. ◆◇◇◇◇ N-COUNT

transmute /trænzmjuːt/ **transmutes, transmuting, transmuted.** If something **transmutes** or **is transmuted** into a different form, it is changed into that form; a formal word. *She ceased to think, as anger transmuted into passion... Scientists transmuted matter into pure energy and exploded the first atomic bomb.* V-ERG =transform V *into* n / V n *into* n / Also V n
♦ **transmutation, transmutations** *...the transmutation of food into energy.* N-VAR: oft N *of* n

transparency /trænspærənsi, AM -per-/ **transparencies** ◆◇◇◇◇
1 A **transparency** is a small piece of photographic film with a frame around it which can be projected onto a screen so that you can see the picture. N-COUNT =slide
2 **Transparency** is the quality that an object or substance has when you can see through it. *Cataracts is a condition that affects the transparency of the lenses.* N-UNCOUNT
3 The **transparency** of a process, situation, or statement is its quality of being easily understood or recognized, for example because there is no secrecy surrounding it, or because it is expressed in a clear way. *The Chancellor emphasised his determination to promote openness and transparency in the Government's economic decision-making.* N-UNCOUNT

transparent /trænspærənt, AM -per-/ ◆◇◇◇◇
1 If an object or substance is **transparent**, you can see through it. *...a sheet of transparent coloured plastic... I looked at his thin face with its almost transparent skin.* ADJ-GRADED ≠opaque
2 If a situation, system, or activity is **transparent**, it is easily understood or recognized. *We are now striving hard to establish a transparent parliamentary democracy... The company has to make its accounts and operations as transparent as possible.* ADJ-GRADED
♦ **transparently** *The system was clearly not functioning smoothly or transparently... The book is remarkably accurate and transparently fair-minded.* ADV-GRADED: ADV with v, ADV adj
3 You use **transparent** to describe a statement or action that is obviously dishonest or wrong, and that you think will not deceive people. *...a transparent effort by officials to blame foreigners... He thought he could fool people with transparent deceptions.* ♦ **transparently** *To force this agreement on the nation is transparently wrong... Her answers were transparently untruthful.* ADJ-GRADED / ADV-GRADED: ADV adj

transpire /trænspaɪəʳ/ **transpires, transpiring, transpired** ◆◇◇◇◇
1 When it **transpires** that something is the case, people discover that it is the case; a formal use. *It transpired that Paolo had left his driving licence at home... As it transpired, the Labour government did not dare go against the pressures exerted by the City.* VERB =turn out *it* V that
2 When something **transpires**, it happens. Some speakers of English consider this use to be incorrect. *Nothing is known as yet about what transpired at the meeting.* VERB V

transplant, transplants, transplanting, transplanted. The noun is pronounced /trænsplɑːnt, -plænt/. The verb is pronounced /trænsplɑːnt, -plænt/. ◆◆◇◇◇
1 A **transplant** is a medical operation in which a part of a person's body is replaced because it is diseased. *He was recovering from a heart transplant operation. ...the controversy over the sale of human organs for transplant.* N-VAR
2 If doctors **transplant** an organ such as a heart or a kidney, they use it to replace a patient's diseased organ. *The operation to transplant a kidney is now fairly routine. ...transplanted organs such as hearts and kidneys.* ♦ **transplantation** /trænzplænteɪʃᵊn/ *...a shortage of kidneys for transplantation... Bone marrow transplantation began 20 years ago.* VERB V n / V-ed / N-UNCOUNT: usu with supp
3 To **transplant** someone or something means to move them to a different place. *Marriage had transplanted Rebecca from London to Manchester... In the 19th century, the Santa Claus tradition seems to have been transplanted back to Europe... Farmers will be able to seed it directly, rather than having to transplant seedlings.* VERB V n *from/to/into* n / V n

transport, transports, transporting, transported. The noun is pronounced /trænspɔːʳt/. The verb is pronounced /trænspɔːʳt/. ◆◆◆◆◇
1 **Transport** refers to any type of vehicle that you can travel in or carry goods in. *Have you got your* N-UNCOUNT

own transport?... Which type of transport do you prefer?

2 Transport is a system for taking people or goods from one place to another, for example using buses or trains. *The extra money could be spent on improving public transport... The sudden onset of winter caused havoc with rail and air transport... An efficient transport system is critical to the long-term future of London.* N-UNCOUNT

3 Transport is the activity of taking goods or people from one place to another in a vehicle. *Local production virtually eliminates transport costs.* N-UNCOUNT

4 To **transport** people or goods somewhere is to take them from one place to another in a vehicle. *There's no petrol, so it's very difficult to transport goods... They use tankers to transport the oil to Los Angeles... The troops were transported to Moscow.* VERB; V n; V n prep/adv

5 If you say that you **are transported** to another place or time, you mean that something causes you to feel that you are living in the other place or at the other time. *Dr Drummond felt that he had been transported into a world that rivalled the Arabian Nights... In a dream you can be transported back in time... This delightful musical comedy transports the audience to the innocent days of 1950s America.* VERB; be V-ed prep/adv; V n prep/adv

6 A military or troop **transport** is a military vehicle, especially a plane, that is used to carry soldiers or equipment. N-COUNT: usu supp N

transportation /trænspɔːʳteɪʃᵊn/ ◆◆◇◇◇

1 Transportation refers to any type of vehicle that you can travel in or carry goods in; used mainly in American English. The usual British word is **transport**. *The company will provide transportation.* N-UNCOUNT =transport

2 Transportation is a system for taking people or goods from one place to another, for example using buses or trains; used in American English. The usual British word is **transport**. *Campuses are usually accessible by public transportation. ...our national transportation policy.* N-UNCOUNT =transport

3 Transportation is the activity of taking goods or people from one place to another in a vehicle. *The baggage was being rapidly stowed away for transportation... Oxfam may also help with the transportation of refugees.* N-UNCOUNT =transport

transporter /trænspɔːʳtəʳ/ **transporters.** A **transporter** is a large vehicle or an aeroplane that is used for carrying very large or heavy objects, for example cars; used mainly in British English. N-COUNT

transpose /trænspoʊz/ **transposes, transposing, transposed**

1 If you **transpose** something from one place or situation to another, you move it there. *Genetic engineers transpose or exchange bits of hereditary material from one organism to the next... The director transposes the action from 16th Century France to post-Civil War America.* ♦ **transposition** /trænspəzɪʃᵊn/ **transpositions** *...a transposition of 'Macbeth' to third century BC China.* VERB =transfer; V n from n to n; Also V n to n, V n; N-VAR: oft N of n

2 If you **transpose** two things, you reverse them or put them in each other's place. *Many people inadvertently transpose digits of the ZIP code. ...a short story in which he transposes the roles of poets and screenwriters.* ♦ **transposition** *His pen name represented the transposition of his initials and his middle name.* VERB =reverse; V n; N-VAR: oft N of n

3 If you **transpose** a piece of music, you perform it or write it in a musical key which is different from the original one: a technical term in music. *She could play any piece of music she heard and transpose it into any key.* VERB; V n into n; Also V n

transsexual /trænsekʃuəl/ **transsexuals.** A **transsexual** is a person who has decided that they want to live as a person of the opposite sex, and so has changed their name and appearance in order to do this. Transsexuals sometimes have an operation to change their sex. N-COUNT

transverse /trænzvɜːʳs/. **Transverse** is used to describe something that is at right angles to something else. ADJ: usu ADJ n

transvestism /trænzvestɪzəm/. **Transvestism** is the practice of wearing clothes normally worn by a person of the opposite sex, usually for pleasure. N-UNCOUNT =cross-dressing

transvestite /trænzvestaɪt/ **transvestites.** A **transvestite** is a person, usually a man, who enjoys wearing clothes normally worn by people of the opposite sex. ◆◇◇◇◇ N-COUNT =cross-dresser

trap /træp/ **traps, trapping, trapped** ◆◆◆◇◇

1 A **trap** is a device which is placed somewhere or a hole which is dug somewhere in order to catch animals or birds. N-COUNT

2 If a person **traps** animals or birds, he or she catches them using traps. *The locals were encouraged to trap and kill the birds.* VERB; V n

3 A **trap** is a trick that is intended to catch or deceive someone. *He failed to keep a rendezvous after sensing a police trap... He was trying to decide whether the question was some sort of a trap.* N-COUNT

4 If you **trap** someone into doing or saying something, you trick them so that they do or say it, although they did not want to. *Were you just trying to trap her into making some admission?... She had trapped him so neatly that he wanted to slap her.* VERB; V n into -ing/n; V n

5 To **trap** someone, especially a criminal, means to capture them; used in journalism. *The police knew that to trap the killer they had to play him at his own game... The couple set up a 24-hour security camera to trap the vandal scratching their car.* VERB; V n

6 A **trap** is an unpleasant situation that you cannot easily escape from. *The Government has found it's caught in a trap of its own making.* N-COUNT: usu sing

7 If you **are trapped** somewhere, something falls onto you or blocks your way and prevents you from moving or escaping. *The train was trapped underground by a fire... The light aircraft then cartwheeled, trapping both men... Until he saw the trapped wagons and animals, he did not realize the full extent of the catastrophe.* VERB; be V-ed; V n; V-ed

8 When something **traps** gas, water, or energy, it prevents it from escaping. *Wool traps your body heat, keeping the chill at bay... The volume of gas trapped on these surfaces can be considerable.* VERB; V n; V-ed

9 A **trap** is a light horse-drawn carriage with two wheels in which people used to travel. N-COUNT

10 See also **trapped**; **booby-trap**, **death trap**, **poverty trap**.

11 If someone **falls into the trap** of doing something, they do something which it would be better for them not to do, especially something which many people make the mistake of doing. *Many people fall into the trap of believing that home decorating must always be done on a large scale... It's a trap too many people fall into.* PHRASES; V inflects, oft PHR of -ing

12 If someone tells you to **shut** your **trap** or **keep** your **trap shut**, they are telling you rudely that you should be quiet and not say anything; an informal expression. V inflects; PRAGMATICS; =shut up

trapdoor, trapdoors /træpdɔːʳ/; also spelled **trap door**. A **trapdoor** is a small horizontal door in a floor, a ceiling, or on a stage. N-COUNT

trapeze /trəpiːz/ **trapezes.** A **trapeze** is a bar of wood or metal hanging from two ropes on which acrobats and gymnasts swing and perform skilful movements. N-COUNT

trapped /træpt/. If you feel **trapped**, you are in an unpleasant situation in which you lack freedom, and you feel you cannot escape from it. *He follows me everywhere and it makes me feel so trapped. ...people who think of themselves as trapped in mundane jobs.* • See also **trap**. ◆◆◇◇◇ ADJ-GRADED: usu v-link ADJ

trapper /træpəʳ/ **trappers.** A **trapper** is a person who traps animals, especially for their fur. N-COUNT

trappings /træpɪŋz/. The **trappings** of power, wealth, or a particular job are the extra things, such as decorations and luxury items, that go with it; used showing disapproval. *The family were in government for several generations and evidently loved the trappings of power.* ◆◇◇◇◇ N-PLURAL: usu N of n; PRAGMATICS

trash /træʃ/ **trashes, trashing, trashed** ◆◇◇◇◇

1 In American English, **trash** consists of unwanted things or waste material such as used paper, empty tins and bottles, and waste food. The British word N-UNCOUNT: also the N is **rubbish**. *The yards are overgrown and cluttered with trash... Mowing lawns and taking out the trash are jobs for the tenant.*

2 If you say that something such as a book, painting, or film is **trash** you mean that it is of very poor quality; an informal use. *Pop music doesn't have to be trash, it can be art... Don't read that awful trash.* N-UNCOUNT =rubbish

3 If someone **trashes** a place or vehicle, they deliberately destroy it or make a great deal of mess in it; an informal use. *Would they trash the place when the party was over?... The building had been trashed and its electricity supply cut.* VERB =wreck V n

4 If you **trash** people or their ideas, you criticize them very strongly and say that they are worthless; an informal use, used mainly in American English. *People asked why the candidates spent so much time trashing each other.* VERB =rubbish V n

5 See also **white trash**.

trash can, trash cans. In American English, a **trash can** is a large round container which people put their rubbish in and which is usually kept outside their house. The British word is **dustbin**. N-COUNT =garbage can

trashy /træʃi/ **trashier, trashiest.** If you describe something as **trashy**, you think it is of very poor quality; an informal word. *I was reading some trashy romance novel.* ADJ-GRADED =rubbishy

trattoria /trætəriːə/ **trattorias.** A **trattoria** is an Italian restaurant. N-COUNT

trauma /trɔːmə, AM traʊmə/ **traumas. Trauma** is a very severe shock or very upsetting experience, which may cause psychological damage. *I'd been through the trauma of losing a house... The officers are claiming compensation for trauma after the disaster.* ◆◆◇◇◇ N-VAR

traumatic /trɔːmætɪk, AM traʊ-/. A **traumatic** experience is very shocking and upsetting, and may cause psychological damage. *I suffered a nervous breakdown. It was a traumatic experience... For a child the death of a pet can be very traumatic.* ◆◇◇◇◇ ADJ-GRADED =distressing, painful

traumatize /trɔːmətaɪz, AM traʊ-/ **traumatizes, traumatizing, traumatized;** also spelled **traumatise** in British English. If someone **is traumatized** by an event or situation, it shocks or upsets them very much, and may cause them psychological damage. *My wife was traumatized by the experience... Did his parents traumatize him?... Traumatising a child with an abnormal fear of strangers probably won't do much good. ...young children traumatised by their parents deaths.* ◆◇◇◇◇ VERB be V-ed V n V n *with* n V-ed

♦ **traumatized** *He left her in the middle of the road, shaking and deeply traumatized... He could not cope alone with two traumatized children.* ADJ-GRADED

travail /træveɪl, AM trəveɪl/ **travails.** You can refer to unpleasant hard work or difficult problems as **travail**; a literary word. *He did whatever he could to ease their travail.* N-VAR

travel /trævᵊl/ **travels, travelling, travelled;** spelled **traveling, traveled** in American English. ◆◆◆◆◇

1 If you **travel**, you go from one place to another, often to a place that is far away. *You had better travel to Helsinki tomorrow... Granny travelled down by train... I've been traveling all day... Students often travel hundreds of miles to get here... I had been travelling at 150 kilometres an hour... He was a charming travelling companion.* VERB V prep/adv V V amount/n V *at* amount V-ing

♦ **travelling** *I love travelling... Getting to and from school involves two hours' travelling a day.* N-UNCOUNT

2 Travel is the activity of travelling. *Information on travel in New Zealand is available at the hotel... He detested air travel. ...a writer of travel books.* N-UNCOUNT

3 If you **travel** the world, the country, or the area, you go to many different places in the world or in a particular country or area. *Dr Ryan travelled the world gathering material for his book... He has had to travel the country in search of work.* VERB V n

4 When light or sound from one place reaches another, you say that it **travels** to the other place. *When sound travels through water, strange things can happen... Light travels at around 300,000,000 metres per second.* VERB V prep/adv V *at* amount

5 When news becomes known by people in different places, you can say that it **travels** to them. *News of his work traveled all the way to Asia... Seems like news travels pretty fast around here.* VERB V adv/prep

6 Someone's **travels** are the journeys that they make to places a long way from their home. *He also collects things for the house on his travels abroad.* N-PLURAL: with poss, usu poss N

7 See also **travelling**, **much-travelled**, **well-travelled.**

8 If you **travel light**, you travel without taking much luggage. PHRASES V inflects

9 If goods such as food products **travel well**, they can be transported a long way without being damaged or their quality being spoiled. *Ripe fruit does not travel well, but unripe fruit can be transported worldwide.* V inflects

10 If you say that an idea, a method, or a style **travels well**, you mean that it can be appreciated or used by people in several different countries, and not just in the country where it originated. *That brand of humour generally travels well.* V inflects

travel agency, travel agencies. A **travel agency** is a business which makes arrangements for people's holidays and journeys. N-COUNT

travel agent, travel agents ◆◇◇◇◇

1 A **travel agent** or **travel agent's** is a shop where you can go to arrange a holiday or journey. *He worked in a travel agent's.* N-COUNT

2 A **travel agent** is a person or business that arranges people's holidays and journeys. N-COUNT

traveller /trævələʳ/ **travellers;** spelled **traveler** in American English. ◆◆◆◇◇

1 A **traveller** is a person who is making a journey or a person who travels a lot. *Many air travellers suffer puffy ankles and feet during long flights.* N-COUNT: oft supp N

2 A **traveller** is a person who travels from place to place, often living in a van or other vehicle, rather than living in one place. • See also **New Age Traveller**. N-COUNT

traveller's cheque, traveller's cheques; spelled **traveler's check** in American English. **Traveller's cheques** are cheques that you buy at a bank and take with you when you travel, for example so that you can exchange them for the currency of the country that you are in. N-COUNT: usu pl

travelling /trævəlɪŋ/; spelled **traveling** in American English. A **travelling** actor or musician, for example, is one who travels around an area or country performing in different places. *...troupes of travelling actors. ...travelling entertainers.* ADJ: ADJ n =itinerant

travelling salesman, travelling salesmen; spelled **traveling salesman** in American English. A **travelling salesman** is a salesman who travels to different places and meets people in order to sell goods or take orders. N-COUNT

travelogue /trævəlɒg, -lɔːg/ **travelogues.** A **travelogue** is a talk or film about travel or about a particular person's travels. N-COUNT

travel sickness. If someone has **travel sickness**, they feel sick as a result of travelling in a vehicle. N-UNCOUNT

traverse /trævɜːʳs, trəvɜːʳs/ **traverses, traversing, traversed.** If someone or something **traverses** an area of land or water, they go across it; a literary word. *I traversed the narrow pedestrian bridge. ...a steep-sided valley traversed by streams.* ◆◇◇◇◇ VERB =cross V n V-ed

travesty /trævəsti/ **travesties.** If you describe something as a **travesty** of another thing, you mean that it is a very bad representation of that other thing. *Her research suggests that Smith's reputation today is a travesty of what he really stood for... If he couldn't prepare his case properly, the trial would be a travesty.* N-COUNT: oft N *of* n

trawl /trɔːl/ **trawls, trawling, trawled** ◆◇◇◇◇

1 In British English, if you **trawl** through a large number of similar things, you search through them looking for something that you want or something that is suitable for a particular purpose. *A team of officers is trawling through the records of thousands of petty thieves... Her private secretary has carefully trawled the West End for a suitable show.* ▶ Also a noun. *Any trawl through the band's interviews will reveal statements that are challenging and incisive.* VERB V *through* n V n N-COUNT: usu sing, usu N prep

2 When fishermen **trawl** for fish, they drag a wide net behind their ship in order to catch fish. *They had seen him trawling and therefore knew that there were fish... We came upon a fishing boat trawling for Dover sole.* VERB V V for n Also V n

trawler /trɔːləʳ/ **trawlers.** A **trawler** is a fishing boat that is used for trawling. ◆◇◇◇◇ N-COUNT

tray /treɪ/ **trays.** A **tray** is a flat piece of wood, plastic, or metal, which usually has raised edges and which is used for carrying things, especially food and drinks. ◆◆◇◇◇ N-COUNT

treacherous /tretʃərəs/ ◆◇◇◇◇

1 If you describe someone as **treacherous**, you mean that they are likely to betray you and cannot be trusted. *He publicly left the party and denounced its treacherous leaders... The President spoke of the treacherous intentions of the enemy.* ADJ-GRADED

2 If you say that something is **treacherous**, you mean that it is very dangerous and unpredictable. *The current of the river is fast flowing and treacherous... They made the treacherous journey across stormy seas in rotten boats.* ADJ-GRADED

treachery /tretʃəri/ **treacheries.** **Treachery** is behaviour or an action in which someone betrays their country or betrays a person who trusts them. *He was deeply wounded by the treachery of close aides and old friends.* ◆◇◇◇◇ N-UNCOUNT: also N in pl

treacle /triːkəl/. In British English, **treacle** is a thick, sweet, sticky liquid that is obtained when sugar is refined. It is used in making cakes and puddings. The usual American word is **molasses**. N-UNCOUNT

tread /tred/ **treads, treading, trod, trodden** ◆◆◇◇◇

1 If you **tread on** something, you put your foot on it when you are walking or standing. *Oh, sorry, I didn't mean to tread on your foot... I had white rugs on the floor, but people were scared to tread on them in case they marked.* VERB V on n

2 If you **tread** in a particular way, you walk that way; a literary use. *She trod casually, enjoying the touch of the damp grass on her feet.* VERB V adv

3 A person's **tread** is the sound that they make with their feet as they walk; used in written English. *We could now very plainly hear their heavy tread and an occasional loud, coarse laugh.* N-SING: supp N, N of n

4 If you **tread** carefully, you behave carefully or cautiously. *If you are hoping to form a new relationship tread carefully and slowly to begin with... There are three reasons for treading warily in such matters.* VERB V adv

5 The **tread** of a step or stair is its flat upper surface. *He walked up the stairs. The treads were covered with a kind of rubber and very quiet.* N-COUNT

6 The **tread** of a tyre or shoe is the pattern of grooves on it that stops it slipping. *The fat, broad tyres had a good depth of tread.* N-VAR

7 If someone is **treading a** fine **line** or **path**, they are acting carefully because they have to avoid a serious mistake, especially in a situation where they have to deal with two opposing demands which cannot both be satisfied easily. *They have to tread the delicate path between informing children and boring them... The President will therefore have to tread a very fine line when he addresses the parliament.* PHRASES V inflects, oft PHR *between* pl-n

8 If you **tread** a particular **path**, you take a particular course of action or do something in a particular way. *He continues to tread an unconventional path... Stylistically, Weller is treading a similar path to that of Lenny Kravitz.* V inflects

9 If someone who is in deep water **treads water**, they stay afloat in an upright position by moving their legs slightly. V inflects

10 If you say that someone **is treading water**, you mean that they are in an unsatisfactory situation where they are not progressing, but are just continuing doing the same things. *I could either tread water until I was promoted, which looked to be a few years away, or I could change what I was doing.* V inflects

11 • to **tread on** someone's **toes**: see **toe**.

treadle /tredəl/ **treadles.** The **treadle** on a spinning wheel or sewing machine is a lever that you operate with your foot in order to turn a wheel in the machine. N-COUNT

treadmill /tredmɪl/ **treadmills** ◆◇◇◇◇

1 You can refer to a task or a job as a **treadmill** when you have to keep doing it although it is unpleasant and exhausting. *Mr Stocks can expect a gruelling week on the publicity treadmill.* N-COUNT: usu sing

2 A **treadmill** is a piece of equipment, for example an exercise machine, consisting of a wheel with steps around its edge or a continuous moving belt. The weight of a person or animal walking on it causes the wheel or belt to turn. N-COUNT

treason /triːzən/. **Treason** is the crime of betraying your country, for example by helping its enemies or by trying to overthrow its government. ◆◇◇◇◇ N-UNCOUNT

treasonable /triːzənəbəl/. **Treasonable** activities are criminal activities which someone carries out with the intention of helping their country's enemies or overthrowing its government. *They were brought to trial for treasonable conspiracy.* ADJ

treasure /treʒəʳ/ **treasures, treasuring, treasured** ◆◆◇◇◇

1 In children's stories, **treasure** is a collection of valuable old objects, such as gold coins and jewels. *It was here, the buried treasure, she knew it was.* N-UNCOUNT

2 **Treasures** are valuable objects, especially works of art and items of historical value. *The house was large and full of art treasures.* N-COUNT: usu pl

3 If you **treasure** something that you have, you keep or preserve it carefully because it gives you great pleasure and you think it is very special. *She treasures her memories of those joyous days.* ► Also a noun. *His greatest treasure is his collection of rock records.* ♦ **treasured** *These books are still among my most treasured possessions.* VERB =cherish V n N-COUNT ADJ-GRADED: ADJ n

4 If you say that someone is a **treasure**, you mean that they are very helpful and useful to you; an informal use. *Charlie? Oh, he's a treasure, loves children.* N-COUNT =gem

treasurer /treʒərəʳ/ **treasurers.** The **treasurer** of a society or organization is the person who is in charge of its finances and keeps its accounts. ◆◇◇◇◇ N-COUNT: oft N of n

treasure trove, treasure troves

1 If you describe something or someone as a **treasure trove of** a particular thing, you mean that they are a very good or rich source of that thing. *The dictionary is a vast treasure trove of information... This Islington shop is a treasure trove of beautiful bridalwear.* N-COUNT: usu sing, N of n

2 You can refer to a collection of valuable objects as a **treasure trove**. *Windsor Castle is quite literally an antique treasure trove... The society's archives are a treasure trove for scholars.* N-COUNT: usu sing, oft N for n

treasury /treʒəri/ **treasuries** ◆◆◆◇◇

1 In Britain and some other countries, the **Treasury** is the government department that deals with the country's finances. *The Treasury has long been predicting an upturn in consumer spending.* N-COUNT-COLL: usu *the* N in sing

2 The **treasury** in a building such as a castle or a cathedral is a room where valuable objects are displayed or stored. N-COUNT

treat /triːt/ **treats, treating, treated** ◆◆◆◆◇

1 If you **treat** someone or something in a particular way, you behave towards them or deal with them in that way. *Artie treated most women with indifference... Police say they're treating it as a case of attempted murder... She adored Paddy but he didn't treat her well... The issues should be treated separately.* VERB V n with n V n as/like n V n adv

2 When a doctor or nurse **treats** a patient or an illness, he or she tries to make the patient well again. *Doctors treated her with aspirin... The boy was treated for a minor head wound... An experienced nurse treats all minor injuries.* VERB V n with n V n for n V n

3 If something **is treated** with a particular substance, the substance is put onto or into it in order to clean it, to protect it, or to give it special properties. *About 70% of the cocoa acreage is treated with insecticide... It was many years before the city began to treat its sewage.* VERB be V-ed with n V n

4 If you **treat** someone to something special which they will enjoy, you buy it or arrange it for them. *She was always treating him to ice cream... Tomorrow I'll treat myself to a day's gardening... If you want to treat yourself, the Malta Hilton offers high international standards.* VERB V n to n, V pron-refl to n, V pron-refl, Also V n

5 If you give someone a **treat**, you buy or arrange something special for them which they will enjoy. *Lettie had never yet failed to return from town without some special treat for him.* N-COUNT

6 If you say that something is your **treat**, you mean that you are paying for it as a treat for someone else; used in spoken English. N-SING: poss N PRAGMATICS

7 If you say, for example, that something looks or works **a treat**, you mean that it looks very good or works very well; an informal expression. *The first part of the plan works a treat... The apricots would go down a treat.* ● to **treat** someone **like dirt**: see **dirt**. PHRASE: PHR after v

treatable /triːtəbᵊl/. A **treatable** disease is one which can be cured or controlled, usually by the use of drugs. *This is a treatable condition... Depression is treatable.* ADJ-GRADED =curable

treatise /triːtɪz, AM -tɪs/ **treatises.** A **treatise** is a long, formal piece of writing about a particular subject. *...Locke's Treatise on Civil Government.* ◆◇◇◇◇ N-COUNT: usu with supp, oft N on n

treatment /triːtmənt/ **treatments** ◆◆◆◆◇

1 **Treatment** is medical attention given to a sick or injured person or animal. *Many patients are not getting the medical treatment they need. ...a veterinary surgeon who specialises in the treatment of cage birds. ...an effective treatment for eczema.* N-VAR: oft supp N, N of/for n

2 Your **treatment** of someone is the way you behave towards them or deal with them. *We don't want any special treatment... Ginny's initial rage at his treatment of Chris had simmered down to resentment.* N-UNCOUNT: usu supp N, N of n

3 **Treatment** of something involves putting a particular substance onto or into it, in order to clean it, to protect it, or to give it special properties. *There should be greater treatment of sewage before it is discharged... As with all oily hair treatments, shampoo needs to be applied first.* N-VAR: usu N of n, supp N

4 If you say that someone is given **the full treatment**, you mean either that they are treated extremely well or that they are treated extremely harshly; an informal expression. *If you've got friends or family coming to stay, make it really special by giving them the full treatment... She'll be interrogated, jailed, interrogated again, get what's usually known as the full treatment.* PHRASE: PHR after v

treaty /triːti/ **treaties.** A **treaty** is a written agreement between countries in which they agree to do a particular thing or to help each other. *...the Treaty of Rome, which established the European Community. ...negotiations over a 1992 treaty on global warming.* ◆◆◆◆◇ N-COUNT

treble /trebᵊl/ **trebles, trebling, trebled** ◆◇◇◇◇

1 If something **trebles** or if you **treble** it, it becomes three times greater in number or amount than it was. *They will have to pay much more when rents treble in January... The city has trebled the number of its prisoners to 21,000.* ♦ **trebling** *A new threat to Bulgaria's stability is the week-old miners' strike for a trebling of minimum pay.* V-ERG =triple, V, V n; N-SING: oft N of n

2 If one thing is **treble** the size or amount of another thing, it is three times greater in size or amount. *More than 7 million shares changed hands, treble the normal daily average.* PREDET: PREDET det n =triple

3 A **treble** is a boy with a very high singing voice. N-COUNT

4 In sport, a **treble** is three successes one after the other, for example winning three horse races on the same day, or winning three competitions in the same season; used mainly in British journalism. *The win completed a treble for them – they already claimed a league and cup double this year.* N-COUNT

tree /triː/ **trees** ◆◆◆◆◇

1 A **tree** is a tall plant that has a hard trunk, branches, and leaves. *I planted those apple trees. ...a variety of shrubs and trees.* ● See also **Christmas tree, family tree.** N-COUNT: oft n N

2 If you say that someone **is barking up the wrong tree**, you mean that they are following the wrong course of action because their beliefs or ideas about something are incorrect; an informal expression. *Scientists in Switzerland realised that most other researchers had been barking up the wrong tree.* PHRASES V inflects, usu cont

3 In British English, if you say that someone **can't see the wood for the trees**, you mean that they are so involved in the details of something that they forget or do not realize the real purpose or importance of the thing as a whole. The usual American expression is **can't see the forest for the trees.** V inflects

4 ● **the top of the tree**: see **top.**

treeless /triːləs/. A **treeless** area or place has no trees in it. *No shelter was available for miles around in this treeless landscape.* ADJ-GRADED

tree-lined. A **tree-lined** road or street has trees on either side. *...the broad, tree-lined avenues.* ADJ: usu ADJ n

treetop /triːtɒp/ **treetops;** also spelled **tree tops.** The **treetops** are the top branches of the trees in a wood or forest. *All they heard was the wind whispering through the treetops.* N-COUNT: usu pl

tree trunk, tree trunks. A **tree trunk** is the wide central part of a tree, from which the branches grow. N-COUNT

trek /trek/ **treks, trekking, trekked** ◆◆◇◇◇

1 If you **trek** somewhere, you go on a journey across difficult terrain, usually on foot. *...trekking through the jungles... This year we're going trekking in Nepal.* ► Also a noun. *He is on a trek through the South Gobi desert.* VERB V prep/adv, V-ing, Also V; N-COUNT

2 If you **trek** somewhere, you go there rather slowly and unwillingly, usually because you are tired. *They trekked from shop to shop in search of white knee-length socks.* ► Also a noun. *The World Trade Centre is a bit of a trek from Soho, but it's worth it.* VERB V prep/adv; N-COUNT: usu sing

trellis /trelɪs/ **trellises.** A **trellis** is a frame which supports climbing plants. N-VAR

tremble /trembᵊl/ **trembles, trembling, trembled** ◆◆◇◇◇

1 If you **tremble**, you shake slightly because you are frightened or cold. *His mouth became dry, his eyes widened, and he began to tremble all over... Gil was white and trembling with anger... With trembling fingers, he removed the camera from his coat pocket.* ► Also a noun. *I will never forget the look on the patient's face, the tremble in his hand.* VERB =shake, V, V with n, V-ing; N-SING: usu N in/of n

2 If something **trembles**, it shakes slightly; a literary use. *He felt the earth tremble under him... The leaves trembled in the trees.* VERB =shake, V

3 If your voice **trembles**, it sounds unsteady and hesitant, usually because you are upset or nervous; a literary use. *His voice trembled, on the verge of tears.* ► Also a noun. *'Please understand this,' she began, a tremble in her voice.* VERB =shake, V; N-SING: usu N in/of n

tremendous /trɪmendəs/ ◆◆◆◇◇

1 You use **tremendous** to emphasize how strong a feeling or quality is, or how large an amount is; an informal use. *I felt a tremendous pressure on my chest... There's tremendous tension between the local population and the refugees... That's a tremendous amount of information.* ♦ **tremendously** *I thought they played tremendously well, didn't you?... I enjoyed it tremendously.* ADJ-GRADED: usu ADJ n PRAGMATICS =terrific; ADV: ADV adj/adv/-ed, ADV after v

2 You can describe someone or something as **tremendous** when you think they are very good or very impressive; an informal use. *He was a tremendous person... I thought the film was absolutely tremendous.* ADJ-GRADED =terrific

tremolo /treməloʊ/. If someone's singing or speaking voice has a **tremolo** in it, it moves up and down instead of staying on the same note. N-UNCOUNT: also a N

tremor /tremᵊr/ **tremors** ◆◇◇◇◇

1 A **tremor** is a small earthquake. N-COUNT

2 If an event causes a **tremor** in a group or organization, it threatens the stability of that group or organization. *News of 160 redundancies had sent tremors through the community... Overproduction and consequent low market prices for wine caused economic tremors.* N-COUNT: usu with supp

3 A **tremor** is a shaking of your body or voice that you cannot control. *He felt a tremor in his arms...* N-COUNT

He felt a tremor of apprehension... The dangerous, excitable tremor was still in her voice.

tremulous /tremjʊləs/. If someone's voice, smile, or actions are **tremulous**, they are unsteady because the person is uncertain, afraid, or upset; a literary word. *She fidgeted in her chair as she took a deep, tremulous breath.* ♦ **tremulously** *'He was so good to me,' she said tremulously.* ADJ-GRADED; ADV-GRADED: ADV with v

trench /trentʃ/ **trenches** ◆◇◇◇◇

1 A **trench** is a long narrow channel that is cut into the ground, for example for drainage or in order to lay pipes. N-COUNT

2 A **trench** is a long narrow channel in the ground used by soldiers as a defensive position. People often refer to the battle grounds of the First World War in Northern France and Belgium as **the trenches**. *We fought with them in the trenches. ...trench warfare.* N-COUNT: usu *the* N in pl, N n

trenchant /trentʃənt/. You can use **trenchant** to describe something such as a criticism or comment that is very clear, effective, and forceful; a formal word. *He was shattered and bewildered by this trenchant criticism... His comment was trenchant and perceptive.* ADJ-GRADED

trench coat, trench coats; also spelled **trenchcoat**. A **trench coat** is a type of raincoat with pockets and a belt. Trench coats are often similar in design to military coats. N-COUNT

trend /trend/ **trends** ◆◆◆◇◇

1 A **trend** is a change or development towards something new or different. *This is a growing trend. ...a trend towards part-time employment. ...the downward trend in gasoline prices.* N-COUNT =tendency

2 If someone or something sets a **trend**, they do something that becomes accepted or fashionable, and that a lot of other people copy. *The record has already proved a success and may well start a trend.* N-COUNT: usu sing

trend-setter, trend-setters; also **trendsetter**. A **trend-setter** is a person or institution that starts a new fashion or trend. N-COUNT

trendy /trendi/ **trendier, trendiest; trendies** ◆◇◇◇◇

1 If you say that something or someone is **trendy**, you mean that they are very fashionable and modern; an informal use. *...a trendy London night club. ...middle-class kids in trendy clothes. ...women who want to look trendy.* ► A **trendy** is someone who is **trendy**. *...a lively and informal city-based television network dedicated to the urban trendy.* ADJ-GRADED; N-COUNT

2 You can describe someone who follows new ideas as **trendy** to show that you disapprove of them because they are more interested in being up to date than in thinking seriously about the implications of such ideas; an informal use. *Trendy teachers are denying children the opportunity to study classic texts.* ► A **trendy** is someone who is **trendy**. *...another example of what happens when you get a few trendies in power.* ADJ-GRADED: usu ADJ n PRAGMATICS; N-COUNT

trepidation /trepɪdeɪʃən/. **Trepidation** is fear or anxiety about something that you are going to do or experience; a formal word. *It was with some trepidation that I viewed the prospect of cycling across Uganda.* N-UNCOUNT: oft *with* N =anxiety

trespass /trespəs/ **trespasses, trespassing, trespassed** ◆◇◇◇◇

1 If someone **trespasses**, they go onto someone else's land without their permission. *They were trespassing on private property... You're trespassing!* ► **Trespass** is the act of trespassing. *You could be prosecuted for trespass. ...trespasses and demonstrations on privately-owned land.* ♦ **trespasser, trespassers** *Trespassers will be prosecuted.* VERB V prep V; N-VAR; N-COUNT

2 If you say that someone **is trespassing** on something, you mean that they are involving themselves in an area of activity where they are not wanted because it is someone else's concern. *In language, rhythm and imagination Naomi Wallace is trespassing on traditional male preserves.* VERB V prep Also V

tress /tres/ **tresses.** A woman's **tresses** are her long flowing hair; a literary word. N-COUNT: usu pl

trestle /tresəl/ **trestles.** A **trestle** is a wooden or metal structure that is used, for example, as one of the supports for a table. It has two pairs of sloping legs which are joined by a flat piece across the top. N-COUNT

trestle table, trestle tables. A **trestle table** is a table made of a long board that is supported on trestles. N-COUNT

tri- /traɪ-/. **Tri-** is used at the beginning of nouns and adjectives that have 'three' as part of their meaning. *...a tri-partite meeting... It was triangular in shape.* PREFIX

triad /traɪæd/ **triads;** also spelled **Triad** for meaning 1. ◆◇◇◇◇

1 The **Triads** are Chinese secret societies that are often associated with organized crime. *Chinese gangs from Hong Kong, known as the Triads, have a presence in the UK too.* N-COUNT: usu pl, oft N n

2 A **triad** is a group of three similar things; a formal word. *For the faculty, there exists the triad of responsibilities: teaching, research, and service.* N-COUNT: oft N *of* n

trial /traɪəl/ **trials** ◆◆◆◆◇

1 A **trial** is a formal meeting in a law court, at which a judge and jury listen to evidence and decide whether a person is guilty of a crime. *New evidence showed the police lied at the trial... He's awaiting trial in a military court on charges of plotting against the state... They believed that his case would never come to trial.* N-VAR

2 A **trial** is an experiment in which you test something by using it or doing it for a period of time to see how well it works. If something is **on trial**, it is being tested in this way. *They have been treated with this drug in clinical trials... I took the car out for a trial on the roads... The robots have been on trial for the past year... We plan to release a prototype this autumn for trial in hospitals.* N-VAR

3 If someone gives you a **trial** for a job, they let you do it for a short period of time to see if you are suitable for it. If you are **on trial**, you are doing a job for a short period so that someone can see if you are suitable for it. *He had just given a trial to a young woman who said she had previous experience... The 26-year old fullback has been on trial at the club for ten days.* N-COUNT: usu sing, also *on* N

4 If you refer to the **trials** of a situation, you mean the unpleasant things that you experience in it. *...the trials of adolescence.* N-COUNT: usu pl, N *of* n

5 In some sports or outdoor activities, **trials** are a series of contests that test a competitor's skill and ability. *He has been riding in horse trials for less than a year. ...Dovedale Sheepdog Trials.* N-COUNT: usu pl, supp N

6 If you do something by **trial and error**, you try several different methods of doing it until you find the method that works properly. *Many drugs were found by trial and error... She feels that raising her children has been a matter of trial and error.* PHRASES oft *by/through* PHR

7 If someone is **on trial**, they are being tried in a court of law. *He is currently on trial accused of serious drugs charges... He will go on trial later this month charged with murder... Two skinheads were put on trial for those murders last week.* v-link PHR, PHR after v

8 If you say that someone or something is **on trial**, you mean that they are in a situation where people are observing them to see whether they succeed or fail. *The President will be drawn into a damaging battle in which his credentials will be on trial.* v-link PHR, PHR after v

9 If someone **stands trial**, they are tried in court for a crime they are accused of. *He was found to be mentally unfit to stand trial... Five people are to stand trial for murder.* V inflects, oft PHR *for* n

trial run, trial runs. A **trial run** is a first attempt at doing something to make sure you can do it properly. N-COUNT

triangle /traɪæŋgəl/ **triangles** ◆◇◇◇◇

1 A **triangle** is an object, arrangement, or flat shape with three straight sides and three angles. *This design is in pastel colours with three rectangles and three triangles... Its outline roughly forms an equilateral triangle. ...triangles of fried bread. ...the great triangle of the Lancashire textile towns, stretching from Manchester up as far as Burnley and across to Accrington.* N-COUNT

2 The **triangle** is a musical instrument that con- N-COUNT:

sists of a piece of metal shaped like a triangle. You play it by hitting it with a short metal bar. usu sing, the N

3 If you describe a group of three people as a **triangle**, you mean that they are all connected with each other in a particular situation, but often have different interests. *She plays a French woman in a love triangle with Jonathan Pryce and Christopher Walken. ...the classic triangle of husband, wife and mistress.* • See also **eternal triangle**. N-COUNT: usu sing, with supp

triangular /traɪæŋgjʊləʳ/ ◆◇◇◇◇

1 Something that is **triangular** is in the shape of a triangle. *...cottages around a triangular green. ...triangular bandages to make slings.* ADJ

2 You can describe a relationship or situation as **triangular** if it involves three people or things. *One particular triangular relationship became the model of Simone's first novel.* ADJ

triathlon /traɪæθlɒn/ **triathlons.** A **triathlon** is an athletics competition in which each competitor takes part in three different events; swimming, cycling, and marathon running. N-COUNT: usu sing

tribal /traɪbəl/. **Tribal** is used to describe things relating to or belonging to tribes and the way that they are organized. *They would go back to their tribal lands. ...their rich heritage of ancient tribal customs.* ◆◆◇◇◇ ADJ: usu ADJ n

tribalism /traɪbəlɪzəm/

1 Tribalism is the state of existing as a tribe. *Apartheid used tribalism as the basis of its 'divide-and-rule' homeland policies.* N-UNCOUNT

2 You can use **tribalism** to refer to the loyalties that people feel towards particular social groups and to the way these loyalties affect their behaviour and their attitudes towards others; used showing disapproval. *His argument was that multi-party systems encourage tribalism. ...the evils of tribalism, disunity and disintegration.* N-UNCOUNT PRAGMATICS

tribe /traɪb/ **tribes** ◆◆◇◇◇

1 Tribe is sometimes used to refer to a group of people of the same race, language, and customs, especially in a developing country. Some people disapprove of this use. *...three-hundred members of the Xhosa tribe. ...a map of Maryland marked with the names of Indian tribes.* N-COUNT-COLL

2 You can use **tribe** to refer to a group of people who are all doing the same thing or who all behave in the same way; an informal, often humorous use. *...tribes of bicyclists. ...the particularly unpleasant tribe who argue over the splitting of restaurant and bar bills.* N-COUNT-COLL: usu N of n, adj N

tribesman /traɪbzmən/ **tribesmen.** A **tribesman** is a man who belongs to a tribe. N-COUNT

tribulation /trɪbjʊleɪʃən/ **tribulations.** You can refer to the suffering or difficulty that you experience in a particular situation as **tribulations**; a formal word. *...the trials and tribulations of everyday life.* N-VAR

tribunal /traɪbjuːnəl/ **tribunals.** A **tribunal** is a special court or committee that is appointed to deal with particular problems. *His case comes before an industrial tribunal in March. ...when a tribunal finds that an employee has been unfairly dismissed.* ◆◆◇◇◇ N-COUNT-COLL

tributary /trɪbjʊtəri, AM -teri/ **tributaries.** A **tributary** is a stream or river that flows into a larger one. *...the Napo river, a tributary of the Amazon. ...a small tributary river.* N-COUNT: oft N n

tribute /trɪbjuːt/ **tributes** ◆◆◇◇◇

1 A **tribute** is something that you say, do, or make to show your admiration and respect for someone. *The song is a tribute to Roy Orbison... He paid tribute to the organising committee... Over nine-thousand ex-servicemen and women marched past in tribute to their fallen comrades.* N-VAR: usu N to n

2 If one thing is a **tribute** to another, the first thing is the result of the second and shows how good it is. *His success has been a tribute to hard work, to professionalism... It is a tribute to Mr Chandler's skill that he has fashioned a fascinating book out of such unpromising material.* N-SING: a N, usu N to n, N to n that

trice /traɪs/. If someone does something **in a trice**, they do it very quickly. *He will sew it up in a trice... She was back in a trice.* PHRASE: PHR with v, PHR with cl

triceps /traɪseps/; **triceps** is both the singular and the plural form. Your **triceps** is the muscle in the back part of your upper arm. N-COUNT

trick /trɪk/ **tricks, tricking, tricked** ◆◆◆◇◇

1 A **trick** is an action that is intended to deceive someone. *We are playing a trick on a man who keeps bothering me.* N-COUNT

2 If someone **tricks** you, they deceive you, often in order to make you do something. *Stephen is going to be pretty upset when he finds out how you tricked him... His family tricked him into going to Pakistan, and once he was there, they took away his passport... His real purpose is to trick his way into your home to see what he can steal.* VERB V n, V n into -ing/n, V way prep/adv

3 A **trick** is a clever or skilful action that someone does in order to entertain people. *He shows me card tricks.* N-COUNT

4 A **trick** is a clever way of doing something. *Everything I cooked was a trick of my mother's... It is not just a little trick you can pick up in half an hour.* N-COUNT

5 See also **confidence trick**, **conjuring trick**, **hat-trick**.

6 If something **does the trick**, it achieves what you wanted; an informal expression. *Sometimes a few choice words will do the trick.* PHRASES V inflects

7 If someone tries **every trick in the book**, they try every possible thing that they can think of in order to achieve something; an informal expression. *Companies are using every trick in the book to stay one step in front of their competitors.* v PHR

8 If you say that something is a **trick of the light**, you mean that what you are seeing is an effect caused by the way that the light falls on things, and does not really exist in the way that it appears. *Her head appears to be on fire but that is only a trick of the light.* v-link PHR

9 If you say that someone does not **miss a trick**, you mean that they always know what is happening and take advantage of every situation; an informal expression. *When it comes to integrating their transport systems, the French don't miss a trick.* V inflects, with brd-neg

10 The **tricks of the trade** are the quick and clever ways of doing something that are known by people who regularly do a particular activity. *To get you started, we have asked five successful writers to reveal some of the tricks of the trade.* *trick* inflects

11 If you say that someone is **up to** their **tricks** or **up to** their **old tricks**, you disapprove of them because they are behaving in the dishonest or deceitful way in which they typically behave; an informal expression. *I have no respect for my father who, having remarried, is still up to his old tricks.* v-link PHR PRAGMATICS

12 • **you can't teach an old dog new tricks**: see **dog**.

trickery /trɪkəri/. **Trickery** is the use of dishonest methods in order to achieve something. *They are notorious for resorting to trickery in order to impress their clients.* N-UNCOUNT

trickle /trɪkəl/ **trickles, trickling, trickled** ◆◇◇◇◇

1 When a liquid **trickles**, or when you **trickle** it, it flows slowly in very small amounts. *A tear trickled down the old man's cheek... Trickle water gently over the back of your baby's head... The trickling stream glistened in the sunlight.* ► Also a noun. *There was not so much as a trickle of water.* V-ERG V prep/adv, V n, V-ing, Also V; N-COUNT: usu sing

2 When people or things **trickle** in a particular direction, they move there slowly in small groups or amounts, rather than all together. *Some donations are already trickling in.* ► Also a noun. *The flood of cars has now slowed to a trickle... A trickle of refugees began to flee the country.* VERB V adv/prep; N-COUNT: usu sing

trickle-down. The **trickle-down** theory is the theory that benefits given to people at the top of a system will eventually be passed on to people lower down the system. For example, if the rich receive tax cuts, they will pass these benefits on to the poor by creating jobs. *The government is not simply relying on trickle-down economics to tackle poverty.* ADJ: ADJ n

trick or treat. **Trick or treat** is an activity in which children knock on the doors of houses at Halloween and shout 'trick or treat'. If the person who answers the door does not give the children a treat, such as sweets, they play a trick on him or her. N-UNCOUNT

trick question, trick questions. If someone asks you a **trick question**, they ask you a question which is very difficult to answer sensibly, for example because it is based on a false assumption or because the answer that seems obvious is not the correct one. N-COUNT

trickster /trɪkstəʳ/ **tricksters.** A **trickster** is a person who deceives or cheats people, often in order to get money from them; an informal use. N-COUNT

tricky /trɪki/ **trickier, trickiest** ◆◆◇◇◇

1 If you describe a task or problem as **tricky**, you mean that it is difficult to do or deal with. *Parking can be tricky in the town centre... It's a very tricky problem, but I think there are a number of things you can do.* ADJ-GRADED =awkward

2 If you describe a person as **tricky**, you mean that they are likely to deceive you or cheat you. ADJ-GRADED: usu ADJ n

tricolour /trɪkələʳ/ **tricolours;** also spelled **tricolor.** A **tricolour** is a flag which is made up of blocks of three different colours. N-COUNT

tricycle /traɪsɪkᵊl/ **tricycles.** A **tricycle** is a cycle with three wheels, two at the back and one at the front. Tricycles are usually ridden by children. N-COUNT

tried /traɪd/. **Tried** is used in the expressions **tried and tested**, **tried and trusted**, and **tried and true**, which describe a product or method that has already been used and has been found to be successful. *...over 1000 tried-and-tested recipes... Follow the tried and trusted methods that have stood the test of time. ...a good source of tried and true tips on how to cope with the various aspects of the illness.* • See also **try**; **well-tried.** ◆◇◇◇◇ ADJ: ADJ *and* adj

trier /traɪəʳ/ **triers.** In British English, if you say that someone is a **trier**, you approve of them because they try very hard at things that they do, although they are not often successful. *He may not always achieve greatness but at least he's a trier.* N-COUNT PRAGMATICS

trifle /traɪfᵊl/ **trifles, trifling, trifled** ◆◇◇◇◇

1 You can use **a trifle** to mean slightly or to a small extent, especially in order make something you say seem less extreme. *As a photographer, he'd found both locations just a trifle disappointing... 'There we go,' said Diane, a trifle too cheerily... His uniform made him look a trifle out of place.* PHRASE: PHR adj/adv/prep =a little, a bit

2 A **trifle** is something that is considered to have little importance, value, or significance. *He had no money to spare on trifles... Believe me, it's the least I can do, a mere trifle.* N-COUNT

3 **Trifle** is a cold British dessert made of layers of sponge cake, jelly, fruit, and custard, and usually covered with cream. N-VAR

trifle with. If you say that someone is not a person to **be trifled with**, you are indicating to other people that they must treat that person with respect. *He was not someone to be trifled with... No man in Tabriz trifled with the executioner.* PHRASAL VERB usu with brd-neg *be* V-ed P V P n

trifling /traɪfəlɪŋ/. A **trifling** matter is small and unimportant. *The guests had each paid £125, no trifling sum... Outside California these difficulties may seem fairly trifling. ...a comparatively trifling 360 yards.* ADJ-GRADED: oft *a* ADJ amount =trivial

trigger /trɪgəʳ/ **triggers, triggering, triggered** ◆◆◆◇◇

1 The **trigger** of a gun is a small lever which you pull to fire it. *A man pointed a gun at them and pulled the trigger.* N-COUNT

2 The **trigger** of a bomb is the device which causes it to explode. *...trigger devices for nuclear weapons.* N-COUNT: oft N n

3 To **trigger** a bomb or system means to cause it to work. *The thieves must have deliberately triggered the alarm and hidden inside the house... The one thousand pound bomb was triggered by a wire. ...nuclear triggering devices.* VERB =set off, activate V n V-ing

4 If something **triggers** an event or situation, it causes it to begin to happen or exist. *...the incident which triggered the outbreak of the First World War... The current recession was triggered by a slump in consumer spending... Even a problem as simple as a bad back often has an underlying triggering factor.* ▶ **Trigger off** means the same as **trigger.** *It is still not clear what events triggered off the demonstrations.* VERB V n V-ing PHRASAL VERB V P n (not pron) Also V n P

5 If something acts as a **trigger** for another thing such as an illness, event, or situation, the first thing causes the second thing to begin to happen or exist. *Stress may act as a trigger for these illnesses.* N-COUNT: oft N *for* n

trigger-happy; also spelled **trigger happy.** If you describe someone as **trigger-happy**, you disapprove of them because they are too ready and willing to use violence and weapons, especially guns; an informal word. *They were gunned down by members of the trigger-happy National Guard... Some of them are a bit trigger-happy – they'll shoot at anything that moves.* ADJ-GRADED PRAGMATICS

trigonometry /trɪgənɒmɪtri/. **Trigonometry** is the branch of mathematics that is concerned with calculating the angles of triangles or the lengths of their sides. N-UNCOUNT

trike /traɪk/ **trikes.** A **trike** is a child's tricycle; an informal word. N-COUNT

trilby /trɪlbi/ **trilbies.** In British English, a **trilby** or a **trilby hat** is a man's hat which is made of felt and has a groove along the top from front to back. N-COUNT

trill /trɪl/ **trills, trilling, trilled**

1 If a bird **trills**, it sings with short, high-pitched, repeated notes. *At one point a bird trilled in the Conservatory.* VERB V

2 If you say that a woman **trills**, you mean that she talks or laughs in a high-pitched voice which sounds rather musical but which also sounds rather irritating. *'How adorable!' she trills.* VERB V with quote

3 A **trill** is the playing of two musical notes repeatedly and quickly one after the other; a technical term in music. N-COUNT

trillion /trɪljən/ **trillions** The plural form is **trillion** after a number, or after a word or expression referring to a number, such as 'several' or 'a few'. A **trillion** is a million million. *Between July 1st and October 1st, the central bank printed over 2 trillion roubles. ...the idea that we are the culmination of fifteen billion years of cosmic evolution across trillions of galaxies.* ◆◆◇◇◇ NUM: usu *a*/num NUM

trilogy /trɪlədʒi/ **trilogies.** A **trilogy** is a series of three books, plays, films, or operas that have the same subject or the same characters. *...Laurie Lee's trilogy of autobiographical novels.* ◆◇◇◇◇ N-COUNT: oft N *of* n, supp N

trim /trɪm/ **trimmer, trimmest; trims, trimming, trimmed** ◆◆◇◇◇

1 Something that is **trim** is neat, tidy, and attractive. *The neighbours' gardens were trim and neat. ...the trim houses.* ADJ-GRADED

2 If you describe someone's figure as **trim**, you mean that it is attractive because there is no extra fat on their body. *The driver was a trim young woman of perhaps thirty.* ADJ-GRADED PRAGMATICS

3 If you **trim** something, for example someone's hair, you cut off small amounts of it in order to make it look neater and tidier. *My friend trims my hair every eight weeks... Grass shears are specially made to trim grass growing in awkward places.* ▶ Also a noun. *His hair needed a trim.* VERB V n N-SING

4 If a government or other organization **trims** something such as a plan, policy, or amount, they reduce it slightly in extent or size. *American companies looked at ways they could trim these costs... We trimmed the marketing department.* VERB V n

5 If something such as a piece of clothing **is trimmed** with a type of material or design, it is decorated with it, usually along its edges. *...jackets, which are then trimmed with crocheted flowers... I am wearing a plaid nightgown trimmed with white lace.* ♦ **-trimmed** *He wears a fur-trimmed coat. ...gold-trimmed fitted furniture.* VB: usu passive *be* V-ed *with* n V-ed COMB in ADJ

6 The **trim** on something such as a piece of clothing is a decoration, for example along its edges, that is in a different colour or material. *...a white* N-VAR =trimming

satin scarf with black trim... The saddles feature a reflective trim for night time visibility.

7 When people are **in trim** or **in good trim**, they are in good physical condition. *He is already getting in trim for the big day... It is an excellent way of keeping my voice in trim.* PHRASE: v-link PHR, PHR after v

trim away or **trim off.** If you **trim away** or **trim off** parts of something, you cut them off, because they are not needed. *Neatly trim away old flowers on shrubs... Trim the fat off the ham... Butchers recommend cooking meat with the fat and trimming it away later.* PHRASAL VERB =cut away V P n (not pron) V n P n V n P

trimaran /traɪməræn/ **trimarans.** A **trimaran** is a fast sailing boat similar to a catamaran, but with three hulls instead of two. N-COUNT

trimming /trɪmɪŋ/ **trimmings** ◆◇◇◇◇

1 The **trimming** on something such as a piece of clothing is the decoration, for example along its edges, that is in a different colour or material. *...the lace trimming on her satin nightgown.* N-VAR: usu supp N =trim

2 **Trimmings** are pieces of something, usually food, which are left over after you have cut what you need. *Use any pastry trimmings to decorate the apples.* N-PLURAL

3 If you say that something comes with **all the trimmings**, you mean that it has many extra things added to it to make it more special. *They were married with all the trimmings, soon after graduation. ...a Thanksgiving dinner of turkey and all the trimmings.* PHRASE: with/and PHR

Trinity /trɪnɪti/. In the Christian religion, **the Trinity** or **the Holy Trinity** is the union of the Father, the Son, and the Holy Spirit in one God. ◆◇◇◇◇ N-PROPER: the N

trinket /trɪŋkɪt/ **trinkets.** A **trinket** is a pretty piece of jewellery or small ornament that is inexpensive. *She sold trinkets to tourists.* N-COUNT

trio /triːoʊ/ **trios.** A **trio** is a group of three people together, especially musicians or singers, or a group of three things that have something in common. *...classy American songs from a Texas trio... The trio are part of Sotheby's sale of Works of Art.* ◆◆◇◇◇ N-COUNT-COLL

trip /trɪp/ **trips, tripping, tripped** ◆◆◆◆◇

1 A **trip** is a journey that you make to a place and back again. *On the Thursday we went out on a day trip... Mark was sent to the Far East on a business trip.* ● See also **round trip**. N-COUNT

2 If you **trip** when you are walking, you knock your foot against something and fall or nearly fall. *She tripped and fell last night and broke her hip... He tried to follow Jack's footsteps in the snow and tripped on a rock... The cables are all bright yellow to prevent you tripping over them.* ► **Trip up** means the same as **trip**. *I tripped up and hurt my foot... Make sure trailing flexes are kept out of the way so you don't trip up over them.* VERB V V on/over n PHRASAL VERB V P V P on/over n

3 If you **trip** someone who is walking, you put your foot or something else in front of them, so that they knock their own foot against it and fall or nearly fall. *One guy stuck his foot out and tried to trip me.* ► **Trip up** means the same as **trip**. *He made a sudden dive for Uncle Jim's legs to try to trip him up... He was tripped up by a passer-by.* VERB V n PHRASAL VERB V n P be V-ed P

4 A **trip** is an imaginary experience caused by taking hallucinogenic drugs; an informal use. *An anxious or depressed person can experience a really bad trip.* N-COUNT

5 If someone **is tripping**, they are having an imaginary experience caused by taking hallucinogenic drugs; an informal use. *One night I was tripping on acid.* VB: usu cont V on n Also V

6 If someone **trips** somewhere, they walk there with light, quick steps; a literary use. *A girl in a red smock tripped down the hill... They tripped along with scarcely a care in the world.* VERB V prep/adv

trip up. If someone or something **trips** someone **up** or they **trip up**, someone or something causes them to fail or make a mistake. *Your own lies will trip you up... He will do all he can to trip up the new right-wing government... The two occasions she tripped up tell you nothing about how often she got away with it.* ● See also **trip** 2, 3. PHRASAL VERB ERG V n P V P n (not pron) V P

tripartite /traɪpɑːʳtaɪt/. You can use **tripartite** to describe something that has three parts or that involves three groups of people; a formal word. *...tripartite meetings between Government ministers, trades union leaders and industrialists.* ADJ: usu ADJ n

tripe /traɪp/

1 **Tripe** is the stomach of a pig, cow, or ox which is eaten as food. N-UNCOUNT

2 You refer to something that someone has said or written as **tripe** when you think that it is silly and worthless; an informal use. *I've never heard such a load of tripe in all my life.* N-UNCOUNT =rubbish

triple /trɪpəl/ **triples, tripling, tripled** ◆◆◇◇◇

1 **Triple** means consisting of three things or parts. *...a triple somersault... In 1882 Germany, Austria, and Italy formed the Triple Alliance.* ADJ: ADJ n

2 If something **triples** or if you **triple** it, it becomes three times as large in size or number. *I got a fantastic new job and my salary tripled... The Exhibition has tripled in size from last year... The merger puts the firm in a position to triple its earnings.* V-ERG =treble V V in n V n

3 If something is **triple the** amount or size of another thing, it is three times as large. *The mine reportedly had an accident rate triple the national average... The kitchen is triple the size it once was.* PREDET: PREDET the n =three times

triple jump. The **triple jump** is an athletic event in which competitors have to jump as far as they can, and are allowed to touch the ground once with each foot in the course of the jump. N-SING: usu the N

triplet /trɪplət/ **triplets. Triplets** are three children born at the same time to the same mother. N-COUNT: usu pl

tripod /traɪpɒd/ **tripods.** A **tripod** is a stand with three legs that is used to support something such as a camera or a telescope. ◆◇◇◇◇ N-COUNT

tripper /trɪpəʳ/ **trippers.** A **tripper** is a person who is on a trip or on holiday; used mainly in informal British English. *...when the shops shut and the trippers go home.* ● See also **day-tripper**. N-COUNT

triptych /trɪptɪk/ **triptychs.** A **triptych** is a painting or a carving on three panels that are usually joined together by hinges. N-COUNT

tripwire /trɪpwaɪəʳ/ **tripwires;** also **trip wire.** A **tripwire** is a wire stretched just above the ground, which triggers a trap or an explosion if someone touches it. N-COUNT

trite /traɪt/. If you say that something such as an idea, remark, or story is **trite**, you mean that it is dull and boring because it has been said or told too many times. *The movie is teeming with obvious and trite ideas... The simple concepts he had been taught now sounded trite and naive.* ADJ-GRADED =clichéd

triumph /traɪʌmf/ **triumphs, triumphing, triumphed** ◆◆◆◇◇

1 A **triumph** is a great success or achievement, often one that has been gained with a lot of skill or effort. *The championships proved to be a personal triumph for the coach, Dave Donovan... Cataract operations are a triumph of modern surgery, with a success rate of more than 90 percent... In the moment of triumph I felt uneasy.* N-VAR

2 **Triumph** is a feeling of great satisfaction and pride resulting from a success or victory. *Her sense of triumph was short-lived... He was laughing with triumph.* N-UNCOUNT

3 If someone or something **triumphs**, they gain complete success, control, or victory, often after a long or difficult struggle. *President Yeltsin has triumphed at the polls... The whole world looked to her as a symbol of good triumphing over evil.* VERB V V over n

triumphal /traɪʌmfəl/. **Triumphal** is used to describe things that are done or made to celebrate a victory or great success. *He made a triumphal entry into the city... The triumphal arch commemorates Caesar's victory over Pompey.* ADJ-GRADED: usu ADJ n

triumphalism /traɪʌmfəlɪzəm/. People sometimes refer to behaviour which celebrates a great victory or success as **triumphalism**, especially when this behaviour is intended to upset the people they have defeated; used mainly in British journalism. *There was a touch of triumphalism about the occasion.* N-UNCOUNT

triumphalist /traɪʌmfəlɪst/. **Triumphalist** behaviour is behaviour in which politicians or organizations celebrate a victory or a great success, especially when this is intended to upset the people they have defeated; used mainly in British journalism. *...a triumphalist celebration of their supremacy.* ADJ-GRADED: ADJ n

triumphant /traɪʌmfənt/. Someone who is **triumphant** has gained a victory or succeeded in something and feels very happy about it. *Duncan and his triumphant soldiers celebrate their military victory... The captain's voice was triumphant... This trip was not like his first triumphant return home in 1990.* ◆◇◇◇◇ ADJ-GRADED =exultant ♦ **triumphantly** *'I thought so,' Evelina said triumphantly... They marched triumphantly into the capital.* ADV-GRADED: ADV with v, ADV with cl

triumvirate /traɪʌmvɪrət/. A **triumvirate** is a group of three people who work together, especially when they are in charge of something; a formal word. *...the triumvirate of women who worked together on the TV dramatisation of the novel.* N-SING-COLL: oft N *of* n

trivia /trɪviə/ ◆◇◇◇◇
1 **Trivia** is unimportant facts or details that are considered to be amusing rather than serious or useful. *The two men chatted about such trivia as their favourite kinds of fast food... The newspaper is now weighted in favour of trivia.* N-UNCOUNT
2 A **trivia** game or quiz is one where the competitors are tested on their knowledge of interesting but unimportant facts on many subjects. *...a pub trivia game.* ADJ: ADJ n

trivial /trɪviəl/. If you describe something as **trivial**, you think that it is unimportant and not serious. *The director tried to wave aside these issues as trivial details that could be settled later... I don't like to visit the doctor just for something trivial.* ◆◇◇◇◇ ADJ-GRADED =insignificant

triviality /trɪviælɪti/ **trivialities.** If you refer to something as a **triviality**, you think that it is unimportant and not serious. *He accused me of making a great fuss about trivialities... Interviews with politicians were juxtaposed with news items of quite astonishing triviality.* N-VAR

trivialize /trɪviəlaɪz/ **trivializes, trivializing, trivialized;** also spelled **trivialise** in British English. If you say that someone **trivializes** something important, you disapprove of them because they make it seem less important, serious, and complex than it is. *It never ceases to amaze me how the business world continues to trivialize the world's environmental problems.* VERB PRAGMATICS V n

trod /trɒd/. **Trod** is the past tense of **tread**.

trodden /trɒdᵊn/. **Trodden** is the past participle of **tread**.

troglodyte /trɒglədaɪt/ **troglodytes**
1 A **troglodyte** is someone who lives in a cave; a technical use. N-COUNT
2 If you refer to someone as a **troglodyte**, you mean that they are ignorant and unsophisticated. *He dismissed advocates of a completely free market as economic troglodytes with no concern for the social consequences.* N-COUNT

troika /trɔɪkə/ **troikas.** Journalists sometimes refer to a group of three powerful politicians or states as a **troika**. *...leader of the troika of past, present and future presidents... The press regard her as merely one of a ruling troika. ...the current troika, Luxembourg, Holland, and Portugal.* N-COUNT: usu sing, oft N *of* n

Trojan horse /troʊdʒən hɔːʳs/ **Trojan horses.** If you describe something or someone as a **Trojan horse**, you mean that they are being used to conceal someone's true purpose or intentions, and you disapprove of this. *There are accusations that his presidential opponent is a Trojan horse for old guard Communists... Both factions accused each other of using the organization as a Trojan horse to advance their causes.* N-COUNT: usu sing, oft N *for/of* n PRAGMATICS

troll /trɒl, troʊl/ **trolls.** In Scandinavian mythology, **trolls** are creatures who look like ugly people. They live in caves or on mountains and steal children. N-COUNT

trolley /trɒli/ **trolleys** ◆◇◇◇◇
1 In British English, a **trolley** is an object with wheels that you use to transport heavy things such as shopping or luggage. The American word is **cart**. *A porter relieved her of the three large cases she had been pushing on a trolley. ...supermarket trolleys.* N-COUNT
2 In British English, a **trolley** is a small table on wheels which is used for serving drinks or food. The American word is **wagon**. *The waiter had brought the sweet trolley.* N-COUNT
3 In American English, a **trolley** is an electric vehicle for carrying people which travels on rails in the streets of a town. The British word is **tram**. *He took a northbound trolley on State Street.* N-COUNT =streetcar
4 In British English, if you say that someone is **off** their **trolley**, you mean that their ideas or behaviour are very strange; an informal expression. *Is she off her trolley or what?* PHRASE: usu v-link PHR =mad

trolley bus, trolley buses. A **trolley bus** is a bus that is driven by electric power taken from cables above the street. N-COUNT: also *by* N

trombone /trɒmboʊn/ **trombones.** A **trombone** is a large musical instrument of the brass family. It consists of two long oval tubes, one of which can be pushed backwards and forwards to play different notes. N-VAR: oft *the* N

trombonist /trɒmboʊnɪst/ **trombonists.** A **trombonist** is someone who plays the trombone. N-COUNT

troop /truːp/ **troops, trooping, trooped** ◆◆◆◆◇
1 **Troops** are soldiers, especially when they are in a large organized group and on a particular mission. *The next phase of the operation will involve the deployment of more than 35,000 troops from a dozen countries... There were reports of troop movements.* N-PLURAL
2 A **troop** is a group of soldiers within a cavalry or armoured regiment. *...a troop of enemy cavalry trotting towards the Dutch right flank.* N-COUNT-COLL
3 A **troop** of scouts or guides is a local group of them that meets regularly. *...a Scout troop.* N-COUNT: usu with supp
4 A **troop of** people or animals is a group of them. *Amy was aware of the little troop of travellers watching the two of them... Out of beams and cracks came troops of beetles, ants and spiders.* N-COUNT: N *of* n
5 If people **troop** somewhere, they walk there in a group, often sadly or wearily; an informal use. *They all trooped back to the house for a rest... The men trooped into work with resignation.* VERB V adv/prep

trooper /truːpəʳ/ **troopers** ◆◇◇◇◇
1 A **trooper** is a soldier of low rank in the cavalry or in an armoured regiment in the army. *...a trooper from the 7th Cavalry... 'Where to, Corporal?' asked Trooper Fane respectfully.* N-COUNT; N-TITLE
2 In the United States, a **trooper** is a police officer in a state police force. *Once long ago he had considered becoming a state trooper.* N-COUNT
3 See also **storm trooper**.

troopship /truːpʃɪp/ **troopships;** also spelled **troop ship**. A **troopship** is a ship on which large numbers of soldiers are taken from one place to another. N-COUNT

trophy /troʊfi/ **trophies** ◆◆◇◇◇
1 A **trophy** is a prize, for example a silver cup or shield, that is given to the winner of a competition or race. N-COUNT
2 **Trophy** is used in the names of some competitions and races in which the winner receives a trophy. *He finished third in the Tote Gold Trophy.* N-IN-NAMES
3 A **trophy** is something that you keep in order to show that you have done something very difficult. *His office was lined with animal heads, trophies of his hunting hobby.* N-COUNT

tropical /trɒpɪkᵊl/ ◆◆◇◇◇
1 **Tropical** means belonging to or typical of the tropics. *...tropical diseases. ...a plan to preserve the world's tropical forests.* ADJ: ADJ n
2 **Tropical** weather is hot and humid weather that people believe to be typical of the tropics. ADJ-GRADED

tropics /trɒpɪks/. **The tropics** are the parts of the world that lie between two lines of latitude, the tropic of Cancer, 23½° north of the equator, and the tropic of Capricorn, 23½° south of the equator. ◆◇◇◇◇ N-PLURAL: *the* N

trot /trɒt/ **trots, trotting, trotted** ◆◇◇◇◇
1 If you **trot** somewhere, you move fairly fast at a speed between walking and running, taking small quick steps. *I trotted down the steps and out to the shed... They trotted along behind him... He was almost trotting, and the supermarket bag flapped against his trouser leg.* [VERB: V prep/adv, V] ▶ Also a noun. *He walked briskly, but without breaking into a trot.* [N-SING]
2 When an animal such as a horse **trots**, it moves fairly fast, taking quick small steps. You can also say that the rider of the animal **is trotting**. *Alan took the reins and the small horse started trotting... Pete got on his horse and started trotting across the field.* [VERB: V, V prep/adv] ▶ Also a noun. *As they started up again, the horse broke into a brisk trot.* [N-SING]
3 If something happens several times **on the trot**, it happens that number of times without a break; an informal expression. *She lost five games on the trot... Sales of new cars rose in May for the second month on the trot.* [PHRASE: PHR after v =in a row]
trot out. If you say that a person **trots out** old ideas or information, you are criticizing him or her for repeating them in a way that is not new or interesting; an informal expression. *Was it really necessary to trot out the same old stereotypes about Ireland?* [PHRASAL VERB, PRAGMATICS: V P n (not pron), Also V n P]

Trotskyist /trɒtskiɪst/ **Trotskyists.** A **Trotskyist** is someone who supports the revolutionary left-wing ideas of Leon Trotsky. [N-COUNT]

trotter /trɒtər/ **trotters**
1 In British English, **trotters** are pig's feet which you can cook and eat. [N-COUNT: usu pl]
2 A **trotter** is a horse that has been trained to trot fast and to pull a carriage in races. [N-COUNT]

troubadour /tru:bədɔ:r/ **troubadours**
1 **Troubadours** were poets and singers who used to travel around and perform to noble families in Italy and France in the twelfth and thirteenth centuries. [N-COUNT]
2 People sometimes refer to popular singers as **troubadours**, especially when the words of their songs are an important part of their music. [N-COUNT]

trouble /trʌbəl/ **troubles, troubling, troubled** ◆◆◆◆◇
1 You can refer to problems or difficulties as **trouble**. *I had trouble parking... You've caused us a lot of trouble... The plane developed engine trouble soon after taking off... The crew are in serious trouble in 50-knot winds and huge seas... The Sullivans continued to have financial troubles.* [N-UNCOUNT: oft *in* N, also N in pl]
2 If you say that one aspect of a situation is the **trouble**, you mean that it is the aspect which is causing problems or making the situation unsatisfactory. *The trouble is that these restrictions have remained while other things have changed... Your trouble is that you can't take rejection.* [N-SING: usu *the* N =problem]
3 Your **troubles** are the things that you are worried about. *She tells me her troubles. I tell her mine... She kept her troubles to herself.* [N-PLURAL: usu poss N =problems]
4 If you have kidney **trouble** or back **trouble**, for example, there is something wrong with your kidneys or your back. *An unsuitable bed is the most likely cause of back trouble... Her husband had never before had any heart trouble... He began to have trouble with his right knee.* [N-UNCOUNT: n N, N *with* n]
5 If there is **trouble** somewhere, especially in a public place, there is fighting or rioting there. *Riot police are being deployed throughout the city to prevent any trouble... Fans who make trouble during the World Cup will be severely dealt with. ...the first victim of the troubles in Northern Ireland.* [N-UNCOUNT: also N in pl]
6 If you tell someone that it is no **trouble** to do something for them, you are saying politely that you can or will do it, because it is easy or convenient for you. *It's no trouble at all; on the contrary, it will be a great pleasure to help you... Will it be any trouble to get over here that quickly?* [N-UNCOUNT: with brd-neg, oft N to-inf, PRAGMATICS =bother]
7 If you say that a person or animal is no **trouble**, you mean that they are very easy to look after. *My little grandson is no trouble at all, but his 6-year-old elder sister is rude and selfish.* [N-UNCOUNT: with brd-neg]
8 If something **troubles** you, it makes you feel rather worried. *Is anything troubling you?... He was troubled by the lifestyle of his son.* [VERB: V n] ♦ **troubling** *But most troubling of all was the simple fact that nobody knew what was going on.* [ADJ-GRADED]
9 If a part of your body **troubles** you, it causes you physical pain or discomfort. *The ulcer had been troubling her for several years.* [VERB: V n]
10 If you say that someone does not **trouble** to do something or does not **trouble** himself or herself to do something, you are critical of them because they do not do something that they should do, and that you think would require very little effort. *He yawns, not troubling to cover his mouth... He hadn't troubled himself to check his mirrors... He seemed to be a naturally solitary person, troubling himself about only a few friends.* [VB: with brd-neg, PRAGMATICS =bother: V to-inf, V pron-refl to-inf, V pron-refl *about/with* n]
11 You use **trouble** in expressions such as **I'm sorry to trouble you** when you are apologizing to someone for disturbing them in order to ask them something. *I'm sorry to trouble you, but I wondered if by any chance you know where he is... I hate to trouble you, but Aunt Lina's birthday is coming up and I would like to buy something nice for her.* [VERB, PRAGMATICS =bother]
12 If someone is **in trouble**, they are in a situation in which someone in authority is angry with them or is likely to punish them because they have done something which they shouldn't have done. *He was in trouble with his teachers... The person who loaned them to me got into terrible trouble for it. ...a charity that helps women in trouble with the law.* [PHRASES: usu v-link PHR, PHR after v]
13 If you **take the trouble** to do something, you do something which requires a small amount of additional effort. *It is worth taking the trouble to sieve the fruit by hand... He did not take the trouble to see the film before he attacked it.* [V inflects, usu PHR to-inf, oft with brd-neg]
14 If you say that someone or something is **more trouble than they are worth**, you mean that they cause you a lot of problems or take a lot of time and effort and you do not achieve or gain very much in return. *Some grumbled that Johnson was more trouble than he was worth... Learning more about it always seemed more trouble than it was worth.* [V inflects, v-link PHR]

troubled /trʌbəld/ ◆◆◇◇◇
1 Someone who is **troubled** is worried because they have problems. *Rose sounded deeply troubled... She was conscious of a troubled expression on Ann's face.* [ADJ-GRADED]
2 A **troubled** place, situation, organization, or time has many problems or conflicts. *There is much we can do to help this troubled country... Anyone who has been in a troubled relationship will sympathise with Sue... But these are troubled times and many people fear for the future.* [ADJ-GRADED: usu ADJ n]
3 ● to **pour oil on troubled waters**: see **oil**.

trouble-free. Something that is **trouble-free** does not cause any problems or difficulties. *The carnival got off to a virtually trouble-free start with the police reporting only one arrest.* [ADJ-GRADED]

troublemaker /trʌbəlmeɪkər/ **troublemakers.** If you refer to someone as a **troublemaker**, you mean that they cause unpleasantness, quarrels, or fights, especially by encouraging people to rebel against authority. *The regional governor has been given powers to outlaw strikes and expel suspected troublemakers.* [N-COUNT]

troubleshooter /trʌbəlʃu:tər/ **troubleshooters;** also spelled **trouble-shooter**. A **troubleshooter** is a person whose job is to solve major problems or difficulties that occur in a company or government. [N-COUNT]

troubleshooting /trʌbəlʃu:tɪŋ/. **Troubleshooting** is the activity or process of solving major problems or difficulties that occur in a company or government. [N-UNCOUNT]

troublesome /trʌbəlsəm/ ◆◇◇◇◇
1 You use **troublesome** to describe something or someone that causes annoying problems or difficulties. *He needed surgery to cure a troublesome back injury... Parents may find that a troublesome teenager becomes unmanageable.* [ADJ-GRADED]
2 A **troublesome** situation or issue is full of complicated problems or difficulties. *The economy has be-* [ADJ-GRADED]

come a troublesome issue for the Conservative Party.

trouble spot, trouble spots; also spelled **trouble-spot**. A **trouble spot** is a country or an area of a country where there is repeated fighting between two or more groups of people.
N-COUNT

trough /trɒf, AM trɔːf/ **troughs**
◆◇◇◇◇

1 A **trough** is a long narrow container from which farm animals drink or eat. *The old stone cattle trough still sits by the main entrance.*
N-COUNT

2 A **trough** is a low area between two big waves on the sea. *The boat rolled heavily in the troughs between the waves.*
N-COUNT

3 A **trough** is a low point in a pattern that has regular high and low points, for example a period of low productivity in business. *Looking back afterwards you will see that this was not a terminal trough in your career... American bank shares have risen by 60% since their trough last October.*
N-COUNT

4 A **trough** of low pressure is a long narrow area of low air pressure between two areas of higher pressure; a technical term in meteorology. *The trough of low pressure extended over about 1000 kilometres.*
N-COUNT

trounce /traʊns/ **trounces, trouncing, trounced.** If you **trounce** someone in a competition or contest, you defeat them easily or by a large score; an informal word. *In Rugby League, Australia trounced France by sixty points to four.*
VERB =thrash
V n

troupe /truːp/ **troupes.** A **troupe** is a group of actors, singers, or dancers who work together and often travel around together, performing in different places. *...troupes of travelling actors.*
◆◇◇◇◇ N-COUNT-COLL: oft N *of* n =company

trouper /truːpəʳ/ **troupers.** You can refer to an actor or other performer as a **trouper**, especially when you want to suggest that they have a lot of experience and can deal with difficult situations in a professional way. *Like the old trouper he is, he timed his entry to perfection.*
N-COUNT

trousers /traʊzəʳz/; the form **trouser** is used as a modifier. In British English, **trousers** are a piece of clothing that you wear over your body from the waist downwards, and that cover each leg separately. The usual American word is **pants**. *He was smartly dressed in a shirt, dark trousers and boots... Alexander rolled up his trouser legs.* ♦ **-trousered** *I smoothed his khaki-trousered leg.* ● to **wear the trousers**: see **wear**.
◆◆◇◇◇ N-PLURAL: also *a pair of* N
COMB in ADJ

trouser suit, trouser suits. In British English, a **trouser suit** is a woman's outfit consisting of a pair of trousers and a jacket which are made from the same material. Trouser suits are worn by women. The usual American term is **pant suit**.
N-COUNT

trousseau /truːsoʊ/ **trousseaux.** A **trousseau** is a collection of clothes, linen, and other possessions that a bride uses for her marriage; an old-fashioned word.
N-COUNT

trout /traʊt/ **trouts.** The plural can be either **trout** or **trouts**. A **trout** is a fairly large fish that lives in rivers and streams. ► **Trout** is this fish eaten as food.
◆◇◇◇◇ N-VAR
N-UNCOUNT

trove /troʊv/. See **treasure trove**.

trowel /traʊəl/ **trowels**

1 A **trowel** is a garden tool that is rather like a small rounded spade. You hold it in one hand and use it for digging small holes or removing weeds.
N-COUNT

2 A **trowel** is a small tool with a flat blade that you use for spreading things such as cement and plaster onto walls and other surfaces.
N-COUNT

truancy /truːənsi/. **Truancy** is the practice of children staying away from school without permission. *Schools need to reduce levels of truancy.*
N-UNCOUNT

truant /truːənt/ **truants, truanting, truanted**

1 A **truant** is a pupil who stays away from school without permission.
N-COUNT

2 If a pupil **truants**, he or she stays away from school without permission. *In his fourth year he was truanting regularly.* ♦ **truanting** *Truanting is a small but growing problem in primary schools.*
VERB
V
N-UNCOUNT =truancy

3 If a pupil **plays truant**, he or she stays away from school without permission. *She was getting into trouble over playing truant from school.*
PHRASE: V inflects, oft PHR *from* n

truce /truːs/ **truces.** A **truce** is an agreement between two people or groups of people to stop fighting or quarrelling for a short time. *The fighting of recent days has given way to an uneasy truce between the two sides... Let's call a truce.*
◆◆◇◇◇ N-COUNT

truck /trʌk/ **trucks, trucking, trucked**
◆◆◆◇◇

1 A **truck** is a large vehicle that is used to transport goods by road; used mainly in American English. The usual British word is **lorry**. *Now and then they heard the roar of a heavy truck.*
N-COUNT =lorry

2 In British English, a **truck** is an open vehicle used for carrying goods on a railway. *They were loaded on the railway trucks to go to Liverpool.*
N-COUNT: usu supp N

3 When something or someone **is trucked** somewhere, they are driven there in a lorry; used mainly in American English. *The liquor was sold legally and trucked out of the state.*
VB: usu passive
be V-ed prep/adv

4 If you say that you will **have no truck with** someone or something, you are refusing to be involved with them in any way. *He would have no truck with deceit... As an American, she had no truck with the painful formality of English life.*
PHRASE: V inflects, PHR n

trucker /trʌkəʳ/ **truckers.** A **trucker** is someone who drives a truck as their job; used mainly in American English. The usual British term is **lorry driver**.
◆◇◇◇◇ N-COUNT

trucking /trʌkɪŋ/. **Trucking** is the activity of transporting goods from one place to another using trucks; used mainly in American English. The usual British word is **haulage**. *...the deregulation of the trucking industry.*
N-UNCOUNT: usu N n

truckload /trʌkloʊd/ **truckloads;** also spelled **truck load**. A **truckload** of goods or people is the amount of them that a truck can carry. *Truckloads of food, blankets, and other necessities reached the city.*
N-COUNT: usu N *of* n

truculent /trʌkjʊlənt/. If you say that someone is **truculent**, you mean that they are bad-tempered and aggressive. ♦ **truculence** /trʌkjʊləns/ *'Your secretary said you'd be wanting a new cleaner,' she announced with her usual truculence.*
ADJ-GRADED =belligerent
N-UNCOUNT =belligerence

trudge /trʌdʒ/ **trudges, trudging, trudged.** If you **trudge** somewhere, you walk there slowly and with heavy steps, especially because you are tired or unhappy. *We had to trudge up the track back to the station.* ► Also a noun. *We were reluctant to start the long trudge home.*
◆◇◇◇◇ VERB
V prep/adv
N-SING

true /truː/ **truer, truest**
◆◆◆◆◇

1 If something is **true**, it is based on facts rather than being invented or imagined, and is accurate and reliable. *Everything I had heard about him was true... He said it was true that a collision had happened... The film tells the true story of a group who survived in the Andes in sub-zero temperatures.*
ADJ-GRADED: oft *it* v-link ADJ that ≠untrue, false

2 You use **true** to emphasize that something is genuine or sincere, but is often not expressed or acknowledged. *Sometimes it is a little difficult for them to express their true feelings... The true cost often differs from that which had first been projected... He argues that he is the true candidate of change.*
ADJ: ADJ n PRAGMATICS =real

3 If you use **true** to describe something or someone, you approve of them because they have all the characteristics or qualities that such a person or thing typically has. *This country professes to be a true democracy... Maybe one day you'll find true love... The ability to work collaboratively is a true test of leadership... I think he's a true genius.*
ADJ: ADJ n PRAGMATICS =real

4 If you say that a fact is **true** of a particular person or situation, you mean that it is valid or relevant for them. *I accept that the romance may have gone out of the marriage, but surely this is true of many couples... Expenditure on health in most of these countries has gone down, and the same is true for education.*
ADJ-GRADED: v-link ADJ *of/for* n

5 You can use **true** in order to admit that a fact or opinion is real or valid before indicating that you think that it is not important or relevant in the circumstances. *It's true she gets madly impatient with*
ADJ-GRADED: usu *it* v-link ADJ PRAGMATICS

him, but what mother doesn't?... The state, it is true, gave money towards their wages. Nevertheless the whole process had not been organized properly... 'Things are a bit different in my country.' 'True, true, but we're not in your country, are we?'

6 If you are **true to** someone, you remain committed and loyal to them. If you are **true to** an idea or promise, you remain committed to it and continue to act according to it. *David was true to his wife... India has remained true to democracy... She's been true to her word from day one.* ADJ: v-link ADJ *to* n =faithful

7 If a dream, wish, or prediction **comes true**, it actually happens. *Many of his predictions are coming true... Owning a place of their own is a dream come true for the couple.* PHRASES V inflects

8 If a general statement **holds true** in particular circumstances, or if your previous statement **holds true** in different circumstances, it is true or valid in those circumstances; a formal expression. *This law is known to hold true for galaxies at a distance of at least several billion light years.* V inflects, oft PHR *for* n

9 If you say that something seems **too good to be true**, you are suspicious of it because it seems better than you had expected, and you think there may something wrong with it that you have not noticed. *On the whole the celebrations were remarkably good-humoured and peaceful. Indeed, it seemed almost too good to be true.* v-link PHR

10 If you say that something such as a story or a film is **true to life**, you approve of it because it seems real. *The opening scenes of this movie are just not true to life.* v-link PHR PRAGMATICS

11 • **true colours**: see **colour**. • **true to form**: see **form**. • **ring true**: see **ring**. • **tried and true**: see **tried**.

true-blue; also spelled **true blue**. If you describe someone as **true-blue**, you mean that they are right-wing in their ideas and opinions. *Her husband is a true blue Tory.* ADJ

truffle /trʌfᵊl/ **truffles** ◆◇◇◇◇

1 A **truffle** is a soft round sweet made with chocolate and usually flavoured with rum. N-COUNT

2 A **truffle** is a round mushroom-like fungus which is expensive and considered very good to eat. N-COUNT

trug /trʌg/ **trugs.** In British English, a **trug** is a wide, shallow, oval basket used for carrying garden tools, flowers, or plants. N-COUNT

truism /truːɪzəm/ **truisms.** A **truism** is a statement that is generally accepted as obviously true and is repeated so often that it has become boring. *Orpington seems an example of the truism that nothing succeeds like success... Whilst this might sound like a truism, it is nevertheless a crucial problem to address.* N-COUNT =platitude

truly /truːli/ ◆◆◆◇◇

1 You use **truly** to emphasize that something has all the features or qualities of a particular thing, or is the case to the fullest possible extent. *...a truly democratic system... Not all doctors truly understand the reproductive cycle... Spain was truly a European nation.* ADV: ADV group, ADV before v

2 You can use **truly** in order to emphasize your description of something. *...a truly splendid man... They were truly appalling.* ADV: ADV adj PRAGMATICS

3 You use **truly** to emphasize that feelings are genuine and sincere. *Believe me, Susan, I am truly sorry... He truly loved his children.* ADV: ADV adj, ADV before v

4 You can use **truly** in order to emphasize that what you are saying is true. *I truly never minded caring for Rusty... I do not expect a war between my country and yours. Truly I do not.* ADV: ADV with cl =honestly

5 • **well and truly**: see **well**.

6 You write **Yours truly** at the end of a formal letter to someone you do not know very well. You write your signature after the words 'Yours truly'. *Yours truly, Phil Turner.* PHRASES CONVENTION =Yours sincerely

7 You can say **yours truly** as a humorous way of referring to yourself; an informal expression. *Yours truly was awoken by a shout: 'Ahoy there!'*

trump /trʌmp/ **trumps, trumping, trumped** ◆◇◇◇◇

1 In a game of cards, **trumps** is the suit which is chosen to have the highest value in one particular game. *Hearts are trumps. ...the ace of trumps.* N-UNCOUNT-COLL

2 In a game of cards, a **trump** is a playing card which belongs to the suit which has been chosen as trumps. *He played a trump.* N-COUNT

3 If you **trump** something that someone has said or done, you beat it by saying or doing something else that seems better. *The Socialists tried to trump this with their slogan... The Hong Kong and Shanghai Bank has trumped Lloyds by raising its offer.* VERB V n

4 Your **trump card** is something powerful that you can use or do, which gives you an advantage over someone. *Mr Amato's trump card is his colleagues' fear of an early election... She could threaten to play her trump card, an autobiography of embarrassing disclosures.* PHRASES poss PHR

5 If you say that someone **came up trumps**, you mean that they did something successfully, often when they were not expected to; used mainly in British English. *Sylvester Stallone has come up trumps at the US box office with his new movie Cliffhanger.* V inflects

trumped-up. **Trumped-up** charges are untrue, and are deliberately made up in order to punish someone unfairly. ADJ: usu ADJ n =false

trumpet /trʌmpɪt/ **trumpets, trumpeting, trumpeted** ◆◆◇◇◇

1 A **trumpet** is a musical instrument of the brass family which plays quite high notes. N-VAR: oft *the* N

2 If someone **trumpets** something that they are proud of or that they think is important, they speak about it publicly in a very forceful way. *The Conservative government has been trumpeting tourism as a growth industry. ...Mark Morris, who is trumpeted as the dance talent of his generation... It was trumpeted that the nation's health was improving. ...the much trumpeted 'tax cuts' in the 1980s.* VERB V n *as* n, V *about* n, *it be* V-ed that, V-ed, Also V n

3 When an elephant **trumpets**, it makes a loud sound. *The elephants trumpeted and stamped their feet at their approach.* VERB V

4 If you **blow** your **own trumpet**, you boast about yourself. *Hollywood cameramen have good reason to blow their own trumpets.* PHRASE: V and N inflect

trumpeter /trʌmpɪtəʳ/ **trumpeters.** A **trumpeter** is someone who plays a trumpet. ◆◇◇◇◇ N-COUNT

truncated /trʌŋkeɪtɪd, AM trʌŋkeɪtɪd/. A **truncated** version of something is one that has been shortened. *The review body has produced a truncated version of its annual report. ...a rock about eight feet high, shaped like a truncated cone.* ADJ-GRADED: usu ADJ n

truncheon /trʌntʃən/ **truncheons.** A **truncheon** is a short, thick stick that is carried as a weapon by policeman in Britain. N-COUNT

trundle /trʌndᵊl/ **trundles, trundling, trundled** ◆◇◇◇◇

1 If a vehicle **trundles** somewhere, it moves there slowly, often with difficulty or an irregular movement. *The truck was trundling along the escarpment of the Zambesi valley... A few horse-drawn carts still trundle through the dilapidated mining villages... The train eventually trundled in at 7.54.* VERB V prep/adv

2 If you **trundle** something somewhere, especially a small, heavy object with wheels, you move or roll it along slowly. *The old man lifted the barrow and trundled it away... They trundled his mowers outside and dumped them.* VERB V n adv/prep

3 If you say that someone **is trundling**, you mean that they are walking slowly, often in a tired way or with heavy steps. *Girls trundle in, a book bag on one shoulder, a diaper bag on the other.* VERB V adv/prep

trunk /trʌŋk/ **trunks** ◆◆◇◇◇

1 The **trunk** of a tree is the large main stem from which the branches grow. *...the gnarled trunk of a birch tree. ...toadstools growing on fallen tree trunks.* N-COUNT: usu N *of* n, n N

2 A **trunk** is a large, strong case or box used for storing things or for taking on a journey. N-COUNT

3 An elephant's **trunk** is its very long nose that it uses to lift food and water to its mouth. N-COUNT: usu with poss

4 In American English, the **trunk** of a car is a covered space at the back or front in which you put luggage or other things. The usual British word is **boot**. N-COUNT

5 **Trunks** are shorts that a man wears when he goes swimming. *I wear these trunks because they have a streamline effect in the water.* N-PLURAL =swimming trunks

6 Your **trunk** is the central part of your body, from your neck to your waist; a formal use. N-COUNT: usu sing

trunk road, trunk roads. In British English, a **trunk road** is a major road that has been specially built for travelling long distances. A trunk road is not as wide or as fast as a motorway. N-COUNT

truss /trʌs/ **trusses, trussing, trussed**

1 To **truss** someone means to tie them up very tightly so that they cannot move; used in written English. *She trussed him quickly with stolen bandage, and gagged his mouth.* ▶ **Truss up** means the same as **truss**. *She was trussed up with yellow nylon rope.* VERB =bind V n PHRASAL VERB: usu passive *be* V-ed P Also V n P

2 If you **truss** a piece of poultry, you prepare it for cooking by tying its legs and wings. *Put stuffing into the cavity and truss the bird.* ▶ **Truss up** means the same as **truss**. *Some people like to truss up the turkey.* VERB V n PHRASAL VERB V P n (not pron) Also V n P

3 A **truss** is a special belt with a pad that a man wears when he has a hernia in order to prevent it from getting worse. N-COUNT

truss up. See **truss** 1, 2. PHRASAL VERB

trust /trʌst/ **trusts, trusting, trusted** ◆◆◆◆◇

1 If you **trust** someone, you believe that they are honest and sincere and will not deliberately do anything to harm you. *'I trust you completely,' he said... He did argue in a general way that the president can't be trusted.* ♦ **trusted** *After speaking to a group of her most trusted advisers, she turned her anger into action.* VERB V n Also V ADJ-GRADED: ADJ n

2 Your **trust** in someone is your belief that they are honest and sincere and will not deliberately do anything to harm you. *He destroyed me and my trust in men... You've betrayed their trust... There's a feeling of warmth and trust here.* N-UNCOUNT: oft poss N *in* n

3 If you **trust** someone to do something, you believe that they will do it. *That's why I must trust you to keep this secret... They argued that the ruling party could not be trusted to oversee its own removal from power.* VERB V n to-inf

4 If you **trust** someone **with** something important or valuable, you allow them to look after it or deal with it. *This could make your superiors hesitate to trust you with a major responsibilities... I'd trust him with my life.* ▶ Also a noun. *She was organizing and running a large household, a position of trust which was generously paid... Although I didn't betray a trust, I feel I behaved shabbily.* VERB V n *with* n N-UNCOUNT: also a N

5 If you do not **trust** something, you feel that it is not safe or reliable. *She nodded, not trusting her own voice... For one thing, he didn't trust his legs to hold him up... I still can't trust myself to remain composed in their presence.* VERB V n V n to-inf V pron-refl to-inf

6 If you **trust** someone's judgement or advice, you believe that it is good or right. *Jake has raised two smashing kids and I trust his judgement... I blame myself and will never be able to trust my instinct again.* VERB V n

7 If you say you **trust that** something is true, you mean you hope and expect that it is true; a formal use. *I trust you will take the earliest opportunity to make a full apology... We trust that he and his department are considering our suggestion.* VERB V that

8 If you **trust in** someone or something, you believe strongly in them, and do not doubt their powers or their good intentions; a formal use. *For a believer, replies to all the questions about life and work are far different because he trusts in God... Don't blindly trust in the good faith of any government official.* VERB =have faith V *in* n

9 A **trust** is a financial arrangement in which a group of people or an organization keeps and invests money for someone. *You could also set up a trust so the children can't spend any inheritance until they are a certain age... The money will be put in trust until she is 18.* N-COUNT: also *in* N

10 A **trust** is a group of people or an organization that has control of an amount of money or property and invests it on behalf of other people or as a charity. *He had set up two charitable trusts... The National Childbirth Trust has recently conducted a survey of 1,271 new mothers.* N-COUNT: supp N, oft in names

11 In Britain, a **trust** or a **trust hospital** is a public hospital that receives its funding directly from the national government. It has its own board of governors and is not controlled by the local health authority. *St Mary's Hospital in Paddington became a self-governing trust this week.* N-COUNT: supp N, N n

12 See also **trusting; unit trust.**

13 If something valuable is kept **in trust**, it is held and protected by a group of people or an organization on behalf of other people. *The British Library holds its collection in trust for the nation... Works of art are in trust to us during our lifetime.* PHRASES PHR after v, v-link PHR, oft PHR *for* n

14 If you **take** something **on trust** after having heard or read it, you believe it completely without checking it. *I decided to take the Bible on trust, and live as if it were true.* V inflects

15 ● **tried and trusted**: see **tried.**

trust to. If you **trust to** luck or instinct, you hope that it will enable you to achieve what you are trying to do, because you have nothing else to help you. *I clambered over the gate and set off for the valley, trusting to luck... Gardiner is simply trusting to instinct and experience.* PHRASAL VERB no passive =rely on V P n

trustee /trʌstiː/ **trustees.** A **trustee** is someone with legal control of money or property that is kept or invested for another person, company, or organization. ◆◆◇◇◇ N-COUNT

trust fund, trust funds. A **trust fund** is an amount of money or property that someone owns, usually after inheriting it, but which is kept and invested for them. ◆◇◇◇◇ N-COUNT

trusting /trʌstɪŋ/. A **trusting** person believes that people are honest and sincere and do not intend to harm him or her. *She has an open, trusting nature... Perhaps I was too trusting.* ◆◇◇◇◇ ADJ-GRADED

trustworthy /trʌstwɜːʳði/. A **trustworthy** person is reliable, responsible, and can be trusted completely. *He is a trustworthy and level-headed leader.* ♦ **trustworthiness** *He wrote a reference for him, describing his reliability and trustworthiness as 'above questioning'.* ◆◇◇◇◇ ADJ-GRADED N-UNCOUNT

trusty /trʌsti/. **Trusty** things, animals, or people are reliable and have always worked well in the past. *She still drives her trusty black Corvette.* ADJ-GRADED: ADJ n =faithful

truth /truːθ/ **truths** ◆◆◆◆◇

1 The **truth** about something is all the facts about it, rather than things that are imagined or invented. *Is it possible to separate truth from fiction?... I must tell you the truth about this business... The truth of the matter is that we had no other choice... In the town very few know the whole truth. ...judgements of truth or falsity.* N-UNCOUNT

2 If you say that there is some **truth** in a statement or story, you mean that it is true, or at least partly true. *There is no truth in this story... Is there any truth to the rumors?... The criticisms have at least an element of truth and validity.* N-UNCOUNT: oft N *of/in* n

3 A **truth** is something that is believed to be true. *It is an almost universal truth that the more we are promoted in a job, the less we actually exercise the skills we initially used to perform it.* N-COUNT

4 See also **home truth, moment of truth.**

5 You say **in truth** in order to indicate that you are giving your honest opinion about something. *In truth, we were both unhappy.* PHRASES PHR with cl

6 You say **to tell you the truth** or **truth to tell** in order to indicate that you are telling someone something in an open and honest way, without trying to hide anything. *To tell you the truth, I was afraid to see him... Truth to tell, John did not want Veronica at his wedding.* PHR with cl =to be honest

truthful /truːθfʊl/. If a person or their comments are **truthful**, they are honest and do not tell any lies. *Most religions teach you to be truthful... We've all learnt to be fairly truthful about our personal lives... She could not give him a truthful answer.* ♦ **truthfully** *I answered all their questions truthfully.* ♦ **truthfulness** *I can say,* ◆◇◇◇◇ ADJ-GRADED =untruthful ADV-GRADED: ADV with v N-UNCOUNT *with absolute truthfulness, that I did not injure her.*

try /traɪ/ **tries, trying, tried** ◆◆◆◆◆

1 If you **try** to do something, you want to do it, and you take action which you hope will help you to do it. *He secretly tried to block her advancement in the Party... Try to make the effort to work your way through all of your tasks one at a time... Does it annoy you if others do things less well than you would, or don't seem to try hard enough?... I tried calling him when I got here but he wasn't at home... No matter how bad you feel, keep trying.* [VERB; V to-inf; V adv; V -ing; V] ▶ Also a noun. *It wasn't that she'd really expected to get any money out of him; it had just seemed worth a try... After a few tries Patrick had given up any attempt to reform his brother.* [N-COUNT]

2 To **try** and do something means to try to do it; an informal use. *He has started a privatisation programme to try and win support from the business community... I must try and see him.* [VERB; V and inf]

3 If you **try for** something, you make an effort to get it or achieve it. *My partner and I have been trying for a baby for two years... He said he was going to try for first place next year.* [VERB; V for n]

4 If you **try** something new or different, you use it, do it, or experience it in order to discover its qualities or effects. *It's best not to try a new recipe for the first time on such an important occasion... I've tried everything from herbal cigarettes to chewing gum... I have tried painting the young shoots with weed poisoner, but this does not kill them off.* [VERB; V n; V -ing] ▶ Also a noun. *If you're still sceptical about exercising, we can only ask you to trust us and give it a try.* [N-COUNT: usu sing]

5 If you **try** a particular place or person, you go to that place or person because you think that they may be able to provide you with what you want. *Have you tried the local music shops?* [VERB; V n]

6 If you **try** a door or window, you try to open it. *Bob tried the door. To his surprise it opened.* [VERB; V n]

7 When a person **is tried**, he or she has to appear in a law court and is found innocent or guilty after the judge and jury have heard the evidence. When a legal case **is tried**, it is considered in a court of law. *He suggested that those responsible should be tried for crimes against humanity... Whether he is innocent or guilty is a decision that will be made when the case is tried in court... The military court which tried him excluded two of his lawyers... Why does it take 253 days to try a case of fraud?* [VERB; be V-ed for n; be V-ed; V n]

8 In the game of rugby, a **try** is the action of scoring by putting the ball down behind the goal line of the opposing team. *The French, who led 21-3 at half time, scored eight tries.* [N-COUNT]

9 See also **tried, trying.**

10 If you say that something fails but not **for want of trying** or not **for lack of trying**, you mean that everything possible was done to make it succeed. *Not all is perfect, but it isn't for want of trying.* [PHRASE: with neg, it v-link PHR, PHR with cl]

11 • to **try** your **best**: see **best**. • to **try** your **hand**: see **hand**. • to **try** your **luck**: see **luck**. • to **try** someone**'s patience**: see **patience**.

try on [PHRASAL VERB]

1 If you **try on** a piece of clothing, you put it on to see if it fits you or if it looks nice. *Try on clothing and shoes to make sure they fit.* [V P n (not pron); Also V n P]

2 In informal British English, if you say that someone **is trying it on**, you mean that they are trying to obtain something or to impress someone, often in a slightly dishonest way or without much hope of success. *They're just trying it on – I don't believe they'll go this far.* [usu cont; V it P; Also V it P with n]

try out. If you **try** something **out**, you test it in order to find out how useful or effective it is or what it is like. *She knew I wanted to try the boat out at the weekend... London Transport hopes to try out the system in September.* [PHRASAL VERB; V n P; V P n (not pron)]

try out for. If you **try out for** a sports team or an acting role, you compete or audition in an attempt to be chosen for it; used mainly in American English. *He should have tried out for the Olympic 100 metres squad.* [PHRASAL VERB; V P P n]

trying /traɪɪŋ/. If you describe something or someone as **trying**, you mean that they are difficult to deal with and make you feel impatient or annoyed. *Support from those closest to you is vital in these trying times... The whole business has been very trying.* • See also **try**. [◆◇◇◇◇; ADJ-GRADED]

tryout /traɪaʊt/ **tryouts;** also spelled **try-out**.

1 If you give something a **tryout**, you try it or test it to see how useful it is. *The recycling scheme gets its first try-out in rural Dorset.* [N-COUNT; =trial]

2 If an athlete or a performer is given a **tryout**, they are given a test or an audition. *...tryouts for the U.S. junior national athletics team.* [N-COUNT; =trial]

tryst /trɪst/ **trysts.** A **tryst** is a meeting between lovers in a quiet secret place; a literary word. [N-COUNT; =assignation]

tsar /zɑːʳ/ **tsars;** also spelled **czar**. In former times, the **tsar** was the king of Russia. [◆◇◇◇◇; N-COUNT; N-TITLE]

tsarina /zɑːriːnə/ **tsarinas;** also spelled **czarina**. In former times, a **tsarina** was the queen of Russia or the wife of the tsar. [N-COUNT; N-TITLE]

tsarist /zɑːrɪst/; also spelled **czarist**. **Tsarist** means belonging to or supporting the system of government by a tsar, especially in Russia before 1917. [ADJ: usu ADJ n]

tsetse fly /tsetsi flaɪ/ **tsetse flies;** also spelled **tsetse**. A **tsetse fly** or a **tsetse** is an African fly that feeds on blood and can cause serious diseases in the people and animals that it bites. [N-VAR]

T-shirt, T-shirts; also spelled **tee-shirt**. A **T-shirt** is a cotton shirt with no collar or buttons. T-shirts usually have short sleeves. [◆◆◇◇◇; N-COUNT]

tsp., tsps. In a recipe, **tsp.** is a written abbreviation for **teaspoon**.

tub /tʌb/ **tubs** ◆◇◇◇◇

1 A **tub** is a deep container of any size. *He peeled the paper top off a little white tub and poured the cream into his coffee... Shrubs can be grown in tubs or large containers.* [N-COUNT] ▶ A **tub of** something is the amount of it contained in a tub. *She would eat four tubs of ice cream in one sitting.* [N-COUNT: N of n]

2 In American English, a **tub** is the same as a **bathtub**. *She lay back in the tub.* [N-COUNT; =bath]

3 See also **hot tub**.

tuba /tjuːbə, AM tuː-/ **tubas.** A **tuba** is a large musical instrument of the brass family which produces very low notes. It consists of a long metal tube folded round several times with a wide funnel at the end. [N-VAR: oft the N]

tubby /tʌbi/ **tubbier, tubbiest.** If you describe someone as **tubby**, you mean that they are rather fat; an informal word. [ADJ-GRADED; =chubby]

tube /tjuːb, AM tuːb/ **tubes** ◆◆◆◇◇

1 A **tube** is a long hollow object that is usually round, like a pipe. *He is fed by a tube that enters his nose. ...a cardboard tube.* [N-COUNT]

2 A **tube** of something such as paste is a long, thin container which you squeeze in to order to force the paste out. *I went out today and bought a tube of toothpaste. ...a small tube of moisturizer.* [N-COUNT: oft N of n]

3 Some long, thin, hollow parts in your body are referred to as **tubes**. *The lungs are in fact constructed of thousands of tiny tubes.* [N-COUNT]

4 In British English, **the tube** is the underground railway system in London. *I took the tube then the train and came straight here... He travelled by tube.* [N-SING: the N, also by N]

5 In American English, you can refer to the television as **the tube**; an informal use. The British word is **the box**. *The only baseball he saw was on the tube.* [N-COUNT: the N; =TV]

6 If a business, economy, or institution **goes down the tubes** or **goes down the tube**, it fails or collapses completely; used mainly in American English. *The country was going down the tubes economically... When I was dieting, that was when my social life started going down the tube.* [PHRASE: V inflects]

7 See also **bronchial tube, cathode-ray tube, fallopian tube, inner tube, test tube.**

tuber /tjuːbəʳ, AM tuː-/ **tubers.** A **tuber** is the swollen underground stem particular types of plants. [◆◇◇◇◇; N-COUNT]

tubercular /tjuːbɜːʳkjʊləʳ, AM tuː-/. **Tubercular** means suffering from, relating to, or causing tu- [ADJ] berculosis. ...*tubercular patients... He died of tubercular meningitis. ...tubercular bacteria.*

tuberculosis /tjuːbɜːʳkjʊloʊsɪs, AM tuː-/. **Tuberculosis** is a serious infectious disease that affects someone's lungs and other parts of their body. The abbreviation 'TB' is also used. ◆◇◇◇◇ N-UNCOUNT

tubing /tjuːbɪŋ, AM tuː-/. **Tubing** is plastic, rubber, or another material in the shape of a tube. ...*metres of plastic tubing.* ◆◇◇◇◇ N-UNCOUNT

tubular /tjuːbjʊləʳ, AM tuː-/. Something that is **tubular** is long, round, and hollow in shape, like a tube. ...*a modern table with chrome tubular legs.* ◆◇◇◇◇ ADJ

TUC /tiː juː siː/. In Britain, the **TUC** is an organization which represents trade unions, and to which most trade unions belong. **TUC** is an abbreviation for 'Trades Union Congress'. ◆◇◇◇◇ N-PROPER: *the* N

tuck /tʌk/ **tucks, tucking, tucked** ◆◆◇◇◇

1 If you **tuck** something somewhere, you put it there so that it is safe, comfortable, or neat. *He tried to tuck his flapping shirt inside his trousers... She found a rose tucked under the windscreen wiper of her car one morning.* VERB V n prep V-ed

2 In British English, **tuck** is food that children eat as a snack at school; an informal, old-fashioned use. *He stole a Mars bar from the school tuck shop.* N-UNCOUNT: oft N n

3 You can use **tuck** to refer to a form of plastic surgery which involves reducing the size of a part of someone's body. *She'd undergone 13 operations, including a tummy tuck.* N-COUNT: usu supp N

tuck away PHRASAL VERB

1 If you **tuck away** something such as money, you store it in a safe place. *The extra income has meant Phillippa can tuck away the rent... I tucked the box away in the linen drawer.* =stash away V P n (not pron) V n P

2 If someone or something **is tucked away**, they are well hidden in a quiet place where very few people go. *We were tucked away in a secluded corner of the room... His home in Bexley is tucked away in a miniature forest.* usu passive *be* V-ed P

tuck in PHRASAL VERB

1 If you **tuck in** a piece of material, you secure it in position by placing the edge of it behind or under something else. For example, if you **tuck in** your shirt, you place the bottom part of it behind the front of your trousers. *'Probably,' I said, tucking in my shirt... Tuck the sheets in firmly.* V P n (not pron) V n P

2 If you **tuck** a child **in** bed or **tuck** them **in**, you make them comfortable by straightening the sheets and blankets and pushing the loose ends under the mattress. *I read Lili a story and tucked her in her own bed... Tuck me in, turn out the lights and tiptoe out.* V n P n V n P

tuck into or **tuck in.** If someone **tucks into** a meal or **tucks in**, they start eating enthusiastically or hungrily; used in informal British English. *She tucked into a breakfast of bacon and eggs... Tuck in, it's the last hot food you'll get for a while.* PHRASAL VERB V P n V P

tuck up. If you **tuck** a child **up** in bed, you tuck them in; used in British English. *She tucked them up in bed... He mostly stayed at home tucking up the children... She had gone to work believing Helen was safely tucked up in bed.* PHRASAL VERB V n P V P n (not pron) V-ed P

Tues.; also spelled **Tue.. Tues.** or **Tue.** is a written abbreviation for **Tuesday**. ◆◆◇◇◇

Tuesday /tjuːzdeɪ, -di, AM tuːz-/ **Tuesdays. Tuesday** is the day after Monday and before Wednesday. *He phoned on Tuesday, just before you came... Talks are likely to start next Tuesday... On Tuesdays and Saturdays the market comes to town.* ◆◆◆◆◇ N-VAR

tuft /tʌft/ **tufts.** A **tuft** of something such as hair or grass is a small section of it which has strands that grow closely together or that are held together at the bottom. *He had a small tuft of hair on his chin. ...tufts of wool torn from sheep by bushes and brambles.* N-COUNT: oft N *of* n =clump

tufted /tʌftɪd/. Something that is **tufted** has a tuft or tufts on it. ADJ

tug /tʌg/ **tugs, tugging, tugged** ◆◆◇◇◇

1 If you **tug** something or **tug** at it, you give it a quick and usually strong pull. *A little boy came running up and tugged at his sleeve excitedly... She kicked him, tugging his thick hair.* ► Also a noun. *Bobby gave her hair a tug... I felt a tug at my sleeve.* VERB =yank V *at* n V n Also V N-COUNT

2 A **tug** or a **tug boat** is a small powerful boat which pulls large ships, usually when they come into a port. N-COUNT

tug-of-love. In British English, journalists sometimes use **tug-of-love** to refer to a situation in which the parents of a child are divorced and the parent who does not have custody tries to get the child, for example by kidnapping it. *A mother yesterday won a tug-of-love battle for custody of her twin daughters.* N-SING: usu N n

tug-of-war, tugs-of-war; also spelled **tug of war.**

1 A **tug-of-war** is a sports event in which two teams test their strength by pulling against each other on opposite ends of a rope. *The sailors won at tug-of-war. ...the European Tug of War Championships.* N-VAR

2 You can use **tug-of-war** to refer to a situation in which two people or groups both want the same thing and are fairly equally matched in their struggle to get it. *Adolescence is a tortuous tug-of-war between the dictates of society and the pull of one's emotions. ...the tug of war between government departments.* N-VAR

tuition /tjuɪʃᵊn, AM tu-/ ◆◇◇◇◇

1 If you are given **tuition** in a particular subject, you are taught about that subject. *The courses will give the beginner personal tuition in all types of outdoor photography.* N-UNCOUNT: oft supp N, N *in* n

2 You can use **tuition** to refer to the amount of money that you have to pay for being taught particular subjects, especially in a university, college, or private school. *Angela's $7,000 tuition at University this year will be paid for with scholarships.* N-UNCOUNT

tulip /tjuːlɪp, AM tuː-/ **tulips. Tulips** are flowers that grow in the spring, and have a lot of oval or pointed petals packed closely together. ◆◇◇◇◇ N-COUNT

tulle /tjuːl, AM tuːl/. **Tulle** is a soft nylon or silk cloth similar to net, that is used for making evening dresses and veils. N-UNCOUNT

tum /tʌm/ **tums.** Your **tum** is your stomach; an informal British word. N-COUNT =tummy

tumble /tʌmbᵊl/ **tumbles, tumbling, tumbled** ◆◆◇◇◇

1 If someone or something **tumbles** somewhere, they fall there with a rolling or bouncing movement. *A small boy tumbled off a third floor fire escape... The dog had tumbled down the cliff... He fell to the ground, and the gun tumbled out of his hand.* ► Also a noun. *He injured his ribs in a tumble from his horse.* VERB V prep/adv N-COUNT: usu sing

2 If prices **are tumbling**, they are decreasing rapidly; used by journalists. *House prices have tumbled by almost 30 per cent in real terms since mid-1989... Share prices continued to tumble today on the Tokyo stock market. ...tumbling inflation.* ► Also a noun. *Oil prices took a tumble yesterday.* VERB V *by/from/to* amount V V-ing N-COUNT: usu sing

3 If water **tumbles**, it flows quickly over an uneven surface with a lot of splashing. *Waterfalls crash and tumble over rocks. ...the aromatic pines and tumbling streams of the Zonba Plateau.* VERB V prep V-ing Also V

4 If you say that someone **tumbles** into a situation or place, you mean that they get into it without being fully in control of themselves or knowing what they are doing; used mainly in British English. *Many mothers and children tumble into poverty after divorce... There's no thought more pleasing than the prospect of tumbling into my apartment and slamming the door.* VERB V *into* n

5 See also **rough and tumble**.

tumble down. If a building **tumbles down**, it collapses or parts of it fall off, usually because it is old and neglected. *The outer walls looked likely to tumble down in a stiff wind... If the foundations are flawed the house will come tumbling down.* PHRASAL VERB V P

tumble over. If someone or something **tumbles over**, they fall, often with a rolling or bouncing movement. *The man tumbled over backwards.* PHRASAL VERB V P

tumbledown /tʌmbᵊldaʊn/. A **tumbledown** building is in such a bad condition that it is partly falling down or has holes in it. ADJ-GRADED: usu ADJ n =ramshackle

tumble dryer, tumble dryers; also spelled **tumble drier**. A **tumble dryer** is an electric machine which dries washing by turning it over and over inside a drum and blowing warm air onto it. N-COUNT

tumbler /tʌmblər/ **tumblers**
1 A **tumbler** is a drinking glass with straight sides. *He took a tumbler from a cupboard.* ► The contents of a tumbler can be referred to as a **tumbler** of something. *Add a few drops to half a tumbler of water.* N-COUNT; N-COUNT: usu N of n
2 A **tumbler** is an acrobat who performs on the ground, often with other members of a group. N-COUNT

tummy /tʌmi/ **tummies** ◆◇◇◇◇
1 Your **tummy** is the part of the front of your body below your waist. **Tummy** is often used by children or by adults talking to children. *Your baby's tummy should feel warm, but not hot.* N-COUNT =stomach
2 You can use **tummy** to refer to the parts inside your body where food is digested. **Tummy** is often used by children or by adults talking to children. *I've got a sore tummy... It's easy to get a tummy upset from river water.* N-COUNT =stomach

tumour /tjuːmər, AM tuː-/ **tumours;** spelled **tumor** in American English. A **tumour** is a mass of diseased or abnormal cells that has grown in a person's or animal's body. ◆◆◇◇◇ N-COUNT

tumult /tjuːmʌlt, AM tuː-/
1 A **tumult** is a state of great confusion or excitement. *A tumult of feelings inside her fought for supremacy. ...the recent tumult in global financial markets.* N-SING: also no det, oft N of n
2 A **tumult** is a lot of noise made by a crowd of people. *Round one ends, to a tumult of whistles, screams and shouts.* N-SING: also no det, oft N of n

tumultuous /tjuːmʌltʃuəs, AM tuː-/ ◆◇◇◇◇
1 A **tumultuous** event or period of time involves many exciting and confusing events or feelings. *...the tumultuous changes in Eastern Europe... It's been a tumultuous day at the international trade negotiations in Brussels.* ADJ-GRADED: usu ADJ n
2 A **tumultuous** reaction to something is very noisy, because the people involved are very happy or excited. *A tumultuous welcome from a 2,000 strong crowd greeted the champion... Delegates greeted the news with tumultuous applause.* ADJ: usu ADJ n

tuna /tjuːnə, AM tuːnə/ **tunas.** The plural can be either **tuna** or **tunas. Tuna** or **tuna fish** are large fish that live in warm seas and are caught for food. ► **Tuna** or **tuna fish** is this fish eaten as food. *She began opening a tin of tuna.* ◆◇◇◇◇ N-VAR; N-UNCOUNT

tundra /tʌndrə/ **tundras. Tundra** is one of the large flat areas of land in the north of Europe, Asia, and America. The ground below the top layer of soil is always frozen and no trees grow there. N-VAR

tune /tjuːn, AM tuːn/ **tunes, tuning, tuned** ◆◆◆◇◇
1 A **tune** is a series of musical notes that is pleasant and easy to remember. *She was humming a merry little tune.* N-COUNT =melody
2 You can refer to a song or a short piece of music as a **tune**. *She'll also be playing your favourite pop tunes.* N-COUNT
3 When someone **tunes** a musical instrument, they adjust it so that it produces the right notes. *'We do tune our guitars before we go on,' he insisted.* ► **Tune up** means the same as **tune**. *Others were quietly tuning up their instruments.* VERB V n; PHRASAL VERB V P n (not pron)
4 When an engine or machine **is tuned**, it is adjusted so that it works well. *Drivers are urged to make sure that car engines are properly tuned.* ► **Tune up** means the same as **tune**. *The shop charges up to $500 to tune up a Porsche.* VB: usu passive be V-ed; PHRASAL VERB V P n (not pron)
5 If your radio or television **is tuned** to a particular broadcasting station, you are listening to or watching the programmes being broadcast by that station. *A small colour television was tuned to an afternoon soap opera.* VB: usu passive be V-ed to n
6 See also **fine-tune, signature tune, tuning fork**.
7 If you say that a person or organization **is calling the tune**, you mean that they are in a position of power or control in a particular situation. *Who would then be calling the tune in Parliament?* PHRASES V inflects
8 If you say that someone **has changed** their **tune**, you are criticizing them because they have changed their opinion or way of doing things. *You've changed your tune since this morning, haven't you?... Yesterday he changed his tune, saying the fare increase was experimental.* V inflects PRAGMATICS
9 If you say that someone is **dancing to** someone else's **tune**, you mean that they are allowing themselves to be controlled by the other person and are doing what they are told to do by that person; used showing disapproval. *The danger of commercialism is that the churches end up dancing to the tune of their big business sponsors.* V inflects PRAGMATICS
10 A person or musical instrument that is **in tune** produces exactly the right notes. A person or musical instrument that is **out of tune** does not produce exactly the right notes. *It was just an ordinary voice, but he sang in tune... Many of the notes are out of tune... It's no wonder the piano kept going out of tune.* PHR after v, v-link PHR
11 If you are **in tune with** a group of people, you are in agreement or sympathy with them. If you are **out of tune with** them, you are not in agreement or sympathy with them. *Today, his change of direction seems more in tune with the times... The peace campaigners were probably out of tune with most Britons.* v-link PHR, PHR n
12 **To the tune of** a particular amount of money means to the extent of that amount. *They've been sponsoring the World Cup to the tune of a million and a half pounds.* PREP: PREP amount
13 ● **he who pays the piper calls the tune**: see **piper**.

tune in PHRASAL VERB
1 If you **tune in** to a particular television or radio station or programme, you watch or listen to it. *More than six million youngsters tune in to Blockbusters every day... The idea that people plan their radio listening is absolute nonsense; most tune in impulsively.* V P to n; V P
2 If you **tune in** to something such as your own or other people's feelings, you become aware of them. *You can start now to tune in to your own physical, social and spiritual needs.* ● See also **tuned in**. V P to n

tune out. If you **tune out**, you stop listening or paying attention to what is being said. *Whatever you're talking about, children rapidly tune out if you go beyond them... Rose heard the familiar voice, but tuned out the words.* PHRASAL VERB V P; V P n (not pron) Also V n P

tune up. When a group of musicians **tune up**, they adjust their instruments so that they produce the right notes. *I could hear the sound of a band tuning up.* ● See also **tune** 3, 4. PHRASAL VERB V P

tuned in. If someone is **tuned in** to something, they are aware of it and concentrating on it. *He's just not tuned in to the child's world, the child's feelings... They were tuned in to their own needs and didn't care about the feelings of other people.* ADJ-GRADED: usu v-link ADJ to n

tuneful /tjuːnfʊl, AM tuːn-/. A piece of music that is **tuneful** has a pleasant tune. ADJ-GRADED

tuneless /tjuːnləs, AM tuːn-/. **Tuneless** music and voices do not sound pleasant. *Someone walked by, singing a tuneless song.* ♦ **tunelessly** *My dad whistled tunelessly through his teeth.* ADJ-GRADED: usu ADJ n; ADV-GRADED: ADV after v

tuner /tjuːnər, AM tuːn-/ **tuners.** The **tuner** in a radio or television set is the part which you adjust to receive the radio signals or television signals at the right wavelength, so that you can watch or listen to the programme that you want. N-COUNT: oft supp N

tungsten /tʌŋstən/. **Tungsten** is a greyish-white metal. N-UNCOUNT

tunic /tjuːnɪk, AM tuː-/ **tunics.** A **tunic** is a sleeveless garment that is worn on the top part of your body. ◆◇◇◇◇ N-COUNT

tuning fork, tuning forks. A **tuning fork** is a small steel instrument which is used to tune instruments by striking it against something to produce a note of fixed musical pitch. N-COUNT

Tunisian /tjuːnɪziən, AM tuːn-/ **Tunisians** ◆◆◆◆◇
1 **Tunisian** means belonging to or relating to Tuni- ADJ

sia, or to its people or culture. ...*the Tunisian coast.* ...*the Tunisian Foreign Minister.*
2 A **Tunisian** is a Tunisian citizen, or a person of Tunisian origin. N-COUNT

tunnel /tʌnəl/ **tunnels, tunnelling, tunnelled;** spelled **tunneling, tunneled** in American English. ◆◆◆◇◇
1 A **tunnel** is a long passage which has been made under the ground, usually through a hill or under the sea. ...*two new railway tunnels through the Alps.* ...*the motorway tunnels under the Hudson river.* N-COUNT: oft supp N
2 To **tunnel** somewhere means to make a tunnel there. *The rebels tunnelled out of a maximum security jail... The caterpillars tunnel into the fruit to grow and mature.* VERB V prep/adv Also V
3 See also **wind tunnel.** • **light at the end of the tunnel**: see **light.**

tunnel vision
1 If you suffer from **tunnel vision**, you are unable to see things that are not straight in front of you. N-UNCOUNT
2 If you say that someone has **tunnel vision**, you disapprove of them because they are concentrating completely on achieving a particular aim, and do not notice or consider all the different aspects of what they are doing. N-UNCOUNT PRAGMATICS

tuppence /tʌpəns/. In Britain, **tuppence** was two old pence; an informal use. N-UNCOUNT

turban /tɜːʳbən/ **turbans.** A **turban** is a type of headgear worn by Sikh men and by some Hindu and Muslim men. It consists of a long piece of cloth wound round and round the head. N-COUNT

turbine /tɜːʳbaɪn, AM -bɪn/ **turbines.** A **turbine** is a machine or engine which uses a stream of air, gas, water, or steam to turn a wheel and produce power. ◆◇◇◇◇ N-COUNT

turbo /tɜːʳbou/ **turbos.** A **turbo** is a fan in the engine of a car or plane that improves its performance by using exhaust gases to blow fuel vapour into the engine. ◆◇◇◇◇ N-COUNT

turbo-charged; also spelled **turbocharged.** A **turbo-charged** engine or vehicle is fitted with a turbo. ADJ: usu ADJ n

turbot /tɜːʳbət/; **turbot** is both the singular and the plural. **Turbot** are a type of edible flat fish that live in European seas. ► **Turbot** is this fish eaten as food. ...*a fillet of turbot with mushrooms.* N-VAR N-UNCOUNT

turbulence /tɜːʳbjʊləns/ ◆◇◇◇◇
1 **Turbulence** is a state of confusion and constant disorganized change. *The 1960s and early 1970s were a time of change and turbulence.* ...*a region often beset by political turbulence.* N-UNCOUNT
2 **Turbulence** is violent and uneven movement within a particular area of air, liquid, or gas. *His plane encountered severe turbulence and winds of nearly two-hundred miles an hour.* N-UNCOUNT

turbulent /tɜːʳbjʊlənt/ ◆◇◇◇◇
1 A **turbulent** time, place, or relationship is one in which there is a lot of change, confusion, and disturbance. *They had been together for five or six turbulent years of rows and reconciliations... The turbulent world of Middle Eastern politics defies prediction.* ADJ-GRADED: usu ADJ n
2 **Turbulent** water or air contains strong currents which change direction suddenly. *I had to have a boat that could handle turbulent seas.* ADJ-GRADED: usu ADJ n

turd /tɜːʳd/ **turds**
1 A **turd** is a lump of faeces; an informal use. N-COUNT
2 People sometimes insult someone they do not like by referring to them as a **turd**; an informal and offensive use. N-COUNT PRAGMATICS

tureen /tjʊəriːn, AM tʊr-/ **tureens.** A **tureen** is a large bowl with a lid from which you can serve soup or vegetables. N-COUNT

turf /tɜːʳf/ **turfs, turfing, turfed** ◆◇◇◇◇
1 **Turf** is short, thick, even grass. *They shuffled slowly down the turf towards the cliff's edge.* N-UNCOUNT: also the N
2 A **turf** is a small rectangular piece of grass which you lay on the ground in order to make a lawn. *Lift the turfs carefully – they can be re-used elsewhere.* N-COUNT
3 Someone's **turf** is the area which is most familiar to them or where they feel most confident. *Their turf was Paris: its streets, theaters, homes, and parks... On its home turf, the combined bank would be unrivalled.* N-UNCOUNT: usu poss N =territory

turf out. If someone **is turfed out** of a place or position, they are forced to leave; used in informal British English. *We hear stories of people being turfed out and ending up on the streets... The party was turfed out of office after 15 years.* ...*the right wing landslide which has turfed out the Socialist government.* PHRASAL VERB be V-ed P be V-ed P of n V P n (not pron) Also V n P

turgid /tɜːʳdʒɪd/. If you describe something such as a piece of writing or a film as **turgid**, you think it is pompous, boring, and difficult to understand. *He used to make extremely dull, turgid and frankly boring speeches... The rest of the arts scene looks increasingly turgid by comparison.* ADJ-GRADED

Turk /tɜːʳk/ **Turks.** A **Turk** is a Turkish citizen, or a person of Turkish origin. ◆◆◇◇◇ N-COUNT

turkey /tɜːʳki/ **turkeys.** A **turkey** is a large bird that is kept on a farm for its meat. ► **Turkey** is the flesh of this bird eaten as food. *It's a proper Christmas dinner, with turkey and bread sauce.* • See also **cold turkey.** ◆◇◇◇◇ N-COUNT N-UNCOUNT

Turkish /tɜːʳkɪʃ/ ◆◆◆◆◇
1 **Turkish** means belonging or relating to Turkey, or to its people, language, or culture. ...*the Turkish capital, Ankara.* ...*the Turkish government.* ADJ
2 **Turkish** is the main language spoken in Turkey. N-UNCOUNT

Turkish bath, Turkish baths
1 A **Turkish bath** is a type of bath in which you sit in a very hot steamy room, then wash, have a massage, and finally swim or shower in very cold water. N-COUNT
2 A **Turkish bath** a place where you can have a Turkish bath. N-COUNT

Turkish delight, Turkish delights. Turkish delight is a jelly-like sweet that is covered with powdered sugar or chocolate. N-VAR

turmeric /tɜːʳmərɪk/. **Turmeric** is a yellow spice that is used to flavour hot food such as curry. N-UNCOUNT

turmoil /tɜːʳmɔɪl/ **turmoils. Turmoil** is a state of confusion, disorder, uncertainty, or great anxiety. ...*the political turmoil of 1989... Her marriage was in turmoil... Your mind is in such a turmoil you do not know what you are saying.* ◆◆◇◇◇ N-VAR: usu with supp, oft in N

turn /tɜːʳn/ **turns, turning, turned** ◆◆◆◆◆
1 When you **turn** or when you **turn** part of your body, you move your body or part of your body so that it is facing in a different or opposite direction. *He turned abruptly and walked away... He turned to his publicist and jokingly asked, 'What's next?'... He sighed, turning away and surveying the sea... He turned his head left and right... He waited for the woman to turn her face back to the road.* ► **Turn around** or **turn round** means the same as **turn.** *I felt a tapping on my shoulder and I turned around... Turn your upper body round so that your shoulders are facing to the side.* VERB V V prep/adv V n adv/prep Also V n PHRASAL VERB V P V n P
2 When you **turn** something, you move it so that it is facing in a different or opposite direction, or is in a very different position. *They turned their telescopes towards other nearby galaxies... Turn the cake the right way up on to a wire rack... I turned my jacket inside out... She had turned the bedside chair to face the door... The lid, turned upside down, served as a coffee table.* VERB V n prep/adv V n to-inf V-ed
3 When something such as a wheel **turns,** or when you **turn** it, it continually moves around in a particular direction. *As the wheel turned, the potter shaped the clay... The engine turned a propeller.* V-ERG V V n
4 When you **turn** something such as a key, knob, or switch, or when it **turns**, you hold it and twist your hand, in order to open something or make it start working. *Turn a special key, press the brake pedal, and your car's brakes lock... Turn the heat to very low and cook for 20 minutes... I tried the doorknob and it turned.* V-ERG V n V n prep/adv V
5 When you **turn** in a particular direction or **turn** a corner, you change the direction in which you are moving or travelling. *He turned into the narrow terraced street where he lived... Now turn right to follow West Ferry Road... The man with the umbrella* VERB V prep/adv V n

turned the corner again. ▶ Also a noun. *You can't do a right-hand turn here.* N-COUNT

6 The point where a road, path, or river **turns**, is the point where it has a bend or curve in it. *...the corner where Tenterfield Road turned into the main road.* ▶ Also a noun. *...a sharp turn in the road.* VERB V prep/adv Also V N-COUNT

7 When the tide **turns**, it starts coming in or going out. *There was not much time before the tide turned.* VERB V

8 When someone **turns** a cartwheel or a somersault, they do a cartwheel or somersault. *They were still doing wild acrobatics in the yard, turning somersaults and cartwheels.* VERB V n

9 When you **turn** a page of a book or magazine, you move it so that is flat against the previous page, and you can read the next page. *He turned the pages of a file in front of him.* VERB V n

10 If you **turn** a weapon or an aggressive feeling **on** someone, you point it at them or direct it at them. *He tried to turn the gun on me... The crowd than turned their anger on Prime Minister James Mitchell.* VERB V n *on* n

11 If you **turn to** a particular page in a book or magazine, you open it at that page. *To order, turn to page 236.* VERB V *to* n

12 If you **turn** your attention or thoughts **to** a particular person or thing or if you **turn to** them, you start thinking about them or discussing them. *We turned our attention to the practical matters relating to forming a company ... We turn now to the British news.* VERB V n *to* n V *to* n

13 If you **turn to** someone, you ask for their help or advice. *For assistance, they turned to one of the city's most innovative museums... There was no one to turn to, no one to tell.* VERB V *to* n

14 If you **turn** to a particular activity, job, or way of doing something, you start doing or using it. *These communities are now turning to recycling in large numbers... The Superpowers turned to the harder task of cutting their nuclear arsenals... Universities are turning from academic to commercial sponsorship.* VERB V *to/from* n/-ing

15 When something **turns** into something else or when you **turn** it into something else, it becomes something different. *A prince turns into a frog in this cartoon fairytale... Their grief turned to hysteria when the funeral procession arrived at the cemetery... The hated dictator had turned his country into one of the poorest police states in Europe... He soon turned his dreams to reality. ...an MP turned diplomat.* V-ERG V *into/to* n V n *into/to* n V-ed

16 You can use **turn** before an adjective to indicate that something or someone changes by acquiring the quality described by the adjective. *Czechoslovakia flew home its diplomats, fearing that the refugee affair might turn dangerous... She announced that she was going to turn professional.* V-LINK =become V adj

17 If something **turns** a particular colour or if something **turns** it a particular colour, it becomes that colour. *The sea would turn pale pink and the sky blood red... Her contact lenses turned her eyes green.* V-LINK-ERG V colour V n colour

18 You can use **turn** to indicate that there is a change to a particular kind of weather. For example, if it **turns** cold, the weather starts being cold. *If it turns cold, cover plants... The weather had turned warm and thundery overnight.* V-LINK V adj

19 If a situation or trend takes a particular kind of **turn**, it changes so that it starts developing in a different or opposite way. *The scandal took a new turn over the weekend. ...the latest turn in the fighting... Retailers have given up waiting for a turn in the housing market.* N-COUNT: with supp, oft N *in* n

20 In sport, if a game **turns**, or if someone or something **turns** it, something significant happens which changes the way the game is developing; used in British journalism. *The game turned in the 56th minute. ...the Gareth Edwards try which turned the game between France and Wales in Paris in 1971.* V-ERG V V n

21 In American English, if a business **turns** a profit, it earns more money than it spends. The usual British word is **make**. *The firm will be able to service debt and still turn a modest profit... He says the fares are just too low to turn profits.* VB: no passive V n

22 When someone **turns** a particular age, they pass that age. When it **turns** a particular time, it passes that time. *It was his ambition to accumulate a million dollars before he turned thirty... It had just turned twelve o'clock.* VERB V n

23 **Turn** is used in expressions such as **the turn of the century** and **the turn of the year** to refer to a period of time when one century or year is ending and the next one is beginning. *They fled to South America around the turn of the century.* N-SING: *the* N *of* n

24 When someone **turns** a wooden or metal object that they are making, they shape it using a lathe. *...the joys of making a living from turning wood. ...finely-turned metal.* VERB V n V-ed

25 If it is your **turn** to do something, you now have the duty, chance, or right to do it, when other people have done it before you or will do it after you. *Tonight it's my turn to cook... Let each child have a turn at fishing... Students are expected to take their turn leading the study group.* N-COUNT: usu with poss, oft N to-inf, N *at*-ing, N -ing

26 In British English, if you say that someone is having a **turn**, you mean they feel suddenly very unwell for a short period of time; an informal use. *He is having one of his turns... He gets funny turns, you know. It's his age.* N-COUNT

27 See also **turning**.

28 You can use **by turns** to indicate that someone has two particular emotions or qualities, one after the other. *His tone was by turns angry and aggrieved.* PHRASES PHR with group, PHR with v

29 If there is a particular **turn of events**, a particular series of things happen. *They were horrified at this unexpected turn of events.*

30 If you say that something happens **at every turn**, you are emphasizing that it happens frequently or all the time, usually so that it prevents you from achieving what you want. *Its operations were hampered at every turn by inadequate numbers of trained staff... At every turn smoke and flame stopped efforts to get into the living quarters.* PHR after v, PHR with cl

31 If you do someone **a good turn**, you do something that helps or benefits them. *He did you a good turn by resigning... One good turn deserves another.* usu PHR after v

32 If someone **turns** a place **inside out** or **upside down**, they search it very thoroughly and usually make it very untidy. *They hadn't found a scrap of evidence though they had turned his flat inside out.* V inflects

33 If something such as a system or way of life **is turned inside out** or **upside down**, it is changed completely, making people confused or upset. *He felt too shocked to move. His world had been turned upside down.* V inflects

34 You use **in turn** to refer to actions or events that are in a sequence one after the other, for example because one causes the other. *One of the members of the surgical team leaked the story to a fellow physician who, in turn, confided in a reporter.* PHR with cl/group

35 If each person in a group does something **in turn**, they do it one after the other in a fixed or agreed order. *There were cheers for each of the women as they spoke in turn.* PHR after v

36 If someone is of a particular **turn of mind**, they have that kind of mind or character. *She was of a rational turn of mind.*

37 If you **speak out of turn** or **talk out of turn**, you say something that you do not have the right or authority to say. *I hope I haven't spoken out of turn.* V inflects

38 If a person, animal, or vehicle has a good **turn of speed**, they have the ability to move fast; used in British English. PHR after v

39 If two or more people **take turns** to do something or **take it in turns** to do it, they do it one after the other several times, rather than do it together. *We took turns to drive the car... Ted and I took it in turns to go into hospital and sit with Emma.* V inflects, oft PHR to-inf

40 If a situation **takes a turn for the worse**, it suddenly becomes worse. If a situation **takes a turn** V inflects

for the better, it suddenly becomes better. *Her condition took a sharp turn for the worse.*

41 Turn is used in a large number of other expressions which are explained under other words in the dictionary. For example, the expression 'turn over a new leaf' is explained at **leaf**.

turn against. PHRASAL VERB ERG

If you **turn against** someone or something, or if something **turns** you **against** them, you stop supporting them, trusting them, or liking them. *A kid I used to be friends with turned against me after being told that I'd been insulting him... Workers may turn against reform... Working with the police has turned me against the use of violent scenes as entertainment.*
VPn
VnPn

turn around or **turn round** PHRASAL VERB

1 See **turn** 1.

2 If you **turn** something **around**, or if it **turns around**, it is moved so that it faces the opposite direction. *Bud turned the truck around, and started back for Dalton Pond... He had reached over to turn round a bottle of champagne so that the label didn't show... There was enough room for a wheelchair to get in but not to turn round.*
ERG
VnP
VPn (not pron)
VP

3 If something such as a business or economy **turns around**, or if someone **turns** it **around**, it becomes successful, after being unsuccessful for a period of time. *Turning the company around won't be easy... In his long career at BP, Horton turned around two entire divisions... If the economy turned round the Prime Minister's authority would quickly increase.*
ERG
VnP
VPn (not pron)
VP

4 If you say that someone **turns around** and says something, you are indicating that they say it unexpectedly or angrily, especially in order to criticize someone or defend themselves; an informal expression. *I feel that if I say how tired I get, David will turn around and say, 'I told you so'.*
VP *and* v

5 If you **turn around** a question, sentence, or idea, you change the way in which it is expressed, in order to consider it differently. *Now turn the question around and start looking not for what you did wrong in the past, but for what you can do to make things better in the future... It's an example of how you can turn around the sentence and create a whole new meaning.*
VnP
VPn (not pron)

6 See also **turnaround**.

turn away PHRASAL VERB

1 If you **turn** someone **away**, you do not allow them to enter your country, home, or other place. *Turning boat people away would be an inhumane action... Hard times are forcing community colleges to turn away students.*
VnP
VPn (not pron)

2 To **turn away** from something such as a method or an idea means to stop using it or to become different from it. *Japanese corporations have been turning away from production and have diverted into finance and real estate... Medicine began to turn away from botany in the scientific revolution of the 17th and 18th centuries.*
VP *from* n

turn back PHRASAL VERB

1 If you **turn back** or if someone **turns** you **back** when you are going somewhere, you change direction and go towards where you started from. *She turned back towards the crossroads... They were very nearly forced to turn back... Police attempted to turn back protesters marching towards the offices of President Ershad.*
ERG
VP prep/adv
VP
VPn (not pron)
Also VnP

2 If you cannot **turn back**, you cannot change your plans and decide not to do something, because the action you have already taken makes it impossible. *The administration has now endorsed the bill and can't turn back.*
with brd-neg
VP

turn down PHRASAL VERB

1 If you **turn down** a person or their request or offer, you refuse their request or offer. *Before this I'd have smiled and turned her down... I thanked him for the offer but turned it down... Would you turn down $7,000,000 to appear nude in a magazine?*
=refuse
VnP
VPn (not pron)

2 When you **turn down** a radio, heater, or other piece of equipment, you reduce the amount of sound or heat being produced, by adjusting the controls. *He kept turning the central heating down... She could not bear the relentless music and turned down the volume.*
≠turn up
VnP
VPn (not pron)

3 If the rate or level of something **turns down**, it decreases; used in British journalism. *The divorce rate turned down in the 1950s.*
VP

turn in PHRASAL VERB

1 When you **turn in**, you go to bed; an informal expression. *Would you like some tea before you turn in?*
VP

2 If you **turn** someone **in**, you take them to the police because they are suspected of committing a crime. If you **turn** yourself **in**, you go voluntarily to the police because you are suspected of committing a crime. *He has been given until noon today to turn himself in to authorities... There would be strong incentives to turn someone in... He seems to be making all the arrangements necessary so that he can continue trafficking in drugs when he turns himself in... I might today hesitate to turn in a burglar.*
VnP *to* n
VnP
VPn (not pron)
Also VPn (not pron) *to* n

3 When you **turn in** a completed piece of work, especially written work, you give it to the person who asked you to do it. *Now we wait for them to turn in their contracts... I want everybody to turn a report in on Zanzibar.*
=hand in
VPn (not pron)
VnP

4 If you **turn** something **in**, you return it to the place or person you borrowed it from; used mainly in American English. *I went back to the station-house to turn in my badge and gun... The official showed up to tell her to turn in her library books.*
=return
VPn (not pron)
Also VnP

turn off PHRASAL VERB

1 If you **turn off** the road or path you are going along, you start going along a different road or path which leads away from it. *The truck turned off the main road along the gravelly track which led to the farm... He turned off only to find he was trapped in a town square with no easy exit.*
VPn (not pron)
VP

2 When you **turn off** a piece of equipment or a supply of something, you stop heat, sound, or water being produced by adjusting the controls. *The light's a bit too harsh. You can turn it off... I have to get up and turn off the radio... Their water was turned off weeks ago without explanation.*
=switch off
≠turn on
VnP
VPn (not pron)

3 If something **turns** you **off** a particular subject or activity, it makes you have no interest in it. *What turns teenagers off science and technology?... Teaching off a blackboard is boring, and undoubtedly turns people off.* • See also **turn-off**.
VnPn
VnP
Also VPn (not pron)

4 If something or someone **turns** you **off**, you do not find them sexually attractive or they stop you feeling sexually excited; an informal expression. *Aggressive men turn me off completely.* • See also **turn-off**.
≠turn on
VnP
Also VPn (not pron)

turn on PHRASAL VERB

1 When you **turn on** a piece of equipment or a supply of something, you cause heat, sound, or water to be produced by adjusting the controls. *I want to turn on the television... She asked them why they hadn't turned the lights on.*
=switch on
≠turn off
VPn (not pron)
VnP

2 If someone or something **turns** you **on**, they attract you and make you feel sexually excited; an informal expression. *The body that turns men on doesn't have to be perfect.* • See also **turn-on**.
≠turn off
VnP
Also VPn (not pron)

3 If you say that someone **turns on** a particular way of behaving, you mean that they suddenly start behaving in that way, and you are often also suggesting that this is insincere; an informal use. *He could also turn on the style when the occasion demanded.*
VPn (not pron)
Also VnP

4 If someone **turns on** you, they attack you or speak angrily to you. *Demonstrators turned on police, overturning vehicles and setting fire to them... He turned on Pete and accused him of being mixed up in drugs.*
VPn

5 If something **turns on** a particular thing, its success or truth depends on that thing. *The plot turns on whether Ilsa will choose her lover or her husband.*
=rest on
VPn

turn out PHRASAL VERB

1 If something **turns out** a particular way, it happens in that way or has the result or degree of success indicated. *If I had known my life was going to turn out like this, I would have let them kill me...*
LINK
=work out
VP prep
VPn
VP adj

Sometimes things don't turn out the way we think they're going to... I was positive things were going to turn out fine.

2 When you are commenting on pleasant weather, you can say that is has **turned out** nice or fine, especially if this is unexpected; an informal use, mainly in British English. *It's turned out nice again.* LINK PRAGMATICS *it* V P adj

3 If something **turns out** to be a particular thing, it is discovered to be that thing. *Cosgrave's forecast turned out to be quite wrong... It turned out that I knew the person who got shot.* V P to-inf *it* V-ed P that

4 When you **turn out** something such as a light or gas, you move the switch or knob that controls it so that it stops giving out light or heat. *I'll just play until the janitor comes round to turn the lights out.* =turn off V n P Also V P n (not pron)

5 If a business or other organization **turns out** something, it produces it. *They have been turning out great blades for 400 years.* V P n (not pron) Also V n P

6 If you **turn** someone **out** of a place, especially the place where they have been living, you force them to leave that place. *Surely nobody would suggest turning him out of the house... They were turned out of the hotel... It was previously a small monastery but the authorities turned all the monks out.* =throw out V n P *of/from* n V n P Also V P n (not pron)

7 If you **turn out** the contents of a container, you empty it by removing them or letting them fall out. *Turn out the dough on to a floured surface... Turn the plants out of their pots.* V P n (not pron) V n P *of/from* n Also V n P

8 If people **turn out** for a particular event or activity, they go and take part in it or watch it. *Thousands of people turned out for the funeral... It was no wonder the fans turned out. The matches yielded 259 goals.* V P *for* n V P

9 See also **turnout, turned out**.

turn over PHRASAL VERB

1 If you **turn** something **over**, or if it **turns over**, it is moved so that the top part is now facing downwards. *Liz picked up the blue envelope and turned it over curiously... I turned him over on his back... I don't suppose you thought to turn over the tape, did you?... The buggy turned over and Nancy was thrown out.* ERG V n P V P n (not pron) V P

2 If you **turn over**, for example when you are lying in bed, you move your body so that you are lying in a different position. *Ann turned over in her bed once more.* =roll over V P

3 If you **turn** something **over** in your mind, you think carefully about it. *Even when she didn't say anything you could see her turning things over in her mind.* V n P *in* n

4 If you **turn** something **over** to someone, you give it to them when they ask for it, because they have a right to it. *I would, indeed, turn the evidence over to the police... The lawyer immediately turned over the release papers.* =hand over V n P (not pron) *to* n V P n (not pron) Also V n P

5 If you **turn over** a job or responsibility that you have, you give it to someone else, so that you no longer have it. *The King may turn over some of his official posts to his son... Parliamentarians were eager to turn over responsibility for the decision.* V P n (not pron) *to* n V P n (not pron) Also V n P

6 If you **turn over** when you are watching television, you change to another channel. *Whenever he's on TV, I turn over.* =switch over V P

7 See also **turnover**.

turn over to. If you **turn** something **over to** a different function or use, you change its function or use. *When he first leased the land in the late 1970s, he planned to turn it over to cereal production.* PHRASAL VERB V n P P n Also V P n (not pron) P n

turn round. See **turn around.** PHRASAL VERB

turn up PHRASAL VERB

1 If you say that someone or something **turns up**, you mean that they arrive, often unexpectedly or after you have been waiting a long time. *Richard had turned up on Christmas Eve with Tony... This is similar to waiting for a bus that never turns up.* =show up V P

2 If you **turn** something **up** or if it **turns up**, you find, discover, or notice it. *Investigations have never turned up any evidence. ...a very rare 15th-Century spoon, which turned up in an old house in Devon.* ERG V P n (not pron) V P Also V n P

3 When you **turn up** a radio, heater, or other piece of equipment, you increase the amount of sound, heat, or power being produced, by adjusting the controls. *Bill would turn up the TV in the other room... I turned the volume up... Turn the heat up high.* ≠turn down V P n (not pron) V n P V n P adj

turnabout /tɜːʳnəbaut/. A **turnabout** is a complete change in opinion, attitude, or method. *As her confidence grows you may well see a considerable turnabout in her attitude.* N-SING: oft N *in* n =turnaround

turnaround /tɜːʳnəraund/ **turnarounds** ◆◇◇◇◇

1 A **turnaround** is a complete change in opinion, attitude, or method. *I have personally never done such a complete turnaround in my opinion of a person... I don't see any vast turnarounds in the way we do business.* N-COUNT: oft N *in* n

2 A **turnaround** is a sudden improvement, especially in the success of a business or a country's economy. *The deal marks a turnaround in the fortunes of South Wales Electricity... A new survey shows signs of a turnaround in Northern California's housing market.* N-COUNT: usu sing, oft N *in* n

3 The **turnaround** or **turnaround time** of a task, for example the unloading of an aircraft or ship, is the amount of time that it takes. *It is possible to produce a result within 24 hours but the standard turnaround is 12 days... The agency should reduce turnaround time by 11 per cent.* N-VAR

turncoat /tɜːʳnkout/ **turncoats.** If you describe someone as a **turncoat**, you disapprove of them and think they are disloyal or hypocritical, because they have left their party or organization and joined an opposing one. *His one-time admirers now accuse him of being a turncoat.* N-COUNT PRAGMATICS

turned out. If you are well **turned out** or smartly **turned out**, you are dressed smartly. *...a well-turned-out young chap in a black suit. ...a woman, smartly turned out in patterned skirt and green top.* ◆◆◆◇◇ ADJ: adv ADJ

turning /tɜːʳnɪŋ/ **turnings.** If you take a particular **turning**, you go along a road which leads away from the side of another road. *Take the next turning on the right.* • See also **turn**. ◆◇◇◇◇ N-COUNT =turn

turning point, turning points. A **turning point** is a time at which an important change takes place which affects the future of a person or thing. *The vote yesterday appears to mark something of a turning point in the war... Hungary's opening of the border was a turning point for the refugees.* ◆◇◇◇◇ N-COUNT: usu sing, oft N *in/for* n

turnip /tɜːʳnɪp/ **turnips.** A **turnip** is a round vegetable with a greenish-white skin that is the root of a crop. ◆◇◇◇◇ N-VAR

turn-off, turn-offs

1 A **turn-off** is a road leading away from a major road or a motorway. N-COUNT

2 Something that is a **turn-off** causes you to lose interest or sexual excitement; an informal use. N-COUNT: usu sing

turn-on, turn-ons. Something or someone that is a **turn-on** is sexually exciting; an informal use. N-COUNT: usu sing

turnout /tɜːʳnaut/ **turnouts;** also spelled **turn-out**. ◆◇◇◇◇

1 The **turnout** at an event is the number of people who go to it or take part in it. *On the big night there was a massive turnout... It was a marvellous afternoon with a huge turnout of people.* N-COUNT: usu sing, oft supp N

2 The **turnout** in an election is the number of people who vote in it, as a proportion of the number of people who have the right to vote in it. *In 1988 the turnout was 50%... Election officials said the turnout of voters was low... A high turnout was reported at the polling booths.* N-COUNT: usu sing

turnover /tɜːʳnouvəʳ/ **turnovers** ◆◆◇◇◇

1 The **turnover** of a company is the value of the goods or services sold during a particular period of time. *Her annual turnover is around £45,000... The company had a turnover of £3.8 million.* N-VAR: usu with supp, supp N, N *of* n

2 The **turnover** of people in an organization or place is the rate at which people leave and are replaced. *Short-term contracts increase staff turnover... The industry has a high turnover of young people.* N-VAR: usu with supp, supp N, N *of* n

turnpike /tɜːʳnpaɪk/ **turnpikes.** In American English, a **turnpike** is a road, especially an expressway, which people have to pay to drive on. N-COUNT

turnround /tɜːʳnraʊnd/. A **turnround** is the same as a **turnaround.** N-SING

turnstile /tɜːʳnstaɪl/ **turnstiles.** A **turnstile** is a mechanical barrier at the entrance to a place such as a zoo or a football ground. Turnstiles have metal arms that you push round as you enter the area or building. N-COUNT

turntable /tɜːʳnteɪbəl/ **turntables.** A **turntable** is the flat, round part of a record player on which a record is put when it is played. N-COUNT

turn-up, turn-ups. In British English, the **turn-ups** on a pair of trousers or pants are the parts at the ends of the legs, which are folded over. The American expression is **cuff.** N-COUNT: usu pl

turpentine /tɜːʳpəntaɪn/. **Turpentine** is a colourless liquid used, for example, for cleaning paint off brushes. N-UNCOUNT

turpitude /tɜːʳpɪtjuːd, AM -tuːd/. **Turpitude** is very immoral behaviour; a formal word. N-UNCOUNT: usu supp N

turquoise /tɜːʳkwɔɪz/ **turquoises** ◆◇◇◇◇
1 **Turquoise** or **turquoise blue** is used to describe things that are of a light greenish-blue colour. *...a clear turquoise sea.* COLOUR
2 **Turquoise** is a bright blue stone that is often used in jewellery. *...beautiful silver and turquoise jewelry and pottery.* N-VAR: oft N n

turret /tʌrɪt, AM tɜːr-/ **turrets** ◆◇◇◇◇
1 A **turret** is a small narrow tower on top of a building or a larger tower. N-COUNT
2 The **turret** on a tank or warship is the part where the guns are fixed, which can be turned to point in any direction. N-COUNT: oft n N

turtle /tɜːʳtəl/ **turtles** ◆◇◇◇◇
1 In British English, a **turtle** is a large reptile which has a thick shell covering its body and which lives in the sea most of the time. The usual American term is **sea turtle.** N-COUNT
2 In American English, a **turtle** is any reptile that has a thick shell around its body, for example a tortoise or terrapin. N-COUNT
3 If a boat **turns turtle**, it turns upside down when it is in the water. *The tug nearly turned turtle twice, but I managed to keep her upright.* PHRASE: V inflects =capsize

turtle dove, turtle doves; also spelled **turtledove.** A **turtle dove** is a type of light-brown dove which makes a soft cooing sound and which is said to behave very affectionately towards its mate and its young. N-COUNT

turtleneck /tɜːʳtəlnek/ **turtlenecks.** A **turtleneck** or **turtleneck sweater** is a sweater with a short round collar that fits closely around your neck. N-COUNT

tusk /tʌsk/ **tusks.** The **tusks** of an elephant, wild boar, or walrus are its two very long, curved, pointed teeth. N-COUNT

tussle /tʌsəl/ **tussles, tussling, tussled** ◆◇◇◇◇
1 If one person **tussles** with another, or if they **tussle**, they grab hold of and struggle with each other. *They ended up ripping down perimeter fencing and tussling with the security staff... He grabbed my microphone and we tussled over that... James and Elliott tussled.* ► Also a noun. *The referee booked him for a tussle with the goalie.* V-RECIP; V *with* n; pl-n V *over* n; pl-n V; N-COUNT
2 If one person **tussles** with another for something, or if they **tussle** for it, they try to beat each other in order to get it; used in journalism. *Pezzo tussled for fourth place with Orvosova... Officials tussled over who had responsibility for the newly fashionable unemployment agenda.* ► Also a noun. *...a legal tussle over who gets custody of the children.* V-RECIP =battle; V *for* n *with* n; pl-n V *for/over* n; N-COUNT: usu with supp
3 If someone **tussles with** a difficult problem or issue, they try hard to solve it; used in journalism. *He is tussling with the problem of what to do about inflation.* VERB =wrestle; V *with* n

tussock /tʌsək/ **tussocks.** A **tussock** is a small clump of grass which is much longer and thicker than the grass around it. N-COUNT: oft N *of* n

tut /tʌt/ **tuts, tutting, tutted**
1 **Tut** is used in writing to represent a clicking sound that you make with your tongue to indicate disapproval, annoyance, or sympathy.
2 If someone **tuts**, they make a clicking sound with their tongue to indicate disapproval, annoyance, or sympathy. *He tutted and shook his head.* VERB; V

tutelage /tjuːtɪlɪdʒ, AM tuːt-/. If one person, group, or country does something **under the tutelage of** another, they do it while they are being taught or guided by them; a formal word. N-UNCOUNT: usu *under* N

tutor /tjuːtəʳ, AM tuːt-/ **tutors, tutoring, tutored** ◆◆◇◇◇
1 A **tutor** is a teacher at a British university or college. *He is course tutor in archaeology at the University of Southampton... Liam surprised his tutors by twice failing a second year exam.* N-COUNT
2 A **tutor** is someone who gives private lessons to one pupil or a very small group of pupils. N-COUNT
3 If someone **tutors** a person or a subject, they teach that person or subject. *The old man was tutoring her in the stringed instruments. ...at the college where I tutored a two-day Introduction to Chairmaking course... I tutored in economics.* VERB; V n *in* n; V n; V *in* n; Also V
♦ **tutoring** *He made his living by a mixture of tutoring and journalism.* N-UNCOUNT

tutorial /tjuːtɔːriəl, AM tuːt-/ **tutorials** ◆◇◇◇◇
1 In a university or college, a **tutorial** is a regular meeting between a tutor and one or several students, for discussion of a subject that is being studied. *The methods of study include lectures, tutorials, case studies and practical sessions. ...teaching in small tutorial groups.* N-COUNT: oft N n
2 **Tutorial** means relating to a tutor or tutors, especially one at a university or college. *Students may decide to seek tutorial guidance. ...the tutorial staff.* ADJ: ADJ n

tut-tut, tut-tuts, tut-tutting, tut-tutted; also spelled **tut tut.**
1 **Tut-tut** is used in writing to represent a clicking sound that you make with your tongue to indicate disapproval, annoyance, or sympathy. CONVENTION PRAGMATICS =tut
2 If you **tut-tut** about something, you express your disapproval about it, especially by clicking your tongue. *We all spent a lot of time tut-tutting about Angie and her lifestyle... The doctor tut-tutted, dismissing my words as excuses.* VERB =tut; V *about* n; V

tutu /tuːtuː/ **tutus.** A **tutu** is a costume worn by female ballet dancers. It has a very short stiff skirt made of many layers of material that sticks out from the waist. N-COUNT

tuxedo /tʌksiːdoʊ/ **tuxedos.** A **tuxedo** is a black or white jacket worn by men for formal social events; used mainly in American English. The usual British expression is **dinner jacket.** N-COUNT

TV /tiː viː/ **TVs. TV** means the same as **television.** *The TV was on... I prefer going to the cinema to watching TV. ...a TV commercial.* ◆◆◆◆◇ N-VAR

TV dinner, TV dinners. TV dinners are complete meals that are sold in a single package. They can be heated up quickly and eaten from the package they are cooked in. N-COUNT

twaddle /twɒdəl/. If you refer to something that someone says as **twaddle**, you mean that it is silly or untrue; an informal word. N-UNCOUNT =drivel

twang /twæŋ/ **twangs, twanging, twanged** ◆◇◇◇◇
1 If you **twang** something such as a tight string or elastic band, or if it **twangs**, it makes a fairly loud, resonating sound because it has been pulled and then released. *...people who thought it was clever to sit at the back of class and twang an elastic band for hours... His guitar makes a noise like a wooden ruler being twanged upon a desk... The song is a fiery mix of twanging guitar with relentless drumming.* ► Also a noun. *Something gave a loud discordant twang... He fitted a pebble into the catapult and pulled back the elastic. Twang!* V-ERG; V n; V-ing; Also V; N-COUNT; SOUND
2 A **twang** is a nasal quality in someone's way of speaking. *...the nasal twang of his voice. ...her broad Australian twang.* N-COUNT: usu sing

twat /twɒt/ **twats**
1 If someone calls another person a **twat**, they are insulting them and expressing contempt for them; a very rude and offensive word which you should avoid using. N-COUNT PRAGMATICS

2 Some people use the word **twat** to refer to a woman's vagina; a very rude and offensive use which you should avoid. N-COUNT

tweak /twiːk/ **tweaks, tweaking, tweaked**

1 If you **tweak** something, especially part of someone's body, you hold it between your finger and thumb and twist it or pull it. *He tweaked Guy's ear roughly... 'A handsome offer', she replied, tweaking his cheek.* VERB; V n

2 If you **tweak** something such as a system or a design, you improve it by making a slight change; an informal use. *He expects the system to get even better as the engineers tweak its performance.* ► Also a noun. *Regular readers may notice a few changes in this issue – nothing too radical, just a tweak here and there.* VERB; V n; N-COUNT

twee /twiː/. In British English, if you say that something is **twee**, you disapprove of it because it is pretty or sentimental in a way that you think is excessive or tasteless. ADJ-GRADED: usu v-link ADJ; PRAGMATICS

tweed /twiːd/ **tweeds** ◆◇◇◇◇

1 **Tweed** is a thick woollen cloth, often woven from different coloured threads. *...shooting coats in tweed or rubberised cotton. ...my husband's old tweed cap.* N-MASS

2 Someone who is wearing **tweeds** is wearing a tweed suit. *...an academic, dressed in tweeds and smoking a pipe.* N-PLURAL

tweedy /twiːdi/

1 If you describe someone as **tweedy**, you mean that they have an upper-class but plain appearance, and look as if they live in the country, for example because they are wearing tweed. *An older woman, pink-cheeked and tweedy, appeared in the doorway.* ADJ-GRADED

2 **Tweedy** clothes are made from tweed. ADJ-GRADED

tweet /twiːt/ **tweets.** A **tweet** is a short, high-pitched sound made by a small bird. N-COUNT; SOUND

tweezers /twiːzərz/. **Tweezers** are a small tool that you use for tasks such as pulling out hairs or splinters and picking up small objects. N-PLURAL: oft *a pair of* N

twelfth /twelfθ/ **twelfths** ◆◆◆◆◇

1 The **twelfth** item in a series is the one that you count as number twelve. *...the twelfth anniversary of the April revolution. ...a twelfth-century church.* ORD

2 A **twelfth** is one of twelve equal parts of something. *She is entitled to a twelfth of the cash.* FRACTION

twelve /twelv/ **twelves. Twelve** is the number 12. ◆◆◆◆◆ NUM

twentieth /twentiəθ/ **twentieths** ◆◆◆◆◇

1 The **twentieth** item in a series is the one that you count as number twenty. *...the twentieth century.* ORD

2 A **twentieth** is one of twenty equal parts of something. *A few twentieths of a gram can be critical.* FRACTION

twenty /twenti/ **twenties.** ◆◆◆◆◆

1 **Twenty** is the number 20. NUM

2 When you talk about the **twenties**, you are referring to numbers between 20 and 29. For example, if you are **in your twenties**, you are aged between 20 and 29. If the temperature is **in the twenties**, the temperature is between 20 and 29 degrees. *They're both in their twenties and both married with children of their own.* N-PLURAL

3 **The twenties** is the decade between 1920 and 1929. *It was written in the Twenties, but it still really stands out.* N-PLURAL: *the* N

twerp /twɜːrp/ **twerps.** If you call someone a **twerp**, you are insulting them and saying that they are silly or stupid; an informal word. N-COUNT; PRAGMATICS; =twit

twice /twaɪs/ ◆◆◆◆◆

1 If something happens **twice**, there are two actions or events of the same kind. *He visited me twice that fall and called me on the telephone often... The government has twice declined to back the scheme... Thoroughly brush teeth and gums twice daily... Twice before he had been in New York with Gladys on summer vacations. ...Foster, who is twice the world champion.* ADV: ADV with v, ADV adv, ADV n

2 You use **twice** in expressions such as **twice a day** and **twice a week** to indicate that two events or actions of the same kind happen in each day or week. *I phoned twice a day, leaving messages with his wife... This famous horse race has taken place here twice a year since 1310.* ADV: ADV *a* n

3 If one thing is, for example, **twice as** big or old as another, the first thing is bigger or older by an amount equal to the second thing. People sometimes say that one thing is **twice as** good or hard as another when they mean the first thing is much better or harder than the second. *The figure of seventy-million pounds was twice as big as expected. ...a report claiming that teachers could be twice as effective if they returned to traditional classroom methods.* ► Also a predeterminer. *Unemployment in Northern Ireland is twice the national average... Double cream contains approximately twice the quantity of fat-soluble vitamins as single cream.* ADV: ADV *as* adj/adv; PREDET: PREDET *the* n

4 If you **think twice** about doing something, you reconsider it and may decide to do it differently or not to do it at all. *She'd better shut her mouth and from now on think twice before saying stupid things.* PHRASE: V inflects

5 ● **once or twice**: see **once**. ● **twice over**: see **over**.

twiddle /twɪdəl/ **twiddles, twiddling, twiddled**

1 If you **twiddle** something, you twist it or turn it quickly with your fingers. *He twiddled a knob on the dashboard... She had sat there twiddling nervously with the clasp of her handbag.* VERB; V n; V *with* n

2 ● **to twiddle** your **thumbs**: see **thumb**.

twig /twɪg/ **twigs, twigging, twigged** ◆◇◇◇◇

1 A **twig** is a very small thin branch that grows out from a main branch of a tree or bush. N-COUNT

2 In British English, if you **twig**, you suddenly realize or understand something; an informal use. *Then I twigged that they were illegal immigrants... By the time she'd twigged what it was all about it was too late.* VERB; V that; V wh; Also V

twilight /twaɪlaɪt/ ◆◇◇◇◇

1 **Twilight** is the time just before night when the daylight has almost gone but when it is not completely dark. *They returned at twilight, and set off for one of the promenade bars.* N-UNCOUNT =dusk

2 **Twilight** is the dim light that there is outside just after sunset. *...the deepening autumn twilight.* N-UNCOUNT

3 **The twilight of** a period of time is the final stages of it, when the most important events have already happened, and there is a state of weakness or decline. *Now both men are in the twilight of their careers... I am getting old. I am in the twilight of my life. ...the twilight years of the Habsburg empire.* N-SING: *the* N *of* n, N n

4 A **twilight** state or a **twilight** zone is a situation of confusion or uncertainty, which seems to exist between two different states or categories. *They fell into that twilight zone between military personnel and civilian employees.* ADJ: ADJ n

twill /twɪl/. **Twill** is cloth, usually cotton, that is woven in a way which produces diagonal lines across it. N-UNCOUNT

twin /twɪn/ **twins, twinning, twinned** ◆◆◆◇◇

1 If two people are **twins**, they have the same mother and were born on the same day. *Sarah was looking after the twins... I think there are many positive aspects to being a twin... She had a twin brother and a younger brother.* N-COUNT: oft N n

2 **Twin** is used to describe a pair of things that look the same and are close together. *...the twin spires of the cathedral. ...the world's largest twin-engined aircraft.* ADJ: ADJ n

3 **Twin** is used to describe two things or ideas that are similar or connected in some way. *...the twin concepts of liberty and equality... Nothing was done to save these women from the twin evils of begging or the workhouse.* ADJ: ADJ n

4 When a place or organization in one country **is twinned** with a place or organization in another country, a special relationship is formally established between them. *Five Polish banks are to be twinned with counterparts in Western Europe... The borough is twinned with Kasel in Germany.* ♦ **twinning** *The twinning of Leeds and St Mary was formalised at a function held last week.* VB: usu passive; be V-ed *with* n; V-ed; N-UNCOUNT

5 **Twin** towns or cities are twinned with each other. *This led Zagreb's twin town, Mainz, to donate £70,000-worth of high-quality equipment.* ADJ: ADJ n

6 See also **identical twin, Siamese twin.**

twin bed, twin beds. Twin beds are two single beds in one bedroom. N-COUNT: usu pl

twin-bedded; also spelled **twin bedded**. A **twin-bedded** room, for example in a hotel, has twin beds; used mainly in British English. ADJ: ADJ n

twine /twaɪn/ **twines, twining, twined**

1 **Twine** is strong string used especially in gardening and farming. N-UNCOUNT

2 If you **twine** one thing around another, or if one thing **twines** around another, the first thing is twisted or wound around the second. *He had twined his chubby arms around Vincent's neck... He twined his fingers into hers... These strands of molecules twine around each other to form cable-like structures.* V-ERG; V n prep; V prep

twinge /twɪndʒ/ **twinges**

1 A **twinge** is a sudden sharp feeling or emotion, usually an unpleasant one. *I would have twinges of guilt occasionally... For a moment, Arnold felt a twinge of sympathy for Mr Wilson.* N-COUNT: with supp, usu N *of* n =pang

2 A **twinge** is a sudden sharp pain. *He felt a slight twinge in his damaged hamstring. ...the occasional twinge of indigestion.* N-COUNT

twinkle /twɪŋkəl/ **twinkles, twinkling, twinkled** ◆◇◇◇◇

1 If a star or a light **twinkles**, it shines with an unsteady light which rapidly and constantly changes from bright to faint. *At night, lights twinkle in distant villages across the valleys. ...a band of twinkling diamonds.* VERB; V; V-ing

2 If you say that someone's eyes **twinkle**, you mean that their face expresses good humour, amusement, or mischief. *She saw her grandmother's eyes twinkle with amusement.* ► Also a noun. *A kindly twinkle came into her eyes.* VERB; V; N-SING

twinset /twɪnset/ **twinsets;** also spelled **twin set** or **twin-set**. In British English, a **twinset** is a set of women's clothing, consisting of a matching cardigan and sweater of the same colour. N-COUNT

twirl /twɜːrl/ **twirls, twirling, twirled** ◆◇◇◇◇

1 If you **twirl** something or if it **twirls**, it turns round and round with a smooth, fairly fast movement. *Bonnie twirled her empty glass in her fingers... All around me leaves twirl to the ground.* V-ERG =spin; V n; V prep/adv; Also V

2 If you **twirl**, you move round and round rapidly, for example when you are dancing. *Several hundred people twirl around the ballroom dance floor.* VERB =whirl; V prep/adv

3 If you **twirl** something such as your hair, you twist it around your finger. *Sarah lifted her hand and started twirling a strand of hair.* VERB; V n

twist /twɪst/ **twists, twisting, twisted** ◆◆◆◇◇

1 If you **twist** something, you turn it to make a spiral shape, for example by turning the two ends of it in opposite directions. *Her hands began to twist the handles of the bag she carried... Twist the string carefully around the second stem with the other hand... She twisted her hair into a bun and pinned it at the back of her head.* VERB; V n; V n adv/prep

2 If you **twist** something, especially a part of your body, or if it **twists**, it moves into a strange, uncomfortable, or distorted shape or position, for example as a result of violence or strong emotion. *He twisted her arms behind her back and clipped a pair of handcuffs on her wrists... Sophia's face twisted in perplexity... Her hands twisted in her lap... The body was twisted, its legs at an awkward angle... The car was left a mess of twisted metal.* V-ERG; V n prep; V; V-ed

3 If you **twist** part of your body such as your head or your shoulders, you turn that part while keeping the rest of your body still. *She twisted her head sideways and looked towards the door... Susan twisted round in her seat until she could see Graham and Sabrina behind her... Holding your arms straight out in front of you, twist to the right and left.* VERB; V n adv; V adv/prep

4 If you **twist** a part of your body such as your ankle or wrist, you injure it by turning it too sharply, or in an unusual direction. *He fell and twisted his ankle... Rupert Moon is out of today's session with a twisted knee.* VERB; V n; V-ed

5 If you **twist** something, you turn it so that it moves around in a circular direction. *She was staring down at her hands, twisting the ring on her finger... She twisted the handle and opened the door... Reaching up to a cupboard he takes out a jar and twists the lid off.* ► Also a noun. *The bag is resealed with a simple twist of the valve.* VERB; V n; V n with adv; N-COUNT: oft N *of* n

6 If a road or river **twists**, it has a lot of sudden changes of direction in it. *The roads twist round hairpin bends... The lane twists and turns between pleasant but unspectacular cottages.* ► Also a noun. *It allows the train to maintain a constant speed through the twists and turns of existing track.* VERB; V prep; V; N-COUNT: usu pl

7 If you say that someone **has twisted** something that you have said, you disapprove of them because they have repeated it in a way that changes its meaning, in order to harm you or benefit themselves. *It's a shame the way that the media can twist your words and misrepresent you... Even remarks that were quite innocent could be twisted to produce an unintended effect.* VERB PRAGMATICS =distort; V n

8 A **twist** in something is an unexpected and significant development. *...the twists and turns of economic policy... The battle of the sexes also took a new twist... Roger Hardy of the BBC looks at this latest twist in the political crisis in Algeria... As so often happens, this little story has a twist in the tail.* N-COUNT

9 A **twist** is the shape that something has when it has been twisted. *...bunches of violets in twists of paper... A thin twist of smoke curled from the cottage's single chimney.* N-COUNT: usu N *of* n

10 **The twist** is a dance that was popular in the 1960's, in which you twist your body and move your hips vigorously. N-SING: *the* N

11 If something happens by **a twist of fate**, it happens by chance, and it is strange, interesting, or unfortunate in some way; an expression used by journalists. *By a curious twist of fate, cricket was also my favourite sport... In a cruel twist of fate, Ann's husband Bill is also suffering from the disease.* PHRASE: *twist* inflects, usu *by/in* PHR

12 See also **twisted.** • **to twist** someone**'s arm**: see **arm.** • **to get** your **knickers in a twist**: see **knickers.** • **to twist the knife**: see **knife.**

twisted /twɪstɪd/. If you describe a person as **twisted**, you dislike them because you think they are strange in an unpleasant way. *He has been described as bitter and twisted, a man scorned... The letter showed horribly clearly the workings of a twisted mind.* ADJ-GRADED PRAGMATICS =warped

twisty /twɪsti/. A **twisty** road, track, or river has a lot of sharp bends and corners. *The drive required going down a quite twisty road.* ADJ-GRADED

twit /twɪt/ **twits.** If you call someone as a **twit**, you are insulting them and saying that they are silly or stupid; an informal word, used mainly in British English. N-COUNT PRAGMATICS =twerp

twitch /twɪtʃ/ **twitches, twitching, twitched.** ◆◇◇◇◇ If something, especially a part of your body, **twitches** or you **twitch** it, it makes a little jerking movement. *When I stood up to her, her right cheek would begin to twitch... His left eyelid twitched involuntarily... As they turned to leave, they saw the curtains twitch in the house next door... Stern twitched his shoulders.* ► Also a noun. *He developed a nervous twitch and began to blink constantly.* V-ERG; V; V; V n; N-COUNT

twitcher /twɪtʃər/ **twitchers.** In British English, a **twitcher** is an enthusiastic bird-watcher; an informal word. N-COUNT

twitchy /twɪtʃi/. If you are **twitchy**, you are anxious or uneasy about something and so are behaving in a rather nervous, unpredictable way; an informal word. *He was still twitchy and we awaited Ann's return anxiously... Afraid of bad publicity, the department had suddenly become very twitchy about journalists.* ADJ-GRADED =jumpy

twitter /twɪtər/ **twitters, twittering, twittered**

1 When birds **twitter**, they make a lot of short high-pitched sounds. *There were birds twittering in the eucalyptus trees. ...a tree filled with twittering birds.* ► Also a noun. *Naomi would waken to the twitter of birds.* VERB; V; V-ing; N-UNCOUNT: usu N *of* n

2 If you say that someone **is twittering** about VERB

something, you mean that they are speaking about silly or unimportant things, usually rather fast or in a high-pitched voice. *...debutantes twittering excitedly about Christian Dior dresses... She laughs, blushes and twitters: 'Oh, doesn't Giles have just the most charming sense of humour?'* =prattle V *about* n V with quote Also V

two /tuː/ **twos** ◆◆◆◆◆
1 **Two** is the number 2. NUM
2 If you say **it takes two** or **it takes two to tango**, you mean that a situation or argument involves two people and they are both therefore responsible for it. *Divorce is never the fault of one partner; it takes two... It takes two to tango and so far our relationship has been one-sided.* PHRASES
3 If you **put two and two together**, you work out the truth about something for yourself, by using the clues available to you. *Putting two and two together, I assume that this was the car he used.* V inflects
4 ● to **kill two birds with one stone**: see **bird**.
● **two a penny**: see **penny**.

two-dimensional; also spelled **two dimensional**.
1 A **two-dimensional** object or figure is flat rather than solid and can be measured only in the dimensions of length and width. *...new software, which generates both two-dimensional drawings and three-dimensional images.* ADJ: usu ADJ n
2 If you describe fictional characters as **two-dimensional**, you are critical of them because they are very simple and not realistic enough to be taken seriously. *I found the characters very two-dimensional, not to say dull.* ADJ-GRADED PRAGMATICS

two-faced. If you describe someone as **two-faced**, you are critical of them because they say they do or believe one thing when their behaviour or words show that they do not do it or do not believe it. *He had been devious and two-faced... The scientists saw the public as being particularly two-faced about animal welfare in view of the way domestic animals are treated.* ADJ-GRADED: usu v-link ADJ PRAGMATICS

twofold /tuːfould/; also spelled **two-fold**. You can use **twofold** to introduce a topic that has two equally important parts; a formal word. *The purpose of the ambassador's visit is twofold – to step up pressure on the invaders to withdraw peacefully, and to intensify preparations for war if that pressure fails.* ADJ PRAGMATICS

two-handed. A **two-handed** blow or catch is done using both hands. *...a brilliant two-handed catch by Atherton.* ADJ: usu ADJ n, also ADJ after v

two-piece, two-pieces; also spelled **two piece**. ◆◇◇◇◇
1 You can use **two-piece** to describe something, especially a set of clothing, that is in two parts. *She was wearing a simple light-grey two-piece suit. ...a two-piece bathing suit. ...a two-piece telescopic truncheon made of aluminium.* ADJ: ADJ n
2 A **two-piece** is a woman's suit which consists of a jacket and a skirt or pair of trousers. *...a woman in a check two-piece.* N-COUNT

twosome /tuːsəm/ **twosomes.** A **twosome** is a group of two people. N-COUNT

two-thirds; also spelled **two thirds**. **Two-thirds of** something is an amount that is two out of three equal parts of it. *Two-thirds of householders in this country live in a mortgaged home... Stir the chopped chocolate, fruit and nuts into two-thirds of the cheese mixture.* ◆◆◇◇◇ QUANT: QUANT *of* n
► Also a pronoun. *The United States and Russia hope to conclude a treaty to cut their nuclear arsenals by two-thirds.* PRON
► Also an adverb. *Do not fill the container more than two-thirds full... A second book has already been commissioned and is two-thirds finished.* ADV: ADV adj/-ed
► Also an adjective. *...the two thirds majority in parliament needed to make constitutional changes.* ADJ: ADJ n

two-way ◆◇◇◇◇
1 **Two-way** means moving or working in two opposite directions or allowing something to move or work in two opposite directions. *The bridge is now open to two-way traffic... Two-way trade between the two countries increased by more than forty per cent last year... They were spied on via a two-way mirror.* ADJ: usu ADJ n
2 A **two-way** radio or transmitter can both send and receive signals. ADJ: ADJ n
3 If there is **two-way** co-operation or learning, two people or groups are both helping the other or both learning from the other. *Education is a two-way process... Trust is a two-way thing.* ADJ: ADJ n =mutual

tycoon /taɪkuːn/ **tycoons.** A **tycoon** is a person who is successful in business and so has become rich and powerful. *...a self-made Australian property tycoon.*  N-COUNT =magnate

tyke /taɪk/ **tykes.** You can refer to a child, especially a naughty or mischievous one, as a **tyke** when you want to show affection for them; an informal word. N-COUNT PRAGMATICS

type 1 sort or kind

type /taɪp/ **types** ◆◆◆◆◇
1 A **type** of something is a group of those things that have particular features in common. *...several types of lettuce... There are various types of the disease... In 1990, 25% of households were of this type.* N-COUNT: usu with supp, oft N *of* n =sort, kind
2 If you refer to a particular thing or person as a **type** of something more general, you are considering that thing or person as an example of that more general group. *Have you done this type of work before?... Rates of interest for this type of borrowing can be high... I am a very determined type of person.* N-COUNT: with supp, usu N *of* n =sort, kind
3 If you refer to a person as a particular **type**, you mean that they have that particular appearance, character, or type of behaviour. *It's the first time I, a fair-skinned, freckly type, have sailed in the sun without burning... I was rather an outdoor type... Miranda was certainly not the type to murder her husband.* N-COUNT: usu supp N =sort
4 If you say that someone is **not** your **type**, you mean that they are not the sort of person who you usually find attractive; an informal expression. *At first I thought he was rather ordinary looking, a little chubby, not my type... I'm not his type. I am probably too strong a character.* PHRASE: v-link PHR
5 See also **blood type**.

type 2 writing and printing

type /taɪp/ **types, typing, typed** ◆◆◆◆◇
1 If you **type** something, you use a typewriter or word processor to write it. *I can type your essays for you... I had never really learnt to type properly... The letter consists of six closely typed pages.* VERB V n V V-ed
2 **Type** is printed text as it appears in a book or newspaper, or the small pieces of metal that are used to create this. *The correction had already been set in type.* N-UNCOUNT
3 See also **typing**.

type in or **type into.** If you **type** information **into** a computer or **type** it **in**, you press keys on the keyboard so that the computer stores or processes the information. *Officials type each passport number into a computer... You have to type in commands, such as 'help' and 'print'... You type things in, and it responds.* PHRASAL VERB V n P n V P n (not pron) V n P

type out. If you **type** something **out**, you write it in full using a typewriter or word processor. *The two of us stood by while two typists typed out the whole document again... I read it down the phone to a man called Dave, who typed it out.* PHRASAL VERB =type V P n (not pron) V n P

type up. If you **type up** a handwritten text, you produce a typed copy of it. *They didn't get around to typing up the letter... When the first draft was completed, Nichols typed it up.* PHRASAL VERB V P n (not pron) V n P

typecast /taɪpkɑːst, -kæst/ **typecasts, typecasting;** the form **typecast** is used in the present tense and is the past tense and past participle. If an actor **is typecast**, they play the same type of character in every play or film that they are in. *I didn't want to be typecast and I think I've maintained a large variety in the roles I've played... African-Americans were often typecast as servants, entertainers or criminals.* VB: usu passive *be* V-ed *be* V-ed *as* n
♦ **typecasting** *She was always keen to shake off the early typecasting as the empty-headed sex symbol.* N-UNCOUNT

typeface /taɪpfeɪs/ **typefaces.** In printing, a **typeface** is a set of alphabetical, numerical, and other characters that share a common design. There are many different typefaces. N-COUNT

typescript /taɪpskrɪpt/ **typescripts.** A **typescript** is a typed copy of an essay, article, or literary work. N-VAR

typewriter /taɪpraɪtəʳ/ **typewriters.** A **typewriter** is a machine with keys which are pressed in order to print letters, numbers, or other characters onto paper. ◆◇◇◇◇ N-COUNT

typewritten /taɪprɪtᵊn/. A **typewritten** document has been typed on a typewriter or word processor. ADJ

typhoid /taɪfɔɪd/. **Typhoid** or **typhoid fever** is a serious infectious disease that produces fever and diarrhoea and can cause death. It is spread by dirty water or food. N-UNCOUNT

typhoon /taɪfuːn/ **typhoons.** A **typhoon** is a very violent tropical storm. ◆◇◇◇◇ N-COUNT

typhus /taɪfəs/. **Typhus** is a serious infectious disease that produces a skin rash, a high fever, and a severe headache. N-UNCOUNT

typical /tɪpɪkᵊl/ ◆◆◆◇◇

1 You use **typical** to describe someone or something that shows the most usual characteristics of a particular type of person or thing, and is therefore a good example of that type. *Cheney is everyone's image of a typical cop: a big white guy, six foot, 220 pounds... Carole goes in for such typical schoolgirl pastimes as horse-riding and watching old films... Horrigan was typical of the new-generation executive Sticht had brought into the company.* ADJ-GRADED

2 If a particular action or feature is **typical** of someone or something, it shows their usual qualities or characteristics. *This reluctance to move towards a democratic state is typical of totalitarian regimes... This is not typical of Chinese, but is a feature of the Thai language... With typical energy he found new journalistic outlets.* ADJ-GRADED: usu v-link ADJ, oft ADJ *of* n =characteristic

3 If you say that something is **typical** of a person, situation, or thing, you are criticizing or complaining about them and saying that they are just as bad or disappointing as you expected them to be. *She threw her hands into the air. 'That is just typical of you, isn't it?'... 'Typical!' Hattie slammed down the receiver. 'Absolutely typical!'* ADJ-GRADED: usu v-link ADJ, oft ADJ *of* n PRAGMATICS

typically /tɪpɪkəli/ ◆◆◇◇◇

1 You use **typically** to say that something usually happens in the way that you are describing. *Typically, parents apply to several schools and settle, if need be, for their fourth or fifth choice... It typically takes a day or two, depending on size... Today's organic wine producer is typically a small, quality-conscious family concern... Female migrants are typically very young.* ADV-GRADED: ADV with cl/group =normally

2 You use **typically** to say that something shows all the most usual characteristics of a particular type of person or thing. *The main course was typically Swiss... Philip paced the floor, a typically nervous expectant father.* ADV-GRADED: ADV adj =characteristically

3 You use **typically** to indicate that someone has behaved in the way that they normally do. *Typically, the Norwegians were on the mountain two hours before anyone else... Robbins is typically cool in his pronouncements about his future.* ADV-GRADED: ADV with cl, ADV adj =characteristically

typify /tɪpɪfaɪ/ **typifies, typifying, typified.** If something or someone **typifies** a situation or type of thing or person, they have all the usual characteristics of it and are a typical example of it. *These two buildings typify the rich extremes of Irish architecture. ...a reaction against the achievements of science, as typified by the development of nuclear weapons. ...a more intelligent and articulate breed of disc jockeys, typified by university graduate Simon Mayo.* ◆◇◇◇◇ VERB =epitomize; V n

typing /taɪpɪŋ/ ◆◇◇◇◇

1 Typing is the work or activity of typing something by means of a typewriter or word processor. *She didn't do any typing till the evening.* N-UNCOUNT

2 Typing is the skill of using a typewriter or keyboard quickly and accurately. *My typing is quite dreadful... Ginny tried to sharpen up some rusty typing skills.* N-UNCOUNT: usu with supp, oft poss N

typist /taɪpɪst/ **typists.** A **typist** is someone who works in an office typing letters and other documents. N-COUNT

typographical /taɪpəgræfɪkᵊl/. **Typographical** relates to the way in which printed material is presented. *Owing to a typographical error, the town of Longridge was spelt as Longbridge.* ADJ: ADJ n

typography /taɪpɒgrəfi/. **Typography** is the way in which written material is arranged and prepared for printing. N-UNCOUNT

typology /taɪpɒlədʒi/ **typologies.** A **typology** is a system for dividing things into different types, especially in science and the social sciences; a formal word. N-COUNT

tyrannical /tɪrænɪkᵊl/

1 If you describe someone as **tyrannical**, you mean that they are severe or unfair towards the people that they have authority over. *He killed his tyrannical father with a blow to the head... His behavior grew more unpredictable by the day, and increasingly tyrannical.* ADJ-GRADED

2 If you describe a government or organization as **tyrannical**, you mean that it acts without considering the wishes of its people and treats them cruelly or unfairly. *...one of the world's most oppressive and tyrannical regimes.* ADJ-GRADED

tyrannize /tɪrənaɪz/ **tyrannizes, tyrannizing, tyrannized;** also spelled **tyrannise** in British English. If you say that one person **tyrannizes** another, you mean that the first person uses their power over the second person in order to treat them very cruelly and unfairly. *...fathers who tyrannize their families... Armed groups use their power to tyrannise over civilians.* VERB; V n; V *over* n; Also V

tyranny /tɪrəni/ **tyrannies** ◆◇◇◇◇

1 A **tyranny** is a cruel, unfair, and oppressive regime in which a person or small group of people have absolute power over everyone else. *He described these regimes as tyrannies and dictatorships... Self-expression and individuality are the greatest weapons against tyranny.* N-VAR

2 If you describe someone's behaviour and treatment of others that they have authority over as **tyranny**, you mean that they are severe with them or unfair to them. *I'm the sole victim of Mother's violence and tyranny.* N-UNCOUNT

3 You can describe something that you have to use or have as a **tyranny** if you think it is undesirable or unpleasant. *The telephone is one of the great tyrannies of modern life.* N-COUNT: oft N *of* n

tyrant /taɪərənt/ **tyrants.** You can use **tyrant** to refer to someone who treats the people they have authority over in a cruel and unfair way. *Since 1804 the country has mostly been ruled by tyrants. ...households where the father was a tyrant.* ◆◇◇◇◇ N-COUNT

tyre /taɪəʳ/ **tyres;** spelled **tire** in American English. A **tyre** is a thick piece of rubber which is fitted onto the wheels of vehicles such as cars, buses, and bicycles. • See also **spare tyre**. ◆◆◇◇◇ N-COUNT

tyro /taɪroʊ/ **tyros.** A **tyro** is someone who is just beginning to learn something or who has very little experience of something; used mainly in journalism. *...a tyro journalist.* N-COUNT: oft N n

U u

U, u, U's, u's /juː/
1 **U** is the twenty-first letter of the English alphabet. N-VAR
2 **U** or **u** is used as an abbreviation for words beginning with the letter 'u', such as 'unit', 'united', or 'University'.

ubiquitous /juːbɪkwɪtəs/. If you describe something or someone as **ubiquitous**, you mean that they are so widespread that they seem to be everywhere at the same time. *Sugar is ubiquitous in the diet... In the US, the camcorder has become ubiquitous... She is one of the wealthiest, most ubiquitous media personalities around.* ◆◇◇◇◇ ADJ-GRADED

ubiquity /juːbɪkwɪti/. If you talk about the **ubiquity** of something, you mean that it is so widespread that it seems to be everywhere at the same time. N-UNCOUNT: oft N *of* n

udder /ʌdəʳ/ **udders.** A cow's **udder** is the organ that hangs below its body and produces milk. N-COUNT

UFO /juː ef oʊ, juːfoʊ/ **UFOs.** A **UFO** is an object seen in the sky or landing on earth which cannot be identified and which is often believed to be from another planet. It is an abbreviation for 'unidentified flying object'. *There has been a surge of UFO sightings in America.* N-COUNT

Ugandan /juːgændən/ **Ugandans** ◆◆◆◆◇
1 **Ugandan** means belonging or relating to Uganda or to its people or culture. *...the Ugandan capital, Kampala.* ADJ
2 A **Ugandan** is a Ugandan citizen, or a person of Ugandan origin. N-COUNT

ugh. **Ugh** is used in writing to represent the sound that people make if they think something is unpleasant, horrible, or disgusting. *Ugh - it was horrible.* ◆◇◇◇◇ EXCLAM

ugly /ʌgli/ **uglier, ugliest** ◆◆◇◇◇
1 If you say that someone or something is **ugly**, you mean that they are very unattractive and unpleasant to look at. *...an ugly little hat... She makes me feel dowdy and ugly.* ♦ **ugliness** *...the raw ugliness of his native city.* ADJ-GRADED ≠beautiful; N-UNCOUNT ≠beauty
2 If you refer to an event, situation, or issue as **ugly**, you mean that it is very unpleasant, usually because it involves violence or aggression. *There have been some ugly scenes... The confrontation turned ugly. ...an ugly publicity stunt.* ♦ **ugliness** *...the subtlety and ugliness of sexual harassment.* ADJ-GRADED; N-UNCOUNT: usu with supp
3 ● **to rear** its **ugly head**: see **head**.

ugly duckling, ugly ducklings. If you say that someone, especially a child, is an **ugly duckling**, you mean that they are unattractive or awkward now, but will probably develop into an attractive and successful person. *She was a shy, ugly duckling of a child.* N-COUNT: usu sing

UHF /juː eɪtʃ ef/. **UHF** is used of a range of radio waves which allows a radio or television receiver to produce a good quality of sound. It is an abbreviation for 'ultra-high frequency'. *...Boston UHF channels.* N-UNCOUNT: oft N n

uh huh; also spelled **uh-huh**. **Uh huh** is used in written English to represent a sound that people make when they are agreeing with you, when they want to show that they understand what you are saying, or when they are answering 'yes' to a question; used in informal English. *'Did she?'—'Uh huh.'... 'Oh that one'—'Uh huh.'* ◆◆◇◇◇ CONVENTION PRAGMATICS

UHT /juː eɪtʃ tiː/. **UHT** is used to describe milk which has been treated at a very high temperature so that it can be kept for a long time if the container is not opened. It is an abbreviation for 'ultra-heat-treated'. ADJ: usu ADJ n =long-life

UK /juː keɪ/. **The UK** is Great Britain and Northern Ireland. It is an abbreviation for 'United Kingdom'. ◆◆◆◆◇ N-PROPER: *the* N

ukulele /juːkəleɪli/ **ukuleles;** also spelled **ukelele.** A **ukulele** is a small guitar with four strings. N-COUNT

ulcer /ʌlsəʳ/ **ulcers.** An **ulcer** is a sore area on a part of your body which is very painful and may bleed, or which may produce an unpleasant poisonous substance. Ulcers can be outside your body or inside, for example in your mouth or stomach. *In addition to headaches, you may develop stomach ulcers as well.* ◆◇◇◇◇ N-COUNT

ulcerated /ʌlsəreɪtɪd/. If a part of someone's body is **ulcerated**, ulcers have developed on it. *They are used to cure ulcerated mouths and various throat infections... Every inch of his arms and legs was ulcerated.* ADJ

ulterior /ʌltɪəriəʳ/. If you say that someone has **ulterior** motives for doing something, you believe that they have hidden reasons for what they are doing. *Sheila had an ulterior motive for trying to help Stan... Posing for the camera pleased him more than anything else. No doubt with the ulterior object of catching votes.* ADJ: ADJ n

ultimate /ʌltɪmət/ ◆◆◆◇◇
1 You use **ultimate** to describe the final result or aim of a long series of events. *He said it is still not possible to predict the ultimate outcome... The ultimate aim is to expand the network further.* ADJ: ADJ n =final, eventual
2 You use **ultimate** to describe the original source or cause of something. *Plants are the ultimate source of all foodstuffs... The ultimate cause of what's happened seems to have been the advertising campaign.* ADJ: ADJ n =fundamental
3 You use **ultimate** to describe the most important or powerful thing of a particular kind. *...the ultimate power of the central government... Of course, the ultimate authority remained the presidency... My experience as player, coach and manager has prepared me for this ultimate challenge.* ADJ: ADJ n
4 You use **ultimate** to describe the most extreme and unpleasant example of a particular thing. *Bringing back the death penalty would be the ultimate abuse of human rights... Treachery was the ultimate sin... Coleman lives in fear of the ultimate disgrace.* ADJ: ADJ n =worst
5 You use **ultimate** to describe the best possible example of a particular thing. *He is the ultimate English gentleman... Caviar and oysters on ice are generally considered the ultimate luxury foods.* ADJ: ADJ n =best
6 **The ultimate in** something is the best or most advanced example of it. *Ballet is the ultimate in human movement... This hotel is the ultimate in luxury... Working from home offers the ultimate in flexible life styles.* PHRASE: PHR n/-ing, usu v-link PHR, PHR after v

ultimately /ʌltɪmətli/ ◆◆◆◇◇
1 **Ultimately** means finally, after a long and often complicated series of events. *Whatever the scientists ultimately conclude, all of their data will immediately be disputed. ...a tough but ultimately worthwhile struggle.* ADV: ADV with v, ADV adj =in the end
2 You use **ultimately** to indicate that what you are saying is the most important point in a discussion. *Ultimately, Bismarck's revisionism scarcely affected or damaged British interests at all.* ADV: ADV with cl PRAGMATICS

ultimatum /ʌltɪmeɪtəm/ **ultimatums.** An **ultimatum** is a warning to someone that unless they act in a particular way, action will be taken against them. *They issued an ultimatum to the police to rid an area of racist attackers, or they* ◆◇◇◇◇ N-COUNT *will take the law into their own hands. ...a 48-hour ultimatum.*

ultra- /ʌltrə-/. **Ultra-** is added to adjectives to form other adjectives that emphasize that something or someone has a quality to an extreme degree. *...a wide range of ultra-modern equipment. ...an ultra-ambitious executive.* PREFIX PRAGMATICS

ultramarine /ʌltrəməriːn/. **Ultramarine** is used to describe things that are very bright blue in colour. *...an ultramarine sky.* COLOUR

ultrasonic /ʌltrəsɒnɪk/. **Ultrasonic** sounds have very high frequencies, which human beings cannot hear. ADJ: usu ADJ n

ultrasound /ʌltrəsaʊnd/. **Ultrasound** is used to refer to sound waves which travel at such a high frequency that they cannot be heard by humans. Ultrasound is used in medicine to perform scans of people's bodies. *I had an ultrasound scan to see how the pregnancy was progressing.* ◆◇◇◇◇ N-UNCOUNT: usu N n

ultraviolet /ʌltrəvaɪələt/. **Ultraviolet** light or radiation is what causes your skin to become darker in colour after you have been in sunlight. In large amounts ultraviolet light is harmful. *The sun's ultraviolet rays are responsible for both tanning and burning.* ◆◇◇◇◇ ADJ: usu ADJ n

ululate /juːljʊleɪt, AM ʌl-/ **ululates, ululating, ululated.** To **ululate** means to howl or wail loudly; a literary word. *They ululated like Red Indians... He let out this long ululating moan.* VERB V V-ing

um. **Um** is used in writing to represent a sound that people make when they are hesitating, usually while deciding what they want to say next. *'What are you doing here, Mrs Stebbing?' Millson asked sternly.'Um .. well ..I thought I'd pop in and empty Janet's fridge.'* ◆◇◇◇◇ PRAGMATICS

umber /ʌmbəʳ/. **Umber** is used to describe things that are yellowish or reddish brown in colour. *...umber paint.* COLOUR

umbilical cord /ʌmbɪlɪkəl kɔːʳd/ **umbilical cords**

1 An **umbilical cord** is the tube connecting an unborn baby to its mother, through which it receives oxygen and nutrients. N-COUNT: usu sing

2 If you say that one person, organization, or country has **cut** its **umbilical cord** with another, you mean that they have done something that makes them more independent. *The referendum will bring Puerto Rico one step closer to cutting the island's umbilical cord to the United States... I will never forget all you've done for me, but it's time to cut the umbilical cord.* PHRASE: V and N inflect

umbrage /ʌmbrɪdʒ/. If you say that someone **takes umbrage**, you mean that they are offended or upset by something that someone says or does to them, often without sufficient reason. *He takes umbrage against anyone who criticises him.* PHRASE: V inflects =take offence

umbrella /ʌmbrelə/ **umbrellas** ◆◆◇◇◇

1 An **umbrella** is an object which you use to protect yourself from the rain or hot sun. It consists of a long stick with a folding frame covered in cloth. *Harry held an umbrella over Dawn.* N-COUNT

2 **Umbrella** is used to refer to a single group or description that includes a lot of different organizations or ideas. *Does coincidence come under the umbrella of the paranormal? ...Socialist International, an umbrella group comprising almost a hundred Social Democrat parties... Within the umbrella term 'dementia' there are many different kinds of disease.* N-SING: usu N of n, supp N, N n

3 **Umbrella** is used to refer to a system or agreement which protects a country or group of people. *These Cambodians are under the protective umbrella of the United Nations... Britain cannot avoid being under the US nuclear umbrella, whether it wants to or not.* N-SING: N of n, supp N

umlaut /ʊmlaʊt/ **umlauts.** An **umlaut** is a symbol that is written over vowels in German and some other languages to indicate the way in which they should be pronounced. For example, the word 'über' has an umlaut over the 'u'. N-COUNT

umpire /ʌmpaɪəʳ/ **umpires, umpiring, umpired** ◆◆◇◇◇

1 An **umpire** is a person whose job is to make sure that a sports match or contest is played fairly and that the rules are not broken. *The umpire's decision is final.* N-COUNT

2 To **umpire** means to be the umpire in a sports match or contest. *He umpired baseball games... He umpired for school football matches until he was in his late 50s.* VERB V n V

umpteen /ʌmptiːn/. **Umpteen** can be used to refer to an extremely large number of things or people; an informal word. *He was interrupted by applause umpteen times... He has produced umpteen books, plays and television series.* DET: DET pl-n =countless

umpteenth /ʌmptiːnθ/. You use **umpteenth** to indicate that an occasion, thing, or person happens or comes after many others; an informal word. *He checked his watch for the umpteenth time... She was now on her umpteenth gin.* ORD

un- /ʌn-/

1 **Un-** is added to the beginning of adjectives, adverbs, and nouns, in order to form words that have the opposite meaning. *My father was an unemployed labourer... He had sensed his mother's unhappiness.* PREFIX

2 **Un-** is added to the beginning of a verb that describes a process, in order to form another verb that describes the reverse of that process. *He undressed and draped his clothes neatly over the back of the chair... She was anxious for me to unwrap the other gifts.* PREFIX

3 **Un-** is added to the beginning of the past participle of a verb, in order to form an adjective that means that the process described by the verb has not happened. *The theory remains untested... Dealers across the country continue to complain about huge stocks of unsold cars.* PREFIX

UN /juː en/. The **UN** is the same as the **United Nations**. *...a UN peacekeeping mission.* ◆◆◆◆◇ N-PROPER

unabashed /ʌnəbæʃt/. If you describe someone as **unabashed**, you mean that they are not ashamed, embarrassed, or shy about something, especially when you think most people would be. *He seems unabashed by his recent defeat... He's an unabashed, old-fashioned romantic.* ADJ

unabated /ʌnəbeɪtɪd/. If something continues **unabated**, it continues without any reduction in intensity or amount. *The fighting has continued unabated for over 24 hours. ...his unabated enthusiasm for cinema.* ADJ: usu ADJ after v, also ADJ n, v-link ADJ

unable /ʌneɪbəl/. If you are **unable** to do something, it is impossible for you to do it, for example because you do not have the necessary skill or knowledge, or because you do not have enough time or money. *The military may feel unable to hand over power to a civilian President next year... Unable any longer to keep from breaking in she said, 'I simply cannot believe you're serious.'* ◆◆◆◇◇ ADJ: v-link ADJ to-inf ≠able

unabridged /ʌnəbrɪdʒd/. An **unabridged** piece of writing, for example a book or article, is complete and not shortened in any way. *...the unabridged version of 'War and Peace'.* ADJ =full-length

unacceptable /ʌnəkseptəbəl/. If you describe something as **unacceptable**, you strongly disapprove of it or object to it and feel that it should not be allowed to continue. *It is totally unacceptable for children to swear... Joanna left her husband because of his unacceptable behaviour.* ◆◆◇◇◇ ADJ-GRADED

♦ **unacceptably** /ʌnəkseptəbli/ *The reform program has brought unacceptably high unemployment and falling wages.* ADV-GRADED: usu ADV adj, also ADV after v

unaccompanied /ʌnəkʌmpənid/

1 If someone is **unaccompanied**, they are alone. *It is estimated that every year 50 unaccompanied children arrive in Britain... Kelly's too young to go unaccompanied.* ADJ: ADJ n, ADJ after v, v-link ADJ

2 **Unaccompanied** luggage or goods are being sent or transported separately from their owner. *Unaccompanied bags are either searched or removed.* ADJ: ADJ n

3 An **unaccompanied** voice or instrument sings or plays alone, with no other instruments playing at the same time. *...an unaccompanied flute... The piece is most often sung unaccompanied.* ADJ: ADJ n, ADJ after v

unaccountable /ʌnəkaʊntəbᵊl/
1 Something that is **unaccountable** does not seem to have any sensible explanation. *For some unaccountable reason, it struck me as extremely funny... He had an unaccountable change of mind.* ADJ-GRADED: usu ADJ n =inexplicable
♦ **unaccountably** /ʌnəkaʊntəbli/ *And then, unaccountably, she giggled... Leonard felt unaccountably happy.* ADV-GRADED
2 If you describe a person or organization as **unaccountable**, you are critical of them because they are not responsible to anyone for their actions, or do not feel they have to explain their actions to anyone. *Economic policy in Europe should not be run by an unaccountable committee of governors of central banks. ...an arrogant, unaccountable police chief.* ADJ-GRADED PRAGMATICS ≠accountable

unaccounted for /ʌnəkaʊntɪd fɔːʳ/. If people or things are **unaccounted for**, you do not know where they are or what has happened to them. *5,000 American servicemen who fought in Korea are still unaccounted for... About £50 million from the robbery five years ago is unaccounted for.* ADJ: v-link ADJ

unaccustomed /ʌnəkʌstəmd/
1 If you are **unaccustomed to** something, you do not know it very well or have not experienced it very often; used in written English. *They were unaccustomed to such military setbacks... It is a part of Britain as yet largely unaccustomed to tourists.* ADJ-GRADED: v-link ADJ *to* n/-ing =unused ≠accustomed
2 If you describe someone's behaviour or experiences as **unaccustomed**, you mean that they do not usually behave like this or have experiences of this kind; used in written English. *He began to comfort me with such unaccustomed gentleness... His nose had been reddened by unaccustomed exposure to the California sun.* ADJ-GRADED: ADJ n

unacknowledged /ʌnæknɒlɪdʒd/
1 If you describe something or someone as **unacknowledged**, you mean that people ignore their existence or presence, or are not aware of it. *Unresolved or unacknowledged fears can trigger sleepwalking.* ADJ: usu ADJ n
2 If you describe something or someone as **unacknowledged**, you mean that their existence or importance is not recognized officially or publicly. *This tradition goes totally unacknowledged in official guidebooks... Johnny and Guy are the greatest unacknowledged pop songwriters in Britain.* ADJ-GRADED

unacquainted /ʌnəkweɪntɪd/. If you are **unacquainted with** something, you do not know about it or do not have not any experience of it. *Professor Baker is unacquainted with the idea of representative democracy... I was then totally unacquainted with his poems.* ADJ-GRADED: v-link ADJ *with* n =unfamiliar

unadorned /ʌnədɔːʳnd/. Something that is **unadorned** is plain, rather than having decorations or being artistically designed. *The room is typically simple and unadorned, with white walls and a tiled floor.* ADJ

unadulterated /ʌnədʌltəreɪtɪd/
1 Something that is **unadulterated** is completely pure and has had nothing added to it. *Organic food is unadulterated food produced without artificial chemicals or pesticides.* ADJ ≠adulterated
2 You can also use **unadulterated** to emphasize a particular quality, often a bad quality. *It was pure, unadulterated hell.* ADJ: ADJ n PRAGMATICS

unaffected /ʌnəfektɪd/ ◆◇◇◇◇
1 If someone or something is **unaffected** by an event or occurrence, they are not changed by it in any way. *She seemed totally unaffected by what she'd drunk... The strike shut down 50 airports, but most international flights were unaffected.* ADJ-GRADED: v-link ADJ, oft ADJ *by* n
2 If you describe someone as **unaffected**, you approve of them because they are natural and genuine in their behaviour, and not snobbish or pretentious. *...this unaffected, charming couple.* ADJ-GRADED PRAGMATICS =genuine

unafraid /ʌnəfreɪd/. If you are **unafraid** to do something, you are confident and not at all nervous about doing it. *He is a man with a reputation for being tough and unafraid of unpopular decisions... She was a forceful intellectual unafraid to speak her mind.* ADJ: v-link ADJ, ADJ after v, oft ADJ *of* n, ADJ to-inf ≠afraid

unaided /ʌneɪdɪd/. If you do something **unaided**, you do it without help from anyone or anything else. *There have been at least thirteen previous attempts to reach the North Pole unaided... She brought us up completely unaided. ...the smallest speck of matter visible to the unaided eye.* ADJ: usu ADJ after v, also ADJ n

unalloyed /ʌnəlɔɪd/. If you describe a feeling such as happiness or relief as **unalloyed**, you are emphasizing that it is perfect and complete; a literary word. *...an occasion of unalloyed joy.* ADJ: usu ADJ n PRAGMATICS

unalterable /ʌnɔːltərəbᵊl/. Something that is **unalterable** cannot be changed. *...an unalterable fact of life.* ADJ: usu ADJ n =unchangeable

unaltered /ʌnɔːltəʳd/. Something that remains **unaltered** has not changed or been changed. *The rest of the apartment had fortunately remained unaltered since that time... These were my opinions, and they continue unaltered.* ADJ: v-link ADJ, ADJ after v, ADJ n =unchanged

unambiguous /ʌnæmbɪgjuəs/. If you describe a message or comment as **unambiguous**, you mean that it is clear and cannot be misunderstood. *...an election result that sent the party an unambiguous message... The close-up photography and commentary are clear and unambiguous.* ◆◇◇◇◇ ADJ-GRADED ≠ambiguous
♦ **unambiguously** *He has failed to dissociate himself clearly and unambiguously from the attack.* ADV-GRADED: usu ADV with v, also ADV adj

unambitious /ʌnæmbɪʃəs/
1 An **unambitious** person is not particularly interested in improving their position in life or in being successful, rich, or powerful. *He was a reliable, unambitious officer who did as he was told.* ADJ-GRADED ≠ambitious
2 An **unambitious** idea or plan is not very risky or adventurous, and is easy to carry out successfully. *This was not by any means a daring expedition into the outback, it was a very unambitious exploration.* ADJ-GRADED ≠ambitious

unanimity /juːnənɪmɪti/. When there is **unanimity** among a group of people, they all agree about something or all vote for the same thing. *All decisions would require unanimity.* ◆◇◇◇◇ N-UNCOUNT

unanimous /juːnænɪməs/ ◆◆◇◇◇
1 When a group of people are **unanimous**, they all agree about something or all vote for the same thing. *Editors were unanimous in their condemnation of the proposals... They were unanimous that Chortlesby Manor must be preserved.* ADJ-GRADED: usu v-link ADJ, oft ADJ *in* n, ADJ that
♦ **unanimously** *Today its executive committee voted unanimously to reject the proposals... The board of ministers unanimously approved the project last week.* ADV: ADV with v
2 A **unanimous** vote, decision, or agreement is one in which all the people involved agree. *...the unanimous vote for Hungarian membership... Their decision was unanimous.* ADJ

unannounced /ʌnənaʊnst/. If someone arrives or does something **unannounced**, they do it unexpectedly and without anyone having being told about it beforehand. *He had just arrived unannounced from South America... My first night in Saigon I paid an unannounced visit to my father's cousins.* ◆◇◇◇◇ ADJ: usu ADJ after v, ADJ n, also v-link ADJ

unanswerable /ʌnɑːnsərəbᵊl, -æns-/
1 If you describe a question as **unanswerable**, you mean that it has no possible answer or that a particular person cannot possibly answer it. *They would ask their mother unanswerable questions.* ADJ
2 If you describe a case or argument as **unanswerable**, you think that it is obviously true or correct and that nobody could disagree with it. *He actually became convinced that the nurses had an unanswerable case... The argument for recruiting McGregor was unanswerable.* ADJ

unanswered /ʌnɑːnsəʳd, -æns-/. Something such as a question or letter that is **unanswered** has not been answered. *Some of the most important questions remain unanswered... Readers should send a copy of unanswered letters to their MP... He had always had difficulty leaving questions unanswered.* ◆◇◇◇◇ ADJ: v-link ADJ, ADJ n, ADJ after v

unappealing /ʌnəpiːlɪŋ/. If you describe someone or something as **unappealing**, you find them unpleasant and unattractive. *He's wearing a deeply unappealing baseball hat... The town is scruffy and unappealing.* ADJ-GRADED ≠appealing

unappetizing /ʌnæpɪtaɪzɪŋ/; also spelled **unappetising** in British English. If you describe food as **unappetizing**, you think it will be unpleasant to eat because of its appearance. *...cold and unappetizing chicken.* ADJ-GRADED ≠appetizing

unapproachable /ʌnəproutʃəbᵊl/. If you describe someone as **unapproachable**, you mean that they seem to be difficult to talk to and not very friendly. *She was somewhat unapproachable but I'm sure she wanted to be friendly.* ADJ-GRADED ≠approachable

unarguable /ʌnɑːʳgjuəbᵊl/. If you describe a statement or opinion as **unarguable**, you think that it is obviously true or correct and that nobody could disagree with it. *He is making the unarguable point that our desires and preferences have a social component.* ADJ ≠arguable ♦ **unarguably** /ʌnɑːʳgjuəbli/ *He is unarguably an outstanding man.* ADV: ADV with cl/group

unarmed /ʌnɑːʳmd/. If a person or vehicle is **unarmed**, they are not carrying any weapons. *The soldiers concerned were unarmed at the time... Thirteen unarmed civilians died in that attack.* ◆◇◇◇◇ ADJ ▶ Also an adverb. *He says he walks inside the prison without guards, unarmed.* ADV: ADV after v

unashamed /ʌnəʃeɪmd/. If you describe someone's behaviour or attitude as **unashamed**, you mean that they are open and honest about things that other people might find embarrassing or shocking. *I grinned at him in unashamed delight. ...a man rightly unashamed of his own talent.* ◆◇◇◇◇ ADJ ♦ **unashamedly** /ʌnəʃeɪmɪdli/ *Drugs are sold unashamedly in broad daylight. ...an unashamedly traditional view of geology.* ADV: ADV with v, ADV adj/n

unasked /ʌnɑːskt, -æskt/

1 An **unasked** question is one that has not been asked, although people are wondering what the answer is. *She was undernourished, an observation that prompted yet another unasked question... Significant questions will go unasked.* ADJ

2 If someone says or does something **unasked**, they say or do it without being asked to do it. *His advice, offered to her unasked, was to stay home and make the best of things.* ADJ: ADJ after v =unprompted

unassailable /ʌnəseɪləbᵊl/. If you describe something or someone as **unassailable**, you mean that nothing can alter, destroy, or challenge them. *That was enough to give Mansell an unassailable lead... His legal position is unassailable... Mrs Thatcher was apparently unassailable. And yet only 40 days later she had resigned.* ADJ-GRADED =invulnerable

unassisted /ʌnəsɪstɪd/. If you do something **unassisted**, you do it on your own and no-one helps you. *He overcame his addictions unassisted... At other times, he'd force her to walk totally unassisted. ...a mother who has had an unassisted delivery.* ADJ: ADJ after v, ADJ n =unaided

unassuming /ʌnəsjuːmɪŋ, AM -suːm-/. If you describe a person or their behaviour as **unassuming**, you approve of them because they have a modest or quiet character. *He's a man of few words, very polite and unassuming... She has a gentle, unassuming manner.* ADJ-GRADED PRAGMATICS

unattached /ʌnətætʃt/. Someone who is **unattached** is not married or does not have a girlfriend or boyfriend. *I knew only two or three unattached men.* ADJ =single

unattainable /ʌnəteɪnəbᵊl/. If you say that something is **unattainable**, you mean that it cannot be achieved or is not available. *There are those who argue that true independent advice is unattainable. ...an unattainable dream.* ADJ-GRADED

unattended /ʌnətendɪd/. When people or things are left **unattended**, they are not being watched or looked after. *Never leave young children unattended near any pool or water tank... An unattended bag was spotted near the platform at Gatwick... The mob broke into the family house while it was unattended and started four fires.* ADJ: ADJ after v, ADJ n, v-link ADJ

unattractive /ʌnətræktɪv/ ◆◇◇◇◇

1 **Unattractive** people and things are unpleasant in appearance. *I'm 27, have a nice flat, a good job and I'm not unattractive. ...an unattractive shade of orange. ...an unattractive and uninteresting city.* ADJ-GRADED ≠attractive

2 If you describe something as **unattractive**, you mean that people do not like it and do not want to be involved with it. *The market is still unattractive to many insurers... It is not an unattractive option to make programmes for other companies.* ADJ-GRADED =unappealing ≠attractive

unauthorized /ʌnɔːθəraɪzd/; also spelled **unauthorised** in British English. If something is **unauthorized**, it has been produced or is happening without official permission. *...a new unauthorized biography of the Russian President. ...the unauthorized use of a military vehicle... It has also been made quite clear that the trip was unauthorised.* ◆◇◇◇◇ ADJ =unofficial

unavailable /ʌnəveɪləbᵊl/. When things or people are **unavailable**, you cannot obtain them, meet them, or talk to them. *Mr Icke is out of the country and so unavailable for comment... Basic food products are frequently unavailable in the state shops.* ◆◇◇◇◇ ADJ: usu v-link ADJ ≠available

unavailing /ʌnəveɪlɪŋ/. An **unavailing** attempt to do something does not succeed. *Efforts to reach the people named in the report proved unavailing... He died after a brave but unavailing fight against a terminal illness.* ADJ =unsuccessful

unavoidable /ʌnəvɔɪdəbᵊl/. If something is **unavoidable**, it cannot be avoided or prevented. *Managers said the job losses were unavoidable... The recession has resulted in an unavoidable increase in spending on unemployment benefit.* ◆◇◇◇◇ ADJ-GRADED ≠avoidable ♦ **unavoidably** /ʌnəvɔɪdəbli/ *Prince Khalid was unavoidably detained in Saudi Arabia and watched the race on television.* ADV-GRADED

unaware /ʌnəweəʳ/. If you are **unaware** of something, you do not know about it. *Many people are unaware of just how much food and drink they consume... She was unaware that she was being filmed.* ◆◆◇◇◇ ADJ: v-link ADJ, usu ADJ of n, ADJ that ≠aware

unawares /ʌnəweəʳz/. If something **catches** you **unawares** or **takes** you **unawares**, it happens when you are not expecting it. *Investors and currency dealers were caught completely unawares by the Bundesbank's action... The suspect was taken unawares, without the chance to dispose of the evidence.* PHRASE: V inflects =off guard

unbalance /ʌnbæləns/ **unbalances, unbalancing, unbalanced**

1 If something **unbalances** a relationship, system, or group, it disturbs or upsets it so that it is no longer successful or functioning properly. *The opposition alliance will further unbalance Mr Kohl's already shaky coalition.* VERB =destabilize V n

2 To **unbalance** something means to make it unsteady and likely to tip over. *Her whole body began to buckle, unbalancing the ladder... Don't lean in – you're unbalancing the horse.* VERB V n

unbalanced /ʌnbælənst/ ◆◇◇◇◇

1 If you describe someone as **unbalanced**, you mean that they appear disturbed and upset or they seem to be slightly mad. *I knew how unbalanced Paula had been since my uncle Peter died... He was shown to be mentally unbalanced.* ADJ-GRADED =disturbed

2 If you describe something such as a report or argument as **unbalanced**, you think that it is unfair or inaccurate because it emphasizes some things and ignores others. *UN officials argued that the report was unbalanced. ...unbalanced and unfair reporting.* ADJ-GRADED =biased ≠balanced

unbearable /ʌnbeərəbᵊl/. If you describe something as **unbearable**, you mean that it is so unpleasant, painful, or upsetting that you feel unable to accept it or deal with it. *War has made life almost unbearable for the civilians remaining in the capital... I was in terrible, unbearable pain.* ◆◇◇◇◇ ADJ-GRADED =intolerable ♦ **unbearably** /ʌnbeərəbli/ *By the evening it had become unbearably hot.* ADV-GRADED: usu ADV adj/-ed

unbeatable /ʌnbiːtəbəl/ ◆◇◇◇◇
1 If you describe something as **unbeatable**, you mean that it is the best thing of its kind. *These resorts, like Magaluf and Arenal, remain unbeatable in terms of price. ...unbeatable Italian cars.* ADJ PRAGMATICS
2 In a game or competition, if you describe a person or team as **unbeatable**, or say that they are in an **unbeatable** position, you mean that they are winning, succeeding, or performing so well that they are unlikely to lose. *The opposition was unbeatable... With two more days of competition to go China is in an unbeatable position.* ADJ

unbeaten /ʌnbiːtən/. In sport, if a person or their performance is **unbeaten**, nobody else has performed well enough to beat them. *He's unbeaten in 20 fights... Sampdoria lost their unbeaten record with a 2-1 home defeat against Genoa.* ◆◆◇◇◇ ADJ =undefeated

unbecoming /ʌnbɪkʌmɪŋ/
1 If you describe things such as clothes as **unbecoming**, you mean that they look unattractive; an old-fashioned use. *...the unbecoming dress hurriedly stitched from cheap cloth.* ADJ-GRADED ≠becoming
2 If you describe a person's behaviour or remarks as **unbecoming**, you mean that they are shocking and unsuitable for that person; a formal word. *His conduct was totally unbecoming to an officer in the British armed services... Those involved had performed acts unbecoming of university students.* ADJ-GRADED: oft ADJ *to/of* n

unbeknown /ʌnbɪnoʊn/. The form **unbeknownst** /ʌnbɪnoʊnst/ is also used. If something happens **unbeknown to** you or **unbeknownst to** you, you do not know about it. *I am appalled that children can mount up debts unbeknown to their parents... Unbeknownst to her father, she began taking dancing lessons.* PHR-PREP

unbelievable /ʌnbɪliːvəbəl/ ◆◆◇◇◇
1 If you say that something is **unbelievable**, you are emphasizing that it is very good, impressive, intense, or extreme. *His guitar solos are just unbelievable... The pressure they put us under there was unbelievable... It was an unbelievable moment when Chris won the gold medal.* ADJ-GRADED PRAGMATICS =incredible, amazing ♦ **unbelievably** /ʌnbɪliːvəbli/ *It was unbelievably dramatic as lightning crackled all round the van... Our car was still going unbelievably well... He beamed: 'Unbelievably, we have now made it to the final twice.'* ADV-GRADED: ADV with cl/group =incredibly
2 You can use **unbelievable** to emphasize that you think something is very bad or shocking. *I find it unbelievable that people can accept this sort of behaviour... Yes, the music library burned, three or four double basses burned. It's just unbelievable.* ADJ: oft *it* v-link ADJ that PRAGMATICS ♦ **unbelievably** *What you did was unbelievably stupid... Unbelievably, our Government are now planning to close this magnificent institution.* ADV-GRADED: ADV with cl/group
3 If an idea or theory is **unbelievable**, it is so unlikely or so illogical that you cannot believe it. *I still find this story both fascinating and unbelievable... I know it sounds unbelievable but I never wanted to cheat.* ADJ =incredible ♦ **unbelievably** *Lainey was, unbelievably, pregnant again... Most unbelievably of all, it only has three moving parts!* ADV-GRADED: ADV with cl/group

unbeliever /ʌnbɪliːvər/ **unbelievers.** People who do not believe in a particular religion are sometimes referred to as **unbelievers.** N-COUNT ≠believer

unbelieving /ʌnbɪliːvɪŋ/. If you describe someone as **unbelieving**, you mean that they do not believe something that they have been told. *He looked at me with unbelieving eyes.* ADJ =sceptical

unbend /ʌnbend/ **unbends, unbending, unbent.** If someone **unbends**, their attitude becomes less strict than it was. *In her dying days the old Queen unbent a little.* VERB V

unbending /ʌnbendɪŋ/. If you describe a person or their behaviour as **unbending**, you mean that they have very strict beliefs and attitudes, which they are unwilling to change. *He was rigid and unbending. ...her unbending opposition to Communist rule.* ADJ-GRADED =rigid

unbiased /ʌnbaɪəst/; also spelled **unbiassed.** If you describe someone or something as **unbiased**, you mean they are fair and do not show prejudice or favouritism. *There is no clear and unbiased information available for consumers... The researchers were expected to be unbiased. ...an unbiased jury.* ADJ-GRADED =impartial ≠biased

unbidden /ʌnbɪdən/. If something happens **unbidden**, it happens without you expecting or wanting it to happen; a literary word. *The name came unbidden to Cook's mind – Ashley Stoker... Unbidden, his thoughts turned to his wife, who had died two years ago.* ADJ: ADJ after v, v-link ADJ, ADJ n

unbind /ʌnbaɪnd/ **unbinds, unbinding, unbound.** If you **unbind** something or someone, you untie a piece of cloth, string, or rope that has been tied round them. *She became very well known for her reforming zeal in unbinding the feet of Chinese women... Many cultures still have fairly strict rules about women displaying unbound hair.* VERB V n V-ed

unblemished /ʌnblemɪʃt/
1 If you describe something such as someone's record, reputation, or character as **unblemished**, you mean it has not been harmed or spoiled. *Ghana does not have an unblemished record on human rights. ...Lee's unblemished reputation as a man of honor and principle.* ADJ: usu ADJ n =untarnished
2 If you describe something as **unblemished**, you mean that it has no marks or imperfections on its surface. *Be sure to select firm, unblemished fruit. ...an open field of unblemished snow.* ADJ: usu ADJ n

unblinking /ʌnblɪŋkɪŋ/. If you describe someone's eyes or expression as **unblinking**, you mean that they are looking steadily at something without blinking; a literary use. *He stared into Leo's unblinking eyes. ...an expressionless, unblinking stare.* ADJ ♦ **unblinkingly** *She looked at him unblinkingly.* ADV: usu ADV after v

unborn /ʌnbɔːrn/. An **unborn** child has not yet been born and is still inside its mother's womb. *...her unborn baby... They will affect generations of Britons still unborn.* ◆◇◇◇◇ ADJ ▶ **The unborn** are children who are not born yet. N-PLURAL: *the* N

unbound /ʌnbaʊnd/. **Unbound** is the past tense and past participle of **unbind**.

unbounded /ʌnbaʊndɪd/. If you describe something as **unbounded**, you mean that it has, or seems to have, no limits. *...an unbounded capacity to imitate and adopt the new... His advice was always sensible and his energy unbounded.* ADJ =boundless

unbreakable /ʌnbreɪkəbəl/
1 Unbreakable objects cannot be broken, usually because they are made of a very strong material. *Tableware for outdoor use should ideally be unbreakable.* ADJ
2 If you say that a rule or limit is **unbreakable**, you mean that it must be obeyed or adhered to. *The unbreakable rule of the seminar is that nobody whose name is not in the box may listen to the talk.* ADJ

unbridgeable /ʌnbrɪdʒəbəl/. When journalists refer to an **unbridgeable** gap or divide between two sides in an argument, they are saying that they do not think it is likely that the argument will end because they think the two sides will never agree. *...the apparently unbridgeable gulf between the SIS and the Security Service... The gap between the President and his opponents is unbridgeable.* ADJ

unbridled /ʌnbraɪdəld/. If you describe behaviour or feelings as **unbridled**, you mean that they are not controlled or limited in any way. *...the unbridled greed of the 1980s. ...a tale of lust and unbridled passion.* ADJ: usu ADJ n

unbroken /ʌnbroʊkən/. If something is **unbroken**, it is continuous or complete and has not been interrupted or broken. *...an unbroken run of 38 match wins... We've had ten days of almost unbroken sunshine... Labour support remained strong and unbroken by the depression.* ◆◇◇◇◇ ADJ

unbuckle /ʌnbʌkəl/ **unbuckles, unbuckling, unbuckled.** If you **unbuckle** something such as a belt or a shoe, you unfasten it by releasing the buckle on it. *He unbuckled his seat belt... She bent over and unbuckled her sandals.* VERB V n

unburden /ʌnbɜːʳdᵊn/ **unburdens, unburdening, unburdened.** If you **unburden** yourself or your problems to someone, you tell them about something which you have been secretly worrying about. *At this time Diana was unburdening herself to her closest friends... Somehow he had to unburden his soul to somebody, and it couldn't be to Laura... Some students unburden themselves of emotional problems that faculty members feel ill equipped to handle.*
VERB; V pron-refl *to* n; V n *to* n; V pron-refl *of* n; Also V pron-refl, V n

unbutton /ʌnbʌtᵊn/ **unbuttons, unbuttoning, unbuttoned.** If you **unbutton** an item of clothing, you unfasten the buttons on it. *She had begun to unbutton her blouse. ...his unbuttoned blue coat.*
VERB; V n; V-ed

uncalled for /ʌnkɔːld fɔːʳ/. If you describe a remark or criticism as **uncalled for**, you feel it should not have been made, because it was unkind or unfair. *I'm sorry. That was uncalled for. ...Leo's uncalled-for remarks about her cousin.*
ADJ-GRADED; =unwarranted

uncanny /ʌnkæni/. If you describe something as **uncanny**, you mean that it is strange and difficult to explain. *The hero, Danny, bears an uncanny resemblance to Kirk Douglas... I had this uncanny feeling that Alice was warning me.* ♦ **uncannily** /ʌnkænɪli/. *They have uncannily similar voices... It fits Orwell's guidelines almost uncannily.*
◆◇◇◇◇ ADJ-GRADED; ADV-GRADED: usu ADV adj/adv

uncared for /ʌnkeəʳd fɔːʳ/. If you describe people or animals as **uncared for**, you mean that they have not been looked after properly and as a result are hungry, dirty, or ill. *...people who feel unwanted, unloved, and uncared for.*
ADJ: usu v-link ADJ

uncaring /ʌnkeərɪŋ/. If you describe someone as **uncaring**, you are critical of them for not caring about other people's suffering and hardship. *It portrays him as cold and uncaring. ...this uncaring attitude towards the less well off.*
ADJ-GRADED; PRAGMATICS; ≠caring

unceasing /ʌnsiːsɪŋ/ If you describe something as **unceasing**, you are emphasizing that it continues without stopping. *...the unceasing quest for more speed. ...his unceasing labours.* ♦ **unceasingly** *Paul talked unceasingly from dawn to dusk.*
ADJ: usu ADJ n; ADV: ADV with v

unceremoniously /ʌnserɪmoʊniəsli/. Something that is done **unceremoniously** is done in a sudden or rude way that lacks in dignity. *She was unceremoniously dumped to be replaced by a leader who could win the election... He had to be bundled unceremoniously out of the way.*
ADV: ADV with v

uncertain /ʌnsɜːʳtᵊn/
◆◆◇◇◇

1 If you are **uncertain** about something, you do not know what you should do, what is going to happen, or what the truth is about something. *He was uncertain about his brother's intentions... They were uncertain of the total value of the transaction... He stopped, uncertain how to put the question tactfully... With some hesitation and an uncertain smile, she held out her hand.* ♦ **uncertainly** *He entered the hallway and stood uncertainly.*
ADJ-GRADED: usu v-link ADJ, oft ADJ *about/of* n, ADJ wh/that; =unsure; ≠certain; ADV-GRADED: usu ADV after v

2 If something is **uncertain**, it is not known or definite. *How far the republics can give practical help, however, is uncertain... It's uncertain whether they will accept the plan... Students all over the country are facing an uncertain future.*
ADJ-GRADED: usu v-link ADJ, oft *it* v-link ADJ wh

3 If you say that someone tells a person something **in no uncertain terms**, you are emphasizing that they say it strongly and clearly so that there is no doubt about what they mean. *She told him in no uncertain terms to go away.*
PHRASE: PHR after v; PRAGMATICS

uncertainty /ʌnsɜːʳtᵊnti/ **uncertainties. Uncertainty** is a state of doubt about the future or about what is the right thing to do. *...a period of political uncertainty. ...the uncertainties of life on the West Coast.*
◆◆◇◇◇ N-VAR

unchallenged /ʌntʃælɪndʒd/
◆◇◇◇◇

1 When something goes **unchallenged** or is **unchallenged**, people accept it without asking questions about whether it is right or wrong. *These views have not gone unchallenged... She couldn't let that pass unchallenged. ...the unchallenged principle of parliamentary sovereignty... His integrity was unchallenged.*
ADJ: ADJ after v, ADJ n, v-link ADJ

2 If you say that someone's leadership or authority is **unchallenged**, you mean that it is secure and that no one is able to compete with them. *He is the unchallenged leader of the strongest republic. ...the man who has led his party unchallenged for over thirty years.*
ADJ: ADJ n, ADJ after v, v-link ADJ

3 If you do something **unchallenged**, nobody stops you and asks you questions, for example about who you are or why you are doing it. *I managed to walk around unchallenged for 10 minutes before an alert nurse spotted me.*
ADJ: ADJ after v

unchangeable /ʌntʃeɪndʒəbᵊl/. Something that is **unchangeable** cannot be changed at all. *The doctrine is unchangeable. ...a thoroughly organised and almost unchangeable system of laws and customs.*
ADJ; =unalterable

unchanged /ʌntʃeɪndʒd/. If something is **unchanged**, it has stayed the same for a particular period of time. *For many years prices have remained virtually unchanged... In July Belgium's jobless rate was unchanged at 8.2% of the workforce.*
◆◆◇◇◇ ADJ: usu v-link ADJ

unchanging /ʌntʃeɪndʒɪŋ/. Something that is **unchanging** always stays the same. *...eternal and unchanging truths... The ground beneath us, however, appears solid and unchanging.*
ADJ-GRADED

uncharacteristic /ʌnkærɪktərɪstɪk/. If you describe something as **uncharacteristic** of someone, you mean that it is not typical of them. *It was uncharacteristic of her father to disappear like this. ...an uncharacteristic lack of modesty.* ♦ **uncharacteristically** /ʌnkærɪktərɪstɪkli/ *Lord Owen has been uncharacteristically silent... Cassandra's tone was uncharacteristically cautious... Uncharacteristically for Keegan, he decided to have a snooze.*
◆◇◇◇◇ ADJ-GRADED: oft ADJ *of* n; ≠typical; ADV-GRADED: usu ADV adj, also ADV with v, ADV with cl

uncharitable /ʌntʃærɪtəbᵊl/. If you describe someone's remarks, thoughts, or behaviour as **uncharitable**, you think they are being unkind or unfair to someone. *Don't be uncharitable... This was an uncharitable assessment of the reasons for the failure.*
ADJ-GRADED; =mean

uncharted /ʌntʃɑːʳtɪd/. If you describe a situation, experience, or activity as **uncharted** territory or waters, you mean that it is new or unfamiliar. *Carter's fourth album definitely moves into uncharted territory. ...a largely uncharted area of medical science.*
ADJ: usu ADJ n; =unexplored

unchecked /ʌntʃekt/. If something harmful or undesirable is left **unchecked**, nobody controls it or prevents it from growing or developing. *If left unchecked, weeds will flourish. ...a world in which brutality and lawlessness are allowed to go unchecked... This provision gives the president total and unchecked power.*
◆◇◇◇◇ ADJ: ADJ after v, ADJ n, v-link ADJ

uncivilized /ʌnsɪvɪlaɪzd/; also spelled **uncivilised** in British English. If you describe someone's behaviour as **uncivilized**, you disapprove of it and find it unacceptable, for example because it is very cruel or very rude. *The campaign has abounded in mutual accusations of uncivilised behaviour... I think any sport involving animals where the animals do not have a choice is barbaric and uncivilized.*
ADJ-GRADED; PRAGMATICS

unclaimed /ʌnkleɪmd/. If something is **unclaimed**, nobody has claimed it or said that it belongs to them. *Her luggage remained unclaimed at Frankfurt Departures. ...unclaimed prizes.*
ADJ

unclassified /ʌnklæsɪfaɪd/. If information or a document is **unclassified**, it is not secret and is available to the general public; used mainly in American English. *The material consisted only of already published, unclassified information.*
ADJ; ≠classified

uncle /ʌŋkᵊl/ **uncles.** Someone's **uncle** is the brother of their mother or father, or the husband of their aunt. *My uncle was the mayor of Memphis... A telegram from Uncle Fred arrived... Uncle, pa wants to see you.*
◆◆◆◇◇ N-FAMILY; N-TITLE

unclean /ʌnkliːn/

1 Something that is **unclean** is dirty and likely to
ADJ-GRADED

cause disease. *...the Western attitude to insects as being dirty and unclean... By bathing in unclean water, they expose themselves to contamination.* [=dirty ≠clean]

2 If you describe someone or something as **unclean**, you consider them to be spiritually or morally bad. *They felt as though they had done something discreditable and unclean. ...unclean thoughts.* [ADJ]

unclear /ʌnklɪəʳ/ ◆◆◇◇◇

1 If something is **unclear**, it is not known or not certain. *It is unclear how much popular support they have among the island's population... Just what the soldier was doing in Bireij is unclear... His itinerary is still unclear.* [ADJ-GRADED: usu v-link ADJ, oft *it* v-link ADJ wh =uncertain]

2 If you are **unclear** about something, you do not understand it properly or are not sure about it. *He is still unclear about his own future... Experts remain unclear as to why the danger appears to have been steadily increasing.* [ADJ-GRADED: v-link ADJ, oft ADJ *about* n/wh, ADJ *as to* wh/n, ADJ wh]

Uncle Sam /ʌŋkəl sæm/. Some people, especially Americans, refer to the United States of America or its government as **Uncle Sam**, usually when they are criticizing it. *They are ready to defend themselves against Uncle Sam's imperialist policies... For years we were taught that Uncle Sam and foreign investment were the problem.* [N-PROPER PRAGMATICS]

Uncle Tom, Uncle Toms. In the past, some people used **Uncle Tom** to refer to a black man when they disapproved of him because he was always humble and obedient to white people; an offensive term. *To the radical blacks of the Sixties, he was an Uncle Tom.* [N-COUNT PRAGMATICS]

unclothed /ʌnkloʊðd/. If someone is **unclothed**, they are not wearing any clothes; a formal word. *He learned how to draw the unclothed human frame... It's considered improper to be unclothed in public, yet some families feel it's OK at home.* [ADJ: ADJ n, v-link ADJ, ADJ after v =naked]

uncluttered /ʌnklʌtəʳd/. If you describe something as **uncluttered**, you mean that it is simple and does not contain or consist of a lot of unnecessary things. *If you keep a room uncluttered it makes it seem lighter and bigger... The portraits are simple, uncluttered compositions.* [ADJ-GRADED ≠cluttered]

uncoil /ʌnkɔɪl/ **uncoils, uncoiling, uncoiled.** If something **uncoils** or if you **uncoil** it, it becomes straight when it has been in a coil or curled up. If someone **uncoils**, or **uncoils** part of their body, they straighten out from being curled up. *He uncoiled the hose and gave them a thorough drenching... Dan played with the tangerine peel, letting it uncoil and then coil again... Mack seemed to uncoil slowly up into a standing position.* [V-ERG; V n; V]

uncombed /ʌnkoʊmd/. If you describe a person or their hair as **uncombed**, you mean that their hair is untidy because it has not been brushed or combed. *Her hair is uncombed, and she is chewing bubble gum. ...his uncombed appearance.* [ADJ]

uncomfortable /ʌnkʌmftəbəl/ ◆◆◇◇◇

1 If you are **uncomfortable**, you are slightly worried or embarrassed, and not relaxed and confident. *The request for money made them feel uncomfortable... If you are uncomfortable with your counsellor or therapist, you must discuss it... I feel uncomfortable lying.* [ADJ-GRADED: usu v-link ADJ, oft ADJ *with/about* n, ADJ -ing =awkward] ♦ **uncomfortably** /ʌnkʌmftəbli/ *Sandy leaned across the table, his face uncomfortably close to Brad's... I became uncomfortably aware that the people at the next table were watching me... He smiled uncomfortably.* [ADV-GRADED: usu ADV adj/-ed, also ADV after v]

2 Something that is **uncomfortable** makes you feel slight pain or physical discomfort when you experience it or use it. *Wigs are hot and uncomfortable to wear constantly... The Metro journey back to the centre of the town was hot and uncomfortable. ...an uncomfortable chair.* [ADJ-GRADED: oft ADJ to-inf] ♦ **uncomfortably** *The water was uncomfortably cold.* [ADV-GRADED: ADV adj]

3 If you are **uncomfortable**, you are not physically content and relaxed, and feel slight pain or discomfort. *I sometimes feel uncomfortable after eating in the evening... People living or working with smokers can find it uncomfortable to wear contact lenses because the smoke causes irritation.* [ADJ-GRADED: usu v-link ADJ] ♦ **uncomfortably** *He felt uncomfortably hot... He awoke to find himself lying uncomfortably on a pile of firewood.* [ADV-GRADED: ADV adj, ADV after v]

4 You can describe a situation or fact as **uncomfortable** when it is difficult to deal with and causes problems and worries. *It is uncomfortable to think of our own death, but we need to... Such questions are uncomfortable to answer... The decree put the president in an uncomfortable position... This book will make their life uncomfortable back at the office.* [ADJ-GRADED: oft *it* v-link ADJ to-inf, ADJ to-inf]

uncommitted /ʌnkəmɪtɪd/. Someone who is **uncommitted** is unwilling to show support and loyalty for a particular idea, belief, group, or person. *The allegiance of uncommitted voters will be crucial... I was still uncommitted to the venture when we reached Kanpur.* [ADJ ≠committed] ► **The uncommitted** are people who are uncommitted. *It is the uncommitted that Labour needs to reach.* [N-PLURAL: *the* N]

uncommon /ʌnkɒmən/ ◆◇◇◇◇

1 If you describe something as **uncommon**, you mean that it does not happen often or is not often seen. *Cancer of the breast in young women is uncommon... A 15-year lifespan is not uncommon for a dog.* [ADJ-GRADED: usu v-link ADJ =rare ≠common]

2 If you describe a quality, usually a good quality, as **uncommon**, you mean that it is unusually great in degree or amount; a literary word. *Both are blessed with uncommon ability to fix things... She read Cecelia's last letter with uncommon interest.* [ADJ: ADJ n =rare] ♦ **uncommonly** *Mary Whitehouse was uncommonly good at tennis.* [ADV: usu ADV adj/adv]

uncommunicative /ʌnkəmjuːnɪkətɪv/. If you describe someone as **uncommunicative**, you are critical of them because they do not talk to other people very much and are unwilling to express opinions or give information. *My daughter is very difficult, uncommunicative and moody.* [ADJ-GRADED PRAGMATICS]

uncomplaining /ʌnkəmpleɪnɪŋ/. If you describe someone as **uncomplaining**, you approve of them because they do difficult or unpleasant things and do not complain about them. *He was a cheerful and uncomplaining travel companion.* [ADJ PRAGMATICS]

uncomplicated /ʌnkɒmplɪkeɪtɪd/. If you describe someone or something as **uncomplicated**, you approve of them because they are simple and straightforward. *She is a beautiful, uncomplicated girl. ...good, fresh British cooking with its uncomplicated, direct flavours.* [◆◇◇◇◇ ADJ PRAGMATICS ≠complicated]

uncomprehending /ʌnkɒmprɪhendɪŋ/. If you describe someone as **uncomprehending**, you mean that they do not understand what is happening or what someone has said. *He gave the bottle a long, uncomprehending look.* [ADJ]

uncompromising /ʌnkɒmprəmaɪzɪŋ/ ◆◇◇◇◇

1 If you describe someone as **uncompromising**, you mean that they are determined not to change their opinions or aims in any way. *Mrs Thatcher was a tough and uncompromising politician.* [ADJ-GRADED =unyielding] ♦ **uncompromisingly** *The company had once been uncompromisingly socialist... He states uncompromisingly that he is opposed to any practices which oppress animals.* [ADV-GRADED: usu ADV adj, also ADV after v]

2 If you describe something as **uncompromising**, you mean that it does not attempt to make something that is shocking or unpleasant any more acceptable to people. *...a film of uncompromising brutality.* [ADJ-GRADED] ♦ **uncompromisingly** *...the uncompromisingly modern decor.* [ADV-GRADED: ADV adj]

unconcealed /ʌnkənsiːld/. An **unconcealed** emotion is one that someone has made no attempt to hide. *His message was received with unconcealed anger. ...their unconcealed dislike of each other.* [ADJ: usu ADJ n =open]

unconcern /ʌnkənsɜːʳn/. Someone's **unconcern** is their lack of interest or anxiety about something, often something that most people would be concerned about. *...the terrorists' increasing unconcern about civilian casualties... Suzanne's feelings about food and eating had gone from blithe unconcern to anxiety.* [N-UNCOUNT ≠concern]

unconcerned /ʌnkənsɜːʳnd/. If someone is **unconcerned** about something, usually something [ADJ-GRADED: usu v-link ADJ, oft ADJ *about/*]

that most people would care about, they are not interested in it or worried about it. *Paul was unconcerned about what he had done... He seems totally unconcerned by real dangers.*
by n
≠concerned

unconditional /ʌnkəndɪʃənəl/. If you describe something as **unconditional**, you mean that it has no conditions or limitations attached to it. *Children need unconditional love... The leader of the revolt made an unconditional surrender early this morning.* ♦ **unconditionally** *The hostages were released unconditionally.*
◆◆◇◇◇
ADJ: usu ADJ n
≠conditional
ADV: ADV with v
≠conditionally

unconfirmed /ʌnkənfɜːʳmd/. If a report or a rumour is **unconfirmed**, there is no definite proof as to whether it is true or not. *There are unconfirmed reports of several small villages buried by mudslides.*
◆◇◇◇◇
ADJ
≠confirmed

uncongenial /ʌnkəndʒiːniəl/. If you describe a person or place as **uncongenial**, you mean that they are unfriendly and unpleasant. *He continued to find the Simpsons uncongenial bores... Hollywood was an uncongenial place to work.*
ADJ-GRADED
≠congenial

unconnected /ʌnkənektɪd/. If one thing is **unconnected** with another or the two things are **unconnected**, the things are not related to each other in any way. *She was known to have had personal problems unconnected with her marriage... I can't believe that those two murders are unconnected.*
ADJ-GRADED: oft ADJ *with/to* n
=unrelated

unconscionable /ʌnkɒnʃənəbəl/. If you describe something as **unconscionable**, you mean that the person responsible for it ought to be ashamed of it, especially because its effects are so great or severe; a literary word. *It's unconscionable for the government to do anything for a man who admits to smuggling 135 tons of cocaine into the United States.*
ADJ

unconscious /ʌnkɒnʃəs/
◆◆◇◇◇

1 Someone who is **unconscious** is in a state similar to sleep, usually as the result of a serious injury or a lack of oxygen. *By the time ambulancemen arrived he was unconscious... He was dragged from his van and beaten unconscious by a gang of salmon poachers.* ♦ **unconsciousness** *He knew that he might soon lapse into unconsciousness.*
ADJ: v-link ADJ, ADJ n, ADJ after v
N-UNCOUNT

2 If you are **unconscious of** something, you are unaware of it. *He himself seemed totally unconscious of his failure... Mr Battersby was apparently quite unconscious of their presence.* ♦ **unconsciously** *'I was very unsure of myself after the divorce,' she says, unconsciously sweeping back the curls from her forehead.*
ADJ-GRADED: v-link ADJ *of* n
=oblivious
ADV: usu ADV with v, also ADV adj

3 If feelings or attitudes are **unconscious**, you are not aware that you have them, but they show in the way that you behave. *Unconscious envy manifests itself very often as this kind of arrogance... 'You're well out of it,' Christopher said with unconscious brutality.* ♦ **unconsciously** *Many women whose fathers left home unconsciously expect to be betrayed by their own mates... I think racism is unconsciously inherent in practically everyone.*
ADJ
ADV: ADV with v, ADV adj

4 Your **unconscious** is the part of your mind that contains feelings and ideas that you do not know about or cannot control. *In examining the content of the unconscious, Freud called into question some deeply-held beliefs.*
N-SING: *the*/poss N

unconstitutional /ʌnkɒnstɪtjuːʃənəl, AM -tuː-/. If something is **unconstitutional**, it breaks the rules of a political system. *The Moldavian parliament has declared the elections unconstitutional... Banning cigarette advertising would be unconstitutional, since selling cigarettes is legal.*
◆◇◇◇◇
ADJ
≠constitutional

uncontrollable /ʌnkəntroʊləbəl/
◆◇◇◇◇

1 If you describe a feeling or physical action as **uncontrollable**, you mean that you cannot control it or prevent yourself from feeling or doing it. *It had been a time of almost uncontrollable excitement... William was seized with uncontrollable rage... He burst into uncontrollable laughter at something I'd said.* ♦ **uncontrollably** /ʌnkəntroʊləbli/ *I started shaking uncontrollably and began to cry.*
ADJ: usu ADJ n
ADV: usu ADV after v

2 If you describe a person as **uncontrollable**, you mean that their behaviour is bad and that nobody can make them behave more sensibly. *Mark was withdrawn and uncontrollable... Uncontrollable children grow into young criminals.*
ADJ
=unmanageable

3 If you describe a situation or series of events as **uncontrollable**, you believe that nothing can be done to control them or to prevent things from getting worse. *If political and ethnic problems are not resolved the situation could become uncontrollable.*
ADJ

uncontrolled /ʌnkəntroʊld/
◆◇◇◇◇

1 If you describe someone's behaviour as **uncontrolled**, you mean they appear unable to stop it or to make it less extreme. *His uncontrolled behavior disturbed the entire class... Julia blows her nose, but her sobbing goes on uncontrolled.*
ADJ-GRADED: ADJ n, ADJ after v, v-link ADJ

2 If a situation or activity is **uncontrolled**, no-one is controlling it or preventing it from continuing or growing. *The capital, Nairobi, is choking on uncontrolled immigration. ...the central bank's uncontrolled printing of money.*
ADJ-GRADED
=unchecked

unconventional /ʌnkənvenʃənəl/
◆◇◇◇◇

1 If you describe a person or their attitude or behaviour as **unconventional**, you mean that they do not behave in the same way as most other people in their society. *Linus Pauling is an unconventional genius... He was known for his unconventional behaviour... He had rather unconventional work habits, preferring to work through the night.*
ADJ-GRADED

2 An **unconventional** way of doing something is not the usual way of doing it, and may be rather surprising. *The vaccine had been produced by an unconventional technique... Despite his unconventional methods, he has inspired pupils more than anyone else... Their marriage was unconventional.*
ADJ-GRADED

unconvinced /ʌnkənvɪnst/. If you are **unconvinced** that something is true or right, you are not at all certain that it is true or right. *Most consumers seem unconvinced that the recession is over... Many academics remain unconvinced of the need for change.*
◆◇◇◇◇
ADJ: usu v-link ADJ, oft ADJ that

unconvincing /ʌnkənvɪnsɪŋ/
◆◇◇◇◇

1 If you describe something such as an argument or explanation as **unconvincing**, you do not believe it is true or valid. *Mr Patel phoned the University for an explanation, and he was given the usual unconvincing excuses... To many readers it sounded unconvincing.* ♦ **unconvincingly** *'It's not that I don't believe you, Meg,' Jack said, unconvincingly.*
ADJ-GRADED
ADV-GRADED: ADV with v

2 If you describe a story or a character in a story as **unconvincing**, you think they are not real or believable. *...an unconvincing love story.*
ADJ-GRADED

uncooked /ʌnkʊkt/. **Uncooked** food has not yet been cooked. *Don't use pickled beetroot, but buy it uncooked and cook it yourself.*
ADJ
=raw

uncooperative /ʌnkoʊɒpərətɪv/. If you describe someone as **uncooperative**, you mean that they make no effort at all to help other people or to make other people's lives easier. *She became uncooperative: unwilling to do her homework or help with any household chores. ...a bunch of stupid, cranky, uncooperative old fools.*
ADJ-GRADED: usu v-link ADJ
=unhelpful
≠cooperative

uncoordinated /ʌnkoʊɔːʳdɪneɪtɪd/; also spelled **unco-ordinated**.

1 If you describe someone as **uncoordinated** you mean that their movements are jerky and they are not in proper control of them. *They were unsteady on their feet and rather uncoordinated. ...an uncoordinated toddler.*
ADJ-GRADED

2 If you describe actions or plans as **uncoordinated**, you mean they are not well-organized. *Government action has been half-hearted and uncoordinated. ...late, uncoordinated and piecemeal enemy responses.*
ADJ-GRADED

uncork /ʌnkɔːʳk/ **uncorks, uncorking, uncorked.** When you **uncork** a bottle, you open it by pulling the cork out of it. *Steve uncorked bottles of champagne to toast the achievement.*
VERB
=open
V n

uncorroborated /ʌnkərɒbəreɪtɪd/. An **uncorroborated** statement or claim is not supported by any evidence or information. *Uncorroborated confessions should no longer be accepted by courts.*
ADJ: usu ADJ n

uncountable noun /ʌnkaʊntəbᵊl naʊn/ **uncountable nouns.** An **uncountable noun** is the same as an **uncount noun.** N-COUNT

uncount noun /ʌnkaʊnt naʊn/ **uncount nouns.** An **uncount noun** is a noun such as 'gold', 'information', or 'furniture' which has only one form and can be used without a determiner. N-COUNT

uncouth /ʌnkuːθ/. If you describe a person as **uncouth**, you mean they are bad-mannered, and that their behaviour is unpleasant and unacceptable. *...that oafish, uncouth person.* ADJ-GRADED =coarse

uncover /ʌnkʌvəʳ/ **uncovers, uncovering, uncovered** ◆◆◇◇◇

1 If you **uncover** something, especially something that has been kept secret, you discover or find out about it. *Auditors said they had uncovered evidence of fraud... A specific plot to kill him was uncovered in the past couple of weeks.* VERB =discover V n

2 When archaeologists **uncover** something, they find a thing or a place that has been under the ground for a long time. *Archaeologists have uncovered an 11,700-year-old hunting camp in Alaska.* VERB =unearth V n

3 To **uncover** something means to remove something that is covering it. *When the seedlings sprout, uncover the tray.* VERB V n

uncovered /ʌnkʌvəʳd/. Something that is left **uncovered** does not have anything covering it. *Minor cuts and grazes can usually be left uncovered to heal by themselves... The uncovered bucket in the corner stank.* ADJ: ADJ after v, ADJ n, v-link ADJ

uncritical /ʌnkrɪtɪkᵊl/. If you describe a person or their behaviour as **uncritical**, you mean that they do not judge whether someone or something is good or bad or right or wrong. *...the conventional notion of women as uncritical purchasers of heavily advertised products. ...that uncritical view of history.* ADJ-GRADED ≠discriminating ♦ **uncritically** /ʌnkrɪtɪkli/ *Politicians want a lap-dog press which will uncritically report their propaganda.* ADV-GRADED: usu ADV with v, also ADV adj

unctuous /ʌŋktʃuəs/

1 If you describe someone as **unctuous**, you are critical of them because they seem to be full of praise, kindness, or interest, but are obviously insincere; a formal word. *...the kind of unctuous tone that I've heard often at diplomatic parties.* ADJ-GRADED PRAGMATICS

2 If you describe food or drink as **unctuous**, you mean that it is creamy or oily; a formal use. *...unctuous but firm aubergines... Our helping at The Canteen was unctuous and sweet.* ADJ-GRADED

uncultivated /ʌnkʌltɪveɪtɪd/. If land is **uncultivated**, there are no crops growing on it. *...the flat, largely uncultivated plains. ...an area left uncultivated to attract insects and small animals.* ADJ: ADJ n, ADJ after v, v-link ADJ

uncultured /ʌnkʌltʃəʳd/. If you describe someone as **uncultured**, you are critical of them because they do not seem to know much about art, literature, and other cultural topics. *He comes from a completely uncultured, lower middle-class family.* ADJ-GRADED PRAGMATICS

uncut /ʌnkʌt/

1 Something that is **uncut** has not been cut. *...a patch of uncut grass... Trees were to be left uncut, roads unpaved.* ADJ

2 An **uncut** book, play, or film has not been shortened or censored. *We saw the uncut version of 'Caligula' when we were in Europe.* ADJ: usu ADJ n

3 **Uncut** diamonds and other precious stones have not been cut into a regular shape. ADJ: usu ADJ n

undamaged /ʌndæmɪdʒd/. Something that is **undamaged** has not been damaged or spoilt in any way. *The Korean ship was apparently undamaged... Choose a golden-orange-coloured pineapple with undamaged leaves.* ADJ-GRADED ≠damaged

undated /ʌndeɪtɪd/. Something that is **undated** does not have a date written on it. *In each packet there are batches of letters, most of which are undated.* ADJ ≠dated

undaunted /ʌndɔːntɪd/. If you are **undaunted**, you are not at all afraid or worried about dealing with something, especially something that would frighten or worry most people. *Undaunted by the scale of the job, Lesley set about planning how each room should look.* ADJ-GRADED: usu v-link ADJ, oft ADJ *by* n =undeterred

undecided /ʌndɪsaɪdɪd/. If someone is **undecided**, they cannot decide about something or have not yet decided about it. *After university she was still undecided as to what career she wanted to pursue... He says he's counting on undecided voters to help him win next week's election.* ◆◇◇◇◇ ADJ-GRADED

undefeated /ʌndɪfiːtɪd/. If a sports player or team is **undefeated**, nobody has beaten them over a particular period of time. *She was undefeated for 12 years... The two London clubs are the only undefeated teams in the division.* ADJ =unbeaten

undemanding /ʌndɪmɑːndɪŋ/

1 If you describe something such as a job as **undemanding**, you mean that it does not require you to work very hard or to think a great deal about it. *Over a tenth of the population have secure, undemanding jobs... The book is an enjoyable and undemanding read.* ADJ-GRADED: usu ADJ n ≠challenging

2 If you describe someone as **undemanding**, you mean they are easy to be with and do not ask other people to do a great deal for them. *...an undemanding companion.* ADJ-GRADED ≠demanding

undemocratic /ʌndeməkrætɪk/. A system, process, or decision that is **undemocratic** is one that is controlled or made by one person or a small number of people, rather than by all the people involved. *...the undemocratic rule of the former communist establishment... Opponents denounced the decree as undemocratic and unconstitutional. ...the undemocratic seizure of power by the military.* ◆◇◇◇◇ ADJ-GRADED ≠democratic

undemonstrative /ʌndɪmɒnstrətɪv/. Someone who is **undemonstrative** does not often show affection. *Lady Ainslie is an undemonstrative woman who rarely touches even her own son.* ADJ-GRADED =reserved

undeniable /ʌndɪnaɪəbᵊl/. If you say that something is **undeniable**, you mean that it is definitely true. *Her charm is undeniable. ...the undeniable fact that she was driving with almost twice the legal limit of alcohol in her blood.* ◆◇◇◇◇ ADJ =incontrovertible ♦ **undeniably** /ʌndɪnaɪəbli/ *Bringing up a baby is undeniably hard work.* ADV

under /ʌndəʳ/ ◆◆◆◆◆

In addition to the uses shown below, **under** is also used in phrasal verbs such as 'go under' and 'knuckle under'.

1 If a person or thing is **under** something, they are at a lower level than that thing, and may be covered or hidden by it. *They found a labyrinth of tunnels under the ground. ...swimming in the pool or lying under an umbrella reading... Under a wide shelf that holds coffee jars stands a pile of magazines... She buried her head under the covers, pretending to be asleep... A path runs under the trees.* PREP

2 In a place such as a sea, river, or swimming pool, if someone or something is **under** the water, they are fully in the water and covered by it. *They said he'd been held under the water and drowned... Goldfish were swimming lazily in a group just under the surface.* PREP ► Also an adverb. *When the water was up to his neck, a hand came from behind and pushed his head under.* ADV: ADV after v

3 If you go **under** something, you move from one side to the other of something that is at a higher level than you. *He went under a brick arch... A river boat passed under the bridge.* PREP

4 Something that is **under** a layer of something, especially clothing, is covered by that layer. *I was wearing two sweaters under the green army jacket... He had no shirt on under his thin jumper... It was hard to see the colours under the layer of dust.* PREP

5 You can use **under** before a noun to indicate that a person or thing is being affected by something or is going through a particular process. *...fishermen whose livelihoods are under threat... I'm rarely under pressure and my co-workers are always nice to me... Firemen said they had the blaze under control... The cause of the crash was under investigation... He was rushed to court yesterday under armed guard.* PREP

6 If something happens **under** particular circumstances or conditions, it happens when those circumstances or conditions exist. *His best friend was killed by police under extremely questionable circumstances... Under normal conditions, only about 20 to 40 per cent of vitamin E is absorbed... Most doctors and nurses live under stressful conditions.* PREP

7 If something happens **under** a law, agreement, or system, it happens because that law, agreement, or system says that it should happen. *Under law, your employer has the right to hire a temporary worker to replace you... We believe an offence was committed under EC regulations... Under the Constitution, you cannot be tried twice for the same crime.* PREP

8 If something happens **under** a particular person or government, it happens when that person or government is in power. *There would be no new taxes under his leadership. ...the realities of life under a brutal dictatorship... The North has been under Communist rule since 1954.* PREP

9 If you study or work **under** a particular person, that person is your teacher or boss. *Kiefer was just one of the artists who had studied under Beuys in the early Sixties... General Lewis Hyde had served under General 'Billy' Mitchell... I am the new manager and you will be working under me.* PREP

10 If you do something **under** a particular name, you use that name instead of your real name. *Were any of your books published under the name Amanda Fairchild?... The patient was registered under a false name.* PREP

11 You use **under** to say which section of a list, book, or system something is classified in. *This study is described under 'General Diseases of the Eye'. ...a parental rights order under section 4 of the Family Law Reform Act... 'Where would it be?'—'Filed under C, second drawer down.'* PREP

12 If something or someone is **under** a particular age or amount, they are less than that age or amount. *...jobs for those under 65... Nearly half of mothers with children under five have a job... Expenditure this year should be just under 15 billion pounds.* ▶ Also an adverb. *...free childminding service for 5's and under.* PREP: PREP amount ≠over; ADV: amount *and* ADV

13 ● **under canvas**: see **canvas**. ● **under wraps**: see **wrap**.

under- /ʌndəʳ-/

1 Under- is used to form words that express the idea that there is not enough of something or that something has not been done or has not happened as much or as well as is needed. For example if people are underfed, they are not getting enough food. *Make sure that you are not underinsured... Victorian cut glass is perhaps the most underpriced area of the antique glass market.* PREFIX

2 Under- is added to the beginning of nouns that refer to a job or rank in order to form nouns that refer to a more junior job or rank. *...the new under-secretary of education. ...clients who wouldn't deal with an undermanager.* PREFIX

underachieve /ʌndərətʃiːv/ **underachieves, underachieving, underachieved.** If someone **underachieves** in something such as school work or a job, they do not perform as well as they could. *Some people might think I've underachieved in my job.* ♦ **underachiever, underachievers** *He just wanted people to stop calling him disadvantaged, an underachiever.* VERB ≠excel; V; N-COUNT

under age; also spelled **underage**.

1 A person who is **under age** is legally too young to do something, for example to drink alcohol, have sex, or vote. *Underage youths can obtain alcohol from their older friends. ...girls who have babies when they are under age.* ADJ

2 Under age activities such as drinking or smoking are carried out by people who are legally too young to do something, for example to vote or drink alcohol. *...his efforts to stop under age drinking and drug abuse.* ADJ: ADJ n

underarm /ʌndərɑːʳm/ **underarms**

1 You use **underarm** to refer to your armpits. *Use underarm deodorants sparingly to avoid skin irritations.* ▶ Also a noun. *She wanted to shave her legs and underarms.* ADJ: ADJ n; N-COUNT: usu pl

2 You use **underarm** to describe actions that you do, such as throwing a ball, in which you do not stretch your arm over your shoulder. *...an underarm throw from the athletic Curran.* ▶ Also an adverb. *All the Arsenal goalkeeper could do was fend it off underarm.* ADJ: ADJ n ≠overarm; ADV: ADV after v ≠overarm

underbelly /ʌndəʳbeli/ **underbellies**

1 The **underbelly** of something is the part of it that can be most easily attacked or criticized. *The ANC are attacking rugby because it is the soft underbelly of South African sport... Inadvertent disclosures by judges sometimes offer an extraordinary glimpse of the legal system's underbelly.* N-COUNT: usu with supp, usu N *of* n

2 The **underbelly** of an animal or a vehicle is the underneath part of it. *...the underbelly of a fish... The missiles emerge from the underbelly of the transport plane.* N-COUNT: usu with supp, usu N *of* n

underbrush /ʌndəʳbrʌʃ/. In American English, **underbrush** consists of bushes and plants growing close together under trees in a forest or jungle. The British word is **undergrowth**. *...the cool underbrush of the rain forest... The trail was steep and thick with underbrush.* N-UNCOUNT

undercarriage /ʌndəʳkærɪdʒ/ **undercarriages.** The **undercarriage** of an aeroplane is the part, including the wheels, which supports the aeroplane when it is on the ground and when it is landing or taking off; used mainly in British English. N-COUNT

underclass /ʌndəʳklɑːs, -klæs/ **underclasses.** ◆◇◇◇◇ A particular country's **underclass** consists of those members of its population who are poor, and who have little chance of improving their situation. *The basic problems of the inner-city underclass are inadequate housing and lack of jobs... Welfare has become identified with the long-term poor, the underclass.* N-COUNT: usu sing

underclothes /ʌndəʳkloʊðz/. Your **underclothes** are the items of clothing that you wear next to your skin and under your other clothes. *...from multi-patterned sweaters to attractive underclothes.* N-PLURAL =underwear

underclothing /ʌndəʳkloʊðɪŋ/. **Underclothing** is the same as **underclothes**. *...a common brand of men's underclothing.* N-UNCOUNT =underwear

undercoat /ʌndəʳkoʊt/ **undercoats.** An **undercoat** is a covering of paint or varnish put onto a surface as a base for a final covering of paint or varnish. ● See also **topcoat**. N-VAR

undercover /ʌndəʳkʌvəʳ/. ◆◇◇◇◇ **Undercover** work involves secretly obtaining information for the government or the police. *...an undercover operation designed to catch drug smugglers. ...undercover FBI agents. ...undercover reporters.* ▶ Also an adverb. *Swanson persuaded Hubley to work undercover to capture the killer.* ADJ: usu ADJ n; ADV: ADV after v

undercurrent /ʌndəʳkʌrənt, -kɜːr-/ **undercurrents** ◆◇◇◇◇

1 If there is an **undercurrent** of a feeling, you are hardly aware of the feeling, but it influences the way you think or behave. *...a deep undercurrent of racism in British society.* N-COUNT: usu with supp, usu N *of* n =undertow

2 An **undercurrent** is a strong current of water that is moving below the surface current and in a different direction to it. *Colin tried to swim after him but the strong undercurrent swept them apart.* N-COUNT =undertow

undercut /ʌndəʳkʌt/ **undercuts, undercutting** ◆◇◇◇◇

The form **undercut** is used in the present tense and is also the past tense and past participle.

1 If you **undercut** someone or **undercut** their prices, you sell a product more cheaply than they do. *The firm will be able to undercut its competitors whilst still making a profit. ...promises to undercut air fares on some routes by 40 per cent... Prices were undercut and profits collapsed.* VERB; V n

2 If your attempts to achieve something **are undercut** by something, that thing prevents your attempts from being effective. *The appeal in Miller's pictures of Indian women is undercut at times by* VB: usu passive =undermine; *be* V-ed *what the artist writes about them... Popular support would be undercut by political developments.*

underdeveloped /ʌndəʳdɪ veləpt/. An **underdeveloped** country or region does not have modern industries and usually has a low standard of living. Some people dislike this term and prefer to use **developing**. *Underdeveloped countries should be assisted by allowing them access to modern technology. ...public-health problems in the underdeveloped world.*

ADJ: usu ADJ n =developing

underdog /ʌndəʳdɒg, AM -dɔːg/ **underdogs.** **The underdog** in a competition or situation is the person who seems least likely to succeed or win. *Most of the crowd were cheering for the underdog to win just this one time. ...Webb, the underdog in this race.*
◆◇◇◇◇ N-COUNT: usu *the* N

underdone /ʌndəʳdʌn/. **Underdone** food has been cooked for less time than necessary, and so is not pleasant to eat. *The second batch of bread came out underdone. ...underdone meat.*
ADJ-GRADED ≠overdone

underemployed /ʌndərɪmplɔɪd/. If someone is **underemployed**, they have not got enough work to do, or their work does not make full use of their skills or abilities. *He was underemployed and not satisfied with his work.*
ADJ

underestimate /ʌndərestɪmeɪt/ **underestimates, underestimating, underestimated**
◆◆◇◇◇

1 If you **underestimate** something, you do not realize how large or great it is or will be. *None of us should ever underestimate the degree of difficulty women face in career advancement... Never underestimate what you can expect to learn from a group of like-minded people.* ♦ **underestimation** /ʌndərestɪmeɪʃən/ *...a serious underestimation of harm to the environment.*
VERB V n V wh; N-UNCOUNT: also *a* N

2 If you **underestimate** someone, you do not realize what they are capable of doing. *I think a lot of people still underestimate him... The first lesson I learnt as a soldier was never to underestimate the enemy.*
VERB V n

underexposed /ʌndərɪkspoʊzd/. If photographic film is **underexposed**, it has not been exposed to enough light during the developing process, and so the photos are darker than they should be. *Photos taken by compact cameras are often dark because they're slightly underexposed.*
ADJ-GRADED ≠overexposed

underfed /ʌndəʳfed/. People who are **underfed** do not get enough food to eat. *Kate still looks pale and underfed. ...ill-trained and underfed young soldiers.*
ADJ-GRADED

underfinanced /ʌndəʳfaɪnænst/; also spelled **under-financed**. **Underfinanced** means the same as **underfunded**. *From the beginning, the project was underfinanced.*
ADJ-GRADED: usu v-link ADJ =underfunded

underfoot /ʌndəʳfʊt/

1 You describe something as being **underfoot** when you are standing or walking on it. *...a room, high and square with carpet underfoot and tapestries on the walls... It was still wet underfoot.*
ADV: ADV after v, n ADV

2 If you trample or crush something **underfoot**, you spoil or destroy it by treading on it. *Morgan dropped his cigarette and crushed it underfoot. ...half-ripe apples that were being trampled underfoot.*
ADV: ADV after v

underfunded /ʌndəʳfʌndɪd/; also spelled **under-funded**. An organization or institution that is **underfunded** does not have enough money to spend, and so it cannot function properly. *For years we have argued that the health service is underfunded... Most adults believe state schools are underfunded. ...underfunded pensions.*
ADJ-GRADED: usu v-link ADJ =underfinanced

undergarment /ʌndəʳgɑːʳmənt/ **undergarments.** **Undergarments** are items of clothing that you wear next to your skin and under your other clothes; an old-fashioned word. *...Rigby and Peller, who make undergarments for women.*
N-COUNT: usu pl =underwear, underclothes

undergo /ʌndəʳgoʊ/ **undergoes, undergoing, underwent, undergone.** If you **undergo** something necessary or unpleasant, it happens to you and you endure it. *New recruits have been undergoing training in recent weeks... He underwent an agonising 48-hour wait for the results of tests.*
◆◆◇◇◇ VERB =go through V n

undergraduate /ʌndəʳgrædʒuət/ **undergraduates.** An **undergraduate** is a student at a university or college who is studying for his or her first degree. *Economics undergraduates are probably the brightest in the university. ...undergraduate degree programmes.*
◆◇◇◇◇ N-COUNT: oft N n

underground. The adverb is pronounced /ʌndəʳgraʊnd/. The noun and adjective are pronounced /ʌndəʳgraʊnd/.
◆◆◆◇◇

1 Something that is **underground** is below the surface of the ground. *Solid low-level waste will be disposed of deep underground... The plane hit so hard that one engine was buried 16 feet underground.* ► Also an adjective. *...a run-down shopping area with an underground car park. ...underground water pipes.*
ADV: ADV after v; ADJ: ADJ n

2 In British English, the **underground** in a city is the railway system in which electric trains travel below the ground in tunnels. The American word is **subway**. *...a woman alone in the underground waiting for a train... He crossed London by underground... The underground is ideal for getting to work in Milan.*
N-SING: *the* N, also *by* N =tube

3 In a country which is occupied by another country, or which has a dictatorship, **the underground** is an organized group of people who are involved in illegal activities against the government in power. *These US dollars were smuggled into the country during the war, to aid the underground.*
N-SING: *the* N

4 **Underground** activities are done secretly because they are unofficial and illegal and are usually directed against the government. *...the underground Kashmir Liberation Front... His mother took him to Hong Kong where she worked in the underground communist movement.*
ADJ: ADJ n

5 If you go **underground**, you hide from the authorities or the police because your political ideas or activities are illegal. *After the violent clashes of 1981 they either went underground or left the country. ...opposition leaders, who are working underground because of the threat of arrest.*
ADV: ADV after v

undergrowth /ʌndəʳgroʊθ/. In British English, **undergrowth** consists of bushes and plants growing together under the trees in a forest or jungle. The American word is **underbrush**. *...plunging through the undergrowth.*
◆◇◇◇◇ N-UNCOUNT

underhand /ʌndəʳhænd/. If an action is **underhand** or if it is done in an **underhand** way, it is done secretly and dishonestly; used showing disapproval. *The Prime Minister himself had been involved in underhand financial deals. ...a sneaky and underhand way of doing business... Mr Dobson apparently accused the government of being underhand.*
ADJ-GRADED: usu ADJ n PRAGMATICS

underlay, underlays. The noun is pronounced /ʌndəʳleɪ/. The verb is pronounced /ʌndəʳleɪ/.

1 In British English, **underlay** is a thick material that you place between a carpet and the floor for extra warmth and in order to protect the carpet. *...foam-rubber type of carpet underlay... A good quality carpet can be ruined by a poor underlay.*
N-MASS

2 **Underlay** is the past tense of **underlie**.

underlie /ʌndəʳlaɪ/ **underlies, underlying, underlay, underlain.** If something **underlies** a feeling or situation, it is the cause or basis of it. *Try to figure out what feeling underlies your anger. ...the energy which seems to underlie all human success.* ● See also **underlying**.
◆◇◇◇◇ VERB V n

underline /ʌndəʳlaɪn/ **underlines, underlining, underlined**
◆◆◇◇◇

1 If one thing, for example an action or an event, **underlines** another, it draws attention to it and emphasizes its importance; used mainly in British English. *The report underlined his concern that standards were at risk... The decision to keep him in hospital for a second night underlines the seriousness of his injury... All this underlines how important it was for Mr Gorbachev to conclude some sort of agreement with the republics.*
VERB =underscore V n V wh Also V that, V *the fact* that

2 If you **underline** something such as a word or a sentence, you draw a line underneath it in order to make people notice it or to give it extra impor-
VERB =underscore

tance; used mainly in British English. *Underline the following that apply to you... Take two coloured pens and underline the positive and negative words.* — V n

underling /ʌndəʳlɪŋ/ **underlings.** You refer to someone as an **underling** when they are inferior in rank or status to someone else and take orders from them. You use this word to show that you do not respect someone. *Every underling feared him. ...underlings who do the dirty work.* — N-COUNT, PRAGMATICS, =minion

underlying /ʌndəʳlaɪɪŋ/ ◆◆◇◇◇

1 The **underlying** features of an object, event, or situation are not obvious, and it may be difficult to discover or reveal them. *To stop a problem you have to understand its underlying causes... I think that the underlying problem is education, unemployment and bad housing.* — ADJ: ADJ n, =root

2 You describe something as **underlying** when it is below the surface of something else. *...hills with the hard underlying rock poking through the turf... Cars were covered with clear-coat finish at the factory to protect the underlying paint from fading.* — ADJ: ADJ n

3 See also **underlie.**

undermanned /ʌndəʳmænd/. If an organization is **undermanned**, it does not have enough employees to function properly. *In some stores we were undermanned and customer service was suffering.* — ADJ-GRADED: usu v-link ADJ, =understaffed

undermine /ʌndəʳmaɪn/ **undermines, undermining, undermined** ◆◆◆◇◇

1 If you **undermine** something such as a feeling or a system, you make it less strong or less secure than it was before, often by a gradual process or by repeated efforts. *Offering advice on each and every problem will undermine her feeling of being adult... Western intelligence agencies are accused of trying to undermine the government.* — VERB, V n

2 If you **undermine** someone, or **undermine** their position or authority, you make their authority or position less secure, often by indirect methods. *She undermined him and destroyed his confidence in his own talent... The conversations were designed to undermine her authority so she felt that she could no longer work for the company.* — VERB, V n

3 If you **undermine** someone's efforts, or **undermine** their chances of achieving something, you do something which makes them less likely to succeed. *The continued fighting threatens to undermine efforts to negotiate an agreement. ...political groups who maintained that a Walesa presidency would undermine the chances for creating a modern democratic Poland.* — VERB, V n

underneath /ʌndəʳniːθ/ ◆◆◇◇◇

1 If one thing is **underneath** another, it is directly below or beneath it, and may be covered or hidden by it. *The device exploded underneath a van. ...using dogs to locate people trapped underneath collapsed buildings. ...a table for two underneath the olive trees... Her apartment was underneath a bar, called 'The Lift'.* ► Also an adverb. *Russell wore his shirt open to reveal a white vest underneath. ...if we could maybe pull back a bit of this carpet to see what's underneath... The shooting-range is lit from underneath by rows of ruby-red light fittings.* — PREP, =beneath; ADV: n ADV, ADV after v, be ADV, from ADV

2 The part of something which is **underneath** is the part which normally touches the ground or faces towards the ground. *Check the actual construction of the chair by looking underneath... The sand martin is a brown bird with white underneath... His bare feet were smooth on top and rough-skinned underneath.* ► Also an adjective. *Some objects had got entangled with the underneath mechanism of the engine.* ► Also a noun. *Now I know what the underneath of a car looks like.* — ADV: ADV after v, n/adj ADV; ADJ: ADJ n; N-SING: the N

3 You use **underneath** when talking about feelings and emotions that people do not show in their behaviour. *He was as violent as Nick underneath... Underneath, Sofia was deeply committed to her husband.* ► Also a preposition. *Underneath his outgoing behaviour Luke was shy.* — ADV: ADV with cl; PREP

undernourished /ʌndəʳnʌrɪʃt, AM -nɜːr-/. If someone is **undernourished**, they are weak and unhealthy because they have not been eating enough food, or because the food they have been eating does not contain all the nutrients they need. *People who are undernourished also lack reserves of energy when faced with physical or mental crises. ...undernourished children.* — ADJ-GRADED: usu v-link ADJ, =underfed, malnourished

undernourishment /ʌndəʳnʌrɪʃmənt, AM -nɜːr-/. If someone is suffering from **undernourishment**, they have poor health because they are not eating enough food or are eating the wrong kind of food. *Forty per cent of children under five in developing countries are short for their age because of undernourishment.* — N-UNCOUNT, =malnutrition

underpaid /ʌndəʳpeɪd/. People who are **underpaid** are not paid enough money for the job that they do. *Women are frequently underpaid for the work that they do. ...underpaid factory workers.* — ADJ-GRADED: usu v-link ADJ, ≠overpaid

underpants /ʌndəʳpænts/. **Underpants** are a piece of underwear which have two holes to put your legs through and elastic around the top to hold them up round your waist or hips. In British English, **underpants** refers to only men's underwear but in American English it refers to both men's and women's. — ◆◇◇◇◇ N-PLURAL: also *a pair of* N

underpass /ʌndəʳpɑːs, -pæs/ **underpasses.** An **underpass** is a road or footpath that goes underneath a railway or another road. *The Hanger Lane underpass was closed through flooding.* — N-COUNT

underpin /ʌndəʳpɪn/ **underpins, underpinning, underpinned.** If one thing **underpins** another, it helps the other thing to continue or succeed by supporting and strengthening it. *...mystical themes that underpin all religions... ...the beliefs underpinning Tibetan art. ...a style of life extensively underpinned by public money.* — ◆◇◇◇◇ VERB, V n

♦ **underpinning, underpinnings** *...the economic underpinning of ancient Mexican society. ...the violent woman-hating underpinnings of films like 'Cape Fear'.* — N-VAR

underplay /ʌndəʳpleɪ/ **underplays, underplaying, underplayed.** If you **underplay** something, you make it seem less important than it really is; used mainly in British English. *We often underplay the skills we have... The problem of alcoholism was, and still is, often underplayed.* — VERB, =play down, downplay, V n

underpopulated /ʌndəʳpɒpjʊleɪtɪd/. You describe a country or region as **underpopulated** when it could support a much larger population than it has. *Many of the islands are mainly wild and underpopulated.* — ADJ, ≠overpopulated

underprivileged /ʌndəʳprɪvɪlɪdʒd/. **Underprivileged** people have less money and fewer possessions and opportunities than other people in their society. *...helping underprivileged children to learn to read. ...the hideous effects of government cuts on underprivileged families.* ► **The underprivileged** are people who are underprivileged. *...government plans to make more jobs available to the underprivileged.* — ADJ: usu ADJ n, =deprived, disadvantaged; N-PLURAL: the N

underrate /ʌndəʳreɪt/ **underrates, underrating, underrated.** If you **underrate** someone or something, you do not recognize how clever, important, or significant they are. *We women have a lot of good business skills, although we tend to underrate ourselves... He underrated the seriousness of William's head injury.* ♦ **underrated** *He is a very underrated poet... The most important and underrated Alpine wine country is Austria.* — ◆◇◇◇◇ VERB, ≠overrate, V n; ADJ-GRADED: usu ADJ n

underscore /ʌndəʳskɔːʳ/ **underscores, underscoring, underscored** ◆◇◇◇◇

1 If something such as an action or an event **underscores** another, it draws attention to the other thing and emphasizes its importance; used mainly in American English. *The Labor Department figures underscore the shaky state of the economic recovery... The rash of accidental shootings underscores how difficult it will be to restore order here.* — VERB, =underline, V n, V wh, Also V that, V *the fact* that

2 If you **underscore** something such as a word or a sentence, you draw a line underneath it in order to make people notice it or give it extra importance; — VERB, =underline used mainly in American English. *He heavily underscored his note to Shelley.* — V n

undersea /ʌndəʳsiː/. **Undersea** things or activities exist or happen below the surface of the sea. *...an undersea pipeline running to Europe. ...undersea exploration.* — ADJ: ADJ n

under-secretary, under-secretaries. An **under-secretary** is a senior official with an important post in a government department. *...Under-Secretary of State Reginald Bartholomew. ...the under-secretary for Foreign Affairs.* — ◆◇◇◇◇ N-COUNT

undershirt /ʌndəʳʃɜːʳt/ **undershirts.** In American English, an **undershirt** is a piece of clothing worn for warmth on the top part of your body next to your skin. The British word is **vest**. *He put on a pair of short pants and an undershirt.* — N-COUNT

underside /ʌndəʳsaɪd/ **undersides.** The **underside** of something is the part of it which normally faces towards the ground. *...the underside of the car. ...the underside of the eyelid.* — ◆◇◇◇◇ N-COUNT: usu with supp, N of n =underneath

undersigned /ʌndəʳsaɪnd/. On a legal document, the **undersigned** people are the ones who have signed their names at the bottom of the document; a legal term. *The undersigned buyers agree to pay a 5,000 pound deposit.* — ADJ: ADJ n ▶ **The undersigned** are the people who have signed a legal document. *...we the undersigned, all prominent doctors in our fields.* — N-PLURAL: the N

undersized /ʌndəʳsaɪzd/. **Undersized** people or things are smaller than usual, or smaller than they should be. *...undersized and underweight babies... They squashed into an undersized reception room... He was undersized, as were all the Tibetan children I was to meet.* — ADJ: usu ADJ n ≠oversized

understaffed /ʌndəʳstɑːft, -stæft/. If an organization is **understaffed**, it does not have enough employees to do its work properly. *Many institutions offering child care are understaffed and underequipped. ...an understaffed police force.* — ADJ-GRADED: usu v-link ADJ =undermanned

understand /ʌndəʳstænd/ **understands, understanding, understood** — ◆◆◆◆◆

1 If you **understand** someone or **understand** what they are saying, you know what they mean. *I think you heard and also understand me... Rusty nodded as though she understood the old woman... I don't understand what you are talking about... He was speaking poor English, trying to make himself understood.* — VB: no cont; V n; V wh; make pron-refl V-ed

2 If you **understand** a language, you know what someone is saying when they are speaking that language. *I couldn't read or understand a word of Yiddish, so I asked him to translate.* — VB: no cont; V n

3 To **understand** someone means to know how they feel and why they behave in the way that they do. *It would be nice to have someone who really understood me, a friend... Trish had not exactly understood his feelings... She understands why I get tired and grumpy.* — VB: no cont; V n; V wh

4 You say that you **understand** something when you know why or how it happens. *They are too young to understand what is going on... She didn't understand why the TV was kept out of reach of the patients... In the effort to understand AIDS, attention is moving from the virus to the immune system.* — VB: no cont; V wh; V n

5 If you **understand** that something is the case, you think it is the case because you have heard or read that it is. You can say that something **is understood** to be the case to mean that people generally think it is the case. *We understand that she's in the studio recording her second album... I understand you've heard about David... As I understand it, you came round the corner by the cricket field and there was the man in the road... The management is understood to be very unwilling to agree to this request... It is understood that the veteran reporter had a heart attack.* — VB: no cont; V that; V it; be V-ed to-inf; it be V-ed that/to-inf

6 If someone **is given to understand** that something is the case, it is communicated to them that it is the case, usually without them being told directly. *I am given to understand that he was swearing throughout the game at our fans.* — PHRASES: give inflects, usu PHR that

7 You can use **understand** in expressions like **do you understand?** or **is that understood?** after you have told someone what you want or told them what to do, to make sure that they have understood you and will obey you. *You do not hit my grandchildren, do you understand?... I don't need it, understand?... I don't want to hear another word about it. Is that understood, Emma?* — CONVENTION PRAGMATICS

understandable /ʌndəʳstændəbəl/ — ◆◆◇◇◇

1 If you describe someone's behaviour or feelings as **understandable**, you think that they have reacted to a situation in a natural way or in the way you would expect. *His unhappiness was understandable.* — ADJ-GRADED ♦ **understandably** /ʌndəʳstændəbli/ *The duke is understandably proud of Lady Helen and her achievements... Most organizations are, quite understandably, suspicious of new ideas.* — ADV-GRADED: ADV adj, ADV with cl

2 If you say that something such as a statement or theory is **understandable**, you mean that people can easily understand it. *Roger Neuberg writes in a simple and understandable way.* — ADJ-GRADED =comprehensible

understanding /ʌndəʳstændɪŋ/ **understandings** — ◆◆◆◇◇

1 If you have an **understanding of** something, you know how it works or know what it means. *They have to have a basic understanding of computers in order to use the advanced technology.* — N-VAR: N of n =grasp

2 If you are **understanding** towards someone, you are kind and forgiving. *Her boss, who was very understanding, gave her time off... Fortunately for John, he had an understanding wife.* — ADJ-GRADED =sympathetic

3 If you show **understanding**, you sympathise with other people's feelings and forgive them if they hurt or disappoint you. *We would like to thank them for their patience and understanding.* — N-UNCOUNT

4 If there is **understanding** between people, they are friendly towards each other and trust each other. *There was complete understanding between Wilson and myself.* — N-UNCOUNT: usu N between pl-n

5 An **understanding** is an informal agreement about something. *We had not set a date for marriage but there was an understanding between us.* — N-COUNT: N prep

6 If you say that it is your **understanding** that something is the case, you mean that you believe it to be the case because you have heard or read that it is. *It is my understanding that this torture has been going on for many years... Our understanding is that they wanted to be in Washington.* — N-SING: poss N, oft N that

7 If you agree to do something **on the understanding that** something else will be done, you do it because you have been told that the other thing will definitely be done. *Poverty forced her to surrender him to foster families, but only on the understanding that she could eventually regain custody.* — PHR-CONJ-SUBORD =on condition that

understate /ʌndəʳsteɪt/ **understates, understating, understated.** If you **understate** something, you describe it in a way that suggests that it is less important or serious than it really is. *The government chooses deliberately to understate the increase in prices... That understates my commitment to the orchestra.* — ◆◇◇◇◇ VERB ≠overstate, exaggerate; V n

understated /ʌndəʳsteɪtɪd/. If you describe a style, colour, or effect as **understated**, you mean that it is not obvious. *I have always liked understated clothes – simple shapes which take a lot of hard work to get right. ...his typically understated humour.* — ◆◇◇◇◇ ADJ: ADJ n =subtle

understatement /ʌndəʳsteɪtmənt/ **understatements** — ◆◇◇◇◇

1 If you say that a statement is an **understatement**, you mean that it does not fully express the extent to which something is true. *To say I'm disappointed is an understatement... He was getting very hard to live with, and that's the understatement of the year.* — N-COUNT ≠overstatement

2 **Understatement** is the practice of suggesting that things have much less of a particular quality than they really have. *He informed us with massive understatement that he was feeling disappointed. ...typical British understatement.* — N-UNCOUNT ≠overstatement

understood /ʌndəʳstʊd/. **Understood** is the past tense and past participle of **understand**.

understudy /ʌndəʳstʌdi/ **understudies.** An actor's or actress's **understudy** is the person who — N-COUNT has learned their part in a play and can act the part if the actor or actress is ill. *He was an understudy to Charlie Chaplin on a tour of the USA.*

undertake /ʌndəʳteɪk/ **undertakes, undertaking, undertook, undertaken** ◆◆◇◇◇

1 When you **undertake** a task or job, you start doing it and accept responsibility for it. *She undertook the arduous task of monitoring the elections.* VERB V n

2 If you **undertake** to do something, you promise that you will do it. *He undertook to edit the text himself.* VERB V to-inf

undertaker /ʌndəʳteɪkəʳ/ **undertakers.** An **undertaker** is a person whose job is to deal with the bodies of people who have died and to arrange funerals. ◆◇◇◇◇ N-COUNT =funeral director

undertaking /ʌndəʳteɪkɪŋ/ **undertakings** ◆◇◇◇◇

1 An **undertaking** is a task or job, especially a large or difficult one. *Organizing the show has been a massive undertaking.* N-COUNT

2 If you give an **undertaking** to do something, you formally promise to do it. *British Coal gave an undertaking to the High Court that it was maintaining the 10 pits in a state of production.* N-COUNT: oft N to-inf

undertone /ʌndəʳtoʊn/ **undertones**

1 If you say something **in** an **undertone**, you say it very quietly. *'What d'you think?' she asked in an undertone... Well-dressed clients were talking in polite undertones as they ate.* N-COUNT: in N

2 If something has **undertones** of a particular kind, it suggests ideas or attitudes of this kind without expressing them directly. *The sobbing voice had an undertone of anger. ...a witty, racy story with surprisingly serious undertones.* N-COUNT: with supp

undertook /ʌndəʳtʊk/. **Undertook** is the past tense of **undertake**.

undertow /ʌndəʳtoʊ/ **undertows**

1 If there is an **undertow** of a feeling, that feeling exists in such a weak form that you are hardly aware of it, but it influences the way you think or behave. *The existence of an emotional undertow is an aspect of all politics. ...an undertow of sadness.* N-COUNT: usu with supp =undercurrent

2 An **undertow** is a strong current of water that is moving below the surface current and in a different direction to it. *Dangerous undertows make swimming unsafe along most of the coastline.* N-COUNT =undercurrent

underused /ʌndəʳjuːzd/; also spelled **underused**. Something useful that is **underused** is not used as much for people's benefit as it could be. *At present many schools' sports grounds are grossly underused. ...areas where muscles are underused and underdeveloped. ...underused land.* ADJ-GRADED =underutilized

underutilized /ʌndəʳjuːtɪlaɪzd/; also spelled **underutilised** in British English. **Underutilized** is a more formal word for **underused**. *They had to sell off 10 percent of all underutilized farmland.* ADJ-GRADED: usu ADJ n =underused

undervalue /ʌndəʳvæljuː/ **undervalues, undervaluing, undervalued.** If you **undervalue** something or someone, you fail to recognize how valuable or important they are. *We must never undervalue freedom... Many companies deal with their female employees in a way that undervalues them.* ◆◇◇◇◇ VERB =underrate V n ♦ **undervalued** *...greatly undervalued German wines... Even the best teacher can feel undervalued.* ADJ-GRADED =underrated

underwater /ʌndəʳwɔːtəʳ/ ◆◇◇◇◇

1 Something that exists or happens **underwater** exists or happens below the surface of the sea, a river, or a lake. *...giant submarines able to travel at high speeds underwater... Some stretches of beach are completely underwater at high tide... State television showed film of vast areas of farmland underwater.* ► Also an adjective. *...underwater exploration. ...underwater fishing with harpoons. ...a retired underwater photographer.* ADV: ADV after v, n ADV; ADJ: ADJ n

2 **Underwater** devices are specially made so that they can work in water. *...underwater camera equipment. ...a pool of clear water lit by underwater lights.* ADJ: ADJ n

underway /ʌndəʳweɪ/. If an activity is **underway**, it has already started. If an activity gets **underway**, it starts. *An investigation is underway to find out how the disaster happened... It was a cold evening, winter well underway... The conference gets underway later today with a debate on the family.* ◆◆◇◇◇ ADJ: v-link ADJ

underwear /ʌndəʳweəʳ/. **Underwear** is clothing such as vests and pants which you wear next to your skin under your other clothes. *...a couple who went for a late-night swim in their underwear. ...a change of underwear.* ◆◇◇◇◇ N-UNCOUNT =underclothes

underweight /ʌndəweɪt/. If someone is **underweight**, they are too thin, and therefore not healthy. *Nearly a third of the children were severely underweight.* ADJ-GRADED: usu v-link ADJ ≠overweight

underwent /ʌndəʳwent/. **Underwent** is the past tense of **undergo**.

underwhelmed /ʌndəʳʰwelmd/. If you are **underwhelmed** by something, you are not impressed or excited by it; an informal word. *He was underwhelmed by the prospect of meeting the Queen.* ADJ-GRADED: usu v-link ADJ, oft ADJ by n ≠overwhelmed

underwhelming /ʌndəʳʰwelmɪŋ/. If you use **underwhelming** to describe the response or reaction to something, you mean that people were not very impressed or excited by it; an informal word. *...the distinctly underwhelming response to their second album... He met with underwhelming applause.* ADJ-GRADED

underworld /ʌndəʳwɜːʳld/ ◆◇◇◇◇

1 The **underworld** in a city is the organized crime there and the people who are involved in it. *...a Spanish Harlem underworld of gangs, drugs and violence... He was involved in the terrorist underworld. ...a wealthy businessman with underworld connections.* N-SING: oft N n, n N

2 In many ancient religions and legends, **the underworld** is a place under the earth's surface where people go after they die. *...Persephone, goddess of the underworld.* N-SING: the N

underwrite /ʌndəʳraɪt/ **underwrites, underwriting, underwrote, underwritten.** If an institution or company **underwrites** an activity or **underwrites** the cost of it, they agree to provide any money that is needed to cover losses or buy special equipment, often for an agreed fee; a technical term. *...58,500 dollars to underwrite a new home... The government will have to create a special agency to underwrite small business loans... Projects included a pilot scheme, underwritten by the trade department.* ◆◆◇◇◇ VERB V n

underwriter /ʌndəʳraɪtəʳ/ **underwriters** ◆◇◇◇◇

1 An **underwriter** is someone whose job involves agreeing to provide money for a particular activity or to pay for any losses that are made; a technical use. *If the market will not buy the shares, the underwriter buys them... Global 2000 became an underwriter for small farmers.* N-COUNT

2 In insurance, an **underwriter** is someone whose job is to assess the risks involved in certain activities and decide how much it will cost to insure something or someone. *Underwriters assess the risks involved in insuring property or liability.* N-COUNT

undeserved /ʌndɪzɜːʳvd/. If you describe something such as a reaction, treatment, or result as **undeserved**, you mean that the person who experiences it has not earned it and should not really have it. *Douglas Hurd has an undeserved reputation for being dull and dry... Jim's treatment was harsh and undeserved.* ADJ =unmerited

undesirable /ʌndɪzaɪərəbᵊl/ **undesirables** ◆◇◇◇◇

1 If you describe something or someone as **undesirable**, you think they will have harmful effects. *Inflation is considered to be undesirable because of its adverse effects on income distribution... A large group of undesirable strangers crashed her party.* ADJ-GRADED

2 **Undesirables** are people who a particular government considers to be dangerous or a threat to society, and therefore wants to get rid of. *The Home Office is usually quick to deport undesirables.* N-COUNT

undetected /ʌndɪtektɪd/. If you are **undetected** or if you do something **undetected**, people do not find out where you are or what you are doing. *...the spy ring had a fifth member as yet still* ADJ: ADJ after v, ADJ n, v-link ADJ *undetected... They managed to get away from the coast undetected... She had had an undetected cancer and the end was swift.*

undeveloped /ʌndɪveləpt/

1 An **undeveloped** country or region does not have modern industries and usually has a low standard of living. *The big losers will be the undeveloped countries, especially sub-Saharan Africa.* ADJ-GRADED: usu ADJ n

2 **Undeveloped** land has not been built on or used for activities such as mining and farming. *Vast tracts of the country are wild and undeveloped... St Lucia is still mercifully undeveloped as a tourist destination. ...the world's largest undeveloped gold deposit outside of South Africa.* ADJ-GRADED

undid /ʌndɪd/. **Undid** is the past tense of **undo**.

undies /ʌndiz/. You can refer to someone's underwear as their **undies**; an informal word. N-PLURAL: oft poss N

undignified /ʌndɪgnɪfaɪd/. If you describe someone's actions as **undignified**, you mean they are foolish or embarrassing. *It is sad to see a county confine its activities to undignified public bickering... There followed an undignified slamming of doors... All this public outpouring is so undignified.* ADJ-GRADED ≠dignified

undiluted /ʌndaɪluːtɪd/

1 If you describe someone's feelings or characteristics as **undiluted**, you are emphasizing that they are very strong and not mixed with any other feeling or quality. *I will look back at this one with undiluted pleasure... The report had not been received with undiluted enthusiasm... Her Irish accent, after thirty-odd years in London, is undiluted.* ADJ: usu ADJ n

2 A liquid that is **undiluted** has not been made weak by mixing it with water. ADJ

undisciplined /ʌndɪsɪplɪnd/. If you describe someone as **undisciplined**, you mean that they behave badly or show a lack of self-control. *...a noisy and undisciplined group of students... Teachers often view youth workers as undisciplined and ineffectual.* ADJ-GRADED

undisclosed /ʌndɪsklouzd/. **Undisclosed** information is not revealed to the public. *The company has been sold for an undisclosed amount... They are now in hiding at an undisclosed address.* ◆◇◇◇◇ ADJ: usu ADJ n

undiscovered /ʌndɪskʌvəʳd/. Something that is **undiscovered** has not been discovered or noticed. *The name Vulcan was given to the undiscovered planet... This site remained undiscovered, though long sought, until recent times.* ADJ

undisguised /ʌndɪsgaɪzd/. If you describe someone's feelings as **undisguised**, you mean that they show them openly and do not make any attempt to hide them. *...undisguised glee... Hean looked down at Bauer in undisguised disgust... By mid-season the hostility between the two was undisguised.* ADJ: usu ADJ n

undismayed /ʌndɪsmeɪd/. If you say that someone is **undismayed** by something unpleasant or unexpected, you mean that they do not feel any fear, worry, or sadness about it; a formal word. *He was undismayed by the prospect of failure.* ADJ-GRADED: v-link ADJ =undaunted

undisputed /ʌndɪspjuːtɪd/ ◆◇◇◇◇

1 If you describe a fact or opinion as **undisputed**, you are trying to persuade someone that it is generally accepted as true or correct. *...the undisputed fact that he had broken the law. ...his undisputed genius. ...in spite of the undisputed challenges of the job.* ADJ =irrefutable

2 If you describe someone as the **undisputed** leader or champion, you mean that everyone accepts their position as leader or champion, although they may have past or future rivals or critics. *Seles won 10 tournaments, and was the undisputed world champion... At 78 years of age, he's still undisputed leader of his country. ...after 10 years of undisputed power.* ADJ

undistinguished /ʌndɪstɪŋgwɪʃt/. If you describe someone or something as **undistinguished**, you mean they are not attractive, interesting, or successful. *...his short and undistinguished career as an art student. ...this rather undistinguished, grimy industrial town.* ADJ-GRADED =mediocre

undisturbed /ʌndɪstɜːʳbd/ ◆◇◇◇◇

1 Something that remains **undisturbed** is not touched, moved, or used by anyone. *The desk looked undisturbed... Peonies react badly to being moved and are best left undisturbed.* ADJ: v-link ADJ, ADJ after v, ADJ n =untouched

2 A place that is **undisturbed** is peaceful and has not been affected by changes that have happened in other places. *In the Balearics pockets of rural life and inland villages are undisturbed... The war had not left Bargate undisturbed.* ADJ: v-link ADJ, ADJ after v, ADJ n

3 If you are **undisturbed** in something that you are doing, you are able to continue doing it and are not affected by something that is happening. *I can spend the whole day undisturbed at the warehouse... There was a small restaurant on Sullivan Street where we could talk undisturbed... They want undisturbed rest.* ADJ: ADJ after v, ADJ n, v-link ADJ =uninterrupted

4 If someone is **undisturbed** by something, it does not affect, bother, or upset them. *Victoria was strangely undisturbed by this symptom, even though her husband and family were frightened.* ADJ: usu v-link ADJ *by* n =unconcerned

undivided /ʌndɪvaɪdɪd/

1 If you give someone or something your **undivided** attention, you concentrate on them fully and do not think about anything else. *Eldest children are the only ones to have experienced the undivided attention of their parents... Adults rarely give the television their undivided attention. ... any task that requires undivided concentration.* ADJ: usu ADJ n

2 **Undivided** feelings are ones that are very strong and not mixed with other feelings. *The paintings she produced in those months won undivided admiration... He has my undivided loyalty.* ADJ: usu ADJ n =wholehearted

3 An **undivided** country or organization is one that is not separated into smaller parts or groups. *Mandela said, 'We want a united, undivided South Africa'. ...the goal of an undivided Church.* ADJ

undo /ʌnduː/ **undoes, undoing, undid, undone** ◆◇◇◇◇

1 If you **undo** something that is closed, tied, or held together, you unfasten, loosen, or untie it. *I managed secretly to undo a corner of the parcel... I undid the bottom two buttons of my yellow and grey shirt... Some clamps that had held the device together came undone.* VERB V n V-ed

2 To **undo** something that has been done is to reverse its effect. *A heavy-handed approach from the police could undo that good impression... She knew it would be difficult to undo the damage that had been done... If Michael won, he would undo everything I have fought for.* VERB V n

3 If a person, organization, or plan **is undone by** something, that thing causes their failure. *They were undone by a goal from John Barnes... Macbeth is the story of a Scottish soldier who becomes king but is undone by his own ambition.* VB: usu passive *be* V-ed *by* n

4 See also **undoing undone**..

undoing /ʌnduːɪŋ/. If something is someone's **undoing**, it is the cause of their failure. *His lack of experience may prove to be his undoing... Issues of national defense have been the undoing of Democratic candidates.* N-SING: with poss =downfall

undone /ʌndʌn/

1 Work that is **undone** has not yet been done. *He left nothing undone that needed attention.* ADJ: ADJ after v

2 See also **undo**.

undoubted /ʌndaʊtɪd/. You can use **undoubted** to emphasize that something exists or is true. *The event was an undoubted success. ...a man of your undoubted ability. ...a player whose fitness is suspect, despite his undoubted talent.* ◆◆◇◇◇ ADJ: usu ADJ n PRAGMATICS

♦ **undoubtedly** *Undoubtedly, political and economic factors have played their part... Hanley is undoubtedly a great player... These sort of statistics are undoubtedly alarming... She undoubtedly met Captain Waite at sea.* ADV: ADV with cl/group, ADV before v

undreamed of /ʌndriːmd ɒv, AM ʌv/. The form **undreamt of** is also used in British English. If you describe something as **undreamed of**, you are emphasizing that it is much better, worse, or more unusual than you thought was possible. *This new design will offer undreamed-of levels of* ADJ PRAGMATICS *comfort, safety and speed... This project has complications undreamed of when the letter came through the door... They have freedoms that were undreamed-of even ten years ago.*

undress /ʌndres/ **undresses, undressing, undressed** ◆◇◇◇◇
1 When you **undress** or **undress** someone, you take off your clothes or someone else's clothes. *She went out, leaving Rachel to undress and have her shower... She undressed the child before putting her in the tin bath.* VERB V V n
2 If someone is **in a state of undress**, they do not have all their clothes on. *Every cover showed a woman in a state of undress.* PHRASE

undressed /ʌndrest/. If you are **undressed**, you are wearing no clothes or your night clothes. If you get **undressed**, you take off your clothes. *Fifteen minutes later he was undressed and in bed... He got undressed in the bathroom.* ADJ

undue /ʌndjuː, AM -duː/. If you describe something bad as **undue**, you mean that it is greater or more extreme than you think is reasonable or appropriate. *This would help the families to survive the drought without undue suffering... It might give the Commission undue influence over the coming negotiations... It is unrealistic to put undue pressure on ourselves by saying we are the best.* ◆◇◇◇◇ ADJ: ADJ n =excessive

undulate /ʌndʒʊleɪt/ **undulates, undulating, undulated.** Something that **undulates** has gentle curves or slopes, or moves gently and slowly up and down or from side to side in an attractive manner; a literary word. *As we travel south, the countryside begins to undulate as the rolling hills sweep down to the riverbanks... His body slowly undulated in time to the music.* ♦ **undulating** *...gently undulating hills.* ◆◇◇◇◇ VERB V Also V n ADJ-GRADED

unduly /ʌndjuːli, AM -duːli/. If you say that something does not happen or is not done **unduly**, you mean that it does not happen or is not done to an excessive or unnecessary extent. *'But you're not unduly worried about doing this report?'—'No.'... This will achieve greater security without unduly burdening the consumers or the economy... He appealed to firms not to increase their prices unduly.* ◆◇◇◇◇ ADV: ADV with v, ADV adj, oft with brd-neg =excessively

undying /ʌndaɪɪŋ/. If you refer to someone's **undying** feelings, you mean that the feelings are very strong and are unlikely to change; a literary word. *Dianne declared her undying love for Sam... He had won her undying gratitude... You need an undying belief in your own ability.* ADJ: usu ADJ n =eternal

unearned income /ʌnɜːʳnd ɪŋkʌm/. **Unearned income** is money that people gain from interest or profit from property or investment, rather than money that they earn from a job. *Mr Smith did spring some surprises, including the scrapping of his controversial 'savings tax' on unearned income.* N-UNCOUNT

unearth /ʌnɜːʳθ/ **unearths, unearthing, unearthed** ◆◇◇◇◇
1 If someone **unearths** facts or evidence about something bad, they discover them with difficulty, usually because they were being kept secret or were being lied about. *Researchers have unearthed documents indicating her responsibility for the forced adoption of children... No evidence has yet been unearthed to link the incident to terrorists. ...the sensational unearthing of a plot to assassinate the President.* VERB =uncover V n V-ing
2 If someone **unearths** something that is buried, they find it by digging in the ground. *Fossil hunters have unearthed the bones of an elephant believed to be 500,000 years old. ...saying that the treasure had been unearthed on his property... More human remains have been unearthed in the north.* VERB V n
3 If you say that someone **has unearthed** something, you mean that they have found it after it had been hidden or lost for some time. *From somewhere, he had unearthed a black silk suit... Today I unearthed a copy of '90 Minutes' and had a chuckle at your article. ...his reputation for unearthing talent from the most unlikely sources.* VERB V n

unearthly /ʌnɜːʳθli/
1 You use **unearthly** to describe something that seems very strange and unnatural. *For a few seconds we watched the unearthly lights on the water... The sound was so serene that it seemed unearthly.* ADJ: usu ADJ n
2 If you refer to a time as an **unearthly** hour, you are emphasizing that it is unreasonably early. *They arranged to meet in Riverside Park at the unearthly hour of seven in the morning.* ADJ: ADJ n PRAGMATICS =ungodly
3 An **unearthly** noise is unpleasant because it sounds menacing and unnatural. *She heard the sirens scream their unearthly wail.* ADJ: usu ADJ n

unease /ʌniːz/ ◆◇◇◇◇
1 If you have a feeling of **unease**, you feel rather anxious or afraid, because you think that something is wrong. *Sensing my unease about the afternoon ahead, he told me, 'These men are pretty easy to talk to.'... We left with a deep sense of unease, because we knew something was being hidden from us... Garland tried to appear casual, but he couldn't conquer his unease.* N-UNCOUNT: oft with poss =anxiety
2 If you say that there is **unease** in a situation, you mean that people are dissatisfied or angry, but have not yet started to take any action. *He faces growing unease among the Democrats about the likelihood of war. ...the depth of public unease about the economy... There is, however, unease in feminist circles.* N-UNCOUNT

uneasy /ʌniːzi/ ◆◆◇◇◇
1 If you are **uneasy**, you feel anxious, afraid, or embarrassed, because you think that something is wrong or that there is danger. *He said nothing but gave me a sly grin that made me feel terribly uneasy... He looked uneasy and refused to answer questions... I had an uneasy feeling that he was going to spoil it.* ♦ **uneasily** /ʌniːzɪli/ *Meg shifted uneasily on her chair... He laughed uneasily... 'Well,' she said a little uneasily, 'what is it?'... He was uneasily aware of another watcher in the bushes.* ♦ **uneasiness** *With a small degree of uneasiness, he pushed it open and stuck his head inside.* ADJ-GRADED =uncomfortable ADV-GRADED: usu ADV after v, also ADV adj N-UNCOUNT
2 If you are **uneasy** about doing something, you are not sure that it is correct or wise. *Richard was uneasy about how best to approach his elderly mother... Scientists feel uneasy about giving a positive answer.* ♦ **uneasiness** *I felt a great uneasiness about meeting her again.* ADJ-GRADED: usu v-link ADJ *about* n N-UNCOUNT
3 If you describe a situation or relationship as **uneasy**, you mean that the situation is not settled and may not last; used mainly in journalism. *An uneasy calm has settled over Los Angeles... The uneasy alliance between these two men offered a glimmer of hope... There is an uneasy relationship between us and the politicians.* ♦ **uneasily** *Democracy and entrepreneurial flair often sit uneasily together... The people have always co-existed uneasily since their country came into being. ...a country whose component parts fit uneasily together.* ADJ-GRADED: usu ADJ n ADV-GRADED: usu ADV after v, also ADV adj
4 If you describe a book or music as **uneasy**, you are critical of it because it is difficult to read or listen to; used in journalism. *'Rid Of Me' is harrowing, uneasy listening... This is an uneasy travel book. ...an uneasy mix of thudding bass, drums and screaming guitar.* ADJ PRAGMATICS

uneconomic /ʌniːkənɒmɪk, -ek-/
1 If you describe something such as an industry or business as **uneconomic**, you mean that it does not produce enough profit. *...the closure of uneconomic factories... The company said the service was uneconomic.* ADJ-GRADED =unprofitable ≠profitable
2 If you say that an action or plan is **uneconomic**, you think it will cost a lot of money and not be successful or not be worth the expense. *It would be uneconomic to try and repair it... Sending a replacement jet would have been uneconomic.* ADJ-GRADED: v-link ADJ ≠cost-effective

uneconomical /ʌniːkənɒmɪkᵊl, -ek-/. If you say that an action, a method, or a product is **uneconomical**, you mean that it does not make a profit. *It would be uneconomical to send a brand new tape... The methods employed are old-* ADJ-GRADED PRAGMATICS =unprofitable *fashioned and uneconomical... Even the successful flying boats proved, in the end, uneconomical. ...the uneconomical duplication of jobs.*

uneducated /ʌnedʒʊkeɪtɪd/. Someone who is **uneducated** has not received much education. *Though an uneducated man, Chavez was not a stupid one.* ▶ **The uneducated** are people who are uneducated. *The poor and uneducated did worst under these reforms.* ADJ-GRADED ≠educated; N-PLURAL: the N

unemotional /ʌnɪmoʊʃənᵊl/. If you describe someone as **unemotional**, you mean that they do not show any feelings. *British men are often seen as being reserved and unemotional... She began to read in a brisk, unemotional voice... I know it's nothing serious and I feel quite unemotional about it.* ♦ **unemotionally** *'I'd like to have their names,' said Johnson unemotionally... McKinnon looked at him unemotionally.* ADJ-GRADED ≠emotional; ADV-GRADED: ADV after v

unemployable /ʌnɪmplɔɪəbᵊl/. Someone who is **unemployable** does not have a job and is unlikely to get a job, because they do not have the skills or abilities that an employer might want. *He freely admits he is unemployable and will probably never find a job.* ADJ

unemployed /ʌnɪmplɔɪd/. Someone who is **unemployed** does not have a job. *The problem is millions of people are unemployed... This workshop helps young unemployed people in Grimsby... Have you been unemployed for over six months?* ▶ **The unemployed** are people who are unemployed. *We want to create jobs for the unemployed.* ◆◆◇◇◇ ADJ; N-PLURAL: the N

unemployment /ʌnɪmplɔɪmənt/. **Unemployment** is the fact that people who want jobs cannot get them. *...an area that had the highest unemployment rate in western Europe... Unemployment is so damaging both to individuals and to communities.* ◆◆◆◇◇ N-UNCOUNT

unemployment benefit, unemployment benefits. Unemployment benefit is money that some people receive from the state when they do not have a job and are unable to find one. *In 1986 more than three million were receiving unemployment benefit... Unemployment benefits are directly related to previous earnings.* ◆◇◇◇◇ N-UNCOUNT: also N in pl

unemployment line, unemployment lines. In American English, when people talk about the **unemployment line**, they are talking about the state of being unemployed, especially when saying how many people are unemployed. The usual British expression is **dole queue**. *Many white-collar workers, like stock brokers and investment bankers, find themselves in the unemployment lines.* N-COUNT

unending /ʌnendɪŋ/. If you describe something as **unending**, you mean that it continues without stopping for a very long time. *I do not recall any formal training, just endless work and an unending stream of people!. ...the country's seemingly unending cycle of political violence. ...a source of unending pleasure and delight.* ADJ: usu ADJ n =endless

unendurable /ʌnɪndjʊərəbᵊl, AM -dʊr-/. If you describe a bad situation as **unendurable**, you mean that it is so extremely unpleasant that you have to end it; a formal word. *Isaac had found the work unendurable and walked out of the job... He had not expected the pain to be unendurable... It has placed an almost unendurable strain on their marriage.* ADJ =intolerable ≠bearable

unenviable /ʌnenviəbᵊl/. If you describe a situation or task as **unenviable**, you mean that nobody would enjoy dealing with it because it is very difficult, dangerous, or unpleasant. *She had the unenviable task of making the first few phone calls... It put me in the unenviable position of having to lie.* ADJ-GRADED: usu ADJ n ≠enviable

unequal /ʌniːkwəl/ ◆◇◇◇◇

1 An **unequal** system or situation is unfair because it gives more power or privileges to one person or group of people than to others. *This country still had a deeply oppressive, unequal and divisive political system. ...the unequal power relationships between men and women. ...unequal pay.* ♦ **unequally** *...unequally distributed assets... The victims were treated unequally.* ADJ-GRADED: usu ADJ n =unfair; ADV-GRADED: ADV with v

2 If someone is **unequal to** a task, they are incapable of doing it well; a formal use. *Her critics say she has proved unequal to the task... He felt unequal to the job and wished there were someone he could go to for advice.* ADJ: v-link ADJ *to* n

3 Unequal means being different in size, strength, or amount. *The Egyptians probably measured their day in twenty-four hours of unequal length.* ADJ

unequalled /ʌniːkwəld/; spelled **unequaled** in American English. If you describe something as **unequalled**, you mean that it is greater, better, or more extreme than anything else of the same kind. *This record figure was unequalled for 13 years... We offer the very finest properties, and an unequalled level of service. ...a feat unequaled in the history of polar exploration.* ADJ =unparalleled

unequivocal /ʌnɪkwɪvəkᵊl/. If you describe someone's attitude as **unequivocal**, you mean that it is completely clear and very firm; a formal word. *...Richardson's unequivocal commitment to fair play... Yesterday, the message to him was unequivocal: 'Get out.'* ♦ **unequivocally** /ʌnɪkwɪvəkli/ *He stated unequivocally that the French forces were ready to go to war... Temperature records have unequivocally confirmed the existence of global warming.* ◆◇◇◇◇ ADJ-GRADED; ADV-GRADED: ADV with v, ADV adj

unerring /ʌnɜːrɪŋ/. If you describe someone's judgement or ability as **unerring**, you mean that they are always correct and never mistaken. *These designs demonstrate her unerring eye for colour and detail... Paul is a thoroughly likeable man with an unerring sense of comedy... She has an unerring instinct for people's weak spots.* ♦ **unerringly** *It was wonderful to watch her fingers moving deftly and unerringly... She had seized unerringly on the fact that most disturbed him... The man could unerringly select the parts that were necessary to his task... An unerringly professional team greet and treat clients.* ADJ: usu ADJ n =unfailing; ADV: ADV with v, ADV adj

unescorted /ʌnɪskɔːtɪd/. If someone or something is **unescorted**, they are not protected or supervised. *Unescorted children are not allowed beyond this point... He worked as a dancing partner for unescorted ladies at Manhattan cabarets... The President's unescorted vehicle was ambushed just outside the capital... They advise against foreign delegates wandering unescorted in various parts of town.* ADJ: ADJ n, ADJ after v, v-link ADJ

unethical /ʌneθɪkᵊl/. If you describe someone's behaviour as **unethical**, you think it is wrong and unacceptable according to a society's rules or people's beliefs; a formal word. *It's simply unethical to promote and advertise such a dangerous product... I thought it was unethical for doctors to operate upon their wives. ...to investigate widespread unethical and illegal practices in banking. ...accusations of unethical conduct.* ADJ-GRADED ≠ethical

uneven /ʌniːvᵊn/ ◆◇◇◇◇

1 An **uneven** surface or edge is not smooth, flat, or straight. *He staggered on the uneven surface of the car park... She gazed round the church at the grey uneven walls and the vivid stained glass windows. ...uneven teeth.* ♦ **unevenly** *...wearing dresses that pinched at the armholes, that hung as unevenly as flags... My cuticles were split and ragged, and my nails unevenly bitten.* ADJ-GRADED ≠even; ADV-GRADED: ADV with v

2 Something that is **uneven** is not regular or consistent. *He could hear that her breathing was uneven... Business activity in Hong Kong is staggering along at an uneven pace.* ♦ **unevenly** *Winds are generated by the sun as it unevenly heats the earth's surface... The steaks were unevenly cooked.* ADJ-GRADED; ADV-GRADED: ADV with v

3 If you describe something as **uneven**, you think it is not very good because it is not consistent in quality. *This was, for him, an oddly uneven performance... The acting is wildly uneven.* ADJ-GRADED =patchy

4 An **uneven** system or situation is unfairly arranged or organized. *Some of the victims are complaining loudly about the uneven distribution of* ADJ-GRADED: usu ADJ n =unequal

emergency aid... It was an uneven contest. ♦ **unevenly** *Within a free enterprise capitalist society, resources are very unevenly distributed.* ADV-GRADED: ADV with v

uneventful /ʌnɪventfʊl/. If you describe a period of time as **uneventful**, you mean that nothing interesting, exciting, or important happened during it. *The return journey was uneventful, the car running perfectly... It was rare for her to have an opportunity to discuss her dull, uneventful life.* ♦ **uneventfully** *The five years at that school passed fairly uneventfully.* ADJ-GRADED =unremarkable; ADV-GRADED: ADV after v

unexceptionable /ʌnɪksepʃənəbəl/. If you describe someone or something as **unexceptionable**, you mean that it is unlikely to be criticized or objected to, but is not exciting or new, or may have some hidden bad qualities; a formal word. *The candidate was quite unexceptionable, a well-known travel writer and TV personality... The school's unexceptionable purpose is to involve parents more closely in the education of their children.* ADJ

unexceptional /ʌnɪksepʃənəl/. If you describe something as **unexceptional**, you mean that it is ordinary, not very interesting, and often disappointing. *Since then, Michael has lived an unexceptional life. ...a pretty unexceptional bunch of players... The photographs are fairly predictable and unexceptional... The rest of the summer was unexceptional.* ADJ-GRADED =unremarkable ≠exceptional

unexciting /ʌnɪksaɪtɪŋ/. If you describe someone or something as **unexciting**, you think they are rather boring, and not likely to shock or surprise you in any way. *He is regarded as very capable but unexciting. ...an unexciting but likeable painter. ...a quiet woman with a stable but equally unexciting career... It was a methodical, unexciting chore.* ADJ-GRADED ≠exciting

unexpected /ʌnɪkspektɪd/. If an event or someone's behaviour is **unexpected**, it surprises you because you did not think that it was likely to happen. *His death was totally unexpected... He made a brief, unexpected appearance at the office... Help may also come from some unexpected places... 'Hello,' he said. 'This is an unexpected pleasure.'* ♦ **unexpectedly** *Moss had clamped an unexpectedly strong grip on his arm... The Indians came out unexpectedly, catching the soldiers off-guard.* ◆◆◆◇◇ ADJ-GRADED; ADV-GRADED: ADV adj, ADV with v

unexplained /ʌnɪkspleɪnd/. If you describe something as **unexplained**, you mean that the reason for it or cause of it is unclear or is not known. *The demonstrations were provoked by the unexplained death of an opposition leader... Soon after leaving Margate, for some unexplained reason, the train was brought to a standstill... How such extensive damage could have been sustained so quickly remains unexplained.* ◆◇◇◇◇ ADJ: usu ADJ n

unfailing /ʌnfeɪlɪŋ/. If you describe someone's good qualities or behaviour as **unfailing**, you mean that they never change. *He had the unfailing care and support of Erica, his wife. ...a man of unfailing courtesy and kindness... He continued to appear in the office with unfailing regularity thereafter.* ♦ **unfailingly** *He was unfailingly polite to customers... Foreigners unfailingly fall in love with the place.* ADJ: usu ADJ n =unerring; ADV: usu ADV adj, also ADV with v

unfair /ʌnfeəʳ/ ◆◆◆◇◇

1 An **unfair** action or situation is not right or just. *She was awarded £5,000 in compensation for unfair dismissal... America decided that imported steel had an unfair advantage over steel made at home... It was unfair that he should suffer so much... The union said it was unfair to ask workers to adopt a policy of wage restraint.* ♦ **unfairly** *An industrial tribunal has no jurisdiction to decide whether an employee was fairly or unfairly dismissed... He unfairly blamed Frances for the failure.* ADJ-GRADED: oft *it* v-link ADJ that/to-inf; ADV-GRADED: ADV adj, ADV with v

2 An **unfair** system or situation does not give equal treatment or equal opportunities to everyone involved. *The American plane makers continue to accuse Airbus of unfair competition... Some have been sentenced to long prison terms after unfair trials.* ♦ **unfairness** *I must complain about the unfairness of the penalty shoot-out in the FA Cup semi-final.* ADJ-GRADED: usu ADJ n; N-UNCOUNT

unfaithful /ʌnfeɪθfʊl/. If someone is **unfaithful** to their lover or to the person they are married to, they have a sexual relationship with someone else. *James had been unfaithful to Christine for the entire four years they'd been together... She was frequently left alone by her unfaithful husband.* ◆◇◇◇◇ ADJ-GRADED: oft ADJ *to* n

unfamiliar /ʌnfəmɪliəʳ/ ◆◇◇◇◇

1 If something is **unfamiliar** to you, you know nothing or very little about it, because you have not seen or experienced it before. *She grew many wonderful plants that were unfamiliar to me... I was alone in an unfamiliar city.* ♦ **unfamiliarity** /ʌnfəmɪliærɪti/ *...problems which arise from the newness of the approach and its unfamiliarity to prisoners.* ADJ-GRADED: oft ADJ *to* n; N-UNCOUNT: oft with poss ≠familiarity

2 If you are **unfamiliar with** something, it is unfamiliar to you. *She speaks no Japanese and is unfamiliar with Japanese culture.* ♦ **unfamiliarity** *...her unfamiliarity with the politics of the region.* ADJ-GRADED: v-link ADJ *with* n; N-UNCOUNT: N *with* n

unfashionable /ʌnfæʃənəbəl/. If something is **unfashionable**, it is not approved of or done by most people. *Wearing fur has become deeply unfashionable... The couple hold the unfashionable view that marriage is a sacred union.* ♦ **unfashionably** *He wears his blonde hair unfashionably long.* ◆◇◇◇◇ ADJ-GRADED ≠fashionable; ADV-GRADED: usu ADV adj

unfasten /ʌnfɑːsən, -fæsən/ **unfastens, unfastening, unfastened.** If you **unfasten** something that is holding another thing in place, for example buttons or zips on clothing, you loosen them or separate their parts, for example so that you can remove the clothing. *When Ted was six we decided that he needed to know how to fasten and unfasten his seat belt... Reaching down, he unfastened the latch on the gate... He once emerged from the toilets with his flies unfastened.* VERB =undo ≠fasten; V n; V-ed

unfathomable /ʌnfæðəməbəl/

1 If you describe something as **unfathomable**, you mean that it cannot be understood or explained, usually because it is very strange or complicated. *An iron gate hung open, with a blue shirt, for some unfathomable reason, jammed between two upright bars... How odd life was, how unfathomable, how profoundly unjust.* ADJ-GRADED =inexplicable

2 If you use **unfathomable** to describe a person or the expression on their face, you mean that you cannot tell what they are thinking or what they intend to do; a literary use. *...a strange, unfathomable and unpredictable individual. ...the dark eyes that right now seemed opaque and unfathomable.* ADJ =inscrutable

unfavourable /ʌnfeɪvərəbəl/; spelled **unfavorable** in American English. ◆◇◇◇◇

1 **Unfavourable** conditions or circumstances cause problems for you and reduce your chances of success. *Unfavourable economic conditions were blocking a recovery of the American insurance market... We've got a fairly unfavourable exchange rate at the moment... Unfavourable weather has had damaging effects on this year's harvest... Mr Markovic told parliament that the situation in the country was 'extremely unfavourable'.* ADJ-GRADED: usu ADJ n =poor ≠favourable

2 If you have an **unfavourable** reaction to something, you do not like it. *A more unfavourable response was given today by the Prime Minister... President Mubarak was particularly unfavourable to the idea... First reactions have been distinctly unfavourable.* ♦ **unfavourably** /ʌnfeɪvərəbli/ *When the body reacts unfavourably to food, the pulse rate will go up.* ADJ-GRADED ≠favourable; ADV-GRADED: ADV after v

3 If you make an **unfavourable** comparison between two things, you say that one thing seems worse than the other. *He makes unfavourable comparisons between British and French cooking... A younger child will benefit more from an older sister's help than from an unfavourable comparison between their progress.* ♦ **unfavourably** *Childcare facilities in Britain compare unfavourably with other European countries.* ADJ: ADJ n ≠favourable; ADV-GRADED: ADV with v

unfeasible /ʌnfiːzɪbəl/. If you say that something is **unfeasible**, you mean that you do not think it can be done, made, or achieved. *The weather made it unfeasible to be outdoors... The board said the idea was unfeasible.* ADJ ≠feasible

unfeeling /ʌnfiːlɪŋ/. If you describe someone as **unfeeling**, you are criticizing them for their cruelty or lack of sympathy for other people; used in written English. *He was branded an unfeeling bully who used his huge size to frighten people... There's no way anyone could accuse this woman of being cold and unfeeling... It was a flippant and unfeeling remark.* ADJ-GRADED PRAGMATICS =insensitive

unfettered /ʌnfetəʳd/. If you describe something as **unfettered**, you mean that it is not controlled or limited by anyone or anything; a formal word. *Unfettered free trade is an ideal, never achieved... Unfettered by the bounds of reality, my imagination flourished... A load is lifted from your subconscious, enabling you to forge ahead unfettered.* ADJ: ADJ n, v-link ADJ, ADJ after v =unconstrained

unfinished /ʌnfɪnɪʃt/. If you describe something such as a work of art or a piece of work as **unfinished**, you mean that it is not complete, for example because it was abandoned or there was no time to complete it. *...Jane Austen's unfinished novel... The cathedral was eventually completed in 1490, though the Gothic facade remains unfinished... He left the sentence unfinished.* ◆◇◇◇◇ ADJ: ADJ n, v-link ADJ, ADJ after v

unfit /ʌnfɪt/ ◆◇◇◇◇

1 If you are **unfit**, your body is not in good condition because you have not been taking regular exercise. *Many children are so unfit they are unable to do even basic exercises.* ADJ-GRADED: usu v-link ADJ =out of shape ≠fit

2 If someone is **unfit** for something, he or she is unable to do it because of injury or illness. *He had a third examination and was declared unfit for duty... Mr Abel's doctor has said he is unfit to travel.* ADJ-GRADED: usu v-link ADJ, ADJ *for* n, ADJ to-inf

3 If you say that someone or something is **unfit** for a particular purpose or job, you are criticizing them because they are not good enough for that purpose or job. *Existing houses are becoming totally unfit for human habitation... They were utterly unfit to govern America... She is an unfit mother.* ADJ-GRADED: oft ADJ *for* n, ADJ to-inf PRAGMATICS ≠fit

unflagging /ʌnflægɪŋ/. If you describe something such as support, effort, or enthusiasm as **unflagging**, you mean that it is constant and strong. *He was sustained by the unflagging support of his family. ...unflagging optimism... The book is not one word too long and its narrative pace is unflagging.* ADJ PRAGMATICS =unfaltering

unflappable /ʌnflæpəbəl/. Someone who is **unflappable** is always calm and never panics or gets upset or angry. ADJ-GRADED

unflattering /ʌnflætərɪŋ/. If you describe something as **unflattering**, you mean that it makes someone or something seem less attractive than they really are. *He depicted the town's respectable families in an unflattering light... The knee-length dresses were unflattering and ugly.* ADJ-GRADED ≠flattering

unflinching /ʌnflɪntʃɪŋ/. You can use **unflinching** in expressions such as **unflinching honesty** and **unflinching support** to indicate that a good quality which someone has is strong and steady, and never weakens. *...the armed forces, all of whom had pledged their unflinching support and loyalty to the government.* ♦ **unflinchingly** *They were unflinchingly loyal to their friends.* ADJ; ADV-GRADED

unfocused /ʌnfoʊkəst/; also spelled **unfocussed**.

1 If someone's eyes are **unfocused**, they are open, but not looking at anything. *Her eyes were unfocused, as if she were staring inside at her memories of the day. ...his unfocused gaze.* ADJ

2 If you describe someone's feelings or plans as **unfocused**, you are criticizing them because they do not seem to be clearly formed or have any clear purpose. *But for now, she is in the grip of a blind, unfocused anger... It is not perhaps surprising that the administration now appears so indecisive and unfocused.* ADJ-GRADED PRAGMATICS

unfold /ʌnfoʊld/ **unfolds, unfolding, unfolded** ◆◆◇◇◇

1 If a situation **unfolds**, it develops and becomes known or understood. *The outcome depends on conditions as well as how events unfold... The facts started to unfold before them.* VERB V

2 If a story **unfolds** or someone **unfolds** it, it is told to someone else. *Don's story unfolded as the cruise got under way... Mr Wills unfolds his story with evident enjoyment.* V-ERG V V n

3 If someone **unfolds** something which has been folded or if it **unfolds**, it is opened out and becomes flat. *He quickly unfolded the blankets and spread them on the mattress... When the bird lifts off into flight, its wings unfold to an impressive six-foot span.* V-ERG ≠fold V n V

unforeseeable /ʌnfɔːʳsiːəbəl/. An **unforeseeable** problem or unpleasant event is one which you did not expect and could not have predicted. *...severe unforeseeable weather conditions... This is such an unforeseeable situation that anything could happen.* ADJ-GRADED

unforeseen /ʌnfəʳsiːn/. If something that has happened was **unforeseen**, it was not expected to happen or known about beforehand. *Radiation may damage cells in a way that was previously unforeseen... Unfortunately, due to unforeseen circumstances, this year's show has been cancelled... Ring regularly to check that no unforeseen problems have arisen.* ◆◇◇◇◇ ADJ =unexpected

unforgettable /ʌnfəʳgetəbəl/. If you describe something as **unforgettable**, you mean that it is, for example, extremely beautiful, enjoyable, or unusual, so that you remember it for a long time. You can also refer to extremely unpleasant things as **unforgettable**. *A visit to the Museum is an unforgettable experience... A bright shooting star, or meteor, is an unforgettable sight. ...those unforgettable songs we love to hate. ...the leisure activities that will make your holiday unforgettable.* ♦ **unforgettably** /ʌnfəʳgetəbli/. *...an unforgettably unique performer.* ◆◇◇◇◇ ADJ-GRADED =memorable; ADV-GRADED: usu ADV cl/group

unforgivable /ʌnfəʳgɪvəbəl/. If you say that something is **unforgivable**, you mean that it is very bad, cruel, or socially unacceptable. *These people are animals and what they did was unforgivable... I also suspect that I'm becoming a bore, which is something unforgivable in anybody, but especially in a journalist.* ADJ-GRADED =inexcusable

unforgiving /ʌnfəʳgɪvɪŋ/

1 If you describe someone as **unforgiving**, you mean that they are unwilling to forgive other people; a formal use. *He was an unforgiving man who never forgot a slight... He finds human foibles endearing, but is unforgiving of pretension.* ADJ ≠forgiving

2 If you describe a situation or activity as **unforgiving**, you mean that it causes a lot of people to experience great difficulty or failure, even people who deserve to succeed. *Business is a competitive activity. It is very fierce and very unforgiving.* ADJ-GRADED

unformed /ʌnfɔːʳmd/. If you describe someone or something as **unformed**, you mean that they are in an early stage of development and not fully formed or matured; a formal word. *The market for which they are competing is still unformed. ...the unformed minds of children.* ADJ =undeveloped

unfortunate /ʌnfɔːʳtʃʊnət/ **unfortunates** ◆◆◇◇◇

1 If you describe someone as **unfortunate**, you mean that something unpleasant or unlucky has happened to them. You can also describe the unpleasant things that happen to them as **unfortunate**. *Some unfortunate person passing below could all too easily be seriously injured... Apparently he had been unfortunate enough to fall victim to a gang of thugs... Through some unfortunate accident, the information reached me a day late... It was unfortunate for Davey that his teacher did not take kindly to him.* ADJ-GRADED =unlucky

2 If you describe something that has happened as **unfortunate**, you think that it is inappropriate, embarrassing, awkward, or undesirable. *It really is desperately unfortunate that this should have happened just now. ...the unfortunate incident of the upside-down Canadian flag... He made the un-* ADJ-GRADED =regrettable

fortunate mistake of promising he would quit if the budget deficit was still out of control.

3 You can describe someone as **unfortunate** when they are poor, deprived, or have a difficult life. *Every year we have charity days to raise money for unfortunate people. ...the unfortunate inhabitants of the East End slums.* ► An **unfortunate** is someone who is unfortunate. *Dorothy was another of life's unfortunates.* ADJ-GRADED N-COUNT

unfortunately /ʌnfɔːʳtʃʊnətli/. You can use **unfortunately** to introduce or refer to a statement when you consider that it is sad or disappointing, or when you want to express regret. *Unfortunately, my time is limited... Unfortunately for the Prince, his title brought obligations as well as privileges... The enclosed photograph is unfortunately not good enough to reproduce.* ◆◆◆◇◇ ADV-GRADED: ADV with cl, oft ADV *for* n PRAGMATICS =regrettably

unfounded /ʌnfaʊndɪd/. If you describe a rumour, belief, or feeling as **unfounded**, you mean that it is wrong and is not based on facts or evidence. *There were unfounded rumours of alcohol abuse... The allegations were totally unfounded... However, these fears proved unfounded.* ◆◇◇◇◇ ADJ =groundless

unfriendly /ʌnfrendli/. If you describe a person, organization, or their behaviour as **unfriendly**, you mean that they behave towards you in an unkind or rather hostile way. *It is not fair for him to be permanently unfriendly to someone who has hurt him... People always complain that the big banks and big companies are unfriendly and unhelpful... To hide her embarrassment, Judy spoke in a loud, rather unfriendly voice.* ◆◇◇◇◇ ADJ-GRADED ≠friendly

-unfriendly /-ʌnfrendli/. **-unfriendly** combines with nouns, and sometimes adverbs, to form adjectives which describe something which is harmful, inconvenient, or unsuitable in relation to the specified thing. *It's couched in such very user-unfriendly terminology. ...this harsh, and environmentally-unfriendly, action. ...Polly's patent camera-unfriendly glum expression.* COMB in ADJ-GRADED ≠-friendly

unfruitful /ʌnfruːtfʊl/. If you describe something as **unfruitful**, you mean that it does not produce results or success; a formal word. *His search for financial support has so far been unfruitful... It was proving a decidedly unfruitful day.* ADJ-GRADED =unproductive, fruitless ≠fruitful

unfulfilled /ʌnfʊlfɪld/ ◆◇◇◇◇

1 If you use **unfulfilled** to describe something such as a promise, ambition, or need, you mean that what was promised, hoped for, or needed has not happened. *Do you have any unfulfilled ambitions? ...angry at unfulfilled promises of jobs and decent housing... The election had raised hopes that remain unfulfilled.* ADJ: usu ADJ n ≠fulfilled

2 If you describe someone as **unfulfilled**, you mean that they feel dissatisfied with life or with what they have done. *You must let go of the idea that to be single is to be unhappy and unfulfilled... There is a lot more good stuff in the 17 chapters and yet at the end you still feel unfulfilled.* ADJ-GRADED: usu v-link ADJ

unfunny /ʌnfʌni/. If you describe something or someone as **unfunny**, you mean that they do not make you laugh, although this was their intention or purpose. *We became increasingly fed up with his increasingly unfunny and unintelligent comments. ...another unfunny pair of comedians.* ADJ-GRADED ≠funny

unfurl /ʌnfɜːʳl/ **unfurls, unfurling, unfurled** ◆◇◇◇◇

1 If you **unfurl** something such as an umbrella, sail, or flag, or if it **unfurls**, you unroll or unfold it so that it is flat or spread out, and can be used or seen. *Once outside the inner breakwater, we began to unfurl all the sails. ...two weeks later when the leaves unfurl.* V-ERG V n V

2 If you say that events, stories, or scenes **unfurl** before you, you mean that you are aware of them or can see them as they happen or develop. *...as the dramatic changes in Europe continue to unfurl.* VERB =unfold V

unfurnished /ʌnfɜːʳnɪʃt/. If you rent an **unfurnished** flat or house, no furniture is provided by the owner. ADJ: usu ADJ n, also ADJ after v, v-link ADJ

ungainly /ʌngeɪnli/. If you describe a person, animal, or vehicle as **ungainly**, you mean that they look awkward or clumsy, often because they are big. *The dog, an ungainly mongrel pup, was loping about the road... Paul swam in his ungainly way to the side of the pool.* ADJ-GRADED =clumsy

ungenerous /ʌndʒenərəs/

1 If you describe someone's remarks, thoughts, or actions as **ungenerous**, you mean that they judge or treat people unfairly or harshly; a formal use. *This was a typically ungenerous response, even if tinged with truth.* ADJ-GRADED ≠generous

2 You can use **ungenerous** when you are describing a person or organization that is selfish or unwilling to give much money to other people; a formal use. *The company had a good scheme for the salaried employees and an ungenerous scheme for the hourly paid.* ADJ-GRADED ≠generous

ungodly /ʌngɒdli/

1 If you describe someone or something as **ungodly**, you mean that you think they are sinful. *Such a view implies that our bodies and sexual nature are inherently ungodly.* ADJ-GRADED =unholy

2 If you refer to a time as an **ungodly** hour, you are emphasizing that it is unreasonably early. *...at the ungodly hour of 4.00am.* ADJ: ADJ n PRAGMATICS =unearthly

3 If you refer to the amount or volume of something as **ungodly**, you mean that it is excessive or unreasonable. *...a power struggle of ungodly proportions.* ADJ: ADJ n

ungovernable /ʌngʌvəʳnəbəl/

1 If you describe a country or region as **ungovernable**, you mean that it seems impossible to control or govern it effectively, for example because of violence or conflict among the population. *Beset by ethnic strife, the province remains ungovernable... The country has become virtually ungovernable.* ADJ: usu v-link ADJ

2 If you describe feelings as **ungovernable**, you mean that they are so strong that they cannot be controlled. *He was filled with an ungovernable rage. ...ungovernable passions.* ADJ: usu ADJ n =uncontrollable

ungracious /ʌngreɪʃəs/. If you describe a person or their behaviour as **ungracious**, you mean that they are not polite or friendly in their speech or behaviour; a formal word. *...his ungracious behaviour during the Queen's recent visit... I was often rude and ungracious in refusing help.* ADJ-GRADED =discourteous, uncivil

ungraded /ʌngreɪdɪd/. In this dictionary, an **ungraded** adjective or adverb is one which is not normally used with an adverb or phrase indicating degree. 'Absent' is an example of a graded adjective. ADJ: usu ADJ n

ungrateful /ʌngreɪtfʊl/. If you describe someone as **ungrateful**, you are criticizing them for not showing thanks or for being unkind to someone who has given them something or done something for them. *I thought it was rather ungrateful... You ungrateful brat.* ADJ-GRADED PRAGMATICS ≠grateful

unguarded /ʌngɑːʳdɪd/

1 If something is **unguarded**, nobody is protecting it or looking after it. *I should not leave my briefcase and camera bag unguarded.* ADJ: ADJ after v, v-link ADJ, ADJ n

2 If you do or say something in an **unguarded** moment, you do or say it carelessly and without thinking, especially when it is something that you did not want anyone to see or know. *The photographers managed to capture Jane in an unguarded moment... He was ambushed by a reporter into an unguarded comment.* ADJ: usu ADJ n

unhampered /ʌnhæmpəʳd/. If you are **unhampered** by a problem or obstacle, you are free from it, and so you are able to do what you want to; used in written English. *...her belief that things go best if businessmen are allowed to make money unhampered by any kind of regulations.* ADJ-GRADED: usu ADJ after v, ADJ *by* n =unconstrained

unhappily /ʌnhæpɪli/. You use **unhappily** to introduce or refer to a statement when you consider it is sad and wish that it was different. *On May 23rd, unhappily, the little boy died... Unhappily the facts do not wholly bear out the theory... Unhappily for Berkowitz, he never got a penny.* ADV: ADV with cl PRAGMATICS =unfortunately

unhappy /ʌnhæpi/ **unhappier, unhappiest** ◆◆◆◇◇

1 If you are **unhappy**, you are sad and depressed. *Her marriage is in trouble and she is desperately unhappy... He was a shy, sometimes unhappy* ADJ-GRADED =miserable ≠happy

man... I thought of my father's unhappy boyhood. ♦ **unhappily** *'I don't have your imagination,' King said unhappily. ...an unhappily married woman.* ADV-GRADED: usu ADV with v ♦ **unhappiness** *There was a lot of unhappiness in my adolescence.* N-UNCOUNT

2 If you are **unhappy** about something, you are not pleased about it or not satisfied with it. *He has been unhappy with his son's political leanings... I suspect he isn't altogether unhappy about my absence... A lot of Republicans are unhappy that the government isn't doing more.* ADJ-GRADED: v-link ADJ, oft ADJ *about*/*at* n/-ing, ADJ that ♦ **unhappiness** *He has, by submitting his resignation, signalled his unhappiness with the government's decision.* N-UNCOUNT: oft N *with*/*about* n, N that

3 An **unhappy** situation or choice is not satisfactory or desirable. *It is our hope that this unhappy chapter in the history of relations between our two countries will soon be closed... The legislation represents in itself an unhappy compromise. ...unhappy experiences of writing for television.* ADJ: ADJ n

unharmed /ʌnhɑːʳmd/. If someone or something is **unharmed** after an accident or violent incident, they are not hurt or damaged in any way. *The car was a write-off, but everyone escaped unharmed... His eleven-year-old daughter was unharmed in the attack... The nine crew on the Boeing 747 were released unharmed.* ◆◇◇◇◇ ADJ: ADJ after v, v-link ADJ =unscathed

unhealthy /ʌnhelθi/ **unhealthier, unhealthiest** ◆◇◇◇◇

1 Something that is **unhealthy** is likely to cause illness or poor health. *Avoid unhealthy foods such as hamburger and chips... He worked in the notoriously unhealthy environment of a coal mine.* ADJ-GRADED ≠healthy

2 If you are **unhealthy**, you are not very fit or well. *I'm quite unhealthy really. ...a poorly dressed, unhealthy looking fellow with a poor complexion.* ADJ-GRADED ≠healthy

3 An **unhealthy** economy or company is financially weak and unsuccessful. *The redundancy of skilled and experienced workers is a terrible waste and a clear sign of an unhealthy economy.* ADJ-GRADED =weak ≠strong

4 If you describe someone's behaviour or interests as **unhealthy**, you do not consider them to be normal and think they may be psychologically harmful. *Frank has developed what I would term an unhealthy relationship with these people... Beatlemania became an unhealthy obsession... MacGregor believes it is unhealthy to lead a life with no interests beyond politics.* ADJ-GRADED ≠healthy

unheard /ʌnhɜːʳd/

1 If you say that a person or their words go **unheard**, you are expressing criticism because someone refuses to pay attention to what is said or take it into consideration; used in written English. *His impassioned pleas went unheard... She had not waited for any explanation but had condemned him unheard.* ADJ: usu v-link ADJ, ADJ after v, also ADJ n PRAGMATICS

2 If you describe spoken comments or pieces of music as **unheard**, you mean that most people are not familiar with them because they have not been expressed or performed in public. *A vast treasure-trove of virtually unheard melody awaits discovery by this new audience. ...a country where social criticism was largely unheard until this year.* ADJ

3 If someone's words or cries go **unheard**, nobody can hear them, or a particular person cannot hear them; used in written English. *Martin's weak cries for help went unheard until 6.40pm yesterday.* ADJ: usu v-link ADJ

unheard of ◆◇◇◇◇

1 You can say that an event or situation is **unheard of** when it never happens. *Meals are taken communally with other guests in the dining-room. Private bathrooms and toilets are unheard of... It's almost unheard of in France for a top politician not to come from the social elite.* ADJ: v-link ADJ

2 You can say that an event or situation is **unheard of** when it happens for the first time and is very surprising or shocking. *Long lines of people had queued up to buy at the unheard-of rate of two bottles of rum for $3... Mom announced that she was going to visit her family for a couple of weeks, which was absolutely unheard of.* ADJ

unheeded /ʌnhiːdɪd/. If you say that something such as a warning or danger goes **unheeded**, you mean that it has not been taken seriously or dealt with; used in written English. *The advice of experts went unheeded... He warned of the serious threat to global ecology which is going unheeded. ...a damning picture of lax banking standards and unheeded warnings.* ADJ: usu v-link ADJ, also ADJ n, ADJ after v =ignored

unhelpful /ʌnhelpfʊl/. If you say that someone or something is **unhelpful**, you mean that they do not help you or improve a situation, and may even make things worse. *The criticism is both unfair and unhelpful. ...unhelpful hotel staff.* ◆◇◇◇◇ ADJ-GRADED ≠helpful

unheralded /ʌnherəldɪd/

1 If you describe an artist or sports player as **unheralded**, you mean that people have not recognized their talent or ability; used in journalism. *They are inviting talented, but unheralded film-makers to submit examples of their work. ...the unheralded 22-year-old German qualifier Marc Gollner.* ADJ: usu ADJ n =unsung ≠acclaimed

2 If you describe something that happens as **unheralded**, you mean that you did not expect it, because nobody mentioned it beforehand; used in written English. *...Sandi's unheralded arrival on her doorstep... The complete reversal of this policy was unheralded.* ADJ

unhesitatingly /ʌnhezɪteɪtɪŋli/. If you say that someone does something **unhesitatingly**, you mean that they do it immediately and confidently, without any doubt or anxiety. *I would unhesitatingly choose the latter option... So is there any taboo she wouldn't touch? Unhesitatingly she replies, 'Politics.'* ADV: usu ADV with v, also ADV with cl =readily

unhinge /ʌnhɪndʒ/ **unhinges, unhinging, unhinged.** If you say that an experience **has unhinged** someone, you mean that it has affected them so deeply that they have become mentally ill. *The stress of war temporarily unhinged him.* VERB =unbalance V n ♦ **unhinged** *...feelings that make you feel completely unhinged and crazy.* ADJ-GRADED

unhinged /ʌnhɪndʒd/. If you describe someone's behaviour or performance as **unhinged**, you are critical of it because it seems wild and uncontrollable; used in journalism. *The phrase 'yeah yeah yeah' can rarely have been delivered with so much unhinged passion.* ADJ-GRADED PRAGMATICS

unholy /ʌnhoʊli/

1 You use **unholy** to emphasize how unreasonable or unpleasant you think something is. *She protested that it wasn't traditional jazz at all, but an unholy row... The economy is still an unholy mess.* ADJ: ADJ n PRAGMATICS =horrendous

2 If you refer to two or more people or groups that have come together for a common purpose as an **unholy** alliance, you mean that it is very surprising that these people or groups who usually oppose each other are working together, and that you find it worrying or undesirable that they are doing so. *The military will have to be persuaded to end its unholy alliance with the terrorists... Westerners charged that the party was run by an unholy coalition between North and South.* ADJ: ADJ n

3 If you describe something as **unholy**, you mean that it is wicked or sinful. *'This ought to be fun,' he told Alex, eyes gleaming with an almost unholy relish... He screamed unholy things at me.* ADJ-GRADED: usu ADJ n

unhook /ʌnhʊk/ **unhooks, unhooking, unhooked**

1 If you **unhook** a piece of clothing that is fastened with hooks, such as a bra or dress, you unfasten it. *She unhooked her dress.* VERB V n

2 If you **unhook** something that is held in place by hooks, you open it or remove it by undoing the hooks. *Chris unhooked the shutters and went out on the balcony.* VERB V n

unhurried /ʌnhʌrɪd/. If you describe something as **unhurried**, you approve of it because it is relaxed and slow, and is not rushed or anxious. *The islands are green, peaceful, and incredibly beautiful, with an unhurried pace of life.* ADJ-GRADED PRAGMATICS =leisurely ♦ **unhurriedly** *She walked unhurriedly away.* ADV: ADV with v

unhurt /ʌnhɜːʳt/. If someone who has been attacked, or involved in an accident, is **unhurt**, they are not injured. *The lorry driver escaped unhurt, but a pedestrian was injured... The two girls* ◆◇◇◇◇ ADJ: ADJ after v, v-link ADJ =unharmed ≠hurt *suddenly emerged from among the trees. Both seemed to be calm and unhurt.*

unhygienic /ʌnhaɪdʒiːnɪk, AM -dʒienɪk/. If you describe something as **unhygienic**, you mean that it is dirty and likely to cause infection or disease. *Parts of the shop were very dirty, unhygienic, and an ideal breeding ground for bacteria. ...unhygienic conditions.* ADJ-GRADED =insanitary ≠hygienic

unicorn /juːnɪkɔːʳn/ **unicorns.** In stories and legends, a **unicorn** is an imaginary animal that looks like a white horse and has a horn growing from its forehead. N-COUNT

unidentifiable /ʌnaɪdentɪfaɪəbᵊl/. If something or someone is **unidentifiable**, you are not able to say exactly what it is or who they are. *...unidentifiable howling noises... All the bodies were totally unidentifiable.* ADJ-GRADED =unrecognizable

unidentified /ʌnaɪdentɪfaɪd/ ◆◆◆◇◇

1 If you describe someone or something as **unidentified**, you mean that nobody knows who or what they are. *He was shot this morning by unidentified intruders at his house. ...unidentified cancer-causing substances in the environment.* ADJ: usu ADJ n =unknown

2 If you use **unidentified** to describe people, groups, and organizations, you do not want to give their names; used in journalism. *...his claims, which were based on the comments of anonymous and unidentified sources.* ADJ: usu ADJ n =unnamed

unification /juːnɪfɪkeɪʃᵊn/. **Unification** is the process by which two or more countries join together and become one country. *...the process of general European unification.* ◆◆◇◇◇ N-UNCOUNT

uniform /juːnɪfɔːʳm/ **uniforms** ◆◆◆◇◇

1 A **uniform** is a special set of clothes which some people, for example soldiers or the police, wear to work in and which some children wear at school. *The town police wear dark blue uniforms and flat caps... Philippe was in uniform, wearing a pistol holster on his belt... She will probably take great pride in wearing school uniform.* N-VAR

2 You can refer to the particular style of clothing which a group of people wear to show they belong to a group or a movement as their **uniform**. *Mark's is the uniform of the young male traveller – green Army trousers, T-shirt and shirt.* N-COUNT: with supp

3 If something is **uniform**, it does not vary, but is even and regular throughout. *Chips should be cut into uniform size and thickness... All flowing water, though it appears to be uniform, is actually divided into extensive inner surfaces, or layers, moving against one another... The price rises will not be uniform across the country.* ♦ **uniformity** /juːnɪfɔːʳmɪti/ *...the caramel that was used to maintain uniformity of color in the brandy.* ♦ **uniformly** *Beyond the windows, a November midday was uniformly grey... Microwaves heat water uniformly.* ADJ-GRADED; N-UNCOUNT; ADV-GRADED: ADV adj, ADV with v

4 If you describe a number of things as **uniform**, you mean that they are all the same. *Along each wall stretched uniform green metal filing cabinets... Shrimp are raised in long uniform ponds, frozen in the nearby packing plant and shipped north.* ♦ **uniformity** *...the dull uniformity of the houses.* ♦ **uniformly** *They are all about twenty years old, serious, smart, a bit conventional perhaps, but uniformly pleasant... The natives uniformly agreed on this important point.* ADJ-GRADED: usu ADJ n =identical; N-UNCOUNT; ADV-GRADED: ADV adj, ADV with v

uniformed /juːnɪfɔːʳmd/. If you use **uniformed** to describe someone who does a particular job, you mean that they are wearing a uniform. *...uniformed policemen.* ◆◇◇◇◇ ADJ: usu ADJ n

uniformity /juːnɪfɔːʳmɪti/. If there is **uniformity** in something such as a system, organization, or group of countries, the same rules, ideas, or methods are applied in all parts of it. *Spanish liberals sought to create linguistic as well as administrative uniformity... It is unlikely that the Maastricht treaty will produce uniformity of policy.* • See also **uniform**. ◆◇◇◇◇ N-UNCOUNT

unify /juːnɪfaɪ/ **unifies, unifying, unified.** If someone **unifies** different things or parts, or if the things or parts **unify**, they are brought together to form one thing. *A flexible retirement age is being considered by Ministers to unify men's and women's pension rights... Mr Major said his main job will be to unify the Conservative Party... The plan has been for the rival armies to demobilise, to unify, and then to hold elections to decide who rules... Helmut Kohl completed the task of unifying thriving West Germany with the old communist state of East Germany. ...the benefits of unifying with the West.* ♦ **unified** *...a unified German state. ...a unified system of taxation.* ◆◆◇◇◇ V-RECIP-ERG =unite; V pl-n; V n; pl-n V; V n with n; V with n; ADJ-GRADED: usu ADJ n

unilateral /juːnɪlætərᵊl/. A **unilateral** decision or action is taken by only one of the groups, organizations, or countries that are involved in a particular situation, without the agreement of the others. *...unilateral nuclear disarmament.* ♦ **unilaterally** *The British Government was careful not to act unilaterally.* ◆◇◇◇◇ ADJ: usu ADJ n; ADV: ADV with v

unilateralism /juːnɪlætərəlɪzəm/

1 Unilateralism is the belief that one country should get rid of all its own nuclear weapons, without waiting for other countries to do the same. N-UNCOUNT

2 Unilateralism is used to refer to a policy in which one country or group involved in a situation takes a decision or action on its own, without the agreement of the other countries or groups involved. *...the recent history of American aggressive unilateralism on trade.* N-UNCOUNT

unimaginable /ʌnɪmædʒɪnəbᵊl/. If you describe something as **unimaginable**, you are emphasizing that it is difficult to imagine or understand properly, because it is not part of people's normal experience. *The scale of the fighting is almost unimaginable... The children here have lived through unimaginable horrors.* ♦ **unimaginably** /ʌnɪmædʒɪnəbli/ *Conditions in prisons out there are unimaginably bad.* ◆◇◇◇◇ ADJ-GRADED PRAGMATICS =unbelievable; ADV-GRADED: ADV adj

unimaginative /ʌnɪmædʒɪnətɪv/

1 If you describe someone as **unimaginative**, you are criticizing them because they are not original or creative in what they do. *Her second husband was a steady, unimaginative, corporate lawyer. ...unimaginative teachers.* ADJ-GRADED PRAGMATICS ≠imaginative

2 If you describe something as **unimaginative**, you mean that it is boring or unattractive because very little imagination or effort has been used on it. *...unimaginative food... Film critics called it a monumentally unimaginative movie.* ADJ-GRADED: usu ADJ n PRAGMATICS ≠imaginative

unimpaired /ʌnɪmpeəʳd/. If something is **unimpaired** after something bad or unpleasant has happened to it, it is not damaged or made worse; a formal word. *His health and vigour were unimpaired by a stroke... By the time he had reached Japan he had reassured himself that their love affair would survive unimpaired.* ADJ: v-link ADJ, ADJ after v, ADJ n =unharmed

unimpeachable /ʌnɪmpiːtʃəbᵊl/. If you describe someone as **unimpeachable**, you mean that they are completely honest and reliable; a formal word. *He said all five were men of unimpeachable character. ...an unimpeachable source.* ADJ =reliable

unimpeded /ʌnɪmpiːdɪd/. If something moves or happens **unimpeded**, it continues without being stopped or interrupted by anything; a formal word. *We drove, unimpeded by anyone, to Arras... He promised to allow justice to run its course unimpeded... U.N. aid convoys have unimpeded access to the city.* ADJ: ADJ after v, ADJ n, v-link ADJ

unimportant /ʌnɪmpɔːʳtᵊnt/. If you describe something or someone as **unimportant**, you mean that they do not have much influence, effect, or value, and are therefore not worth serious consideration. *It was an unimportant job, and paid very little... When they had married, six years before, the difference in their ages had seemed unimportant.* ◆◇◇◇◇ ADJ-GRADED =insignificant ≠important

unimpressed /ʌnɪmprest/. If you are **unimpressed** by something or someone, you do not think they are very good, useful, or worthy of serious consideration. *He was also very unimpressed by his teachers... Graham Fletcher was unimpressed with the idea of filling in a lengthy questionnaire.* ◆◇◇◇◇ ADJ-GRADED: v-link ADJ, oft ADJ *by/with* n ≠impressed

unimpressive /ʌnɪmpre̲sɪv/. If you describe someone or something as **unimpressive**, you mean they appear very ordinary, without any special or exciting qualities. *...even though Manchester United have looked unimpressive over recent weeks... Rainey was an unimpressive, rather dull lecturer.* ADJ-GRADED ≠impressive

uninformed /ʌnɪnfɔ̲ːʳmd/. If you describe someone as **uninformed**, you mean that they have very little knowledge or information about a particular situation or subject. *He could not complain that he was uninformed about the true nature of the regime... 'Dumb, uninformed critics,' he replies, 'do not realise that even a great artist can have a bad day.'.* ADJ-GRADED ≠informed

uninhabitable /ʌnɪnhæ̲bɪtəbᵊl/. If a place is **uninhabitable**, it is impossible for people to live there, for example because it is dangerous or unhealthy. *About 90 percent of the city's single-family homes are uninhabitable... As parts of the world become uninhabitable, millions of people will try to migrate to more hospitable areas. ...a young couple turning an uninhabitable wreck into their first home.* ADJ ≠habitable

uninhabited /ʌnɪnhæ̲bɪtɪd/. An **uninhabited** place is one where nobody lives. *...an uninhabited island in the North Pacific... The area is largely uninhabited. ...a charred, uninhabited farmhouse.* ADJ =deserted

uninhibited /ʌnɪnhɪ̲bɪtɪd/. If you describe a person or their behaviour as **uninhibited**, you mean that they express their opinions and feelings openly, and behave as they want to, without worrying what other people think. *...a commanding and uninhibited entertainer... The dancing is uninhibited and as frenzied as an aerobics class... Mason was uninhibited in his questions about Foster's family.* ADJ-GRADED

uninitiated /ʌnɪnɪ̲ʃieɪtɪd/. You can refer to people who have no knowledge or experience of a particular subject or activity as **the uninitiated**. *For the uninitiated, Western Swing is a fusion of jazz, rhythm & blues, rock & roll and country music... Its appeal may not be immediately obvious to the uninitiated.* ► Also an adjective. *For those uninitiated in scientific ocean drilling, the previous record was a little over 4 km... This may not be visible to the uninitiated eye, but the experienced quarryman sees it.* N-PLURAL: the N; ADJ

uninspired /ʌnɪnspa̲ɪəʳd/. If you describe something or someone as **uninspired**, you are criticizing them because they do not seem to have any original or exciting qualities. *The script was singularly uninspired. ...an honest if uninspired leader... Food in the dining car was adequate, if uninspired.* ADJ-GRADED PRAGMATICS =unexceptional ≠inspired

uninspiring /ʌnɪnspa̲ɪərɪŋ/. If you describe something or someone as **uninspiring**, you are criticizing them because they have no special or exciting qualities, and make you feel bored. *The series of speeches on the economy was uninspiring and a rehash of old subjects... The house had a tiny kitchen with an uninspiring view. ...his image as a dull and uninspiring leader.* ADJ-GRADED PRAGMATICS ≠inspiring

unintelligent /ʌnɪnte̲lɪdʒᵊnt/. If you describe a person as **unintelligent**, you mean that they are stupid, or do not show any sensible ideas or thoughts. *He believes him to be a weak and unintelligent man... He certainly was not unintelligent.* ADJ-GRADED ≠intelligent

unintelligible /ʌnɪnte̲lɪdʒɪbᵊl/. **Unintelligible** speech or writing is impossible to understand, for example because it is not written or pronounced clearly, or because its meaning is confused or complicated. *He muttered something unintelligible... I did my best to join in, but the conversation was largely unintelligible. ...the unintelligible phrases and images of his earlier poems.* ◆◇◇◇◇ ADJ-GRADED =incomprehensible

unintended /ʌnɪnte̲ndɪd/. **Unintended** results were not planned to happen, although they happened. *...the unintended consequences of human action. ...unintended pregnancies.* ADJ ≠intended

unintentional /ʌnɪnte̲nʃənᵊl/. Something that is **unintentional** is not done deliberately, but happens by accident. *Perhaps he had slightly misled them, but it was quite unintentional... There are moments of unintentional humour.* ◆◇◇◇◇ ADJ =inadvertent
♦ **unintentionally** *...an overblown and unintentionally funny adaptation of 'Dracula'. ...a scientist who unintentionally absorbed a small quantity of the mind-altering drug through the skin on his fingers.* ADV: ADV adj, ADV with v

uninterested /ʌnɪ̲ntrəstɪd/. If you are **uninterested** in something or someone, you do not want to know any more about them, because you think they have no special or exciting qualities. *I was so uninterested in the result that I didn't even bother to look at it. ...unhelpful and uninterested shop staff.* ADJ-GRADED: usu v-link ADJ, oft ADJ *in* n/-ing

uninteresting /ʌnɪ̲ntrəstɪŋ/. If you describe something or someone as **uninteresting**, you mean they have no special or exciting qualities. *Their media has earned the reputation for being rather dull and uninteresting... Why did he choose these pale, nerveless, uninteresting people?* ADJ-GRADED =boring, dull

uninterrupted /ʌnɪntərʌ̲ptɪd/ ◆◇◇◇◇

1 If something is **uninterrupted**, it is continuous and has no breaks or interruptions in it. *This enables the healing process to continue uninterrupted... His hearing remained good, so that his contact with the world was uninterrupted. ...five years of rapid and uninterrupted growth.* ADJ: ADJ after v, v-link ADJ, ADJ n

2 An **uninterrupted** view of something is a clear view of it, without any obstacles in the way. *Diners can enjoy an uninterrupted view of the garden.* ADJ: usu ADJ n

uninvited /ʌnɪnva̲ɪtɪd/. If someone does something or goes somewhere **uninvited**, they do it or go there without being asked, often when their action or presence is not wanted. *He came uninvited to one of Stein's parties. ...a hundred invited guests and many more who were uninvited. ...an uninvited question from a reporter.* ADJ: ADJ after v, v-link ADJ, ADJ n ≠invited

union /ju̲ːnjən/ **unions** ◆◆◆◆◆

1 A **union** is a workers' organization which represents its members and which aims to improve things such as their working conditions and pay. *I feel that women in all types of employment can benefit from joining a union. ...union officials.* N-COUNT =trade union

2 When the **union** of two or more things occurs, they are joined together and become one thing. *In 1918 the Romanian majority in this former tsarist province voted for union with Romania.* N-UNCOUNT: oft N *with/of* n

3 When two or more things, for example countries or organizations have been joined together to form one thing, you can refer to them as a **union**. *Tanzania is a union of the states of Tanganyika and Zanzibar. ...the question of which countries should join the currency union.* N-SING: usu with supp, oft N *of* pl-n =coalition

4 The marriage of two people is sometimes referred to as a **union**; a formal use. *Even Louis began to think their union was not blessed in the eyes of God.* N-COUNT: usu sing

5 **Union** is used in the name of some clubs, societies, and organizations. *The naming of stars is at the discretion of the International Astronomical Union. ...the Mothers' Union.* N-IN-NAMES

unionism /ju̲ːnjənɪzəm/ ◆◇◇◇◇

1 **Unionism** is any set of political principles based on the idea that two or more political or national units should be joined or remain together, for example the political belief that Northern Ireland should remain part of the United Kingdom. N-UNCOUNT
♦ **unionist, unionists** *...traditional unionists fearful of home rule.* N-COUNT

2 **Unionism** is the same as **trade unionism**. N-UNCOUNT
♦ **unionist** *As a former unionist, he'll be more sensitive to the demands of the people.* N-COUNT

unionization /ju̲ːnjənaɪze̲ɪʃᵊn/; also spelled **unionisation** in British English. The **unionization** of workers or industries is the process of workers becoming members of trade unions. *Increasing unionization led to demands for higher wages and shorter hours.* N-UNCOUNT

unionized /juːnjənaɪzd/; also spelled **unionised** in British English. **Unionized** workers belong to trade unions. If a workplace is **unionized**, most of the workers there belong to trade unions. *The contract would give unionized workers a 12 percent pay raise over three years... The company is unionized.* ADJ

Union Jack, Union Jacks. The **Union Jack** is the national flag of the United Kingdom. It consists of a blue background with red and white crosses on it. ◆◇◇◇◇ N-COUNT: usu sing, oft *the* N

unique /juːniːk/ ◆◆◆◇◇

1 Something that is **unique** is the only one of its kind. *Each person's signature is unique... The area has its own unique language, Catalan.* ♦ **uniquely** *Because of the extreme cold, the Antarctic is a uniquely fragile environment... Uniquely among the great world religions, Buddhism is rooted only in the universal experience of suffering known to all human beings.* ♦ **uniqueness** *...the uniqueness of China's own experience.* ADJ; ADV: ADV group, ADV with v; N-UNCOUNT

2 You can use **unique** to describe things that you admire because they are very unusual and special. *Brett's vocals are just unique... Kauffman was a woman of unique talent and determination.* ♦ **uniquely** *There'll never be a shortage of people who consider themselves uniquely qualified to be president of the United States. ...a festival ambience that is uniquely conducive to the absorption of serious music.* ADJ-GRADED PRAGMATICS; ADV: ADV group, ADV with v

3 If something is **unique to** one thing, person, group, or place, it concerns or belongs only to that thing, person, group, or place. *No one knows for sure why adolescence is unique to humans... This interesting and charming creature is unique to Borneo.* ♦ **uniquely** *The problem isn't uniquely American.* ADJ: v-link ADJ *to* n; ADV: ADV adj

unisex /juːnɪseks/. **Unisex** is used to describe things, usually clothes or hairdressing salons, which are designed for use by both men and women rather than by only one sex. *...the classic unisex hair salon... A lot of the longer jackets are unisex.* ADJ

unison /juːnɪsən, -zən/ ◆◇◇◇◇

1 If two or more people do something **in unison**, they do it together at the same time. *The students gave him a rapturous welcome, chanting in unison: 'We want the king!'... Michael and the landlady nodded in unison.* PHRASES PHR after v =in concert

2 If people or organizations act **in unison**, they act the same way because they agree with each other or because they want to achieve the same aims. *For churches not normally noted for their ability to act in unison, today's unprecedented move was all the more remarkable... The international community is ready to work in unison against him.* PHR after v =in harmony

unit /juːnɪt/ **units** ◆◆◆◆◇

1 If you consider something as a **unit**, you consider it as a single, complete thing. *Agriculture was based in the past on the family as a unit.* N-COUNT

2 A **unit** is a group of people who work together at a specific job, often in a particular place. *...the health services research unit... The results from this unit are staggering.* N-COUNT

3 A **unit** is a small machine which has a particular function, often part of a larger machine. *The unit plugs into any TV set.* N-COUNT

4 A **unit** of measurement is a fixed standard quantity, length, or weight that is used for measuring things. The litre, the centimetre, and the ounce are all units. N-COUNT

5 A **unit** is one of the parts that a coursebook is divided into. N-COUNT =module

unitary /juːnɪtri, AM -teri/. A **unitary** country or organization is one in which two or more areas or groups in it have joined together, have the same aims, and are controlled by a single government or group of people. *...a call for the creation of a single unitary state.* ◆◇◇◇◇ ADJ: ADJ n

unite /juːnaɪt/ **unites, uniting, united.** If a group of people or things **unite** or if something **unites** them, they join together and act as a group. *The two parties have been trying to unite since the New Year... The vast majority of nations have agreed to unite their efforts to bring peace.* ◆◆◇◇◇ V-ERG; V; V n

united /juːnaɪtɪd/ ◆◆◆◇◇

1 When people are **united** about something, they agree about it and act together. *Every party is united on the need for parliamentary democracy... A united effort is always more effective than an isolated complaint.* ADJ-GRADED

2 **United** is used to describe a country which has been formed from two or more countries or states. *...the first elections to be held in a united Germany for fifty eight years.* ADJ

United Kingdom. **The United Kingdom** is the official name for the country consisting of Great Britain and Northern Ireland. ◆◆◇◇◇ N-PROPER: *the* N

United Nations. **The United Nations** is a worldwide organization which most countries belong to. Its role is to encourage international peace, cooperation, and friendship. ◆◆◆◆◇ N-PROPER: *the* N

unit trust, unit trusts. In British English, a **unit trust** is an organization which invests money in many different types of business and which offers units for sale to the public as an investment. You can also refer to an investment of this type as a **unit trust**. The American term is **mutual fund**. ◆◇◇◇◇ N-COUNT

unity /juːnɪti/ ◆◆◆◇◇

1 **Unity** is the state of different areas or groups being joined together to form a single country or organization. *Senior politicians met today to discuss the future of European economic unity. ...German unity.* N-UNCOUNT: oft adj N =union

2 When there is **unity**, people are in agreement and act together for a particular purpose. *...a renewed unity of purpose... Speakers at the rally mouthed sentiments of unity... The choice was meant to create an impression of party unity.* N-UNCOUNT

Univ. **Univ** is a written abbreviation for 'University' which is used especially in the names of some universities. *...the Wharton School, Univ of Pennsylvania.* ◆◇◇◇◇

universal /juːnɪvɜːʳsəl/ **universals** ◆◆◇◇◇

1 Something that is **universal** relates to everyone in the world or everyone in a particular group or society. *The insurance industry has produced its own proposals for universal health care... The desire to look attractive is universal.* ♦ **universality** /juːnɪvɜːʳsælɪti/ *I have been amazed at the universality of all of our experiences, whatever our origins, sex or age.* ADJ: usu ADJ n; N-UNCOUNT: oft N *of* n

2 Something that is **universal** affects or relates to every part of the world or the universe. *...universal diseases.* ADJ

3 A **universal** is a principle that applies in all cases or a characteristic that is present in all members of a particular class. *There are simply no economic universals.* N-COUNT

universally /juːnɪvɜːʳsəli/ ◆◇◇◇◇

1 If something is **universally** believed or accepted, it is believed or accepted by everyone with no disagreement. *...a universally accepted point of view... The scale of these problems is now universally recognised.* ADV: usu ADV -ed/adj

2 If something is **universally** true, it is true everywhere in the world or in all situations. *The disadvantage is that it is not universally available... Nor is acid rain always, and universally, a bad thing.* ADV: usu ADV adj, also ADV with v, *be* ADV n

universe /juːnɪvɜːʳs/ **universes** ◆◆◆◇◇

1 The **universe** is the whole of space and all the stars, planets, and other forms of matter and energy in it. *Einstein's equations showed the Universe to be expanding... Early astronomers thought that our planet was the centre of the universe.* N-COUNT: usu *the* N in sing

2 If you talk about someone's **universe**, you are referring to the whole of their experience or an important part of it. *Good writers suck in what they see of the world, re-creating their own universe on the page... They marked out the boundaries of our visual universe... Behind his eyes was a whole universe of pain.* N-COUNT: usu sing, oft with poss =world

3 If you say that something is, for example, the best PHRASE:

or biggest thing of its kind **in the universe**, you are emphasizing that you think it is bigger or better than anything else of its kind; an informal expression. *According to my friends I am the coolest, thinnest, cleverest, funniest journalist in the universe.*
PHR after superl
PRAGMATICS

university /juːnɪvɜːʳsɪti/ **universities.** A **university** is an institution where students study for degrees and where academic research is done. *Patrick is now at London University... They want their daughter to go to university, but they are also keen that she get a summer job... The university refused to let Dick Gregory speak on campus.*
◆◆◆◆◆
N-VAR: oft in names

unjust /ʌndʒʌst/. If you describe an action, system, or law as **unjust**, you think that it treats a person or group badly in a way that they do not deserve. *The attack on Charles was deeply unjust... He spent 25 years campaigning against racist and unjust immigration laws.* ♦ **unjustly** *She was unjustly accused of stealing money and then given the sack.*
◆◇◇◇◇
ADJ-GRADED =unfair
ADV-GRADED: usu ADV with v

unjustifiable /ʌndʒʌstɪfaɪəbᵊl, ʌndʒʌstɪfaɪəbᵊl/. If you describe an action, especially one that harms someone, as **unjustifiable**, you mean there is no good reason for it. *Using these missiles to down civilian aircraft is simply immoral and totally unjustifiable.* ♦ **unjustifiably** *The press invade people's privacy unfairly and unjustifiably every day.*
ADJ-GRADED ≠justifiable
ADV-GRADED ≠justifiably

unjustified /ʌndʒʌstɪfaɪd/. If you describe a belief or action as **unjustified**, you think that there is no good reason for having it or doing it. *Your report last week was unfair. It was based upon wholly unfounded and totally unjustified allegations... The commission concluded that the police action was unjustified.*
◆◇◇◇◇
ADJ

unkempt /ʌnkempt/. If you describe something or someone as **unkempt**, you mean that they are untidy, and not looked after carefully or kept neat. *His hair was unkempt and filthy. ...the unkempt grass. ...an unkempt old man.*
ADJ-GRADED =messy

unkind /ʌnkaɪnd/ **unkinder, unkindest**
◆◇◇◇◇

1 If someone is **unkind**, they behave in an unpleasant, unfriendly, or slightly cruel way. You can also describe someone's words or actions as **unkind**. *All last summer he'd been unkind to her... No one has an unkind word to say about him... Without wishing to be unkind, she's not the most interesting company... I think it's a bit unkind to describe the ship in those terms.* ♦ **unkindly** *Several viewers commented unkindly on her costumes... 'He's a bit of an eccentric old fatty,' Thomas thought, unkindly.* ♦ **unkindness** *He realized the unkindness of the remark and immediately regretted having hurt her with it.*
ADJ-GRADED: oft ADJ *to*n, *it* v-link ADJ to-inf =hurtful ≠kind
ADV-GRADED: ADV with v, ADV with cl ≠kindly
N-UNCOUNT ≠kindness

2 If you describe something bad that happens to someone as **unkind**, you mean that they do not deserve it; used in written English. *The weather was unkind to those pipers who played in the morning. ...a shared conviction that some unkind fate or chance is keeping them apart.*
ADJ-GRADED: oft ADJ *to* n ≠kind

unknowable /ʌnnoʊəbᵊl/. If you describe something as **unknowable**, you mean that it is impossible for human beings to know anything about it; used in written English. *Any investment in shares is a bet on an unknowable future flow of profits... The specific impact of the greenhouse effect is unknowable, at least at this point.*
ADJ

unknowing /ʌnnoʊɪŋ/. If you describe a person as **unknowing**, you mean that they are not aware of what is happening or of what they are doing. *Some governments have been victims and perhaps unknowing accomplices in the bank's activities.*
ADJ: usu ADJ n =unwitting

unknowingly /ʌnnoʊɪŋli/. If someone does something **unknowingly**, they do it without being aware of it. *...if people unknowingly move into more contaminated areas of the river. ...the extent to which the workforce colludes knowingly or unknowingly with such criminal activity... Art often imitates nature unknowingly.*
ADV: ADV with v, ADV with cl ≠knowingly

unknown /ʌnnoʊn/ **unknowns**
◆◆◆◇◇

1 If something is **unknown** to you, you have no knowledge of it. *An unknown number of demonstrators were arrested... How did you expect us to proceed on such a perilous expedition, through unknown terrain... The motive for the killing is unknown.* ► An **unknown** is something that is unknown. *The length of the war is one of the biggest unknowns.*
ADJ ≠known
N-COUNT

2 An **unknown** person is someone whose name you do not know or whose character you do not know anything about. *Unknown thieves had forced their way into the apartment... I could not understand how someone with so many awards could be unknown to me.*
ADJ

3 An **unknown** person is not famous or publicly recognized. *He was an unknown writer. ...a popular environment where both established and unknown artists can meet, talk and drink.* ► An **unknown** is a person who is unknown. *Within a short space of time a group of complete unknowns had established a wholly original form of humour.*
ADJ-GRADED
N-COUNT

4 If you say that a particular problem or situation is **unknown**, you mean that it never occurs. *A hundred years ago coronary heart disease was virtually unknown in Europe and America.*
ADJ: usu v-link ADJ =unheard of

5 **The unknown** refers generally to things or places that people do not know about or understand. *Ignorance of people brings fear, fear of the unknown.*
N-SING: *the*N

unlawful /ʌnlɔːfʊl/. If something is **unlawful**, the law does not allow you to do it; a formal word. *...employees who believe their dismissal was unlawful... A pushed-in window indicated unlawful entry.* ♦ **unlawfully** *...the councils' assertion that the government acted unlawfully in imposing the restrictions.*
◆◇◇◇◇
ADJ =illegal ≠lawful
ADV: ADV with v

unlawful killing, unlawful killings. Unlawful killing is used to refer in a general way to crimes such as murder and manslaughter; a legal expression.
N-VAR

unleaded /ʌnledɪd/. **Unleaded** fuels contain a reduced amount of lead in order to reduce the pollution caused when they are burned. *The new Metro is designed to run on unleaded fuel.* ► Also a noun. *All its V8 engines will run happily on unleaded.*
◆◇◇◇◇
ADJ
N-UNCOUNT

unlearn /ʌnlɜːʳn/ **unlearns, unlearning, unlearned;** also spelled **unlearnt** in British English. If you **unlearn** something that you have learned, you try to forget it or ignore it, often because it is wrong or it is having a bad influence on you. *They learn new roles and unlearn old ones... Before you know it, you will have unlearned the debt habit.*
VERB ≠learn
V n

unleash /ʌnliːʃ/ **unleashes, unleashing, unleashed.** If you say that someone or something **unleashes** a powerful movement, force, or feeling, you mean that it starts suddenly and has an immediate strong effect. *There's a real risk that food rationing will unleash a new stream of refugees... Then he unleashed his own, unstoppable, attack. ...the power unleashed by their leg muscles.*
◆◆◇◇◇
VERB =let loose
V n
V-ed

unleavened /ʌnlevᵊnd/. **Unleavened** bread or dough is made without any yeast.
ADJ: usu ADJ n

unless /ʌnles/. You use **unless** to introduce the only circumstances in which an event you are mentioning will not take place or in which a statement you are making is not true. *Unless you are trying to lose weight to please yourself, it's going to be tough to keep your motivation level high... We cannot understand disease unless we understand the person who has the disease... I'm not happy unless I ride or drive every day.*
◆◆◆◆◇
CONJ-SUBORD
PRAGMATICS

unlike /ʌnlaɪk/
◆◆◆◇◇

1 If one thing is **unlike** another thing, the two things have different qualities or characteristics from each other. *This was a foreign country, so unlike San Jose... She was unlike him in every way except for her coal black eyes.*
PREP =dissimilar to ≠like

2 You can use **unlike** to contrast two people, things, or situations, and show how they are different. *Unlike aerobics, walking entails no expensive fees for classes or clubs.*
PREP =in contrast to, as opposed to ≠like

3 If you describe something that a particular person has done as being **unlike** them, you mean that you are surprised by it because it is not typical of their character or normal behaviour. *It was so unlike him to say something like that, with such intensity, that I was astonished... 'We'll all be arrested!' Thomas yelled, which was most unlike him.* PREP

unlikely /ʌnlaɪkli/ **unlikeliest.** If you say that something is **unlikely** to happen or **unlikely** to be true, you believe that it will not happen or that it is not true, although you are not completely sure. *A military coup seems unlikely... As with many technological revolutions, you are unlikely to be aware of it... It's now unlikely that future parliaments will bring back the death penalty... In the unlikely event of anybody phoning, could you just scribble a message down?* ◆◆◆◆◇ ADJ-GRADED: usu v-link ADJ, oft ADJ to-inf, *it* v-link ADJ that ≠likely

unlimited /ʌnlɪmɪtɪd/. If there is an **unlimited** quantity of something, you can have as much or as many of that thing as you want. *An unlimited number of copies can still be made from the original... You'll also have unlimited access to the swimming pool... Career prospects are virtually unlimited.* ◆◇◇◇◇ ADJ =limitless ≠limited

unlisted /ʌnlɪstɪd/. In American English, if a person or his or her telephone number is **unlisted**, the number is not listed in the telephone directory, and the telephone company will refuse to give it to people who ask for it. The usual British word is **ex-directory**. ADJ

unlit /ʌnlɪt/
1 An **unlit** fire or cigarette has not been set alight. ADJ
2 An **unlit** street or building is dark because there are no lights switched on in it. ADJ

unload /ʌnloʊd/ **unloads, unloading, unloaded** ◆◇◇◇◇
1 If you **unload** goods from a vehicle, or you **unload** a vehicle, you remove the goods from the vehicle, usually after they have been transported from one place to another. *Unload everything from the boat and clean it thoroughly... They were reported to be unloading trucks filled with looted furniture.* VERB V n *from* n V n
2 If someone **unloads** investments, they get rid of them or sell them; used in business journalism. *Since March, he has unloaded 1.3 million shares.* VERB V n

unlock /ʌnlɒk/ **unlocks, unlocking, unlocked** ◆◇◇◇◇
1 If you **unlock** something such as a door, a room, or a container that has a lock, you open it using a key. *He unlocked the car and threw the coat on to the back seat... She unlocked the case and carefully lifted out the vase.* VERB ≠lock V n
2 If you **unlock** the potential or the secrets of something or someone, you release them. *Education and training is the key that will unlock our nation's potential. ...the man who dedicated his life to unlocking the secrets of the universe.* VERB V n

unlovable /ʌnlʌvəbᵊl/. If someone is **unlovable**, they are not likely to be loved by anyone, because they do not have any attractive qualities. ADJ-GRADED ≠lovable

unloved /ʌnlʌvd/. If someone feels **unloved**, they feel that nobody loves them. *I think she feels desperately wounded and unloved at the moment. ...a lonely, unloved child.* ADJ-GRADED ≠loved

unlovely /ʌnlʌvli/. If you describe something as **unlovely**, you mean that it is unattractive or unpleasant in some way. *She found a small, inexpensive motel on the outskirts of the town; it was barren and unlovely.* ADJ-GRADED =ugly

unloving /ʌnlʌvɪŋ/. If you describe a person as **unloving**, you believe that they do not love, or show love to, the people they ought to love. *The overworked, overextended parent may be seen as unloving, but may simply be exhausted.* ADJ-GRADED ≠loving

unluckily /ʌnlʌkɪli/. You use **unluckily** as a comment on something bad or unpleasant that happens to someone, in order to suggest sympathy for them or that it was not their fault. *Unluckily for him, the fraud officers were watching this flight too... Some people unluckily achieve suicide when they only meant to attempt it.* ADV: ADV with cl, ADV with v, oft ADV *for* n =unfortunately ≠luckily

unlucky /ʌnlʌki/ **unluckier, unluckiest** ◆◇◇◇◇
1 If someone is **unlucky**, they have bad luck. *Cantona was unlucky not to score on two occasions... Others were unlucky victims of falling debris.* ADJ-GRADED: oft ADJ to-inf ≠lucky
2 You can use **unlucky** to describe unpleasant things which happen to someone, especially when you feel that the person does not deserve them. *...Argentina's unlucky defeat by Ireland.* ADJ-GRADED ≠lucky
3 **Unlucky** is used to describe something that is thought to cause bad luck. *Some people think it is unlucky to look at a new moon through glass.* ADJ-GRADED ≠lucky

unmade /ʌnmeɪd/. An **unmade** bed has not had the bedclothes neatly arranged after it was last slept in. ADJ

unmanageable /ʌnmænɪdʒəbᵊl/
1 If you describe something as **unmanageable**, you mean that is difficult to use, deal with, or control. *People were visiting the house every day, sometimes in unmanageable numbers. ...her freckles and unmanageable hair.* ADJ-GRADED ≠manageable
2 If you describe someone, especially a young person, as **unmanageable**, you mean that they behave in an unacceptable way and are difficult to control. *The signs are that indulged children tend to become unmanageable when they reach their teens.* ADJ-GRADED =unruly

unmanly /ʌnmænli/. If you describe a boy's or man's behaviour as **unmanly**, you are critical of the fact that they are behaving in a way that you think is inappropriate for a man. *Your partner can feel the loss as acutely as you, but may feel that it is unmanly to cry.* ADJ-GRADED: usu v-link ADJ PRAGMATICS =effeminate

unmanned /ʌnmænd/
1 **Unmanned** vehicles such as spacecraft do not have any crew and are operated automatically or by remote control. *...a special unmanned spacecraft. ...unmanned rockets.* ADJ: usu ADJ n
2 If a place is **unmanned**, there is nobody working there. *The fare from the last unmanned station is probably less than a pound... Unmanned post offices meant millions of letters went unsorted.* ADJ

unmarked /ʌnmɑːʳkt/ ◆◇◇◇◇
1 Something that is **unmarked** has no marks on it. *Her shoes are still white and unmarked.* ADJ: usu v-link ADJ
2 Something that is **unmarked** has no marking on it which identifies what it is or whose it is. *He had seen them come out and get into the unmarked police car... He lies in an unmarked grave at Elmton.* ADJ: usu ADJ n
3 In a sport such as football, hockey, or basketball, if a player is **unmarked**, there are no players from the opposing team who are waiting to challenge them when they have control of the ball. *Sheringham was unmarked as he met Anderton's free kick and headed in after nine minutes.* ADJ: usu v-link ADJ, also ADJ after v

unmarried /ʌnmærid/. Someone who is **unmarried** is not married. *They refused to rent an apartment to an unmarried couple.* ◆◇◇◇◇ ADJ

unmask /ʌnmɑːsk, -mæsk/ **unmasks, unmasking, unmasked.** If you **unmask** someone or something bad, you show or make known their true nature or character, when they had previously been thought to be good. *Elliott unmasked and confronted the master spy and traitor Kim Philby... He managed to pass top secret documents to East Berlin for many years before he was unmasked in 1974.* VERB =expose V n

unmatched /ʌnmætʃt/. If you describe something as **unmatched**, you are emphasizing that it is better or greater than all other things of the same kind. *...a landscape of unmatched beauty... Brian's old-fashioned cuisine was unmatched for flavour.* ADJ =unrivalled

unmentionable /ʌnmenʃənəbᵊl/. If you describe something as **unmentionable**, you mean that it is too embarrassing or unpleasant to talk about. *Has he got some unmentionable disease?* ADJ

unmercifully /ʌnmɜːʳsɪfʊli/. If you do something **unmercifully**, you do it a lot, showing no mercy or pity. *Uncle Sebastian used to tease Mother and Daddy unmercifully that all they could produce was girls.* ADV: usu ADV with v, also ADV adj =mercilessly

unmet /ʌnmet/. **Unmet** needs or demands are not satisfied. *...the unmet demand for quality family planning services... This need routinely goes unmet.*
ADJ: ADJ n, v-link ADJ, ADJ after v

unmissable /ʌnmɪsəbᵊl/. In British English, when journalists say that something such as an event or a film is **unmissable**, they are emphasizing that it is so good that everyone should try to go to it or see it; an informal word. *His new show is unmissable... Book your place on this unmissable conference.*
ADJ

unmistakable /ʌnmɪsteɪkəbᵊl/; also spelled **unmistakeable**. If you describe something as **unmistakable**, you mean that it is so obvious that it cannot be mistaken for anything else. *He didn't give his name, but the voice was unmistakable. ...the unmistakable smell of marijuana drifted down.* ♦ **unmistakably** /ʌnmɪsteɪkəbli/ *It's still unmistakably a Minnelli movie... She's unmistakably Scandinavian... He had unmistakably been waving his flag to attract the referee's attention.*
◆◇◇◇◇ ADJ
ADV: usu ADV group, also ADV with v

unmitigated /ʌnmɪtɪgeɪtɪd/. You use **unmitigated** to emphasize that a bad situation or quality is totally bad. *Last year's cotton crop was an unmitigated disaster... She leads a life of unmitigated misery.*
ADJ: ADJ n =absolute, utter

unmolested /ʌnməlestɪd/. If someone does something **unmolested**, they do it without being stopped or interfered with. *Like many fugitives, he lived in Argentina unmolested for many years... The trouble started when a few men chose to ignore the wishes of a few women who wanted to dance unmolested at the front.*
ADJ: usu ADJ after v, also v-link ADJ, ADJ n

unmoved /ʌnmuːvd/. If you are **unmoved** by something, you are not emotionally affected by it. *Mr Bird remained unmoved by the corruption allegations... His face was unmoved, but on his lips there was a trace of displeasure.*
◆◇◇◇◇ ADJ-GRADED: v-link ADJ ≠moved

unmusical /ʌnmjuːzɪkᵊl/

1 An **unmusical** sound is unpleasant to listen to. *Lainey had a terrible voice, unmusical and sharp.*
ADJ-GRADED ≠sweet

2 An **unmusical** person cannot play or appreciate music. *They're completely unmusical.*
ADJ-GRADED

unnamed /ʌnneɪmd/
◆◇◇◇◇

1 **Unnamed** people or things are talked about but their names are not mentioned. *An unnamed man collapsed and died while he was walking near Dundonald... The cash comes from an unnamed source.*
ADJ: usu ADJ n

2 **Unnamed** things have not been given a name. *...unnamed comets and asteroids.*
ADJ: usu ADJ n

unnatural /ʌnnætʃərᵊl/
◆◇◇◇◇

1 If you describe something as **unnatural**, you mean that it is strange and often frightening, because it is different from what you normally expect. *The aircraft rose with unnatural speed on take-off... The altered landscape looks unnatural and weird.* ♦ **unnaturally** *The house was unnaturally silent. ...unnaturally cold conditions.*
ADJ-GRADED
ADV-GRADED: ADV adj

2 Behaviour that is **unnatural** seems artificial and not normal or spontaneous. *She gave him a bright, determined smile which seemed unnatural.* ♦ **unnaturally** *Try to avoid shouting or speaking unnaturally.*
ADJ-GRADED: usu v-link ADJ =strained
ADV-GRADED: ADV with v

unnaturally /ʌnnætʃərəli/. You can use **not unnaturally** to indicate that the situation you are describing is exactly as you would expect in the circumstances. *It was a question that Roy not unnaturally found impossible to answer... Not unnaturally, Jane greatly resented Harry's interference.* • See also **unnatural**.
PHRASE: PHR with cl ≠naturally

unnecessary /ʌnnesəsri, AM -seri/. If you describe something as **unnecessary**, you mean that it is not needed or does not have to be done, and is undesirable. *The slaughter of whales is unnecessary and inhuman... He accused Diana of making an unnecessary fuss.* ♦ **unnecessarily** /ʌnnesəserɪli/ *I didn't want to upset my husband or my daughter unnecessarily... A bad keyboard can make life unnecessarily difficult.*
◆◆◇◇◇ ADJ-GRADED =needless ≠necessary
ADV-GRADED: ADV with v, ADV adj ≠necessarily

unnerve /ʌnnɜːʳv/ **unnerves, unnerving, unnerved.** If you say that something **unnerves** you, you mean that it worries or troubles you. *The news about Dermot had unnerved me... Tony was unnerved by the uncanny familiarity of her face.*
◆◇◇◇◇ VERB
V n

unnerving /ʌnnɜːʳvɪŋ/. If you describe something as **unnerving**, you mean that it is startling or very worrying. *It is very unnerving to find out that someone you see every day is carrying a potentially deadly virus. ...her unnerving habit of continuously touching people she was speaking to.* ♦ **unnervingly** *...a table decorated, unnervingly, by African fertility symbols... The driver was very quiet, unnervingly quiet.*
◆◇◇◇◇ ADJ-GRADED =disconcerting
ADV-GRADED: ADV with v, ADV adj

unnoticed /ʌnnoʊtɪst/. If something happens or passes **unnoticed**, it is not seen or noticed by anyone. *I tried to slip up the stairs unnoticed... Her forty-fourth birthday had just passed, unnoticed by all but herself.*
◆◇◇◇◇ ADJ: usu ADJ after v, also v-link ADJ, ADJ n

unobserved /ʌnəbzɜːʳvd/. If you do something **unobserved**, you do it without being seen by other people. *Looking round to make sure he was unobserved, he slipped through the door... John had been sitting, unobserved, in the darkness.*
ADJ: v-link ADJ, ADJ after v, ADJ n =unseen

unobtainable /ʌnəbteɪnəbᵊl/. If something or someone is **unobtainable**, you cannot get them. *...an unobtainable married man... Fish was unobtainable in certain sections of Tokyo.*
ADJ =available

unobtrusive /ʌnəbtruːsɪv/. If you describe something or someone as **unobtrusive**, you mean that they are not easily noticed or do not draw attention to themselves; a formal word. *The coffee-table is glass, to be as unobtrusive as possible... He managed the factory with unobtrusive efficiency.* ♦ **unobtrusively** *They slipped away unobtrusively... Unobtrusively, the other actors filed into the lounge.*
◆◇◇◇◇ ADJ-GRADED
ADV-GRADED: usu ADV with v

unoccupied /ʌnɒkjʊpaɪd/. If a building is **unoccupied**, there is nobody in it. *The house was unoccupied at the time of the explosion... The fire broke out in two unoccupied cabins.*
ADJ: v-link ADJ, ADJ n, ADJ after v

unofficial /ʌnəfɪʃᵊl/. An **unofficial** action or statement is not authorized, approved, or organized by a person in authority. *Staff voted to continue an unofficial strike in support of seven colleagues who were dismissed last week... Official reports put the death toll at under one hundred, but unofficial estimates speak of at least two hundred dead.* ♦ **unofficially** *Some workers are legally employed, but the majority work unofficially with neither health nor wage security.*
◆◆◇◇◇ ADJ: usu ADJ n ≠official
ADV: usu ADV with v, also ADV with cl

unopened /ʌnoʊpənd/. If something is **unopened**, it has not been opened yet. *...unopened bottles of olive oil... The letter lay unopened in the travel firm's pigeonhole... Catherine put all the envelopes aside unopened.*
ADJ: ADJ n, v-link ADJ, ADJ after v

unopposed /ʌnəpoʊzd/. In something such as an election or a war, if someone is **unopposed**, there are no opponents competing or fighting against them. *...President Suharto, who has been elected five times unopposed since he first came to power in 1967... The next day, 1st Army armoured cars drove unopposed into Tunis.*
ADJ: usu ADJ after v, also v-link ADJ, ADJ n

unorthodox /ʌnɔːʳθədɒks/
◆◇◇◇◇

1 If you describe someone's behaviour, beliefs, or customs as **unorthodox**, you mean that they are different from what is generally accepted. *She spent an unorthodox girlhood travelling with her father throughout Europe... His methods were unorthodox, and his lifestyle eccentric.*
ADJ-GRADED =unusual ≠orthodox

2 If you describe ways of doing things as **unorthodox**, you are criticizing them because they are illegal or unethical. *The charity says the journalists appear to have obtained confidential documents in an unorthodox manner.*
ADJ-GRADED PRAGMATICS =irregular ≠orthodox

unpack /ʌnpæk/ **unpacks, unpacking, unpacked**
◆◇◇◇◇

1 When you **unpack** a suitcase, box, or similar container, or you **unpack** the things inside it, you take the things out of the container. *He unpacked his bag... Our guide unpacked a picnic of ham sandwiches and offered us tea.*
VERB ≠pack
V n
Also V

2 If you **unpack** an idea or problem, you analyse it and consider it in detail. *A lot of ground has been*
VERB =analyse
V n

covered in unpacking the issues central to achieving this market-led strategic change.

unpaid /ʌnpeɪd/ ◆◇◇◇◇

1 If you do **unpaid** work or you are an **unpaid** volunteer, for example, you do a job without receiving any money for it. *Even unpaid work for charity is better than nothing... The unpaid volunteers do the work because they love it.* ADJ: ADJ n ≠paid

2 **Unpaid** taxes or bills, for examples, are bills or taxes which have not been paid yet. *The taxman caught up with him and demanded £17,000 in unpaid taxes... The bills remained unpaid because of a dispute over the quality of the company's work.* ADJ =outstanding

unpalatable /ʌnpælɪtəbᵊl/

1 If you describe an idea as **unpalatable**, you mean that you find it unpleasant and difficult to accept. *It is an unpalatable fact that rape makes a good news story... It was only then that I began to learn the unpalatable truth about John.* ADJ-GRADED =distasteful

2 If you describe food as **unpalatable**, you mean that it is so unpleasant that you can hardly eat it. *...a lump of dry, unpalatable cheese.* ADJ-GRADED

unparalleled /ʌnpærəleld/. If you describe something as **unparalleled**, you are emphasizing that it is, for example, bigger, better, or worse than anything else of its kind, or anything that has happened before. *Germany's unparalleled prosperity is based on wise investments... The country is facing a crisis unparalleled since the Second World War.* ◆◇◇◇◇ ADJ: oft ADJ *since/in* n

unpardonable /ʌnpɑːʳdənəbᵊl/. If you say that someone's behaviour is **unpardonable**, you mean that it is very wrong or offensive, and completely unacceptable. *...an unpardonable lack of discipline... I must ask a question you may find unpardonable.* ADJ =unforgivable, inexcusable

unpick /ʌnpɪk/ **unpicks, unpicking, unpicked**

1 If you **unpick** a piece of sewing, you remove the stitches from it. *You can always unpick the hems on the dungarees if you don't like them.* VERB =undo V n

2 If someone **unpicks** a plan or policy, they disagree with it and examine it thoroughly in order to find any mistakes that they can use to defeat it; used in British English. *A statesman who ought to know better wants to unpick last year's reform of Europe's common agricultural policy.* VERB V n

unplayable /ʌnpleɪəbᵊl/. In some sports, if you describe a player as **unplayable**, you mean that they are playing extremely well and are difficult to beat. If you describe a ball as **unplayable**, you mean it is difficult to hit, because it was thrown with great skill or speed, or because of its position. ADJ-GRADED

unpleasant /ʌnplezᵊnt/ ◆◆◇◇◇

1 If something is **unpleasant**, it gives you bad feelings, for example by making you feel upset or uncomfortable. *The symptoms can be uncomfortable, unpleasant and serious... The vacuum has an unpleasant smell... It was a very unpleasant and frightening attack.* ♦ **unpleasantly** *The water moved darkly around the body, unpleasantly thick and brown... The smell was unpleasantly strong... My heart was hammering unpleasantly.* ADJ-GRADED ≠pleasant; ADV: ADV adj, ADV with v ≠pleasantly

2 An **unpleasant** person is very unfriendly and rude. *She thought him an unpleasant man... Don't start giving me problems otherwise I'll have to be very unpleasant indeed. ...a thoroughly unpleasant person.* ♦ **unpleasantly** *Melissa laughed unpleasantly... The Heidlers are an unpleasantly hypocritical pair.* ♦ **unpleasantness** *There had to be a reason for the unpleasantness some people habitually displayed.* ADJ-GRADED =disagreeable ≠pleasant; ADV-GRADED ≠pleasantly; N-UNCOUNT ≠pleasantness

unplug /ʌnplʌg/ **unplugs, unplugging, unplugged.** If you **unplug** an electrical device or telephone, you pull a wire out of a socket so that it stops working. *I had to unplug the phone.* VERB V n

unplugged /ʌnplʌgd/. If a pop group or musician performs **unplugged**, they perform without any electrically amplified instruments; used in journalism. *At a time when many rock musicians are playing unplugged, Tangerine Dream remains resolutely connected to electric sockets.* ADJ: ADJ after v, ADJ n

unpolluted /ʌnpəluːtɪd/. Something that is **unpolluted** is free from pollution. ADJ ≠polluted

unpopular /ʌnpɒpjʊləʳ/. If something or someone is **unpopular**, most people do not like them. *It was a painful and unpopular decision... In high school, I was very unpopular, and I did encounter a little prejudice... The Chancellor is deeply unpopular with voters.* ♦ **unpopularity** /ʌnpɒpjʊlærɪti/ *...his unpopularity among his colleagues. ...the unpopularity of the new tax.* ◆◆◇◇◇ ADJ-GRADED: oft ADJ *with* n ≠popular; N-UNCOUNT: usu with poss ≠popularity

unprecedented /ʌnpresɪdentɪd/ ◆◆◇◇◇

1 If something is **unprecedented**, it has never happened before. *Such a move is rare, but not unprecedented... In 1987 the Socialists took the unprecedented step of appointing a civilian to command the force.* ADJ

2 If you describe something as **unprecedented**, you are emphasizing that it is very great in quality, amount, or scale. *Each home boasts an unprecedented level of quality throughout... The scheme has been hailed as an unprecedented success.* ADJ-GRADED: usu ADJ n

unpredictable /ʌnprɪdɪktəbᵊl/. If you describe someone or something as **unpredictable**, you mean that you cannot tell what they are going to do or how they are going to behave. *He is utterly unpredictable. ...Britain's notoriously unpredictable weather.* ♦ **unpredictably** *Monthly costs can rise or fall unpredictably. ...her husband's unpredictably violent behavior to others.* ♦ **unpredictability** /ʌnprɪdɪktəbɪlɪti/ *...the unpredictability of the weather. ...a reputation for unpredictability.* ◆◆◇◇◇ ADJ-GRADED ≠reliable; ADV-GRADED: usu ADV with v, ADV adj; N-UNCOUNT: oft with poss

unprepared /ʌnprɪpeəʳd/ ◆◇◇◇◇

1 If you are **unprepared** for something, you are not ready for it, and you are therefore surprised or at a disadvantage when it happens. *I was totally unprepared for the announcement on the next day... Faculty members complain that their students are unprepared to do college-level work... We were caught completely unprepared.* ADJ-GRADED: usu v-link ADJ, oft ADJ *for* n ≠prepared

2 If you are **unprepared** to do something, you are not willing to do it. *They are unprepared to accept the real reasons for their domestic and foreign situation... He was unprepared to co-operate, or indeed to communicate.* ADJ-GRADED: v-link ADJ to-inf

unprepossessing /ʌnpriːpəzesɪŋ/. If you describe someone or something as **unprepossessing**, you mean that they look rather plain or ordinary, although they may have good or special qualities that are hidden; a formal word. *We found the tastiest and most imaginative paella and tapas in the most unprepossessing bars and cafés.* ADJ-GRADED

unpretentious /ʌnprɪtenʃəs/. If you describe a place, person, or thing as **unpretentious**, you approve of them because they are simple in appearance or character, rather than sophisticated or luxurious. *The Tides Inn is both comfortable and unpretentious. ...good, unpretentious pop music... Linda is totally unpretentious about herself.* ◆◇◇◇◇ ADJ-GRADED PRAGMATICS =unassuming

unprincipled /ʌnprɪnsɪpᵊld/. If you describe a person or their actions as **unprincipled**, you are criticizing them for their lack of moral principles and because they do things which are immoral or dishonest. *It is a market where people can be very unprincipled and unpleasant. ...the unprincipled behaviour of the prosecutor's office during the crisis.* ADJ-GRADED PRAGMATICS =unscrupulous ≠principled

unprintable /ʌnprɪntəbᵊl/. If you describe something that someone has said or done as **unprintable**, you mean that it is so rude or shocking that you do not want to say exactly what it was. *Her reply was unprintable. ...some quite unprintable stories.* ADJ

unproductive /ʌnprədʌktɪv/. Something that is **unproductive** does not produce any good results. *Research workers are well aware that much of their time and effort is unproductive. ...increasingly unproductive land.* ◆◇◇◇◇ ADJ-GRADED ≠productive

unprofessional /ʌnprəfeʃənᵊl/. If you use **unprofessional** to describe someone's behaviour at ADJ-GRADED PRAGMATICS ≠professional work, you are criticizing them for not behaving according to the standards that are expected of a person in their profession. *What she did was very unprofessional. She left abruptly about 90 minutes into the show... He was also fined $150 for unprofessional conduct.*

unprofitable /ʌnprɒfɪtəbᵊl/ ◆◇◇◇◇
1 An industry, company, or product that is **unprofitable** does not make any profit or does not make enough profit. *...unprofitable state-owned industries... The newspaper is believed to have been unprofitable for at least the past decade.* ADJ-GRADED ≠profitable
2 **Unprofitable** activities or efforts do not produce any useful or helpful results. *...an endless, unprofitable argument... The day proved frustratingly unprofitable.* ADJ =fruitless ≠constructive

unpromising /ʌnprɒmɪsɪŋ/. If you describe something as **unpromising**, you think that it is unlikely to be successful or produce anything good in the future. *In fact, his business career had distinctly unpromising beginnings... Their land looked so unpromising that the colonists eventually gave most of it back.* ADJ-GRADED ≠promising

unpronounceable /ʌnprənaʊnsəbᵊl/. An **unpronounceable** word or name is very difficult to say or impossible to say. ADJ-GRADED

unprotected /ʌnprətektɪd/ ◆◇◇◇◇
1 An **unprotected** person or place is not looked after or defended, and so they may be harmed or attacked. *What better target than an unprotected girl, going along that river walkway in the dark... The landing beaches would be unprotected.* ADJ: ADJ n, v-link ADJ, ADJ after v =defenceless
2 If something is **unprotected**, it is not covered or treated with anything, and so it may easily be damaged. *Exposure of unprotected skin to the sun carries the risk of developing skin cancer... This leaves fertile soil unprotected and prone to erosion.* ADJ: ADJ n, v-link ADJ, ADJ after v ≠protected
3 If two people have **unprotected** sex, they do not use a condom when they have intercourse. ADJ: ADJ n

unprovoked /ʌnprəvoʊkt/. If someone makes an **unprovoked** attack, they attack someone who has not tried to harm them in any way. ADJ

unpublished /ʌnpʌblɪʃt/. An **unpublished** book, letter, or report has never been published. ◆◇◇◇◇ ADJ

unpunished /ʌnpʌnɪʃt/. If a criminal or crime goes **unpunished**, the criminal is not punished. *Persistent criminals who have gone unpunished by the courts have been dealt with by local people... I have been amazed at times that cruelty can go unpunished.* ADJ: v-link ADJ, ADJ n, ADJ after v

unqualified /ʌnkwɒlɪfaɪd/ ◆◇◇◇◇
1 If you are **unqualified**, you do not have any qualifications, or you do not have the right qualifications for a particular job. *She was unqualified for the job... Unqualified members of staff at the hospital were not sufficiently supervised.* ADJ ≠qualified
2 **Unqualified** means total, unlimited, and complete. *The event was an unqualified success... Egypt has given almost unqualified backing to the proposal from Washington.* ADJ: usu ADJ n =unconditional

unquestionable /ʌnkwestʃənəbᵊl/. If you describe something as **unquestionable**, you are emphasizing that it is so obviously true or real that nobody can doubt it. *He inspires affection and respect as a man of unquestionable integrity... There is an unquestionable link between job losses and deteriorating services.* ◆◇◇◇◇ ADJ =unequivocal ≠questionable
♦ **unquestionably** /ʌnkwestʃənəbli/ *They have seen the change as unquestionably beneficial to the country... He is unquestionably a star.* ADV-GRADED: ADV with cl/group

unquestioned /ʌnkwestʃənd/
1 You use **unquestioned** to emphasize that something is so obvious, real, or great that nobody can doubt it or disagree with it. *His commitment has been unquestioned... The play was an immediate and unquestioned success in London.* ADJ =unequivocal ≠questionable
2 If something or someone is **unquestioned**, they are accepted by everyone, without anyone doubting or disagreeing. *Stalin was the unquestioned ruler of the Soviet Union from the late 1920s until his death in 1953.* ADJ =undisputed
3 If you describe someone's belief or attitude as **unquestioned**, you are emphasizing that they accept something without any doubt or disagreement. *Royalty is regarded with unquestioned reverence.* ADJ: ADJ n =unquestioning

unquestioning /ʌnkwestʃənɪŋ/. If you describe a person or their beliefs as **unquestioning**, you are emphasizing that they accept something without any doubt or disagreement. *Isabella had been taught unquestioning obedience... For the last 20 years, I have been an unquestioning supporter of comprehensive schools.* ADJ-GRADED: usu ADJ n
♦ **unquestioningly** *She supported him unquestioningly.* ADV: ADV with v

unquote /ʌnkwoʊt/
1 In spoken English, you can say **unquote** to mark the end of a quotation, especially one which you have introduced with the word 'quote'. *Stalin's history of the Communist Party was, quote, 'full of lies', unquote.* PRAGMATICS
2 In spoken English, you can say **quote, unquote** before or after words you are using to show that you are quoting someone's words or that the words do not reflect what you believe. *We've only had an 'average', quote, unquote, kind of recession... He drowned in a boating quote 'accident' unquote.* PHRASE PRAGMATICS

unravel /ʌnrævᵊl/ **unravels, unravelling, unravelled;** spelled **unraveling, unraveled** in American English. ◆◇◇◇◇
1 If something such as a plan or system **unravels**, it breaks up or begins to fail. *His government began to unravel because of a banking scandal... When she returned to America, the marriage unravelled.* VERB V
2 If you **unravel** a mystery or puzzle, or it **unravels**, it gradually becomes clearer and you can work out the answer to it. *A young mother has flown to Iceland to unravel the mystery of her husband's disappearance... Gradually, with an intelligent use of flashbacks, Yves' story unravels.* V-ERG V n V
3 If you **unravel** something that is knotted, twisted, woven, or knitted, or if it **unravels**, it separates into its different threads or strands. *He was good with his hands and could unravel a knot or untangle yarn that others wouldn't even attempt... The stairway carpet is so frayed it threatens to unravel.* V-ERG V n V

unread /ʌnred/. If a book or other piece of writing is **unread**, you or other people have not read it, for example because it is boring or because you have no time. *All his unpublished writing should be destroyed unread... He caught up on months of unread periodicals.* ADJ: ADJ after v, ADJ n, v-link ADJ

unreadable /ʌnriːdəbᵊl/
1 If you use **unreadable** to describe a book or other piece of writing, you are criticizing it because it is very boring, complicated, or difficult to understand. *For some this is the greatest novel in the world. For others it is unreadable... Most computer ads used to be loaded with technical specifications, virtually unreadable to the average consumer.* ADJ-GRADED PRAGMATICS =unintelligible
2 If a piece of writing is **unreadable**, it is impossible to read because the letters are unclear, especially because it has been damaged in some way. *...if contracts are unreadable because of the microscopic print... I always cover my licence with sticky-backed plastic, but even then it can turn mouldy and unreadable.* ADJ: usu v-link ADJ =illegible
3 If someone's face or expression is **unreadable**, it is impossible to tell what they are thinking or feeling; a literary use. *He looked back at the woman for approval, but her face was unreadable.* ADJ-GRADED =impenetrable

unreal /ʌnriːl/ ◆◇◇◇◇
1 If you say that a situation is **unreal**, you mean that it is so strange that you find it difficult to believe it is happening. *It was unreal. Like some crazy childhood nightmare... It felt so unreal to be talking about our son like this.* ADJ-GRADED: v-link ADJ =bizarre ♦ **unreality** /ʌnriælɪti/ *To his surprise he didn't feel too weak. Light-headed certainly, and with a sense of unreality, but able to walk.* N-UNCOUNT
2 If you use **unreal** to describe something that exists or is talked about, you are critical of it because you think that is does not correspond to reality or ADJ-GRADED PRAGMATICS =phoney

to the truth. *It is an unreal capital, little more than an overgrown village. ...unreal financial targets... Almost all fictional detectives are unreal.*

3 Some people use **unreal** to express the feeling of liking something very much; an informal use. *Oh, I can't explain it. It's just unreal. Everybody is so happy.* ADJ-GRADED: usu v-link ADJ

unrealistic /ʌnriəlɪstɪk/. If you say that someone is being **unrealistic**, you mean that they do not recognize the truth about a situation, especially about the difficulties involved in something they want to achieve. *There are many who feel that the players are being completely unrealistic in their demands... It would be unrealistic to expect such a process ever to be completed. ...their unrealistic expectations of parenthood.* ◆◇◇◇◇ ADJ-GRADED: oft *it* v-link ADJ to-inf =over-optimistic ≠realistic

♦ **unrealistically** /ʌnriəlɪstɪkli/ *Tom spoke unrealistically of getting a full-time job that paid an enormous sum. ...unrealistically high standards of expectation.* ADV-GRADED: ADV with v, ADV adj ≠realistically

unreasonable /ʌnriːzənəbəl/ ◆◇◇◇◇

1 If you say that someone is being **unreasonable**, you mean that they are behaving in a way that is not fair or sensible. *The strikers were being unreasonable in their demands, having rejected the deal two weeks ago... It was her unreasonable behaviour with a Texan playboy which broke up her marriage... It's unreasonable to expect your child to behave in a caring way if you behave selfishly.* ADJ-GRADED ≠reasonable

♦ **unreasonably** /ʌnriːzənəbli/ *We unreasonably expect near perfect behaviour from our children.* ADV

2 An **unreasonable** decision, action, price, or amount seems unfair and difficult to justify. *...unreasonable increases in the price of petrol... One in four consumers now say water prices are very unreasonable.* ♦ **unreasonably** *The banks' charges are unreasonably high.* ADJ-GRADED ≠reasonable; ADV: usu ADV adj

unreasoning /ʌnriːzənɪŋ/. **Unreasoning** feelings or actions are not logical, sensible, or controlled; a literary word. *At this moment of success I found only an unreasoning sense of futility... Niki's voice provoked a new bout of unreasoning anger.* ADJ: ADJ n =irrational

unrecognizable /ʌnrekəgnaɪzəbl, -naɪz-/; also spelled **unrecognisable** in British English. If someone or something is **unrecognizable**, they have become impossible to recognize or identify, for example because they have been greatly changed or damaged. *The corpses of the prisoners were nearly unrecognizable from the number of bullet wounds they'd received... The new town would have been unrecognisable to the original inhabitants.* ADJ: oft ADJ *to* n ≠recognizable

unrecognized /ʌnrekəgnaɪzd/; also spelled **unrecognised** in British English.

1 If someone does something **unrecognized**, nobody knows or recognizes them while they do it. *He is believed to have worked unrecognised as a doorman at East End clubs... I actually knew her, but in overalls I passed unrecognised.* ADJ: ADJ after v, v-link ADJ

2 If something is **unrecognized**, people are not aware of it. *There is the possibility that hypothermia can go unrecognized... There must be many vases, bowls or bottles sitting unrecognised in people's homes... Until comparatively recently, dyslexia remained largely unrecognised.* ADJ: ADJ after v, v-link ADJ, ADJ n =unnoticed

3 If you or your achievements or qualities are **unrecognized**, you have not been properly appreciated or acknowledged by other people for what you have done. *Hard work and talent so often go unrecognised and unrewarded... She became ill and died with her life's work unrecognised... There really is a wealth of unrecognised talent out there.* ADJ: ADJ after v, v-link ADJ, ADJ n

4 An **unrecognized** meeting, agreement, or political party is not formally acknowledged as legal or valid by the authorities. *...the unrecognised communist Workers Party... Local authorities are likely to refuse to hire facilities to unrecognised martial arts organisations.* ADJ: usu ADJ n

unreconstructed /ʌnriːkənstrʌktɪd/. If you describe systems, beliefs, policies, or people as **unreconstructed**, you are critical of them because they have not changed at all, in spite of new ideas and circumstances. *...the unreconstructed racism of the official opposition... It was the unreconstructed communists who continued in charge.* ADJ-GRADED: usu ADJ n PRAGMATICS

unrecorded /ʌnrɪkɔːʳdɪd/. You use **unrecorded** to describe something that has not been written down or recorded officially, especially when it should have been. *The statistics don't reveal of course unrecorded crime... Much of Poland's private industry goes unrecorded... Nothing is left unrecorded.* ADJ: ADJ n, v-link ADJ, ADJ after v

unrefined /ʌnrɪfaɪnd/. An **unrefined** food or other substance is in its natural state and has not been processed. *Unrefined carbohydrates include brown rice and other grains. ...the price of unrefined oil as it comes out of the ground.* ADJ: usu ADJ n ≠refined

unrehearsed /ʌnrɪhɜːʳst/. **Unrehearsed** activities or performances have not been prepared, planned, or practised beforehand. *...'Talking Point,' an unrehearsed program presenting inside opinions and forecasts on major issues of the day.* ADJ

unrelated /ʌnrɪleɪtɪd/ ◆◇◇◇◇

1 If one thing is **unrelated** to another, there is no connection between them. You can also say that two things are **unrelated**. *My line of work is entirely unrelated to politics... Two of them died from apparently unrelated causes.* ADJ-GRADED: oft ADJ *to* n =unconnected ≠related

2 If one person is **unrelated** to another, they are not members of the same family. You can also say that two people are **unrelated**. Used in written English. *Jimmy is adopted and thus unrelated to Beth by blood.* ADJ: oft ADJ *to* n ≠related

unrelenting /ʌnrɪlentɪŋ/ ◆◇◇◇◇

1 If you describe someone's behaviour as **unrelenting**, you mean that they are continuing to do something in a very determined way, often without caring whether they hurt or embarrass other people. *She established her authority with unrelenting thoroughness... In the face of severe opposition and unrelenting criticism, the task seemed overwhelming.* ADJ =relentless

2 If you describe something unpleasant as **unrelenting**, you mean that it is continuing without stopping, and that you have no relief or rest from it. *...an unrelenting downpour of rain. ...the unrelenting hardship of everyday life in medieval Europe.* ADJ-GRADED =ceaseless

unreliable /ʌnrɪlaɪəbəl/. If you describe a person, machine, or method as **unreliable**, you are mean that you cannot trust them to do or provide what you want. *Diplomats can be a notoriously unreliable and misleading source of information... His judgement was unreliable... He had an unreliable car.* ♦ **unreliability** /ʌnrɪlaɪəbɪlɪti/ *...his lateness and unreliability.* ◆◇◇◇◇ ADJ-GRADED ≠reliable; N-UNCOUNT

unrelieved /ʌnrɪliːvd/. If you describe something unpleasant as **unrelieved**, you mean that it is very severe and is not replaced by anything better, even for a short time. *...unrelieved misery... The sun baked down on the concrete, unrelieved by any breeze.* ADJ: oft ADJ *by* n

unremarkable /ʌnrɪmɑːʳkəbəl/. If you describe someone or something as **unremarkable**, you mean that they are very ordinary, without many exciting, original, or attractive qualities. *...a tall, lean man, with an unremarkable face. ...the unremarkable town of Athens, Georgia.* ADJ-GRADED ≠remarkable

unremarked /ʌnrɪmɑːʳkt/. If something happens or goes **unremarked**, people say nothing about it, because they consider it normal or do not notice it; a formal word. *His departure, in fact, went almost unremarked... It did not pass unremarked that three-quarters of the petitions were instituted by women.* ADJ: v-link ADJ, ADJ after v, ADJ n =unnoticed

unremitting /ʌnrɪmɪtɪŋ/. Something that is **unremitting** continues without stopping or becoming less intense; a formal word. *I was sent to boarding school, where I spent six years of unremitting misery... He watched her with unremitting attention.* ♦ **unremittingly** *The weather was unremittingly awful.* ADJ: usu ADJ n; ADV-GRADED: usu ADV adj

unrepentant /ʌnrɪpentənt/. If you are **unrepentant**, you are not ashamed of your beliefs or actions. *Pamela was unrepentant about her strong language and abrasive remarks. ...an unrepentant believer in the final victory of socialism.* ADJ =unabashed

unrepresentative /ʌnreprɪzentətɪv/. If you describe a group of people as **unrepresentative**, you mean that their views are not typical of the community or society to which they belong. *The President denounced the demonstrators as unrepresentative of the Romanian people.* ADJ-GRADED: oft ADJ *of* n ≠representative

unrepresented /ʌnreprɪzentɪd/. If you are **unrepresented** in something such as a parliament, law court, or meeting, there is nobody there speaking or acting for you, for example to give your opinions or instructions. *...groups who feel they've been officially unrecognized or unrepresented in international councils.* ADJ ≠represented

unrequited /ʌnrɪkwaɪtɪd/. If you have **unrequited** love for someone, they do not love you; a literary word. *...his unrequited love for a married woman.* ADJ

unreserved /ʌnrɪzɜːʳvd/. An **unreserved** opinion or statement is one that expresses a feeling or opinion completely and without any doubts. *Charles displays unreserved admiration for his grandfather... Jones' lawyers are seeking an unreserved apology from the newspaper.* ADJ: usu ADJ n

♦ **unreservedly** /ʌnrɪzɜːʳvɪdli/ *We apologise unreservedly for any imputation of incorrect behaviour by Mr Taylor.* ADV: ADV with v =wholeheartedly

unresolved /ʌnrɪzɒlvd/. If a problem or difficulty is **unresolved**, no satisfactory solution has been found to it; a formal word. *The murder remains unresolved. ...unresolved issues.* ◆◇◇◇◇ ADJ: v-link ADJ, ADJ n, ADJ after v

unresponsive /ʌnrɪspɒnsɪv/

1 An **unresponsive** person does not react or pay enough attention to something, for example to an urgent situation or to people's needs; a formal use. *He was totally unresponsive to the pressing social and economic needs of the majority of the population... In my opinion, Peter Doyle was a cold, unresponsive man.* ADJ-GRADED: oft ADJ *to* n ≠responsive

2 If a person or their body is **unresponsive**, they do not react to anything or make any movements, because they are dead or unconscious; a formal use. *I found her in a coma, totally unresponsive.* ADJ

unrest /ʌnrest/. If there is **unrest** in a particular place or society, people are expressing anger and dissatisfaction about something, often by demonstrating or rioting; used in journalism. *The real danger is civil unrest in the east of the country... There is growing unrest among students in several major cities.* ◆◆◇◇◇ N-UNCOUNT

unrestrained /ʌnrɪstreɪnd/. If you describe someone's behaviour as **unrestrained**, you mean that it is extreme or intense, for example because they are expressing their feelings strongly or loudly. *There was unrestrained joy on the faces of the people... His campaign has been unrestrained and often vulgar.* ADJ ≠restrained

unrestricted /ʌnrɪstrɪktɪd/ ◆◇◇◇◇

1 If an activity is **unrestricted**, you are free to do it in the way that you want, without being limited by any rules. *Freedom to pursue extra-curricular activities is totally unrestricted... The Commissioner has absolutely unrestricted access to all the files.* ADJ =unlimited

2 If you have an **unrestricted** view of something, you can see it fully and clearly, because there is nothing in the way. *Nearly all seats have an unrestricted view.* ADJ

unrewarded /ʌnrɪwɔːʳdɪd/. You can say that someone goes **unrewarded**, or that their activities go **unrewarded**, when they do not achieve what they are trying to achieve. *The jockey rushed back from America to ride at Nottingham on Monday but went unrewarded. ...a long and unrewarded struggle.* ADJ

unrewarding /ʌnrɪwɔːʳdɪŋ/. If you describe an activity as **unrewarding**, you mean that it does not give you any feelings of achievement or pleasure. *...dirty and unrewarding work... Listening to it in its entirety is also fairly unrewarding.* ADJ-GRADED ≠rewarding

unripe /ʌnraɪp/. **Unripe** fruit or vegetables are not yet ripe. *I was only ill once and that came of eating an unripe pear.* ADJ ≠ripe

unrivalled /ʌnraɪvəld/; spelled **unrivaled** in American English. If you describe something as **unrivalled**, you are emphasizing that it is better than anything else of the same kind. *He had an unrivalled knowledge of south Arabian society, religion, law and customs... It's a team unrivalled in stature, expertise and credibility.* ADJ =unmatched

unroll /ʌnroʊl/ **unrolls, unrolling, unrolled.** If you **unroll** something such as a sheet of paper or cloth, or if it **unrolls**, it opens up and becomes flat when it was previously rolled in a cylindrical shape. *I unrolled my sleeping bag as usual... Guests bring movies on tape, and show them on the screen that unrolls from the ceiling.* V-ERG V n V

unruffled /ʌnrʌfəld/. If you describe someone as **unruffled**, you mean that they are calm and do not seem to be affected by surprising or frightening events. *Anne had remained unruffled, very cool and controlled.* ADJ-GRADED =unperturbed

unruly /ʌnruːli/ ◆◇◇◇◇

1 If you describe people, especially children, as **unruly**, you mean that they behave badly and are difficult to control. *It's not good enough just to blame the unruly children. ...unruly behaviour.* ADJ-GRADED =uncontrollable

2 Unruly hair is difficult to keep tidy. *The man had a huge head of remarkably black, unruly hair.* ADJ-GRADED: usu ADJ n

unsafe /ʌnseɪf/ ◆◇◇◇◇

1 If a building, machine, activity, or area is **unsafe**, it is dangerous. *Critics claim the trucks are unsafe... She was also warned it was unsafe to run early in the morning in the neighbourhood.* ADJ-GRADED =dangerous ≠safe

2 If you are **unsafe**, you are in danger of being harmed. *In the larger neighbourhood, I felt very unsafe.* ADJ-GRADED: v-link ADJ ≠safe

3 If a criminal conviction is **unsafe**, it is based on inadequate or false evidence. *An appeal court decided their convictions were unsafe.* ADJ-GRADED

unsaid /ʌnsed/. If something is **left unsaid** or **goes unsaid** in a particular situation, it is not said, although you might have expected it to be said. *Some things, Donald, are better left unsaid... What she and her characters leave unsaid is often more important than what they actually put into words... Bill Bradley says too much is going unsaid between blacks and whites.* ADJ: usu ADJ after v, also v-link ADJ, ADJ n

unsaleable /ʌnseɪləbəl/; spelled **unsalable** in American English. If something is **unsaleable**, it cannot be sold because nobody wants to buy it. *Most developers reserve the right to turn down a property they think is virtually unsaleable.* ADJ

unsanitary /ʌnsænɪtri, AM -teri/. Something that is **unsanitary** is dirty and unhealthy, so that you may catch a disease from it. *...diseases caused by unsanitary conditions... Discharge of raw sewage into the sea is unsanitary and unsafe.* ADJ-GRADED =unhygienic, insanitary

unsatisfactory /ʌnsætɪsfæktəri/. If you describe something as **unsatisfactory**, you mean that it is not as good as it should be, and cannot be considered acceptable. *The inspectors said just under a third of lessons were unsatisfactory... He asked a few more questions, to which he received unsatisfactory answers.* ◆◇◇◇◇ ADJ-GRADED =unacceptable ≠adequate

unsatisfied /ʌnsætɪsfaɪd/

1 If you are **unsatisfied** with something, you are disappointed because you have not got what you hoped to get. *The game ended a few hours too early, leaving players and spectators unsatisfied... The centre helps people who are unsatisfied with the solicitors they are given.* ADJ-GRADED: usu v-link ADJ, oft ADJ *with* n =dissatisfied

2 If a need or demand is **unsatisfied**, it is not dealt with. *The poll suggests that the strongest unsatisfied appetite for home computers isn't among the richest consumers.* ADJ-GRADED: usu ADJ n

unsatisfying /ʌnsætɪsfaɪɪŋ/. If you find something **unsatisfying**, you do not get any satisfaction from it. *Rose says so far the marriage has been unsatisfying... The boredom is caused as* ADJ-GRADED =unrewarding ≠satisfying

much by people's unsatisfying home lives as by lack of work.*

unsavoury /ʌnseɪvəri/; spelled **unsavory** in American English. ADJ-GRADED: usu ADJ n =distasteful If you describe a person, place, or thing as **unsavoury**, you mean that you find them unpleasant or morally unacceptable. *The sport has long been associated with illegal wagers and unsavoury characters.*

unscathed /ʌnskeɪðd/. ◆◇◇◇◇ ADJ-GRADED: ADJ after v, v-link ADJ =unharmed If you are **unscathed** after a dangerous experience, you have not been injured or harmed by it. *Tony emerged unscathed apart from a severely bruised finger... East Los Angeles was left relatively unscathed by the riots... The tobacco industry escaped unscathed from its toughest legal challenge.*

unscheduled /ʌnʃedjuːld, AM -skedʒ-/. ADJ: usu ADJ n An **unscheduled** event was not planned to happen, but happens unexpectedly or because someone changes their plans at a late stage. *...an unscheduled meeting with Nelson Mandela... The ship made an unscheduled stop at Hawaii.*

unschooled /ʌnskuːld/. ADJ-GRADED An **unschooled** person has had no formal education; a literary word. *...unskilled work done by unschooled people... He was almost completely unschooled.*

unscientific /ʌnsaɪəntɪfɪk/. ADJ-GRADED A method, experiment, or process that is **unscientific** may be unreliable because is not based on facts or is not objective. *No member of the team was medically qualified and its methods were considered totally unscientific. ...this small, unscientific sample of voters.*

unscramble /ʌnskræmbᵊl/ **unscrambles, unscrambling, unscrambled.** VERB To **unscramble** things that are in a state of confusion or disorder means to arrange them in an orderly way so that you can understand them. V n *All you have to do to win is unscramble the words here to find four names of birds. ...electronic circuits which can be programmed to allow the user to unscramble transmitted signals.*

unscrew /ʌnskruː/ **unscrews, unscrewing, unscrewed**

1 V-ERG If you **unscrew** something such as a lid, or if it **unscrews**, you keep turning it until you can remove it. V n *She unscrewed the cap of her water bottle and gave him a drink...* V *A wick soaks up the petrol, and the head of the candle unscrews for refilling.*

2 VERB If you **unscrew** something such as a sign or mirror which is fastened to something by screws, you remove it by taking out the screws. V n *He unscrewed the back of the telephone and started connecting it to the cable.*

unscripted /ʌnskrɪptɪd/. ADJ: usu ADJ n An **unscripted** talk or speech is spoken without a previously prepared script. *...a witty, chatty and unscripted speech. ...unscripted radio programmes.*

unscrupulous /ʌnskruːpjʊləs/. ◆◇◇◇◇ ADJ-GRADED PRAGMATICS =unprincipled If you describe a person as **unscrupulous**, you are critical of the fact that they are prepared to act in a dishonest or immoral way in order to get what they want. *These kids are being exploited by very unscrupulous people. ...the unscrupulous use of hostages.*

unseasonably /ʌnsiːzənəbli/. ADV: ADV adj **Unseasonably** warm, cold, or mild weather is warmer, colder, or milder than it usually is at the time of year. *...a spell of unseasonably warm weather... It was unseasonably mild for late January.*

unseat /ʌnsiːt/ **unseats, unseating, unseated** ◆◇◇◇◇

1 VERB When people try to **unseat** a person who is in an important job or position, they try to remove him or her from that job or position. V n *It is still not clear who was behind Sunday's attempt to unseat the President... Only two US representatives were unseated.*

2 VERB =throw If a horse **unseats** its rider, it causes him or her to fall off. V n *Crystal Spirit unseated his rider in the Berkshire Hurdle at Newbury... She was unseated on her first ride.*

unsecured /ʌnsɪkjʊəʳd/. ◆◇◇◇◇ ADJ: usu ADJ n ≠secured **Unsecured** is used to describe loans or debts that are not guaranteed by a particular asset such as a person's home. *We can arrange unsecured loans for any amount from £500 to £7,500.*

unseeded /ʌnsiːdɪd/. ◆◇◇◇◇ ADJ ≠seeded In sports competitions such as tennis or badminton, an **unseeded** player is someone who has not been ranked amongst the top 16 players by the tournament's organizers. *Rajchrtova of Czechoslovakia will be the only other unseeded player in the quarter-finals.*

unseeing /ʌnsiːɪŋ/. ADJ: ADJ n, ADJ after v, v-link ADJ If you describe a person or their eyes as **unseeing**, you mean that they are not looking at anything, or not noticing something, although their eyes are open; a literary word. *In the hallway Greenfield was staring at the wood panelling with unseeing eyes... He stared unseeing out of the window.*

unseemly /ʌnsiːmli/. ADJ-GRADED PRAGMATICS =improper If you say that someone's behaviour is **unseemly**, you disapprove of it because it is not polite or not suitable for a particular situation or occasion; a literary word. *It would be unseemly for judges to receive pay increases when others are having to tighten their belts. ...unseemly drinking, brawling and gambling.*

unseen /ʌnsiːn/ ◆◇◇◇◇

1 ADJ If you describe something as **unseen**, you mean that it has not been seen for a long time. *...a spectacular ballroom, unseen by the public for over 30 years... We print a selection of previously unseen photos from the Spanish rider's early years.*

2 ADJ: ADJ n, ADJ after v You can use **unseen** to describe things which people cannot see. *For me, a performance is in front of a microphone, over the radio, to an unseen audience... There was barely time for the two boys to escape unseen.*

unselfish /ʌnselfɪʃ/. ADJ-GRADED PRAGMATICS =selfless ≠selfish If you describe someone as **unselfish**, you approve of the fact that they regard other people's wishes and interests as more important than their own. *She started to get a reputation as an unselfish girl with a heart of gold... As a player he was unselfish, a true team man.* ♦ **unselfishly** ADV-GRADED: ADV with v *She has loyally and unselfishly spent every day at her husband's side.* ♦ **unselfishness** N-UNCOUNT *...acts of unselfishness and care.*

unsentimental /ʌnsentɪmentᵊl/. ADJ-GRADED If you describe someone as **unsentimental**, you mean that they do not allow emotions like pity or affection to interfere with their work or decisions. *She was a practical, unsentimental woman... They are unsentimental about their impact on employees.*

unsettle /ʌnsetᵊl/ **unsettles, unsettling, unsettled.** ◆◇◇◇◇ VERB =disturb If something **unsettles** you, it causes you to feel restless, dissatisfied, or rather worried. V n *The presence of the two policemen unsettled her... But what unsettled the market most was the serious slump in demand.*

unsettled /ʌnsetᵊld/ ◆◇◇◇◇

1 ADJ-GRADED =unstable In an **unsettled** situation, there is a lot of uncertainty about what will happen. *Britain's unsettled political scene also worries some investors... The junk market has been unsettled for the past seven months.*

2 ADJ-GRADED: v-link ADJ If you are **unsettled**, you cannot concentrate on anything because you are worried. *A lot of people wake up every day with a sense of being unsettled and disturbed... To tell the truth, I'm a bit unsettled tonight.*

3 ADJ =unresolved An **unsettled** argument or dispute has not yet been resolved. *They were in the process of resolving all the unsettled issues... Can one even talk of stability in the Middle East as long as the conflict is still unsettled?*

4 ADJ: usu ADJ n **Unsettled** places are places where no people have yet lived. *Until very recently Texas was an unsettled frontier.*

5 ADJ-GRADED **Unsettled** weather is unpredictable and changes a lot. *Despite the unsettled weather, we had a marvellous weekend.*

unsettling /ʌnsetəlɪŋ/.  ADJ-GRADED If you describe something as **unsettling**, you mean that it causes you to feel restless, dissatisfied, or rather worried. *The prospect of change of this kind has an unsettling effect on any organisation... His sense of* *humour was really unsettling.* ♦ **unsettlingly** *It was unsettlingly quiet.* ADV: ADV adj

unshaded /ʌnʃeɪdɪd/. An **unshaded** light or light bulb has no shade fitted to it. *...a solitary, unshaded bulb dangling from a long flex.* ADJ: ADJ n =naked

unshakeable /ʌnʃeɪkəbᵊl/; also spelled **unshakable**. If you describe someone's beliefs as **unshakeable**, you are emphasizing that they are so strong that they cannot be destroyed or altered. *William has acquired an unshakeable belief in himself... She had an unshakeable faith in human goodness and natural honesty.* ADJ: usu ADJ n

unshaken /ʌnʃeɪkən/
1 If your beliefs are **unshaken**, you still have those beliefs, although they have been attacked or challenged. *His faith that men such as the Reverend John Leale tried to do their best is unshaken.* ADJ: usu v-link ADJ =firm
2 If you are **unshaken** by something, you are not emotionally affected by it. *Mona remains unshaken by her ordeal and is matter-of-fact about her courage.* ADJ: usu v-link ADJ

unshaven /ʌnʃeɪvᵊn/. If a man is **unshaven**, he has not shaved recently and there are short hairs on his face or chin. *His hair was disheveled, and his face was unshaven and gray.* ADJ

unsightly /ʌnsaɪtli/. If you describe something as **unsightly**, you mean that it is unattractive to look at. *My mother has had unsightly varicose veins for years... The Polish market in Berlin was considered unsightly and shut down.* ◆◇◇◇◇ ADJ-GRADED =ugly

unsigned /ʌnsaɪnd/
1 An **unsigned** document does not have anyone's signature on it. *The envelope contained a typed, unsigned letter demanding £175,000 in cash.* ADJ
2 An **unsigned** band has not signed a contract with a company to produce records. *Fugazi are America's biggest unsigned alternative band.* ADJ: usu ADJ n

unskilled /ʌnskɪld/ ◆◇◇◇◇
1 People who are **unskilled** do not have any special training for a job. *He went to Paris in search of work as an unskilled labourer... Most of those who left the province to work abroad were unskilled.* ADJ
2 **Unskilled** work does not require any special training. *In the US, minorities and immigrants have generally gone into low-paid, unskilled jobs.* ADJ: usu ADJ n

unsmiling /ʌnsmaɪlɪŋ/. An **unsmiling** person is not smiling, and looks serious or unfriendly; a literary word. *He was unsmiling and silent. ...the unsmiling woman in the ticket booth.* ADJ =dour

unsociable /ʌnsoʊʃəbᵊl/. Someone who is **unsociable** does not like talking to other people and tries to avoid meeting them. *My marriage has broken up. It has made me reclusive and unsociable... I am by no means an unsociable person.* ADJ-GRADED ≠sociable

unsocial /ʌnsoʊʃᵊl/. If someone works **unsocial** hours, they work late at night, early in the morning, at weekends, or on public holidays. In Britain, people are usually paid extra for working unsocial hours. ADJ

unsold /ʌnsoʊld/. **Unsold** goods have been available for people to buy but nobody has bought them. *...piles of unsold books... Thirteen per cent of Christie's coin and banknote auction went unsold.* ◆◇◇◇◇ ADJ

unsolicited /ʌnsəlɪsɪtɪd/. Something that is **unsolicited** has been given without being asked for and may not have been wanted. *'If I were you,' she adds by way of some unsolicited advice, 'I'd watch out for that girl of yours.'* ADJ: usu ADJ n

unsolved /ʌnsɒlvd/. An **unsolved** mystery or problem has never been solved. *...America's unsolved problems of poverty and racism... David's murder remains unsolved.* ◆◇◇◇◇ ADJ

unsophisticated /ʌnsəfɪstɪkeɪtɪd/
1 **Unsophisticated** people do not have a wide range of experience or knowledge and have simple tastes. *It was music of a rather crude kind which unsophisticated audiences enjoyed listening to... She was quite unsophisticated in the ways of the world.* ADJ-GRADED
2 An **unsophisticated** method or device is very simple and often not very effective. *...an unsophisticated alarm system.* ADJ-GRADED =crude ≠sophisticated

unsound /ʌnsaʊnd/
1 If a conclusion or method is **unsound**, it is based on ideas that are wrong. *The thinking is good-hearted, but muddled and fundamentally unsound... The national tests were educationally unsound.* ADJ-GRADED: usu v-link ADJ ≠sound
2 If something or someone is **unsound**, they are unreliable. *No sensible person would put his money in a bank he knew to be unsound.* ADJ-GRADED =unreliable
3 If you say that something is **unsound** in some way, you mean that it is damaging in that way or to the thing mentioned. *The project is environmentally unsound... A diet extremely low in calories can also be a diet that is nutritionally unsound.* ADJ-GRADED: usu v-link ADJ, usu adv ADJ
4 If a building or other structure is **unsound**, it is in poor condition and is likely to collapse. *The church was structurally unsound.* ADJ-GRADED: usu v-link ADJ

unspeakable /ʌnspiːkəbᵊl/. If you describe something as **unspeakable**, you are emphasizing that it is extremely unpleasant. *...the unspeakable horrors of chemical weapons... The pain is unspeakable. ...unspeakable crimes.* ◆◇◇◇◇ ADJ-GRADED =terrible
♦ **unspeakably** /ʌnspiːkəbli/ *The novel was unspeakably boring.* ADV-GRADED: usu ADV adj

unspecified /ʌnspesɪfaɪd/. You say that something is **unspecified** when you are not told exactly what it is. *The government said an unspecified number of bandits were killed... He was arrested on unspecified charges.* ◆◇◇◇◇ ADJ: usu ADJ n

unspectacular /ʌnspektækjʊləʳ/. If you describe something as **unspectacular**, you mean that it is rather dull and not remarkable in any way. *His progress at school had been unspectacular compared to his brother. ...pleasant, if largely unspectacular, countryside.* ADJ-GRADED

unspoiled /ʌnspɔɪld/; also spelled **unspoilt** /ʌnspɔɪlt/. If you describe a place as **unspoiled**, you think it is beautiful because it has not been changed or built on for a long time. *The port is quiet and unspoiled... On a rest day I made the offshore trip to the unspoiled island of Cozumel.* ADJ-GRADED

unspoken /ʌnspoʊkən/ ◆◇◇◇◇
1 If your thoughts, wishes, or feelings are **unspoken**, you do not speak about them. *His face was expressionless, but Alex felt the unspoken criticism... The other unspoken fear here is of an outbreak of hooliganism.* ADJ
2 When there is an **unspoken** agreement or understanding between people, their behaviour shows that they agree about something or understand it, even though they have never spoken about it. *There had been an unspoken agreement between them that he would not call for her at Seymour House... Most designers share the unspoken belief that fashion is a valid form of visual art.* ADJ: ADJ n

unsporting /ʌnspɔːʳtɪŋ/. If you describe someone playing a game as **unsporting**, you are critical of them because they have behaved in a selfish way that is unfair to their opponent. *Players are warned, fined and can even be disqualified for unsporting actions in the heat of contest.* ADJ-GRADED PRAGMATICS

unstable /ʌnsteɪbᵊl/ ◆◇◇◇◇
1 You can describe something as **unstable** if it is likely to change suddenly, especially if this creates difficulty or danger. *After the fall of Pitt in 1801 there was a decade of unstable government... The situation is unstable and potentially dangerous.* ADJ-GRADED =volatile
2 **Unstable** objects are likely to move or fall. *Both clay and sandstone are unstable rock formations.* ADJ-GRADED
3 If people are **unstable**, their emotions and behaviour keep changing because their minds are disturbed or upset. *He was emotionally unstable... Coleridge was also a highly unstable person.* ADJ-GRADED ≠stable

unstated /ʌnsteɪtɪd/. You say that something is **unstated** when it has not been expressed in words. *The implication was plain, if left unstated... An additional, unstated reason for his resignation may have been a lawsuit filed against him.* ADJ

unsteady /ʌnstedi/
1 If you are **unsteady**, you have difficulty doing ADJ-GRADED

something, for example walking, because you cannot completely control your legs or your body. *The boy was very unsteady and had staggered around when he got up... He poured coffee into the mugs, and with an unsteady hand, held one of them out to David.* ♦ **unsteadily** /ʌnstedɪli/ *She pulled herself unsteadily from the bed to the dresser.*

≠steady
ADV-GRADED: ADV with v

2 If you describe something as **unsteady**, you mean that it is not regular or stable, but unreliable or unpredictable. *His voice was unsteady and only just audible... She knew first-hand the impact an unsteady parent could have on a sensitive young girl.*

ADJ-GRADED

3 **Unsteady** objects are not held, fixed, or balanced securely. *...a slightly unsteady item of furniture.*

ADJ-GRADED: usu ADJ n

unstick /ʌnstɪk/ **unsticks, unsticking, unstuck.** If you **unstick** something or if it **unsticks**, it becomes separated from the thing that it was stuck to. *Mike shook his head, to unstick his hair from his sweating forehead... The stewards' badges are made so they do not unstick from a car and therefore cannot be passed around.*

V-ERG
V n
V

unstinting /ʌnstɪntɪŋ/. **Unstinting** help, care, or praise is great in amount or degree and is given generously. *The task of producing the text was made easier by the unstinting help and generosity extended to me. ...her unstinting charity work.*

ADJ: usu ADJ n

unstoppable /ʌnstɒpəbᵊl/. Something that is **unstoppable** cannot be prevented from continuing or developing. *The progress of science is unstoppable. ...China's seemingly unstoppable economy.*

◆◇◇◇◇
ADJ

unstressed /ʌnstrest/. If a word or syllable is **unstressed**, it is pronounced without emphasis; a technical term in language teaching. *...the unstressed syllable of words like 'above', 'surround' or 'arrive'.*

ADJ
≠stressed

unstructured /ʌnstrʌktʃəʳd/. Something such as a meeting, interview, or activity that is **unstructured** is not organized in a complete or detailed way. *Our aim was that these meetings be unstructured and informal... As seminars go, these are loose, unstructured affairs. ...the highly unstructured nature of the graduate recruitment procedures.*

ADJ-GRADED

unstuck /ʌnstʌk/

1 If something **comes unstuck**, it becomes separated from the thing that it was attached to. *Cecelia tugged the bracelets until the tape came unstuck.*

PHRASES
V inflects

2 If a plan or system **comes unstuck**, it fails; an informal expression. *Where economics comes unstuck is when it doesn't take account of the anticipated actions of human beings.*

V inflects
=fail

3 If someone **comes unstuck**, they fail badly at something that they are trying to achieve; an informal expression. *Those who come unstuck are the ones who cannot sell the properties on fast enough.*

V inflects

unsubstantiated /ʌnsəbstænʃieɪtɪd/. A claim, accusation, or story that is **unsubstantiated** has not been proved to be valid or true. *I do object to their claim, which I find totally unsubstantiated. ...unsubstantiated rumours about his private life.*

ADJ
=unconfirmed

unsuccessful /ʌnsəksesfʊl/

◆◆◇◇◇

1 Something that is **unsuccessful** does not achieve what it was intended to achieve. *His efforts were unsuccessful. ...a second unsuccessful operation on his knee... There were reports last month of unsuccessful negotiations between guerrillas and commanders.* ♦ **unsuccessfully** *He has been trying unsuccessfully to sell the business in one piece since early last year.*

ADJ-GRADED
≠successful
ADV-GRADED: ADV with v
≠successfully

2 Someone who is **unsuccessful** does not achieve what they intended to achieve, especially in their career. *The difference between successful and unsuccessful people is that successful people put into practice the things they learn... He and his friend Boris were unsuccessful in getting a job.*

ADJ-GRADED
≠successful

unsuitable /ʌnsuːtəbᵊl/. Someone or something that is **unsuitable** for a particular purpose or situation does not have the right qualities for it. *Amy's shoes were unsuitable for walking any distance. ...taking heavy traffic out of unsuitable towns and villages.*

◆◇◇◇◇
ADJ-GRADED: oft ADJ for n/-ing
≠suitable

unsuited /ʌnsuːtɪd/

1 If someone or something is **unsuited** to a particular job, situation, or place, they do not have the right qualities or characteristics for it. *He's totally unsuited to the job... The snow cruiser proved hopelessly unsuited to Antarctic conditions.*

ADJ-GRADED: oft ADJ to n/-ing
=inappropriate
≠suited

2 If two people, especially a man and a woman, are **unsuited** to each other, they have different personalities or interests, and so are unlikely to have a successful relationship. *By the end of that first year, I knew how totally unsuited we were to each other.*

ADJ-GRADED: oft ADJ to n
=incompatible
≠suited

unsullied /ʌnsʌlid/. If something is **unsullied**, it has not been spoiled or made less pure by the addition of something unpleasant or unacceptable; a literary word. *She had the combined talents of toughness, intellect, experience and unsullied reputation... He smiled, unsullied by doubt.*

ADJ-GRADED
=untainted
≠sullied, tainted

unsung /ʌnsʌŋ/. **Unsung** is used to describe people, things, or places that are not appreciated or praised, although you think they deserve to be. *They are among the unsung heroes of our time... It is little known, unsung and one of the grandest little towns you could ever wish to see.*

ADJ
=unacclaimed

unsupported /ʌnsəpɔːʳtɪd/

1 If a statement or theory is **unsupported**, there is no evidence which proves that it is true or correct. *It was a theory unsupported by evidence... The letters contained unsupported allegations.*

ADJ
=insubstantiated

2 An **unsupported** person does not have anyone to provide them with money and the things they need. *Unsupported mothers are one of the fastest-growing groups of welfare claimants.*

ADJ: usu ADJ n

3 An **unsupported** building or person is not being physically supported or held up by anything. *...the vast unsupported wall of the Ajuda Palace in Lisbon. ...the child's first unsupported step.*

ADJ: usu ADJ n

unsure /ʌnʃʊəʳ/

◆◇◇◇◇

1 If you are **unsure** of yourself, you lack confidence. *He made her feel hot, and awkward, and unsure of herself... The evening show was terrible, with hesitant unsure performances from all.*

ADJ-GRADED: usu v-link ADJ, oft ADJ of n
≠confident, sure

2 If you are **unsure** about something, you feel uncertain about it. *Fifty-two per cent were unsure about the idea... Scientists are becoming increasingly unsure of the validity of this technique.*

ADJ-GRADED: v-link ADJ, oft ADJ about/of n
≠certain

unsurpassed /ʌnseʳpɑːst, -pæst/. If you describe something as **unsurpassed**, you are emphasizing that it is better or greater than anything else of its kind. *The quality of Smallbone furniture is unsurpassed... They enjoy a living standard unsurpassed in the Soviet bloc.*

ADJ
=unrivalled
≠surpassed

unsurprising /ʌnsəʳpraɪzɪŋ/. If something is **unsurprising**, you are not surprised by it because you would expect it to happen or be like it is. *It is unsurprising that he remains so hated... His choice was unsurprising.* ♦ **unsurprisingly** *Unsurprisingly, not everyone agrees that things are better... The proposals were swiftly and unsurprisingly rejected by Western ministers.*

◆◇◇◇◇
ADJ-GRADED: usu v-link ADJ, oft ADJ that
≠surprising
ADV: ADV with cl, ADV with v
≠surprisingly

unsuspected /ʌnsəspektɪd/. If you describe something as **unsuspected**, you mean that people do not realize it or are not aware of it. *A surprising number of ailments are caused by unsuspected environmental factors... He died in 1984 of an unsuspected brain tumour.*

ADJ: usu ADJ n

unsuspecting /ʌnsəspektɪŋ/. You can use **unsuspecting** to describe someone who is not at all aware of something that is happening or going to happen. *The co-defendants are charged with selling worthless junk bonds to thousands of unsuspecting depositors. ...his unsuspecting victim.*

◆◇◇◇◇
ADJ: usu ADJ n
=unwary

unsweetened /ʌnswiːtᵊnd/. **Unsweetened** food or drink does not have any sugar or other sweet substance added to it.

ADJ: usu ADJ n
≠sweetened

unswerving /ʌnswɜːʳvɪŋ/. If you describe someone's attitude, feeling, or way of behaving as **unswerving**, you mean that it is strong and firm and does not weaken or change. *In his diary of 1944 he proclaims unswerving loyalty to the*

ADJ: usu ADJ n
=unflagging, staunch

monarchy. ...her unswerving belief in her father's innocence.

unsympathetic /ʌnsɪmpəθetɪk/
1 If someone is **unsympathetic**, they are not kind or helpful to a person in difficulties. *Her husband was unsympathetic and she felt she had no one to turn to. ...an unsympathetic doctor.* ADJ-GRADED ≠sympathetic
2 An **unsympathetic** person is unpleasant and difficult to like. *...a very unsympathetic main character... He's unsympathetic, but charismatic and complex.* ADJ-GRADED
3 If you are **unsympathetic to** a particular idea or aim, you are not willing to support it. *I'm highly unsympathetic to what you are trying to achieve.* ADJ-GRADED: v-link ADJ *to* n

untamed /ʌnteɪmd/. An **untamed** area or place is wild or unmanageable because it has not been greatly changed or influenced by modern things. *...the wild, untamed undergrowth... The interior of Corsica is high and untamed.* ADJ

untangle /ʌntæŋgəl/ **untangles, untangling, untangled**
1 If you **untangle** something, especially something that consists of long strands twisted together, you undo the knots in it or free the twisted parts. *He was found desperately trying to untangle several reels of film. ...a light, non-sticky mousse which untangles hair and adds brilliant shine.* VERB =disentangle V n
2 If you **untangle** something complicated or confusing, you make it understandable or work out what it means. *Lawyers and accountants began trying to untangle the complex affairs of the bank... The problem took three hours to untangle.* VERB =straighten out V n

untapped /ʌntæpt/. An **untapped** supply or source of something is available but has not yet been used or exploited. *Mongolia, although poor, has considerable untapped resources of oil and minerals... There is enormous, acknowledged and untapped potential in the Indian stock markets.* ADJ: usu ADJ n ≠exploited

untenable /ʌntenəbəl/. An argument, theory, or position that is **untenable** cannot be defended successfully against criticism or attack. *This argument is untenable from an intellectual, moral and practical standpoint... He claimed the charges against him were untenable.* ◆◇◇◇◇ ADJ-GRADED: usu v-link ADJ =indefensible ≠tenable

untested /ʌntestɪd/
1 If something or someone is **untested**, they have not yet been tried out or have not yet experienced a particular situation, so you do not know what they will be like. *The Egyptian Army remained an untested force... All of us were untested for what lay ahead.* ADJ =untried
2 If you describe something such as a drug or chemical as **untested**, you mean that it has not been subject to scientific tests to find out if it is safe to use. *...the dangers of giving untested drugs to people.* ADJ: usu ADJ n

unthinkable /ʌnθɪŋkəbəl/ ◆◇◇◇◇
1 If you say that something is **unthinkable**, you are emphasizing that it cannot possibly be accepted or imagined as a possibility. *Her strong Catholic beliefs made abortion unthinkable.* ▶ **The unthinkable** is something that is unthinkable. *Edward VIII had done the unthinkable and abdicated the throne.* ADJ: usu v-link ADJ =inconceivable; N-SING: *the* N
2 You can use **unthinkable** to describe a situation, event, or action which is extremely unpleasant to imagine or remember. *This place is going to be unthinkable without you. ...Monday's unthinkable tragedy.* ADJ

unthinking /ʌnθɪŋkɪŋ/. If you say that someone is **unthinking**, you are critical of them because you consider that they do not think carefully about the effects of their behaviour. *He doesn't say those silly things that unthinking people say... Bruce was no unthinking vandal.* ♦ **unthinkingly** *Many motor accidents are the result of unthinkingly mixing speed and alcohol.* ADJ-GRADED PRAGMATICS =thoughtless; ADV-GRADED: usu ADV with v, also ADV adj

untidy /ʌntaɪdi/ ◆◇◇◇◇
1 If you describe something as **untidy**, you mean that it is messy and disordered and not neat or well arranged. *The place quickly became untidy. ...a thin man with untidy hair... Clothes were thrown in the luggage in an untidy heap.* ♦ **untidily** /ʌntaɪdɪli/ *Her long hair tumbles untidily around her shoulders. ...the desk piled untidily with books and half-finished homework.* ♦ **untidiness** *The dust and untidiness in her room no longer bothered her.* ADJ-GRADED ≠tidy; ADV-GRADED: usu ADV with v, also ADV adj ≠tidily; N-UNCOUNT ≠tidiness
2 If you describe a person as **untidy**, you mean that they do not care about whether things are neat and well arranged, for example in their house. *I'm untidy in most ways.* ADJ-GRADED

untie /ʌntaɪ/ **unties, untying, untied** ◆◇◇◇◇
1 If you **untie** something that is tied to another thing or if you **untie** two things that are tied together, you remove the string or rope that holds them or that has been tied round them. *If you have a trailer, untie the horse before lifting the front bars... Just untie my hands.* VERB V n
2 If you **untie** something such as string or rope, you undo it so that there is no knot or so that it is no longer tying something. *She hurriedly untied the ropes binding her ankles... Then she untied her silk scarf.* VERB V n
3 When you **untie** your shoelaces or your shoes, you loosen or undo the laces of your shoes. *She untied the laces on one of her sneakers... Your boot lace is untied.* VERB =undo V n V-ed

until /ʌntɪl/ ◆◆◆◆◆
1 If something happens **until** a particular time, it happens during the period before that time and stops at that time. *Until 1971, he was a high-ranking official in the Central Communist Committee. ...consumers who have waited until after the Christmas holiday to do that holiday shopping.* ▶ Also a conjunction. *I waited until it got dark... Stir with a metal spoon until the sugar has dissolved.* PREP: PREP n/prep =till; CONJ-SUBORD =till
2 You use **until** with a negative to emphasize the moment in time after which the rest of your statement becomes true, or the condition which would make it true. *The traffic laws don't take effect until the end of the year... It was not until 1911 that the first of the vitamins was identified.* ▶ Also a conjunction. *The EC will not lift its sanctions until that country makes political changes.* PREP: PREP after neg =till; CONJ-SUBORD: CONJ after neg =till
3 • **up until**: see **up**.

untimely /ʌntaɪmli/
1 If you describe an event as **untimely**, you mean that it happened earlier than it should, or sooner than you expected. *His mother's untimely death had a catastrophic effect on him... Her untimely return could spoil Miss Melville's entire programme for the evening.* ADJ: usu ADJ n =premature
2 You can describe something as **untimely** if it happens at an unsuitable time. *...an untimely visit from the milkman... I am sure your readers would have seen the article as at best untimely.* ADJ =ill-timed

untiring /ʌntaɪərɪŋ/. If you describe a person or their efforts as **untiring**, you approve of them because they continue what they are doing without slowing down or stopping. *...an untiring fighter for justice, democracy and tolerance.* ADJ: usu ADJ n PRAGMATICS =tireless

unto /ʌntu/ ◆◇◇◇◇
1 **Unto** was used to indicate that something was done or given to someone; an old-fashioned, literary use. *And he said unto him, 'Who is my neighbor?'... I will do unto others what they did to me.* PREP =to
2 **Unto** was used to indicate that something continued until a particular time; an old-fashioned, literary use. *Be ye faithful unto the end.* PREP =until

untold /ʌntoʊld/ ◆◇◇◇◇
1 You can use **untold** to emphasize how bad or unpleasant something is. *The demise of the industry has caused untold misery to thousands of hard-working tradesmen... This might do untold damage to her health.* ADJ: ADJ n
2 You can use **untold** to emphasize that an amount or quantity is very large, especially when you are not sure how large it is. *...the nation's untold millions of anglers. ...the glittering prospect of untold riches.* ADJ: ADJ n =countless

untouchable /ʌntʌtʃəbəl/ **untouchables** ◆◇◇◇◇
1 Some people refer to members of the lowest N-COUNT

Hindu caste as **untouchables**. *He was born an untouchable in a very poor village in south India.*

2 If you say that someone is **untouchable**, you mean that they cannot be affected or punished in any way. *I want to make it clear, however, that no one is untouchable in this investigation.* ▶ An **untouchable** is someone who is untouchable. *He will be put in charge of a new force of 'untouchables' to deal with narcotics and terrorism.*
ADJ-GRADED
N-COUNT

3 If you describe someone, especially a sports player or entertainer, as **untouchable**, you are emphasizing that they are better than anyone else in what they do. *A lot of the players began to feel they were untouchable.*
ADJ

untouched /ʌntʌtʃt/ ◆◇◇◇◇

1 Something that is **untouched** by something else is not affected by it. *Asian airlines remain untouched by the deregulation that has swept America... Vested interests were left untouched.*
ADJ: v-link ADJ, ADJ after v

2 If something is **untouched**, it is not damaged in any way, although it has been in a situation where it could easily have been damaged. *Michael pointed out to me that amongst the rubble, there was one building that remained untouched... The desk had been rifled for money, some banknotes taken but cheque-book and credit cards left untouched.*
ADJ: v-link ADJ, ADJ after v

3 An **untouched** area or place is thought to be beautiful because it is still in its original state and has not been changed or damaged in any way. *Ducie is one of the world's last untouched islands, nearly 5,000km from Australia. ...a relatively untouched cottage within only an hour or so's drive of London.*
ADJ: ADJ n, v-link ADJ, ADJ after v

4 If food or drink is **untouched**, none of it has been eaten or drunk. *The coffee was untouched, the toast had cooled... He murmured something, then, food left untouched, went into the sitting-room.*
ADJ: v-link ADJ, ADJ after v, ADJ n

untoward /ʌntəwɔːʳd, AM -tɔːʳd/. If you say that something **untoward** happens, you mean that something happens that is unexpected and causes difficulties; a formal word. *The surveyor's report didn't highlight anything untoward... Tampering with a single enzyme can lead to untoward effects elsewhere.*
ADJ: pron-indef ADJ, ADJ n

untrained /ʌntreɪnd/

1 Someone who is **untrained** has not been taught the skills that they need for a particular job, activity, or situation. *It is a nonsense to say we have untrained staff dealing with emergencies... Our Intelligence Service was untrained, cumbersome, and almost wholly ineffectual.*
ADJ

2 If you describe a voice or a mind, for example, as **untrained**, you mean that it has not been developed through formal education or training. *It was often said that he had the best untrained mind in politics.*
ADJ: usu ADJ n ≠trained

untrammelled /ʌntræməld/; spelled **untrammeled** in American English. Someone who is **untrammelled** is able to act freely in the way they want to, rather than being restricted by rules, conventions, or circumstances; a literary word. *...the only place where the royal family could really relax and lead an untrammelled domestic life... She thought of herself as a free woman, untrammelled by family relationships.*
ADJ: oft ADJ *by* n =unconstrained

untreated /ʌntriːtɪd/ ◆◇◇◇◇

1 If an injury or illness is left **untreated**, it is not given medical treatment. *If left untreated the condition may become chronic. ...the consequences of untreated tuberculosis.*
ADJ: ADJ after v, ADJ n, v-link ADJ

2 **Untreated** materials, water, or chemicals are harmful and have not been made safe. *...the dumping of nuclear waste and untreated sewage.*
ADJ: usu ADJ n

3 **Untreated** materials are in their natural or original state, often before being prepared for use in a particular process. *All the bedding is made of simple, untreated cotton... In its untreated state the carbon fibre material is rather like cloth.*
ADJ: usu ADJ n

untried /ʌntraɪd/. If someone or something is **untried**, they have not yet experienced certain situations or have not yet been tried out, so you do not know what they will be like. *He was young and untried, with no reputation of his own. ...a long legal battle through untried areas of law.*
ADJ =untested

untroubled /ʌntrʌbəld/. If you are **untroubled** by something, you are not affected or worried by it. *She is untroubled by the fact that she didn't win. ...an untroubled night's sleep.*
ADJ-GRADED ≠troubled

untrue /ʌntruː/. If a statement or idea is **untrue**, it is false and not based on facts. *The allegations were completely untrue... It was untrue to say that all political prisoners have been released... Such remarks are both offensive and untrue.*
◆◇◇◇◇ ADJ: usu v-link ADJ ≠true

untrustworthy /ʌntrʌstwɜːʳði/. If you say that someone is **untrustworthy**, you think they are unreliable and cannot be trusted. *I think he is shallow, vain and untrustworthy... His opponents still say he's a fundamentally untrustworthy figure.*
ADJ-GRADED

untruth /ʌntruːθ/ **untruths** /ʌntruːðz/. An **untruth** is a lie; a formal word. *The Advertising Standards Authority accused estate agents of using blatant untruths... I have never uttered one word of untruth.*
N-VAR =falsehood, lie

untruthful /ʌntruːθfʊl/. If someone is **untruthful** or if they say **untruthful** things, they are dishonest and say things that they know are not true. *He must not be untruthful, or a coward... Some people may be tempted to give untruthful answers.*
ADJ-GRADED ≠truthful

untutored /ʌntjuːtəʳd, AM -tuːt-/. If someone is **untutored**, they have not been formally trained to do something, although they may be quite skilled at it; a formal word. *This untutored mathematician had an obsession with numbers... They had left school at fifteen and were quite untutored in writing.*
ADJ

untypical /ʌntɪpɪkəl/. If someone or something is **untypical** of a particular type of person or thing, they are not usual and therefore not a good example of the way that type of person or thing normally is. People sometimes say something is **not untypical** to mean that it is quite normal. *Anita Loos was in many respects untypical of the screenwriting trade... I believe our results are not untypical.* ♦ **untypically** /ʌntɪpɪkli/ *I was working untypically hard... Untypically for a man in that situation he became interested in Buddhism.*
ADJ-GRADED: usu v-link ADJ
ADV-GRADED: ADV adj/-ed, ADV with cl =unusually

unusable /ʌnjuːzəbəl/. Something that is **unusable** is not in a good enough state or condition to be used. *Bombing had made roads and railways unusable.*
ADJ

unused. Pronounced /ʌnjuːzd/ for meaning 1, and /ʌnjuːst/ for meaning 2. ◆◇◇◇◇

1 Something that is **unused** has not been used or is not being used at the moment. *...unused containers of food and drink... The insurance on his BMW has run out, and the car stands unused.*
ADJ: ADJ n, ADJ after v, v-link ADJ

2 If you are **unused to** something, you have not often done it or experienced it before, so it feels unusual and unfamiliar to you. *Mother was entirely unused to such hard work.*
ADJ-GRADED: v-link ADJ *to* n =unaccustomed

unusual /ʌnjuːʒuəl/ ◆◆◆◇◇

1 If something is **unusual**, it does not happen very often or you do not see it or hear it very often. *They have replanted many areas with rare and unusual plants... To be appreciated as a parent is quite unusual.*
ADJ-GRADED

2 If you describe someone as **unusual**, you think that they have extraordinary and remarkable qualities. *He was an unusual man with great business talents.*
ADJ-GRADED

unusually /ʌnjuːʒuəli/ ◆◆◇◇◇

1 You use **unusually** to emphasize that someone or something has more of a particular quality than is usual. *He was an unusually complex man. ...this year's unusually harsh winter.*
ADV-GRADED: ADV adj PRAGMATICS

2 You can use **unusually** to suggest that something is not what normally happens. *Unusually among British prime ministers, he was not a man of natural authority.*
ADV-GRADED: ADV with cl, oft ADV *for* n

unutterable /ʌnʌtərəbəl/. You can use **unutterable** to emphasize that something, especially a
ADJ-GRADED: ADJ n PRAGMATICS

bad quality, is great in degree or intensity. *I am at the beginning of a new and unutterable loneliness. ...unutterable rubbish.* ♦ **unutterably** /ʌnʌtərəbli/. *I suddenly felt unutterably depressed.* ADV-GRADED: usu ADV adj

unvarying /ʌnveəriɪŋ/. If you describe something as **unvarying**, you mean that it stays the same and never changes. *...her unvarying refusal to make public appearances.* ADJ: usu ADJ n

unveil /ʌnveɪl/ **unveils, unveiling, unveiled** ◆◆◇◇◇

1 If someone formally **unveils** something such as a new statue or painting, they draw back the curtain which is covering it. *...a ceremony to unveil a monument to the victims.* ♦ **unveiling** *...the unveiling of a monument to one of the Croatian heroes of the past.* VERB; V n; N-UNCOUNT: oft N of n

2 If you **unveil** a plan, new product, or some other thing that has been kept secret, you introduce it to the public. *Mr Werner unveiled his new strategy this week... Companies from across Europe are here to unveil their latest models.* ♦ **unveiling** *...the unveiling of a detailed peace plan.* VERB =reveal; V n; N-UNCOUNT: oft N of n

unwaged /ʌnweɪdʒd/. In British English, you can refer to people who do not have a paid job as the **unwaged**. *There are special rates for the under 18s, full-time students, over 60's and the unwaged... Individual membership costs £13 (£7 unwaged).* ► Also an adjective. *...the effect on male wage-earners, unwaged females, and children.* N-PLURAL: usu the N; ADJ

unwanted /ʌnwɒntɪd/. If you say that something or someone is **unwanted**, you mean that you do not want them, or that nobody wants them. *...the misery of unwanted pregnancies... She felt unwanted... Every year thousands of unwanted animals are abandoned.* ◆◆◇◇◇ ADJ-GRADED

unwarranted /ʌnwɒrəntɪd, AM -wɔːr-/. If you describe something as **unwarranted**, you are critical of it because it is unnecessary and unjustified; a formal word. *Any attempt to discuss the issue of human rights was rejected as an unwarranted interference in the country's internal affairs... He accused the police of using unwarranted brutality.* ◆◇◇◇◇ ADJ PRAGMATICS =gratuitous

unwary /ʌnweəri/. If you describe someone as **unwary**, you mean that they are not cautious or experienced and are therefore likely to be harmed or deceived; a formal word. *With its quicksands the river usually drowns a few unwary visitors every season.* ► **The unwary** are people who are unwary. *Specialist subjects are full of pitfalls for the unwary.* ADJ-GRADED: usu ADJ n; N-SING: the N

unwashed /ʌnwɒʃt/

1 **Unwashed** people or objects are dirty and need to be washed. *They looked pale and unhealthy, with unwashed hair and sunken cheeks... Leftover food and unwashed dishes cover the dirty counters.* ADJ =grubby

2 **The unwashed** or **the great unwashed** is a humorous way of referring to poor or uneducated people. *A scowling man briskly led the Queen's husband away from the great unwashed.* PHRASE =the masses

unwavering /ʌnweɪvərɪŋ/. If you describe a feeling or attitude as **unwavering**, you mean that it is strong and firm and does not weaken. *She has been encouraged by the unwavering support of her family. ...his unwavering commitment to public education... His attitude was unwavering.* ADJ =unswerving

unwelcome /ʌnwelkəm/ ◆◇◇◇◇

1 An **unwelcome** experience is one that you do not like and did not want. *The media has brought more unwelcome attention to the Royal Family... A colleague made unwelcome sexual advances towards her.* ADJ-GRADED =unwanted

2 If you say that a visitor is **unwelcome**, you mean that you did not want them to come. *...an unwelcome guest... She was, quite deliberately, making him feel unwelcome.* ADJ-GRADED

unwelcoming /ʌnwelkəmɪŋ/

1 If someone is **unwelcoming**, or if they behave in an **unwelcoming** way, they are unfriendly or hostile when you visit or approach them. *His manner was cold and unwelcoming... Both women were unwelcoming, making little attempt to put Kathryn at her ease.* ADJ-GRADED PRAGMATICS

2 If you describe a place as **unwelcoming**, you mean that it looks unattractive or difficult to live or work in. *My room was cold and unwelcoming.* ADJ-GRADED

unwell /ʌnwel/. If you are **unwell**, you are ill. *He had been riding in Hyde Park, but felt unwell as he was being driven back to his office late this afternoon.* ◆◇◇◇◇ ADJ-GRADED: v-link ADJ

unwholesome /ʌnhoʊlsəm/

1 **Unwholesome** food or drink is not healthy or good for you. *The fish were unwholesome and old.* ADJ-GRADED =unhealthy

2 If you describe someone's feelings or behaviour as **unwholesome**, you are critical of it because it is unpleasant or unnatural. *My desire to be rich was an insane, unwholesome, oppressive desire.* ADJ-GRADED PRAGMATICS

unwieldy /ʌnwiːldi/ ◆◇◇◇◇

1 If you describe an object as **unwieldy**, you mean that it is difficult to move or carry because it is so big or heavy. *They came panting up to his door with their unwieldy baggage.* ADJ-GRADED =cumbersome

2 If you describe a system as **unwieldy**, you mean that it does not work very well as a result of it being too large or badly organized. *His firm must contend with the unwieldy Russian bureaucracy. ...an unwieldy legal system.* ADJ-GRADED

unwilling /ʌnwɪlɪŋ/ ◆◆◇◇◇

1 If you are **unwilling** to do something, you do not want to do it and will not agree to do it. *Initially the government was unwilling to accept the defeat... For months I had been either unwilling or unable to go through with it.* ♦ **unwillingness** *...their unwillingness to accept responsibility for mistakes. ...the unwillingness of banks to grant loans.* ADJ-GRADED: usu v-link, usu ADJ to-inf =disinclined ≠willing; N-UNCOUNT: oft N to-inf ≠willingness

2 You can use **unwilling** to describe someone who does not really want to do something so they do it unenthusiastically and often with caution. *A youthful teacher, he finds himself an unwilling participant in school politics... She was certainly an unwilling victim of circumstances.* ♦ **unwillingly** *My beard had started to grow, and I had unwillingly complied with the order to shave it off... Unwillingly, she moved aside.* ADJ-GRADED: usu ADJ n =reluctant; ADV-GRADED: ADV with v, ADV with cl =reluctantly

unwind /ʌnwaɪnd/ **unwinds, unwinding, unwound** ◆◇◇◇◇

1 When you **unwind**, you relax after you have done something that makes you tense or tired. *It helps them to unwind after a busy day at work... Singing is a nice way of unwinding.* VERB; V

2 If you **unwind** something that is wrapped round something else or that is in a ball, or if it **unwinds**, you undo it or straighten it out. *One of them unwound a length of rope from around his waist... I want to try to unwind the ball of wool... The thread unwound a little more.* V-ERG; V n; V

unwise /ʌnwaɪz/. If you describe something as **unwise**, you think that it is foolish and likely to lead to a bad result. *It would be unwise to expect too much... I think this is extremely unwise. ...a series of unwise investments in plastics and shipping.* ♦ **unwisely** *She accepted that she had acted unwisely and mistakenly... We unwisely chose not to go on a coach excursion to Trondheim.* ◆◇◇◇◇ ADJ-GRADED: oft it v-link ADJ to-inf =ill-advised ≠sensible; ADV-GRADED: usu ADV with v, also ADV with cl

unwitting /ʌnwɪtɪŋ/. If you describe a person or their actions as **unwitting**, you mean that the person does something or is involved in something without realizing it. *We're unwitting victims of the system... It had been an unwitting blunder on Blair's part.* ♦ **unwittingly** *He was unwittingly caught up in the confrontation.* ◆◇◇◇◇ ADJ: usu ADJ n; ADV: usu ADV with v

unworkable /ʌnwɜːʳkəbəl/. If you describe something such as a plan, law, or system as **unworkable**, you believe that it cannot be successful. *There is the strong possibility that such cooperation will prove unworkable... Washington is unhappy with the peace plan which it views as unworkable.* ◆◇◇◇◇ ADJ-GRADED: usu v-link ADJ

unworldly /ʌnwɜːʳldli/

1 If you describe someone as **unworldly**, you mean that they have not experienced many things and are therefore innocent and naive. *She was so* ADJ-GRADED =naive

young, so unworldly... He is a little unworldly about such matters.

2 If you describe someone as **unworldly**, you mean that they are not interested in having a lot of money or possessions. *Kitty's family was unworldly, unimpressed by power, or money.*
ADJ-GRADED ≠worldly

unworthy /ʌnwɜːʳði/ ◆◇◇◇◇

1 If someone or something is **unworthy** of something good, they do not deserve it; a literary use. *You may feel unworthy of the attention and help people offer you... He felt unworthy of being married to such an attractive woman.*
ADJ-GRADED: oft ADJ *of* n/-ing, ADJ to-inf ≠worthy

2 If you say that an action is **unworthy** of someone, you mean that it is not a nice thing to do and someone with their reputation or position should not do it; a literary use. *Miss Melville could not resist asking, although she knew it was unworthy of her... His accusations are unworthy of a prime minister.*
ADJ-GRADED: oft ADJ *of* n

unwound /ʌnwaʊnd/. **Unwound** is the past tense and past participle of **unwind**.

unwrap /ʌnræp/ **unwraps, unwrapping, unwrapped.** When you **unwrap** something, you take off the paper, plastic, or other covering that is around it. *I untied the bow and unwrapped the small box... Vacuum-packed ham slices should be unwrapped 30 minutes before serving.*
◆◇◇◇◇ VERB ≠wrap V n

unwritten /ʌnrɪtᵊn/ ◆◇◇◇◇

1 Something such as a book that is **unwritten** has not been printed or written down. *Universal have agreed to pay £2.5 million for Grisham's next, as yet unwritten, novel.*
ADJ: usu ADJ n

2 An **unwritten** rule, law, or agreement is one that is understood and accepted by everyone, although it may not have been formally or officially established. *They obey the one unwritten rule that binds them all - no talking.*
ADJ: usu ADJ n

unyielding /ʌnjiːldɪŋ/

1 You describe someone as **unyielding** when they have very strong, fixed ideas about something and are unlikely to change their mind; used in written English. *The authorities proved unyielding on one crucial opposition demand... His unyielding attitude on this subject was that since he had done it, so could everyone.*
ADJ-GRADED

2 If a barrier or surface is **unyielding**, it is very solid or hard; a literary use. *...the troopers, who had to build roads through those unyielding mountains... He sat on the edge of an unyielding armchair, a cup of tea in his hand.*
ADJ-GRADED

unzip /ʌnzɪp/ **unzips, unzipping, unzipped.** When you **unzip** something which is fastened by a zip or when it **unzips**, you open it by pulling open the zip. *James unzipped his bag... Wrap up warmly in this dramatic trenchcoat with tie belt and detachable leather collar. The lining unzips for milder days.*
V-ERG V n V

up 1 preposition, adverb, and adjective uses

up. The preposition is pronounced /ʌp/. The adverb and adjective are pronounced /ʌp/. ◆◆◆◆◆

Up is often used with verbs of movement such as 'jump' and 'pull', and also in phrasal verbs such as 'give up' and 'wash up'.

1 If someone or something goes **up** something such as a slope, ladder, or chimney, they move away from the ground or to a higher position. *They were climbing up a narrow mountain road... I ran up the stairs and saw Alison lying at the top... The heat disappears straight up the chimney.* ► Also an adverb. *Finally, after an hour, I went up to Jeremy's room... Intense balls of flame rose up into the sky... He put his hand up.*
PREP ≠down
ADV: ADV after v, oft ADV prep/adv ≠down

2 If someone or something is **up** something such as a ladder or a mountain, they are near the top of it. *He was up a ladder sawing off the tops of his apple trees... The Newton Hotel is halfway up a steep hill.* ► Also an adverb. *...a research station perched 4000 metres up on the lip of the crater.*
PREP ≠down
ADV: ADV after v

3 You use **up** to indicate that you are looking or facing in a direction that is away from the ground or towards a higher level. *Paul answered, without looking up... Keep your head up, and look around you from time to time.*
ADV: ADV after v ≠down

4 If someone stands **up**, they move so that they are standing. *He stood up and went to the window... He got up and went out into the foyer.*
ADV: ADV after v

5 If you go or look **up** something such as a road or river, you go or look along it. If you are **up** a road or river, you are somewhere along it. *Chinese tanks came up the road from Lhasa... We leaned on the wooden rail of the bridge and looked up the river... He had a relation who lived up the road.*
PREP: v PREP n ≠down

6 If you are travelling to a particular place, you can say that you are going **up** to that place, especially if you are going towards the north or to a higher level of land. If you are already in such a place, you can say that you are **up** there. Used in spoken English. *I'll be up to see you tomorrow... He was living up North... I live here now, but I've spent all my time up in Swaziland.*
ADV: ADV after v, *be* ADV, oft ADV prep/adv

7 If you go **up** to something or someone, you move to the place where they are and stop there. *The girl ran the rest of the way across the street and up to the car... On the way out a boy of about ten came up on roller skates... He brought me up to the bar and introduced me to Dave.*
ADV: ADV after v, usu ADV *to* n

8 If an amount of something goes **up**, it increases. If an amount of something is **up**, it has increased and is at a higher level than it was. *They recently put my rent up... Tourism is up, jobs are up, individual income is up... Western Germany's rate has also risen sharply, up from 3 percent in 1989 to 4.5 percent... Over the decade, women in this category went up by 120%.*
ADV: ADV after v, *be* ADV, oft ADV *to/by* amount ≠down

9 If you are **up**, you are not in bed. *Are you sure you should be up?... These days all sorts of people were up at the crack of dawn... Soldiers are up at seven for three hours of exercises.*
ADJ: v-link ADJ

10 If a period of time is **up**, it has come to an end. *The moment the half-hour was up, Brooks rose... When the six weeks were up, everybody was sad that she had to leave.*
ADJ: v-link ADJ =over

11 In British English, you say that a road is **up** when it is being repaired and cannot be used. *Men and equipment were moved in and the road was up... Half the road was up in Leadenhall Street, so their taxi was obliged to make a detour.*
ADJ: v-link ADJ

12 People sometimes say **'Up yours!'** as an insult when you have said something to annoy them or make them angry; an informal expression which some people find offensive. *'Up yours,' said the reporter and stormed out into the street.*
EXCLAM PRAGMATICS

13 If someone who has been in bed for some time, for example because they have been ill, is **up and about**, they are now out of bed and living their normal life. *How are you Lennox? Good to see you up and about.*
PHRASES v-link PHR

14 If you say that **something is up**, you mean that something is wrong or that something worrying is happening; an informal expression. *What is it then? Something's up, isn't it?... Mr. Gordon stopped talking, and his friends knew something was up.*
V inflects

15 If you say to someone **'What's up?'** or if you tell them **what's up**, you are asking them or telling them what is wrong or what is worrying them; an informal expression. *'What's up?', I said to him.—'Nothing much,' he answered... Let's sit down and then you can say what's up.*
PRAGMATICS

16 If you move **up and down** somewhere, you move there repeatedly in one direction and then in the opposite direction. *He continued to jump up and down like a boy at a football match... I strolled up and down thoughtfully before calling a taxi... There's a lot of rushing up and down the gangways.*
PHR after v

17 If you have **ups and downs**, you experience a mixture of good things and bad things. *Every relationship has a lot of ups and downs... The organisation has had its ups and downs. ...the ups and downs of parenthood.*

18 • **up in arms**: see **arm**.

up 2 used in combination as a preposition

up /ʌp/ ◆◆◆◆◆

1 If you feel **up to** doing something, you are well enough to do it. *Those patients who were up to it*
PHR-PREP: PREP n/-ing

could move to the adjacent pool... He wasn't at all sure Sarah was up to that... His fellow-directors were not up to running the business without him.

2 If you say that someone is **up to** something, you mean that they are secretly doing something that they should not be doing; an informal use. *Why did you need a room unless you were up to something?... They must they must have known what their father was up to... Look at what they are getting up to.*
PHR-PREP

3 If you say that it is **up to** someone to do something, you mean that it is their responsibility to do it. *It was up to him to make it right, no matter how long it took... I'm sure I'd have spotted him if it had been up to me... The choice was up to Paula.*
PHR-PREP: oft v-link PREP n to-inf

4 **Up until** or **up to** are used to indicate the latest time at which something can happen, or the end of the period of time that you are referring to. *Please feel free to call me any time up until half past nine at night... Up to 1979, the growth of per capita income averaged 1 per cent per year.*
PHR-PREP

5 You use **up to** to say how large something can be or what level it has reached. *Up to twenty thousand students paid between five and six thousand dollars... It could be up to two years before the process is complete.*
PHR-PREP: PREP amount

6 In informal British English, if you say that something is **not up to much**, you mean that it is of poor quality. *My own souffles aren't up to much... This business isn't up to much.*
PHRASE: v-link PHR

7 If someone or something is **up for** election, review, or examination, they are about to be considered or judged. *A third of the Senate and the entire House are up for re-election.*
PHR-PREP

8 If you are **up against** something, you have a very difficult situation or problem to deal with. *The chairwoman is up against the greatest challenge to her position... They were up against a good team but did very well.*
PHR-PREP =facing

9 • **up to your ears**: see **ear**. • **up to par**: see **par**. • **up to scratch**: see **scratch**. • **up to the mark**: see **mark**.

up 3 verb uses

up /ʌp/ **ups, upping, upped** ◆◆◇◇◇

1 If you **up** something such as the amount of money you are offering for something, you increase it. *He upped his offer for the company... Chemist stores upped sales by 63 percent... We are talking about upping everybody's pay.*
VERB =increase V n

2 If you **up** and leave a place, you go away from it, often suddenly or unexpectedly. *A man who for months had been dropping amorous hints about a long-term relationship upped and disappeared to America... One day he just upped and left.*
VERB V *and* v

up-and-coming. ◆◇◇◇◇ **Up-and-coming** people are likely to be successful in the future. *...up and coming stars Joelle Obadia and Josef Nadj... Mr Hurford is an up and coming player.*
ADJ: ADJ n

upbeat /ʌpbiːt/ **upbeats** ◆◇◇◇◇

1 If people or their opinions are **upbeat**, they are cheerful and optimistic about a situation; an informal use. *The Defense Secretary gave an upbeat assessment of the war so far... Neil's colleagues say he was actually in a joking, upbeat mood... Scientists remain upbeat about the information that will be gathered.*
ADJ-GRADED: usu ADJ n =positive ≠downbeat

2 In music, the **upbeat** is the beat before the first beat of the bar.
N-COUNT ≠downbeat

upbraid /ʌpbreɪd/ **upbraids, upbraiding, upbraided.** If you **upbraid** someone, you tell them that they have done something wrong and criticize them for doing it; a formal word. *Eleanor upbraided him for things he'd left undone... His wife set about upbraiding him for neglecting the children.*
VERB =reproach ≠praise V n V n *for* n/-ing

upbringing /ʌpbrɪŋɪŋ/. ◆◇◇◇◇ Your **upbringing** is the way that your parents treat you and the things that they teach you when you are growing up. *Martin's upbringing shaped his whole life... Sam's mother said her son had a good upbringing and schooling.*
N-UNCOUNT: usu with supp

upcoming /ʌpkʌmɪŋ/. ◆◇◇◇◇ **Upcoming** events will happen in the near future. *...the upcoming Asian Games in Peking... We'll face a tough fight in the upcoming election.*
ADJ: ADJ n

upcountry /ʌpkʌntri/; also spelled **up-country.** **Upcountry** places are in the more remote or far northern areas of a large country. *...a collection of upcountry hamlets.* ► Also an adverb. *The Ussuri reserves is 30 miles upcountry from Vlad. ...going up-country.*
ADJ: ADJ n
ADV: *be* ADV, ADV after v

update /ʌpdeɪt/ **updates, updating, updated.** ◆◆◇◇◇ The verb is pronounced /ʌpdeɪt/. The noun is pronounced /ʌpdeɪt/.

1 If you **update** something, you make it more modern, usually by adding new parts to it or giving new information. *He was back in the office, updating the work schedule on the computer... Airlines would prefer to update rather than retrain crews. ...an updated edition of the book.*
VERB V n V V-ed

2 An **update** is a news item which has been rewritten so that it includes the latest developments in a situation. *She had heard the news-flash on a TV channel's news update. ...a weather update. ...football results update.*
N-COUNT: usu with supp

3 If you **update** someone **on** a situation, you tell them the latest developments in that situation. *We'll update you on the day's top news stories... I would just update them on any news we might have.*
VERB V n *on* n

upend /ʌpend/ **upends, upending, upended.** If you **upend** something, you turn it upside down. *He upended the beer, and swallowed. ...upended flower pots.*
VERB V n V-ed

up front; also spelled **up-front.** ◆◇◇◇◇

1 If you are **up front** about something, you act openly or publicly so that people know what you are doing or what you believe; an informal use. *You can't help being biased so you may as well be up front about it... They tended to have a much more up-front attitude.*
ADJ-GRADED: usu v-link ADJ =direct, frank

2 If a payment is made **up front**, it is made in advance and openly, so that the person being paid can see that the money is there. *For the first time the government's actually put some money up front... Some companies charge a fee up front, but we don't think that's right.* ► Also an adjective. *The eleven percent loan has no up-front costs. ...up-front charges.*
ADV: ADV after v
ADJ: ADJ n

upgrade /ʌpgreɪd/ **upgrades, upgrading, upgraded** ◆◆◇◇◇

1 If equipment or services **are upgraded**, they are improved or made more efficient. *Helicopters have been upgraded and modernized... Medical facilities are being reorganized and upgraded. ...upgraded catering facilities.* ► Also a noun. *...equipment which needs expensive upgrades. ...upgrades in the level of security.*
VB: usu passive =improve *be* V-ed V-ed
N-COUNT: usu pl

2 If someone **is upgraded**, their job or status is changed so that they become more important or receive more money. *He was upgraded to security guard.*
VB: usu passive =promote ≠downgrade *be* V-ed *to* n

upheaval /ʌphiːvəl/ **upheavals.** ◆◇◇◇◇ An **upheaval** is a big change which causes a lot of trouble, confusion, and worry. *Algeria has been going through political upheaval for the past two months... Having a baby will mean the greatest upheaval in your life.*
N-COUNT: usu adj N

upheld /ʌpheld/. **Upheld** is the past tense and past participle of **uphold**.

uphill /ʌphɪl/ ◆◇◇◇◇

1 If something or someone is **uphill** or is moving **uphill**, they are near the top of a hill or are going up a slope. *He had been running uphill a long way... The man was no more than ten yards away and slightly uphill. ...trees that ran in a ragged line uphill from the ledge.* ► Also an adjective. *...a long, uphill journey... The walk from the village to Greystones was uphill all the way.*
ADV: ADV after v, *be* ADV, ADV *from* n ≠downhill
ADJ: usu ADJ n ≠downhill

2 If you refer to something as an **uphill** struggle or an **uphill** battle, you mean that it requires a great deal of effort and determination, but it should be possible to achieve it. *It had been an uphill struggle*
ADJ: ADJ n

to achieve what she had wanted... It's an uphill battle but I think we're going to win.

uphold /ʌphəʊld/ **upholds, upholding, upheld** ◆◆◇◇◇
1 If you **uphold** something such as a law, a principle, or a decision, you support and maintain it. *Our policy has been to uphold the law... It is the responsibility of every government to uphold certain basic principles. ...upholding the artist's right to creative freedom.* VERB V n
2 If a court of law **upholds** a legal decision that has already been made, it decides that it was the correct decision. *The crown court, however, upheld the magistrate's decision.* VERB V n

upholder /ʌphəʊldər/ **upholders.** An **upholder** of a particular tradition or system is someone who believes strongly in it and will support it when it is threatened; a formal word. *...upholders of the traditional family unit.* N-COUNT

upholstered /ʌphəʊlstərd/. **Upholstered** chairs and sofas have a soft covering that makes them comfortable to sit on. *All of their furniture was upholstered in flowery materials.* ◆◇◇◇◇ ADJ: oft ADJ *in* n

upholsterer /ʌphəʊlstərər/ **upholsterers.** An **upholsterer** is someone whose job is to make and fit the soft covering on chairs and sofas. N-COUNT

upholstery /ʌphəʊlstəri/. **Upholstery** is the soft covering on chairs and sofas that makes them more comfortable to sit on. *...white leather upholstery... Simon rested his head against the upholstery.* ◆◇◇◇◇ N-UNCOUNT

upkeep /ʌpkiːp/ ◆◇◇◇◇
1 The **upkeep** of a building or place is the continual process of keeping it in good condition. *The money will be used for the estate's upkeep... The maintenance department is responsible for the general upkeep of the park.* N-UNCOUNT: usu with poss =maintenance
2 The **upkeep** of a group of people or services is the process of providing them with the things that they need. *He offered to pay £100 a month towards his son's upkeep. ...subsidies for the upkeep of kindergartens and orphanages.* N-UNCOUNT: usu with poss =maintenance

upland /ʌplənd/ **uplands** ◆◇◇◇◇
1 **Upland** places are situated on high land. *...San Marino, the tiny upland republic... It's important that these upland farms continue to survive.* ADJ: ADJ n
2 **Uplands** are areas of high land. *Flooding was caused by water gushing into rivers from uplands. ...a deep valley ringed about by green uplands.* N-PLURAL ≠lowlands

uplift, uplifts, uplifting, uplifted. The verb is pronounced /ʌplɪft/. The noun is pronounced /ʌplɪft/. If something **uplifts** people, it helps them to have a better life, for example by making them feel happy or by improving their social conditions; a literary word. *We need a little something to help sometimes, to uplift us and make us feel better... Art was created to uplift the mind and the spirit.* ▶ Also a noun. *...an uplift in the economy.* VERB V n N-UNCOUNT

uplifted /ʌplɪftɪd/
1 If people's faces or arms are **uplifted**, they are pointing them upwards or are holding them up; a literary use. *The men support the ballerinas, who pose with their uplifted arms. ...her white, uplifted chin.* ADJ: usu ADJ n =raised
2 If something makes you feel **uplifted**, it makes you feel very cheerful and happy. *...people whose presence left you feeling uplifted, happy and full of energy. ...a smile so radiant that he felt uplifted by it.* ADJ-GRADED: v-link ADJ, oft ADJ *by* n

uplifting /ʌplɪftɪŋ/. You describe something as **uplifting** when it makes you feel very cheerful and happy. *...a charming and uplifting love story... I like a film to be uplifting.* ◆◇◇◇◇ ADJ-GRADED

upmarket /ʌpmɑːrkɪt/; also spelled **up-market.** **Upmarket** products or services are expensive, of good quality, and intended to appeal to people in a high social class; used mainly in British English. The usual American word is **upscale**. *Anne chose an upmarket agency aimed at professional people. ...restaurants which years ago weren't quite so upmarket as they are today.* ▶ Also an adverb. *Japanese firms have moved steadily upmarket... He promised a move upmarket and a drive to improve service and quality.* ◆◇◇◇◇ ADJ-GRADED: usu ADJ n ≠downmarket ADV: ADV after v ≠downmarket

upon /əpɒn/ ◆◆◆◆◇
In addition to the uses shown below, **upon** is used in phrasal verbs such as 'come upon' and 'look upon', and after some other verbs such as 'decide' and 'depend'.
1 If one thing is **upon** another, it is on it; a formal use. *He set the tray upon the table... He bent forward and laid a kiss softly upon her forehead... I imagined the eyes of the others in the room upon me.* PREP =on
2 You use **upon** when mentioning an event that is followed immediately by another event; a formal use. *The door on the left, upon entering the church, leads to the Crypt of St Issac... Upon conclusion of these studies, the patient was told that she had a severe problem.* PREP: PREP -ing/n =on
3 You use **upon** between two occurrences of the same noun in order to say that there are large numbers of the thing mentioned. *Row upon row of women surged forwards... I looked across the mountains, ridge upon ridge.* PREP: n PREP n
4 If an event is **upon** you, it is just about to happen. *The long-threatened storm was upon us... The wedding season is upon us... They had to conserve the candles now with winter upon them.* PREP: PREP pron

upper /ʌpər/ **uppers** ◆◆◆◇◇
1 You use **upper** to describe something that is above something else. *There is a smart restaurant on the upper floor... Students travel the cheap lower deck and tourists the upper.* ADJ-COMPAR: ADJ n, *the* ADJ ≠lower
2 You use **upper** to describe the higher part of something. *...the upper part of the foot. ...the muscles of the upper back and chest. ...the upper rungs of the ladder.* ADJ-COMPAR: ADJ n ≠lower
3 If you have **the upper hand** in a situation, you have more power than the other people involved and can make decisions about what happens. *The government was beginning to gain the upper hand... It was easy to see who had the upper hand.* PHRASE: PHR after v
4 The **upper** of a shoe is the top part of it, which is attached to the sole and the heel. *Wear well-fitting, lace-up shoes with soft uppers... Leather uppers allow the feet to breath.* N-COUNT: usu pl
5 **Uppers** are drugs that make you feel very happy, excited, and full of energy; an informal use. *...people crazy on alcohol and cocaine and uppers and downers... I'd taken a handful of uppers.* N-COUNT ≠downer
6 • **a stiff upper lip**: see **lip**.

upper case. **Upper case** letters are capital letters. *Most schools teach children lower case letters first, and upper case letters later.* ▶ Also a noun. *I'm wondering if 'per capita' ought to have upper case, or should it be lower case?* ADJ: usu ADJ n ≠lower case N-UNCOUNT ≠lower case

upper class, upper classes; also spelled **upper-class**. The **upper class** or the **upper classes** are the group of people in a society who own the most property and have the highest social status, and who may not need to work for money. *...goods specifically designed to appeal to the tastes of the upper class... Many of the British upper classes are no longer very rich.* ▶ Also an adjective. *All of them came from wealthy, upper class families. ...different styles of upper-class speech.* ◆◇◇◇◇ N-COUNT-COLL: usu *the* N ≠lower class ADJ: usu ADJ n ≠lower class

upper crust; also spelled **upper-crust**. The **upper crust** are the upper classes; an informal word. *...the kind of lifestyle of the privileged upper crust.* ▶ Also an adjective. *Sergeant Parrott normally spoke with an upper-crust accent.* N-SING-COLL ADJ: ADJ n

uppercut /ʌpərkʌt/ **uppercuts.** An **uppercut** is a type of punch used in boxing. It is a hard upward blow to the opponent's chin. *He was knocked down by an uppercut from Eubank.* N-COUNT

Upper House, Upper Houses ◆◇◇◇◇
1 In Britain, the **Upper House** is the **House of Lords**. *The decision was announced after objections were raised in the Upper House of Parliament.* N-PROPER
2 In countries other than Britain where the government is divided into two debating chambers, the **Upper House** is one of these chambers, and is N-PROPER

often called the Senate. *The Upper House of the German parliament is to meet today in Berlin.*

upper lip, upper lips ◆◇◇◇◇
1 Your **upper lip** is the part of your face between your mouth and your nose. *The beginnings of a moustache showed on his upper lip.* N-COUNT: usu sing
2 Your **upper lip** is the higher of your two lips. *His upper lip was flat, but the lower one sagged.* ● **keep a stiff upper lip**: see **lip**. N-COUNT ≠lower lip

uppermost /ʌpəʳmoʊst/ ◆◇◇◇◇
1 The **uppermost** part of something is the part that is higher than the rest of it. The **uppermost** thing is the highest one of a group of things. *John was on the uppermost floor of the three-storey gatehouse... The rain spattered on the uppermost leaves.* ► Also an adverb. *She placed her hands palm uppermost in her lap... Lift the fish and carefully place it on a large board, flat side uppermost.* ADJ: usu ADJ n =topmost; ADV: n ADV =up
2 If something is **uppermost** in a particular situation, it is the most important thing in that situation. *The economy appears to be uppermost in people's minds... Protection of sites, habitats and landscapes is of uppermost priority.* ADJ: usu v-link ADJ =paramount

uppity /ʌpɪti/. If you say that someone is **uppity**, you mean that they are behaving as if they were very important and you do not think that they are important; an informal word. *If you just tried to show normal dignity, you were viewed as uppity.* ADJ-GRADED

upraised /ʌpreɪzd/. If your hand or an object is **upraised**, you are holding it up in the air. *A soldier stood on the centre line of the road, his arm upraised. ...the landlady's upraised glass.* ADJ

upright /ʌpraɪt/ **uprights.** ◆◆◇◇◇
1 If you are sitting or standing **upright**, you are sitting or standing with your back straight, rather than bending or lying down. *Helen sat upright in her chair. ...those who had managed to remain upright... Jerrold pulled himself upright on the bed... He moved into an upright position.* ADJ: usu ADJ after v, v-link ADJ, also ADJ n
2 An **upright** vacuum cleaner or freezer stands vertically and is taller than it is wide. *...the latest state-of-the-art upright vacuum cleaners.* ADJ: ADJ n
3 An **upright** chair has a straight back and no arms. *He was sitting on an upright chair beside his bed, reading.* ADJ
4 You can refer to vertical posts or the vertical parts of an object as **uprights**. *...the uprights of a four-poster bed.* N-COUNT
5 You can describe people as **upright** when they are careful to follow acceptable rules of behaviour and behave in a moral way. *...a very upright, trustworthy man.* ADJ-GRADED: usu ADJ n =virtuous

upright piano, upright pianos. An **upright piano** is a piano in which the strings are laid out vertically rather than horizontally as in a grand piano. N-COUNT

uprising /ʌpraɪzɪŋ/ **uprisings.** When there is an **uprising**, a group of people start fighting against the people who are in power in their country, because they want to bring about a political change. *...a popular uprising against the authoritarian government... Isolated attacks in the north-east of the country have now turned into a full-scale uprising.* ◆◆◇◇◇ N-COUNT: usu sing =rebellion, revolt

up-river; also spelled **upriver**. Something that is moving **up-river** is moving towards the source of a river, from a point further down the river. Something that is **up-river** is further towards the source of a river than where you are. *Heavy goods could be brought up-river in barges... He has a house down there but it's miles up river... The vineyards of Anjou extend from west of Angers to up-river of Saumur. ...La Reole, up-river from St-Macaire.* ► Also an adjective. *...an upriver trip in Central Africa.* ADV: ADV after v, be ADV, oft ADV *of/from* n ≠down-river; ADJ: ADJ n

uproar /ʌprɔːʳ/ ◆◇◇◇◇
1 If there is **uproar**, there is a lot of shouting and noise because people are very angry or upset about something. *The announcement caused uproar in the crowd... The courtroom was in an uproar.* N-UNCOUNT: also *a* N, oft *in* N
2 You can also use **uproar** to refer to a lot of public criticism and debate about something that has made people angry. *The town is in uproar over the dispute... The surprise announcement could cause an uproar in the United States.* N-UNCOUNT: also *a* N

uproarious /ʌprɔːriəs/. When events or people are **uproarious**, they make people laugh in a very noisy way; a literary word. *He had spent several uproarious evenings at the Embassy Club... The noise of talk and laughter was uproarious.* ♦ **uproariously** *Bob laughed uproariously, delighted and amused. ...an uproariously funny story.* ADJ; ADV: ADV after v, ADV adj

uproot /ʌpruːt/ **uproots, uprooting, uprooted** ◆◇◇◇◇
1 If you **uproot** yourself or if you **are uprooted**, you leave, or are made to leave, a place where you have lived for a long time. *...the trauma of uprooting themselves from their homes... He had no wish to uproot Dena from her present home. ...refugees who were uprooted during Ethiopia's civil war.* VERB V pron-refl V n *be* V-ed
2 If someone **uproots** a tree or plant, or if the wind **uproots** it, it is pulled out of the ground. *They had been forced to uproot their vines and plant wheat. ...fallen trees which have been uprooted by the storm. ...uprooted trees.* VERB V n V-ed

upscale /ʌpskeɪl/. In American English, **upscale** is used to describe products or services that are expensive, of good quality, and intended to appeal to people in a high social class. The British word is **upmarket**. *Vodka has acquired an upscale image in the US. ...upscale department-store chains such as Bloomingdale's and Saks Fifth Avenue.* ► Also an adverb. *T-shirts, the epitome of American casualness, have moved upscale.* ADJ-GRADED: usu ADJ n; ADV: ADV after v

upset, upsets, upsetting, upset. Pronounced /ʌpset/ when it is a verb, or an adjective. Pronounced /ʌpset/ when it is a noun. ◆◆◆◇◇
1 If you are **upset**, you are unhappy or disappointed because something unpleasant has happened to you. *After she died I felt very, very upset... Marta looked upset... She sounded upset when I said you couldn't give her an appointment... They are terribly upset by the break-up of their parents' marriage.* ► Also a noun. *...stress and other emotional upsets.* ADJ-GRADED: usu v-link ADJ, oft ADJ *by/about* n =distressed; N-COUNT
2 If something **upsets** you, it makes you feel worried or unhappy. *The whole incident had upset me and my fiancee terribly... She warned me not to say anything to upset him... Don't upset yourself, Ida.* ♦ **upsetting** *Childhood illness can be upsetting for children and parents alike... I will never see him again and that is a terribly upsetting thought.* VERB =distress V n V pron-refl; ADJ-GRADED: usu v-link ADJ =distressing
3 If events **upset** something such as a procedure or a state of affairs, they cause it to go wrong. *Political problems could upset agreements between Moscow and Kabul... House prices are easily upset by factors which have nothing to do with property.* ► Also a noun. *Markets are very sensitive to any upsets in the Japanese economic machine.* VERB =mess up, disrupt V n; N-COUNT =disruption
4 If you **upset** an object, you accidentally knock or push it over so that it scatters over a large area. *Don't upset the piles of sheets under the box. ...bumping into him, and almost upsetting the ginger ale.* VERB V n
5 A stomach **upset** is a slight illness in your stomach caused by an infection or by something that you have eaten. *Paul was unwell last night with a stomach upset... It wasn't anything serious. A mild stomach upset, that's all.* ► Also an adjective. *Larry is suffering from an upset stomach.* N-COUNT: supp N; ADJ: ADJ n
6 ● to **upset the apple cart**: see **applecart**.

upshot /ʌpʃɒt/. **The upshot** of a series of events or discussions is the final result of them, usually a surprising result. *The upshot is that we have lots of good but not very happy employees... So the upshot is we're going for lunch on Friday.* N-SING: *the* N =outcome

upside down /ʌpsaɪd daʊn/; also spelled **upside-down.** ◆◇◇◇◇
1 If something has been moved **upside down**, it has been turned round so that the part that is usually lowest is above the part that is usually highest. *The painting was hung upside down... Salter held the bag by the corners and shook it upside* ADV: ADV after v, n ADV

down. ► Also an adjective. *His eyes were open and everything he saw was upside down... Tony had an upside-down map of Britain on his wall.* ADJ
2 • to **turn** something **upside down**: see **turn**.

upstage /ʌpsteɪdʒ/ **upstages, upstaging, upstaged** ◆◇◇◇◇
1 When an actor is **upstage** or moves **upstage**, he or she is or moves towards the back part of the stage; a technical use. *Upstage and right of centre, Robert Morris stands with his back to the audience... Position a camera upstage... They slowly moved from upstage left into the centre.* ► Also an adjective. *...the large upstage box that Noble used for his 1990 production of King Lear.* ADV: ADV after v, *be* ADV, prep ADV ≠downstage; ADJ: ADJ n ≠downstage
2 If someone **upstages** you, they draw attention away from you by being more attractive or interesting. *He had a younger brother who always publicly upstaged him... He upstages her by flirting with other women.* VERB =outshine; V n

upstairs /ʌpsteə^r^z/ ◆◆◇◇◇
1 If you go **upstairs** in a building, you go up a staircase towards a higher floor. *He went upstairs and changed into fresh clothes... I walked upstairs and unlocked my front door.* ADV: ADV after v ≠downstairs
2 If something or someone is **upstairs** in a building, they are on a floor that is higher than the ground floor. *The restaurant is upstairs and consists of a large, open room... The boys are curled asleep in the small bedroom upstairs.* ADV: *be* ADV, n ADV ≠downstairs
3 An **upstairs** room or object is situated on a floor of a building that is higher than the ground floor. *Marsani moved into the upstairs apartment. ...an upstairs balcony.* ADJ: ADJ n
4 **The upstairs** of a building is the floor or floors that are higher than the ground floor. *Together we went through the upstairs... Frances invited them to occupy the upstairs of her home.* N-SING: *the* N ≠downstairs

upstanding /ʌpstændɪŋ/. **Upstanding** people behave in a morally acceptable way; a formal word. *...a fine, upstanding and decent Irish citizen... You look like a nice upstanding young man.* ADJ-GRADED: usu ADJ n =upright

upstart /ʌpstɑː^r^t/ **upstarts.** You can refer to someone as an **upstart** when they behave as if they are important, but you think that they are too new in a place or job to be treated as important. *Many prefer a familiar authority figure to a young upstart. ...an upstart who had come from nowhere.* ◆◇◇◇◇ N-COUNT PRAGMATICS

upstate /ʌpsteɪt/. **Upstate** means belonging or relating to the parts of a state that are furthest to the north or furthest from the centre; used mainly in American English. *...an idyllic village in upstate New York.* ► Also an adverb. *These buses will carry families upstate to visit relatives in prison... The park was created to preserve some of the forests upstate.* ADJ: ADJ n; ADV: ADV after v, n ADV

upstream /ʌpstriːm/. Something that is moving **upstream** is moving towards the source of a river, from a point further down the river. Something that is **upstream** is towards the source of a river. *The water rose high enough for them to continue upstream. ...the river police, whose headquarters are just upstream of the Isle St Louis... Cities upstream use the river to get rid of sewage... He lives about 60 miles upstream from Oahe, near Gettysburg, South Dakota.* ► Also an adjective. *Steps lead down to the subway from the upstream side.* ◆◇◇◇◇ ADV: ADV after v, *be* ADV, n ADV, oft ADV *of/from* n ≠downstream; ADJ: ADJ n ≠downstream

upsurge /ʌpsɜː^r^dʒ/. If there is an **upsurge** in something, there is a sudden, large increase in it; a formal word. *...the upsurge in oil prices... Saudi bankers say there's been an upsurge of business confidence since the end of the war.* ◆◇◇◇◇ N-SING: oft N *in/of* n

upswing /ʌpswɪŋ/ **upswings.** An **upswing** is a sudden improvement in something such as an economy, or an increase in an amount or level. *...an upswing in the economy... Violent crime is on the upswing.* N-COUNT: usu sing, oft N *in* n, *on the* N ≠downswing

uptake /ʌpteɪk/
1 A person's **uptake** of something is the amount of it that they use; a technical use. *The drug increases the number of red cells in the blood, enhancing oxygen uptake by 10 percent. ...research in relation to the uptake of nitrate into vegetables.* N-SING: usu with supp =intake
2 You say that someone is **quick on the uptake** when they understand things quickly. You say that someone is **slow on the uptake** when they have difficulty understanding simple or obvious things. *She is not an intellectual, but is quick on the uptake... Carol was absent-minded and a little slow on the uptake.* PHRASE: v-link PHR

up-tempo; also spelled **uptempo**. An **up-tempo** piece of music has a fast beat. *...an up-tempo arrangement of 'Some Enchanted Evening'.* ADJ: usu ADJ n

uptight /ʌptaɪt/. Someone who is **uptight** is tense, nervous, or annoyed about something and so is difficult to be with; an informal word. *Penny never got uptight about exams... I tend to get very uptight during a match.* ADJ-GRADED: usu v-link ADJ =edgy

up to date; also spelled **up-to-date**. ◆◆◇◇◇
1 If something is **up-to-date**, it is the newest thing of its kind. *...Germany's most up to date electric power station. ...enhancing the system and bringing it up to date... This production is bang up-to-date.* ADJ-GRADED ≠out of date
2 If you are **up-to-date** about something, you have the latest information about it. *We'll keep you up to date with any news... I am very up to date on this sort of thing because I listen to the news.* ADJ-GRADED: usu v-link ADJ =informed

up-to-the-minute; also spelled **up to the minute. Up-to-the-minute** information is the latest information that you can get about something. *...24 hours a day up-to-the-minute instant news... Computers give them up-to-the-minute information on sales and stocks.* ADJ-GRADED: usu ADJ n

uptown /ʌptaʊn/. In American English, if you go **uptown**, or go to a place **uptown**, you go away from the centre of a town or city towards one of its suburbs. *He rode uptown and made his way to Bob's apartment... Susan continued to live uptown... There's a skating rink uptown.* ► Also an adjective. *...uptown clubs. ...a small uptown radio station. ...uptown New York.* ◆◇◇◇◇ ADV: ADV after v ≠downtown; ADJ: ADJ n ≠downtown

uptrend /ʌptrend/. An **uptrend** is a general improvement in something such as a market or the economy. *Racal Electronics shares have been in a strong uptrend... Many analysts think the dollar is on an uptrend.* N-SING ≠downtrend

upturn /ʌptɜː^r^n/ **upturns.** If there is an **upturn** in the economy or in a company or industry, it improves or becomes more successful. *They do not expect an upturn in the economy until the end of the year... There has been a modest upturn in most parts of the industry.* ◆◇◇◇◇ N-COUNT: oft N *in* n ≠downturn

upturned /ʌptɜː^r^nd/
1 Something that is **upturned** points upwards. *...the rain splashing down on her upturned face. ...his eyes closed and his palms upturned.* ADJ: usu ADJ n
2 Something that is **upturned** is upside down. *...upturned buckets... He clung to the upturned boat, screaming for help.* ADJ: usu ADJ n

upward /ʌpwə^r^d/ ◆◆◇◇◇
1 An **upward** movement or look is directed towards a higher place or a higher level. *She started once again on the steep upward climb... Oil prices continued an upward swing in New York this morning... She gave him a quick, upward look, then lowered her eyes.* ADJ: ADJ n ≠downward
2 If you refer to an **upward** trend or an **upward** spiral, you mean that something is increasing in quantity or price. *...the Army's concern that the upward trend in the numbers avoiding military service may continue. ...if prices continue their inexorably upward spiral.* ADJ: ADJ n ≠downward

upwardly mobile. If you describe someone as **upwardly mobile**, you mean that they are moving, have moved, or are trying to move to a higher social position. *The Party has been unable to attract upwardly mobile voters.* ► **The upwardly mobile** are people who are upwardly mobile. *...the large detached houses of the upwardly mobile with their double garages and array of cars.* ADJ; N-PLURAL: *the* N

upwards /ʌpwəʳdz/; also spelled **upward**. ◆◆◇◇◇
In American English, **upward** is the more usual form.

1 If someone moves or looks **upwards**, they move or look up towards a higher place. *'There,' said Jack, pointing upwards... They climbed upward along the steep cliffs surrounding the village... Hunter nodded again and gazed upwards in fear... Lie face upwards with a cushion under your head.* ADV: ADV after v, n ADV ≠downwards

2 If an amount or rate moves **upwards**, it increases. *...with prices soon heading upwards in high street stores... Unemployment will continue upward for much of this year... The share price is likely to leap upwards.* ADV: ADV after v ≠downwards

3 A quantity that is **upwards of** a particular number is more than that number. *...projects worth upwards of 200 million pounds... It costs upward of $40,000 a year to keep some prisoners in prison.* PHR-PREP: PREP amount =over ≠less than

upwind /ʌpwɪnd/. If something moves **upwind**, it moves in the opposite direction to the wind. If something is **upwind**, the wind is blowing away from it. *...riding a bike upwind... The rich went to live in the west of London, upwind of the smell of people and industry.* ► Also an adjective. *...big trees at the forest's upwind edge.* ADV: ADV after v, *be* ADV, oft ADV *of* n ≠downwind ADJ: ADJ n

uranium /jʊreɪniəm/. **Uranium** is a naturally occurring radioactive metal that is used to produce nuclear energy and weapons. ◆◆◇◇◇ N-UNCOUNT

urban /ɜːʳbən/. **Urban** means belonging to, or relating to, a town or city. *Most of the population is an urban population. ...most urban areas are close to a park. ...urban planning.* ◆◆◆◇◇ ADJ-GRADED: usu ADJ n ≠rural

urbane /ɜːʳbeɪn/. Someone who is **urbane** is well-mannered, relaxed, and appears comfortable in social situations. *She describes him as urbane and charming... In conversation, he was suave and urbane.* ♦ **urbanity** /ɜːʳbænɪti/ *Fearey had all the charm and urbanity of the trained diplomat.* ADJ-GRADED =cultured ≠gauche N-UNCOUNT =refinement

urbanization /ɜːʳbənaɪzeɪʃᵊn/; also spelled **urbanisation** in British English. **Urbanization** is the process of creating towns in country areas. ◆◇◇◇◇ N-UNCOUNT

urbanized /ɜːʳbənaɪzd/; also spelled **urbanised** in British English.

1 An **urbanized** country or area has many buildings and a lot of industry and business. *Zambia is black Africa's most urbanised country... All the nice areas in Florida are becoming more and more urbanized.* ADJ-GRADED: usu ADJ n

2 An **urbanized** population consists of people who live and work in a town. *...a large urbanized industrial population.* ADJ-GRADED

urchin /ɜːʳtʃɪn/ **urchins.** You can refer to a young child who is dirty and poorly dressed as an **urchin**; an old-fashioned word. *We were in the bazaar with all the little urchins watching us.* N-COUNT
• See also **sea urchin**.

Urdu /ʊəʳduː, ɜːʳ-/. **Urdu** is an official language of Pakistan. Urdu is also spoken in India. N-UNCOUNT

urge /ɜːʳdʒ/ **urges, urging, urged** ◆◆◆◆◇

1 If you **urge** someone to do something, you try hard to persuade them to do it. *They urged parliament to approve plans for their reform programme... He urged employers and trade unions to adapt their pay settlements to the economic circumstances.* VERB V n to-inf

2 If you **urge** someone somewhere, you make them go there by touching them or talking to them. *He slipped his arm around her waist and urged her away from the window... 'Come on, Grace,' he was urging her, 'don't wait, hurry up.'* VERB V n prep/adv V n

3 If you **urge** a course of action, you strongly advise that it should be taken. *He urged restraint on the security forces... We urge vigorous action to be taken immediately.* VERB V n on n V n

4 If you have an **urge** to do or have something, you have a strong wish to do or have it. *He had an urge to open a shop of his own... I have often talked about why we want to be mothers, but none of us can describe the urge exactly.* N-COUNT: oft N to-inf

urge on. If you **urge** someone **on**, you encourage them to do something. *She had a strong and supportive sister who urged her on... Western visitors remember a lean, cheerful figure on horseback urging on his men.* PHRASAL VERB =encourage V n P V P n (not pron)

urgent /ɜːʳdʒᵊnt/ ◆◆◆◇◇

1 If something is **urgent**, it needs to be dealt with as soon as possible. *There is an urgent need for food and water... He had urgent business in New York.* ♦ **urgency** *The urgency of finding a cure attracted some of the best minds in medical science... It is a matter of utmost urgency.* ♦ **urgently** *Red Cross officials said they urgently needed bread and water... The money was most urgently required.* ADJ-GRADED =pressing N-UNCOUNT ADV-GRADED: ADV with v

2 If you speak in an **urgent** way, you show that you are anxious for people to notice something or to do something. *His voice was low and urgent... His mother leaned forward and spoke to him in urgent undertones.* ♦ **urgency** *She was surprised at the urgency in his voice... 'Daniel,' Pat said, her voice harsh with urgency. 'Come out here immediately.'* ♦ **urgently** *They hastened to greet him and asked urgently, 'Did you find it?'.* ADJ-GRADED N-UNCOUNT ADV-GRADED: ADV with v

urinal /jʊraɪnᵊl, AM jʊrɪnᵊl/ **urinals.** A **urinal** is a bowl or trough fixed to the wall of men's public lavatories for men to urinate in. N-COUNT

urinary /jʊərɪnəri, AM -neri/. **Urinary** means belonging to or related to the parts of a person's body through which urine flows; a medical term. *...urinary tract infections.* ◆◇◇◇◇ ADJ: ADJ n

urinate /jʊərɪneɪt/ **urinates, urinating, urinated.** When someone **urinates**, they get rid of urine from their body. ◆◇◇◇◇ VERB: V

urine /jʊərɪn/. **Urine** is the liquid that you get rid of from your body when you go to the toilet. ◆◆◇◇◇ N-UNCOUNT

urn /ɜːʳn/ **urns** ◆◇◇◇◇

1 An **urn** is a container in which the ashes of a cremated person are kept. N-COUNT

2 An **urn** is a metal container used for making a large quantity of tea or coffee and keeping it hot. N-COUNT: usu supp N

us /əs STRONG ʌs/ ◆◆◆◆◆
Us is the third person plural pronoun. **Us** is usually used as the object of a verb or a preposition.

1 A speaker or writer uses **us** to refer both to himself or herself and to one or more other people as a group. In conversation, **us** can also include someone who is not present. You can use **us** before a noun to make it clear which group of people you are referring to. *Neither of us forgot about it... Heather went to the kitchen to get drinks for us... The invention of Beckett's 'Play' is that it includes us, the audience, in a different way than does traditional theater... He showed us aspects of the game that we had never seen before... Another time of great excitement for us boys was when war broke out.* PRON-PLURAL: v PRON, prep PRON

2 **Us** is sometimes used to refer to people in general. *All of us will struggle fairly hard to survive if we are in danger... Each of us will have our own criteria for success.* PRON-PLURAL: v PRON, prep PRON

3 In fairly formal English, a speaker or writer may use **us** instead of 'I' in order to include the listeners or readers in what he or she is saying, especially when talking about how the book or talk is organized. *So that gets us to the end of chapter nine.* PRON-PLURAL: v PRON, prep PRON

4 In non-standard spoken British English, **us** is sometimes used instead of 'me'. *'Hang on a bit,' said Eileen. 'I'm not finished yet. Give us a chance.'* PRON-SING: v PRON, prep PRON

US /juː es/. **US** is an abbreviation for 'United States'. *The first time I saw TV was when I arrived in the US in 1956... His niece and nephew are each to inherit 100,000 US dollars.* ◆◆◆◆◆ N-PROPER: *the* N, N n

USA /juː es eɪ/. The **USA** an abbreviation for the 'United States of America'. *In the USA you can ring Social Security or the Department of Welfare and ask what help is available.* ◆◆◆◇◇ N-PROPER: *the* N

usable /juːzəbᵊl/. If something is **usable**, it is in a good enough state or condition to be used. *Charity shops and jumble sales welcome usable clothes... Half of the island's population has no usable English.* ◆◇◇◇◇ ADJ-GRADED ≠unusable

USAF /juː es eɪ ef/. **USAF** is an abbreviation for 'United States Air Force'. N-PROPER: usu *the* N

usage /juːsɪdʒ/ **usages** ◆◇◇◇◇

1 **Usage** is the way in which words are actually used N-UNCOUNT:

in particular contexts, especially with regard to their meanings. *The word 'undertaker' had long been in common usage... He was a stickler for the correct usage of English.*
usu with supp =use

2 A **usage** is a meaning that a word has or a way in which it can be used. *It's very definitely a usage which has come over to Britain from America.*
N-COUNT =use

3 **Usage** is the degree to which something is used or the way in which it is used. *Parts of the motor wore out because of constant usage... If your water usage is very small it may be worthwhile opting for a meter.*
N-UNCOUNT: usu with supp

use 1 verb uses

use /ju:z/ **uses, using, used** ◆◆◆◆◆

1 If you **use** something, you do something with it in order to do a job or to achieve a particular result or effect. *Trim off the excess pastry using a sharp knife... He had simply used a little imagination... Officials used loud hailers to call for calm... The show uses Zondo's trial and execution as its framework.*
VERB — V n; V n to-inf; V n prep

2 If you **use** a supply of something, you finish it so that none of it is left. *You used all the ice cubes and didn't put the ice trays back... They've never had anything spare – they've always used it all.* ► To **use up** something means the same as to **use** it. *It isn't them who use up the world's resources... We were breathing really fast, and using the air up quickly.*
VERB — V n; PHRASAL VERB — V P n (not pron); V n P

3 If someone **uses** drugs, they take drugs regularly, especially illegal ones. *He denied he had used drugs... You'll find that most people that don't use heroin don't like people that do.*
VERB =take, do — V n

4 You can say that someone **uses** the toilet or bathroom as a polite way of saying that they go to the toilet. *Wash your hands after using the toilet... He asked whether he could use my bathroom.*
VERB PRAGMATICS — V n

5 If you **use** a particular word or expression, you say or write it, because it has the meaning that you want to express. *The judge liked using the word 'wicked' of people he had sent to jail... When Johnson talks about cuts, he uses words like 'target price' and 'efficiency payments'.*
VERB — V n

6 If you **use** a particular name, you call yourself by that name, especially when it is not the name that you usually call yourself. *Now I use a false name if I'm meeting people for the first time... I didn't want to use my married name because we've split.*
VERB — V n

7 If you say that someone **uses** people, you disapprove of them because they make others do things for them in order to benefit or gain some advantage from it, and not because they care about the other people. *Be careful she's not just using you... Why do I have the feeling I'm being used again?*
VERB PRAGMATICS =exploit — V n

8 See also **used**.

use 2 noun uses

use /ju:s/ **uses** ◆◆◆◆◇

1 Your **use** of something is the action or fact of your using it. *The treatment does not involve the use of any artificial drugs. ...research related to microcomputers and their use in classrooms... We are denied use of the land by the ruling classes... He would support a use of force if the UN deemed it necessary.*
N-UNCOUNT: also a N, usu N of n

2 If you have **a use for** something, you need it or can find something to do with it. *You will no longer have a use for the magazines... They both loved the fabric, but couldn't find a use for it.*
N-SING: a N for n

3 If something has a particular **use**, it is intended for a particular purpose. *Infrared detectors have many uses... It's an interesting scientific phenomenon, but of no practical use whatever... French furniture was designed for every use... The report outlined possible uses for the new weapon. ...Elderflower Water for use as an eye and skin lotion... We need to recognize that certain uses of the land upon which we live are simply wrong.*
N-VAR: with supp, oft adj N, N of/for n, N as/in n

4 If you have the **use** of something, you have the permission or ability to use it. *She will have the use of the car one night a week. ...young people who at some point in the past have lost the use of their limbs... You will have full use of all the new leisure club facilities.*
N-UNCOUNT: also the N, usu N of n

5 A **use** of a word is a particular meaning that it has or a particular way in which it can be used. *There are new uses of words coming in and old uses dying out.*
N-COUNT: with supp, oft N of n

6 Your **use of** a particular name is the fact of your calling yourself by it. *Police have been hampered by Mr Urquhart's use of bogus names.*
N-UNCOUNT: N of n

7 If something is **for the use of** a particular person or group of people, it is for that person or group to use. *The leisure facilities are there for the use of guests... He raises crops mainly for the use of his family.*
PHRASES — PHR n

8 If you say that being something or knowing someone **has** its **uses**, you mean that it makes it possible for you to do something you otherwise would not be able to do; an informal expression. *Being a hospital Sister had its uses.*
V inflects

9 If something such as a technique, building, or machine is **in use**, it is used regularly by people. If it has gone **out of use**, it is no longer used regularly by people. *...the methods of making Champagne which are still in use today... The site has been out of use for many years.*
usu v-link PHR

10 If you **make use of** something, you do something with it in order to do a job or achieve a particular result or effect; used in written English. *Not all nursery schools make use of the opportunities open to them. ...making use of the same bottle time after time.*
V inflects, PHR n

11 You use expressions such as **it's no use**, **there's no use** and **what's the use** to indicate that an action is pointless and will not achieve anything. *It's no use arguing with a drunk... There's no use you asking me any more questions about that because I won't answer... What's the use? There is nothing I can do.*
V inflects, usu PHR -ing

12 If you say **it's no use**, you mean that you have failed to do something and realize that it is useless to continue trying because it is impossible. *It's no use. Let's hang up and try for a better line.*
V inflects

13 If something or someone is **of use**, they are useful. If they are **no use**, they are not at all useful. *The contents of this booklet should be of use to all students... I'm sorry, I've been no use to you.*
usu v-link PHR, oft PHR to n

used 1 modal uses and phrases

used /ju:st/ 

1 If something **used to** be done or **used to** be the case, it was done regularly in the past or was the case in the past. *People used to come and visit him every day... He used to be one of the professors at the School of Education... I feel more compassion and less anger than I used to.*
PHR-MODAL

2 If something **used not to** be done or **used not to** be the case, it was not done in the past or was not the case in the past. The forms **did not use to** and **did not used to** are also found, especially in spoken English. *Borrowing used not to be recommended... At some point kids start doing things they didn't use to do. They get more independent... He didn't used to like anyone walking on the lawns in the back garden.*
PHR-MODAL: with neg

3 If you **are used to** something, you are familiar with it because you have done it or experienced it many times before. *I'm used to having my sleep interrupted... It doesn't frighten them. They're used to it.*
PHRASE: V inflects, PHR n/-ing

4 If you **get used to** something or someone, you become familiar with it or get to know someone, so that you no longer feel that the thing or person is unusual or surprising. *This is how we do things here. You'll soon get used to it... He took some getting used to... You quickly get used to using the brakes.*
PHRASE: V inflects

used 2 adjective uses

used /ju:zd/ ◆◇◇◇◇

1 A **used** handkerchief, glass, or other object is dirty or spoiled because it has been used and needs to be thrown away or washed. *...a used cotton ball stained with makeup... He took a used envelope bearing an Irish postmark.*
ADJ: usu ADJ n ≠clean

2 A **used** car has already had one or more owners. *Would you buy a used car from this man?... His only big purchase has been a used Ford.*
ADJ: usu ADJ n =second-hand

useful /juːsfʊl/ ◆◆◆◆◇

1 If something is **useful**, you can use it to do something or to help you in some way. *The slow cooker is very useful for people who go out all day... Hypnotherapy can be useful in helping you give up smoking... The police gained a great deal of useful information about the organization.* ♦ **usefully** *...the problems to which computers could be usefully applied... We need to find ways of dealing creatively and usefully with our feelings.* ♦ **usefulness** *His interest lay in the usefulness of his work, rather than in any personal credit.*

ADJ-GRADED ≠useless; ADV-GRADED: ADV with v; N-UNCOUNT

2 If an object or skill **comes in useful**, it can help you achieve something in a particular situation. *The accommodation is some distance from the clubhouse, so a hire car comes in useful.*

PHRASE: V inflects

useless /juːsləs/ ◆◆◇◇◇

1 If something is **useless**, you cannot use it. *He realised that their money was useless in this country... Computers would be useless without software writers.* ♦ **uselessly** *His right arm hung rather uselessly.* ♦ **uselessness** *The car had rusted almost to the point of uselessness.*

ADJ-GRADED: usu v-link ADJ ≠useful; ADV-GRADED; N-UNCOUNT

2 If something is **useless**, it does not achieve anything helpful or beneficial. *She knew it was useless to protest. ...a useless punishment which fails to stop drug trafficking.* ♦ **uselessly** *Uselessly, he checked the same pockets he'd checked before.* ♦ **uselessness** *...the uselessness of their research.*

ADJ-GRADED: oft *it* v-link ADJ to-inf =pointless; ADV-GRADED; N-UNCOUNT

3 If you say that someone or something is **useless**, or **useless** at something, you are emphasizing that they are no good at all; an informal use. *Their education system is useless... He was useless at any game with a ball.*

ADJ-GRADED: oft ADJ *at* n =hopeless

4 If someone feels **useless**, they feel worthless and unhelpful to other people. *She sits at home all day, watching TV and feeling useless.* ♦ **uselessness** *...the sense of uselessness and the boredom of empty days.*

ADJ-GRADED; N-UNCOUNT

user /juːzəʳ/ **users.** A **user** is a person or thing that uses something such as a place, facility, product, or machine. *Beach users have complained that the bikes are noisy. ...a regular user of Holland's health-care system. ...a user of electric current, such as an electric motor, a lamp, or a toaster.*

◆◆◆◇◇ N-COUNT: with supp

user-friendly. If you describe something such as a machine or system as **user-friendly**, you mean that it is well designed and easy to use. *This an entirely computer operated system which is very user friendly. ...user-friendly libraries.*

◆◇◇◇◇ ADJ-GRADED

usher /ʌʃəʳ/ **ushers, ushering, ushered** ◆◇◇◇◇

1 If you **usher** someone somewhere, you show them where they should go, often by going with them. *I ushered him into the office... They were quickly ushered away.*

VERB; V n prep/adv

2 An **usher** is a person who shows people where to sit, for example at a wedding or at a concert. *He did part-time work as an usher in a theatre.*

N-COUNT

3 An **usher** is a person who organises people attending a law court.

N-COUNT

usher in. If one thing **ushers in** another thing, it indicates that the other thing is about to begin; a formal expression. *...a unique opportunity to usher in a new era of stability in Europe.*

PHRASAL VERB =herald; V P n (not pron)

usherette /ʌʃəret/ **usherettes.** An **usherette** is a woman who shows people where to sit in a cinema or theatre and who sells refreshments or programmes; an old-fashioned word.

N-COUNT

usu. **usu.** is a written abbreviation for **usually**.

usual /juːʒuəl/ ◆◆◆◆◇

1 **Usual** is used to describe what happens or what is done most often in a particular situation. *It is a neighborhood beset by all the usual inner-city problems... She's smiling her usual friendly smile... After lunch there was a little more clearing up to do than usual... We've had more press coverage in the last three weeks than in the usual three years... It is usual to tip waiters, porters, guides and drivers.* ▶ Also a noun. *The stout barman in a bow tie presented himself to take their order. 'Good morning, sir. The usual?'*

ADJ: det ADJ, v-link ADJ, oft *it* v-link ADJ to-inf; N-SING: *the* N

2 You use **as usual** to indicate that you are describing something that normally happens or that is normally the case. *As usual there will be the local and regional elections on June the twelfth... The front pages are, as usual, a mixture of domestic and foreign news.*

PHRASES; PHR with cl

3 If something happens **as usual**, it happens in the way that it normally does, especially when other things have changed. *When somebody died everything went on as usual, as if it had never happened... With medication, life at home goes on as usual.*

PHR after v =as normal

4 ● **business as usual**: see **business**.

usually /juːʒuəli/ ◆◆◆◆◇

1 If something **usually** happens, it is the thing that most often happens in a particular situation. *The best information about hotels usually comes from friends and acquaintances who have been there... They ate, as they usually did, in the kitchen... Usually, the work is boring... Offering only one loan, usually an installment loan, is part of the plan.*

ADV: ADV before v, ADV with cl/group =generally, normally

2 You use **more than usually** to show that something shows even more of a particular quality than it normally does. *She felt more than usually hungry after her excursion... He was more than usually depressed by problems at work.*

PHRASE: v-link PHR adj =unusually

usurp /juːzɜːʳp/ **usurps, usurping, usurped.** If you say that someone **usurps** a job, role, title, or position, they take it from someone when they have no right to do this; a formal word. *Did she usurp his place in his mother's heart?... The Congress wants to reverse the reforms and usurp the power of the presidency.*

◆◇◇◇◇ VERB; V n

usurper /juːzɜːʳpəʳ/ **usurpers.** A **usurper** is someone who takes another person's title or position when they have no right to; a formal word.

N-COUNT

usury /juːʒəri/. **Usury** is the practice of lending money at unacceptably high interest rates; used showing disapproval.

N-UNCOUNT PRAGMATICS

utensil /juːtensəl/ **utensils. Utensils** are tools or objects that you use in order to help you to cook or to do other tasks in your home. *...utensils such as bowls, steamers and frying pans... The best carving utensil is a long, sharp, flexible knife.*

◆◇◇◇◇ N-COUNT: usu pl

uterine /juːtəraɪn, AM -rɪn/. **Uterine** means relating to the uterus of a woman or female mammal; a medical term.

ADJ

uterus /juːtərəs/ **uteruses.** The **uterus** of a woman or female mammal is her womb; a technical term in biology. *...an ultrasound scan of the uterus.*

◆◇◇◇◇ N-COUNT

utilise /juːtɪlaɪz/. See **utilize**.

utilitarian /juːtɪlɪteəriən/ **utilitarians** ◆◇◇◇◇

1 **Utilitarian** views or ideas are based on the notion that the morally correct course of action is one that produces benefit for the greatest number of people; a technical use in philosophy. *It was James Mill who was the best publicist for utilitarian ideas on government.* ▶ A **utilitarian** is someone with utilitarian views. *One of the greatest utilitarians was Claude Helvetius.*

ADJ; N-COUNT

2 **Utilitarian** objects and buildings are designed to be useful rather than attractive. *Bruce's office is a corner one, utilitarian and unglamorous.*

ADJ-GRADED =functional

utilitarianism /juːtɪlɪteəriənɪzəm/. **Utilitarianism** is the doctrine that the morally correct course of action is one that produces benefit for the greatest number of people; a technical term in philosophy.

N-UNCOUNT

utility /juːtɪlɪti/ **utilities** ◆◆◇◇◇

1 The **utility** of something is its usefulness; a formal use. *Belief in the utility of higher education is shared by students nationwide... He inwardly questioned the utility of his work.*

N-UNCOUNT: with supp =usefulness

2 A **utility** is an important service such as water, electricity, or gas that is provided for everyone, and that everyone pays for. *...public utilities such as gas, electricity and phones.*

N-COUNT

utility room, utility rooms. A **utility room** is a room in a house which is usually connected to

N-COUNT

the kitchen and which contains things such as a washing machine, sink, and cleaning equipment.

utilize /juːtɪlaɪz/ **utilizes, utilizing, utilized;** also spelled **utilise** in British English. If you **utilize** something, you use it; a formal use. *Sound engineers utilize a range of techniques to enhance the quality of the recordings... Minerals can be absorbed and utilized by the body in a variety of different forms.* ♦ **utilization** /juːtɪlaɪzeɪʃən/ *...the utilisation of human resources. ...land utilization on large farms.* ◆◆◇◇◇ VERB =use V n; N-UNCOUNT: usu N of n, n N

utmost /ʌtmoust/ ◆◇◇◇◇

1 You can use **utmost** to emphasize the importance or seriousness of something or to emphasize the way that it is done. *It is a matter of the utmost urgency to find out what has happened to these people... Security matters are treated with the utmost seriousness... You should proceed with the utmost caution... Utmost care must be taken not to spill any of the contents.* ADJ: ADJ n PRAGMATICS =uttermost

2 If you say that you are doing your **utmost** to do something, you are emphasizing that you are trying as hard as you can to do it; a formal use. *He would have done his utmost to help her, of that she was certain... He will try his utmost to help them by means of his conventional medical knowledge.* N-SING: poss N PRAGMATICS

3 If you say that something is done to the **to the utmost**, you are emphasizing that it is done to the greatest extent, amount, or degree possible. *My limited diplomatic skills were tested to the utmost... The best plan is to continue to attack him to the utmost of our power.* PHRASE: usu PHR after v

utopia /juːtoupiə/ **utopias.** If you refer to an imaginary situation as a **utopia**, you mean that it is one in which society is perfect and everyone is happy, but which you feel is not possible. *We weren't out to design a contemporary utopia. ...the writer in search of utopia. ...his criticism of communist utopias.* ◆◇◇◇◇ N-VAR

utopian /juːtoupiən/ **utopians** ◆◇◇◇◇

1 If you describe a plan or idea as **utopian**, you are criticizing it because it is unrealistic and shows a belief that things can be improved much more than is possible. *He was pursuing a utopian dream of world prosperity... A complete absence of national border controls is as utopian today as the vision of world government.* ► A **utopian** is someone with utopian ideas. *Kennedy had no time for lost causes or famous failures, no patience with dreamers or liberal utopians.* ADJ-GRADED PRAGMATICS =idealist; N-COUNT =idealist

2 **Utopian** is used to describe political or religious philosophies which claim that it is possible to build a new and perfect society in which everyone is happy; a formal use. *His was a utopian vision of nature in its purest form.* ► A **utopian** is someone with utopian beliefs. *...a group of utopians who immigrated in the 1920s and '30s.* ADJ: usu ADJ n; N-COUNT

utter /ʌtəʳ/ **utters, uttering, uttered** ◆◆◇◇◇

1 If someone **utters** sounds or words, they say them; a literary use. *He uttered a snorting laugh... They departed without uttering a word.* VERB V n

2 You use **utter** to emphasize that something is great in extent, degree, or amount. *This, of course, is utter nonsense. ...this utter lack of responsibility... A look of utter confusion swept across his handsome face.* ADJ: ADJ n PRAGMATICS =absolute, total

utterance /ʌtərəns/ **utterances** ◆◇◇◇◇

1 Someone's **utterances** are the things that they say; a formal use. *...the Queen's public utterances. ...a host of admirers who hung on her every utterance.* N-COUNT: oft poss N

2 **Utterance** is the expression in words of ideas, thoughts, and feelings; a formal use. *She could choose her own partner in matrimony, as long as she gave no utterance to her passions and emotions.* N-UNCOUNT

utterly /ʌtəʳli/. You use **utterly** to emphasize that something is very great in extent, degree, or amount. *China is utterly different... The new laws coming in are utterly ridiculous... Such an allegation is utterly without foundation.* ◆◆◇◇◇ ADV: ADV adj/prep, ADV with v PRAGMATICS =totally

uttermost /ʌtəʳmoust/. **Uttermost** means the same as **utmost**; a literary word. ADJ

U-turn, U-turns ◆◇◇◇◇

1 If you make a **U-turn** when you are driving or cycling, you turn in a half circle in one movement, so that you are then going in the opposite direction. *Making a sharp U-turn, she headed back... Eventually, he turned off the main route and suddenly did a U-turn.* N-COUNT

2 If you describe the change of a politician's policy, plans, or actions as a **U-turn**, you mean that it is a complete change and are suggesting that they made the change because they are weak or were wrong. *...a humiliating U-turn by the Prime Minister. ...the U-turns he made on economic policy and pit closures.* N-COUNT

V v

V, v /viː/ **V's, v's**

1 **V** is the twenty-second letter of the English alphabet. N-VAR

2 **V** or **v** is an abbreviation for words beginning with v, such as 'verse', 'versus', 'very', and 'volt'. *...Newcastle United v Leicester City.*

vac /væk/ **vacs**

1 In informal British English, a **vac** is a period of the year when universities and colleges are officially closed. It is an abbreviation for **vacation**. *During the summer vac she asked me to help her entertain her little nephew.* N-COUNT: usu sing

2 In informal British English, a **vac** is an electric machine which sucks up dust and dirt from carpets. It is an abbreviation for **vacuum cleaner**. *We found the vac easy to push.* N-COUNT

vacancy /veɪkənsi/ **vacancies** ◆◇◇◇◇

1 A **vacancy** is a job or position which has not been filled. *They had a short-term vacancy for a person on the foreign desk... Most vacancies are at senior level, requiring appropriate qualifications.* N-COUNT

2 If there are **vacancies** at a building such as a hotel, some of the rooms are available to rent. *This year hotels that usually are jammed had vacancies all summer.* N-COUNT

vacant /veɪkənt/ ◆◇◇◇◇

1 If something is **vacant**, it is not being used by anyone. *Half way down the coach was a vacant seat... In every major city there are more vacant buildings than there are homeless people.* ADJ: usu ADJ n =empty

2 If a job or position is **vacant**, no one is doing it or in it at present, and people can apply for it. *A number of senior people were regarded as likely to occupy the now vacant post... The post of chairman has been vacant for some time.* ADJ

3 A **vacant** look or expression is one that suggests that someone does not understand something or that they are not thinking about anything in particular. *She had a kind of vacant look on her face.* ♦ **vacantly** *He looked vacantly out of the window. ...African children, vacantly staring into a bleak world.* ADJ-GRADED =blank; ADV: ADV after v

vacate /veɪkeɪt, AM veɪkeɪt/ **vacates, vacating, vacated.** If you **vacate** a place or a job, you leave it or give it up, making it available for other people; a formal word. *He vacated the flat and* ◆◇◇◇◇ VERB =leave V n *went to stay with an uncle... He recently vacated his post as NHS Personnel Director... Chris slumped down in the chair Mrs Tennant had just vacated.*

vacation /vəkeɪʃᵊn, AM veɪ-/ **vacations, vacationing, vacationed** ◆◆◇◇◇

1 A **vacation** is a period of the year when universities or colleges are officially closed. *During his summer vacation he visited Russia... Did you have a lot of reading during the vacation?* N-COUNT =holiday

2 In American English, a **vacation** is a period of time during which you relax and enjoy yourself away from home. The British word is **holiday**. *They planned a late summer vacation in Europe... We went on vacation to Puerto Rico.* N-COUNT: also *on/from* N

3 In American English, if you have a particular number of days' or weeks' **vacation**, you do not have to go to work for that number of days or weeks. The usual British word is **holiday**. *The French get five to six weeks vacation a year.* N-UNCOUNT

4 In American English, if you **are vacationing** in a place away from home, you are on vacation there. The British word is **holiday**. *Myles vacationed in Jamaica... He was vacationing and couldn't be reached for comment.* VERB V prep/adv V

vacationer /veɪkeɪʃənəʳ/ **vacationers.** In American English, **vacationers** are people who are on holiday in a particular place. The usual British word is **holidaymakers**. N-COUNT: usu pl

vaccinate /væksɪneɪt/ **vaccinates, vaccinating, vaccinated.** If a person or animal **is vaccinated**, they are given a vaccine, usually by injection, to prevent them from getting a disease. *Dogs must be vaccinated against distemper... Have you had your child vaccinated against whooping cough?... Measles, mumps and whooping cough are spreading again because children are not being vaccinated.* ◆◇◇◇◇ VB: usu passive =inoculate be V-ed *against* n have n V-ed *against* n be/get V-ed

♦ **vaccination** /væksɪneɪʃᵊn/ **vaccinations** *Parents were too frightened to bring their children for vaccination... Anyone who wants to avoid the flu should consider getting a vaccination.* N-VAR

vaccine /væksiːn, AM væksiːn/ **vaccines.** A **vaccine** is a substance containing a harmless form of the germs that cause a particular disease. It is given to people, usually by injection, to prevent them getting that disease. *Anti-malarial vaccines are now undergoing trials... Seven million doses of vaccine are annually given in sugar to British children. ...the rabies vaccine.* ◆◆◇◇◇ N-MASS

vacillate /væsɪleɪt/ **vacillates, vacillating, vacillated.** If you **vacillate** between two alternatives or choices, you keep changing your mind; a formal word. *She vacillates between men twice her age and men younger than she... We cannot vacillate on the question of the party's leadership.* VERB =waver V *between* pl-n V

♦ **vacillation** /væsɪleɪʃᵊn/ **vacillations** *He accused President Carter of vacillation and retreat. ...Stalin's miscalculations and vacillations.* N-VAR

vacuity /vækjuːɪti/. If you refer to the **vacuity** of something or someone, you are critical of them because they lack intelligent thought or ideas; a formal word. *His vacuity was a handicap in these debates. ...a campaign notable for its intellectual vacuity and personal nastiness.* N-UNCOUNT: usu with poss PRAGMATICS =vapidity

vacuous /vækjuəs/. If you describe a person or their comments as **vacuous**, you are critical of them because they lack intelligent thought or ideas. *Male models are not always so vacuous as they are made out to be. ...the usual vacuous comments by some faceless commentator.* ADJ-GRADED PRAGMATICS =vapid

vacuum /vækjuːm, -juːəm/ **vacuums, vacuuming, vacuumed** ◆◆◇◇◇

1 If someone or something creates a **vacuum**, they leave a place or position which then needs to be filled by someone or something else. *The collapse of the army left a vacuum in the area... His presence should fill the power vacuum which has been developing over the past few days.* N-COUNT: usu sing, oft supp N

2 If something is done **in a vacuum**, it is done whilst being isolated from all the other things which you would normally expect to have an influence on it. *Moral values cannot be taught in a vacuum. Schools can only reflect what the child gets from its family background... We lived in a vacuum – no life, no news, no books.* PHRASE: PHR after v

3 If you **vacuum** something, you clean it using a vacuum cleaner. *I vacuumed the carpets today... It's important to vacuum regularly.* VERB V n V

4 A **vacuum** is a space that contains no air or other gas. *Wind is a current of air caused by a vacuum caused by hot air rising... The spinning turbine creates a vacuum.* N-COUNT: usu sing

vacuum cleaner, vacuum cleaners; also spelled **vacuum-cleaner.** A **vacuum cleaner** or a **vacuum** is an electric machine which sucks up dust and dirt from carpets. ◆◇◇◇◇ N-COUNT

vacuum flask, vacuum flasks. In British English, a **vacuum flask** is a container which is used to keep hot drinks hot or cold drinks cold. It has two thin silvery glass walls with a vacuum between them. The usual American term is **Thermos bottle** or **Thermos**. N-COUNT

vacuum-packed. Food that is **vacuum-packed** is packed in a container or packet from which most of the air has been removed, in order to keep the food fresh. ADJ

vagabond /vægəbɒnd/ **vagabonds.** A **vagabond** is someone who wanders from place to place and has no home or job; an old-fashioned word. N-COUNT =tramp, vagrant

vagary /veɪgəri/ **vagaries. Vagaries** are unexpected and unpredictable changes in a situation or in someone's behaviour which you have no control over; a formal word. *I take an assortment of clothes on holiday, as a provision against the vagaries of the weather. ...the perplexing vagaries of politics.* ◆◇◇◇◇ N-COUNT: usu pl, usu N *of* n

vagina /vədʒaɪnə/ **vaginas.** A woman's **vagina** is the passage connecting her outer sex organs to her womb. ◆◇◇◇◇ N-COUNT

vaginal /vədʒaɪnᵊl/. **Vaginal** means relating to or involving the vagina. *The creams have been used to reduce vaginal infections.* ◆◇◇◇◇ ADJ: ADJ n

vagrancy /veɪgrənsi/. **Vagrancy** is a way of life in which someone moves a lot from place to place because they have no permanent home or job, and have to beg or steal in order to live. *Vagrancy and begging has become common-place in London.* N-UNCOUNT

vagrant /veɪgrənt/ **vagrants.** A **vagrant** is someone who moves a lot from place to place because they have no permanent home or job, and have to beg or steal in order to live. *He lived on the street as a vagrant.* N-COUNT =tramp

vague /veɪg/ **vaguer, vaguest** ◆◆◇◇◇

1 If something written or spoken is **vague**, it does not explain or express things clearly. *A lot of the talk was apparently vague and general... The description was pretty vague. ...vague information.* ADJ-GRADED ≠precise

♦ **vaguely** *'I'm not sure,' Liz said vaguely... They issued a vaguely worded statement.* ADV ♦ **vagueness** *...the vagueness of the language in the text.* N-UNCOUNT: oft N *of* n

2 If you have a **vague** memory or idea of something, the memory or idea is not clear. *They have only a vague idea of the amount of water available... Waite's memory of that first meeting was vague.* ♦ **vaguely** *Judith could vaguely remember her mother lying on the sofa.* ADJ-GRADED =faint ADV: ADV with v

3 If you are **vague** about something, you deliberately do not tell people much about it. *He was vague, however, about just what U.S. forces might actually do... Democratic leaders under election pressure tend to respond with vague promises of action... Christopher's answer was deliberately vague.* ADJ-GRADED

4 If you describe someone as **vague**, you mean that they do not seem to be thinking clearly. *She had married a charming but rather vague Englishman... His eyes were always so vague when he looked at her.* ♦ **vaguely** *He looked vaguely around the room as he spoke, his mind elsewhere.* ♦ **vagueness** *...a girl wandering in the blissful vagueness of someone in love.* ADJ-GRADED ADV: ADV with v N-UNCOUNT

5 If something such as a **feeling** is vague, you experience it only slightly. *He was conscious of that* ADJ-GRADED: usu ADJ n

vague feeling of irritation again... He had a vague impression of rain pounding on the packed earth.

6 A **vague** shape or outline is not clear and is therefore not easy to see. *He looked at her vague shape through the frosted glass... The bus was a vague shape in the distance.* ADJ-GRADED: usu ADJ n

vaguely /veɪgli/. ◆◇◇◇◇

1 **Vaguely** means to some degree but not to a very large degree. *The voice on the line was vaguely familiar, but Crook couldn't place it at first... Arnold felt vaguely embarrassed... Most farm workers were only vaguely aware that there was a storm on its way.* ADV-GRADED: ADV adj PRAGMATICS =slightly

2 See also **vague**.

vain /veɪn/ **vainer, vainest** ◆◆◇◇◇

1 A **vain** attempt or action is one that fails to achieve what was intended. *The drafting committee worked through the night in a vain attempt to finish on schedule... I was singing in a vain effort to cheer him up.* ♦ **vainly** *He hunted vainly through his pockets for a piece of paper.* ADJ: ADJ n =fruitless; ADV: ADV with v

2 If you describe a hope that something will happen as a **vain** hope, you mean that there is no chance of it happening. *He married his fourth wife, Susan, in the vain hope that she would improve his health.* ♦ **vainly** *He then set out for Virginia for what he vainly hoped would be a peaceful retirement.* ADJ: ADJ n; ADV: ADV with v

3 If you describe someone as **vain**, you are critical of their extreme pride in their own beauty, intelligence, or other good qualities. *I think he is shallow, vain and untrustworthy.* ADJ-GRADED PRAGMATICS =conceited

4 If you do something **in vain**, you do not succeed in achieving what you intend. *He stopped at the door, waiting in vain for her to acknowledge his presence... It became obvious that all her complaints were in vain.* PHRASES PHR after v, v-link PHR

5 If you say that something such as someone's death, suffering, or effort was **in vain**, you mean that it was pointless because it did not achieve anything. *He wants the world to know his son did not die in vain.* PHR after v, v-link PHR

vainglorious /veɪnglɔːriəs/. If you describe someone's behaviour as **vainglorious**, you are critical of it because it is very boastful or proud and you find it ridiculous; a literary word. ADJ: ADJ n PRAGMATICS

valance /væləns/ **valances**

1 A **valance** is a decorative frill that hangs down from the sides of a bed. N-COUNT

2 In American English, a **valance** is a long narrow piece of wood or fabric which is fitted at the top of a window for decoration and to hide the curtain rail. The British word is **pelmet**. N-COUNT

vale /veɪl/ **vales.** A **vale** is a valley; a literary word. *...a small vale, sheltering under mist-shrouded hills.* ◆◇◇◇◇ N-COUNT: oft in names

valedictory /vælɪdɪktəri/. A **valedictory** speech, letter, or performance is one that is intended as a way of saying goodbye when someone leaves another person, a place, or a job; a formal word. *Kinnock made his valedictory speech as Labour's leader a few days later. ...her valedictory aria, sung as she leaves her lover.* ADJ: usu ADJ n =farewell

valentine /væləntaɪn/ **valentines.** A **valentine** or a **valentine card** is a greetings card that you send to someone who you are in love with or are attracted to, usually without signing your name, on St Valentine's Day, the 14th of February. *How many valentines did you get then?* N-COUNT

valet /væleɪ, -lɪt/ **valets.** A **valet** is a male servant who looks after his employer by doing things such as caring for his clothes and cooking for him. N-COUNT

valiant /væliənt/. A **valiant** action is very brave and determined, though it may lead to failure or defeat. *Despite valiant efforts by the finance minister, inflation rose to 36%. ...a valiant attempt to keep the business going.* ♦ **valiantly** *He suffered further heart attacks and strokes, all of which he fought valiantly.* ◆◇◇◇◇ ADJ-GRADED: usu ADJ n; ADV-GRADED: ADV with v =bravely

valid /vælɪd/ ◆◆◇◇◇

1 A **valid** argument, comment, or idea is based on sensible reasoning. *They put forward many valid reasons for not exporting... It is valid to consider memory the oldest mental skill, from which all others derive... He recognized the valid points that both sides were making.* ♦ **validity** /vælɪdɪti/ *The editorial in the Financial Times says this argument has lost much of its validity.* ADJ-GRADED: oft it v-link ADJ to-inf; N-UNCOUNT: usu with poss

2 Something that is **valid** is important or serious enough to make it worth saying or doing. *Most designers share the unspoken belief that fashion is a valid form of visual art.* ♦ **validity** *...the validity of making children wear cycle helmets.* ADJ-GRADED; N-UNCOUNT: usu N of n/-ing

3 If a ticket or other document is **valid**, it can be used and will be accepted by people in authority. *For foreign holidays you will need a valid passport... All tickets are valid for two months.* ADJ

4 See also **validity**.

validate /vælɪdeɪt/ **validates, validating, validated** ◆◇◇◇◇

1 To **validate** something such as a claim or statement means to prove or confirm that it is true or correct; a formal word. *This discovery seems to validate the claims of popular astrology. ...how that evidence was evaluated and validated by historians.* ♦ **validation** /vælɪdeɪʃən/ **validations** *Some thought must be given to the method of validation... This validation process ensures that the data conforms to acceptable formats.* VERB =substantiate, corroborate V n; N-VAR

2 To **validate** a person, state, or system means to prove or confirm that they are valuable or worthwhile. *She is looking for an image that validates her... The Academy Awards appear to validate his career.* ♦ **validation** *I think the film is a validation of our lifestyle.* VERB V n; N-VAR: usu N of n

validity /vəlɪdɪti/. The **validity** of something such as a result or a piece of information is whether it can be trusted or believed. *Shocked by the results of the elections, they now want to challenge the validity of the vote... Tibet, of course, denied the validity of any such claim. ...if a defence lawyer challenges the validity of a computer assisted identification.* • See also **valid**. N-UNCOUNT: usu the N of n

Valium /væliəm/. **Valium** is both the singular and the plural form. **Valium** is a drug given to people to calm their nerves when they are very depressed or upset. **Valium** is a trademark. ◆◇◇◇◇ N-VAR

valley /væli/ **valleys.** A **valley** is a low stretch of land between hills, especially one that has a river flowing through it. *...a wooded valley set against the backdrop of Monte Rosa. ...the Loire valley.* ◆◆◆◇◇ N-COUNT: oft in names

valour /vælər/; spelled **valor** in American English. **Valour** is great bravery, especially in battle; a literary word. *He was himself decorated for valour in the war.* • **discretion is the better part of valour**: see **discretion**. N-UNCOUNT =gallantry

valuable /væljuəbəl/ ◆◆◆◇◇

1 If you describe something or someone as **valuable**, you mean that they are very useful and can help someone a great deal. *Many of our teachers also have valuable academic links with Heidelberg University... If you decide to do you own make-up, here are a few valuable tips that will help you look your best... The experience was very valuable.* ADJ-GRADED

2 **Valuable** objects are objects which are worth a lot of money. *Just because a camera is old does not mean it is valuable. ...valuable books.* ADJ-GRADED

valuables /væljuəbəlz/. **Valuables** are things that you own that are worth a lot of money, especially small objects such as jewellery. *Leave your valuables in the hotel safe.* ◆◇◇◇◇ N-PLURAL

valuation /væljueɪʃən/ **valuations.** A **valuation** is a judgement that someone makes about how much money something is worth. *...an independent valuation of the company... The valuations reflect prices at 1 April 1991... Valuation lies at the heart of all takeovers.* ◆◇◇◇◇ N-VAR

value /væljuː/ **values, valuing, valued** ◆◆◆◆◆

1 The **value** of something such as a quality, attitude, or method is its importance or usefulness. If you place a particular **value** on something, that is the importance or usefulness you think it has. *The value of this work experience should not be under-* N-UNCOUNT: also a N, usu with supp

estimated... Further studies will be needed to see if these therapies have any value... Ronnie put a high value on his appearance. • If something is **of value**, it is useful or important. If it is **of no value**, it has no usefulness or importance. *This weekend course will be of value to everyone interested in the Pilgrim Route... Current sales figures tell us something of value about what is really going on.* PHRASE: v-link PHR

2 If you **value** something or someone, you think that they are important and you appreciate them. *I've done business with Mr Weston before. I value the work he gives me... If you value your health then you'll start being a little kinder to yourself.* ♦ **valued** *As you are a valued customer, I am writing to you to explain the situation... Why were spices so highly valued in late 15th-century Europe?* VERB V n; ADJ-GRADED

3 The **value** of something is how much money it is worth. *The value of his investment has risen by more than $50,000... The company's market value rose to $5.5 billion... Italy's currency went down in value by 3.5 per cent... That cup is priceless. You can't put a value on it.* • If something is **of value**, it is worth a lot of money. If it is **of no value**, it is worth very little money. *...a brooch which is really of no value... It might contain something of value.* N-VAR; PHRASE: v-link PHR

4 When experts **value** something, they decide how much money it is worth. *Your lender will then send their own surveyor to value the property... I asked him if he would have my jewellery valued for insurance purposes... Spanish police have seized cocaine valued at around $53 million.* VERB V n; *have* n V-ed; V-ed

5 You use **value** in certain expressions to say whether something is worth the money that it costs. For example, if something is or gives **good value**, it is worth the money that it costs. *The restaurant is informal, stylish and extremely good value... Both offer excellent value at around £50 for a double room... This wine highlights the quality and value for money of South African wines.* N-UNCOUNT

6 The **values** of a person or group are the moral principles and beliefs that they think are important. *The countries of South Asia also share many common values... The Health Secretary called for a return to traditional family values. ...young Muslims who feel little sympathy for the values of their adopted country.* N-PLURAL: with supp, oft with poss, supp N

7 **Value** is used after another noun when mentioning an important or noticeable feature about something. *The script has lost all of its shock value over the intervening 24 years... Having a mid-morning party certainly adds novelty value.* N-UNCOUNT: n N

8 A **value** is a particular number or quantity that can replace a general expression such as 'x' or 'y' in a particular case; a technical term in maths. N-COUNT

9 See also **face value**.

value added tax. In British English, **value added tax** is a tax that is added to the price of goods or services. The abbreviation **VAT** is also used. N-UNCOUNT

value judgement, value judgements; spelled **value judgment** in American English. If you make a **value judgement** about something, you form an opinion about it based on your principles and beliefs and not on facts which can be checked or proved. *Social scientists have grown extremely unwilling to make value judgments about cultures... That isn't a value judgement, it's a fact.* N-COUNT

valueless /vælju:ləs/. If you describe something as **valueless**, you mean that it is not at all useful. *Such attitudes are valueless unless they reflect inner cognition and certainty. ...commercially valueless trees.* ADJ =worthless

valuer /vælju:əʳ/ **valuers.** In British English, a **valuer** is someone whose job is to estimate the cost or value of something, for example a house, or objects that are going to be sold in an auction. The usual American word is **appraiser.** N-COUNT

valve /vælv/ **valves** ◆◆◇◇◇

1 A **valve** is a device attached to a pipe or a tube which controls the flow of air or liquid through the pipe or tube. N-COUNT

2 A **valve** is a small flap of tissue in your heart or in a vein which controls the flow of blood and keeps it flowing in one direction only. *He also has problems with a heart valve.* N-COUNT

3 See also **safety valve**.

vamp /væmp/ **vamps.** If you describe a woman as a **vamp**, you disapprove of her because she uses her sexual attractiveness to get what she wants from men. N-COUNT PRAGMATICS

vampire /væmpaɪəʳ/ **vampires.** A **vampire** is a creature in legends and horror stories. Vampires are said to come out of graves at night and suck the blood of living people. ◆◇◇◇◇ N-COUNT

vampire bat, vampire bats. A **vampire bat** is a bat from South America which feeds by sucking the blood of other animals. N-COUNT

vampirism /væmpɪrɪzəm/. **Vampirism** is used to describe what vampires do when they suck people's blood. N-UNCOUNT

van /væn/ **vans** ◆◆◆◇◇

1 A **van** is a small or medium-sized road vehicle with one row of seats and a space for carrying goods behind. N-COUNT

2 In British English, a **van** is a railway carriage with a roof and sides, often without windows, which is used to carry luggage, goods, or mail. *In the guard's van lay my tin trunk.* N-COUNT: usu supp N

vandal /vændəl/ **vandals.** A **vandal** is someone who deliberately damages things, especially public property. *All information systems that have been fitted at Ashford station have now been destroyed by vandals.* ◆◇◇◇◇ N-COUNT

vandalise /vændəlaɪz/. See **vandalize.**

vandalism /vændəlɪzəm/. **Vandalism** is the deliberate damaging of things, especially public property. *...acts of vandalism. ...a housing estate with a reputation for violence and vandalism.* ◆◇◇◇◇ N-UNCOUNT

vandalize /vændəlaɪz/ **vandalizes, vandalizing, vandalized;** also spelled **vandalise** in British English. If something such as a building or part of a building **is vandalized** by someone, it is damaged on purpose. *The walls had been horribly vandalized with spray paint... About 1,000 rioters vandalized buildings and looted stores.* VERB be V-ed; V n

vane /veɪn/ **vanes.** A **vane** is a flat blade which pushes or is pushed by wind or water, and forms part of a machine such as a fan, a windmill, or a ship's propeller. • See also **weather vane.** N-COUNT

vanguard /væŋgɑːʳd/ ◆◇◇◇◇

1 If someone is **in the vanguard of** something such as a revolution or an area of research, they are involved in the most advanced part of it. You can also refer to the people themselves as **the vanguard.** *Students and intellectuals have been in the vanguard of revolutionary change in China... Sir James was an immensely distinguished architect in the vanguard of his profession. ...the role of the Party as the political vanguard.* N-SING: usu *the* N, oft *in the* N *of* n

2 **The vanguard** of an army is the part of it that goes into battle first. *...a force of mobile reserve units that could strike quickly and effectively at the vanguard of an invading army.* N-SING: *the* N

vanilla /vənɪlə/. ◆◇◇◇◇

1 **Vanilla** is a flavouring used in ice cream and other sweet food. *I added a dollop of vanilla ice-cream to the pie. ...vanilla essence.* N-UNCOUNT: usu N n

2 If you describe a person or thing as **vanilla**, you mean that they are ordinary, with no special or extra features. *...just plain vanilla couples like me and Tony... The tensions of the Nixon presidency were replaced by the plain vanilla administration of a friendly, middle-aged, middle-class man from the Middle West.* ADJ

vanish /vænɪʃ/ **vanishes, vanishing, vanished** ◆◆◇◇◇

1 If someone or something **vanishes**, they disappear suddenly or in a way that cannot be explained. *He just vanished and was never seen again... The aircraft vanished without trace... Anne vanished from outside her home last Wednesday... The gunmen paused only to cut the wires to the house, then vanished into the countryside.* VERB =disappear V; V *from* n; V *into* n

2 If something such as a species of animal or a tra- VERB

dition **vanishes**, it ceases to exist. *Near the end of Devonian times, thirty percent of all animal life vanished... In the past two years, one-party rule has vanished from Eastern Europe.* =disappear V V from n

vanishing point, vanishing points
1 The **vanishing point** is the point in the distance where parallel lines seem to meet. *The highway stretched out ahead of me until it narrowed to a vanishing point some miles away.* N-COUNT: usu sing
2 If you say that something has reached **vanishing point**, you mean it has become very small or unimportant. *By 1973, this gap had narrowed almost to vanishing point... Everybody accepts that the threat has now shrunk to vanishing point.* N-UNCOUNT

vanity /vænɪti/ **vanities.** If you refer to someone's **vanity**, you are critical of them because they take great pride in their appearance or abilities. *Men who use steroids are motivated by sheer vanity... With my usual vanity, I thought he might be falling in love with me.* ◆◇◇◇◇ N-UNCOUNT: also N in pl PRAGMATICS =conceit

vanquish /væŋkwɪʃ/ **vanquishes, vanquishing, vanquished.** To **vanquish** someone means to defeat them completely in a battle or a competition; a literary word. *A happy ending is only possible because the hero has first vanquished the dragons... With knowledge and wisdom, evil could be vanquished on this earth.* VERB =conquer V n

vantage point /vɑːntɪdʒ pɔɪnt, vænt-/ **vantage points** ◆◇◇◇◇
1 A **vantage point** is a place from which you can see a lot of things. *From a concealed vantage point, he saw a car arrive... The warden took us to a vantage point on the slopes where we saw herring gulls on the rocks below.* N-COUNT =viewpoint
2 If you view a situation from a particular **vantage point**, you have a clear understanding of it because of the particular period of time you are in. *The rules of Sparta seem needlessly cruel from the vantage point of the twentieth century... From the vantage point of the present he saw the unquestioning love and support that had been lavished upon him for his first twenty-five years.* N-COUNT: oft with poss =viewpoint

vapid /væpɪd/. If you describe someone or something as **vapid**, you are critical of them because they are dull and uninteresting and contain nothing stimulating or challenging. *...the Minister's young and rather vapid wife... She made a vapid comment about the weather.* ADJ-GRADED PRAGMATICS =vacuous

vapor /veɪpəʳ/. See **vapour**.

vaporize /veɪpəraɪz/ **vaporizes, vaporizing, vaporized;** also spelled **vaporise** in British English. If a liquid or solid **vaporizes** or if you **vaporize** it, it changes into vapour or gas. *The benzene vaporized and formed a huge cloud of gas... The blast may have vaporised the meteorite.* V-ERG V V n

vapour /veɪpəʳ/ **vapours;** spelled **vapor** in American English. **Vapour** consists of tiny drops of water or other liquids in the air, which appear as mist. *...water vapour.* ◆◇◇◇◇ N-VAR

vapour trail, vapour trails. A **vapour trail** is a white trail of water vapour left in the sky by an aeroplane, a rocket, or a missile. N-COUNT

variable /veəriəbᵊl/ **variables** ◆◆◇◇◇
1 Something that is **variable** changes quite often, and there usually seems to be no fixed pattern to these changes. *The potassium content of foodstuffs is very variable... There was a bit of a wind and it was blowing onshore, variable, but quite strong. ...a variable rate of interest.* ♦ **variability** /veəriəbɪlɪti/ *There's a great deal of variability between individuals. ...the variability in the climate.* ADJ-GRADED N-UNCOUNT
2 A **variable** is a factor, which can change in quality, quantity, or size, which you have to take into account in a situation. *Decisions could be made on the basis of price, delivery dates, after-sales service or any other variable... Other variables in making forecasts for the industry include the weather and the general economic climate.* N-COUNT
3 A **variable** is a quantity that can have any one of a set of values; a technical term in mathematics. *It is conventional to place the independent variable on the right-hand side of an equation.* N-COUNT

variance /veəriəns/ **variances** ◆◇◇◇◇
1 If one thing is **at variance** with another, the two things seem to contradict each other; a formal use. *Many of his statements were at variance with the facts... This idealistic concept is at variance with reality.* PHRASE: v-link PHR, oft PHR with n =at odds
2 The **variance** between things, is the difference between them; a formal use. *...the variances in the stock price. ...total revenue variance.* N-VAR: usu with supp =variation

variant /veəriənt/ **variants.** A **variant** of a particular thing is something that has a different form to that thing, although it is related to it. *The quagga was a strikingly beautiful variant of the zebra... An intriguing variant to pipelines would be to carry the water using the existing system of canals... There are so many variant spellings of his name.* ◆◇◇◇◇ N-COUNT: usu with supp, oft N of n

variation /veərieɪʃᵊn/ **variations** ◆◆◇◇◇
1 A **variation on** something is the same thing presented in a slightly different form. *This delicious variation on an omelette is quick and easy to prepare... Many theories on punishment exist, all of which are variations on a theme.* N-COUNT: usu N on n
2 A **variation** is a change or slight difference in a level, amount, or quantity. *The survey found a wide variation in the prices charged for canteen food... Every day without variation my grandfather ate a plate of cold ham.* N-VAR

varicose vein /værɪkoʊs veɪn/ **varicose veins. Varicose veins** are swollen and painful veins in a person's legs, which sometimes require a medical operation. N-COUNT: usu pl

varied /veərid/. Something that is **varied** consists of things of different types, sizes, or qualities. *It is essential that your diet is varied and balanced... Before his election to the presidency, Mitterrand had enjoyed a long and varied career.* • See also **vary**. ◆◆◇◇◇ ADJ-GRADED =diverse

variegated /veəriəgeɪtɪd/ ◆◇◇◇◇
1 A **variegated** leaf or plant has different coloured markings on it. *The leaves are a variegated red.* ADJ: usu ADJ n
2 If you describe something as **variegated**, you mean that it is varied and diverse; a formal use. *...our variegated dialects.* ADJ-GRADED =varied

variety /vəraɪɪti/ **varieties** ◆◆◆◆◇
1 If something has **variety**, it consists of things which are different from each other. *Susan's idea of freedom was to have variety in her life style... I know no store anywhere in the world that has such variety and display... The music itself has so much variety.* N-UNCOUNT =diversity
2 A **variety** of things is a number of different kinds or examples of the same thing. *West Hampstead has a variety of good shops and supermarkets... The island offers such a wide variety of scenery and wildlife... People change their mind for a variety of reasons.* N-SING: usu N of n =range
3 A **variety** of something is a type of it. *I'm always pleased to try out a new variety... She has 12 varieties of old-fashioned roses.* N-COUNT: oft N of n =kind
4 **Variety** is a type of entertainment which includes many different kinds of acts in the same show. *...a variety show of music, comedy, and magic.* N-UNCOUNT: usu N n =vaudeville

various /veəriəs/ ◆◆◆◆◇
1 If you say that there are **various** things, you mean there are several different things of the type mentioned. *His plan is to spread the capital between various building society accounts... The school has received various grants from the education department.* ADJ: usu ADJ n
2 If a number of things are described as **various**, they are very different from one another. *The methods are many and various. ...the country's rich and various heritage.* ADJ =varied

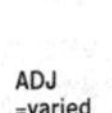

variously /veəriəsli/. You can use **variously** introduce a number of different ways in which something can be described. *...the crowds, which were variously estimated at two to several thousand... The family has been described variously as crass, bigoted, racist and plain boring.* ◆◇◇◇◇ ADV: usu ADV with v, also ADV adj

varnish /vɑːʳnɪʃ/ **varnishes, varnishing, varnished** ◆◇◇◇◇
1 **Varnish** is an oily liquid which is painted onto N-MASS

wood or other material to give it a hard, clear, shiny surface. *The varnish comes in six natural wood shades.*

2 The **varnish** on an object is the hard, clear, shiny surface that it has when it has been painted with varnish. *He brought out the fiddle, its varnish cracked and blistered.* N-SING

3 If you **varnish** something, you paint it with varnish. *Varnish the table with two or three coats of water-based varnish... The floors have been varnished. ...the varnished floorboards.* VERB V n V-ed

4 See also **nail varnish**.

varsity /vɑːʳsɪti/. People sometimes use **varsity** to describe things that relate to universities, especially sports activities or teams at a university or competitions between universities; used mainly by journalists. *The school has not given them the same opportunities to participate in varsity sports that men receive.* ADJ: ADJ n

vary /veəri/ **varies, varying, varied** ◆◆◆◇◇

1 If things **vary**, they are different from each other in size, amount, or degree. *As they're handmade, each one varies slightly... The text varies from the earlier versions... Different writers will prepare to varying degrees.* VERB =differ V V from n V-ing

2 If something **varies** or if you **vary** it, it becomes different or changed. *The cost of the alcohol duty varies according to the amount of wine in the bottle... You are welcome to vary the diet.* V-ERG =change V V n

3 See also **varied**.

vascular /væskjʊləʳ/. **Vascular** is used to describe the channels and veins through which fluids pass in the bodies of animals and plants; a technical term in biology and anatomy. *...the oldest known vascular plants. ...vascular diseases of the legs.* ADJ: ADJ n

vase /vɑːz, AM veɪs/ **vases.** A **vase** is a jar, usually made of glass or pottery, used for holding cut flowers or as an ornament. *...a vase of red roses. ...lead crystal vases.* ◆◇◇◇◇ N-COUNT

vasectomy /vəsektəmi/ **vasectomies.** A **vasectomy** is a surgical operation in which the tube that carries sperm to a man's penis is cut, usually as a means of contraception. N-VAR

Vaseline /væsəliːn/. **Vaseline** is a soft clear jelly made from petroleum, which is used as an ointment or as grease. **Vaseline** is a trademark. N-UNCOUNT =petroleum jelly

vassal /væsəl/ **vassals**

1 In feudal society, a **vassal** was a man who gave military service to a lord in return for which he was protected by the lord and received land to live on. N-COUNT

2 If you say that one country is a **vassal** of another, you mean that it is dominated by it; used showing disapproval. *Opponents of the treaty argue that monetary union will turn France into a vassal of Germany.* N-COUNT: usu sing PRAGMATICS

vast /vɑːst, væst/ **vaster, vastest.** Something that is **vast** is extremely large. *...Afrikaner farmers who own vast stretches of land... The vast majority of the eggs would be cracked.* ♦ **vastness** *...the vastness of the desert.* ◆◆◆◇◇ ADJ-GRADED: usu ADJ n =huge N-UNCOUNT

vastly /vɑːstli, væst-/. **Vastly** means to an extremely great degree or extent. *The jury has heard two vastly different accounts of what happened. ...cars that are vastly more competitive.* ◆◇◇◇◇ ADV: usu ADV compar

vat /væt/ **vats.** A **vat** is a large barrel or tank in which liquids can be stored. N-COUNT

VAT /viː eɪ tiː, væt/. In British English, **VAT** is a tax that is added to the price of goods or services. **VAT** is an abbreviation for 'value-added tax'. ◆◆◇◇◇ N-UNCOUNT

Vatican /vætɪkən/. **The Vatican** is the city state in Rome over which the Pope has sovereignty and where the central administration of the Roman Catholic Church has its offices. You can also use **the Vatican** to refer to the Pope or his officials. *The president had an audience with the Pope in the Vatican... The Vatican resumed relations with the Soviet Union after a gap of seventy years.* ◆◆◇◇◇ N-PROPER: *the* N, N n

vatman /vætmæn/; also spelled **VAT man.** In Britain, you can refer to the government department which advises and checks the accounts of people who have to pay VAT as **the vatman**; an informal word. *If you have had a problem with the vatman, let us know.* N-SING: *the* N

vaudeville /vɔːdəvɪl/. **Vaudeville** is a type of theatrical entertainment consisting of short acts, such as comedy, acrobatics, singing, and dancing. **Vaudeville** was especially popular in the early part of this century. *In 1901, he broke out of vaudeville and set his sights on Broadway.* N-UNCOUNT

vault /vɔːlt/ **vaults, vaulting, vaulted** ◆◇◇◇◇

1 A **vault** is a secure room where money and other valuable things can be kept safely. *Most of the money was in storage in bank vaults... The gold that has been recovered so far is being held in a vault at a secret location.* N-COUNT

2 A **vault** is a room underneath a church or in a cemetery where people are buried, usually the members of a single family. *He ordered that Matilda's body should be buried in the family vault.* N-COUNT =tomb

3 A **vault** is an arched roof or ceiling. *...the vault of a great cathedral.* N-COUNT

4 If you **vault** something or **vault** over it, you jump quickly onto or over it, especially by putting a hand on top of it to help you balance while you jump. *He could easily vault the wall... Ned vaulted over a fallen tree... He ran to the door and vaulted into the saddle.* VERB =leap V n V prep

vaunted /vɔːntɪd/. If something is **vaunted** or **much vaunted**, it is described, praised, or displayed in a boastful or pompous way; a formal word. *Its vaunted security procedures hadn't worked... Simpson's much vaunted discoveries are in fact commonplace in modern sociology.* ADJ: usu ADJ n

vb. **Vb** is a written abbreviation for **verb**.

VC /viː siː/ **VCs** ◆◇◇◇◇

1 The **VC** is a medal awarded to soldiers, sailors, and airmen in Britain and the Commonwealth for acts of great bravery in battle. **VC** is an abbreviation for 'Victoria Cross'. ► A **VC** is a soldier who has been awarded a Victoria Cross. *Aren't you the boy whose father was a VC in the war?* N-COUNT N-COUNT

2 **VC** is a written abbreviation for **vice-chancellor**.

VCR /viː siː ɑːʳ/ **VCRs.** A **VCR** is a machine that can be used to record television programmes or films onto video tapes, so that people can play them back and watch them later on a television set. **VCR** is an abbreviation for 'video cassette recorder'. ◆◇◇◇◇ N-COUNT =video

VD /viː diː/. **VD** is used to refer to diseases such as syphilis and gonorrhoea which are passed on by sexual intercourse. It is an abbreviation for **venereal disease**. N-UNCOUNT

VDU /viː diː juː/ **VDUs.** A **VDU** is a machine with a screen which is used to display information from a computer. **VDU** is an abbreviation for 'visual display unit'. N-COUNT =monitor

veal /viːl/. **Veal** is meat from a calf. ◆◇◇◇◇ N-UNCOUNT

vector /vektəʳ/ **vectors**

1 A **vector** is a variable quantity, such as force, that has magnitude and direction; a technical term in maths and science. N-COUNT

2 A **vector** is an insect or other organism that causes a disease by carrying a germ or parasite from one person or animal to another; a technical term in medicine. N-COUNT

veer /vɪəʳ/ **veers, veering, veered** ◆◇◇◇◇

1 If something **veers** in a certain direction, it suddenly moves in that direction. *The plane veered off the runway and careered through the perimeter fence... Horrified commuters saw the lorry veer across the motorway and overturn.* VERB =swerve V prep/adv

2 If someone or something **veers** in a certain direction, they change their position or direction in a particular situation. *He is unlikely to veer from his boss's strongly held views... I veered away from the set menu and went for the day's special of queen scallops... Her image veers towards the untidily romantic.* VERB V prep/adv

3 When the wind **veers**, it changes direction. *The wind had veered from the west to north-by-west... As it strengthened the wind was veering southerly.* VERB V prep/adv Also V

veg /vedʒ/; **veg** is both the singular and the plural form. **Veg** are plants such as cabbages, potatoes, and onions which you can cook and eat. It is an abbreviation for **vegetables**. *...fruit and veg. ...youngsters who prefer burgers to meat and two veg.* ◆◇◇◇◇ N-VAR

vegan /viːgən/ **vegans**. Someone who is **vegan** never eats meat or any animal products such as milk, butter, or cheese. *The menu changes weekly and usually includes a vegan option... I'd been vegan for a long time.* ► A **vegan** is someone who is vegan. *...vegetarians and vegans.* ◆◇◇◇◇ ADJ; N-COUNT

vegeburger /vedʒibɜːʳgəʳ/ **vegeburgers;** also spelled **veggieburger**. **Vegeburgers** are flat round cakes of food made from vegetables mixed with flour and flavourings. You grill or fry them. N-COUNT

vegetable /vedʒtəbəl/ **vegetables** ◆◆◆◇◇

1 **Vegetables** are plants such as cabbages, potatoes, and onions which you can cook and eat. *A good general diet should include plenty of fresh vegetables. ...traditional Caribbean fruit and vegetables. ...vegetable soup.* N-COUNT

2 **Vegetable** matter comes from plants; a formal use. *...compounds, of animal, vegetable or mineral origin. ...decayed vegetable matter.* ADJ: usu ADJ n

3 If someone refers to a very sick or disabled person as a **vegetable**, they mean that they are so severely brain-damaged or physically unwell that they cannot do anything or enjoy anything; an offensive use. N-COUNT: usu sing =cabbage

vegetarian /vedʒɪteəriən/ **vegetarians** ◆◆◇◇◇

1 Someone who is **vegetarian** never eats meat. *Yasmin sticks to a strict vegetarian diet... Over 1.5 million people in Britain are vegetarian.* ► A **vegetarian** is someone who is vegetarian. *...a special menu for vegetarians.* ADJ; N-COUNT

2 **Vegetarian** food does not contain any animal products. *...vegetarian lasagnes... The cheese is vegetarian and the eggs free-range.* ADJ

vegetarianism /vedʒɪteəriənɪzəm/. If someone practises **vegetarianism**, they never eat meat. *Vegetarianism is on the increase in Britain.* N-UNCOUNT

vegetate /vedʒɪteɪt/ **vegetates, vegetating, vegetated**. If someone **vegetates**, they spend their time doing boring or worthless things, so that their mind is not stimulated. *He spends all his free time at home vegetating in front of the TV.* VERB; V

vegetated /vedʒɪteɪtɪd/. If an area is **vegetated**, it is covered with plants and trees; a formal word. *That part of Castle Walk is not thickly vegetated.* ADJ: usu adv ADJ

vegetation /vedʒɪteɪʃən/. Plants, trees, and flowers can be referred to as **vegetation**; a formal word. *The inn has a garden of semi-tropical vegetation. ...a smell of gently-rotting vegetation.* ◆◇◇◇◇ N-UNCOUNT: usu with supp

vegetative /vedʒɪtətɪv, AM -teɪt-/

1 If someone who is in a coma is in a **vegetative** state, they are unable to do anything and their condition is not likely to improve; a medical use. *She was in what was described as a vegetative state.* ADJ: usu ADJ n

2 **Vegetative** growth or development is the growth or development of plantlife; a formal use. *The harshness of the climate makes vegetative growth extremely slow.* ADJ: ADJ n

veggie /vedʒi/ **veggies**. If someone is **veggie**, they never eat meat; an informal word. *You can cook a cheap veggie chilli in 15 minutes... Going veggie can be tasty, easy and healthy too.* ► A **veggie** is someone who is vegetarian. *...a strict veggie, not eating any product of slaughter.* ADJ =vegetarian; N-COUNT

vehement /viːəmənt/. If a person or their actions or comments are **vehement**, the person has very strong feelings or opinions and expresses them forcefully. *She suddenly became very vehement and agitated, jumping around and shouting... One vehement critic is Michael Howard... She lowered her voice to a vehement whisper.* ◆◇◇◇◇ ADJ-GRADED

♦ **vehemence** *He spoke more loudly and with more vehemence than he had intended.* N-UNCOUNT

♦ **vehemently** *Krabbe has always vehemently denied using drugs... I'm vehemently against any form of censorship.* ADV: ADV with v, ADV prep/adj

vehicle /viːɪkəl/ **vehicles** ◆◆◆◆◇

1 A **vehicle** is a machine with an engine, for example a bus, car, or truck, that carries people or things from place to place. *The vehicle would not have the capacity to make the journey on one tank of fuel. ...a vehicle which was somewhere between a tractor and a truck.* N-COUNT

2 You can use **vehicle** to refer to something that you use in order to achieve a particular purpose. *Her art became a vehicle for her political beliefs... The vehicle that permitted both communication and acceptability was social revolution.* N-COUNT: usu with supp, oft N *for* n =medium

vehicular /vɪhɪkjʊləʳ/. **Vehicular** is used to describe something which relates to vehicles and traffic; a formal word. *Village streets were actually broad pedestrian malls, closed to vehicular traffic... There is no vehicular access.* ADJ: usu ADJ n

veil /veɪl/ **veils** ◆◇◇◇◇

1 A **veil** is a piece of thin soft cloth that women sometimes wear over their heads and which can also cover their face. *She's got long fair hair but she's got a veil over it... She swathes her face in a veil of decorative muslin.* N-COUNT

2 You can refer to something that hides or partly hides a situation or activity as a **veil**. *The country is ridding itself of its disgraced prime minister in a veil of secrecy... The chilling facts behind this veil of silence were slow to emerge.* N-COUNT: usu sing, N *of* n

3 You can refer to something that you can partly see through, for example a mist, as a **veil**; a literary use. *The eruption has left a thin veil of dust in the upper atmosphere... He recognized the coast of England through a veil of mist... He retreated behind a veil of cigarette smoke.* N-COUNT: oft N *of* n =haze

4 If you **draw a veil over** something, you stop talking about it because it is too unpleasant to talk about. *The clamour to draw a veil over the minister's extra-marital activities reeks of hypocrisy.* PHRASE: V inflects, PHR n

veiled /veɪld/ ◆◇◇◇◇

1 A **veiled** comment is expressed in a disguised form rather than directly and openly. *He made only a veiled reference to international concerns over human rights issues... This last clause is a thinly-veiled threat to those who might choose to ignore the decree.* ADJ-GRADED: ADJ n

2 A woman or girl who is **veiled** is wearing a veil. *A veiled woman gave me a kindly smile.* ADJ

vein /veɪn/ **veins** ◆◆◇◇◇

1 Your **veins** are the thin tubes in your body through which your blood flows towards your heart. *Many veins are found just under the skin.* ● See also **varicose vein**. N-COUNT: usu pl

2 Something that is written or spoken in a particular **vein** is written or spoken in that style or mood. *It is one of his finest works in a lighter vein... The girl now replies in similar vein.* N-COUNT: usu sing, with supp, usu adj N

3 A **vein** of a particular quality is evidence of that quality which someone often shows in their behaviour or work. *The striker's rich vein of form this season has seen him net 32 goals... This is perhaps the album's most abandoned track; venomous, with a vein of humour running right through it.* N-COUNT: usu sing, with supp =streak

4 A **vein** of a particular metal or mineral is a layer of it lying in rock. *...a vein of copper. ...a rich and deep vein of limestone.* N-COUNT: N *of* n =seam

5 The **veins** on a leaf are the thin lines on it. *...the serrated edges and veins of the feathery leaves.* N-COUNT

veined /veɪnd/

1 **Veined** skin has a lot of veins showing through it. *Helen's hands were thin and veined.* ► Also a combining form. *...a man who had blue-veined cheeks.* ADJ; COMB in ADJ

2 Something that is **veined** has a pattern or colouring like that of veins showing through skin. *...a bronze ashtray shaped like a veined leaf.* ► Also a combining form. *...this distinctive blue-veined cheese.* ADJ; COMB in ADJ

velcro /velkroʊ/. **Velcro** is a material consisting of two strips of nylon fabric which press together to form a strong bond. It is used to open and close parts of clothes and bags. **Velcro** is a trademark. N-UNCOUNT: oft N n

veldt /velt/; spelled **veld** in American English. The **veldt** is a high area of flat grassland with very few trees in southern Africa. *...a gang of hyenas, stalking about the veldt.* N-SING: usu *the*N

vellum /veləm/. **Vellum** is strong good-quality paper for writing on. N-UNCOUNT

velocity /vɪlɒsɪti/ **velocities.** **Velocity** is the speed at which something moves in a particular direction; a technical term in physics. *...the velocity of light. ...the velocities at which the stars orbit. ...high velocity rifles.* ◆◇◇◇◇ N-VAR

velour /vəlʊəʳ/. **Velour** is a silk or cotton fabric similar to velvet. *...black velour hats. ...a gold Mercedes with red velour seats.* N-UNCOUNT: usu N n

velvet /velvɪt/ **velvets.** **Velvet** is soft material made from cotton, silk, or nylon, which has a thick layer of short cut threads on one side. *...a charcoal-gray overcoat with a velvet collar... She looked pretty and rather fragile, dressed in black velvet.* ◆◆◇◇◇ N-MASS: usu N n

velveteen /velvɪtiːn/. **Velveteen** is a soft fabric which looks and feels like velvet and is sometimes used as a cheaper alternative to velvet. *...a black velveteen coat. ...loose blouses of bright-coloured velveteen.* N-UNCOUNT: usu N n

velvety /velvɪti/. If you describe something as **velvety**, you mean that it is pleasantly soft to touch and has the appearance or quality of velvet. *The grass grew thick and velvety... I rubbed the velvety grooves inside the calf's ears.* ADJ-GRADED

venal /viːnəl/. If you describe someone as **venal**, you disapprove of them because they are prepared to do almost anything in return for money, even things which are dishonest or immoral. *Ian Trimmer is corrupt and thoroughly venal. ...venal politicians.* ADJ-GRADED PRAGMATICS

vendetta /vendetə/ **vendettas.** If one person has a **vendetta** against another, the first person wants revenge for something the second person did to them in the past. *The vice president said the cartoonist has a personal vendetta against him... His murder was a vendetta killing.* ◆◇◇◇◇ N-VAR: oft N *against* n

vending machine, vending machines. A **vending machine** is a machine from which you can get things such as cigarettes, chocolate, or coffee by putting in money and pressing a button. N-COUNT

vendor /vendəʳ/ **vendors** ◆◇◇◇◇

1 A **vendor** is someone who sells things such as newspapers, cigarettes, or hamburgers from a small stall or cart. *...ice-cream vendors.* N-COUNT: usu supp N =seller

2 The **vendor** of a house or piece of land is the person who owns it and is selling it; a legal use. *The estate agent is working for the vendor, from whom he will be receiving his commission.* N-COUNT =seller

veneer /vɪnɪəʳ/ **veneers** ◆◇◇◇◇

1 If you refer to the pleasant way that someone behaves or that something appears as a **veneer**, you are critical of them because you believe that their true character or feelings are unpleasant, and this is being hidden. *He was able to fool the world with his veneer of education... They made him acting president, hoping to give their actions a veneer of constitutional authority.* N-SING: usu with supp, oft N *of*n, adj N PRAGMATICS =facade

2 **Veneer** is a thin layer of wood or plastic which is used to improve the appearance of something. *The wood was cut into large sheets of veneer... Only the finest timbers and veneers are used.* N-VAR

venerable /venərəbəl/ ◆◇◇◇◇

1 A **venerable** person deserves respect because they are old and wise. *Her Chinese friends referred to the Empress as their venerable ancestor. ...a venerable old man with white hair.* ADJ-GRADED: usu ADJ n

2 Something that is **venerable** is impressive because it is old or important historically. *May Day has become a venerable institution... Venerable dailies such as the Tokyo Times have shut down.* ADJ-GRADED: usu ADJ n

venerate /venəreɪt/ **venerates, venerating, venerated.** If you **venerate** someone or something, you value them or feel great respect for them; a formal word. *My father venerated General Eisenhower.* ♦ **venerated** *Jerusalem is Christianity's most venerated place.* ♦ **veneration** *Churchill was held in near veneration during his lifetime.* ◆◇◇◇◇ VERB =revere V n ADJ-GRADED N-UNCOUNT

venereal disease /vɪnɪəriəl dɪziːz/ **venereal diseases.** **Venereal disease** is used to refer to diseases such as syphilis and gonorrhoea which are passed on by sexual intercourse. The abbreviation **VD** is also used. N-VAR

Venetian blind /vəniːʃən blaɪnd/ **Venetian blinds.** A **Venetian blind** is a window blind made of thin horizontal strips which can be adjusted to let in more or less light. N-COUNT

vengeance /vendʒəns/ ◆◇◇◇◇

1 **Vengeance** is the act of killing, injuring, or harming someone because they have harmed you. *He swore vengeance on everyone involved in the murder... She cried aloud to the gods for vengeance for the loss of her daughter.* N-UNCOUNT =revenge

2 If you say that something happens **with a vengeance**, you are emphasizing that it happens to a much greater extent than was expected. *It began to rain again with a vengeance... Once Gretchen had left the office, her doubts would return with a vengeance.* PHRASE: PHR after v PRAGMATICS

vengeful /vendʒfʊl/. If you describe someone as **vengeful**, you are critical of them because they feel a great desire for revenge. *He was stabbed to death by his vengeful wife... He did not think he was any more cruel, any more vengeful than other men.* ADJ-GRADED PRAGMATICS

venison /venɪzən/. **Venison** is the meat of a deer. ◆◇◇◇◇ N-UNCOUNT

venom /venəm/ **venoms** ◆◇◇◇◇

1 You can use **venom** to refer to someone's feelings of great bitterness and anger towards someone. *He reserved particular venom for critics of his foreign policy... There was no mistaking the venom in his voice.* N-UNCOUNT =malice

2 The **venom** of a snake, scorpion, or spider is the poison that it injects into you when it bites or stings you. *...snake handlers who grow immune to snake venom.* N-MASS =poison

venomous /venəməs/

1 If you describe a person or their behaviour as **venomous**, you mean that they show great bitterness and anger towards someone. *...his terrifying and venomous Aunt Bridget... He heaped abuse on Waite and made venomous personal attacks... He was surprised by the venomous tone of the anonymous calls.* ♦ **venomously** *'You betrayed me first!' she answered venomously.* ADJ-GRADED: usu ADJ n =malevolent ADV-GRADED: ADV with v

2 A **venomous** snake, scorpion, or spider uses poison to attack its enemy or prey. *The adder is Britain's only venomous snake.* ADJ =poisonous

venous /viːnəs/. **Venous** is used to describe something which is related to veins; a medical term. *...venous blood.* ADJ: ADJ n

vent /vent/ **vents, venting, vented** ◆◇◇◇◇

1 A **vent** is a hole in something through which air can come in and smoke, gas, or smells can go out. *Quite a lot of steam escaped from the vent at the front of the machine... There was a small air vent in the ceiling.* N-COUNT =duct

2 If you **vent** your feelings, you express them forcefully. *She telephoned her best friend to vent her frustration... The rioters were prevented from venting their anger on the police.* VERB V n V n *on* n

3 If you **give vent to** your feelings, you express them forcefully; a formal expression. *She gave vent to her anger and jealousy.* PHRASES V inflects

4 If you **give vent to** a noise, you make a particular type of noise, especially suddenly or as a reaction to something; a literary expression. *He squatted on the floor and gave vent to a deep sigh... The cabby gave vent to an angry shout.* V inflects =let out

ventilate /ventɪleɪt/ **ventilates, ventilating, ventilated** ◆◇◇◇◇

1 If you **ventilate** a room or building, you allow fresh air to get into it. *Ventilate the room properly when paint stripping... The pit is ventilated by a steel fan. ...badly ventilated rooms.* ♦ **ventilation** VERB V n V-ed N-UNCOUNT

/ventɪleɪʃᵊn/ *The only ventilation comes from tiny sliding windows.*
2 If you **ventilate** your ideas or feelings, you talk about them or express them freely in front of other people; a formal use. *He did not think it the job of officials to ventilate their doubts or daydreams.* VERB =air V n

ventilator /ventɪleɪtəʳ/ **ventilators**
1 A **ventilator** is a machine that helps people breathe when they cannot breathe naturally, for example because they are very ill or have been seriously injured. N-COUNT
2 A **ventilator** is a device that lets fresh air into a room or building and lets stale air out. N-COUNT

ventricle /ventrɪkᵊl/ **ventricles.** A **ventricle** is a chamber of the heart that pumps blood to the arteries; a technical term in anatomy. N-COUNT

ventriloquist /ventrɪləkwɪst/ **ventriloquists.** A **ventriloquist** is someone who can speak without moving their lips and who entertains people by making their words appear to be spoken by a puppet or dummy. N-COUNT

venture /ventʃəʳ/ **ventures, venturing, ventured** ◆◆◆◇◇
1 A **venture** is a project or activity which is new, exciting, and difficult because it involves the risk of failure. *...his latest writing venture. ...a Russian-American joint venture.* N-COUNT: usu supp N
2 If you **venture** somewhere, you go somewhere that might be dangerous. *People are afraid to venture out for fear of sniper attacks... Few Europeans who had ventured beyond the Himalayas had returned to tell the tale.* VERB =go V adv/prep
3 If you **venture** a question or statement, you say it in a cautious hesitant manner because you are afraid it might be stupid or wrong; used in written English. *'So you're Leo's girlfriend?' he ventured... He ventured that plants draw part of their nourishment from the air... He didn't venture to tell his mother what had happened... Stephen ventured a few more sentences in halting Welsh.* VERB V with quote V that V to-inf V n
4 If you **venture into** an activity, you do something that involves the risk of failure because it is new and different. *He enjoyed little success when he ventured into business.* VERB V into n

venturesome /ventʃəʳsəm/. If you describe someone as **venturesome**, you mean that they are willing to take risks and try out new things; a formal use. *...the venturesome graduate who is determined to succeed.* ADJ-GRADED =adventurous

venue /venjuː/ **venues.** The **venue** for an event or activity is the place where it will happen. *Birmingham's International Convention Centre is the venue for a three-day arts festival... Peace talks failed to take place because of a dispute over the venue.* ◆◆◆◇◇ N-COUNT

veracity /vəræsɪti/. **Veracity** is the quality of being true or the habit of telling the truth; a formal word. *We have total confidence in the veracity of our research... He was shocked to find his veracity questioned.* N-UNCOUNT =truthfulness

veranda /vərændə/ **verandas;** also spelled **verandah**. A **veranda** is a roofed platform along the outside of a house. *They had their coffee and tea on the veranda.* N-COUNT

verb /vɜːʳb/ **verbs.** A **verb** is a word such as 'sing', 'feel', or 'die' which is used with a subject to say what someone or something does or what happens to them, or to give information about them. • See also **phrasal verb**. ◆◇◇◇◇ N-COUNT

verbal /vɜːʳbᵊl/ ◆◆◇◇◇
1 You use **verbal** to indicate that something is expressed in speech rather than in writing or action. *They were jostled and subjected to a torrent of verbal abuse... We have a verbal agreement with her... The West must back up its verbal support with substantial economic aid.* ♦ **verbally** *My girlfriend and myself were verbally abused several times by skinheads... Twins often have difficulty expressing themselves verbally.* ADJ: usu ADJ n ADV
2 You use **verbal** to indicate that something is connected with words and the use of words. *The test has scores for verbal skills, mathematical skills, and abstract reasoning skills... Wayne has great verbal dexterity.* ADJ: ADJ n
3 In grammar, **verbal** means relating to a verb. *...a verbal noun..* ADJ: usu ADJ n

verbalize /vɜːʳbəlaɪz/ **verbalizes, verbalizing, verbalized;** also spelled **verbalise** in British English. If you **verbalize** your feelings, thoughts, or ideas, you express them in words; a formal word. *...his inability to verbalize his feelings.* VERB V n Also V
♦ **verbalization** /vɜːʳbəlaɪzeɪʃᵊn/ **verbalizations** *...a level of support and trust which encourages the verbalization of doubts and fears.* N-VAR

verbatim /vəʳbeɪtɪm/. If you repeat something **verbatim**, you use exactly the same words as were used originally. *The President's speeches are regularly reproduced verbatim in the state-run newspapers.* ► Also an adjective. *I was treated to a verbatim report of every conversation she's taken part in over the past week.* ADV: ADV after v ADJ: ADJ n

verb group, verb groups. A **verb group** or **verbal group** consists of a verb, or of a main verb following a modal or one or more auxiliaries. Examples are 'walked', 'can see', and 'had been waiting'. N-COUNT

verbiage /vɜːʳbiɪdʒ/. If you refer to someone's speech or writing as **verbiage**, you are critical of them because they use too many words, which makes their speech or writing difficult to understand; a formal word. *Stripped of their pretentious verbiage, his statements come dangerously close to inviting racial hatred.* N-UNCOUNT PRAGMATICS =waffle

verbose /vɜːʳbous/. If you describe a person or a piece of writing as **verbose**, you are critical of them because they use more words than are necessary, and so make you feel bored or annoyed. *...verbose politicians... His writing is diffuse and often verbose.* ♦ **verbosity** /vəʳbɒsɪti/ *Truscott's verbosity made it hard to separate plain fact from decorative embellishment.* ADJ-GRADED PRAGMATICS =long-winded N-UNCOUNT

verdant /vɜːʳdᵊnt/. If you describe a place as **verdant**, you mean that it is covered with green grass, trees, and plants; a literary word. *...a small verdant garden with a view out over Paris.* ADJ-GRADED =lush

verdict /vɜːʳdɪkt/ **verdicts** ◆◆◆◇◇
1 In a court of law, the **verdict** is the decision that is given by the jury or judge at the end of a trial. *The jury returned a unanimous guilty verdict... Three judges will deliver their verdict in October.* N-COUNT
2 Someone's **verdict** on something is their opinion of it, after thinking about it or investigating it. *The doctor's verdict was that he was entirely healthy... The critics were too quick to give their verdict on us.* N-COUNT: oft with poss, oft N on n

verdigris /vɜːʳdɪgrɪs, -griːs/. **Verdigris** is a greenish-blue substance that forms on copper, brass, or bronze after it has been left in wet or damp conditions. N-UNCOUNT

verge /vɜːʳdʒ/ **verges, verging, verged** ◆◆◇◇◇
1 If you are **on the verge of** something, you are going to do it very soon or it is likely to happen or begin very soon. *The country was on the verge of becoming prosperous and successful... Carole was on the verge of tears.* PHR-PREP: v-link PREP -ing/n =brink
2 The **verge** of a road is a narrow piece of ground by the side of a road, which is usually covered with grass or flowers; used mainly in British English. N-COUNT
verge on. If someone or something **verges on** a particular state or quality, they are almost the same as that state or quality. *...a fury that verged on madness... Her speaking voice verges on the ridiculous.* PHRASAL VERB =border on V P n (not pron)

verifiable /verɪfaɪəbᵊl/. Something that is **verifiable** can be proved to be true or genuine. *This is not a romantic notion but verifiable fact... It is crucial that all documents presented are authentic and easily verifiable.* ADJ

verify /verɪfaɪ/ **verifies, verifying, verified** ◆◇◇◇◇
1 If you **verify** something, you check that it is true by careful examination or investigation. *I verified the source from which I had that information... A clerk simply verifies that the payment and invoice amount match.* ♦ **verification** /verɪfɪkeɪʃᵊn/ *All charges against her are dropped pending the* VERB V n V that N-UNCOUNT: oft N of n

verification of her story. ...the agency's verification procedures.

2 If you **verify** something, you state or confirm that it is true. *The government has not verified any of those reports... I can verify that it takes about thirty seconds.* VB: no cont =confirm V n V that

verily /verɪli/. **Verily** is an old-fashioned or religious word meaning 'truly'. It is used to emphasize a statement or opinion. *Verily she is the best cook in the parish... Verily I say unto you, that one of you shall betray me.* ADV: usu ADV with cl, also ADV adj/adv =truly

verisimilitude /verɪsɪmɪlɪtjuːd, AM -tuːd/. **Verisimilitude** is the quality of seeming to be true or real; a formal word. *At the required level of visual verisimilitude, computer animation is costly.* N-UNCOUNT =authenticity

veritable /verɪtəbᵊl/. You can use **veritable** to emphasize the size, amount, or nature of something. *...a veritable feast of pre-match entertainment. ...a veritable army of security guards.* ◆◇◇◇◇ ADJ: usu a ADJ n PRAGMATICS =positive

verity /verɪti/ **verities.** The **verities** of something are all the things that are believed to be true about it. *...some verities of human nature.* N-COUNT: usu pl, usu with supp

vermilion /vəʳmɪliən/. **Vermilion** is used to describe things that are bright red in colour; a literary word. *...her vermilion lip gloss... The furniture on it is glossy vermilion.* COLOUR

vermin /vɜːʳmɪn/. **Vermin** are small animals such as rats and mice which cause problems to humans by carrying disease and damaging crops or food. *From 1066 to the 17th century the fox was looked upon as vermin. ...vermin control.* N-PLURAL

vermouth /vɜːʳməθ/ **vermouths. Vermouth** is a strong alcoholic drink made from red or white wine flavoured with herbs. N-MASS

vernacular /vəʳnækjʊləʳ/ **vernaculars**

1 The **vernacular** is the language or dialect that is most widely spoken by ordinary people in a region or country. *...books or plays written in the vernacular... To use the vernacular of the period, Peter was square... Most of these new sermons were recorded in literary Sanskrit, rather than in vernacular language.* N-COUNT: usu *the*N in sing

2 Vernacular architecture is the style of architecture in which ordinary people's houses are built in a particular region; a formal use. *...the island's vernacular architecture. ...the untouched vernacular buildings in superb limestone.* ADJ: ADJ n

verruca /vəruːkə/ **verrucas.** A **verruca** is a kind of wart which occurs on the sole of the foot; used mainly in British English. N-COUNT

versatile /vɜːʳsətaɪl, AM -tᵊl/ ◆◆◇◇◇

1 If you say that a person is **versatile**, you approve of them because they have many different skills. *He had been one of the game's most versatile athletes.* ♦ **versatility** /vɜːʳsətɪlɪti/ *Aileen stands out for her incredible versatility as an actress.* ADJ-GRADED PRAGMATICS N-UNCOUNT

2 A tool, machine, or material that is **versatile** can be used for many different purposes. *Never before has computing been so versatile. ...a versatile blue chambray skirt.* ♦ **versatility** *Velvet is not known for its versatility.* ADJ-GRADED N-UNCOUNT

verse /vɜːʳs/ **verses** ◆◆◇◇◇

1 Verse is writing arranged in lines which have rhythm and which often rhyme at the end. *...a slim volume of verse... I have been moved to write a few lines of verse.* ● See also **blank verse.** N-UNCOUNT =poetry

2 A **verse** is one of the parts into which a poem, a song, or a chapter of the Bible or the Koran is divided. *This verse describes three signs of spring... The choir has sung only two verses of the last hymn.* N-COUNT

3 ● **chapter and verse**: see **chapter.**

versed /vɜːʳst/. If you are **versed in** or **well versed in** something, you know a lot about it. *Page is well versed in many styles of jazz. ...experts more versed in the economics of taxes than the politics of taxes.* ADJ-GRADED: v-link ADJ *in* n, adv ADJ

version /vɜːʳʃᵊn, -ʒᵊn/ **versions** ◆◆◆◆◇

1 A **version** of something is a particular form of it in which some details are different from earlier or later forms. *...an updated version of his book... Ludo is a version of an ancient Indian racing game... The second-hand version is a poor copy of the original.* N-COUNT: oft N *of*n

2 Someone's **version** of an event is their own description of it, especially when it is different to other people's. *Yesterday afternoon the White House put out a new version of events... She and her friends wanted to go public with their version of the incident... There have been widely differing versions in the newspapers about the prison siege.* N-COUNT: with supp, oft poss N, N *of*n =account

versus /vɜːʳsəs/ ◆◆◇◇◇

1 You use **versus** to indicate that two figures, ideas, or choices are opposed. *Only 18.8% of the class of 1982 had some kind of diploma four years after high school, versus 45% of the class of 1972. ...bottle-feeding versus breastfeeding.* PREP =as opposed to

2 Versus is used to indicate that two teams or people are competing against each other in a sporting event. *Italy versus Japan is turning out to be a surprisingly well matched competition. ...the Lennox Lewis versus Frank Bruno boxing confrontation.* PREP =against

vertebra /vɜːʳtɪbrə/ **vertebrae** /vɜːʳtɪbreɪ/. **Vertebrae** are the small circular bones that form the backbone of a human being or animal. ◆◇◇◇◇ N-COUNT: usu pl

vertebrate /vɜːʳtɪbrɪt/ **vertebrates.** A **vertebrate** is a creature which has a backbone. Mammals, birds, reptiles, amphibians, and most fish are vertebrates. *Both groups share two attributes normally associated with vertebrates. ...the ears of vertebrate animals.* N-COUNT: oft N n ≠invertebrate

vertical /vɜːʳtɪkᵊl/ **verticals** ◆◆◇◇◇

1 Something that is **vertical** stands or points straight upwards. *The climber inched up a vertical wall of rock... The gadget can be attached to any vertical or near vertical surface... The rock was quite vertical and very smooth at the base.* ♦ **vertically** *Cut each bulb in half vertically.* ADJ ADV: ADV after v

2 The vertical is the direction that points straight up, at an angle of 90 degrees to a flat surface. *Pluto seems to have suffered a major collision that tipped it 122 degrees from the vertical.* N-SING: *the*N =perpendicular

3 A **vertical** is a line or structure that is vertical. *As long as the verticals align, the design will look regular.* N-COUNT

vertiginous /vɜːʳtɪdʒɪnəs/. **Vertiginous** is used to describe a very high cliff or path, from which the ground falls away steeply, and which could cause you to suffer from vertigo; a literary word. *...vertiginous cliffs that rise out of the Baltic.* ADJ: usu ADJ n

vertigo /vɜːʳtɪgoʊ/. **Vertigo** is a feeling of dizziness and sickness caused by looking down from a high place. *If you have vertigo it seems as if the whole room is spinning round you... He had a dreadful attack of vertigo.* N-UNCOUNT

verve /vɜːʳv/. **Verve** is lively and forceful enthusiasm; used in written English. *He looked for the dramatic, like the sunset in this painting, and painted it with great verve... She revelled in big MGM musicals with their colour and verve.* ◆◇◇◇◇ N-UNCOUNT =gusto

very /veri/ ◆◆◆◆◆

1 Very is used to give emphasis to an adjective or adverb. *The problem and the answer are very simple... It is very, very strong evidence indeed... I'm very sorry... They are getting the hang of it very quickly... Thank you very much... The men were very much like my father.* ADV: ADV adj/adv

2 Not very is used with an adjective or adverb to say that something is not at all true, or that it is true only to a small degree. *She's not very impressed with them... I'm not very good at explaining myself... It's obviously not used very much... 'How well do you know her?'—'Not very.'* PHRASE: usu PHR adj/adv

3 You use **very** to give emphasis to an adjective that is not usually graded, when you want to say that a quality is very obvious. *Janet looked very pregnant... His taste strikes the English as very French... If you think I'm happy with what's left, you're very wrong.* ADV: ADV adj

4 You use **very** to give emphasis to a superlative adjective or adverb. For example, if you say that something is **the very best**, you are emphasizing that it is the best. *They will be helped by the very latest in navigation aids... I am feeling in the very best of spirits... At the very least, the Government must* ADV: ADV superl *offer some protection to mothers who fear domestic violence.*

5 You use **very** with certain nouns in order to specify an extreme position or extreme point in time. *At the very back of the yard, several feet from Lenny, was a wooden shack... I turned to the very end of the book, to read the final words... The opening of a Euro-Disneyland in the very heart of France is a potent symbol... He was wrong from the very beginning... We still do not have enough women at the very top.* ADJ: ADJ n

6 You use **very** with nouns to emphasize that something is exactly the right one or exactly the same one. *Everybody says he is the very man for the case... She died in this very house... In my view, it only perpetuates the very problem that it sets out to cure... 'Most secret', he called it. Those were his very words.* ADJ: ADJ n =exact

7 You use **very** with nouns to emphasize the importance or seriousness of what you are saying. *At one stage his very life was in danger... The very basis of Indian politics has been transformed... Mr Campbell said such programmes were by their very nature harmful... History is taking place before your very eyes.* ADJ: ADJ n

8 Very good is used to tell someone in authority that you agree to carry out a suggestion or order; a rather formal expression. *'Now give me some account of your voyage.'—'Very good, sir.'* PHRASES CONVENTION PRAGMATICS =certainly

9 The expression **very much so** is an emphatic way of answering 'yes' to something or saying that it is true or correct. *'Are you enjoying your holiday?'—'Very much so.'.* PHR as reply, cl PHR PRAGMATICS

10 Very well is used to say that you agree to do something or you accept someone's answer, even though you might not be completely satisfied with it. *'We need proof, sir.' Another pause. Then, 'Very well.'... Very well, please yourself.* CONVENTION PRAGMATICS =all right

11 If you say that you **cannot very well** do something, you mean that it would not be right or possible to do it. *He couldn't very well go to her office and force her to write a check... I said yes. I can't very well say no.* V inflects, PHR inf =can hardly

vespers /vespəʳz/. In some Christian churches, **vespers** is a service in the evening. N-UNCOUNT

vessel /vesəl/ **vessels** ◆◆◆◇◇

1 A **vessel** is a ship or large boat; a formal use. *A Moroccan fishing vessel and a South Korean cargo ship collided in rough seas. ...a New Zealand navy vessel.* N-COUNT

2 A **vessel** is a bowl or other container in which liquid is kept; a formal use. *He makes decorative vessels in copper, stainless steel and silver. ...storage vessels.* N-COUNT

3 See also **blood vessel**.

vest /vest/ **vests, vesting, vested** ◆◆◇◇◇

1 In British English, a **vest** is a piece of underwear which you can wear on the top half of your body in order to keep warm. The American word is **undershirt**. N-COUNT

2 In American English, a **vest** is a sleeveless piece of clothing with buttons which people usually wear over a shirt. The British word is **waistcoat**. N-COUNT

3 If something **is vested** in you, or if you **are vested** with it, it is given to you as a right or responsibility; a formal use. *All authority was vested in the woman, who discharged every kind of public duty... The mass media have been vested with significant power as social and political agents in modern developed societies... There's an extraordinary amount of power vested in us.* VB: usu passive; be V-ed in n; be V-ed with n; V-ed

vested interest, vested interests. If you have a **vested interest** in something, you have a very strong reason for acting in a particular way, for example to protect your money, power, or reputation. *Only those with vested interests in the current system could ignore the need for change... The administration has no vested interest in proving public schools good or bad.* ◆◇◇◇◇ N-VAR: usu N in n/-ing

vestibule /vestɪbjuːl/ **vestibules.** A **vestibule** is an enclosed area between the outside door of a building and the inner door; a formal word. N-COUNT =entrance hall

vestige /vestɪdʒ/ **vestiges.** A **vestige** of something is a very small part that still remains of something that was once much larger or more important; a formal word. *We represent the last vestige of what made this nation great – hard work.* ◆◇◇◇◇ N-COUNT: usu N of n

vestigial /vestɪdʒiəl/. **Vestigial** is used to describe the small amounts of something that still remain of a larger or more important thing; a formal word. *Vestigial remains of these plays are now seen in the Christmas pantomime.* ADJ: usu ADJ n

vestments /vestmənts/. **Vestments** are the special clothes worn by priests during church ceremonies. N-PLURAL

vestry /vestri/ **vestries.** A **vestry** is a room in a church which the clergy use as an office or to change into their ceremonial clothes for church services. N-COUNT

vet /vet/ **vets, vetting, vetted** ◆◆◇◇◇

1 In British English, a **vet** is someone who is qualified to treat sick or injured animals. **Vet** is also used in American English with this meaning, but the more usual word is **veterinarian**. N-COUNT

2 In American English, a **vet** is someone who has served in the armed forces of their country, especially during a war; an informal use. *The New England Shelter in Boston will serve Christmas dinner for 200 vets... All three are Vietnam vets.* N-COUNT: oft supp N =veteran

3 If something **is vetted**, it is checked carefully to make sure that it is acceptable to people in authority; used mainly in British English. *He can find no trace of a rule requiring research to be vetted before publication... All objects are vetted by a distinguished panel of experts... He had not been allowed to read any book until his mother had vetted it.* VERB be V-ed; V n

4 In British English, if someone **is vetted**, they are investigated fully before being given a particular job, role, or position, especially one which involves military or political secrets. *She was secretly vetted before she ever undertook any work for me... People who marry into the Royal Family will have to be vetted much more carefully in future.* ♦ **vetting** *The government is to make major changes to the procedure for carrying out security vetting.* VB: usu passive =screen; be V-ed; N-UNCOUNT

vetch /vetʃ/ **vetches.** **Vetch** is a climbing or creeping plant found in temperate climates. N-MASS

veteran /vetərən/ **veterans** ◆◆◆◇◇

1 A **veteran** is someone who has served in the armed forces of their country, especially during a war. *They approved a $1.1 billion package of pay increases for the veterans of the Persian Gulf War.* N-COUNT: oft N of n

2 You use **veteran** to refer to someone who has been involved in a particular activity for a long time. *The veteran television campaigner Mary Whitehouse described the ban as splendid news.* N-COUNT: usu N n

veterinarian /vetərɪneəriən/ **veterinarians.** In American English, a **veterinarian** is a person who is qualified to treat sick or injured animals. The usual British word is **vet**. N-COUNT

veterinary /vetərənəri, AM -neri/. **Veterinary** is used to describe the work of a person whose job is to treat sick or injured animals, or to describe the medical treatment of animals. *It was decided that our veterinary screening of horses at events should be continued.* ◆◇◇◇◇ ADJ: ADJ n

veterinary surgeon, veterinary surgeons. In formal British English, a **veterinary surgeon** is someone who is qualified to treat sick or injured animals. The usual American word is **veterinarian**. N-COUNT =vet

veto /viːtou/ **vetoes, vetoing, vetoed** ◆◆◇◇◇

1 If someone in authority **vetoes** something, they forbid it, or stop it being put into action. *De Gaulle vetoed Britain's application to join the EEC... The President vetoed the economic package passed by Congress.* ► Also a noun. *The veto was a calculated political risk taken by a President beset by rising domestic troubles.* VERB =block V n; N-COUNT

2 Veto is the right that someone in authority has to forbid something. *...the President's power of veto.* N-UNCOUNT

vex /veks/ **vexes, vexing, vexed.** If someone or something **vexes** you, they make you feel VERB =annoy annoyed, puzzled, and frustrated. *It vexed me to think of others gossiping behind my back... Everything about her vexed him.* ♦ **vexed** *Exporters, farmers and industrialists alike are vexed and blame the government.* ♦ **vexing** *There remains, however, another and more vexing problem.* • See also **vexed**. V n; ADJ-GRADED: usu v-link ADJ; ADJ-GRADED

vexation /vekseɪʃᵊn/ **vexations. Vexation** is a feeling of being annoyed, puzzled, and frustrated; a formal word. *He kicked the broken machine in vexation.* N-UNCOUNT: also N in pl =annoyance

vexed /vekst/. A **vexed** problem or question is very difficult and causes people a lot of trouble. *European Community ministers have begun work on the vexed issue of economic union... Later Mr Moi raised the vexed question of refugees.* • See also **vex**. ADJ-GRADED: usu ADJ n =thorny

VHF /viː eɪtʃ ef/. **VHF** is used to refer to a range of frequencies that is often used for transmitting radio broadcasts in stereo. **VHF** is an abbreviation for 'very high frequency'. N-UNCOUNT: oft N n

via /vaɪə, viːə/ ◆◆◆◇◇

1 If you go somewhere **via** a particular place, you go through that place on the way to your destination. *We drove via Lovech to the old Danube town of Ruse... Mr Baker will return home via Britain and France.* PREP =by way of

2 If you do something **via** a particular means or person, you do it by making use of that means or person. *The technology to allow relief workers to contact the outside world via satellite already exists... Translators can now work from home, via electronic mail systems... The executive's meeting had finished and Sir Marcus had reported its conclusions to the prime minister via Richard Ryder.* PREP

viable /vaɪəbᵊl/ ◆◆◇◇◇

1 Something that is **viable** is capable of doing what it is intended to do. *Cash alone will not make Eastern Europe's banks viable... The goal has been to establish and sustain a nation of viable family farms. ...commercially viable products.* ♦ **viability** /vaɪəbɪlɪti/ *...the shaky financial viability of the nuclear industry.* ADJ-GRADED; N-UNCOUNT

2 Foetuses, seeds, or eggs are described as **viable** if they are capable of developing into living beings without outside help; a technical use in biology. *Five viable pregnancies were established.* ADJ

viaduct /vaɪədʌkt/ **viaducts.** A **viaduct** is a long, high bridge that carries a road or a railway across a valley. N-COUNT

vial /vaɪəl/ **vials.** A **vial** is a very small bottle which is used to hold something such as perfume or medicine; a formal word. N-COUNT =phial

vibe /vaɪb/ **vibes** ◆◇◇◇◇

1 Vibes are the good or bad atmosphere that you sense with a person or in a place; an informal use. *Sorry, Chris, but I have bad vibes about this guy... You don't see a vibe like you see in Manchester on a Saturday night in any other city in western Europe.* N-COUNT: usu pl

2 The **vibes** are the same as the **vibraphone**; an informal use. *...a variety of other instruments, including vibes, cello, bass, accordion and clarinet.* N-PLURAL

vibrant /vaɪbrənt/ ◆◇◇◇◇

1 Someone or something that is **vibrant** is full of life, energy, and enthusiasm. *Tom felt himself being drawn towards her vibrant personality. ...Shakespeare's vibrant language... Orlando itself is vibrant, full of affordable accommodation and great places to eat.* ♦ **vibrancy** /vaɪbrənsi/ *She was a woman with extraordinary vibrancy and extraordinary knowledge.* ADJ-GRADED; N-UNCOUNT =vitality

2 Vibrant colours are very bright and clear. *Horizon Blue, Corn Yellow and Pistachio Green are just three of the vibrant colours in this range... The grass was a vibrant green. ...vibrant turquoise scarfs.* ♦ **vibrantly** *...a selection of vibrantly coloured French cast-iron saucepans.* ADJ-GRADED: usu ADJ n =brilliant; ADV: ADV adj

vibraphone /vaɪbrəfoʊn/ **vibraphones.** A **vibraphone** is an electronic musical instrument which consists of a set of metal bars in a frame. When you hit the bars they produce vibrating notes that do not fade away immediately. N-COUNT

vibrate /vaɪbreɪt, AM vaɪbreɪt/ **vibrates, vibrating, vibrated.** If something **vibrates** or if you **vibrate** it, it shakes with repeated small, quick movements. *The ground shook and the cliffs seemed to vibrate... The noise vibrated the table.* ♦ **vibration** /vaɪbreɪʃᵊn/ **vibrations** *The vibrations of the vehicles rattled the shop windows.* ◆◇◇◇◇ V-ERG; V; V n; N-VAR

vibrato /vɪbrɑːtoʊ/ **vibratos. Vibrato** is a rapidly repeated slight variation in the pitch of a musical note. Singers and musicians use vibrato to make the music more expressive. *I encourage oboe and clarinet players to use plenty of vibrato.* N-VAR

vibrator /vaɪbreɪtəʳ, AM vaɪbreɪtər/ **vibrators.** A **vibrator** is an electric device which vibrates. It is used in massage to give relief from pain or to give sexual pleasure. N-COUNT

vicar /vɪkəʳ/ **vicars.** In most parishes of the Church of England, the **vicar** is the priest who is in charge of the church and the parish; used mainly in British English. ◆◆◇◇◇ N-COUNT; N-VOC

vicarage /vɪkərɪdʒ/ **vicarages.** A **vicarage** is a house in which a vicar lives; used mainly in British English. ◆◇◇◇◇ N-COUNT

vicarious /vɪkeəriəs, AM vaɪkær-/. A **vicarious** pleasure or feeling is experienced by watching, listening to, or reading about other people doing something, rather than by doing it yourself. *She invents fantasy lives for her own vicarious pleasure... Lots of people use television as their vicarious form of social life.* ♦ **vicariously** *...a father who lived vicariously through his sons' success.* ADJ: ADJ n; ADV: usu ADV with v

vice /vaɪs/ **vices;** spelled **vise** in American English for meaning 3. ◆◆◆◇◇

1 A **vice** is a habit which is regarded as a weakness in someone's character, but not usually as a serious fault. *His only vice is to get drunk on champagne after concluding a successful piece of business... Intellectual pretension was never one of his vices.* N-COUNT

2 Vice refers to criminal activities, especially those connected with pornography or prostitution. *He said those responsible for offences connected with vice, gaming and drugs should be deported on conviction. ...allegations of how she worked in a 'seedy vice den'.* N-UNCOUNT

3 A **vice** or **vise** is a tool with a pair of jaws that hold an object tightly while you do work on it. N-COUNT

vice- /vaɪs-/. **Vice-** is used before a rank or title to indicate that someone is next in importance to the person who holds the rank or title mentioned. *Mr Yeltsin's vice-president, Alexander Rutskoi, called for an economic state of emergency... Tim Munton becomes the new vice-captain.* PREFIX

vice-chancellor, vice-chancellors. In a British university, the **vice-chancellor** is the head of academic and administrative matters. ◆◇◇◇◇ N-COUNT

viceroy /vaɪsrɔɪ/ **viceroys.** In former times, a **viceroy** was the person who ruled a colony on behalf of his king, queen, or government. N-COUNT

vice squad, vice squads. The **vice squad** is the section of a police force that deals with crime relating to pornography, prostitution, and gambling. *...members of the vice squad. ...ten vice-squad officers.* N-COUNT: usu *the* N in sing, N n

vice versa /vaɪsə vɜːʳsə/. **Vice versa** is used to indicate that the reverse of what you have said is true. For example 'women may bring their husbands with them, and vice versa' means that men may also bring their wives with them. *Teachers qualified to teach in England are not accepted in Scotland and vice versa.* ◆◇◇◇◇ PHRASE: usu *and/or/not* PHR

vicinity /vɪsɪnɪti/. If something is in **the vicinity** of a place, it is in the nearby area. *There were a hundred or so hotels in the vicinity of the railway station... The police roadblocks are still in place and the immediate vicinity of the house remains cordoned off.* ◆◇◇◇◇ N-SING: *the* N, oft *in* N, N *of* n

vicious /vɪʃəs/ ◆◆◇◇◇

1 A **vicious** person is violent and cruel. *He was a cruel and vicious man... He suffered a vicious attack by a gang of white youths... The blow was so sudden and vicious that he dropped to his knees.* ADJ-GRADED =brutal

♦ **viciously** *She had been viciously attacked with a hammer.* ♦ **viciousness** *...the intensity and viciousness of these attacks.* ADV-GRADED: usu ADV with v, also ADV adj N-UNCOUNT

2 A **vicious** remark is cruel and intended to upset someone. *It is a deliberate, nasty and vicious attack on a young man's character. ...her shrewish temperament and vicious tongue.* ♦ **viciously** *'He deserved to die,' said Penelope viciously.* ADJ-GRADED =savage ADV-GRADED: ADV with v

vicious circle, vicious circles. A **vicious circle** is a problem or difficult situation that has the effect of creating new problems which then cause the original problem or situation to occur again. *The more pesticides are used, the more resistant the insects become so the more pesticides have to be used. It's a vicious circle. ...the vicious circle of poverty.* ◆◇◇◇◇ N-COUNT: usu sing, oft N of n

vicissitudes /vɪsɪsɪtjuːdz, AM -tuːdz/. You use **vicissitudes** to refer to changes, especially unpleasant ones, that happen to someone or something at different times in their life or development; a formal word. *Whatever the vicissitudes of her past life, Jill now seems to have come through.* N-PLURAL: oft N of n

victim /vɪktɪm/ **victims** ◆◆◆◆◇

1 A **victim** is someone who has been hurt or killed by someone or something. *Not all the victims survived... Statistically our chances of being the victims of violent crime are remote.* N-COUNT

2 A **victim** is someone who has suffered as a result of someone else's actions or beliefs, or as a result of unpleasant circumstances. *He was a victim of racial prejudice... He described himself and Altman as victims rather than participants in the scandal... Infectious diseases are spreading among many of the flood victims.* N-COUNT

3 If you **fall victim to** something or someone, you suffer as a result of them, or you are killed by them. *In the early 1960s, Blyton fell victim to Alzheimer's disease... At Brussels airport he fell victim to pickpockets who pinched his wallet.* PHRASE: V inflects, PHR n =fall prey to

victimize /vɪktɪmaɪz/ **victimizes, victimizing, victimized;** also spelled **victimise** in British English. If someone **is victimized**, they are deliberately treated unfairly. *He felt that the students had been victimized because they'd voiced their opposition to the government.* ♦ **victimization** /vɪktɪmaɪzeɪʃən/ *...society's cruel victimization of women.* ◆◆◆◇◇ VERB be V-ed Also V n N-UNCOUNT

victor /vɪktəʳ/ **victors.** In literary English, a **victor** in a battle or contest is the person who wins. ◆◆◇◇◇ N-COUNT

Victorian /vɪktɔːriən/ **Victorians** ◆◆◇◇◇

1 **Victorian** means belonging to, connected with, or typical of Britain in the middle and last parts of the 19th century, when Victoria was Queen. *We have a lovely old Victorian house. ...a Victorian-style family portrait. ...The Early Victorian Period.* ADJ: usu ADJ n

2 You can use **Victorian** to describe people who have old-fashioned qualities, especially in relation to discipline and morals. *Victorian values are much misunderstood... My grandfather was very Victorian.* ADJ-GRADED

3 The **Victorians** were the people who lived in the reign of Queen Victoria. N-COUNT: usu pl

Victoriana /vɪktɔːriɑːnə/. Interesting or valuable objects made during the reign of Queen Victoria are sometimes referred to as **Victoriana**. N-UNCOUNT

victorious /vɪktɔːriəs/. You use **victorious** to describe someone who has won a victory in a struggle, war, or competition. *In 1978 he played for the victorious Argentinian side in the World Cup. ...the three victorious allied powers: France, Britain, and the United States.* ◆◇◇◇◇ ADJ =triumphant ≠losing

victory /vɪktəri/ **victories** ◆◆◆◆◇

1 A **victory** is a success in a struggle, war, or competition. *The underlying truth is not that Labour came very near to winning, but that it is still far from victory. ...the former Welsh rugby union skipper who led Great Britain to victory over France.* N-VAR ≠defeat

2 If you say that someone has won a **moral victory**, you mean that although they have officially lost a contest or dispute, they have succeeded in showing they are right about something. *She said her party had won a moral victory... We stood up to the West, and that's a moral victory.* PHRASE: N inflects, PHR after v, v-link PHR

video /vɪdioʊ/ **videos, videoing, videoed** ◆◆◆◆◇

1 A **video** is a film or television programme recorded on video tape for people to watch on a television set. *We were watching videos with her. ...the makers of films and videos.* N-COUNT

2 **Video** is the recording and showing of films and events, using a video recorder, videotapes, and a television set. *She has watched the race on video. ...manufacturers of audio and video equipment. ...lessons which use video and film.* N-UNCOUNT: oft on N

3 A **video** is a machine that you can use to record and play videotapes on a television set. *He'd set the video for 8.00.* N-COUNT =video recorder, VCR

4 If you **video** something, you record it on magnetic tape using a video recorder or camera, in order to watch it later. *She had been videoing the highlights of the Test series... The club specialises in videoing its student golfers to correct their faults.* VERB =videotape V n

video cassette, video cassettes. A **video cassette** is a cassette containing video tape, on which you can record or watch films and television programmes. N-COUNT =videotape

video conferencing /vɪdioʊ kɒnfrənsɪŋ/; also spelled **video-conferencing**. **Video conferencing** is a system that enables people in various places around the world to have a meeting by seeing and hearing each other on a screen. N-UNCOUNT

video nasty, video nasties. In British English, a **video nasty** is an extremely violent or horrific film which has been released on video. N-COUNT

videophone /vɪdioʊfoʊn/ **videophones;** also spelled **video phone**. A **videophone** is a telephone with a camera and screen so that each caller can see video images of the other. N-COUNT

video recorder, video recorders. A **video recorder** or a **video cassette recorder** is the same as a **VCR**. ◆◇◇◇◇ N-COUNT =video

videotape /vɪdioʊteɪp/ **videotapes, videotaping, videotaped;** also spelled **video tape**. ◆◆◇◇◇

1 **Videotape** is magnetic tape that is used to record pictures and sounds to be shown on television. N-UNCOUNT

2 A **videotape** is the same as a **video cassette**. N-COUNT

3 If you **videotape** something, you record it on magnetic tape using a video recorder or camera, in order to watch or show it on television later. *She videotaped the entire trip.* VERB =video V n

vie /vaɪ/ **vies, vying, vied.** If one person **vies** with another to do something or if they **vie** to do it, they both try hard to do it sooner or better than the other person; a formal word. *California is vying with other states to capture a piece of the growing communications market... Four rescue plans are vying to save the zoo... He will vie with Mr Clinton for the votes of the young... The two are vying for the support of New York voters.* ◆◇◇◇◇ V-RECIP =compete, struggle V with n to-inf pl-n V to-inf V with n for n pl-n V for n

view /vjuː/ **views, viewing, viewed** ◆◆◆◆◆

1 Your **views** on something are the beliefs or opinions that you have about it, for example whether you think it is good, bad, right, or wrong. *Washington and Moscow are believed to have similar views on Kashmir... I take the view that she should be stopped as soon as possible... My own view is absolutely clear. What I did was right... You should also make your views known to your local MP.* N-COUNT: usu with supp, oft N on n, N that =opinion

2 Your **view** of a particular subject is the way that you understand and think about it. *The drama takes an idealistic, even a naive view of the subject... The whole point was to get away from a Christian-centred view of religion... In the old animistic world view, people believed that nature was organised by invisible souls.* N-SING: with supp, oft N of n

3 If you **view** something in a particular way, you think of it in that way. *First-generation Americans view the United States as a land of golden opportunity... Abigail's mother Linda views her daughter's talent with a mixture of pride and worry... Sectors in the economy can be viewed in a variety of ways... We would view favourably any sensible suggestion for maintaining the business.* VERB =regard V n as n/-ing V n with/in n V n with adv

4 The **view** from a window or high place is everything which can be seen from that place, especially when it is considered to be beautiful. *The view from our window was one of beautiful green countryside... Each of the rooms has a superb view of Pissouri Bay.* N-COUNT

5 If you have a **view** of something, you can see it. *He stood up to get a better view of the blackboard... He stopped in the doorway, blocking her view.* N-SING: with supp, oft N *of* n, poss N

6 You use **view** in expressions to do with being able to see something. For example, if something is **in view**, you can see it. If something is **in full view of everyone**, everyone can see it. *She was lying there in full view of anyone who walked by... A group of riders came into view on the dirt road... On South Main Street, a huge brick building looms into view.* N-UNCOUNT: *in/into* N

7 If you **view** something, you inspect it or look at it for a particular purpose; a formal use. *They came back to view the house again... Twenty-five thousand mourners passed to view the body.* VERB V n

8 If you **view** a television programme, video, or film, you watch it; a formal use. *We have viewed the video recording of the incident... 'Elizabeth R', a TV portrait of the Queen, had record viewing figures.* VERB =watch V n V-ing

9 If you take **a dim view** or **a poor view** of someone or something, you disapprove of them or have a low opinion of them. *They took a dim view of local trade unionists... The judge took a dim view and I spent six years in prison.* PHRASES v PHR, usu PHR *of* n =disapprove

10 You use **in my view** when you want to indicate that you are stating a personal opinion, which other people might not agree with. *In my view things won't change... There is, in my view, a simple explanation... It's not cheating in my view.* PHR with cl PRAGMATICS =in my opinion

11 You use **in view of** when you are taking into consideration facts that have just been mentioned or are just about to be mentioned. *In view of the fact that Hobson was not a trained economist his achievements were remarkable... In view of this, the decision may not be easy.* PREP: PREP n PRAGMATICS =considering

12 If you have something **in view**, you are aware of it and your actions are aimed towards it. *They have very clear career aims in view... Ackroyd worked out this whole plot with one objective in view.* usu PHR after v =in mind

13 If you **take the long view**, you consider what is likely to happen in the future over a long period, rather than thinking only about the immediate effects of something. *Some Taiwanese investors are taking the long view... Taking a long view of the project, I began to think in terms of the rehearsal schedules required.* V inflects, oft PHR *of* n

14 If something such as a work of art is **on view**, it is shown in public for people to look at. *A significant exhibition of contemporary sculpture will be on view at the Portland Gallery.* usu v-link PHR =on show

15 If you do something **with a view to** doing something else, you do it because you hope it will result in that other thing being done. *He has called a meeting of all parties tomorrow, with a view to forming a national reconciliation government.* PHR -ing/n

viewer /vju̲ːəʳ/ **viewers** ◆◆◇◇◇

1 Viewers are people who watch television, or who are watching a particular programme on television. *These programmes are each watched by around 19 million viewers every week.* N-COUNT: usu pl

2 A **viewer** is someone who is looking carefully at a picture, antique, or other interesting object. *...the relationship between the art object and the viewer.* N-COUNT

3 A **viewer** is a box-like object with a magnifying lens, used for looking at transparent colour photographs. *This special viewer is simple to use and comes with 70 full-colour slides.* N-COUNT

viewfinder /vju̲ːfaɪndəʳ/ **viewfinders.** A **viewfinder** is a small square of glass in a camera that you look through in order to see what you are going to photograph. ◆◇◇◇◇ N-COUNT

viewpoint /vju̲ːpɔɪnt/ **viewpoints** ◆◆◇◇◇

1 Someone's **viewpoint** is the way that they think about things in general, or the way they think about a particular thing. *The novel is shown from the girl's viewpoint... To include as many viewpoints as possible, the editor reserves the right to shorten letters.* N-COUNT: usu with supp =point of view, vantage point

2 A **viewpoint** is a place from which you can get a good view of something. *You have to know where to stand for a good viewpoint.* N-COUNT: with supp

vigil /vɪ̲dʒɪl/ **vigils.** A **vigil** is a period of time when people remain quietly in a place, especially at night, for example because they are praying or are making a political protest. *A prayer vigil is being held in the cathedral in memory of the bishop... Protesters are holding a twenty-four hour vigil outside the socialist party headquarters.* ● If someone **keeps a vigil** or **keeps vigil** somewhere, they remain there quietly for a period of time, especially at night, for example because they are praying or are making a political protest. *She kept a vigil at Patrick's bedside. ...protesters who kept vigil at the border last night.* ◆◇◇◇◇ N-COUNT PHRASE: V inflects, usu PHR prep/adv

vigilant /vɪ̲dʒɪlənt/. Someone who is **vigilant** gives careful attention to a particular problem or situation and concentrates on noticing any danger or trouble that there might be. *He warned the public to be vigilant and report anything suspicious... All but one of these letter bombs had been intercepted by vigilant post office staff.* ♦ **vigilance** *Drugs are a problem that requires constant vigilance.* ◆◇◇◇◇ ADJ-GRADED =watchful N-UNCOUNT

vigilante /vɪ̲dʒɪlæ̲nti/ **vigilantes. Vigilantes** are people who organize themselves into an unofficial group to protect their community and to catch and punish criminals. *The vigilantes dragged the men out. ...vigilante patrols.* ◆◇◇◇◇ N-COUNT

vignette /vɪnje̲t/ **vignettes.** A **vignette** is a short description, an illustration, or piece of acting, which expresses very clearly and neatly the typical characteristics of the thing that it represents; a formal word. *The book is an excellent vignette of some of the major debates in science.* N-COUNT: oft N *of* n

vigorous /vɪ̲gərəs/ ◆◆◇◇◇

1 Vigorous physical activities involve using a lot of energy, usually to do short and repeated actions. *Very vigorous exercise can increase the risk of heart attacks... African dance is vigorous, but full of subtlety.* ♦ **vigorously** *He shook his head vigorously... She shivered and rubbed her arms vigorously.* ADJ-GRADED ADV-GRADED: ADV after v

2 You use **vigorous** to describe people who take part in a campaign or activity with great energy or enthusiasm, or to describe the campaign or activity. *Sir Robert was a strong and vigorous politician. ...the most vigorous critics of the government... They will take vigorous action to recover the debts. ...a vigorous campaign by local Communists.* ♦ **vigorously** *The police vigorously denied that excessive force had been used.* ADJ-GRADED: usu ADJ n =dynamic ADV-GRADED: ADV with v

3 A **vigorous** person is strong and healthy and full of energy. *He was a vigorous, handsome young man... He and Elaine were alike: vigorous, smart, independent.* ADJ-GRADED =hearty

vigour /vɪ̲gəʳ/; spelled **vigor** in American English. **Vigour** is physical or mental energy and enthusiasm. *His body lacks the bounce and vigour of a normal two-year-old... He blew his nose with great vigour.* ◆◇◇◇◇ N-UNCOUNT

Viking /va̲ɪkɪŋ/ **Vikings.** The **Vikings** were groups of seamen from Scandinavia who attacked villages in most parts of north-western Europe from the 8th to the 11th centuries. ◆◇◇◇◇ N-COUNT

vile /va̲ɪl/ **viler, vilest.** If you say that someone or something is **vile**, you mean that they are very unpleasant. *The weather was consistently vile... She was in too vile a mood to work.* ◆◇◇◇◇ ADJ-GRADED =foul

vilify /vɪ̲lɪfaɪ/ **vilifies, vilifying, vilified.** If you **are vilified** by someone, they say or write very unpleasant things about you, so that people will have a low opinion of you; a formal word. *The agency has been vilified by some doctors for being unnecessarily slow to approve life-saving drugs... He was vilified, hounded, and forced into exile by the FBI.* ♦ **vilification** /vɪlɪfɪke̲ɪʃən/ *Clare did not deserve the vilification she had been subjected to.* VERB =malign be V-ed *for* -ing/n be V-ed Also V n, V n *as* n N-UNCOUNT

villa /vɪ̲lə/ **villas.** A **villa** is a fairly large house, especially one that is used for holidays in Medi- ◆◆◇◇◇ N-COUNT terranean countries. *He lives in a secluded five-bedroom luxury villa.*

village /vɪlɪdʒ/ **villages.** A **village** consists of a group of houses, together with other buildings such as a church and a school, in a country area. *He lives quietly in the country in a village near Lahti. ...the village school.* ◆◆◆◆◇ N-COUNT

villager /vɪlɪdʒəʳ/ **villagers.** You refer to the people who live in a village, especially the people who have lived there for most or all of their lives, as the **villagers**. *Soon the villagers couldn't afford to buy food for themselves.* ◆◆◇◇◇ N-COUNT: usu pl

villain /vɪlən/ **villains** ◆◇◇◇◇

1 A **villain** is someone who deliberately harms other people or breaks the law in order to get what he or she wants. N-COUNT

2 The **villain** in a novel, film, or play is the main bad character. N-COUNT

3 If you say that someone is **the villain of the piece**, you are saying in a slightly humorous way that they are seen by some people as the cause of all trouble in a particular situation. *If Mr Denny is indeed the villain of the piece, as the police claim he is, he should have been more carefully watched.* PHRASE: *villain* inflects PRAGMATICS

villainous /vɪlənəs/. A **villainous** person is very bad and willing to harm other people or break the law in order to get what he or she wants. *...her villainous father.* ADJ-GRADED: usu ADJ n

villainy /vɪləni/. **Villainy** is very bad or criminal behaviour; a formal word. *They justify every villainy in the name of high ideals.* N-UNCOUNT

vinaigrette /vɪnɪgret/ **vinaigrettes. Vinaigrette** is a dressing made by mixing oil, vinegar, salt, pepper, and herbs, which is put on salad. N-MASS

vindicate /vɪndɪkeɪt/ **vindicates, vindicating, vindicated.** If a person or their decisions, actions, or ideas **are vindicated**, they are proved to be correct, after people have said that they were wrong; a formal word. *The director said he had been vindicated by the experts' report... Ministers and officials are confident their decision will be vindicated.* ♦ **vindication** /vɪndɪkeɪʃᵊn/ *He called the success a vindication of his party's free-market economic policy.* ◆◇◇◇◇ VERB; *be* V-ed; Also V n; N-UNCOUNT: also *a* N, usu N *of* n

vindictive /vɪndɪktɪv/. If you say that someone is **vindictive**, you are critical of them because they deliberately try to upset or cause trouble for someone who they think has done them harm. *How can you be so vindictive? ...a vindictive woman desperate for revenge against the man who loved and left her.* ♦ **vindictiveness** *...a dishonest person who is operating completely out of vindictiveness.* ◆◇◇◇◇ ADJ-GRADED PRAGMATICS =spiteful; N-UNCOUNT

vine /vaɪn/ **vines.** A **vine** is a climbing or trailing plant, especially one which produces grapes. *Every square metre of soil was used, mainly for olives, vines, and almonds.* ◆◆◇◇◇ N-VAR =grapevine

vinegar /vɪnɪgəʳ/ **vinegars. Vinegar** is a sharp-tasting liquid, usually made from sour wine or malt, which is used to make things such as salad dressing. ◆◆◇◇◇ N-MASS

vinegary /vɪnɪgəri/. If something has a **vinegary** taste or smell, it tastes or smells of vinegar. *The salads taste too vinegary.* ADJ-GRADED

vineyard /vɪnjəʳd/ **vineyards.** A **vineyard** is an area of land where grape vines are grown in order to produce wine. You can also use **vineyard** to refer to the set of buildings in which the wine is produced. ◆◆◇◇◇ N-COUNT

vintage /vɪntɪdʒ/ **vintages** ◆◆◇◇◇

1 The **vintage** of a good quality wine is the year and place that it was made before being stored to improve it. You can also use **vintage** to refer to the wine that was made in a certain year. *Many predict 1991 will rival the great vintage of 1965... This wine is from one of the two best vintages of the decade in this region... The 1985 vintage has a stronger bouquet and slight caramelly flavour.* N-COUNT

2 **Vintage** wine is good quality wine that has been stored for several years in order to improve its quality. *If you can buy only one case at auction, it should be vintage port. ...a vintage bottle of wine.* ADJ: ADJ n

3 **Vintage** cars or aeroplanes are old but are admired because they are considered to be the best of their kind. *The museum will have a permanent exhibition of 60 vintage, classic and racing cars.* ADJ: ADJ n

4 You can use **vintage** to describe something which is the best and most typical of its kind. *At the press conference, James is on vintage form... This is vintage comedy at its best.* ADJ: usu ADJ n =classic

vintner /vɪntnəʳ/ **vintners**

1 A **vintner** is someone whose job is to buy and sell wine; a formal use. N-COUNT

2 A **vintner** is someone who grows grapes and makes wine; a formal use. N-COUNT

vinyl /vaɪnɪl/ **vinyls** ◆◆◇◇◇

1 **Vinyl** is a strong plastic used for making things such as floor coverings and furniture. *...a modern vinyl floor covering. ...a reclining chair upholstered in shiny blue vinyl.* N-MASS: oft N n

2 You can use **vinyl** to refer to records, especially in contrast to cassettes or compact discs. *This compilation was first issued on vinyl in 1984. ...the vinyl format of the album.* N-UNCOUNT: oft *on* N

viol /vaɪəl/ **viols. Viols** are a family of musical instruments that are made of wood and have six strings. You play the viol with a bow while holding it on your lap or between your legs. N-VAR: oft *the* N

viola /vioʊlə/ **violas** ◆◇◇◇◇

1 A **viola** is a musical instrument with four strings that is played with a bow. It is like a violin, but is slightly larger and can play lower notes. N-VAR: oft *the* N

2 **Violas** are small plants with white, yellow, mauve, or purple flowers. N-COUNT

violate /vaɪəleɪt/ **violates, violating, violated** ◆◆◆◇◇

1 If someone **violates** an agreement, law, or promise, they break it; a formal use. *They went to prison because they violated the law... They violated the ceasefire agreement.* ♦ **violation** /vaɪəleɪʃᵊn/ **violations** *To deprive the boy of his education is a violation of state law... He was in violation of his contract.* ♦ **violator, violators** *...a government which is a known violator of human rights.* VERB =break V n; N-VAR: usu N *of* n; N-COUNT

2 If you **violate** someone's privacy or peace, you disturb it; a formal use. *These men were violating her family's privacy.* VERB V n

3 If someone **violates** a special place, for example a tomb, they damage it or treat it with disrespect. *Detectives are still searching for those who violated the graveyard.* ♦ **violation** *The violation of the graves is not the first such incident.* VERB =desecrate V n; N-UNCOUNT: usu N *of* n

violence /vaɪələns/ ◆◆◆◆◇

1 **Violence** is behaviour which is intended to hurt, injure, or kill people. *Twenty people were killed in the violence... They threaten them with violence. ...domestic violence between husband and wife.* N-UNCOUNT =aggression

2 If you do or say something with **violence**, you use a lot of force and energy in doing or saying it, often because you are angry; a literary use. *'There's no need,' Amy said, with sudden violence... The violence in her tone gave Alistair a shock.* N-UNCOUNT

violent /vaɪələnt/ ◆◆◆◇◇

1 If someone is **violent**, or if they do something which is **violent**, they use physical force or weapons to hurt, injure, or kill other people. *A quarter of current inmates have committed violent crimes. ...violent anti-government demonstrations... When I first came here, I was very violent... Sometimes the men get violent.* ♦ **violently** *Some opposition activists have been violently attacked.* ADJ-GRADED =aggressive; ADV-GRADED: ADV with v

2 A **violent** event happens suddenly and with great force. *A violent impact hurtled her forward... A violent explosion seemed to jolt the whole ground.* ♦ **violently** *A nearby volcano erupted violently, sending out a hail of molten rock and boiling mud.* ADJ-GRADED: usu ADJ n; ADV-GRADED: ADV with v

3 If you describe something as **violent**, you mean that it is said, done, or felt very strongly. *Violent opposition to the plan continues... He had violent stomach pains. ...an outburst of violent emotion.* ♦ **violently** *He was violently scolded.* ADJ-GRADED: usu ADJ n =intense; ADV-GRADED

4 **Violent** changes are extreme changes from one state to another. *Larry began suffering severe headaches and violent mood swings.* ADJ-GRADED: usu ADJ n =dramatic

5 A **violent** death is painful and unexpected, ADJ-GRADED

usually because the person who dies has been murdered. *...an innocent man who had met a violent death.* ♦ **violently** *...a girl who had died violently nine years earlier.* ADV-GRADED: ADV with v

6 A **violent** film or television programme contains a lot of scenes which show violence. *It was the most violent film that I have ever seen.* ADJ-GRADED

7 If you describe a colour as **violent**, you mean that it is extremely, and often unpleasantly, bright. *...the violent red of dying sunset.* ADJ-GRADED: ADJ n

8 **Violent** weather is extremely stormy and windy. *A violent storm had struck the area.* ADJ-GRADED: usu ADJ n

violet /vaɪəlɪt/ **violets** ◆◇◇◇◇

1 A **violet** is a small purple or white flower that blooms in spring. N-COUNT

2 Something that is **violet** is a bluish-purple colour. *The light was beginning to drain from a violet sky.* COLOUR

3 If you say that someone is no **shrinking violet**, you mean that they are not shy or timid at all. *When it comes to expressing himself he is no shrinking violet... None of the women he paints, however, could be described as shrinking violets.* PHRASE: usu with brd-neg, N inflects, v-link PHR

violin /vaɪəlɪn/ **violins.** A **violin** is a musical instrument. Violins are made of wood and have four strings. You play the violin by holding it under your chin and moving a bow across the strings. *Lizzie used to play the violin. ...the Brahms violin concerto in D.* ◆◇◇◇◇ N-VAR: oft *the* N

violinist /vaɪəlɪnɪst/ **violinists.** A **violinist** is someone who plays the violin. ◆◇◇◇◇ N-COUNT

VIP /viː aɪ piː/ **VIPs.** A **VIP** is someone who is given better treatment than ordinary people because they are famous, influential, or important. **VIP** is an abbreviation for 'very important person'. *...such VIPs as Prince Charles and Richard Nixon... She waited in the VIP lounge.* ◆◇◇◇◇ N-COUNT

viper /vaɪpəʳ/ **vipers.** A **viper** is a small poisonous snake found mainly in Europe. N-COUNT =adder

viral /vaɪərəl/. A **viral** disease or infection is caused by a virus. *...a 65-year-old patient suffering from severe viral pneumonia.* ◆◇◇◇◇ ADJ: usu ADJ n

virgin /vɜːʳdʒɪn/ **virgins** ◆◆◇◇◇

1 A **virgin** is someone, especially a woman or girl, who has never had sex. *I was a virgin until I was thirty years old... They were both virgins when they met and married.* ♦ **virginity** /vəʳdʒɪnɪti/ *She lost her virginity when she was 20.* N-COUNT / N-UNCOUNT

2 You use **virgin** to describe something such as land that has never been used or spoiled. *Within 40 years there will be no virgin forest left. ...a sloping field of virgin snow.* ADJ: usu ADJ n =untouched

3 If you say that a situation is **virgin territory**, you mean that you have no experience of it and it is completely new for you. PHRASE: v-link PHR, PHR after v

virginal /vɜːʳdʒɪnᵊl/

1 If you describe someone as **virginal**, you mean that they look young and innocent, as if they have had no experience of sex. *Somehow she'd always been a child in his mind, pure and virginal... And Julie married Alec, dressed appropriately in virginal white.* ADJ-GRADED =pure

2 Something that is **virginal** looks new and clean, as if it has not been used or spoiled. *...abandoning worn-out land to cultivate virginal pasture.* ADJ-GRADED

Virgo /vɜːʳgoʊ/ **Virgos** ◆◆◇◇◇

1 **Virgo** is one of the twelve signs of the zodiac. Its symbol is a young woman. People who are born approximately between the 23rd of August and the 22nd of September come under this sign. N-UNCOUNT

2 A **Virgo** is a person whose sign of the zodiac is Virgo. N-COUNT

virile /vɪraɪl, AM -rᵊl/ ◆◇◇◇◇

1 If you describe a man as **virile**, you mean that he has the qualities that a man is traditionally expected to have, such as strength and sexuality. *He wanted his sons to become strong, virile, and athletic like himself. ...a tall, virile man with rugged good looks.* ♦ **virility** /vɪrɪlɪti/ *Children are also considered proof of a man's virility.* ADJ-GRADED =red-blooded / N-UNCOUNT

2 Something that is described as **virile** is considered to be very strong and forceful. *...Prokofiev's most virile, aggressive music. ...a virile approach to difficulties.* ♦ **virility** *The strength of national electronics industries has become the new test of industrial virility.* ADJ-GRADED / N-UNCOUNT

virtual /vɜːʳtʃuəl/. You can use **virtual** to indicate that something is so nearly true that for most purposes it can be regarded as true. *Argentina came to a virtual standstill while the game was being played... The Communist take-over culminated in the virtual banning of religion. ...conditions of virtual slavery.* ◆◆◇◇◇ ADJ: ADJ n

virtually /vɜːʳtʃuəli/. You can use **virtually** to indicate that something is so nearly true that for most purposes it can be regarded as true. *Virtually all cooking was done over coal-fired ranges... It would have been virtually impossible to research all the information.* ◆◆◆◇◇ ADV: ADV with group =almost

virtual reality. **Virtual reality** is an environment which is produced by a computer and seems very like reality to the person experiencing it. *One day virtual reality will revolutionize the entertainment industry. ...the launch of the first virtual reality computer in the UK.* ◆◇◇◇◇ N-UNCOUNT

virtue /vɜːʳtʃuː/ **virtues** ◆◆◇◇◇

1 **Virtue** is thinking and doing what is right and avoiding what is wrong. *Virtue is not confined to the Christian world... She could have established her own innocence and virtue easily enough.* N-UNCOUNT =goodness ≠vice

2 A **virtue** is a good quality or way of behaving. *His virtue is patience... Her flaws were as large as her virtues... Humility is considered a virtue.* N-COUNT

3 The **virtue** of something is an advantage or benefit that it has, especially in comparison with something else. *There was no virtue in returning to Calvi the way I had come... It's other great virtue, of course, is its hard-wearing quality.* N-COUNT =advantage

4 You use **by virtue of** to explain why something happens or is true; a formal expression. *The article stuck in my mind by virtue of one detail... Mr Olaechea has British residency by virtue of his marriage.* PHR-PREP =because of

5 If you **make a virtue of** something, you pretend that you did it out of goodness or choice, although in fact you did it because you had to. *The movie makes a virtue out of its economy.* PHRASE: V inflects, PHR n

virtuosity /vɜːʳtʃuɒsɪti/. The **virtuosity** of someone such as an artist or sportsman is their exceptional skill. The **virtuosity** of a performance or creation is the exceptional skill with which it has been done. *At that time, his virtuosity on the trumpet had no parallel in jazz.* N-UNCOUNT: oft with poss

virtuoso /vɜːʳtʃuoʊzoʊ/ **virtuosos** or **virtuosi** /vɜːʳtʃuoʊzi/ ◆◇◇◇◇

1 A **virtuoso** is someone who is exceptionally good at something, especially at playing a musical instrument. *He was gaining a reputation as a remarkable virtuoso.* N-COUNT

2 A **virtuoso** performance or display shows exceptional skill. *England's football fans are hoping for a virtuoso performance against Cameroon.* ADJ

virtuous /vɜːʳtʃuəs/ ◆◇◇◇◇

1 A **virtuous** person behaves in a moral and correct way. *Louis was shown as an intelligent, courageous and virtuous family man.* ADJ-GRADED =good

2 If you describe someone as **virtuous**, you mean that they feel very pleased with their own good behaviour; often used showing disapproval. *She was unlike the virtuous wives and mothers... I cleaned the flat, which left me feeling virtuous.* ♦ **virtuously** *'I've already done that,' said Ronnie virtuously.* ADJ-GRADED =self-righteous / ADV-GRADED: usu ADV with v, also ADV adj

virtuous circle. If you describe a situation as a **virtuous circle**, you mean that once one good thing starts happening, other good things happen, which cause the first thing to continue happening. *Exercise creates its own virtuous circle. Once you start a programme and do it regularly, you'll feel so good you'll want to continue. ...a virtuous circle of investment and growth.* N-SING

virulence /vɪrjʊləns/

1 **Virulence** is strong bitterness and hostility that is N-UNCOUNT:

directed against someone; a formal use. *The virulence of the café owner's anger had appalled her.* oft N *of* n
2 The **virulence** of a disease or poison is its ability to harm or kill people or animals. *Medical authorities were baffled, both as to its causes and its virulence.* N-UNCOUNT

virulent /vɪrjʊlənt/ ◆◇◇◇◇
1 **Virulent** feelings or actions are extremely bitter and hostile. *Now he faces virulent attacks from the Italian media... Friends spoke of 'a virulent personal campaign' being waged against him.* ADJ-GRADED: usu ADJ n =vicious
♦ **virulently** *The talk was virulently hostile to the leadership.* ADV: usu ADV adj
2 A **virulent** disease or poison is extremely powerful and dangerous. *A very virulent form of the disease appeared in Belgium. ...a particularly virulent strain of the virus.* ADJ-GRADED

virus /vaɪərəs/ **viruses** ◆◆◆◇◇
1 A **virus** is a kind of germ that can cause disease. *There are many different strains of flu virus. ...HIV, the virus believed to cause AIDS.* N-COUNT
2 In computer technology, a **virus** is a program that introduces itself into a system, altering or destroying the information stored in the system. *Hackers are said to have started a computer virus.* N-COUNT

visa /viːzə/ **visas.** A **visa** is an official document, or a stamp put in your passport, which allows you to enter or leave a particular country. *His visitor's visa expired. ...an exit visa. ...a tightening of U.S. visa requirements.* ◆◆◇◇◇ N-COUNT: oft supp N =permit

visage /vɪzɪdʒ/ **visages.** Someone's **visage** is their face; a literary word. *...his milky-white innocent visage.* N-COUNT: oft with poss =face

vis-à-vis /viːz ɑː viː/. You use **vis-à-vis** when you are considering a relationship or comparison between two things or quantities; a formal word. *Each currency is given a value vis-à-vis the other currencies. ...Poland's economic weakness vis-à-vis Germany.* PREP =in comparison with

viscera /vɪsərə/. **Viscera** are the large organs inside the body, such as the heart, liver, and stomach; a medical term. N-PLURAL

visceral /vɪsərəl/. **Visceral** feelings and emotions are deep and instinctive rather than rational and carefully thought out; a literary word. *I never overcame a visceral antipathy for the monarchy. ...the sheer visceral joy of being alive.* ADJ-GRADED: usu ADJ n =deep-seated

viscose /vɪskoʊs/. In British English, **viscose** is a smooth man-made fabric that is made from cellulose. The usual American word is **rayon**. *...a black viscose floral dress.* N-UNCOUNT: oft N n

viscosity /vɪskɒsɪti/. **Viscosity** is the quality that some liquids have of being thick and sticky. *...the viscosity of the paint.* N-UNCOUNT: oft N *of* n

viscount /vaɪkaʊnt/ **viscounts.** A **viscount** is a British nobleman who is below an earl and above a baron in rank. *...a biography of Viscount Mourne.* ◆◇◇◇◇ N-COUNT; N-TITLE

viscountess /vaɪkaʊntɪs/ **viscountesses.** A **viscountess** is either the wife of a viscount or a woman who holds the same position as a viscount. *...Viscount and Viscountess Osborne.* N-COUNT; N-TITLE

viscous /vɪskəs/. A **viscous** liquid is thick and sticky. *...dark, viscous blood.* ADJ-GRADED

vise /vaɪs/. See **vice**.

visibility /vɪzɪbɪlɪti/ ◆◇◇◇◇
1 **Visibility** means how far or how clearly you can see in particular weather conditions. *Visibility was poor.* N-UNCOUNT
2 If you refer to the **visibility** of something such as a situation or problem, you mean how much it is seen or noticed by other people. *The plight of the Kurds gained global visibility.* N-UNCOUNT

visible /vɪzɪbəl/ ◆◆◆◇◇
1 If something is **visible**, it can be seen. *The warning lights were clearly visible... They found a bacterium visible to the human eye... The meadows are hardly visible from the house.* ADJ-GRADED: usu v-link ADJ, oft ADJ *to/from* n
2 You use **visible** to describe something or someone that people notice or recognize. *The most visible sign of the intensity of the crisis is unemployment... He was making a visible effort to control himself... Miss Amiel has become a highly visible columnist and was voted the 1989 Woman of Distinction.* ADJ-GRADED
♦ **visibly** /vɪzɪbli/ *The Russians were visibly wavering... They emerged visibly distressed and weeping.* ADV-GRADED: ADV with v, ADV adj

vision /vɪʒən/ **visions** ◆◆◆◇◇
1 Your **vision** of a future situation or society is what you imagine or hope it would be like, if things were very different from the way they are now. *I have a vision of a society that is free of exploitation and injustice... That's my vision of how the world could be... Turning that vision into a practical reality is not easy.* N-COUNT: usu N *of* n
2 If you have a **vision** of someone in a particular situation, you imagine them in that situation, for example because you are worried that it might happen, or hope that it will happen. *He had a vision of Cheryl, slumped on a plastic chair in the waiting-room... Maybe you had visions of being surrounded by happy, smiling children.* N-COUNT: usu N *of* n =image
3 A **vision** is an unusual experience that you have, in which you see things that other people cannot see, as a result of divine inspiration, madness, or taking drugs. *It was on 24th June 1981 that young villagers first reported seeing the Virgin Mary in a vision.* N-COUNT =hallucination
4 Your **vision** is your ability to see clearly with your eyes. *It causes blindness or serious loss of vision... In spite of his otherwise excellent vision, he found he was colour-blind.* N-UNCOUNT =sight
5 Your **vision** is everything that you can see from a particular place or position. *Jane blocked Cross's vision and he could see nothing... I saw other indistinct shapes that stayed out of vision.* N-UNCOUNT =view
6 See also **tunnel vision**.

visionary /vɪʒənri, AM -neri/ **visionaries** ◆◇◇◇◇
1 If you refer to someone as a **visionary**, you mean that they have strong, original ideas about how things might be different in the future, especially about how things might be improved. *Visionaries are constantly fighting conventional wisdom because they see the world ahead in terms of what it can be... An entrepreneur is more than just a risk taker. He is a visionary.* N-COUNT
2 You use **visionary** to describe the strong, original ideas of a visionary. *Many are hailing Rendell's ideas as visionary. ...the visionary architecture of Etienne Boulleé.* ADJ-GRADED

visit /vɪzɪt/ **visits, visiting, visited** ◆◆◆◆◆
1 If you **visit** someone, you go to see them and spend time with them. *He wanted to visit his brother in Worcester... He was visited by an old friend from Iraq... Bill would visit on weekends.* ► Also a noun. *Helen had recently paid him a visit.* VERB V n V N-COUNT
2 If you **visit** a place, you go there for a short time. *He'll be visiting four cities including Cagliari in Sardinia... Caroline visited all the big stores. ...a visiting truck driver.* ► Also a noun. *...the Pope's visit to Canada... I paid a visit to my local print shop.* VERB V n V-ing N-COUNT: usu N *to* n
3 In British English, if you **visit** a professional person such as a doctor or solicitor, you go and see them in order to get professional advice. If they **visit** you, they come to see you in order to give you professional advice. *If necessary the patient can then visit his doctor for further advice... A doctor will visit you in your apartment.* ► Also a noun. *You may have regular home visits from a neonatal nurse.* VERB =see V n V n N-COUNT: usu with supp
4 If something very unpleasant **is visited** upon you, it happens to you; a formal use. *Violence is visited upon us every day... Death and suffering had been visited on thousands of innocents.* V-PASSIVE =be inflicted *be* V-ed *upon/on* n
visit with. In American English, if you **visit with** someone, you go to see them and spend time with them. *I visited with him in San Francisco.* PHRASAL VERB V P n

visitation /vɪzɪteɪʃən/ **visitations**
1 A **visitation** is an event which is thought to be a message from God, an angel, or some other divine force. *The young people have claimed almost daily visitations from the Virgin Mary.* N-COUNT
2 People sometimes refer humorously to a visit from someone, especially from someone in N-COUNT

authority, as a **visitation**. *They had another visitation from Essex police.*

3 **Visitation** is the act of officially visiting someone. *House-to-house visitation has been carried on, under the regulations of the General Board of Health... I had visitation rights.* — N-UNCOUNT: usu with supp

visitor /vɪzɪtəʳ/ **visitors.** A **visitor** is someone who is visiting a person or place. *The other day we had some visitors from Switzerland... As a student I lived in Oxford but was a frequent visitor to Belfast.* — ◆◆◆◇◇ N-COUNT: oft N *from/to* n

visor /vaɪzəʳ/ **visors**

1 A **visor** is a movable part of a helmet which can be pulled down to protect a person's eyes or face. *He pulled on a battered old crash helmet with a scratched visor.* — N-COUNT

2 A **visor** is a piece of plastic or other material fixed above the windscreen inside a car, which can be turned down to protect the driver's eyes from bright sunshine. *I put down the sun visor to shade my eyes from the light.* — N-COUNT: usu n N

vista /vɪstə/ **vistas** — ◆◇◇◇◇

1 A **vista** is a view from a particular place, especially a beautiful view from a high place; used in written English. *From my bedroom window I looked out on a crowded vista of hills and rooftops. ...an endless fascinating vista of snow peaks and shadowed valleys.* — N-COUNT: with supp =panorama

2 A **vista** is a vision of a situation or of a range or possibilities. *These uprisings come from desperation and a vista of a future without hope. ...a vista of future business that was blinding in its promised magnificence.* — N-COUNT =vision

visual /vɪʒuəl/ **visuals** — ◆◆◇◇◇

1 **Visual** means relating to sight, or to things that you can see. *...the graphic visual depiction of violence. ...music, film, dance, and the visual arts. ...visual jokes.* — ADJ: usu ADJ n ♦ **visually** *...visually handicapped boys and girls.* — ADV: usu ADV adj

2 A **visual** is a piece of display material, such as a photograph or film, that is used to illustrate or explain something. *Remember you want your visuals to reinforce your message, not detract from what you are saying.* — N-COUNT

visual aid, visual aids. **Visual aids** are things that you can look at, such as a film, model, map, or slides, to help you understand something or to remember information. — N-COUNT: usu pl

visualize /vɪʒuəlaɪz/ **visualizes, visualizing, visualized;** also spelled **visualise** in British English. If you **visualize** something, you imagine what it is like by forming a mental picture of it. *Susan visualized her wedding day and saw herself walking down the aisle on her father's arm... He could not visualize her as old... She visualized him stomping to his car, the picture of self-righteousness... It was hard to visualize how it could have been done.* — ◆◆◇◇◇ VERB =picture, imagine; V n; V n prep; V n-ing; V wh ♦ **visualization** /vɪʒuəlaɪzeɪʃən/ **visualizations** *...a perfect visualization of reality. ...meditation and visualization techniques.* — N-VAR

vital /vaɪtəl/ — ◆◆◆◇◇

1 If you say that something is **vital**, you mean that it is necessary or very important. *The port is vital to supply relief to millions of drought victims... Nick Wileman is a school caretaker so it is vital that he gets on well with young people... After her release she was able to give vital information about her kidnapper.* — ADJ-GRADED =crucial ♦ **vitally** *Lesley's career in the church is vitally important to her.* — ADV-GRADED: usu ADV adj, also ADV with v

2 If you describe someone or something as **vital**, you mean that they are very energetic and full of life. *They are both very vital people and a good match... They have something important to say and vital and radical ways of saying it.* — ADJ-GRADED =lively

vitality /vaɪtælɪti/. If you say that someone or something has **vitality**, you mean that they have great energy and liveliness. *Without continued learning, graduates will lose their intellectual vitality... Mr Li said China's reforms had brought vitality to its economy.* — ◆◇◇◇◇ N-UNCOUNT =vigour

vital statistics

1 The **vital statistics** of a population are statistics such as the number of births, deaths, or marriages which take place in it. — N-PLURAL: usu with poss

2 Someone's **vital statistics**, especially a woman's, are the measurements of their body at certain points, for example at their chest, waist, and hips. — N-PLURAL: usu with poss

vitamin /vɪtəmɪn, AM vaɪt-/ **vitamins.** **Vitamins** are organic substances in food which you need in order to remain healthy. You can also refer to tablets or medicines containing these substances as **vitamins**. *Lack of vitamin D is another factor to consider... Healthy people do not need vitamin supplements.* — ◆◆◆◇◇ N-COUNT: oft N n

vitiate /vɪʃieɪt/ **vitiates, vitiating, vitiated.** If something **is vitiated**, its effectiveness is spoiled or weakened; a formal word. *Strategic policy during the War was vitiated because of a sharp division between 'easterners' and 'westerners'... But this does not vitiate his scholarship.* — VERB; *be* V-ed; V n

vitreous /vɪtriəs/. **Vitreous** means made of glass or resembling glass; a technical term. — ADJ: usu ADJ n

vitriol /vɪtrioʊl/. If you refer to what someone says or writes as **vitriol**, you disapprove of it because it is full of bitterness and hate, and so causes a lot of distress and pain. *The vitriol he hurled at members of the press knew no bounds... He has been no stranger to controversy and vitriol during a tumultuous political career.* — N-UNCOUNT PRAGMATICS =acrimony, venom

vitriolic /vɪtriɒlɪk/. If you describe someone's language or behaviour as **vitriolic**, you disapprove of it because it is full of bitterness and hate, and so causes a lot of distress and pain. *There was a vicious and vitriolic attack on him in one of the Sunday newspapers two weeks ago.* — ADJ-GRADED: usu ADJ n PRAGMATICS =vituperative, venomous

vitro /viːtroʊ/. See **in vitro**.

vituperation /vɪtjuːpəreɪʃən, AM vaɪtuːp-/ **vituperations.** **Vituperation** is language that is full of hate, anger, or insults; a formal word. — N-UNCOUNT: also N in pl

vituperative /vɪtjuːpərətɪv, AM vaɪtuːp-/. **Vituperative** remarks are full of hate, anger, or insults; a formal word. *He is often the victim of vituperative remarks concerning his wealth. ...one of journalism's most vituperative critics.* — ADJ-GRADED: ADJ n PRAGMATICS =vitriolic, virulent

viva, vivas. Pronounced /vaɪvə/ for meaning 1, and /viːvə/ for meaning 2. — ◆◇◇◇◇

1 In British English, a **viva** is an oral examination, especially in a university. — N-COUNT

2 People in crowds sometimes shout **'Viva!'** before the name of a person or thing as a way of showing their support for them. *Viva Gorbachev!* — EXCLAM

vivacious /vɪveɪʃəs/. If you describe someone as **vivacious**, you mean that they are lively, exciting, and attractive; used in written English. *She's beautiful, vivacious, and charming.* — ADJ-GRADED

vivacity /vɪvæsɪti/. If you say that someone has **vivacity**, you mean that they are lively, exciting, and attractive; used in written English. *...her exceptional vitality, vivacity and wit.* — N-UNCOUNT

vivid /vɪvɪd/ 

1 If you describe memories and descriptions as **vivid**, you mean that they are very clear and detailed. *People of my generation who lived through World War II have vivid memories of confusion and incompetence... On Wednesday night I had a very vivid dream which really upset me.* — ADJ-GRADED ♦ **vividly** *He vividly remembers seeing his first match at the Baseball Ground.* — ADV-GRADED: usu ADV with v, also ADV adj ♦ **vividness** *The vividness of the characterisation came as a complete surprise.* — N-UNCOUNT: oft *the* N *of* n

2 Something that is **vivid** is very bright in colour. *...a vivid blue sky.* — ADJ-GRADED ♦ **vividly** *...vividly coloured birds.* — ADV-GRADED: ADV -ed/adj

vivisection /vɪvɪsekʃən/. **Vivisection** is the practice of using live animals for scientific experiments. *...a fierce opponent of vivisection.* — N-UNCOUNT

vixen /vɪksən/ **vixens.** A **vixen** is a female fox. — N-COUNT

viz. viz. is used in written English to introduce a list of specific items or examples. *The school offers two modules in Teaching English as a Foreign Language, viz. Principles and Methods of Language Teaching and Applied Linguistics.* — =namely

V-neck, V-necks. A **V-neck** or a **V-neck** sweater is a sweater with a neck that is in the shape of the letter V. N-COUNT: oft N n

vocabulary /voʊkæbjʊləri, AM -leri/ **vocabularies** ◆◇◇◇◇

1 Your **vocabulary** is the total number of words you know in a particular language. *His speech is immature, his vocabulary limited... We read to improve our vocabularies.* N-VAR: oft with poss

2 The **vocabulary** of a language is all the words in it. *...a new word in the German vocabulary.* N-SING =lexicon

3 The **vocabulary** of a subject is the group of words that are typically used when discussing it. *...the vocabulary of natural science.* N-VAR: with supp

vocal /voʊkᵊl/ ◆◆◇◇◇

1 You say that people are **vocal** when they speak forcefully about something that they feel strongly about. *He has been very vocal in his displeasure over the results... A public inquiry earlier this year produced vocal opposition from residents.* ADJ-GRADED ♦ **vocally** *Both these proposals were resisted by the developed countries, most vocally by the United States.* ADV-GRADED: usu ADV with v

2 **Vocal** means involving the use of the human voice, especially in singing. *...a wider range of vocal styles. ...vocal training.* ADJ: ADJ n ♦ **vocally** *Vocally, it is often a very accomplished performance... I then begin to improvise melodies vocally.* ADV: ADV with cl/group, ADV with v

vocal cords; also spelled **vocal chords.** Your **vocal cords** are the part of your throat that vibrates when you speak. *She wanted to scream, but her vocal cords seemed paralysed.* N-PLURAL

vocalist /voʊkəlɪst/ **vocalists.** A **vocalist** is a singer who sings with a pop group. *He and Carla Torgerson take turns as the band's lead vocalist.* ◆◇◇◇◇ N-COUNT =singer

vocalize /voʊkəlaɪz/ **vocalizes, vocalizing, vocalized;** also spelled **vocalise** in British English.

1 If you **vocalize** a feeling or an idea, you express it in words. *Archbishop Hunthausen also vocalized his beliefs that women and homosexuals should be more active in the church.* VERB =express V n

2 When you **vocalize** a sound, you use your voice to make it, especially by singing it. *In India and Bali students learn to vocalize music before ever picking up instruments.* VERB V n Also V

vocals /voʊkᵊlz/. In a pop song, the **vocals** are the singing, in contrast to the playing of instruments. *Johnson now sings backing vocals for Mica Paris.* ◆◆◇◇◇ N-PLURAL

vocation /voʊkeɪʃᵊn/ **vocations** ◆◇◇◇◇

1 If you have a **vocation**, you have a strong feeling that you are especially suited to do a particular job or to fulfil a particular role in life, especially one which involves serving other people. *It could well be that he has a real vocation... Diana was a young mission school teacher convinced of her vocation to provide support for her schoolgirl pupils.* N-VAR =calling

2 If you refer to your job or profession as your **vocation**, you feel that you are particularly suited to it. *Her vocation is her work as an actress... She has no vocation for teaching.* N-VAR: oft poss N

vocational /voʊkeɪʃənᵊl/. **Vocational** training and skills are the training and skills needed for a particular job or profession. *...a course designed to provide vocational training in engineering... Vocational courses are often given more respect and funding than arts or philosophy.* ◆◇◇◇◇ ADJ: usu ADJ n ♦ **vocationally** *...a variety of vocationally oriented courses.* ADV: ADV -ed/adj

vocative /vɒkətɪv/ **vocatives.** A **vocative** is a word such as 'darling' or 'madam' which is used to address someone or attract their attention. N-COUNT

vociferous /vəsɪfərəs, AM voʊs-/. If you describe someone as **vociferous**, you mean that they speak with great energy and determination, because they want their views to be heard. *He was a vociferous opponent of communism... Slovak resentment over rule from Prague was becoming more vociferous.* ◆◇◇◇◇ ADJ-GRADED =strident ♦ **vociferously** *He vociferously opposed the state of emergency imposed by the government.* ADV-GRADED: usu ADV with v, also ADV adj

vodka /vɒdkə/ **vodkas. Vodka** is a strong, clear, alcoholic drink. ◆◇◇◇◇ N-MASS

vogue /voʊg/ ◆◆◇◇◇

1 If there is a **vogue** for something, it is very popular and fashionable. *Despite the vogue for so-called health teas, there is no evidence that they are any healthier... In Britain there's been something of a vogue for these books.* N-SING: oft N *for* n =trend, fad

2 If something is **in vogue**, is very popular and fashionable. If it comes **into vogue**, it becomes very popular and fashionable. *Pale colours are much more in vogue than autumnal bronzes and coppers. ...the hippie-ethnic look which came into vogue in the late 60s.* PHRASE: v-link PHR, PHR after v =in fashion

voice /vɔɪs/ **voices, voicing, voiced** ◆◆◆◆◇

1 When someone speaks or sings, you hear their **voice**. *Miriam's voice was strangely calm... 'The police are here,' she said in a low voice... There was a sound of loud voices from the kitchen... I ended up with bronchitis and no voice.* N-COUNT: oft poss N, adj N

2 Someone's **voice** is their opinion on a particular topic and what they say about it. *What does one do when a government simply refuses to listen to the voice of the opposition?... There was no disagreement, there were no dissenting voices.* N-COUNT

3 If you have a **voice in** something, you have the right to express an opinion on it. *Egypt is once again accepted as an important voice in Arab politics... But your partners will have no voice in how you operate your company.* N-SING: N *in* n =say

4 If you **voice** something such as an opinion or an emotion, you say what you think or feel. *Some scientists have voiced concern that the disease could be passed on to humans... The predominant opinion voiced by Detroit's Arab population seems to be one of frustration.* VERB =express V n V-ed

5 In grammar, if a verb is in **the active voice**, the person who performs the action is the subject of the verb. If a verb is in **the passive voice**, the thing or person affected by the action is the subject of the verb. N-SING: *the* adj N

6 If someone **finds** their **voice**, they start to speak in spite of fear or surprise or difficult circumstances. *'Kurt Kohn was my paternal grandfather's name,' Laura said when she found her voice.* PHRASES V inflects

7 If you say that a writer **finds** his or her **voice**, you mean that he or she finds a style and subject matter that are personal and original. *The poems which he wrote in the trenches are generally agreed to be those in which he found his true voice.* V inflects

8 If you **give voice to** an opinion, a need, or a desire, you express it aloud. *...a community radio run by the Catholic Church which gave voice to the protests of the slum-dwellers.* V inflects, PHR n =express

9 If someone tells you to **keep** your **voice down**, they are asking you to speak more quietly. *Keep your voice down, for goodness sake.* V inflects PRAGMATICS

10 If you **lose** your **voice**, you cannot speak for a while because of an illness. *I had to be careful not to get a sore throat and lose my voice.* V inflects

11 If you **raise** your **voice**, you speak more loudly. If you **lower** your **voice**, you speak more quietly. *He raised his voice for the benefit of the other two women... She'd lowered her voice until it was barely audible.* V inflects

12 If you say something **at the top of** your **voice**, you say it as loudly as possible. *'Damn!' he yelled at the top of his voice.* Ns inflect

13 If a number of people say something **with one voice**, they all express the same opinion about something. *This would enable the community to speak with one voice in world affairs.*

voice box, voice boxes. Your **voice box** is the top part of the passage that leads from your throat to your lungs and contains your vocal cords. N-COUNT =larynx

voiced /vɔɪst/. A **voiced** speech sound is one that is produced with vibration of the vocal cords; a technical term in linguistics. ADJ

voiceless /vɔɪsləs/

1 A **voiceless** speech sound is one that is produced ADJ

without vibration of the vocal cords; a technical use in linguistics. *...the voiceless 'th'.*

2 Someone who is **voiceless** is unable to speak; used in written English. *His voiceless lips formed the words 'Thank you'.* ADJ =dumb

voice mail. Voice mail is a system of sending messages over the telephone. Calls are answered by a machine which connects you to the person you want to leave a message for, and they can listen to their messages later. N-UNCOUNT

voice-over, voice-overs; also spelled **voiceover**. A **voice-over** is a commentary or explanation in a film or television programme which is spoken by someone who is not seen. *89% of advertisements had a male voice-over.* N-COUNT

void /vɔɪd/ **voids, voiding, voided** ◆◇◇◇◇

1 If you describe a situation or a feeling as a **void**, you mean that it seems empty because there is nothing interesting or worthwhile about it. *His death has left a void in the cricketing world which can never be filled. ...an aching void of loneliness.* N-COUNT: usu sing

2 You can describe a large or frightening space as a **void**. *He stared into the dark void where the battle had been fought... The ship moved silently through the black void... Observers have recently found in the Universe giant voids about 500,000,000 light-years across.* N-COUNT

3 Something that is **void** or **null and void** is officially considered to have no value or authority. *The original elections were declared void by the former military ruler... The agreement will be considered null and void.* ADJ: v-link ADJ =invalid

4 If you are **void of** something, you do not have any of it; a formal or literary use. *He rose, his face void of emotion as he walked towards the door... The treaty is now void of absolute commitments.* ADJ: v-link ADJ *of*n

5 To **void** something means to make it ineffective or to remove its authority or validity. *The Supreme Court threw out the confession and voided his conviction for murder.* VERB =nullify V n

voile /vɔɪl/. **Voile** is thin material which is used for making women's clothing, for example dresses, blouses, and scarves. N-UNCOUNT: oft N n

vol., vols. Vol. is used as a written abbreviation for **volume** when you are referring to one or more books in a series of books. ◆◆◆◇◇

volatile /vɒlətaɪl, AM -təl/ ◆◆◇◇◇

1 A situation that is **volatile** is liable to change suddenly and unexpectedly. *There have been riots before and the situation is volatile... The international oil markets have been highly volatile since the early 1970s... Armed soldiers guard the streets in this volatile atmosphere.* ♦ **volatility** /vɒlətɪlɪti/ *He is keen to see a general reduction in arms sales given the volatility of the region. ...current stock market volatility.* ADJ-GRADED =unstable; N-UNCOUNT =instability

2 Someone who is **volatile** is liable to change their mood or attitude quickly and frequently. *Their relationship was always volatile... He has a volatile temper.* ADJ-GRADED

3 A **volatile** liquid or substance is one that will quickly change into a gas; a technical use in chemistry. *It's thought that the blast occurred when volatile chemicals exploded.* ADJ-GRADED

volcanic /vɒlkænɪk/. **Volcanic** means coming from or created by volcanoes. *Over 200 people have been killed by volcanic eruptions... Mount Unzen has been spewing out volcanic ash, gas, and rock today... St Vincent is a lush, volcanic island.* ◆◇◇◇◇ ADJ: usu ADJ n

volcano /vɒlkeɪnoʊ/ **volcanoes.** A **volcano** is a mountain from which hot melted rock, gas, steam, and ash from inside the earth sometimes burst. *The volcano erupted last year killing about 600 people... Etna is Europe's most active volcano.* ◆◆◇◇◇ N-COUNT

vole /voʊl/ **voles.** A **vole** is a small animal that looks like a mouse but has very small ears and a short tail. Voles usually live in fields or near rivers. • See also **water vole**. N-COUNT

volition /vəlɪʃən, AM voʊl-/

1 Your **volition** is the power you have to decide something for yourself; a formal use. *We like to think that everything we do and everything we think is a product of our volition... He felt as though he were in the grip of Fate and had no volition of his own.* N-UNCOUNT =free will

2 If you do something **of** your **own volition**, you do it because you have decided for yourself that you will do it and not because someone else has told you to do it; a formal expression. *Makin said Mr Coombes had gone to the police of his own volition.* PHRASE: PHR after v =by choice

volley /vɒli/ **volleys, volleying, volleyed** ◆◇◇◇◇

1 In sport, if someone **volleys** the ball, they hit it before it touches the ground. *He volleyed the ball spectacularly into the far corner of the net... McNeil volleyed more effectively in the second set.* ► Also a noun. *She hit most of the winning volleys.* VERB V n prep/adv V; N-COUNT

2 A **volley** of gunfire is a lot of bullets that travel through the air at the same time. *It's still not known how many died in the volleys of gunfire... Three mounted officers rode into the field after the volley.* N-COUNT: oft N *of*n =salvo

volleyball /vɒlibɔːl/. **Volleyball** is a game in which two teams hit a large ball with their hands backwards and forwards over a high net. If you allow the ball to touch the ground, the other team wins a point. ◆◇◇◇◇ N-UNCOUNT

volt /voʊlt/ **volts.** A **volt** is a unit used to measure the force of an electric current. ◆◇◇◇◇ N-COUNT:

voltage /voʊltɪdʒ/ **voltages.** The **voltage** of an electrical current is its force measured in volts. *The systems are getting smaller and using lower voltages. ...high-voltage power lines.* ◆◇◇◇◇ N-VAR

volte-face /vɒlt fɑːs/ **volte-faces.** If you say that someone's behaviour is a **volte-face**, you mean that they have changed their opinion or decision completely, so that it is the opposite of what it was before; a formal word. *The day's events were a remarkable volte-face.* N-COUNT: usu sing =about-face

voluble /vɒljʊbəl/. If you say that someone is **voluble**, you mean that they talk a lot with great energy and enthusiasm; a formal word. *She was voluble with excitement... Bert is a voluble, gregarious man.* ♦ **volubly** /vɒljʊbli/. *In the next booth along he could see an elderly lady, talking volubly.* ADJ-GRADED; ADV-GRADED: ADV with v

volume /vɒljuːm/ **volumes** ◆◆◆◆◇

1 The **volume** of something is the amount of it that there is. *Senior officials will be discussing how the volume of sales might be reduced. ...the sheer volume of traffic and accidents.* N-COUNT: usu sing, usu N *of*n

2 The **volume** of an object is the amount of space that it contains or occupies. *It is 2,300 metres above sea level, so a given volume of air contains only about one-third as much oxygen as it would at sea level... When egg whites are beaten they can rise to seven or eight times their original volume.* N-COUNT: usu sing

3 A **volume** is a book; a formal use. *...a 125-page volume.* N-COUNT

4 A **volume** is one book in a series of books. *...the first volume of his autobiography.* N-COUNT: usu supp N

5 A **volume** is a collection of several issues of a magazine or journal, for example all the issues for one year. *...bound volumes of the magazine.* N-COUNT: usu with supp

6 The **volume** of a radio, TV, or sound system is the amount of sound it produces. *He turned down the volume... He came to complain about the volume of the music.* N-UNCOUNT

7 If you say that something **speaks volumes** about someone or something, you mean that it gives you a lot of information about them. *What you wear speaks volumes about you... Their absence spoke volumes.* PHRASE: V inflects, oft PHR *about*n

voluminous /vəluːmɪnəs/. If you describe something as **voluminous**, you mean that it is very large in size or quantity; a formal word. *...a voluminous trench coat... The FBI kept a voluminous file on Pablo Picasso.* ADJ-GRADED: usu ADJ n =huge

voluntary /vɒləntri, AM -teri/ ◆◆◆◇◇

1 **Voluntary** actions or activities are done because someone chooses to do them and not because they have been forced to do them. *Attention is drawn to a special voluntary course in Commercial French... The scheme, due to begin next month, will be voluntary.* ♦ **voluntarily** /vɒləntrəli, AM -terɪli/ *I would* ADJ ≠obligatory; ADV:

only leave here voluntarily if there was a big chance to play abroad. ADV with v

2 **Voluntary** work is done by people who are not paid for it, but who do it because they want to do it. *In her spare time she does voluntary work... He'd been working at the local hostel for the handicapped on a voluntary basis.* ADJ: usu ADJ n

3 A **voluntary** worker is someone who does work without being paid for it, because they want to do it. *Apna Arts has achieved more with voluntary workers in three years than most organisations with paid workers have achieved in ten... We depend solely upon our voluntary helpers.* ADJ: usu ADJ n

4 A **voluntary** organization is controlled and organized by the people who have chosen to work for it, often without being paid, rather than receiving help or money from the government. *Some local authorities and voluntary organizations also run workshops for disabled people... It has been largely through the voluntary sector that the needs of victims have been met. ...a voluntary hostel for ex-offenders.* ADJ: ADJ n

volunteer /vɒləntɪəʳ/ **volunteers, volunteering, volunteered** ◆◆◆◇◇

1 A **volunteer** is someone who does work without being paid for it, because they want to do it. *She now helps in a local school as a volunteer three days a week... Mike was a member of the local volunteer fire brigade.* N-COUNT

2 A **volunteer** is someone who offers to do a particular task or job without being forced to do it. *Right. What I want now is two volunteers to come down to the front... Any volunteers?* N-COUNT

3 If you **volunteer** to do something, you offer to do it without being forced to do it. *Aunt Mary volunteered to clean up the kitchen... He volunteered for the army in 1939... She volunteered as a nurse in a soldiers' rest-home... He's volunteered his services as a chauffeur.* VERB V to-inf V *for* n V *as* n V n Also V

4 If you **volunteer** information, you tell someone something without being asked; a formal use. *The room was quiet; no one volunteered any further information... 'They were both great supporters of Franco,' Ryle volunteered... The next week, Phillida volunteered that they were getting on better.* VERB V n V with quote V that

5 A **volunteer** is someone who chooses to join the armed forces, especially in wartime, as opposed to someone who is forced to join by law. *They fought as volunteers with the Afghan guerrillas... Victory in the civil war had been achieved by a mainly volunteer army.* N-COUNT

voluptuous /vəlʌptʃuəs/ ◆◇◇◇◇

1 If you describe a woman as **voluptuous**, you mean that she has large breasts and hips and is considered attractive in a sexual way. *...a voluptuous, well-rounded lady with glossy black hair.* ADJ-GRADED

2 Something that is **voluptuous** gives you a great deal of pleasure from the rich way it is experienced through your senses. *'Opium' is a provocative, sensual, and voluptuous fragrance which makes all your senses vibrate.* ♦ **voluptuously** *She paints voluptuously, breathing through her nostrils.* ♦ **voluptuousness** *It is a magnificent wine a soft voluptuousness more reminiscent of old-fashioned burgundy.* ADJ-GRADED =sensuous; ADV-GRADED; N-UNCOUNT

vomit /vɒmɪt/ **vomits, vomiting, vomited** ◆◇◇◇◇

1 If you **vomit**, food and drink comes back up from your stomach and out through your mouth. *Any product made from cow's milk made him vomit... She began to vomit blood a few days before she died... He vomited up all he had just eaten.* ♦ **vomiting** *Nausea, diarrhoea, and vomiting may accompany migraine.* VERB =be sick V V n V n with *up*; N-UNCOUNT

2 **Vomit** is partly digested food and drink that has come back up from someone's stomach and out through their mouth. N-UNCOUNT =sick

voodoo /vuːduː/. **Voodoo** is a form of religion involving witchcraft practised by some inhabitants of the West Indies, especially Haiti. N-UNCOUNT

voracious /vəreɪʃəs, AM vɔːr-/. If you describe a person, or their appetite for something, as **voracious**, you mean that they want a lot of it; a literary word. *Joseph Smith was a voracious book collector. ...the band's voracious appetite for fun.* ♦ **voraciously** *He read voraciously.* ADJ-GRADED: usu ADJ n =insatiable; ADV-GRADED

vortex /vɔːʳteks/ **vortexes** or **vortices** /vɔːʳtɪsiːz/ ◆◇◇◇◇

1 A **vortex** is a mass of wind or water that spins round so fast that it pulls objects down into its empty centre. *The polar vortex is a system of wintertime winds. ...the spiralling vortex air-flow that slows the plane.* N-COUNT

2 If you refer to a situation as a **vortex**, you feel that you are being forced into it without being able to prevent it. *When marriages break down children are swept into the vortex of their parents' embittered emotions. ...a self-destructive vortex of alcoholic binges and blackouts.* N-COUNT: usu sing, with supp

vote /vout/ **votes, voting, voted** ◆◆◆◆◆

1 A **vote** is a choice made by a particular person or group in a meeting or an election. *He walked to the local polling centre to cast his vote... The government got a massive majority – well over 400 votes... Mr Reynolds was re-elected by 102 votes to 60.* N-COUNT

2 A **vote** is an occasion when a group of people make a decision by each person indicating his or her choice. The choice that most people support is accepted by the group. *Why do you think we should have a vote on that?... They took a vote and decided not to do it.* N-COUNT: usu *a* N in sing

3 The **vote** is the total number of votes or voters in an election, or the number of votes received or cast by a particular group. *Opposition parties won about fifty-five per cent of the vote... The vote was overwhelmingly in favour of the Democratic Party. ...a huge majority of the white male vote.* N-SING: usu *the* N

4 If you have the **vote** in an election, or have a **vote** in a meeting, you have the legal right to indicate your choice. *And of course we didn't even have the vote, did we?... Before that, women did not have a vote at all... People with disabilities have got a vote as well, you know.* N-SING

5 When you **vote**, you indicate your choice officially at a meeting or in an election, for example by raising your hand or writing on a piece of paper. *Two-thirds of the national electorate had the chance to vote in these elections... I mean, are they going to vote for George Bush?... Both chambers plan to vote on that policy before January 15th... The residents of Leningrad voted to restore the city's original name of St Petersburg... The parliament has voted by an overwhelming majority to suspend its declaration of independence... The Bridgeport Common Council voted 9:8 for a five percent tax increase.* ♦ **voting** *Voting began about two hours ago.* VERB V V prep V to-inf V *by* n to-inf/prep V num prep/to-inf; N-UNCOUNT

6 If you **vote** a particular political party or leader, or **vote** yes or no, you make that choice with the vote that you have. *52.5% of those questioned said they'd vote Labour... I probably would have voted that way anyway... A single candidate is put forward and the people vote yes or no.* VERB V n V *yes/no*

7 If a government or other organization **votes** money for something or to do something, they decide to spend the money in that way. *The General Court had voted $250 for a monument to be erected to his memory... The Parliament voted more funds to help maintain American forces.* VERB =allot V n *for/to* n V n to-inf Also V n n

8 If people **vote** someone a particular title, they choose that person to have that title. *His class voted him the man 'who had done the most for Yale.'... Michael has been voted Player of the Year.* VERB =elect V n n

9 See also **block vote**.

10 If you **vote with** your **feet**, you show that you do not support something by leaving the place where it is happening or leaving the organization that is supporting it. *Thousands of citizens are already voting with their feet, and leaving the country... Authors still have power to vote with their feet by leaving to join smaller companies.* PHRASES V inflects

11 If you say **'I vote'** that a particular thing should happen, you are suggesting that this is what should happen; an informal expression. *I vote that we all go to Holland immediately... I vote that you try to pick out the trail for us.* PHR that PRAGMATICS =I suggest

12 One man one vote or **one person one vote** is a system of voting in which every person in a group or country has the right to cast their vote, and in which each individual's vote is counted and has equal value. *Mr Gould called for a move towards 'one man one vote'... The African National Congress insists on a one-man, one-vote system.*

vote down. If people **vote down** a person or their proposal, they reject that person or proposal, usually as a result of a formal vote. *The Congress voted down a motion to change the union's structure... If he demands too much, the unions will vote him down.* PHRASAL VERB; V P n (not pron); V n P

vote in. If people **vote in** a particular person or political party, they give enough votes to that person or party in an official election for them to hold a position of power. *If he fails, then he will have little excuse in the eyes of those who voted him in... The members of the national assembly will vote in a prime minister by a simple majority.* PHRASAL VERB =elect; V n P; V P n (not pron)

vote out. If people **vote out** a particular person or political party, they give that person or party so few votes in an official election that they no longer hold a position of power. *And if the President doesn't make things better, other voters say, we'll vote him out, too... They cannot join forces to vote her out of office. ...Nicaragua, whose people voted out the pro-Soviet Sandinista government.* PHRASAL VERB; V n P; V n P *of* n; V P n (not pron)

vote of confidence, votes of confidence ◆◇◇◇◇

1 A **vote of confidence** is a vote in which members of a group are asked to indicate that they still support the person or group in power, usually the government. *The Indian Prime Minister, V P Singh, lost a vote of confidence in the Indian parliament.* N-COUNT: usu sing

2 A **vote of confidence** is something that you say or do which shows that you approve of or support a person or a group. *The ten-year deal is a vote of confidence in a coal-fired station at a time when such plants face a loss of the market share to gas-fired ones.* N-COUNT: usu sing

vote of no confidence, votes of no confidence. ◆◇◇◇◇ A **vote of no confidence** is a vote in which members of a group are asked to indicate that they do not support the person or group in power, usually the government. *The opposition has called for a vote of no confidence in the government.* N-COUNT: usu sing

vote of thanks, votes of thanks. A **vote of thanks** is an official speech in which the speaker formally thanks a person for doing something. *I would like to propose a vote of thanks to our host.* N-COUNT: usu sing

voter /voʊtəʳ/ **voters.** ◆◆◆◆◇ **Voters** are people who have the legal right to vote in elections, or people who are voting in a particular election. *The turnout was at least 62 percent of registered voters... Austrian voters went to the polls this weekend to elect a successor to the President.* N-COUNT: usu pl

vouch /vaʊtʃ/ **vouches, vouching, vouched**

vouch for PHRASAL VERB

1 If you say that you can or will **vouch for** someone, you mean that you can guarantee their good behaviour. *Kim's mother agreed to vouch for Maria and get her a job.* V P n

2 If you say that you can **vouch for** something, you mean that you have evidence from your own personal experience that it is true or correct. *He cannot vouch for the accuracy of the story.* =swear to; V P n

voucher /vaʊtʃəʳ/ **vouchers.** ◆◆◇◇◇ A **voucher** is a ticket or piece of paper that can be used instead of money to pay for something. *The winners will each receive a voucher for a pair of cinema tickets. ...gift vouchers.* N-COUNT: usu N *for* n, n N

vouchsafe /vaʊtʃseɪf/ **vouchsafes, vouchsafing, vouchsafed.** If you **are vouchsafed** something or it **is vouchsafed** to you, you are given or granted it; a formal word. *As we approached the summit we were vouchsafed a rare vision... Eric gritted his teeth and vouchsafed them a few more drops of brandy... 'He drives like a madman,' was all the information he vouchsafed.* VERB; *be* V-ed n; V n n; V n; Also V n *to* n

vow /vaʊ/ **vows, vowing, vowed** ◆◆◇◇◇

1 If you **vow** to do something, you make a solemn promise or decision that you will do it. *While many models vow to go back to college, few do... I solemnly vowed that someday I would return to live in Europe... 'I'll kill him,' she vowed... They have vowed a quick and decisive response.* VERB; V to-inf; V that; V with quote; V n

2 A **vow** is a solemn promise or decision to do a particular thing. *I made a silent vow to be more careful in the future... I had to admire David's vow that he would leave the programme.* N-COUNT: oft N to-inf, N that =resolution

3 Vows are a particular set of solemn promises and decisions, such as the promises two people make when they are getting married. *I took my marriage vows and kept them. ...a nun who had taken final vows... He had broken his vow of poverty.* N-COUNT: usu pl, with supp =oath

vowel /vaʊəl/ **vowels.** ◆◇◇◇◇ A **vowel** is a sound such as the ones represented in writing by the letters 'a', 'e' 'i', 'o' and 'u', which you pronounce with your mouth open, allowing the air to flow through it. Compare **consonant**. *The vowel in words like 'my' and 'thigh' is not very difficult. ...English vowel sounds.* N-COUNT

vox pop /vɒks pɒp/ **vox pops.** In a radio or television programme, a **vox pop** is an item consisting of a series of short interviews with ordinary members of the public; used mainly in British journalism. *The film also made use of newsreel footage and vox pop.* N-VAR

voyage /vɔɪɪdʒ/ **voyages, voyaging, voyaged** ◆◆◇◇◇

1 A **voyage** is a long journey on a ship or in a spacecraft. *He aims to follow Columbus's voyage to the West Indies. ...the first space shuttle voyage to be devoted entirely to astronomy.* N-COUNT: usu sing, usu with supp =journey

2 To **voyage** to a place means to travel there, especially by sea. *The Greenpeace flagship is voyaging through the Arctic cold of the Barents Sea.* VERB =journey, travel; V prep/adv

♦ **voyager, voyagers** *...fifteenth-century voyagers to the lands now called America and the Caribbean.* N-COUNT

♦ **voyaging** *Our boat would not have been appropriate for ocean voyaging.* N-UNCOUNT: supp N

voyeur /vwaɪɜːʳ, AM vɔɪ-/ **voyeurs**

1 A **voyeur** is someone who gets sexual pleasure from secretly watching other people having sex or from watching them undress. N-COUNT

2 If you describe someone as a **voyeur**, you disapprove of them because you think they enjoy watching other people's sufferings or problems. *The media has made unfeeling voyeurs of all of us.* N-COUNT PRAGMATICS

voyeurism /vwaɪərɪzəm, AM vɔɪɜːr-/

1 Voyeurism is the practice of obtaining sexual pleasure by secretly watching other people having sex or undressing. N-UNCOUNT

2 If you describe someone's behaviour as **voyeurism**, you disapprove of them because you think they enjoy watching other people's sufferings or problems. *The BBC yesterday defended a series featuring dramatic crime reconstructions against suggestions of voyeurism.* N-UNCOUNT PRAGMATICS

voyeuristic /vwaɪərɪstɪk, AM vɔɪ-/

1 Voyeuristic behaviour involves obtaining sexual pleasure from secretly watching other people having sex or undressing. ADJ-GRADED

2 If you describe someone's behaviour as **voyeuristic**, you disapprove of them because you think they enjoy watching other people's sufferings or problems. *We as a society are growing more commercial and voyeuristic all the time.* ADJ-GRADED PRAGMATICS

vs. vs. is a written abbreviation for **versus**. *...England vs. Brazil in the U.S. Cup.* ◆◆◇◇◇

V-sign, V-signs

1 In Britain, a **V-sign** is a rude gesture which is made by sticking up your first two fingers in a V shape, with the palm of your hand facing you. N-COUNT

2 In Britain, a **V-sign** is a gesture which is made by sticking up your first two fingers in a V shape, with the palm of your hand facing away from you, as a sign of victory. *They were waving V signs for victory.* N-COUNT

VSO /viː es oʊ/. **VSO** is a British organization that sends skilled people to developing countries to work on projects that help the local commu- N-PROPER nity. **VSO** is an abbreviation for 'Voluntary Service Overseas'.

vulgar /vʌlgəʳ/ ◆◇◇◇◇

1 If you describe something as **vulgar**, you think it is in bad taste or of poor artistic quality. *I think it's a very vulgar house... The film is tasteless, vulgar and even badly shot... It's vulgar to be famous.* ADJ-GRADED PRAGMATICS =tasteless
♦ **vulgarity** /vʌlgærɪti/ *I hate the vulgarity of this room.* N-UNCOUNT

2 If you describe pictures, gestures, or remarks as **vulgar**, you dislike them because they refer to sex or other bodily functions in a way you find distasteful. *The women laughed coarsely at some vulgar jokes... The lyrics were vulgar.* ADJ-GRADED PRAGMATICS =crude ♦ **vulgarity** *There's a good deal of vulgarity.* N-UNCOUNT

3 If you describe a person or their behaviour as **vulgar**, you mean that they lack taste or behave rudely. *He was a vulgar old man, but he never swore in front of a woman... 'Don't be vulgar,' she reprimanded.* ADJ-GRADED PRAGMATICS =crude ♦ **vulgarity** *It's his vulgarity that I can't take.* N-UNCOUNT

vulnerable /vʌlnərəbᵊl/ ◆◆◆◇◇

1 Someone who is **vulnerable** is weak and without protection, with the result that they are easily hurt physically or emotionally. *Old people are particularly vulnerable members of our society. ...vulnerable children... I consider my daughter very vulnerable.* ADJ-GRADED ♦ **vulnerability** /vʌlnərəbɪlɪti/ **vulnerabilities** *David accepts his own vulnerability.* N-VAR

2 If someone is **vulnerable** to a particular illness, they are more likely to get it than other people. *People with high blood pressure are especially vulnerable to diabetes... As we come to the end of our natural life cycle, we become more vulnerable to the stress of disease.* ADJ-GRADED: usu v-link ADJ *to* n =prone, susceptible ♦ **vulnerability** *Taking long-term courses of certain medicines may increase vulnerability to infection.* N-UNCOUNT

3 If someone is **vulnerable** to doing something wrong, they are easily influenced to do it because they are weak, innocent, or in a difficult position. *Their homelessness made them vulnerable to getting involved in crime. ...a way of spotting people who are especially vulnerable to alcoholism.* ADJ-GRADED: usu v-link ADJ *to*-ing/n

4 Something such as a country or a company that is **vulnerable** is weak, especially economically or financially, and therefore likely to fail. *Hotels and restaurants are acutely vulnerable to recession... Goodyear could be vulnerable in a prolonged economic slump... The company would be in a vulnerable position.* ADJ-GRADED: oft ADJ *to* n

5 When a country or place is **vulnerable**, it is not very well defended and is therefore an easy target to attack. *Their tanks would be vulnerable to attack from the air. ...the latest in a series of attacks on vulnerable targets.* ADJ-GRADED: oft ADJ *to* n ♦ **vulnerability** *...anxieties about the country's vulnerability to invasion.* N-UNCOUNT

vulture /vʌltʃəʳ/ **vultures.** A **vulture** is a large bird which lives in hot countries and eats the flesh of dead animals. ◆◇◇◇◇ N-COUNT

vulva /vʌlvə/ **vulvas.** The **vulva** is the outer part of a woman's sexual organs; a technical term. N-COUNT

vying /vaɪɪŋ/. **Vying** is the present participle of **vie**.

Ww

W, w /dʌbᵊlju:/ **W's, w's**

1 **W** is the twenty-third letter of the English alphabet. N-VAR

2 **W** or **w** is an abbreviation for words beginning with w, such as 'west' or 'watt'.

wacko /wækoʊ/. If you say that someone is **wacko**, you are saying in an unkind way that you think they are strange and eccentric; an informal word. *Lampley was obviously completely wacko.* ADJ PRAGMATICS =mad

wacky /wæki/ **wackier, wackiest;** also spelled **whacky**. If you describe something or someone as **wacky**, you mean that they are eccentric, unusual, and often funny; an informal word. *...a wacky new television comedy series... Wacky ideas are commonplace among space scientists.* ◆◇◇◇◇ ADJ-GRADED =offbeat

wad /wɒd/ **wads.** A **wad** of something such as paper, cloth, or money is a thick, tightly packed bundle or ball of it. *...a wad of cotton soaked in cleaning fluid. ...a wad of banknotes.* ◆◇◇◇◇ N-COUNT: oft N *of* n

wadding /wɒdɪŋ/. **Wadding** is soft material which is put around things to protect them, for example in packing. N-UNCOUNT

waddle /wɒdᵊl/ **waddles, waddling, waddled.** VERB
To **waddle** somewhere means to walk there with short, quick steps, swaying slightly from side to side. A person or animal that waddles usually has short legs and a fat body. *McGinnis pushed himself laboriously out of the chair and waddled to the window... In the evenings, ducks waddle up to the front door to be fed.* V prep/adv Also V

wade /weɪd/ **wades, wading, waded** ◆◇◇◇◇

1 If you **wade** through something that makes it difficult to walk, usually water or mud, you walk through it. *Her mother came to find them, wading across a river to reach them... Spencer waded through the debris of broken chairs and beer bottles... We had to wade the river Genal and then climb out of the valley to get to Juzcar.* VERB V prep/adv V n

2 To **wade through** a lot of information or correspondence means to spend a lot of time and effort reading it or dealing with it. *It has taken a long time to wade through the 'incredible volume' of evidence... It could be a tremendous tool for scientists who have to wade through tons of data.* VERB =trawl through V *through* n

wade in or **wade into.** If someone **wades in** or **wades into** something, they intervene in something in a very determined and forceful way, often without thinking enough about the consequences of their actions. *They don't just listen sympathetically, they wade in with remarks like, 'If I were you ..'... I waded in to help, but got kicked to the ground... Police waded into a crowd of protesters.* PHRASAL VERB V P V P n

wader /weɪdəʳ/ **waders**

1 A **wader** is a bird with long legs and a long neck, which lives near water and feeds on fish. There are several different kinds of waders. N-COUNT

2 **Waders** are long rubber boots which cover all of the legs and are worn by fishermen when they are standing in water. N-COUNT: usu pl

wadi /wɒdi/ **wadis.** A **wadi** is a river in North Africa and Arabia which is dry except in the rainy season; a technical term in geography. N-COUNT

wafer /weɪfəʳ/ **wafers** ◆◇◇◇◇

1 A **wafer** is a thin crisp biscuit which is usually eaten with ice cream. N-COUNT

2 A **wafer** is a circular, thin piece of special bread which the priest gives people to eat in the Christian service of Holy Communion. N-COUNT

wafer-thin

1 **Wafer-thin** means extremely thin and flat. *Cut the fennel into wafer-thin slices. ...how to slice radishes wafer thin.* ADJ: ADJ n, v-link ADJ, ADJ after v

2 If you succeed by a **wafer-thin** margin, you succeed by a very small amount. *...a prime minister with a divided party and a wafer-thin majority.* ADJ =narrow

waffle /wɒfᵊl/ **waffles, waffling, waffled** ◆◇◇◇◇

1 In British English, if you say that someone **waffles**, you are critical of them because they talk or VERB PRAGMATICS write a lot without actually making any clear or important points; an informal use. *My wife often tells me I waffle... There was some bloke waffling about an airline ticket on the phone.* ▸ **Waffle on** means the same as **waffle**. *Whenever I open my mouth I don't half waffle on... That's all I had to say on the subject – we don't want to waffle on about it all day.* ▸ Also a noun. *He writes smug, sanctimonious waffle.* — V; V about n; PHRASAL VERB; V P; V P about n; N-UNCOUNT

2 In American English, if someone **waffles** on an issue or question, they cannot decide what to do or what their opinion is about it. *He's waffled on abortion and gay rights... He kept waffling and finding excuses not to close the deal.* ♦ **waffling** *Bush called this waffling; Clinton calls it an ability to see issues from all sides.* — VERB =waver; V on/about/over n; V; N-UNCOUNT

3 A **waffle** is a thick crisp pancake with squares marked on it. Waffles are usually eaten with syrup poured over them. — N-COUNT

waft /wɒft, wæft/ **wafts, wafting, wafted.** ◆◇◇◇◇ If sounds, scents, or smoke **waft** through the air, or if something such as a light wind **wafts** them, they move gently through the air. *The scent of climbing roses wafts through the window... The music from the party wafts out to the terrace... A slight breeze rose, wafting the heavy scent of flowers past her.* ▸ Also a noun. *A waft of perfume drifted into Ingrid's nostrils.* — V-ERG =drift; V prep/adv; V n prep/adv; N-COUNT: N of n

wag /wæɡ/ **wags, wagging, wagged** ◆◇◇◇◇

1 When a dog **wags** its tail, it repeatedly waves its tail from side to side. *The dog was biting, growling and wagging its tail.* — VERB; V n

2 If you **wag** your finger, you shake it repeatedly and quickly from side to side, usually because you are annoyed with someone. *He wagged a disapproving finger... She wagged a finger under his nose in a taunting gesture.* — VERB =waggle; V n; V n prep

3 If you **wag** your head, you move it from side to side or up and down, often as a gesture of disbelief or unhappiness. *He wags his head unhappily... He wagged his head up and down.* — VERB =shake; V n; V n adv

4 A **wag** is someone who makes jokes; an old-fashioned word that is now used humorously. *He's a bit of a wag, his dad... There was a moose head on the wall. Some wag had put a cigarette in its mouth.* — N-COUNT =wit

5 If **tongues are wagging**, people are gossiping about other people and their behaviour; an informal expression. *What set tongues wagging was the age difference between the two partners.* — PHRASE: V inflects

6 • **the tail is wagging the dog**: see **tail**.

wage /weɪdʒ/ **wages, waging, waged** ◆◆◆◇◇

1 Someone's **wages** are the amount of money that is regularly paid to them for the work that they do. *His wages have gone up... This may end efforts to set a minimum wage well above the poverty line.* — N-COUNT

2 If a person, group, or country **wages** a campaign or a war, they start it and continue it over a period of time. *The government, along with the three factions that had been waging a civil war, signed a peace agreement... They waged a price war.* — VERB =engage in; V n

wage packet, wage packets. People's wages can be referred to as their **wage packet**; used mainly in British English. *They work long hours in order to take home a fat wage packet.* — N-COUNT

wager /weɪdʒəʳ/ **wagers, wagering, wagered** ◆◇◇◇◇

1 If you **wager** on the result of a horse race, football match, or other event, you give someone a sum of money which they give you back with extra money if the result is what you predicted, or which they keep if it is not; used mainly in journalism. *Just because people wagered on the Yankees did not mean that they liked them... Golfers had wagered a good deal of money on Nick Faldo winning the championship.* ▸ Also a noun. *There have been various wagers on certain candidates since the Bishop announce his retirement.* — VERB =bet, gamble; V on n; V n on n; N-COUNT

2 If you say that you will **wager** that something is the case, you mean you are confident that it is the case. *She knew his type, and she was willing to wager that he didn't own the apartment he lived in... I'll wager she'll still make the same impact when she's 70.* — VERB =bet; V that

waggle /wæɡəl/ **waggles, waggling, waggled.** If you **waggle** something, or if something **waggles**, it moves up and down or from side to side with short quick movements. *He was waggling his toes in his socks... His hand waggled beneath Mallory's face.* — V-ERG =wiggle; V n; V

wagon /wæɡən/ **wagons;** also spelled **waggon** in British English. ◆◆◇◇◇

1 A **wagon** is a strong vehicle with four wheels, usually pulled by horses or oxen and used for carrying heavy loads. — N-COUNT =cart

2 A **wagon** is a large container on wheels which is pulled by a train; used mainly in British English. — N-COUNT

3 Someone who is **on the wagon** has stopped drinking alcohol; an informal expression. *I'm on the wagon for a while. Cleaning out my system.* — PHRASE: v-link PHR, PHR after v

4 See also **station wagon**.

wagtail /wæɡteɪl/ **wagtails.** A **wagtail** is a type of small bird which moves its tail quickly up and down as it walks. — N-COUNT

waif /weɪf/ **waifs.** If you refer to a child or young woman as a **waif**, you mean that they are very thin and look as if they have nowhere to live. *She was an emaciated waif with eyes of pure fright... The director wants a waif-like, teenage girl with long, dark hair for the role.* — N-COUNT

wail /weɪl/ **wails, wailing, wailed** ◆◇◇◇◇

1 If someone **wails**, they make long, loud, high-pitched cries which express sorrow or pain. *The women began to wail in mourning... A mother wailing for her lost child.* ▸ Also a noun. *Wails of grief were heard as visitors filed past the site of the disaster.* ♦ **wailing** *Mace still remembers the pitiful wailing of the trapped and the wounded.* — VERB; V; V for n; N-COUNT: oft N of n; N-UNCOUNT

2 If you **wail** something, you say it in a loud, high-pitched voice that shows that you are unhappy or in pain. *'Now look what you've done!' Shirley wailed... Primrose, stupefied by tiredness, began to wail that she was hungry.* — VERB; V with quote; V that; Also V about n

3 If something such as a siren or an alarm **wails**, it makes long, high-pitched, piercing sounds. *Police cars, their sirens wailing, accompanied the lorries... The wind wailed outside the closed windows.* ▸ Also a noun. *The wail of the bagpipe could be heard in the distance.* ♦ **wailing** *Our artillery opened up and we heard a fearful wailing and screeching.* — VERB; V; N-UNCOUNT; N-UNCOUNT

waist /weɪst/ **waists** ◆◆◇◇◇

1 Your **waist** is the middle part of your body where it narrows slightly above your hips. *Ricky kept his arm round her waist... He was stripped to the waist.* ♦ **-waisted** *Sarah looked slender-waisted, fragile and very beautiful.* — N-COUNT: oft poss N; COMB in ADJ-GRADED

2 The **waist** of a garment such as a dress, coat, or pair of trousers is the part of it which covers the middle part of your body. ♦ **-waisted** *...high-waisted dresses.* — N-COUNT; COMB in ADJ-GRADED

waistband /weɪstbænd/ **waistbands.** A **waistband** is a narrow piece of material which is sewn on to a pair of trousers, a skirt, or other item of clothing at the waist in order to strengthen it. — N-COUNT

waistcoat /weɪstkoʊt, weskət/ **waistcoats.** In British English, a **waistcoat** is a sleeveless piece of clothing with buttons, which people wear over a shirt. The American word is **vest**. — ◆◇◇◇◇ N-COUNT

waistline /weɪstlaɪn/ **waistlines**

1 Your **waistline** is your waist measurement. *A passion for cooking does not necessarily have to be bad for your waistline.* — N-COUNT: oft poss N =waist

2 The **waistline** of a piece of clothing is the place where the upper and lower parts are sewn together, which is near to your waist when you wear it. — N-COUNT =waist

wait /weɪt/ **waits, waiting, waited** ◆◆◆◆◆

1 When you **wait** for something or someone, you spend some time, usually doing very little, because you cannot act until that thing happens or that person arrives. *I walk to a street corner and wait for the school bus... Stop waiting for things to happen. Make them happen... I waited to see how she responded... Angus got out of the car to wait... We will have to wait a week or so before we know whether the operation is a success... He told waiting journal-* — VB: no passive; V for n; V for n to-inf; V to-inf; V; V n; V-ing; Also V n for n ists that he did not expect a referendum to be held for several months. ♦ **waiting** The waiting became almost unbearable. N-UNCOUNT

2 A **wait** is a period of time in which you do very little, before something happens or before you can do something or see someone. *...the four-hour wait for the organizers to declare the result.* N-COUNT: usu sing

3 If something **is waiting** for you, it is ready for you to use, have, or do. *There'll be a car waiting for you... When we came home we had a meal waiting for us... Ships with unfurled sails wait to take them aboard... Three-hundred railway wagons were waiting to be unloaded... He had a taxi waiting to take him to the train... The President had his plane waiting, 20 minutes' drive away.* VB: usu cont; V for n; have n V-ing for n; V to-inf; have n V-ing; to-inf; have n V-ing; Also V

4 If you say that something can **wait**, you mean that it is not important or urgent and so you will deal with it or do it later. *I want to talk to you, but it can wait... Any changes will have to wait until sponsors can be found.* VB: no cont; V

5 You can use **wait** when you are telling someone something that you expect them to find exciting, reassuring, or threatening. *If you think this all sounds very exciting, just wait until you read the book... As soon as you get some food inside you, you'll feel more cheerful. Just you wait.* VB: only imper; V until cl/n; V

6 **Wait** is used in expressions such as **wait a minute**, **wait a second**, and **wait a moment** to interrupt someone when they are speaking, for example because you object to what they are saying or because you want them to repeat something. *'Wait a minute!' he broke in. 'This is not giving her a fair hearing!'* VB: only imper; PRAGMATICS; =hold on, hang on; V n

7 If an employee **waits** on you, for example in a restaurant or hotel, they take orders from you and bring you what you want. *There were plenty of servants to wait on her... Each student is expected to wait at table for one week each semester.* VERB; V on n; V at n

8 If you say that you **can't wait** to do something or **can hardly wait** to do it, you are emphasizing that you are very excited about it and eager to do it; used in spoken English. *We can't wait to get started... It's gonna be great. I can hardly wait... I could hardly wait to get out of there.* PHRASES; oft PHR to-inf; PRAGMATICS

9 In British English, you say **'wait for it'** to stop someone from doing something too soon because you have not yet given them the command to do it. *Arms bend. Arms upward. Wait for it. Stretch.* CONVENTION; PRAGMATICS

10 You can use **'wait for it'** to indicate that you are about to say something that is amusing or surprising; an informal British expression. *A cool $500,000 is to be spent on obtaining genuine 17th-century air from the inside of, wait for it, an occupied lead coffin.* PHR with group; PRAGMATICS

11 If you tell someone to **wait and see**, you tell them that they must be patient or that they must not worry about what is going to happen in the future because they have no control over it. *We'll have to wait and see what happens. ...a wait-and-see attitude.* oft PHR n, PHR wh

12 If you say to someone **'What are you waiting for?'** you are telling them to hurry up and do something. *Well, what are you waiting for? Do I have to ask you for a kiss?* PRAGMATICS

13 • **an accident waiting to happen**: see **accident**. • **ready and waiting**: see **ready**.

wait around; the form **wait about** is also used in British English. If you **wait around** or **wait about**, you stay in the same place, usually doing very little, because you cannot act before something happens or before someone arrives. *The attacker may have been waiting around for an opportunity to strike... I waited around to speak to the doctor. ...the ghastly tedium of waiting about at the airport.* PHRASAL VERB; =hang around; V P for n; V P to-inf; V P

wait in. If you **wait in**, you deliberately stay at home and do not go out, for example because someone is coming to see you; used mainly in British English. *If I'd waited in for you I could have waited all day... There's no need to wait in all day.* PHRASAL VERB; =stay in; V P for n; V P n

wait on. In informal American English, if you **are waiting on** something, you are waiting for it to happen, for example before you do or decide anything. *Since then I've been waiting on events and till now fortune hasn't favored us... We cannot wait on the government to make changes at its own pace.* PHRASAL VERB; =await; V P n

wait up PHRASAL VERB

1 If you **wait up**, you deliberately do not go to bed, especially because you are expecting someone to return home late at night. *I hope he doesn't expect you to wait up for him... Don't wait up.* =stay up; V P for n; V P

2 In informal American English, if you ask someone to **wait up**, you are asking them to go more slowly or to stop and wait for you. *I was running down the hill shouting, 'Michael, Michael, man, wait up'.* usu imper; =wait; V P

waiter /weɪtəʳ/ **waiters.** A **waiter** is a man who works in a restaurant, serving people with food and drink. • See also **dumb waiter**. ◆◆◇◇◇ N-COUNT

waiting game, waiting games. If you play a **waiting game**, you deal with a situation by deliberately not doing anything, because you believe you will gain an advantage by acting later, or because you are waiting to see how the other people involved are going to act. *He's playing a waiting-game. He'll hope to hang on as long as possible until the pressure is off.* N-COUNT: usu sing

waiting list, waiting lists. A **waiting list** is a list of people who have asked for something which cannot be given to them immediately, for example medical treatment, housing, or training, and who must therefore wait until it is available. *There were 20,000 people on the waiting list for a home.* ◆◇◇◇◇ N-COUNT: oft on N

waiting room, waiting rooms; also spelled **waiting-room.** A **waiting room** is a room in a place such as a railway station or a doctor's surgery, where people can sit down while they wait. ◆◇◇◇◇ N-COUNT

waitress /weɪtrəs/ **waitresses, waitressing, waitressed** ◆◇◇◇◇

1 A **waitress** is a woman who works in a restaurant, serving people with food and drink. N-COUNT

2 A woman who **waitresses** works in a restaurant serving food and drink. *She had been working in a pub, cooking and waitressing.* ♦ **waitressing** *She does a bit of waitressing as a part-time job.* VERB; V; N-UNCOUNT

waive /weɪv/ **waives, waiving, waived** ◆◇◇◇◇

1 If you **waive** your right to something, for example legal representation, or if someone else **waives** it, you no longer have the right to receive it. *He pled guilty to the murders of three boys and waived his right to appeal.* VERB; V n

2 If someone **waives** a rule, they decide not to enforce it in a particular situation. *The art gallery waives admission charges on Sundays... The authorities had agreed to waive normal requirements for permits to cross the border.* VERB; V n

waiver /weɪvəʳ/ **waivers.** A **waiver** is when a person, government, or organization agrees to give up a right or claim or decides not to enforce a particular rule or law. *...a waiver of constitutional rights... Non-members do not qualify for the tax waiver normally applied to members.* ◆◇◇◇◇ N-COUNT: usu with supp

wake /weɪk/ **wakes, waking, woke, woken;** the form **waked** is used in American English for the past tense. ◆◆◆◇◇

1 When you **wake** or when someone or something **wakes** you, you become conscious again after being asleep. *It was cold and dark when I woke at 6.30... Bob woke slowly to sunshine pouring in his window... She woke to find her dark room lit by flashing lights... She went upstairs to wake Milton.* V-ERG; V; V to n; V to-inf; V n

► **Wake up** means the same as **wake**. *One morning I woke up and felt something was wrong... At dawn I woke him up and said we were leaving.* PHRASAL VERB; ERG; V P; V n P

2 The **wake** of a boat or other object moving in water is the track of waves that it makes behind it as it moves through the water. *The ride was smooth until they got into the merchant ship's wake... Dolphin sometimes play in the wake of the boats.* N-COUNT: usu sing, with poss

3 A **wake** is a gathering of people who have collected together to mourn someone's death. *A funeral wake was in progress.* N-COUNT: usu sing

4 If one thing follows **in the wake of** another, it happens after the other thing is over, often as a re- PHR-PREP; =following sult of it. *The governor has enjoyed a huge surge in the polls in the wake of last week's convention... The company is in bankruptcy proceedings in the wake of a strike that began last spring.*

5 Your **waking hours** are the times when you are awake rather than asleep. *It was work which consumed most of his waking hours... Most of their waking hours are spent eating.* — PHRASES usu with poss

6 If you leave something or someone **in** your **wake**, you leave them behind you as you go. *Adam stumbles on, leaving a trail of devastation in his wake... The tanks left burning vehicles in their wake as they ploughed through makeshift barricades.* — PHR after v

7 If you are following **in** someone's **wake** , you are following them or their example. *In his wake came a waiter wheeling a trolley. ...the endless stream of female artists who released albums in her wake.* — PHR after v

wake up. If something such as an activity **wakes** you **up**, it makes you more alert and ready to do things after you have been lazy or inactive. *A cool shower wakes up the body and boosts circulation.* • See also **wake** 1. — PHRASAL VERB; V P n (not pron); Also V n P

wake up to. If you **wake up to** something, you become aware of it. *Lithuanians are waking up to a world of increasing shortages... People should wake up to the fact that people with disabilities have got a vote as well.* — PHRASAL VERB; V P P n

wakeful /weɪkfʊl/. Someone who is **wakeful** finds it difficult to get to sleep and wakes up very often when they should be sleeping. *Wakeful babies will often continue to need little sleep as they grow older.* ♦ **wakefulness** *It is never a good idea to take sleeping tablets regularly for this kind of wakefulness.* — ADJ-GRADED; N-UNCOUNT

waken /weɪkən/ **wakens, wakening, wakened.** When you **waken**, or when someone or something **wakens** you, you wake from sleep; a literary word. *The noise of a door slamming wakened her... Women are much more likely than men to waken because of noise.* ▶ **Waken up** means the same as **waken**. *'Drink this coffee – it will waken you up.'... If you do waken up during the night, start the exercises again.* — V-ERG =wake; V n; V; PHRASAL VERB ERG; V n P; V P

walk /wɔːk/ **walks, walking, walked** ♦♦♦♦♦

1 When you **walk**, you move forward by putting one foot in front of the other on the ground at a regular, fairly slow pace. *Rosanna and Forbes walked in silence for some while... We walked into the foyer... She turned and walked away... They would stop the car and walk a few steps... When I was your age I walked five miles to school.* — VERB; V; V prep/adv; V n; V n *to* n

2 A **walk** is a journey that you make by walking, usually for pleasure. *I went for a walk... He often took long walks in the hills.* — N-COUNT

3 A **walk** of a particular distance is the distance which a person has to walk to get somewhere. *It was only a three-mile walk to Kabul from there... The church is a short walk from Piazza Dante.* — N-SING: supp N, N *of* n

4 A **walk** is a route suitable for walking along for pleasure. *There is a 2 mile coastal walk from Craster to Newton.* — N-COUNT

5 **A walk** is the action of walking rather than running. *She slowed to a steady walk.* — N-SING: *a* N

6 Someone's **walk** is the way that they walk. *George, despite his great height and gangling walk, was a keen dancer.* — N-SING: poss N =gait

7 If you **walk** someone somewhere, you walk there with them in order to show politeness or to make sure that they get there safely. *She walked me to my car... 'What a nice gentleman you are, to walk Hilary home,' her mother said.* — VERB =escort; V n prep/adv

8 If you **walk** your dog, you take it for a walk in order to keep it healthy. *I walk my dog each evening around my local streets.* — VERB; V n

9 • to be **walking on air**: see **air**. • to **walk tall**: see **tall**.

walk away. If you **walk away** from a problem or a difficult situation, you do nothing about it or do not face any bad consequences from it. *The most appropriate strategy may simply be to walk away from the problem... No one knows you're a part of this. You can just walk away.* — PHRASAL VERB; V P *from* n; V P

walk away with. If you **walk away with** something such as a prize, you win it or achieve it very easily; used mainly in journalism. *Enter our competition and you could walk away with £1,000.* — PHRASAL VERB =walk off with; V P P n

walk in on. If you **walk in on** someone, you enter the room that they are in while they are doing something private, and this creates an embarrassing situation. *His wife walked in on him making love.* — PHRASAL VERB; V P P n

walk into — PHRASAL VERB

1 If you **walk into** an unpleasant situation, you become involved in it without expecting to, especially because you have been careless. *He's walking into a situation that he absolutely can't control.* — V P n

2 If you **walk into** a job, you manage to get it very easily; an informal expression. *When I left school, I could walk into any job.* — V P n

walk off with — PHRASAL VERB

1 If someone **walks off with** something that does not belong to them, they take it without permission; an informal expression. *I'll bet you walked off with my coat, too.* — =go off with; V P P n

2 If you **walk off with** something such as a prize, you win it or achieve it very easily; used mainly in journalism. *The delighted pensioner walked off with a £1,000 prize.* — =walk away with; V P P n

walk out — PHRASAL VERB

1 If you **walk out** of a meeting, a performance, or an unpleasant situation, you leave it suddenly, usually in order to show that you are angry or bored. *Several dozen councillors walked out of the meeting in protest... Mr. Mason walked out during the performance.* — V P *of* n; V P

2 If someone **walks out** on their family or their partner, they leave them suddenly and go to live somewhere else. *Her husband walked out on her... She had walked out and gone to live in Bath with her granny.* — V P *on* n; V P

3 If workers **walk out**, they stop doing their work for a period of time, usually in order to try to get better pay or conditions for themselves. *Nationwide industrial action began earlier this week, when staff at most banks walked out.* — =go on strike; V P

walk over. If someone **walks over** you, they treat you very badly; an informal expression. *Do you think you can walk over me? Well, you won't, ever!... You let your children walk all over you.* — PHRASAL VERB; V P n

walkabout /wɔːkəbaʊt/ **walkabouts.** A **walkabout** is a walk by a king, queen, or other important person through a public place in order to meet people in an informal way; used mainly in British English. *He was ambushed by angry protesters during a walkabout in Bolton.* • If a king, queen, or other important person **goes walkabout** or **goes on a walkabout**, he or she walks through crowds in a public place in order to meet people in an informal way; used mainly in British English. *The Prime Minister insisted on going walkabout in Belfast.* — N-COUNT; PHRASE: V inflects

walker /wɔːkəʳ/ **walkers** ♦◇◇◇◇

1 A **walker** is a person who walks, especially in the countryside for pleasure or in order to keep healthy. — N-COUNT

2 A **walker** is a special kind of frame which is designed to help babies or disabled or ill people to walk. *She eventually used a cane, then a walker, and finally was confined to the house.* — N-COUNT: oft supp N

walkie-talkie /wɔːki tɔːki/ **walkie-talkies.** A **walkie-talkie** is a small portable radio which you can talk into and hear messages through so that you can communicate with someone far away. — N-COUNT

walking /wɔːkɪŋ/ ♦◇◇◇◇

1 **Walking** is the activity of taking walks for exercise or pleasure, especially in the country. *Recently I've started to do a lot of walking and cycling. ...a walking holiday.* — N-UNCOUNT =hiking

2 You can use **walking** in expressions like **a walking disaster** or **a walking dictionary** in order to emphasize in a humorous way a particular attribute that someone has, for example the fact that they cause a lot of disasters or that they know a lot of difficult words. *He was a walking encyclopae-* — ADJ: ADJ n; PRAGMATICS *dia... If you ever get any ailments there's no problem as he is like a walking chemist's shop.*

walking stick, walking sticks. A **walking stick** is a long wooden stick which a person can lean on while walking. N-COUNT

Walkman /wɔːkmən/ **Walkmans.** A **Walkman** is a small cassette player with very light headphones which people carry around so that they can listen to music while they are doing something. **Walkman** is a trademark. ◆◇◇◇◇ N-COUNT =personal stereo

walk of life, walks of life. The **walk of life** that you come from is the position that you have in society and the kind of job you have. *One of the greatest pleasures of this job is meeting people from all walks of life.* ◆◇◇◇◇ N-COUNT: usu pl =background

walk-on. A **walk-on** part in a play or film is a very small part which usually does not involve any speaking. *He and his family have walk-on parts in the latest film.* ◆◇◇◇◇ ADJ: ADJ n =bit

walkout /wɔːkaʊt/ **walkouts** ◆◇◇◇◇

1 A **walkout** is a strike. N-COUNT

2 If there is a **walkout** during a meeting, some or all of the people attending it leave in order to show their disapproval of something that has happened at the meeting. *The commission's proceedings have been wrecked by tantrums and walkouts.* N-COUNT

walkover /wɔːkoʊvəʳ/ **walkovers.** If you say that a competition or contest is a **walkover**, you mean that it is won very easily. N-COUNT: usu sing

walk-up, walk-ups. In American English, a **walk-up** is a tall apartment block which has no lift. You can also refer to an apartment in such a block as a **walk-up**. *She lives in a tiny fifth floor walk-up in New York's East Village.* ◆◇◇◇◇ N-COUNT

walkway /wɔːkweɪ/ **walkways.** A **walkway** is a passage or pathway for pedestrians to use. Walkways are often raised above the ground. ◆◇◇◇◇ N-COUNT

wall /wɔːl/ **walls, walling, walled** ◆◆◆◆◆

1 A **wall** is one of the vertical sides of a building or room. *Kathryn leaned against the wall of the church... The bedroom walls would be papered with chintz... She checked the wall clock.* ♦ **-walled** *...a glass-walled elevator... Our bedroom was white-walled with yellow silk curtains.* N-COUNT; COMB in ADJ

2 A **wall** is a long narrow vertical structure made of stone or brick that surrounds or divides an area of land. *He sat on the wall in the sun... The well is surrounded by a wall only 12 inches high.* N-COUNT

3 The **wall** of something that is hollow is its side. *He ran his fingers along the inside walls of the box.* N-COUNT: with supp

4 A **wall** of something is a large amount of it forming a high vertical barrier. *She gazed at the wall of books... I was just hit by a wall of water.* N-COUNT: with supp, usu N *of* n

5 You can describe something as a **wall** of a particular kind when it acts as a barrier preventing people from understanding something or someone. *The police say they met the usual wall of silence... Despite its prevalence, schizophrenia has existed behind a wall of secrecy for years.* N-COUNT: with supp, usu N *of* n

6 See also **cavity wall, dry-stone wall, fly-on-the-wall, hole-in-the-wall, off-the-wall, retaining wall, sea wall, stonewall, wall-to-wall.**

7 If you say that you **are banging your head against a wall**, you are emphasizing that you are frustrated because someone is stopping you from making progress in something; an informal expression. *I appealed for help but felt I was always banging my head against a wall... I wondered if I was banging my head against a brick wall.* PHRASES V inflects, usu cont PRAGMATICS

8 If you have your **back to the wall**, you are in a very difficult situation and can see no way out of it; an informal expression. *Their threat to hire replacement workers has the union with its back to the wall.* *back* inflects

9 If you say that you **are climbing the walls**, you are emphasizing that you feel very frustrated, nervous, or anxious. *Sitting at home would only have had him climbing the walls with frustration.* V inflects, usu cont PRAGMATICS

10 If you say that something or someone **is driving** you **up the wall**, you are emphasizing that they annoy and irritate you; an informal expression. *The heat is driving me up the wall... I sang in the bath and drove my parents up the wall.* V inflects PRAGMATICS =drive mad

11 If a person or company **goes to the wall**, they lose all their money and their business fails; an informal expression. *Even quite big companies are going to the wall these days.* V inflects

12 ● **fly on the wall**: see **fly**. ● **the writing is on the wall**: see **writing**.

wall in. If someone or something **is walled in**, they are surrounded or enclosed by a wall or barrier. *He is walled in by a mountain of papers in his cluttered Broadway office.* PHRASAL VERB usu passive *be* V-ed P

wall off. If part of a place **is walled off**, it is separated from the rest of the place by a wall. *The side alley was walled off from the back garden. ...a ring of cliffs that walled off the surrounding wilderness.* PHRASAL VERB *be* V-ed P *from* n; V P n (not pron)

wall up. If someone **walls up** a room, or if someone **is walled up** in it, every exit to the room is blocked by walls so that nobody can get in or out. *They had walled up her room because of the fear that things might be infected.* PHRASAL VERB V P n (not pron) Also V n P

wallaby /wɒləbi/ **wallabies.** A **wallaby** is an animal similar to a small kangaroo. Wallabies live in Australia and New Guinea. N-COUNT

wallcovering /wɔːlkʌvərɪŋ/ **wallcoverings;** also spelled **wall covering**. **Wallcovering** is material such as wallpaper that is used to decorate the walls on the inside of a building. N-VAR

walled /wɔːld/. If an area of land or a city is **walled**, it is surrounded or enclosed by a wall. *The city was walled and built upon a rock. ...a walled rose garden.* ◆◇◇◇◇ ADJ

wallet /wɒlɪt/ **wallets.** A **wallet** is a small flat folded case, usually made of leather or plastic, where you can keep banknotes and credit cards. ◆◇◇◇◇ N-COUNT: oft poss N

wallflower /wɔːlflaʊəʳ/ **wallflowers**

1 A **wallflower** is a plant that is grown in gardens and has sweet-smelling yellow, red, orange, or purple flowers. N-COUNT

2 If you say that someone is a **wallflower**, you mean that they are shy and do not get involved in dancing or talking to people at social events. *I was something of a wallflower; I was terribly shy.* N-COUNT

wallop /wɒləp/ **wallops, walloping, walloped.** To **wallop** someone or something means to hit them very hard, often causing a dull thudding sound; an informal use. *Once, she walloped me over the head with a frying pan... There was a thud as a chunk of rubber flew out and walloped the mechanic.* ► Also a noun. *With one brutal wallop, Clarke flattened him.* VERB =clout V n prep; V n; N-COUNT: usu sing; SOUND

wallow /wɒloʊ/ **wallows, wallowing, wallowed** ◆◇◇◇◇

1 If you say that someone **is wallowing in** an unpleasant situation, you are criticizing them for being deliberately unhappy. *His tired mind continued to wallow in self-pity... I wanted only to wallow in my own grief.* VERB PRAGMATICS V *in* n

2 If a person or animal **wallows** in water or mud, they lie or roll about in it slowly for pleasure. *Never have I had such a good excuse for wallowing in deep warm baths... Dogs love splashing in mud and hippos wallow in it.* VERB V *in* n

wallpaper /wɔːlpeɪpəʳ/ **wallpapers, wallpapering, wallpapered** ◆◆◇◇◇

1 **Wallpaper** is thick coloured or patterned paper that is used for covering and decorating the walls of rooms. *...the wallpaper in the bedroom.* N-MASS

2 If someone **wallpapers** a room, they cover the walls with wallpaper. *We were going to wallpaper that room anyway. ...a wallpapered bedroom.* VERB V n; V-ed

3 If you describe music, television, or art as **wallpaper**, you are critical of it because there is nothing interesting or difficult to understand about it, so that people find it pleasant and soothing but do not pay any attention to it. *...bland, wallpaper music.* N-UNCOUNT: oft N n PRAGMATICS

Wall Street. **Wall Street** is a street in New York where the Stock Exchange and important banks are. **Wall Street** is often used to refer to the financial business carried out there and to the people who work there. *On Wall Street, stocks* ◆◆◆◆◇ N-PROPER *closed at their second highest level today... Wall Street seems to be ignoring other indications that consumers are spending less.*

wall-to-wall
1 A **wall-to-wall** carpet covers the floor of a room completely. ADJ: usu ADJ n
2 You can use **wall-to-wall** to describe something that fills or seems to fill all the available space. *...television's wall-to-wall soccer coverage... There were wall-to-wall people, all invited guests and celebrities.* ADJ: usu ADJ n

wally /wɒli/ **wallies.** In British English, if you refer to someone as a **wally** you think that they are stupid or foolish; an informal word. N-COUNT PRAGMATICS =twit

walnut /wɔːlnʌt/ **walnuts** ◆◇◇◇◇
1 **Walnuts** are edible nuts which have a wrinkled shape and a very hard round shell that is light brown in colour. *...chopped walnuts.* N-VAR
2 A **walnut tree** or a **walnut** is a tree on which walnuts grow. ► **Walnut** is the wood of this tree. *The stool comes in several sizes in walnut or mahogany. ...a handsome walnut desk.* N-VAR N-UNCOUNT

walrus /wɔːlrəs/ **walruses.** A **walrus** is an animal which lives in the sea. It has long whiskers and two tusks pointing downwards. N-COUNT

waltz /wɔːlts/ **waltzes, waltzing, waltzed** ◆◇◇◇◇
1 A **waltz** is a piece of music with a rhythm of three beats in each bar, which people can dance to. *...Tchaikovsky's 'Waltz of the Flowers'.* N-COUNT: oft in names
2 A **waltz** is a dance in which two people hold each other and move around the floor doing special steps in time to waltz music. *Arthur Murray taught the foxtrot, the tango and the waltz.* N-COUNT
3 If you **waltz** with someone, you dance a waltz with them. *'Waltz with me,' he said, taking her hand... Couples are waltzing round the wooden floor... She seized her mother round the waist and waltzed her round the kitchen.* V-RECIP; V *with* n; pl-n V adv/prep; V n prep (non-recip); Also V
4 If you say that someone **waltzes** somewhere, you mean that they do something in a relaxed and confident way; an informal use. *She's probably got herself a new man and gone waltzing off with him... My cousin Henry, he waltzes in a few months later at three times the salary.* VERB; V adv/prep

wan /wɒn/. If you describe someone as **wan**, you mean that they look pale and tired; a literary word. *He looked wan and tired... All she could manage was a thin, wan smile.* ♦ **wanly** *Marcia smiled wanly and shook her head.* ◆◇◇◇◇ ADJ-GRADED =washed out; ADV-GRADED: usu ADV after v

wand /wɒnd/ **wands.** A **wand** is the same as a **magic wand**. *You can't simply wave a wand and get rid of nuclear weapons.* ◆◇◇◇◇ N-COUNT

wander /wɒndəʳ/ **wanders, wandering, wandered** ◆◆◇◇◇
1 If you **wander** in a place, you walk around there in a casual way, often without intending to go in any particular direction. *When he got bored he wandered around the fair... They wandered off in the direction of the nearest store... Those who do not have relatives to return to are left to wander the streets and sleep rough.* ► Also a noun. *A wander around any market will reveal stalls piled high with vegetables.* VERB; V prep/adv; V n; N-SING: a N =stroll
2 If a person or animal **wanders** from a place where they are supposed to stay, they move away from the place without going in a particular direction. *Because Mother is afraid we'll get lost, we aren't allowed to wander far... To keep their bees from wandering, beekeepers feed them sugar solutions.* VERB =stray; V adv/prep; V
3 If your mind **wanders** or your thoughts **wander**, you stop concentrating on something and start thinking about other things. *His mind would wander, and he would lose track of what he was doing... Jarvis found his attention wandering... Grace allowed her mind to wander to other things.* VERB =stray; V; V prep/adv
4 If your eyes **wander**, you stop looking at one thing and start looking around at other things. *His eyes wandered restlessly around the room... His eyes kept wandering to the picture... Read their body language. Are their eyes wandering or are they drumming the desk with their fingers?* VERB; V prep/adv; V

wanderer /wɒndərəʳ/ **wanderers.** A **wanderer** is a person who travels around rather than settling in one place. N-COUNT =drifter

wandering /wɒndərɪŋ/. **Wandering** is used to describe people who travel around rather than staying in one place for a long time; a literary use. *...a band of wandering musicians.* ADJ: ADJ n =itinerant

wanderings /wɒndərɪŋz/. Someone's **wanderings** are journeys that they make from place to place without staying in one place for a long time. *On his wanderings he's picked up Spanish, Italian, French and a smattering of Russian.* N-PLURAL: usu with poss

wanderlust /wɒndəʳlʌst/. Someone who has **wanderlust** has a strong desire to travel. *His wanderlust would not allow him to stay long in one spot.* N-UNCOUNT

wane /weɪn/ **wanes, waning, waned** ◆◇◇◇◇
1 If a condition, attitude, or emotion **wanes**, it becomes gradually weaker, often so that it eventually disappears. *While his interest in these sports began to wane, a passion for rugby developed. ...her mother's waning strength.* ● **wax and wane** see **wax**. VERB =fade; V; V-ing
2 If a condition, attitude, or emotion is **on the wane**, it is becoming weaker. *The influence of the Communist Party was clearly on the wane... In 1982, with his career prospects on the wane, he sold a script for £5,000.* PHRASE: v-link PHR =diminishing
3 When the moon **is waning**, it is showing a smaller area of brightness each day as it changes from a full moon to a new moon. *The moon was waning, and each day it rose later. ...a sky silvered by a waning moon.* VB: usu cont; V; V-ing

wangle /wæŋgəl/ **wangles, wangling, wangled.** If you **wangle** something that you want, you manage to get it by being clever or persuasive; an informal word. *We managed to wangle a few days' leave... He had wangled his way into the country without a visa... I asked the Captain to wangle us three tickets to Athens... Amanda had wangled a job for Robyn with the council.* VERB; V n; V *way* prep/adv; V n n; V n *for* n

wank /wæŋk/ **wanks, wanking, wanked.** In British English, to **wank** means to masturbate; a rude and offensive word. ► Also a noun. VERB; N-SING

wanker /wæŋkəʳ/ **wankers.** In British English, if someone calls a man a **wanker**, they do not like him and they think he is very stupid or unpleasant; a rude and offensive word which you should avoid using. N-COUNT PRAGMATICS

wanna /wɒnə/. **Wanna** is used in written English to represent the words **want to** when they are pronounced informally. *I wanna be married to you. Do you wanna be married to me?*

wannabe /wɒnəbiː/ **wannabes;** also spelled **wannabee**. If you call someone a **wannabe**, you are saying in an unkind way that they are trying very hard to be like another person or group of people; an informal word. *...a feeble James Dean wannabe. ...wannabe musicians who don't know which way up to hold their guitars.* N-COUNT: usu n N, N n PRAGMATICS

want /wɒnt/ **wants, wanting, wanted** ◆◆◆◆◆
1 If you **want** something, you feel a desire or a need for it. *I want a drink... Ian knows exactly what he wants in life and is determined to get it... People wanted to know who this talented designer was... They began to want their father to be the same as other daddies... They didn't want people staring at them as they sat on the lawn, so they put up high walls... He wanted his power recognised... I want my car this colour... I want my boy alive. I don't want him to be just a painful memory.* VB: no cont, no passive; V n; V to-inf; V n to-inf; V n -ing; V n -ed; V n n; V n adj/prep
2 You can say that you **want** to say something to indicate that you are about to say it. *I want to say how really delighted I am that you're having a baby... Look, I wanted to apologize for today. I think I was a little hard on you.* VB: no cont, no passive PRAGMATICS; V to-inf
3 If you ask someone if they **want** something or **want** to do something, you are offering them something or inviting them to do something. *Do you want another cup of coffee?... Do you want to leave your bike here?* VB: no cont, no passive PRAGMATICS; V n; V to-inf
4 If you say to someone that you **want** something or you **want** them to do something, or ask them if VB: no cont, no passive PRAGMATICS

they **want** to do it, you are firmly telling them what you want or what you want them to do. *I want an explanation from you, Jeremy... If you have a problem with that, I want you to tell me right now... Do you want to tell me what all this is about?... I want my money back!* V n / V n to-inf / V to-inf / V n adv/prep

5 If you say that something **wants** doing, you think that it needs to be done; used mainly in informal British English. *The windows wanted cleaning... Her hair wants cutting.* VB: no cont, no passive =need V -ing

6 If you tell someone that they **want** to do a particular thing, you are advising them to do it; an informal use. *You want to be very careful not to have a man like Crevecoeur for an enemy... You want to look where you're going, mate.* VB: no cont, no passive PRAGMATICS =ought V to-inf

7 If someone **is wanted** by the police, the police are searching for them because they are thought to have committed a crime. *They were wanted by the police... He has killed many in his time, and is wanted in at least three countries... He was wanted for the murder of a magistrate.* ♦ **wanted** *He is one of the most wanted criminals in Europe.* VB: usu passive be V-ed / be V-ed for n / ADJ-GRADED: ADJ n

8 If you **want** someone, you have a great desire to have sex with them. *Come on, darling. I want you.* VERB V n

9 If a child **is wanted**, its mother or another person loves it and is willing to look after it. *Children should be wanted and planned... I want this baby very much, because it certainly will be the last.* VERB be V-ed / V n

10 If someone **wants** you in a particular place or role, they desire you to be in that place or role. *Albie wants you in his office... They didn't want her as attorney general... This is my territory. I want you out of here.* VB: no cont V n prep/adv

11 A **want of** something is a lack of it; a formal use. *...a want of manners and charm... The men were daily becoming weaker from want of rest.* N-SING: also no det, N of n =lack

12 **Want** is the same as poverty; a formal word. *He said they were fighting for freedom of speech, freedom of worship, and freedom from want.* N-UNCOUNT

13 Your **wants** are the things that you want. *She couldn't lift a spoon without a servant anticipating her wants and getting it for her... Supermarkets often claim that they are responding to the wants of consumers by providing packaged foods.* N-PLURAL: usu with poss

14 If you do something **for want of** something else, you do it because the other thing is not available or not possible. *Many of them had gone into teaching for want of anything better to do... There was another emotion, and for want of a better word he called it grief.* PHRASES PHR n, PHR with v

15 You say **if you want** when you are making or agreeing to an offer or suggestion in a casual way. *Mary says you're welcome to stay the night if you want... 'Do you want to go through it all?'—'Yeah, if you want.'* PHR with cl PRAGMATICS

16 People sometimes say '**I don't want to** be rude', for example, or '**without wanting to** be rude' as a way of apologising or warning you in advance when they are going to say something which they think might upset, annoy, or worry you. *'I don't want to appear big-headed,' explains Loubet, 'but I would say there is a 95% chance of success.'... Without wanting to sound mean about it, these things all have to come from a budget.* PHR inf PRAGMATICS

17 If you say to someone **'what do you want?'**, you are asking them in a rather rude or angry way why they have come to the place where you are or why they want to speak to you. *'What do you want!' she whispered savagely. 'Get out.'... 'Bernie's been on the 'phone.'—'What does he want?'* PRAGMATICS

want out. If you **want out**, you no longer want to be involved in a plan, project, or situation that you are part of; an informal expression. *We've had enough, John. We want out... I just want out of the relationship.* PHRASAL VERB V P / V P of n

wanting /wɒntɪŋ/. If you find something or someone **wanting**, they are not of as high a standard as you think they should be. *He analysed his game and found it wanting... Eleanor was scrutinized, too, and often found wanting... He is wanting in moral constraints.* ADJ-GRADED: v-link ADJ, oft ADJ in n =deficient

wanton /wɒntən/ ◆◇◇◇◇

1 A **wanton** action deliberately causes harm, damage, or waste without having any reason to. *...this unnecessary and wanton destruction of our environment?... Wanton violence is now becoming a regular feature of urban life.* ♦ **wantonly** *His diaries were wantonly destroyed.* ADJ: usu ADJ n / ADV-GRADED: ADV with v

2 If someone describes a woman as **wanton**, they disapprove of her because she behaves in an immoral or immodest way. *It is all right for a man to be sexual but a woman behaving in the same way is still considered wanton and a tart.* ADJ-GRADED PRAGMATICS

war /wɔːʳ/ **wars** ◆◆◆◆◆

1 A **war** is a period of fighting or conflict between countries or states. *He spent part of the war in the National Guard. ...matters of war and peace... They've been at war for the last fifteen years.* N-VAR ≠peace

2 **War** is intense economic competition between countries or organizations. *The most important thing is to reach an agreement and to avoid a trade war.* N-VAR: usu with supp

3 If you make **war** on someone or something that you are opposed to, you do things to stop them succeeding. *She has been involved in the war against organised crime. ...if the United States is to be successful in its war on drugs.* N-VAR: oft N *against/on* n

4 See also **warring**, **civil war**, **Cold War**, **council of war**.

5 If someone **has been in the wars**, they have been injured, for example in a fight or in an accident; an informal expression. *Ben has also been in the wars. He is still in plaster after breaking a leg.* PHRASES V inflects

6 If a country **goes to war**, it starts fighting a war. *Do you think this crisis can be settled without going to war?* V inflects

7 If two people, countries, or organizations have a **war of words**, they criticize each other because they strongly disagree about something; used mainly in journalism. *Animal rights activists have been engaged in an increasingly bitter war of words with many of the nation's zoos.* oft PHR *between/with* n

warble /wɔːʳbəl/ **warbles, warbling, warbled**

1 When a bird **warbles**, it sings pleasantly. *The bird continued to warble... A flock of birds was already warbling a cheerful morning chorus.* VERB V / V n

2 If someone **warbles**, they sing, often with a high-pitched or quavering voice. *She warbled as she worked. ...singers warbling 'Over the Rainbow'.* ► Also a noun. *...the soft warble of her speaking voice.* VERB V / V n / N-SING

3 When machines such as telephones **warble**, they make a soft, low sound on two alternating notes. *The telephone on his desk warbled.* VERB V

warbler /wɔːʳbləʳ/ **warblers.** **Warblers** are a family of small birds that have a pleasant song. N-COUNT: usu supp N

war chest, war chests. A **war chest** is a fund to finance a project such as a political campaign. *Governor Caperton has the largest campaign war chest.* N-COUNT

ward /wɔːʳd/ **wards, warding, warded** ◆◆◇◇◇

1 A **ward** is a room in a hospital which has beds for many people, often people who need similar treatment. *A toddler was admitted to the emergency ward with a wound in his chest.* N-COUNT

2 A **ward** is a district which forms part of a political constituency or local council. *...the marginal wards of Reading Kentwood and Tilehurst West.* N-COUNT

3 A **ward** or a **ward of court** is a child who is being looked after by an appointed guardian or by a court of law, either because their parents are dead or they are considered to be in need of protection. *Alex was made a ward of court.* N-COUNT

ward off. To **ward off** a danger or illness means to prevent it from affecting you or harming you. *She may have put up a fight to try to ward off her assailant... Mass burials are now under way in an effort to ward off an outbreak of cholera.* PHRASAL VERB V P n (not pron) Also V n P

warden /wɔːʳdən/ **wardens** ◆◇◇◇◇

1 A **warden** is a person who is responsible for a particular place or thing, and for making sure that the laws or regulations that relate to it are obeyed. *He was a warden at the local parish church... Game* N-COUNT: usu with supp *wardens were appointed to enforce hunting laws in New Hampshire.* • See also **traffic warden**.

2 A **warden** is someone who works in a prison supervising the prisoners; used mainly in British English. *The siege began on Sunday, when the prisoners seized three wardens.* N-COUNT =warder

3 In American English, the **warden** of a prison is the person in charge of it. The usual British word is **governor**. *A new warden took over the prison.* N-COUNT

warder /wɔːʳdəʳ/ **warders.** In British English, a **warder** is a person who works in a prison and is in charge of prisoners. The usual American word is **guard**. N-COUNT

wardrobe /wɔːʳdroʊb/ **wardrobes** ◆◆◇◇◇

1 A **wardrobe** is a tall cupboard in which you can hang your clothes. N-COUNT

2 Someone's **wardrobe** is the total collection of clothes that they have. *Her wardrobe consists primarily of huge cashmere sweaters and tiny Italian sandals.* N-COUNT: oft poss N

3 The **wardrobe** in a theatre company is the actors' and actresses' costumes. *In the wardrobe department were rows of costumes.* N-UNCOUNT: also *the* N

ware /weəʳ/ **wares** ◆◇◇◇◇

1 **-ware** combines with nouns to refer to objects that are made of a particular material or that are used for a particular domestic purpose. *...the sparkle of fine German crystal ware. ...copper and porcelain cooking ware.* COMB in N-UNCOUNT

2 Someone's **wares** are the things that they sell, usually in the street or in a market; an old-fashioned use. *Vendors displayed their wares in baskets or on the ground.* N-PLURAL

warehouse /weəʳhaʊs/ **warehouses.** A **warehouse** is a large building where raw materials or manufactured goods are stored until they are exported to other countries or distributed to shops to be sold. ◆◆◇◇◇ N-COUNT

warehouse club, warehouse clubs. A **warehouse club** is a shop which offers goods for sale at reduced prices to people who pay an annual subscription. N-COUNT

warehousing /weəʳhaʊzɪŋ/. **Warehousing** is the act or process of storing large quantities of goods so that they can be sold or used at a later date. *All donations go towards the cost of warehousing. ...a major warehousing and distribution group.* N-UNCOUNT

warfare /wɔːʳfeəʳ/ ◆◆◇◇◇

1 **Warfare** is the activity of fighting a war. *...the threat of chemical warfare.* N-UNCOUNT: oft supp N

2 **Warfare** is sometimes used to refer to any violent struggle or conflict. *Much of the violence is related to drugs and gang warfare... At times party rivalries have broken out into open warfare.* N-UNCOUNT: oft supp N

warhead /wɔːʳhed/ **warheads.** A **warhead** is the front part of a bomb or missile where the explosives are carried. *...nuclear warheads.* ◆◇◇◇◇ N-COUNT

warhorse /wɔːʳhɔːʳs/ **warhorses.** You can refer to someone such as an old soldier or politician who is still active and aggressive as a **warhorse**. N-COUNT

warlike /wɔːʳlaɪk/

1 **Warlike** people seem aggressive and eager to start a war. *The Scythians were a fiercely warlike people. ...hopes of a peaceful solution despite increased warlike rhetoric from both sides.* ADJ-GRADED: usu ADJ n =aggressive

2 A **warlike** object or activity relates to fighting a war. *They were armed with spears and other warlike implements. ...the warlike preparations of Mr Churchill.* ADJ: ADJ n

warlord /wɔːʳlɔːʳd/ **warlords.** If you describe a leader of a country or organization as a **warlord**, you are critical of them because they have achieved power by behaving in an aggressive and violent way. *He had been a dictator and a warlord who had oppressed and degraded the people of the South. ...a drug warlord.* ◆◇◇◇◇ N-COUNT PRAGMATICS

warm /wɔːʳm/ **warmer, warmest; warms, warming, warmed** ◆◆◆◆◇

1 Something that is **warm** has some heat but not enough to be hot. *Wheat is grown in places which have cold winters and warm, dry summers... Because it was warm, David wore only a white cotton shirt... Dissolve the salt in the warm water.* ADJ-GRADED: oft *it* v-link ADJ ≠cool

2 **Warm** clothes and blankets are made of a material such as wool which protects you from the cold. *They have been forced to sleep in the open without food or warm clothing... The bed had clean sheets and warm blankets.* ♦ **warmly** *Remember to wrap up warmly on cold days... The men were warmly dressed and wore mufflers about their throats.* ADJ-GRADED ≠cool; ADV-GRADED: ADV after v, ADV -ed

3 **Warm** colours have red or yellow in them rather than blue or green, and make you feel comfortable and relaxed. *We hope the colour gives the house a warm and inviting feel... The basement hallway is painted a warm yellow.* ADJ-GRADED: usu ADJ n ≠cool

4 A **warm** person is friendly and shows a lot of affection or enthusiasm in their behaviour. *She was a warm and loving mother... 'Wonderful!' he exclaimed, in the familiar warm voice that made everybody who knew him feel welcome... I would like to express my warmest thanks to the doctors.* ♦ **warmly** *New members are warmly welcomed... He greeted me warmly.* ADJ-GRADED; ADV-GRADED: ADV with v

5 If you **warm** a part of your body or if something hot **warms** it, it stops feeling cold and starts to feel hotter. *The sun had come out to warm his back... She went to warm her hands by the log fire.* VERB V n

6 If you **warm to** a person or an idea, you become fonder of the person or more interested in the idea. *Those who got to know him better warmed to his openness and honesty... Elizabeth warmed to her theme as the letter continued with her favourite lament about being left alone.* VERB V *to* n

warm up PHRASAL VERB

1 If you **warm** something **up** or if it **warms up**, it gets hotter. *He blew on his hands to warm them up... All that she would have to do was warm up the pudding... The weather had warmed up.* ERG V n P, V P n (not pron), V P

2 If you **warm up** for an event such as a race, you prepare yourself for it by doing exercises or by practising just before it starts. *In an hour the drivers will be warming up for the main event... Carl slipped a disc in his back while warming up.* • See also **warm-up**. =limber up; V P

3 When a machine or engine **warms up** or someone **warms** it **up**, it becomes ready for use a little while after being switched on or started. *He waited for his car to warm up... We spent a frustrating five minutes while the pilot warmed up the engines.* ERG V P, V P n (not pron), Also V n P

4 If a comedian or speaker **warms up** an audience or the audience **warms up**, the audience is prepared for the main act or speaker by being told jokes or funny stories, so that they are in a good mood. *They would always come out and warm up the audience... The crowd began to warm up.* ERG V P n (not pron), V P

warm-blooded. A **warm-blooded** animal, for example a bird or a mammal, has a relatively high body temperature which remains constant and is not usually affected by the surrounding temperature. ADJ

warm-hearted. A **warm-hearted** person is friendly and affectionate. ADJ-GRADED

warmonger /wɔːʳmʌŋgəʳ/ **warmongers.** If you describe a politician or leader as a **warmonger**, you disapprove of them because you think they are encouraging people to start or join a war. N-COUNT PRAGMATICS

warmth /wɔːʳmθ/ ◆◆◇◇◇

1 The **warmth** of something is the heat that it has or produces. *She went further into the room, drawn by the warmth of the fire... June had brought with it the first of the summer warmth.* N-UNCOUNT ≠cold

2 The **warmth** of something such as a garment or blanket is the protection that it gives you against the cold. *The blanket will provide additional warmth and comfort in bed.* N-UNCOUNT

3 Someone who has **warmth** is friendly and enthusiastic in their behaviour towards other people. *He greeted us both with warmth and affection.* N-UNCOUNT

warm-up, warm-ups. A **warm-up** is something that prepares you for an activity or event, usually because it is a short practice or example of what the activity or event will involve. *The exercises* ◆◇◇◇◇ N-COUNT: usu sing, oft N *for* n, N n

can be fun and a good warm-up for the latter part of the programme... The criticism was merely a warm-up for what is being prepared for the finance minister... In a warm-up game for the World Cup, Uruguay have beaten England.

warn /wɔːʳn/ **warns, warning, warned** ◆◆◆◆◇

1 If you **warn** someone about something such as a possible danger or problem, you tell them about it so that they are aware of it. *When I had my first baby friends warned me that children were expensive... They warned him of the dangers of sailing alone... Analysts warned that Europe's most powerful economy may be facing trouble... He also warned of a possible anti-Western backlash.* VERB V n that V n *of/about* n V that V *of* n

2 If you **warn** someone not to do something, you advise them not to do it so that they can avoid possible danger or punishment. *Mrs. Blount warned me not to interfere... Children must be warned to stay away from main roads... 'Don't do anything yet,' he warned. 'Too risky.'... 'Keep quiet, or they'll all come out,' they warned him... I wish I'd listened to the people who warned me against having the operation... Mr Lowe warned against complacency.* VERB V n to-inf V with quote V n with quote V n *against* n/-ing V *against* n/-ing

3 If someone says to you **'be warned'**, they are advising you to be cautious, because there are risks that you may not have thought about. *But be warned: this is not a cheap option.* CONVENTION PRAGMATICS

warn away. If you **warn** someone **away**, you tell them to go away or to stop doing something because of possible danger or punishment. *Soon an official appeared to warn them away... Analysts warn us away from drawing any conclusions.* PHRASAL VERB =warn off V n P V n P *from* n/-ing

warn off. If you **warn** someone **off**, you tell them to go away or to stop doing something because of possible danger or punishment. *The police warned the intruder off... He pressed for a full investigation, but was warned off... He spends his spare time visiting schools to warn pupils off drugs.* PHRASAL VERB =warn away V n P V n P n/-ing Also V P n (not pron)

warning /wɔːʳnɪŋ/ **warnings** ◆◆◆◇◇

1 A **warning** is something which is said or written to tell people of a possible danger, problem, or other unpleasant thing that might happen. *The minister gave a warning that if war broke out, it would be catastrophic... He was killed because he ignored a warning to put stronger cords on his parachute... The government has unveiled new health warnings for cigarette packets.* N-COUNT: oft N that, N to-inf

2 A **warning** is an advance notice of something that will happen, often something unpleasant or dangerous. *The soldiers opened fire without warning... With no warning, he was fired from his job... He said Mr Rocard had met him on Tuesday and given him advance warning of his speech.* N-VAR: oft *without* N

3 Warning actions or signs give a warning. *She ignored the warning signals and did not check the patient's medical notes... Some fog warning signs had been put up with flashing yellow lights.* ADJ: ADJ n

war of nerves. A **war of nerves** is a conflict in which the opposing sides try to weaken each other psychologically, for example by making each other frightened or telling lies about each other. *...the continuing war of nerves between the army and the leadership.* N-SING

warp /wɔːʳp/ **warps, warping, warped** ◆◇◇◇◇

1 If something **warps** or **is warped**, it becomes damaged by bending or curving, often because of the effect of heat or water. *Left out in the heat of the sun, tapes easily warp or get stuck in their cases... It should have prevented rain water warping the door trim... The door, warped by seasons and sea-changes, split slightly.* ► Also an adjective. *The key was fractionally warped.* V-ERG V V n V-ed ADJ-GRADED: v-link ADJ

2 If something **warps** someone's character, it damages them or it influences them in a bad way. *I never had any toys, my father thought that they would warp my personal values... Their lives have been warped by war.* ► Also an adjective. *The individual's whole personality appears to be permanently warped. ...a person with a very warped mind.* VERB V n ADJ-GRADED

3 A **warp** in time or space is an imaginary break or sudden change in the normal experience of time or space. *When a divorced woman re-enters the world of dating and romance, she's likely to feel as though she has entered a time warp.* N-COUNT: n N

4 In weaving, **the warp** in a piece of woven material is the threads which are held along a loom while other threads are passed across them. N-SING: *the* N

war paint; also spelled **warpaint**. **War paint** is the paint which some tribal people use to decorate their faces and bodies before they fight a battle. N-UNCOUNT

warpath /wɔːʳpɑːθ, -pæθ/. If you say that someone is or has gone **on the warpath**, you mean that they are angry and getting ready for a fight or conflict; an informal expression. *I had warned the children that daddy was on the warpath.* PHRASE: PHR after v, oft v-link PHR

warplane /wɔːʳpleɪn/ **warplanes;** also spelled **war plane**. A **warplane** is an aeroplane that is specially designed to be used in warfare, for example to attack other aeroplanes or to drop bombs on buildings. ◆◇◇◇◇ N-COUNT

warrant /wɒrənt, AM wɔːr-/ **warrants, warranting, warranted** ◆◆◇◇◇

1 If something **warrants** a particular action, it makes the action seem necessary or appropriate for the circumstances. *The allegations are serious enough to warrant an investigation... No matter was too small to warrant his attention.* ♦ **warranted** *Do you think this fear is warranted?* VERB =merit V n ADJ

2 A **warrant** is a legal document that allows or orders someone to do something, especially one that is signed by a judge or magistrate and gives the police permission to arrest someone or search their house. *Police confirmed that they had issued a warrant for his arrest. ...a search warrant?... Equipment is allocated by warrant.* N-COUNT: oft N *for* n, also *by* N

3 If you say that there is no **warrant** for something, you mean that there is no good reason to justify it; a formal use. *There is some warrant for holding back on full-scale aid.* N-UNCOUNT: oft with brd-neg, usu N *for* n/-ing

4 If you **warrant** that something is true or will happen, you say officially that it is true, or guarantee that it will happen; a formal use. *All entrants must warrant that their entry is entirely their own work... The contract warrants that an experienced person is on board all the time.* VERB V that

5 See also **death warrant.**

warrant officer, warrant officers. A **warrant officer** is a person in the army, the air force, or the marines, who is above the rank of sergeant and below the rank of lieutenant. N-COUNT

warranty /wɒrənti, AM wɔːr-/ **warranties.** A **warranty** is a written promise by a company that, if you find faults or defects in something that they have sold you within a certain time, they will repair it or replace it free of charge. *...a twelve month warranty... The equipment is still under warranty.* ◆◇◇◇◇ N-COUNT: also *under* N

warren /wɒrən, AM wɔːr-/ **warrens**

1 A **warren** is a group of holes in the ground which are connected by tunnels and which rabbits live in. N-COUNT: oft n N

2 If you describe a building or an area of a city as a **warren**, you mean that the conditions are crowded and that there are many narrow passages, corridors, or streets. *...a warren of narrow streets.* N-COUNT: usu with supp, oft N *of* n =maze

warring /wɔːrɪŋ/. **Warring** is used to describe groups of people who are involved in a conflict or quarrel with each other. *An official said the warring factions have not yet turned in all their heavy weapons. ...warring husbands and wives.* ◆◆◇◇◇ ADJ: ADJ n

warrior /wɒriəʳ, AM wɔːr-/ **warriors.** A **warrior** is a fighter or soldier, especially one in former times who was very brave and experienced in fighting. ◆◆◇◇◇ N-COUNT

warship /wɔːʳʃɪp/ **warships.** A **warship** is a ship with guns that is used for fighting in wars. ◆◇◇◇◇ N-COUNT

wart /wɔːʳt/ **warts** ◆◇◇◇◇

1 A **wart** is a small lump which grows on your skin and which is usually caused by a virus. N-COUNT

2 If you describe someone or accept them **warts and all**, you describe them or accept them as they are, including all their faults. *Lyn loves him warts and all... He gives us a portrait of the real Gandhi,* PHRASE: PHR after v, PHR n *warts and all... 'Edinburgh in Focus' provides a warts-and-all look at the city.*

warthog /wɔːʳthɒg, AM -hɔːg/ **warthogs.** A **warthog** is a wild pig with two small tusks. Warthogs live in Africa. N-COUNT

wartime /wɔːʳtaɪm/; also spelled **war-time. Wartime** is a period of time when a war is being fought. *The government will commandeer ships only in wartime. ...his wartime experiences in France.* ◆◆◇◇◇ N-UNCOUNT: oft *in* N, N n

war widow, war widows. A **war widow** is a woman whose husband was killed while he was in the armed forces during a war. N-COUNT

wary /weəri/ **warier, wariest** ◆◆◇◇◇

1 If you are **wary** of something or someone, you are cautious because you do not know much about them and you believe they may be dangerous or cause problems. *People did not teach their children to be wary of strangers... They were very wary about giving him a contract.* ♦ **warily** /weərɪli/ *She studied me warily, as if I might turn violent.* ADJ-GRADED: usu v-link ADJ, oft ADJ *of/about* n/-ing; ADV-GRADED: usu ADV with v

2 If you keep **a wary eye** on something or someone, you are cautious about them and watch them to see what they will do or what will happen to them. *Bankers are keeping a wary eye on the outcome.* PHRASE: usu PHR *on* n, usu v PHR, also *with* PHR

was /wəz, STRONG wɒz, AM wʌz/. **Was** is the first and third person singular of the past tense of **be**.

wash /wɒʃ/ **washes, washing, washed** ◆◆◆◇◇

1 If you **wash** something, you clean it, usually with water and soap or detergent. *He got a job washing dishes in a pizza parlour... The colours gently fade each time you wash the shirt... It took a long time to wash the mud out of his hair... Rub down the door and wash off the dust before applying the varnish.* ► Also a noun. *That coat could do with a wash... The treatment leaves hair glossy and lasts 10 to 16 washes.* VERB V n V n prep V n with adv; N-COUNT

2 If you **wash** or if you **wash** part of your body, especially your hands and face, you clean part of your body using soap and water. *They looked as if they hadn't washed in days... She washed her face with cold water... You are going to have your dinner, get washed, and go to bed.* ► Also a noun. *She had a wash and changed her clothes.* VERB V V n *get* V-ed; N-COUNT: usu *a* N in sing

3 If a sea or river or something carried by a sea or river **washes** somewhere or **is washed** there, it flows there gently. *The sea washed against the shore... The oil washed ashore on roughly 1000 miles of coastline... The force of the water washed him back into the cave.* V-ERG V prep/adv V n with adv Also V n prep

4 **The wash** in a sea or river is water which has a lot of waves and froth, for example because a boat has just passed. *...the wash from large ships.* N-SING: *the* N

5 If a feeling **washes** over you, you suddenly feel it very strongly and cannot control it; used in written English. *A wave of self-consciousness can wash over her when someone new enters the room... Overpowering despair that he'd fought so hard to keep at bay, washed through the boy.* VERB V *over/through* n

6 A **wash** of something such as light or colour is a thin layer of it; used in written English. *The lights from the truck sent a wash of pale light over the snow.* N-COUNT: usu N *of* n

7 If you say that an excuse or idea will not **wash**, you mean that people will not accept or believe it; an informal use. *He said her policies didn't work and the excuses didn't wash... If they believe that solution would wash with the Haitian people, they are making a dramatic error.* VB: usu with brd-neg V V *with* n

8 See also **washing**.

9 If you say that something will **come out in the wash**, you mean that people will eventually find out the truth about it; an informal expression. *This will all come out in the wash – I promise you.* PHRASES V inflects

10 If you say that something such as an item of clothing **is in the wash**, you mean that it is being washed, waiting to be washed, or has just been washed and can therefore not be worn or used; an informal expression. *Your jeans are in the wash.* V inflects

11 • to **wash** your **dirty linen in public**: see **dirty**. • to **wash** your **hands of** something: see **hand**.

wash away. If rain or floods **wash away** something, they destroy it and carry it away. *Flood waters washed away one of the main bridges in Pusan... This causes environmental damage when the topsoil is washed away by the rains.* PHRASAL VERB V P n (not pron) Also V n P

wash down PHRASAL VERB

1 If you **wash** something, especially food, **down** with a drink, you drink the drink after eating the food, especially to make the food easier to swallow or digest. *He took two aspirin immediately and washed them down with three cups of water. ...a massive beef sandwich washed down by a bottle of beer.* V n P V-ed P Also V P n (not pron)

2 If you **wash down** an object, you wash it all, from top to bottom. *The prisoner started to wash down the walls of his cell.* V P n (not pron) Also V n P

wash out PHRASAL VERB

1 If you **wash out** a container, you wash the inside of it. *It was my job to wash out the fish tank.* =clean out V P n (not pron)

2 If dye or dirt **washes out**, it can be removed by washing. *With permanent tints you can go any colour you want, but the result won't wash out.* V P

3 If rain **washes out** a sports match or other event, it spoils it or prevents it from continuing. *Rain washed out five of the last seven games.* V P n (not pron)

4 See also **washed-out, washout**.

wash over. If something someone does or says **washes over** you, you do not notice it or it does not affect you in any way. *The television headlines seemed to wash over her without meaning anything.* PHRASAL VERB V P n (not pron)

wash up PHRASAL VERB

1 If you **wash up**, you wash the plates, cups, knives, forks, and other utensils which have been used in cooking and eating a meal; used mainly in British English. *I ran some hot water and washed up... I bet you make breakfast and wash up their plates, too.* V P V P n (not pron) Also V n P

2 In American English, if you **wash up**, you clean part of your body with soap and water, especially your hands and face. *He headed to the bathroom to wash up.* V P

3 If something **is washed up** on a piece of land, it is carried by a river or sea and left there. *Thousands of herring and crab are washed up on the beaches during every storm... The fossils appear to be an early form of seaweed washed up on a beach.* usu passive *be* V-ed P prep/adv V-ed P

4 See also **washed up, washing-up**.

washable /wɒʃəbᵊl/. **Washable** clothes or materials can be washed in water without being damaged. *Choose washable curtains.* ADJ

washbasin /wɒʃbeɪsᵊn/ **washbasins;** also spelled **wash basin**. A **washbasin** is a large bowl, usually with taps for hot and cold water, for washing your hands and face. N-COUNT

washcloth /wɒʃklɒθ, AM -klɔːθ/ **washcloths.** In American English, a **washcloth** is a small cloth that you use for washing yourself. The British word is **flannel**. N-COUNT

washed-out; also spelled **washed out**.

1 **Washed-out** colours are pale and dull rather than vivid. *He stared at me out of those washed-out blue eyes. ...suits in washed-out pastels.* ADJ-GRADED: usu ADJ n =pale

2 If someone looks **washed-out**, they look very tired and lacking in energy. *She looked washed out and listless.* ADJ-GRADED: usu v-link ADJ

washed up; also spelled **washed-up**. If you say that someone is **washed up**, you mean that they are at the end of their career with no prospects for the future; an informal expression. *He's all washed up, but he still yells at everyone.* ADJ-GRADED

washer /wɒʃəʳ/ **washers** ◆◇◇◇◇

1 A **washer** is a thin flat ring of metal, plastic, or other substance, which is placed over a bolt before the nut is screwed on. N-COUNT

2 A **washer** is the same as a **washing machine**; an informal use. N-COUNT

washing /wɒʃɪŋ/. **Washing** is a collection of clothes, sheets, and other things which are waiting to be washed, are being washed, or have just been washed. *...plastic bags full of dirty washing... They were anxious to bring the washing in before it rained.* ◆◇◇◇◇ N-UNCOUNT =laundry

washing machine, washing machines. A **washing machine** is a machine that you use to wash clothes in. ◆◇◇◇◇ N-COUNT

washing powder, washing powders. In British English, **washing powder** is powdered detergent that you use to wash clothes. The usual American terms are **soap powder** or **laundry detergent**. N-MASS

washing-up ◆◇◇◇◇

1 In British English, to do the **washing-up** means to wash the plates, cups, cutlery, and pans which have been used in cooking and eating a meal. *Martha volunteered to do the washing-up.* N-UNCOUNT

2 In British English, **washing-up** is the plates, cups, cutlery, and pans which you have to wash after a meal. *You are faced with a brimming bowl of washing-up.* N-UNCOUNT

washing-up liquid, washing-up liquids. In British English, **washing-up liquid** is a thick soapy liquid which you add to hot water to clean dirty dishes. N-MASS

washout /wɒʃaʊt/ **washouts.** If an event or plan is a **washout**, it fails completely; an informal word. *The mission was a washout.* N-COUNT =disaster

washroom /wɒʃruːm/ **washrooms.** A **washroom** is a room with toilets and washing facilities, situated in a large building such as a factory or an office block. N-COUNT

washstand /wɒʃstænd/ **washstands.** A **washstand** is a piece of furniture designed to hold a basin and other things for washing your face and hands, especially one that was used in former times, before wash basins were connected to water pipes. *...a Victorian marble-topped washstand.* N-COUNT

wasn't /wɒzᵊnt, AM wʌz-/. In informal English, **was not** is usually said or written as **wasn't**.

wasp /wɒsp/ **wasps.** A **wasp** is an insect with wings and yellow and black stripes across its body. Wasps have a painful sting like a bee but do not produce honey. ◆◇◇◇◇ N-COUNT

waspish /wɒspɪʃ/. A **waspish** remark or sense of humour is sharp and critical. *...a lawyer with an inventive mind and a waspish sense of humour.* ADJ-GRADED

wastage /weɪstɪdʒ/

1 **Wastage** of something is the act of wasting it or the amount of it that is wasted. *...a series of measures to prevent the wastage of water... There was a lot of wastage and many wrong decisions were hastily taken.* N-UNCOUNT =waste

2 **Wastage** is the process of deterioration and weakening that takes place in the body of someone who is very ill or starving. *This can lead to bodily weakness and muscle wastage. ...the terrible wastage of his lungs.* N-UNCOUNT =wasting

3 **Wastage** refers to a number of people who leave a job or an educational establishment, especially before they have completed their education or training; used mainly in British English. *British universities have very little wastage and their graduates are good... Wages are low and the wastage rate of staff is high.* ● See also **natural wastage**. N-UNCOUNT

waste /weɪst/ **wastes, wasting, wasted** ◆◆◆◆◇

1 If you **waste** something such as time, money, or energy, you use too much of it doing something that is not important or necessary, or is unlikely to succeed. *There could be many reasons and he was not going to waste time speculating on them... I resolved not to waste money on a hotel... The system wastes a large amount of water.* ► Also a noun. *It is a waste of time going to the doctor with most mild complaints... I think that is a total waste of money.* VERB V n-ing V n on n V n N-SING: a N of n

2 **Waste** is the use of money or other resources on things that do not need it. *The packets are measured to reduce waste... I hate waste. Two weeks was reasonable, but this is far too much.* N-UNCOUNT

3 **Waste** is material which has been used and is no longer wanted, for example because the valuable or useful part of it has been taken out. *Congress passed a law that regulates the disposal of waste... Up to 10 million tonnes of toxic wastes are produced every year in the UK. ...the process of eliminating body waste.* N-UNCOUNT: also N in pl

4 If you **waste** an opportunity for something, you do not take advantage of it when it is available. *Let's not waste an opportunity to see the children... It was a wasted opportunity.* VERB V n V-ed

5 If you say that something **is wasted on** someone, you mean that there is no point giving it or telling it to them as they will not appreciate, understand, or pay any attention to it. *All the well-meant, sincere advice is largely wasted on him.* VB: usu passive =be lost on be V-ed on n

6 **Waste** land is land, especially in or near a city, which is not used or looked after by anyone, and so is covered by wild plants and rubbish. *There was a patch of waste land behind the church... Yarrow can be found growing wild in fields and on waste ground.* ADJ: usu ADJ n

7 **Wastes** are a large area of land, for example a desert, in which there are very few people, plants, or animals. *...the barren wastes of the Sahara.* N-PLURAL: adj N, N of n

8 See also **wasted**.

9 If something **goes to waste** it remains unused or has to be thrown away. *So much of his enormous effort and talent will go to waste if we are forced to drop one hour of the film... Mexican cookery is economical, she says. Nothing goes to waste.* PHRASES V inflects =be wasted

10 If something or someone **lays waste** an area or town or **lays waste to** it, they completely destroy it. *The war has laid waste large regions of the countryside. ...cities laid waste by the decline of traditional industries... The aphid is now laying waste to the wheat and barley fields.* V inflects, PHR n =annihilate

11 The expression **waste not, want not** means that if you do not use too much of something now you will have some left later when you need it. *...a nation that prides itself on its 'waste not, want not' thrift and its environmental conscience.*

12 ● to **waste your breath**: see **breath**. ● to **waste no time**: see **time**.

waste away. If someone **wastes away**, they become extremely thin or weak because they are ill or worried and they are not eating properly. *Persons dying from cancer grow thin and visibly waste away.* PHRASAL VERB V P

wastebasket /weɪstbɑːskɪt, -bæsk-/ **wastebaskets.** A **wastebasket** is the same as a **wastepaper basket**; used mainly in American English. N-COUNT

wasted /weɪstɪd/

1 A **wasted** action is one that is unnecessary. *I'm sorry you had a wasted journey.* ADJ =unnecessary

2 Someone who is **wasted** is very tired and weak, often because of an illness. *They look too wasted to care about much.* ADJ-GRADED

wasteful /weɪstfʊl/. Action that is **wasteful** uses too much of something valuable such as time, money, or energy. *This kind of training is ineffective, and wasteful of scarce resources... Try to avoid wasteful duplication of effort.* ◆◇◇◇◇ ADJ-GRADED

♦ **wastefully** *The law should impose penalties on companies that use energy wastefully.* ADV-GRADED: ADV with v

wasteland /weɪstlænd/ **wastelands** ◆◇◇◇◇

1 A **wasteland** is an area of land which cannot be used, for example because it is infertile or because it has been misused by people. *The pollution has already turned vast areas into a wasteland. ...a £3 billion scheme which was to transform the wasteland of London's docks. ...an industrial wasteland.* N-VAR: oft adj N, N of n

2 If you refer to a place, situation, or period in time as a **wasteland**, you are criticizing it because you think it has no life or excitement at all. *...the cultural wasteland of Franco's repressive rule... Everything was wrong, his life seemed to be a wasteland.* N-COUNT: oft adj N, N of n PRAGMATICS =desert

wastepaper basket, wastepaper baskets. A **wastepaper basket** is a container for rubbish, especially paper, which is usually placed on the floor in the corner of a room or next to a desk. N-COUNT

wasting /weɪstɪŋ/. A **wasting** disease is one which makes you gradually become thinner and weaker. ADJ: ADJ n

wastrel /weɪstrəl/ **wastrels.** If you describe someone as a **wastrel** you mean that they are lazy and spend their time and money on foolish N-COUNT things; a literary word. *Her father wouldn't let her marry a wastrel.*

watch 1 looking and paying attention

watch /wɒtʃ/ **watches, watching, watched** ◆◆◆◆◆

1 If you **watch** someone or something, you look at them, usually for a period of time, and pay attention to what is happening. *The man was standing in his doorway watching him... He watched the barman prepare the beer he had ordered... Chris watched him sipping his brandy... I watched as Amy ate a few nuts.* VERB =observe V n V n inf V n -ing V

2 If you **watch** something on television or an event such as a sports match, you spend time looking at it, especially when you see it from the beginning to the end. *I'd stayed up late to watch the film... They spent a great deal of time watching television.* VERB V n

3 If you **watch** a situation or event, you pay attention to it or you are aware of it, but you are not participating in it. *Human rights groups have been closely watching the case... Annoyed commuters could only watch as the departure time ticked by.* VERB =observe V n V

4 If you **watch** people, especially children or animals, you are responsible for them, and make sure that they are not in danger. *Parents can't be expected to watch their children 24 hours a day.* VERB =watch over V n

5 If you **watch** someone, you follow them secretly or spy on them. *Ella was scared that someone was watching her... I always had the feeling we were being watched.* VERB V n

6 If you tell someone to **watch** a particular person or thing, you are warning them to be careful that the person or thing does not get out of control or do something unpleasant. *You really ought to watch these quiet types... If you're watching the calories, don't have mayonnaise.* VERB PRAGMATICS =keep an eye on V n

7 The **watch** is the job of carefully looking around, usually when other people are asleep, so that you can warn them of danger or an attack. *I had the first watch that May evening.* N-COUNT

8 If someone **keeps watch**, they look around all the time, usually when other people are asleep, so that they can warn the others of danger or an attack. *Jose, as usual, had climbed a tree to keep watch.* PHRASES V inflects

9 If you **keep watch** on events or a situation, you pay attention to what is happening, so that you can take action at the right moment. *US officials have been keeping close watch on the situation.* V inflects, usu PHR *on* n

10 You say **'watch it'** in order to warn someone to be careful, especially when you want to threaten them about what will happen if they are not careful. *'Now watch it, Patsy,' the Sergeant told her.* PRAGMATICS

11 If someone is **on watch**, they have the job of carefully looking around, usually when other people are asleep, so that they can warn them of danger or an attack. *Apart from two men on watch in the engine-room, everyone was asleep.* v-link PHR, PHR after v

12 If you are **on the watch** for something, you are expecting it to happen and you therefore pay attention to events so that you will notice it when it does happen. *Environmentalists will be on the watch for damage to wildlife.* v-link PHR, oft PHR *for* n =on the lookout

13 If someone is being kept **under watch**, they are being guarded or observed all the time. PHR after v, v-link PHR

14 You say to someone **'you watch'** or **'just watch'** when you are predicting that something will happen, and you are very confident that it will happen as you say. *You watch. Things will get worse before they get better.*

15 • **watch this space**: see **space**. • **watch** your **step**: see **step**.

watch for or **watch out for.** If you **watch for** something or **watch out for** it, you pay attention so that you notice it, either because you do not want to miss it or because you want to avoid it. *We'll be watching for any developments... He called out to them to watch out for the unexploded mine.* PHRASAL VERB =look out for V P n V P P n

watch out. If you tell someone to **watch out**, you are warning them to be careful, because something unpleasant might happen to them or they might get into difficulties. *You have to watch out because there are land mines all over the place... The casinos in Las Vegas had better watch out since I'm obviously on a lucky streak!* PHRASAL VERB PRAGMATICS =look out V P

watch out for. See **watch for.** PHRASAL VERB

watch over. If you **watch over** someone or something, you pay attention to them to make sure that nothing bad happens to them. *The guards were originally hired to watch over the houses as they were being built.* PHRASAL VERB =watch V P n

watch 2 instrument that tells the time

watch /wɒtʃ/ **watches.** A **watch** is a small clock which you wear on a strap on your wrist or on a chain. ◆◆◆◇◇ N-COUNT

watchdog /wɒtʃdɒg, AM -dɔːg/ **watchdogs.** A **watchdog** is a person or committee whose job is to make sure that companies do not act illegally or irresponsibly. *...an anti-crime watchdog group funded by New York businesses.* ◆◇◇◇◇ N-COUNT: oft supp N, N n

-watcher /-wɒtʃəʳ/ **-watchers. -watcher** combines with nouns to form other nouns that refer to people who are interested in a group of animals or people, and who study them closely. *The bird-watchers crept silently about in the bushes... Royal-watcher Mary Hayes said: 'It looks like it is going to be an unhappy time for the Queen.'* COMB in N-COUNT

watchful /wɒtʃfʊl/ ◆◇◇◇◇

1 Someone who is **watchful** notices everything that is happening. *The best thing is to be watchful and see the family doctor for any change in your normal health... He looked tall and powerful and, with his dark, watchful face, a little threatening.* ADJ-GRADED =alert

2 If you do something **under the watchful eye of** someone who has authority over you, they watch you carefully to make sure there are no problems. *There were demonstrations in the streets today, under the watchful eye of police... Children swim at the pool, under the watchful eye of lifeguards.* PHRASES N inflects, PHR n

3 If you **keep a watchful eye on** someone or something, you watch carefully to make sure there are no problems. *Keep a watchful eye on babies and toddlers.* V inflects, PHR n

-watching /-wɒtʃɪŋ/. **-watching** combines with nouns to form other nouns which refer to the activity of looking at a group of animals or people and studying them because they interest you. *Whale-watching has become a growth leisure industry... He is said to have invented the sport of celebrity-watching.* COMB in N-UNCOUNT

watchman /wɒtʃmən/ **watchmen.** A **watchman** is a person whose job is to guard a building or area. • See also **nightwatchman.** ◆◇◇◇◇ N-COUNT

watchtower /wɒtʃtaʊəʳ/ **watchtowers.** A **watchtower** is a high building which gives a sentry a good view of the area around a place that is being guarded. N-COUNT

watchword /wɒtʃwɜːʳd/ **watchwords.** Someone's **watchword** is a word or phrase that sums up their attitude or approach to a particular subject or to things in general. *Caution has been one of Mr Allan's watchwords... You don't have to deny yourself everything that's nice when you're pregnant. Moderation is the watchword.* N-COUNT: oft with poss

water /wɔːtəʳ/ **waters, watering, watered** ◆◆◆◆◆

1 Water is a clear thin liquid that has no colour or taste when it is pure. It falls from clouds as rain and enters rivers and seas. All animals and people need water in order to live. *Get me a glass of water. ...the sound of water hammering on the metal roof. ...a trio of children playing along the water's edge.* N-UNCOUNT

2 You use **waters** to refer to a large area of sea, especially the area of sea which is near to a country and which is regarded as belonging to it. *The ship will remain outside Chinese territorial waters. ...the open waters of the Arctic Ocean.* N-PLURAL: with supp

3 You sometimes use **waters** to refer to a situation which is very complex or difficult. *...the man brought in to guide him through troubled waters... The British Government may be in stormy economic waters.* N-PLURAL: adj N

4 If you **water** plants, you pour water over them in order to help them to grow. *He went out to water the plants.* VERB V n

5 If your eyes **water**, tears build up in them be- VERB cause they are hurting or because you are upset. *His eyes watered from cigarette smoke.* V

6 If you say that your mouth **is watering**, you mean that you can smell or see some appetizing food and you might mean that you mouth is actually producing saliva. ...*cookies to make your mouth water.* • See also **mouth-watering**. VERB =salivate V

7 When a pregnant woman's **waters break**, the fluid in her womb that surrounds the baby passes out of her body, showing that the baby is ready to be born. A midwife can **break** a woman's **waters** so that the birth can begin. *My waters broke at 6 in the morning and within four hours Jamie was born.* PHRASES ERG: V inflects

8 If you say that an event or incident is **water under the bridge**, you mean that it has happened and cannot now be changed, so there is no point in worrying about it any more. *He was relieved his time in jail was over and regarded it as water under the bridge.* v-link PHR

9 If you are **in deep water**, you are in a difficult or awkward situation. *You certainly seem to be in deep water... I could tell that we were getting off the subject and into deep water.*

10 If an argument or theory does not **hold water**, it does not seem to be reasonable or be in accordance with the facts. *This argument simply cannot hold water in Europe.* V inflects, usu with brd-neg

11 If you are **in hot water**, you are in trouble; an informal expression. *The company has already been in hot water over high prices this year.* v-link PHR, PHR after v

12 If you **pour cold water on** an idea or suggestion, you show that you have a low opinion of it. *City economists pour cold water on the idea that the economic recovery has begun.* V inflects, PHR n

13 If you **test the water** or **test the waters**, you try to find out what reaction an action or idea will get before you do it or tell it to people. *You should be cautious when getting involved and test the water before committing yourself.* V and N inflect

14 • **like water off a duck's back**: see **duck**. • to **take to something like a duck to water**: see **duck**. • **like a fish out of water**: see **fish**. • to **keep** your **head above water**: see **head**. • to **pour oil on troubled waters**: see **oil**.

water down PHRASAL VERB

1 If you **water down** a substance, for example food or drink, you add water to it to make it weaker. *You can water down a glass of wine and make it last twice as long... I bought a water-based paint, then decided to water it down even more.* =dilute V P n (not pron) V n P

2 If something, especially a proposal, speech, or statement **is watered down**, it is made much weaker and less forceful or less controversial. *Proposed European Community legislation affecting bird-keepers has been watered down.* • See also **watered-down**. VERB =tone down *be* V-ed P

waterbed /wɔːtəʳbed/ **waterbeds;** also spelled **water bed**. A **waterbed** is a bed whose mattress consists of a plastic case filled with water. N-COUNT

water bird, water birds. A **water bird** is a bird that swims or wades in water, especially freshwater. There are many kinds of water bird. N-COUNT

water-borne; also spelled **waterborne**.

1 **Water-borne** disease or infection is passed on through contact with infected water. *UN officials are warning of an outbreak of cholera and other water-borne diseases.* ADJ: ADJ n

2 Something that is **water-borne** travels or is transported on water. ...*a waterborne safari down the Nile... Environmental pressures are strengthening the case for waterborne freight.* ADJ: ADJ n

water bottle, water bottles. A **water bottle** is a small container for carrying water to drink on a long journey. • See also **hot-water bottle**. N-COUNT

water buffalo, water buffaloes; water buffalo can also be used as the plural form. A **water buffalo** is an animal like a large cow with long horns that curve upwards. In some countries water buffalo are kept for their milk and are used to draw ploughs. N-COUNT =buffalo

water butt, water butts. In British English, a **water butt** is a large barrel for collecting rain as it flows off a roof. The usual American word is **rain barrel**. N-COUNT

water cannon, water cannons; water cannon can also be used as the plural form. A **water cannon** is a machine which shoots out a large, powerful jet of water. It is used by police to break up crowds of people who are demonstrating. N-COUNT

water chestnut, water chestnuts. A **water chestnut** is the thick bottom part of the stem of a plant which grows in China. It is frequently used in Chinese cookery. N-COUNT

watercolour /wɔːtəʳkʌləʳ/ **watercolours;** spelled **watercolor** in American English. ◆◇◇◇◇

1 **Watercolours** are coloured paints, used for painting pictures, which you apply with a wet brush or dissolve in water first. ...*a collection of rich paintings in watercolour, acrylic and oil.* N-VAR

2 A **watercolour** is a picture which has been painted with watercolours. ...*a lovely watercolour by J. M. W. Turner.* N-COUNT

watercourse /wɔːtəʳkɔːʳs/ **watercourses;** also spelled **water course**. A **watercourse** is a stream or river, or the channel that it flows along; a formal word. N-COUNT

watercress /wɔːtəʳkres/. **Watercress** is a small plant with white flowers which grows in streams and pools. Its leaves taste hot and are eaten raw in salads. ◆◇◇◇◇ N-UNCOUNT

watered-down; also spelled **watered down**. If you describe something such as a proposal, speech, or statement as **watered down**, you mean that it is weaker or less forceful or controversial than its original form. *The British government introduced a watered-down version of the proposals.* • See also **water**. ◆◇◇◇◇ ADJ-GRADED =toned down

waterfall /wɔːtəʳfɔːl/ **waterfalls.** A **waterfall** is a place where water flows over the edge of a steep, high cliff in hills or mountains, and falls into a pool below. ...*Angel Falls, the world's highest waterfall.* ◆◇◇◇◇ N-COUNT

waterfowl /wɔːtəʳfaʊl/; **waterfowl** is both the singular and the plural form. **Waterfowl** are birds that swim in water, especially ducks, geese, and swans. N-COUNT

waterfront /wɔːtəʳfrʌnt/ **waterfronts.** A **waterfront** is a street or piece of land which is next to an area of water, for example a harbour or the sea. *They went for a stroll along the waterfront.* ◆◇◇◇◇ N-COUNT: usu sing

water hole, water holes; also spelled **waterhole**. In a desert or other dry area, a **water hole** is a pond or pool where animals can find water to drink. N-COUNT

watering can, watering cans. A **watering can** is a container with a long spout which is used to water plants. N-COUNT

watering hole, watering holes. You can refer to a pub or bar where people go to drink and meet their friends as a **watering hole**. *I was in my favorite watering hole, waiting for the game to start.* N-COUNT

water jump, water jumps. A **water jump** is a fence with a pool of water on the far side of it, which people or horses jump over as part of a race or competition. N-COUNT

water lily, water lilies; also spelled **waterlily**. A **water lily** is a plant with large flat leaves and colourful flowers which floats on the surface of lakes and rivers. N-COUNT

waterline /wɔːtəʳlaɪn/ **waterlines;** also spelled **water line**. The **waterline** is a line, either real or imaginary, on the side of a ship representing the level the water reaches when the ship is at sea. *Ray painted below the waterline with a special anti-rust paint.* N-COUNT: usu sing

waterlogged /wɔːtəʳlɒgd, AM -lɔːgd/; also spelled **water-logged**. Something such as soil or land that is **waterlogged** is so wet that it cannot absorb any more water, so that a layer of water remains on its surface. *The match between Brighton and Leicester is off because of a waterlogged pitch.* ADJ-GRADED

water main, water mains. A **water main** is a very large underground pipe used for supplying water to houses and factories. *A water main burst and the street was flooded.* N-COUNT

watermark /wɔːtəʳmɑːʳk/ **watermarks.** A **watermark** is a design which is put into paper by the people who make it, and which you can only see if you hold the paper up to the light. Banknotes often have a watermark, to make them harder to forge. • See also **high-water mark.** N-COUNT

water meadow, water meadows. Water meadows are wet fields of grass near a river, which are often flooded; used mainly in British English. N-COUNT: usu pl

watermelon /wɔːtəmelən/ **watermelons.** A **watermelon** is a large round fruit with green skin, pink flesh, and black seeds. N-VAR

watermill /wɔːtəʳmɪl/ **watermills;** also spelled **water mill.** A **watermill** is a mill powered by a water wheel. N-COUNT

water pistol, water pistols. A **water pistol** is a small toy gun which shoots out water. N-COUNT

water polo. Water polo is a game played in a swimming pool in which two teams of swimmers try to score goals with a ball. N-UNCOUNT

waterproof /wɔːtəʳpruːf/ **waterproofs, waterproofing, waterproofed** ◆◇◇◇◇

1 Something which is **waterproof** does not let water pass through it. *Take waterproof clothing – Orkney weather is unpredictable... Designed to be completely waterproof, the lights are manufactured from heavy duty plastic.* ADJ

2 In British English, **waterproofs** are items of clothing which do not let water in. *For staying dry you'll want nice lightweight waterproofs to wear over your leathers.* N-COUNT: usu pl

3 If something **is waterproofed**, it is treated so that water cannot pass through it or damage it. *The whole boat has been totally waterproofed... Waterproofed fabric pants are more expensive than plastic pants.* VB: usu passive be V-ed V-ed

water rate, water rates. In Britain, the charges made for the use of water from the public water supply are known as the **water rates.** N-COUNT: usu pl

water-resistant. Something that is **water-resistant** does not allow water to pass through it easily, or is not easily damaged by water. *Microfibre fabrics are both water resistant and windproof... The personal stereo has a water-resistant outer case.* ADJ-GRADED

watershed /wɔːtəʳʃed/ **watersheds** ◆◇◇◇◇

1 If something such as an event is a **watershed** in the history or development of something, it is very important because it represents the beginning of a new stage in it. *Many observers expected this election to be a watershed in Malaysia's political history... Tonight could prove to be a watershed for the international career of Barnes.* N-COUNT: usu sing, oft N *in* n =turning point

2 In Britain, the **watershed** is a time before which television broadcasters have agreed not to show programmes unsuitable for children, for example programmes that contain scenes of sex or violence. *Bad language before the watershed is widely resented... The advert should only be shown after the 9pm watershed.* N-COUNT: usu *the* N in sing

3 A **watershed** is an area of high ground which divides two or more river systems, so that all streams on one side flow into one river and those on the other side flow into a different river; a technical use in geography. N-COUNT

waterside /wɔːtəʳsaɪd/. The **waterside** is the area beside a stretch of water such as a river or lake. *Her garden stretches down to the waterside. ...pretty waterside hotels.* N-SING: oft N n =waterfront

water-ski, water-skis, water-skiing, water-skied; also spelled **waterski.** If you **water-ski**, you stand on skis in the water while being pulled along by a boat. *The staff will be happy to help arrange for you to swim, sail, or water-ski.* ♦ **water-skiing** *He offered to teach them water-skiing.* VERB V N-UNCOUNT

water-soluble; also spelled **water soluble.** Something that is **water-soluble** dissolves in water. *Vitamin C is water soluble. ...oat bran and other water-soluble fibres.* ADJ

water supply, water supplies. The **water supply** in an area is the water which is collected and passed through pipes to buildings for people to use. *The town is without electricity and the water supply has been cut off.* ◆◇◇◇◇ N-COUNT

water table, water tables. The **water table** is the level below the surface of the ground where water can be found. *Environmentalists say that diverting water from the river will lower the water table and dry out wells.* N-COUNT: usu *the* N

watertight /wɔːtəʳtaɪt/; also spelled **water-tight.**

1 Something that is **watertight** does not allow water to pass through it, for example because it is tightly sealed. *The flask is completely watertight, even when laid on its side... The batteries are safely enclosed in a watertight compartment.* ADJ =unassailable

2 A **watertight** case, argument, or agreement is one that has been so carefully put together that nobody will be able to find a fault in it. *The police had a watertight case. They even got his fingerprints from that glass cabinet. ...a legally watertight agreement.* ADJ-GRADED

water tower, water towers. A **water tower** is a large tank of water which is placed on a high metal structure so that water can be supplied at a steady pressure to surrounding buildings. N-COUNT

water vole, water voles. A **water vole** is a small rat-like animal that can swim. Water voles live in holes in the banks of rivers. N-COUNT

waterway /wɔːtəʳweɪ/ **waterways.** A **waterway** is a canal, river, or narrow channel of sea which ships or boats can sail along. ◆◇◇◇◇ N-COUNT

water wheel, water wheels; also spelled **waterwheel.** A **water wheel** is a large wheel which is turned by water flowing through it. Water wheels are used to provide power to drive machinery. N-COUNT

waterworks /wɔːtəʳwɜːʳks/; **waterworks** is both the singular and the plural form. A **waterworks** is a building where a supply of water is stored and cleaned before being distributed to the public. N-COUNT

watery /wɔːtəri/ ◆◇◇◇◇

1 Something that is **watery** is weak or pale. *A watery light began to show through the branches... Martha managed to produce a dim, watery smile.* ADJ-GRADED: usu ADJ n =feeble

2 If you describe food or drink as **watery**, you dislike it because it contains too much water or is thin or tasteless like water. *...a plateful of watery soup. ...watery beer.* ADJ-GRADED: usu ADJ n PRAGMATICS

3 Something that is **watery** contains, resembles, or consists of water. *There was a watery discharge from her ear... Diana's eyes went red and watery.* ADJ-GRADED

watt /wɒt/ **watts.** A **watt** is a unit of measurement of electrical power. *Use a 3 amp fuse for equipment up to 720 watts. ...a 100-watt lightbulb.* ◆◇◇◇◇ N-COUNT: usu num N

wattage /wɒtɪdʒ/. The **wattage** of a piece of electrical equipment is the amount of electrical power, expressed in watts, which it generates or uses. N-UNCOUNT

wattle /wɒtᵊl/. **Wattle** is a framework made by weaving thin sticks and twigs over thick sticks, which is used for making fences and walls. *...the native huts of mud and wattle. ...wattle fencing.* N-UNCOUNT

wave /weɪv/ **waves, waving, waved** ◆◆◆◆◇

1 If you **wave** or **wave** your hand, you move your hand from side to side in the air, usually in order to say hello or goodbye to someone. *Jessica caught sight of Lois and waved to her... He waved at the waiter, who rushed to the table... He grinned, waved, and said, 'Hi!'... Elaine turned and waved her hand lazily and left.* ► Also a noun. *Steve stopped him with a wave of the hand... Paddy spotted Mary Ann and gave her a cheery wave.* VERB V *to/at* n V V n Also V n prep N-COUNT: usu with supp

2 If you **wave** someone away or **wave** them on, you make a movement with your hand to indicate that they should move in a particular direction. *Leshka waved him away with a show of irritation... He waited for a policeman to stop the traffic and wave* VERB V n adv/prep

the people on... He waved the servants out of the tent.

3 If you **wave** something, you hold it up and move it rapidly from side to side. *Hospital staff were outside to welcome him, waving flags and applauding... She was apt to raise her voice and wave her hands about.* ♦ **-waving** *Hundreds of banner-waving demonstrators took to the streets. ...a flag-waving crowd.* ♦ **-waving** *There will be marching bands and plenty of flag-waving.*
VERB V n V n adv/prep COMB in ADJ COMB in N-UNCOUNT

4 If something **waves**, it moves gently from side to side or up and down. *...grass and flowers waving in the wind.*
VERB =sway V

5 A **wave** is a raised mass of water on the surface of water, especially the sea, which is caused by the wind or by tides making the surface of the water rise and fall. *...the sound of the waves breaking on the shore.*
N-COUNT

6 If someone's hair has **waves**, it curves slightly instead of being straight.
N-COUNT

7 A **wave** is a sudden increase in heat or energy that spreads out from an earthquake, eruption, or explosion. *The shock waves of the earthquake were felt in Teheran... The blast wave crushed the breath from Neil, but he survived.*
N-COUNT: with supp

8 **Wave** is used to refer to the way in which things such as sound, light, and radio signals travel. *Regular repeating actions such as sound waves, light waves, or radio waves have a certain frequency, or number of waves per second.*
N-COUNT: usu pl, oft supp N

9 If you refer to a **wave** of a particular feeling, you mean that it increases quickly and becomes very intense, and then often decreases again. *She felt a wave of panic, but forced herself to leave the room calmly... A wave of sympathy for her swept Ireland... The loneliness and grief comes in waves.*
N-COUNT: usu N *of* n =surge

10 A **wave** is a sudden increase in a particular activity or type of behaviour, especially an undesirable or unpleasant one. *...the current wave of violence. ...an even newer crime wave. ...the shortages of bread, meat and gasoline that have hit Moscow in waves over the summer.*
N-COUNT: usu N *of* n

11 A **wave** is a sudden increase in the number of people moving somewhere. *A wave of immigrants is washing over Western Europe.*
N-COUNT: usu sing, oft N *of* n

12 In American English, if a crowd of people do a **wave**, each person in the crowd stands up and puts their arms in the air after the person to one side of them, creating a continuous rolling motion through the crowd. The British term is **Mexican wave**.
N-COUNT

13 See also **long wave**, **medium wave**, **Mexican wave**, **new wave**, **short wave**, **tidal wave**.

wave aside. If you **wave aside** something such as a suggestion, explanation, or idea, you decide that it is not important enough to consider seriously. *Wolfe waved my suggestion aside... Rachel waved aside the explanation.*
PHRASAL VERB =dismiss, brush aside V n P V P n (not pron)

wave down. If someone **waves down** a vehicle, they wave their hand as a signal to the driver to stop the vehicle. *He was frustrated by his inability to wave down a taxi... He turned the corner a little too fast, narrowly missing the boy who ran into the road to wave him down.*
PHRASAL VERB =flag down V P n (not pron) V n P

waveband /weɪvbænd/ **wavebands.** A **waveband** is a group of radio waves of similar length which are used for particular types of radio transmission.
N-COUNT

wavelength /weɪvleŋθ/ **wavelengths** ◆◇◇◇◇

1 A **wavelength** is the distance between the same point on consecutive cycles of a wave of energy such as light or sound. *Sunlight consists of different wavelengths of radiation... Blue light has a shorter wavelength than red.*
N-COUNT: usu with supp

2 A **wavelength** is the size of radio wave which a particular radio station uses to broadcast its programmes. *She found the wavelength of their broadcasts, and left the radio tuned to their station.*
N-COUNT: with supp

3 If two people are **on the same wavelength**, they find it easy to understand each other and they tend to agree, because they share similar interests or opinions. *We could complete each other's sentences because we were on the same wavelength.*
PHRASE: v-link PHR

wavelet /weɪvlət/ **wavelets.** **Wavelets** are small waves on the surface of a sea or lake; a literary word.
N-COUNT: usu pl

waver /weɪvər/ **wavers, wavering, wavered** ◆◇◇◇◇

1 If you **waver**, you are uncertain or indecisive about something. *Some military commanders wavered over whether to support the coup... Coleman has never wavered in his claim that he is innocent... Today on the streets of Montreal, opinion seems still to waver... He told wavering colleagues the country must back the Government's stance.*
VERB V V-ing

2 If something **wavers**, it shakes with very slight movements or changes. *The shadows of the dancers wavered continually... This time his voice wavered badly... She draws another wavering breath.*
VERB =tremble V V-ing

wavy /weɪvi/ **wavier, waviest**

1 **Wavy** hair is not straight or curly, but curves slightly. *She had short, wavy brown hair.*
ADJ-GRADED

2 A **wavy** line has a series of regular curves along it. *The boxes were decorated with a wavy gold line. ...leaves with wavy edges.*
ADJ-GRADED: usu ADJ n

wax /wæks/ **waxes, waxing, waxed** ◆◆◇◇◇

1 **Wax** is a solid, slightly shiny substance made of fat or oil which is used to make candles and polish. It melts when it is heated. *There were coloured candles which had spread pools of wax on the furniture... She loved the scent in the house of wax polish.*
N-MASS

2 If you **wax** a surface, you put a thin layer of wax onto it, especially in order to polish it. *We'd have long talks while she helped me wax the floor. ...all those Sundays spent washing and waxing the car.*
VERB V n

3 If you have your legs **waxed**, you have the hair removed from your legs by having wax put on them and then pulled off quickly. *She has just had her legs waxed at the local beauty parlour... She could go shopping, and wax her legs.*
VERB have n V-ed V n

4 **Wax** is the sticky yellow substance found in your ears.
N-UNCOUNT

5 If you say that someone, for example, **waxes** lyrical or **waxes** indignant about a subject, you mean that they talk a lot in a lyrical or indignant way about it. *He waxed lyrical about the skills and commitment of his employees... My mother waxed eloquent on the theme of wifely duty.*
VERB V adj

6 If something **waxes and wanes**, it first increases and then decreases over a period of time. *Portugal and Spain had possessed vast empires that waxed and waned.*
PHRASE: V inflect

waxed paper. **Waxed paper** is the same as **wax paper**.
N-UNCOUNT

waxen /wæksən/. A **waxen** face is very pale and looks very unhealthy; a literary word. *Her eyes were fixed on the waxen face of her son, willing him to live.*
ADJ

wax paper. **Wax paper** is paper that has been covered with a thin layer of wax in order to make it waterproof.
N-UNCOUNT

waxwork /wækswɜːrk/ **waxworks**

1 A **waxwork** is a model of a person, especially a famous person, made out of wax.
N-COUNT

2 A **waxworks** is a place where waxworks are displayed for the public to look at. **Waxworks** is both the singular and the plural form.
N-COUNT

waxy /wæksi/. Something that is **waxy** looks or feels like wax. *Choose small waxy potatoes for the salad. ...the waxy coating on the insect's body.*
ADJ-GRADED: usu ADJ n

way /weɪ/ **ways** ◆◆◆◆◆

1 If you refer to a **way** of doing something, you are referring to how you can do it, for example the action you can take or the method you can use to achieve it. *Freezing isn't a bad way of preserving food... Another way of making new friends is to go to an evening class... I worked myself into a frenzy plotting ways to make him jealous... I can't think of a worse way to spend my time... There just might be a way... 'All right, Mrs Bates,' she said. 'We'll do it your way'.*
N-COUNT: oft N *of* -ing, N to-inf

2 If you talk about the **way** someone does something, you are talking about the qualities their action has. *She smiled in a friendly way... He had a*
N-COUNT: usu sing, usu adj N

strange way of talking... I also used to love the smooth way in which the foreigner operated.

3 If a general statement or description is true in a particular **way**, that is a particular manner or form that it takes in a specific case. *Computerized reservation systems help airline profits in several ways... She was afraid in a way that was quite new to her... To be female is not a disability; it is just a particular way of being human.* N-COUNT: with supp, oft *in* N

4 You use **way** in expressions such as **in some ways, in many ways**, and **in every way** to indicate the degree or extent to which a statement is true. *In some ways, the official opening is a formality... She described her lover as 'perfect in every way'.* N-COUNT: *in* N with supp =respect

5 The **ways** of a particular person or group of people are their customs or their usual behaviour. *He denounces people who urge him to alter his ways... I think you've been too long in Cornwall. You've forgotten the ways of the city... He said he was against returning to old authoritarian ways.* N-PLURAL: with supp

6 If you refer to someone's **way**, you are referring to their usual or preferred type of behaviour. *She is now divorced and, in her usual resourceful way, has started her own business... Direct confrontation was not his way.* N-SING: with poss

7 You use **way** to refer to one particular opinion or interpretation of something, when others are possible. *I suppose that's one way of looking at it... With most of Dylan's lyrics, however, there are other ways of interpreting the words... Sometimes, the bank manager just doesn't see it your way.* N-COUNT: with supp

8 You use **way** when mentioning one of a number of possible, alternative results or decisions. *There is no indication which way the vote could go... The judge could have decided either way.* N-COUNT: with supp

9 The **way** you feel about something is your attitude to it or your opinion about it. *I'm terribly sorry – I had no idea you felt that way.* N-SING: with supp

10 If you mention the **way** that something happens, you are mentioning the fact that it happens. *I hate the way he manipulates people... You may remember the way each scene ended with someone looking pensive or significant.* N-SING: *the* N that

11 You use **way** in expressions such as **push your way, work your way**, or **eat your way**, followed by a prepositional phrase, in order to suggest an idea of movement, progress, or force as well as the action described by the verb. *She thrust her way into the crowd... He thought we were trying to buy our way into his company... Start at the bottom and try to work your way up.* N-SING: poss N

12 The **way** somewhere consists of the different places that you go through or the route that you take in order to get there. *Does anybody know the way to the bathroom?... I'm afraid I can't remember the way... We're not even a third of the way there... We'll go out the back way.* N-COUNT: usu *the* N in sing, oft N *to* n

13 If you go or look a particular **way**, you go or look in that direction. *As he strode into the kitchen, he passed Pop coming the other way... They paused at the top of the stairs, doubtful as to which way to go next... Could you look this way?* N-SING: with supp

14 You can refer to the direction you are travelling in as your **way**; used in spoken English. *It's not very far out of his way... She would say she was going my way and offer me a lift.* N-SING: poss N

15 If you lose your **way**, you take a wrong or unfamiliar route, so that you do not know how to get to the place that you want to go to. If you find your **way**, you manage to get to the place that you want to go to. *The men lost their way in a sandstorm and crossed the border by mistake... They've changed a lot of the old street names, and people can't find their way anymore.* N-SING: poss N

16 You talk about people going their different **ways** in order to say that their lives develop differently and they have less contact with each other. *It wasn't until we each went our separate ways that I began to learn how to do things for myself... You go your way and I'll go mine.* N-COUNT: poss N

17 If something comes your **way**, you get it or receive it. *Take advantage of the opportunities coming your way in a couple of months... If I run into anything that might interest you, I'll send it your way.* N-SING: poss N

18 If someone or something is in the **way**, they prevent you from moving forward or seeing clearly. *'You're standing in the way,' she said. 'Would you mind moving aside'... Get out of my way!* N-SING: *the*/poss N, *in/out of* N

19 **Way** is used in the names of some roads, and also in the names of some long-distance walking paths in the countryside. *Silvertown Way, was that the road? ...the well-trodden 250-mile Pennine Way.* N-IN-NAMES: n N

20 You can use **way** to refer to the area near where someone lives or near a specified place; an informal use. *If you speak standard English anywhere round our way, people tend to view you with suspicion. ...somebody from Newcastle way.* N-UNCOUNT: supp N

21 You use **way** in expressions like **the right way up** and **the other way round** to refer to one of two or more possible positions or arrangements that something can have. *The flag was held the wrong way up by some spectators... It's important to fit it the right way round.* N-SING: with supp

22 You can use **way** to emphasize, for example, that something is a great distance away or is very much below or above a particular level or amount. *Way down in the valley to the west is the town of Freiburg... These exam results are way above average... I have to decide my plan way in advance.* ADV: ADV adv/prep

23 If you split something a number of **ways**, you divide it into a number of different parts or quantities, usually fairly equal in size. *The region was split three ways, between Greece, Serbia and Bulgaria... Splitting the price six ways had still cost them each a bundle.* ► Also a combining form. *...a simple three-way division.* N-PLURAL: num N; COMB in ADJ: ADJ n

24 **Way** is used in expressions such as **a long way, a little way**, and **quite a way**, to say how far away something is or how far you have travelled. *Some of them live in places quite a long way from here... A little way further down the lane we passed the driveway to a house... We've a fair way to go yet.* N-SING: *a* N, usu supp N

25 **Way** is used in expressions such as **a long way, a little way**, and **quite a way**, to say how far away in time something is. *Success is still a long way off... August is still an awfully long way away.* N-SING: *a* N, usu supp N

26 You use **way** in expressions such as **all the way, most of the way** and **half the way** to refer to the extent to which an action has been completed. *He had unscrewed the caps most of the way... When was the last time you listened to an album all the way through?* N-SING: predet/quant *the* N

PHRASES

27 If something is **across the way**, it is nearby, especially on the opposite side of a road or area; an informal use. *...the big gabled house across the way.*

28 You use **all the way** to emphasize how long a distance is. *He had to walk all the way home... That dress came all the way from New York.* usu PHR after v, oft PHR adv/prep

29 You can use **all the way** to emphasize that your remark applies to every part of a situation, activity, or period of time. *Having started a revolution we must go all the way... I'll support him all the way.* PHR after v

30 You can use **as is the way** to say that a particular situation or example of behaviour is typical and you would not expect it to be different. *As is the way with these gatherings, the declarations were largely drafted before the delegations arrived.* usu PHR *with/of* n

31 If you say that someone is **in a bad way**, you mean they are in a poor state of health; an informal expression. *He's in a bad way, but able to talk.* v-link PHR

32 If you say that something exists, happens, or develops **in a big way**, you are emphasizing its great degree or importance; an informal expression. *The man who took over a few weeks later has also helped further her career in a big way... Soccer in the States has never taken off in a big way.* PHR after v

33 If someone says that you **can't have it both ways**, they are telling you that you have to choose between two things and cannot do or have them both. *Countries cannot have it both ways: the cost of a cleaner environment may sometimes be fewer jobs* V inflects

in dirty industries... Make up your mind, you can't have it both ways.

34 You say **by the way** when you add something to what you are saying, especially something that you have just thought of; used in spoken English. *The name Latifah, by the way, means 'delicate'... By the way, how did your seminar go?*
PHR with cl PRAGMATICS =incidentally

35 You use **by way of** when you are explaining the purpose of something that you have said or are about to say. For example, if you say something **by way of an introduction**, you say it as an introduction. *By way of contrast, Manchester United will travel slightly more than 1,200 miles... 'I get very superstitious about things like that,' she said by way of explanation.*
PREP: PREP n PRAGMATICS

36 If you do something **by way of** a particular method, you use that method to do it; used in written English. *I teach psychology by way of a range of traditional lectures, practicals and tutorials.*
PREP: PREP n

37 If you go somewhere **by way of** a particular place, you go through that place in order to get to where you want. *The path goes under the river by way of the tunnel.*
PREP: PREP n =via

38 If someone **changes** their **ways** or **mends** their **ways**, they permanently improve their behaviour or their way of doing something. *What can be done to encourage convicted offenders to change their ways?*
V inflects =reform

39 If you **clear the way**, **open the way**, or **prepare the way** for something, you create an opportunity for it to happen. *The talks are meant to clear the way for formal negotiations on a new constitution... The decision could open the way for other children to sue their parents.*
V inflects, usu PHR *for* n

40 If you say that someone takes **the easy way out**, you disapprove of them because they do what is easiest for them in a difficult situation, rather than dealing with it properly. *As soon as things got difficult he took the easy way out... It is the easy way out to blame others for our failure.*
PHR after v, v-link PHR PRAGMATICS

41 You use **either way** in order to introduce a statement which is true in each of the two possible or alternative cases that you have just mentioned. *The sea may rise or the land may fall; either way the sand dunes will be gone in a short time.*
PHR with cl

42 If you say that a particular type of action or development is **the way forward**, you approve of it or recommend it because it is likely to lead to success. *...people who genuinely believe that anarchy is the way forward... Young players have got to be the way forward for every club.*
usu v-link PHR

43 If someone **gets** their **way** or **has** their **way**, nobody stops them doing what they want to do. You can also say that someone **gets** their **own** way or **has** their **own way**. *She is very good at using her charm to get her way.*
V inflects

44 If one thing **gives way to** another, the first thing is replaced by the second. *First he had been numb. Then the numbness gave way to anger... The last houses give way to soybean fields.*
V inflects, PHR n

45 If an object that is supporting something **gives way**, it breaks or collapses, so that it can no longer support that thing. *The hook in the ceiling had given way and the lamp had fallen blazing on to the table.*
V inflects

46 If you **give way** to someone or something that you have been resisting, you stop resisting and allow yourself to be persuaded or controlled by them; used in written English. *It seems the President has given way to pressure from the hard-liners... He finally gave way to an impulse and pulled her toward him.*
V inflects, usu PHR *to* n =give in, yield

47 In British English, if a moving person or a vehicle or its driver **gives way**, they slow down or stop in order to allow other people or vehicles to pass in front of them. The usual American word is **yield**. *Give way to traffic coming from the left, especially at roundabouts.*
V inflects, oft PHR *to* n

48 If you say that someone or something **has a way of** doing a particular thing, you mean that they often do it, especially when you are warning someone to expect them to do it. *Bosses have a way of always finding out about such things.*
V inflects, PHR -ing =have a habit of

49 If you say that a person **has a way with** something or someone, you mean that that person seems to have a natural skill or instinct for dealing with them; used in spoken English showing approval. *Constance doesn't have a way with words the way you do... He seems to have had a way with foreigners.*
V inflects, PHR n PRAGMATICS

50 If you say **have it your way** or **have it your own way**, you are telling someone in an annoyed way that you will agree with or accept their suggestion even though you do not think they are right. *All right then, have it your way. Be like that.*
PRAGMATICS

51 You use **in no way** or **not in any way** to emphasize that a statement is not at all true. *In no way am I going to adopt any of his methods... A spokesman insisted the two events were 'in no way related'... 'He hasn't become more boring has he?' she laughs. 'No. Not in any way.'*
PRAGMATICS

52 If you say that something is true **in a way**, you mean that although a statement is not completely true, it is true to a limited extent or in certain respects. You use **in a way** to reduce the force of a statement. *In a way, I suppose I'm frightened of failing... It made things very unpleasant in a way.*
PHR with cl PRAGMATICS

53 If you say that someone does something or contributes to something **in a small way**, you mean that although they do not do very much, their actions are useful or significant. *...demonstrations against corruption, which began in a small way last week... By doing this you will, in a small way, help win the victory.*
PHR after v, PHR with cl

54 If you say that someone **gets in the way**, or **is in the way**, you are annoyed because their presence or their actions stop you doing something properly. *'We wouldn't get in the way,' Suzanne promised. 'We'd just stand quietly in a corner.'*
V inflects

55 To **get in the way** of something means to make it difficult for it to happen, continue, or be appreciated properly. *She had a job which never got in the way of her leisure interests.*
V inflects, oft PHR *of* n

56 If you **know** your **way around** a particular subject, system, or job, or if you **know** your **way about** it, you know all the procedures and facts about it. *He knows his way around the intricate maze of European law... He knows his way about the system better than do most ministers.*
V inflects, PHR n

57 If you say that someone **is laughing all the way to the bank**, you mean that they are making a lot of money very easily; an informal expression. *The lucrative contract with television means that England's wealthy football clubs will now be laughing all the way to the bank.*
V inflects

58 If you **lead the way** along a particular route, you go along it in front of someone in order to show them where to go. *She grabbed his suitcase and led the way.*
V inflects

59 If a person or group **leads the way** in a particular activity, they are the first person or group to do it or they make the most new developments in it. *Sony has also led the way in shrinking the size of compact-disc players.*
V inflects, usu PHR *in* -ing/n

60 If you say that someone or something **has come a long way**, you mean that they have developed, progressed, or become very successful. *He has come a long way since the days he could only afford one meal a day.*
have inflects, oft PHR *since* n

61 You can use **by a long way** to emphasize that something is, for example, much better, worse, or bigger than any other thing of that kind. *It was, by a long way, the worst meeting I have ever attended... Our favourite by a long way was the supermarkets' own brand.*
PHR with cl, compar/superl PHR PRAGMATICS =easily

62 If you say that something is **a long way from** being true, you are emphasizing that it is definitely not true. *She is a long way from being the richest person in Britain... That's a long way from the truth.*
v-link PHR n/-ing PRAGMATICS =far from

63 If you say that something **goes a long way** towards doing a particular thing, you mean that it is an important factor in achieving that thing. *Al-*
V inflects, usu PHR *towards/to* -ing/n

though by no means a cure, it goes a long way towards making the patient's life more tolerable.

64 If you say that someone has **lost** their **way**, you are criticizing them because they do not have any good ideas any more, or seem to have become unsure about what to do. *Why has the White House lost its way on tax and budget policy?*
V inflects

65 When you **make** your **way** somewhere, you walk or travel there. *He made his way to the market-place, as he had been instructed to do... He made his way home at last.*
V inflects, PHR prep/adv

66 If one person or thing **makes way** for another, the first is replaced by the second. *He said he was prepared to make way for younger people in the party... A number of houses would have to be demolished to make way for the new building.*
V inflects, usu PHR *for* n

67 If you say **there's no way** that something will happen, you are emphasizing that you think it will definitely not happen. *There was absolutely no way that we were going to be able to retrieve it.*
V inflects, usu PHR that PRAGMATICS

68 You can say **no way** as an emphatic way of saying no; an informal expression. *Mike, no way am I playing cards with you for money... That was not the life Jack Hewitt planned to live. No way!*
PRAGMATICS

69 You use **in the way of** or **by way of** in order to specify the kind of thing you are talking about. *Latvia is a country without much in the way of natural resources... Meetings held today produced little in the way of an agreement... The man with whom she maintains a relationship provides nothing by way of support.*
PHR n, usu amount/n PHR n =as regards

70 If you **are on** your **way**, you have started your journey somewhere. *He has been allowed to leave China and is on his way to Britain... By sunrise tomorrow we'll be on our way.*
v-link PHR, oft PHR prep/adv

71 If you **go on** your **way**, you continue with your journey. *She picked up her bag, and went on her way.*
V inflects

72 If something happens **on the way** or **along the way**, it happens during the course of a particular event or process. *You may have to learn a few new skills along the way.*

73 If you are **on** your **way** or **well on** your **way** to something, you have made so much progress that you are almost certain to achieve that thing. *I am now out of hospital and well on the way to recovery.*
usu v-link PHR *to* n/-ing

74 If something is **on the way**, it is due to come in the near future. *The forecasters say more snow is on the way... She is married with twin sons and a third child on the way.*
v-link PHR, *with/have* n PHR

75 You can use **one way or another** or **one way or the other** when you want to say that something definitely happens, but without giving any details about how it happens. *...those who had entered Germany one way or another during the war... You know pretty well everyone here, one way or the other.*
PHR after v, PHR with cl

76 You use **one way or the other** or **one way or another** to refer to two possible decisions or conclusions that have previously been mentioned, without stating which one is reached or preferred. *We've got to make our decision one way or the other... I didn't really care one way or another.*
PHR after v

77 You say **in more ways than one** to indicate that what you have said is intended to have more than one meaning. *These local elections may prove a turning point in more ways than one.*
PHR with cl

78 You use **the other way around** or **the other way round** to refer to the opposite of what you have just said. *You'd think you were the one who did me the favor, and not the other way around.*

79 If something or someone is **on the way out**, or **on** their **way out**, they are likely to disappear or to be replaced very soon. *There are encouraging signs that cold war attitudes are on the way out... The ban on Sunday shopping could be on its way out before Christmas... He is rumoured to be on the way out of professional cycling following a disastrous season.*
usu v-link PHR

80 If you **go out of** your **way** to do something, for example to help someone, you make a special effort to do it. *He was very kind to me and seemed to go out of his way to help me.*
V inflects, usu PHR to-inf

81 If you **keep out of** someone's **way** or **stay out of** their **way**, you avoid them or do not get involved with them. *I'd kept out of his way as much as I could... He warned the army to stay out of the way of the relief effort.*
V inflects

82 When something is **out of the way**, it has finished or you have dealt with it, so that it is no longer a problem or needs no more time spent on it. *The plan has to remain confidential at least until the local elections are out of the way... It would have been better to have got it out of the way earlier.*
v-link PHR, PHR after v =over with

83 If you **go** your **own way**, you do what you want rather than what everyone else does or expects. *In school I was a loner. I went my own way.*
V inflects

84 You use **in the same way** to introduce a situation that you are comparing with one that you have just mentioned, because there is a strong similarity between them. *There is no reason why a gifted aircraft designer should also be a capable pilot. In the same way, a brilliant pilot can be a menace behind the wheel of a car.*
PHR with cl PRAGMATICS =likewise

85 If you say that someone is **set in** their **ways**, you mean that they have been behaving in the same way for many years and do not want to change. *He was too set in his ways to make any real changes.*
v-link PHR

86 You can use **that way** and **this way** to refer to a statement or comment that you have just made. *Some of us have habits few people know about and we keep it this way... We have a beautiful city and we pray it stays that way... I've never found it hard to make friends so I suppose I was lucky that way.*
PHR after v, adj PHR =like that, like this

87 You can use **that way** or **this way** to refer to an action or situation that you have just mentioned, when you go on to mention the likely consequence or effect of it. *Keep the soil moist. That way, the seedling will flourish... I know it's unfair that I am left holding the baby; but at least this way I know that she's being well looked after.*
PHR with cl PRAGMATICS

88 You can use **the way things are going** to indicate that you expect something to happen because of the way the present situation is developing. *The way things are going, perhaps he won't come at all.*
be inflects, PHR with cl

89 You add **to** my **way of thinking** to a statement in order to indicate that you are giving your opinion. *To my way of thinking, it didn't seem as if it ought to be so terribly complicated.*
PHR with cl PRAGMATICS

90 If you say that there are **no two ways about it**, you are emphasizing that there is no doubt at all about the situation or how it should be interpreted; used in spoken English. *You stay here, you die. No two ways about it.*
usu v-link PHR PRAGMATICS

91 If an activity or plan is **under way**, it has begun and is now taking place. *A full-scale security operation is now under way... The court case got under way last autumn.*
usu v-link PHR

92 Every which way and **any which way** are used to emphasize that something happens, or might happen, in a lot of different ways, or using a lot of different methods; used in American English or informal British English. *He re-ran the experiment every which way he could... They are just happy to sell their inventory any which way they can.*
PHR after v, oft PHR cl PRAGMATICS

93 Every which way is used to emphasize that things move in a lot of different directions or are arranged in a lot of different positions; used in American English or informal British English. *...cars parked every which way.*
PHR after v PRAGMATICS

94 • to see **the error of** your **ways**: see **error**. • to **look the other way**: see **look**.

-way /-weɪ/. **-way** combines with numbers to form adjectives that describe a means of communication that functions or takes place between the stated number of people. *...a two-way radio. ...a system of three-way communication.* • See also **one-way, two-way**.
COMB in ADJ

waylay /weɪleɪ, AM -leɪ/ **waylays, waylaying, waylaid.** If someone **waylays** you, they stop you when you are going somewhere, for example in order to talk to you, to steal something from you, or to attack you. *She was forever waylaying him in odd holes and corners of the hotel... The trucks*
VERB V n *get* V-ed

are being waylaid by bandits... I'm sorry, Nick, I got waylaid.

way of life, ways of life ◆◆◇◇◇

1 A **way of life** is the behaviour and habits that are typical of a particular person or group, or that are chosen by them. *Mining activities have totally disrupted the traditional way of life of the Yanomami Indians.* N-COUNT: usu sing, oft poss N, adj N

2 If you describe a particular activity as a **way of life** for someone, you mean that it has become a very important and regular thing in their life, rather than something they do or experience occasionally. *She likes it so much it's become a way of life for her. ...cities where violence is a way of life.* N-COUNT: usu sing

way-out. If you describe someone or something as **way-out**, you are critical of them because they are very unusual or different from other things or people, especially if they are very modern or fashionable; an informal word. *They will not allow your more way-out ideas to pass unchallenged... Didn't you find her a little way-out for you, a bit too arty?* ◆◆◇◇◇ ADJ-GRADED PRAGMATICS =weird

wayside /weɪsaɪd/ **waysides**

1 The **wayside** is the side of the road; a literary use. *...groups of men playing cards by lamplight at the wayside. ...a wayside drinking fountain.* N-COUNT: usu *the* N in sing =roadside

2 If a person or plan **falls by the wayside**, they fail or stop before they complete what they set out to do. *Amateurs fall by the wayside when the going gets tough... In the mid 70s, Morrison planned a comedy album. The project fell by the wayside.* PHRASE: V inflects

way station, way stations. A **way station** is a place where people stop to eat and rest when they are on a long journey. N-COUNT

wayward /weɪwəʳd/. If you describe a person or their behaviour as **wayward**, you mean that they are likely to change suddenly, are often selfish or stubborn, and are therefore difficult to control. *...wayward children with a history of severe emotional problems.* ♦ **waywardness** *...the curiosity, caprice and waywardness of children.* ◆◇◇◇◇ ADJ-GRADED: usu ADJ n =unruly, unmanageable; N-UNCOUNT: oft with poss

WC /dʌbəljuː siː/ **WCs.** In British English, a toilet is sometimes referred to as a **WC**, especially on signs or in advertisements for houses, flats, or hotels. **WC** is an abbreviation for 'water closet'. N-COUNT =toilet

we /wɪ, STRONG wiː/ ◆◆◆◆◆

We is the first person plural pronoun. **We** is used as the subject of a verb.

1 A speaker or writer uses **we** to refer both to himself or herself and to one or more other people as a group. In conversation, **we** can also include someone who is not present. You can use **we** before a noun to make it clear which group of people you are referring to. *We both swore we'd be friends ever after... We ordered another bottle of champagne... Don't you think we should ask this young man some technical questions?... We students outnumbered our teachers.* PRON-PLURAL

2 **We** is sometimes used to refer to people in general. *We need to take care of our bodies. ...the withdrawal symptoms that we all experience at the end of a long, close relationship.* PRON-PLURAL

3 A speaker or writer may use **we** instead of 'I' in order to include the listeners or readers in what he or she is saying, especially when talking about how a book or talk is organized; a formal use. *We will now consider the raw materials from which the body derives energy.* PRON-PLURAL

weak /wiːk/ **weaker, weakest** ◆◆◆◆◇

1 If someone is **weak**, they are not healthy or do not have good muscles, so that they cannot move quickly or carry heavy things. *I was too weak to move or think or speak... His arms and legs were weak.* ♦ **weakly** *'I'm all right,' Max said weakly, but his breathing came in jagged gasps... He weakly pressed his arms against her sides.* ♦ **weakness** *Symptoms of anaemia include weakness, fatigue and iron deficiency.* ADJ-GRADED ≠strong; ADV-GRADED: ADV with v; N-UNCOUNT

2 If someone has an organ or sense that is **weak**, it is not very effective or powerful, or is likely to fail. *Until the beating, Cantanco's eyesight had been weak, but adequate... She tired easily and had a weak heart.* ADJ-GRADED

3 If you describe someone as **weak**, you mean that they are not very confident or determined, so that they are often frightened or worried, or easily influenced by other people. *He was a nice doctor, but a weak man who wasn't going to stick his neck out... You have been conditioned to believe that it is weak to be scared.* ♦ **weakness** *Many people felt that admitting to stress was a sign of weakness.* ADJ-GRADED ≠strong; N-UNCOUNT

4 If you describe someone's voice or smile as **weak**, you mean that it not very loud or big, suggesting that the person lacks confidence, enthusiasm, or physical strength. *His weak voice was almost inaudible... He managed a weak smile.* ♦ **weakly** *He smiled weakly at reporters.* ADJ-GRADED =feeble; ADV-GRADED: ADV after v

5 If an object or surface is **weak**, it breaks easily and cannot support a lot of weight or resist a lot of strain. *The owner said the bird may have escaped through a weak spot in the aviary... Swimming is helpful for bones that are porous and weak.* ADJ-GRADED ≠strong

6 A **weak** physical force does not have much power or intensity. *The molecules in regular liquids are held together by relatively weak bonds... Strong winds can turn boats when the tide is weak. ...the weak winter sun.* ♦ **weakly** *The mineral is weakly magnetic... Down through the trees the wind whooshed weakly, like a sick child.* ADV-GRADED ≠strong; ADV-GRADED: ADV adj/-ed, ADV after v

7 If individuals or groups are **weak**, they do not have any power or influence. *The council was too weak to do anything about it.* ► **The weak** are people who are weak. *He voiced his solidarity with the weak and defenceless.* ♦ **weakness** *It made me feel patronised, in a position of weakness.* ADJ-GRADED =powerless; N-PLURAL: *the* N; N-UNCOUNT =impotence

8 A **weak** government or leader does not have much control, and is not prepared or able to act firmly or severely. *The changes come after mounting criticism that the government is weak and indecisive... The chief editorial writer also blames weak leadership for the current crisis.* ♦ **weakly** *...the weakly-led movement for reform.* ♦ **weakness** *Officials fear that he might interpret the emphasis on diplomacy as a sign of weakness.* ADJ-GRADED ≠strong; ADV-GRADED; N-UNCOUNT

9 If you describe something such a country's currency, economy, industry, or government as **weak**, you mean that it is not successful, and may be likely to fail or collapse. *The weak dollar means American goods are relative bargains for foreigners... When the economy is weak, it's very hard for suppliers to raise their prices.* ♦ **weakness** *The weakness of his regime is showing more and more... The pound's weakness compounded the widespread gloom in the City.* ADJ-GRADED ≠strong; N-UNCOUNT: usu with poss

10 If something such as an argument or case is **weak**, it is not convincing or there is little evidence to support it. *Do you think the prosecution made any particular errors, or did they just have a weak case?... The claim exposed a weak point in the structure of facts upon which his argument rested... The evidence against him was weak and insufficient.* ♦ **weakly** *The doctor also rather weakly puts the case that the mother-to-be has many relatives.* ♦ **weakness, weaknesses** *...the strengths and weaknesses of the government's case... The Law recognises the weakness of claims based on retrospective knowledge.* ADJ-GRADED =flimsy ≠strong; ADV-GRADED: ADV before v; N-VAR

11 A **weak** drink, chemical, or drug contains very little of a particular substance, for example because it has been diluted with a lot of water. *Grace poured a cup of weak tea... You can neutralise the smell by wiping the plaster with a very weak bleach solution.* ADJ-GRADED ≠strong

12 Your **weak** points are the qualities or talents you do not possess, or the things you are not very good at. *You may very well be asked what your weak points are. Don't try to claim you don't have any... Geography was my weak subject... His short stories tend to be weak on plot.* ♦ **weakness** *His only weakness is his temperament... There's some weakness in their teaching ability.* ADJ-GRADED: oft ADJ *on* n ≠strong; N-VAR

13 You can say that someone has **weak** features to mean that they do not have very distinctive facial ADJ-GRADED ≠strong

features, especially when you want to suggest that they do not have a strong character. *She was a plain-looking woman with a weak chin.*

14 See also **weakness**.

weaken /wiːkən/ **weakens, weakening, weakened** ◆◆◆◇◇

1 If you **weaken** something or if it **weakens**, it becomes less strong or less powerful. *The recession has weakened so many firms that many can no longer survive... The Prime Minister's opponents believe that her authority has been fatally weakened... Family structures are weakening and breaking up.* V-ERG ≠strengthen V n V

2 If your resolve **weakens** or if something **weakens** it, you become less determined or less certain about taking a particular course of action that you had previously decided to take. *I looked at the list and felt my resolve weakening... Jennie weakened, and finally relented... The verdict hasn't weakened his resolve to fight the charges against him.* V-ERG V V n

3 If something **weakens** you, it causes you to lose some of your physical strength. *Malnutrition obviously weakens the patient.* VERB =debilitate V n

4 If something **weakens** an object, it does something to it which causes it to become less firm and more likely to break. *A bomb blast had weakened an area of brick on the back wall... Never dry underwear over direct heat; it will weaken the fabric.* VERB V n

weak-kneed. If you describe someone as **weak-kneed**, you mean that they are unable or unwilling to do anything because they are influenced by a strong emotion such as fear; an informal word. *He would need all his authority to keep the weak-kneed volunteers from bolting.* ADJ-GRADED

weakling /wiːklɪŋ/ **weaklings**

1 If you describe a person or an animal as a **weakling**, you mean that they are physically weak; used showing disapproval. N-COUNT PRAGMATICS

2 If you describe someone as a **weakling**, you mean that they are weak or cowardly in character; used showing disapproval. *...a moral weakling.* N-COUNT PRAGMATICS =wimp

weakness /wiːknəs/ **weaknesses.** If you have a **weakness** for something, you like it very much, although this is perhaps surprising or undesirable. *Stephen himself had a weakness for cats... His one weakness, apart from aeroplanes, is ice cream.* • See also **weak**. ◆◆◇◇◇ N-COUNT: usu sing, oft N *for* n

weal /wiːl/ **weals.** In British English, a **weal** is a swelling made on someone's skin by a blow, especially from something sharp or thin such as a sword or whip. *...the red weals left across his chest by the strap.* N-COUNT =welt

wealth /welθ/ ◆◆◆◇◇

1 Wealth is the possession of a large amount of money, property, or other valuable things. You can also refer to a particular person's money or property as their **wealth**. *Economic reform has brought relative wealth to peasant farmers... His own wealth grew.* N-UNCOUNT =affluence

2 If you say that someone or something has **a wealth of** good qualities or attributes, you are emphasizing that they have a very large number or amount of them; a formal use. *...such a wealth of creative expertise... The city boasts a wealth of beautiful churches.* N-SING: *a* N *of* n PRAGMATICS =abundance

wealthy /welθi/ **wealthier, wealthiest.** Someone who is **wealthy** has a large amount of money, property, or valuable possessions. *...a wealthy international businessman.* ► **The wealthy** are people who are wealthy. *...a measure to raise income taxes on the wealthy.* ◆◆◇◇◇ ADJ-GRADED =affluent, rich N-PLURAL: *the* N =the rich

wean /wiːn/ **weans, weaning, weaned** ◆◇◇◇◇

1 When a baby or baby animal **is weaned**, its mother stops feeding it milk and starts giving it other food, especially solid food. *The baby would be weaned and she would bring it home... When would be the best time to start weaning my baby?... Phil took the labrador home and is weaning him off milk on to meat... Once weaned, the piglets may be put in pens.* ♦ **weaning** *Weaning should be a gradual process.* VERB *be* V-ed V n V n *off/from* n V-ed N-UNCOUNT

2 If you **wean** someone off a habit or something they like, you gradually make them stop doing it or liking it, especially when you think is bad for them. *He was mellowed by a wife who weaned him off violence and drink... You are given capsules or pills with small quantities of nicotine to wean you from the habit... Children should be weaned off television... It's two years since I've seen Iain. I'm still trying to wean myself off him but it's hard.* VERB V n *off/from* n V pron-refl *off/from* n

weapon /wepən/ **weapons** ◆◆◆◆◇

1 A **weapon** is an object such as a gun, a knife, or a missile, which is used to kill or hurt people in a fight or a war. *...nuclear weapons.* N-COUNT

2 A **weapon** is something such as knowledge about a particular subject, which you can use to protect yourself or to get what you want in a difficult situation. *I attack politicians with the one weapon they don't have, a sense of humor.* N-COUNT

weaponry /wepənri/. **Weaponry** is all the weapons that a group or country has or that are available to it. *...rich nations, armed with superior weaponry.* ◆◇◇◇◇ N-UNCOUNT

wear /weə^r/ **wears, wearing, wore, worn** ◆◆◆◆◇

1 When you **wear** something such as clothes, shoes, or jewellery, you have them on your body or on part of your body. *He was wearing a brown uniform... I sometimes wear contact lenses... She can't make her mind up what to wear.* VERB V n

2 If you **wear** your hair or beard in a particular way, you have it cut or styled in that way. *She wore her hair in a long braid... He wore a full moustache.* VERB V n prep/adv V n

3 If you **wear** a particular expression, that expression is on your face and shows the emotions that you are feeling. *When we drove through the gates, she wore a look of amazement... Millson's face wore a satisfied expression.* VERB V n

4 You use **wear** to refer to clothes that are suitable for a certain time or place. For example, **evening wear** is clothes suitable for the evening. *The shop stocks an extensive range of beach wear... Bring informal casual wear.* N-UNCOUNT: supp N

5 Wear is the amount or type of use that something has over a period of time. *You'll get more wear out of a hat if you choose one in a neutral colour... Rugs in the bedrooms got much less wear.* N-UNCOUNT =use

6 Wear is the damage or change that is caused by something being used a lot or for a long time. *...a large, well-upholstered armchair which showed signs of wear.* N-UNCOUNT

7 If something **wears**, it becomes thinner or weaker because it is constantly being used over a long period of time. *The stone steps, dating back to 1855, are beginning to wear... Your horse needs new shoes if the shoe has worn thin or smooth.* VERB V V adj

8 You can use **wear** to talk about how well something lasts over a period of time. For example, if something **wears well**, it still seems quite new or useful after a long time or a lot of use. *Casual shoes need to wear well... Ten years on, the original concept was wearing well.* VERB V adv

9 In informal British English, if you say that one person in a married couple **wears the trousers**, especially the wife, you mean that they are the one who makes all the decisions. The American expression is **wear the pants**. *She may give the impression that she wears the trousers but it's Tim who makes the final decisions.* PHRASES V inflects

10 If your patience or temper **is wearing thin**, you are beginning to lose patience or lose your temper, and are likely to become angry soon. *Her husband was sympathetic at first but his patience soon wore thin.* V inflects, usu cont

11 If you say that something **is wearing thin**, you mean that people do not find it funny or interesting any more and are becoming annoyed with it, because they have seen or heard it so many times. *Some of Wilson's eccentricities are beginning to wear thin.* V inflects, usu cont

12 If you say that someone is **the worse for wear**, you mean that they are tired, ill, or in a bad state because they have been very active, been through a difficult experience, or been drinking alcohol; an informal expression. *He arrived in Britain on January 9, disheveled and much the worse for wear.* v-link PHR

wear away. If you **wear** something **away** or if it **wears away**, it becomes thin and eventually disappears because it is used a lot or rubbed a lot. *It had a saddle with springs sticking out, which wore away the seat of my pants... The softer rock wears away.* PHRASAL VERB ERG V P n (not pron) V P Also V n P

wear down PHRASAL VERB

1 If you **wear** something **down** or if it **wears down**, it becomes flatter or smoother as a result of constantly rubbing against something else. *Pipe smokers sometimes wear down the tips of their teeth where they grip their pipes... The machines start to wear down, they don't make as many nuts and bolts as they used to... Although the tusk grows throughout the life of the elephant, they're wearing it down faster than they can grow it.* ERG V P n (not pron) V P V n P

2 If you **wear** someone **down**, you make them gradually weaker or less determined until they eventually do what you want, by being more persistent than they are. *None can match your sheer will-power and persistence in wearing down the opposition... They hoped the waiting and the uncertainty would wear down my resistance... He believed that he could wear her down if he only asked often enough.* V P n (not pron) V n P

wear off. If a sensation or feeling **wears off**, it disappears slowly until it no longer exists or has any effect. *For many the philosophy was merely a fashion, and the novelty soon wore off... Now that the initial shock was wearing off, he was in considerable pain... The contraceptive effect wears off in two days.* PHRASAL VERB V P

wear on. If you say that time **wears on**, you mean that it passes, especially when it seems to pass slowly. *As the day wore on Brand found himself increasingly impressed... The summer days wore on and life returned to its boring routine.* PHRASAL VERB =go on V P

wear out PHRASAL VERB

1 When something **wears out** or when you **wear** it **out**, it is used so much that it becomes thin or weak and unable to be used any more. *Every time she consulted her watch, she wondered if the batteries were wearing out... Horses used for long-distance riding tend to wear their shoes out more quickly... He wore out his shoes wandering around Mexico City.* ERG V P V n P V P n (not pron)

2 If something **wears** you **out**, it makes you feel extremely tired; an informal use. *The past few days had really worn him out... The young people run around kicking a ball, wearing themselves out... The effect of the two severe defeats, and the continuous attacks, has been to wear out his troops.* =tire out, exhaust V n P V pron-refl P V P n (not pron)

3 If someone **wears out** their welcome with you, or if it **wears out**, they spend a lot of time with you and you are no longer happy that they are with you. You can also say that a feeling **wears out** or **is worn out**. *'Could you not stay with us while you are solving your mystery?'—'Oh, we don't want to wear out our welcome.'... His stubborn resistance to anything new eventually wore out the patience of his superiors... No matter how often they turn up, their welcome never wears out.* ERG V P n (not pron) V P n (not pron) V P Also V n P

4 See also **worn out**.

wearable /weərəbəl/. **Wearable** clothes are practical, comfortable, and suitable for ordinary people to wear, rather than being very unusual or extreme. *It's fashionable but wearable, and it's easy to look after.* ADJ-GRADED

wear and tear /weər ən teəʳ/. **Wear and tear** is the damage or change that is caused to something when it is being used normally. *...the problem of wear and tear on the equipment in the harsh desert conditions.* N-UNCOUNT

wearer /weərəʳ/ **wearers.** You can use **wearer** to indicate that someone is wearing a certain thing on a particular occasion or that they often wear a certain thing. *These suits are designed to protect the wearer from cold shock as they enter the water... The mascara is suitable for contact lens wearers.* ◆◇◇◇◇ N-COUNT: oft N *of* n, n N

wearing /weərɪŋ/. If you say that a situation or activity is **wearing**, you mean that it requires a lot of energy and makes you feel mentally or physically tired. *She finds the continual confrontation very wearing... Being in demand can be rather wearing.* ADJ-GRADED: usu v-link ADJ =tiring, exhausting

wearisome /wɪərɪsəm/. If you describe something as **wearisome**, you mean that it is very tiring and boring or frustrating; a formal word. *...a long and wearisome journey... Sympathising with him eventually becomes somewhat wearisome.* ADJ-GRADED =tiresome

weary /wɪəri/ **wearier, weariest; wearies, wearying, wearied** ◆◆◇◇◇

1 If you are **weary**, you are very tired. *Rachel looked pale and weary. ...a weary traveller... He managed a weary smile.* ♦ **wearily** /wɪərɪli/ *I sighed wearily... Hector trudged wearily down Arthur Street.* ♦ **weariness** *Despite his weariness, Brand mustered a wan smile... He showed absolutely no signs of weariness.* ADJ-GRADED =exhausted ADV-GRADED: ADV after v N-UNCOUNT

2 If you are **weary of** something, you have become tired of it and have lost your enthusiasm for it. *They're getting awfully weary of this silly war... She was weary of being alone.* ♦ **wearily** *'I'm not Mrs Reynolds,' she said wearily... Measures like these sound wearily familiar.* ADJ-GRADED: v-link ADJ *of* n/-ing =tired ADV-GRADED: usu ADV after v, also ADV adj

3 If you **weary** of something or it **wearies** you, you become tired of it and lose your enthusiasm for it; a formal use. *The public had wearied of his repeated warnings of a revolution that never seemed to start... He had wearied of teaching in state universities... The political hysteria soon wearied him and he dropped the newspaper to the floor.* VERB =tire V *of* n/-ing V n

weasel /wiːzəl/ **weasels.** A **weasel** is a small wild animal with a long thin body, a tail, short legs, and reddish-brown fur. ◆◇◇◇◇ N-COUNT

weather /weðəʳ/ **weathers, weathering, weathered** ◆◆◆◆◇

1 The **weather** is the condition of the atmosphere in one area at a particular time, for example if it is raining, hot, or windy. *The weather was bad... I like cold weather... Fishing is possible in virtually any weather. ...the weather conditions.* ● If you say that someone does something **in all weathers**, you mean that they do it regularly whether the weather is good or bad. *They go out in all weathers.* N-UNCOUNT PHRASE: PHR after v, v-link PHR

2 If something such as wood or rock **weathers** or **is weathered**, it changes colour or shape as a result of the wind, sun, rain, or frost. *Unpainted wooden furniture weathers to a grey colour... This rock has been weathered and eroded.* ♦ **weathered** *The facade of the building was a little weathered... The man had a worn, weathered face.* V-ERG V *be* V-ed Also V n ADJ-GRADED =weather-beaten

3 If you **weather** a difficult time or a difficult situation, you survive it and are able to continue normally after it has passed or ended. *The company has weathered the recession... The government has weathered its worst political crisis intact.* VERB V n

● to **weather the storm**: see **storm**.

4 If you **keep a weather eye on** someone or something, you stay alert so that you will notice if anything unpleasant happens. *Street committees keep a weather eye on the families in their district.* PHRASES V inflects, PHR n

5 In British English, if you say that someone **is making heavy weather of** a task, you are critical of them because they are doing it in an inefficient way and are making it seem more difficult than it really is. *Some of the riders in this section made heavy weather of the cross-country race.* V inflects, PHR n PRAGMATICS

6 If you say that you are **under the weather**, you mean that you feel slightly ill. *I was still feeling a bit under the weather.* v-link PHR =below par, unwell

weather-beaten; also spelled **weatherbeaten**.

1 If your face or skin is **weather-beaten**, it is rough with deep lines because you have spent a lot of time outside in bad weather. *...a stout man with a ruddy, weather-beaten face.* ADJ-GRADED: usu ADJ n =weathered

2 Something that is **weather-beaten** has become roughened and slightly damaged after being out in the weather for a long time. *They would look out through the cracks of their weather-beaten door.* ADJ-GRADED =weathered

weather forecast, weather forecasts. A **weather forecast** is a statement saying what the weather will be like the next day or for the next few days. N-COUNT

weather forecaster, weather forecasters. A **weather forecaster** is a person whose job is to study weather conditions and make reports predicting what the weather will be like for the next few days. N-COUNT

weatherman /weðəʳmæn/ **weathermen.** A **weatherman** is a man who makes weather forecasts at regular times on television or radio. N-COUNT

weatherproof /weðəʳpruːf/. Something that is **weatherproof** is made of material which protects it from the weather or keeps out wind and rain. *Use a weatherproof rucksack to carry your camera and lenses around in.* ADJ

weather station, weather stations. A **weather station** is a building that is used for studying and recording facts about the weather, so that weather forecasts can be made. N-COUNT

weather vane, weather vanes. A **weather vane** is a metal object on the roof of a building which turns round as the wind blows. It is used to show the direction of the wind. N-COUNT

weave /wiːv/ **weaves, weaving, wove, woven.** The form **weaved** is used for the past tense and past participle for meaning 4. ◆◆◇◇◇

1 If you **weave** cloth or a carpet, you make it by crossing the threads over and under each other using a machine called a loom. *They would spin and weave cloth, cook and attend to the domestic side of life... In one room, young mothers weave while babies doze in their laps.* ♦ **woven** *...woven cotton fabrics.* ♦ **weaving** *When I studied weaving, I became intrigued with natural dyes.* VERB; V n; V; ADJ: usu ADJ n; N-UNCOUNT

2 A particular **weave** is the way in which the threads are arranged in a cloth or carpet. *Fabrics with a close weave are ideal for painting.* N-COUNT: usu supp N

3 If you **weave** something such as a basket, you make it by crossing long plant stems or fibres over and under each other. *Jenny weaves baskets from willow she grows herself.* ♦ **woven** *The floors are covered with woven straw mats.* VERB; V n; ADJ: usu ADJ n

4 If you **weave** your way somewhere, you move between and around things as you go there. *The cars then weaved in and out of traffic at top speed... He weaved around the tables to where she sat with Bob... He weaves his way through a crowd.* VERB; V prep; V *way* prep/adv

5 If you **weave** a story or a tale, you invent a complicated story or tale; used in written English. *Jan Roberts weaves a compelling tale which traps a young woman in a world run by the Mafia.* VERB; V n

6 If you **weave** details into a story or design, you include them, so that they are closely linked together or so that they exist alongside each other; used in written English. *She weaves imaginative elements into her poems... Bragg weaves together the histories of his main characters.* VERB; V n *into* n; V pl-n with *together*

weaver /wiːvəʳ/ **weavers.** A **weaver** is a person who weaves cloth, carpets, or baskets. N-COUNT

web /web/ **webs** ◆◇◇◇◇

1 A **web** is the thin net made by a spider from a sticky substance which it produces in its body. *...the spider's web in the window.* N-COUNT =cobweb

2 A **web** is a complicated pattern of connections or relationships, sometimes considered as an obstacle or a danger. *He's forced to untangle a complex web of financial dealings... They accused him of weaving a web of lies and deceit. ...the complex web of life on this planet.* ● If you refer to a situation as **a tangled web**, you are emphasizing that it is very confused. *Relationships are often a tangled web at the best of times.* N-COUNT: usu sing, oft N *of* n; PHRASE: N inflects PRAGMATICS

3 The Web is the same as **the World-Wide Web**. N-PROPER

webbed /webd/. **Webbed** feet or toes have a piece of skin between the toes. Water birds such as ducks have webbed feet. ADJ: ADJ n

webbing /webɪŋ/. **Webbing** is strong material which is woven in strips and used to make belts or straps, or used in seats to support the springs. N-UNCOUNT

wed /wed/ **weds, wedded.** The form **wed** is used in the present tense and is the past tense. The past participle can be either **wed** or **wedded.** If one person **weds** another or if two people **wed** or **are wed**, they get married; an old-fashioned use that also occurs in tabloid newspapers and informal broadcast news. *In 1952 she wed film director Roger Vadim... The couple wed late at night in front of just nine guests... They were wed at Amiens last August... His cousin was about to wed.* ● See also **newlyweds, wedded.** ◆◆◇◇◇ V-RECIP-ERG: no cont =marry; V n; pl-n V; *be* V-ed; V (non-recip)

Wed.; also spelled **Weds.**. **Wed.** or **Weds.** is a written abbreviation for **Wednesday**. *Our big task for tomorrow (Wed) is to get them exit visas.* ◆◆◇◇◇

we'd /wɪd, STRONG wiːd/

1 We'd is the usual spoken form of 'we had', especially when 'had' is an auxiliary verb. *Come on, George, we'd better get back now... At the time we'd really nothing to tell the police.*

2 We'd is the usual spoken form of 'we would'. *If we smoked, we'd light a cigarette and let her try it out... I don't know how we'd have managed without her!*

wedded /wedɪd/

1 If you are **wedded to** something such as an idea, you support it so strongly or like it so much that you are unable to give it up; a formal use. *Conservationists are mostly wedded to preserving diversity in nature.* ADJ-GRADED: v-link ADJ *to* n =committed

2 Wedded means the same as married; a formal use. *He proposed she become his lawfully wedded wife... She clings to a romantic fantasy of wedded bliss.* ADJ: ADJ n

wedding /wedɪŋ/ **weddings.** A **wedding** is a marriage ceremony and the party or special meal that often takes place after the ceremony. *Most Britons want a traditional wedding. ...a wedding present. ...the couple's 22nd wedding anniversary.* ◆◆◆◇◇ N-COUNT

wedding band, wedding bands. A **wedding band** is the same as a **wedding ring**. N-COUNT

wedding ring, wedding rings. A **wedding ring** is a plain ring that you wear to show that you are married. N-COUNT =wedding band

wedge /wedʒ/ **wedges, wedging, wedged** ◆◆◇◇◇

1 If you **wedge** something, you force it to remain in a particular position by holding it there tightly or by fixing something next to it to prevent it from moving. *I shut the shed door and wedged it with a log of wood... We slammed the gate after them, wedging it shut with planks.* VERB; V n; V n adj

2 If you **wedge** something somewhere, you fit it there tightly. *Wedge the plug into the hole... The hotel's wedged right between the two airports.* VERB; V n prep; V-ed

3 A **wedge** is an object with one pointed edge and one thick edge, which you put under a door to keep it firmly in position. N-COUNT

4 A **wedge** is a piece of metal with a pointed edge which is used for splitting a material such as stone or wood, by being hammered into a crack in the material. N-COUNT

5 A **wedge** of something such as fruit or cheese is a piece of it that has a thick triangular shape. N-COUNT: usu N *of* n

6 If someone **drives a wedge** between two people who are close, they cause ill feelings between them in order to weaken their relationship. *I started to feel Toby was driving a wedge between us.* PHRASES; V inflects, usu PHR *between* pl-n

7 If you say that something is **the thin end of the wedge**, you mean that it appears to be unimportant at the moment, but that it is the beginning of a harmful development. *I think it's the thin end of the wedge when you have armed police permanently on patrol round a city.* v-link PHR, PHR after v

wedlock /wedlɒk/

1 Wedlock is the state of being married; an old-fashioned use. N-UNCOUNT =marriage

2 If a baby is born **in wedlock**, it is born while its parents are married. If it is born **out of wedlock**, it is born at a time when its parents are not married; a formal expression. PHRASE: PHR after v

Wednesday /wenzdeɪ, -di/ **Wednesdays.** **Wednesday** is the day after Tuesday and before Thursday. *Come and have supper with us on Wednesday, if you're free... Did you happen to see her leave last Wednesday?... David always collects Alistair from school on Wednesdays.* 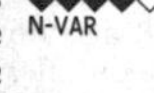 N-VAR

wee /wiː/ **wees, weeing, weed** ◆◆◇◇◇

1 In informal English, especially in Scotland, **wee** ADJ:

means small in size or extent. *I've got a wee kitten in the flat... He just needs to calm down a wee bit.* ADJ n =little

2 In British English, to **wee** means to urinate; an informal word used especially by children. *He said he wanted to wee.* ► Also a noun. *The baby has done a wee in his potty... I put him on his pot, he did some wee.* VERB V N-VAR =pee

weed /wiːd/ **weeds, weeding, weeded** ◆◆◇◇◇

1 A **weed** is a wild plant that grows in gardens or fields of crops and prevents the cultivated plants from growing properly. *With repeated applications of weedkiller, the weeds were overcome.* N-COUNT

2 Weed is a flowerless plant that grows in water and usually forms a thick floating mass. There are many different kinds of weed. *Large, clogging banks of weed are the only problem.* N-VAR

3 If you **weed** an area, you remove the weeds from it. *Caspar was weeding the garden... The Hodges are busy weeding and planting.* ♦ **weeding** *She taught me to do the weeding.* VERB V n V N-UNCOUNT

4 People sometimes refer to tobacco or marijuana as **weed**; an informal use. *Two and a half years ago I gave up the evil weed.* N-UNCOUNT: also *the* N

weed out. If you **weed out** things or people that are useless or unwanted in a group, you find them and get rid of them. *He is keen to weed out the many applicants he believes may be frauds... A small group of neo-Nazis have infiltrated the ranks. We must weed them out as soon as possible.* PHRASAL VERB =root out V P n (not pron) V n P

weedkiller /wiːdkɪləʳ/ **weedkillers. Weedkiller** is a substance you put on your garden to kill weeds. N-MASS

weedy /wiːdi/ **weedier, weediest**

1 A **weedy** place is full of weeds. *The car was parked in the small weedy lot next to the hotel.* ADJ: usu ADJ n

2 In British English, if you describe someone as **weedy**, you are criticizing them or laughing at them because they are thin and physically weak; an informal use. ADJ-GRADED PRAGMATICS =puny

week /wiːk/ **weeks** ◆◆◆◆◆

1 A **week** is a period of seven days. Some people consider that a week starts on Monday and ends on Sunday. *I had a letter from my mother last week... This has been on my mind all week... I know a wonderful restaurant where we can have lunch next week.* N-COUNT

2 A **week** is a period of about seven days. *Her mother stayed for another two weeks... Only 12 weeks ago he underwent major heart transplant surgery... Three million people will visit theatres in the annual six-week season.* N-COUNT

3 Your working **week** is the hours that you spend at work during a week. *It is not unusual for women to work a 40-hour week. ...workers on a three-day week because of the sales slump.* N-COUNT: usu supp N

4 The week is the part of the week that does not include Saturday and Sunday. *...the hard work of looking after the children during the week... They arrived at the weekend and gave three concerts in the week.* N-SING: *the* N ≠the weekend

5 You use **week** in expressions such as 'a week on Monday', 'a week next Tuesday', and 'tomorrow week' to mean exactly one week after the day that you mention. *The deadline to publish the document is a week tomorrow... The 800 metre final is on Monday week.* N-COUNT

6 You use **week** in expressions such as **'a week last Monday'**, **'a week ago this Tuesday'**, and **'a week ago yesterday'** to mean exactly one week before the day that you mention. *'That's the time you weren't well, wasn't it?'—'Yes, that's right, that was a week ago yesterday.'* N-COUNT

7 If you say that something happens **week in week out**, you do not like it because it happens all the time, and never seems to change. *...stars who appear on television week in week out.* • **weeks on end**: see **end**. PHRASE PRAGMATICS

weekday /wiːkdeɪ/ **weekdays.** A **weekday** is any of the days of the week except Saturday and Sunday. *If you want to avoid the crowds, it's best to come on a weekday... Visitor Centre and shop open 9 a.m. – 5 p.m. weekdays; 10 a.m. – 5 p.m. weekends.* ◆◇◇◇◇ N-COUNT

weekend /wiːkend/ **weekends.** A **weekend** is Saturday and Sunday. *She had agreed to have dinner with him in town the following weekend... He told me to give you a call over the weekend.* ◆◆◆◆◇ N-COUNT

weekender /wiːkendəʳ, AM -endər/ **weekenders.** A **weekender** is someone who goes to a place or lives at a place only at weekends. *He converted his barns into cottages for weekenders.* N-COUNT: usu pl

weekly /wiːkli/ **weeklies** ◆◆◆◇◇

1 A **weekly** event or publication happens or appears once a week or every week. *Each course comprises 10-12 informal weekly meetings... We go and do the weekly shopping every Thursday... His story was published in a weekly newspaper.* ► Also an adverb. *The group meets weekly. ...a magazine published weekly since 2 January 1909.* ADJ: ADJ n ADV: ADV after v

2 Weekly quantities or rates relate to a period of one week. *Working wives get an average weekly wage of £153.* ADJ: ADJ n

3 A **weekly** is a newspaper or magazine that is published once a week. *Two of the four national daily papers are to become weeklies.* N-COUNT

weep /wiːp/ **weeps, weeping, wept** ◆◆◇◇◇

1 If someone **weeps**, they cry; a literary use. *She wanted to laugh and weep all at once... The weeping family hugged and comforted each other... She wept tears of joy.* ► Also a noun. *There are times when I sit down and have a good weep.* VERB V V-ing V n N-SING: *a* N

2 If a wound **weeps**, pus or blood comes from it because it is not healing properly. *In severe cases, the skin can crack and weep. ...little blisters which develop into weeping sores.* VERB V V-ing

weeping willow, weeping willows. A **weeping willow** is a type of willow tree. It has long thin branches that hang down to the ground. N-COUNT

weepy /wiːpi/ **weepies**

1 Someone who is **weepy** is sad and likely to cry easily. *I suddenly felt very weepy. ...weepy moods.* ADJ-GRADED =tearful

2 A **weepy** is a film or a story which is sentimental and makes you cry; an informal use. N-COUNT

weevil /wiːvɪl/ **weevils.** A **weevil** is a small beetle which feeds on grain and seeds, and destroys crops. N-COUNT

weft /weft/. The **weft** of a piece of woven material is the threads which are passed sideways in and out of the threads held in the loom. N-SING: usu *the* N

weigh /weɪ/ **weighs, weighing, weighed** ◆◆◆◇◇

1 If someone or something **weighs** a particular amount, this amount is how heavy they are. *I weighed 22 stone at the time... This little ball of gold weighs a quarter of an ounce... You always weigh less in the morning.* VB: no cont V amount

2 If you **weigh** something or someone, you measure how heavy they are. *The scales can be used to weigh other items such as parcels.* VERB V n

3 If you **weigh** the facts about a situation, you consider them very carefully before you make a decision, especially by comparing the various facts involved. *She weighed her options... He is weighing the possibility of filing criminal charges against the doctor... She spoke very slowly, weighing what she would say.* ► **Weigh up** means the same as **weigh**; used mainly in British English. *Nirex will be able to weigh up the environmental pros and cons of each site... You have to weigh up whether a human life is more important than an animal's life.* VERB =evaluate V n V wh PHRASAL VERB V P n (not pron) V P wh Also V n P

4 If you **weigh** your words, you think very carefully before you say something. *He said the words very slowly, as if weighing each one of them.* VERB V n

5 If a problem **weighs** on you, it makes you worried or unhappy. *The separation weighed on both of them... She knows how your brother's disappearance weighs upon you.* VERB V *on/upon* n

6 Something that **weighs** heavily in a situation has a strong influence or important effect on it. *Current economic hardships weigh heavily in young women's decisions to find salaried work... Human life weighed more with him than purity of policy... There are many factors weighing against the meeting happening.* VERB V adv prep V *against* n/-ing

weigh down PHRASAL VERB
1 If something that you are wearing or carrying **weighs** you **down**, it stops you moving easily by making you heavier. *He wrenched off his sneakers. If they had to swim, he didn't want anything weighing him down... These nests increase in size each year, and can eventually weigh down the branch. ...soldiers weighed down by their heavy packs.* V n P; V P n (not pron); V-ed P
2 If you **are weighed down** by something, it makes you extremely worried or causes you great problems. *The merchant bank is being weighed down by a £1.3 billion book of bad debts. ...the depression that weighed him down each morning.* =burden; be V-ed by/with n; V n P ♦ **weighed down** *I was too weighed down by guilt to eat the sweet.* ADJ-GRADED: v-link ADJ

weigh in PHRASAL VERB
1 If you **weigh in** on a plan, decision, or discussion, you make a significant or important contribution to it; used in journalism. *Clinton's political advisers also weighed in on the plan... Cranston and others were improperly trying to weigh in on the decision.* V P on n; Also V P
2 If someone **weighs in at** a particular weight, for example before competing in a sports competition, their weight is measured at that amount; used in journalism. *He weighed in on Friday night at around 19 stone... Their daughter Renee weighed in at 8lb 3oz.* V P at amount ● See also **weigh-in**.

weigh out. If you **weigh** something **out**, you measure a certain weight of it to make sure you have the correct amount. *I agreed to help him weigh it out... I learned how to weigh out packages of seed.* PHRASAL VERB; V n P; V P n (not pron)

weigh up PHRASAL VERB
1 See **weigh** 3.
2 If you **weigh** someone **up**, you try and find out what they are like and form an opinion of them, especially when you are suspicious of them; used mainly in British English. *She looked at me the way my Marine recruiting sergeant weighed me up when I first walked into his office.* V n P; Also V P n (not pron)

weigh-in, weigh-ins. When there is a **weigh-in** on the day of a boxing match or a horse race, each competitor is weighed to check their weight shortly before the event. N-COUNT: usu sing

weight /weɪt/ **weights, weighting, weighted** ♦♦♦♦◇
1 The **weight** of a person or thing is how heavy they are, measured in units such as kilos, pounds, or tons. *What is your height and weight?... This reduced the weight of the load... Turkeys can reach enormous weights of up to 50 pounds.* N-VAR: oft amount in N, with poss, N of amount ● If someone **loses weight**, they become lighter. If they **gain weight** or **put on weight**, they become heavier. *I'm lucky really as I never put on weight... He lost two stone in weight during his time there.* PHRASE: V inflects
2 A person's or thing's **weight** is the fact that they are very heavy. *His weight was harming his health... Despite the vehicle's size and weight it is not difficult to drive.* N-UNCOUNT: with poss
3 If you move your **weight**, you change position so that most of the pressure of your body is on a particular part of your body. *He shifted his weight from one foot to the other... He kept the weight from his left leg.* N-SING: poss/the N
4 **Weights** are objects which weigh a known amount and which people lift as a form of fitness training. *I was in the gym lifting weights.* N-COUNT: usu pl
5 **Weights** are metal objects which weigh a known amount and which are used on a set of scales to weigh other things. N-COUNT
6 You can refer to a heavy object as a **weight**, especially when you have to lift it. *Straining to lift heavy weights can lead to a rise in blood pressure.* N-COUNT
7 If you **weight** something, you make it heavier by adding something to it, for example in order to stop it from moving easily. *It can be sewn into curtain hems to weight the curtain and so allow it to hang better.* VERB; V n
8 If you **weight** things, you give them different values according to how important or significant they are. *...a computer program which weights the different transitions according to their likelihood... This takes account of the number of countries in which a company wins approval for a new drug, weighted by the size of each country's market.* VERB; V n; V-ed
9 If something is given a particular **weight**, it is given a particular value according to how important or significant it is. *The scientists involved put different weight on the conclusions of different models... We had this understanding that courses were roughly the same weight.* N-VAR =weighting
10 If you talk about **the weight of** something, you think it is large in amount or has great power, which means that it is difficult to contradict or fight against. *The weight of expectation was getting to them... Companies found themselves collapsing under the weight of debts.* N-UNCOUNT: the N of n =burden
11 If someone or something gives **weight** to something that someone says, thinks, or does, they emphasize its significance. *The fact that he is gone has given more weight to fears that he may try to launch a civil war... Do you think, perhaps, that what happened today might lend weight to that criticism?* N-UNCOUNT
12 If you give something or someone **weight**, you consider them to be very important or influential in a particular situation. *Consumers generally place more weight on negative information than on the positive when deciding what to buy. ...the overwhelming weight Freud assigned to parents in our development.* N-UNCOUNT
13 If you feel a **weight** on you, you have a problem or a responsibility that is difficult for you to manage and that you are very worried about. *The relief was indescribable. It was freedom after years of slavery. A great weight lifted from me.* N-SING =burden
14 See also **weighting**; **dead weight**.
15 If a person or their opinion **carries weight**, they are respected and are able to influence people. *That argument no longer carries as much weight... They know that Senator Kerrey carries considerable weight in Washington.* PHRASES V inflects
16 If you say that someone or something is **worth** their **weight in gold**, you are emphasizing that they are so useful, helpful, or valuable that you feel you could not manage without them. *Any successful manager is worth his weight in gold.* v-link PHR PRAGMATICS
17 If you **pull** your **weight**, you work as hard as everyone else who is involved in the same task or activity. *He accused the team of not pulling their weight.* V inflects
18 If someone **throws** their **weight around** or **throws** their **weight about**, they act aggressively and use their authority over other people more than they need to. V inflects
19 If you **throw** your **weight behind** a person, plan, or campaign, you use all your influence and do everything you can to support them; used in written English. *The administration is throwing its full weight behind the U.N plan.* V inflects =back
20 ● **a weight off** your **mind**: see **mind**.

weight down. If you **weight** something **down**, you put something heavy on it or in it in order to prevent it from moving easily. *Put some tins on top to weight it down.* PHRASAL VERB; V n P

weighted /weɪtɪd/. A system that is **weighted** in favour of a particular person or group is organized so that this person or group has an advantage. *The current electoral law is still heavily weighted in favour of the ruling party... They say the peace process is so heavily weighted against them that it will never achieve results.* ADJ-GRADED: usu v-link ADJ prep =biased

weighting /weɪtɪŋ/ **weightings**
1 A **weighting** is a value which is given to something according to how important or significant it is. *Each country's currency is given a weighting in the ECU.* N-COUNT
2 A **weighting** is an advantage that a particular group of people receives in a system, especially an extra sum of money that people receive if they work in a city where the cost of living is very high. *I get an extra £2,700-a-year London weighting.* N-COUNT: usu sing
3 See also **weight**.

weightless /weɪtləs/
1 Something that is **weightless** weighs nothing or ADJ-GRADED

seems to weigh nothing. *Photons have no mass – they are weightless. ...weightless silk curtains.*
2 A person or object is **weightless** when they are in space and the earth's gravity does not affect them, so that they float around. *Helen gave graphic descriptions of life in a weightless environment during her period in space.* ♦ **weightlessness** *...the human body's response to weightlessness.* ADJ / N-UNCOUNT

weightlifter /weɪtlɪftəʳ/ **weightlifters.** A **weightlifter** is a person who does weightlifting. N-COUNT

weightlifting /weɪtlɪftɪŋ/; also **weight-lifting. Weightlifting** is a sport in which the competitor who can lift the heaviest weight wins. N-UNCOUNT

weighty /weɪti/ **weightier, weightiest** ◆◇◇◇◇
1 If you describe something such as an issue or a concept as **weighty**, you mean that it seems serious or important; a formal use. *Surely such weighty matters merit a higher level of debate?* ADJ-GRADED: usu ADJ n =serious, important
2 You use **weighty** to describe something, especially a book, that is heavy or heavier than you would expect; a literary use. *Simon lifted a weighty volume from the shelf.* ADJ-GRADED =hefty

weir /wɪəʳ/ **weirs** ◆◇◇◇◇
1 A **weir** is a low dam which is built across a river in order to control or direct the flow of water. N-COUNT
2 A **weir** is a wooden fence which is built across a stream in order to create a pool for catching fish. N-COUNT

weird /wɪəʳd/ **weirder, weirdest.** If you describe something or someone as **weird**, you mean that they are strange and peculiar; an informal word. *That first day was weird... He's different. He's weird... Drugs can make you do all kinds of weird things... It must be really weird to be rich... It felt weird going back to Liverpool.* ♦ **weirdly** *...weirdly wonderful sculptures. ...difficult men who dressed weirdly.* ♦ **weirdness** *The weirdness of Hollywood suits him well.* ◆◆◇◇◇ ADJ-GRADED: oft *it* v-link ADJ to-inf/-ing =strange, bizarre / ADV-GRADED / N-UNCOUNT

weirdo /wɪəʳdoʊ/ **weirdos.** If you describe someone as a **weirdo**, you disapprove of them because they behave in an unusual way which you find difficult to understand or to accept as normal; an informal word, used mainly in spoken English. N-COUNT PRAGMATICS =crackpot

welcome /welkəm/ **welcomes, welcoming, welcomed** ◆◆◆◆◇
1 If you **welcome** someone, you greet them in a friendly way when they arrive somewhere. *Several people came by to welcome me... She was there to welcome him home from war... The delegates received a welcoming speech by the President.* ► Also a noun. *There would be a fantastic welcome awaiting him back here.* VERB / V n / V n adv/prep / V-ing / N-COUNT: usu sing
2 You use **welcome** in expressions such as **welcome home**, **welcome to London**, and **welcome back** when you are greeting someone who has just arrived somewhere. *Welcome to Washington... Welcome back, Deborah – It's good to have you here.* CONVENTION PRAGMATICS
3 If you **welcome** an action, decision, or situation, you approve of it and are pleased that it has occurred. *She welcomed this move but said that overall the changes didn't go far enough... The European decision was welcomed by President Bush.* ► Also a noun. *Environmental groups have given a guarded welcome to the Prime Minister's proposal.* VERB / V n / N-COUNT: usu sing
4 If you describe something as **welcome**, you mean that people wanted it and are happy that it has occurred. *This was certainly a welcome change of fortune... The new 25 metre pool for more serious swimmers is a welcome addition... Any progress in reducing chemical weapons is welcome.* ADJ-GRADED
5 If you say that you **welcome** certain people or actions, you are inviting and encouraging people to do something, for example to come to a particular place. *We welcome you to join us on a special tour which explores this unique Australian attraction... We would welcome your views about the survey.* VERB PRAGMATICS / V n
6 If you say that someone is **welcome** in a particular place, you are encouraging them to go there by assuring them that they will be accepted. *New members are always welcome... I told him he wasn't welcome in my home.* ADJ-GRADED: usu v-link ADJ
7 If you tell someone that they are **welcome** to do something, you are encouraging them to do it by assuring them that they are allowed to do it. *You are welcome to visit the hospital at any time. ...a conservatory which guests are welcome to use.* ADJ-GRADED: v-link ADJ, usu ADJ to-inf PRAGMATICS
8 If you say that someone is **welcome to** something, you mean that you do not want it yourself because you do not like it and you are very willing for them to have it. *If women want to take on the business world they are welcome to it as far as I'm concerned.* ADJ-GRADED: v-link ADJ *to* n
9 See also **welcoming**.
10 If you **make** someone **welcome** or **make** them **feel** welcome, you make them feel happy and accepted in a new place. PHRASES *make* inflects
11 If you say that someone **outstays** their **welcome** or **overstays** their **welcome**, you mean that they stay somewhere longer than they are wanted or expected to. *After the kindness that had been shown to him, he didn't want to outstay his welcome.* V inflects
12 You say **'You're welcome'** to someone who has thanked you for something in order to acknowledge their thanks in a polite way. *'Thank you for the information.'—'You're welcome.'* CONVENTION PRAGMATICS

welcoming /welkəmɪŋ/
1 If someone is **welcoming** or if they behave in a **welcoming** way, they are friendly to you when you arrive somewhere, so that you feel happy and accepted. *When we arrived at her house Susan was very welcoming... Her face spread in a welcoming smile.* ADJ-GRADED =cordial
2 A **welcoming** building or room is pleasantly decorated and furnished and you feel as though you would be happy spending time there. *The restaurant is small and green and very welcoming.* ADJ-GRADED

weld /weld/ **welds, welding, welded** ◆◇◇◇◇
1 To **weld** one piece of metal to another means to join them by heating the edges and putting them together so that they cool and harden into one piece. *It's possible to weld stainless steel to ordinary steel... They will also be used on factory floors to weld things together... Where did you learn to weld?* ♦ **welding** *All the welding had been done from inside the car... This repair was done with the help of a friend using welding equipment.* VERB / V n *to* n / V n with *together* / V / Also V n / N-UNCOUNT
2 A **weld** is a join where two pieces of metal have been welded together. N-COUNT
3 If you **weld** people together, you join them together to form a united organization; a formal use. *She has both the authority and the personality to weld the party together... The miracle was that Rose had welded them into a team.* VERB / V n with *together* / V n *into* n

welder /weldəʳ/ **welders.** A **welder** is a person whose job is welding metal. N-COUNT

welfare /welfeəʳ/ ◆◆◆◇◇
1 The **welfare** of a person or group is their health, comfort, and prosperity. *I do not think he is considering Emma's welfare... He was the head of a charity for the welfare of children.* N-UNCOUNT: usu with poss
2 **Welfare** services are provided to help with people's living conditions and financial problems. *Child welfare services are well established and comprehensive... He has urged complete reform of the welfare system.* ADJ: usu ADJ n
3 In the United States, **welfare** is money that is paid by the government to people who are unemployed, poor, or ill. *States such as Michigan and Massachusetts are making deep cuts in welfare... If she does find a job through the training program she may have less money than now when she's on welfare.* N-UNCOUNT

welfare state. In Britain and some other countries, the **welfare state** is a system in which the government provides free social services such as health and education and gives money to people when they are unable to work, for example because they are old, unemployed, or sick. ◆◇◇◇◇ N-SING

well 1 discourse uses

well /wel/. ◆◆◆◆◆
Well is used mainly in spoken English.
1 You say **well** to indicate that you are about to say something. *Sylvia shook hands. 'Well, you go get* ADV: ADV cl PRAGMATICS

yourselves some breakfast.'... Well, I don't like the look of that.

2 You say **well** to indicate that you intend or want to carry on speaking. *You can lose your perspective. You know, get paranoid? Well, that's something I really try and avoid... The trouble with City is that they do not have enough quality players. Well, that can easily be rectified.* ADV: ADV cl PRAGMATICS

3 You say **well** to indicate that you are changing the topic, and are either going back to something that was being discussed earlier or are going on to something new. *Thank you Lionel, for singing that for us. Well, we'd better tell you what's on the show between nine and midnight... Well, let's press on.* ADV: ADV cl PRAGMATICS =anyway, so

4 You say **well** to indicate that you have reached the end of a conversation. *'I'm sure you will be an asset,' she finally added. 'Well, I see it's just about time for lunch.'... Well, thank you for speaking with us.* ADV: ADV cl PRAGMATICS

5 You say **well** to make a suggestion, criticism, or correction seem less definite or rude. *Well, maybe it would be easier to start with a smaller problem... Well, let's wait and see... Well, I thought she was a bit unfair about me.* ADV: ADV cl PRAGMATICS

6 You say **well** just before or after you pause, especially to give yourself time to think about what you are going to say, or because you want to rephrase something that you have just said. *Look, I'm really sorry I woke you, and, well, I just wanted to tell you I was all right.* ADV: ADV cl PRAGMATICS =you know

7 You say **well** when you are modifying or correcting something that you have just said. *The comet is going to come back in 2061 and we are all going to be able to see it. Well, our offspring are, anyway... There was a note. Well, not really a note.* ADV: ADV cl/group PRAGMATICS =at least

8 You say **well** to express your doubt about something that someone has said. *'But finance is far more serious.'—'Well I don't know really.'... 'Go on, Dennis.'—'Well, if you're sure.'* ADV: ADV cl PRAGMATICS

9 You say **well** to express your surprise or anger at something that someone has just said or done. *'Imelda,' said Mrs Kennerly. 'That's my name, Tom.' 'Well,' said Tom. 'Imelda. I never knew.'... Well, honestly! They're like an old married couple at times.* EXCLAM PRAGMATICS

10 You say **well** to indicate that you are waiting for someone to say something or explain something, and often to express your irritation with them. *'Well?' asked Barry, 'what does it tell us?'... 'Well, why don't you ask me?' he said finally.* CONVENTION PRAGMATICS =so

11 You use **well** to indicate that you are amused by something you have heard or seen, and often to introduce a comment on it. *Well, well, well, look at you. Ethel, look at this little fat girl... Bob peered at it. 'Well, well!' he said, 'I haven't seen Spam since the war!' and laughed.* CONVENTION PRAGMATICS

12 You say **oh well** to indicate that you accept a situation or that someone else should accept it, even though you or they are not very happy about it, because it is not too bad and cannot be changed. *Oh well, it could be worse... 'I called her and she said no.'—'Oh well.'* CONVENTION PRAGMATICS =never mind

13 ● **very well**: see **very**.

well 2 adverb uses

well /wel/ **better, best** ◆◆◆◆◆

1 If you do something **well**, you do it to a high standard or to a great extent. *All the Indian batsmen played well... He speaks English better than I do... It is a formula that worked very well indeed... I don't really know her very well.* ADV-GRADED: ADV after v

2 If you do something **well**, you do it thoroughly and completely. *Mix all the ingredients well... Wash your hands well with soap.* ADV-GRADED: ADV after v =thoroughly

3 If you speak or think **well** of someone, you say or think favourable things about them. *'He speaks well of you.'—'I'm glad to hear that.'... It might help people think better of him.* ADV-GRADED: ADV after v =highly

4 **Well** is used in front of past participles to indicate that something is done to a high standard or to a great extent. Many of the commonest combinations are treated as separate headwords in this dictionary. *Helen is a very well-known novelist in Australia... People live longer nowadays, and they are better educated... British nurses were among the best trained in Europe.* COMB in ADJ-GRADED

5 You use **well** to ask or talk about the extent or standard of something. *How well do you remember your mother, Franzi?... This new career doesn't pay nearly as well as the old one... Their captain said his team had played as well as it possibly could... He wasn't dressed any better than me.* ADV-GRADED: how ADV, as ADV as, ADV-compar than

6 You use **well** in front of a prepositional phrase to emphasize it. For example, if you say that one thing happened **well before** another, you mean that it happened a long time before it. *Franklin did not turn up until well after midnight... We often plan our meals well in advance... They had remained silent until they were well away from the house... There are well over a million Muslims in Britain.* ADV: ADV prep PRAGMATICS

7 You use **well** before certain adjectives to emphasize them. *She has a close group of friends who are very well aware of what she has suffered... Men are generally better able to express anger... The show is well worth a visit.* ADV-GRADED: ADV adj PRAGMATICS

8 You use **well** after adverbs such as 'perfectly', 'jolly', or 'damn' in order to emphasize an opinion or the truth of what you are saying. *You know perfectly well I can't be blamed for the failure of that mission... I'd got myself into this marriage and I jolly well had to get myself out of it.* ADV: adv ADV, ADV with v PRAGMATICS

9 You use **well** after verbs such as 'may' and 'could' when you are saying what you think is likely to happen. *Our instinct tells us that the murderer may well come from the estate... Ours could well be the last generation for which moviegoing has a sense of magic.* ADV: modal ADV =very likely

well 3 phrases

well /wel/ ◆◆◆◆◆

1 You use **as well** when mentioning something which happens in the same way as something else already mentioned, or which should be considered at the same time as something else already mentioned. *It is most often diagnosed in women in their thirties and forties, although I've seen it in many younger women, as well... 'What do you like about it then?'—'Erm, the history, the shops – people are quite friendly as well.'... Andy's face paled with disappointment; perhaps with anger as well.* PHRASES cl PHR =too

2 You use **as well as** when you want to mention another item connected with the subject you are discussing. *She published historical novels, as well as a non-fiction study of women in the British Empire... It is in his best interests as well as yours... Wearing the right shoes and clothes as well as being fit can make all the difference... As well as a good academic record I look for people who've climbed mountains or been captain of a team.* PREP =in addition to

3 If you say, after stating that something has happened or is the case, **as well it might** or **as well it may**, you mean that this is not at all surprising or is quite appropriate. *This caused a few gasps, as well it might... You can see he's terrified, as well he might be after what we've been through.* PRAGMATICS

4 If you say that something that has happened **is just as well**, you mean that it is fortunate that it happened in the way it did. *Blue asbestos is far less common in buildings, which is just as well because it's the more dangerous than white asbestos... Judging from everything you've said, it was just as well she wasn't there.* V inflects, oft *it* PHR that

5 You say **it is as well to** think or do something when you are advising someone to think in a particular way or to take a particular action. *It is as well to bear in mind that laughter is a great releaser of tension.* V inflects, PHR inf PRAGMATICS

6 If you say that someone **would do well to** do something, you mean that you advise or recommend that they do it. *The new president would do well to remember that he wouldn't have made it without the support of America's Black voters... Investors would do well to take a look at the Swiss economy.* MODAL PRAGMATICS

7 If you say that something, usually something bad, **might as well** be true or **may as well** be true, PHR inf you mean that the situation is the same or almost the same as if it were true. *The couple might as well have been strangers... We might just as well be in prison for all the quality our lives have at present.*

8 If you say that you **might as well** do something, or that you **may as well** do it, you mean that you will do it although you do not have a strong desire to do it and may even feel slightly reluctant about it. *If I've got to go somewhere I may as well go to Birmingham... Anyway, you're here; you might as well stay... I'll come with you if you like. I might as well.* — usu PHR inf; PRAGMATICS

9 If you say that something is **all well and good,** you are suggesting that it has faults or disadvantages, although it may appear to be correct or reasonable. *It's all well and good for him to say he's sorry for dropping you, but has he told you why he did it?* — usu v-link PHR, oft PHR *for* n, PHR to-inf; PRAGMATICS; =all very well

10 You say **well and good** or **all well and good** to indicate that if something is true or happens you will be pleased in general, but you think that it probably is not true or will not happen, or you are aware of disadvantages. *If they arrive before I leave, well and good. If not, the responsibility will be mine... This is all well and good, but we have to look at the situation in the long term.* — usu PHR with cl, v-link PHR, *it* v-link PHR to-inf/-ing

11 If you say to someone who is no longer involved in a situation that they **are well out of it,** you mean that it is a good thing they are no longer involved and they should be pleased about this. *I hated the Cold War. I think we're very well out of it.* — V inflects

12 If you say that something is **well and truly** finished, gone, or done, you are emphasizing that it is completely finished or gone, or thoroughly done; used mainly in British English. *The war is well and truly over. ...the relief of knowing that a problem was well and truly solved... The greenhouse effect is well and truly with us.* — PHR group; PRAGMATICS

13 If you say that you like something or someone **well enough,** you mean that you quite like them or find them reasonably acceptable. *Nancy liked it well enough, but complained about the color... Crook liked her well enough, but remained indifferent to her feminine charms.* — PHR after v

14 • **all very well**: see **all.** • to **know full well**: see **full.** • to **leave well alone**: see **leave.** • to **mean well**: see **mean.** • **pretty well**: see **pretty.**

well 4 adjective use

well /wel/. If you are **well,** you are healthy and not ill. *I'm not very well today, I can't come in... I hope you're well.* — ◆◆◆◆◆ ADJ-GRADED: usu v-link ADJ ≠ill

well 5 noun uses

well /wel/ **wells** — ◆◆◇◇◇

1 A **well** is a hole in the ground from which a supply of water is extracted. *I had to fetch water from the well.* — N-COUNT

2 A **well** is an oil well. *About 650 wells are on fire.* — N-COUNT

well 6 verb uses

well /wel/ **wells, welling, welled** — ◆◇◇◇◇

1 If liquids, for example tears, **well,** they come to the surface and form a pool. *Tears welled in her eyes... He fell back, blood welling from a gash in his thigh.* ► **Well up** means the same as **well.** *Tears welled up in Anni's eyes.* — VERB; V; PHRASAL VERB; V P

2 If an emotion **wells** in you, it suddenly becomes stronger, to the point where you have to express it. *Gratitude welled in Chryssa... Her love for him welled stronger than ever.* ► **Well up** means the same as **well.** *He could feel the anger welling up inside him... Hope welled up.* — VERB =surge; V *in/inside* n; V; PHRASAL VERB =surge up; V P *in/inside* n; V P

we'll /wɪl, STRONG wiːl/. **We'll** is the usual spoken form of 'we shall' or 'we will'. *Whatever you want to chat about, we'll do it tonight... Will there be anything else? – If there is, we'll let you know.*

well-adjusted; also spelled **well adjusted.** A **well-adjusted** person has a mature personality and can control their emotions and deal with problems without becoming anxious. *...a happy, loving and well adjusted family.* — ADJ-GRADED ≠maladjusted

well advised; also spelled **well-advised.** If someone says that you would be **well advised** to do a particular thing, they are advising you to do it. *Moderates believe the party would be well advised to talk to the government.* — ADJ-GRADED: v-link ADJ to-inf; PRAGMATICS; =wise ≠ill advised

well-appointed. A **well-appointed** room or building is equipped or furnished to a very high standard; a formal word. *Guestrooms are commodious and well-appointed.* — ADJ-GRADED

well-balanced; also spelled **well balanced.** — ◆◇◇◇◇

1 If you describe someone as **well-balanced,** you mean that they are sensible and do not have many emotional problems. *...a fun-loving, well-balanced individual.* — ADJ-GRADED =stable

2 If you describe something that is made up of several elements or parts as **well-balanced,** you mean that the way that the different elements or parts are put together is good, because there is not too much or too little of any one element or part. *...a well balanced diet.* — ADJ-GRADED

well-behaved; also spelled **well behaved.** If you describe someone, especially a child, as **well-behaved,** you mean that they behave in a way that adults generally like and think is correct. *...well-behaved little boys... The troops have been remarkably well-behaved so far.* — ADJ-GRADED

well-being; also spelled **wellbeing.** Someone's **well-being** is their health and happiness. *Singing can create a sense of wellbeing... His work emphasised the emotional as well as the physical well-being of children.* — ◆◆◇◇◇ N-UNCOUNT: usu with supp

well-born. Someone who is **well-born** belongs to an upper-class family. — ADJ-GRADED

well-bred. A **well-bred** person is very polite and has good manners. *She was too well bred to want to hurt the little boy's feelings.* — ADJ-GRADED =well-mannered

well-brought-up; also spelled **well brought up.** If you say that someone, especially a child, is **well-brought-up,** you mean that they are very polite because they have been taught good manners. *He's just a well-brought-up, middle-class boy.* — ADJ-GRADED

well-built; also spelled **well built.** A **well-built** person, especially a man, is strong and muscular. *Mitchell is well built, of medium height, with a dark complexion.* — ADJ-GRADED

well-connected; also spelled **well connected.** Someone who is **well-connected** has important or influential relatives or friends. — ADJ-GRADED

well-defined; also spelled **well defined.** Something that is **well-defined** is clear and precise and therefore easy to recognize or understand. *Can you look back and see a well-defined path, or simply an aimless series of job moves with no coherent structure?... Today's pawnbrokers operate within well-defined financial regulations.* — ◆◇◇◇◇ ADJ-GRADED

well disposed; also spelled **well-disposed.** If you are **well disposed** to a person, plan, or activity, you are likely to agree with them or support them. *They are likely to be well disposed to an offer of a separate peace deal... He felt well disposed towards her.* — ADJ-GRADED: usu ADJ *to/towards* n

well done — ◆◇◇◇◇

1 You say **'Well done'** to indicate that you are pleased that someone has got something right or done something good. *'Well done,' said Claud in admiration... 'Daddy! I came second in history'—'Well done, sweetheart!'* — CONVENTION; PRAGMATICS; =Congratulations

2 If something that you have cooked, especially meat, is **well done,** it has been cooked thoroughly. *Allow an extra 10-15 min if you prefer lamb well done.* — ADJ-GRADED

well-dressed; also spelled **well dressed.** Someone who is **well-dressed** is wearing smart or elegant clothes. *She's always well dressed.* — ◆◇◇◇◇ ADJ-GRADED =smart

well-earned; also spelled **well earned.** You can use **well-earned** to indicate that you think something is deserved, usually because the person who gets it has been working very hard. *Take a well-earned rest and go out and enjoy yourself. ...his well-earned win in Sunday's race.* — ADJ-GRADED: usu ADJ n =well-deserved

well-established; also **well established.** If you say that something is **well-established,** you mean that it has been in existence for quite a long time and is successful. *The University has a* —  ADJ-GRADED

well-established tradition of welcoming post-graduate students from overseas. ...well-established companies such as Compaq and Olivetti.

well-fed; also spelled **well fed**. If you say that someone is **well-fed**, you mean they get good food regularly. *...his well-fed children.* ADJ-GRADED

well-founded; also spelled **well founded**. If you say that a report, opinion, or feeling is **well-founded**, you mean that it is based on facts and can therefore be justified. *If the reports are well founded, the incident could seriously aggravate relations between the two nations... We must respond to well-founded criticism with a willingness to change.* ADJ-GRADED =justifiable

well-groomed; also spelled **well groomed**. A **well-groomed** person is very neat and tidy, and looks as if they have taken care over their appearance. *...well-groomed young men in expensive suits.* ADJ-GRADED

well-heeled. Someone who is **well-heeled** is wealthy. ADJ-GRADED =wealthy

well-informed, **better-informed**; also spelled **well informed**. If you say that someone is **well-informed**, you mean that they know a lot about many different subjects or about one particular subject. *...a lending library to encourage members to become as well informed as possible... This is a subject for serious, well-informed discussion, not tabloid headlines.* ◆◇◇◇◇ ADJ-GRADED

wellington /welɪŋtən/ **wellingtons**. **Wellingtons** or **wellington boots** are long rubber boots which you wear to keep your feet dry; used mainly in British English. The usual American term is **rubber boots**. N-COUNT: usu pl

well-intentioned; also spelled **well intentioned**. If you say that a person or their actions or remarks are **well-intentioned**, you mean that they intend to be helpful or kind but they are unsuccessful or cause unfortunate results. *He is well-intentioned but a poor administrator. ...rules that, however well-intentioned, are often hopelessly impractical.* ADJ-GRADED =well-meaning

well-kept; also spelled **well kept**.

1 A **well-kept** building, street, garden, or other place is always neat and tidy because it is carefully looked after. *...two idyllic thatched cottages with well-kept gardens. ...broad, well-kept streets.* ADJ-GRADED

2 A **well-kept** secret has not been told or made known to anyone, or has been told or made known to only a small number of people. *His resignation was such a well-kept secret that only Leavis knew about it in advance.* ADJ-GRADED: usu ADJ n

well-known; also spelled **well known**. ◆◆◆◇◇

1 A **well-known** person or thing is known about by a lot of people and is therefore famous or familiar. If someone is **well-known** for a particular activity, a lot of people know about them because of their involvement with that activity. *It entertains him to surround himself with attractive, intelligent, or well-known people... He is well-known to the local police... Hubbard was well known for his work in the field of drug rehabilitation.* ADJ-GRADED

2 A **well-known** fact is a fact that is known by people in general. *It may be a well-known fact, but I didn't know it... It is well known that bamboo shoots are a panda's staple diet.* ADJ-GRADED

well-mannered. Someone who is **well-mannered** is polite and has good manners. ADJ-GRADED

well-meaning; also spelled **well meaning**. If you say that a person or their actions or remarks are **well-meaning**, you mean that they intend to be helpful or kind but they are unsuccessful or cause unfortunate results. *He is a well-meaning but ineffectual leader... Even well-meaning attempts at conservation can bring problems.* ◆◇◇◇◇ ADJ-GRADED =well-intentioned

well-meant; also spelled **well meant**. A **well-meant** decision, action, or comment is intended to be helpful or kind but is unsuccessful or causes unfortunate results. *Any decision taken by them now, however well meant, could complicate the peace process. ...a well-meant experiment gone wrong.* ADJ-GRADED =well-intentioned

well-nigh; also spelled **well nigh**. **Well-nigh** means almost, but not completely or exactly. *Finding a rug that's just the colour, size and price you want can be well-nigh impossible. ...a hierarchical structure that was well-nigh unassailable.* ADV: ADV adj =practically

well-off; also spelled **well off**. Someone who is **well-off** is rich enough to be able to do and buy most of the things that they want; an informal expression. *My grandparents were quite well off.* ◆◇◇◇◇ ADJ-GRADED =well-to-do

▶ **The well-off** are people who are well-off. *Higher tax rates on the well-off would be phased in gradually.* N-PLURAL: the N

well-oiled. Journalists sometimes refer to a system or organization that is operating very efficiently as a **well-oiled** machine. *...a well-oiled publicity machine... Just as important, it has a well-oiled organization.* ADJ: ADJ n

well-paid; also spelled **well paid**. If you say that a person or their job is **well-paid**, you mean that they receive a lot of money for the work that they do. *Kate was well paid and enjoyed her job... I have an interesting, well-paid job, with opportunities to travel.* ◆◇◇◇◇ ADJ-GRADED

well-preserved; also spelled **well preserved**.

1 If you describe a middle-aged or old person as **well-preserved**, you mean that they look good for their age. *Annie is a well-preserved 50-year-old.* ADJ-GRADED

2 A **well-preserved** object or building does not show any signs of its age. *...well-preserved fossils... Although many of the stones have fallen out, the monument remains very well preserved.* ADJ-GRADED

well-read /wel red/; also spelled **well read**. A **well-read** person has read a lot of books and has learnt a lot from them. *He was clever, well-read and interested in the arts.* ADJ-GRADED

well-spoken; also spelled **well spoken**. A **well-spoken** person speaks in a polite correct way and with an accent which is considered socially acceptable. *I remember her as a quiet, hard-working and well-spoken girl.* ADJ-GRADED

well-thumbed. A book or magazine that is **well-thumbed** is creased and marked because it has been read so often. ADJ-GRADED

well-timed; also spelled **well timed**. A **well-timed** action or comment is done or made at the most appropriate or suitable time. *He built the company through a string of well-timed acquisitions... One well-timed word from you will be all it needs.* ADJ-GRADED =timely

well-to-do. A **well-to-do** person is rich enough to be able to do and buy most of the things that they want. *...a rather well-to-do family of diamond cutters. ...two well educated girls from well-to-do homes.* ◆◇◇◇◇ ADJ-GRADED =well-off

▶ **The well-to-do** are people who are well-to-do. *...a firm that installed stereo equipment in homes of the well-to-do.* N-PLURAL: the N

well-travelled; spelled **well-traveled** in American English. A **well-travelled** person has travelled a lot in foreign countries. ADJ-GRADED =much-travelled

well-tried; also spelled **well tried**. A **well-tried** treatment, product, or method is one that has been used many times before and so is known to work well or to be successful. *There are a number of well-tried remedies which are perfectly safe to take... It's a well-tried tactic to play down public expectations in advance of a superpower summit.* ADJ-GRADED =tried and tested

well-trodden

1 A **well-trodden** path is used regularly by a large number of people, and therefore looks worn and is easy to see. *He made his way along a well-trodden path towards the shed.* ADJ-GRADED: usu ADJ n

2 You can use **well-trodden**, especially in expressions such as **a well-trodden path** and **well-trodden ground**, to indicate that a plan or course of action has been tried or done by a lot of people and so the result of it is easy to predict. *Political power has long been a well-trodden path to personal wealth... These working parties will be going over well-trodden ground.* ADJ-GRADED: usu ADJ n

well versed; also spelled **well-versed**. If someone is **well versed** in a particular subject, they know a lot about it. *Page is well versed in many styles of jazz.* ADJ-GRADED: usu v-link ADJ in n

well-wisher, well-wishers; also spelled **wellwisher**. **Well-wishers** are people who hope that a particular person or thing will be successful, and who show this by their behaviour. *The main street was lined with well-wishers.* N-COUNT: usu pl

well-worn; also spelled **well worn**.
1 A **well-worn** expression, remark, or idea has been used so often that it no longer seems to have much meaning or to be interesting. *To use a well-worn cliche, it is packed with information. ...well-worn party dogma and ideology.* ADJ-GRADED =hackneyed
2 A **well-worn** object or piece of clothing has been worn or used so frequently that it looks rather old and untidy. *He was dressed casually in a sweater, blue trousers and well-worn brown shoes.* ADJ-GRADED

welly /weli/ **wellies.** In British English, **wellies** are long rubber boots which you wear to keep your feet dry; an informal word. N-COUNT: usu pl =wellington

Welsh /welʃ/ ◆◆◆◆◇
1 Welsh means belonging or relating to Wales, or to its people, language, or culture. *...the Welsh city of Cardiff. ...a full Welsh choir.* ► The **Welsh** are the people of Wales. *The Welsh eat more potatoes than anyone else.* ADJ; N-PLURAL: usu the N
2 Welsh is the language that is spoken in some parts of Wales. N-UNCOUNT

Welshman /welʃmən/ **Welshmen.** A **Welshman** is a man who was born in Wales and considers himself to be Welsh. ◆◇◇◇◇ N-COUNT

welt /welt/ **welts.** A **welt** is a mark which is made on someone's skin, usually by a blow from something such as a whip or sword. *He had a reddening welt on his temple and his nose was bleeding.* N-COUNT =weal

welter /weltəʳ/. A **welter of** something is a large quantity of it which occurs suddenly or in a confusing way; used in written English. *...patients with a welter of confusing symptoms. ...the welter of publicity that followed his engagement.* QUANT: QUANT of pl-n/n-uncount

wench /wentʃ/ **wenches.** A **wench** was a girl or young woman who worked as a servant or waitress; an old-fashioned use. *...a serving wench called Petunia.* N-COUNT

wend /wend/ **wends, wending, wended.** If you **wend** your **way** in a particular direction, you walk, especially slowly, casually, or carefully, in that direction; a literary expression. *...sleepy-eyed commuters were wending their way to work.* PHRASE: V inflects, usu PHR prep/adv =make your way

wendy house, wendy houses. In British English, a **wendy house** is a small toy house for a child to play in. The usual American word is **playhouse**. N-COUNT

went /went/. **Went** is the past tense of **go**.

wept /wept/. **Wept** is the past tense and past participle of **weep**.

were /wəʳ, STRONG wɜːʳ/
1 Were is the plural and the second person singular of the past tense of **be**.
2 In formal English, **were** is sometimes used instead of 'was' in certain structures, for example in conditional clauses or after the verb 'wish'. *He told a diplomat that he might withdraw if he were allowed to keep part of a disputed oil field... He believes in atheism as though it were a new religion.*
3 ● **as it were**: see **as**.

we're /wiːəʳ/. **We're** is the usual spoken form of 'we are'. *I'm married, but we're separated... We're thinking of going to a jazz club tonight.*

weren't /wɜːʳnt/. In informal English, **were not** is usually said or written as **weren't**.

werewolf /weəʳwulf/ **werewolves.** In folklore, horror stories, and films, a **werewolf** is a person who changes into a wolf. N-COUNT

west /west/; also spelled **West**. ◆◆◆◆◆
1 The **west** is the direction which you look towards in the evening in order to see the sun set. *I pushed on towards Flagstaff, a hundred miles to the west... The sun crosses the sky from east to west.* N-UNCOUNT: also the N
2 The **west** of a place, country, or region is the part of it which is in the west. *...physicists working at Bristol University in the west of England.* N-SING: usu the N, oft N of n
3 If you go **west**, you travel towards the west. *We are going West to California.* ADV: ADV after v
4 Something that is **west** of a place is positioned to the west of it. *...their home town of Paisley, several miles west of Glasgow.* ADV: usu ADV of n
5 The **west** part of a place, country, or region is the part which is towards the west. *...a small island off the west coast of South Korea.* ADJ: ADJ n
6 West is used in the names of some countries, states, and regions in the west of a larger area. *Mark has been working in West Africa for about six months. ...his West London home.* ADJ: ADJ n
7 A **west** wind blows from the west. ADJ
8 The West is used to refer to the United States, Canada, and the countries of Western, Northern, and Southern Europe. *Gorbachev was never as popular in the Soviet Union as he was in the West.* N-SING: the N

westbound /westbaʊnd/. **Westbound** roads or vehicles lead to the west or are travelling towards the west. *Traffic is slow on the westbound carriageway of the M4. ...the last westbound train to leave Chicago.* ADJ: ADJ n

westerly /westəʳli/ ◆◇◇◇◇
1 A **westerly** point, area, or direction is to the west or towards the west. *...Finisterre, Spain's most westerly point... They set out in a westerly direction along the riverbank.* ADJ-GRADED: usu ADJ n
2 A **westerly** wind blows from the west. *...a prevailing westerly wind.* ADJ: usu ADJ n

western /westəʳn/ **westerns;** also spelled **Western**. ◆◆◆◆◇
1 Western means in or from the west of a region or country. *...hand-made rugs from Western and Central Asia. ...Moi University, in western Kenya.* ADJ: ADJ n
2 Western is used to describe things, people, ideas, or ways of life that come from or are associated with the United States, Canada, and the countries of Western, Northern, and Southern Europe. *Mexico had the support of the big western governments... It seems that those statements have never been reported in the Western media.* ADJ: usu ADJ n
3 A **western** is a book or film about life in the west of America in the nineteenth century, especially the life of cowboys. N-COUNT

westerner /westəʳnəʳ/ **westerners;** also spelled **Westerner**. A **westerner** is a person who was born in or lives in the United States, Canada, or Western, Northern, or Southern Europe. *It's the first time a Westerner has been convicted for a drug-related offence in recent years in China.* ◆◇◇◇◇ N-COUNT

westernization /westəʳnaɪzeɪʃᵊn/; also spelled **westernisation** in British English. The **westernization** of a country, place, or person is the process of them adopting ideas and behaviour that are typical of Europe and North America, rather than preserving the ideas and behaviour traditional in their culture. *...fundamentalists unhappy with the westernization of Afghan culture... The explosive growth in casinos is one of the most conspicuous signs of Westernisation.* N-UNCOUNT

westernized /westəʳnaɪzd/; also spelled **westernised** in British English. A **westernized** country, place, or person has adopted ideas and behaviour typical of Europe and North America, rather than preserving the ideas and behaviour that are traditional in their culture. *Rapid urbanisation brings with it a more westernised and generally more sugary diet... We must stop our country becoming Westernized.* ADJ-GRADED

westernmost /westəʳnmoʊst/. The **westernmost** part of something is the part that is farther towards the west than any other. *...a village in the westernmost province of North Sudan.* ADJ-SUPERL: ADJ n

West German, West Germans ◆◆◆◇◇
1 West German means belonging or relating to the part of Germany that was known as the Federal Republic of Germany before the reunification of Germany in 1990. **West German** also means belonging or relating to the people or culture of this part of ADJ

Germany. *...the West German capital, Bonn. ...Willy Brandt, the former West German chancellor.*
2 A **West German** is someone who was a citizen of the part of Germany that was known as the Federal Republic of Germany before the reunification of Germany in 1990, or a person of West German origin. *Many West Germans are anxious about the potential cost of unification.* N-COUNT

West Indian, West Indians ◆◆◆◆◇
1 **West Indian** means belonging or relating to the West Indies, or to its people or culture. *The future quality of West Indian cricket looks promising... Barbadian-born Frank Collymore was at the heart of the West Indian literary renaissance in the '40s and '50s.* ADJ
2 A **West Indian** is a citizen of the West Indies or a person of West Indian origin. N-COUNT

westward /wɛstwəʳd/. The form **westwards** is also used. **Westward** or **westwards** means towards the west. *He sailed westward from Palos de la Frontera... Within hours, she was free to resume her journey westward.* ► Also an adjective. *...the one-hour westward flight over the Andes to Lima.* ◆◇◇◇◇ ADV: usu ADV after v, also n ADV; ADJ: ADJ n

wet /wɛt/ **wetter, wettest; wets, wetting, wetted.** The forms **wet** and **wetted** are both used as the past tense and past participle of the verb. ◆◆◆◇◇
1 If something is **wet**, it is covered in water, rain, sweat, tears, or another liquid. *He towelled his wet hair... I lowered myself to the water's edge, getting my feet wet... My gloves were soaking wet... I saw his face was wet with tears.* ♦ **wetly** *Her hair clung wetly to her head.* ♦ **wetness** *Anti-perspirants stop wetness, deodorants stop odour.* ADJ-GRADED ≠dry; ADV-GRADED; N-UNCOUNT ≠dryness
2 To **wet** something means to get water or some other liquid over it. *When assembling the pie, wet the edges where the two crusts join... Fielding nervously wet his lips and tried to smile.* VERB V n
3 If the weather is **wet**, it is raining. *If the weather is wet or cold choose an indoor activity... It was a miserable wet day.* ► **The wet** is used to mean wet weather. *They had come in from the cold and the wet... Braking in the wet in heavy traffic is never fun.* ADJ-GRADED =rainy ≠dry; N-SING: the N =the rain
4 If something such as paint, ink, or cement is **wet**, it is not yet dry or solid. *I lay the painting flat to stop the wet paint running... She rendered the walls in cement and, while it was still wet, applied the shells.* ADJ ≠dry
5 If a child or its nappy or clothing is **wet**, its nappy or clothing is soaked in urine. *Change him when he's wet... Avoid changing a nappy unless it's dirty or very wet.* ADJ-GRADED
6 If people, especially children, **wet** their beds or clothes or **wet** themselves, they urinate in their beds or clothes because they cannot control their bladder. *A quarter of 4-year-olds frequently wet the bed... To put it plainly, they wet themselves.* VERB V n V pron-refl
7 In British English, **wet** fish is fish that is sold fresh and uncooked, and not frozen or dried. ADJ: ADJ n
8 If you say that someone is **wet**, you have a low opinion of them because you think they are weak and lacking in enthusiasm, energy, or confidence; used in informal British English. *Don't be so wet, Charles.* ADJ-GRADED PRAGMATICS =pathetic
9 In British English, a **wet** is a Conservative politician who supports moderate political policies and opposes extreme ones. *Other Tory wets are not completely satisfied.* N-COUNT
10 If you say that someone is still **wet behind the ears**, you mean that they have only recently arrived in a new place or job, and are therefore still inexperienced or naive. PHRASE: v-link PHR
11 ● to **wet** your **whistle**: see **whistle**.

wet blanket, wet blankets. If you say that someone is a **wet blanket**, you are criticizing them because they refuse to join other people in an enjoyable activity or because they want to stop other people enjoying themselves; an informal expression. N-COUNT PRAGMATICS =spoilsport

wet dream, wet dreams
1 If a man has a **wet dream**, he has an erotic dream which causes him to ejaculate while he is asleep. N-COUNT
2 If someone says that a person or thing is a particular person's **wet dream**, they are saying in an unkind and mocking way that they think that this person or thing would give that person a lot of pleasure; an informal use which some people find offensive. *His wet dream is to score the winning goal for England in the World Cup Final.* N-COUNT: usu poss N

wetland /wɛtlænd/ **wetlands.** A **wetland** is an area of very wet, muddy land with wild plants growing in it. You can also refer to a wetland as **wetlands**. *...a scheme that aims to protect the wilderness of the wetlands... There are some areas of wetland which are of ancient origin. ...wetland habitats rich in plants, insects and birds.* ◆◇◇◇◇ N-VAR: oft N n

wet nurse, wet nurses; also spelled **wet-nurse**. In former times, a **wet nurse** was a woman who was paid to breast-feed another woman's baby. N-COUNT

wet suit, wet suits; also spelled **wetsuit**. A **wet suit** is a close-fitting rubber suit which a diver or underwater swimmer wears in order to keep his or her body warm. N-COUNT

we've /wɪv, STRONG wiːv/. **We've** is the usual spoken form of 'we have', especially when 'have' is an auxiliary verb. *'Hello, I don't think we've met,' Robert introduced himself... It's the first time for years that we've been to the cinema together as a family.*

whack /ʰwæk/ **whacks, whacking, whacked** ◆◇◇◇◇
1 If you **whack** someone or something, you hit them hard; an informal use. *You really have to whack the ball... Someone whacked him on the head.* ► Also a noun. *He gave the donkey a whack across the back with his stick... He took his ax and struck the trunk of the tree. Whack. Whack. Whack.* VERB V n V n prep; N-COUNT; SOUND
2 In informal British English, your **whack** of something is your share of it. *The majority of people in this country pay their whack... We need to win a fair whack of the contracts.* N-SING: oft poss N =share
3 If something is **out of whack**, it is not working properly, often because its natural balance has been upset; an informal expression, used mainly in American English. *The ecosystem will be thrown out of whack.* PHRASE: PHR after v, oft v-link PHR

whacking /ʰwækɪŋ/. In British English, you can use **whacking** to emphasize how big something is; an informal use. *The supermarkets may be making whacking profits.* ► Also an adverb. *...a whacking great hole.* ADJ: ADJ n PRAGMATICS =enormous; ADV: ADV adj

whacky /ʰwæki/. See **wacky**.

whale /ʰweɪl/ **whales** ◆◆◇◇◇
1 **Whales** are very large mammals that live in the sea. ● See also **killer whale, sperm whale**. N-COUNT
2 If you say that someone **is having a whale of a time**, you mean that they are enjoying themselves very much; an informal expression. *I had a whale of a time in Birmingham.* PHRASE: V inflects

whaler /ʰweɪləʳ/ **whalers**
1 A **whaler** is a ship which is used in hunting whales. N-COUNT
2 A **whaler** is someone who works on a ship which is used in hunting whales. N-COUNT

whaling /ʰweɪlɪŋ/. **Whaling** is the activity of hunting and killing whales. *...a ban on commercial whaling. ...the whaling industry.* ◆◇◇◇◇ N-UNCOUNT: oft N n

wham /ʰwæm/. You use **wham** to indicate that something happens suddenly or forcefully; an informal word. *Then I met someone and wham, bam, I was completely in love... There you are driving along and wham! You hit a pothole.* EXCLAM

whammy /ʰwæmi/. Journalists use **whammy** in expressions such as **double whammy** and **triple whammy** to indicate that two or three unpleasant or difficult situations occur at the same time, or occur one after the other. *This is a double whammy for public sector workers... We're suffering a triple whammy at the moment.* N-SING: adj N

wharf /ʰwɔːʳf/ **wharves** or **wharfs.** A **wharf** is a platform by a river or the sea where ships can be tied up. ◆◆◇◇◇ N-COUNT =jetty, quay

what /ʰwɒt/; usually pronounced /ʰwɒt/ for meanings 2, 4, 5 and 18. ◆◆◆◆◆

1 You use **what** in questions when you ask for specific information about something that you do not know. *What do you want?... What did she tell you, anyway?... 'Has something happened?'—'Indeed it has.'—'What?'... What are the greatest sources of conflict in the Middle East?... Hey! What are you doing?* ► Also a determiner. *What time is it?... What crimes are the defendants being charged with?... 'The heater works.'—'What heater?'... What kind of poetry does he like?* QUEST; DET-QUEST

2 You use **what** after certain words, especially verbs and adjectives, when you are referring to a situation that is unknown or has not been specified. *You can imagine what it would be like driving a car into a brick wall at 30 miles an hour... I want to know what happened to Norman... Do you know what those idiots have done?... We had never seen anything like it before and could not see what to do next... She turned scarlet from embarrassment, once she realized what she had done.* ► Also a determiner. *I didn't know what college I wanted to go to... I didn't know what else to say. ...an inspection to ascertain to what extent colleges are responding to the needs of industry.* CONJ-SUBORD; DET

3 You use **what** at the beginning of a clause in structures where you are changing the order of the information to give special emphasis to something. *What precisely triggered off yesterday's riot is still unclear... What I want to tell you is of the deep love and respect that I have for my husband... What she does possess is the ability to get straight to the core of a problem.* CONJ-SUBORD PRAGMATICS

4 You use **what** in expressions such as **what is called** and **what amounts to** when you are giving a possible description or identification of something. *She had been in what doctors described as an irreversible vegetative state for five years... The packed 38,900 Sydney crowd could not help but applaud what may be their last view of Botham in an England shirt.* CONJ-SUBORD

5 You use **what** to indicate that you are talking about the whole of an amount that is available to you. *He drinks what is left in his glass as if it were water... He moved carefully over what remained of partition walls.* ► Also a determiner. *They had had to use what money they had.* CONJ-SUBORD; DET =whatever

6 You say **'What?'** to tell someone who has indicated that they want to speak to you that you have heard them and are inviting them to continue. *'Dad?'—'What?'—'Can I have the car tonight?'* CONVENTION PRAGMATICS

7 You say **'What?'** when you ask someone to repeat the thing that they have just said because you did not hear or understand it properly. 'What?' is more informal and less polite than expressions such as 'Pardon?' and 'Excuse me?'. *'They could paint this place,' she said. 'What?' he asked.* CONVENTION PRAGMATICS

8 You say **'What'** to express surprise or disbelief. *'Adolphus Kelling, I arrest you on a charge of trafficking in narcotics.'—'What?'... 'We've got the car that killed Myra Moss.'—'What!'* CONVENTION PRAGMATICS

9 You use **what** in exclamations to emphasize an opinion or reaction. *What a horrible thing to do... What a busy day.* ► Also a determiner. *What ugly things; throw them away, throw them away... What great news, Jakki.* PREDET PRAGMATICS; DET

10 You use **what** to indicate that you are making a guess about something such as an amount or value. *It's, what, eleven years or more since he's seen him... This piece is, what, about an hour long?* ADV: ADV n

11 You say **guess what** or **do you know what** to introduce a piece of information which is surprising, which is not generally known, or which you want to emphasize. *Guess what? I'm going to dinner at Mrs. Combley's tonight... Do you know what? I'm going to the circus this afternoon.* PHRASES CONVENTION PRAGMATICS

12 In conversation, you say **or what?** after a question as a way of stating an opinion forcefully and showing that you expect other people to agree. *Look at that moon. Is that beautiful or what?... Am I wasting my time here, or what?* cl PHR PRAGMATICS

13 You say **so what?** or **what of it?** to indicate that the previous remark seems unimportant, uninteresting, or irrelevant to you. *'I skipped off school today,'—'So what? What's so special about that?'... 'This is Hollywood, U.S.A., where they make all the movies, remember.'—'What of it?'* CONVENTION PRAGMATICS =so?

14 You say **'Tell you what'** to introduce a suggestion or offer. *Tell you what, let's stay here another day and go to the fair.* PHR cl PRAGMATICS =I know

15 You use **what about** at the beginning of a question when you make a suggestion, offer, or request. *'What about Sunday evening at Frank's?'—'Sure. What time?'... 'What about selling me the car?'—'Sorry matey, can't be done.'* PHR n/-ing PRAGMATICS =how about

16 You use **what about** or **what of** when you introduce a new topic or a point which seems relevant to a previous remark. *Now you've talked about work on daffodils, what about other commercially important flowers, like roses?... And what about when you were in the fifth year, did people give you careers advice on coming to college?... And what of the effect on U.S domestic opinion?... 'I don't like being in the house on my own.'—'What about at night? Do you mind being by yourself at night?'* PHR group/cl PRAGMATICS

17 You say **what about** a particular person or thing when you ask someone to explain why they have asked you about that person or thing. *'This thing with the Corbett woman.'—'Oh, yeah. What about her?'... 'You're talking to yourself.'—'Well, what of it?'* PHR n PRAGMATICS

18 You say **what have you** at the end of a list in order to refer generally to other things of the same kind. *So many things are unsafe these days – milk, cranberry sauce, what have you... My great-grandfather, who had the forge in town, made horseshoes and nails and what have you.* n PHR, n *and/or* PHR =et cetera

19 You say **what if** at the beginning of a question when you ask about the consequences of something happening, especially something undesirable. *What if this doesn't work out?... What if he was going to die!... What if relations between you and your neighbour have reached deadlock, and their behaviour is still unacceptable?* PHR cl PRAGMATICS

20 If you know **what's what**, you know the important things that need to be known about a situation. *You have to know what's what and when to draw the line... You should come across the river with us. Then you will really see what's what.* PHR after v

21 You say **what with** in order to introduce the reasons for a particular situation, especially an undesirable one. *Maybe they are tired, what with all the sleep they're losing staying up night after night... What with one thing and another, it was fairly late in the day when we returned to Shrewsbury.* PREP PRAGMATICS

22 In informal conversation, people say **you what?** to indicate that they do not believe or accept the remark that someone has just made, or that they have not heard or understood it properly. *'I'm going to have problems sleeping tonight.'—'You what?'... 'What are you doing here?'—'Oh I work here now.'—'You what?'* CONVENTION PRAGMATICS =what

23 • **what's more**: see **more**.

whatever /ʰwɒtevəʳ/ ◆◆◆◆◇

1 You use **whatever** to refer to anything or everything of a particular type. *Franklin was free to do pretty much whatever he pleased... When you're older I think you're better equipped mentally to cope with whatever happens... He's good at whatever he does.* ► Also a determiner. *Whatever doubts he might have had about Ingrid were all over now.* CONJ-SUBORD; DET =any

2 You use **whatever** to say that something is the case in all circumstances. *We shall love you whatever happens, Diana... People will judge you whatever you do... She runs on average about 15 miles a day every day, week in week out, whatever the circumstances, whatever the weather.* CONJ-SUBORD =no matter what

3 You use **whatever** after a noun group in order to emphasize a negative statement. *There is no evidence whatever that competition in broadcasting has ever reduced costs... I have nothing whatever to say.* ADV: with brd-neg, n ADV PRAGMATICS =whatsoever

4 You use **whatever** to ask in an emphatic way QUEST

about something which you are very surprised about. *Whatever can you mean? Whatever is the matter with you both?*
PRAGMATICS =what

5 You use **whatever** when you are indicating that you do not know the precise identity, meaning, or value of the thing just mentioned. *I thought that my upbringing was 'normal', whatever that is... 'I love you,' he said.—'Whatever that means,' she said.*
CONJ-SUBORD

6 You say **or whatever** to refer generally to something else of the same kind as the thing or things that you have just mentioned; an informal expression. *You may like a Malt whisky that is peatier, or smokier, or sweeter, or whatever.*
PHRASE: cl/group PHR

7 You say **'whatever you say'** to indicate that you accept what someone has said, even though you do not really believe them or do not think it is a good idea. *'We'll go in your car, Billy.'—'Whatever you say.'*
CONVENTION PRAGMATICS

8 You say **whatever** you **do** when giving advice or warning someone about something. *Whatever you do, don't look for a pay increase when you know the company is going through some difficulty... Whatever you do, don't upset the women.*
PHRASE: PHR cl PRAGMATICS

whatnot /ʰwɒtnɒt/. People sometimes say **'and whatnot'** or **'or whatnot'** after mentioning one or more things, to refer in a vague way to other things which are similar; used in informal spoken English. *The women were there in their jeans and T-shirts and overalls and whatnot... The council can send messages or letters or whatnot in Spanish to their constituents.*
PHRASE: cl/group PHR =whatever

what's /ʰwɒts/. **What's** is the usual spoken form of 'what is' or 'what has', especially when 'has' is an auxiliary verb.

whatshername /ʰwɒtsəʳneɪm/; also spelled **whatsername**. You say **whatshername** instead of a woman's name when you cannot remember it or are trying to remember it. *That's the thing that whatshername gave me.*
PRON

whatshisname /ʰwɒtsɪzneɪm/; also spelled **whatsis name**. You say **whatshisname** instead of a man's name when you cannot remember it or are trying to remember it. *...the new junior minister, whatsisname, Donald Sinclair.*
PRON

whatsit /ʰwɒtsɪt/ **whatsits.** You use **whatsit** instead of a noun or name which you cannot remember or which you do not want to say because it is rude. *We wanted to be here early in case the whatsit, maintenance supervisor had forgotten to deal with it... He's got that fiery temper which scares the whatsit out of everybody.*
N-VAR

whatsoever /ʰwɒtsoʊevəʳ/. You use **whatsoever** after a noun group in order to emphasize a negative statement. *My school did nothing whatsoever in the way of athletics... I don't think they'll have any idea how I'm feeling. None whatsoever... There is absolutely no doubt whatsoever that this woman was a totally devoted and caring mother.*
◆◆◇◇◇ ADV: usu with brd-neg, n ADV PRAGMATICS =at all

wheat /ʰwiːt/ **wheats. Wheat** is a cereal crop grown for food. **Wheat** is also used to refer to the grain of this crop, which is usually ground into flour and used to make bread. *...farmers growing wheat, corn, or other crops. ...wheat flour.* ● to **separate the wheat from the chaff**: see **chaff**.
◆◆◇◇◇ N-MASS

wheatgerm /ʰwiːtdʒɜːʳm/; also spelled **wheat germ. Wheatgerm** is the middle part of a grain of wheat which is rich in vitamins and is often added to other food.
N-UNCOUNT

wheedle /ʰwiːdəl/ **wheedles, wheedling, wheedled.** If you say that someone **wheedles**, you mean they try to persuade someone to do or give them what they want, for example by saying nice things that they do not mean; used showing disapproval. *Cross decided to beg and wheedle a bit... He managed to wheedle his way into the offices. ...an opportunity to wheedle more money out of Wilson... 'Why don't you try to read on past page 21,' I wheedled and sat down again.*
VERB; V; V *way* prep; V n *out of/from* n; V with quote; Also V n

wheel /ʰwiːl/ **wheels, wheeling, wheeled**
◆◆◆◇◇

1 The **wheels** of a vehicle are the circular objects which are fixed underneath it and which enable it to move along the ground. *The car wheels spun and slipped on some oil on the road.* ● Something **on wheels** has wheels attached to the bottom, so that it can be moved easily. *...a trolley on wheels... The stove is on wheels so it can be shuffled around easily.*
N-COUNT; PHRASE: n PHR, v-link PHR

2 A **wheel** is a circular object which forms a part of a machine, usually a moving part. *The wheels of whetstone grinders are usually fairly large.*
N-COUNT

3 The wheel of a car or other vehicle is the circular object that is used to steer it. **The wheel** is used in expressions to talk about who is driving a vehicle. For example, if someone is **at the wheel** of a car, they are driving it. *My co-pilot suddenly grabbed the wheel... Curtis got behind the wheel and they started back toward the cottage... Roberto handed Flynn the keys and let him take the wheel.*
N-COUNT: usu sing, *the* N =steering wheel

4 People sometimes refer to a car as **wheels**; an informal use. *'Do you own a house?'—'No. But I have wheels.'*
N-PLURAL

5 If you **wheel** an object that has wheels somewhere, you push it along. *He wheeled his bike into the alley at the side of the house... They wheeled her out on the stretcher.*
VERB; V n prep/adv

6 If something such as a group of animals or birds **wheels**, it moves in a circle; a literary use. *A flock of crows wheeled overhead.*
VERB; V

7 If you **wheel** round, you turn round suddenly on the place where you are standing, often because you are surprised, shocked, or angry. *He wheeled around to face her... She wheeled sharply and headed for the check-out counter.*
VERB; V adv; V

8 You use **wheel** in expressions such as **the wheel of fortune** to refer to the changes that take place in life, especially when you are referring to the fact that the same situations occur more than once. *The wheel of fortune will swing round again; in politics, it always does... In his view the wheel of history could not be turned back.*
N-SING: *the* N *of* n

9 People talk about **the wheels of** an organization or system to mean the way in which it operates. *He knows the wheels of administration turn slowly.* ● to **oil the wheels**: see **oil**.
N-PLURAL: *the* N *of* n

10 If you say that there are **wheels within wheels**, you mean that there are a number of different influences, reasons, and actions which together make a situation complicated and difficult to understand. *Our culture is more complex than he knows. Wheels within wheels.*
PHRASE

11 See also **catherine wheel, meals on wheels, potter's wheel, spare wheel, spinning wheel, steering wheel, water wheel.**

wheel and deal, wheels and deals, wheeling and dealing, wheeled and dealed. If you say that someone **wheels and deals**, you mean that they use a lot of different methods and contacts to achieve what they want in business or politics, often in a way which you consider dishonest. *He still wheels and deals around the globe. ...a fisherman's son who wheeled and dealed his way to the most senior public position.* ♦ **wheeling and dealing** *He hates the wheeling and dealing associated with conventional political life.*
VERB; V; V *way* prep; N-UNCOUNT

wheelbarrow /ʰwiːlbæroʊ/ **wheelbarrows.** A **wheelbarrow** is a small open cart with one wheel and handles that is used for carrying things, for example in the garden.
N-COUNT

wheelbase /ʰwiːlbeɪs/ **wheelbases.** The **wheelbase** of a car or other vehicle is the distance between its front and back wheels.
N-COUNT: usu sing

wheelchair /ʰwiːltʃeəʳ/ **wheelchairs.** A **wheelchair** is a chair with wheels that you use in order to move about in if you cannot walk properly, for example because you are disabled or sick.
◆◆◇◇◇ N-COUNT

wheeler-dealer, wheeler-dealers. If you refer to someone, especially in business or politics, as a **wheeler-dealer**, you disapprove of the way that they try to succeed or to get what they want, often by dishonest or unfair methods.
N-COUNT PRAGMATICS

wheelhouse /ʰwiːlhaʊs/ **wheelhouses.** A **wheelhouse** is a small room or shelter on a ship or boat, where the wheel used for steering the boat is situated.
N-COUNT

wheelwright /ʰwiːlraɪt/ **wheelwrights.** A **wheelwright** is someone who makes and repairs wooden wheels and other wooden things such as carts, carriages, and gates. N-COUNT

wheeze /ʰwiːz/ **wheezes, wheezing, wheezed** ◆◇◇◇◇
1 If someone **wheezes**, they breathe with difficulty, making a hissing or whistling sound. *He had quite serious problems with his chest and wheezed and coughed all the time... 'Boy,' wheezed old Pop Ryan.* VERB V V with quote
2 In British English is a **wheeze** is a clever idea, joke, or trick; an old-fashioned, informal use. *He came up with what seemed like a clever wheeze. ...the temptation to boost profits through accounting wheezes.* N-COUNT: usu with supp, oft adj N =trick

wheezy /ʰwiːzi/. A **wheezy** cough or laugh comes from someone who has difficulty in breathing, so it has hissing or whistling in it. ADJ-GRADED

whelk /ʰwelk/ **whelks.** A **whelk** is a creature like a snail that is found in the sea near the shore. Whelks have hard shells and very soft bodies which can be eaten. N-COUNT

whelp /ʰwelp/ **whelps.** A **whelp** is the young offspring of an animal, especially a dog or a wolf; an old-fashioned word. N-COUNT

when /ʰwen/ ◆◆◆◆◆
1 You use **when** to ask questions about the time at which things happen. *When are you going home?... When did you get married?... When is the press conference?... When were you in this house last?... 'I'll be there this afternoon.'—'When?'* QUEST
2 If something happens **when** something else is happening, the two things are happening at the same time. *When eating a whole cooked fish, you should never turn it over to get at the flesh on the other side... Mustard is grown in the field when weeds are there, rather than when the growing crops are there.* CONJ-SUBORD
3 You use **when** to introduce a clause in which you mention something which happens at some point during an activity, event, or situation. *When I met the Gills, I had been gardening for nearly ten years.* CONJ-SUBORD
4 You use **when** to introduce a clause where you mention the circumstances under which the event in the main clause happened or will happen. *When he brought Imelda her drink she gave him a genuine, sweet smile of thanks... I'll start to think about it when I have to write my report.* CONJ-SUBORD
5 You use **when** after certain words, especially verbs and adjectives, to introduce a clause where you mention the time at which something happens. *I asked him when he'd be back to pick me up... I don't know when the decision was made... It is important to check when the laboratory can do the tests.* CONJ-SUBORD
6 You use **when** to introduce a clause which specifies or refers to the time at which something happens. *He could remember a time when he had worked like that himself... She remembered clearly that day when she'd gone exploring the rockpools... In 1973, when he lived in Rome, his sixteen-year-old son was kidnapped.* PRON-REL
7 You use **when** to introduce the reason for an opinion, comment, or question. *How can I love myself when I look like this?... Emerald starlings are fairly small when compared with other such birds.* CONJ-SUBORD PRAGMATICS
8 You use **when** in order to introduce a fact or comment which makes the other part of the sentence rather surprising or unlikely. *Our mothers sat us down to read and paint, when all we really wanted to do was to make a mess... The temperature sensor is making the computer think the engine is cold when, in fact, it's hot.* CONJ-SUBORD PRAGMATICS =although

whence /ʰwens/. **Whence** means from where; an old-fashioned or literary word. *We looked down to the river whence we'd climbed, and nobody complained of the effort as I had anticipated... He was educated at Quakers' Yard Grammar School, whence he took a mathematics scholarship to Jesus College, Oxford.* ► Also a question. *Whence then come the lofty Olympian ideals of fair play?* ► Also a conjunction. *Asked whence he had come, he said in the broadest of accents, 'Lancashire'... Hunter is dead and his remains have long since returned to the earth from whence they came.* ◆◇◇◇◇ PRON-REL QUEST CONJ-SUBORD

whenever /ʰwenevəʳ/ ◆◆◆◇◇
1 You use **whenever** to refer to any time or every time that something happens or is true. *She always called at the vicarage whenever she was in the area... You can have my cottage whenever you like... I recommend that you avoid processed foods whenever possible.* CONJ-SUBORD
2 You use **whenever** to mean an unspecified time. *He married Miss Vancouver in 1963, or whenever it was.* CONJ-SUBORD

where /ʰweəʳ/; usually pronounced /ʰweəʳ/ for meanings 2 and 3. ◆◆◆◆◆
1 You use **where** to ask questions about the place something is in, or is coming from or going to. *Where did you meet him?... Where's Anna?... Where are we going?... 'You'll never believe where Julie and I are going.'—'Where?'* QUEST
2 You use **where** after certain words, especially verbs and adjectives, to introduce a clause in which you mention the place in which something is situated or happens. *People began looking across to see where the noise was coming from... He knew where Henry Carter had gone... If he's got something on his mind he knows where to find me... Ernest Brown lives about a dozen blocks from where the riots began.* ► Also a relative pronoun. *Conditions which apply to your flight are available at the travel agency where you book your holiday... Wanchai boasts the Academy of Performing Arts, where everything from Chinese Opera to Shakespeare is performed.* CONJ-SUBORD PRON-REL
3 You use **where** to ask questions about a situation, a stage in something, or an aspect of something. *Where will it all end?... If they get their way, where will it stop?... It's not so simple. They'll have to let the draft board know, and then where will we be?* QUEST
4 You use **where** after certain words, especially verbs and adjectives, to introduce a clause in which you mention a situation, a stage in something, or an aspect of something. *It's not hard to see where she got her feelings about herself... She had a feeling she already knew where this conversation was going to lead... I didn't know where to start.* ► Also a relative pronoun. *...that delicate situation where a friend's confidence can easily be betrayed... The government is at a stage where it is willing to talk to almost anyone.* CONJ-SUBORD PRON-REL
5 You use **where** to introduce a clause that contrasts with the other parts of the sentence. *Where some people learned to play the accordion for dances in their community, others took music lessons... Sometimes a teacher will be listened to, where a parent might not.* CONJ-SUBORD PRAGMATICS =whereas

whereabouts. Pronounced /ʰweərəbaʊts/ for meaning 1, and /ʰweərəbaʊts/ for meanings 2 and 3. ◆◇◇◇◇
1 If you refer to the **whereabouts** of a particular person or thing, you mean the place where that person or thing may be found. *The police are anxious to hear from anyone who may know the whereabouts of the firearms... Once he knew his father's name, finding his whereabouts proved surprisingly easy.* N-SING-COLL: with poss =location
2 You use **whereabouts** in questions when you are asking precisely where something is. *Whereabouts in Liverpool are you from?... Whereabouts are you living?... 'I actually live near Chester.'—'Whereabouts?'* QUEST
3 You use **whereabouts** after certain words, especially verbs and adjectives, to introduce a clause in which you mention precisely where something is situated or happens. *I live in a village near to Germaine Greer and know whereabouts she lives.* CONJ-SUBORD

whereas /ʰweəræz/. You use **whereas** to introduce a comment which contrasts with what is said in the main clause. *These fixed-price menus for two or three courses can cost as little as 50f, whereas the à la carte is always more expensive... Whereas the population of working age increased* ◆◆◆◇◇ CONJ-SUBORD PRAGMATICS =while *by 1 million between 1981 and 1986, today it is barely growing.*

whereby /ʰweəʳbaɪ/. A system or action **whereby** something happens is one that makes that thing happen; a formal word. *The system whereby Britons choose their family doctors and the government pays those doctors, has been reasonably successful... They voted to accept a deal whereby the union will receive nearly three-quarters of a million pounds from the International Miners Organisation.* ◆◆◇◇◇ PRON-REL

wherefores /ʰweəʳfɔːʳz/. **The whys and wherefores** of something are the reasons for it. *Even successful bosses need to be queried about the whys and wherefores of their actions.* PHRASE: usu PHR *of* n

wherein /ʰweərɪn/ ◆◇◇◇◇

1 Wherein means in which place or thing; a formal, literary, or old-fashioned use. *...a riding school wherein we could learn the art of horsemanship... Adequate housing is possible in developed, mixed economies wherein the interests of the poor have prevailed.* PRON-REL

2 Wherein means in which part or respect; a formal use. *Wherein lies the truth?* ► Also a conjunction. *It is difficult to know wherein Mr Ritchie hoped to find salvation for his country.* QUEST / CONJ-SUBORD

whereupon /ʰweərəpɒn/. You use **whereupon** to say that one thing happens immediately after another thing, and usually as a result of it; a formal word. *Mr Muite refused to talk to them except in the company of his legal colleagues, whereupon the police officers departed... 'Well, get on with it then,' said Dobson, whereupon Davies started to explain.* ◆◇◇◇◇ CONJ-COORD PRAGMATICS =at which

wherever /ʰweərevəʳ/ ◆◆◇◇◇

1 You use **wherever** to indicate that something happens or is true in any place or situation. *Some people enjoy themselves wherever they are... Jack believed in finding happiness wherever possible... By simply planning a route, you can explore at will and stop whenever and wherever you like.* CONJ-SUBORD

2 You use **wherever** when you indicate that you do not know where a person or place is. *I'd like to leave as soon as possible and join my children, wherever they are... 'Till we meet again, wherever that it,' said the chairman.* CONJ-SUBORD

3 You use **wherever** in questions as an emphatic form of 'where', usually when you are surprised about something. *Wherever did you get that idea?... Wherever have you been?* QUEST PRAGMATICS

4 You use **or wherever** to say that something might happen in a place other than the place you have mentioned, but that you are not able to specify where; an informal use. *The next day she was gone to Lusaka, Kampala, or wherever. ...language which will allow the students in class or wherever to express their opinions.* PHRASE: n-proper/prep PHR

wherewithal /ʰweəʳwɪðɔːl/. If you have **the wherewithal** for something, you have the means, especially the money, that you need for it. *She didn't have the financial wherewithal to do it... Some of the companies illegally sent the wherewithal for making chemical weapons.* N-SING: *the* N, oft N to-inf, N *for* n/-ing =means

whet /ʰwet/ **whets, whetting, whetted.** If someone or something **whets** your **appetite** for a particular thing, they increase your desire to have it or know about it, especially by giving you an idea of what it is like. *A really good catalogue can also whet customers' appetites for merchandise. ...lectures he hopes might whet the appetite and keep students' enthusiasm.* PHRASE: V and N inflect, oft PHR *for* n

whether /ʰweðəʳ/ ◆◆◆◆◆

1 You use **whether** when you are talking about a choice or doubt between two or more alternatives. *To this day, it's unclear whether he shot himself or was murdered... Whether it turns out to be a good idea or a bad idea, we'll find out... They now have two weeks to decide whether or not to buy... The council is considering whether to approve of the use of firearms... I don't know whether they've found anybody yet.* CONJ-SUBORD

2 You use **whether** to say that something is true in any of the circumstances that you mention. *This happens whether the children are in two-parent or one-parent families... Whether they say it aloud or not, most men expect their wives to be faithful. ...beers and lagers of all kinds, whether bottled or draught.* CONJ-SUBORD

whetstone /ʰwetstoun/ **whetstones.** A **whetstone** is a stone which is used for sharpening knives, chisels, or other tools. N-COUNT: usu sing

whew. **Whew** is used in writing to represent a sound that you make when you breathe out quickly, for example because you are very hot, very relieved, or very surprised. *'Whew,' he said. 'It's hot.'... You were just in time. Whew! What a close call... 'Whew! What is that terrible smell?' she cried.* EXCLAM PRAGMATICS

whey /ʰweɪ/. **Whey** is the watery liquid that is separated from the curds in sour milk, for example when you are making cheese. N-UNCOUNT

which /ʰwɪtʃ/; usually pronounced /ʰwɪtʃ/ for meanings 2, 3 and 4. ◆◆◆◆◆

1 You use **which** in questions when there are two or more possible answers or alternatives. *Which do they want me to do, declare war or surrender?... Which are the ones you really like? Which are the good adverts for you?* ► Also a determiner. *Which woman or man do you most admire?... 'You go down that passageway over there.'—'Which one?'... Which vitamin supplements are good value?* QUEST / DET-QUEST

2 You use **which** to refer to a choice between two or more possible answers or alternatives. *I wanted to know which school it was you went to... I can't remember which teachers I had... Scientists have long wondered which parts of the brain are involved in musical tasks.* ► Also a conjunction. *In her panic she couldn't remember which was Mr Grainger's cabin... There are so many diets on the market, how do you know which to choose?* DET / CONJ-SUBORD

3 You use **which** at the beginning of a relative clause when specifying the thing that you are talking about or when giving more information about it. *Soldiers opened fire on a car which failed to stop at an army checkpoint... He's based in Banja Luka, which is the largest city in northern Bosnia... Colic describes a whole variety of conditions in which a horse suffers abdominal pain... I'm no longer allowed to smoke in any room which he currently occupies.* PRON-REL

4 You use **which** to refer back to an idea or situation expressed in a previous sentence or sentences, especially when you want to give your opinion about it. *They ran out of drink. Which actually didn't bother me because I wasn't drinking... Since we started in September we have raised fifty thousand pounds, which is pretty good going... Visited Park West. Viewed a flat, no. 76. Which I like.* ► Also a determiner. *The chances are you haven't fully decided what you want from your career at the moment, in which case you're definitely not cut out to be a boss yet!* PRON-REL / DET: DET sing-n

5 If you cannot tell the difference between two things, you can say that you do not know **which is which**. *They all look so alike to me that I'm never sure which is which... It's essential to know which is which as treatments will be quite different.* PHRASE: V inflects

6 • **any which way**: see **way**. • **every which way**: see **way**.

whichever /ʰwɪtʃevəʳ/ ◆◇◇◇◇

1 You use **whichever** in order to indicate that it does not matter which of the possible alternatives happens or is chosen. *Whichever way you look at it, nuclear power is the energy of the future... Israel offers automatic citizenship to all Jews who want it, whatever colour they are and whichever language they speak.* ► Also a conjunction. *If you are unhappy with anything you have bought from us, we will gladly exchange your goods, or refund your money, whichever you prefer.* DET: DET sing-n =whatever / CONJ-SUBORD =whatever

2 You use **whichever** to specify which of a number of possibilities is the right one or the one you mean. *Learning to relax by whichever method suits you best is a positive way of contributing to your* DET *overall good health.* ► Also a conjunction. *Fishing is from 6 am to dusk or 10.30pm, whichever is sooner... In the second year, management has offered 7 per cent or the rate of inflation, whichever is higher... Whichever of the fitness classes you opt for, trained instructors are there to help you.* CONJ-SUBORD

whiff /hwɪf/ **whiffs** ◆◇◇◇◇

1 If there is a **whiff** of a particular smell, you smell it faintly or for only a brief period of time, for example as you walk past someone or something. *He caught a whiff of her perfume.* N-COUNT: usu sing, usu N *of* n

2 A **whiff** of something bad or harmful is a slight sign of it. *Not a whiff of scandal has ever tainted his private life... The TV show had the whiff of hypocrisy and pomposity.* N-COUNT: usu sing, usu N *of* n

Whig /hwɪg/ **Whigs.** A **Whig** was a member of an English political party that in the 18th and 19th centuries was in favour of political and social reforms. ◆◇◇◇◇ N-COUNT

while 1 conjunction uses

while /hwaɪl/; usually pronounced /hwaɪl/ for meaning 4. The form **whilst** is also used in formal or literary English, especially British English. ◆◆◆◆◆

1 If something happens **while** something else is happening, the two things are happening at the same time. *They were grinning and watching while one man laughed and poured beer over the head of another... I sat on the settee to unwrap the package while he stood by... Racing was halted for an hour while the track was repaired... Her parents could help with child care while she works.* CONJ-SUBORD

2 If something happens **while** something else happens, the first thing happens at some point during the time that the second thing is happening. *The two ministers have yet to meet, but may do so while in New York... Never apply water to a burn from an electric shock while the casualty is still in contact with the electric current.* CONJ-SUBORD

3 You use **while** at the beginning of a clause to introduce information which contrasts with information in the main clause. *Marianne was tempted to turn the large rooms into traditional French-style salons, while Howard was in favour of a typically English look... The first two services are free, while the third costs £35.00.* CONJ-SUBORD PRAGMATICS =whereas

4 You use **while** when you admit in the clause that something is the case but say that it does not affect the truth of the other part of the sentence, although the two statements partly conflict. *While the numbers of such developments are relatively small, the potential market is large... While the modelling business is by no means easy to get into, the good model, male or female, will always be in demand... While the news, so far, has been good, there may be days ahead when it is bad.* CONJ-SUBORD PRAGMATICS =although

while 2 noun and verb uses

while /hwaɪl/ **whiles, whiling, whiled** ◆◆◆◆◇

1 A **while** is a period of time. *They walked on in silence for a while... He was married a little while ago... Working at low intensity means that you can continue to perform the activity for a long while.* N-SING: *a* N, usu adj N =time

2 You use **all the while** in order to say that something happens continually or that it happens throughout the time when something else is happening. *All the while the people at the next table watched me eat.* PHRASE: PHR with cl

3 ● **once in a while**: see **once**. ● **to make it worth your while**: see **worth**.

while away. If you **while away** the time in a particular way, you spend time in that way, often just talking, because you are waiting for something, or because you have nothing else to do. *Miss Bennett whiled away the hours playing old films on her video-recorder.* PHRASAL VERB V P n (not pron) Also V n P

whilst /hwaɪlst/. **Whilst** means the same as **while** when it is a conjunction; a formal or literary word, used mainly in British English. ◆◆◆◇◇ CONJ-SUBORD

whim /hwɪm/ **whims.** A **whim** is a wish to do or have something which seems to have no serious reason or purpose behind it, and often occurs suddenly. *We decided, more or less on a whim, to sail to Morocco... You have to remember that the premium can increase at the whim of the insurers... Lately, the president has been sacking and picking new ministers at whim.* ◆◇◇◇◇ N-VAR: oft *on/at* N

whimper /hwɪmpəʳ/ **whimpers, whimpering, whimpered** ◆◇◇◇◇

1 If someone **whimpers**, they make quiet unhappy or frightened sounds, as if they are about to start crying. *She lay at the bottom of the stairs, whimpering in pain... He made another pathetic whimpering sound.* ► Also a noun. *David's crying subsided to a whimper.* VERB V V-ing N-COUNT

2 If someone **whimpers** something, they say it in an unhappy or frightened way. *'Let me go,' she whimpered. 'You're hurting me.'... She whimpered something inaudible.* VERB V with quote V n

3 If you say that something happens **not with a bang but a whimper**, you mean that it is less effective or exciting than was expected or intended. *He bowed out of world politics not with a bang but a whimper... The festival started with a whimper rather than a bang.* PHRASE: PHR after v

whimsical /hwɪmzɪkəl/. A **whimsical** person or idea is unusual, playful, and unpredictable, rather than serious and practical. *McGrath remembers his offbeat sense of humor, his whimsical side... His graphic art became slighter and more whimsical.* ◆◇◇◇◇ ADJ-GRADED =quirky

whimsy /hwɪmzi/; also spelled **whimsey**. **Whimsy** is behaviour which is unusual, playful, and unpredictable, rather than having any serious reason or purpose behind it. N-UNCOUNT

whine /hwaɪn/ **whines, whining, whined** ◆◇◇◇◇

1 If something or someone **whines**, they make a long, high-pitched noise, especially one which sounds sad or unpleasant. *He could hear her dog barking and whining in the background... The engines whined.* ► Also a noun. *...the whine of air-raid sirens.* VERB V N-COUNT: usu sing

2 If you say that someone **is whining** about something, you mean they are complaining in an annoying way about something unimportant. *They come to me to whine about their troubles. ...children who whine that they are bored... 'Why can't you tell me?' I whined... It's just a scratch. Stop whining. ...a pleading, whining voice.* VERB =moan V *about* n/-ing V that V with quote V V-ing

whinge /hwɪndʒ/ **whinges, whingeing, whinging, whinged.** If you say that someone **is whingeing** about something, you think that they are complaining in an annoying way about something unimportant; used in informal British English. *...people who whine and whinge about their alleged misfortunes... All she ever does is whinge and complain... Stop whingeing and get on with it.* ► Also a noun. *It must be really depressing listening to everybody's whinges.* ◆◇◇◇◇ VERB =moan, whine V *about* n/-ing V Also V with quote N-COUNT

whinger /hwɪndʒəʳ/ **whingers.** If you call someone a **whinger**, you are critical of them because they complain about things all the time; used in informal British English. *Shut up, you moaning whinger.* N-COUNT PRAGMATICS

whinny /hwɪni/ **whinnies, whinnying, whinnied.** When a horse **whinnies**, it neighs softly. *The girl's horse whinnied.* ► Also a noun. *...with a terrified whinny the horse shied.* VERB V N-COUNT

whip /hwɪp/ **whips, whipping, whipped** ◆◆◆◇◇

1 A **whip** is a long thin piece of material such as leather or rope, fastened to a stiff handle. It is used for hitting people or animals. N-COUNT

2 If someone **whips** a person or animal, they beat them or hit them with a whip or something like a whip. *Eye-witnesses claimed Mr Melton whipped the horse up to 16 times... He was whipped with a studded belt.* ♦ **whipping, whippings** *He threatened to give her a whipping.* VERB =beat V n N-COUNT =beating

3 If something, for example the wind, **whips** something, it strikes it sharply; a literary use. *A terrible wind whipped our faces... A branch whipped her across the cheek.* VERB V n

4 If something flexible **whips** in a particular way, it moves sharply when it is affected by a force, for example by the wind; a literary use. *Blond strands of hair whipped in the wind.* VERB V prep/adv

5 If someone **whips** something out or **whips** it off, they take it out or take it off very quickly and suddenly. *Bob whipped out his notebook... Players were whipping their shirts off... My waitress whipped the plate away and put down my bill.* VERB V n with adv V n adv

6 If something or someone **whips** somewhere, they move there or go there very quickly. *The wind out here is whipping along at about 30 miles an hour... I whipped into a parking space.* VERB V adv/prep

7 When you **whip** something liquid such as cream or an egg, you stir it very fast until it is thick and frothy or stiff. *Whip the cream until thick... Whip the eggs, oils and honey together. ...strawberries and whipped cream.* VERB V n V n adv/prep V-ed

8 If you **whip** people **into** an emotional state, you deliberately cause and encourage them to be in that state. *He could whip a crowd into hysteria... Politicians and businessmen have whipped themselves into a panic.* VERB V n *into* n

9 A **whip** is a member of a particular party in a parliament, who is responsible for making sure that party members are present to vote on important issues and to vote in the appropriate way. *The Whips have the job of making sure MPs toe the line.* N-COUNT

10 In British English, a **whip** is a notice which tells the members of a particular party in parliament that it is important for them to vote in a particular way on an important issue. • See also **three-line whip**. N-COUNT

11 If you have **the whip hand**, you have power over someone else in a particular situation. *These days the shopper has the whip hand, and will not buy if stores fail to lower their prices.* PHRASE: PHR after v

12 • **a fair crack of the whip**: see **crack**.

whip up PHRASAL VERB

1 If someone **whips up** an emotion, especially a dangerous one such as hatred, or if they **whip** people **up** into a state of hatred, they deliberately cause and encourage people to feel that emotion. *He accused politicians of whipping up anti-foreign sentiments in order to win right-wing votes... Joe McCarthy whipped up Americans into a frenzy of anti-Communist activity in the Fifties.* =stir up V P n (not pron) V P n (not pron) *into* n Also V n P *into* n

2 If a force such as the wind **whips up** dust or water, it makes it rise up. *In 1346 a hurricane whipped up the sea to destroy the town. ...clouds of smoke and sand whipped up by a strong wind.* V P n (not pron) Also V n P

3 If you **whip up** something, especially a meal, you make it quickly; an informal use. *I used to entertain at home quite a lot, and I can still whip up a fairly decent dinner party.* V P n (not pron) Also V n P

whiplash /ʰwɪplæʃ/. **Whiplash** is a neck injury caused by the head suddenly jerking forwards and then back again, for example in a car accident. *His wife suffered whiplash and shock... Four police officers were taken to the nearby hospital with whiplash injuries.* N-UNCOUNT: oft N n

whippersnapper /ʰwɪpəʳsnæpəʳ/ **whippersnappers.** If you refer to a young person as a **whippersnapper**, you disapprove of them because you think that they are behaving more confidently and boldly than they should; an informal, old-fashioned word. *...this bunch of irresponsible young whippersnappers.* N-COUNT PRAGMATICS

whippet /ʰwɪpɪt/ **whippets.** A **whippet** is a small thin dog which looks like a greyhound. Some whippets take part in races. N-COUNT

whipping boy, whipping boys. If someone or something is a **whipping boy** for a particular situation, they get all the blame for it. *He has become a convenient whipping boy for the failures of the communist regime.* N-COUNT =scapegoat

whipping cream. **Whipping cream** is cream that becomes stiff when it is stirred very fast. N-UNCOUNT

whip-round. When a group of people have a **whip-round**, money is collected from each person so that it can be used to buy something for all of them or for someone they all know; an informal word. N-SING

whir /ʰwɜːʳ/. See **whirr**.

whirl /ʰwɜːʳl/ **whirls, whirling, whirled** ◆◇◇◇◇

1 If something or someone **whirls** round or if you **whirl** them round, they move round or turn round very quickly. *Not receiving an answer, she whirled round... He was whirling Anne around the floor... The smoke began to whirl and grew into a monstrous column.* ► Also a noun. *...the barely audible whirl of wheels.* V-ERG =spin V adv/prep V n adv/prep V N-COUNT

2 You can refer to a lot of intense activity as a **whirl** of activity. *In half an hour's whirl of activity she does it all... Your life is such a social whirl.* N-COUNT: usu sing, with supp

3 If a person or their mind is **in a whirl**, they are very confused or excited; a literary expression. *My thoughts are in a whirl.* PHRASES v-link PHR

4 If you decide to **give** an activity **a whirl**, you do it even though it is something that you have never tried before; an informal expression. *Why not give acupuncture a whirl?... We decided to give it a whirl.* V inflects

whirlpool /ʰwɜːʳlpuːl/ **whirlpools** ◆◇◇◇◇

1 A **whirlpool** is a small area in a river or the sea where the water is moving quickly round and round, so that objects floating near it are pulled into its centre. N-COUNT

2 You can describe a situation in which a lot of unpleasant or complicated things are happening, and from which it is very difficult to escape, as a **whirlpool**. *They felt they were being sucked into a whirlpool of publicity... She became caught in a whirlpool of hate.* N-COUNT: usu sing, with supp, usu N *of* n

3 A **whirlpool bath** or a **whirlpool** is a bath that is specially designed so that the water moves round and round. *...a luxurious whirlpool bath with gold taps... There's also an outdoor whirlpool.* N-COUNT: usu N n

whirlwind /ʰwɜːʳlwɪnd/ **whirlwinds** ◆◇◇◇◇

1 A **whirlwind** is a tall column of air which spins round and round very fast and moves across the land or sea. N-COUNT

2 You can describe a situation in which a lot of things happen very quickly and are very difficult for someone to control as a **whirlwind**. *I had been running around southern England in a whirlwind of activity... He had been swept aside in the whirlwind of reform and anarchy.* N-COUNT: usu sing, with supp, usu N *of* n

3 A **whirlwind** event or action happens or is done much more quickly than normal. *He got married after a whirlwind romance. ... a whirlwind tour of France.* ADJ: ADJ n

whirr /ʰwɜːʳ/ **whirrs, whirring, whirred;** also spelled **whir**. When something such as a machine or an insect's wing **whirrs**, it makes a series of low sounds so quickly that they seem like one continuous sound. *The camera whirred and clicked. ...the whirring sound of the film projector.* ► Also a noun. *He could hear the whirr of a vacuum cleaner... Whirr, click, whirr, click – step by step the scan probed deeper.* ♦ **whirring** *The silence was broken by the whirring of a helicopter.* VERB V V-ing N-COUNT; SOUND N-UNCOUNT: with supp

whisk /ʰwɪsk/ **whisks, whisking, whisked** ◆◆◇◇◇

1 If you **whisk** someone or something somewhere, you take them or move them there quickly. *He whisked her across the dance floor... I was whisked away in a police car.* VERB V n prep/adv

2 If you **whisk** something such as eggs or cream, you stir it very fast, often with an electric device, so that it becomes light and fluffy. *Just before serving, whisk the cream... Gently fold in the whisked egg whites... In a separate bowl, whisk together the remaining sugar and the yolks.* VERB V n V-ed V pl-n with *together*

3 A **whisk** is a kitchen tool used for whisking eggs or cream. *Using a whisk, mix the yolks and sugar to a smooth paste. ...an electric whisk.* N-COUNT

whisker /ʰwɪskəʳ/ **whiskers** ◆◇◇◇◇

1 The **whiskers** of an animal such as a cat or a mouse are the long stiff hairs that grow near its mouth. N-COUNT: usu pl

2 You can refer to the hair on a man's face, especially on the sides of his face, as his **whiskers**. *...wild, savage-looking fellows, with large whiskers, unshaven beards, and dirty faces.* N-PLURAL

3 You can use **whisker** in expressions such as **by a whisker** or **within a whisker of** to indicate that something happened or is true, but only by a very small amount or degree. *Lennox Lewis beat Frank* N-SING

Bruno only by a whisker... She came within a whisker of taking a gold medal... Unemployment is now a whisker away from three million.

whiskery /ʰwɪskəri/. If you describe someone as **whiskery**, you mean that they have lots of little bristles or hairs on their face. *...a whiskery old man.* ADJ-GRADED

whiskey /ʰwɪski/ **whiskeys.** **Whiskey** is whisky that is made in Ireland or the United States. *...a tumbler with about an inch of whiskey in it.* ► A **whiskey** is a glass of whiskey. ◆◇◇◇◇ N-MASS; N-COUNT

whisky /ʰwɪski/ **whiskies.** **Whisky** is a strong alcoholic drink made, especially in Scotland, from grain such as barley or rye. *...a bottle of whisky. ...expensive whiskies and brandies.* ► A **whisky** is a glass of whisky. *She handed him a whisky.* ◆◆◇◇◇ N-MASS; N-COUNT

whisper /ʰwɪspər/ **whispers, whispering, whispered** ◆◆◆◇◇

1 When you **whisper**, you say something very quietly, using your breath rather than your throat, so that only one person can hear you. *'Keep your voice down,' I whispered... She sat on Rossi's knee as he whispered in her ear... He whispered the message to David... Somebody whispered that films like that were illegal... She whispered his name.* ► Also a noun. *Men were talking in whispers in every office.* VERB; V with quote; V prep; V n prep; V that; V n; N-COUNT

2 If people **whisper** about a piece of information, they talk about it, although it might not be true or accurate, or might be a secret. *For years English football has whispered about how transfer transactions are used to hide perks for players and managers... It is whispered that he intended to resign... But don't whisper a word of that.* ► Also a noun. *I've heard a whisper that the Bishop intends to leave.* N-COUNT; V *about* wh/n; *it be* V-ed that; V n; N-COUNT =rumour

3 If something **whispers**, it makes a low quiet sound which can only just be heard; a literary use. *The cold breeze moved through the bushes around him, whispering just loud enough to obscure the chanting... The car's tires whispered through the puddles. ...whispering ceiling fans.* ► Also a noun. *They heard the whisper of leaves.* VERB; V; V prep/adv; V-ing; N-COUNT: usu sing

whist /ʰwɪst/. **Whist** is a card game in which people play in pairs against each other. N-UNCOUNT

whistle /ʰwɪsəl/ **whistles, whistling, whistled** ◆◆◇◇◇

1 When you **whistle** or when you **whistle** a tune, you make a series of notes by forcing your breath out between your lips, or your teeth. *He whistled and sang snatches of songs... He was whistling softly to himself... As he washed he whistled a tune.* VERB; V; V n

2 When someone **whistles**, they make a sound by forcing their breath out between their lips, or their teeth. People sometimes whistle when they are surprised or shocked, or to call a dog, or to show that they are impressed. *He whistled, surprised but not shocked... Jenkins whistled through his teeth, impressed at last... Women don't enjoy being whistled at.* ● See also **wolf-whistle**. ► Also a noun. *Jackson gave a low whistle.* VERB; V; V prep; N-COUNT: oft supp N

3 If something such as a train or a kettle **whistles**, it makes a loud, high sound. *Somewhere a train whistled... Over the whistling car radio the brass band music stopped.* ♦ **whistling** *...the whistling of the wind.* VERB; V; V-ing; N-SING: oft *the* N *of* n

4 If something such as the wind or a bullet **whistles** somewhere, it moves, making a loud, high sound. *The wind was whistling through the building... As I stood up a bullet whistled past my back.* VERB; V prep

5 A **whistle** is a loud sound produced by air or steam being forced through a small opening, or by something moving quickly through the air. *Hugh listened to the whistle of a train. ...the whistle of the wind. ...a shrill whistle from the boiling kettle.* N-COUNT: oft N *of* n

6 A **whistle** is a small metal tube which you blow in order to produce a loud sound and attract someone's attention. *On the platform, the guard blew his whistle... The referee blew his whistle for a penalty.* N-COUNT

7 Some factories and other places where people work have a **whistle** which signals the beginning and the end of the working day. *Every night you could hear the whistles of the steel mill.* N-COUNT

8 A **whistle** is a simple musical instrument in the shape of a metal pipe with holes. ● See also **tin whistle**. N-COUNT

9 If you **blow the whistle** on someone, or on something secret or illegal, you tell another person, especially someone in authority, what is happening. *Companies should protect employees who blow the whistle on dishonest workmates and work practices.* ● See also **whistle-blower**. PHRASES; V inflects, usu PHR *on* n =inform

10 If you say that someone **can whistle for** a particular thing, you mean that you are not willing or able to give it to them; an informal expression. *'He wants a police escort.' 'Well, he can whistle for that.'* V inflects

11 If you describe something as **clean as a whistle**, you mean that it is completely clean. v-link PHR

12 If you describe someone as **clean as a whistle**, you mean that they are not guilty of having done anything wrong. *'His private life is as clean as a whistle,' says McSmith.* v-link PHR

13 If you say that someone **is whistling in the dark**, you mean that they are trying to keep their courage up and convince themselves that the situation is not as bad as it really is. *The Times says Mr Gorbachev continues to be politically isolated and vulnerable, describing his warning to Mr Yeltsin as whistling in the dark.* V inflects

14 To **wet** your **whistle** means to have a drink; an old-fashioned use. V inflects

15 If you describe someone as **whistling in the wind**, you mean that they are trying unsuccessfully to stop something which cannot be stopped or to change something which cannot be changed. *The leader of the Liberal Democrats accused the Prime Minister of whistling in the wind to raise Conservative party morale.* V inflects

whistle-blower, whistle-blowers; also spelled **whistleblower**. A **whistle-blower** is someone who finds out that the organization they are working for is doing something immoral or illegal and tells the authorities or the public about it; used in journalism. *He has been a prominent victim of alleged witch-hunts against whistle-blowers in the NHS.* N-COUNT

whistle-stop. If someone, especially a politician, goes on a **whistle-stop** tour, they visit a lot of different places in a short time. *From Iran, Benazir Bhutto flew to neighbouring Turkey, the next leg on her whistle-stop tour of eight countries in nine days.* ADJ: ADJ n

whit /ʰwɪt/

1 You say **not a whit** or **not one whit** to emphasize that something is not the case at all; a rather old-fashioned, formal use. *He cared not a whit for the social, political or moral aspects of literature... It does not matter one whit to the customer.* PHRASE: with neg, PHR after v =not at all

2 **Whit** means the same as **Whitsun**. *The orchestra gave its first performance on Whit Monday.* N-UNCOUNT: usu N n

white /ʰwaɪt/ **whites; whiter, whitest** ◆◆◆◆◆

1 Something that is **white** is the colour of snow or milk. *He had nice square white teeth... Issa's white beach hat gleamed in the harsh lights... He was dressed in white from head to toe.* ♦ **whiteness** *Her scarlet lipstick emphasized the whiteness of her teeth.* ● to **bleed** someone **white**: see **bleed**. COLOUR; N-UNCOUNT

2 A **white** person has a pale skin and belongs to a race which is of European origin. *Working with white people hasn't been a problem for me or for them... He was white, with brown shoulder-length hair and a moustache.* ► **Whites** are white people. *It's a school that's brought blacks and whites and Hispanics together.* ADJ; N-COUNT: usu pl

3 If someone goes **white**, the skin on their face becomes very pale, for example because of fear, shock, anger, or illness. *Richard had gone very white, but he stood his ground... He turned white and began to stammer... His face was white with fury.* ● If someone looks **white as a sheet** or **as white as a sheet**, they look very frightened, shocked, or ill. *He appeared in the doorway, white as a sheet, eyes wide with horror.* ADJ-GRADED: usu v-link ADJ =pale; PHRASE: v-link PHR

4 **White** wine is pale yellowish or pale greenish in colour. *Gregory poured another glass of white wine* ADJ

and went back to his bedroom. ► You can refer to white wine as **white**. *I bought a bottle of Californian white.* N-MASS

5 White coffee has had milk or cream added to it; used in British English. *Wayne has a Coca-Cola and a large white coffee in front of him.* ADJ

6 White blood cells are the cells in your blood which your body uses to fight infection. ADJ: ADJ n

7 The **white** of an egg, especially a hen's egg, is the transparent liquid that surrounds the yolk. N-VAR

8 The **white** of someone's eye is the white part of their eyeball. N-COUNT: usu N of n

9 In British English, **whites** are white-coloured clothes that you wear for playing some sports, for example tennis or cricket. *There was a Frenchman sitting at the next table, immaculate in tennis whites.* N-PLURAL

whiteboard /ʰwaɪtbɔːʳd/ **whiteboards.** A **whiteboard** is a shiny white board on which people draw or write using special pens. Whiteboards are often used at schools for teaching or presentations. N-COUNT

white Christmas, white Christmases. A **white Christmas** is a Christmas when it snows. *London has only had eight white Christmases this century.* N-COUNT

white-collar; also spelled **white collar.** ◆◇◇◇◇

1 White-collar workers work in offices rather than doing manual work in industry. *White-collar workers now work longer hours.* ADJ: ADJ n

2 White-collar crime is committed by people who work in offices, and involves stealing from companies by fraud, rather than taking money or goods directly from a person or place. ADJ: ADJ n

white elephant, white elephants. If you describe something as a **white elephant**, you mean that it is a waste of money because it is completely useless. *The pavilion has become a £14 million steel and glass white elephant.* N-COUNT

white goods. In British English, people in business sometimes refer to fridges, washing machines, and other large pieces of electrical household equipment as **white goods**. N-PLURAL

white-haired. Someone who is **white-haired** has white hair, usually because they are old. ADJ

Whitehall /ʰwaɪthɔːl/. **Whitehall** is the name of a street in London in which there are many government offices. You can also use **Whitehall** to mean the British Government itself. *...people with banners marching down Whitehall... Whitehall said that it hoped to get the change through by the end of June.* ◆◆◇◇◇ N-PROPER

white-hot. If something is **white-hot**, it is extremely hot. *It is important to get the coals white-hot before you start.* ADJ

White House. **The White House** is the official home in Washington DC of the President of the United States. You can also use **the White House** to refer to the President of the United States and his or her officials. *He drove to the White House... The White House has not participated in any talks.* ◆◆◆◇◇ N-PROPER: the N, N n

white lie, white lies. If you refer to an untrue statement as a **white lie**, you mean that it is made to avoid hurting someone's feelings or to avoid trouble, and not for an evil purpose. N-COUNT

white meat, white meats. **White meat** is meat such as chicken and pork, which is pale in colour after it has been cooked. N-UNCOUNT: also N in pl

whiten /ʰwaɪtᵊn/ **whitens, whitening, whitened.** When something **whitens** or when you **whiten** it, it becomes whiter or paler in colour. *Her knuckles whiten as she clenches her hands harder. ...toothpastes that whiten teeth.* V-ERG V V n

white noise. **White noise** is sound, especially of a loud, continuous, or unpleasant kind, that seems to have no pattern or rhythm. *They were made to listen to white noise, such as static of the sort you might pick up between radio stations.* N-UNCOUNT

White Paper, White Papers. In Britain, Australia, Canada, and some other countries, a **White Paper** is an official report which gives the policy of the Government on a particular subject. ◆◆◇◇◇ N-COUNT

white pepper. **White pepper** is pepper which has been made from the dried insides of the fruits of the pepper plant. N-UNCOUNT

white sauce, white sauces. **White sauce** is a thick, white-coloured sauce that is usually made from milk, flour, and butter. N-MASS

white spirit. In British English, **white spirit** is a colourless liquid that is made from petrol and is used, for example, to make paint thinner or to clean surfaces. N-UNCOUNT

white trash. Some people use **white trash** to refer to poor white people who they think are corrupt or worthless. Some people find this expression offensive. *...a place peopled by illiterate poor white trash.* N-UNCOUNT-COLL

whitewash /ʰwaɪtwɒʃ/ **whitewashes, whitewashing, whitewashed** ◆◇◇◇◇

1 Whitewash is a mixture of lime or chalk and water that is used for painting walls white. N-UNCOUNT

2 If a wall or building **has been whitewashed**, it has been painted white with whitewash. *The walls had been whitewashed. ...a town of picturesque whitewashed cottages.* VERB be V-ed V-ed

3 If you say that people **whitewash** something, you are accusing them of hiding the unpleasant facts or truth about it in order to make it acceptable. *The administration is whitewashing the regime's actions... 'The whole incident was whitewashed,' he claimed yesterday.* VERB =cover up V n

4 Whitewash is an attempt to hide the unpleasant facts or truth about someone or something; used showing disapproval. *He pledged that there would be no whitewash and that the police would carry out a full investigation... The report's findings were condemned as total whitewash.* N-UNCOUNT: also a N PRAGMATICS =cover-up

5 In sport, if a player or team **whitewashes** an opponent, they win very easily, and the opponent does not get any points at all; an informal use. *Not since 1988 had she whitewashed an opponent in her opening match... Their leading players were being whitewashed 4-0.* VERB =thrash V n

white wedding, white weddings. A **white wedding** is a wedding where the bride wears white and the ceremony takes place in a church. N-COUNT

whither /ʰwɪðəʳ/. **Whither** means to where; an old-fashioned or literary word. *Who are you and whither are you bound?* ► Also a conjunction. *They knew not whither they went.* ► Also a relative pronoun. *The letter came from the Lagoon, whither she had gone to be the nearer to her husband.* QUEST =where CONJ-SUBORD PRON-REL

whiting /ʰwaɪtɪŋ/ **whitings.** The plural can be either **whitings** or **whiting**. A **whiting** is a black and silver fish that lives in the sea. *...fishing boats which normally catch a mix of cod, haddock and whiting.* ► **Whiting** is this fish eaten as food. *He ordered stuffed whiting.* N-VAR N-UNCOUNT

whitish /ʰwaɪtɪʃ/. **Whitish** means very pale and almost white in colour. *...a whitish dust.* COLOUR

Whitsun /ʰwɪtsᵊn/. **Whitsun** is the seventh Sunday after Easter, and the week that follows that Sunday; used mainly in British English. N-UNCOUNT

Whit Sunday. **Whit Sunday** is a Christian festival that takes place on the seventh Sunday after Easter and celebrates the sending of the Holy Spirit to the first apostles. N-UNCOUNT =Pentecost

whittle /ʰwɪtᵊl/ **whittles, whittling, whittled.** If you **whittle** something from a piece of wood, you carve it by cutting or shaving parts off the wood with a penknife or other small tool. *He whittled a new handle for his ax... Chitty sat in his rocking-chair whittling wood.* ◆◇◇◇◇ VERB =carve V n

whittle away. To **whittle away** something or **whittle away** at it means to gradually make it smaller, weaker, or less effective. *I believe that the Government's general aim is to whittle away the Welfare State... Their approach is to whittle away at the evidence to show reasonable doubt.* PHRASAL VERB V P n (not pron) V P at n

whittle down. To **whittle** something **down** means to gradually make it smaller or less exten- PHRASAL VERB sive. *He had whittled eight interviewees down to two... By September, they will have whittled the list down to a winner... The president has agreed to whittle down his proposal.* V n P to/from num/n V P n (not pron) Also V n P

whizz /hwɪz/ **whizzes, whizzing, whizzed** ◆◇◇◇◇

1 If something **whizzes** somewhere, it moves there very fast; an informal use. *Stewart felt a bottle whizz past his head... A car whizzed past.* VERB V prep/adv

2 If you are a **whizz** at something, you are very good at it; an informal use. *Simon's a whizz at card games.* N-COUNT: oft a N at/with/on n

whizz-kid, whizz-kids; also spelled **whizzkid** or **whizz kid**. If you refer to a young person as a **whizz-kid**, you mean that they have achieved success at a young age because they are very clever and very good at something, especially making money; an informal word. *...a financial whizz kid. ...a whizz-kid physics student.* N-COUNT: usu with supp

who /huː/; usually pronounced /huː/ for meanings 2 and 3. ◆◆◆◆◆

Who is used as the subject or object of a verb. See entries at **whom** and **whose**.

1 You use **who** in questions when you ask about the name or identity of a person or group of people. *Who's there?... Who is the least popular man around here?... Who do you work for?... Who do you suppose will replace her on the show?... 'You reminded me of somebody.'—'Who?'* QUEST

2 You use **who** after certain words, especially verbs and adjectives, to introduce a clause where you talk about the identity of a person or a group of people. *Police have not been able to find out who was responsible for the forgeries... I went over to start up a conversation, asking her who she knew at the party... You know who these people are.* CONJ-SUBORD

3 You use **who** at the beginning of a relative clause when specifying the person or group of people you are talking about or when giving more information about them. *There are those who eat out for a special occasion, or treat themselves... The woman, who needs constant attention, is cared for by relatives... The hijacker gave himself up to police, who are now questioning him.* PRON-REL

whoa /hwoʊ/

1 **Whoa** is a command that you give to a horse to slow down or stop. EXCLAM

2 You can say **whoa** to someone who is talking to you, to indicate that you think they are going too fast or assuming things that may not be true; an informal use. *Slow down! Whoa!* EXCLAM PRAGMATICS

who'd /huːd, huːd/

1 **Who'd** is the usual spoken form of 'who had', especially when 'had' is an auxiliary verb.

2 **Who'd** is a spoken form of 'who would'.

whodunnit /huːdʌnɪt/ **whodunnits;** also spelled **whodunit**. A **whodunnit** is a novel, film, or play which is about a murder and in which the identity of the murderer is kept a mystery until the end; an informal word. N-COUNT

whoever /huːevəʳ/ ◆◆◇◇◇

1 You use **whoever** to refer to someone when their identity is not yet known. *Whoever did this will sooner or later be caught and will be punished... Whoever wins the election is going to have a tough job getting the economy back on its feet... Ben, I want whoever's responsible to come forward.* CONJ-SUBORD

2 You use **whoever** to indicate that the actual identity of the person who does something will not affect a situation. *You can have whoever you like to visit you... Everybody who goes into this region, whoever they are, is at risk of being taken hostage.* CONJ-SUBORD

3 You use **whoever** in questions as an emphatic way of saying 'who', usually when you are surprised about something. *Whoever thought up that joke?... Ridiculous! Whoever suggested such a thing?* QUEST PRAGMATICS =who

4 You say **or whoever** to refer vaguely to someone, especially when you are not sure if you are talking about the right person; an informal expression. *We're not just some big business like Mobil or IBM or whoever... The police, or whoever, would not think of looking for him here.* PHRASE: n PHR PRAGMATICS

whole /hoʊl/ **wholes** ◆◆◆◆◆

1 If you refer to **the whole of** something, you mean all of it. *He has said he will make an apology to the whole of Asia for his country's past behaviour... I was cold throughout the whole of my body. ...the whole of August.* ► Also an adjective. *He'd been observing her the whole trip... We spent the whole summer in Italy that year.* QUANT: QUANT of def-n ADJ: ADJ n =entire

2 A **whole** is a single thing which contains several different parts. *An atom itself is a complete whole, with its electrons, protons and neutrons and other elements... Taken as a percentage of the whole, the mouth has to be a fairly minor body part.* N-COUNT: usu sing

3 If something is **whole**, it is in one piece and is not broken or damaged. *Much of the temple was ruined, but the front was whole, as well as a large hall behind it... I struck the glass with my fist with all my might; yet it remained whole... Small bones should be avoided as the dog may swallow them whole and risk internal injury.* ADJ: v-link ADJ, v n ADJ =complete, intact

4 You use **whole** to emphasize what you are saying; an informal use. *It was like seeing a whole different side of somebody... His father had helped invent a whole new way of doing business.* ► Also an adjective. *That saved me a whole bunch of money... There's a whole group of friends he doesn't want you to meet.* ADV: ADV adj PRAGMATICS =totally ADJ: ADJ n

5 If you refer to something **as a whole**, you are referring to it generally and as a single unit. *He described the move as a victory for the people of South Africa as a whole... As a whole we do not eat enough fibre in Britain.* PHRASES n PHR, PHR with cl =in general

6 You use **on the whole** to indicate that what you are saying is true in general and may not be true in every case, or that you are giving a general opinion or summary of something. *On the whole, people miss the opportunity to enjoy leisure... The wine towns encountered are, on the whole, quiet and modest.* PHR with cl PRAGMATICS =generally

wholefood /hoʊlfuːd/ **wholefoods. Wholefoods** are foods which have had very little refining or processing and which do not contain additives or artificial ingredients; used mainly in British English. *It pays to avoid food additives and eat only wholefoods... A healthy diet should consist of wholefood.* N-MASS

wholegrains /hoʊlgreɪnz/; the form **wholegrain** is used as a modifier. **Wholegrains** are the whole unprocessed grains of cereals such as wheat and maize. *Fruits, vegetables, and wholegrains are rich in potassium. ...crusty wholegrain bread.* N-PLURAL

wholehearted /hoʊlhɑːʳtɪd/; also spelled **whole-hearted**. If you support or agree to something in a **wholehearted** way, you support or agree to it enthusiastically and completely. *The Government deserves our wholehearted support for having taken a step in this direction.* ◆ **wholeheartedly** *That's exactly right. I agree wholeheartedly with you.* ◆◇◇◇◇ ADJ-GRADED ADV-GRADED: usu ADV with v

wholemeal /hoʊlmiːl/ ◆◇◇◇◇

1 In British English, **wholemeal** flour is made from the complete grain of the wheat plant, including the husk. **Wholemeal** bread or pasta is made from wholemeal flour. The American word is **wholewheat**. *...a slice of wholemeal toast.* ADJ: usu ADJ n

2 In British English, **wholemeal** means wholemeal bread or wholemeal flour. *...one slice of white and one of wholemeal.* N-UNCOUNT

wholeness /hoʊlnəs/. **Wholeness** is the quality of being complete or a single unit and not broken or divided into parts. *...the need for wholeness and harmony in mind, body and spirit.* N-UNCOUNT

whole number, whole numbers. A **whole number** is an exact number such as 1, 7, and 24, as opposed to a number with fractions or decimals. N-COUNT =integer

wholesale /hoʊlseɪl/ ◆◆◇◇◇

1 **Wholesale** is the activity of buying and selling goods in large quantities and therefore at cheaper prices, usually to shopkeepers who then sell them to the public. Compare **retail**. *Warehouse clubs al-* N-UNCOUNT: usu N n

low members to buy goods at wholesale prices... I am in the wholesale trade.

2 If something is sold **wholesale**, it is sold in large quantities and at cheaper prices, usually to shopkeepers. *The fabrics are sold wholesale to retailers, fashion houses, and other manufacturers.* ADV: ADV after v

3 If you describe a change, for example, as a **wholesale** change, you are emphasizing the completeness or the severity of it. *They are only doing what is necessary to prevent wholesale destruction of vegetation... It was wholesale slaughter of women and children.* ► Also an adverb. *...a government which kills wholesale and guerrillas who kill selectively.* ADJ: ADJ n PRAGMATICS; ADV: ADV after v

wholesaler /hoʊlseɪləʳ/ **wholesalers.** A **wholesaler** is a person whose business is buying large quantities of goods and selling them in smaller amounts, for example to shops. ◆◇◇◇◇ N-COUNT =distributor

wholesaling /hoʊlseɪlɪŋ/. **Wholesaling** is the activity of buying or selling goods in large amounts, especially in order to sell them in shops or supermarkets. N-UNCOUNT

wholesome /hoʊlsəm/ ◆◇◇◇◇

1 If you describe something as **wholesome**, you approve of it because you think it is likely to have a positive influence on people's behaviour or mental state, especially because it does not involve anything sexually immoral. *...good, wholesome fun. ...a very decent and wholesome bunch of lads.* ADJ-GRADED PRAGMATICS ≠unwholesome

2 If you describe food as **wholesome**, you approve of it because you think it is good for your health. *...fresh, wholesome ingredients... The food is filling and wholesome.* ADJ-GRADED PRAGMATICS =healthy

wholewheat /hoʊlʰwiːt/; also spelled **whole wheat.**

1 **Wholewheat** flour is made from the complete grain of the wheat plant, including the husk. **Wholewheat** bread or pasta is made from wholewheat flour. *...vegetables with wholewheat noodles.* ADJ: usu ADJ n

2 **Wholewheat** means wholewheat bread or wholewheat flour. *...a chicken salad sandwich on whole wheat.* N-UNCOUNT

who'll /huːl, huːl/. **Who'll** is a spoken form of 'who will' or 'who shall'.

wholly /hoʊlli/. You use **wholly** to emphasize the extent or degree to which something is the case. *While the two are only days apart in age they seem to belong to wholly different generations... For urban areas this approach was wholly inadequate... The accusation is wholly without foundation.* ◆◆◇◇◇ ADV: ADV adj, ADV with cl/group PRAGMATICS =completely, entirely

whom /huːm/ ◆◆◆◆◇

Whom is used in formal or written English instead of 'who' when it is the object of a verb or preposition.

1 You use **whom** in questions when you ask about the name or identity of a person or group of people. *'I want to send a telegram.' 'Fine, to whom?'... Whom did he expect to answer his phone?... 'You're too sensitive.'—'Too sensitive for whom?'* QUEST =who

2 You use **whom** after certain words, especially verbs and adjectives, to introduce a clause where you talk about the name or identity of a person or a group of people. *He asked whom I'd told about his having been away... He likes to know whom you've met... I have resigned, and they have a free hand to appoint whom they like in my place.* CONJ-SUBORD =who

3 You use **whom** at the beginning of a relative clause when specifying the person or group of people you are talking about or when giving more information about them. *One writer in whom I had taken an interest was Immanuel Velikovsky... The Homewood residents whom I knew had little money and little free time. ...generations of women for whom work provided an escape from family life.* PRON-REL: oft prep PRON

whomever /huːmevəʳ/. **Whomever** is a formal word for **whoever** when it is the object of a verb or preposition. CONJ-SUBORD =whoever

whoop /ʰwuːp, AM huːp/ **whoops, whooping, whooped** ◆◇◇◇◇

1 If you **whoop**, you shout loudly in a very happy or excited way; used in written English. *She whoops with delight at a promise of money.* ► Also a noun. *Scattered groans and whoops broke out in the crowd.* VERB V; N-COUNT

2 See also **whoops.**

whoopee /ʰwʊpiː/. People sometimes shout **'whoopee'** when they are very happy or excited; an informal word. *I can have a lie in tomorrow. Whoopee!* EXCLAM PRAGMATICS =hooray

whooping cough /huːpɪŋ kɒf, AM - kɔːf/. **Whooping cough** is a serious infectious disease which causes people to cough and make a loud noise when they breathe in. N-UNCOUNT

whoops /ʰwʊps/. People say **'whoops'** when they have had a slight accident or made a mistake; used in spoken English. *Whoops, that was a mistake... Whoops, it's past 11, I'd better be off home.* EXCLAM PRAGMATICS

whoosh /ʰwʊʃ, AM hwuːʃ/ **whooshes, whooshing, whooshed**

1 People sometimes say **'whoosh'** when they are emphasizing the fact that something happens very suddenly or very fast. *Then came the riders amid even louder cheers and whoosh! It was all over.* EXCLAM PRAGMATICS

2 If something **whooshes** somewhere, it moves there quickly or suddenly; an informal use. *Cool air whooshes up through the grates on the street... Kites whooshed above the beach at intervals.* VERB V adv/prep

3 A **whoosh** of air or water is a sudden rush of it; a literary use. *...the whoosh and murmur of the wind through the trees... They drove home with their windshield wipers going whoosh whoosh.* N-SING: oft N of n; SOUND

whopper /ʰwɒpəʳ/ **whoppers**

1 If you describe a lie as a **whopper**, you mean that it is very far from the truth; an informal use. *...the biggest whopper the president told.* N-COUNT

2 If you refer to something as a **whopper**, you mean that it is an unusually large example of the thing mentioned; an informal use. *As comets go, it is a whopper.* N-COUNT

whopping /ʰwɒpɪŋ/. If you describe an amount as **whopping**, you are emphasizing that it is large; an informal word. *The Russian leader won a whopping 89.9 percent yes vote... Planned spending amounts to a whopping $31.4 billion.* ► Also an adverb. *Footballers in whopping great, studded boots walk over the pitch.* ADJ: ADJ n, usu *a* ADJ amount PRAGMATICS; ADV: ADV adj

whore /hɔːʳ/ **whores** ◆◇◇◇◇

1 A **whore** is the same as a **prostitute**. N-COUNT

2 If you call a woman a **whore**, you disapprove of her because you consider her sexual behaviour to be immoral or unacceptable; an offensive word. N-COUNT PRAGMATICS

who're /huːəʳ, huːəʳ/. **Who're** is a spoken form of 'who are'. *I've got loads of friends who're unemployed... Who're you going to the pictures with?*

whorehouse /hɔːʳhaʊs/ **whorehouses.** A **whorehouse** is the same as a **brothel**; an informal word. N-COUNT =brothel

whorl /ʰwɜːʳl, AM hwɔːʳl/ **whorls.** A **whorl** is a spiral shape, for example the pattern on the tips of your fingers; a literary word. *He stared at the whorls and lines of her fingertips. ...dense whorls of red-purple flowers.* N-COUNT

who's /huːz, huːz/. **Who's** is the usual spoken form of 'who is' or 'who has', especially when 'has' is an auxiliary verb.

whose /huːz/; usually pronounced /huːz/ for meanings 2 and 3. ◆◆◆◆◆

1 You use **whose** at the beginning of a relative clause where you mention something that belongs to or is associated with the person or thing mentioned in the previous clause. *I saw a man shouting at a driver whose car was blocking the street. ...a speedboat, whose fifteen-strong crew claimed to belong to China's navy. ...tourists whose vacations included an unexpected adventure.* PRON-REL

2 You use **whose** in questions to ask about the person or thing that something belongs to or is associated with. *Whose was the better performance?... 'Whose is this?'—'Mick's stuff.'... 'It wasn't your fault, John.'—'Whose, then?'* ► Also a determiner. *Whose car were they in?... Whose daughter is she?* QUEST; DET-POSS-QUEST

3 You use **whose** after certain words, especially DET-POSS

verbs and adjectives, to introduce a clause where you talk about the person or thing that something belongs to or is associated with. *I'm wondering whose mother she is then... I can't remember whose idea it was for us to meet again.* ▶ Also a conjunction. *I wondered whose the coat was... That kind of person likes to spend money, it doesn't matter whose it is.* CONJ-SUBORD

whosoever /huːsoʊevəʳ/. **Whosoever** means the same as **whoever**; an old-fashioned, literary word. *They can transfer or share the contract with whosoever they choose.* CONJ-SUBORD =whoever

who've /huːv, huːv/. **Who've** is the usual spoken form of 'who have,' especially when 'have' is an auxiliary verb.

why /ʰwaɪ/. The conjunction and the pronoun are usually pronounced /ʰwaɪ/. ◆◆◆◆◆

1 You use **why** in questions when you ask about the reasons for something. *Why hasn't he brought the whisky?... Why didn't he stop me?... Why can't I remember the exact year we married?... 'I just want to see him.'—'Why?'... Why should I leave?* QUEST

2 You use **why** at the beginning of a clause in which you talk about the reasons for something. *He still could not throw any further light on why the elevator could have become jammed... Experts wonder why the US government is not taking similarly strong actions against AIDS in this country... I can't understand why they don't want us.* CONJ-SUBORD ▶ Also an adverb. *I don't know why... It's obvious why... Here's why.* ADV: ADV after v, *be* ADV

3 You use **why** to introduce a relative clause after the word 'reason'. *There's a reason why women don't read this stuff; it's not funny... Unless you're ill, there's no reason why you can't get those 15 minutes of walking in daily.* PRON-REL ▶ Also an adverb. *He confirmed that the city had been closed to foreigners, but gave no reason why.* ADV: n ADV

4 You use **why** with 'not' in questions in order to introduce a suggestion. *Why not give Claire a call?... Why don't you come home with me until you sort things out?... Why don't we talk it through?* QUEST PRAGMATICS

5 You use **why** with 'not' in questions in order to express your annoyance or anger. *You clumsy stupid woman! Why don't you look out what you're doing?... Why don't they cheer up a bit, the miserable buggers?* QUEST PRAGMATICS

6 You say **why not** in order to agree with what someone has suggested. *'Want to spend the afternoon with me?'—'Why not?'... 'Shall I tell them about poor Mrs Blair?'—'Why not?'* CONVENTION PRAGMATICS

7 People say **'Why!'** to indicate their surprise, shock, or indignation; used mainly in American English. *Why hello, Tom... Why, this is nothing but common vegetable soup... Why, I wouldn't give the end off one of my fingers for all the money you've got!* EXCLAM PRAGMATICS

8 • **the whys and wherefores**: see **wherefores**.

wick /wɪk/ **wicks**

1 The **wick** of a candle is the piece of string in it which burns when it is lit. N-COUNT

2 The **wick** of a paraffin lamp or cigarette lighter is the part which supplies the fuel to the flame when it is lit. N-COUNT

3 In informal British English, if you say that someone or something **gets on** your **wick**, you mean that they annoy and irritate you. *The Professor was beginning to get on Molly's wick.* PHRASE: V inflects

wicked /wɪkɪd/ ◆◆◇◇◇

1 You use **wicked** to describe someone or something that is very bad in a way that is deliberately harmful to people. *She described the shooting as a wicked attack... She flew at me, shouting how wicked and evil I was.* ADJ-GRADED =evil ♦ **wickedness** *...moral arguments about the wickedness of nuclear weapons.* N-UNCOUNT

2 If you describe someone or something as **wicked**, you mean that they are rather mischievous, but in a way that you find attractive or enjoyable. *She had a wicked sense of humour... I adore white chocolate, as it has such a sweet taste and I always feel very wicked when eating it.* ADJ-GRADED ♦ **wickedly** *This collection of letters is affectionate, candid and wickedly funny... Michael grinned wickedly.* ADV: usu ADV adj, also ADV after v

wicker /wɪkəʳ/. **Wicker** is material made by weaving canes, twigs, or reeds together, which is used to make baskets and furniture. *...a wicker basket.* ◆◇◇◇◇ N-UNCOUNT: usu N n =wickerwork

wickerwork /wɪkəʳwɜːʳk/. **Wickerwork** is the same as **wicker**. N-UNCOUNT: usu N n

wicket /wɪkɪt/ **wickets** ◆◆◆◇◇

1 In cricket, a **wicket** is a set of three upright sticks with two small sticks on top of them at which the ball is bowled. There are two wickets on a cricket pitch. N-COUNT

2 In cricket, a **wicket** is the area of grass in between the two wickets on the pitch. N-COUNT

3 In cricket, when a **wicket** falls or is taken, a batsman is out. N-COUNT

wicket-keeper, wicket-keepers; also spelled **wicket keeper.** A **wicket-keeper** is the player in a cricket team who stands behind the wicket in order to stop balls that the batsman misses or to catch balls that the batsman hits. N-COUNT

wide /waɪd/ **wider, widest** ◆◆◆◆◆

1 Something that is **wide** measures a large distance from one side or edge to the other. *All worktops should be wide enough to allow plenty of space for food preparation. ...a wide-brimmed sunhat.* ADJ-GRADED ≠narrow

2 A **wide** smile is one in which your mouth is stretched because you are very pleased or amused. *It brought a wide smile to his face and laughter to his eyes... His face broke into a wide grin.* ADJ-GRADED: usu ADJ n =broad ♦ **widely** *He was grinning widely, waving to her as he ran.* ADV-GRADED: ADV after v

3 If you open or spread something **wide**, you open or spread it as far as possible or to the fullest extent. *Open your mouth wide... 'It was huge,' he announced, spreading his arms wide... His eyes were wide in disbelief... He fell over this time, flat on his back with his legs wide.* ADJ: usu v n ADJ, v-link ADJ, also ADJ n

4 You use **wide** to talk or ask about how much something measures from one side or edge to the other. *...a corridor of land 10 kilometres wide... The road is only one track wide. ...a desk that was almost as wide as the room... Stand tall with your feet slightly wider than shoulder distance apart.* ADJ: amount ADJ, *as* ADJ *as*, ADJ-compar *than*, *how* ADJ

5 You use **wide** to describe something that includes a large number of different things or people. *The brochure offers a wide choice of hotels, apartments and holiday homes... The proposed constitution gives him much wider powers than his predecessor. ...a major event which brought together a wide range of interest groups.* ADJ-GRADED: usu ADJ n =broad ≠narrow ♦ **widely** *He published widely in scientific journals... He was widely travelled.* ADV-GRADED: usu ADV after v

6 You use **wide** to say that something is found, believed, known, or supported by many people or throughout a large area. *The case has attracted wide publicity... I suspect this book will have the widest appeal of all... As pope he won wide support for his strict orthodoxy.* ADJ-GRADED: usu ADJ n =extensive ♦ **widely** *At present, no widely approved vaccine exists for malaria. ...the group which is widely blamed for having planted the bomb.* ADV-GRADED: ADV with v

7 A **wide** difference or gap between two things, ideas, or qualities is a large difference or gap. *Research shows a wide difference in tastes around the country... There are wide variations caused by different academic programme structures.* ADJ-GRADED: usu ADJ n =great ♦ **widely** *The treatment regime may vary widely depending on the type of injury. ...children from widely different backgrounds.* ADV-GRADED: ADV after v, ADV adj

8 **Wider** is used to describe something which relates to the most important or general parts of a situation, rather than to the smaller parts or to details. *He emphasised the wider issue of superpower cooperation... Oakley locates housework in the wider context of economic, social and political structures.* ADJ-GRADED: ADJ n =broader

9 If something such as a shot or punch is **wide**, it does not hit its target but lands to the right or left of it. *The shot was wide anyway... Nearly half the missiles landed wide.* ADJ-GRADED: usu v-link ADJ

10 • **wide awake**: see **awake**. • **far and wide**: see

far. • wide of the mark: see **mark**. • **wide open**: see **open**.

-wide /-waɪd/. **-wide** combines with nouns to form adjectives which indicate that something exists or happens throughout the place or area that the noun refers to. *...a Europe-wide conference on security and cooperation... Is the problem one that's industry-wide?* ▶ Also combines to form adverbs. *Employers want to be sure recruits understand business Europe-wide... Country-wide, a total of 22 political parties are competing for the voters' allegiance.* COMB in ADJ; COMB in ADV: n ADV, ADV with cl, ADV after v

wide-angle lens, wide-angle lenses. A **wide-angle lens** is a lens which allows you to photograph a wider view than a normal lens. N-COUNT

wide awake. If you are **wide awake**, you are completely awake. *I could not relax and still felt wide awake.* ADJ: usu v-link ADJ

wide-eyed ◆◇◇◇◇

1 If you describe someone as **wide-eyed**, you mean that they seem inexperienced, and may be rather naive and easily impressed. *Her wide-eyed innocence soon exposes the pretensions of the art world. ...a wide-eyed boy ready to explore.* ADJ: usu ADJ n

2 If you describe someone as **wide-eyed**, you mean that their eyes are more open than usual, especially because they are surprised or frightened. *She is wide-eyed with astonishment. ...an expression of wide-eyed amazement.* ▶ Also an adverb. *Trevor was staring wide-eyed at me.* ADJ; ADV-GRADED: ADV after v

widen /waɪdᵊn/ **widens, widening, widened** ◆◆◇◇◇

1 If you **widen** something or if it **widens**, it becomes greater in measurement from one side or edge to the other. *He had an operation last year to widen a heart artery... The river widens considerably as it begins to turn east.* ♦ **widening** *They have ordered the widening of the road where the incident took place.* V-ERG =broaden; V n; V; N-UNCOUNT: oft N *of* n

2 If you **widen** something or if it **widens**, it becomes greater in range or variety or includes or affects a larger number of people or things. *U.S. prosecutors have widened a securities-fraud investigation... The search for my brother widened... Newspapers enjoyed a widening circle of readers.* V-ERG =extend; V n; V; V-ing

3 If your eyes **widen**, they open more. *His eyes widened as he spoke the words.* VERB; V

4 If a difference or gap **widens** or if something **widens** it, it becomes greater. *Wage differences in the two areas are widening... The US trade deficit widened to $7.59 billion in November. ...policies that widen the gap between the rich and the poor.* V-ERG; V; V *to/from/by* amount; V n

wide-ranging. If you describe something as **wide-ranging**, you mean it deals with or affects a great variety of different things. *...a wide-ranging debate about the party's goals. ...a package of wide-ranging economic reforms... The aims of the redesign are wide-ranging but simple.* ◆◇◇◇◇ ADJ-GRADED =far-reaching

widespread /waɪdspred/. Something that is **widespread** exists or happens over a large area, or to a great extent. *Mr Pasqua's proposals have attracted widespread support... Food shortages are widespread.* ◆◆◆◇◇ ADJ-GRADED =extensive

widget /wɪdʒɪt/ **widgets.** You can refer to any small device as a **widget** when you do not know exactly what it is or how it works; an informal word. *The secret is a little widget in the can.* N-COUNT

widow /wɪdoʊ/ **widows.** A **widow** is a woman whose husband has died and who has not married again. ◆◆◇◇◇ N-COUNT

widowed /wɪdoʊd/. If someone **is widowed**, their husband or wife has died and they have not married again. *More and more young men are widowed by cancer... She was widowed in 1967... Imogen stayed with her widowed sister.* ◆◇◇◇◇ V-PASSIVE; *be* V-ed; V-ed

widower /wɪdoʊəʳ/ **widowers.** A **widower** is a man whose wife has died and who has not married again. N-COUNT

widowhood /wɪdoʊhʊd/. **Widowhood** is the state of being a widow or widower, or the period of time during which someone is a widow or widower. *Nothing can prepare you for the shock and grief of widowhood.* N-UNCOUNT

width /wɪdθ/ **widths** ◆◇◇◇◇

1 The **width** of something is the distance it measures from one side or edge to the other. *Measure the full width of the window... The road was reduced to 18ft in width by adding parking bays... Saddles are made in a wide range of different widths.* N-VAR: oft N *of* n =breadth

2 The **width** of something is its quality of being wide. *The best utensil for steaming is a wok because its width easily accommodates a whole fish.* N-UNCOUNT: usu with poss =breadth

3 A **width** is the distance from one side of a swimming pool to the other. *We swam several widths.* N-COUNT

wield /wiːld/ **wields, wielding, wielded** ◆◇◇◇◇

1 If you **wield** a weapon, tool, or piece of equipment, you carry and use it. *...a lone assailant wielding a kitchen knife.* VERB; V n

2 If someone **wields** power, they have it and are able to use it. *He remains chairman, but wields little power at the company.* VERB; V n

wife /waɪf/ **wives.** A man's **wife** is the woman he is married to. *He married his wife Jane 37 years ago... The woman was the wife of a film director.* • See also **old wives' tale**. ◆◆◆◆◆ N-COUNT: usu with poss

wifely /waɪfli/. **Wifely** is used to describe things that are supposed to be typical of a good wife. *She strove to perform all her wifely functions perfectly. ...the ideology of wifely duty.* ADJ: usu ADJ n

wig /wɪg/ **wigs.** A **wig** is a mass of false hair which you wear on your head, for example because you are bald or because you want to cover up your own hair. ◆◆◇◇◇ N-COUNT

wiggle /wɪgᵊl/ **wiggles, wiggling, wiggled.** If you **wiggle** something or if it **wiggles**, it moves up and down or from side to side in small quick movements. *She wiggled her finger... His ears wiggled if you scratched his chin... Your baby will try to shuffle or wiggle along the floor.* ▶ Also a noun. *...a wiggle of the hips.* ◆◇◇◇◇ V-ERG; V n; V; V prep/adv; N-COUNT

wigwam /wɪgwæm, AM -wɑːm/ **wigwams.** A **wigwam** is the same as a **tepee**. N-COUNT =tepee

wild /waɪld/ **wilds; wilder, wildest** ◆◆◆◆◇

1 **Wild** animals or plants live or grow in natural surroundings and are not looked after by people. *We saw two more wild cats creeping towards us in the darkness... The lane was lined with wild flowers.* ADJ: usu ADJ n

2 **Wild** land is natural and not cultivated. *Elmley is one of the few wild areas remaining in the South East.* ♦ **wildness** *...the wildness of the mountains and the soft hues of the fields.* ADJ-GRADED: usu ADJ n; N-UNCOUNT

3 **The wilds** are remote areas, far away from towns. *They went canoeing in the wilds of Canada.* N-PLURAL: *the* N

4 **Wild** is used to describe the weather or the sea when it is stormy. *The wild weather did not deter some people from taking an unseasonable dip in the sea.* ADJ-GRADED: usu ADJ n =stormy

5 **Wild** behaviour is uncontrolled, excited, or energetic. *The children are wild with joy... As George himself came on stage they went wild... They marched into town to the wild cheers of the inhabitants.* ♦ **wildly** *As she finished each song, the crowd clapped wildly.* ADJ-GRADED: oft v-link ADJ *with* n; ADV-GRADED: ADV with v

6 If you describe someone or something as **wild**, you mean that they lack discipline and control. *When angry or excited, however, he could be wild, profane, and terrifying... She lived a wild and incredible life... The house is in a mess after a wild party.* ♦ **wildly** *Five people were injured as Reynolds slashed out wildly with a kitchen knife.* ♦ **wildness** *He had come to love the danger and the wildness of his life.* ADJ-GRADED; ADV-GRADED: ADV with v; N-UNCOUNT

7 If someone is **wild**, they are very angry; an informal use. *For a long time I daren't tell him I knew, and when I did he went wild.* ADJ-GRADED: usu v-link ADJ =mad, crazy

8 If you say that someone has **wild** eyes or a **wild** look, you mean that their eyes are wide open and staring because they are frightened, angry, or insane. *She could see his face now, his eyes wild and his skin glistening with perspiration... I could not forget the wild look in his eyes.* ♦ **wildness** *She stared at him with wildness in her eyes.* ADJ-GRADED; N-UNCOUNT

9 A **wild** idea or guess is unusual and made without much thought. *I was just a kid and full of all sorts of* ADJ-GRADED: ADJ n

wild ideas... Browning's prediction is no better than a wild guess. ♦ **wildly** *'Thirteen?' he guessed wildly.* ADV-GRADED

10 See also **wildly**; **wild child**.

11 If you **are wild about** someone or something, you like them very much; an informal expression. *I'm just wild about Peter, and he's just wild about me... Irene was wild about the play.* PHRASES V inflects =be crazy about

12 Animals that live **in the wild** live in a free and natural state and are not looked after by people. *Fewer than a thousand giant pandas still live in the wild.* PHR after v, v-link PHR ≠in captivity

13 If something or someone, especially a child, **runs wild**, they behave in a natural, free, or uncontrolled way. *Everything that could grow was running wild for lack of attention... Molly has let that girl run wild.* V inflects

14 • **beyond** your **wildest dreams**: see **dream**. • **in** your **wildest dreams**: see **dream**. • **to sow** your **wild oats**: see **oat**.

wild boar, wild boars. The plural can be either **wild boar** or **wild boars**. A **wild boar** is a large fierce pig which has tusks and a lot of hair and which lives in forests. N-COUNT

wild card, wild cards

1 If you refer to someone or something as a **wild card** in a particular situation, you mean that they cause uncertainty because you do not know how they will behave. *The wild card in the picture is eastern Europe.* N-COUNT: oft N *in* n =loose cannon

2 If a sports player is given a **wild card** for a particular competition, they are allowed to play in it, although they have not qualified for it in the usual way. You can also use **wild card** to refer to a player who enters a competition in this way. *Andre Agassi has accepted a wild card to play in the Stockholm Open.* N-COUNT

wildcat /waɪldkæt/ **wildcats**

1 A **wildcat** is a cat which is very fierce and lives especially in mountains and forests. *A giant wildcat is being hunted after 58 lambs were butchered.* N-COUNT

2 A **wildcat** strike happens suddenly, as a result of a decision by a group of workers, and is not officially approved by a trade union. *Frustration, anger and desperation have led to a series of wildcat strikes. ...wildcat stoppages on public transport.* ADJ: ADJ n

3 A **wildcat** scheme, project, or business is risky and likely to fail, usually because there has not been enough planning. *It was a wildcat plan by some of our members.* ADJ: ADJ n

wild child. In British English, journalists sometimes use **wild child** to refer a young teenage girl who looks very attractive and grown-up and who behaves in an undisciplined way. N-SING

wildebeest /wɪldɪbiːst, vɪl-/; **wildebeest** is both the singular and the plural form. A **wildebeest** is a large African antelope which has a hairy tail, short curved horns, and hair under its neck that looks like a beard. Wildebeest usually live in large herds. N-COUNT

wilderness /wɪldərnes/ **wildernesses** ◆◆◇◇◇

1 A **wilderness** is a desert or other area of natural land which is not cultivated. *...the icy Canadian wilderness... He is proud of the garden he made from a wilderness. ...one of the largest wilderness areas in North America.* N-COUNT: usu sing

2 If politicians or other well-known people spend time **in the wilderness**, they are not in an influential position or very active in their profession for that time. *...a party released from 12 years in the wilderness... For so long he had waited in the wilderness for a recall to Test cricket.* PHRASE: n PHR, PHR after v, v-link PHR

wildfire /waɪldfaɪər/ **wildfires**

1 A **wildfire** is a fire that starts, usually by itself, in a wild area such as a forest, and spreads rapidly, causing great damage. *...a wildfire in Montana that's already burned thousands of acres of rich grassland.* N-COUNT

2 If something, especially news or a rumour, **spreads like wildfire**, it spreads extremely quickly. *These stories are spreading like wildfire through the city.* PHRASE: V inflects

wild flower, wild flowers. Wild flowers are plants and their flowers which grow naturally, for example in the countryside, rather than being grown by people in gardens or nurseries. ◆◇◇◇◇ N-COUNT

wildfowl /waɪldfaʊl/. **Wildfowl** are birds such as ducks, pheasants, and quails which some people hunt and shoot. N-PLURAL =game birds

wild goose chase, wild goose chases. If you are on a **wild goose chase**, you waste a lot of time searching for something that you have little chance of finding, because you have been given misleading information. *Harry wondered if Potts had deliberately sent him on a wild goose chase.* N-COUNT: usu *on* N

wildlife /waɪldlaɪf/. You can use **wildlife** to refer to the animals and other living things that live in the wild. *People were concerned that pets or wildlife could be affected by the pesticides.* ◆◆◇◇◇ N-UNCOUNT

wildly /waɪldli/. You use **wildly** to emphasize the degree, amount, or intensity of something. *Here again, the community and police have wildly different stories of what happened... The island's hotels vary wildly.* • See also **wild**. ◆◆◇◇◇ ADV-GRADED: usu ADV adj, also ADV after v PRAGMATICS

Wild West. The **Wild West** is used to refer to the western part of the United States during the time when Europeans were first settling there. N-SING: *the* N

wiles /waɪlz/. **Wiles** are clever tricks that people, especially women, use to persuade other people to do something. *She claimed that women 'use their feminine wiles to get on.'* N-PLURAL: usu supp N, N *of* n

wilful /wɪlfʊl/; spelled **willful** in American English. ◆◇◇◇◇

1 If you describe actions or attitudes as **wilful**, you are critical of them because they are done or expressed deliberately, especially with the intention of causing someone harm. *Wilful neglect of our manufacturing industry has caused this problem... A jury found the airline guilty of wilful misconduct because its lax security allowed a suitcase bomb on to the plane.* ♦ **wilfully** *There were claims that the Front has wilfully perverted democracy... West was wilfully blind to the abuse that took place.* ADJ: ADJ n PRAGMATICS =deliberate; ADV-GRADED: ADV with v, ADV adj

2 If you describe someone as **wilful**, you mean that they are stubborn and determined to have their own way. *He is a wilful and indeed rather spiteful young man.* ♦ **wilfulness** *I refuse to stand by and see the company allowed to run aground because of one woman's wilfulness.* ADJ-GRADED =headstrong; N-UNCOUNT

will 1 modal verb uses

will /wɪl/ ◆◆◆◆◆

Will is a modal verb. It is used with the base form of a verb. In spoken English and informal written English, the form **won't** is often used in negative statements.

1 You use **will** to indicate that you hope, think, or have evidence that something is going to happen or be the case in the future. *The Prime Minister is now 64 years old and in all probability this will be the last election that he is likely to contest... I'm sure we will find a wide variety of choices available in school cafeterias... It is hoped that representatives from across the horse industry will attend the meeting... It has been estimated that 70 per cent of airports in the Far East will have to be upgraded... Will you ever feel at home here?... The ship will not be ready for a month.* MODAL

2 You use **will** in order to make statements about official arrangements in the future. *The show will be open to the public at 2pm; admission will be 50p... When will I be released, sir?* MODAL

3 You use **will** in order to make promises and threats about what is going to happen or be the case in the future. *I'll call you tonight... Price quotes on selected product categories will be sent on request... If she refuses to follow rules about car safety, she won't be allowed to use the car.* MODAL PRAGMATICS

4 You use **will** to indicate someone's intention to do something. *I will say no more on these matters, important though they are... In this section we will describe common myths about cigarettes, alcohol, and marijuana... 'Dinner's ready.'—'Thanks, Carrie, but we'll have a drink first.'... He will be devoting more time to writing, broadcasting and lec-* MODAL *turing... What will you do next?... Where will you stay when you get to San Francisco?... Will you be remaining in the city?*

5 You use **will** in questions in order to make polite invitations or offers. *Will you stay for supper?... Will you join me for a drink?... Won't you sit down?*
MODAL PRAGMATICS

6 You use **will** in questions in order to ask or tell someone to do something. *Will you drive me home?... Will you listen again, Andrew?... Wipe the jam off my mouth, will you?*
MODAL PRAGMATICS =would

7 You can use **will** in statements to give an order to someone; a formal use. *You will do as I request, if you please... You will now maintain radio silence... You will not make jokes about him. He has been very good to me... You will not discuss this matter with anyone.*
MODAL PRAGMATICS

8 You use **will** to say that someone is willing to do something. You use **will not** or **won't** to indicate that someone refuses to do something. *All right, I'll forgive you... I'll answer the phone... If you won't let me pay for a taxi, then at least allow me to lend you something... He has insisted that his organisation will not negotiate with the government.* • See also **willing**.
MODAL PRAGMATICS

9 You use **will** to say that someone or something is able to do something in the future. *How the country will defend itself in the future has become increasingly important... How will I recognize you?*
MODAL

10 You use **will** to indicate that an action usually happens in the particular way mentioned. *The thicker the material, the less susceptible the garment will be to wet conditions... There's no snake known that will habitually attack human beings unless threatened with its life... Art thieves will often hide an important work for years after it has been stolen.*
MODAL

11 You use **will** in the main clause of some 'if' and 'unless' sentences to indicate something that you consider to be fairly likely to happen. *If you overcook the pancakes they will be difficult to roll... If a nuclear war breaks out, every living thing will be wiped off the face of the Earth... China won't stop burning coal unless the West provides more modern energy-producing technology.*
MODAL

12 You use **will** to say that someone insists on behaving or doing something in a particular way and you cannot change them. You emphasize the word **will** when you use it in this way. *He will leave his socks lying all over the place and it drives me mad.*
MODAL PRAGMATICS

13 You use **will have** with a past participle when you are saying that you are fairly certain that something will be true by a particular time in the future. *By the year two-thousand ten-million more babies will have been infected with HIV... He will have left by January the fifteenth.*
MODAL

14 You use **will have** with a past participle to indicate that you are fairly sure that something is the case. *If someone has been in captivity for a long time, he will have changed as a result of his experience... The holiday will have done him the world of good.*
MODAL

will 2 wanting something to happen

will /wɪl/ **wills, willing, willed** ◆◆◆◆◇

1 **Will** is the determination to do something. *He was said to have lost his will to live. ...the inevitable battle of wills as your child realises that he can't do or have everything he wants... He who was usually so full of questions lacked the will to confront her with them.* • See also **free will**.
N-VAR: oft N to-inf

2 If something is the **will** of a person or group of people with authority, they want it to happen. *He has submitted himself to the will of God... Democracy responds and adjusts to the will of the people... The parliament didn't deserve to represent the nation's will.*
N-SING: with poss

3 If you **will** something to happen, you try to make it happen by using mental effort rather than physical effort. *I looked at the telephone, willing it to ring... He was watching her fixedly, willing her to look at him.*
VERB V n to-inf

4 A **will** is a document in which you declare what you want to happen to your money and property when you die. *Attached to his will was a letter he had written to his wife just days before his death.*
N-COUNT

5 If you **will** something to someone, you say in your will that they should have it when you die. *The large sum of money that came to him when she died was a shock, and he had not spent a penny of it on himself. He had, however, willed it to Frank.*
VERB V n to n

6 If something is done **against** your **will**, it is done even though you do not want it to be done. *Ambassador Kurt Murkel became the first European diplomat to be moved to Baghdad against his will.*
PHRASES PHR after v

7 If you can do something **at will**, you can do it when you want and as much as you want. *...scientists who can adjust their experiments at will.*
PHR after v

8 If you do something **with a will**, you do it with a lot of enthusiasm and energy. *Set to work with a will and be pleased with the amount you get done... It was an easy opening circuit, but the riders attacked it with a will.*
PHR after v =eagerly

willful. See **wilful**.

willie /wɪli/. See **willy**.

willing /wɪlɪŋ/ ◆◆◆◆◇

1 If someone is **willing** to do something, they do not mind doing it or have no objection to doing it. *The military now say they're willing to hold talks with the political parties... There are, of course, questions which she will not be willing to answer.* ♦ **willingly** *I am glad you have come here so willingly... I won't willingly let you go.* ♦ **willingness** *I had to prove my willingness to work hard and accept the university's authority.*
ADJ-GRADED: v-link ADJ to-inf =prepared ≠unwilling
ADV-GRADED: ADV with v
N-UNCOUNT =readiness

2 **Willing** is used to describe someone who does something fairly enthusiastically and because they want to do it rather than because they are forced to do it. *Have the party on a Saturday, when you can get your partner and other willing adults to help... Although he had had no formal engineering training he was a natural and willing pupil.* ♦ **willingly** *Most companies willingly correct what went wrong or, if that is impossible, explain why the situation occurred.* ♦ **willingness** *Self-discipline, willingness, enthusiasm, that's what you must depend on.*
ADJ-GRADED: usu ADJ n ≠unwilling, reluctant
ADV-GRADED: ADV with v =readily
N-UNCOUNT

3 • **God willing**: see **god**.

will-o'-the-wisp /wɪl ə ðə wɪsp/ **will-o'-the-wisps.** You can refer to someone or something that keeps disappearing or that is impossible to catch or reach as a **will-o'-the-wisp**.
N-COUNT: usu sing

willow /wɪloʊ/ **willows.** A **willow** or a **willow tree** is a type of tree with long branches and long narrow leaves that grows near water. ▸ **Willow** is the wood of this tree. *...willow furniture.*
◆◇◇◇◇ N-COUNT
N-UNCOUNT: oft N n

willowy /wɪloʊi/. A person who is **willowy** is tall, thin, and graceful.
ADJ-GRADED =slender

willpower /wɪlpaʊəʳ/; also spelled **will-power** or **will power**. **Willpower** is a very strong determination to do something. *I know I've got the willpower to do it... He came in for help after his attempts to stop smoking by willpower alone failed.*
◆◇◇◇◇ N-UNCOUNT =resolve

willy /wɪli/ **willies;** also spelled **willie**.

1 In informal British English, a boy's or man's **willy** is his penis; a word used mainly by children.
N-COUNT

2 If someone or something **gives** you **the willies** they make you feel nervous or frightened; an informal expression.
PHRASE: V inflects

willy-nilly /wɪli nɪli/; also spelled **willy nilly**.

1 If something happens to you **willy-nilly**, it happens whether you like it or not. *The government were dragged willy-nilly into the confrontation.*
ADV: usu ADV with v, also ADV with cl

2 If someone does something **willy-nilly**, they do it in a careless and haphazard way, without planning or choosing things in advance. *Clerks bundled papers into files willy-nilly.*
ADV: usu ADV after v, also ADV with cl

wilt /wɪlt/ **wilts, wilting, wilted** ◆◇◇◇◇

1 If a plant **wilts**, it gradually bends downwards and becomes weak because it needs more water or is dying. *The roses wilted the day after she bought them... Remove any damaged or wilted leaves.*
VERB V V-ed

2 If someone **wilts**, they become weak or tired, or lose confidence. *She soon wilted in the morning heat... The government wilted in the face of such powerful pressure.*
VERB V

wily /waɪli/ **wilier, wiliest.** If you describe someone or someone's behaviour as **wily**, you mean that they are clever and cunning, especially in ways that involve deceiving people. *His appointment as prime minister owed much to the wily manoeuvring of the President.* ◆◇◇◇◇ ADJ-GRADED =cunning ≠artless

wimp /wɪmp/ **wimps.** If you call someone a **wimp**, you disapprove of them because they lack confidence or determination, or because they are often afraid of things; an informal word. ◆◇◇◇◇ N-COUNT PRAGMATICS =drip, nerd

wimpish /wɪmpɪʃ/. **Wimpish** means the same as **wimpy**. ADJ-GRADED PRAGMATICS

wimpy /wɪmpi/. If you describe a person or their behaviour as **wimpy**, you disapprove of them because they are weak and seem to lack confidence and determination; an informal word. *...a wimpy unpopular schoolboy... This portrays her as wimpy, but she has a very strong character.* ADJ-GRADED PRAGMATICS =drippy, wet

win /wɪn/ **wins, winning, won** ◆◆◆◆◆

1 If you **win** something such as a competition, battle, or argument, you defeat those people you are competing or fighting against, or you do better than everyone else involved. *He does not have any realistic chance of winning the election... The NCAA basketball championship was won by North Carolina. ...when Napoleon was winning his great battles in Italy... The top four teams all won... Sanchez Vicario won 2-6, 6-4, 6-3.* ▶ Also a noun. *...Arsenal's dismal league run of eight games without a win... The voters gave a narrow win to Vargas Llosa.* VERB ≠lose; V n; V; V amount; Also V n amount; N-COUNT =victory ≠defeat

2 If something **wins** you something such as an election, competition, battle, or argument, it causes you to defeat the people competing with you or fighting you, or to do better than everyone else involved. *They believed that better economic news, would win Mr Bush the election... Graham is more determined than ever to win the club its third Championship under his command.* VERB ≠lose; V n n

3 If you **win** something such as a prize or medal, you get it because you have defeated everyone else in something such as an election, competition, battle, or argument, or have done very well in it. *The first correct entry wins the prize... She won bronze for Great Britain in the European Championships.* VERB; V n

4 If you **win** something that you want or need, you succeed in getting it. *...moves to win the support of the poor... British Aerospace has won an order worth 340 million dollars.* VERB =gain ≠lose; V n

5 If something **wins** you a prize or **wins** you something else that you want, it causes you to get it. *The feat won them a prize of £85,000... Good weather leading to good grain harvests should win the country relief from food shortages.* VERB ≠lose; V n n

6 See also **winning**.

7 If you say that someone **can't win** in a particular situation, you mean that they are certain to fail or to suffer whatever they do; an informal expression. *If you're too assertive they regard you as an aggressive hysterical woman. I mean, you can't win!* PHRASES

8 You say **'you win'** when you have been having a slight argument with someone and you are indicating that you agree to do what they want or that you accept their suggestion, even though you do not really want to. *'All right', I said. 'You win'.* CONVENTION PRAGMATICS

9 ● **lost the battle but won the war**: see **battle**. ● to **win the day**: see **day**. ● to **win hands down**: see **hand**.

win back. If you **win back** something that you have lost, you get it again, especially as a result of a great effort. *The Government will have to work hard to win back the confidence of the people... So he went and filed a suit and won his job back.* PHRASAL VERB; V P n (not pron); V n P

win out or **win through.** If something or someone **wins out** or **wins through**, they are successful or gain an advantage over others, after a competition or struggle. *Sometimes perseverance does win out... Stick to your principles, and you will win through... Here is a chance for greengrocers to win out over the supermarkets by selling local produce.* PHRASAL VERB; V P; V P *over/against* n

win over or **win round.** If you **win** someone **over** or **win** them **round**, you persuade them to support you or agree with you. *By the end of the day President Gorbachev had won over the crowd... They still hope to win him round.* PHRASAL VERB; V P n (not pron); V n P

win through. See **win out.** PHRASAL VERB

win through to. If you **win through to** a particular position or stage of a competition, you succeed in achieving it after a great effort or by defeating opponents. *...Sabatini, who won through to the final after defeating the world number one.* PHRASAL VERB =get through to; V P P n

wince /wɪns/ **winces, wincing, winced.** If you **wince**, the muscles of your face tighten suddenly because you have felt a pain or because you have just seen, heard, or remembered something unpleasant. *Every time he put any weight on his left leg he winced in pain... He winced at the thought of dining with Camilla... 'Shh!' Sunny winced.* ▶ Also a noun. *He suppressed a wince as motion renewed the pain.* ◆◇◇◇◇ VERB =grimace; V; V with quote; N-COUNT: usu sing

winch /wɪntʃ/ **winches, winching, winched** ◆◇◇◇◇

1 A **winch** is a machine which is used to lift heavy objects or people who need to be rescued. It consists of a drum around which a rope or chain is wound. N-COUNT

2 If you **winch** an object or person somewhere, you lift or lower them using a winch. *He would attach a cable around the chassis of the car and winch it up on to the canal bank... The crew members were winched to safety by helicopters.* VERB; V n with adv/prep

wind 1 air

wind /wɪnd/ **winds, winding, winded** ◆◆◆◆◇

1 A **wind** is a current of air that is moving across the earth's surface. *There was a strong wind blowing... Then the wind dropped and the surface of the sea was still... The leaves rustled in the wind... During the night a gust of wind had blown the pot over.* N-VAR

2 Journalists often refer to a trend or factor that influences events as a **wind** of some kind. *The winds of change are blowing across the country... The world's entire aerospace industry is feeling the chill winds of recession.* N-COUNT: N *of* n

3 If you **are winded** by something such as a blow, the air is suddenly knocked out of your lungs so that you have difficulty breathing for a short time. *He was winded and shaken... The cow stamped on his side, winding him.* VERB; *be* V-ed; V n

4 **Wind** is the air that you sometimes swallow with food or drink, or gas that is produced in your intestines, which causes an uncomfortable feeling. N-UNCOUNT

5 If you **wind** a baby, you pat its back in order to help it to release air from its stomach; a fairly informal use. *If he cries when you put him down after a feed, try winding him.* VERB =burp; V n

6 The **wind** section of an orchestra or band is the group of people who produce musical sounds by blowing into their instruments. ADJ: ADJ n

7 If someone **breaks wind**, they release gas from their intestines through their anus; a polite expression. PHRASES; V inflects

8 If you **get wind of** something, you hear about it, especially when someone else did not want you to know about it; a fairly informal expression. *I don't want the public, and especially not the press, to get wind of it at this stage.* V inflects, PHR n

9 If something is **in the wind**, it is likely to happen. *By the mid-1980s, change was in the wind again.* v-link PHR

10 If something or someone **puts the wind up** you, they frighten or worry you; used in informal British English. *'I heard you had some funny phone calls.'—'Yeah, that's why yours rather put the wind up me.'* V inflects, PHR n =alarm

11 If you **sail close to the wind**, you take a risk by doing or saying something that may get you into trouble. *Max warned her she was sailing dangerously close to the wind and risked prosecution.* V inflects

12 If something **takes the wind out of** your **sails**, it suddenly makes you much less confident in what you are doing or saying. V inflects =deflate

13 If you realize or find out **which way the wind is blowing** or **how the wind is blowing**, you realize or find out what is likely to happen, for example whether something is likely to succeed. *He didn't* V inflects, PHR after v

like to make pronouncements before he was sure which way the wind was blowing.
14 ● to **throw caution to the wind**: see **caution**.

wind 2 turning or wrapping

wind /waɪnd/ **winds, winding, wound** ◆◆◆◆◇
1 If a road, river, or line of people **winds** in a particular direction, it goes in that direction with a lot of bends or twists in it. *The Moselle winds through some 160 miles of tranquil countryside... The road winds uphill... The convoy wound its way through the West Bank. ...a narrow winding road* VERB V prep/adv V *way* prep/adv V-ing
2 When you **wind** something flexible round something else, you wrap it around it several times. *The horse jumped forwards and round her, winding the rope round her waist.* VERB =coil V n prep/adv
3 When you **wind** a mechanical device, for example a watch or a clock, you turn a knob, key, or handle on it round and round in order to make it operate. *I still hadn't wound my watch so I didn't know the time.* ► **Wind up** means the same as **wind**. *I wound up the watch and listened to it tick... Frances took the tiny music box from her trunk and wound it up.* VERB V n PHRASAL VERB V P n (not pron) V n P
4 To **wind** a tape or film **back** or **forward** is to make it move nearer to its starting or ending position using a device such as a tape recorder or camera. *The camcorder winds the tape back or forward at high speed.* VERB V n adv

wind down PHRASAL VERB
1 When you **wind down** something such as the window of a car, you make it move downwards by turning a handle. *Glass motioned to him to wind down the window... If a stranger stops you, just wind the window down a fraction.* =roll down ≠wind up V P n (not pron) V n P
2 If you **wind down**, you relax after doing something that has made you feel tired or tense; an informal use. *I regularly have a drink to wind down.* =unwind V P
3 If someone **winds down** a business or activity, they gradually reduce the amount of work that is done or the number of people that are involved, usually before closing or stopping it completely. *Foreign aid workers have already begun winding down their operation... In 1991 the Ada plant began to wind down.* ERG V P n (not pron) V P Also V n P

wind up PHRASAL VERB
1 When you **wind up** an activity, you finish it or stop doing it. *President Bush is about to wind up his visit to Somalia... Winding up the debate, she said: 'It would immediately put up interest rates.'* V P n (not pron) Also V n P
2 When someone **winds up** a business or other organization, they stop running it and close it down completely. *The Bank of England seems determined to wind up the company.* V P n (not pron) Also V n P
3 If you **wind up** in a particular place, situation, or state, you are in it at the end of a series of actions, events, or experiences, even though you did not originally intend to be. *He could wind up in gaol... Little did I know that I would actually wind up being on the staff... Both partners of the marriage wound up unhappy.* =finish up, end up V P prep/adv V P -ing V P adj/n
4 When you **wind up** something such as the window of a car, you make it move upwards by turning a handle. *He started winding the window up but I grabbed the door and opened it.* =roll up ≠wind down V n P
5 If you **wind** someone **up**, you deliberately say things which annoy them; used in informal British English. *This woman really wound me up. She kept talking over me.* =annoy V n P Also V P n (not pron)
6 If you **wind** someone **up**, you say untrue things in order to trick them; used in informal British English. *You're joking. Come on, you're winding me up.* V n P
7 See also **wind** 3, **wind-up**, **wound up**.

windbag /wɪndbæg/ **windbags.** If you call someone a **windbag**, you are saying in a fairly rude way that you think they talk a great deal in a boring way; an informal word. N-COUNT

wind-blown /wɪnd bloʊn/; also spelled **windblown.**
1 You can use **wind-blown** to indicate that something has been blown from one place to another by the wind. *...the wind-blown sand which forms the 60 ft dunes.* ADJ
2 If something such as someone's hair is **wind-blown**, it is untidy because it has been blown about by the wind. *His blond hair was windblown.* ADJ-GRADED

windbreak /wɪndbreɪk/ **windbreaks.** A **windbreak** is something such as a line of trees or a fence which gives protection against the wind. N-COUNT

windbreaker /wɪndbreɪkər/ **windbreakers.** A **windbreaker** is a warm waterproof jacket, with a neck and cuffs that fit closely; used mainly in American English. N-COUNT =anorak

windfall /wɪndfɔːl/ **windfalls** ◆◇◇◇◇
1 A **windfall** is a sum of money that you receive unexpectedly or by luck, for example if you win a lottery. N-COUNT
2 A **windfall** is a fruit, especially an apple, that has fallen from a tree. N-COUNT

wind farm /wɪnd fɑːrm/ **wind farms.** A **wind farm** is a kind of power station where special windmills are used to convert the power of the wind into electricity. N-COUNT

wind instrument /wɪnd ɪnstrʊmənts/ **wind instruments.** A **wind instrument** is a musical instrument that you blow into in order to produce sounds, such as a flute, a clarinet, or a recorder. N-COUNT

windlass /wɪndləs/ **windlasses.** A **windlass** is a mechanical device for lifting heavy objects, which uses a motor to pull a rope or chain around a cylinder. N-COUNT =winch

windless /wɪndləs/. If the air is **windless**, or if it is a **windless** day, it is very calm and still. ADJ ≠windy

windmill /wɪndmɪl/ **windmills.** A **windmill** is a building with large sails on the outside which turn round as the wind blows. This provides energy for a machine which crushes corn or wheat. ◆◇◇◇◇ N-COUNT

window /wɪndoʊ/ **windows** ◆◆◆◆◇
1 A **window** is a space in the wall of a building or in the side of a vehicle, which has glass in it so that light can come in and you can see out. *He stood at the window, moodily staring out... The room felt very hot and she wondered why someone did not open a window... That's the second time I've had my car window smashed in the last two weeks.* N-COUNT
2 A **window** is a large piece of glass along the front of a shop, behind which some of the goods that the shop sells are displayed. *I stood for a few moments in front of the nearest shop window.* N-COUNT
3 A **window** is a glass-covered opening above a counter, for example in a bank, post office, railway station, or museum, which the person serving you sits behind. *The woman at the ticket window told me that the admission fee was $17.50.* N-COUNT
4 On a computer screen, a **window** is one of the work areas that the screen can be divided into. N-COUNT
5 See also **French window**, **picture window**, **rose window**.
6 If you say that something such as a plan, or a particular way of thinking or behaving **has gone out of the window** or **has flown out of the window**, you mean that it has disappeared completely. *By now all logic had gone out of the window... When he went, our happiness and our security flew out of the window.* PHRASES V inflects
7 If you say that there is a **window of opportunity** for something, you mean that there is an opportunity to do something but that this opportunity will only last for a short time and so it needs to be taken advantage of quickly; used mainly in journalism. *The king said there was now a window of opportunity for peace.* *window* inflects, oft PHR *for* n, PHR to-inf

window box, window boxes. A **window box** is a long narrow container on a window-sill in which plants are grown. N-COUNT

window-dressing; also spelled **window dressing.**
1 **Window-dressing** is the skill of arranging objects attractively in a window, especially a shop window, or the way in which they are arranged. N-UNCOUNT
2 If you refer to something as **window-dressing**, you are critical of it because it is done in order to create a good impression and to prevent people N-UNCOUNT PRAGMATICS

from realizing the real or more unpleasant nature of someone's activities. *The measures are little more than window dressing that will fade fast once investors take a hard look at them.*

window frame, window frames. A **window frame** is a frame round the edges of a window, which glass is fixed into. N-COUNT

windowpane /wɪndoʊpeɪn/ **windowpanes;** also spelled **window pane.** A **windowpane** is a piece of glass in the window of a building. N-COUNT

window seat, window seats
1 A **window seat** is a seat which is fixed to the wall underneath a window in a room. N-COUNT
2 On a train, bus, or aeroplane, a **window seat** is a seat next to a window. N-COUNT

window shopping; also spelled **window-shopping.** If you do some **window shopping**, you spend time looking at the goods in the windows of shops without intending to buy anything. N-UNCOUNT

windowsill /wɪndoʊsɪl/ **windowsills;** also spelled **window sill.** A **windowsill** is a ledge along the bottom of a window, either inside or outside a building. N-COUNT =trachea

windpipe /wɪndpaɪp/ **windpipes.** Your **windpipe** is the tube in your body that carries air into your lungs when you breathe. N-COUNT =trachea

windscreen /wɪndskriːn/ **windscreens.** In British English, the **windscreen** of a car or other vehicle is the glass window at the front through which the driver looks. The usual American word is **windshield.** ◆◇◇◇◇ N-COUNT

windscreen wiper, windscreen wipers. In British English a **windscreen wiper** is a device that wipes rain from a vehicle's windscreen. The usual American word is **windshield wiper.** N-COUNT: usu pl

windshield /wɪndʃiːld/ **windshields.** In American English, the **windshield** of a car or other vehicle is the glass window at the front through which the driver looks. The usual British word is **windscreen.** N-COUNT

windshield wiper, windshield wipers. See **windscreen wiper.**

windsurfer /wɪndsɜːʳfəʳ/ **windsurfers**
1 A **windsurfer** is a long narrow board with a sail attached to it. You stand on a windsurfer in the sea or on a lake and are blown along by the wind. N-COUNT
2 A **windsurfer** is a person who rides on a windsurfer. N-COUNT

windsurfing /wɪndsɜːʳfɪŋ/. **Windsurfing** is a sport in which you move along the surface of the sea or a lake on a long narrow board with a sail on it. N-UNCOUNT

windswept /wɪndswept/. A **windswept** place has no shelter and is not protected against strong winds. *...the remote and windswept hillside.* ADJ

wind tunnel /wɪnd tʌnəl/ **wind tunnels.** A **wind tunnel** is a room or passage which is designed so that air can be made to flow through it at controlled speeds. Wind tunnels are used to test new or experimental equipment or machinery, especially cars or aeroplanes. N-COUNT

wind-up /waɪnd ʌp/, **wind-ups** ◆◇◇◇◇
1 A **wind-up** device has a mechanism that is operated by clockwork. *...an old-fashioned wind-up gramophone.* ADJ: ADJ n
2 In informal British English, a **wind-up** is a joke or trick in which someone deliberately tells you something untrue to annoy you. *At first I couldn't believe it. I thought it was a wind-up by one of my mates.* N-COUNT: usu sing, usu *a* N

windward /wɪndwəʳd/
1 **Windward** is used to describe the side of something, especially a ship, which is facing the wind. *...the windward side of the quarterdeck... Gardens on the windward side of a hill receive more rain than those on the lee side.* ADJ: ADJ n ≠leeward
2 If a ship sails **to windward**, it sails towards the place from which the wind is blowing; a technical expression in sailing. PHRASE: PHR after v ≠to leeward

windy /wɪndi/ **windier, windiest.** If it is **windy**, the wind is blowing a lot. *It was windy and Jake felt cold.* ◆◇◇◇◇ ADJ-GRADED =blustery ≠windless

wine /waɪn/ **wines, wining, wined** ◆◆◆◆◇
1 **Wine** is an alcoholic drink which is made from grapes. You can also refer to alcoholic drinks made from other fruits or vegetables as **wine.** *...a bottle of white wine... This is a nice wine. ...homemade parsnip wine.* N-MASS
2 **Wine** is used to describe things that are very dark red in colour. *She wore her wine-coloured gaberdine raincoat. ...an olive and wine wool sweater.* COLOUR
3 If you **wine and dine**, or if someone **wines and dines** you, you go out, for example to expensive restaurants, and spend a lot of money. *Colleagues were furious at doing her work while she wined and dined... A lot of money went on wining and dining prospective clients.* PHR-ERG: Vs inflect

wine bar, wine bars. A **wine bar** is a place where people can buy and drink wine, and sometimes eat food as well. ◆◇◇◇◇ N-COUNT

wine glass, wine glasses. A **wine glass** is a glass, usually with a narrow stem, which you use for drinking wine. N-COUNT

winery /waɪnəri/ **wineries.** In American English, a **winery** is a place where wine is made. The usual British word is **vineyard.** N-COUNT

wing /wɪŋ/ **wings, winging, winged** ◆◆◆◆◇
1 The **wings** of a bird or insect are the two parts of its body that it uses for flying. *The bird flapped its wings furiously... She saw the occasional glimmer of a moth's wings.* ♦ **-winged** *...black-winged birds.* N-COUNT; COMB in ADJ
2 The **wings** of an aeroplane are the long flat parts sticking out of its side which support it while it is flying. ♦ **-winged** *...a wide-winged plane.* N-COUNT; COMB in ADJ
3 A **wing** of a building is a part of it which sticks out from the main part. *We were given an office in the empty west wing. ...in the Child Psychiatry wing of London's Royal Free Hospital.* N-COUNT: usu with supp
4 A **wing** of an organization, especially a political organization, is a group within it which has a particular function or particular beliefs. *...the military wing of the African National Congress. ...the liberal wing of the Democratic Party.* • See also **left-wing, right-wing.** N-COUNT: with supp, usu supp N =section
5 In a theatre, **the wings** are the sides of the stage which are hidden from the audience by curtains or scenery. *Most nights I watched the start of the play from the wings.* N-PLURAL: *the* N
6 In a game such as football or hockey, the **left wing** and the **right wing** are the areas on the far left and the far right of the pitch. You can also refer to the players who play in these positions as the **left wing** and the **right wing.** N-COUNT: usu supp N
7 In British English, a **wing** of a car is the part of its bodywork which is over a wheel. The American word is **fender.** N-COUNT
8 When a pilot gets his or her **wings**, he or she becomes qualified to fly aeroplanes. *He had no sooner got his wings than the Korean conflict broke out.* N-PLURAL: usu poss N
9 If you say that something or someone **wings their way** somewhere or **wings** somewhere, you mean that they go there quickly, especially by plane. *A few moments later they were airborne and winging their way south... A bumper cash bonanza of £1.4bn will be winging its way to the 600,000 members of their pension scheme in the New Year... The first of the airliners winged westwards and home.* VERB: V *way* adv/prep; V adv/prep
10 If you say that something or someone **clips** your **wings**, you mean that they restrict your freedom to do what you want; an informal expression. *...legislation aimed at clipping the president's political wings.* PHRASES: V inflects
11 If you say that someone is waiting **in the wings**, you mean that they are ready and waiting for the opportunity to take action. *There are now more than 20 big companies waiting in the wings to take over some of its business.* usu v PHR
12 If you **spread** your **wings**, you do something new and rather difficult or move to a new place, because you feel more confident in your abilities than you used to and you want to gain wider experience. *I led a very confined life in my village so I suppose that I wanted to spread my wings.* V inflects

13 If you **take** someone **under** your **wing**, you look after them, help them, and protect them. *Her boss took her under his wing after fully realising her potential.* V inflects

wing commander, wing commanders. A **wing commander** is a senior officer in the air force. *...Wing Commander Christopher Moran.* N-COUNT; N-TITLE

winged /wɪŋd/. A **winged** insect or other creature has wings. *Flycatchers feed primarily on winged insects.* ◆◇◇◇◇ ADJ: usu ADJ n

winger /wɪŋəʳ/ **wingers.** In a game such as football or hockey, a **winger** is an attacking player who plays mainly on the far left or the far right of the pitch. ◆◆◇◇◇ N-COUNT

wingspan /wɪŋspæn/ **wingspans;** also spelled **wing span**. The **wingspan** of a bird, insect, or aeroplane is the distance from the end of one wing to the end of the other wing. *...a glider with an 18-foot wingspan.* N-COUNT: usu sing, usu with supp

wink /wɪŋk/ **winks, winking, winked** ◆◇◇◇◇

1 When you **wink** at someone, you look towards them and close one eye very briefly, usually as a signal that something is a joke or a secret. *Brian winked at his bride-to-be... He smiled, winked and nodded, giving his seal of approval.* ▶ Also a noun. *I gave her a wink.* VERB V at n V N-COUNT: usu sing

2 If a lamp **winks**, it shines or reflects light in short flashes. *From the hotel window, they could see lights winking on the bay.* VERB =twinkle V

3 If you say that you **did not sleep a wink** or **did not get a wink of sleep**, you mean that you tried to go to sleep but could not; an informal expression. *I didn't get a wink of sleep on the aeroplane.* PHRASE: V inflects

winkle /wɪŋkᵊl/ **winkles, winkling, winkled.** In British English, a **winkle** is a small sea-snail with a hard shell and a soft body which you can eat. N-COUNT

winkle out PHRASAL VERB

1 If you **winkle** information **out** of someone, you get it from them when they do not want to give it to you, often by tricking them; used in informal British English. *My research boys winkle out everything... The detective was trying to winkle information out of her.* =worm out V P n (not pron) V n P of n Also V n P

2 If you **winkle** someone **out** of a place where they are hiding or which they do not want to leave, you make them leave it; used in informal British English. *He somehow managed to winkle Picard out of his room... Political pressure finally winkled him out and on to a plane bound for Berlin... It will not be easy to winkle out the old guard and train younger replacements.* =flush out V n P of n V n P V P n (not pron)

winner /wɪnəʳ/ **winners** ◆◆◆◆◇

1 The **winner** of a prize, race, or competition is the person, animal, or thing that wins it. *She will present the trophies to the award winners... The winner was a horse called Last Town.* N-COUNT ≠loser

2 If you say that something or someone is **a winner**, you mean that they are popular and successful, or that they are likely to be popular and successful; an informal use. *They think the appeal is a winner... Selling was my game and I intended to be a winner.* N-COUNT: usu sing, a N =success, hit ≠failure

3 The **winners** in a particular situation are the people who have benefited from it and are in a better position than they previously were because of it. *There are clear winners when a dam is built. Farmers get irrigation water, businesses get electricity... The real winners of the election, he said, were the Hungarian people.* N-COUNT: usu pl ≠loser

4 In games such as football or tennis, **the winner** is the goal or shot that wins a particular match or point. *Gough scored the winner in extra time.* N-SING: the N

winning /wɪnɪŋ/ ◆◆◆◇◇

1 You can use **winning** to describe a person or thing that wins something such as a competition, game, or election. *The leader of the winning party took her oath of office as prime minister... Hill has never been on the winning side... Donovan scored the winning goal.* ADJ: ADJ n

2 You can use **winning** to describe actions or qualities that please other people and make them feel friendly towards you. *She gave him another of her winning smiles... He had much charm and a winning personality.* ♦ **winningly** *Livingstone smiled again, winningly.* ADJ: ADJ n =engaging ADV-GRADED: ADV with v, ADV adj

3 See also **win**.

winnings /wɪnɪŋz/. You can use **winnings** to refer to the money that someone wins in a competition or by gambling. *I have come to collect my winnings.* ◆◇◇◇◇ N-PLURAL: oft poss N

winnow /wɪnoʊ/ **winnows, winnowing, winnowed.** If you **winnow** a group of things or people, you reduce its size by separating the ones that are useful or relevant from those that are not. *Administration officials have winnowed the list of candidates to three.* VERB V n

winnow out. If you **winnow out** part of a group of things or people, you identify the part that is not useful or relevant and the part that is; used in written English. *The committee will need to winnow out the nonsense and produce more practical proposals if it is to achieve results... Time has winnowed out certain of the essays as superior.* PHRASAL VERB V P n (not pron)

wino /waɪnoʊ/ **winos.** Some people refer to alcoholics as **winos**, especially if the alcoholics are poor or homeless; an informal word which some people find offensive. N-COUNT =drunk

winsome /wɪnsəm/. If you describe a person or their actions or behaviour as **winsome**, you mean that they are attractive and charming. *...a winsome young screen star... She gave him her best winsome smile.* ADJ-GRADED =charming

winter /wɪntəʳ/ **winters, wintering, wintered** ◆◆◆◇◇

1 **Winter** is the season between autumn and spring. In the winter the weather is usually cold. *In winter the nights are long and cold. ...the winter months. ...the late winter of 1941.* N-VAR

2 If an animal or plant **winters** somewhere or **is wintered** there, it spends the winter there. *Once fully acclimatised the birds will winter outside in an aviary... The young seedlings are usually wintered in a cold frame. ...one of the most important sites for wintering wildfowl.* V-ERG V adv/prep be V-ed prep/adv V-ing Also V n prep/adv

3 If you **winter** somewhere, you spend the winter there; a formal use. *The family decided to winter in Nice again.* VERB V prep/adv

winter sports. **Winter sports** are sports that take place on ice or snow, for example skating, skiing, or bobsleigh racing. N-PLURAL

wintertime /wɪntəʳtaɪm/; also spelled **winter time**. **Wintertime** is the period of time during which winter lasts. N-UNCOUNT

wintry /wɪntri/

1 **Wintry** weather is cold and has features that are typical of winter. *Wintry weather continues to sweep across Britain... A wintry wind was blowing. ...a dark wintry day.* ADJ-GRADED: usu ADJ n

2 If you describe someone's attitude or behaviour as **wintry**, you mean that they seem very unfriendly. *He was, according to witnesses, extremely wintry with Her Royal Highness.* ADJ-GRADED =frosty ≠warm

wipe /waɪp/ **wipes, wiping, wiped** ◆◆◆◇◇

1 If you **wipe** something, you rub its surface to remove dirt or liquid from it. *I'll just wipe the table... When he had finished washing he began to wipe the basin clean... Lainey wiped her hands on the towel.* ▶ Also a noun. *Tomorrow I'm going to give the toys a good wipe as some seem a bit greasy.* VERB V n V n with adj V n on n N-COUNT: usu sing

2 If you **wipe** dirt or liquid from something, you remove it, for example by using a cloth or your hand. *Gleb wiped the sweat from his face... He shook his head and wiped his tears with a tissue.* VERB V n prep V n

3 If you say that something **wipes the smile off** someone's **face**, you mean that it suddenly spoils their enjoyment or removes an advantage that they had and that you are pleased about it; an informal expression. *Tony Holmes wiped the smile off the faces of his rivals with a solo 30-second win.* PHRASE: V and Ns inflect PRAGMATICS

4 ● to **wipe the floor with** someone: see **floor.** ● to **wipe the slate clean**: see **slate.**

wipe away or **wipe off.** If you **wipe away** or **wipe off** dirt or liquid from something, you remove it, for example by using a cloth or your hand. *He wiped* PHRASAL VERB V P n (not pron) *away the blood with a paper napkin... She applied a little lipstick, wiped it off, but it left a pink tinge.*

wipe down. If you **wipe down** something, you wash or dry its surface completely. *The girls took it in turn to wipe down the tables after meals... Ben will have to wipe down that wall if you leave any marks.* PHRASAL VERB V P n (not pron) Also V n P

wipe off. See **wipe away**. PHRASAL VERB

wipe out. To **wipe out** something such as a place or a group of people or animals means to destroy them completely. *Experts say if the island is not protected, the spill could wipe out the Gulf's turtle population... The man is a fanatic who is determined to wipe out any opposition to the way he conducts himself.* PHRASAL VERB =destroy V P n (not pron) Also V n P

wipe up. If you **wipe up** dirt or liquid from something, you remove it using a cloth. *I spilled my coffee all over the table and Mom leaned across me to wipe it up... Wipe up spills immediately.* PHRASAL VERB V n P V P n (not pron)

wiper /waɪpəʳ/ **wipers.** A **wiper** is the same as a **windscreen wiper.** N-COUNT: usu pl

wire /waɪəʳ/ **wires, wiring, wired** ◆◆◆◇◇

1 A **wire** is a long thin piece of metal that is used to fasten things or to carry electric current. *...fine copper wire. ...gadgets which detect electrical wires, pipes and timbers in walls.* N-VAR

2 A **wire** is a cable which carries power or signals from one place to another. *I ripped out the telephone wire that ran through to his office. ...the voltage of the overhead wires.* N-COUNT: usu supp N =cable

3 If you **wire** something such as a building or piece of equipment, you install or connect wires inside it so that electricity or signals can pass into or through it. *...learning to wire and plumb the house herself... Lamps should be safely wired... 95% of all American households will be wired for cable in the year 2000. ...a badly wired appliance.* ► **Wire up** means the same as **wire**. *He was helping wire up the Channel Tunnel last season... Wire the thermometers up to trigger off an alarm bell if the temperature drops... Security experts wired up dozens of expensive plants to the main alarm system at his mansion.* VERB V n be V-ed *for* n V-ed PHRASAL VERB V P n (not pron) V n P V P n *to/into* n Also V n P *to/into* n

4 In American English, a **wire** is the same as a **telegram.** N-COUNT =telegram

5 In American English, if you **wire** a person, you send them a telegram. *He wired the chairman immediately... They wired back a long list of books... If I get another tummy ache, I will wire you to come.* VERB V n V n with *back* V n to-inf Also V

6 In American English, if you **wire** an amount of money to a person or place, you instruct a bank to send it to the person or place by a telegram message. *I'm wiring you some money... They arranged to wire the money from the United States... Investigators say nearly $100,000 was wired into the suspect's bank accounts.* VERB V n n V n prep Also V n

7 See also **barbed wire, high wire, hot wire, live wire.**

wire up. See **wire** 3. PHRASAL VERB

wired /waɪəʳd/

1 In American English, if someone is **wired**, they are tense, nervous, and unable to relax; an informal use. *Tonight he is manic, wired and uptight.* ADJ-GRADED: usu v-link ADJ =edgy, uptight

2 Wired is used to describe material or clothing that has wires sewn into it in order to keep it stiff. *...a length of wired ribbon.* ADJ: usu ADJ n

wireless /waɪəʳləs/ **wirelesses** ◆◇◇◇◇

1 Wireless is a system by which messages are sent over a distance by radio signals; an old-fashioned use. *...the development of wireless and radar... They confirmed by wireless that she was picking up survivors.* N-UNCOUNT =radio

2 A **wireless** or **wireless set** is a radio; an old-fashioned use. N-COUNT =radio

wiretap /waɪəʳtæp/ **wiretaps, wiretapping, wiretapped;** also spelled **wire-tap.** In American English, if someone **wiretaps** your telephone, they attach a special device to the line so that they can secretly listen to your conversations. The usual British word is **tap.** *The coach said his club had wire-tapped the hotel room of a player during a road trip.* ► Also a noun. *...tapes of telephone conversations that can have been obtained only by illegal wiretaps.* ♦ **wiretapping** *The legislator criticized the report for failing to investigate allegations of wiretapping.* VERB =bug V n N-COUNT N-UNCOUNT

wire wool. In British English, **wire wool** consists of very thin pieces of wire twisted together, often in the form of small pads. These are used to clean wooden and metal objects. The American term is **steel wool.** N-UNCOUNT =steel wool

wiring /waɪərɪŋ/. The **wiring** in a building or machine is the system of wires that supply electricity to the different parts of it. ◆◇◇◇◇ N-UNCOUNT

wiry /waɪəri/

1 Someone who is **wiry** is rather thin but is also strong. *His body is wiry and athletic.* ADJ =sinewy ≠flabby

2 Something such as hair or grass that is **wiry** is stiff and rough to touch. *Her wiry hair was pushed up on top of her head in an untidy bun.* ADJ =coarse ≠soft

wisdom /wɪzdəm/ **wisdoms** ◆◆◇◇◇

1 Wisdom is the ability to use your experience and knowledge in order to make sensible decisions or judgements. *...the patience and wisdom that comes from old age. ...a great man, who spoke words of great wisdom.* N-UNCOUNT

2 Wisdom is the store of knowledge that a society or culture has collected over a long period of time. *...a folksy piece of wisdom. ...this church's original Semitic wisdom, religion and faith. ...a simpler and more humane approach, based on ancient wisdoms and 'natural' mechanisms.* N-VAR

3 If you talk about **the wisdom of** a particular decision or action, you are talking about how sensible it is. *Many Lithuanians have expressed doubts about the wisdom of the decision.* N-SING: *the* N *of* n/-ing

4 You can use **wisdom** to refer to ideas that are accepted by a large number of people. *Health education wisdom in the UK differs from that of the United States... Unchallenged wisdoms flow swiftly among the middle classes.* N-VAR: supp N

wisdom tooth, wisdom teeth. Your **wisdom teeth** are the four large teeth at the back of your mouth which usually grow much later than your other teeth. N-COUNT

wise /waɪz/ **wises, wising, wised; wiser, wisest** ◆◆◆◇◇

1 A **wise** person is able to use their experience and knowledge in order to make sensible decisions and judgements. *She has the air of a wise woman... You're a wise old man: tell me what to do.* ♦ **wisely** *The three of us stood around the machine nodding wisely.* ADJ-GRADED ≠foolish ADV-GRADED: ADV with v

2 A **wise** action or decision is sensible. *It's never wise to withhold evidence... She had made a very wise decision... It is wise to seek help and counsel as soon as possible.* ♦ **wisely** *They've invested their money wisely... Our man had wisely decided to be picked up at the farm.* ADJ-GRADED: oft *it* v-link ADJ to-inf =sensible ADV-GRADED: usu ADV with v

3 If someone says to you that it **would be wise** to do something, they are advising you to do it, because it is the most sensible and reasonable action or decision in a particular situation. *It would be wise to get his eyes checked to ensure there is no problem.* PHRASES PHR to-inf PRAGMATICS

4 If you **get wise to** something, you find out about it, especially when someone has been trying to keep it secret; an informal expression. *Dealers have already got wise to the trend and increased their prices accordingly.* V inflects, PHR n =wise up to

5 If you say that someone is **none the wiser** after an event or an explanation, or that nobody is **any the wiser** after it, you mean that they have failed to understand it, or are not fully aware of what happened. *The brewers are still none the wiser about the shape the Government envisages for the industry... We could have stolen the original from the warehouse without you being any the wiser.* v-link PHR

wise up. If someone **wises up** to a situation or state of affairs, they become aware of it and take appropriate action; an informal use. *Some insurers have wised up to the fact that their clients were getting very cheap insurance... It's time to wise up and tell those around you that enough is enough.* PHRASAL VERB =get wise V P to n V P

-wise /-waɪz/

1 **-wise** is added to nouns to form adverbs indicating that something is the case when considering the particular thing mentioned. *Career-wise, this illness couldn't have come at a worse time... It was a much better day weather-wise... Because the work was voluntary it was flexible, time-wise.* COMB in ADV: ADV with cl

2 **-wise** is added to nouns to form adverbs indicating that someone behaves in the same way as the person or thing that is mentioned. *We were housed student-wise in dormitory rooms... Kenny, struggling with too many chairs, moved crabwise towards the door.* COMB in ADV: ADV after v =-like

wisecrack /waɪzkræk/ **wisecracks.** A **wisecrack** is a clever remark that is intended to be amusing, but is often rather unkind. N-COUNT =quip

wisecracking /waɪzkrækɪŋ/; also spelled **wise-cracking**. You can use **wisecracking** to describe someone who keeps making wisecracks. *...a wisecracking private eye.* ADJ: usu ADJ n

wise guy, wise guys; also spelled **wiseguy**. If you say that someone is a **wise guy**, you dislike the fact that they think they are very clever and always have an answer for everything; an informal expression, used showing disapproval. N-COUNT PRAGMATICS =smart alec

wish /wɪʃ/ **wishes, wishing, wished** ◆◆◆◆◇

1 A **wish** is a desire or strong feeling that you want to have something or do something. *She was sincere and genuine in her wish to make amends for the past... Clearly she had no wish for conversation... She wanted to go everywhere in the world. She soon got her wish... The decision was made against the wishes of the party leader.* • See also **death wish**. N-COUNT: oft with poss =desire

2 If you **wish** to do something or to have it done for you, you want to do it or have it done; a formal use. *If you wish to go away for the weekend, our office will be delighted to make hotel reservations... We can dress as we wish now... There were the collaborators, who wished for a German victory.* VERB V to-inf V for n

3 **Wish** is used in expressions such as **I don't wish to be rude** or **without wishing to be rude** as a way of apologising or warning someone in advance when you are going to say something which might upset, annoy, or worry them. *I don't wish to sound callous, but I am glad I wasn't here... Without wishing to be unkind, you must admit, she's not the most interesting company.* VB: no cont, with brd-neg PRAGMATICS V to-inf

4 If you **wish** something were true, you would like it to be true, even though you know that it is impossible or unlikely. *I wish I could do that... I wish it weren't true... Pa, I wish you wouldn't shout... The world is not always what we wish it to be.* VB: no cont V that V n to-inf

5 If you **wish for** something, you express the desire silently to yourself. In fairy stories, when someone wishes for something, it often happens by magic. *We have all wished for men who are more like women... A philosopher once said, 'Be careful what you wish for; you might get it.'* ► Also a noun. *The custom is for people to try and eat 12 grapes as the clock strikes midnight. Those who are successful can make a wish.* VERB V for n N-COUNT

6 **Wish** is used in sentences such as **I could not wish for anything better** to indicate that you are very pleased with what you have and could not imagine anything better. *I really could not have wished for a better teacher... Who could wish for a better opportunity?.* VB: no cont, usu with brd-neg =ask V for n

7 If you say that you would not **wish** something **on** someone, you mean that it is so unpleasant that you would not want them to be forced to experience or deal with it. *It's a horrid experience and I wouldn't wish it on my worst enemy.* VB: no cont, with brd-neg V n on n

8 If you **wish** someone something such as luck or happiness, you express the hope that they will be lucky or happy. *I wish you both a very good journey... Goodbye, Hanu. I wish you well.* VERB V n n V n adv

9 If you express your good **wishes** towards someone, you are politely expressing your friendly feelings towards them and your hope that they will be successful or happy. *I found George's story very sad. Please give him my best wishes... Western leaders sent good wishes to the new American president.* N-PLURAL: adj N PRAGMATICS

wishbone /wɪʃboʊn/ **wishbones.** A **wishbone** is a V-shaped bone in chickens, turkeys, and other birds. N-COUNT

wishful thinking. If you say that an idea, wish, or hope is **wishful thinking**, you mean that it has failed to come true or is unlikely to come true. *It is wishful thinking to expect deeper change under his leadership.* ◆◇◇◇◇ N-UNCOUNT

wish list, wish lists. If you refer to someone's **wish list**, you mean the things which they would ideally like to happen or be given to them, although this is often unlikely in reality; an informal expression. *Every Christmas there seems to be one special toy that tops the wish list of every child... The resolution that was passed was a wish list that nobody could deliver.* N-COUNT: oft with poss

wishy-washy /wɪʃi wɒʃi/. If you say that someone is **wishy-washy**, you are critical of them because their ideas are not firm or clear; an informal word. *If there's anything I can't stand it's an indecisive, wishy-washy customer.* ADJ-GRADED PRAGMATICS

wisp /wɪsp/ **wisps** ◆◇◇◇◇

1 A **wisp** of hair is a small, thin, untidy bunch of it. *She smoothed away a wisp of hair from her eyes.* N-COUNT: usu N of n

2 A **wisp** of something such as smoke or cloud is an amount of it in a long thin shape. *A thin wisp of smoke straggled up through the trees. ...an occasional wisp of white cloud.* N-COUNT: usu N of n

wispy /wɪspi/

1 If someone has **wispy** hair, their hair is thin and grows in fine strands. *...grey wispy hair straggled down to her shoulders.* ADJ-GRADED =straggly

2 A **wispy** cloud is thin or faint. *The half moon is hidden behind some wispy clouds.* ADJ-GRADED: usu ADJ n

wisteria /wɪstɪəriə/. **Wisteria** is a type of climbing plant, usually with mauve or white flowers. N-UNCOUNT

wistful /wɪstfʊl/. Someone who is **wistful** is rather sad because they want something and know that they cannot have it. *I can't help feeling slightly wistful about the perks I'm giving up... He has a wistful look.* ♦ **wistfully** *'I wish I had a little brother,' said Daphne wistfully.* ♦ **wistfulness** *I sensed her wistfulness when she talked about vacations her relatives took.* ◆◇◇◇◇ ADJ-GRADED ADV-GRADED: usu ADV with v N-UNCOUNT

wit /wɪt/ **wits** ◆◆◇◇◇

1 **Wit** is the ability to use words or ideas in an amusing, clever, and imaginative way. *Boulding was known for his biting wit... They love her practical attitude to life, her zest and wit.* N-UNCOUNT

2 If you describe someone as a **wit**, you mean they have the ability to use words or ideas in an amusing, clever, and imaginative way. *Holmes was gregarious, a great wit, a man of wide interests.* N-COUNT

3 If you say that someone has **the wit** to do something, you mean they have the intelligence and understanding to make the right decision or take the right action in a particular situation. *The information is there and waiting to be accessed by anyone with the wit to use it.* N-SING: the N to-inf =sense, gumption

4 You can refer to your ability to think quickly and cleverly in a difficult situation as your **wits**. *She has used her wits to progress to the powerful position she holds today.* N-PLURAL: usu poss N

5 You can use **wits** in expressions such as **frighten someone out of their wits** and **scare the wits out of someone** to emphasize that someone or something worries or frightens someone very much. *You scared us out of our wits. We heard you had an accident. ...a huge bass drum which frightened the wits out of the organist each time it was banged.* N-PLURAL: usu out of poss N PRAGMATICS =terrify

6 If you **have your wits about** you or **keep your wits about** you, you are alert and ready to act in a difficult situation. *Travellers need to keep their wits about them.* PHRASES V inflects

7 If you say that you are **at your wits' end**, you are emphasizing that you are so worried and exhausted by problems or difficulties that you do not know what to do next. *We row a lot and we never have time on our own. I'm at my wit's end.* usu v-link PHR PRAGMATICS

8 If you **pit** your **wits against** someone, you V inflects,

compete against them in a test of knowledge or intelligence. *He has to pit his wits against an adversary who is cool, clever and cunning.* PHR n

9 To wit is used to indicate that you are about to state or describe something more precisely; a literary expression. *He'd like 'happiness' to be given a new and more scientifically descriptive label, to wit 'Major affective disorder, pleasant type'.* PHR with cl, PHR n PRAGMATICS =namely

10 ● **battle of wits**: see **battle**.

witch /wɪtʃ/ **witches** ◆◆◇◇◇

1 In fairy tales, a **witch** is a woman, usually an old woman with a pointed black hat, who has evil magic powers. N-COUNT

2 A **witch** is a man or woman who claims to have magic powers and to be able to use them for good or bad purposes. N-COUNT

witchcraft /wɪtʃkrɑːft, -kræft/. **Witchcraft** is the use of magic powers, especially evil ones. ◆◇◇◇◇ N-UNCOUNT =sorcery

witch doctor, witch doctors; also spelled **witch-doctor**. A **witch doctor** is a person in some societies, for example in Africa, who is thought to have magic powers which can be used to heal people. N-COUNT

witch hazel. **Witch hazel** is a liquid that you put on your skin if it is sore or bruised, in order to heal it. N-UNCOUNT

witch-hunt, witch-hunts. A **witch-hunt** is an attempt to find and punish a particular group of people who are being blamed for something, often simply because of their opinions and not because they have actually done anything wrong; used showing disapproval. N-COUNT: oft N *against* n PRAGMATICS

with /wɪð, wɪθ/; pronounced /wɪð/ for meanings 20 and 21. ◆◆◆◆◆

In addition to the uses shown below, **with** is used after some verbs, nouns and adjectives in order to introduce extra information. **With** is also used in most reciprocal verbs, such as 'agree' or 'fight', and in some phrasal verbs, such as 'deal with' and 'dispense with'.

1 If one person is **with** another, they are together in one place. *With her were her son and daughter-in-law... She is currently staying with her father at his home.* PREP

2 If something is put **with** or is **with** something else, they are used at the same time. *Serve hot, with pasta or rice and French beans... Cookies are just the thing to serve with tall glasses of real lemonade.* PREP

3 If you do something **with** someone else, you both do it together or are both involved in it. *Parents will be given reports on their child's progress and the right to discuss it with a teacher... He walked with her to the front door.* PREP

4 If you fight, argue, or compete **with** someone, you oppose them. *About a thousand students fought with riot police in the capital... He was in an argument with his landlord downstairs.* PREP

5 If you do something **with** a particular tool, object, or substance, you do it using that tool, object, or substance. *Remove the meat with a fork and divide it among four plates... Pack the fruits and nuts into the jars and cover with brandy... Doctors are treating him with the drug AZT.* PREP

6 If someone stands or goes somewhere **with** something, they are carrying it. *A man came round with a tray of chocolates... A young woman came in with a cup of coffee.* PREP

7 Someone or something **with** a particular feature or possession has that feature or possession. *He was in his early forties, tall and blond with bright blue eyes... Someone with an income of $34,895 can afford this loan.* PREP

8 Someone **with** an illness has that illness. *I spent a week in bed with flu.* PREP

9 If something is filled or covered **with** a substance or **with** things, it has that substance or those things in it or on it. *His legs were caked with dried mud... They sat at a Formica table cluttered with dirty tea cups. ...rivers teeming with salmon and trout.* PREP

10 If you are, for example, pleased or cross **with** someone or something, you have that feeling towards them. *He was still a little angry with her... After sixteen years of marriage they have grown bored with each other... I am happy with that decision.* PREP: adj/n PREP n

11 You use **with** to indicate what a state, quality, or action relates to, involves, or affects. *Our aim is to allow student teachers to become familiar with the classroom... He still has a serious problem with money... Depression lowers the human ability to cope with disease.* PREP

12 You use **with** when indicating the way something is done or the feeling that someone has when they do something. *...teaching her to read music with skill and sensitivity... He agreed, but with reluctance.* PREP

13 You use **with** when indicating a sound, gesture, or facial expression that is made at the same time as an action. *With a sigh, she leant back and closed her eyes... The front door closed with a crash behind him... Her eyes stared into his with an expression of absolute honesty.* PREP

14 You use **with** to indicate the feeling that makes someone have a particular appearance or type of behaviour. *Gil was white and trembling with anger... I felt sick to my stomach with sadness for them... His father's body was hot with fever.* PREP

15 You use **with** when mentioning the position or appearance of someone or something at the time that they do something, or what someone else is doing at that time. *Joanne stood with her hands on the sink, staring out the window... Michelle had fallen asleep with her head against his shoulder... She walked back to the bus stop, with him following her.* PREP: PREP n prep/-ing

16 You use **with** to introduce a current situation that is a factor affecting another situation. *With all the night school courses available, there is no excuse for not getting some sort of training... With the win, the US reclaimed the cup for the first time since 1985.* PREP PRAGMATICS

17 You use **with** when making a comparison or contrast between the situations of different people or things. *We're not like them. It's different with us... Skiing, camping, hiking, and wind surfing are all activities through which I've met athletic, fun people. The same with most team sports.* PREP PRAGMATICS

18 If something increases or decreases **with** a factor, it changes as that factor changes. *The risk of developing heart disease increases with the number of cigarettes smoked... Blood pressure decreases with exercise.* PREP: v PREP n

19 If something moves **with** a wind or current, it moves in the same direction as the wind or current. *...a piece of driftwood carried down with the current... We left him there to float off with the tide, and told him to follow the coast.* PREP ≠against

20 If someone says that they are **with** you, they mean that they understand what you are saying; an informal use. *Yes, I know who you mean. Yes, now I'm with you... I'm not with you. Tell me what you mean.* PREP: v-link PREP n PRAGMATICS

21 If someone says that they are **with** you, they mean that they support or approve of what you are doing. *'I'm with you all the way.'—'Thank you.'* PREP: v-link PREP n =behind

withdraw /wɪðdrɔː/ **withdraws, withdrawing, withdrew, withdrawn** ◆◆◆◆◇

1 If you **withdraw** something from a place, you remove it or take it away; a formal use. *He reached into his pocket and withdrew a sheet of notepaper... Cassandra withdrew her hand from Roger's.* VERB =remove V n V n *from* n

2 When groups of people such as troops **withdraw** or when someone **withdraws** them, they leave the place where they are fighting or where they are based and return nearer home. *He stated that all foreign forces would withdraw as soon as the crisis ended... The United States has announced it is to withdraw forty-thousand troops from Western Europe in the next year... Troops withdrew from the north east of the country last March.* V-ERG V V n *from* n V *from* n Also V *to* n

3 If you **withdraw** money from a bank account, you take it out of that account. *Open a savings account that does not charge ridiculous fees to withdraw money... They withdrew 100 dollars from a bank account after checking out of their hotel.* VERB V n V n *from* n

4 If you **withdraw** to another room, you go there; a formal use. *He and the others withdrew to their rented rooms... He poured the wine and then withdrew again... Kenworthy withdrew into his bedroom, washed and shaved.* VERB V to n V V into n

5 If you **withdraw** from an activity or organization, you stop taking take part in it. *The African National Congress threatened to withdraw from the talks.* VERB V from n Also V

6 If you **withdraw** a remark or statement that you have made, you say that you want people to ignore it; a formal use. *He withdrew his remarks and explained that he had meant to say 'discreet' instead of 'decent'.* VERB =retract V n

withdrawal /wɪðdrɔːəl/ **withdrawals** ◆◆◆◇◇

1 The **withdrawal** of something is the act or process of removing it, or ending it; a formal use. *...withdrawal of friendship... If you experience any unusual symptoms after withdrawal of the treatment then contact your doctor. ...allied troop withdrawal from the north of the country.* N-VAR: usu N of n

2 Someone's **withdrawal** from an activity or an organization is their decision to stop taking part in it. *...his withdrawal from government in 1946.* N-UNCOUNT: usu with supp

3 A **withdrawal** is an amount of money that you take from your bank account. N-COUNT ≠deposit

4 The **withdrawal of** a remark or statement that you have made is the act of saying that you want people to ignore it. *The charity says it wants a withdrawal of the comments.* N-SING: N of n =retraction

5 **Withdrawal** is the period during which someone feels ill after they have stopped taking a drug which they were addicted to. *Withdrawal from heroin is actually like a severe attack of gastric flu.* N-UNCOUNT

6 **Withdrawal** is behaviour in which someone prefers to be alone and does not want to talk to other people. *...an inability to cope with emotional problems except by retreating into withdrawal.* N-UNCOUNT

withdrawal symptoms. When someone has **withdrawal symptoms**, they feel ill after they have stopped taking a drug which they were addicted to. *If these drugs are stopped abruptly then some withdrawal symptoms may occur.* N-PLURAL

withdrawn /wɪðdrɔːn/ ◆◇◇◇◇

1 **Withdrawn** is the past participle of **withdraw**.

2 Someone who is **withdrawn** is very quiet, and does not want to talk to other people. *Her husband had become withdrawn and moody.* ADJ-GRADED: v-link ADJ =introverted

withdrew /wɪðdruː/. **Withdrew** is the past tense of **withdraw**.

wither /wɪðəʳ/ **withers, withering, withered** ◆◇◇◇◇

1 If someone or something **withers**, they become very weak. *When he went into retirement, he visibly withered... The question now is whether the railways will flourish or wither in the hands of the private sector.* ▶ **Wither away** means the same as **wither**. *To see my body literally wither away before my eyes was exasperating.* VERB V PHRASAL VERB V P

2 If a flower or plant **withers**, it shrinks, dries up, and dies. *The flowers in Isabel's room had withered... Farmers in the Midwest have watched their crops wither because of drought conditions.* ♦ **withered** *...a mound of withered leaves... His fridge was bare apart from three very withered tomatoes.* VERB V ADJ-GRADED: usu ADJ n

3 The highest part of a horse's back, behind its neck, is referred to as its **withers**. N-PLURAL

wither away. See **wither** 1. PHRASAL VERB

withered /wɪðəʳd/

1 If you describe a person or a part of their body as **withered**, you mean that their skin is very wrinkled and dry, and looks old. *Diana grasped his face in her withered hands. ...the bartender's withered face.* ADJ-GRADED: usu ADJ n =wizened

2 **Withered** is used to describe someone's leg, arm, or other part of their body when it is thin and weak because of disease or paralysis. *She has one slightly withered leg, noticeably thinner than the other.* ADJ: usu ADJ n

withering /wɪðərɪŋ/. A **withering** look or remark is very angry or scornful, and is often intended to make someone feel ashamed or stupid. *Deborah Jane's mother gave her a withering look... She launched a withering attack on the Press.* ADJ-GRADED: usu ADJ n

withhold /wɪðhoʊld/ **withholds, withholding, withheld** /wɪðheld/. If you **withhold** something that someone wants, you do not let them have it; a formal word. *Police withheld the dead boy's name yesterday until relatives could be told... Financial aid for Britain has been withheld... The captain decided to withhold the terrible news even from his officers.* ♦ **withholding** *The withholding of property from the market may cause prices to be higher than normal.* ◆◆◇◇◇ VERB V n V n from n Also V from n/-ing N-UNCOUNT: usu the N of n

within /wɪðɪn/ ◆◆◆◆◆

1 If something is **within** a place, area, or object, it is inside it or surrounded by it; a formal use. *Clients are entertained within private dining rooms... An olive-coloured tent stood within a thicket of trees. ...a 1987 agreement which would recognise Quebec as a distinct society within Canada.* ▶ Also an adverb. *A small voice called from within. 'Yes, just coming.'* PREP =in, inside ≠outside ADV: usu from ADV, also ADV after v

2 Something that happens or exists **within** a society, organization, or system, happens or exists inside it or to something that is part of it. *The motives that attract people to work within a social service are variable. ...the spirit of self-sacrifice within an army... Within criminal law almost anything could be defined as 'crime'.* ▶ Also an adverb. *The Church of England, with threats of split from within, has still to make up its mind.* PREP =in ADV: usu from ADV, also ADV after v

3 If you experience a particular feeling, you can say that it is **within** you; a literary use. *He's coping much better within himself... You've got to identify these inadequacies within yourself.* ▶ Also an adverb. *'God!' cried Dennis from within. 'Oh, my God!'* PREP: PREP pron =in ADV: usu from ADV, also ADV after v

4 If something is **within** a particular limit or set of rules, it does not go beyond it or is not more than what is allowed. *Troops have agreed to stay within specific boundaries to avoid confrontations... Exercise within your comfortable limit... The film will be finished within its budget.* PREP =inside

5 If you are **within** a particular distance of a place, you are less than that distance from it. *The man was within a few feet of him... It was within easy walking distance of the hotel... The rebels have advanced to within 150 kms of the capital.* PREP

6 **Within** a particular length of time means before that length of time has passed. *About 40% of all students entering as freshmen graduate within 4 years... Yasir Arafat is said to be planning to go to Syria within 48 hours.* PREP: PREP amount

7 If something is **within sight**, **within earshot**, or **within reach**, you can see it, hear it, or reach it. *His twenty-five-foot boat was moored within sight of West Church. ...her heels clicking on the tiled floor, probably an irritating noise to other people within earshot... Amy looked to see if there was anything within reach that she could give him to ease the pain.* PREP ≠out of

8 • **within reason**: see **reason**.

without /wɪðaʊt/ ◆◆◆◆◆

In addition to the uses shown below, **without** is used in the phrasal verbs 'do without', 'go without', and 'reckon without'.

1 You use **without** to indicate that someone or something does not have or use the thing mentioned. *I don't like myself without a beard... She wore a brown shirt pressed without a wrinkle. ...a meal without barbecue sauce.* PREP ≠with

2 If one thing happens **without** another thing, or if you do something **without** doing something else, the second thing does not happen or occur. *He was offered a generous pension provided he left without a fuss... They worked without a break until about eight in the evening... Alex had done this without consulting her.* PREP: PREP n/-ing

3 If you do something **without** a particular feeling, you do not have that feeling when you do it. *Janet Magnusson watched his approach without enthusiasm... 'Hello, Swanson,' he said without surprise.* PREP ≠with

4 If you do something **without** someone else, they are not in the same place as you are or are not involved in the same action as you. *I told Franklin he would have to start dinner without me... How can I* PREP ≠with *rebuild my life without my husband?... We would never go anywhere without you.*

withstand /wɪðstæ̱nd/ **withstands, withstanding, withstood** /wɪðstʊ̱d/. If something or someone **withstands** a force or action, they survive it or do not give in to it; a formal word. *...armoured vehicles designed to withstand chemical attack... Exercise really can help you withstand stresses and strains more easily.* ◆◇◇◇◇ VERB =stand up to V n

witless /wɪ̱tləs/. If you describe something or someone as **witless**, you think they are very foolish or stupid. *...a witless, nasty piece of gutter journalism.* ADJ PRAGMATICS =mindless, stupid

witness /wɪ̱tnəs/ **witnesses, witnessing, witnessed** ◆◆◆◇◇

1 A **witness** to an event such as an accident or crime is a person who saw it. *Witnesses to the crash say they saw an explosion just before the disaster... No witnesses have come forward.* N-COUNT: oft N to n =eye-witness

2 If you **witness** something, you see it happen. *Anyone who witnessed the attack should call the police... It was the quickest swimming lesson I'd ever witnessed.* VERB =see V n

3 A **witness** is someone who appears in a court of law to say what they know about a crime or other event. *In the next three or four days, eleven witnesses will be called to testify.* N-COUNT: oft N for n

4 A **witness** is someone who writes their name on a document that you have signed, to confirm that it really is your signature. N-COUNT

5 If someone **witnesses** your signature on a document, they write their name after it, to confirm that it really is your signature. *Ask a friend, (not your spouse), to witness your signature.* VERB V n

6 If you say that a place or period of time **witnessed** a particular event or change, you mean that it happened in that place or during that period of time. You can also say that a person **witnessed** an event or change, meaning that it happened during that person's lifetime. *India has witnessed many political changes in recent years... The year 1886 witnessed the first extended translation into English of the writings of Eliphas Levi... At present, we are witnessing another building boom.* VERB =see V n

7 You use **witness** to introduce an example of what you have just been talking about; a formal use. *Americans are a generous people: witness the increase in charitable giving, even during the recession of the 1980s.* VB: only imper PRAGMATICS V n

8 If you **are witness to** something, you see it happen; a fairly formal expression. *Too often children are witness to a disturbing amount of violence.* PHRASES V inflects, PHR n

9 If something or someone **bears witness to** something else, they show or say that it exists or happened; a formal expression. *Many of these poems bear witness to his years spent in India, England, California and China... Many veterans believe it is their job to bear witness to the horrors of war that they personally experienced.* V inflects, PHR n =testify

wi̱tness box. In British English, **the witness-box** in a court of law is the place where people stand or sit when they are giving evidence. The usual American expression is **witness stand**. N-SING: the N

witter /wɪ̱təʳ/ **witters, wittering, wittered.** In informal British English, if you say that someone **is wittering** about something, you mean that they are talking a lot about things that you think are silly and boring. *They just sat there wittering about what lectures they had tomorrow.* ► **Witter on** means the same as **witter**. *They started wittering on about their last trip to Provence.* VERB PRAGMATICS =prattle V about n Also V PHRASAL VERB V P about n Also V P

witticism /wɪ̱tɪsɪzəm/ **witticisms.** A **witticism** is a witty remark or joke; a formal word. N-COUNT =quip

wittingly /wɪ̱tɪŋli/. If you do something **wittingly**, you are fully aware of what you are doing and what its consequences will be; a formal word. *When she had an affair with her friend's husband, she wittingly set off a chain of crises.* ADV: usu ADV with v, also ADV adj ≠unwittingly

witty /wɪ̱ti/ **wittier, wittiest.** Someone or something that is **witty** is amusing in a clever way. *His plays were very good, very witty... He is one of those genuinely witty speakers to whom one could listen for hours.* ♦ **wittily** *The play deals wittily and intelligently with the pain of betrayal... 'Count Dracula, I presume,' I said wittily.* ◆◆◇◇◇ ADJ-GRADED; ADV-GRADED: usu ADV with v, also ADV adj

wives /wa̱ɪvz/. **Wives** is the plural of **wife**.

wizard /wɪ̱zəʳd/ **wizards** ◆◇◇◇◇

1 In legends and fairy stories, a **wizard** is a man who has magic powers. N-COUNT

2 If you admire someone because they are very good at doing a particular thing, you can say they are a **wizard**. *...a financial wizard... Accountant John Talbot is a wizard with numbers.* N-COUNT: with supp PRAGMATICS

wizardry /wɪ̱zəʳdri/. You can refer to a very clever achievement or piece of work as **wizardry**, especially when you do not understand how it is done. *...a piece of technical wizardry.* N-UNCOUNT

wizened /wɪ̱zᵊnd/. A **wizened** person is old and has very wrinkled skin. *...a little wizened old fellow with no teeth.* ADJ-GRADED

wk, wks. wk is a written abbreviation for **week**. *...6 wks holiday.* =week

wobble /wɒ̱bᵊl/ **wobbles, wobbling, wobbled** ◆◇◇◇◇

1 If something or someone **wobbles**, they make small movements from side to side, for example because they are unsteady. *A gravitational wave made the spacecraft wobble... Just then, Bart returned, wobbling on his skates... I narrowly missed a cyclist who wobbled into my path... He placed one hand heavily on a fragile, wobbling table.* ► Also a noun. *We might look for a tiny wobble in the position of a star.* VERB V V prep/adv V-ing N-VAR

2 If a person or government **wobbles**, they suddenly appear less secure or less sure about something; used in journalism. *The coach began to wobble when some of his team selections provoked much baffled comment.* ► Also a noun. *Even a small wobble will hurt its banks, which have roughly $120 billion in outstanding property loans.* VERB V N-VAR

wobbly /wɒ̱bli/ ◆◇◇◇◇

1 Something that is **wobbly** moves unsteadily from side to side. *I was sitting on a wobbly plastic chair. ...a wobbly green jelly. ...wobbly teeth.* ADJ-GRADED

2 If you feel **wobbly** or if your legs feel **wobbly**, you feel weak and have difficulty standing up, especially because you are afraid, ill, or exhausted. *She could not maintain her balance and moved in a wobbly fashion... Ryan was exhausted by the flight and walked off with wobbly legs to find Clark.* ADJ-GRADED

3 If a person's voice is **wobbly**, it sounds weak and keeps varying in pitch, for example because the person is about to cry. *'So that's why I want to go home,' he said in a wobbly voice.* ADJ-GRADED =quavering

4 If you describe an organization, economy, or plan as **wobbly**, you think it is not very good or will not be successful. *...cheap deals on wobbly airlines... Both countries suffer from soaring unemployment, large budget deficits and wobbly financial sectors.* ADJ-GRADED =unstable

wodge /wɒ̱dʒ/ **wodges.** In British English, a **wodge** of something is a large amount of it or a large piece of it; an informal word. *...a wodge of syrupy sponge.* N-COUNT: usu N of n

woe /wo̱ʊ/ **woes** ◆◇◇◇◇

1 **Woe** is very great sadness; a literary use. *He listened to my tale of woe... All around women wailed their woe or screamed abuse.* N-UNCOUNT ≠joy

2 You can refer to someone's problems or misfortunes as their **woes**; used in written English. *He did not tell his relatives and friends about his woes.* N-PLURAL: usu with poss

3 • **woe betide**: see **betide**.

woebegone /wo̱ʊbɪgɒn/. Someone who is **woebegone** is very sad; used in written English. *She sniffed and looked woebegone.* ADJ-GRADED =miserable ≠joyful

woeful /wo̱ʊfʊl/ ◆◇◇◇◇

1 If someone or something is **woeful**, they are very sad. *...a woeful ballad.* ♦ **woefully** *He said woefully: 'I love my country, but it does not give a damn about me.'* ADJ-GRADED; ADV-GRADED: ADV with v

2 You can use **woeful** to emphasize that something is very bad or undesirable. *Such attitudes are the product of woeful ignorance. ...the woeful state of the economy.* ♦ **woefully** *Public expenditure on* ADJ-GRADED: usu ADJ n PRAGMATICS; ADV-GRADED:

the arts is woefully inadequate... Most of the ships were woefully short of ammunition. usu ADV adj, also ADV before v

wog /wɒg/ **wogs. Wog** is an extremely offensive word for anyone whose skin is not white; used in British English. N-COUNT

wok /wɒk/ **woks.** A **wok** is a large bowl-shaped pan which is used for Chinese-style cooking. N-COUNT

woke /woʊk/. **Woke** is the past tense of **wake**.

woken /woʊkən/. **Woken** is the past participle of **wake**.

wolf /wʊlf/ **wolves; wolfs, wolfing, wolfed** ◆◇◇◇◇

1 A **wolf** is a wild animal that looks like a large dog. N-COUNT

2 If someone **wolfs** their food, they eat it all very quickly and greedily; an informal use. *I was back in the changing-room wolfing tea and sandwiches.* VERB =gobble V n
▶ **Wolf down** means the same as **wolf**. *He wolfed down the rest of the biscuit and cheese... She bought a hot dog from a stand on a street corner and wolfed it down.* PHRASAL VERB V P n (not pron) V n P

3 If someone **cries wolf**, they say that there is a problem when there is not, with the result that people do not believe them when there really is a problem. PHRASES V inflects

4 If you **keep the wolf from the door**, you succeed in providing food and other necessary things for yourself or your family; an informal expression. *A lot of the lads took small jobs to help keep the wolf from the door.* V inflects

wolf down. See **wolf** 2. PHRASAL VERB

wolfhound /wʊlfhaʊnd/ **wolfhounds.** A **wolfhound** is a type of very large dog. N-COUNT

wolf-whistle, wolf-whistles, wolf-whistling, wolf-whistled. If someone **wolf-whistles**, they make a whistling sound with a short rising note and a longer falling note. Some men wolf-whistle at a woman to show that they think she is attractive, and some women find this offensive. *They wolf-whistled at me, and I was so embarrassed I tripped up.* ▶ Also a noun. *Her dancing brought loud cheers, wolf whistles and applause.* VERB V at n Also V N-COUNT

wolves /wʊlvz/. **Wolves** is the plural of **wolf**.

woman /wʊmən/ **women** ◆◆◆◆◆

1 A **woman** is an adult female human being. *...a young Lithuanian woman named Dayva. ...men and women over 75 years old. ...a woman doctor.* N-COUNT

2 You can refer to women in general as **woman**. *...the oppression of woman.* N-UNCOUNT

3 If you say that a woman is, for example, a gambling **woman** or an outdoors **woman**, you mean that she likes gambling or outdoor activities. *She is an avid outdoors woman... I'm too old to have a dog now. I'm a cat woman.* • **a woman about town**: see **town**. N-COUNT: supp N

4 If you say that a woman is, for example, a London **woman** or an Oxford **woman**, you mean that she comes from London or Oxford, or went to university there. *...a 38-year-old London woman... The headmistress was an Oxford woman.* N-COUNT: n-proper N

5 Some people refer to a man's wife, lover, or girlfriend as his **woman**; an informal use. *I know my woman will never leave me.* N-COUNT: poss N

6 You can refer to a female representative of a company or organization as that company or organization's **woman**. *Yet another successful Labour woman took her seat... That's Judith Croft, the CND woman.* N-COUNT: with supp

7 People sometimes address a woman as **woman** when they are ordering her to do something or when they are angry or impatient with her; an offensive use. *Do you realize, woman, the scandal and publicity that will be involved?* N-VOC PRAGMATICS

8 See also **career woman**.

9 If you say that a woman **is** her **own woman**, you approve of the fact that she makes her plans and decisions herself, and does not depend on other people. *She knew she had made the right decision. She was her own woman again.* PHRASES V inflects PRAGMATICS

10 • **woman of the world**: see **world**.

-woman /-wʊmən/. **-woman** combines with numbers to indicate that something involves the number of women mentioned. *The Squash Association yesterday selected Sue Wright for its four-woman squad.* COMB in ADJ: ADJ n

womanhood /wʊmənhʊd/

1 **Womanhood** is the state of being a woman rather than a girl, or the period of a woman's adult life. *Here she is on the threshold of womanhood... Pregnancy is a natural part of womanhood.* N-UNCOUNT

2 You can refer to women in general or the women of a particular country or community as **womanhood**. *She symbolised for me the best of Indian womanhood. ...the changing condition of womanhood in the closing decades of this century.* N-UNCOUNT

womanizer /wʊmənaɪzəʳ/ **womanizers;** also spelled **womaniser**. If you describe a man as a **womanizer**, you disapprove of him because he likes to have many short sexual relationships with women. N-COUNT PRAGMATICS =philanderer

womanizing /wʊmənaɪzɪŋ/; also spelled **womanising**.

1 If you talk about a man's **womanizing**, you disapprove of him because he likes to have many short sexual relationships with women. N-UNCOUNT PRAGMATICS =philandering

2 A **womanizing** man likes to have many short sexual relationships with women; used showing disapproval. *He plays a womanising car salesman.* ADJ: ADJ n PRAGMATICS =philandering

womankind /wʊmənkaɪnd/. You can refer to all women as **womankind** when considering them as a group; a formal word. N-UNCOUNT

womanly /wʊmənli/. People describe a woman's behaviour, character, or appearance as **womanly** when they like it because they think it is typical of, or suitable for, a woman rather than a man or girl. *She had a classical, womanly shape. ...womanly tenderness.* ADJ-GRADED PRAGMATICS =feminine

woman-to-woman; also spelled **woman to woman**. If you talk about a **woman-to-woman** conversation, you are talking about an honest and open discussion between two women. *She had had a woman-to-woman chat with Mrs Hardie.* ▶ Also an adverb. *Maybe she would talk to her mother one day, woman to woman.* ADJ: ADJ n ADV: ADV after v

womb /wuːm/ **wombs.** A woman's **womb** is the part inside her body where a baby grows before it is born. ◆◇◇◇◇ N-COUNT: oft *the* N, poss N

wombat /wɒmbæt/ **wombats.** A **wombat** is a type of furry animal which has very short legs and eats plants. Wombats are found in Australia. N-COUNT

women /wɪmɪn/. **Women** is the plural of **woman**.

womenfolk /wɪmɪnfoʊk/. Some people refer to the women of a particular community as its **womenfolk**, especially when the community is ruled or organized by men. *Men never notice anything in a house run by their womenfolk.* N-PLURAL: oft poss N

women's group, women's groups. A **women's group** is a group of women who meet regularly, usually in order to organize campaigns. ◆◇◇◇◇ N-COUNT

Women's Lib. Women's Lib is the same as **Women's Liberation**; an informal word. N-UNCOUNT

Women's Liberation. Women's Liberation is the ideal that women should have the same social and economic rights and privileges as men; an old-fashioned expression. ◆◇◇◇◇ N-UNCOUNT: oft N n =feminism

women's movement. The **women's movement** is a social and political movement which aims to achieve equality for women by organizing groups and campaigns, and by causing individuals to change their attitudes. ◆◇◇◇◇ N-SING: usu *the* N

won /wʌn/. **Won** is the past tense and past participle of **win**.

wonder /wʌndəʳ/ **wonders, wondering, wondered** ◆◆◆◆◇

1 If you **wonder** about something, you think about it, either because it interests you and you want to know more about it, or because you are worried or suspicious about it. *I wondered what that noise was... 'He claims to be her father,' said Max. 'We've been wondering about him.'... It makes you wonder about the effect on men's behaviour... 'Why does she want to get in there?' Pete wondered... But there was something else, too. Not hard evidence, but it made me wonder.* VERB V wh V *about* n V with quote V

2 If you **wonder** at something, you are surprised and amazed about it. *He liked to sit and wonder at all that had happened... Walk down Castle Street, admire our little jewel of a cathedral, then wonder at the castle... We all wonder you're still alive.*
VERB
V at n
V that

3 If you say that it is a **wonder** that something happened, you mean that it is very surprising and unexpected. *It's a wonder that it took almost ten years... The wonder is that Olivier was not seriously hurt.*
N-SING

4 **Wonder** is a feeling of surprise, pleasure, or amusement that you have, for example when you see something that is very beautiful, or when something happens that you thought was impossible. *'That's right!' Bobby exclaimed in wonder. 'How did you remember that?'... I was expressing some amazement and wonder at her good fortune... Cross shook his head in wonder.*
N-UNCOUNT
=awe

5 The **wonder** of something is a quality in it that causes people to feel astonishment or great admiration. *...a lecture on the wonders of space and space exploration. ...the wonder of seeing his name in print... The East Window is a wonder of medieval glazing.*
N-COUNT:
usu *the* N *of* n/-ing

6 If you refer, for example, to a young man as a **wonder** boy, or to a new product as a **wonder** drug, you mean that other people admire or praise them for their qualities, although you yourself may not yet be convinced that they are very good. *Mickelson was hailed as the wonder boy of American golf... Dr Williams describes it as a potential wonder drug.*
ADJ:
ADJ n

7 In British English, if you say that someone or something is **a** nine-**day wonder**, you disapprove of the fact that they are attracting so much interest and attention, because you think their popularity will only last for a very short time. *Harry dismissed his old friend's speech as 'a nine-day wonder'... Some supernova researchers wondered if it might be just a nine-day wonder.*
PHRASES
v-link PHR

8 You can say **'I wonder'** if you want to be very polite when you are asking someone to do something, or when you are asking someone to give you information or their opinion about something. *I was just wondering if you could help me... I just wonder what you make of all that... I'm wondering if that was the spirit in the courtroom, too.*
V inflects,
usu PHR wh
PRAGMATICS

9 If you say **'no wonder'**, **'little wonder'**, or **'small wonder'**, you mean that you are not surprised by something that has happened. *No wonder my brother wasn't feeling well... Under such circumstances, it is little wonder that they experience difficulties... Small wonder that he decided to take no part in the debate.*
PHR that
PRAGMATICS

10 You can say **'No wonder'** to express your satisfaction when you find out the answer to something that has been puzzling you for some time. *Brad was Jane's brother! No wonder he reminded me so much of her!*
PHR that
PRAGMATICS

11 If you say that something or someone **works wonders** or **does wonders**, you mean that they have a very good effect on something. *A few moments of relaxation can work wonders... Rushton has done wonders for the industry.*
V inflects,
oft PHR *for* n/-ing,
PHR *with/on* n

wonderful /wʌndəʳfʊl/. If you describe something or someone as **wonderful**, you think they are extremely good. *The cold, misty air felt wonderful on his face... It's wonderful to see you... I've always thought he was a wonderful actor.* ♦ **wonderfully** *It's a system that works wonderfully well... The weather was wonderfully warm.*
◆◆◆◆◇
ADJ-GRADED:
oft *it* v-link ADJ to-inf/that
=fantastic
≠awful
ADV-GRADED:
usu ADV adv/adj/-ed

wonderland /wʌndəʳlænd/ **wonderlands**
◆◇◇◇◇

1 **Wonderland** is an imaginary world that exists in fairy tales.
N-UNCOUNT

2 You can refer to a place as a **wonderland** when it is strange and very beautiful or exciting. *Children find Lake George Village a wonderland of amusement parks.*
N-COUNT:
usu sing,
usu with supp,
oft N *of* n

wonderment /wʌndəʳmənt/. **Wonderment** is a feeling of pleasant amazement. *His big blue eyes opened wide in wonderment.*
N-UNCOUNT:
oft *in* N
=astonishment

wondrous /wʌndrəs/. If you describe something as **wondrous**, you mean it is strange and beautiful or impressive; a literary word. *We were driven across this wondrous vast land of lakes and forests.* ♦ **wondrously** *Ever since they had set eyes on each other they had been wondrously happy.*
◆◇◇◇◇
ADJ-GRADED:
usu ADJ n
ADV-GRADED:
usu ADV adj/adv

wonky /wɒŋki/. If something is **wonky**, it is not steady, not straight, or not evenly balanced; used in informal British English. *...a tiny house with lots of little rooms, wonky floors and doors... The wheels keep going wonky.*
ADJ-GRADED

wont /wəʊnt, AM wɔːnt/

1 If someone is **wont** to do something, they often or regularly do it; used in written English. *Both have committed their indiscretions, as human beings are wont to do.*
ADJ:
v-link ADJ to-inf
=inclined

2 If you say that someone does something **as is** their **wont**, you mean that it is something that they often or regularly do; used in written English. *Paul woke early, as was his wont.*
PHRASE:
V inflects

won't /wəʊnt/. **Won't** is the usual spoken form of 'will not'. *The space shuttle Discovery won't lift off the launch pad until Sunday at the earliest.*

woo /wuː/ **woos, wooing, wooed**
◆◆◇◇◇

1 If you **woo** people, you try to encourage them to help you, support you, or vote for you, for example by promising them things which they would like. *They wooed customers by offering low interest rates... They are trying to woo back electoral support.* ♦ **wooing** *This election has been marked so far by the candidates' wooing of each other's traditional political bases.*
VERB
V n
V n with adv
N-UNCOUNT:
oft poss N,
N *of* n

2 If a man **woos** a woman, he spends time with her and tries to persuade her to marry him; an old-fashioned use. *The penniless author successfully wooed and married Fanny.* ♦ **wooing** *...the hero's rapturous wooing of his beautiful cousin Roxanne.*
VERB
=court
V n
N-UNCOUNT:
oft poss N,
N *of* n

wood /wʊd/ **woods**
◆◆◆◆◇

1 **Wood** is the material which forms the trunks and branches of trees. *Their dishes were made of wood... There was a smell of damp wood and machine oil. ...a short piece of wood.*
N-MASS

2 A **wood** is a fairly large area of trees growing near each other. You can refer to one or several of these areas as **woods**. *After dinner Alice slipped away for a walk in the woods with Artie... About a mile to the west of town he came upon a large wood.*
N-COUNT

3 See also **dead wood**.

4 If something or someone is **not out of the woods** yet, they are still having difficulties or problems; an informal expression. *The nation's economy is not out of the woods yet.*
PHRASES
v-link PHR

5 In British English, you can say **'touch wood'** to indicate that you hope to have good luck in something you are doing and that nothing will go wrong, usually after saying that so far you have not had bad luck with it. The American expression is **knock on wood** . *She's never even been to the doctor's, touch wood... Touch wood, I've been lucky enough to avoid any other serious injuries.*
CONVENTION

6 • your **neck of the woods**: see **neck**. • **can't see the wood for the trees**: see **tree**.

wood carving, wood carvings. A **wood carving** is a decorative piece of wood that has been carved in an artistic way.
N-VAR

woodcock /wʊdkɒk/ **woodcocks.** The plural can be either **woodcocks** or **woodcock**. A **woodcock** is a small brown bird with a long beak. Woodcock are sometimes shot for sport or food.
N-COUNT

woodcutter /wʊdkʌtəʳ/ **woodcutters.** A **woodcutter** is someone who cuts down trees or who chops wood as a job; an old-fashioned word.
N-COUNT

wooded /wʊdɪd/. A **wooded** area is covered in trees. *...a wooded valley.*
◆◇◇◇◇
ADJ-GRADED

wooden /wʊdən/
◆◆◆◇◇

1 **Wooden** objects are made of wood. *...the shop's bare brick walls and faded wooden floorboards.*
ADJ:
ADJ n

2 If you describe an actor as **wooden**, you are critical of them because their performance is not at all lively or natural.
ADJ-GRADED
PRAGMATICS

wooden spoon, wooden spoons
1 A **wooden spoon** is a spoon that is used for stirring sauces and for mixing ingredients in cooking. It is made of wood and has a long handle. N-COUNT
2 In British English, if someone gets the **wooden spoon**, they come last in a race or competition. *Jarvis took the wooden spoon in the first tournament.* N-COUNT: usu *the* N in sing
woodland /wʊdlənd/ **woodlands. Woodland** is land which is mostly covered with trees. ◆◆◇◇◇ N-VAR
woodlouse /wʊdlaʊs/ **woodlice** /wʊdlaɪs/. A **woodlouse** is a very small grey creature with a hard shell and fourteen legs. It lives in damp places. N-COUNT
woodpecker /wʊdpekəʳ/ **woodpeckers.** A **woodpecker** is a type of bird with a long sharp beak. Woodpeckers use their beaks to make holes in tree trunks. N-COUNT
woodpile /wʊdpaɪl/ **woodpiles.** A **woodpile** is a pile of firewood. N-COUNT: usu sing
wood pulp. **Wood pulp** is wood that has been cut up into small pieces and crushed. Wood pulp is used to make paper. N-UNCOUNT
woodshed /wʊdʃed/ **woodsheds.** A **woodshed** is a small building which is used for storing firewood. N-COUNT
woodwind /wʊdwɪnd/ **woodwinds. Woodwind** instruments are musical instruments such as flutes, clarinets, and recorders that are played by blowing into them. N-VAR: oft N n
woodwork /wʊdwɜːʳk/ ◆◇◇◇◇
1 You can refer to the doors and other wooden parts of a house as the **woodwork**. *I love the living room, with its dark woodwork, oriental rugs, and chunky furniture... He could see the glimmer of fresh paint on the woodwork.* N-UNCOUNT
2 **Woodwork** is the activity or skill of making things out of wood. *I have done woodwork for many years... Joseph instructs a class in woodwork.* N-UNCOUNT =carpentry
3 If you say that people **are coming out of the woodwork**, you are criticizing them for suddenly appearing in public or revealing their opinions when previously they did not make themselves known. *When a song gets to the top, someone will come out of the woodwork and claim to have written it.* PHRASE: V inflects PRAGMATICS
woodworm /wʊdwɜːʳm/ **woodworms.** The plural can be either **woodworms** or **woodworm**.
1 **Woodworm** are the larvae of certain types of beetle which make holes in wood by feeding on it. N-COUNT
2 **Woodworm** is damage caused to wood, especially to the wooden parts of a house or to furniture, by woodworm making holes in the wood. *...treating the ground floor of a house for woodworm.* N-UNCOUNT
woody /wʊdi/
1 **Woody** plants have very hard stems. *Care must be taken when trimming around woody plants like shrubs and trees... Trim any tough or woody stalks from the asparagus.* ADJ-GRADED: usu ADJ n
2 A **woody** area has a lot of trees in it. *...the wet and woody Vosges mountains.* ADJ-GRADED: usu ADJ n
3 Something that smells **woody** smells like wood. *This oil has a lovely woody fragrance.* ADJ
woof /wʊf/. A **woof** is the sound that a dog makes when it barks; an informal word, especially used by children. *The dogs sat there without even a woof... She started going 'woof woof'.* N-SING
wool /wʊl/ **wools** ◆◆◇◇◇
1 **Wool** is the hair that grows on sheep and on some other animals. N-UNCOUNT
2 **Wool** is a material made from animal's wool that is used to make things such as clothes, blankets, and carpets. *...a wool overcoat... The carpets are made in wool and nylon.* N-MASS
3 See also **cotton wool**, **steel wool**, **wire wool**.
4 If you say that someone is **pulling the wool over** your **eyes**, you mean that they are trying to deceive you, in order to have an advantage over you. *Stop trying to pull the wool over my eyes! What were you two fighting about just now?* PHRASE: V inflects
woollen /wʊlən/ **woollens;** spelled **woolen** in American English. ◆◇◇◇◇
1 **Woollen** clothes or materials are made from wool or from a mixture of wool and artificial fibres. *...thick woollen socks.* ADJ: usu ADJ n
2 **Woollens** are clothes, especially sweaters, that are made of wool. *...winter woollens.* N-PLURAL
woolly /wʊli/ **woollies;** spelled **wooly** in American English. ◆◇◇◇◇
1 Something that is **woolly** is made of wool or looks like wool. *She wore this woolly hat with pompoms.* ADJ: usu ADJ n
2 In British English, a **woolly** is a woollen piece of clothing, especially a pullover; an informal use. N-COUNT
3 If you describe a person or their aims or ideas as **woolly**, you are criticising them for being inconsistent or confused. *...a weak and woolly Government... It is no good setting vague and woolly goals – you will not know whether or not you have really achieved them.* ADJ-GRADED PRAGMATICS
woozy /wuːzi/. If you feel **woozy** you feel rather weak and unsteady and cannot think clearly; an informal word. *The fumes made them woozy.* ADJ-GRADED: usu v-link ADJ ≠alert
word /wɜːʳd/ **words, wording, worded** ◆◆◆◆◆
1 A **word** is a single unit of language that can be represented in writing or speech. In English, a word has a space on either side of it when it is written. *The words stood out clearly on the page... The word 'ginseng' comes from the Chinese word 'Shenseng'. ...swear words... Do you enjoy word puzzles?* N-COUNT
2 Someone's **words** are what they say or write. *I was devastated when her words came true... The words of the young woman doctor echoed in his ears... Allied military leaders have said they want actions, not words.* N-PLURAL: oft with poss
3 The **words** of a song consist of the text that is sung, in contrast to the music that is played. *Can you hear the words on the album?.* N-PLURAL: usu *the* N =lyrics
4 If you have **a word** with someone, you have a short conversation with them; used in spoken English. *I think it's time you had a word with him... James, could I have a quiet word?... It's the detective-sergeant. He wants a word.* N-SING: *a* N
5 If you offer someone a **word of** something such as warning, advice, or praise, you warn, advise, or praise them. *A word of warning. Don't stick too precisely to what it says in the book... May I also say a word of thanks to all the people who sent letters.* N-COUNT: N *of* n
6 If you say that someone does not hear, understand, or say **a word**, you are emphasizing that they hear, understand, or say nothing at all. *I can't understand a word she says... I bet he doesn't remember a single word... Not a word was spoken.* N-SING: *a* N, with brd-neg PRAGMATICS
7 You can use **word** after a letter of the alphabet to refer politely or humorously to a word beginning with that letter which people find offensive or are embarrassed to use. *He uses the f-word and other expletives freely... Politicians began to use the dreaded R-word: recession.* N-COUNT: usu sing, *the* n N
8 If there is **word** of something, people receive news or information about it. *There is no word from the authorities on the reported attack... Word has been spreading fast of the incidents on the streets... Both men sent word that they had retired for the evening.* N-UNCOUNT: also *the* N
9 If you give your **word**, you make a sincere promise to someone. *...an adult who gave his word the boy would be supervised... He simply cannot be trusted to keep his word.* N-SING: poss N
10 If someone gives **the word** to do something, they give an order to do it. *I want nothing said about this until I give the word.* N-SING: *the* N
11 To **word** something in a particular way means to choose or use particular words to express it. *If I had written the letter, I might have worded it differently.* ♦ **-worded** *...a strongly-worded statement. ...a carefully-worded speech.* VERB V n adv/prep; COMB in ADJ-GRADED
12 See also **wording**, **code word**, **four-letter word**, **play on words**, **printed word**, **spoken word**, **written word**.
13 If you say that people consider something to be a **dirty word**, you mean that they disapprove of it. *So many people think feminism is a dirty word.* PHRASES usu v-link PHR
14 If you say that someone has to **eat** their **words**, you mean that they have to admit that they were V inflects

wrong about something they said in the past, especially when this makes them look foolish. *He has had to eat his words about the company being recession-proof.*

15 A person **of few words** says very little, especially about their opinions or feelings. *He's a man of few words, very polite and unassuming.*
n PHR

16 If you do something **from the word go**, you do it from the very beginning of a period of time or situation. *It's essential you make the right decisions from the word go.*
PHR with cl

17 If you **hang on** someone's **every word**, you listen very intently to what they have to say, because you admire or respect them. *Melina was hanging on his every word, fascinated.*
V inflects

18 You can use expressions such as **never have a good word to say** or **never have a bad word to say** to emphasize that someone always criticizes someone or something or that they never criticize them. *The press never has a good word to say about them... She doesn't have a kind word for anyone.*
V inflects, usu PHR prep PRAGMATICS

19 If one person **has words with** another, or if two or more people **have words**, they have a serious discussion or argument, especially because one has complained about the other's behaviour. *We had words and she stormed out... I shall have words with these stupid friends of mine!*
RECIP: V inflects, pl-n PHR, PHR *with* n

20 You can use **in** someone's **words** or **in** someone's **own words** to indicate that you are reporting something someone said using the exact words that they used. *Even the Assistant Secretary of State had to admit that previous policy did not, in his words, produce results.*
PHR with cl

21 You use **in a word** to indicate that you are summarizing what you have just been saying. *'Shouldn't he be given the leading role?' 'In a word – No'... Victor, in a word, got increasingly fed up.*
PHR with cl PRAGMATICS =in short

22 If someone has **the last word** or **the final word** in a discussion, argument, or disagreement, they are the one who wins it or who makes the final decision. *She does like to have the last word in any discussion... The final word will still come from the Secretary of State.*

23 If you say that something is **the last word in** luxury, comfort, or some other quality, you are emphasizing that it has a great deal of this quality. *The spa is the last word in luxury and efficiency.*
PHR n, usu v-link PHR PRAGMATICS

24 If someone is **lost for words**, they cannot think of anything to say, especially because they are very surprised by something. *I'm lost for words – it's fantastic... She was gaping at it, lost for words.*
usu v-link PHR =dumbstruck

25 If you say that someone has said something, but **not in so many words**, you mean that they said it or expressed it, but in a very indirect way. *'And has she agreed to go with you'. – Not in so many words. But I read her thoughts.*
usu with brd-neg, usu PHR after v, PHR with cl

26 If you say **'mark my words'** to someone, you are emphasizing that something you have just warned them about is very likely to happen, especially when you think they should change their attitude or behaviour to prevent it. *That's what you'll end up with, you mark my words.*
usu PHR with cl PRAGMATICS

27 If news or information passes by **word of mouth**, people tell it to each other rather than it being printed in written form. *The story has been passed down by word of mouth.*
oft *by/through* PHR

28 If you say that someone **is putting words into** your **mouth** or **is putting words in** your **mouth,** you mean that they are suggesting that you mean one thing when you really mean something else or something different.
V inflects

29 If you refer to someone as **a man of his word** or **a woman of her word**, you mean that they always keep their promises and can be relied on.

30 You say **in other words** in order to introduce a different, and usually simpler, explanation or interpretation of something that has just been said. *The mobile library services have been reorganised – in other words, they visit fewer places.*
PHR with cl PRAGMATICS

31 If you say something **in your own words**, you express it in your own way, without copying or repeating someone else's description. *Now tell us in your own words about the events of Saturday.*
PHR after v, PHR with cl

32 If you **pass the word**, you tell someone something that another person has told you. *Friends passed the word that the miners wanted to see him.*
V inflects, oft PHR that

33 If someone **says the word**, they give their approval as a sign that something should start to happen. *When I say the word, follow me down.*
V inflects

34 If you **spread the word**, you tell people about something. *The community reacted quickly and spread the word about safe sex.*
V inflects, oft PHR *about* n, PHR that

35 If you **take** someone **at their word**, you believe what they say, when they did not really mean it or when they meant something slightly different. *They're willing to take him at his word when he says, 'Oh, I made mistakes and now I'll change.'*
V inflects

36 If you say to someone **'take** my **word for it'**, you mean that they should believe you because you are telling the truth. *You'll buy nothing but trouble if you buy that house, take my word for it.*
V inflects

37 You can use expressions such as **too silly for words, too awful for words**, and **too ridiculous for words** to emphasize that someone or something is extremely silly, awful, or ridiculous. *It's too stupid for words not having the machines switched on when they're most needed... I feel simply too devastated for words.*
v-link PHR PRAGMATICS

38 If you are **true to** your **word** or **as good as** your **word**, you do what you say you will do. *How do I know that he will be true to his word?... They were as good as their word and stayed away.*
v-link PHR, PHR with cl

39 If you repeat something **word for word**, you repeat it exactly as it was originally said or written. *I don't try to memorize speeches word for word.*
PHR after v =verbatim

40 • **not get a word in edgeways**: see **edgeways**. • **not mince** your **words**: see **mince.** • **the operative word**: see **operative.** • **actions speak louder than words**: see **speak.** • **war of words**: see **war.**

word class, word classes. A **word class** is a group of words that have the same basic behaviour, for example nouns, adjectives, or verbs.
N-COUNT

wording /wɜːʳdɪŋ/. The **wording** of a piece of writing or a speech are the words used in it, especially when these are chosen to have a particular effect. *The two sides to agree on the wording of a final report... The wording is so vague that no one actually knows what it means.*
◆◇◇◇◇ N-UNCOUNT: also *a* N

wordless /wɜːʳdləs/

1 You say that someone is **wordless** when they do not say anything, especially at a time when they are expected to say something; a literary use. *She stared back, now wordless... Here and there, husbands sit in wordless despair.* ♦ **wordlessly** *Gil downed his food wordlessly, his attention far away.*
ADJ =silent; ADV: ADV with v

2 If someone makes a **wordless** sound, they make a sound that do not seem to contain any words; a literary use. *...a wordless chant... He shrieked a long, wordless cry.*
ADJ: usu ADJ n

wordplay /wɜːʳdpleɪ/; also spelled **word play. Wordplay** involves making jokes by using the meanings of words in an amusing or clever way.
N-UNCOUNT

word processing; also spelled **word-processing. Word processing** is the work or skill of producing printed material using a computer or word processor.
N-UNCOUNT: oft N n

word processor, word processors. A **word processor** is a computer or piece of software which is used to produce printed material such as documents, letters, and books.
◆◇◇◇◇ N-COUNT

wordy /wɜːʳdi/. If you describe a person's speech or something that they write as **wordy**, you disapprove of the fact that they use too many words, especially words which are very long, formal, or literary. *The chapter is mostly wordy rhetoric.*
ADJ-GRADED PRAGMATICS =verbose

wore /wɔːʳ/. **Wore** is the past tense of **wear**.

work /wɜːʳk/ **works, working, worked**
◆◆◆◆◆

1 People who **work** have a job, usually one which they are paid to do. *Weiner works for the US Department of Transport... I started working in a recording studio... Where do you work?... He worked as*
VERB V prep/adv V as n V

a bricklayer's mate... I want to work, I don't want to be on welfare.

2 People who have **work** or who are **in work** have a job, usually one which they are paid to do. *Fewer and fewer people are in work... I was out of work at the time... She'd have enough money to provide for her children until she could find work... What kind of work do you do?*
N-UNCOUNT: oft *in/out of* N

3 When you **work**, you do the things that you are paid or required to do in your job. *I can't talk to you right now – I'm working... He was working at his desk... Some firms expect the guards to work twelve hours a day.*
VERB V, V n

4 Your **work** consists of the things you are paid or required to do in your job. *We're supposed to be running a business here. I've got work to do... I used to take work home, but I don't do it any more... There have been days when I have finished work at 2pm. ...an image of teaching which highlighted the stressful and difficult aspects of the teacher's work.*
N-UNCOUNT

5 When you **work**, you spend time and effort doing a task that needs to be done or trying to achieve something. *Linda spends all her time working on the garden... While I was working on my letter the telephone rang... Leonard was working at his German. His mistakes made her laugh... The most important reason for coming to university is to work for a degree... The government expressed hope that all the sides will work towards a political solution.* ▸ Also a noun. *There was a lot of work to do on their house... We knew we would have to organise the wedding but we hadn't appreciated how much work was involved... He said that the peace plan would be rejected because it needed more work.*
VERB V prep; N-UNCOUNT

6 Work is the place where you do your job. *Many people travel to work by car... She told her friends at work that she was trying to lose weight.*
N-UNCOUNT: usu *to/at* N

7 Work is something which you produce as a result of an activity or as a result of doing your job. *It can help to have an impartial third party look over your work... Tidiness in the workshop is really essential for producing good work... That's a beautiful piece of work. You should be proud of it.*
N-UNCOUNT: oft poss/adj N

8 A **work** is something such as a painting, book, or piece of music, produced by an artist, writer, or composer. *In my opinion, this is Rembrandt's greatest work... Under his arm, there was a book which looked like the complete works of Shakespeare... The church has several valuable works of art.*
N-COUNT: usu with supp

9 If a researcher **is working on** a particular subject or question, they are studying or researching it. *Professor Bonnet has been working for many years on molecules of this type.* ▸ Also a noun. *Their work shows that one-year-olds are much more likely to have allergies if either parent smokes.*
VERB V *on* n; N-UNCOUNT

10 If you **work** with a person or a group of people, you spend time and effort trying to help them in some way. *She spent a period of time working with people dying of cancer... He knew then that he wanted to work among the poor.* ▸ Also a noun. *...a highly respected priest who is noted for his work with the poor... She became involved in social and relief work among the refugees.*
VERB V *with/among* n; N-UNCOUNT: with supp, usu poss N, N *with/among* n

11 If a machine or piece of equipment **works**, it operates and performs a particular function. *The pump doesn't work and we have no running water... Is the telephone working today?... Ned turned on the lanterns, which worked with batteries... How does the gun work?*
VERB V, V prep/adv

12 If an idea, system, or way of doing something **works**, it is successful, effective, or satisfactory. *95 per cent of these diets do not work... If lust is all there is to hold you together, the relationship will never work... I shouldn't have come, I knew it wouldn't work... A methodical approach works best.*
VERB V, V adv

13 If a drug or medicine **works**, it produces a particular physical effect. *I wake at 6am as the sleeping pill doesn't work for more than nine hours... The drug works by increasing levels of serotonin in the brain.*
VERB V, V prep/adv

14 If something **works** in your favour, it helps you in some way. If something **works** to your disadvantage, it causes problems for you in some way. *One factor thought to have worked in his favour is his working class image... This obviously works against the interests of the child.*
VERB V prep

15 If something or someone **works** their magic or **works** their charms on someone, they have a powerful positive effect on them. *Nevertheless, she is always optimistic about the possibilities and can work her charm on the disenchanted... Our spirits rallied as the bitter-sweet alcohol worked its magic.*
VERB V n *on* n, V n

16 If your mind or brain **is working**, you are thinking about something or trying to solve a problem. *My mind was working frantically, running over the events of the evening.*
VERB V

17 If you **work on** an assumption or idea, you act as if it were true or base other ideas on it, until you have more information. *We are working on the assumption that it was a gas explosion.*
VERB V *on* n

18 If you **work** a particular area or type of place, you travel around that area or work in those places as part of your job, for example trying to sell something there. *Brand has been working the clubs and the pubs since 1986, developing her comedy act... This is the seventh year that he has worked the streets of Manhattan.*
VERB V n

19 If you **work** someone, you make them spend time and effort doing a particular activity or job. *They're working me too hard. I'm too old for this... They didn't take my father away, but kept him in the village and worked him to death.*
VERB V n adv/prep, Also V n

20 If you **work** the land, you cultivate it and do all the various tasks involved in growing and harvesting crops. *Farmers worked the fertile valleys.*
VERB =farm V n

21 When a mine or quarry **is worked**, it is in use, and minerals such as coal are removed from it. *The mines had first been worked in 1849, when gold was discovered... Only an agreed number of men was allowed to work any given seam at any given time.*
VERB *be* V-ed, V n

22 If you **work** a machine or piece of equipment, you use or control it. *Many adults still depend on their children to work the video.*
VERB =operate V n

23 If something **works** into a particular state or condition, it gradually moves so that it is in that state or condition. *It's important to put a locking washer on that last nut, or it can work loose.*
VERB V adj

24 If you **work** something, you mould, press, and squeeze it to make it have a particular shape, form, or consistency. *Work the dough with the palm of your hand until it is very smooth... Remove rind from the cheese and work it to a firm paste, with a fork.*
VERB V n, V n prep/adv

25 If you **work** a material such as metal, leather, or stone, you cut, sew, or shape it in order to make something or to create a design. *...the machines needed to extract and work the raw stone. ...a long, cool tunnel of worked stone.*
VERB V n, V-ed

26 If you **work with** a particular substance or material, you use it in order to make something or to create a design. *He studied sculpture because he enjoyed working with clay.*
VERB V *with/in* n

27 If you **work** a part of your body, or if it **works**, you move it. *Each position will work the muscles in a different way... Her mouth was working in her sleep.*
V-ERG V n, V

28 In British English, a **works** is a place where something is manufactured or where an industrial process is carried out. **Works** is used to refer to one or to more than one of these places. *The steel works, one of the landmarks of Stoke-on-Trent, could be seen for miles. ...a recycling works. ...the works canteen.*
N-COUNT-COLL: usu n N, N n

29 Works are activities such as digging the ground or building on a large scale. *...six years of disruptive building works, road construction and urban development.*
N-PLURAL: usu supp N

30 You can say **the works** after listing things such as someone's possessions or requirements, to emphasize that they possess or require everything you can think of in a particular category; an informal use. *Amazing place he's got there – squash courts, swimming pool, jacuzzi, the works.*
N-SING: *the* N, PRAGMATICS, =the lot

31 See also **working.**

32 If someone is **at work** they are doing their job or are busy doing a particular activity. *The salvage teams are already hard at work trying to deal with the spilled oil... He is currently at work on a novel... Television cameras were invited in to film him at work.* PHRASES usu v-link PHR

33 If a force or process is **at work**, it is having a particular influence or effect. *The report suggested that the same trend was at work in politics... It is important to understand the powerful economic and social forces at work behind our own actions.* usu v-link PHR

34 If you say that you will **have your work cut out** to do something, you mean that it will be a very difficult task. *The new administration has its work cut out for it. Creating jobs in this kind of environment is not going to be easy... He will have his work cut out to get into the team.* V inflects, oft PHR *for* n, PHR to-inf

35 You can use **work** to talk about how easily or quickly a particular task is done. For example, if someone or something **makes** short **work of** doing something or **makes** light **work of** it, they do it quickly and easily. *An aerosol spray will make short work of painting awkward objects... This horse made light work of the cross-country course... Australia made hard work of beating them.* V inflects, PHR -ing/n

36 If you describe someone as **a nasty piece of work**, you think they are very unpleasant or cruel; an informal expression. *Underneath I think he's actually a rather nasty piece of work.* usu v-link PHR

37 If you **put** someone **to work** or **set** them **to work**, you give them a job or task to do. *By stimulating the economy, we're going to put people to work... Instead of sending them to prison, we have set them to work helping the lemon growers.* V inflects, oft PHR prep, PHR -ing

38 If you **get to work, go to work**, or **set to work** on a job, task, or problem, you start doing it or dealing with it. *He promised to get to work on the state's massive deficit... He returned to America where he set to work on a new novel.* V inflects, oft PHR *on* n

39 If you **work** your **way** somewhere, you move or progress there slowly, and with a lot of effort or work. *Rescuers were still working their way towards the trapped men... Many personnel managers started as secretaries or personnel assistants and worked their way up.* V inflects, PHR prep/adv

40 You can say to someone **'nice work'** or **'good work'** in order to thank or congratulate them for doing something well or quickly. *Nice work, Matthew. I knew you could do it... 'Good work!' said Jack.* CONVENTION PRAGMATICS

41 • to **throw a spanner in the works**: see **spanner**.

work in or **work into.** If you **work** one substance **into** another or **work** it **in**, you add it to the other substance and mix the two together thoroughly. *Gradually pour the liquid into the flour, working it in carefully with a wooden spoon... Work in the potato and milk until the mixture comes together... Work the oil gradually into the yolks with a wooden spoon.* PHRASAL VERB V n P, V P n (not pron), V n P n

work off PHRASAL VERB

1 If you **work off** energy, aggression, or anger, you get rid of it by doing something that requires a lot of physical effort. *Cleaning my kitchen really works off frustration if I've had a row with someone... If I've had a bad day I'll work it off by cooking.* V P n (not pron), V n P

2 If you **work off** a debt, you repay it by working. *The report proposes that students be allowed to work off their debt through community service... There were heavy debts. It would take half Edward's lifetime to work them off.* V P n (not pron), V n P

work out PHRASAL VERB

1 If you **work out** a solution to a problem or mystery, you manage to find the solution by thinking or talking about it. *Negotiators are due to meet later today to work out a compromise... It took me some time to work out what was causing this... 'How will you contact me?'—'We haven't worked that out yet.'* V P n (not pron), V P wh, V n P

• If you **have** something **all worked out**, you have thought about it carefully, and know exactly what you are going to do or exactly what you want. *I had the ideal man all worked out in my mind.* PHRASE *have* inflects

2 If you **work out** the answer to a mathematical problem, you calculate it. *It is proving hard to work out the value of bankrupt firms' assets... When asked what a £30.35 meal for five people would cost each diner, they were unable to work it out.* =calculate V P n (not pron), V n P

3 If something **works out** at a particular amount, it is calculated to be that amount after all the facts and figures have been considered. *The price per pound works out at £3.20... It will probably work out cheaper to hire a van and move your own things.* V P *at* amount, V P adj

4 If a situation **works out** well or **works out**, it happens or progresses in a satisfactory way. *Things just didn't work out as planned... I hope it will work out well... The deal just isn't working out the way we were promised... One of the ways people experience loss is when relationships don't work out.* V P prep/adv, V P n (not pron), V P

5 If a process **works** itself **out**, it reaches a conclusion or satisfactory end. *People involved in it think it's a nightmare, but I'm sure it will work itself out.* V pron-refl P

6 If you **work out** your service or your notice, you continue to work at your job until you have completed a specified period of time. *There was an interim before her successor actually came because she had to work out her notice.* V P n (not pron), Also V n P

7 If you **work out**, you do physical exercises in order to make your body fit and strong. *Work out at a gym or swim twice a week.* =exercise V P

8 See also **workout**.

work over. To **work** someone **over** means to beat them very violently; an informal expression. *The gang worked me over.* PHRASAL VERB =beat up V n P

work up PHRASAL VERB

1 If you **work** yourself **up**, you make yourself feel very upset or angry about something. *She worked herself up into a bit of a state... Don't just lie there working yourself up, do something about it.* • See also **worked up**. V pron-refl P *into/to* n, V pron-refl P

2 If you **work up** the enthusiasm or courage to do something, you succeed in making yourself feel it. *Your creative talents can also be put to good use, if you can work up the energy... Malcolm worked up the nerve to ask Grandma Rose for some help.* =summon up V P n (not pron)

3 If you **work up** a sweat or an appetite, you make yourself sweaty or hungry by doing exercise or hard work. *The hills are inspiring as well as peaceful, and you can really work up a sweat... It was around seven when I finished at the library. I wasn't hungry, but I'd worked up a thirst.* V P n (not pron)

4 If you **work up** something such as a piece of writing, you spend time and effort preparing it. *I sketched the layout of a prototype store and worked up a business plan... They asked me to work up some sample drawings and bring them down.* V P n (not pron)

workable /wɜːʳkəbᵊl/. A **workable** idea or system is realistic and practical, and likely to be effective. *Investors can simply pay cash, but this isn't a workable solution in most cases.* ◆◇◇◇◇ ADJ-GRADED =practicable ≠unworkable

workaday /wɜːʳkədeɪ/. **Workaday** means ordinary and not especially interesting or unusual. *Enough of fantasy, the workaday world awaited him.* ADJ: usu ADJ n =everyday

workaholic /wɜːkəhɒlɪk, AM -hɔːl-/ **workaholics.** A **workaholic** is a person who works most of the time and finds it difficult to stop working in order to do other things; an informal word. ◆◇◇◇◇ N-COUNT

workbench /wɜːʳkbentʃ/ **workbenches.** A **workbench** is a heavy wooden table on which people use tools such as a hammer and nails to make or repair things. N-COUNT

workbook /wɜːʳkbʊk/ **workbooks.** A **workbook** is a textbook that has questions in it with spaces for the answers. N-COUNT

workday /wɜːʳkdeɪ/ **workdays**

1 A **workday** is the amount of time during a day which you spend doing your job; used mainly in American English. *His workday starts at 3.30 a.m. and lasts 12 hours.* N-COUNT: usu sing =working day

2 A **workday** is a day on which people go to work. *What's he doing home on a workday?* N-COUNT

worked up. If someone is **worked up**, they are angry or upset. *Steve shouted at her. He was really worked up now.* ADJ-GRADED: v-link ADJ

worker /wɜːʳkəʳ/ **workers** ◆◆◆◆◆

1 A particular kind of **worker** does the kind of work mentioned. *She ate her sandwich alongside several other office workers taking their break... The society was looking for a capable research worker. ...aid workers in Somalia.* N-COUNT: with supp, usu n N

2 **Workers** are people who are employed in industry or business and who are not managers. *Wages have been frozen and workers laid off. ...a call for the workers of the world to unite... The agreement encourages worker participation in management decisions.* N-COUNT: usu pl

3 You can use **worker** to say how well or badly someone works. *He is a hard worker and a skilled gardener... A first-class worker, she operated the difficult Jacquard looms.* • See also **care worker**, **caseworker**, **dock worker**, **social worker**, **teleworker**, **youth worker**. N-COUNT: usu adj N

workforce /wɜːʳkfɔːʳs/ **workforces** ◆◆◇◇◇

1 The **workforce** is the total number of people in a country or region who are physically able to do a job and are available for work. *...a country where half the workforce is unemployed.* N-COUNT: usu sing

2 The **workforce** is the total number of people who are employed by a particular company. *...an employer of a very large workforce.* N-COUNT: usu sing =staff

workhorse /wɜːʳkhɔːʳs/ **workhorses**

1 A **workhorse** is a horse which is used to do a job, for example to pull a plough. N-COUNT

2 If you describe a person or a machine as a **workhorse**, you mean that they can be relied upon to do a large amount of work, especially work that is dull or routine. *...the Wellington bomber, the great workhorse of the war... My husband never even looked at me. I was just a workhorse bringing up three children.* N-COUNT: usu with supp

workhouse /wɜːʳkhaʊs/ **workhouses.** A **workhouse** was a place where, in the seventeenth to nineteenth centuries in Britain, very poor people who had no money and nowhere to live did unpleasant jobs in return for food and shelter. People also say **the workhouse** when they are referring to these places in general. *...a struggling Shropshire family which lived in constant fear of the workhouse.* N-COUNT =poorhouse

working /wɜːʳkɪŋ/ **workings** ◆◆◆◆◆

1 **Working** people have jobs which they are paid to do. *Like working women anywhere, Asian women are buying convenience foods.* ADJ: ADJ n

2 **Working** people are ordinary people who do not have professional or very highly paid jobs. *The needs and opinions of ordinary working people were ignored... One or two, in blue suits, might have been bank officials. Others were clearly working men.* ADJ: ADJ n =working class

3 A **working** day or week is the number of hours that you work during a day or a week. *For doctors the working day often has no end... Automation would bring a shorter, more flexible working week.* ADJ: ADJ n

4 A **working** day is a day on which people normally have to do their job. *The full effect will not be apparent until Tuesday, the first working day after the three day holiday weekend.* ADJ: ADJ n

5 Your **working** life is the period of your life in which you have a job or are of a suitable age to have a job. *He started his working life as a truck driver.* ADJ: ADJ n

6 The **working** population of an area consists of all the people in that area who have a job or who are of a suitable age to have a job. *Almost 13 per cent of the working population is already unemployed.* ADJ: ADJ n

7 **Working** conditions or practices are ones which you have in your job. *The strikers are demanding higher pay and better working conditions.* ADJ: ADJ n

8 **Working** clothes are designed for doing work in, and they are intended to be practical rather than attractive. ADJ: ADJ n

9 If you have a **working** relationship with someone, you work well together, though you may not know each other personally. *A working relationship turned into a very close friendship... The vice-president seems to have a good working relationship with the president.* ADJ: ADJ n

10 A **working** farm or business exists to do normal work and make a profit, and not only for tourists or as someone's hobby. ADJ: ADJ n

11 The **working** parts of a machine are the parts which move and operate the machine, in contrast to the outer case or container which encloses them. ADJ: ADJ n

12 A **working** model is one that has parts that move. ADJ: ADJ n

13 A **working** knowledge or majority is not very great, but is enough to be useful. *This book was designed in order to provide a working knowledge of finance and accounts... Neither candidate won a working majority.* ADJ: ADJ n

14 A **working** title or definition is one which you use as the basis for a particular job or piece of research, but which you are likely to change or improve. *His working title for the script was 'Trust the People'.* ADJ: ADJ n

15 The **workings** of a piece of equipment, an organization, or a system are the ways in which it operates and the processes which are involved in it. *Neural networks are computer systems which mimic the workings of the brain... The bill would give people the right to much more information about the workings of government.* N-PLURAL: usu N *of* n

16 You can use **workings** to refer to a mine or quarry which has been dug in the ground in order to remove metals or stone. *...housing which was built above old mine workings.* N-PLURAL

17 • **in working order**: see **order**.

working capital. **Working capital** is money which is available for use immediately, rather than money which is invested in land or equipment; a technical term in business. ◆◇◇◇◇ N-UNCOUNT

working class, working classes. **The working class** or **the working classes** are the group of people in a society who do not own much property, who have low social status, and who do jobs which involve using physical skills rather than intellectual skills. *A quarter of the working class voted for him. ...increased levels of home ownership among the working classes.* ▶ Also an adjective. *...a self-educated man from a working class background... The group is mainly black, mainly working-class.* ◆◆◇◇◇ N-COUNT-COLL: *the* N; ADJ: usu ADJ n

working group, working groups. A **working group** is the same as a **working party**. *...the European Community's working group on health and nutrition.* ◆◇◇◇◇ N-COUNT-COLL

working party, working parties. In British English, a **working party** is a committee which is established to investigate a particular situation or problem and to produce a report containing its opinions and recommendations about what should be done. The usual American term is **working group**. *They set up a working party to look into the issue. ...a finance working party.* ◆◇◇◇◇ N-COUNT-COLL =working group

workload /wɜːʳkloʊd/ **workloads;** also spelled **work load**. The **workload** of a person or organization is the amount of work that has to be done by them. *The sudden cancellation of Mr Major's trip was due to his heavy workload... This office's resources and staff would have to be increased to cope with the extra workload.* ◆◇◇◇◇ N-COUNT: oft supp N

workman /wɜːʳkmən/ **workmen.** A **workman** is a man who works with his hands, for example a builder or plumber. *In University Square workmen are building a steel fence... Millson saw the workman, Terry, descending the ladder.* ◆◇◇◇◇ N-COUNT

workmanlike /wɜːʳkmənlaɪk/. If you describe something as **workmanlike**, you mean that it has been done quite well and sensibly, but not in a particularly imaginative or original way. *Really it's a workmanlike conference rather than a dramatic one... The script was workmanlike at best.* ADJ-GRADED

workmanship /wɜːʳkmənʃɪp/. **Workmanship** is the skill with which something is made and which affects the appearance and quality of the N-UNCOUNT: oft supp N =craftsmanship finished object. *The problem may be due to poor workmanship... The standard of workmanship is very high.*

workmate /wɜːʳkmeɪt/ **workmates.** Your **workmates** are the people you work with; an informal word. *My workmates, and, even more, the management, didn't want me to leave.* N-COUNT: usu pl, usu supp N =colleague

work of art, works of art ◆◇◇◇◇

1 A **work of art** is a painting or piece of sculpture which is of high quality. *...a collection of works of art of international significance.* N-COUNT

2 A **work of art** is something which is very complex or which has been skilfully made or produced. *The actual nest is a work of art.* N-COUNT

workout /wɜːʳkaʊt/ **workouts.** A **workout** is a period of physical exercise or training. *Give your upper body a workout by using handweights. ...a 35-minute aerobic workout.* ◆◇◇◇◇ N-COUNT

workplace /wɜːʳkpleɪs/ **workplaces;** also spelled **work place**. Your **workplace** is the place where you work. *...the difficulties facing women in the workplace... Their houses were workplaces as well as dwellings... Workplace canteens are offering healthier foods than ever before.* ◆◆◇◇◇ N-COUNT

workroom /wɜːʳkruːm/ **workrooms.** A person's **workroom** is a room where they work, especially when their work involves making things. N-COUNT

worksheet /wɜːʳkʃiːt/ **worksheets.** A **worksheet** is a specially prepared page of exercises designed to improve your knowledge or understanding of a particular subject. N-COUNT

workshop /wɜːʳkʃɒp/ **workshops** ◆◆◇◇◇

1 A **workshop** is a period of discussion or practical work on a particular subject in which a group of people share their knowledge or experience. *Trumpeter Marcus Belgrave ran a jazz workshop for young artists... The Jamaica Festival is planning a series of workshops and business seminars.* N-COUNT: oft supp N

2 A **workshop** is a room or building which contains tools or machinery for making or repairing things, especially using wood or metal. *...a modestly equipped workshop. ...the railway workshops.* N-COUNT

work-shy; also spelled **workshy**. If you describe someone as **work-shy**, you disapprove of them because you think they are lazy and do not want to work. *He is a morose, work-shy layabout.* ADJ-GRADED: usu ADJ n PRAGMATICS =lazy

workstation /wɜːʳksteɪʃᵊn/ **workstations;** also spelled **work station**. A **workstation** is a part of a computerized office system consisting of a display screen and a keyboard. ◆◇◇◇◇ N-COUNT

work surface, work surfaces; also spelled **worksurface**. A **work surface** is the same as a **worktop**. N-COUNT

worktop /wɜːʳktɒp/ **worktops.** A **worktop** is a flat surface in a kitchen which is easily cleaned and on which you can prepare food. N-COUNT =work surface

world /wɜːʳld/ **worlds** ◆◆◆◆◆

1 **The world** is the planet that we live on. *It's a beautiful part of the world... More than anything, I'd like to drive around the world... The satellite enables us to calculate their precise location anywhere in the world.* N-SING: *the* N

2 The **world** refers to all the people who live on this planet, and our societies, institutions, and ways of life. *The world was, and remains, shocked... He wants to show the world that anyone can learn to be an ambassador... His personal contribution to world history is likely to have been incidental. ...inflationary pressures in the world economy.* N-SING: *the* N, N n

3 You can use **world** to describe someone or something that is one of the most important or significant of its kind on earth. *Abroad, Mr Bush was seen as a world statesman... Like Japan, China has emerged as a world power... He was one of Newcastle's most distinguished medical men, a world authority on heart-diseases.* ADJ: ADJ n

4 You can use **world** in expressions such as **the Arab world, the western world,** and **the ancient world** to refer to a particular group of countries or a particular period in history. *Athens had strong ties to the Arab world. ...the developing world... Dogs were also associated with healing in the ancient world.* N-SING: *the* supp N

5 Someone's **world** is the life they lead, the people they have contact with, and the things they experience. *His world seemed so different from mine... I lost my job and it was like my world collapsed... I tried to understand the adult world and could not.* N-COUNT: oft poss N

6 You can use **world** to refer to a particular field of activity, and the people involved in it. *The publishing world had certainly never seen an event quite like this. ...the latest news from the world of finance.* N-SING: *the* N, with supp, oft N *of* n

7 You can use **world** to refer to a place or way of life by describing its strongest features. *...a golf course set in a hidden world of parkland, forest and lakes... The patient must re-enter a world full of problems and stresses.* N-COUNT: with supp, oft N *of* n

8 You can use **world** in expressions such as **this world, the next world,** and **the world to come** to refer to the state of being alive or a state of existence after death. *Good fortune will follow you, both in this world and the next.* N-SING: with supp

9 You can use **world** to refer to a particular group of living things, for example **the animal world, the plant world,** and **the insect world.** N-SING: *the* n N

10 A **world** is a planet. *He looked like something from another world... Man was drawing closer to the stars, opening new worlds.* N-COUNT

11 See also **brave new world, New World, real world, Third World.**

12 If you say that two people or things are **worlds apart**, you are emphasizing that they are very different from each other. *Intellectually, this man and I are worlds apart... The novel is worlds apart from his academic writings.* PHRASES usu v-link PHR, oft PHR *from* n PRAGMATICS =poles apart

13 If you say that someone has **the best of both worlds**, you mean that they have only the benefits of two things and none of the disadvantages. *Her living room provides the best of both worlds, with an office at one end and comfortable sofas at the other.* PHR after v, v-link PHR

14 If a woman **brings** a child **into the world,** she gives birth to a baby. You can also say that doctors or midwives who deliver babies **bring** children **into the world**. *I never felt I achieved a great deal in my life, apart from bringing my children into the world.* V inflects

15 If you say that there is **a world of difference** between one thing and another, you are emphasizing that they are very different from each other. *There's a world of difference between an amateur video and a slick Hollywood production.* v-link PHR, oft PHR *between* pl-n PRAGMATICS

16 If you say that you would not do something **for the world**, you are emphasizing that you definitely would not do it. *I wouldn't have missed this for the world.* with brd-neg, PHR after v PRAGMATICS =for anything

17 If you say that something **has done** someone **the world of good** or **a world of good,** you mean that it has made them feel better or improved their life; an informal expression. *A sleep will do you the world of good. ...a mature performance which must have done his career prospects a world of good.* V inflects

18 You use **in the world** to emphasize a statement that you are making. *The saddest thing in the world is a little baby nobody wants... He had no one in the world but her.* oft PHR after superl PRAGMATICS

19 You can use **in the world** in expressions such as **what in the world** and **who in the world** to emphasize a question, especially when expressing surprise, anger, or despair. *What in the world is he doing?... Where in the world were you when I was struggling for my life?* quest PHR PRAGMATICS =on earth

20 You can use **in an ideal world** or **in a perfect world** when you are talking about things that you would like to happen, although you realize that they are not likely to happen. *In an ideal world Karen Stevens says she would love to stay at home with her two-and-half-year old son... In a perfect world, there would be the facilities and money to treat every sick person.* PHR with cl =ideally

21 If you say that someone thinks that **the world owes** them **a living**, you are criticizing them because they think it is their right to have a comfort- V inflects PRAGMATICS

able life without having to make any effort at all. *All young people must face up to reality and not kid themselves that the world owes them a living.*

22 If you say that someone is **a man of the world** or **a woman of the world**, you mean that they are experienced and knowledgeable about life, and are not easily shocked, for example by immoral or dishonest things. *Look, we are both men of the world, would anyone really mind? ...an elegant, clever and tough woman of the world.* man/woman inflects

23 If you say that something is **out of this world**, you are emphasizing that it is extremely good or impressive; an informal expression. *These new trains are out of this world.* v-link PHR PRAGMATICS

24 You can use **the outside world** to refer to all the people who do not live in a particular place or who are not involved in a particular situation. *For many, the post office is the only link with the outside world... This, at least, was the situation as it appeared to the outside world.*

25 If you say that something happens or exists **the world over**, you mean that it happens or exists in every part of the world. *Some problems are the same the world over... Governments the world over should do something about it.* PHR after v, n PHR =everywhere

26 If you say that someone is **in a world of** their **own**, you mean that they seem not to notice other people or the things going on around them. *When I'm swimming I'm in a world of my own... Sarah was nine years old and until that moment she had been locked in a world of her own.* v-link PHR, PHR after v

27 If you **think the world of** someone, you like them or care about them very much. *I think the world of him, but something tells me it's not love... We were really close. We thought the world of each other.* V inflects, PHR n

28 If you say that someone **has gone up in the world**, you mean they have become richer or have a higher social status than before. If you say they **have come down in the world**, you mean they have become poorer or have a lower social status; used mainly in British English. *When they started to go up in the world, they moved to a flat in London. ...young women of middle class families which had come down in the world.* V inflects

29 • **not be the end of the world**: see **end**. • **the world is** your **oyster**: see **oyster**. • **on top of the world**: see **top**.

world beater, world beaters; also spelled **world-beater**. In British English, if you describe a person or thing as a **world beater**, you are mean that they are better than most other people or things of their kind. N-COUNT

world-class. A **world-class** sportsperson or competitor is one of the best in the world at what they do; used in journalism. *He was determined to become a world-class player. ...some of Britain's few world-class companies.* ◆◇◇◇◇ ADJ: usu ADJ n

world-famous. Someone or something that is **world-famous** is known about by people all over the world. *...the world-famous Hollywood Bowl... Harefield Hospital has become world-famous for its pioneering heart transplant surgery.* ◆◇◇◇◇ ADJ

worldly /wɜːʳldli/ ◆◇◇◇◇

1 **Worldly** is used to describe things relating to the ordinary activities of life, rather than to spiritual things; a literary use. *I think it is time you woke up and focused your thoughts on more worldly matters... He has repeatedly criticized Western churches as too worldly and too entrenched in consumerism.* ADJ-GRADED

2 Someone who is **worldly** is experienced and knowledgeable about the practical aspects of life rather than about spiritual things. *He was different from anyone I had known, very worldly, everything that Dermot was not... He was worldly and sophisticated.* ♦ **worldliness** *To Betty, Joe had an air of worldliness.* ADJ-GRADED: usu v-link ADJ; N-UNCOUNT

3 **Worldly** is used to describe things relating to success, wealth, and possessions: a literary use. *Today the media drive athletes to the view that the important thing is to gain worldly success.* ADJ: ADJ n

4 You can refer to someone's possessions as their **worldly** goods or possessions; a literary use. *...a man who had given up all his worldly goods... They are willing to sign away their entire worldly possessions to pay off their debts.* ADJ: ADJ n

worldly-wise. If you describe someone as **worldly-wise**, you mean they are experienced and knowledgeable about life, and are not easily shocked or impressed. ADJ-GRADED

world view, world views; also spelled **worldview**. A person's **world view** is the way they see and understand the world, especially regarding issues such as politics, philosophy, and religion. *...their Christian world view... Many artists express their world view in their work.* ◆◇◇◇◇ N-COUNT: with supp

world war, world wars. A **world war** is a war that involves countries all over the world. *Many senior citizens have been though two world wars... At the end of the second world war he was working as a docker... There is a risk of world war.* ◆◆◆◇◇ N-VAR

world-weary. A **world-weary** person no longer feels excited or enthusiastic about anything. ADJ-GRADED =jaded

worldwide /wɜːʳldwaɪd/; also spelled **world-wide**. If something exists or happens **worldwide**, it exists or happens throughout the world. *His books have sold more than 20 million copies worldwide... Every day the newspapers tell stories of children worldwide who are abused... Worldwide, an enormous amount of research effort goes into military technology.* ► Also an adjective. *Today, doctors are fearing a worldwide epidemic.* ◆◆◆◇◇ ADV: ADV after v, n ADV, ADV with cl; ADJ: usu ADJ n

World-Wide Web. **The World-Wide Web** is a system which links documents and pictures into an information database that is stored in computers in many different parts of the world and which can be accessed with a single program. **World-Wide Web** is often abbreviated to **WWW** or **Web**. N-PROPER: *the* N

worm /wɜːʳm/ **worms, worming, wormed** ◆◆◇◇◇

1 A **worm** is a small animal with a long thin body, no bones and no legs. N-COUNT

2 If animals or people have **worms**, small, thin parasites are living in their intestines. N-PLURAL

3 If you **worm** an animal, you give it medicine in order to kill the parasites that are in its intestines. *I worm all my birds in early spring... All adult dogs are routinely wormed at least every six months.* VERB Vn

4 If you **worm** your **way** somewhere, you move there slowly and with difficulty. *I had to worm my way out sideways from the bench in a ridiculous, undignified fashion... The kitten wormed its way through the just-open door.* VERB =inch V *way* adv/prep

5 If you say that someone **is worming** their **way** to success, or **is worming** their **way** into someone else's affection, you disapprove of the way that they are gradually making someone trust them or like them, often in order to deceive them or gain some advantage. *She never misses a chance to worm her way into the public's hearts... Everyone knows people who have wormed their way up on old school connections.* VERB PRAGMATICS V *way* prep/adv

6 If you call a person a **worm**, you are insulting them by saying that they have a very weak or unpleasant character and you have no respect for them. N-SING PRAGMATICS

7 If you say that someone or something is opening **a can of worms**, you are warning them that they are planning to do or talk about something which is more complicated, unpleasant, and difficult than they realize and which might be better left alone. *You've opened up a whole new can of worms here I think. We could have a whole debate on student loans and grants... Drug abuse is a can of worms nobody wants to open at sporting events.* PHRASES PHR after v, v-link PHR PRAGMATICS

8 If you say that **the worm turns**, you mean that someone who is usually very patient and passive has unexpectedly changed their behaviour and done something bold and daring. *Now the worm turns, and his wife Elizabeth chucks him out and takes a lover herself.* V inflects

worm out of. If you **worm** information **out of** someone, you gradually find it out by constantly PHRASAL VERB

asking them about it. *It took me weeks to worm the facts out of him... It didn't take long before she'd wormed out of him confessions of his other moments of infidelity.*
V n P P n
V P P n n (not pron)

wormwood /wɜːʳmwʊd/. **Wormwood** is a plant that has a very bitter taste and is used in making medicines and alcoholic drinks.
N-UNCOUNT

worn /wɔːʳn/ ◆◇◇◇◇
1 **Worn** is the past participle of **wear**.
2 **Worn** is used to describe something that is damaged or thin because it is old and has been used a lot. *Worn rugs increase the danger of tripping... Most of the trek is along worn paths.*
ADJ-GRADED: usu ADJ n
3 If someone looks **worn**, they look tired and old. *She was looking very haggard and worn.*
ADJ-GRADED: v-link ADJ
4 See also **well-worn**.

worn out; also spelled **worn-out**. ◆◇◇◇◇
1 Something that is **worn out** is so old, damaged, or thin from use that it cannot be used any more. *Car buyers tend to replace worn-out tyres with the same brand. ...faded bits of worn-out clothing.*
ADJ
2 Someone who is **worn out** is extremely tired after hard work or a difficult or unpleasant experience. *Before the race, he is fine. But afterwards he is worn out.*
ADJ-GRADED: usu v-link ADJ =exhausted
3 If you describe something such as an idea as **worn out**, you mean that it is no longer relevant or interesting because it is old and has been repeated many times; used showing disapproval. *Mr Hurd said it was time to set aside worn out arguments about sanctions.*
ADJ: ADJ n PRAGMATICS

worried /wʌrid, AM wɜːrid/. When you are **worried**, you are unhappy because you keep thinking about problems that you have or about unpleasant things that might happen in the future. *He seemed very worried... If you're at all worried about his progress, do discuss it with one of his teachers... The unions are worried that at least 100,000 jobs will disappear as a result of privatization.* ♦ **worriedly** *'You don't have to go, you know,' she said worriedly.*
◆◆◆◇◇
ADJ-GRADED: oft ADJ about n, ADJ that =anxious
ADV-GRADED: usu ADV with v

worrier /wʌriəʳ, AM wɜːriər/ **worriers.** If you describe someone as a **worrier**, you mean that they spend a lot of time thinking about problems that they have or unpleasant things that might possibly happen.
N-COUNT

worrisome /wʌrɪsəm, AM wɜːr-/. Something that is **worrisome** causes people to worry or should cause them to worry; used mainly in American English.
ADJ-GRADED =worrying

worry /wʌri, AM wɜːri/ **worries, worrying, worried** ◆◆◆◆◇
1 If you **worry**, you keep thinking about problems that you have or about unpleasant things that might happen. *Don't worry, your luggage will come on afterwards by taxi... I worry about her constantly... I work in a school so I don't have to worry about finding someone to look after my little boy... They worry that extremists might gain control.*
VERB
V
V about n/-ing
V that
2 If someone or something **worries** you, they make you anxious because you keep thinking about problems or unpleasant things that might be connected with them. *I'm still in the early days of my recovery and that worries me... 'Why didn't you tell us?'—'I didn't want to worry you.'... The English, worried by the growing power of Prince Henry, sent a raiding party to Scotland to kill him... Does it worry you that the Americans are discussing this?*
VERB
V n
V-ed
it V n that/to-inf
3 If someone or something does not **worry** you, you do not dislike them or you are not annoyed by them; used in spoken English. *The cold doesn't worry me... It wouldn't worry me if he came to my house, but I don't know if I would go out of my way to ask him.*
VB: oft with neg =bother
V n
it V n if
4 **Worry** is the state or feeling of anxiety and unhappiness caused by the problems that you have or by thinking about unpleasant things that might happen. *The admission shows the depth of worry among the Tories over the state of the economy... His last years were overshadowed by financial worry.*
N-UNCOUNT
5 A **worry** is a problem that you keep thinking about and that makes you unhappy. *My main worry was that Madeleine Johnson would still be there... The worry is that the use of force could make life impossible for the UN peacekeepers... His wife Cheryl said she had no worries about his health.*
N-COUNT
6 You say **not to worry** to someone to indicate that you are not upset or angry when something has gone wrong; an informal expression. *'Not to worry, Baby,' he said, and kissed her tenderly.*
PHRASES CONVENTION PRAGMATICS

worrying /wʌriɪŋ, AM wɜːriɪŋ/. If something is **worrying**, it causes people to worry. *It is very worrying that petrol bombs have been brought into a fight between two secondary schools. ...a new and worrying report about smoking.* ♦ **worryingly** *The rate of assaults was worryingly high... Worryingly for those in favour of competition, the Minister has been resistant to this argument.*
◆◆◇◇◇
ADJ-GRADED: oft it v-link ADJ that =worrisome
ADV-GRADED: ADV adj, ADV with cl

worse /wɜːʳs/ ◆◇◇◇◇
1 **Worse** is the comparative of **bad**.
2 **Worse** is the comparative of **badly**.
3 **Worse** is used to form the comparative of compound adjectives beginning with 'bad' and 'badly.' For example, the comparative of 'badly off' is 'worse off'.
4 If a situation **goes from bad to worse**, it becomes even more unpleasant or unsatisfactory. *For the past couple of years my life has gone from bad to worse.*
PHRASES V inflects
5 If you tell someone that they **could do worse** than do a particular thing, you are advising them that it would be quite a good thing to do. *Scientists in search of a challenging career could do worse than consider forensic science.*
oft PHR than inf/n PRAGMATICS
6 If a situation changes **for the worse**, it becomes more unpleasant or more difficult. *The grandparents sigh and say how things have changed for the worse.*
PHR after v
7 If someone or something is **the worse for** something, they have been harmed or badly affected by it. If they are **none the worse** for it, they have not been harmed or badly affected by it. *Father came home from the pub very much the worse for drink... They are all apparently fit and well and none the worse for the fifteen hour journey.*
PHR after v, PHR n
8 ● **for better or worse**: see **better**.

worsen /wɜːʳsən/ **worsens, worsening, worsened.** If a bad situation **worsens** or if something **worsens** it, it becomes more difficult, unpleasant, or unacceptable. *The security forces had to intervene to prevent the situation worsening... These options would actually worsen the economy and add to the deficit... They remain stranded in freezing weather and rapidly worsening conditions.* ♦ **worsening** *This latest incident is bound to lead to a further worsening of relations between the two countries.*
◆◆◇◇◇
V-ERG ≠improve
V
V n
V-ing
N-SING: usu N of n

worship /wɜːʳʃɪp/ **worships, worshipping, worshipped;** spelled **worshiping, worshiped** in American English. ◆◆◇◇◇
1 If you **worship** a god, you show your respect to the god, for example by saying prayers. *I enjoy going to church and worshipping God. ...Jews worshipping at the Wailing Wall.* ► Also a noun. *...the worship of the ancient Roman gods... St Jude's church is a public place of worship.* ♦ **worshipper, worshippers** *At the end of the service, scores of worshippers streamed down to the alter.*
VERB
V n
V
N-UNCOUNT
N-COUNT
2 If you **worship** someone or something, you love them or admire them very much. *She had worshipped him for years... They worship James Brown, Bob Marley and Jimi Hendrix.*
VERB
V n

worshipful /wɜːʳʃɪpfʊl/. If someone has a **worshipful** attitude to someone or something, they show a very great amount of respect and admiration for them. *...Franklin's almost worshipful imitation of his cousin.*
ADJ: ADJ n =reverential

worst /wɜːʳst/ ◆◇◇◇◇
1 **Worst** is the superlative of **bad**.
2 **Worst** is the superlative of **badly**.
3 **The worst** is the most unpleasant or unfavourable thing that could happen or does happen. *Though mine safety has much improved, miners'*
N-SING: the N, oft N of n ≠best

families still fear the worst... The country had come through the worst of the recession.
4 Worst is used to form the superlative of compound adjectives beginning with 'bad' and 'badly'. For example, the superlative of 'badly-affected' is 'worst-affected'.
5 You say **worst of all** to indicate that what you are about to mention is the most unpleasant or has the most disadvantages out of all the things you are mentioning. *The people most closely affected are the passengers who were injured and, worst of all, those who lost relatives.* PHRASES PHR with cl PRAGMATICS
6 You use **at worst** or **at the worst** to indicate that you are considering a situation in the most unfavourable or most pessimistic way. *At best Nella would be an invalid; at worst she would die... At the worst he would be there by the following night.* PHR with cl/group
7 If someone is **at their worst**, they are behaving as unpleasantly or doing something as unsuccessfully as it is possible for them to do. *This was their mother at her worst. Her voice was strident, she was ready to be angry at anyone.* n PHR, PHR after v, v-link PHR
8 If you say that you might do something **if the worst comes to the worst**, you mean that you might do it if the situation develops in the most unfavourable way. *If the worst comes to the worst I guess I can always ring Jean... He was asked whether he would walk out if the worst came to the worst.* V inflects, PHR with cl
9 If someone **does their worst**, they do everything unpleasant that they can possibly do. You can say **'do your worst'** to show someone that you are not frightened even if they do everything unpleasant that they can possibly do. *I think it was dangerous to say: look, we've got an army now – do your worst.* V inflects PRAGMATICS

worsted /wʊstɪd/ **worsteds. Worsted** is a kind of woollen cloth. N-MASS

worth /wɜːʳθ/ ◆◆◆◆◇
1 If something is **worth** a particular amount of money, it can be sold for that amount or is considered to have that value. *These books might be worth £50 or £60 or more to a collector... His mother inherited a farm worth 15,000 dollars a year... The contract was worth £25 million a year.* v-link *worth* amount
2 Worth combines with amounts of money, so that when you talk about a particular amount of money's **worth of** something, you mean the quantity of it that you can buy for that amount of money. *I went and bought about six dollars' worth of potato chips... Large numbers of deer now roam the forests and are causing thousands of millions of roubles-worth of damage.* ► Also a pronoun. *'How many do you want?'—'I'll have a pound's worth.'* COMB in QUANT: QUANT *of* n; PRON
3 Worth combines with time expressions, so you can use **worth** when you are saying how long an amount of something will last. For example, a week's **worth of** food is the amount of food that will last you for a week. *You've got three years' worth of research money to do what you want with... After an hour and a quarter's-worth of cleansing, toning and pampering, the difference to the way my skin felt was remarkable.* ► Also a pronoun. *There's really not very much food down there. About two weeks' worth.* COMB in QUANT: QUANT *of* n; PRON
4 If you say that something is **worth** having, you mean that it is pleasant or useful, and therefore a good thing to have. *He's decided to get a look at the house and see if it might be worth buying... If this was what his job required, then the job wasn't really worth having... Most things worth having never come easy.* v-link *worth* -ing
5 If something is **worth** a particular action, or if an action is **worth** doing, it is considered to be important enough for that action. *No one is worth a great deal of sacrifice... I am spending a lot of money and time on this boat, but it is worth it... This restaurant is well worth a visit... It is worth pausing to consider these statements from Mr Wigley.* v-link *worth* n/-ing
6 Someone's **worth** is the value, usefulness, or importance that they are considered to have; a formal use. *He had never met a woman like her, nor had he ever had a woman of her worth as a friend... The team would have need of a driver of his worth.* N-UNCOUNT: usu with poss
7 If you do something **for all** you **are worth**, you do it with a lot of energy and enthusiasm. *We both began waving to the crowd for all we were worth... Push for all you're worth!* PHRASES V inflects
8 If someone does something **for all it is worth**, they do it as much as possible and for as long as they can get benefit from it. *You get anywhere with legal aid only by playing the system for all it is worth. ...taking an idea and exploiting it for all it's worth.* V inflects
9 If you add **for what it's worth** to something that you say, you are suggesting that what you are saying or referring to may not be very valuable or helpful, especially because you do not want to appear arrogant. *Personal preference will dictate how you drink your whisky. For what it's worth, my feeling is that ice is fine... I've brought my notes, for what it's worth.* PHR with cl
10 If an action or activity is **worth** someone's **while**, it will be helpful, useful, or enjoyable for them if they do it, even though it requires some effort. *It might be worth your while to go to court and ask for the agreement to be changed... You'll find it well worth your while to learn something of each island's special features before visiting them.* v-link PHR =worthwhile
11 ● **worth your weight in gold**: see **weight**.

worthless /wɜːʳθləs/ ◆◇◇◇◇
1 Something that is **worthless** is of no real value or use. *The guarantee could be worthless if the firm goes out of business... Training is worthless unless there is proof that it works. ...a worthless piece of old junk.* ADJ-GRADED =useless
2 Someone who is described as **worthless** is considered to have no good qualities or skills. *You feel you really are completely worthless and unlovable.* ADJ-GRADED: usu v-link ADJ
♦ **worthlessness** *...feelings of worthlessness and inadequacy.* N-UNCOUNT

worthwhile /wɜːʳθʰwaɪl/. If something is **worthwhile**, it is enjoyable or useful, and worth the time, money, or effort that is spent on it. *The President's trip to Washington this week seems to have been worthwhile. ...a worthwhile movie that was compelling enough to watch again... It might be worthwhile to consider your attitude to an insurance policy.* ◆◆◇◇◇ ADJ-GRADED: oft *it* v-link ADJ to-inf

worthy /wɜːʳði/ **worthier, worthiest; worthies** ◆◆◇◇◇
1 If someone or something is **worthy** of something, they deserve it because they have the qualities or abilities required; a formal use. *The bank might think you're worthy of a loan... The Minister says the idea is worthy of consideration... I hope he was worthy of her.* ♦ **worthily** *I have not achieved my goal in becoming chief constable, a rank I know I could have worthily held.* ♦ **worthiness** *Some people are afraid to take risks because their belief in their own worthiness is so low.* ADJ-GRADED: usu v-link ADJ, usu ADJ *of* n ≠unworthy; ADV: ADV with v; N-UNCOUNT =worth
2 A **worthy** person or thing is approved of by most people in society and considered to be morally respectable or correct. *...worthy members of the community... They thought the feminist label was too worthy.* ► You can refer to worthy people as **worthies**. *...the commission, which brought together worthies from big corporations, universities and state governments.* ADJ-GRADED; N-COUNT

-worthy /-wɜːʳði/. **-worthy** can be added to words to form adjectives which indicate that someone or something deserves or merits a particular thing or action. For example, if a remark or person is **quote-worthy**, they are worth quoting. *It was not the transparency of Ms Westwood's outfit that was most comment-worthy... You may see yourself as useless, incompetent and blameworthy... Candidates deemed vote-worthy will be rewarded with campaign funds.* ● See also **airworthy**, **creditworthy**, **newsworthy**, **noteworthy**, **praiseworthy**, **seaworthy**, **trustworthy**. COMB in ADJ-GRADED

wot. In British English, **wot** is sometimes used in writing to represent **'what'**, to show that someone is speaking very informally or that they are being humorous. *'Cor, wot brilliant prizes!'*

would /wəd STRONG wʊd/ ◆◆◆◆◆
Would is a modal verb. It is used with the base

form of a verb. In spoken English, **would** is often abbreviated to **'d**.

1 You use **would** when you are saying what someone believed, hoped, or expected to happen or be the case. *No one believed the soldiers stationed at the border would actually open fire... Would he always be like this?... Once inside, I found that the flat would be perfect for my life in Paris... He expressed the hope that on Monday elementary schools would be reopened... A report yesterday that said British unemployment would continue to rise... I don't think that he would take such a decision.* MODAL

2 You use **would** when saying what someone intended to do. *The statement added that although there were a number of differing views, these would be discussed by both sides... George decided it was such a rare car that he would only use it for a few shows... He did not think he would marry Beth.* MODAL

3 You use **would** when you are referring to the result or effect of a possible situation. *Ordinarily it would be fun to be taken to fabulous restaurants... It would be wrong to suggest that police officers were not annoyed by acts of indecency... It would cost very much more for the four of us to go from Italy. ...identity cards without which fans would not be able to get into stadiums.* MODAL

4 You use **would**, or **would have** with a past participle, to indicate that you are assuming or guessing that something is true, because you have good reasons for thinking it. *You wouldn't know him... His fans would already be familiar with Caroline... That would have been Della's car... He made a promise to his great-grandfather? That would have been a long time ago... It was half seven; her mother would be annoyed because he was so late.* MODAL

5 You use **would** in the main clause of some 'if' and 'unless' sentences to indicate something you consider to be fairly unlikely to happen. *If only I could get some sleep, I would be able to cope... Foreign troops would withdraw from Saudi Arabia if his government asked them to do so... I think if I went to look at more gardens, I would be better on planning and designing them... A policeman would not live one year if he obeyed these regulations... the targets would not be achieved unless other departments showed equal commitment.* MODAL

6 You use **would** to say that someone was willing to do something. You use **would not** to indicate that someone refused to do something. *They said they would give the police their full cooperation... She indicated that she would help her husband... David would not accept this... He wouldn't say where he had picked up the information.* MODAL

7 You use **would not** to indicate that something did not happen, often in spite of a lot of effort. *He kicked, pushed, and hurled his shoulder at the door. It wouldn't open... He kept trying to start the car and the battery got flatter and flatter, until it wouldn't turn the engine at all... The paint wouldn't stick to the wallpaper.* MODAL

8 You use **would**, especially with verbs such as 'like', 'love', and 'wish' when saying that someone wants to do or have something or wants something to happen. *She asked me what I would like to do and mentioned a particular job... Right now, your mom would like a cup of coffee... Ideally, she would love to become pregnant again... He wished it would end... Anne wouldn't mind going to Italy or France to live.* • **would rather**: see **rather**. MODAL

9 You use **would** with 'if' clauses in questions when you are asking for permission to do something. *Do you think it would be all right if I smoked?... Mr. Cutler, would you mind if I asked a question?* MODAL PRAGMATICS

10 You use **would**, usually in questions, when you are politely offering someone something or inviting someone to do something. *Would you like a drink?... Would you like to stay?... Perhaps you would like to pay a visit to London.* MODAL PRAGMATICS

11 You use **would**, usually in questions, when you are politely asking someone to do something. *Would you do me a favour and get rid of this letter I've just received?... Would you come in here a moment, please?... Would you excuse us for a minute, Cassandra?... Oh dear, there's the doorbell. See who it is, would you, darling.* MODAL PRAGMATICS =could

12 You say that someone **would** do something when it is typical of them and you are critical of it. You emphasize the word **would** when you use it in this way. *I was amazed, during a 'Women In Rock' debate, to be told, 'Well, you would say that: you're a man.'... 'Well then Francesca turned round and said, "That's a stupid question."'—'She would, wouldn't she.'* MODAL PRAGMATICS

13 You use **would**, or sometimes **would have** with a past participle, when you are expressing your opinion about something or seeing if people agree with you, especially when you are not certain that what you are saying is correct or when you are pretending to be uncertain in order to be polite. *I think you'd agree he's a very respected columnist... I would have thought it a proper job for the Army to fight rebellion... 'Was it much different for you when you started at the Foreign Office?'—'Worse, I'd expect.'... I would imagine that you can't grow seeds actually in these big plastic bags.* MODAL PRAGMATICS

14 You use **I would** when you are giving someone advice in an informal way. *If I were you, Mrs Gretchen, I just wouldn't worry about it... I would not, if I were you, be inclined to discuss private business with the landlady... There could be more unrest, but I wouldn't exaggerate the problems.* MODAL PRAGMATICS

15 You use **you would** in negative sentences with verbs such as 'guess' and 'know' when you want to say that something is not obvious, especially something surprising. *Chris is so full of artistic temperament you'd never think she was the daughter of a banker... Inside, he admits, his emotions may be churning, but you would never guess it.* MODAL

16 You use **would** to talk about something which happened regularly in the past but which no longer happens. *Sunday mornings my mother would bake. I'd stand by the fridge and help... 'Beauty is only skin deep.' my mother would say.* MODAL =used to

17 You use **would have** with a past participle when you are saying what was likely to have happened by a particular time. *Within ten weeks of the introduction, 34 million people would have been reached by our television commercials.* MODAL

18 You use **would have** with a past participle when you are referring to the result or effect of a possible event in the past. *My daughter would have been 17 this week if she had lived... If I had known how he felt, I would never have let him adopt those children... If I had not been enjoying the work, I would not have done so much of it.* MODAL

19 If you say that someone **would have** liked or preferred something, you mean that they wanted to do it or have it but were unable to. *I would have liked a life in politics... She would have liked to ask questions, but he had moved on to another topic... He also had made it a practice to dine there regularly, though he would have preferred being at home.* MODAL

20 You use **would**, usually in negative sentences, to criticize something that someone has done and to express your disapproval of it. *I would never have done what they did.* MODAL PRAGMATICS

21 If you say **'would that'** something were the case, you are saying that you wish it were the case; a formal expression. *Would that he could have listened to his father.* PHRASE: PHR cl PRAGMATICS =if only

would-be. You can use **would-be** to describe someone who wants or attempts to do a particular thing. For example, a **would-be** writer is someone who wants to be a writer. *...a book that provides encouragement for would-be writers who cannot get their novel into print. ...a would-be rock star.* ADJ: ADJ n

wouldn't /wʊdᵊnt/. **Wouldn't** is written to represent the usual spoken form of 'would not'. *They wouldn't allow me to smoke.*

would've /wʊdəv/. **Would've** is written to represent a spoken form of 'would have', when 'have' is an auxiliary verb. *I knew deep down that my mum would've loved one of us to go to college.*

wound 1 verb form of 'wind'
wound /waʊnd/. **Wound** is the past tense and past participle of **wind** 2.
wound 2 injury
wound /wuːnd/ **wounds, wounding, wounded** ◆◆◆◆◇
1 A **wound** is damage to part of your body, especially a cut or a hole in your flesh, which is caused by a gun, knife, or other weapon. *The wound is healing nicely and the patient is healthy... Six soldiers are reported to have died from their wounds.* N-COUNT =injury
2 If a weapon or something sharp **wounds** you, it damages your body. *A bomb exploded in a hotel, killing six people and wounding another five... The driver of an evacuation bus was wounded by shrapnel... The two wounded men were taken to a nearby hospital.* ► **The wounded** are people who are wounded. *Hospitals said they could not cope with the wounded... They were told to carry their wounded and leave their dead.* VERB =injure V n V-ed N-PLURAL =injured
3 A **wound** is a lasting bad effect on someone's mind or feelings caused by a very upsetting experience; a literary use. *She has been so deeply hurt it may take forever for the wounds to heal.* N-COUNT =scar
4 If you **are wounded** by what someone says or does, your feelings are deeply hurt. *He was deeply wounded by the treachery of close aides... My children have wounded me in the past.* ♦ **wounded** *I think she feels desperately wounded and unloved.* VERB =hurt be V-ed V n ADJ-GRADED: usu v-link ADJ =hurt
5 If you say that someone is **licking** their **wounds** you mean that they are recovering after being thoroughly defeated or humiliated. *The British team was returning home yesterday to lick its wounds after defeat by India.* PHRASES V inflects
6 Something that **opens old wounds** or **reopens old wounds** reminds someone about an upsetting experience in the past which they would prefer to forget. *Courts have been reluctant to reopen old wounds by trying crimes that are decades old.* V inflects
7 ● to **rub salt into the wound**: see **salt**.
wound up /waʊnd ʌp/. If someone is **wound up** they are very tense and nervous or angry. ◆◇◇◇◇ ADJ-GRADED: usu v-link ADJ
wove /woʊv/. **Wove** is the past tense of **weave**.
woven /woʊvᵊn/. **Woven** is a past participle of **weave**.
wow /waʊ/ **wows, wowing, wowed** ◆◇◇◇◇
1 You can say **'wow'** when you are very impressed, surprised, or pleased; an informal word. *I thought, 'Wow, what a good idea'.* EXCLAM PRAGMATICS
2 In informal English, you say that someone **wows** you when they give an impressive performance and fill you with enthusiasm and admiration. *Ben Tankard wowed the crowd with his jazz.* VERB V n
WPC /dʌbᵊljuː piː siː/ **WPCs.** In Britain, a **WPC** is a female police officer of the lowest rank. **WPC** is an abbreviation for 'woman police constable'. N-COUNT; N-TITLE
wraith /reɪθ/ **wraiths.** A **wraith** is a ghost; a literary word. *That child flits about like a wraith.* N-COUNT
wrangle /ræŋgᵊl/ **wrangles, wrangling, wrangled.** If you say that someone **is wrangling** with someone over something, or they **are wrangling** over it, you mean that they are arguing angrily for quite a long time about it. *The two sides have spent most of their time wrangling over procedural problems... A group of MPs is still wrangling with the government over the timing of elections.* ► Also a noun. *The party was torn apart by wrangles over fiscal policy... He was involved in a legal wrangle with the Health Secretary.* ♦ **wrangling, wranglings** *There was some wrangling between creditors about who was to blame.* ◆◇◇◇◇ V-RECIP pl-n V over n V with n over n Also pl-n V, V with n N-COUNT N-UNCOUNT: also N in pl
wrap /ræp/ **wraps, wrapping, wrapped** ◆◆◆◇◇
1 When you **wrap** something, you fold paper or cloth tightly round it to cover it completely, for example in order to protect it or so that you can give it to someone as a present. *Harry had carefully bought and wrapped presents for Mark to give them... Mexican Indians used to wrap tough meat in leaves from the papaya tree.* ► **Wrap up** means the same as **wrap**. *Diana is taking the opportunity to wrap up the family presents.* VERB ≠unwrap V n V n in n PHRASAL VERB V P n (not pron) Also V n P
2 **Wrap** is the material that something is wrapped in. *I tucked some plastic wrap around the sandwiches to keep them from getting stale. ...gift wrap.* N-UNCOUNT: usu supp N
3 When you **wrap** something such as a piece of paper or cloth round another thing, you put it around it. *She wrapped a handkerchief around her bleeding palm... Then she stood up, wrapping her coat around her angrily... Wrap the foil over the fish.* VERB V n around/over n
4 If someone **wraps** their arms, fingers, or legs around something, they put them firmly around it. *He wrapped his arms around her.* VERB V n around n
5 A **wrap** is a piece of clothing which women wear round their shoulders, either to keep them warm when wearing an evening dress, or for decoration over a coat. N-COUNT
6 See also **wrapping**.
7 If you keep something **under wraps**, you keep it secret, often until you are ready to announce it at some time in the future. *The bids were submitted in May and were meant to have been kept under wraps until October... The date and venue of the game must remain under wraps... You can never keep a launch as big as ours completely under wraps.* PHRASE: v-link PHR, PHR after v
wrap up PHRASAL VERB
1 If you **wrap up**, you put warm clothes on. *Markus has wrapped up warmly in a woolly hat... Kids just love being able to romp around in the fresh air without having to wrap up warm... I love crisp wintry days when you wrap up in cosy winter clothes.* V P adv/adj/prep Also V P
2 If you **wrap up** something such as a job or an agreement, you complete it in a satisfactory way. *NATO defense ministers wrap up their meeting in Brussels today... Seeing Sticht was keeping him from his golf game, and he hoped they could wrap it up quickly.* V P n (not pron) V n P
3 See also **wrap** 1; **wrapped up**.
wrapped up. If someone is **wrapped up** in something or someone, they spend nearly all their time thinking about them, so that they forget about other things which may be important. *He's too serious and dedicated, wrapped up in his career... New mothers can get very wrapped up in their baby without realising it.* ◆◇◇◇◇ ADJ-GRADED: v-link ADJ in/with n
wrapper /ræpəʳ/ **wrappers.** A **wrapper** is a piece of paper, plastic, or foil which covers and protects something that you buy, especially something perishable such as food. *I emptied the sweet wrappers from the ashtray. ...an unsmoked cigar in its cellophane wrapper.* N-COUNT: oft supp N
wrapping /ræpɪŋ/ **wrappings. Wrapping** is something such as paper or plastic which is used to cover and protect something. *Nick asked for the tile to be delivered in waterproof wrapping... He raced into the living room with his package, excitedly pulling at the wrappings.* ◆◇◇◇◇ N-VAR
wrapping paper, wrapping papers. Wrapping paper is special paper which is used for wrapping presents. N-MASS
wrath /rɒθ, AM ræθ/. **Wrath** means the same as anger. *He incurred the wrath of the authorities in speaking out against government injustices.* ◆◇◇◇◇ N-UNCOUNT: oft with poss
wreak /riːk/ **wreaks, wreaking, wreaked; wrought** can also be used as the past participle. ◆◇◇◇◇
1 Something or someone that **wreaks** havoc or destruction causes a great amount of disorder or damage; a literary or journalistic use. *Violent storms wreaked havoc on the French Riviera, leaving three people dead and dozens injured... The mountains are studded with dams, any one of which could wreak destruction in the valley below. ...the devastation wrought by a decade of fighting.* VERB V n
2 If you **wreak** revenge or vengeance on someone, you do something that will harm them very much to punish them for the harm they have done to you; a literary or journalistic use. *He threatened to wreak vengeance on the men who toppled him a year ago.* VERB V n
3 See also **wrought**.
wreath /riːθ/ **wreaths** ◆◇◇◇◇
1 A **wreath** is an arrangement of flowers and leaves, usually in the shape of a circle, which is put onto a grave or by a statue as a sign of remembrance for the dead. *The coffin lying before the altar* N-COUNT

was bare, except for a single wreath of white roses... The British, Australian and Turkish Prime Ministers laid wreaths at the war memorial.

2 A **wreath** is a circle of leaves or flowers which someone wears around their head. N-COUNT

3 A **wreath** is a circle of leaves and flowers which some people hang on the front door of their house at Christmas. N-COUNT

wreathe /riːð/ **wreathes, wreathing, wreathed**

1 If something **is wreathed** in smoke or mist, it is surrounded by it; a literary use. *The ship was wreathed in smoke... Fog wreathes the temples.* VERB =shroud *be* V-ed *in* n V n

2 If something **is wreathed** with flowers or leaves, it has a circle or chain of flowers or leaves put round it. *Its huge columns were wreathed with laurel and magnolia.* VB: usu passive *be* V-ed *with/in* n

wreck /rek/ **wrecks, wrecking, wrecked** ◆◆◇◇◇

1 If someone or something **wrecks** something, they completely destroy or ruin it. *He wrecked the garden... A coalition could have defeated the government and wrecked the treaty... His life has been wrecked by the tragedy. ...missed promotions, lost jobs, wrecked marriages.* ♦ **wrecker, wreckers** *They may be remembered as the wreckers of a fine company.* VERB V n V-ed N-COUNT

2 If a ship **is wrecked**, it is damaged so much that it sinks or can no longer sail. *The ship was wrecked by an explosion. ...a wrecked cargo ship.* VB: usu passive *be* V-ed V-ed

3 A **wreck** is something such as a ship, car, plane, or building which has been destroyed, usually in an accident. *...the wreck of a sailing ship... The car was a total wreck... We thought of buying the house as a wreck, doing it up, then selling it.* N-COUNT

4 In American English, a **wreck** is an accident in which a moving vehicle hits something and is damaged or destroyed. The British word is **crash**. *He was killed in a car wreck. ...the little girl that survived that plane wreck... What would he tell his parents if he had a wreck?* N-COUNT: usu supp N =crash

5 If you say that someone is a **wreck**, you mean that they are very exhausted or unhealthy; an informal use. *You look a wreck... It was embarrassing and sad to see this man reduced to a mumbling wreck.* N-COUNT: usu sing

• See also **nervous wreck**.

wreckage /rekɪdʒ/ ◆◇◇◇◇

1 When something such as a plane, car, or building has been destroyed, you can refer to what remains as **wreckage** or **the wreckage**. *Mark was dragged from the burning wreckage of his car.* N-UNCOUNT: also *the* N

2 If something such as a plan has failed or been spoilt completely, you can refer to what remains as **the wreckage** of it. *New states were born out of the wreckage of old colonial empires.* N-SING: *the* N, usu N *of* n

wren /ren/ **wrens.** A **wren** is a very small brown bird. There are several kinds of wren. ◆◇◇◇◇ N-COUNT

wrench /rentʃ/ **wrenches, wrenching, wrenched** ◆◇◇◇◇

1 If you **wrench** something that is fixed in a particular position, you pull or twist it violently, in order to move or remove it. *He felt two men wrench the suitcase from his hand... He wrenched off his sneakers... They wrenched open the passenger doors and jumped into her car.* VERB V n prep V n with adv V n with adj

2 If you **wrench** yourself free from someone who is holding you, you get away from them by suddenly twisting the part of your body that is being held. *She wrenched herself from his grasp... He wrenched his arm free... She tore at one man's face as she tried to wrench free... I wrenched my hand away from my attacker.* VERB =tear V pron-refl prep V n adj V adj V n adv

3 If you **wrench** a limb or one of your joints, you twist it and injure it. *He had wrenched his ankle badly from the force of the fall.* VERB V n

4 If you say that leaving someone or something is a **wrench**, you feel very sad about it. *I always knew it would be a wrench to leave Essex after all these years... Many of the things are of great sentimental value and it is going to be a wrench parting with them... Although it would be a wrench, we would all accept the challenge of moving abroad.* N-SING: usu *a* N to-inf/-ing

5 A **wrench** or **monkey wrench** is an adjustable metal tool used for tightening or loosening nuts and bolts. N-COUNT

6 In American English, if someone **throws a wrench** or **throws a monkey wrench** into a process, they prevent something happening smoothly in the way that it was planned, by deliberately causing a problem or difficulty. The British expression is to **throw a spanner in the works**. *Their delegation threw a giant monkey wrench into the process this week by raising all sorts of petty objections.* PHRASE: V inflects, PHR *in/into* n

wrest /rest/ **wrests, wresting, wrested** ◆◇◇◇◇

1 If you **wrest** something from someone else, you take it from them with effort or unlawfully; a literary or journalistic use. *For the past year he has been trying to wrest control from the central government... The men had returned to wrest back power.* VERB =seize V n *from* n V n with *away/back*

2 If you **wrest** something from someone who is holding it, you take it from them by pulling or twisting it violently; a literary use. *He wrested the suitcase from the chauffeur... He was attacked by a security man who tried to wrest away a gas cartridge.* VERB V n *from* n V n with *away*

wrestle /resᵊl/ **wrestles, wrestling, wrestled** ◆◇◇◇◇

1 When you **wrestle** with a difficult problem, you try to deal with it. *Delegates wrestled with the problems of violence and sanctions... We're wrestling with a recession... What he liked to do was to take an idea and wrestle it by finding every possible consequence.* VERB V *with* n V n

2 If you **wrestle** with someone, you fight them by forcing them into painful positions or throwing them to the ground, rather than by hitting them. Some people wrestle as a sport. *They taught me to wrestle... The bridesmaids and pageboys squealed and wrestled with each other in the garden.* VERB V V *with* n Also V n

3 If you **wrestle** someone or something somewhere, you move them there using a lot of force, for example by twisting a part of someone's body into painful positions. *We had to physically wrestle the child from the man's arms... The stationmaster pounced and wrestled the gun from him... Marshals tried to wrestle the demonstrator out of the room.* VERB V n prep

4 See also **wrestling**.

wrestler /resləʳ/ **wrestlers.** A **wrestler** is someone who wrestles as a sport, usually for money. ◆◇◇◇◇ N-COUNT

wrestling /reslɪŋ/. **Wrestling** is a sport in which two people wrestle and try to throw each other to the ground. *...a championship wrestling match.* ◆◇◇◇◇ N-UNCOUNT

wretch /retʃ/ **wretches**

1 You can refer to someone as a **wretch** when you feel sorry for them because they are unhappy or unfortunate; a literary use. *Before the poor wretch had time to speak, he was shot.* N-COUNT

2 You can refer to someone as a **wretch** when you think that they are wicked or if they have done something you are angry about; a literary use. *Oh, what have you done, you wretch!* N-COUNT

wretched /retʃɪd/ ◆◇◇◇◇

1 You describe someone as **wretched** when you feel sorry for them because they are in an unpleasant situation or have suffered unpleasant experiences; a formal use. *You have built up a huge property empire by buying from wretched people who had to sell or starve.* ♦ **wretchedly** *The country's 37 million people are wretchedly poor. ...prisoners living in wretchedly overcrowded conditions.* ♦ **wretchedness** *He does deserve some good luck after so much wretchedness.* ADJ-GRADED =pitiable ADV: ADV adj/-ed, ADV after v N-UNCOUNT

2 Someone who feels **wretched** feels very unhappy; a formal use. *I feel really confused and wretched... The wretched look on the little girl's face made him sorry.* ♦ **wretchedly** *His marriage was wretchedly unhappy... 'I made it all up,' she said wretchedly.* ♦ **wretchedness** *...their shared wretchedness at Werner's death.* ADJ-GRADED =miserable ADV-GRADED: ADV adj, ADV after v N-UNCOUNT

3 If you describe something as **wretched**, you are emphasizing that it is very bad or of very poor quality; a formal use. *What a wretched excuse... The pay has always been wretched.* ADJ-GRADED PRAGMATICS =atrocious, awful

4 You use **wretched** to describe someone or something that you dislike or feel angry with; an informal use. *Wretched woman, he thought, why the hell* ADJ: ADJ n PRAGMATICS =stupid

can't she wait?... Theft is something that really disgusts me. It makes me feel hateful towards this whole wretched island.

wriggle /rɪgəl/ **wriggles, wriggling, wriggled** ◆◇◇◇◇

1 If you **wriggle** or **wriggle** part of your body, you twist and turn with quick movements, for example because you are uncomfortable. *The babies are wriggling on their tummies... They were fidgeting and wriggling in their seats... She pulled off her shoes and stockings and wriggled her toes. ...wriggling worms.* VERB; V; V n; V-ing

2 If you **wriggle** somewhere, for example through a small gap, you move there by twisting and turning your body. *He clutched the child tightly as she again tried to wriggle free... Bauman wriggled into the damp coverall.* VERB; V adv/prep

wriggle out of. If you say that someone has **wriggled out of** doing something, you disapprove of the fact that they have managed to avoid doing it, although they should have done it. *The Government has tried to wriggle out of any responsibility for providing childcare for working parents.* PHRASAL VERB; PRAGMATICS; V P P n/-ing

wring /rɪŋ/ **wrings, wringing, wrung** ◆◇◇◇◇

1 If you **wring** something out of someone, you manage to make them give it to you even though they do not want to. *Buyers use different ruses to wring free credit out of their suppliers... In this way, he hoped to put pressure on the British and thus to wring concessions from them.* VERB; =squeeze; V n *out of/from* n

2 If someone **wrings** their **hands**, they hold them together and twist and turn them, usually because they are very worried or upset about something. You can also say that someone is **wringing** their **hands** when they are expressing sorrow that a situation is so bad but are saying that they are powerless to change it. *The Government has got to get a grip. Wringing its hands and saying it is a world problem just isn't good enough.* PHRASES; V inflects

3 If you say that you will **wring** someone**'s neck** or that you would like to **wring** their **neck**, you mean that you are very angry or exasperated with them; an informal expression. *That crazy Debbie! He could wring her neck for this!... I still love you even though I'd like to wring your neck.* V inflects

wring out. When you **wring out** a wet cloth or a wet piece of clothing, you squeeze the water out of it by twisting it strongly. *He turned away to wring out the wet shirt... Soak a small towel in the liquid, wring it out, then apply to the abdomen.* PHRASAL VERB; V P n (not pron); V n P

wringer /rɪŋər/. If you say that someone has **been put through the wringer** or has **gone through the wringer**, you mean that they have suffered a very difficult or unpleasant experience; an informal expression. PHRASE: V inflects

wrinkle /rɪŋkəl/ **wrinkles, wrinkling, wrinkled** ◆◇◇◇◇

1 Wrinkles are lines which form on someone's face as they grow old. *His face was covered with wrinkles... Some deep wrinkles furrow his lower forehead.* N-COUNT: usu pl

2 When someone's skin **wrinkles** or when something **wrinkles** it, lines start to form in it because the skin is getting old or damaged. *The skin on her cheeks and around her eyes was beginning to wrinkle. ...protection against the sun's rays that age and wrinkle the skin.* ♦ **wrinkled** *I did indeed look older and more wrinkled than ever.* V-ERG; V; V n; ADJ-GRADED

3 A **wrinkle** is a raised fold in something such as a piece of cloth or thin paper, usually one made unintentionally. *He noticed a wrinkle in her stocking.* N-COUNT

4 If something such as cloth **wrinkles**, or if someone or something **wrinkles** it, it gets folds or lines in it. *Her stockings wrinkled at the ankles... I wrinkled the velvet.* ♦ **wrinkled** *His suit was wrinkled and he looked very tired.* V-ERG; V; V n; ADJ-GRADED; =crumpled

5 When you **wrinkle** your nose or forehead, or when it **wrinkles**, you tighten the muscles in your face so that the skin folds. *Frannie wrinkled her nose at her daughter... Ellen's face wrinkles as if she is about to sneeze.* V-ERG; V n; V

wrinkly /rɪŋkli/ **wrinklies**

1 A **wrinkly** surface has a lot of wrinkles on it. *...wrinkly cotton and wool stockings. ...a smallish, greying man, with a wrinkly face.* ADJ-GRADED: usu ADJ n

2 In informal British English, young people sometimes refer to older people as **wrinklies**, especially when they are teasing them or making fun of the way they behave. N-COUNT; PRAGMATICS

wrist /rɪst/ **wrists.** Your **wrist** is the part of your body between your hand and your arm which bends when you move your hand. ◆◆◇◇◇ N-COUNT

wristwatch /rɪstwɒtʃ/ **wristwatches.** A **wristwatch** is a watch with a strap which you wear round your wrist. N-COUNT

writ /rɪt/ **writs** ◆◇◇◇◇

1 A **writ** is a legal document that orders a person to do a particular thing. *He issued a writ against one of his accusers.* N-COUNT: oft N *for/against* n

2 If you say that something is **writ large**, you mean that it is very obvious; a literary expression. *They now have to cope with the legacy of their past incompetence writ large on their balance sheets.* PHRASES; v-link PHR, n PHR, usu PHR *in/on* n

3 If you say that one thing is another thing **writ large**, you mean that the first thing is a larger or more exaggerated version of the second thing; a literary expression. *Her life was her personality writ large.* n PHR

write /raɪt/ **writes, writing, wrote, written** ◆◆◆◆◆

1 When you **write** something on a surface, you use something such as a pen or pencil to produce words, letters, or numbers on it. *If you'd like one, simply write your name and address on a postcard and send it to us... They were still trying to teach her to read and write... He wrote the word 'fingerprints' and put a query.* VERB; V n adv/prep; V; V n

2 If you **write** something such as a book, a poem, an essay, or a piece of music, you create it and record it on paper or perhaps on a computer. *I had written quite a lot of orchestral music in my student days... Finding a volunteer to write the computer program isn't a problem... Thereafter she wrote articles for papers and magazines in Paris... Jung Lu wrote me a poem once.* VERB; V n; V n *for* n; V n n

3 Someone who **writes** creates books, stories, or articles, usually for publication. *Jay wanted to write... She writes for many papers, including the Sunday Times... He now works in industry and writes on science in his spare time.* VERB; V; V *for* n; V *on/about* n

4 When you **write** to someone or **write** them a letter, you give them information, ask them something, or express your feelings in a letter. In American English, you can also **write** someone. *Apparently she had written to her aunt in Holland asking for artistic advice... She had written him a note a couple of weeks earlier... I wrote a letter to the car rental agency, explaining what had happened... Why didn't you write, call, anything?... He had written her in Italy but received no reply.* • **nothing to write home about**: see **home**. VERB; V *to* n; V n n; V n *to* n; V; V n

5 If someone **writes** that something is the case, they say it in a letter, book, or article. *'Some six months later,' Freud writes, 'Hans had got over his jealousy.'... A few days later he wrote that he had hopes of a staff job.* VERB; V with quote; V that

6 When someone **writes** something such as a cheque, receipt, or prescription, they put the necessary information on it and usually sign it. *Snape wrote a receipt with a gold fountain pen... I'll write you a cheque in a moment.* ► **Write out** means the same as **write**. *We went straight to the estate agent and wrote out a cheque... Get my wife to write you out a receipt before you leave.* VERB; V n; V n n; Also V n *for* n; PHRASAL VERB; V P n (not pron); V n P n; Also V n P

7 See also **writing, written.**

write back. If you **write back** to someone who has sent you a letter, you write them a letter in reply. *Macmillan wrote back saying that he could certainly help... I wrote back to Meudon at once to fix up a meeting.* PHRASAL VERB; V P; V P *to* n

write down. When you **write** something **down**, you record it on a piece of paper using a pen or pencil. *On the morning before starting the fast, write down your starting weight... Only by writing things down could I bring some sort of order to the confusion.* PHRASAL VERB; =note down; V P n (not pron); V n P

write in PHRASAL VERB
1 If you **write in** to an organization, you send them a letter. *What's the point in writing in when you only print half the letter anyway?... So there's another thing that you might like to write in to this programme about.* VP; VP *to* n
2 In the United States, if someone who is voting in an election **writes in** a person whose name is not on the list of candidates, they write that person's name on the voting paper and vote for him or her. *I think I'll write in Pat Wilson... I'm going to write him in on my ballot next year.* VP n (not pron); V n P
write into. If a rule or detail **is written into** a contract, law, or agreement, it is included in it when the contract, law, or agreement is made. *They insisted that a guaranteed supply of Chinese food was written into their contracts... The President has encouraged companies to allow unpaid leave for workers with family emergencies, but has opposed writing it into the law.* PHRASAL VERB; *be* V-ed P n; V n P n
write off PHRASAL VERB
1 If you **write off** to a company or organization, you send them a letter, usually asking for something. *He wrote off to the New Zealand Government for these pamphlets about life in New Zealand.* =write; VP *to* n; Also V P
2 If someone **writes off** a debt or an amount of money that has been spent on a project, they accept that they are never going to get the money back. *It was the president who persuaded the West to write off Polish debts... He had long since written off the money.* VP n (not pron); Also V n P
3 If you **write** someone or something **off**, you decide that they are unimportant or useless and that they are not worth further serious attention. *He is fed up with people writing him off because of his age... His critics write him off as too cautious to succeed... Most voters care more about jobs and therefore the Government can write off voters motivated by environmental issues... These people are difficult to write off as malingering employees.* =dismiss; V n P; V n P *as* n/adj; V P n (not pron); V P n (not pron) *as* n/adj
4 If someone **writes off** a vehicle, they have a crash in it and it is so badly damaged that it is not worth repairing. *John's written off four cars. Now he sticks to public transport... One of Pete's friends wrote his car off there.* V P n (not pron); V n P
5 If you **write off** a plan or project, you accept that it is not going to be successful and do not continue with it. *We decided to write off the rest of the day and go shopping... The prices were much higher. So we decided to write that off... It's too soon to write off the whole consultation process as a failure... They've stopped the project and will write this off as part of the growing pains of a new organization.* V P n (not pron); V n P; V P n (not pron) *as* n; V n P *as* n
6 See also **write-off**.
write out PHRASAL VERB
1 When you **write out** something fairly long such as a report or a list, you write it on paper. *We had to write out a list of ten jobs we'd like to do... If there's a particularly good recipe, write it out on decorative paper and take photocopies to sell.* V P n (not pron); V n P
2 If a character in a drama series **is written out**, he or she is taken out of the series. *When Angie was written out of 'Eastenders' her character went to Spain to open a bar... Maybe soon the scriptwriters will have to write her out of the series.* *be* V-ed P *of* n; V n P *of* n; Also V n P
3 See **write** 6.
write up. If you **write up** something that has been done or said, you record it on paper in a neat and complete form, usually using notes that you have made. *He wrote up his visit in a report of over 600 pages... Mr Sadler conducted interviews, and his girlfriend wrote them up.* • See also **write-up**. PHRASAL VERB; V P n (not pron); V n P
write-off, write-offs ◆◇◇◇◇
1 Something such as a vehicle that is a **write-off** has been so badly damaged in an accident that it is not worth repairing. *The car was a write-off, but everyone escaped unharmed.* N-COUNT
2 A **write-off** is the decision by a company or government to accept that they will never recover a debt or an amount of money that has been spent on something. *Mr James persuaded the banks to accept a large write-off of debt.* N-COUNT
3 If you describe a plan or period of time as a **write-off**, you mean that it has been a failure and you have achieved nothing; an informal use. *Today was really a bit of a write-off for me... For him, the rest of the decade was a creative write-off.* N-SING
writer /raɪtə^r/ **writers** ◆◆◆◆◇
1 A **writer** is a person who writes books, stories, or articles as a job. *Turner is a writer and critic. ...detective stories by American writers. ...novelist and travel writer Paul Theroux. ...Frank Keating, this paper's respected sports writer.* N-COUNT: oft supp N
2 The **writer** of a particular article, report, letter, or story is the person who wrote it. *No-one is to see the document without the permission of the writer of the report... I can't agree with the letter writer who claims bringing back the death penalty would be an abuse of human rights.* N-COUNT: usu with supp
write-up, write-ups. A **write-up** is an article in a newspaper or magazine, in which someone gives their opinion of something such as a film, restaurant, or new product. *The show received a good write-up... The guide book contains a short write-up of each hotel.* N-COUNT: usu with supp =review
writhe /raɪð/ **writhes, writhing, writhed.** If you **writhe**, your body twists and turns violently backwards and forwards, usually because you are in great pain or discomfort. *He was writhing in agony... The subject makes her writhe with embarrassment... The shark was writhing around wildly, trying to get free.* ◆◇◇◇◇ VERB; V; V adv/prep
writing /raɪtɪŋ/ **writings** ◆◆◆◆◇
1 **Writing** is something that has been written or printed. *'It's from a notebook,' the sheriff said, 'And there's writing on it.'... If you have a complaint about your holiday, please inform us in writing.* N-UNCOUNT
2 You can refer to any piece of written work as **writing**, especially when you are considering the style of language used in it. *The writing is brutally tough and savagely humorous... It was such a brilliant piece of writing.* N-UNCOUNT
3 **Writing** is the activity of writing, especially of writing books for money. *She had begun to be a little bored with novel writing... There are a number of good pre-school work-books with activities to help prepare children for writing.* N-UNCOUNT
4 Your **writing** is the way that you write with a pen or pencil, which can usually be recognized as belonging to you. *It was a little difficult to read your writing... I think it's due to being left handed that he's got terrible writing.* N-UNCOUNT: usu poss N =handwriting
5 An author's **writings** are all the things that he or she has written, especially on a particular subject. *Althusser's writings are focused mainly on France... The pieces he is reading are adapted from the writings of playwright and author Michael Frayn.* N-PLURAL: usu with poss
6 If you say that **the writing is on the wall**, you mean that there are clear signs that a situation is going to become very difficult or unpleasant. *The writing is clearly on the wall. If we do nothing about it, we shall only have ourselves to blame.* PHRASE: V inflects
writing desk, writing desks. A **writing desk** is a piece of furniture with drawers, an area for keeping writing materials, and a surface on which you can rest your paper while writing. N-COUNT
writing paper, writing papers. Writing paper is paper for writing letters on. It is usually of good, smooth quality. N-MASS
written /rɪt^{ə}n/ ◆◆◆◇◇
1 **Written** is the past participle of **write**.
2 A **written** test or piece of work is one which involves writing rather than doing something practical or giving spoken answers. *Learners may have to take a written exam before they pass their driving test... Amy discovered that the theoretical and written work came easily to her.* ADJ: usu ADJ n
3 A **written** agreement, rule, or law has been officially written down. *The newspaper broke a written agreement not to sell certain photographs... We're waiting for written confirmation from the Americans.* ADJ: ADJ n ≠unwritten
4 • **be written all over** someone's **face**: see **face**.

written word. You use **the written word** to refer to language expressed in writing, especially when contrasted with speech or with other forms of expression such as painting or film. *Even in the 18th century scholars continued to give primacy to the written word.* [N-SING: usu the N]

wrong /rɒŋ, AM rɔːŋ/ **wrongs, wronging, wronged** ◆◆◆◆◇

1 If you say there is something **wrong**, you mean there is something unsatisfactory about the situation, person, or thing you are talking about. *Pain is the body's way of telling us that something is wrong... Nobody seemed to notice anything wrong. ...a relationship that felt wrong from the start... He sensed that something was very wrong... What's wrong with him?* [ADJ-GRADED: v-link ADJ, oft ADJ with n ≠right]

2 If you choose the **wrong** thing, person, or method, you make a mistake and do not choose the one that you really want. *He went to the wrong house... The wrong man had been punished... Could you have given them the wrong drug by mistake?... There is no right or wrong way to do these exercises.* [ADJ: usu ADJ n ≠right] ▶ Also an adverb. *You've done it wrong... I must have dialed wrong.* [ADV: ADV after v ≠right]

3 If something such as a decision, choice, or action is the **wrong** one, it is not the best or most suitable one. *I really made the wrong decision there... The wrong choice of club might limit your chances of success... We got married when I was 30 for all the wrong reasons.* [ADJ: ADJ n ≠right]

4 If something is **wrong**, it is incorrect and not in accordance with the facts. *How do you know that this explanation is wrong?... 20 per cent of the calculations are wrong. ...a clock which showed the wrong time... Lots of people got the questions wrong.* [ADJ ≠right] ▶ Also an adverb. *I must have added it up wrong, then... It looks like it's spelled wrong... I can see exactly where he went wrong.* [ADV: ADV after v] ♦ **wrongly** *A child was wrongly diagnosed as having a bone tumour... Civilians assume, wrongly, that everything in the military runs smoothly.* [ADV: ADV with v]

5 If something is **wrong** or goes **wrong** with a machine or piece of equipment, it stops working properly. *We think there's something wrong with the computer... Something must have gone wrong with the satellite link.* [ADJ: v-link ADJ, usu ADJ with n]

6 If you are **wrong** about something, what you say or think about it is not correct. *I was wrong about it being a casual meeting... Am I wrong in thinking that?... It would be wrong to assume that rich countries will always be able to insulate themselves with drugs against the ravages of new diseases... He was wrong to call it science... I'm sure you've got it wrong. Kate isn't like that... It's been very nice to prove them wrong.* [ADJ: v-link ADJ, oft ADJ about n, ADJ in -ing, it v-link ADJ to-inf, ADJ to-inf ≠right]

7 You can use **wrong** in expressions such as **you thought wrong** and **you heard wrong** to tell someone that what they thought or were told is incorrect, usually when you are annoyed. *I thought you and I were going to spend the night together,' he whispered. 'You thought wrong,' Nancy whispered back.* [ADV: ADV after v PRAGMATICS ≠right]

8 If you think that someone was **wrong** to do something, you think that they should not have done it because it was bad or immoral. *She was wrong to leave her child alone... We don't consider we did anything wrong.* [ADJ-GRADED: ADJ to-inf ≠right] ▶ Also a noun. *...a man who believes that he has done no wrong.* [N-UNCOUNT]

9 **Wrong** is used to refer to activities or actions that are considered to be morally bad and unacceptable. *Is it wrong to try to save the life of someone you love?... It is wrong that we have to tell ill people to go somewhere else to look for treatment... They thought slavery was morally wrong... You mustn't do that. It's wrong... The only thing I consider wrong is when you hurt someone... There is nothing wrong with journalists commenting on the attractiveness of artists.* [ADJ-GRADED: v-link ADJ, oft it v-link ADJ to-inf/that] ▶ Also a noun. *Johnson didn't seem to be able to tell the difference between right and wrong.* [N-UNCOUNT ≠right]

10 A **wrong** is an unfair or immoral action. *I intend to right that wrong... The insurance company should not be held liable for the wrongs of one of its agents.* [N-COUNT =misdeed]

11 If someone **wrongs** you, they treat you in an unfair way. *You have wronged my mother... She felt she'd been wronged... Those who have wronged must be ready to say: 'We have hurt you by this injustice.'* [VERB Vn V]

12 You use **wrong** to describe something which is not thought to be socially acceptable or desirable. *If you went to the wrong school, you won't get the job... The prospect of easy profits has attracted the wrong kind of businessman.* [ADJ: ADJ n]

13 You say **'Don't get me wrong'** when you want to make sure that someone does not misunderstand what you are doing or saying, or why you are doing or saying it. *Don't get me wrong, it's interesting work. But it's not permanent... I mean, don't get me wrong. Joanie's my best friend, but she can be kind of a pain sometimes.* [PHRASES PRAGMATICS]

14 If a situation **goes wrong**, it stops progressing in the way that you expected or intended, and becomes much worse. *It all went horribly wrong... Nearly everything that could go wrong has gone wrong.* [V inflects]

15 If someone who is involved in an argument or dispute has behaved in a way which is morally or legally wrong, you can say that they are **in the wrong**. *He didn't press charges because he was in the wrong... She was the one in the wrong.* [usu v-link PHR]

16 If someone says **'Two wrongs don't make a right'**, they mean that you should not do harm to a person who has done harm to you, even if you think that person deserves it. [CONVENTION PRAGMATICS]

17 • **won't go far wrong**: see **wrong**. • **get off on the wrong foot**: see **foot**. • to **get hold of the wrong end of the stick**: see **stick**. • to **be barking up the wrong tree**: see **tree**.

wrongdoer /rɒŋduːəʳ, AM rɔːŋ-/ **wrongdoers.** A **wrongdoer** is a person who does things that are immoral or illegal; a word used by journalists. [N-COUNT]

wrongdoing /rɒŋduːɪŋ, AM rɔːŋ-/ **wrongdoings. Wrongdoing** is behaviour that is illegal or immoral. *The city attorney's office hasn't found any evidence of criminal wrongdoing.* ◆◇◇◇◇ [N-VAR]

wrong-foot, wrong-foots, wrong-footing, wrong-footed; also spelled **wrong foot**. If you **wrong-foot** someone, you surprise them by putting them into an unexpected or difficult situation; used mainly in British English. *He has surprised his supporters and wrong-footed his opponents with his latest announcement.* • to **get off on the wrong foot**: see **foot**. [VERB Vn]

wrongful /rɒŋfʊl, AM rɔːŋ-/. A **wrongful** act is one that is illegal, immoral, or unjust. *He is on hunger strike in protest at what he claims is his wrongful conviction for murder... One of her employees sued her for wrongful dismissal.* ◆◇◇◇◇ [ADJ: usu ADJ n] ♦ **wrongfully** *The criminal justice system is in need of urgent reform to prevent more people being wrongfully imprisoned.* [ADV: ADV with v =unjustly]

wrong-headed. If you describe someone as **wrong-headed**, you mean that although they act in a determined way, their actions and ideas are based on wrong judgements. [ADJ-GRADED]

wrote /rəʊt/. **Wrote** is the past tense of **write**.

wrought /rɔːt/

1 If something has **wrought** a change, it has made it happen; a literary or journalistic use. *Events in Paris wrought a change in British opinion towards France and Germany.* [VB: only past Vn]

2 If something is **wrought** in a particular material or in a particular way, it has been created in that material or way; a literary use. *...a walking stick with a gold head wrought in the form of the cap of liberty. ...remnants of finely wrought ironwork.* [ADJ]

3 See also **wreak**.

wrought iron; also spelled **wrought-iron**. **Wrought iron** is a pure type of iron that is formed into decorative shapes and used especially for making gates and railings. ◆◇◇◇◇ [N-UNCOUNT]

wrung /rʌŋ/. **Wrung** is the past tense of **wring**.

wry /raɪ/ ◆◇◇◇◇

1 If someone has a **wry** expression, it shows that they find a bad or difficult situation slightly amusing or ironic. *Matthew allowed himself a wry smile... She cast a wry glance in her grandmother's direction.* ADJ-GRADED: usu ADJ n

♦ **wryly** *She studied him for the longest time, looking wryly amused.* ADV-GRADED

2 A **wry** remark or piece of writing refers to a bad or difficult situation in an amusing or ironic way. *The play is a rueful, wry observation about the way we are all subject to the ravages of time... There is a wry sense of humour in his work.* ADJ-GRADED: usu ADJ n ♦ **wryly** *When asked if he would be visiting his family, Becker said wryly: 'I hope I don't have time.'* ADV-GRADED: ADV with v, ADV adj/-ed

wt. **Wt** is a written abbreviation for **weight**.

XYZ xyz

X, x /eks/ **X's, x's**

1 **X** is the twenty-fourth letter of the English alphabet. N-VAR

2 When writing down the size of something, you can use **x** in between the measurements to mean 'by'. *The conservatory measures approximately 13ft x 16ft.*

3 **X** can be used to represent the name of a person when you do not know their real name, or when you are trying to keep their real name a secret. *...Dr. X.* N-PROPER

4 You can use **X** or **x** to refer to a number or amount when the exact number or amount is not known or is not important. *You can only make X amount of dollars a year.*

5 **x** is used to represent a kiss at the end of a letter or written message.

6 People sometimes write **X** on a map to mark a precise position that they want to refer to.

X chromosome, X chromosomes. An **X chromosome** is one of an identical pair of chromosomes found in a woman's cells, or one of a non-identical pair found in a man's cells. X chromosomes are associated with female characteristics. Compare **Y chromosome**. N-COUNT

xenophobia /zenəfoʊbiə/. **Xenophobia** is strong and unreasonable dislike or fear of people from other countries. N-UNCOUNT

xenophobic /zenəfoʊbɪk/. If you describe someone as **xenophobic**, you disapprove of them because they show strong dislike or fear of people from other countries. *Xenophobic nationalism is on the rise in some West European countries... Stalin was obsessively xenophobic.* ADJ-GRADED

Xerox /zɪərɒks/ **Xeroxes, Xeroxing, Xeroxed** ◆◇◇◇◇

1 A **Xerox** is a machine that can make copies of pieces of paper which have writing or other marks on them. **Xerox** is a trademark. *The rooms are crammed with humming Xerox machines.* N-COUNT: usu N n

2 A **Xerox** is a copy of something written or printed on a piece of paper, which has been copied on a Xerox machine. *I had to make Xerox copies of the letters.* N-COUNT

3 If you **Xerox** a document, you make a copy of it using a Xerox machine. *I should have simply Xeroxed this sheet for you.* VERB Vn

Xmas. **Xmas** is used in informal written English to represent the word **Christmas**. *It would be nice to have my Dad home for Xmas.*

X-ray **X-rays, X-raying, X-rayed** ◆◆◇◇◇

1 An **X-ray** is a type of radiation that can pass through most solid materials. X-rays are commonly used by doctors to examine the bones or organs inside your body and at airports to see inside people's luggage. N-COUNT: usu pl

2 An **X-ray** is a picture made by sending X-rays through something, usually someone's body. *She was advised to have an abdominal X-ray.* N-COUNT

3 If someone or something **is X-rayed**, an x-ray picture is taken of them. *All hand baggage would be x-rayed... They took my pulse, took my blood pressure, and X-rayed my jaw.* VERB be V-ed Vn

xylophone /zaɪləfoʊn/ **xylophones.** A **xylophone** is a musical instrument which consists of a row of wooden bars of different lengths. You play the xylophone by hitting the bars with special hammers. N-COUNT: oft *the* N

Y, y /waɪ/ **Y's, y's**

1 **Y** is the twenty-fifth letter of the English alphabet. N-VAR

2 In American English, a YMCA or YWCA hostel is sometimes referred to as **the Y**; an informal use. *I took him to the Y.* N-SING: *the* N

-y /-i/ **-ies, -ier, -iest**

1 **-y** is added to nouns in order to form adjectives that describe something or someone as having the characteristics of what the noun refers to. *He watched from the corner of a smoky pub... She picked and tasted the juicy ripe berries... The process results in a much fruitier wine.* SUFFIX

2 **-y** is added to colours in order to form adjectives that describe something as being roughly that colour or having some of that colour in it. *...a rich, reddy, brown wood... Her eyes were the bluey-green colour that often went with red hair.* SUFFIX

3 **-y** is added to a name or a noun in order to give it a more affectionate or familiar form. *'How are you, Mikey?'... Move the little doggy.* SUFFIX

yacht /jɒt/ **yachts.** A **yacht** is a large boat with sails or a motor, used for racing or pleasure trips. *His 36ft yacht sank suddenly last summer. ...a round-the-world yacht race.* ◆◆◆◇◇ N-COUNT

yachting /jɒtɪŋ/. **Yachting** is the sport or activity of sailing a yacht. *...the joys of yachting. ...the Olympic yachting regatta.* ◆◇◇◇◇ N-UNCOUNT

yachtsman /jɒtsmən/ **yachtsmen.** A **yachtsman** is a man who sails a yacht. ◆◇◇◇◇ N-COUNT

yachtswoman /jɒtswʊmən/ **yachtswomen.** A **yachtswoman** is a woman who sails a yacht. N-COUNT

yahoo, yahoos. Pronounced /jɑːhuː/ for meaning 1, and /jɑːhuː/ for meaning 2.

1 People sometimes shout **'yahoo!'** when they are very happy or excited about something. EXCLAM

2 In informal British English, some people refer to young rich people as **yahoos** when they disapprove of them because they behave in a noisy, extravagant, and unpleasant way. *...a typical City merchant banking yahoo.* N-COUNT PRAGMATICS

yak /jæk/ **yaks.** The plural can be either **yaks** or **yak**. A **yak** is a type of cattle that has long hair and long horns. Yaks live mainly in the Himalayan mountains and in Tibet. N-COUNT

yam /jæm/ **yams.** A **yam** is a root vegetable which grows in tropical regions. It is similar to a potato in appearance and texture. N-VAR

yank /jæŋk/ **yanks, yanking, yanked.** If you **yank** someone or something somewhere, you pull them there suddenly and with a lot of force. *She yanked open the drawer... She yanked the child back into the house... He yanked a handkerchief out of his pocket... A quick-thinking ticket inspector yanked an emergency cord.* ◆◇◇◇◇ VERB V n with adj, V n with adv, V n prep, V n, Also V *at* n ▸ Also a noun. *Grabbing his ponytail, Shirley gave it a yank.* N-COUNT

Yank, Yanks. Some people refer to people from the United States of America as **Yanks**; an informal use which many people find offensive. ◆◇◇◇◇ N-COUNT =Yankee

Yankee /jæŋki/ **Yankees** ◆◇◇◇◇
1 A **Yankee** is a person from a northern or northeastern state of the United States; used mainly in American English. N-COUNT
2 Some speakers of British English people refer to anyone from the United States as a **Yankee**; an informal use which many people find offensive. N-COUNT =Yank

yap /jæp/ **yaps, yapping, yapped**
1 If a small dog **yaps**, it barks a lot with a high-pitched sound. *The little dog yapped frantically. ...two yapping cairn terriers.* VERB V V-ing
2 If you say that someone **yaps**, you mean that they talk continuously in an annoying way; an informal use. *The guy just loves to yap, and will do so at length... She keeps yapping at me about Joe.* VERB V V at/about n

yard /jɑːʳd/ **yards** ◆◆◆◆◇
1 A **yard** is a unit of length equal to thirty-six inches or approximately 91.4 centimetres. *The incident took place about 500 yards from where he was standing... A few yards away, José Vargas stands beside his small home. ...a long narrow strip of linen two or three yards long. ...a yard of silk.* N-COUNT: num N, oft N of n
2 A **yard** is a flat area of concrete or stone that is next to a building and often has a wall around it. *I saw him standing in the yard.* N-COUNT =courtyard
3 You can refer to a large open area where a particular type of work is done as a **yard**. *...a railway yard. ...a ship repair yard.* N-COUNT: usu supp N
4 In American English, a **yard** is a piece of land next to someone's house where they grow flowers, vegetables, or other plants, and may have a lawn. The usual British word is **garden**. *He dug a hole in our yard on Edgerton Avenue to plant a maple tree when I was born.* N-COUNT

Yardie /jɑːʳdi/ **Yardies.** In British English, a **Yardie** is a member of a secret criminal organization, based in Jamaica, which is especially associated with drug dealing. N-COUNT

yard sale yard sales. In American English, a **yard sale** is a sale where people sell things they own and do not want from a little stall or from the back of their car. The usual British word is **car boot sale**. *...clothes he'd picked up at yard sales.* N-COUNT

yardstick /jɑːʳdstɪk/ **yardsticks.** If you use someone or something as a **yardstick**, you use them as a standard for comparison when you are judging other people or things. *She had never had a real boyfriend before and so had no yardstick by which to compare Charles's behaviour... The best yardstick was to measure traffic against the 1990 figures.* ◆◇◇◇◇ ADJ

yarn /jɑːʳn/ **yarns** ◆◇◇◇◇
1 **Yarn** is thread used for knitting or making cloth. *She still spins the yarn and knits sweaters for her family. ...vegetable-dyed yarns.* N-MASS
2 A **yarn** is a story that someone tells, often a true story with invented details which make it more interesting. *Doug has a yarn or two to tell me about his trips into the bush.* ● If you say that someone **spins a yarn**, you mean that they tell a story that is not true, often in an interesting or inventive way. *Rukmeni's a great storyteller, so she'll probably spin them a yarn about some prince or god.* N-COUNT PHRASE: V and N inflect

yaw /jɔː/ **yaws, yawing, yawed.** If an aircraft or a ship **yaws**, it turns to one side so that it changes the direction in which it is moving; a technical term in aviation and sailing. *As the plane climbed to 370 feet, it started yawing... He spun the steering-wheel so that we yawed from side to side.* VERB V V prep/adv

yawn /jɔːn/ **yawns, yawning, yawned** ◆◇◇◇◇
1 If you **yawn**, you open your mouth very wide and breathe in more air than usual, often when you are tired or when you are not interested in something. *She yawned, and stretched lazily... They looked bored and yawned at the speeches.* ► Also a noun. *Rosanna stifled a huge yawn.* VERB V N-COUNT
2 If you describe something such as a book or a film as **a yawn**, you think it is very boring; an informal use. *The debate was a mockery. A big yawn... The concert was a predictable yawn.* N-SING: a N =bore
3 A gap or opening that **yawns** is large and wide, and often frightening; a literary use. *The gulf between them yawned wider than ever... Liddie's doorway yawned blackly open at the end of the hall.* VERB V V adj

Y chromosome, Y chromosomes. A **Y chromosome** is the single chromosome in a man's cells which will produce a male baby if it joins with an X chromosome during the reproductive process. Y chromosomes are associated with male characteristics. Compare **X chromosome**. N-COUNT

yd, yds. yd is a written abbreviation for **yard**. *The entrance is on the left 200 yds further on up road.*

ye /jiː/ ◆◇◇◇◇
1 **Ye** is an old-fashioned, poetic, or religious word for **you** when you are talking to more than one person. *Abandon hope all ye who enter here.* PRON-PLURAL
2 **Ye** is sometimes used in imitation of an old written form of the word 'the'. *...Ye Olde Tea Shoppe.* DET

yea /jeɪ/
1 **Yea** is an old-fashioned, poetic, or religious word for 'yes'. CONVENTION =yes
2 **Yea** is sometimes used to mean 'yes' when people are talking about voting for or giving their consent for something. *The House of Commons can merely say yea or nay to the executive judgment.* CONVENTION

yeah /jeə/. **Yeah** is used in written English to represent the way **yes** is pronounced in informal speech. *'Bring us something to drink.'—'Yeah, yeah.'* ◆◆◆◆◆ CONVENTION =yes

year /jɪəʳ/ **years** ◆◆◆◆◆
1 A **year** is a period of twelve months or 365 or 366 days, beginning on the first of January and ending on the thirty-first of December. *The year was 1840... We had an election last year. ...the number of people on the planet by the year 2050.* N-COUNT
2 A **year** is any period of twelve months. *The museums attract more then two and a half million visitors a year... She's done quite a bit of work this past year... The school has been empty for ten years.* N-COUNT
3 **Year** is used to refer to the age of a person. For example, if someone or something is twenty **years** old or twenty **years** of age, they have lived or existed for twenty years. *He's 58 years old... I've been in trouble since I was eleven years of age... This column is ten years old today.* N-COUNT: num N adj/prep
4 A school **year** is the period of time in each twelve months when the school is open and students are studying there. In Britain, the school year runs from September to July, and is divided into three terms. *...the 1990/91 academic year... The twins didn't have to repeat their second year at school.* N-COUNT: usu adj/ord N
5 In British English, you can refer to someone who is, for example, in their first year at school or university as a first **year**. *The first years and second years got a choice of French, German and Spanish.* N-COUNT: ord N
6 A financial or business **year** is an exact period of twelve months which businesses or institutions use as a basis for organizing their finances. *He announced big tax increases for the next two financial years... The company admits it will make a loss for the year ending September.* N-COUNT: with supp
7 You can use **years** to emphasize that you are referring to a long time. *I haven't laughed so much in years... It took him years to get up the courage... People hold onto letters for years and years.* N-PLURAL PRAGMATICS =ages
8 You can refer to the time you spend in a place or doing an activity as your **years** there or your **years** of doing that activity. *The joy turned to tragedy during his years in Cyprus. ...his years as Director of the Manchester City Art Gallery.* N-PLURAL: poss N, usu N prep
9 See also **calendar year, fiscal year**.
10 If something happens **year after year**, it happens regularly every year. *Regulars return year after year... You keep on amazing me, year after year, the same old ways.* PHRASES PHR after v
11 If something changes **year by year**, it changes gradually each year. *This problem has increased year by year... The department has been shrinking year by year because of budget cuts.* PHR after v

12 If something happens **year in, year out**, it happens every year without changing and is often boring. *Year in, year out, nothing changes... With stockbroking it was the same thing, year in year out.* PHR with cl

13 You can say **a man of his years** or **a woman of her years** to refer to that person's age in relation to something else you are talking about. *He was moving with surprising speed for a man of his years... A young man of his years needed to have a separate room.*

14 If you say that something such as an experience or a way of dressing **has put years on** someone, you mean that it has made them look or feel much older; an informal expression. *I always turn adversity and defeat into victories, but it's probably put ten years on me.* V inflects

15 If you say something happens **all year round** or **all the year round**, it happens continually throughout the year. *Town gardens are ideal because they produce flowers nearly all year round... Drinking and driving is a problem all the year round.* PHR after v, PHR with cl

16 If you say that something such as an experience or a way of dressing **has taken years off** someone, you mean that it has made them look or feel much younger; an informal expression. *Changing your hairstyle can take ten years off you.* V inflects, PHR n

17 • **donkey's years**: see **donkey**.

yearbook /jɪəʳbʊk/ **yearbooks.** A **yearbook** is a book that is published once a year and that contains information about the events and achievements of the previous year, usually concerning a particular place or organization. *...an American college yearbook for 1955.* N-COUNT

year-long. **Year-long** is used to describe something that lasts for a year. *The miners ended their year-long strike in March 1985.* ◆◇◇◇◇ ADJ: ADJ n

yearly /jɪəʳli/ ◆◇◇◇◇

1 A **yearly** event happens once a year or every year. *The seven major industrial countries will have their yearly meeting in London.* ▶ Also an adverb. *Clients normally pay fees in advance, monthly, quarterly, or yearly.* ADJ: ADJ n; ADV: ADV after v

2 You use **yearly** to describe something such as an amount that relates to a period of one year. *In Holland, the government sets a yearly budget for health care.* ▶ Also an adverb. *Novello says college students will spend $4.2 billion yearly on alcoholic beverages.* ADJ: ADJ n; ADV: ADV after v

yearn /jɜːʳn/ **yearns, yearning, yearned.** If someone **yearns** for something that they are unlikely to get, they want it very much. *He yearned for freedom... I yearned to be a movie actor.* VERB =long; V *for* n; V to-inf

yearning /jɜːʳnɪŋ/ **yearnings.** A **yearning** for something is a very strong desire for it. *He spoke of his yearning for another child... He always had a yearning to be a schoolteacher.* N-VAR: oft N *for* n, N to-inf =longing

-year-old /-jɪər-oʊld/ **-year-olds.** **-year-old** combines with numbers to describe the age of people or things. *She has a six-year-old daughter. ...their 200-year-old farmhouse in Ohio.* ▶ Also combines to form nouns. *Snow Puppies is a ski school for 3- to 6-year-olds.* COMB in ADJ: ADJ n; COMB in N-COUNT

year-round. **Year-round** is used to describe something that happens, exists, or is done throughout the year. *Cuba has a tropical climate with year-round sunshine.* ▶ Also an adverb. *They work 7 days a week year-round.* ◆◇◇◇◇ ADJ: ADJ n; ADV: ADV with cl

yeast /jiːst/ **yeasts.** **Yeast** is a kind of fungus which is used to make bread rise, and in making alcoholic drinks such as beer. N-MASS

yeast extract, yeast extracts. **Yeast extract** is a brown sticky food that is obtained from yeast. It can be used in cooking or spread on bread. N-MASS

yeasty /jiːsti/. Something that is **yeasty** tastes or smells strongly of yeast. ADJ-GRADED

yell /jel/ **yells, yelling, yelled** ◆◆◇◇◇

1 If you **yell**, you shout loudly, usually because you are excited, angry, or in pain. *'Eva!' he yelled... I'm sorry I yelled at you last night... Christian pushed him away, yelling abuse... He was out there shouting and yelling.* ▶ **Yell out** means the same as **yell**. *'Are you coming or not?' they yelled out after him.* VERB; V with quote; V *at* n; V n; V; PHRASAL VERB V P

2 A **yell** is a loud shout given by someone who is afraid or in pain. *Something brushed past Bob's face and he let out a yell.* N-COUNT =cry

yell out. See **yell** 1. PHRASAL VERB

yellow /jeloʊ/ **yellows, yellowing, yellowed** ◆◆◆◇◇

1 Something that is **yellow** is the colour of lemons or egg yolks. *The walls have been painted bright yellow... Kim opted for cooler blues and yellows in the master bedroom.* COLOUR

2 If something **yellows**, it becomes yellow in colour, often because it is old. *The flesh of his cheeks seemed to have yellowed... She sat scanning the yellowing pages until she heard a knock on the door.* VERB; V; V-ing

yellow fever. **Yellow fever** is a serious infectious disease that people can catch in tropical countries. N-UNCOUNT

yellowish /jeloʊɪʃ/. Something that is **yellowish** is slightly yellow in colour. *...a small yellowish cauliflower.* ▶ Also a combining form. *The yellowish brown smoke fumed up and swirled.* ADJ; COMB in COLOUR

yellow pages. The **Yellow Pages** are a telephone directory or part of a directory, in which companies and people are listed and grouped according to the kind of business they are involved in. **Yellow Pages** is a trademark. N-PLURAL

yellowy /jeloʊi/. Something that is **yellowy** is slightly yellow in colour. *She had long hair she'd bleached herself, all yellowy and orangey.* ▶ Also a combining form. *...black ink, fading now to a yellowy brown.* ADJ =yellowish; COMB in COLOUR

yelp /jelp/ **yelps, yelping, yelped.** If a person or dog **yelps**, they give a sudden short cry, often because of fear or pain. *Her dog yelped and came to heel.* ▶ Also a noun. *I had to bite back a yelp of surprise.* VERB; V; N-COUNT: oft N *of* n

Yemeni /jemɪni/ **Yemenis** ◆◆◆◆◇

1 **Yemeni** means belonging or relating to the Yemen, or to its people or culture. *...the Yemeni capital, Sanaa. ...the Yemeni ambassador.* ADJ

2 A **Yemeni** is a Yemeni citizen, or a person of Yemeni origin. N-COUNT

yen /jen/; **yen** is both the singular and the plural form. ◆◆◆◇◇

1 The **yen** is the unit of currency used in Japan. *She's got a part-time job for which she earns 2,000 yen a month.* ▶ **The yen** is also used to refer to the Japanese currency system. *...sterling's devaluation against the dollar and the yen.* N-COUNT: usu num N; N-SING: *the* N

2 If you have a **yen** to do something, you have a strong desire to do it. *Mike had a yen to try cycling... He's a natural with any kind of engine but he has an unfortunate yen for speed.* N-SING: usu *a* N, N to-inf, N *for* n =yearning

yeoman /joʊmən/ **yeomen.** In former times, a **yeoman** was a man who was free and not a servant, and who cultivated his own land. N-COUNT

yes /jes/ **yeses** ◆◆◆◆◆

Yes is used mainly in spoken English. In informal English, **yes** is often pronounced in a casual way that is usually written as **yeah**.

1 You use **yes** to give a positive response to a question. *'Are you a friend of Nick's?'—'Yes.'... 'You actually wrote it down, didn't you?'—'Yes.'... Will she say yes when I ask her out?* CONVENTION PRAGMATICS ≠no

2 You use **yes** to accept an offer or request, or to give permission. *'More wine?'—'Yes please.'... 'Will you take me there?'—'Yes, I will.'... 'Can I ask you something?'—'Yes, of course.'* CONVENTION PRAGMATICS ≠no

3 You use **yes** to tell someone that what they have said is correct. *'Well I suppose it is based on the old lunar months isn't it.'—'Yes that's right.'... 'That's a type of whitefly, is it?'—'Yes, it is a whitefly.'* CONVENTION PRAGMATICS ≠no

4 You use **yes** to show that you are ready or willing to speak to the person who wants to speak to you, for example when you are answering a telephone or doorbell. *He pushed a button on the intercom. 'Yes?' came a voice... Yes, can I help you?* CONVENTION PRAGMATICS

5 You use **yes** to indicate that you agree with, accept, or understand what the previous speaker has said. *'A lot of people find it very difficult indeed to give up smoking.'—'Oh yes. I used to smoke nearly* CONVENTION PRAGMATICS *sixty a day.'... 'It's a fabulous opportunity.'—'Yeah. I know.'*

6 You use **yes** to encourage someone to continue speaking. *'I remembered something funny today.'—'Yeah?'* CONVENTION PRAGMATICS

7 You use **yes** as a polite way of introducing an objection to what the previous speaker has just said. *'She is entitled to her personal allowance which is three thousand pounds of income.'—'Yes, but she doesn't earn any money.'... Ah yes, but think of all the family life they're missing.* CONVENTION PRAGMATICS

8 You use **yes** to say that a negative statement or question that the previous speaker has made is wrong or untrue. *'That is not possible,' she said. 'Oh, yes, it is!' Mrs Gruen insisted... 'I don't know what you're talking about.'—'Yes, you do.'* CONVENTION PRAGMATICS

9 You can use **yes** to suggest that you do not believe or agree with what the previous speaker has said, especially when you want to express your annoyance about it. *'There was no way to stop it.'—'Oh yes? Well, here's something else you won't be able to stop.'* CONVENTION PRAGMATICS

10 You use **yes** to indicate that you had forgotten something and have just remembered it. *What was I going to say. Oh yeah, we've finally got our second computer.* CONVENTION PRAGMATICS

11 You use **yes** to emphasize and confirm a statement that you are making. *He collected the £10,000 first prize. Yes, £10,000.* CONVENTION PRAGMATICS

12 You say **yes and no** in reply to a question when you cannot give a definite answer, because in some ways the answer is yes and in other ways the answer is no. *'Was it strange for you, going back after such a long absence?'—'Yes and no.'* CONVENTION PRAGMATICS

13 A **yes** is a person who has answered 'yes' to a question or who has voted in favour of something, or the answer or vote they have made. *The no-votes are leading the yeses... The noes have 50 percent, the yeses 35 percent and the rest are undecided.* N-COUNT ≠no

yes-man, yes-men. If you describe a man as a **yes-man**, you dislike the fact that he seems always to agree with people who have authority over him, in order to gain favour. N-COUNT PRAGMATICS

yesterday /jestərdeɪ, -di/ **yesterdays** ◆◆◆◆◆

1 You use **yesterday** to refer to the day before today. *She left yesterday... Yesterday she announced that she is quitting her job.* ► Also a noun. *In yesterday's games, Switzerland beat the United States two-one.* ADV: ADV with cl; N-UNCOUNT

2 You can refer to the past, especially the recent past, as **yesterday**. *The worker of today is different from the worker of yesterday. ...a world without yesterdays or tomorrows.* N-UNCOUNT: also N in pl

yesteryear /jestərjɪər/. You use **yesteryear** to refer to the past, often a period in the past with a set of values or a way of life that no longer exists; a literary word. *The modern-day sex symbol has now taken the place of the old-fashioned hero of yesteryear.* N-UNCOUNT

yet /jet/ ◆◆◆◆◆

1 You use **yet** in negative statements to indicate that something has not happened up to the present time, although it probably will happen. You can also use **yet** in questions to ask if something has happened up to the present time. In British English the simple past tense is not normally used in this sense. *They haven't finished yet... No decision has yet been made... She hasn't yet set a date for her marriage... 'Has the murderer been caught?'–'Not yet.'... Have you met my husband yet?... Hammer-throwing for women is not yet a major event.* ADV: usu with brd-neg, ADV with v, ADV group =as yet

2 You use **yet** with a negative statement when you are talking about the past, to report something that was not the case then, although it became the case later. *There was so much that Sam didn't know yet... He had asked around and learned that Billy was not yet here.* ADV: usu with brd-neg, ADV with v, ADV group

3 If you say that something should not or cannot be done **yet**, you mean that it should not or cannot be done now, although it will have to be done at a later time. *Don't get up yet... The hostages cannot go home just yet... We should not yet abandon this option for the disposal of highly radioactive waste.* ADV: with brd-neg, ADV with v

4 You use **yet** after a superlative to indicate, for example, that something is the worst or the best of its kind up to the present time. *This is the BBC's worst idea yet... Her latest novel is her best yet. ...one of the toughest warnings yet delivered.* ADV: n ADV, ADV adv/-ed, ADV after superl

5 You can use **yet** to say that there is still a possibility that something will happen. *Like the best stories, this one may yet have a happy end... A negotiated settlement might yet be possible.* ADV: ADV before v =still

6 You can use **yet** after expressions which refer to a period of time, when you want to say how much longer a situation will continue for. *Unemployment will go on rising for some time yet... Nothing will happen for a few years yet... They'll be ages yet.* ADV: n ADV

7 If you say that you have **yet** to do something, you mean that you have never done it, especially when this is surprising or bad. *She has yet to spend a Christmas with her husband... He has been nominated three times for the Oscar but has yet to win.* ADV: ADV to-inf

8 You can use **yet** to introduce a fact which is rather surprising after the previous fact you have just mentioned. *I don't eat much, yet I am a size 16... They were terrified James would die – yet there were moments when they almost wished he would... It is completely waterproof, yet light and comfortable.* CONJ-COORD PRAGMATICS =but

9 You can use **yet** to emphasize a word, especially when you are saying that something is surprising because it is more extreme than previous things of its kind, or a further case of them. *Yet bigger satellites will be sent up into orbit... I saw yet another doctor... They would criticize me, or worse yet, pay me no attention... By then governments may have woken up to a yet more radical option... It is plain to see we will not have anything to eat yet again.* ADV: ADV with adj/n/adv, usu ADV with compar PRAGMATICS

10 You use **as yet** with negative statements to describe a situation that has existed up until the present time; a formal use. *As yet it is not known whether the crash was the result of an accident... We have not as yet received a response.* PHRASE: PHR with cl

yew /juː/ **yews.** A **yew** or a **yew tree** is an evergreen tree. It has sharp leaves which are broad and flat, and red berries. ► **Yew** is the wood of this tree. ◆◇◇◇◇ N-VAR; N-UNCOUNT

Y-fronts. **Y-fronts** are men's or boys' underpants with an opening at the front. **Y-fronts** is a trademark; used mainly in British English. N-PLURAL

Yiddish /jɪdɪʃ/. **Yiddish** is a language spoken by many Jewish people of European origin, which is derived mainly from German. N-UNCOUNT

yield /jiːld/ **yields, yielding, yielded** ◆◆◆◇◇

1 If you **yield** to someone or something, you stop resisting them; a formal use. *Carmen yielded to general pressure and grudgingly took the child to a specialist... I yielded to an impulse... If the government does not yield, it should face sufficient military force to ensure its certain and swift defeat.* VERB =give in V to n V

2 If you **yield** something that you have control of or responsibility for, you allow someone else to have control or responsibility for it; a formal use. *He may yield control... The President is now under pressure to yield power to the republics.* ► **Yield up** means the same as **yield**. *Giulio Andreotti yielded up the prime ministership last summer.* VERB =surrender V n V n to n; PHRASAL VERB V P n (not pron)

3 If one thing **yields** to another thing, it is replaced by this other thing; a formal use. *Boston's traditional drab brick was slow to yield to the modern glass palaces of so many American urban areas.* VERB =give way to V to n

4 In American English, if a moving person or a vehicle or its driver **yields**, they slow down or stop in order to allow other people or vehicles to pass in front of them. The usual British expression is **give way**. *When entering a trail or starting a descent, yield to other skiers. ...examples of common signs like No Smoking or Yield.* VERB V to n V

5 If something **yields**, it breaks or moves position because force or pressure has been put on it. *He reached the massive door of the barn and pushed. It yielded.* VERB V

6 If an area of land or a number of animals **yields** a particular amount of food or plants, this amount of VERB =produce food or plants is produced by the land or animals. *Last year 400,000 acres of land yielded a crop worth $1.75 billion.* ▸ **Yield up** means the same as **yield**. *The shallow sea bed yields up an abundance of food.* Vn PHRASAL VERB V P n (not pron)

7 A **yield** is the amount of food produced on an area of land or by a number of animals. *...improving the yield of the crop... Polluted water lessens crop yields.* N-COUNT: with supp

8 If a tax or investment **yields** an amount of money or profit, this money or profit is obtained from it. *It yielded a profit of at least $36 million.* VERB Vn

9 A **yield** is the amount of money or profit produced by an investment; a technical term in finance. *...a yield of 4%... The lira strengthened because of high yields available in the Italian cash market. ...the yield on a bank's investments.* N-COUNT: with supp, oft N of amount, N on n

10 If something **yields** a result or piece of information, it produces it. *This research has been in progress since 1961 and has yielded a great number of positive results... His trip to Melbourne had yielded a lot of information.* VERB Vn

yield up. If you **yield up** a secret, you reveal it; a formal use. *...asking law firms to yield up their deepest secrets.* • See also **yield** 2, 5. PHRASAL VERB V P n (not pron)

yielding /jɪəldɪŋ/. A **yielding** surface or object is quite soft and will move or bend rather than staying stiff if you put pressure on it. *...the yielding ground. ...the soft yielding cushions.* ADJ-GRADED

yippee /jɪpiː/. People sometimes shout **yippee** when they are very pleased or excited. EXCLAM

YMCA /waɪ em siː eɪ/ **YMCAs.** A **YMCA** is a hostel run by the YMCA organization where men can stay. YMCA is an abbreviation for 'Young Men's Christian Association'. N-COUNT: usu *the* N in sing

yob /jɒb/ **yobs.** If you call a boy or a man a **yob**, you disapprove of him because he behaves in a noisy, bad-mannered, and perhaps violent way in public; used in informal British English. *Violent and dangerous yobs deserve to be locked up.* N-COUNT: usu with supp PRAGMATICS =lout

yobbo /jɒbou/ **yobbos.** A **yobbo** is the same as a **yob**; used in informal British English. N-COUNT =lout

yodel /joudᵊl/ **yodels, yodelling, yodelled;** spelled **yodeling, yodeled** in American English. When someone **yodels**, they sing normal notes with very high quick notes in between. *You also yodel and tap-dance. Do I have that right?* ♦ **yodelling** *Switzerland isn't all cow bells and yodelling, you know.* VERB V N-UNCOUNT

yoga /jougə/ ◆◇◇◇◇

1 **Yoga** is a type of exercise in which you move your body into various positions in order to become more fit or flexible, to improve your breathing, and to relax your mind. N-UNCOUNT

2 **Yoga** is a philosophy which first developed in India, in which physical exercises and meditation are believed to help people to become calmer and gradually united in spirit with a Supreme Being. N-UNCOUNT

yoghurt /jɒgəʳt, AM jou-/. See **yogurt**.

yogi /jougi/ **yogis.** A **yogi** is a person who has spent many years practising the philosophy of yoga, and is considered to have reached an advanced state of spiritual awareness. N-COUNT

yogurt /jɒgəʳt, AM jou-/ **yogurts;** also spelled **yoghurt**. **Yogurt** is a food in the form of a thick, slightly sour liquid that is made by adding bacteria to milk. A **yogurt** is a small pot of yogurt. ◆◇◇◇◇ N-VAR

yoke /jouk/ **yokes, yoking, yoked**

1 If you say that people are under the **yoke** of a bad thing or person, you mean they are forced to live in a difficult or unhappy state because of that thing or person; a literary use. *People are still suffering under the yoke of slavery... With the Cold War abruptly over, Eastern Europe was cast free from the communist yoke.* N-SING: usu N of n, adj N

2 A **yoke** is a long piece of wood which is tied across the necks of two animals such as oxen, in order to make them walk close together when they are pulling a plough. N-COUNT

3 If two or more people or things **are yoked** together, they are forced to be closely linked with each other. *Finally, let me close by yoking together a further pair of extremes, the personal with the global... The Auto Pact signed in 1965 yoked Ontario into the United States economy... Farmers and politicians are yoked by money and votes.* VERB V pl-n with together V n to/into n be V-ed

yokel /joukᵊl/ **yokels.** If you refer to someone as a **yokel**, you think they are uneducated and stupid because they come from the countryside. N-COUNT PRAGMATICS =country bumpkin

yolk /jouk/ **yolks.** The **yolk** of an egg is the yellow part in the middle. *Only the yolk contains cholesterol. ...buttered toast dipped in egg yolk.* ◆◇◇◇◇ N-VAR

Yom Kippur /jɒm kɪpuəʳ/. **Yom Kippur** is a Jewish holiday which is a day of fasting and prayers of repentance. It is in September or October. N-UNCOUNT

yon /jɒn/. **Yon** means 'that' or 'those'; an old-fashioned word or a word that is used in some dialects of English. *Don't let yon dog nod off.* DET
• **hither and yon**: see **hither**.

yonder /jɒndəʳ/. **Yonder** means over there; an old-fashioned word or a word which is used in some dialects of English. *Now look yonder, just beyond the wooden post there.* ▸ Also a determiner. *His wife, Claudia, lies under yonder tree.* ADV: ADV with v DET

yonks /jɒŋks/. In informal British English, you can use **yonks** to mean a very long time. *He's been here for yonks. Everyone knows him.* N-PLURAL =ages

yore /jɔːʳ/. **Of yore** is used to refer to a period of time in the past; a literary or journalistic expression. *The images provoked strong surges of nostalgia for the days of yore... Suburbia is a sadder place than of yore.* PHRASE: n PHR, *than* PHR =of old

Yorkshire pudding /jɔːʳkʃəʳ pudɪŋ/ **Yorkshire puddings.** **Yorkshire pudding** is a British food which is made by baking a thick liquid mixture of flour, milk, and eggs. It is often eaten with roast beef. N-VAR

you /juː/ **yous** ◆◆◆◆◆

You is the second person pronoun. **You** can refer to one or more people and is used as the subject of a verb or the object of a verb or preposition.

1 A speaker or writer uses **you** to refer to the person or people that he or she is talking or writing to. You can use **you** before a noun to make it clear which group of people you are referring to. *When I saw you across the room I knew I'd met you before... You two seem very different to me... I could always talk to you about anything in the world... What is alternative health care? What can it do for you?... What you kids need is more exercise.* PRON

2 In spoken English and informal written English, a speaker or writer sometimes uses **you** to refer to people in general. *Veal is good value when compared with minced beef, and gives you a greater cooked yield... 'I didn't want to go into nursing,' she said, 'but my dad told me to, and in those days you did what you were told.'* PRON

3 In some dialects of English, **yous** is sometimes used instead of 'you' when talking to two or more people. *'Yous two are no' gettin' paid,' he said. 'Ye're too lazy!'* PRON-PLURAL

you'd /juːd/

1 **You'd** is the usual spoken form of 'you had', especially when 'had' is an auxiliary verb. *I think you'd better tell us why you're asking these questions.*

2 **You'd** is the usual spoken form of 'you would'. *With your hair and your beautiful skin, you'd look good in red and other bright colors.*

you'll /juːl/. **You'll** is the usual spoken form of 'you will'. *Promise me you'll take very special care of yourself... I think you'll find everything you need here.*

young /jʌŋ/ **younger** /jʌŋgəʳ/ **youngest** /jʌŋgəst/ ◆◆◆◆◆

1 A **young** person, animal, or plant has not lived or existed for very long and is not yet mature. *In Scotland, young people can marry at 16... You weren't so very young when she died; you were old enough to remember... I crossed the hill, and found myself in a field of young barley... He played with his younger brother.* ▸ **The young** are people who are young. *The association is advising pregnant women, the very young and the elderly to avoid such foods.* ADJ-GRADED ≠old N-PLURAL: *the* N

2 You use **young** to describe a time when a person or thing was young. *In her younger days my mother had been a successful fashionwear saleswoman.* ADJ-GRADED: ADJ n

3 Someone who is **young** in appearance or behaviour looks or behaves as if they are young. *I was twenty-three, I suppose, and young for my age... He seemed to me very young and very lonely.* ADJ-GRADED

4 The **young** of an animal are its babies. *The hen may not be able to feed its young.* N-PLURAL

youngish /jʌŋɪʃ/. If you describe someone as **youngish**, you mean they are fairly young. *...a smart, dark-haired, youngish man.* ADJ

youngster /jʌŋstəʳ/ **youngsters.** Young people, especially children, are sometimes referred to as **youngsters**. *Other youngsters are not so lucky... I was only a youngster in 1935.* ◆◆◆◇◇ N-COUNT

your /jɔːʳ, jʊəʳ/ ◆◆◆◆◆

Your is the second person possessive determiner. **Your** can refer to one or more people.

1 A speaker or writer uses **your** to indicate that something belongs or relates to the person or people that he or she is talking or writing to. *Emma, I trust your opinion a great deal... I left all of your messages on your desk... If you are unable to obtain the information you require, consult your telephone directory.* DET-POSS

2 In spoken English and informal written English, a speaker or writer sometimes uses **your** to indicate that something belongs to or relates to people in general. *Pain-killers are very useful in small amounts to bring your temperature down... I then realized how possible it was to overcome your limitations.* DET-POSS

3 In spoken English, a speaker sometimes uses **your** before an adjective such as 'typical' or 'normal' to indicate that the thing referred to is a typical example of its type. *Stan Reilly is not really one of your typical Brighton Boys... It's just your average wooden door.* DET-POSS

you're /jɔːʳ, jʊəʳ/. **You're** is the usual spoken form of 'you are'. *Go to him, tell him you're sorry... I think you're expecting too much of me.*

yours /jɔːʳz, jʊəʳz/ ◆◆◆◇◇

Yours is the second person possessive pronoun. **Yours** can refer to one or more people.

1 A speaker or writer uses **yours** to refer to something that belongs or relates to the person or people that he or she is talking or writing to. *I'll take my coat upstairs. Shall I take yours, Roberta?... I believe Paul was a friend of yours... If yours is a high-stress job, it is important that you learn how to cope.* PRON-POSS

2 People write **yours**, **yours sincerely**, or **yours faithfully** at the end of a letter before they sign their name. *With best regards, Yours, George... Yours faithfully, Michael Moore, London Business School... Waiting to hear from you, Yours sincerely, William Faulkner.* ● **yours truly** see **truly**. CONVENTION

yourself /jɔːʳself, jʊəʳ-/ **yourselves** ◆◆◆◆◇

Yourself is the second person reflexive pronoun.

1 A speaker or writer uses **yourself** to refer to the person that he or she is talking or writing to. **Yourself** is used when the object of a verb or preposition refers to the same person as the subject of the verb. *Have the courage to be honest with yourself and about yourself... Your baby depends on you to look after yourself properly while you are pregnant... Treat yourselves to a glass of wine to help you relax at the end of the day.* PRON-REFL: v PRON, prep PRON

2 You use **yourself** to emphasize the person that you are referring to. *They mean to share the business between them, after you yourself are gone, Sir... I've been wondering if you yourselves have any idea why she came.* PRON-REFL-EMPH PRAGMATICS

3 You use **yourself** instead of 'you' for emphasis or in order to be more polite when 'you' is the object of a verb or preposition. *A wealthy man like yourself is bound to make an enemy or two along the way... I wouldn't want to cause such important people as yourselves any bother.* ● **by yourself**: see **by**. PRON-REFL-EMPH: v PRON, prep PRON PRAGMATICS

youth /juːθ/ **youths** /juːðz/ ◆◆◆◆◇

1 Someone's **youth** is the period of their life during which they are a child, before they are a fully mature adult. *In my youth my ambition had been to be an inventor. ...the comic books of my youth.* N-UNCOUNT: usu poss N

2 Youth is the quality or state of being young and perhaps immature and inexperienced. *Gregory was still enchanted with Shannon's youth and joy and beauty... The team is now a good mixture of experience and youth.* N-UNCOUNT

3 Journalists often refer to young men as **youths**, especially when they are reporting that the young men have caused trouble. *...gangs of youths who broke windows and looted shops... A 17-year-old youth was remanded in custody yesterday.* N-COUNT

4 The **youth** are young people considered as a group. *He represents the opinions of the youth of today... She's not a very good influence on the youth of this country.* N-PLURAL: usu with poss

youth club, youth clubs. A **youth club** is a club where young people can go to meet each other and take part in various leisure activities. Youth clubs are often run by a church or local authority. *...the youth club disco.* N-COUNT

youthful /juːθfʊl/. Someone who is **youthful** behaves as if they are young or younger than they really are. *I'm a very youthful 50. ...youthful enthusiasm and high spirits... Gary Glitter, 48, revealed the secret of his youthful looks.* ♦ **youthfulness** *His youthfulness was as striking as hers.* ◆◇◇◇◇ ADJ-GRADED N-UNCOUNT

youth hostel youth hostels. A **youth hostel** is a place where young people can stay cheaply when they are travelling. *Can you tell us where the youth hostel is?* N-COUNT

youth worker, youth workers. A **youth worker** is a person whose job involves providing support and social activities for young people, especially young people from underprivileged backgrounds; used mainly in British English. N-COUNT

you've /juːv/. **You've** is the usual spoken form of 'you have', especially when 'have' is an auxiliary verb. *Now you've got your degree, what will you do?... Many of the fruits you've tasted on your holidays can be found in supermarkets.*

yowl /jaʊl/ **yowls, yowling, yowled.** If a person or an animal **yowls**, they make a loud wailing noise. *The dog began to yowl.* ► Also a noun. *Patsy could hardly be heard above the baby's yowls.* ♦ **yowling** *I couldn't stand that yowling.* VERB V N-COUNT N-UNCOUNT

yo-yo /joʊ joʊ/ **yo-yos.** A **yo-yo** is a toy made of a round piece of wood or plastic attached to a piece of string. You play with the yo-yo by letting it rise and fall on the string. ◆◇◇◇◇ N-COUNT

yr, yrs. yr is a written abbreviation for **year**. *Their imaginations are quite something for 2 yr olds.*

yuan /juːæn, AM -ɑːn/. **Yuan** is both the singular and the plural form. The **yuan** is the unit of money used in the People's Republic of China. *For most events, tickets cost one, two or three yuan.* ► **The yuan** is also used to refer to the Chinese currency system. *The yuan recovered a little; it now hovers around 8.2 to the dollar.* N-COUNT: num N N-SING: the N

Yugoslav /juːgəslɑːv/ **Yugoslavs. Yugoslav** means belonging or relating to the former Yugoslavia, or to its people or culture. *...the former Yugoslav republics. ...the Yugoslav Embassy in Washington.* ► A **Yugoslav** was a Yugoslav citizen, or a person of Yugoslav origin. ◆◆◆◇◇ ADJ N-COUNT

Yugoslavian /juːgəslɑːviən/. **Yugoslavian** means the same as **Yugoslav**. ◆◆◆◆◇ ADJ

yuk /jʌk/. Some people say **'yuk'** when they think something is very unpleasant or disgusting; an informal word. *'It's corned beef and cabbage,' said Malone. 'Yuk,' said Maureen.* EXCLAM

Yule /juːl/. **Yule** is an old-fashioned word for **Christmas**. N-UNCOUNT

Yuletide /juːltaɪd/. **Yuletide** is the period of several days around and including Christmas Day. *...ideas for Yuletide food, drink and decorations.* N-UNCOUNT: oft N n

yum /jʌm/. People sometimes say **'yum'** or **'yum yum'** to show that they think something tastes or smells very good; an informal word. EXCLAM

yummy /jʌmi/. **Yummy** means delicious; an informal word. *I'll bet they have yummy ice cream... It smells yummy.* ADJ-GRADED

yuppie /jʌpi/ **yuppies.** A **yuppie** is a young middle-class person with a well-paid job, who likes to show that they have a lot of money by buying expensive things and doing expensive activities; used showing disapproval. *A lot of people think, 'You've got a car phone, you must be a yuppie.' ...an ambitious yuppie lawyer.* ◆◇◇◇◇ N-COUNT

YWCA /waɪ dʌbəlju: si: eɪ/ **YWCAs.** A **YWCA** is a hostel run by the YWCA organization where women can stay. YWCA is an abbreviation for 'Young Women's Christian Association'. N-COUNT: usu *the* N in sing

Z, z /zed, AM zi:/ **Z's, z's.** Z is the twenty-sixth and last letter of the English alphabet. N-VAR

zany /zeɪni/ **zanier, zaniest. Zany** humour or a **zany** person is strange or eccentric in an amusing way; an informal word. *...the zany humour of the Marx Brothers.* ADJ-GRADED: usu ADJ n =wacky

zap /zæp/ **zaps, zapping, zapped** ◆◇◇◇◇

1 To **zap** someone or something means to kill, destroy, or hit them, usually using a gun, spray, or laser; an informal use. *A guard zapped him with the stun gun. ...throat spray, which absolutely zaps any remnant of my sore throat.* VERB V n

2 If you **zap** channels while watching television, you change channels using the remote control; an informal use. *Men like to zap the TV channels, something that can drive certain women berserk.* VERB V n

zeal /zi:l/. **Zeal** is great enthusiasm, especially in connection with work, religion, or politics. *...his zeal for teaching... Mr Lopez approached his task with a religious zeal.* ◆◇◇◇◇ N-UNCOUNT

zealot /zelət/ **zealots.** If you describe someone as a **zealot**, you think that their views and actions are extreme or fanatical, especially in following a political or religious ideal. *He was forceful, but by no means a zealot.* N-COUNT

zealous /zeləs/. Someone who is **zealous** spends a lot of time or energy in supporting something that they believe in very strongly, especially a political or religious ideal. *She was a zealous worker for charitable bodies... He was a recent Catholic convert, and very zealous.* ◆◇◇◇◇ ADJ-GRADED
♦ **zealously** *Details of its past activities were zealously guarded.* ADV-GRADED: usu ADV with v

zebra /zebrə, zi:-/ **zebras.** The plural can be either **zebras** or **zebra**. A **zebra** is an African wild horse which has black and white stripes. ◆◇◇◇◇ N-COUNT

zebra crossing, zebra crossings. In Britain, a **zebra crossing** is a place on the road that is marked with black and white stripes, where vehicles are supposed to stop so that people can walk across. N-COUNT

zeitgeist /zaɪtgaɪst/. The **zeitgeist** of a particular place during a particular period in history is the attitudes and ideas that are generally common there at that time, especially the attitudes and ideas shown in literature, philosophy, and politics. *He has caught the zeitgeist of rural life in the 1980s very well indeed.* N-SING

Zen /zen/. **Zen** or **Zen Buddhism** is a form of the Buddhist religion that concentrates on meditation rather than on studying religious writings. ◆◇◇◇◇ N-UNCOUNT

zenith /zenɪθ, AM zi:-/

1 The **zenith** of something is the time when it is most successful or powerful. *His career is now at its zenith... The zenith of Perugia's influence came with the defeat of Siena in 1358.* N-SING: usu with poss =peak ≠nadir

2 The **zenith** is the point at which the sun or moon is directly above you and seems to be at its highest. *The sun rises, reaches its zenith and sets.* N-SING ≠nadir

zephyr /zefəʳ/ **zephyrs.** A **zephyr** is a gentle wind; a literary word. N-COUNT

zero /zɪərou/ **zeros** or **zeroes, zeroing, zeroed** ◆◆◇◇◇

1 **Zero** is the number 0. *Visibility at the city's airport came down to zero, bringing air traffic to a standstill. ...a scale ranging from zero to seven.* NUM =nought, nil

2 **Zero** is freezing point on the Centigrade scale. It is often written as 0°C. *The temperature is a little above absolute zero... That night the mercury fell to thirty degrees below zero.* N-UNCOUNT

3 You can use **zero** to say that there is none at all of the thing mentioned. *This new ministry was being created with zero assets and zero liabilities. ...zero inflation... His chances are zero.* ADJ =nil

zero in on PHRASAL VERB

1 To **zero in on** a target means to aim at it or move towards it. *He raised the binoculars again and zeroed in on an eleventh-floor room.* =home in on V P P n

2 If you **zero in on** a problem or subject, you give it your full attention. *Many of the other major daily newspapers have not really zeroed in on the problem... Critics have zeroed in on his plan to raise gasoline taxes 10 cents a gallon.* =home in on V P P n

zero-sum game. If you refer to a situation as a **zero-sum game**, you mean that if one person gains an advantage from it, someone else involved must suffer an equivalent disadvantage. *They believe they're playing a zero-sum game, where both must compete for the same paltry resources.* N-SING

zest /zest/ **zests** ◆◇◇◇◇

1 **Zest** is a feeling of pleasure and enthusiasm. *He retired from professional chess because he had lost the zest for winning... He has a zest for life and a quick intellect.* N-UNCOUNT: also *a* N, oft N *for* n

2 **Zest** is a quality in an activity or situation which you find exciting. *Live interviews add zest and a touch of the unexpected to any piece of research. ...the zest and charm of this beautiful comic opera.* N-UNCOUNT

3 The **zest** of a lemon, orange, or lime is the rind when it is grated to give flavour to something such as a cake or a drink. *Mix the rest of the olive oil with the zest and juice of the lemon... Finely grate about a teaspoon of orange zest and put aside.* N-UNCOUNT: also N in pl, usu N *of* n, n N

zigzag /zɪgzæg/ **zigzags, zigzagging, zigzagged;** also spelled **zig-zag.**

1 A **zigzag** is a line which has a series of angles in it like a continuous series of 'W's. *They staggered in a zigzag across the tarmac. ...a zigzag pattern.* N-COUNT

2 If you **zigzag**, you move forward by going at an angle first to one side then to the other. *I zigzagged down a labyrinth of alleys... Expertly he zigzagged his way across the field, avoiding the deeper gullies and making good time.* VERB V prep V *way* prep Also V

zilch /zɪltʃ/. **Zilch** means nothing; an informal word. *Nothing's happened Connie. Zilch... At the moment these shares are worth zilch.* PRON-INDEF-NEG =nothing

zillion /zɪljən/ **zillions.** If you talk about a **zillion** people or things you are emphasizing that there is an extremely large number of them; an informal word. *It's been a zillion years since I've seen her.* NUM PRAGMATICS ▶ Also a quantifier. *There are zillions of things to look at or try out.* QUANT: QUANT *of* pl-n

Zimmer frame /zɪməʳ freɪm/ **Zimmer frames.** In British English, a **Zimmer frame** or a **Zimmer** is a frame that old or ill people sometimes use to help them walk. **Zimmer** is a trademark. N-COUNT

zinc /zɪŋk/. **Zinc** is a bluish-white metal which is used to make other metals such as brass or to cover other metals such as iron to stop them rusting. ◆◆◇◇◇ N-UNCOUNT

zing /zɪŋ/. If you refer to the **zing** in someone or something, you mean the quality that makes them lively or interesting; an informal word. *He just lacked that extra zing... There's nothing like fresh basil to put a zing into a tomato sauce.* N-UNCOUNT: also *a* N

Zionism /zaɪənɪzəm/. **Zionism** is a movement which was originally concerned with establishing a political and religious state in Palestine for Jewish people, and is now concerned with the development of Israel. N-UNCOUNT

Zionist /zaɪənɪst/ **Zionists** ◆◇◇◇◇

1 A **Zionist** is someone who believes in Zionism. *He was an ardent Zionist.* N-COUNT

2 **Zionist** means relating to Zionism. *...the Zionist movement.* ADJ: usu ADJ n

zip /zɪp/ **zips, zipping, zipped** ◆◇◇◇◇

1 In British English, a **zip** or **zip fastener** is a device used to open and close parts of clothes and bags. It consists of two rows of metal or plastic teeth which N-COUNT

separate or fasten together as you pull a small tag along them. The usual American word is **zipper**. *He pulled the zip of his leather jacket down slightly.*

2 When you **zip** something, you fasten it using a zip. *She zipped her jeans... I slowly zipped and locked the heavy black nylon bags.* VERB V n

3 If you say that something or someone **zips** somewhere, you mean that they move there very quickly; an informal use. *My craft zipped across the bay... Max zips back and forth across the living room.* VERB V prep/adv

4 If you say that someone or something has **zip**, you mean that they show a lot of energy and enthusiasm; an informal use. *Share options will play a bigger role in future, putting zip into the performance of middle managers... Tommy Tune gives the choreography his usual class and zip.* N-UNCOUNT =verve

zip up. If you **zip up** something such as a piece of clothing or if it **zips up**, you are able to fasten it using its zip. *He zipped up his jeans... My jeans wouldn't zip up.* PHRASAL VERB ERG V P n (not pron) V P Also V n P

zip code, zip codes. In American English, your **zip code** is a short sequence of letters and numbers at the end of your address, which helps the post office to sort the mail. The British term is **postcode**. N-COUNT

zipper /zɪpəʳ/ **zippers.** In American English, a **zipper** is the same as a **zip**. N-COUNT

zit /zɪt/ **zits. Zits** are spots or pimples on someone's skin; an informal word. N-COUNT =spot

zither /zɪðəʳ/ **zithers.** A **zither** is a musical instrument which consists of two sets of strings stretched over a flat box. You play the zither by plucking the strings with both hands. N-COUNT

zodiac /zoʊdiæk/. **The zodiac** is a diagram used by astrologers to represent the positions of the planets and stars. It is divided into twelve sections, each with a special name and symbol. The zodiac is used by astrologers to help calculate the influence of the planets. *...the twelve signs of the zodiac.* ◆◇◇◇◇ N-SING: the N

zombie /zɒmbi/ **zombies**

1 You can describe someone as a **zombie** if their face or behaviour shows no feeling, understanding, or interest in what is going on around them. *I didn't want to do anything, I just sat at home and vegetated. I became a total zombie... Without sleep you will become a zombie at work.* N-COUNT

2 In horror stories and some religions, a **zombie** is a dead person who has been brought back to life. N-COUNT

zone /zoʊn/ **zones, zoning, zoned** ◆◆◆◇◇

1 A **zone** is an area that has particular features or characteristics. *Many people have stayed behind in the potential war zone... The area has been declared a disaster zone. ...time zones.* N-COUNT: oft n N

2 If an area of land **is zoned**, it is formally set aside for a particular purpose. *The land was not zoned for commercial purposes... Most of the private land in the park wasn't zoned or protected in any way.* VB: usu passive be V-ed

♦ **zoning** *...the use of zoning to preserve agricultural land... Local zoning laws prohibit building near property lines.* N-UNCOUNT

zonked /zɒŋkt/. If someone is **zonked** or **zonked out**, they are not capable of doing anything because they are very tired, drunk, or drugged; an informal word. ADJ-GRADED

zoo /zuː/ **zoos.** A **zoo** is a park where live animals are kept so that people can look at them. *He took his son Christopher to the zoo. ...the penguin pool at London Zoo.* ◆◆◇◇◇ N-COUNT; N-IN-NAMES

zoology /zuːɒlədʒi, zoʊ-/. **Zoology** is the scientific study of animals. ♦ **zoological** *...zoological specimens.* ♦ **zoologist** /zuːɒlədʒɪst, zoʊ-/ **zoologists** *...a renowned zoologist and writer.*  N-UNCOUNT ADJ: ADJ n N-COUNT

zoom /zuːm/ **zooms, zooming, zoomed** ◆◆◇◇◇

1 If you **zoom** somewhere, you go there very quickly; an informal use. *We zoomed through the gallery... A police car zoomed by very close to them.* VERB =speed V prep/adv

2 If prices or sales **zoom**, they increase greatly in a very short time. *The economy shrank and inflation zoomed... Profits zoomed from nil in 1981 to about 16 million last year.* VERB =soar V

3 A **zoom** is the same as a **zoom lens**. N-COUNT

zoom in. If a camera **zooms in** on something that is being filmed or photographed, it gives a close-up picture of it. *...a tracking system which can follow a burglar round a building and zoom in on his face... He trained his camera on nature, sometimes zooming in to examine single leaves.* PHRASAL VERB V P on n V P

zoom off. If you **zoom off**, you leave very quickly; an informal expression. *The bikers zoomed off.* PHRASAL VERB V P

zoom lens, zoom lenses. A **zoom lens** is a lens that you can attach to a camera, which allows you to make the details larger or smaller while always keeping the picture clear. N-COUNT

zucchini /zuːkiːni/ **zucchinis.** The plural can be either **zucchini** or **zucchinis**. In American English, **zucchini** are long thin green vegetables that you usually chop into slices and boil in water before eating. The British word is **courgette**. N-VAR

Zulu /zuːluː/ **Zulus** ◆◆◇◇◇

1 A **Zulu** is a member of a race of black people who live in Southern Africa. N-COUNT

2 **Zulu** is the language spoken by Zulus and also by many other black South Africans. N-UNCOUNT